Kentucky

Holt McDougal

ALGEBRA 2

Built for Kentucky

Featuring:

- Kentucky Standards Pacing Guide
- Kentucky Table of Contents
- Kentucky Student Guide
- KCCT Chapter Support
- Additional Standards Based Lessons
- Full Standards Correlation

About the Authors

Ron Larson is a professor of mathematics at Penn State University at Erie, where he has taught since receiving his Ph.D. in mathematics from the University of Colorado. Dr. Larson is well known as the author of a comprehensive program for mathematics that spans middle school, high school, and college courses.Dr. Larson's numerous professional activities keep him in constant touch with the needs of teachers and supervisors. He closely follows developments in mathematics standards and assessment.

Laurie Boswell is a mathematics teacher at The Riverside School in Lyndonville, Vermont, and has taught mathematics at all levels, elementary through college. A recipient of the Presidential Award for Excellence in Mathematics Teaching, she was also a Tandy Technology Scholar. She served on the NILM Board of Directors (2002–2005), and she speaks frequently at regional and national conferences on topics related to instructional strategies and course content.

Timothy D. Kanold is the superintendent of Adlai E. Stevenson High School District 125 in Lincolnshire, Illinois. Dr. Kanold served as a teacher and director of mathematics for 17 years prior to becoming superintendent. He is the recipient of the Presidential Award for Excellence in Mathematics and Science Teaching, and a past president of the Council for Presidential Awardees in Mathematics. Dr. Kanold is a frequent speaker at national and international mathematics meetings.

Lee Stiff is a professor of mathematics education in the College of Education and Psychology of North Carolina State University at Raleigh and has taught mathematics at the high school and middle school levels. He served on the NILM Board of Directors and was elected President of NILM for the years 2000–2002. He is a recipient of the W. W. Rankin Award for Excellence in Mathematics Education presented by the North Carolina Council of Teachers of Mathematics.

Printed in Canada

ISBN-13: 978-0-547-11753-9
ISBN-10: 0-547-11753-1

1 2 3 4 5 6 7 8 9—TBQC—12 11 10 09 08

Kentucky

Holt McDougal

ALGEBRA 2

GREAT LESSONS BEGIN

- When your students are active and involved
- When you teach the way you want to teach
- When assessment informs your daily instruction

Great lessons begin when
your students are active and involved

Integrated print and technology captures the imagination and helps your students connect to essential math concepts.

Animated Algebra

Animated Algebra helps you answer the why and how of math with interactive, animated problem-solving graphics that capture your students' imagination.

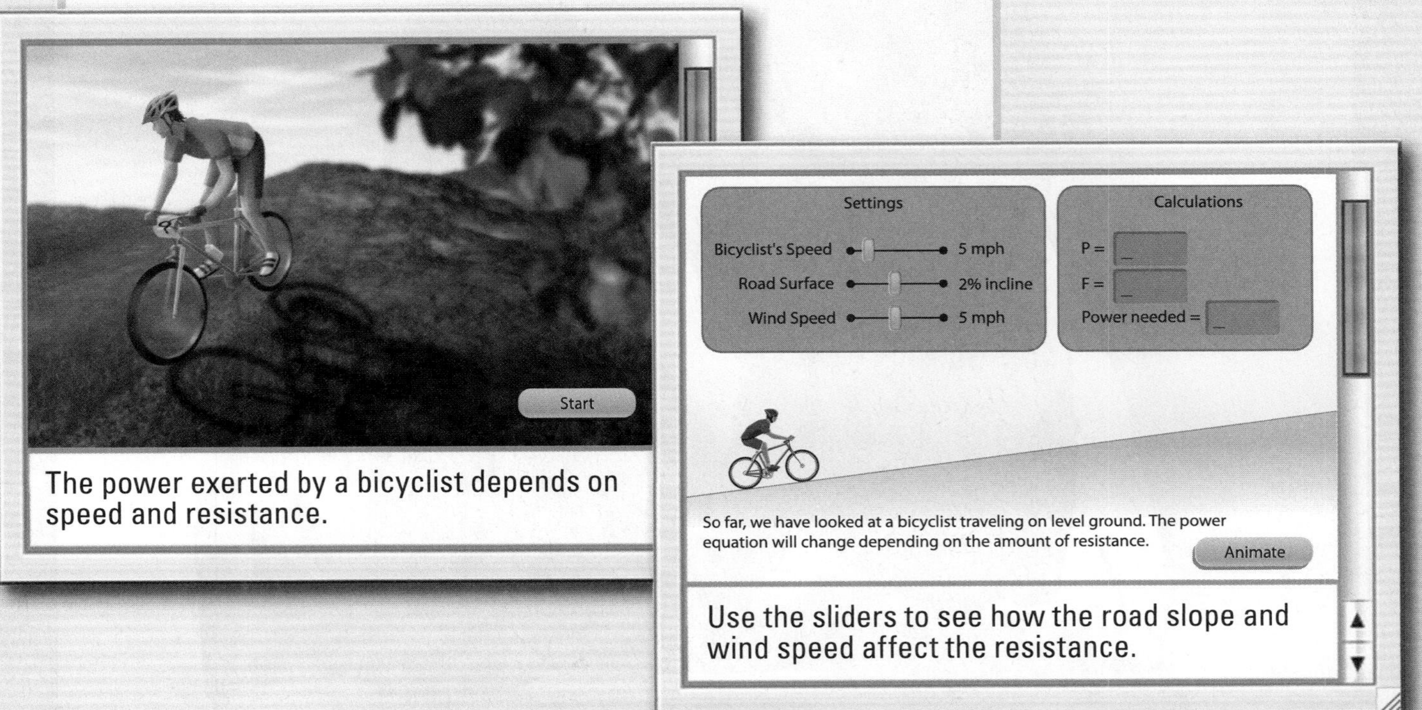
Start
The power exerted by a bicyclist depends on speed and resistance.
Settings
Bicyclist's Speed
5 mph
Road Surface
2% incline
Wind Speed
5 mph
Calculations
P =
F =
Power needed =
So far, we have looked at a bicyclist traveling on level ground. The power equation will change depending on the amount of resistance.
Animate
Use the sliders to see how the road slope and wind speed affect the resistance.

Capture the imagination and provide a vital link to real-life problem solving with hands-on **Investigating Algebra Activities** to motivate the lesson.

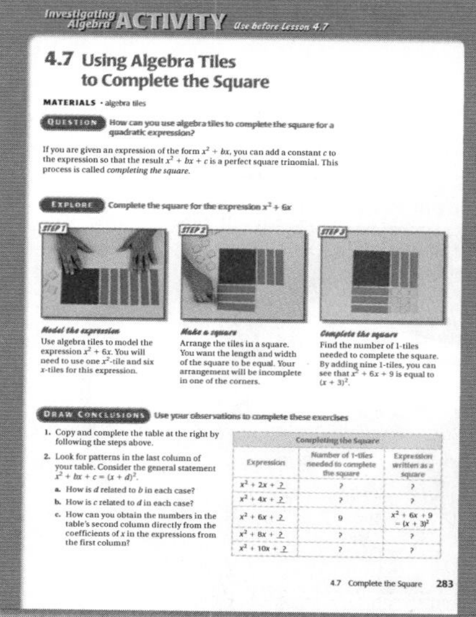

Investigating Algebra ACTIVITY *Use before Lesson 4.7*

4.7 Using Algebra Tiles to Complete the Square

MATERIALS • algebra tiles

QUESTION How can you use algebra tiles to complete the square for a quadratic expression?

If you are given an expression of the form $x^2 + bx$, you can add a constant c to the expression so that the result $x^2 + bx + c$ is a perfect square trinomial. This process is called *completing the square.*

EXPLORE Complete the square for the expression $x^2 + 6x$

STEP 1 *Model the expression*
Use algebra tiles to model the expression $x^2 + 6x$. You will need to use one x^2-tile and six x-tiles for this expression.

STEP 2 *Make a square*
Arrange the tiles in a square. You want the length and width of the square to be equal. Your arrangement will be incomplete in one of the corners.

STEP 3 *Complete the square*
Find the number of 1-tiles needed to complete the square. By adding nine 1-tiles, you can see that $x^2 + 6x + 9$ is equal to $(x + 3)^2$.

DRAW CONCLUSIONS Use your observations to complete these exercises

1. Copy and complete the table at the right by following the steps above.
2. Look for patterns in the last column of your table. Consider the general statement $x^2 + bx + c = (x + d)^2$.
   a. How is d related to b in each case?
   b. How is c related to d in each case?
   c. How can you obtain the numbers in the table's second column directly from the coefficients of x in the expressions from the first column?

Completing the Square

Expression	Number of 1-tiles needed to complete the square	Expression written as a square
$x^2 + 2x + \underline{?}$	?	?
$x^2 + 4x + \underline{?}$	?	?
$x^2 + 6x + \underline{?}$	9	$x^2 + 6x + 9 = (x + 3)^2$
$x^2 + 8x + \underline{?}$	?	?
$x^2 + 10x + \underline{?}$	?	?

4.7 Complete the Square 283

The **@Home Tutor CD-ROM** makes it easier than ever for students to focus on the math, enabling them to be more prepared for class.

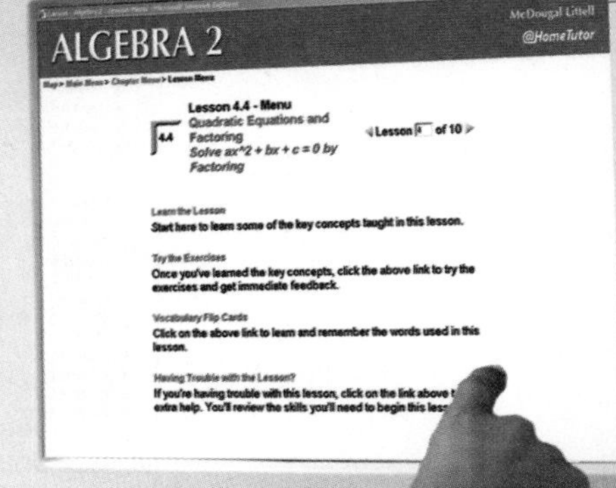

Great lessons begin when
you teach the way you want to teach

Flexible teaching tools help you reduce your preparation time and maximize your goals, while giving you the freedom to teach your way every day.

Power Presentations

The Electronic Classroom CD-ROM is the all-in-one source for dynamic teaching tools that save time and help you deliver the interactive lessons your students will remember.

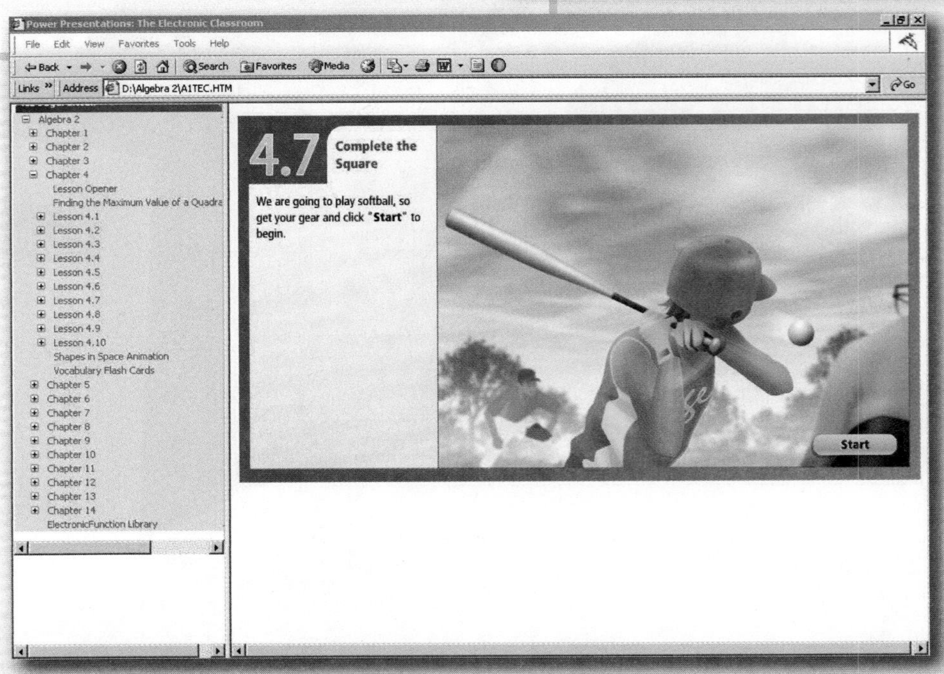

The **Electronic Function Library** is an easy-to-use graphing tool that makes it simple to incorporate everything from dynamic function families to colorful number lines.

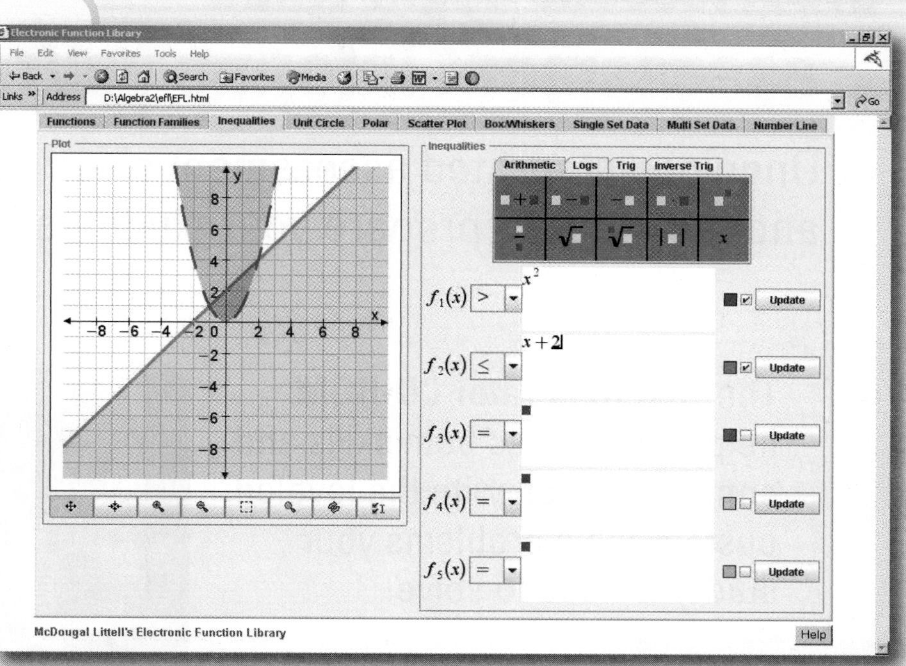

The **Activity Generator CD-ROM** gets students thinking with easily customized and leveled hands-on activities that are aligned to chapter content and to your state standards.

Editable Classroom Activities

High School Activity Generator STATE SPECIFIC

Pre-Algebra

Geometry

Algebra 2

Algebra 1

Get students thinking with editable hands-on activities aligned to your state standards.

New Version

This CD contains:

- Over 1000 editable, engaging activities
- Leveled activities designed to meet the needs of ALL students
- Hands-on, concept and calculator activities for every lesson in the program
- Activities correlated to your state standards

McDougal Littell

Great lessons begin when
assessment informs your daily instruction

Ongoing, integrated assessment gives you the power, flexibility and feedback to prepare your students for success.

The **Test Generator CD-ROM** helps you assess both skills and comprehension with the leveled, customizable problems your students need to solve.

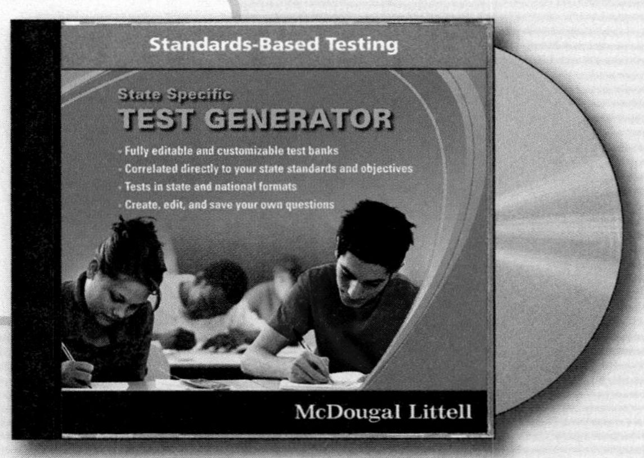

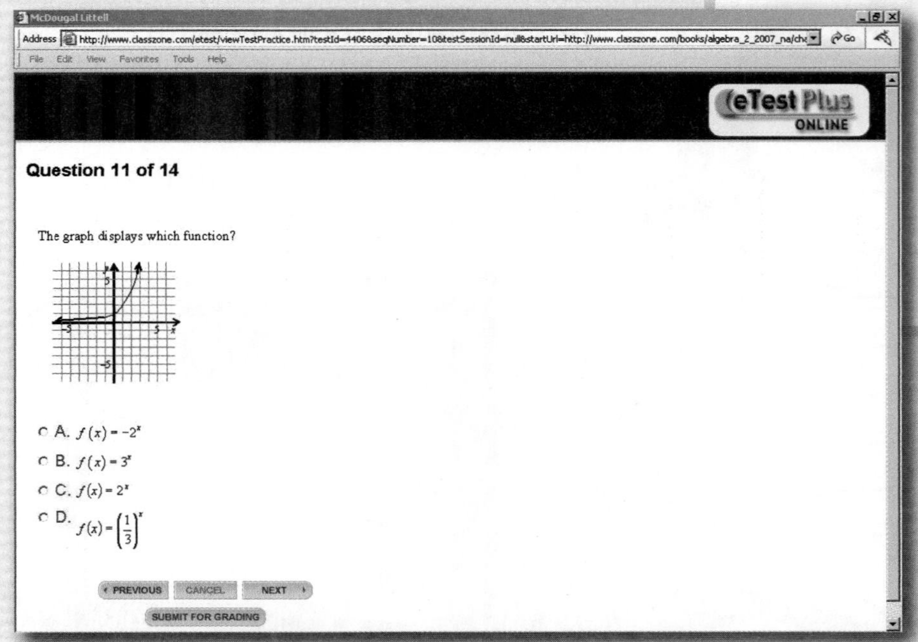

Online support at classzone.com provides online quizzes and chapter tests, instructional test practice, extra examples, and at-home tutorials just a click away.

McDougal Littell
Assessment System

The **McDougal Littell Assessment System** is the full-circle assessment and remediation solution that helps you track, record, and accurately address each student's individual progress.

TEST
Unique testing is custom built to Kentucky Standards.

REPORT
Diagnostic reports show you what Kentucky Standards were missed.

SCORE
Automatic scoring gives you results in minutes.

RETEACH
Personalized remediation helps you target reteaching.

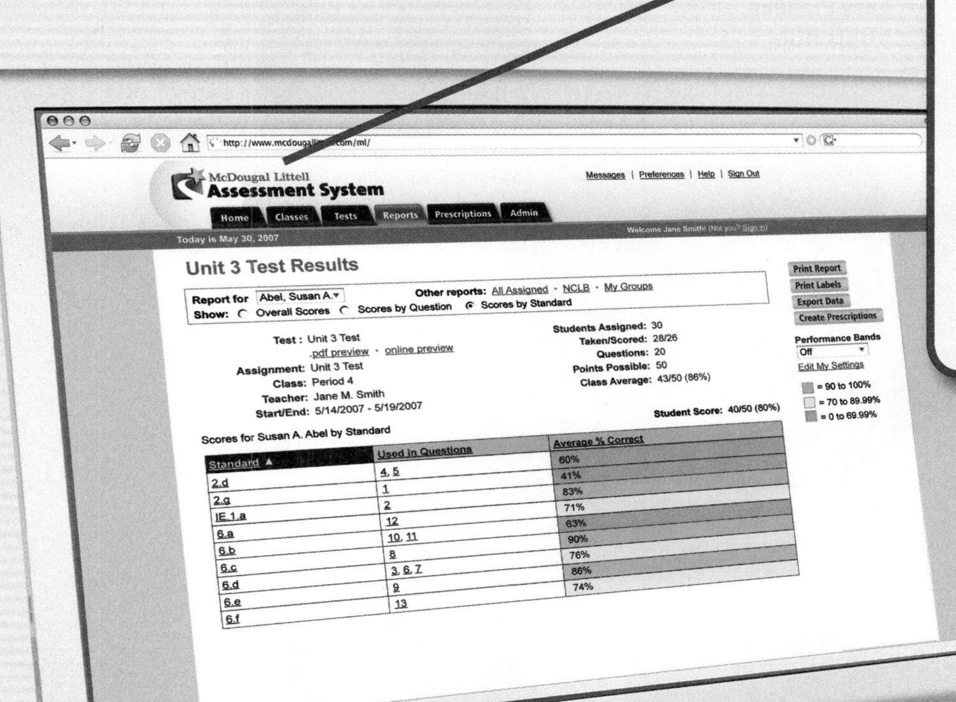

ALGEBRA 2 provides a complete set of resources organized for ease of use.

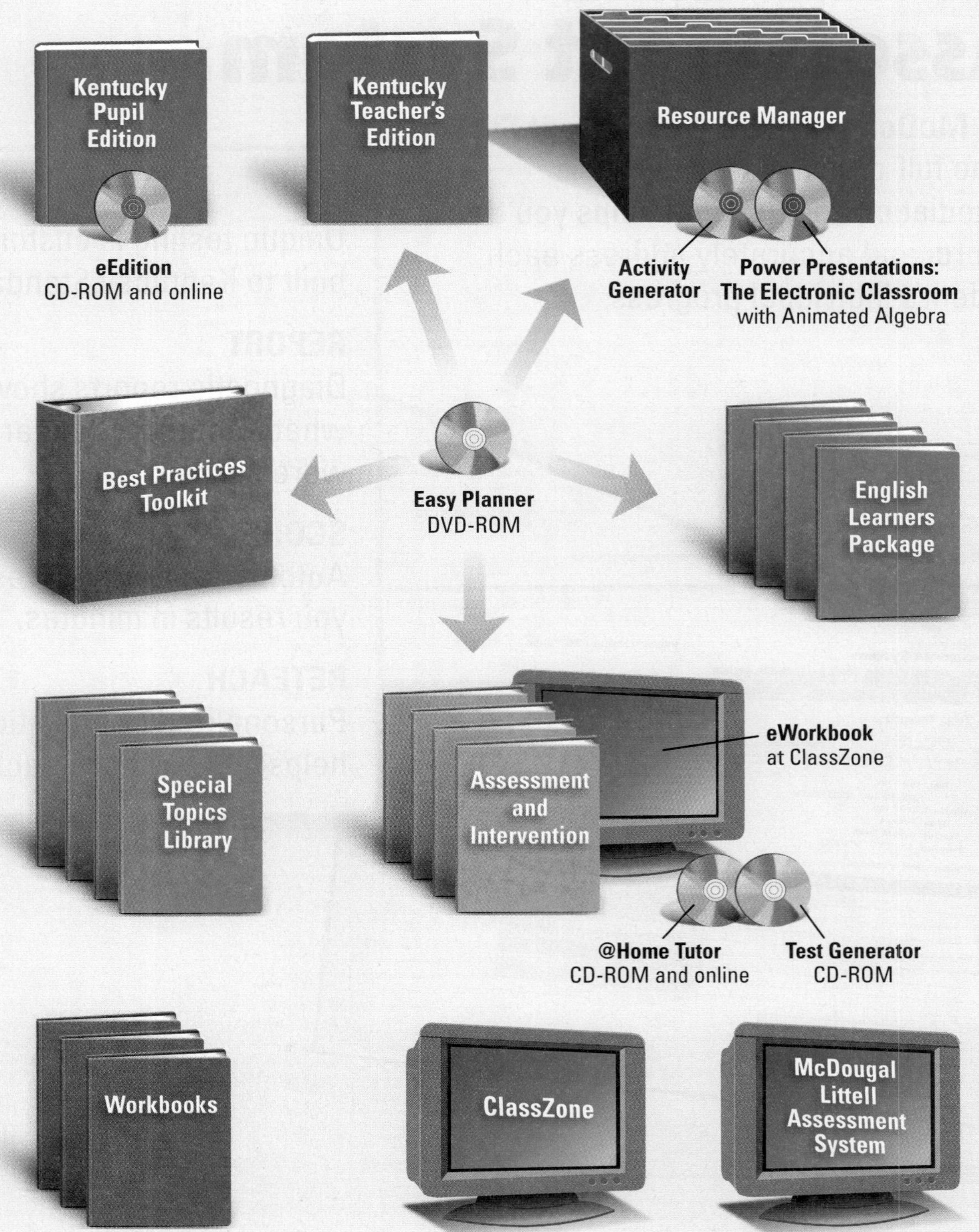

Guide to the
Kentucky Program of Studies for Mathematics and the Kentucky Core Content for Mathematics Assessment Version 4.1

- Daily practice in every lesson
- Weekly practice in the mid-chapter mixed review
- Summative practice in the end-of-chapter assessment

Horse farm near Lexington, Kentucky © David R. Frazier Photolibrary, Inc./Alamy

KENTUCKY STANDARDS PACING GUIDE

The following table gives a suggested pacing for presenting the textbook material so that the necessary content is covered for the state test in about 160 instructional days. The Mixed Review for Preparation and Practice material can be distributed throughout the course, as shown below, or you may wish to present it in the weeks immediately before the state test.

Day	Pages	Lesson or Feature	Kentucky Standards
1	2–9	1.1 Apply Properties of Real Numbers	**MA-HS-1.1.2, MA-HS-1.4.1 (DOK 2), MA-HS-1.5.1, MA-HS-2.1.3 (DOK 3), MA-HS-2.2.1**
2	10–16	1.2 Evaluate and Simplify Algebraic Expressions	**MA-HS-1.5.1, MA-HS-3.1.12 (DOK 3), MA-HS-5.2.1 (DOK 1), MA-HS-5.2.2**
	17	1.2 Graphing Calculator Activity	**MA-HS-5.2.2**
3	18–24	1.3 Solve Linear Equations	**MA-HS-1.4.1 (DOK 2), MA-HS-1.5.1, MA-HS-5.3.1 (DOK 2)**
	25	1.3 Graphing Calculator Activity	**MA-HS-5.3.1 (DOK 2)**
4	26–32	1.4 Rewrite Formulas and Equations	**MA-HS-3.1.3 (DOK 2), MA-HS-5.3.1 (DOK 2), MA-HS-5.3.2**
	33	Mixed Review for 1.1–1.4	**MA-HS-5.3.1 (DOK 2)**
5	34–40	1.5 Use Problem Solving Strategies and Models	**MA-HS-1.4.1 (DOK 2), MA-HS-2.1.3 (DOK 3), MA-HS-5.2.2, MA-HS-5.3.1 (DOK 2), MA-HS-5.3.2**
6	41–47	1.6 Solve Linear Inequalities	**MA-HS-2.1.2 (DOK 3), MA-HS-5.1.3, MA-HS-5.3.1 (DOK 2)**
	48–49	1.6 Problem Solving Workshop	**MA-HS-5.3.1 (DOK 2)**
7	50–58	1.7 Solve Absolute Value Equations and Inequalities	**MA-HS-3.1.5 (DOK 2), MA-HS-5.3.1 (DOK 2)**
8	59	Mixed Review for 1.5–1.7	**MA-HS-3.1.5 (DOK 2), MA-HS-5.3.1 (DOK 2)**
9	60–64	Chapter Summary and Review	**MA-HS-1.5.1, MA-HS-2.1.1 (DOK 2), MA-HS-5.2.1 (DOK 1), MA-HS-5.3.1 (DOK 2), MA-HS-5.3.2**
10	65	Chapter Test	**MA-HS-1.5.1, MA-HS-2.1.1 (DOK 2), MA-HS-5.2.1 (DOK 1), MA-HS-5.3.1 (DOK 2), MA-HS-5.3.2**
11	66–69	Test Preparation and Practice	**MA-HS-5.3.1 (DOK 2)**
12	72–79	2.1 Represent Relations and Functions	**MA-HS-5.1.1 (DOK 2), MA-HS-5.1.5 (DOK 2), MA-HS-5.3.3 (DOK 2)**
	80–81	2.1 Extension: Use Discrete and Continuous Functions	**MA-HS-5.1.1 (DOK 2)**
13	82–88	2.2 Find Slope and Rate of Change	**MA-HS-1.4.1 (DOK 2), MA-HS-2.1.3 (DOK 3), MA-HS-3.3.1 (DOK 2), MA-HS-5.3.1 (DOK 2)**
14	89–96	2.3 Graph Equations of Lines	**MA-HS-1.2.1, MA-HS-2.1.1 (DOK 2), MA-HS-3.1.7 (DOK 2), MA-HS-3.3.1 (DOK 2), MA-HS-5.1.1 (DOK 2), MA-HS-5.1.3, MA-HS-5.1.8 (DOK 2), MA-HS-5.3.3 (DOK 2)**
	97	2.3 Graphing Calculator Activity	**MA-HS-5.1.1 (DOK 2), MA-HS-5.1.8 (DOK 2), MA-HS-5.3.3 (DOK 2)**
15	98–104	2.4 Write Equations of Lines	**MA-HS-3.1.5 (DOK 2), MA-HS-5.1.1 (DOK 2), MA-HS-5.3.3 (DOK 2)**
	105	2.4 Problem Solving Workshop	**MA-HS-5.1.1 (DOK 2), MA-HS-5.3.3 (DOK 2)**
	106	Mixed Review for 2.1–2.4	**MA-HS-5.1.1 (DOK 2), MA-HS-5.1.5 (DOK 2), MA-HS-5.3.3 (DOK 2)**
16	107–111	2.5 Model Direct Variation	**MA-HS-1.4.1 (DOK 2), MA-HS-5.1.1 (DOK 2), MA-HS-5.1.3, MA-HS-5.1.7, MA-HS-5.3.3 (DOK 2)**
17	112–120	2.6 Draw Scatter Plots and Best-Fitting Lines	**MA-HS-4.1.1 (DOK 3), MA-HS-4.1.2 (DOK 2), MA-HS-4.2.1 (DOK 2), MA-HS-4.2.3 (DOK 3), MA-HS-5.1.1 (DOK 2), MA-HS-5.1.7, MA-HS-5.3.3 (DOK 2)**
18	121–129	2.7 Use Absolute Value Functions and Transformations	**MA-HS-2.1.3 (DOK 3), MA-HS-5.1.1 (DOK 2), MA-HS-5.1.8 (DOK 2), MA-HS-5.2.1 (DOK 1), MA-HS-5.3.3 (DOK 2)**
	130–131	2.7 Extension: Use Piecewise Functions	**MA-HS-5.1.1 (DOK 2), MA-HS-5.1.2, MA-HS-5.1.5 (DOK 2), MA-HS-5.3.3 (DOK 2)**
19	132–138	2.8 Graph Linear Inequalities in Two Variables	**MA-HS-2.1.3 (DOK 3), MA-HS-5.1.1 (DOK 2), MA-HS-5.1.8 (DOK 2), MA-HS-5.3.3 (DOK 2)**
20	139	Mixed Review for 2.5–2.8	**MA-HS-4.1.2 (DOK 2), MA-HS-5.1.1 (DOK 2), MA-HS-5.1.7, MA-HS-5.3.3 (DOK 2)**
21	140–144	Chapter Summary and Review	**MA-HS-3.3.1 (DOK 2), MA-HS-4.1.2 (DOK 2), MA-HS-4.2.3 (DOK 3), MA-HS-5.1.1 (DOK 2), MA-HS-5.1.3, MA-HS-5.1.5 (DOK 2), MA-HS-5.1.7, MA-HS-5.1.8 (DOK 2), MA-HS-5.3.3 (DOK 2)**
22	145	Chapter Test	**MA-HS-3.3.1 (DOK 2), MA-HS-4.2.3 (DOK 3), MA-HS-5.1.1 (DOK 2), MA-HS-5.1.3, MA-HS-5.1.5 (DOK 2), MA-HS-5.1.8 (DOK 2), MA-HS-5.3.3 (DOK 2)**
23	146–149	Test Preparation and Practice	**MA-HS-1.4.1 (DOK 2), MA-HS-3.3.1 (DOK 2), MA-HS-5.1.1 (DOK 2), MA-HS-5.1.5 (DOK 2), MA-HS-5.1.7, MA-HS-5.3.3 (DOK 2)**
24	152–158	3.1 Solve Linear Systems by Graphing	**MA-HS-1.2.1, MA-HS-3.1.7 (DOK 2), MA-HS-5.1.1 (DOK 2), MA-HS-5.3.3 (DOK 2), MA-HS-5.3.4 (DOK 3)**
	159	3.1 Graphing Calculator Activity	**MA-HS-5.3.4 (DOK 3)**

Day	Pages	Lesson or Feature	Kentucky Standards
25	160–167	3.2 Solve Linear Systems Algebraically	MA-HS-5.1.5 (DOK 2), MA-HS-5.3.4 (DOK 3)
26	168–173 174–176	3.3 Graph Systems of Linear Inequalities 3.3 Extension: Use Linear Programming	MA-HS-1.4.1 (DOK 2), MA-HS-5.3.5
27	177–185 186	3.4 Solve Systems of Linear Equations in Three Variables Mixed Review for 3.1–3.4	MA-HS-3.3.1 (DOK 2) MA-HS-5.3.4 (DOK 3)
28	187–193 194	3.5 Perform Basic Matrix Operations 3.5 Graphing Calculator Activity	MA-HS-4.1.3, MA-HS-5.1.5 (DOK 2), MA-HS-5.3.5 MA-HS-4.1.3
29	195–202	3.6 Multiply Matrices	MA-HS-1.4.1 (DOK 2), MA-HS-2.1.3 (DOK 3), MA-HS-4.1.3, MA-HS-5.1.5 (DOK 2)
30	203–209	3.7 Evaluate Determinants and Apply Cramer's Rule	MA-HS-2.2.1, MA-HS-3.1.9 (DOK 2), MA-HS-3.3.1 (DOK 2), MA-HS-5.3.1 (DOK 2), MA-HS-5.3.4 (DOK 3)
31, 32	210–217 218–219 220	3.8 Use Inverse Matrices to Solve Linear Systems 3.8 Problem Solving Workshop Mixed Review for 3.5–3.8	MA-HS-5.3.1 (DOK 2), MA-HS-5.3.4 (DOK 3)
33	221–226	Chapter Summary and Review	MA-HS-4.1.3, MA-HS-5.3.4 (DOK 3), MA-HS-5.3.5
34	227	Chapter Test	MA-HS-5.3.4 (DOK 3), MA-HS-5.3.5
35	228–231	Test Preparation and Practice	MA-HS-3.3.1 (DOK 2), MA-HS-4.2.3 (DOK 3), MA-HS-5.3.4 (DOK 3), MA-HS-5.3.5
36	232–233	Cumulative Review, Chapters 1–3	MA-HS-3.3.1 (DOK 2), MA-HS-4.2.3 (DOK 3), MA-HS-5.1.1 (DOK 2), MA-HS-5.1.3, MA-HS-5.1.5 (DOK 2), MA-HS-5.1.7, MA-HS-5.2.1 (DOK 1), MA-HS-5.3.1 (DOK 2), MA-HS-5.3.2, MA-HS-5.3.3 (DOK 2), MA-HS-5.3.4 (DOK 3), MA-HS-5.3.5
37	236–243 244	4.1 Graph Quadratic Functions in Standard Form 4.1 Graphing Calculator Activity	MA-HS-5.1.1 (DOK 2), MA-HS-5.1.3, MA-HS-5.1.5 (DOK 2), MA-HS-5.1.8 (DOK 2), MA-HS-5.3.3 (DOK 2), MA-HS-5.3.6 (DOK 2) MA-HS-5.1.1 (DOK 2), MA-HS-5.1.5 (DOK 2)
38	245–251	4.2 Graph Quadratic Functions in Vertex or Intercept Form	MA-HS-1.4.1 (DOK 2), MA-HS-5.1.1 (DOK 2), MA-HS-5.1.3, MA-HS-5.1.5 (DOK 2), MA-HS-5.3.6 (DOK 2)
39	252–258	4.3 Solve $x^2 + bx + c = 0$ by Factoring	MA-HS-5.1.5 (DOK 2), MA-HS-5.2.3 (DOK 2), MA-HS-5.2.4, MA-HS-5.3.4 (DOK 3), MA-HS-5.3.6 (DOK 2)
40	259–265	4.4 Solve $ax^2 + bx + c = 0$ by Factoring	MA-HS-1.4.1 (DOK 2), MA-HS-5.1.1 (DOK 2), MA-HS-5.1.3, MA-HS-5.1.5 (DOK 2), MA-HS-5.3.6 (DOK 2)
41	266–271 272–273 274	4.5 Solve Quadratic Equations by Finding Square Roots 4.5 Problem Solving Workshop Mixed Review for 4.1–4.5	MA-HS-5.1.3, MA-HS-5.3.3 (DOK 2), MA-HS-5.3.6 (DOK 2) MA-HS-5.3.6 (DOK 2) MA-HS-1.4.1 (DOK 2), MA-HS-5.3.3 (DOK 2), MA-HS-5.3.6 (DOK 2)
42	275–282	4.6 Perform Operations with Complex Numbers	MA-HS-5.1.5 (DOK 2), MA-HS-5.3.3 (DOK 2)
43	283–291	4.7 Complete the Square	MA-HS-3.3.1 (DOK 2), MA-HS-5.3.3 (DOK 2), MA-HS-5.3.6 (DOK 2)
44	292–299	4.8 Use the Quadratic Formula and the Discriminant	MA-HS-5.1.3, MA-HS-5.3.1 (DOK 2), MA-HS-5.3.4 (DOK 3), MA-HS-5.3.6 (DOK 2)
45	300–307	4.9 Graph and Solve Quadratic Inequalities	MA-HS-5.3.3 (DOK 2)
46, 47	308–315 316	4.10 Write Quadratic Functions and Models Mixed Review for 4.6–4.10	MA-HS-5.1.1 (DOK 2), MA-HS-5.3.3 (DOK 2), MA-HS-5.3.6 (DOK 2) MA-HS-5.1.5 (DOK 2), MA-HS-5.3.1 (DOK 2), MA-HS-5.3.3 (DOK 2), MA-HS-5.3.6 (DOK 2)
48	317–322	Chapter Summary and Review	MA-HS-5.1.1 (DOK 2), MA-HS-5.1.5 (DOK 2), MA-HS-5.3.6 (DOK 2)
49	323	Chapter Test	MA-HS-5.1.1 (DOK 2), MA-HS-5.2.3 (DOK 2), MA-HS-5.2.4, MA-HS-5.3.6 (DOK 2)
50	324–327	Test Preparation and Practice	MA-HS-5.1.3, MA-HS-5.1.5 (DOK 2), MA-HS-5.3.2, MA-HS-5.3.6 (DOK 2)
51	330–335	5.1 Use Properties of Exponents	MA-HS-1.1.3, MA-HS-1.2.1, MA-HS-2.1.1 (DOK 2), MA-HS-2.1.2 (DOK 3), MA-HS-3.1.3 (DOK 2), MA-HS-5.2.1 (DOK 1)
52	336–344 345	5.2 Evaluate and Graph Polynomial Functions 5.2 Graphing Calculator Activity	MA-HS-5.1.1 (DOK 2), MA-HS-5.3.1 (DOK 2), MA-HS-5.3.3 (DOK 2)
53	346–352	5.3 Add, Subtract, and Multiply Polynomials	MA-HS-2.1.1 (DOK 2), MA-HS-3.1.6, MA-HS-5.1.1 (DOK 2), MA-HS-5.2.1 (DOK 1), MA-HS-5.2.3 (DOK 2), MA-HS-5.3.3 (DOK 2)
54	353–359 360–361	5.4 Factor and Solve Polynomial Equations 5.4 Problem Solving Workshop	MA-HS-5.2.3 (DOK 2)
55	362–368 369	5.5 Apply the Remainder and Factor Theorems Mixed Review for 5.1–5.5	MA-HS-5.1.5 (DOK 2), MA-HS-5.3.4 (DOK 3) MA-HS-1.1.3, MA-HS-5.1.1 (DOK 2), MA-HS-5.3.6 (DOK 2)
56	370–377 378	5.6 Find Rational Zeros 5.6 Spreadsheet Activity	MA-HS-1.4.1 (DOK 2), MA-HS-5.2.1 (DOK 1)

KENTUCKY STANDARDS PACING GUIDE

Day	Pages	Lesson or Feature	Kentucky Standards
57	379–386	5.7 Apply the Fundamental Theorem of Algebra	**MA-HS-5.3.4 (DOK 3)**
58	387–392	5.8 Analyze Graphs of Polynomial Functions	**MA-HS-1.2.1, MA-HS-5.1.8 (DOK 2)**
59, 60	393–399	5.9 Write Polynomial Functions and Models	**MA-HS-5.1.1 (DOK 2), MA-HS-5.1.3, MA-HS-5.3.4 (DOK 3), MA-HS-5.3.6 (DOK 2)**
	400	Mixed Review for 5.6–5.9	
61	401–406	Chapter Summary and Review	**MA-HS-1.1.3, MA-HS-5.1.1 (DOK 2), MA-HS-5.2.1 (DOK 1), MA-HS-5.2.3 (DOK 2)**
62	407	Chapter Test	**MA-HS-2.1.1 (DOK 2), MA-HS-5.1.1 (DOK 2), MA-HS-5.2.3 (DOK 2)**
63	408–411	Test Preparation and Practice	**MA-HS-5.2.1 (DOK 1)**
64	414–419	6.1 Evaluate *n*th Roots and Use Rational Exponents	**MA-HS-1.2.1, MA-HS-2.1.3 (DOK 3), MA-HS-5.2.1 (DOK 1)**
65	420–427	6.2 Apply Properties of Rational Exponents	**MA-HS-2.1.1 (DOK 2), MA-HS-2.1.2 (DOK 3), MA-HS-3.3.1 (DOK 2), MA-HS-5.3.1 (DOK 2)**
66	428–434	6.3 Perform Function Operations and Composition	**MA-HS-5.1.1 (DOK 2), MA-HS-5.2.1 (DOK 1), MA-HS-5.3.3 (DOK 2)**
67	435	6.3 Graphing Calculator Activity	
	436	Mixed Review for 6.1–6.3	**MA-HS-2.1.1 (DOK 2)**
68	437–445	6.4 Use Inverse Functions	**MA-HS-5.1.5 (DOK 2), MA-HS-5.3.4 (DOK 3)**
69	446–451	6.5 Graph Square Root and Cube Root Functions	**MA-HS-3.1.12 (DOK 3), MA-HS-5.1.1 (DOK 2), MA-HS-5.1.3, MA-HS-5.3.3 (DOK 2)**
70, 71	452–459	6.6 Solve Radical Equations	**MA-HS-5.1.5 (DOK 2), MA-HS-5.3.3 (DOK 2)**
	460–461	6.6 Problem Solving Workshop	
	462–463	6.6 Extension: Solve Radical Inequalities	
	464	Mixed Review for 6.4–6.6	**MA-HS-1.4.1 (DOK 2), MA-HS-5.3.3 (DOK 2)**
72	465–468	Chapter Summary and Review	
73	469	Chapter Test	
74	470–473	Test Preparation and Practice	**MA-HS-5.1.5 (DOK 2)**
75	474–475	Cumulative Review, Chapters 1–6	**MA-HS-5.1.1 (DOK 2), MA-HS-5.2.1 (DOK 1), MA-HS-5.2.3 (DOK 2), MA-HS-5.3.1 (DOK 2), MA-HS-5.3.3 (DOK 2), MA-HS-5.3.4 (DOK 3), MA-HS-5.3.6 (DOK 2)**
76	478–485	7.1 Graph Exponential Growth Functions	**MA-HS-1.2.1, MA-HS-5.1.1 (DOK 2), MA-HS-5.1.3, MA-HS-5.1.4, MA-HS-5.1.8 (DOK 2)**
77	486–491	7.2 Graph Exponential Decay Functions	**MA-HS-1.2.1, MA-HS-1.4.1 (DOK 2), MA-HS-3.2.1 (DOK 3), MA-HS-5.1.1 (DOK 2), MA-HS-5.1.4**
78	492–498	7.3 Use Functions Involving *e*	**MA-HS-1.2.1, MA-HS-3.1.5 (DOK 2), MA-HS-5.1.1 (DOK 2)**
79	499–505	7.4 Evaluate Logarithms and Graph Logarithmic Functions	**MA-HS-5.1.3**
	506	Mixed Review for 7.1–7.4	**MA-HS-5.1.1 (DOK 2), MA-HS-5.1.4**
80	507–513	7.5 Apply Properties of Logarithms	**MA-HS-2.1.3 (DOK 3), MA-HS-5.1.5 (DOK 2)**
	514	7.5 Graphing Calculator Activity	
81	515–522	7.6 Solve Exponential and Logarithmic Equations	**MA-HS-3.1.3 (DOK 2), MA-HS-5.1.8 (DOK 2)**
	523–525	7.6 Problem Solving Workshop	
	526–527	7.6 Extension: Exponential and Logarithmic Inequalities	
82	528–536	7.7 Write and Apply Exponential and Power Functions	**MA-HS-5.1.1 (DOK 2), MA-HS-5.1.4, MA-HS-5.3.3 (DOK 2)**
	537	Mixed Review for 7.5–7.7	**MA-HS-5.1.1 (DOK 2), MA-HS-5.1.4**
83	538–542	Chapter Summary and Review	**MA-HS-5.1.1 (DOK 2), MA-HS-5.1.8 (DOK 2)**
84	543	Chapter Test	**MA-HS-1.2.1, MA-HS-5.1.1 (DOK 2), MA-HS-5.1.4**
85	544–547	Test Preparation and Practice	**MA-HS-5.1.4, MA-HS-5.1.5 (DOK 2)**
86	550–557	8.1 Model Inverse and Joint Variation	**MA-HS-1.2.1, MA-HS-2.1.3 (DOK 3), MA-HS-3.1.9 (DOK 2), MA-HS-5.1.3, MA-HS-5.1.7**
87	558–563	8.2 Graph Simple Rational Functions	**MA-HS-5.1.1 (DOK 2), MA-HS-5.1.3, MA-HS-5.3.3 (DOK 2)**
	564	8.2 Graphing Calculator Activity	
88	565–571	8.3 Graph General Rational Functions	**MA-HS-5.1.3, MA-HS-5.1.7**
	572	Mixed Review for 8.1–8.3	**MA-HS-5.1.7**
89	573–580	8.4 Multiply and Divide Rational Expressions	**MA-HS-1.4.1 (DOK 2), MA-HS-2.1.1 (DOK 2), MA-HS-5.2.3 (DOK 2)**
	581	8.4 Graphing Calculator Activity	
90	582–588	8.5 Add and Subtract Rational Expressions	**MA-HS-2.1.3 (DOK 3), MA-HS-5.2.5 (DOK 1), MA-HS-5.3.4 (DOK 3)**
91	589–595	8.6 Solve Rational Equations	**MA-HS-3.1.3 (DOK 2), MA-HS-3.1.5 (DOK 2), MA-HS-5.1.5 (DOK 2), MA-HS-5.3.3 (DOK 2)**
	596–597	8.6 Problem Solving Workshop	

Day	Pages	Lesson or Feature	Kentucky Standards
92	598–600 601	8.6 Extension: Solve Rational Inequalities Mixed Review for 8.4–8.6	
93	602–606	Chapter Summary and Review	**MA-HS-5.1.7**
94	607	Chapter Test	**MA-HS-5.1.7**
94	608–611	Test Preparation and Practice	**MA-HS-5.1.1 (DOK 2), MA-HS-5.1.7, MA-HS-5.2.3 (DOK 2), MA-HS-5.3.3 (DOK 2)**
95	614–619	9.1 Apply the Distance and Midpoint Formulas	**MA-HS-2.1.1 (DOK 2), MA-HS-2.2.1, MA-HS-3.3.1 (DOK 2), MA-HS-5.1.5 (DOK 2)**
96	620–625	9.2 Graph and Write Equations of Parabolas	**MA-HS-2.1.3 (DOK 3), MA-HS-2.2.1, MA-HS-5.3.1 (DOK 2)**
97	626–632 633	9.3 Graph and Write Equations of Circles 9.3 Graphing Calculator Activity	**MA-HS-2.2.1, MA-HS-3.3.1 (DOK 2), MA-HS-5.3.4 (DOK 3)**
98	634–639 640 641	9.4 Graph and Write Equations of Ellipses 9.4 Problem Solving Workshop Mixed Review for 9.1–9.4	**MA-HS-2.1.1 (DOK 2), MA-HS-5.2.1 (DOK 1)**
99	642–648	9.5 Graph and Write Equations of Hyperbolas	
100	649–657	9.6 Translate and Classify Conic Sections	**MA-HS-3.1.5 (DOK 2)**
101, 102	658–664 665–666 667	9.7 Solve Quadratic Systems 9.7 Extension: Determine Eccentricity of Conic Sections Mixed Review for 9.5–9.7	**MA-HS-5.3.1 (DOK 2), MA-HS-5.3.3 (DOK 2)**
103	668–672	Chapter Summary and Review	**MA-HS-3.3.1 (DOK 2)**
104	673	Chapter Test	
105	674–677	Test Preparation and Practice	**MA-HS-3.3.1 (DOK 2)**
106	678–679	Cumulative Review, Chapters 1–9	**MA-HS-1.4.1 (DOK 2), MA-HS-3.3.1 (DOK 2), MA-HS-5.1.4, MA-HS-5.1.7, MA-HS-5.3.1 (DOK 2), MA-HS-5.3.3 (DOK 2), MA-HS-5.3.4 (DOK 3), MA-HS-5.3.6 (DOK 2)**
107	682–689	10.1 Apply the Counting Principle and Permutations	**MA-HS-1.4.1 (DOK 2), MA-HS-4.4.2, MA-HS-5.3.6 (DOK 2)**
108	690–697	10.2 Use Combinations and Binomial Theorem	**MA-HS-4.4.2, MA-HS-5.3.4 (DOK 3)**
109	698–704 705	10.3 Define and Use Probability Mixed Review for 10.1–10.3	**MA-HS-3.3.1 (DOK 2), MA-HS-4.4.1 (DOK 3), MA-HS-4.4.3 MA-HS-4.4.1 (DOK 3), MA-HS-4.4.2, MA-HS-4.4.3**
110	706–713 714 715–716	10.4 Find Probabilities of Disjoint and Overlapping Events 10.4 Problem Solving Workshop 10.4 Extension: Apply Set Theory	**MA-HS-4.4.1 (DOK 3), MA-HS-4.4.3, MA-HS-5.3.1 (DOK 2) MA-HS-4.4.3, MA-HS-4.4.4**
111	717–723	10.5 Find Probabilities of Independent and Dependent Events	**MA-HS-4.4.1 (DOK 3), MA-HS-4.4.3, MA-HS-5.1.5 (DOK 2), MA-HS-5.3.6 (DOK 2)**
112, 113	724–730 731 732	10.6 Construct and Interpret Binomial Distributions 10.6 Graphing Calculator Activity Mixed Review for 10.4–10.6	**MA-HS-4.2.1 (DOK 2), MA-HS-4.4.1 (DOK 3), MA-HS-4.4.3, MA-HS-5.1.1 (DOK 2), MA-HS-5.3.1 (DOK 2), MA-HS-5.3.3 (DOK 2) MA-HS-4.2.1 (DOK 2) MA-HS-4.4.1 (DOK 3), MA-HS-4.4.3**
114	733–736	Chapter Summary and Review	**MA-HS-4.2.1 (DOK 2), MA-HS-4.4.1 (DOK 3), MA-HS-4.4.2, MA-HS-4.4.3**
115	737	Chapter Test	**MA-HS-4.4.1 (DOK 3), MA-HS-4.4.2, MA-HS-4.4.3**
116	738–741	Test Preparation and Practice	**MA-HS-4.4.1 (DOK 3), MA-HS-4.4.2, MA-HS-4.4.3**
117	744–749 750	11.1 Find Measures of Central Tendency and Dispersion 11.1 Graphing Calculator Activity	**MA-HS-3.3.1 (DOK 2), MA-HS-4.1.1 (DOK 3), MA-HS-4.2.1 (DOK 2), MA-HS-5.1.1 (DOK 2), MA-HS-5.1.8 (DOK 2), MA-HS-5.3.3 (DOK 2) MA-HS-4.1.1 (DOK 3), MA-HS-4.2.1 (DOK 2)**
118	751–755 756	11.2 Apply Transformations to Data Mixed Review for 11.1–11.2	**MA-HS-3.1.12 (DOK 3), MA-HS-4.2.1 (DOK 2), MA-HS-4.4.2 MA-HS-4.1.1 (DOK 3), MA-HS-4.2.1 (DOK 2)**
119	757–762	11.3 Use Normal Distributions	**MA-HS-4.1.1 (DOK 3), MA-HS-4.2.2, MA-HS-5.2.2**
120	763–765	11.3 Extension: Approximate Binomial Distributions and Test Hypotheses	**MA-HS-4.1.1 (DOK 3), MA-HS-4.2.2**
121	766–771 772–773	11.4 Select and Draw Conclusions from Samples 11.4 Extension: Design Surveys and Experiments	**MA-HS-3.1.5 (DOK 2), MA-HS-4.3.1 (DOK 2), MA-HS-5.3.6 (DOK 2) MA-HS-4.3.2**
122, 123	774–780 781 782	11.5 Choose the Best Model for Two-Variable Data 11.5 Problem Solving Workshop Mixed Review for 11.3–11.5	**MA-HS-2.1.1 (DOK 2), MA-HS-4.1.2 (DOK 2), MA-HS-4.2.2, MA-HS-4.2.3 (DOK 3), MA-HS-5.3.3 (DOK 2) MA-HS-1.2.1, MA-HS-4.1.2 (DOK 2), MA-HS-4.2.3 (DOK 3) MA-HS-4.2.1 (DOK 2), MA-HS-4.2.3 (DOK 3), MA-HS-4.3.1 (DOK 2)**
124	783–786	Chapter Summary and Review	**MA-HS-4.1.1 (DOK 3), MA-HS-4.1.2 (DOK 2), MA-HS-4.2.1 (DOK 2), MA-HS-4.2.2, MA-HS-4.2.3 (DOK 3), MA-HS-4.3.1 (DOK 2)**

KENTUCKY STANDARDS PACING GUIDE

Day	Pages	Lesson or Feature	Kentucky Standards
125	787	Chapter Test	MA-HS-4.1.1 (DOK 3), MA-HS-4.2.1 (DOK 2), MA-HS-4.2.2, MA-HS-4.2.3 (DOK 3)
126	788–791	Test Preparation and Practice	MA-HS-4.1.2 (DOK 2), MA-HS-4.2.1 (DOK 2), MA-HS-4.2.3 (DOK 3), MA-HS-4.3.1 (DOK 2)
127	794–800 801	12.1 Define and Use Sequences and Series 12.1 Graphing Calculator Activity	MA-HS-3.3.1 (DOK 2), MA-HS-5.1.1 (DOK 2), MA-HS-5.3.3 (DOK 2)
128	802–809	12.2 Analyze Arithmetic Sequences and Series	MA-HS-1.3.2 (DOK 3), MA-HS-3.3.1 (DOK 2), MA-HS-4.4.1 (DOK 3)
129	810–817	12.3 Analyze Geometric Sequences and Series	MA-HS-1.3.2 (DOK 3), MA-HS-1.3.3, MA-HS-1.3.4, MA-HS-5.1.8 (DOK 2), MA-HS-5.3.4 (DOK 3)
130	818	Mixed Review for 12.1–12.3	MA-HS-1.3.2 (DOK 3), MA-HS-1.3.3
131	819–825	12.4 Find Sums of Infinite Geometric Series	MA-HS-2.1.3 (DOK 3)
132	826–833 834–835 836–837	12.5 Use Recursive Rules with Sequences and Functions 12.5 Problem Solving Workshop 12.5 Extension: Prove Statements Using Mathematical Induction	MA-HS-5.3.1 (DOK 2)
133	838	Mixed Review for 12.4–12.5	MA-HS-1.3.2 (DOK 3)
134	839–842	Chapter Summary and Review	MA-HS-1.3.2 (DOK 3), MA-HS-1.3.3
135	843	Chapter Test	MA-HS-1.3.2 (DOK 3), MA-HS-1.3.3
136	844–847	Test Preparation and Practice	MA-HS-1.3.2 (DOK 3), MA-HS-1.3.3
137	848–849	Cumulative Review, Chapters 1–12	MA-HS-1.3.2 (DOK 3), MA-HS-1.3.3, MA-HS-1.4.1 (DOK 2), MA-HS-2.2.1, MA-HS-4.1.1 (DOK 3), MA-HS-4.2.1 (DOK 2), MA-HS-4.4.2, MA-HS-5.1.1 (DOK 2), MA-HS-5.1.7, MA-HS-5.3.3 (DOK 2), MA-HS-5.3.6 (DOK 2)
138	852–858	13.1 Use Trigonometry with Right Triangles	MA-HS-2.1.3 (DOK 3), MA-HS-2.2.1, MA-HS-3.3.1 (DOK 2), MA-HS-5.3.6 (DOK 2)
139	859–865	13.2 Define General Angles and Use Radian Measure	MA-HS-2.1.3 (DOK 3), MA-HS-2.2.1, MA-HS-5.1.1 (DOK 2), MA-HS-5.3.3 (DOK 2)
140	866–872	13.3 Evaluate Trigonometric Functions of Any Angle	MA-HS-1.2.1, MA-HS-2.1.3 (DOK 3), MA-HS-2.2.1, MA-HS-5.1.5 (DOK 2)
141	873	Mixed Review for 13.1–13.3	MA-HS-2.1.3 (DOK 3), MA-HS-2.2.1
142	874–880	13.4 Evaluate Inverse Trigonometric Functions	MA-HS-2.1.3 (DOK 3), MA-HS-2.2.1, MA-HS-5.1.5 (DOK 2)
143	881 882–888	13.5 Geometry Software Activity 13.5 Apply the Law of Sines	 MA-HS-1.2.1, MA-HS-2.2.1
144	889–894 895	13.6 Apply the Law of Cosines 13.6 Problem Solving Workshop	MA-HS-2.1.1 (DOK 2), MA-HS-2.2.1, MA-HS-3.3.1 (DOK 2), MA-HS-5.3.3 (DOK 2) MA-HS-2.2.1
145	896	Mixed Review for 13.4–13.6	MA-HS-2.1.3 (DOK 3), MA-HS-2.2.1
146	897–900	Chapter Summary and Review	MA-HS-2.1.3 (DOK 3)
147	901	Chapter Test	MA-HS-2.1.3 (DOK 3), MA-HS-2.2.1
148	902–905	Test Preparation and Practice	MA-HS-1.1.3, MA-HS-1.2.1, MA-HS-2.1.3 (DOK 3), MA-HS-2.2.1
149	908–914	14.1 Graph Sine, Cosine, and Tangent Functions	MA-HS-2.2.1, MA-HS-3.3.1 (DOK 2)
150	915–922	14.2 Translate and Reflect Trigonometric Graphs	MA-HS-2.1.1 (DOK 2), MA-HS-4.2.1 (DOK 2)
151	923–930	14.3 Verify Trigonometric Identities	MA-HS-3.2.1 (DOK 3)
152	931–937 938–939	14.4 Solve Trigonometric Equations 14.4 Problem Solving Workshop	MA-HS-5.1.1 (DOK 2), MA-HS-5.1.5 (DOK 2), MA-HS-5.3.3 (DOK 2)
153	940	Mixed Review for 14.1–14.4	
154	941–947 948	14.5 Write Trigonometric Functions and Models 14.5 CBL Activity	MA-HS-3.1.11
155	949–954	14.6 Apply Sum and Difference Formulas	MA-HS-5.3.1 (DOK 2)
156	955–962	14.7 Apply Double-Angle and Half-Angle Formulas	MA-HS-3.1.3 (DOK 2)
157	963	Mixed Review for 14.5–14.7	
158	964–968	Chapter Summary and Review	
159	969	Chapter Test	
160	970–973	Test Preparation and Practice	

Kentucky Core Content for Mathematics Assessment Version 4.1 (CCA 4.1) High School

Bold – State Assessment Content Standard
Italics – Supporting Content Standard
Plain Text – ADP Benchmarks Supporting Content Standard

Number Properties and Operations

High school students should enter high school with a strong background in rational numbers and numerical operations and expand this to real numbers. Solving quadratic equations produces a working knowledge of complex numbers. This becomes the foundation for algebra and working with algebraic symbols. They understand large and small numbers and their representations, powers and roots. They compare and contrast properties of numbers and number systems and develop strategies to estimate the results of operations on real numbers. Students will use and understand the limitations of graphing calculators and computer spreadsheets appropriately as learning tools.

Standard	Description	Program	Pages
NUMBER SENSE			
MA-HS-1.1.1	*Students will compare real numbers using order relations (less than, greater than, equal to) and represent problems using real numbers.*	HOLT ALGEBRA 1	Z24, 18, 24, 29, 35, S50
		LARSON ALGEBRA 1	909
		LARSON GEOMETRY	328–334
		LARSON ALGEBRA 2	2–3, 6, 8, 16
MA-HS-1.1.2	*Students will demonstrate the relationships between different subsets of the real number system.*	HOLT ALGEBRA 1	32–37, 59, 64, 98
		LARSON ALGEBRA 1	64–65, 120
		LARSON ALGEBRA 2	2
MA-HS-1.1.3	*Students will use scientific notation to express very large or very small quantities.*	HOLT ALGEBRA 1	452–457
		LARSON ALGEBRA 1	512–518, 519
		LARSON ALGEBRA 2	333, 334, 369, 402, 904, 982
ESTIMATION			
MA-HS-1.2.1	*Students will estimate solutions to problems with real numbers (including very large and very small quantities) in both real-world and mathematical problems, and use the estimations to check for reasonable computational results.*	HOLT ALGEBRA 1	33, 79, 88, 89, 95, 110, 122, 128, 130, 138, 139, 142, 178, 255, 268, 307, 316, 396, 499, 570, 616, 638, 717, 798
		LARSON ALGEBRA 1	111, 114, 115, 252, 336–341, 342, 348, 653, 655, 659, 805
		LARSON GEOMETRY	32, 692
		LARSON ALGEBRA 2	91, 153, 156, 335, 390, 484, 485, 488, 490, 491, 494, 497, 557, 781, 870, 887
NUMBER OPERATIONS			
MA-HS-1.3.1	**Students will solve real-world and mathematical problems to specified accuracy levels by simplifying expressions with real numbers involving addition, subtraction, multiplication, division, absolute value, integer exponents, roots (square, cube) and factorials. DOK 2**	HOLT ALGEBRA 1	46–51, 59, 65, 98, 173, 208, 363, 571, 743
		LARSON ALGEBRA 1	2–7, 8–12, 13, 66–70, 73, 74–79, 80–84, 85, 87, 88–93, 103–108, 110–116, 488, 489–494, 495–501, 502, 503–508, 509–510, 719–726, 914, 915
		LARSON GEOMETRY	870–872, 874
		LARSON ALGEBRA 2	983
MA-HS-1.3.2	**Students will: • describe and extend arithmetic and geometric sequences; • determine a specific term of a sequence given an explicit formula; • determine an explicit rule for the *n*th term of an arithmetic sequence and • apply sequences to solve real-world problems. DOK 3**	HOLT ALGEBRA 1	272–277, 279, 283, 411, 466, 529, 766–771, 778
		LARSON ALGEBRA 1	14, 309–310, 539–540
		LARSON GEOMETRY	72, 75
		LARSON ALGEBRA 2	802–804, 805, 806, 807, 808, 809, 810, 813, 814, 815, 816, 817, 818
MA-HS-1.3.3	*Students will write an explicit rule for the* n*th term of a geometric sequence.*	HOLT ALGEBRA 1	766–771, 778, 797, 865
		LARSON ALGEBRA 1	540
		LARSON ALGEBRA 2	811–812, 814, 815, 816, 817, 818

MA-HS-1.3.4	Students will recognize and solve problems that can be modeled using a finite geometric series, such as home mortgage problems and other compound interest problems.	**HOLT ALGEBRA 1** **LARSON ALGEBRA 1** **LARSON ALGEBRA 2**	782, 785, 787, 803 523,527 813, 815, 816, 817
RATIOS AND PROPORTIONAL REASONING			
MA-HS-1.4.1	**Students will apply ratios, percents and proportional reasoning to solve real-world problems (e.g., those involving slope and rate, percent of increase and decrease) and will explain how slope determines a rate of change in linear functions representing real-world problems. DOK 2**	**HOLT ALGEBRA 1** **LARSON ALGEBRA 1** **LARSON GEOMETRY** **LARSON ALGEBRA 2**	121–126, 132, 154, 179, 251, 302, 310–317, 333, 369, 466, 499, 788, 872 162, 164, 166–167, 170, 172, 180– 181, 238, 240–241 177, 349, 362, 366, 369 5, 7, 8, 9, 24, 40, 82, 83, 85, 87, 88, 111, 173, 202, 251, 265, 274, 377, 491, 580, 689
PROPERTIES OF NUMBERS AND OPERATIONS			
MA-HS-1.5.1	*Students will identify real number properties (commutative properties of addition and multiplication, associative properties of addition and multiplication, distributive property of multiplication over addition and subtraction, identity properties of addition and multiplication and inverse properties of addition and multiplication) when used to justify a given step in simplifying an expression or solving an equation.*	**HOLT ALGEBRA 1** **LARSON ALGEBRA 1** **LARSON GEOMETRY** **LARSON ALGEBRA 2**	21, 46, 79, 86, 98, 165, 174, 180, 181 75–76, 89, 103 105–111 3, 6, 12, 13, 20, 62, 65
MA-HS-1.5.2	*Students will use equivalence relations (reflexive, symmetric, transitive).*	**LARSON GEOMETRY**	107–108, 109

Measurement

High school students continue to measure and estimate measurements including fractions and decimals. They use formulas to find surface areas and volumes. They use US Customary and metric units of measurement. They use the Pythagorean theorem and other right triangle relationships to solve realistic problems.

MEASURING PHYSICAL ATTRIBUTES			
MA-HS-2.1.1	**Students will determine the surface area and volume of right rectangular prisms, pyramids, cylinders, cones and spheres in real-world and mathematical problems. DOK 2**	**HOLT ALGEBRA 1** **LARSON ALGEBRA 1** **LARSON GEOMETRY** **LARSON ALGEBRA 2**	500, 779, S66, S67 927–928 802, 803–809, 810–817, 819–825, 826–827, 828, 829–836, 837, 838–845 335, 350, 427, 436, 580, 619, 993
MA-HS-2.1.2	**Students will describe how a change in one or more dimensions of a geometric figure affects the perimeter, area and volume of the figure. DOK 3**	**HOLT ALGEBRA 1** **LARSON ALGEBRA 1** **LARSON GEOMETRY** **LARSON ALGEBRA 2**	53, 123, 779 282, 764 737, 741, 846, 848–853 47, 332, 335, 427
MA-HS-2.1.3	**Students will apply definitions and properties of right triangle relationships (right triangle trigonometry and the Pythagorean theorem) to determine length and angle measures to solve real-world and mathematical problems. DOK 3**	**HOLT ALGEBRA 1** **LARSON ALGEBRA 1** **LARSON GEOMETRY** **LARSON ALGEBRA 2**	641, 643, 807, S59, S68 736, 737–742, 753 432, 433–439, 440, 441–447, 457–464, 466–472, 473–480, 481–482, 483–489, 490–491 9, 40, 88, 129, 138, 138, 202, 419, 513, 557, 588, 625, 825, 850, 852–858, 865, 873, 877, 878, 879, 880, 896, 995
MA-HS-2.1.4	Students will apply special right triangles and the converse of the Pythagorean theorem to solve real-world problems.	**LARSON ALGEBRA 1** **LARSON GEOMETRY** **LARSON ALGEBRA 2**	739 445, 446, 463 995

SYSTEMS OF MEASUREMENTS			
MA-HS-2.2.1	*Students will continue to apply to both real-world and mathematical problems U.S. customary and metric systems of measurement.*	**HOLT ALGEBRA 1** **LARSON ALGEBRA 1** **LARSON GEOMETRY** **LARSON ALGEBRA 2**	122, 301, 345, 456, 562, 770, S53 924–928,929, A2–A3 53, 54, 63, 69, 177, 437, 475, 722, 767, 803–809, 810–817, 820–825, 829–836, 839–845, 850–851, A2–A3 5, 7–8, 208, 209 616, 618, 619, 622, 624, 625, 628, 855, 857–858, 862–865, 869–873, 879–880, 885, 887–888, 891, 893–896, 981, A2–A3

Geometry

High school students expand analysis of two-dimensional figures and three-dimensional objects. They translate figures in a coordinate plane. They extend work with congruent and similar figures, including proportionality.

SHAPES AND RELATIONSHIPS			
MA-HS-3.1.1	**Students will analyze and apply spatial relationships (not using Cartesian coordinates) among points, lines and planes (e.g., betweenness of points, midpoint, segment length, collinear, coplanar, parallel, perpendicular, skew). DOK 2**	**HOLT ALGEBRA 1** **LARSON GEOMETRY** **LARSON ALGEBRA 2**	S56 2–8, 10–13, 15–16, 19, 22, 81, 147–152, 153, 154–160 99, 102, 145, 148–149, 167, 258, 271, 723
MA-HS-3.1.2	Students will use spatial relationships to prove basic theorems.	**LARSON GEOMETRY**	118, 121, 129, 130, 137, 160, 168, 177, 196
MA-HS-3.1.3	**Students will analyze and apply angle relationships (e.g., linear pairs, vertical, complementary, supplementary, corresponding and alternate interior angles) in real-world and mathematical problems. DOK 2**	**HOLT ALGEBRA 1** **LARSON GEOMETRY** **LARSON ALGEBRA 2**	121, 681, S56, S57, S59 35–41, 59, 62, 64, 128, 132,137, 144, 149, 150–151, 154–160, 165, 170, 202, 203, 204, 206, 212 32, 335, 522, 595, 962, 994
MA-HS-3.1.4	Students will use angle relationships to prove basic theorems.	**LARSON GEOMETRY**	129, 130, 159, 168
MA-HS-3.1.5	**Students will classify and apply properties of two-dimensional geometric figures (e.g., number of sides, vertices, length of sides, sum of interior and exterior angle measures). DOK 2**	**HOLT ALGEBRA 1** **LARSON ALGEBRA 1** **LARSON GEOMETRY** **LARSON ALGEBRA 2**	S58, S63 919–920 42–47, 63–64 217–224, 239, 507–513, 515–521, 533–540, 542–549, 552–557, 910–911 58, 59, 104, 498, 595, 657, 771, 850
MA-HS-3.1.6	Students will know the definitions and basic properties of a circle and will use them to prove basic theorems and solve problems.	**HOLT ALGEBRA 1** **LARSON ALGEBRA 1** **LARSON GEOMETRY** **LARSON ALGEBRA 2**	S62 926 650, 651–658, 659–663, 664–670, 671, 672–679, 680–686, 687, 688, 689–695, 696 352, 992
MA-HS-3.1.7	**Students will solve real-world and mathematical problems by applying properties of triangles (e.g., Triangle Sum theorem and Isosceles Triangle theorems). DOK 2**	**LARSON GEOMETRY** **LARSON ALGEBRA 2**	216, 219–224, 248, 264–270 96, 158, 995
MA-HS-3.1.8	Students will use the properties of triangles to prove basic theorems.	**LARSON GEOMETRY**	223, 224, 269
MA-HS-3.1.9	**Students will classify and apply properties of three-dimensional geometric figures. DOK 2**	**HOLT ALGEBRA 1** **LARSON ALGEBRA 1** **LARSON GEOMETRY** **LARSON ALGEBRA 2**	S64 927–928 794–801 209, 557
MA-HS-3.1.10	*Students will describe the intersection of a plane with a three-dimensional figure.*	**LARSON GEOMETRY**	797,799, 800, 839, 842
MA-HS-3.1.11	Students will visualize solids and surfaces in three-dimensional space when given two-dimensional representations (e.g., nets, multiple views) and create two-dimensional representations for the surfaces of three-dimensional objects.	**HOLT ALGEBRA 1** **LARSON GEOMETRY** **LARSON ALGEBRA 2**	874–875, S67 792–793, 802, 805, 806, 811–812, 816, 828 947

MA-HS-3.1.12	**Students will apply the concepts of congruence and similarity to solve real-world and mathematical problems. DOK 3**	**HOLT ALGEBRA 1** **LARSON ALGEBRA 1** **LARSON GEOMETRY** **LARSON ALGEBRA 2**	S63 174–175 11–12, 26–27, 127, 138, 225–231, 283, 372–379, 380, 383, 449–456, 737–743, 744, 846, 847–853 16, 451, 755
MA-HS-3.1.13	Students will prove triangles congruent and similar.	**LARSON GEOMETRY**	230, 231, 240–246, 249–255, 260, 263, 386, 395, 429
TRANSFORMATIONS OF SHAPES			
MA-HS-3.2.1	**Students will identify and describe properties of and apply geometric transformations within a plane to solve real-world and mathematical problems. DOK 3**	**HOLT ALGEBRA 1** **LARSON ALGEBRA 1** **LARSON GEOMETRY** **LARSON ALGEBRA 2**	360, 616 213–214, 396–397, 922–923 271, 272–279, 408, 409–415, 572–579, 584, 585, 587, 588, 589–596, 597, 598–605, 606, 607, 608–615, 625, 626–632, 633 491, 930, 988–989
COORDINATE GEOMETRY			
MA-HS-3.3.1	**Students will apply algebraic concepts and graphing in the coordinate plane to analyze and solve problems (e.g., finding the final coordinates for a specified polygon, midpoints, between-ness of points, parallel and perpendicular lines, the distance between two points, the slope of a segment). DOK 2**	**HOLT ALGEBRA 1** **LARSON ALGEBRA 1** **LARSON GEOMETRY** **LARSON ALGEBRA 2**	309, 310–317, 349–355, 642–643, 802, S68 206–212, 213–214, 215–221, 222, 223–224, 225–232, 235–242, 243, 244–250, 251–252, 262–268, 270, 271–274, 283–284, 292–293, 302–303, 311–314, 319–324, 345–347, 743, 744–750, 753 12, 17–19, 20, 53, 171–178, 179, 180–187, 193, 198–199, 235, 271, 274–275, 276–277, 294, 297, 298–299, 526, 527, 546 82–88, 96, 142, 145, 185, 204, 208, 209, 291, 427, 614–619, 632, 704, 749, 800, 809, 858, 894, 914, 988–989
FOUNDATIONAL STATEMENTS			
MA-HS-3.4.1	Students will identify definitions, axioms and theorems, explain the necessity for them and give examples of them.	**LARSON GEOMETRY**	9–10, 24–25, 96, 113, 124–126, 148, 154–155, 161–162, 164, 172, 190–192, 218, 220, 227–228, 234, 240–241, 249, 264–265, 295, 303, 305, 310, 312, 319–320, 328, 330, 335, 374, 381, 388, 390, 397–398, 433, 441–442, 449, 452, 457, 459, 507, 509, 515, 517, 522–523, 533, 535, 543–545, 573, 591, 601, 609–610, 653–654, 660, 664–666, 672–675, 680–681, 689–691, 720–721, 730–731, 737, 746–747, 755–756, 763, 795, 804–805, 811–812, 819–821, 829, 838, 840, 848
MA-HS-3.4.2	Students will recognize that there are geometries, other than Euclidean geometry, in which the parallel postulate is not true.	**LARSON ALGEBRA 1** **LARSON GEOMETRY** **LARSON ALGEBRA 2**	A5–A6 753 A5–A6
MA-HS-3.4.3	*Students will be able to perform constructions such as a line parallel to a given line through a point not on the line, the perpendicular bisector of a line segment and the bisector of an angle.*	**LARSON GEOMETRY**	33–34, 152, 169, 195, 235, 261, 305, 307, 314, 317, 323, 401, 767

Data Analysis and Probability

High school students extend data representations, interpretations and conclusions. They describe data distributions in multiple ways and connect data gathering issues with data interpretation issues. They relate curve-of-best-fit with two-variable data and determine a line-of-best-fit for a given set of data. They distinguish between combinations and permutations and compare and contrast theoretical and experimental probability.

DATA REPRESENTATIONS			
MA-HS-4.1.1	**Students will analyze and make inferences from a set of data with no more than two variables, and will analyze problems for the use and misuse of data representations. DOK 3**	**HOLT ALGEBRA 1** **LARSON ALGEBRA 1** **LARSON GEOMETRY** **LARSON ALGEBRA 2**	678–686, 687–693, 702–707 875, A18–A19, A24–A25 14, 48, 74, 77, 89, 103, 301, 387, 480, 557, 679, 695, 888–889, A12–A13, A18–A19 113, 114, 117, 744–749, 750, 756, 757–762, 763–765, A12–A13, A18–A19
MA-HS-4.1.2	**Students will construct data displays for data with no more than two variables. DOK 2**	**HOLT ALGEBRA 1** **LARSON ALGEBRA 1** **LARSON GEOMETRY** **LARSON ALGEBRA 2**	262, 681–682, 688, 700–701 881–885, 886, 887–892, 893, 895, 900 48, 363, 488, 760, 888–889, A18–A19, A24–A25 112, 115, 118, 119, 139, 143, 774, 775–777, 778, 779, 781, A18–A19, A24–A25
MA-HS-4.1.3	*Students will represent real-world data using matrices and will use matrix addition, subtraction, multiplication (with matrices no larger than 2 × 2) and scalar multiplication to solve real-world problems.*	**HOLT ALGEBRA 1** **LARSON ALGEBRA 1** **LARSON GEOMETRY** **LARSON ALGEBRA 2**	746–749 94–95 583, 586, 587, 597 189, 192, 194, 198, 200, 201, 202
CHARACTERISTICS OF DATA SETS			
MA-HS-4.2.1	**Students will describe and compare data distributions and make inferences from the data based on the shapes of graphs, measures of center (mean, median, mode) and measures of spread (range, standard deviation). DOK 2**	**HOLT ALGEBRA 1** **LARSON ALGEBRA 1** **LARSON GEOMETRY** **LARSON ALGEBRA 2**	694–699, 711, 718 104, 400, 875–878, 879–880 84, 363, 887, A8 113–114, 117, 118, 119, 120, 727, 728, 730, 731, 744–749, 750, 755, 756, 848, 849, 922, A8
MA-HS-4.2.2	Students will know the characteristics of the Gaussian normal distribution (bell-shaped curve).	**LARSON ALGEBRA 2**	757–762, 763–765, 780
MA-HS-4.2.3	**Students will:** • **identify an appropriate curve of best fit (linear, quadratic, exponential) for a set of two-variable data;** • **determine a line of best fit equation for a set of linear two-variable data and** • **apply a line of best fit to make predictions within and beyond a given set of two-variable data.** **DOK 3**	**LARSON ALGEBRA 1** **LARSON ALGEBRA 2**	327–331, 332–333, 334, 335–341, 342 112, 115–116, 117, 118, 119, 233, 774, 775–780, 781
MA-HS-4.2.4	Students will recognize when arguments based on data confuse correlation and causation.	**LARSON ALGEBRA 1** **LARSON GEOMETRY** **LARSON ALGEBRA 2**	A24–A25 A24–A25 A24–A25
EXPERIMENTS AND SAMPLES			
MA-HS-4.3.1	**Students will recognize potential for bias resulting from the misuse of sampling methods (e.g., non-random sampling, polling only a specific group of people, using limited or extremely small sample sizes) and explain why these samples can lead to inaccurate inferences. DOK 2**	**HOLT ALGEBRA 1** **LARSON ALGEBRA 1** **LARSON GEOMETRY** **LARSON ALGEBRA 2**	708–709, S73 871–874 890 766–767, 769, 770, 782
MA-HS-4.3.2	Students will design simple experiments or investigations to collect data to answer questions of interest.	**HOLT ALGEBRA 1** **LARSON ALGEBRA 1** **LARSON GEOMETRY** **LARSON ALGEBRA 2**	708–709, S73 A14 A14, A15 772–773

MA-HS-4.3.3	Students will explain the differences between randomized experiments and observational studies.	HOLT ALGEBRA 1 LARSON ALGEBRA 1 LARSON ALGEBRA 2	708–709, S73 871–874 766–770
PROBABILITY			
MA-HS-4.4.1	**Students will:** • **determine theoretical and experimental (from given data) probabilities;** • **make predictions and draw inferences from probabilities;** • **compare theoretical and experimental probabilities and** • **determine probabilities involving replacement and non-replacement.** **DOK 3**	HOLT ALGEBRA 1 LARSON ALGEBRA 1 LARSON GEOMETRY LARSON ALGEBRA 2	713–718, 720–725, 726–733, 734–735, 745, 752–753 842, 844–848, 849–850, 861–867, 868–869, A14–A15, A16–A17 770, 771–777, 893, A16–A17, A20, A21 698, 699, 700, 701, 702, 703, 704, 705, 713, 719, 722, 730, 732, 742, 809 A14–A15, A16–A17, A20, A21
MA-HS-4.4.2	*Students will recognize and identify the differences between combinations and permutations and use them to count discrete quantities.*	HOLT ALGEBRA 1 LARSON ALGEBRA 1 LARSON GEOMETRY LARSON ALGEBRA 2	736–743, 745, 753 851–855, 856–859, 860 891–892 684–685, 686, 687–690, 694–697, 705, 755
MA-HS-4.4.3	*Students will represent probabilities in multiple ways, such as fractions, decimals, percentages and geometric area models.*	HOLT ALGEBRA 1 LARSON ALGEBRA 1 LARSON GEOMETRY LARSON ALGEBRA 2	713–718, 720–725, 726–733, 734–735, 745, 752–753 843–848, 861–867, 868–869, A14–A15, A16–A17 770, 771–777, 893 698–704, 705, 706, 707–713, 714, 717–723, 724–725, 726, 727–729, 732, A14–A15, A16–A17, A20, A21
MA-HS-4.4.4	Students will explain how the law of large numbers can be applied in simple examples.	LARSON ALGEBRA 1 LARSON GEOMETRY LARSON ALGEBRA 2	A17 A17 714, A17

Big Idea: Algebraic Thinking

High school students extend analysis and use of functions and focus on linear, quadratic, absolute value and exponential functions. They explore parametric changes on graphs of functions. They use rules and properties to simplify algebraic expressions. They combine simple rational expressions and simple polynomial expressions. They factor polynomial expressions and quadratics of the form $1x^2 + bx + c$.

PATTERNS, RELATIONS AND FUNCTIONS			
MA-HS-5.1.1	**Students will identify multiple representations (tables, graphs, equations) of functions (linear, quadratic, absolute value, exponential) in real-world or mathematical problems. DOK 2**	HOLT ALGEBRA 1 LARSON ALGEBRA 1 LARSON GEOMETRY LARSON ALGEBRA 2	236–242, 245–251, 252–258, 259, 261, 280–282, 295, 296–302, 360, 366–367, 590–597, 599–605, 606–611, 612, 772–778, 789–795 35–39, 41, 42, 43–48, 223–224, 262–268, 396–397, 520–527, 528–529, 530, 531–538, 628–634, 635–640, 641–642, 669–670, 710–716, 717, 775–782, 830, A22–A23 565, 882–883, 884, A22–A23 73–75, 76–79, 80–81, 89–96, 97, 98–104, 105, 106, 107–111, 115–116, 117–120, 121–122, 123–129, 130–131, 138, 158, 236–243, 244, 245–251, 265, 308, 309–315, 337, 338, 339–340, 341, 342–344, 352, 369, 393–399, 434, 451, 478–485, 486–491, 498, 506, 528, 529–530, 531, 533, 535, 536, 563, 730, 749, 800, 865, 937, A22–A23
MA-HS-5.1.2	*Students will identify, relate and apply representations (graphs, equations, tables) of a piecewise function (such as long distance telephone rates) from mathematical or real-world information.*	LARSON ALGEBRA 2	130–131

Standard	Description	Textbook	Pages
MA-HS-5.1.3	*Students will demonstrate how equations and graphs are models of the relationship between two real-world quantities (e.g., the relationship between degrees Celsius and degrees Fahrenheit).*	HOLT ALGEBRA 1 LARSON ALGEBRA 1 LARSON GEOMETRY LARSON ALGEBRA 2	252–258, 261, 269, 282, 347, 355 186, 255, 263, 285, 294–295, 304–305, 313, 522–523, 528–529, 534, 631, 637, 713, 768, 778, 111, 835 44, 91, 94, 95, 96, 108, 109, 110, 111, 239, 242, 247, 250, 262, 270, 295, 298, 396, 398, 399, 447, 450, 480, 484, 485, 500, 501, 504, 552, 553, 556, 560, 562, 570, 571
MA-HS-5.1.4	Students will recognize and solve problems that can be modeled using an exponential function, such as compound interest problems.	HOLT ALGEBRA 1 LARSON ALGEBRA 1 LARSON ALGEBRA 2	*772–778, 781–788,* 791, 797, 803 522–523, 525–527, 528–529, 530, 534, 537–538, 687 480–481, 483–485, 488–491, 530–537
MA-HS-5.1.5	**Students will:** • **determine if a relation is a function;** • **determine the domain and range of a function (linear and quadratic);** • **determine the slope and intercepts of a linear function;** • **determine the maximum, minimum, and intercepts (roots/zeros) of a quadratic function and** • **evaluate a function written in function notation for a specified rational number.** **DOK 2**	HOLT ALGEBRA 1 LARSON ALGEBRA 1 LARSON GEOMETRY LARSON ALGEBRA 2	236–242, 243, 247–250, 251, 261, 281, 296–302, 303–308, 310–317, 320–325, 334–340, 355, 396, 420, 451, 489, 537, 554, 564, 605, 611, 628–629, 651, 686, 699, 725, 803, 810, 857, 872 35–40, 44–46, 49–50, 207, 210, 217, 218, 219, 220, 221. 235–242, 243, 262, 265, 266, 268, 273, 631, 637, 641–642, 645, 647, 650–651 181–185, 879 73–79, 130–131, 167, 232, 238–239, 241–244, 246–247, 249–251, 253–258, 368, 445, 459
MA-HS-5.1.6	*Students will find the domain and range for absolute value functions.*	HOLT ALGEBRA 1 LARSON ALGEBRA 1 LARSON ALGEBRA 2	366–367 396–397 121–122, 123–129, 138
MA-HS-5.1.7	*Students will apply and use direct and inverse variation to solve real-world and mathematical problems.*	HOLT ALGEBRA 1 LARSON ALGEBRA 1 LARSON ALGEBRA 2	326–331, 333, 340 253–259, 260–261, 768, 771 107–111, 120, 550, 551–553, 555–556, 571
MA-HS-5.1.8	**Students will identify the changes and explain how changes in parameters affect graphs of functions (linear, quadratic, absolute value, exponential) (e.g., compare $y = x^2$, $y = 2x^2$, $y = (x - 4)^2$, and $y = x^2 + 3$). DOK 2**	HOLT ALGEBRA 1 LARSON ALGEBRA 1 LARSON GEOMETRY LARSON ALGEBRA 2	236–242, 245–251, 252–258, 259, 261, 280–282, 296–302, 360, 366–367, 590–597, 599–605, 606–611, 612, 772–778, 789–795 264, 266, 268, 396–397, 521, 524, 532, 535, 536, 545, 629–630, 632, 633 565, 882–883, 884 89–90, 93, 97, 121–122, 123–128, 138, 236–237, 240, 392, 478–479, 485, 522, 817
VARIABLES, EXPRESSIONS, AND OPERATIONS			
MA-HS-5.2.1	**Students will apply order of operations, real number properties (identity, inverse, commutative, associative, distributive, closure) and rules of exponents (integer) to simplify algebraic expressions. DOK 1**	HOLT ALGEBRA 1 LARSON ALGEBRA 1 LARSON GEOMETRY LARSON ALGEBRA 2	21, 46, 79, 86, 98, 165, 174, 180, 181, S78 96–101,489–494, 495–501, 503–508 139, 870–873 12–14,16, 129, 330–334, 352, 377, 419, 434, 639
MA-HS-5.2.2	Students will evaluate polynomial and rational expressions and expressions containing radicals and absolute values at specified values of their variables.	HOLT ALGEBRA 1 LARSON ALGEBRA 1 LARSON GEOMETRY LARSON ALGEBRA 2	476–481, 499, 509, 512, 686, 9, 13, 53, 66 870 11,13–17, 40, 762
MA-HS-5.2.3	**Students will:** • **add, subtract and multiply polynomial expressions;** • **factor polynomial expressions using the greatest common monomial factor and** • **factor quadratic polynomials of the form $ax^2 + bx + c$, when $a = 1$ and b and c are integers.** **DOK 2**	HOLT ALGEBRA 1 LARSON ALGEBRA 1 LARSON GEOMETRY LARSON ALGEBRA 2	482–483, 484–489, 490–491, 492–499, 501–507, 509, 512–513, 529, 530, 531–537, 547, 548–554, 557, 566–571, 576, 651, 803, 821 555–559, 561, 562–568, 569–574, 576, 582, 583–589 641, 713, 873 252–253, 255–256, 346–352, 353–354, 356, 548, 580, 680

MA-HS-5.2.4	*Students will factor quadratic polynomials, such as perfect square trinomials and quadratic polynomials of the form $ax^2 + bx + c$ when $a \neq 1$ and b and c are integers.*	**HOLT ALGEBRA 1** **LARSON ALGEBRA 1** **LARSON GEOMETRY** **LARSON ALGEBRA 2**	558–564, 778 582, 583–589 713 252–253, 255–256, 548
MA-HS-5.2.5	**Students will add, subtract, multiply and divide simple rational expressions with monomial first-degree denominators and integer numerators (e.g., $\frac{3}{5x} + \frac{4}{3y}, \frac{9}{2a} - \frac{-7}{4b}, \frac{3}{-5x} \times \frac{-4}{7y}, \frac{5}{2c} \div \frac{9}{-11d}$),and will express the results in simplified form. DOK 1**	**HOLT ALGEBRA 1** **LARSON ALGEBRA 1** **LARSON GEOMETRY** **LARSON ALGEBRA 2**	885–891, 893–899, 907, 912–913 802, 812 139 582, 586
EQUATIONS AND INEQUALITIES			
MA-HS-5.3.1	**Students will model, solve and graph first degree, single variable equations and inequalities, including absolute value, based in real-world and mathematical problems and graph the solutions on a number line. DOK 2**	**HOLT ALGEBRA 1** **LARSON ALGEBRA 1** **LARSON GEOMETRY** **LARSON ALGEBRA 2**	76, 77–82, 84–90, 91, 113, 143, 152, 174–179, 180–185, 188–193, 194–200, 235, 325, 366–367, 388 21–26, 132–133, 134–140, 141–146, 147, 148–153, 154–159, 160, 356–361, 362, 363–368, 369–374, 375–376, 377–378, 390–395, 398–403 65, 105–106, 109, 287, 785, 875, 876, 899 18–24, 25, 32–39, 40–49, 50, 51–59, 88, 209, 217, 299, 316, 344, 427, 625, 664, 713, 730, 792, 833, 954
MA-HS-5.3.2	*Students will solve for a specified variable in a multivariable equation.*	**HOLT ALGEBRA 1** **LARSON ALGEBRA 1** **LARSON GEOMETRY** **LARSON ALGEBRA 2**	107–111, 113, 120, 153, 179, 331 184–189, 253 109, 877 26–32, 40, 70, 412
MA-HS-5.3.3	**Students will model, solve and graph first degree, two-variable equations and inequalities in real-world and mathematical problems. DOK 2**	**HOLT ALGEBRA 1** **LARSON ALGEBRA 1** **LARSON GEOMETRY** **LARSON ALGEBRA 2**	298–299, 304–305, 306–307, 326–331, 447, 449, 343–344, 346, 348, 414–420, 429, 433, 499 215–221, 222, 223–224, 225–232, 245, 251–252, 254–255, 257–259, 260–261, 263–268, 292–299, 300–301, 302–310, 311–316, 319–324, 375–376, 377–378, 405–412 180–187, 188–189, 881 74–75, 77–78, 89–96, 97, 98–106, 107–111, 112, 113–120, 121–122, 123–129, 130–131, 132–138, 139, 150, 158, 243, 271, 274, 282, 291, 307, 315, 316, 344, 352, 434, 451, 459, 464, 536, 563, 595, 664, 678, 679, 730, 749, 780, 800, 865, 894, 937
MA-HS-5.3.4	**Students will model, solve and graph systems of two linear equations in real-world and mathematical problems. DOK 3**	**HOLT ALGEBRA 1** **LARSON ALGEBRA 1** **LARSON GEOMETRY** **LARSON ALGEBRA 2**	400–403, 406–411, 413, 430, 481, 611 426, 427–433, 434, 435–441, 442, 443, 444–450, 451–457, 459–465 183, 186, 188–189, 880 152, 153–158, 159, 160–167, 186, 205, 207–208, 212–213, 215–217, 258, 299, 368, 386, 399, 445, 588, 612, 632, 679, 697, 792, 817
MA-HS-5.3.5	*Students will write, graph, and solve systems of two linear inequalities based on real-world or mathematical problems and interpret the solution.*	**HOLT ALGEBRA 1** **LARSON ALGEBRA 1** **LARSON GEOMETRY** **LARSON ALGEBRA 2**	421–426, 427, 429, 433, 554 466–472 881 168–173, 193
MA-HS-5.3.6	**Students will model, solve and graph quadratic equations in real-world and mathematical problems. DOK 2**	**HOLT ALGEBRA 1** **LARSON ALGEBRA 1** **LARSON GEOMETRY** **LARSON ALGEBRA 2**	622–627, 630–635, 636–641, 645–651, 652–659, 661, 662–665, 795, 857, 865, 891 575–580, 585, 628–634, 635–640, 641–642, 643–649, 652–658, 659–660, 664–668, 669–670, 671–676, 727–728 423, 499, 641, 882–883 236–237, 238, 240–243, 245–247, 249–250, 253–254, 256–258, 261–271, 272–274, 285 –286, 288–291, 292–299, 315, 316, 369, 399, 476, 612, 689, 723, 771, 858

Kentucky Program of Studies (POS) High School

Big Idea: Number Properties and Operations

High school students should enter high school with a strong background in rational numbers and numerical operations and expand this to real numbers. This becomes the foundation for algebra and working with algebraic symbols. They understand large and small numbers and their representations, powers, and roots. They compare and contrast properties of numbers and number systems and develop strategies to estimate the results of operations on real numbers. Students will use, and understand the limitations of graphing calculators and computer spreadsheets appropriately as learning tools.

Academic Expectations

2.7 Students understand number concepts and use numbers appropriately

2.8 Students understand various mathematical procedures and use them appropriately and accurately.

2.12 Students understand mathematical structure concepts including the properties and logic of various mathematical systems

Standard	Program	Pages
NUMBER SENSE		
MA-HS-NPO-S-NS1 Students will compare real numbers using order relations.	**HOLT ALGEBRA 1**	33, 37, 131, S50
	LARSON ALGEBRA 1	62, 64–65, 67–70, 84, 515–516, 518, 909, 939
	LARSON GEOMETRY	328–334, 905
	LARSON ALGEBRA 2	2–3, 6, 8, 33, 742
MA-HS-NPO-S-NS2 Students will locate the position of a real number on the number line, find its distance from the origin (absolute value/magnitude) and find the distance between two numbers on the number line (the absolute value of their difference)	**HOLT ALGEBRA 1**	14, 17–18, 37, 148, S50
	LARSON ALGEBRA 1	64–69, 939
	LARSON GEOMETRY	12, 20
	LARSON ALGEBRA 2	2–3, 6–7, 16, 742, 1010
MA-HS-NPO-S-NS3 Students will determine the relative position on the number line of real numbers, including very large and very small numbers, and the relative magnitude of numbers expressed in fractional form, in decimal form, as roots or in scientific notation.	**HOLT ALGEBRA 1**	33, 35, 37, 169, 454–457, 511, S50
	LARSON ALGEBRA 1	64–65, 67–70, 112, 114, 513, 515, 516, 518, 909,
	LARSON GEOMETRY	12, 20
	LARSON ALGEBRA 2	2–3, 6–7, 16, 742, 1010
MA-HS-NPO-S-NS4 Students will explore vectors and matrices as systems that have some of the properties of the real number system.	**HOLT ALGEBRA 1**	746–749
	LARSON ALGEBRA 1	94–95
	LARSON GEOMETRY	586
	LARSON ALGEBRA 2	188
MA-HS-NPO-S-NS5 Students will compare and contrast number systems, including complex numbers as solutions to quadratic equations that do not have real solutions.	**HOLT ALGEBRA 1**	34–37
	LARSON ALGEBRA 1	64, 67, 111–112
	LARSON ALGEBRA 2	2, 276, 279
ESTIMATION		
MA-HS-NPO-S-E1 Students will use calculators appropriately and regularly make estimations without a calculator to detect potential errors.	**HOLT ALGEBRA 1**	Z12, 33, 91, 178, 908
	LARSON ALGEBRA 1	111, 252, 378, 653, 718, 778
	LARSON GEOMETRY	48, 122–123, 153, 179, 247, 326–327, 387, 396, 440, 514, 541, 633, 688, 845
	LARSON ALGEBRA 2	975, 976, 977, 978–979, 982, 983
MA-HS-NPO-S-E2 Students will estimate solutions to problems with real numbers (including very large and very small quantities) in both realistic and mathematical situations.	**HOLT ALGEBRA 1**	Z9–Z11, 30, 50, 110, 130, 134, 142, 178, 185, 250, 316, 465, 499, 570, 697, 717, 856, 898
	LARSON ALGEBRA 1	40, 111, 114–115, 252, 308, 336–341, 342, 395, 525, 526, 538, 633, 653, 655, 659, 780, 790, 805, 842
	LARSON GEOMETRY	13, 32, 54, 169, 178, 315, 333, 369, 378, 394, 471, 751–752, 774, 776, 816, 824, 834
	LARSON ALGEBRA 2	335, 557, 904
MA-HS-NPO-S-E3 Students will establish and apply benchmarks for real numbers in context.	**HOLT ALGEBRA 1**	Z10–Z11, 130, 134, 717
	LARSON ALGEBRA 1	74–79, 80–84, 88–93, 103–108
	LARSON ALGEBRA 2	976
NUMBER OPERATIONS		
MA-HS-NPO-S-NO1 Students will add, subtract, multiply and divide real numbers.	**HOLT ALGEBRA 1**	Z12–Z13, Z14–Z16, Z30–Z31, Z32–Z33, 14–19, 20–25, 31, 37, 39, 45, 63, 66, S4, S28
	LARSON ALGEBRA 1	73, 74–79, 80–84, 85, 87, 88–93, 101, 914, 915
	LARSON GEOMETRY	869, 870, 874
	LARSON ALGEBRA 2	975, 979

Standard	Program	Pages
MA-HS-NPO-S-NO2 Students will add, subtract and multiply complex numbers.	**LARSON ALGEBRA 2**	276–277, 278–280, 291, 321, 323, 327, 1013
MA-HS-NPO-S-NO3 Students will multiply and divide numbers expressed in scientific notation.	**HOLT ALGEBRA 1** **LARSON ALGEBRA 1** **LARSON ALGEBRA 2**	457, 461, 464–466, 468, 471, 473, 474, 475, 511–512, S16, S34 513, 516–517, 519 331, 333–334, 369, 1014
MA-HS-NPO-S-NO4 Students will apply absolute value, integer exponents, roots and factorials to solve problems.	**HOLT ALGEBRA 1** **LARSON ALGEBRA 1** **LARSON GEOMETRY** **LARSON ALGEBRA 2**	Z20, 18, 26–31, 32–37, 39, 63–64, 66, 446–451, 452–457, 458–459, 460–466, 467–473, 475, 481, 738–743, 745, 805–810, 811–815, 816–821, 831, 832–835, 838–839, 840 3–6, 8–13, 20, 53–54, 66–69, 110–111, 113–115, 852, 854 139, 423, 870–871, 874 10, 11, 55, 330–335, 352, 414–415, 417, 421–422, 424, 427, 469, 684–689, 690–691, 694, 697, 737, 1015, 1019
MA-HS-NPO-S-NO5 Students will determine a specific term of a sequence given an explicit formula.	**HOLT ALGEBRA 1** **LARSON ALGEBRA 1** **LARSON GEOMETRY** **LARSON ALGEBRA 2**	276, 770 309–310, 539–540 72–78 794, 798–799, 801, 843
MA-HS-NPO-S-NO6 Students will describe and extend arithmetic and geometric sequences.	**HOLT ALGEBRA 1** **LARSON ALGEBRA 1** **LARSON GEOMETRY** **LARSON ALGEBRA 2**	272–277, 279, 283, 284, 766–771, 778, 836, 840, S11, S24, S31, S38 309–310, 539–540, 683 72, 75–76, 212, 898 802, 806, 843, 846–847
MA-HS-NPO-S-NO7 Students will determine an explicit rule for the *n*th term of an arithmetic sequence.	**HOLT ALGEBRA 1** **LARSON ALGEBRA 1** **LARSON GEOMETRY** **LARSON ALGEBRA 2**	276, 770–771 310 72–78 803–804, 805–808, 817, 1021
MA-HS-NPO-S-NO8 Students will apply sequences and arithmetic and geometric series to solve realistic problems.	**HOLT ALGEBRA 1** **LARSON ALGEBRA 1** **LARSON GEOMETRY** **LARSON ALGEBRA 2**	274–277, 279, 283, 284, 768–771, 840, S31, S38 540 77 795, 799–800, 805, 808–809, 813, 815–818, 838, 846
MA-HS-NPO-S-NO9 Students will solve realistic problems to a specified degree of accuracy.	**HOLT ALGEBRA 1** **LARSON ALGEBRA 1** **LARSON GEOMETRY** **LARSON ALGEBRA 2**	114–118, 129, 131, 153, 155, 156, 472, 638, 640, 649–650, 665, 666, 830, 834–835, 769 108, 115, 516, 648, 655, 657–658, 665–668, 676, 682, 691, 725, 731, 733–734, 738, 741–742, 749, 826 726, 735, 739, 747, 749, 760, 767, 825, 844, 865, 867 273, 418, 983
MA-HS-NPO-S-NO10 Students will judge the effects of multiplication, division and computing powers and roots on the magnitudes of quantities.	**HOLT ALGEBRA 1** **LARSON ALGEBRA 1** **LARSON GEOMETRY** **LARSON ALGEBRA 2**	20–21, 24, 30, 32, 53 87, 88, 92, 104, 110 869, 871, 874 10, 414–415, 975
MA-HS-NPO-S-NO11 Students will develop an understanding of the properties and representations for the addition and multiplication of vectors and matrices.	**HOLT ALGEBRA 1** **LARSON ALGEBRA 1** **LARSON GEOMETRY** **LARSON ALGEBRA 2**	746–749 94–95 581–587, 597, 912 187–193, 194, 195–202, 217, 220, 227, 475, 1012
MA-HS-NPO-S-NO12 Students will develop fluency in operations with real numbers and matrices, using mental computation or paper-and-pencil calculations for simple cases and calculators and/or computers for more-complicated cases.	**HOLT ALGEBRA 1** **LARSON ALGEBRA 1** **LARSON GEOMETRY** **LARSON ALGEBRA 2**	Z12–Z13, Z14–Z16, 14–19, 20–25, 31, 37, 39, 40–45, 46–47, 49, 63–64, 66, 126, 746–749, S4–S5, S28 74–79, 80–86, 88–93, 94–95, 102, 104–108, 116, 122, 126–129 581–587, 597, 869, 912 10, 11, 13, 187–193, 194, 195–202, 217, 220, 225, 227, 975, 977, 979
MA-HS-NPO-S-NO13 Students will use concrete, pictorial and abstract models to develop and/or generalize a procedure.	**HOLT ALGEBRA 1** **LARSON ALGEBRA 1** **LARSON GEOMETRY** **LARSON ALGEBRA 2**	14, 16–18, 26, 76, 91, 169, 244, 382, 389, 445, 482–483, 490–491, 493, 530, 538–539 64, 65, 73, 74, 96, 132–133, 443, 561, 582, 592, 662 122–123, 153, 216, 326–327, 371, 396, 432, 440, 506, 514, 541, 650, 671, 688, 729, 802, 828 258, 283–285

RATIOS AND PROPORTIONAL REASONING		
MA-HS-NPO-S-RP1 Students will calculate and apply ratios, proportions, rates and percentages to solve problems.	**HOLT ALGEBRA 1**	114–120, 121–126, 127–132, 133–137, 138–143, 144–145, 146, 147, 154–155, 156, 157, 160–161, S7, S29
	LARSON ALGEBRA 1	162–167, 168–173, 174–175, 176–181, 182–183, 189 194–197, 212, 221, 261, 268, 368, 374, 494, 580, 676, 859
	LARSON GEOMETRY	131, 173–174, 176–178, 197, 263, 270, 349, 356–363, 364–370, 372–379, 380, 387, 388–395, 396, 397–403, 405, 415–416, 422, 424–425, 426–429, 450–456, 464–465, 736–743, 745, 761, 809, 846, 847–854, 855, 906–908, 916, 919
	LARSON ALGEBRA 2	5, 7, 9, 24, 40, 85, 87–88, 108–109, 111, 173, 265, 491, 580, 872, 977, 1010
MA-HS-NPO-S-RP2 Students will translate real-world proportional relationships into mathematical expressions and vice versa.	**HOLT ALGEBRA 1**	116, 118–120, 122, 124–126, 129, 154–155, 156, S29
	LARSON ALGEBRA 1	164, 166–167, 169–170, 172–173, 175
	LARSON GEOMETRY	359, 362–363, 365–369, 374, 376, 378, 387, 398–399, 402–403, 405, 416, 736
	LARSON ALGEBRA 2	291, 689
MA-HS-NPO-S-RP3 Students will represent slope graphically, numerically and symbolically and relate it to a graph of an equation based on a realistic situation.	**HOLT ALGEBRA 1**	311–317, 318–319, 320–325, 331, 332, 333, 369, 372, 373, S12, S32
	LARSON ALGEBRA 1	234, 235–242, 243, 244, 247, 250
	LARSON GEOMETRY	171–178, 213, 429, 901
	LARSON ALGEBRA 2	82–88, 94–95, 258, 1011
PROPERTIES OF NUMBERS AND OPERATIONS		
MA-HS-NPO-S-PNO1 Students will identify and apply real number properties.	**HOLT ALGEBRA 1**	21–23, 46–51, 59, 61, 65, 66, 67, 132, 208, S5, S28
	LARSON ALGEBRA 1	75–78, 89–91, 96–101, 103–104, 106
	LARSON GEOMETRY	65, 70, 106, 108–109, 212, 873, 899
	LARSON ALGEBRA 2	3–4, 6, 12–13, 16, 20, 28, 202, 253–258, 265, 323, 1033
MA-HS-NPO-S-PNO2 Students will use equivalence relations of real numbers to solve problems.	**HOLT ALGEBRA 1**	77–82, 84–90, 92–98, 100–106, 113, 120, 143, 152–153, 156, 174–179, 180–185, 186, 187, 188–193, 194–200, 208, 211, 217–219, 220, S6, S8–S9, S29, S30
	LARSON GEOMETRY	65, 70, 105–111, 212, 899
	LARSON ALGEBRA 2	18–24, 26–32, 40, 42–43, 44–47, 65, 1010
MA-HS-NPO-S-PNO3 Students will compare and contrast the number systems according to their properties.	**HOLT ALGEBRA 1**	34, 36–37
	LARSON ALGEBRA 1	64, 67, 112, 120
	LARSON ALGEBRA 2	2, 18, 188, 197, 253, 266, 420, 465, 1033, 1034
MA-HS-NPO-S-PNO4 Students will justify the solution steps in simplifying expressions or solving an equation.	**HOLT ALGEBRA 1**	48, 50–51, 61, S5
	LARSON ALGEBRA 1	90–91, 100, 118, 172, 493, 499
	LARSON GEOMETRY	105–106, 108–111, 899
	LARSON ALGEBRA 2	11–13, 18–20, 34–36, 254, 261, 267–269, 285–287, 292–293, 295, 319–321, 452–455, 468, 515–519, 589–592, 606

Big Idea: Measurement

High school students continue to measure and estimate measurements including fractions and decimals. They use formulas to find surface areas and volumes. They use US Customary and metric units of measurement. They use the Pythagorean theorem and other right triangle relationships to solve realistic problems.

Academic Expectations

2.9 Students understand space and dimensionality concepts and use them appropriately and accurately.
2.10 Students understand measurement concepts and use measurements appropriately and accurately.

MEASURING PHYSICAL ATTRIBUTES		
MA-HS-M-S-MPA1 Students will apply units of measurements of physical quantities correctly in expressions, equations and problem solutions that involve measurement.	**HOLT ALGEBRA 1**	10, 18–19, 38, 39, 60, 61, 63–64, 66, 81, 86, 88–89, 97, 104, 110, 112, 113, 116, 118, 122, 124–126, 150–151, 153–154, 156, 176, 626, 634, 638–641, 647–648, 650, 660, 827–828, 830, 831, 904, 909
	LARSON ALGEBRA 1	4, 6–7, 12, 32–33, 170, 172, 175, 188–189, 192, 195–197, 231, 255, 738, 740–742, 748–750, 759
	LARSON GEOMETRY	9, 10, 12–13, 25, 28, 48, 49–56, 58, 720–726, 727–728, 730–736, 737–743, 744, 745–752, 754–761, 762–768, 777, 784, 788–789, 803–809, 810–818, 819–825, 826–827, 829–836, 837, 838–845, 848, 850–855, 865–867, 916–919
	LARSON ALGEBRA 2	31–33, 35, 39–40, 54–55, 57–58, 85, 88, 334–335, 373, 376, 426, 450, 475, 570, 622–625, 631, 636, 638–639, 644, 891, 893, 895–896, 901
MA-HS-M-S-MPA2 Students will analyze precision, accuracy and approximate error in measurement situations.	**HOLT ALGEBRA 1**	S54, S55
	LARSON GEOMETRY	727–728

Standard	Program	Pages
MA-HS-M-S-MPA3 Students will determine the surface area and volume of right rectangular prisms, pyramids, cylinders, cones and spheres in realistic problems.	**HOLT ALGEBRA 1** **LARSON ALGEBRA 1** **LARSON GEOMETRY** **LARSON ALGEBRA 2**	500, S66, S67 4, 6, 7, 927–928 32, 270, 805, 807–809, 813–814, 816–818, 820, 822–827, 830–831, 834–835, 838, 840–842, 844, 848, 852–853, 855 96, 332, 335, 386, 427, 436, 639, 780, 922
MA-HS-M-S-MPA4 Students will describe how change in one or more dimensions of a geometric figure or object affects the perimeter, circumference, area and/or volume of the figure or object.	**HOLT ALGEBRA 1** **LARSON ALGEBRA 1** **LARSON GEOMETRY** **LARSON ALGEBRA 2**	53, 779 180, 282, 455, 689, 690 47, 160, 374, 376–377, 380, 740–743, 745, 846, 848, 850–852, 854–855, 919 332, 335
MA-HS-M-S-MPA5 Students will explore the relationships between the right triangle trigonometric functions, using technology (e.g., graphing calculator) as appropriate.	**HOLT ALGEBRA 1** **LARSON GEOMETRY** **LARSON ALGEBRA 2**	908–909 466–472, 473–480, 481–482, 483–489, 492, 790, 909 852–858, 865, 872–873, 901, 1022
MA-HS-M-S-MPA6 Students will apply definitions and properties of right triangle relationships (basic right triangle trigonometry and the Pythagorean theorem) to determine length and angle measures to solve realistic problems.	**HOLT ALGEBRA 1** **LARSON ALGEBRA 1** **LARSON GEOMETRY** **LARSON ALGEBRA 2**	36, 641, 643, 807–809, 908–909, S68 738, 741–742, 756 41, 432, 433–439, 440, 441–447, 457–464, 465, 466–472, 473–480, 481–482, 483–489, 496–497, 498, 500–501, 502–503, 587, 646, 648, 790, 908–909 40, 88, 138, 202, 419, 464, 625, 833, 855, 857–858, 877, 879–880, 898–899, 901, 903–904
MA-HS-M-S-MPA7 Students will apply special right triangles and the converse of the Pythagorean theorem to solve realistic problems.	**HOLT ALGEBRA 1** **LARSON ALGEBRA 1** **LARSON GEOMETRY** **LARSON ALGEBRA 2**	641, S68 739, 741, 742 41, 443, 445–446, 459–461, 463, 465, 503 995
MA-HS-M-S-MPA8 Students will explore periodic real-world phenomena, using technology (e.g., graphing calculator) as appropriate.	**LARSON ALGEBRA 2**	910–911, 913–914, 916, 918–919, 921–922
SYSTEMS OF MEASUREMENT		
MA-HS-M-S-SM1 Students will convert a measurement using one unit of measurement to another unit of measurement given the relationship between the units (e.g., miles per hour to feet per second, °F to °C).	**HOLT ALGEBRA 1** **LARSON ALGEBRA 1** **LARSON GEOMETRY** **LARSON ALGEBRA 2**	115, 117, 301, 456, S53 115, 186, 929 51, 54, 739, 886 5, 7–9, 981
MA-HS-M-S-SM2 Students will apply to both real world and mathematical situations US Customary and metric systems of measurement.	**HOLT ALGEBRA 1** **LARSON ALGEBRA 1** **LARSON GEOMETRY** **LARSON ALGEBRA 2**	Z3–Z4, 115, 117, S53, S54, S60, S61, S62, S66, S67 4, 6–7, 12, 32, 33, 170, 174–175, 185, 188–189, 231, 255, 738, 740–742, 748–750 9, 10, 12–13, 25, 28, 49–56, 58, 63–64, 68–69, 720–726, 730–736, 737–743, 744, 745–752, 754–761, 762–768, 777, 784, 788–789, 803–809, 810–818, 820–825, 826–827, 829–836, 837, 838–845, 848, 850–855, 865–867, 916–919 31–33, 35, 39–40, 54–55, 57–59, 85, 88, 334–335, 373, 376, 426, 450, 475, 567, 570, 622–625, 631, 636, 638–639, 644, 891, 893, 895–896, 901, 961
MA-HS-M-S-SM3 Students will make decisions about units and scales that are appropriate for problem solving situations involving measurement.	**HOLT ALGEBRA 1** **LARSON ALGEBRA 1** **LARSON GEOMETRY** **LARSON ALGEBRA 2**	Z3–Z4, S53, S54, S60, S61, S62, S66, S67 A2, A3 A2, A3 A2, A3
MA-HS-M-S-SM4 Students will use unit analysis to check measurement computations.	**HOLT ALGEBRA 1** **LARSON ALGEBRA 1** **LARSON GEOMETRY** **LARSON ALGEBRA 2**	115 17, 185 51, 722, 739 5, 7, 34
MA-HS-M-S-SM5 Students will compare and contrast the use of US Customary and metric systems of measurement.	**HOLT ALGEBRA 1** **LARSON ALGEBRA 1** **LARSON GEOMETRY** **LARSON ALGEBRA 2**	S53 A2–A3 A2, A3 A2, A3

Big Idea: Geometry

High school students expand analysis of two-dimensional figures and three-dimensional objects. They translate figures in a coordinate plane. They extend work with congruent and similar figures, including proportionality.

Academic Expectations

2.9 Students understand space and dimensionality concepts and use them appropriately and accurately.
2.10 Students understand measurement concepts and use them appropriately and accurately.
2.12 Students understand mathematical structure concepts including the properties and logic of various mathematical systems.

SHAPES AND RELATIONSHIPS

Standard	Program	Pages
MA-HS-G-S-SR1 Students will identify and apply the definitions, properties and theorems about line segments, rays and angles and use them to prove theorems in Euclidean geometry, solve problems and perform basic geometric constructions using a straight edge and a compass.	**HOLT ALGEBRA 1**	56, S57
	LARSON GEOMETRY	3, 6–7, 24–25, 28–29, 33–34, 112–119, 120–121, 131, 258, 899
MA-HS-G-S-SR2 Students will identify and apply properties and theorems about parallel and perpendicular lines and use them to prove theorems and to perform constructions.	**HOLT ALGEBRA 1**	351, S56
	LARSON ALGEBRA 1	246, 248, 319–324
	LARSON GEOMETRY	152–153, 154–160, 161–169, 170, 178, 190–197, 206, 210–212, 900–901
MA-HS-G-S-SR3 Students will analyze and apply angle relationships (e.g., linear pairs, vertical, complementary, supplementary, corresponding and alternate interior angles) in real-world or mathematical situations.	**HOLT ALGEBRA 1**	81, 120, 395, S57
	LARSON GEOMETRY	35–41, 58, 64, 68, 69, 70, 127–128, 132, 143–144, 149–151,154–160, 161–162, 165–166, 170, 178, 206, 212, 255, 866, 897, 899–900
	LARSON ALGEBRA 2	32, 522, 595, 962, 994
MA-HS-G-S-SR4 Students will use the definitions, properties and theorems about congruent and similar triangles and other figures to prove additional theorems and apply these to solve real-world problems.	**HOLT ALGEBRA 1**	122, 124–126, 154, S29, S59
	LARSON ALGEBRA 1	174
	LARSON GEOMETRY	226, 230, 236–239, 242, 245, 248, 250–251, 254, 256–257, 261–262, 383, 386, 390, 393–395, 416
	LARSON ALGEBRA 2	996–997
MA-HS-G-S-SR5 Students will use the definitions and basic properties of a circle (e.g., arcs, chords, central angles, inscribed angles) to prove basic theorems and solve problems.	**LARSON GEOMETRY**	650, 651–658, 659–663, 664–670, 671, 672–679, 680–686, 687, 688, 689–695, 696, 705–706, 712, 716–717, 914–915
MA-HS-G-S-SR6 Students will analyze and apply spatial relationships (not using Cartesian coordinates) among points, lines and planes (e.g., "betweenness" of points, midpoint, segment length, collinear, coplanar, parallel, perpendicular, skew).	**HOLT ALGEBRA 1**	S56
	LARSON GEOMETRY	2–8, 11–13, 15–16, 19–23, 64, 81, 83, 144, 147–148, 150–152, 170, 896
	LARSON ALGEBRA 2	148, 149, 299
MA-HS-G-S-SR7 Students will classify, determine attributes of, analyze and apply properties of two-dimensional geometric figures and three-dimensional objects.	**HOLT ALGEBRA 1**	874–875, S63, S64
	LARSON ALGEBRA 1	919–920
	LARSON GEOMETRY	42–47, 56, 58, 506, 507–513, 514, 515–521, 522–529, 530–531, 532, 533–540, 541, 542–549, 552–557, 558, 560–563, 564, 566–567, 568–569, 650, 651–658, 659–663, 664–670, 671, 672–679, 680–686, 687, 688, 689–695, 696, 705–706, 712, 714–715, 716–717, 794–801, 818, 857, 902, 910–911, 914, 915, 918
	LARSON ALGEBRA 2	58, 59, 104, 185, 209, 299, 498, 557, 595, 614–615, 617, 657, 771, 850
MA-HS-G-S-SR8 Students will describe the intersection of lines, planes and solids and visualize three-dimensional objects and spaces from different perspectives and analyze their cross sections.	**HOLT ALGEBRA 1**	874–875, 939, S65
	LARSON GEOMETRY	6–7, 23, 797, 799–801, 818, 839, 842, 853
	LARSON ALGEBRA 2	178, 649, 657

Standard	Program	Pages
MA-HS-G-S-SR9 Students will classify and apply properties of three-dimensional geometric figures.	**HOLT ALGEBRA 1** **LARSON ALGEBRA 1** **LARSON GEOMETRY** **LARSON ALGEBRA 2**	500, 779, 874–875, S64, S65 4, 6–7, 188–189, 811, 924, 927–928 794–801, 817–818, 861, 918 209, 557
MA-HS-G-S-SR10 Students will visualize solids and surfaces in three-dimensional space when given two-dimensional representations and create two-dimensional representations for the surfaces of three-dimensional objects.	**HOLT ALGEBRA 1** **LARSON ALGEBRA 1** **LARSON GEOMETRY** **LARSON ALGEBRA 2**	874–875, S65 457, 599 4–6, 8, 231, 798, 804–809, 811–812, 815–817, 836 178, 649, 657, 947
MA-HS-G-S-SR11 Students will draw and construct representations of two-dimensional figures and three-dimensional objects using a variety of tools.	**HOLT ALGEBRA 1** **LARSON GEOMETRY** **LARSON ALGEBRA 2**	57, 874–875, S65 218, 235, 307, 322–324, 326–327, 387, 396, 440, 510, 512, 514, 519–520, 528–529, 535, 537, 541, 547–548, 550–551, 555–556, 724, 767, 798, 804, 806–807, 809, 815 881
MA-HS-G-S-SR12 Students will use geometric models and ideas to gain insights into and answer questions in other areas of mathematics and into other disciplines and areas of interest, such as art and architecture.	**HOLT ALGEBRA 1** **LARSON ALGEBRA 1** **LARSON GEOMETRY** **LARSON ALGEBRA 2**	10, 30, 36, 43–45, 50–51, 57, 81, 88, 96, 104, 109, 120, 183, 192, 197, 199, 240, 302, 350–351, 353–355, 395, 402, 419, 464–465, 473, 479–480, 487–489, 496–499, 500, 505, 509, 514, 529, 536–537, 545, 552–553, 563, 571, 626, 634–635, 638–641, 648–651, 725, 733, 770, 801, 812–815, 819–821, 825–827, 835, 871–872, 898–899 6, 32, 115, 197, 485, 741 40, 46, 69, 152, 165, 169, 219–222, 229, 299, 311, 313–314, 324, 332, 339, 389, 392, 414, 445, 508, 511, 515, 518–519, 538, 631, 656, 667–668, 676, 684, 689, 722–724, 734, 820, 822–823, 830, 832 23–24, 31–32, 78, 108–109, 204, 208–209, 232, 254, 257–258, 261, 264, 283–285, 290–291, 298, 319, 334–335, 351, 358–361, 373, 376–377, 386, 389, 392, 399, 404, 419, 427, 569–571, 574 578–580, 594, 616, 618–619, 622–625, 631–632, 636, 638–640, 644, 646–647, 649, 657, 663–664, 673, 701, 703, 737, 799, 809, 837, 855, 857–858, 862, 864–865, 1019
MA-HS-G-S-SR13 Students will explore geometry to make and test conjectures using geometric tools and technology.	**HOLT ALGEBRA 1** **LARSON GEOMETRY** **LARSON ALGEBRA 2**	209, 779 73, 75, 122–123, 153, 216, 269, 294, 371, 396, 432, 440, 480, 488, 514, 541, 615, 650, 671, 688, 769, 802, 828 881
TRANSFORMATIONS OF SHAPES		
MA-HS-G-S-TS1 Students will understand and represent transformations within a plane (translations, reflections, rotations and dilations) of figures by using sketches, coordinates, vectors, function notation, matrices and technology.	**HOLT ALGEBRA 1** **LARSON ALGEBRA 1** **LARSON GEOMETRY** **LARSON ALGEBRA 2**	357–363, 749, S69, S70 213–214, 922–923 56, 271–279, 280 309, 341, 408–415, 421–422, 427, 489, 572–579, 581, 584–585, 587–588, 589–597, 598–605, 606, 607, 608–615, 625, 626–632, 633, 634, 640, 642–643, 644–645, 647, 912–913 202, 291, 491, 930, 988–989
MA-HS-G-S-TS2 Students will use various representations, including electronic displays, to understand the effects of simple transformations within a plane and compositions of transformation.	**HOLT ALGEBRA 1** **LARSON ALGEBRA 1** **LARSON GEOMETRY** **LARSON ALGEBRA 2**	357–363, 749, S69, S70 213–214, 922–923 56, 271–280, 285–286, 289–291, 309, 341, 408–415, 421–422, 427, 489, 572–279, 581, 584–585, 588, 589–597, 598–605, 606, 607, 608–615, 625, 626–634, 640, 642–643, 644–645, 647, 912–913 988–989
COORDINATE GEOMETRY		
MA-HS-G-S-CG1 Students will express the intuitive concept of the "slant" of a line as slope, use the coordinates of two points on a line to determine its slope and use slope to express the parallelism and perpendicularity of lines.	**HOLT ALGEBRA 1** **LARSON ALGEBRA 1** **LARSON GEOMETRY** **LARSON ALGEBRA 2**	311–317, 320–325, 333, 349–355, 363, 365, 369, 371, 372, S12–S13 234, 235–242, 246 248, 250, 319–320, 321–322, 331 171–178, 204, 206, 210–211, 213, 379, 579, 879, 901 82–88, 96, 145, 147–149, 167, 232, 271, 315, 344, 427, 723, 894, 1011
MA-HS-G-S-CG2 Students will describe a line by a linear equation.	**HOLT ALGEBRA 1** **LARSON ALGEBRA 1** **LARSON GEOMETRY** **LARSON ALGEBRA 2**	335, 337–340, 342–343, 345–347, 352–355, 364, 365, 370–371, 372, S13 219, 230, 247, 283–289, 292–299, 302–308, 311–316, 319, 321–323 180–187, 197, 206, 209, 213, 246, 255, 429, 901 98–104, 105–106, 120, 138, 145, 1011
MA-HS-G-S-CG3 Students will find the distance between two points using their coordinates and the Pythagorean theorem or the distance formula.	**HOLT ALGEBRA 1** **LARSON ALGEBRA 1** **LARSON GEOMETRY** **LARSON ALGEBRA 2**	642–643, 802 743, 744–750, 756 17–18, 20–23, 50–51, 53, 297–298, 896 614–615, 617–619, 632, 673–674, 677–678, 749, 914, 1018
MA-HS-G-S-CG4 Students will find the equation of a circle given its center and radius; given the equation of a circle, find its center and radius.	**LARSON GEOMETRY** **LARSON ALGEBRA 2**	700, 702, 705, 711–712, 915 626–627, 629, 632, 1018

Standard	Program	Pages
MA-HS-G-S-CG5 Students will find the midpoint of a segment when the coordinates of the endpoints are identified.	**HOLT ALGEBRA 1** **LARSON ALGEBRA 1** **LARSON GEOMETRY** **LARSON ALGEBRA 2**	S68 745–747, 749–750, 756 16–17, 19, 22, 214, 896 615–617, 632, 648, 673, 678, 704, 1018
MA-HS-G-S-CG6 Students will use Cartesian coordinates and other coordinate systems (e.g., navigational, polar, spherical systems) to analyze geometric situations.	**HOLT ALGEBRA 1** **LARSON ALGEBRA 1** **LARSON GEOMETRY** **LARSON ALGEBRA 2**	57, 59, 350–351, 353–355, 419 210, 323, 746–747, 749, 751 A4–A6 17–23, 30, 32, 46, 50–51, 53, 58, 64, 211, 214, 218, 221–222, 235, 237, 239, 253, 260, 296–300, 322, 353, 385, 444, 447, 517–519, 525–527, 529–532, 538, 542, 546–547, 555, 558, 564, 569, 896–897, 901–902, 910–911, A4–A6 185, 204, 208–209, 614–615, 617, 679, 704, 809, 858, 872, A4–A6
MA-HS-G-S-CG7 Students will investigate conjectures and solve problems involving two-dimensional figures and three-dimensional objects represented graphically.	**HOLT ALGEBRA 1** **LARSON ALGEBRA 1** **LARSON GEOMETRY** **LARSON ALGEBRA 2**	57, 59, 350–351, 353–355 210 46, 50–51, 53, 218, 221–222, 235, 237, 239, 253, 260, 296–301, 322, 385, 444, 447, 517–519, 525–527, 529–532, 538, 542, 546–547, 555, 558, 897, 902–903, 910–911 129, 614–617, 619
MA-HS-G-S-CG8 Students will use a variety of technological tools to explore and test conjectures about slope, midpoints and other geometric ideas that can be expressed using the Cartesian plane	**HOLT ALGEBRA 1** **LARSON ALGEBRA 1** **LARSON GEOMETRY** **LARSON ALGEBRA 2**	320–325, 642–643, S68 290–291 179, 633 82–88, 614–619
FOUNDATIONAL STATEMENTS		
MA-HS-G-S-FS1 Students will identify, explain the necessity of and give examples of definitions, axioms and theorems.	**LARSON GEOMETRY**	9–10, 24–25, 96, 113, 124–126, 148, 154–155, 161–162, 164, 172, 190–192, 218, 220, 227–228, 234, 240–241, 249, 264–265, 295, 303, 305, 310, 312, 319–320, 328, 330, 335, 374, 381, 388, 390, 397–398, 433, 441–442, 449, 452, 457, 459, 507, 509, 515, 517, 522–523, 533, 535, 543–545, 573, 591, 601, 609–610, 653–654, 660, 664–666, 672–675, 680–681, 689–691, 720–721, 730–731, 737, 746–747, 755–756, 763, 795, 804–805, 811–812, 819–821, 829, 838, 840, 848
MA-HS-G-S-FS2 Students will explore geometries other than Euclidean geometry, in which the parallel postulate is not true.	**LARSON GEOMETRY** **LARSON ALGEBRA 2**	753–754 A5–A6
MA-HS-G-S-FS3 Students will establish the validity of geometric conjectures using deduction, prove theorems and critique arguments made by others.	**LARSON ALGEBRA 1** **LARSON GEOMETRY** **LARSON ALGEBRA 2**	239, 740, 748 76, 91, 117, 122, 124–126, 129–130, 156–157, 159–160, 163, 166, 168, 191, 196, 219, 222–223, 230, 233, 252, 254, 259, 267, 269, 299–300, 307–308, 315–316, 334, 340–341, 389, 395, 402–403, 446, 455–456, 463, 512, 520–521, 526, 528–529, 531, 536, 539–540, 548–549, 658, 662, 668–670, 678, 685, 694, 736 1000–1001
MA-HS-G-S-FS4 Students will perform constructions such as a line parallel to a given line through a point not on the line, the perpendicular bisector of a line segment and the bisector of an angle.	**LARSON GEOMETRY**	33–34, 152, 169, 195, 235, 307, 314, 323, 401, 767

Big Idea: Data Analysis and Probability

High school students extend data representations, interpretations and conclusions. They describe data distributions in multiple ways and connect data gathering issues with data interpretation issues. They relate curve-of-best-fit with two-variable data and determine a line-of-best-fit for a given set of data. They distinguish between combinations and permutations and compare and contrast theoretical and experimental probability.

Academic Expectations

2.8 Students understand various mathematical procedures and use them appropriately and accurately.
2.13 Students understand and appropriately use statistics and probability.

Standard	Program	Pages
DATA REPRESENTATIONS		
MA-HS-DAP-S-DR1 Students will be familiar with the definitions of measurement data and categorical data, univariate and bivariate data and the term variable.	**HOLT ALGEBRA 1** **LARSON ALGEBRA 1** **LARSON GEOMETRY** **LARSON ALGEBRA 2**	676–677, 678–686, 687–693, 700–701 325–331, 332–333, 334, 335–341, 342, 881–885, 886, 887–892, 893, 933, 934, 935 887, 888–889 112, 113–120, 724, 1006–1007, 1008–1009

Standard	Program	Pages
MA-HS-DAP-S-DR2 Students will apply histograms, parallel box plots and scatterplots to display data.	**HOLT ALGEBRA 1**	262, 266–269, 270–271, 278, 279, 283, 284, 688, 691–692, 696–698, 701, 710, 711, 751, 754, 759, S22, S37
	LARSON ALGEBRA 1	42, 326–330, 332–333, 334, 335, 338–341, 687, 688, 690, 882–884, 886, 893, A18, A19, A24–A25
	LARSON GEOMETRY	48, 363, 488, 888–889, A18, A19, A24–A25
	LARSON ALGEBRA 2	112, 113–120, 888, 1008–1009, A18, A19, A24–A25
MA-HS-DAP-S-DR3 Students will display the distribution, analyze patterns and describe relationships in paired data for univariate measurement data.	**HOLT ALGEBRA 1**	262–269, 270, 271, 277, 278, 279, 283, 284, 678–686, 687–693, 696–699, 700–701, 707, 710, 711, 750–751, 754, S11, S22, S31, S37
	LARSON ALGEBRA 1	881–885, 886, 887–892, 893–894, 950, A18, A19, A24–A25
	LARSON GEOMETRY	888–889, A18, A19, A24–A25
	LARSON ALGEBRA 2	1006–1007, 1008–1009
MA-HS-DAP-S-DR4 Students will display a scatterplot and describe its shape for bivariate data	**HOLT ALGEBRA 1**	262–263, 266–269, 270, 271, 277, 278, 279, 283, 284, S11
	LARSON ALGEBRA 1	42, 326–330, 332–335, 338–341, 687, 688, 690 A18, A19, A24–A25
	LARSON GEOMETRY	48, 363, 488, A18, A19, A24–A25
	LARSON ALGEBRA 2	112–115, 117–119, 311, 314, 774, 775–780, 781, A18, A19, A24–A25
MA-HS-DAP-S-DR5 Students will display and discuss bivariate data where at least one variable is categorical.	**HOLT ALGEBRA 1**	676–677, 679, 680–686, 693, 700, 711, 750, S22, S37
	LARSON ALGEBRA 1	933
	LARSON GEOMETRY	888–889
	LARSON ALGEBRA 2	1006–1007
MA-HS-DAP-S-DR6 Students will organize and display data using appropriate methods (e.g., spreadsheets and graphing calculators) to detect patterns and departures from patterns.	**HOLT ALGEBRA 1**	267–269, 279, 283, 284
	LARSON ALGEBRA 1	325–331, 332–333, 334, 335–343, A18–A19
	LARSON GEOMETRY	32, 48, 363, 488, 888–889, 891–892, A18–A19
	LARSON ALGEBRA 2	116–119, 311, 314, 774, 775–780, 781, A18–A19, A24–A25
MA-HS-DAP-S-DR7 Students will identify and explain misleading uses of data displays.	**HOLT ALGEBRA 1**	702–707, 711, 752, 754, S22
	LARSON ALGEBRA 1	A12–A13
	LARSON GEOMETRY	742, A12–A13
	LARSON ALGEBRA 2	A12–A13
CHARACTERISTICS OF DATA SETS		
MA-HS-DAP-S-CDS1 Students will understand the distinction between a statistic and a parameter.	**LARSON ALGEBRA 1**	A7–A8
	LARSON GEOMETRY	A7, A8
	LARSON ALGEBRA 2	A7, A8
MA-HS-DAP-S-CDS2 Students will describe the shape and select and calculate summary statistics for univariate measurement data, using technological tools as necessary.	**HOLT ALGEBRA 1**	694–695, 697–699, 701, 711, 751, 754, S22, S37
	LARSON ALGEBRA 1	875–878, 879–880, 881, 888, 892
	LARSON GEOMETRY	887
	LARSON ALGEBRA 2	727–728, 742, 744–749, 750, 755–756, 787, 790–791, 848–849, 1005, 1020, A8
MA-HS-DAP-S-CDS3 Students will recognize how linear transformations of univariate data affect shape, center and spread.	**HOLT ALGEBRA 1**	699
	LARSON ALGEBRA 1	875–878, 879–880
	LARSON GEOMETRY	887
	LARSON ALGEBRA 2	751–756, 787, 791, 1020
MA-HS-DAP-S-CDS4 Students will determine regression coefficients, regression equations and correlation coefficients for bivariate data using technological tools.	**HOLT ALGEBRA 1**	270
	LARSON ALGEBRA 1	332–333, 335–340, 692–693
	LARSON GEOMETRY	48, 363, 488, A24–A25
	LARSON ALGEBRA 2	114, 116–119
MA-HS-DAP-S-CDS5 Students will apply line-of-best fit equations for a set of two-variable data to make predictions.	**HOLT ALGEBRA 1**	265, 267–269, 270, 279, 283, 284
	LARSON ALGEBRA 1	334, 336–340, 342
	LARSON GEOMETRY	48, A24–A25
	LARSON ALGEBRA 2	116–117, 119, 139, 233, 475, 791
MA-HS-DAP-S-CDS6 Students will collect, organize and display bivariate data and use a curve of best fit as a model to make predictions.	**HOLT ALGEBRA 1**	262–269, 270
	LARSON ALGEBRA 1	687, 690, 692–693
	LARSON GEOMETRY	48, 363, 488, A24–A25
	LARSON ALGEBRA 2	308, 311, 314, 774, 775–780, 781–782, 1020, A18, A19, A24–A25
MA-HS-DAP-S-CDS7 Students will identify trends in bivariate data and find functions that model the data or transform the data, so that they can be modeled.	**HOLT ALGEBRA 1**	263, 265–269, 270, 271, 277, 279, 283, 284, S11, S31
	LARSON ALGEBRA 1	325–331, 332–333, 335–341, 342, 684–691, 692–693
	LARSON GEOMETRY	48, A24–A25
	LARSON ALGEBRA 2	115–116, 118–120, 139, 308, 311, 314, 774, 775–780, 781–782, 1011, 1020

Standard	Program	Pages
MA-HS-DAP-S-CDS8 Students will understand how simple statistics reflect the values of population parameters and use sampling distributions as the basis for informal inference.	**HOLT ALGEBRA 1** **LARSON ALGEBRA 1** **LARSON GEOMETRY** **LARSON ALGEBRA 2**	708 A7–A8 A7–A8 A7–A8
MA-HS-DAP-S-CDS9 Students will explore how basic statistical techniques monitor process characteristics in the workplace.	**HOLT ALGEBRA 1** **LARSON ALGEBRA 1** **LARSON GEOMETRY** **LARSON ALGEBRA 2**	684, 701 A8 A8 A8
MA-HS-DAP-S-CDS10 Students will compare data sets using graphs and summary statistics.	**HOLT ALGEBRA 1** **LARSON ALGEBRA 1** **LARSON GEOMETRY** **LARSON ALGEBRA 2**	679–680, 683–686, 697, 750 876, 878, 888, 893, 887, 888–889 744–745, 749, 791, 849
MA-HS-DAP-S-CDS11 Students will know the characteristics of the Gaussian normal distribution (bell-shaped curve).	**HOLT ALGEBRA 1** **LARSON ALGEBRA 2**	S74 757–762, 763–765, 780, 782, 787, 789–791, 1020
MA-HS-DAP-S-CDS12 Students will evaluate reports based on data published in the media by considering the source of the data, the design of the study and the way the data are displayed and analyzed.	**HOLT ALGEBRA 1** **LARSON ALGEBRA 1** **LARSON GEOMETRY** **LARSON ALGEBRA 2**	702, 704–706, 711, 752, 754, S22 A9–A11 A9–A11 A9–A11
MA-HS-DAP-S-CDS13 Students will identify and explain misleading uses of data.	**HOLT ALGEBRA 1** **LARSON ALGEBRA 1** **LARSON GEOMETRY** **LARSON ALGEBRA 2**	702–707, 711, 743, 752, 754, S22, S37 A12–A13 742, A12–A13 A12–A13
EXPERIMENTS AND SAMPLES		
MA-HS-DAP-S-ES1 Students will understand and explain the differences among various kinds of studies (e.g., randomized experiments and observational studies) and which types of inferences can be legitimately be drawn from each.	**HOLT ALGEBRA 1** **LARSON ALGEBRA 1** **LARSON ALGEBRA 2**	708–709 842, 871–874 766–767, 769–770, 772–774
MA-HS-DAP-S-ES2 Students will know the characteristics of well-designed studies, including the role of randomization in surveys and experiments.	**HOLT ALGEBRA 1** **LARSON ALGEBRA 1** **LARSON ALGEBRA 2**	708–709, S73 871–874 766–767, 769–770, 772–774
MA-HS-DAP-S-ES3 Students will use simulations to explore the variability of sample statistics from a known population and to construct sampling distributions.	**HOLT ALGEBRA 1** **LARSON ALGEBRA 1** **LARSON GEOMETRY** **LARSON ALGEBRA 2**	712 A14–A15 A14–A15 A14–A15
MA-HS-DAP-S-ES4 Students will evaluate published reports that are based on interpretations of data by examining the design of the study, the appropriateness of the data analysis and the validity of the conclusions.	**HOLT ALGEBRA 1** **LARSON ALGEBRA 1** **LARSON GEOMETRY** **LARSON ALGEBRA 2**	703–707, 709, 711, S22, S37 A9–A11 A9–A11 A9–A11
MA-HS-DAP-S-ES5 Students will explain the impact of sampling methods, bias and the phrasing of questions asked during data collection and the conclusions that can be justified.	**HOLT ALGEBRA 1** **LARSON ALGEBRA 1** **LARSON GEOMETRY** **LARSON ALGEBRA 2**	709, S73 871–874 890 766–767, 769, 772–773
MA-HS-DAP-S-ES6 Students will design and conduct simple experiments or investigations to collect data to answer student-generated questions.	**HOLT ALGEBRA 1** **LARSON ALGEBRA 1** **LARSON ALGEBRA 2**	234, 316, 617 842, 849–850 772–773

PROBABILITY		
MA-HS-DAP-S-P1 Students will design and conduct probability simulations and interpret the results.	**HOLT ALGEBRA 1** **LARSON ALGEBRA 1** **LARSON GEOMETRY** **LARSON ALGEBRA 2**	712, 719 849–850, A14, A15 A14, A15 714, A14, A15
MA-HS-DAP-S-P2 Students will apply the concepts of sample space and probability distribution to construct sample spaces and distributions in simple cases.	**HOLT ALGEBRA 1** **LARSON ALGEBRA 1** **LARSON GEOMETRY** **LARSON ALGEBRA 2**	713, 716 843, 846, 847, A15 A15 724–731, A15
MA-HS-DAP-S-P3 Students will design simulations to construct empirical probability distributions and report/ interpret the results.	**HOLT ALGEBRA 1** **LARSON ALGEBRA 1** **LARSON GEOMETRY** **LARSON ALGEBRA 2**	719 849–850, A14–A15 A14, A15 A14, A15
MA-HS-DAP-S-P4 Students will compute and interpret the expected value of random variables in simple cases.	**HOLT ALGEBRA 1** **LARSON ALGEBRA 1** **LARSON GEOMETRY** **LARSON ALGEBRA 2**	720–721, 723–725 A21 A21 A21
MA-HS-DAP-S-P5 Students will apply the concepts of conditional probability and independent events and be able to compute those probabilities.	**HOLT ALGEBRA 1** **LARSON ALGEBRA 1** **LARSON GEOMETRY** **LARSON ALGEBRA 2**	726–728, 730–732, 753, S23 862–863, 864–867, 898 893 717–723, 730, 732, 849, 1019
MA-HS-DAP-S-P6 Students will compute the probability of a compound event.	**HOLT ALGEBRA 1** **LARSON ALGEBRA 1** **LARSON GEOMETRY** **LARSON ALGEBRA 2**	734–735 861–867, 868–869, 898 893 707–713, 732, 762, 848, 1019
MA-HS-DAP-S-P7 Students will explain how probability quantifies the likelihood that an event occurs in terms of numbers.	**HOLT ALGEBRA 1** **LARSON ALGEBRA 1** **LARSON GEOMETRY** **LARSON ALGEBRA 2**	713 843, 846 893 698, 742
MA-HS-DAP-S-P8 Students will explain how the relative frequency of a specified outcome of an event can be used to estimate the probability of the outcome.	**HOLT ALGEBRA 1** **LARSON ALGEBRA 1** **LARSON GEOMETRY** **LARSON ALGEBRA 2**	714, 718, 720 842, A20–A21 893, A20–A21 700, 702, 735, A20–A21
MA-HS-DAP-S-P9 Students will explain how the law of large numbers can be applied in simple examples.	**HOLT ALGEBRA 1** **LARSON ALGEBRA 1** **LARSON GEOMETRY** **LARSON ALGEBRA 2**	714, 717, 719 A17 A17 A17
MA-HS-DAP-S-P10 Students will determine and compare theoretical and experimental probabilities.	**HOLT ALGEBRA 1** **LARSON ALGEBRA 1** **LARSON GEOMETRY** **LARSON ALGEBRA 2**	714–718, 719, 720–721, 723–725, 733, 752, 754, 755, S23, S37 842, 844–848, 853–855, 857, 859, 861–867, 868–869, A16, A17 770, A16, A17 698, 700–705, 713, 740–742, 809, 1019, A16–A17, A20 –A21
MA-HS-DAP-S-P11 Students will determine the probability of an event and the probability of its complement.	**HOLT ALGEBRA 1** **LARSON ALGEBRA 1** **LARSON GEOMETRY** **LARSON ALGEBRA 2**	721, 723–725, 754, S23, S37 865, A16, A17 85, 334, 615, 770, 771–777, 893, 917, A16, A17 709–710, 712, 736
MA-HS-DAP-S-P12 Students will make predictions and draw inferences from probabilities. And apply probability concepts to practical situations to make informed decisions.	**HOLT ALGEBRA 1** **LARSON ALGEBRA 1** **LARSON GEOMETRY** **LARSON ALGEBRA 2**	715–718, 732, 752, 754 842, 848, 859 778 698–704, 707–713, 717–723
MA-HS-DAP-S-P13 Students will determine probabilities involving replacement and non-replacement.	**HOLT ALGEBRA 1** **LARSON ALGEBRA 1** **LARSON GEOMETRY** **LARSON ALGEBRA 2**	727–733, 745, 753, S23, S37 862, 863–865 893 719, 722, 730, 865, 1019
MA-HS-DAP-S-P14 Students will recognize and identify the differences between combinations and permutations and use them to count discrete quantities.	**HOLT ALGEBRA 1** **LARSON ALGEBRA 1** **LARSON GEOMETRY** **LARSON ALGEBRA 2**	737–743, 744, 745, 753, 754, S23 851–855, 856–859, 860, 867 891–892 684–690, 694 –697, 705, 737, 755, 1019

Standard	Program	Pages
MA-HS-DAP-S-P15 Students will represent probabilities in multiple ways (e.g., fractions, decimals, percentages, geometric area models).	**HOLT ALGEBRA 1**	714–718, 719, 720–721, 723–725, 726–733, 734–735, 742–743, 744, 745, 752–753, 754, 755, 890, S23, S37
	LARSON ALGEBRA 1	842, 844–848, 853–855, 857, 859, 861–867, 868–869, 874, A16, A17, A20, A21
	LARSON GEOMETRY	85, 334, 615, 770, 771–777, 893, 917, A16, A17, A20–A21
	LARSON ALGEBRA 2	698–704, 706, 707–713, 714, 717–723, 724–730, 731, 732, 737, 742, 1019, A14–A17, A20–A21
Big Idea: Algebraic Thinking High school students extend analysis and use of functions and focus on linear, quadratic, absolute value and exponential functions. They explore parametric changes on graphs of functions. They use rules and properties to simplify algebraic expressions. They combine simple rational expressions and simple polynomial expressions. They factor polynomial expressions and quadratics of the form $1x^2 + bx + c$. **Academic Expectations** 2.7 Students underst and number concepts and use numbers appropriately and accurately. 2.8 Students understand various mathematical procedures and use them appropriately and accurately. 2.11 Students understand mathematical change concepts and use them appropriately and accurately. 2.12 Students understand mathematical structure concepts including the properties and logic of various mathematical systems.		
PATTERNS, RELATIONS AND FUNCTIONS		
MA-HS-AT-S-PRF1 Students will use explicitly-defined or recursively defined functions to generalize patterns.	**HOLT ALGEBRA 1**	245, 249–251, 261, 276, 282, 770, S10
	LARSON ALGEBRA 1	37, 39, 40, 44–47
	LARSON GEOMETRY	76–78, 200, 325, 736, 752
	LARSON ALGEBRA 2	37–40, 107–111, 112, 113–120, 143, 145, 311, 314, 322–323, 396–399, 774, 775–780, 781, 803–804, 806–812, 814–817, 826, 828–829, 831–833, 838, 843–844, 846–848, 1021
MA-HS-AT-S-PRF2 Students will understand relations and functions and use various representations for them.	**HOLT ALGEBRA 1**	55–59, 61, 65, 66, 236–242, 243, 245–251, 252–258, 259, 260, 261, 269, 281–282, 284, 285, 296–302, 303–308, 334–340, 341–347, 355, 364, 365, 366–367, 368, 370, 372, 591, 594–597, 606–611, 619, 621, 662–663, 666, 773–778, 788, 795, 797, 800–803, 829, 836, 838, 840, 860–865, 873, 877, 905, 911, S10–S11, S12–S13, S20, S24, S26
	LARSON ALGEBRA 1	35–40, 41, 42, 43–48, 49–50, 262–268, 283–289, 290–291, 292–299, 302–308, 311–316, 396–397, 520–527, 528–529, 530, 531–538, 628–634, 635–640, 641–642, 710–716, 717, 734, 773–774, 775–782, A22–A23
	LARSON GEOMETRY	14, 76–78, 200, 325, 415, 565, 736, 752, 768, A22–A23
	LARSON ALGEBRA 2	72–79, 80–81, 89–96, 97, 98–104, 105, 107–111, 121–122, 123–129, 130–131, 145, 236–238, 239–243, 245–251, 265, 270–271, 272–273, 287, 289–291, 297, 309–315, 323, 340–344, 352, 356, 358, 360–361, 368–369, 376, 386, 387–392, 393–399, 406, 407, 446–451, 459, 465, 468–469, 478–485, 486–491, 493–498, 502–505, 513–514, 529–536, 543, 558–563, 564, 565–571, 589–590, 594, 607, 775–780, 781, 786–787, 908–914, 915–922, 941–947, 969, 1011, 1013–1017, 1020, 1023, A22–A23
MA-HS-AT-S-PRF3 Students will analyze functions by investigating rates of change, intercepts, zeros, asymptotes and local and global behavior.	**HOLT ALGEBRA 1**	303–308, 311–317, 318–319, 320–325, 331, 332, 333, 369, 372, 599–600, 603–605, 611, 620, 621, 663, 666, 859–860, 862–865, 911, 914, S12, S20, S26
	LARSON ALGEBRA 1	225–232, 239, 243, 244, 247, 250, 337–341, 642, 645–646, 647, 649, 651, 767, 773–774, 779
	LARSON GEOMETRY	171, 175, 204, 206, 211
	LARSON ALGEBRA 2	82–88, 89–96, 120, 255–257, 339, 342, 344, 369, 379–386, 387–392, 399–400, 407, 410–411, 459, 478–479, 483, 486–487, 490, 610, 1013–1014
MA-HS-AT-S-PRF4 Students will transform functions (e.g., arithmetically combining, composing and inverting commonly used functions), using technology on more complicated symbolic expressions.	**HOLT ALGEBRA 1**	356, 357–360, 612, 613–619, 799–800, 804
	LARSON ALGEBRA 1	556, 558–559, 567–568, 805, 807, 808, 809
	LARSON ALGEBRA 2	428–434, 435–437, 438–445, 469, 474, 1015
MA-HS-AT-S-PRF5 Students will understand and compare the properties of classes of functions (e.g., absolute value, step, exponential, polynomial, rational, logarithmic, periodic).	**HOLT ALGEBRA 1**	296–302, 308, 366, 368, 372, 590, 594–597, 605, 662, 666, 772, 776, 858, 862
	LARSON ALGEBRA 1	263, 265, 396, 523, 533, 628, 635, 710, 713, 775
	LARSON GEOMETRY	499, 565
	LARSON ALGEBRA 2	80–81, 121–122, 123–129, 130–131,446–451, 478–485, 486–491, 492–498, 499–505, 507–513, 514, 540–541, 543, 558–563, 564, 565–571, 607, 678

Standard	Text	Pages
MA-HS-AT-S-PRF6 Students will interpret representations of functions of two variables.	**HOLT ALGEBRA 1**	55–59, 61, 65, 237–241, 243, 245, 248–251, 252–258, 260, 261, 296–302, 303–308, 332, 333, 336–339, 343–346, 366–367, 368–369, 372, 590–597, 599–605, 606–611, 772–778, 789–795, 797, 798–803, 840, 858–865
	LARSON ALGEBRA 1	45, 47–48, 208, 211, 218–222, 224, 227–228, 230–232, 262–269, 285, 288–289, 294–295, 298, 299, 308, 313, 315, 521–522, 524–526, 532, 534–535, 537, 538, 631, 635–640, 642, 650–651, 670, 710–716, 717, 776–778, 781
	LARSON GEOMETRY	41, 76–77, 111, 378, 513
	LARSON ALGEBRA 2	72–79, 80–81, 89–96, 97, 98–104, 105, 107–111, 121–122, 123–129, 130–131, 145, 236–243, 245–251, 265, 270–273, 287, 289–291, 297, 309–315, 323, 340–344, 352, 356, 358, 360–361, 368–369, 376, 386, 387–392, 393–399, 407, 446–451, 459, 469, 478–485, 486–491, 493–498, 502–505, 513–514, 529–536, 543, 558–563, 564, 565–571, 589–590, 594, 607 775–780, 781, 908–914, 915–922, 941–947, 969, 1011, 1013–1017, 1020, 1023
MA-HS-AT-S-PRF7 Students will use a variety of symbolic representations, including recursive and parametric equations, for functions and relations.	**HOLT ALGEBRA 1**	55, 57–58, 61, 65, 66, 245–251, 257, 260, 261, 307, 332, 335–339, 342–347, 370, 372, 781–787, 796, 797, 837, 840, 864, S13, S32, S38
	LARSON ALGEBRA 1	283–289, 290–291, 292–299, 304, 305, 307–308, 319, 321–324, 327–331, 335–336, 338–343, 522, 525–526, 528–530, 534, 537–538, 634, 640, 778, 780–782, 839, A22–A23
	LARSON GEOMETRY	76–78, 200, 325, 378, 447, 736, 752, 768, A22–A23
	LARSON ALGEBRA 2	37–40, 107–111, 112, 113–120, 145, 311, 314, 396–399, 563, 774, 775–780, 781, 803– 804, 806–812, 814–817, 827, 828–829, 831–833, 843, A22–A23
MA-HS-AT-S-PRF8 Students will identify essential quantitative relationships in a situation and determine the class or classes of functions that might model the relationship.	**HOLT ALGEBRA 1**	301, 307, 332, 337–339, 343–346, 781–788, 789–795, 796, 797, 837, 840, 864, S32, S38
	LARSON ALGEBRA 1	327–331, 333, 334. 335–336, 338–341, 684–691, 692–693
	LARSON GEOMETRY	*Not addressed in this text.*
	LARSON ALGEBRA 2	115–116, 118–120, 139, 308, 311, 314, 774, 775–780, 781, 782, 1011, 1020
MA-HS-AT-S-PRF9 Students will determine whether a relationship given in symbolic or graphical form is a function.	**HOLT ALGEBRA 1**	237–242, 243, 251, 261, 281, 284, S10
	LARSON ALGEBRA 1	49–50
	LARSON ALGEBRA 2	73–74, 77–78, 128, 232
MA-HS-AT-S-PRF10 Students will determine the domain of a function represented in either symbolic or graphical form.	**HOLT ALGEBRA 1**	237–242, 260, 261, 281, 284, 299, 301, 366–367, 596, 621, 799–803, 815, 829, 838, 840, 841, 853, 856–857, 861, 863–864, S10, S25
	LARSON ALGEBRA 1	44–46, 218, 220–221, 232, 263, 267–268, 521, 524, 526, 532, 535, 631, 633, 710–711, 712–716, 717, 734, 776, 779, 782
	LARSON ALGEBRA 2	78–79, 81, 96, 391, 446–450, 459, 464, 476, 478–479, 482, 484, 487–489, 493–494, 496, 498, 503–504, 513, 543, 558–559, 560–562, 565, 607, 611, 792, 1015–1017
MA-HS-AT-S-PRF11 Students will understand functional notation and evaluate a function at a specified point in its domain.	**HOLT ALGEBRA 1**	247–251, 261, 282, 284, 285, 772, 777, S10
	LARSON ALGEBRA 1	262, 265–266, 268
	LARSON ALGEBRA 2	75, 78, 130–131, 338, 341, 445, 472
MA-HS-AT-S-PRF12 Students will combine functions by addition, subtraction, multiplication and compositions.	**HOLT ALGEBRA 1**	356, 357–360, 612, 613–619, 799–800, 804
	LARSON ALGEBRA 1	556, 558–559, 567–568, 805, 807, 808, 809
	LARSON ALGEBRA 2	428–434, 435, 436, 445, 469, 474, 792, 1015
MA-HS-AT-S-PRF13 Students will graph linear, absolute value, quadratic and exponential functions and identify their key characteristics.	**HOLT ALGEBRA 1**	252–258, 259, 261, 282, 284, 298–302, 303–308, 325, 333, 334, 336, 338, 341, 345, 347, 365, 366–367, 368, 370, 372, 606–611, 619, 621, 662–663, 666, 773–778, 788, 795, 797, 836, 840, S11, S12, S20, S24
	LARSON ALGEBRA 1	43, 46, 48, 216–221, 222, 226–232, 245, 248–250, 254, 257, 263–268, 396–397, 521, 524–526, 532, 535, 537–538, 628–634, 635–640, 641–642, 643–649, 650–651, 669–670, 696–697
	LARSON GEOMETRY	41, 77, 111, 378, 499, 513, 565, 884
	LARSON ALGEBRA 2	89–96, 97, 103–104, 107, 109, 121–122, 123–124, 125–131, 145, 150, 236–243, 244, 245–251, 265, 292–294, 299, 323, 328, 478–480, 482–485, 486–491, 498, 543–544, 546, 612, 1011, 1013, 1016
MA-HS-AT-S-PRF14 Students will recognize and solve problems that can be modeled using linear, absolute value, quadratic or exponential functions.	**HOLT ALGEBRA 1**	301, 304, 306–307, 337–338, 343–346, 368, 596, 602, 604–605, 607–610, 621, 663, 666, 781–788, 789–795, 796, 797, 837, 840, S32, S36, S38
	LARSON ALGEBRA 1	37, 39–40, 220–221, 230, 285, 288–289, 294–295, 298–299, 522, 525–526, 534, 537–538, 541, 631, 633–634, 637, 639–640
	LARSON GEOMETRY	41, 78, 378, 513, 884
	LARSON ALGEBRA 2	91, 94–95, 100–101, 103–106, 107–111, 112, 115–116, 117, 119–120, 125–126, 128–129, 131, 139, 145, 239, 241–243, 246–247, 250–251, 254, 256–258, 261–262, 264–265, 268–274, 287, 289–290, 295, 298–299, 311, 314–315, 480–485, 488–491, 543, 546–547, 730, 775–780, 781, 787, 849, 954

Standard	Correlations
MA-HS-AT-S-PRF15 Students will extend the ideas of transformations and parametric changes of linear function, such as vertical and horizontal shifts, to transformations of non-linear functions.	**HOLT ALGEBRA 1** 613–619, 621, 627, 664, 666, S20 **LARSON ALGEBRA 1** 521, 524, 532, 535, 629–633, 649, 710–714, 734, 775–776, 779 **LARSON GEOMETRY** 579, 686, 845 **LARSON ALGEBRA 2** 121–122, 123–124, 125–128, 138, 236–237, 240, 392, 478–479, 485, 522, 539–540, 749, 817, 1011
MA-HS-AT-S-PRF16 Students will see the patterns in arithmetic and geometric sequences using recursion.	**HOLT ALGEBRA 1** 272–273, 275–277, 279, 283, 284, 766–771, 778, 797, 836, 840, 841, S11, S24, S38 **LARSON ALGEBRA 1** 309–310, 539–540 **LARSON GEOMETRY** 72, 75–76, 134, 138, 898 **LARSON ALGEBRA 2** 826, 827–833, 834–835, 1021
MA-HS-AT-S-PRF17 Students will see patterns in other sequences (e.g., quadratic, cubic).	**HOLT ALGEBRA 1** 276, 771 **LARSON ALGEBRA 1** 309–310, 539–540 **LARSON GEOMETRY** 72, 76, 78, 119, 898 **LARSON ALGEBRA 2** 795
MA-HS-AT-S-PRF18 Students will relate the patterns in arithmetic sequences to linear functions.	**HOLT ALGEBRA 1** 273–274, 276 **LARSON ALGEBRA 1** 310 **LARSON GEOMETRY** 76, 78 **LARSON ALGEBRA 2** 803–804, 806–808, 817, 1021
MA-HS-AT-S-PRF19 Students will relate the patterns in geometric sequences to exponential functions.	**HOLT ALGEBRA 1** 767–768, 770–771 **LARSON ALGEBRA 1** 540 **LARSON GEOMETRY** 72, 75, 134, 898 **LARSON ALGEBRA 2** 811–812, 814–818, 1021
MA-HS-AT-S-PRF20 Students will solve problems that have direct or inverse relationships for any variable.	**HOLT ALGEBRA 1** 328–331, 333, 370, 373, 853–857, 876, 877, 910, 914, S13, S26, S39 **LARSON ALGEBRA 1** 253, 255, 257–259, 269, 767–771, 949 **LARSON ALGEBRA 2** 108–110, 120, 139, 145–146, 233, 548, 551–553, 555–556, 571–572, 607, 611, 848, 1011, 1017
VARIABLES, EXPRESSIONS AND OPERATIONS	
MA-HS-AT-S-VE01 Students will write expressions, equations, inequalities and relations in equivalent forms.	**HOLT ALGEBRA 1** 48–51, 52–53, 59, 61, 65, 66, 107–111, 113, 153, 156, 173, 179, 203, 212–214, 530, 531–537, 538–539, 540–547, 548–554, 555, 556, 557, 558–564, 566–571, 572, 573, 575–577, 578, 579, S5, S18–S19, S35 **LARSON ALGEBRA 1** 96–101, 105–106, 116, 149, 184–189, 381, 391, 488, 489–494, 495–501, 505–506, 555–559, 561, 562–568, 569–574, 582, 583–589, 592, 593–599, 600–605, 606–613, 719–726, 734, 794–800, 802–809, 810–811, 812–819, 826 **LARSON GEOMETRY** 160, 187, 871–873, 877 **LARSON ALGEBRA 2** 12, 14, 16, 26–32, 40, 51–58, 65, 129, 248–249, 252–253, 255–256, 259–260, 263–265, 323, 328, 331–334, 352–357, 407, 411–412, 419, 423, 425, 427, 469, 472–474, 492–493, 495–496, 498–499, 501, 503–504, 508, 510, 513, 548580, 678, 1010, 1013–1016
MA-HS-AT-S-VE02 Students will use symbolic algebra to represent and explain mathematical relationships.	**HOLT ALGEBRA 1** 6–11, 25, 62, 66, 79–82, 86–90, 94–98, 102–105, 113, 137, 150–151, 152–153, 170–173, 175–179, 182–185, 186, 187, 190–193, 195, 197–200, 276–277, S4, S29, S30 **LARSON ALGEBRA 1** 14, 15, 18, 20, 21, 24–25, 142, 144, 151, 158–159, 356–357, 359–360, 366, 372–373, 385, 394, 401, 410, 448, 455, 470, 667, 675 **LARSON GEOMETRY** 36–37, 39–41, 76–78, 180–187, 189, 200, 210–211, 213, 220, 325, 378, 447, 736, 752, 768, 901 **LARSON ALGEBRA 2** 11, 13, 15–16, 20–21, 23–24, 32–33, 34–40, 42, 44, 46–47, 54–55, 57–59, 81, 95, 100–101, 103–106, 108–111, 115–117, 119–120, 125–126, 128–129, 134–135, 137–139, 145, 147–149, 239, 242–243, 250–251, 262, 265, 268–271, 274, 311, 314, 396, 398–399, 405, 407, 439, 441–442, 444, 451, 469, 480, 483–485, 488, 490–491, 530–537, 542–543, 546–547, 552–553, 553–557, 560–562, 564, 567, 569–572, 606–607, 611, 775–780, 781–782, 910–911, 913–914, 942–947, 969
MA-HS-AT-S-VE03 Students will use symbolic expressions, including iterative and recursive forms, to represent relationships among various contexts.	**HOLT ALGEBRA 1** 6–11, 25, 62, 66, 105, 137, 198, S4 **LARSON ALGEBRA 1** 14, 15–20 **LARSON GEOMETRY** 78 **LARSON ALGEBRA 2** 11, 13, 15–16, 62, 65, 984
MA-HS-AT-S-VE04 Students will judge the meaning, utility and reasonableness of the results of symbol manipulations, including those carried out using technology.	**HOLT ALGEBRA 1** 79–82, 88–89, 95, 97, 104, 118, 120, 122, 124, 128, 131, 176, 255, 344, 798 **LARSON ALGEBRA 1** 139, 143, 146, 153, 155, 159, 360, 371, 374, 436, 456, 654, 664, 667, 672, 676, 730–731, 820–826 **LARSON GEOMETRY** 894–895 **LARSON ALGEBRA 2** 157, 158, 166, 184, 186, 254, 261, 269, 286, 290, 295, 356, 359, 434, 484, 491, 560, 592

Standard	Text	Pages
MA-HS-AT-S-VE05 Students will understand the properties of integer exponents and roots and apply these properties to simplify algebraic expressions.	**HOLT ALGEBRA 1** **LARSON ALGEBRA 1** **LARSON GEOMETRY** **LARSON ALGEBRA 2**	460–466, 467–473, 475, 481, 489, 511–512, 514, 805–810, 821, 838, 840, S16, S25 489–494, 495–501, 505–506, 719–721, 723–724, 734 139, 160, 187, 292, 549, 871–872 330–334, 352, 377, 402, 407, 411–412, 423, 425, 427, 434, 467, 469, 472–474, 1014–1015
MA-HS-AT-S-VE06 Students will add, subtract and multiply polynomials.	**HOLT ALGEBRA 1** **LARSON ALGEBRA 1** **LARSON GEOMETRY** **LARSON ALGEBRA 2**	482–483, 484–489, 490–491, 492–499, 500, 501–507, 509, 513, 514, S17, S34 555–559, 561, 562–568, 569–574 152, 187, 549, 872, 873 346–352, 407, 474, 548, 1014
MA-HS-AT-S-VE07 Students will divide a polynomial by a first-degree polynomial.	**HOLT ALGEBRA 1** **LARSON ALGEBRA 1** **LARSON GEOMETRY** **LARSON ALGEBRA 2**	892, 893–899, 907, 913, 914, S27 783, 784–791, 800, 809 *Not addressed in this text.* 363–364, 366, 377, 1014
MA-HS-AT-S-VE08 Students will factor polynomials by removing the greatest common factor.	**HOLT ALGEBRA 1** **LARSON ALGEBRA 1** **LARSON GEOMETRY** **LARSON ALGEBRA 2**	531–537, 575, 578, S18, S35 576, 578–579, 599, 607–608, 610, 613, 706, 762, 946 713 260, 263, 353–354, 356, 678, 1014
MA-HS-AT-S-VE09 Students will factor quadratic polynomials.	**HOLT ALGEBRA 1** **LARSON ALGEBRA 1** **LARSON GEOMETRY** **LARSON ALGEBRA 2**	530, 531–532, 535–536, 538–539, 540–547, 548–554, 555, 556, 557, 558–564, 566–571, 572, 573, 575–577, 578, 579, S18–S19, S35 582, 583–589, 592, 593–599, 600–605, 613 713 252–253, 255–256, 259–260, 263, 323, 328, 548, 678, 1013
MA-HS-AT-S-VE010 Students will determine when an expression is undefined.	**HOLT ALGEBRA 1** **LARSON ALGEBRA 1** **LARSON GEOMETRY** **LARSON ALGEBRA 2**	866–867, 870, 872, 877, 891, 911, 914, S26 794–796, 797–798, 800 139 428–432, 445, 469, 558–563, 564, 565–571, 576–579, 581, 582–585, 586–587, 607, 1015, 1017
MA-HS-AT-S-VE011 Students will add, subtract, multiply, divide and simplify rational expressions.	**HOLT ALGEBRA 1** **LARSON ALGEBRA 1** **LARSON GEOMETRY** **LARSON ALGEBRA 2**	878–884, 885–891, 899, 907, 912, 914, S27 795–800, 802–809, 812–819, 826 139 573–580, 581, 582–588, 595, 601, 607, 678, 1017
MA-HS-AT-S-VE012 Students will evaluate polynomial and rational expressions and expressions containing radicals and absolute values at specified values of their variables.	**HOLT ALGEBRA 1** **LARSON ALGEBRA 1** **LARSON GEOMETRY** **LARSON ALGEBRA 2**	478, 480–481, 509, 807, 809–810, 881–883, 888–891 2–7, 9, 11, 13, 20, 66–68, 77, 82, 84, 91, 114 870 10, 14, 16–17, 65, 1010
EQUATIONS AND INEQUALITIES		
MA-HS-AT-S-EI1 Students will write equivalent forms of equations, inequalities and systems of equations and inequalities and solve them with fluency - mentally or with paper and pencil in simple cases and using technology in all cases.	**HOLT ALGEBRA 1** **LARSON ALGEBRA 1** **LARSON GEOMETRY** **LARSON ALGEBRA 2**	76, 77–82, 84–90, 92–98, 99, 100–106, 111, 113, 152–153, 156, 174–179, 180–185, 186, 187, 188–193, 194–200, 203–204, 206–208, 210, 211, 389, 390–396, 397–403, 404–405, 406–407, 409–411, 412, 413, 416, 418–420, 424, 426, 427, 429, 430–433, 434, 630–635, 636–641, 646–651, 822–829, 831, 839, 840, 900–905, 907, 913, 914 134–140, 141–146, 148–153, 154–159, 161, 192–193, 356–361, 363–368, 369–374, 381–387, 390–395, 398–403, 435–441, 444–450, 451–457, 459–465, 479, 575–580, 585, 586, 597, 599, 602, 603, 608–609, 611, 613 643–649, 652–658, 659–660, 664–668, 671–676, 698–699, 729–734, 820–826 65, 105–106, 109, 111, 212, 214, 287, 292, 423, 428, 785, 875, 876, 880–883, 899 18–24, 25, 26–32, 33–40, 41–47, 48–49, 50, 51–58, 59, 64–65, 66–67, 68–70, 88, 152, 153–158, 159, 160–167, 177, 178–185, 186, 193, 205–209, 213, 215–217, 227–233, 236–238, 240–243, 245–247, 249–250, 253–254, 256–258, 261–265, 267–271, 272–274, 285–286, 288–291, 292–299, 315–317, 323–327, 344, 368–369, 386, 399, 412, 427, 445, 474–476, 588, 612, 625, 632, 664, 678,–679, 689, 697, 713, 723, 730, 771, 792, 833, 848, 858, 954, 1010, 1012–1013
MA-HS-AT-S-EI2 Students will draw reasonable conclusions about a situation being modeled.	**HOLT ALGEBRA 1** **LARSON ALGEBRA 1** **LARSON GEOMETRY** **LARSON ALGEBRA 2**	79–82, 86–90, 94–98, 102–106, 113, 152–153, 385–388, 393–396, 400–403, 404–405, 408, 410, 412, 413, 416, 418–419, 423–425, 428, 429, 430–433, 434, 622–626, 632–634, 638–641, 647–651, 660, 661, 663–665, 666, S6, S29, S33, S36 25–26, 33, 139–140, 145, 152, 159, 208, 211, 221, 227, 249–250, 331, 361, 368, 374, 395, 433, 440, 657, 690, 781 65 271, 306, 433, 458, 505, 563, 570, 647

Standard	Program	Pages
MA-HS-AT-S-EI3 Students will solve one-variable equations and inequalities using manipulatives, symbols, procedures and graphing, including graphing the solution set on a number line.	**HOLT ALGEBRA 1**	77–82, 84–90, 91, 92–98, 99, 100–106, 111, 113, 120, 143, 148–151, 152–153, 156, 157, 174–179, 180–185, 186, 187, 188–193, 194–200, 203–204, 206–208, 212–215, 217–219, 220, 622–627, 628–629, 630–635, 636–641, 646–651, 652–653, 655–659, 660, 661, 664–665, 666, 822–829, 831, 839, 840, 900–905, 907, 913, 914
	LARSON ALGEBRA 1	132–133, 134–140, 141–146, 147, 148–153, 154–159, 160, 173, 357–361, 362, 363–368, 369–374, 377–378, 390–395, 398–403, 412, 414, 575–578, 585–586, 597, 599, 602–603, 608–609, 611, 613, 643–649, 652–658, 659–660, 664–668, 671–676, 698–699, 706–707, 729–734, 820–826
	LARSON GEOMETRY	65, 105–106, 109, 111, 212, 214, 287, 292, 785, 875, 876, 882–883, 899
	LARSON ALGEBRA 2	18–24, 25, 32–34, 39–40, 41–47, 48–49, 50, 51–58, 59, 65–69, 70, 209, 217, 232, 253–254, 256–258, 261–262, 263–265, 267–274, 284–286, 288–291, 292–299, 315–316, 323–324, 344, 355–358, 399, 404, 427, 452–459, 460–461, 462–463, 473–475, 515–522, 523–525, 526–527, 536, 589–595, 596–597, 598–600, 606, 607, 611–612, 625, 664, 678, 713, 723, 730, 771, 792, 833, 954, 1010, 1013, 1015–1017
MA-HS-AT-S-EI4 Students will solve linear equations and inequalities in one variable including those involving the absolute value of a linear function.	**HOLT ALGEBRA 1**	77–82, 84–90, 91, 92–98, 99, 100–106, 111, 113, 120, 143, 148–151, 152–153, 156, 157, 174–179, 180–185, 186, 187, 188–193, 194–200, 203–204, 206–208, 212–215, 217–219, 220, S6, S8–S9, S29, S30
	LARSON ALGEBRA 1	132–133, 134–140, 141–146, 147, 148–153, 154–159, 160, 173, 357–361, 362, 363–368, 369–374, 377–378, 390–395, 398–403, 412, 834
	LARSON GEOMETRY	65, 105–106, 109, 111, 138, 212, 214, 287, 292, 428, 785, 875, 876, 899
	LARSON ALGEBRA 2	18–24, 25, 32–33, 34–39, 40, 41–47, 48–49, 50, 51–58, 59, 65–67, 68–70, 150, 173, 209, 217, 232, 234, 344, 427, 474, 664, 678, 730, 792, 833, 954, 1010
MA-HS-AT-S-EI5 Students will solve an equation involving several variables for one variable in terms of the others.	**HOLT ALGEBRA 1**	107–111, 113, 120, 153, 156, 157, S7, S29
	LARSON ALGEBRA 1	184–189, 212, 247
	LARSON GEOMETRY	106, 109–111, 877
	LARSON ALGEBRA 2	26–32, 40, 65, 70, 233, 327, 412, 1010
MA-HS-AT-S-EI6 Students will solve systems of two linear equations in two variables.	**HOLT ALGEBRA 1**	384–388, 389, 390–396, 397–403, 404–405, 406–411, 412, 413, 420, 430–432, 434, 439, S14, S33
	LARSON ALGEBRA 1	426, 427–433, 434, 435–441, 442, 443, 444–450, 451–457, 459–465, 472, 479, 480–481
	LARSON GEOMETRY	183, 186, 255, 447, 615, 761, 880
	LARSON ALGEBRA 2	152, 153–158, 159, 160–167, 186, 205, 207–208, 217, 227–228, 230–232, 258, 299, 368, 386, 399, 445, 474475, 588, 612, 632, 679, 697, 792, 817, 1012
MA-HS-AT-S-EI7 Students will solve systems of three linear equations in three variables.	**HOLT ALGEBRA 1**	396
	LARSON ALGEBRA 1	448
	LARSON GEOMETRY	880
	LARSON ALGEBRA 2	178–185, 193, 206–208, 213, 215–216, 227, 229, 231, 1012
MA-HS-AT-S-EI8 Students will solve quadratic equations in one variable.	**HOLT ALGEBRA 1**	622–627, 628–629, 630–635, 636–641, 646–651, 652–659, 660, 661, 664–665, 666, 667, S21, S36
	LARSON ALGEBRA 1	575, 576–578, 585, 586, 597, 599, 602–603, 618–619, 643–649, 652–658, 659–660, 661, 664–668, 671–676
	LARSON GEOMETRY	22, 363, 423, 499, 743, 882–883
	LARSON ALGEBRA 2	253–258, 261–262, 263–265, 267–271, 272–274, 285–286, 288–291, 292–299, 316, 323–324, 399, 474, 612, 678, 723, 771, 1013
MA-HS-AT-S-EI9 Students will approximate and interpret rates of change from graphical and numerical data.	**HOLT ALGEBRA 1**	310–317, 318–319, 321–324, 332, 333, 369, 372, S12, S32
	LARSON ALGEBRA 1	237, 238, 240–242
	LARSON GEOMETRY	171–178, 206, 211, 213, 379, 879
	LARSON ALGEBRA 2	82–88, 96, 106, 145–146, 149, 1011
MA-HS-AT-S-EI10 Students will graph a linear equation and demonstrate that it has a constant rate of change.	**HOLT ALGEBRA 1**	297–301, 311, 318–319, 321–322, 324, 328, 332
	LARSON ALGEBRA 1	207, 210, 216–221, 222, 226–232, 245, 248–250, 263–268, 270, 272–273
	LARSON GEOMETRY	182–183, 185–187, 211
	LARSON ALGEBRA 2	89–96, 97, 145, 232, 474, 536, 1011
MA-HS-AT-S-EI11 Students will relate the coefficients of a linear equation and the slope and *x*- and *y*-intercepts of its graph.	**HOLT ALGEBRA 1**	335–340, 342–347, 355, 365, 370, 372, S13, S32
	LARSON ALGEBRA 1	225–232, 243, 244–250
	LARSON GEOMETRY	180–187, 879
	LARSON ALGEBRA 2	89–96, 98–106, 145, 147, 149, 167, 193, 258, 368, 595, 648, 749, 800, 872, 880, 937, 1011

Standard	Program	Pages
MA-HS-AT-S-EI12 Students will relate a solution of a system of two linear equations in two variables and the graphs of the corresponding lines.	**HOLT ALGEBRA 1** **LARSON ALGEBRA 1** **LARSON GEOMETRY** **LARSON ALGEBRA 2**	384–388, 404, 406–411, 413, 430, 432, 434, S14 427–433, 434, 436, 441, 454, 459–460, 462, 472 183, 186, 255 153–158, 159, 167, 227, 1012
MA-HS-AT-S-EI13 Students will graph the solution set of a linear inequality and identify whether the solution set is an open or closed half-plane.	**HOLT ALGEBRA 1** **LARSON ALGEBRA 1** **LARSON GEOMETRY** **LARSON ALGEBRA 2**	414, 415–420, 426, 429, 433, 434, S15, S33 406–412, 414, 418 207, 881 132–138, 139, 150, 232, 271, 1011
MA-HS-AT-S-EI14 Students will graph the solution set of a system of two or three linear inequalities.	**HOLT ALGEBRA 1** **LARSON ALGEBRA 1** **LARSON GEOMETRY** **LARSON ALGEBRA 2**	422–426, 428, 429, 433, 434, S15, S33 466–472, 944 102, 881 168–173, 174–176, 227, 233, 1012
MA-HS-AT-S-EI15 Students will read information and draw conclusions from graphs and identify properties of a graph that provide useful information about the original problem.	**HOLT ALGEBRA 1** **LARSON ALGEBRA 1** **LARSON GEOMETRY** **LARSON ALGEBRA 2**	254–258, 260, 261, 263, 265, 267–269, 270, 271, 278, 279, 282–283, 284, 304, 306–308, 337–339, 346, 365, 372, 608, 610, 616–618, 620, 621, 663, 666, 863–864, S31, S32, S36 220–221, 222, 227, 230–232, 241–242, 323–324, 408, 410–413, 432–433, 537–538, 633, 713, 715–716, 778, 781 178, 183, 186–187 91, 94–96, 128–129, 131, 134, 137, 155, 157–159, 170, 172–173, 175–176, 239, 242–243, 246–247, 250–251, 326, 389, 391–392, 447, 450–451, 480, 484–485, 488, 490–491, 494, 497, 560, 562–564, 567, 570–571
MA-HS-AT-S-EI16 Students will graph a quadratic function and understand the relationship between its real zeros and the *x*-intercepts of the graph.	**HOLT ALGEBRA 1** **LARSON ALGEBRA 1** **LARSON GEOMETRY** **LARSON ALGEBRA 2**	622–627, 628–629, 631, 635, 638, 653–655, 661, 664, 666, S21 628–634, 636–640, 641–642, 643–649 499, 882–883 236–243, 244, 245–251, 265, 323, 326–328, 335, 411, 474, 612, 619, 1013
MA-HS-AT-S-EI17 Students will write and solve linear sentences, describing real-world situations by using and relating formulas, tables, graphs and equations.	**HOLT ALGEBRA 1** **LARSON ALGEBRA 1** **LARSON GEOMETRY** **LARSON ALGEBRA 2**	337–339, 343–346, S32 137, 139–140, 143, 145–146, 147, 150, 152–153, 158–159 106, 111, 186, 206 19–21, 23–24, 29, 31–40, 65, 68–69, 101, 103–104, 108–111, 115–116, 117, 119–120, 139, 143, 145, 148–149, 451
MA-HS-AT-S-EI18 Students will recognize and solve problems that can be modeled using a linear equation in one variable, a quadratic equation or a system of linear equations.	**HOLT ALGEBRA 1** **LARSON ALGEBRA 1** **LARSON GEOMETRY** **LARSON ALGEBRA 2**	79–82, 86–90, 94–98, 102–106, 113, 152–153, 385–388, 393–396, 400–403, 404–405, 408, 410, 412, 413, 430–432, 434, 622–626, 632–634, 638–641, 647–651, 660, 661, 663–665, 666, S6, S29, S33, S36 137, 139–140, 143, 145–146, 150–153, 155, 158–159, 429–430, 432–433, 437–438, 440, 441, 442, 446, 449, 450, 453, 456–457, 461, 464–465, 646, 648–649, 654–655, 657–658, 665, 667–668, 672–673, 675–676 183, 186–189, 206, 211 19–21, 23–24, 47, 58–59, 62, 65, 155, 157–159, 162–163, 165–167, 181, 184–186, 206, 208–209, 213, 215–217, 220, 254, 256–258, 261–262, 264–265, 269–273, 290, 295, 298–299, 321, 323,344, 368–369, 399, 475, 563, 678
MA-HS-AT-S-EI19 Students will use the skills learned to solve linear equations and inequalities to solve numerically, graphically or symbolically non-linear equations (e.g., absolute value, quadratic, exponential equations).	**HOLT ALGEBRA 1** **LARSON ALGEBRA 1** **LARSON GEOMETRY** **LARSON ALGEBRA 2**	148–149, 622–627, 628–629, 630–635, 636–641, 646–651, 652–653, 655–659, 660, 661, 664–665, 666, 667, 822–829, 831, 839, 840, S21, S25, S36, S38 390–395, 412, 575–580, 585–586, 595–597, 599, 602–603, 608–609, 611, 613, 643–649, 652–658, 659–660, 664–668, 671–676, 729–734, 820–826, 828, 834 287, 423, 499, 641, 882–883 51–53, 54–56, 58, 65, 254, 256, 261–264, 267–268, 270, 275, 279, 284–286, 288–289, 291, 323, 355–357, 452–459, 460–461, 468–469, 474, 515–522, 523–525, 542–543, 547, 589–595, 596–597, 606, 607, 611–612, 678, 848, 1010, 1013, 1015–1017
MA-HS-AT-S-EI20 Students will use graphing technology to explore the meaning of quadratic equations with complex solutions.	**HOLT ALGEBRA 1** **LARSON ALGEBRA 1** **LARSON GEOMETRY** **LARSON ALGEBRA 2**	623, 625 679 882–883 293

KENTUCKY

ALGEBRA 2

Ron Larson
Laurie Boswell
Timothy D. Kanold
Lee Stiff

About *Algebra 2*

The content of *Algebra 2* is organized around families of functions, including linear, quadratic, exponential, logarithmic, radical, and rational functions. As you study each family of functions, you will learn to represent them in multiple ways—as verbal descriptions, equations, tables, and graphs. You will also learn to model real-world situations using functions in order to solve problems arising from those situations.

In addition to its algebra content, *Algebra 2* includes lessons on probability and data analysis as well as numerous examples and exercises involving geometry and trigonometry. These math topics often appear on standardized tests, so maintaining your familiarity with them is important. To help you prepare for standardized tests, *Algebra 2* provides instruction and practice on standardized test questions in a variety of formats—multiple choice, short response, extended response, and so on. Technology support for both learning algebra and preparing for standardized tests is available at classzone.com.

ISBN-13: 978-0-547-11774-4
ISBN-10: 0-547-11774-4

1 2 3 4 5 6 7 8 9—DWO—12 11 10 09 08

About the Authors

Ron Larson is a professor of mathematics at Penn State University at Erie, where he has taught since receiving his Ph.D. in mathematics from the University of Colorado. Dr. Larson is well known as the author of a comprehensive program for mathematics that spans middle school, high school, and college courses. Dr. Larson's numerous professional activities keep him in constant touch with the needs of teachers and supervisors. He closely follows developments in mathematics standards and assessment.

Laurie Boswell is a mathematics teacher at The Riverside School in Lyndonville, Vermont, and has taught mathematics at all levels, elementary through college. A recipient of the Presidential Award for Excellence in Mathematics Teaching, she was also a Tandy Technology Scholar. She served on the NCTM Board of Directors (2002–2005), and she speaks frequently at regional and national conferences on topics related to instructional strategies and course content.

Timothy D. Kanold is the superintendent of Adlai E. Stevenson High School District 125 in Lincolnshire, Illinois. Dr. Kanold served as a teacher and director of mathematics for 17 years prior to becoming superintendent. He is the recipient of the Presidential Award for Excellence in Mathematics and Science Teaching, and a past president of the Council for Presidential Awardees in Mathematics. Dr. Kanold is a frequent speaker at national and international mathematics meetings.

Lee Stiff is a professor of mathematics education in the College of Education and Psychology of North Carolina State University at Raleigh and has taught mathematics at the high school and middle school levels. He served on the NCTM Board of Directors and was elected President of NCTM for the years 2000–2002. He is a recipient of the W. W. Rankin Award for Excellence in Mathematics Education presented by the North Carolina Council of Teachers of Mathematics.

Advisers and Reviewers

Kentucky Advisers and Reviewers

Janice A. Eaves
Owensboro Middle School
Owensboro, KY

Mary Eschels
Ballard High School
Louisville, KY

Jane Markham
Daviess County High School
Owensboro, KY

Kathy V. Zwanzig
duPont Manual High School
Louisville, KY

Curriculum Advisers and Reviewers

Craig Edward Auten
Mathematics Teacher
Walled Lake Central High School
Walled Lake, MI

Cindy L. Blair
Curriculum Instructional Coordinator
Thomas Jefferson High School
San Antonio, TX

Michael Bolling
Instructional Specialist for Mathematics
Chesterfield County Public Schools
Chesterfield, VA

Barbara J. Brooks
Mathematics Teacher
Mumford High School
Detroit, MI

Ronnee Sue Carpenter
Mathematics Teacher
Flint Southwestern Academy High School
Flint, MI

Brian Croston
Mathematics Teacher
Frisco Centennial High School
Frisco, TX

Randy Daniels
Mathematics Teacher
Ankeny High School
Ankeny, IA

Bonnie Davis
Mathematics Consultant (retired)
Gilmer Independent School District
Gilmer, TX

Brett Duffney
Mathematics Teacher
Preble High School
Green Bay, WI

Robert W. Ewing
Mathematics Teacher
Austin High School
El Paso, TX

Diana Faoro
Mathematics Teacher
Romeo Engineering and Technology Center
Washington, MI

Nancy L. Fisher
Mathematics Teacher
Hilliard Davidson High School
Hilliard, OH

KY 4

Curriculum Advisers and Reviewers

Kristen Karbon
Mathematics Teacher
Troy High School
Troy, MI

Kathryn Laster
Mathematics Teacher
Lake Highlands High School
Dallas, TX

Kelly Leal
Mathematics Teacher
The Colony High School
The Colony, TX

Jamie K. Lipsey
Mathematics Teacher
Skyline High School
Dallas, TX

Lois M. McCarty
Mathematics Chair and Teacher
Midland Independent School District
Midland, TX

Mohammad Moshfeghian
Mathematics Department Chair
Homer Hanna High School
Brownsville, TX

Susan B. Nelson
Team Leader
Spring High School
Spring, TX

Anne Papakonstantinou
Director, School Mathematics Project
Rice University
Houston, TX

Richard Parr
Director of Educational Technology, School Mathematics Project
Rice University
Houston, TX

Joseph F. Pawloski
Mathematics Teacher
Brighton High School
Brighton, MI

Donald J. Pratt
Mathematics Teacher
Huron High School
Ann Arbor, MI

Wayne Rumple
Mathematics Teacher
Monroe Senior High School
Monroe, MI

Michael Schulte
Mathematics Consultant
Warren Mott High School
Warren, MI

Shirley K. Ward
Mathematics Teacher
Westside High School
Houston, TX

Denise Weatherford
Mathematics Teacher
Central High School
Beaumont, TX

Peggy S. Winfree White
Mathematics Teacher
Caprock High School
Amarillo, TX

Dianne Young
Mathematics Department Chair
Robert E. Lee Freshman High School
Midland, TX

KY 5

KENTUCKY

Overview
Kentucky Student Edition

Horse farm near Lexington, Kentucky © David R. Frazier Photolibrary, Inc./Alamy

Chapter 1 Summary

Chapter 1 focuses on a review of algebraic concepts, including the use of **variables**, writing and evaluating **algebraic expressions**, and **simplifying expressions**. Students use **properties of equality** to solve simple **linear equations** and **rewrite formulas** to solve for variables. Students also review several **problem solving strategies**, such as *use a formula*, *look for a pattern*, and *draw a diagram*. The chapter concludes by extending solving methods to **linear inequalities in one variable** and **absolute value equations and inequalities**, including the representations of their solutions **as graphs on a number line**.

Standards

MA-HS-1.5.1 Students will identify real number properties (commutative properties of addition and multiplication, associative properties of addition and multiplication, distributive property of multiplication over addition and subtraction, identity properties of addition and multiplication and inverse properties of addition and multiplication) when used to justify a given step in simplifying an expression or solving an equation.

MA-HS-5.2.1 Students will apply order of operations, real number properties (identity, inverse, commutative, associative, distributive, closure) and rules of exponents (integer) to simplify algebraic expressions. DOK 1

MA-HS-5.3.1 Students will model, solve and graph first degree, single variable equations and inequalities, including absolute value, based in real-world and mathematical problems and graph the solutions on a number line. DOK 2

MA-HS-5.3.2 Students will solve for a specified variable in a multivariable equation.

CHAPTER 1

Unit 1

Linear Equations, Inequalities, Functions, and System

Kentucky

Work Rates, p. 20

$\frac{1}{8}t + \frac{1}{6}t = 7$

Equations and Inequalities

Kentucky

ASSESSMENT

- Kentucky Practice Examples, 3, 19, 36
- Kentucky Daily Practice, 9, 16, 24, 32, 40, 47, 58
- Kentucky Preparation and Practice, 6, 8, 9, 14, 15, 21, 23, 24, 29, 30, 31, 32, 33, 37, 38, 45, 46, 47, 55, 56, 59, 66
- Writing, 6, 13, 21, 30, 37, 44, 55

PROBLEM SOLVING

- Kentucky Mixed Review, 33, 59
- Multiple Representations, 15, 24, 35, 39, 48, 57
- Multi-Step Problems, 8, 23, 32, 33, 39, 47, 57, 59
- Using Alternative Methods, 48
- Real-World Problem Solving Examples, 3, 5, 11, 13, 19, 20, 29, 35, 36, 42, 44, 54

TECHNOLOGY

At classzone.com:

- Animated Algebra, 1, 5, 11, 20, 27, 34, 42, 53
- @Home Tutor, 8, 15, 17, 23, 25, 31, 38, 46, 57, 61
- Online Quiz, 9, 16, 24, 32, 40, 47, 58
- State Test Practice, 33, 59, 69

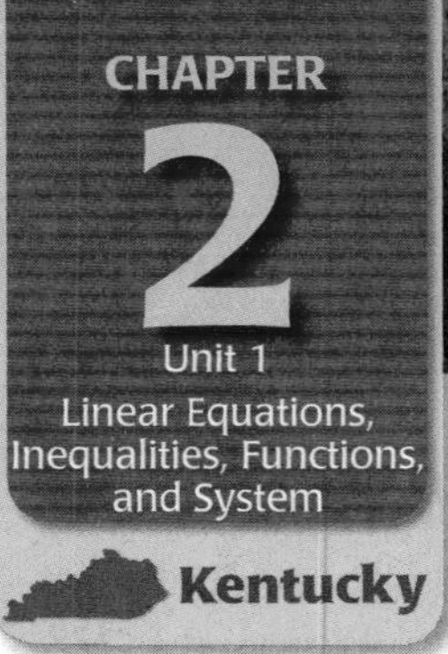

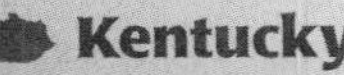

Linear Functions, p. 76
$P(d) = 1 + 0.03d$

Linear Equations and Functions

Kentucky

ASSESSMENT
- Kentucky Practice Examples, 82, 132
- Kentucky Daily Practice, 79, 88, 96, 104, 111, 120, 129, 138
- Kentucky Preparation and Practice, 77, 78, 79, 85, 86, 87, 88, 91, 93, 94, 95, 102, 103, 106, 109, 110, 111, 118, 119, 127, 128, 129, 134, 136, 137, 139, 146
- Writing, 76, 86, 93, 101, 109, 117, 127, 128, 135, 136

PROBLEM SOLVING
- Kentucky Mixed Review, 106, 139
- Multiple Representations, 95, 104, 105, 119, 129
- Multi-Step Problems, 78, 88, 95, 103, 106, 137, 139
- Using Alternative Methods, 105
- Real-World Problem Solving Examples, 74, 76, 85, 91, 100, 108, 115, 125, 134

TECHNOLOGY

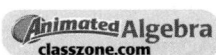

At classzone.com:
- Animated Algebra, 71, 73, 86, 90, 95, 98, 102, 107, 115, 133
- @Home Tutor, 70, 78, 87, 94, 97, 103, 110, 119, 121, 128, 137, 141
- Online Quiz, 79, 88, 96, 104, 111, 120, 129, 138
- Electronic Function Library, 140
- State Test Practice, 106, 139, 149

Chapter 2 Summary

Chapter 2 focuses on **linear equations in two variables** and developing the idea of a **function**. Students review the use of **slope** and its relation to rate of change. Students **graph and write equations of lines** in **slope-intercept form** and in **standard form**. Students write equations for real-life situations that exhibit **direct variation**, and examine **scatter plots** and use **best-fitting lines** to model real-life situations with linear equations. Students apply **transformations** (translations, stretches, and reflections) to **absolute value functions**. The chapter concludes by showing students how to **graph linear inequalities and absolute value inequalities in two variables** in a coordinate plane.

Standards

MA-HS-5.1.5 Students will: determine if a relation is a function; determine the domain and range of a function (linear and quadratic); determine the slope and intercepts of a linear function; determine the maximum, minimum, and intercepts (roots/zeros) of a quadratic function and evaluate a function written in function notation for a specified rational number. DOK 2

MA-HS-5.3.3 Students will model, solve and graph first degree, two-variable equations and inequalities in real-world and mathematical problems. DOK 2

MA-HS-5.1.7 Students will apply and use direct and inverse variation to solve real-world and mathematical problems.

MA-HS-4.2.3 Students will: identify an appropriate curve of best fit (linear, quadratic, exponential) for a set of two-variable data; determine a line of best fit equation for a set of linear two-variable data and apply a line of best fit to make predictions within and beyond a given set of two-variable data. DOK 3

MA-HS-5.1.8 Students will identify the changes and explain how changes in parameters affect graphs of functions (linear, quadratic, absolute value, exponential) (e.g., compare $y = x^2$, $y = 2x^2$, $y = (x - 4)^2$, and $y = x^2 + 3$). DOK 2

Chapter 3 Summary

Chapter 3 focuses on **solving systems of linear equations**. Students solve **systems of two equations in two variables** by **graphing**, by **substitution**, and by **elimination**. The substitution and elimination methods are later extended to solve **systems of three equations in three variables**. Students also learn how to graph **systems of linear inequalities**. In the second half of the chapter, students learn how to add, subtract, and multiply **matrices**. Then they use **determinants** and **Cramer's rule** to solve systems of equations. The chapter ends by showing students how to use **inverse matrices** (calculated by hand and using technology) to solve systems.

Standards

MA-HS-5.3.4 Students will model, solve and graph systems of two linear equations in real-world and mathematical problems. DOK 3

MA-HS-5.3.5 Students will write, graph, and solve systems of two linear inequalities based on real-world or mathematical problems and interpret the solution.

MA-HS-4.1.3 Students will represent real-world data using matrices and will use matrix addition, subtraction, multiplication (with matrices no larger than 2x2) and scalar multiplication to solve real-world problems.

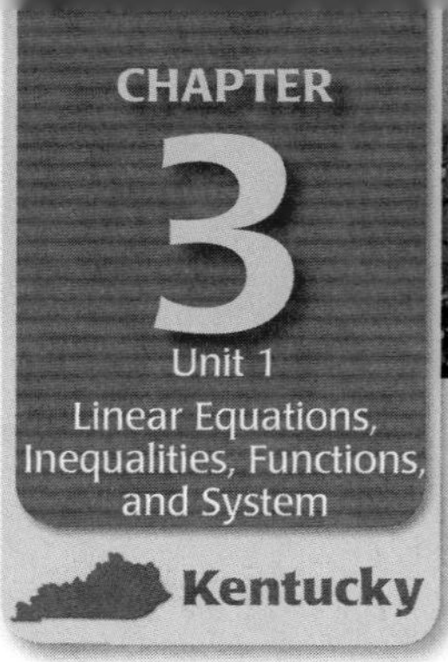

CHAPTER 3

Unit 1 Linear Equations, Inequalities, Functions, and System

Kentucky

Linear Systems, p. 155
$y = x + 30$; $y = 2.5x$

Linear Systems and Matrices

Kentucky

ASSESSMENT

- Kentucky Practice Examples, 155, 162
- Kentucky Daily Practice, 158, 167, 173, 185, 193, 202, 209, 217
- Kentucky Preparation and Practice, 156, 157, 158, 165, 166, 170, 171, 172, 173, 183, 184, 185, 186, 189, 191, 192, 199, 200, 201, 202, 206, 207, 208, 209, 213, 214, 215, 216, 220, 228
- Writing, 156, 164, 171, 182, 190, 199, 207, 214, 222

PROBLEM SOLVING

- Kentucky Mixed Review, 186, 220
- Multiple Representations, 157, 173, 216, 218
- Multi-Step Problems, 184, 186, 200, 201, 209, 216, 220
- Using Alternative Methods, 218
- Real-World Problem Solving Examples, 155, 162, 170, 181, 189, 198, 206, 213

TECHNOLOGY

At *classzone.com*:

- Animated Algebra, 151, 161, 168, 196, 211
- @Home Tutor, 150, 157, 159, 165, 172, 184, 192, 194, 200, 208, 215, 222
- Online Quiz, 158, 167, 173, 185, 193, 202, 209, 217
- State Test Practice, 186, 220, 231

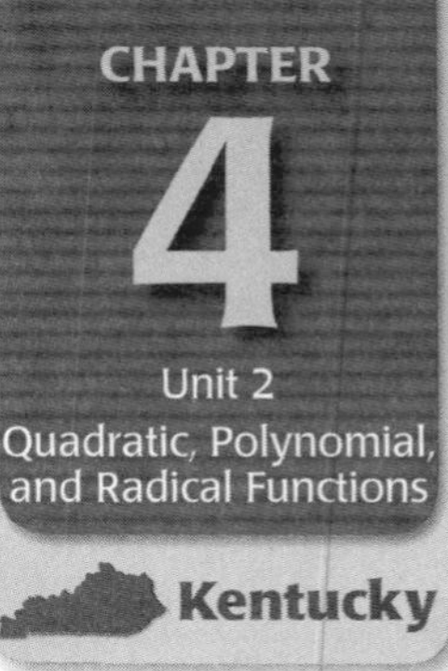

Complex Numbers, p. 281
$f(z) = z^2 + c$

Quadratic Functions and Factoring

Kentucky Standards

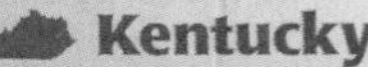
Kentucky

ASSESSMENT
- Kentucky Practice Examples, 254, 268, 286
- Kentucky Daily Practice, 243, 251, 258, 265, 271, 282, 291, 299, 307, 315
- Kentucky Preparation and Practice, 239, 241, 242, 249, 250, 251, 256, 257, 258, 262, 263, 264, 270, 271, 274, 280, 281, 282, 288, 289, 290, 296, 297, 298, 299, 305, 306, 311, 312, 313, 315, 316, 324

PROBLEM SOLVING
- Kentucky Mixed Review, 274, 316
- Multiple Representations, 242, 258, 272, 290, 306, 314
- Multi-Step Problems, 250, 257, 274, 298, 307, 314, 316
- Using Alternative Methods, 272
- Real-World Problem Solving Examples, 239, 246, 254, 262, 277, 287, 295, 303, 311

TECHNOLOGY

At classzone.com:
- Animated Algebra, 235, 238, 247, 269, 279, 287, 300
- @Home Tutor, 234, 242, 244, 250, 257, 264, 270, 281, 290, 298, 306, 308, 314, 318,
- Online Quiz, 243, 251, 258, 265, 271, 282, 291, 299, 307, 315
- Electronic Function Library, 317
- State Test Practice, 274, 316, 327

Chapter 4 Summary

Chapter 4 focuses on **graphing quadratic functions** and **solving quadratic equations**. Students graph quadratic functions in standard form $y = ax^2 + bx + c$, vertex form $y = a(x - h)^2 + k$, and intercept form $y = a(x - p)(x - q)$. Next, students solve quadratic equations using **factoring** and **square roots**. A lesson introducing **complex numbers** prepares students for the general approach to solving quadratic equations. Students learn the method of **completing the square** and see how this yields the **quadratic formula**. The chapter concludes by having students graph and solve **quadratic inequalities**, as well as use **quadratic regression** and other techniques to find quadratic models for data.

Standards

MA-HS-5.3.6 Students will model, solve and graph quadratic equations in real-world and mathematical problems. DOK 2

Chapter 5 Summary

Chapter 5 focuses on **graphing polynomial functions** and **solving polynomial equations**. The chapter begins with a review of **properties of exponents** and the use of **scientific notation**. Students evaluate polynomial functions by direct and **synthetic substitution**, and they observe how the **end behavior** of a graph depends on the degree and leading coefficient of the function. Students perform **operations on polynomials**, solve polynomial equations **by factoring**, and use **polynomial long division** and **synthetic division** to find factors. Students find **real zeros** and **complex zeros** of polynomial functions. At the end of the chapter, students graph polynomial functions by finding their ***x*-intercepts** and **local maximums and minimums**. They use **finite differences** and **cubic regression** to model real-life data with polynomial functions.

Standards

MA-HS-5.2.1 Students will apply order of operations, real number properties (identity, inverse, commutative, associative, distributive, closure) and rules of exponents (integer) to simplify algebraic expressions. DOK 1

MA-HS-5.1.5 Students will: determine if a relation is a function; determine the domain and range of a function (linear and quadratic); determine the slope and intercepts of a linear function; determine the maximum, minimum, and intercepts (roots/zeros) of a quadratic function and evaluate a function written in function notation for a specified rational number. DOK 2

MA-HS-5.2.3 Students will: add, subtract and multiply polynomial expressions; factor polynomial expressions using the greatest common monomial factor and factor quadratic polynomials of the form $ax^2 + bx + c$, when $a = 1$ and b and c are integers. DOK 2

MA-HS-5.1.1 Students will identify multiple representations (tables, graphs, equations) of functions (linear, quadratic, absolute value, exponential) in real-world or mathematical problems. DOK 2

CHAPTER 5

Unit 2
Quadratic, Polynomial, and Radical Functions

Kentucky

Polynomial Functions, p. 340
$E = 0.0029s^4$

Polynomials and Polynomial Functions

Kentucky

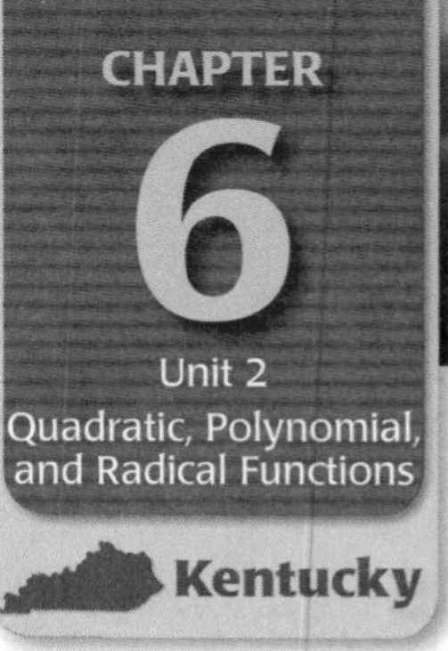

Kentucky

Square Root Functions, p. 451

$v_t = 33.7\sqrt{\frac{W}{A}}$

Rational Exponents and Radical Functions

Kentucky

ASSESSMENT

- Kentucky Practice Examples, 430, 453
- Kentucky Daily Practice, 419, 427, 434, 445, 451, 459
- Kentucky Preparation and Practice, 417, 419, 424, 425, 426, 427, 429, 431, 432, 433, 436, 439, 443, 444, 447, 449, 450, 456, 457, 458, 464
- Writing, 417, 424, 432, 442, 449, 456

PROBLEM SOLVING

- Kentucky Mixed Review, 436, 464
- Multiple Representations, 434, 451, 460
- Multi-Step Problems, 418, 433, 436, 444, 458, 464
- Using Alternative Methods, 460
- Real-World Problem Solving Examples, 416, 421, 429, 441, 447, 453

TECHNOLOGY

At classzone.com:

- Animated Algebra, 413, 431, 444, 448, 458
- @Home Tutor, 412, 418, 426, 433, 435, 444, 457, 458, 466
- Online Quiz, 419, 427, 434, 445, 451
- Electronic Function Library, 465
- State Test Practice, 436, 464, 473

Chapter 6 Summary

Chapter 6 focuses on **using rational exponents**, **graphing radical functions**, and **solving radical equations**. Students see that the properties of integral exponents can be extended to rational exponents. The idea of **composition** of functions is introduced to prepare for a formal presentation of **inverse functions**. Square root and cube root functions are presented as inverses of quadratic and cubic functions, and their graphs are understood in terms of this inverse relationship. Students **graph radical functions** and perform **transformations** on the graphs. Students solve radical equations algebraically and check for **extraneous solutions**.

Standards

MA-HS-1.3.1 **Students will solve real-world and mathematical problems to specified accuracy levels by simplifying expressions with real numbers involving addition, subtraction, multiplication, division, absolute value, integer exponents, roots (square, cube) and factorials. DOK 2**

MA-HS-5.2.1 **Students will apply order of operations, real number properties (identity, inverse, commutative, associative, distributive, closure) and rules of exponents (integer) to simplify algebraic expressions. DOK 1**

MA-HS-5.1.5 **Students will: determine if a relation is a function; determine the domain and range of a function (linear and quadratic); determine the slope and intercepts of a linear function; determine the maximum, minimum, and intercepts (roots/zeros) of a quadratic function and evaluate a function written in function notation for a specified rational number. DOK 2**

Chapter 7 Summary

Chapter 7 focuses on **exponential and logarithmic functions** and graphs. Students see how the graph of $y = ab^x$ depends on the values of *a* and *b* and solve real-life problems involving exponential **growth** and **decay**. Next, students learn about the **natural base *e*** and graph natural base exponential and logarithmic functions. They also evaluate logarithms and graph logarithmic functions with bases other than *e*. Students learn the **properties of logarithms** and use them to solve **exponential and logarithmic equations**. The chapter ends with a lesson about **modeling real-life data using exponential and power functions.**

Standards

MA-HS-5.1.4 Students will recognize and solve problems that can be modeled using an exponential function, such as compound interest problems.

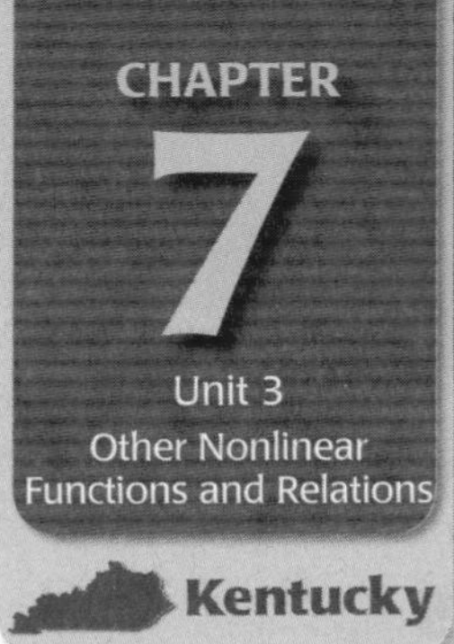

Power Functions, p. 532
$y = 0.0784x^{2.5}$

Exponential and Logarithmic Functions

Kentucky

ASSESSMENT

- Kentucky Practice Examples, 508, 518
- Kentucky Daily Practice, 485, 491, 498, 505, 513, 522, 536
- Kentucky Preparation and Practice, 480, 482, 483, 484, 485, 488, 489, 490, 491, 494, 495, 496, 497, 504, 505, 506, 510, 511, 512, 520, 521, 522, 534, 535, 537, 544
- Writing, 482, 489, 495, 503, 510, 519, 533

PROBLEM SOLVING

- Kentucky Mixed Review, 506, 537
- Multiple Representations, 485, 521, 523
- Multi-Step Problems, 484, 491, 497, 505, 506, 535, 537,
- Using Alternative Methods, 523
- Real-World Problem Solving Examples, 480, 488, 494, 500, 509, 516, 530

TECHNOLOGY

At classzone.com:

- Animated Algebra, 477, 480, 487, 502, 519
- @Home Tutor, 476, 484, 512, 514, 521, 528, 534, 535, 539
- Online Quiz, 485, 491, 498, 505, 513, 522, 536
- Electronic Function Library, 538
- State Test Practice, 506, 537, 547

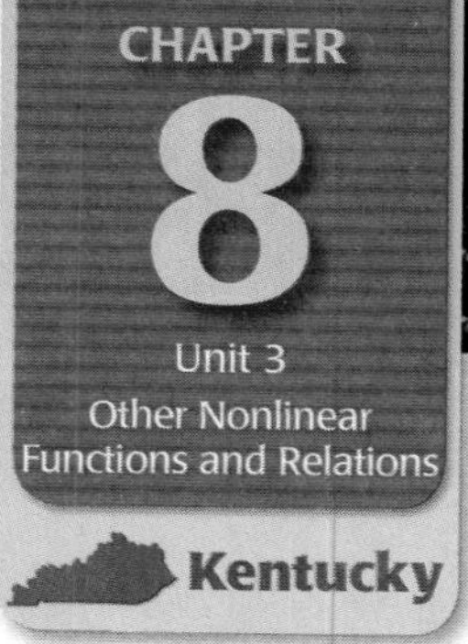

Rational Equations, p. 562
$t = \frac{1000}{0.6T + 331}$

Rational Functions

Kentucky

ASSESSMENT

- Kentucky Practice Examples, 575, 590
- Kentucky Daily Practice, 557, 563, 571, 580, 588, 595
- Kentucky Preparation and Practice, 555, 556, 557, 560, 561, 562, 563, 567, 568, 569, 570, 572, 574, 578, 579, 580, 587, 588, 593, 594, 601, 608
- Writing, 555, 561, 568, 577, 586, 592

PROBLEM SOLVING

- Kentucky Mixed Review, 572, 601
- Multiple Representations, 562, 570
- Multi-Step Problems, 556, 570, 572, 580, 601
- Using Alternative Methods, 596
- Real-World Problem Solving Examples, 552, 560, 567, 574, 585, 592

TECHNOLOGY

At *classzone.com*:

- Animated Algebra, 549, 554, 559, 568, 587
- @Home Tutor, 548, 556, 562, 564, 569, 570, 579, 581, 587, 594, 603
- Online Quiz, 557, 563, 571, 580, 588, 595
- Electronic Function Library, 602
- State Test Practice, 572, 601, 611

Chapter 8 Summary

Chapter 8 focuses on **graphing rational functions**, performing **operations with rational expressions**, and **solving rational equations**. Students graph simple **inverse variation** functions and examine the effect of translations on the graph of the function and its **asymptotes**. Then students learn how to graph the quotient of any two polynomials, using **zeros**, vertical and horizontal asymptotes, and **end behavior** analysis. The second half of the chapter emphasizes operations with rational expressions, and demonstrates how to **solve rational equations** and check for extraneous solutions.

Standards

MA-HS-5.1.7 Students will apply and use direct and inverse variation to solve real-world and mathematical problems.

MA-HS-5.1.3 Students will demonstrate how equations and graphs are models of the relationship between two real-world quantities (e.g., the relationship between degrees Celsius and degrees Fahrenheit).

MA-HS-5.2.5 Students will add, subtract, multiply and divide simple rational expressions with monomial first-degree denominators and integer numerators (e.g., +; −; ×; ÷), and will express the results in simplified form. DOK 1

Chapter 9 Summary

Chapter 9 focuses on the graphs of equations of **conic sections**. It begins with a review of the **distance formula** and **midpoint formula**. Building on their understanding of **parabolas** from Chapter 4, students now graph parabolas using information about the **focus**, **directrix**, and **axis of symmetry**. The distance formula is used to generate the standard equation of a **circle**, and students graph and write equations of circles. Next, students examine the standard equation of an **ellipse** to find values they can use to draw its **vertices, major and minor axes**, and **foci**. Students also see the standard equation of a **hyperbola** and use it to draw **transverse axes, asymptotes, vertices**, and **foci** of hyperbolas. Real-life applications are emphasized throughout. The chapter ends with material on **translations** of conic sections, classification of conics by their **discriminants**, and solving **quadratic systems**.

Standards

MA-HS-3.3.1 Students will apply algebraic concepts and graphing in the coordinate plane to analyze and solve problems (e.g., finding the final coordinates for a specified polygon, midpoints, betweenness of points, parallel and perpendicular lines, the distance between two points, the slope of a segment). DOK 2

MA-HS-5.3.6 Students will model, solve and graph quadratic equations in real-world and mathematical problems. DOK 2

MA-HS-3.1.6 Students will know the definitions and basic properties of a circle and will use them to prove basic theorems and solve problems.

MA-HS-3.1.5 Students will classify and apply properties of two-dimensional geometric figures (e.g., number of sides, vertices, length of sides, sum of interior and exterior angle measures). DOK 2

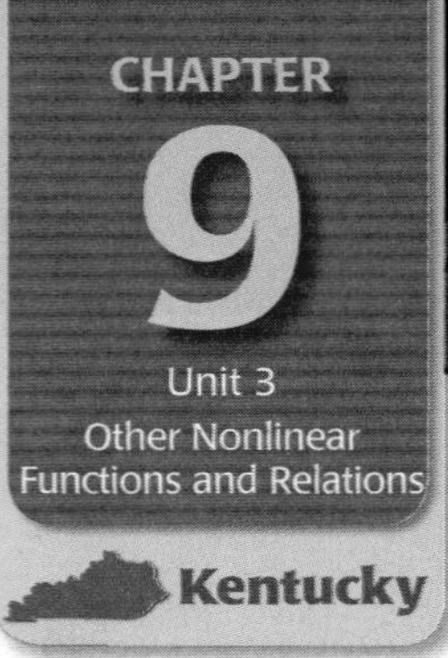

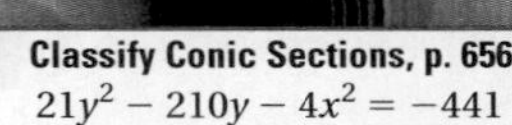

Quadratic Relations and Conic Sections

Kentucky

ASSESSMENT

- Kentucky Practice Examples, 614, 627
- Kentucky Daily Practice, 619, 625, 632, 639, 648, 657, 664
- Kentucky Preparation and Practice, 616, 617, 619, 623, 624, 625, 629, 630, 631, 636, 638, 639, 641, 644, 645, 646, 647, 654, 655, 656, 657, 661, 662, 663, 667, 674
- Writing, 617, 623, 624, 629, 637, 645, 655, 661

PROBLEM SOLVING

- Kentucky Mixed Review, 641, 667
- Multiple Representations, 631, 640, 647
- Multi-Step Problems, 619, 625, 631, 641, 647, 663, 667
- Using Alternative Methods, 640
- Real-World Problem Solving Examples, 616, 622, 628, 636, 644, 654, 660

TECHNOLOGY

At classzone.com:

- Animated Algebra, 613, 615, 621, 625, 635, 643, 649, 651
- @Home Tutor, 612, 618, 624, 630, 633 638, 646, 656, 662, 663, 669
- Online Quiz, 619, 625, 632, 639, 648, 657, 664
- State Test Practice, 641, 667, 677

Kentucky

Independent Events, p. 718
$P(A \text{ and } B \text{ and } C) = \frac{1}{8} \cdot \frac{1}{8} \cdot \frac{1}{8}$

Counting Methods and Probability

Kentucky

ASSESSMENT
- Kentucky Practice Examples, 708, 717
- Kentucky Daily Practice, 689, 697, 704, 713, 723, 730
- Kentucky Preparation and Practice, 687, 688, 691, 695, 696, 702, 704, 705, 710, 711, 712, 720, 721, 722, 723, 728, 730, 732, 738, 739
- Writing, 686, 694, 701, 710, 721, 727

PROBLEM SOLVING
- Kentucky Mixed Review, 705, 732
- Multiple Representations, 703, 714, 729
- Multi-Step Problems, 688, 696, 705, 712, 732
- Using Alternative Methods, 714
- Real-World Problem Solving Examples, 683, 685, 691, 699, 700, 708, 709, 719, 720, 726

TECHNOLOGY

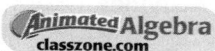

At classzone.com:
- Animated Algebra, 681, 701, 711, 716, 722, 726
- @Home Tutor, 680, 688, 696, 703, 711, 722, 729, 731, 734
- Online Quiz, 689, 697, 704, 713, 723, 730
- State Test Practice, 705, 732, 741

Chapter 10 Summary

Chapter 10 focuses on **permutations, combinations**, and **probability**. Using tree diagrams, the fundamental counting principle, and **factorial notation**, students learn the formulas for the number of **permutations** and **combinations** of *n* objects taken *r* at a time. The formula for combinations is linked to the values of **Pascal's triangle** and the coefficients in the **binomial expansion** of $(a + b)^n$. In the second half of the chapter, students learn how to find the **probabilities** of simple events, **overlapping** and **disjoint** compound events, and **independent** and **dependent** events. The chapter concludes by considering a type of **probability distribution** called a **binomial distribution**, and explains how binomial probabilities are related to combinations.

Standards

MA-HS-4.4.2 Students will recognize and identify the differences between combinations and permutations and use them to count discrete quantities.

MA-HS-4.4.1 Students will: determine theoretical and experimental (from given data) probabilities; make predictions and draw inferences from probabilities; compare theoretical and experimental probabilities and determine probabilities involving replacement and non-replacement. DOK 3

MA-HS-4.2.1 Students will describe and compare data distributions and make inferences from the data based on the shapes of graphs, measures of center (mean, median, mode) and measures of spread (range, standard deviation). DOK 2

Chapter 11 Summary

Chapter 11 focuses on **statistics** and **analyzing data**. It begins with a review of **mean, median, mode,** and **range**, and then develops the definition of **standard deviation**. Students see how transforming data by adding constants or multiplying by constants affects these **measures of central tendency and dispersion**. Students learn how standard deviation is used to find areas under bell-shaped **normal curves** that are used to model **normal distributions**. They use ***z*-scores** and the **standard normal table** to find probabilities associated with such distributions. The chapter concludes with material on **sampling** and a lesson on **using regression** to find mathematical models for data.

Standards

MA-HS-4.2.1 Students will describe and compare data distributions and make inferences from the data based on the shapes of graphs, measures of center (mean, median, mode) and measures of spread (range, standard deviation). DOK 2

MA-HS-4.2.2 Students will know the characteristics of the Gaussian normal distribution (bell-shaped curve).

MA-HS-4.3.1 Students will recognize potential for bias resulting from the misuse of sampling methods (e.g., non-random sampling, polling only a specific group of people, using limited or extremely small sample sizes) and explain why these samples can lead to inaccurate inferences. DOK 2

MA-HS-4.2.3 Students will: identify an appropriate curve of best fit (linear, quadratic, exponential) for a set of two-variable data; determine a line of best fit equation for a set of linear two-variable data and apply a line of best fit to make predictions within and beyond a given set of two-variable data. DOK 3

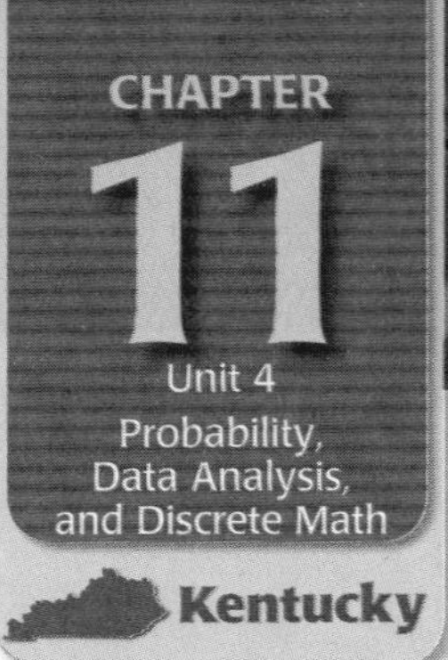

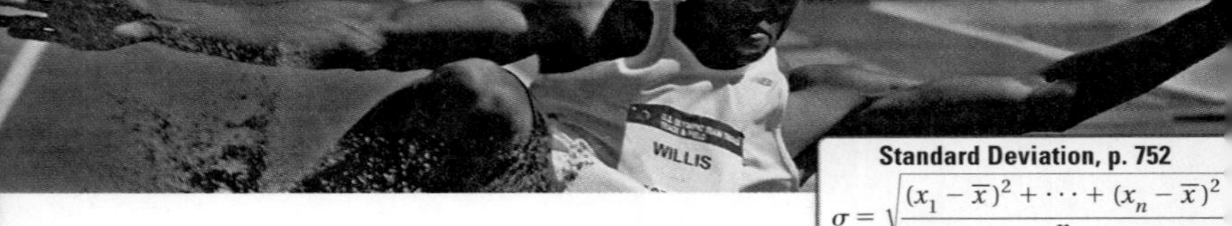

Standard Deviation, p. 752

$$\sigma = \sqrt{\frac{(x_1 - \overline{x})^2 + \cdots + (x_n - \overline{x})^2}{n}}$$

Data Analysis and Statistics

Kentucky

ASSESSMENT
- Kentucky Practice Examples, 745, 769
- Kentucky Daily Practice, 749, 755, 762, 771, 780
- Kentucky Preparation and Practice, 747, 748, 749, 753, 754, 756, 760, 761, 762, 770, 771, 778, 779, 782, 788
- Writing, 747, 753, 760, 769, 778, 784

PROBLEM SOLVING
- Kentucky Mixed Review, 756, 782
- Multiple Representations, 754, 779, 781
- Multi-Step Problems, 748, 756, 761, 771, 782
- Using Alternative Methods, 781
- Real-World Problem Solving Examples, 746, 752, 759, 767, 776

TECHNOLOGY

At classzone.com:
- Animated Algebra, 743, 744, 754, 757, 776
- @Home Tutor, 742, 748, 750, 753, 761, 770, 774, 779, 784
- Online Quiz, 749, 755, 762, 771, 780
- State Test Practice, 756, 782, 791

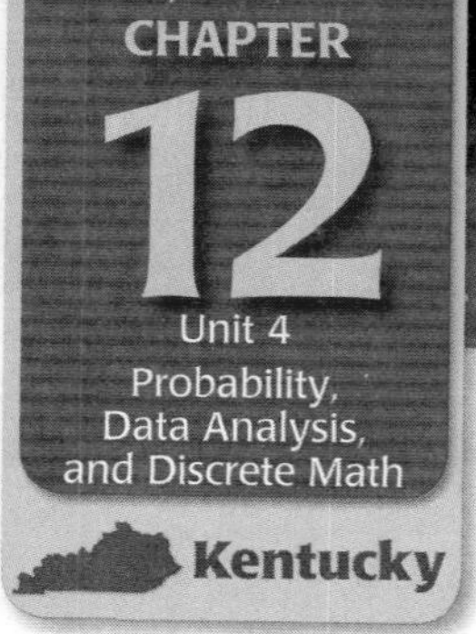

Kentucky

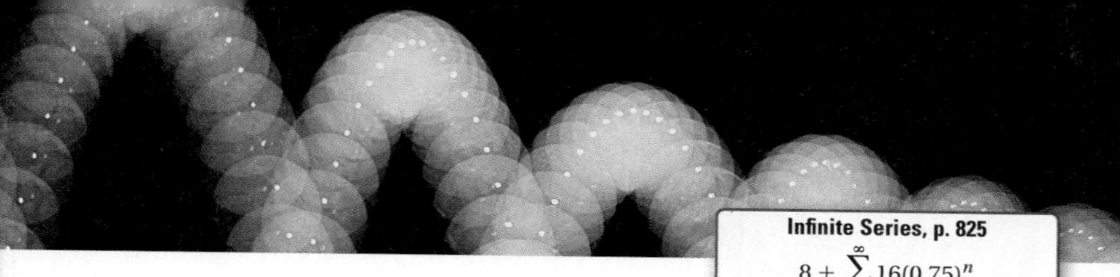

Infinite Series, p. 825

$$8 + \sum_{n=1}^{\infty} 16(0.75)^n$$

Sequences and Series

Kentucky

ASSESSMENT

- Kentucky Daily Practice, 805, 821
- Kentucky Preparation and Practice, 795, 798, 799, 800, 806, 807, 809, 814, 815, 816, 818, 823, 824, 825, 829, 830, 831, 832, 844
- Writing, 798, 806, 807, 814, 823, 830

PROBLEM SOLVING

- Kentucky Mixed Review, 818, 838
- Multiple Representations, 808, 816
- Multi-Step Problems, 800, 818, 838
- Using Alternative Methods, 834
- Real-World Problem Solving Examples, 795, 805, 813, 822, 829

TECHNOLOGY

At classzone.com:

- Animated Algebra, 793, 805, 811, 820, 832
- @Home Tutor, 792, 799, 801, 808, 815, 824, 826, 832, 840
- Online Quiz, 800, 809, 817, 825, 833
- State Test Practice, 756, 838, 847

Chapter 12 Summary

Chapter 12 focuses on **sequences** and **series**. Students analyze **arithmetic and geometric sequences and series** and find how to generate terms in sequences and use formulas for the sums of finite series. Students study **infinite geometric series** and find partial sums and the sums of such infinite series when they exist. Students then compare the definitions of sequences using **explicit rules** and **recursive rules**.

Standards

MA-HS-1.3.2 Students will: describe and extend arithmetic and geometric sequences; determine a specific term of a sequence given an explicit formula; determine an explicit rule for the nth term of an arithmetic sequence and apply sequences to solve real-world problems. DOK 3

MA-HS-1.3.4 Students will recognize and solve problems that can be modeled using a finite geometric series, such as home mortgage problems and other compound interest problems.

Chapter 13 Summary

Chapter 13 focuses on **right triangle trigonometry** and **trigonometric functions**. The basic ratios of *sine*, *cosine*, *tangent*, *cosecant*, *secant*, and *cotangent* are developed in the context of right triangles. Next, students learn about **radian measure** of angles and its relation to degree measure. The **trigonometric functions** are then defined for all angles (including angles with negative measures and measures greater than 90°) by using **reference angles**. The chapter concludes with a presentation of the **law of sines** and **law of cosines** and has students use these laws to solve for the lengths and angle measures of triangles.

Standards

MA-HS-2.1.3 Students will apply definitions and properties of right triangle relationships (right triangle trigonometry and the Pythagorean theorem) to determine length and angle measures to solve real-world and mathematical problems. DOK 3

MA-HS-2.2.1 Students will continue to apply to both real-world and mathematical problems U.S. customary and metric systems of measurement.

MA-HS-3.1.7 Students will solve real-world and mathematical problems by applying properties of triangles (e.g., Triangle Sum theorem and Isosceles Triangle theorems). DOK 2

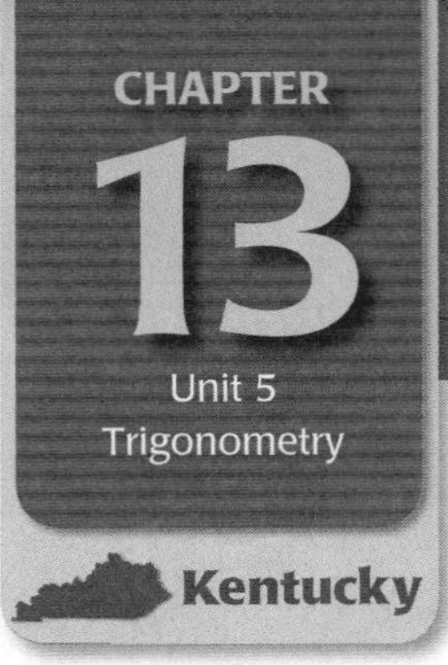

Kentucky

Law of Cosines, p. 893
$a^2 = b^2 + c^2 - 2bc \cos A$

Trigonometric Ratios and Functions

Kentucky

ASSESSMENT
- Kentucky Practice Examples, 853, 877
- Kentucky Daily Practice, 858, 865, 872, 880, 888, 894
- Kentucky Preparation and Practice, 856, 857, 858, 862, 863, 864, 870, 871, 872, 873, 878, 879, 886, 887, 888, 891, 892, 893, 894, 896, 902
- Writing, 856, 862, 870, 878, 886, 892

PROBLEM SOLVING
- Kentucky Mixed Review, 873, 896
- Multiple Representations, 857, 887, 895
- Multi-Step Problems, 864, 872, 873, 888, 893, 896
- Using Alternative Methods, 895
- Real-World Problem Solving Examples, 855, 862, 869, 877, 885, 890

TECHNOLOGY

At classzone.com:
- Animated Algebra, 851, 854, 867, 884
- @Home Tutor, 850, 857, 864, 871, 879, 881, 887, 893, 898
- Online Quiz, 858, 865, 872, 880, 888, 894
- Electronic Function Library, 897
- State Test Practice, 873, 896, 905

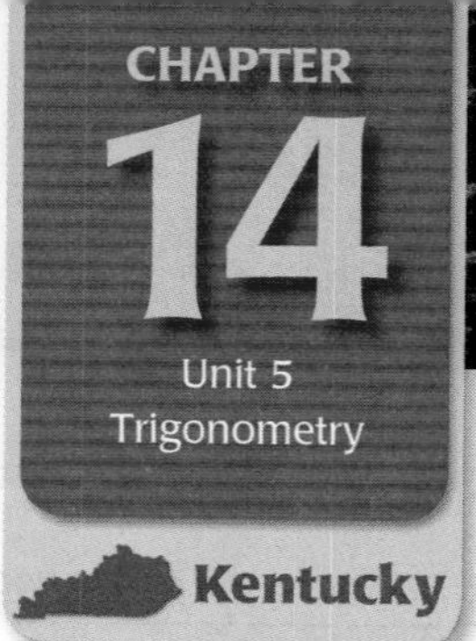

Kentucky

Difference Formulas, p. 954

$$\tan(a - b) = \frac{\tan a - \tan b}{1 + \tan a \tan b}$$

Trigonometric Graphs, Identities, and Equations

Kentucky

ASSESSMENT

- Kentucky Practice Examples, 933, 956
- Kentucky Daily Practice, 914, 922, 930, 937, 947, 954, 962
- Kentucky Preparation and Practice, 913, 914, 920, 921, 922, 928, 929, 930, 935, 936, 940, 944, 945, 946, 951, 952, 954, 959, 960, 961, 962, 963
- Writing, 912, 919, 927, 935, 944, 945, 952, 959

PROBLEM SOLVING

- Kentucky Mixed Review, 940, 963
- Multiple Representations, 914, 929, 937
- Multi-Step Problems, 921, 940, 946, 954, 961, 963
- Using Alternative Methods, 938
- Real-World Problem Solving Examples, 910, 916, 927, 932, 942, 951, 957

TECHNOLOGY

At classzone.com:

- Animated Algebra, 907, 912, 917, 961
- @Home Tutor, 906, 913, 921, 923, 929, 936, 945, 953, 961
- Online Quiz, 914, 922, 930, 937, 947, 954, 962
- Electronic Function Library, 964
- State Test Practice, 940, 963, 973

Chapter 14 Summary

Chapter 14 focuses on **graphing trigonometric functions**, using **trigonometric identities**, and **solving trigonometric equations**. Students graph the functions by considering **amplitude, period, maximums**, and **minimums**. They also apply transformations such as **translations** and **reflections** to graphs. Next, students **simplify trigonometric expressions** and **verify trigonometric identities**. In the middle of the chapter, students **solve trigonometric equations** and use trigonometric functions to **model real-life data**. The chapter concludes with **sum and difference formulas** and **double-angle and half-angle formulas** and their applications.

Standards

MA-HS-5.1.3 Students will demonstrate how equations and graphs are models of the relationship between two real-world quantities (e.g., the relationship between degrees Celsius and degrees Fahrenheit).

MA-HS-5.3.6 Students will model, solve and graph quadratic equations in real-world and mathematical problems. DOK 2

Contents of Student Resources

KENTUCKY

Student Guide to the Standards

Kentucky Program of Studies for Mathematics and Core Content for Mathematics Assessment Version 4.1

- The Kentucky Program of Studies for Mathematics are goals set by the state to ensure that you are being taught a thoughtful, complete curriculum.
- The Core Content for Mathematics Assessment Version 4.1 is a subset of the content standards in the Kentucky Program of Studies for Mathematics. They represent the content standards that are tested on the state assessment.
- The Core Content for Mathematics Assessment Version 4.1 also includes the Depth of Knowledge (DOK) that is appropriate for each grade level for the state assessment.
- Teachers and other educators use the standards when developing courses and tests.
- Lessons in your book connect to a standard, which is listed next to the lesson in the table of contents beginning on KY8. These standards are also shown on the first page of each lesson throughout the book.

Kentucky Program of Studies for Mathematics and Core Content for Mathematics Assessment Version 4.1
page S1

Horse farm near Lexington, Kentucky © David R. Frazier Photolibrary, Inc./Alamy

KENTUCKY STUDENT GUIDE

Guide to the Kentucky Program of Studies for Mathematics

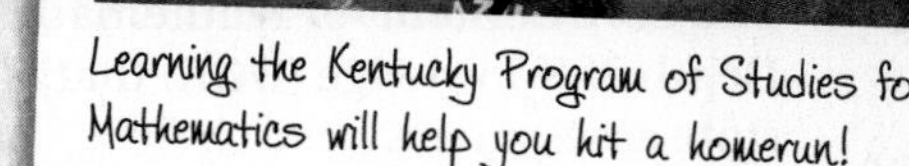
Learning the Kentucky Program of Studies for Mathematics will help you hit a homerun!

Did you know . . .

. . . that baseball and math standards have some things in common?

. . . and, that your math standards have been written as a commitment to you, the Kentucky student?

So . . .

. . . "What are Math Standards and what do they have in common with baseball?"

Compare the standards to a set of rules that must be followed in a sport event. For example, in a baseball game, the batter must move from first base to second base and then third base before proceeding to the home plate to score a run. Learning this rule enables the team to win the game.

Without the knowledge of how a baseball game is played, the team will not have the fundamental concepts to compete.

Math standards, like the rules in baseball, help you focus on a common foundation of mathematical concepts that you will use in everyday life and later in the workplace.

And . . .

. . . How will learning the Kentucky Program of Studies for Mathematics make a difference for you, the student?

It is important to learn material that is closely aligned to the math standards because they are what you will be tested on when it comes time to take your state test.

The Kentucky state standards have been written as a commitment to you, the student, to help you focus on the proper content to achieve both depth and understanding of mathematical knowledge.

Kentucky High School Mathematics Standards Decoder

The information from the parts will help you break the standard code!

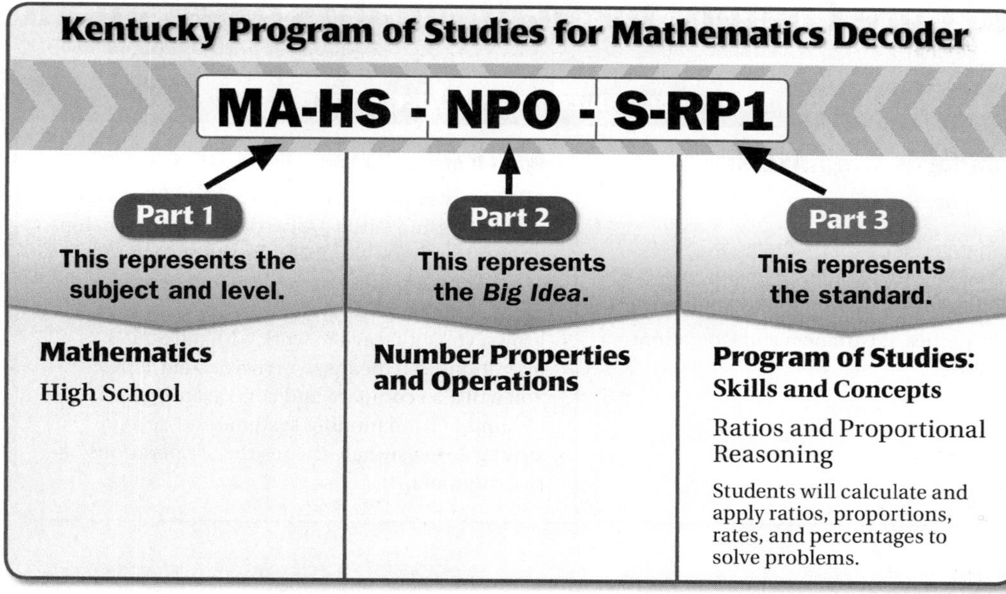

Kentucky Program of Studies for Mathematics Decoder
MA-HS - NPO - S-RP1
Part 1
This represents the subject and level.
Mathematics
High School
Part 2
This represents the *Big Idea*.
Number Properties and Operations
Part 3
This represents the standard.
Program of Studies: Skills and Concepts
Ratios and Proportional Reasoning
Students will calculate and apply ratios, proportions, rates, and percentages to solve problems.

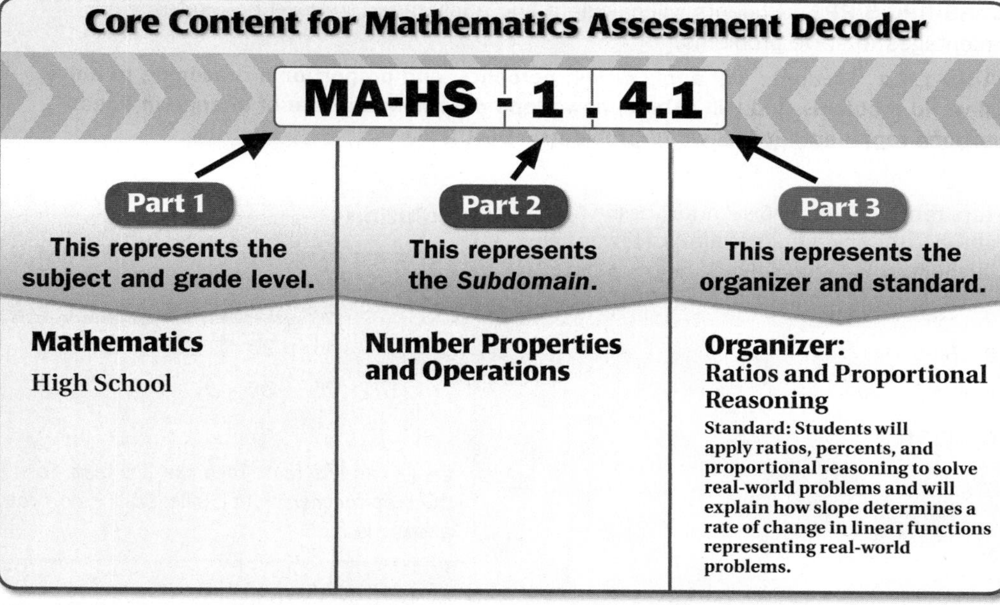

The Process Standards for Kentucky are a central focus of this course and they can be found throughout the book. They include problem solving, mathematical communication, mathematical connections, mathematical reasoning, and multiple representations.

Kentucky Program of Studies for Mathematics and Core Content for Mathematics Assessment

Big Idea/Subdomain 1: Number Properties and Operations

Standards/Organizers:

1. Number Sense
2. Estimation
3. Number Operations
4. Ratios and Proportional Reasoning
5. Properties of Numbers and Operations

What It Means To You

All students studying math should develop an understanding of the properties and relationships among numbers. Numbers are the cornerstone of any mathematics curriculum and permeate all areas of life. As your understanding of numbers grows, you will learn to work with particular operations as a means to arrive at solutions. You will also compare and contrast properties of numbers and number systems and develop strategies to estimate the results of operations on real numbers.

Here is what a question might look like on the KCCT:

MA-HS-NPO-S-RP1 Students will calculate and apply ratios, proportions, rates, and percentages to solve problems.

MA-HS-1.4.1 Students will apply ratios, percents, and proportional reasoning to solve real-world problems and will explain how slope determines a rate of change in linear functions representing real-world problems. DOK 2

Tara ran 175 feet in 35 seconds. Leslie ran at the same rate for 25 seconds. How much farther did Tara run than Leslie?

A. 25 ft

B. 50 ft

C. 75 ft

D. 125 ft

Solution

Write and solve a proportion to find the distance d that Leslie ran.

$$\frac{175}{35} = \frac{d}{25} \quad \begin{matrix} \leftarrow \text{distance} \\ \leftarrow \text{time} \end{matrix}$$

$$175 \cdot 25 = 35 \cdot d$$

$$125 = d$$

Leslie ran 125 feet. Tara ran 175 feet. Tara ran 50 feet farther than Leslie, so the correct answer is B.

Big Idea/Subdomain 2: Measurement

Standards/Organizers:	*What It Means To You*
1. Measuring Physical Attributes 2. Systems of Measurement	High school students continue to measure and estimate measurements including fractions and decimals. You will learn how to use formulas to find surface areas and volumes. You will also learn about the connection between the US Customary and metric units of measurement. Additionally, you will use the Pythagorean theorem and other right triangle relationships to solve realistic problems.

Here is what a question might look like on the KCCT:

MA-HS-M-S-MPA3 Students will determine the surface area and volume of right rectangular prisms, pyramids, cylinders, cones and spheres in realistic problems.

MA-HS-2.1.1 Students will determine the surface area and volume of right rectangular prisms, pyramids, cylinders, cones and spheres in real-world and mathematical problems. DOK 2

A farmer is planning to paint the roof of his silo, which is cone-shaped as shown. What is the best estimate for the number of square feet the farmer must paint?

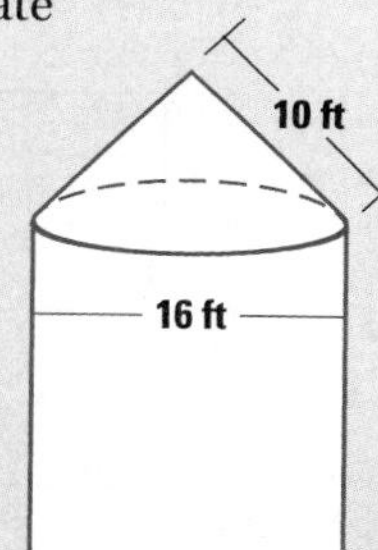

A. 250 ft^2

B. 500 ft^2

C. 750 ft^2

D. 1000 ft^2

Solution

Because only the lateral surface of the cone is to be painted, use the formula for the lateral surface area of a cone.

$$S = \pi r l$$
$$= \pi(8)(10)$$
$$\approx 251$$

So, the area he must paint is about 251 square feet. The correct answer is A.

Big Idea/Subdomain 3: Geometry

Standards/Organizers:

1. Shapes and Relationships
2. Transformations of Shapes
3. Coordinate Geometry

What It Means To You

Geometry is the study of the properties, measurement, and relationships of points, lines, angles, surfaces, and solids. Geometry also includes the aspect of spatial visualization, which is the ability to visualize, draw, and compare shapes in various positions. You will learn how to translate figures in a coordinate plane. You will also learn how to expand analysis of two-dimensional figures and three-dimensional objects and work with congruent and similar figures, including proportionality.

Here is what a question might look like on the KCCT:

MA-HS-G-S-SR4 Students will use the definitions, properties and theorems about congruent and similar triangles and other figures to prove additional theorems and apply these to solve real-world problems.

MA-HS-3.1.13 Students will prove triangles congruent and similar.

Which coordinates are the vertices of a triangle congruent to $\triangle RST$?

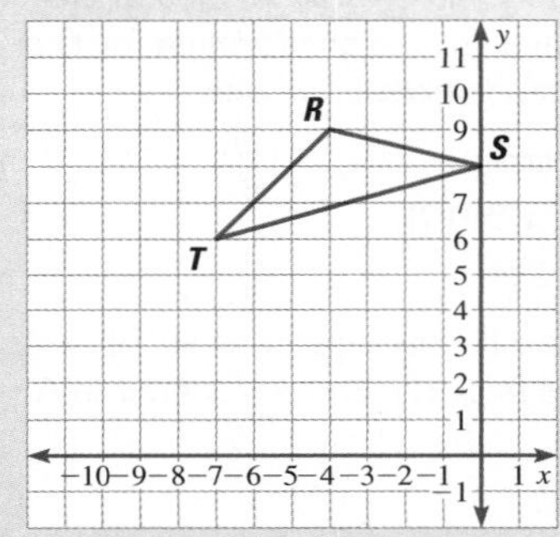

A. $(-3, -1)$, $(-5, -4)$, and $(-1, -4)$

B. $(-3, 2)$, $(0, -1)$, and $(4, 0)$

C. $(2, -2)$, $(5, -2)$, and $(2, -6)$

D. $(3, 3)$, $(4, 5)$, and $(-3, 5)$

Solution

Sketch each triangle in a coordinate plane.

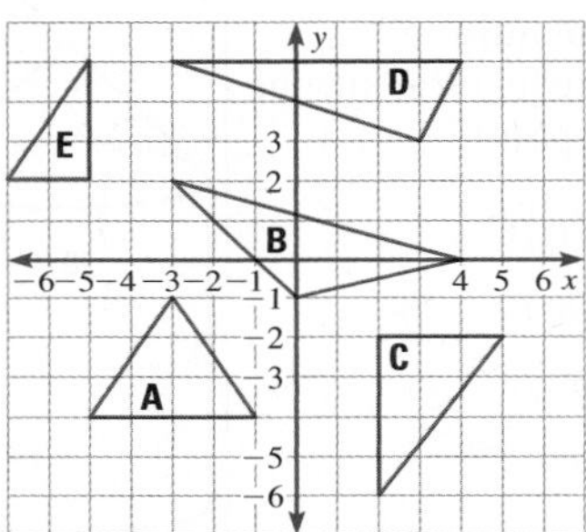

Choice B describes the only triangle with the same size and shape as $\triangle RST$.

The correct answer is B.

Big Idea/Subdomain 4: Data Analysis and Probability

Standards/Organizers:

1. Data Representations
2. Characteristics of Data Sets
3. Experiments and Samples
4. Probability

What It Means To You

Data analysis involves using data and statistics to solve problems that come up in work and in life. Probability is the study of the likelihood that a given event will occur. You will learn how to extend data representations, interpretations, and conclusions and describe data in multiple ways. Also, you will learn how to distinguish between combinations and permutations and compare and contrast theoretical and experimental probability.

Here is what a question might look like on the KCCT:

MA-HS-DAP-S-CDS8 Students will understand how simple statistics reflect the values of population parameters and use sampling distributions as the basis for informal inference.

MA-HS-4.2.1 Students will describe and compare data distributions and make inferences from the data based on the shapes of graphs, measures of center (mean, median, mode) and measures of spread (range, standard deviation). DOK 2

The ages of 8 people living on the same floor of an apartment complex are 52, 17, 9, 27, 49, 16, 16, and 38. The nine year old and one of the sixteen year olds share the same birthday, which is the next birthday to be celebrated. On their birthday, which measure of central tendency remains the same?

A. Mean

B. Median

C. Mode

D. Range

Solution

Current age order: 9, 16, 16, 17, 27, 38, 49, 52

Mean $\frac{224}{8} = 28$ Median $\frac{17 + 27}{2} = 22$

Mode 16 Range $52 - 9 = 43$

Order on birthday: 10, 16, 17, 17, 27, 38, 49, 52

Mean $\frac{226}{8} = 28.25$ Median $\frac{17 + 27}{2} = 22$

Mode 17 Range $52 - 10 = 42$

The median remains the same, so the correct answer is B.

STANDARDS

KY 29

Big Idea/Subdomain 5: Algebraic Thinking

Standards/Organizers:

1. Patterns, Relations, and Functions
2. Variables, Expressions, and Operations
3. Equations and Inequalities

What It Means To You

Algebra is the branch of mathematics in which symbols, usually letters, are used to represent numbers and quantities. Thinking algebraically includes recognizing and analyzing patterns, studying and representing relationships, making generalizations, and analyzing how things change. Algebra emphasizes learning about functions, which helps develop the ability to form generalizations that lay the foundation for studying other areas of math such as geometry and data analysis.

Here is what questions might look like on the KCCT:

MA-HS-AT-S-VE06 Students will add, subtract and multiply polynomials.

MA-HS-5.2.3 Students will:

- **add, subtract and multiply polynomial expressions;**
- **factor polynomial expressions using the greatest common monomial factor and**
- **factor quadratic polynomials of the form $ax^2 + bx + c$, when $a = 1$ and b and c are integers. DOK 2**

Which statement about the parabola is true?

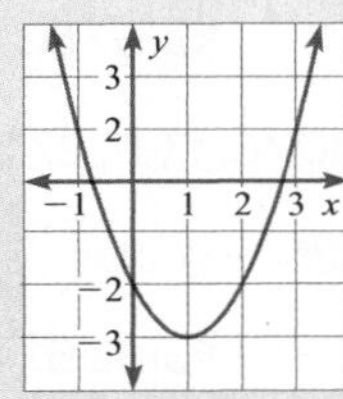

A. The vertex is $(-3, 1)$.

B. The maximum value is 1.

C. The minimum value is -2.

D. The axis of symmetry is the line $x = 1$.

Solution

The vertex of the parabola is $(1, -3)$. The minimum value is -3. The parabola does not have a maximum value. The axis of symmetry is the line $x = 1$.

So, the correct answer is D.

KY 30

KENTUCKY

Countdown to the KCCT

What is the KCCT?

- The Kentucky state test is called the Kentucky Core Content Test. The KCCT is given in the spring to students in the 11th grade.
- The test is made up of multiple-choice and open-response questions that evaluate your knowledge of the Kentucky Program of Studies for Mathematics and the Core Content for Mathematics Assessment Version 4.1.

Getting Ready

You can use the questions on the following pages to practice for the KCCT. Each question addresses an organizer/standard.

The questions are in the same format as those on the KCCT, and are organized by the big idea/subdomain. For example, the first big idea/subdomain is *Number Properties and Operations.*

If you need practice with a particular organizer/standard under the big idea/subdomain, use the chart on the next page to find which questions address that organizer/standard. If you need additional preparation, the chart lists lessons that you can review.

You will have more opportunities to practice for the KCCT in every lesson and chapter throughout the book.

Horse farm near Lexington, Kentucky © David R. Frazier Photolibrary, Inc./Alamy

COUNTDOWN TO KCCT

Countdown Reference Chart

This chart lists what questions address which standards for the Kentucky Core Content for Mathematics Assessment Version 4.1. The content standards for the state assessment are in **bold print.** Additionally, the depth of knowledge (DOK) is listed with each standard within the countdown. *Italics* represent a supporting content standard and plain text is an American Diploma Project benchmark supporting content standard. Lesson support is referenced and the full text of the standards is available on S1.

KY Standard Code	Practice Questions for the KCCT	Lesson-by-Lesson KCCT Support
Subdomain 1: Number Properties and Operations		
MA-HS-1.1.1	*1, 2*	*1.1*
MA-HS-1.1.3	*3, 4, 5*	*5.1*
MA-HS-1.2.1	*6*	*1.3*
MA-HS-1.2.1	*7*	*2.3*
MA-HS-1.3.1	**8**	**4.5**
MA-HS-1.3.1	**9**	**5.1**
MA-HS-1.3.1	**10, 11**	**1.2, 1.7**
MA-HS-1.3.2	**12, 13, 14, 15, 110**	**12.1, 12.2, 12.3**
MA-HS-1.3.3	*16, 17*	*12.3*
MA-HS-1.3.4	18	7.1
MA-HS-1.4.1	**19, 21, 111**	**2.2, 2.3**
MA-HS-1.4.1	**20**	**1.1**
MA-HS-1.5.1	22, 23	1.1
Subdomain 2: Measurement		
MA-HS-2.1.1	**24, 25, 26, 27**	**Skills Review Handbook**
MA-HS-2.1.3	**28, 29, 30, 31, 112, 113**	**13.1, 13.4**
MA-HS-2.1.4	32, 33	13.1
MA-HS-2.2.1	*34, 35*	*1.1*
MA-HS-2.2.1	*36*	*Skills Review Handbook*
Subdomain 3: Geometry		
MA-HS-3.1.3	**37, 38**	**Skills Review Handbook**
MA-HS-3.1.6	39, 40	13.2
MA-HS-3.1.6	41, 42	9.3
MA-HS-3.1.7	**43**	**Skills Review Handbook**
MA-HS-3.1.10	*44, 45, 46*	*9.6*
MA-HS-3.1.12	**47, 48, 114**	**Skills Review Handbook**
MA-HS-3.2.1	**49, 50, 51, 52, 53, 54**	**Skills Review Handbook**
MA-HS-3.3.1	**55, 56, 57, 60, 115**	**9.1**
MA-HS-3.3.1	**58, 59**	**2.2, 2.4**

KY 32

KY Standard Code	Practice Questions for the KCCT	Lesson-by-Lesson KCCT Support
Subdomain 4: Data Analysis and Probability		
MA-HS-4.1.1	**61**	**11.4**
MA-HS-4.1.1	**62**	**Skills Review Handbook**
MA-HS-4.1.2	**116**	**11.5**
MA-HS-4.1.3	*63, 64, 65*	*3.5*
MA-HS-4.2.1	**66, 67, 68, 70**	**11.1, 11.2**
MA-HS-4.2.1	**69**	**2.6**
MA-HS-4.2.2	71, 72	11.3
MA-HS-4.2.3	**73**	**2.6**
MA-HS-4.2.3	**74, 117, 118**	**11.5**
MA-HS-4.3.1	**75, 76**	**11.4**
MA-HS-4.4.1	**77, 78, 79, 80**	**10.3, 10.5**
MA-HS-4.4.2	*81, 82*	*10.1, 10.2*
Subdomain 5: Algebraic Thinking		
MA-HS-5.1.1	**83**	**2.7**
MA-HS-5.1.1	**84**	**7.1**
MA-HS-5.1.1	**85**	**11.5**
MA-HS-5.1.1	**86**	**1.5**
MA-HS-5.1.2	*87*	*2.7 Extension*
MA-HS-5.1.4	88, 89	7.1, 7.3
MA-HS-5.1.5	**90, 91, 92, 93**	**2.1, 2.3, 2.4**
MA-HS-5.1.5	**94**	**4.1**
MA-HS-5.1.6	*95*	*2.7*
MA-HS-5.1.7	*96*	*2.5*
MA-HS-5.1.8	**97**	**4.1**
MA-HS-5.1.8	**98**	**2.7**
MA-HS-5.2.1	**99, 100**	**1.2**
MA-HS-5.2.1	**101**	**5.1**
MA-HS-5.2.3	**102, 103, 104, 105, 106**	**5.3, 5.4**
MA-HS-5.2.5	**107, 108, 109**	**8.4, 8.5**
MA-HS-5.3.1	**119**	**1.5**
MA-HS-5.3.3	**120**	**1.5**
MA-HS-5.3.4	**121**	**3.1**
MA-HS-5.3.6	**122**	**4.7**

1. C
2. C
3. C
4. B
5. B

Subdomain 1 Number Properties and Operations

MA-HS-1.1.1 Students will compare real numbers using order relations (less than, greater than, equal to) and represent problems using real numbers.

Use the information below to answer question 1.

The table shows the average daily temperatures in Anchorage, Alaska, during a recent workweek.

Day	Mon.	Tues.	Wed.	Thurs.	Fri.
Average Temperature	−15°F	3°F	5°F	−8°F	0°F

1. Which list shows the average temperatures in order from least to greatest? *(p. 6, prob. 9–10)*

A. $0, 3, 5, -8, -15$

B. $-15, -8, 5, 3, 0$

C. $-15, -8, 0, 3, 5$

D. $-8, -15, 0, 3, 5$

2. Between which two numbers on a number line will $\sqrt{8}$ lie? *(p. 6, prob. 3–8)*

A. between 0 and 1

B. between 1 and 2

C. between 2 and 3

D. between 3 and 4

MA-HS-1.1.3 Students will use scientific notation to express very large or very small quantities.

3. What is the product of $(3.7 \times 10^7)(7.4 \times 10^3)$ in scientific notation? *(p. 333, prob. 15–23)*

A. 27.38×10^{21}

B. 11.1×10^{21}

C. 2.738×10^{11}

D. 1.11×10^{11}

4. Simplify: $\dfrac{(6.8 \times 10^8)}{(1.7 \times 10^2)}$ *(p. 333, prob. 15–23)*

A. 4.0×10^4

B. 4.0×10^6

C. 5.1×10^6

D. 5.1×10^4

5. A large rectangular park has a perimeter of 1.6×10^3 meters. If the length of the park is 6.2×10^2 meters, what is the width? *(p. 333, prob. 15–23)*

A. 4.6×10^1 m

B. 1.8×10^2 m

C. 4.6×10^2 m

D. 1.8×10^3 m

Go On 

Countdown to KCCT

6. D
7. A
8. D
9. C
10. B
11. D

Subdomain 1 Number Properties and Operations

MA-HS-1.2.1 Students will estimate solutions to problems with real numbers (including very large and very small quantities) in both real-world and mathematical problems, and use the estimations to check for reasonable computational results.

6. It takes you 20 minutes to complete a set of chores. It takes your sister 18 minutes to complete the same chores. Which shows a reasonable estimate of the amount of time it will take you and your sister to complete the chores if you work together? *(p. 24, prob. 75)*

A. 38 minutes

B. 19 minutes

C. 18 minutes

D. 10 minutes

7. You are reading a book with 540 pages. The function $P(d) = -30d + 540$ describes the number P of pages you have left to read after d days. What is a reasonable range for the real-life function? *(p. 94, prob. 62)*

A. $0 \leq P \leq 540$

B. $0 \leq P \leq \infty$

C. $0 \leq P \leq 30$

D. $0 \leq P \leq 17$

MA-HS-1.3.1 Students will solve real-world and mathematical problems to specified accuracy levels by simplifying expressions with real numbers involving addition, subtraction, multiplication, division, absolute value, integer exponents, roots (square, cube) and factorials. DOK 2

8. The area of a square garden is 216 meters. What is the length of each side as a decimal to the nearest tenth? *(p. 269, prob. 3–5)*

A. 14.6 m

B. 14.69 m

C. 14.696 m

D. 14.7 m

9. Which of the following shows the product of $3^6 \cdot 3^{-2}$? *(p. 333, prob. 10–14)*

A. 3^{-12}

B. 3^{-3}

C. 3^4

D. 9^4

10. What is the value of $2 - 3 \cdot (5 + 1)$? *(p. 14, prob. 16–23)*

A. -18 B. -16

C. -6 D. 6

11. What is the value of $|1 - 7|$? *(p. 55, prob. 3–8)*

A. -8 B. -6

C. 1 D. 6

Go On 

COUNTDOWN to KCCT

12. A
13. D
14. B
15. A

Subdomain 1 Number Properties and Operations

MA-HS-1.3.2 Students will:
- **describe and extend arithmetic and geometric sequences;**
- **determine a specific term of a sequence given an explicit formula;**
- **determine an explicit rule for the nth term of an arithmetic sequence and**
- **apply sequences to solve real-world problems.**

DOK 3

12. Look at the sequence below:

1.25, 0.75, 0.25, −0.25, . . .

Which of the following is true?
(p. 806, prob. 3–11)

A. The sequence is arithmetic with a common difference of −0.5.

B. The sequence is arithmetic with a common difference of −0.25.

C. The sequence is arithmetic with a common difference of 0.5.

D. The sequence is not arithmetic.

13. The second term of a geometric sequence is 8 and the first term is 2. What is the fifth term? *(p. 814, prob. 28–36)*

A. 26

B. 32

C. 128

D. 512

Use the sequence below to answer questions 14–15.

1, 5, 9, 13, . . .

14. What is the next term in the sequence?
(p. 798, prob. 15–26)

A. 15

B. 17

C. 21

D. 25

15. What is the rule for the *n*th term?
(p. 798, prob. 15–26)

A. $a_n = 4n - 3$

B. $a_n = 3n + 1$

C. $a_n = 4(n - 1)$

D. $a_n = 3n^2 + 1$

Go On 

Countdown to KCCT

16. C
17. D
18. C

Subdomain 1 Number Properties and Operations

MA-HS-1.3.3 Students will write an explicit rule for the nth term of a geometric sequence.

16. Find the rule for the nth term of the geometric sequence. *(p. 814, prob. 15–27)*

$$4, 8, 16, 32, \ldots$$

A. $a_n = (n - 1)^2$

B. $a_n = 2(n - 1)$

C. $a_n = 4(2)^{n-1}$

D. $a_n = 2^{n-1}$

17. Find a rule for the nth term of the following geometric sequence. *(p. 815, prob. 39–47)*

$$a_2 = 21, a_5 = 567$$

A. $a_n = \frac{44 - n}{n}$

B. $a_n = 81(7)^{n-1}$

C. $a_n = 63(81)^n$

D. $a_n = 7(3)^{n-1}$

MA-HS-1.3.4 Students will recognize and solve problems that can be modeled using a finite geometric series, such as home mortgage problems and other compound interest problems.

18. Leah deposited $500 in a bank account. If the account pays 4% annual interest compounded every six months, what is the balance after 3 years? *(p. 484, prob. 37)*

A. $518.64

B. $540.48

C. $563.08

D. $632.66

COUNTDOWN to KCCT

Go On 

19. D
20. C
21. A
22. C
23. A

Subdomain 1 | Number Properties and Operations

MA-HS-1.4.1 Students will apply ratios, percents and proportional reasoning to solve real-world problems (e.g., those involving slope and rate, percent of increase and decrease) and will explain how slope determines a rate of change in linear functions representing real-world problems. DOK 2

19. The temperature in a laboratory refrigerator is lowered from 58° to 31° over a 12-hour period. What is the average rate of change in the temperature? *(p. 87, prob. 45)*

A. −7.42°/hour

B. −3.25°/hour

C. −3.08°/hour

D. −2.25°/hour

20. You cycle for 38.25 miles at an average speed of 17 miles per hour. How many hours does your ride take? *(p. 7, prob. 30)*

A. 2 h

B. 2.2 h

C. 2.25 h

D. 2.4 h

21. A road's *grade* is its slope expressed as a percent. If a road rises 12 feet over a horizontal distance of 2400 feet, what is the grade of the road? *(p. 87, prob. 43)*

A. 0.5% B. 2%

C. 5% D. 200%

MA-HS-1.5.1 Students will identify real number properties (commutative properties of addition and multiplication, associative properties of addition and multiplication, distributive property of multiplication over addition and subtraction, identity properties of addition and multiplication and inverse properties of addition and multiplication) when used to justify a given step in simplifying an expression or solving an equation.

22. When solving the equation $4(x - 3) = 2(x + 8)$, a student wrote $4x - 12 = 2x + 16$. Which property of real numbers guarantees that the equations are equivalent? *(p. 6, prob. 15)*

A. Symmetric property

B. Identity property of multiplication

C. Distributive property

D. Commutative property of multiplication

23. Which property of real numbers is illustrated by the equation $3 \cdot (9 \cdot 12) = (3 \cdot 9) \cdot 12$? *(p. 6, prob. 16)*

A. Associative property of multiplication

B. Commutative property of multiplication

C. Inverse property of multiplication

D. Identity property of multiplication

Go On 

24. A
25. D
26. C
27. A

Subdomain 2 Measurement

MA-HS-2.1.1 Students will determine the surface area and volume of right rectangular prisms, pyramids, cylinders, cones and spheres in real-world and mathematical problems. DOK 2

24. Rosa purchased a wooden storage chest for her bedroom. The height of the chest is 20 inches, the depth of the chest is 22 inches, and the width of the chest is 45 inches. What is the volume of the storage chest? Use the formula $V = \ell wh$. *(p. 993, prob.1–6)*

A. 19,800 in.^3

B. 9900 in.^3

C. 1980 in.^3

D. 1340 in.^3

25. A chef uses a cylinder-shaped tool to form pastry shells. The tool has a diameter of 3 centimeters and a height of 8 centimeters. What is the surface area of the pastry tool? *(p. 993, prob. 1–6)*

A. about 51.81 cm^2

B. about 56.52 cm^2

C. about 86.78 cm^2

D. about 89.49 cm^2

26. What is the volume of the solid? *(p. 993, prob. 5)*

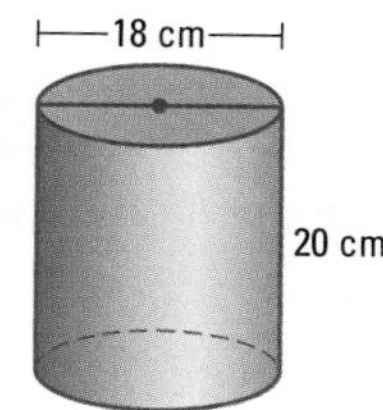

A. $180\pi\ \text{cm}^3$

B. $360\pi\ \text{cm}^3$

C. $1620\pi\ \text{cm}^3$

D. $6480\pi\ \text{cm}^3$

27. What is the surface area of the solid? *(p. 993, prob. 3)*

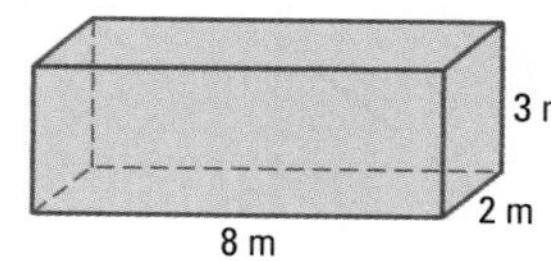

A. 92 m^2

B. 84 m^2

C. 80 m^2

D. 48 m^2

Go On 

COUNTDOWN to KCCT

28. C
29. A
30. D
31. B

MA-HS-2.1.3 Students will apply definitions and properties of right triangle relationships (right triangle trigonometry and the Pythagorean theorem) to determine length and angle measures to solve real-world and mathematical problems. DOK 3

28. Frank is standing 10 feet from the base of a tree. The angle of elevation from Frank's feet to the top of the tree is 65°. What is the height of the tree to the nearest tenth of a foot? *(p. 857, prob. 30)*

A. 11.0 ft

B. 17.8 ft

C. 21.4 ft

D. 64.3 ft

29. Solve $\triangle ABC$ using the diagram. *(p. 857, prob. 21–28)*

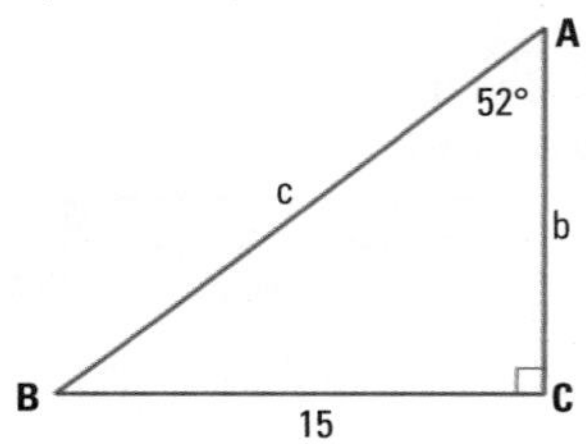

A. $B = 38°, b = 11.72, c = 19.04$

B. $B = 38°, b = 19.2, c = 11.82$

C. $B = 38°, b = 19.2, c = 24.3$

D. $B = 38°, b = 11.72, c = 24.3$

30. What is the measure of θ in the triangle below? *(p. 878, prob. 27–29)*

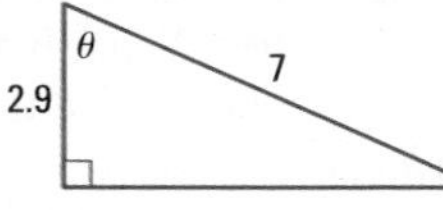

A. 22.5°

B. 24.5°

C. 62.5°

D. 65.5°

31. The Washington Mountaineering Club is currently hiking Mount Rainier. Their current altitude is 1200 feet above sea level and 2500 feet directly from their base camp. What is the angle of depression from their current position? *(p. 879, prob. 36)*

A. 25.6°

B. 28.7°

C. 61.3°

D. 64.4°

Go On

32.	C
33.	A
34.	A
35.	D
36.	B

Subdomain 2 Measurement

MA-HS-2.1.4 Students will apply special right triangles and the converse of the Pythagorean theorem to solve real-world problems.

32. A tree casts the shadow shown. What is the exact length of the shadow? *(p. 857, prob. 30)*

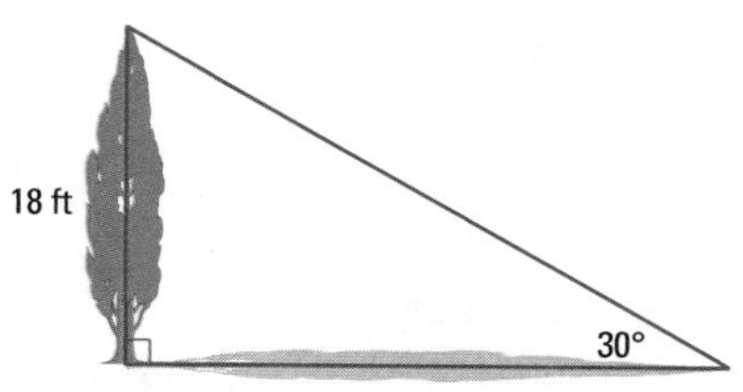

A. 9 ft

B. $9\sqrt{3}$ ft

C. $18\sqrt{3}$ ft

D. 36 ft

33. What are the exact values of x and y? *(p. 856, prob. 17–19)*

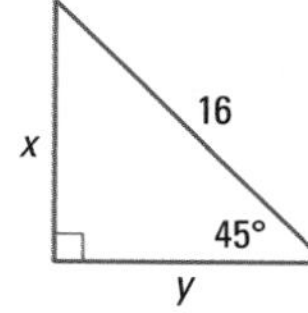

A. $x = 8\sqrt{2}, y = 8\sqrt{2}$

B. $x = 8\sqrt{3}, y = 8$

C. $x = 16\sqrt{2}, y = 16\sqrt{2}$

D. $x = 16\sqrt{3}, y = 8$

MA-HS-2.2.1 Students will continue to apply to both real-world and mathematical problems U.S. customary and metric systems of measurement.

34. A snail crawled 5 centimeters in 30 seconds. What is its average speed in inches per minute? *(p. 7, prob. 47–48)*

A. about 4 in./min

B. about 6 in./min

C. about 10 in./min

D. about 20 in./min

35. About how many kilometers long is 50 miles? *(p. 7, prob. 43–44)*

A. about 30 km

B. about 60 km

C. about 80 km

D. about 120 km

36. A circle has a diameter of 9 cm. What is its approximate area? *(p. 992, prob. 1–12)*

A. 28 cm^2

B. 64 cm^2

C. 127 cm^2

D. 254 cm^2

COUNTDOWN to KCCT

Go On

37. B
38. B
39. B
40. C

MA-HS-3.1.3 Students will analyze and apply angle relationships (e.g., linear pairs, vertical, complementary, supplementary, corresponding and alternate interior angles) in real-world and mathematical problems. DOK 2

37. $\angle ABD$ and $\angle DBC$ are supplementary. The measure of $\angle ABD$ is $2x + 5$. The measure of $\angle DBC$ is $3x$. What is the value of x? *(p. 994, prob. 7–9)*

A. $x = 85$

B. $x = 35$

C. $x = 19$

D. $x = 17$

38. $\angle ABD$ and $\angle DBC$ are complementary. What is the value of x? *(p. 994, prob. 4–6)*

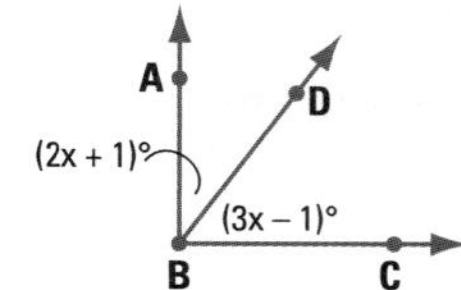

A. 16

B. 18

C. 24

D. 32

MA-HS-3.1.6 Students will know the definitions and basic properties of a circle and will use them to prove basic theorems and solve problems.

39. What is the arc length and area of a sector whose radius is 8 and central angle is $\frac{\pi}{3}$? *(p. 863, prob. 32–37)*

A. about 8.37; about 16.75

B. about 8.37; about 33.49

C. about 25.12; about 16.75

D. about 25.12; about 33.49

40. A playground sandbox forms a sector with a radius of 4.5 feet and a central angle of 90°. What is the area of the sandbox? *(p. 863, prob. 32–37)*

A. 3.53 ft^2

B. 7.95 ft^2

C. 15.90 ft^2

D. 31.79 ft^2

Go On 

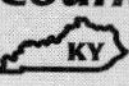

Countdown to KCCT

41. A
42. D
43. B

Subdomain 3 Geometry

MA-HS-3.1.6 Students will know the definitions and basic properties of a circle and will use them to prove basic theorems and solve problems.

41. What is the equation in standard form of the circle that passes through $(4, -8)$ and is centered at the origin?
(p. 630, prob. 31–42)

A. $x^2 + y^2 = 80$

B. $x^2 + y^2 = \sqrt{80}$

C. $x^2 + y^2 = 32$

D. $x^2 + y^2 = \sqrt{32}$

42. Which equation represents the graph of the circle below? *(p. 629, prob. 3–8)*

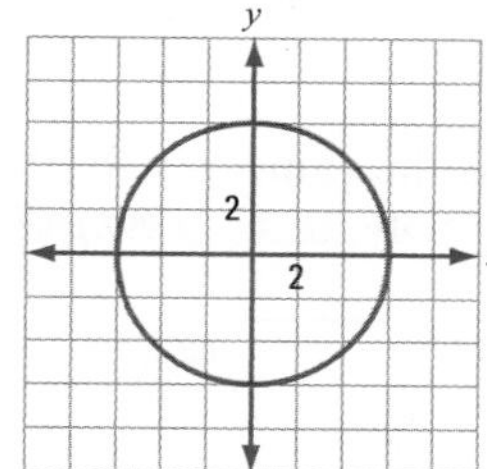

A. $x^2 + y^2 = 3$

B. $x^2 + y^2 = 6$

C. $x^2 + y^2 = 9$

D. $x^2 + y^2 = 36$

MA-HS-3.1.7 Students will solve real-world and mathematical problems by applying properties of triangles (e.g., Triangle Sum theorem and Isosceles Triangle theorems). DOK 2

43. Find the value of x. *(p. 995, prob. 1–4)*

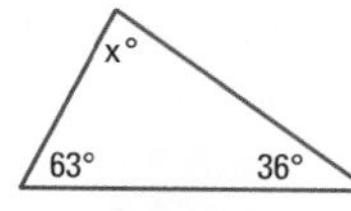

A. 71

B. 81

C. 91

D. 101

Go On

44. D
45. B
46. A
47. A
48. C

Subdomain 3 Geometry

MA-HS-3.1.10 Students will describe the intersection of a plane with a three-dimensional figure.

44. When a plane cuts through a cone perpendicular to the cone's base as shown, which figure is formed on the plane? *(p. 655, prob. 1)*

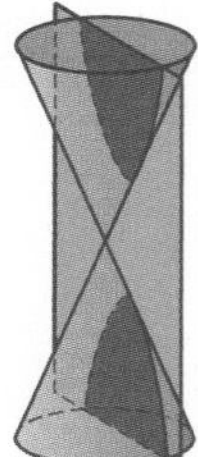

A. circle
B. ellipse
C. parabola
D. hyperbola

45. When a plane cuts through a cone at an angle greater than 0° and less than 90°, which figure is formed on the plane? *(p. 655, prob. 1)*

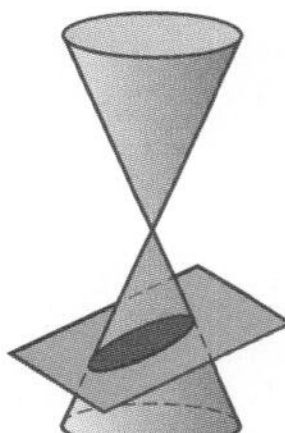

A. circle
B. ellipse
C. parabola
D. hyperbola

46. When a plane cuts through the middle of a cone parallel to the cone's base, what is formed on the plane? *(p. 655, prob. 1)*

A. circle
B. ellipse
C. parabola
D. hyperbola

MA-HS-3.1.12 Students will apply the concepts of congruence and similarity to solve real-world and mathematical problems. DOK 3

47. What is the value of x for the two similar polygons? *(p. 997, prob. 10–18)*

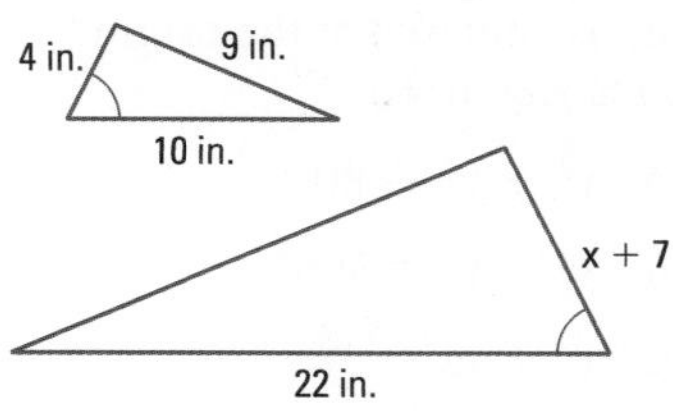

A. 1.8 in.
B. 15.8 in.
C. 48 in.
D. 56 in.

48. What is the value of x for the two similar polygons? *(p. 997, prob. 10–18)*

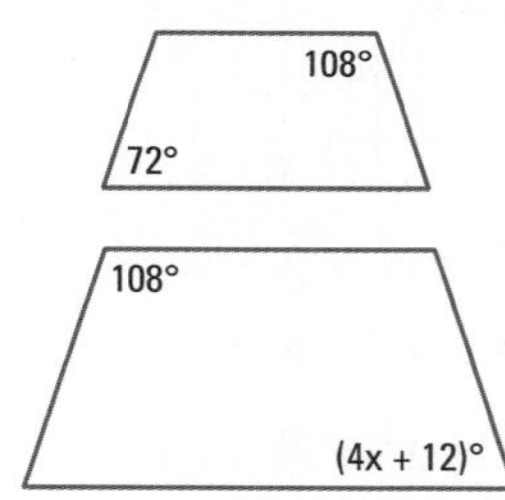

A. 10
B. 12
C. 15
D. 24

Go On

Subdomain 3 Geometry

MA-HS-3.2.1 Students will identify and describe properties of and apply geometric transformations within a plane to solve real-world and mathematical problems. DOK 3

Use the graph below to answer questions 49–51.

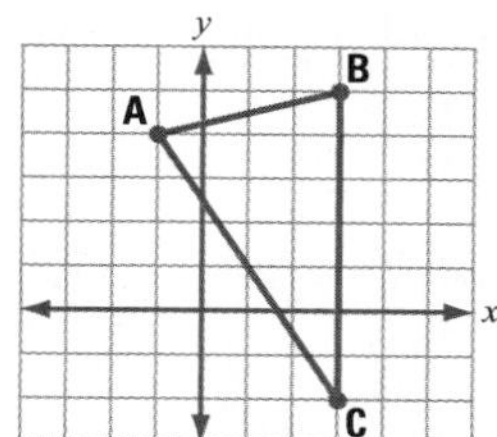

49. If $\triangle ABC$ is rotated 180° around the origin, what are the coordinates of vertex A after the rotation? *(p. 989, prob. 9–18)*

A. $(-1, 4)$ B. $(1, 4)$
C. $(1, -4)$ D. $(-1, -4)$

50. If $\triangle ABC$ is translated left 2 units and up 1 unit, what are the coordinates of vertex B after the translation? *(p. 989, prob. 9–18)*

A. $(6, 1)$ B. $(5, 4)$
C. $(5, 3)$ D. $(3, 1)$

51. If $\triangle ABC$ is reflected in the y-axis, what are the coordinates of vertex C after the reflection? *(p. 989, prob. 9–18)*

A. $(-3, 2)$ B. $(-3, -2)$
C. $(2, -3)$ D. $(2, 3)$

Use the graph below to answer questions 52–53.

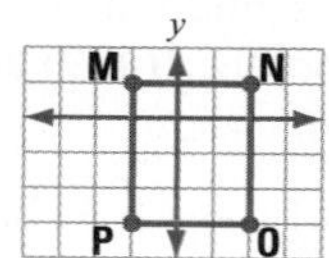

52. What is the coordinate of vertex M when rectangle $MNOP$ is dilated using a scale factor of 3? *(p. 989, prob. 19–23)*

A. $(3, -3)$ B. $(-3, 3)$
C. $\left(\frac{1}{3}, -\frac{1}{3}\right)$ D. $\left(-\frac{1}{3}, \frac{1}{3}\right)$

53. What scale factor was used to dilate rectangle $MNOP$ in order for vertex O to be located at $(1, -1.5)$? *(p. 989, prob. 19–23)*

A. 2 B. $\frac{1}{2}$
C. $\frac{1}{3}$ D. $-\frac{1}{2}$

54. What scale factor was used to dilate $\triangle DEF$? *(p. 989, prob. 19–23)*

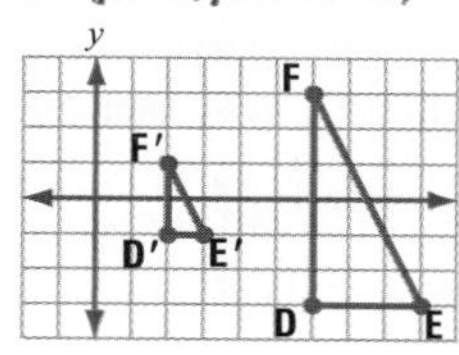

A. 3 B. 2
C. $\frac{1}{2}$ D. $\frac{1}{3}$

Go On

COUNTDOWN to KCCT

Countdown to KCCT

49. C
50. D
51. B
52. B
53. B
54. D

55. B
56. B
57. A
58. B
59. A
60. C

Subdomain 3 Geometry

MA-HS-3.3.1 Students will apply algebraic concepts and graphing in the coordinate plane to analyze and solve problems (e.g., finding the final coordinates for a specified polygon, midpoints, betweenness of points, parallel and perpendicular lines, the distance between two points, the slope of a segment). DOK 2

55. What is the midpoint of the segment with endpoints $A(4, 9)$ and $B(2, 7)$? *(p. 617, prob. 3)*

A. (6, 16) B. (3, 8)
C. (2, 2) D. (5, 5)

56. A triangle has vertices at $E(4, -2)$, $F(-1, 5)$, and $G(6, 10)$. What is the classification of triangle EFG by the lengths of its sides? *(p. 617, prob. 27)*

A. scalene
B. isosceles
C. equilateral
D. right

57. A line segment has endpoints (6, 16) and (8, 18). What is the equation of the line that is the perpendicular bisector of the segment? *(p. 617, prob. 31)*

A. $y = -x + 24$
B. $y = x + 10$
C. $y = -x - 10$
D. $y = x + 24$

58. What is the slope of the line passing through (4, 1) and (7, −3)? *(p. 86, prob. 6)*

A. $-\frac{2}{3}$
B. $-\frac{4}{3}$
C. $-\frac{3}{2}$
D. $-\frac{3}{4}$

59. What is the equation of the line that passes through $P(8, 2)$ and is parallel to $y = 4x - 3$? *(p. 102, prob. 20)*

A. $y = 4x - 30$
B. $y = 4x$
C. $y = 4x + 2$
D. $y = 4x + 8$

60. A rescue ship located at (−800, 2000), on a coordinate grid, must sail to a fishing boat located at (0, 500). If the coordinates are in meters, how far does the rescue ship have to travel? *(p. 618, prob. 47)*

A. 500 meters
B. 800 meters
C. 1700 meters
D. 2000 meters

Go On 

Countdown to KCCT

61. B
62. C
63. A
64. D
65. D

Subdomain 4 Data Analysis and Probability

MA-HS-4.1.1 Students will analyze and make inferences from a set of data with no more than two variables, and will analyze problems for the use and misuse of data representations. DOK 3

61. A company randomly asked 500 people from all over the country what their favorite brand of gum is. They claim that 40% of respondents said that they did not chew gum with a margin of error of 3%. What is the *best* description of this claim? *(p. 770, prob. 15–22)*

A. The question is biased.

B. The sample size is not large enough to have the claimed margin of error.

C. The convenience sample is not representative.

D. The claim is accurate and reasonable.

62. How many more students chose comedy as their favorite type of movie than romance? *(p. 1007, prob. 6–8)*

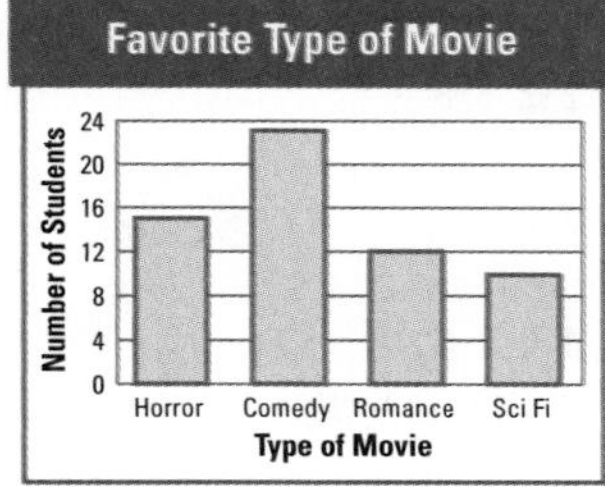

A. 3

B. 8

C. 11

D. 15

MA-HS-4.1.3 Students will represent real-world data using matrices and will use matrix addition, subtraction, multiplication (with matrices no larger than 2×2) and scalar multiplication to solve real-world problems.

Use the two matrices below to answer questions 63–64.

$$M = \begin{bmatrix} 3 & 7 \\ 9 & -2 \end{bmatrix} \qquad N = \begin{bmatrix} 2 & -3 \\ -1 & 4 \end{bmatrix}$$

63. What is $M + N$? *(p. 191, prob. 16)*

A. $\begin{bmatrix} 5 & 4 \\ 8 & 2 \end{bmatrix}$ B. $\begin{bmatrix} 5 & -4 \\ -8 & 2 \end{bmatrix}$

C. $\begin{bmatrix} 1 & 4 \\ 2 & 8 \end{bmatrix}$ D. $\begin{bmatrix} -1 & 4 \\ -8 & 2 \end{bmatrix}$

64. What is $M - N$? *(p. 191, prob. 17)*

A. $\begin{bmatrix} 1 & 4 \\ 8 & 2 \end{bmatrix}$ B. $\begin{bmatrix} 5 & 4 \\ -8 & 2 \end{bmatrix}$

C. $\begin{bmatrix} 1 & 4 \\ 10 & -6 \end{bmatrix}$ D. $\begin{bmatrix} -1 & -10 \\ -10 & 6 \end{bmatrix}$

65. Perform the indicated operation. *(p. 191, prob. 10)*

$$-2\begin{bmatrix} 3 & 2 \\ 0 & -2 \end{bmatrix}$$

A. $\begin{bmatrix} 6 & 4 \\ 0 & -4 \end{bmatrix}$ B. $\begin{bmatrix} -4 & -6 \\ 4 & 0 \end{bmatrix}$

C. $\begin{bmatrix} 1 & 0 \\ 0 & -4 \end{bmatrix}$ D. $\begin{bmatrix} -6 & 4 \\ 0 & -4 \end{bmatrix}$

COUNTDOWN to KCCT

Go On 

66. B
67. D
68. C
69. A
70. D

Subdomain 4 | Data Analysis and Probability

MA-HS-4.2.1 Students will describe and compare data distributions and make inferences from the data based on the shapes of graphs, measures of center (mean, median, mode) and measures of spread (range, standard deviation). DOK 2

66. On a geography test, Ms. Hemingway's class had a mean score of 80.5 and Mr. Walsh's class had a mean score of 75. If Mr. Walsh has 20 students and the average of the two classes combined is 78, how many students are in Ms. Hemingway's class? *(p. 754, prob. 19–23)*

A. 20

B. 24

C. 38

D. 44

67. The winning scores for the first ten football games for your school are: 14, 10, 14, 21, 17, 10, 13, 18, 24, and 17. What is the standard deviation of the winning scores? *(p. 748, prob. 29–30)*

A. 15.80

B. 13.55

C. 9.18

D. 4.28

68. The range of the set of scores for a player in his last golf game was 5. In the next game the player took 2 more strokes to get the ball in each hole. What is the range of his scores on the second game? *(p. 753, prob. 16)*

A. 2

B. 3

C. 5

D. 7

69. Which is the best approximation of the correlation coefficient for the data in the scatter plot? *(p. 117, prob. 9)*

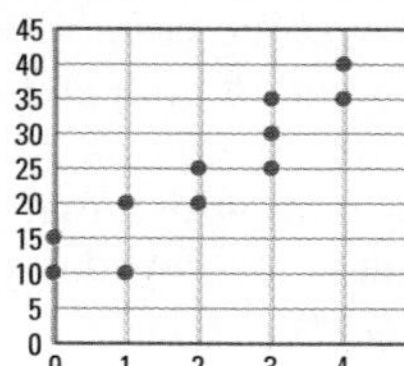

A. 1

B. 0

C. −0.5

D. −1

70. The stem-and-leaf plot shows the ages of people attending a family reunion. What is the median age? *(p. 749, prob. 30)*

Stem	Leaves
0	2 3 9
1	4 4 4 9
2	0 2 2 5 8
3	2 5
4	6 9 9
5	0
6	2 4 6 6 9
7	6 8

A. 14

B. 25

C. 28

D. 32

Go On

Subdomain 4 Data Analysis and Probability

MA-HS-4.2.2 Students will know the characteristics of the Gaussian normal distribution (bell-shaped curve).

71. What is the percent of the area under the normal curve represented by the shaded region? *(p. 760, prob. 9–10)*

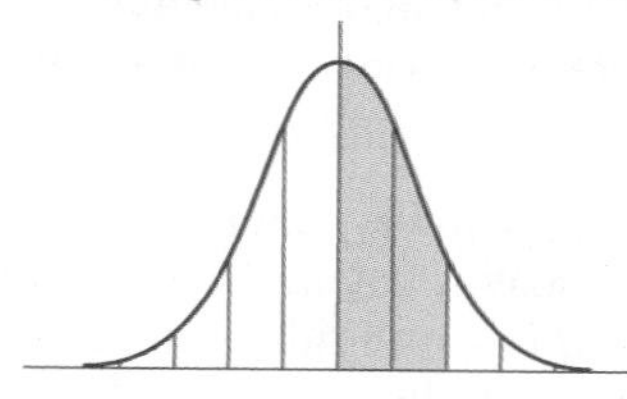

A. 68%

B. 47.5%

C. 36.35%

D. 34%

72. The fuel economy of a certain model of car is determined to be normally distributed with a mean of 32 miles per gallon. If the standard deviation is 2, what is the probability that a car of this model will get less than 34 miles per gallon? *(p. 760, prob. 9–10)*

A. 0.16

B. 0.68

C. 0.84

D. 0.975

MA-HS-4.2.3 Students will:

- **identify an appropriate curve of best fit (linear, quadratic, exponential) for a set of two-variable data;**
- **determine a line of best fit equation for a set of linear two-variable data and**
- **apply a line of best fit to make predictions within and beyond a given set of two-variable data.**

DOK 3

73. Which equation best models the data? *(p. 118, prob. 19–20)*

x	0	5	10	15	20	25
y	63	54	48	33	21	13

A. $y = 2.08x + 64.7$

B. $y = -2.08x + 64.7$

C. $y = -64.7x + 2.08$

D. $y = 1.2x + 63$

74. What type of function best models the data points? *(p. 778, prob. 5)*

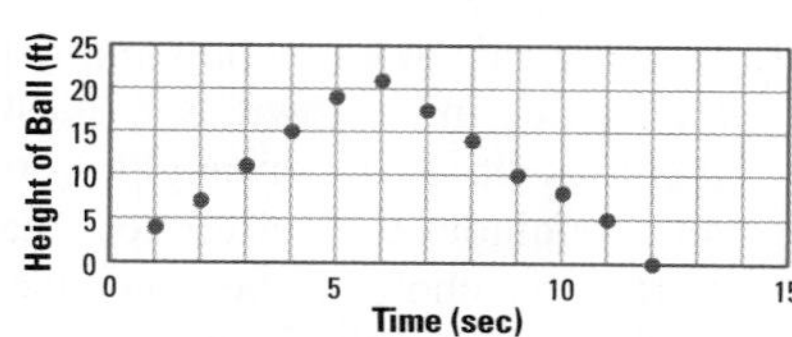

A. linear

B. exponential

C. quadratic

D. cubic

Go On 

COUNTDOWN to KCCT

Countdown to KCCT

71. B
72. C
73. B
74. C

75. B
76. C
77. A
78. B

Subdomain 4 Data Analysis and Probability

MA-HS-4.3.1 Students will recognize potential for bias resulting from the misuse of sampling methods (e.g., non-random sampling, polling only a specific group of people, using limited or extremely small sample sizes) and explain why these samples can lead to inaccurate inferences. DOK 2

75. Justin wants to find out how often people go to the movie theater. He decides to survey people at his local movie theater on Friday and Saturday night to find out how often they have seen a movie at a theater during the past 6 months. Why might Justin's method be biased? *(p. 769, prob. 3–5)*

A. He is only asking on Friday and Saturday night, when more people go to the movies.
B. He is taking the survey at the theater, where everyone is going to see a movie.
C. Six months is too long. He should ask how often over the past 3 months.
D. Nothing is biased about Justin's method.

76. Sonya wants to know how many people have a dog in her town. She questions the households in her neighborhood and concludes that a little less than half of the households in her town have a dog since 12 of the 25 homes she went to had a dog. Is Sonya's survey valid? If not, why? *(p. 769, prob. 3–5)*

A. Yes, her survey is a valid survey.
B. No, because she should have gone to the dog park and counted the number of dog owners.
C. No, because her sample is just one small part of her town.
D. No, she should have asked students in her school if they have a dog.

MA-HS-4.4.1 Students will:
- **determine theoretical and experimental (from given data) probabilities;**
- **make predictions and draw inferences from probabilities;**
- **compare theoretical and experimental probabilities and**
- **determine probabilities involving replacement and non-replacement.**

DOK 3

77. The probability that it will rain on Thursday is 0.4 and the probability that it will rain on Friday is 0.75. What is the probability of rain on Thursday and Friday? *(p. 721, prob. 3–8)*

A. 0.3
B. 0.35
C. 0.58
D. 0.79

78. The results of spinning a spinner 120 times are shown. From the table, what is the experimental probability of spinning an even number? (Assume the outcomes are equally likely.)
(p. 702, prob. 28–32)

Spin	1	2	3	4	5	6	7	8
Number of Occurences	14	16	5	12	11	25	10	27

A. $\frac{1}{2}$
B. $\frac{2}{3}$
C. $\frac{3}{4}$
D. $\frac{5}{6}$

Go On

Countdown to KCCT

79. A
80. C
81. A
82. B

Subdomain 4 Data Analysis and Probability

MA-HS-4.4.1 Students will:

- **determine theoretical and experimental (from given data) probabilities;**
- **make predictions and draw inferences from probabilities;**
- **compare theoretical and experimental probabilities and**
- **determine probabilities involving replacement and non-replacement.**

DOK 3

79. There are 12 chips in a blue bag. The chips are numbered 1 through 12. You randomly select two chips without replacement. What is the probability that the first chip is a prime number and the second chip is a multiple of 4? *(p. 721, prob. 26–31)*

A. $\frac{1}{12}$ B. $\frac{1}{11}$

C. $\frac{2}{11}$ D. $\frac{5}{12}$

80. A survey was conducted to find out how 10th graders at Oliver School go to school. The results are shown in the bar graph. What is the experimental probability that a randomly selected 10th grader gets to school by public transportation? *(p. 702, prob. 28–31)*

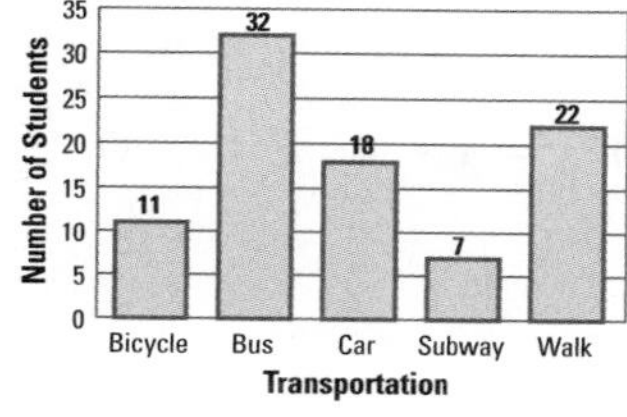

A. about 0.2 B. about 0.356

C. about 0.433 D. about 0.756

MA-HS-4.4.2 Students will recognize and identify the differences between combinations and permutations and use them to count discrete quantities.

81. A race is run with 10 people. You are required to find how many different ways the race can be won. Which of the following requires combinations to find the answer? *(p. 695, prob. 38–39)*

A. The top 3 runners win a blue ribbon.

B. Different prizes are awarded for 1st, 2nd, and 3rd place.

C. Blue ribbons are awarded for first place. Red ribbons are awarded for second place.

D. A medal is awarded for 1st place and a ribbon is awarded for second place.

82. What is the number of distinguishable permutations of the letters in the word GREEN? *(p. 687, prob. 43–55)*

A. 6

B. 7

C. 12

D. 16

Go On 

COUNTDOWN to KCCT

83. A
84. B
85. B
86. B

MA-HS-5.1.1 Students will identify multiple representations (tables, graphs, equations) of functions (linear, quadratic, absolute value, exponential) in real-world or mathematical problems. DOK 2

83. Which is the equation for the graph shown? *(p. 127, prob. 3–14)*

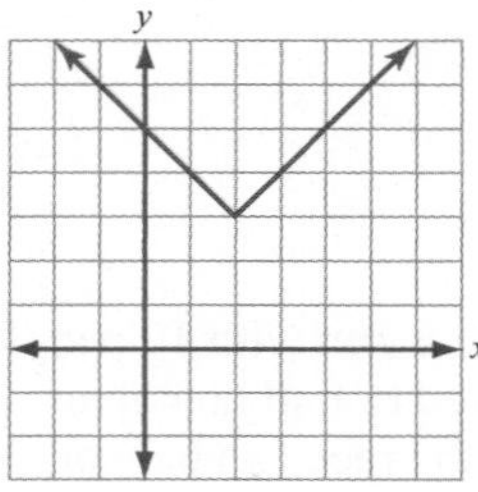

A. $y = |x - 2| + 3$

B. $y = |x + 2| - 3$

C. $y = |x + 3| - 2$

D. $y = |x - 3| + 2$

84. The graph of which function is shown? *(p. 482, prob. 15–23)*

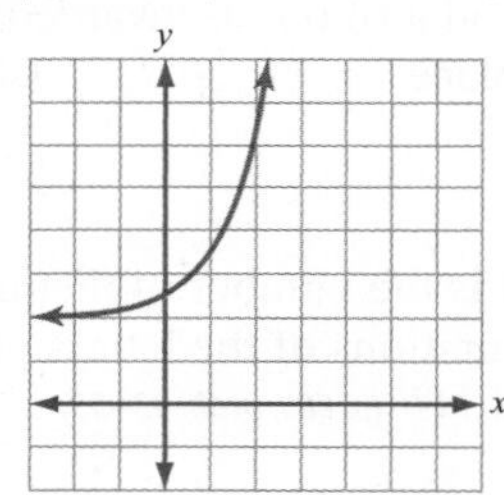

A. $y = 2 \cdot 3^x + 0.5$

B. $y = 0.5 \cdot 3^x + 2$

C. $y = (2.5)^x$

D. $y = 2 \cdot 3^x + 2$

85. The table shows the height in feet y of a hot air balloon after x number of hours of being in the air.

x	1	2	3	4	5	6	7
y	26	350	890	1270	900	640	31

What type of function does this data represent? *(p. 778, prob. 5)*

A. linear

B. quadratic

C. cubic

D. exponential

86. Which equation represents the data from the table below? *(p. 37, prob. 11–15)*

x	1	2	3	4	5	6
y	5	7	9	11	13	15

A. $y = 2(x + 3)$

B. $y = 2x + 3$

C. $y = 2^x + 3$

D. $y = x + 4$

Go On 

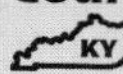

Subdomain 5 Algebraic Thinking

MA-HS-5.1.2 Students will identify, relate and apply representations (graphs, equations, tables) of a piecewise function (such as long distance telephone rates) from mathematical or real-world information.

87. Which is the graph of the following step function? *(p.131, prob. 7)*

$$f(x) = \begin{cases} 4, & 0 \le x < 3 \\ 2, & 3 \le x < 5 \\ 6, & 5 \le x < 8 \end{cases}$$

A.

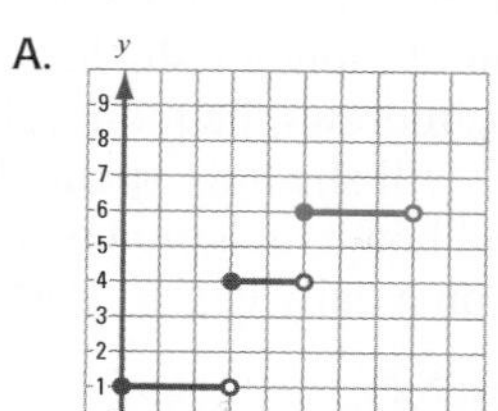

B.

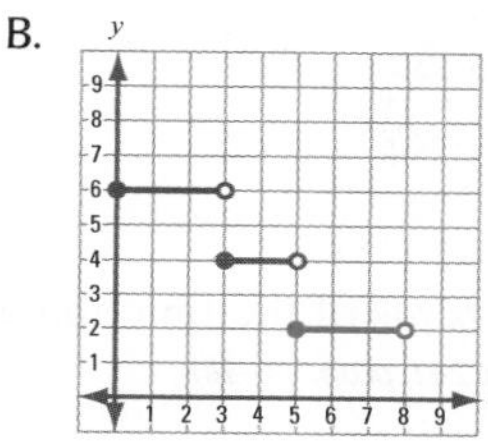

C.

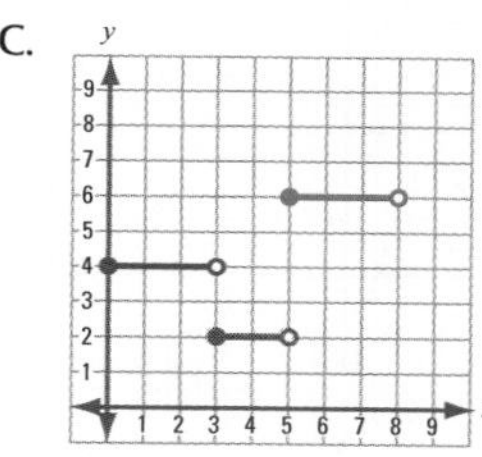

D.

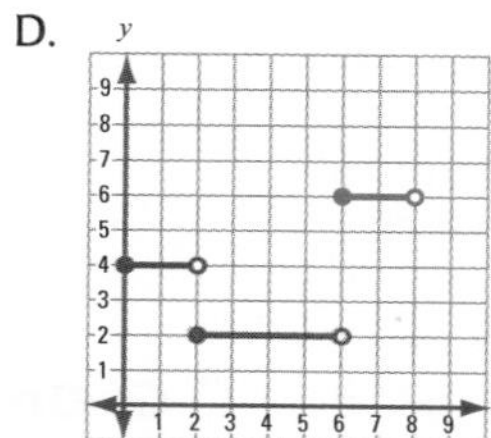

MA-HS-5.1.4 Students will recognize and solve problems that can be modeled using an exponential function, such as compound interest problems.

88. The population P of a town was 5200 in 2001 and has increased by 5% per year since then. Which exponential growth model gives the town's population in terms of t, where t is the number of years since 2001? *(p. 482, prob. 25)*

A. $P = 1.05(5200)^t$

B. $P = 0.5(5200)^t$

C. $P = 5200(1.05)^t$

D. $P = 5200(0.05)^t$

89. Interest is compounded continuously at an annual rate of 4% on a money market account at your local bank. If you make an initial deposit of $3500, what will be the balance after 2 years? Use the formula $A = Pe^{rt}$.
(p. 497, prob. 57–58)

A. $3642.83

B. $3791.50

C. $5221.38

D. $7789.39

Go On

COUNTDOWN to KCCT

87. C
88. C
89. B

90. C
91. C
92. B
93. C
94. B

Subdomain 5 Algebraic Thinking

MA-HS-5.1.5 Students will:

- **determine if a relation is a function;**
- **determine the domain and range of a function (linear and quadratic);**
- **determine the slope and intercepts of a linear function;**
- **determine the maximum, minimum, and intercepts (roots/zeros) of a quadratic function and**
- **evaluate a function written in function notation for a specified rational number.**

DOK 2

90. The relation given by the ordered pairs $(-2, 3)$, $(6, 1)$, $(4, -8)$, and $(0, 3)$ is a function. Which ordered pair could be included in this relation so that it is still a function? *(p. 77, prob. 16–20)*

A. $(0, 4)$

B. $(6, 1)$

C. $(3, 0)$

D. $(-2, 8)$

91. What is the y-intercept of the line that is parallel to $x + 2y = 1$ and passes through $(3, -5)$? *(p. 102, prob. 20)*

A. $\left(0, \frac{7}{2}\right)$

B. $(0, 3)$

C. $\left(0, -\frac{7}{2}\right)$

D. $\left(0, \frac{1}{2}\right)$

92. Is the function $f(x) = 5$ linear, and what is its value at $x = 2$? *(p. 78, prob. 34–39)*

A. linear; 2 B. linear; 5

C. not linear; 2 D. not linear; 5

93. Betty withdraws \$25 from her bank account for spending money. The equation $y = -5x + 25$ represents the amount of money y she has x days after she withdraws the money. In how many days will she have spent all the money, and how much money does she withdraw on a daily basis? *(p. 95, prob. 68)*

A. 3 days; \$2

B. 4 days; \$6

C. 5 days; \$5

D. 6 days; \$4

94. What are zeros of the function graphed below? *(p. 241, prob. 33–38)*

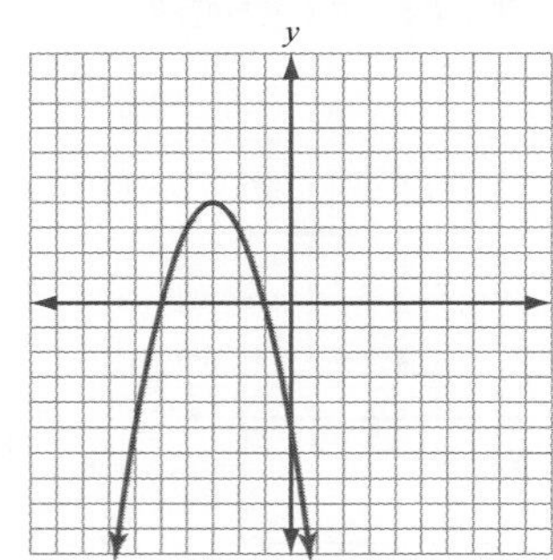

A. $1, 5$

B. $-5, -1$

C. $-3, 4$

D. $-5, 4$

Go On

Subdomain 5 Algebraic Thinking

MA-HS-5.1.6 Students will find the domain and range for absolute value functions.

95. What is the domain of the function below? *(p. 127, prob. 3–14)*

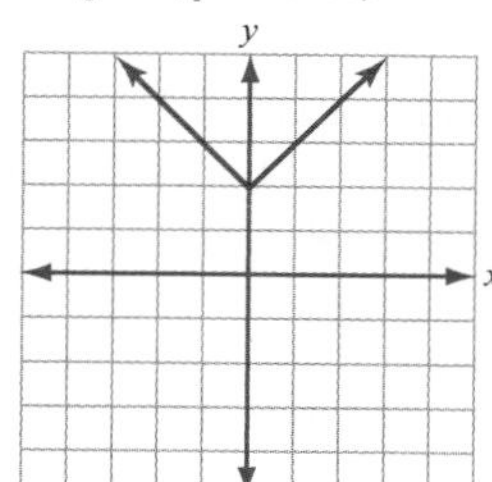

A. Domain: $x \geq 0$; Range: $y \geq 0$

B. Domain: $x \geq 1$; Range: all real numbers

C. Domain: $x \leq 2$; Range: $y \geq 1$

D. Domain: all real numbers; Range: $y \geq 2$

MA-HS-5.1.7 Students will apply and use direct and inverse variation to solve real-world and mathematical problems.

96. Your weight M on the moon varies directly with your weight E on Earth. If you weigh 120 pounds on Earth, you would weigh 20 pounds on the moon. Which equation relates E and M? *(p. 110, prob. 40)*

A. $20M = 120E$

B. $M = \frac{6}{1}E$

C. $M = E - 100$

D. $M = \frac{1}{6}E$

MA-HS-5.1.8 Students will identify the changes and explain how changes in parameters affect graphs of functions (linear, quadratic, absolute value, exponential) (e.g., compare $y = x^2$, $y = 2x^2$, $y = (x - 4)^2$, and $y = x^2 + 3$). DOK 2

97. How does the graph of $y = 5x^2 + 2$ compare to the graph of $y = x^2$? *(p. 240, prob. 7–18)*

A. It is wider and shifted up by two units.

B. It is wider and shifted to the left by two units.

C. It is narrower and shifted up by two units.

D. It is narrower and shifted down by two units.

98. How does the graph of $y = -\frac{1}{3}|x|$ compare to the graph of $y = |x|$? *(p. 127, prob. 3–14)*

A. It is wider and shifted to the left by $\frac{1}{3}$.

B. It is narrower and shifted to the right by $\frac{1}{3}$.

C. It is narrower and reflected over the y-axis.

D. It is wider and reflected over the x-axis.

COUNTDOWN to KCCT

Go On 

Countdown to KCCT

95. D
96. D
97. C
98. D

99. D
100. B
101. B
102. B
103. C
104. C

Subdomain 5 Algebraic Thinking

MA-HS-5.2.1 Students will apply order of operations, real number properties (identity, inverse, commutative, associative, distributive, closure) and rules of exponents (integer) to simplify algebraic expressions.
DOK 1

99. Which expression is equivalent to $11y^2 - 8y + 2y - y^2$? *(p. 14, prob. 25–32)*

A. $12y^2 + 6y$

B. $10y^2 + 6y$

C. $12y^2 - 6y$

D. $10y^2 - 6y$

100. Which expression is equivalent to $-5(p + 7) - 9(p - 1)$? *(p. 14, prob. 25–32)*

A. $14p + 26$

B. $-14p - 26$

C. $14p - 44$

D. $-14p + 6$

101. Multiply: $r^2s \cdot r^3s^5 \cdot rs^4$.
(p. 333, prob. 24–35)

A. r^6s^{20}

B. r^6s^{10}

C. rs^{16}

D. rs^{120}

MA-HS-5.2.3 Students will:
- **add, subtract and multiply polynomial expressions;**
- **factor polynomial expressions using the greatest common monomial factor and**
- **factor quadratic polynomials of the form $ax^2 + bx + c$, when $a = 1$ and b and c are integers.**

DOK 2

102. What is the sum of $(2x^6 + 7x^2 + 1) + (x^6 - 5x^2 - 3)$?
(p. 349, prob. 3–14)

A. $5x^8 - 1$

B. $3x^6 + 2x^2 - 2$

C. $3x^{12} + 2x^4 - 2$

D. $5x^{16} - 2$

103. Simplify: $(a^2 + 3a - 2) - (2a^2 + 4)$.
(p. 349, prob. 3–14)

A. $3a^2 + 3a - 6$

B. $-a^2 + 3a - 2$

C. $-a^2 + 3a - 6$

D. $-a^2 + 3a + 2$

104. Multiply: $-2x^2(x - 2)$. *(p. 349, prob. 16–25)*

A. $-2x^3 - 4x^2$

B. $-2x^3 - 2x^2$

C. $-2x^3 + 4x^2$

D. $-2x^3 - 2$

Go On 

Subdomain 5 Algebraic Thinking

MA-HS-5.2.3 Students will:
- **add, subtract and multiply polynomial expressions;**
- **factor polynomial expressions using the greatest common monomial factor and**
- **factor quadratic polynomials of the form $ax^2 + bx + c$, when $a = 1$ and b and c are integers.**

DOK 2

105. What is the complete factorization of $9x^4y^2 - 144x^4$? *(p. 356, prob. 3–8)*

A. $(3x^2y + 12x^2)(3x^2y - 12x^2)$

B. $9x^4(y + 4)(y - 4)$

C. $3x^4(y + 4)(3y - 12)$

D. $9x^4(y^2 - 16)$

106. What is the complete factorization of $x^2 + 9x - 36$? *(p. 356, prob. 3–8)*

A. $(x - 2)(x + 18)$

B. $(x + 4)(x - 9)$

C. $(x + 9)(x - 4)$

D. $(x + 12)(x - 3)$

MA-HS-5.2.5 Students will add, subtract, multiply and divide simple rational expressions with monomial first-degree denominators and integer numerators (e.g., $\frac{3}{5x} + \frac{4}{3y}$; $\frac{9}{2a} - \frac{-7}{4b}$; $\frac{3}{-5x} \times \frac{-4}{7y}$; $\frac{5}{2c} \div \frac{9}{-11d}$), and will express the results in simplified form. DOK1

107. Which of the following is equivalent to $\frac{3}{4x} + \frac{7}{5x}$? *(p. 586, prob. 16–24)*

A. $\frac{10}{9x}$

B. $\frac{10}{9x^2}$

C. $\frac{43}{9x}$

D. $\frac{43}{20x}$

108. Which of the following is equivalent to $-\frac{2}{3m} \div \frac{12}{9n}$? *(p. 578, prob. 34–35)*

A. $-\frac{n}{2m}$ B. $-\frac{24}{27mn}$

C. $\frac{8}{9mn}$ D. $-\frac{2m}{n}$

109. Which is the equivalent expression to $\frac{4}{14p} \bullet \frac{30}{10q}$? *(p. 578, prob. 24–25)*

A. $\frac{2q}{21p}$ B. $\frac{7p}{2q}$

C. $\frac{6}{7pq}$ D. $\frac{2}{35pq}$

Go On 

COUNTDOWN to KCCT

105. B
106. D
107. D
108. A
109. C

110.

a. $a_3 = a_1 + (3 - 1)d$

$40 = a_1 + 2d$

Solve for a_1.

$40 - 2d = a_1 + 2d - 2d$

$a_1 = -2d + 40$

$a_8 = a_1 + (8 - 1)d$

$85 = a_1 + 7d$

Substitute $a_1 = -2d + 40$.

$85 = (-2d + 40)d + 7d$

Solve for d.

$85 = 5d + 40$

$85 - 40 = 5d + 40 - 40$

$45 = 5d$

$\frac{45}{5} = \frac{5d}{5}$

$d = 8$

Solve for a_1.

$40 = a_1 + 2(9)$

$40 = a_1 + 18$

$a_1 = 22$

Rule for the nth term is

$a_n = a_1 + (n - 1)d$

$= 22 + (n - 1)9$

$= 22 + 9n - 9$

$= 13 + 9n$

b. 22, 31, 40, 49, 58, 67, 76;

Term (n)	1	2	3	4	5	6	7
$a_n = 13 + 9n$	22	31	40	49	58	67	76

111. a. Graph the red line using equation $y = 4x$.

Graph the dark yellow line using equation $y = 2x + 4$.

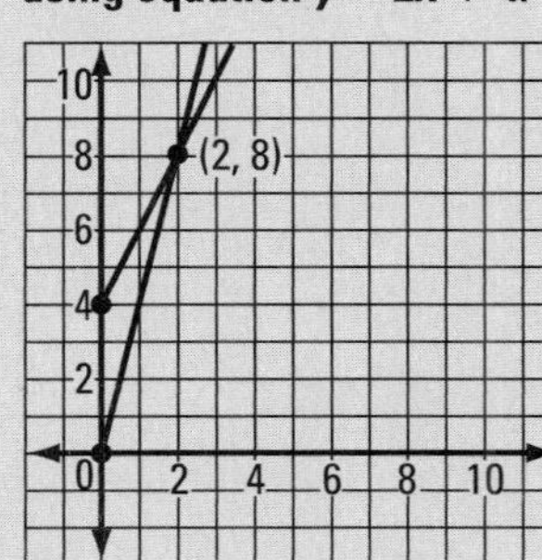

b. Monthly memberships:

Monthly memberships cost $12 by the third month, whereas annual memberships cost $10.

c. Annual memberships:

The cost of annual memberships changes from $g(x) = 2x + 4$ to $g(x) = 3x + 4$.

Annual memberships cost $40 by the twelfth month, whereas monthly memberships cost $48.

Subdomain 1 Number Properties and Operations

MA-HS-1.3.2 Students will:

- **describe and extend arithmetic and geometric sequences;**
- **determine a specific term of a sequence given an explicit formula;**
- **determine an explicit rule for the nth term of an arithmetic sequence and**
- **apply sequences to solve real-world problems.**

DOK 3

110. (OR) The following numbers are terms of an arithmetic sequence. *(p. 807, prob. 30–38)*

$$a_3 = 40,\ a_8 = 85,\ a_{11} = 128$$

a. Find a rule for the nth term of the arithmetic sequence. Show your procedure.

b. What are the first seven terms of the sequence? Justify your answer.

MA-HS-1.4.1 Students will apply ratios, percents and proportional reasoning to solve real-world problems (e.g., those involving slope and rate, percent of increase and decrease) and will explain how slope determines a rate of change in linear functions representing real-world problems. DOK 2

111. (OR) The Rowing Club offers both monthly and annual memberships. Monthly memberships are described by the cost function $f(x) = 4x$, whereas annual memberships are described by $g(x) = 2x + 4$. The cost (in dollars) is dependent on x month(s) of membership. *(p. 95, prob. 68)*

a. Graph both $f(x)$ and $g(x)$.

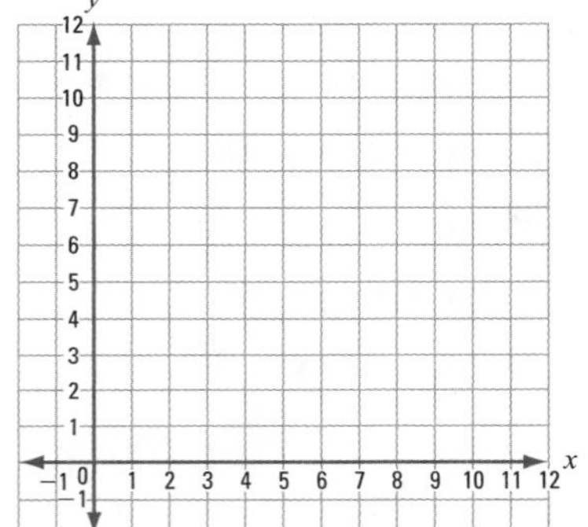

b. Based on the graph, which type of membership is more expensive by the third month?

c. By increasing the monthly rate of annual memberships to $3 per month, which type of membership is more cost effective for one year? Justify your answer.

Go On 

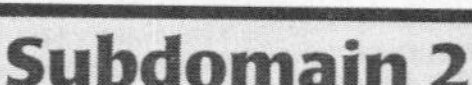

Subdomain 2 Measurement

MA-HS-2.1.3 Students will apply definitions and properties of right triangle relationships (right triangle trigonometry and the Pythagorean theorem) to determine length and angle measures to solve real-world and mathematical problems. DOK 3

112. (OR) A wheelchair ramp 18 feet long forms a 19° angle of elevation. *(p. 857, prob. 34)*

a. Make a sketch to represent the situation.

b. How much vertical distance does a person travel by using the ramp? Justify your answer.

113. (OR) An airplane is flying at an altitude of 29,040 feet when it begins its descent for landing. The runway is 200 miles away. *(p. 879, prob. 36)*

a. Make a sketch to represent the situation.

b. What distance does the plane travel during its descent?

c. What is the angle of descent? Justify your answer.

Go On

COUNTDOWN *to* KCCT

Countdown to KCCT

112. Sample sketch is shown.

a.

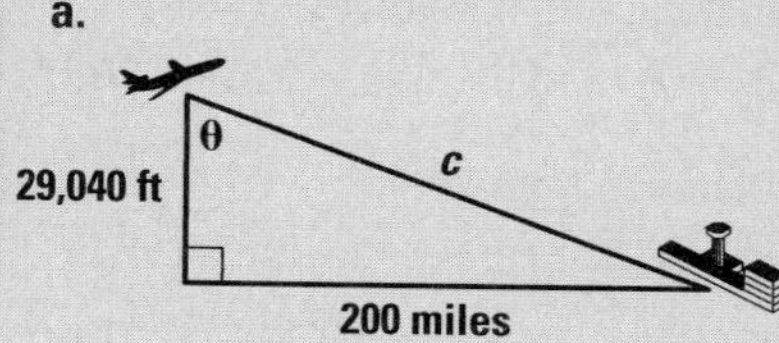

b. $\sin 19° = \frac{x}{18}$

$0.3256 \approx \frac{x}{18}$

$0.3256 \cdot 18 \approx x$

$5.8608 \approx x$

A person travels about 5.86 feet of vertical distance by using the ramp.

113. Sample is shown.

a.

29,040 ft, θ, c, 200 miles

b. $\left(\frac{29040}{5280}\right)^2 + 200^2 = c^2$

$(5.5)^2 + 200^2 = c^2$

$40030.25 = c^2$

$200 \approx c$

The plane travels about 200 miles during its descent.

c. $\tan\theta = \frac{200}{5.5}$

$\tan\theta = 36.36$

$\theta = 88.4247$

The angle of descent is 90° – 88.4247°, or about 1.58°.

114. a. 16:

$$(3x + 6)° + (2x + 4)° + 90° = 180°$$
$$5x + 100 = 180$$
$$5x = 180$$
$$x = 16$$

b. 54°:

$m\angle A + (3x + 6)° = (3(16) + 6)° = (48 + 6)° = 54°$

c. 36°:

$m\angle Q + (2x + 4)° = (2(16) + 4)° = (32 + 4)° = 36°$

115.

a. $M = \left(\frac{-4+7}{2}, \frac{-2+9}{2}\right) = (1.5, 3.5);$

b.

Distance from M to W:

$d = \sqrt{(7-1.5)^2 + (9-3.5)^2} \approx 7.78;$

Distance from W to F:

$d = \sqrt{(9-7)^2 + (-3-9)^2} \approx 12.17$

Total distance: about 7.78 + 12.17 or about 19.95 units. Since each unit is 0.2 miles, the total distance is about 3.99 miles.

MA-HS-3.1.12 Students will apply the concepts of congruence and similarity to solve real-world and mathematical problems. DOK 3

114. (OR) Triangle ABC is similar to triangle PQT. *(p. 997, prob. 10–18)*

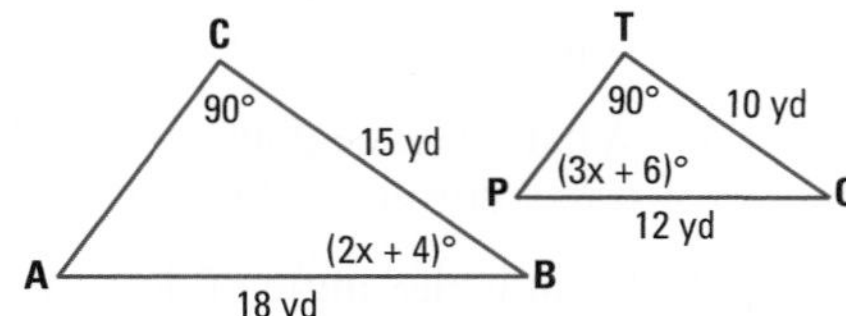

a. Find the value of x for the two similar triangles. Justify your answer.

b. Find the measure of angle A.

c. Find the measure of angle Q.

MA-HS-3.3.1 Students will apply algebraic concepts and graphing in the coordinate plane to analyze and solve problems (e.g., finding the final coordinates for a specified polygon, midpoints, betweenness of points, parallel and perpendicular lines, the distance between two points, the slope of a segment). DOK 2

115. (OR) The diagram shows part of a road race course. Each unit is 0.2 mile. The course starts at S, continues toward a water station at W, then heads toward the finish line at F. *(p. 619, prob. 53)*

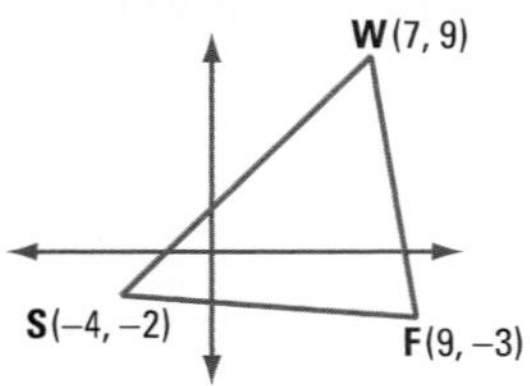

a. A runner stops to tie his shoe at a point M halfway between the starting line and the water station. What are his coordinates at M? Justify your answer.

b. After tying his shoe at M, the runner finishes the course. How far does he run between M and the finish line F? Give your answer in miles.

Subdomain 4 Data Analysis and Probability

MA-HS-4.1.2 Students will construct data displays for data with no more than two variables. DOK 2

116. **(OR)** A temporary employee at a shoe manufacturing company kept track of the number of hours x she worked and the number of shoes y she was able to produce. *(p. 779, prob. 10–11)*

x	2	5	3	4	3	6
y	5	15	10	12	8	18

a. Make a scatter plot of the data.

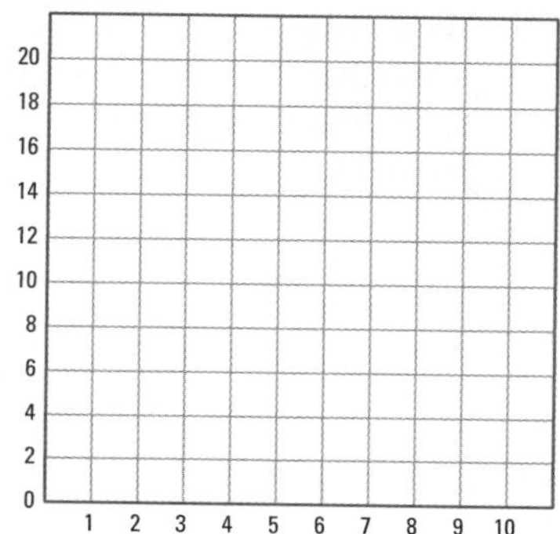

b. Find the function that models the data. Justify your answer.

MA-HS-4.2.3 Students will:

- **identify an appropriate curve of best fit (linear, quadratic, exponential) for a set of two-variable data;**
- **determine a line of best fit equation for a set of linear two-variable data and**
- **apply a line of best fit to make predictions within and beyond a given set of two-variable data.**

DOK 3

117. **(OR)** A restaurant kept track of the number of desserts y it sold depending on the price of the dessert. *(p. 779, prob. 13)*

x	\$.50	\$1.00	\$2.00	\$3.50	\$4.00	\$4.50	\$6.00
y	25	24	23	19	17	15	7

a. Using your calculator, what is the quadratic function that best models this data?

b. About how many desserts will be sold if the price is \$3.25 per dessert? Justify your answer.

118. **(OR)** David is trying a new entrée at two of his restaurants. The table below shows the number of orders of this entrée each day for the past 6 days. *(p. 779, prob. 13)*

x	1	2	3	4	5	6
y	3	8	7	12	13	16

a. Approximate the line of best fit for the data. Show your procedure.

b. Use your equation to determine how many orders of the entrée he can expect to receive on day 8.

Go On 

COUNTDOWN to KCCT

Countdown to KCCT

116. a.

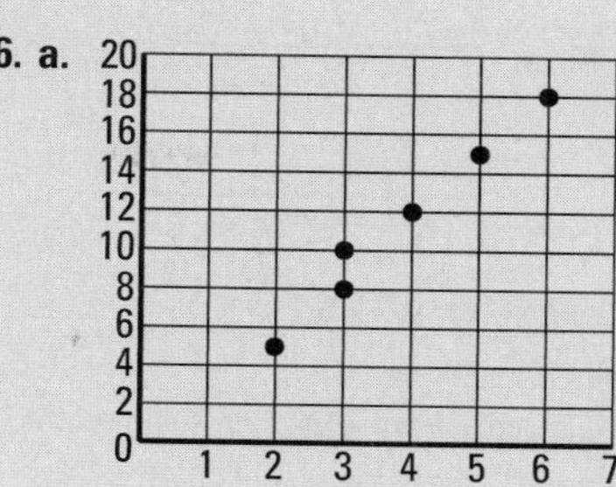

b. $y = 3.2x - 0.8$

117. a. $y = -0.51x^2 + 0.11x + 24.8$

b. about 20:

$y = -0.51(3.25)^2 + 0.11(3.25) + 24.8 = 19.77 \approx 20$

118. a. $y = 2.4x - 1.3$

b. 17.9:

$y = 2.4(8) - 1.3 = 17.9$

119. a.

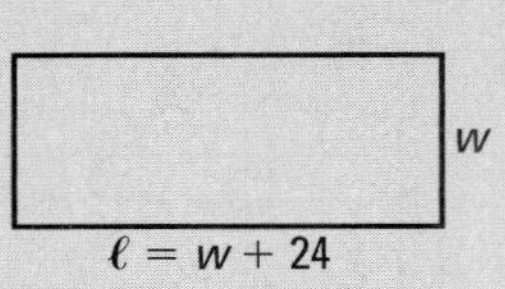

Length (ℓ): $w + 24$
Width (w): w
Perimeter (P): 136

$P = 2w + 2\ell$

$136 = 2w + 2(w + 24)$
$136 = 2x + 2w + 48$
$136 = 4w + 48$

b. 22 feet:

$136 = 4w + 48$
$88 = 4w$
$22 = w$

c. 46 feet:

$\ell = w + 24 = 22 + 24 = 46$

120. a. $A = 200 - 2x$

b. 61 minutes:

$A = 200 - 2x$
$78 = 200 - 2x$
$-122 = -2x$
$x = 61$

Subdomain 5 Algebraic Thinking

MA-HS-5.3.1 Students will model, solve and graph first degree, single variable equations and inequalities, including absolute value, based in real-world and mathematical problems and graph the solutions on a number line. DOK 2

119. (OR) The perimeter of a rectangular garden is 136 feet. The width of the garden is 24 feet less than the length. *(p. 39, prob. 28–30)*

a. Find an equation that can be used to determine the width, *w*, of the garden. Write the equation in terms of *w*. Show your procedure.

b. What is the width of the garden?

c. Determine the length, *l*, of the garden. Justify your answer.

MA-HS-5.3.3 Students will model, solve and graph first degree, two-variable equations and inequalities in real-world and mathematical problems. DOK 2

120. (OR) A large water tank is filled with 200 gallons of water. The water is then released from the tank at a steady rate of 2 gallons per minute. *(p. 39, prob. 28–30)*

a. What equation can be used to find the number of gallons of water, *A*, in the tank *x* minutes after the water is released?

b. How many minutes have elapsed when there are 78 gallons of water left in the tank? Show your procedure.

Go On

Subdomain 5 Algebraic Thinking

MA-HS-5.3.4 Students will model, solve and graph systems of two linear equations in real-world and mathematical problems. DOK 3

121. (OR) The market analyst at Chicago Investments has done research on the two best stocks to buy for an investor. The stocks are Phototronics and Maple Technology. *(p. 157–158, prob. 38–40)*

a. Phototronics sells for \$15 per share, whereas Maple Technoogy sells for \$20 per share. Write a system of linear equations if given \$1200 to invest in 70 shares of stock.

b. Graph the system of equations.

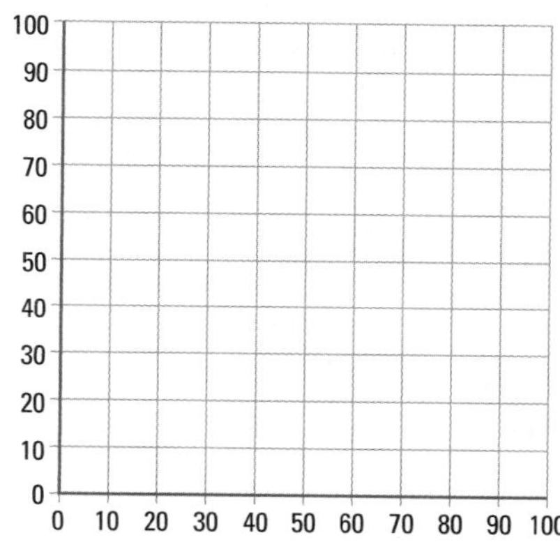

c. Determine the point of intersection algebraically. Show your work.

d. Based on parts (b) and (c), explain the meaning of the intersection with regards to how many shares of stock are to be bought.

MA-HS-5.3.6 Students will model, solve and graph quadratic equations in real-world and mathematical problems. DOK 2

122. (OR) A projectile is shot into the air. The height y of the projectile (in feet) after t seconds can be modeled by $y = -16t^2 + 64t + 6$. *(p. 290, prob. 62)*

a. Complete the square to find the vertex of the parabola with the given equation. What is the vertex of the graph of the equation? Show your procedure.

b. What is the maximum height of the projectile? Justify your answer.

STOP

COUNTDOWN to KCCT

Countdown to KCCT

121.

a.

Number of Photonics shares: x
Number of Maple Technology shares: y
Cost of a Photonics share: \$15
Cost of a Maple Technology share: \$20

$15x + 20y = 1200$

$x + y = 70$

b.

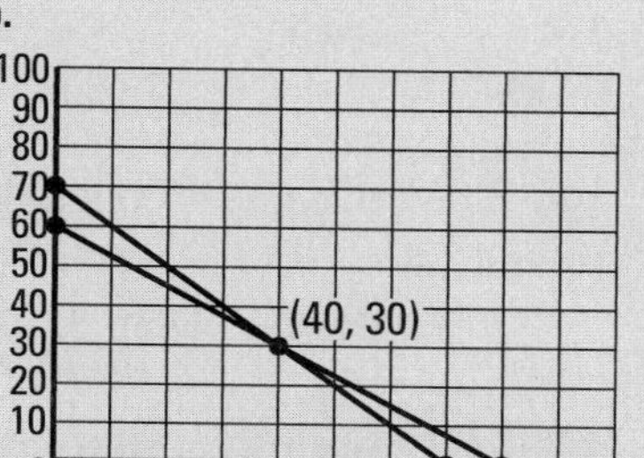

c.

Solve $x + y = 70$ for y.

$x - x + y = -x + 70$

$y = -x + 70$

Substitute $y = -x + 70$ into $15x + 20y = 1200$.

$15x + 20(-x + 70) = 1200$

Solve for x.

$15x - 20x + 1400 = 1200$

$-5x + 1400 = 1200$

$-5x + 1400 - 1400 = 1200 - 1400$

$\frac{-5x}{-5} = \frac{-200}{-5}$

$x = 40$

Now solve for y.

$y = -40 + 70 = 30$

The point of intersection is (40, 30).

d. The intersection represents the number of shares of stock to be bought that satisfy the system of equations. Based on both the graph (part b) and algebraic solution (part c), the analyst would recommend buying 40 shares of Photonics and 30 shares of Maple Technology.

122. a. $y = -16t^2 + 64t + 6$

$y - 64 = -16(t^2 - 4t + 4) + 6;$

$y - 64 = -16(t - 2)^2 + 6$

$y = -16(t - 2)^2 + 70$

The vertex of the graph of the equation is (2, 70).

b. The maximum height of the graph is at 70 feet.

At $t = 2$ seconds,

$y = -16(t - 2)^2 + 70$

$= -16(2 - 2)^2 + 70$

$= -16(0) + 70$

$= 0 + 70$

$= 70$

1 Pacing and Assignment Guide

REGULAR SCHEDULE

Pre-AP For pacing and assignments for a Pre-AP course, see the *Algebra 2 Toolkit.*

Lesson	Les. Day	BASIC	AVERAGE	ADVANCED
1.1 *MA-HS-1.5.1*	Day 1	SRH p. 975 Exs. 1–10; pp. 6–9 Exs. 1–5, 9–13, 17–37 odd, 39–44, 57–60	pp. 6–9 Exs. 1, 2, 6–10, 14–16, 20–24, 28–30, 35–43, 47–55, 58–61, 64	pp. 6–9 Exs. 1, 2, 7–10, 15, 16, 21–24, 29, 30, 37–40, 44–56*, 59–62*
1.2 **MA-HS-5.2.1**	Day 1	SRH p. 984 Exs. 1–6; pp. 13–16 Exs. 1–9, 17–23 odd, 24–29, 33, 34–40 even, 57–61, 64	pp. 13–16 Exs. 1–3, 10–14 even, 16–18, 24, 29–33, 35–51 odd, 52–54, 58–62, 65	pp. 13–16 Exs. 1, 2, 11–15 odd, 20–24 even, 30–33, 36–50 even, 51–56*, 59–63*
1.3 **MA-HS-5.3.1**	Day 1	SRH p. 976 Exs. 16–20; pp. 21–24 Exs. 1–10, 19–25, 32–36, 41–46, 68–73, 79	pp. 21–24 Exs. 1, 2, 11–19 odd, 26–32 even, 37–42, 43–65 odd, 68–77, 80	pp. 21–24 Exs. 1, 2, 12–18 even, 19, 27–31 odd, 32, 38–42, 48–62 even, 63–67*, 70–78*
1.4 *MA-HS-5.3.2*	Day 1	SRH p. 991 Exs. 1–4; pp. 30–32 Exs. 1–6, 18–20	pp. 30–32 Exs. 1–6, 18–20, 40–42	pp. 30–32 Exs. 1–6, 18–20, 32*, 40–42
	Day 2	pp. 30–32 Exs. 7–17, 21, 22, 33–36, 40–42	pp. 30–32 Exs. 11–17, 21–29, 33–38	pp. 30–32 Exs. 12–15, 21–31, 35–39*
1.5 **MA-HS-5.3.1**	Day 1	SRH p. 981 Exs. 1–15 odd; pp. 37–40 Exs. 1–12, 15–19, 24–32, 34–36	pp. 37–40 Exs. 1, 2, 4–6, 8–10, 12–22*, 24–32, 35	pp. 37–40 Exs. 1, 2, 5, 6, 9, 10, 12–33*, 34–36
1.6 **MA-HS-5.3.1**	Day 1	pp. 44–47 Exs. 1–6, 11–18, 22–27	pp. 44–47 Exs. 1, 2, 7–15, 19–27	pp. 44–47 Exs. 1, 2, 7–21 odd, 22–27, 52, 53
	Day 2	pp. 44–47 Exs. 28–39, 43, 44, 52–57, 61–62	pp. 44–47 Exs. 28–36, 37–47 odd, 50–59*, 61	pp. 44–47 Exs. 28–33, 37–51*, 54–62*
1.7 **MA-HS-5.3.1**	Day 1	SRH p. 1005 Exs. 1–4; pp. 55–58 Exs. 1–5, 9–14, 21–29, 33–42	pp. 55–58 Exs. 1, 2, 6–8, 12–17, 24–42	pp. 55–58 Exs. 1, 2, 6–8, 15–20, 24–42
	Day 2	pp. 55–58 Exs. 43–58, 74–80, 83–84	pp. 55–58 Exs. 49–65, 74–81, 83–84	pp. 55–58 Exs. 53–73*, 75–82*, 84
Review	Day 1	pp. 61–64 Exs. 1–47	pp. 61–64 Exs. 1–47	pp. 61–64 Exs. 1–47
Assess	Day 1	Chapter 1 Test	Chapter 1 Test	Chapter 1 Test
Yearly Pacing		Chapter 1 Total – 12 days	Chapter 1 Total – 12 days	Remaining – 148 days

*Challenge Exercises EP = Extra Practice SRH = Skills Review Handbook

BLOCK SCHEDULE

DAY 1	DAY 2	DAY 3	DAY 4	DAY 5	DAY 6
1.1	**1.3**	**1.4 (CONT.)**	**1.6**	**1.7**	**REVIEW**
pp. 6–9 Exs. 1, 2, 6–10, 14–16, 20–24, 28–30, 35–43, 47–55, 58–61, 64	pp. 21–24 Exs. 1, 2, 11–19 odd, 26–32 even, 37–42, 43–65 odd, 68–77, 80	pp. 30–32 Exs. 11–17, 21–29, 33–38	pp. 44–47 Exs. 1, 2, 7–15, 19–36, 37–47 odd, 50–59*, 61	pp. 55–58 Exs. 1, 2, 6–8, 12–17, 24–42, 49–65, 74–81, 83–84	pp. 61–64 Exs. 1–47
1.2	**1.4**	**1.5**			**ASSESS**
pp. 13–16 Exs. 1–3, 10–14 even, 16–18, 24, 29–33, 35–51 odd, 52–54, 58–62, 65	pp. 30–32 Exs. 1–6, 18–20, 40–42	pp. 37–40 Exs. 1, 2, 4–6, 8–10, 12–22*, 24–32, 35			Chapter 1 Test
Yearly Pacing	Chapter 1 Total – 6 days	Chapter 1 Total – 6 days	Remaining – 74 days		

Chapter Resource Guide 1

RESOURCE MANAGER

Chapter Resource Book

CHAPTER SUPPORT							
Parents as Partners (Chapter Overview with home involvement exercises and activity)						p. 1	
LESSON SUPPORT **Standards**	1.1 *MA-HS-1.5.1*	1.2 **MA-HS-5.2.1**	1.3 **MA-HS-5.3.1**	1.4 *MA-HS-5.3.2*	1.5 **MA-HS-5.3.1**	1.6 **MA-HS-5.3.1**	1.7 **MA-HS-5.3.1**
Teaching Guide/Lesson Plan	p. 3	p. 14	p. 25	p. 36	p. 50	p. 60	p. 71
Activity Masters	p. 5			p. 38		p. 62	
Technology Activities & Keystrokes		p. 16	p. 27	p. 39			p. 73
Activity Support Masters							
Practice (3 levels)	p. 6	p. 17	p. 28	p. 41	p. 52	p. 63	p. 75
Study Guide	p. 9	p. 20	p. 31	p. 44	p. 55	p. 66	p. 78
Catch-Up for Absent Students	p. 11	p. 22	p. 33	p. 46	p. 57	p. 68	p. 80
Problem Solving/Application	p. 12	p. 23	p. 34	p. 47	p. 58	p. 69	p. 81
Challenge Practice	p. 13	p. 24	p. 35	p. 49	p. 59	p. 70	p. 82

REVIEW

Chapter Review Games and Activities	p. 83	Cumulative Practice	p. 85
Project with Rubric	p. 84	Resource Book Answers	A1

Transparencies	1.1	1.2	1.3	1.4	1.5	1.6	1.7
Warm-Up/Daily Homework Quiz	✔	✔	✔	✔	✔	✔	✔
Notetaking Guide	✔	✔	✔	✔	✔	✔	✔
Teacher Support						✔	✔
Answer Transparencies	✔	✔	✔	✔	✔	✔	✔

ASSESSMENT BOOK

Quizzes	p. 1	SAT/ACT Chapter Test	p. 12
Chapter Tests (3 levels)	p. 4	Alternative Assessment with Rubric	p. 14
Standardized Chapter Test	p. 10		

TECHNOLOGY

- Easy Planner
- Test and Practice Generator
- Power Presentations
- @HomeTutor
- Activity Generator
- Animated Algebra
- Classzone.com
- eEdition Plus Online
- eWorkbook Plus Online
- ML Assessment System

ADDITIONAL RESOURCES

Kentucky

- Additional Lesson A Measurement
- Additional Lesson B Other Coordinate Systems
- Worked-Out Solution Key
- Notetaking Guide

- Practice Workbook
- Algebra 2 Toolkit
- Benchmark Tests
- Remediation Workbook
- Spanish Study Guide
- Spanish Assessment Book
- Spanish Resources in Spanish
- Multi-Language Visual Glossary

1 Lesson Practice Level B

LESSON 1.1
Practice B
For use with pages 2–9

Graph the numbers on a number line. Decide which number is greater and use the symbol < or > to show the relationship.

1. -5 and -6 $\quad -5 > -6$

2. $-\sqrt{3}$ and 0.75 $\quad -\sqrt{3} < 0.75$

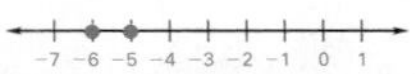

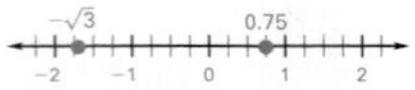

Write the numbers in increasing order. 3. $-\frac{3}{2}, -\frac{3}{7}, 0.75, 2$ 4. $-1.5, \frac{3}{4}, 3, \sqrt{10}$ 5. $-\sqrt{2}, 0, \sqrt{5}, \frac{13}{4}$

3. $2, -\frac{3}{7}, 0.75, -\frac{3}{2}$ **4.** $3, \sqrt{10}, \frac{3}{4}, -1.5$ **5.** $0, -\sqrt{2}, \sqrt{5}, \frac{13}{4}$

Identify the property that the statement illustrates.

6. $(-3)(1) = -3$ identity property of multiplication

7. $5(4 + (-5)) = 5 \cdot 4 + 5 \cdot (-5)$ distributive property

8. $1 + (3 + 2) = 1 + (2 + 3)$ commutative property of addition

9. $a + (b + c) = (a + b) + c$ associative property of addition

10. $a \cdot \frac{1}{a} = 1$ inverse property of multiplication

11. $a \cdot b = b \cdot a$ commutative property of multiplication

Select and perform an operation to answer the question.

12. What is the sum of -3 and 2? -1

13. What is the sum of -6 and -2? -8

14. What is the difference of 4 and 9? -5

15. What is the difference of -4 and -3? -1

16. What is the product of -4 and 5? -20

17. What is the product of -6 and -3? 18

18. What is the quotient of 49 and -7? -7

19. What is the quotient of -21 and $-\frac{7}{3}$? 9

Give the answer with the appropriate unit of measure.

20. $-5\frac{1}{4}$ inches $-2\frac{2}{3}$ inches $\quad -7\frac{11}{12}$ in.

21. $-3\frac{1}{3}$ miles $+ 1\frac{2}{3}$ miles $\quad -1\frac{2}{3}$ mi

22. Gas Mileage A car can travel 25 miles per gallon of gas. The gas tank contains 9 gallons. How far can the car travel without refueling? 225 mi

23. Touchdown A football team scored 24 of their 28 points from touchdowns. A touchdown is worth 6 points. How many touchdowns did the team score? 4

24. Birthday Cake Ten classmates are going to share a birthday cake after school. The rectangular birthday cake is 5 pieces long and 4 pieces wide. Each person eats the same number of pieces. How many pieces does each person eat? 2

25. Mile Run Jim runs one mile by running four laps around the track. The times in seconds for each lap are shown in the table. What is his total mile time in minutes and seconds? What is his average lap time in seconds? 6 min 38 sec; 99.5 sec

Lap	1	2	3	4
Time (sec)	91	103	106	98

LESSON 1.1

LESSON 1.2
Practice B
For use with pages 10–16

Write the expression using exponents.

1. $a \cdot a \cdot a$ $\quad a^3$

2. $(-7) \cdot (-7) \cdot (-7) \cdot (-7)$ $\quad (-7)^4$

3. $(-x)(-x)(-x)(-x)(-x)$ $\quad (-x)^5$

4. $(2x \cdot 2x \cdot 2x) + 5$ $\quad (2x)^3 + 5$

5. $(3a \cdot 3a) - (b \cdot b \cdot b \cdot b)$ $\quad (3a)^2 - b^4$

6. 2 to the nth power $\quad 2^n$

Evaluate the expression.

7. $(-4)^2$ $\quad 16$

8. -2^4 $\quad 16$

9. $3 - (4 - 2) \cdot 5$ $\quad -7$

10. $1 + (5^2 - 10) \div 5$ $\quad 4$

11. $(6 - 5)^3 + 14 \div (2 + 5)$ $\quad 3$

12. $24 - (1 + 1)^4 \div 4$ $\quad 20$

Evaluate the expression for the given value of x.

13. $x(x - 3)$ when $x = 7$ $\quad 28$

14. $3x - 0.5(x - 2x)$ when $x = 4$ $\quad 14$

15. $3x^2 - 2x$ when $x = -2$ $\quad 16$

16. $2x^2 \div (4 - 2x) + 2$ when $x = 4$ $\quad -6$

17. $35 - \frac{2}{3}x^2 \div x$ when $x = 9$ $\quad 29$

18. $7 - x^3\left(\frac{1}{2x}\right)$ when $x = -2$ $\quad 5$

Evaluate the expression for the given values of x and y.

19. $x^2 + 2y^2$ when $x = 3, y = 2$ $\quad 17$

20. $-3x^2 + (3y)^4$ when $x = -5, y = 1$ $\quad 6$

21. $\frac{3x + y - 1}{2x - y}$ when $x = 3, y = 4$ $\quad 6$

22. $\frac{(2x - 2)^3}{-y^3 - 3}$ when $x = 2, y = -2$ $\quad \frac{8}{5}$

Write an expression for the area of the figure. Evaluate the expression for the given values of the variables.

23. $x = 3, y = 3$ $\quad 2xy^2 + 2x; 60$

24. $x = 2, y = 5$ $\quad \frac{1}{2}(x^3y^2 - x^3y); 80$

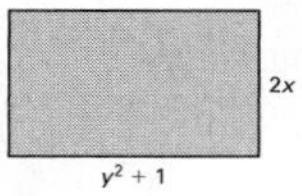

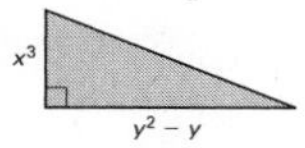

25. Photography Studio A photography studio advertises a session with a sitting fee of \$8.95 per person. The standard package of pictures costs \$29.95. Write an expression that gives the total cost of a session plus the purchase of one standard package. Evaluate the expression if a family of four purchases this package. $8.95x + 29.95$; \$65.75

26. Books You want to buy either a paperback or hard covered book as a gift for five friends. Paperbacks cost \$6.95 each and hard covered books cost \$24.99 each. Write and simplify an expression for the total amount you spend if x of the books are paperback. Evaluate the expression if three of your friends get a paperback. $124.95 - 18.04x$; \$70.83

LESSON 1.2

LESSON 1.3
Practice B
For use with pages 18–24

Solve the equation. Check your solution.

1. $x - 9 = 12$ $\quad 21$

2. $3x - 2 = 16$ $\quad 6$

3. $3 - x = 2$ $\quad 1$

4. $-4 = x - 1$ $\quad -3$

5. $3 = 2 + x$ $\quad 1$

6. $-14 + 2x = 6$ $\quad 10$

7. $6x = 24$ $\quad 4$

8. $-4x = -14$ $\quad \frac{7}{2}$

9. $\frac{3}{2}x + 1 = 13$ $\quad 8$

10. $\frac{2}{5}x + 10 = 0$ $\quad -25$

11. $\frac{4}{3}x + 2 = 6$ $\quad 3$

12. $x + 6 = 3(5 - x)$ $\quad \frac{9}{4}$

13. $x + \frac{3}{2} = \frac{3}{4}\left(x - \frac{1}{2}\right)$ $\quad -\frac{15}{2}$

14. $3(x - 2) = 2(2x - 3)$ $\quad 0$

15. $x + \frac{3}{5} = \frac{7}{5}(x + 1)$ $\quad -2$

16. $\frac{1}{2}(14x + 2) = 3(2 - 3x)$ $\quad \frac{5}{16}$

17. $5x = \frac{4}{5}(5x - 2)$ $\quad -\frac{8}{5}$

18. $x + 6 = 3(3 - x)$ $\quad \frac{3}{4}$

19. $\frac{5}{4}(4x + 2) = 3$ $\quad \frac{1}{10}$

20. $27 - 2x = 2(x + 1)$ $\quad \frac{25}{4}$

21. $x + 4 = 2x - 8\left(\frac{1}{4}x - \frac{1}{4}\right)$ $\quad -2$

22. Perimeter The perimeter of the rectangle below is 78 feet. Find its dimensions. length: 23 ft, width: 16 ft

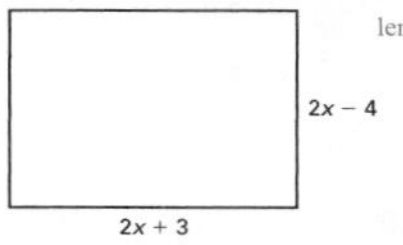

23. Movie Tickets A movie ticket costs \$6.50. You have \$35.00 to buy tickets and popcorn for four people. How much money is left to buy popcorn after the tickets are paid for? \$9.00

24. Pay Rate You need to earn \$475 per week to afford the new car you want to purchase. Your work week is 45 hours. You get 1.5 times the regular hourly rate for overtime (anything over 40 hours). How much does your hourly rate need to be? \$10.00/h

25. Car Bill The bill for your automobile repairs was \$265.74. The cost for labor was \$52.00 per hour. The cost for materials was \$135.74. How many hours did the mechanic work on your automobile? 2.5 h

26. Road Trip On Friday, you drove 145 miles to stay at your grandmother's house. On Sunday, you returned home and calculated that the round trip travel time was 5 hours. What was your average speed? 58 mi/h

LESSON 1.3

LESSON 1.4
Practice B
For use with pages 26–32

Substitute the given value of x into the equation. Then solve the equation for y.

1. $7x - 3y = 6; x = 3$ $\quad 5$

2. $6x + 5y = -7; x = -2$ $\quad 1$

3. $xy = 12 + 3x; x = 4$ $\quad 6$

4. $\frac{2}{3}x = 2y - \frac{2}{5}; x = -9$ $\quad -\frac{14}{5}$

5. $\frac{2}{3}y + \frac{1}{2}x = 1; x = 12$ $\quad -\frac{15}{2}$

6. $x - 2y = 3xy + 1; x = -2$ $\quad \frac{3}{4}$

Solve the equation for y. Then find the value of y for the given value of x.

7. $3x - 6y = 6; x = 2$ $\quad 0$

8. $-2x + 2 = 5y - 1; x = 5$

9. $2xy + 1 = xy + 3; x = 2$ $\quad 1$

10. $\frac{1}{2}x - y = \frac{2}{3}x - 3; x = 7$ $\quad -4$

11. $\frac{3}{4}x + \frac{4}{7}y = \frac{5}{4}x - 1; x = 8$

12. $\frac{3}{5}y - 4x = 3 - 2y; x = 9$ $\quad 15$

8. $-\frac{7}{5}$ 11. $\frac{21}{4}$

Solve the formula for the indicated variable.

13. *Fahrenheit to Celsius* $\quad F = \frac{9}{5}C + 32$
Solve for F: $C = \frac{5}{9}(F - 32)$

14. *Perimeter of a Parallelogram* $\quad b = \frac{P - 2s}{2}$
Solve for b: $P = 2b + 2s$

15. *Perimeter of a Triangle* $\quad c = P - a - b$
Solve for c: $P = a + b + c$

16. *Area of a Rhombus* $\quad d_1 = \frac{2A}{d_2}$
Solve for d_1: $A = \frac{1}{2}d_1d_2$

17. *Area of a Trapezoid* $\quad b_1 = \frac{2A}{h} - b_2$
Solve for b_1: $A = \frac{1}{2}(b_1 + b_2)h$

18. *Volume of a Right Circular Cylinder* $\quad h = \frac{V}{\pi r^2}$
Solve for h: $V = \pi r^2 h$

19. *Lateral Surface Area of a Right Circular Cylinder* $\quad h = \frac{S}{2\pi r}$
Solve for h: $S = 2\pi rh$

20. *Volume of a Right Circular Cone* $\quad h = \frac{3V}{\pi r^2}$
Solve for h: $V = \frac{\pi r^2 h}{3}$

Solve the formula for the indicated variable. Then use the given information to find the value of the variable. Include units of measure in the answer.

21. *Area of a Parallelogram* $\quad h = \frac{A}{b}$; 9 cm
Solve for h: $A = bh$
Find h when $A = 81$ cm^2 and $b = 9$ cm.

22. *Celsius to Fahrenheit* $\quad C = \frac{5}{9}(F - 32)$; 25°C
Solve for C: $F = \frac{9}{5}C + 32$
Find C when $F = 77$°F.

Basketball A regulation size basketball has a volume of 455.9 cubic inches. Use this information to answer the following questions. Approximate your answers to the nearest tenth.

23. The formula for the volume of a sphere is $V = \frac{4}{3}\pi r^3$. What is the radius of the basketball? 4.8 in.

24. What is the diameter of the basketball? 9.6 in.

25. The formula for the circumference of the basketball is $C = 2\pi r$. If the circumference of a basketball is 29 inches, is it a regulation size basketball? no

LESSON 1.4

LESSON 1.5

Practice B

For use with pages 34–39

Use the formula $d = rt$ for distance traveled to solve for the missing variable.

1. $d =$ __?__, $r = 55$ mi/h, $t = 3$ h   165 mi
2. $d = 240$ mi, $r = 60$ mi/h, $t =$ __?__   4 h
3. $d = 552$ mi, $r =$ __?__, $t = 8$ h   69 mi/h
4. $d = 247.5$ mi, $r = 45$ mi/h, $t =$ __?__   5.5 h

Use the formula $A = bh$ for the area of a parallelogram to solve for the missing variable.

5. $A =$ __?__, $b = 6$ ft, $h = 3$ ft   18 ft^2
6. $A = 34$ ft^2, $b =$ __?__, $h = 4$ ft   8.5 ft
7. $A = 175$ m^2, $b = 25$ m, $h =$ __?__   7 m
8. $A =$ __?__, $b = 23$ cm, $h = 15$ cm   345 cm^2

Look for a pattern in the table. Then write an equation that represents the table.

9. $y = 5x + 5$

x	0	1	2	3
y	5	10	15	20

10. $y = 3x + 22$

x	0	1	2	3
y	22	25	28	31

11. $y = 17 - x$

x	0	1	2	3
y	17	16	15	14

12. $y = 89 - 7x$

x	0	1	2	3
y	89	82	75	68

13. **Fastest Solar Powered Vehicle** The highest speed reached by a solar powered vehicle is 48.71 miles per hour. This record was set by a car called Sunraycer on June 24, 1988 in Mesa, Arizona. How far could Sunraycer travel in 2.5 hours at this speed? 121.775 mi

14. **Cable Bill** Your local cable company charges $29.99 per month for basic cable service. Premium channels are available for a surcharge of $5.95 per channel. You have $70 per month budgeted for cable. How many premium channels can you purchase? 6

15. **Sharing the Drive** You and a friend take turns driving on a 450 mile trip. Your friend drives for 3.5 hours at an average speed of 60 miles per hour. What must your average speed be for the remainder of the trip if you want to reach your hotel in 4 more hours? 60 mi/h

16. **Parking Lot** A five gallon bucket of tar can seal 3500 square feet of blacktop. If a parking lot is 15,000 square feet, how many buckets of tar must be purchased in order to seal it? 5

LESSON 1.5

LESSON 1.6

Practice B

For use with pages 41–47

Graph the solution of the inequality.

1. $0 < x < 3$ $0 < x < 3$

2. $x \le -2$ or $x > 1$ $x \le -2$ or $x > 1$

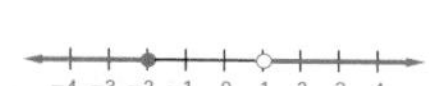

Solve the inequality.

3. $x - 5 > 9$ $x > 14$
4. $4x \le 48$ $x \le 12$
5. $-3 < 7 + 2x$ $x > -5$
6. $3x \le 8 + x$ $x \le 4$
7. $7x + 3 > 10$ $x > 1$
8. $\frac{1}{4}x - 2 < -1$ $x < 4$
9. $-x + 4 \ge -2$ $x \le 6$
10. $5 - 5x \le 10$ $x \ge -1$
11. $-3x + 7 < -8$ $x > 5$
12. $4 < 3 - x$ $x < -1$
13. $-3x + 6 \le 6$ $x \ge 0$
14. $x + 8 \le 2x - 2$ $x \ge 10$
15. $-3 < x - 3 < 0$ $0 < x < 3$
16. $2 \le x + 3 \le 5$ $-1 \le x \le 2$
17. $x + 2 \le -1$ or $x - 2 \ge 1$ $x \le -3$ or $x \ge 3$
18. $x - 3 < -4$ or $x - 1 > 5$ $x < -1$ or $x > 6$
19. $3 \le \frac{1}{3}x - 2 \le 4$ $15 \le x \le 18$
20. $2(x + 3) > -4$ $x > -5$

Solve the inequality and then graph the solution.

21. $2 - x > 3x + 10$ $x < -2$
22. $3(x + 2) \ge 15$ $x \ge 3$

23. **Population of Hawaii** From 2000 to 2003, Hawaii's population grew approximately by 3.8% from 1,211,537 to 1,257,608. Write an inequality that represents the number of people living in Hawaii during this time period. $1{,}211{,}537 \le x \le 1{,}257{,}608$

24. **NBA** The all time leading scorer in NBA history is Kareem Abdul-Jabbar with 38,387 points. The tenth player on this list is John Havlicek with 26,395 points. Write an inequality that represents range of points scored by the top ten all time leading scorers in NBA history. $26{,}395 \le x \le 38{,}387$

25. **Speed Limit** On some sections of the German Autobahn there are no speed limits. Write an inequality that represents the various distances that you could travel in 2.5 hours if your maximum speed was 135 miles per hour during this time period. Solve the inequality. $x \le 135(2.5)$; $x \le 337.5$ mi

26. **Exam Grades** The grades for a course are based on 5 exams and 1 final. All six of these tests are worth 100 points. To receive an A in the course, you must earn at least 552 points. Your grades on the 5 exams are as follows: 88, 96, 93, 91, and 89. Write an inequality that represents the various grades you can earn on the final and still get an A. Solve the inequality. $x + 457 \ge 552$, $x \ge 95$

LESSON 1.6

LESSON 1.7

Practice B

For use with pages 51–58

Decide whether the number is a solution of the equation.

1. $|2x + 3| = 7; 2$ yes
2. $|3x - 5| = 2; -1$ no
3. $|2x - 7| = 3; 2$ yes
4. $|4 - 3x| = 10; 2$ no
5. $\left|\frac{1}{3}x + 3\right| = 6; -9$ no
6. $\left|2 - \frac{1}{2}x\right| = 5; -6$ yes

Solve the equation.

7. $|x - 3| = 5$ $-2, 8$
8. $|2x + 6| = 12$ $-9, 3$
9. $|3x - 3| = 8$ $-\frac{5}{3}, \frac{11}{3}$
10. $|1 - 2x| = 9$ $-4, 5$
11. $\left|\frac{2}{3}x + 2\right| = 0$ -3
12. $|9x - 2| = 7$ $-\frac{5}{9}, 1$
13. $|2x - 3| = 3$ $0, 3$
14. $\left|1 - \frac{1}{5}x\right| = 3$ $-10, 20$
15. $|5 - 6x| = 7$ $-\frac{1}{3}, 2$

Solve the inequality.

16. $|x - 3| < 8$ $-5 < x < 11$
17. $|2x - 3| \ge 5$ $x \le -1$ or $x \ge 4$
18. $|3 - x| \le 3$ $0 \le x \le 6$
19. $|x + 7| > 3$
20. $|4x - 7| < 9$ $-\frac{1}{2} < x < 4$
21. $|4 - x| \le 8$ $-4 \le x \le 12$
22. $\left|\frac{1}{3}x + 4\right| > 1$ $x < -15$ or $x > -9$
23. $\left|4 - \frac{1}{2}x\right| \le 6$ $-4 \le x \le 20$
24. $|2 - 3x| \ge \frac{2}{3}$ $x \le \frac{4}{9}$ or $x \ge \frac{8}{9}$

19. $x < -10$ or $x > -4$

25. **Golfing** You plan on going golfing this weekend with a friend. You can either go to your favorite course which is 14 miles north of your house or to your friend's favorite course which is 14 miles south of your house. Write an absolute value inequality that represents all the distances you may be from your house. $|x| \le 14$

26. **Garter Snake** The garter snake is a common species in North America. There are various subspecies and coloration schemes depending on the geographical location. Typical adult garter snakes range in length from 46 to 130 cm. Write an absolute value inequality that represents the range of lengths of adult garter snakes. $|x - 88| \le 42$

27. **Homework** On a slow weekday, you spend at least two hours on homework. On a busy weekday, you spend as much as five hours on homework. Write an absolute value inequality that represents the number of hours you spend doing homework on a typical weekday. $|x - 3.5| \le 1.5$

28. **African Elephant** The African elephant is the heaviest land animal on the planet. Their mass varies from 3600 to 6000 kg. Write an absolute value inequality that represents the mass range of the African elephant. $|x - 4800| \le 1200$

LESSON 1.7

1 Assessment

CHAPTER 1 Quiz 1
For use after Lessons 1.1–1.2

Graph the numbers on a number line.

1. $\frac{7}{2}, -4, 1, -\sqrt{7}, \frac{5}{4}$

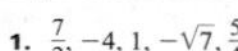

2. $\frac{2}{3}, \frac{11}{4}, -7, \sqrt{5}, -\frac{7}{2}$

Identify the property that the statement illustrates.

3. $3(9 + 4) = 3(9) + 3(4)$

4. $(-3 + 2) + 6 = -3 + (2 + 6)$

Perform the indicated conversion.

5. 45 yards to feet　　**6.** 11,000 pounds to tons

Evaluate the power.

7. -5^3　　**8.** $(-11)^2$

9. 7^1　　**10.** $(-3)^3$

Evaluate the expression for the given value of the variable(s).

11. $-5k + 9$ when $k = 2$

12. $(11 - r)^3 - 6s$ when $r = 8$ and $s = 2$

Simplify the expression.

13. $4r^2 + 9r - 5r^2 + 3r$　　**14.** $5(x - 2y) + 9(3 - y)$

15. Tickets for a concert cost $25 each. You have $180 to spend. Write an expression for the money that you have left after purchasing t tickets. Evaluate the expression to find the amount of money left after purchasing 6 tickets.

Answers

1. See left.
2. See left.
3. distributive property
4. associative property
5. 135 ft
6. 5.5 tons
7. -125
8. 121
9. 7
10. -27
11. -1
12. 15
13. $-r^2 + 12r$
14. $5x - 19y + 27$
15. $180 - 25t$; $30

CHAPTER 1 Quiz 2
For use after Lessons 1.3–1.5

Solve the equation.

1. $7n + 9 = 44$

2. $2(8 - 3q) = 4q - 9$

3. $\frac{8}{9}z - \frac{1}{2} = -\frac{2}{3}z + \frac{1}{6}$

Solve the equation for *y*.

4. $4x + y = 17$　　**5.** $xy - 7y = 49$

Solve the equation for *y*. Then find the value of *y* for the given value of *x*.

6. $32x - 16y = 96; x = 15$　　**7.** $13y - xy = 17; x = -4$

Use the formula $d = rt$ for the distance traveled to solve for the missing variables.

8. $d =$ ___?___, $r = 35$ mi/h, $t = 5$ h

9. $d = 520$ mi, $r =$ ___?___, $t = 8$ h

Look for a pattern in the table. Then write an equation that represents the table.

10.

x	0	1	2	3
y	1500	1250	1000	750

11.

x	0	1	2	3
y	−22	−11	0	11

12. It takes you 45 minutes to clean the fish tank and it takes your sister 30 minutes. How long does it take the two of you working together to clean the fish tank?

13. You buy 15 articles of clothing at a local clothing store. Each shirt costs $3.00 and each pair of pants costs $10.00. The total cost is $94. How many shirts and how many pants did you buy?

Answers

1. 5
2. 2.5
3. $\frac{3}{7}$
4. $y = 17 - 4x$
5. $y = \frac{49}{x - 7}$
6. $y = -6 + 2x$; 24
7. $y = \frac{17}{13 - x}$; 1
8. 175 mi
9. 65 mi/h
10. $y = 1500 - 250x$
11. $y = 11x - 22$
12. 18 min
13. 8 shirts, 7 pairs of pants

CHAPTER 1 Quiz 3
For use after Lessons 1.6–1.7

Graph the inequality.

1. $x > 6$

2. $-2 \le x < 5$

3. $x < -3$ or $x \ge 7$

Solve the inequality. Then graph the solution.

4. $-x + 5 < 12$　　**5.** $3(x - 5) \le 7 - 3x$

6. $-2 \le \frac{1}{5}x - 2 < 3$　　**7.** $2x - 6 < 4$ or $\frac{3}{2}x - 6 > 6$

Evaluate the expression for the given value of the variable.

8. $|w - 15|; w = -2$　　**9.** $|4 - 5x|; x = 9$

Solve the equation.

10. $|q - 13| = 5$　　**11.** $\left|\frac{1}{8}x - 4\right| = 12$

Solve the inequality. Then graph the solution.

12. $|x - 9| \ge 6$　　**13.** $|4x - 5| < 15$

14. One weight class that will be wrestling at a wrestling match consists of wrestlers that weigh between 152 pounds and 160 pounds, inclusive. Write an absolute value inequality describing the acceptable weight in this class.

Answers

1. See left.
2. See left.
3. See left.
4. $x > -7$; See left.
5. $x \le \frac{11}{3}$; See left.
6. $0 \le x < 25$; See left.
7. $x < 5$ or $x > 8$; See left.
8. 17
9. 41
10. 8, 18
11. -64, 128
12. $x \le 3$ or $x \ge 15$; See left.
13. $-\frac{5}{2} < x < 5$; See left.
14. $|x - 156| \le 4$

CHAPTER 1 Chapter Test B
For use after Chapter 1

Graph the numbers on a number line.

1. $-\frac{3}{4}, -4, 3, \frac{4}{3}, 4$　　**2.** $2, \pi, \sqrt{5}, -2.5, -1$

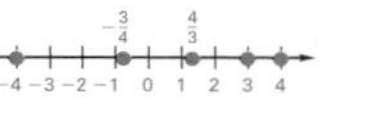

Identify the property that the statement illustrates.

3. $c + (-c) = 0$　　**4.** $(g + 2) + b = g + (2 + b)$

Convert the rate into the given units.

5. 100 kilometers per hour to miles per hour

6. 2 tons per hour to ounces per second

Evaluate the expression for the given value of the variable.

7. $3x^2 - 1; x = -1$　　**8.** $\sqrt{16t^2}; x = -4$

In Exercises 9 and 10, use the following information.

You have $20 to spend on strawberries, which are sold for $3 a pint.

9. Write an expression for the amount of money you have left after purchasing n pints of strawberries.

10. Evaluate the expression to find the amount of money you have left after purchasing 3 pints of strawberries.

Solve the equation.

11. $\frac{2}{5}r - 9 = 1$　　**12.** $q \div \frac{2}{3} + 9 = 3$

13. You purchased a CD player and paid a total of $54, including the 8% sales tax. What was the price of the CD player without the tax?

14. One lawn care worker can mow 3 lawns in 60 minutes, and another worker can mow 5 lawns in 75 minutes. How long will it take them to mow 7 lawns?

Answers

1. See left.
2. See left.
3. inverse property of addition
4. associative property of addition
5. 62.1 mi/h
6. $17.\overline{7}$ oz/sec
7. 2
8. 16
9. $20 - 3n$
10. $11
11. 25
12. -4
13. $50
14. 60 min

CHAPTER 1

Chapter Test B *continued*

For use after Chapter 1

15. The volume of a rectangular box can be found with the formula $V = \ell \cdot w \cdot h$. Solve for ℓ, and find the length of the rectangular box when $w = 6$ inches, $h = 7$ inches, and $V = 210$ cubic inches.

Solve the equation for *y*. Then find the value of *y* for the given value of *x*.

16. $\frac{2y}{5x} = 2 + 4x; x = 2$ **17.** $y + 0.5xy = x + 2; x = 1$

18. You travel on the highway at a speed of 60 miles per hour for 2.5 hours. How far did you travel?

19. A ferry connects an island to the mainland. The island is 47 miles away, and a one-way trip on the ferry takes 2.5 hours. What is the average speed of the ferry?

20. The table shows temperatures starting at 9 P.M. If the trend continues, what will the temperature be at 5 A.M.?

Time	9 P.M.	10 P.M.	11 P.M.	12 A.M.
Temperature	57°F	55°F	53°F	51°F

Graph the inequality.

21. $x \le -2.5$ **22.** $-3 > x > -6$

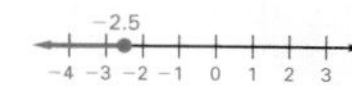

Solve the inequality.

23. $0.25x + 5 \ge 10$ **24.** $12x + 21 < 3x - 6$

25. $|5x + 5| > 15$ **26.** $|3x + 5| \le 20$

Answers

15. $\ell = \frac{V}{w \cdot h}$; 5 in.
16. $y = 10x^2 + 5x$; 50
17. $y = \frac{x + 2}{1 + 0.5x}$; 2
18. 150 mi
19. 18.8 mi/h
20. 41°F
21. See left.
22. See left.
23. $x \ge 20$
24. $x < -3$
25. $x < -4$ or $x > 2$
26. $-\frac{25}{3} \le x \le 5$

CHAPTER 1

Standardized Test

For use after Chapter 1

Multiple Choice

1. Which list shows the numbers in decreasing order? B

Ⓐ $-1.75, -\sqrt{3}, \frac{1}{4}, \frac{2}{7}, 2$

Ⓑ $2, \frac{2}{7}, \frac{1}{4}, -\sqrt{3}, -1.75$

Ⓒ $2, \frac{1}{4}, \frac{2}{7}, -\sqrt{3}, -1.75$

Ⓓ $2, \frac{2}{7}, \frac{1}{4}, -1.75, -\sqrt{3}$

2. Which of the following statements illustrates the distributive property? C

Ⓐ $(4 \cdot 2) \cdot 9 = 4 \cdot (2 \cdot 9)$

Ⓑ $5 \cdot 3 = 3 \cdot 5$

Ⓒ $3(2) + 3(3) = 3(2 + 3)$

Ⓓ $7 + (-7) = 0$

3. 72 feet is equal to how many yards? C

Ⓐ 6 Ⓑ 18

Ⓒ 24 Ⓓ 216

4. What is the value of $2g - (3g + 1)^2$ when $g = -2$? A

Ⓐ −29 Ⓑ −21

Ⓒ 21 Ⓓ 29

5. Which of the following polynomials is the simplified expression of $8p^2 - q^2 + 2 + 3q^2 - 2p^2$? B

Ⓐ $8p^2q^2 + 2$

Ⓑ $6p^2 + 2q^2 + 2$

Ⓒ $10p^2 - 4q^2 + 2$

Ⓓ $10p^2 + 2q^2 + 2$

6. What is the solution of $-3m - 2 = 10$? A

Ⓐ −4 Ⓑ $-\frac{8}{3}$

Ⓒ 9 Ⓓ 15

7. Which equation is represented by the table below? D

x	0	1	2	3
y	2	11	20	29

Ⓐ $y = 2x + 9$ Ⓑ $y = 3x + 5$

Ⓒ $y = 5x - 3$ Ⓓ $y = 9x + 2$

8. Your softball team is ordering equipment from a catalog. Each bat costs \$42. The cost of shipping is \$12 no matter how much you order. The total cost is \$348. How many bats did your team order? A

Ⓐ 8 Ⓑ 9 Ⓒ 10 Ⓓ 11

9. You can mow your lawn in 2 hours. Your friend can mow your lawn in 3 hours. How long will it take to mow your lawn if the two of you work together? C

Ⓐ 0.2 hour Ⓑ 1 hour

Ⓒ 1.2 hours Ⓓ 2.2 hours

10. What equation do you obtain when you solve the formula $h = \frac{V^2}{2g}$ for g? A

Ⓐ $g = \frac{V^2}{2h}$ Ⓑ $g = \sqrt{\frac{V^2}{2}}$

Ⓒ $g = 2V^2h$ Ⓓ $g = \frac{V_2}{2} - h$

11. What is the value of $\left|\frac{2}{3} - z\right|$ if $z = 3$? C

Ⓐ $\frac{1}{3}$ Ⓑ 1

Ⓒ $\frac{7}{3}$ Ⓓ $\frac{11}{3}$

CHAPTER 1

Standardized Test *continued*

For use after Chapter 1

12. Which inequality represents the solution to $7x + 2 \le -x + 18$? A

Ⓐ $x \le 2$ Ⓑ $x \ge 2$

Ⓒ $x \le 3$ Ⓓ $x \ge 3$

13. The weekly salary for a salesperson is \$225 plus a 5% commission on total sales. The salesperson would like to earn at least \$650 per week. What is the least amount the salesperson must sell in order to produce the desired salary? C

Ⓐ \$85 Ⓑ \$8400

Ⓒ \$8500 Ⓓ \$8501

14. What is (are) the solution(s) to $|6x - 8| = 2x$? D

Ⓐ 1 only Ⓑ 2 only

Ⓒ −1 and 2 Ⓓ 1 and 2

15. Which compound inequality is shown by the graph below? C

Ⓐ $x \ge 2$ or $x \le -5$

Ⓑ $-5 \le x \le 2$

Ⓒ $-5 < x \le 2$

Ⓓ $-5 \le x < 2$

Gridded Answer

16. What is the solution of the equation $3(c - 2) + 5 = 2(c + 1)$? 3

Short Response

17. The formula for the surface area of a rectangular prism with a square base is $S = 2w^2 + 4wh$, where,

S = Surface area

w = Length of sides of square base

h = Height

a. Solve the formula for h. $h = \frac{S - 2w^2}{4w}$

b. What is the height of a prism having a surface area of 24 square centimeters and a square base with a side length of 2 centimeters? 2 cm

Extended Response

18. A cell phone company offers you a plan that charges a flat rate of \$25 per month for 200 minutes of airtime. The rate for any time in excess of 200 minutes is \$.12 per minute.

a. Write an expression for the monthly dollar amount spent for the cell phone service if you use x minutes of airtime in excess of 200 minutes. $0.12x + 25$

b. Write an inequality which indicates that you have budgeted no more than \$40 per month to spend on the service.

c. Determine the maximum number of minutes you can use in excess of 200 minutes so that you do not exceed your \$40 per month budget. 125 min

18. b. $0.12x + 25 \le 40$

CHAPTER 1

Alternative Assessment and Math Journal

For use after Chapter 1

Journal **1.** Explain the importance of an agreed-upon order of operations. Write an example to illustrate. A four-function calculator can only perform the operations of addition, subtraction, multiplication, and division. Describe the order in which as expression is evaluated using a four-function calculator. How does this differ from the way an expression is evaluated using a scientific or graphing calculator?

Multi-Step Problem **2.** An adult's normal body temperature ranges from 97.6°F to 99.6°F, inclusive.

a. Write the range of normal body temperature as a compound inequality. Then graph the inequality.

b. Find the average normal body temperature and the tolerance.

c. Write an absolute value inequality that describes the range of normal body temperature.

d. Write an absolute value inequality that describes the body temperatures outside the normal range. Then graph the inequality.

e. If a fever is defined to be a body temperature that is higher than normal, write an inequality that describes a fever.

f. Writing Explain why the inequality from part (e) can not be written as a compound or absolute value inequality. What information would be necessary in order for the inequality in part (e) to be written as a compound or absolute value inequality?

1. Complete answers should include: an explanation that an agreed-upon order of operations is the only way to guarantee that the evaluation of a expression will always result in the same value; an example of an expression that when evaluated with two different order of operations results in two different values; an explanation that a four-function calculator evaluates the expression from left to right as it is inputted without regard for which operation is being performed. A scientific or graphing calculator does not evaluate the expression until it has been completely inputted and so will do the multiplication and division operations from left to right first, before doing the addition and subtraction operations.

2. a. $97.6 \le t \le 99.6$;

b. 98.6°F; 1°F **c.** $|t - 98.6| \le 1$

d. $|t - 98.6| > 1$;

e. $t > 99.6$ **f.** *Sample answer:* In order for the inequality from part (e) to be written as a compound or absolute value inequality, it would need a second condition that limits how large t can be.

PLAN AND PREPARE

Main Ideas

In Chapter 1, students will review the relationships between the subsets of real numbers, as well as reviewing the properties of real numbers. They will use the properties of real numbers and the order of operations to evaluate and simplify algebraic expressions, including expressions containing exponents. Then, students will use the properties of equality to solve linear equations and to rewrite formulas and equations. They will use verbal models and problem solving strategies to solve problems. Finally, students will learn to solve and graph linear inequalities and to solve absolute value equations and inequalities.

Prerequisite Skills

- Simplifying numerical expressions
- Finding the area of a geometric figure
- Writing algebraic expressions

Additional resources for reviewing prerequisite skills are:

- Skills Review Handbook, pp. 975–1009
- @HomeTutor

1 Equations and Inequalities

MA-HS-1.5.1	1.1 Apply Properties of Real Numbers
MA-HS-5.2.1	1.2 Evaluate and Simplify Algebraic Expressions
MA-HS-5.3.1	1.3 Solve Linear Equations
MA-HS-5.3.2	1.4 Rewrite Formulas and Equations
MA-HS-5.3.1	1.5 Use Problem Solving Strategies and Models
MA-HS-5.3.1	1.6 Solve Linear Inequalities
MA-HS-5.3.1	1.7 Solve Absolute Value Equations and Inequalities

Before

In previous courses, you learned the following skills, which you'll use in Chapter 1: simplifying numerical expressions, using formulas, and writing algebraic expressions.

Prerequisite Skills

VOCABULARY CHECK

Copy and complete the statement.

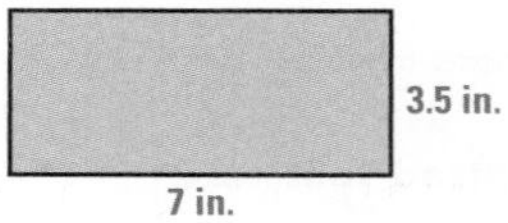

1. The **area** of the rectangle is _?_. 24.5 in.^{2}
2. The **perimeter** of the rectangle is _?_. 21 in.
3. The **opposite** of any number a is _?_. $-a$

(Rectangle: 7 in. by 3.5 in.)

SKILLS CHECK

Perform the indicated operation. *(Review p. 975 for 1.1, 1.2.)*

4. $5 \cdot (-3)$ -15 5. $3 + (-4)$ -1 6. $-28 \div (-7)$ 4 7. $8 - (-15)$ 23

Find the area of the figure. *(Review pp. 991–992 for 1.4.)*

8. A square with side length 7 ft 49 ft^2 9. A circle with radius 3 m about 28.3 m^2

Write an expression to answer the question. *(Review p. 984 for 1.5.)*

10. How much is a 15% tip on a restaurant bill of x dollars? $0.15x$
11. You have \$15 and buy r raffle tickets for \$.50 each. How much money do you have left? $15 - 0.5r$

Chapter Planning Guide

Chapter 1 Resource Book
- Teaching Guide/Lesson Plan (pp. 3, 14, 25, 36, 50, 60, 71)
- Project with Rubric (p. 84)

Assessment and Intervention
- Assessment Book (pp. 1–15)
- Benchmark Tests
- Remediation Book

Interactive Technology
- Easy Planner
- Power Presentations CD-ROM
- Activity Generator CD-ROM
- Animated Algebra
- Test Generator CD-ROM
- Online Quizzes
- eWorkbook
- eEdition
- @HomeTutor

Resources for English Learners
- Quick Reference for English Learners
- Spanish Study Guide
- Multi-Language Visual Glossary
- Student Resources in Spanish

Now

In Chapter 1, you will apply the big ideas listed below and reviewed in the Chapter Summary on page 60. You will also use the key vocabulary listed below.

Big Ideas

1. **Using properties to evaluate and simplify expressions**
2. **Using problem solving strategies and verbal models**
3. **Solving linear and absolute value equations and inequalities**

KEY VOCABULARY

- reciprocal, *p. 4*
- power, *p. 10*
- exponent, *p. 10*
- base, *p. 10*
- variable, *p. 11*
- coefficient, *p. 12*
- like terms, *p. 12*
- equivalent expressions, *p. 12*
- linear equation, *p. 18*
- equivalent equations, *p. 18*
- solve for a variable, *p. 26*
- linear inequality, *p. 41*
- compound inequality, *p. 41*
- absolute value, *p. 51*
- extraneous solution, *p. 52*

Why?

You can use equations to solve problems about work rates. For example, if two people complete a job at different rates, you can find how long it will take them if they work together.

Animated Algebra

The animation illustrated below for Exercise 76 on page 24 helps you answer this question: If two people paint a community mural at different rates, how long will it take them to complete the mural if they work together?

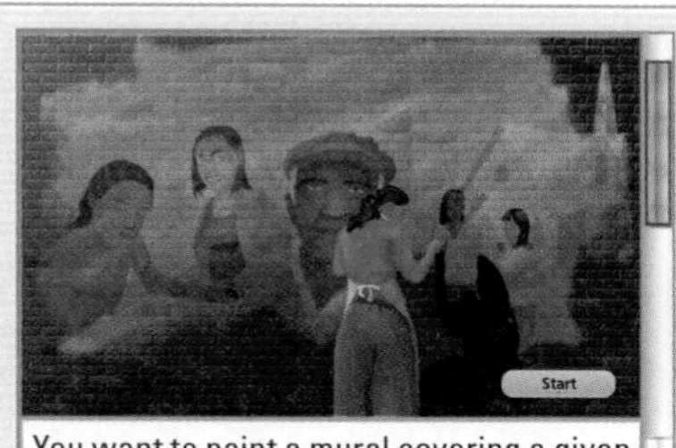

You want to paint a mural covering a given area. You can work with a friend.

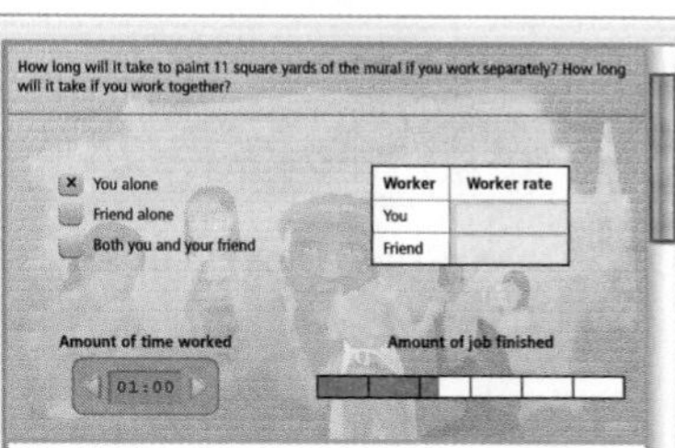

Enter your work rates, then find how long it takes working alone or with your friend.

Animated Algebra at classzone.com

Other animations for Chapter 1: pages 5, 11, 20, 27, 34, 42, and 53

Algebra 2 Toolkit

- Reading Strategies for Chapter 1, pp. 9–10
- Differentiated Instruction Notes, pp. 51–54
- English Learners Notes, pp. 101–102
- Inclusion Notes, pp. 135–136
- Teaching Strategies with Sample Worksheets, pp. 163–186
- Using Technology in the Classroom, pp. 187–192
- Tips for New Teachers, pp. 193–194
- Math Background Notes, pp. 221–223
- Pre-AP Strategies and Copymasters, pp. 311–312, 339–346
- Teacher Survival Activities, pp. 469–470, 497–498
- Bulletin Board Idea, p. 525
- Teacher Tool Transparencies, following p. 538

1 PLAN AND PREPARE

Warm-Up Exercises

Transparency Available

1. $18 + (-25) = \underline{?}$ -7

2. $\left(-\frac{1}{2}\right)\left(-\frac{4}{3}\right) = \underline{?}$ $\frac{2}{3}$

3. What is the difference between a daily low temperature of $-5°F$ and a daily high temperature of $18°F$? $23°F$

Notetaking Guide

Transparency Available

Promotes interactive learning and notetaking skills, pp. 1–3.

Pacing

Basic: 1 day

Average: 1 day

Advanced: 1 day

Block: 0.5 block with 1.2

• See *Teaching Guide/Lesson Plan.*

2 FOCUS AND MOTIVATE

Essential Question

Big Idea 1, p. 1

How are addition and subtraction related and how are multiplication and division related? Tell students they will learn how to answer this question by studying the properties of addition and multiplication.

1.1 Apply Properties of Real Numbers

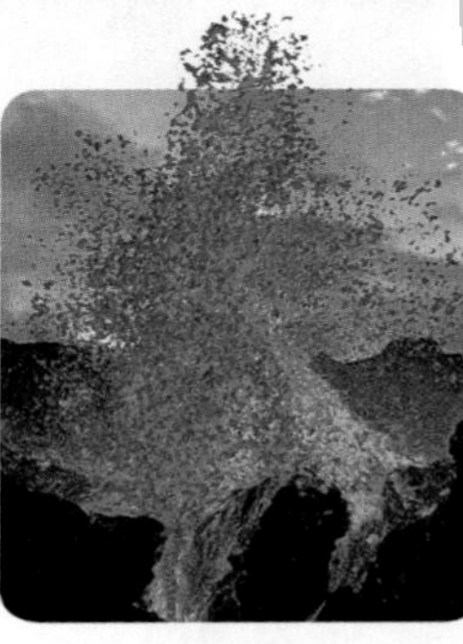

MA-HS-1.5.1

Before You performed operations with real numbers.

Now You will study properties of real numbers.

Why? So you can order elevations, as in Ex. 58.

Key Vocabulary
- opposite
- reciprocal

MA-HS-1.5.1
Students will identify real number properties (commutative properties of addition and multiplication, associative properties of addition and multiplication, distributive property of multiplication over addition and subtraction, identity properties of addition and multiplication and inverse properties of addition and multiplication) when used to justify a given step in simplifying an expression or solving an equation.

KEY CONCEPT — *For Your Notebook*

Subsets of the Real Numbers

The *real numbers* consist of the *rational numbers* and the *irrational numbers*. Two subsets of the rational numbers are the *whole numbers* (0, 1, 2, 3, . . .) and the *integers* (. . . , −3, −2, −1, 0, 1, 2, 3, . . .).

REAL NUMBERS

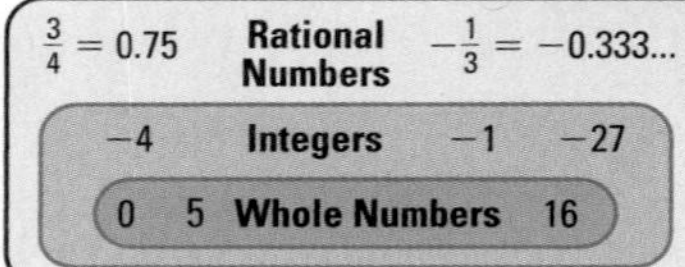

Rational Numbers
- can be written as quotients of integers
- can be written as decimals that terminate or repeat

Irrational Numbers
- cannot be written as quotients of integers
- cannot be written as decimals that terminate or repeat

NUMBER LINE Real numbers can be graphed as points on a line called a *real number line,* on which numbers increase from left to right.

EXAMPLE 1 Graph real numbers on a number line

Graph the real numbers $-\frac{5}{4}$ and $\sqrt{3}$ on a number line.

Solution

Note that $-\frac{5}{4} = -1.25$. Use a calculator to approximate $\sqrt{3}$ to the nearest tenth: $\sqrt{3} \approx 1.7$. (The symbol $\approx$ means *is approximately equal to.*)

So, graph $-\frac{5}{4}$ between −2 and −1, and graph $\sqrt{3}$ between 1 and 2, as shown on the number line below.

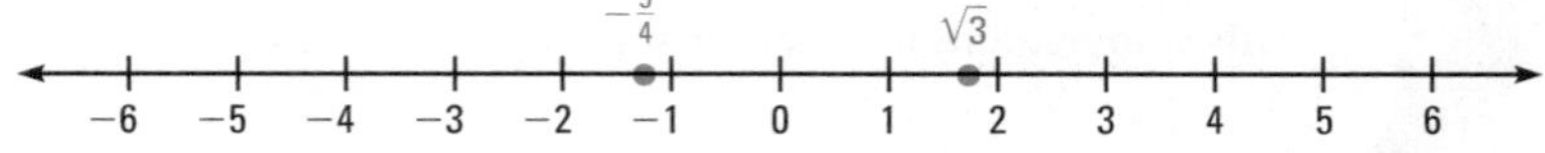

Resource Planning Guide

Chapter Resource Book
- Teaching Guide/Lesson Plan (pp. 3–4)
- Activity Master (p. 5)
- Practice levels A, B, C (pp. 6–8)
- Study Guide (pp. 9–10)
- Catch-up for Absent Students (p. 11)
- Application (p. 12)
- Challenge (p. 13)

Workbooks
- Notetaking Guide (pp. 1–3)
- Practice Workbook (pp. 1–2)

Teaching Options
- **Power Presentations CD-ROM** provides dynamic electronic teaching resources for the classroom.
- **Activity Generator CD-ROM** provides editable activities for all ability levels.

Interactive Technology
- Easy Planner
- Power Presentations CD-ROM
- Activity Generator CD-ROM
- Animated Algebra
- Test Generator CD-ROM
- Online Quiz
- eWorkbook
- eEdition
- @HomeTutor

Resources for English Learners
- Quick Reference for English Learners
- Spanish Study Guide
- Multi-Language Visual Glossary
- Student Resources in Spanish

See also the *Algebra 2 Toolkit* for more strategies for meeting individual needs.

EXAMPLE 2 Standardized Test Practice

The table shows the lowest elevations of six continents. Which list shows the elevations from lowest to highest?

Continent	Africa	Asia	Australia	Europe	North America	South America
Lowest elevation	−156 m	−408 m	−16 m	−28 m	−86 m	−40 m

Ⓐ −408, −156, −86, −28, −40, −16 Ⓑ −408, −156, −28, −86, −40, −16

Ⓒ −16, −28, −40, −86, −156, −408 Ⓓ −408, −156, −86, −40, −28, −16

ELIMINATE CHOICES
The problem asks for the elevations from lowest to highest, not from highest to lowest. So, you can eliminate choice C.

Solution

From lowest to highest, the elevations are −408, −156, −86, −40, −28, and −16.

▶ The correct answer is D. Ⓐ Ⓑ Ⓒ Ⓓ

✓ GUIDED PRACTICE for Examples 1 and 2

1. Graph the numbers $-0.2, \frac{7}{10}, -1, \sqrt{2}$, and -4 on a number line. See margin.

2. Which list shows the numbers in increasing order? C

Ⓐ $-0.5, 1.5, -2, -0.75, \sqrt{7}$ Ⓑ $-0.5, -2, -0.75, 1.5, \sqrt{7}$

Ⓒ $-2, -0.75, -0.5, 1.5, \sqrt{7}$ Ⓓ $\sqrt{7}, 1.5, -0.5, -0.75, -2$

PROPERTIES OF REAL NUMBERS You learned in previous courses that when you add or multiply real numbers, there are several properties you can use.

KEY CONCEPT *For Your Notebook*

Properties of Addition and Multiplication

Let a, b, and c be real numbers.

Property	Addition	Multiplication
Closure	$a + b$ is a real number.	ab is a real number.
Commutative	$a + b = b + a$	$ab = ba$
Associative	$(a + b) + c = a + (b + c)$	$(ab)c = a(bc)$
Identity	$a + 0 = a, 0 + a = a$	$a \cdot 1 = a, 1 \cdot a = a$
Inverse	$a + (-a) = 0$	$a \cdot \frac{1}{a} = 1, a \neq 0$

The following property involves both addition and multiplication.

Distributive $a(b + c) = ab + ac$

Motivating the Lesson

Using unit analysis is useful when you are working with rates. For example, when looking for the best buy among several brands or sizes at the supermarket, you might want to find the price per ounce.

3 TEACH

Extra Example 1

Graph the real numbers $-\sqrt{5}$ and $\frac{7}{2}$ on a number line.

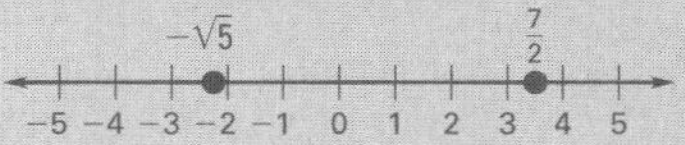

Key Questions to Ask for Example 1

- How do you know whether to place a number to the right or left of 0 on the number line? **If the number is negative, place it to the left of 0. If it is positive, place it to the right of 0.**
- How do you know where to place a number whose value you do not know exactly? **Place it based on its approximate value found using a calculator.**

Extra Example 2

The table shows the record low temperatures for several states. Which list shows the temperatures from highest to lowest? C

AK	CA	FL
−80°F	−45°F	−2°F
HI	**OR**	**TN**
12°F	−54°F	−32°F

Ⓐ −80, −54, −45, −32, −2, 12
Ⓑ −80, −54, −45, −32, 12, −2
Ⓒ 12, −2, −32, −45, −54, −80
Ⓓ 12, −2, −32, −54, −45, −80

1. 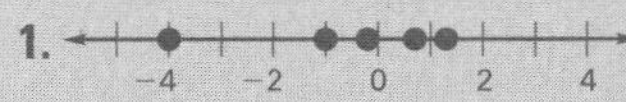

Differentiated Instruction

Below Level Some students may not remember the meaning of the square root symbol or the concept of a square root. Although these students may be able to approximate a square root by pushing the buttons on a calculator, it is important to make sure that they understand the meaning of the number given by their calculator. Emphasize that $a = \sqrt{b}$ if and only if $a^2 = b$.

See also the *Algebra 2 Toolkit* for more strategies.

Extra Example 3

Identify the property that the statement illustrates.

a. $5 + (9 + 12) = (5 + 9) + 12$ **Associative property of addition**

b. $250 \cdot 1 = 250$ **Identity property of multiplication**

Key Question to Ask for Example 3

- What is the difference between the commutative and associative properties? **The commutative properties say that you can change the order of two numbers when adding or multiplying without changing the result, while the associative properties say that you can change the grouping of three or more numbers when adding or multiplying without changing the result.**

Extra Example 4

Use properties and definitions of operations to show that $(10 \div c) \cdot c = 10$ when $c \neq 0$. Justify each step.

$(10 \div c) \cdot c = \left(10 \cdot \frac{1}{c}\right) \cdot c$ **[Definition of division]**

$= 10 \cdot \left(\frac{1}{c} \cdot c\right)$ **[Associative property of multiplication]**

$= 10 \cdot 1$ **[Inverse property of multiplication]**

$= 10$ **[Identity property of multiplication]**

Key Question to Ask for Example 4

- In Example 4, why is the definition of subtraction used in the first step? **The definition of subtraction is used to change the subtraction to an addition so that you can apply the addition properties.**

EXAMPLE 3 Identify properties of real numbers

Identify the property that the statement illustrates.

a. $7 + 4 = 4 + 7$

b. $13 \cdot \frac{1}{13} = 1$

Solution

a. Commutative property of addition

b. Inverse property of multiplication

KEY CONCEPT *For Your Notebook*

Defining Subtraction and Division

Subtraction is defined as *adding the opposite*. The **opposite**, or *additive inverse*, of any number b is $-b$. If b is positive, then $-b$ is negative. If b is negative, then $-b$ is positive.

$a - b = a + (-b)$ **Definition of subtraction**

Division is defined as *multiplying by the reciprocal*. The **reciprocal**, or *multiplicative inverse*, of any nonzero number b is $\frac{1}{b}$.

$a \div b = a \cdot \frac{1}{b}, b \neq 0$ **Definition of division**

EXAMPLE 4 Use properties and definitions of operations

Use properties and definitions of operations to show that $a + (2 - a) = 2$. Justify each step.

Solution

$a + (2 - a) = a + [2 + (-a)]$	Definition of subtraction
$= a + [(-a) + 2]$	Commutative property of addition
$= [a + (-a)] + 2$	Associative property of addition
$= 0 + 2$	Inverse property of addition
$= 2$	Identity property of addition

✓ GUIDED PRACTICE for Examples 3 and 4

3. Associative property of multiplication
4. Identity property of addition
5. Distributive property
6. Identity property of multiplication

Identify the property that the statement illustrates.

3. $(2 \cdot 3) \cdot 9 = 2 \cdot (3 \cdot 9)$

4. $15 + 0 = 15$

5. $4(5 + 25) = 4(5) + 4(25)$

6. $1 \cdot 500 = 500$

Use properties and definitions of operations to show that the statement is true. *Justify* each step. 7, 8. See margin.

7. $b \cdot (4 \div b) = 4$ when $b \neq 0$

8. $3x + (6 + 4x) = 7x + 6$

7. $b \cdot (4 \div b) = b \cdot \left(4 \cdot \frac{1}{b}\right)$ Def. of division
$= b \cdot \left(\frac{1}{b} \cdot 4\right)$ Comm. prop. of multiplication
$= \left(b \cdot \frac{1}{b}\right) \cdot 4$ Assoc. prop. of multiplication
$= 1 \cdot 4$ Inverse prop. of multiplication
$= 4$ Identity prop. of multiplication

8. $3x + (6 + 4x) = 3x + (4x + 6)$ Comm. prop. of addition
$= (3x + 4x) + 6$ Assoc. prop. of addition
$= 7x + 6$ Combine like terms.

UNIT ANALYSIS When you use operations in real-life problems, you should use *unit analysis* to check that the units in your calculations make sense.

EXAMPLE 5 Use unit analysis with operations

a. You work 4 hours and earn \$36. What is your earning rate?

b. You travel for 2.5 hours at 50 miles per hour. How far do you go?

c. You drive 45 miles per hour. What is your speed in feet per second?

Solution

a. $\frac{36 \text{ dollars}}{4 \text{ hours}} = 9$ dollars per hour

b. $(2.5 \text{ hours})\left(\frac{50 \text{ miles}}{1 \text{ hour}}\right) = 125$ miles

c. $\left(\frac{45 \text{ miles}}{1 \text{ hour}}\right)\left(\frac{1 \text{ hour}}{60 \text{ minutes}}\right)\left(\frac{1 \text{ minute}}{60 \text{ seconds}}\right)\left(\frac{5280 \text{ feet}}{1 \text{ mile}}\right) = 66$ feet per second

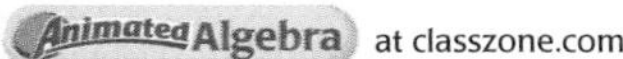 at classzone.com

EXAMPLE 6 Use unit analysis with conversions

DRIVING DISTANCE The distance from Montpelier, Vermont, to Montreal, Canada, is about 132 miles. The distance from Montreal to Quebec City is about 253 kilometers.

a. Convert the distance from Montpelier to Montreal to kilometers.

b. Convert the distance from Montreal to Quebec City to miles.

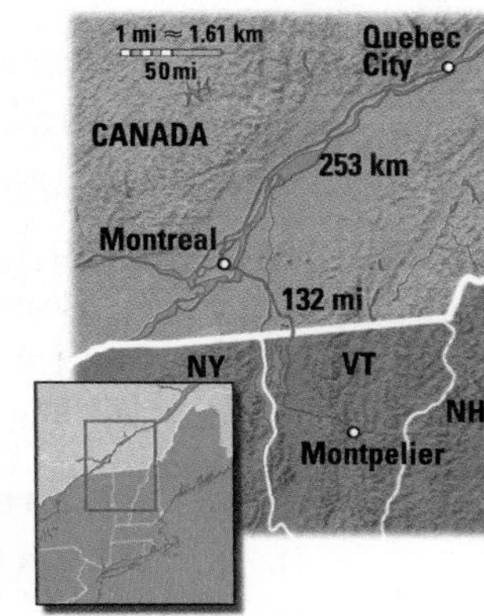

Solution

a. $132 \text{ miles} \cdot \frac{1.61 \text{ kilometers}}{1 \text{ mile}} \approx 213$ kilometers

b. $253 \text{ kilometers} \cdot \frac{1 \text{ mile}}{1.61 \text{ kilometers}} \approx 157$ miles

✓ GUIDED PRACTICE for Examples 5 and 6

Solve the problem. Use unit analysis to check your work.

9. You work 6 hours and earn \$69. What is your earning rate? **\$11.50/h**

10. How long does it take to travel 180 miles at 40 miles per hour? **4.5 h**

11. You drive 60 kilometers per hour. What is your speed in miles per hour? **about 37 mph**

Perform the indicated conversion.

12. 150 yards to feet **450 ft**

13. 4 gallons to pints **32 pints**

14. 16 years to seconds **504,576,000 sec**

REVIEW MEASURES
For help with converting units, see the Table of Measures on p. 1025.

Extra Example 5

a. You work 8 hours and earn \$60. What is your earning rate? **\$7.50 per hour**

b. You buy 18 gallons of gasoline at \$2.65 per gallon. What is your total cost? **\$47.70**

c. You drive 90 kilometers per hour. What is your speed in meters per second? **25 m/sec**

An **Animated Algebra** activity is available on-line for **Example 5**. This activity is also available on the **Power Presentations CD-ROM**.

Extra Example 6

The driving distance between Minneapolis, Minnesota, and Winnipeg, Manitoba, Canada, is about 450 miles. The driving distance between Vancouver, British Columbia, Canada, and Seattle, Washington, is about 325 kilometers.

a. Convert the distance from Minneapolis to Winnipeg to kilometers. **about 725 km**

b. Convert the distance from Vancouver to Seattle to miles. **about 202 mi**

Closing the Lesson

Have students summarize the major points of the lesson and answer the Essential Question: How are addition and subtraction related and how are multiplication and division related?

- **Real numbers can be graphed on a number line.**
- **The properties and definitions of operations can be used to justify an algebraic statement.**

Subtraction is defined as adding the opposite of the number being subtracted. Division is defined as multiplying by the reciprocal of the divisor.

Differentiated Instruction

English Learners Some students find mathematical terminology overwhelming, especially since there are often different ways to express the same thing. For example, some students may be more familiar with calling the reciprocal of a number its "inverse" rather than its *multiplicative inverse.* Have students maintain a glossary of key terms in their notes, listing the terms and any synonyms in the student's native language.

See also the *Algebra 2 Toolkit* for more strategies.

Assignment Guide

Answer Transparencies available for all exercises

Basic:
Day 1: SRH p. 975 Exs. 1–10
pp. 6–9
Exs. 1–5, 9–13, 17–37 odd, 39–44, 57–60, 63

Average:
Day 1: pp. 6–9
Exs. 1, 2, 6–10, 14–16, 20–24, 28–30, 35–43, 47–55, 58–61, 64

Advanced:
Day 1: pp. 6–9
Exs. 1, 2, 7–10, 15, 16, 21–24, 29, 30, 37–40, 44–56*, 59–62*

Block:
pp. 6–9
Exs. 1, 2, 6–10, 14–16, 20–24, 28–30, 35–43, 47–55, 58–61, 64 (with 1.2)

Differentiated Instruction

See *Algebra 2 Best Practices Toolkit* for suggestions on addressing the needs of a diverse classroom.

Homework Check

For a quick check of student understanding of key concepts, go over the following exercises:

Basic: 4, 9, 12, 25, 33
Average: 6, 9, 15, 20, 60
Advanced: 8, 16, 22, 59, 61

Extra Practice

- Student Edition, p. 1010
- Chapter 1 Resource Book: Practice levels A, B, C, pp. 6–8

Practice Worksheet

An easily-readable reduced practice page (with answers) for this lesson can be found on p. 1C.

1.1 EXERCISES

HOMEWORK KEY
○ = **WORKED-OUT SOLUTIONS on p. WS1 for Exs. 21, 31, and 59**
★ = **STANDARDIZED TEST PRACTICE Exs. 2, 9, 10, 23, 24, 60, and 61**

SKILL PRACTICE

A

1. **VOCABULARY** Copy and complete: The __?__ of any nonzero number b is $\frac{1}{b}$. reciprocal

2. ★ **WRITING** Express the associative property of addition in words. See margin.

2. Sample answer: If three numbers are being added together, it does not matter which two numbers are added together first.

EXAMPLE 1 on p. 2 for Exs. 3–8

GRAPHING NUMBERS **Graph the numbers on a number line.** 3–8. See margin.

3. $-\frac{3}{4}, 5, \frac{9}{2}, -2, -1$
4. $-3, \frac{5}{2}, 2, -\frac{9}{4}, 4$
5. $1, \sqrt{3}, -\frac{2}{3}, -\frac{5}{4}, 2$
6. $6, -\sqrt{5}, 2.7, -2, \frac{7}{3}$
7. $-0.4, \frac{3}{2}, 0, \sqrt{10}, -1$
8. $-1.7, 5, \frac{9}{2}, -\sqrt{8}, -3$

EXAMPLE 2 on p. 3 for Exs. 9–10

ORDERING NUMBERS **In Exercises 9 and 10, use the table of elevations below.**

State	Alabama	California	Kentucky	Louisiana	Tennessee
Highest elevation	2407 ft	14,494 ft	4145 ft	535 ft	6643 ft
Lowest elevation	0 ft	−282 ft	257 ft	−8 ft	178 ft

Louisiana bayou

9. ★ **MULTIPLE CHOICE** Which list shows the highest elevations in order from least to greatest? B
   (A) 2407; 14,494; 4145; 535; 6643
   (B) 535; 2407; 4145; 6643; 14,494
   (C) 14,494; 2407; 4145; 535; 6643
   (D) 14,494; 6643; 4145; 2407; 535

10. ★ **MULTIPLE CHOICE** Which list shows the lowest elevations in order from greatest to least? D
   (A) 0, −8, 178, 257, −282
   (B) −282, −8, 0, 178, 257
   (C) −282, 257, 178, −8, 0
   (D) 257, 178, 0, −8, −282

EXAMPLE 3 on p. 4 for Exs. 11–16

IDENTIFYING PROPERTIES **Identify the property that the statement illustrates.**

11. $(4 + 9) + 3 = 4 + (9 + 3)$ Associative property of addition
12. $15 \cdot 1 = 15$ Identity property of multiplication
13. $6 \cdot 4 = 4 \cdot 6$ Commutative property of multiplication
14. $5 + (-5) = 0$ Inverse property of addition
15. $7(2 + 8) = 7(2) + 7(8)$ Distributive property
16. $(6 \cdot 5) \cdot 7 = 6 \cdot (5 \cdot 7)$ Associative property of multiplication

EXAMPLE 4 on p. 4 for Exs. 17–22

USING PROPERTIES **Use properties and definitions of operations to show that the statement is true.** ***Justify*** **each step.** 17–22. See margin.

17. $6 \cdot (a \div 3) = 2a$
18. $15 \cdot (3 \div b) = 45 \div b$
19. $(c - 3) + 3 = c$
20. $(a + b) - c = a + (b - c)$
21. $7a + (4 + 5a) = 12a + 4$
22. $(12b + 15) - 3b = 15 + 9b$

23. ★ **OPEN-ENDED MATH** Find values of a and b such that a is a whole number, b is a rational number but not an integer, and $a \div b = -8$. *Sample answer:* $a = -2, b = \frac{1}{4}$

24. ★ **OPEN-ENDED MATH** Write three equations using integers to illustrate the distributive property.

24. Sample answer: $3(4 + 8) = 3 \cdot 4 + 3 \cdot 8 = 36$, $(1 + 8) \cdot 5 = 1 \cdot 5 + 8 \cdot 5 = 45$, $-6(4 - 7) = -6 \cdot 4 + (-6) \cdot (-7) = 18$

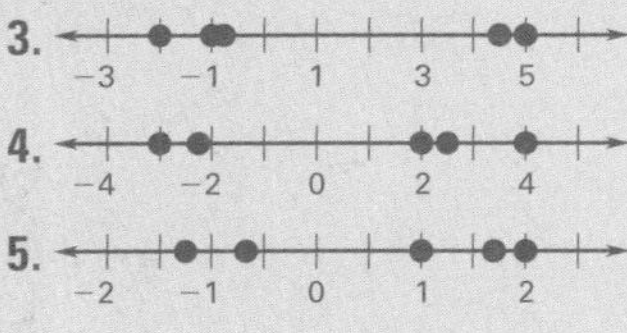

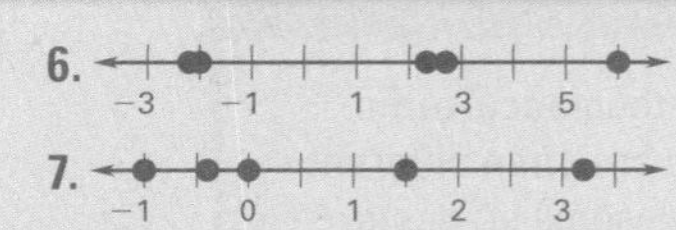

17–22. See Additional Answers beginning on p. AA1.

EXAMPLE 5
on p. 5
for Exs. 25–30

OPERATIONS AND UNIT ANALYSIS Solve the problem. Use unit analysis to check your work.

25. You work 10 hours and earn \$85. What is your earning rate? **\$8.50/h**

26. You travel 60 kilometers in 1.5 hours. What is your average speed? **40 km/h**

27. You work for 5 hours at \$7.25 per hour. How much do you earn? **\$36.25**

28. You buy 6 gallons of juice at \$1.25 per gallon. What is your total cost? **\$7.50**

29. You drive for 3 hours at 65 miles per hour. How far do you go? **195 mi**

30. You ride in a train for 175 miles at an average speed of 50 miles per hour. How many hours does the trip take? **3.5 h**

EXAMPLE 6
on p. 5
for Exs. 31–40

CONVERSION OF MEASUREMENTS Perform the indicated conversion.

31. 350 feet to yards **$116\frac{2}{3}$ yd**
32. 15 meters to millimeters **15,000 mm**
33. 2.2 kilograms to grams **2200 g**
34. 5 hours to minutes **300 min**
35. 7 quarts to gallons **1.75 gal**
36. 3.5 tons to pounds **7000 lb**
37. 56 ounces to tons **0.00175 ton**
38. 6800 seconds to hours **$1\frac{8}{9}$ h**

Animated Algebra at classzone.com

B

ERROR ANALYSIS *Describe* and correct the error in the conversion.

39.

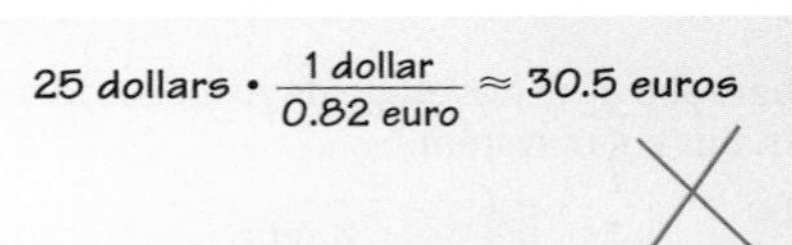

25 dollars • 1 dollar / 0.82 euro ≈ 30.5 euros

40.

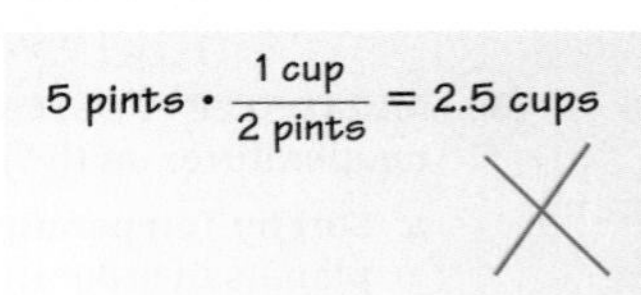

39. The unit multiplier should be $\frac{0.82 \text{ euro}}{1 \text{ dollar}}$; 25 dollars • $\frac{0.82 \text{ euro}}{1 \text{ dollar}}$ = 20.5 euros.

40. The unit multiplier should be $\frac{2 \text{ cups}}{1 \text{ pint}}$; 5 pints • $\frac{2 \text{ cups}}{1 \text{ pint}}$ = 10 cups.

CONVERSION OF RATES Convert the rate into the given units.

41. 20 mi/h to feet per second **about 29.3 ft/sec**
42. 6 ft/sec to miles per hour **about 4.1 mi/h**
43. 50 km/h to miles per hour **about 31.1 mi/h**
44. 40 mi/h to kilometers per hour **64.4 km/h**
45. 1 gal/h to ounces per second **about 0.04 oz/sec**
46. 6 oz/sec to gallons per hour **168.75 gal/h**

47. **ROCKET SLED** On a track at an Air Force base in New Mexico, a rocket sled travels 3 miles in 6 seconds. What is the average speed in miles per hour? **1800 mi/h**

48. **ELEVATOR SPEED** The elevator in the Washington Monument takes 60 seconds to rise 500 feet. What is the average speed in miles per hour? **about 5.7 mi/h**

REASONING Tell whether the statement is *always, sometimes,* or *never* true for real numbers *a, b,* and *c. Explain* your answer. **49–54. See margin.**

49. $(a + b) + c = a + (b + c)$
50. $(a \cdot b) \cdot c = a \cdot (b \cdot c)$
51. $(a - b) - c = a - (b - c)$
52. $(a \div b) \div c = a \div (b \div c)$
53. $a(b - c) = ab - ac$
54. $a(b \div c) = ab \div ac$

C

55. **REASONING** Show that $\frac{a}{b} \div \frac{c}{d} = \frac{a}{c} \div \frac{b}{d}$ for nonzero real numbers a, b, c, and d. *Justify* each step in your reasoning. **See margin.**

56. **CHALLENGE** Let $\frac{a}{b}$ and $\frac{c}{d}$ be two distinct rational numbers. Find the rational number that lies exactly halfway between $\frac{a}{b}$ and $\frac{c}{d}$ on a number line. **$\frac{ad + bc}{2bd}$**

Vocabulary

Exercise 23 To help students remember the meaning of the term *rational number*, point out that the word *rational* contains the word *ratio*.

An **Animated Algebra** activity is available on-line for **Exercises 31–38**. This activity is also available on the **Power Presentations CD-ROM**.

Avoiding Common Errors

Exercises 41, 42, 45, 46, 48 Each of these exercises requires more than one unit conversion, one conversion involving units of distance or volume, and one or two other conversions involving units of time. Some students make errors because they try to do all the conversions at once. Guide them in using unit analysis, one step at a time, as illustrated in the solution for Example 5.

Teaching Strategy

Exercises 49–54 Many students do not know where to begin when working on exercises like these. To guide them, first ask them if they have seen any of these statements before. Refer students to the list of properties on page 3 and the definitions of subtraction and division on page 4 if necessary. This should lead them to conclude that the statements in Exercises 49, 50, and 53 are *always* true. For the others, students will have to test several cases using different types of numbers. Ask them what *types* of numbers they think they should try and how many different cases they think they will need to try.

Differentiated Instruction

Below Level If students are having trouble knowing when to multiply and when to divide while doing **Exercises 26, 29, and 30**, have them start by writing the distance-rate-time formula, $d = rt$. See also the *Algebra 2 Toolkit* for more strategies.

49. Always; this represents the associative property of addition, which is true for all real numbers.

50. Always; this represents the associative property of multiplication, which is true for all real numbers.

51. Sometimes; it is true when $c = 0$.

52. Sometimes; it is true when $c = 1$ or $c = -1$.

53. Always; this represents the distributive property, which is true for all real numbers.

54. Sometimes; it is true when $a = 1$.

55. See Additional Answers beginning on p. AA1.

Teaching Strategy

Exercise 57 Some students may not be familiar with miniature golf, so you may need to explain the scoring system of positive and negative numbers representing strokes above and below par. You will also need to explain that the nine scores for each player represent their score for each of the nine holes. Then, ask students if they can think of a quick way to add the scores for each player without using a calculator. Students should be able to do this easily with mental math. Some students may find it useful to cross out pairs of numbers that are opposites, such as −1 and 1 in the first line, and then add the remaining scores.

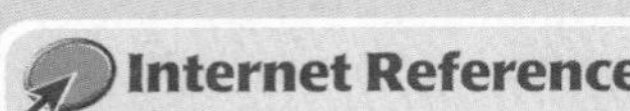

Exercise 59 More information about the planets in our solar system can be found at NASA's website pds.jpl.nasa.gov/planets/welcome.htm

PROBLEM SOLVING

EXAMPLE 2 A on p. 3 for Exs. 57–59

57. MINIATURE GOLF The table shows the scores of people playing 9 holes of miniature golf.

Lance	+2	+1	0	0	−1	+1	+3	0	0
Darcy	−1	+3	0	−1	+1	0	0	+1	−1
Javier	+1	0	+1	0	0	−1	+1	0	+1
Sandra	−1	−1	0	0	+1	−1	0	0	0

a. Find the sum of the scores for each player. **Lance: 6, Darcy: 2, Javier: 3, Sandra: −2**

b. List the players from best (lowest) to worst (highest) total score. **Sandra, Darcy, Javier, Lance**

@HomeTutor for problem solving help at classzone.com

58. VOLCANOES The following list shows the elevations (in feet) of several volcano summits above or below sea level.

641, 3976, 610, −59, 1718, 1733, −137

Order the elevations from lowest to highest. **−137, −59, 610, 641, 1718, 1733, 3976**

@HomeTutor for problem solving help at classzone.com

59. MULTI-STEP PROBLEM The chart shows the average daytime surface temperatures on the planets in our solar system.

a. **Sort by Temperature** List the planets in order from least to greatest daytime surface temperature.

b. **Sort by Distance** List the planets in order from least to greatest distance from the sun.

c. **Find Patterns** What pattern do you notice between surface temperature and distance from the sun?

d. **Analyze** Which planet does not follow the general pattern you found in part (c)? **Mercury or Venus**

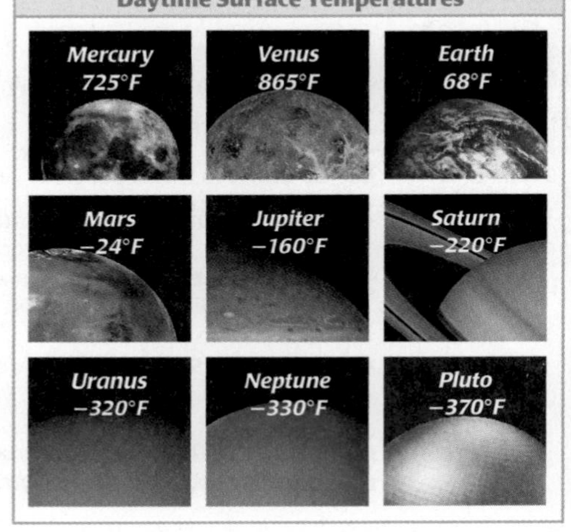

59a. Pluto, Neptune, Uranus, Saturn, Jupiter, Mars, Earth, Mercury, Venus

59b. Mercury, Venus, Earth, Mars, Jupiter, Saturn, Uranus, Neptune, Pluto

59c. *Sample answer:* The planets are in opposite orders in parts (a) and (b) with the exception of Mercury and Venus.

EXAMPLES B **5 and 6** on p. 5 for Exs. 60–61

60. ★ EXTENDED RESPONSE The average weight of the blue whale (the largest mammal) is 120 tons, and the average weight of the bumblebee bat (the smallest mammal) is 0.07 ounce.

a. **Convert** Convert the weight of the blue whale from tons to pounds. Convert the weight of the bumblebee bat from ounces to pounds. **240,000 lb; 0.004375 lb**

b. **Compare** About how many times as heavy as the bat is the blue whale? **about 54,857,143 times**

c. **Find a Method** Besides converting the weights to pounds, what is another method for comparing the weights of the mammals?
Sample answer: **You could convert the weights to ounces and then compare them.**

○ = WORKED-OUT SOLUTIONS on p. WS1 ★ = STANDARDIZED TEST PRACTICE

61. ★ **SHORT RESPONSE** The table shows the maximum speeds of various animals in miles per hour or feet per second.

Animal	Speed (mi/h)	Speed (ft/s)
Cheetah	70	? 102.67
Three-toed sloth	? 0.15	0.22
Squirrel	12	? 17.6
Grizzly bear	? 30	44

Three-toed sloth

a. Copy and complete the table.

b. *Compare* the speeds of the fastest and slowest animals in the table.
Sample answer: The cheetah is about 467 times faster than the three-toed sloth.

C 62. **CHALLENGE** A newspaper gives the exchange rates of some currencies with the U.S. dollar, as shown below. Copy and complete the statements.

	1 USD	in USD
Australian dollar	1.31234	0.761998
Canadian dollar	1.1981	0.834655
Hong Kong dollar	7.7718	0.12867
New Zealand dollar	1.43926	0.694801
Singapore dollar	1.6534	0.604814

This row indicates that $1 U.S. ≈ $1.31 Australian and $1 Australian ≈ $.76 U.S.

a. 1 Singapore dollar ≈ _?_ Canadian dollar(s) 0.724628

b. 1 Hong Kong dollar ≈ _?_ New Zealand dollar(s) 0.185190

KENTUCKY MIXED REVIEW

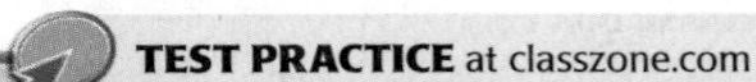

63. Susan purchased a television on sale for $315. The original price of the television was $370. Which expression can be used to determine the percent of the original price that Susan saved on the purchase of this television? **D**

Ⓐ $\frac{315}{370} \times 100$

Ⓑ $\frac{370}{315} \times 100$

Ⓒ $\frac{370 - 315}{315 \times 100}$

Ⓓ $\frac{370 - 315}{370} \times 100$

64. In the figure, what is the length of $\overline{QR}$ in inches? **D**

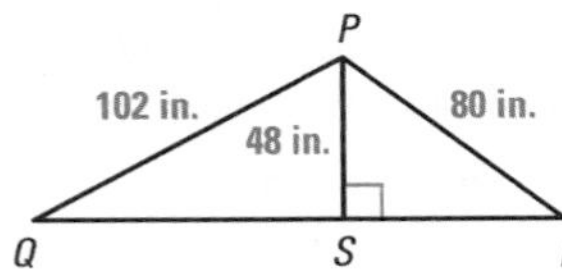

Ⓐ 86 in. Ⓑ 90 in. Ⓒ 122 in. Ⓓ 154 in.

5 ASSESS AND RETEACH

Daily Homework Quiz

Transparency Available

1. Graph the real numbers $\sqrt{13}$, $-\frac{12}{7}$, and −2.8 on a number line.

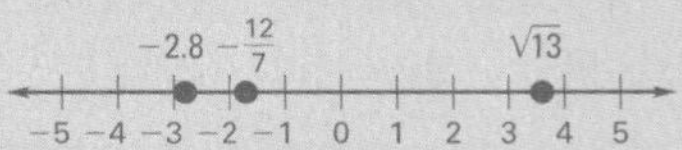

2. Arrange the numbers 82, −60, 54, −58, and 0 in increasing order. −60, −58, 0, 54, 82
3. Identify the property illustrated by the statement 19(6 + 8) = 19(6) + 19(8). Distributive property
4. You drive 60 miles per hour. What is your speed in feet per second? 88 ft/sec

Available at **classzone.com**

Diagnosis/Remediation

- Practice A, B, C in Chapter 1 Resource Book, pp. 6–8
- Study Guide in Chapter 1 Resource Book, pp. 9–10
- Practice Workbook, pp. 1–2
- @HomeTutor

Challenge

Additional challenge is available in the Chapter 1 Resource Book, p. 13.

1 PLAN AND PREPARE

Warm-Up Exercises

Transparency Available

Use the distributive property to rewrite the expression.

1. $7(4a - 8)$ $28a - 56$
2. $-9(5x - 9y)$ $-45x + 81y$
3. Jill has enough money for a total of 32 table decorations and wall decorations. If n is the number of table decorations, write an expression for the number of wall decorations she can buy. $32 - n$

Notetaking Guide

Transparency Available

Promotes interactive learning and notetaking skills, pp. 4–6.

Pacing

Basic: 1 day

Average: 1 day

Advanced: 1 day

Block: 0.5 block with 1.1

- See *Teaching Guide/Lesson Plan.*

2 FOCUS AND MOTIVATE

Essential Question

Big Idea 1, p. 1

When an expression involves more than one operation, in what order do you do the operations? Tell students they will learn how to answer this question by learning the order of operations.

1.2 Evaluate and Simplify Algebraic Expressions

MA-HS-5.2.1

Before	You studied properties of real numbers.
Now	You will evaluate and simplify expressions involving real numbers.
Why?	So you can estimate calorie use, as in Ex. 60.

Key Vocabulary
- power
- variable
- term
- coefficient
- identity

A **numerical expression** consists of numbers, operations, and grouping symbols. An expression formed by repeated multiplication of the same factor is a **power**.

A power has two parts: an *exponent* and a *base*. The **exponent** represents the number of times the **base** is used as a factor. In the power shown below, the base 7 is used as a factor 3 times.

exponent

$$\text{base} \rightarrow \underbrace{7^3}_{\text{power}} = 7 \cdot 7 \cdot 7$$

You do not usually write the exponent when it is 1. For instance, you can write 8^1 simply as 8.

MA-HS-5.2.1 Students will apply order of operations, real number properties (identity, inverse, commutative, associative, distributive, closure) and rules of exponents (integer) to simplify algebraic expressions. DOK 1

EXAMPLE 1 Evaluate powers

a. $(-5)^4 = (-5) \cdot (-5) \cdot (-5) \cdot (-5) = 625$

b. $-5^4 = -(5 \cdot 5 \cdot 5 \cdot 5) = -625$

In Example 1, notice how parentheses are used in part (a) to indicate that the base is -5. In part (b), the base of the power is 5, not -5. An *order of operations* helps avoid confusion when evaluating expressions.

KEY CONCEPT *For Your Notebook*

Order of Operations

	Steps	Example
STEP 1	**First**, do operations that occur within grouping symbols.	$1 + 7^2 \cdot (5 - 3)$
STEP 2	**Next**, evaluate powers.	$= 1 + 7^2 \cdot 2$
STEP 3	**Then**, do multiplications and divisions from left to right.	$= 1 + 49 \cdot 2$
STEP 4	**Finally**, do additions and subtractions from left to right.	$= 1 + 98$ $= 99$

Resource Planning Guide

Chapter Resource Book
- Teaching Guide/Lesson Plan (pp. 14–15)
- Practice levels A, B, C (pp. 17–19)
- Study Guide (pp. 20–21)
- Catch-up for Absent Students (p. 22)
- Application (p. 23)
- Challenge (p. 24)

Workbooks
- Notetaking Guide (pp. 4–6)
- Practice Workbook (pp. 3–4)

Teaching Options
- **Power Presentations CD-ROM** provides dynamic electronic teaching resources for the classroom.
- **Activity Generator CD-ROM** provides editable activities for all ability levels.

Interactive Technology
- Easy Planner
- Power Presentations CD-ROM
- Activity Generator CD-ROM
- Animated Algebra
- Test Generator CD-ROM
- Online Quiz
- eWorkbook
- eEdition
- @HomeTutor

Resources for English Learners
- Quick Reference for English Learners
- Spanish Study Guide
- Multi-Language Visual Glossary
- Student Resources in Spanish

See also the *Algebra 2 Toolkit* for more strategies for meeting individual needs.

VARIABLES A **variable** is a letter that is used to represent one or more numbers. An expression involving variables is called an **algebraic expression**. When you substitute a number for each variable in an algebraic expression and simplify, you are *evaluating* the algebraic expression.

EXAMPLE 2 Evaluate an algebraic expression

Evaluate $-4x^2 - 6x + 11$ when $x = -3$.

$-4x^2 - 6x + 11 = -4(-3)^2 - 6(-3) + 11$	**Substitute −3 for *x*.**
$= -4(9) - 6(-3) + 11$	**Evaluate power.**
$= -36 + 18 + 11$	**Multiply.**
$= -7$	**Add.**

Animated Algebra at classzone.com

EXAMPLE 3 Use a verbal model to solve a problem

CRAFT FAIR You are selling homemade candles at a craft fair for \$3 each. You spend \$120 to rent the booth and buy materials for the candles.

- Write an expression that shows your profit from selling *c* candles.
- Find your profit if you sell 75 candles.

Solution

STEP 1 **Write** a verbal model. Then write an algebraic expression. Use the fact that profit is the difference between income and expenses.

Price per candle (dollars/candle)	·	Number of candles sold (candles)	−	Expenses (dollars)
↓		↓		↓
3	·	***c***	−	**120**

An expression that shows your profit is $3c - 120$.

STEP 2 **Evaluate** the expression in Step 1 when $c = 75$.

$3c - 120 = 3(75) - 120$	**Substitute 75 for *c*.**
$= 225 - 120$	**Multiply.**
$= 105$	**Subtract.**

▶ Your profit is \$105.

GUIDED PRACTICE for Examples 1, 2, and 3

Evaluate the expression.

1. 6^3 216
2. -2^6 −64
3. $(-2)^6$ 64
4. $5x(x - 2)$ when $x = 6$ 120
5. $3y^2 - 4y$ when $y = -2$ 20
6. $(z + 3)^3$ when $z = 1$ 64
7. **WHAT IF?** In Example 3, find your profit if you sell 135 candles. \$285

Motivating the Lesson

Your high school band is planning to sell miniature school mascots as a fundraiser. You can write, simplify, and evaluate an algebraic expression to find the profit the band will make for any specific number of mascots that are sold.

3 TEACH

Extra Example 1

Evaluate.

a. -13^2 −169

b. $(-13)^2$ 169

Key Question to Ask for Example 1

- If a is a positive number and n is a positive integer, for what values of the exponent n would the expressions $(-a)^n$ and $-a^n$ be equal? They will be equal if n is an odd number.

Extra Example 2

Evaluate $3m^2 + 5m - 12$ when $m = -4$. 16

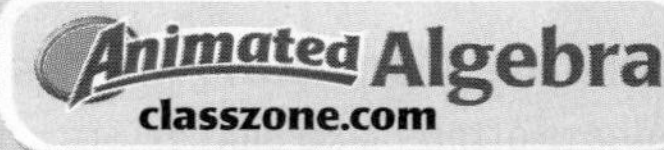

An **Animated Algebra** activity is available on-line for **Example 2**. This activity is also available on the **Power Presentations CD-ROM**.

Extra Example 3

You are selling fresh-squeezed lemonade at a county fair for \$2.50 per glass. You spend \$180 to rent the stand and buy the ingredients and supplies you need. Write an expression that shows your profit from selling g glasses of lemonade. Find your profit if you sell 268 glasses of lemonade.
$2.5g - 180$; \$490

Vocabulary

To help students remember the meaning of the term *coefficient*, break the word into two parts: *co-* and *efficient*. Point out that *co-* means "together," as in "cooperate," while *efficient* describes something that works well. Suggest that in algebra, a *coefficient* and a variable work well together as a single term.

Extra Example 4

Simplify the expression.

a. $12n - 7n$ $5n$

b. $8r^3 + 6r^2 - 9r^3$ $-r^3 + 6r^2$

c. $9(t - 4) - 6(t + 7)$ $3t - 78$

d. $15a - 8b - 20a + 14b$ $-5a + 6b$

Key Question to Ask for Example 4

- What is the difference between the way the distributive property is used in Examples 4a and 4c? **In Example 4a, the distributive property is used to factor out the common factor x. In Example 4c, it is used to remove parentheses, that is, to rewrite $a(b + c)$ as $ab + ac$.**

Avoiding Common Errors

Students often make sign errors when using the distributive property, such as writing -28 rather than $+28$ at the end of the first line in part (c) of Example 4. Stress that they are "distributing" -4 to both terms inside the parentheses, not just 4. Consider having them write an intermediate step to show how the distributive property is used, rewriting $-4(y - 7)$ as $(-4)(y) + (-4)(-7)$.

KEY CONCEPT *For Your Notebook*

Terms and Coefficients

In an expression that can be written as a sum, the parts added together are called **terms**.

A term that has a variable part is called a **variable term**. A term that has no variable part is called a **constant term**.

When a term is a product of a number and a power of a variable, the number is called the **coefficient** of the power.

$3x^2 + 5x + (-7)$ — variable terms: $3x^2$, $5x$; constant term: -7; coefficients: 3, 5

SIMPLIFYING An expression is simplified if it contains no grouping symbols and all *like terms* are combined. **Like terms** are terms that have the same variable parts. (Constant terms are also considered like terms.) The distributive property allows you to *combine like terms* by adding coefficients.

EXAMPLE 4 Simplify by combining like terms

a. $8x + 3x = (8 + 3)x$ **Distributive property**

$= 11x$ **Add coefficients.**

b. $5p^2 + p - 2p^2 = (5p^2 - 2p^2) + p$ **Group like terms.**

$= 3p^2 + p$ **Combine like terms.**

AVOID ERRORS
The terms $3p^2$ and p are not like terms. They use the same variable but different exponents, so the terms cannot be combined.

c. $3(y + 2) - 4(y - 7) = 3y + 6 - 4y + 28$ **Distributive property**

$= (3y - 4y) + (6 + 28)$ **Group like terms.**

$= -y + 34$ **Combine like terms.**

d. $2x - 3y - 9x + y = (2x - 9x) + (-3y + y)$ **Group like terms.**

$= -7x - 2y$ **Combine like terms.**

IDENTITIES Two algebraic expressions are **equivalent expressions** if they have the same value for all values of their variable(s). For instance, in part (a) of Example 4, the expressions $8x + 3x$ and $11x$ are equivalent. A statement such as $8x + 3x = 11x$ that equates two equivalent expressions is called an **identity**.

✓ **GUIDED PRACTICE** for Example 4

8. Identify the terms, coefficients, like terms, and constant terms in the expression $2 + 5x - 6x^2 + 7x - 3$. Then simplify the expression.

8. terms: 2, $5x$, $-6x^2$, $7x$, -3, coefficients: 5, -6, 7, like terms: $5x$ and $7x$, 2 and -3, constant terms: 2 and -3; $-6x^2 + 12x - 1$

Simplify the expression.

9. $15m - 9m$ $6m$

10. $2n - 1 + 6n + 5$ $8n + 4$

11. $3p^3 + 5p^2 - p^3$ $2p^3 + 5p^2$

12. $2q^2 + q - 7q - 5q^2$ $-3q^2 - 6q$

13. $8(x - 3) - 2(x + 6)$ $6x - 36$

14. $-4y - x + 10x + y$ $9x - 3y$

Differentiated Instruction

English Learners Students may confuse the terms *equal* and *equivalent*. Equivalent expressions have the same value for all values of the variable, while equal expressions have the same value for only some values of the variable. Try using the following algebraic examples: $12y - 7y$ is *equivalent* to $5y$ because both expressions have the same value for all values of y; $12y - 7$ is *equal* to 5 only when $y = 1$.

See also the *Algebra 2 Toolkit* for more strategies.

EXAMPLE 5 Simplify a mathematical model

DIGITAL PHOTO PRINTING You send 15 digital images to a printing service that charges \$.80 per print in large format and \$.20 per print in small format. Write and simplify an expression that represents the total cost if n of the 15 prints are in large format. Then find the total cost if 5 of the 15 prints are in large format.

Solution

Write a verbal model. Then write an algebraic expression.

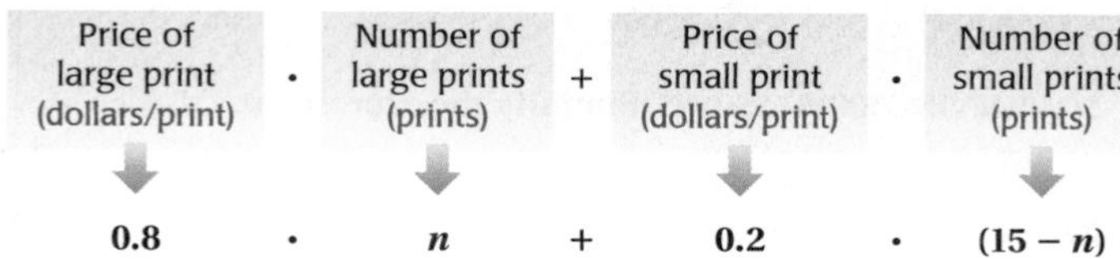

$$0.8 \cdot n + 0.2 \cdot (15 - n)$$

INTERPRET EXPRESSIONS The total number of prints is 15, so if n are in large format, then $15 - n$ are in small format.

An expression for the total cost is $0.8n + 0.2(15 - n)$.

$0.8n + 0.2(15 - n) = 0.8n + 3 - 0.2n$	**Distributive property**
$= (0.8n - 0.2n) + 3$	**Group like terms.**
$= 0.6n + 3$	**Combine like terms.**

▶ When $n = 5$, the total cost is $0.6(5) + 3 = 3 + 3 = \$6$.

GUIDED PRACTICE for Example 5

15. **WHAT IF?** In Example 5, write and simplify an expression for the total cost if the price of a large print is \$.75 and the price of a small print is \$.25. $0.75n + 0.25(15 - n)$; $0.5n + 3.75$

1.2 EXERCISES

HOMEWORK KEY

○ = **WORKED-OUT SOLUTIONS** on p. WS1 for Exs. 21, 29, and 59

★ = **STANDARDIZED TEST PRACTICE** Exs. 2, 24, 33, 51, and 59

◆ = **MULTIPLE REPRESENTATIONS** Ex. 61

SKILL PRACTICE

A

1. **VOCABULARY** Copy 12^7 and label the base and the exponent. base: 12, exponent: 7

2. ★ **WRITING** *Explain* what it means for terms to be like terms. Like terms have the same variable raised to the same power.

3. **ERROR ANALYSIS** *Describe* and correct the error in evaluating the power shown at the right.

$-3^4 = 81$ ✗

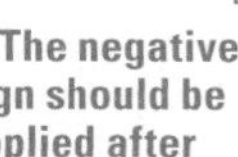

3. The negative sign should be applied after evaluating the power, $-3^4 = -81$.

EXAMPLE 1 on p. 10 for Exs. 4–15

EVALUATING POWERS Evaluate the power.

4. 2^3 8	5. 3^4 81	6. 4^3 64	7. 7^2 49
8. -5^2 −25	9. -2^5 −32	10. -8^3 −512	11. -10^4 −10,000
12. $(-3)^2$ 9	13. $(-4)^3$ −64	14. $(-2)^8$ 256	15. $(-8)^2$ 64

Extra Example 5

Yesterday, a store sold 60 recordable DVDs. The Brand A DVDs sell for \$15 each, and the Brand B DVDs sell for \$12 each. Write and simplify an expression that represents the store's total income for the DVD sales yesterday if x represents the number of Brand A DVDs sold. Then find the total income if 38 of the 60 DVDs were Brand A. $15x + 12(60 - x)$, or $3x + 720$; \$834

Closing the Lesson

Have students summarize the major points of the lesson and answer the Essential Question: When an expression involves more than one operation, in what order do you do the operations?

- The order of operations tells you the order to follow when an expression involves more than one operation.
- Algebraic expressions can be simplified by applying the distributive property, and by grouping and combining like terms.

1) Do operations that occur within grouping symbols. 2) Evaluate powers. 3) Do multiplications and divisions from left to right. 4) Do additions and subtractions from left to right.

4 PRACTICE AND APPLY

Assignment Guide

Answer Transparencies available for all exercises

Basic:
Day 1: SRH p. 984 Exs. 1–6
pp. 13–16
Exs. 1–9, 17–23 odd, 24–29, 33, 34–40 even, 57–61, 64

Average:
Day 1: pp. 13–16
Exs. 1–3, 10–14 even, 16–18, 24, 29–33, 35–51 odd, 52–54, 58–62, 65

Advanced:
Day 1: pp. 13–16
Exs. 1, 2, 11–15 odd, 20–24 even, 30–33, 36–50 even, 51–56*, 59–63*

Block:
pp. 13–16
Exs. 1–3, 10–14 even, 16–18, 24, 29–33, 35–51 odd, 52–54, 58–62, 65 (with 1.1)

Differentiated Instruction

See *Algebra 2 Best Practices Toolkit* for suggestions on addressing the needs of a diverse classroom.

Homework Check

For a quick check of student understanding of key concepts, go over the following exercises:

Basic: 6, 17, 26, 57, 60

Average: 12, 18, 30, 58, 61

Advanced: 13, 22, 32, 59, 62

Extra Practice

- Student Edition, p. 1010
- Chapter 1 Resource Book: Practice levels A, B, C, pp. 17–19

Practice Worksheet

An easily-readable reduced practice page (with answers) for this lesson can be found on p. 1C.

EXAMPLE 2 on p. 11 for Exs. 16–24

ORDER OF OPERATIONS **Evaluate the expression for the given value of the variable.**

16. $5d - 6$ when $d = 7$ **29**

17. $-10f + 15$ when $f = 2$ **−5**

18. $6h \div 2 + h$ when $h = 4$ **16**

19. $5j - 3j \cdot 5$ when $j = 10$ **−100**

20. $(k + 2)^2 - 6k$ when $k = 5$ **19**

(21.) $8m + (2m - 9)^3$ when $m = 6$ **75**

22. $n^3 - 4n + 10$ when $n = -3$ **−5**

23. $2x^4 - 4x^3$ when $x = -1$ **6**

Animated Algebra at classzone.com

24. ★ **MULTIPLE CHOICE** What is the value of $2x^2 - 6x + 15$ when $x = -2$? **C**

Ⓐ 11 Ⓑ 19 Ⓒ 35 Ⓓ 43

EXAMPLE 4 on p. 12 for Exs. 25–33

SIMPLIFYING EXPRESSIONS **Simplify the expression.**

25. $9x - 4x + 5$ **$5x + 5$**

26. $y^2 + 2y + 3y^2$ **$4y^2 + 2y$**

27. $5z^2 - 2z + 8z^2 + 10$ **$13z^2 - 2z + 10$**

28. $10w^2 - 4w + 3w^2 + 18w$ **$13w^2 + 14w$**

(29.) $7(m - 3) + 4(m + 5)$ **$11m - 1$**

30. $10(n^2 + n) - 6(n^2 - 2)$ **$4n^2 + 10n + 12$**

31. $4p^2 - 12p - 9p^2 + 3(4p + 7)$ **$-5p^2 + 21$**

32. $6(q - 2) - 2(q^2 + 6q)$ **$-2q^2 - 6q - 12$**

33. ★ **MULTIPLE CHOICE** Which terms are like terms? **D**

Ⓐ $2x, 2y$ Ⓑ $3x^2, 4x$ Ⓒ x^2, y^2 Ⓓ $10x^3, 2x^3$

B

GEOMETRY **Write a simplified expression for the perimeter of the figure. Then evaluate the expression for the given value(s) of the variable(s).**

34. $a = 3, b = 10$ **$10a + 3b$; 60**

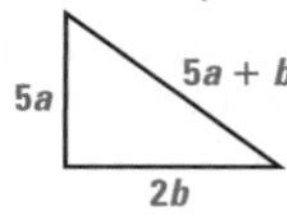

35. $n = 2$ **$10n + 24$; 44**

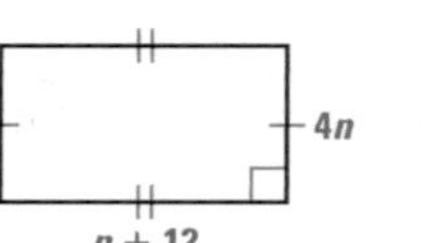

36. $g = 5, h = 4$ **$4g + 8h$; 52**

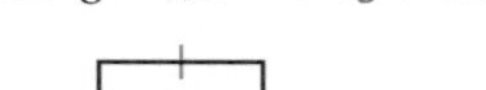

EVALUATING EXPRESSIONS **Evaluate the expression for the given values of *x* and *y*.**

37. $5x + 6y$ when $x = 16$ and $y = -9$ **26**

38. $16x + 11y$ when $x = -2$ and $y = -3$ **−65**

39. $x^3 + 5y$ when $x = 4$ and $y = -3$ **49**

40. $(3x)^2 - y^3$ when $x = 4$ and $y = 5$ **19**

41. $\frac{x - y}{x + y}$ when $x = 10$ and $y = 8$ **$\frac{1}{9}$**

42. $\frac{x + 2y}{4x - y}$ when $x = -3$ and $y = 4$ **$-\frac{5}{16}$**

HINT Fraction bars are grouping symbols.

SIMPLIFYING EXPRESSIONS **Simplify the expression.**

43. $16c - 10d + 3d - 5c$ **$-7d + 11c$**

44. $9j + 4k - 2j - 7k$ **$7j - 3k$**

45. $2m^2 - 5n^2 + 6n^2 - 8m$ **$2m^2 + n^2 - 8m$**

46. $p^3 + 3q^2 - q + 3p^3$ **$4p^3 + 3q^2 - q$**

47. $10m^2 + 3n - 8 + 3m^2 - 3n + 3$ **$13m^2 - 5$**

48. $3y^2 + 5x - 12x + 9y^2 - 5$ **$12y^2 - 7x - 5$**

49. $8(s - t) + 16(t - s)$ **$-8s + 8t$**

50. $3(x^2 - y) + 9(x^2 + 2y)$ **$12x^2 + 15y$**

51. ★ **OPEN-ENDED MATH** Write an algebraic expression that includes three coefficients, two like terms, and one constant term. Then simplify the expression. ***Sample answer:* $3k + 4k + (-8) - 2j$; $7k - 8 - 2j$**

○ = WORKED-OUT SOLUTIONS on p. WS1 ★ = STANDARDIZED TEST PRACTICE  = MULTIPLE REPRESENTATIONS

Differentiated Instruction

Below Level Many students think only of parentheses when they think of grouping symbols and may not recognize that the fraction bars in **Exercises 41 and 42** are grouping symbols. Explain that in cases like this, Step 1 in the order of operations means you need to do all operations in the numerator, then do all operations in the denominator, and finally divide the numerator by the denominator. Suggest that students remember this sequence as Numerator–Denominator–Divide, or NDD.

See also the *Algebra 2 Toolkit* for more strategies.

C **GROUPING SYMBOLS** **Add parentheses to make a true statement.**

52. $9 + 12 \div 3 - 1 = 15$ $9 + 12 \div (3 - 1) = 15$

53. $4 + 3 \cdot 5 - 2 = 21$ $(4 + 3) \cdot (5 - 2) = 21$

54. $8 + 5^2 - 6 \div 3 = 9$ $(8 + 5^2 - 6) \div 3 = 9$

55. $3 \cdot 4^2 - 2^3 + 3^2 = 23$ $(3 \cdot 4)^2 - (2^3 + 3)^2 = 23$

56. CHALLENGE Under what conditions are the expressions $(x + y)^2$ and $x^2 + y^2$ equal? Are the expressions equivalent? *Explain.*
If $x = 0$ or $y = 0$; no; $(x + y)^2 = x^2 + 2xy + y^2$, which is not equivalent to $x^2 + y^2$.

PROBLEM SOLVING

EXAMPLE 3 **A** on p. 11 for Exs. 57–59

57. MOVIE COSTS In the United States, the average movie ticket price (in dollars) since 1974 can be modeled by $0.131x + 1.89$ where x is the number of years since 1974. What values of x should you use to find the ticket prices in 1974, 1984, 1994, and 2004? Find the ticket prices for those years. 0, 10, 20, 30; \$1.89, \$3.20, \$4.51, \$5.82

@HomeTutor for problem solving help at classzone.com

58. MILEAGE You start driving a used car when the odometer reads 96,882. After a typical month of driving, the reading is 97,057. Write an expression for the reading on the odometer after m months, assuming the amount you drive each month is the same. Predict the reading after 12 months. $175m + 96{,}882$; 98,982 mi

@HomeTutor for problem solving help at classzone.com

59. $270 - 4.5x$; no; when $x > 60$ there will be a negative balance on the card, which means you will have spent more than what you had on the card.

59. ★ **SHORT RESPONSE** A student has a debit card with a prepaid amount of \$270 to use for school lunches. The cafeteria charges \$4.50 per lunch. Write an expression for the balance on the card after buying x lunches. Does your expression make sense for all positive integer values of x? *Explain.*

EXAMPLE 5 on p. 13 for Exs. 60–62

60. CROSS-TRAINING You exercise for 60 minutes, spending w minutes walking and the rest of the time running. Use the information in the diagram below to write and simplify an expression for the number of calories burned. Find the calories burned if you spend 20 minutes walking. $600 - 6w$; 480 cal

Walking burns
4 calories per minute.
Running burns
10 calories per minute.

B **61.** ◆ **MULTIPLE REPRESENTATIONS** A theater has 30 rows of seats with 20 seats in each row. Tickets for the seats in the n rows closest to the stage cost \$45 and tickets for the other rows cost \$35.

a. **Visual Thinking** Make a sketch of the theater seating. See margin.

b. **Modeling** Write a verbal model for the income if all seats are sold.

c. **Simplifying** Write and simplify an expression for the income. $200n + 21{,}000$

d. **Making a Table** Make a table for the income when $n = 5$, 10, and 15. See margin.

61b. price for closest seats • number of close seats + price of other seats • number of other seats

62. COMPUTERS A company offers each of its 80 workers either a desktop computer that costs \$900 or a laptop that costs \$1550. Write and simplify an expression for the cost of all the computers when n workers choose desktop computers. Find the cost if 65 workers choose desktop computers. $124{,}000 - 650n$; \$81,750

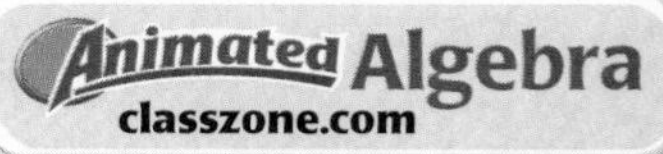
Animated Algebra
classzone.com

An **Animated Algebra** activity is available on-line for **Exercises 16–23**. This activity is also available on the **Power Presentations CD-ROM**.

Avoiding Common Errors

Exercises 22, 23, 37–39, 42 Students may make sign errors when substituting negative numbers for variables in algebraic expressions. To avoid this error, instruct students to first replace every variable with a pair of parentheses and then place the value into the "slots" that are created by the parentheses.

61a. See Additional Answers beginning on p. AA1.

61d.

n number of rows closest to stage	5	10	15
Income (dollars)	22,000	23,000	24,000

5 ASSESS AND RETEACH

Daily Homework Quiz

Transparency Available

1. Evaluate $-2x^3 - 5x^2 + 21$ when $x = -3$. **30**

Simplify the expression.

2. $11z^2 - z - 12z^2 + z$ $-z^2$
3. $5(w + 6) - 9(w - 4)$ $-4w + 66$
4. You are selling cakes at a bake sale for $6.75 each. You spend $86 to buy ingredients and supplies. There is no charge to have a table at the sale. Write an expression that shows your profit from selling n cakes. Then find the profit if you sell 25 cakes. $6.75n - 86$; $82.75

Online Quiz

Available at **classzone.com**

Diagnosis/Remediation

- Practice A, B, C in Chapter 1 Resource Book, pp. 17–19
- Study Guide in Chapter 1 Resource Book, pp. 20–21
- Practice Workbook, pp. 3–4
- @HomeTutor

Challenge

Additional challenge is available in the Chapter 1 Resource Book, p. 24.

Quiz

An easily-readable reduced copy of the quiz (with answers) on Lessons 1.1–1.2 from the Assessment Book can be found on p. 1E.

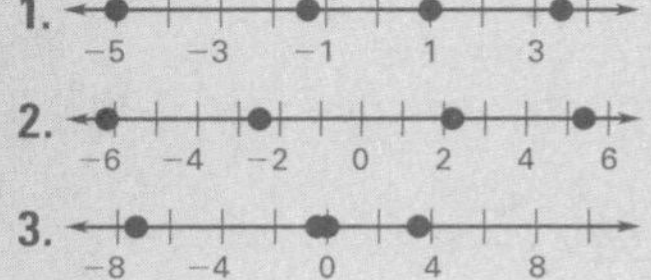

C **63. CHALLENGE** You want to buy 25 fish for an aquarium. You decide to buy danios, tetras, and rainbowfish.

Write and simplify an expression for the total cost of x danios, y tetras, and the rest rainbowfish. You buy 8 danios, 10 tetras, and the rest rainbowfish. What is the total cost? **$-6.5x - 6y + 200$; $88**

KY KENTUCKY MIXED REVIEW

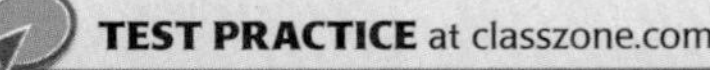

TEST PRACTICE at classzone.com

64. A roadside fruit stand sells three apples for a total of $0.79. The total cost, c, of purchasing n apples can be found by— **B**

Ⓐ multiplying n by c Ⓑ multiplying n by the cost of 1 apple
Ⓒ dividing n by c Ⓓ dividing c by the cost of 1 apple

65. A rectangle has a length of 6 feet and a perimeter of 22 feet. What is the perimeter of a similar rectangle with a width of 20 feet? **C**

Ⓐ 52 ft Ⓑ 82 ft Ⓒ 88 ft Ⓓ 100 ft

QUIZ *for Lessons 1.1–1.2*

Graph the numbers on a number line. *(p. 2)* **1–3. See margin.**

1. $-5, \frac{7}{2}, 1, -\frac{4}{3}$ **2.** $-6.2, 5.4, \sqrt{5}, -2.5$ **3.** $0, -7.3, -\frac{2}{5}, 2\sqrt{3}$

Identify the property that the statement illustrates. *(p. 2)*

4. $6(4 + 9) = 6(4) + 6(9)$ **Distributive property**
5. $-5 \cdot 8 = 8 \cdot (-5)$ **5. Commutative property of multiplication**
6. $17 + (-17) = 0$ **Inverse property of addition**

Evaluate the expression for the given value of the variable. *(p. 10)*

7. $10m + 32$ when $m = -5$ **−18** **8.** $12 + (8 - n)^3$ when $n = 5$ **39** **9.** $p^3 - 3p^2$ when $p = -2$ **−20**

Simplify the expression. *(p. 10)*

10. $8x + 6x^2 - 9x^2 - 4x$ **$-3x^2 + 4x$** **11.** $5(x + 9) - 2(4 - x)$ **$7x + 37$** **12.** $24x - 6y + 15y - 18x$ **$6x + 9y$**

13. CD COSTS CDs are on sale for $8 each and you have a gift card worth $100. Write an expression for the amount of money left on the gift card after purchasing n CDs. Evaluate the expression to find the amount of money left after purchasing 6 CDs. *(p. 10)* **$100 - 8n$; $52**

EXTRA PRACTICE for Lesson 1.2, p. 1010

ONLINE QUIZ at classzone.com

Graphing Calculator ACTIVITY *Use after Lesson 1.2*

@HomeTutor
classzone.com
Keystrokes

1.2 Evaluate Expressions

QUESTION How can you use a calculator to evaluate expressions?

You can use a scientific calculator or a graphing calculator to evaluate expressions. Keystrokes for evaluating several expressions are shown below.

Note that to enter a negative number, you use the [+/-] key on a scientific calculator or the [(-)] key (not the [−] key) on a graphing calculator.

EXAMPLE Evaluate expressions

	EXPRESSION	CALCULATOR	KEYSTROKES	RESULT
a.	$-4^2 + 6$	Scientific	4 [x²] [+/-] [+] 6 [=]	−10
	$-4^2 + 6$	Graphing	[(-)] 4 [x²] [+] 6 [ENTER]	−10
b.	$(-4)^2 + 6$	Scientific	4 [+/-] [x²] [+] 6 [=]	22
	$(-4)^2 + 6$	Graphing	[(] [(-)] 4 [)] [x²] [+] 6 [ENTER]	22
c.	$(39 \div 3)^3$	Scientific	[(] 39 [÷] 3 [)] [yˣ] 3 [=]	2197
	$(39 \div 3)^3$	Graphing	[(] 39 [÷] 3 [)] [^] 3 [ENTER]	2197
d.	$\frac{64 - 5 \cdot 8}{4}$	Scientific	[(] 64 [−] 5 [×] 8 [)] [÷] 4 [=]	6
	$\frac{64 - 5 \cdot 8}{4}$	Graphing	[(] 64 [−] 5 [×] 8 [)] [÷] 4 [ENTER]	6

PRACTICE

Use a calculator to evaluate the expression.

1. $50.2 - 15 \div 3$ 45.2
2. $-11(20) - 66$ −286
3. $21(-8) + 51$ −117
4. $(-4)^4$ 256
5. $7(44.5 - 8^2)$ −136.5
6. $\frac{9.2 - 15.9}{-19 + 14}$ 1.34

Use a calculator to evaluate the expression when $x = -3$, $y = 5$, and $z = -6$.

7. $7z + y$ −37
8. x^6 729
9. $6y - z^3$ 246
10. $\frac{10x}{2z - 3}$ 2
11. $(x + y)^2 + 3z$ −14
12. $(-4x + 9) \div (y + 2)$ 3
13. **ERROR ANALYSIS** A student evaluated the expression $7 + (-4)^3$ on a graphing calculator by pressing 7 [+] [(] [−] 4 [)] [^] 3 [ENTER]. The calculator displayed an error message. *Describe* and correct the error. The student used the minus sign instead of the negative symbol for −4; see margin for art.

13. 7 [+] [(] [(-)] 4 [)] [^] 3 [ENTER]

1 PLAN AND PREPARE

Learn the Method

- Students will learn how to use calculators to evaluate numerical expressions, giving them an alternative to evaluating expressions by hand using the order of operations in Lesson 1.2.

Keystroke Help

Keystrokes for several models of calculators are available in blackline format in the *Chapter 1 Resource Book*.

2 TEACH

Tips for Success

Students may have trouble knowing when to use parentheses when entering an expression into their calculators. Point out that when evaluating an expression that involves a fraction, parentheses are necessary around any numerator or denominator containing more than one term.

Alternative Strategy

Instead of showing students the keystrokes, let them experiment with their calculators to see what sequence of keystrokes will give the same answer that they obtain by evaluating an expression by hand.

Extra Example

Use a calculator to evaluate the expression.

a. $-2^6 + 5 \cdot 9$ −19
b. $(-2)^6 + 5 \cdot 9$ 109
c. $(144 \div 9)^2$ 256
d. $\frac{75 - 6 \cdot 2}{3}$ 21

3 ASSESS AND RETEACH

Use a calculator to evaluate the expression when $a = -6$, $b = -2$, and $c = 3$.

1. $7c - a + 2b^2$ 35
2. $(4 - 3a) \div (8 + c)$ 2
3. $(5b + c)^2 + 9a$ −5

1.3 Solve Linear Equations

MA-HS-5.3.1

Before	You simplified algebraic expressions.
Now	You will solve linear equations.
Why?	So you can solve problems about earnings, as in Example 2.

1 PLAN AND PREPARE

Warm-Up Exercises

Transparency Available

Simplify the expression.

1. $8b - 3(4 - b)$ $11b - 12$
2. $-6(m - 9) + 14m - 20$ $8m + 34$
3. You bought a pair of jeans for n dollars in a city where the sales tax rate is 5%. Write an expression for the total cost of the jeans, including sales tax. $n + 0.05n$, or $1.05n$

Notetaking Guide

Transparency Available

Promotes interactive learning and notetaking skills, pp. 7–9.

Pacing

Basic: 1 day
Average: 1 day
Advanced: 1 day
Block: 0.5 block with 1.4
• See *Teaching Guide/Lesson Plan.*

2 FOCUS AND MOTIVATE

Essential Question

Big Idea 3, p. 1

What are the steps for solving linear equations? Tell students they will learn how to answer this question by learning how to transform a linear equation into an equivalent equation.

Key Vocabulary
- equation
- linear equation
- solution
- equivalent equations

An **equation** is a statement that two expressions are equal. A **linear equation** in one variable is an equation that can be written in the form $ax + b = 0$ where a and b are constants and $a \neq 0$.

A number is a **solution** of an equation in one variable if substituting the number for the variable results in a true statement. Two equations are **equivalent equations** if they have the same solution(s).

MA-HS-5.3.1 Students will model, solve and graph first degree, single variable equations and inequalities, including absolute value, based in real-world and mathematical problems and graph the solutions on a number line. DOK 2

KEY CONCEPT — *For Your Notebook*

Transformations That Produce Equivalent Equations

Addition Property of Equality	*Add* the same number to each side.	If $a = b$, then $a + c = b + c$.
Subtraction Property of Equality	*Subtract* the same number from each side.	If $a = b$, then $a - c = b - c$.
Multiplication Property of Equality	*Multiply* each side by the same nonzero number.	If $a = b$ and $c \neq 0$, then $a \cdot c = b \cdot c$.
Division Property of Equality	*Divide* each side by the same nonzero number.	If $a = b$ and $c \neq 0$, then $a \div c = b \div c$.

EXAMPLE 1 Solve an equation with a variable on one side

ANOTHER WAY
You can also solve the equation in Example 1 by multiplying each side by 5 first.

$$5\left(\frac{4}{5}x + 8\right) = 5(20)$$
$$4x + 40 = 100$$
$$4x = 60$$
$$x = 15$$

Solve $\frac{4}{5}x + 8 = 20$.

$\frac{4}{5}x + 8 = 20$	**Write original equation.**
$\frac{4}{5}x = 12$	**Subtract 8 from each side.**
$x = \frac{5}{4}(12)$	**Multiply each side by $\frac{5}{4}$, the reciprocal of $\frac{4}{5}$.**
$x = 15$	**Simplify.**

▶ The solution is 15.

CHECK Check $x = 15$ in the original equation.

$$\frac{4}{5}x + 8 = \frac{4}{5}(15) + 8 = 12 + 8 = 20 \checkmark$$

Resource Planning Guide

Chapter Resource Book
- Teaching Guide/Lesson Plan (pp. 25–26)
- Practice levels A, B, C (pp. 27–30)
- Study Guide (pp. 31–32)
- Catch-up for Absent Students (p. 33)
- Problem Solving Workshop (p. 34)
- Challenge (p. 35)

Workbooks
- Notetaking Guide (pp. 7–9)
- Practice Workbook (pp. 5–6)

Teaching Options
- **Power Presentations CD-ROM** provides dynamic electronic teaching resources for the classroom.
- **Activity Generator CD-ROM** provides editable activities for all ability levels.

Interactive Technology
- Easy Planner
- Power Presentations CD-ROM
- Activity Generator CD-ROM
- Animated Algebra
- Test Generator CD-ROM
- Online Quiz
- eWorkbook
- eEdition
- @HomeTutor

Resources for English Learners
- Quick Reference for English Learners
- Spanish Study Guide
- Multi-Language Visual Glossary
- Student Resources in Spanish

See also the *Algebra 2 Toolkit* for more strategies for meeting individual needs.

EXAMPLE 2 Write and use a linear equation

RESTAURANT During one shift, a waiter earns wages of \$30 and gets an additional 15% in tips on customers' food bills. The waiter earns \$105. What is the total of the customers' food bills?

Solution

Write a verbal model. Then write an equation. Write 15% as a decimal.

Income (dollars)	=	Wages (dollars)	+	Percent for tips	·	Food bills (dollars)
105	=	**30**	+	**0.15**	·	x

$105 = 30 + 0.15x$ **Write equation.**

$75 = 0.15x$ **Subtract 30 from each side.**

$500 = x$ **Divide each side by 0.15.**

▸ The total of the customers' food bills is \$500.

GUIDED PRACTICE for Examples 1 and 2

Solve the equation. Check your solution.

1. $4x + 9 = 21$ 3
2. $7x - 41 = -13$ 4
3. $-\frac{3}{5}x + 1 = 4$ −5
4. **REAL ESTATE** A real estate agent's base salary is \$22,000 per year. The agent earns a 4% commission on total sales. How much must the agent sell to earn \$60,000 in one year? \$950,000

EXAMPLE 3 Standardized Test Practice

What is the solution of $7p + 13 = 9p - 5$?

Ⓐ −9 Ⓑ −4 Ⓒ 4 Ⓓ 9

Solution

$7p + 13 = 9p - 5$ **Write original equation.**

$13 = 2p - 5$ **Subtract $7p$ from each side.**

$18 = 2p$ **Add 5 to each side.**

$9 = p$ **Divide each side by 2.**

▸ The correct answer is D. Ⓐ Ⓑ Ⓒ Ⓓ

CHECK $7p + 13 = 9p - 5$ **Write original equation.**

$7(9) + 13 \stackrel{?}{=} 9(9) - 5$ **Substitute 9 for p.**

$63 + 13 \stackrel{?}{=} 81 - 5$ **Multiply.**

$76 = 76$ ✓ **Solution checks.**

Motivating the Lesson

Many salespeople are paid a combination of an hourly rate and a commission that depends on the total value of the merchandise they sell. As a salesperson, you can use linear equations to determine the value of the merchandise you must sell in order to meet your earnings goal.

3 TEACH

Extra Example 1

Solve $\frac{2}{3}x - 7 = 5$. 18

Extra Example 2

Your total cost for a book, including 6% sales tax, is \$23.32. What was the price of the book before the sales tax was added? \$22.00

Key Question to Ask for Example 2

- When setting up the equation for Example 2, how do you decide what the variable should represent? **The variable x should represent the total of the customers' food bills since this is what the problem asks you to determine.**

Extra Example 3

What is the solution of $8y - 16 = 13y + 9$? A

Ⓐ −5 Ⓑ $-\frac{7}{5}$

Ⓒ $-\frac{25}{21}$ Ⓓ 5

Differentiated Instruction

Advanced When discussing the properties of equality in the **Key Concept** box on page 18, ask advanced students to explain to their classmates why the restriction $c \neq 0$ is necessary in both the multiplication and division properties of equality, but not in the addition and subtraction properties.

See also the *Algebra 2 Toolkit* for more strategies.

Extra Example 4

Solve $4(2x - 9) + 5x = -3(10 - x)$. $\frac{3}{5}$

Extra Example 5

It takes you 45 minutes to mow your lawn and it takes your brother 30 minutes to mow the lawn. How long does it take you to mow the lawn if you have two mowers and work together? **18 min**

An **Animated Algebra** activity is available on-line for **Example 5**. This activity is also available on the **Power Presentations CD-ROM**.

Closing the Lesson

Have students summarize the major points of the lesson and answer the Essential Question: What are the steps for solving linear equations?

- **You can transform an equation into an equivalent one by using the properties of equality.**
- **You can solve many real-world problems by first writing verbal models, and then writing and solving linear equations.**

If the equation involves an expression in parentheses, remove the parenthese by using the distributive property. Then use the properties of equality to obtain equivalent equations in a series of steps until you obtain an equation of the form $x = a$.

EXAMPLE 4 Solve an equation using the distributive property

Solve $3(5x - 8) = -2(-x + 7) - 12x$.

$3(5x - 8) = -2(-x + 7) - 12x$	**Write original equation.**
$15x - 24 = 2x - 14 - 12x$	**Distributive property**
$15x - 24 = -10x - 14$	**Combine like terms.**
$25x - 24 = -14$	**Add $10x$ to each side.**
$25x = 10$	**Add 24 to each side.**
$x = \frac{2}{5}$	**Divide each side by 25 and simplify.**

▶ The solution is $\frac{2}{5}$.

CHECK

$3\left(5 \cdot \frac{2}{5} - 8\right) \stackrel{?}{=} -2\left(-\frac{2}{5} + 7\right) - 12 \cdot \frac{2}{5}$	**Substitute $\frac{2}{5}$ for x.**
$3(-6) \stackrel{?}{=} \frac{4}{5} - 14 - \frac{24}{5}$	**Simplify.**
$-18 = -18$ ✓	**Solution checks.**

EXAMPLE 5 Solve a work problem

CAR WASH It takes you 8 minutes to wash a car and it takes a friend 6 minutes to wash a car. How long does it take the two of you to wash 7 cars if you work together?

Solution

STEP 1 **Write** a verbal model. Then write an equation.

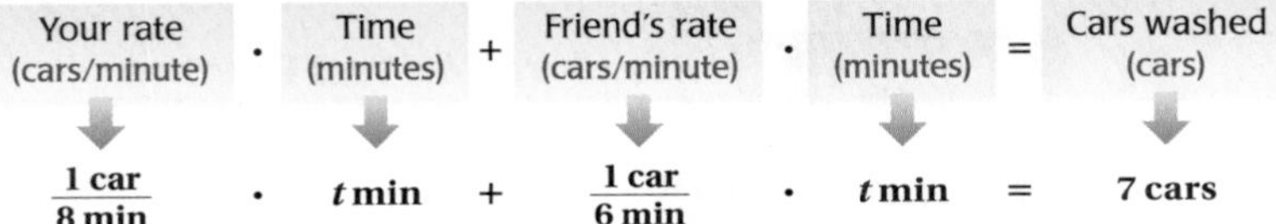

Your rate (cars/minute)
·
Time (minutes)
+
Friend's rate (cars/minute)
·
Time (minutes)
=
Cars washed (cars)

$\frac{1 \text{ car}}{8 \text{ min}} \cdot t \text{ min} + \frac{1 \text{ car}}{6 \text{ min}} \cdot t \text{ min} = 7 \text{ cars}$

STEP 2 **Solve** the equation for t.

$\frac{1}{8}t + \frac{1}{6}t = 7$	**Write equation.**
$24\left(\frac{1}{8}t + \frac{1}{6}t\right) = 24(7)$	**Multiply each side by the LCD, 24.**
$3t + 4t = 168$	**Distributive property**
$7t = 168$	**Combine like terms.**
$t = 24$	**Divide each side by 7.**

AVOID ERRORS
Be sure to multiply *both* sides of the equation by the LCD, not just one side.

▶ It will take 24 minutes to wash 7 cars if you work together.

CHECK You wash $\frac{1}{8} \cdot 24 = 3$ cars and your friend washes $\frac{1}{6} \cdot 24 = 4$ cars in 24 minutes. Together, you wash 7 cars. ✓

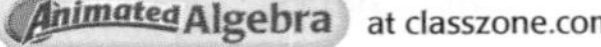

at classzone.com

Differentiated Instruction

Visual Learners Parallel structure often reinforces learning. For instance, some students may find it easier to construct the verbal model in **Example 5** as follows.

Your rate	+	Friend's rate	=	Total rate
$\frac{1 \text{ car}}{8 \text{ min}}$	+	$\frac{1 \text{ car}}{6 \text{ min}}$	=	$\frac{7 \text{ cars}}{t \text{ min}}$

See also the *Algebra 2 Toolkit* for more strategies.

✓ GUIDED PRACTICE for Examples 3, 4, and 5

Solve the equation. Check your solution.

5. $-2x + 9 = 2x - 7$ 4
6. $10 - x = -6x + 15$ 1
7. $3(x + 2) = 5(x + 4)$ −7
8. $-4(2x + 5) = 2(-x - 9) - 4x$ −1
9. $\frac{1}{4}x + \frac{2}{5}x = 39$ 60
10. $\frac{2}{3}x + \frac{5}{6} = x - \frac{1}{2}$ 4
11. **WHAT IF?** In Example 5, suppose it takes you 9 minutes to wash a car and it takes your friend 12 minutes to wash a car. How long does it take the two of you to wash 7 cars if you work together? 36 min

1.3 EXERCISES

HOMEWORK KEY

○ = **WORKED-OUT SOLUTIONS** on p. WS1 for Exs. 23, 43, and 71

★ = **STANDARDIZED TEST PRACTICE** Exs. 2, 19, 32, 72, and 77

◆ = **MULTIPLE REPRESENTATIONS** Ex. 74

SKILL PRACTICE

A

1. **VOCABULARY** Copy and complete: If a number is substituted for a variable in an equation and the resulting statement is true, the number is called a(n) _?_ of the equation. solution

2. ★ **WRITING** Give an example of two equivalent equations. How do you know they are equivalent? *Sample answer:* $3x - 7 = 11$ and $3x = 18$; they have the same solution.

EXAMPLE 1 on p. 18 for Exs. 3–19

VARIABLE ON ONE SIDE Solve the equation. Check your solution.

3. $x + 8 = 11$ 3
4. $y - 4 = 7$ 11
5. $z - 13 = -1$ 12
6. $-3 = w + 5$ −8
7. $5d = 30$ 6
8. $4 = \frac{2}{5}g$ 10
9. $\frac{9}{2}h = -1$ $-\frac{2}{9}$
10. $-16k = -8$ 0.5
11. $6m - 3 = 21$ 4
12. $4n - 10 = 12$ 5.5
13. $3 = 2p + 5$ −1
14. $-3q + 4 = 13$ −3
15. $1 = \frac{1}{3}a - 5$ 18
16. $\frac{3}{11}b + 5 = 5$ 0
17. $7 - \frac{5}{3}c = 22$ −9
18. $3 + \frac{8}{7}d = -1$ $-3\frac{1}{2}$
19. ★ **MULTIPLE CHOICE** What is the solution of $4x - 7 = -15$? B

Ⓐ −12 Ⓑ −2 Ⓒ 2 Ⓓ $\frac{11}{2}$

EXAMPLE 3 on p. 19 for Exs. 20–32

VARIABLE ON BOTH SIDES Solve the equation. Check your solution.

20. $3a + 4 = 2a + 15$ 11
21. $5w + 2 = 2w + 5$ 1
22. $6x + 7 = 2x + 59$ 13
23. $5b - 4 = 2b + 8$ 4
24. $3y + 7 = y - 3$ −5
25. $2z - 3 = 6z + 25$ −7
26. $4n - 7 = 5 - 2n$ 2
27. $2c + 14 = 6 - 4c$ $-1\frac{1}{3}$
28. $5m - 2 = -m - 2$ 0
29. $p + 5 = 25 - 4p$ 4
30. $6 - 5q = q + 9$ $-\frac{1}{2}$
31. $17 - 6r = 25 - 3r$ $-2\frac{2}{3}$
32. ★ **MULTIPLE CHOICE** What is the solution of $7t - 5 = 3t + 11$? D

Ⓐ $-\frac{3}{2}$ Ⓑ $\frac{3}{2}$ Ⓒ $\frac{8}{5}$ Ⓓ 4

4 PRACTICE AND APPLY

Assignment Guide

Answer Transparencies available for all exercises

Basic:
Day 1: SRH p. 976 Exs. 16–20
pp. 21–24
Exs. 1–10, 19–25, 32–36, 41–46, 68–73, 79

Average:
Day 1: pp. 21–24
Exs. 1, 2, 11–19 odd, 26–32 even, 37–42, 43–65 odd, 68–77, 80

Advanced:
Day 1: pp. 21–24
Exs. 1, 2, 12–18 even, 19, 27–31 odd, 32, 38–42, 48–62 even, 63–67*, 70–78*

Block:
pp. 21–24
Exs. 1, 2, 11–19 odd, 26–32 even, 37–42, 43–65 odd, 68–77, 80 (with 1.4)

Differentiated Instruction

See *Algebra 2 Best Practices Toolkit* for suggestions on addressing the needs of a diverse classroom.

Homework Check

For a quick check of student understanding of key concepts, go over the following exercises:

Basic: 6, 22, 34, 44, 68
Average: 15, 28, 38, 45, 70
Advanced: 16, 29, 40, 48, 71

Extra Practice

- Student Edition, p. 1010
- Chapter 1 Resource Book: Practice levels A, B, C, pp. 27–30

Practice Worksheet

An easily-readable reduced practice page (with answers) for this lesson can be found on p. 1C.

Avoiding Common Errors

Exercises 43–46 Because the right side of each of these equations does not contain fractions, some students forget that they must multiply *both* sides of the equation by the least common denominator. To avoid this error, have students carefully reread the multiplication property of equality.

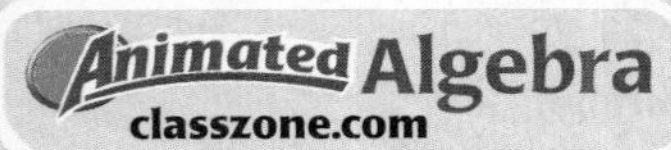

An **Animated Algebra** activity is available on-line for **Exercises 43–50**. This activity is also available on the **Power Presentations CD-ROM**.

Teaching Strategy

Exercises 55–62 Show students that equations involving decimals can be solved either by working with the decimals all the way through (as in Example 2) or by "clearing the decimals" in the first step by multiplying by the appropriate power of 10 needed to transform all the numerical values in the equation into integers. Have students try to solve a few of these equations by both methods so they can see which method they prefer.

EXAMPLE 4 on p. 20 for Exs. 33–40

THE DISTRIBUTIVE PROPERTY Solve the equation. Check your solution.

33. $2(b + 3) = 4b - 2$ **4**

34. $5d + 17 = 4(d + 3)$ **−5**

35. $3(m - 5) = 6(m + 1)$ **−7**

36. $-4(n + 2) = 3(n - 4)$ $\mathbf{\frac{4}{7}}$

37. $12(r + 3) = 2(r + 5) - 3r$ **−2**

38. $7(t - 3) = 2(t - 9) + 2t$ **1**

39. $10(w - 4) = 4(w + 4) + 4w$ **28**

40. $3(2x - 5) - x = -7(x + 3)$ $\mathbf{-\frac{1}{2}}$

ERROR ANALYSIS *Describe* and correct the error in solving the equation.

41.

$\frac{3}{7}x + 2 = 17$

$\frac{3}{7}x = 15$

$x = 15 - \frac{3}{7}$

$x = 14\frac{4}{7}$

42.

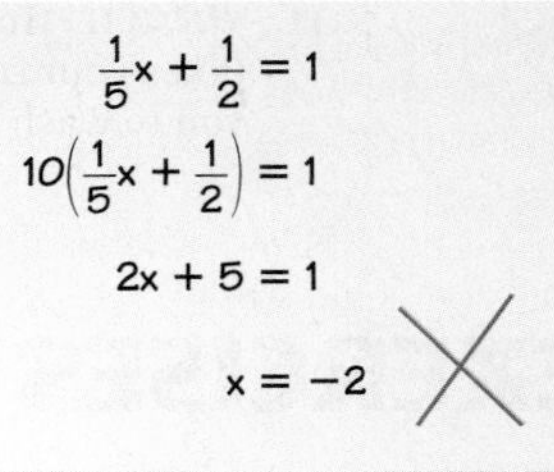

41. Both sides of the equations should be divided by $\frac{3}{7}$ instead of subtracting $\frac{3}{7}$ from the right side; $\frac{3}{7}x = 15$, $x = 15 \div \frac{3}{7}$, $x = 35$.

42. Both sides of the equation should be multiplied by 10; $10\left(\frac{1}{5}x + \frac{1}{2}\right) = 10 \cdot 1$; $2x + 5 = 10$; $2x = 5$; $x = 2\frac{1}{2}$.

EXAMPLE 5 on p. 20 for Exs. 43–50

EQUATIONS WITH FRACTIONS Solve the equation. Check your solution.

(43.) $\frac{1}{2}t + \frac{1}{3}t = 10$ **12**

44. $\frac{1}{5}d + \frac{1}{8}d = 2$ $\mathbf{6\frac{2}{13}}$

45. $\frac{2}{3}m - \frac{3}{5}m = 4$ **60**

46. $\frac{4}{7}z + \frac{2}{3}z = 13$ $\mathbf{10\frac{1}{2}}$

47. $\frac{3}{7}w - \frac{2}{9} = \frac{4}{9}w + \frac{1}{7}$ **−23**

48. $\frac{1}{2}x + 4 = -\frac{2}{3}x + \frac{1}{2}$ **−3**

49. $\frac{2}{5}k + \frac{1}{6} = \frac{3}{10}k + \frac{1}{3}$ $\mathbf{1\frac{2}{3}}$

50. $\frac{2}{3}q - \frac{1}{12} = q + \frac{1}{8}$ $\mathbf{-\frac{5}{8}}$

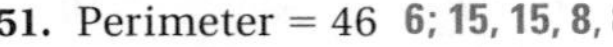

at classzone.com

B

GEOMETRY Solve for x. Then find the length of each side of the figure.

51. Perimeter = 46 **6; 15, 15, 8, 8**

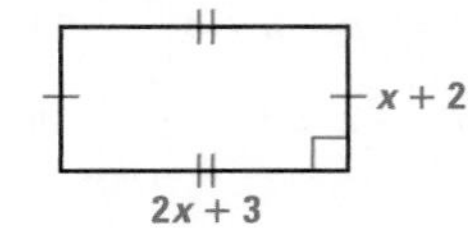

52. Perimeter = 26 **4; 9, 11, 6**

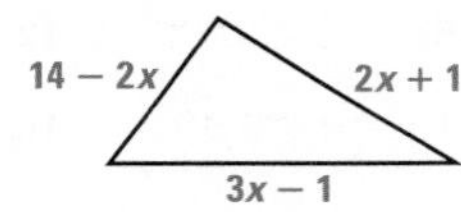

53. Perimeter = 15 **2; 6, 6, 3**

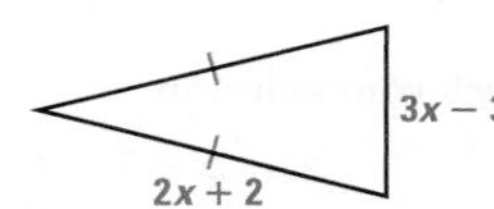

54. Perimeter = 26 **5; 8, 8, 5, 5**

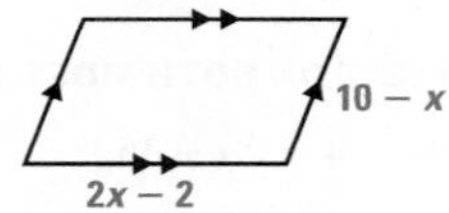

EQUATIONS WITH DECIMALS Solve the equation. Check your solution.

55. $0.6g + 0.5 = 2.9$ **4**

56. $1.1h + 1.3 = 6.8$ **5**

57. $0.4k - 0.6 = 1.3k + 1.2$ **−2**

58. $6.5m + 1.5 = 4.3m - 0.7$ **−1**

59. $3.8w + 3.2 = 2.3(w + 4)$ **4**

60. $1.7(x + 5) = 2.1x + 9.7$ **−3**

61. $2.25b + 3.81 = 1.75b + 5.26$ **2.9**

62. $18.13 - 5.18c = 6.32c - 8.32$ **2.3**

○ = **WORKED-OUT SOLUTIONS** on p. WS1

★ = **STANDARDIZED TEST PRACTICE**

Differentiated Instruction

Below Level In order to complete **Exercise 54**, some students may need help in remembering that the markings on the figure indicate that opposite sides are parallel (meaning the figure is a parallelogram) and that opposites sides of a parallelogram have the same length. Prepare a transparency that quickly reviews this geometry information.

See also the *Algebra 2 Toolkit* for more strategies.

C **SPECIAL EQUATIONS** **Solve the equation. If there is no solution, write *no solution*. If the equation is always true, write *all real numbers*.**

63. $5(x - 4) = 5x + 12$ **no solution**

64. $3(x + 5) = 3x + 15$ **all real numbers**

65. $5(2 - x) = 3 - 2x + 7 - 3x$ **all real numbers**

66. $-2(4 - 3x) + 7 = 6(x + 1)$ **no solution**

67. CHALLENGE Solve the equation $ax + b = cx + d$ for x in terms of a, b, c, and d. Under what conditions is there no solution? Under what conditions are all real numbers solutions? $x = \frac{d - b}{a - c}$; $a = c$ and $b \neq d$; $a = c$ and $b = d$

PROBLEM SOLVING

EXAMPLE 2 on p. 19 for Exs. 68–71

A **68. CATALOG PURCHASE** You are ordering T-shirts from a catalog. Each T-shirt costs \$15. The cost of shipping is \$6 no matter how many you order. The total cost is \$111. How many T-shirts did you order? **7 T-shirts**

@HomeTutor for problem solving help at classzone.com

69. BICYCLE REPAIR The bill for the repair of your bicycle was \$180. The cost of parts was \$105. The cost of labor was \$25 per hour. How many hours did the repair work take? **3 h**

@HomeTutor for problem solving help at classzone.com

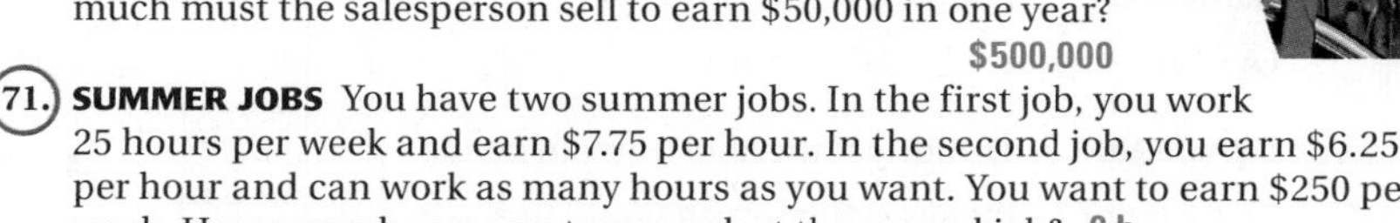

70. CAR SALES A salesperson at a car dealership has a base salary of \$25,000 per year and earns a 5% commission on total sales. How much must the salesperson sell to earn \$50,000 in one year? **\$500,000**

71. SUMMER JOBS You have two summer jobs. In the first job, you work 25 hours per week and earn \$7.75 per hour. In the second job, you earn \$6.25 per hour and can work as many hours as you want. You want to earn \$250 per week. How many hours must you work at the second job? **9 h**

72. ★ SHORT RESPONSE Your friend bought a total of 10 CDs and DVDs as gifts for \$199. The price per CD was \$15 and the price per DVD was \$22. Write and solve an equation to find how many CDs and how many DVDs your friend bought. How would your answer change if the total cost of the CDs and DVDs was \$185? *Explain.*

72. $15c + 22(10 - c) = 199$; 3 CDs and 7 DVDs; you would be able to buy 5 CDs and 5 DVDs, solve $15c + 22(10 - c) = 185$.

B **73. MULTI-STEP PROBLEM** You are working on the layout of a yearbook. The page is 9 inches wide, has $\frac{1}{2}$ inch margins, and has three columns of equal width.

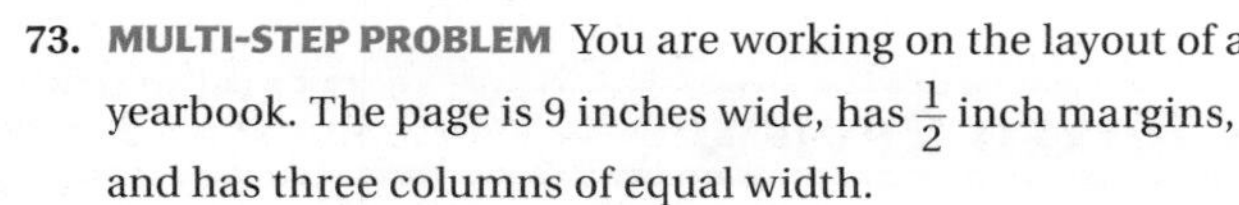

a. Write and simplify an equation that relates the column width c and the gap g between columns to the total width of the page. $3c + 2g = 8$

b. Copy and complete the table by substituting the given value into your equation from part (a) and solving to find the unknown value.

Gap, g (in.)	$\frac{5}{8}$	? $\frac{1}{2}$	$\frac{3}{8}$	? $\frac{1}{4}$
Column width, c (in.)	? $2\frac{1}{4}$	$2\frac{1}{3}$	? $2\frac{5}{12}$	$2\frac{1}{2}$

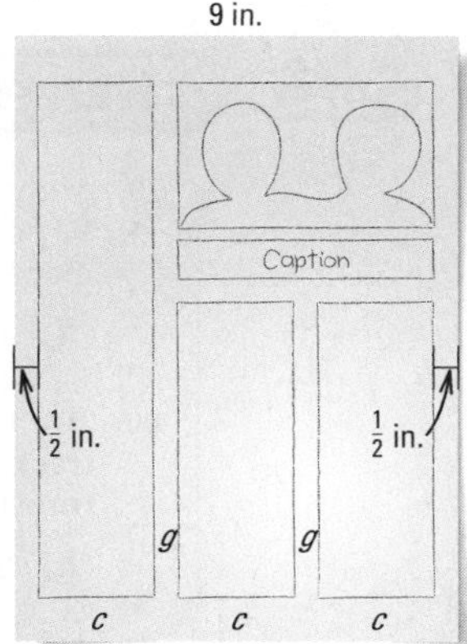

Study Strategy

Exercise 72 If students are having trouble organizing the information given in the problem, guide them in setting up a table. Suggest using Number, Price of Each Item, and Total Price as the column headings. For the row headings, use CDs and DVDs. Then show the students how they can use information from the table and the verbal model Cost of CDs + Cost of DVDs = Total Cost to write an equation that can be used to solve the problem.

5 ASSESS AND RETEACH

Daily Homework Quiz

Transparency Available

Solve the equation.

1. $9 - \frac{4}{5}x = -23$ 40
2. $-8t + 12 = 4t + 48$ −3
3. $6(2x - 4) = 3(-x + 7) + 9x$ 7.5
4. You can type 7 pages in 2 hours, and your classmate can type 8 pages in 3 hours. If you have two computers and can work at the same time, how long will it take the two of you to type 37 pages? 6 h

Available at **classzone.com**

Diagnosis/Remediation

- Practice A, B, C in Chapter 1 Resource Book, pp. 27–30
- Study Guide in Chapter 1 Resource Book, pp. 31–32
- Practice Workbook, pp. 5–6
- @HomeTutor

Challenge

Additional challenge is available in the Chapter 1 Resource Book, p. 35.

74b.

x	Perimeter (in.) $18x + 8$
1.5	35
2	44
2.5	53
3	62
3.5	71

The perimeter is 53 inches when $x = 2.5$.

74. **MULTIPLE REPRESENTATIONS** You want to enlarge a 4 inch by 5 inch photo to fit into a 1 inch wide frame that has an outer perimeter of 53 inches.

a. **Using a Diagram** Write an expression for the outer perimeter of the picture frame. $18x + 8$

b. **Making a Table** Evaluate the perimeter expression when $x = 1.5, 2, 2.5, 3,$ and 3.5. Make a table of your results. For what value of x is the perimeter 53 inches? See margin.

c. **Using an Equation** Write and solve an equation to find x. *Explain* what the value of x tells you about how much you should enlarge the original photo. $18x + 8 = 53$, $x = 2.5$; the photo should be enlarged 2.5 times.

EXAMPLE 5 on p. 20 for Exs. 75–77

75. **RAKING LEAVES** It takes you 30 minutes to rake the leaves in your yard and it takes your brother 45 minutes. How long does it take the two of you to rake the leaves when working together? 18 min

76. **MURAL PAINTING** You paint 2 square yards of a community mural in 3 hours and a friend paints 4 square yards in 5 hours. How long does it take the two of you to paint 11 square yards when working together? 7.5 h

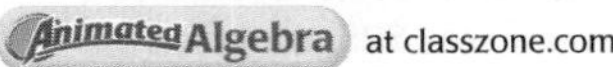

77. ★ **MULTIPLE CHOICE** Three students use calligraphy pens to write the names of graduating seniors on their diplomas. One writes 7 names in 6 minutes, another writes 17 names in 10 minutes, and the third writes 23 names in 15 minutes. How long, to the nearest minute, will the students take to write names on 440 diplomas if they work together? B

(A) 97 minutes (B) 100 minutes (C) 103 minutes (D) 290 minutes

C **78.** **CHALLENGE** A cylindrical thermos with an inside diameter of $2\frac{1}{2}$ inches is filled with liquid to a height of 9 inches. If the liquid is poured into a cylindrical travel mug with an inside diameter of $3\frac{1}{2}$ inches, what will be the height h of the liquid? about 4.6 in.

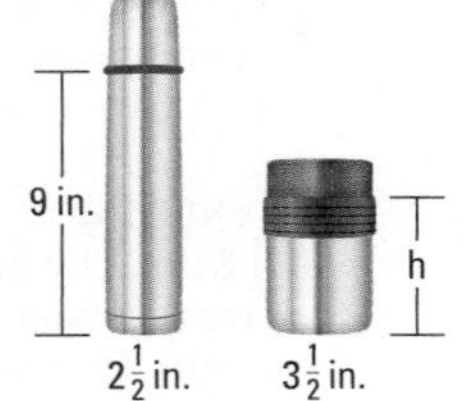

KENTUCKY MIXED REVIEW

79. Andy is saving money for a digital music player that costs \$350. He makes \$7 per hour as a lifeguard. How many hours must he work to earn enough money to buy the digital music player if he uses a coupon for 20% off? C

(A) 10 h (B) 25 h (C) 40 h (D) 43 h

80. Two runners are running at constant speeds in the same direction around a track. The faster runner travels 8 miles per hour and completes 4 laps each time the slower runner completes 3 laps. What is the slower runner's speed? C

(A) 2 mph (B) 4 mph (C) 6 mph (D) 7 mph

@HomeTutor
classzone.com
Keystrokes

1.3 Use Tables to Solve Equations

QUESTION How can you use tables to solve linear equations?

You can use the *table* feature of a graphing calculator to solve linear equations.

EXAMPLE Solve a linear equation

Use the *table* feature of a graphing calculator to solve the equation $3x + 8 = 9x - 16$.

STEP 1 *Enter expressions*

Press [Y=]. Enter the left side of the equation as $y_1 = 3x + 8$. Enter the right side of the equation as $y_2 = 9x - 16$.

STEP 2 *Make a table*

Press [2nd] [TBLSET]. Set the starting x-value TblStart to 0 and the step value ΔTbl (the value by which the x-values increase) to 1.

STEP 3 *Identify solution*

Press [2nd] [TABLE] to display the table. Scroll through the table until you find an x-value for which both sides of the equation have the same value.

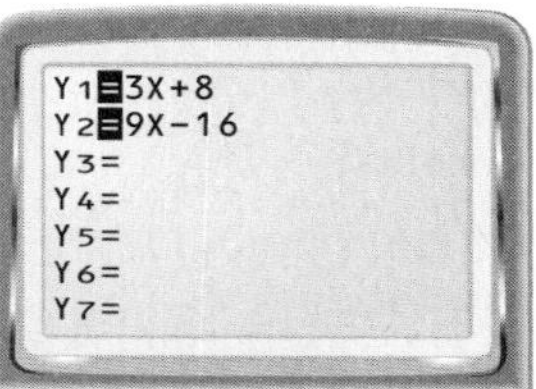

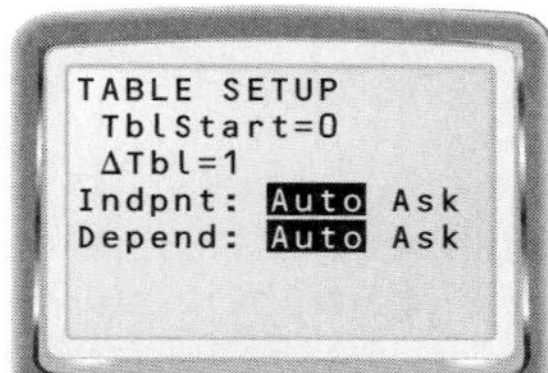

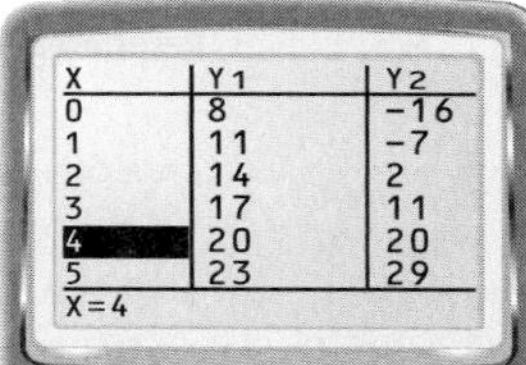

Both sides of the equation have a value of 20 when $x = 4$. So, the solution of $3x + 8 = 9x - 16$ is 4.

PRACTICE

Use the *table* feature of a graphing calculator to solve the equation.

1. $7x - 3 = -x + 13$ 2
2. $-6x + 8 = 12 - 5x$ -4
3. $-2x - 13 = -3x - 5$ 8
4. $22 + 15x = -9x - 2$ -1
5. $4x + 27 = -8 + 11x$ 5
6. $7 - 8x = -9 - 10x$ -8
7. **REASONING** Consider the equation $4x + 18 = 9x - 9$.
   a. Attempt to solve the equation using the *table* feature of a graphing calculator with step value ΔTbl = 1. Between what two integers does the solution lie? How do you know? See margin.
   b. Use a smaller value of ΔTbl to find the exact solution. 5.4
8. **WRITING** Solve the equation $3x + 8 = 9x - 16$ by writing it in the form $ax + b = 0$, entering $y_1 = ax + b$ on a graphing calculator, and using a table to find the x-value for which $y_1 = 0$. What are the advantages and disadvantages of this method compared to the method shown above? See margin.

1 PLAN AND PREPARE

Learn the Method

- Students will learn how to use the *table* feature of a graphing calculator to solve linear equations. This will provide an alternate method for solving the various types of linear equations that students solved in Lesson 1.3.

Keystroke Help

Keystrokes for several models of calculators are available in blackline format in the *Chapter 1 Resource Book*.

2 TEACH

Tips for Success

Students may have trouble finding a solution because they are not looking in the right range on the table for the x-value. Make sure they understand that they should try to find a portion of the table where the two y-values are getting closer and closer together. Also, make sure they understand that they can scroll up from the TblStart value to look at smaller values of x.

Extra Example

Use the *table* feature of a graphing calculator to solve the equation $7x - 18 = 13x + 18$. -6

3 ASSESS AND RETEACH

What type of solution is easiest to find by using the *table* feature of a graphing calculator? an integer solution

7a. 5 and 6; at $x = 5$ the left side of the equation has a greater output and at $x = 6$ the right side of the equation has a greater output. So, somewhere between 5 and 6 the two outputs must be equal.

8. 4. *Sample answer:* An advantage of rewriting the equation is that it is easier to locate the 0 in the table rather than compare the two numbers. A disadvantage is that the equation has to be rewritten.

1 PLAN AND PREPARE

Warm-Up Exercises

Transparency Available

1. Evaluate $\frac{45 - 3(9)}{4}$. $\frac{9}{2}$ or 4.5
2. Evaluate $\frac{x + y}{x - 2y}$ when $x = 3$ and $y = 5$. $-\frac{8}{7}$
3. Use the distributive property to rewrite $xy - 5y$ as a product. $y(x - 5)$

Notetaking Guide

Transparency Available

Promotes interactive learning and notetaking skills, pp. 10–12.

Pacing

Basic: 2 days
Average: 2 days
Advanced: 2 days
Block: 0.5 block with 1.3
0.5 block with 1.5

- See *Teaching Guide/Lesson Plan.*

2 FOCUS AND MOTIVATE

Essential Question

Big Idea 3, p. 1

What are formulas, and how are they used? **Tell students they will learn how to answer this question by using formulas to solve real-world problems.**

1.4 Rewrite Formulas and Equations

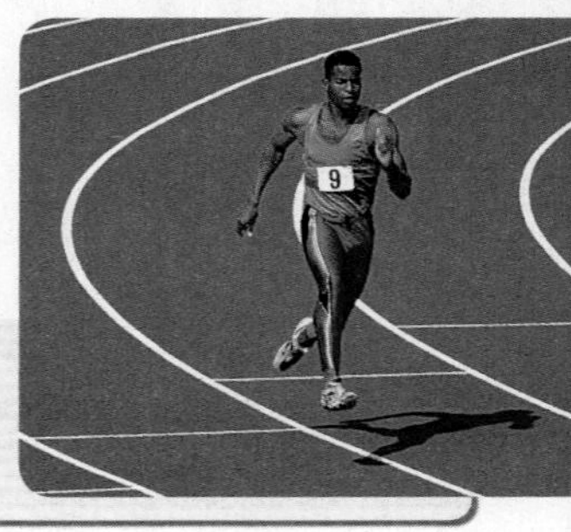

MA-HS-5.3.2 *Students will solve for a specified variable in a multivariable equation.*

Before You solved equations.
Now You will rewrite and evaluate formulas and equations.
Why? So you can apply geometric formulas, as in Ex. 36.

Key Vocabulary
- **formula**
- **solve for a variable**

A **formula** is an equation that relates two or more quantities, usually represented by variables. Some common formulas are shown below.

Quantity	Formula	Meaning of variables
Distance	$d = rt$	d = distance, r = rate, t = time
Temperature	$F = \frac{9}{5}C + 32$	F = degrees Fahrenheit, C = degrees Celsius
Area of a triangle	$A = \frac{1}{2}bh$	A = area, b = base, h = height
Area of a rectangle	$A = \ell w$	A = area, ℓ = length, w = width
Perimeter of a rectangle	$P = 2\ell + 2w$	P = perimeter, ℓ = length, w = width
Area of a trapezoid	$A = \frac{1}{2}(b_1 + b_2)h$	A = area, b_1 = one base, b_2 = other base, h = height
Area of a circle	$A = \pi r^2$	A = area, r = radius
Circumference of a circle	$C = 2\pi r$	C = circumference, r = radius

READING
The variables b_1 and b_2 are read as "b sub one" and "b sub two." The small lowered numbers are called *subscripts.*

To **solve for a variable** means to rewrite an equation as an equivalent equation in which the variable is on one side and does not appear on the other side.

EXAMPLE 1 Rewrite a formula with two variables

Solve the formula $C = 2\pi r$ for r. Then find the radius of a circle with a circumference of 44 inches.

Solution

STEP 1 **Solve** the formula for r.

$C = 2\pi r$ **Write circumference formula.**

$\frac{C}{2\pi} = r$ **Divide each side by 2π.**

STEP 2 **Substitute** the given value into the rewritten formula.

$r = \frac{C}{2\pi} = \frac{44}{2\pi} \approx 7$ **Substitute 44 for C and simplify.**

▸ The radius of the circle is about 7 inches.

Resource Planning Guide

Chapter Resource Book
- Teaching Guide/Lesson Plan (pp. 36–37)
- Activity Master (p. 38)
- Practice levels A, B, C (pp. 41–43)
- Study Guide (pp. 44–45)
- Catch-up for Absent Students (p. 46)
- Problem Solving Workshop (p. 47)
- Challenge (p. 49)

Workbooks
- Notetaking Guide (pp. 10–12)
- Practice Workbook (pp. 7–8)

Teaching Options
- **Power Presentations CD-ROM** provides dynamic electronic teaching resources for the classroom.
- **Activity Generator CD-ROM** provides editable activities for all ability levels.

Interactive Technology
- Easy Planner
- Power Presentations CD-ROM
- Activity Generator CD-ROM
- Animated Algebra
- Test Generator CD-ROM
- Online Quiz
- eWorkbook
- eEdition
- @HomeTutor

Resources for English Learners
- Quick Reference for English Learners
- Spanish Study Guide
- Multi-Language Visual Glossary
- Student Resources in Spanish

See also the *Algebra 2 Toolkit* for more strategies for meeting individual needs.

GUIDED PRACTICE for Example 1

1. Find the radius of a circle with a circumference of 25 feet. **about 4 ft**
2. The formula for the distance d between opposite vertices of a regular hexagon is $d = \frac{2a}{\sqrt{3}}$ where a is the distance between opposite sides. Solve the formula for a. Then find a when $d = 10$ centimeters. $a = \frac{d\sqrt{3}}{2}$; $5\sqrt{3}$

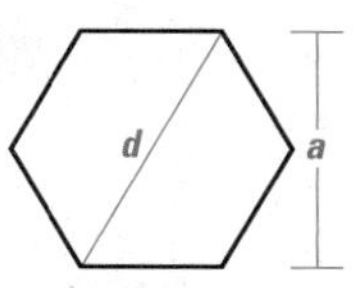

EXAMPLE 2 Rewrite a formula with three variables

Solve the formula $P = 2\ell + 2w$ for w. Then find the width of a rectangle with a length of 12 meters and a perimeter of 41 meters.

P = 41 m   w

12 m

Solution

STEP 1 **Solve** the formula for w.

$P = 2\ell + 2w$ **Write perimeter formula.**

$P - 2\ell = 2w$ **Subtract 2ℓ from each side.**

$\frac{P - 2\ell}{2} = w$ **Divide each side by 2.**

STEP 2 **Substitute** the given values into the rewritten formula.

$w = \frac{41 - 2(12)}{2}$ **Substitute 41 for P and 12 for ℓ.**

$w = 8.5$ **Simplify.**

▶ The width of the rectangle is 8.5 meters.

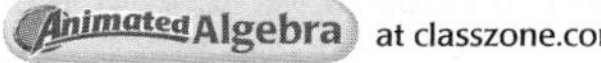 at classzone.com

GUIDED PRACTICE for Example 2

3. Solve the formula $P = 2\ell + 2w$ for ℓ. Then find the length of a rectangle with a width of 7 inches and a perimeter of 30 inches. $\ell = \frac{P - 2w}{2}$; 8 in.
4. Solve the formula $A = \ell w$ for w. Then find the width of a rectangle with a length of 16 meters and an area of 40 square meters. $w = \frac{A}{\ell}$; 2.5 m

Solve the formula for the variable in red. Then use the given information to find the value of the variable.

5. $A = \frac{1}{2}bh$ $h = \frac{2A}{b}$; 14 m

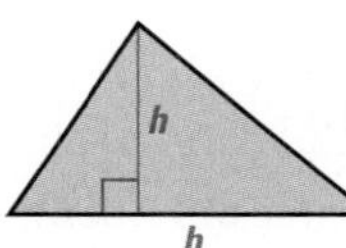

Find h if $b = 12$ m and $A = 84\ m^2$.

6. $A = \frac{1}{2}bh$ $b = \frac{2A}{h}$; 6 cm

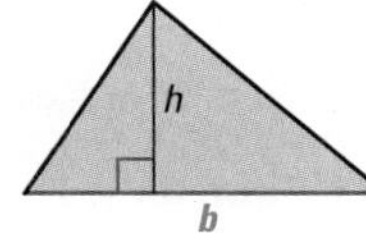

Find b if $h = 3$ cm and $A = 9\ cm^2$.

7. $A = \frac{1}{2}(b_1 + b_2)h$ $h = \frac{2A}{b_1 + b_2}$; 10 in.

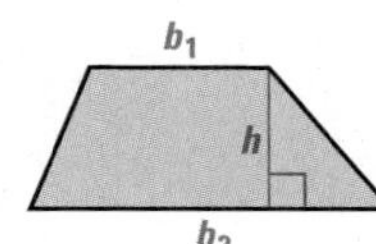

Find h if $b_1 = 6$ in., $b_2 = 8$ in., and $A = 70\ in.^2$

Motivating the Lesson

Ask students to give examples of situations in which they have used formulas in their other classes, especially science classes. Also ask them for examples of formulas they used outside of school.

3 TEACH

Extra Example 1

Solve the formula $d = rt$ for t. Then find the time it takes to travel 312 miles at an average rate of 48 miles per hour. $t = \frac{d}{r}$; 6.5 h

Key Question to Ask for Example 1

- What is the most accurate way to find a numerical answer when working with a formula that involves π? **Use the π key on a calculator.**

Extra Example 2

Solve the formula $A = \frac{1}{2}(b_1 + b_2)h$ for b_2. Then find the length of the other base of a trapezoid if the length of one base is 13 centimeters, the height is 10 centimeters, and the area is 105 square centimeters.

$b_2 = \frac{2A}{h} - b_1$ or $b_2 = \frac{2A - hb_1}{h}$; 8 cm

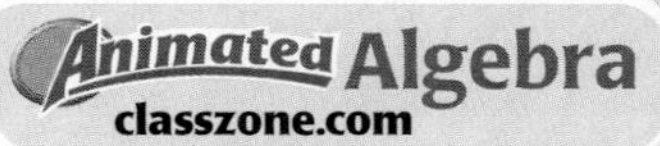

An **Animated Algebra** activity is available on-line for **Example 2**. This activity is also available on the **Power Presentations CD-ROM**.

Differentiated Instruction

Below Level When you are discussing **Example 1**, some students may not remember the significance of the constant π. Demonstrate this concept by wrapping a piece of string around a circle, measuring the length of the string and the diameter of the circle with a ruler, and then asking students to divide the circumference by the diameter. Repeat this process with a second circle of a different size. Make sure that students understand that whenever a decimal value is written for π, it is only an approximation.

See also the *Algebra 2 Toolkit* for more strategies.

Extra Example 3

Solve $5x + 3y = 8$ for y. Then find the value of y when $x = -5$.

$y = \frac{8}{3} - \frac{5}{3}x$ or $y = -\frac{5}{3}x + \frac{8}{3}$; 11

Key Question to Ask for Example 3

- What does it mean to "solve an equation for y?" **It means to rewrite the equation so that y is by itself on one side of the equation.**

Extra Example 4

Solve $2xy - 5y = 8$ for y. Then find the value of y when $x = 3$.

$y = \frac{8}{2x - 5}$; 8

Key Question to Ask for Example 4

- In Example 4, why is it necessary to use the distributive property? **In the given equation, there are two terms that involve y. In order to solve the given equation for y, you need to separate y from the variable x and also from the constant 2. This can be done by using the distributive property to factor out y.**

REWRITING EQUATIONS The approach you use to solve a formula for a variable can be applied to other algebraic equations.

EXAMPLE 3 Rewrite a linear equation

Solve $9x - 4y = 7$ for y. Then find the value of y when $x = -5$.

Solution

STEP 1 **Solve** the equation for y.

$9x - 4y = 7$	Write original equation.
$-4y = 7 - 9x$	Subtract $9x$ from each side.
$y = -\frac{7}{4} + \frac{9}{4}x$	Divide each side by -4.

AVOID ERRORS
When dividing each side of an equation by the same number, remember to divide every term by the number.

STEP 2 **Substitute** the given value into the rewritten equation.

$y = -\frac{7}{4} + \frac{9}{4}(-5)$	Substitute -5 for x.
$y = -\frac{7}{4} - \frac{45}{4}$	Multiply.
$y = -13$	Simplify.

CHECK

$9x - 4y = 7$	Write original equation.
$9(-5) - 4(-13) \stackrel{?}{=} 7$	Substitute -5 for x and -13 for y.
$7 = 7$ ✓	Solution checks.

EXAMPLE 4 Rewrite a nonlinear equation

Solve $2y + xy = 6$ for y. Then find the value of y when $x = -3$.

Solution

AVOID ERRORS
If you rewrite the equation as $y = \frac{6 - 2y}{x}$, then you have not solved for y because y still appears on both sides of the equation.

STEP 1 **Solve** the equation for y.

$2y + xy = 6$	Write original equation.
$(2 + x)y = 6$	Distributive property
$y = \frac{6}{2 + x}$	Divide each side by $(2 + x)$.

STEP 2 **Substitute** the given value into the rewritten equation.

$y = \frac{6}{2 + (-3)}$	Substitute -3 for x.
$y = -6$	Simplify.

✓ GUIDED PRACTICE for Examples 3 and 4

Solve the equation for y. Then find the value of y when $x = 2$.

8. $y - 6x = 7$ $y = 7 + 6x$; 19 **9.** $5y - x = 13$ **10.** $3x + 2y = 12$

11. $2x + 5y = -1$ **12.** $3 = 2xy - x$ $y = \frac{3 + x}{2x}$; $1\frac{1}{4}$ **13.** $4y - xy = 28$

9. $y = \frac{1}{5}x + \frac{13}{5}$; 3
10. $y = -\frac{3}{2}x + 6$; 3
11. $y = -\frac{2}{5}x - \frac{1}{5}$; -1
13. $y = \frac{28}{4 - x}$; 14

EXAMPLE 5 Solve a multi-step problem

MOVIE RENTAL A video store rents new movies for one price and older movies for a lower price, as shown at the right.

- Write an equation that represents the store's monthly revenue.
- Solve the revenue equation for the variable representing the number of new movies rented.
- The owner wants $12,000 in revenue per month. How many new movies must be rented if the number of older movies rented is 500? 1000?

Solution

STEP 1 **Write** a verbal model. Then write an equation.

Monthly revenue (dollars)	=	Price of new movies (dollars/movie)	·	Number of new movies (movies)	+	Price of older movies (dollars/movie)	·	Number of older movies (movies)
R	=	5	·	n_1	+	3	·	n_2

An equation is $R = 5n_1 + 3n_2$.

STEP 2 **Solve** the equation for n_1.

$R = 5n_1 + 3n_2$ **Write equation.**

$R - 3n_2 = 5n_1$ **Subtract $3n_2$ from each side.**

$\frac{R - 3n_2}{5} = n_1$ **Divide each side by 5.**

STEP 3 **Calculate** n_1 for the given values of R and n_2.

If $n_2 = 500$, then $n_1 = \frac{12{,}000 - 3 \cdot 500}{5} = 2100$.

If $n_2 = 1000$, then $n_1 = \frac{12{,}000 - 3 \cdot 1000}{5} = 1800$.

▶ If 500 older movies are rented, then 2100 new movies must be rented. If 1000 older movies are rented, then 1800 new movies must be rented.

✓ GUIDED PRACTICE for Example 5

14. **WHAT IF?** In Example 5, how many new movies must be rented if the number of older movies rented is 1500? **1500 new movies**

15. **WHAT IF?** In Example 5, how many new movies must be rented if customers rent *no* older movies at all? **2400 new movies**

16. Solve the equation in Step 1 of Example 5 for n_2. $n_2 = \frac{R - 5n_1}{3}$

Extra Example 5

A campus bookstore sells T-shirts for $15 each and sweatshirts for $22 each.

- Write an equation for the bookstore's revenue R from selling m T-shirts and n sweatshirts. $R = 15m + 22n$
- Solve the equation for m. $m = \frac{R - 22n}{15}$
- In order for the bookstore to have $6660 in revenue from sales of these two items during the fall semester, how many T-shirts must be sold if 150 sweatshirts are sold? **224 T-shirts**

Closing the Lesson

Have students summarize the major points of the lesson and answer the Essential Question: What are formulas, and how are formulas used?

- **A formula can be solved for any one of its variables in terms of the other variables.**
- **Once a formula has been solved for one of its variables, known values of the other variables can be substituted to solve problems.**

Formulas are equations that relate two or more quantities, usually represented by variables. Formulas can be used to solve many real-world problems, such as problems about investment, temperature, perimeter, area, and volume.

Differentiated Instruction

Auditory Learners To help students write an equation for **Example 5**, ask students to first identify the known and unknown quantities. The known quantities are the price per rental of new and older movies. The unknown quantities are the number of new and older movies and the monthly revenue. Next ask students to identify the relationship between the known and unknown quantities.

See also the *Algebra 2 Toolkit* for more strategies.

4 PRACTICE AND APPLY

Assignment Guide

Answer Transparencies available for all exercises

Basic:
Day 1: SRH p. 991 Exs. 1–4
pp. 30–32
Exs. 1–6, 18–20, 48–53
Day 2: pp. 30–32
Exs. 7–17, 21, 22, 33–36, 40–42

Average:
Day 1: pp. 30–32
Exs. 1–6, 18–20, 40–42
Day 2: pp. 30–32
Exs. 11–17, 21–29, 33–38

Advanced:
Day 1: pp. 30–32
Exs. 1–6, 18–20, 32*, 40–42
Day 2: pp. 30–32
Exs. 12–15, 21–31, 35–39*

Block:
pp. 30–32
Exs. 1–6, 18–20, 40–42 (with 1.3)
pp. 30–32
Exs. 11–17, 21–29, 33–38 (with 1.5)

Differentiated Instruction

See *Algebra 2 Best Practices Toolkit* for suggestions on addressing the needs of a diverse classroom.

Homework Check

For a quick check of student understanding of key concepts, go over the following exercises:

Basic: 3, 6, 10, 22, 34
Average: 4, 5, 12, 24, 36
Advanced: 4, 6, 14, 26, 37

Extra Practice

- Student Edition, p. 1010
- Chapter 1 Resource Book: Practice levels A, B, C, pp. 41–43

Practice Worksheet

An easily-readable reduced practice page (with answers) for this lesson can be found on p. 1C.

1.4 EXERCISES

HOMEWORK KEY
○ = **WORKED-OUT SOLUTIONS** on p. WS1 for Exs. 3, 9, and 35
★ = **STANDARDIZED TEST PRACTICE** Exs. 2, 6, 15, 27, 36, and 38

SKILL PRACTICE

A

1. **VOCABULARY** Copy and complete: A(n) __?__ is an equation that relates two or more quantities. formula

2. ★ **WRITING** What does it mean to solve for a variable in an equation? See margin.

EXAMPLES 1 and 2 on pp. 26–27 for Exs. 3–6

REWRITING FORMULAS **Solve the formula for the indicated variable. Then use the given information to find the value of the variable.**

3. Solve $A = \ell w$ for ℓ. Then find the length of a rectangle with a width of 50 millimeters and an area of 250 square millimeters. $\ell = \frac{A}{w}$; 5 mm

4. Solve $A = \frac{1}{2}bh$ for b. Then find the base of a triangle with a height of 6 inches and an area of 24 square inches. $b = \frac{2A}{h}$; 8 in.

5. Solve $A = \frac{1}{2}(b_1 + b_2)h$ for h. Then find the height of a trapezoid with bases of lengths 10 centimeters and 15 centimeters and an area of 75 square centimeters. $h = \frac{2A}{b_1 + b_2}$; 6 cm

6. ★ **MULTIPLE CHOICE** What equation do you obtain when you solve the formula $A = \frac{1}{2}(b_1 + b_2)h$ for b_1? A

   (A) $b_1 = \frac{2A}{h} - b_2$ (B) $b_1 = \frac{A}{2h} - b_2$
   (C) $b_1 = 2A - b_2h$ (D) $b_1 = \frac{2A}{h - b_2}$

2. Rewrite an equation as an equivalent equation in which the variable is on one side and does not appear on the other side.

EXAMPLE 3 on p. 28 for Exs. 7–17

REWRITING EQUATIONS **Solve the equation for y. Then find the value of y for the given value of x.**

7. $3x + y = 26; x = 7$ $y = 26 - 3x$; 5
8. $4y + x = 24; x = 8$ $y = -\frac{1}{4}x + 6$; 4
9. $6x + 5y = 31; x = -4$ $y = -\frac{6}{5}x + \frac{31}{5}$; 11
10. $15x + 4y = 9; x = -3$ $y = -\frac{15}{4}x + \frac{9}{4}$; $13\frac{1}{2}$
11. $9x - 6y = 63; x = 5$ $y = \frac{3}{2}x - \frac{21}{2}$; -3
12. $10x - 18y = 84; x = 6$ $y = \frac{5}{9}x - \frac{14}{3}$; $-1\frac{1}{3}$
13. $8y - 14x = -22; x = 5$ $y = \frac{7}{4}x - \frac{11}{4}$; 6
14. $9y - 4x = -30; x = 8$ $y = \frac{4}{9}x - \frac{10}{3}$; $\frac{2}{9}$

15. ★ **MULTIPLE CHOICE** What equation do you obtain when you solve the equation $4x - 5y = 20$ for y? C

   (A) $x = \frac{5}{4}y + 5$ (B) $y = -\frac{4}{5}x + 4$ (C) $y = \frac{4}{5}x - 4$ (D) $y = \frac{4}{5}x - 20$

16. All of the terms need to be divided by 5; $5y = 7x + 2$, $y = \frac{7}{5}x + \frac{2}{5}$.

17. The variable y should only appear on one side of the equation, not both; $4y - xy = 9$, $y(4 - x) = 9$, $y = \frac{9}{4 - x}$.

ERROR ANALYSIS ***Describe*** **and correct the error in solving the equation for y.**

16.

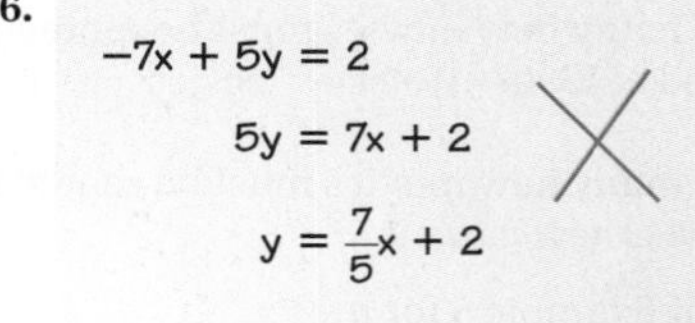

17.

$4y - xy = 9$
$4y = 9 + xy$
$y = \frac{9 + xy}{4}$

B **GEOMETRY** **Solve the formula for the variable in red. Then use the given information to find the value of the variable. Round to the nearest tenth.**

18. Area of a circular ring

$A = 2\pi rw$

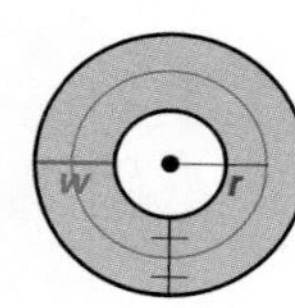

$r = \frac{A}{2\pi w}$; about 4.77 ft

Find r if $w = 4$ ft and $A = 120$ ft^2.

19. Lateral surface area of a truncated cylinder

$S = \pi r(h + k)$

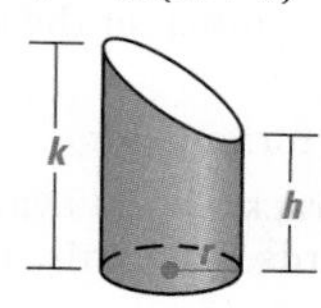

$h = \frac{S}{\pi r} - k$; about 4.96 cm

Find h if $r = 2$ cm, $k = 3$ cm, and $S = 50$ cm^2.

20. Volume of an ellipsoid

$V = \frac{4}{3}\pi abc$

$c = \frac{3V}{4\pi ab}$; about 1.19 in.

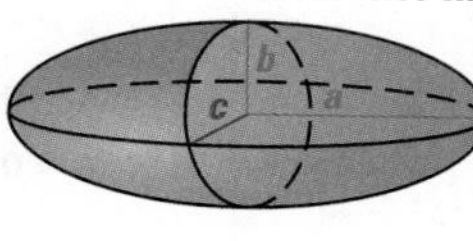

Find c if $a = 4$ in., $b = 3$ in., and $V = 60$ in.^{3}

EXAMPLE 4 on p. 28 for Exs. 21–26

REWRITING EQUATIONS **Solve the equation for y. Then find the value of y for the given value of x.**

21. $xy - 3x = 40; x = 5$ $y = \frac{40 + 3x}{x}$; 11

22. $7x - xy = -18; x = -4$ $y = \frac{7x + 18}{x}$; $2\frac{1}{2}$

23. $3xy - 28 = 16x; x = 4$ $y = \frac{16x + 28}{3x}$; $7\frac{2}{3}$

24. $9y + 6xy = 30; x = -6$ $y = \frac{30}{6x + 9}$; $-1\frac{1}{9}$

25. $y - 2xy = 15; x = -1$ $y = \frac{15}{1 - 2x}$; 5

26. $4x + 7y + 5xy = 0; x = 1$ $y = -\frac{4x}{7 + 5x}$; $-\frac{1}{3}$

27. ★ **SHORT RESPONSE** Consider the equation $15x - 9y = 27$. To find the value of y when $x = 2$, you can use two methods. Method 1: $y = \frac{5}{3}x - 3, y = \frac{5}{3} \cdot 2 - 3, y = \frac{1}{3}$

Method 1 *Solve the original equation for y and then substitute 2 for x.*

Method 2 *Substitute 2 for x and then solve the resulting equation for y.*

Method 2: $15 \cdot 2 - 9y = 27, 30 - 9y = 27, -9y = -3, y = \frac{1}{3}$

Show the steps of the two methods. Which method is more efficient if you need to find the value of y for several values of x? *Explain.*

Sample answer: Method 1 is more efficient because it is already solved for y.

C **REASONING** **Solve for the indicated variable.**

28. Solve $xy = x + y$ for y. $y = \frac{x}{x - 1}$

29. Solve $xyz = x + y + z$ for z. $z = \frac{x + y}{xy - 1}$

30. Solve $\frac{1}{x} + \frac{1}{y} = 1$ for y. $y = \frac{x}{x - 1}$

31. Solve $\frac{1}{x} + \frac{1}{y} + \frac{1}{z} = 1$ for z. $z = \frac{xy}{xy - y - x}$

32. **CHALLENGE** Write a formula giving the area of a circle in terms of its circumference. $A = \frac{C^2}{4\pi}$

PROBLEM SOLVING

EXAMPLE 5 on p. 29 for Exs. 33–38

A

33. **TREE DIAMETER** You can estimate the diameter of a tree without boring through it by measuring its circumference. Solve the formula $C = \pi d$ for d. Then find the diameter of an oak that has a circumference of 113 inches. $d = \frac{C}{\pi}$; about 36 in.

@HomeTutor for problem solving help at classzone.com

34. **DESIGN** The fabric panels on a kite are rhombuses. For the panel shown, a formula for the length of the long diagonal d is $d = s\sqrt{3}$ where s is the length of a side. Solve the formula for s. Then find the value of s when $d = 15$ inches.

@HomeTutor for problem solving help at classzone.com

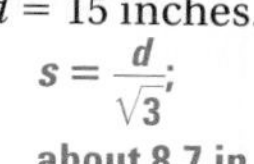

$s = \frac{d}{\sqrt{3}}$; about 8.7 in.

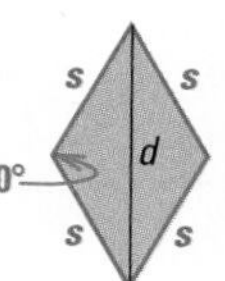

Avoiding Common Errors

Exercise 5 Some students will automatically apply the distributive property to remove parentheses. Doing so will create two terms containing both h and another variable, which is a step in the wrong direction since the goal is to solve for h. Remind these students that they want to get h alone on one side of the equation, so they should *not* apply the distributive property in this situation.

Teaching Strategy

Exercises 28–31 Ask students to write a list of steps to follow in solving equations like these for the indicated variable. Work to develop a consensus among all students about the list of steps.

5 ASSESS AND RETEACH

Daily Homework Quiz

Transparency Available

1. The formula $V = \pi r^2 h$ gives the volume of a cylinder with radius r and height h. Solve this formula for h and then find the height of a cylinder with radius 8 centimeters and volume 704π cubic centimeters. **$h = \frac{V}{\pi r^2}$; 11 cm**
2. Solve $5x + 2y = 8$ for y. Then find the value of y when $x = -8$. **$y = 4 - \frac{5}{2}x$ or $y = -\frac{5}{2}x + 4$; 24**
3. Solve $3y - xy = 21$ for y. **$y = \frac{21}{3 - x}$**

Available at **classzone.com**

Diagnosis/Remediation

- Practice A, B, C in Chapter 1 Resource Book, pp. 41–43
- Study Guide in Chapter 1 Resource Book, pp. 44–45
- Practice Workbook, pp. 7–8
- @HomeTutor

Challenge

Additional challenge is available in the Chapter 1 Resource Book, p. 49.

36c. About 70 yd, 0 yd; the greatest value of r occurs when $x = 0$, and the least value is 0 because x must be nonnegative.

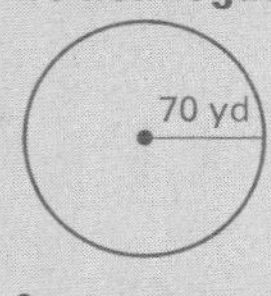

36b. about 46.2 yd, about 38.2 yd, about 31.8 yd, about 22.3 yd

37. $R = 80c + 150d$; $d = \frac{R - 80c}{150}$; 80 designer tuxedos; 160 designer tuxedos; 240 designer tuxedos

35. **TEMPERATURE** The formula for converting temperatures from degrees Celsius to degrees Fahrenheit is $F = \frac{9}{5}C + 32$. Solve the formula for C. Then find the temperature in degrees Celsius that corresponds to 50°F. **$C = \frac{5}{9}(F - 32)$; 10°C**

B

36. ★ **EXTENDED RESPONSE** A quarter mile running track is shaped as shown. The formula for the inside perimeter is $P = 2\pi r + 2x$.

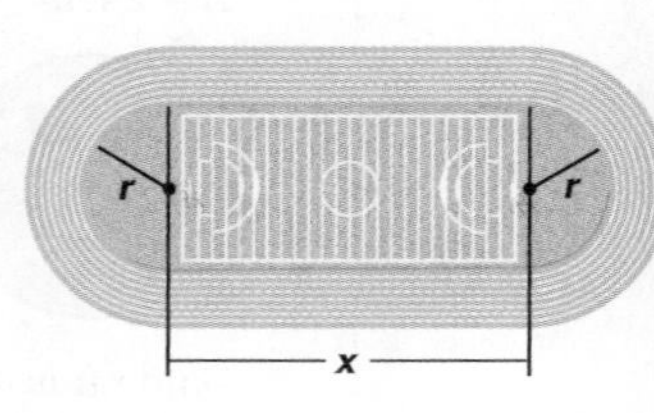

a. Solve the perimeter formula for r. **$r = \frac{P - 2x}{2\pi}$**

b. For a quarter mile track, $P = 440$ yards. Find r when $x = 75$ yards, 100 yards, 120 yards, and 150 yards.

c. What are the greatest and least possible values of r if $P = 440$ yards? *Explain* how you found the values, and sketch the track corresponding to each extreme value. **See margin.**

37. **MULTI-STEP PROBLEM** A tuxedo shop rents classic tuxedos for \$80 and designer tuxedos for \$150. Write an equation that represents the shop's revenue. Solve the equation for the variable representing the number of designer tuxedos rented. The shop owner wants \$60,000 in revenue during prom season. How many designer tuxedos must be rented if the number of classic tuxedos rented is 600? 450? 300?

38. ★ **OPEN-ENDED MATH** The volume of a donut-like shape called a *torus* is given by the formula $V = 2\pi^2 r^2 R$ where r and R are the radii shown and $r \le R$.

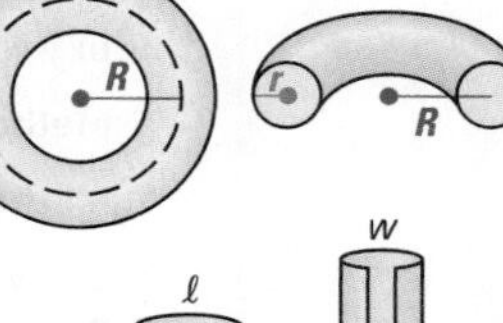

a. Solve the formula for R. **$R = \frac{V}{2\pi^2 r^2}$**

b. A metal ring in the shape of a torus has a volume of 100 cubic centimeters. Choose three possible values of r, and find the corresponding values of R.

***Sample answer:* $r = 1.5, R = 2.25$; $r = 1.15, R = 3.83$; $r = 0.849, R = 7.03$**

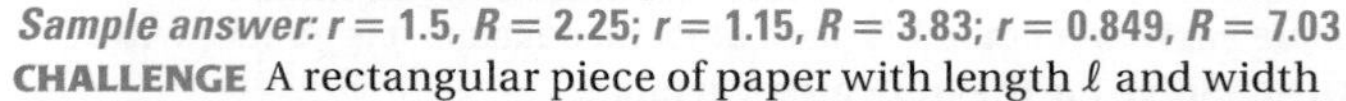

C

39. **CHALLENGE** A rectangular piece of paper with length ℓ and width w can be rolled to form the lateral surface of a cylinder in two ways, assuming no overlapping. Write a formula for the volume of each cylinder in terms of ℓ and w. **$V = \frac{\ell^2 w}{4\pi}$; $V = \frac{w^2 \ell}{4\pi}$**

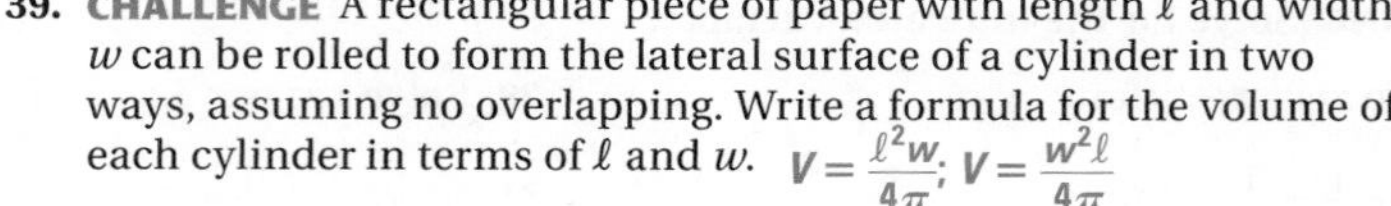

KENTUCKY MIXED REVIEW

40. Jill is mailing a gift in a rectangular box that is 14 inches by 10 inches by 8 inches. She wants to mail this box in a larger box that is 18 inches by 15 inches by 10 inches. How many cubic inches of packing material does she need to surround the gift? **B**

   Ⓐ 1120 in.^{3} Ⓑ 1580 in.^{3} Ⓒ 2700 in.^{3} Ⓓ 3820 in.^{3}

41. If $\angle A$ and $\angle B$ are supplementary angles and $m\angle A$ is 56°, what is $m\angle B$? **C**

   Ⓐ 34° Ⓑ 112° Ⓒ 124° Ⓓ 306°

42. What is the solution of the equation $3(r - 1) = -2(r + 7) + 1$? **B**

   Ⓐ −3 Ⓑ −2 Ⓒ 2 Ⓓ 3

Lessons 1.1–1.4

1. **CAR RENTALS** There is a $50 fee to join an urban car rental service. Using the car costs $8.50 per hour. What is the cost to join and drive for 20 hours?

   A. $119
   B. $135
   C. $170
   D. $220

2. **MUSEUM COSTS** You visit a museum. You have $50 to spend. Admission to the museum is $15. Admission to each special exhibit inside the museum is $10. What is the maximum number of special exhibits you can include in your visit?

   A. 2 B. 3
   C. 6 D. 7

3. **HOCKEY STATISTICS** In hockey, each player has a statistic called plus/minus, which is the difference between the number of goals scored by the player's team and the number of goals scored by the other team when the player is on the ice. Which list shows the players in order from least to greatest plus/minus?

Player	Plus/Minus
Vincent Lecavalier	23
Dave Andreychuk	−9
Ruslan Fedotenko	14
Martin St. Louis	35
Cory Sarich	5
Tim Taylor	−5

   A. Andreychuk, Taylor, Sarich, Fedotenko, Lecavalier, St. Louis
   B. St. Louis, Lecavalier, Fedotenko, Andreychuk, Sarich, Taylor
   C. Taylor, Andreychuk, Sarich, Fedotenko, Lecavalier, St. Louis
   D. St. Louis, Lecavalier, Fedotenko, Sarich, Taylor, Andreychuk

4. **PRINTING MONEY** In one year, the Bureau of Engraving and Printing printed $10 and $20 bills with a total value of $66,368,000. The total number of $10 and $20 bills printed was 3,577,600. What was the number of $20 bills printed?

   A. 172,800 B. 518,400
   C. 3,059,200 D. 3,404,800

5. **SCHOOL PICNIC SUPPLIES** You are in charge of buying food for a school picnic. You have $45 to spend on ground beef and chicken. Ground beef costs $1.80 per pound and chicken costs $1.00 per pound. You want to buy equal amounts of ground beef and chicken. About how many total pounds of meat can you buy?

   A. 16.07 pounds B. 25 pounds
   C. 32.14 pounds D. 112.5 pounds

6. **SUMMER JOBS** You have two summer jobs. You mow lawns for $20 per hour. You also work at a restaurant for $7.50 per hour. In one week, you earn $825 working a total of 50 hours. Which equation can be used to find the number of hours you mowed lawns?

   A. $825 = 20x + 7.5x$
   B. $825 = 20x + 7.5(50 - x)$
   C. $825 = 20x + 7.5(x - 50)$
   D. $825 = 20(x + 50) + 7.5x$

7. **OPEN-RESPONSE** You work 45 hours per week for a construction company during the summer. You earn $8 per hour for office work and $9 per hour for outside work. You earn $399 one week.

	Hours	Earnings
office work	x	$8x$
outside work	?	?
Total	45	$399

   a. Find the missing values in the table in terms of x.
   b. Write and solve an equation to find the number of hours you worked in the office and the number of hours you worked outside.
   c. Compare the number of hours you worked in the office to the number hours you worked outside.

Kentucky Mixed Review

1. D
2. B
3. A
4. C
5. C
6. B
7. a. $45 - x$, $9(45 - x)$
b. $8x + 9(45 - x) = \$399$, 6 hours office, 39 hours outside
c. ***Sample answer:*** The total number of hours worked outside was more than 6 times the number of hours worked in the office.

1.5 Use Problem Solving Strategies and Models

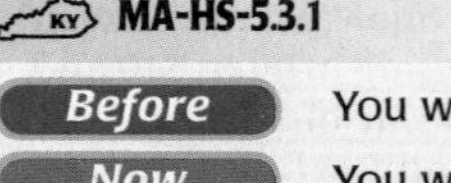

Before You wrote and solved equations.
Now You will solve problems using verbal models.
Why? So you can solve constant rate problems, as in Ex. 26.

1 PLAN AND PREPARE

Warm-Up Exercises

Transparency Available

Solve the equation.

1. $780 = 12.5r$ 62.4
2. $9x + 25 = 178$ 17
3. $636 = 40g + 28(18 - g)$ 11
4. A balloon is released from a height of 5 feet above the ground. Its altitude (in feet) after t minutes is given by the expression $5 + 82t$. What is the altitude of the balloon after 6 minutes? 497 ft

Notetaking Guide

Transparency Available

Promotes interactive learning and notetaking skills, pp. 13–15.

Pacing

Basic: 1 day
Average: 1 day
Advanced: 1 day
Block: 0.5 block with 1.4
- See *Teaching Guide/Lesson Plan.*

2 FOCUS AND MOTIVATE

Essential Question

Big Idea 2, p. 1

How can problem solving strategies be used to find verbal and algebraic models? Tell students they will learn how to answer this question by working with three problem solving strategies.

Key Vocabulary
- verbal model

MA-HS-5.3.1
Students will model, solve and graph first degree, single variable equations and inequalities, including absolute value, based in real-world and mathematical problems and graph the solutions on a number line. DOK 2

As you have seen in this chapter, it is helpful when solving real-life problems to write an equation in words *before* you write it in mathematical symbols. This word equation is called a **verbal model.**

Sometimes problem solving strategies can be used to write a verbal or algebraic model. Examples of such strategies are *use a formula, look for a pattern,* and *draw a diagram.*

EXAMPLE 1 Use a formula

HIGH-SPEED TRAIN The Acela train travels between Boston and Washington, a distance of 457 miles. The trip takes 6.5 hours. What is the average speed?

Solution

You can use the formula for distance traveled as a verbal model.

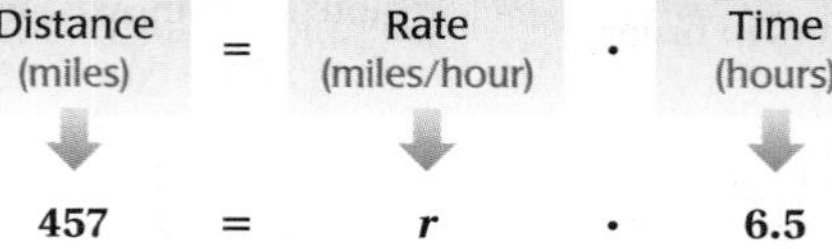

457 = r · 6.5

An equation for this situation is $457 = 6.5r$. Solve for r.

$457 = 6.5r$ **Write equation.**

$70.3 \approx r$ **Divide each side by 6.5.**

▸ The average speed of the train is about 70.3 miles per hour.

CHECK You can use unit analysis to check your answer.

$$457 \text{ miles} \approx \frac{70.3 \text{ miles}}{1 \text{ hour}} \cdot 6.5 \text{ hours}$$

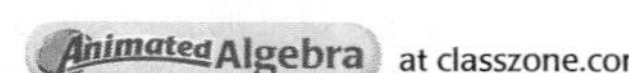

GUIDED PRACTICE for Example 1

1. **AVIATION** A jet flies at an average speed of 540 miles per hour. How long will it take to fly from New York to Tokyo, a distance of 6760 miles? about 12.5 h

Resource Planning Guide

Chapter Resource Book
- Teaching Guide/Lesson Plan (pp. 50–51)
- Practice levels A, B, C (pp. 52–54)
- Study Guide (pp. 55–56)
- Catch-up for Absent Students (p. 57)
- Problem Solving Workshop (p. 58)
- Challenge (p. 59)

Workbooks
- Notetaking Guide (pp. 13–15)
- Practice Workbook (pp. 9–10)

Teaching Options
- **Power Presentations CD-ROM** provides dynamic electronic teaching resources for the classroom.
- **Activity Generator CD-ROM** provides editable activities for all ability levels.

Interactive Technology
- Easy Planner
- Power Presentations CD-ROM
- Activity Generator CD-ROM
- Animated Algebra
- Test Generator CD-ROM
- Online Quiz
- eWorkbook
- eEdition
- @HomeTutor

Resources for English Learners
- Quick Reference for English Learners
- Spanish Study Guide
- Multi-Language Visual Glossary
- Student Resources in Spanish

See also the *Algebra 2 Toolkit* for more strategies for meeting individual needs.

EXAMPLE 2 Look for a pattern

PARAMOTORING A paramotor is a parachute propelled by a fan-like motor. The table shows the height h of a paramotorist t minutes after beginning a descent. Find the height of the paramotorist after 7 minutes.

Time (min), t	0	1	2	3	4
Height (ft), h	2000	1750	1500	1250	1000

Solution

The height decreases by 250 feet per minute.

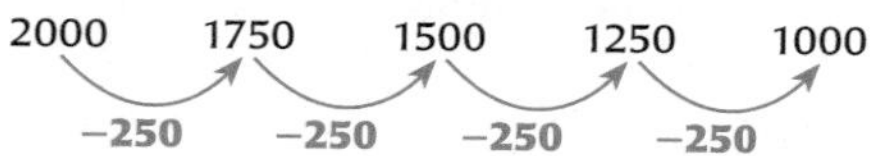

You can use this pattern to write a verbal model for the height.

Height (feet)	=	Initial height (feet)	−	Rate of descent (feet/minute)	•	Time (minutes)
h	=	2000	−	250	•	t

An equation for the height is $h = 2000 - 250t$.

▶ So, the height after 7 minutes is $h = 2000 - 250(7) = 250$ feet.

EXAMPLE 3 Draw a diagram

BANNERS You are hanging four championship banners on a wall in your school's gym. The banners are 8 feet wide. The wall is 62 feet long. There should be an equal amount of space between the ends of the wall and the banners, and between each pair of banners. How far apart should the banners be placed?

Solution

Begin by drawing and labeling a diagram, as shown below.

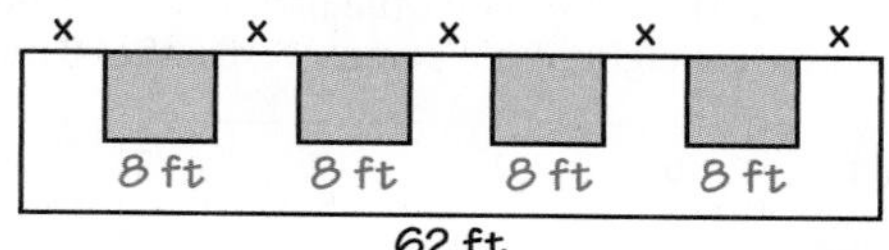

From the diagram, you can write and solve an equation to find x.

$x + 8 + x + 8 + x + 8 + x + 8 + x = 62$ **Write equation.**

$5x + 32 = 62$ **Combine like terms.**

$5x = 30$ **Subtract 32 from each side.**

$x = 6$ **Divide each side by 5.**

▶ The banners should be placed 6 feet apart.

REVIEW STRATEGIES
For help with other problem solving strategies, see p. 998.

Motivating the Lesson

Ask students to describe real-life problems they solved by looking for a pattern or making a diagram.

3 TEACH

Extra Example 1

The driving distance between Boston, Massachusetts, and Cleveland, Ohio, is about 660 miles. If you drive this trip in a total of 12.5 hours, what is your average speed? 52.8 mi/h

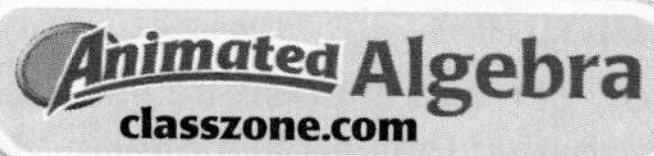

An **Animated Algebra** activity is available on-line for **Example 1**. This activity is also available on the **Power Presentations CD-ROM**.

Extra Example 2

The table shows the number of seats in each of the first four rows of an auditorium. The remaining 10 rows follow the same pattern.

Row	1	2	3	4
Seats	12	14	16	18

Find the number of seats in the last row of the auditorium. 38 seats

Extra Example 3

You are hanging three pictures on a wall in your home that is 16 feet wide. The widths of the three pictures are 2 feet, 3 feet, and 4 feet. You want the space between the pictures to be the same, and for the spaces to the left and right of the group of pictures to each be 6 inches more than the space between adjacent pictures. How should you position the pictures? Place the first picture 2 feet from the left end of the wall and place the pictures 1.5 feet (or 18 inches) apart.

Differentiated Instruction

Inclusion Some students may have difficulty with the alignment of numbers in the construction of a difference pattern shown in **Example 2**. Ruled notebook paper rotated 90° (so that the ruled lines are vertical) may help to align the numbers into "columns." See also the *Algebra 2 Toolkit* for more strategies.

Extra Example 4

Your long-distance telephone plan charges 8 cents per minute for weekday, daytime calls, and 5 cents per minute for night and weekend calls. If you made a total of 220 minutes of long-distance calls during one billing cycle and your bill was $13.16, not including taxes and fees, how many minutes of night and weekend calls did you make? **C**

Ⓐ 72 min Ⓑ 110 min
Ⓒ 148 min Ⓓ 165 min

Key Question to Ask for Example 4

- How can unit analysis be used to verify that the verbal model in the solution for Example 4 is set up correctly? **Use the unit labels to see that miles/gallon • gallons = miles, and miles + miles = miles.**

Closing the Lesson

Have students summarize the major points of the lesson and answer the Essential Question: How can problem solving strategies be used to find verbal and algebraic models?

- **A formula can be used as a verbal model for distance-rate-time problems, geometry problems, and other kinds of problems involving more than one variable.**
- **Looking for a pattern can be used to write a verbal model and then an equation involving more than one variable.**
- **Drawing a diagram can be used to write an algebraic equation.**

The problem solving strategies *use a formula* and *look for a pattern* can be used to write verbal models which can then be used to write algebraic models. The strategy *draw a diagram* can be used to write an algebraic model directly.

EXAMPLE 4 Standardized Test Practice

A car used 16 gallons of gasoline and traveled a total distance of 460 miles. The car's fuel efficiency is 30 miles per gallon on the highway and 25 miles per gallon in the city. How many gallons of gasoline were used on the highway?

Ⓐ 8 gallons Ⓑ 12 gallons Ⓒ $15\frac{1}{3}$ gallons Ⓓ 16 gallons

Solution

STEP 1 **Write** a verbal model. Then write an equation.

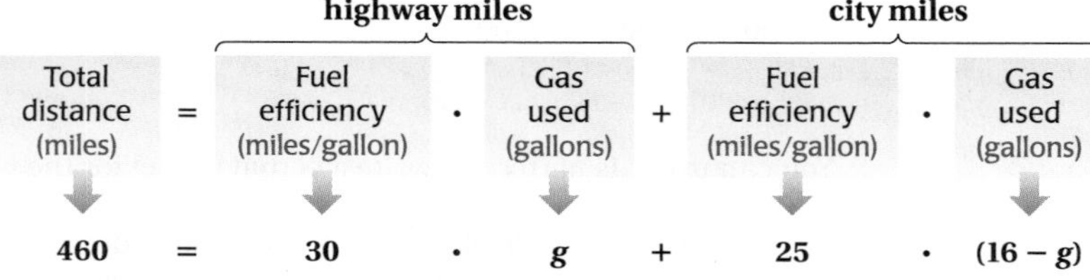

highway miles
city miles
Total distance (miles) = Fuel efficiency (miles/gallon) • Gas used (gallons) + Fuel efficiency (miles/gallon) • Gas used (gallons)
460 = 30 • g + 25 • (16 − g)

An equation for the situation is $460 = 30g + 25(16 - g)$.

STEP 2 **Solve** for g to find the number of gallons used on the highway.

$460 = 30g + 25(16 - g)$	**Write equation.**
$460 = 30g + 400 - 25g$	**Distributive property**
$460 = 5g + 400$	**Combine like terms.**
$60 = 5g$	**Subtract 400 from each side.**
$12 = g$	**Divide each side by 5.**

The car used 12 gallons on the highway.

▶ The correct answer is B. Ⓐ Ⓑ Ⓒ Ⓓ

CHECK $30 \cdot 12 + 25(16 - 12) = 360 + 100 = 460$ ✓

GUIDED PRACTICE for Examples 2, 3, and 4

2. **PARAMOTORING** The table shows the height h of a paramotorist after t minutes. Find the height of the paramotorist after 8 minutes. **720 ft**

Time (min), t	0	1	2	3	4
Height (ft), h	2400	2190	1980	1770	1560

3. **WHAT IF?** In Example 3, how would your answer change if there were only three championship banners? **The space between the banners and walls and banners would increase to 9.5 feet.**

4. **FUEL EFFICIENCY** A truck used 28 gallons of gasoline and traveled a total distance of 428 miles. The truck's fuel efficiency is 16 miles per gallon on the highway and 12 miles per gallon in the city. How many gallons of gasoline were used in the city? **5 gal**

1.5 EXERCISES

HOMEWORK KEY

○ = **WORKED-OUT SOLUTIONS** on p. WS2 for Exs. 3, 11, and 27

★ = **STANDARDIZED TEST PRACTICE** Exs. 2, 15, 16, 21, and 27

◆ = **MULTIPLE REPRESENTATIONS** Ex. 28

SKILL PRACTICE

A

1. **VOCABULARY** Copy and complete: A word equation that represents a real-life problem is called a(n) __?__. verbal model

2. ★ **WRITING** Give an example of how a problem solving strategy can help you write an equation that models a real-life problem. *Sample answer:* You can look for a pattern in a table to write a verbal model for a problem and then use the verbal model to write an equation.

EXAMPLE 1 on p. 34 for Exs. 3–10

USING A FORMULA **Use the formula $d = rt$ for distance traveled to solve for the missing variable.**

3. $d = 20$ mi, $r = 40$ mi/h, $t =$ __?__ 0.5 h
4. $d = 300$ mi, $r =$ __?__, $t = 4$ h 75 mi/h
5. $d =$ __?__, $r = 30$ mi/h, $t = 3$ h 90 mi
6. $d = 250$ mi, $r = 50$ mi/h, $t =$ __?__ 5 h

GEOMETRY **Use the formula $P = 2\ell + 2w$ for the perimeter of a rectangle to solve for the missing variable.**

7. $P =$ __?__, $\ell = 15$ ft, $w = 12$ ft 54 ft
8. $P = 46$ in., $\ell =$ __?__, $w = 4$ in. 19 in.
9. $P = 100$ m, $\ell = 30$ m, $w =$ __?__ 20 m
10. $P = 25$ cm, $w = 5$ cm, $\ell =$ __?__ 7.5 cm

EXAMPLE 2 on p. 35 for Exs. 11–15

USING PATTERNS **Look for a pattern in the table. Then write an equation that represents the table.**

11.

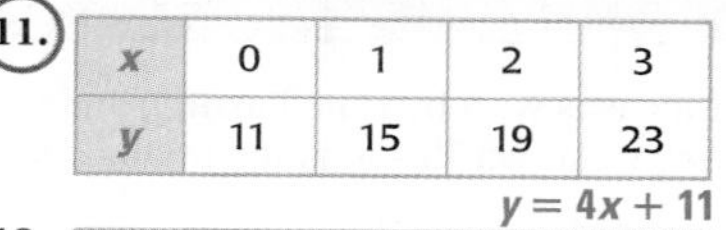

x	0	1	2	3
y	11	15	19	23

$y = 4x + 11$

12.

x	0	1	2	3
y	60	45	30	15

$y = 60 - 15x$

13.

x	0	1	2	3
y	46	36	26	16

$y = 46 - 10x$

14.

x	0	1	2	3
y	57	107	157	207

$y = 50x + 57$

15. ★ **MULTIPLE CHOICE** Which equation represents the table at the right? D

Ⓐ $y = 5x + 7$ Ⓑ $y = 7x + 5$

Ⓒ $y = 12x - 5$ Ⓓ $y = 7x + 12$

x	0	1	2	3
y	12	19	26	33

16. ★ **SHORT RESPONSE** The first story of a building is 24 feet high, and each additional story is 18 feet high. Write an expression for the height to the top of the nth story. *Explain* the meaning of each term in the expression.

16. *Sample answer:* $24 + 18(n - 1)$, or $18n + 6$; in the expression, 24 represents the height of the first story and $18(n - 1)$ represents the height of the other $n - 1$ stories.

EXAMPLE 3 on p. 35 for Exs. 17–18

USING DIAGRAMS **Write and solve an equation to find x.**

17.

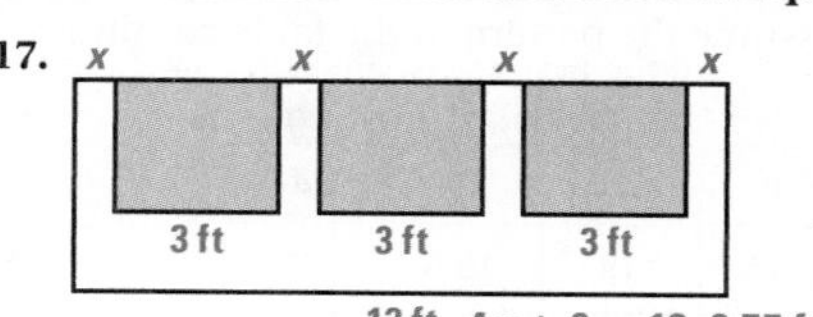

$4x + 9 = 12$, 0.75 ft

18.

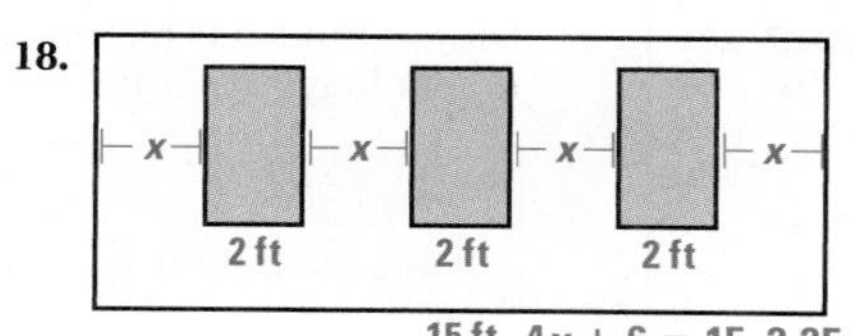

$4x + 6 = 15$, 2.25 ft

4 PRACTICE AND APPLY

Assignment Guide

Answer Transparencies available for all exercises

Basic:
Day 1: SRH p. 981 Exs. 1–15 odd
pp. 37–40
Exs. 1–12, 15–19, 24–32, 34–36 even

Average:
Day 1: pp. 37–40
Exs. 1, 2, 4–6, 8–10, 12–22*, 24–32, 35

Advanced:
Day 1: pp. 37–40
Exs. 1, 2, 5, 6, 9, 10, 12–33*, 34–36 even

Block:
pp. 37–40
Exs. 1, 2, 4–6, 8–10, 12–22*, 24–32, 35 (with 1.4)

Differentiated Instruction

See *Algebra 2 Best Practices Toolkit* for suggestions on addressing the needs of a diverse classroom.

Homework Check

For a quick check of student understanding of key concepts, go over the following exercises:

Basic: 6, 12, 18, 25, 31
Average: 14, 24, 27, 29, 31
Advanced: 18, 25, 28, 30, 32

Extra Practice

- Student Edition, p. 1010
- Chapter 1 Resource Book: Practice levels A, B, C, pp. 52–54

Practice Worksheet

An easily-readable reduced practice page (with answers) for this lesson can be found on p. 1C.

Teaching Strategy

Exercises 11–14 If students have difficulty deciding where to begin, tell them that they need to look at each table and answer three questions: 1) What is y when x is 0? 2) Do the values of y increase or decrease as x increases? 3) By how much does the value of y increase or decrease whenever x increases by 1? If students need more help, guide them in translating their answers to these three questions into the desired equation.

Avoiding Common Errors

Exercise 16 Some students are likely to write $24 + 18n$, rather than $24 + 18(n - 1)$ or $6 + 18n$. Ask them which story of the building is the first with a height of 18 feet. Since it is the second story, this question may prompt them to correct their error. Also, you can suggest representing the relationship between the story number and the height to the top of that story with a table and checking whether their equation matches their table for the first several values of n.

Mathematical Reasoning

Exercises 22–23 Ask students how these tables are different from those given for Exercises 11–15. What information that they used to write the equations in those exercises is not obvious from each of these tables? How might they find this information? Challenge students to think about how graphical representations might be used to find the information needed to write these equations.

Exercise 24 For more information about the Daytona 500, visit www.daytona500.com

B **ERROR ANALYSIS** ***Describe*** **and correct the error in writing the equation.**

19.

x	0	1	2	3
y	75	65	55	45

An equation that represents the table is $y = 75x - 10$. ✗

20.

x	0	5	10	15
y	7	17	27	37

An equation that represents the table is $y = 7 + 10x$. ✗

19. The pattern shows the output is decreased by 10 each time; an equation that represents the table is $y = 75 - 10x$.

20. In the table the inputs increase by 5; an equation that represents the table is $y = 2x + 7$.

21. ★ **MULTIPLE CHOICE** A car used 15 gallons of gasoline and traveled a total distance of 350 miles. The car's fuel efficiency is 25 miles per gallon on the highway and 20 miles per gallon in the city. Which equation can you solve to find h, the number of gallons that were used on the highway? **B**

Ⓐ $350 = 25(15 - h) + 20h$ Ⓑ $25h + 20(15 - h) = 350$

Ⓒ $350 = \left(\frac{25 + 20}{2}\right)h$ Ⓓ $15 = \frac{350}{25h} + \frac{350}{20h}$

C **CHALLENGE** **Write an equation that represents the table.**

22.

x	0	3	6	9
y	12	30	48	66

$y = 6x + 12$

23.

x	4	5	6	7
y	12	19	26	33

$y = 7x - 16$

PROBLEM SOLVING

EXAMPLE 1 A on p. 34 for Exs. 24–26

24. DAYTONA 500 A recent Daytona 500 race was won by Dale Earnhardt, Jr. He completed the 500 mile race in 3.2 hours. What was his average racing speed? **156.25 mi/h**

@HomeTutor for problem solving help at classzone.com

25. MAGLEV TRAIN A magnetic levitation (maglev) train travels between the city center of Shanghai, China, and Pudong International Airport. The trip covers 30 kilometers in just 8 minutes. What is the average speed of the train? **3.75 km/min**

@HomeTutor for problem solving help at classzone.com

26. SCUBA DIVING A scuba diver is returning to the surface from a depth of 165 feet. The safe ascent rate for a diver is 30 feet per minute. How many minutes will it take for the diver to return to the surface? **5.5 min**

EXAMPLE 2 on p. 35 for Exs. 27–28

(27.) ★ **SHORT RESPONSE** The table shows the height of a bamboo shoot during a period of fast growth. Use the table to write an equation modeling the growth. Do you think it is reasonable to assume the pattern in the table continues indefinitely? *Explain.* **$y = 1.5x + 15$; no; the bamboo shoot will eventually slow its growth rate and stop growing.**

Day	0	1	2	3	4
Bamboo height (ft)	15	16.5	18	19.5	21

○ = WORKED-OUT SOLUTIONS on p. WS1 ★ = STANDARDIZED TEST PRACTICE

= MULTIPLE REPRESENTATIONS

B 28. **MULTIPLE REPRESENTATIONS** Your cell phone plan costs $40 per month plus $.10 per text message. You receive a bill for $53.80.

a. **Making a Table** Copy and complete the table below. Use the table to estimate how many text messages you sent. **$45; $50; $55; $60.** ***Sample answer:*** **140 text messages**

Text messages	0	50	100	150	200
Monthly bill	$40	?	?	?	?

b. **Writing a Model** Write an equation for the situation. Solve it to find exactly how many text messages you sent. **$53.8 = 0.1x + 40$; 138 text messages**

c. **Comparing Answers** Is your estimate from part (a) compatible with the exact answer from part (b)? *Explain.* ***Sample answer:*** **Yes; the estimate in part (a) was comparable to the exact answer in part (b).**

EXAMPLE 3 on p. 35 for Exs. 29–30

29. **WOOD SHOP** You have a piece of wood that is 72 inches long. You cut the wood into three pieces. The second piece is 6 inches longer than the first piece. The third piece is 6 inches longer than the second piece. Draw a diagram and then write and solve an equation to find the lengths of the three pieces. **See margin.**

30. **POSTERS** You want to tape five posters on a wall so that the spaces between posters are the same. You also want the spaces at the left and right of the group of posters to be three times the space between any two adjacent posters. The wall is 15 feet wide and the posters are 1.5 feet wide. Draw a diagram and then write and solve an equation to find how to position the posters. **See margin.**

EXAMPLE 4 on p. 36 for Exs. 31–32

31. **PACKING WEIGHT** A moving company weighs 20 boxes you have packed that contain either books or clothes and says the total weight is 404 pounds. You know that a box of books weighs 40 pounds and a box of clothes weighs 7 pounds. Write and solve an equation to find how many boxes of books and how many boxes of clothes you packed. **Let x represent the number of boxes of books, $40x + 7(20 - x) = 404$, 8 boxes of books, 12 boxes of clothes.**

32a. total running distance + biking distance = race distance

32b. Let t represent the time biking, $12\left(2\frac{7}{12} - t\right) + 30t = 55$.

32c. running: 1 h 15 min; biking: 1 h 20 min

32d. total running distance: 15 km; biking distance: 40 km; 15 + 40 = 55 km

32. **MULTI-STEP PROBLEM** A duathlon consists of a run, a bike ride, and a second run. Use the information below about the average rates of one participant who completed a 55 kilometer duathlon in 2 hours 35 minutes.

a. **Model** Write a verbal model that shows the race distance as the sum of the total running distance and the biking distance.

b. **Translate** Write an equation based on the verbal model.

c. **Solve** Solve the equation to find how much time the participant spent running and how much time the participant spent biking.

d. **Check** Find the total running distance and the biking distance, and verify that their sum is 55 kilometers.

C 33. **CHALLENGE** You are hanging fliers around a cylindrical kiosk that has a diameter of 5 feet. You want to hang 15 fliers that are 8.5 inches wide so they are evenly spaced. How far apart should the fliers be placed? **about 4.07 in.**

Study Strategy

Exercises 29–30 Students are instructed to draw a diagram to help them write appropriate equations to solve these problems. Ask students to also solve these problems by writing a verbal model instead of drawing a diagram, and then ask them which strategy they prefer.

29.

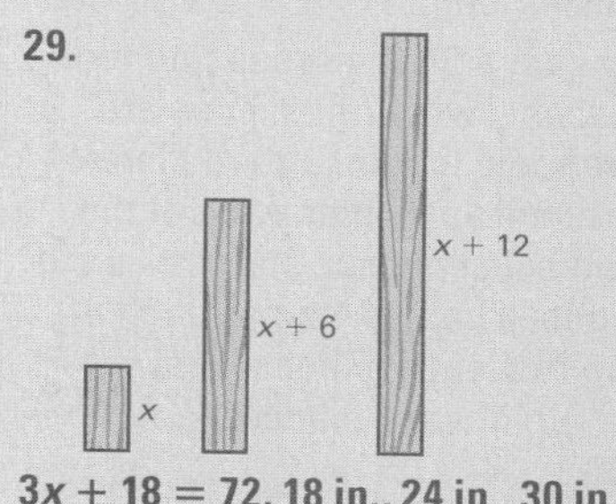

$3x + 18 = 72$, 18 in., 24 in., 30 in.

30.

1.5 feet 1.5 feet 1.5 feet 1.5 feet 1.5 feet

3x x x x x 3x

15 feet

$10x + 7.5 = 15$, $x = 0.75$ so the posters should be 0.75 foot apart and the spaces on the left and right should be 2.25 feet.

5 ASSESS AND RETEACH

Daily Homework Quiz

 **Transparency Available**

1. If you hike at an average speed of 2.8 miles per hour, how long will it take you to hike a trail that is 7 miles long? **2.5 h, or 2 h 30 min**
2. You cut a 54-inch rope into four pieces. Two of the pieces are the same length, a third piece is twice as long as each of the two equal pieces, and the fourth piece is half as long as each of the two equal pieces. Find the length of each piece. **12 in., 12 in., 24 in., 6 in.**

Online Quiz

Available at **classzone.com**

Diagnosis/Remediation

- Practice A, B, C in Chapter 1 Resource Book, pp. 52–54
- Study Guide in Chapter 1 Resource Book, pp. 55–56
- Practice Workbook, pp. 9–10
- @HomeTutor

Challenge

Additional challenge is available in the Chapter 1 Resource Book, p. 59.

Quiz

An easily-readable reduced copy of the quiz (with answers) on Lessons 1.3–1.5 from the Assessment Book can be found on p. 1E.

KENTUCKY MIXED REVIEW

 **TEST PRACTICE** at classzone.com

34. Curtis takes a bag of trail mix on a camping trip. On the first day, he eats one fourth of the trail mix. On the second day, he eats half of the remaining trail mix. On the third day, he eats one third of the remaining trail mix. When Curtis goes home, he has one-half pound of trail mix. How many pounds of trail mix did Curtis take on the camping trip? **A**

Ⓐ 2 lb Ⓑ 4 lb Ⓒ 8 lb Ⓓ 12 lb

35. The number of students participating in extracurricular activities at Alexander High School this year is 25% higher than the previous year's participation of 740 students. What percent of this year's participation is last year's participation? **D**

Ⓐ 20% Ⓑ 57% Ⓒ 75% Ⓓ 80%

36. How many yards of rope are needed to rope off a rectangular region having a width of 9 yards and a diagonal of 15 yards? **D**

Ⓐ 24 yd Ⓑ 33 yd Ⓒ 36 yd Ⓓ 42 yd

QUIZ *for Lessons 1.3–1.5*

Solve the equation. Check your solution. *(p. 18)*

1. $5b - 2 = 8$ **2**
2. $2d - 3 = 8d + 15$ **−3**
3. $2(m - 4) = m + 2$ **10**
4. $\frac{2}{3}k + \frac{2}{7} = \frac{3}{7}k + \frac{1}{2}$ $\frac{9}{10}$

Solve the equation for *y*. Then find the value of *y* for the given value of *x*. *(p. 26)*

5. $4x + y = 12; x = 4$ $y = 12 - 4x; -4$
6. $3x - 2y = 14; x = 6$ $y = \frac{3}{2}x - 7; 2$
7. $3xy - 4x = 19; x = 2$ $y = \frac{4x + 19}{3x}; 4\frac{1}{2}$
8. $11y + 2xy = 9; x = -5$ $y = \frac{9}{11 + 2x}; 9$

Look for a pattern in the table. Then write an equation that represents the table. *(p. 34)*

9.

x	0	1	2	3
y	0	13	26	39

$y = 13x$

10.

x	0	1	2	3
y	−5	−2	1	4

$y = 3x - 5$

11. **TUTORING FEE** A chess tutor charges a fee for the first lesson that is 1.5 times the fee for later lessons. You spend $315 for 10 lessons. How much does the first lesson cost? How much does a later lesson cost? *(p. 34)* **$45; $30**

12. **FLOWER PRICES** You buy some calla lilies and peonies at a flower store. Calla lilies cost $3.50 each and peonies cost $5.50 each. The total cost of 12 flowers is $52. How many calla lilies and how many peonies did you buy? *(p. 34)* **7 calla lilies, 5 peonies**

EXTRA PRACTICE for Lesson 1.5, p. 1010

 **ONLINE QUIZ** at classzone.com

1.6 Solve Linear Inequalities

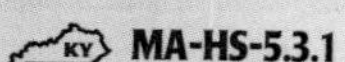
MA-HS-5.3.1

Before You solved linear equations.

Now You will solve linear inequalities.

Why? So you can describe temperature ranges, as in Ex. 54.

Key Vocabulary
- linear inequality
- compound inequality
- equivalent inequalities

MA-HS-5.3.1
Students will model, solve and graph first degree, single variable equations and inequalities, including absolute value, based in real-world and mathematical problems and graph the solutions on a number line.
DOK 2

A **linear inequality** in one variable can be written in one of the following forms, where a and b are real numbers and $a \neq 0$:

$$ax + b < 0 \qquad ax + b > 0 \qquad ax + b \leq 0 \qquad ax + b \geq 0$$

A **solution** of an inequality in one variable is a value that, when substituted for the variable, results in a true statement. The **graph** of an inequality in one variable consists of all points on a number line that represent solutions.

EXAMPLE 1 Graph simple inequalities

a. Graph $x < 2$.

The solutions are all real numbers less than 2.

An open dot is used in the graph to indicate 2 is *not* a solution.

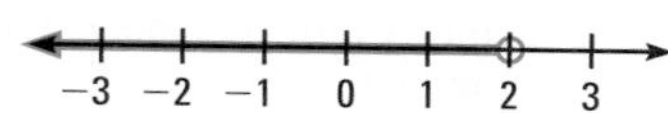

b. Graph $x \geq -1$.

The solutions are all real numbers greater than or equal to −1.

A solid dot is used in the graph to indicate −1 *is* a solution.

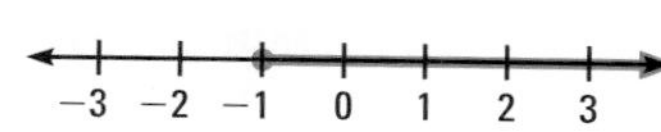

COMPOUND INEQUALITIES A **compound inequality** consists of two simple inequalities joined by "and" or "or."

EXAMPLE 2 Graph compound inequalities

READ INEQUALITIES
The compound inequality $-1 < x < 2$ is another way of writing "$x > -1$ **and** $x < 2$."

a. Graph $-1 < x < 2$.

The solutions are all real numbers that are greater than −1 **and** less than 2.

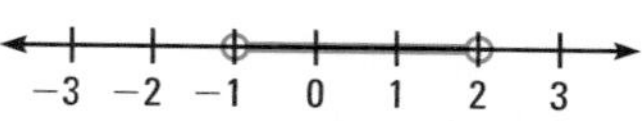

b. Graph $x \leq -2$ or $x > 1$.

The solutions are all real numbers that are less than or equal to −2 **or** greater than 1.

−3 −2 −1 0 1 2 3

✓ **GUIDED PRACTICE** for Examples 1 and 2

Graph the inequality. 1–4. See margin.

1. $x > -5$
2. $x \leq 3$
3. $-3 \leq x < 1$
4. $x < 1$ or $x \geq 2$

1 PLAN AND PREPARE

Warm-Up Exercises

Transparency Available

Solve the equation.

1. $0.4x + 1.5 = 0.6x + 3$ −7.5
2. $5(x - 8) = 9x + 20$ −15
3. Solve the equation $440 = C + 200$ for r after using the formula $C = 2\pi r$ to substitute for the variable C. $r = \frac{120}{\pi}$

Notetaking Guide

Transparency Available

Promotes interactive learning and notetaking skills, pp. 16–19.

Pacing

Basic: 2 days
Average: 2 days
Advanced: 2 days
Block: 1 block
- See *Teaching Guide/Lesson Plan.*

2 FOCUS AND MOTIVATE

Essential Question

Big Idea 3, p. 1

How are the rules for solving linear inequalities similar to those for solving linear equations, and how are they different? Tell students they will learn how to answer this question by learning and using the rules for solving linear inequalities.

Resource Planning Guide

Chapter Resource Book
- Teaching Guide/Lesson Plan (pp. 60–61)
- Activity Master (p. 62)
- Practice levels A, B, C (pp. 63–65)
- Study Guide (pp. 66–67)
- Catch-up for Absent Students (p. 68)
- Application (p. 69)
- Challenge (p. 70)

Workbooks
- Notetaking Guide (pp. 16–19)
- Practice Workbook (pp. 11–12)

Teaching Options
- **Power Presentations CD-ROM** provides dynamic electronic teaching resources for the classroom.
- **Activity Generator CD-ROM** provides editable activities for all ability levels.

Interactive Technology
- Easy Planner
- Power Presentations CD-ROM
- Activity Generator CD-ROM
- Animated Algebra
- Test Generator CD-ROM
- Online Quiz
- eWorkbook
- eEdition
- @HomeTutor

Resources for English Learners
- Quick Reference for English Learners
- Spanish Study Guide
- Multi-Language Visual Glossary
- Student Resources in Spanish

See also the *Algebra 2 Toolkit* for more strategies for meeting individual needs.

Motivating the Lesson

Near the end of the semester, students often ask their teachers what scores they must get on the final exam in order to earn a particular grade in the course. Tell students that they can use linear inequalities to answer this question.

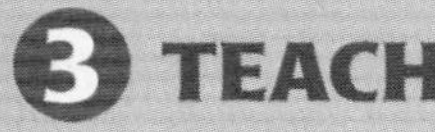

Extra Example 1

a. Graph $x > -3$.

b. Graph $x \leq 0$.

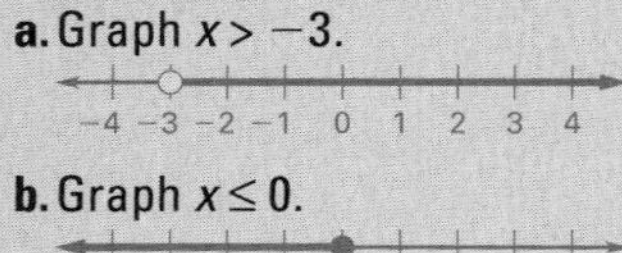

Extra Example 2

a. Graph $-2 \leq x < 3$.

b. Graph $x < -1$ or $x \geq 1$.

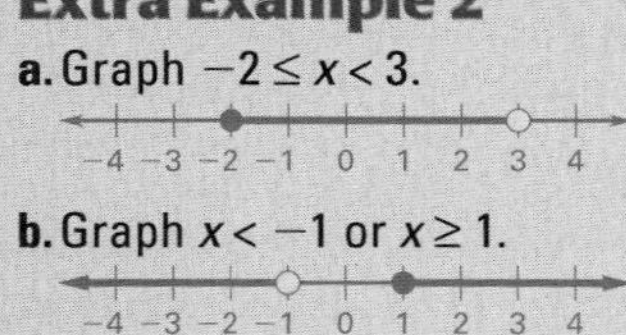

Extra Example 3

You have budgeted \$66 a month to spend on yoga classes. Your yoga studio charges a \$22 per month membership fee, plus \$5.50 per class attended. Describe the possible number of classes you can attend each month. **You can take 8 classes or fewer.**

An **Animated Algebra** activity is available on-line for **Example 3**. This activity is also available on the **Power Presentations CD-ROM**.

SOLVING INEQUALITIES To solve a linear inequality in one variable, you isolate the variable using transformations that produce **equivalent inequalities**, which are inequalities that have the same solutions as the original inequality.

KEY CONCEPT *For Your Notebook*

Transformations That Produce Equivalent Inequalities

Transformation applied to inequality	Original inequality	Equivalent inequality
Add the same number to each side.	$x - 7 < 4$	$x < 11$
Subtract the same number from each side.	$x + 3 \geq -1$	$x \geq -4$
Multiply each side by the same *positive* number.	$\frac{1}{2}x > 10$	$x > 20$
Divide each side by the same *positive* number.	$5x \leq 15$	$x \leq 3$
Multiply each side by the same *negative* number and *reverse* the inequality.	$-x < 17$	$x > -17$
Divide each side by the same *negative* number and *reverse* the inequality.	$-9x \geq 45$	$x \leq -5$

EXAMPLE 3 Solve an inequality with a variable on one side

FAIR You have \$50 to spend at a county fair. You spend \$20 for admission. You want to play a game that costs \$1.50. Describe the possible numbers of times you can play the game.

ANOTHER WAY
For alternative methods for solving the problem in Example 3, turn to page 48 for the **Problem Solving Workshop**.

Solution

STEP 1 **Write** a verbal model. Then write an inequality.

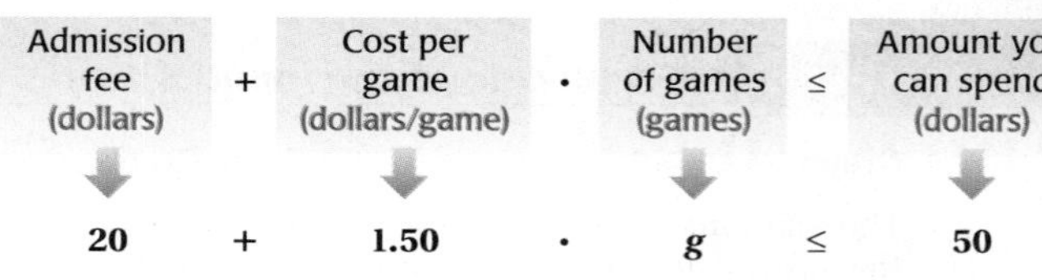

Admission fee (dollars)
+
Cost per game (dollars/game)
·
Number of games (games)
≤
Amount you can spend (dollars)
20
+
1.50
·
g
≤
50

An inequality is $20 + 1.5g \leq 50$.

STEP 2 **Solve** the inequality.

$20 + 1.5g \leq 50$ **Write inequality.**

$1.5g \leq 30$ **Subtract 20 from each side.**

$g \leq 20$ **Divide each side by 1.5.**

▶ You can play the game 20 times or fewer.

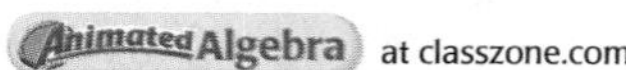

at classzone.com

Differentiated Instruction

Below Level When students see number lines on which the integers are marked, some of them may think that the solutions to the inequalities are made up only of integers. For example, they may think that the solutions of $x > 2$ are 3, 4, 5, ... Use a number line to illustrate that numbers such as 2.1, $\frac{7}{2}$, and π are all solutions of $x > 2$ and ask students to give you additional solutions. See also the *Algebra 2 Toolkit* for more strategies.

EXAMPLE 4 Solve an inequality with a variable on both sides

Solve $5x + 2 > 7x - 4$. Then graph the solution.

$5x + 2 > 7x - 4$	Write original inequality.
$-2x + 2 > -4$	Subtract $7x$ from each side.
$-2x > -6$	Subtract 2 from each side.
$x < 3$	Divide each side by -2 and reverse the inequality.

▶ The solutions are all real numbers less than 3. The graph is shown below.

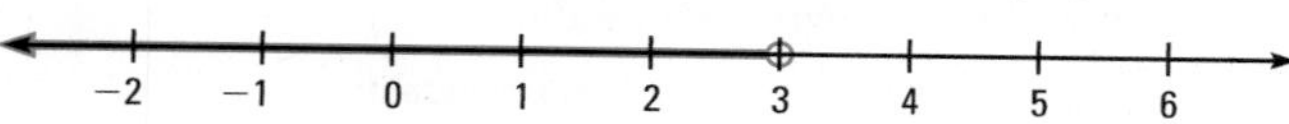

AVOID ERRORS

Don't forget to reverse the inequality symbol if you multiply or divide each side of an inequality by a negative number.

GUIDED PRACTICE for Examples 3 and 4

Solve the inequality. Then graph the solution. 5–8. See margin for art.

5. $4x + 9 < 25$ $x < 4$
6. $1 - 3x \geq -14$ $x \leq 5$
7. $5x - 7 \leq 6x$ $x \geq -7$
8. $3 - x > x - 9$ $x < 6$

EXAMPLE 5 Solve an "and" compound inequality

Solve $-4 < 6x - 10 \leq 14$. Then graph the solution.

$-4 < 6x - 10 \leq 14$	Write original inequality.
$-4 + 10 < 6x - 10 + 10 \leq 14 + 10$	Add 10 to each expression.
$6 < 6x \leq 24$	Simplify.
$1 < x \leq 4$	Divide each expression by 6.

▶ The solutions are all real numbers greater than 1 and less than or equal to 4. The graph is shown below.

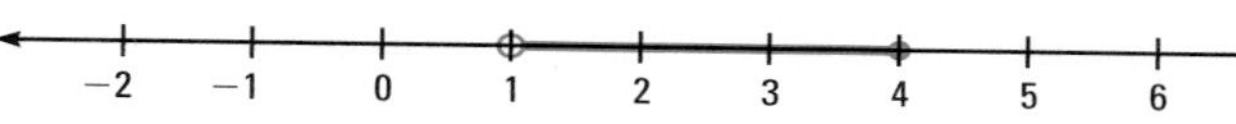

EXAMPLE 6 Solve an "or" compound inequality

Solve $3x + 5 \leq 11$ or $5x - 7 \geq 23$. Then graph the solution.

Solution

A solution of this compound inequality is a solution of *either* of its parts.

First Inequality		**Second Inequality**	
$3x + 5 \leq 11$	Write first inequality.	$5x - 7 \geq 23$	Write second inequality.
$3x \leq 6$	Subtract 5 from each side.	$5x \geq 30$	Add 7 to each side.
$x \leq 2$	Divide each side by 3.	$x \geq 6$	Divide each side by 5.

▶ The graph is shown below. The solutions are all real numbers less than or equal to 2 or greater than or equal to 6.

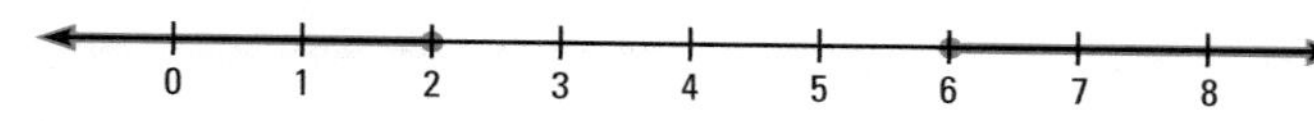

Extra Example 4

Solve $4x + 3 \leq 6x - 5$. Then graph the solution. $x \geq 4$

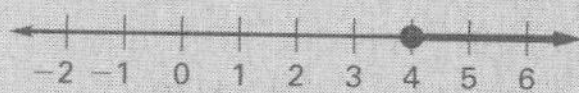

Key Question to Ask for Example 4

- If you start by subtracting $5x$ from each side, rather than $7x$, and then add 4 to each side, what inequality will you get in the final step? Is this the same as $x < 3$? $3 > x$; yes

Extra Example 5

Solve $-10 < 3x + 5 \leq 8$. Then graph the solution. $-5 < x \leq 1$

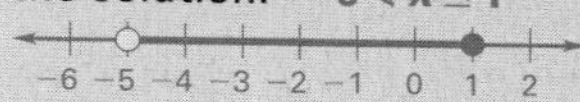

Extra Example 6

Solve $2x - 1 \leq -7$ or $4x + 3 \geq 7$. Then graph the solution. $x \leq -3$ or $x \geq 1$

−4 −3 −2 −1 0 1 2 3 4

Key Question to Ask for Example 6

- Compare the inequalities given in Examples 5 and 6. What can you tell about how their graphs will differ without actually solving the inequalities? The inequality in Example 5 is an "and" compound inequality, so its graph will consist of a single segment on the number line, while the inequality in Example 6 is an "or" inequality, so its graph will consist of two non-overlapping rays going in opposite directions. Also, the inequality symbols tell you that the graph for Example 5 will contain only one of the endpoints, while the graph for Example 6 will contain both endpoints.

Differentiated Instruction

Advanced After discussing **Examples 5 and 6**, give a brief introduction of *set-builder notation.* Explain that this notation is a short symbolic representation of the solutions to linear inequalities like those in these examples. For instance, the result in Example 5 can be written as $\{x \mid 1 < x \leq 4\}$, which is read "the set of all numbers x such that x is greater than 1 and less than or equal to 4." Show the result of Example 6 as $\{x \mid x \leq 2 \text{ or } x \geq 6\}$, which is read "the set of all numbers x such that x is less than or equal to 2 or greater than or equal to 6."

See also the *Algebra 2 Toolkit* for more strategies.

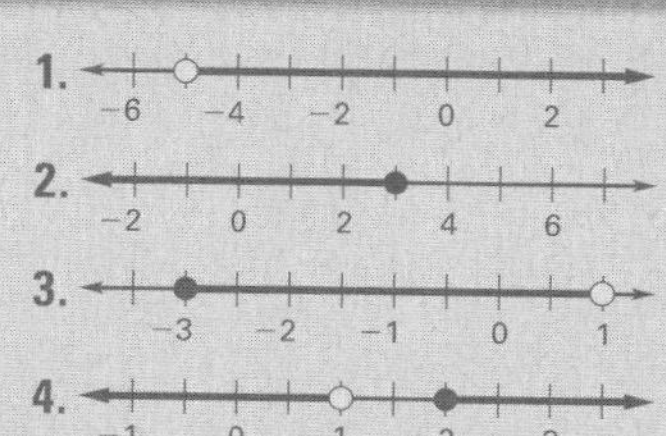

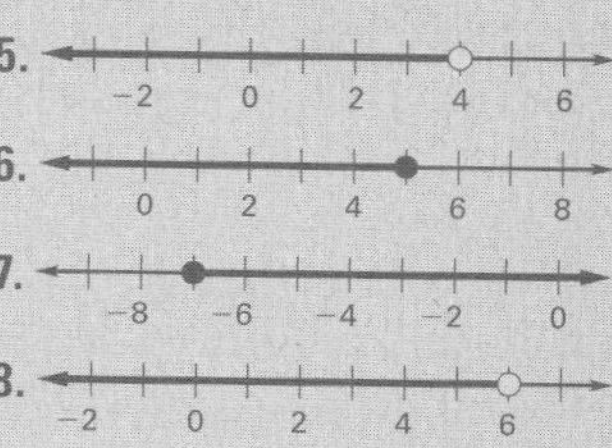

Extra Example 7

In Illinois, the lowest temperature on record is −36°F in January, 1999, in Congerville, while the highest temperature on record is 117°F in July, 1954, in East St. Louis. Write the range of temperatures as an inequality. Then write an inequality giving the temperature range in degrees Celsius.
$-36 \le F \le 117$; $-37.8 \le C \le 47.2$

Closing the Lesson

Have students summarize the major points of the lesson and answer the Essential Question: How are the rules for solving linear inequalities similar to those for solving linear equations, and how are they different?

- Inequalities can be solved by a series of steps that each result in an inequality which is equivalent to the preceding one.
- A number line can be used to graph the solution of an inequality.

The addition and subtraction properties are the same, but if you multiply or divide both sides of an inequality by a negative number, the inequality symbol must be reversed.

Guided Practice

Skill Practice

2. See below.

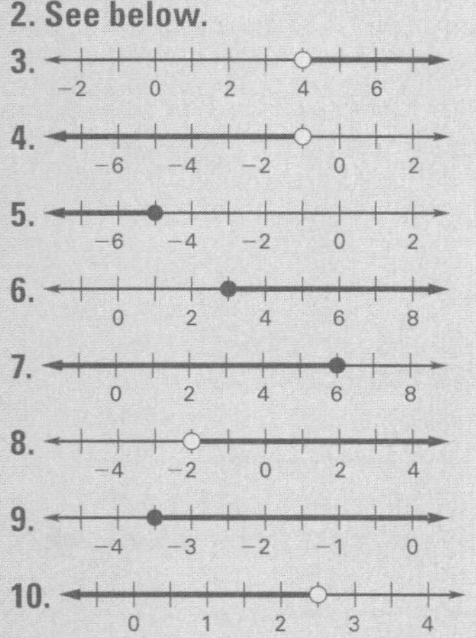

EXAMPLE 7 Write and use a compound inequality

BIOLOGY A monitor lizard has a temperature that ranges from 18°C to 34°C. Write the range of temperatures as a compound inequality. Then write an inequality giving the temperature range in degrees Fahrenheit.

Monitor lizard

Solution

The range of temperatures C can be represented by the inequality $18 \le C \le 34$. Let F represent the temperature in degrees Fahrenheit.

USE A FORMULA
In Example 7, use the temperature formula $C = \frac{5}{9}(F - 32)$.

$18 \le C \le 34$	Write inequality.
$18 \le \frac{5}{9}(F - 32) \le 34$	Substitute $\frac{5}{9}(F - 32)$ for C.
$32.4 \le F - 32 \le 61.2$	Multiply each expression by $\frac{9}{5}$, the reciprocal of $\frac{5}{9}$.
$64.4 \le F \le 93.2$	Add 32 to each expression.

▶ The temperature of the monitor lizard ranges from 64.4°F to 93.2°F.

GUIDED PRACTICE for Examples 5, 6, and 7

Solve the inequality. Then graph the solution. 9–12. See margin for art.

9. $-1 < 2x + 7 < 19$ $-4 < x < 6$
10. $-8 \le -x - 5 \le 6$ $-11 \le x \le 3$
11. $x + 4 \le 9$ or $x - 3 \ge 7$ $x \le 5$ or $x \ge 10$
12. $3x - 1 < -1$ or $2x + 5 \ge 11$ $x < 0$ or $x \ge 3$
13. **WHAT IF?** In Example 7, write a compound inequality for a lizard whose temperature ranges from 15°C to 30°C. Then write an inequality giving the temperature range in degrees Fahrenheit. $15 \le C \le 30$; $59 \le F \le 86$

1.6 EXERCISES

HOMEWORK KEY
○ = **WORKED-OUT SOLUTIONS** on p. WS2 for Exs. 13, 25, and 55
★ = **STANDARDIZED TEST PRACTICE** Exs. 2, 15, 36, 56, and 59

SKILL PRACTICE

1. **VOCABULARY** Copy and complete: The set of all points on a number line that represent solutions of an inequality is called the _?_ of the inequality. graph
2. ★ **WRITING** The first transformation on page 42 can be written as follows:

   If a, b, and c are real numbers and $a > b$, then $a + c > b + c$.

   Write similar statements for the other transformations listed on page 42. See margin.

EXAMPLE 1 on p. 41 for Exs. 3–10

GRAPHING INEQUALITIES Graph the inequality. 3–10. See margin.

3. $x > 4$
4. $x < -1$
5. $x \le -5$
6. $x \ge 3$
7. $6 \ge x$
8. $-2 < x$
9. $x \ge -3.5$
10. $x < 2.5$

2. *Sample answer:* If a, b, and c are real numbers and $a > b$, then $a - c > b - c$. If a, b, and c are real numbers with $c > 0$ and $a > b$, then $ac > bc$. If a, b, and c are real numbers with $c > 0$ and $a > b$, then $\frac{a}{c} > \frac{b}{c}$. If a, b, and c are real numbers with $c < 0$ and $a > b$, then $ac < bc$. If a, b, and c are real numbers with $c < 0$ and $a > b$, then $\frac{a}{c} < \frac{b}{c}$.

EXAMPLE 2
on p. 41
for Exs. 11–21

WRITING COMPOUND INEQUALITIES **Write the compound inequality that is represented by the graph.**

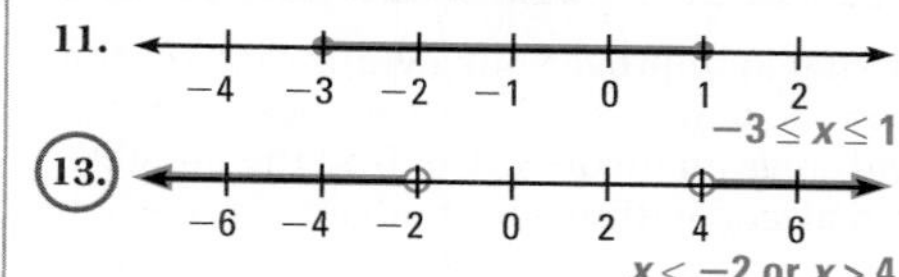

11. $-3 \le x \le 1$

13. $x < -2$ or $x > 4$

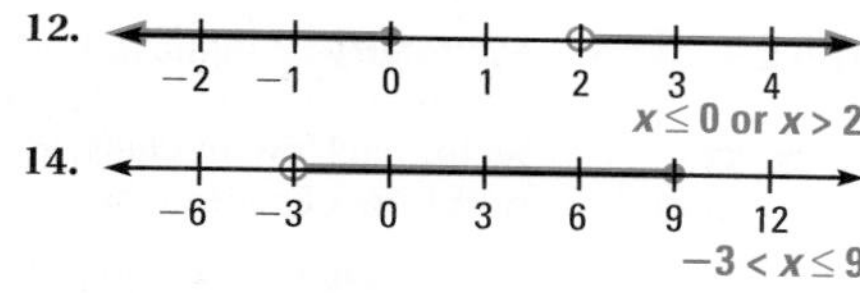

12. $x \le 0$ or $x > 2$

14. $-3 < x \le 9$

15. ★ **MULTIPLE CHOICE** What compound inequality is graphed below? C

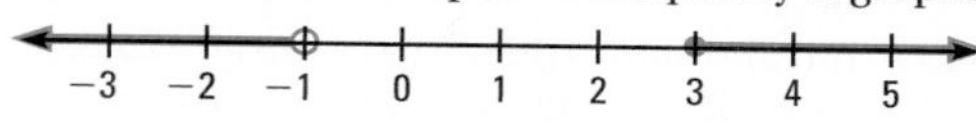

Ⓐ $-1 < x < 3$ Ⓑ $x \le -1$ or $x > 3$

Ⓒ $x < -1$ or $x \ge 3$ Ⓓ $x > -1$ or $x \le 3$

GRAPHING COMPOUND INEQUALITIES **Graph the compound inequality.** 16–21. See margin.

16. $2 \le x \le 5$ 17. $-3 < x < 4$ 18. $5 \le x < 10$

19. $x < 0$ or $x > 2$ 20. $x \le -1$ or $x > 1$ 21. $x > -2$ or $x < -5$

EXAMPLES 3 and 4
on pp. 42–43
for Exs. 22–35

SOLVING INEQUALITIES **Solve the inequality. Then graph the solution.** 22–33. See margin for art.

22. $x + 4 > 10$ $x > 6$ 23. $x - 3 \le -5$ $x \le -2$ 24. $4x - 8 \ge -4$ $x \ge 1$

25. $15 - 3x > 3$ $x < 4$ 26. $11 + 8x \ge 7$ $x \ge -\frac{1}{2}$ 27. $4 + \frac{3}{2}x \le 13$ $x \le 6$

28. $2x - 6 > 3 - x$ $x > 3$ 29. $4x + 14 < 3x + 6$ $x < -8$ 30. $5 - 8x \le 19 - 10x$ $x \le 7$

31. $21x + 7 < 3x + 16$ $x < \frac{1}{2}$ 32. $18 + 2x \le 9x + 4$ $x \ge 2$ 33. $2(x - 4) > 4x + 6$ $x < -7$

ERROR ANALYSIS ***Describe*** **and correct the error in solving the inequality.**

34.

$2x + 8 \le 6x - 4$

$-4x \le -12$

$x \le 3$

35.

$10 + 3x > 5x$

$10 < 2x$

$5 < x$

34. The inequality symbol should be switched when dividing by a negative number; $x \ge 3$.

35. The inequality symbol should not be reversed when subtracting; $10 > 2x$, $5 > x$.

36. ★ **OPEN-ENDED MATH** Write two different inequalities of the form $ax + b > c$ that have a solution of $x > 5$. *Sample answer:* $4x + 2 > 22$, $3x + 12 > 27$

EXAMPLE 5 B
on p. 43
for Exs. 37–42

"AND" COMPOUND INEQUALITIES **Solve the inequality. Then graph the solution.** 37–42. See margin for art.

37. $-5 < x + 1 < 4$ $-6 < x < 3$ 38. $2 \le x - 3 \le 6$ $5 \le x \le 9$ 39. $-3 < 4 - x \le 3$ $1 \le x < 7$

40. $2 < 3x - 1 \le 6$ $1 < x \le 2\frac{1}{3}$ 41. $-4 \le 2 + 4x < 0$ $-1\frac{1}{2} \le x < -\frac{1}{2}$ 42. $0 \le \frac{3}{4}x + 3 \le 4$ $-4 \le x \le 1\frac{1}{3}$

EXAMPLE 6
on p. 43
for Exs. 43–48

"OR" COMPOUND INEQUALITIES **Solve the inequality. Then graph the solution.** 43–48. See margin for art.

43. $x + 1 < -3$ or $x - 2 > 0$ $x < -4$ or $x > 2$ 44. $x - 4 \le -6$ or $x + 2 > 5$ $x \le -2$ or $x > 3$

45. $2x - 3 \le -4$ or $3x + 1 \ge 4$ $x \le -\frac{1}{2}$ or $x \ge 1$ 46. $2 + 3x < -13$ or $4 + 2x > 7$ $x < -5$ or $x > 1\frac{1}{2}$

47. $0.3x - 0.5 < -1.7$ or $0.4x \ge 2.4$ $x < -4$ or $x \ge 6$ 48. $-x - 4 \ge 1$ or $2 - 5x \le -8$ $x \le -5$ or $x \ge 2$

C **CHALLENGE** **Solve the inequality. If there is no solution, write *no solution*. If the inequality is always true, write *all real numbers*.**

49. $2(x - 4) > 2x + 1$ no solution 50. $4x - 5 \le 4(x + 2)$ all real numbers 51. $2(3x - 1) > 3(2x + 3)$ no solution

4 PRACTICE AND APPLY

Assignment Guide

Answer Transparencies available for all exercises

Basic:
Day 1: pp. 44–47
Exs. 1–6, 11–18, 22–27
Day 2: pp. 44–47
Exs. 28–39, 43, 44, 52–57, 61–62

Average:
Day 1: pp. 44–47
Exs. 1, 2, 7–15, 19–27
Day 2: pp. 44–47
Exs. 28–36, 37–47 odd, 50–59*, 61

Advanced:
Day 1: pp. 44–47
Exs. 1, 2, 7–21 odd, 22–27, 52, 53
Day 2: pp. 44–47
Exs. 28–33, 37–51*, 54–62*

Block:
pp. 44–47
Exs. 1, 2, 7–15, 19–36, 37–47 odd, 50–59*, 61

Differentiated Instruction

See *Algebra 2 Best Practices Toolkit* for suggestions on addressing the needs of a diverse classroom.

Homework Check

For a quick check of student understanding of key concepts, go over the following exercises:

Basic: 4, 17, 30, 38, 52
Average: 8, 20, 30, 44, 53
Advanced: 9, 21, 32, 46, 53

Extra Practice

- Student Edition, p. 1010
- Chapter 1 Resource Book: Practice levels A, B, C, pp. 63–65

Practice Worksheet

An easily-readable reduced practice page (with answers) for this lesson can be found on p. 1C.

Differentiated Instruction

Advanced Some students may notice that all the graphs for **Exercises 37–42** are segments on the number line, while all the graphs for **Exercises 43–48** are two rays going in opposite directions. However, these are not the only possibilities for the graphs of compound inequalities. Have advanced students explore possibilities where the graph might be a single ray, the entire number line, the entire number line except for one point, or an empty number line.

See also the *Algebra 2 Toolkit* for more strategies.

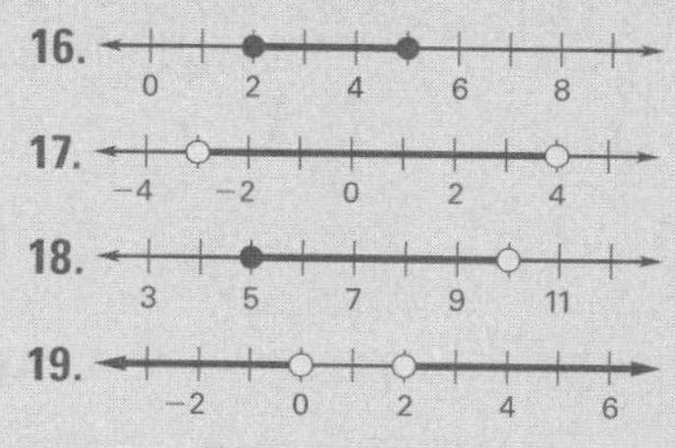

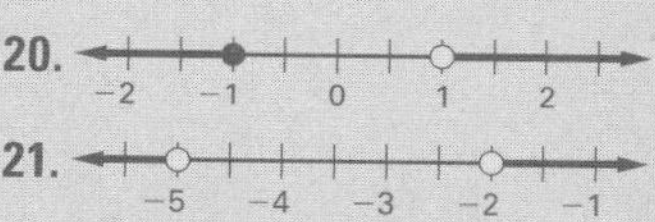

22–33, 37–48. See Additional Answers beginning on p. AA1.

Avoiding Common Errors

Exercises 22–33 An error that many students make when solving linear inequalities is neglecting to reverse the inequality symbol when multiplying or dividing by a negative number. A related error that some students make is to reverse the symbol even when adding or subtracting. To help students remember the properties of inequality correctly, use a number line to illustrate what happens to the relative position of the numbers when you add 2 to each side of $5 > 3$, what happens when you substract 2 from each side, what happens when you multiply each side by 2, and what happens when you multiply each side by -2.

Reading Strategy

Exercises 52–60 In order to solve applied problems involving inequalities, students must correctly interpret the words in the problems that indicate which inequality symbol to use. Students may benefit from making a table of key words or phrases that describe an inequality. Some phrases to look for in their tables are "at least," "at most," "no more than," "no less than," "or better," and "between *x* and *y*, inclusive."

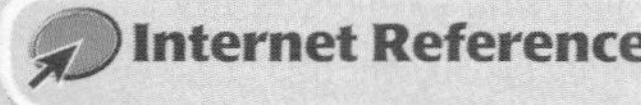

Exercise 55 Additional information about Olympic National Park can be found on the National Park Service's website www.nps.gov/olym

PROBLEM SOLVING

EXAMPLE 3 A on p. 42 for Exs. 52–53

52. SWIMMING You have budgeted \$100 to improve your swimming over the summer. At your local pool, it costs \$50 to join the swim association and \$5 for each swim class. Write and solve an inequality to find the possible numbers of swim classes you can attend within your budget. $5x + 50 \le 100$, $x \le 10$ swim classes

@HomeTutor for problem solving help at classzone.com

53. VIDEO CONTEST You and some friends have raised \$250 to help make a video for a contest. You need \$35 to buy videotapes. It costs \$45 per day to rent the video camera. Write and solve an inequality to find the possible numbers of days you can rent the video camera. $45x + 35 \le 250$, $x \le 4\frac{7}{9}$ days; 4 or fewer days

@HomeTutor for problem solving help at classzone.com

54. WAKEBOARDING What you wear when you wakeboard depends on the air temperature. Copy and complete the table by writing an inequality for each temperature range. Assume each range includes the lower temperature but not the higher temperature. (The first inequality has been written for you.) $65 \le T < 72$; $72 \le T < 80$; $T \ge 80$

Temperature	Gear	Inequality
60°F to 65°F	Full wetsuit	$60 \le T < 65$
65°F to 72°F	Full leg wetsuit	?
72°F to 80°F	Wetsuit trunks	?
80°F or warmer	No special gear	?

(55.) **BOTANY** In Olympic National Park in Washington, different plants grow depending on the elevation, as shown in the diagram. Assume each range includes the lower elevation but not the higher elevation.

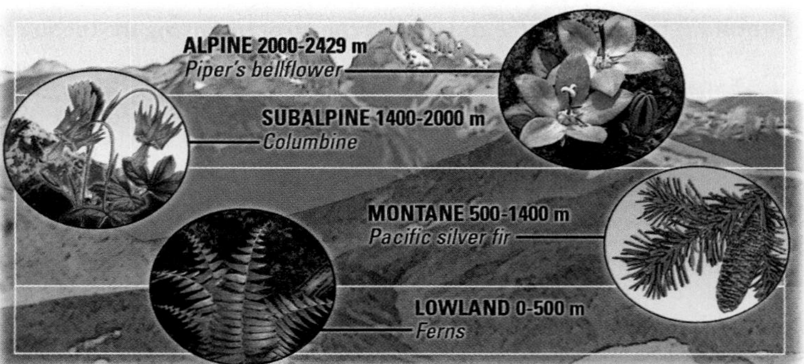

a. Write an inequality for elevations in the lowland zone. $0 \le e < 500$

b. Write an inequality for elevations in the alpine and subalpine zones combined. $1400 \le e < 2429$

c. Write an inequality for elevations *not* in the montane zone. $0 \le e < 500$ or $1400 \le e < 2429$

B

56. ★ MULTIPLE CHOICE Canoe rental costs \$18 for the first two hours and \$3 per hour after that. You want to canoe for more than 2 hours but can spend no more than \$30. Which inequality represents the situation, where *t* is the total number of hours you can canoe? D

Ⓐ $18 + t \le 30$ Ⓑ $18 + 3t \le 30$

Ⓒ $18 + 3(t + 2) \le 30$ Ⓓ $18 + 3(t - 2) \le 30$

○ = WORKED-OUT SOLUTIONS on p. WS1   ★ = STANDARDIZED TEST PRACTICE

EXAMPLE 7 on p. 44 for Exs. 57–58

59a. Amy: $0.65(84) + 0.15(80) + 0.2w \geq 85$, Brian: $0.65(80) + 0.15(100) + 0.2x \geq 85$, Clara: $0.65(75) + 0.15(95) + 0.2y \geq 85$, Dan: $0.65(80) + 0.15(90) + 0.2z \geq 85$

59b. $w \geq 92$; $x \geq 90$; $y \geq 110$; $z \geq 97.5$

59c. Amy, Brian, and Dan; it is impossible to score over 100 points on a test, so Clara will not be able to achieve a grade of 85 or better.

57. **LAPTOP COMPUTERS** A computer manufacturer states that its laptop computer can operate within a temperature range of 50°F to 95°F. Write a compound inequality for the temperature range. Then rewrite the inequality in degrees Celsius. $50 \leq F \leq 95$; $10 \leq C \leq 35$

58. **MULTI-STEP PROBLEM** On a certain highway, there is a minimum speed of 45 miles per hour and a maximum speed of 70 miles per hour.
   a. Write a compound inequality for the legal speeds on the highway. $45 \leq s \leq 70$
   b. Write a compound inequality for the illegal speeds on the highway. $s < 45$ or $s > 70$
   c. Write each compound inequality from parts (a) and (b) so that it expresses the speeds in kilometers per hour. (1 mi ≈ 1.61 km) $72.45 \leq s \leq 112.7$, $s < 72.45$ or $s > 112.7$

59. ★ **EXTENDED RESPONSE** A math teacher announces that grades will be calculated by adding 65% of a student's homework score, 15% of the student's quiz score, and 20% of the student's final exam score. All scores range from 0 to 100 points. See margin.
   a. **Write Inequalities** Write an inequality for each student that can be used to find the possible final exam scores that result in a grade of 85 or better.
   b. **Solve** Solve the inequalities from part (a).
   c. **Interpret** For which students is a grade of 85 or better possible? *Explain.*

Name	Homework	Quiz	Exam
Amy	84	80	*w*
Brian	80	100	*x*
Clara	75	95	*y*
Dan	80	90	*z*

C 60. **CHALLENGE** You are shopping for single-use cameras to hand out at a party. The daylight cameras cost \$2.75 and the flash cameras cost \$4.25. You must buy exactly 20 cameras and you want to spend between \$65 and \$75, inclusive. Write and solve a compound inequality for this situation. Then list all the solutions that involve whole numbers of cameras. See margin.

KENTUCKY MIXED REVIEW

TEST PRACTICE at classzone.com

61. Steve has 6 fewer trading cards than Kevin. Thomas has twice as many trading cards as Steve. The three students have a total of 22 trading cards. Which equation can be used to find the number of trading cards that Kevin has? **C**
   Ⓐ $x - 6x + \frac{1}{2}x = 22$
   Ⓑ $x + (x - 6) + 2x = 22$
   Ⓒ $x + (x - 6) + 2(x - 6) = 22$
   Ⓓ $2x + (x - 6) + (x - 6) = 22$

62. The radius and height of a cylindrical can are doubled. How does the surface area of the new cylindrical can compare with the surface area of the original cylindrical can? **B**
   Ⓐ The new surface area is two times the original surface area.
   Ⓑ The new surface area is four times the original surface area.
   Ⓒ The new surface area is six times the original surface area.
   Ⓓ The new surface area is eight times the original surface area.

5 ASSESS AND RETEACH

Daily Homework Quiz

Transparency Available

Solve the inequality. Then graph the solution.

1. $4x - 7 \leq 12x + 9$ $x \geq -2$

2. $2x + 8 < 0$ or $3x + 5 > 11$
   $x < -4$ or $x > 2$

3. You have budgeted \$120 to rent a moving truck for 2 days. The rental fee is \$39 per day plus \$.25 per mile. Write and solve an inequality to find the possible number of miles you can drive the truck and stay within your budget. $2(39) + 0.25x \leq 120$; $x \leq 168$; you can drive 168 miles or less.

Online Quiz

Available at **classzone.com**

Diagnosis/Remediation

- Practice A, B, C in Chapter 1 Resource Book, pp. 63–65
- Study Guide in Chapter 1 Resource Book, pp. 66–67
- Practice Workbook, pp. 11–12
- @HomeTutor

Challenge

Additional challenge is available in the Chapter 1 Resource Book, p. 70.

60. $65 \leq 2.75x + 4.25(20 - x) \leq 75$, $6\frac{2}{3} \leq x \leq 13\frac{1}{3}$; 7 daylight cameras and 13 flash cameras, 8 daylight cameras and 12 flash cameras, 9 daylight cameras and 11 flash cameras, 10 daylight cameras and 10 flash cameras, 11 daylight cameras and 9 flash cameras, 12 daylight cameras and 8 flash cameras, 13 daylight cameras and 7 flash cameras

Alternative Strategy

Another way to solve the Problem with a graphing calculator is to graph $Y_1 = 20 + 1.5x$ and $Y_2 = 50$ on the same screen. Using the *intersect* feature or the *table* feature, you can see that $Y_1 = Y_2$ when $x = 20$ and that $Y_1 < Y_2$ when $x < 20$. Putting these two results together gives the solution, $x \leq 20$, which translates into saying that you can play 20 games or fewer. This method allows students to visualize the problem in a different way from the algebraic method for solving Example 3 of Lesson 1.6 shown on page 42 or either of the graphing calculator methods shown here.

Teaching Strategy

Be sure students understand that although the calculator table shown in Method 1 shows the exact result that $y = 50$ when $x = 20$, in similar problems, the desired y-value might not actually appear in the table. For example, if you had $49 to spend at the county fair instead of $50, you could not read the answer in the same way. Instead, since $y = 48.5$ when $x = 19$ and $y = 50$ when $x = 20$, you can play the game just 19 or fewer times.

PROBLEM SOLVING WORKSHOP LESSON 1.6

Using ALTERNATIVE METHODS

Another Way to Solve Example 3, page 42

MULTIPLE REPRESENTATIONS Example 3 of Lesson 1.6 involved solving an inequality using algebra. You can also solve an inequality using a table or a graphing calculator's *test* feature, which tells when an inequality is true or false.

PROBLEM

FAIR You have $50 to spend at a county fair. You spend $20 for admission. You want to play a game that costs $1.50. Describe the possible numbers of times you can play the game.

METHOD 1

Using a Table One alternative approach is to make a table of values.

STEP 1 **Write** an expression for the total cost of admission and playing x games.

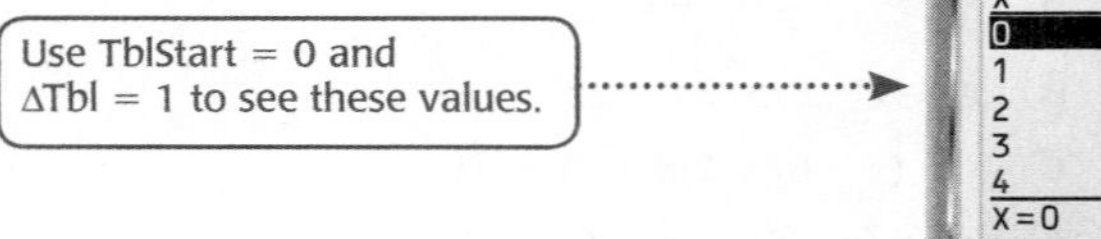

STEP 2 **Enter** the equation $y = 20 + 1.5x$ into a graphing calculator.

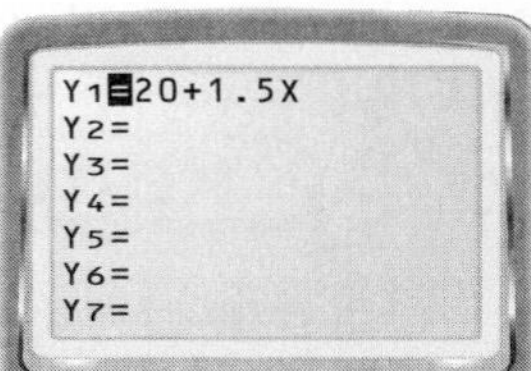

STEP 3 **Make** a table of values for the equation.

Use TblStart = 0 and ΔTbl = 1 to see these values.

X	Y1
0	20
1	21.5
2	23
3	24.5
4	26

X=0

STEP 4 **Scroll** through the table of values to find when the total cost is $50. You can see that $y = 50$ when $x = 20$.

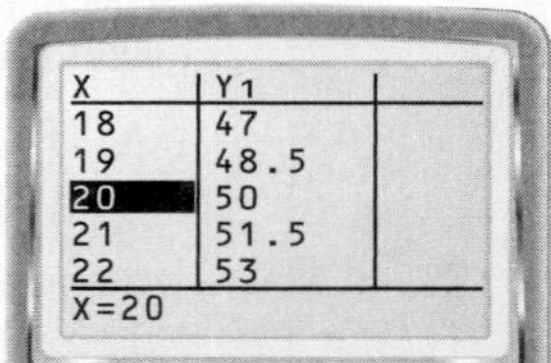

X
Y1
18
47
19
48.5
20
50
21
51.5
22
53
X=20

▶ The table suggests that $20 + 1.5x \leq 50$ when $x \leq 20$. So, you can play the game at the fair 20 times or fewer.

METHOD 2 **Using a Graph** Another approach is to use a graph.

If your graphing calculator has a *test* feature, you can enter the inequality and evaluate its truth for various values of x.

- When the inequality is *true*, the calculator returns a 1.
- When the inequality is *false*, the calculator returns a 0.

STEP 1 **Enter** $y = (20 + 1.5x \le 50)$ into a graphing calculator.

Press 2nd [TEST] 6 to enter the ≤ symbol.

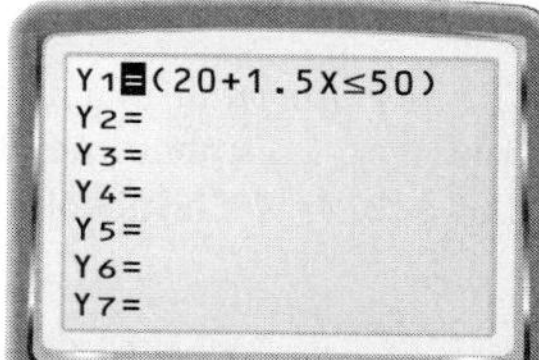

STEP 2 **Graph** the result.

The y-value is 1 for all x-values that make the inequality true.

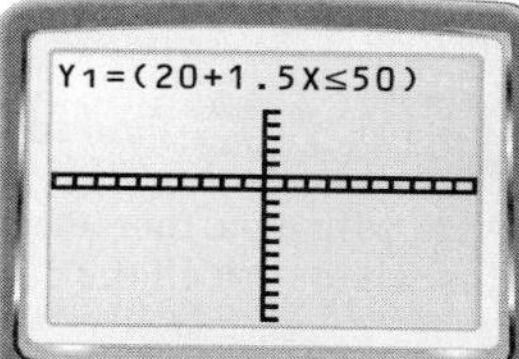

STEP 3 **Find** the point where the inequality changes from true to false by using the *trace* feature.

▶ The graph suggests that the inequality is true when $x \le 20$. So, you can play the game at the fair 20 times or fewer.

PRACTICE

1. **REASONING** Determine the equation that gives the table below. For what x-values is $y < -500$? $y = -35x + 200$; $x > 20$

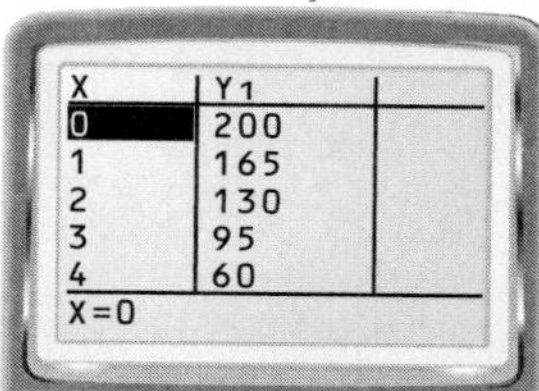

X	Y1	
0	200	
1	165	
2	130	
3	95	
4	60	

X=0

2. **GIFT** You have \$16.50 to spend for a friend's birthday. You spend \$3 on a card and want to buy some chocolates that cost \$.75 each. What are the numbers of chocolates you can buy? Solve using a table and using a graph. $0 \le x \le 18$ chocolates

3. **SALESPERSON** A salesperson has a weekly salary of \$1550 and gets a 5% commission on sales. What are the amounts the salesperson can sell to earn at least \$1900 per week? Solve using a table and using a graph. $x \ge \$7000$

4. **WRITING** *Explain* how to use a table like the one below to solve $0.5x - 1.5 \le 3 - 0.4x$. See margin.

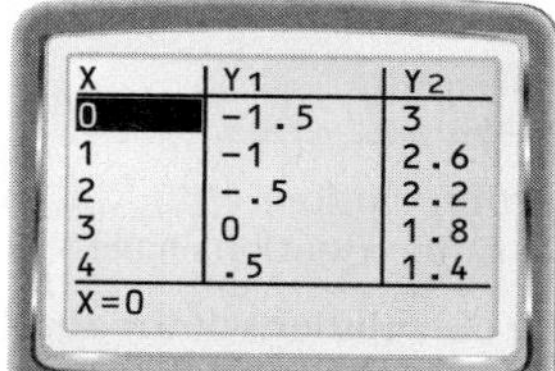

X	Y1	Y2
0	-1.5	3
1	-1	2.6
2	-.5	2.2
3	0	1.8
4	.5	1.4

X=0

Avoiding Common Errors

When using Method 2 to solve this problem, some students may incorrectly conclude that the inequality is *always* true because they have set their viewing window so that Xmax < 20. Encourage them to experiment with different window settings in order to see if and when the y-value changes from 0 to 1.

4. ***Sample answer:*** Compare columns Y_1 and Y_2 and determine for what values of x Y_1 is less than or equal to Y_2.

1 PLAN AND PREPARE

Explore the Concept

- Students will model absolute value equations and inequalities by working with a number line.
- This activity leads into the study of solving absolute value equations and inequalities in Examples 1–5 in Lesson 1.7.

Materials

Each student will need 13 index cards numbered with the integers −6 to 6.

Recommended Time

Work activity: 10 min

Discuss results: 10 min

Grouping

Students should work individually.

2 TEACH

Alternative Strategy

Use masking tape to lay out a number line on the floor, and have students walk along this line to model the solutions of the given equations and inequalities.

Key Discovery

Absolute value equations have at most two solutions, while absolute value inequalities have infinitely many solutions.

3 ASSESS AND RETEACH

1. Are the solutions of an absolute value equation always the same distance from 0? no
2. Did the cards you chose as solutions for the inequalities represent *all* the solutions of these inequalities? Explain. No; there are infinitely many solutions for each of the inequalities.

1.7 Absolute Value Equations and Inequalities

MATERIALS • 13 index cards numbered with the integers from −6 to 6

QUESTION **What does the solution of an absolute value equation or inequality look like on a number line?**

The *absolute value* of a number x, written $|x|$, is the distance the number is from 0 on a number line. Because 2 and −2 are both 2 units from 0, $|2| = 2$ and $|-2| = 2$. The absolute value of a number is never negative.

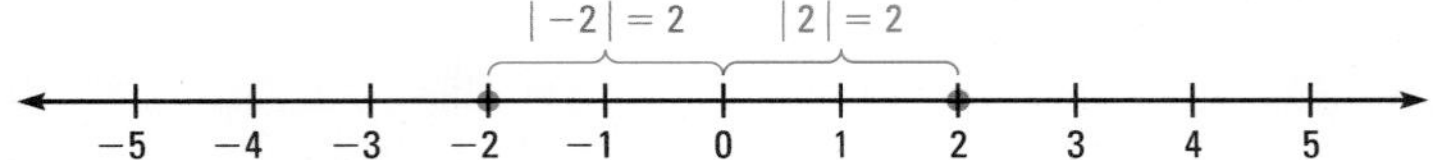

EXPLORE **Find solutions of absolute value equations and inequalities**

Work with a partner. Place the numbered index cards in a row to form a number line. Then turn all the cards face down.

STEP 1

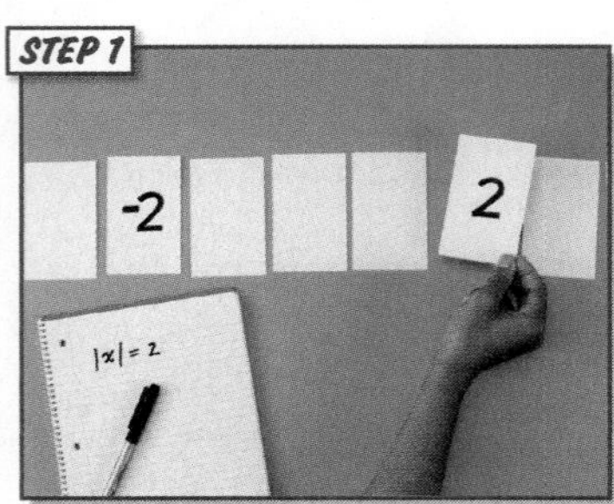

Solve equations Turn over cards to reveal numbers that are solutions of the equations below.

a. $|x| = 2$

b. $|x - 2| = 1$

c. $|x + 1| = 3$

STEP 2

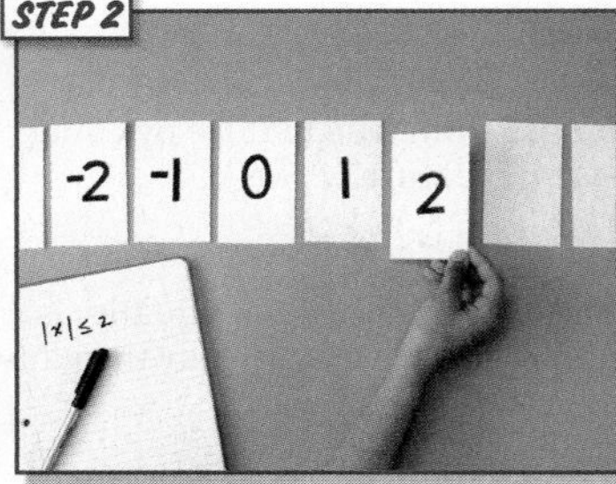

Solve inequalities with ≤ Turn over cards to reveal numbers that are solutions of the inequalities below.

d. $|x| \le 2$

e. $|x - 2| \le 1$

f. $|x + 1| \le 3$

STEP 3

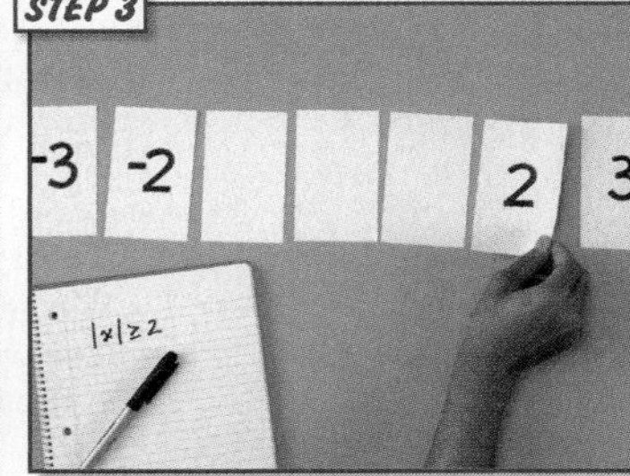

Solve inequalities with ≥ Turn over cards to reveal numbers that are solutions of the inequalities below.

g. $|x| \ge 2$

h. $|x - 2| \ge 1$

i. $|x + 1| \ge 3$

DRAW CONCLUSIONS **Use your observations to complete these exercises** 1, 2. See margin.

1. *Describe* the solutions of the absolute value equations in Step 1. Will all absolute value equations have the same number of solutions? *Explain.*
2. *Compare* the solutions of the absolute value inequalities in Steps 2 and 3. How does the inequality symbol (≤ or ≥) affect the pattern of the solutions?

1. ***Sample answer:*** The solutions in Step 1 are two distinct points; no; the equation $|x| = k$ has only 1 solution if $k = 0$ and has no solutions if k is negative.

2. ***Sample answer:*** In Step 2 the solutions are between the two endpoints. In Step 3 the solutions begin at two points and then go in opposite directions; if the inequality symbol is ≤, the solution will resemble the solution in Step 2. If the inequality symbol is ≥, the solution will resemble the solution in Step 3.

1.7 Solve Absolute Value Equations and Inequalities

MA-HS-5.3.1

Before You solved linear equations and inequalities.
Now You will solve absolute value equations and inequalities.
Why? So you can describe hearing ranges of animals, as in Ex. 81.

Key Vocabulary
- absolute value
- extraneous solution

MA-HS-5.3.1
Students will model, solve and graph first degree, single variable equations and inequalities, including absolute value, based in real-world and mathematical problems and graph the solutions on a number line. DOK 2

Recall that the **absolute value** of a number x, written $|x|$, is the distance the number is from 0 on a number line. This understanding of absolute value can be extended to apply to simple absolute value equations.

$$|x| = \begin{cases} x, & \text{if } x \text{ is positive} \\ 0, & \text{if } x = 0 \\ -x, & \text{if } x \text{ is negative} \end{cases}$$

KEY CONCEPT *For Your Notebook*

Interpreting Absolute Value Equations

Equation	$\lvert x\rvert = \lvert x - 0\rvert = k$	$\lvert x - b\rvert = k$
Meaning	The distance between x and 0 is k.	The distance between x and b is k.
Graph	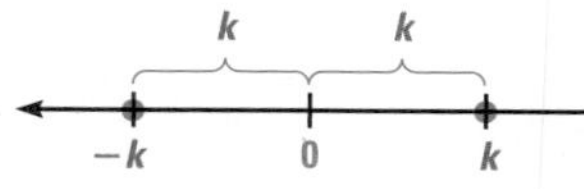	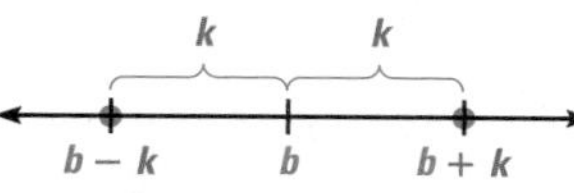
Solutions	$x - 0 = -k$ or $x - 0 = k$ $x = -k$ or $x = k$	$x - b = -k$ or $x - b = k$ $x = b - k$ or $x = b + k$

EXAMPLE 1 Solve a simple absolute value equation

Solve $|x - 5| = 7$. Graph the solution.

Solution

$\lvert x - 5\rvert = 7$	**Write original equation.**
$x - 5 = -7$ or $x - 5 = 7$	**Write equivalent equations.**
$x = 5 - 7$ or $x = 5 + 7$	**Solve for x.**
$x = -2$ or $x = 12$	**Simplify.**

▶ The solutions are -2 and 12. These are the values of x that are 7 units away from 5 on a number line. The graph is shown below.

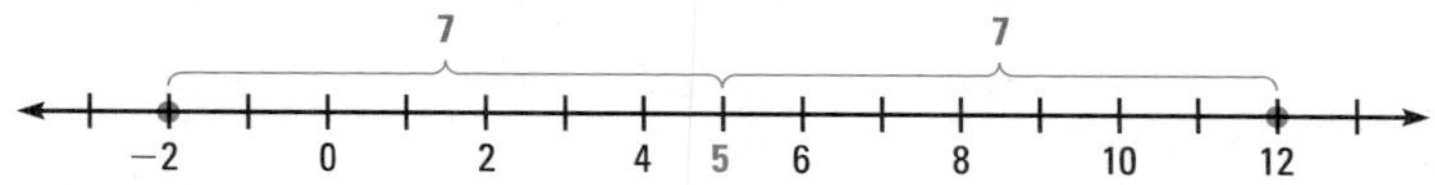

1 PLAN AND PREPARE

Warm-Up Exercises

Transparency Available

Solve the equation or inequality.

1. $3x + 15 = -42$ -19
2. $5x - 8 \le 7$ $x \le 3$
3. $2x + 1 < -3$ or $2x + 1 > 5$ $x < -2$ or $x > 2$
4. In the next 2 weeks you need to work at least 30 hours. If you can work h hours this week and then twice as many hours next week, how many hours must you work this week? at least 10 h

Notetaking Guide

Transparency Available

Promotes interactive learning and notetaking skills, pp. 20–23.

Pacing

Basic: 2 days
Average: 2 days
Advanced: 2 days
Block: 1 block
- See *Teaching Guide/Lesson Plan.*

2 FOCUS AND MOTIVATE

Essential Question

Big Idea 3, p. 1

How are absolute value equations and inequalities like linear equations and inequalities? **Tell students they will learn how to answer this question by learning to solve absolute value equations and inequalities.**

Resource Planning Guide

Chapter Resource Book
- Teaching Guide/Lesson Plan (pp. 71–72)
- Activity Master (p. 73)
- Practice levels A, B, C (pp. 75–77)
- Study Guide (pp. 78–79)
- Catch-up for Absent Students (p. 80)
- Problem Solving Workshop (p. 81)
- Challenge (p. 82)

Workbooks
- Notetaking Guide (pp. 20–23)
- Practice Workbook (pp. 13–14)

Teaching Options
- **Power Presentations CD-ROM** provides dynamic electronic teaching resources for the classroom.
- **Activity Generator CD-ROM** provides editable activities for all ability levels.

Interactive Technology
- Easy Planner
- Power Presentations CD-ROM
- Activity Generator CD-ROM
- Animated Algebra
- Test Generator CD-ROM
- Online Quiz
- eWorkbook
- eEdition
- @HomeTutor

Resources for English Learners
- Quick Reference for English Learners
- Spanish Study Guide
- Multi-Language Visual Glossary
- Student Resources in Spanish

See also the *Algebra 2 Toolkit* for more strategies for meeting individual needs.

Motivating the Lesson

Sporting equipment must be manufactured to meet certain specifications for size and weight. You can use absolute value inequalities to determine whether individual pieces of equipment are close enough to the ideal size and weight to be acceptable for sale.

Extra Example 1

Solve $|2x - 9| = 15$. Graph the solutions. **$-3, 12$**

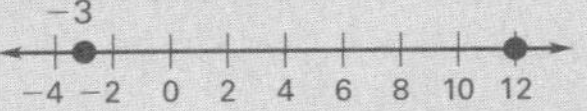

Key Question to Ask for Example 1

- When is the absolute value of a number the same as the number itself? **when the number is greater than or equal to 0**

Extra Example 2

Solve $|4x + 12| = 28$. **$-10, 4$**

Extra Example 3

Solve $|4x + 10| = 6x$. Check for extraneous solutions. **5 (-1 is an extraneous solution.)**

Key Question to Ask for Examples 2 and 3

- Before solving them, how can you tell that the equation in Example 3 might have an extraneous solution while the equation in Example 2 will not? **The equation in Example 2 has only a constant on the right side while the equation in Example 3 contains a variable on the right side.**

KEY CONCEPT *For Your Notebook*

Solving an Absolute Value Equation

Use these steps to solve an absolute value equation $|ax + b| = c$ where $c > 0$.

STEP 1 **Write** two equations: $ax + b = c$ or $ax + b = -c$.

STEP 2 **Solve** each equation.

STEP 3 **Check** each solution in the original absolute value equation.

EXAMPLE 2 Solve an absolute value equation

Solve $|5x - 10| = 45$.

$\|5x - 10\| = 45$			**Write original equation.**
$5x - 10 = 45$	or	$5x - 10 = -45$	**Expression can equal 45 or −45.**
$5x = 55$	or	$5x = -35$	**Add 10 to each side.**
$x = 11$	or	$x = -7$	**Divide each side by 5.**

▶ The solutions are 11 and −7. Check these in the original equation.

CHECK

$\|5x - 10\| = 45$	$\|5x - 10\| = 45$
$\|5(11) - 10\| \stackrel{?}{=} 45$	$\|5(-7) - 10\| \stackrel{?}{=} 45$
$\|45\| \stackrel{?}{=} 45$	$\|-45\| \stackrel{?}{=} 45$
$45 = 45$ ✓	$45 = 45$ ✓

EXTRANEOUS SOLUTIONS When you solve an absolute value equation, it is possible for a solution to be *extraneous*. An **extraneous solution** is an apparent solution that must be rejected because it does not satisfy the original equation.

EXAMPLE 3 Check for extraneous solutions

Solve $|2x + 12| = 4x$. Check for extraneous solutions.

$\|2x + 12\| = 4x$			**Write original equation.**
$2x + 12 = 4x$	or	$2x + 12 = -4x$	**Expression can equal $4x$ or $-4x$.**
$12 = 2x$	or	$12 = -6x$	**Subtract $2x$ from each side.**
$6 = x$	or	$-2 = x$	**Solve for x.**

AVOID ERRORS
Always check your solutions in the original equation to make sure that they are not extraneous.

Check the apparent solutions to see if either is extraneous.

CHECK

$\|2x + 12\| = 4x$	$\|2x + 12\| = 4x$
$\|2(6) + 12\| \stackrel{?}{=} 4(6)$	$\|2(-2) + 12\| \stackrel{?}{=} 4(-2)$
$\|24\| \stackrel{?}{=} 24$	$\|8\| \stackrel{?}{=} -8$
$24 = 24$ ✓	$8 \neq -8$

▶ The solution is 6. Reject −2 because it is an extraneous solution.

Differentiated Instruction

Below Level Some students will be confused by the part of the algebraic definition of absolute value that says "$|x| = -x$ if $x < 0$." Have them read this definition aloud, saying "the absolute value of x is the opposite of x," rather than "the absolute value of x is negative x." Then have them use a number line to practice finding opposites of several positive and negative numbers.

See also the *Algebra 2 Toolkit* for more strategies.

GUIDED PRACTICE for Examples 1, 2, and 3

Solve the equation. Check for extraneous solutions.

1. $|x| = 5$ −5, 5
2. $|x - 3| = 10$ −7, 13
3. $|x + 2| = 7$ −9, 5
4. $|3x - 2| = 13$ $-3\frac{2}{3}$; 5
5. $|2x + 5| = 3x$ 5
6. $|4x - 1| = 2x + 9$ $-1\frac{1}{3}$; 5

INEQUALITIES You can solve an absolute value inequality by rewriting it as a compound inequality and then solving each part.

KEY CONCEPT *For Your Notebook*

Absolute Value Inequalities

Inequality	Equivalent form	Graph of solution
$\|ax + b\| < c$	$-c < ax + b < c$	
$\|ax + b\| \leq c$	$-c \leq ax + b \leq c$	
$\|ax + b\| > c$	$ax + b < -c$ or $ax + b > c$	
$\|ax + b\| \geq c$	$ax + b \leq -c$ or $ax + b \geq c$	

EXAMPLE 4 Solve an inequality of the form $|ax + b| > c$

Solve $|4x + 5| > 13$. Then graph the solution.

Solution

The absolute value inequality is equivalent to $4x + 5 < -13$ or $4x + 5 > 13$.

First Inequality		Second Inequality
$4x + 5 < -13$	**Write inequalities.**	$4x + 5 > 13$
$4x < -18$	**Subtract 5 from each side.**	$4x > 8$
$x < -\frac{9}{2}$	**Divide each side by 4.**	$x > 2$

▸ The solutions are all real numbers less than $-\frac{9}{2}$ or greater than 2. The graph is shown below.

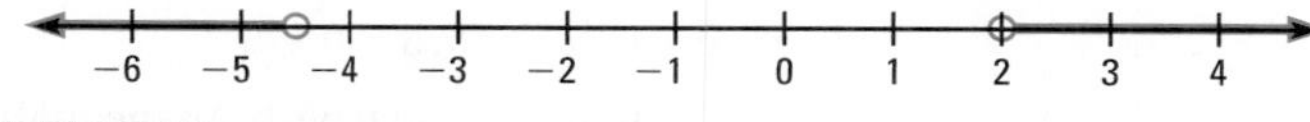

 Animated Algebra at classzone.com

GUIDED PRACTICE for Example 4

Solve the inequality. Then graph the solution. 7–9. See margin for art.

7. $|x + 4| \geq 6$ $x \leq -10$ or $x \geq 2$
8. $|2x - 7| > 1$ $x < 3$ or $x > 4$
9. $|3x + 5| \geq 10$ $x \leq -5$ or $x \geq 1\frac{2}{3}$

Mathematical Reasoning

Multiple Representations The Key Concept box shows three ways to represent an absolute value inequality: two equivalent symbolic (algebraic) forms and a graphical form. Explain that the "equivalent form" shown here is the result of translating the absolute value inequalities into compound inequalities like those studied in Lesson 1.6.

Extra Example 4

Solve $|3x - 7| \geq 5$. Then graph the solution. $x \leq \frac{2}{3}$ or $x \geq 4$

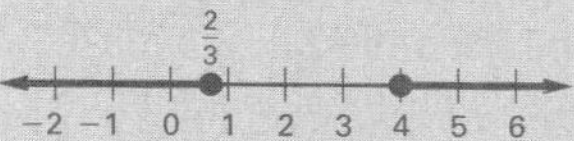

Key Question to Ask for Example 4

- When you graphed the solutions of "or" compound inequalities in Lesson 1.6, sometimes the graph had one open dot and one closed dot. Why doesn't that happen with the graph of an absolute value inequality? **In an absolute value inequality there is only one inequality symbol. If it is < or >, the graph will have two open dots, and if the symbol is ≤ or ≥, the graph will have two closed dots.**

An **Animated Algebra** activity is available on-line for **Example 4**. This activity is also available on the **Power Presentations CD-ROM**.

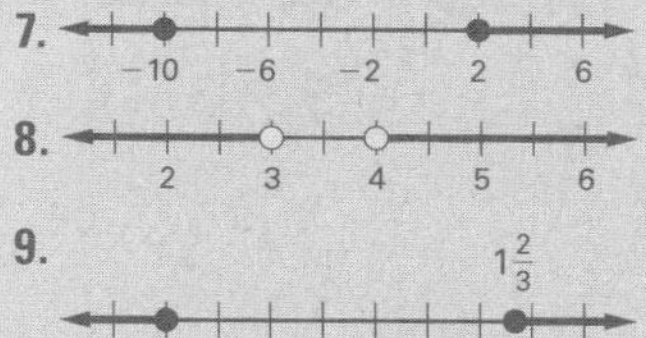

Extra Example 5

A food manufacturer specifies that every family-size box of cereal should have a net weight of 25 ounces, with a tolerance of 1.2 ounces. Write and solve an absolute value inequality that describes the acceptable net weights for the cereal in a family-size box. **$|w - 25| \leq 1.2$; $23.8 \leq w \leq 26.2$; the net weight should be between 23.8 ounces and 26.2 ounces, inclusive.**

Extra Example 6

You have found that your new winter coat is comfortable to wear when the outdoor temperature is between 10°F and 42°F, inclusive. Write an absolute value inequality for this temperature range, where t represents the temperature in degrees Fahrenheit. **$|t - 26| \leq 16$**

Closing the Lesson

Have students summarize the major points of the lesson and answer the Essential Question: How are absolute value equations and inequalities like linear equations and inequalities?

- **An absolute value equation may have 0, 1, or 2 solutions.**
- **The graph of an absolute value inequality will generally be the portion of a number line *between* two numbers, or the portions of the number line *beyond* two numbers.**

An absolute value equation can be rewritten as two linear equations, and an absolute value inequality can be rewritten as two linear inequalities.

EXAMPLE 5 Solve an inequality of the form $|ax + b| \leq c$

READING
Tolerance is the maximum acceptable deviation of an item from some ideal or mean measurement.

BASEBALL A professional baseball should weigh 5.125 ounces, with a *tolerance* of 0.125 ounce. Write and solve an absolute value inequality that describes the acceptable weights for a baseball.

Solution

STEP 1 **Write** a verbal model. Then write an inequality.

Actual weight (ounces)	–	Ideal weight (ounces)	≤	Tolerance (ounces)
w	–	**5.125**	≤	**0.125**

$$|w - 5.125| \leq 0.125$$

STEP 2 **Solve** the inequality.

$|w - 5.125| \leq 0.125$ **Write inequality.**

$-0.125 \leq w - 5.125 \leq 0.125$ **Write equivalent compound inequality.**

$5 \leq w \leq 5.25$ **Add 5.125 to each expression.**

▶ So, a baseball should weigh between 5 ounces and 5.25 ounces, inclusive. The graph is shown below.

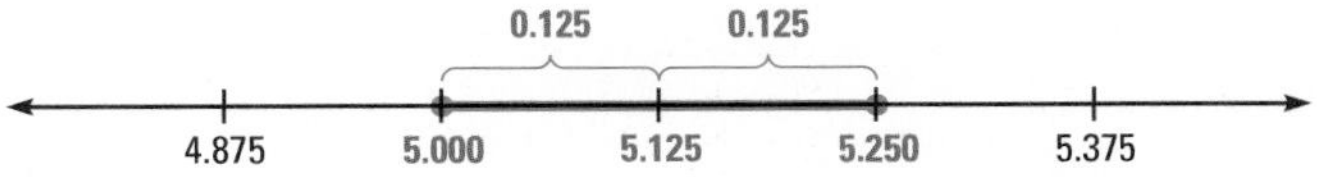

EXAMPLE 6 Write a range as an absolute value inequality

GYMNASTICS The thickness of the mats used in the rings, parallel bars, and vault events must be between 7.5 inches and 8.25 inches, inclusive. Write an absolute value inequality describing the acceptable mat thicknesses.

Solution

REVIEW MEAN
For help with finding a mean, see p. 1005.

STEP 1 **Calculate** the mean of the extreme mat thicknesses.

$$\text{Mean of extremes} = \frac{7.5 + 8.25}{2} = 7.875$$

STEP 2 **Find** the tolerance by subtracting the mean from the upper extreme.

$$\text{Tolerance} = 8.25 - 7.875 = 0.375$$

STEP 3 **Write** a verbal model. Then write an inequality.

Actual thickness (inches)	–	Mean of extremes (inches)	≤	Tolerance (inches)
t	–	**7.875**	≤	**0.375**

▶ A mat is acceptable if its thickness t satisfies $|t - 7.875| \leq 0.375$.

Guided Practice, p. 55

10. 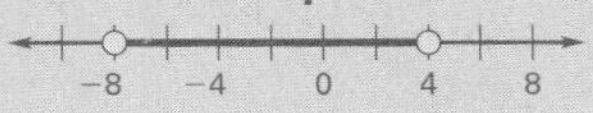

11. 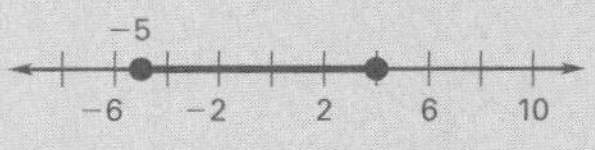

12. 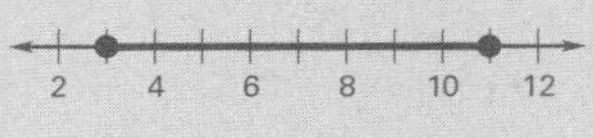

Differentiated Instruction

Visual Learners Some students who think visually may have difficulty beginning with a verbal model; it may be more instructive for them to construct a graph on a number line as the first step. For **Example 5**, students can plot 5.125 on a number line and then mark off the tolerance of 0.125 on both sides of 5.125. This should help them visualize the acceptable weights as the values between 5 and 5.25. Then show students how to construct an inequality based on the graph.

See also the *Algebra 2 Toolkit* for more strategies.

✓ GUIDED PRACTICE for Examples 5 and 6

Solve the inequality. Then graph the solution. 10–12. See margin for art.

10. $|x + 2| < 6$ $-8 < x < 4$ 11. $|2x + 1| \le 9$ $-5 \le x \le 4$ 12. $|7 - x| \le 4$ $3 \le x \le 11$

13. **GYMNASTICS** For Example 6, write an absolute value inequality describing the *unacceptable* mat thicknesses. $|t - 7.875| > 0.375$

1.7 EXERCISES

HOMEWORK KEY
- ○ = **WORKED-OUT SOLUTIONS** on p. WS2 for Exs. 21, 47, and 77
- ★ = **STANDARDIZED TEST PRACTICE** Exs. 2, 33, 40, 63, and 64
- ◆ = **MULTIPLE REPRESENTATIONS** Ex. 78

SKILL PRACTICE

A

1. **VOCABULARY** What is an extraneous solution of an equation?
An apparent solution that must be rejected because it does not satisfy the original equation.

2. ★ **WRITING** The absolute value of a number cannot be negative. How, then, can the absolute value of x be $-x$ for certain values of x?
Sample answer: If x is negative then $-x$ would be positive.

CHECKING SOLUTIONS **Decide whether the given number is a solution of the equation.**

3. $|b - 1| = 14; -13$ solution
4. $|d + 6| = 10; -4$ not a solution
5. $|32 - 6f| = 20; -2$ not a solution
6. $|2m + 6| = 10; -8$ solution
7. $|3n - 7| = 4; 1$ solution
8. $|17 - 8r| = 15; 4$ solution

EXAMPLE 1 on p. 51 for Exs. 9–20

SOLVING EQUATIONS **Solve the equation. Graph the solution.** 9–20. See margin for art.

9. $|x| = 9$ $-9, 9$
10. $|y| = -5$ no solution
11. $|z| = 0$ 0
12. $|f - 5| = 3$ $2, 8$
13. $|g - 2| = 7$ $-5, 9$
14. $|h - 4| = 4$ $0, 8$
15. $|k + 3| = 6$ $3, -9$
16. $|m + 5| = 1$ $-6, -4$
17. $|n + 9| = 10$ $-19, 1$
18. $|6 - p| = 4$ $2, 10$
19. $|5 - q| = 7$ $-2, 12$
20. $|-4 - r| = 4$ $-8, 0$

EXAMPLE 2 on p. 52 for Exs. 21–32

SOLVING EQUATIONS **Solve the equation.**

21. $|2d - 5| = 13$ $-4, 9$
22. $|3g + 14| = 7$ $-7, -2\frac{1}{3}$
23. $|7h - 10| = 4$ $\frac{6}{7}, 2$
24. $|3p - 6| = 21$ $-5, 9$
25. $|2q + 3| = 11$ $-7, 4$
26. $|4r + 7| = 43$ $-12\frac{1}{2}, 9$
27. $|5 + 2j| = 9$ $-7, 2$
28. $|6 - 3k| = 21$ $-5, 9$
29. $|20 - 9m| = 7$ $1\frac{4}{9}; 3$
30. $\left|\frac{1}{4}x - 3\right| = 10$ $-28, 52$
31. $\left|\frac{1}{2}y + 4\right| = 6$ $-20, 4$
32. $\left|\frac{2}{3}z - 6\right| = 12$ $-9, 27$

33. ★ **SHORT RESPONSE** The equation $|5x - 10| = 45$ in Example 2 has two solutions. Does the equation $|5x - 10| = -45$ also have two solutions? *Explain.* No; the equation has no solutions because an absolute value will never be negative.

EXAMPLE 3 on p. 52 for Exs. 34–42

B

EXTRANEOUS SOLUTIONS **Solve the equation. Check for extraneous solutions.**

34. $|3x - 4| = x$ $1, 2$
35. $|x + 24| = -7x$ -3
36. $|8x - 1| = 6x$ $\frac{1}{2}, \frac{1}{14}$
37. $|4x + 5| = 2x + 4$ $-1\frac{1}{2}, -\frac{1}{2}$
38. $|9 - 2x| = 10 + 3x$ $-\frac{1}{5}$
39. $|8 + 5x| = 7 - x$ $-\frac{1}{6}, -3\frac{3}{4}$

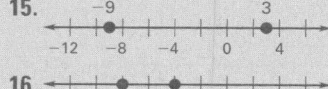

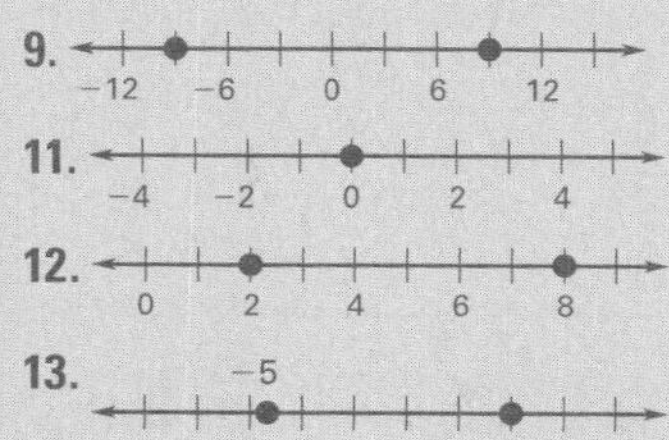

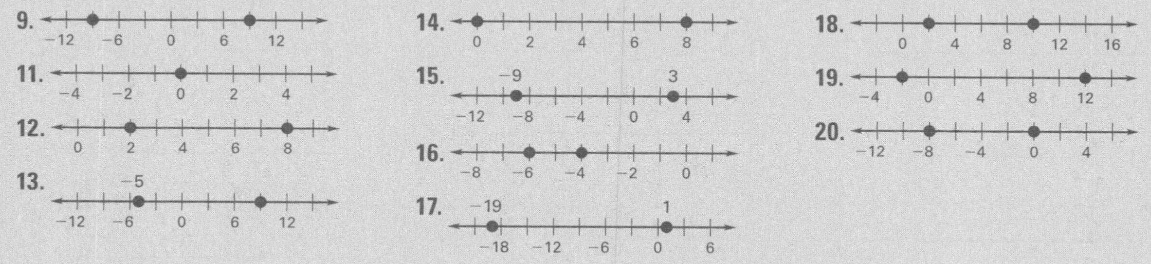

14. (graph: points at 0 and 8)
15. (graph: points at −9 and 3)
16. (graph: points at −6 and −4)
17. (graph: points at −19 and 1)
18. (graph: points at 2 and 10)
19. (graph: points at −2 and 12)
20. (graph: points at −8 and 0)

4 PRACTICE AND APPLY

Assignment Guide

Answer Transparencies available for all exercises

Basic:
Day 1: SRH p. 1005 Exs. 1–4
pp. 55–58
Exs. 1–5, 9–14, 21–29, 33–42
Day 2: pp. 55–58
Exs. 43–58, 74–80, 83–84

Average:
Day 1: pp. 55–58
Exs. 1, 2, 6–8, 12–17, 24–42
Day 2: pp. 55–58
Exs. 49–65, 74–81, 83–84

Advanced:
Day 1: pp. 55–58
Exs. 1, 2, 6–8, 15–20, 24–42
Day 2: pp. 55–58
Exs. 53–73*, 75–82*, 84

Block:
pp. 55–58
Exs. 1, 2, 6–8, 12–17, 24–42, 49–65, 74–81, 83–84

Differentiated Instruction

See *Algebra 2 Best Practices Toolkit* for suggestions on addressing the needs of a diverse classroom.

Homework Check

For a quick check of student understanding of key concepts, go over the following exercises:

Basic: 12, 22, 35, 46, 79
Average: 15, 28, 36, 50, 80
Advanced: 18, 30, 38, 56, 81

Extra Practice

- Student Edition, p. 1010
- Chapter 1 Resource Book: Practice levels A, B, C, pp. 75–77

Practice Worksheet

An easily-readable reduced practice page (with answers) for this lesson can be found on p. 1C.

Mathematical Reasoning

Exercise 40 Rather than checking for extraneous solutions, students can use mathematical reasoning and the definition of absolute value to see that this equation cannot have any negative solutions. Since absolute value can never be negative, the expression on the left side will be greater than or equal to 0 for all values of x, but if x is negative, the value of the right side will be negative. So, choices A and B can be eliminated.

An **Animated Algebra** activity is available on-line for **Exercises 43–62**. This activity is also available on the **Power Presentations CD-ROM**.

Avoiding Common Errors

Exercises 49, 66–69 When students are given absolute value inequalities like these, a common error is to follow the patterns shown in the Key Concept box on page 53 to rewrite them as compound inequalities and then solve the compound linear inequalities. Show these students that $c > 0$, so whenever $c \le 0$, these methods do not apply. Remind students that the absolute value of an expression can *never* be negative.

41. When writing the second equation, the right side of the equation should be $-x - 3$; $5x - 9 = -x - 3$, $6x - 9 = -3$, $6x = 6$, $x = 1$, the solutions are 3 and 1.

42. -3 is an extraneous solution; the solution is 2.

40. ★ **MULTIPLE CHOICE** What is (are) the solution(s) of $|3x + 7| = 5x$? **D**

Ⓐ $-4, -\frac{2}{3}$ Ⓑ $-\frac{7}{8}, \frac{7}{2}$ Ⓒ $\frac{7}{8}, \frac{7}{2}$ Ⓓ $\frac{7}{2}$

ERROR ANALYSIS ***Describe*** **and correct the error in solving the equation.**

41.

$|5x - 9| = x + 3$

$5x - 9 = x + 3$ or $5x - 9 = -x + 3$

$4x - 9 = 3$ or $6x - 9 = 3$

$4x = 12$ or $6x = 12$

$x = 3$ or $x = 2$

The solutions are 3 and 2. ✗

42.

$|n - 7| = 3n - 1$

$n - 7 = 3n - 1$ or $n - 7 = -3n + 1$

$-7 = 2n - 1$ or $4n - 7 = 1$

$-6 = 2n$ or $4n = 8$

$-3 = n$ or $n = 2$

The solutions are -3 and 2. ✗

EXAMPLES 4 and 5 on pp. 53–54 for Exs. 43–63

SOLVING INEQUALITIES **Solve the inequality. Then graph the solution.** **43–62. See margin.**

43. $\|j\| \le 5$	**44.** $\|k\| > 4$	**45.** $\|m - 2\| < 7$	**46.** $\|n - 11\| \ge 1$
(47.) $\|d + 4\| \ge 3$	**48.** $\|f + 6\| < 2$	**49.** $\|g - 1\| > 0$	**50.** $\|h + 10\| \le 10$
51. $\|3w - 15\| < 30$	**52.** $\|2x + 6\| \ge 10$	**53.** $\|4y - 9\| \le 7$	**54.** $\|5z + 1\| > 14$
55. $\|16 - p\| > 3$	**56.** $\|24 - q\| \le 11$	**57.** $\|7 - 2r\| < 19$	**58.** $\|19 - 5t\| > 7$
59. $\left\|\frac{1}{2}x - 10\right\| \le 4$	**60.** $\left\|\frac{1}{3}m - 15\right\| < 6$	**61.** $\left\|\frac{1}{7}y + 2\right\| - 5 > 3$	**62.** $\left\|\frac{2}{5}n - 8\right\| + 4 \ge 12$

Animated Algebra at classzone.com

63. ★ **MULTIPLE CHOICE** What is the solution of $|6x - 9| \ge 33$? **C**

Ⓐ $-4 \le x \le 7$ Ⓑ $-7 \le x \le 4$

Ⓒ $x \le -4$ or $x \ge 7$ Ⓓ $x \le -7$ or $x \ge 4$

64. ★ **MULTIPLE CHOICE** Which absolute value inequality represents the graph shown below? **C**

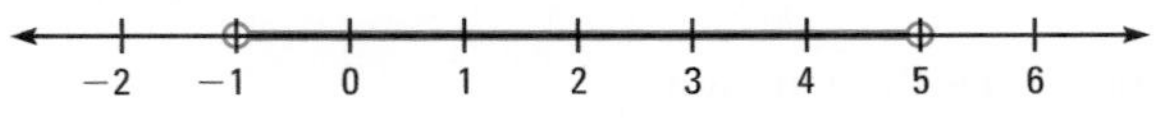

Ⓐ $-1 < |x| < 5$ Ⓑ $|x + 2| < 3$ Ⓒ $|x - 2| < 3$ Ⓓ $|x - 2| < 5$

C **65.** **REASONING** For the equation $|ax + b| = c$ (where a, b, and c are real numbers and $a \ne 0$), describe the value(s) of c that yield two solutions, one solution, and no solution. **$c > 0$, $c = 0$, $c < 0$**

SOLVING INEQUALITIES **Solve the inequality. Then graph the solution.** **66–69. See margin for art.**

66. $|x + 1| \ge -16$ **all real numbers** **67.** $|2x - 1| < -25$ **no solution** **68.** $|7x + 3| \le 0$ $-\frac{3}{7}$ **69.** $|x - 9| > 0$ $x < 9$ **or** $x > 9$

CHALLENGE **Solve the inequality for x in terms of a, b, and c. Assume a, b, and c are real numbers and $c > 0$.**

70. $|ax + b| < c$ where $a > 0$ $\frac{-c-b}{a} < x < \frac{c-b}{a}$ **71.** $|ax + b| \ge c$ where $a > 0$

72. $|ax + b| \le c$ where $a < 0$ $\frac{c-b}{a} \le x \le \frac{-c-b}{a}$ **73.** $|ax + b| > c$ where $a < 0$

71. $x \le \frac{-c-b}{a}$ or $x \ge \frac{c-b}{a}$

73. $x < \frac{c-b}{a}$ or $x > \frac{-c-b}{a}$

○ = WORKED-OUT SOLUTIONS on p. WS1 ★ = STANDARDIZED TEST PRACTICE

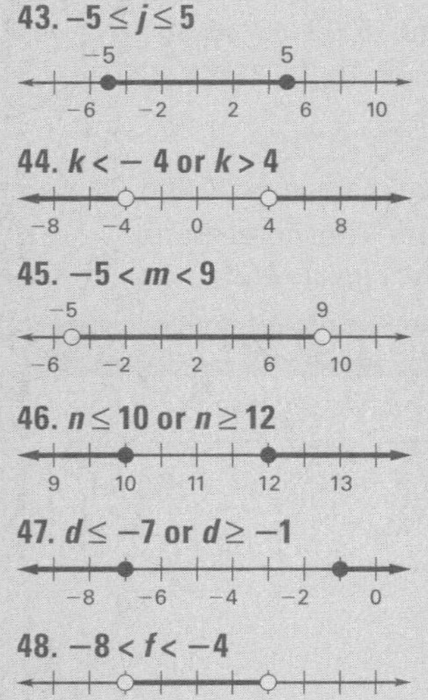

49. $g < 1$ or $g > 1$

50. $-20 \le h \le 0$

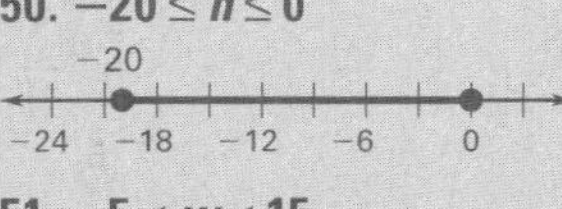

51. $-5 < w < 15$

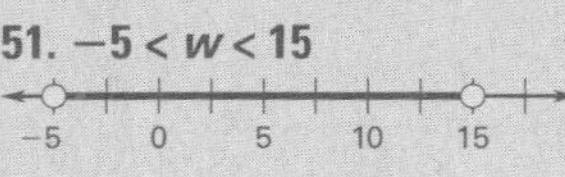

52. $x \le -8$ or $x \ge 2$

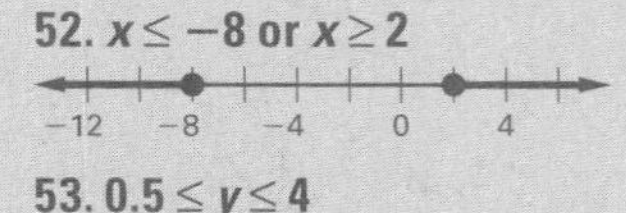

53. $0.5 \le y \le 4$

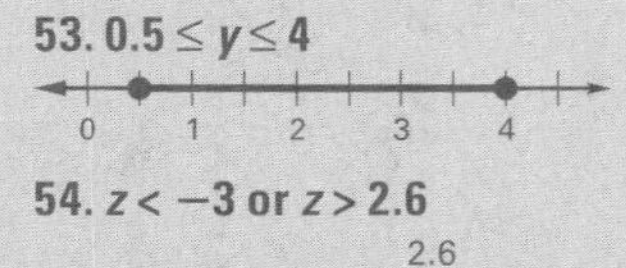

54. $z < -3$ or $z > 2.6$

55. $p < 13$ or $p > 19$

56. $13 \le q \le 35$

57. $-6 < r < 13$

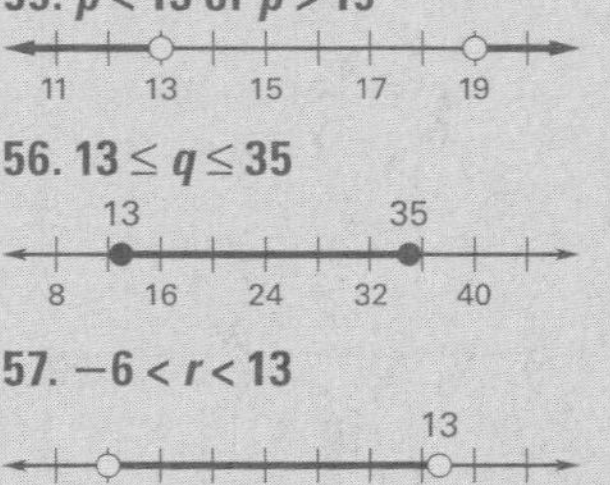

PROBLEM SOLVING

EXAMPLE 5 A on p. 54 for Exs. 74–78

74. GYMNASTICS The horizontal bar used in gymnastics events should be placed 110.25 inches above the ground, with a tolerance of 0.4 inch. Write an absolute value inequality for the acceptable bar heights. $|h - 110.25| \le 0.4$

@HomeTutor for problem solving help at classzone.com

75. SOIL PH LEVELS Cucumbers grow in soil having a pH level of 6.5, with a tolerance of 1 point on the pH scale. Write an absolute value inequality that describes the pH levels of soil in which cucumbers can grow. $|p - 6.5| \le 1$

@HomeTutor for problem solving help at classzone.com

76. MULTI-STEP PROBLEM A baseball has a cushioned cork center called the *pill*. The pill must weigh 0.85 ounce, with a tolerance of 0.05 ounce.

a. Write an absolute value inequality that describes the acceptable weights for the pill of a baseball. $|p - 0.85| \le 0.05$

b. Solve the inequality to find the acceptable weights for the pill. $0.8 \le p \le 0.9$

c. Look back at Example 5 on page 54. Find the minimum and maximum percentages of a baseball's total weight that the pill can make up. about 15.2%; 18%

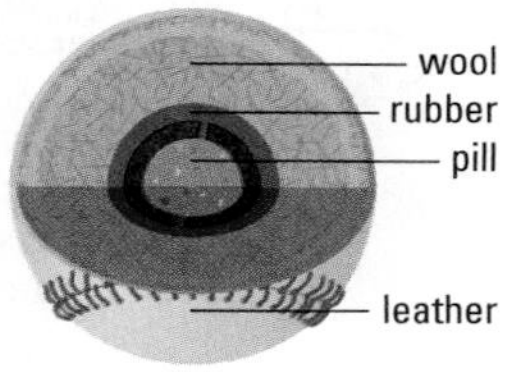

B **(77.) MANUFACTURING** A regulation basketball should weigh 21 ounces, with a tolerance of 1 ounce. Write an absolute value inequality describing the weights of basketballs that should be *rejected*. $|b - 21| > 1$

78. MULTIPLE REPRESENTATIONS The strength of eyeglass lenses is measured in units called *diopters*. The diopter number x is negative for nearsighted vision and positive for farsighted vision.

Nearsightedness (focus is in front of retina)		Farsightedness (focus is behind retina)	
Mild	$\lvert x + 1.5\rvert < 1.5$	Mild	$\lvert x - 1\rvert < 1$
Moderate	$\lvert x + 4.5\rvert < 1.5$	Moderate	$\lvert x - 3\rvert < 1$
Severe	$\lvert x + 7.5\rvert < 1.5$	Severe	$\lvert x - 5\rvert < 1$

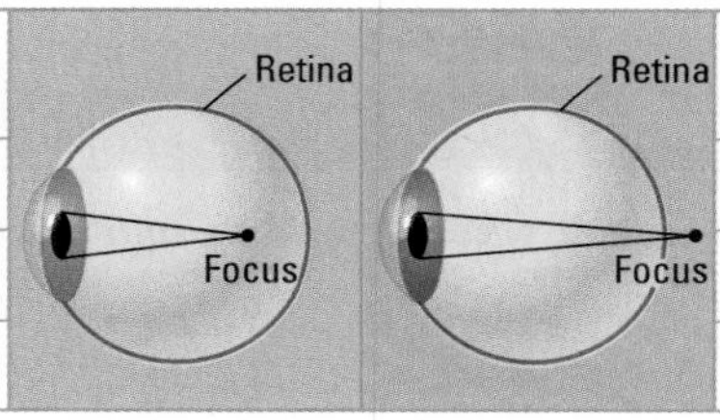

a. Writing Inequalities Write an equivalent compound inequality for each vision category shown above. Solve the inequalities. a, b. See margin.

b. Making a Graph Illustrate the six vision categories by graphing their ranges of diopter numbers on the same number line. Label each range with the corresponding category name.

EXAMPLE 6 on p. 54 for Exs. 79–81

79. SLEEPING BAGS A manufacturer of sleeping bags suggests that one model is best suited for temperatures between 30°F and 60°F, inclusive. Write an absolute value inequality for this temperature range. $|x - 45| \le 15$

80. TEMPERATURE The recommended oven setting for cooking a pizza in a professional brick-lined oven is between 550°F and 650°F, inclusive. Write an absolute value inequality for this temperature range. $|t - 600| \le 50$

Vocabulary

Exercises 74–77 If students have trouble understanding or remembering the meaning of *tolerance* in these contexts, ask them what it means for a parent to tolerate a child's behavior. Since this means that the behavior is within acceptable limits, that is, close enough to what is expected to be acceptable, the tolerance in a manufacturing or science context also means that a measurement is within acceptable limits, that is, close enough to the ideal.

78a. Nearsightedness: Mild: $-1.5 < x + 1.5 < 1.5$, $-3 < x < 0$; **Moderate:** $-1.5 < x + 4.5 < 1.5$, $-6 < x < -3$; **Severe:** $-1.5 < x + 7.5 < 1.5$, $-9 < x < -6$; **Farsightedness: Mild:** $-1 < x - 1 < 1$, $0 < x < 2$; **Moderate:** $-1 < x - 3 < 1$, $2 < x < 4$; **Severe:** $-1 < x - 5 < 1$, $4 < x < 6$

78b.

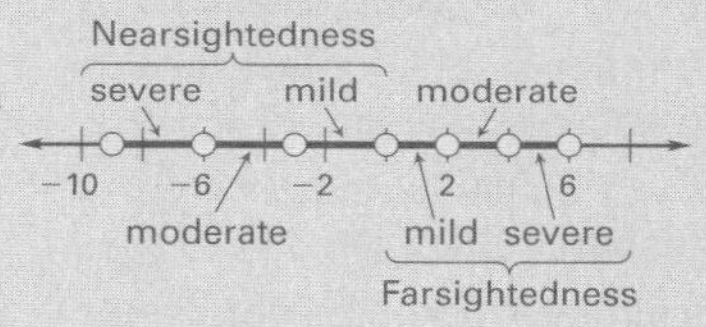

58. $t < 2.4$ or $t > 5.2$

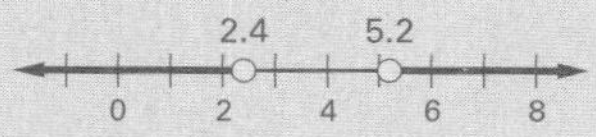

59. $12 \le x \le 28$

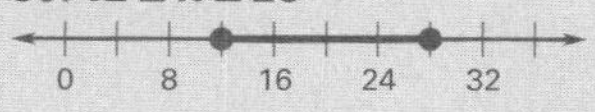

60. $27 < m < 63$

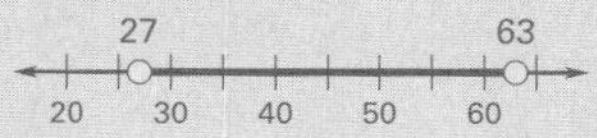

61. $y < -70$ or $y > 42$

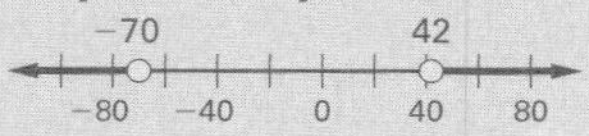

62. $n \le 0$ or $n \ge 40$

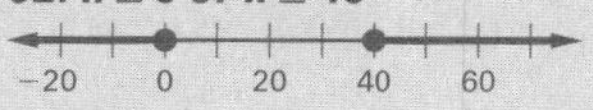

66.

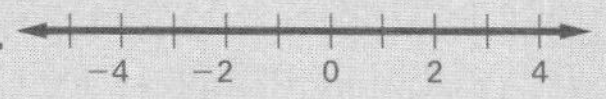

68.

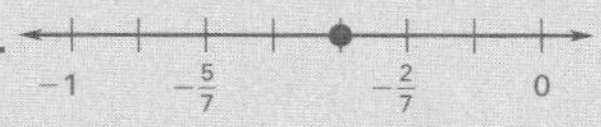

69.

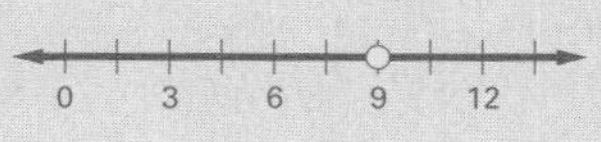

81. **AUDIBLE FREQUENCIES** An elephant can hear sounds with frequencies from 16 hertz to 12,000 hertz. A mouse can hear sounds with frequencies from 1000 hertz to 91,000 hertz. Write an absolute value inequality for the hearing range of each animal. $|e - 6008| \le 5992$, $|m - 46{,}000| \le 45{,}000$

C 82. **CHALLENGE** The depth finder on a fishing boat gives readings that are within 5% of the actual water depth. When the depth finder reading is 250 feet, the actual water depth x lies within a range given by the following inequality:

$$|x - 250| \le 0.05x$$

a. Write the absolute value inequality as a compound inequality. $-0.05x \le x - 250 \le 0.05x$

b. Solve each part of the compound inequality for x. What are the possible actual water depths if the depth finder's reading is 250 feet?

$238 \le x \le 263$; the actual depths are between 238 feet and 263 feet.

KENTUCKY MIXED REVIEW

TEST PRACTICE at classzone.com

83. A car dealership hires Anne to wash cars. She is paid \$28 per day plus \$6 for every car she washes. Anne shares the money equally with a friend who assists her. After five days, Anne's share of the pay is \$130. How many cars did Anne and her friend wash? **B**

(A) 17 (B) 20 (C) 32 (D) 39

84. Pentagon $ABCDE$ is the outline of the front of a cabin. The measure of $\angle ABC$ is 115°. What is the measure of $\angle BCD$? **C**

(A) 90° (B) 115°

(C) 130° (D) 155°

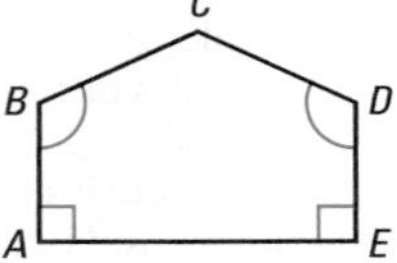

QUIZ *for Lessons 1.6–1.7*

Solve the inequality. Then graph the solution. *(p. 41)* 1–6. See margin for art.

1. $4k - 17 < 27$ $k < 11$
2. $14n - 8 \ge 90$ $n \ge 7$
3. $-9p + 15 \le 96$ $p \ge -9$
4. $-8r - 11 > 45$ $r < -7$
5. $3(x - 7) < 6(10 - x)$ $x < 9$
6. $-25 - 4z > 66 - 17z$ $z > 7$

Solve the equation or inequality. *(p. 51)*

7. $|x - 6| = 9$ $-3, 15$
8. $|3y + 3| = 12$ $-5, 3$
9. $|2z + 5| = -9z$ $-\frac{5}{11}$
10. $|p + 7| > 2$ $p < -9$ or $p > -5$
11. $|2q - 3| \le 3$ $0 \le q \le 3$
12. $|5 - r| \ge 4$ $r \le 1$ or $r \ge 9$

13. **TEST SCORES** Your final grade in a course is 80% of your current grade, plus 20% of your final exam score. Your current grade is 83 and your goal is to get a final grade of 85 or better. Write and solve an inequality to find the final exam scores that will meet your goal. *(p. 41)* $0.8(83) + 0.2e \ge 85$; $e \ge 93$

14. **GROCERY WEIGHTS** A container of potato salad from your grocer's deli is supposed to weigh 1.5 pounds, with a tolerance of 0.025 pound. Write and solve an absolute value inequality that describes the acceptable weights for the container of potato salad. *(p. 51)* $|p - 1.5| \le 0.025$, 1.475 lb $\le p \le$ 1.525 lb

ONLINE QUIZ at classzone.com

5 ASSESS AND RETEACH

Daily Homework Quiz

Transparency Available

1. Decide whether -7 is a solution of $|12 - 4x| = 16$. no
2. Solve $|3x - 9| = 15$. $-2, 8$
3. Solve $|x + 5| \ge 3$. Then graph the solution. $x \le -8$ or $x \ge -2$

−10 −9 −8 −7 −6 −5 −4 −3 −2 −1 0

4. A house plant will grow well in temperatures between 52°F and 78°F, inclusive. Write an absolute value inequality that describes this range, where t is the temperature in degrees Fahrenheit. $|t - 65| \le 13$

Online Quiz

Available at **classzone.com**

Diagnosis/Remediation

- Practice A, B, C in Chapter 1 Resource Book, pp. 75–77
- Study Guide in Chapter 1 Resource Book, pp. 78–79
- Practice Workbook, pp. 13–14
- @HomeTutor

Challenge

Additional challenge is available in the Chapter 1 Resource Book, p. 82.

Quiz

An easily-readable reduced copy of the quiz (with answers) on Lessons 1.6–1.7 from the Assessment Book can be found on p. 1E.

83–88.

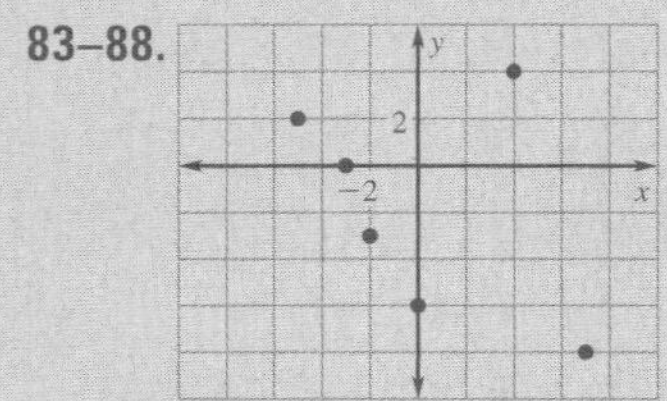

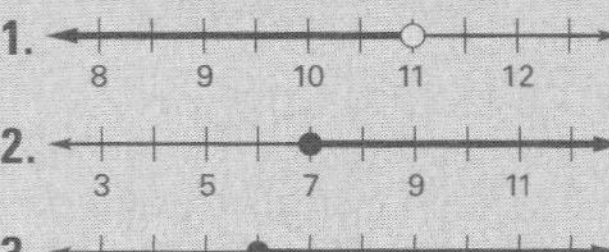

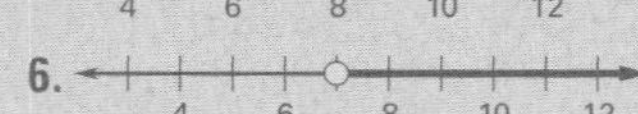

Lessons 1.5–1.7

1. **HYBRID CAR** A hybrid car gets about 60 miles per gallon of gas in the city and about 51 miles per gallon on the highway. During one week, the hybrid uses 12 gallons of gas and travels 675 miles. How much gas was used on the highway?

   A. 4 gallons
   B. 5 gallons
   C. 7 gallons
   D. 8 gallons

2. **POPCORN** A popcorn manufacturer's ideal weight for a bag of microwave popcorn is 3.5 ounces, with a tolerance of 0.25 ounce. What is the range of acceptable weights w (in ounces) of a bag of popcorn?

   A. $w \geq 3.75$
   B. $w \leq 3.25$
   C. $-0.25 \leq w \leq 0.25$
   D. $3.25 \leq w \leq 3.75$

3. **LIQUID OXYGEN** Oxygen exists as a liquid between −369°F and −297°F, inclusive. Which compound inequality gives the range of temperatures T for liquid oxygen?

   A. $-369 \leq T \leq -297$
   B. $-369 < T < -297$
   C. $-297 \leq T \leq -369$
   D. $-297 < T < -369$

4. **FOOTBALL** A football kicker scores 1 point for each extra point and 3 points for each field goal. One season, a kicker made 34 extra points and scored a total of 112 points. How many field goals did the kicker make?

   A. 13
   B. 26
   C. 48
   D. 78

5. **VIDEO RENTAL** A video store rents movies for \$2.95 each. Recently, the store began a special allowing an unlimited number of rentals for \$15.95 per month. How many movies must you rent in a month in order to save money by using the special?

   A. 5 or less B. exactly 6
   C. 6 or more D. 13 or more

6. **SWIMMING POOL** You are draining a swimming pool. The table shows the depth of the water at different times. How long will it take the pool to empty?

Time (h)	0	1	2	3
Depth (ft)	12	10.5	9	7.5

   A. 4.8 hours B. 6.7 hours
   C. 8 hours D. 24 hours

7. **TRIANGLE INEQUALITY** The triangle inequality relationship from geometry states that the sum of the lengths of any two sides of a triangle is greater than the length of the third side. If the lengths of the three sides of a triangle are x, $2x$, and 9, which of the following is a possible value of x?

   A. 2 B. 3 C. 5 D. 10

8. **OPEN-RESPONSE** For a rope trick, a magician cuts a 72 inch piece of rope into three pieces of different lengths. The length of one piece must be the mean of the lengths of the other two pieces, as shown below.

short | long | medium
a | b | $\frac{1}{2}(a + b)$
72 in.

   a. Find the length of the second-longest piece.
   b. Write an equation that relates a and b. Explain what this equation expresses about the lengths of the ropes.
   c. Give a pair of possible lengths for the shortest and longest pieces of rope.

Kentucky Mixed Review

1. B
2. D
3. A
4. B
5. C
6. C
7. C
8. a. 24 inches
   b. $a + b = 48$; The sum of the lengths of the rope must be 48 inches
   c. *Sample answer:* 12 in. and 36 in.

Additional Resources

The following resources are available to help review the materials in this chapter.

Chapter 1 Resource Book

- Chapter Review Games and Activities, p. 83
- Cumulative Practice, Ch. 1, pp. 85–86

Student Resources in Spanish

eWorkbook

@HomeTutor

Vocabulary Practice

Vocabulary practice is available at **classzone.com**

1 CHAPTER SUMMARY

BIG IDEAS *For Your Notebook*

Big Idea 1

Using Properties to Evaluate and Simplify Expressions

	Example	Answer
To **evaluate a numerical expression**, use order of operations and properties of real numbers.	$3 + (-3)^2$	$3 + 9 = 12$
To **evaluate an algebraic expression**, substitute the value(s) of the variable(s) into the expression, and then evaluate the resulting numerical expression.	$4x - 5$ when $x = 1$	$4(1) - 5 = -1$
To **simplify an algebraic expression**, combine like terms.	$3y - 4 + 2y - 6$	$5y - 10$

Big Idea 2

Using Problem Solving Strategies and Verbal Models

You may be able to write a **verbal model** that describes a real-world problem and use it to write an equation or inequality you can solve. To write the verbal model, analyze the information you are given and use a problem solving strategy if appropriate.

If this is what you know...	...try this strategy.
A formula can be applied to the situation.	Use a Formula
Numerical information is given in a table or a list.	Look for a Pattern
There is a geometric or physical context.	Draw a Diagram

Big Idea 3

Solving Linear and Absolute Value Equations and Inequalities

Use the following guidelines when solving equations and inequalities.

Linear Equation

$ax + b = 0$

Use properties of equality to isolate x.

Add or **subtract** the same number from each side of the equation, or **multiply** or **divide** each side by the same nonzero number.

Linear Inequality

$ax + b \leq 0$

Use properties similar to those used in solving equations.

Remember to **reverse the inequality** when multiplying or dividing by a **negative** number.

Absolute Value Equation

$|ax + b| = c$

Rewrite as follows and solve:

$ax + b = c$ or $ax + b = -c$

Check for **extraneous** solutions.

Absolute Value Inequality

$|ax + b| > c$ → Solve $ax + b < -c$ or $ax + b > c$.

$|ax + b| < c$ → Solve $-c < ax + b < c$.

1 CHAPTER REVIEW

@HomeTutor
classzone.com
- Multi-Language Glossary
- Vocabulary practice

REVIEW KEY VOCABULARY

- opposite, *p. 4*
- reciprocal, *p. 4*
- numerical expression, *p. 10*
- power, *p. 10*
- exponent, *p. 10*
- base, *p. 10*
- variable, *p. 11*
- algebraic expression, *p. 11*
- term, *p. 12*
- variable term, *p. 12*
- constant term, *p. 12*
- coefficient, *p. 12*
- like terms, *p. 12*
- equivalent expressions, *p. 12*
- identity, *p. 12*
- equation, *p. 18*
- linear equation, *p. 18*
- solution of an equation, *p. 18*
- equivalent equations, *p. 18*
- formula, *p. 26*
- solve for a variable, *p. 26*
- verbal model, *p. 34*
- linear inequality, *p. 41*
- solution of an inequality, *p. 41*
- graph of an inequality, *p. 41*
- compound inequality, *p. 41*
- equivalent inequalities, *p. 42*
- absolute value, *p. 51*
- extraneous solution, *p. 52*

VOCABULARY EXERCISES

1. Copy and complete: In a power, the _?_ represents the number of times the _?_ is used as a factor. **exponent, base**
2. Copy and complete: If substituting a number for a variable in an equation results in a true statement, then the number is a(n) _?_ of the equation. **solution**
3. Copy and complete: A(n) _?_ is an apparent solution that must be rejected because it does not satisfy the original equation. **extraneous solution**
4. Identify the like terms in the expression $40 + 3x^3 + 3x^2 - 7 - x^2$. **$3x^2$ and $-x^2$, 40 and -7**
5. Give an example of two equivalent algebraic expressions. ***Sample answer:* $3(x - 4)$ and $3x - 12$**
6. **WRITING** *Compare* the procedures for solving a linear equation and a linear inequality. How are they similar? How are they different?

6. *Sample answer:* The methods for using the properties of addition are the same for both methods. The procedures are different when multiplying or dividing an inequality by a negative number, the inequality symbol changes, but this process has no effect on an equation.

REVIEW EXAMPLES AND EXERCISES

Use the review examples and exercises below to check your understanding of the concepts you have learned in each lesson of Chapter 1.

1.1 Apply Properties of Real Numbers

pp. 2–9

EXAMPLE

Identify the property that the statement illustrates.

a. $2(w + \ell) = 2w + 2\ell$ **Distributive property**

b. $6 + (2 + 4) = 6 + (4 + 2)$ **Commutative property of addition**

EXERCISES

EXAMPLE 3 on p. 4 for Exs. 7–9

Identify the property that the statement illustrates.

7. $17 \cdot \frac{1}{17} = 1$
8. $60 + 0 = 60$
9. $3a + 7a = (3 + 7)a$

7. Inverse property of multiplication
8. Identity property of addition
9. Distributive property

Extra Example 1.1

Identify the property that the statement illustrates.

a. $(8 \cdot 9) \cdot 2 = (9 \cdot 8) \cdot 2$ **Commutative property of multiplication**

b. $16 + (-16) = 0$ **Inverse property of addition**

Extra Example 1.2
Simplify the expression $-3(5 - x) + 6(2x + 4)$. $15x + 9$

Extra Example 1.3
Solve $8(3x - 4) = -5(6 - 3x)$. $\frac{2}{9}$

1 CHAPTER REVIEW

1.2 Evaluate and Simplify Algebraic Expressions
pp. 10–16

EXAMPLE

Simplify the expression.

$5(y - 4) - 3(2y - 9) = 5y - 20 - 6y + 27$ **Distributive property**

$= (5y - 6y) + (-20 + 27)$ **Group like terms.**

$= -y + 7$ **Combine like terms.**

EXERCISES

EXAMPLES 3 and 4 on pp. 11–12 for Exs. 10–16

Simplify the expression.

10. $25x + 14 - 17 - 6x$ $19x - 3$

11. $6y + 12x - 12y - 9x$ $3x - 6y$

12. $6(n - 2) - 8n + 40$ $-2n + 28$

13. $5(2b + 3) + 8(b - 6)$ $18b - 33$

14. $3g + 9g^2 - 12g^2 + g$ $-3g^2 + 4g$

15. $7t^4 + 7t^2 - 2t^2 - 9t^4$ $-2t^4 + 5t^2$

16. TAXI RATES A New York City taxi charges \$2.50, plus \$.40 for each fifth of a mile if it is not delayed by traffic. Write an expression for the cost of the ride if you travel x miles in the taxi with no traffic delays. $2x + 2.5$

1.3 Solve Linear Equations
pp. 18–24

EXAMPLE

Solve $-4(3x + 5) = -2(5 - x)$.

$-4(3x + 5) = -2(5 - x)$ **Write original equation.**

$-12x - 20 = -10 + 2x$ **Distributive property**

$-20 = -10 + 14x$ **Add $12x$ to each side.**

$-10 = 14x$ **Add 10 to each side.**

$-\frac{5}{7} = x$ **Divide each side by 14 and simplify.**

EXERCISES

EXAMPLES 1, 2, 3, and 4 on pp. 18–20 for Exs. 17–24

Solve the equation. Check your solution.

17. $24x + 16 = 12$ $-\frac{1}{6}$

18. $-6y + 15 = -9$ 4

19. $4(q - 5) = 16$ 9

20. $7m + 38 = -5m - 16$ -4.5

21. $48j + 25 = 12j - 11$ -1

22. $8(2n - 5) = 3(6n - 2)$ -17

23. SALES TAX You buy a jacket, and the sales tax is 6%. The total cost is \$79.49. Find the cost of the jacket before the tax. \$74.99

24. FOOD SHOPPING At a vegetable stand, you bought 3 pounds of peppers for \$4.50. Green peppers cost \$1 per pound and orange peppers cost \$4 per pound. Find how many pounds of each kind of pepper you bought. 2.5 lb green peppers, 0.5 lb orange peppers

@HomeTutor
classzone.com
Chapter Review Practice

1.4 Rewrite Formulas and Equations *pp. 26–32*

25. $y = -10x + 7$; -23

26. $y = \frac{3}{8}x + \frac{9}{4}$; 3

27. $y = \frac{-15}{x-6}$; 15

28. $y = \frac{2}{3}x - \frac{3}{2}$; $4\frac{1}{2}$

29. $y = \frac{5}{2}x - 5$; -20

30. $y = \frac{x-1}{3x}$; $\frac{2}{5}$

EXAMPLE

Solve $5x - 11y = 7$ for y. Then find the value of y when $x = 4$.

STEP 1 $5x - 11y = 7$ **Write original equation.**

$-11y = 7 - 5x$ **Subtract $5x$ from each side.**

$y = -\frac{7}{11} + \frac{5}{11}x$ **Divide each side by -11.**

STEP 2 $y = -\frac{7}{11} + \frac{5}{11}(4)$ **Substitute 4 for x.**

$y = \frac{13}{11}$ **Simplify.**

EXERCISES

EXAMPLES 2, 3, and 4 on pp. 27–28 for Exs. 25–31

Solve the equation for y. Then find the value of y for the given value of x. 25–30. See margin.

25. $10x + y = 7$; $x = 3$
26. $8y - 3x = 18$; $x = 2$
27. $xy - 6y = -15$; $x = 5$
28. $4x = 6y + 9$; $x = 9$
29. $5x - 2y = 10$; $x = -6$
30. $x - 3xy = 1$; $x = -5$

31. **GEOMETRY** The formula $S = 2\pi rh + 2\pi r^2$ gives the surface area S of a cylinder with height h and radius r. Solve the formula for h. Find h if $r = 5$ centimeters and $S = 400$ square centimeters. $h = \frac{S - 2\pi r^2}{2\pi r}$; about 7.73 cm

1.5 Use Problem Solving Strategies and Models *pp. 34–40*

EXAMPLE

Find the time it takes to drive 525 miles at 50 miles per hour.

Distance (miles)	=	Rate (miles/hour)	•	Time (hours)
525	=	50	•	t

$525 = 50t$ **Write equation.**

$10.5 = t$ **Divide each side by 50.**

▶ It takes 10.5 hours to drive 525 miles at 50 miles per hour.

EXERCISES

EXAMPLES 1 and 4 on pp. 34–36 for Exs. 32–33

32. **AVERAGE SPEED** It takes 3 hours for a train to travel 175 miles. What is the average speed of the train? $58\frac{1}{3}$ mi/h

33. **CAR RENTAL** While on vacation, your family rented a car for $293. The car rental cost $180, plus $.25 for every mile driven over 150 miles. How many miles did you drive while on vacation? 602 mi

Extra Example 1.4

Solve $4x - 3y = 9$ for y. Then find the value of y when $x = 15$.
$y = -3 + \frac{4}{3}x$ or $y = \frac{4}{3}x - 3$; 17

Extra Example 1.5

If you drive 264 miles in 5.5 hours, what is your average speed?
48 mi/h

1 CHAPTER REVIEW

Extra Example 1.6

Solve $18 + 2x > 5x + 6$. Then graph the solution. $x < 4$

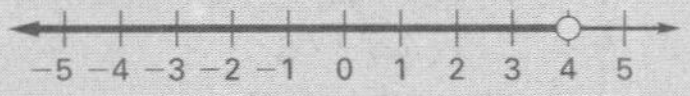

Extra Example 1.7

Solve $|4x - 2| \leq 10$. Then graph the solution. $-2 \leq x \leq 3$

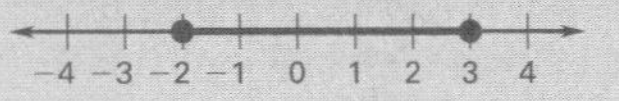

34. 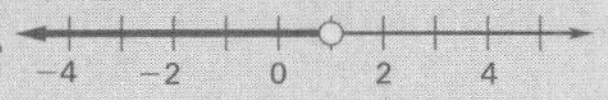

35. 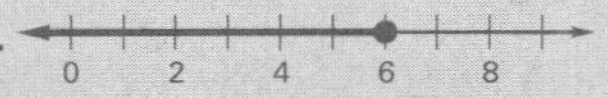

36. 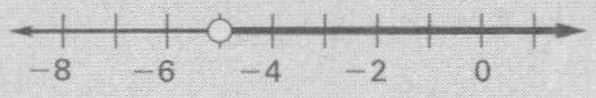

37. 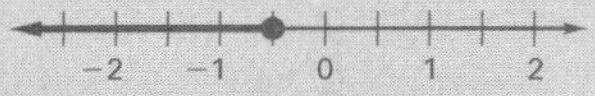

38. 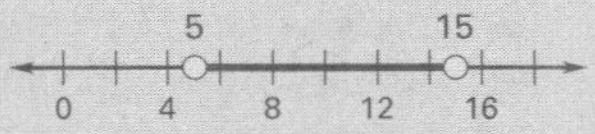

39. 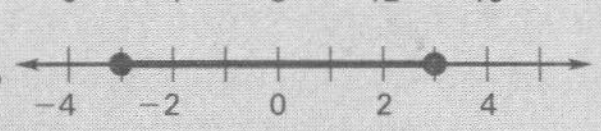

44. 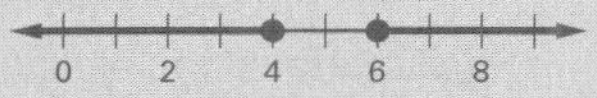

45. 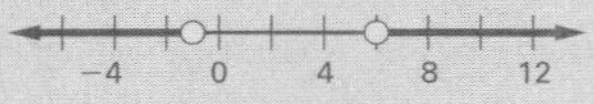

46. 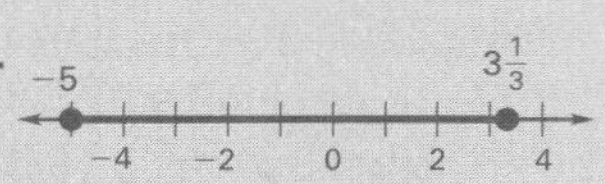

1.6 Solve Linear Inequalities *pp. 41–47*

EXAMPLE

Solve $25 - 3x \leq 10$. Then graph the solution.

$25 - 3x \leq 10$	**Write original inequality.**
$-3x \leq -15$	**Subtract 25 from each side.**
$x \geq 5$	**Divide each side by -3 and reverse the inequality.**
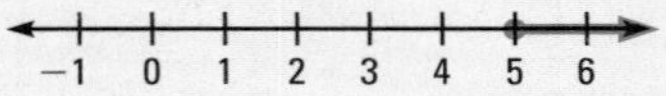	**Graph the solution.**

EXERCISES

EXAMPLES 1, 2, 3, and 4 on pp. 41–43 for Exs. 34–40

Solve the inequality. Then graph the solution. 34–39. See margin for art.

34. $2x - 3 < -1$ $x < 1$

35. $7 - 3x \geq -11$ $x \leq 6$

36. $15x + 8 > 9x - 22$ $x > -5$

37. $13x + 24 \leq 16 - 3x$ $x \leq -\frac{1}{2}$

38. $-5 < 10 - x < 5$ $5 < x < 15$

39. $-8 \leq 3x + 1 \leq 10$ $-3 \leq x \leq 3$

40. **GEOMETRY** A triangle has sides of lengths 10, $2x$, and $3x$. The sum of the lengths of any two sides is greater than the length of the third side. Write and solve three inequalities to find the possible values of x.
$10 + 2x > 3x$, $5x > 10$, $10 + 3x > 2x$; $x < 10$, $x > 2$, $x > -10$; $2 < x < 10$

1.7 Solve Absolute Value Equations and Inequalities *pp. 51–58*

EXAMPLE

Solve $|3x - 7| > 2$. Then graph the solution.

$|3x - 7| > 2$			**Write original inequality.**
$3x - 7 < -2$	or	$3x - 7 > 2$	**Write equivalent compound inequality.**
$3x < 5$	or	$3x > 9$	**Add 7 to each side.**
$x < \frac{5}{3}$	or	$x > 3$	**Divide each side by 3.**
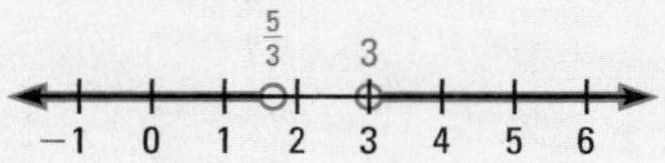			**Graph the solution.**

EXERCISES

EXAMPLES 2, 3, 4, and 5 on pp. 52–54 for Exs. 41–47

Solve the equation. Check for extraneous solutions.

41. $|3p + 2| = 7$ $-3, 1\frac{2}{3}$

42. $|9q - 5| = 2q$ $\frac{5}{7}, \frac{5}{11}$

43. $|8r + 1| = 3r$ no solution

Solve the inequality. Then graph the solution. 44–46. See margin for art.

44. $|x - 5| \geq 1$ $x \leq 4$ or $x \geq 6$

45. $|5 - 2y| > 7$ $y < -1$ or $y > 6$

46. $|6z + 5| \leq 25$ $-5 \leq z \leq 3\frac{1}{3}$

47. **VOLLEYBALL** The circumference of a volleyball should be 26 inches, with a tolerance of 0.5 inch. Write and solve an absolute value inequality that describes the acceptable circumferences of a volleyball. $|v - 26| \leq 0.5$, 25.5 in. $\leq v \leq$ 26.5 in.

1 CHAPTER TEST

Graph the numbers on a number line. 1, 2. See margin.

1. $-2, -\frac{7}{4}, 6.5, \sqrt{30}, \frac{1}{3}$

2. $\frac{9}{2}, 0.8, -5.5, -\sqrt{10}, -\frac{3}{4}$

Use properties and definitions of operations to show that the statement is true. *Justify* each step. 3, 4. See margin.

3. $5 + (x - 5) = x$

4. $(3d + 7) - d + 5 = 2d + 12$

Evaluate the expression for the given values of x and y.

5. $4x - 6y$ when $x = 5$ and $y = -3$ **38**

6. $3x^2 - 9y$ when $x = 2$ and $y = 4$ **−24**

Simplify the expression.

7. $5n + 10 - 8n + 6$ $-3n + 16$

8. $10m - 4(3m + 7) + 6m$ $4m - 28$

9. $11 + q - 3q^2 + 18q^2 - 2$ $15q^2 + q + 9$

10. $9t^2 + 14 - 17t + 6t - 8t^2$ $t^2 - 11t + 14$

11. $5(x - 3y) + 2(4y - x)$ $3x - 7y$

12. $5(2u + 3w) - 2(5u - 7w)$ $29w$

Solve the equation. Check your solution.

13. $5n + 11 = -9$ **−4**

14. $6k + 7 = 4 + 12k$ **0.5**

15. $-t - 2 = 9(t - 8)$ **7**

Solve the equation for y. Then find the value of y for the given value of x.

16. $12x - 28y = 40; x = 6$

17. $x + 4y = 12; x = 2$

18. $15y + 2xy = -30; x = 5$

16. $y = \frac{3}{7}x - \frac{10}{7}$; $1\frac{1}{7}$

17. $y = -\frac{1}{4}x + 3$; $2\frac{1}{2}$

18. $y = \frac{-30}{15 + 2x}$; $-1\frac{1}{5}$

Solve the inequality. Then graph the solution. 19–21. See margin for art.

19. $-5x - 6 < 19$ $x > -5$

20. $x + 22 \geq -3x - 10$ $x \geq -8$

21. $5 < 2x + 3 \leq 11$ $1 < x \leq 4$

Solve the equation. Check for extraneous solutions.

22. $|3d - 4| = 14$ $-3\frac{1}{3}, 6$

23. $|f + 3| = 2f + 4$ -1

24. $|10 - 7g| = 2g$ $1\frac{1}{9}, 2$

Solve the inequality. Then graph the solution. 25–27. See margin for art.

25. $|x - 5| \leq 30$ $-25 \leq x \leq 35$

26. $|3y + 4| > 2$ $y < -2$ or $y > -\frac{2}{3}$

27. $\left|\frac{2}{3}z - 5\right| < 5$ $0 < z < 15$

28. **WIRELESS NETWORK** To set up a wireless network for Internet access at home, you buy a network router for $75. The fee for DSL service is $18 per month. Write an expression for the amount of money you spend in n months. How much money do you spend in 12 months? **$18n + 75$; $291**

29. **CAR REPAIR** The bill for the repair of a car was $420. The cost of parts was $240. The cost of labor was $45 per hour. How many hours did the repair take? **4 h**

30. **HOUSEHOLD CHORES** You can wash one window in 15 minutes and your sister can wash one window in 20 minutes. How many minutes will it take to wash 12 windows if you work together? **about 103 min**

31. **GEOMETRY** The formula $V = \frac{1}{3}\pi r^2 h$ gives the volume V of a cone with height h and base radius r. Solve the formula for h. Then find h when $r = 2$ inches and $V = 45$ cubic inches.

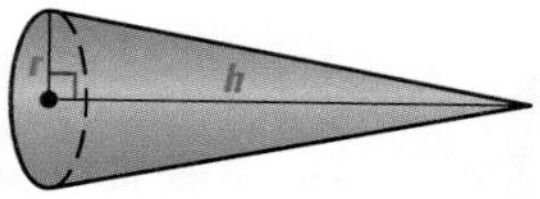

31. $h = \frac{3V}{\pi r^2}$; about 10.7 in.

Additional Resources

Assessment Book

- Chapter Test, Levels A, B, C, pp. 4–9
- Standardized Chapter Test, pp. 10–11
- SAT/ACT Chapter Test, pp. 12–13
- Alternative Assessment, pp. 14–15

Test Generator CD-ROM

Chapter Test

Easily-readable reduced copies (with answers) of Chapter Test B, the Standardized Chapter Test, and the Alternative Assessment from the Assessment Book can be found on pp. 1E–1F.

1.
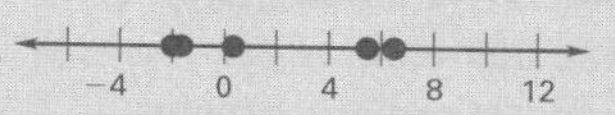

2.
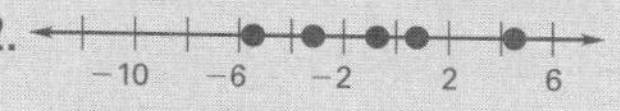

3–4. See below.

19.
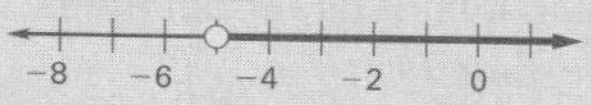

20.
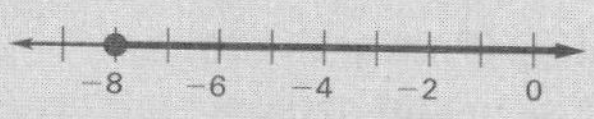

21.
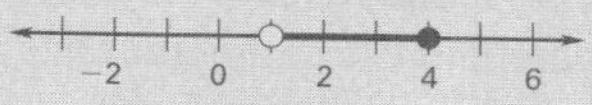

25.
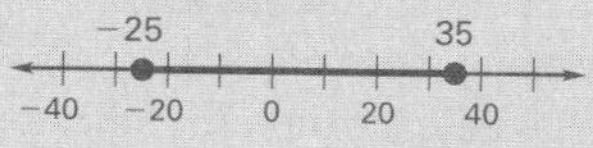

26.
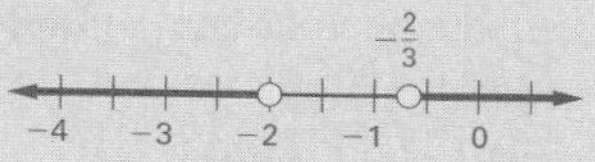

27.
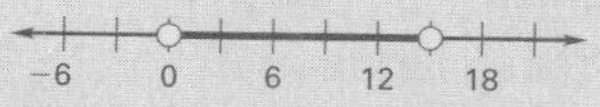

3. $5 + (x - 5) = 5 + (x + (-5))$ Def. of subtraction
$= 5 + ((-5) + x)$ Comm. prop. of addition
$= (5 + (-5)) + x$ Assoc. prop. of addition
$= 0 + x$ Inverse prop. of addition
$= x$ Identity prop. of addition

4. $(3d + 7) - d + 5 = (3d + 7) + (-d) + 5$ Def. of subtraction
$= 3d + (7 + (-d)) + 5$ Assoc. prop. of addition
$= 3d + ((-d) + 7) + 5$ Comm. prop. of addition
$= (3d + (-d)) + (7 + 5)$ Assoc. prop. of addition
$= 2d + 12$ Combine like terms.

Kentucky General Scoring Rubric

4 Points (Full credit)

- You complete all important components of the question and communicate ideas clearly.
- You demonstrate in-depth understanding of the relevant concepts and/or processes.
- Where appropriate, you choose more efficient and/or sophisticated processes.
- Where appropriate, you offer insightful interpretations or extensions (generalizations, applications, analogies).

3 Points (Full or Partial Credit)

- You complete most important components of the question and communicate clearly.
- You demonstrate an understanding of major concepts even though you overlook or misunderstand some less-important ideas or details.

2 Points (Partial Credit)

- You complete some important components of the question and communicate those components clearly.
- You demonstrate that there are gaps in your conceptual understanding.

1 Point (Partial Credit)

- You show minimal understanding of the question.
- You address only a small portion of the question.

0 Points (No Credit)

- Your answer is totally incorrect or irrelevant.

BLANK (No Credit)

- You did not give any answer at all.

TEST PREPARATION

OPEN-RESPONSE QUESTIONS

Scoring Rubric

Full Credit
- solution is complete and correct

Partial Credit
- solution is complete but has errors,

  or
- solution is without error but incomplete

No Credit
- no solution is given,

  or
- solution makes no sense

PROBLEM

A national bank offers a checking account for a fee of \$3.90 per month. The first 10 transactions per month are free, but every additional transaction costs \$.15. A local bank offers a checking account with no monthly fee, but every transaction costs \$.36.

a. When is it less expensive to use the national bank?

b. Justify your answer.

Below are sample solutions to the problem. Read each solution and the comments on the left to see why the sample represents *full credit, partial credit,* or *no credit.*

SAMPLE 1: Full credit solution

If you make 10 transactions or fewer per month, the local bank is less expensive because it costs \$3.60 or less, compared to \$3.90 for the national bank. If the number of transactions is more than 10, you can use the following model, where x is the number of transactions per month.

The verbal model explains how the inequality is obtained.

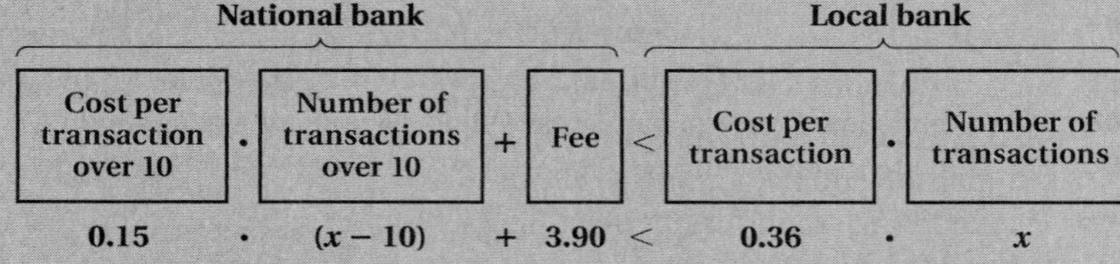

$$0.15 \cdot (x - 10) + 3.90 < 0.36 \cdot x$$

The inequality is solved correctly, step by step.

Solve the inequality to find when it is less expensive to use the national bank.

$$0.15(x - 10) + 3.90 < 0.36x$$

$$0.15x - 1.5 + 3.90 < 0.36x$$

$$2.4 < 0.21x$$

$$11.4 < x$$

The answer is correct. An integer makes sense in this context.

A noninteger answer does not make sense, so round up. The national bank is less expensive if you make 12 or more transactions per month.

SAMPLE 2: Partial credit solution

The inequality is correct when $x > 10$. The case when $x \leq 10$ is not considered.

The student made an error in the last step. The answer is incorrect.

$$0.15(x - 10) + 3.90 < 0.36x$$

$$0.15x - 1.5 + 3.90 < 0.36x$$

$$2.4 < 0.21x$$

$$2.19 < x$$

The national bank is less expensive if you make 3 or more transactions.

Sample 3: Partial credit solution

Calculations are shown for 12 transactions only.

The answer is correct, but it is not justified.

Find the cost for each bank when there are 12 transactions.

National bank: \$3.90 + 2(\$.15) = \$4.20 **Local bank:** 12(\$.36) = \$4.32

The national bank is less expensive when you make 12 or more transactions.

Sample 4: No credit solution

The inequality is incorrect. The national bank does not charge \$.15 for every transaction.

The answer is incorrect.

$$0.15x + 3.90 < 0.36x$$
$$3.9 < 0.21x$$
$$18.6 < x$$

The national bank is less expensive when you make 19 or more transactions.

PRACTICE Apply the Scoring Rubric

Use the rubric on page 66 to score the solution to the problem below as *full credit, partial credit,* or *no credit. Explain* your reasoning.

PROBLEM You plant a 1.5 foot tall sawtooth oak that grows 3.5 feet per year and a 5 foot tall chestnut oak that grows 2 feet per year.

a. When will the sawtooth oak be taller than the chestnut oak?

b. Justify your answer.

1. The sawtooth oak will be taller than the chestnut oak in about 2.33 years.

2. Let x be the number of years.

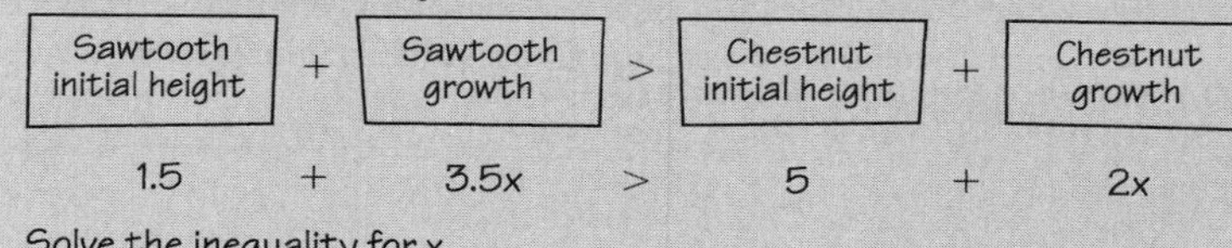

Sawtooth initial height
+
Sawtooth growth
>
Chestnut initial height
+
Chestnut growth
1.5 + 3.5x > 5 + 2x

Solve the inequality for x.

$$1.5 + 3.5x > 5 + 2x$$
$$1.5x > 3.5$$
$$x > 2.33$$

The sawtooth oak will be taller than the chestnut oak after about 2.33 years.

3. $1.5x + 3.5 > 5x + 2$

$1.5 > 3.5x$

$0.43 > x$, so after 0.43 year, the sawtooth oak will be taller.

TEST PREPARATION

Kentucky Test Preparation

1. **Partial credit; the answer is correct, but it is not justified.**
2. **Full credit; the problem is set up correctly and solved correctly.**
3. **No credit; the inequality is incorrect and the answer is incorrect.**

Kentucky Test Practice

1. a. $r < 84$
   b. The online store would be cheaper for $r > 56$ rulers.
2. a. $a = 10$, $h = 2$
   b. *Sample answer:* I used guess and check until I found the right answer.
3. a. *Sample answer:* $24 \cdot 3 + 4x = 100$, $x = 7$
   b. 2128 ft^2; the area of the large rectangle is 4000 square feet, and the height of the white rectangles is $40 - 14 = 26$ feet. So, the area of the shaded region is $4000 - 3 \cdot 26 \cdot 24 = 2128$ square feet.
4. a. Melanie
   b. Yes. *Sample answer:* If one player has 2 assists and 4 goals, her point total is 8. If another player has 1 goal and 6 assists, her point total is also 8.
5. a. 57 people
   b. \$3505
   c. There was $\$25 \cdot 220 = \$5500$ paid in advance. The amount collected at the door is $\$7495 - \$5500 = \$1995$, so the number of people who pay at the door is $\$1995 \div \$35 = 57$. The difference in the amounts is $\$5500 - \$1995 = \$3505$.
6. a. 2 games; they can each bowl 3 games
   b. The total amount spent for all 8 children on each game of bowling is \$21.60, shoe rental is \$10, and snacks are \$22.40. The snacks and shoe rentals will not change according to how many games are bowled, so they must be deducted from the total amount spent to determine how many games of bowling the children can play.

OPEN-RESPONSE

1. A teacher is buying rulers. At an online site, rulers cost \$.89 each plus \$5 for shipping for the entire order. At a store, each ruler costs \$.95.
   a. Under what conditions is the store less expensive?
   b. If there is free shipping for online orders over \$50, how does your answer change?

2. Consider the equation $|x + h| = a$.
   a. For what values of h and a are the solutions of the equation 8 and -12?
   b. *Describe* the method you used to solve the problem.

3. Consider the diagram below.

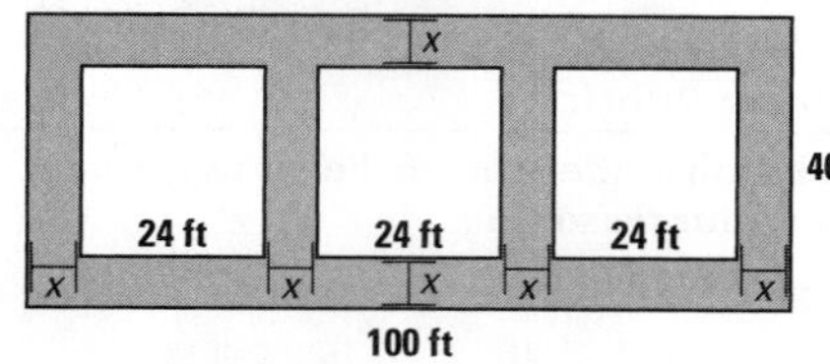

   a. Write and solve an equation to find x.
   b. Then find the area of the shaded region.

4. The table shows the number of goals g and assists a for four players on a girls' varsity soccer team. Each player is assigned a point total given by $p = 2g + a$.

Player	Goals, g	Assists, a
Sandra	2	6
Kim	3	5
Jen	4	1
Melanie	5	2

   a. Which player earned the most points?
   b. Is it possible for two players to earn the same number of points but have different numbers of goals and assists? Justify your answer.

5. A community is having a Taste of the Town event featuring the area's best restaurants. The admission is \$25 in advance and \$35 at the door.
   a. If 220 people pay in advance and the total amount collected is \$7495, how many people pay at the door?
   b. How much more money is collected in advance than at the door?
   c. Show your procedure.

6. Jared and 7 of his friends have a bowling party. Jared's parents pay for bowling, shoe rental, and snacks for all 8 children. The prices of these items are shown in the table. Jared's parents want the total cost to be at most \$80.

Bowling	\$2.70 per person, per game
Shoe rental	\$1.25 per pair
Snacks	\$2.80 per person

   a. If each person bowls the same number of games, what are the possible numbers of games each can bowl?
   b. How does your answer change if Jared's parents decide to pay at most \$100? *Explain.*

7. The volume V of a rectangular prism with a square base is given by $V = s^2h$ where h is the height and s is the length of one side of the base.

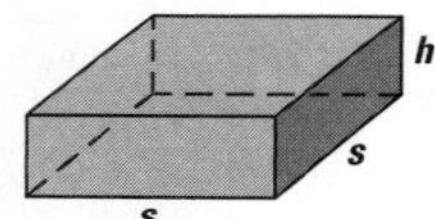

   Suppose such a prism has a volume of 1000 cubic centimeters.
   a. Choose three possible values of s and find the corresponding values of h.
   b. Is there a maximum value that s can have?
   c. Justify your answer.

OPEN-RESPONSE

8. The melting points and boiling points of lithium, carbon, nitrogen, oxygen, and magnesium are shown, to the nearest degree.

	Li	C	N	O	Mg
Melting point (°C)	?	3500	?	−218	?
Melting point (°F)	357	?	−346	?	1202
Boiling point (°C)	1347	?	−196	?	1107
Boiling point (°F)	?	8721	?	−297	?

a. Copy the table. Use the formula $F = \frac{9}{5}C + 32$ to convert the Celsius temperatures in the table to Fahrenheit temperatures. Record the results.

b. Rewrite the formula so that it gives the Celsius temperature in terms of the Fahrenheit temperature. Justify each step.

c. Use the rewritten formula to convert the Fahrenheit temperatures in the table to Celsius temperatures. Record the results.

9. A baseball pitcher's earned run average (ERA) can be calculated using this formula: ERA = 9 • earned runs ÷ innings pitched.

a. During one season, Johan Santana gave up 66 earned runs in 228 innings pitched. To the nearest hundredth, what was his ERA?

b. After pitching 2296 innings, Pedro Martinez had a career ERA of 2.71. Write and solve an equation to find the number of earned runs he allowed in those innings. *Explain* why there are two possible answers.

c. A pitcher who expects to pitch 200 innings in a season wants his ERA to be less than 4.00. Write and solve an inequality to find the possible numbers of earned runs he can allow. *Explain* how you need to round your answer.

MULTIPLE-CHOICE

10. Which graph represents the solution of the inequality $2x - 7 < 11$?

A.
B.

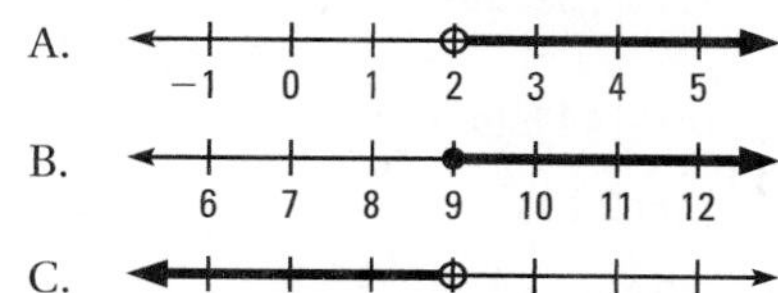

C.
D.

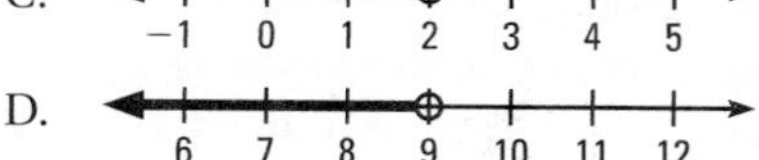

11. Which equation has −5 as a solution?

A. $-3x - 6 = 10$ B. $1.5 + 3x = -14.5$

C. $5 - x = 10$ D. $-9x = -45$

12. What is the solution of the equation $-t + 12 = 5t + 3$?

A. $\frac{4}{9}$ B. $\frac{2}{3}$

C. $\frac{3}{2}$ D. $\frac{9}{4}$

13. What is a solution of the absolute value equation $|x + 5| = 15 - 3x$?

A. −5 B. 2.5

C. 2.5, 10 D. −5, −2.5

14. What is the greatest value of x for which $|2x - 5| \le 7$?

A. −6 B. −1

C. 1 D. 6

TEST PREPARATION

7. a. ***Sample Answers:***
$s = 10$ cm and $h = 10$ cm
$s = 5$ cm and $h = 40$ cm
$s = 20$ cm and $h = 2.5$ cm

b. Yes

c. The length of s cannot be greater than $\sqrt{1000}$. Otherwise, the volume would be greater than 1000 cubic centimeters.

8. a. Row 2: 6332°F, −360.4°F
Row 4: 2456.6°F, −320.8°F, 2024.6°F

b. $F = \frac{9}{5}C + 32$ Given formula
$F - 32 = \frac{9}{5}C$ Subtract 32 from both sides
$\frac{5}{9}(F - 32) = C$ Multiply both sides by $\frac{5}{9}$, the reciprocal of $\frac{9}{5}$.

c. Row 1: 180.6°C, −210°C, 650°C
Row 3: 4827.2°C, −182.8°C

9. a. 2.61 ERA

b. $2.71 = 9 \bullet e \div 2296$; 691 or 692 earned runs. ***Sample answer:*** There are two possible answers because the ERA is only calculated to the nearest hundredth and he has pitched so many innings.

c. $9 \bullet e \div 200 < 4.00$, $e < 88$ earned runs; the answer needs to be rounded down to the nearest integer.

10. D
11. C
12. C
13. B
14. D

2 Pacing and Assignment Guide

KY REGULAR SCHEDULE

Pre-AP For pacing and assignments for a Pre-AP course, see the *Algebra 2 Toolkit*.

Lesson	Les. Day	BASIC	AVERAGE	ADVANCED
2.1 MA-HS-5.1.5	Day 1	SRH p. 987 Exs. 1–10; pp. 76–79 Exs. 1, 2, 3–13 odd, 14–27, 34, 35, 42–48, 51	pp. 76–79 Exs. 1, 2, 6–9, 12–17, 20–24, 28–30, 34–39, 42–49, 52	pp. 76–79 Exs. 1, 2, 7–9, 12, 13, 18–24, 31–50*
2.2 MA-HS-5.1.5	Day 1	SRH p. 975 Exs. 16, 19, 20, 22, 27, 32, 33; pp. 86–88 Exs. 1–17, 41–44, 50–51	pp. 86–88 Exs. 1, 2, 6–17, 29–31, 41–44, 50–51	pp. 86–88 Exs. 1, 2, 6–14, 17, 29–34, 41–44, 51
	Day 2	pp. 86–88 Exs. 18–31, 45–47	pp. 86–88 Exs. 18–28, 32–36, 45–48	pp. 86–88 Exs. 18–28, 35–40*, 45–49*
2.3 MA-HS-5.3.3	Day 1	pp. 93–96 Exs. 1–5, 9–19 odd, 21–23, 59–62, 70–71	pp. 93–96 Exs. 1, 2–20 even, 21–23, 59–62, 70–71	pp. 93–96 Exs. 1, 2, 6–8, 15–20, 23, 59–62, 70–71
	Day 2	pp. 93–96 Exs. 24–30 even, 31–41 odd, 43–48, 63–65	pp. 93–96 Exs. 25–29 odd, 30–42 even, 46–51, 55–57, 63–68	pp. 93–96 Exs. 27–30, 37–42, 46–58*, 63–69*
2.4 MA-HS-5.3.3	Day 1	pp. 101–104 Exs. 1–5, 9–17 odd, 18–23, 26, 27–37 odd, 39–42, 50–55, 59	pp. 101–104 Exs. 1, 2, 4–16 even, 18–26, 28–38 even, 39, 43–47, 50–57, 60	pp. 101–104 Exs. 1, 2, 7, 8, 15–17, 23–26, 33–49*, 51–58*
2.5 *MA-HS-5.1.7*	Day 1	pp. 109–111 Exs. 1–6, 11–13, 17–20, 24–26, 30–32, 38–43, 46	pp. 109–111 Exs. 1, 2, 5–8, 14–17, 21–23, 27–30, 32–35, 38–44, 47	pp. 109–111 Exs. 1, 2, 8–10, 15–17, 22, 23, 27–45*
2.6 MA-HS-4.2.3	Day 1	pp. 117–120 Exs. 1–9, 30–31	pp. 117–120 Exs. 1–9, 30–31	pp. 117–120 Exs. 1, 2, 4–6, 8, 9, 18, 22, 23*, 30–31
	Day 2	pp. 117–120 Exs. 10–19, 24–27	pp. 117–120 Exs. 10–21, 24–28	pp. 117–120 Exs. 12–17, 19–21, 24–29*
2.7 MA-HS-5.1.8	Day 1	SRH p. 989 Exs. 9, 12, 13, 17, 18; pp. 127–129 Exs. 1–14, 36, 37	pp. 127–129 Exs. 1, 2, 4–14, 32, 36, 37	pp. 127–129 Exs. 1, 2, 5–14, 32, 35–37*
	Day 2	pp. 127–129 Exs. 15–29, 38–40, 43–44	pp. 127–129 Exs. 17–31, 33, 38–41, 43–44	pp. 127–129 Exs. 18–31, 33, 34, 38–42*, 44
2.8 MA-HS-5.3.3	Day 1	pp. 135–138 Exs. 1–6, 7–17 odd, 19–25, 28–36 even, 43–47, 50	pp. 135–138 Exs. 1, 2, 5, 6, 8–18 even, 19–21, 22–28 even, 29, 30, 33–35, 39–41, 43–48, 50	pp. 135–138 Exs. 1, 2, 5, 6, 15–18, 21, 25–28, 31, 32, 36–49*, 51
Review	Day 1	pp. 141–144 Exs. 1–34	pp. 141–144 Exs. 1–34	pp. 141–144 Exs. 1–34
Assess	Day 1	Chapter 2 Test	Chapter 2 Test	Chapter 2 Test
Yearly Pacing		Chapter 2 Total – 14 days	Chapters 1–2 Total – 26 days	Remaining – 134 days

*Challenge Exercises EP = Extra Practice SRH = Skills Review Handbook

BLOCK SCHEDULE

DAY 1	DAY 2	DAY 3	DAY 4	DAY 5	DAY 6	DAY 7
2.1	**2.2 (CONT.)**	**2.3 (CONT.)**	**2.5**	**2.6 (CONT.)**	**2.7 (CONT.)**	**REVIEW**
pp. 76–79 Exs. 1, 2, 6–9, 12–17, 20–24, 28–30, 34–39, 42–49, 52	pp. 86–88 Exs. 18–28, 32–36, 45–48	pp. 93–96 Exs. 25–29 odd, 30–42 even, 46–51, 55–57, 63–68	pp. 109–111 Exs. 1, 2, 5–8, 14–17, 21–23, 27–30, 32–35, 38–44, 47	pp. 117–120 Exs. 10–21, 24–28	pp. 127–129 Exs. 17–31, 33, 38–41, 43–44	pp. 141–144 Exs. 1–34
2.2	**2.3**	**2.4**	**2.6**	**2.7**	**2.8**	**ASSESS**
pp. 86–88 Exs. 1, 2, 6–17, 29–31, 41–44, 50–51	pp. 93–96 Exs. 1, 2–20 even, 21–23, 59–62, 70–71	pp. 101–104 Exs. 1, 2, 4–16 even, 18–26, 28–38 even, 39, 43–47, 50–57, 60	pp. 117–120 Exs. 1–9, 30–31	pp. 127–129 Exs. 1, 2, 4–14, 32, 36, 37	pp. 135–138 Exs. 1, 2, 5, 6, 8–18 even, 19–21, 22–28 even, 29, 30, 33–35, 39–41, 43–48, 50	Chapter 2 Test
Yearly Pacing	Chapter 2 Total – 7 days		Chapters 1–2 Total – 13 days		Remaining – 67 days	

RESOURCE MANAGER

Chapter Resource Book

CHAPTER SUPPORT								
Parents as Partners (Chapter Overview with home involvement exercises and activity)							p. 1	
LESSON SUPPORT	**2.1**	**2.2**	**2.3**	**2.4**	**2.5**	**2.6**	**2.7**	**2.8**
Standards	**MA-HS-5.1.5**	**MA-HS-5.1.5**	**MA-HS-5.3.3**	**MA-HS-5.3.3**	*MA-HS-5.1.7*	**MA-HS-4.2.3**	**MA-HS-5.1.8**	**MA-HS-5.3.3**
Teaching Guide/Lesson Plan	p. 3	p. 16	p. 27	p. 41	p. 53	p. 63	p. 78	p. 92
Activity Masters		p. 18		p. 43				
Technology Activities & Keystrokes			p. 29			p. 65	p. 80	p. 94
Activity Support Masters								
Practice (3 levels)	p. 5	p. 19	p. 30	p. 44	p. 55	p. 67	p. 81	p. 96
Study Guide	p. 11	p. 22	p. 36	p. 47	p. 58	p. 73	p. 87	p. 102
Catch-Up for Absent Students	p. 13	p. 24	p. 38	p. 49	p. 60	p. 75	p. 89	p. 104
Problem Solving/Application	p. 14	p. 25	p. 39	p. 50	p. 61	p. 76	p. 90	p. 105
Challenge Practice	p. 15	p. 26	p. 40	p. 52	p. 62	p. 77	p. 91	p. 106

REVIEW			
Chapter Review Games and Activities	p. 107	Cumulative Practice	p. 109
Project with Rubric	p. 108	Resource Book Answers	A1

Transparencies	*2.1*	*2.2*	*2.3*	*2.4*	*2.5*	*2.6*	*2.7*	*2.8*
Warm-Up/Daily Homework Quiz	✔	✔	✔	✔	✔	✔	✔	✔
Notetaking Guide	✔	✔	✔	✔	✔	✔	✔	✔
Teacher Support	✔	✔	✔	✔	✔	✔	✔	✔
Answer Transparencies	✔	✔	✔	✔	✔	✔	✔	✔

ASSESSMENT BOOK

Quizzes	p. 16	SAT/ACT Chapter Test	p. 27
Chapter Tests (3 levels)	p. 19	Alternative Assessment with Rubric	p. 29
Standardized Chapter Test	p. 25		

TECHNOLOGY

- Easy Planner
- Test and Practice Generator
- Power Presentations
- @HomeTutor
- Activity Generator
- Animated Algebra
- Classzone.com
- eEdition Plus Online
- eWorkbook Plus Online
- ML Assessment System

ADDITIONAL RESOURCES

Kentucky

- Worked-Out Solution Key
- Notetaking Guide
- Practice Workbook
- Algebra 2 Toolkit
- Benchmark Tests
- Remediation Workbook
- Spanish Study Guide
- Spanish Assessment Book
- Spanish Resources in Spanish
- Multi-Language Visual Glossary

Lesson Practice Level B

LESSON 2.1 **Practice B** *For use with pages 72–79*

1. domain: {0, 1, 2, 3, 4}; range: {1, 2, 3, 4}; is a function
2. domain: {−2, −1, 0, 1}; range: {−3, −1, 1, 3, 5}; is *not* a function

Identify the domain and range of the given relation. Then tell whether the relation is a function.

1. (0, 3), (1, 1), (2, 2), (3, 4), (4, 2) **2.** (−2, −3), (−1, −1), (0, 1), (0, 3), (1, 5)

Use the vertical line test to determine whether the relation is a function.

3.

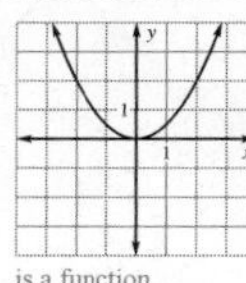

is a function

4.

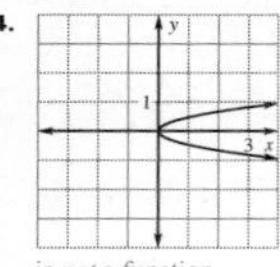

is *not* a function

5.

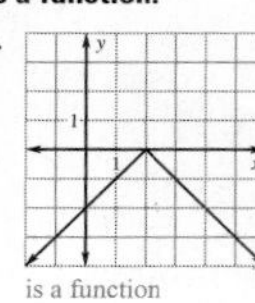

is a function

Graph the equation.

6. $y = 3x + 2$

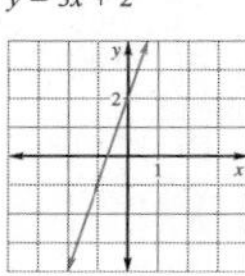

7. $y = -2x - 2$

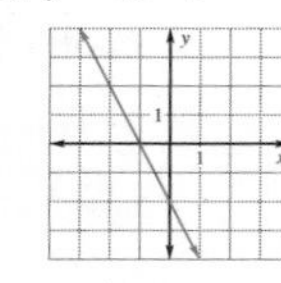

8. $y = -x$

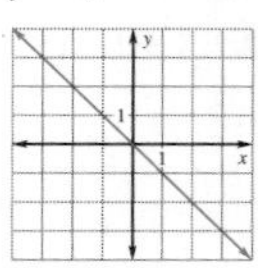

9. $y = -x + 3$

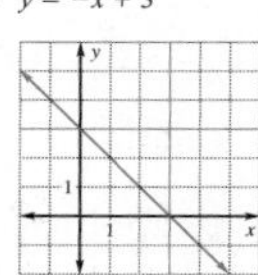

10. $y = \frac{1}{2}x + 2$

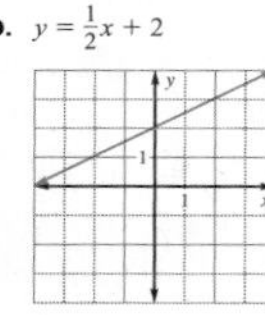

11. $y = 2x - 5$

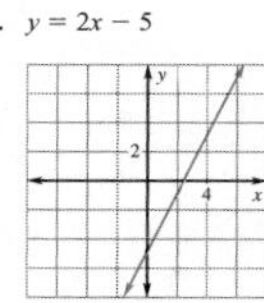

12. $y = x + 2$

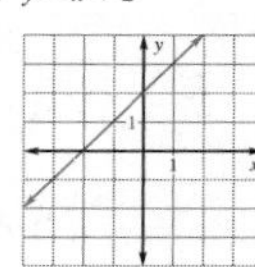

13. $y = -1$

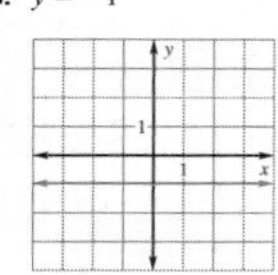

14. $y = -\frac{1}{4}x - 1$

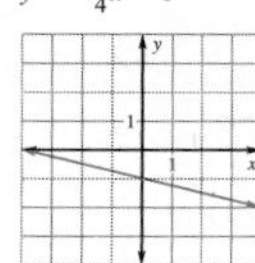

LESSON 2.1

LESSON 2.1 **Practice B** *continued* *For use with pages 72–79*

15. linear; 3 16. not linear; 0 17. linear; −3

Tell whether the function is linear. Then evaluate the function for the given value of *x*.

15. $f(x) = x + 5; f(-2)$ **16.** $f(x) = x^2 + x - 2; f(1)$ **17.** $f(x) = 3 - 3x; f(2)$

18. $f(x) = |x + 2|; f(-4)$ not linear; 2

19. $f(x) = \frac{2}{x - 2}; f(6)$ not linear; $\frac{1}{2}$

20. $f(x) = \frac{2}{3}x - 5; f(9)$ linear; 1

In Exercises 21–23, use the following information.

PGA Money List The table below shows the top five players on the 2005 PGA Tour money list through June 5th along with the number of wins for each player.

Player	Vijay Singh	Phil Mickelson	Tiger Woods	David Toms	Kenny Perry
Wins, *x*	3	3	3	1	2
Dollars, *y* (in millions)	5.3	4.2	4.1	3.3	2.5

21. What is the domain of the relation? domain: {1, 2, 3}

22. What is the range of the relation? range: {2.5, 3.3, 4.1, 4.2, 5.3}

23. Is the amount of money earned a function of the number of wins? no

In Exercises 24–26, use the following information.

Furniture Assembly At the beginning of your 8 hour shift, there were 42 units of furniture that needed assembled. The number of units *n* that still need to be assembled during your shift can be modeled by $n(t) = -3t + 42$ where *t* is the time in hours.

24. Graph the model.

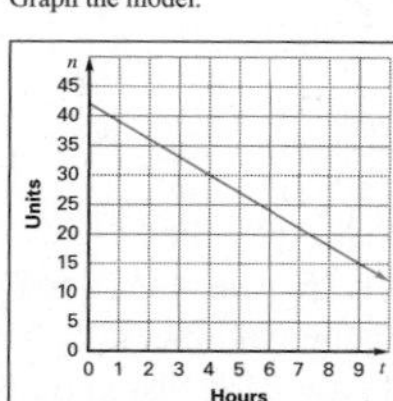

25. What is a reasonable domain and range of the model? domain: $0 \le t \le 8$; range: $18 \le n \le 42$

26. How many units still need to be assembled after you have worked 5 hours of your shift? 27

LESSON 2.1

LESSON 2.2 **Practice B** *For use with pages 82–88*

Find the slope of the line passing through the given points.

1. (2, 1), (6, 9) 2

2. (1, 1), (2, −5) −6

3. (−3, 2), (6, −1) $-\frac{1}{3}$

4. (3, −2), (−1, 7) $-\frac{9}{4}$

5. (0, −5), (−2, −9) 2

6. $\left(\frac{1}{3}, \frac{1}{2}\right), \left(\frac{5}{3}, \frac{5}{2}\right)$ $\frac{3}{2}$

Tell which line is steeper.

7. Line 1: through (−2, 2), (4, 3) Line 2
Line 2: through (2, 3), (6, 4)

8. Line 1: through (5, 2), (7, 12) Line 2
Line 2: through (−3, −1), (−2, 5)

9. Line 1: through (1, 1), (3, 0) Line 2
Line 2: through (4, 2), (8, −2)

10. Line 1: through (3, 8), (6, 17) Line 1
Line 2: through (0, 1), (−3, 7)

Find the slope of the line passing through the given points. Then tell whether the line *rises, falls, is horizontal,* or *is vertical.*

11. (−2, 4), (2, 5) $\frac{1}{4}$; rises

12. (3, 1), (3, −2) undefined; is vertical

13. (8, 15), (12, −1) −4; falls

14. (5, −2), (2, −2) 0; is horizontal

15. (9, −3), (−6, 4) $-\frac{7}{15}$; falls

16. (4, 5), (21, 5) 0; is horizontal

Tell whether the lines are *parallel, perpendicular,* or *neither.*

17. Line 1: through (−6, 2), (3, 5) parallel
Line 2: through (4, 1), (1, 0)

18. Line 1: through (7, 3), (8, 7) perpendicular
Line 2: through (−5, −4), (−1, −5)

19. Line 1: through (5, 2), (1, −7) neither
Line 2: through (−1, 3), (9, −1)

20. Line 1: through (5, 9), (7, 13) parallel
Line 2: through (0, 2), (4, 10)

21. Fuel Efficiency On Friday, you left for a weekend camping trip with 110 miles on the odometer and 14.5 gallons of gas in the tank of your car. When you returned on Sunday, the odometer read 299 miles and you still had 7.5 gallons of gas left. What was the fuel efficiency of your car on this trip? 27 mi/gal

22. Production Rate When you started your shift at 7:00 A.M., 120 steel valves had already been machined and were ready for assembly. At 3:00 P.M., your shift ended and 424 steel valves were now completed and ready for assembly. The target production rate is 36 steel valves per hour. What was the production rate for your shift? Would your supervisor be satisfied with the work pace? 38 steel values/h; yes

LESSON 2.2

LESSON 2.3

Practice B

For use with pages 89–96

Find the slope and y-intercept of the line.

1. $y = 7x + 8$ $m = 7, b = 8$
2. $y = -13x$ $m = -13, b = 0$
3. $2x + y - 2 = 0$ $m = -2, b = 2$
4. $4x + 2y - 5 = 0$ $m = -2, b = \frac{5}{2}$
5. $5x - y + 2 = 0$ $m = 5, b = 2$
6. $-3x + 2y - 4 = 0$ $m = \frac{3}{2}, b = 2$

Find the x- and y-intercepts of the line with the given equation.

7. $y = 4x - 1$ x-intercept: $\frac{1}{4}$, y-intercept: -1
8. $y = -x - 4$ x-intercept: -4, y-intercept: -4
9. $y = -\frac{1}{2}x + 2$ x-intercept: 4, y-intercept: 2
10. $y = \frac{3}{2}x + 1$ x-intercept: $-\frac{2}{3}$, y-intercept: 1
11. $y = \frac{4}{3}x - 2$ x-intercept: $\frac{3}{2}$, y-intercept: -2
12. $y = -\frac{1}{3}x - 3$ x-intercept: -9, y-intercept: -3
13. $x - y - 3 = 0$ x-intercept: 3, y-intercept: -3
14. $2x - 3y + 6 = 0$ x-intercept: -3, y-intercept: 2
15. $-7x - 14y - 5 = 0$ x-intercept: $-\frac{5}{7}$, y-intercept: $-\frac{5}{14}$
16. $4x - 2y = 1$ x-intercept: $\frac{1}{4}$, y-intercept: $-\frac{1}{2}$
17. $6x + 4y = -5$ x-intercept: $-\frac{5}{6}$, y-intercept: $-\frac{5}{4}$
18. $-3x + y = -8$ x-intercept: $\frac{8}{3}$, y-intercept: -8

Graph the equation.

19. $y = 3x + 3$

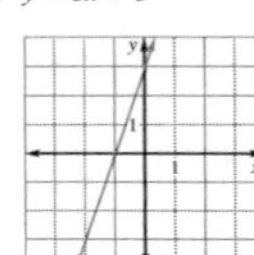

20. $y = -2x - 6$

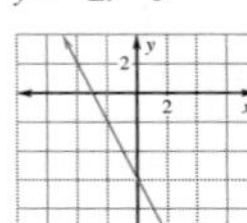

21. $x - 2y + 2 = 0$

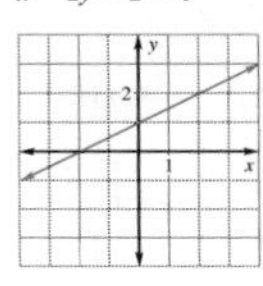

22. $5x + 2y + 6 = 0$

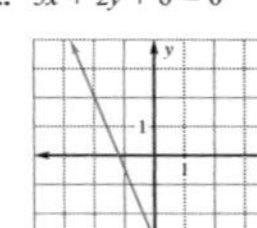

23. $-6x + 3y - 18 = 0$

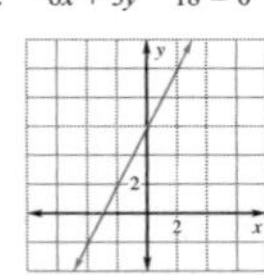

24. $12x - 8y = -24$

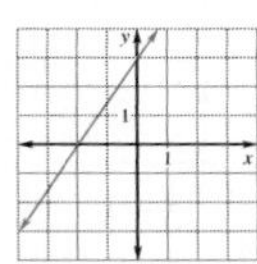

LESSON 2.3

LESSON 2.3

Practice B *continued*

For use with pages 89–96

25. $2x + y = -3$

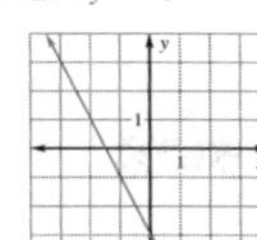

26. $3x + y = 0$

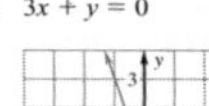

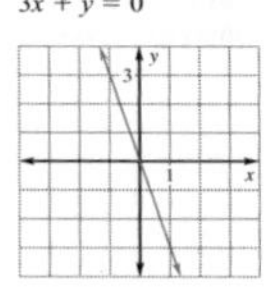

27. $-5x + 3y - 15 = 0$

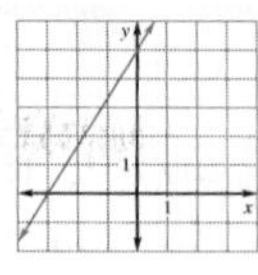

28. $2y = -5x - 4$

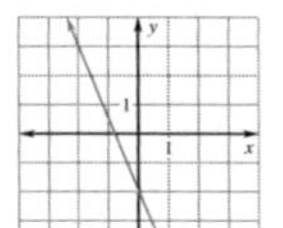

29. $-3y = 6x$

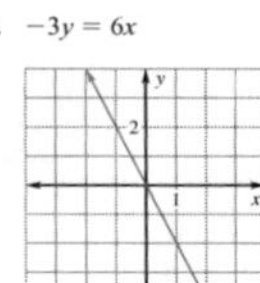

30. $6y - 18 = 0$

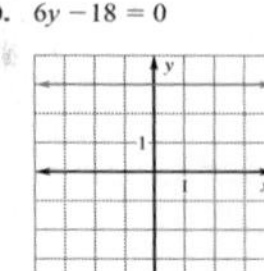

31. **Hot Dogs and Hamburgers** The caterer for your class picnic charges \$1 for each hot dog and \$2 for each hamburger. You have \$48 to spend. Write a model that shows the different numbers of hot dogs and hamburgers that you could purchase. $x + 2y = 48$ where x is the number of hot dogs and y is the number of hamburgers.

32. **Commission** A car salesperson earns 2% on used car sales and 6% on new car sales. The salesperson wants to earn a \$7000 commission this month. Write a model that shows the different sales amounts of used and new cars that can be sold to reach the target commission. $0.02x + 0.06y = 7000$ where x is used cars sales and y is new cars sales.

In Exercises 33–35, use the following information.

Airplane Landing An airplane's altitude is 100 feet as it is descending for a landing on a runway whose touchdown point is 5000 feet away. Let the x-axis represent the distance on the ground and the y-axis represent the airplane's altitude.

33. What is the slope of the airplane's descent? $-\frac{1}{50}$
34. What is the y-intercept of the airplane's descent? 100
35. Write an equation of the line that follows the path of the airplane's descent. $y = -\frac{1}{50}x + 100$

LESSON 2.3

LESSON 2.4

Practice B

For use with pages 98–104

Write an equation of the line that has the given slope and y-intercept.

1. $m = 3, b = -4$ $y = 3x - 4$
2. $m = -4, b = 0$ $y = -4x$
3. $m = 0, b = -5$ $y = -5$

Write an equation of the line that passes through the given point and has the given slope.

4. $(4, 3), m = 1$ $y = x - 1$
5. $(-1, 1), m = -2$ $y = -2x - 1$
6. $(12, 4), m = 0$ $y = 4$
7. $\left(\frac{2}{3}, 1\right), m = -3$ $y = -3x + 3$
8. $\left(-2, \frac{1}{2}\right), m = 8$ $y = 8x + \frac{33}{2}$
9. $\left(\frac{3}{5}, 0\right), m = -5$ $y = -5x + 3$

Write an equation of the line that passes through the given point and satisfies the given condition.

10. $(-2, 3)$; parallel to $y = 4x - 3$ $y = 4x + 11$
11. $(3, 7)$; parallel to $y = -3x + 6$ $y = -3x + 16$
12. $(-1, -4)$; perpendicular to $y = 2x + 5$ $y = -\frac{1}{2}x - \frac{9}{2}$
13. $(6, -2)$; perpendicular to $y = -5x - 7$ $y = \frac{1}{5}x - \frac{16}{5}$

Write an equation of the line that passes through the given points.

14. $(3, 4), (0, 3)$ $y = \frac{1}{3}x + 3$
15. $(-3, -3), (2, 1)$ $y = \frac{4}{5}x - \frac{3}{5}$
16. $(-5, -4), (0, 11)$ $y = 3x + 11$
17. $(1, -4), (-2, 6)$ $y = -\frac{10}{3}x - \frac{2}{3}$
18. $(2, 8), (5, 2)$ $y = -2x + 12$
19. $(-8, -3), (7, 0)$ $y = \frac{1}{5}x - \frac{7}{5}$

Write an equation of the line.

20.

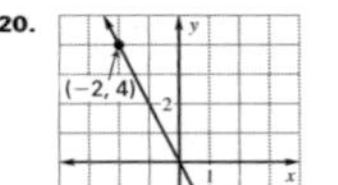

$y = -2x$

21.

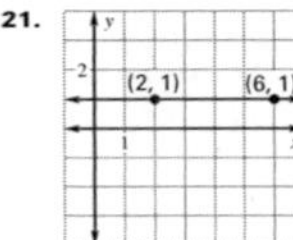

$y = 1$

22.

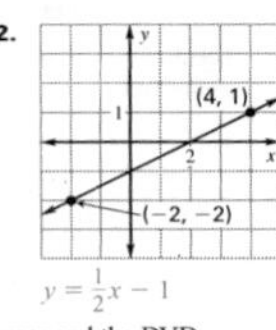

$y = \frac{1}{2}x - 1$

23. **Video Store** The membership to your local video store is \$10 per year and the DVD rental rate is \$3.95 per DVD. Write an equation that models the total amount of money you will spend on DVD rentals this year. $y = 3.95x + 10$

In Exercises 24 and 25, use the following information.

Postal Rates The price for U.S. postage stamps has increased over the years. Since 1975, the price has increased from \$.13 to \$.37 in 2005 at a rate that is approximately linear.

24. Write a linear model for the price of stamps during this time period. Let p represent the price and t represent the number of years since 1975. $p = 0.008t + 0.13$
25. What would you expect the price of a stamp to be in 2015? \$.45

LESSON 2.4

LESSON 2.5

Practice B

For use with pages 107–111

Write and graph a direct variation equation that has the given ordered pair as a solution.

1. $(5, 10)$ $y = 2x$

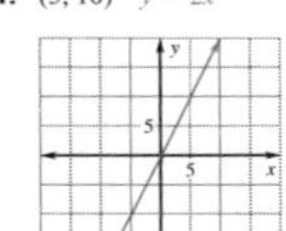

2. $(-6, 3)$ $y = -\frac{1}{2}x$

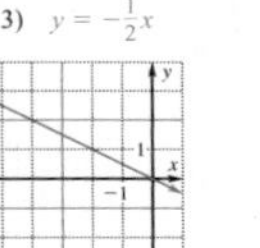

3. $(-5, -2)$ $y = \frac{2}{5}x$

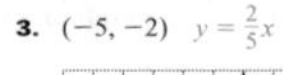

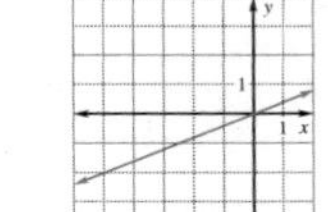

The variables x and y vary directly. Write an equation that relates x and y. Then find y when $x = 3$.

4 $x = 3, y = -9$ $y = -3x; -9$
5 $x = -4, y = -16$ $y = 4x; 12$
6. $x = 2, y = 14$ $y = 7x; 21$
7. $x = -4, y = -20$ $y = 5x; 15$
8. $x = 12, y = -4$ $y = -\frac{1}{3}x; -1$
9. $x = 7, y = 4$ $y = \frac{4}{7}x; \frac{12}{7}$
10. $x = -6, y = -1$ $y = \frac{1}{6}x; \frac{1}{2}$
11. $x = -10, y = -15$ $y = \frac{3}{2}x; \frac{9}{2}$
12. $x = 10, y = 4$ $y = \frac{2}{5}x; \frac{6}{5}$

Tell whether the equation represents direct variation. If it does, give the constant of variation.

13. $y = -3x$ yes; -3
14. $y + 2 = 8x$ no
15. $2y - 6 = 0$ no
16. $6x + y = 2$ no
17. $-6x + 4y = 0$ yes; $\frac{3}{2}$
18. $3y = \frac{9}{2}x$ yes; $\frac{3}{2}$

Tell whether the data in the table show a direct variation. If so, write an equation relating x and y.

19.

x	-2	-1	0	1	2
y	4	3	2	1	0

no

20.

x	-3	-1	1	3	5
y	-2	$-\frac{2}{3}$	$\frac{2}{3}$	2	$\frac{10}{3}$

yes; $y = \frac{2}{3}x$

21. **Reading** The number of pages p a student can read varies directly with the amount of time t in minutes spent reading. The student can read 90 pages in 60 minutes. Write an equation that relates p and t. Predict the number of pages the student can read if 90 minutes is spent reading. $p = \frac{3}{2}t$; 135

22. **Movies** The cost c of going to the movies varies directly with the number n of people attending. A group of four paid \$14 to go to the movies on Friday. Write an equation that relates c and n. How much would it cost for 7 people to go to the movies? $c = \frac{7}{2}n$; \$24.50

LESSON 2.5

2 Lesson Practice Level B

LESSON 2.6 Practice B
For use with pages 113–120

Draw a scatter plot of the data. Tell whether the data have a *positive correlation*, a *negative correlation* or *approximately no correlation*.

1.

x	0	0.5	1.25	2.75	3
y	−3.5	−2	−0.75	1.25	2.5
x	3.5	4.25	4.75	5.25	6
y	3.25	5.5	7	8.25	9.5

positive correlation

2.

x	−1.5	−1	−0.75	0	1.5
y	−5.25	−2.5	4	5.75	−1.75
x	2	2.25	3	3.5	4
y	−3	4.25	5.5	1.75	−1.25

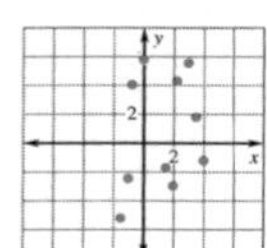

approximately no correlation

3. Answers may vary: $y = -\frac{2}{3}x + \frac{9}{4}$

4. Answers may vary: $y = \frac{7}{4}x - \frac{6}{5}$

Approximate the best-fitting line for the data.

3.

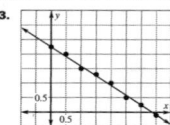

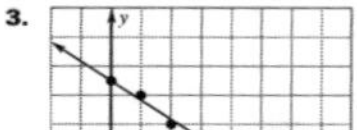

4.

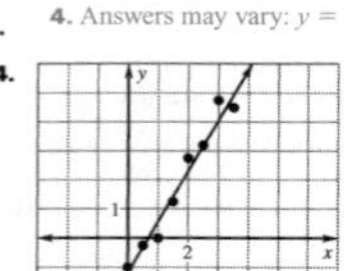

Draw a scatter plot of the data. Approximate the best-fitting line for the data.

5.

x	0.5	1	1.5	2	2.5
y	−2.25	−2.75	−1.7	−0.5	0
x	3	3.5	4	4.5	5
y	−0.6	1.2	1.9	2.5	2.3

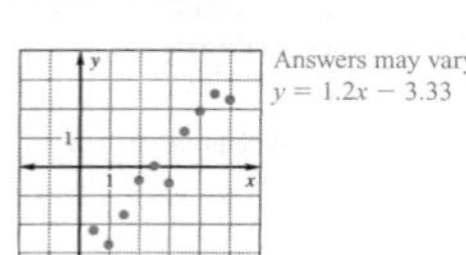

Answers may vary: $y = 1.2x - 3.33$

LESSON 2.6

LESSON 2.6 Practice B *continued*
For use with pages 113–120

6.

x	−4	−3	−2	−1	0
y	2	−0.5	0	−1.5	−4.2
x	1	2	3	4	
y	−5.8	−8.8	−9.5	−11.4	

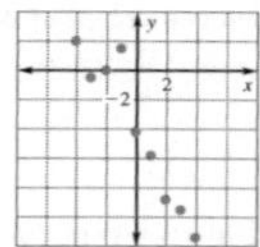

Answers may vary: $y = -1.8x - 4.5$

7.

x	−4	−3	−2	−1	0
y	2.5	3	1.5	2	1
x	1	2	3	4	
y	2	3.5	0.5	2.5	

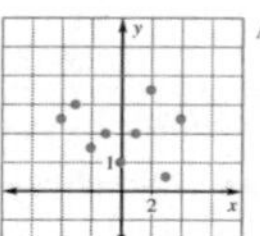

Answers may vary: $y = 2$

In Exercises 8–10, use the following information.

Softball The table shows the number of adult softball teams for the years 1999 to 2003.

Year	1999	2000	2001	2002	2003
Number of teams (in thousands)	163	155	149	143	119

8. Draw a scatter plot for the data. Let t represent the number of years since 1999.

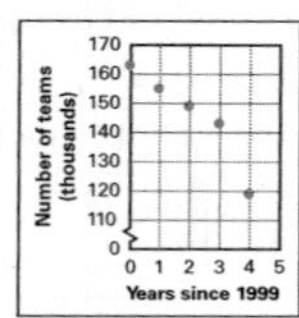

9. Using a graphing calculator, approximate the best-fitting line for the data. Answers may vary: $y = -10x + 165.8$

10. Using this model, predict the number of adult softball teams in 2010. 56 thousand

LESSON 2.6

LESSON 2.7 Practice B
For use with pages 123–129

For the function (a) tell whether the graph *opens up* or *down*, (b) identify the vertex, and (c) tell whether the function is *wider*, *narrower*, or the *same width* as the graph of $y = |x|$. See below.

1. $y = -|x + 1|$

2. $f(x) = 7|x - 3| - 4$

3. $y = -4|x + 2| + 2$

4. $f(x) = 2|x + 2| + 8$

5. $y = -\frac{2}{3}|x + 1|$

6. $f(x) = -|x| - 5$

7. $y = \frac{5}{2}|x + 9| - 1$

8. $f(x) = \frac{7}{8}|x + 3| - 9$

9. $y = -\frac{7}{5}|x - 1| + 1$

Graph the function.

10. $y = |x| - 3$

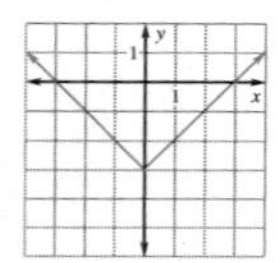

11. $f(x) = |x - 3|$

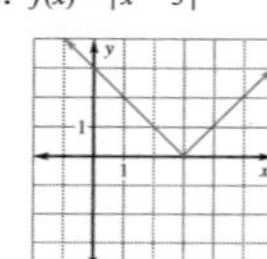

12. $y = |x + 2| + 1$

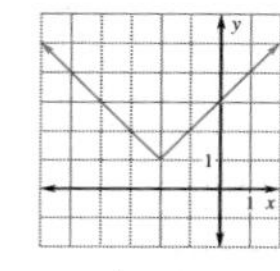

13. $y = 2|x + 1| - 1$

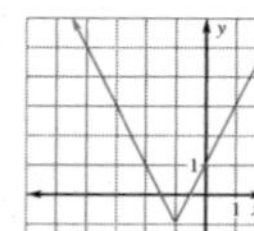

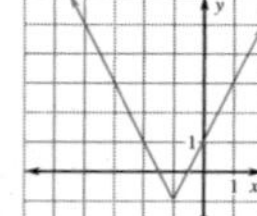

14. $f(x) = \frac{1}{2}|x - 3| + 2$

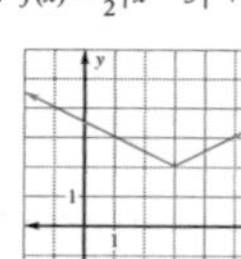

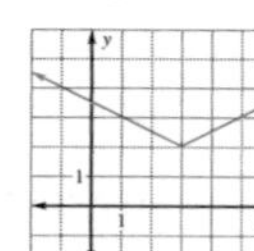

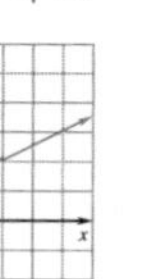

15. $y = -\frac{3}{2}|x - 4| + 2$

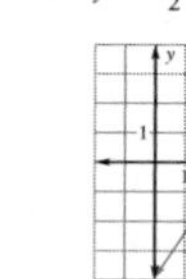

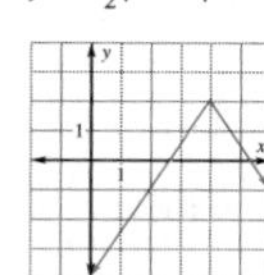

Write an equation of the graph shown.

16.

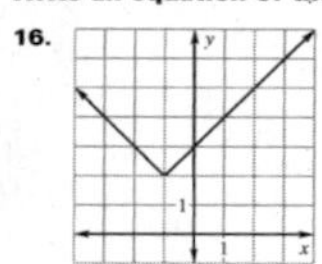

$y = |x + 1| + 2$

17.

$y = -2|x - 2| + 3$

18.

$y = \frac{1}{2}|x + 2| - 3$

1. **a.** down **b.** $(-1, 0)$ **c.** same
2. **a.** up **b.** $(3, -4)$ **c.** narrower
3. **a.** down **b.** $(-2, 2)$ **c.** narrower
4. **a.** up **b.** $(-2, 8)$ **c.** narrower
5. **a.** down **b.** $(-1, 0)$ **c.** wider
6. **a.** down **b.** $(0, -5)$ **c.** same
7. **a.** up **b.** $(-9, -1)$ **c.** narrower
8. **a.** up **b.** $(-3, -9)$ **c.** wider
9. **a.** down **b.** $(1, 1)$ **c.** narrower

LESSON 2.7

LESSON 2.7 Practice B *continued*
For use with pages 123–129

Let $f(x) = x + 2$. Sketch $f(x)$ and then sketch the function y given by the transformation to $f(x)$.

19. $y = f(x) + 1$

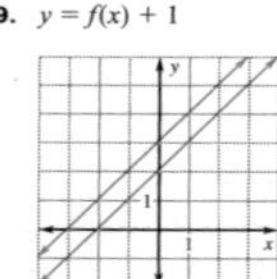

20. $y = f(x - 2)$

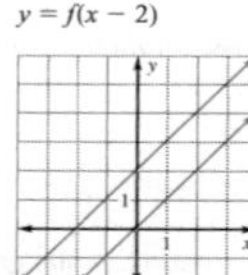

21. $y = -2f(x)$

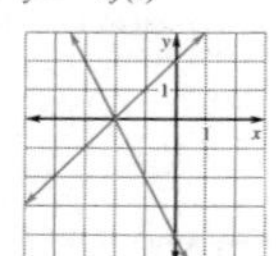

22. $y = \frac{1}{4}f(x)$

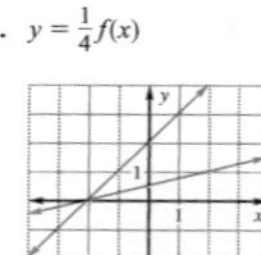

23. $y = 3f(x + 2) - 1$

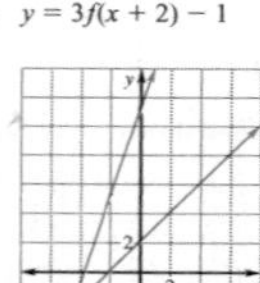

24. $y = -f(x - 1) + 3$

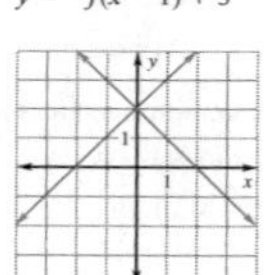

In Exercises 25–27, use the following information.

Speedboats The number of boats B a boat dealer sells in each month of the year can be modeled by the function $B = -15|t - 5| + 120$, where t is the time in months and $t = 1$ represents January.

25. Graph the function for $0 \le t \le 12$.

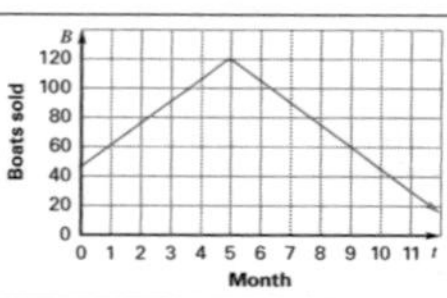

26. What is the maximum number of sales in one month? In what month is the maximum reached? The maximum sold is 120 in month 5.

27. What is the minimum number of sales in one month? In what month is the minimum reached? The minimum sold is 15 in month 12.

LESSON 2.7

LESSON 2.8
Practice B
For use with pages 132–138

Tell whether the given ordered pairs are solutions of the inequality.

1. $x - y < 4$; $(5, 4)$, $(-1, -4)$ yes; yes
2. $2x + 3y \le -3$; $(0, -1)$, $(-3, 2)$ yes; no
3. $4x - 2y > 5$; $(5, 8)$, $(-1, -4)$ no; no
4. $8y - 2x \ge 15$; $(1, 2)$, $(3, 3)$ no; yes
5. $2y < 5x + 10$; $(-2, -1)$, $(-1, 2)$ yes; yes
6. $10x \ge 14 - 8y$; $(2, 4)$, $(4, -3)$ yes; yes

Graph the inequality in a coordinate plane.

7. $x > 2$

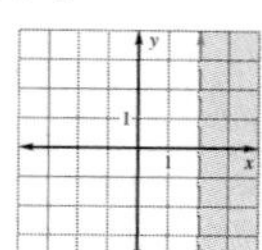

8. $x \le -1$

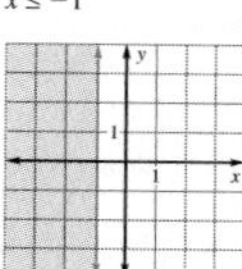

9. $2x \le 8$

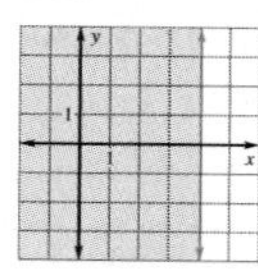

10. $y \ge -2$

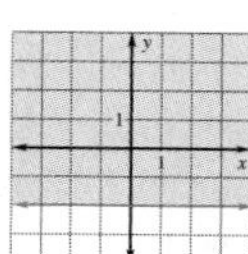

11. $y < 3$

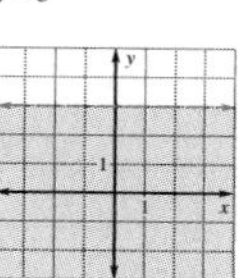

12. $\frac{1}{4}y \le 1$

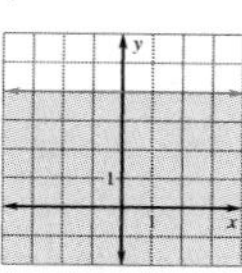

13. $y < 2x - 1$

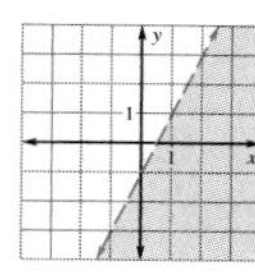

14. $y \ge \frac{1}{2}x + 2$

15. $3x + y > -3$

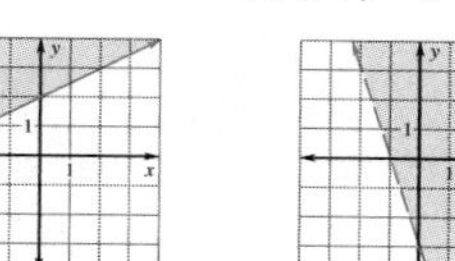

LESSON 2.8
Practice B *continued*
For use with pages 132–138

16. $x + 3y \le 6$

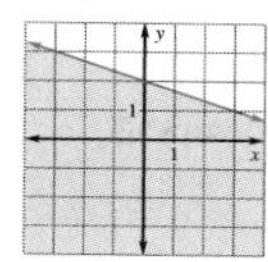

17. $x - 3y > -3$

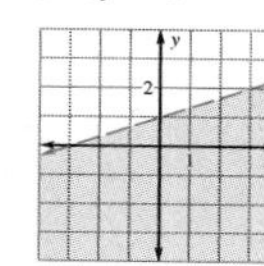

18. $-6x - 2y \le 4$

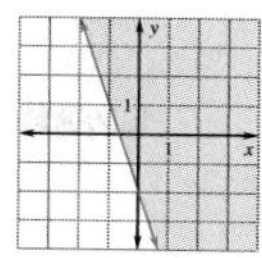

19. $2x - 2y > 8$

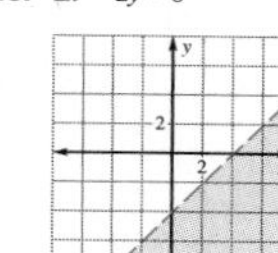

20. $-2x + 6y \ge -4$

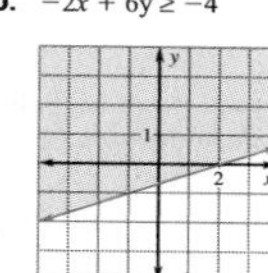

21. $10x + 5y \le 20$

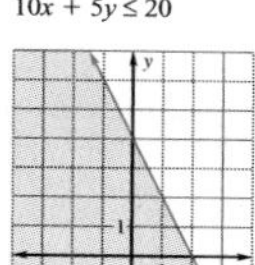

In Exercises 22–24, use the following information.

Summer Job You offer to mow your neighbors' lawns for \$20 or to wash their cars for \$10. Your goal is to earn at least \$1500 this summer.

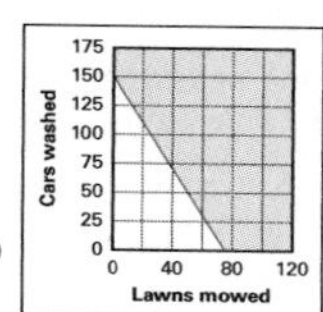

22. Write and graph an inequality that represents the possible number of lawns you would have to mow x and cars you would have to wash y in order to reach your goal. $20x + 10y \ge 1500$
23. What are the coordinates of mowing 50 lawns and washing 65 cars? $(50, 65)$
24. Is the point in Exercise 23 a solution of the inequality? yes

In Exercises 25–27, use the following information.

Music Lessons Your parents have budgeted \$550 for you to take music lessons on the piano for \$25 and on the saxophone for \$20.

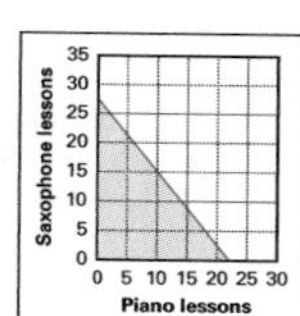

25. Write and graph an inequality that represents the possible number of piano lessons x and saxophone lessons y you can take this summer. $25x + 20y \le 550$
26. Is it possible to take 12 piano lessons and 15 saxophone lessons this summer? no
27. If you take 14 piano lessons, what is the maximum number of saxophone lessons you can take? 10

CHAPTER 2 Quiz 1
For use after Lessons 2.1–2.3

Tell whether the relation is a function.

1. Input Output

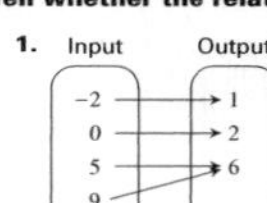

2. (8, 5), (−6, 4), (3, −2), (−6, 7)

Tell whether the function is linear. Then evaluate the function for the given value of *x*.

3. $f(x) = 5x - 10; f(-5)$
4. $f(x) = x^2 - 5x + 4; f(2)$

Find the slope of the line passing through the given points. Then tell whether the line *rises, falls, is horizontal,* or *is vertical.*

5. (3, −2), (−4, −2)
6. (9, 6), (−7, −4)
7. Tell whether the lines are *parallel*, *perpendicular*, or *neither*.

   Line 1: through (4, −2) and (5, −7)

   Line 2: through (2, 3) and (1, 8)

Graph the equation.

8. $y = 2x - 1$

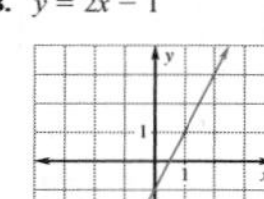

9. $y = -3$

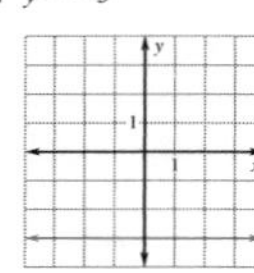

10. You spent $36 buying $9 storage crates and $3 notebooks. This situation can be modeled by the equation $9x + 3y = 36$. Find the *x*- and *y*-intercepts. Graph the equation.

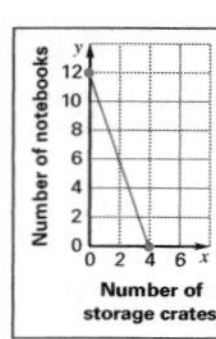

Answers

1. The relation is a function because each input is mapped onto exactly one output.
2. The relation is *not* a function because the input −6 is mapped onto both 4 and 7.
3. yes; −35
4. no; −2
5. $m = 0$; horizontal
6. $m = \frac{5}{8}$; rises
7. parallel
8. See left.
9. See left.
10. *x*-intercept: (4, 0); *y*-intercept: (0, 12) See left.

CHAPTER 2 Quiz 2
For use after Lessons 2.4–2.6

Write an equation of the line that satisfies the given conditions.

1. $m = -2, b = 7$
2. $m = -\frac{3}{4}, b = \frac{1}{8}$
3. $m = -4$, through (7, −2)
4. through (4, 5) and (6, −7)

Write an equation of the line that passes through the given point and satisfies the given conditions.

5. (1, −4); parallel to $y = -3x + 8$
6. (9, −1); perpendicular to $y = \frac{1}{4}x - 7$

The variables *x* and *y* vary directly. Write an equation that relates *x* and *y*. Then find *x* when *y* = −12.

7. $x = 21, y = 7$
8. $x = -2, y = 16$
9. $x = -3, y = 6$
10. $x = \frac{1}{2}, y = 8$

Tell whether the data have a *positive correlation*, a *negative correlation*, or *approximately no correlation*. Then tell whether the correlation coefficient is closest to −1, −0.5, 0, 0.5, or 1.

11.

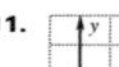

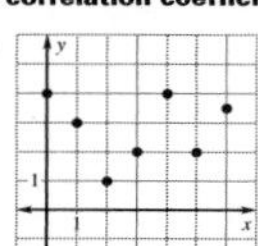

12.

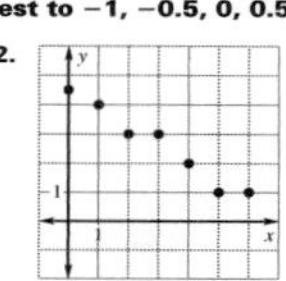

13. The table gives the number *y* (in millions) of sport utility vehicles that were produced in the United States *x* years after 1998. Approximate the best-fitting line for the data.

x	0	1	2	3	4
y	7	12	17	19	22

Answers

1. $y = -2x + 7$
2. $y = -\frac{3}{4}x + \frac{1}{8}$
3. $y = -4x + 26$
4. $y = -6x + 29$
5. $y = -3x - 1$
6. $y = -4x + 35$
7. $y = \frac{1}{3}x; -36$
8. $y = -8x; \frac{3}{2}$
9. $y = -2x; 6$
10. $y = 16x; -\frac{3}{4}$
11. appoximately no correlation; 0
12. negative correlation; −1
13. $y = 3.7x + 8$

CHAPTER 2 Quiz 3
For use after Lessons 2.7–2.8

Graph the function. Compare each graph with the graph of 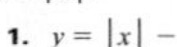 **$y = |x|$.**

1. $y = |x| - 1$

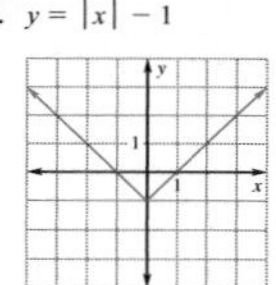

2. $y = -|x - 5| + 6$

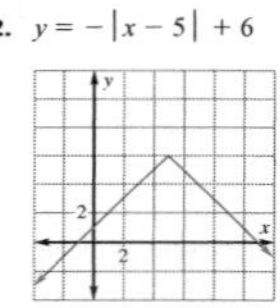

Write an equation of the graph.

3.

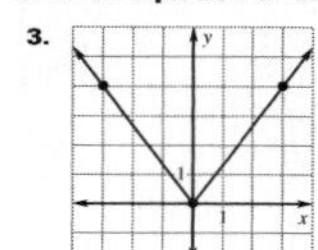

4.

Tell whether the given ordered pair is a solution of the inequality.

5. $y \geq -2x + 11$; (5, 1)
6. $y < \frac{1}{4}x + 9$; (8, 3)

Graph the inequality in a coordinate plane.

7. $x > -3$

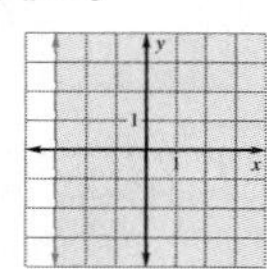

8. $y \leq -3x + 6$

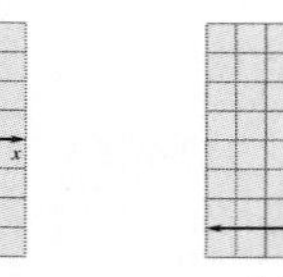

9. $4x + 7y \geq -28$

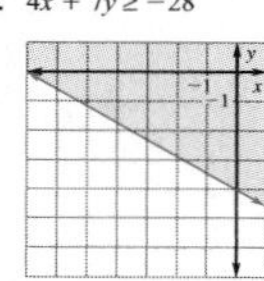

10. $y < |x| + 4$

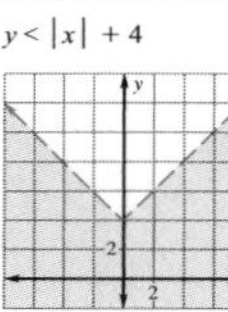

Answers

1. See left. The graphs have the same shape. The graph of $y = |x| - 1$ is the graph of $y = |x|$ translated down 1 unit.
2. See left. The graphs have the same shape. The graph of $y = -|x - 5| + 6$ is the graph of $y = |x|$ reflected in the *x*-axis and then translated 6 units up and 5 units right.
3. $y = \frac{4}{3}|x|$
4. $y = \frac{3}{2}|x + 2| - 3$
5. yes
6. yes
7. See left.
8. See left.
9. See left.
10. See left.

CHAPTER 2 Chapter Test B
For use after Chapter 2

Identify the domain and range of the relation.

1. (0, 2), (1, 0), (3, −2), (−1, 1)
2. (−1, −3), (2, 3), (1, 2), (−1, 2)

Tell whether the function is linear. Then evaluate the function for the given value of *x*.

3. $f(x) = 2x + \frac{3}{2}; f(1)$
4. $f(x) = 2x^2 + x; f(3)$

Find the slope of the line passing through the given points. Then tell whether the line *rises, falls, is horizontal,* or *is vertical.*

5. (2, 4), (0, 4)
6. (−1, −3), (1, −2)
7. You are measuring a bike ramp which is 15 feet wide at its base and 12 feet tall at its tallest point. What is the slope of the bike ramp?

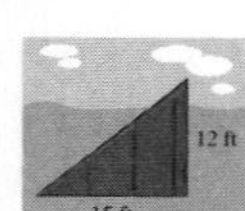

Graph the equation. Label any intercepts.

8. $y = -x + 2$

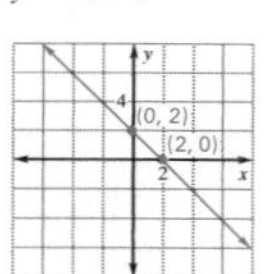

9. $-\frac{1}{3}x - y = -1$

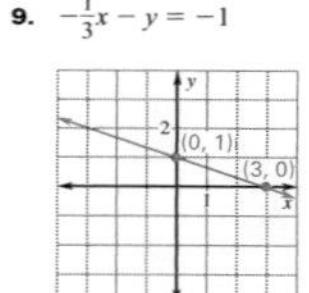

10. A company makes 2 models of snowboards, standard and deluxe. The standard model *s* costs $30 to make, while the deluxe model *d* costs $40. They have $1000 available with which to make snowboards. The number of snowboards that can be made is given by $30s + 40d = 1000$. Give 2 possible combinations where all of the $1000 is used.
11. For first time customers, a bank will open an account with $25 included. This bank also charges a monthly $2.95 service fee on the account. Write an equation that shows the balance *B* after *m* months, assuming no other activity is made on the account. Find the balance in the account after 8 months.

Answers

1. domain: −1, 0, 1, 3; range: −2, 0, 1, 2
2. domain: −1, 1, 2; range: −3, 2, 3
3. linear; 3.5
4. not linear; 21
5. 0; is horizontal
6. $\frac{1}{2}$; rises
7. $\frac{4}{5}$
8. See left.
9. See left.
10. *Sample answer:* $s = 20, d = 10$; $s = 0, d = 25$
11. $B = -2.95m + 25$; $1.40

CHAPTER 2 Chapter Test B *continued*
For use after Chapter 2

12. Write the equation of the line with slope $m = -\frac{1}{3}$ and y-intercept $b = 2$.

The variables *x* and *y* vary directly. Write an equation that relates *x* and *y*. Then find *x* when *y* = 3.

13. $x = 2, y = -4$ **14.** $x = 2, y = -3$

In Exercises 15–18, use the following table.

x	1	2	3
y	−2	−1.5	0
x	4	5	6
y	0	1	1.5

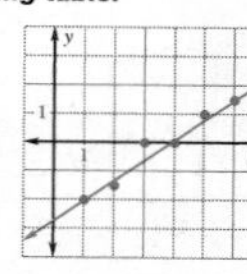

15. Draw a scatter plot of the data.

16. Estimate the correlation coefficient.

17. On the scatter plot, approximate the best fitting line.

18. Estimate y when $x = 8$.

19. Graph $f(x) = -|x + 3| - 2$. **20.** Write an equation of the graph.

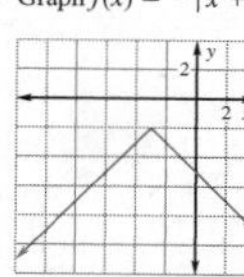

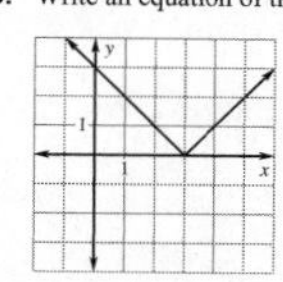

21. Graph the inequality $x + 2y > 3$ in a coordinate plane.

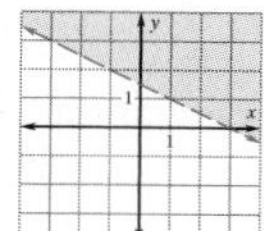

Answers

12. $y = -\frac{1}{3}x + 2$

13. $y = -2x; -\frac{3}{2}$

14. $y = -1.5x; -2$

15. See left.

16. 1

17. See left.

18. about 3

19. See left.

20. $y = |x - 3|$

21. See left.

CHAPTER 2 Standardized Test
For use after Chapter 2

Multiple Choice

1. What is the range of the relation given by the ordered pairs (2, 4), (3, −2), (−3, 7), (5, 2), and (9, 4)? C

Ⓐ −3, 2, 3, 5, and 9
Ⓑ 2, 3, 5, and 9
Ⓒ −2, 2, 4, and 7
Ⓓ −2, 2, 3, 4, and 9

2. Which of the following functions is linear? C

Ⓐ $f(x) = |x| - 2$ Ⓑ $f(x) = x^2 + 3x$
Ⓒ $f(x) = 2x + 4$ Ⓓ $f(x) = x^3 - 1$

3. Which sets of points would produce a line with a slope of $-\frac{3}{2}$? A

Ⓐ (5, 7), (7, 4)
Ⓑ (3, 2), (1, −3)
Ⓒ (−3, 0), (0, −2)
Ⓓ (5, 2), (8, 0)

4. Which represents the slope of a line that is perpendicular to a line with a slope of 4? B

Ⓐ −4 Ⓑ $-\frac{1}{4}$ Ⓒ $\frac{1}{4}$ Ⓓ 4

5. Which is the equation of the line that passes through the point (−4, 4) and is parallel to the line $y = \frac{1}{2}x - 4$? B

Ⓐ $y = 2x + 12$ Ⓑ $y = \frac{1}{2}x + 6$
Ⓒ $y = \frac{1}{2}x - 6$ Ⓓ $y = 2x + 4$

6. Which is the equation of the line that passes through the points (−2, 5) and (−4, −5)? A

Ⓐ $y = 5x + 15$ Ⓑ $y = \frac{1}{5}x - 10$
Ⓒ $y = -2x + 5$ Ⓓ $y = -4x - 5$

7. The variables x and y vary directly. If $x = \frac{1}{2}$ and $y = 6$ what is the direct variation equation? C

Ⓐ $y = 3x$ Ⓑ $y = \frac{1}{12}x$
Ⓒ $y = 12x$ Ⓓ $y = 6x$

8. Which equation best models the data in the scatter plot? D

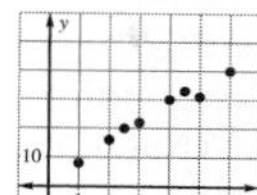

Ⓐ $y = -5x + 7$ Ⓑ $y = -4x - 4$
Ⓒ $y = 4x + 30$ Ⓓ $y = 6x + 4$

9. Which is the equation of the given graph? B

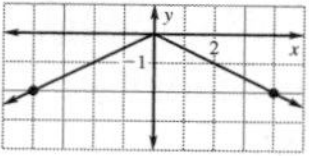

Ⓐ $y = -2|x|$ Ⓑ $y = -\frac{1}{2}|x|$
Ⓒ $y = \frac{1}{2}|x|$ Ⓓ $y = 2|x|$

10. Which equation would show the original function $y = f(x)$ shrunk by a factor of $\frac{1}{5}$, reflected across the x-axis, translated three units left and 4 units down? D

Ⓐ $y = -5f(x + 3) - 4$
Ⓑ $y = \frac{1}{5}f(x - 3) - 4$
Ⓒ $y = 5f(x - 3) + 4$
Ⓓ $y = -\frac{1}{5}f(x + 3) - 4$

CHAPTER 2 Standardized Test *continued*
For use after Chapter 2

11. Which statement is true about the graph of the function $y = 3|x - 2| + 4$? C

Ⓐ Its vertex is at (−6, 0).
Ⓑ Its vertex is at (−2, 4).
Ⓒ Its vertex is at (2, 4).
Ⓓ Its vertex is at (4, 2).

12. Which ordered pair is a solution of $-2x + 3y > 12$? B

Ⓐ (0, 4) Ⓑ (−3, 4)
Ⓒ (6, 0) Ⓓ (7, 4)

13. The graph of which inequality is shown? A

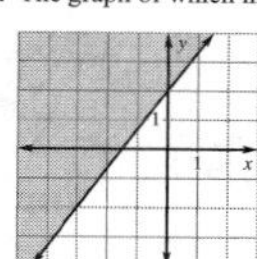

Ⓐ $y \geq \frac{4}{3}x + 2$ Ⓑ $y < \frac{3}{4}x + 2$
Ⓒ $y > \frac{4}{3}x + 2$ Ⓓ $y \geq -\frac{4}{3}x + 2$

Gridded Answer

14. What is the y-intercept of the graph of $2x - 3y = -15$?

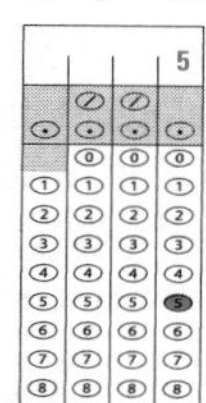

16. a.

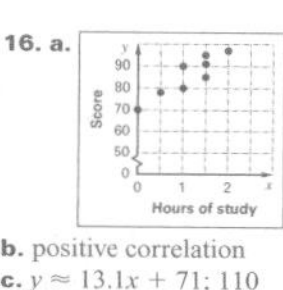

b. positive correlation
c. $y \approx 13.1x + 71$; 110

Short Response

15. The relation given by the ordered pairs (−5, −2), (5, 4), (3, 2), (2, −5), and (0, 5) is a function.

a. Choose an ordered pair that can be included with this relation to form a new relation that is also a function. Why is this new relation a function? *Explain.* See below.

b. Choose an ordered pair that when if added to the previous relation would form a new relation that is *not* a function. Why is this new relation *not* a function? See below.

Extended Response

16. The table shows the number of hours various students studied for their math test and the scores they earned on that test.

Hours of study	0	0.5	1	1
Score	70	78	80	90
Hours of study	1.5	1.5	1.5	2
Score	85	95	91	97

a. Make a scatter plot of the data. Let x represent the hours of study and y represent the score. See left.

b. Describe the correlation shown by the data. See left.

c. Approximate the best-fitting line for the data. Then use this line to predict what score a student might earn after studying for three hours. See left.

15. a. any ordered pair where the first number is *not* −5, 0, 2, 3, or 5; Each input had only one possible output. **b.** any ordered pair where the first number is −5, 0, 2, 3, or 5 and the ordered pair is unique in the relation; The input has 2 possible outputs.

CHAPTER 2 Alternative Assessment and Math Journal
For use after Chapter 2

Journal **1. a.** Compare the graph of $y = |x|$ to the graph of $y = -3|x + 2| - 1$ in terms of transformations.

b. Find the slope of the left and right sides of both graphs in part (a). What do you notice about the slopes of each graph's left and right side?

c. A rotation is a transformation that changes a graph's orientation. If the graph of $y = |x|$ is rotated clockwise 90°, is the relation still a function? Explain. Write an equation for the rotated graph.

Multi-Step Problem **2.** The table shows the average life expectancy (in years) of a person based on their year of birth.

Year of birth	1910	1920	1930	1940	1950
Life expectancy (in years)	50	54.1	59.7	62.9	68.2
Year of birth	1960	1970	1980	1990	2000
Life expectancy (in years)	69.7	70.8	73.7	75.4	77

a. Draw a scatter plot of the data pairs (year of birth, life expectancy).

b. Describe the correlation shown by the scatter plot. Is the correlation coefficient closest to −1, −0.5, 0, 0.5, or 1?

c. Approximate a best-fitting line for the data.

d. Use the *linear regression* feature on a graphing calculator to find an equation of the best-fitting line for the data. Then identify the correlation coefficient.

e. Predict the life expectancy for someone born in 2010 using the best-fitting line from part (c).

f. Writing Is it appropriate to use the best-fitting line to make predictions about the data based on the correlation coefficient? based on the trend in the data?

g. Critical Thinking What factors do you think have contributed to the increase in life expectancy over time? What factors do you think could greatly affect life expectancy in the future?

1. a. vertically stretched, reflected in the x-axis, and then translated left 2 units and down 1 unit; **b.** the slopes of the left and right sides are opposites (−1 and 1, 3 and −3), and the left and right sides of $y = |x|$ are also perpendicular; **c.** not a function because it fails the vertical line test; $y = |x|$

2. a.

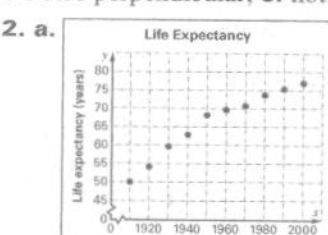

b. positive; 1 **c.** $y = 0.334x - 587.18$ **d.** $y = 0.295x - 511.23$; 0.98 **e.** about 84.2 yr **f.** Because the correlation coefficient is close to 1, it is appropriate to make predicitions using the best-fitting line. If this trend continues, the prediction based on the best-fitting line could be somewhat high. **g.** medical advances, such as vaccinations and organ transplants or sanitation; obesity or future medical advances, such as the use of stem cells

PLAN AND PREPARE

Main Ideas

Students learn that functions are defined as relations that map each value of the domain to a unique value of the range. Students then use slope to graph and write equations for linear functions. They also use slope to identify parallel and perpendicular lines. Students learn how many real world applications can be modeled using direct variation functions, and they learn how correlation coefficients measure how well a line fits a set of data pairs and use best-fitting lines to make predictions based on linear models. They use parent functions to graph absolute value functions. Finally, they graph and interpret solutions of systems of linear inequalities.

Prerequisite Skills

- Evaluating variable expressions for a given value of the variable
- Solving linear equations in one variable
- Solving linear equations in the form $Ax + By = C$ for y

Additional resources for reviewing prerequisite skills are:

- Skills Review Handbook, pp. 975–1009
- @HomeTutor

10. $y = -\frac{2}{3}x + 2$
11. $y = -x - 10$
12. $y = -\frac{1}{4}x - \frac{5}{4}$

2 Linear Equations and Functions

KY

Before

In Chapter 1, you learned the following skills, which you'll use in Chapter 2: evaluating algebraic expressions, solving linear equations, and rewriting equations.

Prerequisite Skills

VOCABULARY CHECK

Copy and complete the statement.

1. A **linear equation** in one variable is an equation that can be written in the form __?__ where a and b are constants and $a \neq 0$. $y = ax + b$
2. The **absolute value** of a real number is the distance the number is from __?__ on a number line. zero

SKILLS CHECK

Evaluate the expression for the given value of x. *(Review p. 10 for 2.1.)*

3. $-2(x + 1)$ when $x = -5$ 8
4. $11x - 14$ when $x = -3$ -47
5. $x^2 + x + 1$ when $x = 4$ 21
6. $-x^2 - 3x + 7$ when $x = 1$ 3

Solve the equation. Check your solution. *(Review p. 18 for 2.3.)*

7. $5x - 2 = 8$ 2
8. $-6x - 10 = 20$ -5
9. $-x + 9 = 2x - 27$ 12

Solve the equation for y. *(Review p. 26 for 2.4.)* 11–13. See margin.

10. $2x + 3y = 6$
11. $-x - y = 10$
12. $x + 4y = -5$

70

Chapter Planning Guide

Chapter 2 Resource Book
- Teaching Guide/Lesson Plan (pp. 3, 16, 27, 41, 53, 63, 78, 92)
- Project with Rubric (p. 108)

Assessment and Intervention
- Assessment Book (pp. 16–30)
- Benchmark Tests
- Remediation Book

Interactive Technology
- Easy Planner
- Power Presentations CD-ROM
- Activity Generator CD-ROM
- Animated Algebra
- Test Generator CD-ROM
- Online Quizzes
- eWorkbook
- eEdition
- @HomeTutor

Resources for English Learners
- Quick Reference for English Learners
- Spanish Study Guide
- Multi-Language Visual Glossary
- Student Resources in Spanish

Now

In Chapter 2, you will apply the big ideas listed below and reviewed in the Chapter Summary on page 140. You will also use the key vocabulary listed below.

Big Ideas

1. **Representing relations and functions**
2. **Graphing linear equations and inequalities in two variables**
3. **Writing linear equations and inequalities in two variables**

KEY VOCABULARY

- domain, range, *p. 72*
- function, *p. 73*
- linear function, *p. 75*
- slope, *p. 82*
- rate of change, *p. 85*
- parent function, *p. 89*
- *y*-intercept, *p. 89*
- slope-intercept form, *p. 90*
- *x*-intercept, *p. 91*
- point-slope form, *p. 98*
- direct variation, *p. 107*
- correlation coefficient, *p. 114*
- best-fitting line, *p. 114*
- absolute value function, *p. 123*
- transformation, *p. 123*
- linear inequality in two variables, *p. 132*

Why?

You can use rates of change to find linear models. For example, you can use an average rate of change to model distance traveled as a function of time.

Animated Algebra

The animation illustrated below for Exercise 44 on page 111 helps you answer this question: If a whale migrates at a given rate, how far will it travel in different periods of time?

Gray whales migrate from Mexico's Baja Peninsula to waters near Alaska.

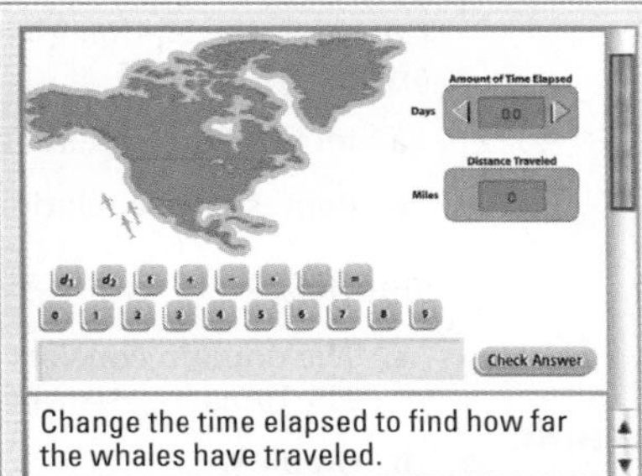

Change the time elapsed to find how far the whales have traveled.

Animated Algebra at classzone.com

Other animations for Chapter 2: pages 73, 86, 90, 95, 98, 102, 107, 115, 133, and 140

Algebra 2 Toolkit

- Reading Strategies for Chapter 2, pp. 11–12
- Differentiated Instruction Notes, pp. 47–50
- English Learners Notes, pp. 103–104
- Inclusion Notes, pp. 137–138
- Teaching Strategies with Sample Worksheets, pp. 163–186
- Using Technology in the Classroom, pp. 187–192
- Tips for New Teachers, pp. 195–196
- Math Background Notes, pp. 224–227
- Pre-AP Strategies and Copymasters, pp. 313–314, 347–358
- Teacher Survival Activities, pp. 471–472, 499–500
- Bulletin Board Idea, p. 526
- Teacher Tool Transparencies, following p. 538

1 PLAN AND PREPARE

Warm-Up Exercises

Transparency Available

Evaluate each expression for the given value of x.

1. $x^2 + 5x$; $x = -2$ -6
2. $4x - 3x^3$; $x = 2$ -16
3. $-x^2 + 3x - 10$; $x = 3$ -10
4. A square flower garden has a perimeter of 24 feet. How long is each side? 6 ft

Notetaking Guide

Transparency Available

Promotes interactive learning and notetaking skills, pp. 26–29.

Pacing

Basic: 1 day
Average: 1 day
Advanced: 1 day
Block: 0.5 block with 2.2

- See *Teaching Guide/Lesson Plan.*

2 FOCUS AND MOTIVATE

Essential Question

Big Idea 1, p. 71

How do you graph relations and functions? **Tell students they will learn how to answer this question by using ordered pairs and tables to create graphs.**

2.1 Represent Relations and Functions

MA-HS-5.1.5

Before You solved linear equations.
Now You will represent relations and graph linear functions.
Why? So you can model changes in elevation, as in Ex. 48.

Key Vocabulary
- relation
- domain
- range
- function
- equation in two variables
- linear function

MA-HS-5.1.5
Students will: determine if a relation is a function; determine the domain and range of a function (linear and quadratic); determine the slope and intercepts of a linear function; determine the maximum, minimum, and intercepts (roots/zeros) of a quadratic function and evaluate a function written in function notation for a specified rational number. DOK 2

A **relation** is a *mapping,* or pairing, of input values with output values. The set of input values is the **domain**, and the set of output values is the **range**.

KEY CONCEPT — *For Your Notebook*

Representing Relations

A relation can be represented in the following ways.

Ordered Pairs

(−2, 2)
(−2, −2)
(0, 1)
(3, 1)

Table

x	y
−2	2
−2	−2
0	1
3	1

Graph

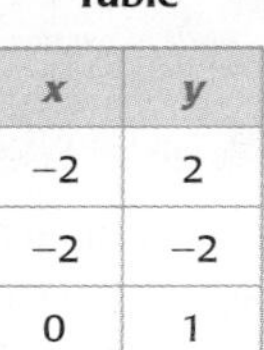

Mapping Diagram

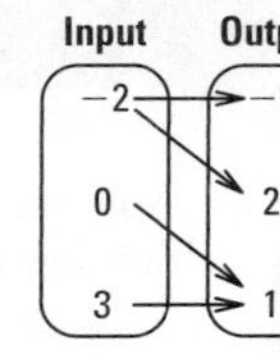

EXAMPLE 1 Represent relations

Consider the relation given by the ordered pairs (−2, −3), (−1, 1), (1, 3), (2, −2), and (3, 1).

a. Identify the domain and range.

b. Represent the relation using a graph and a mapping diagram.

Solution

a. The domain consists of all the x-coordinates: −2, −1, 1, 2, and 3. The range consists of all the y-coordinates: −3, −2, 1, and 3.

REVIEW GRAPHING
For help with plotting points in a coordinate plane, see p. 987.

b. Graph

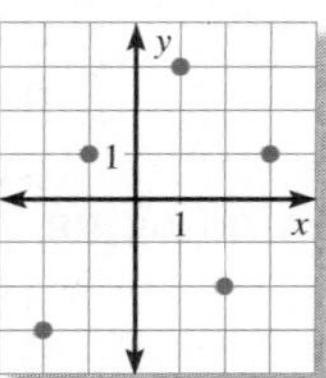

Mapping Diagram

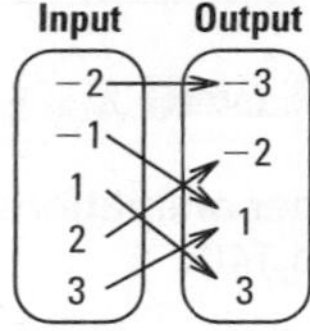

Resource Planning Guide

Chapter Resource Book
- Teaching Guide/Lesson Plan (pp. 3–4)
- Practice levels A, B, C (pp. 5–10)
- Study Guide (pp. 11–12)
- Catch-up for Absent Students (p. 13)
- Application (p. 14)
- Challenge (p. 15)

Workbooks
- Notetaking Guide (pp. 26–29)
- Practice Workbook (pp. 15–17)

Teaching Options
- **Power Presentations CD-ROM** provides dynamic electronic teaching resources for the classroom.
- **Activity Generator CD-ROM** provides editable activities for all ability levels.

Interactive Technology
- Easy Planner
- Power Presentations CD-ROM
- Activity Generator CD-ROM
- Animated Algebra
- Test Generator CD-ROM
- Online Quiz
- eWorkbook
- eEdition
- @HomeTutor

Resources for English Learners
- Quick Reference for English Learners
- Spanish Study Guide
- Multi-Language Visual Glossary
- Student Resources in Spanish

See also the *Algebra 2 Toolkit* for more strategies for meeting individual needs.

FUNCTIONS A **function** is a relation for which each input has exactly one output. If any input of a relation has more than one output, the relation is *not* a function.

EXAMPLE 2 Identify functions

AVOID ERRORS
A relation can map more than one input onto the same output and still be a function.

Tell whether the relation is a function. Explain.

a.

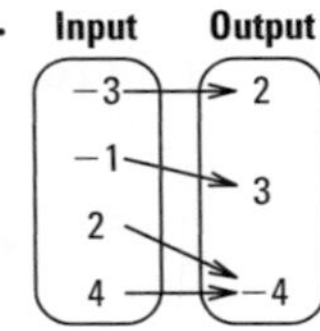

b.

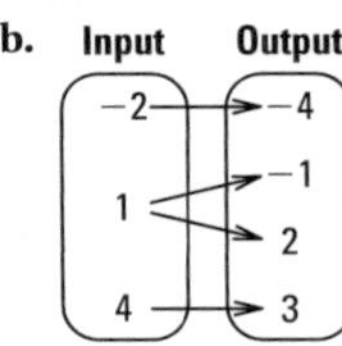

Solution

a. The relation *is* a function because each input is mapped onto exactly one output.

b. The relation *is not* a function because the input 1 is mapped onto both −1 and 2.

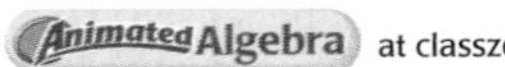

at classzone.com

✓ GUIDED PRACTICE for Examples 1 and 2

1. Consider the relation given by the ordered pairs (−4, 3), (−2, 1), (0, 3), (1, −2), and (−2, −4).
   a. Identify the domain and range. domain: −4, −2, 0, 1, range: −4, −2, 1, 3
   b. Represent the relation using a table and a mapping diagram. See margin.

2. Tell whether the relation is a function. *Explain.*
   Yes; each input has exactly one output.

x	−2	−1	0	1	3
y	−4	−4	−4	−4	−4

VERTICAL LINE TEST You can use the graph of a relation to determine whether it is a function by applying the *vertical line test.*

REVIEW LOGICAL STATEMENTS
For help with "if and only if" statements, see p. 1002.

KEY CONCEPT *For Your Notebook*

Vertical Line Test

A relation is a function if and only if no vertical line intersects the graph of the relation at more than one point.

Function

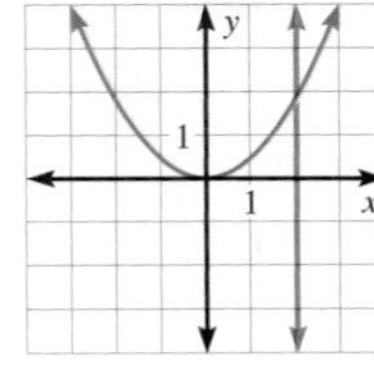

Not a function

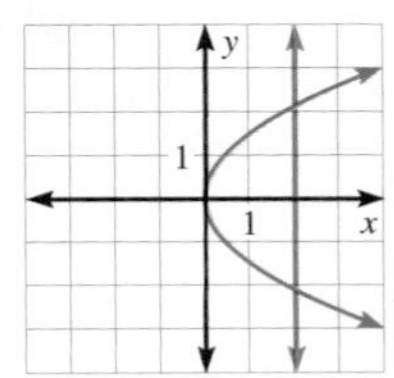

Motivating the Lesson

Knowing how two quantities are related will help you to find one of the quantities when the other is known. For example, you can determine how much more wall space you can cover with ten 10 inch square tiles than you can cover with ten 8 inch square tiles.

3 TEACH

Extra Example 1

Consider the relation given by (3, 2), (−1, 0), (2, −1), (−2, 1), (0, 3).

a. Identify the domain and range.
domain: {−2, −1, 0, 2, 3};
range: {−1, 0, 1, 2, 3}

b. Represent the relation using a graph and a mapping diagram.

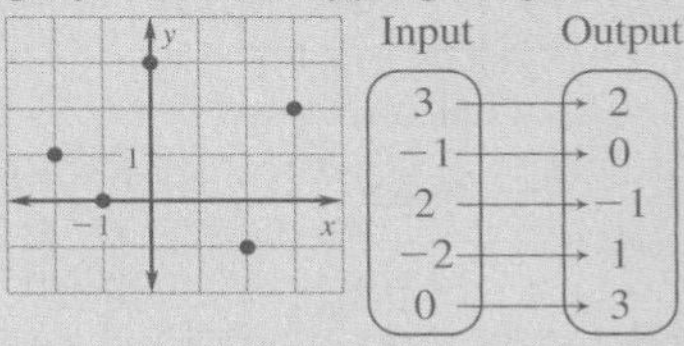

Extra Example 2

Is the relation a function? Explain.

a.

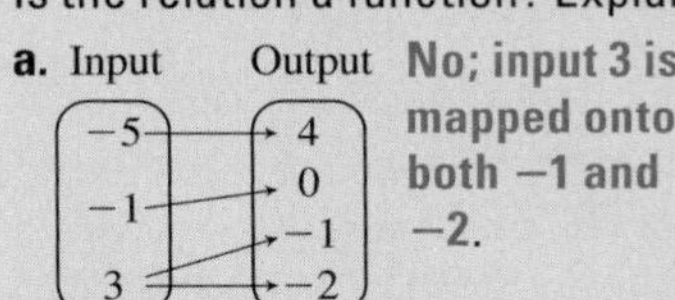

No; input 3 is mapped onto both −1 and −2.

b.

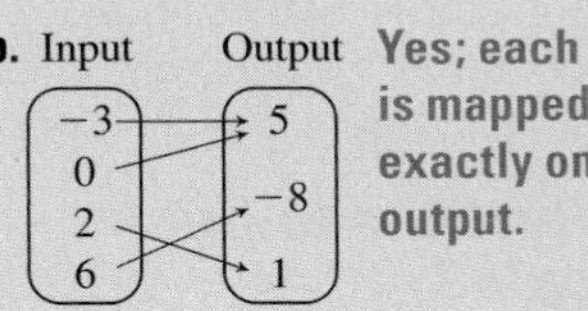

Yes; each input is mapped onto exactly one output.

An **Animated Algebra** activity is available on-line for **Example 2**. This activity is also available on the **Power Presentations CD-ROM**.

1b.

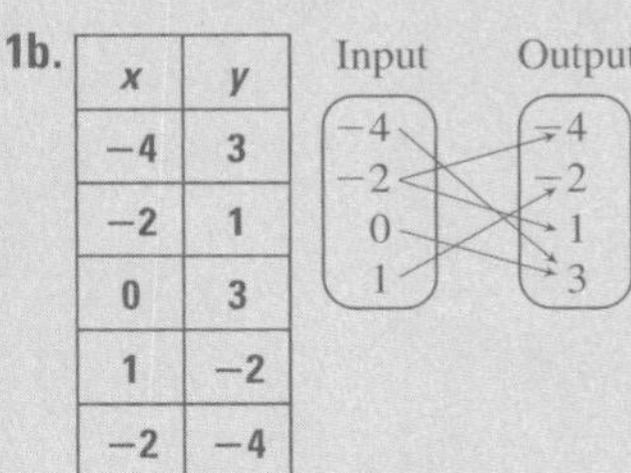

x	y
−4	3
−2	1
0	3
1	−2
−2	−4

Extra Example 3

The first graph below plots the total cost of membership under Plan A at an athletic club at the end of every two months. This plan charges an initial fee plus a $30 monthly fee. The second graph plots the total cost of membership under Plan B at the end of every two months. Plan B has a higher initial fee, but the last three months are free. Are the relations represented by the graphs functions? Explain.

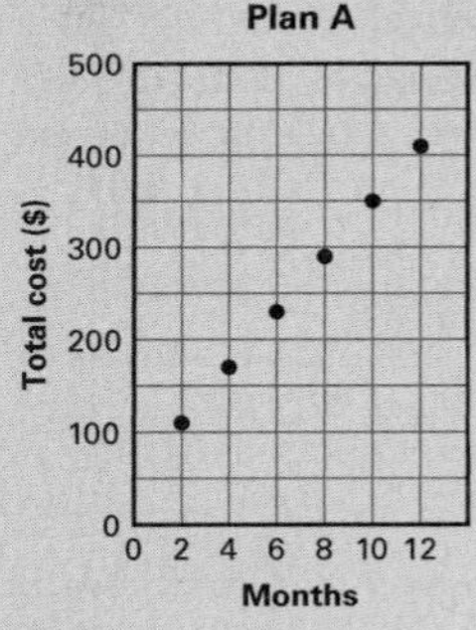

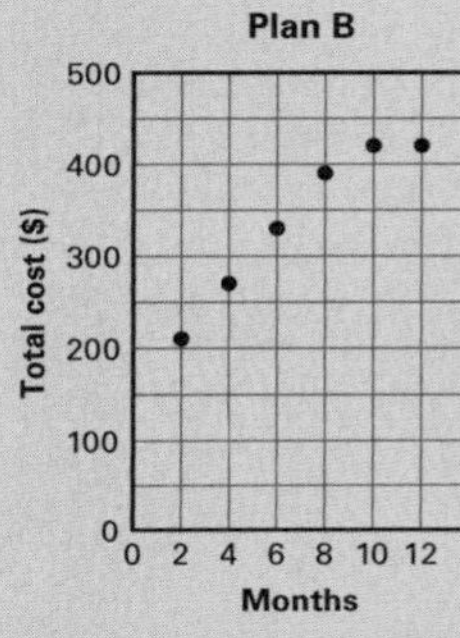

Both graphs represent functions because no vertical line intersects either graph at more than one point.

Key Question to Ask for Example 3

- What were the ages of the Timberwolves members that show the graph is not a function? 28 yr and 29 yr

Vocabulary

The first letter in *domain* precedes the first letter in *range* in the alphabet and the *x*-coordinate precedes the *y*-coordinate in an ordered pair. Students can use this association to remember that the domain of a function consists of all the *x*-coordinates of its ordered pairs.

EXAMPLE 3 Use the vertical line test

BASKETBALL The first graph below plots average points per game versus age at the end of the 2003–2004 NBA regular season for the 8 members of the Minnesota Timberwolves with the highest averages. The second graph plots average points per game versus age for one team member, Kevin Garnett, over his first 9 seasons. Are the relations shown by the graphs functions? Explain.

READING GRAPHS
The zigzag symbol on the horizontal axis of each graph indicates that values of x were skipped.

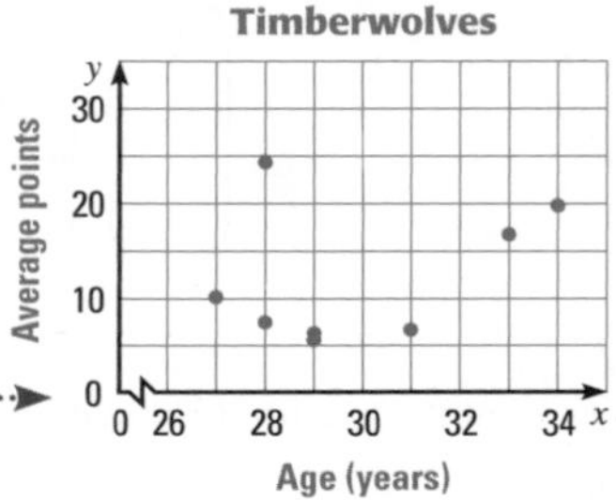

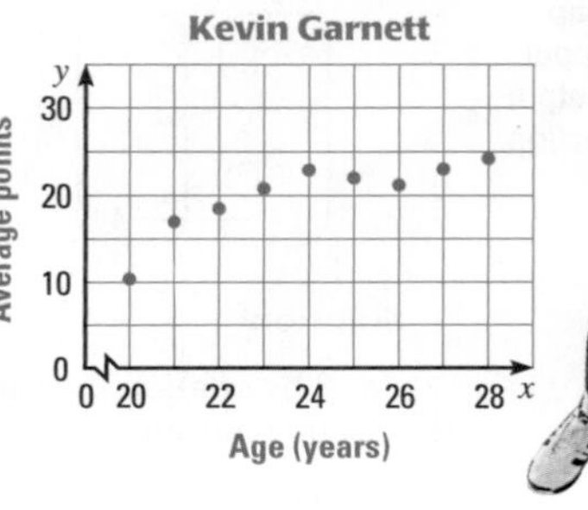

Solution

The team graph *does not* represent a function because vertical lines at $x = 28$ and $x = 29$ each intersect the graph at more than one point. The graph for Kevin Garnett *does* represent a function because no vertical line intersects the graph at more than one point.

✓ GUIDED PRACTICE for Example 3

3. **WHAT IF?** In Example 3, suppose that Kevin Garnett averages 24.2 points per game in his tenth season as he did in his ninth. If the relation given by the second graph is revised to include the tenth season, is the relation still a function? *Explain.* Yes; each input has exactly one output.

EQUATIONS IN TWO VARIABLES Many functions can be described by an **equation in two variables**, such as $y = 3x - 5$. The input variable (in this case, x) is called the **independent variable**. The output variable (in this case, y) is called the **dependent variable** because its value *depends* on the value of the input variable.

An ordered pair (x, y) is a **solution** of an equation in two variables if substituting x and y in the equation produces a true statement. For example, $(2, 1)$ is a solution of $y = 3x - 5$ because $1 = 3(2) - 5$ is true. The **graph** of an equation in two variables is the set of all points (x, y) that represent solutions of the equation.

KEY CONCEPT *For Your Notebook*

Graphing Equations in Two Variables

To graph an equation in two variables, follow these steps:

STEP 1 **Construct** a table of values.

STEP 2 **Plot** enough points from the table to recognize a pattern.

STEP 3 **Connect** the points with a line or a curve.

EXAMPLE 4 Graph an equation in two variables

Graph the equation $y = -2x - 1$.

Solution

STEP 1 **Construct** a table of values.

x	-2	-1	0	1	2
y	3	1	-1	-3	-5

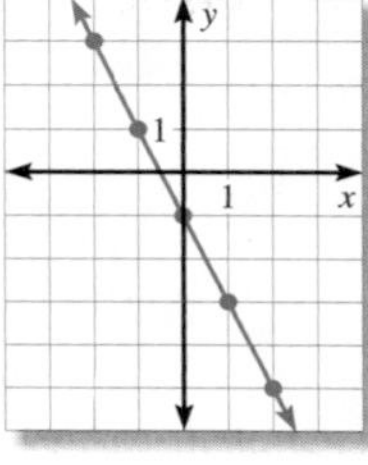

STEP 2 **Plot** the points. Notice that they all lie on a line.

STEP 3 **Connect** the points with a line.

LINEAR FUNCTIONS The function $y = -2x - 1$ in Example 4 is a **linear function** because it can be written in the form $y = mx + b$ where m and b are constants. The graph of a linear function is a line. By renaming y as $f(x)$, you can write $y = mx + b$ using **function notation**.

READING
The parentheses in $f(x)$ do not indicate multiplication. The symbol $f(x)$ does not mean "f times x."

$y = mx + b$ **Linear function in *x-y* notation**

$f(x) = mx + b$ **Linear function in function notation**

The notation $f(x)$ is read "the value of f at x," or simply "f of x," and identifies x as the independent variable. The domain consists of all values of x for which $f(x)$ is defined. The range consists of all values of $f(x)$ where x is in the domain of f.

EXAMPLE 5 Classify and evaluate functions

Tell whether the function is linear. Then evaluate the function when $x = -4$.

a. $f(x) = -x^2 - 2x + 7$ **b.** $g(x) = 5x + 8$

Solution

a. The function f is not linear because it has an x^2-term.

$f(x) = -x^2 - 2x + 7$ **Write function.**

$f(-4) = -(-4)^2 - 2(-4) + 7$ **Substitute −4 for x.**

$= -1$ **Simplify.**

REPRESENT FUNCTIONS
Letters other than f, such as g or h, can also name functions.

b. The function g is linear because it has the form $g(x) = mx + b$.

$g(x) = 5x + 8$ **Write function.**

$g(-4) = 5(-4) + 8$ **Substitute −4 for x.**

$= -12$ **Simplify.**

✓ **GUIDED PRACTICE** for Examples 4 and 5

4. Graph the equation $y = 3x - 2$. **See margin.**

Tell whether the function is linear. Then evaluate the function when $x = -2$.

5. $f(x) = x - 1 - x^3$ **not linear; 5**

6. $g(x) = -4 - 2x$ **linear; 0**

Extra Example 4

Graph the equation $y = 3x - 5$.

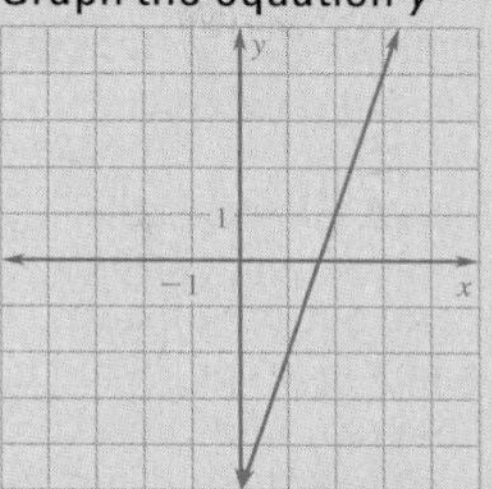

Key Questions to Ask for Example 4

- What is the minimum number of points that you need to graph to a line? **two**
- Where does the graph of $y = -2x - 1$ cross the y-axis? **(0, −1)**

Extra Example 5

Tell whether the function is linear. Then evaluate the function when $x = -3$.

a. $f(x) = -2x^3 + 5$ **not linear; 59**

b. $g(x) = 12 - 8x$ **linear; 36**

Key Questions to Ask for Example 5

- What is the domain of each function? **all real numbers**
- What is the range of $g(x)$? **all real numbers**

Mathematical Reasoning

Multiple Representations In their notebooks, have students record an example of each different representation of a relation (ordered pairs, table, graph, mapping diagram, equation).

4.

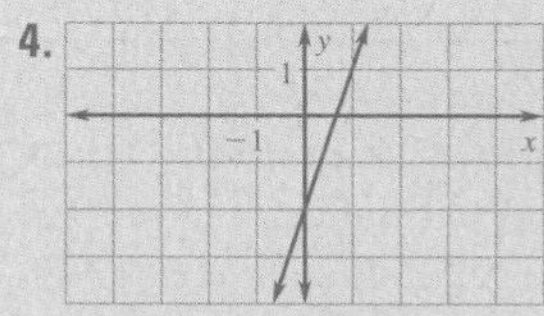

Differentiated Instruction

Inclusion For students with conceptual processing difficulties, function notation can be problematic. Students may mistake $f(x)$ to mean x multiplied by f. Give plenty of examples and emphasize that the letter f is not a variable. Initially, students may remember the meaning of f as function because it is the initial letter of the word "function." When other letters are used to represent functions, such as g and h, be sure to stress again that they are not variables.

See also the *Algebra 2 Toolkit* for more strategies.

Extra Example 6

The length L (in inches) that a spring stretches when a weight up to 20 pounds is attached to it is given by $L(w) = \frac{1}{12}w + 2$, where w is the weight in pounds. Graph the function, and determine a reasonable domain and range. What is the length of the spring when a 10 pound weight is attached?

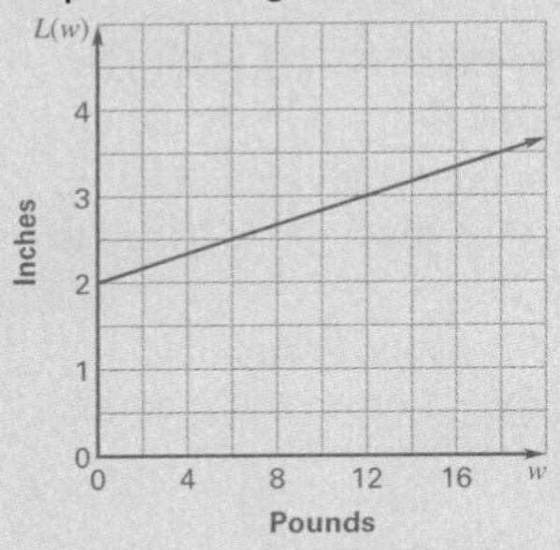

domain: $0 \le w \le 20$; range: $2 \le L \le 3\frac{2}{3}$; $2\frac{5}{6}$ in.

Key Question to Ask for Example 6

- What is represented by the point (0, 1) on the graph? **At the surface, the pressure is 1 atmosphere.**

Closing the Lesson

Have students summarize the major points of the lesson and answer the Essential Question: How do you graph relations and functions?

- **A function is a relation in which each element of the domain is paired with exactly one element of the range.**
- **A linear function can be written in function notation as $f(x) = mx + b$.**

To graph a relation or function, make a table of domain and range values and plot points from the table. If the function represents a linear function, connect the points with a line.

3–8. See Additional Answers beginning on p. AA1.

DOMAINS IN REAL LIFE In Example 5, the domain of each function is all real numbers because there is an output for every real number x. In real life, you may need to restrict the domain so that it is reasonable in the given situation.

EXAMPLE 6 Use a function in real life

DIVING A diver using a Diver Propulsion Vehicle (DPV) descends to a depth of 130 feet. The pressure P (in atmospheres) on the diver is given by $P(d) = 1 + 0.03d$ where d is the depth (in feet). Graph the function, and determine a reasonable domain and range. What is the pressure on the diver at a depth of 33 feet?

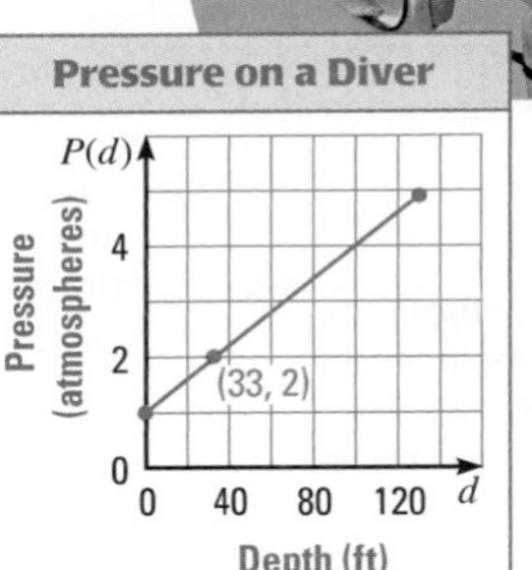

Solution

The graph of $P(d)$ is shown. Because the depth varies from 0 feet to 130 feet, a reasonable domain is $0 \le d \le 130$.

The minimum value of $P(d)$ is $P(0) = 1$, and the maximum value of $P(d)$ is $P(130) = 4.9$. So, a reasonable range is $1 \le P(d) \le 4.9$.

▶ At a depth of 33 feet, the pressure on the diver is $P(33) = 1 + 0.03(33) \approx 2$ atmospheres, which you can verify from the graph.

Pressure on a Diver

✓ GUIDED PRACTICE for Example 6

7. **OCEAN EXPLORATION** In 1960, the deep-sea vessel *Trieste* descended to an estimated depth of 35,800 feet. Determine a reasonable domain and range of the function $P(d)$ in Example 6 for this trip. **domain: $0 \le d \le 35{,}800$; range: $1 \le P(d) \le 1075$**

2.1 EXERCISES

HOMEWORK KEY
○ = **WORKED-OUT SOLUTIONS** on p. WS2 for Exs. 7, 17, and 45
★ = **STANDARDIZED TEST PRACTICE** Exs. 2, 9, 20, 24, 40, 46, and 49

SKILL PRACTICE

A

1. **VOCABULARY** Copy and complete: In the equation $y = x + 5$, x is the _?_ variable and y is the _?_ variable. **independent, dependent**

2. ★ **WRITING** *Describe* how to find the domain and range of a relation given by a set of ordered pairs. **If (x, y) represents each ordered pair, then each x is part of the domain and each y is part of the range.**

EXAMPLE 1 on p. 72 for Exs. 3–9

REPRESENTING RELATIONS Identify the domain and range of the given relation. Then represent the relation using a graph and a mapping diagram. **3–8. See margin.**

3. (−2, 3), (1, 2), (3, −1), (−4, −3)
4. (5, −2), (−3, −2), (3, 3), (−1, −1)
5. (6, −1), (−2, −3), (1, 8), (−2, 5)
6. (−7, 4), (2, −5), (1, −2), (−3, 6)
7.  (5, 20), (10, 20), (15, 30), (20, 30)
8. (4, −2), (4, 2), (16, −4), (16, 4)

. Yes; each put has exactly ne output.

EXAMPLE 2
on p. 73
for Exs. 10–20

. Yes; each put has exactly ne output.

. No; the inputs 1 and 5 have ore than one utput.

. Yes; each put has exactly ne output.

. An output can e mapped to ore than once; e relation ven by the rdered pairs −4, 2), (−1, 5), , 6), and , 2) is a nction because ach input has xactly one utput.

EXAMPLE 3
on p. 74
for Exs. 21–23

EXAMPLE 4
on p. 75
for Exs. 25–33

9. ★ **MULTIPLE CHOICE** What is the domain of the relation given by the ordered pairs $(-4, 2)$, $(-1, -3)$, $(1, 4)$, $(1, -3)$, and $(2, 1)$? **B**

Ⓐ $-3, 1, 2,$ and 4 Ⓑ $-4, -1, 1,$ and 2

Ⓒ $-4, -3, -1,$ and 2 Ⓓ $-4, -3, -1, 1, 2,$ and 4

IDENTIFYING FUNCTIONS **Tell whether the relation is a function.** ***Explain.***

10. Input: −6, −4, −1, 2; Output: 5, 2, 1, −1 (−6 → 5, −4 → 2, −1 → 1, 2 → −1)

11. 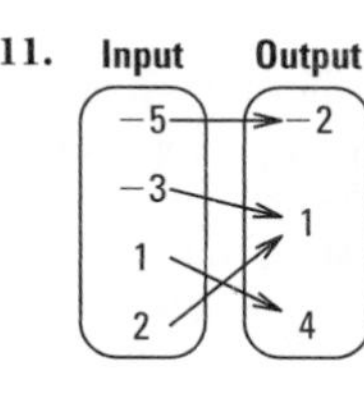

12. 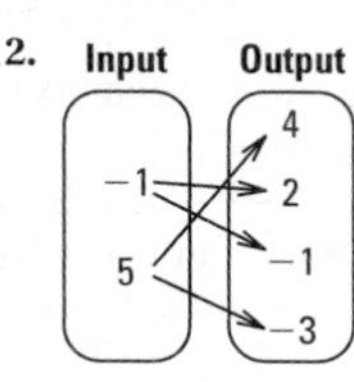

13. 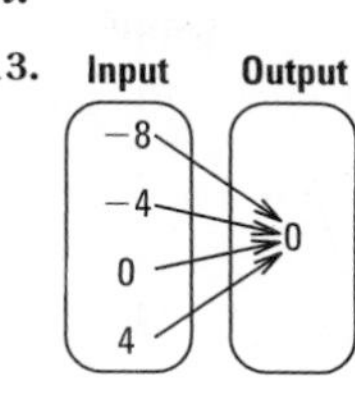

ERROR ANALYSIS ***Describe*** **and correct the error in the student's work.**

14. The relation given by the ordered pairs $(-4, 2)$, $(-1, 5)$, $(3, 6)$, and $(7, 2)$ is not a function because the inputs -4 and 7 are both mapped to the output 2. ✗

15.

x	0	1	2	1	0
y	5	6	7	8	9

The relation given by the table is a function because there is only one value of x for each value of y. ✗

See margin.

IDENTIFYING FUNCTIONS **Tell whether the relation is a function.** ***Explain.***

16. $(3, -2)$, $(0, 1)$, $(1, 0)$, $(-2, -1)$, $(2, -1)$ **Yes; each input has exactly one output.**

17. $(2, -5)$, $(-2, 5)$, $(-1, 4)$, $(-2, 0)$, $(3, -4)$ **No; the input −2 has more than one output.**

18. $(0, 1)$, $(1, 0)$, $(2, 3)$, $(3, 2)$, $(4, 4)$ **Yes; each input has exactly one output.**

19. $(-1, -1)$, $(2, 5)$, $(4, 8)$, $(-5, -9)$, $(-1, -5)$ **No; the input −1 has more than one output.**

20. ★ **MULTIPLE CHOICE** The relation given by the ordered pairs $(-6, 3)$, $(-2, 4)$, $(1, 5)$, and $(4, 0)$ is a function. Which ordered pair can be included with this relation to form a new relation that is also a function? **B**

Ⓐ $(1, -5)$ Ⓑ $(6, 3)$ Ⓒ $(-2, 19)$ Ⓓ $(4, 4)$

VERTICAL LINE TEST **Use the vertical line test to tell whether the relation is a function.**

21. **function**

22. 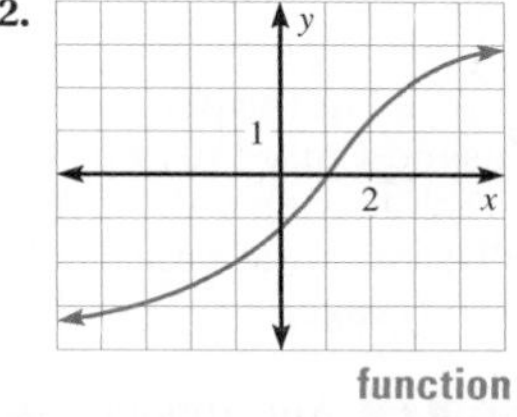

function

23. 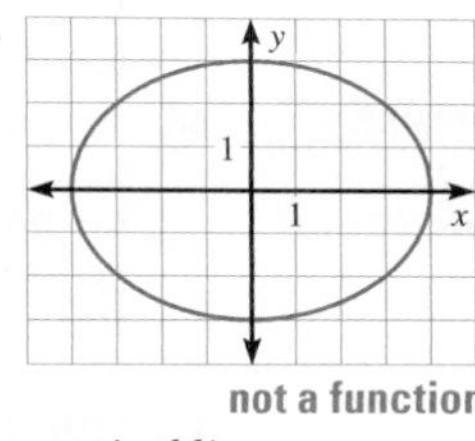

not a function

B 24. ★ **SHORT RESPONSE** *Explain* why a relation is not a function if a vertical line intersects the graph of the relation more than once. See margin.

GRAPHING EQUATIONS **Graph the equation.** 25–33. See margin.

25. $y = x + 2$ 26. $y = -x + 5$ 27. $y = 3x + 1$

28. $y = 5x - 3$ 29. $y = 2x - 7$ 30. $y = -3x + 2$

31. $y = -2x$ 32. $y = \frac{1}{2}x + 2$ 33. $y = -\frac{3}{4}x - 1$

4 PRACTICE AND APPLY

Assignment Guide

Answer Transparencies available for all exercises

Basic:
Day 1: SRH p. 987 Exs. 1–10
pp. 76–79
Exs. 1, 2, 3–13 odd, 14–27, 34, 35, 42–48, 51

Average:
Day 1: pp. 76–79
Exs. 1, 2, 6–9, 12–17, 20–24, 28–30, 34–39, 42–49, 52

Advanced:
Day 1: pp. 76–79
Exs. 1, 2, 7–9, 12, 13, 18–24, 31–50*

Block:
pp. 76–79
Exs. 1, 2, 6–9, 12–17, 20–24, 28–30, 34–39, 42–49, 52 (with 2.2)

Differentiated Instruction

See *Algebra 2 Best Practices Toolkit* for suggestions on addressing the needs of a diverse classroom.

Homework Check

For a quick check of student understanding of key concepts, go over the following exercises:
Basic: 5, 16, 26, 34, 42
Average: 6, 18, 29, 36, 42
Advanced: 8, 19, 32, 38, 43

Extra Practice

- Student Edition, p. 1011
- Chapter 2 Resource Book: Practice levels A, B, C, pp. 5–10

Practice Worksheet

An easily-readable reduced practice page (with answers) for this lesson can be found on p. 70C.

15. *x* is the input and *y* is the output, so there should be one value of *y* for each value of *x*; the relation given by the table is not a function because the inputs 1 and 0 each have more than one output.

24. *Sample answer:* The vertical line represents each input, so if the vertical line crosses the graph more than once, then that input has more than one output and is not a function.

25–33. See Additional Answers beginning on p. AA1.

Teaching Strategy

Exercises 3, 4 Students may assume that they should be able to write an equation that relates the domain and range of a relation. Explain that a mathematical relation does not imply an obvious algebraic relationship between domain and range.

Avoiding Common Errors

Exercises 25–33 Students should graph a minimum of three points to ensure that the points are collinear.

Graphing Calculator

Exercises 44, 45 Students can use their graphing calculators to examine the values of the function in Exercise 44 at $V(4)$ and the function in Exercise 45 at $V(6)$. Have them first graph $y = x^3$, then use the trace function or the calculate function to find the value of y when $x = 4$. They can then graph $y = \frac{4}{3}\pi x^3$ and find the value of y when $x = 6$.

Exercise 48 Additional information about Mount Rainier can be found at www.nps.gov/mora

47a.

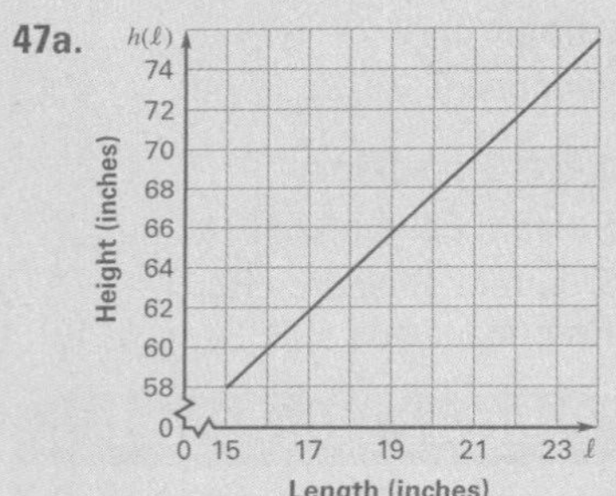

48.

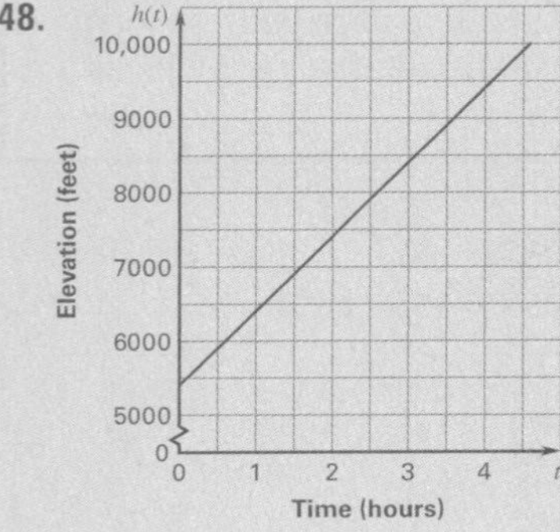

EXAMPLE 5 on p. 75 for Exs. 34–39

EVALUATING FUNCTIONS **Tell whether the function is linear. Then evaluate the function for the given value of x.**

34. $f(x) = x + 15; f(8)$ linear; 23

35. $f(x) = x^2 + 1; f(-3)$ not linear; 10

36. $f(x) = |x| + 10; f(-4)$ not linear; 14

37. $f(x) = 6; f(2)$ linear; 6

38. $g(x) = x^3 - 2x^2 + 5x - 8; g(-5)$ not linear; −208

39. $h(x) = 7 - \frac{2}{3}x; h(15)$ linear; −3

C

40. ★ **SHORT RESPONSE** Which, if any, of the relations described by the equations $y = |x|$, $x = |y|$, and $|y| = |x|$ represent functions? *Explain.*
$y = |x|$. *Sample answer:* This is the only graph that passes the vertical line test.

41. **CHALLENGE** Let f be a function such that $f(a + b) = f(a) + f(b)$ for all real numbers a and b. Show that $f(2a) = 2 \cdot f(a)$ and that $f(0) = 0$.
$f(2a) = f(a + a) = f(a) + f(a) = 2 \cdot f(a)$, $f(0) = f(0 + 0) = f(0) + f(0) = 2f(0)$, $2f(0) = f(0)$, $2f(0) - f(0) = f(0) - f(0)$, $f(0) = 0$

PROBLEM SOLVING

EXAMPLE 3 A on p. 74 for Exs. 42–43

42. No; the inputs 24, 25, and 26 have more than one output.

43. Yes; each input has exactly one output.

46. domain: $0 \le t \le 5$, range: $140.7 \le w(t) \le 172$; over the years 1999–2004 the watermelon acerage ranged from a low of 140,700 in 2004 to a high of 172,000 in 1999.

42. **BICYCLING** The graph shows the ages of the top three finishers in the Mt. Washington Auto Road Bicycle Hillclimb each year from 2002 through 2004. Do the ordered pairs (age, finishing place) represent a function? *Explain.*

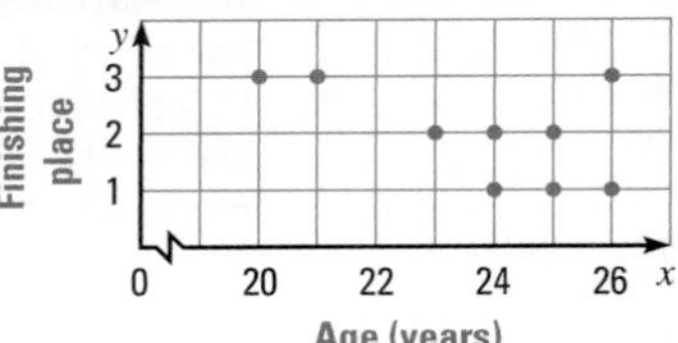

@HomeTutor for problem solving help at classzone.com

43. **BASEBALL** The graph shows the number of games started and the number of wins for each starting pitcher on a baseball team during a regular season. Do the ordered pairs (starts, wins) represent a function? *Explain.*

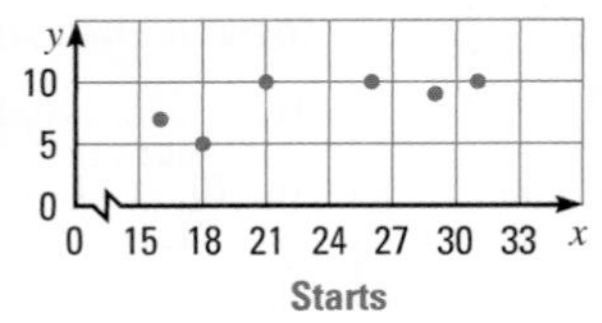

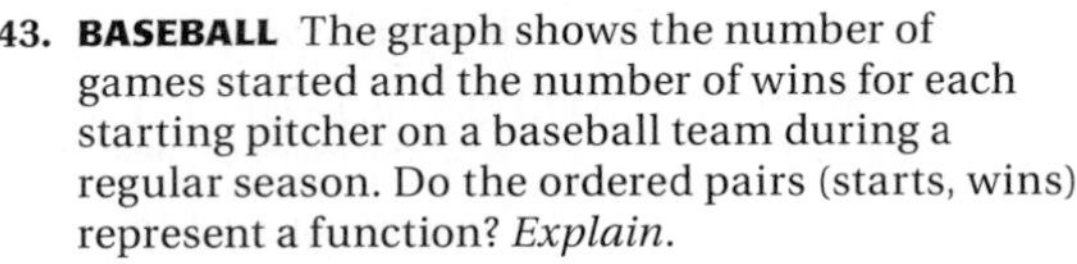

@HomeTutor for problem solving help at classzone.com

44. **GEOMETRY** The volume V of a cube with edge length s is given by the function $V(s) = s^3$. Find $V(4)$. *Explain* what $V(4)$ represents.
64; $V(4)$ represents the volume of a cube with edge length of 4.

(45.) **GEOMETRY** The volume V of a sphere with radius r is given by the function $V(r) = \frac{4}{3}\pi r^3$. Find $V(6)$. *Explain* what $V(6)$ represents.
about 905; $V(6)$ represents the volume of a sphere with radius 6.

EXAMPLE 6 on p. 76 for Exs. 46–48

46. ★ **SHORT RESPONSE** For the period 1999–2004, the average number of acres w (in thousands), used to grow watermelons in the United States can be modeled by the function $w(t) = -6.26t + 172$ where t is the number of years since 1999. Determine a reasonable domain and range for $w(t)$. *Explain* the meaning of the range.

B

47a. domain: $15 \le \ell \le 24$, range: $57.95 \le h(\ell) \le 75.5$.

47. **MULTI-STEP PROBLEM** Anthropologists can estimate a person's height from the length of certain bones. The height h (in inches) of an adult human female can be modeled by the function $h(\ell) = 1.95\ell + 28.7$ where ℓ is the length (in inches) of the femur, or thigh bone. The function is valid for femur lengths between 15 inches and 24 inches, inclusive.

a. Graph the function, and determine a reasonable domain and range. See margin for art.

b. Suppose a female's femur is 15.5 inches long. About how tall was she? 59 in. or 4 ft 11 in.

c. If an anthropologist estimates a female's height as 5 feet 11 inches, about how long is her femur? 21.7 in.

○ = WORKED-OUT SOLUTIONS on p. WS1   ★ = STANDARDIZED TEST PRACTICE

a. domain: ,350,000, ,280,000, ,420,000, ,980,000, ,980,000, ,850,000, ,870,000, nge: 20, 21, , 31, 34, 55

b. Yes; each put p has actly one tput.

c. No; the put 21 has ore than one tput.

a. Yes. *Sample swer:* The ipping cost epends on the erchandise st.

C

b. No. *Sample swer:* The erchandise st does not epend on the ipping cost.

48. **MOUNTAIN CLIMBING** A climber on Mount Rainier in Washington hikes from an elevation of 5400 feet above sea level to Camp Muir, which has an elevation of 10,100 feet. The elevation h (in feet) as the climber ascends can be modeled by $h(t) = 1000t + 5400$ where t is the time (in hours). Graph the function, and determine a reasonable domain and range. What is the climber's elevation after hiking 3.5 hours? **See margin for art; domain: $0 \le t \le 4.7$, range: $5400 \le h(t) \le 10{,}100$; 8900 ft**

49. ★ **EXTENDED RESPONSE** The table shows the populations of several states and their electoral votes in the 2004 and 2008 U.S. presidential elections. The figures are based on U.S. census data for the year 2000.

   a. Identify the domain and range of the relation given by the ordered pairs (p, v).

   b. Is the relation from part (a) a function? *Explain.*

   c. Is the relation given by the ordered pairs (v, p) a function? *Explain.*

State	Population (millions), p	Electoral votes, v
California	33.87	55
Florida	15.98	27
Illinois	12.42	21
New York	18.98	31
Ohio	11.35	20
Pennsylvania	12.28	21
Texas	20.85	34

50. **CHALLENGE** The table shows ground shipping charges for an online retail store.

   a. Is the shipping cost a function of the merchandise cost? *Explain.*

   b. Is the merchandise cost a function of the shipping cost? *Explain.*

Merchandise cost	Shipping cost
\$.01–\$30.00	\$4.50
\$30.01–\$60.00	\$7.25
\$60.01–\$100.00	\$9.50
Over \$100.00	\$12.50

KY KENTUCKY MIXED REVIEW

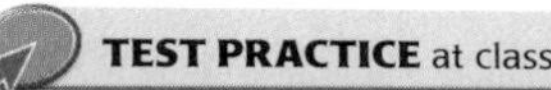

TEST PRACTICE at classzone.com

51. Kate is studying a bacteria culture in biology class. The table shows the number of bacteria, b, in the culture after t hours. How many bacteria are there after 10 hours? **D**

Time (hours), t	0	1	2	3	4	5
Bacteria (billions), b	1	2	4	8	16	32

   (A) 64 billion (B) 128 billion (C) 256 billion (D) 1024 billion

52. What is the area of the composite figure? **C**

   (A) 138 cm^2 (B) 141 cm^2

   (C) 162 cm^2 (D) 210 cm^2

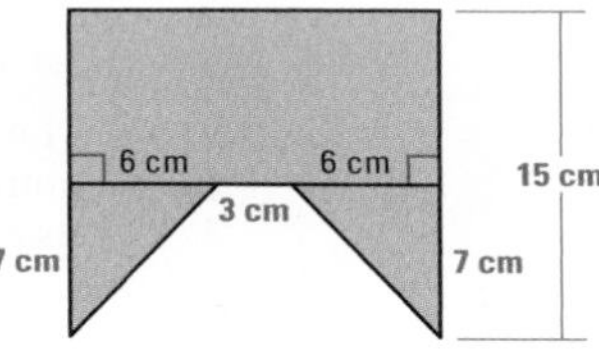

5 ASSESS AND RETEACH

Daily Homework Quiz

Transparency Available

1. Identify the domain and range of the given relation. Then tell whether the relation is a function.

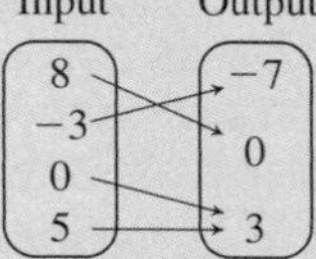

domain: −3, 0, 5, 8, range: −7, 0, 3; function

2. Graph $y = -2x + 2$.

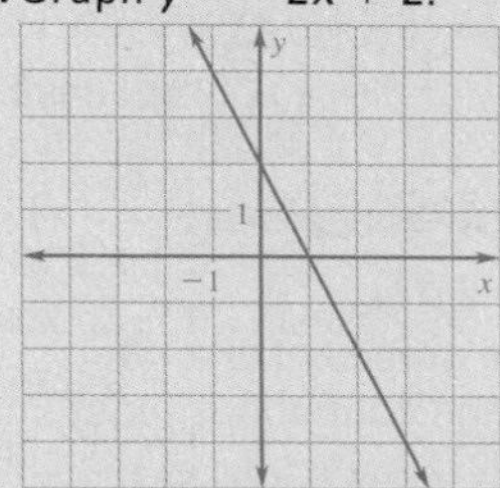

3. Tell whether the function $f(x) = -x^2 + 3$ is linear. Then evaluate the function for $x = -2$. **no; −1**

4. The average daily income of a physical therapist can be modeled by the function $f(c) = 25c - 18$, where c is the number of daily customers. Assume that no more than 10 customers can be seen in 1 day. Determine a reasonable domain and range for $f(c)$ in this situation. **domain: $1 \le c \le 10$; range: $7 \le f(c) \le 232$**

Online Quiz

Available at **classzone.com**

Diagnosis/Remediation

- Practice A, B, C in Chapter 2 Resource Book, pp. 5–10
- Study Guide in Chapter 2 Resource Book, pp. 11–12
- Practice Workbook, pp. 15–17
- @HomeTutor

Challenge

Additional challenge is available in the Chapter 2 Resource Book, p. 15.

① PLAN AND PREPARE

Warm-Up Exercises

Transparency Available

1. Identify the domain and range of $(-7, 2), (-7, 3), (-6, 2), (-6, 3)$. **domain: $-7, -6$; range: $2, 3$**
2. Evaluate $f(x) = 5x$ for $x = 10$. **50**
3. Graph $y = 2x - 1$.

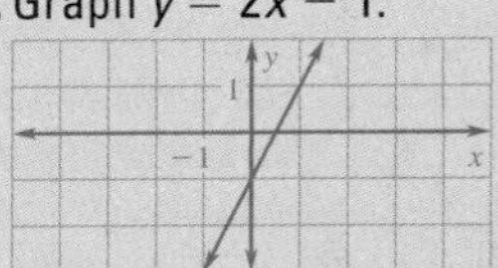

② FOCUS AND MOTIVATE

Essential Question

Big Idea 1, p. 71

How do the graphs of discrete functions and continuous functions differ? **Tell students they will learn how to answer this question by comparing graphs of distinct points with graphs of lines.**

③ TEACH

Extra Example 1

Graph $y = -x + 3$ for $x \geq -1$. Classify the function as *discrete* or *continuous*. Identify the range.

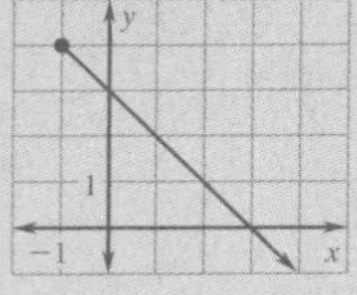

continuous; $y \leq 4$

NCTM STANDARDS

Standard 2: Understand functions; Represent situations using algebraic symbols

---

Extension

Use after Lesson 2.1

Use Discrete and Continuous Functions

GOAL Graph and classify discrete and continuous functions.

Key Vocabulary
- **discrete function**
- **continuous function**

The graph of a function may consist of *discrete*, or separate and unconnected, points in a plane. The graph of a function may also be a *continuous*, or unbroken, line or curve or part of a line or curve.

KEY CONCEPT *For Your Notebook*

Discrete and Continuous Functions

The graph of a **discrete function** consists of separate points.

The graph of a **continuous function** is unbroken.

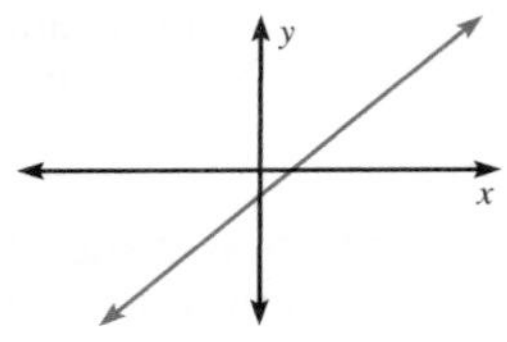

EXAMPLE 1 Graph and classify functions

Graph the function $f(x) = 0.5x + 1$ for the given domain. Classify the function as *discrete* or *continuous* for the domain. Then identify the range.

a. Domain: $x = -2, 0, 2, 4$

b. Domain: $x \geq -3$

Solution

a. Make a table using the x-values in the domain.

x	-2	0	2	4
y	0	1	2	3

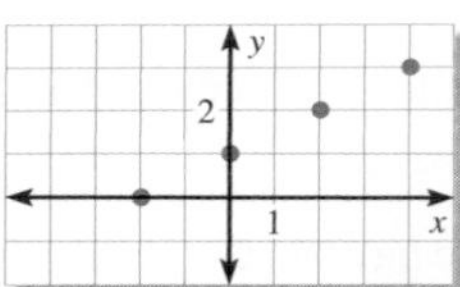

The graph consists of separate points, so the function is discrete. Its range is 0, 1, 2, 3.

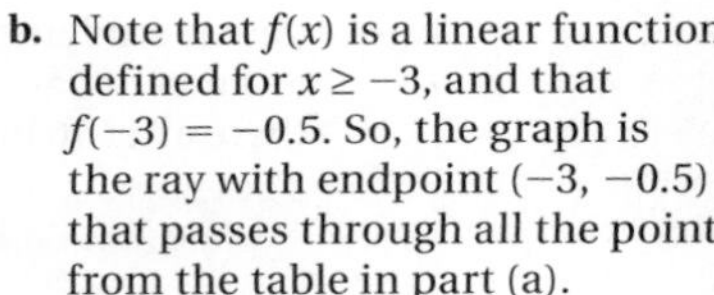

b. Note that $f(x)$ is a linear function defined for $x \geq -3$, and that $f(-3) = -0.5$. So, the graph is the ray with endpoint $(-3, -0.5)$ that passes through all the points from the table in part (a).

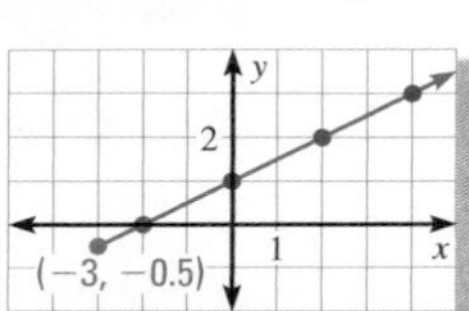

The graph is unbroken, so the function is continuous. Its range is $y \geq -0.5$.

1.

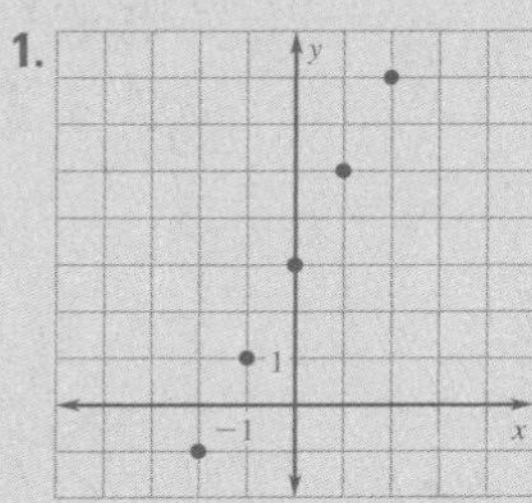

EXAMPLE 2 Graph and classify real-world functions

Write and graph the function described. Determine the domain and range. Then tell whether the function is *discrete* or *continuous*.

a. A student group is selling chocolate bars for \$2 each. The function $f(x)$ gives the amount of money collected after selling x chocolate bars.

b. A low-flow shower head releases 1.8 gallons of water per minute. The function $V(x)$ gives the volume of water released after x minutes.

Solution

a. The function is $f(x) = 2x$. The first four points of the graph of $f(x)$ are shown. Only whole chocolate bars can be sold, so the domain is the set of whole numbers 0, 1, 2, 3, ... From the graph, you can see that the range is 0, 2, 4, 6, ... The graph consists of separate points, so the function is discrete.

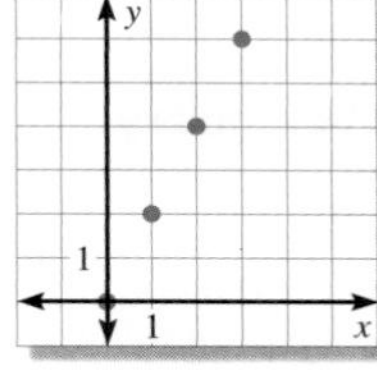

b. The function is $V(x) = 1.8x$. You can run the shower any nonnegative amount of time, so the domain is $x \geq 0$. From the graph, you can see that the range is $y \geq 0$. The graph is unbroken, so the function is continuous.

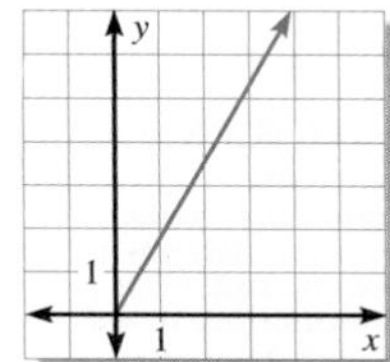

PRACTICE

EXAMPLE 1 on p. 80 for Exs. 1–4

Graph the function for the given domain. Classify the function as *discrete* or *continuous*. Then identify the range of the function. 1–4. See margin for art.

1. $y = 2x + 3$; domain: −2, −1, 0, 1, 2
   discrete; −1, 1, 3, 5, 7
2. $f(x) = 0.5x - 4$; domain: −4, −2, 0, 2, 4
   discrete; −6, −5, −4, −3, −2
3. $y = -3x + 9$; domain: $x < 5$
   continuous; $y > -6$
4. $f(x) = \frac{1}{3}x + 6$; domain: $x \geq -6$
   continuous; $y \geq 4$

EXAMPLE 2 on p. 81 for Exs. 5–8

Write and graph the function described. Determine the domain and range. Then tell whether the function is *discrete* or *continuous*. 5–9. See margin for art.

5. Amanda walks at an average speed of 3.5 miles per hour. The function $d(x)$ gives the distance (in miles) Amanda walks in x hours.
   $d(x) = 3.5x$; domain: $x \geq 0$, range: $d(x) \geq 0$; continuous
6. A token to ride a subway costs \$1.25. The function $s(x)$ gives the cost of riding the subway x times. $s(x) = 1.25x$; domain: whole numbers, range: multiples of 1.25; discrete
7. A family has 3 gallons of milk delivered every Thursday. The function $m(x)$ gives the total amount of milk that is delivered to the family after x weeks.
   $m(x) = 3x$; domain: whole numbers, range: multiples of 3; discrete
8. Steel cable that is $\frac{3}{8}$ inch in diameter weighs 0.24 pound per foot. The function $w(x)$ gives the weight of x feet of steel cable.
   $w(x) = 0.24x$; domain: $x \geq 0$, range: $f(x) \geq 0$; continuous
9. On a number line, the *signed distance* from a number a to a number b is given by $b - a$. The function $d(x)$ gives the signed distance from 3 to any number x.
   $d(x) = x - 3$; domain: all real numbers, range: all real numbers; continuous

2.

3.

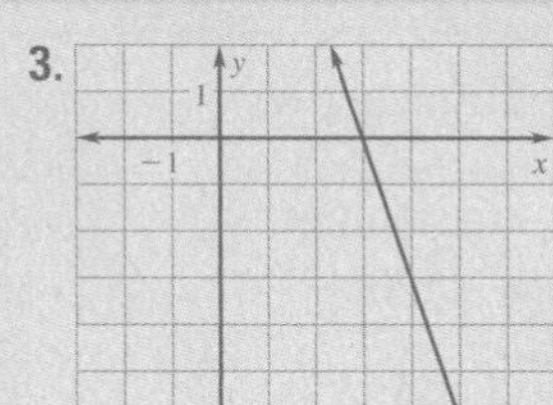

4.

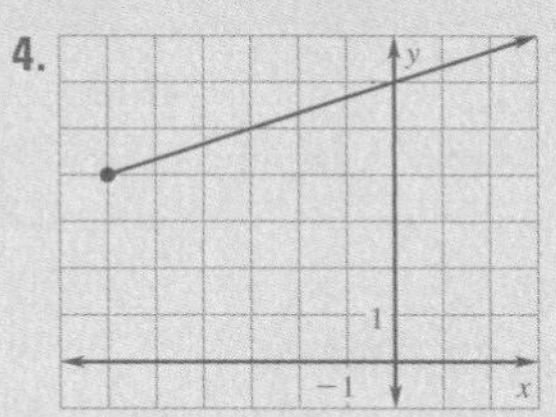

Extra Example 2

Mrs. Malone buys paint for \$20 per gallon. The function $f(x)$ gives the cost of buying x gallons of paint. Write and graph the function described. Determine the domain and range. Then tell whether the function is discrete or continuous.
$f(x) = 20x$

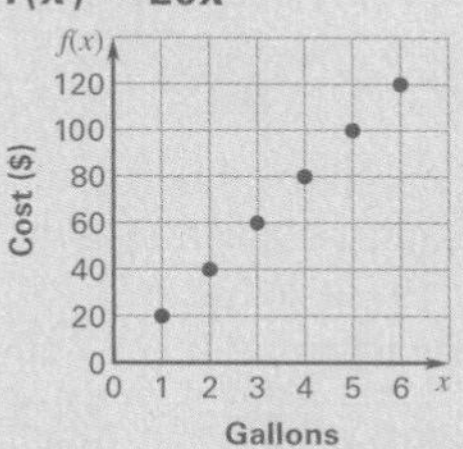

Domain: 0, 1, 2, 3, ...; range: 0, 20, 40, 60, ...; the graph consists of isolated points, so the function is discrete.

Closing the Lesson

Have students summarize the major points of the lesson and answer the Essential Question: How do the graphs of discrete functions and continuous functions differ?

- The graph of a function may be discrete and consist of unconnected points in a plane or it may be continuous and be an unbroken line or curve.

The graph of a discrete function consists of separate points and the graph of a continuous function is unbroken.

4 PRACTICE AND APPLY

Vocabulary

Students may be confused by the word *discrete*, thinking it means "careful or tactful." Tell them that *discreet* and *discrete* are homonyms or homophones; *discreet* means "careful or tactful," and *discrete* means "separate, distinct, or disconnected."

5–9. See Additional Answers beginning on p. AA1.

1 PLAN AND PREPARE

Warm-Up Exercises

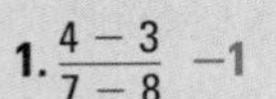 **Transparency Available**

Evaluate each expression.

1. $\frac{4-3}{7-8}$ −1
2. $\frac{8-8}{3-5}$ 0
3. $\frac{2-7}{5-5}$ undefined
4. An Internet company had a profit of $2.6 million in retail sales over the last five years. What was its average annual profit? $520,000

Notetaking Guide

Transparency Available

Promotes interactive learning and notetaking skills, pp. 30–32.

Pacing

Basic: 2 days
Average: 2 days
Advanced: 2 days
Block: 0.5 block with 2.1
0.5 block with 2.3

- See *Teaching Guide/Lesson Plan.*

2 FOCUS AND MOTIVATE

Essential Question

Big Idea 2, p. 71

How do you determine whether two nonvertical lines are parallel or perpendicular? Tell students they will learn how to answer this question by examining the slopes of the lines.

2.2 Find Slope and Rate of Change

KY MA-HS-5.1.5

Before You graphed linear functions.
Now You will find slopes of lines and rates of change.
Why? So you can model growth rates, as in Ex. 46.

Key Vocabulary
- slope
- parallel
- perpendicular
- rate of change
- reciprocal, *p. 4*

MA-HS-5.1.5
Students will: determine if a relation is a function; determine the domain and range of a function (linear and quadratic); determine the slope and intercepts of a linear function; determine the maximum, minimum, and intercepts (roots/zeros) of a quadratic function and evaluate a function written in function notation for a specified rational number. DOK 2

KEY CONCEPT — *For Your Notebook*

Slope of a Line

Words

The **slope** m of a nonvertical line is the ratio of vertical change (the *rise*) to horizontal change (the *run*).

Algebra

$$m = \frac{y_2 - y_1}{x_2 - x_1} = \frac{\text{rise}}{\text{run}}$$

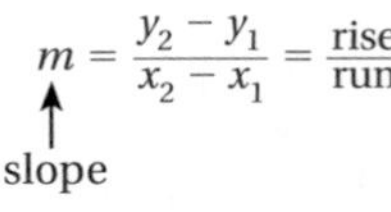

Graph

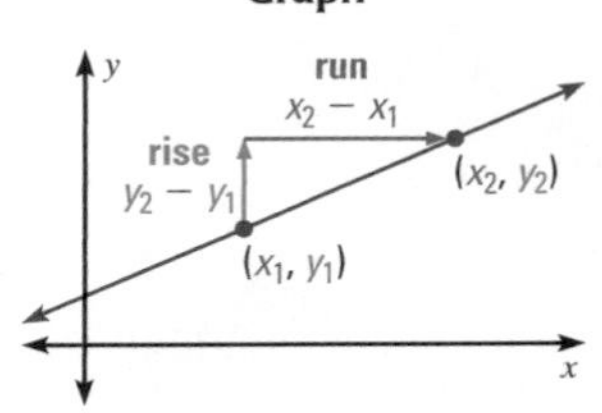

EXAMPLE 1 Find slope in real life

SKATEBOARDING A skateboard ramp has a rise of 15 inches and a run of 54 inches. What is its slope?

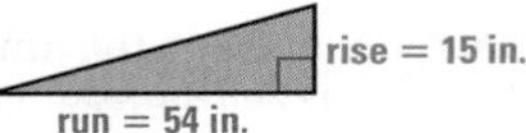

Solution

$$\text{slope} = \frac{\text{rise}}{\text{run}} = \frac{15}{54} = \frac{5}{18}$$

▶ The slope of the ramp is $\frac{5}{18}$.

★ EXAMPLE 2 Standardized Test Practice

What is the slope of the line passing through the points (−1, 3) and (2, −1)?

(A) $-\frac{4}{3}$ (B) $-\frac{3}{4}$ (C) $\frac{3}{4}$ (D) $\frac{4}{3}$

Solution

Let $(x_1, y_1) = (-1, 3)$ and $(x_2, y_2) = (2, -1)$.

$$m = \frac{y_2 - y_1}{x_2 - x_1} = \frac{-1-3}{2-(-1)} = -\frac{4}{3}$$

▶ The correct answer is A. (A) (B) (C) (D)

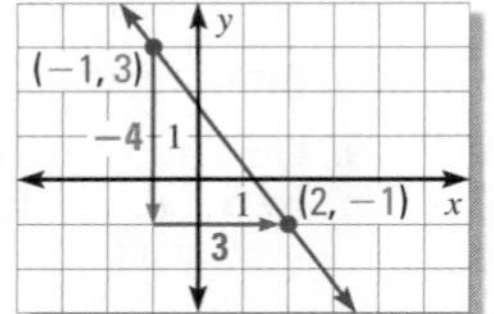

AVOID ERRORS
When calculating slope, be sure to subtract the x- and y-coordinates in a consistent order.

Resource Planning Guide

Chapter Resource Book
- Teaching Guide/Lesson Plan (pp. 16–17)
- Activity Master (p. 18)
- Practice levels A, B, C (pp. 19–21)
- Study Guide (pp. 22–23)
- Catch-up for Absent Students (p. 24)
- Problem Solving Workshop (p. 25)
- Challenge (p. 26)

Workbooks
- Notetaking Guide (pp. 30–32)
- Practice Workbook (pp. 18–19)

Teaching Options
- **Power Presentations CD-ROM** provides dynamic electronic teaching resources for the classroom.
- **Activity Generator CD-ROM** provides editable activities for all ability levels.

Interactive Technology
- Easy Planner
- Power Presentations CD-ROM
- Activity Generator CD-ROM
- Animated Algebra
- Test Generator CD-ROM
- Online Quiz
- eWorkbook
- eEdition
- @HomeTutor

Resources for English Learners
- Quick Reference for English Learners
- Spanish Study Guide
- Multi-Language Visual Glossary
- Student Resources in Spanish

See also the *Algebra 2 Toolkit* for more strategies for meeting individual needs.

✓ GUIDED PRACTICE for Examples 1 and 2

1. **WHAT IF?** In Example 1, suppose that the rise of the ramp is changed to 12 inches without changing the run. What is the slope of the ramp? $\frac{2}{9}$
2. What is the slope of the line passing through the points $(-4, 9)$ and $(-8, 3)$? D

   Ⓐ $-\frac{2}{3}$ Ⓑ $-\frac{1}{2}$ Ⓒ $\frac{2}{3}$ Ⓓ $\frac{3}{2}$

Find the slope of the line passing through the given points.

3. $(0, 3), (4, 8)$ $\frac{5}{4}$
4. $(-5, 1), (5, -4)$ $-\frac{1}{2}$
5. $(-3, -2), (6, 1)$ $\frac{1}{3}$
6. $(7, 3), (-1, 7)$ $-\frac{1}{2}$

KEY CONCEPT *For Your Notebook*

Classification of Lines by Slope

The slope of a line indicates whether the line rises from left to right, falls from left to right, is horizontal, or is vertical.

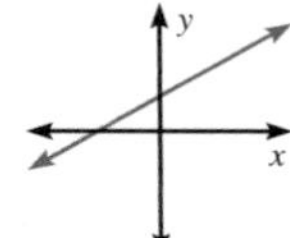

Positive slope
Rises from left to right

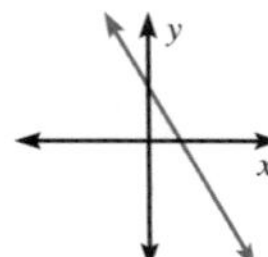

Negative slope
Falls from left to right

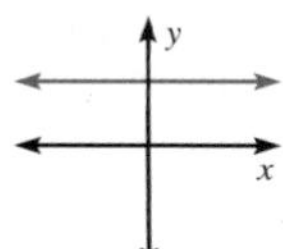

Zero slope
Horizontal

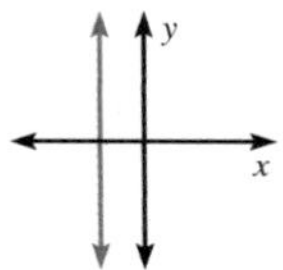

Undefined slope
Vertical

READING
A vertical line has "undefined slope" because for any two points, the slope formula's denominator becomes 0, and division by 0 is undefined.

EXAMPLE 3 Classify lines using slope

Without graphing, tell whether the line through the given points *rises*, *falls*, *is horizontal*, or *is vertical*.

a. $(-5, 1), (3, 1)$ b. $(-6, 0), (2, -4)$ c. $(-1, 3), (5, 8)$ d. $(4, 6), (4, -1)$

Solution

a. $m = \frac{1-1}{3-(-5)} = \frac{0}{8} = 0$ **Because $m = 0$, the line is horizontal.**

b. $m = \frac{-4-0}{2-(-6)} = \frac{-4}{8} = -\frac{1}{2}$ **Because $m < 0$, the line falls.**

c. $m = \frac{8-3}{5-(-1)} = \frac{5}{6}$ **Because $m > 0$, the line rises.**

d. $m = \frac{-1-6}{4-4} = \frac{-7}{0}$ **Because m is undefined, the line is vertical.**

✓ GUIDED PRACTICE for Example 3

Without graphing, tell whether the line through the given points *rises*, *falls*, *is horizontal*, or *is vertical*.

7. $(-4, 3), (2, -6)$ falls
8. $(7, 1), (7, -1)$ is vertical
9. $(3, -2), (5, -2)$ is horizontal
10. $(5, 6), (1, -4)$ rises

Motivating the Lesson

By knowing slope, you can tell how steep an incline is. For example, by knowing the slopes of the water slides at an amusement park, you can tell which is steeper.

3 TEACH

Extra Example 1

The roof of an entryway to an office building has a rise of 40 feet and a run of 100 feet. What is its slope? $\frac{2}{5}$

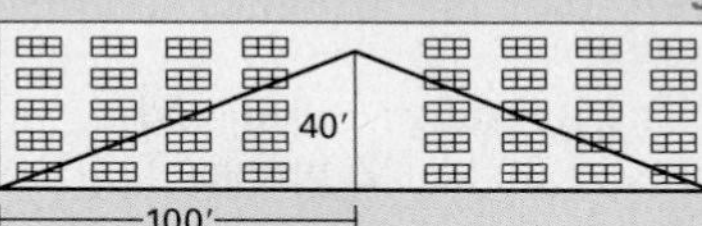

Extra Example 2

What is the slope of the line passing through the points $(-4, -5)$ $(6, -2)$? A

Ⓐ $\frac{3}{10}$ Ⓑ $\frac{7}{10}$

Ⓒ $\frac{10}{7}$ Ⓓ $\frac{10}{3}$

Key Question to Ask for Example 2

- If $(x_1, y_1) = (2, -1)$ and $(x_2, y_2) = (-1, 3)$, would the slope be different? No, you would have $\frac{3-(-1)}{-1-2} = -\frac{4}{3}$.

Extra Example 3

Without graphing, tell whether the line through the given points *rises*, *falls*, *is horizontal*, or *is vertical*.

a. $(1, 6), (8, -1)$ falls
b. $(-4, -3), (7, 1)$ rises
c. $(-5, 3), (-5, 1)$ vertical
d. $(9, 2), (-9, 2)$ horizontal

PARALLEL AND PERPENDICULAR LINES Recall that two lines in a plane are **parallel** if they do not intersect. Two lines in a plane are **perpendicular** if they intersect to form a right angle.

Slope can be used to determine whether two different nonvertical lines are parallel or perpendicular.

KEY CONCEPT *For Your Notebook*

Slopes of Parallel and Perpendicular Lines

Consider two different nonvertical lines ℓ_1 and ℓ_2 with slopes m_1 and m_2.

Parallel Lines The lines are parallel if and only if they have the same slope.

$$m_1 = m_2$$

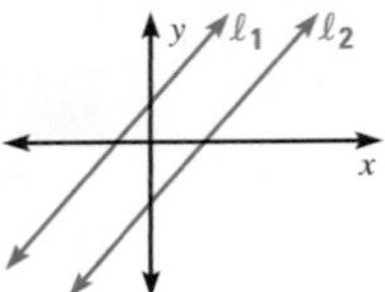

Perpendicular Lines The lines are perpendicular if and only if their slopes are negative reciprocals of each other.

$$m_1 = -\frac{1}{m_2}, \text{ or } m_1 m_2 = -1$$

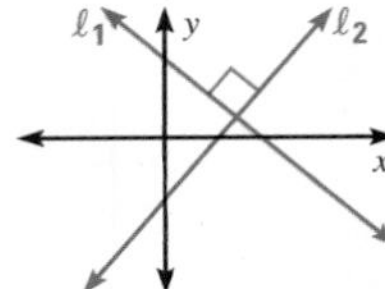

EXAMPLE 4 Classify parallel and perpendicular lines

Tell whether the lines are *parallel, perpendicular,* or *neither.*

a. Line 1: through (−2, 2) and (0, −1)
Line 2: through (−4, −1) and (2, 3)

b. Line 1: through (1, 2) and (4, −3)
Line 2: through (−4, 3) and (−1, −2)

Solution

a. Find the slopes of the two lines.

$$m_1 = \frac{-1 - 2}{0 - (-2)} = \frac{-3}{2} = -\frac{3}{2}$$

$$m_2 = \frac{3 - (-1)}{2 - (-4)} = \frac{4}{6} = \frac{2}{3}$$

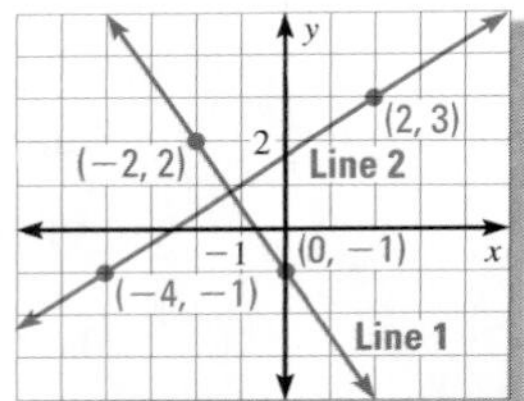

▸ Because $m_1 m_2 = -\frac{3}{2} \cdot \frac{2}{3} = -1$, m_1 and m_2 are negative reciprocals of each other. So, the lines are perpendicular.

b. Find the slopes of the two lines.

$$m_1 = \frac{-3 - 2}{4 - 1} = \frac{-5}{3} = -\frac{5}{3}$$

$$m_2 = \frac{-2 - 3}{-1 - (-4)} = \frac{-5}{3} = -\frac{5}{3}$$

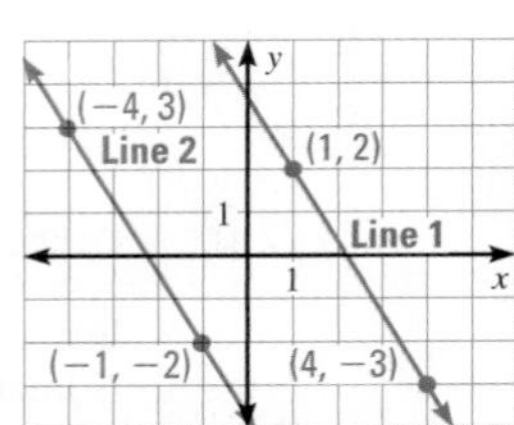

▸ Because $m_1 = m_2$ (and the lines are different), you can conclude that the lines are parallel.

Avoiding Common Errors

Students have trouble remembering which kind of line has zero slope and which has an undefined slope. You can suggest that since *U* and *V* are consecutive letters in the alphabet, they may use this fact to remember that an *U*ndefined slope is associated with a *V*ertical line.

Extra Example 4

Tell whether the lines are *parallel, perpendicular,* or *neither.*

a. Line 1: through (−2, 1) and (0, −5); Line 2: through (0, 1) and (−3, 10) **parallel**

b. Line 1: through (−5, 3) and (−2, −3); Line 2: through (4, 11) and (−4, −5) **neither**

Key Questions to Ask for Example 4

- If two lines are parallel, what do you know about their *y*-intercepts? **They are different.**
- If one of two perpendicular lines has a slope of $\frac{1}{a}$ and $a < 0$, is the slope of the other line positive or negative? **positive**

Reading Strategy

Point out how the slopes of the lines in Example 4a are *negative* reciprocals of each other, which means that they have a product of −1. Note that only one of two perpendicular lines has a negative slope.

Mathematical Reasoning

Multiple Representations Algebraic and graphical representations of slopes of parallel and perpendicular lines are given in Example 4. Students can also count the rise and run units between the given points on the graphs of the lines to determine their slopes.

Differentiated Instruction

Advanced Ask students to consider the meaning of parallel and perpendicular in relation to horizontal and vertical lines. Students should give conditions as to when their lines are parallel or perpendicular.

See also the *Algebra 2 Toolkit* for more strategies.

 **GUIDED PRACTICE** for Example 4

Tell whether the lines are *parallel, perpendicular,* or *neither.*

11. Line 1: through (−2, 8) and (2, −4)
    Line 2: through (−5, 1) and (−2, 2)
    perpendicular

12. Line 1: through (−4, −2) and (1, 7)
    Line 2: through (−1, −4) and (3, 5)
    neither

REVIEW RATES
Remember that a *rate* is a ratio of two quantities that have *different* units.

RATE OF CHANGE Slope can be used to represent an average **rate of change**, or how much one quantity changes, on average, relative to the change in another quantity. A slope that is a real-life rate of change involves units of measure such as miles per hour or degrees per day.

EXAMPLE 5 Solve a multi-step problem

FORESTRY Use the diagram, which illustrates the growth of a giant sequoia, to find the average rate of change in the diameter of the sequoia over time. Then predict the sequoia's diameter in 2065.

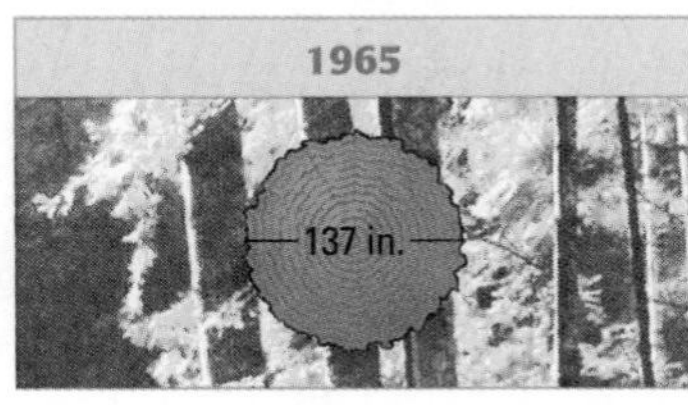

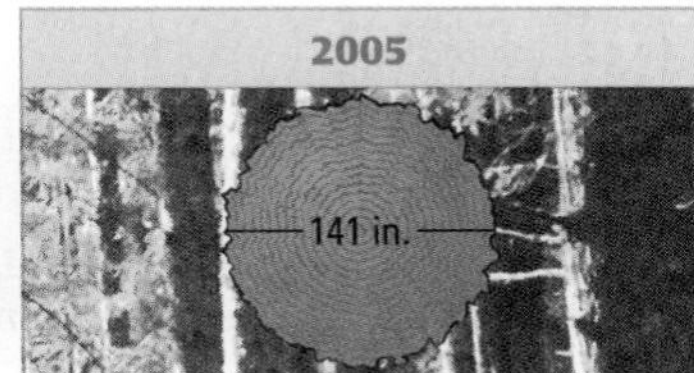

Solution

STEP 1 **Find** the average rate of change.

$$\text{Average rate of change} = \frac{\text{Change in diameter}}{\text{Change in time}}$$

$$= \frac{141 \text{ in.} - 137 \text{ in.}}{2005 - 1965}$$

$$= \frac{4 \text{ in.}}{40 \text{ years}}$$

$$= 0.1 \text{ inch per year}$$

STEP 2 **Predict** the diameter of the sequoia in 2065.

Find the number of years from 2005 to 2065. Multiply this number by the average rate of change to find the total increase in diameter during the period 2005–2065.

Number of years = 2065 − 2005 = 60

Increase in diameter = (60 years)(0.1 inch/year) = 6 inches

▶ In 2065, the diameter of the sequoia will be about 141 + 6 = 147 inches.

 **GUIDED PRACTICE** for Example 5

13. **WHAT IF?** In Example 5, suppose that the diameter of the sequoia is 248 inches in 1965 and 251 inches in 2005. Find the average rate of change in the diameter, and use it to predict the diameter in 2105. **0.075 in. per yr, 258.5 in.**

Differentiated Instruction

Visual Learners When discussing **Example 5**, students may benefit by first plotting the growth of the giant sequoia on a coordinate plane. Have the horizontal axis represent time and the vertical axis represent the diameter, so students can see that the average rate of change will be positive.

See also the *Algebra 2 Toolkit* for more strategies.

Extra Example 5

Use the diagram, which illustrates the decrease in forestland in New Hampshire over time. Then predict the percent of forestland in New Hampshire in 2005. **about 79.8%**

Percent of Forestland in New Hampshire

1983
87% forested

2001
81.1% forested

Key Question to Ask for Example 5

- How do you know that the rate of change must be positive? **The diameter is increasing over time, so the rate of change must be greater than 0.**

Closing the Lesson

Have students summarize the major points of the lesson and answer the Essential Question: How do you determine whether two nonvertical lines are parallel or perpendicular?

- **The slope of a nonvertical line is the ratio of rise to run.**
- **The formula $m = \frac{y_2 - y_1}{x_2 - x_1}$ gives the slope m of a line through the points (x_1, y_1) and (x_2, y_2).**
- **A line with a positive slope rises from left to right. A line with a negative slope falls from left to right. A horizontal line has zero slope. A vertical line has an undefined slope.**
- **The slopes of parallel lines are equal and the slopes of perpendicular lines are negative reciprocals of each other.**

Calculate the slopes of the lines. If the slopes are equal and the lines are different, then the lines are parallel. If the product of the slopes is −1, then the lines are perpendicular.

4 PRACTICE AND APPLY

Assignment Guide

Answer Transparencies available for all exercises

Basic:
Day 1: SRH p. 975 Exs. 16, 19, 20, 22, 27, 32, 33
pp. 86–88
Exs. 1–17, 41–44, 50–51
Day 2: pp. 86–88
Exs. 18–31, 45–47

Average:
Day 1: pp. 86–88
Exs. 1, 2, 6–17, 29–31, 41–44, 50–51
Day 2: pp. 86–88
Exs. 18–28, 32–36, 45–48

Advanced:
Day 1: pp. 86–88
Exs. 1, 2, 6–14, 17, 29–34, 41–44, 51
Day 2: pp. 86–88
Exs. 18–28, 35–40*, 45–49*

Block:
pp. 86–88
Exs. 1, 2, 6–17, 29–31, 41–44, 50–51 (with 2.1)
pp. 86–88
Exs. 18–28, 32–36, 45–48 (with 2.3)

Differentiated Instruction

See *Algebra 2 Best Practices Toolkit* for suggestions on addressing the needs of a diverse classroom.

Homework Check

For a quick check of student understanding of key concepts, go over the following exercises:
Basic: 6, 18, 25, 42, 45
Average: 10, 20, 26, 43, 46
Advanced: 12, 22, 27, 44, 46

Extra Practice

- Student Edition, p. 1011
- Chapter 2 Resource Book: Practice levels A, B, C, pp. 19–21

Practice Worksheet

An easily-readable reduced practice page (with answers) for this lesson can be found on p. 70C.

2.2 EXERCISES

HOMEWORK KEY
○ = **WORKED-OUT SOLUTIONS** on p. WS2 for Exs. 9, 19, and 45
★ = **STANDARDIZED TEST PRACTICE** Exs. 2, 17, 35, 36, 44, 45, and 48

SKILL PRACTICE

A

1. **VOCABULARY** Copy and complete: The __?__ of a nonvertical line is the ratio of vertical change to horizontal change. **slope**

2. ★ **WRITING** How can you use slope to decide whether two nonvertical lines are parallel? whether two nonvertical lines are perpendicular? **See margin.**

EXAMPLES 2 and 3 on pp. 82–83 for Exs. 3–17

2. If two nonvertical lines are parallel, their slopes are equal; if two nonvertical lines are perpendicular, their slopes are negative reciprocals of each other.

FINDING SLOPE **Find the slope of the line passing through the given points. Then tell whether the line *rises, falls, is horizontal,* or *is vertical.***

3. (2, −4), (4, −1) $\frac{3}{2}$; **rises**
4. (8, 9), (−4, 3) $\frac{1}{2}$; **rises**
5. (5, 1), (8, −4) $-\frac{5}{3}$; **falls**
6. (−3, −2), (3, −2) **0; is horizontal**
7. (−1, 4), (1, −4) **−4; falls**
8. (−6, 5), (−6, −5) **undefined; is vertical**
9. (−5, −4), (−1, 3) $\frac{7}{4}$; **rises**
10. (−3, 6), (−7, 3) $\frac{3}{4}$; **rises**
11. (4, 4), (4, 9) **undefined; is vertical**
12. (5, 5), (7, 3) **−1; falls**
13. (0, −3), (4, −3) **0; is horizontal**
14. (1, −1), (−1, −4) $\frac{3}{2}$; **rises**

Animated Algebra at classzone.com

ERROR ANALYSIS ***Describe*** **and correct the error in finding the slope of the line passing through the given points.** **15–16. See margin.**

15. (−4, −3), (2, −1)
$$m = \frac{-1-(-3)}{-4-2} = -\frac{1}{3}$$ ✗

16. (−1, 4), (5, 1)
$$m = \frac{5-(-1)}{1-4} = -2$$ ✗

17. ★ **MULTIPLE CHOICE** What is true about the line through (2, −4) and (5, 1)? **A**
Ⓐ It rises from left to right.
Ⓑ It falls from left to right.
Ⓒ It is horizontal.
Ⓓ It is vertical.

EXAMPLE 4 on p. 84 for Exs. 18–23

CLASSIFYING LINES **Tell whether the lines are *parallel, perpendicular,* or *neither.***

18. Line 1: through (3, −1) and (6, −4)
Line 2: through (−4, 5) and (−2, 7) **perpendicular**
19. Line 1: through (1, 5) and (3, −2)
Line 2: through (−3, 2) and (4, 0) **neither**
20. Line 1: through (−1, 4) and (2, 5)
Line 2: through (−6, 2) and (0, 4) **parallel**
21. Line 1: through (5, 8) and (7, 2)
Line 2: through (−7, −2) and (−4, −1) **perpendicular**
22. Line 1: through (−3, 2) and (5, 0)
Line 2: through (−1, −4) and (3, −3) **neither**
23. Line 1: through (1, −4) and (4, −2)
Line 2: through (8, 1) and (14, 5) **parallel**

EXAMPLE 5 on p. 85 for Exs. 24–27

AVERAGE RATE OF CHANGE **Find the average rate of change in *y* relative to *x* for the ordered pairs. Include units of measure in your answer.**

24. (2, 12), (5, 30) *x* is measured in hours and *y* is measured in dollars **\$6/h**
25. (0, 11), (3, 50) *x* is measured in gallons and *y* is measured in miles **13 mi/gal**
26. (3, 10), (5, 18) *x* is measured in seconds and *y* is measured in feet **4 ft/sec**
27. (1, 8), (7, 20) *x* is measured in seconds and *y* is measured in meters **2 m/sec**

15. The *x*- and *y*-coordinates were not subtracted in the correct order; $\frac{-1-(-3)}{2-(-4)} = \frac{1}{3}$.

16. Slope should be calculated using rise over run, not run over rise; $\frac{1-4}{5-(-1)} = -\frac{1}{2}$.

. No; no. Sample answer: The slope $\overleftrightarrow{PQ} = \frac{2-1}{-3-(-1)} = -\frac{1}{2}$. The slope $\overleftrightarrow{QR} = \frac{1-0}{-1-1} = -\frac{1}{2}$. The slope $\overleftrightarrow{ST} = \frac{-1-(-2)}{3-5} = -\frac{1}{2}$.

B

28. REASONING The Key Concept box on page 84 states that lines ℓ_1 and ℓ_2 must be nonvertical. *Explain* why this condition is necessary. **The slope of vertical lines is undefined.**

FINDING SLOPE Find the slope of the line passing through the given points.

29. $\left(-1, \frac{3}{2}\right), \left(0, \frac{7}{2}\right)$ 2

30. $\left(-\frac{3}{4}, -2\right), \left(\frac{5}{4}, -3\right)$ $-\frac{1}{2}$

31. $\left(-\frac{1}{2}, \frac{5}{2}\right), \left(\frac{5}{2}, 3\right)$ $\frac{1}{6}$

32. (−4.2, 0.1), (−3.2, 0.1) 0

33. (−0.3, 2.2), (1.7, −0.8) $-\frac{3}{2}$

34. (3.5, −2), (4.5, 0.5) $\frac{5}{2}$

35. ★ SHORT RESPONSE Does it make a difference which two points on a line you choose when finding the slope? Does it make a difference which point is (x_1, y_1) and which point is (x_2, y_2) in the formula for slope? Support your answers using three different pairs of points on the line shown.

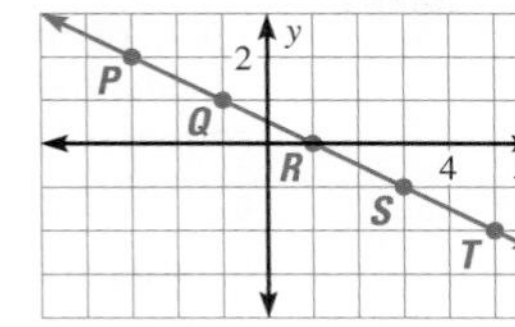

36. ★ OPEN-ENDED MATH Find two additional points on the line that passes through (0, 3) and has a slope of −4. ***Sample answer:* (1, −1), (2, −5)**

C

CHALLENGE Find the value of k so that the line through the given points has the given slope. Check your solution.

37. (2, −3) and $(k, 7)$; $m = -2$ −3

38. $(0, k)$ and (3, 4); $m = 1$ 1

39. $(-4, 2k)$ and $(k, -5)$; $m = -1$ −1

40. $(-2, k)$ and $(2k, 2)$; $m = -0.25$ 5

PROBLEM SOLVING

EXAMPLE 1 on p. 82 for Exs. 41–44

A

41. ESCALATORS An escalator in an airport rises 28 feet over a horizontal distance of 48 feet. What is the slope of the escalator? $\frac{7}{12}$

@HomeTutor for problem solving help at classzone.com

42. INCLINE RAILWAY The Duquesne Incline, a cable car railway, rises 400 feet over a horizontal distance of 685 feet on its ascent to an overlook of Pittsburgh, Pennsylvania. What is the slope of the incline? $\frac{80}{137}$

@HomeTutor for problem solving help at classzone.com

43. ROAD GRADE A road's *grade* is its slope expressed as a percent. A road rises 195 feet over a horizontal distance of 3000 feet. What is the grade of the road? 6.5%

44. ★ SHORT RESPONSE The diagram shows a three-section ramp to a bridge. For a person walking up the ramp, each section has the same positive slope. *Compare* this slope with the slope that a single-section ramp would have if it rose directly to the bridge from the same starting point. *Explain* the benefits of a three-section ramp in this situation.

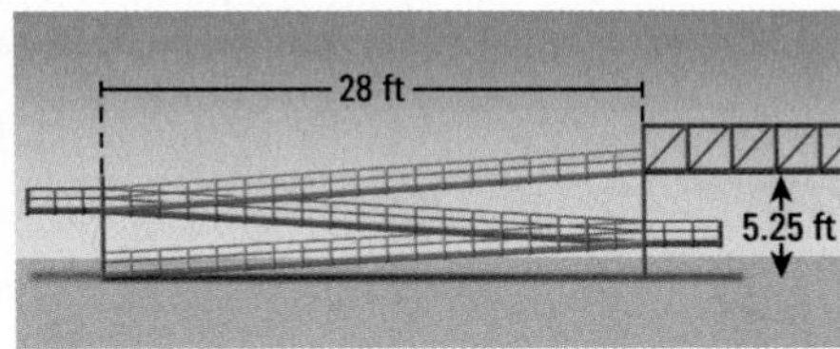

44. Each part of the three-section ramp has a slope of $\frac{1}{16}$, which is one third the single-section ramp's slope of $\frac{3}{16}$. The three-section ramp is easier to climb because the incline is less steep.

EXAMPLE 5 on p. 85 for Exs. 45–46

45. ★ MULTIPLE CHOICE Over a 30 day period, the amount of propane in a tank that stores propane for heating a home decreases from 400 gallons to 214 gallons. What is the average rate of change in the amount of propane? A

Ⓐ −6.2 gallons per day
Ⓑ −6 gallons per day
Ⓒ −0.16 gallon per day
Ⓓ 6 gallons per day

Animated Algebra classzone.com

An **Animated Algebra** activity is available on-line for **Exercises 3–14**. This activity is also available on the **Power Presentations CD-ROM**.

Teaching Strategy

Exercises 3–14 Demonstrate that for a line that rises from left to right, *y* increases as *x* increases, but for a line that falls from left to right, *y* decreases as *x* increases.

Study Strategy

Exercises 24, 26, 27 Suggest that students plot the points on a graph to show change over time. This will help them relate the change in *y* relative to the change in time, as defined by *x*.

Internet Reference

Exercise 42 Additional information about the Duquesne Incline can be found at incline.pghfree.net/historycover.htm

Exercise 46 For more information about the red sea urchin, visit www.dfo-mpo.gc.ca/zone/underwater_sous-marin/red_sea_urchin/urchin_oursin_e.htm

5 ASSESS AND RETEACH

Daily Homework Quiz

Transparency Available

Find the slope of the line passing through the points. Then tell whether the line *rises*, *falls*, *is horizontal*, or *is vertical*.

1. $(-3, 5), (5, -2)$ $-\frac{7}{8}$; falls
2. $(7, 8), (-8, 8)$ 0; horizontal

Tell whether the lines are *parallel*, *perpendicular*, or *neither*.

3. Line 1: through $(5, -1)$ and $(6, -2)$; Line 2: through $(-2, 3)$ and $(4, 8)$ neither
4. Line 1: through $(-9, 3)$ and $(0, 4)$; Line 2: through $(3, -4)$ and $(2, 5)$ perpendicular
5. A handicap ramp has a run of 24 feet and a rise of 2 feet. What is the slope of the ramp? $\frac{1}{12}$

Online Quiz

Available at **classzone.com**

Diagnosis/Remediation

- Practice A, B, C in Chapter 2 Resource Book, pp. 19–21
- Study Guide in Chapter 2 Resource Book, pp. 22–23
- Practice Workbook, pp. 18–19
- @HomeTutor

Challenge

Additional challenge is available in the Chapter 2 Resource Book, p. 26.

46. **BIOLOGY** A red sea urchin grows its entire life, which can last 200 years. The diagram gives information about the growth in the diameter d of one red sea urchin. What is the average growth rate of this urchin over the given period? 0.045 cm/yr

B 47. **MULTI-STEP PROBLEM** A building code requires the minimum slope, or *pitch*, of an asphalt-shingle roof to be a rise of 3 feet for each 12 feet of run. The asphalt-shingle roof of an apartment building has the dimensions shown.

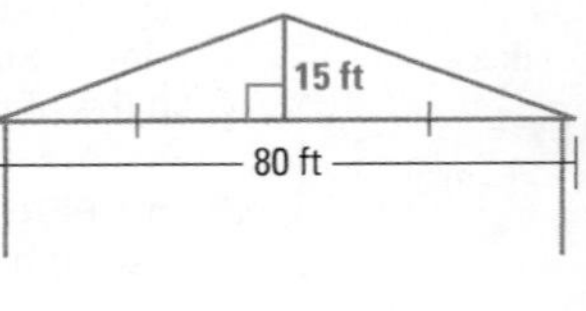

a. **Calculate** What is the slope of the roof? $\frac{3}{8}$

b. **Interpret** Does the roof satisfy the building code? yes

c. **Reasoning** If you answered "no" to part (b), by how much must the rise be increased to satisfy the code? If you answered "yes," by how much does the rise exceed the code minimum? $\frac{1}{8}$

48. ★ **EXTENDED RESPONSE** Plans for a new water slide in an amusement park call for the slide to descend from a platform 80 feet tall. The slide will drop 1 foot for every 3 feet of horizontal distance.

a. What horizontal distance do you cover when descending the slide? 160 ft

b. Use the Pythagorean theorem to find the length of the slide. about 178.9 ft

c. Engineers decide to shorten the slide horizontally by 5 feet to allow for a wider walkway at the slide's base. The plans for the platform remain unchanged. How will this affect the slope of the slide? *Explain.*

48c. The slope of the slide will increase slightly, from $\frac{1}{2}$ to $\frac{16}{31}$. *Sample answer:* The horizontal distance is decreased and the vertical distance remains the same, then the slide must become slightly steeper.

C 49. **CHALLENGE** A car travels 36 miles per gallon of gasoline in highway driving and 24 miles per gallon in city driving. If you drive the car equal distances on the highway and in the city, how many miles per gallon can you expect to average? (*Hint:* The average fuel efficiency for all the driving is the total distance traveled divided by the total amount of gasoline used.) 30 mi/gal

KENTUCKY MIXED REVIEW

TEST PRACTICE at classzone.com

50. A city is building a rectangular playground in a community park. The city has 560 feet of fencing to enclose the playground. The length of the playground should be 40 feet longer than the width. What is the length of the playground if all of the fencing is used? B

Ⓐ 120 ft　Ⓑ 160 ft
Ⓒ 200 ft　Ⓓ 300 ft

51. A computer technician charges \$185 for parts needed to fix a computer and \$45 for each hour that he works on the computer. Which equation best represents the relationship between the number of hours, h, the technician works on the computer and the total charges, c? D

Ⓐ $c = 45 - 185h$　Ⓑ $c = 45 + 185h$
Ⓒ $c = 185 - 45h$　Ⓓ $c = 185 + 45h$

2.3 Graph Equations of Lines

MA-HS-5.3.3 Students will model, solve and graph first degree, two-variable equations and inequalities in real-world and mathematical problems. DOK 2

Before You graphed linear equations by making tables of values.

Now You will graph linear equations in slope-intercept or standard form.

Why? So you can model motion, as in Ex. 64.

Key Vocabulary
- parent function
- *y*-intercept
- slope-intercept form
- standard form of a linear equation
- *x*-intercept

A *family* of functions is a group of functions with shared characteristics. The **parent function** is the most basic function in a family.

KEY CONCEPT *For Your Notebook*

Parent Function for Linear Functions

The parent function for the family of all linear functions is $f(x) = x$. The graph of $f(x) = x$ is shown.

The *y*-intercept of the line $f(x) = x$ is 0.

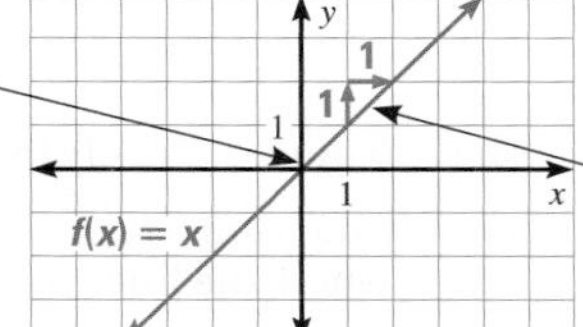

The slope of the line $f(x) = x$ is 1.

In general, a ***y*-intercept** of a graph is the *y*-coordinate of a point where the graph intersects the *y*-axis.

DEFINE *Y*-INTERCEPT

A *y*-intercept is sometimes defined as a *point* where a graph intersects the *y*-axis. Using this definition, the *y*-intercept of the line $f(x) = x$ is (0, 0), not 0.

EXAMPLE 1 Graph linear functions

Graph the equation. Compare the graph with the graph of $y = x$.

a. $y = 2x$ **b.** $y = x + 3$

Solution

a.

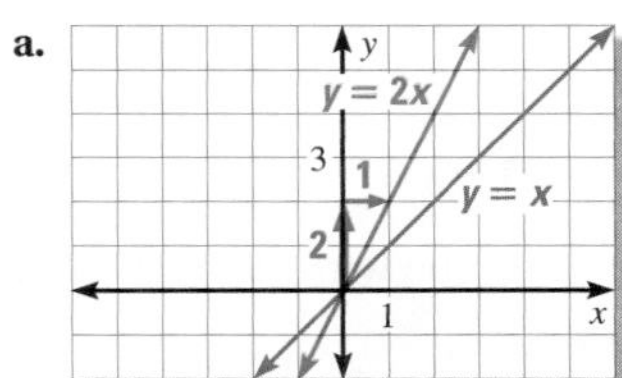

The graphs of $y = 2x$ and $y = x$ both have a *y*-intercept of 0, but the graph of $y = 2x$ has a slope of 2 instead of 1.

b.

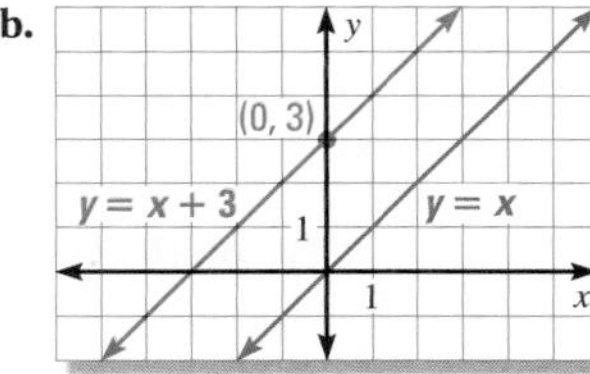

The graphs of $y = x + 3$ and $y = x$ both have a slope of 1, but the graph of $y = x + 3$ has a *y*-intercept of 3 instead of 0.

1 PLAN AND PREPARE

Warm-Up Exercises

Transparency Available

Evaluate each expression for $x = -1, 0$, and 2.

1. $2x + 3$ 1, 3, 7
2. $\frac{2}{3}x - 1$ $-\frac{5}{3}, -1, \frac{1}{3}$
3. In 2005, Carey's Pet Shop had a profit of $55,500. In 2006, profits were $38,700. In a graph of the data, is the slope of the segment between 2005 and 2006 positive or negative? negative

Notetaking Guide

Transparency Available

Promotes interactive learning and notetaking skills, pp. 33–36.

Pacing

Basic: 2 days
Average: 2 days
Advanced: 2 days
Block: 0.5 block with 2.2
0.5 block with 2.4
- See *Teaching Guide/Lesson Plan.*

2 FOCUS AND MOTIVATE

Essential Question

Big Idea 2, p. 71

How do you graph a linear equation? **Tell students they will learn how to answer this question by using slope and *y*-intercept and by finding *x*- and *y*-intercepts.**

Resource Planning Guide

Chapter Resource Book
- Teaching Guide/Lesson Plan (pp. 27–28)
- Practice levels A, B, C (pp. 30–35)
- Study Guide (pp. 36–37)
- Catch-up for Absent Students (p. 38)
- Application (p. 39)
- Challenge (p. 40)

Workbooks
- Notetaking Guide (pp. 33–36)
- Practice Workbook (pp. 20–22)

Teaching Options
- **Power Presentations CD-ROM** provides dynamic electronic teaching resources for the classroom.
- **Activity Generator CD-ROM** provides editable activities for all ability levels.

Interactive Technology
- Easy Planner
- Power Presentations CD-ROM
- Activity Generator CD-ROM
- Animated Algebra
- Test Generator CD-ROM
- Online Quiz
- eWorkbook
- eEdition
- @HomeTutor

Resources for English Learners
- Quick Reference for English Learners
- Spanish Study Guide
- Multi-Language Visual Glossary
- Student Resources in Spanish

See also the *Algebra 2 Toolkit* for more strategies for meeting individual needs.

Motivating the Lesson

When given an equation, you can determine useful information from its graph. For example, suppose your class needed to raise \$2800 for a class trip by selling \$7 baseball caps and \$10 sweatshirts. The graph of the equation $7x + 10y = 2800$ can reveal information about the number of caps and sweatshirts you might sell.

3 TEACH

Extra Example 1

Graph the equation. Compare the graph with the graph of $y = x$.

a. $y = -2x$ The graphs of $y = -2x$ and $y = x$ both have a y-intercept of 0, but the graph of $y = -2x$ has a slope of -2 instead of 1.

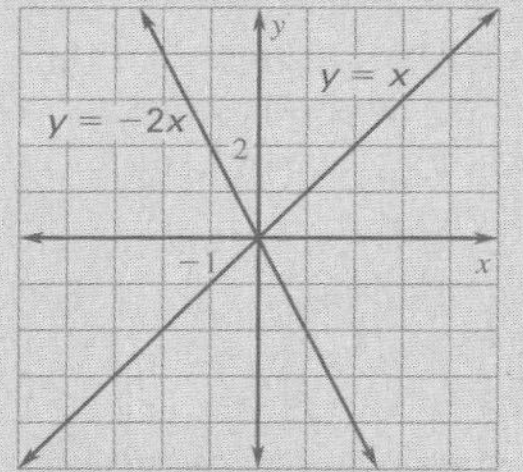

b. $y = x - 1$ The graphs of $y = x - 1$ and $y = x$ both have a slope of 1, but the graph of $y = x - 1$ has a y-intercept of -1 instead of 0.

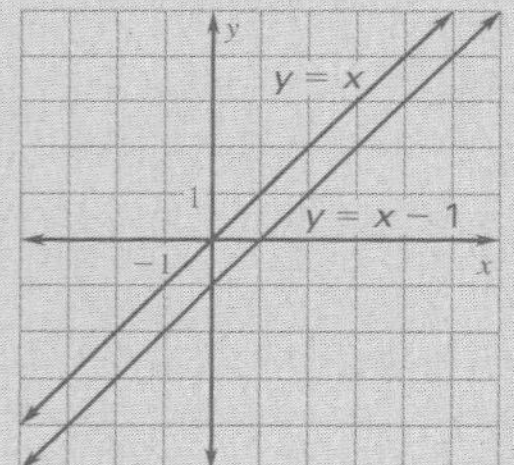

Key Question to Ask for Example 1

- How is the graph of $y = x + a$ related to the graph of $y = x$? The graphs are parallel.

SLOPE-INTERCEPT FORM If you write the equations in Example 1 as $y = 2x + 0$ and $y = 1x + 3$, you can see that the x-coefficients, 2 and 1, are the slopes of the lines, while the constant terms, 0 and 3, are the y-intercepts. In general, a line with equation $y = mx + b$ has slope m and y-intercept b. The equation $y = mx + b$ is said to be in **slope-intercept form**.

KEY CONCEPT *For Your Notebook*

Using Slope-Intercept Form to Graph an Equation

STEP 1 **Write** the equation in slope-intercept form by solving for y.

STEP 2 **Identify** the y-intercept b and use it to plot the point $(0, b)$ where the line crosses the y-axis.

STEP 3 **Identify** the slope m and use it to plot a second point on the line.

STEP 4 **Draw** a line through the two points.

EXAMPLE 2 Graph an equation in slope-intercept form

Graph $y = -\frac{2}{3}x - 1$.

Solution

STEP 1 The equation is already in slope-intercept form.

STEP 2 **Identify** the y-intercept. The y-intercept is -1, so plot the point $(0, -1)$ where the line crosses the y-axis.

STEP 3 **Identify** the slope. The slope is $-\frac{2}{3}$, or $\frac{-2}{3}$, so plot a second point on the line by starting at $(0, -1)$ and then moving down 2 units and right 3 units. The second point is $(3, -3)$.

STEP 4 **Draw** a line through the two points.

ANOTHER WAY
Because $-\frac{2}{3} = \frac{2}{-3}$, you could also plot a second point by moving up 2 units and left 3 units.

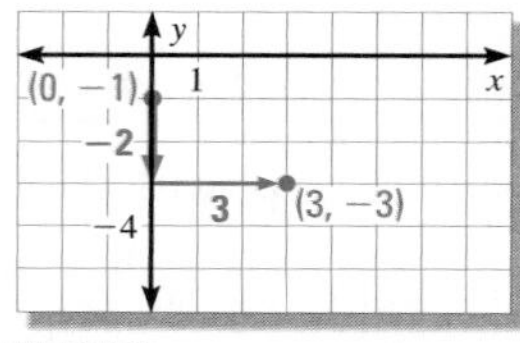

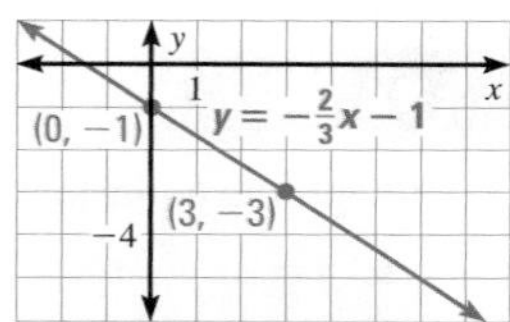

Animated Algebra at classzone.com

✓ GUIDED PRACTICE for Examples 1 and 2

Graph the equation. *Compare* the graph with the graph of $y = x$. 1–3. See margin.

1. $y = -2x$
2. $y = x - 2$
3. $y = 4x$

Graph the equation. 4–9. See margin.

4. $y = -x + 2$
5. $y = \frac{2}{5}x + 4$
6. $y = \frac{1}{2}x - 3$
7. $y = 5 + x$
8. $f(x) = 1 - 3x$
9. $f(x) = 10 - x$

1–9. See Additional Answers beginning on p. AA1.

REAL-LIFE PROBLEMS In a real-life context, a line's slope can represent an average rate of change. The y-intercept in a real-life context is often an initial value.

EXAMPLE 3 Solve a multi-step problem

BIOLOGY The body length y (in inches) of a walrus calf can be modeled by $y = 5x + 42$ where x is the calf's age (in months).

- Graph the equation.
- Describe what the slope and y-intercept represent in this situation.
- Use the graph to estimate the body length of a calf that is 10 months old.

Solution

STEP 1 **Graph** the equation.

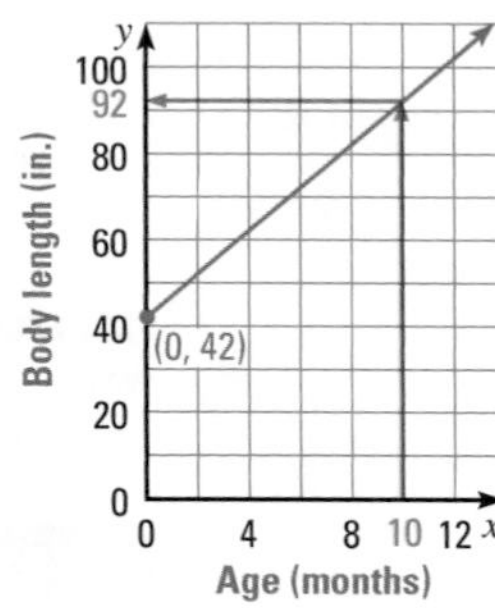

STEP 2 **Interpret** the slope and y-intercept. The slope, 5, represents the calf's rate of growth in inches per month. The y-intercept, 42, represents a newborn calf's body length in inches.

ANOTHER WAY
You can check the result you obtained from the graph by substituting 10 for x in $y = 5x + 42$ and simplifying.

STEP 3 **Estimate** the body length of the calf at age 10 months by starting at 10 on the x-axis and moving up until you reach the graph. Then move left to the y-axis. At age 10 months, the body length of the calf is about 92 inches.

✓ GUIDED PRACTICE for Example 3

10. WHAT IF? In Example 3, suppose that the body length of a fast-growing calf is modeled by $y = 6x + 48$. Repeat the steps of the example for the new model. **See margin.**

DEFINE X-INTERCEPT
An x-intercept is sometimes defined as a *point* where a graph intersects the x-axis, not the x-coordinate of such a point.

STANDARD FORM The **standard form** of a linear equation is $Ax + By = C$ where A and B are not both zero. You can graph an equation in standard form by identifying and plotting the x- and y-intercepts. An **x-intercept** is the x-coordinate of a point where a graph intersects the x-axis.

KEY CONCEPT *For Your Notebook*

Using Standard Form to Graph an Equation

STEP 1 **Write** the equation in standard form.

STEP 2 **Identify** the x-intercept by letting $y = 0$ and solving for x. Use the x-intercept to plot the point where the line crosses the x-axis.

STEP 3 **Identify** the y-intercept by letting $x = 0$ and solving for y. Use the y-intercept to plot the point where the line crosses the y-axis.

STEP 4 **Draw** a line through the two points.

10. Step 1:

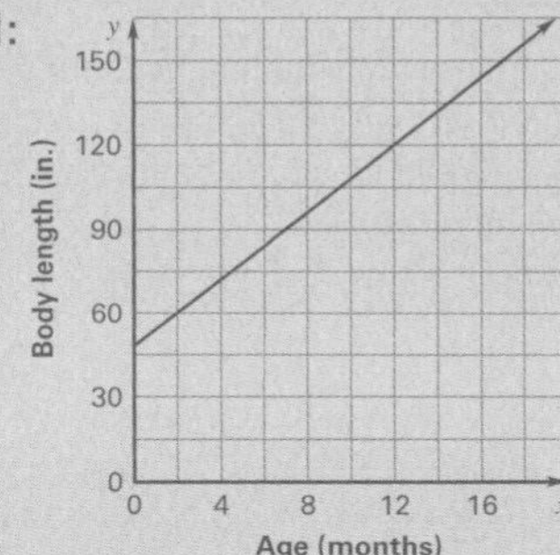

Step 2: The y-intercept, 48, represents the length of the newborn calf's body. The slope, 6, represents the calf's growth rate in inches per month.

Step 3: 108 in.

Extra Example 2

Graph $y = \frac{3}{4}x - 2$.

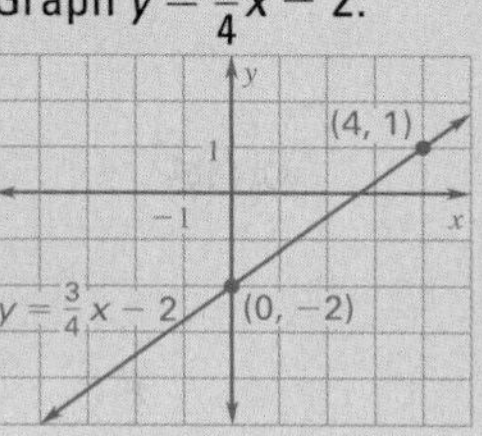

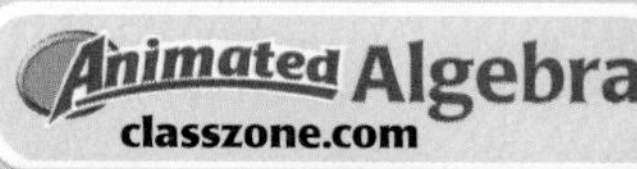

An **Animated Algebra** activity is available on-line for **Example 2**. This activity is also available on the **Power Presentations CD-ROM**.

Extra Example 3

The value y of a copier x years after it was purchased can be modeled by the equation $y = 4000 - 600x$. Graph the equation. Describe what the y-intercept and slope represent in this situation. Use the graph to estimate the value of the copier after 5 years.

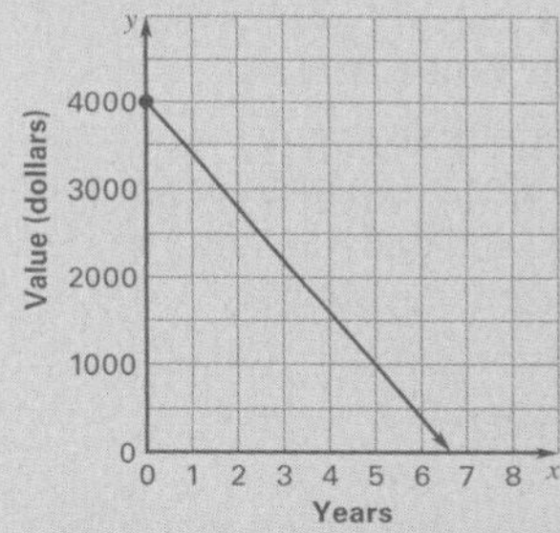

y-intercept: initial price; slope: depreciation per year; $1000

Key Question to Ask for Example 3

- Why is the answer 92 inches an estimate? **The answer was obtained by reading from a graph with a vertical scale marked off by 10s. Since the line from the graph to the vertical scale hits the scale at slightly over 90, the answer must be an estimate. To get an exact answer you must use the equation of the graph and substitute 10 for x.**

Extra Example 4

Graph $-2x - 3y = 6$.

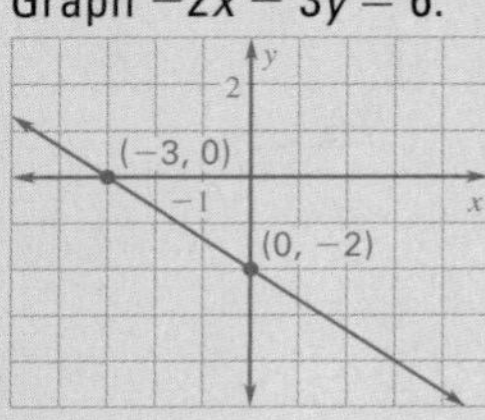

Extra Example 5

Graph (a) $y = -3$ and (b) $x = 4$.

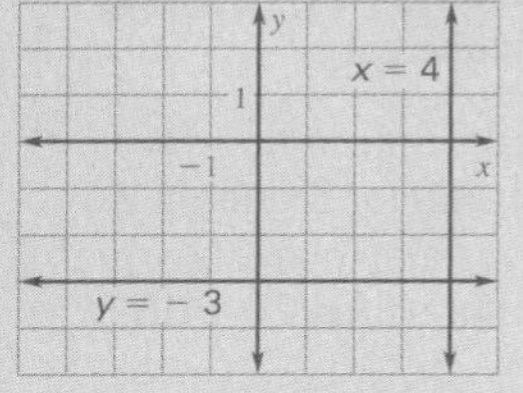

Key Questions to Ask for Example 5

- What is the general form of the coordinates of any point on the line $y = 2$? $(x, 2)$
- What is the general form of the coordinates of any point on the line $x = -3$? $(-3, y)$

Closing the Lesson

Have students summarize the major points of the lesson and answer the Essential Question: How do you graph a linear equation?

- **The parent function for the family of all linear functions is $f(x) = x$.**
- **To graph a linear equation you can use the slope and y-intercept or the x- and y-intercepts.**
- **The graph of $y = c$ is a horizontal line through $(0, c)$. The graph of $x = c$ is a vertical line through $(c, 0)$.**

To graph an equation in slope-intercept form, plot the y-intercept, use the slope to find a second point, and draw a line through the two points. To graph an equation using standard form, solve to identify the intercepts. Plot the intercepts and draw a line through them.

11–14. See Additional Answers beginning on p. AA1.

EXAMPLE 4 Graph an equation in standard form

ANOTHER WAY

You can also graph $5x + 2y = 10$ by first solving for y to obtain $y = -\frac{5}{2}x + 5$ and then using the procedure for graphing an equation in slope-intercept form.

Graph $5x + 2y = 10$.

Solution

STEP 1 The equation is already in standard form.

STEP 2 **Identify** the x-intercept.

$5x + 2(0) = 10$ **Let $y = 0$.**

$x = 2$ **Solve for x.**

The x-intercept is 2. So, plot the point $(2, 0)$.

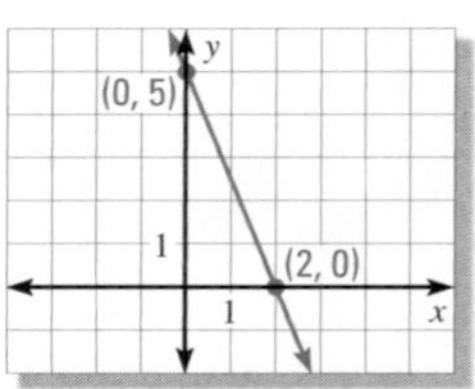

STEP 3 **Identify** the y-intercept.

$5(0) + 2y = 10$ **Let $x = 0$.**

$y = 5$ **Solve for y.**

The y-intercept is 5. So, plot the point $(0, 5)$.

STEP 4 **Draw** a line through the two points.

HORIZONTAL AND VERTICAL LINES The equation of a vertical line cannot be written in slope-intercept form because the slope is not defined. However, every linear equation—even that of a vertical line—can be written in standard form.

KEY CONCEPT *For Your Notebook*

Horizontal and Vertical Lines

Horizontal Lines The graph of $y = c$ is the horizontal line through $(0, c)$.

Vertical Lines The graph of $x = c$ is the vertical line through $(c, 0)$.

EXAMPLE 5 Graph horizontal and vertical lines

Graph (a) $y = 2$ and (b) $x = -3$.

Solution

a. The graph of $y = 2$ is the horizontal line that passes through the point $(0, 2)$. Notice that every point on the line has a y-coordinate of 2.

b. The graph of $x = -3$ is the vertical line that passes through the point $(-3, 0)$. Notice that every point on the line has an x-coordinate of -3.

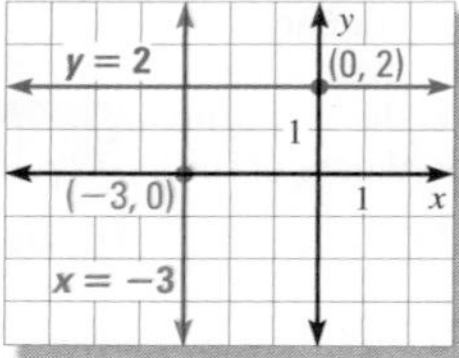

GUIDED PRACTICE for Examples 4 and 5

Graph the equation. 11–14. See margin.

11. $2x + 5y = 10$ **12.** $3x - 2y = 12$ **13.** $x = 1$ **14.** $y = -4$

Differentiated Instruction

Below Level Have students copy the methods for graphing linear equations in slope-intercept and standard form into their notebooks. Each method should be accompanied by an example showing exactly how the method works.

See also the *Algebra 2 Toolkit* for more strategies.

2.3 EXERCISES

HOMEWORK KEY

 = **WORKED-OUT SOLUTIONS** on p. WS3 for Exs. 15, 37, and 61

★ = **STANDARDIZED TEST PRACTICE** Exs. 2, 23, 30, 55, 56, 63, and 68

◆ = **MULTIPLE REPRESENTATIONS** Ex. 67

SKILL PRACTICE

A

1. **VOCABULARY** Copy and complete: The linear equation $y = 2x + 5$ is written in __?__ form. slope-intercept

2. ★ **WRITING** *Describe* how to graph an equation of the form $Ax + By = C$. See margin.

EXAMPLE 1 on p. 89 for Exs. 3–8

GRAPHING LINEAR FUNCTIONS Graph the equation. *Compare* the graph with the graph of $y = x$. 3–8. See margin.

3. $y = 3x$
4. $y = -x$
5. $y = x + 5$
6. $y = x - 2$
7. $y = 2x - 1$
8. $y = -3x + 2$

EXAMPLE 2 on p. 90 for Exs. 9–22

SLOPE-INTERCEPT FORM Graph the equation. 9–20. See margin.

9. $y = -x - 3$
10. $y = x - 6$
11. $y = 2x + 6$
12. $y = 3x - 4$
13. $y = 4x - 1$
14. $y = \frac{2}{3}x - 2$
15. $f(x) = -\frac{1}{2}x - 1$
16. $f(x) = -\frac{5}{4}x + 1$
17. $f(x) = \frac{3}{2}x - 3$
18. $f(x) = \frac{5}{3}x + 4$
19. $f(x) = -1.5x + 2$
20. $f(x) = 3x - 1.5$

2. *Sample answer:* Write the equation in slope intercept form. Then plot the *y*-intercept and use the slope to find a second point on the line. Draw a line through the two points.

ERROR ANALYSIS *Describe* and correct the error in graphing the equation. 21, 22. See margin.

21. $y = 2x + 3$

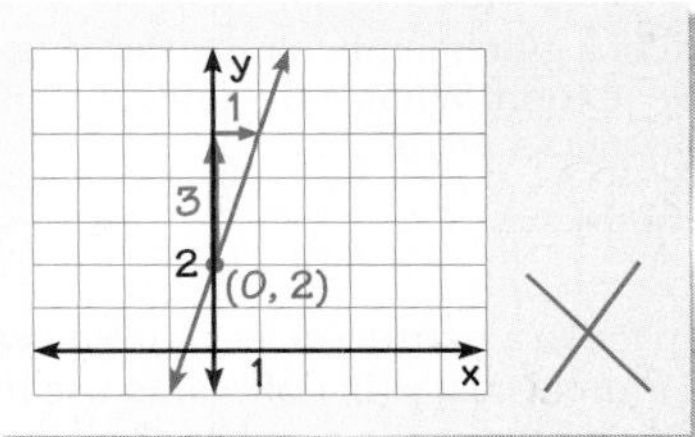

22. $y = 4x - 2$

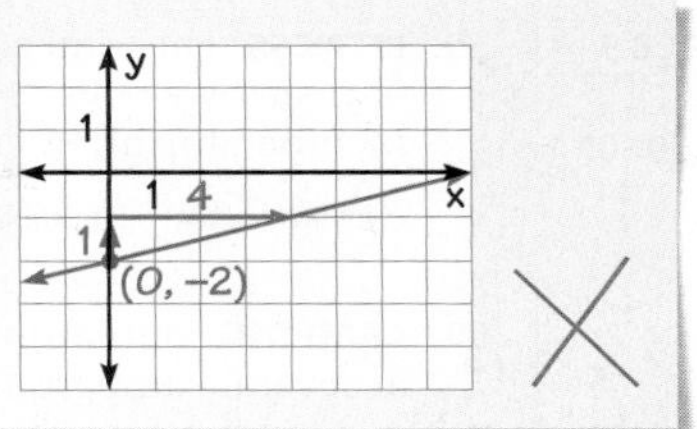

23. ★ **MULTIPLE CHOICE** What is the slope-intercept form of $4x - 3y = 18$? C

Ⓐ $y = \frac{3}{4}x - 6$ Ⓑ $y = -\frac{3}{4}x - 6$ Ⓒ $y = \frac{4}{3}x - 6$ Ⓓ $y = -\frac{4}{3}x + 6$

EXAMPLES 4 and 5 on p. 92 for Exs. 24–42

FINDING INTERCEPTS Find the *x*- and *y*-intercepts of the line with the given equation.

24. $x - y = 4$ *x*-intercept: 4, *y*-intercept: −4
25. $x + 5y = -15$ *x*-intercept: −15, *y*-intercept: −3
26. $3x - 4y = -12$ *x*-intercept: −4, *y*-intercept: 3
27. $2x - y = 10$ *x*-intercept: 5, *y*-intercept: −10
28. $4x - 5y = 20$ *x*-intercept: 5, *y*-intercept: −4
29. $-6x + 8y = -36$ *x*-intercept: 6, *y*-intercept: −4.5

30. ★ **MULTIPLE CHOICE** What is the *x*-intercept of the graph of $5x - 6y = 30$? C

Ⓐ −5 Ⓑ $\frac{5}{6}$ Ⓒ 6 Ⓓ 30

4 PRACTICE AND APPLY

Assignment Guide

Answer Transparencies available for all exercises

Basic:
Day 1: pp. 93–96
Exs. 1–5, 9–19 odd, 21–23, 59–62, 70–71
Day 2: pp. 93–96
Exs. 24–30 even, 31–41 odd, 43–48, 63–65

Average:
Day 1: pp. 93–96
Exs. 1, 2–20 even, 21–23, 59–62, 70–71
Day 2: pp. 93–96
Exs. 25–29 odd, 30–42 even, 46–51, 55–57, 63–68

Advanced:
Day 1: pp. 93–96
Exs. 1, 2, 6–8, 15–20, 23, 59–62, 70–71
Day 2: pp. 93–96
Exs. 27–30, 37–42, 46–58*, 63–69*

Block:
pp. 93–96
Exs. 1, 2–20 even, 21–23, 59–62, 70–71 (with 2.2)
pp. 93–96
Exs. 25–29 odd, 30–42 even, 46–51, 55–57, 63–68 (with 2.4)

Differentiated Instruction

See *Algebra 2 Best Practices Toolkit* for suggestions on addressing the needs of a diverse classroom.

Homework Check

For a quick check of student understanding of key concepts, go over the following exercises:

Basic: 4, 13, 24, 43, 60
Average: 6, 16, 26, 46, 61
Advanced: 8, 18, 28, 48, 62

Extra Practice

- Student Edition, p. 1011
- Chapter 2 Resource Book: Practice levels A, B, C, pp. 30–35

Practice Worksheet

An easily-readable reduced practice page (with answers) for this lesson can be found on p. 70C.

Differentiated Instruction

Kinesthetic Learners Some students may find it confusing that the *x*-axis is horizontal, but $y = c$ is a horizontal line. Explain that because there is no *x*-term in the equation $y = c$, *x* can take on any value. Have students put their fingertip on any point whose *y*-value is *c*. When they vary *x* by moving their fingertip to the left and right, they will discover that $y = c$ is actually a horizontal line. Students can similarly be led to see that $x = c$ is a vertical line.

See also the *Algebra 2 Toolkit* for more strategies.

3–22. See Additional Answers beginning on p. AA1.

Avoiding Common Errors

Exercises 24–29 To avoid confusing the intercepts, discuss the general form $(x, 0)$ of the point associated with the x-intercept and the general form $(0, y)$ of the point associated with the y-intercept with your students before they begin their work.

Mathematical Reasoning

Exercises 31–42 Because a line is determined by any two points on the line, the x- and y-intercepts are sufficient for graphing the equations.

31–54. See Additional Answers beginning on p. AA1.

56. ***Sample:***

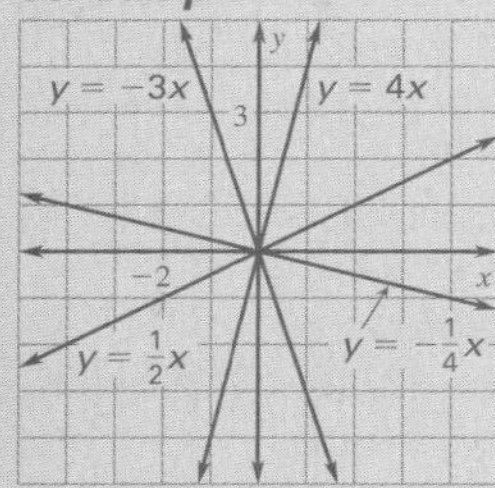

59.

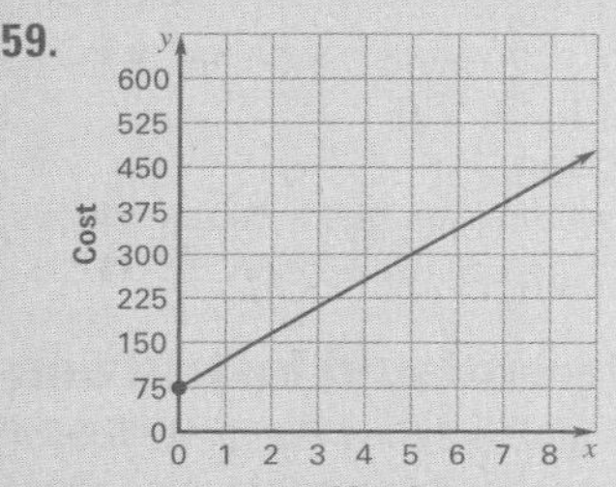

60.

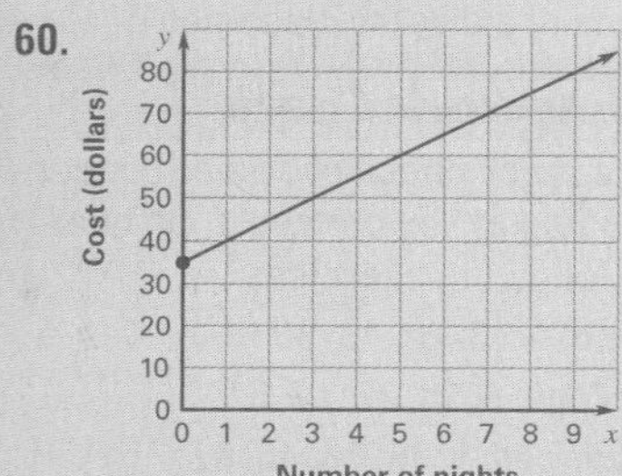

61.

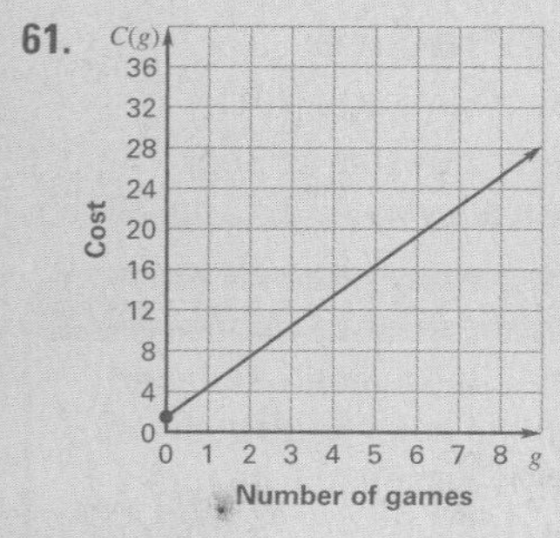

STANDARD FORM Graph the equation. Label any intercepts. **31–42. See margin.**

31. $x + 4y = 8$ 32. $2x - 6y = -12$ 33. $x = 4$

34. $y = -2$ 35. $5x - y = 3$ 36. $3x + 4y = 12$

37. $-5x + 10y = 20$ 38. $-x - y = 6$ 39. $y = 1.5$

40. $2.5x - 5y = -15$ 41. $x = -\frac{5}{2}$ 42. $\frac{1}{2}x + 2y = -2$

B **CHOOSING A METHOD** Graph the equation using any method. **43–54. See margin.**

43. $6y = 3x + 6$ 44. $-3 + x = 0$ 45. $y + 7 = -2x$

46. $4y = 16$ 47. $8y = -2x + 20$ 48. $4x = -\frac{1}{2}y - 1$

49. $-4x = 8y + 12$ 50. $3.5x = 10.5$ 51. $y - 5.5x = 6$

52. $14 - 3x = 7y$ 53. $2y - 5 = 0$ 54. $5y = 7.5 - 2.5x$

55. ★ **OPEN-ENDED MATH** Write equations of two lines, one with an x-intercept but no y-intercept and one with a y-intercept but no x-intercept. ***Sample answer:*** $x = 3$, $y = -2$

56. ★ **SHORT RESPONSE** Sketch $y = mx$ for several values of m, both positive and negative. *Describe* the relationship between m and the steepness of the line. **See margin for art; as m gets closer to zero, the steepness of the line decreases.**

C 57. **REASONING** Consider the graph of $Ax + By = C$ where $B \neq 0$. What are the slope and y-intercept in terms of A, B, and C? **slope: $-\frac{A}{B}$, y-intercept: $\frac{C}{B}$**

58. **CHALLENGE** Prove that the slope of the line $y = mx + b$ is m. (*Hint:* First find two points on the line by choosing convenient values of x.) ***Sample answer:*** **Two points on the line are $(0, b)$ and $(1, m + b)$. Using the slope formula gives $\frac{m + b - b}{1 - 0} = \frac{m}{1} = m$.**

PROBLEM SOLVING

EXAMPLE 3 A on p. 91 for Exs. 59–62

59. **FITNESS** The total cost y (in dollars) of a gym membership after x months is given by $y = 45x + 75$. Graph the equation. What is the total cost of the membership after 9 months? **See margin for art; \$480.**

@HomeTutor for problem solving help at classzone.com

60. **CAMPING** Your annual membership fee to a nature society lets you camp at several campgrounds. Your total annual cost y (in dollars) to use the campgrounds is given by $y = 5x + 35$ where x is the number of nights you camp. Graph the equation. What do the slope and y-intercept represent?

@HomeTutor for problem solving help at classzone.com

See margin for art; slope: cost per night of camping, y-intercept: initial membership fee.

61. **SPORTS** Bowling alleys often charge a fixed fee to rent shoes and then charge for each game you bowl. The function $C(g) = 3g + 1.5$ gives the total cost C (in dollars) to bowl g games. Graph the function. What is the cost to rent shoes? What is the cost per game? **See margin for art; \$1.50; \$3.**

62. **PHONE CARDS** You purchase a 300 minute phone card. The function $M(w) = -30w + 300$ models the number M of minutes that remain on the card after w weeks. *Describe* how to determine a reasonable domain and range. Graph the function. How many minutes per week do you use the card? **See margin.**

○ = WORKED-OUT SOLUTIONS on p. WS1 ★ = STANDARDIZED TEST PRACTICE ◆ = MULTIPLE REPRESENTATIONS

62. A reasonable domain would be greater than or equal to 0 because you cannot have a negative number of weeks. To find the greatest value in the domain, set the function equal to 0 and solve, which gives $0 \leq w \leq 10$. A reasonable range occurs between the minimum value of the domain and the maximum value of the domain, which gives $0 \leq M(w) \leq 300$.

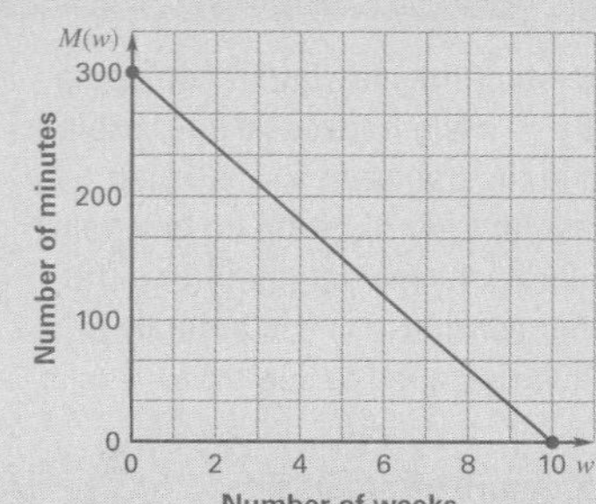

30 min

63. ★ **SHORT RESPONSE** You receive a \$30 gift card to a shop that sells fruit smoothies for \$3. If you graph an equation of the line that represents the money y remaining on the card after you buy x smoothies, what will the y-intercept be? Will the line rise or fall from left to right? *Explain.* **30; fall; the value of the card will decrease after you buy each smoothie, so the line will fall from left to right.**

B 64. **MULTI-STEP PROBLEM** You and a friend kayak 1800 yards down a river. You drift with the current partway at 30 yards per minute and paddle partway at 90 yards per minute. The trip is modeled by $30x + 90y = 1800$ where x is the drifting time and y is the paddling time (both in minutes).

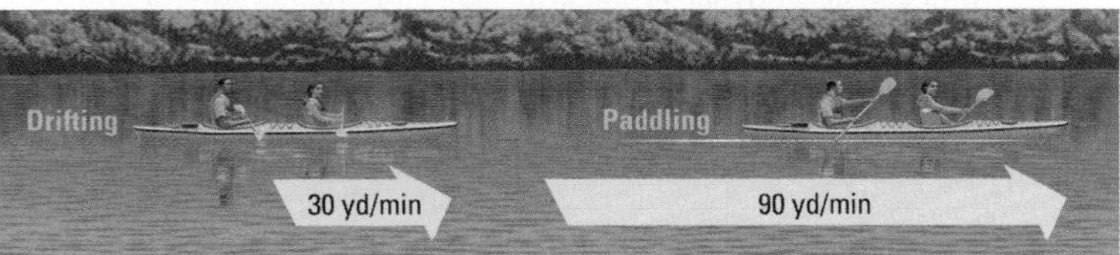

a. Graph the equation, and determine a reasonable domain and range. What do the x- and y-intercepts represent? **See margin.**

b. If you paddle for 5 minutes, what is the total trip time? **50 min**

c. If you paddle and drift equal amounts of time, what is the total trip time? **30 min**

65. **VOLUNTEERING** You participate in a 14 mile run/walk for charity. You run partway at 6 miles per hour and walk partway at 3.5 miles per hour. A model for this situation is $6r + 3.5w = 14$ where r is the time you run and w is the time you walk (both in hours). Graph the equation. Give three possible combinations of running and walking times. **See margin for art. *Sample answer:* $r = 0$ and $w = 4$, $r = 1.75$ and $w = 1$, $r = 0.875$ and $w = 2.5$.**

66. **TICKETS** An honor society has \$150 to buy science museum and art museum tickets for student awards. The numbers of tickets that can be bought are given by $5s + 7a = 150$ where s is the number of science museum tickets (at \$5 each) and a is the number of art museum tickets (at \$7 each). Graph the equation. Give two possible combinations of tickets that use all \$150. **See margin for art. *Sample answer:* $s = 23$ and $a = 5$, $s = 16$ and $a = 10$.**

67. **MULTIPLE REPRESENTATIONS** A hot air balloon is initially 200 feet above the ground. The burners are then turned on, causing the balloon to ascend at a rate of 150 feet per minute.

a. **Making a Table** Make a table showing the height h (in feet) of the balloon t minutes after the burners are turned on where $0 \le t \le 5$. **a–b. See margin.**

b. **Drawing a Graph** Plot the points from the table in part (a). Draw a line through the points for the domain $0 \le t \le 5$.

c. **Writing an Equation** The balloon's height is its initial height plus the product of the ascent rate and time. Write an equation representing this. **$h(t) = 150t + 200$**

Animated Algebra at classzone.com

68. ★ **EXTENDED RESPONSE** You and a friend are each typing your research papers on computers. The function $y = 1400 - 50x$ models the number y of words you have left to type after x minutes. For your friend, $y = 1200 - 50x$ models the number y of words left to type after x minutes.

a. Graph the two equations in the same coordinate plane. *Describe* how the graphs are related geometrically. **See margin.**

b. What do the x-intercepts, y-intercepts, and slopes represent?

c. Who will finish first? *Explain.*

8b. -intercepts: no more words left o type, -intercepts: the number of words each person has o type for the eport, slopes: he words per minute each person types

8c. Your friend. *Sample answer:* The x-intercepts epresent when he paper is inished. It takes you 28 minutes o finish and your riend 24 minutes o finish.

Study Strategy

Exercise 64 Students may find it easier to solve the equivalent equation $x + 3y = 60$ for y.

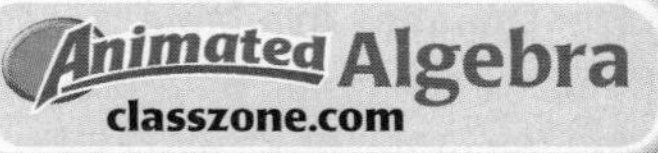

An **Animated Algebra** activity is available on-line for **Exercise 67**. This activity is also available on the **Power Presentations CD-ROM**.

66.

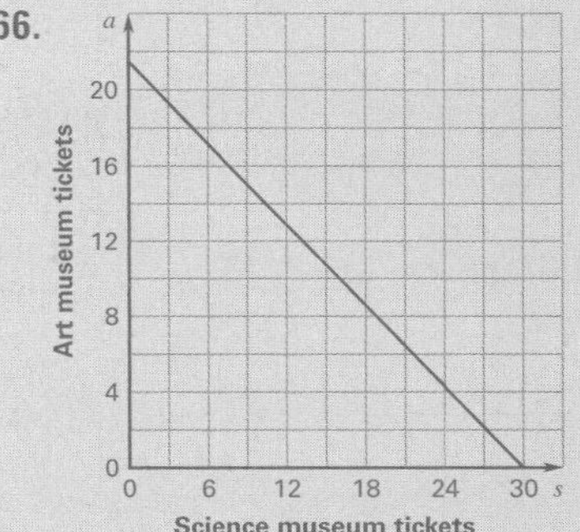

67a.

x (min)	y (ft)
0	200
1	350
2	500
3	650
4	800
5	950

67b.

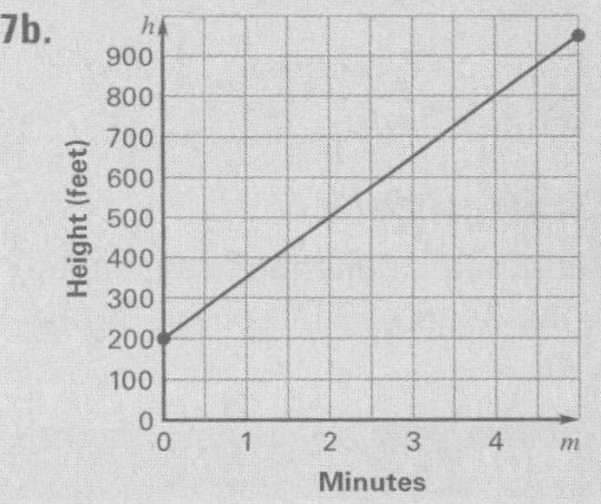

68a.

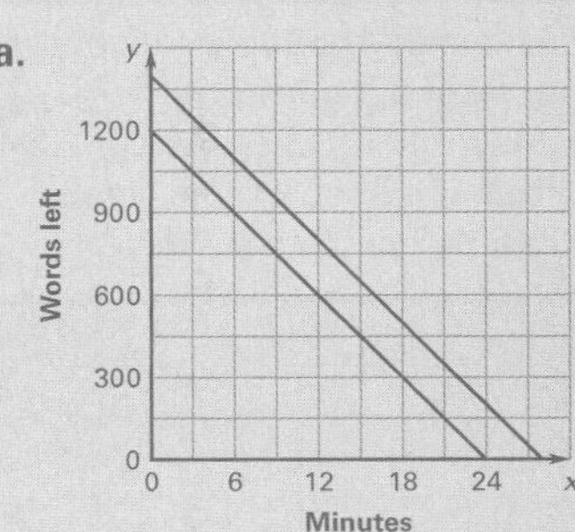

The graphs are parallel to each other.

64a.

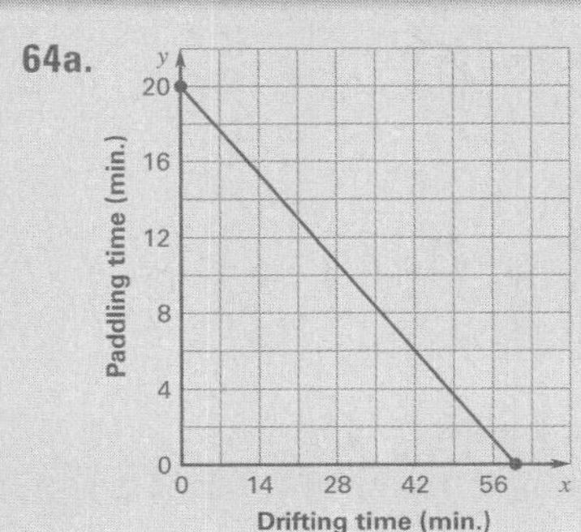

domain: $0 \le x \le 60$, range: $0 \le y \le 20$; x-intercept: the time it would take if you would just drift and not paddle, y-intercept: the time it would take if you would just paddle and not drift

65.

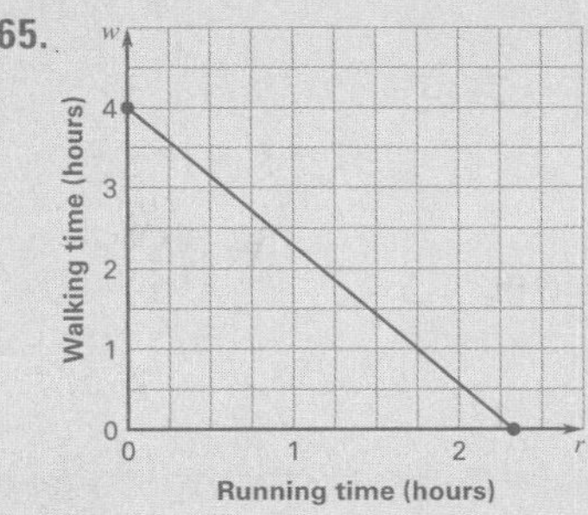

C **69. CHALLENGE** You want to cover a five-by-five grid completely with x three-by-one rectangles and y four-by-one rectangles that do not overlap or extend beyond the grid.

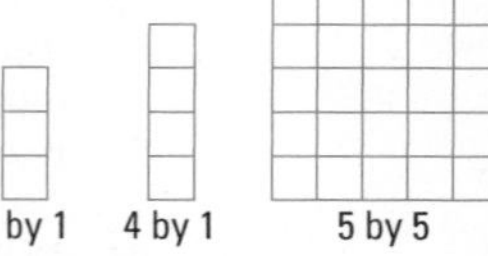

a. *Explain* why x and y must be whole numbers that satisfy the equation $3x + 4y = 25$. **Sample answer: You cannot use partial rectangles.**

b. Find all solutions (x, y) of the equation in part (a) such that x and y are whole numbers. **(3, 4) and (7, 1)**

c. Do all the solutions from part (b) represent combinations of rectangles that can actually cover the grid? Use diagrams to support your answer. **No; see margin for art.**

KENTUCKY MIXED REVIEW

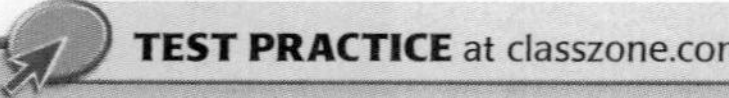

70. In isosceles triangle ABC, the interior angle A measures 110°. The measures of all three interior angles of triangle ABC are— **D**

Ⓐ 110°, 110°, and 140° Ⓑ 110°, 110°, and 110°

Ⓒ 110°, 40°, and 30° Ⓓ 110°, 35°, and 35°

71. A paper cup is shaped like the cone shown. What is the approximate volume of this paper cup? **A**

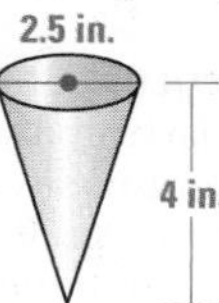

Ⓐ 6.5 in.^{3} Ⓑ 10.5 in.^{3}

Ⓒ 26.2 in.^{3} Ⓓ 41.9 in.^{3}

QUIZ *for Lessons 2.1–2.3*

Tell whether the relation is a function. *Explain.* *(p. 72)*

1. Input: −5, −4, −3, −2; Output: 1. **Function; each input has exactly one output.**

2.

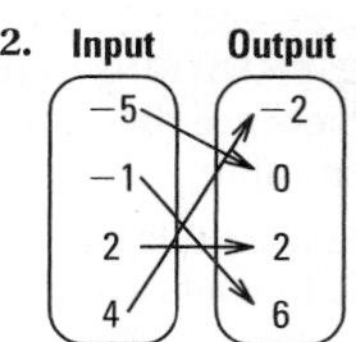

Function; each input has exactly one output.

3.

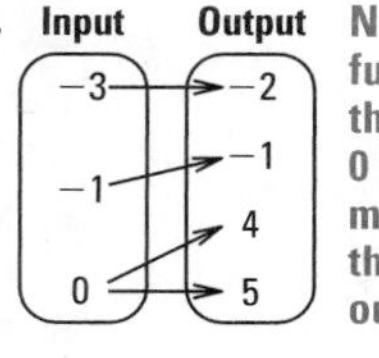

Not a function; the input 0 has more than one output.

Tell whether the lines are *parallel*, *perpendicular*, or *neither*. *(p. 82)*

4. Line 1: through (−3, −7) and (1, 9)
Line 2: through (−1, −4) and (0, −2) **neither**

5. Line 1: through (2, 7) and (−1, −2)
Line 2: through (3, −6) and (−6, −3) **perpendicular**

Graph the equation. *(p. 89)* **6–8. See margin.**

6. $y = -5x + 3$ **7.** $x = 10$ **8.** $4x + 3y = -24$

9. ROWING SPEED In 1999, Tori Murden became the first woman to row across the Atlantic Ocean. She rowed a total of 3333 miles during her crossing. The distance d rowed (in miles) can be modeled by $d = 41t$ where t represents the time rowed (in days) at an average rate of 41 miles per day. Graph the function, and determine a reasonable domain and range. Then estimate how long it took Tori Murden to row 1000 miles. *(p. 72)* **See margin for art; domain: $0 \le t \le \frac{3333}{41}$, range: $0 \le d \le 3333$; about 24 days**

5 ASSESS AND RETEACH

Daily Homework Quiz

Transparency Available

1. Compare the graph of $y = x + 2$ with the graph of $y = x$. **The graphs both have a slope of 1, but the graph of $y = x + 2$ has a y-intercept of 2 and the graph of $y = x$ has a y-intercept of 0.**
2. Graph $2x - 5y = 10$.

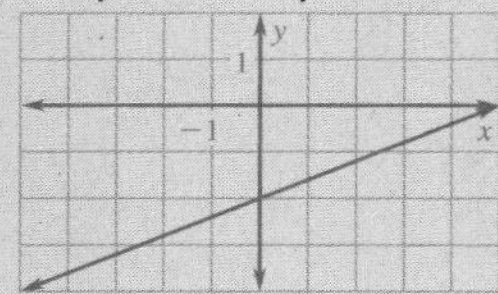

3. Graph $x = 3$.

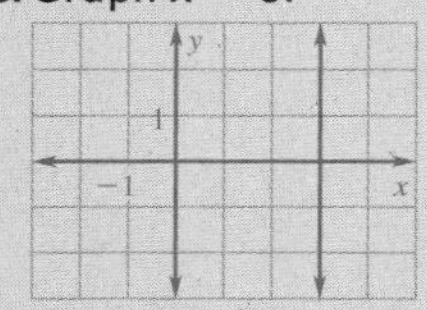

Available at **classzone.com**

Diagnosis/Remediation

- Practice A, B, C in Chapter 2 Resource Book, pp. 30–35
- Study Guide in Chapter 2 Resource Book, pp. 36–37
- Practice Workbook, pp. 20–22
- @HomeTutor

Challenge

Additional challenge is available in the Chapter 2 Resource Book, p. 40.

Quiz

An easily-readable reduced copy of the quiz (with answers) on Lessons 2.1–2.3 from the Assessment Book can be found on p. 70G.

69c.

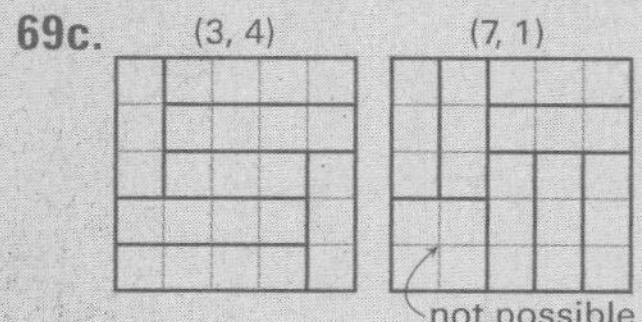

Quiz 6–9. See Additional Answers beginning on p. AA1.

@HomeTutor
classzone.com
Keystrokes

2.3 Graph Equations

QUESTION **How can you use a graphing calculator to graph an equation?**

You can use a graphing calculator to graph equations in two variables. On most calculators, you must first write the equation in the form $y = f(x)$.

EXAMPLE **Graph a linear equation**

Graph the equation $x + 4y = 8$.

STEP 1 ***Solve for y***

First, solve the equation for y so that it can be entered into the calculator.

$$x + 4y = 8$$
$$4y = -x + 8$$
$$y = -\frac{1}{4}x + 2$$

STEP 2 ***Enter equation***

For fractional coefficients, use parentheses. So, enter the equation as $y = -(1/4)x + 2$.

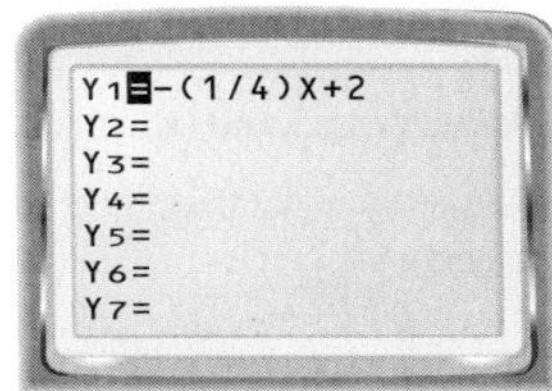

STEP 3 ***Set viewing window and graph***

Enter minimum and maximum x- and y-values and x- and y-scales. The viewing window should show the intercepts. The *standard viewing window* settings and the corresponding graph are shown below.

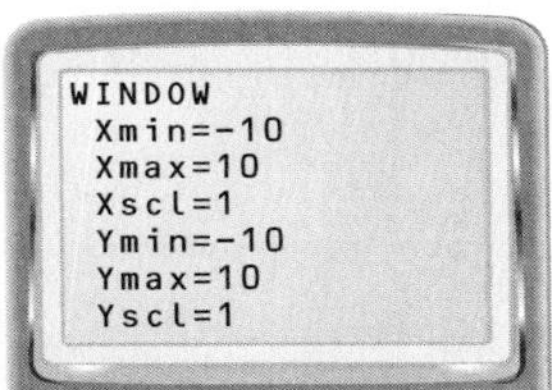

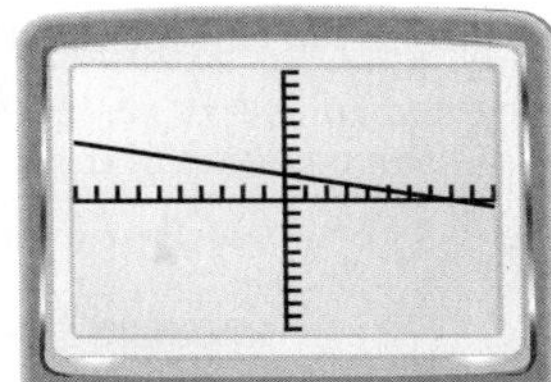

PRACTICE

Graph the equation in a graphing calculator's standard viewing window. 1–3. See margin.

1. $y + 14 = 17 - 2x$
2. $3x - y = 4$
3. $3x - 6y = -18$

Graph the equation using a graphing calculator. Use a viewing window that shows the x- and y-intercepts. 4–6. See margin.

4. $8x = 5y + 16$
5. $4x = 25y - 240$
6. $1.25x + 4.2y = 28.7$

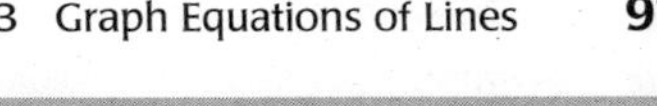

1.
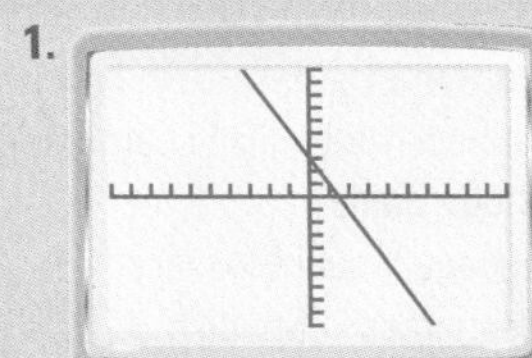

2.
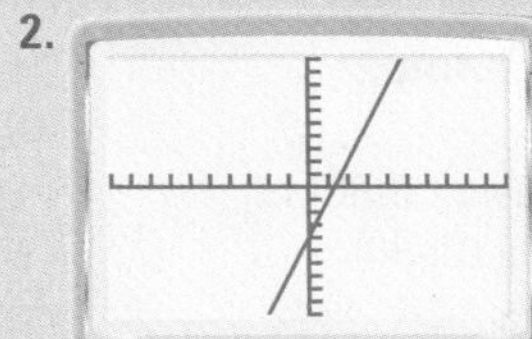

3.
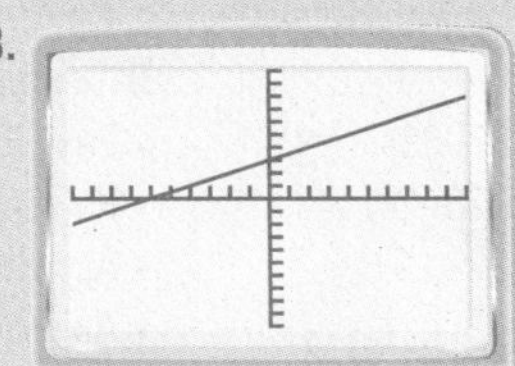

1 PLAN AND PREPARE

Learn the Method

- Students will learn how to graph linear equations in two variables on a graphing calculator.
- Students can use a graphing calculator to check their graphs in Exercises 9–20 and 31–54 in Lesson 2.3.

Keystroke Help

Keystrokes for several models of calculators are available in blackline format in the *Chapter 2 Resource Book.*

2 TEACH

Tips for Success

Make sure students use parentheses if necessary when entering equations into the calculators.

Extra Example

Graph the equation $2x + y = 5$.

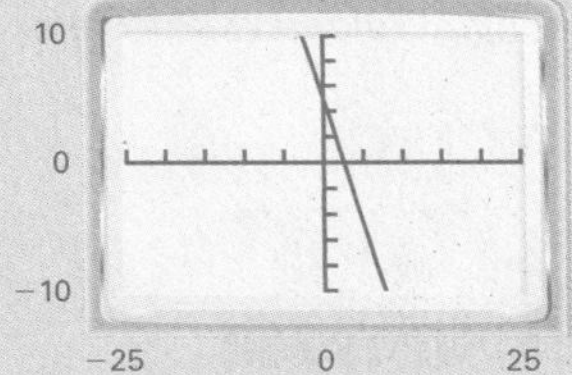

3 ASSESS AND RETEACH

Use the equation $16x - 9y = 200$.

1. Use parentheses to show how you would enter the equation into your graphing calculator. $y = (16/9)x - (200/9)$
2. What viewing window might you use to show the x- and y-intercepts of the graph? *Sample answer:* Xmin = −10, Xmax = 20, Xscl = 5, Ymin = −30, Ymax = 10, Yscl = 5

4–6. See Additional Answers beginning on p. AA1.

1 PLAN AND PREPARE

Warm-Up Exercises

Transparency Available

In a computer generated drawing, a line is represented by the equation $2x - 5y = 15$.

1. Solve the equation for y and identify the slope of the line. $y = \frac{2}{5}x - 3; \frac{2}{5}$
2. What should the slope of a second line in the drawing be if that line must be perpendicular to the first line? $-\frac{5}{2}$

Notetaking Guide

Transparency Available

Promotes interactive learning and notetaking skills, pp. 37–39.

Pacing

Basic: 1 day
Average: 1 day
Advanced: 1 day
Block: 0.5 block with 2.3
• See *Teaching Guide/Lesson Plan.*

2 FOCUS AND MOTIVATE

Essential Question

Big Idea 3, p. 71

How do you write an equation of a line? **Tell students they will learn how to answer this question by using different forms of the equation of a line.**

2.4 Write Equations of Lines

MA-HS-5.3.3 **Students will model, solve and graph first degree, two-variable equations and inequalities in real-world and mathematical problems. DOK 2**

Before You graphed linear equations.
Now You will write linear equations.
Why? So you can model a steady increase or decrease, as in Ex. 51.

Key Vocabulary
• **point-slope form**

KEY CONCEPT — *For Your Notebook*

Writing an Equation of a Line

Given slope m and y-intercept b	Use slope-intercept form: $y = mx + b$
Given slope m and a point (x_1, y_1)	Use **point-slope form**: $y - y_1 = m(x - x_1)$
Given points (x_1, y_1) and (x_2, y_2)	First use the slope formula to find m. Then use point-slope form with either given point.

EXAMPLE 1 Write an equation given the slope and y-intercept

Write an equation of the line shown.

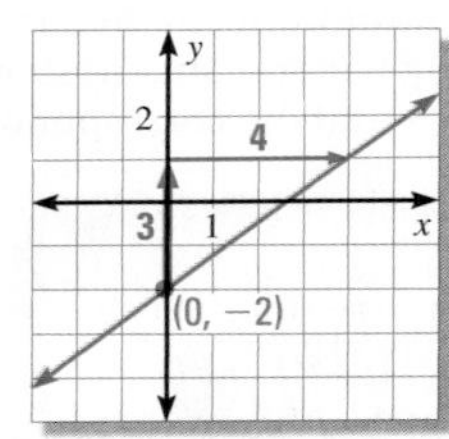

Solution

From the graph, you can see that the slope is $m = \frac{3}{4}$ and the y-intercept is $b = -2$. Use slope-intercept form to write an equation of the line.

$y = mx + b$ — **Use slope-intercept form.**

$y = \frac{3}{4}x + (-2)$ — **Substitute $\frac{3}{4}$ for m and -2 for b.**

$y = \frac{3}{4}x - 2$ — **Simplify.**

 at classzone.com

✓ GUIDED PRACTICE for Example 1

Write an equation of the line that has the given slope and y-intercept.

1. $m = 3, b = 1$ $y = 3x + 1$
2. $m = -2, b = -4$ $y = -2x - 4$
3. $m = -\frac{3}{4}, b = \frac{7}{2}$ $y = -\frac{3}{4}x + \frac{7}{2}$

Resource Planning Guide

Chapter Resource Book
• Teaching Guide/Lesson Plan (pp. 41–42)
• Activity Master (p. 43)
• Practice levels A, B, C (pp. 44–46)
• Study Guide (pp. 47–48)
• Catch-up for Absent Students (p. 49)
• Problem Solving Workshop (p. 50)
• Challenge (p. 52)

Workbooks
• Notetaking Guide (pp. 37–39)
• Practice Workbook (pp. 23–24)

Teaching Options
• **Power Presentations CD-ROM** provides dynamic electronic teaching resources for the classroom.
• **Activity Generator CD-ROM** provides editable activities for all ability levels.

Interactive Technology
• Easy Planner
• Power Presentations CD-ROM
• Activity Generator CD-ROM
• Animated Algebra
• Test Generator CD-ROM
• Online Quiz
• eWorkbook
• eEdition
• @HomeTutor

Resources for English Learners
• Quick Reference for English Learners
• Spanish Study Guide
• Multi-Language Visual Glossary
• Student Resources in Spanish

See also the *Algebra 2 Toolkit* for more strategies for meeting individual needs.

EXAMPLE 2 Write an equation given the slope and a point

Write an equation of the line that passes through (5, 4) and has a slope of −3.

Solution

Because you know the slope and a point on the line, use point-slope form to write an equation of the line. Let $(x_1, y_1) = (5, 4)$ and $m = -3$.

SIMPLIFY EQUATIONS

In this book, equations written in point-slope form will be simplified to slope-intercept form.

$y - y_1 = m(x - x_1)$	**Use point-slope form.**
$y - 4 = -3(x - 5)$	**Substitute for m, x_1, and y_1.**
$y - 4 = -3x + 15$	**Distributive property**
$y = -3x + 19$	**Write in slope-intercept form.**

EXAMPLE 3 Write equations of parallel or perpendicular lines

Write an equation of the line that passes through (−2, 3) and is (a) parallel to, and (b) perpendicular to, the line $y = -4x + 1$.

Solution

a. The given line has a slope of $m_1 = -4$. So, a line parallel to it has a slope of $m_2 = m_1 = -4$. You know the slope and a point on the line, so use the point-slope form with $(x_1, y_1) = (-2, 3)$ to write an equation of the line.

$y - y_1 = m_2(x - x_1)$	**Use point-slope form.**
$y - 3 = -4(x - (-2))$	**Substitute for m_2, x_1, and y_1.**
$y - 3 = -4(x + 2)$	**Simplify.**
$y - 3 = -4x - 8$	**Distributive property**
$y = -4x - 5$	**Write in slope-intercept form.**

b. A line perpendicular to a line with slope $m_1 = -4$ has a slope of $m_2 = -\frac{1}{m_1} = \frac{1}{4}$. Use point-slope form with $(x_1, y_1) = (-2, 3)$.

$y - y_1 = m_2(x - x_1)$	**Use point-slope form.**
$y - 3 = \frac{1}{4}(x - (-2))$	**Substitute for m_2, x_1, and y_1.**
$y - 3 = \frac{1}{4}(x + 2)$	**Simplify.**
$y - 3 = \frac{1}{4}x + \frac{1}{2}$	**Distributive property**
$y = \frac{1}{4}x + \frac{7}{2}$	**Write in slope-intercept form.**

GUIDED PRACTICE for Examples 2 and 3

4. Write an equation of the line that passes through (−1, 6) and has a slope of 4.

5. Write an equation of the line that passes through (4, −2) and is **(a)** parallel to, and **(b)** perpendicular to, the line $y = 3x - 1$.

4. $y = 4x + 10$

5a. $y = 3x - 14$

5b. $y = -\frac{1}{3}x - \frac{2}{3}$

Motivating the Lesson

Some real-life data can be represented by linear equations. By knowing two data points or one point and the slope, it is possible to write the linear equation that represents the data.

3 TEACH

Extra Example 1

Write an equation of the line shown.

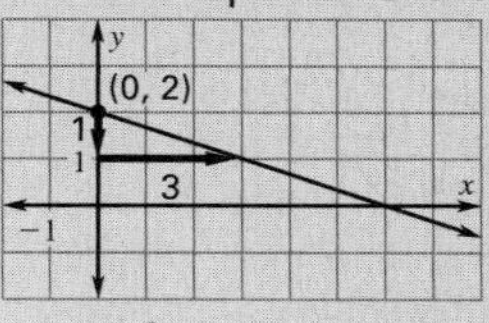

$y = -\frac{1}{3}x + 2$

Animated Algebra classzone.com

An **Animated Algebra** activity is available on-line for **Example 1**. This activity is also available on the **Power Presentations CD-ROM**.

Extra Example 2

Write an equation of the line that passes through (8, −1) and has a slope of $-\frac{1}{2}$. $y = -\frac{1}{2}x + 3$

Extra Example 3

Write an equation of the line that passes through (−2, 1) and is (a) parallel to, and (b) perpendicular to, the line $y = -3x + 1$.

a. $y = -3x - 5$; b. $y = \frac{1}{3}x + \frac{5}{3}$

Key Question to Ask for Example 3

- How are the lines in part (a) and part (b) related? They are perpendicular.

Differentiated Instruction

Auditory Learners Some students find it difficult to remember a concept they cannot verbalize. Mathematical equations with subscripts may be particularly challenging. Remind students to read the point-slope form aloud as "*y* minus *y*-one equals *m* times *x* minus *x*-one" or have them include the term "sub" as in "*y* minus *y* sub one equals *m* times *x* minus *x* sub one" to remember the subscript.

See also the *Algebra 2 Toolkit* for more strategies.

Extra Example 4

Write an equation of the line that passes through (−8, 20) and (−6, 15). $y = -\frac{5}{2}x$

Key Question to Ask for Example 4

- How can you check that $y = -4x + 18$ is the correct equation? **Substitute 5 and 2 for x to check that you get −2 and 10, respectively.**

Mathematical Reasoning

As you discuss Example 4 with your students, point out that the slope-intercept form of a linear equation is a special case of the point-slope form of the equation. Substituting $(0, b)$ for (x_1, y_1) in the point-slope form will yield the slope intercept form of the equation.

Extra Example 5

In a chemistry experiment you record the temperature of a compound to be −5°F one minute after you begin the experiment. Six minutes after you begin the experiment, the temperature is 20°F. Write a linear equation that models the temperature of the compound in relation to elapsed time. $y = 5x - 10$

Key Question to Ask for Example 5

- What does the y-intercept of the equation $y = 0.086x + 2.00$ represent? **2,000,000; the number of females who participated in U.S. high school sports in the school year ending in 1993**

EXAMPLE 4 Write an equation given two points

Write an equation of the line that passes through (5, −2) and (2, 10).

ANOTHER WAY

For an alternative method for solving the problem in Example 4, turn to page 105 for the **Problem Solving Workshop**.

Solution

The line passes through $(x_1, y_1) = (5, -2)$ and $(x_2, y_2) = (2, 10)$. Find its slope.

$$m = \frac{y_2 - y_1}{x_2 - x_1} = \frac{10 - (-2)}{2 - 5} = \frac{12}{-3} = -4$$

You know the slope and a point on the line, so use point-slope form with either given point to write an equation of the line. Choose $(x_1, y_1) = (2, 10)$.

$y - y_1 = m(x - x_1)$	**Use point-slope form.**
$y - 10 = -4(x - 2)$	**Substitute for m, x_1, and y_1.**
$y - 10 = -4x + 8$	**Distributive property**
$y = -4x + 18$	**Write in slope-intercept form.**

EXAMPLE 5 Write a model using slope-intercept form

SPORTS In the school year ending in 1993, 2.00 million females participated in U.S. high school sports. By 2003, the number had increased to 2.86 million. Write a linear equation that models female sports participation.

Solution

STEP 1 **Define** the variables. Let x represent the time (in years) since 1993 and let y represent the number of participants (in millions).

STEP 2 **Identify** the initial value and rate of change. The initial value is 2.00. The rate of change is the slope m.

AVOID ERRORS

Because time is defined in years since 1993 in Step 1, 1993 corresponds to $x_1 = 0$ and 2003 corresponds to $x_2 = 10$.

$$m = \frac{y_2 - y_1}{x_2 - x_1} = \frac{2.86 - 2.00}{10 - 0} = \frac{0.86}{10} = 0.086$$ **Use $(x_1, y_1) = (0, 2.00)$ and $(x_2, y_2) = (10, 2.86)$.**

STEP 3 **Write** a verbal model. Then write a linear equation.

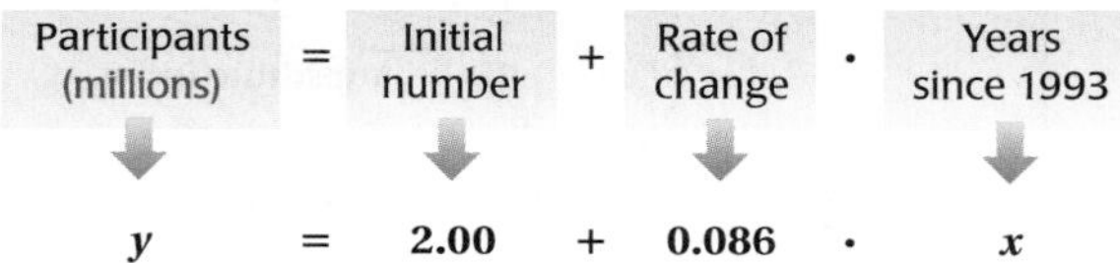

▸ In slope-intercept form, a linear model is $y = 0.086x + 2.00$.

GUIDED PRACTICE for Examples 4 and 5

Write an equation of the line that passes through the given points.

6. (−2, 5), (4, −7) $y = -2x + 1$

7. (6, 1), (−3, −8) $y = x - 5$

8. (−1, 2), (10, 0) $y = -\frac{2}{11}x + \frac{20}{11}$

9. SPORTS In Example 5, the corresponding data for males are 3.42 million participants in 1993 and 3.99 million participants in 2003. Write a linear equation that models male participation in U.S. high school sports. $y = 0.057x + 3.42$

EXAMPLE 6 Write a model using standard form

ONLINE MUSIC You have \$30 to spend on downloading songs for your digital music player. Company A charges \$.79 per song, and company B charges \$.99 per song. Write an equation that models this situation.

Solution

Write a verbal model. Then write an equation.

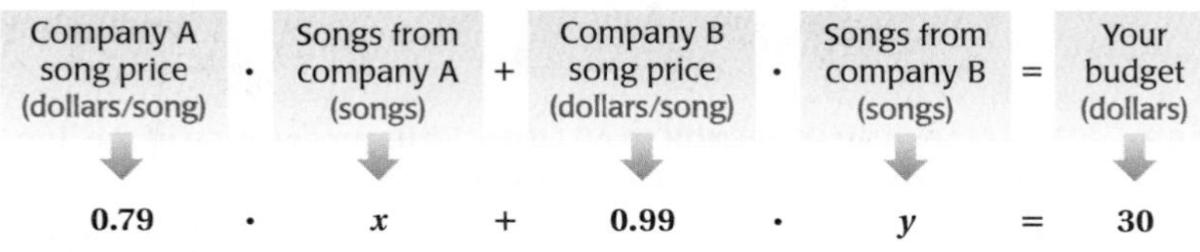

Company A song price (dollars/song)
·
Songs from company A (songs)
+
Company B song price (dollars/song)
·
Songs from company B (songs)
=
Your budget (dollars)
0.79 · x + 0.99 · y = 30

▶ An equation for this situation is $0.79x + 0.99y = 30$.

GUIDED PRACTICE for Example 6

10. **WHAT IF?** In Example 6, suppose that company A charges \$.69 per song and company B charges \$.89 per song. Write an equation that models this situation. $0.69x + 0.89y = 30$

2.4 EXERCISES

HOMEWORK KEY

○ = **WORKED-OUT SOLUTIONS** on p. WS3 for Exs. 15, 35, and 53

★ = **STANDARDIZED TEST PRACTICE** Exs. 2, 26, 39, 47, and 53

◆ = **MULTIPLE REPRESENTATIONS** Ex. 57

SKILL PRACTICE

A

1. **VOCABULARY** Copy and complete: The linear equation $6x + 8y = 72$ is written in _?_ form. standard

2. ★ **WRITING** Given two points on a line, explain how you can use point-slope form to write an equation of the line. First, use the slope formula to find m. Then use the point-slope formula with either point.

EXAMPLE 1 on p. 98 for Exs. 3–8

SLOPE-INTERCEPT FORM **Write an equation of the line that has the given slope and *y*-intercept.**

3. $m = 0, b = 2$ $y = 2$
4. $m = 3, b = -4$ $y = 3x - 4$
5. $m = 6, b = 0$ $y = 6x$
6. $m = \frac{2}{3}, b = 4$ $y = \frac{2}{3}x + 4$
7. $m = -\frac{5}{4}, b = 7$ $y = -\frac{5}{4}x + 7$
8. $m = -5, b = -1$ $y = -5x - 1$

EXAMPLE 2 on p. 99 for Exs. 9–19

POINT-SLOPE FORM **Write an equation of the line that passes through the given point and has the given slope.**

9. $(0, -2), m = 4$ $y = 4x - 2$
10. $(3, -1), m = -3$ $y = -3x + 8$
11. $(-4, 3), m = 2$ $y = 2x + 11$
12. $(-5, -6), m = 0$ $y = -6$
13. $(8, 13), m = -9$ $y = -9x + 85$
14. $(12, 0), m = \frac{3}{4}$ $y = \frac{3}{4}x - 9$
15. $(7, -3), m = -\frac{4}{7}$
16. $(-4, 2), m = \frac{3}{2}$ $y = \frac{3}{2}x + 8$
17. $(9, -5), m = -\frac{1}{3}$

5. $y = -\frac{4}{7}x + 1$

7. $y = -\frac{1}{3}x - 2$

Extra Example 6

You have \$6 to spend on drinks and a salad at the school cafeteria. The drinks cost \$1.25 each and the salad costs \$.20 per ounce. Write an equation that models this situation. $1.25x + 0.20y = 6$

Key Question to Ask for Example 6

- What does the y-intercept of $0.79x + 0.99y = 30$ represent? the number of \$.99 songs you can buy if you do not buy any \$.79 songs

Closing the Lesson

Have students summarize the major points of the lesson and answer the Essential Question: How do you write an equation of a line?

- You can write an equation of a line if you are given the slope and y-intercept, the slope and a point, or two points on a line.

Given the slope m of a line and its y-intercept b, you can use the slope-intercept form $y = mx + b$ to write an equation of the line.

Given a point (x_1, y_1) on a line and the slope m of the line, you can use the point-slope form, $y - y_1 = m(x - x_1)$, to write an equation of the line.

Given two points on a line, you can first find the slope of the line from the points. Then you can use the point-slope form of a linear equation with either point to write an equation of the line.

4 PRACTICE AND APPLY

Assignment Guide

Answer Transparencies available for all exercises

Basic:
Day 1: pp. 101–104
Exs. 1–5, 9–17 odd, 18–23, 26, 27–37 odd, 39–42, 50–55, 59

Average:
Day 1: pp. 101–104
Exs. 1, 2, 4–16 even, 18–26, 28–38 even, 39, 43–47, 50–57, 60

Advanced:
Day 1: pp. 101–104
Exs. 1, 2, 7, 8, 15–17, 23–26, 33–49*, 51–58*

Block:
pp. 101–104
Exs. 1, 2, 4–16 even, 18–26, 28–38 even, 39, 43–47, 50–57, 60 (with 2.3)

Differentiated Instruction

See *Algebra 2 Best Practices Toolkit* for suggestions on addressing the needs of a diverse classroom.

Homework Check

For a quick check of student understanding of key concepts, go over the following exercises:

Basic: 4, 13, 20, 33, 50
Average: 6, 14, 22, 34, 52
Advanced: 8, 16, 24, 36, 54

Extra Practice

- Student Edition, p. 1011
- Chapter 2 Resource Book: Practice levels A, B, C, pp. 44–46

Practice Worksheet

An easily-readable reduced practice page (with answers) for this lesson can be found on p. 70C.

ERROR ANALYSIS ***Describe*** **and correct the error in writing an equation of the line that passes through the given point and has the given slope.**

18, 19. See margin.

18. $(-4, 2)$, $m = 3$

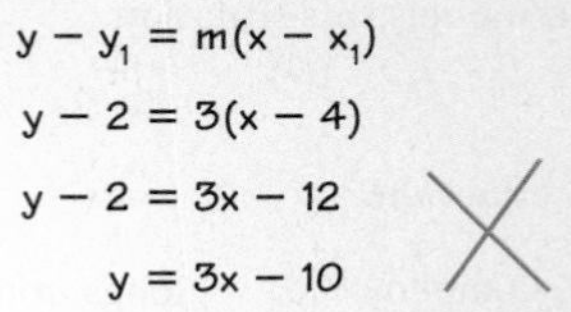

$y - y_1 = m(x - x_1)$
$y - 2 = 3(x - 4)$
$y - 2 = 3x - 12$
$y = 3x - 10$

19. $(5, 1)$, $m = -2$

$y - y_1 = m(x - x_1)$
$y - 5 = -2(x - 1)$
$y - 5 = -2x + 2$
$y = -2x + 7$

EXAMPLE 3 on p. 99 for Exs. 20–26

PARALLEL AND PERPENDICULAR LINES **Write an equation of the line that passes through the given point and satisfies the given condition.**

20. $(-3, -5)$; parallel to $y = -4x + 1$ $y = -4x - 17$

21. $(7, 1)$; parallel to $y = -x + 3$ $y = -x + 8$

22. $(2, 8)$; parallel to $y = 3x - 2$ $y = 3x + 2$

23. $(4, 1)$; perpendicular to $y = \frac{1}{3}x + 3$ $y = -3x + 13$

24. $(-6, 2)$; perpendicular to $y = -2$ $y = \frac{1}{2}x + 5$

25. $(3, -1)$; perpendicular to $y = 4x + 1$ $y = -\frac{1}{4}x - \frac{1}{4}$

26. ★ **MULTIPLE CHOICE** What is an equation of the line that passes through $(1, 4)$ and is perpendicular to the line $y = 2x - 3$? C

Ⓐ $y = 2x + 2$ Ⓑ $y = \frac{1}{2}x + \frac{7}{2}$ Ⓒ $y = -\frac{1}{2}x + \frac{9}{2}$ Ⓓ $y = -\frac{1}{2}x + 4$

EXAMPLE 4 on p. 100 for Exs. 27–38

VISUAL THINKING **Write an equation of the line.**

27.

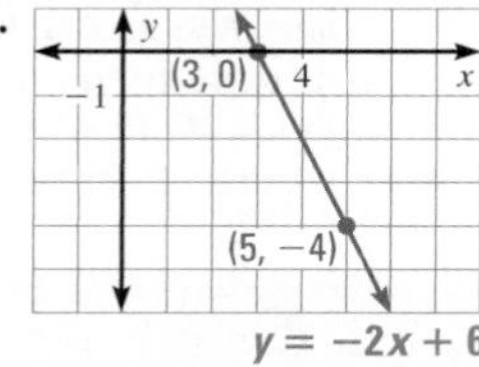

$y = -2x + 6$

28.

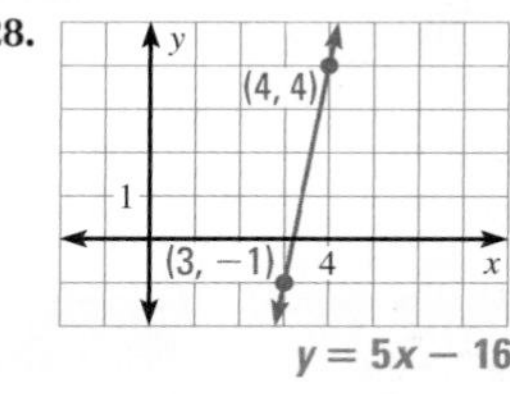

$y = 5x - 16$

29.

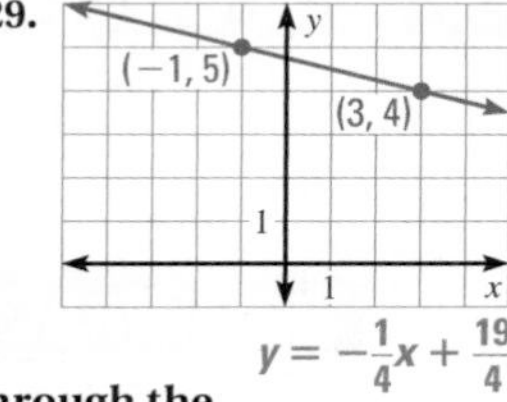

$y = -\frac{1}{4}x + \frac{19}{4}$

WRITING EQUATIONS **Write an equation of the line that passes through the given points.**

30. $(-1, 3)$, $(2, 9)$ $y = 2x + 5$

31. $(4, -1)$, $(6, -7)$ $y = -3x + 11$

32. $(-2, -3)$, $(2, -1)$ $y = \frac{1}{2}x - 2$

33. $(0, 7)$, $(3, 5)$ $y = -\frac{2}{3}x + 7$

34. $(-1, 2)$, $(3, -4)$ $y = -\frac{3}{2}x + \frac{1}{2}$

(35.) $(-5, -2)$, $(-3, 8)$ $y = 5x + 23$

36. $(15, 20)$, $(-12, 29)$ $y = -\frac{1}{3}x + 25$

37. $(3.5, 7)$, $(-1, 20.5)$ $y = -3x + 17.5$

38. $(0.6, 0.9)$, $(3.4, -2.6)$ $y = -1.25x + 1.65$

B

39. ★ **MULTIPLE CHOICE** Which point lies on the line that passes through the point $(9, -5)$ and has a slope of -6? C

Ⓐ $(6, 10)$ Ⓑ $(6, 6)$ Ⓒ $(7, 7)$ Ⓓ $(6, -4)$

STANDARD FORM **Write an equation in standard form $Ax + By = C$ of the line that satisfies the given conditions. Use integer values for A, B, and C.**

40. $m = -3$, $b = 5$ $3x + y = 5$

41. $m = 4$, $b = -3$ $-4x + y = -3$

42. $m = -\frac{3}{2}$, passes through $(4, -7)$ $3x + 2y = -2$

43. $m = \frac{4}{5}$, passes through $(2, 3)$ $4x - 5y = -7$

44. passes through $(-1, 3)$ and $(-6, -7)$ $2x - y = -5$

45. passes through $(2, 8)$ and $(-4, 16)$ $4x + 3y = 32$

Animated Algebra at classzone.com

○ = WORKED-OUT SOLUTIONS on p. WS1 ★ = STANDARDIZED TEST PRACTICE

102

18. Subtracting the x-coordinate in the point gives $x - (-4) = x + 4$; $y - 2 = 3(x + 4)$, $y - 2 = 3x + 12$, $y = 3x + 14$.

19. The x- and y-coordinates were transposed; $y - 1 = -2(x - 5)$, $y - 1 = -2x + 10$, $y = -2x + 11$.

46. **REASONING** Write an equation of the line that passes through (3, 4) and satisfies the given condition.

a. Parallel to $y = -2$ $y = 4$ b. Perpendicular to $y = -2$ $x = 3$

c. Parallel to $x = -2$ $x = 3$ d. Perpendicular to $x = -2$ $y = 4$

47. ★ **OPEN-ENDED MATH** Write an equation of a line ℓ such that ℓ and the lines $y = -3x + 5$ and $y = 2x + 1$ form a right triangle. *Sample answer:* $y = -\frac{1}{2}x + 8$

C 48. **REASONING** Consider two distinct nonvertical lines $A_1x + B_1y = C_1$ and $A_2x + B_2y = C_2$. Show that the following statements are true. **a, b. See margin.**

a. If the lines are parallel, then $A_1B_2 = A_2B_1$.

b. If the lines are perpendicular, then $A_1A_2 + B_1B_2 = 0$.

49. **CHALLENGE** Show that an equation of the line with x-intercept a and y-intercept b is $\frac{x}{a} + \frac{y}{b} = 1$. This is the *intercept form* of a linear equation. **See margin.**

PROBLEM SOLVING

EXAMPLE 5 A on p. 100 for Exs. 50–51

50. **CAR EXPENSES** You buy a used car for \$6500. The monthly cost of owning the car (including insurance, fuel, maintenance, and taxes) averages \$350. Write an equation that models the total cost of buying and owning the car. $c = 350m + 6500$

@HomeTutor for problem solving help at classzone.com

51. **HOUSING** Since its founding, a volunteer group has restored 50 houses. It plans to restore 15 houses per year in the future. Write an equation that models the total number n of restored houses t years from now. $n = 15t + 50$

@HomeTutor for problem solving help at classzone.com

EXAMPLE 6 on p. 101 for Exs. 52–54

52. **GARDENING** You have a rectangular plot measuring 16 feet by 25 feet in a community garden. You want to grow tomato plants that each need 8 square feet of space and pepper plants that each need 5 square feet. Write an equation that models how many tomato plants and how many pepper plants you can grow. How many pepper plants can you grow if you grow 15 tomato plants? $8t + 5p = 400$; 56 pepper plants

53. ★ **SHORT RESPONSE** Concert tickets cost \$15 for general admission, but only \$9 with a student ID. Ticket sales total \$4500. Write and graph an equation that models this situation. *Explain* how to use your graph to find how many student tickets were sold if 200 general admission tickets were sold.

53. $15x + 9y = 4500$, see margin for art; find the point on the line where x is 200, then the corresponding y-coordinate is how many student tickets were sold.

B 54. **MULTI-STEP PROBLEM** A company will lease office space in two buildings. The annual cost is \$21.75 per square foot in the first building and \$17 per square foot in the second. The company has \$86,000 budgeted for rent.

a. Write an equation that models the possible amounts of space rented in the buildings. $21.75x + 17y = 86{,}000$

b. How many square feet of space can be rented in the first building if 2500 square feet are rented in the second? 2000 ft²

c. If the company wants to rent equal amounts of space in the buildings, what is the total number of square feet that can be rented? about 4439 ft²

Avoiding Common Errors

Exercises 9–17 Remind students that when they use the point-slope form of a linear equation, they should substitute the given coordinates of a point for x_1 and y_1 and not for x and y.

Study Strategy

Exercises 30–38 Make sure that students understand that they can use either point to write an equation of the line. Generally they should choose the point that involves the easier computation.

Vocabulary

Exercises 40–45 To help students determine which form of a linear equation to first use, ask them to let the names of the forms guide them. For example, using the slope-intercept form suggests that they know the slope and the y-intercept of the line. Using the point-slope form suggests that they know a point on the line and its slope.

An **Animated Algebra** activity is available on-line for **Exercises 40–45**. This activity is also available on the **Power Presentations CD-ROM**.

49. *Sample answer:* The two points on the line are $(a, 0)$ and $(0, b)$. The slope of the line is $-\frac{b}{a}$, so the equation is $y = -\frac{b}{a}x + b$. Multiplying by a to clear fractions gives $ay = -bx + ab$. Adding bx to both sides gives $bx + ay = ab$, then dividing by ab results in $\frac{x}{a} + \frac{y}{b} = 1$.

53.

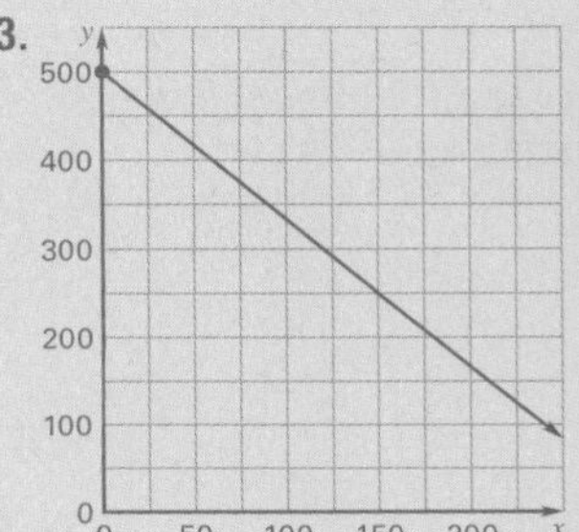

48a. Since the lines are parallel, the slopes must be equal. $m_1 = -\frac{A_1}{B_1}$ and $m_2 = -\frac{A_2}{B_2}$, so $-\frac{A_1}{B_1} = -\frac{A_2}{B_2}$. Cross multiplication gives $A_1B_2 = A_2B_1$.

48b. Since the lines are perpendicular, the slopes must be negative reciprocals of each other. $m_1 = -\frac{A_1}{B_1}$ and $m_2 = -\frac{A_2}{B_2}$, so $-\frac{A_1}{B_1} = \frac{B_2}{A_2}$. Cross multiplication gives $A_1A_2 = -B_1B_2$, then adding B_1B_2 to both sides gives $A_1A_2 + B_1B_2 = 0$.

5 ASSESS AND RETEACH

Daily Homework Quiz

Transparency Available

Write an equation of the line that satisfies the given conditions.

1. passes through (3, 0) and (−5, 2) $y = -\frac{1}{4}x + \frac{3}{4}$
2. passes through (0, 9) and is perpendicular to $y = -\frac{2}{3}x - 1$ $y = \frac{3}{2}x + 9$
3. $m = 4$, passes through (1, −8) $y = 4x - 12$
4. passes through (−2, 3) and is parallel to $y = \frac{1}{4}x - 6$ $y = \frac{1}{4}x + \frac{7}{2}$
5. Your jazz band can spend \$1500 to sew members' names and instruments on their jackets. The sewing cost is \$12 per instrument and \$5 per letter. Write an equation that models this situation. $12x + 5y = 1500$

Online Quiz

Available at **classzone.com**

Diagnosis/Remediation

- Practice A, B, C in Chapter 2 Resource Book, pp. 44–46
- Study Guide in Chapter 2 Resource Book, pp. 47–48
- Practice Workbook, pp. 23–24
- @HomeTutor

Challenge

Additional challenge is available in the Chapter 2 Resource Book, p. 52.

57b–c. See Additional Answers beginning on p. AA1.

55. **CABLE TELEVISION** In 1994, the average monthly cost for expanded basic cable television service was \$21.62. In 2004, this cost had increased to \$38.23. Write a linear equation that models the monthly cost as a function of the number of years since 1994. Predict the average monthly cost of expanded basic cable television service in 2010. $y = 1.66x + 21.62$; \$48.18

56. **TIRE PRESSURE** Automobile tire pressure increases about 1 psi (pound per square inch) for each 10°F increase in air temperature. At an air temperature of 55°F, a tire's pressure is 30 psi. Write an equation that models the tire's pressure as a function of air temperature. $y = \frac{1}{10}x + 24.5$

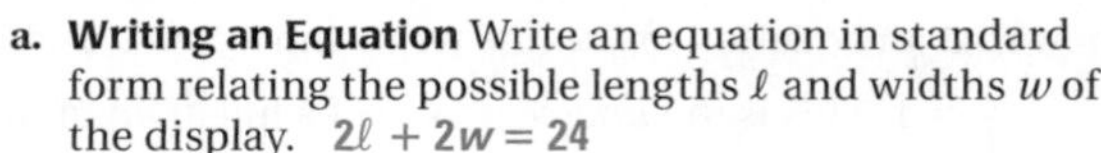

57. **MULTIPLE REPRESENTATIONS** Your class wants to make a rectangular spirit display, and has 24 feet of decorative border to enclose the display

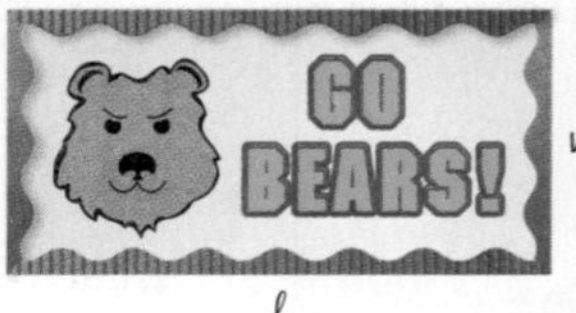

   a. **Writing an Equation** Write an equation in standard form relating the possible lengths ℓ and widths w of the display. $2\ell + 2w = 24$

   b. **Drawing a Graph** Graph the equation from part (a). **b, c. See margin.**

   c. **Making a Table** Make a table of at least five possible pairs of dimensions for the display.

C 58. **CHALLENGE** You are participating in a dance-a-thon to raise money for a class trip. Donors can pledge an amount of money for each hour you dance, a fixed amount of money that does not depend on how long you dance, or both. The table shows the amounts pledged by four donors. Write an equation that models the total amount y of money you will raise from the donors if you dance for x hours. $y = 15x + 70$

Donor	Hourly amount	Fixed amount
Clare	\$4	\$15
Emilia	\$8	None
Julio	None	\$35
Max	\$3	\$20

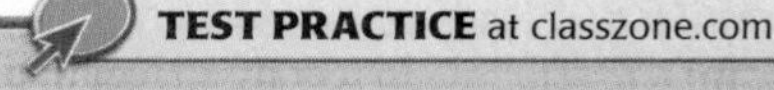

TEST PRACTICE at classzone.com

KENTUCKY MIXED REVIEW

59. At the end of the week, John has \$180 in his bank account. During the week he withdrew \$30 for lunches, deposited a \$125 paycheck, and withdrew \$22 to buy a shirt. How much money did John have in his account at the beginning of the week? **C**

   (A) \$95 (B) \$100 (C) \$107 (D) \$117

60. Use the table to determine the expression that best represents the total measure of the interior angles of any convex polygon having n sides. **B**

Number of sides, n	3	4	5	6	7
Total measure of interior angles (in degrees)	180	360	540	720	900

   (A) $90(n-1)$ (B) $180(n-2)$

   (C) $360(n-3)$ (D) $\frac{360}{n-1}$

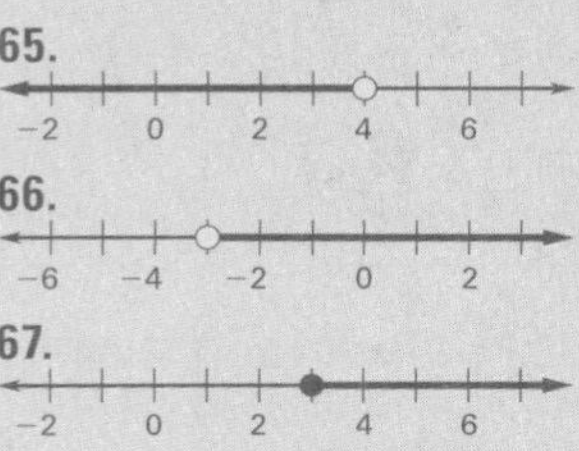

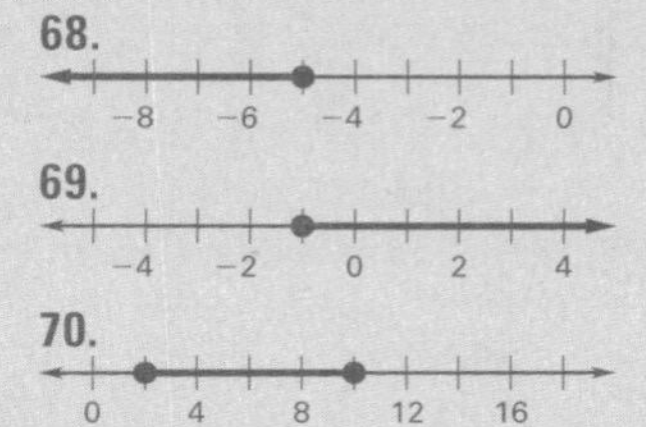

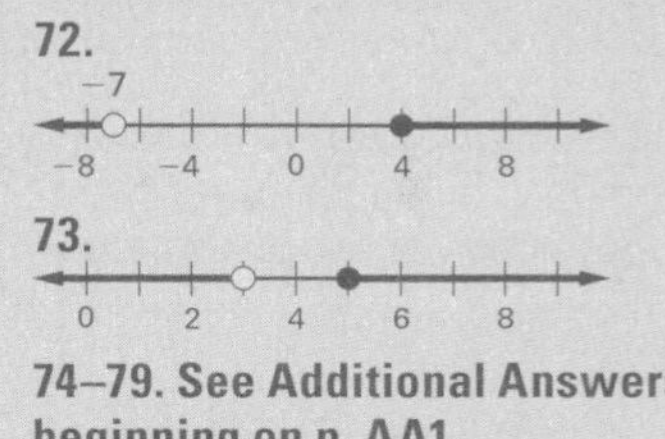

74–79. See Additional Answers beginning on p. AA1.

Using ALTERNATIVE METHODS

Another Way to Solve Example 4, page 100

MULTIPLE REPRESENTATIONS In Example 4 on page 100, you wrote an equation of a line through two given points by first writing the equation in point-slope form and then rewriting it in slope-intercept form. You can also write an equation of a line through two points by using the slope-intercept form to solve for the y-intercept.

PROBLEM

Write an equation of the line that passes through $(5, -2)$ and $(2, 10)$.

METHOD

Solving for the y-Intercept To write an equation of a line through two points, you can substitute the slope and the coordinates of one of the points into $y = mx + b$ and solve for the y-intercept b.

STEP 1 **Find** the slope of the line.

$$m = \frac{10 - (-2)}{2 - 5} = \frac{12}{-3} = -4$$

STEP 2 **Substitute** the slope and the coordinates of one point into the slope-intercept form. Use the point $(5, -2)$.

$$y = mx + b$$
$$-2 = -4(5) + b$$

STEP 3 **Solve** for b.

$$-2 = -20 + b$$
$$18 = b$$

STEP 4 **Substitute** m and b into the slope-intercept form.

$$y = -4x + 18$$

PRACTICE

1. **WRITE AN EQUATION** Use the method above to write an equation of the line that passes through $(2, 15)$ and $(7, 35)$. $y = 4x + 7$

2. **FITNESS** At a speed of 45 yards per minute, a 120 pound swimmer burns 420 calories per hour and a 172 pound swimmer burns 600 calories per hour. Use two different methods to write a linear equation that models the number of calories burned per hour as a function of a swimmer's weight. $y = \frac{45}{13}x + 4.62$

3. **SAFETY** A motorist lights an emergency flare after having a flat tire. After burning for 6 minutes, the flare is 13 inches long. After burning for 20 minutes, it is 6 inches long. Use two different methods to write a linear equation that models the flare's length as a function of time. $y = -\frac{1}{2}x + 16$

4. **SNOWFALL** After 4 hours of snowfall, the snow depth is 8 inches. After 6 hours of snowfall, the snow depth is 9.5 inches. Use two different methods to write a linear equation that models the snow depth as a function of time. $y = \frac{3}{4}x + 5$

5. **ARCHAEOLOGY** Ancient cities often rose in elevation through time as citizens built on top of accumulating rubble and debris. An archaeologist at a site dates artifacts from a depth of 54 feet as 3500 years old and artifacts from a depth of 26 feet as 2600 years old. Use two different methods to write a linear equation that models an artifact's age as a function of depth. $y = 32.14x + 1764.36$

6. **REASONING** Suppose a line has slope m and passes through (x_1, y_1). Write an expression for the y-intercept b in terms of m, x_1, and y_1. $b = -mx_1 + y_1$

Alternative Strategy

The equation in Example 4 on page 100 can be written by solving for the slope and y-intercept. This allows students to see the relationship between the point-slope form of a linear equation and the slope-intercept form of the equation.

Reading Strategy

As they calculate the slope of the equation in Exercise 2, students should see that the speed of 45 yards per minute does not represent a rate of change for this situation.

Kentucky Mixed Review

1. B
2. D
3. A
4. C
5. D
6. A
7. a. $y = -\frac{3}{5}x + 3$
   b. $x = 5$
   c. $y = \frac{5}{3}x + k$ (Students may choose any value k).

Kentucky Mixed Review

Lessons 2.1–2.4

1. **WEBSITES** From January through June, the number of visitors to a news website increased by about 1200 per month. In January, there were 50,000 visitors to the website. Which equation shows the number of visitors v as a function of the number of months t since January?

   A. $v = 50{,}000 - 1200t$

   B. $v = 50{,}000 + 1200t$

   C. $v = 1200 - 50{,}000t$

   D. $v = 1200 + 50{,}000t$

2. **SLOPE** What is the slope of a line parallel to the line $\frac{1}{4}y - 3x = 5$?

   A. -3

   B. $-\frac{3}{4}$

   C. $\frac{1}{4}$

   D. 12

3. **PARALLEL LINES** Which equation represents a line that is parallel to the line $x + 3y = 12$ and contains no points in Quadrant I?

   A. $y = -\frac{1}{3}x - 4$

   B. $y = -\frac{1}{3}x + 8$

   C. $y = -3x - 4$

   D. $y = 3x + 4$

4. **POPULATION** The official population of Baton Rouge, Louisiana, was 219,478 in 1990 and 227,818 in 2000. What is the average rate of change in the population from 1990 to 2000?

   A. -8340 people per year

   B. -834 people per year

   C. 834 people per year

   D. 8340 people per year

5. **FOOTBALL** The costs of general admission and student tickets to a high school football game are shown below. Ticket sales for one game totaled $11,200. Which equation gives the possible numbers of general admission tickets g and student tickets s that were sold?

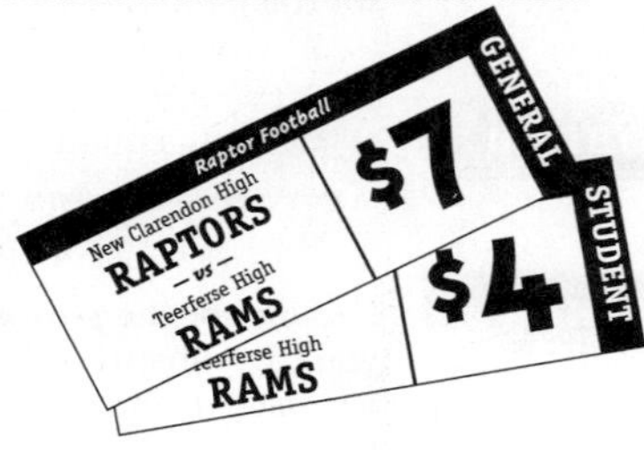

   A. $11{,}200 = 4g - 7s$

   B. $11{,}200 = 4g + 7s$

   C. $11{,}200 = 7g - 4s$

   D. $11{,}200 = 7g + 4s$

6. **PHOTOGRAPHY** Your digital camera has a 512 megabyte memory card. You take pictures at two resolutions, a low resolution requiring 4 megabytes of memory per photo and a high resolution requiring 8 megabytes of memory per photo. Which equation relates the possible numbers of high resolution photos x and low resolution photos y you can take?

   A. $8x + 4y = 512$

   B. $4x + 8y = 512$

   C. $8x - 4y = 512$

   D. $4x - 8y = 512$

7. **OPEN-RESPONSE** Refer to the graph below.

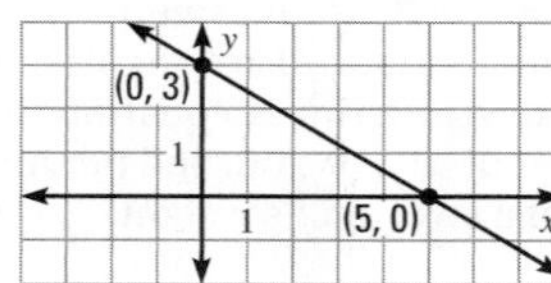

   a. Write the equation of the line.

   b. Write the equation of the vertical line through the x-intercept of the line graphed above.

   c. Write the equation of any line that is perpendicular to the graphed line.

2.5 Model Direct Variation

MA-HS-5.1.7 *Students will apply and use direct and inverse variation to solve real-world and mathematical problems.*

Before You wrote and graphed linear equations.
Now You will write and graph direct variation equations.
Why? So you can model animal migration, as in Ex. 44.

Key Vocabulary
- direct variation
- constant of variation

KEY CONCEPT — *For Your Notebook*

Direct Variation

Equation The equation $y = ax$ represents **direct variation** between x and y, and y is said to *vary directly* with x. The nonzero constant a is called the **constant of variation**.

Graph The graph of a direct variation equation $y = ax$ is a line with slope a and y-intercept 0.

The family of direct variation graphs consists of lines through the origin, such as those shown.

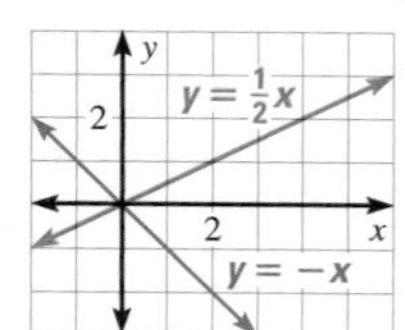

EXAMPLE 1 Write and graph a direct variation equation

Write and graph a direct variation equation that has $(-4, 8)$ as a solution.

Solution

Use the given values of x and y to find the constant of variation.

$y = ax$	Write direct variation equation.
$8 = a(-4)$	Substitute 8 for y and -4 for x.
$-2 = a$	Solve for a.

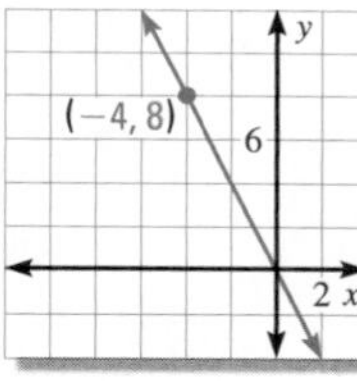

▶ Substituting -2 for a in $y = ax$ gives the direct variation equation $y = -2x$. Its graph is shown.

 at classzone.com

GUIDED PRACTICE for Example 1

Write and graph a direct variation equation that has the given ordered pair as a solution. 1–4. See margin for art.

1. $(3, -9)$ $y = -3x$
2. $(-7, 4)$ $y = -\frac{4}{7}x$
3. $(5, 3)$ $y = \frac{3}{5}x$
4. $(6, -2)$ $y = -\frac{1}{3}x$

1 PLAN AND PREPARE

Warm-Up Exercises

Transparency Available

Solve for a.

1. $10 = 2a$ 5
2. $-5a = -16$ $\frac{16}{5}$
3. Write an equation of the line that passes through the points $(0, 0)$ and $(4, 8)$. $y = 2x$
4. A flower is 4.5 centimeters wide and has a leaf 7.2 centimeters long. What is the ratio of flower width to leaf length? $\frac{5}{8}$

Notetaking Guide

Transparency Available

Promotes interactive learning and notetaking skills, pp. 40–42.

Pacing

Basic: 1 day
Average: 1 day
Advanced: 1 day
Block: 0.5 block with 2.6
- See *Teaching Guide/Lesson Plan.*

2 FOCUS AND MOTIVATE

Essential Question

Big Idea 3, p. 71

What is a constant of variation and how is it related to slope? **Tell students they will learn how to answer this question by studying direct variation.**

Resource Planning Guide

Chapter Resource Book
- Teaching Guide/Lesson Plan (pp. 53–54)
- Practice levels A, B, C (pp. 55–57)
- Study Guide (pp. 58–59)
- Catch-up for Absent Students (p. 60)
- Problem Solving Workshop (p. 61)
- Challenge (p. 62)

Workbooks
- Notetaking Guide (pp. 40–42)
- Practice Workbook (pp. 25–26)

Teaching Options
- **Power Presentations CD-ROM** provides dynamic electronic teaching resources for the classroom.
- **Activity Generator CD-ROM** provides editable activities for all ability levels.

Interactive Technology
- Easy Planner
- Power Presentations CD-ROM
- Activity Generator CD-ROM
- Animated Algebra
- Test Generator CD-ROM
- Online Quiz
- eWorkbook
- eEdition
- @HomeTutor

Resources for English Learners
- Quick Reference for English Learners
- Spanish Study Guide
- Multi-Language Visual Glossary
- Student Resources in Spanish

See also the *Algebra 2 Toolkit* for more strategies for meeting individual needs.

Motivating the Lesson

Have students let x be an arbitrary number of servings of their favorite item from the cafeteria. Then ask them to use the cost per item to write an equation to model the total cost y of x items. Discuss the idea that equations like these model direct variation.

3 TEACH

Extra Example 1

Write and graph a direct variation equation that has $(-3, -9)$ as a solution. $y = 3x$

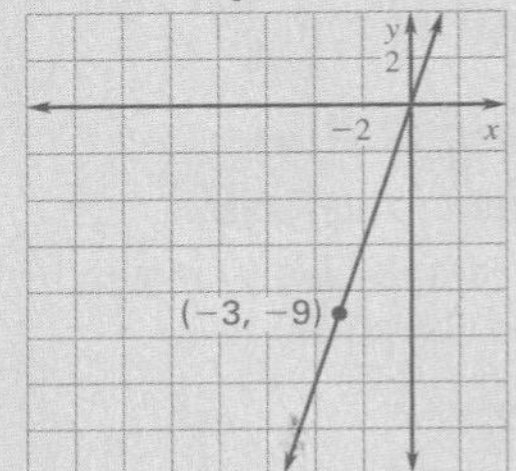

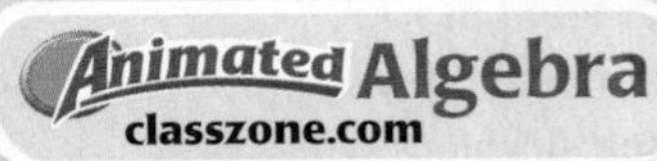

An **Animated Algebra** activity is available on-line for **Example 1**. This activity is also available on the **Power Presentations CD-ROM**.

Extra Example 2

Hooke's Law states that the distance d a spring stretches varies directly with the force f that is applied to it.

a. Suppose a spring stretches 15 inches when a force of 9 pounds is applied. Write an equation that relates d to f. $d = \frac{5}{3}f$

b. Predict the distance that the spring will stretch when a force of 6 pounds is applied. 10 in.

EXAMPLE 2 Write and apply a model for direct variation

METEOROLOGY Hailstones form when strong updrafts support ice particles high in clouds, where water droplets freeze onto the particles. The diagram shows a hailstone at two different times during its formation.

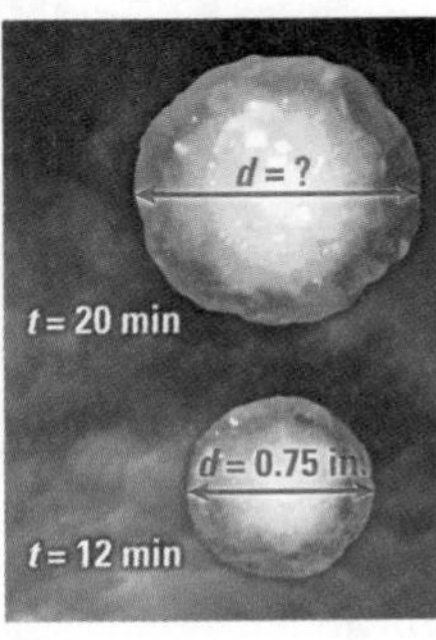

a. Write an equation that gives the hailstone's diameter d (in inches) after t minutes if you assume the diameter varies directly with the time the hailstone takes to form.

b. Using your equation from part (a), predict the diameter of the hailstone after 20 minutes.

Solution

a. Use the given values of t and d to find the constant of variation.

$d = at$ **Write direct variation equation.**

$0.75 = a(12)$ **Substitute 0.75 for d and 12 for t.**

$0.0625 = a$ **Solve for a.**

An equation that relates t and d is $d = 0.0625t$.

b. After $t = 20$ minutes, the predicted diameter of the hailstone is $d = 0.0625(20) = 1.25$ inches.

RATIOS AND DIRECT VARIATION Because the direct variation equation $y = ax$ can be written as $\frac{y}{x} = a$, a set of data pairs (x, y) shows direct variation if the ratio of y to x is constant.

EXAMPLE 3 Use ratios to identify direct variation

SHARKS Great white sharks have triangular teeth. The table below gives the length of a side of a tooth and the body length for each of six great white sharks. Tell whether tooth length and body length show direct variation. If so, write an equation that relates the quantities.

Tooth length, t (cm)	1.8	2.4	2.9	3.6	4.7	5.8
Body length, b (cm)	215	290	350	430	565	695

Solution

Find the ratio of the body length b to the tooth length t for each shark.

AVOID ERRORS
For real-world data, the ratios do not have to be *exactly* the same to show that direct variation is a plausible model.

$\frac{215}{1.8} \approx 119$ $\frac{290}{2.4} \approx 121$ $\frac{350}{2.9} = 121$

$\frac{430}{3.6} \approx 119$ $\frac{565}{4.7} \approx 120$ $\frac{695}{5.8} \approx 120$

▶ Because the ratios are approximately equal, the data show direct variation. An equation relating tooth length and body length is $\frac{b}{t} = 120$, or $b = 120t$.

Differentiated Instruction

English Learners While reading **Exercise 1**, the term *constant of variation* may sound like a contradiction in terms. Explain that it is the one number (constant) that does not change (vary) in a direct variation equation.

See also the *Algebra 2 Toolkit* for more strategies.

✓ **GUIDED PRACTICE** for Examples 2 and 3

5. **WHAT IF?** In Example 2, suppose that a hailstone forming in a cloud has a radius of 0.6 inch. Predict how long it has been forming. 19.2 min

6. **SHARKS** In Example 3, the respective body masses m (in kilograms) of the great white sharks are 80, 220, 375, 730, 1690, and 3195. Tell whether tooth length and body mass show direct variation. If so, write an equation that relates the quantities. not a direct variation

2.5 EXERCISES

HOMEWORK KEY

 = **WORKED-OUT SOLUTIONS** on p. WS3 for Exs. 5, 15, and 41

★ = **STANDARDIZED TEST PRACTICE** Exs. 2, 17, 30, 40, and 44

SKILL PRACTICE

A

1. **VOCABULARY** Define the constant of variation for two variables x and y that vary directly. *Sample answer:* If $y = ax$, then a is the constant of variation. a is a constant ratio of y to x for all ordered pairs (x, y).
2. ★ **WRITING** Given a table of ordered pairs (x, y), describe how to determine whether x and y show direct variation. Find the ratio of y to x for each ordered pair. If the ratios are approximately equal, then it is a direct variation.

EXAMPLE 1 on p. 107 for Exs. 3–10

WRITING AND GRAPHING **Write and graph a direct variation equation that has the given ordered pair as a solution.** 3–10. See margin for art.

3. (2, 6) $y = 3x$
4. (−3, 12) $y = -4x$
5. (6, −21) $y = -3.5x$
6. (4, 10) $y = 2.5x$
7. (−5, −1) $y = 0.2x$
8. (24, −8) $y = -\frac{1}{3}x$
9. $\left(\frac{4}{3}, -4\right)$ $y = -3x$
10. (12.5, 5) $y = 0.4x$

EXAMPLE 2 on p. 108 for Exs. 11–17

WRITING AND EVALUATING **The variables x and y vary directly. Write an equation that relates x and y. Then find y when $x = 12$.**

11. $x = 4, y = 8$ $y = 2x$; 24
12. $x = -3, y = -5$ $y = \frac{5}{3}x$; 20
13. $x = 35, y = -7$ $y = -0.2x$; −2.4
14. $x = -18, y = 4$ $y = -\frac{2}{9}x$; $-2\frac{2}{3}$
15. $x = -4.8, y = -1.6$ $y = \frac{1}{3}x$; 4
16. $x = \frac{2}{3}, y = -10$ $y = -15x$; −180
17. ★ **MULTIPLE CHOICE** Which equation is a direct variation equation that has (3, 18) as a solution? C

Ⓐ $y = 2x^2$ Ⓑ $y = \frac{1}{6}x$ Ⓒ $y = 6x$ Ⓓ $y = 4x + 6$

IDENTIFYING DIRECT VARIATION **Tell whether the equation represents direct variation. If so, give the constant of variation.**

18. $y = -8x$ direct variation; −8
19. $y - 4 = 3x$ not direct variation
20. $3y - 7 = 10x$ not direct variation
21. $2y - 5x = 0$ direct variation; 2.5
22. $5y = -4x$ direct variation; $-\frac{4}{5}$
23. $6y = x$ direct variation; $\frac{1}{6}$

B

WRITING AND SOLVING **The variables x and y vary directly. Write an equation that relates x and y. Then find x when $y = -4$.**

24. $x = 5, y = -15$ $y = -3x$; $\frac{4}{3}$
25. $x = -6, y = 8$ $y = -\frac{4}{3}x$; 3
26. $x = -18, y = -2$ $y = \frac{1}{9}x$; −36
27. $x = -12, y = 84$ $y = -7x$; $\frac{4}{7}$
28. $x = -\frac{20}{3}, y = -\frac{15}{8}$ $y = \frac{9}{32}x$; $-14\frac{2}{9}$
29. $x = -0.5, y = 3.6$ $y = -7.2x$; $\frac{5}{9}$

Extra Example 3

The dimensions of five rectangles, each with an area of 24 square feet are given in the chart. Tell whether length and width show direct variation. If so, write an equation that relates the quantities. no

Length, x	1	2	3	4	5
Width, y	24	12	8	6	4.8

Closing the Lesson

Have students summarize the major points of the lesson and answer the Essential Question: What is a constant of variation?

- Direct variation between x and y is represented by $y = ax$.
- The graph of a direct variation equation $y = ax$ is a line with slope a and y-intercept 0.

The nonzero constant a in the direct variation equation $y = ax$ is called the constant of variation. It represents the slope or rate of change of the direct variation equation.

6.–9.
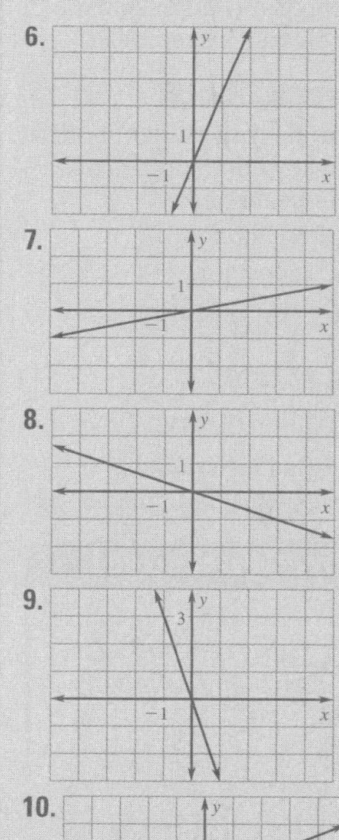

10.
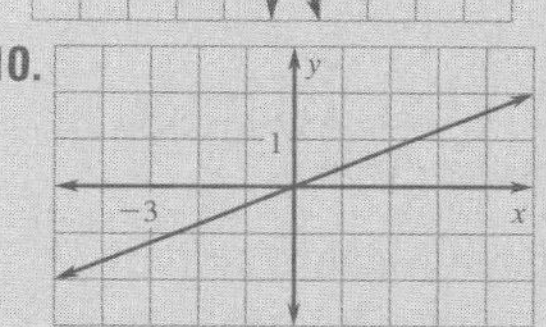

3.
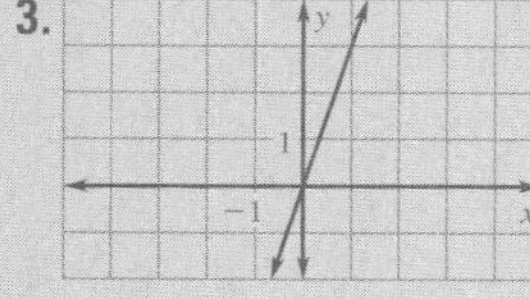

4.
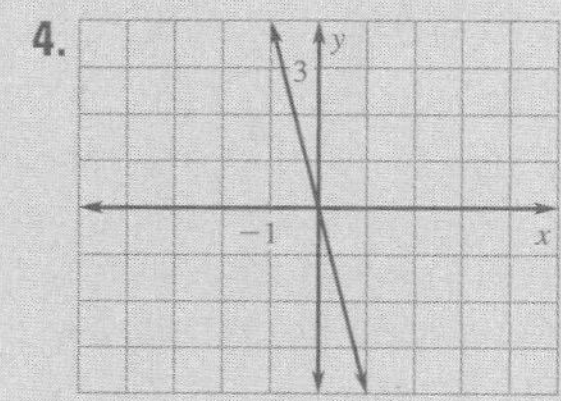

5.
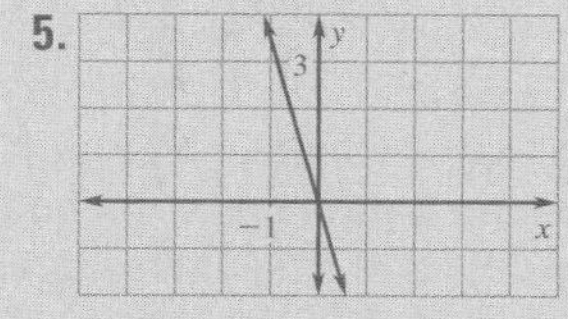

4 PRACTICE AND APPLY

Assignment Guide

Answer Transparencies available for all exercises

Basic:
Day 1: pp. 109–111
Exs. 1–6, 11–13, 17–20, 24–26, 30–32, 38–43, 46

Average:
Day 1: pp. 109–111
Exs. 1, 2, 5–8, 14–17, 21–23, 27–30, 32–35, 38–44, 47

Advanced:
Day 1: pp. 109–111
Exs. 1, 2, 8–10, 15–17, 22, 23, 27–45*

Block:
pp. 109–111
Exs. 1, 2, 5–8, 14–17, 21–23, 27–30, 32–35, 38–44, 47, 64 (with 2.6)

Differentiated Instruction

See *Algebra 2 Best Practices Toolkit* for suggestions on addressing the needs of a diverse classroom.

Homework Check

For a quick check of student understanding of key concepts, go over the following exercises:

Basic: 4, 12, 31, 38, 41
Average: 6, 14, 32, 39, 42
Advanced: 8, 16, 34, 40, 43

Extra Practice

- Student Edition, p. 1011
- Chapter 2 Resource Book: Practice levels A, B, C, pp. 55–57

Practice Worksheet

An easily-readable reduced practice page (with answers) for this lesson can be found on p. 70C.

An **Animated Algebra** activity is available on-line for **Exercise 44**. This activity is also available on the **Power Presentations CD-ROM**.

---

30. ★ **OPEN-ENDED MATH** Give an example of two real-life quantities that show direct variation. *Explain* your reasoning. See margin.

EXAMPLE 3 on p. 108 for Exs. 31–34

IDENTIFYING DIRECT VARIATION **Tell whether the data in the table show direct variation. If so, write an equation relating *x* and *y*.**

31.

x	3	6	9	12	15
y	−1	−2	−3	−4	−5

direct variation; $y = -\frac{1}{3}x$

32.

x	1	2	3	4	5
y	7	9	11	13	15

not direct variation

33.

x	−5	−4	−3	−2	−1
y	20	16	12	8	4

direct variation; $y = -4x$

34.

x	−8	−4	4	8	12
y	8	4	−4	−8	−12

direct variation; $y = -x$

35. **ERROR ANALYSIS** A student tried to determine whether the data pairs (1, 24), (2, 12), (3, 8), and (4, 6) show direct variation. *Describe* and correct the error in the student's work.

$1 \cdot 24 = 24$ $\quad 2 \cdot 12 = 24$
$3 \cdot 8 = 24$ $\quad 4 \cdot 6 = 24$
Because the products xy are constant, y varies directly with x.

35. The quotients need to be compared to each other, not the products; $\frac{24}{1} = 24$, $\frac{12}{2} = 6$, $\frac{8}{3} \approx 2.7$, $\frac{6}{4} = 1.5$, because the ratios are not equal, the data do not show direct variation.

C **36.** **REASONING** Let (x_1, y_1) be a solution, other than (0, 0), of a direct variation equation. Write a second direct variation equation whose graph is perpendicular to the graph of the first equation. $y = \frac{y_1}{x_1}x$; $y = -\frac{x_1}{y_1}x$

37. **CHALLENGE** Let (x_1, y_1) and (x_2, y_2) be any two distinct solutions of a direct variation equation. Show that $\frac{x_2}{x_1} = \frac{y_2}{y_1}$. *Sample answer:* Since the points are a direct variation, $\frac{y_1}{x_1} = \frac{y_2}{x_2}$. An equivalent proportion to this is $\frac{x_2}{x_1} = \frac{y_2}{y_1}$.

PROBLEM SOLVING

EXAMPLE 2 on p. 108 for Exs. 38–40

A **38.** **SCUBA DIVING** The time t it takes a diver to ascend safely to the surface varies directly with the depth d. It takes a minimum of 0.75 minute for a safe ascent from a depth of 45 feet. Write an equation that relates d and t. Then predict the minimum time for a safe ascent from a depth of 100 feet. $t = \frac{1}{60}d$; $1\frac{2}{3}$ min

@HomeTutor for problem solving help at classzone.com

39. **WEATHER** Hail 0.5 inch deep and weighing 1800 pounds covers a roof. The hail's weight w varies directly with its depth d. Write an equation that relates d and w. Then predict the weight on the roof of hail that is 1.75 inches deep. $w = 3600d$; 6300 lb

@HomeTutor for problem solving help at classzone.com

40. ★ **MULTIPLE CHOICE** Your weight M on Mars varies directly with your weight E on Earth. If you weigh 116 pounds on Earth, you would weigh 44 pounds on Mars. Which equation relates E and M? D

Ⓐ $M = E - 72$ Ⓑ $44M = 116E$ Ⓒ $M = \frac{29}{11}E$ Ⓓ $M = \frac{11}{29}E$

EXAMPLE 3 on p. 108 for Exs. 41–43

41. **INTERNET DOWNLOADS** The ordered pairs (4.5, 23), (7.8, 40), and (16.0, 82) are in the form (s, t) where t represents the time (in seconds) needed to download an Internet file of size s (in megabytes). Tell whether the data show direct variation. If so, write an equation that relates s and t. direct variation; $t = 5.1s$

○ = WORKED-OUT SOLUTIONS on p. WS1 ★ = STANDARDIZED TEST PRACTICE

30. *Sample answer:* If you earn an hourly wage, the amount of money you earn varies directly with the number of hours you work. If you work 4 hours and make $28, the equation relating the number of hours h worked and the amount of money m you earn is $m = 7h$. If you are traveling at a constant speed, the distance d you travel varies directly with the time t you travel. If you drive for 4 hours and travel 248 kilometers, the direct variation equation is $d = 62h$.

B **GEOMETRY In Exercises 42 and 43, consider squares with side lengths of 1, 2, 3, and 4 centimeters.**

42. Copy and complete the table.

Side length, s (cm)	1	2	3	4
Perimeter, P (cm)	? 4	? 8	? 12	? 16
Area, A (cm^2)	? 1	? 4	? 9	? 16

43. Tell whether the given variables show direct variation. If so, write an equation relating the variables. If not, explain why not.

a. s and P **direct variation; $P = 4s$** **b.** s and A **c.** P and A

44. ★ **EXTENDED RESPONSE** Each year, gray whales migrate from Mexico's Baja Peninsula to feeding grounds near Alaska. A whale may travel 6000 miles at an average rate of 75 miles per day.

a. Write an equation that gives the distance d_1 traveled in t days of migration. $d_1 = 75t$

b. Write an equation that gives the distance d_2 that remains to be traveled after t days of migration.

c. Tell whether the equations from parts (a) and (b) represent direct variation. *Explain* your answers.

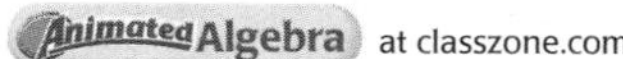 at classzone.com

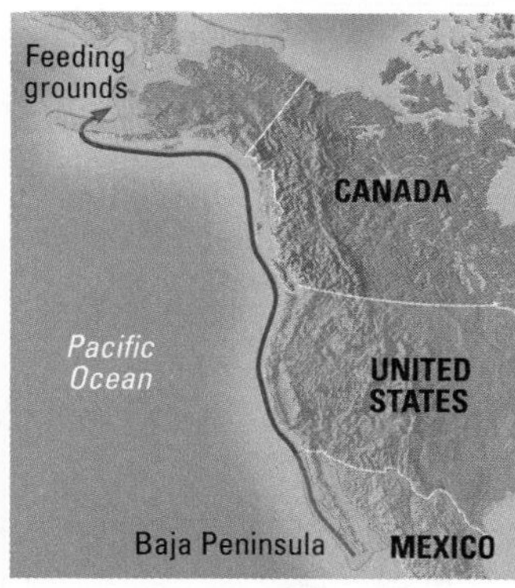

C **45. CHALLENGE** At a jewelry store, the price p of a gold necklace varies directly with its length ℓ. Also, the weight w of a necklace varies directly with its length. Show that the price of a necklace varies directly with its weight. **See margin.**

43b. Not a direct variation; the ratios of A to s are not equal.

43c. Not a direct variation; the ratios of A to P are not equal.

44b. $d_2 = 6000 - 75t$

44c. *Sample answer:* Part a) represents direct variation because the graph goes through the origin. Part b) does not represent direct variation because the graph does not go through the origin.

KY KENTUCKY MIXED REVIEW

TEST PRACTICE at classzone.com

46. An Internet service provider has a 15% off sale on a 6 month subscription. Which statement best represents the functional relationship between the sale price of the subscription and the original price? **B**

Ⓐ The original price is dependent on the sale price.

Ⓑ The sale price is dependent on the original price.

Ⓒ The sale price and the original price are independent of each other.

Ⓓ The relationship cannot be determined.

47. Rose works as a salesperson at a car stereo store. She earns an 8% commission on every sale. She wants to earn $300 from commissions in the next 5 days. What is the average amount of car stereo sales Rose must make per day to reach her goal? **B**

Ⓐ $480 Ⓑ $750 Ⓒ $1000 Ⓓ $3750

5 ASSESS AND RETEACH

Daily Homework Quiz

Transparency Available

1. Write and graph a direct variation equation that has (2, 5) as a solution. **$y = 2.5x$**

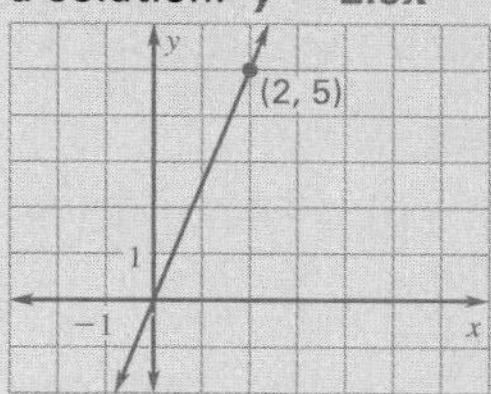

The variables x and y vary directly. Write an equation that relates x and y. Then find y when $x = 14$.

2. $x = 2, y = 10$ **$y = 5x$; 70**

3. $x = -4, y = 7$ **$y = -\frac{7}{4}x$; $-\frac{49}{2}$**

Tell whether the equation represents direct variation. If it does, give the constant of variation.

4. $y = -6x$ **yes; −6**

5. $3 + y = 2x$ **no**

Available at **classzone.com**

Diagnosis/Remediation

- Practice A, B, C in Chapter 2 Resource Book, pp. 55–57
- Study Guide in Chapter 2 Resource Book, pp. 58–59
- Practice Workbook, pp. 25–26
- @HomeTutor

Challenge

Additional challenge is available in the Chapter 2 Resource Book, p. 62.

45. *Sample answer:* Let p be the price of a necklace, ℓ be the length, w be the weight, and a and b be constants of variation. $p = a\ell$ and $w = b\ell$, solve for ℓ in terms of w, $\ell = \frac{w}{b}$, and substitute into the other equation for ℓ, $p = a\left(\frac{w}{b}\right) = \frac{a}{b}w$. Since a and b are constants of variation, $\frac{a}{b}$ is also a constant of variation relating p, the price, to w, the weight.

2.6 Fitting a Line to Data

MATERIALS • overhead projector • overhead transparency • metric ruler • meter stick • graph paper

QUESTION How can you approximate the *best-fitting line* for a set of data?

EXPLORE Collect and record data

STEP 1 ***Set up***
Position an overhead projector a convenient distance from a projection screen. Draw a line segment 15 centimeters long on a transparency, and place the transparency on the projector.

STEP 2 ***Collect data***
Measure the distance, in centimeters, from the projector to the screen and the length of the line segment as it appears on the screen. Reposition the projector several times, each time taking these measurements.

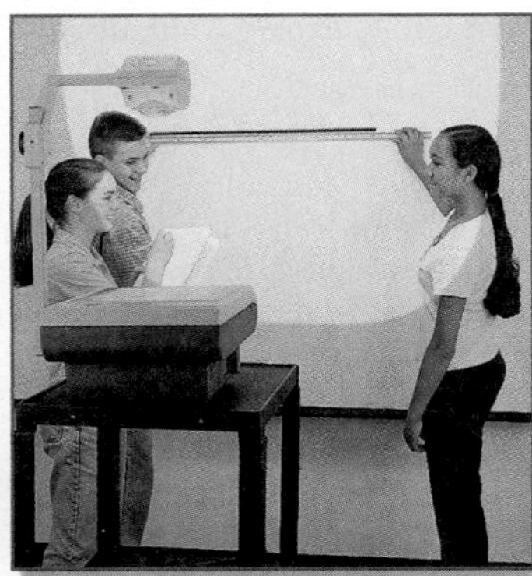

STEP 3 ***Record data***
Record your measurements from Step 2 in a table like the one shown below.

Distance from projector to screen (cm), x	Length of line segment on screen (cm), y
200	?
210	?
220	?
230	?
240	?
250	?
260	?
270	?
280	?
290	?

DRAW CONCLUSIONS Use your observations to complete these exercises

1–5. Check students' work.

1. Graph the data pairs (x, y). What pattern do you observe?
2. Use a ruler to draw a line that lies as close as possible to all of the points on the graph, as shown at the right. The line does not have to pass through any of the points. There should be about as many points above the line as below it.
3. Estimate the coordinates of two points on your line. Use your points to write an equation of the line.
4. Using your equation from Exercise 3, predict the length of the line segment on the screen for a particular projector-to-screen distance less than those in your table and for a particular projector-to-screen distance greater than those in your table.
5. Test your predictions from Exercise 4. How accurate were they?

1 PLAN AND PREPARE

Explore the Concept

- Students will approximate a best-fitting line for a set of data.
- This activity leads into the study of approximating a best-fitting line in Example 3 in Lesson 2.6.

Materials

Each group of students will need:

- metric ruler
- meter stick
- graph paper

Recommended Time

Work activity: 15 min
Discuss results: 10 min

Grouping

Students should work in groups of four. Have one student find the distances, a second sketch the graph and draw a line, a third find the slope of the line, and a fourth find the equation of the line. Then the group can make and test their predictions together.

2 TEACH

Tips for Success

You may wish to have a number of projectors, each with its own transparency, available for a small number of groups to share.

Alternative Strategy

Make the activity into a class demonstration, with students helping to record the data. Use the measurements suggested in Step 3 for the collection of data in Step 2.

Key Discovery

A best-fitting line lies as close as possible to all points in a data set.

3 ASSESS AND RETEACH

Why is it useful to write an equation for a best-fitting line for a set of data? **to help make predictions about points outside the data set**

2.6 Draw Scatter Plots and Best-Fitting Lines

MA-HS-4.2.3

Before	You wrote equations of lines.
Now	You will fit lines to data in scatter plots.
Why?	So you can model sports trends, as in Ex. 27.

Key Vocabulary
- scatter plot
- positive correlation
- negative correlation
- correlation coefficient
- best-fitting line

MA-HS-4.2.3
Students will: identify an appropriate curve of best fit (linear, quadratic, exponential) for a set of two-variable data; determine a line of best fit equation for a set of linear two-variable data and apply a line of best fit to make predictions within and beyond a given set of two-variable data. DOK 3

A **scatter plot** is a graph of a set of data pairs (x, y). If y tends to increase as x increases, then the data have a **positive correlation.** If y tends to decrease as x increases, then the data have a **negative correlation**. If the points show no obvious pattern, then the data have *approximately no correlation*.

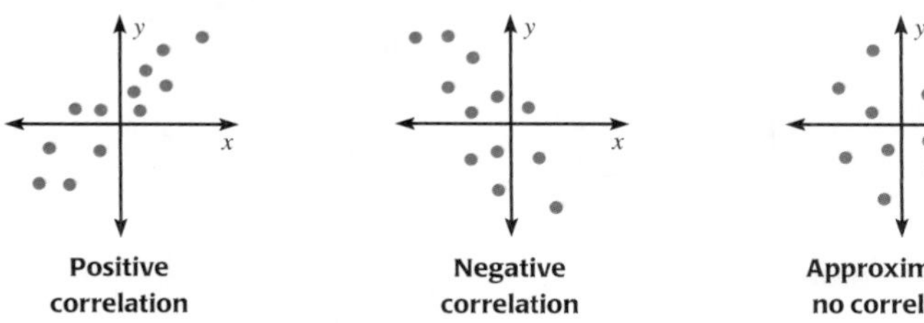

Positive correlation — Negative correlation — Approximately no correlation

EXAMPLE 1 Describe correlation

TELEPHONES Describe the correlation shown by each scatter plot.

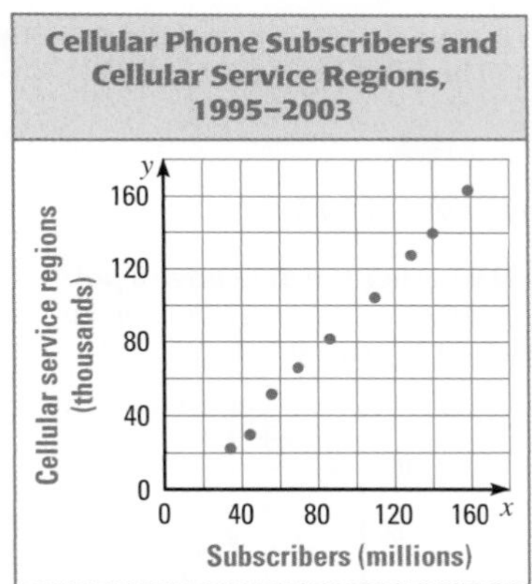

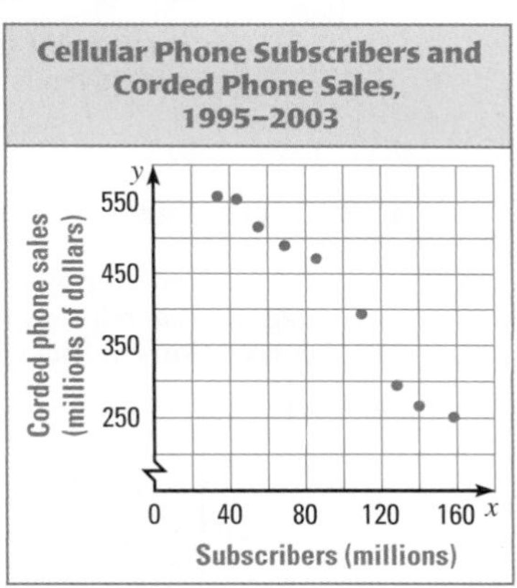

Solution

The first scatter plot shows a positive correlation, because as the number of cellular phone subscribers increased, the number of cellular service regions tended to increase.

The second scatter plot shows a negative correlation, because as the number of cellular phone subscribers increased, corded phone sales tended to decrease.

1 PLAN AND PREPARE

Warm-Up Exercises

Transparency Available

1. Find the slope of the line through $(-5, 1)$ and $(2, -6)$. -1
2. Write an equation of the line through $(-2, 5)$ and $(4, 8)$. $y = \frac{1}{2}x + 6$
3. A line's graph has slope $\frac{2}{3}$ and contains the point $(6, 1)$. Write an equation of the line. $y = \frac{2}{3}x - 3$

Notetaking Guide

Transparency Available

Promotes interactive learning and notetaking skills, pp. 43–45.

Pacing

Basic: 2 days
Average: 2 days
Advanced: 2 days
Block: 0.5 block with 2.5
0.5 block with 2.7

- See *Teaching Guide/Lesson Plan.*

2 FOCUS AND MOTIVATE

Essential Question

Big Idea 3, p. 71

How can you tell if a set of data points can be modeled by a best-fitting line? **Tell students they will learn how to answer this question by using a correlation coefficient.**

Resource Planning Guide

Chapter Resource Book
- Teaching Guide/Lesson Plan (pp. 63–64)
- Practice levels A, B, C (pp. 67–72)
- Study Guide (pp. 73–74)
- Catch-up for Absent Students (p. 75)
- Application (p. 76)
- Challenge (p. 77)

Workbooks
- Notetaking Guide (pp. 43–45)
- Practice Workbook (pp. 27–29)

Teaching Options
- **Power Presentations CD-ROM** provides dynamic electronic teaching resources for the classroom.
- **Activity Generator CD-ROM** provides editable activities for all ability levels.

Interactive Technology
- Easy Planner
- Power Presentations CD-ROM
- Activity Generator CD-ROM
- Animated Algebra
- Test Generator CD-ROM
- Online Quiz
- eWorkbook
- eEdition
- @HomeTutor

Resources for English Learners
- Quick Reference for English Learners
- Spanish Study Guide
- Multi-Language Visual Glossary
- Student Resources in Spanish

See also the *Algebra 2 Toolkit* for more strategies for meeting individual needs.

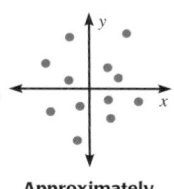

Motivating the Lesson

Your school orchestra is going to rent an auditorium for its concert. They do not want one that is too small or too large. By plotting the attendance figures on a scatter plot and using a line of best fit, they can determine the size they need.

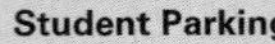

3 TEACH

Extra Example 1

Describe the correlation shown by each scatter plot. first plot: negative correlation; second plot: positive correlation

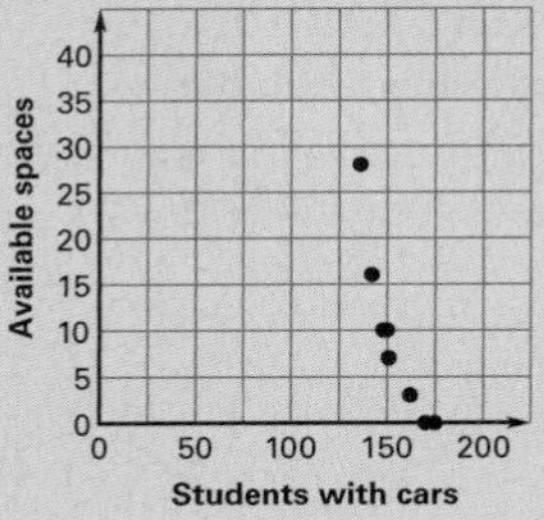

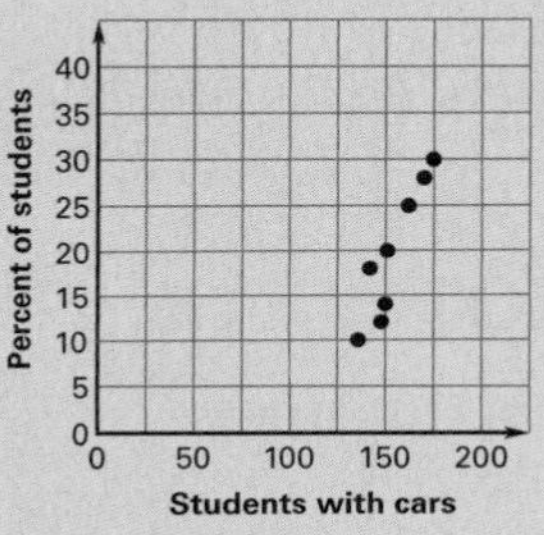

Key Question to Ask for Example 1

If a scatter plot shows a positive correlation, what is the general trend of the data pairs? They rise from left to right.

CORRELATION COEFFICIENTS A **correlation coefficient**, denoted by r, is a number from -1 to 1 that measures how well a line fits a set of data pairs (x, y). If r is near 1, the points lie close to a line with positive slope. If r is near -1, the points lie close to a line with negative slope. If r is near 0, the points do not lie close to any line.

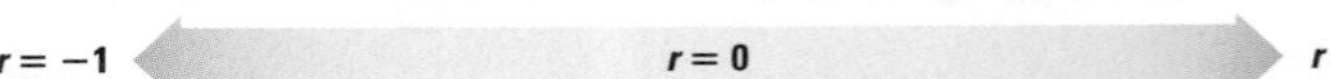

Points lie near line with a negative slope. | **Points do not lie near any line.** | **Points lie near line with positive slope.**

EXAMPLE 2 Estimate correlation coefficients

Tell whether the correlation coefficient for the data is closest to -1, -0.5, 0, 0.5, or 1.

a. 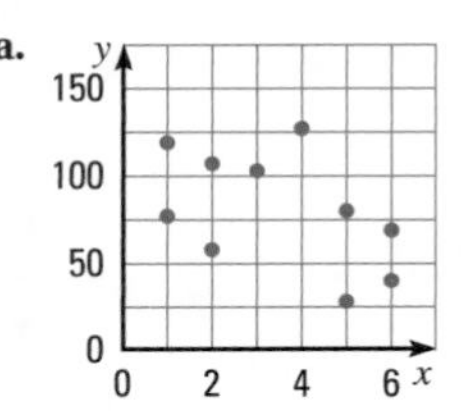

b. 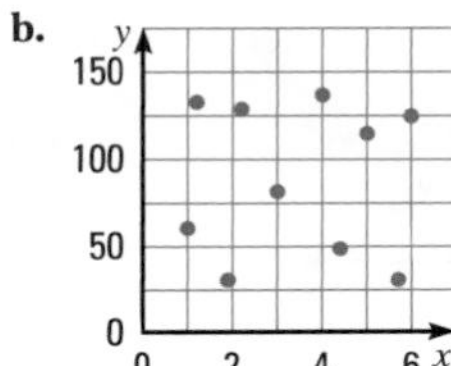

c. 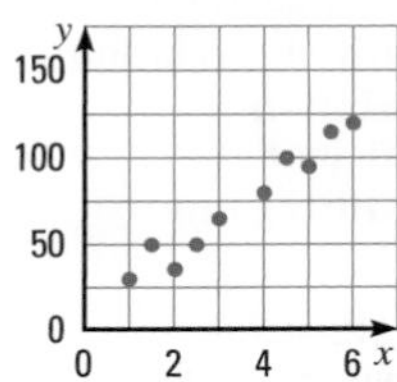

Solution

a. The scatter plot shows a clear but fairly weak negative correlation. So, r is between 0 and -1, but not too close to either one. The best estimate given is $r = -0.5$. (The actual value is $r \approx -0.46$.)

b. The scatter plot shows approximately no correlation. So, the best estimate given is $r = 0$. (The actual value is $r \approx -0.02$.)

c. The scatter plot shows a strong positive correlation. So, the best estimate given is $r = 1$. (The actual value is $r \approx 0.98$.)

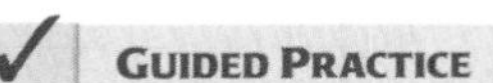

GUIDED PRACTICE for Examples 1 and 2

For each scatter plot, (a) tell whether the data have a *positive correlation*, a *negative correlation*, or *approximately no correlation*, and (b) tell whether the correlation coefficient is closest to -1, -0.5, 0, 0.5, or 1.

1. 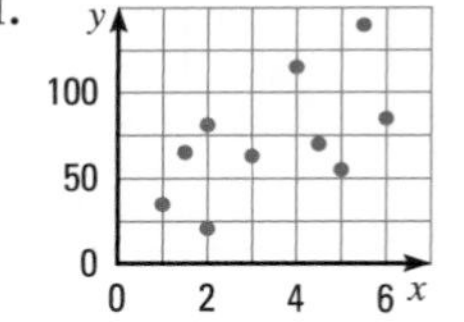

2. 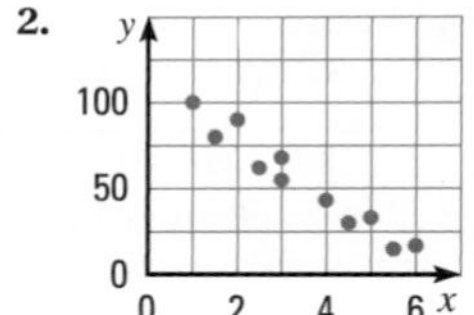

3. 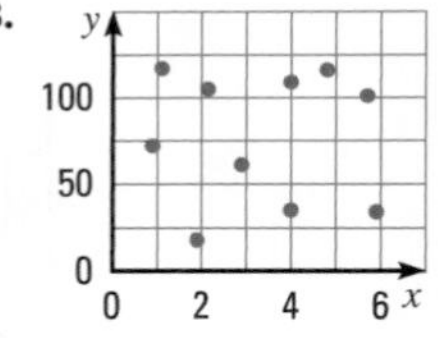

1a. positive correlation
1b. 0.5
2a. negative correlation
2b. −1
3a. no correlation
3b. 0

BEST-FITTING LINES If the correlation coefficient for a set of data is near ± 1, the data can be reasonably modeled by a line. The **best-fitting line** is the line that lies as close as possible to all the data points. You can approximate a best-fitting line by graphing.

Differentiated Instruction

Visual Learners For some students, the correlation coefficient (or "measure of fit") is best understood visually. Suggest that students mentally draw a line through the plotted points. Point out that a perfect fit is 100%, or 1; a rough fit is somewhat less than 100%, or less than 1; and a poor fit is near 0%, or 0. The sign of the correlation coefficient r has the same sign as the slope of the line.

See also the *Algebra 2 Toolkit* for more strategies.

KEY CONCEPT — *For Your Notebook*

Approximating a Best-Fitting Line

STEP 1 **Draw** a scatter plot of the data.

STEP 2 **Sketch** the line that appears to follow most closely the trend given by the data points. There should be about as many points above the line as below it.

STEP 3 **Choose** two points on the line, and estimate the coordinates of each point. These points do not have to be original data points.

STEP 4 **Write** an equation of the line that passes through the two points from Step 3. This equation is a model for the data.

EXAMPLE 3 Approximate a best-fitting line

ALTERNATIVE-FUELED VEHICLES The table shows the number y (in thousands) of alternative-fueled vehicles in use in the United States x years after 1997. Approximate the best-fitting line for the data.

x	0	1	2	3	4	5	6	7
y	280	295	322	395	425	471	511	548

Solution

STEP 1 **Draw** a scatter plot of the data.

STEP 2 **Sketch** the line that appears to best fit the data. One possibility is shown.

STEP 3 **Choose** two points that appear to lie on the line. For the line shown, you might choose (1, 300), which is not an original data point, and (7, 548), which is an original data point.

STEP 4 **Write** an equation of the line. First find the slope using the points (1, 300) and (7, 548).

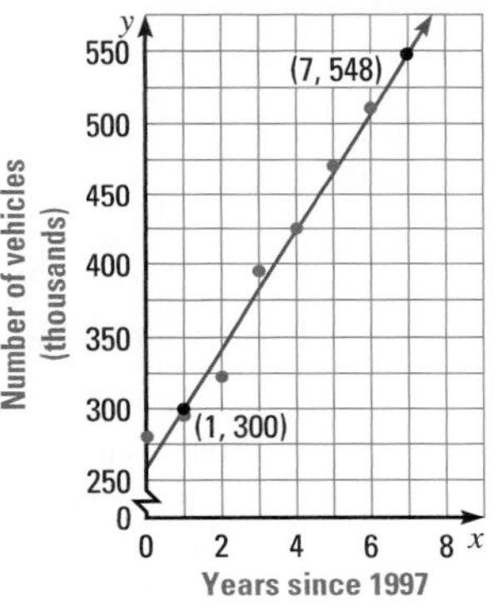

$$m = \frac{548 - 300}{7 - 1} = \frac{248}{6} \approx 41.3$$

Use point-slope form to write the equation. Choose $(x_1, y_1) = (1, 300)$.

$y - y_1 = m(x - x_1)$	**Point-slope form**
$y - 300 = 41.3(x - 1)$	**Substitute for m, x_1, and y_1.**
$y \approx 41.3x + 259$	**Simplify.**

▶ An approximation of the best-fitting line is $y = 41.3x + 259$.

at classzone.com

Extra Example 2

Tell whether the correlation coefficient for the data is closest to −1, −0.5, 0, 0.5, or 1. −1 (actual: −0.94)

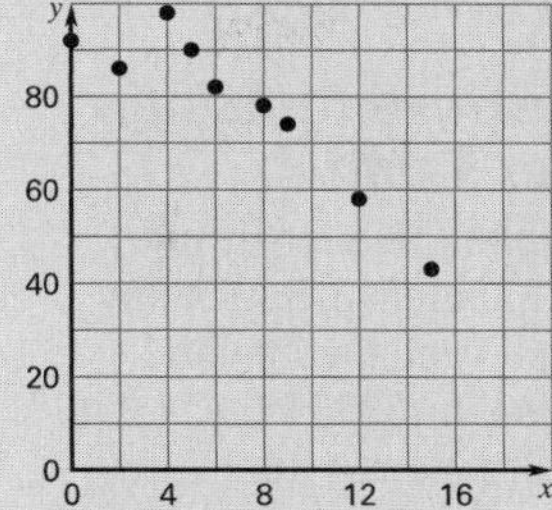

Extra Example 3

The table gives the systolic blood pressure y of patients x years old. Approximate the best-fitting line for the data.

x	43	48	56	61	67	70
y	128	120	135	143	141	152

One approximation for the line would be $y = x + 80$.

Key Questions to Ask for Example 3

- What is the approximate slope between any two of the data pairs? 41.3
- Describe the correlation between the data. a strong positive correlation, close to 1

An **Animated Algebra** activity is available on-line for **Example 3**. This activity is also available on the **Power Presentations CD-ROM**.

Mathematical Reasoning

Students may think that there is only one method of approximating a best-fitting line, the one shown in Example 3. Explain that there are more rigorous algebraic methods for determining a best-fitting line and these methods involve computer software and graphing calculators. An example of such a method is given in Example 5 on page 116.

Extra Example 4

Use the equation from the line of fit from Extra Example 3 to predict the systolic blood pressure of a 75 year old patient. **about 155**

Key Questions to Ask for Examples 3 and 4

- According to the best-fitting model in Example 3, how many alternative-fueled vehicles were in use in 1997? Why is this different from the actual data? **259,000 vehicles; the best-fitting line is an approximation. The actual data point for 1997 is slightly above the line.**
- In Example 4, where would the graph of (13, 796) lie in relation to the best-fitting line? **It lies nearly on the best-fitting line when the line is extended.**

Extra Example 5

Use the linear regression feature on a graphing calculator to find an equation of the best-fitting line for the data in Extra Example 3. $y = 0.96x + 81.05$

Closing the Lesson

Have students summarize the major points of the lesson and answer the Essential Question: How can you tell if a set of data points can be modeled by a best-fitting line?

- **A scatter plot has a positive correlation if *y* tends to increase as *x* increases and a negative correlation if *y* tends to decrease as *x* increases.**
- **A correlation coefficient measures how well a line fits a set of data pairs and is between −1 and 1.**
- **You can draw a line with about as many data points above it as are below it, or use a graphing calculator to approximate a best-fitting line.**

If the correlation coefficient for a set of data points is close to 1 or −1, you can model the data by a best-fitting line.

EXAMPLE 4 Use a line of fit to make a prediction

Use the equation of the line of fit from Example 3 to predict the number of alternative-fueled vehicles in use in the United States in 2010.

Solution

Because 2010 is 13 years after 1997, substitute 13 for x in the equation from Example 3.

$$y = 41.3x + 259 = 41.3(13) + 259 \approx 796$$

▶ You can predict that there will be about 796,000 alternative-fueled vehicles in use in the United States in 2010.

LINEAR REGRESSION Many graphing calculators have a *linear regression* feature that can be used to find the best-fitting line for a set of data.

EXAMPLE 5 Use a graphing calculator to find a best-fitting line

Use the *linear regression* feature on a graphing calculator to find an equation of the best-fitting line for the data in Example 3.

Solution

STEP 1 **Enter** the data into two *lists*. Press STAT and then select Edit. Enter years since 1997 in L_1 and number of alternative-fueled vehicles in L_2.

FIND CORRELATION
If your calculator does not display the correlation coefficient *r* when it displays the regression equation, you may need to select DiagnosticOn from the CATALOG menu.

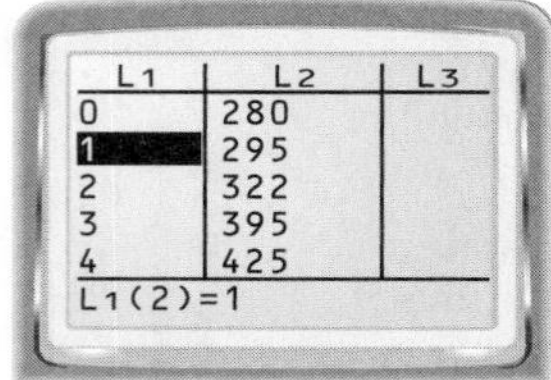

STEP 2 **Find** an equation of the best-fitting (linear regression) line. Press STAT, choose the CALC menu, and select LinReg(ax+b). The equation can be rounded to $y = 40.9x + 263$.

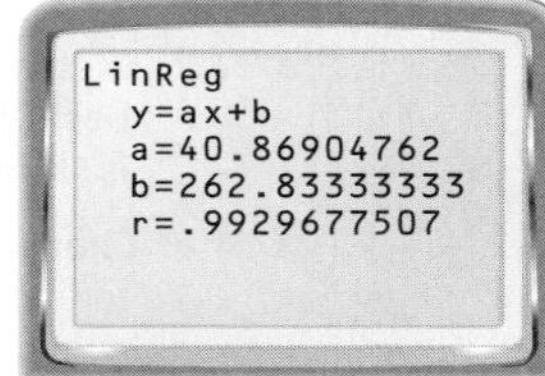

STEP 3 **Make** a scatter plot of the data pairs to see how well the regression equation models the data. Press 2nd [STAT PLOT] to set up your plot. Then select an appropriate window for the graph.

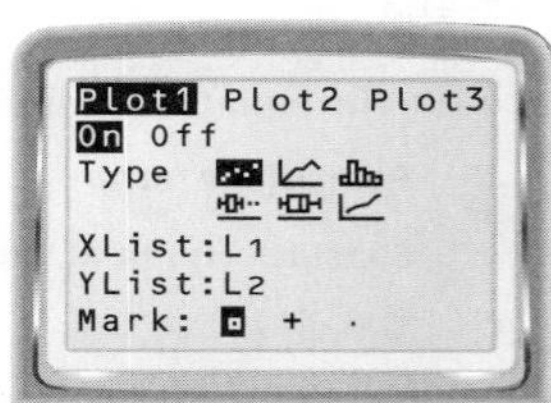

STEP 4 **Graph** the regression equation with the scatter plot by entering the equation $y = 40.9x + 263$. The graph (displayed in the window $0 \le x \le 8$ and $200 \le y \le 600$) shows that the line fits the data well.

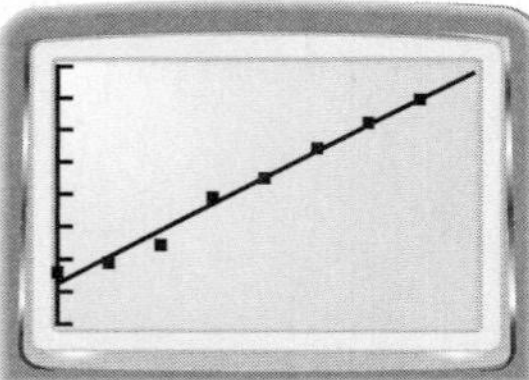

▶ An equation of the best-fitting line is $y = 40.9x + 263$.

Guided Practice
4c. $y = -130x + 6702$

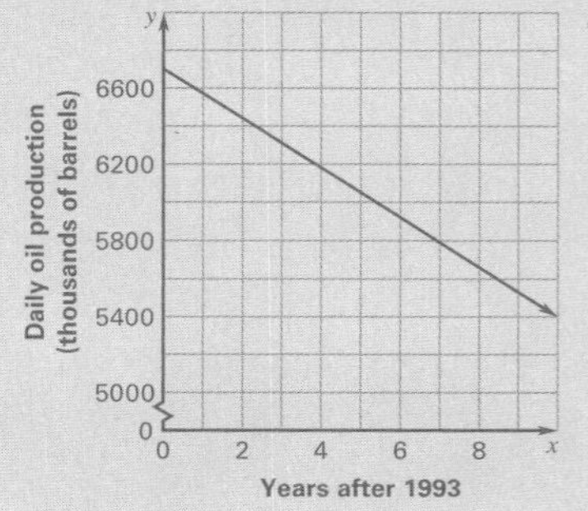

4752 gal

✓ **GUIDED PRACTICE** for Examples 3, 4, and 5

4. **OIL PRODUCTION** The table shows the U.S. daily oil production y (in thousands of barrels) x years after 1994.

x	0	1	2	3	4	5	6	7	8
y	6660	6560	6470	6450	6250	5880	5820	5800	5750

a. Approximate the best-fitting line for the data. *Sample answer:* $y = -130x + 6710$

b. Use your equation from part (a) to predict the daily oil production in 2009. *Sample answer:* 4760 gal

c. Use a graphing calculator to find and graph an equation of the best-fitting line. Repeat the prediction from part (b) using this equation. See margin.

2.6 EXERCISES

HOMEWORK KEY

○ = **WORKED-OUT SOLUTIONS** on p. WS3 for Exs. 9, 11, and 25

★ = **STANDARDIZED TEST PRACTICE** Exs. 2, 16, 18, 21, and 28

◆ = **MULTIPLE REPRESENTATIONS** Ex. 27

SKILL PRACTICE

A

1. **VOCABULARY** Copy and complete: A line that lies as close as possible to a set of data points (x, y) is called the _?_ for the data points. best-fitting line

2. ★ **WRITING** *Describe* how to tell whether a set of data points shows a positive correlation, a negative correlation, or approximately no correlation. See margin.

EXAMPLE 1 on p. 113 for Exs. 3–5

DESCRIBING CORRELATIONS Tell whether the data have a *positive correlation*, a *negative correlation*, or *approximately no correlation*.

3. 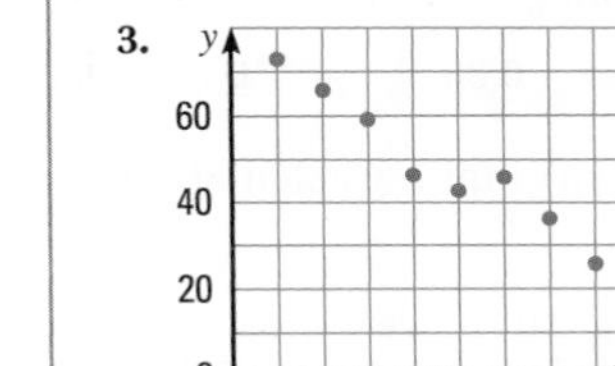
negative correlation

4. 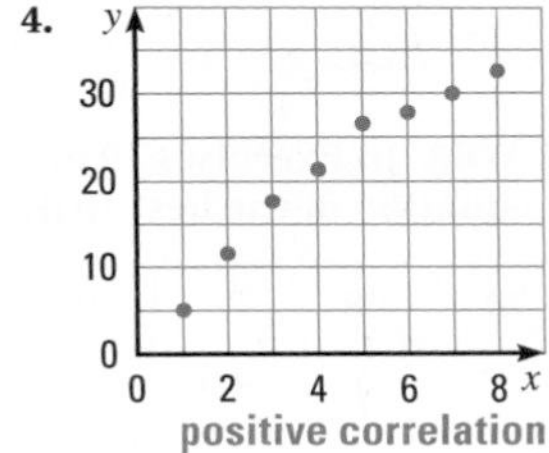
positive correlation

5. 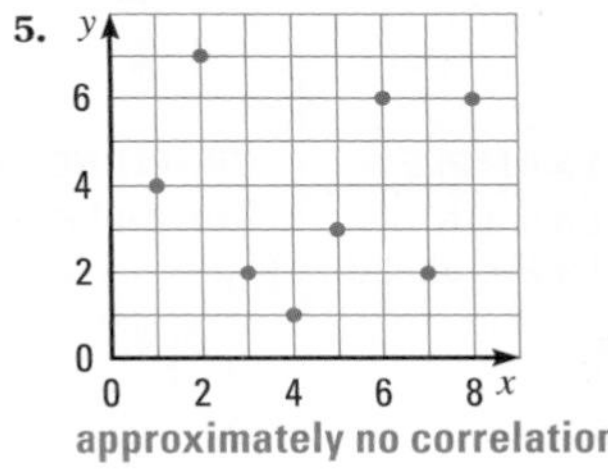
approximately no correlation

6. **REASONING** *Explain* how you can determine the type of correlation for a set of data pairs by examining the data in a table without drawing a scatter plot. See margin.

EXAMPLE 2 on p. 114 for Exs. 7–9

CORRELATION COEFFICIENTS Tell whether the correlation coefficient for the data is closest to −1, −0.5, 0, 0.5, or 1.

7. 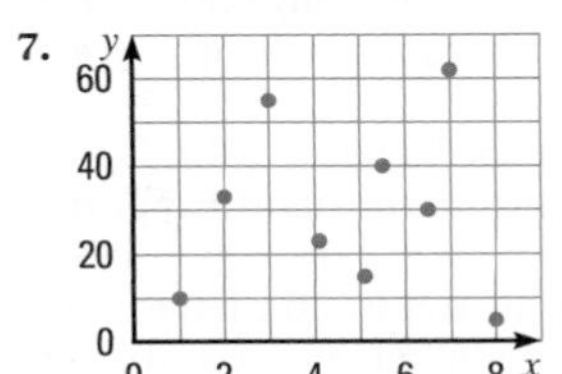
0

8. 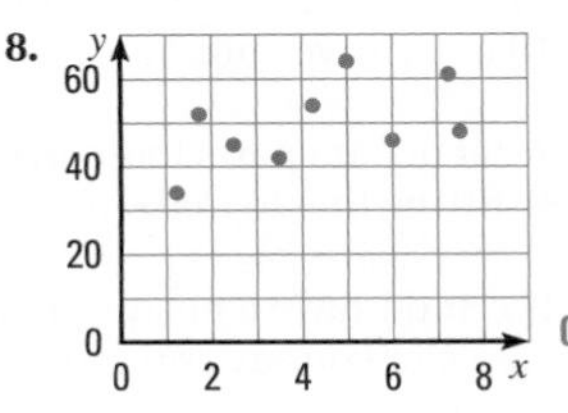
0.5

9. 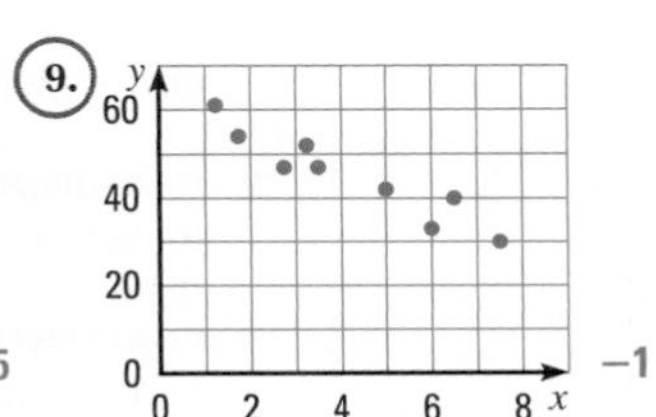
−1

2. *Sample answer:* If the data points show a positive correlation, the points lie close to a line with positive slope. If the data points show a negative correlation, the points lie close to a line with negative slope. If the data points have approximately no correlation, the points do not lie close to any line.

6. *Sample answer:* If the y values increase as the x values increase, then there is a positive correlation. If the y values decrease as the x values increase, there is a negative correlation. If the y values are randomly increasing and decreasing, then there is approximately no correlation.

4 PRACTICE AND APPLY

Assignment Guide

Answer Transparencies available for all exercises

Basic:
Day 1: pp. 117–120
Exs. 1–9, 30–31
Day 2: pp. 117–120
Exs. 10–19, 24–27

Average:
Day 1: pp. 117–120
Exs. 1–9, 30–31
Day 2: pp. 117–120
Exs. 10–21, 24–28

Advanced:
Day 1: pp. 117–120
Exs. 1, 2, 4–6, 8, 9, 18, 22, 23*, 30–31
Day 2: pp. 117–120
Exs. 12–17, 19–21, 24–29*

Block:
pp. 117–120
Exs. 1–9, 30–31 (with 2.5)
pp. 117–120
Exs. 10–21, 24–28 (with 2.7)

Differentiated Instruction

See *Algebra 2 Best Practices Toolkit* for suggestions on addressing the needs of a diverse classroom.

Homework Check

For a quick check of student understanding of key concepts, go over the following exercises:

Basic: 3, 7, 10, 19, 26
Average: 4, 8, 12, 20, 27
Advanced: 5, 9, 14, 24, 28

Extra Practice

- Student Edition, p. 1011
- Chapter 2 Resource Book: Practice levels A, B, C, pp. 67–72

Practice Worksheet

An easily-readable reduced practice page (with answers) for this lesson can be found on p. 70C.

Teaching Strategy

Exercises 10–15 Students may choose different points to approximate best-fitting lines so that their answers to parts b and c may vary. Tell them to document their work so that they can justify their answers during class discussion.

Graphing Calculator

Exercises 19, 20 Point out that the *x*-values represent the domain of the data set and the *y*-values represent the range for each exercise. Understanding this may help students choose an appropriate viewing window.

10–15. See Additional Answers beginning on p. AA1.

17. *Sample:*

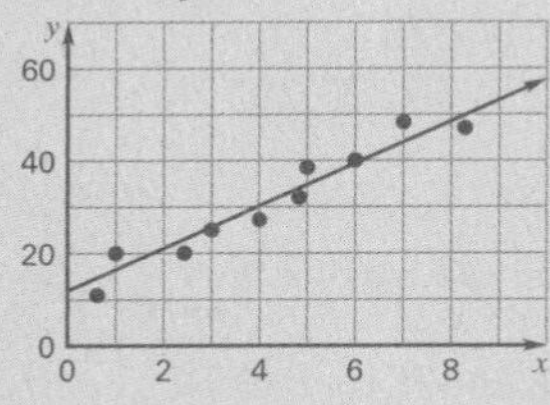

19.

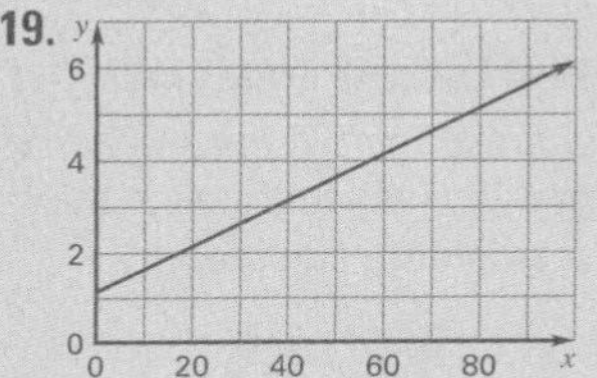

20.

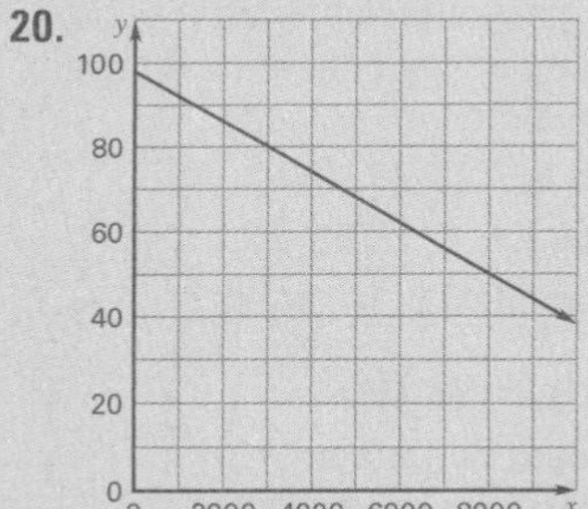

21a. *Sample answer:* Measuring the depth of water at different times while filling a swimming pool; the number of gallons of milk you buy and the total cost

21b. *Sample answer:* The age of a car and its current value; the number of miles you have driven since you last put gas in the tank and the amount of gas left in the tank

---

EXAMPLES 3 and 4 on pp. 115–116 for Exs. 10–15

BEST-FITTING LINES **In Exercises 10–15, (a) draw a scatter plot of the data, (b) approximate the best-fitting line, and (c) estimate y when $x = 20$.** **10–15. See margin.**

10.

x	1	2	3	4	5
y	10	22	35	49	62

(11.)

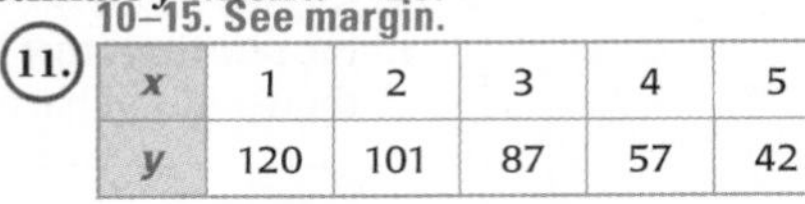

x	1	2	3	4	5
y	120	101	87	57	42

12.

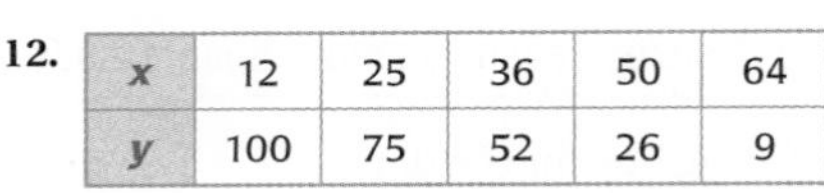

x	12	25	36	50	64
y	100	75	52	26	9

13.

x	3	7	10	15	18
y	16	45	82	102	116

14.

x	5.6	6.2	7	7.3	8.4
y	120	130	141	156	167

15.

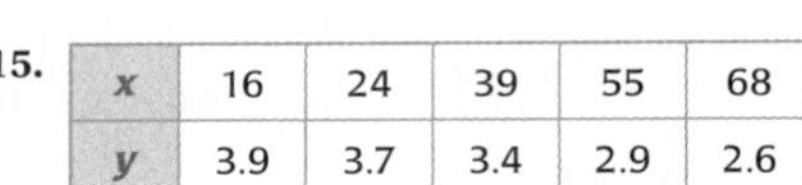

x	16	24	39	55	68
y	3.9	3.7	3.4	2.9	2.6

B

16. ★ **MULTIPLE CHOICE** Which equation best models the data in the scatter plot? **B**

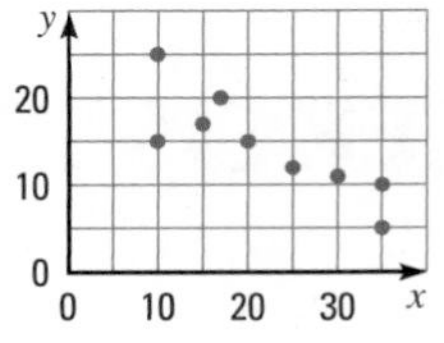

(A) $y = 15$ (B) $y = -\frac{1}{2}x + 26$

(C) $y = -\frac{2}{5}x + 19$ (D) $y = -\frac{4}{5}x + 33$

17. **ERROR ANALYSIS** The graph shows one student's approximation of the best-fitting line for the data in the scatter plot. *Describe* and correct the error in the student's work. **The line should go through the middle of the data points; see margin for art.**

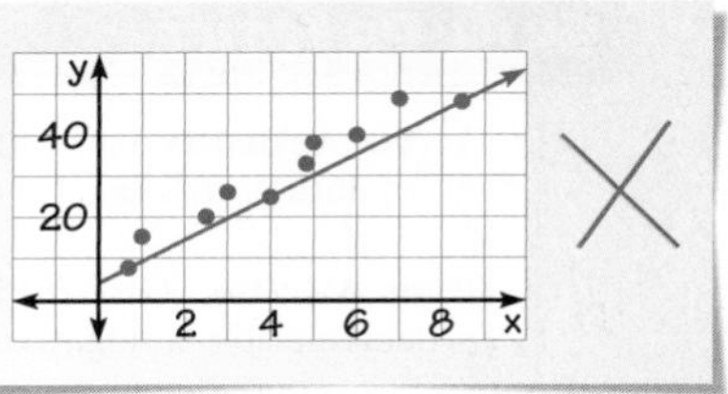

18. ★ **MULTIPLE CHOICE** A set of data has correlation coefficient r. For which value of r would the data points lie closest to a line? **A**

(A) $r = -0.96$ (B) $r = 0$ (C) $r = 0.38$ (D) $r = 0.5$

EXAMPLE 5 on p. 116 for Exs. 19–20

GRAPHING CALCULATOR **In Exercises 19 and 20, use a graphing calculator to find and graph an equation of the best-fitting line.**

19.

x	78	74	68	76	80	84	50	76	55	93
y	5.1	5.0	4.6	4.9	5.3	5.5	3.7	5.0	3.9	5.8

$y = 0.05x + 1.14$, see margin for art.

20.

x	7000	7400	7800	8100	8500	8800	9200	9500	9800
y	56.0	54.5	51.9	50.0	47.3	45.6	43.1	41.6	39.9

$y = -0.006x + 98.1$, see margin for art.

21. ★ **OPEN-ENDED MATH** Give two real-life quantities that have **(a)** a positive correlation, **(b)** a negative correlation, and **(c)** approximately no correlation. **See margin.**

C

22. **REASONING** A set of data pairs has correlation coefficient $r = 0.1$. Is it logical to use the best-fitting line to make predictions from the data? *Explain.* **No; the correlation is close to zero, so it represents a very weak relationship between the two variables.**

23. **CHALLENGE** If x and y have a positive correlation and y and z have a negative correlation, what can you say about the correlation between x and z? *Explain.* **See margin.**

○ = WORKED-OUT SOLUTIONS on p. WS1 ★ = STANDARDIZED TEST PRACTICE  = MULTIPLE REPRESENTATIONS

21c. *Sample answer:* The height of a person and the month they were born; the age of a person and the number of vehicles they own

23. Negative correlation. *Sample answer:* If x and y have a positive correlation, then they are both increasing. If y and z have a negative correlation, then z must be decreasing. So, if x is increasing and z is decreasing, then x and z have a negative correlation.

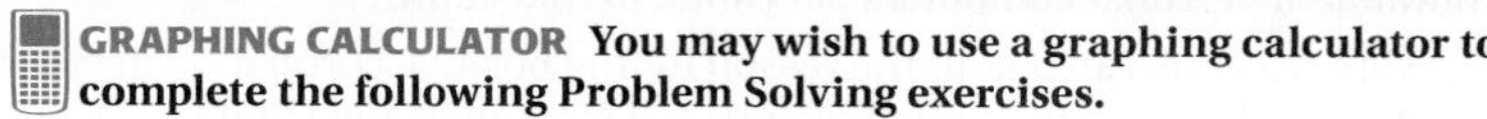

EXAMPLES A **3, 4, and 5** on pp. 115–116 for Exs. 24–28

GRAPHING CALCULATOR You may wish to use a graphing calculator to complete the following Problem Solving exercises.

24. POPULATION The data pairs (x, y) give the population y (in millions) of Texas x years after 1997. Approximate the best-fitting line for the data. ***Sample answer:*** $y = 0.389x + 19.8$

(0, 19.7), (1, 20.2), (2, 20.6), (3, 20.9), (4, 21.3), (5, 21.7), (6, 22.1), (7, 22.5)

@HomeTutor for problem solving help at classzone.com

25. TUITION The data pairs (x, y) give U.S. average annual public college tuition y (in dollars) x years after 1997. Approximate the best-fitting line for the data. ***Sample answer:*** $y = 101.3x + 2236.6$

(0, 2271), (1, 2360), (2, 2430), (3, 2506), (4, 2562), (5, 2727), (6, 2928)

@HomeTutor for problem solving help at classzone.com

26. PHYSICAL SCIENCE The diagram shows the boiling point of water at various elevations. Approximate the best-fitting line for the data pairs (x, y) where x represents the elevation (in feet) and y represents the boiling point (in degrees Fahrenheit). Then use this line to estimate the boiling point at an elevation of 14,000 feet.

6. ***Sample answer:*** $y = -0.001861x + 212.2$; about 186°F

B **27. MULTIPLE REPRESENTATIONS** The table shows the numbers of countries that participated in the Winter Olympics from 1980 to 2002.

Year	1980	1984	1988	1992	1994	1998	2002
Countries	37	49	57	64	67	72	77

a. **Making a List** Use the table to make a list of data pairs (x, y) where x represents years since 1980 and y represents the number of countries. **(0, 37), (4, 49), (8, 57), (12, 64), (14, 67), (18, 72), (22, 77)**

b. **Drawing a Graph** Draw a scatter plot of the data pairs from part (a). **See margin.**

c. **Writing an Equation** Write an equation that approximates the best-fitting line, and use it to predict the number of participating countries in 2014. ***Sample answer:*** $y = 1.8x + 40.7$; **102 countries**

28. ★ EXTENDED RESPONSE The table shows manufacturers' shipments (in millions) of cassettes and CDs in the United States from 1988 to 2002.

Year	1988	1990	1992	1994	1996	1998	2000	2002
Cassettes	450.1	442.2	336.4	345.4	225.3	158.5	76.0	31.1
CDs	149.7	286.5	407.5	662.1	778.9	847.0	942.5	803.3

a. Draw a scatter plot of the data pairs (year, shipments of cassettes). *Describe* the correlation shown by the scatter plot. **See margin for art; negative correlation.**

b. Draw a scatter plot of the data pairs (year, shipments of CDs). *Describe* the correlation shown by the scatter plot. **See margin for art; positive correlation.**

c. *Describe* the correlation between cassette shipments and CD shipments. What real-world factors might account for this? **Negative correlation. *Sample answer:* More people began buying CDs rather than cassettes.**

Study Strategy

Exercises 24–27 Before students calculate best-fitting lines, they should examine the scatter plot of the data and determine the type of correlation for the data set. They can then compare that to the sign of the slope of their best-fitting lines.

Mathematical Reasoning

Exercise 27 Caution students that as they interpret best-fitting lines, they should understand that extrapolating data from a linear model assumes that all variables that affect the model remain constant. This is not likely over a long period of time. For example, the variables that affect participation in the Olympics may change over the long run.

27b.

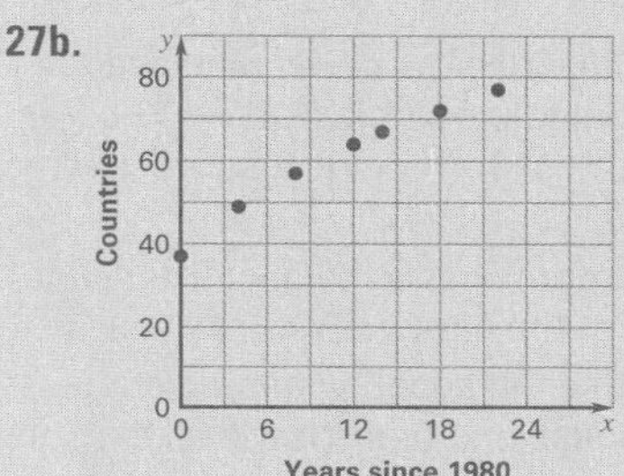

28a.

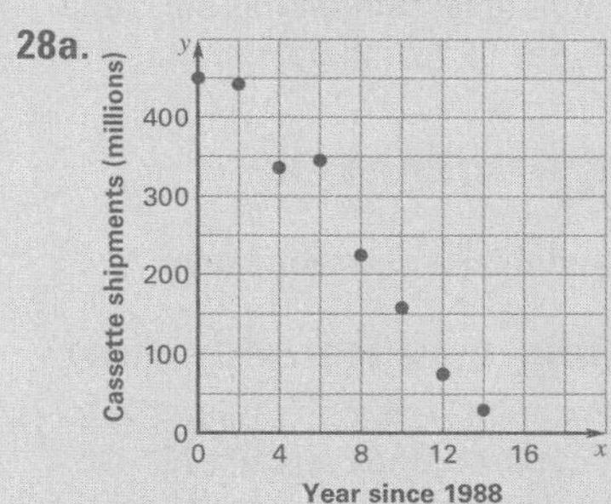

28b.

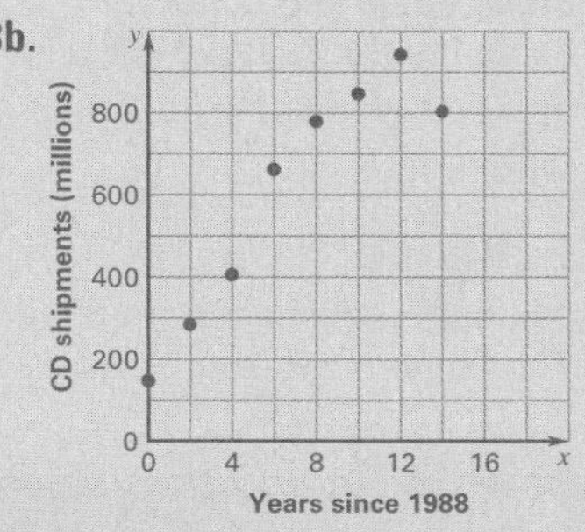

5 ASSESS AND RETEACH

Daily Homework Quiz

Transparency Available

The table gives the number of hours y that it takes a student to learn a new word processing program and the number of words per minute x the student can type.

x	48	74	52	79	83	56
y	7	4	8	3.5	2	6

1. Draw the scatter plot.

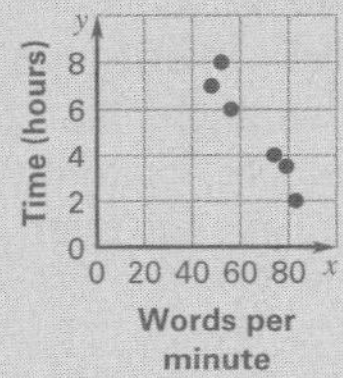

2. Describe the correlation and tell whether it is close to −1, −0.5, 0, 0.5, or 1. **There is a strong negative correlation, close to −1.**
3. Approximate the best fitting line for the data. $y = -0.1x + 11.6$
4. Use the equation to predict the number of hours it will take a student to learn the program if she types 60 words per minute. **5.6 h**

Available at **classzone.com**

Diagnosis/Remediation

- Practice A, B, C in Chapter 2 Resource Book, pp. 67–72
- Study Guide in Chapter 2 Resource Book, pp. 73–74
- Practice Workbook, pp. 27–29
- @HomeTutor

Challenge

Additional challenge is available in the Chapter 2 Resource Book, p. 77.

Quiz

An easily-readable reduced copy of the quiz (with answers) on Lessons 2.4–2.6 from the Assessment Book can be found on p. 70G.

29a, Quiz 7–10. See Additional Answers beginning on p. AA1.

C 29. **CHALLENGE** Data from some countries in North America show a positive correlation between the average life expectancy in a country and the number of personal computers per capita in that country.

a. Make a conjecture about the reason for the positive correlation between life expectancy and number of personal computers per capita. **See margin.**

b. Is it reasonable to conclude from the data that giving residents of a country more personal computers will lengthen their lives? *Explain.* **No.** ***Sample answer:*** **Correlation does not show cause-effect relationships.**

KY KENTUCKY MIXED REVIEW

TEST PRACTICE at classzone.com

30. Ted is planting flowers in a rectangular garden. The length of the garden is 55 feet and the perimeter is 150 feet. What is the area of the garden? **B**

Ⓐ 900 ft^2 Ⓑ 1100 ft^2 Ⓒ 1800 ft^2 Ⓓ 2025 ft^2

31. What is the y-intercept of the line shown? **C**

Ⓐ $-\frac{2}{3}$ Ⓑ $\frac{2}{3}$

Ⓒ 2 Ⓓ 3

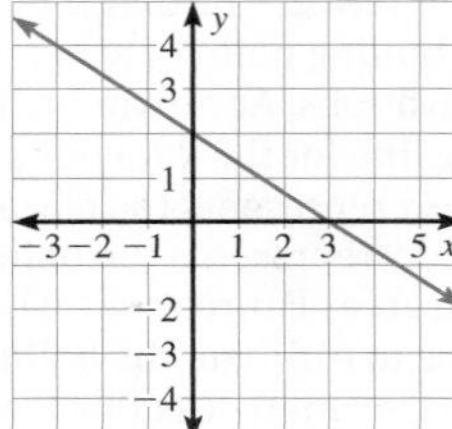

QUIZ *for Lessons 2.4–2.6*

Write an equation of the line that satisfies the given conditions. *(p. 98)*

1. $m = -5, b = 3$ $y = -5x + 3$
2. $m = 2, b = 12$ $y = 2x + 12$
3. $m = 4$, passes through $(-3, 6)$ $y = 4x + 18$
4. $m = -7$, passes through $(1, -4)$ $y = -7x + 3$
5. passes through $(0, 7)$ and $(-3, -2)$ $y = 3x + 7$
6. passes through $(-9, 9)$ and $(-9, 0)$ $x = -9$

Write and graph a direct variation equation that has the given ordered pair as a solution. *(p. 107)* **7–10. See margin for art.**

7. $(1, 2)$ $y = 2x$
8. $(-2, 8)$ $y = -4x$
9. $(5, -16)$ $y = -\frac{16}{5}x$
10. $(12, 4)$ $y = \frac{1}{3}x$

The variables x and y vary directly. Write an equation that relates x and y. Then find y when $x = 8$. *(p. 107)*

11. $x = 4, y = 12$ $y = 3x$; 24
12. $x = -3, y = -8$ $y = \frac{8}{3}x$; $21\frac{1}{3}$
13. $x = 40, y = -5$ $y = -\frac{1}{8}x$; -1
14. $x = 12, y = 2$ $y = \frac{1}{6}x$; $1\frac{1}{3}$

15. **CONCERT TICKETS** The table shows the average price of a concert ticket to one of the top 50 musical touring acts for the years 1999–2004. Write an equation that approximates the best-fitting line for the data pairs (x, y). Use the equation to predict the average price of a ticket in 2010. *(p. 113)*

Years since 1999, x	0	1	2	3	4	5
Ticket price (dollars), y	38.56	44.80	46.69	50.81	51.81	58.71

Sample answer: $y = 3.6x + 39.6$; **about $79.20**

@HomeTutor classzone.com Keystrokes

2.7 Exploring Transformations

MATERIALS • graphing calculator

QUESTION **How are the equation and the graph of an absolute value function related?**

You can investigate families of *absolute value functions* with equations of the form $y = a|x - h| + k$ by varying the values of a, h, and k and then graphing. The resulting graphs are *transformations* of the graph of the parent function $y = |x|$.

EXAMPLE 1 Graph $y = |x| + k$

Graph and describe the family of absolute value functions of the form $y = |x| + k$.

STEP 1 ***Vary the value of k***

Enter $y = |x|$, $y = |x| + 2$, $y = |x| + 5$, and $y = |x| - 3$.

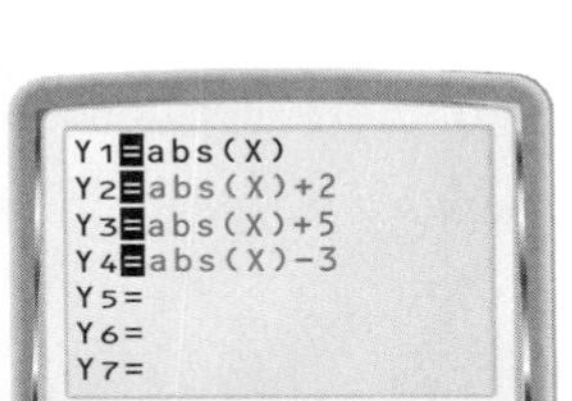

STEP 2 ***Display graphs***

Graph the equations in the standard viewing window by pressing ZOOM 6.

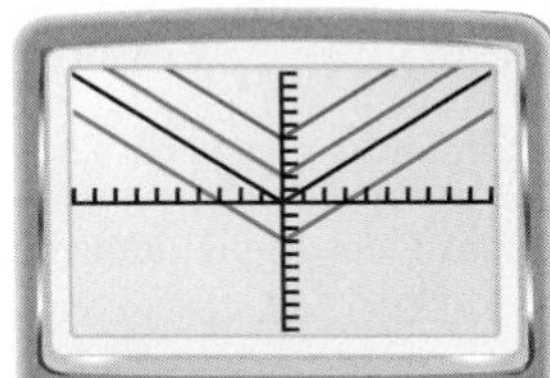

STEP 3 ***Compare graphs***

Describe how the family of graphs of $y = |x| + k$ is related to the graph of $y = |x|$.

The graphs of absolute value functions of the form $y = |x| + k$ have the same shape as the graph of $y = |x|$, but are shifted k units vertically.

EXAMPLE 2 Graph $y = |x - h|$

Graph and describe the family of absolute value functions of the form $y = |x - h|$.

STEP 1 ***Vary the value of h***

Enter $y = |x|$, $y = |x - 2|$, $y = |x - 4|$, and $y = |x + 5|$.

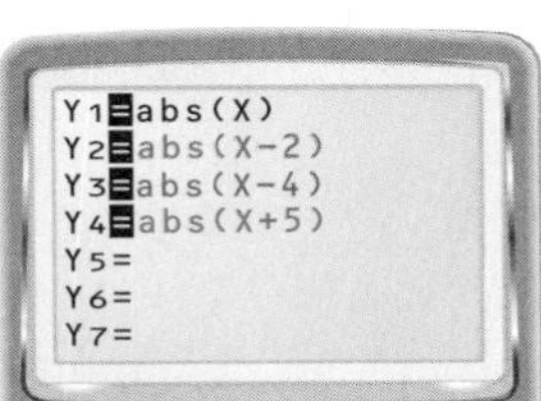

STEP 2 ***Display graphs***

Graph the equations in the standard viewing window by pressing ZOOM 6.

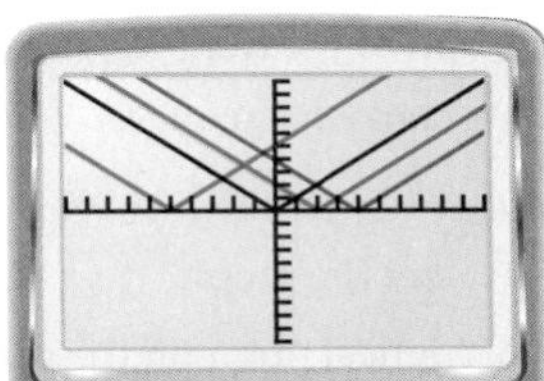

STEP 3 ***Compare graphs***

Describe how the family of graphs of $y = |x - h|$ is related to the graph of $y = |x|$.

The graphs of absolute value functions of the form $y = |x - h|$ have the same shape as the graph of $y = |x|$, but are shifted h units horizontally.

1 PLAN AND PREPARE

Explore the Concept

- Students will explore transformations of the graph of $y = |x|$.
- This activity leads into the study of deriving new absolute value functions from the parent graph in Examples 1–3 in Lesson 2.7.

Materials

Each student will need a graphing calculator.

Recommended Time

Work activity: 10 min

Discuss results: 5 min

Grouping

Students can work individually or in pairs. If students work in pairs, they can take turns graphing the equations.

2 TEACH

Tips for Success

Make sure students know how to find the "abs" notation on their calculators and remember to enclose x in parentheses when entering an equation of the form $y = |x| + k$ in their graphing calculator.

Key Questions

- When is the graph of $y = |x| + k$ shifted upward from the graph of $y = |x|$? **when $k > 0$**
- When is the graph of $y = |x - h|$ shifted to the left of the graph of $y = |x|$? **when $h < 0$**

Key Discovery

The graphs of $y = |x| + k$, $y = |x - h|$ and $y = a|x - h| + k$ are transformations of the graph of $y = |x|$.

3 ASSESS AND RETEACH

1. What is the value of a when the graph of $y = a|x - h| + k$ has the same shape as the graph of $y = |x|$? 1
2. What is the value of a when the graph of $y = a|x|$ is a reflection in the x-axis of the graph of $y = |x|$? -1

1. Step 2:

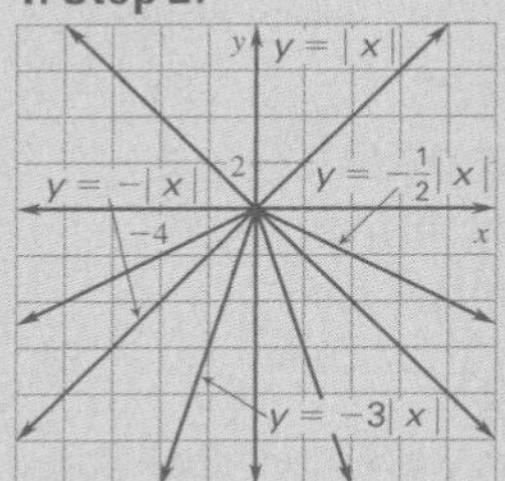

Step 3: When $a < 0$, $y = a|x|$ has its highest point at the origin. If $-1 < a < 0$, the graph is wider than $y = |x|$. If $a < -1$, the graph is narrower than $y = |x|$.

2–10. See Additional Answers beginning on p. AA1.

13. If $a < 0$, then the graph is reflected over the x-axis. If $-1 < a < 1$, then the graph is wider than $y = |x|$. If $a < -1$ or $a > 1$, then the graph is narrower than $y = |x|$.

14. (h, k); if $a < 0$ it is the highest point and if $a > 0$ it is the lowest point.

EXAMPLE 3 Graph $y = a|x|$ where a is a positive number

Graph and describe the family of absolute value functions of the form $y = a|x|$ where $a > 0$.

STEP 1 Vary the value of a
Enter $y = |x|$, $y = 2|x|$, $y = 5|x|$, and $y = \frac{1}{2}|x|$.

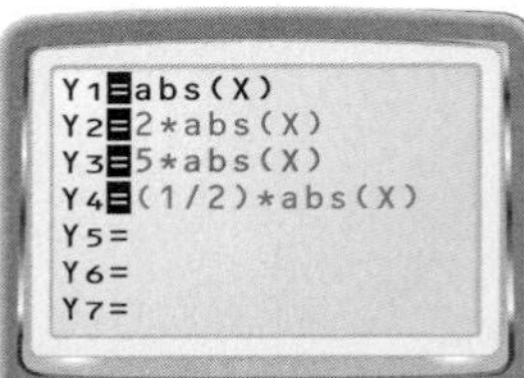

STEP 2 Display graphs
Graph the equations in the standard viewing window by pressing ZOOM 6.

STEP 3 Compare graphs
Describe how the family of graphs of $y = a|x|$ where $a > 0$ is related to the graph of $y = |x|$.

As with $y = |x|$, the graph of $y = a|x|$ $(a > 0)$ has its lowest point at the origin. If $a > 1$, the graph is narrower than that of $y = |x|$. If $0 < a < 1$, the graph is wider than that of $y = |x|$.

PRACTICE

1. Graph and describe the family of absolute value functions of the form $y = a|x|$ where $a < 0$. Follow these steps:

   STEP 1 Enter $y = |x|$, $y = -|x|$, $y = -3|x|$, and $y = -\frac{1}{2}|x|$. Check students' work.

   STEP 2 Graph the equations in the standard viewing window by pressing ZOOM 6. See margin.

   STEP 3 Describe how the family of graphs of $y = a|x|$ where $a < 0$ is related to the graph of $y = |x|$. See margin.

***Describe* how the graph of the given equation is related to the graph of $y = |x|$. Then graph the given equation along with $y = |x|$ to confirm your answer.** 2–10. See margin for art.

2. $y = |x| + 6$ translated up 6 units
3. $y = |x| - 4$ translated down 4 units
4. $y = |x - 3|$ translated right 3 units
5. $y = |x + 2|$ translated left 2 units
6. $y = \frac{2}{3}|x|$ wider than $y = |x|$
7. $y = -6|x|$ reflected over x-axis and narrower than $y = |x|$
8. $y = |x - 1| + 2$ translated up 2 units and right 1 unit
9. $y = 3|x + 2|$ narrower that $y = |x|$ and translated left 2 units
10. $y = -0.5|x + 1| + 7$ reflected over the x-axis and wider than $y = |x|$, translated left 1 unit and up 7 units

DRAW CONCLUSIONS

Answer the following questions about the graph of $y = a|x - h| + k$.

11. How does the value of k affect the graph? shifts the graph vertically
12. How does the value of h affect the graph? shifts the graph horizontally
13. How do the sign and absolute value of a affect the graph? See margin.
14. What are the coordinates of the lowest or highest point on the graph? How can you tell whether this point is the lowest point or the highest point? See margin.

2.7 Use Absolute Value Functions and Transformations

MA-HS-5.1.8

Before You graphed and wrote linear functions.

Now You will graph and write absolute value functions.

Why? So you can model structures, as in Ex. 39.

Key Vocabulary
- absolute value function
- vertex of an absolute value graph
- transformation
- translation
- reflection

MA-HS-5.1.8
Students will identify the changes and explain how changes in parameters affect graphs of functions (linear, quadratic, absolute value, exponential) (e.g., compare $y = x^2$, $y = 2x^2$, $y = (x - 4)^2$, and $y = x^2 + 3$). DOK 2

In Lesson 1.7, you learned that the absolute value of a real number x is defined as follows.

$$|x| = \begin{cases} x, & \text{if } x \text{ is positive} \\ 0, & \text{if } x = 0 \\ -x, & \text{if } x \text{ is negative} \end{cases}$$

You can also define an **absolute value function** $f(x) = |x|$.

KEY CONCEPT *For Your Notebook*

Parent Function for Absolute Value Functions

The parent function for the family of all absolute value functions is $f(x) = |x|$. The graph of $f(x) = |x|$ is V-shaped and is symmetric about the y-axis. So, for every point (x, y) on the graph, the point $(-x, y)$ is also on the graph.

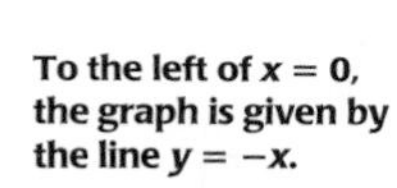

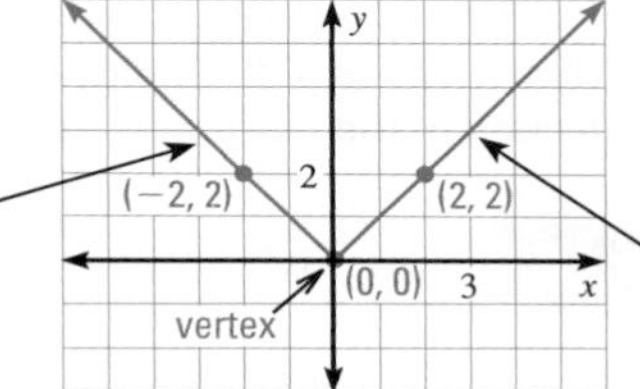

To the right of $x = 0$, the graph is given by the line $y = x$.

The highest or lowest point on the graph of an absolute value function is called the **vertex**. The vertex of the graph of $f(x) = |x|$ is $(0, 0)$.

REVIEW GEOMETRY
For help with transformations, see p. 988.

TRANSLATIONS You can derive new absolute value functions from the parent function through *transformations* of the parent graph.

A **transformation** changes a graph's size, shape, position, or orientation. A **translation** is a transformation that shifts a graph horizontally and/or vertically, but does not change its size, shape, or orientation.

The graph of $y = |x - h| + k$ is the graph of $y = |x|$ translated h units horizontally and k units vertically, as shown in the diagram. The vertex of $y = |x - h| + k$ is (h, k).

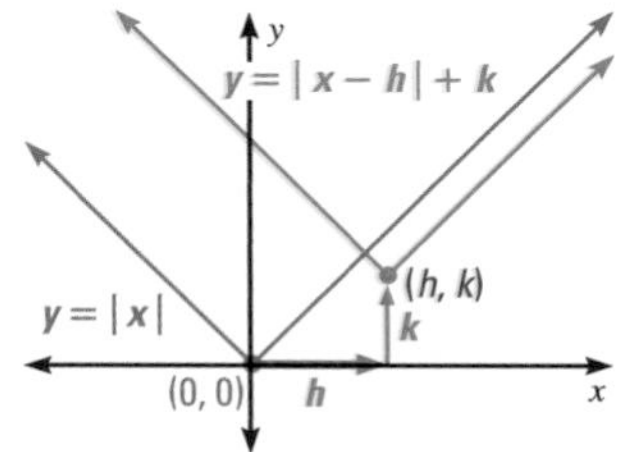

1 PLAN AND PREPARE

Warm-Up Exercises

Transparency Available

Evaluate the expression for $x = -2$.

1. $|x + 5|$ 3
2. $|x - 4| + 8$ 14
3. Ted drove 10 blocks looking for an address. He then had to drive $\frac{1}{2}$ block in reverse to reach it. What expression gives the distance driven? $|10| + \left|-\frac{1}{2}\right|$

Notetaking Guide

Transparency Available

Promotes interactive learning and notetaking skills, pp. 46–50.

Pacing

Basic: 2 days
Average: 2 days
Advanced: 2 days
Block: 0.5 block with 2.6
0.5 block with 2.8
- See *Teaching Guide/Lesson Plan.*

2 FOCUS AND MOTIVATE

Essential Question

Big Idea 3, p. 71

How do the values of a, h, and k affect the graph of $y = a \cdot f(x - h) + k$ in relation to the graph of $y = f(x)$? **Tell students they will learn how to answer this question by graphing transformations of $y = f(x)$.**

Resource Planning Guide

Chapter Resource Book
- Teaching Guide/Lesson Plan (pp. 78–79)
- Practice levels A, B, C (pp. 81–86)
- Study Guide (pp. 87–88)
- Catch-up for Absent Students (p. 89)
- Application (p. 90)
- Challenge (p. 91)

Workbooks
- Notetaking Guide (pp. 46–50)
- Practice Workbook (pp. 30–32)

Teaching Options
- **Power Presentations CD-ROM** provides dynamic electronic teaching resources for the classroom.
- **Activity Generator CD-ROM** provides editable activities for all ability levels.

Interactive Technology
- Easy Planner
- Power Presentations CD-ROM
- Activity Generator CD-ROM
- Animated Algebra
- Test Generator CD-ROM
- Online Quiz
- eWorkbook
- eEdition
- @HomeTutor

Resources for English Learners
- Quick Reference for English Learners
- Spanish Study Guide
- Multi-Language Visual Glossary
- Student Resources in Spanish

See also the *Algebra 2 Toolkit* for more strategies for meeting individual needs.

Motivating the Lesson

Laser beams have many applications: in medicine, space technology, the creating of CDs and DVDs, and the making of 3-dimensional photographs, called *holograms*. Laser beams can be modeled by equations and graphs of absolute value functions and their transformations.

3 TEACH

Extra Example 1

Graph $y = |x - 1| + 3$. Compare the graph with the graph of $y = |x|$.

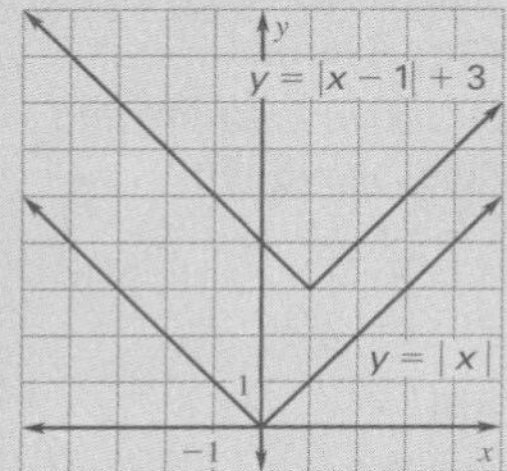

The graph of $y = |x - 1| + 3$ is the graph of $y = |x|$ translated up 3 units and right 1 unit.

Extra Example 2

Graph (a) $y = \frac{1}{3}|x|$ and (b) $y = -2|x|$. Compare each graph with the graph of $y = |x|$.

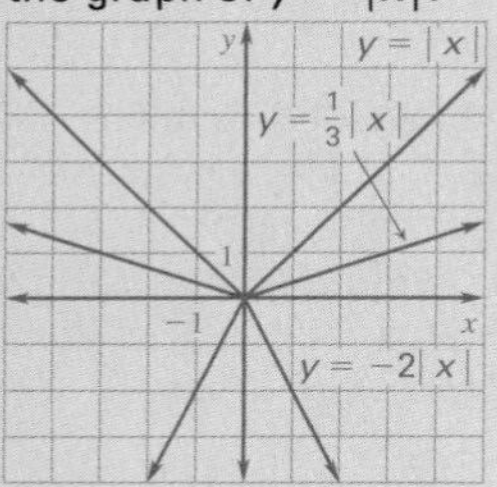

The graph of $y = \frac{1}{3}|x|$ is the graph of $y = |x|$ vertically shrunk by a factor of $\frac{1}{3}$. The graph of $y = -2|x|$ is the graph of $y = |x|$ vertically stretched by a factor of 2 and then reflected in the x-axis.

124

EXAMPLE 1 Graph a function of the form $y = |x - h| + k$

Graph $y = |x + 4| - 2$. Compare the graph with the graph of $y = |x|$.

INTERPRET FUNCTIONS
To identify the vertex, rewrite the given function as $y = |x - (-4)| + (-2)$. So, $h = -4$ and $k = -2$. The vertex is $(-4, -2)$.

Solution

STEP 1 **Identify** and plot the vertex, $(h, k) = (-4, -2)$.

STEP 2 **Plot** another point on the graph, such as $(-2, 0)$. Use symmetry to plot a third point, $(-6, 0)$.

STEP 3 **Connect** the points with a V-shaped graph.

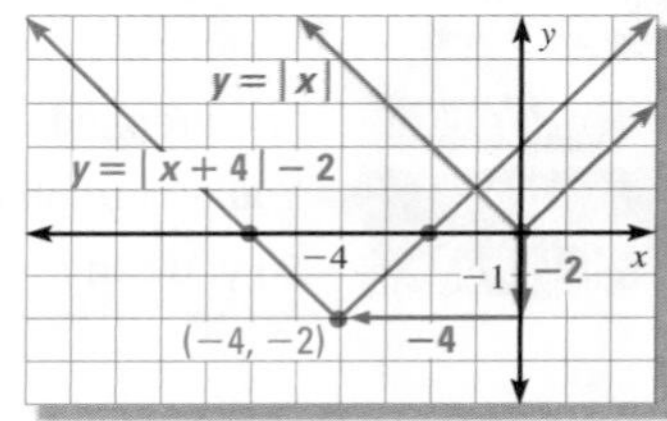

STEP 4 **Compare** with $y = |x|$. The graph of $y = |x + 4| - 2$ is the graph of $y = |x|$ translated down 2 units and left 4 units.

STRETCHES, SHRINKS, AND REFLECTIONS When $|a| \neq 1$, the graph of $y = a|x|$ is a vertical *stretch* or a vertical *shrink* of the graph of $y = |x|$, depending on whether $|a|$ is less than or greater than 1.

For $\|a\| > 1$	For $\|a\| < 1$
• The graph is vertically *stretched*, or elongated.	• The graph is vertically *shrunk*, or compressed.
• The graph of $y = a\|x\|$ is *narrower* than the graph of $y = \|x\|$.	• The graph of $y = a\|x\|$ is *wider* than the graph of $y = \|x\|$.

When $a = -1$, the graph of $y = a|x|$ is a **reflection** in the x-axis of the graph of $y = |x|$. When $a < 0$ but $a \neq -1$, the graph of $y = a|x|$ is a vertical stretch or shrink with a reflection in the x-axis of the graph of $y = |x|$.

EXAMPLE 2 Graph functions of the form $y = a|x|$

Graph (a) $y = \frac{1}{2}|x|$ and (b) $y = -3|x|$. Compare each graph with the graph of $y = |x|$.

Solution

a. The graph of $y = \frac{1}{2}|x|$ is the graph of $y = |x|$ vertically shrunk by a factor of $\frac{1}{2}$. The graph has vertex $(0, 0)$ and passes through $(-4, 2)$ and $(4, 2)$.

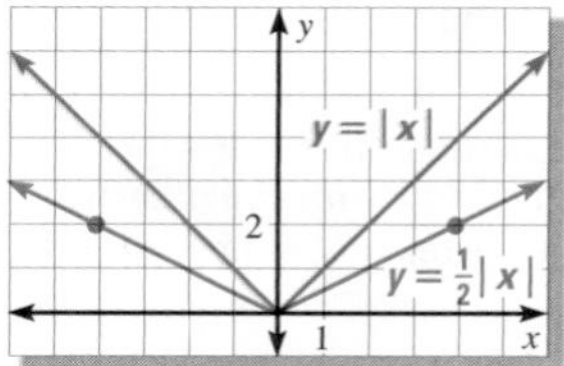

b. The graph of $y = -3|x|$ is the graph of $y = |x|$ vertically stretched by a factor of 3 and then reflected in the x-axis. The graph has vertex $(0, 0)$ and passes through $(-1, -3)$ and $(1, -3)$.

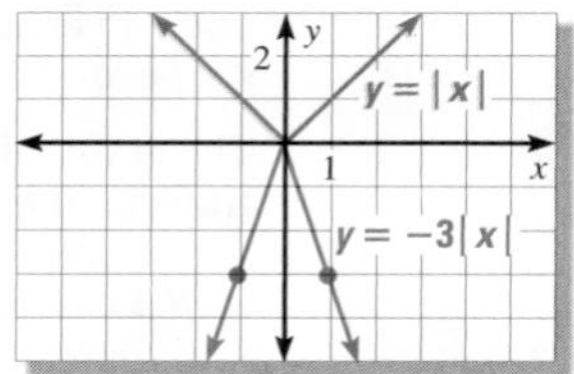

MULTIPLE TRANSFORMATIONS In part (b) of Example 2, graphing $y = -3|x|$ involves both vertically stretching and reflecting the graph of $y = |x|$. A graph may be related to a parent graph by even more than two transformations. For example, the graph of $y = a|x - h| + k$ can involve a vertical stretch or shrink, a reflection, and a translation of the graph of $y = |x|$.

EXAMPLE 3 Graph a function of the form $y = a|x - h| + k$

Graph $y = -2|x - 1| + 3$. Compare the graph with the graph of $y = |x|$.

Solution

STEP 1 **Identify** and plot the vertex, $(h, k) = (1, 3)$.

STEP 2 **Plot** another point on the graph, such as (0, 1). Use symmetry to plot a third point, (2, 1).

STEP 3 **Connect** the points with a V-shaped graph.

STEP 4 **Compare** with $y = |x|$. The graph of $y = -2|x - 1| + 3$ is the graph of $y = |x|$ stretched vertically by a factor of 2, then reflected in the x-axis, and finally translated right 1 unit and up 3 units.

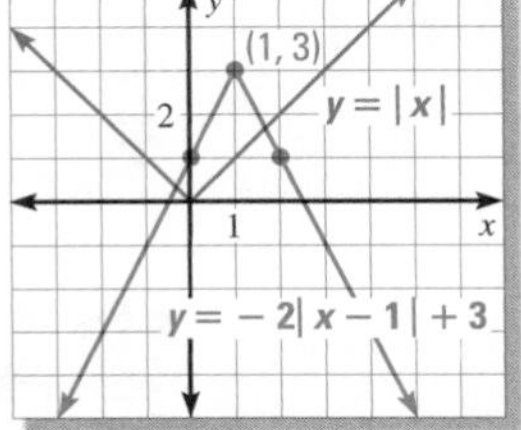

GUIDED PRACTICE for Examples 1, 2, and 3

Graph the function. *Compare* the graph with the graph of $y = |x|$.
1–3. See margin for art.

1. $y = |x - 2| + 5$
translated right 2 units and up 5 units

2. $y = \frac{1}{4}|x|$
shrunk vertically by a factor of $\frac{1}{4}$

3. $f(x) = -3|x + 1| - 2$
reflected over the x-axis, stretched by a factor of 3, translated left 1 unit and down 2 units

EXAMPLE 4 Write an absolute value function

HOLOGRAMS In holography, light from a laser beam is split into two beams, a reference beam and an object beam. Light from the object beam reflects off an object and is recombined with the reference beam to form images on film that can be used to create three-dimensional images. Write an equation for the path of the reference beam.

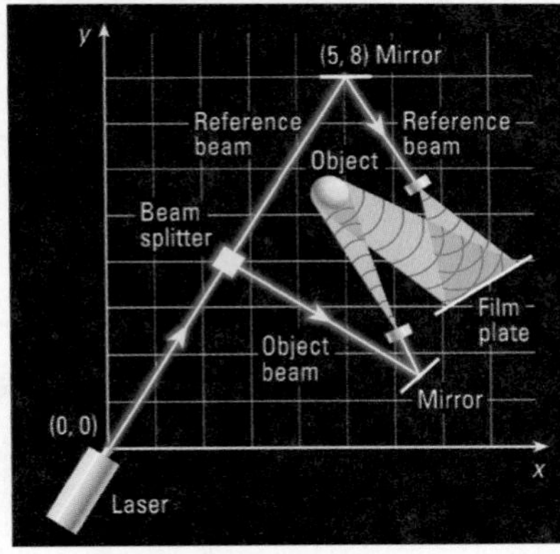

Solution

The vertex of the path of the reference beam is (5, 8). So, the equation has the form $y = a|x - 5| + 8$. Substitute the coordinates of the point (0, 0) into the equation and solve for a.

$0 = a|0 - 5| + 8$ **Substitute 0 for *y* and 0 for *x*.**

$-1.6 = a$ **Solve for *a*.**

▶ An equation for the path of the reference beam is $y = -1.6|x - 5| + 8$.

1. 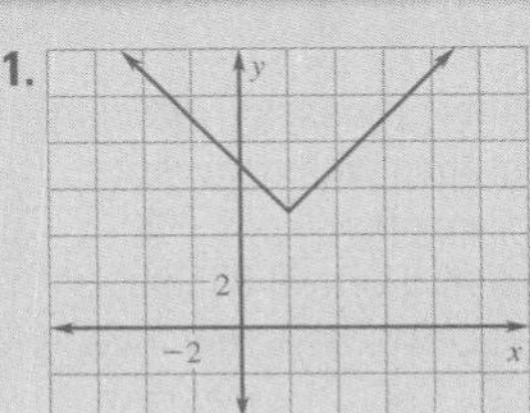

2. 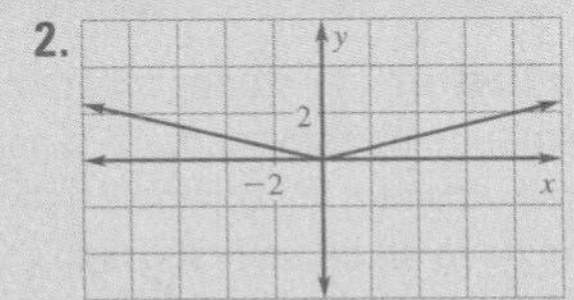

3. 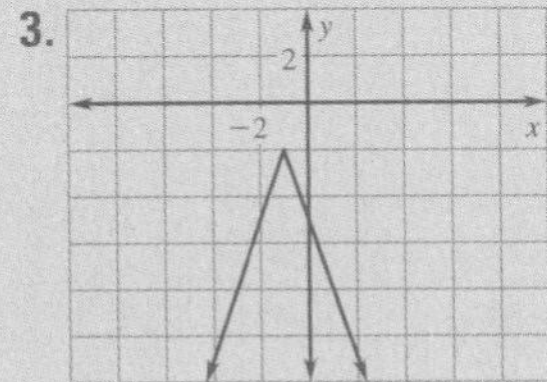

Extra Example 3

Graph $y = \frac{1}{4}|x + 3| - 2$. Compare the graph with the graph of $y = |x|$.

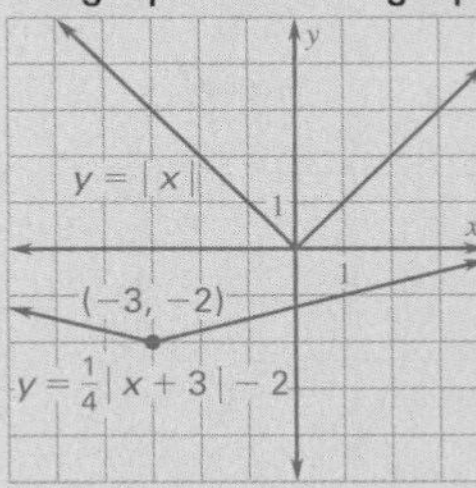

The graph of $y = \frac{1}{4}|x + 3| - 2$ is the graph of $y = |x|$ first vertically shrunk by a factor of $\frac{1}{4}$, then translated left 3 units and down 2 units.

Extra Example 4

A landscaper sketches the design for a triangular shrub protector on graph paper. Write an equation for the shrub protector.

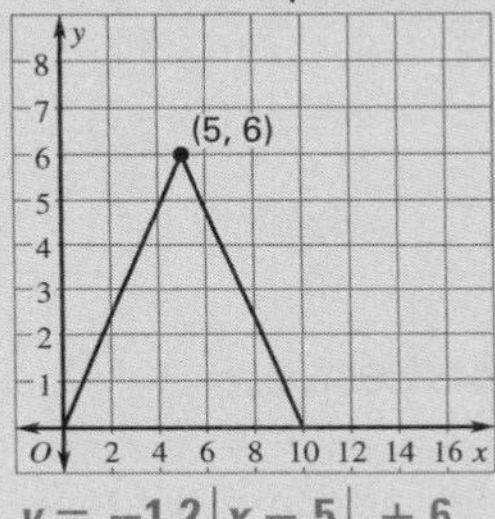

$y = -1.2|x - 5| + 6$

Key Question to Ask for Example 4

- Compare the graph to the graph of $y = |x|$. The graph of $y = -1.6|x - 5| + 8$ is the graph of $y = |x|$ vertically stretched by a factor of 1.6, then reflected in the x-axis, and finally translated 5 units right and 8 units up.

Avoiding Common Errors

Students may confuse the shift of the graph of $y = |x - h|$. Use specific examples, such as 5 and −5, to show that the shift is to the right if h is replaced by a positive number and to the left if replaced by a negative number.

Extra Example 5

The graph of a function $y = f(x)$ is shown. Sketch the graph of the given function.

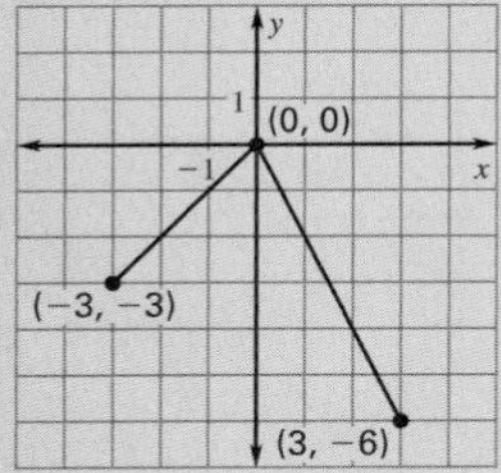

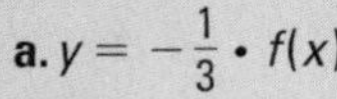

a. $y = -\frac{1}{3} \cdot f(x)$

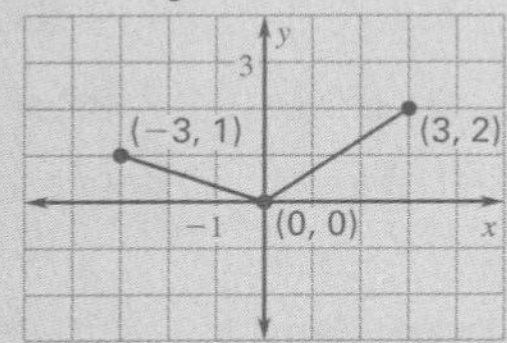

b. $y = f(x - 1) + 3$

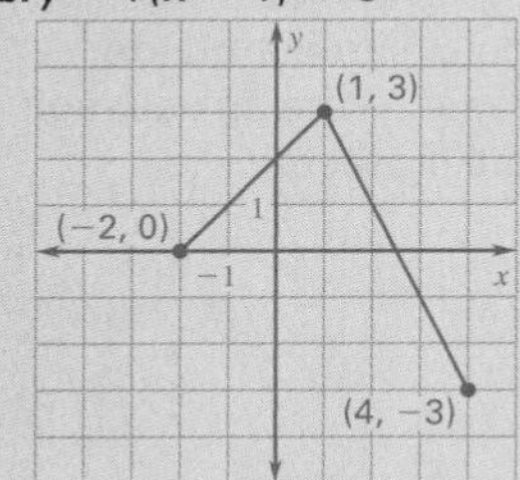

Closing the Lesson

Have students summarize the major points of the lesson and answer the Essential Question: How do the values of a, h, and k affect the graphing of $y = a \cdot f(x - h) + k$ in relation to the graph of $y = f(x)$?

- The graph of $y = |x - h| + k$ is the graph of $y = |x|$ translated h units horizontally and k units vertically with vertex (h, k).
- When $|a| \neq 1$, the graph of $y = a|x|$ is a vertical stretch or a vertical shrink of the graph of $y = |x|$, depending on whether $|a|$ is less than or greater than 1.
- When $a = -1$, the graph of $y = a|x|$ is a reflection in the x-axis of the graph of $y = |x|$.

When $|a| \neq 1$, the value of a cause a vertical shrink or stretch. If $a = -1$, the graph is reflected in the x-axis. The value of h translates the graph horizontally; the value of k translates it vertically.

TRANSFORMATIONS OF ANY GRAPH You can perform transformations on the graph of *any* function f in the same way as for absolute value graphs.

KEY CONCEPT *For Your Notebook*

Transformations of General Graphs

The graph of $y = a \cdot f(x - h) + k$ can be obtained from the graph of any function $y = f(x)$ by performing these steps:

STEP 1 **Stretch or shrink** the graph of $y = f(x)$ vertically by a factor of $|a|$ if $|a| \neq 1$. If $|a| > 1$, stretch the graph. If $|a| < 1$, shrink the graph.

STEP 2 **Reflect** the resulting graph from Step 1 in the x-axis if $a < 0$.

STEP 3 **Translate** the resulting graph from Step 2 horizontally h units and vertically k units.

EXAMPLE 5 Apply transformations to a graph

The graph of a function $y = f(x)$ is shown. Sketch the graph of the given function.

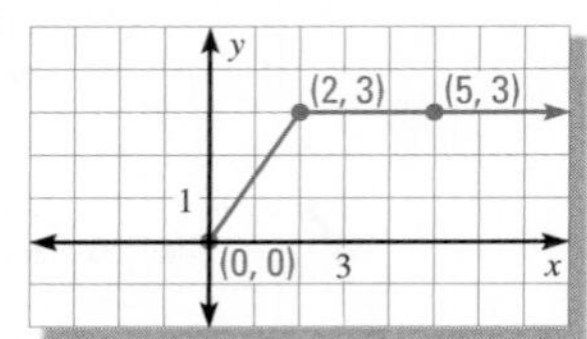

a. $y = 2 \cdot f(x)$

b. $y = -f(x + 2) + 1$

Solution

a. The graph of $y = 2 \cdot f(x)$ is the graph of $y = f(x)$ stretched vertically by a factor of 2. (There is no reflection or translation.) To draw the graph, multiply the y-coordinate of each labeled point on the graph of $y = f(x)$ by 2 and connect their images.

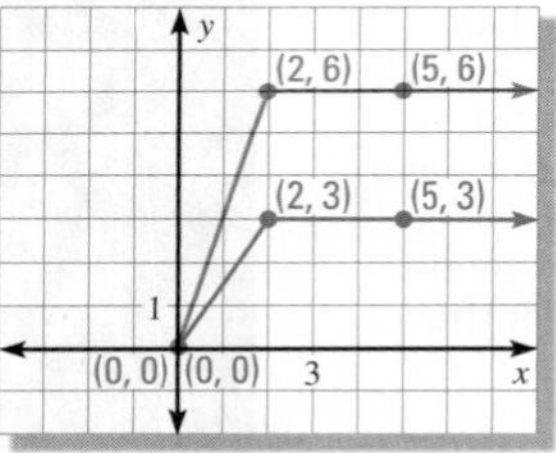

b. The graph of $y = -f(x + 2) + 1$ is the graph of $y = f(x)$ reflected in the x-axis, then translated left 2 units and up 1 unit. To draw the graph, first reflect the labeled points and connect their images. Then translate and connect these points to form the final image.

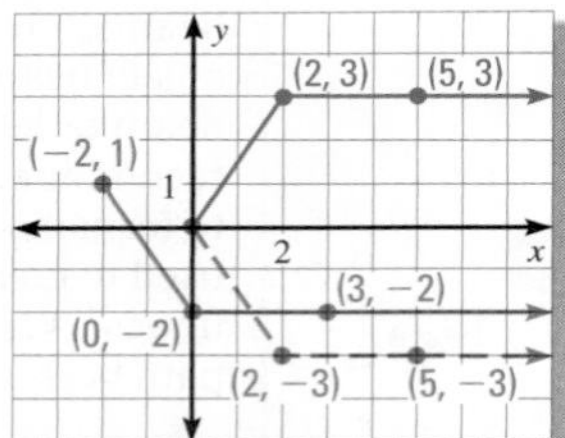

AVOID ERRORS

In Example 5, part (b), the value of h is −2 because $-f(x + 2) + 1 = -f(x - (-2)) + 1$. Because $-2 < 0$, the horizontal translation is to the left.

✓ **GUIDED PRACTICE** for Examples 4 and 5

4. $y = -2|x - 5| + 4$

4. WHAT IF? In Example 4, suppose the reference beam originates at (3, 0) and reflects off a mirror at (5, 4). Write an equation for the path of the beam.

Use the graph of $y = f(x)$ from Example 5 to graph the given function. 5–7. See margin.

5. $y = 0.5 \cdot f(x)$ **6.** $y = -f(x - 2) - 5$ **7.** $y = 2 \cdot f(x + 3) - 1$

Differentiated Instruction

Inclusion For students with conceptual processing difficulty, introduce transformations of general graphs with concrete examples of f. For example, let $f(x) = 2x$ or $f(x) = |x + 3|$ and have students first graph the function. Then give them different values of a, h, and k so they can write the new function $y = a \cdot f(x - h) + k$ to be graphed.

See also the *Algebra 2 Toolkit* for more strategies.

2.7 EXERCISES

HOMEWORK KEY

○ = **WORKED-OUT SOLUTIONS** on p. WS4 for Exs. 13, 19, and 39

★ = **STANDARDIZED TEST PRACTICE** Exs. 2, 27, 28, 31, 32, 33, 38, and 40

◆ = **MULTIPLE REPRESENTATIONS** Ex. 41

SKILL PRACTICE

A

1. **VOCABULARY** The point (h, k) is the __?__ of the graph of $y = a|x - h| + k$. vertex

2. ★ **WRITING** *Describe* three different types of transformations.
Sample answer: Graphs can be stretched vertically, translated left/right, and translated up/down.

EXAMPLES 1, 2, and 3 on pp. 124–125 for Exs. 3–14

GRAPHING FUNCTIONS Graph the function. *Compare* the graph with the graph of $y = |x|$. 3–14. See margin.

3. $y = |x| - 7$
4. $y = |x + 2|$
5. $y = |x + 4| - 2$
6. $f(x) = |x - 1| + 4$
7. $f(x) = 2|x|$
8. $f(x) = -3|x|$
9. $y = -\frac{1}{3}|x|$
10. $y = \frac{3}{4}|x|$
11. $y = 2|x + 1| - 6$
12. $f(x) = -4|x + 2| - 3$
13. $f(x) = -\frac{1}{2}|x - 1| + 5$
14. $f(x) = \frac{1}{4}|x - 4| + 3$

EXAMPLE 4 on p. 125 for Exs. 15–20

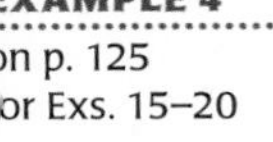

WRITING EQUATIONS Write an equation of the graph.

15. 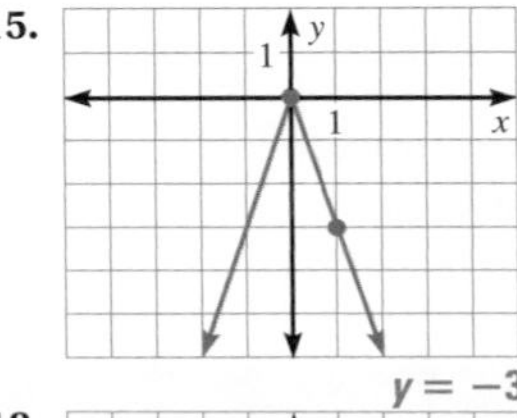
$y = -3|x|$

16. 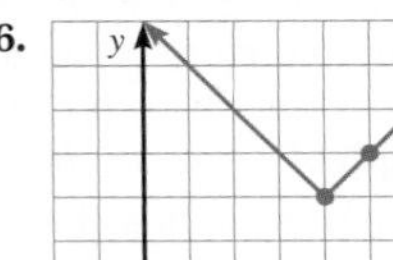
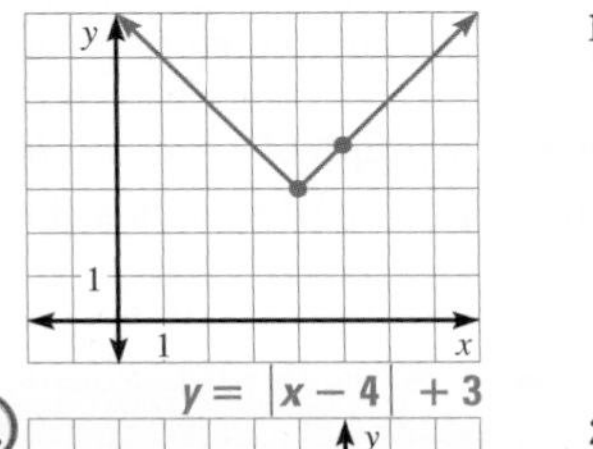
$y = |x - 4| + 3$

17. 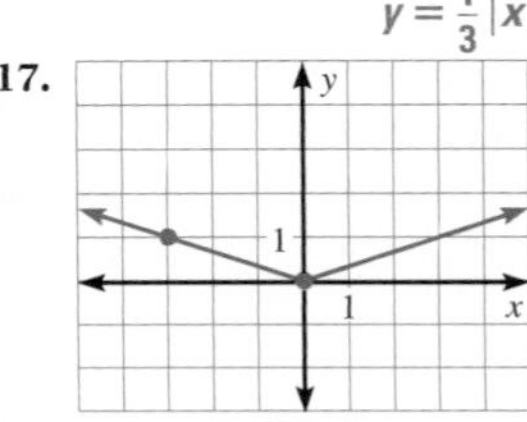
$y = \frac{1}{3}|x|$

18. 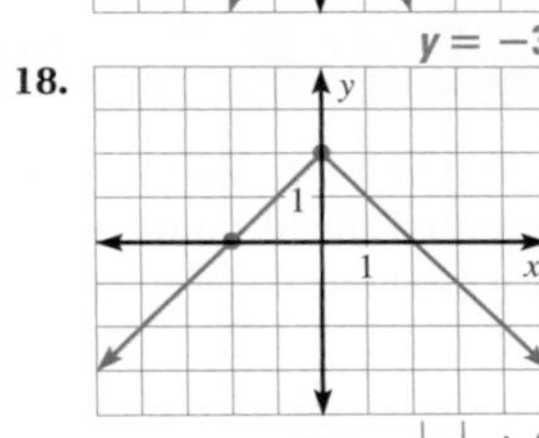
$y = -|x| + 2$

19. 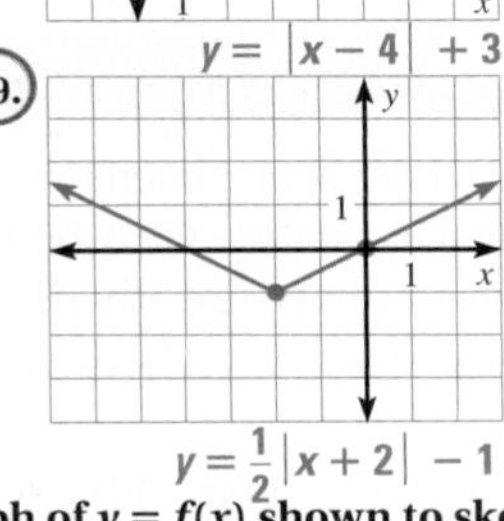
$y = \frac{1}{2}|x + 2| - 1$

20. 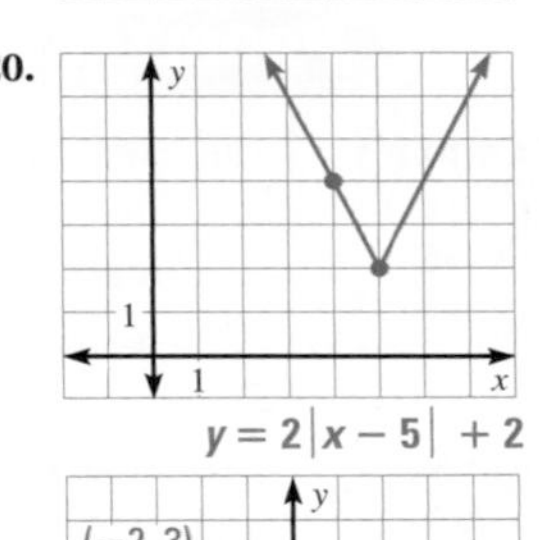
$y = 2|x - 5| + 2$

EXAMPLE 5 on p. 126 for Exs. 21–28

B

TRANSFORMATIONS Use the graph of $y = f(x)$ shown to sketch the graph of the given function. 21–26. See margin.

(Graph of $y = f(x)$ through points $(-2, 3)$, $(1, 2)$, $(2, 0)$.)

21. $y = f(x + 2) - 3$
22. $y = f(x - 4) + 1$
23. $y = \frac{1}{2} \cdot f(x)$
24. $y = -3 \cdot f(x)$
25. $y = -f(x - 1) + 4$
26. $y = 2 \cdot f(x + 3) - 1$

27. ★ **OPEN-ENDED MATH** Create a graph of a function $y = f(x)$. Then sketch the graphs of **(a)** $y = f(x + 3) - 4$, **(b)** $y = 2 \cdot f(x)$, and **(c)** $y = -f(x)$. See margin.

28. ★ **MULTIPLE CHOICE** The highest point on the graph of $y = f(x)$ is $(-1, 6)$. What is the highest point on the graph of $y = 4 \cdot f(x - 3) + 5$? D

Ⓐ $(-11, 6)$ Ⓑ $(8, 11)$ Ⓒ $(-4, 29)$ Ⓓ $(2, 29)$

Guided Practice, p. 126

5. 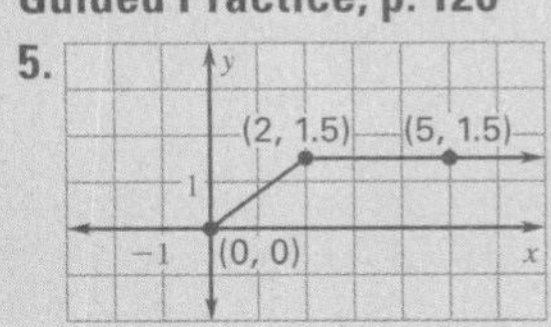

6. 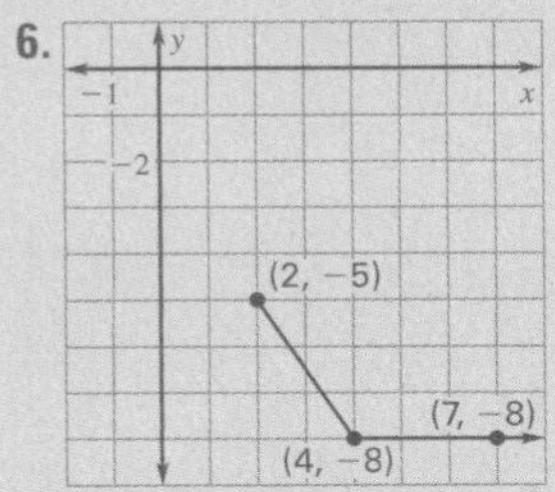

7. 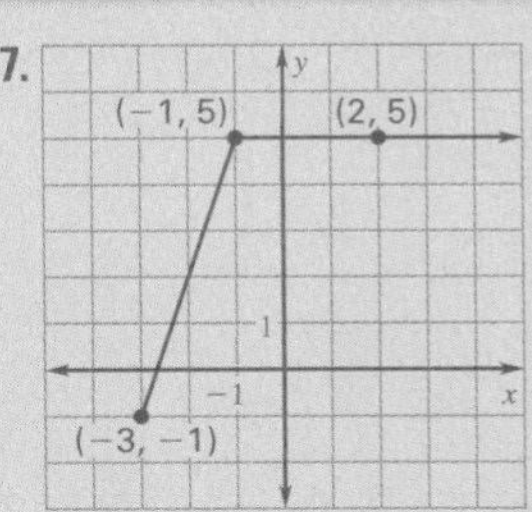

4 PRACTICE AND APPLY

Assignment Guide

Answer Transparencies available for all exercises

Basic:
Day 1: SRH p. 989 Exs. 9, 12, 13, 17, 18
pp. 127–129
Exs. 1–14, 36, 37
Day 2: pp. 127–129
Exs. 15–29, 38–40, 43–44

Average:
Day 1: pp. 127–129
Exs. 1, 2, 4–14, 32, 36, 37
Day 2: pp. 127–129
Exs. 17–31, 33, 38–41, 43–44

Advanced:
Day 1: pp. 127–129
Exs. 1, 2, 5–14, 32, 35–37*
Day 2: pp. 127–129
Exs. 18–31, 33, 34, 38–42*, 44

Block:
pp. 127–129
Exs. 1, 2, 4–14, 32, 36, 37 (with 2.6)
pp. 127–129
Exs. 17–31, 33, 38–41, 43–44 (with 2.8)

Differentiated Instruction

See *Algebra 2 Best Practices Toolkit* for suggestions on addressing the needs of a diverse classroom.

Homework Check

For a quick check of student understanding of key concepts, go over the following exercises:
Basic: 6, 16, 22, 36, 38
Average: 8, 18, 24, 37, 38
Advanced: 10, 20, 26, 37, 39

Extra Practice

- Student Edition, p. 1011
- Chapter 2 Resource Book: Practice levels A, B, C, pp. 81–86

Practice Worksheet

An easily-readable reduced practice page (with answers) for this lesson can be found on p. 70C.

3–14, 21–26, 27. See Additional Answers beginning on p. AA1.

Vocabulary

Exercise 3–26, 32 Suggest that students use the letter h to remember that the variable h in the function $y = a|x - h| + k$ represents the horizontal shift of a graph.

Teaching Strategy

Exercises 36–37 Remind students to choose reasonable domains for their graphs.

Internet Reference

Exercise 39 Additional information about the Leonard P. Zakim Bunker Hill Bridge can be found at www.leonardpzakimbunkerhillbridge.org

29.

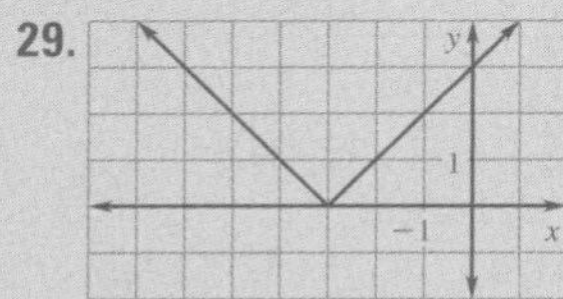

32. *Sample answer:* **The horizontal shift is the opposite sign of h, with negative being translated right and positive being translated left. The vertical shift is the same as k, with positive being translated up and negative being translated down.**

36.

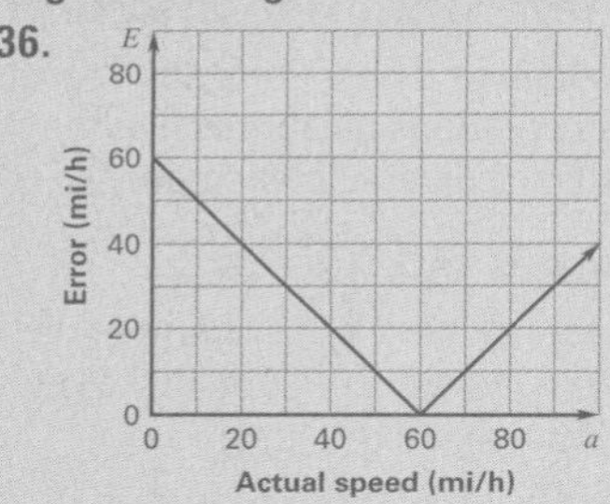

37.

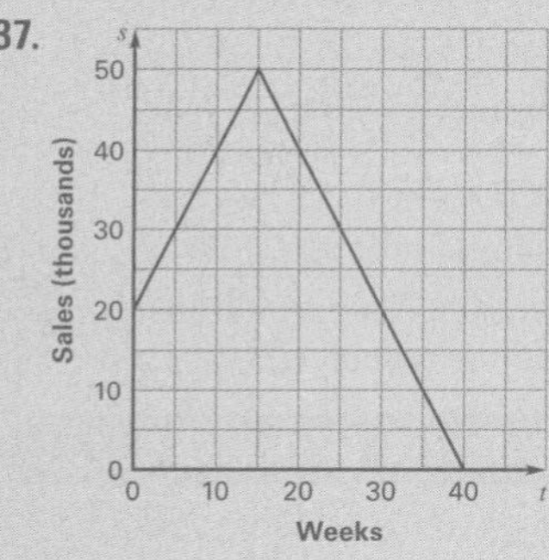

38a. $y = -\frac{4}{3}|x + 1.25| + 5$

29. The graph should have been a translation of $y = |x|$ left 3 units, not right 3 units. See margin for art.

30. The graph should have been a translation of $y = |x|$ left 3 units, not up 3 units. See art for Exercise 29.

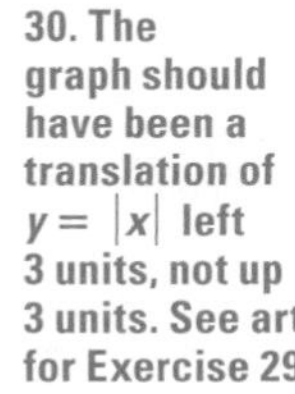

34. No. *Sample answer:* **The graph of $y = |x + h|$ is the graph of $y = |x|$ translated $-h$ units horizontally. The graph of $y = |x| + |h|$ is the graph of $y = |x|$ translated $|h|$ vertically.**

ERROR ANALYSIS ***Describe*** **and correct the error in graphing $y = |x + 3|$.**

29.

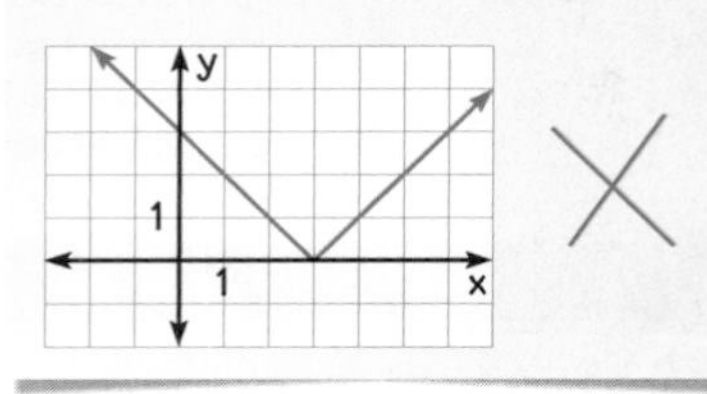

30.

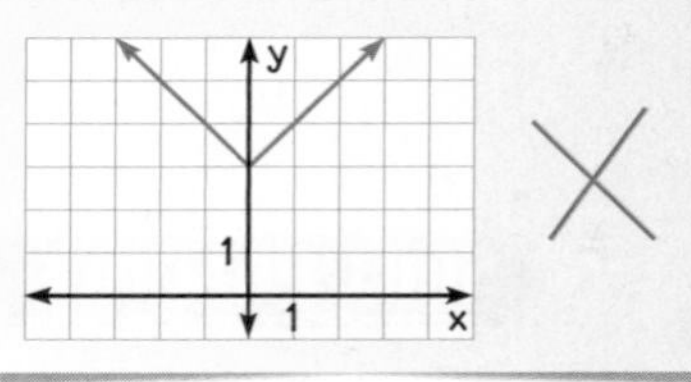

31. ★ **MULTIPLE CHOICE** Which equation has the graph shown? **D**

Ⓐ $y = \frac{3}{2}|x|$ Ⓑ $y = \frac{2}{3}|x|$

Ⓒ $y = -\frac{2}{3}|x|$ Ⓓ $y = -\frac{3}{2}|x|$

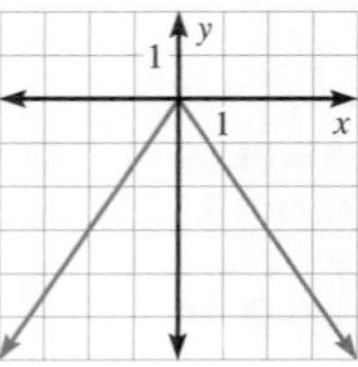

32. ★ **WRITING** *Describe* how the signs of h and k affect how to obtain the graph of $y = f(x - h) + k$ from the graph of $y = f(x)$. **See margin.**

33. ★ **SHORT RESPONSE** The graph of the relation $x = |y|$ is shown at the right. Is the relation a function? *Explain.*
No. *Sample answer:* **It does not pass the vertical line test.**

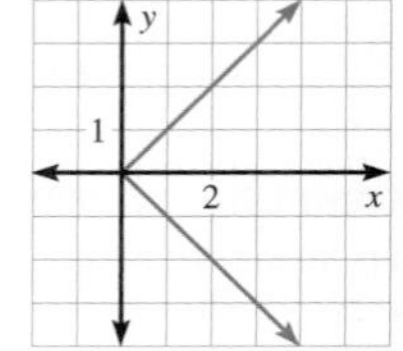

C **34.** **REASONING** Is it true in general that $|x + h| = |x| + |h|$? *Justify* your answer by considering how the graphs of $y = |x + h|$ and $y = |x| + |h|$ are related to the graph of $y = |x|$.

35. **CHALLENGE** The graph of $y = a|x - h| + k$ passes through $(-2, 4)$ and $(4, 4)$. *Describe* the possible values of h and k.
$h = 1$ and k = any real number

PROBLEM SOLVING

EXAMPLE 1 A on p. 124 for Ex. 36

36. **SPEEDOMETER** A car's speedometer reads 60 miles per hour. The error E in this measurement is $E = |a - 60|$ where a is the actual speed. Graph the function. For what value(s) of a will E be 2.5 miles per hour? **See margin for art; 57.5 mi/h, 62.5 mi/h.**

@HomeTutor for problem solving help at classzone.com

EXAMPLE 3 on p. 125 for Ex. 37

37. **SALES** Weekly sales s (in thousands) of a new basketball shoe increase steadily for a while and then decrease as described by the function $s = -2|t - 15| + 50$ where t is the time (in weeks). Graph the function. What is the greatest number of pairs of shoes sold in one week? **See margin for art; 50,000 pairs of shoes.**

@HomeTutor for problem solving help at classzone.com

EXAMPLE 4 on p. 125 for Exs. 38–39

38. ★ **SHORT RESPONSE** On the pool table shown, you bank the five ball off the side at $(-1.25, 5)$. You want the ball to go in the pocket at $(-5, 0)$.

a. Write an equation for the path of the ball. **See margin.**

b. Do you make the shot? *Explain* how you found your answer. **Yes.** *Sample answer:* **$(-5, 0)$ satisfies the equation in part (a).**

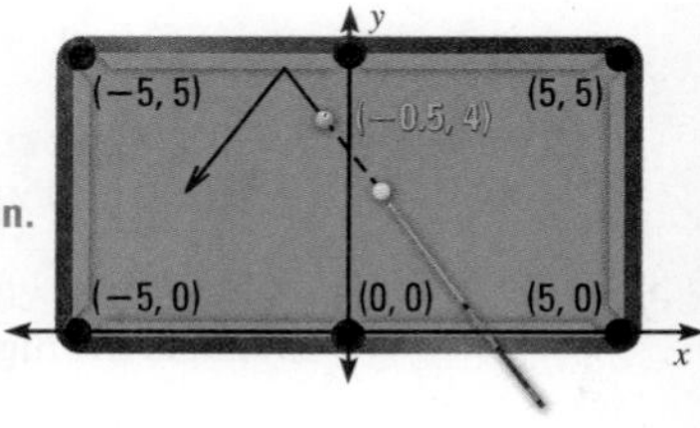

○ = WORKED-OUT SOLUTIONS on p. WS1 ★ = STANDARDIZED TEST PRACTICE

= MULTIPLE REPRESENTATION

40a.

41b.

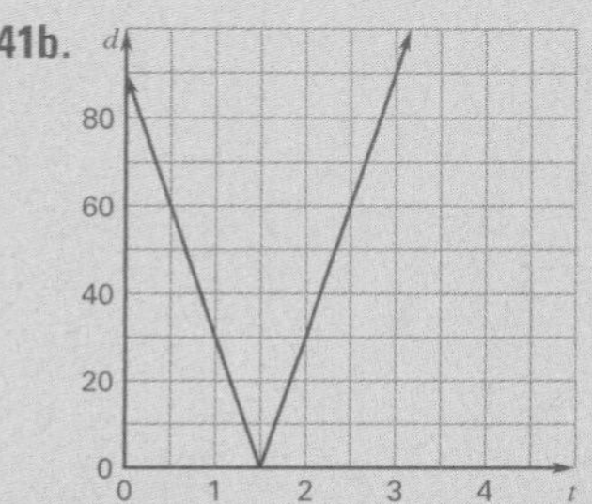

41a.

t	0	0.5	1	1.5	2	2.5	3
d	90	60	30	0	30	60	90

39. **ENGINEERING** The Leonard P. Zakim Bunker Hill Bridge spans the Charles River in Boston. The bridge is suspended from two towers. Each tower has the dimensions shown. Write an absolute value function that represents the inverted V-shaped portion of a tower. $y = -\frac{140}{69}|x - 69| + 140$

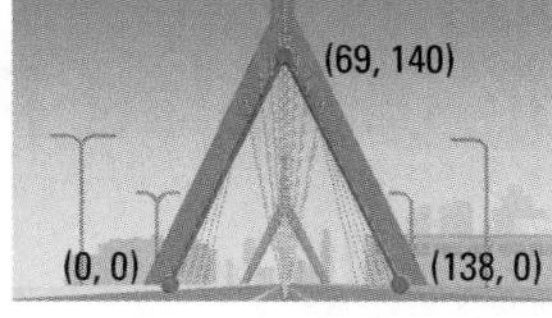

B 40. ★ **EXTENDED RESPONSE** A snowstorm begins with light snow that increases to very heavy snow before decreasing again. The snowfall rate r (in inches per hour) is given by $r(t) = -0.5|t - 4| + 2$ where t is the time (in hours).

a. **Graph** Graph the function. **See margin.**

b. **Interpret** When is the snowfall heaviest? What is the maximum snowfall rate? How are your answers related to the function's graph? **4 h; 2 in./h; it is the vertex of the graph.**

c. **Extend** The total snowfall is given by the area of the triangle formed by the graph of $r(t)$ and the t-axis. What is the total snowfall? **8 in.**

41. **MULTIPLE REPRESENTATIONS** The diagram shows a truck driving toward a radio station transmitter that has a broadcasting range of 50 miles.

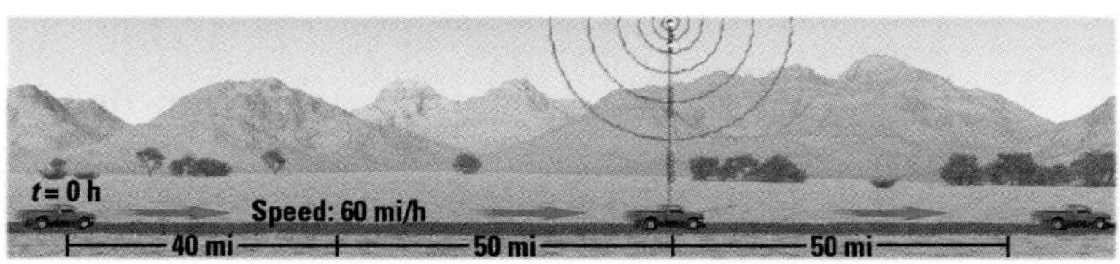

a. **Making a Table** Make a table that shows the truck's distance d (in miles) from the transmitter after $t = 0, 0.5, 1, 1.5, 2, 2.5,$ and 3 hours. **a, b. See margin.**

b. **Drawing a Graph** Use your table from part (a) to draw a graph that shows d as a function of t.

c. **Writing an Equation** Write an equation that gives d as a function of t. During what driving times is the truck within range of the transmitter?

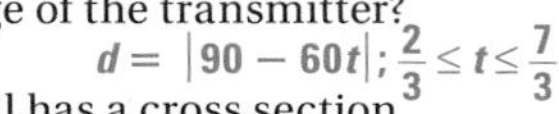

C 42. **CHALLENGE** A hiker walks up and down a hill. The hill has a cross section that can be modeled by $y = -\frac{4}{3}|x - 300| + 400$ where x and y are measured in feet and $0 \le x \le 600$. How far does the hiker walk? **1000 ft**

KENTUCKY MIXED REVIEW

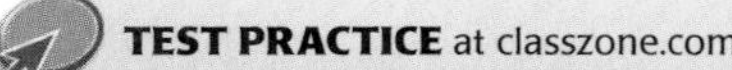

43. Which expression is equivalent to $12(n^2 + n) - 5(n^2 + 3n - 2)$? **B**

Ⓐ $-7n^2 + 3n - 10$ Ⓑ $7n^2 - 3n + 10$

Ⓒ $17n^2 + 27n - 10$ Ⓓ $17n^2 - 13n + 10$

44. In the figure shown, what is the length of $\overline{YX}$ in inches? **C**

Ⓐ 20 in. Ⓑ 36 in.

Ⓒ 56 in. Ⓓ 3136 in.

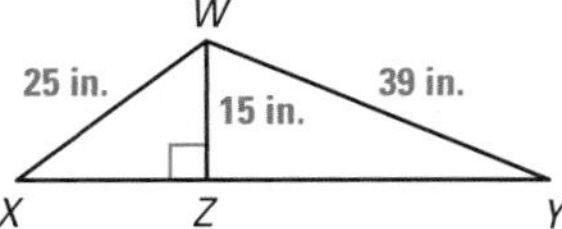

5 ASSESS AND RETEACH

Daily Homework Quiz

Transparency Available

1. Graph $y = 4|x|$ and compare it with the graph of $y = |x|$.

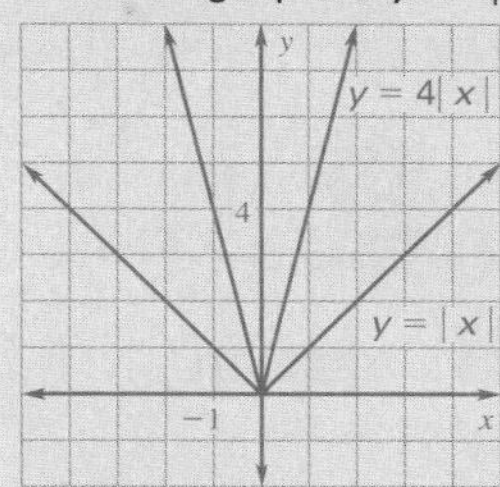

The graph of $y = 4|x|$ is the graph of $y = |x|$ stretched vertically by a factor of 4.

2. Graph $y = -|x + 2| - 2$ and compare it with the graph of $y = |x|$.

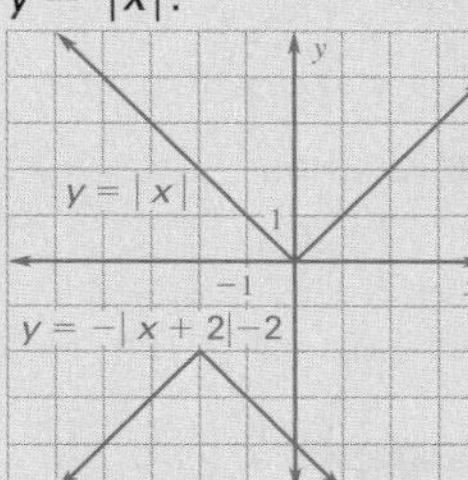

The graph of $y = -|x + 2| - 2$ is the graph of $y = |x|$ first reflected in the x-axis, then translated 2 units down and 2 units left.

Available at **classzone.com**

Diagnosis/Remediation

- Practice A, B, C in Chapter 2 Resource Book, pp. 81–86
- Study Guide in Chapter 2 Resource Book, pp. 87–88
- Practice Workbook, pp. 30–32
- @HomeTutor

Challenge

Additional challenge is available in the Chapter 2 Resource Book, p. 91.

Extension Use Piecewise Functions

Use after Lesson 2.7

1 PLAN AND PREPARE

Warm-Up Exercises

Evaluate each expression.

1. $3x - 1$ for $x = -2$ -7
2. $6 + 5x$ for $x = 4$ 26
3. $-2x + 9$ for $x = -1$ 11

2 FOCUS AND MOTIVATE

Essential Question

Big Idea 3, p. 71

What is a step function? Tell students they will learn how to answer this question by learning about piecewise functions.

3 TEACH

Extra Example 1

Evaluate the function

$$g(x) = \begin{cases} 4x - 3, & \text{if } x > 3 \\ 5x + 2, & \text{if } x \le 3 \end{cases}$$

when $x = -2$ and $x = 5$. $-8, 17$

Extra Example 2

Graph the function

$$f(x) = \begin{cases} x, & \text{if } x < -1 \\ x + 1, & \text{if } -1 \le x \le 2 \\ -1, & \text{if } x > 2 \end{cases}.$$

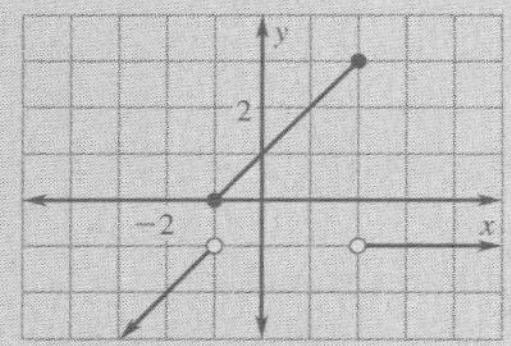

NCTM STANDARDS

Standard 2: Understand functions; Represent situations using algebraic symbols

GOAL Evaluate, graph, and write piecewise functions.

Key Vocabulary
- piecewise function
- step function

A **piecewise function** is defined by at least two equations, each of which applies to a different part of the function's domain. One example of a piecewise function is the absolute value function $f(x) = |x|$, which can be defined by the equations $y = -x$ for $x < 0$ and $y = x$ for $x \ge 0$. Another example is given below.

$$g(x) = \begin{cases} 2x - 1, & \text{if } x \le 1 \\ 3x + 1, & \text{if } x > 1 \end{cases}$$

The equation $y = 2x - 1$ gives the value of $g(x)$ when x is less than or equal to 1, and the equation $y = 3x + 1$ gives the value of $g(x)$ when x is greater than 1.

EXAMPLE 1 Evaluate a piecewise function

Evaluate the function $g(x)$ above when (a) $x = 1$ and (b) $x = 5$.

Solution

a. $g(x) = 2x - 1$ — **Because $1 \le 1$, use first equation.**

$g(1) = 2(1) - 1 = 1$ — **Substitute 1 for x and simplify.**

b. $g(x) = 3x + 1$ — **Because $5 > 1$, use second equation.**

$g(5) = 3(5) + 1 = 16$ — **Substitute 5 for x and simplify.**

EXAMPLE 2 Graph a piecewise function

Graph the function $f(x) = \begin{cases} -\frac{3}{2}x - 1, & \text{if } x < -2 \\ x + 1, & \text{if } -2 \le x \le 1 \\ 3, & \text{if } x > 1 \end{cases}$

Solution

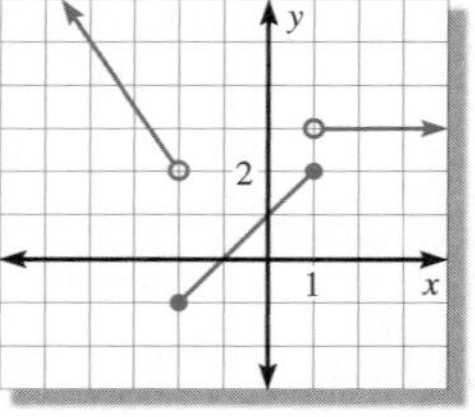

STEP 1 To the left of $x = -2$, graph $y = -\frac{3}{2}x - 1$. Use an open dot at $(-2, 2)$ because the equation $y = -\frac{3}{2}x - 1$ does not apply when $x = -2$.

STEP 2 From $x = -2$ to $x = 1$, inclusive, graph $y = x + 1$. Use solid dots at $(-2, -1)$ and $(1, 2)$ because the equation $y = x + 1$ applies to both $x = -2$ and $x = 1$.

STEP 3 To the right of $x = 1$, graph $y = 3$. Use an open dot at $(1, 3)$ because the equation $y = 3$ does not apply when $x = 1$.

5. 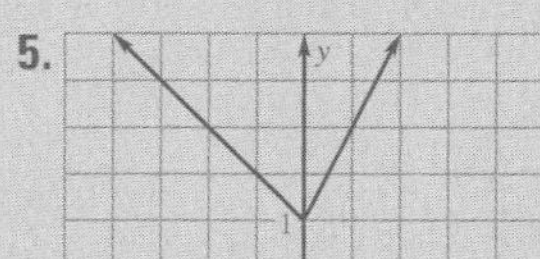

6. 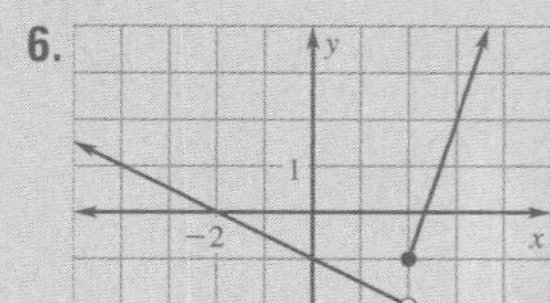

7. 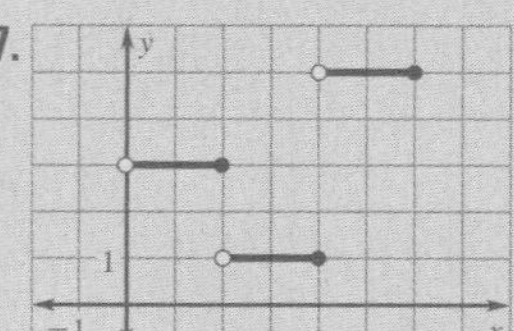

EXAMPLE 3 Write a piecewise function

Write a piecewise function for the graph shown.

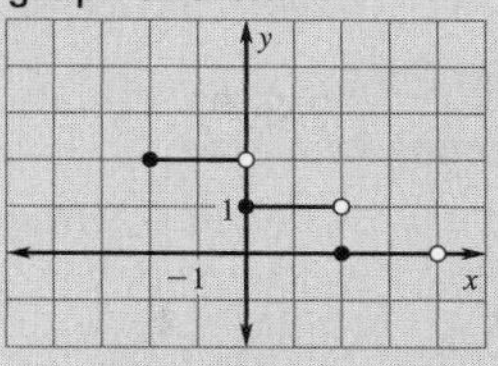

Solution

For x between 0 and 1, including $x = 0$, the graph is the line segment given by $y = 1$.

For x between 1 and 2, including $x = 1$, the graph is the line segment given by $y = 2$.

For x between 2 and 3, including $x = 2$, the graph is the line segment given by $y = 3$. So, a piecewise function for the graph is as follows:

$$f(x) = \begin{cases} 1, & \text{if } 0 \le x < 1 \\ 2, & \text{if } 1 \le x < 2 \\ 3, & \text{if } 2 \le x < 3 \end{cases}$$

STEP FUNCTIONS The piecewise function in Example 3 is called a **step function** because its graph resembles a set of stairs. A step function is defined by a constant value over each part of its domain. The constant values can increase with each "step" as in Example 3, or they can decrease with each step.

PRACTICE

EXAMPLE 1 on p. 130 for Exs. 1–4

EVALUATING FUNCTIONS **Evaluate the function below for the given value of x.**

$$f(x) = \begin{cases} 9x - 4, & \text{if } x > 3 \\ \frac{1}{2}x + 1, & \text{if } x \le 3 \end{cases}$$

1. $f(-4)$ -1
2. $f(2)$ 2
3. $f(3)$ $\frac{5}{2}$
4. $f(5)$ 41

EXAMPLE 2 on p. 130 for Exs. 5–8

GRAPHING FUNCTIONS **Graph the function.** 5–7. See margin.

5. $f(x) = \begin{cases} 2x + 1, & \text{if } x \ge 0 \\ -x + 1, & \text{if } x < 0 \end{cases}$
6. $g(x) = \begin{cases} -\frac{1}{2}x - 1, & \text{if } x < 2 \\ 3x - 7, & \text{if } x \ge 2 \end{cases}$
7. $h(x) = \begin{cases} 3, & \text{if } 0 < x \le 2 \\ 1, & \text{if } 2 < x \le 4 \\ 5, & \text{if } 4 < x \le 6 \end{cases}$

8. **POSTAL RATES** In 2005, the cost C (in dollars) to send U.S. Postal Service Express Mail up to 5 pounds depended on the weight w (in ounces) according to the function at the right.

$$C(w) = \begin{cases} 13.65, & \text{if } 0 < w \le 8 \\ 17.85, & \text{if } 8 < w \le 32 \\ 21.05, & \text{if } 32 < w \le 48 \\ 24.20, & \text{if } 48 < w \le 64 \\ 27.30, & \text{if } 64 < w \le 80 \end{cases}$$

   a. Graph the function. See margin.
   b. What is the cost to send a parcel weighing 2 pounds 9 ounces? \$21.05

EXAMPLE 3 on p. 131 for Exs. 9–10

SPECIAL STEP FUNCTIONS **Write and graph the piecewise function described using the domain $-3 \le x \le 3$.** 9–10. See margin.

9. **Rounding Function** The output $f(x)$ is the input x rounded to the nearest integer. (If the decimal part of x is 0.5, then x is rounded up when x is positive and x is rounded down when x is negative.)
10. **Greatest Integer Function** The output $f(x)$ is the greatest integer less than or equal to the input x.

Extra Example 3

Write a piecewise function for the graph shown.

$$f(x) = \begin{cases} 2, & \text{if } -2 \le x < 0 \\ 1, & \text{if } 0 \le x < 2 \\ 0, & \text{if } 2 \le x < 4 \end{cases}$$

Key Questions to Ask for Example 3

- What is the domain of $f(x)$? $0 \le x < 3$
- What is the range of $f(x)$? 1, 2, 3

Closing the Lesson

Have students summarize the major points of the lesson and answer the Essential Question: What is a step function?

- **A piecewise function is defined by at least two equations, each of which applies to a different part of the function's domain.**
- **To graph a piecewise function, graph each part of the function for its given domain.**

A step function is defined by a constant value over each part of its domain.

4 PRACTICE AND APPLY

Avoiding Common Errors

Remind students that because piecewise functions are in fact functions, their graphs should pass the vertical line test. Performing this test may help them avoid including a point in two or more pieces of the graph of the function.

8a.

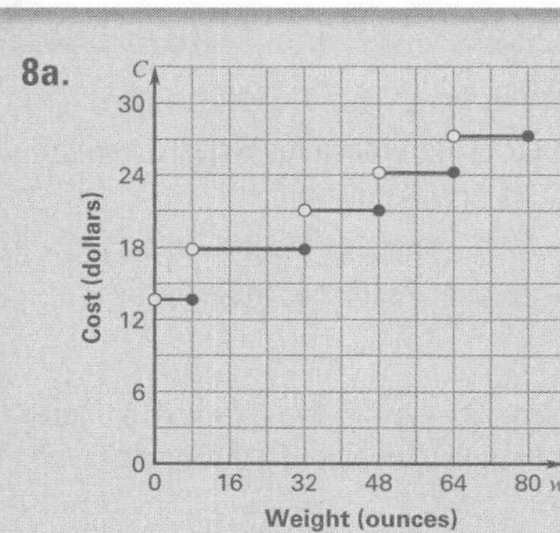

9.

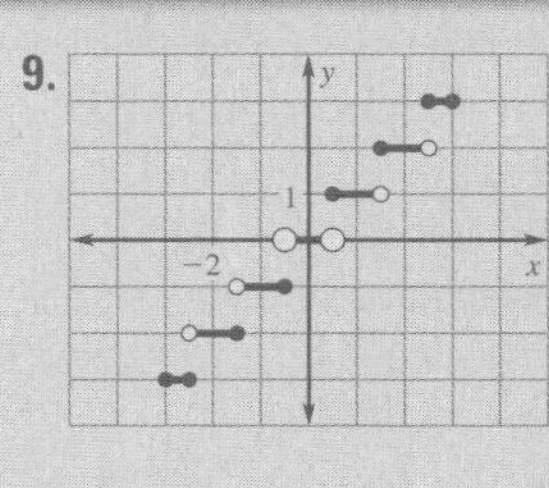

10.

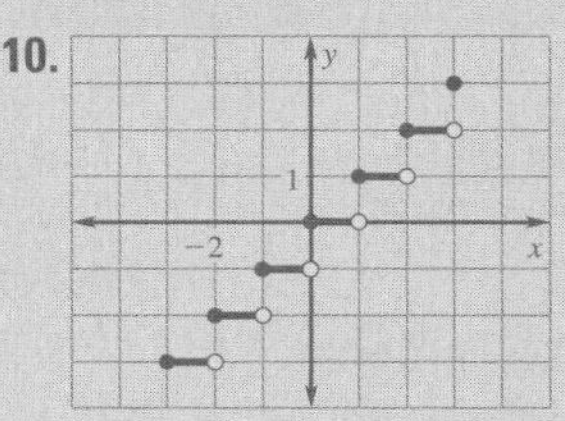

1 PLAN AND PREPARE

Warm-Up Exercises

Transparency Available

Tell whether each statement is *true* or *false* when $x = -2$ and $y = 1$.

1. $2x - y < 5$ **true**
2. $x + 3y \geq 0$ **true**
3. The equation $360x + 600y = 5640$ models the weekly payroll for a small business. Give an example of a solution of the equation. *Sample answer:* (9, 4)

Notetaking Guide

Transparency Available

Promotes interactive learning and notetaking skills, pp. 51–53.

Pacing

Basic: 1 day
Average: 1 day
Advanced: 1 day
Block: 0.5 block with 2.7
• See *Teaching Guide/Lesson Plan.*

2 FOCUS AND MOTIVATE

Essential Question

Big Idea 2, p. 71

What does a dashed boundary line on the graph of an inequality represent? **Tell students they will learn how to answer this question by learning how to graph linear inequalities in two variables.**

2.8 Graph Linear Inequalities in Two Variables

MA-HS-5.3.3 **Students will model, solve and graph first degree, two-variable equations and inequalities in real-world and mathematical problems. DOK 2**

Before You solved linear inequalities in one variable.
Now You will graph linear inequalities in two variables.
Why? So you can model data encoding, as in Example 4.

Key Vocabulary
- linear inequality in two variables
- solution of a linear inequality
- graph of a linear inequality
- half-plane

A **linear inequality in two variables** can be written in one of these forms:

$Ax + By < C$ $\quad Ax + By \leq C$ $\quad Ax + By > C$ $\quad Ax + By \geq C$

An ordered pair (x, y) is a **solution** of a linear inequality in two variables if the inequality is true when the values of x and y are substituted into the inequality.

EXAMPLE 1 ★ Standardized Test Practice

Which ordered pair is a solution of $3x + 4y > 8$?

Ⓐ (6, −3) Ⓑ (0, 2) Ⓒ (−2, −1) Ⓓ (−3, 5)

Solution

Ordered Pair	Substitute	Conclusion
(6, −3)	$3(6) + 4(-3) = 6 \not> 8$	(6, −3) is not a solution.
(0, 2)	$3(0) + 4(2) = 8 \not> 8$	(0, 2) is not a solution.
(−2, −1)	$3(-2) + 4(-1) = -10 \not> 8$	(−2, −1) is not a solution.
(−3, 5)	$3(-3) + 4(5) = 11 > 8$	(−3, 5) is a solution.

▶ The correct answer is D. Ⓐ Ⓑ Ⓒ Ⓓ

✓ GUIDED PRACTICE for Example 1

Tell whether the given ordered pair is a solution of $5x - 2y \leq 6$.

1. (0, −4) **not a solution**
2. (2, 2) **solution**
3. (−3, 8) **solution**
4. (−1, −7) **not a solution**

GRAPHING INEQUALITIES The **graph** of a linear inequality in two variables is the set of all points in a coordinate plane that represent solutions of the inequality.

INTERPRET GRAPHS
A dashed boundary line means that points on the line are *not* solutions. A solid boundary line means that points on the line *are* solutions.

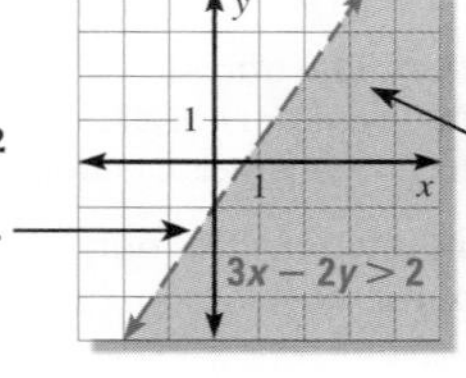

All solutions of $3x - 2y > 2$ lie on one side of the *boundary line* $3x - 2y = 2$.

The boundary line divides the plane into two half-planes. The shaded half-plane is the graph of $3x - 2y > 2$.

Resource Planning Guide

Chapter Resource Book
- Teaching Guide/Lesson Plan (pp. 92–93)
- Activity Master (p. 94)
- Practice levels A, B, C (pp. 96–101)
- Study Guide (pp. 102–103)
- Catch-up for Absent Students (p. 104)
- Problem Solving Workshop (p. 105)
- Challenge (p. 106)

Workbooks
- Notetaking Guide (pp. 51–53)
- Practice Workbook (pp. 33–35)

Teaching Options
- **Power Presentations CD-ROM** provides dynamic electronic teaching resources for the classroom.
- **Activity Generator CD-ROM** provides editable activities for all ability levels.

Interactive Technology
- Easy Planner
- Power Presentations CD-ROM
- Activity Generator CD-ROM
- Animated Algebra
- Test Generator CD-ROM
- Online Quiz
- eWorkbook
- eEdition
- @HomeTutor

Resources for English Learners
- Quick Reference for English Learners
- Spanish Study Guide
- Multi-Language Visual Glossary
- Student Resources in Spanish

See also the *Algebra 2 Toolkit* for more strategies for meeting individual needs.

KEY CONCEPT — For Your Notebook

Graphing a Linear Inequality

To graph a linear inequality in two variables, follow these steps:

STEP 1 **Graph** the boundary line for the inequality. Use a dashed line for < or > and a solid line for ≤ or ≥.

STEP 2 **Test** a point *not* on the boundary line to determine whether it is a solution of the inequality. If it is a solution, shade the half-plane containing the point. If it is not a solution, shade the other half-plane.

EXAMPLE 2 Graph linear inequalities with one variable

Graph (a) $y \le -3$ and (b) $x < 2$ in a coordinate plane.

a. **Graph** the boundary line $y = -3$. Use a solid line because the inequality symbol is ≤.

Test the point (0, 0). Because (0, 0) is *not* a solution of the inequality, shade the half-plane that does not contain (0, 0).

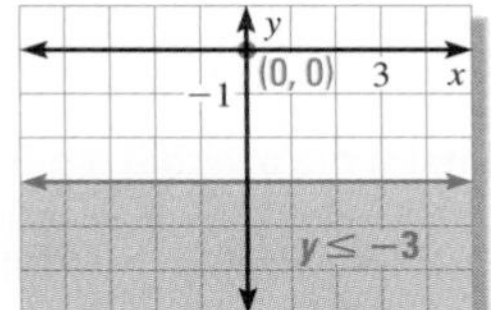

b. **Graph** the boundary line $x = 2$. Use a dashed line because the inequality symbol is <.

Test the point (0, 0). Because (0, 0) *is* a solution of the inequality, shade the half-plane that contains (0, 0).

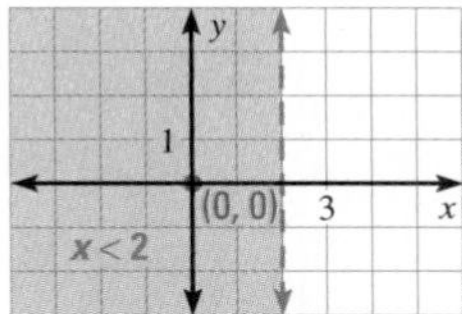

EXAMPLE 3 Graph linear inequalities with two variables

Graph (a) $y > -2x$ and (b) $5x - 2y \le -4$ in a coordinate plane.

a. **Graph** the boundary line $y = -2x$. Use a dashed line because the inequality symbol is >.

Test the point (1, 1). Because (1, 1) *is* a solution of the inequality, shade the half-plane that contains (1, 1).

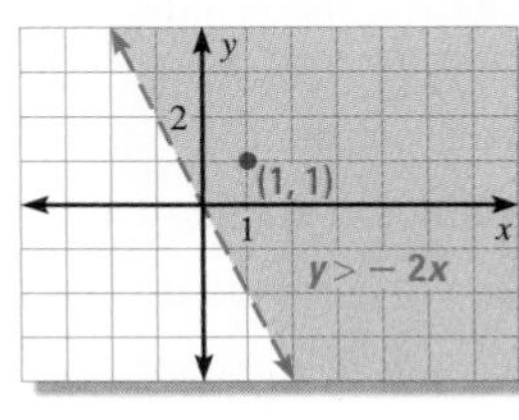

b. **Graph** the boundary line $5x - 2y = -4$. Use a solid line because the inequality symbol is ≤.

Test the point (0, 0). Because (0, 0) is *not* a solution of the inequality, shade the half-plane that does not contain (0, 0).

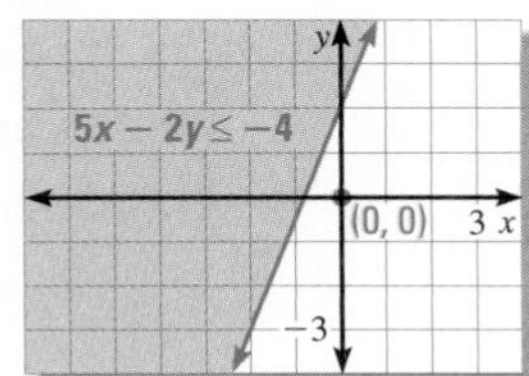

AVOID ERRORS
It is often convenient to use (0, 0) as a test point. However, if (0, 0) lies on the boundary line, you must choose a different test point.

Animated Algebra at classzone.com

Motivating the Lesson

You want to bake brownies and cakes for a bake sale. The brownie recipe uses 2 eggs and the cake recipe uses 3 eggs. A linear inequality in two variables can help tell you how many of each you could make with a dozen eggs.

3 TEACH

Extra Example 1

Which ordered pair is a solution of $5x - 2y \le 6$? A

(A) (0, −3) (B) (5, 5)
(C) (1, −2) (D) (3, 3)

Extra Example 2

Graph $x \le 5$ in a coordinate plane.

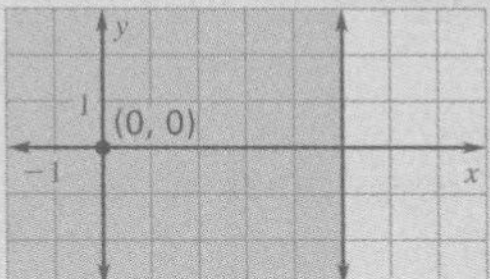

Extra Example 3

Graph $3x - 4y > 12$ in a coordinate plane.

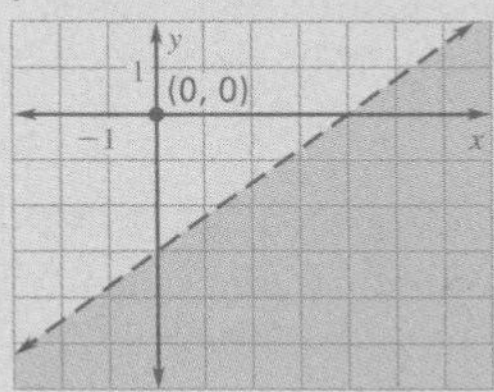

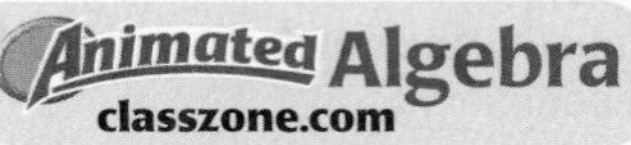

An **Animated Algebra** activity is available on-line for **Example 3**. This activity is also available on the **Power Presentations CD-ROM**.

Differentiated Instruction

Inclusion For a solid line, the inequality symbol is underlined (≤ or ≥). For a dashed line that uses less ink, the inequality symbol has less ink under it (< or >). For students with memory difficulties, this may help them remember the usage of the two symbols in graphing linear inequalities.

See also the *Algebra 2 Toolkit* for more strategies.

Extra Example 4

You have two part-time summer jobs, one that pays \$9 and hour and another that pays \$12 an hour. You would like to earn at least \$240 a week. Write an inequality describing the possible amounts of time you can schedule at both jobs. Graph the inequality. Identify three possible solutions of the inequality. **$9x + 12y \geq 240$; *Sample answers:* 10 hours at \$9 and 13 hours at \$12, 16 hours at \$9 and 9 hours at \$12, or 5 hours at \$9 and 17 hours at \$12**

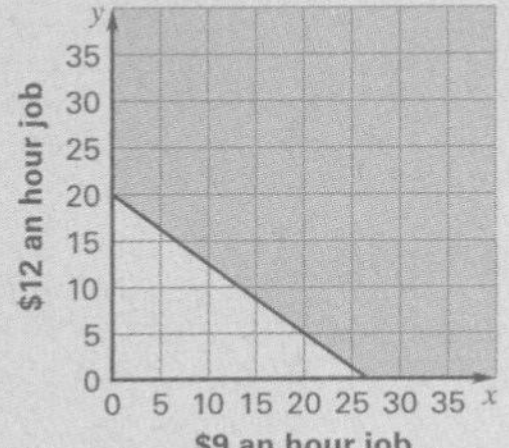

Key Questions to Ask for Example 4

- Why is ≤ used in the inequality? **Each group is allotted up to 300 megabytes.**
- How much total space is represented by the solutions in the shaded region of the graph? **fewer than 300 megabytes**

Avoiding Common Errors

Remind students that when they use a test point to determine which half-plane to shade, they should substitute the point into the given inequality and not the equation for the boundary.

Study Strategy

The origin (0, 0) is a good choice for a test point because computations involving zero are usually easy. If (0, 0) is on the boundary line, choose a test point that is not on the boundary line but does have one coordinate of zero.

GUIDED PRACTICE for Examples 2 and 3

Graph the inequality in a coordinate plane. **5–10. See margin.**

5. $y > -1$	**6.** $x \geq -4$	**7.** $y \geq -3x$
8. $y < 2x + 3$	**9.** $x + 3y < 9$	**10.** $2x - 6y > 12$

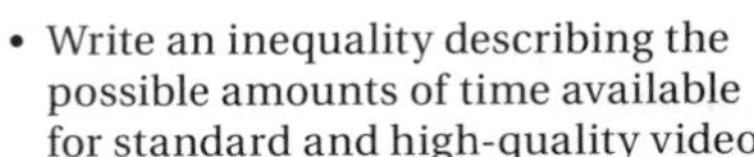

EXAMPLE 4 Solve a multi-step problem

MOVIE RECORDING A film class is recording a DVD of student-made short films. Each student group is allotted up to 300 megabytes (MB) of video space. The films are encoded on the DVD at two different rates: a standard rate of 0.4 MB/sec for normal scenes and a high-quality rate of 1.2 MB/sec for complex scenes.

- Write an inequality describing the possible amounts of time available for standard and high-quality video.
- Graph the inequality.
- Identify three possible solutions of the inequality.

Solution

STEP 1 **Write** an inequality. First write a verbal model.

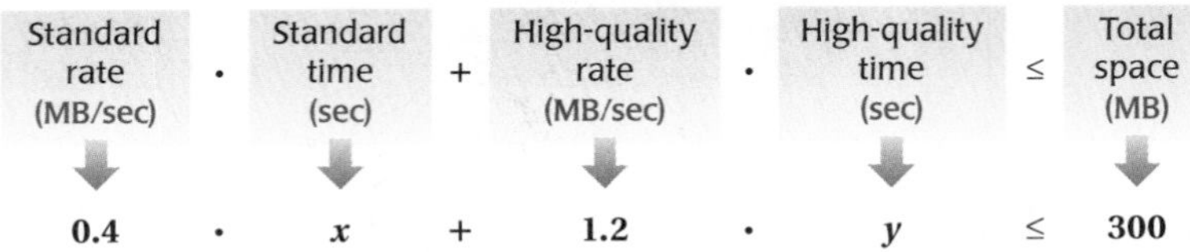

Standard rate (MB/sec)
·
Standard time (sec)
+
High-quality rate (MB/sec)
·
High-quality time (sec)
≤
Total space (MB)
0.4 · x + 1.2 · y ≤ 300

An inequality is $0.4x + 1.2y \leq 300$.

STEP 2 **Graph** the inequality. First graph the boundary line $0.4x + 1.2y = 300$. Use a solid line because the inequality symbol is ≤.

Test the point (0, 0). Because (0, 0) *is* a solution of the inequality, shade the half-plane that contains (0, 0). Because x and y cannot be negative, shade only points in the first quadrant.

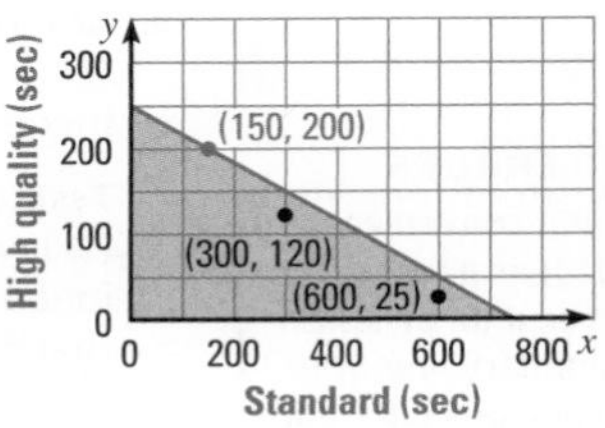

STEP 3 **Identify** solutions. Three solutions are given below and on the graph.

(150, 200) ← 150 seconds of standard and 200 seconds of high quality

(300, 120) ← 300 seconds of standard and 120 seconds of high quality

(600, 25) ← 600 seconds of standard and 25 seconds of high quality

For the first solution, $0.4(150) + 1.2(200) = 300$, so all of the available space is used. For the other two solutions, not all of the space is used.

5.
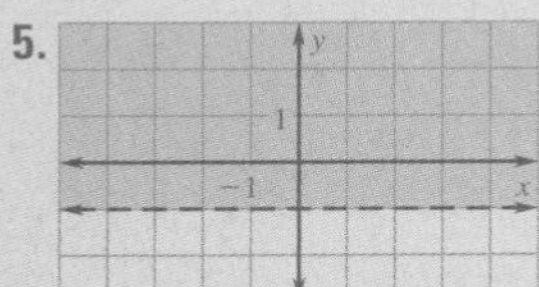

6.
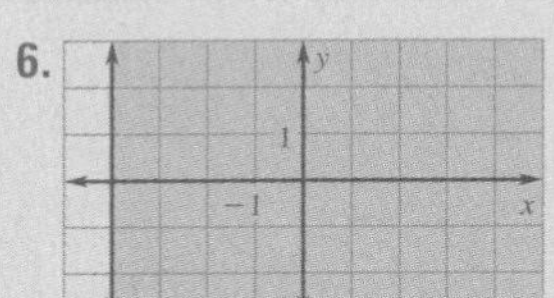

7.
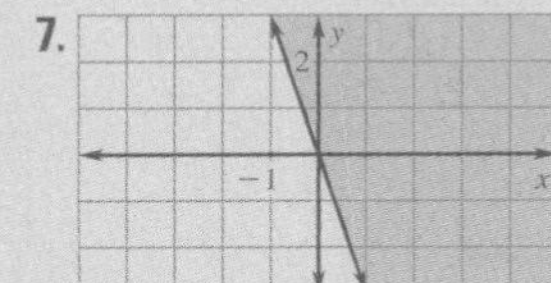

8.
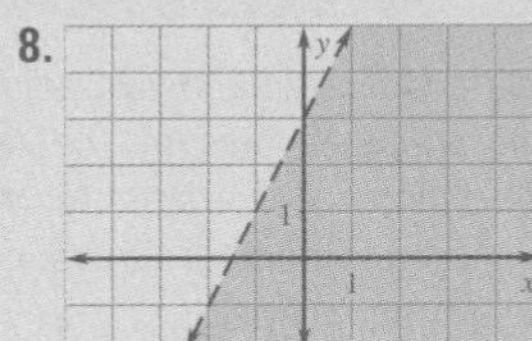

ABSOLUTE VALUE INEQUALITIES Graphing an absolute value inequality is similar to graphing a linear inequality, but the boundary is an absolute value graph.

EXAMPLE 5 Graph an absolute value inequality

Graph $y > -2|x - 3| + 4$ in a coordinate plane.

Solution

STEP 1 **Graph** the equation of the boundary, $y = -2|x - 3| + 4$. Use a dashed line because the inequality symbol is $>$.

STEP 2 **Test** the point (0, 0). Because (0, 0) *is* a solution of the inequality, shade the portion of the coordinate plane outside the absolute value graph.

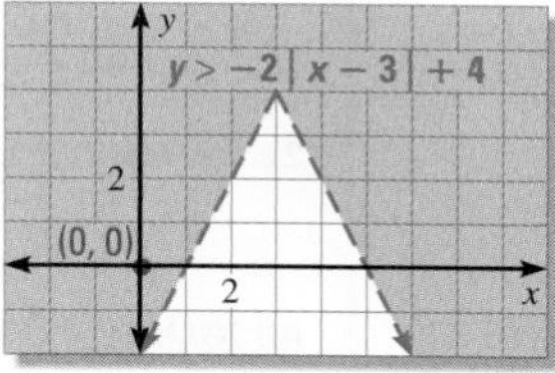

Extra Example 5

Graph $y \le -|x + 2| - 1$ in a coordinate plane.

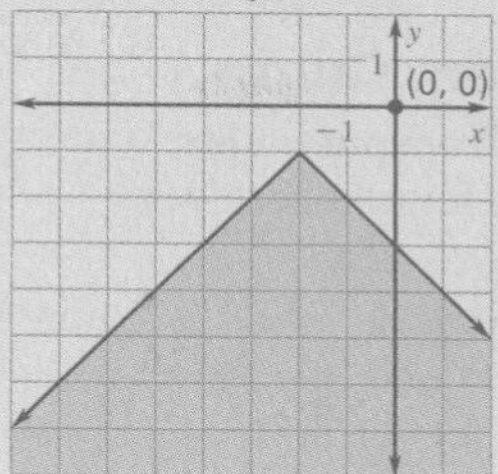

Key Questions to Ask for Example 5

- What is the vertex of the graph? (3, 4)
- Where would you shade the graph of $y < -2|x - 3| + 4$? inside the absolute value graph
- Why is (0, 0) a good test point? It does not lie on either part of the boundary.

Teaching Strategy

As a alternative graphing method, you can suggest that students first solve each inequality for *y*. If the resulting inequality has a greater than symbol, the graph should be shaded above the boundary line. If the resulting inequality has a less than symbol, the graph should be shaded below the line.

Closing the Lesson

Have students summarize the major points of the lesson and answer the Essential Question: What does a dashed boundary line on the graph of an inequality represent?

- An ordered pair is a solution of a linear inequality if the ordered pair makes the inequality true.
- If the inequality symbol is $<$ or $>$, the boundary line is dashed; if the symbol is $\le$ or $\ge$, then the boundary line is solid.
- If a test point is a solution of the inequality, shade the region that contains the test point; otherwise shade the other region.

A dashed boundary line means that the points on that line are not solutions of the inequality.

✓ GUIDED PRACTICE for Examples 4 and 5

11. **WHAT IF?** Repeat the steps of Example 4 if each student group is allotted up to 420 MB of video space. See margin.

Graph the inequality in a coordinate plane. 12–14. See margin.

12. $y \le |x - 2| + 1$
13. $y \ge -|x + 3| - 2$
14. $y < 3|x - 1| - 3$

2.8 EXERCISES

HOMEWORK KEY
○ = **WORKED-OUT SOLUTIONS** on p. WS4 for Exs. 15, 25, and 45
★ = **STANDARDIZED TEST PRACTICE** Exs. 2, 21, 28, 39, 40, 41, 46, and 48

SKILL PRACTICE

A

1. **VOCABULARY** Copy and complete: The graph of a linear inequality in two variables is a(n) __?__. half-plane

2. ★ **WRITING** *Compare* the graph of a linear inequality in two variables with the graph of a linear equation in two variables.
Sample answer: The boundary line of an inequality is the same line as the linear equation.

EXAMPLE 1 on p. 132 for Exs. 3–6

CHECKING SOLUTIONS **Tell whether the given ordered pairs are solutions of the inequality.**

3. $x > -7$; (0, 10), (−8, −5) solution, not a solution
4. $y \le -5x$; (3, 2), (−2, 1) not a solution, solution
5. $y \ge -2x + 4$; (0, 4), (−1, 8) solution, solution
6. $2x - y < 3$; (0, 0), (2, −2) solution, not a solution

EXAMPLES 2 and 3 on p. 133 for Exs. 7–20

GRAPHING INEQUALITIES **Graph the inequality in a coordinate plane.** 7–18. See margin.

7. $x < 3$
8. $x \ge 6$
9. $y > -2$
10. $-2y \le 8$
11. $y \le -2x - 1$
12. $y < 3x + 3$
13. $y > \frac{3}{4}x + 1$
14. $y \ge -\frac{2}{3}x - 2$
15. $2x + y < 6$
16. $x + 4y > -12$
17. $3x - y \ge 1$
18. $2x + 5y \le -10$

Guided Practice

9.
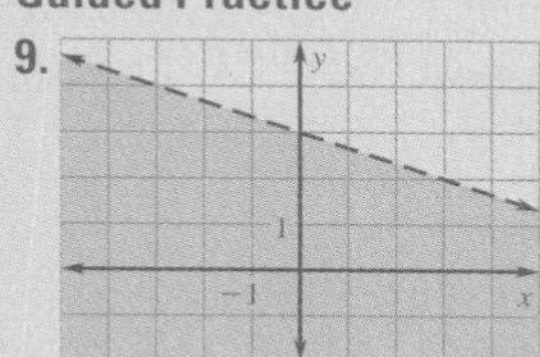

10.
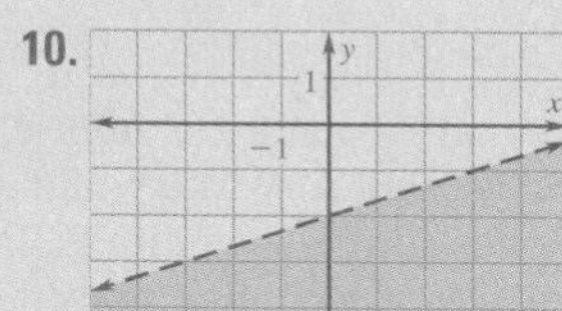

11–14. See Additional Answers beginning on p. AA1.

Skill Practice

7–18. See Additional Answers beginning on p. AA1.

4 PRACTICE AND APPLY

Assignment Guide

Answer Transparencies available for all exercises

Basic:
Day 1: pp. 135–138
Exs. 1–6, 7–17 odd, 19–25, 28–36 even, 43–47, 50

Average:
Day 1: pp. 135–138
Exs. 1, 2, 5, 6, 8–18 even, 19–21, 22–28 even, 29, 30, 33–35, 39–41, 43–48, 50

Advanced:
Day 1: pp. 135–138
Exs. 1, 2, 5, 6, 15–18, 21, 25–28, 31, 32, 36–49*, 51

Block:
pp. 135–138
Exs. 1, 2, 5, 6, 8–18 even, 19–21, 22–28 even, 29, 30, 33–35, 39–41, 43–48, 50

Differentiated Instruction

See *Algebra 2 Best Practices Toolkit* for suggestions on addressing the needs of a diverse classroom.

Homework Check

For a quick check of student understanding of key concepts, go over the following exercises:

Basic: 4, 11, 13, 22, 44
Average: 5, 14, 16, 24, 46
Advanced: 6, 16, 18, 26, 48

Extra Practice

- Student Edition, p. 1011
- Chapter 2 Resource Book: Practice levels A, B, C, pp. 96–101

Practice Worksheet

An easily-readable reduced practice page (with answers) for this lesson can be found on p. 70C.

ERROR ANALYSIS *Describe* and correct the error in graphing the inequality. 19, 20. See margin f

19. $y < 2x + 3$ The boundary line should be a dashed line.

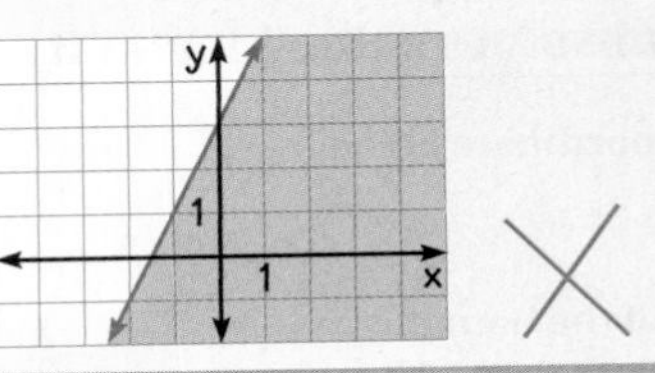

20. $y \geq -3x - 2$ The other side of the boundary line should be shaded.

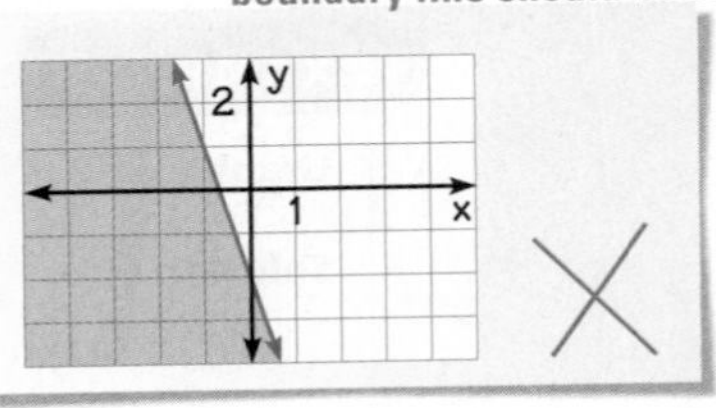

21. ★ **MULTIPLE CHOICE** Which ordered pair is *not* a solution of $3x - 5y < 30$? C

Ⓐ (0, 0) Ⓑ (−1, 7) Ⓒ (1, −7) Ⓓ (−5, −5)

EXAMPLE 5 on p. 135 for Exs. 22–28

ABSOLUTE VALUE INEQUALITIES Graph the inequality in a coordinate plane. 22–27. See margin.

22. $y > |x - 1|$ **23.** $y < |x| + 5$ **24.** $y > |x + 4| - 3$

25. $y \leq -\frac{1}{2}|x - 2| + 1$ **26.** $y < 3|x| + 2$ **27.** $y \geq 2|x - 1| - 4$

28. ★ **MULTIPLE CHOICE** The graph of which inequality is shown? D

Ⓐ $y \leq -2|x + 1| + 3$ Ⓑ $y \geq -2|x - 1| + 3$

Ⓒ $y > -2|x + 1| + 3$ Ⓓ $y \geq -2|x + 1| + 3$

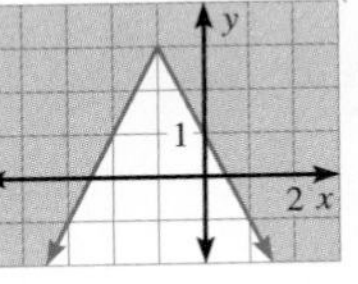

B

CHECKING SOLUTIONS Tell whether the given ordered pairs are solutions of the inequality.

29. $y \geq -\frac{2}{3}x + \frac{1}{2}$; (−6, 8), (−3, −3) solution, not a solution

30. $4.5 + y < 1.6x$; (0.5, 1), (3.8, 0) not a solution, solution

31. $0.2x + 0.7y > -1$; (0.5, −1), (−3, −1.5) solution, not a solution

32. $\frac{1}{4}x - y > 1$; $\left(\frac{4}{3}, 0\right)$, $\left(\frac{2}{3}, -4\right)$ not a solution, solution

GRAPHING INEQUALITIES Graph the inequality in a coordinate plane. 33–38. See margin.

33. $3y < 4.5x + 15$ **34.** $-1.5y - 2x > 3$ **35.** $-y - 0.2 > -0.6x$

36. $\frac{2}{3}x + \frac{1}{2}y > 2$ **37.** $y \geq -\frac{5}{2}|x - 3| - \frac{3}{2}$ **38.** $2y - 4 \leq -3|x + 2|$

39. ★ **OPEN-ENDED MATH** Write a linear inequality in two variables that has (−1, 3) and (1, 6) as solutions, but does not have (4, 0) as a solution. *Sample answer:* $y > x + 3$

40. ★ **WRITING** *Explain* why it is not helpful when graphing a linear inequality in two variables to choose a test point that lies on the boundary line.

40. *Sample answer:* Testing a point on the boundary line would not tell you which side of the line the solutions are on.

C

41. ★ **SHORT RESPONSE** Write an inequality for the graph shown. *Explain* how you came up with the inequality. Then describe a real-life situation that the first-quadrant portion of the graph could represent. See margin.

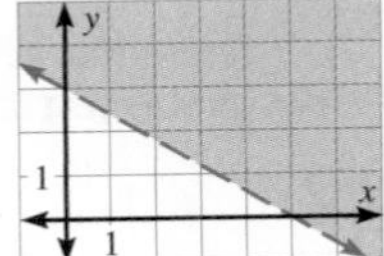

42. **CHALLENGE** Write an absolute value inequality that has exactly one solution in common with $y \geq 2|x - 3| + 5$. The common solution should not be the vertex (3, 5) of the boundary. *Explain* how you found your inequality.

42. *Sample answer:* $x > |y - 9| + 5$; I chose a point on the graph and found another inequality that opened horizontally and had a vertex of the point I chose.

○ = WORKED-OUT SOLUTIONS on p. WS1 ★ = STANDARDIZED TEST PRACTICE

19.

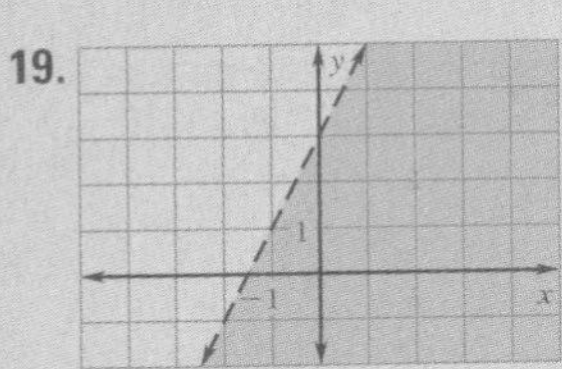

20.

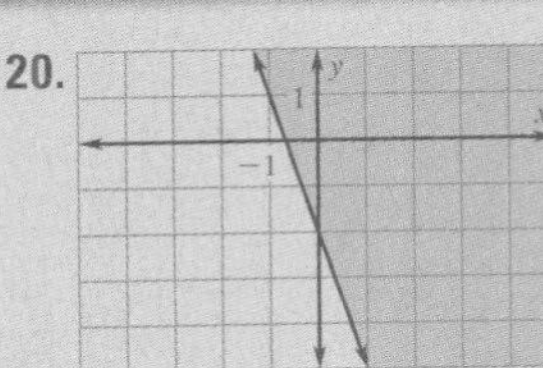

22–27, 33–38. See Additional Answers beginning on p. AA1.

41. $y > -\frac{3}{5}x + 3$; pick two points on the boundary line to find the slope and then use the point-slope form of an equation to find the equation. The boundary line is dashed, so the inequality dos not include points on the boundary. Then choose a point to determine which inequality sign to use. *Sample answer:* You and your sister want to spend at least $15 on your little brother's birthday. You want to buy him some race cars that cost $3 each and some building block sets that cost $5 each.

PROBLEM SOLVING

EXAMPLE 4 A on p. 134 for Exs. 43–48

43. CALLING CARDS You have a \$20 phone card. Calls made using the card cost \$.03 per minute to destinations within the United States and \$.06 per minute to destinations in Brazil. Write an inequality describing the numbers of minutes you can use for calls to U.S. destinations and to Brazil. **$0.03x + 0.06y \le 20$**

@HomeTutor for problem solving help at classzone.com

44. RESTAURANT MANAGEMENT A pizza shop has 300 pounds (4800 ounces) of dough. A small pizza uses 12 ounces of dough and a large pizza uses 18 ounces of dough. Write and graph an inequality describing the possible numbers of small and large pizzas that can be made. Then give three possible solutions.

@HomeTutor for problem solving help at classzone.com

45. CRAFTS Cotton lace costs \$1.50 per yard and linen lace costs \$2.50 per yard. You plan to order at most \$75 of lace for crafts. Write and graph an inequality describing how much of each type of lace you can order. If you buy 24 yards of cotton lace, what are the amounts of linen lace you can buy?
$1.5x + 2.5y \le 75$, see margin for art; $y \le 15.6$ yd.

46. ★ SHORT RESPONSE You sell T-shirts for \$15 each and caps for \$10 each. Write and graph an inequality describing how many shirts and caps you must sell to exceed \$1800 in sales. *Explain* how you can modify this inequality to describe how many shirts and caps you must sell to exceed \$600 in *profit* if you make a 40% profit on shirts and a 30% profit on caps.

B

47. MULTI-STEP PROBLEM On a two week vacation, you and your brother can rent one canoe for \$11 per day or rent two mountain bikes for \$13 each per day. Together, you have \$120 to spend.

a. Write and graph an inequality describing the possible numbers of days you and your brother can canoe or bicycle together. **$11x + 26y \le 120$, see margin for art.**

b. Give three possible solutions of the inequality from part (a).

c. You decide that on one day you will canoe alone and your brother will bicycle alone. Repeat parts (a) and (b) using this new condition.

48. ★ EXTENDED RESPONSE While camping, you and a friend filter river water into two cylindrical containers with the radii and heights shown. You then use these containers to fill the water cooler shown.

a. Find the volumes of the containers and the cooler in cubic inches. **about 48.3 in.^{3}, about 62.8 in.^{3}, about 942 in.^{3}**

b. Using your results from part (a), write and graph an inequality describing how many times the containers can be filled and emptied into the water cooler without the cooler overflowing. **See margin.**

c. Convert the volumes from part (a) to gallons (1 in.$^3 \approx 0.00433$ gal). Then rewrite the inequality from part (b) in terms of these converted volumes.

d. Graph the inequality from part (c). *Compare* the graph with your graph from part (b), and explain why the results make sense. **See margin.**

44. $12x + 18y \le$ 4800, see margin for art. *Sample answer:* 12 large and 382 small, 120 large and 220 small, 0 large and 400 small

46. $15x + 10y >$ 1800, see margin for art; you would have to take the shirt sales, 15x, times 0.4 and the cap sales, 10y, times 0.3. The total sales, 1800, would change to a total profit of 600.

47b. *Sample answer:* 2 days canoeing and 3 days biking, 3 days canoeing and 2 days biking, 2 days canoeing and 2 days biking

47c. $11x + 26y \le$ 96, see margin for art; *Sample answer:* 1 day canoeing and 3 days biking, 4 days canoeing and 2 days biking, 2 days canoeing and 2 days biking.

48c. about 0.209 gal, about 0.272 gal, about 4.08 gal; $0.209x + 0.272y \le 4.08$

Reading Strategy

Exercises 44–48 As students read these exercises, they should keep in mind a reasonable domain for each situation.

47a.

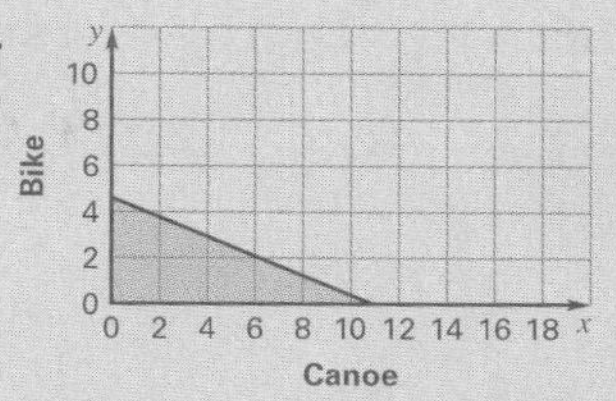

47c.

48. $3x + 62.8y \le 942$

48b.

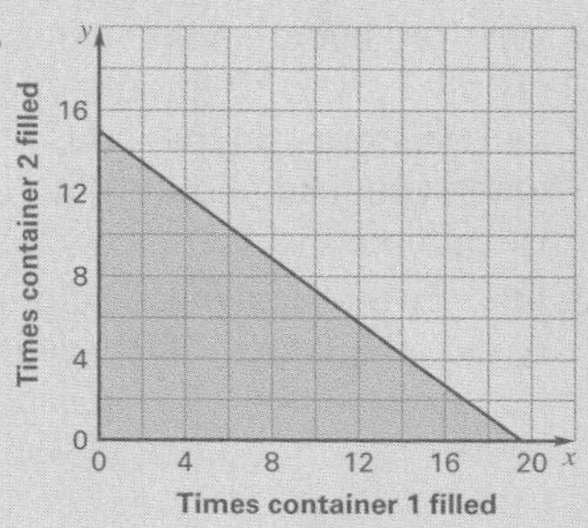

48d.

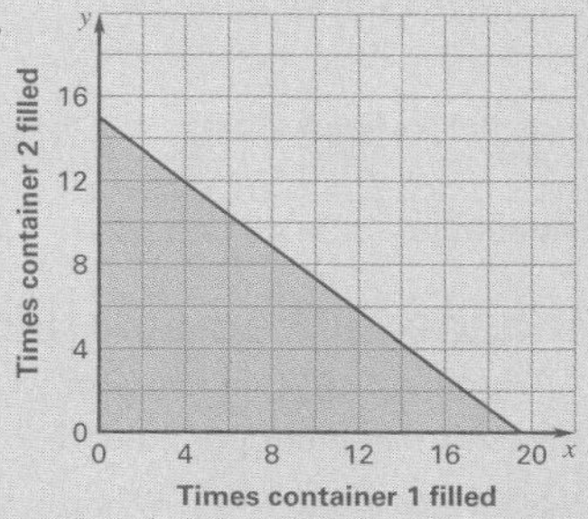

The graphs are identical. *Sample answer:* Converting the volumes does not change the number of times each container must be filled.

44.

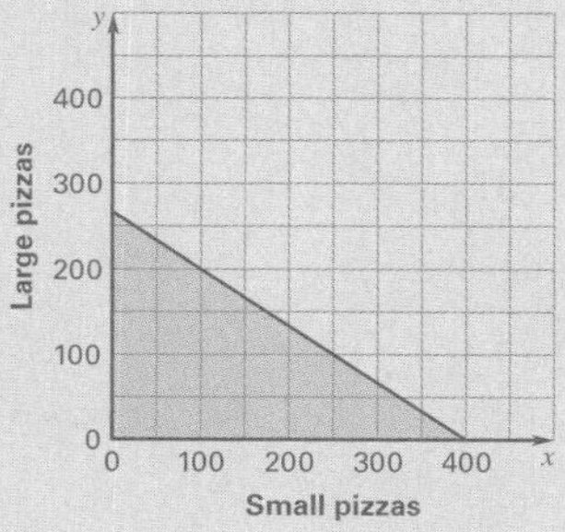

45.

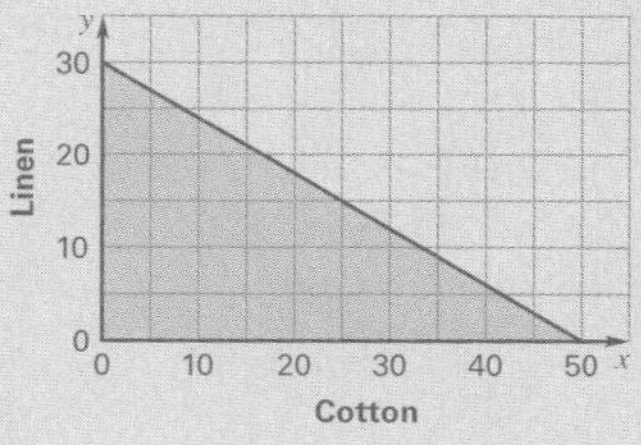

46.

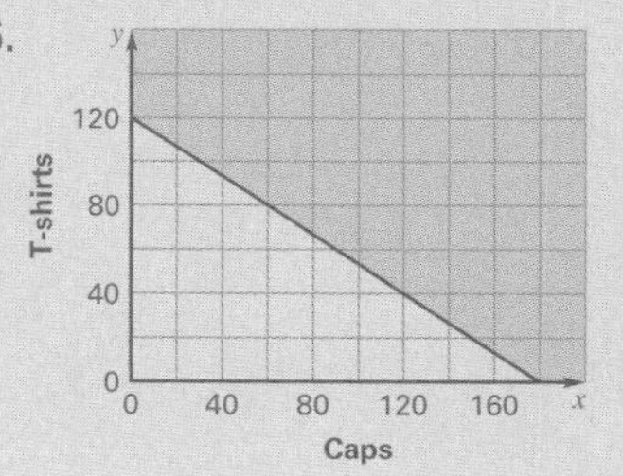

5 ASSESS AND RETEACH

Daily Homework Quiz

Transparency Available

1. Graph $y \le 3|x + 1| - 2$ on the coordinate plane.

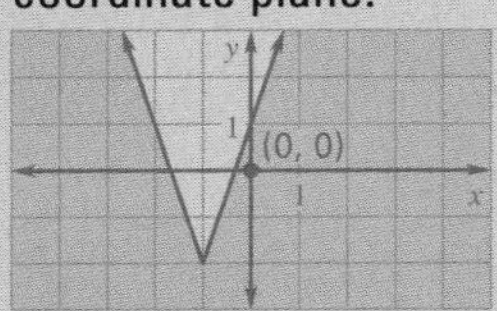

The memory card for your digital camera has 256 megabytes of memory. Each photo uses either 1 megabyte or 2 megabytes of memory, depending on whether you take low resolution or high resolution photos.

2. Write an equation that models the number of photos that can be stored on the card when you take photos at both resolutions. $x + 2y \le 256$
3. Identify three possible solutions of the inequality. 30 low resolution and 113 high resolution, 85 low resolution and 85 high resolution, or 200 low resolution and 28 high resolution

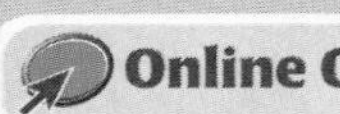

Available at **classzone.com**

Diagnosis/Remediation

- Practice A, B, C in Chapter 2 Resource Book, pp. 96–101
- Study Guide in Chapter 2 Resource Book, pp. 102–103
- Practice Workbook, pp. 33–35
- @HomeTutor

Challenge

Additional challenge is available in the Chapter 2 Resource Book, p. 106.

Quiz

An easily-readable reduced copy of the quiz (with answers) on Lessons 2.7–2.8 from the Assessment Book can be found on p. 70G.

Quiz 1–3, 7–10. See Additional Answers beginning on p. AA1.

C **49. CHALLENGE** A widescreen television image has a width w and a height h that satisfy the inequality $\frac{w}{h} > \frac{4}{3}$.

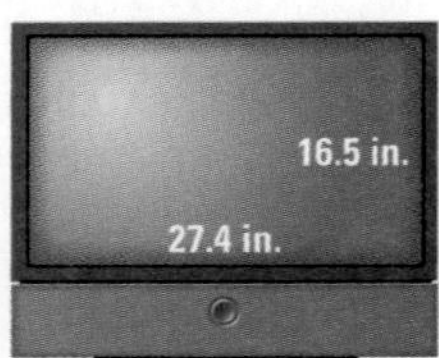

a. Does the television screen shown at the right meet the requirements of a widescreen image? no

b. Let d be the length of a diagonal of a television image. Write an inequality describing the possible values of d and h for a widescreen image. $d > \frac{5}{3}h$

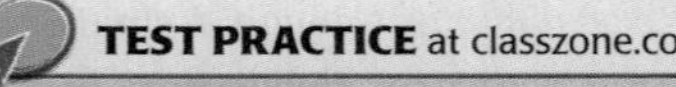

KY KENTUCKY MIXED REVIEW

50. Which equation represents the line that passes through the points (1, 4) and (5, −2)? **C**

Ⓐ $y = -\frac{2}{3}x + \frac{14}{3}$ Ⓑ $y = \frac{2}{3}x + \frac{10}{3}$

Ⓒ $y = -\frac{3}{2}x + \frac{11}{2}$ Ⓓ $y = \frac{3}{2}x + \frac{5}{2}$

51. The map shows two different paths from the library to the cafeteria. How many meters shorter is the walk along the sidewalk than the walk on the covered walkway? **B**

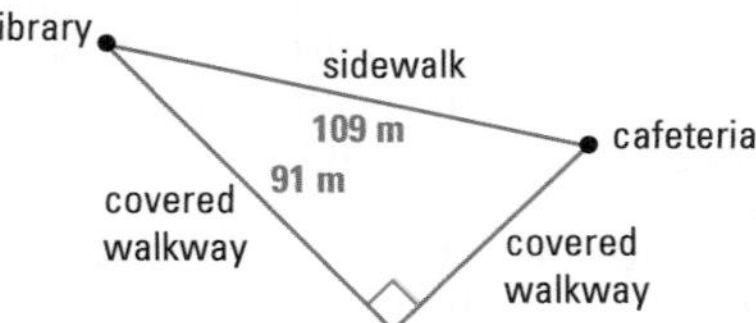

Ⓐ 18 m Ⓑ 42 m

Ⓒ 50 m Ⓓ 60 m

QUIZ for Lessons 2.7–2.8

Graph the function. *Compare* the graph with the graph of $y = |x|$. *(p. 123)* 1–3. See margin.

1. $y = |x + 7| + 4$
2. $y = -2|x + 10| - 1$
3. $f(x) = \frac{1}{2}|x - 1| - 5$

Write an equation of the graph. *(p. 123)*

4. $y = -2|x| - 2$

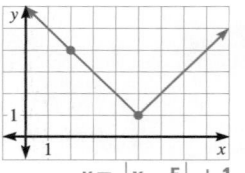

5. 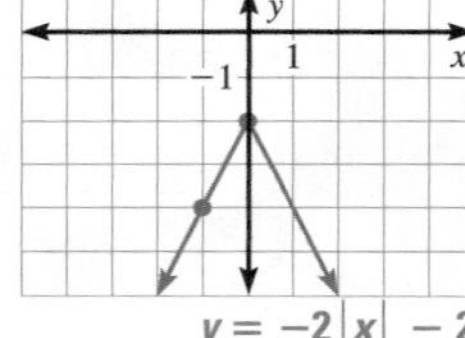
$y = |x - 5| + 1$

6. 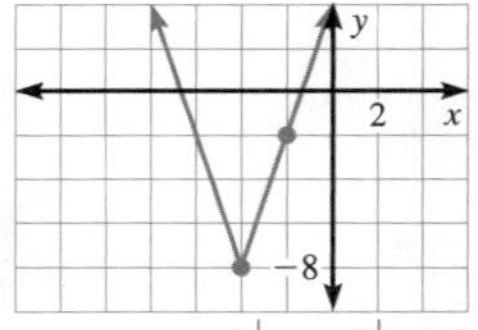
$y = 3|x + 4| - 8$

Graph the inequality in a coordinate plane. *(p. 132)* 7–9. See margin.

7. $y > -2$
8. $y \le 3x + 1$
9. $2x - 5y \ge 10$

10. **MINI-CARS** You have a 20 credit gift pass to a mini-car raceway. It takes 2 credits to drive the cars on the Rally track and 3 credits to drive the cars on the Grand Prix track. Write and graph an inequality describing how many times you can race on the two tracks using your gift pass. Then give three possible solutions. *(p. 132)* See margin.

Lessons 2.5–2.8

1. **ARCHITECTURE** An "A-frame" house is shown below. The coordinates x and y are both measured in feet. Which absolute value function models the front of the house?

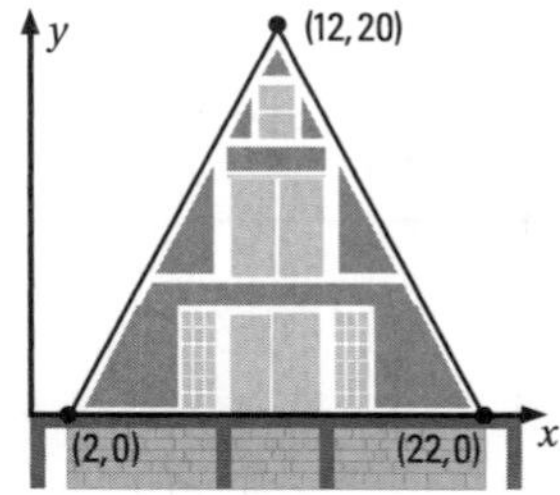

A. $y = -2|x - 12|$

B. $y = 2|x| + 20$

C. $y = -2|x - 12| + 20$

D. $y = 2|x - 12| - 20$

2. **LINEAR INEQUALITIES** The graph of which inequality is shown?

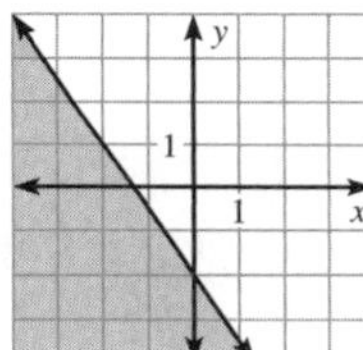

A. $-x + y \geq 2$

B. $3x + 2y \leq -4$

C. $4x + 3y \geq -10$

D. $9x + 4y \leq -24$

3. **INTERNET COST** The cost of an Internet service subscription varies directly with the length of the subscription. A 3 month subscription costs \$32.85. How much does a 12 month subscription cost?

A. \$32.85 B. \$36

C. \$131.40 D. \$133.33

4. **SUNSPOTS** Based on the data in the graph, which conclusion is most accurate?

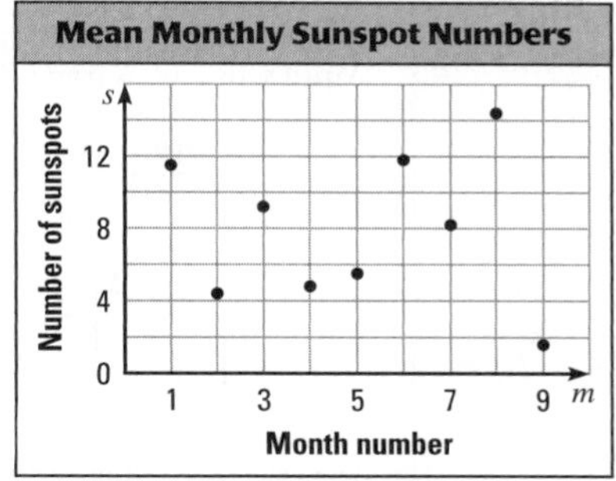

A. The sunspot data show a positive correlation.

B. The sunspot data show a negative correlation.

C. The sunspot data show approximately no correlation.

D. The sunspot data show a strong correlation.

5. **FLOWER SALES** A plant nursery sells marigolds for \$2 per pack and zinnias for \$3 per pack. You have a total of \$30 to spend. Which inequality describes the numbers of packs of marigolds m and zinnias z you can buy?

A. $2m - 3z \leq 30$ B. $2m + 3z \leq 30$

C. $3m - 2z \geq 30$ D. $3m + 2z \geq 30$

6. **OPEN-RESPONSE** The table below shows the number of readers of daily newspapers in the U.S. from 1900 to 2000 in intervals of 20 years.

Year	1900	1920	1940	1960
Readers (millions)	15.1	27.8	41.1	58.9

a. Draw a scatter plot of all (x, y) pairs of the form (years since 1900, readers).

b. Find the equation of the best-fitting line.

c. Use the equation to predict the number of readers in 1980.

d. In 1980, the actual number of readers was 62.2 million. Compare this value to your prediction. What does this indicate about the yearly rate of change of circulation?

Kentucky Mixed Review

1. C
2. B
3. C
4. C
5. B
6. a.

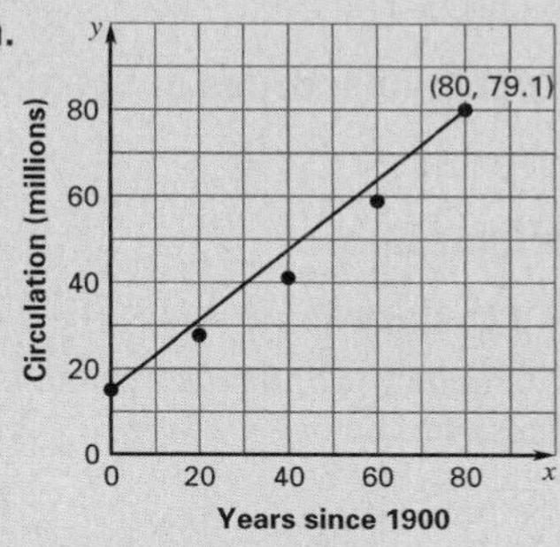

b. $y = 0.72x + 14.02$

c. **71.9 million readers;**

d. ***Sample answer:*** **The yearly rate of change was 0.72 million additional readers per year. This rate must have decreased at some point after 1960, because the actual circulation in 1980 was less than the trend predicted.**

2 CHAPTER SUMMARY

Animated Algebra
classzone.com
Electronic Function Library

BIG IDEAS

For Your Notebook

Big Idea 1 Representing Relations and Functions

A relation pairs input values with output values. A relation is a function if each input value is paired with exactly one output value.

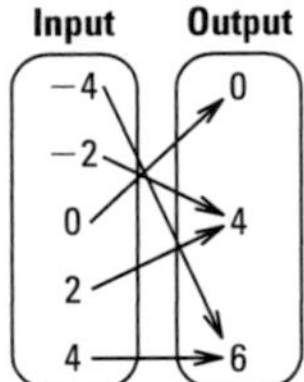

This relation is a function because each input has exactly one output.

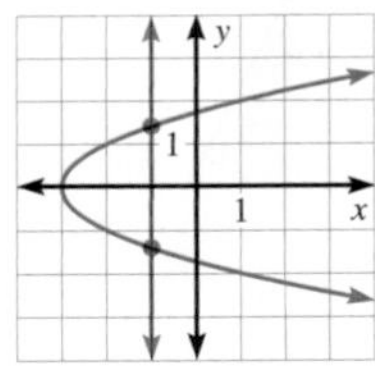

This relation is not a function because a vertical line intersects the graph at more than one point.

Big Idea 2 Graphing Linear Equations and Inequalities in Two Variables

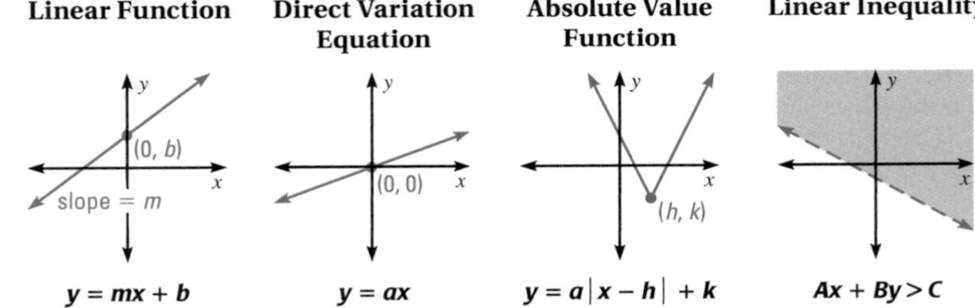

Big Idea 3 Writing Linear Equations and Inequalities in Two Variables

Form	Equation	Key Facts
Slope-intercept form	$y = mx + b$	The graph is a line with slope m and y-intercept b.
Standard form	$Ax + By = C$	The graph is a line with intercepts $x = \frac{C}{A}$ and $y = \frac{C}{B}$.
Point-slope form	$y - y_1 = m(x - x_1)$	The graph is a line that has slope m and passes through (x_1, y_1).
Direct variation	$y = ax, a \neq 0$	The graph is a line that passes through the origin and has slope a (the constant of variation).
Linear inequality	$Ax + By > C$	The graph is a half-plane with boundary line $Ax + By = C$.

Additional Resources

The following resources are available to help review the materials in this chapter.

Chapter 2 Resource Book

- Chapter Review Games and Activities, p. 107
- Cumulative Practice, Chs. 1–2, pp. 109–110

Student Resources in Spanish

eWorkbook

@HomeTutor

Vocabulary Practice

Vocabulary practice is available at **classzone.com**

CHAPTER REVIEW

@HomeTutor
classzone.com
• Multi-Language Glossary
• Vocabulary practice

REVIEW KEY VOCABULARY

- relation, *p. 72*
- domain, range, *p. 72*
- function, *p. 73*
- equation in two variables, *p. 74*
- solution, graph of an equation in two variables, *p. 74*
- independent variable, *p. 74*
- dependent variable, *p. 74*
- linear function, *p. 75*
- function notation, *p. 75*
- slope, *p. 82*
- parallel, perpendicular, *p. 84*
- rate of change, *p. 85*
- parent function, *p. 89*
- *y*-intercept, *p. 89*
- slope-intercept form, *p. 90*
- *x*-intercept, *p. 91*
- standard form of a linear equation, *p. 91*
- point-slope form, *p. 98*
- direct variation, *p. 107*
- constant of variation, *p. 107*
- scatter plot, *p. 113*
- positive correlation, *p. 113*
- negative correlation, *p. 113*
- correlation coefficient, *p. 114*
- best-fitting line, *p. 114*
- absolute value function, *p. 123*
- vertex of an absolute value graph, *p. 123*
- transformation, *p. 123*
- translation, *p. 123*
- reflection, *p. 124*
- linear inequality in two variables, *p. 132*
- solution, graph of a linear inequality in two variables, *p. 132*
- half-plane, *p. 132*

VOCABULARY EXERCISES

1. Copy and complete: The linear equation $5x - 4y = 16$ is written in _?_ form. **standard**
2. Copy and complete: A set of data pairs (x, y) shows a _?_ correlation if y tends to decrease as x increases. **negative**
3. Copy and complete: Two variables x and y show _?_ if $y = ax$ and $a \neq 0$. **direct variation**
4. **WRITING** *Explain* what distinguishes a function from a relation.
Sample answer: **A function has exactly one output for each input, while a relation can have more than one output for each input.**

REVIEW EXAMPLES AND EXERCISES

Use the review examples and exercises below to check your understanding of the concepts you have learned in each lesson of Chapter 2.

2.1 Represent Relations and Functions *pp. 72–79*

EXAMPLE

Tell whether the relation given by the ordered pairs (−6, 3), (−4, 5), (−1, −2), (2, −1), and (2, 3) is a function.

The relation is *not* a function because the input 2 is mapped onto both −1 and 3, as shown in the mapping diagram.

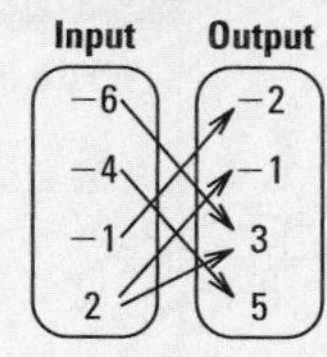

EXERCISES

EXAMPLES 1, 2, and 5 on pp. 72–75 for Exs. 5–7

Consider the relation given by the ordered pairs. Identify the domain and range. Then tell whether the relation is a function.

5. (−2, −2), (−1, 0), (2, 6), (3, 8)
6. (−1, −5), (1, 2), (3, 4), (1, −7)
7. Tell whether $f(x) = 16 - 7x$ is a linear function. Then find $f(-5)$. **linear function; 51**

5. domain: −2, −1, 2, 3, range: −2, 0, 6, 8; function
6. domain: −1, 1, 3, range: −7, −5, 2, 4; not a function

Extra Example 2.1
Tell whether the relation given by the ordered pairs (−2, 3), (5, 0), (3, −1), (−4, −4), and (7, 13) is a function. **yes**

2 CHAPTER REVIEW

Extra Example 2.2

Find the slope of the line passing through (8, 2) and (−5, 1). $\frac{1}{13}$

Extra Example 2.3

Graph $3x + y = 5$.

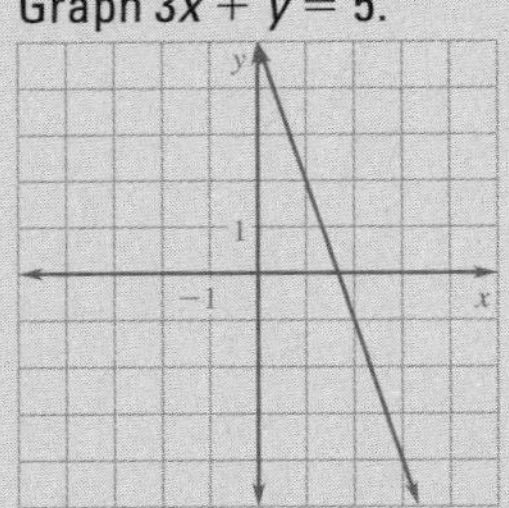

Extra Example 2.4

Write an equation of the line that passes through (−1, 6) and (3, −2). $y = -2x + 4$

12.

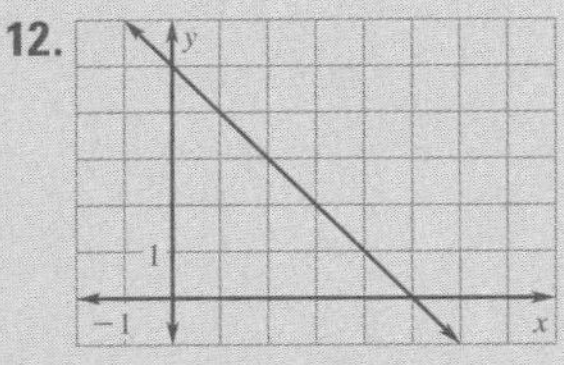

13.

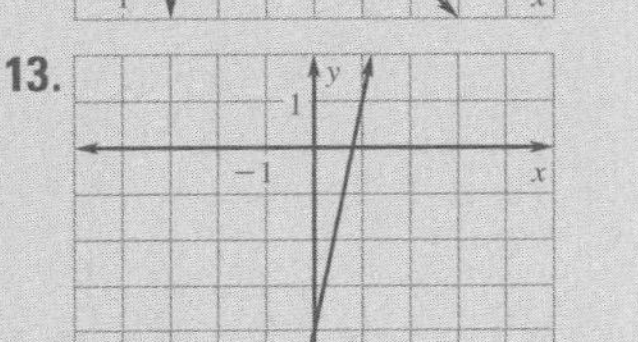

14.

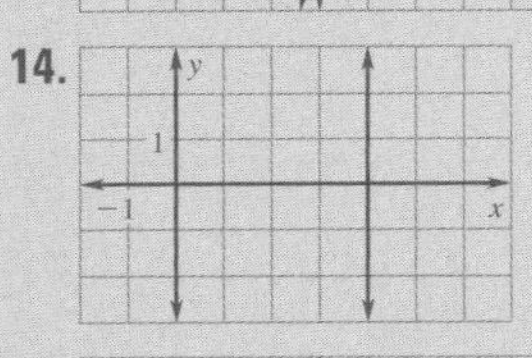

15.

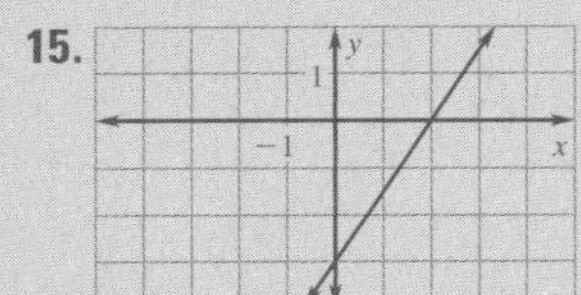

2.2 Find Slope and Rate of Change

pp. 82–88

EXAMPLE

Find the slope m of the line passing through the points (−4, 12) and (3, −2).

$$m = \frac{y_2 - y_1}{x_2 - x_1} = \frac{-2 - 12}{3 - (-4)} = \frac{-14}{7} = -2$$

EXERCISES

EXAMPLE 2 on p. 82 for Exs. 8–11

Find the slope of the line passing through the given points.

8. (−2, −1), (4, 3) $\frac{2}{3}$
9. (1, −5), (1, 2) undefined
10. (5, −3), (1, 7) $-\frac{5}{2}$
11. (6, 2), (−8, 2) 0

2.3 Graph Equations of Lines

pp. 89–96

EXAMPLE

Graph $3 + y = -2x$.

STEP 1 Write the equation in slope-intercept form, $y = -2x - 3$.

STEP 2 The y-intercept is −3. So, plot the point (0, −3).

STEP 3 The slope is −2. Plot a second point by starting at (0, −3) and then moving down 2 units and right 1 unit.

STEP 4 Draw a line through the two points.

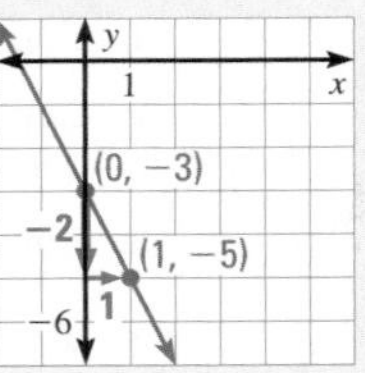

EXERCISES

EXAMPLES 1, 2, and 4 on pp. 89–92 for Exs. 12–15

Graph the equation. 12–15. See margin.

12. $y = 5 - x$
13. $y - 5x = -4$
14. $x = 4$
15. $6x - 4y = 12$

2.4 Write Equations of Lines

pp. 98–104

EXAMPLE

Write an equation of the line that passes through (−2, 5) and (−4, −1).

The slope is $m = \frac{-1 - 5}{-4 - (-2)} = 3$. Use the point-slope form with $(x_1, y_1) = (-2, 5)$.

$y - y_1 = m(x - x_1)$ **Use point-slope form.**

$y - 5 = 3(x - (-2))$ **Substitute for m, x_1, and y_1.**

$y = 3x + 11$ **Write in slope-intercept form.**

16. $y = -2x - 2$
17. $y = -\frac{3}{4}x + 2$
18. $y = -x - 3$

EXERCISES

EXAMPLE 4 on p. 100 for Exs. 16–18

Write an equation of the line that passes through the given points.

16. (−3, 4), (2, −6)
17. (−4, 5), (12, −7)
18. (−4, 1), (3, −6)

@HomeTutor
classzone.com
Chapter Review Practice

2.5 Model Direct Variation

pp. 107–111

EXAMPLE

The variables x and y vary directly, and $y = 76$ when $x = -8$. Write an equation that relates x and y. Then find y when $x = -6$.

$y = ax$	**Write direct variation equation.**
$76 = a(-8)$	**Substitute 76 for y and -8 for x.**
$-9.5 = a$	**Solve for a.**

An equation that relates x and y is $y = -9.5x$. When $x = -6$, $y = -9.5(-6) = 57$.

EXERCISES

EXAMPLE 2
on p. 108
for Exs. 19–22

The variables x and y vary directly. Write an equation that relates x and y. Then find y when $x = 3$.

19. $x = 6, y = -48$
$y = -8x; -24$

20. $x = -9, y = 15$
$y = -\frac{5}{3}x; -5$

21. $x = -3, y = 2.4$
$y = -0.8x; -2.4$

22. PHYSICS Charles's Law states that when pressure is constant, the volume V of a gas varies directly with its temperature T (in kelvins). A gas occupies 4.8 liters at a temperature of 300 kelvins. Write an equation that gives V as a function of T. What is the volume of the gas when the temperature is 420 kelvins? $V = 0.016T$; 6.72 L

2.6 Draw Scatter Plots and Best-Fitting Lines

pp. 113–120

EXAMPLE

The table shows the shoe size x and height y (in inches) for 7 men. Approximate the best-fitting line for the data.

x	9	9.5	10	10.5	11	11.5	12
y	69	70.5	70	71.5	72	74	74

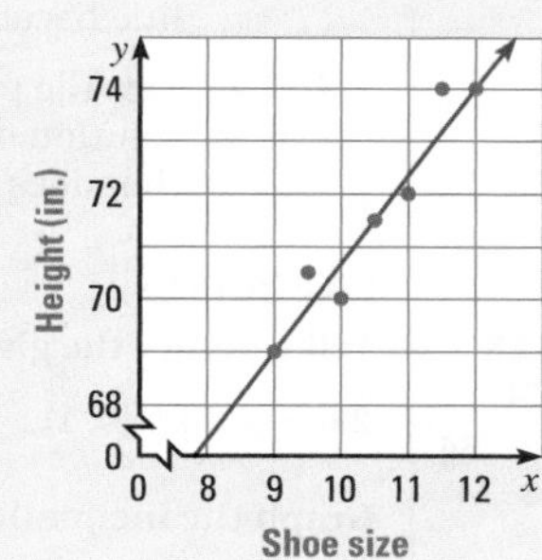

Draw a scatter plot and sketch the line that appears to best fit the data points.

Choose two points on the line, such as (9, 69) and (12, 74). Use the points to find an equation of the line.

The slope is $m = \frac{74 - 69}{12 - 9} = \frac{5}{3} \approx 1.67$.

An equation is $y - 69 = 1.67(x - 9)$, or $y = 1.67x + 54$.

EXERCISES

EXAMPLE 3
on p. 115
for Ex. 23

Approximate the best-fitting line for the data.

23.

x	−2	−1	0	1	2	3	4	5
y	4	3	2.5	2	0.5	−1	−2	−3

Sample answer: $y = -x + 2.3$

Extra Example 2.5

The variables x and y vary directly, and $y = -77$ when $x = -5$. Write and equation that relates x and y. Then find y when $x = 12$. $y = 15.4x$; 184.8

Extra Example 2.6

The table shows the shoe size x and height y (in inches) for 6 women. Approximate the best-fitting line for the data. *Sample answer:* $y = 3.3x + 36$

x	6	8.5	8	8.5	9	9.5
y	57	60	62	65	66	70

2 CHAPTER REVIEW

2.7 Use Absolute Value Functions and Transformations pp. 123–129

EXAMPLE

Graph $y = 3|x - 1| - 4$. Compare the graph with the graph of $y = |x|$.

STEP 1 **Identify** and plot the vertex, $(h, k) = (1, -4)$.

STEP 2 **Plot** another point on the graph, such as $(0, -1)$. Use symmetry to plot a third point, $(2, -1)$.

STEP 3 **Connect** the points with a V-shaped graph.

STEP 4 **Compare** with $y = |x|$. The graph of $y = 3|x - 1| - 4$ is the graph of $y = |x|$ stretched vertically by a factor of 3, then translated right 1 unit and down 4 units.

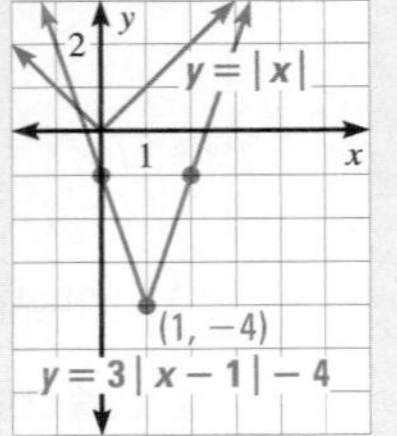

EXERCISES

EXAMPLES 1, 2, 3, and 4 on pp. 123–125 for Exs. 24–27

Graph the function. *Compare* the graph to the graph of $y = |x|$. 24–26. See margin.

24. $y = |x - 3| + 2$

25. $y = \frac{3}{4}|x|$

26. $f(x) = -4|x + 2| + 3$

27. **FINANCE** Analysts predict that a company will report earnings of \$1.50 per share in the next quarter. The function $d = |a - 1.50|$ gives the absolute difference d between the actual earnings a and the predicted earnings. Graph the function. For what value(s) of a will d be \$.25? See margin for art; \$1.75, \$1.25.

2.8 Graph Linear Inequalities in Two Variables pp. 132–138

EXAMPLE

Graph $3x - y \le -2$ in a coordinate plane.

STEP 1 **Graph** the boundary line $3x - y = -2$. Use a solid line because the inequality symbol is $\le$.

STEP 2 **Test** the point $(0, 0)$. Because $(0, 0)$ is *not* a solution of the inequality, shade the half-plane that does not contain $(0, 0)$.

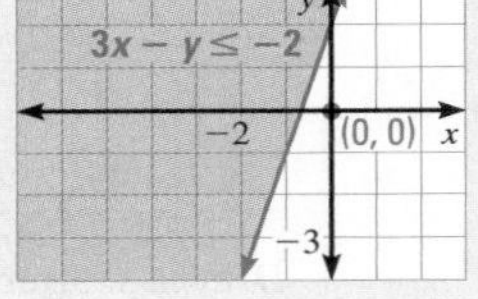

EXERCISES

EXAMPLES 2, 3, and 4 on pp. 132–134 for Exs. 28–34

Tell whether the given ordered pair is a solution of the inequality.

28. $-y \le 5x$; $(0, 1)$ solution

29. $y > -3x - 7$; $(-4, 6)$ solution

30. $3x - 4y < -8$; $(-2, 0)$ not a solution

Graph the inequality in a coordinate plane. 31–33. See margin.

31. $-4y < 16$

32. $y - 2x > 8$

33. $12x - 8y \le 24$

34. **WIND ENERGY** An electric company buys energy from "windmill farms" that have windmills of two sizes, one producing 1.5 megawatts of power and one producing 2.5 megawatts of power. The company wants a total power supply of at least 180 megawatts. Write and graph an inequality describing how many of each size of windmill it takes to supply the electric company. See margin.

Extra Example 2.7

Graph $y = 5|x - 3| + 1$. Compare the graph with the graph of $y = |x|$.

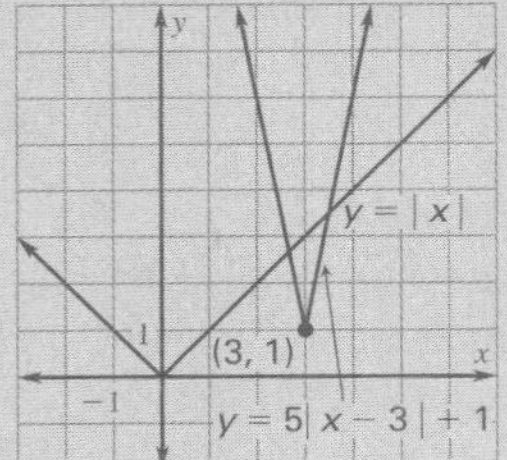

The graph of $y = 5|x - 3| + 1$ is the graph of $y = |x|$ first vertically stretched by a factor of 5, then translated right 3 units and up 1 unit.

Extra Example 2.8

Graph $-4x + y > 6$ in a coordinate plane.

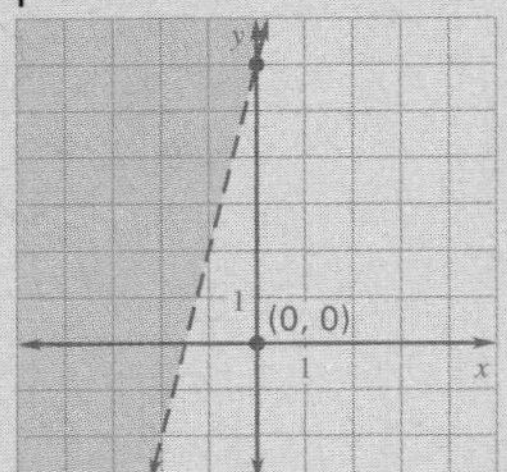

24. 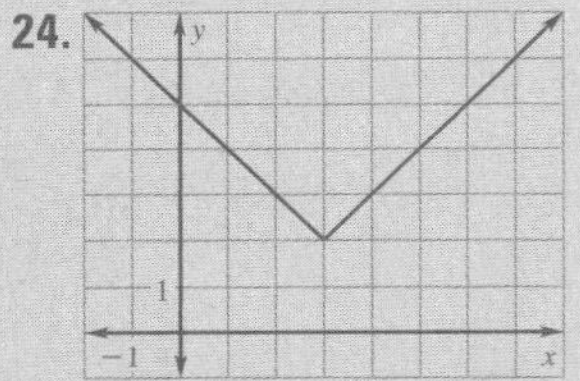

translated right 3 units and up 2 units

25. 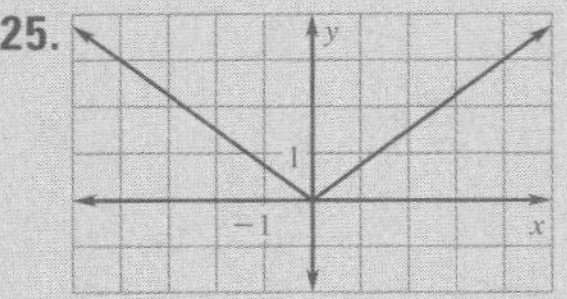

shrunk vertically by a factor of $\frac{3}{4}$

26. 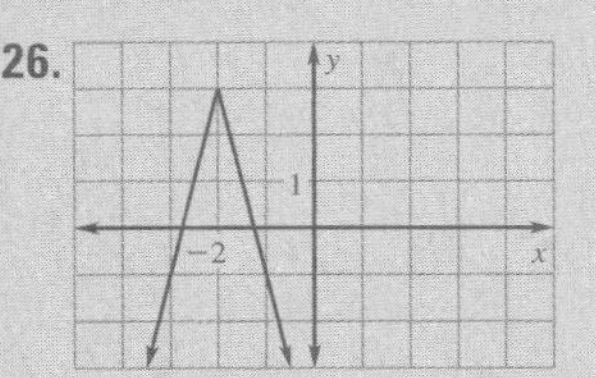

reflected over the x-axis, stretched vertically by a factor of 4, translated left 2 units and up 3 units

27. 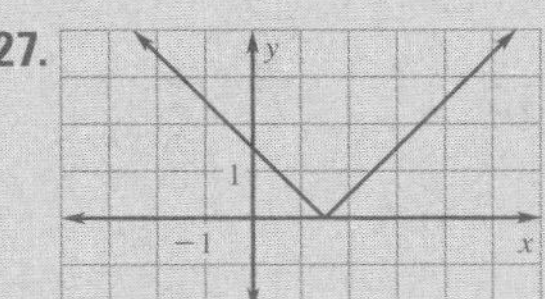

31–34. See Additional Answers beginning on p. AA1.

2 CHAPTER TEST

In Exercises 1 and 2, tell whether the relation is a function. *Explain.*

1. Not a function; the inputs 1 and 2 each have more than one output.

1. (1, −5), (0, 4), (2, 3), (−1, 2), (2, 7), (1, 2)

2. (−3, 4), (2, 5), (1, 0), (0, 4), (−2, −3), (3, 6) Function; each input has exactly one output.

3. Evaluate $f(x) = 3x^2 - 2x + 11$ when $x = -6$. 131

Find the slope of the line passing through the given points. Then tell whether the line *rises, falls, is horizontal,* or *is vertical.*

4. (3, −2), (5, 4) 3; rises

5. (6, −7), (13, −7) 0; is horizontal

6. (−2, 1), (1, −4) $-\frac{5}{3}$; falls

7. (−4, 9), (−4, 8) undefined; is vertical

Graph the equation. 8–11. See margin.

8. $x = 4$

9. $y = \frac{3}{2}x + 3$

10. $x + 2y = 6$

11. $3y = 2x - 12$

Write an equation of the line that passes through the given point and satisfies the given condition.

12. (9, −1); parallel to $y = -\frac{1}{3}x - 8$ $y = -\frac{1}{3}x + 2$

13. (10, 2); perpendicular to $y = -5x + 7$ $y = \frac{1}{5}x$

The variables x and y vary directly. Write an equation that relates x and y. Then find x when $y = 6$.

14. $x = 4, y = -8$ $y = -2x$; −3

15. $x = -2, y = -1$ $y = \frac{1}{2}x$; 12

16. $x = 8, y = 18$ $y = \frac{9}{4}x$; $2\frac{2}{3}$

17. $x = 16, y = -6$ $y = -\frac{3}{8}x$; −16

In Exercises 18 and 19, (a) draw a scatter plot of the data, (b) approximate the best-fitting line for the data, and (c) estimate the value of y when $x = 10$. 18, 19. See margin.

18.

x	1	2	3	4	5
y	18	40	55	73	91

19.

x	1	2	3	4	5
y	97	91	87	81	75

20. Graph $y = -3|x + 1| + 3$. *Compare* the graph with the graph of $y = |x|$. See margin.

Graph the inequality in a coordinate plane. 21–24. See margin.

21. $y \geq -2x + 4$

22. $2x - 4y \leq 16$

23. $y < |x - 3| + 1$

24. $y > -2|x| - 3$

25. TIRE WEAR A new set of car tires has a tread depth of 8 millimeters. The tread depth decreases 0.12 millimeter per thousand miles driven. Write an equation that gives the tread depth as a function of the distance driven. Then predict at what distance the tread depth will be 2 millimeters. $d = 8 - 0.00012m$; 50,000 mi

26. PAINTING The amount of paint an electric paint sprayer applies varies directly with time. A sprayer is set to apply 0.5 gallon in 2.5 minutes. Write an equation that gives the amount p of paint as a function of the time t. How much paint is applied if the sprayer is operated for 20 minutes? $p = 0.2t$; 4 gal

27. COMPUTER CHIPS The table shows the number x of transistors (in millions) and the speed y (in gigahertz) for several computer processors. Approximate the best-fitting line for the data. $y = 0.03x + 0.20$

x	3.1	9.5	28	37	42	55	106	125
y	0.06	0.45	0.5	1.5	1.5	2	2.4	3.6

8. 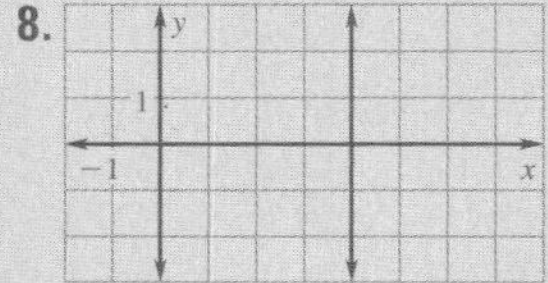

9. 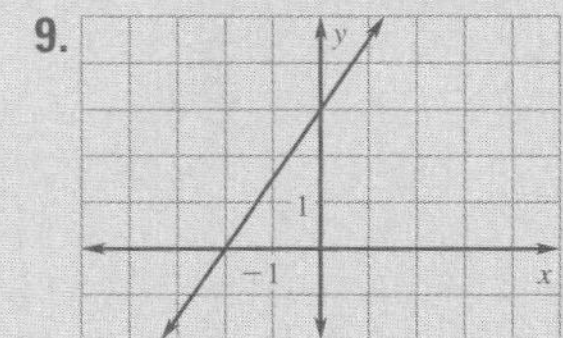

10. 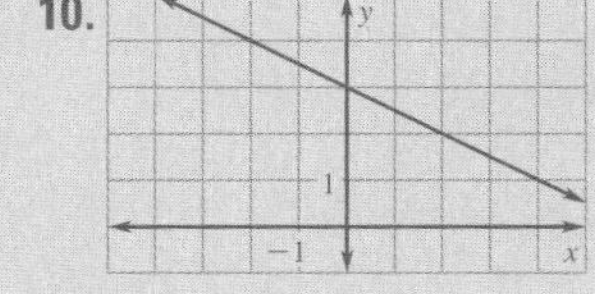

Additional Resources

Assessment Book

- Chapter Test, Levels A, B, C, pp. 19–24
- Standardized Chapter Test, pp. 25–26
- SAT/ACT Chapter Test, pp. 27–28
- Alternative Assessment, pp. 29–30

Test Generator CD-ROM

Chapter Test

Easily-readable reduced copies (with answers) of Chapter Test B, the Standardized Chapter Test, and the Alternative Assessment from the Assessment Book can be found on pp. 70G–70H.

11. 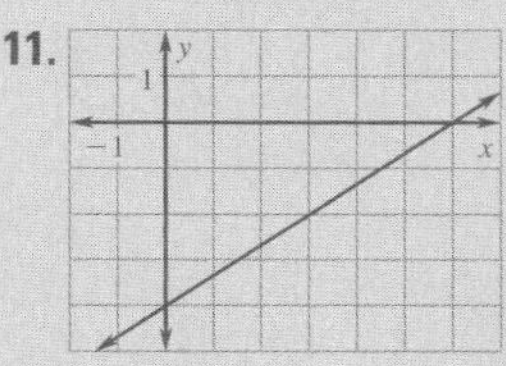

18a. 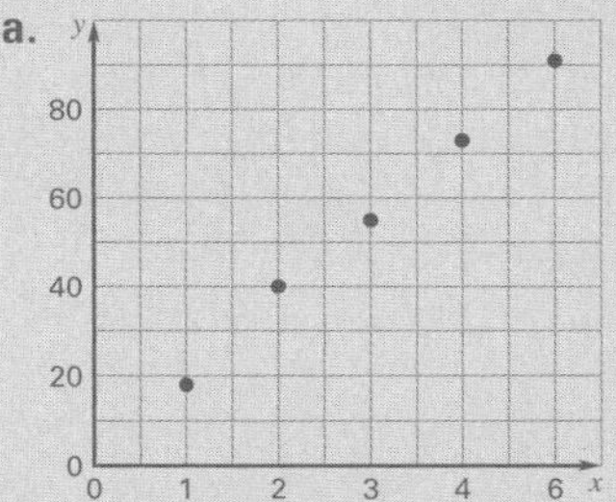

18b. *Sample answer:* $y = 18x + 1.7$

18c. about 182

19a. 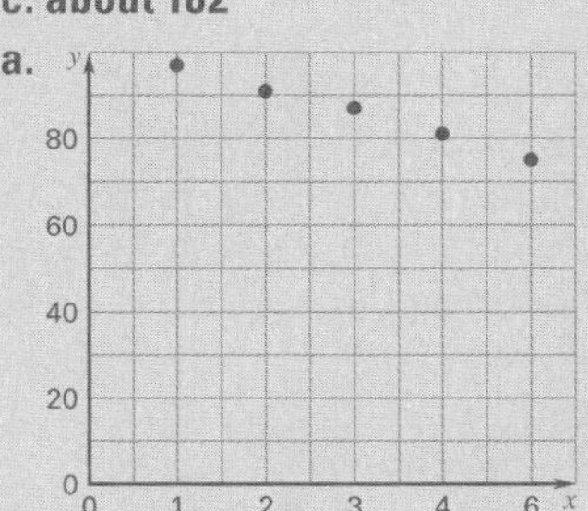

19b. *Sample answer:* $y = -5.4x + 102$

19c. about 48

20–24. See Additional Answers beginning on p. AA1.

TEST PREPARATION

MULTIPLE-CHOICE QUESTIONS

If you have difficulty solving a multiple-choice problem directly, you may be able to use another approach. First, eliminate as many wrong answers as you can. Then, make an educated guess from among the remaining choices.

PROBLEM 1

You are baking cookies and preheat the oven. The oven temperature starts at room temperature (68°F) and takes 8 minutes to reach the baking temperature (350°F). If the relationship between time and temperature is approximately linear for this oven, how much longer will it take the oven to heat to 425°F?

A. 1 minute B. 2 minutes C. 3 minutes D. 5 minutes

METHOD 1

SOLVE DIRECTLY First, use the information in the problem to write an equation for the line.

STEP 1 **Compute** the rate of change, which is also the slope of the line.

$$\text{Rate of Change} = \frac{\text{Change in Temp.}}{\text{Change in Time}} = \frac{350^\circ\text{F} - 68^\circ\text{F}}{8 \text{ minutes}} = \frac{35.25^\circ\text{F}}{\text{minute}}$$

STEP 2 **Write** an equation that relates the temperature (F) in degrees Fahrenheit to the time (t) in minutes. The slope is the rate of change, 35.25°F/minute, and the initial value is 68°F. So, the equation is

$$F = 35.25t + 68$$

STEP 3 **Substitute** $\frac{1}{2} - x$ for y in Equation 1 and solve for x.

$425 = 35.25x + 68$

$357 = 35.25x$

$x \approx 10$ minutes, which is the same as 2 additional minutes.

▸ The correct answer is B.

METHOD 2

ELIMINATE CHOICES Compare the given final temperature to the final temperature for each answer choice.

STEP 1 **Compute** the rate of change.

$$\text{Rate of Change} = \frac{\text{Change in Temp.}}{\text{Change in Time}} = \frac{350^\circ\text{F} - 68^\circ\text{F}}{8 \text{ minutes}} = \frac{35.25^\circ\text{F}}{\text{minute}}$$

STEP 2 **Compute** the possible oven temperature for each answer choice. Add the possible increase in temperature to 350°F. Multiply 35.25°F/min by the number of minutes; then add the product to 350°F to find each possible temperature.

Choice A: 350°F + 1(35.25°F) ≈ 385°F ✗

Choice B: 350°F + 2(35.25°F) ≈ 420°F ✓

Choice C: 350°F + 3(35.25°F) ≈ 456°F ✗

Choice D: 350°F + 5(35.25°F) ≈ 526°F ✗

▸ The correct answer is B.

PROBLEM 2

What is the y-intercept of the line that passes through the point (20, 180) and has a slope of -5?

A. -45 B. 80 C. 180 D. 280

METHOD 1

SOLVE DIRECTLY Use the information in the problem to write the equation of the line in point-slope form. Then convert to slope-intercept form.

STEP 1 **Write** the equation using the slope of -5 and the point (20, 180).

$$y - 180 = -5(x - 20)$$

STEP 2 **Rewrite** the equation in slope intercept form.

$$y - 180 = -5(x - 20)$$

$$y = -5(x - 20) + 180$$

$$y = -5x + 100 + 180$$

$$y = -5x + 280$$

The y-intercept is 280.

▶ The correct answer is D.

METHOD 2

ELIMINATE CHOICES Another method is to write an equation for each answer choice and test whether $y = 180$ when $x = 20$.

STEP 1 **Write** an equation using the slope of -5 and the y-intercept of the answer choice.

Choice A: $y = -5x - 45$

Choice B: $y = -5x + 80$

Choice C: $y = -5x + 180$

Choice D: $y = -5x + 280$

STEP 2 **Compute** y for $x = 20$ and compare this value to $y = 180$.

Choice A: If $x = 20$, $y = -5(20) - 45 = -145$

Choice B: If $x = 20$, $y = -5(20) + 80 = -20$

Choice C: If $x = 20$, $y = -5(20) + 180 = 80$

Choice D: If $x = 20$, $y = -5(20) + 280 = 180$

▶ The correct answer is D.

TEST PREPARATION

PRACTICE

Explain why you can eliminate the highlighted answer choice.

1. Which line below is parallel to $y = -\frac{1}{3}x + 4$?

A. $y = 3x + 7$ B. ✗ $y = -3x + 7$ C. $3y = -x + 7$ D. $3x = -y + 7$

2. Mara hikes up a mountain at a rate of 2 miles each hour. Which equation below relates Mara's distance hiked in miles, m, to the number of hours, h, she has hiked?

A. $m = 2h$ B. $m = 2 + h$ 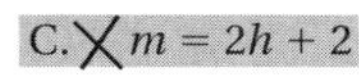 C. ✗ $m = 2h + 2$ D. $m = \frac{h}{2}$

Kentucky Test Preparation

1. The slopes of the lines must be the same, but $-3 \neq -\frac{1}{3}$.

2. Mara hikes 0 miles in 0 hours, so the point (0, 0) must be part of this function. However, $0 \neq 2(0) + 2$.

Kentucky Test Practice

1. A
2. B
3. B
4. B
5. B
6. D
7. D
8. D

TEST PREPARATION

Kentucky Test Practice

MULTIPLE-CHOICE

1. Which equation below does not represent a function?

A. $x = 4$ B. $y = \pi$

C. $y = |x|$ D. $y = x^2 + 4$

2. Water boils at 100° Celsius at sea level. The boiling temperature changes depending on altitude. For each increase of 1 kilometer in altitude, the water boils at about 3.5°C lower. Which equation relates the boiling temperature (C) in degrees Celsius to the altitude (a) in kilometers?

A. $C = -3.5a$ B. $C = 100 - 3.5a$

C. $C = 100 - |3.5a|$ D. $C = 3.5a + 100$

3. The scatter plot shows the ages of the winners of professional golf's annual Masters Tournament for the years 1934–2005. (There was no tournament in the years 1943–1945.) What type of correlation does the graph show?

A. The age of the winner is positively correlated to the year.

B. The age of the winner is not correlated to the year.

C. The age of the winner is negatively correlated to the year.

D. The correlation of the age of the winner to the year is undefined.

4. The Wellness Center increased the number of holistic medicine providers between 2003 and 2007, as shown in the table below. If the trend continues, how many providers will there be x years after 2007?

Year	Number of Providers
2003	32
2004	34
2005	36
2006	38
2007	40

A. $32x$ B. $32 + 2x$

C. $40 + 2x$ D. $42 + 2x$

5. A house's roof has a length of 25 feet from its peak to its lowest edge. The height of the roof at the peak is 15 feet. A special chimney protrudes perpendicularly from the roof. What is the slope of the chimney?

A. $\frac{5}{3}$ B. $\frac{3}{4}$

C. $\frac{4}{3}$ D. $\frac{3}{5}$

6. Which of the ordered pairs below is not on the graph of $-3x + 2y = 12$?

A. $(-4, 0)$ B. $(0, 6)$

C. $(2, 9)$ D. $(6, -3)$

7. A direct variation equation $y = ax$ includes the point $(-3, -6)$. What is the value of the constant of variation?

A. -2 B. -1

C. 1 D. 2

8. What is the value of k so that the line passing through $(k, 2)$ and $(2, 7)$ has a slope of -1?

A. -5 B. -3

C. 3 D. 7

MULTIPLE-CHOICE

9. Which ordered pair is a solution of the inequality $-x + 2y > 10$?

A. $(-10, 0)$ B. $(0, 5)$
C. $(5, 5)$ D. $(5, 10)$

10. The graph of which equation passes through the point $(1, -3)$ and is perpendicular to the line $x + y = 10$?

A. $x + y = -2$ B. $x - y = -2$
C. $x + y = 4$ D. $x - y = 4$

11. What is the slope of the line passing through the points $(0, -4)$ and $(-3, 2)$?

A. -2 B. $-\frac{1}{2}$
C. $\frac{1}{2}$ D. 2

12. Which is the x-intercept of the graph of $2x + 3y = 36$?

A. 6 B. 12
C. 18 D. 36

13 Which choice best describes the relationship between the lines $y = x + 2$ and $y = -x + 2$?

A. The lines are perpendicular.
B. The lines are parallel.
C. The lines have the same x-intercept.
D. The lines are the same.

14. The graph of $g(x) = -3 \cdot f(x) + 5$ is obtained from the graph of $y = f(x)$ through several transformations. The point $(-7, -6)$ lies on the graph of $y = f(x)$. What is $g(-7)$?

A. 18 B. 21
C. 23 D. 26

OPEN-RESPONSE

15. The number of women elected to the U.S. House of Representatives has increased nearly every Congress since 1985. In the 99th Congress beginning in 1985, there were 22 female representatives. In the 109th Congress beginning in 2005, there were 68 female representatives.

a. Write a linear equation that models the number y of female members of the House of Representatives x years after 1985.

b. Given that the number of representatives is fixed at 435, is it reasonable to think that the model could be a fairly accurate predictor of the number of female representatives in 2030? Justify your answer.

16. A park trail leading up a hill has been improved by building steps from wooden timbers, as shown in the diagram of a section of the trail. Each timber measures 8 inches on a side.

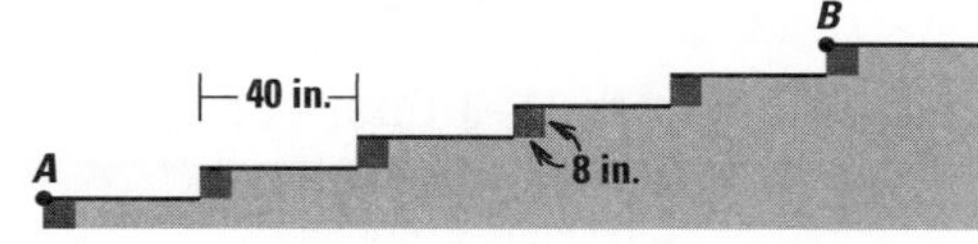

a. What is the average rate of change in elevation on the trail from point A to point B?

b. If the trail continues as shown up a hill that is 120 feet high, what is the horizontal distance covered by climbing the trail?

c. If the trail had used 6-inch timbers for each step instead of 8-inch timbers, what horizontal distance would each step cover? Justify your answer.

TEST PREPARATION

9. D
10. D
11. A
12. C
13. A
14. C
15. a. $y = 2.3x + 22$
b. Yes. ***Sample answer:*** Substituting 45 for x in the equation gives 126 female representatives, which is a reasonable estimate.
16. a. $\frac{1}{5}$
b. 600 feet
c. 30 inches; since the average rate of change is $\frac{1}{5}$, solve the proportion $\frac{1}{5} = \frac{6}{x}$.

3 Pacing and Assignment Guide

REGULAR SCHEDULE

Pre-AP For pacing and assignments for a Pre-AP course, see the *Algebra 2 Toolkit*.

Lesson	Les. Day	BASIC	AVERAGE	ADVANCED
3.1 MA-HS-5.3.4	Day 1	EP p. 1011 Exs. 11–14; pp. 156–158 Exs. 1, 2, 3–15 odd, 16–22, 35–38, 41	pp. 156–158 Exs. 1, 2, 6–11, 15, 16, 20–25, 28–31, 35–39, 42	pp. 156–158 Exs. 1, 2, 10–15, 23–40*
3.2 MA-HS-5.3.4	Day 1	SRH p. 984 Exs. 7–12; pp. 164–167 Exs. 1–8, 15–20, 27–33, 40–45, 55–60, 64	pp. 164–167 Exs. 1, 2, 6–10, 18–22, 27, 31–35, 40–51, 55–62, 65	pp. 164–167 Exs. 1, 2, 11–14, 23–26, 36–54*, 57–63*, 66
3.3 *MA-HS-5.3.5*	Day 1	EP p. 1011 Exs. 39–42; pp. 171–173 Exs. 1–9, 16–22, 34–38, 41	pp. 171–173 Exs. 1–3, 8–12, 16, 21–27, 29, 31, 34–39, 42	pp. 171–173 Exs. 1–3, 12–15, 21–33*, 35–40*, 42
3.4	Day 1	pp. 182–185 Exs. 1, 2, 3–19 odd, 21–29, 42–45, 49	pp. 182–185 Exs. 1, 2, 4–20 even, 21–24, 28–30, 34–36, 42–47, 50	pp. 182–185 Exs. 1, 2, 7, 8, 13, 14, 19, 20, 23, 24, 31–41*, 43–48*, 50
3.5 *MA-HS-4.1.3*	Day 1	SRH p. 975 Exs. 12, 15, 21, 25, 31; pp. 190–193 Exs. 1–7, 10–13, 16–24, 31–33, 37	pp. 190–193 Exs. 1–3, 7–9, 13–15, 18–29, 31–34, 36	pp. 190–193 Exs. 1, 2, 8, 9, 14, 15, 19–35*
3.6 *MA-HS-4.1.3*	Day 1	pp. 199–202 Exs. 1–15, 46–47	pp. 199–202 Exs. 1, 2, 6–18, 46–47	pp. 199–202 Exs. 1, 2, 6–9, 13–21, 46–47
	Day 2	pp. 199–202 Exs. 19–28, 37–42	pp. 199–202 Exs. 19–21, 24–34, 37–44	pp. 199–202 Exs. 22–36*, 38–45*
3.7 *MA-HS-4.1.3*	Day 1	pp. 207–209 Exs. 1–8, 11–16, 19–21, 23–27 odd, 28–31, 40–43, 48	pp. 207–209 Exs. 1, 2, 7–10, 15–21, 22–28 even, 29–34, 38, 40–45, 48	pp. 207–209 Exs. 1, 2, 8–10, 16–18, 21, 25–28, 32–46*
3.8 *MA-HS-4.1.3*	Day 1	SRH p. 984 Exs. 13–19; pp. 214–217 Exs. 1–18	pp. 214–217 Exs. 1–18	pp. 214–217 Exs. 1, 2, 5–10, 12–18, 41, 57–61
	Day 2	pp. 214–217 Exs. 19–30, 34–36, 43–46, 51–53	pp. 214–217 Exs. 19–24, 28–41, 43–48, 51–53	pp. 214–217 Exs. 22–24, 28–50*, 52
Review	Day 1	pp. 222–226 Exs. 1–35	pp. 222–226 Exs. 1–35	pp. 222–226 Exs. 1–35
Assess	Day 1	Chapter 3 Test	Chapter 3 Test	Chapter 3 Test
Yearly Pacing		Chapter 3 Total – 12 days	Chapters 1–3 Total – 38 days	Remaining – 122 days

*Challenge Exercises EP = Extra Practice SRH = Skills Review Handbook

BLOCK SCHEDULE

DAY 1	DAY 2	DAY 3	DAY 4	DAY 5	DAY 6
3.1	**3.3**	**3.5**	**3.6 (CONT.)**	**3.8**	**REVIEW**
pp. 156–158 Exs. 1, 2, 6–11, 15, 16, 20–25, 28–31, 35–39, 42	pp. 171–173 Exs. 1–3, 8–12, 16, 21–27, 29, 31, 34–39, 42	pp. 190–193 Exs. 1–3, 7–9, 13–15, 18–29, 31–34, 36	pp. 199–202 Exs. 19–21, 24–34, 37–44	pp. 214–217 Exs. 1–24, 28–41, 43–48, 51–53	pp. 222–226 Exs. 1–35
3.2	**3.4**	**3.6**	**3.7**		**ASSESS**
pp. 164–167 Exs. 1, 2, 6–10, 18–22, 27, 31–35, 40–51, 55–62, 65	pp. 182–185 Exs. 1, 2, 4–20 even, 21–24, 28–30, 34–36, 42–47, 50	pp. 199–202 Exs. 1, 2, 6–18, 46–47	pp. 207–209 Exs. 1, 2, 7–10, 15–21, 22–28 even, 29–34, 38, 40–45, 48		Chapter 3 Test
Yearly Pacing	Chapter 3 Total – 6 days	Chapters 1–3 Total – 19 days	Remaining – 61 days		

Chapter Resource Guide 3

RESOURCE MANAGER

Chapter Resource Book								
CHAPTER SUPPORT								
Parents as Partners (Chapter Overview with home involvement exercises and activity)							p. 1	
LESSON SUPPORT Standards	3.1 MA-HS-5.3.4	3.2 MA-HS-5.3.4	3.3 MA-HS-5.3.5	3.4	3.5 MA-HS-4.1.3	3.6 MA-HS-4.1.3	3.7 MA-HS-4.1.3	3.8 MA-HS-4.1.3
Teaching Guide/Lesson Plan	p. 3	p. 19	p. 32	p. 46	p. 58	p. 69	p. 79	p. 91
Activity Masters		p. 21	p. 34					p. 93
Technology Activities & Keystrokes	p. 5	p. 23			p. 60		p. 81	p. 94
Activity Support Masters				p. 48				
Practice (3 levels)	p. 8	p. 24	p. 35	p. 49	p. 61	p. 71	p. 83	p. 95
Study Guide	p. 14	p. 27	p. 41	p. 52	p. 64	p. 74	p. 86	p. 98
Catch-Up for Absent Students	p. 16	p. 29	p. 43	p. 54	p. 66	p. 76	p. 88	p. 100
Problem Solving/Application	p. 17	p. 30	p. 44	p. 55	p. 67	p. 77	p. 89	p. 101
Challenge Practice	p. 18	p. 31	p. 45	p. 57	p. 68	p. 78	p. 90	p. 102
REVIEW								
Chapter Review Games and Activities		p. 103		Cumulative Practice			p. 105	
Project with Rubric		p. 104		Resource Book Answers			A1	

Transparencies	3.1	3.2	3.3	3.4	3.5	3.6	3.7	3.8
Warm-Up/Daily Homework Quiz	✔	✔	✔	✔	✔	✔	✔	✔
Notetaking Guide	✔	✔	✔	✔	✔	✔	✔	✔
Teacher Support	✔		✔					
Answer Transparencies	✔	✔	✔	✔	✔	✔	✔	✔

ASSESSMENT BOOK

Quizzes	p. 31	SAT/ACT Chapter Test	p. 42
Chapter Tests (3 levels)	p. 34	Alternative Assessment with Rubric	p. 44
Standardized Chapter Test	p. 40		

TECHNOLOGY

- Easy Planner
- Test and Practice Generator
- Power Presentations
- @HomeTutor
- Activity Generator
- Animated Algebra
- Classzone.com
- eEdition Plus Online
- eWorkbook Plus Online
- ML Assessment System

ADDITIONAL RESOURCES

KY Kentucky

- Worked-Out Solution Key
- Notetaking Guide
- Practice Workbook
- Algebra 2 Toolkit
- Benchmark Tests
- Remediation Workbook
- Spanish Study Guide
- Spanish Assessment Book
- Spanish Resources in Spanish
- Multi-Language Visual Glossary

3 Lesson Practice Level B

LESSON 3.1 Practice B *For use with pages 153–158*

1. C; consistent and independent
2. A; consistent and dependent
3. B; inconsistent

Match the linear system with its graph. Then classify the system as *consistent and independent, consistent and dependent, or inconsistent.* See above.

1. $3x - 2y = 2$; $-2x + y = -2$
2. $4x - y = 3$; $-8x + 2y = -6$
3. $x + 3y = 2$; $-3x - 9y = 18$

A. 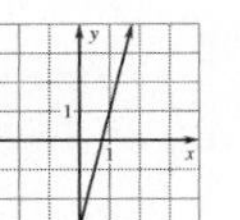
B. 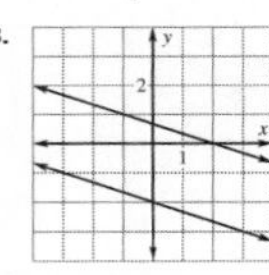
C. 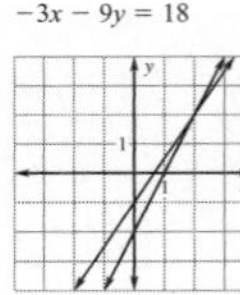

Graph the linear system and estimate the solution. Then check the solution algebraically.

4. $2x + 3y = 8$ (4, 0); $-x + y = -4$
5. $3x + 5y = -4$ (−3, 1); $2x - y = -7$
6. $x - 2y = 4$ (2, −1); $4x + 2y = 6$

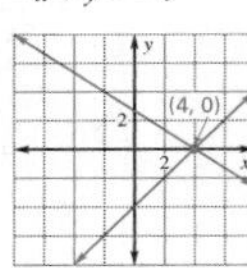

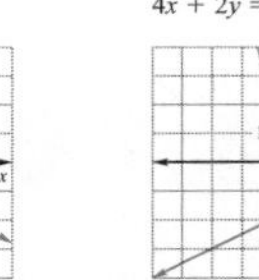

7. $3x + y = 3$ (0, 3); $-2x + y = 3$
8. $5x - 2y = -1$ (−1, −2); $x - 3y = 5$
9. $x - 2y = -5$ (3, 4); $-2x + 6y = 18$

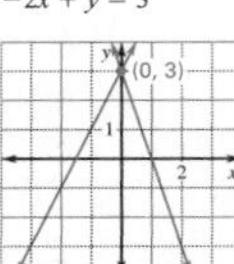

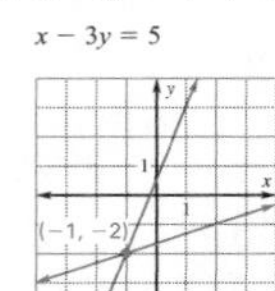

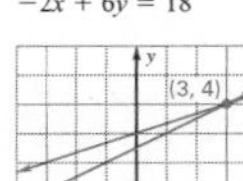

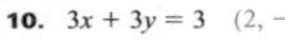

LESSON 3.1 Practice B *continued* *For use with pages 153–158*

10. $3x + 3y = 3$ (2, −1); $x + 2y = 0$
11. $2x - 4y = 2$ (−3, −2); $-2x + 3y = 0$
12. $5x - 3y = -17$ (−1, 4); $4x + 5y = 16$

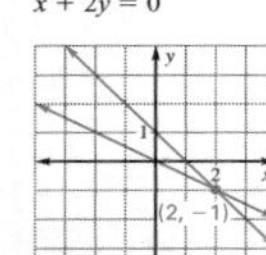

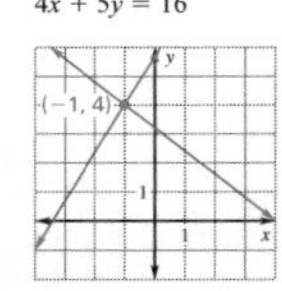

Solve the system. Then classify the system as *consistent and independent, consistent and dependent, or inconsistent.*

13. $x - 2y = 5$; $2x - 4y = 10$ infinitely many solutions; consistent and dependent
14. $5x + y = 16$; $-3x + y = 0$ (2, 6); consistent and independent
15. $2x + \frac{1}{2}y = 4$; $12x - 6y = -12$ (1, 4); consistent and independent
16. **Concert** A vendor sold 200 tickets for an upcoming rock concert. Floor seats were \$36 and stadium seats were \$28. The vendor sold \$6080 in tickets. How many \$36 and \$28 tickets did the vendor sell? 60 tickets at \$36; 140 tickets at \$28

In Exercises 17–20, use the following information.

Break-Even Analysis You purchase a music store for \$115,000. The estimated monthly revenue is \$5500 and expected monthly costs are \$3200.

17. Let R represent the revenue during the first t months. Write a linear model for R. $R = 5500t$
18. Let C represent the costs during the first t months including the purchase price. Write a linear model for C. $C = 3200t + 115{,}000$
19. Graph the revenue and cost linear models on the same coordinate plane.

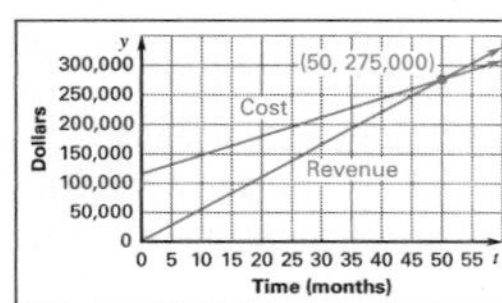

20. How many months will it take until revenue and costs are equal (the "break-even point")? 50

LESSON 3.2 Practice B *For use with pages 160–166*

Solve the system using the substitution method.

1. $x + 2y = 6$ (2, 2); $3x - 2y = 2$
2. $x + 3y = 3$ (3, 0); $2x - 4y = 6$
3. $4x + y = 7$ (2, −1); $2x + 5y = -1$
4. $2x - 3y = 3$ $\left(\frac{9}{4}, \frac{1}{2}\right)$; $-2x + y = -4$
5. $3x + 2y = -2$ $\left(\frac{2}{3}, -2\right)$; $6x - y = 6$
6. $8x + 2y = 2$ (−1, 5); $x + 3y = 14$

Solve the system using the elimination method.

7. $-3x + 3y = 3$ (2, 3); $3x + y = 9$
8. $5x - y = -9$ (−1, 4); $2x + y = 2$
9. $-5x + 12y = 20$ (−16, −5); $x - 2y = -6$
10. $4x - 2y = -2$ $\left(\frac{1}{2}, 2\right)$; $6x + y = 5$
11. $3x + 2y = 1$ $\left(-\frac{4}{5}, \frac{17}{10}\right)$; $4x + 6y = 7$
12. $7x - 3y = 6$ (0, −2); $-2x + 5y = -10$

Solve the system using any algebraic method.

13. $5x + 7y = -2$ (1, −1); $2x - 7y = 9$
14. $x + 3y = 1$ (−2, 1); $3x + 7y = 1$
15. $4x + 6y = 8$ no solution; $2x + 3y = 3$
16. $8x - 5y = -17$ $\left(-\frac{13}{2}, -7\right)$; $-2x + y = 6$
17. $3x - 8y = 0$ (16, 6); $-2x + 5y = -2$
18. $4x - 6y = 2$ $\left(\frac{2}{7}, -\frac{1}{7}\right)$; $5x + 3y = 1$
19. $2x - 5y = 3$; $-4x + 10y = -6$ infinitely many solutions
20. $8x + 3y = 10$ $\left(\frac{23}{13}, -\frac{18}{13}\right)$; $-6x + y = -12$
21. $5x + 4y = -18$ (6, −12); $2x + 3y = -24$
22. **CDs and Cassettes** From 1990 to 1998, the manufacturer's shipments for audio cassettes, A (in millions), and compact discs, C (in millions), can be modeled by the equations

    $A = -31.8t + 322$ Audio cassette shipments

    $C = 42.8t + 110$ Compact disc shipments

    where t is the number of years since 1990. During what year did the number of compact discs shipped surpass the number of audio cassettes shipped? 1992
23. **Hair Salon** A hair salon receives a shipment of 84 bottles of hair conditioner to use and sell to customers. The two types of conditioners received are type A, which is used for regular hair, and type B, which is used for frizzy hair. Type A costs \$6.50 per bottle and type B costs \$8.25 per bottle. The hair salon's invoice for the conditioner is \$588. How many of each type of conditioner are in the shipment? 60 of type A, 24 of type B
24. **Birthday Gift** You and your sister decide to combine your weekly overtime earnings to buy a birthday gift for your mother. Your overtime rate is \$18 per hour and your sister's overtime rate is \$24 per hour. The total amount earned for the gift was \$288. If you worked two more hours of overtime than your sister, how many overtime hours did each of you work? you: 8 h, your sister: 6 h

LESSON 3.3

Practice B

For use with pages 168–173

Match the system of inequalities with its graph.

1. $x + y > 1$ B
   $-2x + 3y \geq -6$
2. $x + y < 1$ C
   $-2x + 3y < -6$
3. $x + y \leq 1$ A
   $-2x + 3y > -6$

A. 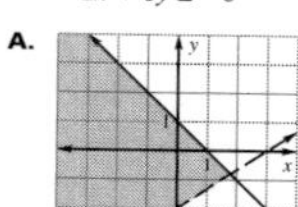

B. 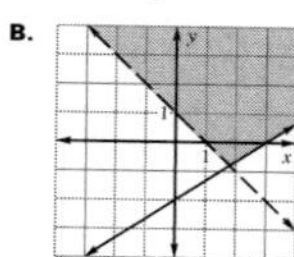

C. 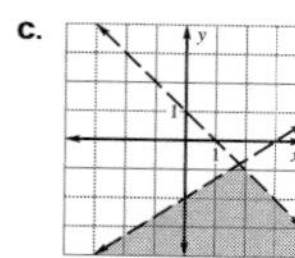

Graph the system of inequalities.

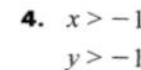

4. $x > -1$
   $y > -1$

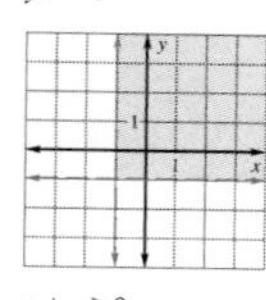

5. $x \geq -2$
   $y < 1$

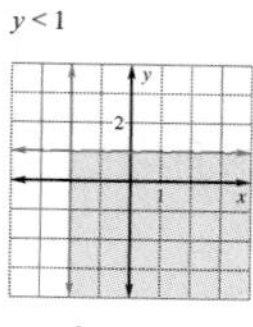

6. $y \leq 3$
   $y > 1$

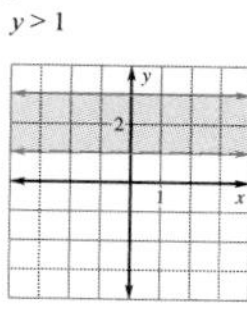

7. $x + y \geq 0$
   $-x + y \geq 0$

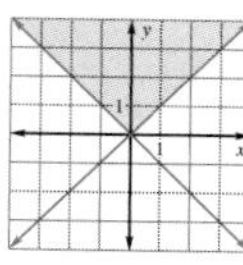

8. $y > -2x$
   $2x - y > 1$

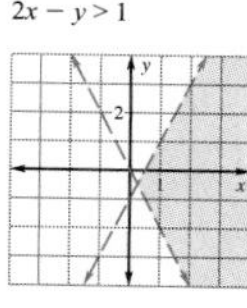

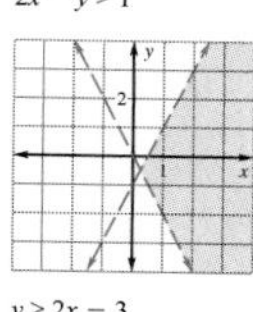

9. $2x + y < 5$
   $y > 2|x - 1|$

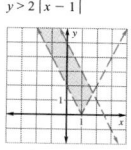

10. $x + 2y < 2$
    $3x + y \leq 3$

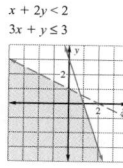

11. $y > 2x - 3$
    $x > -1$
    $y < 3$

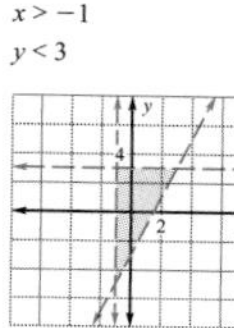

12. $y \leq |x| + 4$
    $x < 2$
    $y \geq 2$

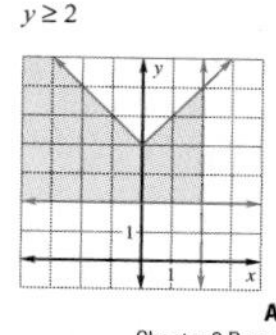

LESSON 3.3

LESSON 3.3

Practice B *continued*

For use with pages 168–173

13. $y < \frac{1}{2}x + 3$
    $y \geq -2x - 3$
    $x \leq 3$

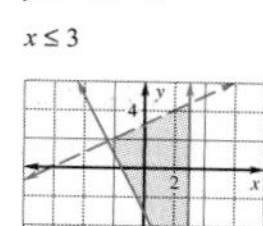

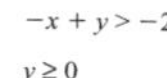

14. $x + y > -2$
    $-x + y > -2$
    $y \geq 0$

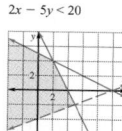

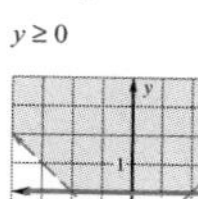

15. $y \leq -\frac{1}{3}x + 2$
    $y > 3x - 3$
    $x > -1$

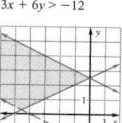

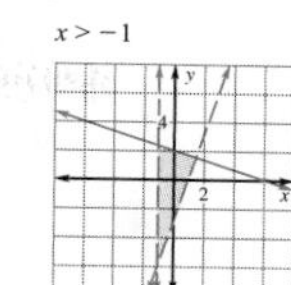

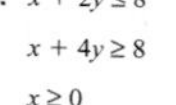

16. $x + 2y \leq 8$
    $x + 4y \geq 8$
    $x \geq 0$

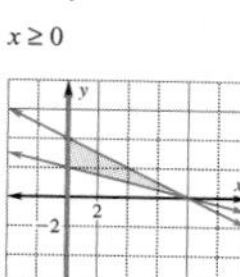

17. $x + 2y \leq 10$
    $2x + y \leq 8$
    $2x - 5y < 20$

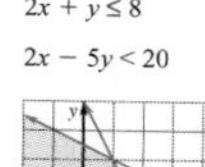

18. $x + 2y \leq 5$
    $2x - 4y \leq -10$
    $3x + 6y > -12$

19. The diagram at the right shows the graph of a system of two inequalities. Write a system of inequalities that represents the graph.
    $y \geq |x - 1| + 1$
    $y < 4$

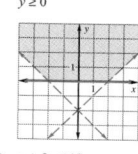

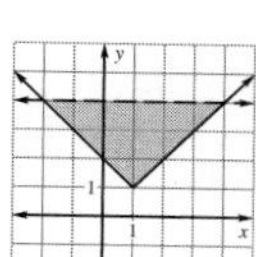

In Exercises 20 and 21, use the following information.

Distance During a family trip, you share the driving with your dad. At most, you are allowed to drive for three hours. While driving, your maximum speed is 55 miles per hour.

20. Write a system of inequalities describing the possible number of hours t and distance d you may have driven. $t \leq 3$, $d \leq 55t$

21. Is it possible for you to have driven 160 miles? yes

LESSON 3.3

LESSON 3.4

Practice B

For use with pages 178–185

7. $(-43, -2, -8)$ 11. $(1, 6, -2)$
13. $(-2, -3, 4)$ 14. $\left(-\frac{5}{2}z + \frac{19}{2}, 2z - 12, z\right)$

Tell whether the given ordered triple is a solution of the system.

1. $(2, 1, 3)$ yes
   $2x - y + 5z = 16$
   $x - 3y + 2z = 5$
   $x + 2y + z = 7$
2. $(5, -2, 2)$ no
   $2x - y + z = 5$
   $x + 2y - z = -1$
   $-2x + y - 3z = -15$
3. $(3, 3, 4)$ no
   $x + 2y - 2z = 1$
   $7x - 4y + z = 11$
   $2x - 3y + 2z = 5$
4. $(1, -1, 3)$ yes
   $4x + 2y + 3z = 11$
   $x - 2y + z = 6$
   $2x + y + 2z = 7$
5. $(0, 0, 2)$ no
   $2x - 4y - 2z = -4$
   $2x + 5y + 8z = 16$
   $6x - 3y - z = 2$
6. $(5, -2, 3)$ yes
   $3x + 4y - 2z = 1$
   $2x + 3y - z = 1$
   $4x + 8y - z = 1$

Solve the system using any algebraic method.

7. $x + y - 5z = -5$ See above.
   $y - 2z = 14$
   $4y - 2z = 8$
8. $x - y + z = 5$ $(2, 1, 4)$
   $2y + 3z = 14$
   $-3y + 2z = 5$
9. $-3x + y - z = -2$ $(-1, 0, 5)$
   $2x - y - 2z = -12$
   $4x + 2y + z = 1$
10. $x - 2y + z = -1$ $(3, 1, -2)$
    $x + 2y - z = 7$
    $x + y + z = 2$
11. $x - 2y + 4z = -19$
    $2x + y - 3z = 14$ See above.
    $3x + y + 2z = 5$
12. $x - 2y - 3z = -7$ $(5, -3, 6)$
    $4x + 5y - 2z = -7$
    $-2x + y + z = -7$
13. $8x - 2y + z = -6$
    $-x + 3y - 2z = -15$
    $3x - y + 4z = 13$ See above.
14. $2x + 2y + z = -5$
    $2x + y + 3z = 7$ See above.
    $-4x - 2y - 6z = -14$
15. $3x - 4y - 4z = 8$ $\left(2, \frac{1}{2}, -1\right)$
    $4x + 2y - 2z = 11$
    $-5x + 8y + 3z = -9$

16. **Harvest Yields** A farmer makes three deliveries to the feed mill during one harvest. The harvest produced 2885 bushels of corn, 1335 bushels of wheat and 1230 bushels of soybeans. Use the table to write and solve a system of equations to find the total number of bushels in each delivery.

Crop	1st Delivery	2nd Delivery	3rd Delivery
Corn	50%	75%	40%
Wheat	30%	10%	30%
Soybeans	20%	15%	30%

$0.5x + 0.75y + 0.4z = 2885$
$0.3x + 0.1y + 0.3z = 1335$
$0.2x + 0.15y + 0.3z = 1230$;
1st delivery: 1800, 2nd delivery: 1500, 3rd delivery: 2150

17. **Harvest Earnings** The feed mill pays a farmer $6930.00 for the 1st delivery, $5475.00 for the 2nd delivery and $8879.50 for the 3rd delivery. The table shows the number of bushels included in each delivery. Use the table to write and solve a system of equations to find the price per bushel that the farmer received for each crop.

Delivery	Corn	Wheat	Soybeans
1st Delivery	900	540	360
2nd Delivery	1125	150	225
3rd Delivery	860	645	645

$900x + 540y + 360z = 6930$
$1125x + 150y + 225z = 5475$
$860x + 645y + 645z = 8879.5$;
corn: $3.20, wheat: $3.50, soybean: $6.00

LESSON 3.5

Practice B

For use with pages 187–193

Perform the indicated operation, if possible. If not possible, state the reason.

1. $\begin{bmatrix} 2 & 1 \\ 6 & 4 \end{bmatrix} - \begin{bmatrix} -2 & 1 \\ -4 & 0 \end{bmatrix}$ $\begin{bmatrix} 4 & 0 \\ 10 & 4 \end{bmatrix}$

2. $\begin{bmatrix} 5 & 2 \\ -1 & 4 \\ -3 & 6 \end{bmatrix} + \begin{bmatrix} -2 & 4 \\ 6 & -2 \\ 7 & -5 \end{bmatrix}$ $\begin{bmatrix} 3 & 6 \\ 5 & 2 \\ 4 & 1 \end{bmatrix}$

3. $\begin{bmatrix} 6 & 4 & 3 \\ 1 & -3 & 2 \\ 8 & 7 & 1 \end{bmatrix} - \begin{bmatrix} 4 & 5 & -4 \\ 5 & 1 & 0 \\ 6 & 4 & 7 \end{bmatrix}$ See below.

4. $\begin{bmatrix} -4 & 2 & 3 \end{bmatrix} + \begin{bmatrix} -2 \\ 0 \\ -1 \end{bmatrix}$ Not possible because the matrices do not have the same dimensions.

5. $\begin{bmatrix} 10 & -5 & 7 \\ 2 & -12 & 0 \\ 8 & -4 & 6 \end{bmatrix} + \begin{bmatrix} -7 & 14 & 6 \\ 0 & 12 & -4 \\ 2 & 7 & 3 \end{bmatrix}$ See below.

6. $\begin{bmatrix} 10 & -7 & 14 \\ -5 & -10 & 0 \\ 9 & -3 & -7 \end{bmatrix} - \begin{bmatrix} -1 & -3 & 8 \\ -12 & 0 & 6 \\ 10 & -5 & 5 \end{bmatrix}$ See below.

Perform the indicated operation.

7. $-3\begin{bmatrix} 4 & 2 \\ 3 & 2 \end{bmatrix}$ $\begin{bmatrix} -12 & -6 \\ -9 & -6 \end{bmatrix}$

8. $-2\begin{bmatrix} 3 & 0 & -1 \\ 0.5 & -6 & 4 \\ 7 & -1.25 & 9 \end{bmatrix}$ See below.

9. $-4\begin{bmatrix} 4 & 1 \\ -5 & 0 \\ 1 & -3 \end{bmatrix}$ See below.

Solve the matrix equation for *x* and *y*.

10. $\begin{bmatrix} -2x & 6 \\ 3y & 9 \end{bmatrix} = \begin{bmatrix} -8 & 6 \\ -12 & 9 \end{bmatrix}$ $x = 4, y = -4$

11. $\begin{bmatrix} 4 & 5x \\ -2 & 5 \end{bmatrix} + \begin{bmatrix} -11 & 2 \\ 6 & 5 \end{bmatrix} = \begin{bmatrix} y & 12 \\ 4 & 10 \end{bmatrix}$ $x = 2, y = -7$

In Exercises 12–15, use the following information.

Book Prices The matrices below show the number of books sold and the average price (in dollars) for the years 2002, 2003, and 2004.

	2002 (A) Sold	2002 (A) Price	2003 (B) Sold	2003 (B) Price	2004 (C) Sold	2004 (C) Price
Book A	125,000	52.00	110,000	55.50	90,000	47.50
Book B	85,000	83.50	95,000	85.50	100,000	89.00
Book C	190,000	45.60	210,000	56.25	225,000	75.25

12. You purchased book A in 2002, book C in 2003 and book B in 2004. How much did you spend on these three books? $197.25

13. How many more (or less) volumes of book B were sold in 2004 than in 2002? 15,000 more

14. How much more (or less) is the price of book A in 2004 than in 2002? $4.50 less

15. In 2005, would you expect book C sales to be *more* or *less* than 100,000? more

3. $\begin{bmatrix} 2 & -1 & 7 \\ -4 & -4 & 2 \\ 2 & 3 & -6 \end{bmatrix}$ 5. $\begin{bmatrix} 3 & 9 & 13 \\ 2 & 0 & -4 \\ 10 & 3 & 9 \end{bmatrix}$ 6. $\begin{bmatrix} 11 & -4 & 6 \\ 7 & -10 & -6 \\ -1 & 2 & -12 \end{bmatrix}$

8. $\begin{bmatrix} -6 & 0 & 2 \\ -1 & 12 & -8 \\ -14 & 2.5 & -18 \end{bmatrix}$ 9. $\begin{bmatrix} -16 & -4 \\ 20 & 0 \\ -4 & 12 \end{bmatrix}$

LESSON 3.6 Practice B

For use with pages 195–202

4. $\begin{bmatrix} 1 & -4 \\ 5 & -2 \end{bmatrix}$ 7. $\begin{bmatrix} -5 & 15 & -11 \\ 4 & 10 & 20 \\ 8 & 6 & 16 \end{bmatrix}$

State the dimensions of each matrix and determine whether the product *AB* is defined. If so, give the dimensions of *AB*.

1. $A = \begin{bmatrix} 2 & 1 \\ 5 & 0 \\ 1 & 2 \end{bmatrix}, B = \begin{bmatrix} 2 & 1 & 5 \end{bmatrix}$
   A: 3×2; B: 1×3; *not* defined

2. $A = \begin{bmatrix} 2 & -3 & 4 \\ -2 & 1 & 0 \end{bmatrix}, B = \begin{bmatrix} 1 & 2 & 0 \\ 5 & 4 & 3 \\ -4 & 2 & -5 \end{bmatrix}$
   A: 2×3; B: 3×3; defined; 2×3

Find the product. If it is not defined, state the reason.

3. $\begin{bmatrix} 3 & 2 \end{bmatrix}\begin{bmatrix} 1 \\ 4 \end{bmatrix}$ $\begin{bmatrix} 11 \end{bmatrix}$

4. $\begin{bmatrix} 1 & -1 \\ 2 & 1 \end{bmatrix}\begin{bmatrix} 2 & -2 \\ 1 & 2 \end{bmatrix}$ See above.

5. $\begin{bmatrix} 2 \\ -1 \\ 3 \end{bmatrix}\begin{bmatrix} -1 & 3 \end{bmatrix}$ $\begin{bmatrix} -2 & 6 \\ 1 & -3 \\ -3 & 9 \end{bmatrix}$

6. $\begin{bmatrix} 3 & 5 \\ -2 & 4 \end{bmatrix}\begin{bmatrix} 2 & -1 \\ 4 & 0 \end{bmatrix}$ $\begin{bmatrix} 26 & -3 \\ 12 & 2 \end{bmatrix}$

7. $\begin{bmatrix} 5 & 1 & 0 \\ -2 & 3 & 1 \\ 0 & 2 & 4 \end{bmatrix}\begin{bmatrix} -1 & 2 & -3 \\ 0 & 5 & 4 \\ 2 & -1 & 2 \end{bmatrix}$ See above.

8. $\begin{bmatrix} 2 \\ 1 \end{bmatrix}\begin{bmatrix} 1 & 2 & 4 \\ -2 & 3 & 1 \end{bmatrix}$ See below.

9. $\begin{bmatrix} -1 & 6 & 2 & 4 \end{bmatrix}\begin{bmatrix} 1 \\ -1 \\ 4 \\ 0 \end{bmatrix}$ $\begin{bmatrix} 1 \end{bmatrix}$

10. $\begin{bmatrix} 2 & -3 \\ 4 & -2 \\ 0 & -1 \end{bmatrix}\begin{bmatrix} 2 & 1 & -1 \\ 5 & 3 & 2 \end{bmatrix}$ $\begin{bmatrix} -11 & -7 & -8 \\ -2 & -2 & -8 \\ -5 & -3 & -2 \end{bmatrix}$

11. $\begin{bmatrix} 0 & 1 & 0 \\ 2 & 3 & -1 \\ -2 & 4 & 0 \\ 5 & 0 & -2 \end{bmatrix}\begin{bmatrix} 2 \\ -3 \\ 1 \end{bmatrix}$ $\begin{bmatrix} -3 \\ -6 \\ -16 \\ 8 \end{bmatrix}$

Using the given matrices, evaluate the expression.

$A = \begin{bmatrix} 2 & -1 \\ 3 & 2 \end{bmatrix}, B = \begin{bmatrix} 1 & 0 \\ 3 & -2 \end{bmatrix}, C = \begin{bmatrix} 3 & -2 \\ -1 & 4 \end{bmatrix}$

12. $-2BC$
13. $AC - AB$
14. $BA + BC$

12. $\begin{bmatrix} -6 & 4 \\ -22 & 28 \end{bmatrix}$ 13. $\begin{bmatrix} 8 & -10 \\ -2 & 6 \end{bmatrix}$ 14. $\begin{bmatrix} 5 & -3 \\ 11 & -21 \end{bmatrix}$

15. **Football** Tickets to the football game cost $2.50 for students, $5.00 for adults and $4.00 for senior citizens. Attendance for the first game of the postseason was 120 students, 185 adults and 34 senior citizens. Attendance for the second game of the postseason was 150 students, 210 adults and 50 senior citizens. Use matrix multiplication to find the revenue from ticket sales for each game.

Game 1 $\begin{bmatrix} \$1361 \end{bmatrix}$
Game 2 $\begin{bmatrix} \$1625 \end{bmatrix}$

8. The matrices cannot be multiplied because the number of columns in $\begin{bmatrix} 2 \\ 1 \end{bmatrix}$ does not equal the number of rows in $\begin{bmatrix} 1 & 2 & 4 \\ -2 & 3 & 1 \end{bmatrix}$.

LESSON 3.6

LESSON 3.7 Practice B

For use with pages 203–209

Evaluate the determinant of the matrix.

1. $\begin{bmatrix} 5 & -2 \\ 4 & -4 \end{bmatrix}$ -12

2. $\begin{bmatrix} 3 & -5 \\ -2 & -3 \end{bmatrix}$ -19

3. $\begin{bmatrix} \frac{1}{2} & \frac{2}{3} \\ 6 & 5 \end{bmatrix}$ $-\frac{3}{2}$

Evaluate the determinant of the matrix.

4. $\begin{bmatrix} 5 & -1 & 3 \\ 4 & 0 & 2 \\ 1 & -2 & -5 \end{bmatrix}$ -26

5. $\begin{bmatrix} 3 & 2 & 9 \\ 0 & 1 & -4 \\ 5 & -1 & 2 \end{bmatrix}$ -91

6. $\begin{bmatrix} 1 & 15 & 2 \\ 0 & 1 & 3 \\ 2 & 12 & 2 \end{bmatrix}$ 52

7. $\begin{bmatrix} 12 & -8 & 3 \\ -1 & 2 & 0 \\ -15 & 1 & 3 \end{bmatrix}$ 135

8. $\begin{bmatrix} 7 & 5 & 6 \\ 3 & 4 & 5 \\ 6 & 1 & 4 \end{bmatrix}$ 41

9. $\begin{bmatrix} 3 & 0 & -2 \\ 0 & 7 & 0 \\ -5 & -4 & 6 \end{bmatrix}$ 56

Find the area of the triangle with the given vertices.

10. 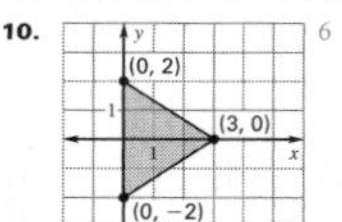

6

11. 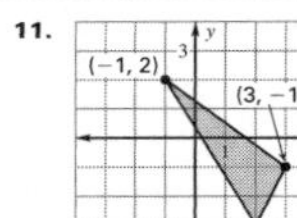

5.5

12. 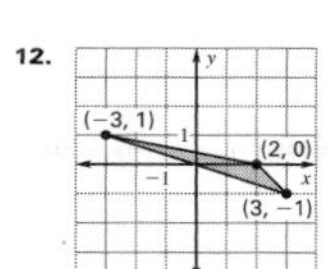

2

Use Cramer's rule to solve the linear system.

13. $x - 5y = -1$ $(4, 1)$
$-2x + 5y = -3$

14. $x + 2y = 1$ $(-5, 3)$
$-3x - 7y = -6$

15. $2x + 6y = 12$ $(6, 0)$
$-x + 7y = -6$

16. $2x + 2y + z = 2$ $(1, -1, 2)$
$-x + 3y + z = -2$
$3x + 2z = 7$

17. $2x - 5y + 2z = 2$ $(3, 0, -2)$
$-3x + y - 6z = 3$
$x + y + z = 1$

18. $3x + 2y + 3z = -1$ $\left(\frac{1}{2}, \frac{1}{4}, -1\right)$
$2x - 8y + 2z = -3$
$x + 6y + 4z = -2$

In Exercises 19 and 20, use the following information.

Gasoline You fill up your car with 15 gallons of premium gasoline and fill up a 5 gallon gas can with regular gasoline for various appliances around the house. You pay the cashier $42. The price of regular gasoline, y, is 20 cents less per gallon than the price of premium gasoline, x.

19. Write a system of linear equations that models the price per gallon for regular and premium gasoline. $15x + 5y = 42$
$x - y = 0.2$

20. Use Cramer's rule to find the price per gallon of regular and premium gasoline.
$x = \$2.15, y = \$1.95$

LESSON 3.7

LESSON 3.8 Practice B

For use with pages 210–217

20. $\begin{bmatrix} 1 & 1 & 1 \\ 1 & 2 & 3 \\ 1 & -1 & 0 \end{bmatrix}\begin{bmatrix} x \\ y \\ z \end{bmatrix} = \begin{bmatrix} 1011 \\ 1669 \\ -305 \end{bmatrix}$

Find the inverse of the matrix, if it exists.

1. $\begin{bmatrix} 4 & 7 \\ 1 & 2 \end{bmatrix}$ $\begin{bmatrix} 2 & -7 \\ -1 & 4 \end{bmatrix}$

2. $\begin{bmatrix} 3 & 2 \\ 4 & 2 \end{bmatrix}$ $\begin{bmatrix} -1 & 1 \\ 2 & -\frac{3}{2} \end{bmatrix}$

3. $\begin{bmatrix} 4 & -2 \\ 3 & 1 \end{bmatrix}$ $\begin{bmatrix} \frac{1}{10} & \frac{1}{5} \\ -\frac{3}{10} & \frac{2}{5} \end{bmatrix}$

4. $\begin{bmatrix} 7 & 14 \\ 3 & 6 \end{bmatrix}$ no inverse

5. $\begin{bmatrix} -4 & -2 \\ 5 & 2 \end{bmatrix}$ $\begin{bmatrix} 1 & 1 \\ -\frac{5}{2} & -2 \end{bmatrix}$

6. $\begin{bmatrix} 3 & -3 \\ -3 & -2 \end{bmatrix}$ $\begin{bmatrix} \frac{2}{15} & -\frac{1}{5} \\ -\frac{1}{5} & -\frac{1}{5} \end{bmatrix}$

Use a graphing calculator to find the inverse of the matrix.

7. $\begin{bmatrix} 1 & 3 & 5 \\ 0 & 3 & 5 \\ 0 & 0 & 5 \end{bmatrix}$ $\begin{bmatrix} 1 & -1 & 0 \\ 0 & \frac{1}{3} & -\frac{1}{3} \\ 0 & 0 & \frac{1}{5} \end{bmatrix}$

8. $\begin{bmatrix} 0 & 1 & 0 \\ 2 & 1 & -2 \\ 0 & 2 & 2 \end{bmatrix}$ $\begin{bmatrix} -\frac{3}{2} & \frac{1}{2} & \frac{1}{2} \\ 1 & 0 & 0 \\ -1 & 0 & \frac{1}{2} \end{bmatrix}$

Solve the matrix equation.

9. $\begin{bmatrix} 2 & 1 \\ 3 & 2 \end{bmatrix}X = \begin{bmatrix} 5 & 1 \\ 2 & 1 \end{bmatrix}$ $\begin{bmatrix} 8 & 1 \\ -11 & -1 \end{bmatrix}$

10. $\begin{bmatrix} 4 & 3 \\ 2 & 2 \end{bmatrix}X = \begin{bmatrix} -2 & 3 \\ -1 & 2 \end{bmatrix}$ $\begin{bmatrix} -\frac{1}{2} & 0 \\ 0 & 1 \end{bmatrix}$

11. $\begin{bmatrix} 3 & 1 \\ 6 & 3 \end{bmatrix}X = \begin{bmatrix} 1 & 4 & -2 \\ 6 & 0 & -3 \end{bmatrix}$ $\begin{bmatrix} -1 & 4 & -1 \\ 4 & -8 & 1 \end{bmatrix}$

12. $\begin{bmatrix} 6 & 2 \\ 5 & 1 \end{bmatrix}X = \begin{bmatrix} 9 & 12 & 6 \\ -4 & 3 & 8 \end{bmatrix}$ $\begin{bmatrix} -\frac{17}{4} & -\frac{3}{2} & \frac{5}{2} \\ \frac{69}{4} & \frac{21}{2} & -\frac{9}{2} \end{bmatrix}$

Use an inverse matrix to solve the linear system.

13. $3x - 2y = 2$ $(2, 2)$
$2x - y = 2$

14. $5x + 3y = 4$ $(-4, 8)$
$2x + 2y = 8$

15. $-x + 6y = 20$ $\left(-36, -\frac{8}{3}\right)$
$x - 9y = -12$

16. $2x + z = 2$ $(2, 3, -2)$
$5x - y + z = 5$
$-x + 2y + 2z = 0$

17. $3x + y + 2z = 9$ $(1, -2, 4)$
$-2x + 2y + 3z = 6$
$2x - y + z = 8$

18. $3x + 3y + 3z = -12$ $(-3, 5, -6)$
$5x + 2y + 2z = -17$
$2x - 4y - z = -20$

In Exercises 19–21, use the following information.

NBA During the 2004–2005 NBA season, Shaquille O'Neal scored 1669 points while making 1011 shots. Shaq's points were a combination of 3-point field goals, 2-point field goals and 1-point free throws. He made 305 more 2-point field goals than free throws.

19. Write a system of equations for the number of shots made during the season.
$x + y + z = 1011$
$x + 2y + 3z = 1669$
$x - y = -305$

20. Write the system of equations from Exercise 19 as a matrix equation $AX = B$.
See above.

21. Use an inverse matrix to solve the system of equations. How many of each type of shot did Shaq make during the season? 3-point: 353, 2-point: 658, 1-point: 0

LESSON 3.8

CHAPTER 3 Quiz 1
For use after Lessons 3.1–3.2

Graph the linear system and estimate the solution.

1. $3x + y = 9$
   $x - 2y = 10$

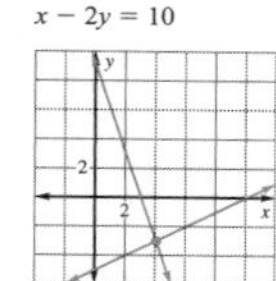

2. $4x - 3y = 12$
   $2x + 3y = 18$

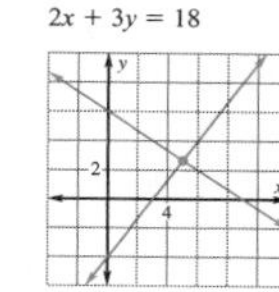

Solve the system. Then classify the system as *consistent and independent*, *consistent and dependent*, or *inconsistent*.

3. $3x - 5y = 9$
   $6x - 10y = 18$
4. $4x - y = 12$
   $y = -8 + 4x$

Solve the system using the substitution method.

5. $3x - 11y = 16$
   $x + y = 3$
6. $6x - 12y = 16$
   $3x - 6y = 8$
7. $4x - y = 4$
   $x + 2y = 10$

Solve the system using the elimination method.

8. $7x - 2y = 15$
   $7x + 2y = 13$
9. $3x + 7y = 11$
   $2x - 3y = -8$
10. $9x + 5y = 24$
    $3x + 2y = 9$

Answers

1. See left.
   $(4, -3)$
2. See left.
   $\left(5, \frac{8}{3}\right)$
3. infinitely many solutions; consistent and dependent
4. no solution; inconsistent
5. $\left(\frac{7}{2}, -\frac{1}{2}\right)$
6. infinitely many solutions
7. $(2, 4)$
8. $\left(2, -\frac{1}{2}\right)$
9. $(-1, 2)$
10. $(1, 3)$

CHAPTER 3 Quiz 2
For use after Lessons 3.3–3.5

Graph the system of inequalities.

1. $y < 3$
   $x + y > -4$

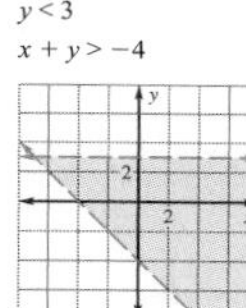

2. $x - 2y \le 6$
   $x + 5y \ge 10$

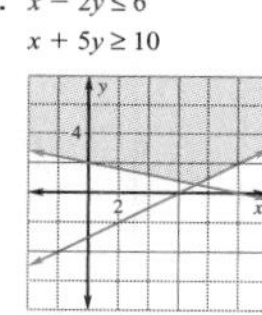

Solve the system using any algebraic method.

3. $2x - 3y + z = 10$
   $3x - 8y + 2z = 11$
   $-x + 5y + 3z = 15$
4. $3x - 7y + 4z = 11$
   $x + y - z = 4$
   $2x - 6y + z = 15$
5. $2x + 5y - 3z = 9$
   $4x - 3y + 3z = 7$
   $x - 5y + 3z = 12$

Use matrices *A*, *B*, and *C* to evaluate the matrix expression, if possible. If not possible, state the reason.

$A = \begin{bmatrix} 5 & -7 \\ -3 & 9 \end{bmatrix}$ $B = \begin{bmatrix} -3 & 11 \\ -4 & 2 \end{bmatrix}$ $C = \begin{bmatrix} 1 & 6 \\ 2 & 9 \\ -4 & 5 \end{bmatrix}$

6. $B + A$
7. $C + A$
8. $2A - B$
9. $\frac{2}{5}C$
10. You have \$33 to spend on 24 Mylar balloons. Birthday balloons cost \$1.50 each, congratulation balloons cost \$1.00 each, and get well balloons cost \$2.00. You want twice as many birthday balloons as the other two kinds combined. Write and solve a system of equations to find how many of each type you should buy.

Answers

1. See left.
2. See left.
3. $(9, 0, -8)$
4. $(3, -2, -3,$
5. $(7, -13, -20)$
6. $\begin{bmatrix} 2 & 4 \\ -7 & 11 \end{bmatrix}$
7. not possible; The dimensions are not equivalent.
8. $\begin{bmatrix} 13 & -25 \\ -2 & 16 \end{bmatrix}$
9. $\begin{bmatrix} \frac{2}{5} & \frac{12}{5} \\ \frac{4}{5} & \frac{18}{5} \\ -\frac{8}{5} & 2 \end{bmatrix}$
10. $b + c + g = 24$
    $1.5b + 1.00c + 2g = 33$
    $b = 2(c + g)$;
    $b = 16, c = 7, g = 1$

CHAPTER 3 Quiz 3
For use after Lessons 3.6–3.8

Using the given matrices, evaluate the expression.

$A = \begin{bmatrix} 2 & -5 \\ 7 & 2 \end{bmatrix}$ $B = \begin{bmatrix} 4 & -1 \\ 1 & -3 \end{bmatrix}$ $C = \begin{bmatrix} -9 & -2 \\ 5 & 0 \end{bmatrix}$

1. $3AB$
2. $A(B + C)$
3. $(A - B)C$

Evaluate the determinant of the matrix.

4. $\begin{bmatrix} 3 & -9 \\ 4 & 2 \end{bmatrix}$
5. $\begin{bmatrix} 0 & 1 & -7 \\ -2 & -4 & 2 \\ 3 & 5 & 1 \end{bmatrix}$
6. $\begin{bmatrix} -1 & -2 & 3 \\ 1 & 4 & 1 \\ 2 & 5 & 2 \end{bmatrix}$

Use an inverse matrix to solve the linear system.

7. $3x + 5y = -7$
   $x - 3y = 7$
8. $-2x + 5y = 11$
   $3x - 4y = 15$
9. $8x + y = 11$
   $3x + y = 6$
10. You are designing a triangular flower garden. The vertices of the garden are $(0, 4)$, $(11, 4)$, and $(11, 24)$ where the coordinates are measured in feet. Find the area of the garden.

Answers

1. $\begin{bmatrix} 9 & 39 \\ 90 & -39 \end{bmatrix}$
2. $\begin{bmatrix} -40 & 9 \\ -23 & -27 \end{bmatrix}$
3. $\begin{bmatrix} -2 & 4 \\ -29 & -12 \end{bmatrix}$
4. 42
5. -6
6. -12
7. $(1, -2)$
8. $(17, 9)$
9. $(1, 3)$
10. 110

CHAPTER 3 Chapter Test B
For use after Chapter 3

1. Graph the linear system and estimate the solution

$y = -x - 2$

$y = 2x + 1$

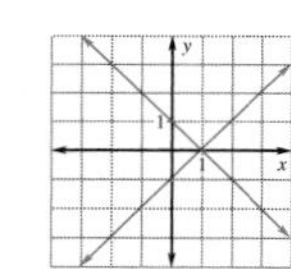

2. Solve the system by graphing. Then classify the system as *consistent and independent*, *consistent and dependent*, or *inconsistent*.

$y = -x + 1$

$y = x - 1$

Solve the system using any algebraic method.

3. $x + 2y = 5$
   $-2x + 3y = -3$

4. $5x - 2y = -7$
   $-3x + 2y = 5$

5. $0.1x + -0.1y = 2$
   $0.7x + 0.7y = 7$

6. $-2x - 3y = 7$
   $4x + y = 1$

7. At a local market, 3 apples and 2 pears cost \$2.70. Three apples cost the same as 4 pears. How much do apples and pears cost?

8. Graph the system of inequalities.

$y > -2x$

$y < -2x + 2$

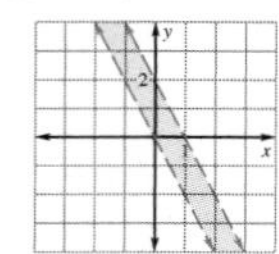

Solve the system using any algebraic method.

9. $4x + 2y - z = 4$
   $2x - 3y + 2z = 4$
   $x + y - z = -1$

10. $2x - 3y + z = 2$
    $x - y - z = -4$
    $-3x + 2y - z = 1$

11. **Cargo** An ant and its cargo weigh 76 milligrams. The cargo is 18 times heavier than the ant. Use a linear system and Cramer's Rule to find the weight of the ant and its cargo.

Answers

1. See left. $(-1, -1)$
2. See left. $(1, 0)$; consistent and independent
3. $(3, 1)$
4. $(-1, 1)$
5. $(15, -5)$
6. $(1, -3)$
7. apples: \$.60, pears: \$.45
8. See left.
9. $(1, 2, 4)$
10. $(-2, -1, 3)$
11. ant: 4 mg, cargo: 72 mg

CHAPTER 3 Chapter Test B *continued*
For use after Chapter 3

Perform the indication operation, if possible. If not possible, state the reason.

12. $\begin{bmatrix} 2 & 4 & 3 \\ 1 & 3 & -5 \end{bmatrix} + \begin{bmatrix} 2 & 3 \\ 1 & 1 \end{bmatrix}$

13. $2\begin{bmatrix} -1 & 2 & 3 \\ 3 & 0 & -4 \end{bmatrix}$

Solve the matrix equation for *x* and *y*.

14. $\begin{bmatrix} 7 & 3 \\ 5 & 1 \end{bmatrix} - x\begin{bmatrix} 2 & 0 \\ -1 & 1 \end{bmatrix} = \begin{bmatrix} y & 3 \\ 8 & -2 \end{bmatrix}$

Find the product. If it is not defined, state the reason.

15. $\begin{bmatrix} -1 \\ 3 \\ -4 \end{bmatrix}\begin{bmatrix} 1 & 0 & -2 \end{bmatrix}$

16. $\begin{bmatrix} 1 & 0 \\ -1 & -2 \\ 3 & 5 \end{bmatrix}\begin{bmatrix} -4 \\ 1 \end{bmatrix}$

Using the given matrix, find $A^2 = AA$ and $A^3 = AAA$.

17. $A = \begin{bmatrix} 1 & -2 \\ 2 & -1 \end{bmatrix}$

18. **Community Service** A school cleaned up the banks of several nearby waters. In all, 11 miles of Silver Stream, 13 miles of Broken Brook, and 22 miles of Crooked Creek were cleaned. It took 35 minutes per mile for Silver Stream; 45 minutes per mile for Broken Brook, and 25 minutes per mile for Crooked Creek. Organize the information using matrices. Then use matrix multiplication to find the total amount of time spent cleaning nearby waters last year.

Evaluate the determinant of the matrix.

19. $\begin{bmatrix} 2 & 4 \\ -1 & -2 \end{bmatrix}$

20. $\begin{bmatrix} 1 & 3 & -2 \\ 3 & -1 & -6 \\ 4 & 2 & -8 \end{bmatrix}$

Use an inverse matrix to solve the linear system.

21. $2x - y = 5$
    $-x + 2y = -1$

22. $2x + 3y = 12$
    $3x - 2y = 5$

Answers

12. not possible; dimensions not compatible
13. $\begin{bmatrix} -2 & 4 & 6 \\ 6 & 0 & -8 \end{bmatrix}$
14. $x = 3, y = 1$
15. $\begin{bmatrix} -1 & 0 & 2 \\ 3 & 0 & -6 \\ -4 & 0 & 8 \end{bmatrix}$
16. $\begin{bmatrix} -4 \\ 2 \\ -7 \end{bmatrix}$
17. $A^2 = \begin{bmatrix} -3 & 0 \\ 0 & -3 \end{bmatrix}$, $A^3 = \begin{bmatrix} -3 & 6 \\ -6 & 3 \end{bmatrix}$
18. 1520 min, or 25 h and 20 min
19. 0
20. 0
21. $(3, 1)$
22. $(3, 2)$

CHAPTER 3 Standardized Test
For use after Chapter 3

Multiple Choice

1. The graph of a linear system is shown. How can you classify the system? A

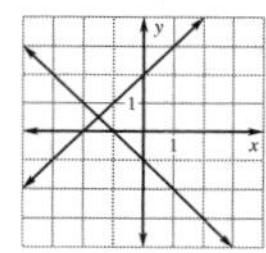

Ⓐ consistent and independent
Ⓑ consistent and dependent
Ⓒ inconsistent
Ⓓ inconsistent and independent

2. How many solutions does the system in Exercise 1 have? B

Ⓐ none Ⓑ one
Ⓒ two Ⓓ infinitely many

3. What is the solution of the system of equations below? C

$3x + 4y = -6$
$x - 2y = 8$

Ⓐ $(-2, -3)$ Ⓑ $(-2, 3)$
Ⓒ $(2, -3)$ Ⓓ $(2, 3)$

4. You have \$123.50 in quarters and dimes. There are 1202 coins altogether. Which system of equations can you use to find the number of each type of coin you have? A

Ⓐ $x + y = 1202$
$0.1x + 0.25y = 123.5$

Ⓑ $x + y = 123.5$
$0.1x + 0.25y = 1202$

Ⓒ $x + y = 1202$
$0.1x + 0.25y = 12{,}350$

Ⓓ $x + y = 1202$
$10x + 25y = 123.5$

5. What is the solution of the system of equations below? D

$x = 7y + 12$
$2x - 14y = 11$

Ⓐ $(12.5, 1)$ Ⓑ $(5, -1)$
Ⓒ many solutions Ⓓ no solution

6. Which system of inequalities is represented by the graph below? B

Ⓐ $x + y < 3$
$-4x + 2y > 1$

Ⓑ $x + y \geq 3$
$-4x + 2y \leq 1$

Ⓒ $x + y \geq 3$
$-4x + 2y > 1$

Ⓓ $x + y \leq 3$
$-4x + 2y \geq 1$

7. What is the solution of the system of equations below? C

$-x + 3y - 2z = 19$
$2x + y - z = 5$
$-3x - y + 2z = -7$

Ⓐ $(-1, -4, -3)$ Ⓑ $(-1, -4, 3)$
Ⓒ $(-1, 4, -3)$ Ⓓ $(1, 4, 3)$

8. A high school's enrollment is 950 students, which includes sophomores, juniors, and seniors. Twice the sophomore enrollment is three times the senior enrollment, and the total number of juniors and seniors enrolled is 200 more than the number of sophomores enrolled. How many seniors are enrolled? A

Ⓐ 250 seniors Ⓑ 325 seniors
Ⓒ 375 seniors Ⓓ 400 seniors

CHAPTER 3 Standardized Test *continued*
For use after Chapter 3

9. What is the sum of the matrices? D

$\begin{bmatrix} 7 & 3 \\ 1 & -2 \end{bmatrix} + \begin{bmatrix} -9 & -4 \\ 1 & 11 \end{bmatrix}$

Ⓐ $\begin{bmatrix} 2 & 1 \\ 2 & 9 \end{bmatrix}$ Ⓑ $\begin{bmatrix} -2 & -1 \\ 2 & 13 \end{bmatrix}$

Ⓒ $\begin{bmatrix} 2 & -1 \\ 2 & 13 \end{bmatrix}$ Ⓓ $\begin{bmatrix} -2 & -1 \\ 2 & 9 \end{bmatrix}$

10. What is the product? C

$-3\begin{bmatrix} -3 & 5 \\ 1 & 0 \\ 4 & -6 \end{bmatrix}$

Ⓐ $\begin{bmatrix} -6 & 2 \\ -2 & -3 \\ 1 & 18 \end{bmatrix}$ Ⓑ $\begin{bmatrix} -6 & 3 \end{bmatrix}$

Ⓒ $\begin{bmatrix} 9 & -15 \\ -3 & 0 \\ -12 & 18 \end{bmatrix}$ Ⓓ $\begin{bmatrix} -3 & 5 \\ -3 & 0 \\ 4 & -6 \end{bmatrix}$

11. What is the determinant of the matrix? D

$\begin{bmatrix} 1 & -3 & 4 \\ 2 & -1 & 3 \\ -2 & 5 & 2 \end{bmatrix}$

Ⓐ -3 Ⓑ 3 Ⓒ 23 Ⓓ 45

Gridded Answer

12. You earned \$141 last week babysitting and cleaning. You earned \$5 per hour babysitting and \$7 per hour cleaning. You worked 9 more hours babysitting than cleaning. How many hours did you work last week?

		2	5

Short Response

13. Matrix *M* gives the number of minutes Amy and Renee spent on three types of long distance calls last month. Matrix *C* gives the cost per minute for each type of call. Which product is defined, *MC* or *CM*? *Explain.* Find this matrix and explain what its elements represent. See above.

Matrix *M*

	Amy	Renee
Local	25	75
State	20	40
International	10	5

Matrix *C*

	Local	State	International
Cost per min	0.05	0.1	1.2

13. *CM* is defined. It is possible to multiply a 1×3 matrix by a 3×2 matrix, but not the other way around. *CM* represents the dollar amount spent by Amy and Renee on all long distance calls.

Extended Response

14. The student council is having a bake sale. They spend \$40 for the ingredients to make brownies and cookies. It costs \$1.25 to make a dozen brownies and \$1.50 to make a dozen cookies. The brownies sell for \$6 per dozen and the cookies sell for \$7.50 per dozen. The student council sells a total of \$195 in baked goods.

a. Write a system of linear equations with two equations and two variables to represent the situation. What do the variables represent? See below.

b. Use an inverse matrix to solve the system of linear equations. See below.

c. What profit did the student council make for the brownies sold? for the cookies sold? \$95 profit for the brownies; \$60 profit for the cookies

14. a. $1.25x + 1.5y = 40$; $6x + 7.5y = 195$; *x* represents the dozens of brownies sold, *y* represents the dozens of cookies sold
b. $x = 20$ dozen; $y = 10$ dozen

Alternative Assessment and Math Journal

For use after Chapter 3

Journal 1. Identify three methods you can use to solve a system of equations and explain when to use each method. Write example systems that illustrate when to use each method.

Multi-Step Problem 2. As a participant in your school's community service project, you volunteer a total of 40 hours over the course of the school year. Your volunteer hours include serving at a soup kitchen, picking up trash at several local parks, and collecting toys for needy children. You spend 4 times as many hours collecting toys as picking up trash, and 2 hours less serving at the soup kitchen than picking up trash.

a. Write a system of equations to represent the given information. Define your variables as s, p, and c for the hours of serving at a soup kitchen, picking up trash, and collecting toys, respectively.

b. Use substitution to determine how many hours you spend doing each volunteer activity.

c. Solve the system using elimination.

d. Solve the system using Cramer's rule.

e. Write the system as a matrix equation and solve using an inverse matrix.

f. **Writing** Which method do you prefer for solving this system? Explain.

g. **Critical Thinking** Suppose you cannot remember the total number of hours you volunteered. From the remaining information, can you still determine how many hours you spend doing each volunteer activity? Why or why not?

1. Complete answers should include: a list of three of the five solution methods presented in Chapter 3 (graphing, substitution, elimination, Cramer's rule, inverse matrices); an explanation of when to use each of the three chosen methods (see the Chapter Summary for Chapter 3 in the text); an example system for each chosen method that illustrates the student's explanation of when to use the method.

2. a. $s + p + c = 40$
$c = 4p$
$s = p - 2$

b. You spend 5 hours serving at a soup kitchen, 7 hours picking up trash, and 28 hours collecting toys. **c., d.** same answer as part (b)

e. $\begin{bmatrix}1 & 1 & 1\\0 & -4 & 1\\1 & -1 & 0\end{bmatrix}\begin{bmatrix}s\\p\\c\end{bmatrix} = \begin{bmatrix}40\\0\\-2\end{bmatrix}$;

same answer as part (b) **f.** Answers will vary. **g.** *Sample answer:* No. Because there are three variables and you have no relationship between s, the number of hours you served at a soup kitchen, and c, the number of hours you collected toys, you cannot determine how many hours you picked up trash.

Alternative Assessment Rubric *continued*

For use after Chapter 3

Journal Solution 1. Complete answers should include:

- a list of three of the five solution methods presented in Chapter 3 (graphing, substitution, elimination, Cramer's rule, inverse matrices).
- an explanation of when to use each of the three chosen methods (see the Chapter Summary for Chapter 3 in the text).
- an example system for each chosen method that illustrates the student's explanation of when to use the method.

Multi-Step Problem Solution 2. **a.** $s + p + c = 40$
$c = 4p$
$s = p - 2$

b. You spend 5 hours serving at a soup kitchen, 7 hours picking up trash, and 28 hours collecting toys.

c., d. same answer as part (b)

e. $\begin{bmatrix}1 & 1 & 1\\0 & -4 & 1\\1 & -1 & 0\end{bmatrix}\begin{bmatrix}s\\p\\c\end{bmatrix} = \begin{bmatrix}40\\0\\-2\end{bmatrix}$; same answer as part (b)

f. Answers will vary.

g. *Sample answer:* No. Because there are three variables and you have no relationship between s, the number of hours you served at a soup kitchen, and c, the number of hours you collected toys, you cannot determine how many hours you picked up trash.

Multi-Step Problem Rubric

4 The student answers all parts of the problem correctly and completely. The student shows all work. The student's work is neat.

3 The student answers all parts of the problem. The student's work may contain one or two errors in the calculations, matrix equation, or explanations. The student shows most work. The student's work is neat.

2 The student answers all parts of the problem. The student's work contains more than two errors in the calculations, matrix equation, or explanations. The student shows some work. The student's work is sloppy.

1 The student does not complete all parts of the problem. The student's work has several errors in the calculations, matrix equation, or explanations. The student's work is sloppy, or no work is shown.

PLAN AND PREPARE

Main Ideas

In this chapter, students will work with systems of equations, systems of inequalities, and matrices. For equations, students will solve systems graphically and algebraically, including systems with many solutions and systems with no solutions. The algebraic methods students will use include the methods of substitution and elimination. For inequalities, they will solve systems by graphing, including absolute value inequalities. For matrices, students will perform addition, subtraction, multiplication, and scalar multiplication. Also, students will use operations to solve matrix equations, find determinants and inverses, and use Cramer's Rule to solve a linear system.

Prerequisite Skills

- Graphing an equation in two variables
- Solving an equation
- Graphing an inequality in the coordinate plane

Additional resources for reviewing prerequisite skills are:

- Skills Review Handbook, pp. 975–1009
- @HomeTutor

3 Linear Systems and Matrices

KY

Before

In previous chapters, you learned the following skills, which you'll use in Chapter 3: graphing equations, solving equations, and graphing inequalities.

Prerequisite Skills

VOCABULARY CHECK

Copy and complete the statement.

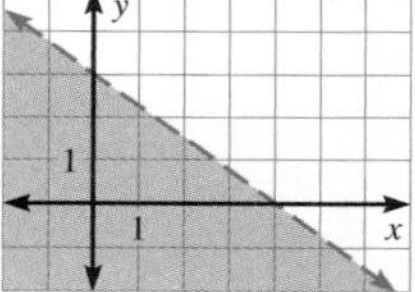

1. The **linear inequality** that represents the graph shown at the right is _?_. $y < -\frac{3}{4}x + 3$
2. The **graph of a linear inequality** in two variables is the set of all points in a coordinate plane that are _?_ of the inequality. solutions

SKILLS CHECK

Graph the equation. *(Review p. 89 for 3.1.)* 3–5. See margin.

3. $x + y = 4$
4. $y = 3x - 3$
5. $-2x + 3y = -12$

Solve the equation. *(Review p. 18 for 3.2, 3.4.)*

6. $2x - 12 = 16$ 14
7. $-3x - 7 = 12$ $-6\frac{1}{3}$
8. $-2x + 5 = 2x - 5$ $2\frac{1}{2}$

Graph the inequality in a coordinate plane. *(Review p. 132 for 3.3.)* 9–11. See margin.

9. $y \geq -x + 2$
10. $x + 4y < -16$
11. $3x + 5y > -5$

150

Chapter Planning Guide

Chapter 3 Resource Book
- Teaching Guide/Lesson Plan (pp. 3, 19, 32, 46, 58, 69, 79, 91)
- Project with Rubric (p. 104)

Assessment and Intervention
- Assessment Book (pp. 31–45)
- Benchmark Tests
- Remediation Book

Interactive Technology
- Easy Planner
- Power Presentations CD-ROM
- Activity Generator CD-ROM
- Animated Algebra
- Test Generator CD-ROM
- Online Quizzes
- eWorkbook
- eEdition
- @HomeTutor

Resources for English Learners
- Quick Reference for English Learners
- Spanish Study Guide
- Multi-Language Visual Glossary
- Student Resources in Spanish

Now

In Chapter 3, you will apply the big ideas listed below and reviewed in the Chapter Summary on page 221. You will also use the key vocabulary listed below.

Big Ideas

1. **Solving systems of equations using a variety of methods**
2. **Graphing systems of equations and inequalities**
3. **Using matrices**

KEY VOCABULARY

- system of two linear equations, *p. 153*
- consistent, *p. 154*
- inconsistent, *p. 154*
- independent, *p. 154*
- dependent, *p. 154*
- substitution method, *p. 160*
- elimination method, *p. 161*
- system of linear inequalities, *p. 168*
- system of three linear equations, *p. 178*
- ordered triple, *p. 178*
- matrix, *p. 187*
- determinant, *p. 203*
- Cramer's rule, *p. 205*
- identity matrix, *p. 210*
- inverse matrices, *p. 210*

Why?

You can use systems of linear equations to solve real-world problems. For example, you can determine which of two payment options for riding a bus is more cost-effective.

Animated Algebra

The animation illustrated below for Example 4 on page 155 helps you answer this question: After how many bus rides will the cost of two payment options be the same?

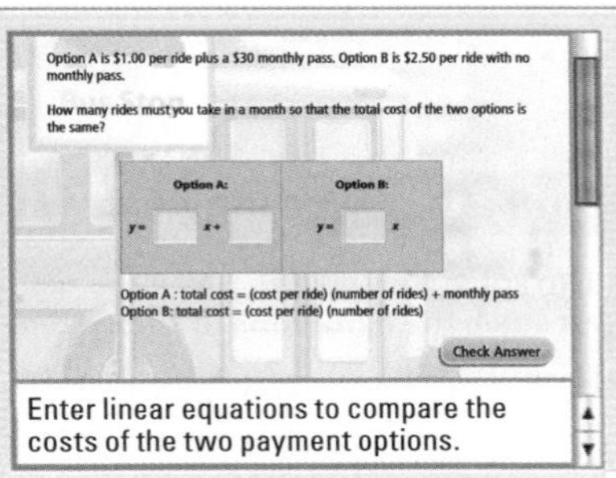

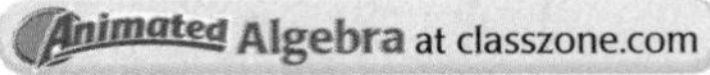

Other animations for Chapter 3: pages 153, 161, 168, 196, 211, and 212

Algebra 2 Toolkit

- Reading Strategies for Chapter 3, pp. 13–14
- Differentiated Instruction Notes, pp. 51–54
- English Learners Notes, pp. 105–106
- Inclusion Notes, pp. 139–140
- Teaching Strategies with Sample Worksheets, pp. 163–186
- Using Technology in the Classroom, pp. 187–192
- Tips for New Teachers, pp. 197–198
- Math Background Notes, pp. 228–230
- Pre-AP Strategies and Copymasters, pp. 315–316, 359–364
- Teacher Survival Activities, pp. 473–474, 501–502
- Bulletin Board Idea, p. 527
- Teacher Tool Transparencies, following p. 538

9.

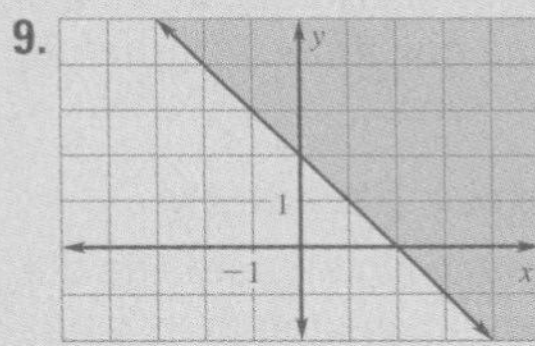

10.

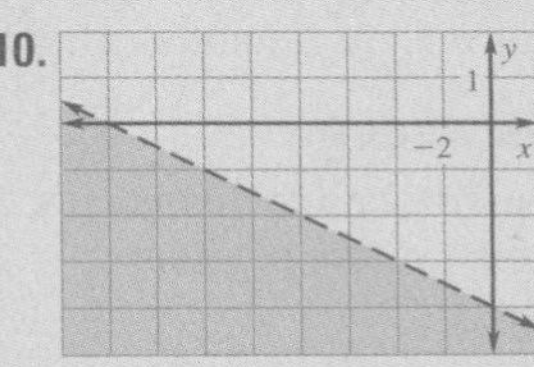

11.

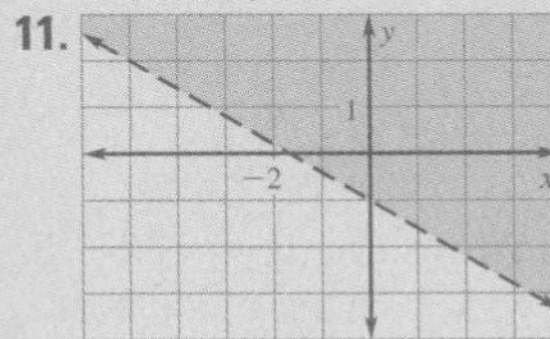

3.

4.

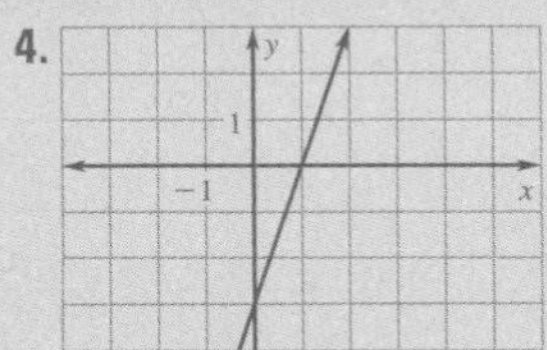

5.

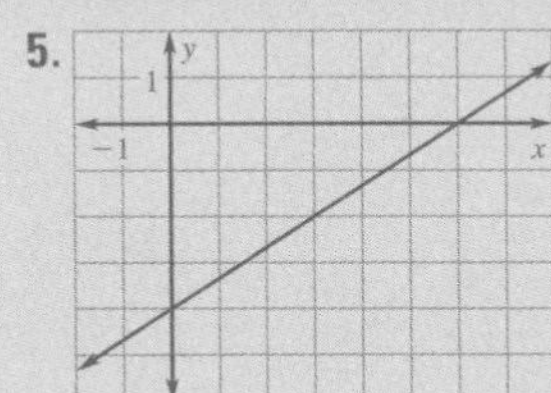

@HomeTutor classzone.com Keystrokes

3.1 Solving Linear Systems Using Tables

MATERIALS • graphing calculator

QUESTION How can you solve a system of linear equations using a table?

An example of a *system of linear equations* in two variables x and y is the following:

$$y = 2x + 4 \quad \text{Equation 1}$$
$$y = -3x + 44 \quad \text{Equation 2}$$

A *solution* of a system of equations in two variables is an ordered pair (x, y) that is a solution of both equations. One way to solve a system is to use the *table* feature of a graphing calculator.

EXPLORE Solve a system

Use a table to solve the system of equations above.

STEP 1 *Enter equations*
Press Y= to enter the equations. Enter Equation 1 as y_1 and Equation 2 as y_2.

```
Y1=2X+4
Y2=-3X+44
Y3=
Y4=
Y5=
Y6=
Y7=
```

STEP 2 *Make a table*
Set the starting x-value of the table to 0 and the step value to 1. Then use the *table* feature to make a table.

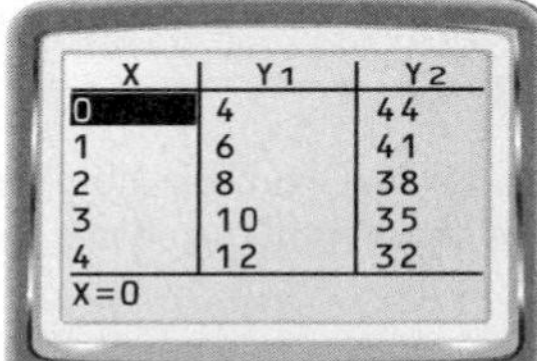

X	Y1	Y2
0	4	44
1	6	41
2	8	38
3	10	35
4	12	32

X=0

STEP 3 *Find the solution*
Scroll through the table until you find an x-value for which y_1 and y_2 are equal. The table shows $y_1 = y_2 = 20$ when $x = 8$.

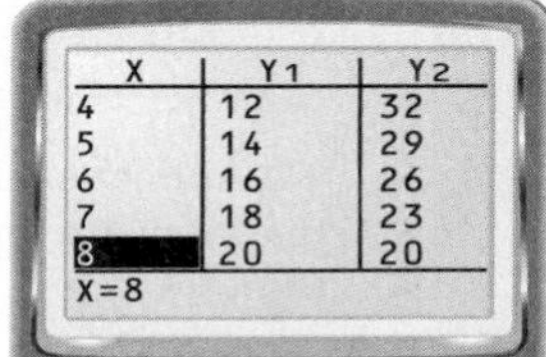

X	Y1	Y2
4	12	32
5	14	29
6	16	26
7	18	23
8	20	20

X=8

▸ The solution of the system is (8, 20).

DRAW CONCLUSIONS Use your observations to complete these exercises

Use a table to solve the system. If you are using a graphing calculator, you may need to first solve the equations in the system for y before entering them.

1. $y = 2x + 5$
   $y = -x + 2$ (−1, 3)
2. $y = 4x + 1$
   $y = 4x - 8$ no solution
3. $y = 4x - 3$
   $y = \frac{3}{2}x + 2$ (2, 5)
4. $8x - 4y = 16$
   $-6x + 3y = 3$ no solution
5. $6x - 2y = -2$
   $-3x - 7y = 17$ (−1, −2)
6. $x + y = 11$
   $-x - y = -11$ infinitely many solutions
7. Based on your results in Exercises 1–6, make a conjecture about the number of solutions a system of linear equations can have.
   Sample answer: A system of linear equations can have one solution, infinitely many solutions, or no solution.

1 PLAN AND PREPARE

Explore the Concept

- Students will solve a system of linear equations using a table.
- This activity leads into the study of solving a linear system of equations by graphing in Lesson 3.1.

Materials

Each student will need a graphing calculator.

Recommended Time

Work activity: 10 min

Discuss results: 5 min

Grouping

Students should work individually.

2 TEACH

Tips for Success

You may want to practice solving two-variable equations for y before starting this lesson.

Alternative Strategy

Rather than having students do the Explore section on their own, you can do it as a class demonstration.

Key Discovery

A table can be used to display the solution to a system of linear equations.

3 ASSESS AND RETEACH

1. A system consists of $y = 2x - 3$ and $y = x + 1$. Use a calculator table to find the y-value for each equation for $x = 3$, 4, and 5. What is the solution to the system? (4, 5)

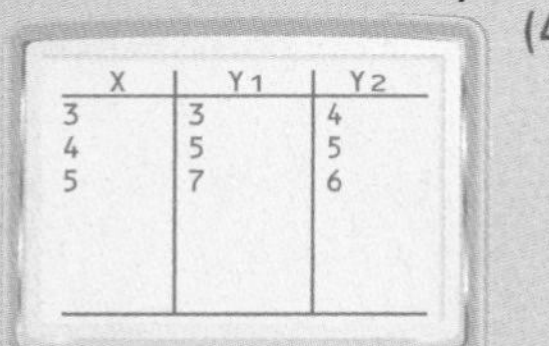

X	Y1	Y2
3	3	4
4	5	5
5	7	6

2. If one of the lines in a table for a system of equations reads X: 0, Y1: 8, Y2: 8, what is a solution to the system? (0, 8)

Guided Practice, p. 153

1.
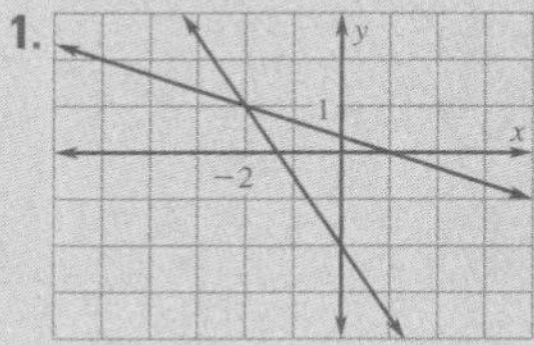

2.
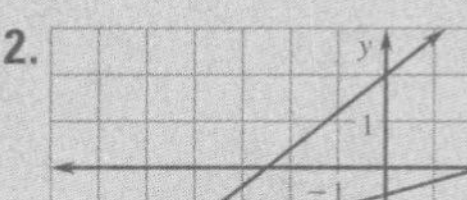

3.
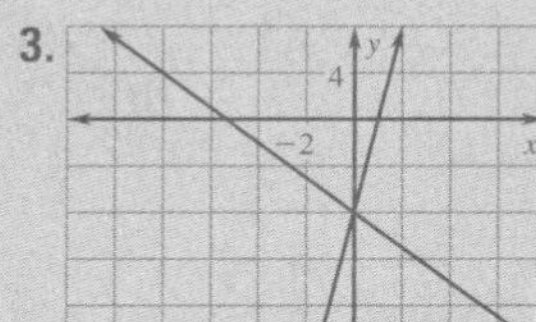

3.1 Solve Linear Systems by Graphing

MA-HS-5.3.4 **Students will model, solve and graph systems of two linear equations in real-world and mathematical problems. DOK 3**

Before You solved linear equations.

Now You will solve systems of linear equations.

Why? So you can compare swimming data, as in Ex. 39.

Key Vocabulary
- system of two linear equations
- solution of a system
- consistent
- inconsistent
- independent
- dependent

A **system of two linear equations** in two variables x and y, also called a *linear system*, consists of two equations that can be written in the following form.

$$Ax + By = C \quad \text{Equation 1}$$
$$Dx + Ey = F \quad \text{Equation 2}$$

A **solution** of a system of linear equations in two variables is an ordered pair (x, y) that satisfies each equation. Solutions correspond to points where the graphs of the equations in a system intersect.

EXAMPLE 1 Solve a system graphically

Graph the linear system and estimate the solution. Then check the solution algebraically.

$$4x + y = 8 \quad \text{Equation 1}$$
$$2x - 3y = 18 \quad \text{Equation 2}$$

Solution

Begin by graphing both equations, as shown at the right. From the graph, the lines *appear* to intersect at $(3, -4)$. You can check this algebraically as follows.

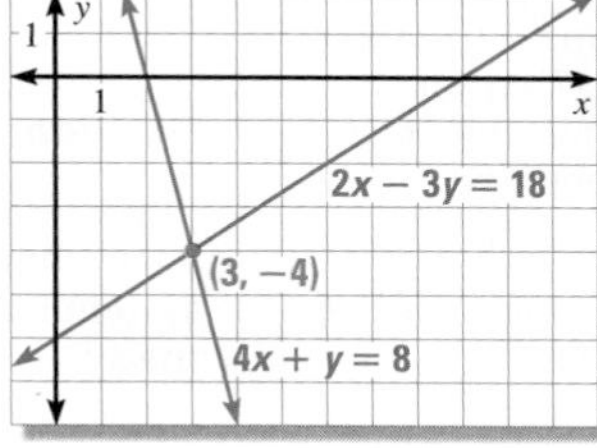

AVOID ERRORS
Remember to check the graphical solution in *both* equations before concluding that it is a solution of the system.

Equation 1	Equation 2
$4x + y = 8$	$2x - 3y = 18$
$4(3) + (-4) \stackrel{?}{=} 8$	$2(3) - 3(-4) \stackrel{?}{=} 18$
$12 - 4 \stackrel{?}{=} 8$	$6 + 12 \stackrel{?}{=} 18$
$8 = 8$ ✓	$18 = 18$ ✓

▶ The solution is $(3, -4)$.

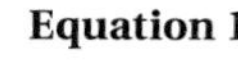 Animated Algebra at classzone.com

✓ **GUIDED PRACTICE** for Example 1

Graph the linear system and estimate the solution. Then check the solution algebraically. 1–3. See margin for art.

1. $3x + 2y = -4$
   $x + 3y = 1$ $(-2, 1)$
2. $4x - 5y = -10$
   $2x - 7y = 4$ $(-5, -2)$
3. $8x - y = 8$
   $3x + 2y = -16$ $(0, -8)$

1 PLAN AND PREPARE

Warm-Up Exercises
Transparency Available
1. Evaluate $5x + 2y$ for $x = 2$ and $y = -4$. 2
2. Find the slope-intercept form of the equation $-3x + 4y = 12$. $y = \frac{3}{4}x + 3$
3. Find the x-intercept of the graph of $y = |x + 1|$. -1
4. Express the cost C of x ball game tickets at a price of $18 per ticket. $C = 18x$

Notetaking Guide
Transparency Available
Promotes interactive learning and notetaking skills, pp. 57–60.

Pacing
Basic: 1 day
Average: 1 day
Advanced: 1 day
Block: 0.5 block with 3.2
- See *Teaching Guide/Lesson Plan*.

2 FOCUS AND MOTIVATE

Essential Question
Big Idea 1, p. 151
How do you solve a system of linear equations graphically? **Tell students they will learn how to answer this question by estimating the solution from a graph and checking the solution algebraically.**

Resource Planning Guide

Chapter Resource Book
- Teaching Guide/Lesson Plan (pp. 3–4)
- Practice levels A, B, C (pp. 8–13)
- Study Guide (pp. 14–15)
- Catch-up for Absent Students (p. 16)
- Application (p. 17)
- Challenge (p. 18)

Workbooks
- Notetaking Guide (pp. 57–60)
- Practice Workbook (pp. 36–38)

Teaching Options
- **Power Presentations CD-ROM** provides dynamic electronic teaching resources for the classroom.
- **Activity Generator CD-ROM** provides editable activities for all ability levels.

Interactive Technology
- Easy Planner
- Power Presentations CD-ROM
- Activity Generator CD-ROM
- Animated Algebra
- Test Generator CD-ROM
- Online Quiz
- eWorkbook
- eEdition
- @HomeTutor

Resources for English Learners
- Quick Reference for English Learners
- Spanish Study Guide
- Multi-Language Visual Glossary
- Student Resources in Spanish

See also the *Algebra 2 Toolkit* for more strategies for meeting individual needs.

Motivating the Lesson

Ask students to describe the possible paths of two ants walking on a sidewalk. **The paths can intersect, be parallel, or be the same if one ant is following the other.**

3 TEACH

Extra Example 1

Graph the linear system and estimate the solution. Then check the solution algebraically.

$5x - 2y = -10$
$2x - 4y = 12$ $(-4, -5)$

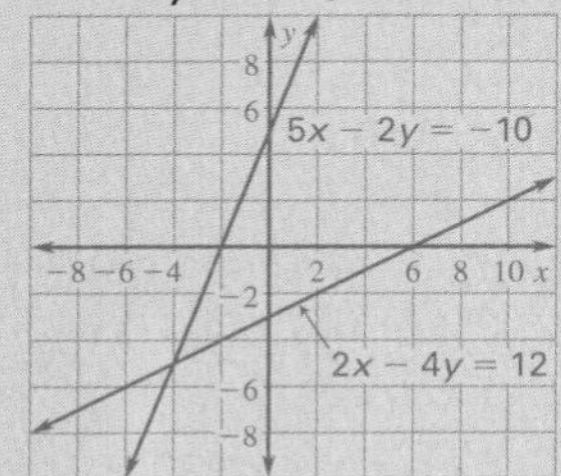

Key Questions to Ask for Example 1

- Why is it important to check the estimated solution algebraically? **to verify the accuracy of the estimate**
- Why do you have the check the solution in both equations? **It has to be a solution to both equations.**

An **Animated Algebra** activity is available on-line for **Example 1**. This activity is also available on the **Power Presentations CD-ROM**.

CLASSIFYING SYSTEMS A system that has at least one solution is **consistent**. If a system has no solution, the system is **inconsistent**. A consistent system that has exactly one solution is **independent**, and a consistent system that has infinitely many solutions is **dependent**. The system in Example 1 is consistent and independent.

KEY CONCEPT *For Your Notebook*

Number of Solutions of a Linear System

The relationship between the graph of a linear system and the system's number of solutions is described below.

Exactly one solution	Infinitely many solutions	No solution
	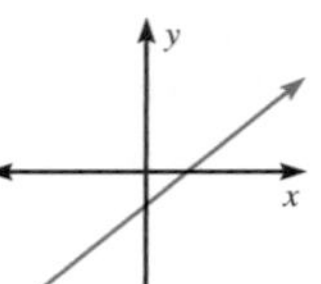	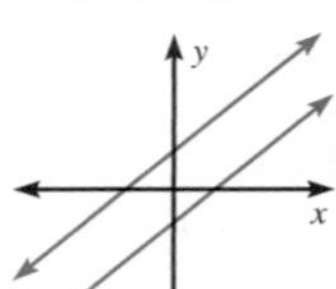
Lines intersect at one point; consistent and independent	Lines coincide; consistent and dependent	Lines are parallel; inconsistent

EXAMPLE 2 Solve a system with many solutions

Solve the system. Then classify the system as *consistent and independent, consistent and dependent,* or *inconsistent.*

$4x - 3y = 8$ **Equation 1**
$8x - 6y = 16$ **Equation 2**

Solution

The graphs of the equations are the same line. So, each point on the line is a solution, and the system has infinitely many solutions. Therefore, the system is consistent and dependent.

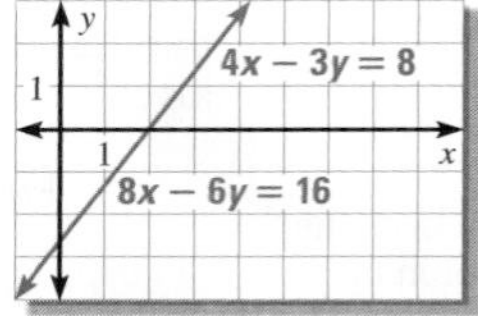

CHECK SOLUTION
To check your solution in Example 2, observe that both equations have the same slope-intercept form:

$$y = \frac{4}{3}x - \frac{8}{3}$$

So the graphs are the same line.

EXAMPLE 3 Solve a system with no solution

Solve the system. Then classify the system as *consistent and independent, consistent and dependent,* or *inconsistent.*

$2x + y = 4$ **Equation 1**
$2x + y = 1$ **Equation 2**

Solution

The graphs of the equations are two parallel lines. Because the two lines have no point of intersection, the system has no solution. Therefore, the system is inconsistent.

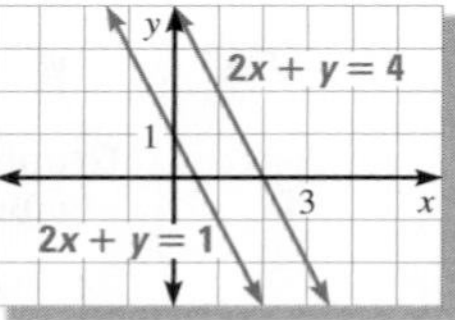

CHECK SOLUTION
To verify that the graphs in Example 3 are parallel lines, write the equations in slope-intercept form and observe that the lines have the same slope, −2, but different *y*-intercepts, 4 and 1.

Differentiated Instruction

Advanced Give students a list of systems of linear equations. Ask them to determine, without solving, if the system is *consistent and independent, consistent and dependent,* or *inconsistent.* Ask students to make a generalization about how to determine what type of system they have without solving the system.

See also the *Algebra 2 Toolkit* for more strategies.

EXAMPLE 4 Standardized Test Practice

You ride an express bus from the center of town to your street. You have two payment options. Option A is to buy a monthly pass and pay \$1 per ride. Option B is to pay \$2.50 per ride. A monthly pass costs \$30. After how many rides will the total costs of the two options be the same?

Ⓐ 12 rides Ⓑ 20 rides Ⓒ 24 rides Ⓓ 28 rides

Solution

Equation 1 (Option A)

Total cost (dollars)	=	Cost per ride (dollars/ride)	·	Number of rides (rides)	+	Monthly fee (dollars)
y	=	1	·	x	+	30

Equation 2 (Option B)

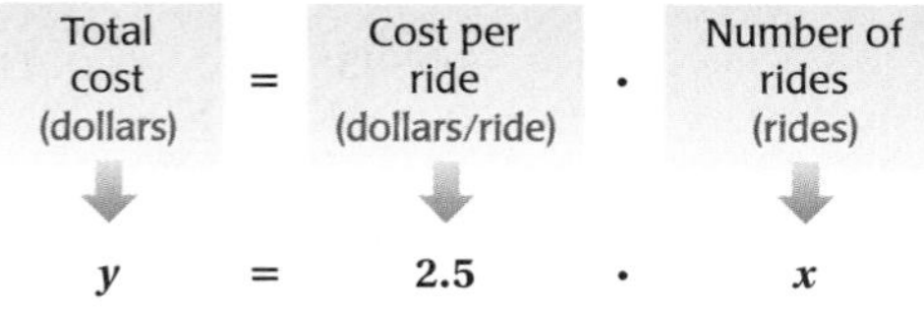

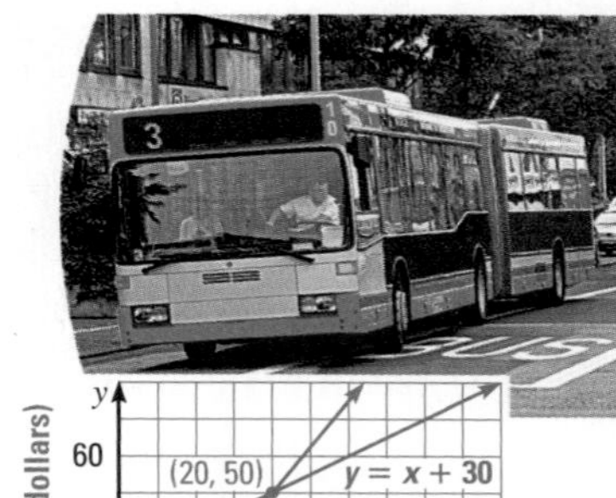

To solve the system, graph the equations $y = x + 30$ and $y = 2.5x$, as shown at the right.

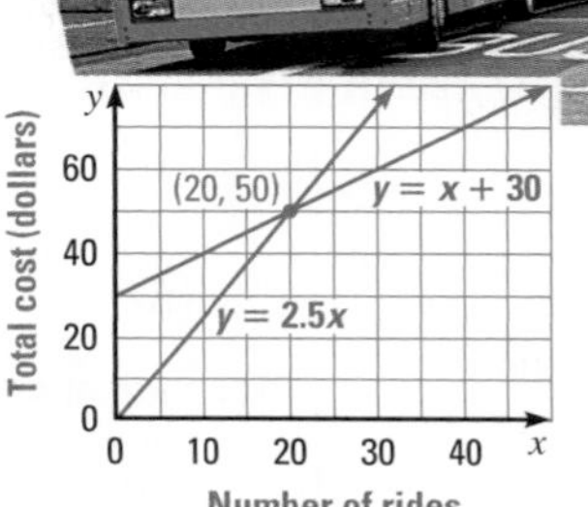

Notice that you need to graph the equations only in the first quadrant because only nonnegative values of x and y make sense in this situation.

The lines appear to intersect at about the point (20, 50). You can check this algebraically as follows.

$50 = 20 + 30$ ✓ **Equation 1 checks.**
$50 = 2.5(20)$ ✓ **Equation 2 checks.**

The total costs are equal after 20 rides.

▶ The correct answer is B. Ⓐ Ⓑ Ⓒ Ⓓ

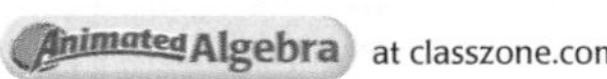 at classzone.com

✓ GUIDED PRACTICE for Examples 2, 3, and 4

Solve the system. Then classify the system as *consistent and independent*, *consistent and dependent*, or *inconsistent*.

4. $2x + 5y = 6$
   $4x + 10y = 12$
   infinitely many solutions; consistent and dependent
5. $3x - 2y = 10$
   $3x - 2y = 2$
   no solution; inconsistent
6. $-2x + y = 5$
   $y = -x + 2$
   (−1, 3); consistent and independent
7. **WHAT IF?** In Example 4, suppose the cost of the monthly pass is increased to \$36. How does this affect the solution? The number of rides increases to 24.

Extra Example 2

Solve the system. Then classify the system as *consistent and independent*, *consistent and dependent*, or *inconsistent*.

$6x - 2y = 8$
$3x - y = 4$

The graphs are the same line; the system is consistent and dependent.

Extra Example 3

Solve the system. Then classify the system as *consistent and independent*, *consistent and dependent*, or *inconsistent*.

$-4x + y = 5$
$-4x + y = -2$

The graphs are two parallel lines; the system is inconsistent.

Extra Example 4

A soccer league offers two options for membership plans. Option *A* includes an initial fee of \$40 and costs \$5 for each game played. Option *B* costs \$10 for each game played. After how many games will the total cost of the two options be the same? C

Ⓐ 2 games Ⓑ 4 games
Ⓒ 8 games Ⓓ 12 games

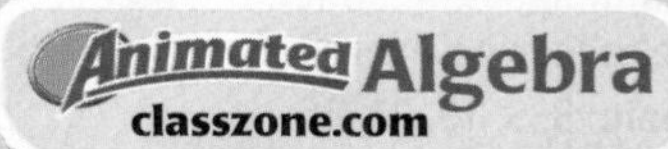

An **Animated Algebra** activity is available on-line for **Example 4.** This activity is also available on the **Power Presentations CD-ROM**.

Closing the Lesson

Have students summarize the major points of the lesson and answer the Essential Question: How do you solve a system of linear equations graphically?

- Systems of linear equations can be solved graphically.
- Systems of linear equations can be *consistent and independent, consistent and dependent,* or *inconsistent.*

To solve a system graphically, you graph the equations, estimate the solution, and check the solution algebraically.

Differentiated Instruction

Below Level Have students use spaghetti and graph paper to graph $y = 2x + 3$. Then give them other linear equations to graph which intersect $y = 2x + 3$, are parallel to it, or are the same line. Ask students to describe the relationship of the two lines and to identify the type of system they represent.

See also the *Algebra 2 Toolkit* for more strategies.

4 PRACTICE AND APPLY

Assignment Guide

Answer Transparencies available for all exercises

Basic:
Day 1: EP p. 1011 Exs. 11–14
pp. 156–158
Exs. 1, 2, 3–15 odd, 16–22, 35–38, 41

Average:
Day 1: pp. 156–158
Exs. 1, 2, 6–11, 15, 16, 20–25, 28–31, 35–39, 42

Advanced:
Day 1: pp. 156–158
Exs. 1, 2, 10–15, 23–40*

Block:
pp. 156–158
Exs. 1, 2, 6–11, 15, 16, 20–25, 28–31, 35–39, 42 (with 3.2)

Differentiated Instruction

See *Algebra 2 Best Practices Toolkit* for suggestions on addressing the needs of a diverse classroom.

Homework Check

For a quick check of student understanding of key concepts, go over the following exercises:

Basic: 3, 9, 19, 21, 35

Average: 6, 12, 20, 28, 36

Advanced: 10, 13, 27, 28, 38

Extra Practice

- Student Edition, p. 1012
- Chapter 3 Resource Book: Practice levels A, B, C, pp. 8–13

Practice Worksheet

An easily-readable reduced practice page (with answers) for this lesson can be found on p. 150C.

3–14. See Additional Answers beginning on p. AA1.

3.1 EXERCISES

HOMEWORK KEY

○ = **WORKED-OUT SOLUTIONS** on p. WS4 for Exs. 9, 21, and 37

★ = **STANDARDIZED TEST PRACTICE** Exs. 2, 15, 29, 30, 37, and 39

◆ = **MULTIPLE REPRESENTATIONS** Ex. 38

SKILL PRACTICE

A

1. **VOCABULARY** Copy and complete: A consistent system that has exactly one solution is called _?_. independent

2. ★ **WRITING** *Explain* how to identify the solution(s) of a system from the graphs of the equations in the system. The solution is the place(s) where the lines intersect.

EXAMPLE 1 on p. 153 for Exs. 3–16

GRAPH AND CHECK **Graph the linear system and estimate the solution. Then check the solution algebraically.** 3–14. See margin for art.

3. $y = -3x + 2$, $y = 2x - 3$ (1, −1)
4. $y = 5x + 2$, $y = 3x$ (−1, −3)
5. $y = -x + 3$, $-x - 3y = -1$ (4, −1)
6. $x + 2y = 2$, $x - 4y = 14$ (6, −2)
7. $y = 2x - 10$, $x - 4y = 5$ (5, 0)
8. $-x + 6y = -12$, $x + 6y = 12$ (12, 0)
9. $y = -3x - 2$, $5x + 2y = -2$ (−2, 4)
10. $y = -3x - 13$, $-x - 2y = -4$ (−6, 5)
11. $x - 7y = 6$, $-3x + 21y = -18$ infinitely many solutions
12. $y = 4x + 3$, $20x - 5y = -15$ infinitely many solutions
13. $5x - 4y = 3$, $3x + 2y = 15$ (3, 3)
14. $7x + y = -17$, $3x - 10y = 24$ (−2, −3)

15. ★ **MULTIPLE CHOICE** What is the solution of the system? C

$$-4x - y = 2$$
$$7x + 2y = -5$$

Ⓐ (2, −6) Ⓑ (−1, 6) Ⓒ (1, −6) Ⓓ (−3, 8)

16. **ERROR ANALYSIS** A student used the check shown to conclude that (0, −1) is a solution of this system:

$$3x - 2y = 2$$
$$x + 2y = 6$$

$3x - 2y = 2$
$3(0) - 2(-1) \stackrel{?}{=} 2$
$2 = 2$

Describe and correct the student's error. The solution was not checked in the second equation; $0 + 2(-1) \stackrel{?}{=} 6$, $-2 \neq 6$, (0, −1) is not a solution to the system.

EXAMPLES 2 and 3 on p. 154 for Exs. 17–29

B

SOLVE AND CLASSIFY **Solve the system. Then classify the system as *consistent and independent*, *consistent and dependent*, or *inconsistent*.**

17. $y = -1$, $3x + y = 5$
18. $2x - y = 4$, $x - 2y = -1$
19. $y = 3x + 2$, $y = 3x - 2$
20. $y = 2x - 1$, $-6x + 3y = -3$
21. $-20x + 12y = -24$, $5x - 3y = 6$
22. $4x - 5y = 0$, $3x - 5y = -5$
23. $3x + 7y = 6$, $2x + 9y = 4$
24. $4x + 5y = 3$, $6x + 9y = 9$
25. $8x + 9y = 15$, $5x - 2y = 17$
26. $\frac{1}{2}x - 3y = 10$, $\frac{1}{4}x + 2y = -2$ (8, −2); consistent and independent
27. $3x - 2y = -15$, $x - \frac{2}{3}y = -5$ infinitely many solutions; consistent and dependent
28. $\frac{5}{2}x - y = -4$, $5x - 2y = \frac{1}{4}$ no solution; inconsistent

17. (2, −1); consistent and independent
18. (3, 2); consistent and independent
19. no solution; inconsistent
20. infinitely many solutions; consistent and dependent
21. infinitely many solutions; consistent and dependent
22. (5, 4); consistent and independent
23. (2, 0); consistent and independent
24. (−3, 3); consistent and independent
25. (3, −1); consistent and independent

Differentiated Instruction

English Learners When working on **Exercises 17–28**, students may have difficulty remembering the difference between an *independent* and a *dependent* system. Remind students that "dependent" means "to rely on another." Since "rely" sounds like "lie," help students make the connection between this sound and the fact that the graph of a dependent linear system has one line that "lies on" the other.

See also the *Algebra 2 Toolkit* for more strategies.

30a. *Sample answer:* $x + 3y = 8$, $x - y = 2$

30b. *Sample answer:* $y = 3x - 4$, $y = 3x + 2$

30c. *Sample answer:* $x - 5y = 10$, $2x - 10y = 20$

29. ★ **MULTIPLE CHOICE** How would you classify the system? A

$$-12x + 16y = 10$$
$$3x + 4y = -6$$

Ⓐ Consistent and independent Ⓑ Consistent and dependent

Ⓒ Inconsistent Ⓓ None of these

30. ★ **OPEN-ENDED MATH** Write a system of two linear equations that has the given number of solutions.

a. One solution **b.** No solution **c.** Infinitely many solutions

C **GRAPH AND CHECK Graph the system and estimate the solution(s). Then check the solution(s) algebraically.** 31–33. See margin for art.

31. $y = |x + 2|$, $y = x$ no solution

32. $y = |x - 1|$, $y = -x + 4$ (2.5, 1.5)

33. $y = |x| - 2$, $y = 2$ (4, 2) and (−4, 2)

34. **CHALLENGE** State the conditions on the constants a, b, c, and d for which the system below is **(a)** consistent and independent, **(b)** consistent and dependent, and **(c)** inconsistent. a–c. See margin.

$$y = ax + b$$
$$y = cx + d$$

PROBLEM SOLVING

EXAMPLE 4 A on p. 155 for Exs. 35–39

35. **WORK SCHEDULE** You worked 14 hours last week and earned a total of \$96 before taxes. Your job as a lifeguard pays \$8 per hour, and your job as a cashier pays \$6 per hour. How many hours did you work at each job? lifeguard: 6 h, cashier: 8 h

@HomeTutor for problem solving help at classzone.com

36. **LAW ENFORCEMENT** During one calendar year, a state trooper issued a total of 375 citations for warnings and speeding tickets. Of these, there were 37 more warnings than speeding tickets. How many warnings and how many speeding tickets were issued? warnings: 206, speeding tickets: 169

@HomeTutor for problem solving help at classzone.com

37. ★ **SHORT RESPONSE** A gym offers two options for membership plans. Option A includes an initiation fee of \$121 and costs \$1 per day. Option B has no initiation fee but costs \$12 per day. After how many days will the total costs of the gym membership plans be equal? How does your answer change if the daily cost of Option B increases? *Explain.*

37. 11 days; the number of days will decrease; the number of days will be divided by a larger number, which will decrease the quotient, which is the number of days.

B 38. **MULTIPLE REPRESENTATIONS** The price of refrigerator A is \$600, and the price of refrigerator B is \$1200. The cost of electricity needed to operate the refrigerators is \$50 per year for refrigerator A and \$40 per year for refrigerator B.

a. Writing Equations Write an equation for the cost of owning refrigerator A and an equation for the cost of owning refrigerator B.

b. Graphing Equations Graph the equations from part (a). After how many years are the total costs of owning the refrigerators equal? See margin for art; 60yr.

c. Checking Reasonableness Is your solution from part (b) reasonable in this situation? *Explain.* No, a refrigerator will not likely last 60 years.

38a. $y = 50x + 600$, where x represents the number of years, and y represents the cost; $y = 40x + 1200$ where x represents the number of years, and y represents the cost.

Teaching Strategy

Exercises 17–28 Remind students that writing each equation in slope-intercept form will help them classify the system as *consistent* or *inconsistent*, and it may make it easier to graph the equations.

Mathematical Reasoning

Exercises 31–33 The graph of $y = |x|$ is in the shape of a "V". Since the second equation in each of these systems is a line, point out that each line may intersect the absolute value graph in more than one point. For Exercise 33, $y = 2$ is a horizontal line that intersects the absolute value graph in two points.

Teaching Strategy

Exercise 37 Ask students to estimate the answer as they plan the solution. Since $120 \div 12 = 10$, the answer has to be at least 10 days.

34a. The values of a and c must be different. The values of b and d can be any number.

34b. The values of a and c must be the same. The values of b and d must also be the same, but not necessarily the same as the value for a and c.

34c. The values of a and c must be the same. The values of b and d must be different.

38b.

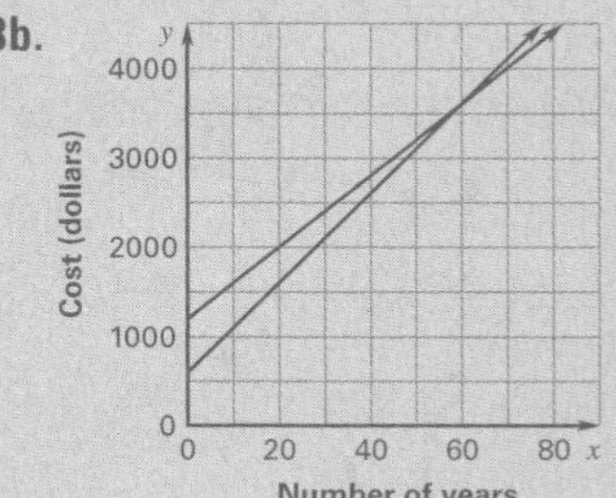

31.

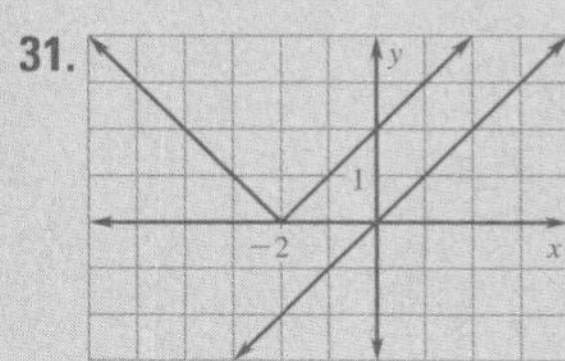

32.

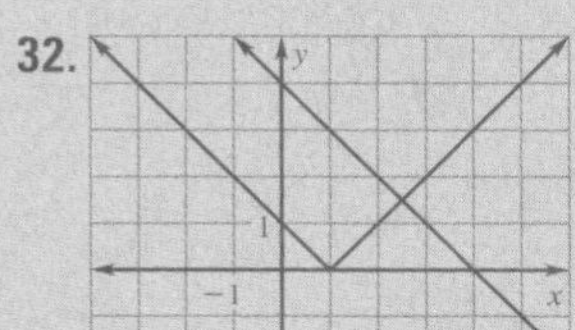

33.

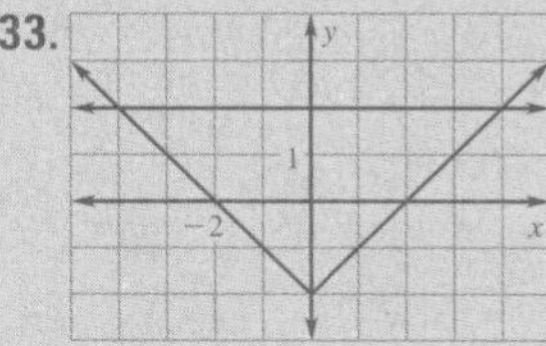

5 ASSESS AND RETEACH

Daily Homework Quiz

Transparency Available

1. Solve the system of equations $3x + 2y = 12$ and $x - y = -1$ graphically. (2, 3)

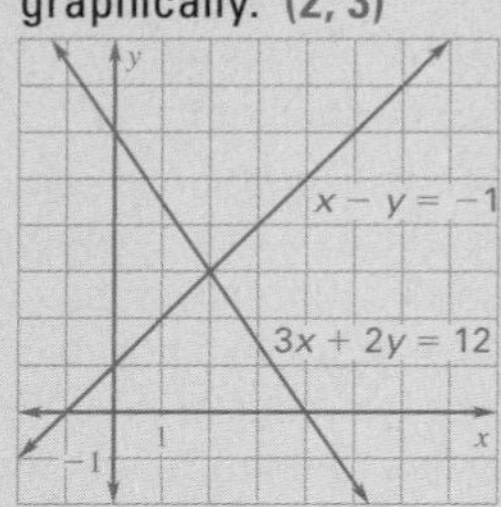

2. Solve the system. Then classify the system as *consistent and independent*, *consistent and dependent*, or *inconsistent*.
$4x + 2y = -8$ no solution;
$-2x - y = 6$ inconsistent

3. The price of air conditioner *A* is \$300, and the electricity costs \$20 per month to operate it. The price of air conditioner *B* is \$240, and the electricity costs \$25 per month to operate it. After how many months are the total costs of buying and operating the air conditioners the same? 12 mo

Available at **classzone.com**

Diagnosis/Remediation

- Practice A, B, C in Chapter 3 Resource Book, pp. 8–13
- Study Guide in Chapter 3 Resource Book, pp. 14–15
- Practice Workbook, pp. 36–38
- @HomeTutor

Challenge

Additional challenge is available in the Chapter 3 Resource Book, p. 18.

40a–b. See Additional Answers beginning on p. AA1.

39d. No. *Sample answer:* It is not likely that women's times will ever catch up to men's times or that the times will continue to decrease infinitely.

39. ★ **EXTENDED RESPONSE** The table below gives the winning times (in seconds) in the Olympic 100 meter freestyle swimming event for the period 1972–2000.

Years since 1972, *x*	0	4	8	12	16	20	24	28
Men's time, *m*	51.2	50.0	50.4	49.8	48.6	49.0	48.7	48.3
Women's time, *w*	58.6	55.7	54.8	55.9	54.9	54.6	54.4	53.8

a. Use a graphing calculator to fit a line to the data pairs (x, m). $m = -0.096x + 50.8$

b. Use a graphing calculator to fit a line to the data pairs (x, w). $w = -0.12x + 57.1$

c. Graph the lines and predict when the women's performance will catch up to the men's performance. in the year 2192

d. Do you think your prediction from part (c) is reasonable? *Explain.*

C **40.** **CHALLENGE** Your house and your friend's house are both on a street that passes by a park, as shown below.

At 1:00 P.M., you and your friend leave your houses on bicycles and head toward the park. You travel at a speed of 25 feet per second, and your friend also travels at a constant speed. You both reach the park at the same time.

a. Write and graph an equation giving your distance *d* (in feet) from the park after *t* seconds. $d = 5000 - 25t$; see margin for art.

b. At what speed does your friend travel to the park? *Explain* how you found your answer. $d = 3000 - 15t$; see margin for art.

c. Write an equation giving your friend's distance *d* (in feet) from the park after *t* seconds. Graph the equation in the same coordinate plane you used for part (a). 15 ft/sec. *Sample answer:* Since we both use the same amount of time and it took me 200 seconds, then it took my friend 200 seconds, so I solved the equation $300 = 200r$.

KENTUCKY MIXED REVIEW

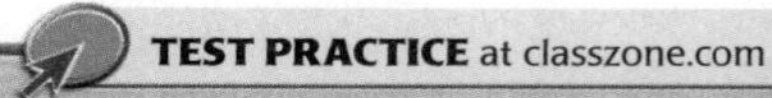

41. A realtor earns a base salary of \$31,000 plus 2.5% of the value of any real estate sold. Which equation best represents the realtor's total salary, *s*, in terms of the value, *x*, of the real estate sold? C

Ⓐ $s = 31{,}000 - 0.025x$ Ⓑ $s = 31{,}000x + 0.025$

Ⓒ $s = 31{,}000 + 0.025x$ Ⓓ $s = 31{,}000 + 2.5x$

42. In $\triangle MNP$, the measure of $\angle M$ is 40°. The measure of $\angle N$ is four times the measure of $\angle P$. What is $m\angle P$? A

Ⓐ 28° Ⓑ 35° Ⓒ 45° Ⓓ 112°

Graphing Calculator **ACTIVITY** *Use after Lesson 3.1*

@HomeTutor
classzone.com
Keystrokes

3.1 Graph Systems of Equations

QUESTION How can you solve a system of linear equations using a graphing calculator?

In Lesson 3.1, you learned to *estimate* the solution of a linear system by graphing. You can use the *intersect* feature of a graphing calculator to get an answer that is very close to, and sometimes *exactly* equal to, the actual solution.

EXAMPLE Solve a system

Use a graphing calculator to solve the system.

$6x - 9y = -20$ Equation 1
$2x + 4y = -52$ Equation 2

STEP 1 *Enter equations*
Solve each equation for y. Then enter the revised equations into a graphing calculator.

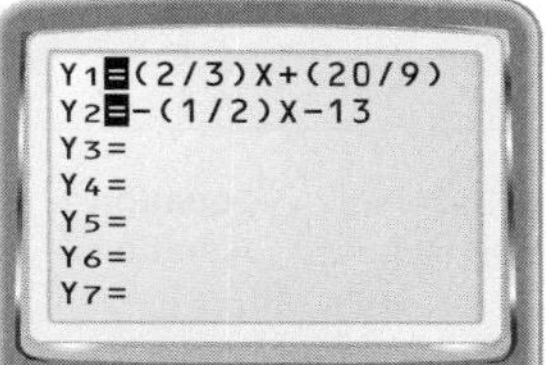

STEP 2 *Graph equations*
Graph the equations in the standard viewing window.

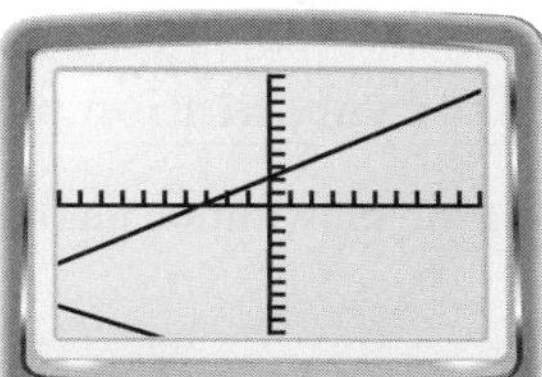

STEP 3 *Find the solution*
Adjust the viewing window, and use the *intersect* feature to find the intersection point.

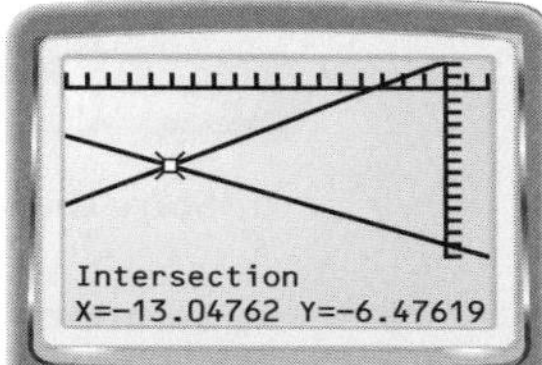

▶ The solution is about (−13.05, −6.48).

PRACTICE

Solve the linear system using a graphing calculator.

1. $y = -x + 2$
   $y = 2x - 5$ $\left(2\frac{1}{3}, -\frac{1}{3}\right)$
2. $y = -2x + 15$
   $y = 5x - 4$ about (2.71, 9.57)
3. $-9x + 7y = 14$
   $-3x + y = -17$ about (11.08, 16.25)
4. $-11x - 6y = -6$
   $4x + 2y = 10$ (24, −43)
5. $5x + 8y = -48$
   $x + 3y = 27$ about (−51.43, 26.14)
6. $-2x + 16y = 56$
   $4x + 7y = -35$ about (−12.21, 1.97)
7. **VACATION** Your family is planning a 7 day trip to Texas. You estimate that it will cost $275 per day in San Antonio and $400 per day in Dallas. Your budget for the 7 days is $2300. How many days should you spend in each city? San Antonio: 4 days, Dallas: 3 days
8. **MOVIE TICKETS** In one day, a movie theater collected $4600 from 800 people. The price of admission is $7 for an adult and $5 for a child. How many adults and how many children were admitted to the movie theater that day? 300 adults, 500 children

1 PLAN AND PREPARE

Learn the Method

- Students will use a graphing calculator to solve a system of linear equations.
- Students can use this method to check their solutions to Exercises 17–28 on page 156.

Keystroke Help

Keystrokes for several models of calculators are available in blackline format in the *Chapter 3 Resource Book*.

2 TEACH

Tips for Success

Remind students that they need to solve for y in each equation before entering it into their calculator. Point out the use of parentheses in the Example to remind students to enter the equations correctly.

Alternative Strategy

Ask each student to work with a partner. One student can graph the equations, and the other can find the solution using the intersect feature of the calculator. Then have them switch roles.

Extra Example

Use a graphing calculator to solve the system.
$3x - 2y = -11.5$
$2x - y = -2$ (7.5, 17)

3 ASSESS AND RETEACH

Describe the solution to each of the following systems of equations as a single point or no solution. Then give the point of intersection if there is one.

1. $4x - 3y = 12$
   $-8x + 6y = -8$ no solution
2. $-x - 2y = -6$
   $2x + y = 12$ single point; (6, 0)

1 PLAN AND PREPARE

Warm-Up Exercises

Transparency Available

1. Evaluate $-3x - 5y$ for $x = -3$ and $y = 4$. -11
2. Solve the system by graphing.
   $x + y = 2$
   $2x + y = 3$ (1, 1)
3. Twice a number x plus a number y is 3. The number y subtracted from three times the number x is 7. Find x and y by graphing. $(2, -1)$

Notetaking Guide

Transparency Available

Promotes interactive learning and notetaking skills, pp. 61–64.

Pacing

Basic: 1 day
Average: 1 day
Advanced: 1 day
Block: 0.5 block with 3.1

• See *Teaching Guide/Lesson Plan.*

2 FOCUS AND MOTIVATE

Essential Question

Big Idea 1, p. 151

How do you solve a system of linear equations algebraically? **Tell students they will learn how to answer this question by using substitution or elimination to solve a system of equations.**

3.2 Solve Linear Systems Algebraically

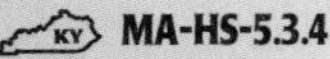 **MA-HS-5.3.4**

Before You solved linear systems graphically.
Now You will solve linear systems algebraically.
Why? So you can model guitar sales, as in Ex. 55.

Key Vocabulary
• **substitution method**
• **elimination method**

MA-HS-5.3.4
Students will model, solve and graph systems of two linear equations in real-world and mathematical problems. DOK 3

In this lesson, you will study two algebraic methods for solving linear systems. The first method is called the **substitution method**.

KEY CONCEPT *For Your Notebook*

The Substitution Method

STEP 1 **Solve** one of the equations for one of its variables.

STEP 2 **Substitute** the expression from Step 1 into the other equation and solve for the other variable.

STEP 3 **Substitute** the value from Step 2 into the revised equation from Step 1 and solve.

EXAMPLE 1 Use the substitution method

Solve the system using the substitution method.

$2x + 5y = -5$ **Equation 1**
$x + 3y = 3$ **Equation 2**

Solution

STEP 1 **Solve** Equation 2 for x.

$x = -3y + 3$ **Revised Equation 2**

STEP 2 **Substitute** the expression for x into Equation 1 and solve for y.

$2x + 5y = -5$ **Write Equation 1.**

$2(-3y + 3) + 5y = -5$ **Substitute $-3y + 3$ for x.**

$y = 11$ **Solve for y.**

STEP 3 **Substitute** the value of y into revised Equation 2 and solve for x.

$x = -3y + 3$ **Write revised Equation 2.**

$x = -3(11) + 3$ **Substitute 11 for y.**

$x = -30$ **Simplify.**

▶ The solution is $(-30, 11)$.

CHECK Check the solution by substituting into the original equations.

$2(-30) + 5(11) \stackrel{?}{=} -5$ **Substitute for x and y.** $-30 + 3(11) \stackrel{?}{=} 3$

$-5 = -5$ ✓ **Solution checks.** $3 = 3$ ✓

Resource Planning Guide

Chapter Resource Book
• Teaching Guide/Lesson Plan (pp. 19–20)
• Activity Master (p. 21)
• Practice levels A, B, C (pp. 24–26)
• Study Guide (pp. 27–28)
• Catch-up for Absent Students (p. 29)
• Application (p. 30)
• Challenge (p. 31)

Workbooks
• Notetaking Guide (pp. 61–64)
• Practice Workbook (pp. 39–40)

Teaching Options
• **Power Presentations CD-ROM** provides dynamic electronic teaching resources for the classroom.
• **Activity Generator CD-ROM** provides editable activities for all ability levels.

Interactive Technology
• Easy Planner
• Power Presentations CD-ROM
• Activity Generator CD-ROM
• Animated Algebra
• Test Generator CD-ROM
• Online Quiz
• eWorkbook
• eEdition
• @HomeTutor

Resources for English Learners
• Quick Reference for English Learners
• Spanish Study Guide
• Multi-Language Visual Glossary
• Student Resources in Spanish

See also the *Algebra 2 Toolkit* for more strategies for meeting individual needs.

ELIMINATION METHOD Another algebraic method that you can use to solve a system of equations is the **elimination method**. The goal of this method is to eliminate one of the variables by adding equations.

KEY CONCEPT *For Your Notebook*

The Elimination Method

STEP 1 **Multiply** one or both of the equations by a constant to obtain coefficients that differ only in sign for one of the variables.

STEP 2 **Add** the revised equations from Step 1. Combining like terms will eliminate one of the variables. Solve for the remaining variable.

STEP 3 **Substitute** the value obtained in Step 2 into either of the original equations and solve for the other variable.

EXAMPLE 2 Use the elimination method

Solve the system using the elimination method.

$3x - 7y = 10$ **Equation 1**
$6x - 8y = 8$ **Equation 2**

Solution

STEP 1 **Multiply** Equation 1 by **−2** so that the coefficients of x differ only in sign.

$3x - 7y = 10$ → × −2 → $-6x + 14y = -20$
$6x - 8y = 8$ → $6x - 8y = 8$

STEP 2 **Add** the revised equations and solve for y.

$6y = -12$
$y = -2$

STEP 3 **Substitute** the value of y into one of the original equations. Solve for x.

$3x - 7y = 10$ **Write Equation 1.**

$3x - 7(-2) = 10$ **Substitute −2 for y.**

$3x + 14 = 10$ **Simplify.**

$x = -\frac{4}{3}$ **Solve for x.**

▸ The solution is $\left(-\frac{4}{3}, -2\right)$.

CHECK You can check the solution algebraically using the method shown in Example 1. You can also use a graphing calculator to check the solution.

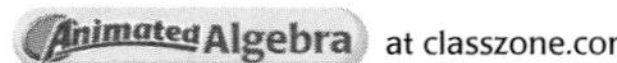 at classzone.com

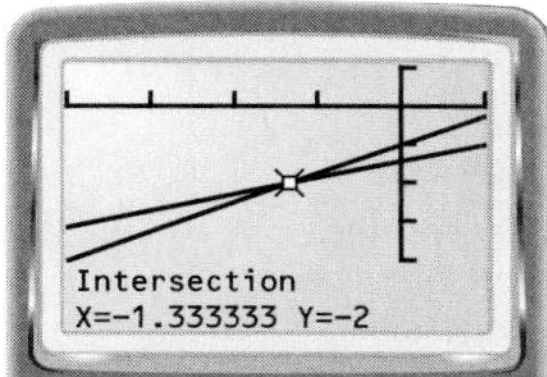

SOLVE SYSTEMS
In Example 2, one coefficient of x is a multiple of the other. In this case, it is easier to eliminate the x-terms because you need to multiply only one equation by a constant.

 **GUIDED PRACTICE** for Examples 1 and 2

Solve the system using the substitution or the elimination method.

1. $4x + 3y = -2$
$x + 5y = -9$ (1, −2)

2. $3x + 3y = -15$
$5x - 9y = 3$ (−3, −2)

3. $3x - 6y = 9$
$-4x + 7y = -16$ (11, 4)

Motivating the Lesson

Graph $x - y = 5.8$ and $x + y = 10.4$ in the same coordinate plane. Discuss with students whether they can tell the exact solution from the graph.

 **TEACH**

Extra Example 1

Solve the system using the substitution method.
$3x + 2y = 1$
$-2x + y = 4$ (−1, 2)

Teaching Strategy

Make sure that students understand that the substitution method is used when one equation can be easily solved for one variable (as when a coefficient is 1). Emphasize the importance of writing the solution as a pair of coordinates and checking the solution in each equation.

Extra Example 2

Solve the system using the elimination method.
$8x + 2y = 4$
$-2x + 3y = 13$ $\left(-\frac{1}{2}, 4\right)$

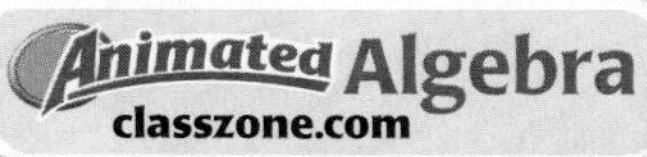

An **Animated Algebra** activity is available on-line for **Example 2**. This activity is also available on the **Power Presentations CD-ROM**.

Reading Strategy

Ask students to read and interpret the *Solve Systems* note with Example 2. The elimination method will be easier if you first eliminate the variable whose coefficients are multiples of each other.

Extra Example 3

At a pizza restaurant it costs \$4 to make a small pizza that sells for \$12, and it costs \$6 to make a large pizza that sells for \$15. In one week, the restaurant spent a total of \$1100 making pizzas and sold all of them for \$2910. How many small pizzas were sold? A

Ⓐ 80 Ⓑ 130
Ⓒ 210 Ⓓ 275

★ EXAMPLE 3 Standardized Test Practice

To raise money for new football uniforms, your school sells silk-screened T-shirts. Short sleeve T-shirts cost the school \$5 each and are sold for \$8 each. Long sleeve T-shirts cost the school \$7 each and are sold for \$12 each. The school spends a total of \$2500 on T-shirts and sells all of them for \$4200. How many of the short sleeve T-shirts are sold?

Ⓐ 50 Ⓑ 100 Ⓒ 150 Ⓓ 250

Solution

STEP 1 **Write** verbal models for this situation.

Equation 1

Short sleeve cost (dollars/shirt)	•	Short sleeve shirts (shirts)	+	Long sleeve cost (dollars/shirt)	•	Long sleeve shirts (shirts)	=	Total cost (dollars)
5	•	x	+	7	•	y	=	2500

Equation 2

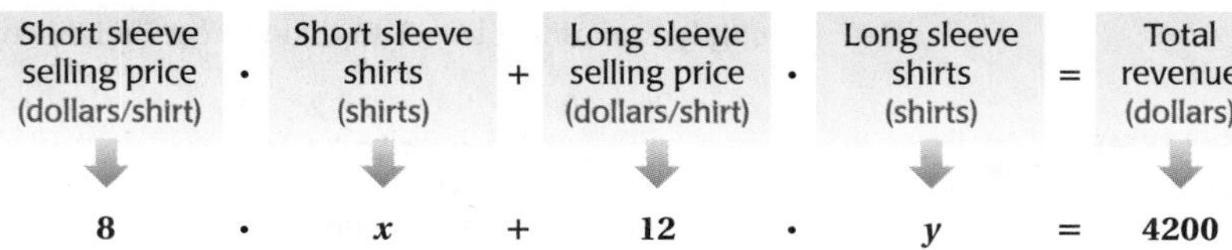

STEP 2 **Write** a system of equations.

Equation 1 $5x + 7y = 2500$ **Total cost for all T-shirts**
Equation 2 $8x + 12y = 4200$ **Total revenue from all T-shirts sold**

STEP 3 **Solve** the system using the elimination method.

Multiply Equation 1 by **−8** and Equation 2 by **5** so that the coefficients of x differ only in sign.

$5x + 7y = 2500$ → × −8 → $-40x - 56y = -20{,}000$

$8x + 12y = 4200$ → × 5 → $40x + 60y = 21{,}000$

Add the revised equations and solve for y.

$$4y = 1000$$
$$y = 250$$

Substitute the value of y into one of the original equations and solve for x.

$5x + 7y = 2500$ **Write Equation 1.**

$5x + 7(250) = 2500$ **Substitute 250 for *y*.**

$5x + 1750 = 2500$ **Simplify.**

$x = 150$ **Solve for *x*.**

The school sold 150 short sleeve T-shirts and 250 long sleeve T-shirts.

▸ The correct answer is C. Ⓐ Ⓑ Ⓒ Ⓓ

AVOID ERRORS

Choice D gives the number of *long* sleeve T-shirts, but the question asks for the number of *short* sleeve T-shirts. So you still need to solve for x in Step 3.

Differentiated Instruction

Inclusion While discussing the steps of the solution in **Example 3**, some students may wish to choose their own variables in order to be better connected with the situation. They may have a difficult time relating x and y to the number of short sleeve and long sleeve T-shirts, respectively. Students might be more comfortable using the variables s and ℓ, for example, to represent these two unknown values. Demonstrate that doing so still leads to a correct result.

See also the *Algebra 2 Toolkit* for more strategies.

✓ **GUIDED PRACTICE** for Example 3

4. **WHAT IF?** In Example 3, suppose the school spends a total of \$3715 on T-shirts and sells all of them for \$6160. How many of each type of T-shirt are sold? 365 short sleeve T-shirts, 270 long sleeve T-shirts

CHOOSING A METHOD In general, the substitution method is convenient when one of the variables in a system of equations has a coefficient of 1 or −1, as in Example 1. If neither variable in a system has a coefficient of 1 or −1, it is usually easier to use the elimination method, as in Examples 2 and 3.

EXAMPLE 4 Solve linear systems with many or no solutions

Solve the linear system.

a. $x - 2y = 4$
$3x - 6y = 8$

b. $4x - 10y = 8$
$-14x + 35y = -28$

Solution

a. Because the coefficient of x in the first equation is 1, use the substitution method.

Solve the first equation for x.

$x - 2y = 4$ **Write first equation.**

$x = 2y + 4$ **Solve for x.**

Substitute the expression for x into the second equation.

$3x - 6y = 8$ **Write second equation.**

$3(2y + 4) - 6y = 8$ **Substitute 2y + 4 for x.**

$12 = 8$ **Simplify.**

▶ Because the statement $12 = 8$ is never true, there is *no solution.*

b. Because no coefficient is 1 or −1, use the elimination method.

AVOID ERRORS
When multiplying an equation by a constant, make sure you multiply each term of the equation by the constant.

Multiply the first equation by **7** and the second equation by **2**.

$4x - 10y = 8$ × 7 $28x - 70y = 56$

$-14x + 35y = -28$ × 2 $-28x + 70y = -56$

Add the revised equations. $0 = 0$

▶ Because the equation $0 = 0$ is always true, there are *infinitely many solutions.*

✓ **GUIDED PRACTICE** for Example 4

Solve the linear system using any algebraic method.

5. $12x - 3y = -9$
$-4x + y = 3$
infinitely many solutions

6. $6x + 15y = -12$
$-2x - 5y = 9$
no solution

7. $5x + 3y = 20$
$-x - \frac{3}{5}y = -4$
infinitely many solutions

8. $12x - 2y = 21$
$3x + 12y = -4$ $\left(\frac{122}{75}, -\frac{37}{50}\right)$

9. $8x + 9y = 15$
$5x - 2y = 17$ (3, −1)

10. $5x + 5y = 5$
$5x + 3y = 4.2$ (0.6, 0.4)

Extra Example 4

Solve the linear system.

a. $2x - 3y = 4$
$6x - 9y = 8$ no solution

b. $x - y = 4$
$-6x + 6y = -24$ infinitely many solutions

Key Questions to Ask for Example 4

- How would the graph of the system in part (a) look? The graphs are parallel.
- How would the graph of the solution in part (b) look? The graphs are the same line.

Avoiding Common Errors

In Example 4, part (a), students may substitute $2y + 4$ for x back into the first equation, get $4 = 4$, and then answer "infinitely many solutions". Caution students that if they solve for a variable in one equation, they must substitute it into the *other* equation.

Closing the Lesson

Have students summarize the major points of the lesson and answer the Essential Question: How do you solve a system of linear equations algebraically?

- You can solve a system of linear equations using substitution or elimination.
- You can check a solution by substituting it back into the original equations.

You can use substitution or elimination to solve a system of equations. To use substitution, solve one equation for one variable and substitute it into the other equation. To use elimination, multiply one or both equations by constants to get opposite coefficients for one variable, then add the equations. In both cases, substitute the value of the variable you find first into either one of the original equations to find the value of the second variable.

Differentiated Instruction

Below Level Ask students to work in groups to analyze the Guided Practice problems. They should tell each other which method they prefer and explain why they made that choice. Also, have students write a summary of how to solve a system of equations by substitution or elimination. Ask them to explain how to tell when there are no solutions or infinitely many solutions.

See also the *Algebra 2 Toolkit* for more strategies.

4 PRACTICE AND APPLY

Assignment Guide

Answer Transparencies available for all exercises

Basic:
Day 1: SRH p. 984 Exs. 7–12
pp. 164–167
Exs. 1–8, 15–20, 27–33, 40–45, 55–60, 64

Average:
Day 1: pp. 164–167
Exs. 1, 2, 6–10, 18–22, 27, 31–35, 40–51, 55–62, 65

Advanced:
Day 1: pp. 164–167
Exs. 1, 2, 11–14, 23–26, 36–54*, 57–63*, 66

Block:
pp. 164–167
Exs. 1, 2, 6–10, 18–22, 27, 31–35, 40–51, 55–62, 65 (with 3.1)

Differentiated Instruction

See *Algebra 2 Best Practices Toolkit* for suggestions on addressing the needs of a diverse classroom.

Homework Check

For a quick check of student understanding of key concepts, go over the following exercises:

Basic: 4, 16, 19, 55, 56
Average: 8, 18, 22, 56, 57
Advanced: 12, 24, 26, 58, 59

Extra Practice

- Student Edition, p. 1012
- Chapter 3 Resource Book: Practice levels A, B, C, pp. 24–26

Practice Worksheet

An easily-readable reduced practice page (with answers) for this lesson can be found on p. 150C.

3.2 EXERCISES

HOMEWORK KEY
○ = **WORKED-OUT SOLUTIONS** on p. WS5 for Exs. 5, 29, and 59
★ = **STANDARDIZED TEST PRACTICE** Exs. 2, 40, 50, 57, 58, and 60

SKILL PRACTICE

A

1. **VOCABULARY** Copy and complete: To solve a linear system where one of the coefficients is 1 or −1, it is usually easiest to use the _?_ method. substitution

2. ★ **WRITING** *Explain* how to use the elimination method to solve a linear system. See margin.

EXAMPLES 1 and 4 on pp. 160–163 for Exs. 3–14

SUBSTITUTION METHOD **Solve the system using the substitution method.**

3. $2x + 5y = 7$
 $x + 4y = 2$ $(6, -1)$

4. $3x + y = 16$
 $2x - 3y = -4$ $(4, 4)$

5. $6x - 2y = 5$
 $-3x + y = 7$ no solution

6. $x + 4y = 1$
 $3x + 2y = -12$ $\left(-5, \frac{3}{2}\right)$

7. $3x - y = 2$
 $6x + 3y = 14$ $\left(\frac{4}{3}, 2\right)$

8. $3x - 4y = -5$
 $-x + 3y = -5$ $(-7, -4)$

9. $3x + 2y = 6$
 $x - 4y = -12$ $(0, 3)$

10. $6x - 3y = 15$
 $-2x + y = -5$ infinitely many solutions

11. $3x + y = -1$
 $2x + 3y = 18$ $(-3, 8)$

12. $2x - y = 1$
 $8x + 4y = 6$ $\left(\frac{5}{8}, \frac{1}{4}\right)$

13. $3x + 7y = 13$
 $x + 3y = -7$ $(44, -17)$

14. $2x + 5y = 10$
 $-3x + y = 36$ $(-10, 6)$

EXAMPLES 2 and 4 on pp. 161–163 for Exs. 15–27

ELIMINATION METHOD **Solve the system using the elimination method.**

15. $2x + 6y = 17$
 $2x - 10y = 9$ $\left(7, \frac{1}{2}\right)$

16. $4x - 2y = -16$
 $-3x + 4y = 12$ $(-4, 0)$

17. $3x - 4y = -10$
 $6x + 3y = -42$ $(-6, -2)$

18. $4x - 3y = 10$
 $8x - 6y = 20$ infinitely many solutions

19. $5x - 3y = -3$
 $2x + 6y = 0$ $\left(-\frac{1}{2}, \frac{1}{6}\right)$

20. $10x - 2y = 16$
 $5x + 3y = -12$ $\left(\frac{3}{5}, -5\right)$

21. $2x + 5y = 14$
 $3x - 2y = -36$ $(-8, 6)$

22. $7x + 2y = 11$
 $-2x + 3y = 29$ $(-1, 9)$

23. $3x + 4y = 18$
 $6x + 8y = 18$ no solution

24. $2x + 5y = 13$
 $6x + 2y = -13$ $\left(-\frac{7}{2}, 4\right)$

25. $4x - 5y = 13$
 $6x + 2y = 48$ $(7, 3)$

26. $6x - 4y = 14$
 $2x + 8y = 21$ $\left(\frac{7}{2}, \frac{7}{4}\right)$

27. **ERROR ANALYSIS** *Describe* and correct the error in the first step of solving the system. See margin.

 $3x + 2y = 7$
 $5x + 4y = 15$

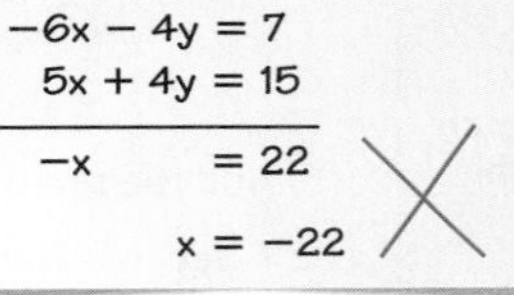

CHOOSING A METHOD **Solve the system using any algebraic method.**

28. $3x + 2y = 11$
 $4x + y = -2$ $(-3, 10)$

29. $2x - 3y = 8$
 $-4x + 5y = -10$ $(-5, -6)$

30. $3x + 7y = -1$
 $2x + 3y = 6$ $(9, -4)$

31. $4x - 10y = 18$
 $-2x + 5y = -9$ infinitely many solutions

32. $3x - y = -2$
 $5x + 2y = 15$ $(1, 5)$

33. $x + 2y = -8$
 $3x - 4y = -24$ $(-8, 0)$

34. $2x + 3y = -6$
 $3x - 4y = 25$ $(3, -4)$

35. $3x + y = 15$
 $-x + 2y = -19$ $(7, -6)$

36. $4x - 3y = 8$
 $-8x + 6y = 16$ no solution

37. $4x - y = -10$
 $6x + 2y = -1$ $\left(-\frac{3}{2}, 4\right)$

38. $7x + 5y = -12$
 $3x - 4y = 1$ $(-1, -1)$

39. $2x + y = -1$
 $-4x + 6y = 6$ $\left(-\frac{3}{4}, \frac{1}{2}\right)$

2. *Sample answer:* Multiply one or both of the equations by a number so that one of the variables will be eliminated when you add them. After adding, solve the resulting equation for the remaining variable. Substitute the value of the variable found in the previous step into one of the original equations and solve for the other variable.

27. Failed to multiply the constant by −2.

$$\begin{aligned} -6x - 4y &= -14 \\ 5x + 4y &= 15 \\ \hline -x &= 1 \\ x &= -1 \end{aligned}$$

40. ★ **MULTIPLE CHOICE** What is the solution of the linear system? B

$$3x + 2y = 4$$
$$6x - 3y = -27$$

(A) $(-2, -5)$ (B) $(-2, 5)$ (C) $(2, -5)$ (D) $(2, 5)$

B **GEOMETRY** **Find the coordinates of the point where the diagonals of the quadrilateral intersect.**

41. 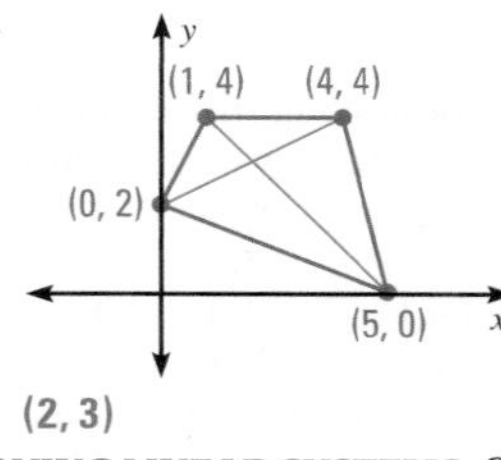

(2, 3)

42. 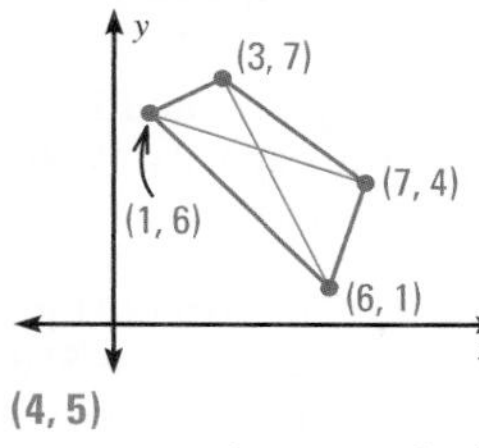

(4, 5)

43. 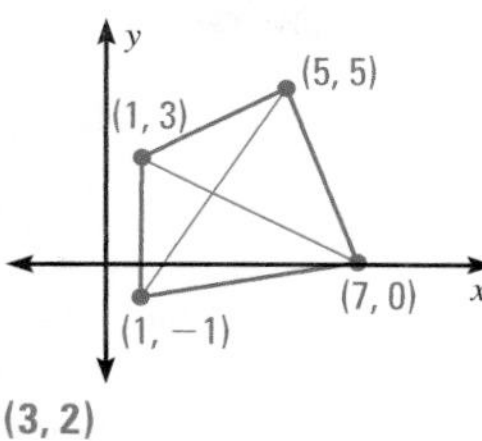

(3, 2)

SOLVING LINEAR SYSTEMS **Solve the system using any algebraic method.**

44. $0.02x - 0.05y = -0.38$
$0.03x + 0.04y = 1.04$ (16, 14)

45. $0.05x - 0.03y = 0.21$
$0.07x + 0.02y = 0.16$ about (2.90, −2.16)

46. $\frac{2}{3}x + 3y = -34$
$x - \frac{1}{2}y = -1$ (−6, −10)

47. $\frac{1}{2}x + \frac{2}{3}y = \frac{5}{6}$
$\frac{5}{12}x + \frac{7}{12}y = \frac{3}{4}$ (−1, 2)

48. $\frac{x+3}{4} + \frac{y-1}{3} = 1$
$2x - y = 12$ (5, −2)

49. $\frac{x-1}{2} + \frac{y+2}{3} = 4$
$x - 2y = 5$ (7, 1)

50. ★ **OPEN-ENDED MATH** Write a system of linear equations that has $(-1, 4)$ as its only solution. Verify that $(-1, 4)$ is a solution using either the substitution method or the elimination method. *Sample answer:* $y = -2x + 2$ and $y = \frac{4}{3}x + \frac{16}{3}$

C **SOLVING NONLINEAR SYSTEMS** **Use the elimination method to solve the system.**

51. $7y + 18xy = 30$
$13y - 18xy = 90$ $\left(-\frac{1}{9}, 6\right)$

52. $xy - x = 14$
$5 - xy = 2x$ $\left(-3, -\frac{11}{3}\right)$

53. $2xy + y = 44$
$32 - xy = 3y$ (5, 4)

54. **CHALLENGE** Find values of r, s, and t that produce the indicated solution(s).

$$-3x - 5y = 9$$
$$rx + sy = t$$

a. No solution
Sample answer: $r = -6$, $s = -10$, $t = 9$

b. Infinitely many solutions
Sample answer: $r = 9$, $s = 15$, $t = -27$

c. A solution of $(2, -3)$
Sample answer: $r = 2$, $s = -3$, $t = 13$

PROBLEM SOLVING

EXAMPLE 3 on p. 162 for Exs. 55–59 A

55. **GUITAR SALES** In one week, a music store sold 9 guitars for a total of \$3611. Electric guitars sold for \$479 each and acoustic guitars sold for \$339 each. How many of each type of guitar were sold? 5 acoustic, 4 electric

@HomeTutor for problem solving help at classzone.com

56. **COUNTY FAIR** An adult pass for a county fair costs \$2 more than a children's pass. When 378 adult and 214 children's passes were sold, the total revenue was \$2384. Find the cost of an adult pass. \$4.75

@HomeTutor for problem solving help at classzone.com

Teaching Strategy

Exercises 28–39 Remind students that the substitution method is more easily used when the coefficient of one of the variables is 1 or −1.

Avoiding Common Errors

Exercises 41–43 Students may recall from a previous course that the diagonals of a parallelogram intersect at their midpoints and incorrectly apply that to *all* quadrilaterals. Remind students that this concept applies *only* to parallelograms.

Exercise 59 Additional information about table tennis can be found at www.usatt.org/index.shtml

Mathematical Reasoning

Exercise 62 Students can simplify this exercise by understanding that if the plane flies 1000 in 5 hours with the wind, then it flies 200 miles in one hour. By a similar simplification, the plane flies 100 miles in one hour against the wind. Then they can use these distances to write simpler equations based on the formula $d = r \cdot t$.

p. 167, Quiz

1.
2.
3.

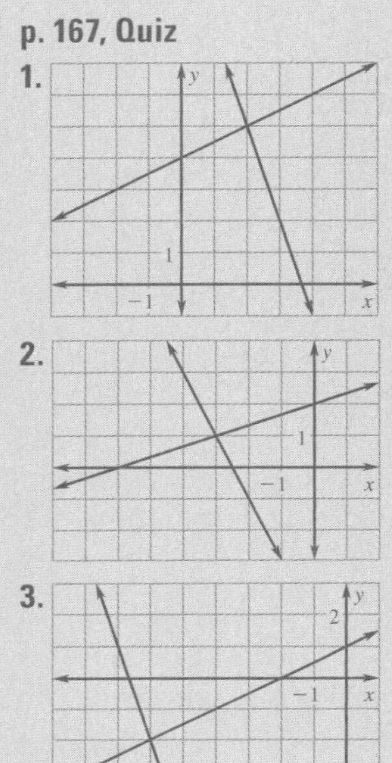

60d. Start 1 hour and 40 minutes after Martha; change her speed to $6\frac{2}{3}$ miles per hour; both answers are reasonable, she could change her starting time and she could increase her speed by $\frac{2}{3}$ mile per hour.

57. ★ **SHORT RESPONSE** A company produces gas mowers and electric mowers at two factories. The company has orders for 2200 gas mowers and 1400 electric mowers. The production capacity of each factory (in mowers per week) is shown in the table.

	Factory A	Factory B
Gas mowers	200	400
Electric mowers	100	300

Describe how the company can fill its orders by operating the factories simultaneously at full capacity. Write and solve a linear system to support your answer. **The company can fill its orders by operating Factory A for 5 weeks and Factory B for 3 weeks.**

58. ★ **MULTIPLE CHOICE** The cost of 11 gallons of regular gasoline and 16 gallons of premium gasoline is \$58.55. Premium costs \$.20 more per gallon than regular. What is the cost of a gallon of premium gasoline? **B**

Ⓐ \$2.05 Ⓑ \$2.25 Ⓒ \$2.29 Ⓓ \$2.55

59. **TABLE TENNIS** One evening, 76 people gathered to play doubles and singles table tennis. There were 26 games in progress at one time. A doubles game requires 4 players and a singles game requires 2 players. How many games of each kind were in progress at one time if all 76 people were playing? **12 doubles games, 14 singles games**

B

60. ★ **EXTENDED RESPONSE** A local hospital is holding a two day marathon walk to raise funds for a new research facility. The total distance of the marathon is 26.2 miles. On the first day, Martha starts walking at 10:00 A.M. She walks 4 miles per hour. Carol starts two hours later than Martha but decides to run to catch up to Martha. Carol runs at a speed of 6 miles per hour.

 a. Write an equation to represent the distance Martha travels. $d = 4t$

 b. Write an equation to represent the distance Carol travels. $d = 6(t - 2)$

 c. Solve the system of equations to find when Carol will catch up to Martha. **4:00 P.M.**

 d. Carol wants to reduce the time she takes to catch up to Martha by 1 hour. How can she do this by changing her starting time? How can she do this by changing her speed? *Explain* whether your answers are reasonable.

61. **BUSINESS** A nut wholesaler sells a mix of peanuts and cashews. The wholesaler charges \$2.80 per pound for peanuts and \$5.30 per pound for cashews. The mix is to sell for \$3.30 per pound. How many pounds of peanuts and how many pounds of cashews should be used to make 100 pounds of the mix? **80 pounds of peanuts, 20 pounds of cashews**

62. **AVIATION** Flying with the wind, a plane flew 1000 miles in 5 hours. Flying against the wind, the plane could fly only 500 miles in the same amount of time. Find the speed of the plane in calm air and the speed of the wind. **plane: 150 mi/h, wind: 50 mi/h**

C

63. **CHALLENGE** For a recent job, an electrician earned \$50 per hour, and the electrician's apprentice earned \$20 per hour. The electrician worked 4 hours more than the apprentice, and together they earned a total of \$550. How much money did each person earn? **apprentice: \$100, electrician: \$450**

◯ = **WORKED-OUT SOLUTIONS** on p. WS1 ★ = **STANDARDIZED TEST PRACTICE**

p. 167, Quiz

13. \$12. *Sample answer:* Write an equation for the cost of the 6-foot cable, $2c + 6f = 15.50$, and an equation for the cost of the 3-foot cable, $2c + 3f = 10.25$. Solve the system of equations by subtracting them to find $f = 1.75$ and $c = 2.50$. So 4 feet of cable will cost $2(2.50) + 4(1.75) = \$12$.

64. What is the y-intercept of the line shown? **B**

Ⓐ $b = -18$

Ⓑ $b = -12$

Ⓒ $b = -8$

Ⓓ $b = -4$

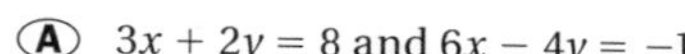

65. Which two lines are parallel? **B**

Ⓐ $3x + 2y = 8$ and $6x - 4y = -18$

Ⓑ $2x + 6y = 9$ and $4x + 12y = -15$

Ⓒ $3x + 2y = 8$ and $2x + 3y = 10$

Ⓓ $2x + 6y = 9$ and $-4x + 12y = 12$

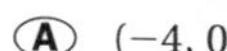

66. Which ordered pair represents the x-intercept of the equation $4x - 5y = 20$? **D**

Ⓐ $(-4, 0)$ Ⓑ $(0, -4)$ Ⓒ $(0, 5)$ Ⓓ $(5, 0)$

QUIZ for Lessons 3.1–3.2

Graph the linear system and estimate the solution. Then check the solution algebraically. *(p. 153)* 1–3. See margin for art.

1. $3x + y = 11$
   $x - 2y = -8$ (2, 5)
2. $2x + y = -5$
   $-x + 3y = 6$ (−3, 1)
3. $x - 2y = -2$
   $3x + y = -20$ (−6, −2)

Solve the system. Then classify the system as *consistent and independent, consistent and dependent,* or *inconsistent.* *(p. 153)*

4. $4x + 8y = 8$
   $x + 2y = 6$
   no solution; inconsistent
5. $-5x + 3y = -5$
   $y = \frac{5}{3}x + 1$
   no solution; inconsistent
6. $x - 2y = 2$
   $2x - y = -5$
   (−4, −3); consistent and independent

Solve the system using the substitution method. *(p. 160)*

7. $3x - y = -4$
   $x + 3y = -28$ (−4, −8)
8. $x + 5y = 1$
   $-3x + 4y = 16$ (−4, 1)
9. $6x + y = -6$
   $4x + 3y = 17$ (−2.5, 9)

Solve the system using the elimination method. *(p. 160)*

10. $2x - 3y = -1$
    $2x + 3y = -19$ (−5, −3)
11. $3x - 2y = 10$
    $-6x + 4y = -20$
    infinitely many solutions
12. $2x + 3y = 17$
    $5x + 8y = 20$ (76, −45)

13. **HOME ELECTRONICS** To connect a VCR to a television set, you need a cable with special connectors at both ends. Suppose you buy a 6 foot cable for \$15.50 and a 3 foot cable for \$10.25. Assuming that the cost of a cable is the sum of the cost of the two connectors and the cost of the cable itself, what would you expect to pay for a 4 foot cable? *Explain* how you got your answer. See margin.

5 ASSESS AND RETEACH

Daily Homework Quiz

Transparency Available

1. Solve the system of equations by substitution.
   $x - 2y = 16$
   $2x + y = 12$ (8, −4)
2. Solve the system of equations by elimination.
   $-6x - 5y = 12$
   $3x + 2y = -3$ (3, −6)
3. The home team fans for a football game bought five times as many tickets as the visiting team fans. The total number of tickets sold was 1440. How many tickets did the home team fans buy? **1200 tickets**

Online Quiz

Available at **classzone.com**

Diagnosis/Remediation

- Practice A, B, C in Chapter 3 Resource Book, pp. 24–26
- Study Guide in Chapter 3 Resource Book, pp. 27–28
- Practice Workbook, pp. 39–40
- @HomeTutor

Challenge

Additional challenge is available in the Chapter 3 Resource Book, p. 31.

Quiz

An easily-readable reduced copy of the quiz (with answers) on Lessons 3.1–3.2 from the Assessment Book can be found on p. 150F.

1 PLAN AND PREPARE

Warm-Up Exercises

Transparency Available

1. Graph $y \leq x + 2$.

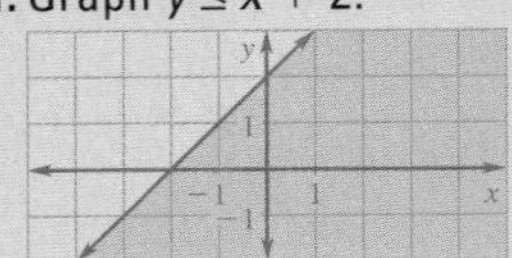

2. Graph $y \geq |x|$.

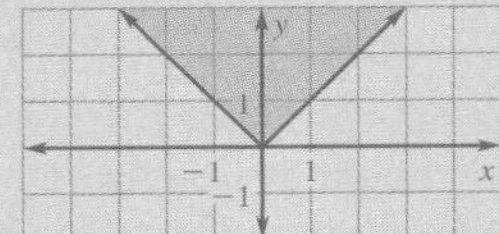

Notetaking Guide

Transparency Available

Promotes interactive learning and notetaking skills, pp. 65–67.

Pacing

Basic: 1 day
Average: 1 day
Advanced: 1 day
Block: 0.5 block with 3.4

- See *Teaching Guide/Lesson Plan.*

2 FOCUS AND MOTIVATE

Essential Question

Big Idea 2, p. 151

How do you find the solution to a system of linear inequalities? **Tell students they will learn how to answer this question by graphing a system of linear inequalities.**

3.3 Graph Systems of Linear Inequalities

KY MA-HS-5.3.5 *Students will write, graph, and solve systems of two linear inequalities based on real-world or mathematical problems and interpret the solution.*

Before You graphed linear inequalities.

Now You will graph systems of linear inequalities.

Why? So you can model heart rates during exercise, as in Ex. 39.

Key Vocabulary
- system of linear inequalities
- solution of a system of inequalities
- graph of a system of inequalities

The following is an example of a **system of linear inequalities** in two variables.

$x + y \leq 8$ **Inequality 1**
$4x - y > 6$ **Inequality 2**

A **solution** of a system of inequalities is an ordered pair that is a solution of each inequality in the system. For example, $(5, -2)$ is a solution of the system above. The **graph** of a system of inequalities is the graph of all solutions of the system.

KEY CONCEPT — *For Your Notebook*

Graphing a System of Linear Inequalities

To graph a system of linear inequalities, follow these steps:

STEP 1 **Graph** each inequality in the system. You may want to use colored pencils to distinguish the different half-planes.

STEP 2 **Identify** the region that is common to all the graphs of the inequalities. This region is the graph of the system. If you used colored pencils, the graph of the system is the region that has been shaded with every color.

EXAMPLE 1 Graph a system of two inequalities

Graph the system of inequalities.

$y > -2x - 5$ **Inequality 1**
$y \leq x + 3$ **Inequality 2**

REVIEW INEQUALITIES
For help with graphing linear inequalities in two variables, see p. 132.

Solution

STEP 1 **Graph** each inequality in the system. Use red for $y > -2x - 5$ and blue for $y \leq x + 3$.

STEP 2 **Identify** the region that is common to both graphs. It is the region that is shaded **purple**.

The graph of the system is the intersection of the red and blue regions.

Animated Algebra at classzone.com

Resource Planning Guide

Chapter Resource Book
- Teaching Guide/Lesson Plan (pp. 32–33)
- Activity Master (p. 34)
- Practice levels A, B, C (pp. 35–40)
- Study Guide (pp. 41–42)
- Catch-up for Absent Students (p. 43)
- Problem Solving Workshop (p. 44)
- Challenge (p. 45)

Workbooks
- Notetaking Guide (pp. 65–67)
- Practice Workbook (pp. 41–43)

Teaching Options
- **Power Presentations CD-ROM** provides dynamic electronic teaching resources for the classroom.
- **Activity Generator CD-ROM** provides editable activities for all ability levels.

Interactive Technology
- Easy Planner
- Power Presentations CD-ROM
- Activity Generator CD-ROM
- Animated Algebra
- Test Generator CD-ROM
- Online Quiz
- eWorkbook
- eEdition
- @HomeTutor

Resources for English Learners
- Quick Reference for English Learners
- Spanish Study Guide
- Multi-Language Visual Glossary
- Student Resources in Spanish

See also the *Algebra 2 Toolkit* for more strategies for meeting individual needs.

EXAMPLE 2 Graph a system with no solution

Graph the system of inequalities.

$2x + 3y < 6$ **Inequality 1**

$y \geq -\frac{2}{3}x + 4$ **Inequality 2**

Solution

STEP 1 **Graph** each inequality in the system. Use red for $2x + 3y < 6$ and blue for $y \geq -\frac{2}{3}x + 4$.

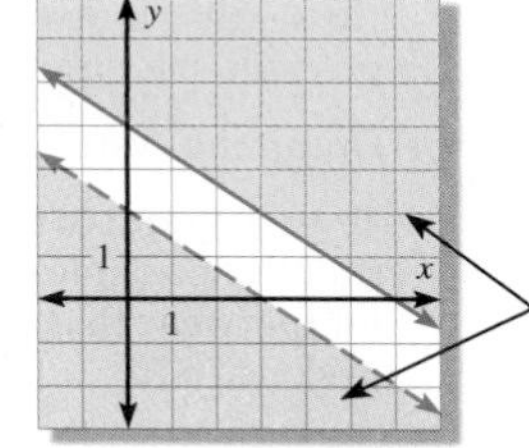

The red and blue regions do not intersect.

STEP 2 **Identify** the region that is common to both graphs. There is no region shaded both red and blue. So, the system has no solution.

EXAMPLE 3 Graph a system with an absolute value inequality

Graph the system of inequalities.

$y \leq 3$ **Inequality 1**

$y > |x + 4|$ **Inequality 2**

REVIEW ABSOLUTE VALUE
For help with graphing absolute value inequalities, see p. 132.

Solution

STEP 1 **Graph** each inequality in the system. Use red for $y \leq 3$ and blue for $y > |x + 4|$.

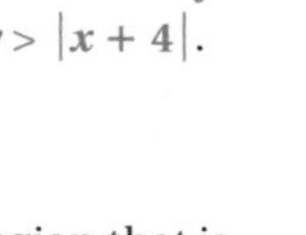

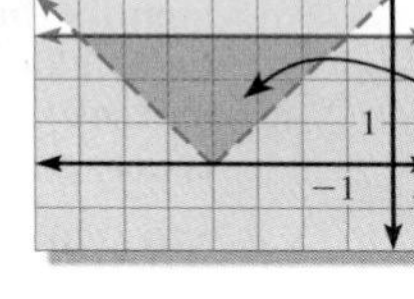

The graph of the system is the intersection of the red and blue regions.

STEP 2 **Identify** the region that is common to both graphs. It is the region that is shaded **purple**.

✓ GUIDED PRACTICE for Examples 1, 2, and 3

Graph the system of inequalities. 1–6. See margin.

1. $y \leq 3x - 2$
   $y > -x + 4$
2. $2x - \frac{1}{2}y \geq 4$
   $4x - y \leq 5$
3. $x + y > -3$
   $-6x + y < 1$
4. $y \leq 4$
   $y \geq |x - 5|$
5. $y > -2$
   $y \leq -|x + 2|$
6. $y \geq 2|x + 1|$
   $y < x + 1$

Differentiated Instruction

Advanced Extend **Example 3** by having students solve systems involving two absolute value inequalities. Ask students to conjecture what types of solutions they could get. See if any student comes up with the possibility of a one-point solution or an all-points solution.

See also the *Algebra 2 Toolkit* for more strategies.

Motivating the Lesson

An airline restricts the size of baggage so that the maximum total linear dimensions (length plus width plus height) is no more than 62 inches. If the height of a bag is 8 inches, you can use a system of linear inequalities to describe all possible values for the length and width.

3 TEACH

Extra Example 1

Graph the system of inequalities.

$y \leq 3x + 2$; $y > -x + 4$

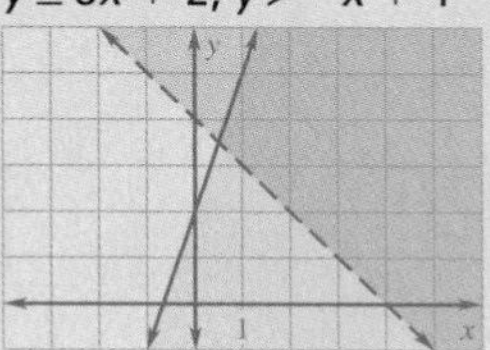

Animated Algebra
classzone.com

An **Animated Algebra** activity is available on-line for **Example 1**. This activity is also available on the **Power Presentations CD-ROM**.

Teaching Strategy

Remind students that the boundary is dashed if the inequality symbol is < or >, and it is solid if the inequality symbol is ≤ or ≥.

Extra Example 2

Graph the system of inequalities.

$4x + 2y \geq 8$; $y < -2x - 3$

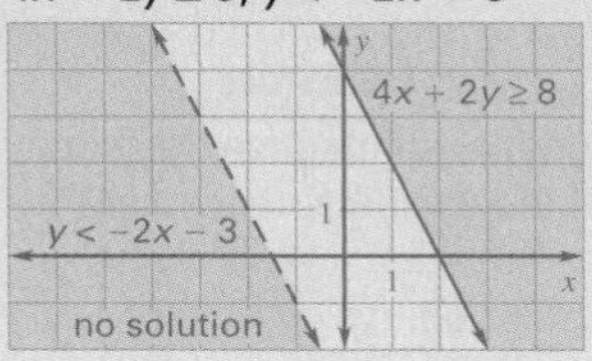

4x + 2y ≥ 8
y < −2x − 3
no solution

1–6. See Additional Answers beginning on p. AA1.

SYSTEMS OF THREE OR MORE INEQUALITIES You can also graph a system of three or more linear inequalities, as shown in Example 4.

EXAMPLE 4 Solve a multi-step problem

SHOPPING A discount shoe store is having a sale, as described in the advertisement shown.

- Use the information in the ad to write a system of inequalities for the regular footwear prices and possible sale prices.
- Graph the system of inequalities.
- Use the graph to estimate the range of possible sale prices for footwear that is regularly priced at $70.

Solution

STEP 1 **Write** a system of inequalities. Let x be the regular footwear price and let y be the sale price. From the information in the ad, you can write the following four inequalities.

$x \geq 20$	**Regular price must be at least $20.**
$x \leq 80$	**Regular price can be at most $80.**
$y \geq 0.4x$	**Sale price is at least (100 − 60)% = 40% of regular price.**
$y \leq 0.9x$	**Sale price is at most (100 − 10)% = 90% of regular price.**

STEP 2 **Graph** each inequality in the system. Then identify the region that is common to all the graphs. It is the region that is shaded.

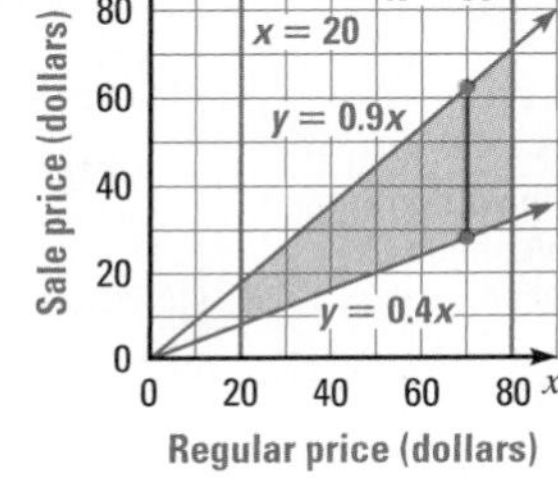

STEP 3 **Identify** the range of possible sale prices for $70 footwear. From the graph you can see that when $x = 70$, the value of y is between these values:

$$0.4(70) = 28 \text{ and } 0.9(70) = 63$$

So, the value of y satisfies $28 \leq y \leq 63$.

▶ Therefore, footwear regularly priced at $70 sells for between $28 and $63, inclusive, during the sale.

✓ **GUIDED PRACTICE** for Example 4

7. **WHAT IF?** In Example 4, suppose the advertisement showed a range of discounts of 20%–50% and a range of regular prices of $40–$100.
   a. Write and graph a system of inequalities for the regular footwear prices and possible sale prices. $x \geq 40$, $x \leq 100$, $y \geq 0.5x$, $y \leq 0.8x$; see margin for art.
   b. Use the graph to estimate the range of possible sale prices for footwear that is regularly priced at $60. $30 \leq y \leq 48$

Extra Example 3

Graph the system of inequalities.

$y < 2$; $y \geq |x - 1|$

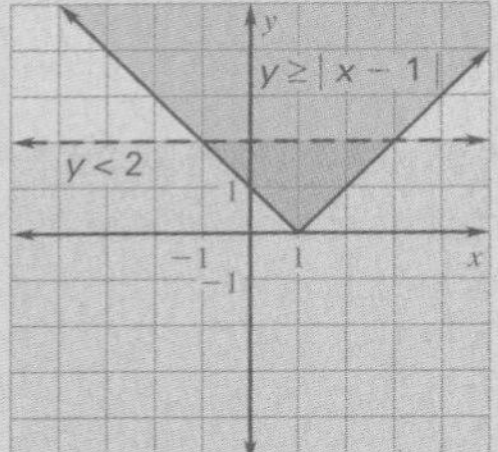

Key Question to Ask for Example 3

- Is the point (−4, 0) a solution to the system? Explain. No, (−4, 0) is not a solution to $y > |x + 4|$ so it is not a solution of the system.

Extra Example 4

Graph the system of inequalities.

$x \geq 10$; $x \leq 70$; $y \leq \frac{8}{7}x$; $y \geq \frac{2}{7}x$

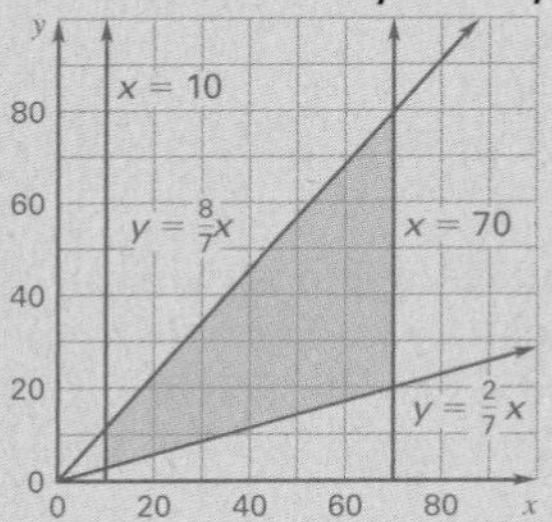

Avoiding Common Errors

In Example 4, students may find it difficult to relate the information in the ad to the system of inequalities. Ask them to write a verbal sentence for each item of information in the ad and then translate it into an inequality.

Closing the Lesson

Have students summarize the major points of the lesson and answer the Essential Question: How do you find the solution to a system of linear inequalities?

- To solve a system of linear inequalities, graph each inequality in the same coordinate plane.

The solution to a system of linear inequalities is found by graphing each inequality. The solution is the overlapping shaded region.

7a.

Sale prices (dollars)

Regular prices (dollars)

Differentiated Instruction

Advanced Inform students that the set-builder notation mentioned in the Differentiated Instruction note on page 43 in Chapter 1 can also be used to represent solutions of a system of inequalities. For example, the solution of the system in **Example 1** on page 168 can written as $\{(x, y) \mid y > -2x - 5 \text{ and } y \leq x + 3\}$. This is read "the set of all ordered pairs (x, y) such that y is greater than $-2x - 5$ and y less than or equal to $x + 3$."

See also the *Algebra 2 Toolkit* for more strategies.

3.3 EXERCISES

HOMEWORK KEY

○ = **WORKED-OUT SOLUTIONS** on p. WS5 for Exs. 9, 19, and 37

★ = **STANDARDIZED TEST PRACTICE** Exs. 2, 3, 26, 27, 36, and 39

◆ = **MULTIPLE REPRESENTATIONS** Ex. 37

SKILL PRACTICE

A

1. **VOCABULARY** What must be true in order for an ordered pair to be a solution of a system of linear inequalities? The ordered pair must satisfy each inequality of the system.

2. ★ **WRITING** *Describe* how to graph a system of linear inequalities. See margin.

EXAMPLES 1, 2, and 3 on pp. 168–169 for Exs. 3–16

. *Sample* *nswer:* Graph ach inequality n the same oordinate lane. The olution to the ystem is the egion of the lane where all he shadings verlap.

3. ★ **MULTIPLE CHOICE** Which system of inequalities is represented by the graph? D

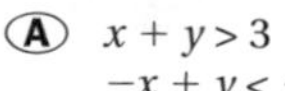

Ⓐ $x + y > 3$, $-x + y < -4$

Ⓑ $-x + y \geq -4$, $x + y \leq 3$

Ⓒ $-2x + y > -4$, $2x + y < 3$

Ⓓ $-x + y > -4$, $x + y < 3$

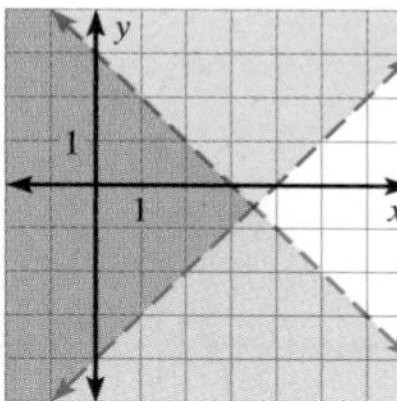

SYSTEMS OF TWO INEQUALITIES **Graph the system of inequalities.** 4–15. See margin.

4. $x > -1$, $x < 3$
5. $x \leq 2$, $y \leq 5$
6. $y \geq 5$, $y \leq 1$
7. $-x + y < -3$, $-x + y > 4$
8. $y < 10$, $y > |x|$
9. $4x - 4y \geq -16$, $-x + 2y \geq -4$
10. $-x \geq y$, $-x + y \geq -5$
11. $y > |x| - 4$, $3y < -2x + 9$
12. $x + y \geq -3$, $-6x + 4y < 14$
13. $2y < -5x - 10$, $5x + 2y > -2$
14. $3x - y > 12$, $-x + 8y > -4$
15. $x - 4y \leq -10$, $y \leq 3|x - 1|$

16. **ERROR ANALYSIS** *Describe* and correct the error in graphing the system of inequalities.

$$y \geq -3$$
$$y \leq 2x - 2$$

The shading of the second inequality is incorrect; see margin for art.

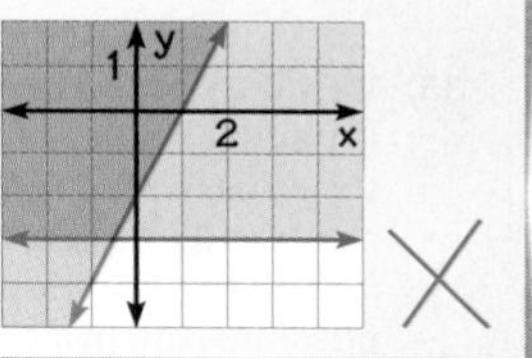

EXAMPLE 4 on p. 170 for Exs. 17–25

B

SYSTEMS OF THREE OR MORE INEQUALITIES **Graph the system of inequalities.** 17–25. See margin.

17. $x < 6$, $y > -1$, $y < x$
18. $x \geq -8$, $y \leq -1$, $y < -2x - 4$
19. $3x + 2y > -6$, $-5x + 2y > -2$, $y < 5$
20. $x + y < 5$, $2x - y > 0$, $-x + 5y > -20$
21. $x \geq 2$, $-3x + y < -1$, $4x + 3y < 12$
22. $y \geq x$, $x + 3y < 5$, $2x + y \geq -3$
23. $y \geq 0$, $x > 3$, $x + y \geq -2$, $y < 4x$
24. $x + y < 5$, $x + y > -5$, $x - y < 4$, $x - y > -2$
25. $x \leq 10$, $x \geq -2$, $3x + 2y < 6$, $6x + 4y > -12$

4 PRACTICE AND APPLY

Assignment Guide

Answer Transparencies available for all exercises

Basic:
Day 1: EP p. 1011 Exs. 39–42
pp. 171–173
Exs. 1–9, 16–22, 34–38, 41

Average:
Day 1: pp. 171–173
Exs. 1–3, 8–12, 16, 21–27, 29, 31, 34–39, 42

Advanced:
Day 1: pp. 171–173
Exs. 1–3, 12–15, 21–33*, 35–40*, 42

Block:
pp. 171–173
Exs. 1–3, 8–12, 16, 21–27, 29, 31, 34–39, 42 (with 3.4)

Differentiated Instruction

See *Algebra 2 Best Practices Toolkit* for suggestions on addressing the needs of a diverse classroom.

Homework Check

For a quick check of student understanding of key concepts, go over the following exercises:

Basic: 5, 7, 20, 34, 35
Average: 10, 12, 22, 36, 37
Advanced: 14, 15, 24, 38, 39

Extra Practice

- Student Edition, p. 1012
- Chapter 3 Resource Book: Practice levels A, B, C, pp. 35–40

Practice Worksheet

An easily-readable reduced practice page (with answers) for this lesson can be found on p. 150C.

4–15. See Additional Answers beginning on p. AA1.

16.

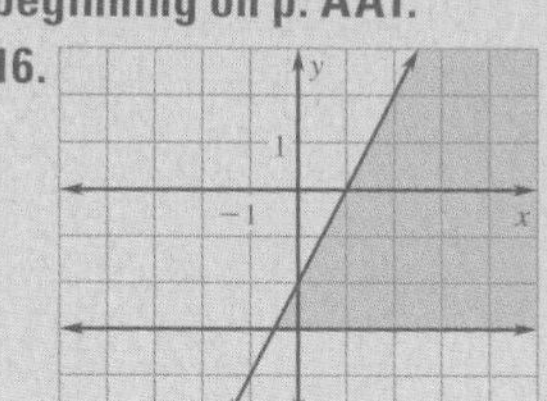

17–25. See Additional Answers beginning on p. AA1.

Avoiding Common Errors

Exercises 8, 11, 15, 28–30 Some students may have a problem graphing an absolute value inequality. Students should follow the same steps as for other inequalities: identify the boundary, decide whether the boundary is solid or dashed, and decide which side of the boundary to shade.

Mathematical Reasoning

Exercises 31–33 Remind students that many of the graphs in these exercises are vertical and horizontal line segments which can be represented by inequalities like $x \le a$, $x \ge b$, $y \le c$, or $y \ge d$.

Internet Reference

Exercise 39 To learn more about maximum heart rates, visit the American Heart Association's website at www.americanheart.org and do a search for "target heart rates."

28., 29., 30.

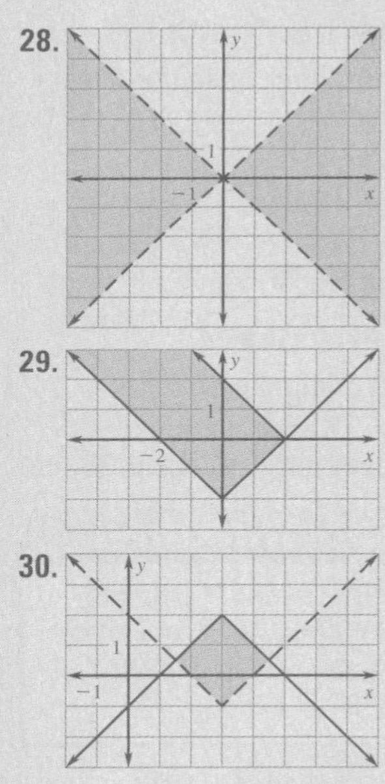

35.

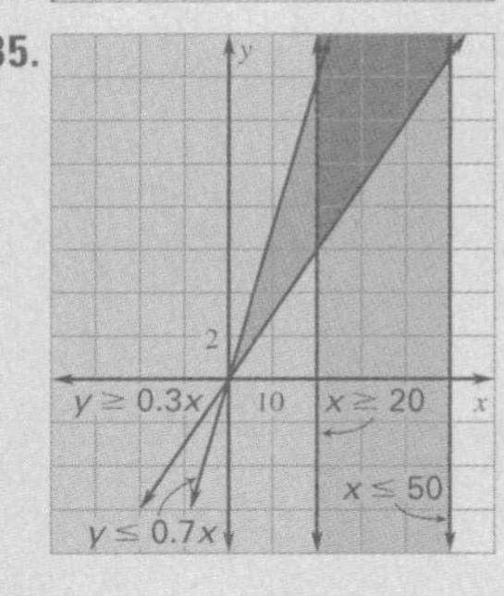

26. ★ **MULTIPLE CHOICE** Which quadrant of the coordinate plane contains no solutions of the system of inequalities? **B**

$$y \le -|x - 3| + 2$$
$$4x - 5y \le 20$$

Ⓐ Quadrant I Ⓑ Quadrant II Ⓒ Quadrant III Ⓓ Quadrant IV

27. ★ **OPEN-ENDED MATH** Write a system of two linear inequalities that has (2, −1) as a solution. ***Sample answer:*** $y < x - 1$, $y < -\frac{3}{4}x + 4$

C **ABSOLUTE VALUE SYSTEMS** **Graph the system of inequalities.** **28–30. See margin.**

28. $y < |x|$, $y > -|x|$

29. $y \le |x - 2|$, $y \ge |x| - 2$

30. $y \le -|x - 3| + 2$, $y > |x - 3| - 1$

CHALLENGE **Write a system of linear inequalities for the shaded region.**

32. $x \ge -2$, $x \le 2$, $y \ge -\frac{1}{2}x - 3$, $y \le \frac{1}{2}x + 3$

31.

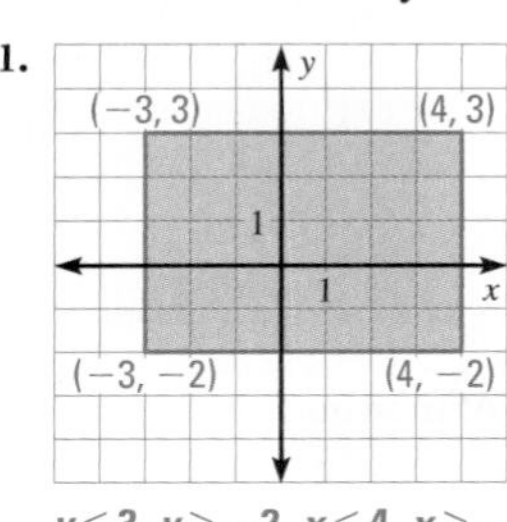

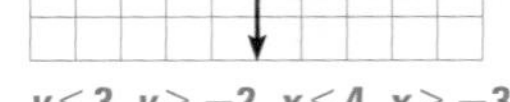

$y \le 3$, $y \ge -2$, $x \le 4$, $x \ge -3$

32.

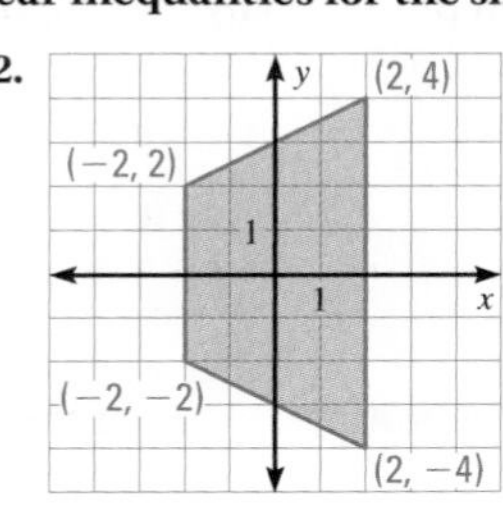

33.

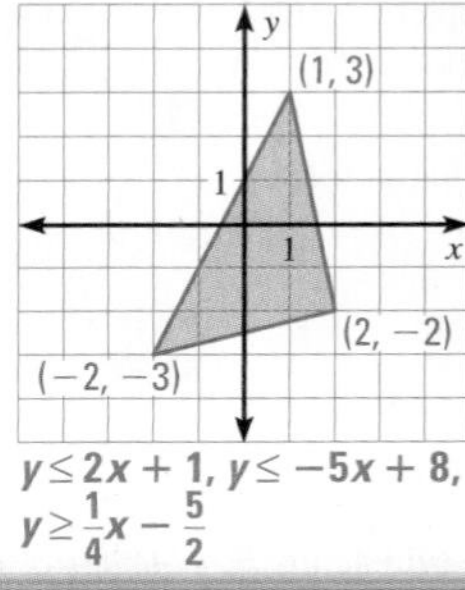

$y \le 2x + 1$, $y \le -5x + 8$, $y \ge \frac{1}{4}x - \frac{5}{2}$

PROBLEM SOLVING

EXAMPLE 4 A on p. 170 for Exs. 34–39

34. SUMMER JOBS You can work at most 20 hours next week. You need to earn at least \$92 to cover your weekly expenses. Your dog-walking job pays \$7.50 per hour and your job as a car wash attendant pays \$6 per hour. Write a system of linear inequalities to model the situation. **$7.5x + 6y \ge 92$, $x + y \le 20$, where x represents the dog walking job and y represents the car wash attendant job**

@HomeTutor for problem solving help at classzone.com

35. $x \ge 20$, $x \le 50$, $y \ge 0.3x$, $y \le 0.7x$, where x represents the regular price and y represents the sale price; see margin for art; $6 \le y \le 14$

35. VIDEO GAME SALE An online media store is having a sale, as described in the ad shown. Use the information in the ad to write and graph a system of inequalities for the regular video game prices and possible sale prices. Then use the graph to estimate the range of possible sale prices for games that are regularly priced at \$20.

@HomeTutor for problem solving help at classzone.com

36. ★ **SHORT RESPONSE** A book on the care of tropical fish states that the pH level of the water should be between 8.0 and 8.3 pH units and the temperature of the water should be between 76°F and 80°F. Let x be the pH level and y be the temperature. Write and graph a system of inequalities that describes the proper pH level and temperature of the water. *Compare* this graph to the graph you would obtain if the temperatures were given in degrees Celsius. **$x > 8.0$, $x < 8.3$, $y > 76°$, $y < 80°$, see margin for art; the graphs look the same, the axes are just incremented differently.**

○ = WORKED-OUT SOLUTIONS on p. WS1 ★ = STANDARDIZED TEST PRACTICE ◆ = MULTIPLE REPRESENTATIONS

36.

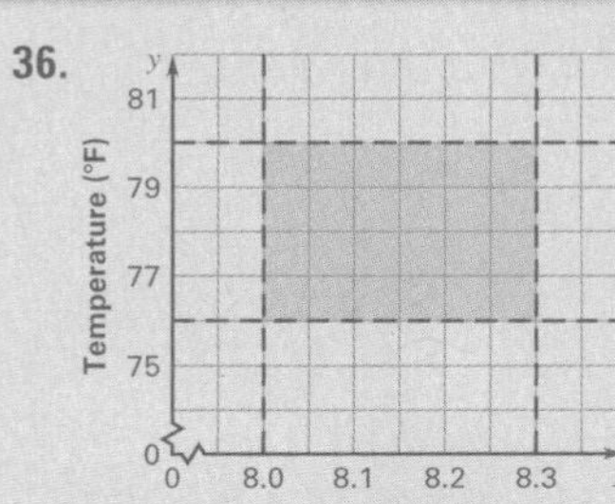

37b.

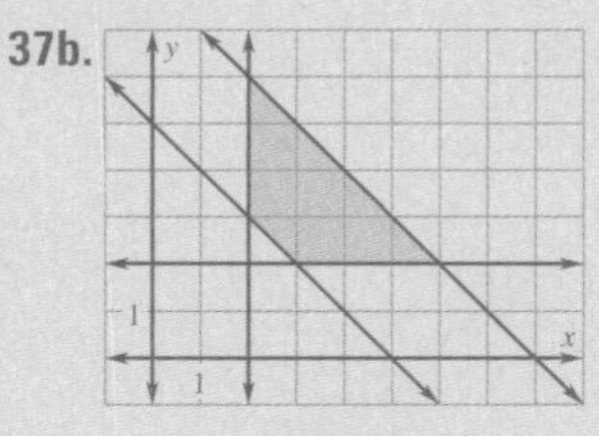

38.

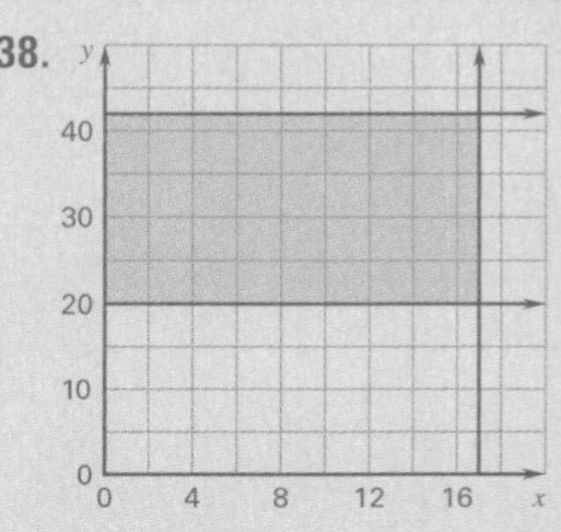

 (37.) ◆ **MULTIPLE REPRESENTATIONS** The Junior-Senior Prom Committee must consist of 5 to 8 representatives from the junior and senior classes. The committee must include at least 2 juniors and at least 2 seniors. Let x be the number of juniors and y be the number of seniors.

a. **Writing a System** Write a system of inequalities to describe the situation. $x \geq 2, y \geq 2, x + y \leq 8, x + y \geq 5$

b. **Graphing a System** Graph the system you wrote in part (a). See margin.

c. **Finding Solutions** Give two possible solutions for the numbers of juniors and seniors on the prom committee. 3 juniors, 4 seniors; 4 juniors, 4 seniors

B 38. **BASEBALL** In baseball, the strike zone is a rectangle the width of home plate that extends from the batter's knees to a point halfway between the shoulders S and the top T of the uniform pants. The width of home plate is 17 inches. Suppose a batter's knees are 20 inches above the ground and the point halfway between his shoulders and the top of his pants is 42 inches above the ground. Write and graph a system of inequalities that represents the strike zone. $y \geq 20, y \leq 42, x \geq 0, x \leq 17$, see margin for art.

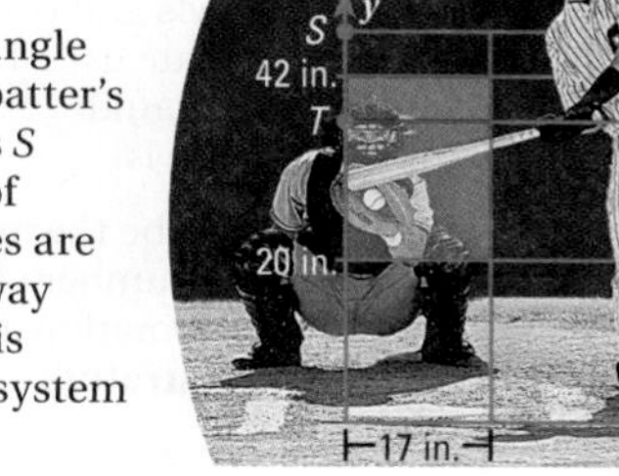

39. ★ **EXTENDED RESPONSE** A person's theoretical maximum heart rate (in heartbeats per minute) is $220 - x$ where x is the person's age in years $(20 \leq x \leq 65)$. When a person exercises, it is recommended that the person strive for a heart rate that is at least 50% of the maximum and at most 75% of the maximum. $x \geq 20, x \leq 65, y \geq 0.5(220 - x), y \leq 0.75(220 - x)$

a. Write a system of linear inequalities that describes the given information.

b. Graph the system you wrote in part (a). See margin.

c. A 40-year-old person has a heart rate of 158 heartbeats per minute when exercising. Is the person's heart rate in the target zone? *Explain.* See margin.

C 40. **CHALLENGE** You and a friend are trying to guess the number of pennies in a jar. You both agree that the jar contains at least 500 pennies. You guess that there are x pennies, and your friend guesses that there are y pennies. The actual number of pennies in the jar is 1000. Write and graph a system of inequalities describing the values of x and y for which your guess is closer than your friend's guess to the actual number of pennies. $500 \leq x, x \leq 1000, 500 \leq y, y \leq 1000, x \geq y + 1$, see margin for art.

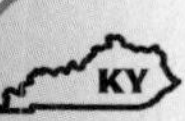

KENTUCKY MIXED REVIEW

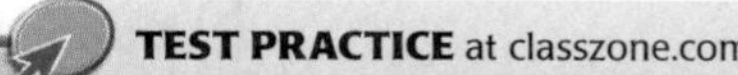

41. What is the value of x in the equation $-6(-2x + 1) = -12(x - 3) - 6x$? **C**

Ⓐ -7 Ⓑ $-\frac{7}{5}$ Ⓒ $\frac{7}{5}$ Ⓓ 7

42. Rick enlarges a 4 inch by 6 inch digital photo using his computer. The dimensions of the resulting photo are 175% of the dimensions of the original photo. What are the dimensions of the enlarged photo? **C**

Ⓐ 4.1 in. by 6.15 in. Ⓑ 5.3 in. by 8 in.

Ⓒ 7 in. by 10.5 in. Ⓓ 11 in. by 16.5 in.

5 ASSESS AND RETEACH

Daily Homework Quiz

Transparency Available

Graph the system of inequalities.

1. $y > -x - 4$; $y \leq 2x + 2$

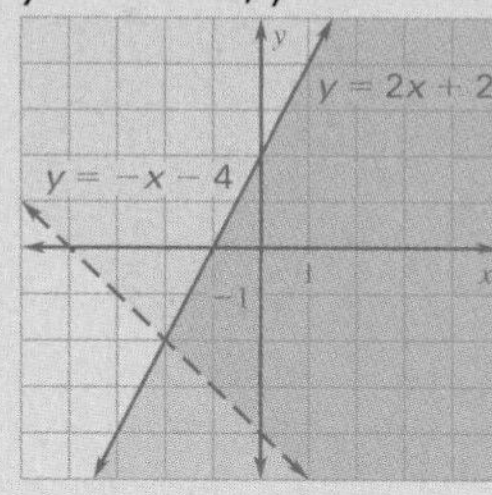

2. $2x - 4y \leq 8$; $y < -\frac{1}{3}x + 4$

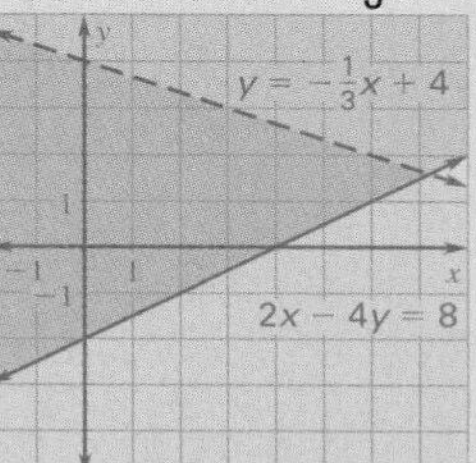

3. $y > |x + 2|$; $y \leq 4$; $x \leq -1$

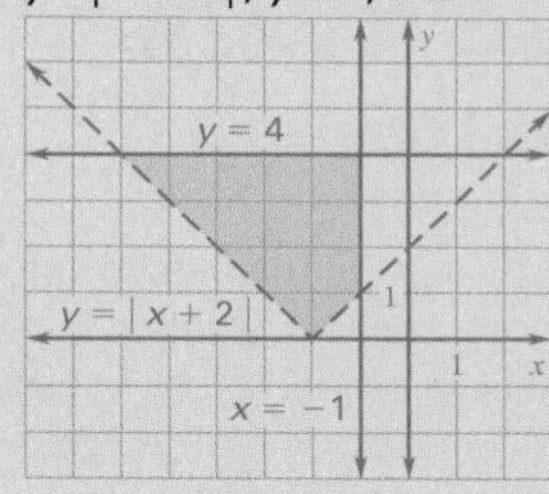

Available at **classzone.com**

Diagnosis/Remediation

- Practice A, B, C in Chapter 3 Resource Book, pp. 35–40
- Study Guide in Chapter 3 Resource Book, pp. 41–42
- Practice Workbook, pp. 41–43
- @HomeTutor

Challenge

Additional challenge is available in the Chapter 3 Resource Book, p. 45.

39b–c, 40. See Additional Answers beginning on p. AA1.

1 PLAN AND PREPARE

Warm-Up Exercises

Graph the system of inequalities.

1. $y \geq -2$; $x \leq 0$

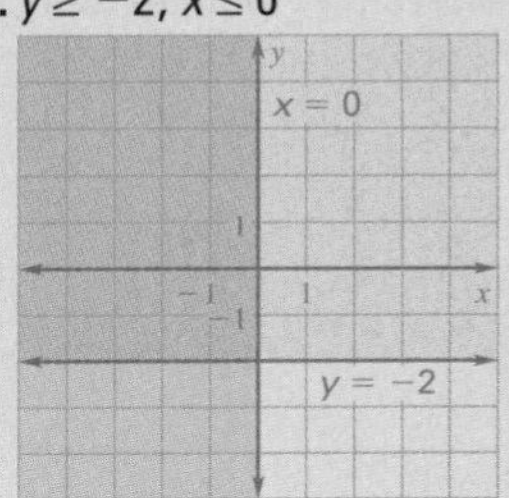

2. $y \leq 2x + 3$; $y \geq 0$; $x \geq 0$

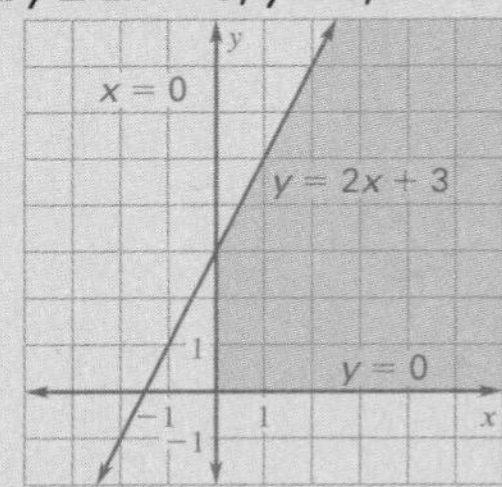

2 FOCUS AND MOTIVATE

Essential Question

Big Idea 2, p. 151

How do you use inequalities to solve a linear programming problem?

Tell students they will learn how to answer this question by graphing the inequalities and finding the vertices of the common region.

NCTM STANDARDS

Standard 2: Use models to represent relationships

Standard 9: Grasp how mathematical ideas interconnect

Extension Use Linear Programming

Use after Lesson 3.3

GOAL Solve linear programming problems.

Key Vocabulary
- **constraints**
- **objective function**
- **linear programming**
- **feasible region**

BUSINESS A potter wants to make and sell serving bowls and plates. A bowl uses 5 pounds of clay. A plate uses 4 pounds of clay. The potter has 40 pounds of clay and wants to make at least 4 bowls.

Let x be the number of bowls made and let y be the number of plates made. You can represent the information above using linear inequalities called **constraints**.

$x \geq 4$	**Make at least 4 bowls.**
$y \geq 0$	**Number of plates cannot be negative.**
$5x + 4y \leq 40$	**Can use up to 40 pounds of clay.**

The profit on a bowl is \$35 and the profit on a plate is \$30. The potter's total profit P is given by the equation below, called the **objective function**.

$$P = 35x + 30y$$

It is reasonable for the potter to want to maximize profit subject to the given constraints. The process of maximizing or minimizing a linear objective function subject to constraints that are linear inequalities is called **linear programming**.

If the constraints are graphed, all of the points in the intersection are the combinations of bowls and plates that the potter can make. The intersection of the graphs is called the **feasible region**.

The following result tells you how to determine the optimal solution of a linear programming problem.

READING
A feasible region is *bounded* if it is completely enclosed by line segments.

KEY CONCEPT *For Your Notebook*

Optimal Solution of a Linear Programming Problem

If the feasible region for a linear programming problem is bounded, then the objective function has both a maximum value and a minimum value on the region. Moreover, the maximum and minimum values each occur at a vertex of the feasible region.

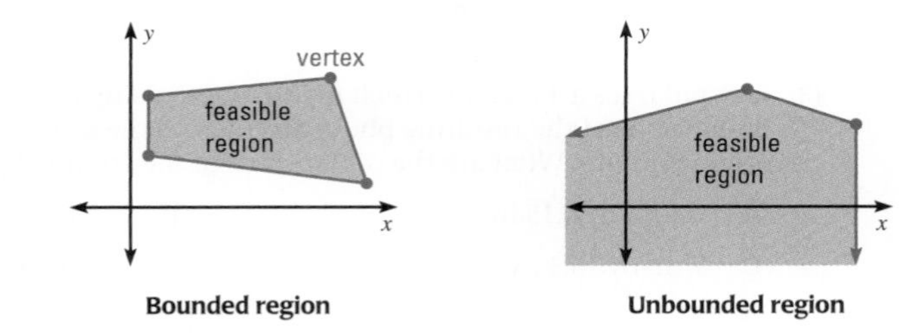

EXAMPLE 1 Use linear programming to maximize profit

BUSINESS How many bowls and how many plates should the potter described on page 174 make in order to maximize profit?

Solution

STEP 1 **Graph** the system of constraints:

$x \geq 4$	**Make at least 4 bowls.**
$y \geq 0$	**Number of plates cannot be negative.**
$5x + 4y \leq 40$	**Can use up to 40 pounds of clay.**

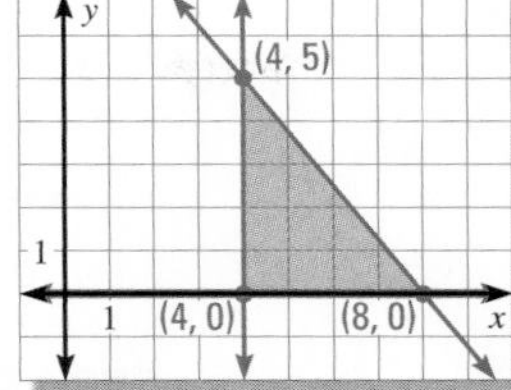

STEP 2 **Evaluate** the profit function $P = 35x + 30y$ at each vertex of the feasible region.

At (4, 0): $P = 35(4) + 30(0) = 140$
At (8, 0): $P = 35(8) + 30(0) = 280$
At (4, 5): $P = 35(4) + 30(5) = 290$ ⟵ **Maximum**

▶ The potter can maximize profit by making 4 bowls and 5 plates.

EXAMPLE 2 Solve a linear programming problem

Find the minimum value and the maximum value of the objective function $C = 4x + 5y$ subject to the following constraints.

$x \geq 0$

$y \geq 0$

$x + 2y \leq 16$

$5x + y \leq 35$

Solution

STEP 1 **Graph** the system of constraints. Find the coordinates of the vertices of the feasible region by solving systems of two linear equations. For example, the solution of the system

$$x + 2y = 16$$
$$5x + y = 35$$

gives the vertex (6, 5). The other three vertices are (0, 0), (7, 0), and (0, 8).

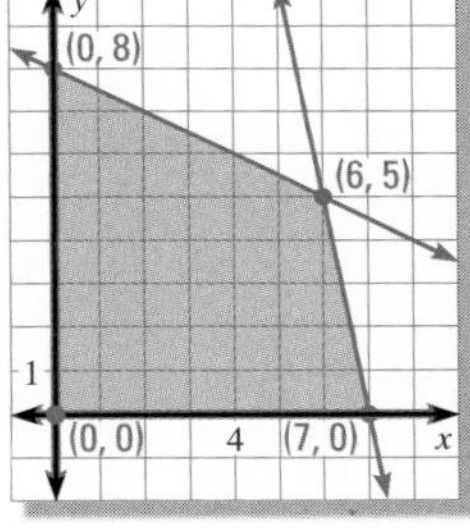

STEP 2 **Evaluate** the function $C = 4x + 5y$ at each of the vertices.

At (0, 0): $C = 4(0) + 5(0) = 0$ ⟵ **Minimum**
At (7, 0): $C = 4(7) + 5(0) = 28$
At (6, 5): $C = 4(6) + 5(5) = 49$ ⟵ **Maximum**
At (0, 8): $C = 4(0) + 5(8) = 40$

▶ The minimum value of C is 0. It occurs when $x = 0$ and $y = 0$. The maximum value of C is 49. It occurs when $x = 6$ and $y = 5$.

3 TEACH

Extra Example 1

The constraints below represent information related to a printing business where x is the number of graphic arts jobs and y is the number of printing jobs. Graph the system and evaluate the profit function $P = 20x + 40y$ at each vertex.
$x \geq 3$; $y \geq 0$; $4x + 6y \leq 24$

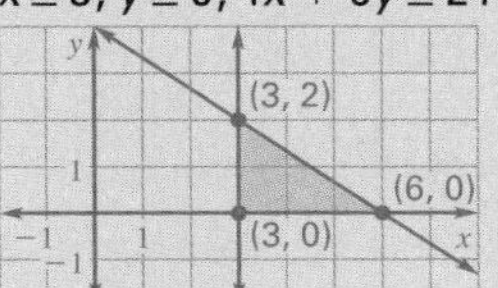

At (3, 0), $P = 60$; at (3, 2), $P = 140$; at (6, 0), $P = 120$. The printing business can maximize profit with 3 graphic arts jobs and 2 printing jobs.

Extra Example 2

Find the minimum and the maximum value of the objective function $C = 3x + 4y$ subject to the following constraints.
$x \geq 0$, $y \geq 0$, $x - 3y \geq -12$, $3x + y \leq 24$

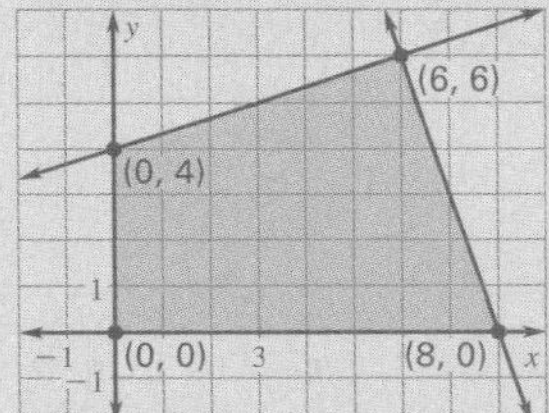

The minimum value $C = 0$ occurs at (0, 0); the maximum $C = 42$ occurs at (6, 6).

Key Question to Ask for Example 2

- How do you find the vertices of the feasible region? **You graph the inequalities and find the intersections of pairs of boundary lines.**

Closing the Lesson

Have students summarize the major points of the lesson and answer the Essential Question: How do you use inequalities to solve a linear programming problem?

- Linear programming problems can be solved by using the vertices of the feasible region given by graphing the problem's constraints.

You graph the inequalities, find the intersection of the graphs, and find the vertices of the feasible region. You evaluate the objective function at each vertex of the feasible region.

4 PRACTICE AND APPLY

Graphing Calculator

Exercises 7–9 Encourage students to graph the boundaries for the constraints and use the intersect feature of their graphing calculator to find the vertices of the feasible region.

10a.

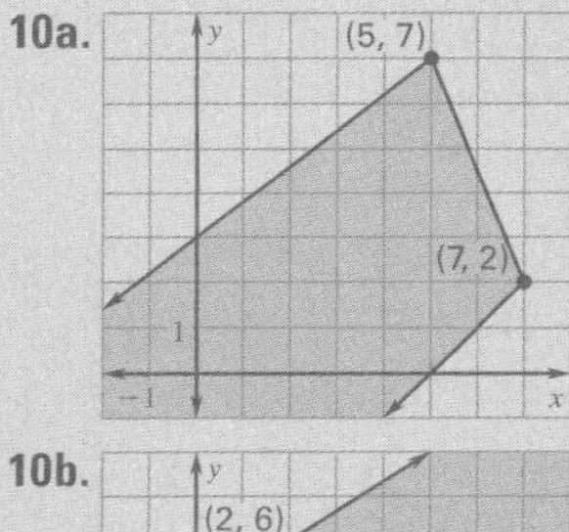

10b.

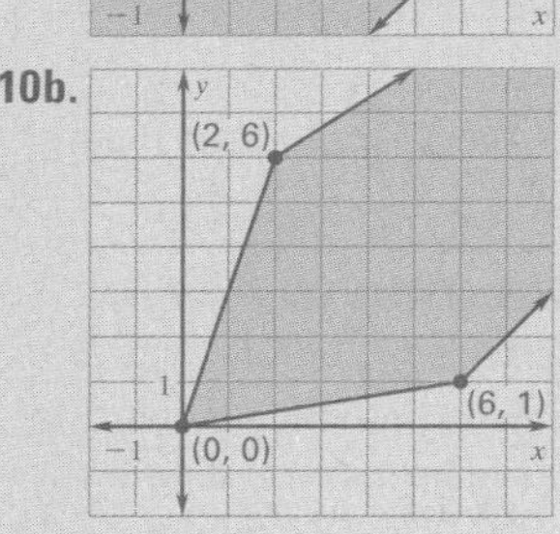

p. 177

1.

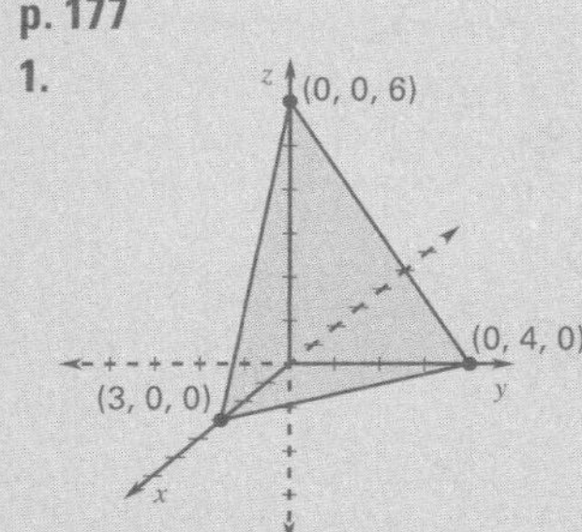

PRACTICE

EXAMPLES 1 and 2 on p. 175 for Exs. 1–9

CHECKING VERTICES Find the minimum and maximum values of the objective function for the given feasible region.

1. $C = x + 2y$

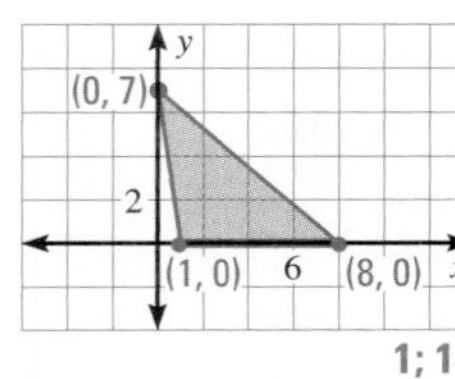

1; 14

2. $C = 4x - 2y$

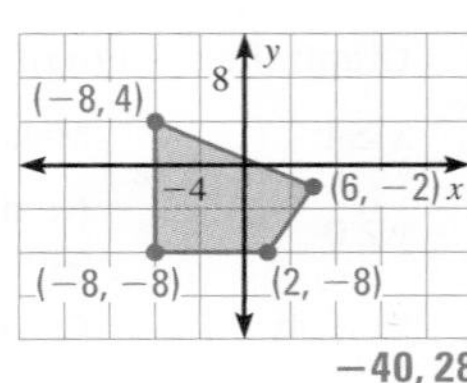

−40, 28

3. $C = 3x + 5y$

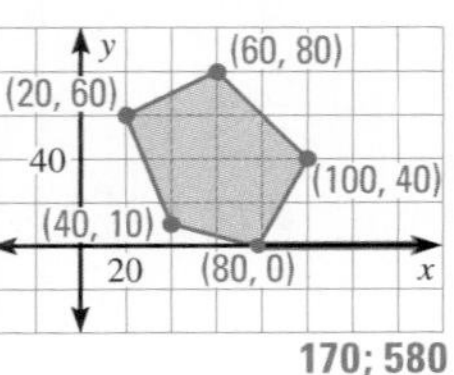

170; 580

FINDING VALUES Find the minimum and maximum values of the objective function subject to the given constraints.

4. **Objective function:**
$C = 3x + 4y$

Constraints:
$x \geq 0$
$y \geq 0$
$x + y \leq 5$ 0; 20

5. **Objective function:**
$C = 2x + 5y$

Constraints:
$x \leq 5$
$y \geq 3$
$-3x + 5y \leq 30$ 5; 55

6. **Objective function:**
$C = 3x + y$

Constraints:
$x \geq 0$
$y \geq -2$
$y \geq -x$
$x - 4y \geq -16$ 0; no maximum

7. **CRAFT FAIR** Piñatas are made to sell at a craft fair. It takes 2 hours to make a mini piñata and 3 hours to make a regular-sized piñata. The owner of the craft booth will make a profit of \$12 for each mini piñata sold and \$24 for each regular-sized piñata sold. If the craft booth owner has no more than 30 hours available to make piñatas and wants to have at least 12 piñatas to sell, how many of each size piñata should be made to maximize profit?
6 mini piñatas, 6 regular-sized piñatas

8. **MANUFACTURING** A company manufactures two types of printers, an inkjet printer and a laser printer. The company can make a total of 60 printers per day, and it has 120 labor-hours per day available. It takes 1 labor-hour to make an inkjet printer and 3 labor-hours to make a laser printer. The profit is \$40 per inkjet printer and \$60 per laser printer. How many of each type of printer should the company make to maximize its daily profit?
30 inkjet printers, 30 laser printers

9. **FARM STAND SALES** You have 140 tomatoes and 13 onions left over from your garden. You want to use these to make jars of tomato sauce and jars of salsa to sell at a farm stand. A jar of tomato sauce requires 10 tomatoes and 1 onion, and a jar of salsa requires 5 tomatoes and $\frac{1}{4}$ onion. You will make a profit of \$2 on every jar of tomato sauce sold and a profit of \$1.50 on every jar of salsa sold. The owner of the farm stand wants at least three times as many jars of tomato sauce as jars of salsa. How many jars of each should you make to maximize profit? 12 jars of tomato sauce, 4 jars of salsa

10. **CHALLENGE** Consider the objective function $C = 2x + 3y$. Draw a feasible region that satisfies the given condition. a, b. See margin.

    a. C has a maximum value but no minimum value on the region.

    b. C has a minimum value but no maximum value on the region.

p. 177

2.

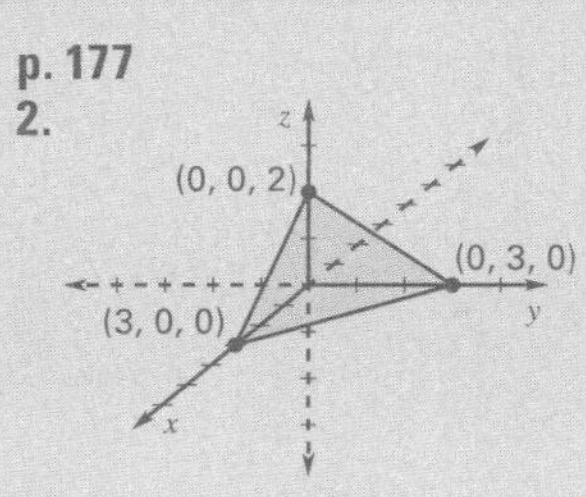

3.

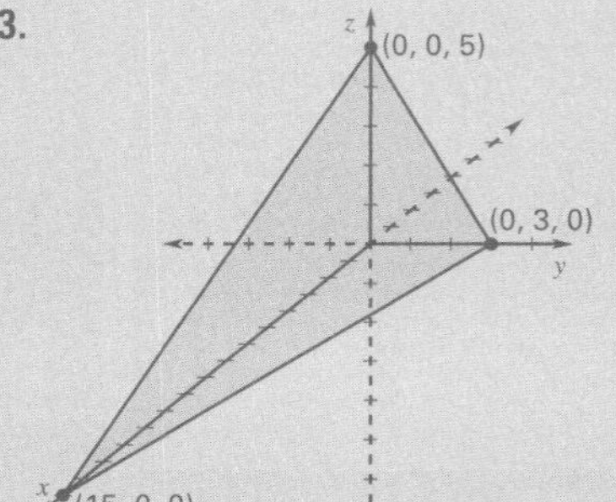

4.

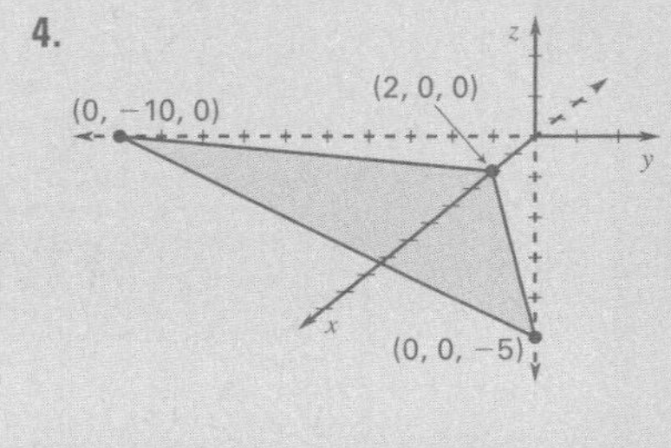

3.4 Graphing Linear Equations in Three Variables

MATERIALS • graph paper • ruler

QUESTION **What is the graph of a linear equation in three variables?**

A *linear equation in three variables* has the form $ax + by + cz = d$. You can graph this type of equation in a three-dimensional coordinate system formed by three axes that divide space into eight *octants*. Each point in space is represented by an *ordered triple* (x, y, z).

The graph of any equation in three variables is the set of all points (x, y, z) whose coordinates make the equation true. For a linear equation in three variables, the graph is a plane.

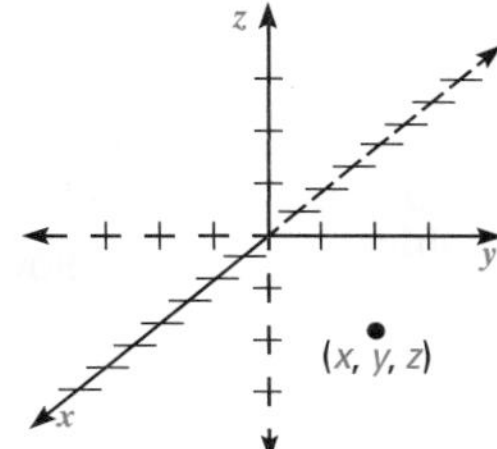

EXPLORE **Graph 3x + 4y + 6z = 12**

STEP 1 ***Find x-intercept***
Find the x-intercept by setting y and z equal to 0 and solving the resulting equation, $3x = 12$. The x-intercept is 4, so plot (4, 0, 0).

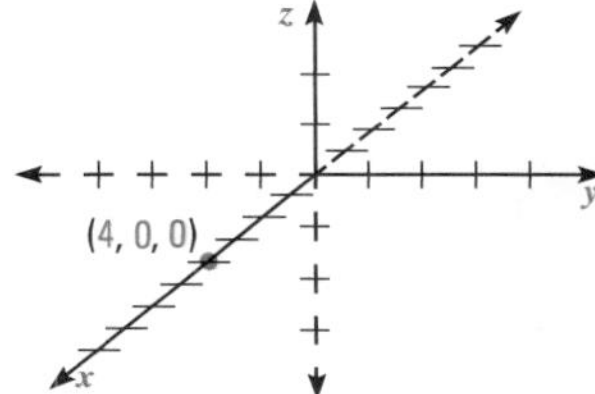

STEP 2 ***Find y-intercept***
Find the y-intercept by setting x and z equal to 0 and solving the resulting equation, $4y = 12$. The y-intercept is 3, so plot (0, 3, 0).

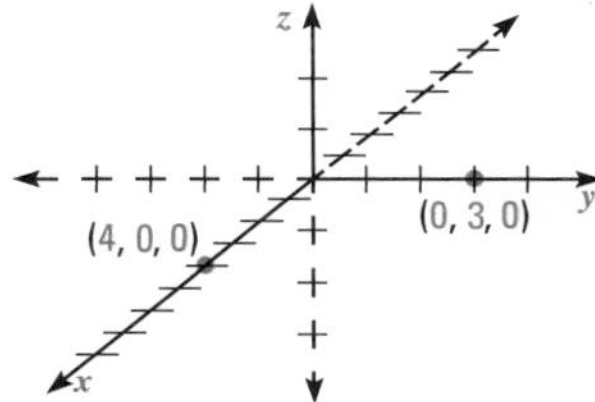

STEP 3 ***Find z-intercept***
Find the z-intercept by setting x and y equal to 0 and solving the resulting equation, $6z = 12$. The z-intercept is 2, so plot (0, 0, 2). Then connect the points.

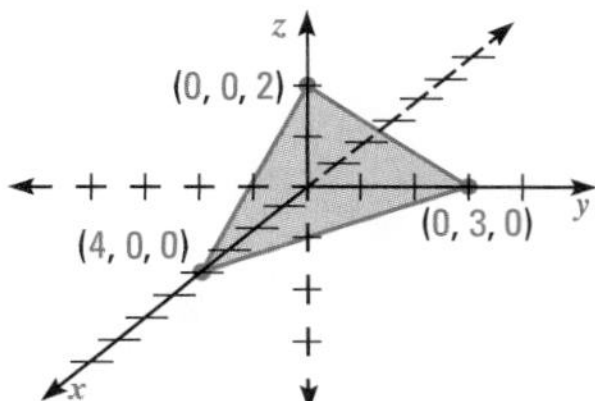

The triangular region shown in Step 3 is the portion of the graph of $3x + 4y + 6z = 12$ that lies in the first octant.

DRAW CONCLUSIONS **Use your observations to complete these exercises**

Sketch the graph of the equation. 1–6. See margin.

1. $4x + 3y + 2z = 12$
2. $2x + 2y + 3z = 6$
3. $x + 5y + 3z = 15$
4. $5x - y - 2z = 10$
5. $-7x + 7y + 2z = 14$
6. $2x + 9y - 3z = -18$
7. Suppose three linear equations in three variables are graphed in the same coordinate system. In how many different ways can the planes intersect? *Explain* your reasoning. See margin.

5.
(0, 0, 7)
(−2, 0, 0)
(0, 2, 0)

6.

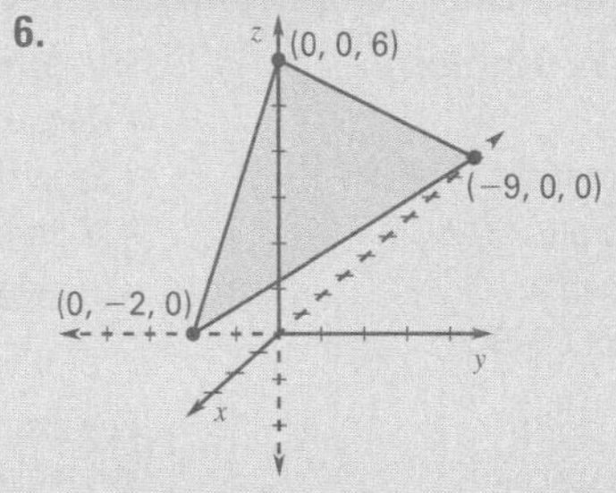

7. 3; the planes can meet at one point therefore having one solution. The planes can be the same or intersect at a line having infinitely many solutions. The planes can have nothing in common and therefore have no solution.

1 PLAN AND PREPARE

Explore the Concept

- Students will graph a linear equation in three variables.
- This activity leads into the study of solving a system of linear equations in three variables in Lesson 3.4, Example 1.

Materials

Each student will need:

- graph paper
- ruler
- Activity Support Master (*Chapter 3 Resource Book*, p. 48)

Recommended Time

Work activity: 10 min
Discuss results: 5 min

Grouping

Students should work individually.

2 TEACH

Tips for Success

Use a model of the 3-dimensional coordinate system to help students see how to graph the point (x, y, z).

Key Question

- What does a linear equation in three variables represent geometrically? **A linear equation of the form $ax + by + cz = d$ represents a plane.**

Alternative Strategy

Ask students to create a 3-dimensional model using straws. Label the straws and use string to represent the triangle determined by the plane's three intercepts.

Key Discovery

The graph of a linear equation in three variables is a plane.

3 ASSESS AND RETEACH

What equation do you solve to find the z-intercept of $2x + 4y + 3z = 12$? Find all three intercepts. **To find the z-intercept, set $x = 0$ and $y = 0$, getting $3z = 12$; (6, 0, 0), (0, 3, 0), (0, 0, 4).**

1 PLAN AND PREPARE

Warm-Up Exercises

Transparency Available

1. Solve by substitution: $x + 2y = -1$; $3x - y = 18$. $(5, -3)$
2. Solve by elimination: $3x + 4y = -25$; $3x - 2y = -1$. $(-3, -4)$
3. At a local store, 4 rolls of film and 2 batteries cost \$20.70. At another store, 6 rolls of film and 1 battery cost \$30.15. What is the price of one roll of film? \$4.95

Notetaking Guide

Transparency Available

Promotes interactive learning and notetaking skills, pp. 68–71.

Pacing

Basic: 1 day

Average: 1 day

Advanced: 1 day

Block: 0.5 block with 3.3

• See *Teaching Guide/Lesson Plan.*

2 FOCUS AND MOTIVATE

Essential Question

Big Idea 1, p. 151

How do you solve a system of linear equations in three variables? **Tell students they will learn how to answer this question by using the elimination method or the substitution method.**

3.4 Solve Systems of Linear Equations in Three Variables

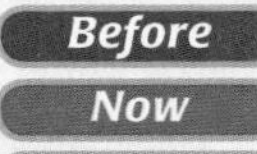

Before You solved systems of equations in two variables.

Now You will solve systems of equations in three variables.

Why? So you can model the results of a sporting event, as in Ex. 45.

Key Vocabulary
- linear equation in three variables
- system of three linear equations
- solution of a system of three linear equations
- ordered triple

A **linear equation in three variables** x, y, and z is an equation of the form $ax + by + cz = d$ where a, b, and c are not all zero.

The following is an example of a **system of three linear equations** in three variables.

$$2x + y - z = 5 \quad \text{Equation 1}$$
$$3x - 2y + z = 16 \quad \text{Equation 2}$$
$$4x + 3y - 5z = 3 \quad \text{Equation 3}$$

A **solution** of such a system is an **ordered triple** (x, y, z) whose coordinates make each equation true.

The graph of a linear equation in three variables is a plane in three-dimensional space. The graphs of three such equations that form a system are three planes whose intersection determines the number of solutions of the system, as shown in the diagrams below.

Exactly one solution

The planes intersect in a single point.

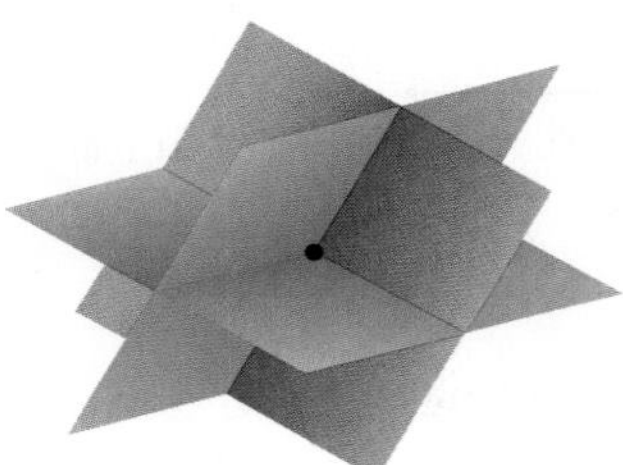

Infinitely many solutions

The planes intersect in a line or are the same plane.

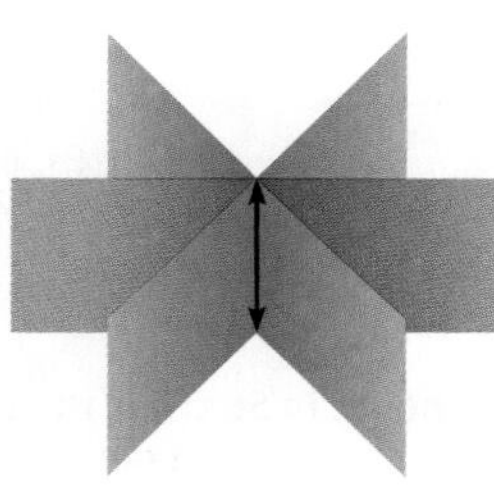

No solution

The planes have no common point of intersection.

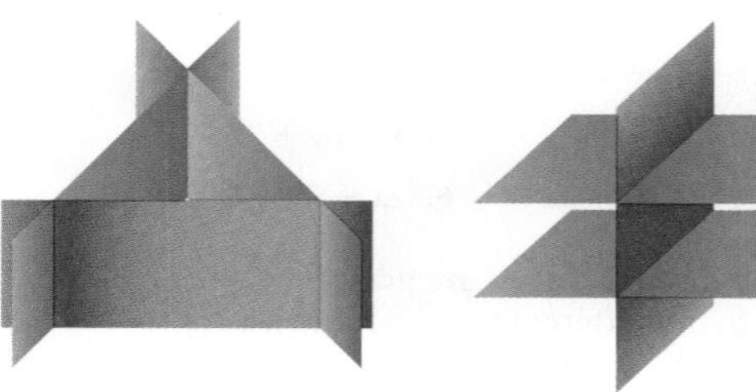

Resource Planning Guide

Chapter Resource Book
- Teaching Guide/Lesson Plan (pp. 46–47)
- Practice levels A, B, C (pp. 49–51)
- Study Guide (pp. 52–53)
- Catch-up for Absent Students (p. 54)
- Problem Solving Workshop (p. 55)
- Challenge (p. 57)

Workbooks
- Notetaking Guide (pp. 68–71)
- Practice Workbook (pp. 44–45)

Teaching Options
- **Power Presentations CD-ROM** provides dynamic electronic teaching resources for the classroom.
- **Activity Generator CD-ROM** provides editable activities for all ability levels.

Interactive Technology
- Easy Planner
- Power Presentations CD-ROM
- Activity Generator CD-ROM
- Animated Algebra
- Test Generator CD-ROM
- Online Quiz
- eWorkbook
- eEdition
- @HomeTutor

Resources for English Learners
- Quick Reference for English Learners
- Spanish Study Guide
- Multi-Language Visual Glossary
- Student Resources in Spanish

See also the *Algebra 2 Toolkit* for more strategies for meeting individual needs.

ELIMINATION METHOD The elimination method you studied in Lesson 3.2 can be extended to solve a system of linear equations in three variables.

KEY CONCEPT *For Your Notebook*

The Elimination Method for a Three-Variable System

STEP 1 **Rewrite** the linear system in three variables as a linear system in two variables by using the elimination method.

STEP 2 **Solve** the new linear system for both of its variables.

STEP 3 **Substitute** the values found in Step 2 into one of the original equations and solve for the remaining variable.

If you obtain a false equation, such as $0 = 1$, in any of the steps, then the system has no solution.

If you do not obtain a false equation, but obtain an identity such as $0 = 0$, then the system has infinitely many solutions.

EXAMPLE 1 Use the elimination method

Solve the system.

$4x + 2y + 3z = 1$ **Equation 1**

$2x - 3y + 5z = -14$ **Equation 2**

$6x - y + 4z = -1$ **Equation 3**

ANOTHER WAY

In Step 1, you could also eliminate x to get two equations in y and z, or you could eliminate z to get two equations in x and y.

Solution

STEP 1 **Rewrite** the system as a linear system in *two* variables.

$4x + 2y + 3z = 1$ **Add 2 times Equation 3**
$12x - 2y + 8z = -2$ **to Equation 1.**

$16x + 11z = -1$ **New Equation 1**

$2x - 3y + 5z = -14$ **Add −3 times Equation 3**
$-18x + 3y - 12z = 3$ **to Equation 2.**

$-16x - 7z = -11$ **New Equation 2**

STEP 2 **Solve** the new linear system for both of its variables.

$16x + 11z = -1$ **Add new Equation 1**
$-16x - 7z = -11$ **and new Equation 2.**

$4z = -12$

$z = -3$ **Solve for z.**

$x = 2$ **Substitute into new Equation 1 or 2 to find x.**

STEP 3 **Substitute** $x = 2$ and $z = -3$ into an original equation and solve for y.

$6x - y + 4z = -1$ **Write original Equation 3.**

$6(2) - y + 4(-3) = -1$ **Substitute 2 for x and −3 for z.**

$y = 1$ **Solve for y.**

▶ The solution is $x = 2$, $y = 1$, and $z = -3$, or the ordered triple $(2, 1, -3)$. Check this solution in each of the original equations.

Motivating the Lesson

Have students draw a coordinate plane on a sheet of paper, then insert a pencil at the origin. Explain that they have now created a three coordinate system and will learn how to solve systems of three equations in three variables.

3 TEACH

Extra Example 1

Solve the system.
$2x - y + 6z = -4$
$6x + 4y - 5z = -7$
$-4x - 2y + 5z = 9$ $(-3, 4, 1)$

Avoiding Common Errors

Focus students' attention on Step 1 of Example 1. Stress that the same variable must be eliminated from the second pair of equations as was eliminated from the first pair.

Reading Strategy

Point out that the solution to a linear system in three variables is an ordered *triple*, not an ordered *pair*. Students tend to read, write, and say pair, rather than triple, because they have had so much previous experience with ordered pairs.

Mathematical Reasoning

In Example 1, notice that the y-variable was eliminated Step 1. You could choose to eliminate any variable first. For example, if you eliminated the x-variable, you would get two equations in y and z.

Differentiated Instruction

Below Level Give students extra practice plotting ordered triples of points to help them visualize points in space. Demonstrate how to plot the point that is the solution to Example 1, along with points in each of the octants, including $(3, 5, -2)$ in octant 4, $(-2, 2, -2)$ in octant 8, and $(5, -3, 1)$ in octant 2.

See also the *Algebra 2 Toolkit* for more strategies.

Extra Example 2

Solve the system.

$x + y - z = 2$
$3x + 3y - 3z = 8$
$2x - y + 4z = 7$ **no solution**

Key Question to Ask for Example 2

- What does "no solution" mean graphically? **The three planes have no point(s) in common.**

Extra Example 3

Solve the system.

$x + y + z = 6$
$x - y + z = 6$
$4x + y + 4z = 24$ **infinitely many solutions**

Key Question to Ask for Example 3

- How does the equation obtained in Example 3 differ from the equation obtained in Example 2? **While neither equation has a variable, the equation in Example 3 is a true statement, whereas the equation in Example 2 is a false statement.**

EXAMPLE 2 Solve a three-variable system with no solution

Solve the system.

$x + y + z = 3$	Equation 1
$4x + 4y + 4z = 7$	Equation 2
$3x - y + 2z = 5$	Equation 3

REVIEW SYSTEMS
For help with solving linear systems with many solutions or no solution, see p. 160.

Solution

When you multiply Equation 1 by -4 and add the result to Equation 2, you obtain a false equation.

$-4x - 4y - 4z = -12$	Add -4 times Equation 1
$4x + 4y + 4z = 7$	to Equation 2.
$0 = -5$	New Equation 1

▶ Because you obtain a false equation, you can conclude that the original system has no solution.

EXAMPLE 3 Solve a three-variable system with many solutions

Solve the system.

$x + y + z = 4$	Equation 1
$x + y - z = 4$	Equation 2
$3x + 3y + z = 12$	Equation 3

Solution

STEP 1 **Rewrite** the system as a linear system in *two* variables.

$x + y + z = 4$	Add Equation 1
$x + y - z = 4$	to Equation 2.
$2x + 2y = 8$	New Equation 1
$x + y - z = 4$	Add Equation 2
$3x + 3y + z = 12$	to Equation 3.
$4x + 4y = 16$	New Equation 2

STEP 2 **Solve** the new linear system for both of its variables.

$-4x - 4y = -16$	Add -2 times new Equation 1
$4x + 4y = 16$	to new Equation 2.
$0 = 0$	

Because you obtain the identity $0 = 0$, the system has infinitely many solutions.

STEP 3 **Describe** the solutions of the system. One way to do this is to divide new Equation 1 by 2 to get $x + y = 4$, or $y = -x + 4$. Substituting this into original Equation 1 produces $z = 0$. So, any ordered triple of the form $(x, -x + 4, 0)$ is a solution of the system.

GUIDED PRACTICE for Examples 1, 2, and 3

Solve the system.

1. $3x + y - 2z = 10$
   $6x - 2y + z = -2$
   $x + 4y + 3z = 7$ **(1, 3, −2)**

2. $x + y - z = 2$
   $2x + 2y - 2z = 6$
   $5x + y - 3z = 8$
   no solution

3. $x + y + z = 3$
   $x + y - z = 3$
   $2x + 2y + z = 6$
   infinitely many solutions

Differentiated Instruction

Visual Learners For the benefit of students who process information visually, rewrite or replace the variables *x*, *y*, and *z* in the equations with colors and/or shapes. Students will be better able to follow the flow of the solution if the variables are written in colored chalk or ink. Also, suggest replacing variables with various shapes (for example, *x* with a triangle, *y* with a square, *z* with a circle) and showing that the solution is still correct.

See also the *Algebra 2 Toolkit* for more strategies.

EXAMPLE 4 Solve a system using substitution

MARKETING The marketing department of a company has a budget of \$30,000 for advertising. A television ad costs \$1000, a radio ad costs \$200, and a newspaper ad costs \$500. The department wants to run 60 ads per month and have as many radio ads as television and newspaper ads combined. How many of each type of ad should the department run each month?

Solution

STEP 1 **Write** verbal models for the situation.

TV ads + Radio ads + Newspaper ads = Total ads — **Equation 1**

1000 · TV ads + 200 · Radio ads + 500 · Newspaper ads = Monthly budget — **Equation 2**

Radio ads = TV ads + Newspaper ads — **Equation 3**

STEP 2 **Write** a system of equations. Let x be the number of TV ads, y be the number of radio ads, and z be the number of newspaper ads.

$x + y + z = 60$ **Equation 1**

$1000x + 200y + 500z = 30{,}000$ **Equation 2**

$y = x + z$ **Equation 3**

STEP 3 **Rewrite** the system in Step 2 as a linear system in *two* variables by substituting $x + z$ for y in Equations 1 and 2.

$x + y + z = 60$ **Write Equation 1.**

$x + (x + z) + z = 60$ **Substitute $x + z$ for y.**

$2x + 2z = 60$ **New Equation 1**

$1000x + 200y + 500z = 30{,}000$ **Write Equation 2.**

$1000x + 200(x + z) + 500z = 30{,}000$ **Substitute $x + z$ for y.**

$1200x + 700z = 30{,}000$ **New Equation 2**

STEP 4 **Solve** the linear system in two variables from Step 3.

$-1200x - 1200z = -36{,}000$ **Add −600 times new Equation 1**

$1200x + 700z = 30{,}000$ **to new Equation 2.**

$-500z = -6000$

$z = 12$ **Solve for z.**

$x = 18$ **Substitute into new Equation 1 or 2 to find x.**

$y = 30$ **Substitute into an original equation to find y.**

▶ The solution is $x = 18$, $y = 30$, and $z = 12$, or (18, 30, 12). So, the department should run 18 TV ads, 30 radio ads, and 12 newspaper ads each month.

AVOID ERRORS

In Example 4, be careful not to write the ordered triple in the order in which you solved for the variables.

(12, 18, 30) ✗

(18, 30, 12) ✓

✓ GUIDED PRACTICE for Example 4

4. **WHAT IF?** In Example 4, suppose the monthly budget is \$25,000. How many of each type of ad should the marketing department run each month?
8 TV ads, 30 radio ads, 22 newspaper ads

Extra Example 4

At a carry-out pizza restaurant, an order of 3 slices of pizza, 4 breadsticks, and 2 juice drinks costs \$13.35. A second order of 5 slices of pizza, 2 breadsticks, and 3 juice drinks costs \$19.50. If four breadsticks and a juice drink cost \$.30 more than a slice of pizza, what is the cost of each item? **pizza: \$2.95; breadstick: \$.50; juice drink: \$1.25**

Avoiding Common Errors

Many students make the common error of using an equation to solve for a variable, then substituting the variable into that same equation. That can lead to the false conclusion that there are no solutions or infinitely many solutions. Encourage students to keep a record of which equation is solved for a variable, and which equation has a substitution, to help avoid this error.

Closing the Lesson

Have students summarize the major points of the lesson and answer the Essential Question: How do you solve a system of linear equations in three variables?

- **The solution to a system of linear equations in three variables is an ordered triple.**
- **A system of linear equations in three variables can be solved by elimination or substitution.**
- **Systems of linear equations in three variables can have one solution, no solutions, or infinitely many solutions.**

Rewrite the system as a linear system in two variables by eliminating or substituting for one variable. Solve that system for each variable. Substitute those two values into an equation in the original system to get the value of the third variable.

4 PRACTICE AND APPLY

Assignment Guide

Answer Transparencies available for all exercises

Basic:
Day 1: pp. 182–185
Exs. 1, 2, 3–19 odd, 21–29, 42–45, 49

Average:
Day 1: pp. 182–185
Exs. 1, 2, 4–20 even, 21–24, 28–30, 34–36, 42–47, 50

Advanced:
Day 1: pp. 182–185
Exs. 1, 2, 7, 8, 13, 14, 19, 20, 23, 24, 31–41*, 43–48*, 50

Block:
pp. 182–185
Exs. 1, 2, 4–20 even, 21–24, 28–30, 34–36, 42–47, 50 (with 3.3)

Differentiated Instruction

See *Algebra 2 Best Practices Toolkit* for suggestions on addressing the needs of a diverse classroom.

Homework Check

For a quick check of student understanding of key concepts, go over the following exercises:

Basic: 5, 9, 17, 42, 43
Average: 6, 12, 18, 44, 45
Advanced: 7, 14, 20, 46, 47

Extra Practice

- Student Edition, p. 1012
- Chapter 3 Resource Book: Practice levels A, B, C, pp. 49–51

Practice Worksheet

An easily-readable reduced practice page (with answers) for this lesson can be found on p. 150C.

3.4 EXERCISES

HOMEWORK KEY
○ = **WORKED-OUT SOLUTIONS** on p. WS5 for Exs. 11, 25, and 45
★ = **STANDARDIZED TEST PRACTICE** Exs. 2, 23, 24, 34, 45, and 47

SKILL PRACTICE

A

1. **VOCABULARY** Write a linear equation in three variables. What is the graph of such an equation? *Sample answer:* $2x - 3y + z = 6$; a plane

2. ★ **WRITING** *Explain* how to use the substitution method to solve a system of three linear equations in three variables. See margin.

EXAMPLES 1, 2, and 3 on pp. 179–180 for Exs. 3–14

CHECKING SOLUTIONS **Tell whether the given ordered triple is a solution of the system.**

3. $(1, 4, -3)$
$2x - y + z = -5$
$5x + 2y - 2z = 19$
$x - 3y + z = -5$ no

4. $(-1, -2, 5)$
$4x - y + 3z = 13$
$x + y + z = 2$
$x + 3y - 2z = -17$ yes

5. $(6, 0, -3)$
$x + 4y - 2z = 12$
$3x - y + 4z = 6$
$-x + 3y + z = -9$ yes

6. $(-5, 1, 0)$
$3x + 4y - 2z = -11$
$2x + y - z = 11$
$x + 4y + 3z = -1$ no

7. $(2, 8, 4)$
$3x - y + 5z = 34$
$x + 3y - 6z = 2$
$-3x + y - 2z = -6$ no

8. $(0, -4, 7)$
$2x + 4y - z = -23$
$x - 5y - 3z = -1$
$-x + y + 4z = 24$ yes

ELIMINATION METHOD **Solve the system using the elimination method.**

9. $3x + y + z = 14$
$-x + 2y - 3z = -9$
$5x - y + 5z = 30$ (1, 5, 6)

10. $2x - y + 2z = -7$
$-x + 2y - 4z = 5$
$x + 4y - 6z = -1$
(−3, −1, −1)

11. $3x - y + 2z = 4$
$6x - 2y + 4z = -8$
$2x - y + 3z = 10$
no solution

12. $4x - y + 2z = -18$
$-x + 2y + z = 11$
$3x + 3y - 4z = 44$ (0, 8, −5)

13. $5x + y - z = 6$
$x + y + z = 2$
$3x + y = 4$ (0, 4, −2)

14. $2x + y - z = 9$
$-x + 6y + 2z = -17$
$5x + 7y + z = 4$ (3, −1, −4)

EXAMPLE 4 on p. 181 for Exs. 15–20

SUBSTITUTION METHOD **Solve the system using the substitution method.**

15. $x + y - z = 4$
$3x + 2y + 4z = 17$
$-x + 5y + z = 8$ (3, 2, 1)

16. $2x - y - z = 15$
$4x + 5y + 2z = 10$
$-x - 4y + 3z = -20$
(5, 0, −5)

17. $4x + y + 5z = -40$
$-3x + 2y + 4z = 10$
$x - y - 2z = -2$
(−6, 4, −4)

18. $x + 3y - z = 12$
$2x + 4y - 2z = 6$
$-x - 2y + z = -6$
no solution

19. $2x - y + z = -2$
$6x + 3y - 4z = 8$
$-3x + 2y + 3z = -6$
(0, 0, −2)

20. $3x + 5y - z = 12$
$x + y + z = 0$
$-x + 2y + 2z = -27$
(9, −4, −5)

ERROR ANALYSIS *Describe* **and correct the error in the first step of solving the system.** 21, 22. See margin.

$2x + y - 2z = 23$
$3x + 2y + z = 11$
$x - y + z = -2$

21.
$2x + y - 2z = 23$
$6x + 2y + 2z = 22$
$8x + 3y = 45$ ✗

22.
$z = 11 + 3x + 2y$
$2x + y - 2(11 + 3x + 2y) = 23$
$-4x - 3y = 45$ ✗

2. *Sample answer:* Solve one of the equations for a variable and then substitute for that variable in the other two equations. The two resulting equations form a system of two linear equations. Solve that system by graphing or algebraically. Substitute the two values found in the previous step into one of the original equations and solve for the remaining variable.

21. In the second equation, the coefficient of y was not multiplied by 2.
$2x + y - 2z = 23$
$6x + 4y + 2z = 22$
$8x + 5y = 45$

22. When solving for z, $3x$ and $2y$ must be subtracted.
$z = 11 - 3x - 2y$
$2x + y - 2(11 - 3x - 2y) = 23$
$8x + 5y = 45$

23. ★ **MULTIPLE CHOICE** Which ordered triple is a solution of the system? A

$$2x + 5y + 3z = 10$$
$$3x - y + 4z = 8$$
$$5x - 2y + 7z = 12$$

Ⓐ (7, 1, −3) Ⓑ (7, −1, −3) Ⓒ (7, 1, 3) Ⓓ (−7, 1, −3)

24. ★ **MULTIPLE CHOICE** Which ordered triple describes all of the solutions of the system? B

$$2x - 2y - z = 6$$
$$-x + y + 3z = -3$$
$$3x - 3y + 2z = 9$$

Ⓐ $(-x, x + 2, 0)$ Ⓑ $(x, x - 3, 0)$ Ⓒ $(x + 2, x, 0)$ Ⓓ $(0, y, y + 4)$

B **CHOOSING A METHOD Solve the system using any algebraic method.**

25. $x + 5y - 2z = -1$; $-x - 2y + z = 6$; $-2x - 7y + 3z = 7$ infinitely many solutions

26. $4x + 5y + 3z = 15$; $x - 3y + 2z = -6$; $-x + 2y - z = 3$ (2, 2, −1)

27. $6x + y - z = -2$; $x + 6y + 3z = 23$; $-x + y + 2z = 5$ (−1, 4, 0)

28. $x + 2y = -1$; $3x - y + 4z = 17$; $-4x + 2y - 3z = -30$ (7, −4, −2)

29. $2x - y + 2z = -21$; $x + 5y - z = 25$; $-3x + 2y + 4z = 6$ (−4, 5, −4)

30. $4x - 8y + 2z = 10$; $-3x + y - 2z = 6$; $2x - 4y + z = 8$ no solution

31. $-x + 5y - z = -16$; $2x + 3y + 4z = 18$; $x + y - z = -8$ (0, −2, 6)

32. $2x - y + 4z = 19$; $-x + 3y - 2z = -7$; $4x + 2y + 3z = 37$ (8, 1, 1)

33. $x + y + z = 3$; $3x - 4y + 2z = -28$; $-x + 5y + z = 23$ (2, 6, −5)

34. ★ **OPEN-ENDED MATH** Write a system of three linear equations in three variables that has the given number of solutions. See margin.

a. One solution b. No solution c. Infinitely many solutions

SYSTEMS WITH FRACTIONS Solve the system using any algebraic method.

35. $x + \frac{1}{2}y + \frac{1}{2}z = \frac{5}{2}$; $\frac{3}{4}x + \frac{1}{4}y + \frac{3}{2}z = \frac{7}{4}$; $\frac{1}{3}x + \frac{3}{2}y + \frac{2}{3}z = \frac{13}{6}$ (2, 1, 0)

36. $\frac{1}{3}x + \frac{5}{6}y + \frac{2}{3}z = \frac{4}{3}$; $\frac{1}{6}x + \frac{2}{3}y + \frac{1}{4}z = \frac{5}{6}$; $\frac{2}{3}x + \frac{1}{6}y + \frac{3}{2}z = \frac{4}{3}$ $\left(-\frac{1}{2}, 1, 1\right)$

C 37. **REASONING** For what values of a, b, and c does the linear system shown have (−1, 2, −3) as its only solution? *Explain* your reasoning. $a = 12$, $b = -4$, $c = 10$; when you substitute −1 for x, 2 for y, and −3 for z into each of the equations, you get the results for a, b, and c.

$$x + 2y - 3z = a$$
$$-x - y + z = b$$
$$2x + 3y - 2z = c$$

CHALLENGE Solve the system of equations. *Describe* each step of your solution. 38–41. See margin.

38. $w + x + y + z = 2$; $2w - x + 2y - z = 1$; $-w + 2x - y + 2z = -2$; $3w + x + y - z = -5$

39. $2w + x - 3y + z = 4$; $w - 3x + y + z = 32$; $-w + 2x + 2y - z = -10$; $w + x - y + 3z = 14$

40. $w + 2x + 5y = 11$; $-2w + x + 4y + 2z = -7$; $w + 2x - 2y + 5z = 3$; $-3w + x = -1$

41. $2w + 7x - 3y = 41$; $-w - 2x + y = -13$; $-2w + 4x + z = 12$; $-w - x + y = -8$

34a. *Sample answer:* $2x - 3y + 5z = 4$; $x + y - 2z = 8$; $3y - z = -2$

34b. *Sample answer:* $-x + 2y + 3z = 12$; $3x - 6y - 9z = 10$; $x + y - z = 5$

34c. *Sample answer:* $x - y + z = 3$; $-2x + 2y - 2z = -6$; $x + y + z = 4$

Avoiding Common Errors

Exercises 3–8 Students sometimes assume that if an ordered triple is a solution to one equation that it will be a solution to all. Caution students to check the ordered triple in all three equations before deciding whether it is a solution to the system.

Exercise 24 Students may have difficulty finding the solution to this system of equations because they will get identities as they work the solution. Suggest that they solve one of the two-variable equations as a literal equation, and use that to help them describe the solution to the system.

Mathematical Reasoning

Exercises 35–36 Encourage students to clear fractions in equations by multiplying each term by the LCD of the fractions.

39. $\left(\frac{76}{7}, -\frac{25}{7}, \frac{43}{7}, \frac{30}{7}\right)$. *Sample answer:* Step 1: Add equation 1 and 2 times equation 3 together, this gives you the new equation 1. Step 2: Add equation 1 and 2 times equation 2 together, this gives you the new equation 2. Step 3: Add equation 1 and 2 times equation 4 together, this gives you the new equation 3. Step 4: Add new equation 1 and new equation 3 together. Step 5: Add 5 times new equation 1 and new equation 2 together. Step 6: Take the results from steps 4 and 5 and solve for x. Step 7: Plug this in and solve for z. Step 8: Plug x and z into one of the "new" equations to get y. Step 9: Plug x, y, and z into one of the original equations to solve for w.

40. $\left(\frac{512}{213}, \frac{441}{71}, -\frac{163}{213}, -\frac{569}{213}\right)$. *Sample answer:* Step 1: Solve equation 4 for x and substitute this into the other 3 equations for x and simplify. Step 2: Add 5 times equation 2 and −2 times equation 3. Step 3: Add this new equation to equation 1 to solve for x. Step 4: Substitute x into equation 1 to find y and into equation 4 to find w. Step 5: Substitute w, x, and y into either equation 2 or 3 to find z.

41. See p. 184.

38. No solution. *Sample answer:* Step 1: Add equations 1 and 2 together to eliminate x and z. Step 2: Add 2 times equation 2 and equation 3 together. Step 3: Subtract the new equations, and the variables are eliminated and you are left with $0 = 3$. Since this is a false statement, the system is inconsistent. Therefore, there is no solution.

Study Strategy

Exercises 42–48 Students may have some difficulty setting up the systems for these equations as writing a linear system in three variables is a new experience. Refer students to Example 4 on page 181 to use as a model.

p. 183

41. (3, 5, 0, −2). *Sample answer:* Step 1: Add equation 2 and −1 times equation 4 together. This solves for *x*. Step 2: Plug *x* into equation 1 and equation 4, then add these equations together to solve for *y*. Step 3: Substitute *x* and *y* into one of the new equations to solve for *w*. Step 4: Substitute *x*, *y*, and *w* into one of the original equations to solve for *z*.

PROBLEM SOLVING

EXAMPLE 4 on p. 181 for Exs. 42–47

A

42. PIZZA SPECIALS At a pizza shop, two small pizzas, a liter of soda, and a salad cost \$14; one small pizza, a liter of soda, and three salads cost \$15; and three small pizzas and a liter of soda cost \$16. What is the cost of one small pizza? of one liter of soda? of one salad? **one small pizza: \$5, liter of soda: \$1, salad: \$3**

@HomeTutor for problem solving help at classzone.com

43. 1st: 300 gal, 2nd: 750 gal, 3rd: 2050 gal

43. HEALTH CLUB The juice bar at a health club receives a delivery of juice at the beginning of each month. Over a three month period, the health club received 1200 gallons of orange juice, 900 gallons of pineapple juice, and 1000 gallons of grapefruit juice. The table shows the composition of each juice delivery. How many gallons of juice did the health club receive in each delivery?

@HomeTutor for problem solving help at classzone.com

Juice	1st delivery	2nd delivery	3rd delivery
Orange	70%	50%	30%
Pineapple	20%	30%	30%
Grapefruit	10%	20%	40%

44a. $c + d + r = 7$, $d = 2c$, $30c + 60d + 60r = 360$, where *c* represents the comedy shows, *d* represents the dramas, and *r* represents the reality shows.

44. MULTI-STEP PROBLEM You make a tape of your friend's three favorite TV shows: a comedy, a drama, and a reality show. An episode of the comedy lasts 30 minutes, while an episode of the drama or the reality show lasts 60 minutes. The tape can hold 360 minutes of programming. You completely fill the tape with 7 episodes and include twice as many episodes of the drama as the comedy.

a. Write a system of equations to represent this situation.

b. Solve the system from part (a). How many episodes of each show are on the tape? **2 comedies, 4 dramas, 1 reality**

c. How would your answer to part (b) change if you completely filled the tape with only 5 episodes but still included twice as many episodes of the drama as the comedy? **This situation is not possible given the 5 episode constraint.**

B

45. ★ **SHORT RESPONSE** The following Internet announcement describes the results of a high school track meet.

MADISON HIGH SCHOOL was the big winner in Saturday's track meet with the help of 20 individual-event placers earning a combined 68 points. A first-place finish earns 5 points, a second-place finish earns 3 points, and a third-place finish earns 1 point. Madison had a strong second-place showing, with as many second-place finishers as first- and third-place finishers combined.

a, b. See margin.

a. Write and solve a system of equations to find the number of athletes who finished in first place, in second place, and in third place.

b. Suppose the announcement had claimed that the Madison athletes scored a total of 70 points instead of 68 points. Show that this claim must be false because the solution of the resulting linear system is not reasonable.

○ = WORKED-OUT SOLUTIONS on p. WS1 ★ = STANDARDIZED TEST PRACTICE

45a. $f + s + t = 20$, $5f + 3s + t = 68$, $s = f + t$, where *f* represents the number of first-place finishes, *s* represents the number of second-place finishes, and *t* represents the number of third-place finishes; 7 first-place finishes, 10 second-place finishes, 3 third-place finishes

45b. When you solve for *f* and *t*, you get a fractional answer and you cannot have fractions of a person.

a. $2.5r +$
$+ 2i = 32,$
$+ \ell + i = 12,$
$= 2(\ell + i)$
here r
presents the
mber of roses,
represents the
mber of lilies,
d i represents
e number of
ses

46. FIELD TRIP You and two friends buy snacks for a field trip. You spend a total of \$8, Jeff spends \$9, and Curtis spends \$9. The table shows the amounts of mixed nuts, granola, and dried fruit that each person purchased. What is the price per pound of each type of snack? **mixed nuts: \$3/lb, granola: \$2/lb, dried fruit: \$4/lb**

	Mixed nuts	Granola	Dried fruit
You	1 lb	0.5 lb	1 lb
Jeff	2 lb	0.5 lb	0.5 lb
Curtis	1 lb	2 lb	0.5 lb

47. ★ EXTENDED RESPONSE A florist must make 5 identical bridesmaid bouquets for a wedding. She has a budget of \$160 and wants 12 flowers for each bouquet. Roses cost \$2.50 each, lilies cost \$4 each, and irises cost \$2 each. She wants twice as many roses as the other two types of flowers combined.

a. **Write** Write a system of equations to represent this situation.

b. **Solve** Solve the system of equations. How many of each type of flower should be in each bouquet? **8 roses, 2 lilies, 2 irises**

c. **Analyze** Suppose there is no limitation on the total cost of the bouquets. Does the problem still have a unique solution? If so, state the unique solution. If not, give three possible solutions. **yes; 8 roses, 2 lilies, 2 irises**

C **48. CHALLENGE** Write a system of equations to represent the first three pictures below. Use the system to determine how many tangerines will balance the apple in the final picture. *Note:* The first picture shows that one tangerine and one apple balance one grapefruit.

$t + a = g$, $t + b = a$, $2g = 3b$ where t represents tangerines, a represents apples, g represents grapefruits, and b represents bananas; 5 tangerines

KENTUCKY MIXED REVIEW

TEST PRACTICE at classzone.com

49. What are the vertices of a triangle congruent to $\triangle PQR$ shown at the right? **A**

Ⓐ (3, 1), (1, −2), (4, −5)
Ⓑ (2, 3), (−1, 1), (2, −2)
Ⓒ (0, 2), (−2, −1), (−3, −4)
Ⓓ (−2, −3), (−4, 1), (−1, 4)

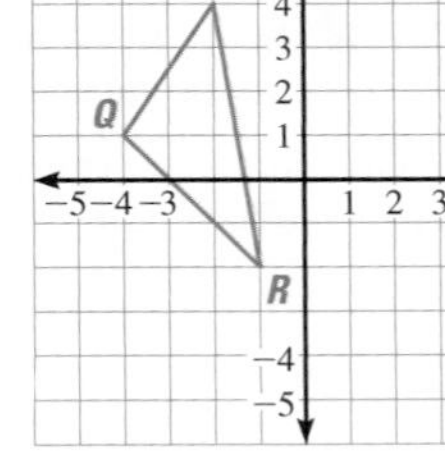

50. What special type of quadrilateral has the vertices $K(-4, 3)$, $L(-7, 3)$, $M(-9, -1)$, and $N(-2, -1)$? **B**

Ⓐ Square
Ⓑ Trapezoid
Ⓒ Kite
Ⓓ Parallelogram

5 ASSESS AND RETEACH

Daily Homework Quiz

Transparency Available

Solve the system.

1. $3x + 2y - z = -5$
$2x - 3y - 3z = -4$
$6x + y + 2z = 12$ **(1, −2, 4)**

2. $-2x + 4y - 3z = -3$
$4x - 8y + 6z = -4$
$x + 2y + 4z = 8$ **no solution**

3. At an entertainment store, 2 music CDs, 3 movie DVDs, and 1 movie VHS cost \$96; 3 music CDs, 3 movie DVDs, and 2 movie VHSs cost \$123; and 4 music CDs, 1 movie DVD, and 2 movie VHSs cost \$102. What is the cost of one CD? of one DVD? of one movie VHS? **CD: \$15; DVD: \$18; VHS: \$12**

Available at **classzone.com**

Diagnosis/Remediation

- Practice A, B, C in Chapter 3 Resource Book, pp. 49–51
- Study Guide in Chapter 3 Resource Book, pp. 52–53
- Practice Workbook, pp. 44–45
- @HomeTutor

Challenge

Additional challenge is available in the Chapter 3 Resource Book, p. 57.

Kentucky Mixed Review

1. D
2. C
3. B
4. B
5. D
6. a. $m = 0.29x + 73.14$
   b. $w = 0.14x + 79.12$
   c. (39.9, 84.7); ***Sample answer:*** The x-coordinate gives the number of years it will take after 1996 to reach the same life expectancy, the y-coordinate, for both men and women. So, if the trend continues, in the year 2036, the life expectancy for men and women will be equal (about 84.7 years).

Lessons 3.1–3.4

1. **JEWELRY** Melinda is making jewelry to sell at a craft fair. The cost of materials is \$3.50 to make one necklace and \$2.50 to make one bracelet. She sells the necklaces for \$9.00 each and the bracelets for \$7.50 each. She spends a total of \$121 on materials and sells all of the jewelry for a total of \$324. Which system of equations relates x, the number of necklaces, and y, the number of bracelets?

   A. $2.5x - 3.5y = 121$
$7.5x - 9y = 324$

   B. $2.5x + 3.5y = 324$
$9x + 7.5y = 121$

   C. $3.5x - 2.5y = 324$
$7.5x + 9y = 121$

   D. $3.5x + 2.5y = 121$
$9x + 7.5y = 324$

2. **GIFT BASKETS** Mike is making gift baskets. Each basket will contain three different kinds of candles: tapers, pillars, and jar candles. Tapers cost \$1 each, pillars cost \$4 each, and jar candles cost \$6 each. Mike puts 8 candles costing a total of \$24 in each basket, and he includes as many tapers as pillars and jar candles combined. How many tapers are in a basket?

   A. 1 taper

   B. 2 tapers

   C. 4 tapers

   D. 5 tapers

3. **BASEBALL** From 1999 through 2002, the average annual salary s of players on two Major League Baseball teams can be modeled by the equations below, where t is the number of years since 1990.

   Florida Marlins: $s = 320{,}000t - 2{,}300{,}000$
   Kansas City Royals: $s = 440{,}000t - 3{,}500{,}000$

   In what year were the average annual salaries of the two baseball teams equal?

   A. 1999   B. 2000

   C. 2001   D. 2002

4. **RESTAURANT SEATING** A restaurant has 20 tables. Each table can seat either 4 people or 6 people. The restaurant can seat a total of 90 people. How many 6 seat tables does the restaurant have?

   A. 1 table   B. 5 tables

   C. 7 tables   D. 15 tables

5. **BUSINESS** A store orders rocking chairs, hand paints them, and sells the chairs for a profit. A small chair costs the store \$51 and sells for \$80. A large chair costs the store \$70 and sells for \$110. The store wants to pay no more than \$2000 for its next order of chairs and wants to sell them all for at least \$2750. What is a possible combination of small and large rocking chairs that the store can buy and sell?

   A. 10 small chairs and 25 large chairs

   B. 12 small chairs and 20 large chairs

   C. 15 small chairs and 20 large chairs

   D. 24 small chairs and 8 large chairs

6. **OPEN-RESPONSE** The table below shows the expected life spans for men and women born in the years 1996–2000.

Years since 1996 (x)	Men's Life Span (years) (m)	Women's Life Span (years) (w)
0	73.0	79.0
1	73.6	79.4
2	73.8	79.5
3	73.9	79.4
4	74.3	79.7

   a. Write an equation for the best-fitting line for the data pairs (x, m).

   b. Write an equation for the best-fitting line for the data pairs (x, w).

   c. Assuming that the trend continues, what is the point of intersection of these two lines? *Explain* what both coordinates of this point represent.

3.5 Perform Basic Matrix Operations

MA-HS-4.1.3

Before	You performed operations with real numbers.
Now	You will perform operations with matrices.
Why?	So you can organize sports data, as in Ex. 34.

Key Vocabulary
- matrix
- dimensions
- elements
- equal matrices
- scalar
- scalar multiplication

MA-HS-4.1.3
Students will represent real-world data using matrices and will use matrix addition, subtraction, multiplication (with matrices no larger than 2 × 2) and scalar multiplication to solve real-world problems.

A **matrix** is a rectangular arrangement of numbers in rows and columns. For example, matrix A below has two rows and three columns. The **dimensions** of a matrix with m rows and n columns are $m \times n$ (read "m by n"). So, the dimensions of matrix A are 2×3. The numbers in a matrix are its **elements**.

$$A = \begin{bmatrix} 4 & -1 & 5 \\ 0 & 6 & 3 \end{bmatrix}$$

2 rows

3 columns

The element in the first row and third column is 5.

Two matrices are **equal** if their dimensions are the same and the elements in corresponding positions are equal.

KEY CONCEPT *For Your Notebook*

Adding and Subtracting Matrices

To add or subtract two matrices, simply add or subtract elements in corresponding positions. You can add or subtract matrices only if they have the same dimensions.

Adding Matrices
$$\begin{bmatrix} a & b \\ c & d \end{bmatrix} + \begin{bmatrix} e & f \\ g & h \end{bmatrix} = \begin{bmatrix} a+e & b+f \\ c+g & d+h \end{bmatrix}$$

Subtracting Matrices
$$\begin{bmatrix} a & b \\ c & d \end{bmatrix} - \begin{bmatrix} e & f \\ g & h \end{bmatrix} = \begin{bmatrix} a-e & b-f \\ c-g & d-h \end{bmatrix}$$

EXAMPLE 1 **Add and subtract matrices**

AVOID ERRORS
Be sure to verify that the dimensions of two matrices are equal before adding or subtracting them.

Perform the indicated operation, if possible.

a. $\begin{bmatrix} 3 & 0 \\ -5 & -1 \end{bmatrix} + \begin{bmatrix} -1 & 4 \\ 2 & 0 \end{bmatrix} = \begin{bmatrix} 3+(-1) & 0+4 \\ -5+2 & -1+0 \end{bmatrix} = \begin{bmatrix} 2 & 4 \\ -3 & -1 \end{bmatrix}$

b. $\begin{bmatrix} 7 & 4 \\ 0 & -2 \\ -1 & 6 \end{bmatrix} - \begin{bmatrix} -2 & 5 \\ 3 & -10 \\ -3 & 1 \end{bmatrix} = \begin{bmatrix} 7-(-2) & 4-5 \\ 0-3 & -2-(-10) \\ -1-(-3) & 6-1 \end{bmatrix} = \begin{bmatrix} 9 & -1 \\ -3 & 8 \\ 2 & 5 \end{bmatrix}$

1 PLAN AND PREPARE

Warm-Up Exercises

Transparency Available

Identify the property of real numbers illustrated by each exercise.

1. $(6 + 4) + (-2) = 6 + [4 + (-2)]$ **Assoc. Property of Addition**
2. $3(5x + 1) = 3 \cdot 5x + 3 \cdot 1$ **Distributive Property**
3. Solve $3x + 9 = 24$. **5**

Notetaking Guide

Transparency Available

Promotes interactive learning and notetaking skills, pp. 72–75.

Pacing

Basic: 1 day
Average: 1 day
Advanced: 1 day
Block: 0.5 block with 3.6
- See *Teaching Guide/Lesson Plan.*

2 FOCUS AND MOTIVATE

Essential Question

Big Idea 3, p. 151

How do you perform the basic matrix operations? **Tell students they will learn how to answer this question by adding or subtracting matrices and by multiplying a matrix by a scalar.**

Resource Planning Guide

Chapter Resource Book
- Teaching Guide/Lesson Plan (pp. 58–59)
- Practice levels A, B, C (pp. 61–63)
- Study Guide (pp. 64–65)
- Catch-up for Absent Students (p. 66)
- Application (p. 67)
- Challenge (p. 68)

Workbooks
- Notetaking Guide (pp. 72–75)
- Practice Workbook (pp. 46–47)

Teaching Options
- **Power Presentations CD-ROM** provides dynamic electronic teaching resources for the classroom.
- **Activity Generator CD-ROM** provides editable activities for all ability levels.

Interactive Technology
- Easy Planner
- Power Presentations CD-ROM
- Activity Generator CD-ROM
- Animated Algebra
- Test Generator CD-ROM
- Online Quiz
- eWorkbook
- eEdition
- @HomeTutor

Resources for English Learners
- Quick Reference for English Learners
- Spanish Study Guide
- Multi-Language Visual Glossary
- Student Resources in Spanish

See also the *Algebra 2 Toolkit* for more strategies for meeting individual needs.

SCALAR MULTIPLICATION In matrix algebra, a real number is often called a **scalar**. To multiply a matrix by a scalar, you multiply each element in the matrix by the scalar. This process is called **scalar multiplication**.

EXAMPLE 2 Multiply a matrix by a scalar

COMPARE ORDER OF OPERATIONS
The order of operations for matrix expressions is similar to that for real numbers. In particular, you perform scalar multiplication before matrix addition and subtraction.

Perform the indicated operation, if possible.

a. $-2\begin{bmatrix} 4 & -1 \\ 1 & 0 \\ 2 & 7 \end{bmatrix} = \begin{bmatrix} -2(4) & -2(-1) \\ -2(1) & -2(0) \\ -2(2) & -2(7) \end{bmatrix} = \begin{bmatrix} -8 & 2 \\ -2 & 0 \\ -4 & -14 \end{bmatrix}$

b. $4\begin{bmatrix} -2 & -8 \\ 5 & 0 \end{bmatrix} + \begin{bmatrix} -3 & 8 \\ 6 & -5 \end{bmatrix} = \begin{bmatrix} 4(-2) & 4(-8) \\ 4(5) & 4(0) \end{bmatrix} + \begin{bmatrix} -3 & 8 \\ 6 & -5 \end{bmatrix}$

$= \begin{bmatrix} -8 & -32 \\ 20 & 0 \end{bmatrix} + \begin{bmatrix} -3 & 8 \\ 6 & -5 \end{bmatrix}$

$= \begin{bmatrix} -8 + (-3) & -32 + 8 \\ 20 + 6 & 0 + (-5) \end{bmatrix}$

$= \begin{bmatrix} -11 & -24 \\ 26 & -5 \end{bmatrix}$

✓ GUIDED PRACTICE for Examples 1 and 2

Perform the indicated operation, if possible. 1–4. See margin.

1. $\begin{bmatrix} -2 & 5 & 11 \\ 4 & -6 & 8 \end{bmatrix} + \begin{bmatrix} -3 & 1 & -5 \\ -2 & -8 & 4 \end{bmatrix}$

2. $\begin{bmatrix} -4 & 0 \\ 7 & -2 \\ -3 & 1 \end{bmatrix} - \begin{bmatrix} 2 & 2 \\ -3 & 0 \\ 5 & -14 \end{bmatrix}$

3. $-4\begin{bmatrix} 2 & -1 & -3 \\ -7 & 6 & 1 \\ -2 & 0 & -5 \end{bmatrix}$

4. $3\begin{bmatrix} 4 & -1 \\ -3 & -5 \end{bmatrix} + \begin{bmatrix} -2 & -2 \\ 0 & 6 \end{bmatrix}$

MATRIX PROPERTIES Many of the properties you have used with real numbers can be applied to matrices as well.

CONCEPT SUMMARY *For Your Notebook*

Properties of Matrix Operations

Let A, B, and C be matrices with the same dimensions, and let k be a scalar.

Associative Property of Addition	$(A + B) + C = A + (B + C)$
Commutative Property of Addition	$A + B = B + A$
Distributive Property of Addition	$k(A + B) = kA + kB$
Distributive Property of Subtraction	$k(A - B) = kA - kB$

Motivating the Lesson

Write two 2×3 matrices on the board. Ask students to suggest ways to add and subtract these numerical arrays. Perform the operations that students suggest, pointing out correct and incorrect methods.

3 TEACH

Extra Example 1

Perform the indicated operation, if possible.

a. $\begin{bmatrix} 2 & 4 \\ 0 & 1 \end{bmatrix} + \begin{bmatrix} -3 & 2 \\ 4 & 0 \end{bmatrix}$ $\begin{bmatrix} -1 & 6 \\ 4 & 1 \end{bmatrix}$

b. $\begin{bmatrix} 4 & 6 \\ -2 & 2 \\ 1 & 5 \end{bmatrix} - \begin{bmatrix} 2 & 3 \\ -4 & 2 \\ -3 & 1 \end{bmatrix}$ $\begin{bmatrix} 2 & 3 \\ 2 & 0 \\ 4 & 4 \end{bmatrix}$

Key Question to Ask for Example 1

- If you have an $m \times n$ matrix and an $n \times m$ matrix, is it possible to add and subtract them? No, the dimensions are not the same. One matrix has m rows and n columns, the other has n rows and m columns.

Extra Example 2

Perform the indicated operation, if possible.

a. $4\begin{bmatrix} 3 & -2 \\ 0 & 3 \\ 1 & 6 \end{bmatrix}$ $\begin{bmatrix} 12 & -8 \\ 0 & 12 \\ 4 & 24 \end{bmatrix}$

b. $-3\begin{bmatrix} -1 & 5 \\ 4 & 0 \end{bmatrix} + \begin{bmatrix} -2 & 1 \\ 5 & -3 \end{bmatrix}$ $\begin{bmatrix} 1 & -14 \\ -7 & -3 \end{bmatrix}$

Differentiated Instruction

Below Level When discussing why two matrices must have the same dimensions in order to add or subtract, write several sample matrices with the same and with different dimensions on overhead transparencies. Then visually "stack" those matrices that can be added or subtracted and stack those that can't be added or subtracted. Students should see that the matrices with different dimensions don't "fit" over each other.

See also the *Algebra 2 Toolkit* for more strategies.

ORGANIZING DATA Matrices are useful for organizing data and for performing the same operations on large numbers of data values.

EXAMPLE 3 Solve a multi-step problem

MANUFACTURING A company manufactures small and large steel DVD racks with wooden bases. Each size of rack is available in three types of wood: walnut, pine, and cherry. Sales of the racks for last month and this month are shown below.

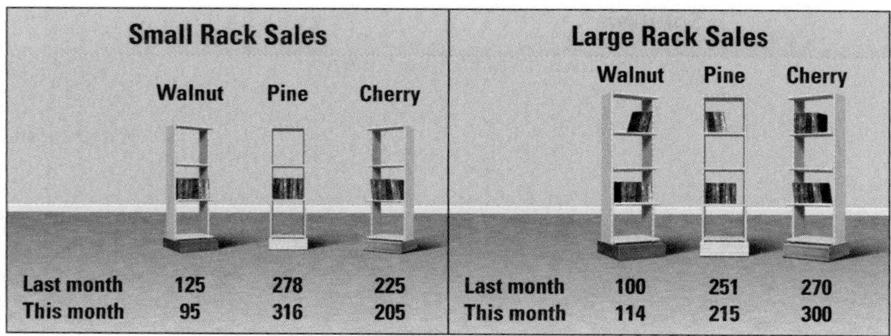

Small Rack Sales	Walnut	Pine	Cherry	Large Rack Sales	Walnut	Pine	Cherry
Last month	125	278	225	Last month	100	251	270
This month	95	316	205	This month	114	215	300

Organize the data using two matrices, one for last month's sales and one for this month's sales. Then write and interpret a matrix giving the average monthly sales for the two month period.

Solution

STEP 1 **Organize** the data using two 3×2 matrices, as shown.

Last Month (A): Small, Large; This Month (B): Small, Large; rows Walnut, Pine, Cherry

$$\begin{bmatrix} 125 & 100 \\ 278 & 251 \\ 225 & 270 \end{bmatrix} \quad \begin{bmatrix} 95 & 114 \\ 316 & 215 \\ 205 & 300 \end{bmatrix}$$

STEP 2 **Write** a matrix for the average monthly sales by first adding A and B to find the total sales and then multipling the result by $\frac{1}{2}$.

$$\frac{1}{2}(A + B) = \frac{1}{2}\left(\begin{bmatrix} 125 & 100 \\ 278 & 251 \\ 225 & 270 \end{bmatrix} + \begin{bmatrix} 95 & 114 \\ 316 & 215 \\ 205 & 300 \end{bmatrix}\right)$$

$$= \frac{1}{2}\begin{bmatrix} 220 & 214 \\ 594 & 466 \\ 430 & 570 \end{bmatrix}$$

$$= \begin{bmatrix} 110 & 107 \\ 297 & 233 \\ 215 & 285 \end{bmatrix}$$

ANOTHER WAY You can also evaluate $\frac{1}{2}(A + B)$ by first using the distributive property to rewrite the expression as $\frac{1}{2}A + \frac{1}{2}B$.

STEP 3 **Interpret** the matrix from Step 2. The company sold an average of 110 small walnut racks, 107 large walnut racks, 297 small pine racks, 233 large pine racks, 215 small cherry racks, and 285 large cherry racks.

Differentiated Instruction

Visual Learners Students may easily forget to multiply *every* element in the matrix by the scalar. Draw an arrow from the scalar to each element in the matrix, and have students do the same until they are comfortable with remembering to multiply all elements by the scalar.

See also the *Algebra 2 Toolkit* for more strategies.

Extra Example 3

A local bakery keeps track of their sales as shown below.

Last Month Store 1: 650 Rolls, 220 Cakes, 32 Pies; Store 2: 540 Rolls, 200 Cakes, 30 Pies

This Month Store 1: 840 Rolls, 250 Cakes, 50 Pies; Store 2: 800 Rolls, 250 Cakes, 42 Pies

Organize the data using matrices. Then write and interpret a matrix giving the number of total bakery items sold per store.

Last Month: Store 1, Store 2; This Month: Store 1, Store 2; rows rolls, cakes, pies

$$\begin{bmatrix} 650 & 540 \\ 220 & 200 \\ 32 & 30 \end{bmatrix} + \begin{bmatrix} 840 & 800 \\ 250 & 250 \\ 50 & 42 \end{bmatrix} = \begin{bmatrix} 1490 & 1340 \\ 470 & 450 \\ 82 & 72 \end{bmatrix};$$

Store 1 sold 1490 rolls, 470 cakes, and 82 pies. Store 2 sold 1340 rolls, 450 cakes, and 72 pies.

Key Questions to Ask for Example 3

- Why do the dimensions of each matrix in Step 1 need to be the same? You can add matrices only if they have the same dimensions.
- Why do you multiply by $\frac{1}{2}$? To find the average of 2 items you divide by the number of items, 2, or multiply by its reciprocal, $\frac{1}{2}$.

Reading Strategy

Point out to students that the "Another Way" note next to Example 3 tells them that they can also multiply the scalar $\frac{1}{2}$ by each matrix, and then add the products.

1. $\begin{bmatrix} -5 & 6 & 6 \\ 2 & -14 & 12 \end{bmatrix}$

2. $\begin{bmatrix} -6 & -2 \\ 10 & -2 \\ -8 & 15 \end{bmatrix}$

3. $\begin{bmatrix} -8 & 4 & 12 \\ 28 & -24 & -4 \\ 8 & 0 & 20 \end{bmatrix}$

4. $\begin{bmatrix} 10 & -5 \\ -9 & -9 \end{bmatrix}$

Extra Example 4

Solve the matrix equation for x and y.

$$2\left(\begin{bmatrix} 2x & -3 \\ 5 & -y \end{bmatrix} + \begin{bmatrix} -1 & 4 \\ 3 & 5 \end{bmatrix}\right) = \begin{bmatrix} 10 & 2 \\ 16 & 14 \end{bmatrix}$$

$x = 3$; $y = -2$

Key Question to Ask for Example 4

- Why can you ignore 15 and 3 in the last matrix equation? **The elements 15 and 3 have no variables associated with them and merely produce the true equations 15 = 15 and 3 = 3.**

Closing the Lesson

Have students summarize the major points of the lesson and answer the Essential Question: How do you perform the basic matrix operations?

- **To add or subtract matrices, the matrices must have the same dimensions.**
- **You can multiply each element of a matrix by a real number called a scalar.**

To add or subtract matrices, you add or subtract corresponding elements of matrices with the same dimensions. To perform scalar multiplication, you multiply each element of a matrix by the scalar.

SOLVING MATRIX EQUATIONS You can use what you know about matrix operations and matrix equality to solve an equation involving matrices.

EXAMPLE 4 Solve a matrix equation

Solve the matrix equation for x and y.

$$3\left(\begin{bmatrix} 5x & -2 \\ 6 & -4 \end{bmatrix} + \begin{bmatrix} 3 & 7 \\ -5 & -y \end{bmatrix}\right) = \begin{bmatrix} -21 & 15 \\ 3 & -24 \end{bmatrix}$$

Solution

Simplify the left side of the equation.

$$3\left(\begin{bmatrix} 5x & -2 \\ 6 & -4 \end{bmatrix} + \begin{bmatrix} 3 & 7 \\ -5 & -y \end{bmatrix}\right) = \begin{bmatrix} -21 & 15 \\ 3 & -24 \end{bmatrix}$$ **Write original equation.**

$$3\begin{bmatrix} 5x+3 & 5 \\ 1 & -4-y \end{bmatrix} = \begin{bmatrix} -21 & 15 \\ 3 & -24 \end{bmatrix}$$ **Add matrices inside parentheses.**

$$\begin{bmatrix} 15x+9 & 15 \\ 3 & -12-3y \end{bmatrix} = \begin{bmatrix} -21 & 15 \\ 3 & -24 \end{bmatrix}$$ **Perform scalar multiplication.**

Equate corresponding elements and solve the two resulting equations.

$15x + 9 = -21$ $\quad$ $-12 - 3y = -24$

$x = -2$ $\quad$ $y = 4$

▸ The solution is $x = -2$ and $y = 4$.

✓ GUIDED PRACTICE for Examples 3 and 4

5. In Example 3, find $B - A$ and explain what information this matrix gives.

6. Solve $-2\left(\begin{bmatrix} -3x & -1 \\ 4 & y \end{bmatrix} + \begin{bmatrix} 9 & -4 \\ -5 & 3 \end{bmatrix}\right) = \begin{bmatrix} 12 & 10 \\ 2 & -18 \end{bmatrix}$ for x and y. **$x = 5, y = 6$**

5. $\begin{bmatrix} -30 & 14 \\ 38 & -36 \\ -20 & 30 \end{bmatrix}$; **the difference in the number of DVD racks sold this month compared to last month**

3.5 EXERCISES

HOMEWORK KEY

 = **WORKED-OUT SOLUTIONS on p. WS6 for Exs. 5, 21, and 33**

★ = **STANDARDIZED TEST PRACTICE Exs. 2, 28, 29, 33, and 34**

SKILL PRACTICE

A

1. **VOCABULARY** Copy and complete: The __?__ of a matrix with 3 rows and 4 columns are 3×4. **dimensions**

2. ★ **WRITING** *Describe* how to determine whether two matrices are equal. **Compare the dimensions and the corresponding elements. If they are the same, the matrices are equal.**

EXAMPLE 1 on p. 187 for Exs. 3–9

3. **ERROR ANALYSIS** *Describe* and correct the error in adding the matrices. **See margin.**

$$\begin{bmatrix} 9 \\ -5 \end{bmatrix} + \begin{bmatrix} 4.1 \\ 3.8 \end{bmatrix} = \begin{bmatrix} 9 & 4.1 \\ -5 & 3.8 \end{bmatrix}$$

3. The corresponding entries were not added together to create a 2×1 matrix; $\begin{bmatrix} 13.1 \\ -1.2 \end{bmatrix}$.

Differentiated Instruction

Advanced Have students prove the properties of matrix operations on page 188 using the matrices in the Key Concept box on page 187. Students should see that the proofs depend on the corresponding properties for real numbers.

See also the *Algebra 2 Toolkit* for more strategies.

ADDING AND SUBTRACTING MATRICES **Perform the indicated operation, if possible. If not possible, state the reason.** 4–9. See margin.

4. $\begin{bmatrix} 5 & 2 \\ -1 & 8 \end{bmatrix} + \begin{bmatrix} -8 & 10 \\ -6 & 3 \end{bmatrix}$

5. $\begin{bmatrix} 10 & -8 \\ 5 & -3 \end{bmatrix} - \begin{bmatrix} 12 & -3 \\ 3 & -4 \end{bmatrix}$

6. $\begin{bmatrix} 4 & -5 \\ 8 & 1 \end{bmatrix} - \begin{bmatrix} 2 \\ -1 \end{bmatrix}$

7. $\begin{bmatrix} 1.2 & 5.3 \\ 0.1 & 4.4 \\ 6.2 & 0.7 \end{bmatrix} + \begin{bmatrix} 2.4 & -0.6 \\ 6.1 & 3.1 \\ 8.1 & -1.9 \end{bmatrix}$

8. $\begin{bmatrix} 8 & 3 \\ 9 & -1 \\ 4 & 5 \end{bmatrix} + \begin{bmatrix} 5 & -1 & 0 \\ 6 & 2 & -3 \\ 8 & -1 & 2 \end{bmatrix}$

9. $\begin{bmatrix} 7 & -3 \\ 12 & 5 \\ -4 & 11 \end{bmatrix} - \begin{bmatrix} 9 & 2 \\ -2 & 6 \\ 6 & 5 \end{bmatrix}$

EXAMPLE 2 on p. 188 for Exs. 10–15

MULTIPLYING BY A SCALAR **Perform the indicated operation.** 10–15. See margin.

10. $2\begin{bmatrix} -1 & 4 \\ 3 & -6 \end{bmatrix}$

11. $-3\begin{bmatrix} 2 & 0 & -5 \\ 4 & 7 & -3 \end{bmatrix}$

12. $-4\begin{bmatrix} 2 & -3 & -2 \\ -\frac{5}{8} & \frac{11}{2} & \frac{7}{4} \end{bmatrix}$

13. $1.5\begin{bmatrix} -2 & 3.4 & 1.6 \\ 5.4 & 0 & -3 \end{bmatrix}$

14. $\frac{1}{2}\begin{bmatrix} -2 & 8 & 12 \\ 20 & -1 & 0 \\ -8 & 10 & 2 \end{bmatrix}$

15. $-2.2\begin{bmatrix} 6 & 3.1 & 4.5 \\ -1 & 0 & 2.5 \\ 5.5 & -1.8 & 6.4 \end{bmatrix}$

B

MATRIX OPERATIONS **Use matrices A, B, C, and D to evaluate the matrix expression.** 16–23. See margin.

$A = \begin{bmatrix} 5 & -4 \\ 3 & -1 \end{bmatrix}$ $B = \begin{bmatrix} 18 & -12 \\ -6 & 0 \end{bmatrix}$ $C = \begin{bmatrix} 1.8 & -1.5 & 10.6 \\ -8.8 & 3.4 & 0 \end{bmatrix}$ $D = \begin{bmatrix} 7.2 & 0 & -5.4 \\ 2.1 & -1.9 & 3.3 \end{bmatrix}$

16. $A + B$
17. $B - A$
18. $4A - B$
19. $\frac{2}{3}B$
20. $C + D$
21. $C + 3D$
22. $D - 2C$
23. $0.5C - D$

EXAMPLE 4 on p. 190 for Exs. 24–27

SOLVING MATRIX EQUATIONS **Solve the matrix equation for x and y.**

24. $\begin{bmatrix} -1 & 3x \\ -4 & 5 \end{bmatrix} = \begin{bmatrix} -1 & -18 \\ 2y & 5 \end{bmatrix}$ $x = -6, y = -2$

25. $\begin{bmatrix} -2x & 6 \\ 1 & -8 \end{bmatrix} + 2\begin{bmatrix} 5 & -1 \\ -7 & 6 \end{bmatrix} = \begin{bmatrix} -9 & 4 \\ -13 & y \end{bmatrix}$ $x = \frac{19}{2}, y = 4$

26. $2\begin{bmatrix} 8 & -x \\ 5 & 6 \end{bmatrix} - \begin{bmatrix} 3 & -9 \\ 10 & -4y \end{bmatrix} = \begin{bmatrix} 13 & 4 \\ 0 & 16 \end{bmatrix}$ $x = \frac{5}{2}, y = 1$

27. $4x\begin{bmatrix} -1 & 2 \\ 3 & 6 \end{bmatrix} = \begin{bmatrix} 8 & -16 \\ -24 & 3y \end{bmatrix}$ $x = -2, y = -16$

28. ★ **MULTIPLE CHOICE** Based on the equation below, what is the value of the expression $3x - 2y$? C

$$\begin{bmatrix} 2x & 0 \\ 0.5 & -0.75 \end{bmatrix} = \begin{bmatrix} 6.4 & 0 \\ 0.5 & 3y \end{bmatrix}$$

(A) 7.15 (B) 9.1 (C) 10.1 (D) 20.7

C

29. ★ **OPEN-ENDED MATH** Find two matrices A and B such that $2A - 3B = \begin{bmatrix} 5 & 0 \\ -1 & 2 \end{bmatrix}$. See margin.

30. **CHALLENGE** Find the matrix X that makes the equation true. a–d. See margin.

a. $X + \begin{bmatrix} -5 & 0 \\ 4 & -3 \end{bmatrix} = \begin{bmatrix} 7 & -8 \\ -3 & 5 \end{bmatrix}$

b. $X - \begin{bmatrix} 2 & 3 \\ 5 & 0 \end{bmatrix} = \begin{bmatrix} 8 & 6 \\ -1 & 3 \end{bmatrix}$

c. $-X + \begin{bmatrix} -3 & 1 \\ 4 & 7 \end{bmatrix} = \begin{bmatrix} 8 & -9 \\ 0 & 10 \end{bmatrix}$

d. $3X - \begin{bmatrix} 11 & -6 \\ 2 & 1 \end{bmatrix} = \begin{bmatrix} -13 & 15 \\ -19 & 2 \end{bmatrix}$

4 PRACTICE AND APPLY

Assignment Guide

Answer Transparencies available for all exercises

Basic:
Day 1: SRH p. 975 Exs. 12, 15, 21, 25, 31
pp. 190–193
Exs. 1–7, 10–13, 16–24, 31–33, 37

Average:
Day 1: pp. 190–193
Exs. 1–3, 7–9, 13–15, 18–29, 31–34, 36

Advanced:
Day 1: pp. 190–193
Exs. 1, 2, 8, 9, 14, 15, 19–35*

Block:
pp. 190–193
Exs. 1–3, 7–9, 13–15, 18–29, 31–34, 36 (with 3.6)

Differentiated Instruction

See *Algebra 2 Best Practices Toolkit* for suggestions on addressing the needs of a diverse classroom.

Homework Check

For a quick check of student understanding of key concepts, go over the following exercises:

Basic: 7, 12, 24, 31, 32
Average: 8, 13, 26, 32, 33
Advanced: 9, 14, 27, 33, 34

Extra Practice

- Student Edition, p. 1012
- Chapter 3 Resource Book: Practice levels A, B, C, pp. 61–63

Practice Worksheet

An easily-readable reduced practice page (with answers) for this lesson can be found on p. 150C.

4. $\begin{bmatrix} -3 & 12 \\ -7 & 11 \end{bmatrix}$

5. $\begin{bmatrix} -2 & -5 \\ 2 & 1 \end{bmatrix}$

6. Not possible; the matrices do not have the same dimensions.

7. $\begin{bmatrix} 3.6 & 4.7 \\ 6.2 & 7.5 \\ 14.3 & -1.2 \end{bmatrix}$

8. Not possible; the matrices do not have the same dimensions.

9. $\begin{bmatrix} -2 & -5 \\ 14 & -1 \\ -10 & 6 \end{bmatrix}$

10–23. See Additional Answers beginning on p. AA1.

29. *Sample answer:*
$A = \begin{bmatrix} 5.5 & -3 \\ -8 & 7 \end{bmatrix}, B = \begin{bmatrix} 2 & -2 \\ -5 & 4 \end{bmatrix}$

30a. $\begin{bmatrix} 12 & -8 \\ -7 & 8 \end{bmatrix}$ 30b. $\begin{bmatrix} 10 & 9 \\ 4 & 3 \end{bmatrix}$

30c. $\begin{bmatrix} -11 & 10 \\ 4 & -3 \end{bmatrix}$ 30d. $\begin{bmatrix} -\frac{2}{3} & 3 \\ -\frac{17}{3} & 1 \end{bmatrix}$

Avoiding Common Errors

Exercises 6, 8 These matrices do not have the same dimensions, so the indicated operation cannot be done. Encourage students to verify that the dimensions of matrices are the same before trying to add or subtract.

Mathematical Reasoning

Exercise 35 This exercise represents a dilation or enlargement of a rectangle by a scale factor of 3. If the rectangles are drawn in the same coordinate plane, the length and width of the second rectangle will be three times the length and width of the first rectangle.

31. $\begin{bmatrix} 0 & 5 & 1 & -1 \\ -7 & -1 & -5 & -2 \\ 1 & -1 & 4 & 10 \end{bmatrix}$

32. $\begin{matrix} \text{Economy} \\ \text{Midsize} \\ \text{Mini-van} \\ \text{SUV} \end{matrix} \begin{bmatrix} 32 & 40 \\ 24 & 34 \\ 18 & 25 \\ 19 & 22 \end{bmatrix}; \begin{bmatrix} 35 & 43 \\ 26 & 37 \\ 19 & 27 \\ 21 & 24 \end{bmatrix}$

33a. $M = \begin{matrix} \text{Model A} \\ \text{Model B} \\ \text{Model C} \end{matrix} \begin{bmatrix} 31 & 22 \\ 42 & 25 \\ 18 & 11 \end{bmatrix},$

$J = \begin{matrix} \text{Model A} \\ \text{Model B} \\ \text{Model C} \end{matrix} \begin{bmatrix} 25 & 38 \\ 36 & 32 \\ 12 & 15 \end{bmatrix}$

35. $\begin{bmatrix} 1 & 1 & 5 & 5 \\ 1 & 4 & 1 & 4 \end{bmatrix}; \begin{bmatrix} 3 & 3 & 15 & 15 \\ 3 & 12 & 3 & 12 \end{bmatrix}$

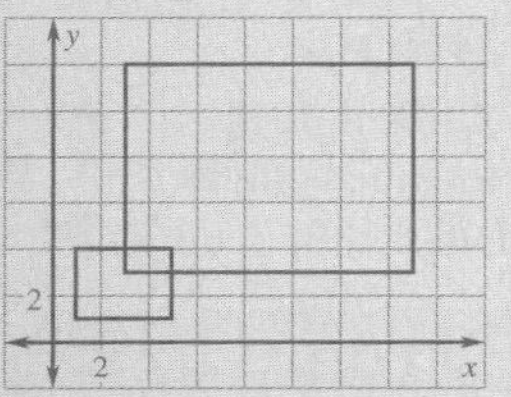

The rectangles are similar to each other and the 3A matrix is a dilation of the A matrix.

33b. $\begin{bmatrix} 56 & 60 \\ 78 & 57 \\ 30 & 26 \end{bmatrix}$; **the sum represents the total sales for May and June.**

33c. $\begin{bmatrix} 28 & 30 \\ 39 & 28.5 \\ 15 & 13 \end{bmatrix}$

34. No; $A + B$ is the total number of athletes and team sizes for each sport for 2000–2002. The team size for 2000–2002 is not correct because it is the sum of two averages and not an average.

PROBLEM SOLVING

EXAMPLE 3 [A] on p. 189 for Exs. 31–34

31. SNOWBOARD SALES A sporting goods store sells snowboards in several different styles and lengths. The matrices below show the number of each type of snowboard sold in 2003 and 2004. Write a matrix giving the change in sales for each type of snowboard from 2003 to 2004. **See margin.**

	Sales for 2003				Sales for 2004			
	150 cm	155 cm	160 cm	165 cm	150 cm	155 cm	160 cm	165 cm
Freeride	32	42	29	20	32	47	30	19
Alpine	12	17	25	16	5	16	20	14
Freestyle	28	40	32	21	29	39	36	31

@HomeTutor for problem solving help at classzone.com

32. FUEL ECONOMY A car dealership sells four different models of cars. The fuel economy (in miles per gallon) is shown below for each model. Organize the data using a matrix. Then write a new matrix giving the fuel economy figures for next year's models if each measure of fuel economy increases by 8%. **See margin.**

Economy car: 32 mpg in city driving, 40 mpg in highway driving

Mid-size car: 24 mpg in city driving, 34 mpg in highway driving

Mini-van: 18 mpg in city driving, 25 mpg in highway driving

SUV: 19 mpg in city driving, 22 mpg in highway driving

@HomeTutor for problem solving help at classzone.com

[B]

(33.) ★ **EXTENDED RESPONSE** In a certain city, an electronics chain has a downtown store and a store in the mall. Each store carries three models of digital camera. Sales of the cameras for May and June are shown.

May Downtown sales: 31 of model A, 42 of model B, 18 of model C
Mall sales: 22 of model A, 25 of model B, 11 of model C

June Downtown sales: 25 of model A, 36 of model B, 12 of model C
Mall sales: 38 of model A, 32 of model B, 15 of model C

a. Organize the information using two matrices M and J that represent the sales for May and June, respectively. **See margin.**

b. Find $M + J$ and describe what this matrix sum represents.

c. Write a matrix giving the average monthly sales for the two month period.

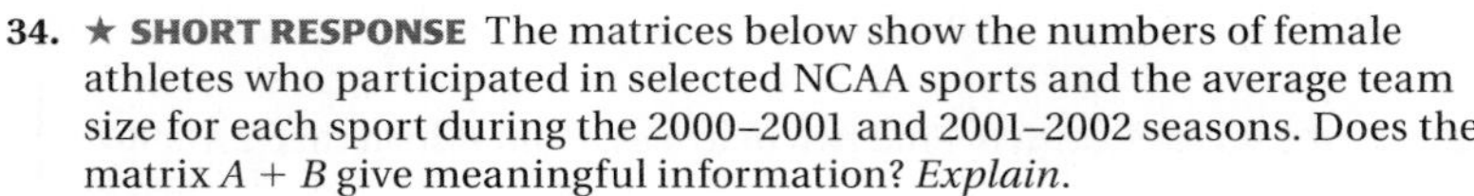

34. ★ **SHORT RESPONSE** The matrices below show the numbers of female athletes who participated in selected NCAA sports and the average team size for each sport during the 2000–2001 and 2001–2002 seasons. Does the matrix $A + B$ give meaningful information? *Explain.*

	2000–2001 (*A*)		2001–2002 (*B*)	
	Athletes	Team size	Athletes	Team size
Basketball	14,439	14.5	14,524	14.3
Gymnastics	1,397	15.7	1,440	16.2
Skiing	526	11.9	496	11.0
Soccer	18,548	22.5	19,467	22.4

◯ = WORKED-OUT SOLUTIONS on p. WS1 ★ = STANDARDIZED TEST PRACTICE

35. CHALLENGE A rectangle has vertices (1, 1), (1, 4), (5, 1), and (5, 4). Write a 2×4 matrix A whose columns are the vertices of the rectangle. Multiply matrix A by 3. In the same coordinate plane, draw the rectangles represented by the matrices A and $3A$. How are the rectangles related? See margin.

KENTUCKY MIXED REVIEW

TEST PRACTICE at classzone.com

36. A health teacher surveyed 100 students to determine their favorite exercise activity or combination of exercise activities. The results are shown at the right. How many of the students surveyed chose only running as their favorite exercise activity? **C**

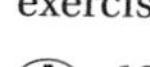

Ⓐ 13 Ⓑ 29

Ⓒ 42 Ⓓ 71

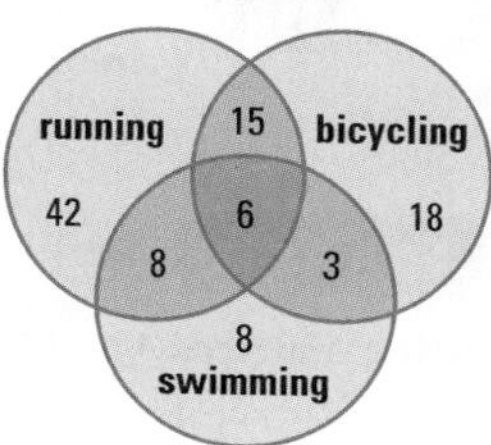

37. Which statement best describes the effect on the graph shown when the y-intercept is decreased by 4? **A**

Ⓐ The x-intercept decreases.

Ⓑ The slope decreases.

Ⓒ The x-intercept increases.

Ⓓ The slope increases.

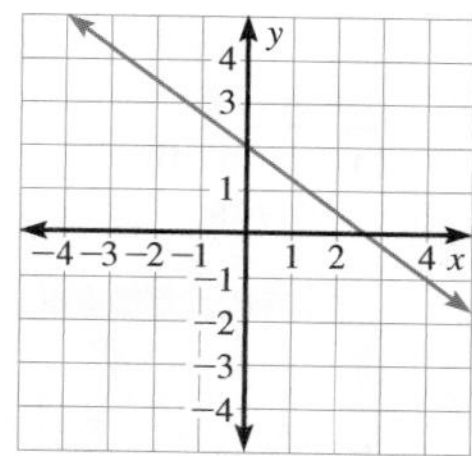

QUIZ *for Lessons 3.3–3.5*

Graph the system of inequalities. *(p. 168)* 1–6. See margin.

1. $y < 6$
 $x + y > -2$

2. $x \geq -1$
 $-2x + y \leq 5$

3. $x + 3y > 3$
 $x + 3y < -9$

4. $x - y \geq 4$
 $2x + 4y \geq -10$

5. $x + 2y \leq 10$
 $y \geq |x + 2|$

6. $-y < x$
 $2y < 5x + 9$

Solve the system using any algebraic method. *(p. 178)*

7. $2x - y - 3z = 5$
 $x + 2y - 5z = -11$
 $-x - 3y = 10$ (2, −4, 1)

8. $x + y + z = -3$
 $2x - 3y + z = 9$
 $4x - 5y + 2z = 16$ (4, −2, −5)

9. $2x - 4y + 3z = 1$
 $6x + 2y + 10z = 19$
 $-2x + 5y - 2z = 2$ $\left(-\frac{1}{2}, 1, 2\right)$

Use matrices *A*, *B*, and *C* to evaluate the matrix expression, if possible. If not possible, state the reason. *(p. 187)*

$A = \begin{bmatrix} 2 & -5 \\ 3 & -1 \end{bmatrix}$ $B = \begin{bmatrix} -4 & 3 \\ 8 & 10 \end{bmatrix}$ $C = \begin{bmatrix} -6 & -2 & 9 \\ 1 & -4 & -1 \end{bmatrix}$

10. $A + B$ $\begin{bmatrix} -2 & -2 \\ 11 & 9 \end{bmatrix}$ **11.** $B - 2A$ $\begin{bmatrix} -8 & 13 \\ 2 & 12 \end{bmatrix}$ **12.** $3A + C$ **13.** $\frac{2}{3}C$

14. APPLES You have $25 to spend on 21 pounds of three types of apples. Empire apples cost $1.40 per pound, Red Delicious apples cost $1.10 per pound, and Golden Delicious apples cost $1.30 per pound. You want twice as many Red Delicious apples as the other two kinds combined. Use a system of equations to find how many pounds of each type you should buy. *(p. 178)* 5 lb empire, 14 lb red delicious, 2 lb golden delicious

12. Not possible; A and C are not the same dimension.

13. $\begin{bmatrix} -4 & -\frac{4}{3} & 6 \\ \frac{2}{3} & -\frac{8}{3} & -\frac{2}{3} \end{bmatrix}$

5 ASSESS AND RETEACH

Daily Homework Quiz

Transparency Available

Perform the indicated operation.

1. $\begin{bmatrix} 5 & -2 \\ 0 & 8 \end{bmatrix} + \begin{bmatrix} -1 & 5 \\ 7 & -1 \end{bmatrix}$ $\begin{bmatrix} 4 & 3 \\ 7 & 7 \end{bmatrix}$

2. $-3\begin{bmatrix} 1 & -4 \\ 3 & 8 \\ \frac{1}{3} & 0 \end{bmatrix}$ $\begin{bmatrix} -3 & 12 \\ -9 & -24 \\ -1 & 0 \end{bmatrix}$

3. Solve for x and y.

$2\left(\begin{bmatrix} 4x & -5 \\ 5 & 10 \end{bmatrix} - \begin{bmatrix} 8 & 7 \\ 4 & -y \end{bmatrix}\right) = \begin{bmatrix} 48 & -24 \\ 2 & 16 \end{bmatrix}$ $x = 8$; $y = -2$

Online Quiz

Available at **classzone.com**

Diagnosis/Remediation

- Practice A, B, C in Chapter 3 Resource Book, pp. 61–63
- Study Guide in Chapter 3 Resource Book, pp. 64–65
- Practice Workbook, pp. 46–47
- @HomeTutor

Challenge

Additional challenge is available in the Chapter 3 Resource Book, p. 68.

Quiz

An easily-readable reduced copy of the quiz (with answers) on Lessons 3.3–3.5 from the Assessment Book can be found on p. 150F.

Quiz 1–6. See Additional Answers beginning on p. AA1.

@HomeTutor
classzone.com
Keystrokes

3.5 Use Matrix Operations

QUESTION How can you use a graphing calculator to perform matrix operations?

EXAMPLE Perform operations with matrices

Using matrices A and B below, find $A + B$ and $3A - 2B$.

$$A = \begin{bmatrix} 8 & -1 & 2 \\ 3 & -7 & 9 \end{bmatrix} \qquad B = \begin{bmatrix} 1 & 0 & -5 \\ -4 & 6 & 10 \end{bmatrix}$$

STEP 1 *Enter matrix A*

Enter the dimensions and elements of matrix A.

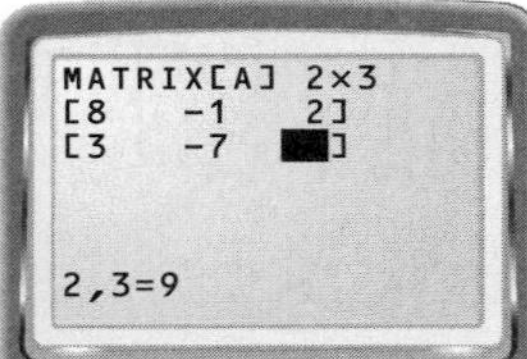

STEP 2 *Enter matrix B*

Enter the dimensions and elements of matrix B.

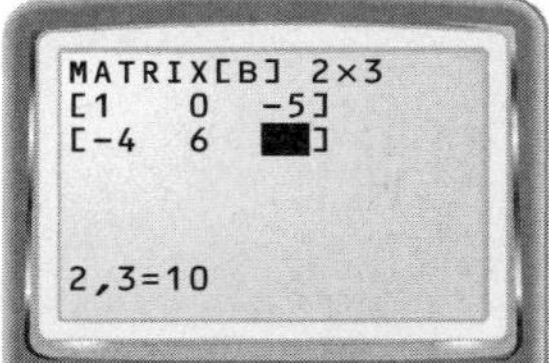

STEP 3 *Perform calculations*

From the home screen, calculate $A + B$ and $3A - 2B$.

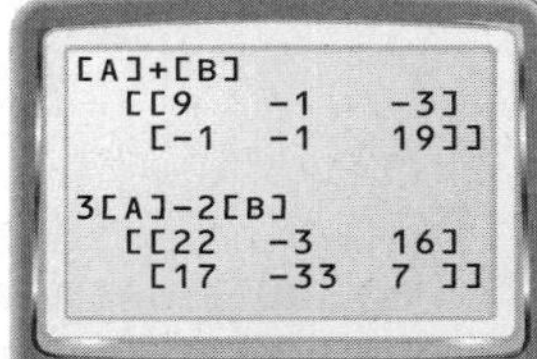

PRACTICE

Use a graphing calculator to perform the indicated operation(s).

1. $\begin{bmatrix} 7 & 3 \\ 5 & -2 \end{bmatrix} + \begin{bmatrix} 12 & -8 \\ 3 & -6 \end{bmatrix}$ $\begin{bmatrix} 19 & -5 \\ 8 & -8 \end{bmatrix}$

2. $2.6\begin{bmatrix} 12.4 & 6.8 & -1.2 \\ -0.8 & 5.6 & -3.2 \end{bmatrix}$ $\begin{bmatrix} 32.24 & 17.68 & -3.12 \\ -2.08 & 14.56 & -8.32 \end{bmatrix}$

3. $\begin{bmatrix} 3 & 1 & -2 \\ -1 & 5 & 6 \\ 4 & 13 & 0 \end{bmatrix} + \begin{bmatrix} -9 & 10 & -3 \\ 0 & 6 & 1 \\ 14 & 7 & -8 \end{bmatrix}$ See margin.

4. $3\begin{bmatrix} 4 & -3 \\ 8 & -7 \\ -1 & 2 \end{bmatrix} - 2\begin{bmatrix} -5 & 8 \\ -7 & 9 \\ 4 & -3 \end{bmatrix}$ $\begin{bmatrix} 22 & -25 \\ 38 & -39 \\ -11 & 12 \end{bmatrix}$

5. **BOOK SALES** The matrices below show book sales (in thousands of dollars) at a chain of bookstores for July and August. The book formats are hardcover and paperback. The categories of books are romance (R), mystery (M), science fiction (S), and children's (C). Find the total sales of each format and category for July and August.

	July R	July M	July S	July C	August R	August M	August S	August C
Hardcover	18	16	21	13	26	20	17	8
Paperback	36	20	14	30	40	24	8	20

Total Sales

	R	M	S	C
Hardcover	44	36	38	21
Paperback	76	44	22	50

3. $\begin{bmatrix} -6 & 11 & -5 \\ -1 & 11 & 7 \\ 18 & 20 & -8 \end{bmatrix}$

1 PLAN AND PREPARE

Learn the Method

- Students will perform matrix operations with a graphing calculator.
- Students can use this method to check their solutions to Exercises 16–23 in Lesson 3.5.

Keystroke Help

Keystrokes for several models of calculators are available in blackline format in the *Chapter 3 Resource Book*.

2 TEACH

Tips for Success

Urge students to check that all the elements have been correctly entered before they perform calculations.

Alternative Strategy

Ask students to work in pairs, with one student doing the practice exercises by hand and one doing the exercises on a graphing calculator. They should switch roles occasionally.

Extra Example

Using the matrices P and Q, find $Q - P$ and $3P + 2Q$.

$$P = \begin{bmatrix} 2 & 1 \\ 7 & -3 \\ 5 & -2 \end{bmatrix} \quad Q = \begin{bmatrix} -2 & 5 \\ 3 & 0 \\ 2 & -2 \end{bmatrix}$$

$\begin{bmatrix} -4 & 4 \\ -4 & 3 \\ -3 & 0 \end{bmatrix}, \begin{bmatrix} 2 & 13 \\ 27 & -9 \\ 19 & -10 \end{bmatrix}$

3 ASSESS AND RETEACH

Use a graphing calculator to find

$$2\begin{bmatrix} 3 & -2 & 4 \\ 5 & 7 & 0 \\ -5 & 8 & -2 \end{bmatrix} + \begin{bmatrix} 4 & -1 & 8 \\ 3 & -5 & 10 \\ -2 & 1 & 0 \end{bmatrix}.$$

$\begin{bmatrix} 10 & -5 & 16 \\ 13 & 9 & 10 \\ -12 & 17 & -4 \end{bmatrix}$

3.6 Multiply Matrices

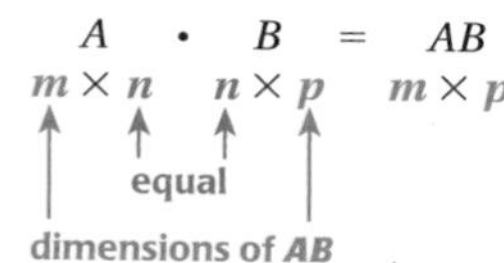

MA-HS-4.1.3

Before You added and subtracted matrices.

Now You will multiply matrices.

Why? So you can calculate the cost of sports equipment, as in Example 4.

Key Vocabulary
- **matrix,** *p. 187*
- **dimensions,** *p. 187*
- **elements,** *p. 187*

MA-HS-4.1.3
Students will represent real-world data using matrices and will use matrix addition, subtraction, multiplication (with matrices no larger than 2 × 2) and scalar multiplication to solve real-world problems.

The product of two matrices A and B is defined provided the number of columns in A is equal to the number of rows in B.

If A is an $m \times n$ matrix and B is an $n \times p$ matrix, then the product AB is an $m \times p$ matrix.

$$\underset{m \times n}{A} \cdot \underset{n \times p}{B} = \underset{m \times p}{AB}$$

equal

dimensions of AB

EXAMPLE 1 Describe matrix products

State whether the product AB is defined. If so, give the dimensions of AB.

a. A: 4×3, B: 3×2 **b.** A: 3×4, B: 3×2

Solution

a. Because A is a 4×3 matrix and B is a 3×2 matrix, the product AB is defined and is a 4×2 matrix.

b. Because the number of columns in A (four) does not equal the number of rows in B (three), the product AB is not defined.

GUIDED PRACTICE for Example 1

State whether the product AB is defined. If so, give the dimensions of AB.

1. A: 5×2, B: 2×2 defined; 5×2

2. A: 3×2, B: 3×2 not defined

KEY CONCEPT *For Your Notebook*

Multiplying Matrices

Words To find the element in the ith row and jth column of the product matrix AB, multiply each element in the ith row of A by the corresponding element in the jth column of B, then add the products.

Algebra

$$\overset{A}{\begin{bmatrix} a & b \\ c & d \end{bmatrix}} \cdot \overset{B}{\begin{bmatrix} e & f \\ g & h \end{bmatrix}} = \overset{AB}{\begin{bmatrix} ae + bg & af + bh \\ ce + dg & cf + dh \end{bmatrix}}$$

1 PLAN AND PREPARE

Warm-Up Exercises

Transparency Available

Use $A = \begin{bmatrix} 2 & -1 \\ 5 & 3 \end{bmatrix}$, $B = \begin{bmatrix} -4 & 6 \\ 0 & 9 \end{bmatrix}$, and $C = \begin{bmatrix} 1 & -8 \\ 3 & 5 \\ -6 & 0 \end{bmatrix}$.

1. Find $A + B$. $\begin{bmatrix} -2 & 5 \\ 5 & 12 \end{bmatrix}$

2. Find $-3C$. $\begin{bmatrix} -3 & 24 \\ -9 & -15 \\ 18 & 0 \end{bmatrix}$

Notetaking Guide

Transparency Available

Promotes interactive learning and notetaking skills, pp. 76–79.

Pacing

Basic: 2 days
Average: 2 days
Advanced: 2 days
Block: 0.5 block with 3.5
0.5 block with 3.7

- See *Teaching Guide/Lesson Plan.*

2 FOCUS AND MOTIVATE

Essential Question

Big Idea 3, p. 151

How do you find each element in the product of two matrices? **Tell students they will learn how to answer this question by multiplying matrices.**

Resource Planning Guide

Chapter Resource Book
- Teaching Guide/Lesson Plan (pp. 69–70)
- Practice levels A, B, C (pp. 71–73)
- Study Guide (pp. 74–75)
- Catch-up for Absent Students (p. 76)
- Application (p. 77)
- Challenge (p. 78)

Workbooks
- Notetaking Guide (pp. 76–79)
- Practice Workbook (pp. 48–49)

Teaching Options
- **Power Presentations CD-ROM** provides dynamic electronic teaching resources for the classroom.
- **Activity Generator CD-ROM** provides editable activities for all ability levels.

Interactive Technology
- Easy Planner
- Power Presentations CD-ROM
- Activity Generator CD-ROM
- Animated Algebra
- Test Generator CD-ROM
- Online Quiz
- eWorkbook
- eEdition
- @HomeTutor

Resources for English Learners
- Quick Reference for English Learners
- Spanish Study Guide
- Multi-Language Visual Glossary
- Student Resources in Spanish

See also the *Algebra 2 Toolkit* for more strategies for meeting individual needs.

Motivating the Lesson

The following matrix represents the inventory of a chain of entertainment stores.

	CDs	DVDs	VHSs	Games
Store 1	2800	550	200	150
Store 2	2600	800	150	120
Store 3	1850	650	190	100

If you know the costs of CDs, DVDs, VHSs, and Games, you can use matrix multiplication to find the total value of the inventory.

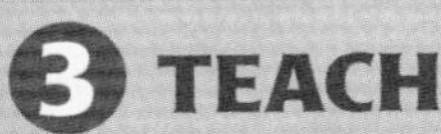

3 TEACH

Extra Example 1

State whether the product *AB* is defined. If so, give the dimensions of *AB*.

a. $A: 3 \times 5$, $B: 5 \times 2$ yes, 3×2

b. $A: 3 \times 4$, $B: 3 \times 2$ no

Study Strategy

An easy way to remember how to find the dimensions of the product of two matrices is to write the dimensions from left to right and then cover the middle two numbers. For example, when you multiply matrices with dimensions 3×5 and 5×2, the product has dimensions 3×2.

Extra Example 2

Find *AB* if $A = \begin{bmatrix} 2 & -3 \\ 1 & 5 \end{bmatrix}$ and $B = \begin{bmatrix} 1 & -4 \\ 3 & -2 \end{bmatrix}$. $\begin{bmatrix} -7 & -2 \\ 16 & -14 \end{bmatrix}$

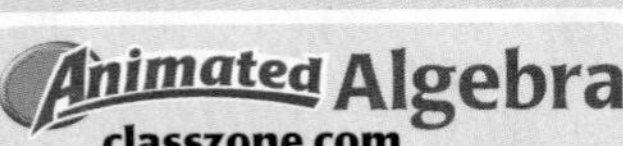

An **Animated Algebra** activity is available on-line for **Example 2**. This activity is also available on the **Power Presentations CD-ROM**.

EXAMPLE 2 Find the product of two matrices

Find *AB* if $A = \begin{bmatrix} 1 & 4 \\ 3 & -2 \end{bmatrix}$ **and** $B = \begin{bmatrix} 5 & -7 \\ 9 & 6 \end{bmatrix}$.

Solution

Because *A* is a 2×2 matrix and *B* is a 2×2 matrix, the product *AB* is defined and is a 2×2 matrix.

AVOID ERRORS
Order is important when multiplying matrices. To find *AB*, write matrix *A* on the left and matrix *B* on the right.

STEP 1 **Multiply** the numbers in the first row of *A* by the numbers in the first column of *B*, add the products, and put the result in the first row, first column of *AB*.

$$\begin{bmatrix} 1 & 4 \\ 3 & -2 \end{bmatrix}\begin{bmatrix} 5 & -7 \\ 9 & 6 \end{bmatrix} = \begin{bmatrix} 1(5) + 4(9) & \\ & \end{bmatrix}$$

STEP 2 **Multiply** the numbers in the first row of *A* by the numbers in the second column of *B*, add the products, and put the result in the first row, second column of *AB*.

$$\begin{bmatrix} 1 & 4 \\ 3 & -2 \end{bmatrix}\begin{bmatrix} 5 & -7 \\ 9 & 6 \end{bmatrix} = \begin{bmatrix} 1(5) + 4(9) & 1(-7) + 4(6) \\ & \end{bmatrix}$$

STEP 3 **Multiply** the numbers in the second row of *A* by the numbers in the first column of *B*, add the products, and put the result in the second row, first column of *AB*.

$$\begin{bmatrix} 1 & 4 \\ 3 & -2 \end{bmatrix}\begin{bmatrix} 5 & -7 \\ 9 & 6 \end{bmatrix} = \begin{bmatrix} 1(5) + 4(9) & 1(-7) + 4(6) \\ 3(5) + (-2)(9) & \end{bmatrix}$$

STEP 4 **Multiply** the numbers in the second row of *A* by the numbers in the second column of *B*, add the products, and put the result in the second row, second column of *AB*.

$$\begin{bmatrix} 1 & 4 \\ 3 & -2 \end{bmatrix}\begin{bmatrix} 5 & -7 \\ 9 & 6 \end{bmatrix} = \begin{bmatrix} 1(5) + 4(9) & 1(-7) + 4(6) \\ 3(5) + (-2)(9) & 3(-7) + (-2)(6) \end{bmatrix}$$

STEP 5 **Simplify** the product matrix.

$$\begin{bmatrix} 1(5) + 4(9) & 1(-7) + 4(6) \\ 3(5) + (-2)(9) & 3(-7) + (-2)(6) \end{bmatrix} = \begin{bmatrix} 41 & 17 \\ -3 & -33 \end{bmatrix}$$

Animated Algebra at classzone.com

For the matrices *A* and *B* in Example 2, notice that the product *BA* is not the same as the product *AB*.

$$BA = \begin{bmatrix} 5 & -7 \\ 9 & 6 \end{bmatrix}\begin{bmatrix} 1 & 4 \\ 3 & -2 \end{bmatrix} = \begin{bmatrix} -16 & 34 \\ 27 & 24 \end{bmatrix} \neq AB$$

In general, matrix multiplication is *not* commutative.

✓ GUIDED PRACTICE for Example 2

3. Find *AB* if $A = \begin{bmatrix} -3 & 3 \\ 1 & -2 \end{bmatrix}$ and $B = \begin{bmatrix} 1 & 5 \\ -3 & -2 \end{bmatrix}$. $\begin{bmatrix} -12 & -21 \\ 7 & 9 \end{bmatrix}$

EXAMPLE 3 Use matrix operations

Using the given matrices, evaluate the expression.

$$A = \begin{bmatrix} 4 & 3 \\ -1 & -2 \\ 2 & 0 \end{bmatrix}, B = \begin{bmatrix} -3 & 0 \\ 1 & -2 \end{bmatrix}, C = \begin{bmatrix} 1 & 4 \\ -3 & -1 \end{bmatrix}$$

a. $A(B + C)$ **b.** $AB + AC$

Solution

a. $$A(B + C) = \begin{bmatrix} 4 & 3 \\ -1 & -2 \\ 2 & 0 \end{bmatrix}\left(\begin{bmatrix} -3 & 0 \\ 1 & -2 \end{bmatrix} + \begin{bmatrix} 1 & 4 \\ -3 & -1 \end{bmatrix}\right)$$

$$= \begin{bmatrix} 4 & 3 \\ -1 & -2 \\ 2 & 0 \end{bmatrix}\begin{bmatrix} -2 & 4 \\ -2 & -3 \end{bmatrix} = \begin{bmatrix} -14 & 7 \\ 6 & 2 \\ -4 & 8 \end{bmatrix}$$

b. $$AB + AC = \begin{bmatrix} 4 & 3 \\ -1 & -2 \\ 2 & 0 \end{bmatrix}\begin{bmatrix} -3 & 0 \\ 1 & -2 \end{bmatrix} + \begin{bmatrix} 4 & 3 \\ -1 & -2 \\ 2 & 0 \end{bmatrix}\begin{bmatrix} 1 & 4 \\ -3 & -1 \end{bmatrix}$$

$$= \begin{bmatrix} -9 & -6 \\ 1 & 4 \\ -6 & 0 \end{bmatrix} + \begin{bmatrix} -5 & 13 \\ 5 & -2 \\ 2 & 8 \end{bmatrix} = \begin{bmatrix} -14 & 7 \\ 6 & 2 \\ -4 & 8 \end{bmatrix}$$

MULTIPLICATION PROPERTIES Notice in Example 3 that $A(B + C) = AB + AC$, which is true in general. This and other properties of matrix multiplication are summarized below.

EVIEW ROPERTIES
or help with properties f real numbers, ee p. 2.

CONCEPT SUMMARY *For Your Notebook*

Properties of Matrix Multiplication

Let A, B, and C be matrices and let k be a scalar.

Associative Property of Matrix Multiplication	$A(BC) = (AB)C$
Left Distributive Property	$A(B + C) = AB + AC$
Right Distributive Property	$(A + B)C = AC + BC$
Associative Property of Scalar Multiplication	$k(AB) = (kA)B = A(kB)$

✓ GUIDED PRACTICE for Example 3

Using the given matrices, evaluate the expression.

$$A = \begin{bmatrix} -1 & 2 \\ -3 & 0 \\ 4 & 1 \end{bmatrix}, B = \begin{bmatrix} 3 & 2 \\ -2 & -1 \end{bmatrix}, C = \begin{bmatrix} -4 & 5 \\ 1 & 0 \end{bmatrix}$$

4. $A(B - C)$ **5.** $AB - AC$ **6.** $-\frac{1}{2}(AB)$

$\begin{bmatrix} -13 & 1 \\ -21 & 9 \\ 25 & -13 \end{bmatrix}$

$\begin{bmatrix} -13 & 1 \\ -21 & 9 \\ 25 & -13 \end{bmatrix}$

$\begin{bmatrix} 3.5 & 2 \\ 4.5 & 3 \\ -5 & -3.5 \end{bmatrix}$

Extra Example 3

Using the given matrices, evaluate the expression. $A = \begin{bmatrix} 3 & -2 \\ 0 & 4 \\ -1 & 5 \end{bmatrix}$, $B = \begin{bmatrix} 2 & -3 \\ 1 & 0 \end{bmatrix}$, and $C = \begin{bmatrix} 2 & 1 \\ -4 & -2 \end{bmatrix}$.

a. $A(B - C)$ $\begin{bmatrix} -10 & -16 \\ 20 & 8 \\ 25 & 14 \end{bmatrix}$

b. $AB - AC$ $\begin{bmatrix} -10 & -16 \\ 20 & 8 \\ 25 & 14 \end{bmatrix}$

Key Questions to Ask for Example 3

- Does $A(B + C) = (B + C)A$ in this example? Explain. **No; the expression on the right side of the equation is not defined.**
- Does $A(B + C) = (B + C)A$ in general? Explain. **No; even if AB, AC, BA, and CA are all defined it is not necessarily true that $AB = BA$ and $AC = CA$.**

Differentiated Instruction

Kinesthetic Learners While discussing **Example 2**, have students write each matrix on a separate sheet of paper, cut or tear out each of the elements, and rearrange them in a new matrix to represent the end result of matrix multiplication. This method will help students be more involved in understanding how the elements in the product are obtained from the elements in the original matrices.

See also the *Algebra 2 Toolkit* for more strategies.

Extra Example 4

The following matrix represents the inventory of a chain of entertainment stores.

	CDs	DVDs	VHSs	Games
Store 1	2800	550	200	150
Store 2	2600	800	150	120
Store 3	1850	650	190	100

If CDs cost \$15, DVDs cost \$20, VHSs cost \$18, and Games cost \$30, the cost of each item is represented by the matrix below.

$$\begin{bmatrix} 15 \\ 20 \\ 18 \\ 30 \end{bmatrix}$$

Find the total value of the inventory for each store. **Store 1: \$61,100; Store 2: \$61,300; Store 3: \$47,170**

Key Question to Ask for Example 4

- Why do you write the cost matrix on the right? **The product of a 2×3 matrix times a 3×1 matrix is defined, but the product 3×1 matrix times a 2×3 matrix is not defined.**

Graphing Calculator

Graphing calculators can simplify the calculations for real world problems. Enter the matrix values as shown in Activity 3.5, page 194, and then use the multiply key to multiply the matrices.

Closing the Lesson

Have students summarize the major points of the lesson and answer the Essential Question: How do you find each element in the product of two matrices?

- **Two matrices *A* and *B* can be multiplied if the number of columns in *A* is equal to the number of rows in *B*.**
- **Matrix multiplication is not commutative.**

You can find each element for the product of two matrices by multiplying elements in a row of the left matrix by elements in a column of the right matrix, and then adding the products.

COST MATRICES Matrix multiplication is useful in business applications because an *inventory* matrix, when multiplied by a *cost per item* matrix, results in a *total cost* matrix.

$$\underset{m \times n}{\begin{bmatrix} \text{Inventory} \\ \text{matrix} \end{bmatrix}} \cdot \underset{n \times p}{\begin{bmatrix} \text{Cost per item} \\ \text{matrix} \end{bmatrix}} = \underset{m \times p}{\begin{bmatrix} \text{Total cost} \\ \text{matrix} \end{bmatrix}}$$

For the total cost matrix to be meaningful, the column labels for the inventory matrix must match the row labels for the cost per item matrix.

EXAMPLE 4 Use matrices to calculate total cost

SPORTS Two hockey teams submit equipment lists for the season as shown.

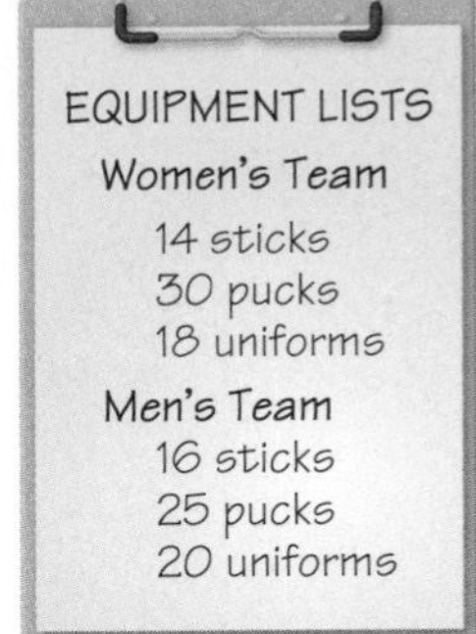

EQUIPMENT LISTS
Women's Team
14 sticks
30 pucks
18 uniforms
Men's Team
16 sticks
25 pucks
20 uniforms

Each stick costs \$60, each puck costs \$2, and each uniform costs \$35. Use matrix multiplication to find the total cost of equipment for each team.

Solution

To begin, write the equipment lists and the costs per item in matrix form. In order to use matrix multiplication, set up the matrices so that the columns of the equipment matrix match the rows of the cost matrix.

Equipment	Sticks	Pucks	Uniforms
Women's team	14	30	18
Men's team	16	25	20

Cost	Dollars
Sticks	60
Pucks	2
Uniforms	35

The total cost of equipment for each team can be found by multiplying the equipment matrix by the cost matrix. The equipment matrix is 2×3 and the cost matrix is 3×1. So, their product is a 2×1 matrix.

$$\begin{bmatrix} 14 & 30 & 18 \\ 16 & 25 & 20 \end{bmatrix}\begin{bmatrix} 60 \\ 2 \\ 35 \end{bmatrix} = \begin{bmatrix} 14(60) + 30(2) + 18(35) \\ 16(60) + 25(2) + 20(35) \end{bmatrix} = \begin{bmatrix} 1530 \\ 1710 \end{bmatrix}$$

The labels for the product matrix are shown below.

Total Cost	Dollars
Women's team	1530
Men's team	1710

▸ The total cost of equipment for the women's team is \$1530, and the total cost for the men's team is \$1710.

✓ GUIDED PRACTICE for Example 4

7. **WHAT IF?** In Example 4, suppose a stick costs \$75, a puck costs \$1, and a uniform costs \$45. Find the total cost of equipment for each team. **women's team: \$1890, men's team: \$2125**

3.6 EXERCISES

HOMEWORK KEY
○ = **WORKED-OUT SOLUTIONS** on p. WS6 for Exs. 13, 23, and 41
★ = **STANDARDIZED TEST PRACTICE** Exs. 2, 9, 21, 35, 41, and 44

SKILL PRACTICE

A

1. VOCABULARY Copy and complete: The product of matrices A and B is defined provided the number of _?_ in A is equal to the number of _?_ in B. **columns; rows**

2. ★ WRITING Suppose A and B are two matrices and AB is defined. *Explain* how to find the element in the first row and first column of AB. **See margin.**

EXAMPLE 1
on p. 195
for Exs. 3–9

MATRIX PRODUCTS **State whether the product AB is defined. If so, give the dimensions of AB.**

3. $A: 2 \times 2, B: 2 \times 2$ **defined; 2 × 2**

4. $A: 3 \times 4, B: 4 \times 2$ **defined; 3 × 2**

5. $A: 2 \times 1, B: 2 \times 2$ **not defined**

6. $A: 1 \times 2, B: 2 \times 3$ **defined; 1 × 3**

7. $A: 4 \times 3, B: 2 \times 3$ **not defined**

8. $A: 2 \times 1, B: 1 \times 5$ **defined; 2 × 5**

9. ★ MULTIPLE CHOICE If A is a 2×3 matrix and B is a 3×2 matrix, what are the dimensions of AB? **A**

Ⓐ 2×2 Ⓑ 3×3 Ⓒ 3×2 Ⓓ 2×3

EXAMPLE 2
on p. 196
for Exs. 10–21

MULTIPLYING MATRICES **Find the product. If the product is not defined, state the reason.**

10. $\begin{bmatrix} 3 & -1 \end{bmatrix} \begin{bmatrix} 5 \\ 7 \end{bmatrix}$ **[8]**

11. $\begin{bmatrix} 1 \\ 4 \end{bmatrix} \begin{bmatrix} -2 & 1 \end{bmatrix} \begin{bmatrix} -2 & 1 \\ -8 & 4 \end{bmatrix}$

12. $\begin{bmatrix} -1 & 0 \\ 5 & 4 \end{bmatrix} \begin{bmatrix} 4 & -6 \end{bmatrix}$

(13.) $\begin{bmatrix} 9 & -3 \\ 0 & 2 \end{bmatrix} \begin{bmatrix} 0 & 1 \\ 4 & -2 \end{bmatrix}$

14. $\begin{bmatrix} 5 & 0 \\ -4 & 1 \end{bmatrix} \begin{bmatrix} -3 & 2 \\ 6 & 2 \end{bmatrix}$

15. $\begin{bmatrix} 5 & 2 \\ 0 & -4 \\ 1 & 6 \end{bmatrix} \begin{bmatrix} 3 & 7 \\ -2 & 0 \end{bmatrix}$

16. $\begin{bmatrix} 0 & -4 \\ 2 & 5 \\ 4 & 0 \end{bmatrix} \begin{bmatrix} 2 & 8 \\ 3 & 0 \\ -5 & -2 \end{bmatrix}$

17. $\begin{bmatrix} 1 & 3 & 0 \\ 2 & 12 & -4 \end{bmatrix} \begin{bmatrix} 9 & 1 \\ 4 & -3 \\ -2 & 4 \end{bmatrix}$

18. $\begin{bmatrix} 2 & 5 \\ -1 & 4 \\ 3 & -7 \end{bmatrix} \begin{bmatrix} 0 & 1 & 5 \\ -3 & 10 & -4 \end{bmatrix}$

2. Not possible; the number of columns in the first matrix does not equal the number of rows in the second matrix.

3. $\begin{bmatrix} -12 & 15 \\ 8 & -4 \end{bmatrix}$

4. $\begin{bmatrix} -15 & 10 \\ 18 & -6 \end{bmatrix}$

5. $\begin{bmatrix} 11 & 35 \\ 8 & 0 \\ -9 & 7 \end{bmatrix}$

6. Not possible; the number of columns in the first matrix does not equal the number of rows in the second matrix.

7. $\begin{bmatrix} 21 & -8 \\ 74 & -50 \end{bmatrix}$

8. $\begin{bmatrix} -15 & 52 & -10 \\ -12 & 39 & -21 \\ 21 & -67 & 43 \end{bmatrix}$

ERROR ANALYSIS *Describe* **and correct the error in finding the element in the first row and first column of the matrix product.** **19, 20. See margin.**

19.

$\begin{bmatrix} 3 & -1 \\ 6 & 2 \end{bmatrix} \begin{bmatrix} 7 & 0 \\ 1 & -6 \end{bmatrix} =$ ✗

$\begin{bmatrix} 3(7) + (-1)(0) & \\ & \end{bmatrix} = \begin{bmatrix} 21 & \\ & \end{bmatrix}$

20.

$\begin{bmatrix} 2 & 5 \\ 1 & 7 \end{bmatrix} \begin{bmatrix} 4 & -8 \\ 3 & -1 \end{bmatrix} =$ ✗

$\begin{bmatrix} 2(4) + 1(-8) & \\ & \end{bmatrix} = \begin{bmatrix} 0 & \\ & \end{bmatrix}$

21. ★ MULTIPLE CHOICE What is the product of $\begin{bmatrix} 1 & -4 \\ 3 & -2 \end{bmatrix}$ and $\begin{bmatrix} 4 & -1 \\ 0 & -3 \end{bmatrix}$? **B**

Ⓐ $\begin{bmatrix} -4 & 12 \\ 3 & -3 \end{bmatrix}$ Ⓑ $\begin{bmatrix} 4 & 11 \\ 12 & 3 \end{bmatrix}$ Ⓒ $\begin{bmatrix} -4 & 11 \\ 12 & -3 \end{bmatrix}$ Ⓓ $\begin{bmatrix} 4 & -11 \\ 0 & 3 \end{bmatrix}$

2. Multiply the first element in the first row of A by the first element in the first column of B. Add this value to the product of the second element in the first row of A and the second element in the first column of B. Continue for the rest of the elements in the first row of A and first column of B.

19. The multiplication should be row 1 of the left matrix by column 1 of the right matrix; $3(7) + (-1)(1) = 20$.

20. The multiplication should be row 1 of the left matrix by column 1 of the right matrix; $2(4) + 5(3) = 23$.

4 PRACTICE AND APPLY

Assignment Guide

Answer Transparencies available for all exercises

Basic:
Day 1: pp. 199–202
Exs. 1–15, 46–47
Day 2: pp. 199–202
Exs. 19–28, 37–42

Average:
Day 1: pp. 199–202
Exs. 1, 2, 6–18, 46–47
Day 2: pp. 199–202
Exs. 19–21, 24–34, 37–44

Advanced:
Day 1: pp. 199–202
Exs. 1, 2, 6–9, 13–21, 46–47
Day 2: pp. 199–202
Exs. 22–36*, 38–45*

Block:
pp. 199–202
Exs. 1, 2, 6–18, 46–47 (with 3.5)
pp. 199–202
Exs. 19–21, 24–34, 37–44 (with 3.7)

Differentiated Instruction

See *Algebra 2 Best Practices Toolkit* for suggestions on addressing the needs of a diverse classroom.

Homework Check

For a quick check of student understanding of key concepts, go over the following exercises:

Basic: 4, 12, 24, 37, 38
Average: 6, 14, 26, 39, 40
Advanced: 8, 16, 28, 41, 42

Extra Practice

- Student Edition, p. 1012
- Chapter 3 Resource Book: Practice levels A, B, C, pp. 71–73

Practice Worksheet

An easily-readable reduced practice page (with answers) for this lesson can be found on p. 150C.

Teaching Strategy

Exercise 21 Tell students they can eliminate choices A and C immediately upon seeing that the element in the upper left corner of the product matrix is 4, not −4.

Avoiding Common Errors

Exercises 22, 23, 28, 29 Some students may think that multiplying a scalar by the product of two matrices means to multiply each matrix by the scalar. Show them this is not the case by using an example from algebra, such as $3xy \neq 3x \cdot 3y$.

Graphing Calculator

Exercises 32–34 Graphing calculators can simplify the calculations for finding A^3. Tell students that they can use the power key of the calculator with matrices.

Avoiding Common Errors

Exercises 37–40 Students may have difficulty with these exercises if they list the matrices in an incorrect order. Encourage them to check that, whenever they write a product of matrices, the product is defined.

22. $\begin{bmatrix} -36 & 33 \\ 48 & -30 \end{bmatrix}$

23. $\begin{bmatrix} 21 & -6 \\ -14 & 1 \end{bmatrix}$

24. $\begin{bmatrix} -54 & 23 \\ 44 & -12 \end{bmatrix}$

25. $\begin{bmatrix} -10 & 7 \\ -8 & 10 \end{bmatrix}$

26. $\begin{bmatrix} 30 & 9 & -28 \\ -24 & 18 & 48 \\ 5 & 11 & 29 \end{bmatrix}$

27. $\begin{bmatrix} -2 & 4 & 0 \\ 5 & 15 & 8 \\ -16 & 17 & 36 \end{bmatrix}$

28. $\begin{bmatrix} -8 & -2 \\ 64 & -20 \end{bmatrix}$

29. $\begin{bmatrix} -204 & 81 \\ 160 & -38 \end{bmatrix}$

32. $\begin{bmatrix} 1 & -3 \\ 0 & 4 \end{bmatrix}, \begin{bmatrix} 1 & -7 \\ 0 & 8 \end{bmatrix}$

EXAMPLE 3 B on p. 197 for Exs. 22–29

EVALUATING EXPRESSIONS **Using the given matrices, evaluate the expression.**

$A = \begin{bmatrix} 5 & -3 \\ -2 & 4 \end{bmatrix}, B = \begin{bmatrix} 0 & 1 \\ 4 & -2 \end{bmatrix}, C = \begin{bmatrix} -6 & 3 \\ 4 & 1 \end{bmatrix}, D = \begin{bmatrix} 1 & 3 & 2 \\ -3 & 1 & 4 \\ 2 & 1 & -2 \end{bmatrix}, E = \begin{bmatrix} -3 & 1 & 4 \\ 7 & 0 & -2 \\ 3 & 4 & -1 \end{bmatrix}$ 22–29. See margin.

22. $3AB$ **(23.)** $-\frac{1}{2}AC$ **24.** $AB + AC$ **25.** $AB - BA$

26. $E(D + E)$ **27.** $(D + E)D$ **28.** $-2(BC)$ **29.** $4AC + 3AB$

SOLVING MATRIX EQUATIONS **Solve for x and y.**

30. $\begin{bmatrix} -2 & 1 & 2 \\ 3 & 2 & 4 \\ 0 & -2 & 4 \end{bmatrix}\begin{bmatrix} 1 \\ x \\ 3 \end{bmatrix} = \begin{bmatrix} 6 \\ 19 \\ y \end{bmatrix}$ $x = 2, y = 8$

31. $\begin{bmatrix} 4 & 1 & 3 \\ -2 & x & 1 \end{bmatrix}\begin{bmatrix} 9 & -2 \\ 2 & 1 \\ -1 & 1 \end{bmatrix} = \begin{bmatrix} y & -4 \\ -13 & 8 \end{bmatrix}$ $x = 3, y = 35$

FINDING POWERS **Using the given matrix, find $A^2 = AA$ and $A^3 = AAA$.** 32–34. See margin.

32. $A = \begin{bmatrix} 1 & -1 \\ 0 & 2 \end{bmatrix}$ **33.** $A = \begin{bmatrix} -4 & 1 \\ 2 & -1 \end{bmatrix}$ **34.** $A = \begin{bmatrix} 2 & 0 & -1 \\ 1 & 3 & 2 \\ -2 & -1 & 0 \end{bmatrix}$

C

35. ★ **OPEN-ENDED MATH** Find two matrices A and B such that $A \neq B$ and $AB = BA$. See margin.

36. **CHALLENGE** Let $A = \begin{bmatrix} a & b \\ c & d \end{bmatrix}$ and $B = \begin{bmatrix} e & f \\ g & h \end{bmatrix}$, and let k be a scalar. Prove the associative property of scalar multiplication for 2×2 matrices by showing that $k(AB) = (kA)B = A(kB)$. See margin.

PROBLEM SOLVING

EXAMPLE 4 A on p. 198 for Exs. 37–42

In Exercises 37 and 38, write an inventory matrix and a cost per item matrix. Then use matrix multiplication to write a total cost matrix.

37. **SOFTBALL** A softball team needs to buy 12 bats, 45 balls, and 15 uniforms. Each bat costs \$21, each ball costs \$4, and each uniform costs \$30. See margin.

@HomeTutor for problem solving help at classzone.com

38. **ART SUPPLIES** A teacher is buying supplies for two art classes. For class 1, the teacher buys 24 tubes of paint, 12 brushes, and 17 canvases. For class 2, the teacher buys 20 tubes of paint, 14 brushes, and 15 canvases. Each tube of paint costs \$3.35, each brush costs \$1.75, and each canvas costs \$4.50. See margin.

@HomeTutor for problem solving help at classzone.com

39. **MULTI-STEP PROBLEM** Tickets to the senior class play cost \$2 for students, \$5 for adults, and \$4 for senior citizens. At Friday night's performance, there were 120 students, 150 adults, and 40 senior citizens in attendance. At Saturday night's performance, there were 192 students, 215 adults, and 54 senior citizens in attendance. Organize the information using matrices. Then use matrix multiplication to find the income from ticket sales for Friday and Saturday nights' performances. See margin.

○ = WORKED-OUT SOLUTIONS on p. WS1 ★ = STANDARDIZED TEST PRACTICE

33. $\begin{bmatrix} 18 & -5 \\ -10 & 3 \end{bmatrix}, \begin{bmatrix} -82 & 23 \\ 46 & -13 \end{bmatrix}$

34. $\begin{bmatrix} 6 & 1 & -2 \\ 1 & 7 & 5 \\ -5 & -3 & 0 \end{bmatrix}, \begin{bmatrix} 17 & 5 & -4 \\ -1 & 16 & 13 \\ -13 & -9 & -1 \end{bmatrix}$

35. *Sample answer:* $\begin{bmatrix} 3 & 7 \\ -2 & 5 \end{bmatrix}\begin{bmatrix} 1 & 0 \\ 0 & 1 \end{bmatrix}$

40. **SUMMER OLYMPICS** The top three countries in the final medal standings for the 2004 Summer Olympics were the United States, China, and Russia. Each gold medal is worth 3 points, each silver medal is worth 2 points, and each bronze medal is worth 1 point. Organize the information using matrices. How many points did each country score? U.S.: 212 points, China: 144 points, Russia: 173 points

Medals Won

	Gold	Silver	Bronze
USA	35	39	29
China	32	17	14
Russia	27	27	38

41. ★ **SHORT RESPONSE** Matrix S gives the numbers of three types of cars sold in February by two car dealers, dealer A and dealer B. Matrix P gives the profit for each type of car sold. Which matrix is defined, SP or PS? Find this matrix and explain what its elements represent. PS; $\begin{bmatrix} 62{,}400 & 57{,}575 \end{bmatrix}$, it shows the profit for all of the cars sold by each dealer.

Matrix S

$$\begin{array}{r} \\ \textbf{Compact} \\ \textbf{Mid-size} \\ \textbf{Full-size} \end{array} \begin{array}{c} \textbf{A} \quad \textbf{B} \\ \begin{bmatrix} 21 & 16 \\ 40 & 33 \\ 15 & 19 \end{bmatrix} \end{array}$$

Matrix P

$$\begin{array}{c} \quad\quad\quad \textbf{Compact} \quad \textbf{Mid-size} \quad \textbf{Full-size} \\ \textbf{Profit} \begin{bmatrix} \$650 & \$825 & \$1050 \end{bmatrix} \end{array}$$

B 42. **GRADING** Your overall grade in math class is a weighted average of three components: homework, quizzes, and tests. Homework counts for 20% of your grade, quizzes count for 30%, and tests count for 50%. The spreadsheet below shows the grades on homework, quizzes, and tests for five students. Organize the information using a matrix, then multiply the matrix by a matrix of weights to find each student's overall grade. Jean: 85.8, Ted: 89.8, Pat: 78.8, Al: 76.3, Matt: 90.2

	A	B	C	D
1	Name	Homework	Quizzes	Test
2	Jean	82	88	86
3	Ted	92	88	90
4	Pat	82	73	81
5	Al	74	75	78
6	Matt	88	92	90

43. **MULTI-STEP PROBLEM** Residents of a certain suburb commute to a nearby city either by driving or by using public transportation. Each year, 20% of those who drive switch to public transportation, and 5% of those who use public transportation switch to driving.

a. The information above can be represented by the *transition matrix*

$$T = \begin{bmatrix} 1-p & q \\ p & 1-q \end{bmatrix} \quad \begin{bmatrix} 0.8 & 0.05 \\ 0.2 & 0.95 \end{bmatrix}$$

where p is the percent of commuters who switch from driving to public transportation and q is the percent of commuters who switch from public transportation to driving. (Both p and q are expressed as decimals.) Write a transition matrix for the given situation.

b. Suppose 5000 commuters drive and 8000 commuters take public transportation. Let M_0 be the following matrix:

$$M_0 = \begin{bmatrix} 5000 \\ 8000 \end{bmatrix} \quad \begin{bmatrix} 4400 \\ 8600 \end{bmatrix}$$; the numbers of commuters after one year.

Find $M_1 = TM_0$. What does this matrix represent?

c. Find $M_2 = TM_1$, $M_3 = TM_2$, and $M_4 = TM_3$. What do these matrices represent? See margin.

Mathematical Reasoning

Exercise 43 Transition matrices are used to analyze and describe change. The elements in each column in matrix T add to 1 because they are percents expressed as decimals. Graphing calculators or computers can perform the computations necessary to use transitions matrices to make predictions. Students will learn in other math classes that the matrices in part (c) are an example of a *Markov chain.*

37. $\begin{array}{r} \text{Bats} \\ \text{Balls} \\ \text{Uniforms} \end{array} \begin{bmatrix} 12 \\ 45 \\ 15 \end{bmatrix}$, $\begin{array}{c} \quad\quad \text{Bat} \quad \text{Ball} \quad \text{Uniform} \\ \text{Cost} \begin{bmatrix} 21 & 4 & 30 \end{bmatrix} \end{array}$; $\begin{array}{c} \quad\quad \text{Cost} \\ \text{Item} \begin{bmatrix} 882 \end{bmatrix} \end{array}$

38. $\begin{array}{c} \quad\quad\quad \text{P} \quad \text{B} \quad \text{C} \\ \begin{array}{r} \text{Class 1} \\ \text{Class 2} \end{array} \begin{bmatrix} 24 & 12 & 17 \\ 20 & 14 & 15 \end{bmatrix} \end{array}$, $\begin{array}{r} \\ \text{Paint} \\ \text{Brushes} \\ \text{Canvases} \end{array} \begin{array}{c} \text{Cost} \\ \begin{bmatrix} 3.35 \\ 1.75 \\ 4.50 \end{bmatrix} \end{array}$; $\begin{array}{r} \\ \text{Class 1} \\ \text{Class 2} \end{array} \begin{array}{c} \text{Cost} \\ \begin{bmatrix} 177.9 \\ 159 \end{bmatrix} \end{array}$

43c. $M_2 = \begin{bmatrix} 3950 \\ 9050 \end{bmatrix}$, the number of commuters after 2 years; $M_3 = \begin{bmatrix} 3612.5 \\ 9387.5 \end{bmatrix}$, the number of commuters after 3 years; $M_4 = \begin{bmatrix} 3359.375 \\ 9640.625 \end{bmatrix}$, the number of commuters after 4 years

36. $A = \begin{bmatrix} a & b \\ c & d \end{bmatrix}$, $B = \begin{bmatrix} e & f \\ g & h \end{bmatrix}$; $k(AB) = \begin{bmatrix} aek + bgk & afk + bhk \\ cek + dgk & cfk + dhk \end{bmatrix}$,

$(kA)B = \begin{bmatrix} aek + bgk & afk + bhk \\ cek + dgk & cfk + dhk \end{bmatrix}$, $A(kB) = \begin{bmatrix} aek + bgk & afk + bhk \\ cek + dgk & cfk + dhk \end{bmatrix}$

Therefore $k(AB) = (kA)B = A(kB)$.

5 ASSESS AND RETEACH

Daily Homework Quiz

Transparency Available

1. State whether the product AB is defined. If so, give the dimensions of AB.

a. A: 2×4, B: 2×4 **no**

b. A: 3×2, B: 2×4 **yes; 3×4**

2. Find AB if $A = \begin{bmatrix} 4 & -1 \\ 3 & 2 \end{bmatrix}$ and $B = \begin{bmatrix} 2 & -5 \\ 4 & 8 \end{bmatrix}$. $\begin{bmatrix} 4 & -28 \\ 14 & 1 \end{bmatrix}$

3. Using the given matrices, evaluate the expression $A(B + C)$.

$A = \begin{bmatrix} 2 & -8 \\ 3 & -1 \\ -6 & 0 \end{bmatrix}$, $B = \begin{bmatrix} 0 & 6 \\ 1 & -2 \end{bmatrix}$, and $C = \begin{bmatrix} -2 & -1 \\ 1 & 3 \end{bmatrix}$.

$\begin{bmatrix} -20 & 2 \\ -8 & 14 \\ 12 & -30 \end{bmatrix}$

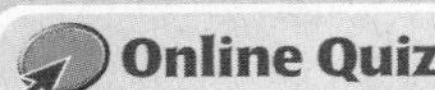

Available at **classzone.com**

Diagnosis/Remediation

- Practice A, B, C in Chapter 3 Resource Book, pp. 71–73
- Study Guide in Chapter 3 Resource Book, pp. 74–75
- Practice Workbook, pp. 48–49
- @HomeTutor

Challenge

Additional challenge is available in the Chapter 3 Resource Book, p. 78.

44a–d, 45a–b. See Additional Answers beginning on p. AA1.

44. ★ **EXTENDED RESPONSE** Two students have a business selling handmade scarves. The scarves come in four different styles: plain, with the class year, with the school name, and with the school mascot. The costs of making each style of scarf are \$10, \$15, \$20, and \$20, respectively. The prices of each style of scarf are \$15, \$20, \$25, and \$30, respectively. **a–d. See margin.**

a. Write a 4×1 matrix C that gives the cost of making each style of scarf and a 4×1 matrix P that gives the price of each style of scarf.

b. The sales for the first three years of the business are shown below.

Year 1: *0 plain, 20 class year, 100 school name, 0 school mascot*

Year 2: *10 plain, 100 class year, 50 school name, 30 school mascot*

Year 3: *20 plain, 300 class year, 100 school name, 50 school mascot*

Write a 3×4 matrix S that gives the sales for the first three years.

c. Find SC and SP. What do these matrices represent?

d. Find $SP - SC$. What does this matrix represent?

C **45.** **CHALLENGE** Matrix A is a 90° rotational matrix. Matrix B contains the coordinates of the vertices of the triangle shown in the graph. **a, b. See margin.**

$$A = \begin{bmatrix} 0 & -1 \\ 1 & 0 \end{bmatrix} \qquad B = \begin{bmatrix} -7 & -4 & -4 \\ 4 & 8 & 2 \end{bmatrix}$$

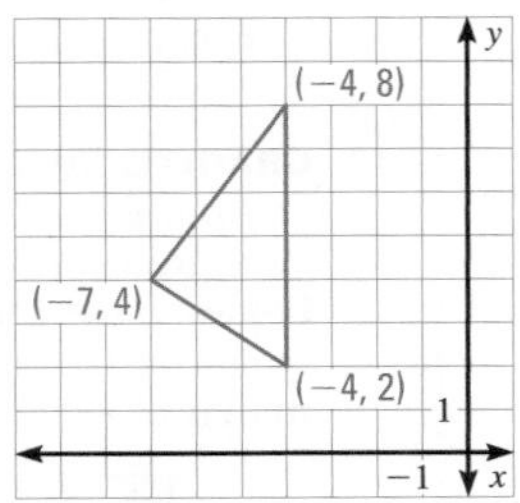

a. Find AB. Draw the triangle whose vertices are given by AB.

b. Find the 180° and 270° rotations of the original triangle by using repeated multiplication of the 90° rotational matrix. What are the coordinates of the vertices of the rotated triangles?

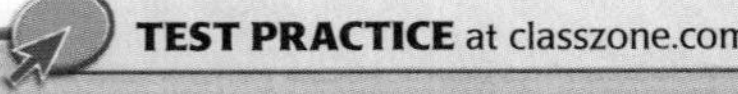

KY KENTUCKY MIXED REVIEW

46. The graph shows the value of a comic book over a period of 9 years. What is a reasonable conclusion about the value of the comic book during the time shown on the graph? **C**

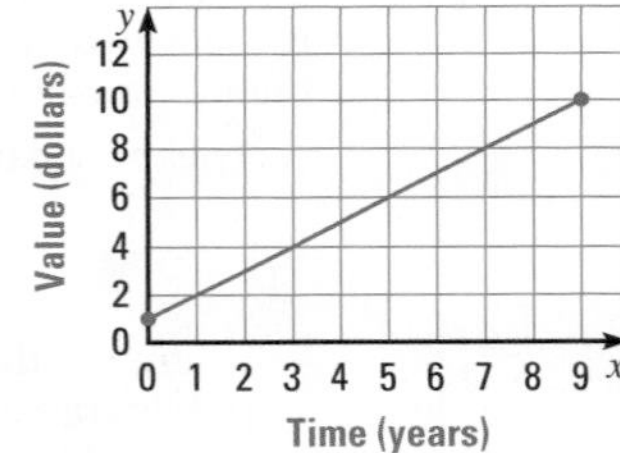

Ⓐ It appreciated \$2 every year.

Ⓑ It appreciated \$3 every 2 years.

Ⓒ Its value at 5 years was twice its value at 2 years.

Ⓓ Its value at 7 years was half its value at 3 years.

47. Use the information in the diagram. What is the distance x across the river? **A**

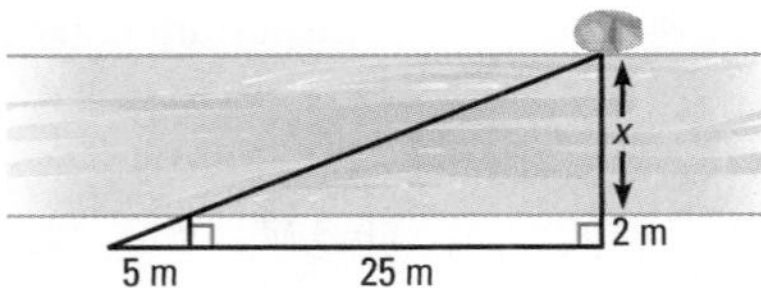

Ⓐ 10 m Ⓑ 12 m

Ⓒ 22 m Ⓓ 30 m

3.7 Evaluate Determinants and Apply Cramer's Rule

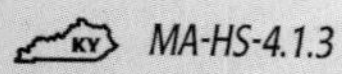 MA-HS-4.1.3

Before	You added, subtracted, and multiplied matrices.
Now	You will evaluate determinants of matrices.
Why?	So you can find areas of habitats, as in Example 2.

Key Vocabulary
- **determinant**
- **Cramer's rule**
- **coefficient matrix**

MA-HS-4.1.3
Students will represent real-world data using matrices and will use matrix addition, subtraction, multiplication (with matrices no larger than 2 × 2) and scalar multiplication to solve real-world problems.

Associated with each square ($n \times n$) matrix is a real number called its **determinant**. The determinant of a matrix A is denoted by det A or by $|A|$.

KEY CONCEPT *For Your Notebook*

The Determinant of a Matrix

Determinant of a 2 × 2 Matrix

$$\det\begin{bmatrix} a & b \\ c & d \end{bmatrix} = \begin{vmatrix} a & b \\ c & d \end{vmatrix} = ad - cb$$

The determinant of a 2 × 2 matrix is the difference of the products of the elements on the diagonals.

Determinant of a 3 × 3 Matrix

STEP 1 **Repeat** the first two columns to the right of the determinant.

STEP 2 **Subtract** the sum of the red products from the sum of the blue products.

$$\det\begin{bmatrix} a & b & c \\ d & e & f \\ g & h & i \end{bmatrix} = \begin{vmatrix} a & b & c \\ d & e & f \\ g & h & i \end{vmatrix}\begin{matrix} a & b \\ d & e \\ g & h \end{matrix} = (aei + bfg + cdh) - (gec + hfa + idb)$$

EXAMPLE 1 Evaluate determinants

Evaluate the determinant of the matrix.

a. $\begin{bmatrix} 5 & 4 \\ 3 & 1 \end{bmatrix}$ **b.** $\begin{bmatrix} 2 & -1 & -3 \\ 4 & 1 & 0 \\ 3 & -4 & -2 \end{bmatrix}$

Solution

a. $\begin{vmatrix} 5 & 4 \\ 3 & 1 \end{vmatrix} = 5(1) - 3(4) = 5 - 12 = -7$

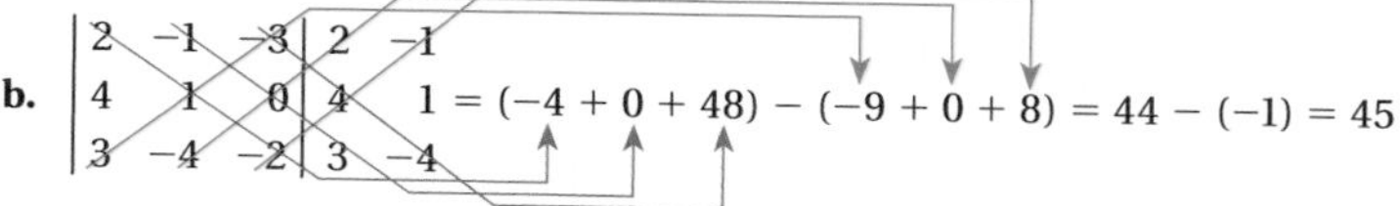

b. $\begin{vmatrix} 2 & -1 & -3 \\ 4 & 1 & 0 \\ 3 & -4 & -2 \end{vmatrix}\begin{matrix} 2 & -1 \\ 4 & 1 \\ 3 & -4 \end{matrix} = (-4 + 0 + 48) - (-9 + 0 + 8) = 44 - (-1) = 45$

1 PLAN AND PREPARE

Warm-Up Exercises

Transparency Available

1. Let $a = 4$, $b = -5$, $c = -2$, and $d = 7$. Find $ad - bc$. 18
2. Solve the linear system.
$2x - 3y = 4$
$-x - 2y = -9$ (5, 2)
3. Does either triple, (2, −1, 3) or (−2, −2, 1), satisfy the equation $2x - 3y + 4z = 6$? **(2, −1, 3) does not satisfy the equation; (−2, −2, 1) does.**

Notetaking Guide

Transparency Available

Promotes interactive learning and notetaking skills, pp. 80–84.

Pacing

Basic: 1 day
Average: 1 day
Advanced: 1 day
Block: 0.5 block with 3.6
- See *Teaching Guide/Lesson Plan.*

2 FOCUS AND MOTIVATE

Essential Question

Big Idea 1, p. 151

How do you solve a system of equations using Cramer's Rule? **Tell students they will learn how to use determinants to solve systems of equations.**

Resource Planning Guide

Chapter Resource Book
- Teaching Guide/Lesson Plan (pp. 79–80)
- Activity Master (p. 81)
- Practice levels A, B, C (pp. 83–85)
- Study Guide (pp. 86–87)
- Catch-up for Absent Students (p. 88)
- Problem Solving Workshop (p. 89)
- Challenge (p. 90)

Workbooks
- Notetaking Guide (pp. 80–84)
- Practice Workbook (pp. 50–51)

Teaching Options
- **Power Presentations CD-ROM** provides dynamic electronic teaching resources for the classroom.
- **Activity Generator CD-ROM** provides editable activities for all ability levels.

Interactive Technology
- Easy Planner
- Power Presentations CD-ROM
- Activity Generator CD-ROM
- Animated Algebra
- Test Generator CD-ROM
- Online Quiz
- eWorkbook
- eEdition
- @HomeTutor

Resources for English Learners
- Quick Reference for English Learners
- Spanish Study Guide
- Multi-Language Visual Glossary
- Student Resources in Spanish

See also the *Algebra 2 Toolkit* for more strategies for meeting individual needs.

Motivating the Lesson

Place a triangle on a coordinate plane on the board. Ask students to find its area. Most will not be able to do this. Then tell them that by creating a square matrix based on the coordinates of the vertices of the triangle, they will be able to find the area directly.

3 TEACH

Extra Example 1

Evaluate the determinant of the matrix.

a. $\begin{bmatrix} 6 & -2 \\ 1 & -4 \end{bmatrix}$ −22

b. $\begin{bmatrix} 4 & -2 & 0 \\ 1 & 1 & -2 \\ 2 & 5 & 3 \end{bmatrix}$ 66

Extra Example 2

The approximate coordinates (in miles) of a triangular region representing a city and its suburbs are (10, 20), (−8, 5), and (−4, −5). Find the area of the region. 120 mi^2

AREA OF A TRIANGLE You can use a determinant to find the area of a triangle whose vertices are points in a coordinate plane.

KEY CONCEPT *For Your Notebook*

Area of a Triangle

The area of a triangle with vertices (x_1, y_1), (x_2, y_2), and (x_3, y_3) is given by

$$\text{Area} = \pm\frac{1}{2}\begin{vmatrix} x_1 & y_1 & 1 \\ x_2 & y_2 & 1 \\ x_3 & y_3 & 1 \end{vmatrix}$$

where the symbol ± indicates that the appropriate sign should be chosen to yield a positive value.

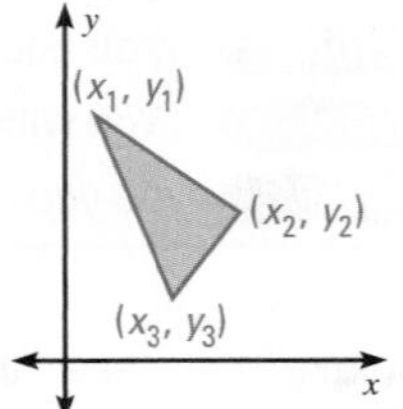

EXAMPLE 2 Find the area of a triangular region

SEA LIONS Off the coast of California lies a triangular region of the Pacific Ocean where huge populations of sea lions and seals live. The triangle is formed by imaginary lines connecting Bodega Bay, the Farallon Islands, and Año Nuevo Island, as shown. (In the map, the coordinates are measured in miles.) Use a determinant to estimate the area of the region.

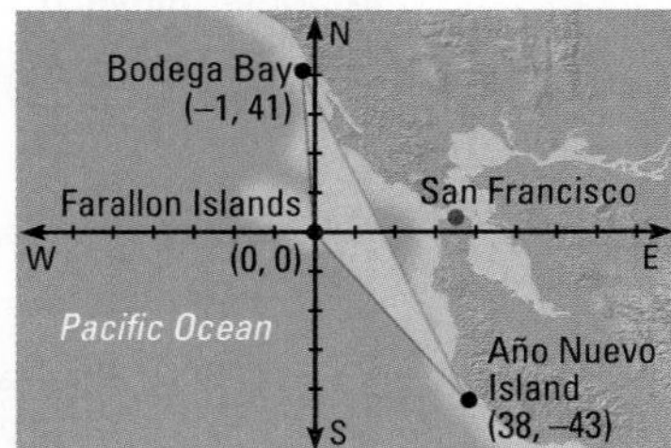

Solution

The approximate coordinates of the vertices of the triangular region are (−1, 41), (38, −43), and (0, 0). So, the area of the region is:

$$\text{Area} = \pm\frac{1}{2}\begin{vmatrix} -1 & 41 & 1 \\ 38 & -43 & 1 \\ 0 & 0 & 1 \end{vmatrix} = \pm\frac{1}{2}\begin{vmatrix} -1 & 41 & 1 \\ 38 & -43 & 1 \\ 0 & 0 & 1 \end{vmatrix}\begin{matrix} -1 & 41 \\ 38 & -43 \\ 0 & 0 \end{matrix}$$

$$= \pm\frac{1}{2}[(43 + 0 + 0) - (0 + 0 + 1558)]$$

$$= 757.5$$

 The area of the region is about 758 square miles.

✓ GUIDED PRACTICE for Examples 1 and 2

Evaluate the determinant of the matrix.

1. $\begin{bmatrix} 3 & -2 \\ 6 & 1 \end{bmatrix}$ 15

2. $\begin{bmatrix} 4 & -1 & 2 \\ -3 & -2 & -1 \\ 0 & 5 & 1 \end{bmatrix}$ −21

3. $\begin{bmatrix} 10 & -2 & 3 \\ 2 & -12 & 4 \\ 0 & -7 & -2 \end{bmatrix}$ 470

4. Find the area of the triangle with vertices $A(5, 11)$, $B(9, 2)$, and $C(1, 3)$. 34

Differentiated Instruction

Advanced Have students generate the formula for finding the area of a triangle with vertices (x_1, y_1), (x_2, y_2), and (x_3, y_3). Students should begin with the determinant formula in the Key Concept box and arrive at $\pm\frac{1}{2}(x_1y_2 - x_2y_1 + x_2y_3 - x_3y_2 + x_3y_1 - x_1y_3)$. Students can share this formula with their classmates.

See also the *Algebra 2 Toolkit* for more strategies.

CRAMER'S RULE You can use determinants to solve a system of linear equations. The method, called **Cramer's rule** and named after the Swiss mathematician Gabriel Cramer (1704–1752), uses the **coefficient matrix** of the linear system.

Linear System	Coefficient Matrix
$ax + by = e$ $cx + dy = f$	$\begin{bmatrix} a & b \\ c & d \end{bmatrix}$

KEY CONCEPT *For Your Notebook*

Cramer's Rule for a 2 × 2 System

Let A be the coefficient matrix of this linear system:

$$ax + by = e$$
$$cx + dy = f$$

If $\det A \neq 0$, then the system has exactly one solution. The solution is:

$$x = \frac{\begin{vmatrix} e & b \\ f & d \end{vmatrix}}{\det A} \quad \text{and} \quad y = \frac{\begin{vmatrix} a & e \\ c & f \end{vmatrix}}{\det A}$$

Notice that the numerators for x and y are the determinants of the matrices formed by replacing the coefficients of x and y, respectively, with the column of constants.

EXAMPLE 3 Use Cramer's rule for a 2 × 2 system

Use Cramer's rule to solve this system: $\quad 9x + 4y = -6$
$\quad 3x - 5y = -21$

ANOTHER WAY
You can also solve the system in Example 3 using the substitution method or the elimination method you learned in Lesson 3.2.

Solution

STEP 1 **Evaluate** the determinant of the coefficient matrix.

$$\begin{vmatrix} 9 & 4 \\ 3 & -5 \end{vmatrix} = -45 - 12 = -57$$

STEP 2 **Apply** Cramer's rule because the determinant is not 0.

$$x = \frac{\begin{vmatrix} -6 & 4 \\ -21 & -5 \end{vmatrix}}{-57} = \frac{30 - (-84)}{-57} = \frac{114}{-57} = -2$$

$$y = \frac{\begin{vmatrix} 9 & -6 \\ 3 & -21 \end{vmatrix}}{-57} = \frac{-189 - (-18)}{-57} = \frac{-171}{-57} = 3$$

▶ The solution is $(-2, 3)$.

CHECK Check this solution in the original equations.

$9x + 4y = -6$	$3x - 5y = -21$
$9(-2) + 4(3) \stackrel{?}{=} -6$	$3(-2) - 5(3) \stackrel{?}{=} -21$
$-18 + 12 \stackrel{?}{=} -6$	$-6 - 15 \stackrel{?}{=} -21$
$-6 = -6$ ✓	$-21 = -21$ ✓

Extra Example 3

Use Cramer's rule to solve this system:
$6x - 2y = -16$
$-3x + 5y = 16$ **(−2, 2)**

Key Question to Ask for Example 3

- When does Cramer's rule allow you to solve a system of equations? **when the determinant is not 0**

Mathematical Reasoning

The slopes of lines whose equations are $ax + by = c$ and $dx + ey = f$ are $-\frac{a}{b}$ and $-\frac{d}{e}$, respectively. If the slopes are equal, then $-\frac{a}{b} = -\frac{d}{e}$, and $ae - bd = 0$. Since $\begin{vmatrix} a & b \\ d & e \end{vmatrix} = ae - bd$, a zero determinant means the lines are either parallel or coincident. In either case, there is no unique solution to the system.

Study Strategy

When using Cramer's rule, students should stop if the determinant is 0, as there is no unique solution. Students should instead determine if the two equations represent parallel lines (no solution) or the same line (infinitely many solutions).

Differentiated Instruction

Visual Learners Students might struggle with writing the coefficient matrix in order to apply Cramer's rule. Have students circle or highlight the coefficients of x and y, and then similarly identify the constants in the linear system, before applying Cramer's rule.

See also the *Algebra 2 Toolkit* for more strategies.

Extra Example 4

Last year, Yolanda invested \$50,000 in stocks, bonds, and a savings account. She earned 4% on the stocks, 5.8% on the bonds, and 3.5% on the savings account. Her total earnings were \$2008. The stocks earned twice as much as the bonds. How much did she invest in each account? **stocks: \$19,952; bonds: \$6,880; bank account: \$23,168**

Key Question to Ask for Example 4

- What is different about each numerator of the fractions in Cramer's rule? **Each numerator represents the coefficient matrix with a column of the matrix replaced by a column of constants.**

Closing the Lesson

Have students summarize the major points of the lesson and answer the Essential Question: How do you solve a system of equations using Cramer's Rule?

- **Every square matrix has a determinant.**
- **Determinants can be used to find the area of a triangle on a coordinate plane, given the coordinates of the vertices of the triangle.**
- **Cramer's rule can be used to solve systems of linear equations.**

If the determinant of the coefficient matrix is not equal to zero, find the determinants formed by replacing each column of the coefficient matrix by the matrix of constants. Divide these by the determinant of the coefficient matrix to determine the value of each variable.

SOLVE SYSTEMS
As with Cramer's rule for a 2×2 system, the numerators for x, y, and z are the determinants of the matrices formed by replacing the coefficients of x, y, and z respectively with the column of constants.

KEY CONCEPT — *For Your Notebook*

Cramer's Rule for a 3×3 System

Let A be the coefficient matrix of the linear system shown below.

Linear System

$$\begin{aligned} ax + by + cz &= j \\ dx + ey + fz &= k \\ gx + hy + iz &= l \end{aligned}$$

Coefficient Matrix

$$A = \begin{bmatrix} a & b & c \\ d & e & f \\ g & h & i \end{bmatrix}$$

If $\det A \neq 0$, then the system has exactly one solution. The solution is:

$$x = \frac{\begin{vmatrix} j & b & c \\ k & e & f \\ l & h & i \end{vmatrix}}{\det A}, \quad y = \frac{\begin{vmatrix} a & j & c \\ d & k & f \\ g & l & i \end{vmatrix}}{\det A}, \quad \text{and} \quad z = \frac{\begin{vmatrix} a & b & j \\ d & e & k \\ g & h & l \end{vmatrix}}{\det A}$$

EXAMPLE 4 Solve a multi-step problem

CHEMISTRY The atomic weights of three compounds are shown. Use a linear system and Cramer's rule to find the atomic weights of carbon (C), hydrogen (H), and oxygen (O).

Compound	Formula	Atomic weight
Glucose	$C_6H_{12}O_6$	180
Carbon dioxide	CO_2	44
Hydrogen peroxide	H_2O_2	34

Solution

STEP 1 **Write** a linear system using the formula for each compound. Let C, H, and O represent the atomic weights of carbon, hydrogen, and oxygen.

$$\begin{aligned} 6C + 12H + 6O &= 180 \\ C \qquad\quad + 2O &= 44 \\ 2H + 2O &= 34 \end{aligned}$$

STEP 2 **Evaluate** the determinant of the coefficient matrix.

$$\begin{vmatrix} 6 & 12 & 6 \\ 1 & 0 & 2 \\ 0 & 2 & 2 \end{vmatrix}\begin{matrix} 6 & 12 \\ 1 & 0 \\ 0 & 2 \end{matrix} = (0 + 0 + 12) - (0 + 24 + 24) = -36$$

STEP 3 **Apply** Cramer's rule because the determinant is not 0.

$$C = \frac{\begin{vmatrix} 180 & 12 & 6 \\ 44 & 0 & 2 \\ 34 & 2 & 2 \end{vmatrix}}{-36} = \frac{-432}{-36} = 12 \qquad H = \frac{\begin{vmatrix} 6 & 180 & 6 \\ 1 & 44 & 2 \\ 0 & 34 & 2 \end{vmatrix}}{-36} = \frac{-36}{-36} = 1 \qquad O = \frac{\begin{vmatrix} 6 & 12 & 180 \\ 1 & 0 & 44 \\ 0 & 2 & 34 \end{vmatrix}}{-36} = \frac{-576}{-36} = 16$$

▶ The atomic weights of carbon, hydrogen, and oxygen are 12, 1, and 16, respectively.

✓ **GUIDED PRACTICE** for Examples 3 and 4

Use Cramer's rule to solve the linear system.

5. $3x - 4y = -15$
$2x + 5y = 13$ (−1, 3)

6. $4x + 7y = 2$
$-3x - 2y = -8$ (4, −2)

7. $3x - 4y + 2z = 18$
$4x + y - 5z = -13$
$2x - 3y + z = 11$
(2, −1, 4)

3.7 EXERCISES

HOMEWORK KEY
○ = **WORKED-OUT SOLUTIONS** on p. WS6 for Exs. 11, 23, and 43
★ = **STANDARDIZED TEST PRACTICE** Exs. 2, 21, 28, 38, 42, and 45

SKILL PRACTICE

1. VOCABULARY Copy and complete: The _?_ of a 2 × 2 matrix is the difference of the products of the elements on the diagonals. determinant

2. ★ WRITING *Explain* Cramer's rule and how it is used. See margin.

EXAMPLE 1
on p. 203
for Exs. 3–21

2 × 2 DETERMINANTS **Evaluate the determinant of the matrix.**

3. $\begin{bmatrix} 2 & -1 \\ 4 & -5 \end{bmatrix}$ −6

4. $\begin{bmatrix} 7 & 1 \\ 0 & 3 \end{bmatrix}$ 21

5. $\begin{bmatrix} -4 & 3 \\ 1 & -7 \end{bmatrix}$ 25

6. $\begin{bmatrix} 1 & -3 \\ 2 & 6 \end{bmatrix}$ 12

7. $\begin{bmatrix} 10 & -6 \\ -7 & 5 \end{bmatrix}$ 8

8. $\begin{bmatrix} 0 & 3 \\ 5 & -3 \end{bmatrix}$ −15

9. $\begin{bmatrix} 9 & -3 \\ 7 & 2 \end{bmatrix}$ 39

10. $\begin{bmatrix} -5 & 12 \\ 4 & 6 \end{bmatrix}$ −78

3 × 3 DETERMINANTS **Evaluate the determinant of the matrix.**

(11.) $\begin{bmatrix} -1 & 12 & 4 \\ 0 & 2 & -5 \\ 3 & 0 & 1 \end{bmatrix}$ −206

12. $\begin{bmatrix} 1 & 2 & 3 \\ 5 & -8 & 1 \\ 2 & 4 & 3 \end{bmatrix}$ 54

13. $\begin{bmatrix} 5 & 0 & 2 \\ -3 & 9 & -2 \\ 1 & -4 & 0 \end{bmatrix}$ −34

14. $\begin{bmatrix} -7 & 4 & 5 \\ 1 & 2 & -4 \\ -10 & 1 & 6 \end{bmatrix}$ 129

15. $\begin{bmatrix} 12 & 5 & 8 \\ 0 & 6 & -8 \\ 1 & 10 & 4 \end{bmatrix}$ 1160

16. $\begin{bmatrix} -4 & 3 & -9 \\ 12 & 6 & 0 \\ 8 & -12 & 0 \end{bmatrix}$ 1728

17. $\begin{bmatrix} -2 & 6 & 0 \\ 8 & 15 & 3 \\ 4 & -1 & 7 \end{bmatrix}$ −480

18. $\begin{bmatrix} 5 & 7 & 6 \\ -4 & 0 & 8 \\ 1 & 8 & 7 \end{bmatrix}$ −260

ERROR ANALYSIS *Describe* **and correct the error in evaluating the determinant.**

19.
$$\left|\begin{matrix} 2 & 0 & -1 \\ 4 & 1 & 6 \\ -3 & 2 & 5 \end{matrix}\right| \begin{matrix} 2 & 0 \\ 4 & 1 \\ -3 & 2 \end{matrix}$$
$= 10 + 0 + (-8) + (3 + 24 + 0)$
$= 2 + 27 = 29$ ✗

20.
$$\begin{matrix} 3 & 0 \\ 2 & 2 \\ -3 & 5 \end{matrix} \left|\begin{matrix} 3 & 0 & 1 \\ 2 & 2 & -3 \\ -3 & 5 & 0 \end{matrix}\right|$$
$= -18 + 0 + 0 - (-18 + 0 - 6)$
$= -18 - (-24) = 6$ ✗

See margin.

19. The sum of the products for the diagonals that go up should be subtracted from the sum of the products for the diagonals that go down; 10 + 0 + (−8) − (3 + 24 + 0) = 2 − 27 = −25.

21. ★ MULTIPLE CHOICE Which matrix has the greatest determinant? D

Ⓐ $\begin{bmatrix} -4 & 1 \\ 6 & 3 \end{bmatrix}$ Ⓑ $\begin{bmatrix} 1 & 6 \\ 3 & 8 \end{bmatrix}$ Ⓒ $\begin{bmatrix} 5 & -3 \\ 7 & -1 \end{bmatrix}$ Ⓓ $\begin{bmatrix} 5 & -2 \\ 1 & 5 \end{bmatrix}$

4 PRACTICE AND APPLY

Assignment Guide

Answer Transparencies available for all exercises

Basic:
Day 1: pp. 207–209
Exs. 1–8, 11–16, 19–21, 23–27 odd, 28–31, 40–43, 48

Average:
Day 1: pp. 207–209
Exs. 1, 2, 7–10, 15–21, 22–28 even, 29–34, 38, 40–45, 48

Advanced:
Day 1: pp. 207–209
Exs. 1, 2, 8–10, 16–18, 21, 25–28, 32–46*

Block:
pp. 207–209
Exs. 1, 2, 7–10, 15–21, 22–28 even, 29–34, 38, 40–45, 48 (with 3.6)

Differentiated Instruction

See *Algebra 2 Best Practices Toolkit* for suggestions on addressing the needs of a diverse classroom.

Homework Check

For a quick check of student understanding of key concepts, go over the following exercises:
Basic: 4, 12, 25, 30, 40
Average: 8, 16, 24, 34, 42
Advanced: 10, 18, 26, 36, 44

Extra Practice

- Student Edition, p. 1012
- Chapter 3 Resource Book: Practice levels A, B, C, pp. 83–85

Practice Worksheet

An easily-readable reduced practice page (with answers) for this lesson can be found on p. 150C.

2. *Sample answer:* Cramer's rule is a method for solving systems of equations using the determinant. Create a coefficient matrix and compute its determinant; this becomes the denominator for each variable in the system. Create a new matrix for each variable in the system by replacing the column that corresponds to the variable in the coefficient matrix with the constants. Compute the determinant of this matrix; this becomes the numerator for each variable.

20. The column extensions go on the right side of the matrix; 61.

Avoiding Common Errors

Exercises 22–28 Some students may forget to add a column of 1's to the coefficient matrix before finding the area of the triangles in these exercises. Remind them that the 1's are necessary because they make the matrix square, and only a square matrix has a determinant.

Mathematical Reasoning

Exercise 43 Point out to students that they do not need to solve another system of equations using Cramer's rule for part (b). After they have found the number of each type of cone in part (a), they can decrease each of those values by 5%, increase each price by 10%, and then substitute the results into the equation for finding the revenue.

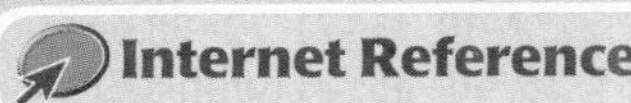

Exercise 45 More information about the Dinosaur Diamond region can be found at www.dinosaurdiamond.org

42. $40x + 25y = 185{,}500$, $x + y = 6700$ where x represents the floor seats and y represents all other seats; 1200 floor seats, 5500 other seats. *Sample answer:* I prefer the elimination method because it uses the least amount of numerical work, so I am less likely to make a mistake.

EXAMPLE 2 **B** on p. 204 for Exs. 22–28

AREA OF A TRIANGLE **Find the area of the triangle with the given vertices.**

22. $A(1, 5), B(4, 6), C(7, 3)$ **6**
23. $A(4, 2), B(4, 8), C(8, 5)$ **12**
24. $A(-4, 6), B(0, 3), C(6, 6)$ **15**
25. $A(-4, -4), B(-1, 2), C(2, -6)$ **21**
26. $A(5, -4), B(6, 3), C(8, -1)$ **9**
27. $A(-6, 1), B(-2, -6), C(0, 3)$ **25**

28. ★ **MULTIPLE CHOICE** What is the area of the triangle with vertices $(-3, 4)$, $(6, 3)$, and $(2, -1)$? **A**

Ⓐ 20 Ⓑ 26 Ⓒ 30 Ⓓ 40

EXAMPLES 3 and 4 on pp. 205–206 for Exs. 29–37

USING CRAMER'S RULE **Use Cramer's rule to solve the linear system.**

29. $3x + 5y = 3$, $-x + 2y = 10$ **(−4, 3)**
30. $2x - y = -2$, $x + 2y = 14$ **(2, 6)**
31. $5x + y = -40$, $2x - 5y = 11$ **(−7, −5)**
32. $-x + y + z = -3$, $4x - y + 4z = -14$, $x + 2y - z = 9$ **(1, 2, −4)**
33. $-x - 2y + 4z = -28$, $x + y + 2z = -11$, $2x + y - 3z = 30$ **(6, −3, −7)**
34. $4x + y + 3z = 7$, $2x - 5y + 4z = -19$, $x - y + 2z = -2$ **(−1, 5, 2)**
35. $5x - y - 2z = -6$, $x + 3y + 4z = 16$, $2x - 4y + z = -15$ **(0, 4, 1)**
36. $x + y + z = -8$, $3x - 3y + 2z = -21$, $-x + 2y - 2z = 11$ **(−5, 0, −3)**
37. $3x - y + z = 25$, $-x + 2y - 3z = -17$, $x + y + z = 21$ **(8, 6, 7)**

38. *Sample answer:* $\begin{bmatrix} 8 & 7 \\ 5 & 5 \end{bmatrix}$

C

38. ★ **OPEN-ENDED MATH** Write a 2×2 matrix that has a determinant of 5.

39. **CHALLENGE** Let $A = \begin{bmatrix} 2 & -1 \\ 1 & 2 \end{bmatrix}$ and $B = \begin{bmatrix} 3 & 5 \\ -2 & -4 \end{bmatrix}$.

a. How is det AB related to det A and det B? **det AB is the product of det A and det B.**

b. How is det kA related to det A if k is a scalar? Give an algebraic justification for your answer. **det $kA = k^2$ det A; det kA = det $k\begin{bmatrix} 2 & -1 \\ 1 & 2 \end{bmatrix}$ = det $\begin{bmatrix} 2k & -k \\ k & 2k \end{bmatrix}$ $= 4k^2 - (-k^2) = 5k^2 = k^2[2(2) - 1(-1)] = k^2$ det A**

PROBLEM SOLVING

EXAMPLE 2 **A** on p. 204 for Exs. 40–41

40. **BERMUDA TRIANGLE** The Bermuda Triangle is a large triangular region in the Atlantic Ocean. The triangle is formed by imaginary lines connecting Bermuda, Puerto Rico, and Miami, Florida. (In the map, the coordinates are measured in miles.) Use a determinant to estimate the area of the Bermuda Triangle. **447,242 mi²**

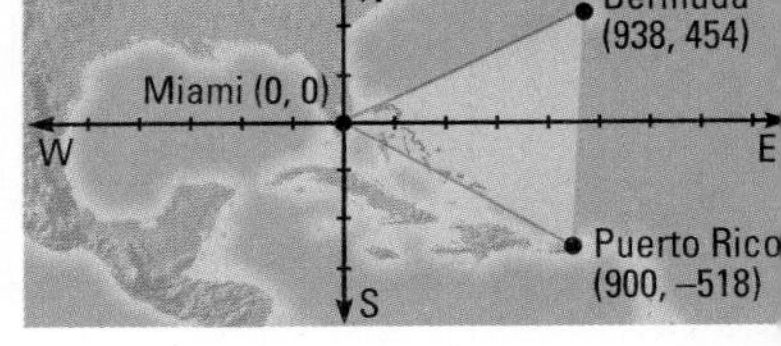

@HomeTutor for problem solving help at classzone.com

41. **GARDENING** You are planning to turn a triangular region of your yard into a garden. The vertices of the triangle are (0, 0), (5, 2), and (3, 6) where the coordinates are measured in feet. Find the area of the triangular region. **12 ft²**

@HomeTutor for problem solving help at classzone.com

EXAMPLES 3 and 4 on pp. 205–206 for Exs. 42–44

42. ★ **SHORT RESPONSE** The attendance at a rock concert was 6700 people. The tickets for the concert cost \$40 for floor seats and \$25 for all other seats. The total income of ticket sales was \$185,500. Write a linear system that models this situation. Solve the system in three ways: using Cramer's rule, using the substitution method, and using the elimination method. *Compare* the methods, and explain which one you prefer in this situation. **See margin.**

○ = WORKED-OUT SOLUTIONS on p. WS1 ★ = STANDARDIZED TEST PRACTICE

B **43.** **MULTI-STEP PROBLEM** An ice cream shop sells the following sizes of ice cream cones: single scoop for \$.90, double scoop for \$1.20, and triple scoop for \$1.60. One day, a total of 120 cones are sold for \$134, as many single-scoop cones are sold as double-scoop and triple-scoop cones combined.

a. Use a linear system and Cramer's rule to find how many of each size of cone are sold. **60 single scoop, 40 double scoop, 20 triple scoop**

b. The next day, the shop raises prices by 10%. As a result, the number of each size of cone sold falls by 5%. What is the revenue from cone sales? **\$140.03**

44. SCIENCE The atomic weights of three compounds are shown in the table. Use a linear system and Cramer's rule to find the atomic weights of fluorine (F), sodium (Na), and chlorine (Cl).

Compound	Formula	Atomic weight
Sodium fluoride	FNa	42
Sodium chloride	NaCl	58.5
Chlorine pentafluoride	ClF_5	130.5

Fluorine (F) 19, Sodium (Na) 23, Chlorine (Cl) 35.5

45. ★ **EXTENDED RESPONSE** In Utah and Colorado, an area called the Dinosaur Diamond is known for containing many dinosaur fossils. The map at the right shows the towns at the four vertices of the diamond. The coordinates given are measured in miles.

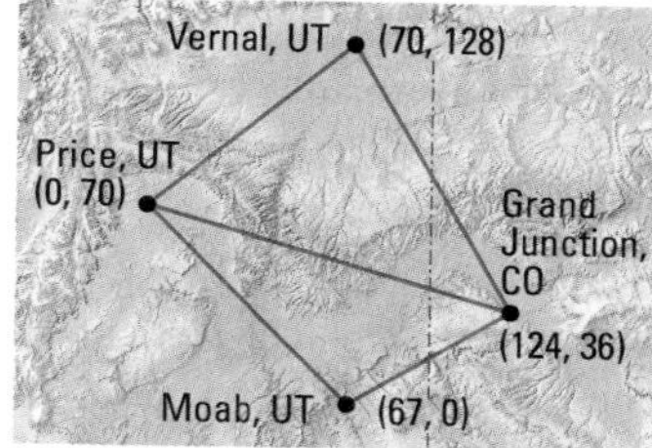

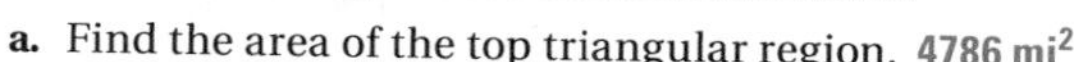

a. Find the area of the top triangular region. **4786 mi^2**

b. Find the area of the bottom triangular region. **3201 mi^2**

c. What is the total area of the Dinosaur Diamond? **7987 mi^2**

d. *Describe* another way in which you can divide the Dinosaur Diamond into two triangles in order to find its area. **Connect Vernal, UT to Moab, UT to create a left and right triangle.**

C **46. CHALLENGE** A farmer is fencing off a triangular region of a pasture, as shown. The area of the region should be 5000 square feet. The farmer has planted the first two fence posts at (0, 0) and (100, 50). He wants to plant the final post along his neighbor's fence, which lies on the horizontal line $y = 120$. At which *two* points could the farmer plant the final post so that the triangular region has the desired area? **(40, 120) or (440, 120)**

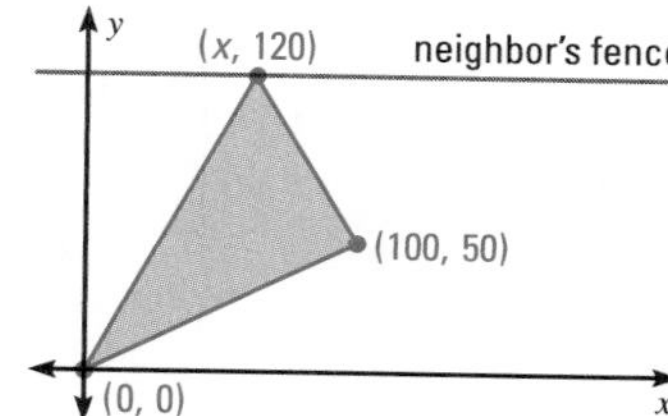

KY KENTUCKY MIXED REVIEW

TEST PRACTICE at classzone.com

47. Nadia's weekly salary is \$390, and she receives a \$5 bonus for each new customer she brings in. Which inequality represents the number of new customers, *c*, she needs to bring in per week to earn at least \$450 per week? **C**

Ⓐ $c < 60$ Ⓑ $c < 12$ Ⓒ $c \geq 12$ Ⓓ $c \geq 60$

48. How many edges does the pentagonal prism have? **C**

Ⓐ 7 Ⓑ 10

Ⓒ 15 Ⓓ 17

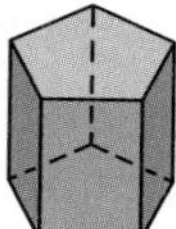

5 ASSESS AND RETEACH

Daily Homework Quiz

Transparency Available

Evaluate the determinant of the matrix.

1. $\begin{bmatrix} -4 & -1 \\ 5 & 3 \end{bmatrix}$ **−7**

2. $\begin{bmatrix} 0 & -5 & 1 \\ -3 & 1 & -2 \\ 2 & 5 & -4 \end{bmatrix}$ **63**

3. Find the area of a triangle with vertices (−2, 5), (5, 7), and (−3, −8). **44.5**

4. Use Cramer's rule to solve the linear system.
$x - 4y = 13$
$-3x + 5y = -32$ **(9, −1)**

Available at **classzone.com**

Diagnosis/Remediation

- Practice A, B, C in Chapter 3 Resource Book, pp. 83–85
- Study Guide in Chapter 3 Resource Book, pp. 86–87
- Practice Workbook, pp. 50–51
- @HomeTutor

Challenge

Additional challenge is available in the Chapter 3 Resource Book, p. 90.

1 PLAN AND PREPARE

Warm-Up Exercises

Transparency Available

1. Find the product $\begin{bmatrix} -2 & 4 \\ 5 & -1 \end{bmatrix} \cdot \begin{bmatrix} 3 \\ 7 \end{bmatrix}$ $\begin{bmatrix} 22 \\ 8 \end{bmatrix}$
2. Solve the linear system.
 $-x - 4y = -21$
 $2x + y = 0$ $(-3, 6)$
3. Find the determinant of $\begin{bmatrix} 3 & -3 \\ -5 & 8 \end{bmatrix}$. 39

Notetaking Guide

Transparency Available

Promotes interactive learning and notetaking skills, pp. 85–88.

Pacing

Basic: 2 days
Average: 2 days
Advanced: 2 days
Block: 1 block
- See *Teaching Guide/Lesson Plan.*

2 FOCUS AND MOTIVATE

Essential Question

Big Idea 1, p. 151

How do you solve a system of two linear equations using inverse matrices? Tell students they will learn how to answer this question by finding and using the inverse of a matrix.

3.8 Use Inverse Matrices to Solve Linear Systems

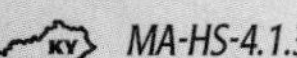

MA-HS-4.1.3

Before You solved linear systems using Cramer's rule.
Now You will solve linear systems using inverse matrices.
Why? So you can find how many batches of a recipe to make, as in Ex. 45.

Key Vocabulary
- identity matrix
- inverse matrices
- matrix of variables
- matrix of constants

MA-HS-4.1.3
Students will represent real-world data using matrices and will use matrix addition, subtraction, multiplication (with matrices no larger than 2 × 2) and scalar multiplication to solve real-world problems.

The $n \times n$ **identity matrix** is a matrix with 1's on the main diagonal and 0's elsewhere. If A is any $n \times n$ matrix and I is the $n \times n$ identity matrix, then $AI = A$ and $IA = A$.

2 × 2 Identity Matrix

$$I = \begin{bmatrix} 1 & 0 \\ 0 & 1 \end{bmatrix}$$

3 × 3 Identity Matrix

$$I = \begin{bmatrix} 1 & 0 & 0 \\ 0 & 1 & 0 \\ 0 & 0 & 1 \end{bmatrix}$$

Two $n \times n$ matrices A and B are **inverses** of each other if their product (in both orders) is the $n \times n$ identity matrix. That is, $AB = I$ and $BA = I$. An $n \times n$ matrix A has an inverse if and only if $\det A \neq 0$. The symbol for the inverse of A is A^{-1}.

KEY CONCEPT — For Your Notebook

The Inverse of a 2 × 2 Matrix

The inverse of the matrix $A = \begin{bmatrix} a & b \\ c & d \end{bmatrix}$ is

$$A^{-1} = \frac{1}{|A|}\begin{bmatrix} d & -b \\ -c & a \end{bmatrix} = \frac{1}{ad - cb}\begin{bmatrix} d & -b \\ -c & a \end{bmatrix} \text{ provided } ad - cb \neq 0.$$

EXAMPLE 1 Find the inverse of a 2 × 2 matrix

CHECK INVERSES
In Example 1, you can check the inverse by showing that $AA^{-1} = I = A^{-1}A$.

Find the inverse of $A = \begin{bmatrix} 3 & 8 \\ 2 & 5 \end{bmatrix}$.

$$A^{-1} = \frac{1}{15 - 16}\begin{bmatrix} 5 & -8 \\ -2 & 3 \end{bmatrix} = -1\begin{bmatrix} 5 & -8 \\ -2 & 3 \end{bmatrix} = \begin{bmatrix} -5 & 8 \\ 2 & -3 \end{bmatrix}$$

GUIDED PRACTICE for Example 1

Find the inverse of the matrix. 1–3. See margin.

1. $\begin{bmatrix} 6 & 1 \\ 2 & 4 \end{bmatrix}$
2. $\begin{bmatrix} -1 & 5 \\ -4 & 8 \end{bmatrix}$
3. $\begin{bmatrix} -3 & -4 \\ -1 & -2 \end{bmatrix}$

Resource Planning Guide

Chapter Resource Book
- Teaching Guide/Lesson Plan (pp. 91–92)
- Activity Master (p. 93)
- Practice levels A, B, C (pp. 95–97)
- Study Guide (pp. 98–99)
- Catch-up for Absent Students (p. 100)
- Problem Solving Workshop (p. 101)
- Challenge (p. 102)

Workbooks
- Notetaking Guide (pp. 85–88)
- Practice Workbook (pp. 52–53)

Teaching Options
- **Power Presentations CD-ROM** provides dynamic electronic teaching resources for the classroom.
- **Activity Generator CD-ROM** provides editable activities for all ability levels.

Interactive Technology
- Easy Planner
- Power Presentations CD-ROM
- Activity Generator CD-ROM
- Animated Algebra
- Test Generator CD-ROM
- Online Quiz
- eWorkbook
- eEdition
- @HomeTutor

Resources for English Learners
- Quick Reference for English Learners
- Spanish Study Guide
- Multi-Language Visual Glossary
- Student Resources in Spanish

See also the *Algebra 2 Toolkit* for more strategies for meeting individual needs.

EXAMPLE 2 Solve a matrix equation

Solve the matrix equation $AX = B$ for the 2 × 2 matrix X.

$$\overbrace{\begin{bmatrix} 2 & -7 \\ -1 & 4 \end{bmatrix}}^{A} X = \overbrace{\begin{bmatrix} -21 & 3 \\ 12 & -2 \end{bmatrix}}^{B}$$

Solution

Begin by finding the inverse of A.

$$A^{-1} = \frac{1}{8-7}\begin{bmatrix} 4 & 7 \\ 1 & 2 \end{bmatrix} = \begin{bmatrix} 4 & 7 \\ 1 & 2 \end{bmatrix}$$

To solve the equation for X, multiply both sides of the equation by A^{-1} *on the left.*

$$\begin{bmatrix} 4 & 7 \\ 1 & 2 \end{bmatrix}\begin{bmatrix} 2 & -7 \\ -1 & 4 \end{bmatrix} X = \begin{bmatrix} 4 & 7 \\ 1 & 2 \end{bmatrix}\begin{bmatrix} -21 & 3 \\ 12 & -2 \end{bmatrix} \qquad A^{-1}AX = A^{-1}B$$

$$\begin{bmatrix} 1 & 0 \\ 0 & 1 \end{bmatrix} X = \begin{bmatrix} 0 & -2 \\ 3 & -1 \end{bmatrix} \qquad IX = A^{-1}B$$

$$X = \begin{bmatrix} 0 & -2 \\ 3 & -1 \end{bmatrix} \qquad X = A^{-1}B$$

Animated Algebra at classzone.com

GUIDED PRACTICE for Example 2

4. Solve the matrix equation $\begin{bmatrix} -4 & 1 \\ 0 & 6 \end{bmatrix} X = \begin{bmatrix} 8 & 9 \\ 24 & 6 \end{bmatrix}$. **See margin.**

INVERSE OF A 3 × 3 MATRIX The inverse of a 3 × 3 matrix is difficult to compute by hand. A calculator that will compute inverse matrices is useful in this case.

EXAMPLE 3 Find the inverse of a 3 × 3 matrix

Use a graphing calculator to find the inverse of A. Then use the calculator to verify your result.

$$A = \begin{bmatrix} 2 & 1 & -2 \\ 5 & 3 & 0 \\ 4 & 3 & 8 \end{bmatrix}$$

Solution

Enter matrix A into a graphing calculator and calculate A^{-1}. Then compute AA^{-1} and $A^{-1}A$ to verify that you obtain the 3 × 3 identity matrix.

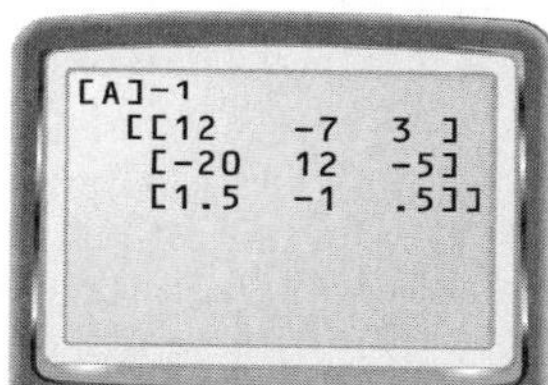

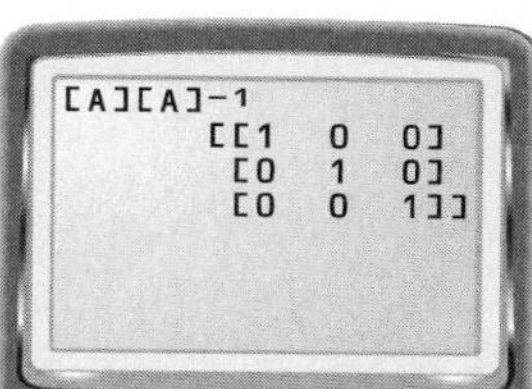

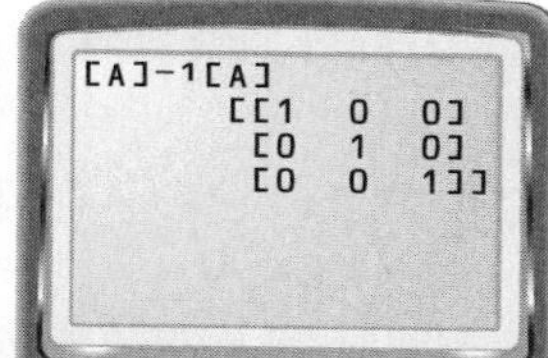

Motivating the Lesson

Write a system of equations such as:
$3x + 4y - z = 12$
$2x - y + 5z = -5$
$x + 3y - 2z = 9$
Tell students they will learn how to use matrices to represent and solve such systems.

3 TEACH

Extra Example 1

Find the inverse of $A = \begin{bmatrix} 5 & -2 \\ 8 & -3 \end{bmatrix}$.

$\begin{bmatrix} -3 & 2 \\ -8 & 5 \end{bmatrix}$

Extra Example 2

Solve the matrix equation $AX = B$ for the 2 × 2 matrix X.

$\begin{bmatrix} 3 & -2 \\ -7 & 5 \end{bmatrix} X = \begin{bmatrix} -2 & 4 \\ 3 & -1 \end{bmatrix}$

$\begin{bmatrix} -4 & 18 \\ -5 & 25 \end{bmatrix}$

Key Questions to Ask for Example 2

- Why is it important to multiply both sides of the equation by A^{-1} on the left? **Matrix multiplication is not commutative, so A^{-1} must be next to A on the left. However, matrix multiplication is associative, so $A^{-1}(AX) = (A^{-1}A)X = IX = X$.**
- What is $A^{-1}A$? **the identity matrix**

An **Animated Algebra** activity is available on-line for **Example 2**. This activity is also available on the **Power Presentations CD-ROM**.

1–4. See Additional Answers beginning on p. AA1.

Differentiated Instruction

Auditory Learners Students may feel compelled to memorize the formula for the inverse of a 2 × 2 matrix A. Have students draw two diagonal lines through the elements of a given matrix. Then have the students verbalize the following steps: exchange the elements on the main diagonal, switch the sign of the elements on the other diagonal, and multiply this transformed matrix by the determinant of the original matrix.

See also the *Algebra 2 Toolkit* for more strategies.

Extra Example 3

Use a graphing calculator to find the inverse of A. Then use the calculator to verify your result.

$A = \begin{bmatrix} 1 & 0 & -2 \\ 3 & 2 & 1 \\ -1 & 1 & 4 \end{bmatrix}$ $\begin{bmatrix} -\frac{7}{3} & \frac{2}{3} & -\frac{4}{3} \\ \frac{13}{3} & -\frac{2}{3} & \frac{7}{3} \\ -\frac{5}{3} & \frac{1}{3} & -\frac{2}{3} \end{bmatrix}$;

$A^{-1}A = AA^{-1} = \begin{bmatrix} 1 & 0 & 0 \\ 0 & 1 & 0 \\ 0 & 0 & 1 \end{bmatrix}$

Reading Strategy

Ask students to read the text carefully for Example 3. They should notice that calculator screens show $AA^{-1} = A^{-1}A$, and both products are equal to the identity matrix.

Extra Example 4

Use an inverse matrix to solve the linear system.

$-2x + 3y = -11$

$5x + y = 19$ (4, −1)

Key Question to Ask for Example 4

- Why does the inverse matrix A^{-1} have fractions in it? The reciprocal of the determinant, which is the fraction $\frac{1}{11}$, is multiplied by the elements of the matrix.

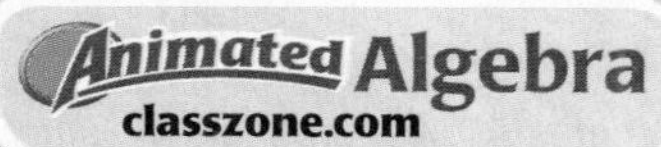

An **Animated Algebra** activity is available on-line for **Example 4**. This activity is also available on the **Power Presentations CD-ROM**.

✓ **GUIDED PRACTICE** for Example 3

Use a graphing calculator to find the inverse of the matrix A. Check the result by showing that $AA^{-1} = I$ and $A^{-1}A = I$. 5–7. See margin.

5. $A = \begin{bmatrix} 2 & -2 & 0 \\ 2 & 0 & -2 \\ 12 & -4 & -6 \end{bmatrix}$ **6.** $A = \begin{bmatrix} -3 & 4 & 5 \\ 1 & 5 & 0 \\ 5 & 2 & 2 \end{bmatrix}$ **7.** $A = \begin{bmatrix} 2 & 1 & -2 \\ 5 & 3 & 0 \\ 4 & 3 & 8 \end{bmatrix}$

KEY CONCEPT *For Your Notebook*

Using an Inverse Matrix to Solve a Linear System

STEP 1 **Write** the system as a matrix equation $AX = B$. The matrix A is the coefficient matrix, X is the **matrix of variables**, and B is the **matrix of constants**.

STEP 2 **Find** the inverse of matrix A.

STEP 3 **Multiply** each side of $AX = B$ by A^{-1} *on the left* to find the solution $X = A^{-1}B$.

EXAMPLE 4 Solve a linear system

Use an inverse matrix to solve the linear system.

$2x - 3y = 19$ Equation 1

$x + 4y = -7$ Equation 2

SOLVE SYSTEMS

You can use the method shown in Example 4 if A has an inverse. If A does not have an inverse, then the system has either no solution or infinitely many solutions.

Solution

STEP 1 **Write** the linear system as a matrix equation $AX = B$.

coefficient matrix (A) · matrix of variables (X) = matrix of constants (B)

$$\begin{bmatrix} 2 & -3 \\ 1 & 4 \end{bmatrix} \cdot \begin{bmatrix} x \\ y \end{bmatrix} = \begin{bmatrix} 19 \\ -7 \end{bmatrix}$$

STEP 2 **Find** the inverse of matrix A.

$$A^{-1} = \frac{1}{8-(-3)}\begin{bmatrix} 4 & 3 \\ -1 & 2 \end{bmatrix} = \begin{bmatrix} \frac{4}{11} & \frac{3}{11} \\ -\frac{1}{11} & \frac{2}{11} \end{bmatrix}$$

STEP 3 **Multiply** the matrix of constants by A^{-1} on the left.

$$X = A^{-1}B = \begin{bmatrix} \frac{4}{11} & \frac{3}{11} \\ -\frac{1}{11} & \frac{2}{11} \end{bmatrix}\begin{bmatrix} 19 \\ -7 \end{bmatrix} = \begin{bmatrix} 5 \\ -3 \end{bmatrix} = \begin{bmatrix} x \\ y \end{bmatrix}$$

▶ The solution of the system is (5, −3).

CHECK $2(5) - 3(-3) = 10 + 9 = 19$ ✓ $5 + 4(-3) = 5 - 12 = -7$ ✓

Animated Algebra at classzone.com

5. $\begin{bmatrix} -1 & -\frac{3}{2} & \frac{1}{2} \\ -\frac{3}{2} & -\frac{3}{2} & \frac{1}{2} \\ -1 & -2 & \frac{1}{2} \end{bmatrix}$ 6. $\begin{bmatrix} -\frac{10}{153} & -\frac{2}{153} & \frac{25}{153} \\ \frac{2}{153} & \frac{31}{153} & -\frac{5}{153} \\ \frac{23}{153} & -\frac{26}{153} & \frac{19}{153} \end{bmatrix}$ 7. $\begin{bmatrix} 12 & -7 & 3 \\ -20 & 12 & -5 \\ \frac{3}{2} & -1 & \frac{1}{2} \end{bmatrix}$

EXAMPLE 5 Solve a multi-step problem

GIFTS A company sells three types of movie gift baskets. A basic basket with 2 movie passes and 1 package of microwave popcorn costs \$15.50. A medium basket with 2 movie passes, 2 packages of popcorn, and 1 DVD costs \$37. A super basket with 4 movie passes, 3 packages of popcorn, and 2 DVDs costs \$72.50. Find the cost of each item in the gift baskets.

ANOTHER WAY
For an alternative method for solving the problem in Example 5, turn to page 218 for the **Problem Solving Workshop**.

Solution

STEP 1 **Write** verbal models for the situation.

2 · Cost of movie pass + Cost of popcorn = Cost of basic basket **Equation 1**

2 · Cost of movie pass + 2 · Cost of popcorn + Cost of DVD = Cost of medium basket **Equation 2**

4 · Cost of movie pass + 3 · Cost of popcorn + 2 · Cost of DVD = Cost of super basket **Equation 3**

STEP 2 **Write** a system of equations. Let m be the cost of a movie pass, p be the cost of a package of popcorn, and d be the cost of a DVD.

$2m + p = 15.50$ **Equation 1**
$2m + 2p + d = 37.00$ **Equation 2**
$4m + 3p + 2d = 72.50$ **Equation 3**

STEP 3 **Rewrite** the system as a matrix equation.

$$\begin{bmatrix} 2 & 1 & 0 \\ 2 & 2 & 1 \\ 4 & 3 & 2 \end{bmatrix}\begin{bmatrix} m \\ p \\ d \end{bmatrix} = \begin{bmatrix} 15.50 \\ 37.00 \\ 72.50 \end{bmatrix}$$

STEP 4 **Enter** the coefficient matrix A and the matrix of constants B into a graphing calculator. Then find the solution $X = A^{-1}B$.

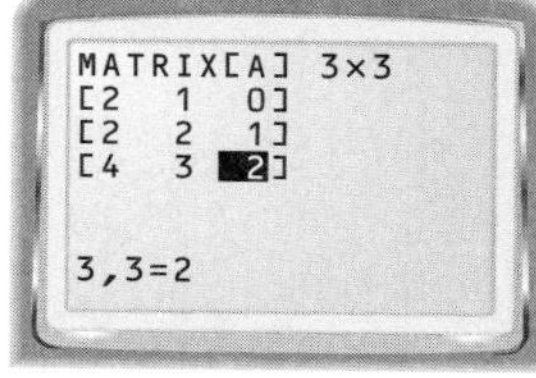

▶ A movie pass costs \$7, a package of popcorn costs \$1.50, and a DVD costs \$20.

✓ GUIDED PRACTICE for Examples 4 and 5

Use an inverse matrix to solve the linear system.

8. $4x + y = 10$
$3x + 5y = -1$ **(3, −2)**

9. $2x - y = -6$
$6x - 3y = -18$
infinitely many solutions

10. $3x - y = -5$
$-4x + 2y = 8$ **(−1, 2)**

11. WHAT IF In Example 5, how does the answer change if a basic basket costs \$17, a medium basket costs \$35, and a super basket costs \$69?
movie pass: \$8, package of popcorn: \$1, DVD: \$17

Extra Example 5

At a video store, the cost of 3 DVDs, 2 video games, and 4 VHS movies is \$130. The cost of 2 DVDs, 1 video game, and 5 VHS movies is \$105. The cost of 3 DVDs, 3 video games, and 3 VHS movies is \$135. Find the cost of each item. **DVD: \$20; game: \$15; movie: \$10**

Closing the Lesson

Have students summarize the major points of the lesson and answer the Essential Question: How do you solve a system of two linear equations using inverse matrices?

- **The $n \times n$ identity matrix has all 1's on its main diagonal and all 0's elsewhere.**
- **Inverse matrices can be used to solve matrix equations and systems of linear equations.**

You write a matrix equation using the coefficient matrix and the matrix of constants. You find the inverse of the coefficient matrix and multiply it on the left on both sides of the matrix equation. The resulting matrix gives the solution to the original system.

4 PRACTICE AND APPLY

Assignment Guide

Answer Transparencies available for all exercises

Basic:
Day 1: SRH p. 984 Exs. 13–19
pp. 214–217
Exs. 1–18
Day 2: pp. 214–217
Exs. 19–30, 34–36, 43–46, 51–53

Average:
Day 1: pp. 214–217
Exs. 1–18
Day 2: pp. 214–217
Exs. 19–24, 28–41, 43–48,
51–53 odd

Advanced:
Day 1: pp. 214–217
Exs. 1, 2, 5–10, 12–18, 41
Day 2: pp. 214–217
Exs. 22–24, 28–50*, 52

Block:
pp. 214–217
Exs. 1–24, 28–41, 43–48,
51–53 odd

Differentiated Instruction

See *Algebra 2 Best Practices Toolkit* for suggestions on addressing the needs of a diverse classroom.

Homework Check

For a quick check of student understanding of key concepts, go over the following exercises:

Basic: 4, 14, 20, 26, 43
Average: 6, 16, 22, 38, 44
Advanced: 8, 18, 24, 39, 46

Extra Practice

- Student Edition, p. 1012
- Chapter 3 Resource Book: Practice levels A, B, C, pp. 95–97

Practice Worksheet

An easily-readable reduced practice page (with answers) for this lesson can be found on p. 150C.

1. matrix of variables: $\begin{bmatrix} x \\ y \end{bmatrix}$,

matrix of constants: $\begin{bmatrix} 4 \\ -2 \end{bmatrix}$

3.8 EXERCISES

HOMEWORK KEY

○ = **WORKED-OUT SOLUTIONS** on p. WS7 for Exs. 3, 25, and 47

★ = **STANDARDIZED TEST PRACTICE** Exs. 2, 12, 34, 41, and 46

◆ = **MULTIPLE REPRESENTATIONS** Ex. 45

SKILL PRACTICE

A

1. **VOCABULARY** Identify the matrix of variables and the matrix of constants in the matrix equation. $\begin{bmatrix} -1 & 2 \\ 3 & 4 \end{bmatrix}\begin{bmatrix} x \\ y \end{bmatrix} = \begin{bmatrix} 4 \\ -2 \end{bmatrix}$ **See margin.**

2. ★ **WRITING** *Explain* how to find the inverse of a 2×2 matrix A where $\det A \neq 0$. **See margin.**

EXAMPLE 1 on p. 210 for Exs. 3–12

FINDING INVERSES **Find the inverse of the matrix.** 3–10. See margin.

3. $\begin{bmatrix} 1 & -5 \\ -1 & 4 \end{bmatrix}$ 4. $\begin{bmatrix} -2 & 3 \\ -3 & 4 \end{bmatrix}$ 5. $\begin{bmatrix} 6 & 2 \\ 5 & 2 \end{bmatrix}$ 6. $\begin{bmatrix} -7 & -9 \\ 2 & 3 \end{bmatrix}$

7. $\begin{bmatrix} -4 & -6 \\ 4 & 7 \end{bmatrix}$ 8. $\begin{bmatrix} 6 & -22 \\ -12 & 20 \end{bmatrix}$ 9. $\begin{bmatrix} -24 & 60 \\ -6 & 30 \end{bmatrix}$ 10. $\begin{bmatrix} \frac{4}{3} & \frac{5}{6} \\ -4 & -1 \end{bmatrix}$

11. **ERROR ANALYSIS** *Describe* and correct the error in finding the inverse of the matrix $\begin{bmatrix} 2 & 4 \\ 1 & 5 \end{bmatrix}$. **See margin.**

$$\begin{bmatrix} 2 & 4 \\ 1 & 5 \end{bmatrix}^{-1} = 6\begin{bmatrix} 5 & -4 \\ -1 & 2 \end{bmatrix} = \begin{bmatrix} 30 & -24 \\ -6 & 12 \end{bmatrix} \times$$

12. ★ **MULTIPLE CHOICE** What is the inverse of the matrix $\begin{bmatrix} 10 & -3 \\ 3 & -1 \end{bmatrix}$? C

Ⓐ $\begin{bmatrix} -10 & 3 \\ -3 & 1 \end{bmatrix}$ Ⓑ $\begin{bmatrix} -1 & 3 \\ -3 & 10 \end{bmatrix}$ Ⓒ $\begin{bmatrix} 1 & -3 \\ 3 & -10 \end{bmatrix}$ Ⓓ $\begin{bmatrix} 10 & -3 \\ 3 & -1 \end{bmatrix}$

EXAMPLE 2 on p. 211 for Exs. 13–18

SOLVING EQUATIONS **Solve the matrix equation.** 13–18. See margin.

13. $\begin{bmatrix} 1 & 1 \\ 4 & 5 \end{bmatrix}X = \begin{bmatrix} 2 & 3 \\ -1 & 6 \end{bmatrix}$ 14. $\begin{bmatrix} 6 & 8 \\ 2 & 3 \end{bmatrix}X = \begin{bmatrix} 4 & 3 \\ 0 & -2 \end{bmatrix}$ 15. $\begin{bmatrix} -1 & 0 \\ 6 & 4 \end{bmatrix}X = \begin{bmatrix} 3 & -1 \\ 4 & 5 \end{bmatrix}$

16. $\begin{bmatrix} -3 & 6 \\ 1 & 2 \end{bmatrix}X = \begin{bmatrix} 5 & -1 \\ 8 & 2 \end{bmatrix}$ 17. $\begin{bmatrix} 1 & 5 \\ 0 & -2 \end{bmatrix}X = \begin{bmatrix} 3 & -1 & 0 \\ 6 & 8 & 4 \end{bmatrix}$ 18. $\begin{bmatrix} -5 & 2 \\ -9 & 3 \end{bmatrix}X = \begin{bmatrix} 4 & 5 & 0 \\ 3 & 1 & 6 \end{bmatrix}$

EXAMPLE 3 on p. 211 for Exs. 19–24

FINDING INVERSES **Use a graphing calculator to find the inverse of matrix A. Check the result by showing that $AA^{-1} = I$ and $A^{-1}A = I$.** 19–24. See margin.

B

19. $A = \begin{bmatrix} 1 & 1 & -2 \\ -2 & 0 & 3 \\ 3 & 1 & 0 \end{bmatrix}$ 20. $A = \begin{bmatrix} 1 & 0 & 2 \\ 2 & 1 & 3 \\ 1 & 4 & 4 \end{bmatrix}$ 21. $A = \begin{bmatrix} 1 & -1 & 2 \\ -2 & 3 & 10 \\ 3 & -1 & 2 \end{bmatrix}$

22. $A = \begin{bmatrix} -2 & 5 & -1 \\ 0 & 8 & 1 \\ 12 & -5 & 0 \end{bmatrix}$ 23. $A = \begin{bmatrix} 3 & -8 & 0 \\ 2 & 4 & 1 \\ -1 & 0 & -6 \end{bmatrix}$ 24. $A = \begin{bmatrix} 4 & 1 & 5 \\ -2 & 2 & 1 \\ 3 & -1 & 6 \end{bmatrix}$

2. *Sample answer:* Compute the determinant of *A*. Use its reciprocal as the scalar multiple for a new matrix where you interchange the values along the main diagonal and compute the product of –1 and the values along the other diagonal. This product is the inverse matrix.

EXAMPLE 4 on p. 212 for Exs. 25–34

SYSTEMS OF TWO EQUATIONS **Use an inverse matrix to solve the linear system.**

25. $4x - y = 10$
$-7x - 2y = -25$ **(3, 2)**

26. $4x + 7y = -16$
$2x + 3y = -4$ **(10, −8)**

27. $3x - 2y = 5$
$6x - 5y = 14$ **(−1, −4)**

28. $x - y = 4$
$9x - 10y = 45$ **(−5, −9)**

29. $-2x - 9y = -2$
$4x + 16y = 8$ **(10, −2)**

30. $2x - 7y = -6$
$-x + 5y = 3$ **(−3, 0)**

31. $6x + y = -2$
$-x + 3y = -25$ **(1, −8)**

32. $2x + y = -2$
$2x + 5y = 38$ **(−6, 10)**

33. $5x + 7y = 20$
$3x + 5y = 16$ **(−3, 5)**

34. ★ **MULTIPLE CHOICE** What is the solution of the system shown? **C**

$3x - 5y = -26$
$-x + 2y = 10$

(A) (3, 7) (B) (7, −1) (C) (−2, 4) (D) (68, 110)

EXAMPLE 5 on p. 213 for Exs. 35–40

SYSTEMS OF THREE EQUATIONS **Use an inverse matrix and a graphing calculator to solve the linear system.**

35. $x - y - 3z = 2$
$5x + 2y + z = -17$
$-3x - y = 8$ **(−9, 19, −10)**

36. $-3x + y - 8z = 18$
$x - 2y + z = -11$
$2x - 2y + 5z = -17$ **(−2, 4, −1)**

37. $2x + 4y + 5z = 5$
$x + 2y + 3z = 4$
$5x - 4y - 2z = -3$ **(−1, −2, 3)**

38. $4x - y - z = -20$
$6x - z = -27$
$-x + 4y + 5z = 23$ **(−4, 1, 3)**

39. $3x + 2y - z = 14$
$-x - 5y + 4z = -48$
$4x + y + z = 2$ **(−2, 10, 0)**

40. $6x + y + 2z = 11$
$x - y + z = -5$
$-x + 4y - z = 14$ **(3, 3, −5)**

C

41. ★ **OPEN-ENDED MATH** Write a 2×2 matrix that has no inverse. ***Sample answer:*** $\begin{bmatrix} 2 & 3 \\ 4 & 6 \end{bmatrix}$

42. **CHALLENGE** Solve the linear system using the given inverse of the coefficient matrix. **(−3, 8, 1, −5)**

$2w + 5x - 4y + 6z = 0$
$2x + y - 7z = 52$
$4w + 8x - 7y + 14z = -25$
$3w + 6x - 5y + 10z = -16$

$$A^{-1} = \begin{bmatrix} -10 & 4 & 27 & -29 \\ 5 & -2 & -16 & 18 \\ 4 & -2 & -17 & 20 \\ 2 & -1 & -7 & 8 \end{bmatrix}$$

PROBLEM SOLVING

EXAMPLES 4 and 5 A on pp. 212–213 for Exs. 43–48

43. single-engine: 150 h, twin-engine: 50 h

43. **AVIATION** A pilot has 200 hours of flight time in single-engine airplanes and twin-engine airplanes. Renting a single-engine airplane costs \$60 per hour, and renting a twin-engine airplane costs \$240 per hour. The pilot has spent \$21,000 on airplane rentals. Use an inverse matrix to find how many hours the pilot has flown each type of airplane.

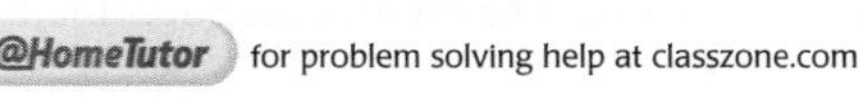

for problem solving help at classzone.com

44. **BASKETBALL** During the 2003–2004 NBA season, Dirk Nowitzki of the Dallas Mavericks made a total of 976 shots and scored 1680 points. His shots consisted of 3-point field goals, 2-point field goals, and 1-point free throws. He made 135 more 2-point field goals than free throws. Use an inverse matrix to find how many of each type of shot he made. **99 3-point field goals, 506 2-point field goals, 371 free throws**

@HomeTutor for problem solving help at classzone.com

Avoiding Common Errors

Exercises 13–16 When an equation has square matrices, students sometimes forget to multiply by the inverse on both sides of the equation.

Exercises 35, 38 Point out to students that they need to add a zero for a coefficient if one variable is missing in an equation. This keeps the variables aligned vertically and helps avoid the error of replacing the wrong coefficient with one of the constants.

Graphing Calculator

Exercise 42 The inverse of a 4×4 matrix is difficult to find without a graphing calculator. Since the inverse is given for this problem, students can use a calculator to multiply on the left by that inverse.

11. The scalar should be $\frac{1}{\det}$;
$\frac{1}{6}\begin{bmatrix} 5 & -4 \\ -1 & 2 \end{bmatrix} = \begin{bmatrix} \frac{5}{6} & -\frac{2}{3} \\ -\frac{1}{6} & \frac{1}{3} \end{bmatrix}$.

13. $\begin{bmatrix} 11 & 9 \\ -9 & -6 \end{bmatrix}$

14. $\begin{bmatrix} 6 & \frac{25}{2} \\ -4 & -9 \end{bmatrix}$

15. $\begin{bmatrix} -3 & 1 \\ \frac{11}{2} & -\frac{1}{4} \end{bmatrix}$

16. $\begin{bmatrix} \frac{19}{6} & \frac{7}{6} \\ \frac{29}{12} & \frac{5}{12} \end{bmatrix}$

17. $\begin{bmatrix} 18 & 19 & 10 \\ -3 & -4 & -2 \end{bmatrix}$

18. $\begin{bmatrix} 2 & \frac{13}{3} & -4 \\ 7 & \frac{40}{3} & -10 \end{bmatrix}$

19–24. See Additional Answers beginning on p. AA1.

3. $\begin{bmatrix} -4 & -5 \\ -1 & -1 \end{bmatrix}$

4. $\begin{bmatrix} 4 & -3 \\ 3 & -2 \end{bmatrix}$

5. $\begin{bmatrix} 1 & -1 \\ -\frac{5}{2} & 3 \end{bmatrix}$

6. $\begin{bmatrix} -1 & -3 \\ \frac{2}{3} & \frac{7}{3} \end{bmatrix}$

7. $\begin{bmatrix} -\frac{7}{4} & -\frac{3}{2} \\ 1 & 1 \end{bmatrix}$

8. $\begin{bmatrix} -\frac{5}{36} & -\frac{11}{72} \\ -\frac{1}{12} & -\frac{1}{24} \end{bmatrix}$

9. $\begin{bmatrix} -\frac{1}{12} & \frac{1}{6} \\ -\frac{1}{60} & \frac{1}{15} \end{bmatrix}$

10. $\begin{bmatrix} -\frac{1}{2} & -\frac{5}{12} \\ 2 & \frac{2}{3} \end{bmatrix}$

45a. $2x + y = 8, 3x + y = 11$ where x represents rolls and y represents muffins

45b. $\begin{bmatrix} 2 & 1 \\ 3 & 1 \end{bmatrix}\begin{bmatrix} x \\ y \end{bmatrix} = \begin{bmatrix} 8 \\ 11 \end{bmatrix}$

45c. 3 batches of rolls, 2 batches of muffins

46a. $2x + 3y = 18, 3x + 5y = 28$ where x represents cheeses and y represents meats; 6 cheeses, 2 meats

46b. $3x + 5y = 28, 7x + 10y = 60$ where x represents cheeses and y represents meats; 4 cheeses, 3.2 meats

46c. *Sample answer:* The larger volume of cheese reduces the price, but the amount of meat is larger and raises the price.

48a. $6.5x + 4.5y + 8.5z = 80,$ $x + y + z = 12, x - y - z = 0$

48b. $\begin{bmatrix} 6.5 & 4.5 & 8.5 \\ 1 & 1 & 1 \\ 1 & -1 & -1 \end{bmatrix}\begin{bmatrix} x \\ y \\ z \end{bmatrix} = \begin{bmatrix} 80 \\ 12 \\ 0 \end{bmatrix}$

48c. $\begin{bmatrix} 0 & 0.5 & 0.5 \\ -0.25 & 1.875 & -0.25 \\ 0.25 & -1.375 & -0.25 \end{bmatrix}\begin{bmatrix} 80 \\ 12 \\ 0 \end{bmatrix}$

$= \begin{bmatrix} 6 \\ 2.5 \\ 3.5 \end{bmatrix}$

49a. $\begin{bmatrix} 1 & 4 & 2 \\ -1 & -3 & -5 \end{bmatrix}, \begin{bmatrix} -1 & -3 & -5 \\ -1 & -4 & -2 \end{bmatrix};$ 90° clockwise rotation

49b. Multiply AAT by A and then again by A.

45. ◆ **MULTIPLE REPRESENTATIONS** A cooking class wants to use up 8 cups of buttermilk and 11 eggs by baking rolls and muffins to freeze. A batch of rolls uses 2 cups of buttermilk and 3 eggs. A batch of muffins uses 1 cup of buttermilk and 1 egg. a–c. See margin.

   a. **Writing a System** Write a system of equations for this situation.

   b. **Writing a Matrix Equation** Write the system of equations from part (a) as a matrix equation $AX = B$.

   c. **Solving a System** Use an inverse matrix to solve the system of equations. How many batches of each recipe should the class make?

B

46. ★ **EXTENDED RESPONSE** A company sells party platters with varying assortments of meats and cheeses. A basic platter with 2 cheeses and 3 meats costs \$18, a medium platter with 3 cheeses and 5 meats costs \$28, and a super platter with 7 cheeses and 10 meats costs \$60. a–c. See margin.

   a. Write and solve a system of equations using the information about the basic platter and the medium platter.

   b. Write and solve a system of equations using the information about the medium platter and the super platter.

   c. *Compare* the results from parts (a) and (b) and make a conjecture about why there is a discrepancy.

47. **NUTRITION** The table shows the calories, fat, and carbohydrates per ounce for three brands of cereal. How many ounces of each brand should be combined to get 500 calories, 3 grams of fat, and 100 grams of carbohydrates? Round your answers to the nearest tenth of an ounce. Bran Crunchies: 2.3 oz, Toasted Oats: 0.8 oz, Whole Wheat Flakes: 1.2 oz

Cereal	Calories	Fat	Carbohydrates
Bran Crunchies	78	1 g	22 g
Toasted Oats	104	0 g	25.5 g
Whole Wheat Flakes	198	0.6 g	23.8 g

48. **MULTI-STEP PROBLEM** You need 9 square feet of glass mosaic tiles to decorate a wall of your kitchen. You want the area of the red tiles to equal the combined area of the yellow and blue tiles. The cost of a sheet of glass tiles having an area of 0.75 square foot is \$6.50 for red, \$4.50 for yellow, and \$8.50 for blue. You have \$80 to spend. a–c. See margin.

   a. Write a system of equations to represent this situation.

   b. Rewrite the system as a matrix equation.

   c. Use an inverse matrix to find how many sheets of each color tile you should buy.

Mosaic tiles

C

49. **GEOMETRY** The columns of matrix T below give the coordinates of the vertices of a triangle. Matrix A is a transformation matrix. a–b. See margin.

$$A = \begin{bmatrix} 0 & 1 \\ -1 & 0 \end{bmatrix} \qquad T = \begin{bmatrix} 1 & 3 & 5 \\ 1 & 4 & 2 \end{bmatrix}$$

   a. Find AT and AAT. Then draw the original triangle and the two transformed triangles. What transformation does A represent?

   b. *Describe* how to use matrices to obtain the original triangle represented by T from the transformed triangle represented by AAT.

50. CHALLENGE Verify the formula on page 210 for the inverse of a 2×2 matrix by showing that $AB = I$ and $BA = I$ for the matrices A and B given below. **See margin.**

$$A = \begin{bmatrix} a & b \\ c & d \end{bmatrix} \qquad B = \frac{1}{ad - cb}\begin{bmatrix} d & -b \\ -c & a \end{bmatrix}$$

KENTUCKY MIXED REVIEW

TEST PRACTICE at classzone.com

51. A grocer wants to mix peanuts worth \$2.50 per pound with 12 pounds of cashews worth \$4.75 per pound. To obtain a nut mixture worth \$4 per pound, how many pounds of peanuts are needed? **B**

Ⓐ 3.6 lb Ⓑ 6 lb Ⓒ 12 lb Ⓓ 18 lb

52. The sum of three numbers is 141. The second number is 5 less than three times the first number. The third number is 2 more than four times the first number. Which equation represents the relationship between the three numbers where n is the first number? **C**

Ⓐ $141 = n - (3n - 5) - (4n + 2)$ Ⓑ $141 = n + (4n - 5) + (3n + 2)$

Ⓒ $141 = n + (3n - 5) + (4n + 2)$ Ⓓ $141 = n + (5 - 3n) + (2 + 4n)$

53. Which ordered pair is the solution of this system of linear equations? **A**

$$5x + y = -17$$
$$2x - 7y = 8$$

Ⓐ $(-3, -2)$ Ⓑ $(-3, 2)$ Ⓒ $\left(3, -\frac{2}{7}\right)$ Ⓓ $(11, 2)$

QUIZ for Lessons 3.6–3.8

Using the given matrices, evaluate the expression. *(p. 195)*

$$A = \begin{bmatrix} 1 & -4 \\ 5 & 2 \end{bmatrix}, B = \begin{bmatrix} 2 & -3 \\ 0 & 1 \end{bmatrix}, C = \begin{bmatrix} -6 & -1 \\ 2 & 4 \end{bmatrix}$$

1. $2AB$ **2.** $AB + AC$ **3.** $A(B + C)$ **4.** $(B - A)C$

1. $\begin{bmatrix} 4 & -14 \\ 20 & -26 \end{bmatrix}$ 2. $\begin{bmatrix} -12 & -24 \\ -16 & -10 \end{bmatrix}$ 3. $\begin{bmatrix} -12 & -24 \\ -16 & -10 \end{bmatrix}$ 4. $\begin{bmatrix} -4 & 3 \\ 28 & 1 \end{bmatrix}$

Evaluate the determinant of the matrix. *(p. 203)*

5. $\begin{bmatrix} 5 & 4 \\ -2 & -3 \end{bmatrix}$ -7 **6.** $\begin{bmatrix} 1 & 0 & -2 \\ -3 & 1 & 4 \\ 2 & 3 & -1 \end{bmatrix}$ 9 **7.** $\begin{bmatrix} 2 & -1 & 5 \\ -3 & 6 & 9 \\ -2 & 3 & 1 \end{bmatrix}$ -12

Use an inverse matrix to solve the linear system. *(p. 210)*

8. $x + 3y = -2$
$2x + 7y = -6$ $(4, -2)$

9. $3x - 4y = 5$
$2x - 3y = 3$ $(3, 1)$

10. $-3x + 2y = -13$
$6x - 5y = 24$ $\left(\frac{17}{3}, 2\right)$

11. $3x - y = -4$
$2x - 2y = -8$ $(0, 4)$

12. $7x + 4y = 6$
$5x + 3y = -25$ $(118, -205)$

13. $4x + y = -2$
$-6x + y = 18$ $(-2, 6)$

14. BOATING You are making a triangular sail for a sailboat. The vertices of the sail are (0, 2), (12, 2), and (12, 26) where the coordinates are measured in feet. Find the area of the sail. *(p. 203)* $144\ ft^2$

5 ASSESS AND RETEACH

Daily Homework Quiz

Transparency Available

1. Find the inverse of $A = \begin{bmatrix} 2 & -3 \\ 1 & 0 \end{bmatrix}$. $\begin{bmatrix} 0 & 1 \\ -\frac{1}{3} & \frac{2}{3} \end{bmatrix}$

2. Solve the matrix equation $AX = B$ for the 2×2 matrix X.
$\begin{bmatrix} -5 & -4 \\ 4 & 3 \end{bmatrix}X = \begin{bmatrix} 4 & -6 \\ 1 & 2 \end{bmatrix}$. $\begin{bmatrix} 16 & -10 \\ -21 & 14 \end{bmatrix}$

3. Use inverses to solve the linear system.
$3x - 2y = 18$
$-2x + 4y = -20$ $(4, -3)$

Online Quiz

Available at **classzone.com**

Diagnosis/Remediation

- Practice A, B, C in Chapter 3 Resource Book, pp. 95–97
- Study Guide in Chapter 3 Resource Book, pp. 98–99
- Practice Workbook, pp. 52–53
- @HomeTutor

Challenge

Additional challenge is available in the Chapter 3 Resource Book, p. 102.

Quiz

An easily-readable reduced copy of the quiz (with answers) on Lessons 3.6–3.8 from the Assessment Book can be found on p. 150F.

50. See Additional Answers beginning on p. AA1.

Alternative Strategy

Example 5 on page 213 can be solved using augmented matrices. This method allows students to better understand the inverse matrix solution given in Lesson 3.8.

Vocabulary

Help students remember the meaning of "augmented matrix" by discussing the meaning of *augment.* To augment is to increase, and an augmented matrix is one that has additional elements to perform row operations. The additional elements are the elements of the matrix of constants.

Avoiding Common Errors

Some students perform a row operation on one side of an augmented matrix and forget to perform it on the other side. Stress the importance of performing the row operation on all elements in the row.

Reading Strategy

As students read through the example, they should notice the gradual emergence of zeros in the matrix below the main diagonal of ones. They should expect that the rows will change as row operations are being performed, and that there may be equations to solve at the end of the process. Stress the importance of keeping track of the row operations used so that work can be checked.

Another Way to Solve Example 5, page 213

MULTIPLE REPRESENTATIONS In Example 5 on page 213, you solved a linear system using an inverse matrix. You can also solve systems using *augmented matrices.* An **augmented matrix** for a system contains the system's coefficient matrix and matrix of constants.

Linear System → **Augmented Matrix**

$$x - 4y = 9$$
$$-6x + 7y = -2$$

$$\left[\begin{array}{cc|c} 1 & -4 & 9 \\ -6 & 7 & -2 \end{array}\right]$$

Recall from Lesson 3.2 that an equation in a system can be multiplied by a constant, or a multiple of one equation can be added to another equation. Similar operations can be performed on the rows of an augmented matrix to solve the corresponding system.

KEY CONCEPT *For Your Notebook*

Elementary Row Operations for Augmented Matrices

Two augmented matrices are *row-equivalent* if their corresponding systems have the same solution(s). Any of these row operations performed on an augmented matrix will produce a matrix that is row-equivalent to the original:

- Interchange two rows.
- Multiply a row by a nonzero constant.
- Add a multiple of one row to another row.

PROBLEM

GIFTS A company sells three types of movie gift baskets. A basic basket with 2 movie passes and 1 package of microwave popcorn costs \$15.50. A medium basket with 2 movie passes, 2 packages of popcorn, and 1 DVD costs \$37. A super basket with 4 movie passes, 3 packages of popcorn, and 2 DVDs costs \$72.50. Find the cost of each item in the gift baskets.

METHOD

Using an Augmented Matrix You need to write a linear system, write the corresponding augmented matrix, and use row operations to transform the augmented matrix into a matrix with 1's along the main diagonal and 0's below the main diagonal. Such a matrix is in *triangular form* and can be used to solve for the variables in the system.

Let m be the cost of a movie pass, p be the cost of a package of popcorn, and d be the cost of a DVD.

STEP 1 **Write** a linear system and then write an augmented matrix.

$$2m + p = 15.5 \qquad \left[\begin{array}{ccc|c} 2 & 1 & 0 & 15.5 \\ 2 & 2 & 1 & 37 \\ 4 & 3 & 2 & 72.5 \end{array}\right]$$
$$2m + 2p + d = 37$$
$$4m + 3p + 2d = 72.5$$

STEP 2 **Add** −2 times the first row to the third row.

$$(-2)R_1 + R_3 \longrightarrow \left[\begin{array}{ccc|c} 2 & 1 & 0 & 15.5 \\ 2 & 2 & 1 & 37 \\ 0 & 1 & 2 & 41.5 \end{array}\right]$$

STEP 3 **Add** −1 times the first row to the second row.

$$(-1)R_1 + R_2 \longrightarrow \left[\begin{array}{ccc|c} 2 & 1 & 0 & 15.5 \\ 0 & 1 & 1 & 21.5 \\ 0 & 1 & 2 & 41.5 \end{array}\right]$$

STEP 4 **Add** −1 times the second row to the third row.

$$(-1)R_2 + R_3 \longrightarrow \left[\begin{array}{ccc|c} 2 & 1 & 0 & 15.5 \\ 0 & 1 & 1 & 21.5 \\ 0 & 0 & 1 & 20 \end{array}\right]$$

STEP 5 **Multiply** the first row by 0.5.

$$0.5R_1 \longrightarrow \left[\begin{array}{ccc|c} 1 & 0.5 & 0 & 7.75 \\ 0 & 1 & 1 & 21.5 \\ 0 & 0 & 1 & 20 \end{array}\right]$$

The third row of the matrix tells you that $d = 20$. Substitute 20 for d in the equation for the second row, $p + d = 21.5$, to obtain $p + 20 = 21.5$, or $p = 1.5$. Then substitute 1.5 for p in the equation for the first row, $m + 0.5p = 7.75$, to obtain $m + 0.5(1.5) = 7.75$, or $m = 7$.

▶ A movie pass costs \$7, a package of popcorn costs \$1.50, and a DVD costs \$20.

PRACTICE

1. **WHAT IF?** In the problem on page 218, suppose a basic basket costs \$17.75, a medium basket costs \$34.50, and a super basket costs \$67.25. Use an augmented matrix to find the cost of each item. **DVD: \$15, popcorn: \$1.75, movie pass: \$8**

2. **FINANCE** You have \$18,000 to invest. You want an overall annual return of 8%. The expected annual returns are 10% for a stock fund, 7% for a bond fund, and 5% for a money market fund. You want to invest as much in stocks as in bonds and the money market combined. Use an augmented matrix to find how much to invest in each fund. **stocks: \$9000, bonds: \$4500, money market: \$4500**

3. **BIRDSEED** A pet store sells 20 pounds of birdseed for \$10.85. The birdseed is made from two kinds of seeds, sunflower seeds and thistle seeds. Sunflower seeds cost \$.34 per pound and thistle seeds cost \$.79 per pound. Use an augmented matrix to find how many pounds of each variety are in the mixture. **11 lbs of sunflower seed, 9 lbs of thistle seed**

4. **REASONING** Solve the given system using an augmented matrix. What can you say about the system's solution(s)? **infinitely many solutions**

$$x - 2y + 4z = -10$$
$$5x + y - z = 24$$
$$3x - 6y + 12z = -30$$

Kentucky Mixed Review

1. B
2. C
3. C
4. C
5. a.

$$\begin{cases} c + s + w = 1700 \\ 2.35c + 5.40s + 3.60w = 4837 \\ -3.25(s + w) + s + w = 0 \end{cases}$$

where c, s, and w are the number of bushels of corn, soybeans, and wheat respectively;

b.

$$\begin{bmatrix} 1 & 1 & 1 \\ 2.35 & 5.40 & 3.60 \\ 1 & -3.25 & -3.25 \end{bmatrix} \begin{bmatrix} c \\ s \\ w \end{bmatrix} = \begin{bmatrix} 1700 \\ 4837 \\ 0 \end{bmatrix}$$

c. 1300 bushels of corn, 190 bushels of soybeans, and 210 bushels of wheat.

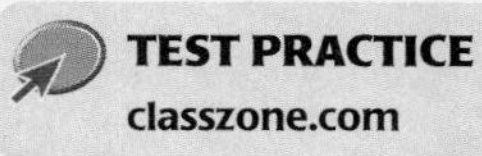

Lessons 3.5–3.8

1. **TV COMMERCIALS** The cost (in thousands of dollars) of a 30 second commercial on two cable TV networks is shown below for two cities. The cost varies based on when the commercial airs: daytime (D), prime time (P), and late night (L).

Costs in City A

	D	P	L
Network 1	4.5	6	2.5
Network 2	5.5	8	2.5

Costs in City B

	D	P	L
Network 1	4	6.5	3.25
Network 2	5	8.5	3.25

If this information is organized using two matrices A and B that give the costs for city A and city B, respectively, what is $B - A$?

A. $\begin{bmatrix} 0.5 & -0.5 & -0.75 \\ 0.5 & -0.5 & -0.75 \end{bmatrix}$

B. $\begin{bmatrix} -0.5 & 0.5 & 0.75 \\ -0.5 & 0.5 & 0.75 \end{bmatrix}$

C. $\begin{bmatrix} -0.5 & -0.5 & 0.75 \\ -0.5 & -0.5 & 0.75 \end{bmatrix}$

D. $\begin{bmatrix} 9.5 & 12.5 & 5.75 \\ 10.5 & 16.5 & 5.75 \end{bmatrix}$

2. **COINS** A person has 85 coins, of which n are nickels, d are dimes, and q are quarters. The value of the coins is $13.25. There are twice as many quarters as dimes. The situation can be modeled using the matrix equation below. How many quarters does the person have?

$$\begin{bmatrix} 1 & 1 & 1 \\ 0.05 & 0.1 & 0.25 \\ 0 & -2 & 1 \end{bmatrix} \begin{bmatrix} n \\ d \\ q \end{bmatrix} = \begin{bmatrix} 85 \\ 13.25 \\ 0 \end{bmatrix}$$

A. 20 B. 25 C. 40 D. 45

3. **SALES COMMISSION** A store has three departments: clothing (C), housewares (H), and electronics (E). Matrix A shows the total sales (in dollars) for two salespeople, Mary and Mark, in each department. Matrix B shows the commission on sales in each department. Which matrix shows the amount of commission for Mary and Mark?

Matrix A (rows C, H, E; columns Mary, Mark)

$$\begin{bmatrix} 175 & 270 \\ 370 & 225 \\ 200 & 255 \end{bmatrix}$$

Matrix B (columns C, H, E)

$$\begin{bmatrix} 3\% & 5\% & 8\% \end{bmatrix}$$

A. $\begin{bmatrix} 13.35 & 29.75 \end{bmatrix}$

B. $\begin{bmatrix} 38.50 & 40.50 \end{bmatrix}$

C. $\begin{bmatrix} 39.75 & 39.75 \end{bmatrix}$

D. $\begin{bmatrix} 397.50 & 397.50 \end{bmatrix}$

4. **ATOMIC WEIGHTS** The atomic weights of three compounds are shown in the table.

Compound	Formula	Atomic weight
Nitric acid	HNO_3	63
Nitrous oxide	N_2O	44
Water	H_2O	18

Let H, N, and O represent the atomic weights of hydrogen, nitrogen, and oxygen, respectively. What is the atomic weight of nitrogen?

A. 1 B. 2 C. 14 D. 16

5. **OPEN-RESPONSE** A farmer harvests his crops and receives $2.35 per bushel of corn, $5.40 per bushel of soybeans, and $3.60 per bushel of wheat. The farmer harvests a total of 1700 bushels of crops and receives a total of $4837. The amount of corn harvested is 3.25 times the combined amount of soybeans and wheat harvested.

a. Write a system of equations that models this situation.

b. Write the system as a matrix equation of the form $AX = B$.

c. Use an inverse matrix to find the number of each type of crop.

3 CHAPTER SUMMARY

BIG IDEAS *For Your Notebook*

ig Idea 1

Solving Systems of Equations Using a Variety of Methods

Method	When to use
Graphing: Graph each equation in the system. A point where the graphs intersect is a solution.	The equations have only two variables and are given in a form that is easy to graph.
Substitution: Solve one equation for one of the variables and substitute into the other equation(s).	One of the variables in the system has a coefficient of 1 or -1.
Elimination: Multiply equations by constants, then add the revised equations to eliminate a variable.	None of the variables in the system have a coefficient of 1 or -1.
Cramer's rule: Use determinants to find the solution.	The determinant of the coefficient matrix is not zero.
Inverse matrices: Write the system as a matrix equation $AX = B$. Multiply each side by A^{-1} on the left to obtain the solution $X = A^{-1}B$.	The determinant of the coefficient matrix is not zero.

ig Idea 2

Graphing Systems of Equations and Inequalities

System of equations with 1 solution

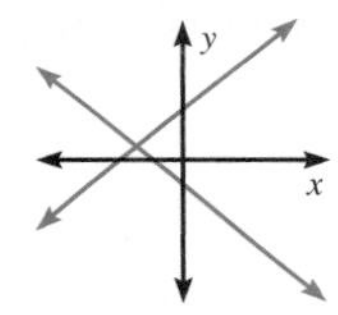

Intersecting lines

System of equations with many solutions

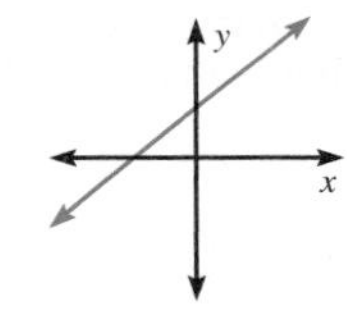

Coinciding lines

System of equations with no solution

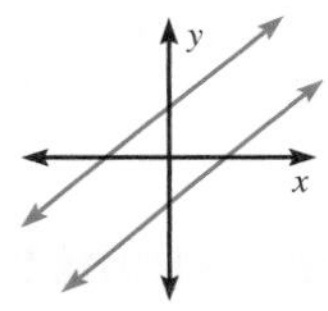

Parallel lines

System of inequalities

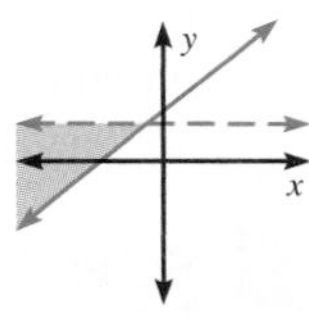

Shaded region

ig Idea 3

Using Matrices

Addition, subtraction, and scalar multiplication	Matrix multiplication	Inverse matrices
$\begin{bmatrix} a & b \\ c & d \end{bmatrix} + \begin{bmatrix} e & f \\ g & h \end{bmatrix} = \begin{bmatrix} a+e & b+f \\ c+g & d+h \end{bmatrix}$ $\begin{bmatrix} a & b \\ c & d \end{bmatrix} - \begin{bmatrix} e & f \\ g & h \end{bmatrix} = \begin{bmatrix} a-e & b-f \\ c-g & d-h \end{bmatrix}$ $k\begin{bmatrix} a & b \\ c & d \end{bmatrix} = \begin{bmatrix} ka & kb \\ kc & kd \end{bmatrix}$	$\begin{bmatrix} a & b \\ c & d \end{bmatrix}\begin{bmatrix} e & f \\ g & h \end{bmatrix} =$ $\begin{bmatrix} ae+bg & af+bh \\ ce+dg & cf+dh \end{bmatrix}$	If $A = \begin{bmatrix} a & b \\ c & d \end{bmatrix}$, then $A^{-1} = \frac{1}{\lvert A \rvert}\begin{bmatrix} d & -b \\ -c & a \end{bmatrix}$ or $A^{-1} = \frac{1}{ad-cb}\begin{bmatrix} d & -b \\ -c & a \end{bmatrix}$.

Additional Resources

The following resources are available to help review the materials in this chapter.

Chapter 3 Resource Book

- Chapter Review Games and Activities, p. 103
- Cumulative Practice, Chs. 1–3, pp. 105–106

Student Resources in Spanish

eWorkbook

@HomeTutor

Vocabulary Practice

Vocabulary practice is available at **classzone.com**

3 CHAPTER REVIEW

@HomeTutor
classzone.com
• Multi-Language Glossary
• Vocabulary practice

Extra Example 3.1
Graph the linear system and estimate the solution. Check the solution algebraically.
$6x + 2y = -6$
$8x - 4y = -8$ $(-1, 0)$

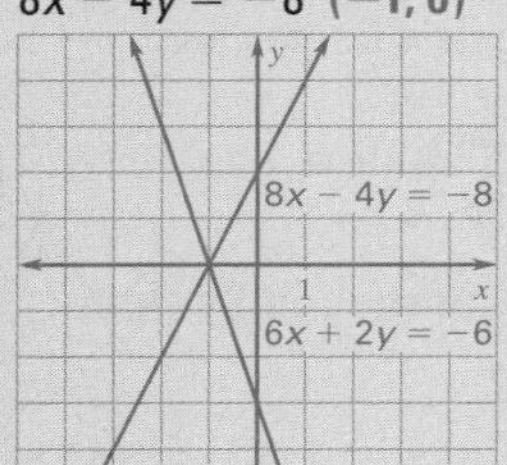

4.
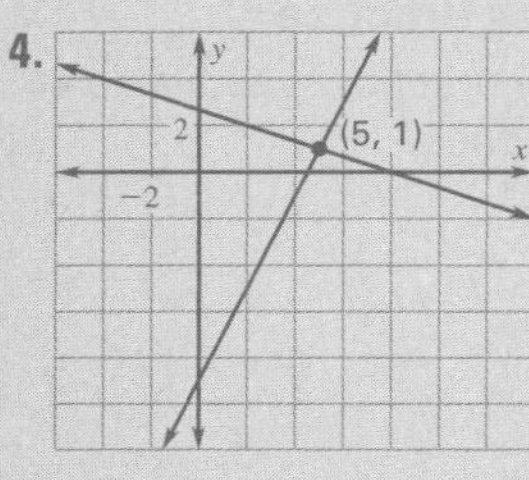

5.
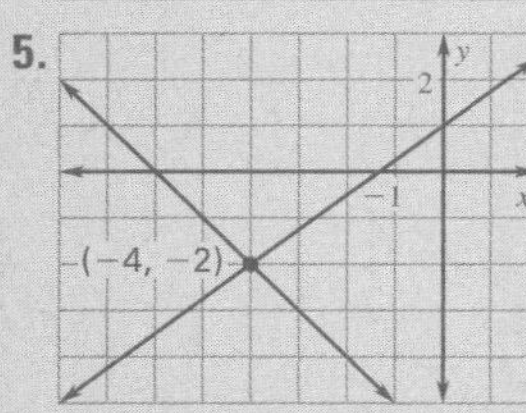

6.
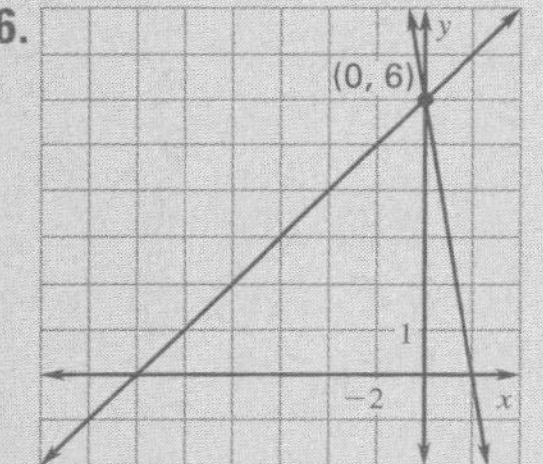

REVIEW KEY VOCABULARY

- system of two linear equations in two variables, *p. 153*
- solution of a system of linear equations, *p. 153*
- consistent, inconsistent, independent, dependent, *p. 154*
- substitution method, *p. 160*
- elimination method, *p. 161*
- system of linear inequalities in two variables, *p. 168*
- solution, graph of a system of inequalities, *p. 168*
- linear equation in three variables, *p. 178*
- system of three linear equations in three variables, *p. 178*
- solution of a system of three linear equations, *p. 178*
- ordered triple, *p. 178*
- matrix, *p. 187*
- dimensions, elements of a matrix, *p. 187*
- equal matrices, *p. 187*
- scalar, *p. 188*
- scalar multiplication, *p. 188*
- determinant, *p. 203*
- Cramer's rule, *p. 205*
- coefficient matrix, *p. 205*
- identity matrix, inverse matrices, *p. 210*
- matrix of variables, *p. 212*
- matrix of constants, *p. 212*

VOCABULARY EXERCISES

1. Copy and complete: A system of linear equations with at least one solution is _?_, while a system with no solution is _?_. **consistent, inconsistent**

2. Copy and complete: A solution (x, y, z) of a system of linear equations in three variables is called a(n) _?_. **ordered triple**

3. **WRITING** *Explain* when the product of two matrices is defined. **The number of columns in the left hand matrix is the same as the number of rows in the right hand matrix.**

REVIEW EXAMPLES AND EXERCISES

Use the review examples and exercises below to check your understanding of the concepts you have learned in each lesson of Chapter 3.

3.1 Solve Linear Systems by Graphing *pp. 153–158*

EXAMPLE

Graph the system and estimate the solution. Check the solution algebraically.

$3x + y = 3$ **Equation 1**
$4x + 3y = -1$ **Equation 2**

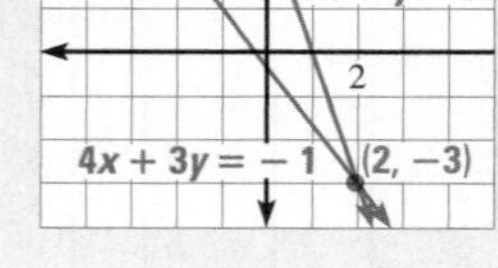

Graph both equations. From the graph, the lines appear to intersect at $(2, -3)$. You can check this algebraically.

$3(2) + (-3) = 3$ ✓ **Equation 1 checks.**

$4(2) + 3(-3) = -1$ ✓ **Equation 2 checks.**

EXERCISES

EXAMPLE 1 on p. 153 for Exs. 4–6

Graph the system and estimate the solution. Check the solution algebraically.
4–6. See margin for art.

4. $2x - y = 9$
$x + 3y = 8$ $(5, 1)$

5. $2x - 3y = -2$
$x + y = -6$ $(-4, -2)$

6. $3x + y = 6$
$-x + 2y = 12$ $(0, 6)$

@HomeTutor
classzone.com
Chapter Review Practice

3.2 Solve Linear Systems Algebraically

pp. 160–167

EXAMPLE

Solve the system using the elimination method.

$2x + 5y = 8$ **Equation 1**
$4x + 3y = -12$ **Equation 2**

Multiply Equation 1 by -2 so that the coefficients of x differ only in sign.

$2x + 5y = 8$ → $\times -2$ → $-4x - 10y = -16$

$4x + 3y = -12$ → $4x + 3y = -12$

Add the revised equations and solve for y. $-7y = -28$

$y = 4$

Substitute the value of y into one of the original equations and solve for x.

$2x + 5(4) = 8$ **Substitute 4 for y in Equation 1.**

$2x = -12$ **Subtract 5(4) = 20 from each side.**

$x = -6$ **Divide each side by 2.**

▶ The solution is $(-6, 4)$.

EXERCISES

EXAMPLES 2 and 3 on pp. 161–162 for Exs. 7–10

Solve the system using the elimination method.

7. $3x + 2y = 5$
$-2x + 3y = 27$ **(−3, 7)**

8. $3x + 5y = 5$
$2x - 3y = 16$ **(5, −2)**

9. $2x + 3y = 9$
$-3x + y = 25$ **(−6, 7)**

10. FUEL COSTS The cost of 14 gallons of regular gasoline and 10 gallons of premium gasoline is \$46.68. Premium costs \$.30 more per gallon than regular. What is the cost per gallon of each type of gasoline? **regular \$1.82, premium \$2.12**

3.3 Graph Systems of Linear Inequalities

pp. 168–173

EXAMPLE

Graph the system of linear inequalities.

$3x - y \le 4$ **Inequality 1**
$x + y > 1$ **Inequality 2**

Graph each inequality in the system. Use a different color for each half-plane. Then identify the region that is common to both graphs. It is the region that is shaded purple.

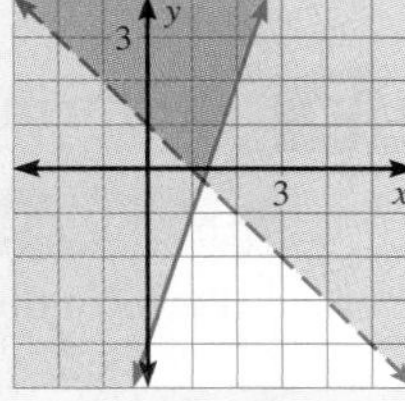

EXERCISES

EXAMPLE 1 on p. 168 for Exs. 11–13

Graph the system of linear inequalities. **11–13. See margin.**

11. $4x + y < 1$
$-x + 2y \le 5$

12. $2x + 3y > 6$
$2x - y \le 8$

13. $x + 3y \ge 5$
$-x + 2y < 4$

Extra Example 3.2

Solve the system using the substitution method.
$-3x - 4y = 1$
$x + 3y = -7$ **(5, −4)**

Extra Example 3.3

Graph the system of linear inequalities.
$3x + y > -1$
$2x - 4y \ge -8$

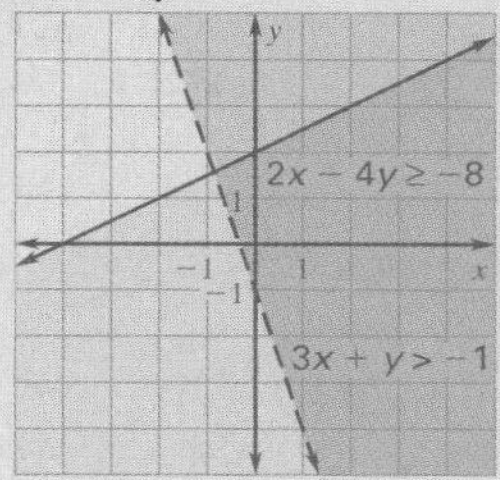

11.

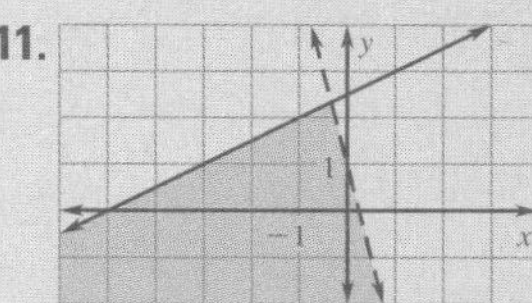

12.

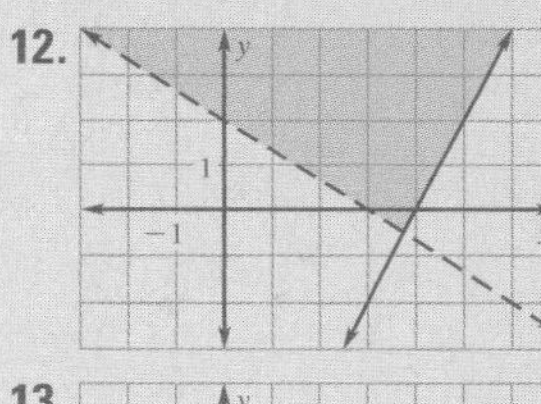

13.

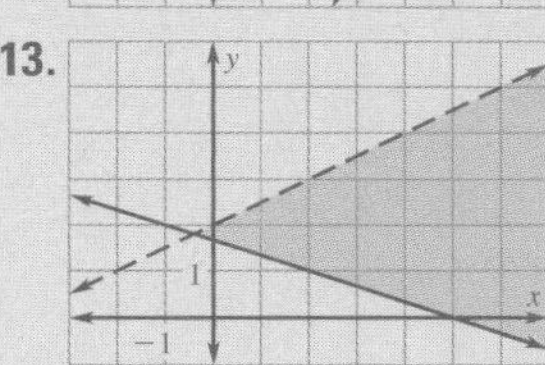

Extra Example 3.4

Solve the system.

$x + 3y + 2z = 10$

$-2x - 5y - 3z = -17$

$4x + 7y - z = 5$ (6, −2, 5)

Extra Example 3.5

Perform the indicated operation.

a. $\begin{bmatrix} 4 & -5 \\ -3 & 7 \end{bmatrix} - \begin{bmatrix} -2 & -6 \\ 5 & 1 \end{bmatrix}$

$\begin{bmatrix} 6 & 1 \\ -8 & 6 \end{bmatrix}$

b. $-3\begin{bmatrix} 2 & -8 \\ -1 & 5 \end{bmatrix}$ $\begin{bmatrix} -6 & 24 \\ 3 & -15 \end{bmatrix}$

3 CHAPTER REVIEW

3.4 Solve Systems of Linear Equations in Three Variables *pp. 178–185*

EXAMPLE

Solve the system.

$$\begin{aligned} 2x + y + 3z &= 5 && \textbf{Equation 1} \\ -x + 3y + z &= -14 && \textbf{Equation 2} \\ 3x - y - 2z &= 11 && \textbf{Equation 3} \end{aligned}$$

Rewrite the system as a linear system in two variables. Add −3 times Equation 1 to Equation 2. Then add Equation 1 and Equation 3.

$$\begin{array}{rl} -6x - 3y - 9z = -15 & \quad 2x + y + 3z = 5 \\ -x + 3y + z = -14 & \quad 3x - y - 2z = 11 \\ \hline -7x \qquad - 8z = -29 & \quad 5x \qquad + z = 16 \end{array}$$

Solve the new linear system for both of its variables.

$$\begin{array}{rl} -7x - 8z = -29 & \textbf{Add new Equation 1 to} \\ 40x + 8z = 128 & \textbf{8 times new Equation 2.} \\ \hline 33x \qquad = 99 & \\ x = 3 & \textbf{Solve for } \boldsymbol{x}\textbf{.} \\ z = 1 & \textbf{Substitute into new Equation 1 or 2 to find } \boldsymbol{z}\textbf{.} \end{array}$$

Substituting $x = 3$ and $z = 1$ into one of the original equations and solving for y gives $y = -4$. The solution is (3, −4, 1).

EXERCISES

EXAMPLES 1 and 4 on pp. 179–181 for Exs. 14–17

Solve the system.

14. $x - y + z = 10$
$4x + y - 2z = 15$
$-3x + 5y - z = -18$
(6, 1, 5)

15. $6x - y + 4z = 6$
$-x - 3y + z = 31$
$2x + 2y - 5z = -42$
(−3, −8, 4)

16. $5x + y - z = 40$
$x + 7y + 4z = 44$
$-x + 3y + z = 16$
(5, 9, −6)

17. MUSIC Fifteen band members from a school were selected to play in the state orchestra. Twice as many students who play a wind instrument were selected as students who play a string or percussion instrument combined. Of the students selected, one fifth play a string instrument. How many of the students selected play each type of instrument?
10 wind instruments, 3 string instruments, 2 percussion instruments

3.5 Perform Basic Matrix Operations *pp. 187–193*

EXAMPLE

Perform the indicated operation.

a. $\begin{bmatrix} 4 & -1 \\ 2 & 5 \end{bmatrix} + \begin{bmatrix} -5 & 2 \\ -3 & 1 \end{bmatrix} = \begin{bmatrix} 4 + (-5) & -1 + 2 \\ 2 + (-3) & 5 + 1 \end{bmatrix} = \begin{bmatrix} -1 & 1 \\ -1 & 6 \end{bmatrix}$

b. $4\begin{bmatrix} -2 & 0 \\ 3 & 5 \end{bmatrix} = \begin{bmatrix} 4(-2) & 4(0) \\ 4(3) & 4(5) \end{bmatrix} = \begin{bmatrix} -8 & 0 \\ 12 & 20 \end{bmatrix}$

@HomeTutor
classzone.com
Chapter Review Practice

EXAMPLES 2 and 3 on pp. 188–189 for Exs. 18–23

EXERCISES

Perform the indicated operation.

18. $\begin{bmatrix} 4 & -5 \\ 2 & 3 \end{bmatrix} + \begin{bmatrix} -1 & 3 \\ -7 & 4 \end{bmatrix}$ $\begin{bmatrix} 3 & -2 \\ -5 & 7 \end{bmatrix}$

19. $\begin{bmatrix} -1 & 8 \\ 2 & -3 \end{bmatrix} + \begin{bmatrix} 7 & -4 \\ 6 & -1 \end{bmatrix}$ $\begin{bmatrix} 6 & 4 \\ 8 & -4 \end{bmatrix}$

20. $\begin{bmatrix} 10 & -4 \\ 5 & 1 \end{bmatrix} - \begin{bmatrix} 0 & 9 \\ 2 & 7 \end{bmatrix}$ $\begin{bmatrix} 10 & -13 \\ 3 & -6 \end{bmatrix}$

21. $\begin{bmatrix} -2 & 3 & 5 \\ -1 & 6 & -2 \end{bmatrix} - \begin{bmatrix} -4 & 7 & 5 \\ -8 & 0 & -9 \end{bmatrix}$ $\begin{bmatrix} 2 & -4 & 0 \\ 7 & 6 & 7 \end{bmatrix}$

22. $-3\begin{bmatrix} 5 & -2 \\ 3 & 6 \end{bmatrix}$ $\begin{bmatrix} -15 & 6 \\ -9 & -18 \end{bmatrix}$

23. $8\begin{bmatrix} 8 & 4 & 5 \\ -1 & 6 & -2 \end{bmatrix}$ $\begin{bmatrix} 64 & 32 & 40 \\ -8 & 48 & -16 \end{bmatrix}$

3.6 Multiply Matrices

pp. 195–202

EXAMPLE

Find AB if $A = \begin{bmatrix} 2 & -3 \\ -1 & 0 \\ 4 & 5 \end{bmatrix}$ and $B = \begin{bmatrix} -2 & 3 \\ 3 & 1 \end{bmatrix}$.

$$AB = \begin{bmatrix} 2 & -3 \\ -1 & 0 \\ 4 & 5 \end{bmatrix}\begin{bmatrix} -2 & 3 \\ 3 & 1 \end{bmatrix} = \begin{bmatrix} 2(-2) + (-3)(3) & 2(3) + (-3)(1) \\ -1(-2) + 0(3) & -1(3) + 0(1) \\ 4(-2) + 5(3) & 4(3) + 5(1) \end{bmatrix}$$

$$= \begin{bmatrix} -13 & 3 \\ 2 & -3 \\ 7 & 17 \end{bmatrix}$$

EXAMPLES 2 and 4 on pp. 196–198 for Exs. 24–28

EXERCISES

Find the product.

24. $\begin{bmatrix} -1 & -1 \end{bmatrix}\begin{bmatrix} 8 & 2 \\ -6 & -9 \end{bmatrix}$ $\begin{bmatrix} -2 & 7 \end{bmatrix}$

25. $\begin{bmatrix} 11 & 7 \\ 1 & -5 \end{bmatrix}\begin{bmatrix} 0 & -5 \\ 4 & -3 \end{bmatrix}$ $\begin{bmatrix} 28 & -76 \\ -20 & 10 \end{bmatrix}$

26. $\begin{bmatrix} 4 & -1 \\ 1 & 7 \end{bmatrix}\begin{bmatrix} 5 & -2 & 4 \\ 3 & 12 & 6 \end{bmatrix}$ $\begin{bmatrix} 17 & -20 & 10 \\ 26 & 82 & 46 \end{bmatrix}$

27. $\begin{bmatrix} -2 & 5 \\ 0 & 3 \end{bmatrix}\begin{bmatrix} 6 & -3 & 5 \\ 2 & 0 & -1 \end{bmatrix}$ $\begin{bmatrix} -2 & 6 & -15 \\ 6 & 0 & -3 \end{bmatrix}$

28. MANUFACTURING A company manufactures three models of flat-screen color TVs: a 19 inch model, a 27 inch model, and a 32 inch model. The TVs are shipped to two warehouses. The numbers of units shipped to each warehouse are given in matrix A, and the prices of the models are given in matrix B. Write a matrix that gives the total value of the TVs in each warehouse. See margin.

Matrix *A*

	19 in.	27 in.	32 in.
Warehouse 1	5,000	6,000	8,000
Warehouse 2	4,000	10,000	5,000

Matrix *B*

	Price
19 inch	$109.99
27 inch	$319.99
32 inch	$549.99

Extra Example 3.6

Find AB if $A = \begin{bmatrix} 3 & -2 \\ 4 & -1 \\ 0 & 5 \end{bmatrix}$ and $B = \begin{bmatrix} 1 & -6 \\ -4 & 5 \end{bmatrix}$. $\begin{bmatrix} 11 & -28 \\ 8 & -29 \\ -20 & 25 \end{bmatrix}$

28.

	Total Value
Warehouse 1	$6,869,810
Warehouse 2	$6,389,810

Extra Example 3.7

Evaluate the determinant of $\begin{bmatrix} 5 & 2 & 8 \\ 3 & 4 & 1 \\ 7 & -1 & 6 \end{bmatrix}$. −145

Extra Example 3.8

Use an inverse matrix to solve the linear system.

$-5x - 4y = 5$
$4x + 3y = -3$ (3, −5)

3 CHAPTER REVIEW

3.7 Evaluate Determinants and Apply Cramer's Rule

pp. 203–209

EXAMPLE

Evaluate the determinant of $\begin{bmatrix} 2 & 1 \\ 5 & 7 \end{bmatrix}$.

$$\begin{vmatrix} 2 & 1 \\ 5 & 7 \end{vmatrix} = 2(7) - 5(1) = 14 - 5 = 9$$

EXERCISES

EXAMPLES 1 and 2 on pp. 203–204 for Exs. 29–32

Evaluate the determinant of the matrix.

29. $\begin{bmatrix} -4 & 2 \\ 5 & 8 \end{bmatrix}$ −42

30. $\begin{bmatrix} 3 & -5 \\ 2 & 6 \end{bmatrix}$ 28

31. $\begin{bmatrix} 3 & 0 \\ 1 & 6 \end{bmatrix}$ 18

32. SCHOOL SPIRIT You are making a large triangular pennant for your school football team. The vertices of the triangle are (0, 0), (0, 50), and (70, 20) where the coordinates are measured in inches. How many square *feet* of material will you need to make the pennant? about 12.2 ft^2

3.8 Use Inverse Matrices to Solve Linear Systems

pp. 210–217

EXAMPLE

Use an inverse matrix to solve the linear system at the right.

$x - 2y = 14$
$2x + y = 8$

Write the linear system as a matrix equation $AX = B$.

$$\begin{bmatrix} 1 & -2 \\ 2 & 1 \end{bmatrix}\begin{bmatrix} x \\ y \end{bmatrix} = \begin{bmatrix} 14 \\ 8 \end{bmatrix}$$

Find the inverse of the coefficient matrix A.

$$A^{-1} = \frac{1}{1 - (-4)}\begin{bmatrix} 1 & 2 \\ -2 & 1 \end{bmatrix} = \begin{bmatrix} 0.2 & 0.4 \\ -0.4 & 0.2 \end{bmatrix}$$

Then multiply the matrix of constants by A^{-1} on the left.

$$X = A^{-1}B = \begin{bmatrix} 0.2 & 0.4 \\ -0.4 & 0.2 \end{bmatrix}\begin{bmatrix} 14 \\ 8 \end{bmatrix} = \begin{bmatrix} 6 \\ -4 \end{bmatrix} = \begin{bmatrix} x \\ y \end{bmatrix}$$

▶ The solution of the system is (6, −4).

EXERCISES

EXAMPLE 4 on p. 212 for Exs. 33–35

Use an inverse matrix to solve the linear system.

33. $x + 4y = 11$
$2x - 5y = 9$ (7, 1)

34. $3x + y = -1$
$-x + 2y = 12$ (−2, 5)

35. $3x + 2y = -11$
$4x - 3y = 8$ (−1, −4)

3 CHAPTER TEST

Graph the linear system and estimate the solution. Then check the solution algebraically. 1–4. See margin for art.

1. $4x + y = 5$
$3x - y = 2$ (1, 1)

2. $x + 2y = -6$
$-6x - 2y = -14$ (4, −5)

3. $2x - 3y = 15$
$x - \frac{3}{2}y = -3$ no solution

4. $3x - y = 12$
$-x + 8y = -4$ (4, 0)

Graph the system of linear inequalities. 5–8. See margin.

5. $2x + y < 6$
$y > -2$

6. $x - 3y \geq 9$
$\frac{1}{3}x - y \leq 3$

7. $x - 2y \leq -14$
$y \geq |x|$

8. $-3x + 4y > -12$
$y < -2|x| + 5$

Solve the system using any algebraic method.

9. $3x + y = -9$
$x - 2y = -10$ (−4, 3)

10. $2x + 3y = -2$
$4x + 7y = -6$ (2, −2)

11. $x + 4y = -26$
$-5x - 2y = -14$ (6, −8)

12. $x - y + z = -3$
$2x - y + 5z = 4$
$4x + 2y - z = 2$ (−1, 4, 2)

13. $x + y + z = 3$
$-x + 3y + 2z = -8$
$5y + z = 2$ (5, 1, −3)

14. $2x - 5y - z = 17$
$x + y + 3z = 19$
$-4x + 6y + z = -20$
$\left(-\frac{4}{3}, -\frac{17}{3}, \frac{26}{3}\right)$

Use the given matrices to evaluate the expression, if possible. If not possible, state the reason.

$$A = \begin{bmatrix} 1 & -2 \\ 4 & -3 \end{bmatrix}, B = \begin{bmatrix} 3 & 5 \\ -1 & 0 \end{bmatrix}, C = \begin{bmatrix} -6 & 8 \\ 10 & 15 \end{bmatrix}, D = \begin{bmatrix} -1 & 3 & -2 \\ 2 & 0 & -1 \end{bmatrix}, E = \begin{bmatrix} 4 & -1 & 3 \\ 6 & -2 & 1 \end{bmatrix}$$

15. $2A + B$ **16.** $C - 3B$ **17.** $A - 2D$ **18.** $4D + E$

19. AC **20.** DE **21.** $(A + B)D$ **22.** $A(C - B)$

15. $\begin{bmatrix} 5 & 1 \\ 7 & -6 \end{bmatrix}$

16. $\begin{bmatrix} -15 & -7 \\ 13 & 15 \end{bmatrix}$

17. Not possible; and D do not ave the same imensions.

18. $\begin{bmatrix} 0 & 11 & -5 \\ 14 & -2 & -3 \end{bmatrix}$

19. $\begin{bmatrix} -26 & -22 \\ -54 & -13 \end{bmatrix}$

20. Not possible; the number of olumns in D oes not equal the number of ows in E.

21. $\begin{bmatrix} 2 & 12 & -11 \\ -9 & 9 & -3 \end{bmatrix}$

22. $\begin{bmatrix} -31 & -27 \\ -69 & -33 \end{bmatrix}$

Evaluate the determinant of the matrix.

23. $\begin{bmatrix} 3 & -2 \\ 4 & 1 \end{bmatrix}$ 11

24. $\begin{bmatrix} -4 & 5 \\ 2 & -1 \end{bmatrix}$ −6

25. $\begin{bmatrix} -1 & 3 & 1 \\ 0 & 2 & -3 \\ 5 & 1 & -2 \end{bmatrix}$ −54

26. $\begin{bmatrix} 2 & 0 & -1 \\ 5 & -3 & 2 \\ 1 & 4 & 6 \end{bmatrix}$ −75

Use an inverse matrix to solve the linear system.

27. $3x + 4y = 6$
$4x + 5y = 7$ (−2, 3)

28. $2x - 7y = -36$
$x - 3y = -16$ (−4, 4)

29. $5x + 3y = -5$
$-9x - 6y = 12$ (2, −5)

30. $3x + 2y = 15$
$-x + 4y = -33$ (9, −6)

31. FINANCE A total of \$15,000 is invested in two corporate bonds that pay 5% and 7% simple annual interest. The investor wants to earn \$880 in interest per year from the bonds. How much should be invested in each bond? \$8500 at 5%, \$6500 at 7%

32. TICKET SALES For the opening day of a carnival, 800 admission tickets were sold. The receipts totaled \$3775. Tickets for children cost \$3 each, tickets for adults cost \$8 each, and tickets for senior citizens cost \$5 each. There were twice as many children's tickets sold as adult tickets. How many of each type of ticket were sold? 450 children tickets, 225 adult tickets, 125 senior citizen tickets

33. BOATING On a certain river, a motorboat can travel 34 miles per hour with the current and 28 miles per hour against the current. Find the speed of the motorboat in still water and the speed of the current.
speed in still water: 31 mi/h, speed of current: 3 mi/h

Additional Resources

Assessment Book

- Chapter Test, Levels A, B, C, pp. 34–39
- Standardized Chapter Test, pp. 40–41
- SAT/ACT Chapter Test, pp. 42–43
- Alternative Assessment, pp. 44–45

Test Generator CD-ROM

Chapter Test

Easily-readable reduced copies (with answers) of Chapter Test B, the Standardized Chapter Test, and the Alternative Assessment from the Assessment Book can be found on pp. 150G–150H.

4.
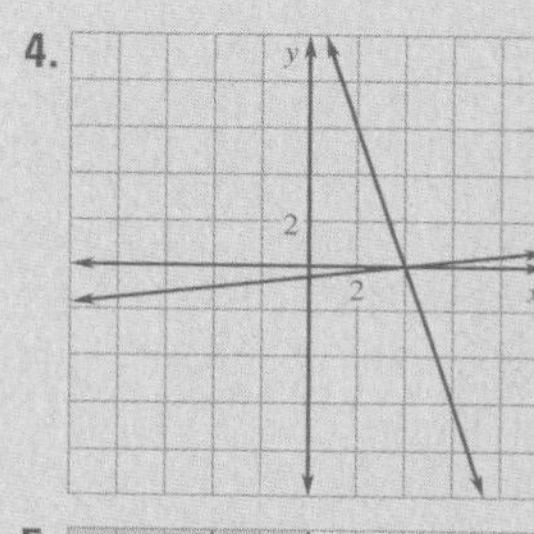

5.
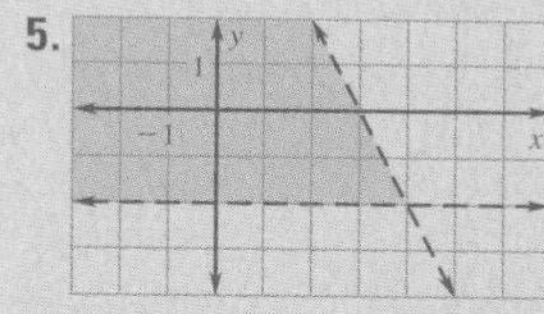

6.
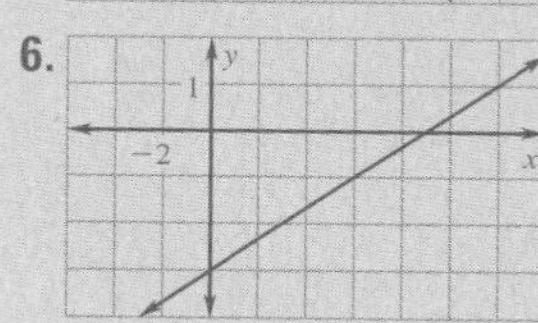

7.
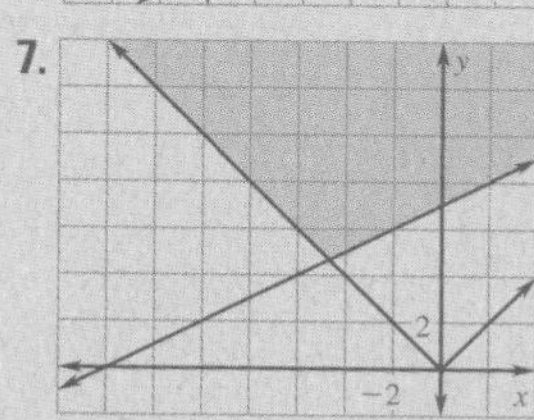

8.
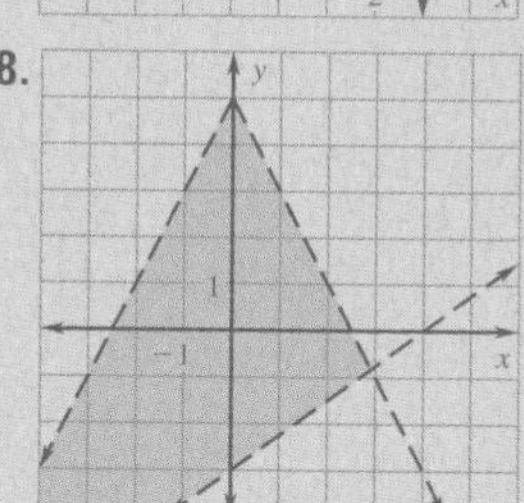

1.
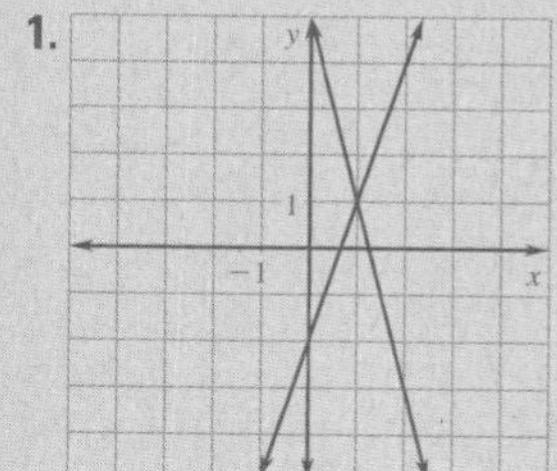

2.
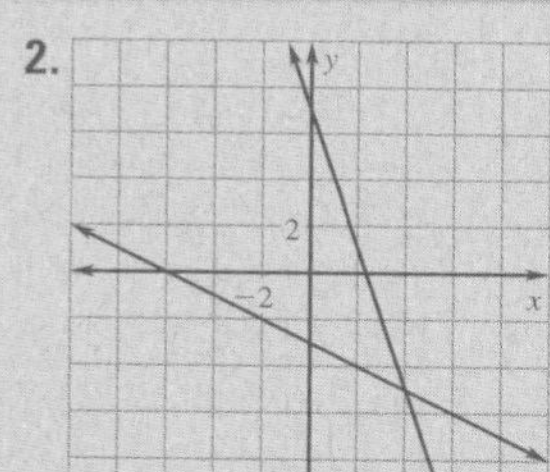

3.
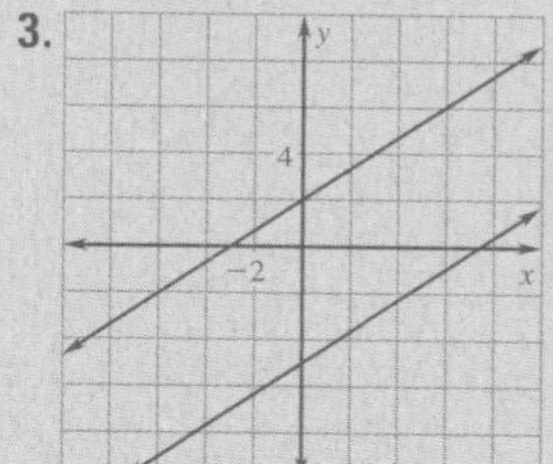

MULTIPLE-CHOICE QUESTIONS

If you have difficulty solving a multiple-choice problem directly, you may be able to use another approach. First, eliminate as many wrong answers as you can. Then, make an educated guess from among the remaining choices.

PROBLEM 1

On a treadmill, Lee jogs at 6 miles per hour and sprints at 8 miles per hour. Lee covers $3\frac{1}{3}$ miles in $\frac{1}{2}$ hour. How long did he spend at each activity?

A. 25 minutes jogging, 5 minutes sprinting

B. 20 minutes jogging, 10 minutes sprinting

C. 10 minutes jogging, 20 minutes sprinting

D. 5 minutes jogging, 25 minutes sprinting

METHOD 1

SOLVE DIRECTLY Write and solve a linear system.

STEP 1 **Write** a system of equations. Let x be the jogging time and y be the sprinting time.

$6x + 8y = 3\frac{1}{3}$ Equation 1 (miles)

$x + y = \frac{1}{2}$ Equation 2 (hours)

STEP 2 **Solve** Equation 2 for y to get $y = \frac{1}{2} - x$.

STEP 3 **Substitute** $\frac{1}{2} - x$ for y in Equation 1 and solve for x.

$$6x + 8\left(\frac{1}{2} - x\right) = 3\frac{1}{3}$$

$$-2x + 4 = 3\frac{1}{3}$$

$$x = \frac{1}{3}$$

STEP 4 **Substitute** the value of x into revised Equation 2 and solve for y.

$$y = \frac{1}{2} - x = \frac{1}{2} - \frac{1}{3} = \frac{1}{6}$$

He jogs for $\frac{1}{3}$ hour, or 20 minutes.

He sprints for $\frac{1}{6}$ hour, or 10 minutes.

▸ The correct answer is B.

METHOD 2

ELIMINATE CHOICES Another method is to eliminate incorrect answer choices by consider what happens if he jogs the entire time or sprin the entire time.

STEP 1 **Find** the distance he covers if he spends the entire time jogging or the entire tim sprinting.

If he jogs the entire time, then he covers $6 \cdot \frac{1}{2} = 3$ miles.

If he sprints the entire time, then he co $8 \cdot \frac{1}{2} = 4$ miles.

Because $3\frac{1}{3}$ is closer to 3 than to 4, he must spend more time jogging than sprinting. So, you can eliminate choice C and D.

STEP 2 **Calculate** the distances for the remainin choices. Use the fact that 5 min $= \frac{1}{12}$ h.

Choice A: $6 \cdot \frac{5}{12} + 8 \cdot \frac{1}{12} = \frac{38}{12} = 3\frac{1}{6}$ mi

Choice B: $6 \cdot \frac{4}{12} + 8 \cdot \frac{2}{12} = \frac{40}{12} = 3\frac{1}{3}$ mil

▸ The correct answer is B.

TEST PRACTICE
classzone.com

Kentucky Test Preparation

1. $-1 + 2 + (-3) \neq 2$, so the coordinates are not a solution of the first equation, and therefore not a solution of the system.
2. The answer cannot be the identity matrix since the two given matrices are not the same.

ROBLEM 2

What is the inverse of $A = \begin{bmatrix} 3 & -3 \\ -7 & 6 \end{bmatrix}$?

A. $\begin{bmatrix} 1 & 0 \\ 0 & 1 \end{bmatrix}$ B. $\begin{bmatrix} 2 & 1 \\ \frac{7}{3} & 1 \end{bmatrix}$ C. $\begin{bmatrix} 1 & -1 \\ -\frac{7}{3} & 2 \end{bmatrix}$ D. $\begin{bmatrix} -2 & -1 \\ -\frac{7}{3} & -1 \end{bmatrix}$

ETHOD 1

VE DIRECTLY Find the inverse of matrix A by ng the formula below.

$$A^{-1} = \frac{1}{|A|}\begin{bmatrix} d & -b \\ -c & a \end{bmatrix}$$

inverse of $A = \begin{bmatrix} 3 & -3 \\ -7 & 6 \end{bmatrix}$ is:

$$A^{-1} = \frac{1}{3(6) - (-7)(-3)}\begin{bmatrix} 6 & 3 \\ 7 & 3 \end{bmatrix}$$

$$= \frac{1}{18 - 21}\begin{bmatrix} 6 & 3 \\ 7 & 3 \end{bmatrix}$$

$$= -\frac{1}{3}\begin{bmatrix} 6 & 3 \\ 7 & 3 \end{bmatrix}$$

$$= \begin{bmatrix} -2 & -1 \\ -\frac{7}{3} & -1 \end{bmatrix}$$

ne correct answer is D.

METHOD 2

ELIMINATE CHOICES Use the fact that $A^{-1}A = I$ to eliminate incorrect answer choices.

Multiply the matrix in each answer choice by matrix A. Eliminate as soon as you realize that the product $A^{-1}A$ is not the identity matrix.

Choice A: $\begin{bmatrix} 1 & 0 \\ 0 & 1 \end{bmatrix}\begin{bmatrix} 3 & -3 \\ -7 & 6 \end{bmatrix} = \begin{bmatrix} 3 & \\ & \end{bmatrix}$ ✗

Choice B: $\begin{bmatrix} 2 & 1 \\ \frac{7}{3} & 1 \end{bmatrix}\begin{bmatrix} 3 & -3 \\ -7 & 6 \end{bmatrix} = \begin{bmatrix} -1 & \\ & \end{bmatrix}$ ✗

Choice C: $\begin{bmatrix} 1 & -1 \\ -\frac{7}{3} & 2 \end{bmatrix}\begin{bmatrix} 3 & -3 \\ -7 & 6 \end{bmatrix} = \begin{bmatrix} 10 & \\ & \end{bmatrix}$ ✗

Choice D: $\begin{bmatrix} -2 & -1 \\ -\frac{7}{3} & -1 \end{bmatrix}\begin{bmatrix} 3 & -3 \\ -7 & 6 \end{bmatrix} = \begin{bmatrix} 1 & 0 \\ 0 & 1 \end{bmatrix}$ ✓

▶ The correct answer is D.

RACTICE

lain why you can eliminate the highlighted answer choice.

What is the solution of the system?

A. (1, −2, 3) B. ✗ (−1, 2, −3) C. (3, −2, 1) D. (1, 3, −2)

What is the solution of the matrix equation? $\begin{bmatrix} 3 & 4 \\ 2 & 3 \end{bmatrix}X = \begin{bmatrix} 4 & -10 \\ 1 & -6 \end{bmatrix}$

A. $\begin{bmatrix} 8 & -6 \\ -5 & 2 \end{bmatrix}$ B. $\begin{bmatrix} 4 & 6 \\ 0 & -1 \end{bmatrix}$ C. $\begin{bmatrix} 3 & -4 \\ -2 & 3 \end{bmatrix}$ D. ✗ $\begin{bmatrix} 1 & 0 \\ 0 & 1 \end{bmatrix}$

TEST PREPARATION

Kentucky Test Practice

1. C
2. C
3. B
4. A
5. D
6. B
7. C
8. D
9. B
10. B

Kentucky Test Practice

MULTIPLE-CHOICE

1. The two top-selling DVDs of 2003 grossed a combined total of \$600.9 million. The top-selling DVD grossed \$39.9 million more than the DVD ranked second. How much did the top-selling DVD gross?

   A. \$240.6 million
   B. \$280.5 million
   C. \$320.4 million
   D. \$561 million

2. Which system has (0, 4) as a solution?

   A. $x + y = 4$, $x - y = 4$
   B. $2x + y = -4$, $x - 2y = 8$
   C. $3x + 2y = 8$, $x - 4y = -16$
   D. $-x + y = 4$, $3x - 2y = 12$

3. Which system of inequalities is graphed below?

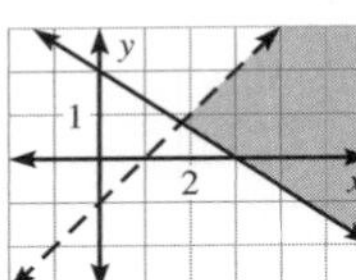

   A. $y > x - 1$, $2x + 3y \leq 6$
   B. $y < x - 1$, $2x + 3y \geq 6$
   C. $y < x - 1$, $3x + 2y \geq 6$
   D. $y \geq x - 1$, $3x + 2y < 6$

4. Julia bought scarves and gloves as gifts for family members. Each scarf costs \$3 less than each pair of gloves. A pair of gloves costs \$9. Julia bought 8 items for \$66. How many scarves did she buy?

   A. 2
   B. 4
   C. 5
   D. 6

5. What is the solution of the matrix equation?

$$\begin{bmatrix} 2 & -3 \\ -5 & 7 \end{bmatrix} X = \begin{bmatrix} 4 & 6 \\ 0 & -1 \end{bmatrix}$$

   A. $\begin{bmatrix} 2 & -2 \\ 0 & -\frac{7}{2} \end{bmatrix}$
   B $\begin{bmatrix} -7 & -3 \\ -5 & -2 \end{bmatrix}$
   C. $\begin{bmatrix} 8 & 15 \\ 20 & 37 \end{bmatrix}$
   D $\begin{bmatrix} -28 & -39 \\ -20 & -28 \end{bmatrix}$

6. A driver's education program consists of a total of 46 hours of classroom instruction, driving, and observation. You must spend 3 times as much time in the classroom as driving, and 4 hours longer driving than observing. How much time do you spend driving?

   A. 6 hours
   B. 10 hours
   C. 14 hours
   D. 30 hours

7. What is the solution of the linear system?

$$2x - 3y = 9$$
$$y = \frac{2}{3}x + 2$$

   A. (6, 6)
   B. (9, 3)
   C. No solution
   D. Infinitely many solutions

8. Which set of vertices forms a triangle having the same area as the triangle with vertices (1, −5), (2, 3), and (12, 2)?

   A. (−1, 5), (2, 3), (−12, 2)
   B. (0, 0), (6, 6), (8, 6)
   C. (1, 1), (8, 1), (−2, −8)
   D. (−1, 0), (5, 9), (8, 0)

9. Madeline paid \$19.43 for 6 packages of bulbs for her flower garden. The cost of 1 package of each type of bulb is shown. She bought twice as many packages of phlox bulbs as lily bulbs. How many packages of lily bulbs did she buy?

Peony bulbs	Phlox bulbs	Lily bulbs
\$3.99	\$2.61	\$2.24

   A. None
   B. 1 package
   C. 2 packages
   D. 3 packages

10. Which matrix has *no* inverse?

   A. $\begin{bmatrix} 6 & 0 \\ 0 & 5 \end{bmatrix}$
   B. $\begin{bmatrix} 4 & 6 \\ -6 & -9 \end{bmatrix}$
   C. $\begin{bmatrix} -2 & 4 \\ 3 & 6 \end{bmatrix}$
   D. $\begin{bmatrix} 1 & 1 \\ 0 & 1 \end{bmatrix}$

TEST PREPARATION

MULTIPLE-CHOICE

11. What is the y-coordinate of the solution of the linear system below?

$$2x - 5y = -10$$
$$x + 4y = 21$$

A. -5 B. -4
C. 4 D. 5

12. For the matrix equation below, what is the value of $x + 4y$?

$$2\begin{bmatrix} 5x & 0 \\ -2 & 3 \end{bmatrix} - \begin{bmatrix} 3 & -1 \\ 4y & -2 \end{bmatrix} = \begin{bmatrix} 17 & 1 \\ -10 & 8 \end{bmatrix}$$

A. $1\frac{1}{2}$ B. 2
C. 8 D. $9\frac{1}{2}$

13. The solution of the linear system below is $(-1, -2, z)$. What is the value of z?

$$x + 2y + 2z = 7$$
$$2x - 3y - z = -2$$
$$-4x + y - 3z = -16$$

A. -6 B. -2
C. -1 D. 6

14. A second-run movie theater sells matinee tickets for \$4 and regular tickets for \$6. During one week, the theater earned \$6000. The theater sold 890 more regular tickets than matinee tickets. How many matinee tickets were sold?

A. 66 B. 84
C. 824 D. 956

OPEN-RESPONSE

15. The table shows U.S. consumer spending on video games and at the box office (in dollars per person per year) for the years 1996 to 2002. Let 1996 = year 0.

Year	0	1	2	3	4	5	6
Video games	11.5	16.5	18.5	24.5	24.7	26.9	30.5
Box office	27.1	28.9	31.2	33.1	32.5	35.5	39.7

a. Approximate the best-fitting line for the video game data.

b. Approximate the best-fitting line for the box office data.

c. Use the best-fitting lines to estimate the year when consumer spending on video games will catch up to consumer spending at the box office. Justify your answer.

16. A triangle has an area of 100 square units. Its vertices are (0, 0), (20, 0), and (x, y).

a. Write an equation involving a determinant that you can use to find the coordinates of the unknown vertex.

b. Solve the equation. Show all of your steps.

c. What does your answer tell you about the coordinates of the unknown vertex?

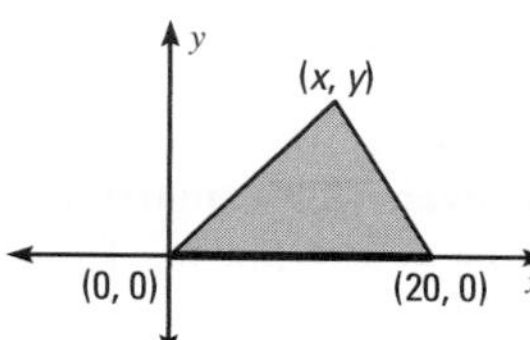

TEST PREPARATION

11. C
12. C
13. D
14. A
15. a. $y = 3x + 12.87$
b. $y = 1.87x + 26.97$
c. During the twelfth year. ***Sample answer:*** By solving the system of equations, the point of intersection is approximately (12.5, 50.4). This means that about one-half of the way into the twelfth year, the video game spending will equal that of the box office spending.

16. a. $\pm\frac{1}{2}\begin{vmatrix} 0 & 0 & 1 \\ 20 & 0 & 1 \\ x & y & 1 \end{vmatrix} = 100$
b. $y = \pm 10$. Eliminate $y = -10$ because the point (x, y) is in the first quadrant.
c. The x-value does not matter as long as the point is on the line $y = 10$.

Additional Resources

The following resources are available to help review the materials in Chapters 1–3.

Chapter Resource Books

- Chapter 1 CRB, Cumulative Review, pp. 85–86
- Chapter 2 CRB, Cumulative Review, pp. 109–110
- Chapter 3 CRB, Cumulative Review, pp. 105–106

10.

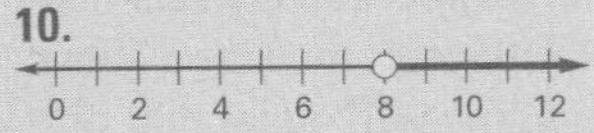

11.

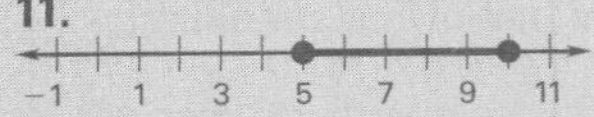

12.

13.

14.

15.

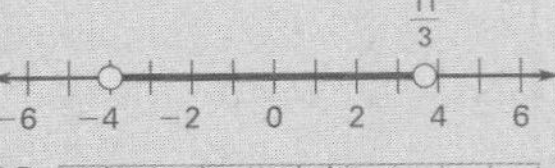

20.

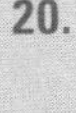

21.

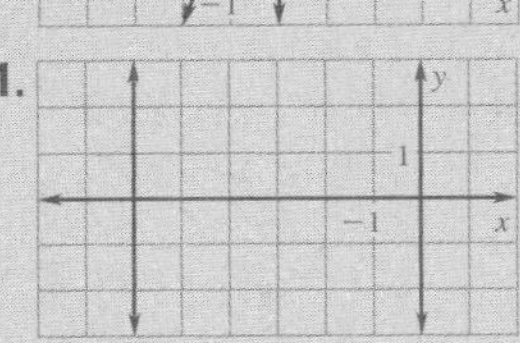

22.

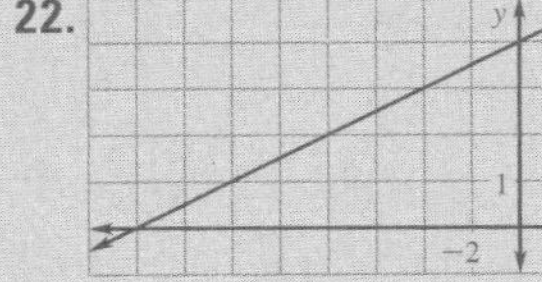

23.

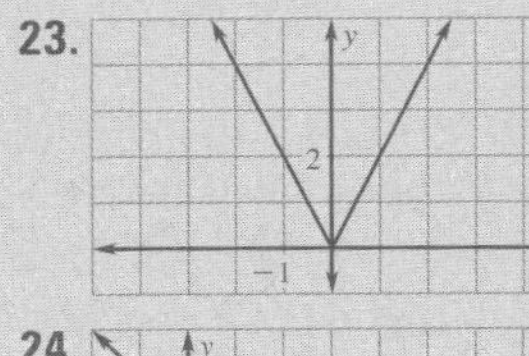

24.

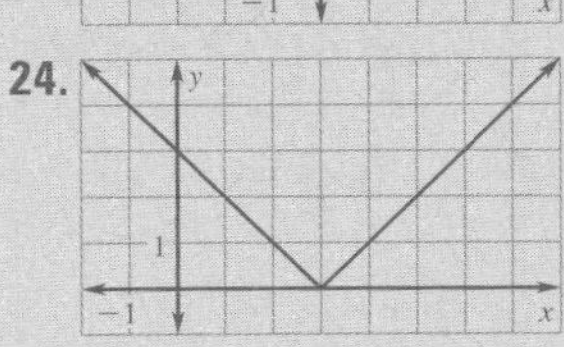

3 CUMULATIVE REVIEW Chapters 1–3

Simplify the expression. *(p. 10)*

1. $3x^2 - 8x + 12x - 5x^2 + 3x$ $\quad -2x^2 + 7x$
2. $15x - 6x + 10y - 3y + 4x$ $\quad 13x + 7y$
3. $3(x + 2) - 4x^2 + 3x + 9$ $\quad -4x^2 + 6x + 15$

Solve the equation. Check your solution.

4. $6x - 7 = -2x + 9$ *(p. 18)* $\quad 2$
5. $4(x - 3) = 16x + 18$ *(p. 18)* $\quad -\frac{5}{2}$
6. $\frac{1}{3}x + 3 = -\frac{7}{2}x - \frac{3}{2}$ *(p. 18)* $\quad -\frac{27}{23}$
7. $|x + 3| = 5$ *(p. 51)* $\quad -8, 2$
8. $|4x - 1| = 27$ *(p. 51)* $\quad -\frac{13}{2}, 7$
9. $|9 - 2x| = 41$ *(p. 51)* $\quad -16, 25$

Solve the inequality. Then graph the solution. 10–15. See margin for art.

10. $6(x - 4) > 2x + 8$ *(p. 41)* $\quad x > 8$
11. $3 \le x - 2 \le 8$ *(p. 41)* $\quad 5 \le x \le 10$
12. $2x < -6$ or $x + 2 > 5$ *(p. 41)* $\quad x < -3$ or $x > 3$
13. $|x - 4| < 5$ *(p. 51)* $\quad -1 < x < 9$
14. $|x + 3| \ge 15$ *(p. 51)* $\quad x \le -18$ or $x \ge 12$
15. $|6x + 1| < 23$ *(p. 51)* $\quad -4 < x < \frac{11}{3}$

Find the slope of the line passing through the given points. Then tell whether the line *rises, falls, is horizontal,* or *is vertical.* *(p. 82)*

16. $(3, 2), (-1, -5)$ $\quad \frac{7}{4}$; rises
17. $(-7, 4), (5, -3)$ $\quad -\frac{7}{12}$; falls
18. $(-4, -6), (-4, 4)$ $\quad$ undefined; is vertical
19. $\left(-\frac{5}{4}, 3\right), \left(\frac{2}{3}, 3\right)$ $\quad$ 0; is horizontal

Graph the equation or inequality. 20–28. See margin.

20. $y = 3x + 5$ *(p. 89)*
21. $x = -6$ *(p. 89)*
22. $-x + 4y = 16$ *(p. 89)*
23. $y = 2|x|$ *(p. 123)*
24. $y = |x - 3|$ *(p. 123)*
25. $y = -4|x| + 5$ *(p. 123)*
26. $y \le x - 7$ *(p. 132)*
27. $2x + y > 1$ *(p. 132)*
28. $2x - 5y \ge -15$ *(p. 132)*

Graph the relation. Then tell whether the relation is a function. *(p. 72)* 29, 30. See margin for art.

29.

x	−4	−2	0	2	4
y	−1	0	1	2	3

function

30.

x	4	−2	1	1	−3
y	−2	0	1	4	3

not a function

Solve the system using any algebraic method.

31. $4x - 3y = 32$, $-2x + y = -14$ *(p. 160)* $\quad (5, -4)$
32. $5x - 2y = -4$, $3x + 6y = 36$ *(p. 160)* $\quad \left(\frac{4}{3}, \frac{16}{3}\right)$
33. $x - y + 2z = -4$, $3x + y - 4z = -6$, $2x + 3y + z = 9$ *(p. 178)* $\quad (-2, 4, 1)$

Use the given matrices to evaluate the expression. *(p. 195)*

$$A = \begin{bmatrix} -2 & 6 \\ 1 & 4 \end{bmatrix}, B = \begin{bmatrix} 3 & -1 \\ 5 & 2 \end{bmatrix}, C = \begin{bmatrix} -4 & 8 \\ -7 & 12 \end{bmatrix}, D = \begin{bmatrix} 1 & 0 & -4 \\ -2 & 3 & -1 \end{bmatrix}$$

35. $\begin{bmatrix} 6 & 2 \\ 19 & 0 \end{bmatrix}$

34. $B - 3A$ $\quad \begin{bmatrix} 9 & -19 \\ 2 & -10 \end{bmatrix}$
35. $2(A + B) - C$
36. $(C - A)B$ $\quad \begin{bmatrix} 4 & 6 \\ 16 & 24 \end{bmatrix}$
37. $(B + C)D$ $\quad \begin{bmatrix} -15 & 21 & -3 \\ -30 & 42 & -6 \end{bmatrix}$

Find the inverse of the matrix. *(p. 210)*

38. $\begin{bmatrix} 5 & 4 \\ 4 & 3 \end{bmatrix}$ $\quad \begin{bmatrix} -3 & 4 \\ 4 & -5 \end{bmatrix}$
39. $\begin{bmatrix} 6 & 9 \\ -3 & -4 \end{bmatrix}$
40. $\begin{bmatrix} -2 & 2 \\ 4 & 1 \end{bmatrix}$
41. $\begin{bmatrix} -5 & 8 \\ 2 & -8 \end{bmatrix}$

39–41. See margin.

42. **CITY PARK** A triangular section of a city park is being turned into a playground. The triangle's vertices are (0, 0), (15, 10), and (8, 25) where the coordinates are measured in yards. Find the area of the playground. *(p. 203)* 147.5 yd^2

25.

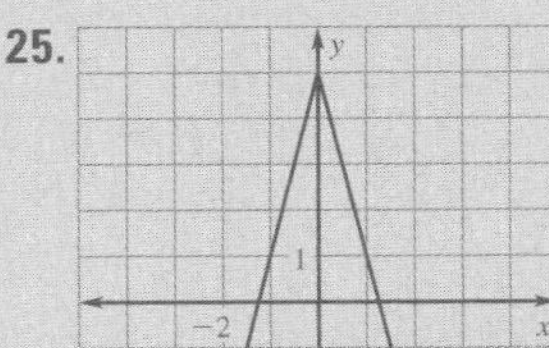

26.

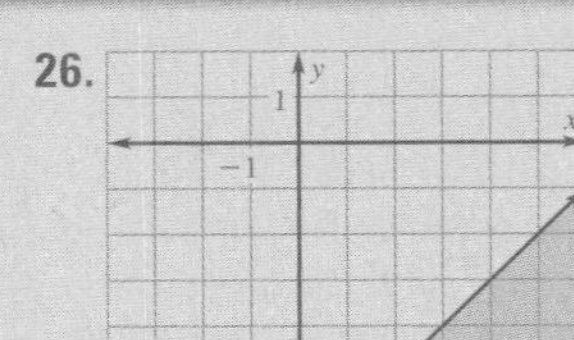

27.

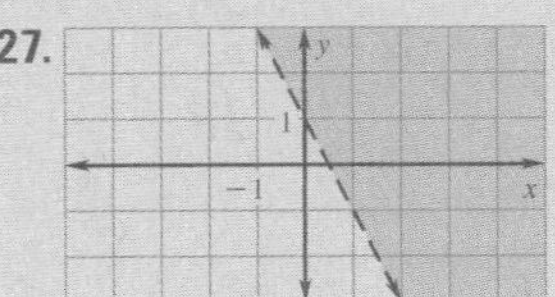

43. **BASEBALL** The Pythagorean Theorem of Baseball is a formula for approximating a team's ratio of wins to games played. Let R be the number of runs the team scores during the season, A be the number of runs allowed to opponents, W be the number of wins, and T be the total number of games played. Then the formula below approximates the team's ratio of wins to games played. *(p. 26)*

$$\frac{W}{T} = \frac{R^2}{R^2 + A^2}$$

a. Solve the formula for W. **$W = \frac{TR^2}{R^2 + A^2}$**

b. In 2004 the Boston Red Sox scored 949 runs and allowed 768 runs. How many of its 162 games would you estimate the team won? *Compare* your answer to the team's actual number of wins, which was 98.
About 98 games; it's the same.

44. **HIGHWAY DRIVING** A sport utility vehicle has a 21 gallon gas tank. On a long highway trip, gas is used at a rate of approximately 4 gallons per hour. Assume the gas tank is full at the start of the trip. *(p. 72)*

a. Write a function giving the number of gallons g of gasoline in the tank after traveling for t hours. **$g = 21 - 4t$**

b. Graph the function from part (a). **See margin.**

c. Identify the domain and range of the function from part (a).
domain: $0 \le t \le 5.25$, range: $0 \le g \le 21$

45. **COMMISSION** A real estate agent's commission c varies directly with the selling price p of a house. An agent made \$3900 in commission after selling a \$78,000 house. Write an equation that gives c as a function of p. Predict the agent's commission if the selling price of a house is \$125,000. *(p. 107)* **$c = \frac{1}{20}p$; \$6250**

46. **WASTE RECOVERY** The table shows the amount of material (in millions of tons) recovered from solid waste in the United States from 1994 to 2001. Make a scatter plot of the data and approximate the best-fitting line. Predict the amount of material that will be recovered from solid waste in 2010. *(p. 113)* **See margin for art; about 92 million tons.**

Years since 1994, t	0	1	2	3	4	5	6	7
Recovered material, m	50.6	54.9	57.3	59.4	61.1	64.8	67.7	68.0

47. **WEIGHTLIFTING RECORDS** The men's world weightlifting records for the 105-kg-and-over weight category are shown in the table. The combined lift is the sum of the snatch lift and the clean and jerk lift. Let s be the weight lifted in the snatch and let j be the weight lifted in the clean and jerk. Write and graph a system of inequalities to describe the weights an athlete could lift to break the records for both the snatch and combined lifts, but *not* the clean and jerk lift. *(p. 168)* **$s > 213$, $j < 263$, $s + j > 472.5$**

Men's 105+ kg World Weightlifting Records		
Snatch	**Clean and Jerk**	**Combined**
213.0	263.0	472.5

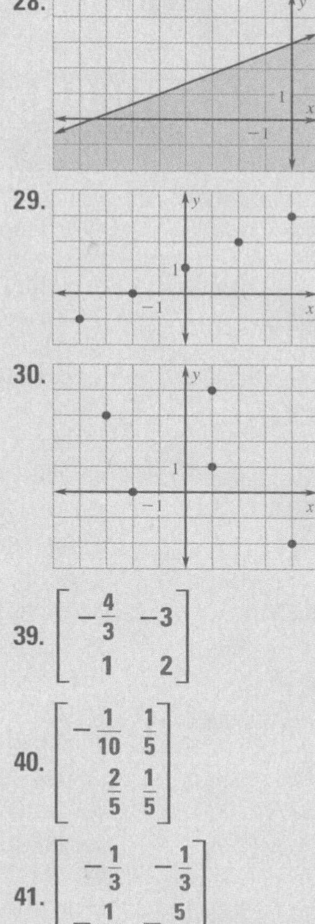

28.

29.

30.

39. $\begin{bmatrix} -\frac{4}{3} & -3 \\ 1 & 2 \end{bmatrix}$

40. $\begin{bmatrix} -\frac{1}{10} & \frac{1}{5} \\ \frac{2}{5} & \frac{1}{5} \end{bmatrix}$

41. $\begin{bmatrix} -\frac{1}{3} & -\frac{1}{3} \\ -\frac{1}{12} & -\frac{5}{24} \end{bmatrix}$

44b.

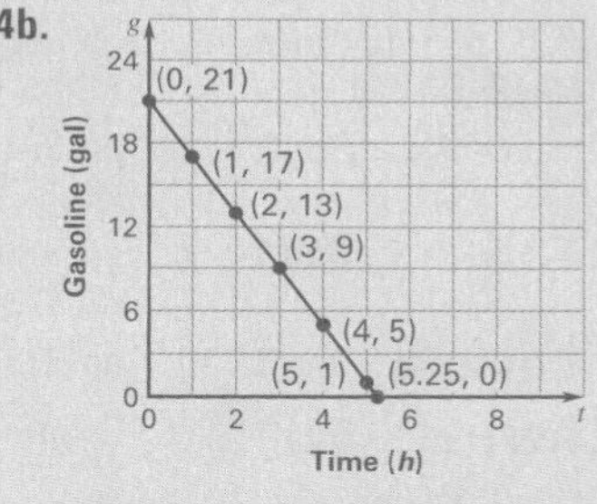

46. An equation for the best-fitting line is $m = 2.5t + 51.725$.

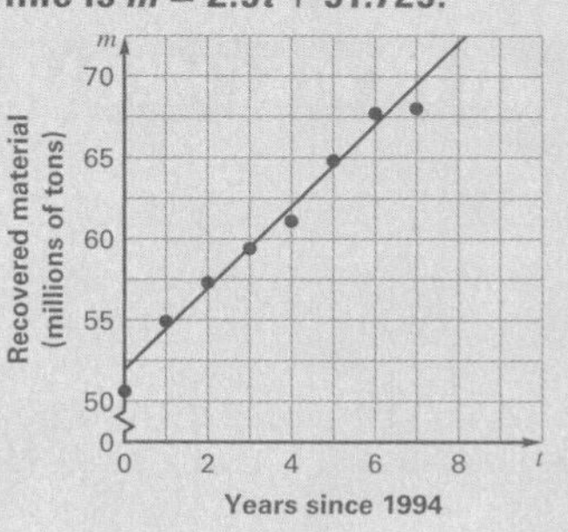

47. Weightlifting Records

Weight in Clean and Jerk

Weight in Snatch

4 Pacing and Assignment Guide

REGULAR SCHEDULE

Pre-AP For pacing and assignments for a Pre-AP course, see the *Algebra 2 Toolkit.*

Lesson	Les. Day	BASIC	AVERAGE	ADVANCED
4.1 MA-HS-5.3.6	Day 1	SRH p. 985 Exs. 1–6; pp. 240–243 Exs. 1–6, 7–15 odd, 19–26, 33–39 odd, 40–46, 55–59, 62	pp. 240–243 Exs. 1, 2, 4–6, 8–18 even, 19, 20, 25–29, 34–38 even, 39–49, 56–60, 63	pp. 240–243 Exs. 1, 2, 5, 6, 11, 12, 14–18, 29–32, 36–54*, 57–61*
4.2 MA-HS-5.3.6	Day 1	EP p. 1010 Exs. 10–15; pp. 249–251 Exs. 1, 2, 4–12 even, 13–21 odd, 22–29, 33–35, 42–44, 51–54, 57	pp. 249–251 Exs. 1, 2, 3–11 odd, 12–22 even, 23, 27–29, 36–38, 42, 45–48, 51–55	pp. 249–251 Exs. 1, 2, 9–12, 19–22, 30–32, 39–50*, 52–56*
4.3 MA-HS-5.3.6	Day 1	pp. 255–258 Exs. 1–6, 15–18, 25–37 odd, 39–47, 56–59, 65–69, 73	pp. 255–258 Exs. 1, 2, 7–11, 18–20, 24–32 even, 39–43, 48–52, 56–62, 65–71, 74	pp. 255–258 Exs. 1, 2, 12–14, 21–23, 34–38 even, 41–43, 53–64*, 66–72*
4.4 MA-HS-5.3.6	Day 1	pp. 263–265 Exs. 1–18	pp. 263–265 Exs. 1–12, 16–21	pp. 263–265 Exs. 1, 2, 5–12, 15–21
	Day 2	pp. 263–265 Exs. 23–39 odd, 41–43, 50–52, 62–65, 69–70	pp. 263–265 Exs. 22–28 even, 31, 32–36 even, 44–46, 50–58, 62–67, 70	pp. 263–265 Exs. 28–30, 38–40, 47–61*, 63–68*
4.5 MA-HS-5.3.6	Day 1	SRH p. 979 Exs. 1–10; pp. 269–271 Exs. 1, 2, 3–19 odd, 20, 21–31 odd, 38–41, 45	pp. 269–271 Exs. 1, 2–18 even, 19–21, 25–30, 34, 35, 38–42, 44	pp. 269–271 Exs. 1, 2, 7–10, 15–19, 25–43*
4.6 MA-HS-5.3.6	Day 1	SRH p. 987 Exs. 11–19 odd; pp. 279–282 Exs. 1–21, 65–67, 77	pp. 279–282 Exs. 1–17, 21, 51, 52, 65–67, 78	pp. 279–282 Exs. 1, 2, 5–11, 14–21, 51, 52, 65–67, 78
	Day 2	pp. 279–282 Exs. 23–33 odd, 34–37, 42–45, 50–53, 68–71	pp. 279–282 Exs. 22–32 even, 37–39, 45–47, 50, 53–55, 57–60, 68–75	pp. 279–282 Exs. 26, 27, 31–33, 39–41, 47–50, 54–64*, 68–76*
4.7 MA-HS-5.3.6	Day 1	pp. 288–291 Exs. 1–6, 12–16, 22–27, 34	pp. 288–291 Exs. 1, 2, 5–8, 12, 15–18, 25–30, 34	pp. 288–291 Exs. 1, 2, 9–12, 18–21, 28–34, 61*
	Day 2	pp. 288–291 Exs. 35–46, 50–55, 62–66, 69–70	pp. 288–291 Exs. 35–40, 43–47, 50, 51, 55–59, 62–67, 69–70	pp. 288–291 Exs. 35–40, 45–49, 55–60, 62–68*, 69–70
4.8 MA-HS-5.3.6	Day 1	EP p. 1010 Exs. 7–9; pp. 296–299 Exs. 1, 2, 4–12 even, 13–21 odd, 22–24, 31–33, 40–42, 49–51, 68–72, 75	pp. 296–299 Exs. 1, 2, 6–8, 12, 16–18, 25–27, 34–36, 43–45, 49–58, 62, 68–73, 76	pp. 296–299 Exs. 1, 2, 9–12, 19–21, 28–30, 37–39, 46–48, 51–67*, 69–74*
4.9 MA-HS-5.3.6	Day 1	pp. 304–307 Exs. 1–5, 7–17 odd, 18–25, 70, 71, 78–79	pp. 304–307 Exs. 1–5, 6–16 even, 18–25, 70, 71, 78–79	pp. 304–307 Exs. 1–5, 12–17, 20–25, 70, 71, 78–79
	Day 2	pp. 304–307 Exs. 26–29, 35–38, 44–51, 58–61, 72–74	pp. 304–307 Exs. 29–31, 38–40, 44, 45, 50–54, 58–67, 72–76	pp. 304–307 Exs. 32–34, 41–45, 54–69*, 72–77*
4.10	Day 1	pp. 312–315 Exs. 1–8, 15–22, 26–29, 31–33, 40, 41, 46–50, 53	pp. 312–315 Exs. 1–3, 9–11, 15–17, 23–27, 34–36, 40–44, 46–51, 54	pp. 312–315 Exs. 1, 2, 5, 12–16, 19, 23–25, 37–52*, 54
Review	Day 1	pp. 318–322 Exs. 1–48	pp. 318–322 Exs. 1–48	pp. 318–322 Exs. 1–48
Assess	Day 1	Chapter 4 Test	Chapter 4 Test	Chapter 4 Test
Yearly Pacing		Chapter 4 Total – 16 days	Chapters 1–4 Total – 54 days	Remaining – 106 days

*Challenge Exercises EP = Extra Practice SRH = Skills Review Handbook

BLOCK SCHEDULE

DAY 1	DAY 2	DAY 3	DAY 4	DAY 5	DAY 6	DAY 7	DAY 8
4.1	4.3	4.4 (CONT.)	4.6	4.7	4.8	4.9 (CONT.)	REVIEW
pp. 240–243 Exs. 1, 2, 4–6, 8–18 even, 19, 20, 25–29, 34–38 even, 39–49, 56–60, 63	pp. 255–258 Exs. 1, 2, 7–11, 18–20, 24–32 even, 39–43, 48–52, 56–62, 65–71, 74	pp. 263–265 Exs. 22–28 even, 31, 32–36 even, 44–46, 50–58, 62–67, 70	pp. 279–282 Exs. 1–17, 21, 22–32 even, 37–39, 45–47, 50–55, 57–60, 65–75, 78	pp. 288–291 Exs. 1, 2, 5–8, 12, 15–18, 25–30, 34–40, 43–47, 50, 51, 55–59, 62–67, 69–70	pp. 296–299 Exs. 1, 2, 6–8, 12, 16–18, 25–27, 34–36, 43–45, 49–58, 62, 68–73, 76	pp. 304–307 Exs. 29–31, 38–40, 44, 45, 50–54, 58–67, 72–76	pp. 318–322 Exs. 1–48
4.2	4.4	4.5			4.9	4.10	ASSESS
pp. 249–251 Exs. 1, 2, 3–11 odd, 12–22 even, 23, 27–29, 36–38, 42, 45–48, 51–55	pp. 263–265 Exs. 1–12, 16–21	pp. 269–271 Exs. 1, 2–18 even, 19–21, 25–30, 34, 35, 38–42, 44			pp. 304–307 Exs. 1–5, 6–16 even, 18–25, 70, 71, 78–79	pp. 312–315 Exs. 1–3, 9–11, 15–17, 23–27, 34–36, 40–44, 46–51, 54	Chapter 4 Test
Yearly Pacing	Chapter 4 Total – 8 days		Chapters 1–4 Total – 27 days		Remaining – 53 days		

Chapter Resource Guide 4

RESOURCE MANAGER

Chapter Resource Book

CHAPTER SUPPORT										
Parents as Partners (Chapter Overview with home involvement exercises and activity)									p. 1	
LESSON SUPPORT **Standards**	**4.1** MA-HS-5.3.6	**4.2** MA-HS-5.3.6	**4.3** MA-HS-5.3.6	**4.4** MA-HS-5.3.6	**4.5** MA-HS-5.3.6	**4.6** MA-HS-5.3.6	**4.7** MA-HS-5.3.6	**4.8** MA-HS-5.3.6	**4.9** MA-HS-5.3.6	**4.10** MA-HS-5.3.6
Teaching Guide/Lesson Plan	p. 3	p. 17	p. 33	p. 44	p. 54	p. 65	p. 75	p. 86	p. 98	p. 114
Activity Masters		p. 19	p. 35					p. 88		
Technology Activities & Keystrokes	p. 5	p. 21							p. 100	p. 116
Activity Support Masters							p. 77			
Practice (3 levels)	p. 6	p. 22	p. 36	p. 46	p. 56	p. 67	p. 78	p. 90	p. 103	p. 117
Study Guide	p. 12	p. 28	p. 39	p. 49	p. 59	p. 70	p. 81	p. 93	p. 109	p. 120
Catch-Up for Absent Students	p. 14	p. 30	p. 41	p. 51	p. 61	p. 72	p. 83	p. 95	p. 111	p. 122
Problem Solving/Application	p. 15	p. 31	p. 42	p. 52	p. 62	p. 73	p. 84	p. 96	p. 112	p. 123
Challenge Practice	p. 16	p. 32	p. 43	p. 53	p. 64	p. 74	p. 85	p. 97	p. 113	p. 124

REVIEW			
Chapter Review Games and Activities	p. 125	Cumulative Practice	p. 127
Project with Rubric	p. 126	Resource Book Answers	A1

Transparencies	*4.1*	*4.2*	*4.3*	*4.4*	*4.5*	*4.6*	*4.7*	*4.8*	*4.9*	*4.10*
Warm-Up/Daily Homework Quiz	✔	✔	✔	✔	✔	✔	✔	✔	✔	✔
Notetaking Guide	✔	✔	✔	✔	✔	✔	✔	✔	✔	✔
Teacher Support	✔	✔							✔	✔
Answer Transparencies	✔	✔	✔	✔	✔	✔	✔	✔	✔	✔

ASSESSMENT BOOK

Quizzes	p. 46	SAT/ACT Chapter Test	p. 57
Chapter Tests (3 levels)	p. 49	Alternative Assessment with Rubric	p. 59
Standardized Chapter Test	p. 55		

TECHNOLOGY

- Easy Planner
- Test and Practice Generator
- Power Presentations
- @HomeTutor
- Activity Generator
- Animated Algebra
- Classzone.com
- eEdition Plus Online
- eWorkbook Plus Online
- ML Assessment System

ADDITIONAL RESOURCES

Kentucky

- Additional Lesson J Parametric Equations
- Worked-Out Solution Key
- Notetaking Guide
- Practice Workbook
- Algebra 2 Toolkit
- Benchmark Tests
- Remediation Workbook
- Spanish Study Guide
- Spanish Assessment Book
- Spanish Resources in Spanish
- Multi-Language Visual Glossary

LESSON 4.1 Practice B
For use with pages 236–243

For the following functions (a) tell whether the graph *opens up* or *opens down*, (b) find the vertex, and (c) find the axis of symmetry. See below.

1. $y = -3x^2 + 1$
2. $y = -2x^2 - 1$
3. $y = 3x^2 - 2x$
4. $y = -4x^2 - 2x + 9$
5. $y = 5x^2 - 5x + 7$
6. $y = -2x^2 - 3x + 3$

Match the equation with its graph.

7. $y = -x^2 + 5x - 2$ C
8. $y = -x^2 - 5x - 2$ A
9. $y = -\frac{1}{4}x^2 + 2$ B

A. 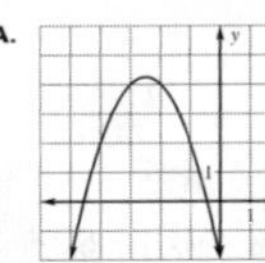

B. 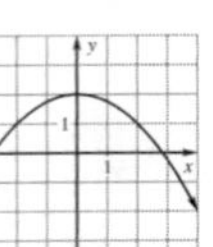

C. 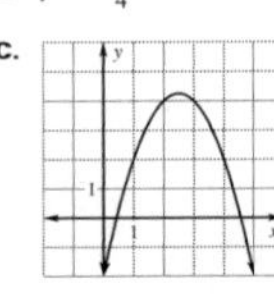

Graph the function. Label the vertex and axis of symmetry.

10. $y = x^2 - 3$

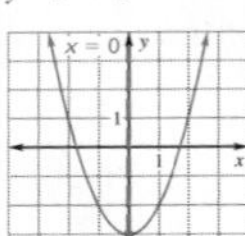

11. $y = -2x^2 + 4x$

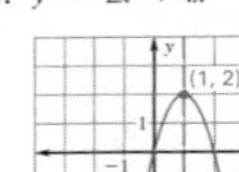

12. $y = 2x^2 + 6x + 1$

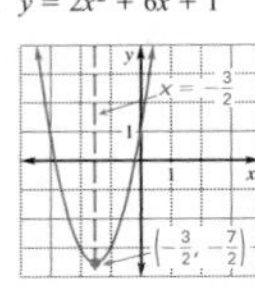

13. $y = 4x^2 - 16x + 3$

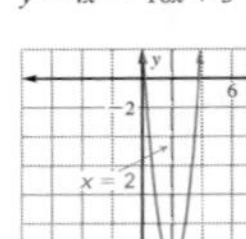

14. $y = -3x^2 - 12x + 1$

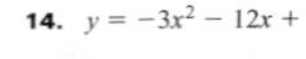

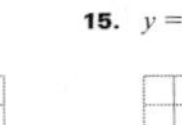

15. $y = \frac{1}{3}x^2 + 2x - 1$

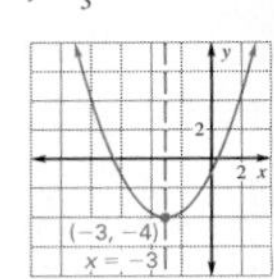

1. a. opens down b. $(0, 1)$ c. $x = 0$
2. a. opens down b. $(0, -1)$ c. $x = 0$
3. a. opens up b. $\left(\frac{1}{3}, -\frac{1}{3}\right)$ c. $x = \frac{1}{3}$
4. a. opens down b. $\left(-\frac{1}{4}, \frac{37}{4}\right)$ c. $x = -\frac{1}{4}$
5. a. opens up b. $\left(\frac{1}{2}, \frac{23}{4}\right)$ c. $x = \frac{1}{2}$
6. a. opens down b. $\left(-\frac{3}{4}, \frac{33}{8}\right)$ c. $x = -\frac{3}{4}$

LESSON 4.1 Practice B *continued*
For use with pages 236–243

16. $y = x^2 + 5x - 1$

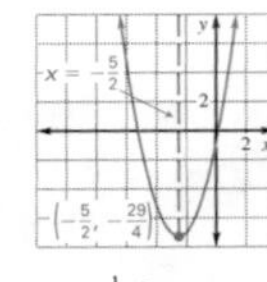

17. $y = 3x^2 + 3x - 2$

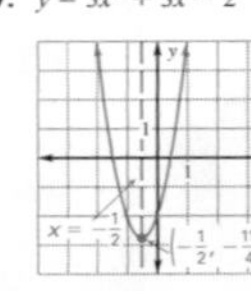

18. $y = -5x^2 + 4x + 2$

19. $y = -\frac{1}{2}x^2 + 3x - 1$

20. $y = -2x^2 - 4x + 3$

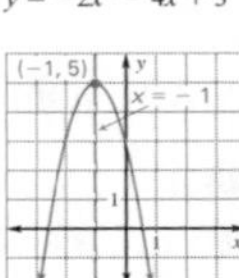

21. $y = 2x^2 - 4x - 2$

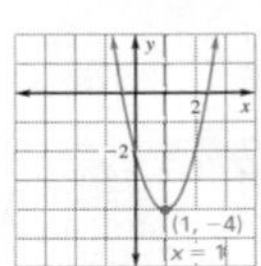

In Exercises 22–24, use the following information.

Minimize Cost A baker has modeled the monthly operating costs for making wedding cakes by the function $y = 0.5x^2 - 12x + 150$ where y is the total cost in dollars and x is the number of cakes prepared.

22. Find the vertex and axis of symmetry. $(12, 78)$; $x = 12$
23. What is the minimum cost? \$78
24. How many cakes should be prepared each month to yield the minimum cost? 12

In Exercises 25 and 26, use the following information.

Maximize Revenue A sports store sells about 50 mountain bikes per month at a price of \$220 each. For each \$20 decrease in price, about 10 more bikes per month are sold.

25. Write a quadratic function in standard form that models the revenue from bike sales. $y = -200x^2 + 1200x + 11{,}000$
26. What price produces the maximum revenue? \$160

LESSON 4.2 Practice B
For use with pages 245–251

Match the equation with its graph.

1. $y = 2(x - 2)^2 + 1$ C
2. $y = -(x - 3)(x - 1)$ B
3. $y = -(x + 1)^2 + 2$ A

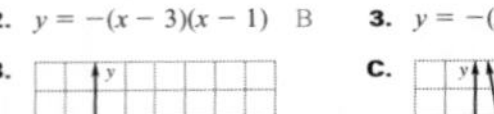

A. 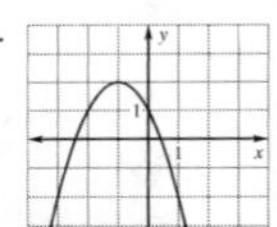

B.

C. 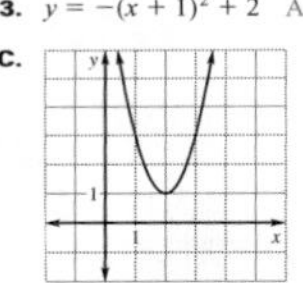

Graph the function. Label the vertex and axis of symmetry.

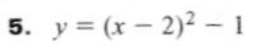

4. $y = (x + 1)^2 + 3$

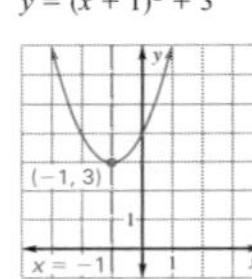

5. $y = (x - 2)^2 - 1$

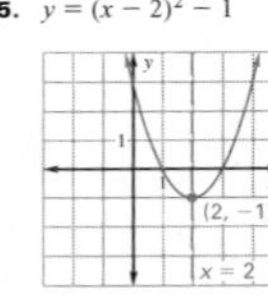

6. $y = (x + 2)^2 - 3$

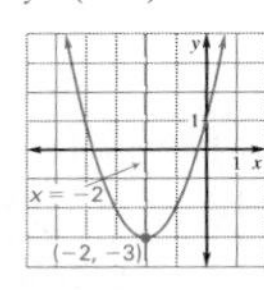

7. $y = -2(x + 1)^2 - 4$

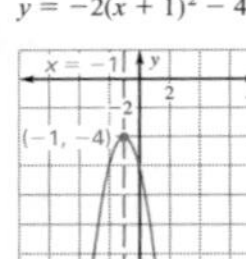

8. $y = 2(x + 2)^2 - 4$

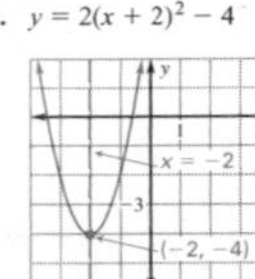

9. $y = -(x - 4)^2 + 8$

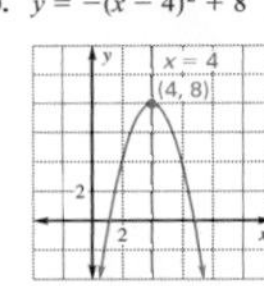

Graph the function. Label the vertex, axis of symmetry and *x*-intercepts.

10. $y = (x + 2)(x - 4)$

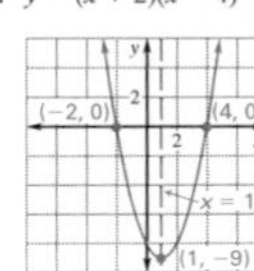

11. $y = (x + 2)(x + 3)$

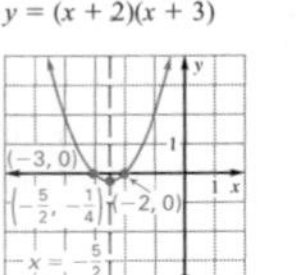

12. $y = (x + 4)(x + 2)$

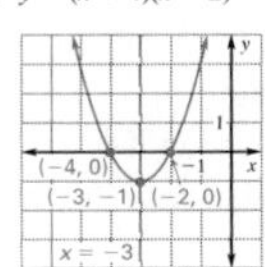

LESSON 4.2 Practice B *continued*
For use with pages 245–251

13. $y = -(x - 3)(x + 1)$

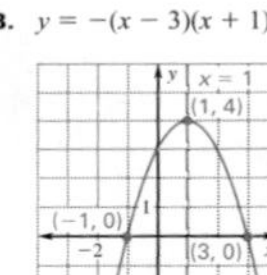

14. $y = 3(x - 1)(x - 4)$

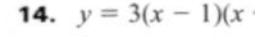

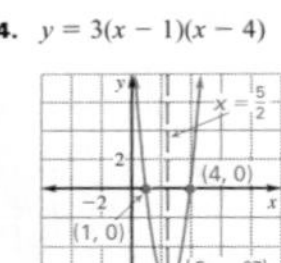

15. $y = -3x(x + 7)$

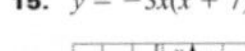

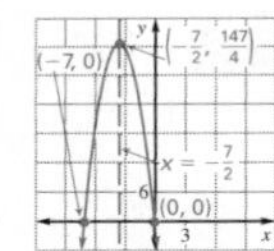

Write the quadratic function in standard form. See below.

16. $y = (x - 2)^2 + 6$
17. $y = -2(x + 1)^2 + 3$
18. $y = 3(x - 3)^2 - 12$
19. $y = (x - 4)(x - 2)$
20. $y = 4(x + 1)(x + 2)$
21. $y = -3(x - 3)(x + 2)$

Find the maximum or the minimum value of the function. See below.

22. $y = (x - 6)^2 + 3$
23. $y = -(x - 3)^2 - 4$
24. $y = 3(x - 3)^2 - 3$
25. $y = (x + 7)(x + 3)$
26. $y = 2(x - 3)(x - 5)$
27. $y = -(x - 1)(x + 4)$

28. **Visual Thinking** Use a graphing calculator to graph $y = a(x - 2)(x - 6)$ where $a = \frac{1}{2}$, 1 and 4. Use the same viewing window for all three graphs. How do the graphs change as a increases? As a increases, the graph becomes more narrow and the vertex moves down.

In Exercises 29 and 30, use the following information.

Golf The flight of a particular golf shot can be modeled by the function $y = -0.001x(x - 260)$ where x is the horizontal distance (in yards) from the impact point and y is the height (in yards).

29. How many yards away from the impact point does the golf ball land? 260
30. What is the maximum height in yards of the golf shot? 16.9

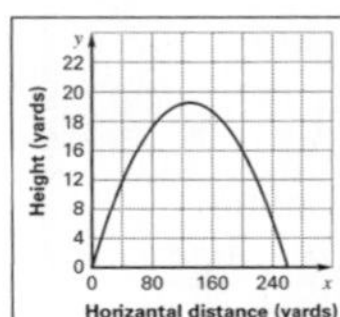

16. $y = x^2 - 4x + 10$
17. $y = -2x^2 - 4x + 1$
18. $y = 3x^2 - 18x + 15$
19. $y = x^2 - 6x + 8$
20. $y = 4x^2 + 12x + 8$
21. $y = -3x^2 + 3x + 18$
22. minimum, 3
23. maximum, -4
24. minimum, -3
25. minimum, -4
26. minimum, -2
27. maximum, $\frac{25}{4}$

LESSON 4.3 Practice B
For use with pages 252–258

Factor the expression. If the expression cannot be factored, say so.

1. $x^2 + 4x - 21$ $(x - 3)(x + 7)$ **2.** $x^2 - 6x + 5$ $(x - 5)(x - 1)$ **3.** $x^2 + 6x + 8$ $(x + 2)(x + 4)$

4. $x^2 - x - 6$ $(x - 3)(x + 2)$ **5.** $x^2 - x - 12$ $(x - 4)(x + 3)$ **6.** $x^2 - 2x - 8$ $(x - 4)(x + 2)$

7. $x^2 - 9x + 20$ $(x - 4)(x - 5)$ **8.** $x^2 + 3x - 18$ $(x - 3)(x + 6)$ **9.** $x^2 - 9$ $(x - 3)(x + 3)$

10. $x^2 + 8x + 16$ $(x + 4)(x + 4)$ **11.** $x^2 - 11x + 28$ See below. **12.** $x^2 - 2x + 2$ cannot factor

13. $x^2 + 4x - 32$ $(x - 4)(x + 8)$ **14.** $x^2 - 3x - 10$ $(x - 5)(x + 2)$ **15.** $x^2 - 25$ $(x - 5)(x + 5)$

16. $x^2 - 9x + 14$ $(x - 7)(x - 2)$ **17.** $x^2 - 100$ $(x - 10)(x + 10)$ **18.** $x^2 - 8x - 15$ cannot factor

11. $(x - 4)(x - 7)$

Solve the equation.

19. $x^2 + x - 6 = 0$ $-3, 2$ **20.** $x^2 + 3x - 10 = 0$ $-5, 2$ **21.** $x^2 - 5x + 6 = 0$ $2, 3$

22. $x^2 - 4x + 4 = 0$ 2 **23.** $x^2 + 7x + 12 = 0$ $-4, -3$ **24.** $x^2 - 3x - 28 = 0$ $-4, 7$

25. $x^2 - 36 = 0$ $-6, 6$ **26.** $x^2 - 2x - 15 = 0$ $-3, 5$ **27.** $x^2 - 11x + 18 = 0$ $2, 9$

28. $3x^2 = 48$ $-4, 4$ **29.** $x^2 - 7x - 4 = -10$ $1, 6$ **30.** $9x - 8 = x^2$ $1, 8$

Find the zeros of the function by rewriting the function in intercept form.

31. $y = x^2 + 8x + 15$ $-5, -3$ **32.** $y = x^2 - 12x + 32$ $4, 8$ **33.** $f(x) = x^2 - 2x - 35$ $-5, 7$

34. $y = x^2 - x - 30$ $-5, 6$ **35.** $g(x) = x^2 + 10x + 9$ $-9, -1$ **36.** $y = x^2 - 6x$ $6, 0$

37. $h(x) = x^2 - 12x + 27$ $3, 9$ **38.** $y = x^2 - 9$ $-3, 3$ **39.** $y = x^2 + 16x + 64$ -8

40. Picture Frame You are making a square frame of uniform width for a square picture that has side lengths of two feet. The total area of the frame is five square feet. What is the length of the sides of the frame? 3 ft

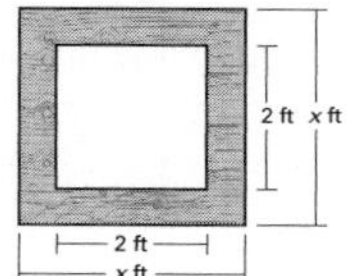

41. Concert Stage The dimensions of the old stage at the concert hall were 30 feet wide and 15 feet deep. The new stage has a total area of 1000 square feet. The dimensions of the new stage were created by adding the same distance x to the width and the depth of the old stage dimensions. What is the value of x? 10 ft

LESSON 4.3

LESSON 4.4 Practice B
For use with pages 259–265

1. $(3x - 2)(x + 4)$ **2.** $(2x - 1)(x + 3)$ **3.** $(2x + 1)(2x + 1)$
4. cannot factor **5.** $(4x - 3)(x + 2)$ **6.** $(2x + 5)(x + 3)$
7. $(3x + 2)(3x + 2)$ **8.** $3(2x - 3)(2x - 1)$ **9.** $2(3x - 1)(3x + 1)$

Factor the expression. If the expression cannot be factored, say so.

1. $3x^2 + 10x - 8$ See above. **2.** $2x^2 + 5x - 3$ See above. **3.** $4x^2 + 4x + 1$ See above.

4. $2x^2 - 5x + 1$ See above. **5.** $4x^2 + 5x - 6$ See above. **6.** $2x^2 + 11x + 15$ See above.

7. $9x^2 + 12x + 4$ See above. **8.** $12x^2 - 24x - 9$ See above. **9.** $18x^2 - 2$ See above.

10. $12x^2 + 17x + 6$ See below. **11.** $15x^2 + 8x - 16$ See below. **12.** $4x^2 - 5$ See below.

13. $12x^2 - 39x + 9$ See below. **14.** $18x^2 - 9x - 14$ See below. **15.** $20x^2 - 54x + 36$ See below.

16. $42x^2 + 35x + 7$ See below. **17.** $-12x^2 - x + 11$ See below. **18.** $80x^2 + 68x + 12$ See below.

LESSON 4.4

Solve the equation.

19. $2x^2 + 3x - 2 = 0$ $-2, \frac{1}{2}$ **20.** $2x^2 - 3x - 9 = 0$ $-\frac{3}{2}, 3$

21. $4x^2 - 8x + 3 = 0$ $\frac{1}{2}, \frac{3}{2}$ **22.** $9x^2 - 4 = 0$ $-\frac{2}{3}, \frac{2}{3}$

23. $8x^2 - 6x + 1 = 0$ $\frac{1}{4}, \frac{1}{2}$ **24.** $18x^2 + 48x = -32$ $-\frac{4}{3}$

25. $9x^2 + 11x + 18 = -10x + 8$ $-\frac{5}{3}, -\frac{2}{3}$ **26.** $5x^2 - 2x - 6 = -3x^2 + 6x$ $-\frac{1}{2}, \frac{3}{2}$

27. $5x^2 - 3x + 3 = -2x^2 + 3$ $0, \frac{3}{7}$ **28.** $25x^2 - 24x - 9 = -7x^2 + 12x - 18$ $\frac{3}{8}, \frac{3}{4}$

Find the zeros of the function by rewriting the function in intercept form.

29. $y = 3x^2 + 2x$ $-\frac{2}{3}, 0$ **30.** $y = 12x^2 + 8x - 15$ $-\frac{3}{2}, \frac{5}{6}$

31. $f(x) = 5x^2 - 25x + 30$ $2, 3$ **32.** $y = 25x^2 + 10x - 24$ $-\frac{6}{5}, \frac{4}{5}$

33. $g(x) = 33x^2 - 9x - 24$ $-\frac{8}{11}, 1$ **34.** $y = 4x^2 + 1$ none

Find the value of x.

35. Area of the triangle = 27 2 **36.** Area of the rectangle = 22 $\frac{3}{2}$

3x
4x + 1

10. $(4x + 3)(3x + 2)$
11. $(5x - 4)(3x + 4)$
12. cannot factor
13. $3(4x - 1)(x - 3)$

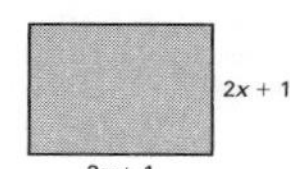

37. Picture Frame You are making a frame of uniform width for a picture that is to be displayed at the local museum. The picture is 3.25 feet tall and 3 feet wide. The museum has allocated 15 square feet of wall space to display the picture. What should the width of the frame be in order to use all of the allocated space? 0.375 ft

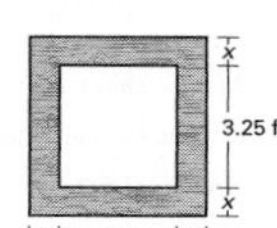

14. $(6x - 7)(3x + 2)$ **15.** $2(5x - 6)(2x - 3)$
16. $7(3x + 1)(2x + 1)$ **17.** $(-12x + 11)(x + 1)$
18. $4(5x + 3)(4x + 1)$

LESSON 4.5 Practice B
For use with pages 266–271

Simplify the expression.

1. $\sqrt{242}$ $11\sqrt{2}$ **2.** $\sqrt{153}$ $3\sqrt{17}$ **3.** $\sqrt{56}$ $2\sqrt{14}$

4. $5\sqrt{24} \cdot 2\sqrt{28}$ $40\sqrt{42}$ **5.** $\sqrt{8} \cdot 3\sqrt{40} \cdot \sqrt{3}$ $24\sqrt{15}$ **6.** $\sqrt{10} \cdot \sqrt{14}$ $2\sqrt{35}$

7. $\sqrt{\frac{121}{225}}$ $\frac{11}{15}$ **8.** $\sqrt{\frac{7}{9}} \cdot \sqrt{\frac{4}{7}}$ $\frac{2}{3}$ **9.** $\sqrt{24} \cdot \sqrt{\frac{80}{192}}$ $\sqrt{10}$

10. $\frac{3}{4 + \sqrt{5}}$ $\frac{12 - 3\sqrt{5}}{11}$ **11.** $\frac{-6}{5 - \sqrt{11}}$ $\frac{-15 - 3\sqrt{11}}{7}$ **12.** $\frac{7 - \sqrt{7}}{10 + \sqrt{3}}$ $\frac{70 - 7\sqrt{3} - 10\sqrt{7} + \sqrt{21}}{97}$

Solve the equation.

13. $x^2 = 289$ ± 17 **14.** $x^2 - 169 = 0$ ± 13 **15.** $2x^2 - 512 = 0$ ± 16

16. $3x^2 - 150 = 282$ ± 12 **17.** $\frac{1}{2}x^2 - 8 = 16$ $\pm 4\sqrt{3}$ **18.** $\frac{2}{3}x^2 - 4 = 12$ $\pm 2\sqrt{6}$

19. $2x^2 + 5 = 5x^2 - 37$ $\pm\sqrt{14}$ **20.** $4(x^2 - 8) = 84$ $\pm\sqrt{29}$ **21.** $3(x^2 + 2) = 18$ ± 2

22. $2(x + 2)^2 = 72$ $-8, 4$ **23.** $3(x - 3)^2 + 2 = 26$ **24.** $(3x + 2)^2 - 49 = 0$ $-3, \frac{5}{3}$

25. $(4x - 5)^2 = 64$ $-\frac{3}{4}, \frac{13}{4}$ **26.** $\frac{1}{2}(x - 4)^2 = 8$ $0, 8$ **27.** $\frac{2}{3}(x + 8)^2 - 66 = 0$

23. $3 \pm 2\sqrt{2}$ **27.** $-8 \pm 3\sqrt{11}$

LESSON 4.5

When an object is dropped, its height h can be determined after t seconds by using the falling object model $h = -16t^2 + s$ where s is the initial height. Find the time it takes an object to hit the ground when it is dropped from a height of s feet.

28. $s = 160$ 3.16 sec **29.** $s = 300$ 4.33 sec

30. $s = 550$ 5.86 sec **31.** $s = 690$ 6.57 sec

32. $s = 900$ 7.5 sec **33.** $s = 1600$ 10 sec

Use the Pythagorean theorem to find x. Round to the nearest hundredth.

34. 9.43

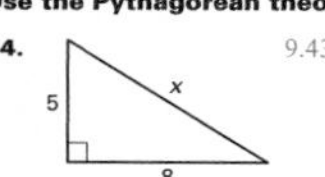

35. 6.63

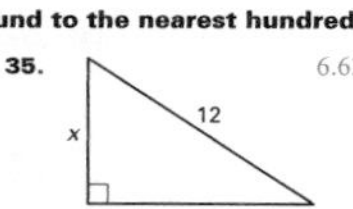

36. Operating Costs For a period of 48 months, the average monthly operating cost for a small business, C (in dollars), can be approximated by the model $C = 0.55t^2 + 550$, where t is the number of months. During which month was the average operating cost $1430? 40

4 Lesson Practice Level B

LESSON 4.6 Practice B
For use with pages 275–282

Solve the equation.

1. $x^2 = -36$ $\pm 6i$
2. $x^2 + 121 = 0$ $\pm 11i$
3. $x^2 + 9 = 4$ $\pm i\sqrt{5}$
4. $x^2 = 2x^2 + 4$ $\pm 2i$
5. $3x^2 + 40 = -x^2 - 56$ 5. $\pm 2i\sqrt{6}$
6. $11x^2 = -5x^2 - 1$ $\pm \frac{1}{4}i$
7. $(x - 3)^2 = -12$ $3 \pm 2i\sqrt{3}$
8. $-2(x - 1)^2 = 36$ $1 \pm 3i\sqrt{2}$
9. $4(x + 2)^2 + 320 = 0$ $-2 \pm 4i\sqrt{5}$

Write the expression as a complex number in standard form.

10. $(1 + i) + (3 + i)$ $4 + 2i$
11. $(4 - 3i) + (2 + 6i)$ $6 + 3i$
12. $(-4 - i) - (4 + 5i)$ $-8 - 6i$
13. $(5 - 3i) + (-3 - 6i)$ $2 - 9i$
14. $3i(4 + 2i)$ $-6 + 12i$
15. $-2i(3 - i)$ $-2 - 6i$
16. $(2 + i)(4 + 2i)$ $6 + 8i$
17. $(5 - 2i)(1 - 3i)$ $-1 - 17i$
18. $-(3 + i)(7 - 3i)$ $-24 + 2i$
19. $-2i(1 + i)(2 + 3i)$ $10 + 2i$
20. $(2 - i)^2$ $3 - 4i$
21. $(5 + 3i)(5 - 3i)$ 34
22. $\frac{5}{3 - 2i}$ $\frac{15}{13} + \frac{10}{13}i$
23. $\frac{2 - i}{3 + 4i}$ $\frac{2}{25} - \frac{11}{25}i$
24. $\frac{1 + 2i}{\sqrt{2} + i}$ $\frac{2 + \sqrt{2}}{3} + \frac{2\sqrt{2} - 1}{3}i$
25. $\frac{3}{2 - 4i} - (3 + 2i)$ $-\frac{27}{10} - \frac{7}{5}i$

Find the absolute value of the complex number.

26. $3 - 4i$ 5
27. $1 - i\sqrt{3}$ 2
28. $\sqrt{5} + 2i\sqrt{2}$ $\sqrt{13}$

Plot the numbers in a complex plane.

29. $3i$
30. $2 + 2i$
31. $-2 - 3i$

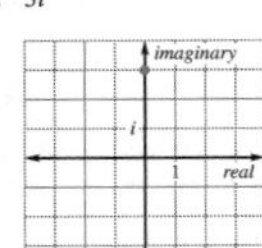

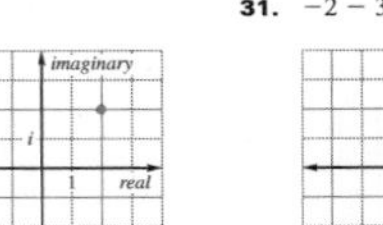

Using the properties of exponents, write the complex number in standard form.

32. $2 + i^2$ 1
33. $3 + i^3$ $3 - i$
34. $5 - i^4$ 4
35. $2 - i^5$ $2 - i$
36. $1 + i^4$ 2
37. $1 + i^8$ 2
38. $1 + i^{12}$ 2
39. $1 + i^{16}$ 2

40. **Pattern Recognition** Using the information from Exercises 36–39, write a general statement about the value of i^n where n is a positive factor of 4. Use this statement to write $2 + i^{207}$ in standard form. If the exponent of i is a factor of 4 the expression can be reduced to 1. To simplify i raised to any natural number, factor out the multiples of 4 in the exponent and simplify the remaining expression; $2 + i^{207} = 2 + (i^{204})(i^3) = 2 + i^3 = 2 - i$

LESSON 4.6

LESSON 4.7 Practice B
For use with pages 284–291

Solve the equation by finding square roots.

1. $x^2 + 8x + 16 = 9$ $-7, -1$
2. $x^2 - 6x + 9 = 25$ $-2, 8$
3. $x^2 - 12x + 36 = 49$ $-1, 13$
4. $2x^2 - 12x + 18 = 32$ $-1, 7$
5. $4x^2 - 4x + 1 = 36$ $-\frac{5}{2}, \frac{7}{2}$
6. $5x^2 - 20x + 20 = 35$ $2 \pm \sqrt{7}$
7. $x^2 - \frac{2}{3}x + \frac{1}{9} = 1$ $-\frac{2}{3}, \frac{4}{3}$
8. $x^2 + \frac{3}{2}x + \frac{9}{16} = 3$ $-\frac{3}{4} \pm \sqrt{3}$
9. $9x^2 + 12x + 4 = 5$ $-\frac{2}{3} \pm \frac{\sqrt{5}}{3}$

Find the value of *c* that makes the expression a perfect square trinomial. Then write the expression as a square of a binomial.

10. $x^2 + 8x + c$ $16; (x + 4)^2$
11. $x^2 - 22x + c$ $121; (x - 11)^2$
12. $x^2 + 16x + c$ $64; (x + 8)^2$
13. $x^2 + 3x + c$ $\frac{9}{4}; \left(x + \frac{3}{2}\right)^2$
14. $x^2 - 9x + c$ $\frac{81}{4}; \left(x - \frac{9}{2}\right)^2$
15. $9x^2 - 12x + c$ $4; (3x - 2)^2$

Solve the equation by completing the square.

16. $x^2 + 4x = 1$ $-2 \pm \sqrt{5}$
17. $x^2 - 10x = -10$ $5 \pm \sqrt{15}$
18. $x^2 - 2x - 9 = 0$ $1 \pm \sqrt{10}$
19. $x^2 + 6x + 10 = 0$ $-3 \pm i$
20. $x^2 + 8x + 4 = 0$ $-4 \pm 2\sqrt{3}$
21. $3x^2 + 36x = -42$ $-6 \pm \sqrt{22}$
22. $x^2 - 24x + 81 = 0$ $12 \pm 3\sqrt{7}$
23. $4x^2 + 20x + 25 = 0$ $-\frac{5}{2}$
24. $3x^2 - 3x + 9 = 0$ $\frac{1}{2} \pm \frac{\sqrt{11}}{2}i$
25. $6x^2 - 12x - 18 = 0$ $-1, 3$

Write the quadratic function in vertex form. Then identify the vertex.

26. $y = x^2 + 14x + 11$ See below.
27. $y = x^2 - 8x + 10$ $y = (x - 4)^2 - 6; (4, -6)$
28. $y = 2x^2 + 4x - 5$ See below.
29. $y = 3x^2 - 9x + 18$ $y = 3\left(x - \frac{3}{2}\right)^2 + \frac{45}{4}; \left(\frac{3}{2}, \frac{45}{4}\right)$

Find the value of *x*.

30. Area of rectangle = 84   7
31. Area of triangle = 20   8

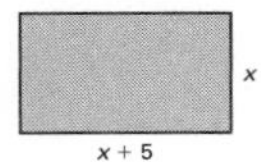

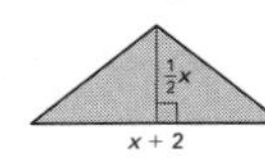

32. **Shot Put** In a track and field event, a contestant had a throw in the shot put that can be modeled by $y = -0.02x^2 + x + 6$ where x is the shot put's horizontal distance (in feet) and y is the corresponding height (in feet). How long was the throw? Round the answer to the nearest tenth. 55.4

26. $y = (x + 7)^2 - 38; (-7, -38)$
28. $y = 2(x + 1)^2 - 7; (-1, -7)$

LESSON 4.7

LESSON 4.8 Practice B
For use with pages 292–299

Find the discriminant of the quadratic equation.

1. $x^2 - 3x + 5 = 0$ -11
2. $2x^2 + x + 2 = 0$ -15
3. $4x^2 - 9x + 2 = 0$ 49
4. $-3x^2 + 6x - 3 = 0$ 0
5. $3x^2 + 3x - 1 = 0$ 21
6. $7x^2 - 4x + 5 = 0$ -124

Find the discriminant and use it to determine if the solution has *one real, two real,* or *two imaginary* number(s).

7. $x^2 + 4x + 3 = 0$ 4; two real
8. $x^2 - 2x + 4 = 0$ −12; two imaginary
9. $x^2 - 2x + 1 = 0$ 0; one real
10. $3x^2 + 2x - 1 = 0$ 16; two real
11. $-x^2 - x = 4$ −15; two imaginary
12. $5x^2 - 4x + 1 = 3x + 4$ 109; two real

Use the quadratic formula to solve the equation.

13. $x^2 + 4x - 2 = 0$ $-2 \pm \sqrt{6}$
14. $2x^2 - 5x - 2 = 0$ $\frac{5}{4} \pm \frac{\sqrt{41}}{4}$
15. $x^2 + 2x = 4x$ $0, 2$
16. $-6x^2 + 3x + 2 = 3$ $\frac{1}{4} \pm \frac{\sqrt{15}}{12}i$
17. $-x^2 + 1 = -5x^2 + 4x$ $\frac{1}{2}$
18. $2(x - 3)^2 = -2x + 9$ $\frac{5}{2} \pm \frac{\sqrt{7}}{2}$
19. $2.5x^2 - 2.8x = 0.4$ $-0.13, 1.25$
20. $4.8x^2 = 5.2x + 2.7$ $-0.38, 1.47$

Solve the equation using the quadratic formula. Then solve the equation by factoring to check your solution(s).

21. $x^2 - 2x - 24 = 0$ $-4, 6$
22. $x^2 - 2x + 1 = 0$ 1
23. $2x^2 - 9x + 9 = 0$ $\frac{3}{2}, 3$
24. $6x^2 + 17x + 5 = 0$ $-\frac{5}{2}, -\frac{1}{3}$
25. $10x^2 + x = 2$ $-\frac{1}{2}, \frac{2}{5}$
26. $6x^2 = 5x + 6$ $-\frac{2}{3}, \frac{3}{2}$

27. **New Carpet** You have new carpeting installed in a rectangular room. You are charged for 28 square yards of carpet and 60 feet (20 yards) of tack strip. Tack strip is used along the perimeter to secure the carpet in place. Do you think these figures are correct? Explain your answer. No. The area of the room is $x(10 - x)$ and can be expressed as $x(10 - x) = 28$ which has no real solutions.

Tack strip
x
10 − x

In Exercises 28–31, use the following information.

Launched Object An object is launched upward with an initial velocity of 64 feet per second from a platform 80 feet high.

28. Write a height model for the object. $h = -16t^2 + 64t + 80$
29. How many seconds until the maximum height is reached?   2 sec
30. What will be the maximum height?   144 ft
31. How many seconds until the object hits the ground?   5 sec

LESSON 4.8

LESSON 4.9

Practice B

For use with pages 300–307

Determine whether the ordered pair is a solution of the inequality.

1. $y < x^2 + 2x + 2, (1, 6)$ not a solution

2. $y > x^2 - 5x, (2, -3)$ solution

3. $y \le 2x^2 - 7x, (4, 4)$ solution

4. $y \ge -2x^2 + 3x - 6, (-1, -12)$ not a solution

Match the inequality with its graph.

5. $y \ge x^2 + 4x - 1$ B

6. $y < -2x^2 + 3x - 5$ A

7. $y \le \frac{1}{2}x^2 - x - 1$ C

A.

B.

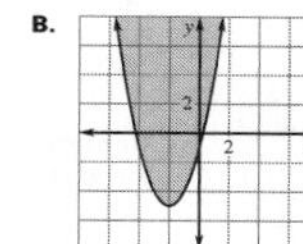

C.

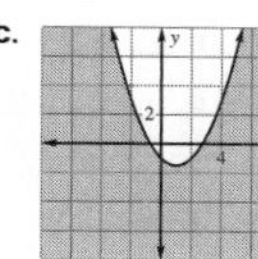

Graph the inequality.

8. $y \ge x^2 - 2$

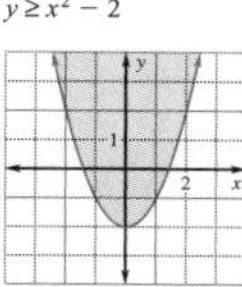

9. $y < -x^2 - 2x + 1$

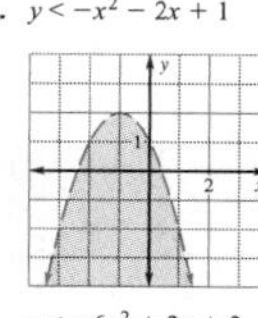

10. $y \le x^2 - 3x + 15$

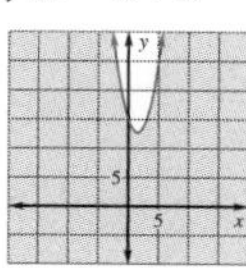

11. $y > 3x^2 - 8x$

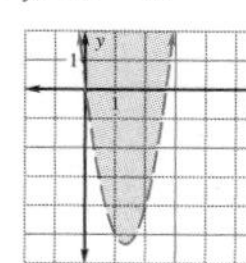

12. $y < -6x^2 + 2x + 3$

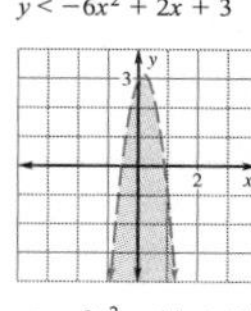

13. $y \ge 4x^2 - x - 7$

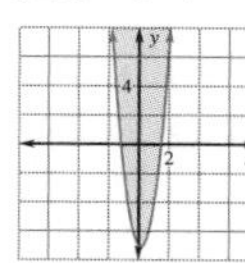

14. $y \ge x^2 + 2x - 8$

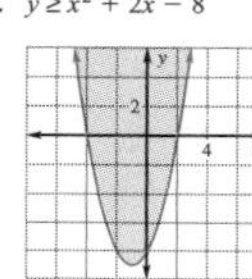

15. $y > -2x^2 - 14x + 21$

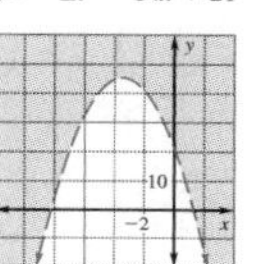

16. $y \le 5x^2 + 2x - 6$

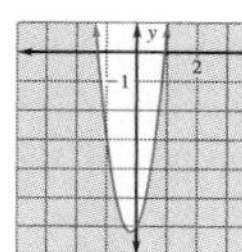

LESSON 4.9

Practice B *continued*

For use with pages 300–307

Match the system of inequalities with its graph.

17. $y > x^2 - 2x - 1$, $y < x^2 + 3x + 1$ A

18. $y \le -2x^2 - x + 2$, $y > \frac{2}{3}x^2 - 3$ C

19. $y \le 3x^2 + x + 2$, $y \ge -x^2 - 3x - 2$ B

A.

B.

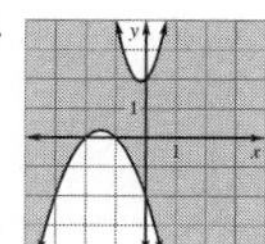

C.

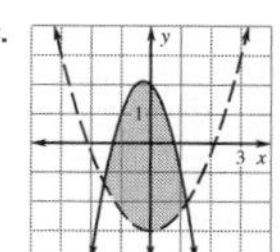

Graph the system of inequalities.

20. $y \ge x^2 + 2x - 3$, $y < -x^2 - x - 2$

21. $y \le -\frac{1}{2}x^2 + 2x + 1$, $y \le -\frac{1}{2}x^2 - 2x + 1$

22. $y < x^2 + 2x - 2$, $y < x^2 - 2x - 2$

Solve the inequality algebraically.

23. $x^2 + x - 12 > 0$ $x < -4$ or $x > 3$

24. $x^2 - 3x - 18 \le 0$ $-3 \le x \le 6$

25. $2x^2 + 13x + 6 < 0$ $-6 < x < -\frac{1}{2}$

In Exercises 26–28, use the following information.

Football The path of a football kicked from the ground can be modeled by $h = -0.02x^2 + 1.2x$ where h is the height (in yards) and x is the horizontal distance (in yards) from where the ball is kicked. The crossbar on a field goal post is 10 feet above the ground.

26. Write an inequality to find the values of x where the ball is high enough to go over the crossbar. $-0.02x^2 + 1.2x > \frac{10}{3}$

27. Solve the inequality. $2.92 < x < 57.08$

28. A player attempts to kick a field goal from 52 yards away. Will the ball have enough height to go over the crossbar from this distance? yes

LESSON 4.10

Practice B

For use with pages 309–315

4. $y = (x + 4)^2 - 2$ **5.** $y = \frac{1}{2}(x - 3)^2 - 2$ **6.** $y = 2(x - 4)^2 - 5$
7. $y = (x - 3)(x - 2)$ **8.** $y = (x + 4)(x - 1)$ **9.** $y = (x + 5)(x - 5)$

Write a quadratic function in vertex form whose graph has the given vertex and passes through the given point.

1. vertex: (0, 0) point: (2, 4) $y = x^2$

2. vertex: (2, 1) point: (4, 5) $y = (x - 2)^2 + 1$

3. vertex: (2, −4) point: (0, 0) $y = (x - 2)^2 - 4$

4. vertex: (−4, −2) See above. point: (−3, −1)

5. vertex: (3, −2) See above. point: (7, 6)

6. vertex: (4, −5) See above. point: (1, 13)

Write a quadratic function in intercept form whose graph has the given x-intercepts and passes through the given point.

7. x-intercepts: 2, 3 See above. point: (4, 2)

8. x-intercepts: −4, 1 point: (−3, −4) See above.

9. x-intercepts: −5, 5 See above. point: (6, 11)

10. x-intercepts: −7, −2 point: (−5, −6) $y = (x + 7)(x + 2)$

11. x-intercepts: 0, 4 point: (−1, 20) $y = 4x(x - 4)$

12. x-intercepts: −3, −2 point: (−4, −6) $y = -3(x + 2)(x + 3)$

Write a quadratic function in standard form whose graph passes through the given points.

13. (1, −2), (−2, 1), (3, 6) $y = x^2 - 3$

14. (2, 6), (−2, −2), (1, 1) $y = x^2 + 2x - 2$

15. (−2, 7), (−1, 3), (3, 7) $y = x^2 - x + 1$

16. (1, 0), (2, 4), (0, 2) $y = 3x^2 - 5x + 2$

17. (2, −4), (3, −7), (1, −3) $y = -x^2 + 2x - 4$

18. (−1, −2), (1, −4), (2, 1) $y = 2x^2 - x - 5$

In Exercises 19 and 20, use the following information.

Population Model The following table shows the population of a town from 1996 to 2004. Assume that t is the number of years since 1996 and P is measured in thousands of people.

Year, t	0	1	2	3	4	5	6	7	8
Population, P	22.8	25.0	26.5	27.1	27.8	28.1	27.9	26.9	26.1

19. Use a graphing calculator to find the best-fitting quadratic model for the data. $P = -0.2t^2 + 2.1t + 23$

20. Using the model, what is the population in 2007? 21,900

In Exercises 21 and 22, use the following information.

Operating Costs The following table shows the operating costs of a small business from 2000 to 2005. Assume that t is the number of years since 2000 and C is the cost in thousands of dollars.

Year, t	0	1	2	3	4	5
Operating costs, C	2.3	2.6	3.1	3.3	4.0	5.2

$C = 0.09t^2 + 0.07t + 2.4$

21. Use a graphing calculator to find the best-fitting quadratic model for the data.

22. Using the model, how much are the operating costs in 2008? $8720

CHAPTER 4 Quiz 1
For use after Lessons 4.1–4.4

Graph the function. Label the vertex and axis of symmetry.

1. $y = x^2 - 6x + 7$

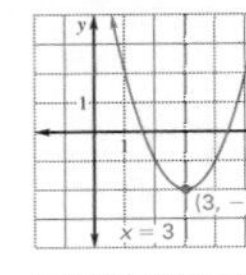

2. $y = 2(x - 1)^2 - 4$

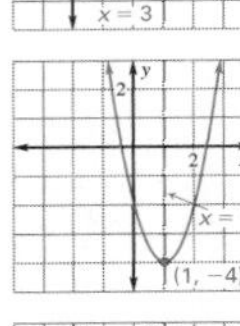

3. $y = -2(x - 4)(x - 2)$

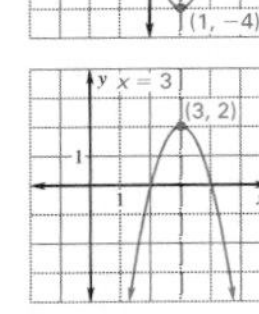

Write the quadratic function in standard form.

4. $y = -2(x - 9)(x + 7)$
5. $y = -4(x + 6)(x - 8)$
6. $y = 3(x - 4)^2 - 8$

Solve the equation.

7. $x^2 + 13x + 36 = 0$
8. $z^2 - 9z + 14 = 0$
9. $3a^2 + 5a - 28 = 0$

10. **Picture Frame** You have a picture that is 5 inches by 7 inches. You want to make a frame for the picture that is of uniform width. Together, the picture and the frame, have an area of 99 inches. What should the width of the frame be?

Answers

1. See left.
2. See left.
3. See left.
4. $y = -2x^2 + 4x + 126$
5. $y = -4x^2 + 8x + 192$
6. $y = 3x^2 - 24x + 40$
7. $-9, -4$
8. $2, 7$
9. $-4, \frac{7}{3}$
10. 2 in.

CHAPTER 4 Quiz 2
For use after lessons 4.5–4.7

Solve the equation.

1. $9x^2 = 36$
2. $5(r - 2)^2 = 35$
3. $-4(k - 8)^2 = 16$

Write the expression as a complex number in standard form.

4. $(7 - 4i) + (8 + 6i)$
5. $(-2 + 15i) - (8 - 3i)$
6. $(5 - i)(9 + 3i)$
7. $\frac{6i}{1 - 2i}$

Write the quadratic function in vertex form. Then, identify the vertex.

8. $x^2 - 16x + 56 = 0$
9. $x^2 - 8x + 11 = 0$
10. Solve $x^2 - 6x + 5 = 0$ by completing the square.
11. **Playground** The area of the playground shown is 96 square units. Complete the square to find the value of x.

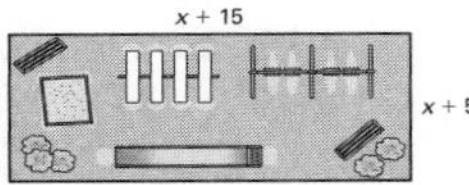

Answers

1. $2, -2$
2. $2 \pm \sqrt{7}$
3. $8 \pm 2i$
4. $15 + 2i$
5. $-10 + 18i$
6. $48 + 6i$
7. $\frac{-12}{5} + \frac{6}{5}i$
8. $y = (x - 8)^2 - 8$; $(8, -8)$
9. $y = (x - 4)^2 - 5$; $(4, -5)$
10. $1, 5$
11. 1 unit

CHAPTER 4 Quiz 3
For use after Lessons 4.8–4.10

Use the quadratic formula to solve the equation.

1. $x^2 - 10x + 25 = 0$
2. $x^2 + 9x - 10 = 0$
3. $2x^2 + 6x + 5 = 0$

Graph the inequality.

4. $y > 7x^2$

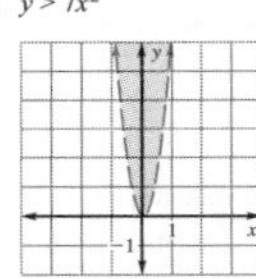

5. $y \le -x^2 + 4x$

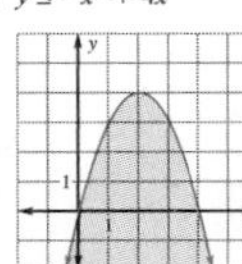

6. $y < x^2 - 4x + 9$

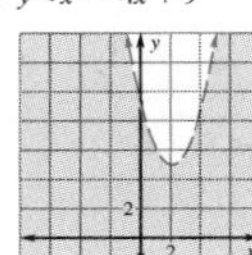

Solve the inequality.

7. $x^2 - 4 \le 0$
8. $x^2 - 10 > -9$

Write a quadratic function whose graph has the given characteristics.

9. vertex: (6, 10)
   point on graph: (5, 8)
10. x-intercepts: $-3, 2$
    point on graph: (11, 63)

Answers

1. 5
2. $-10, 1$
3. $-\frac{3}{2} \pm \frac{1}{2}i$
4. See left.
5. See left.
6. See left.
7. $-2 \le x \le 2$
8. $x < -1$ or $x > 1$
9. $y = -2(x - 6)^2 + 10$
10. $y = \frac{1}{2}(x + 3)(x - 2)$

CHAPTER 4 Chapter Test B
For use after Chapter 4

Graph the function. Label the vertex and the axis of symmetry.

1. $y = -2x^2$

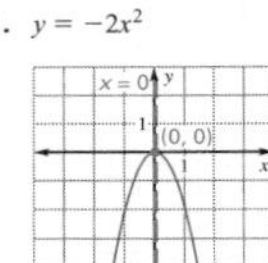

2. $g(x) = \frac{3}{4}x^2 + 3x + \frac{9}{4}$

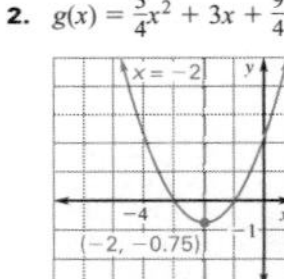

3. **Ball Height** A thrown ball hits the ground and bounces along a parabolic path given by $y = -\frac{2}{9}x^2 + \frac{52}{9}x - \frac{320}{9}$ where x is measured in feet. What is the maximum height that the ball reaches on this bounce?

Graph the function. Label the vertex and the axis of symmetry. For Exercise 5, also label the x-intercepts.

4. $y = \frac{1}{2}(x + 1)^2 - 2$

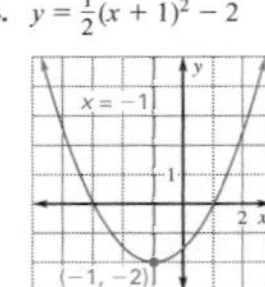

5. $y = -2(x - 1)(x - 2)$

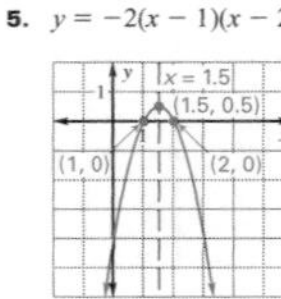

6. Tell whether $y = -3(x + 1)^2 + 4$ has a *minimum value* or a *maximum value*. Then find that value.

Factor the expression.

7. $j^2 - 3j - 10$
8. $-2x^2 + 6x + 56$
9. Solve $-3u = u^2$.
10. **Wilderness Park** A wilderness park is approximately 1 mile wide by 20 miles long. A large expansion project is underway that will give the park 6 times its current area. The same distance x will be added to the width and the length. Write and solve an equation to find the value of x. What will the dimensions of the park be after the expansion project?

Answers

1. See left.
2. See left.
3. 2 ft
4. See left.
5. See left.
6. maximum; 4
7. $(j - 5)(j + 2)$
8. $-2(x - 7)(x + 4)$
9. $-3, 0$
10. 4; 5 mi by 24 mi

CHAPTER 4

Chapter Test B *continued*

For use after Chapter 4

Find the zeros of the function by rewriting in intercept form.

11. $f(x) = 2x^2 - 4x$ **12.** $y = 2x^2 - 11x - 21$

13. Simplify $6 \cdot \sqrt{12} \cdot \sqrt{6} \cdot \sqrt{2}$.

Solve the equation.

14. $25x^2 = 16$ **15.** $x^2 - 3x + 5 = 0$

16. Write $\frac{1 - 3i}{2 + 5i}$ as a complex number in standard form.

17. Find the absolute value of $5 - 12i$.

Solve the equation by completing the square.

18. $x^2 + 9x + 9 = 0$ **19.** $3w^2 - 7w + 19 = 0$

20. Online Retailer An online retailer sells songs for $1. At this rate, they sell about 3000 songs per hour. For each $.10 decrease in price, they sell about 500 more songs. The retailer's revenue can be modeled by $R = (1 - 0.1x)(3000 + 500x)$. Use the vertex form to find how the store can maximize hourly revenue.

21. Solve $r^2 = 18 - 7r$.

22. Find the discriminant of $3p^2 - 6p + 8 = 0$ and give the number and type of solutions to the equation.

23. Graph the system.

$y \le -x^2 + 2x + 4$

$y \ge 2x^2 - 4x - 5$

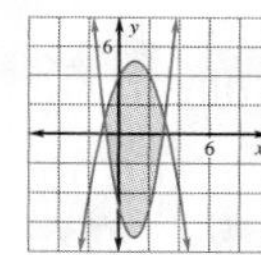

Write a quadratic function whose graph has the given characteristics.

24. vertex: $(-3, 0)$; points on graph: $(0, -9)$

25. x-intercepts: $-4, 2$; points on graph: $(5, -9)$

Answers

11. $0, 2$

12. $-\frac{3}{2}, 7$

13. 72

14. $\pm\frac{4}{5}$

15. $\frac{3}{2} \pm \frac{\sqrt{11}}{2}i$

16. $-\frac{13}{29} - \frac{11}{29}i$

17. 13

18. $-\frac{9}{2} \pm \frac{3\sqrt{5}}{2}$

19. $\frac{7}{6} \pm \frac{\sqrt{179}}{6}i$

20. $.20 price decrease maximizes revenue at $3200/h.

21. $-9, 2$

22. -60; two imaginary solutions

23. See left.

24. $y = -(x + 3)^2$

25. $y = -\frac{1}{3}x^2 - \frac{2}{3}x + \frac{8}{3}$

CHAPTER 4

Standardized Test

For use after Chapter 4

Multiple Choice

1. For the function $y = -x^2 - 6x - 7$, find the vertex and axis of symmetry. C

Ⓐ vertex $(3, -2)$; axis of symmetry $x = 3$

Ⓑ vertex $(-3, 2)$; axis of symmetry $x = 4$

Ⓒ vertex $(-3, 2)$; axis of symmetry $x = -3$

Ⓓ vertex $(3, -2)$; axis of symmetry $x = -4$

2. If the graph of $y = ax^2 + bx + c$ opens down, which of the following must be true? A

Ⓐ $a < 0$ Ⓑ $a > 0$

Ⓒ $c < 0$ Ⓓ $c > 0$

3. Which function does *not* have a maximum value? C

Ⓐ $y = -x^2 - 5x - 6$

Ⓑ $y = -x^2 - x - 6$

Ⓒ $y = 3x^2 - 15x + 2$

Ⓓ $y = 49 - x^2$

4. What is the vertex of $y = -3(x - 2)^2 - 4$? C

Ⓐ $(-2, -4)$ Ⓑ $(-2, 4)$

Ⓒ $(2, -4)$ Ⓓ $(2, 4)$

5. What are the x-intercepts of $y = -2(x - 7)(x + 2)$? B

Ⓐ -7 and 2 Ⓑ 7 and -2

Ⓒ 14 and -4 Ⓓ 14 and -2

6. Factor the expression $m^2 - 4m - 21$. B

Ⓐ $(m - 7)(m - 3)$ Ⓑ $(m - 7)(m + 3)$

Ⓒ $(m + 7)(m - 3)$ Ⓓ $(m + 7)(m + 3)$

7. Which value of c makes the expression $x^2 - 5x + c$ a perfect square trinomial? C

Ⓐ $-\frac{5}{2}$ Ⓑ $\frac{5}{2}$

Ⓒ $\frac{25}{4}$ Ⓓ 25

8. What are the roots of the equation $z^2 + 11z - 42 = 0$? B

Ⓐ $-3, -14$ Ⓑ $3, -14$

Ⓒ $-3, 14$ Ⓓ $3, 14$

9. Factor the expression $8x^2 + 28x + 12$. D

Ⓐ $2(x + 2)(4x + 3)$

Ⓑ $2(x + 3)(2x + 1)$

Ⓒ $4(x + 1)(2x + 3)$

Ⓓ $4(x + 3)(2x + 1)$

10. Simplify the expression $\frac{2}{2 + \sqrt{3}}$. C

Ⓐ $\frac{4}{13}$ Ⓑ 2

Ⓒ $4 - 2\sqrt{3}$ Ⓓ $\frac{4 - 2\sqrt{3}}{-5}$

11. What are the solutions of the equation $w^2 = -9w$? B

Ⓐ $-9, 3$ Ⓑ $0, -9$

Ⓒ $0, 9$ Ⓓ $1, 9$

12. What are the solutions of $23 = 2(x - 3)^2 + 7$? B

Ⓐ ± 3 Ⓑ $3 \pm 2\sqrt{2}$

Ⓒ $\pm 2\sqrt{2}$ Ⓓ $6 \pm 4\sqrt{2}$

13. What are the solutions of $-3 - y^2 = 24$? B

Ⓐ $\pm 3\sqrt{3}$ Ⓑ $\pm 3i\sqrt{3}$

Ⓒ $\pm 9\sqrt{3}$ Ⓓ $\pm 9i\sqrt{3}$

14. What is the standard form of the expression $\frac{i}{2 + i}$? D

Ⓐ $\frac{1}{2}i + 1$ Ⓑ $\frac{2}{3}i - 1$

Ⓒ $\frac{i}{2} + 1$ Ⓓ $\frac{2}{5}i + \frac{1}{5}$

CHAPTER 4

Standardized Test *continued*

For use after Chapter 4

15. What is the absolute value of $3 - 4i$? C

Ⓐ $\sqrt{5}$ Ⓑ $\sqrt{7}$

Ⓒ 5 Ⓓ 25

16. What is the vertex of $y = 3x^2 - 30x + 77$? D

Ⓐ $(-5, -2)$ Ⓑ $(-5, 2)$

Ⓒ $(5, -2)$ Ⓓ $(5, 2)$

17. What is the value of c if the discrimant of $-2x^2 - 3x + c$ is 41? B

Ⓐ -4 Ⓑ 4

Ⓒ $\frac{11}{2}$ Ⓓ $\frac{25}{4}$

18. Which inequality represents the graph below? A

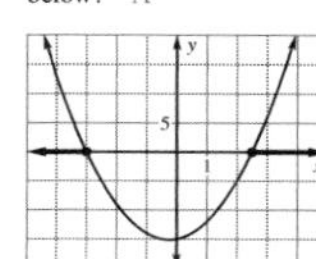

Ⓐ $2x^2 + x - 15 \ge 0$

Ⓑ $-2x^2 + x - 15 \ge 0$

Ⓒ $(2x + 5)(x + 3) \ge 0$

Ⓓ $2x^2 - x - 15 \ge 0$

Gridded Answer

19. How many real number solutions does the equation $7x^2 - 5x + 1 = 0$ have?

0

Short Response **20. a.** $y = -\frac{3}{7}(x - 7)^2 + 21$

20. A bottle rocket travels along a parabolic path and reaches a maximum height of 21 feet after traveling a horizontal distance of 7 feet.

a. Write a quadratic function of the form $y = a(x - h)^2 + k$ that models the bottle rocket's path, assuming it leaves the ground at the point $(0, 0)$. See above.

b. *Describe* how changing the values of a, h, and k affect the flight path of the bottle rocket. Answers will vary.

Extended Response

21. A rectangular garden is 25 feet long by 10 feet wide. You have enough mulch to cover 1000 square feet.

a. You would like to extend both the length and the width of the garden by x feet to use up all of the mulch. Write an equation to represent the area of the new garden. See below.

b. Solve the equation from part (a). See below.

c. Which solution do you have to reject? *Explain.* $x = -50$ because you cannot have a negative length.

21. a. $1000 = (10 + x)(25 + x)$
b. $x = 15, -50$

CHAPTER 4

Alternative Assessment and Math Journal

For use after Chapter 4

Journal **1.** Quadratic equations can have several types of solutions. For a quadratic equation in standard form, $ax^2 + bx + c = 0$, the expression $b^2 - 4ac$ (known as the discriminant), can quickly give some insight into the nature of the solution(s).

For the quadratic equation $2x^2 + bx - 3 = 0$, explain how to find a value of b where the discriminant yields a quadratic equation with the following types of solutions.

a. two imaginary solutions **b.** one real solution
c. two rational solutions **d.** two irrational solutions

Multi-Step Problem **2.** The table shows the per capita egg consumption from 1986 through 2002.

Years since 1986	0	4	8	12	16
Number of eggs	254	234	235	239	255

a. Make a scatter plot of the data.

b. Draw the parabola that you think best fits the data. Estimate the coordinates of three points on the parabola. Use the points to write a quadratic function for the data.

c. Use your function from part (b) to make a table of data for the years listed in the original table above. Compare the numbers of eggs given by your function with the numbers in the original table.

d. Use the *quadratic regression* feature of a graphing calculator to find the best-fitting quadratic model for the data.

e. Describe what the vertex of the best-fitting quadratic model from part (d) represents.

f. Critical Thinking What health-related factors may have affected the trend of egg consumption from 1986 to 2002?

g. Writing Explain why the best-fitting quadratic model from part (d) may not be a reliable predictor of egg consumption in the future. Use examples to illustrate.

1. Complete answers should include a clear explanation that in finding an expression for the discriminant of the quadratic equation $2x^2 + bx + 3 = 0$, one needs to find values of b for which the discriminant will be: **a.** negative. **b.** zero. **c.** a positive value that is a perfect square. **d.** a positive value that is not a perfect square.

2. a.

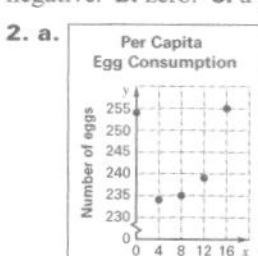

b., c. Answers will vary. **d.** $y = 0.33x^2 - 5.2x + 253$ **e.** The vertex of the best-fitting quadratic model represents when per capita egg consumption reached its minimum. **f.** *Sample answer:* The fact that eggs are a high-cholesterol food may have contributed to the decrease in egg consumption from 1986 to the mid-1990s. Similarly, the low-carb diet trend may have contributed to the recent increase in egg consumption. **g.** *Sample answer:* There are many factors that could greatly affect future egg consumption. Diet research may find that eggs contribute to or prevent certain diseases. A shortage could make the price of eggs to soar, causing people to use them sparingly.

PLAN AND PREPARE

Main Ideas

Students will learn several sets of related skills. They will learn how to graph quadratic functions written in standard form, vertex form, or intercept form, how to graph quadratic inequalities, and how to use the graph of a quadratic inequality to solve it. They will learn how to factor binomials and trinomials and learn how to solve quadratic equations by factoring, finding square roots, completing the square, and using the quadratic formula. Also, students will learn how to use properties of radicals, how to simplify radicals, and how to calculate with the imaginary unit *i* and perform operations with complex numbers.

Prerequisite Skills

- Evaluating expressions
- Graphing functions
- Solving equations

Additional resources for reviewing prerequisite skills are:

- Skills Review Handbook, pp. 975–1009
- @HomeTutor

4 Quadratic Functions and Factoring

KY

Before

In previous chapters, you learned the following skills, which you'll use in Chapter 4: evaluating expressions, graphing functions, and solving equations.

Prerequisite Skills

VOCABULARY CHECK

Copy and complete the statement.

1. The ***x*-intercept** of the line shown is _?_. 3
2. The ***y*-intercept** of the line shown is _?_. 2

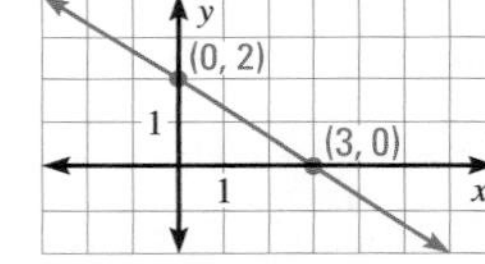

SKILLS CHECK

Evaluate the expression when $x = -3$. *(Review p. 10 for 4.1, 4.7.)*

3. $-5x^2 + 1$ −44
4. $x^2 - x - 8$ 4
5. $(x + 4)^2$ 1
6. $-3(x - 7)^2 + 2$ −298

Graph the function and label the vertex. *(Review p. 123 for 4.2.)* 7–10. See margin.

7. $y = |x| + 2$
8. $y = |x - 3|$
9. $y = -2|x|$
10. $y = |x - 5| + 4$

Solve the equation. *(Review p. 18 for 4.3, 4.4.)*

11. $x + 8 = 0$ −8
12. $3x - 5 = 0$ $1\frac{2}{3}$
13. $2x + 1 = x$ −1
14. $4(x - 3) = x + 9$ 7

Chapter Planning Guide

Chapter 4 Resource Book
- Teaching Guide/Lesson Plan (pp. 3, 17, 33, 44, 54, 65, 75, 86, 98, 114)
- Project with Rubric (p. 126)

Assessment and Intervention
- Assessment Book (pp. 46–60)
- Benchmark Tests
- Remediation Book

Interactive Technology
- Easy Planner
- Power Presentations CD-ROM
- Activity Generator CD-ROM
- Animated Algebra
- Test Generator CD-ROM
- Online Quizzes
- eWorkbook
- eEdition
- @HomeTutor

Resources for English Learners
- Quick Reference for English Learners
- Spanish Study Guide
- Multi-Language Visual Glossary
- Student Resources in Spanish

Now

In Chapter 4, you will apply the big ideas listed below and reviewed in the Chapter Summary on page 317. You will also use the key vocabulary listed below.

Big Ideas

1. **Graphing and writing quadratic functions in several forms**
2. **Solving quadratic equations using a variety of methods**
3. **Performing operations with square roots and complex numbers**

KEY VOCABULARY

- standard form of a quadratic function, *p. 236*
- parabola, *p. 236*
- vertex form, *p. 245*
- intercept form, *p. 246*
- quadratic equation, *p. 253*
- root of an equation, *p. 253*
- zero of a function, *p. 254*
- square root, *p. 266*
- complex number, *p. 276*
- imaginary number, *p. 276*
- completing the square, *p. 284*
- quadratic formula, *p. 292*
- discriminant, *p. 294*
- best-fitting quadratic model, *p. 311*

Why?

You can use quadratic functions to model the heights of projectiles. For example, the height of a baseball hit by a batter can be modeled by a quadratic function.

Animated Algebra

The animation illustrated below for Example 7 on page 287 helps you answer this question: How does changing the ball speed and hitting angle affect the maximum height of a baseball?

A quadratic function models the height of a baseball in flight.

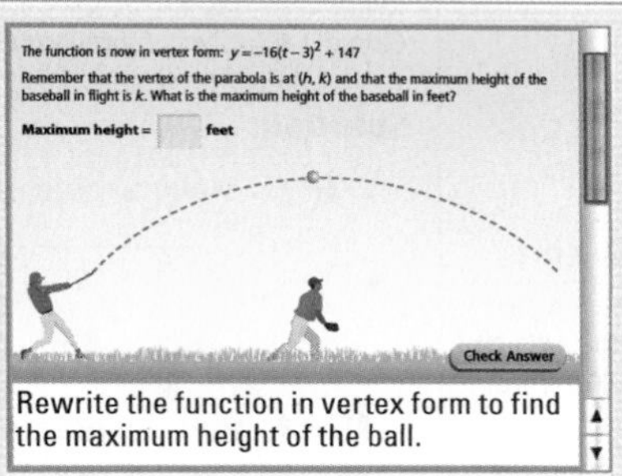

The function is now in vertex form: $y = -16(t-3)^2 + 147$
Remember that the vertex of the parabola is at (h, k) and that the maximum height of the baseball in flight is k. What is the maximum height of the baseball in feet?
Maximum height = feet
Check Answer

Rewrite the function in vertex form to find the maximum height of the ball.

Animated Algebra at classzone.com

Other animations for Chapter 4: pages 238, 247, 269, 279, 300, and 317

Algebra 2 Toolkit

- Reading Strategies for Chapter 4, pp. 15–16
- Differentiated Instruction Notes, pp. 55–58
- English Learners Notes, pp. 107–108
- Inclusion Notes, pp. 141–142
- Teaching Strategies with Sample Worksheets, pp. 163–186
- Using Technology in the Classroom, pp. 187–192
- Tips for New Teachers, pp. 199–200
- Math Background Notes, pp. 231–234
- Pre-AP Strategies and Copymasters, pp. 317–318, 365–376
- Teacher Survival Activities, pp. 475–476, 503–504
- Bulletin Board Idea, p. 528
- Teacher Tool Transparencies, following p. 538

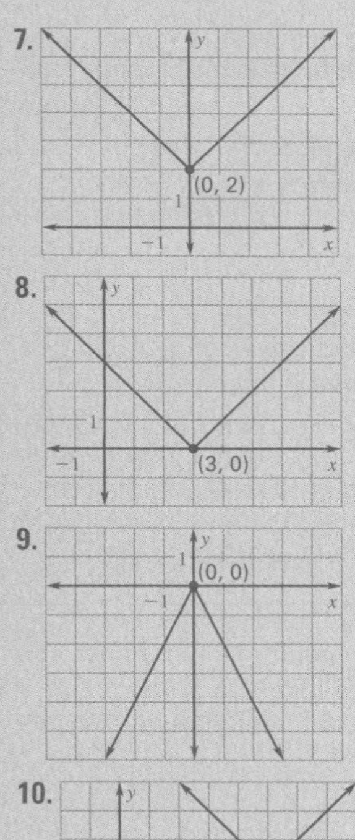

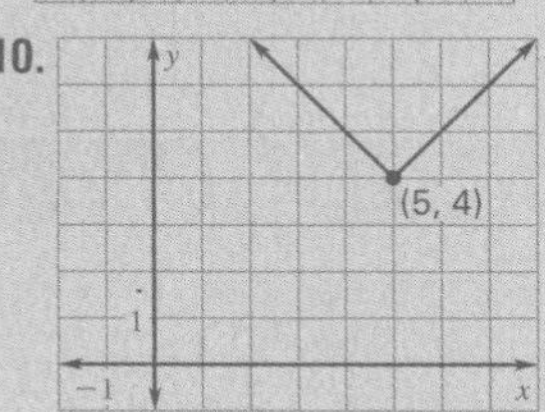

① PLAN AND PREPARE

Warm-Up Exercises

Transparency Available

Find the x-intercept and y-intercept.

1. $3x - 5y = 15$ 5; −3

2. $y = 2x + 7$ $-\frac{7}{2}$; 7

3. A ball is thrown so its height h, in feet, is given by the equation $h = -16t^2 + 10t$, where t is the time in seconds. What is the height when t is $\frac{1}{4}$ second? $1\frac{1}{2}$ ft

Notetaking Guide

Transparency Available

Promotes interactive learning and notetaking skills, pp. 92–95.

Pacing

Basic: 1 day
Average: 1 day
Advanced: 1 day
Block: 0.5 block with 4.2

- See *Teaching Guide/Lesson Plan.*

② FOCUS AND MOTIVATE

Essential Question

Big Idea 1, p. 235

How are the values of a, b, and c in the equation $y = ax^2 + bx + c$ related to the graph of a quadratic function? **Tell students they will learn how to answer this question by comparing the graphs of several functions to the graph of $y = x^2$.**

4.1 Graph Quadratic Functions in Standard Form

MA-HS-5.3.6 **Students will model, solve and graph quadratic equations in real-world and mathematical problems. DOK 2**

Before You graphed linear functions.

Now You will graph quadratic functions.

Why? So you can model sports revenue, as in Example 5.

Key Vocabulary
- **quadratic function**
- **parabola**
- **vertex**
- **axis of symmetry**
- **minimum value**
- **maximum value**

A **quadratic function** is a function that can be written in the **standard form** $y = ax^2 + bx + c$ where $a \neq 0$. The graph of a quadratic function is a **parabola**.

KEY CONCEPT *For Your Notebook*

Parent Function for Quadratic Functions

The parent function for the family of all quadratic functions is $f(x) = x^2$. The graph of $f(x) = x^2$ is the parabola shown below.

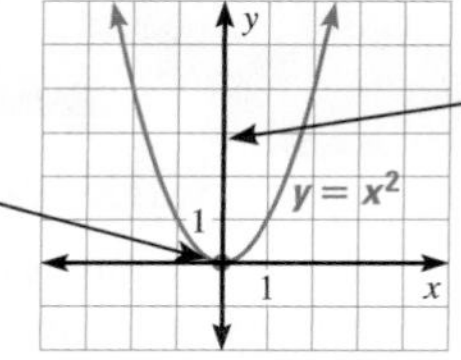

The lowest or highest point on a parabola is the vertex. The vertex for $f(x) = x^2$ is (0, 0).

The axis of symmetry divides the parabola into mirror images and passes through the vertex.

For $f(x) = x^2$, and for any quadratic function $g(x) = ax^2 + bx + c$ where $b = 0$, the vertex lies on the y-axis and the axis of symmetry is $x = 0$.

EXAMPLE 1 Graph a function of the form $y = ax^2$

Graph $y = 2x^2$. Compare the graph with the graph of $y = x^2$.

Solution

STEP 1 **Make** a table of values for $y = 2x^2$.

SKETCH A GRAPH
Choose values of x on *both* sides of the axis of symmetry $x = 0$.

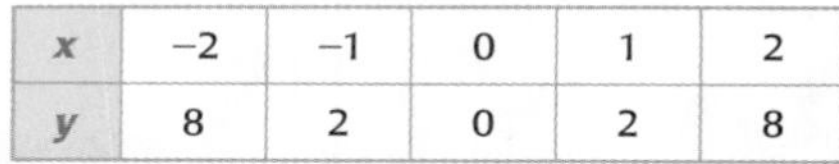

x	−2	−1	0	1	2
y	8	2	0	2	8

STEP 2 **Plot** the points from the table.

STEP 3 **Draw** a smooth curve through the points.

STEP 4 **Compare** the graphs of $y = 2x^2$ and $y = x^2$. Both open up and have the same vertex and axis of symmetry. The graph of $y = 2x^2$ is narrower than the graph of $y = x^2$.

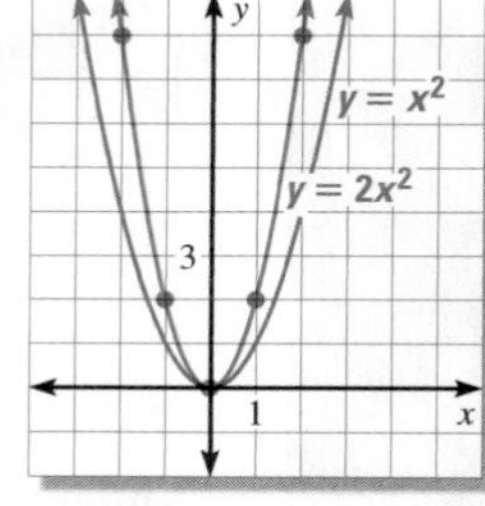

Resource Planning Guide

Chapter Resource Book
- Teaching Guide/Lesson Plan (pp. 3–4)
- Practice levels A, B, C (pp. 6–11)
- Study Guide (pp. 12–13)
- Catch-up for Absent Students (p. 14)
- Application (p. 15)
- Challenge (p. 16)

Workbooks
- Notetaking Guide (pp. 92–95)
- Practice Workbook (pp. 54–56)

Teaching Options
- **Power Presentations CD-ROM** provides dynamic electronic teaching resources for the classroom.
- **Activity Generator CD-ROM** provides editable activities for all ability levels.

Interactive Technology
- Easy Planner
- Power Presentations CD-ROM
- Activity Generator CD-ROM
- Animated Algebra
- Test Generator CD-ROM
- Online Quiz
- eWorkbook
- eEdition
- @HomeTutor

Resources for English Learners
- Quick Reference for English Learners
- Spanish Study Guide
- Multi-Language Visual Glossary
- Student Resources in Spanish

See also the *Algebra 2 Toolkit* for more strategies for meeting individual needs.

EXAMPLE 2 Graph a function of the form $y = ax^2 + c$

Graph $y = -\frac{1}{2}x^2 + 3$. Compare the graph with the graph of $y = x^2$.

Solution

STEP 1 **Make** a table of values for $y = -\frac{1}{2}x^2 + 3$.

SKETCH A GRAPH
Choose values of x that are multiples of 2 so that the values of y will be integers.

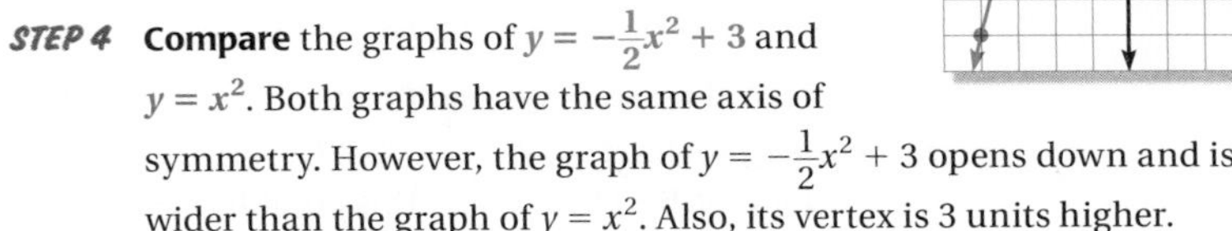

x	−4	−2	0	2	4
y	−5	1	3	1	−5

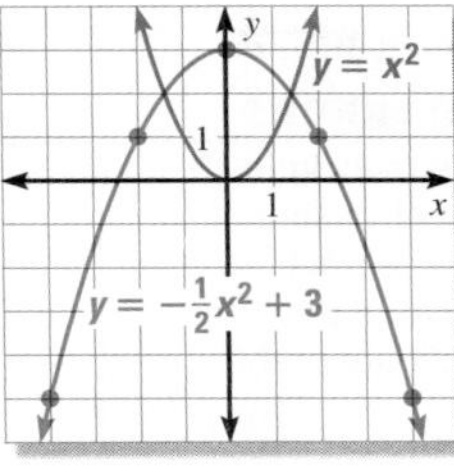

STEP 2 **Plot** the points from the table.

STEP 3 **Draw** a smooth curve through the points.

STEP 4 **Compare** the graphs of $y = -\frac{1}{2}x^2 + 3$ and $y = x^2$. Both graphs have the same axis of symmetry. However, the graph of $y = -\frac{1}{2}x^2 + 3$ opens down and is wider than the graph of $y = x^2$. Also, its vertex is 3 units higher.

✓ GUIDED PRACTICE for Examples 1 and 2

Graph the function. Compare the graph with the graph of $y = x^2$. 1–3. See margin for art.

1. $y = -4x^2$
2. $y = -x^2 - 5$
3. $f(x) = \frac{1}{4}x^2 + 2$

1. same axis of symmetry and vertex, opens down, and is narrower

2. same axis of symmetry, vertex is shifted down 5 units, and opens down

3. same axis of symmetry, vertex is shifted up 2 units, opens up, and is wider

GRAPHING ANY QUADRATIC FUNCTION You can use the following properties to graph *any* quadratic function $y = ax^2 + bx + c$, including a function where $b \neq 0$.

KEY CONCEPT *For Your Notebook*

Properties of the Graph of $y = ax^2 + bx + c$

$y = ax^2 + bx + c, a > 0$

$y = ax^2 + bx + c, a < 0$

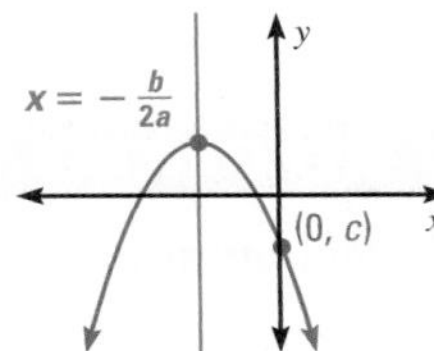

Characteristics of the graph of $y = ax^2 + bx + c$:

- The graph opens up if $a > 0$ and opens down if $a < 0$.
- The graph is narrower than the graph of $y = x^2$ if $|a| > 1$ and wider if $|a| < 1$.
- The axis of symmetry is $x = -\frac{b}{2a}$ and the vertex has x-coordinate $-\frac{b}{2a}$.
- The y-intercept is c. So, the point $(0, c)$ is on the parabola.

Motivating the Lesson

Your high school band has decided to sell band jackets as a fund raiser, and members are trying to decide how much to charge for a jacket. If the price is lowered from what was charged last year, the revenue from each jacket will decrease, but more jackets will be sold. You can use a quadratic function to find the price that will result in the maximum revenue.

3 TEACH

Extra Example 1

Graph $y = \frac{1}{2}x^2$. Compare the graph with the graph of $y = x^2$.

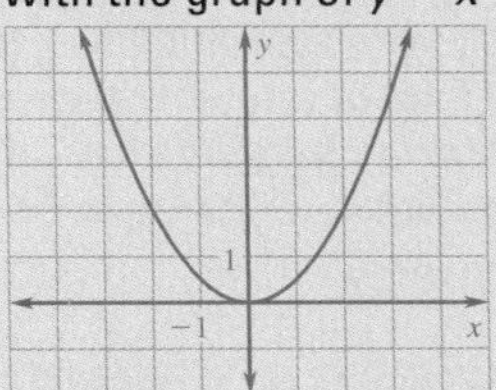

Both graphs open up and have the same vertex and axis of symmetry. The graph of $y = \frac{1}{2}x^2$ is wider than the graph of $y = x^2$.

Extra Example 2

Graph $y = -2x^2 + 4$. Compare the graph with the graph of $y = x^2$.

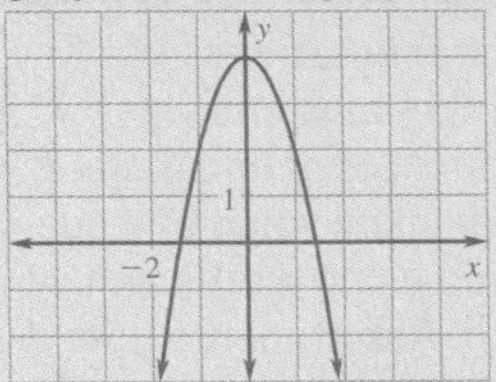

Both graphs have the same axis of symmetry. The graph of $y = -2x^2 + 4$ opens down, is narrower than the graph of $y = x^2$, and its vertex is 4 units higher.

1–3. See Additional Answers beginning on p. AA1.

Extra Example 3

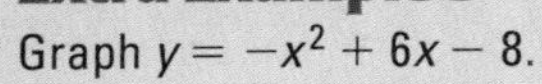

Graph $y = -x^2 + 6x - 8$.

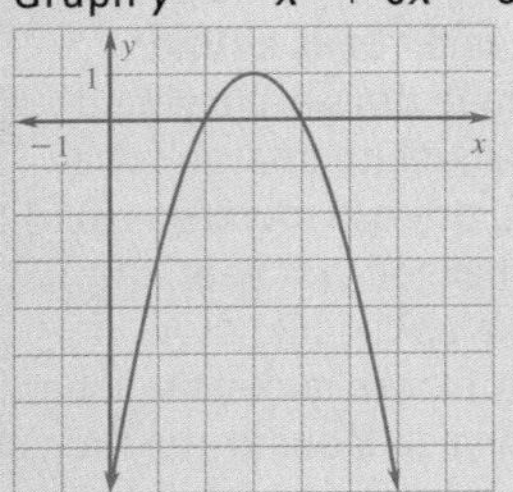

Key Questions to Ask for Example 3

- How is the vertex of a parabola related to its axis of symmetry? **The line of symmetry contains the vertex, so they have the same x-value.**
- Why is it useful to know the axis of symmetry when graphing a parabola? **Except for the vertex, each point on the parabola can be reflected in the axis of symmetry to find another point on the parabola.**

An **Animated Algebra** activity is available on-line for **Example 3**. This activity is also available on the **Power Presentations CD-ROM**.

Mathematical Reasoning

Multiple Representations The Key Concept box explains and illustrates the concepts of minimum value and maximum value of a quadratic function using words and using a graph. Ask students how they might illustrate the same concepts using a table.

Avoiding Common Errors

Some students may think that a maximum or minimum value of a quadratic function is the x-coordinate of the vertex. Make sure that they understand that it is the y-coordinate by emphasizing that they should be looking for the "top" or the "bottom" of the parabola.

EXAMPLE 3 Graph a function of the form $y = ax^2 + bx + c$

Graph $y = 2x^2 - 8x + 6$.

Solution

STEP 1 **Identify** the coefficients of the function. The coefficients are $a = 2$, $b = -8$, and $c = 6$. Because $a > 0$, the parabola opens up.

STEP 2 **Find** the vertex. Calculate the x-coordinate.

$$x = -\frac{b}{2a} = -\frac{(-8)}{2(2)} = 2$$

AVOID ERRORS
Be sure to include the negative sign before the fraction when calculating the x-coordinate of the vertex.

Then find the y-coordinate of the vertex.

$$y = 2(2)^2 - 8(2) + 6 = -2$$

So, the vertex is $(2, -2)$. Plot this point.

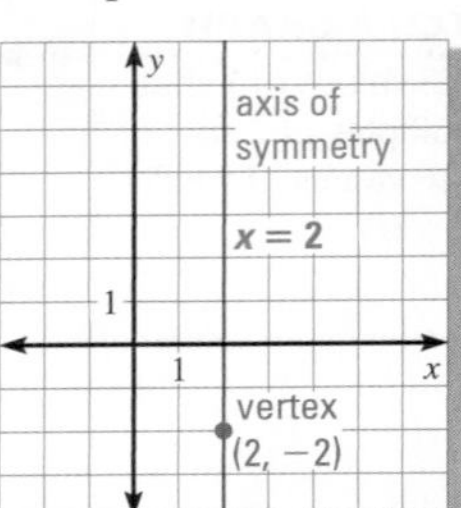

STEP 3 **Draw** the axis of symmetry $x = 2$.

STEP 4 **Identify** the y-intercept c, which is 6. Plot the point $(0, 6)$. Then reflect this point in the axis of symmetry to plot another point, $(4, 6)$.

STEP 5 **Evaluate** the function for another value of x, such as $x = 1$.

$$y = 2(1)^2 - 8(1) + 6 = 0$$

Plot the point $(1, 0)$ and its reflection $(3, 0)$ in the axis of symmetry.

STEP 6 **Draw** a parabola through the plotted points.

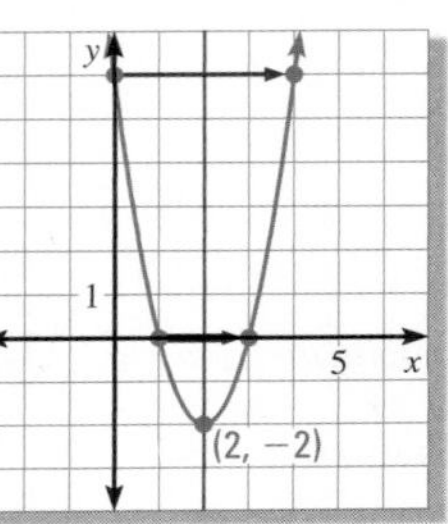

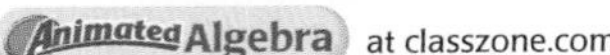

at classzone.com

✓ GUIDED PRACTICE for Example 3

Graph the function. Label the vertex and axis of symmetry. **4–6. See margin.**

4. $y = x^2 - 2x - 1$
5. $y = 2x^2 + 6x + 3$
6. $f(x) = -\frac{1}{3}x^2 - 5x + 2$

KEY CONCEPT *For Your Notebook*

Minimum and Maximum Values

Words For $y = ax^2 + bx + c$, the vertex's y-coordinate is the **minimum value** of the function if $a > 0$ and the **maximum value** if $a < 0$.

Graphs

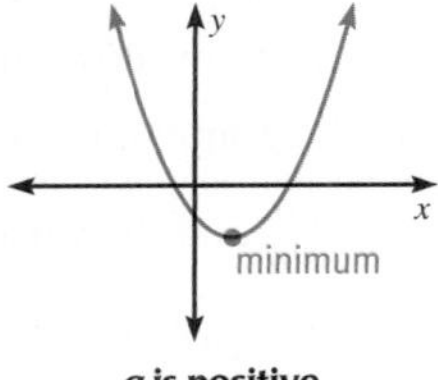

***a* is positive**

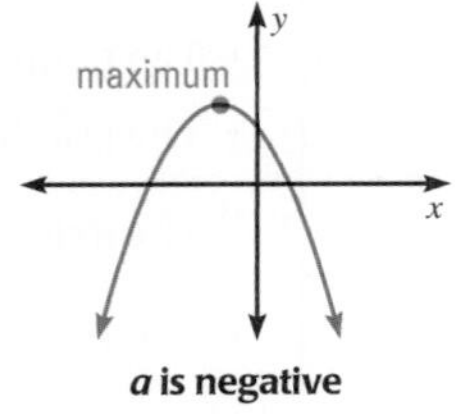

***a* is negative**

4.

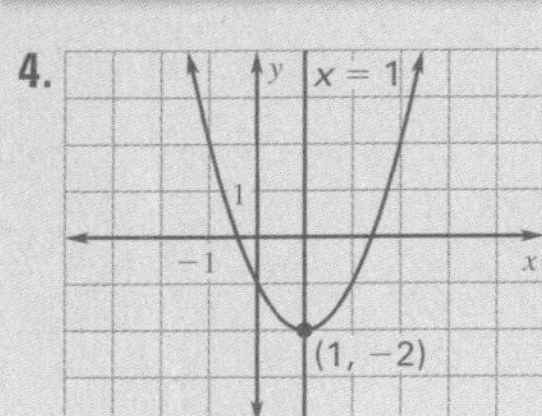

Differentiated Instruction

Visual Learners After writing a quadratic function in standard form, students may want to highlight (in different colors) the values of a, b, and c. When b is zero, students can write the function as $y = ax^2 + 0x + c$, and when c is zero, students can write the function as $y = ax^2 + bx + 0$.

See also the *Algebra 2 Toolkit* for more strategies.

EXAMPLE 4 Find the minimum or maximum value

Tell whether the function $y = 3x^2 - 18x + 20$ has a *minimum value* or a *maximum value*. Then find the minimum or maximum value.

Solution

Because $a > 0$, the function has a minimum value. To find it, calculate the coordinates of the vertex.

$$x = -\frac{b}{2a} = -\frac{(-18)}{2(3)} = 3$$

$$y = 3(3)^2 - 18(3) + 20 = -7$$

▸ The minimum value is $y = -7$. You can check the answer on a graphing calculator.

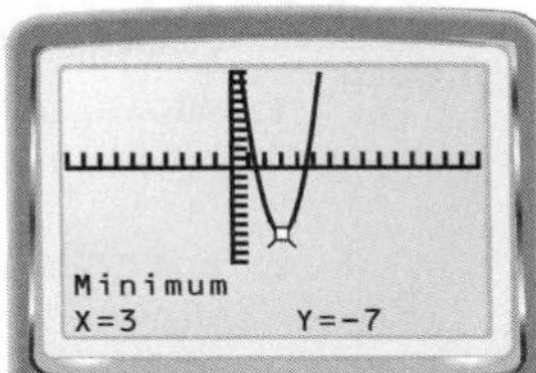

EXAMPLE 5 Solve a multi-step problem

GO-CARTS A go-cart track has about 380 racers per week and charges each racer \$35 to race. The owner estimates that there will be 20 more racers per week for every \$1 reduction in the price per racer. How can the owner of the go-cart track maximize weekly revenue?

Solution

STEP 1 **Define** the variables. Let x represent the price reduction and $R(x)$ represent the weekly revenue.

STEP 2 **Write** a verbal model. Then write and simplify a quadratic function.

Revenue (dollars)	=	Price (dollars/racer)	•	Attendance (racers)
$\mathbf{R(x)}$	=	$\mathbf{(35 - x)}$	•	$\mathbf{(380 + 20x)}$

$$R(x) = 13{,}300 + 700x - 380x - 20x^2$$

$$R(x) = -20x^2 + 320x + 13{,}300$$

INTERPRET FUNCTIONS Notice that $a = -20 < 0$, so the revenue function has a maximum value.

STEP 3 **Find** the coordinates $(x, R(x))$ of the vertex.

$$x = -\frac{b}{2a} = -\frac{320}{2(-20)} = 8 \qquad \textbf{Find } x\textbf{-coordinate.}$$

$$R(8) = -20(8)^2 + 320(8) + 13{,}300 = 14{,}580 \qquad \textbf{Evaluate } R(8).$$

▸ The vertex is (8, 14,580), which means the owner should reduce the price per racer by \$8 to increase the weekly revenue to \$14,580.

GUIDED PRACTICE for Examples 4 and 5

7. Find the minimum value of $y = 4x^2 + 16x - 3$. −19

8. **WHAT IF?** In Example 5, suppose each \$1 reduction in the price per racer brings in 40 more racers per week. How can weekly revenue be maximized?

The vertex is (2.75, 19,802.5), which means the owner should reduce the price per racer by \$2.75 to increase the weekly revenue to \$19,802.50.

Extra Example 4

Tell whether the function $y = -2x^2 + 4x + 3$ has a *minimum value* or a *maximum value*. Then find the minimum or maximum value. **The maximum value is $y = 5$.**

Key Question to Ask for Example 4

- Can a quadratic function have a maximum value AND a minimum value? Explain. **No; a parabola has only one vertex.**

Extra Example 5

A video store sells about 150 DVDs a week at a price of \$20 each. The owner estimates that for each \$1 decrease in price, about 25 more DVDs will be sold each week. How can the owner maximize weekly revenue? **The owner should reduce the price of a CD by \$7 to increase the weekly revenue from CD sales to \$4225.**

Closing the Lesson

Have students summarize the major points of the lesson and answer the Essential Question: How are the values of *a*, *b*, and *c* in the equation $y = ax^2 + bx + c$ related to the graph of a quadratic function?

- **The graph of every quadratic function is a parabola.**
- **The vertex of a parabola is the highest or lowest point on the curve. Its *y*-value gives the maximum or minimum value of the quadratic function.**

The sign of *a* is used to tell whether the parabola opens up or down. The values of *a* and *b* are used to find the equation of the axis of symmetry and the *x*-coordinate of the vertex. The value of *c* is the *y*-intercept.

5.
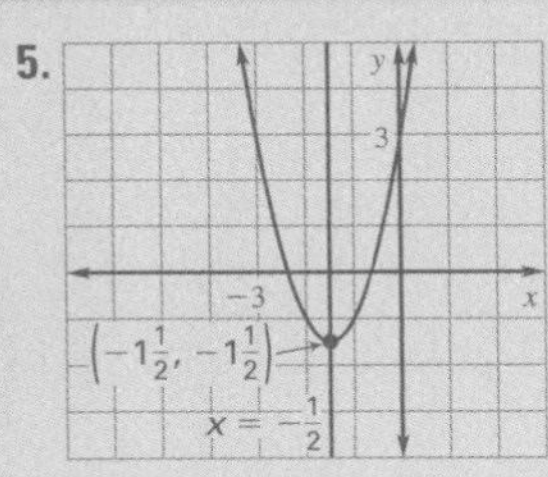

6.
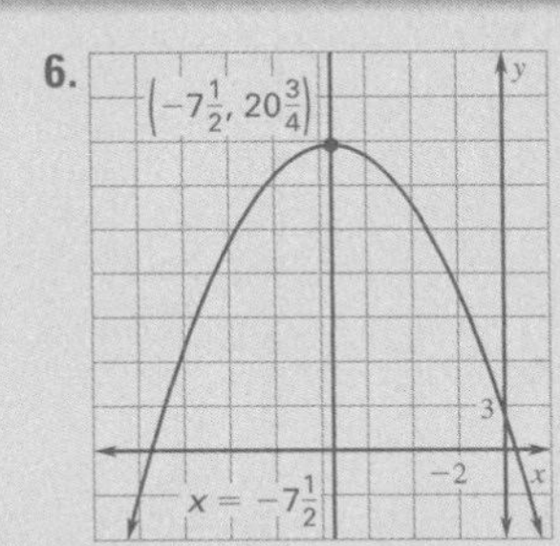

4 PRACTICE AND APPLY

Assignment Guide

Answer Transparencies available for all exercises

Basic:
Day 1: SRH p. 985 Exs. 1–6
pp. 240–243
Exs. 1–6, 7–15 odd, 19–26, 33–39 odd, 40–46, 55–59, 62

Average:
Day 1: pp. 240–243
Exs. 1, 2, 4–6, 8–18 even, 19, 20, 25–29, 34–38 even, 39–49, 56–60, 63

Advanced:
Day 1: pp. 240–243
Exs. 1, 2, 5, 6, 11, 12, 14–18, 29–32, 36–54*, 57–61*

Block:
pp. 240–243
Exs. 1, 2, 4–6, 8–18 even, 19, 20, 25–29, 34–38 even, 39–49, 56–60, 63 (with 4.2)

Differentiated Instruction

See *Algebra 2 Best Practices Toolkit* for suggestions on addressing the needs of a diverse classroom.

Homework Check

For a quick check of student understanding of key concepts, go over the following exercises:

Basic: 9, 13, 22, 34, 55
Average: 10, 16, 24, 36, 56
Advanced: 12, 18, 30, 38, 58

Extra Practice

- Student Edition, p. 1013
- Chapter 4 Resource Book: Practice levels A, B, C, pp. 6–11

Practice Worksheet

An easily-readable reduced practice page (with answers) for this lesson can be found on p. 234C.

7–18, 21–32. See Additional Answers beginning on p. AA1.

4.1 EXERCISES

HOMEWORK KEY
○ = **WORKED-OUT SOLUTIONS** on p. WS7 for Exs. 15, 37, and 57
★ = **STANDARDIZED TEST PRACTICE** Exs. 2, 39, 40, 43, 53, 58, and 60
◆ = **MULTIPLE REPRESENTATIONS** Ex. 59

SKILL PRACTICE

A

1. **VOCABULARY** Copy and complete: The graph of a quadratic function is called a(n) _?_. **parabola**

2. ★ **WRITING** *Describe* how to determine whether a quadratic function has a minimum value or a maximum value. **For the parabola $y = ax^2 + bx + c$ with $a \neq 0$, if $a < 0$ then the function has a maximum value and if $a > 0$ the function has a minimum value.**

EXAMPLE 1 on p. 236 for Exs. 3–12

USING A TABLE Copy and complete the table of values for the function.

3. $y = 4x^2$ **16, 4, 0, 4, 16**

x	−2	−1	0	1	2
y	?	?	?	?	?

4. $y = -3x^2$ **−12, −3, 0, −3, −12**

x	−2	−1	0	1	2
y	?	?	?	?	?

5. $y = \frac{1}{2}x^2$ **8, 2, 0, 2, 8**

x	−4	−2	0	2	4
y	?	?	?	?	?

6. $y = -\frac{1}{3}x^2$ **−12, −3, 0, −3, −12**

x	−6	−3	0	3	6
y	?	?	?	?	?

MAKING A GRAPH Graph the function. *Compare* the graph with the graph of $y = x^2$. **7–18. See margin.**

7. $y = 3x^2$
8. $y = 5x^2$
9. $y = -2x^2$
10. $y = -x^2$
11. $f(x) = \frac{1}{3}x^2$
12. $g(x) = -\frac{1}{4}x^2$

EXAMPLE 2 on p. 237 for Exs. 13–18

13. $y = 5x^2 + 1$
14. $y = 4x^2 + 1$
15. $f(x) = -x^2 + 2$
16. $g(x) = -2x^2 - 5$
17. $f(x) = \frac{3}{4}x^2 - 5$
18. $g(x) = -\frac{1}{5}x^2 - 2$

ERROR ANALYSIS *Describe* and correct the error in analyzing the graph of $y = 4x^2 + 24x - 7$.

19.
The x-coordinate of the vertex is:
$x = \frac{b}{2a} = \frac{24}{2(4)} = 3$

20.
The y-intercept of the graph is the value of c, which is 7.

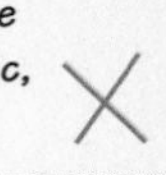

19. The formula for the x-coordinate of the vertex is $-\frac{b}{2a}$; $-\frac{24}{2(4)} = -3$.

20. $c = -7$; The y-intercept of the graph is the value of c, which is −7.

EXAMPLE 3 on p. 238 for Exs. 21–32

MAKING A GRAPH Graph the function. Label the vertex and axis of symmetry. **21–32. See margin.**

21. $y = x^2 + 2x + 1$
22. $y = 3x^2 - 6x + 4$
23. $y = -4x^2 + 8x + 2$
24. $y = -2x^2 - 6x + 3$
25. $g(x) = -x^2 - 2x - 1$
26. $f(x) = -6x^2 - 4x - 5$
27. $y = \frac{2}{3}x^2 - 3x + 6$
28. $y = -\frac{3}{4}x^2 - 4x - 1$
29. $g(x) = -\frac{3}{5}x^2 + 2x + 2$
30. $f(x) = \frac{1}{2}x^2 + x - 3$
31. $y = \frac{8}{5}x^2 - 4x + 5$
32. $y = -\frac{5}{3}x^2 - x - 4$

EXAMPLE 4
on p. 239
for Exs. 33–38

MINIMUMS OR MAXIMUMS **Tell whether the function has a *minimum value* or a *maximum value*. Then find the minimum or maximum value.**

33. $y = -6x^2 - 1$ maximum value; -1

34. $y = 9x^2 + 7$ minimum value; 7

35. $f(x) = 2x^2 + 8x + 7$ minimum value; -1

36. $g(x) = -3x^2 + 18x - 5$ maximum value; 22

37. $f(x) = \frac{3}{2}x^2 + 6x + 4$ minimum value; -2

38. $y = -\frac{1}{4}x^2 - 7x + 2$ maximum value; 51

39. ★ **MULTIPLE CHOICE** What is the effect on the graph of the function $y = x^2 + 2$ when it is changed to $y = x^2 - 3$? D

Ⓐ The graph widens. Ⓑ The graph narrows.

Ⓒ The graph opens down. Ⓓ The vertex moves down the y-axis.

40. ★ **MULTIPLE CHOICE** Which function has the widest graph? C

Ⓐ $y = 2x^2$ Ⓑ $y = x^2$ Ⓒ $y = 0.5x^2$ Ⓓ $y = -x^2$

IDENTIFYING COEFFICIENTS **In Exercises 41 and 42, identify the values of *a*, *b*, and *c* for the quadratic function.**

41. The path of a basketball thrown at an angle of 45° can be modeled by $y = -0.02x^2 + x + 6$. $a = -0.02$, $b = 1$, $c = 6$

42. The path of a shot put released at an angle of 35° can be modeled by $y = -0.01x^2 + 0.7x + 6$. $a = -0.01$, $b = 0.7$, $c = 6$

B **43.** ★ **OPEN-ENDED MATH** Write three different quadratic functions whose graphs have the line $x = 4$ as an axis of symmetry but have different y-intercepts. *Sample answer:* $y = -x^2 + 8x + 3$, $y = 2x^2 - 16x - 1$, $y = x^2 - 8x - 6$

MATCHING **In Exercises 44–46, match the equation with its graph.**

44. $y = 0.5x^2 - 2x$ C

45. $y = 0.5x^2 + 3$ A

46. $y = 0.5x^2 - 2x + 3$ B

A.
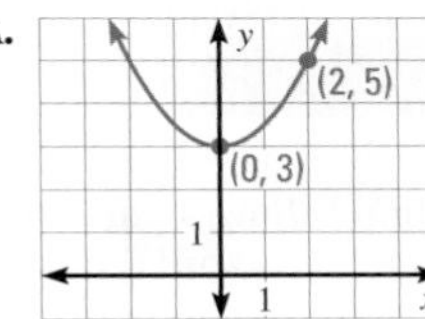

B.
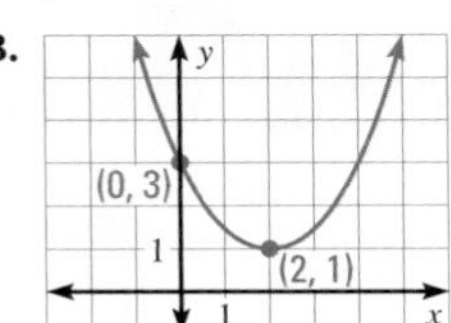

C.
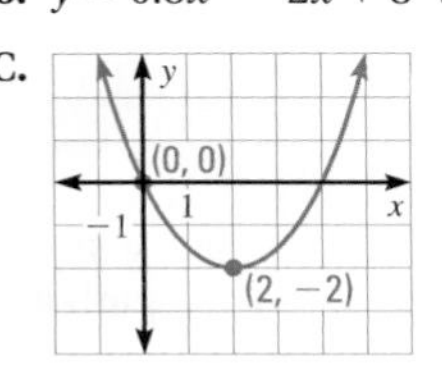

MAKING A GRAPH **Graph the function. Label the vertex and axis of symmetry.** 47–52. See margin.

47. $f(x) = 0.1x^2 + 2$

48. $g(x) = -0.5x^2 - 5$

49. $y = 0.3x^2 + 3x - 1$

50. $y = 0.25x^2 - 1.5x + 3$

51. $f(x) = 4.2x^2 + 6x - 1$

52. $g(x) = 1.75x^2 - 2.5$

C **53.** ★ **SHORT RESPONSE** The points (2, 3) and (−4, 3) lie on the graph of a quadratic function. *Explain* how these points can be used to find an equation of the axis of symmetry. Then write an equation of the axis of symmetry. The axis of symmetry has to lie half way between the two x-coordinates; $x = -1$.

54. **CHALLENGE** For the graph of $y = ax^2 + bx + c$, show that the y-coordinate of the vertex is $-\frac{b^2}{4a} + c$. See margin.

Avoiding Common Errors

Exercises 21–32 Sometimes students confuse the y-intercept with the y-coordinate of the vertex. Reinforce the idea that the y-intercept is the value of y for a point on the y-axis, while the y-value of the vertex is the y-value of a point on the axis of symmetry. Students should realize that the y-coordinate of the vertex and y-intercept will be the same only when the y-axis is the axis of symmetry, which happens when $b = 0$.

47.
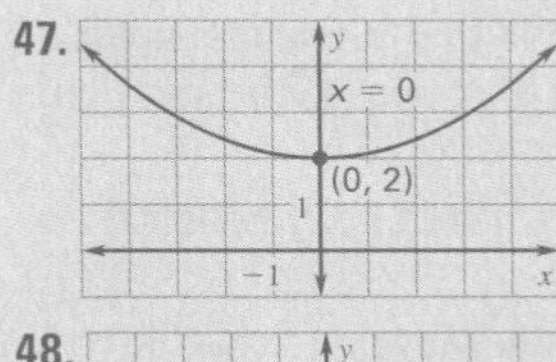

48.
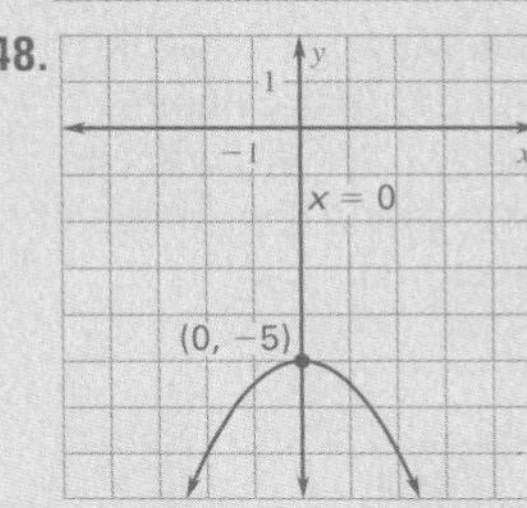

49.
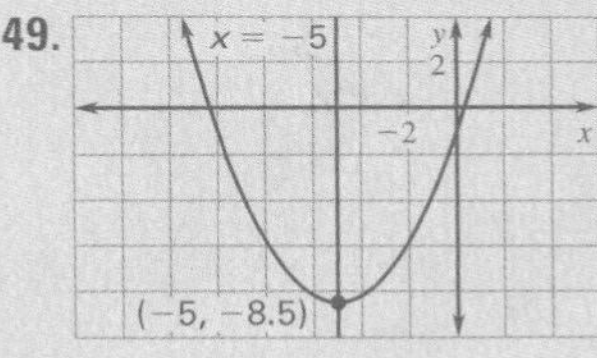

50.
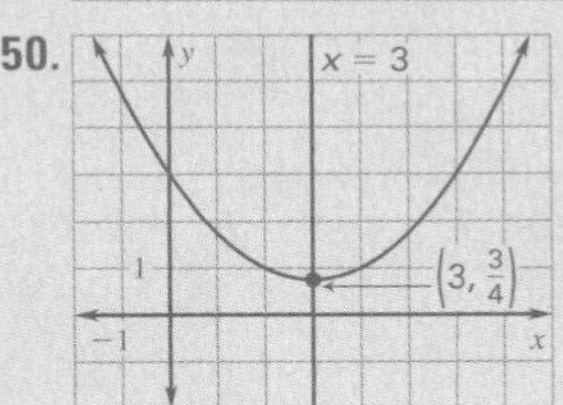

51.
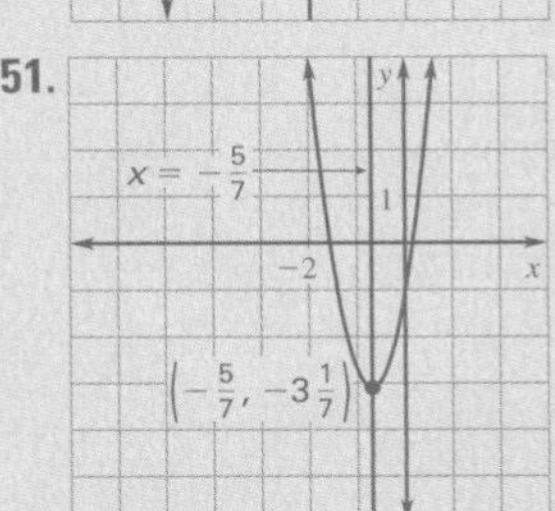

52.
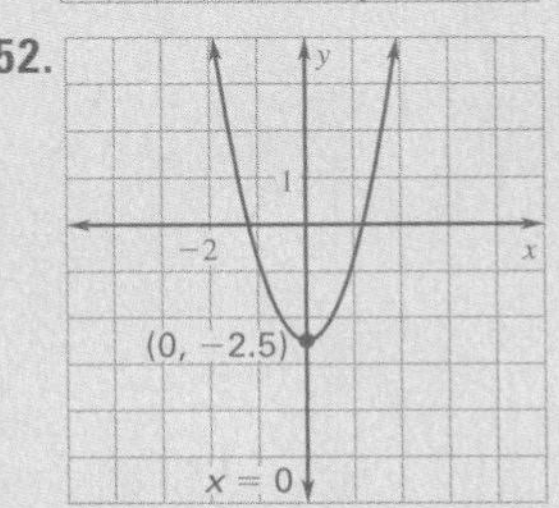

54. The y-coordinate of the vertex is obtained by substituting the x-coordinate of the vertex, $-\frac{b}{2a}$, into the equation for x. So,

$$y = a\left(-\frac{b}{2a}\right)^2 + b\left(-\frac{b}{2a}\right) + c = \frac{ab^2}{4a^2} - \frac{b^2}{2a} + c = \frac{b^2}{4a} - \frac{2b^2}{4a} + c = -\frac{b^2}{4a} + c.$$

Reading Strategy

Exercise 58 If students are having trouble knowing how to approach this problem, suggest that as they read the problem, they translate each piece of given information into a sketch showing the path of the mouse and the bridge. Ask them what would have to be true for the mouse to be able to jump over the fence, and then ask them to translate their answer into language about the maximum value of the quadratic function. Make sure that they are clear on the difference between the real-world meanings of the x- and y-values in this situation.

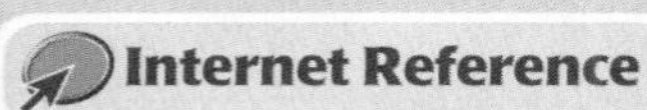

Exercise 60 More information about astronaut Alan Shepard can be found at NASA's website www.jsc.nasa.gov/Bios/htmlbios/shepard-alan.html

59b.

x	$P(x)$
0	1500
1	1540
2	1560
3	1560
4	1540
5	1500

59c.

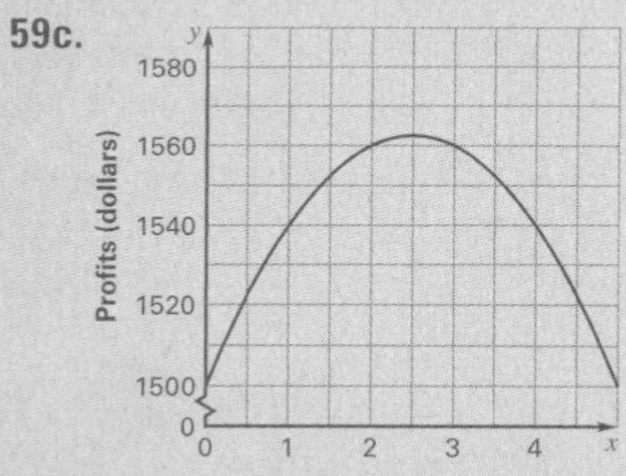

PROBLEM SOLVING

EXAMPLE 5 A on p. 239 for Exs. 55–58

55. ONLINE MUSIC An online music store sells about 4000 songs each day when it charges \$1 per song. For each \$.05 increase in price, about 80 fewer songs per day are sold. Use the verbal model and quadratic function to find how the store can maximize daily revenue. **Raise the price by \$.75 to increase revenue to \$4900 per da**

Revenue (dollars)	=	Price (dollars/song)	·	Sales (songs)
$R(x)$	=	$(1 + 0.05x)$	·	$(4000 - 80x)$

@HomeTutor for problem solving help at classzone.com

56. DIGITAL CAMERAS An electronics store sells about 70 of a new model of digital camera per month at a price of \$320 each. For each \$20 decrease in price, about 5 more cameras per month are sold. Write a function that models the situation. Then tell how the store can maximize monthly revenue from sales of the camera. **$R(x) = (320 - 20x)(70 + 5x)$; decrease the price by \$20 to maximize revenue at \$22,500 per month**

@HomeTutor for problem solving help at classzone.com

57. GOLDEN GATE BRIDGE Each cable joining the two towers on the Golden Gate Bridge can be modeled by the function

$$y = \frac{1}{9000}x^2 - \frac{7}{15}x + 500$$

where x and y are measured in feet. What is the height h above the road of a cable at its lowest point? **about 10 ft**

58. ★ **SHORT RESPONSE** A woodland jumping mouse hops along a parabolic path given by $y = -0.2x^2 + 1.3x$ where x is the mouse's horizontal position (in feet) and y is the corresponding height (in feet). Can the mouse jump over a fence that is 3 feet high? *Explain.* **No; the maximum height the mouse will jump is about 2.1 feet.**

B

59. ◆ **MULTIPLE REPRESENTATIONS** A community theater sells about 150 tickets to a play each week when it charges \$20 per ticket. For each \$1 decrease in price, about 10 more tickets per week are sold. The theater has fixed expenses of \$1500 per week.

a. Writing a Model Write a verbal model and a quadratic function to represent the theater's weekly profit. **profit = price · sales − expenses; $P(x) = (20 - x)(150 + 10x) - 1500$**

b. Making a Table Make a table of values for the quadratic function. **See margin.**

c. Drawing a Graph Use the table to graph the quadratic function. Then use the graph to find how the theater can maximize weekly profit.

59c. See margin for art; reduce the price by \$2.50 to increase profits to \$1562.50 per week.

◯ = WORKED-OUT SOLUTIONS on p. WS1 ★ = STANDARDIZED TEST PRACTICE ◆ = MULTIPLE REPRESENTATIONS

60c. The ratio of the distance traveled on the moon to the distance traveled on Earth is about 6.04 to 1. The ratio of the gravity of the moon to the gravity of Earth is about 1 to 6.04. So, as the gravity increases the distance traveled decreases proportionally.

60. ★ **EXTENDED RESPONSE** In 1971, astronaut Alan Shepard hit a golf ball on the moon. The path of a golf ball hit at an angle of 45° and with a speed of 100 feet per second can be modeled by

$$y = -\frac{g}{10{,}000}x^2 + x$$

where x is the ball's horizontal position (in feet), y is the corresponding height (in feet), and g is the acceleration due to gravity (in feet per second squared).

a. **Model** Use the information in the diagram to write functions for the paths of a golf ball hit on Earth and a golf ball hit on the moon. **Earth: $\frac{-32}{10{,}000}x^2 + x$, moon: $\frac{-5.3}{10{,}000}x^2 + x$**

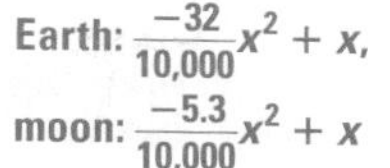

GRAPHING CALCULATOR
In part (b), use the calculator's *zero* feature to answer the questions.

b. **Graphing Calculator** Graph the functions from part (a) on a graphing calculator. How far does the golf ball travel on Earth? on the moon? **312.5 ft; about 1887 ft**

c. **Interpret** *Compare* the distances traveled by a golf ball on Earth and on the moon. Your answer should include the following: **See margin.**
- a calculation of the ratio of the distances traveled
- a discussion of how the distances and values of g are related

C 61. **CHALLENGE** Lifeguards at a beach want to rope off a rectangular swimming section. They have P feet of rope with buoys. In terms of P, what is the maximum area that the swimming section can have? $\frac{P^2}{8}$

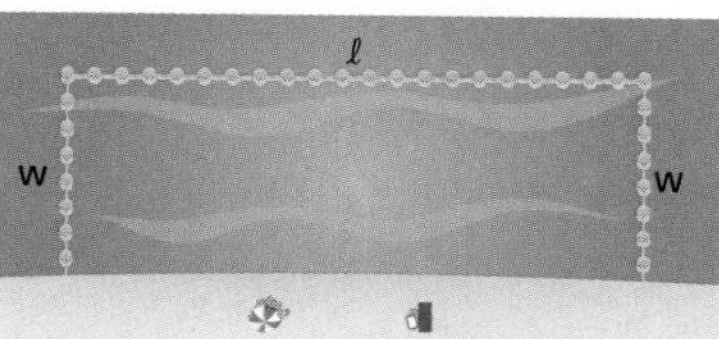

KENTUCKY MIXED REVIEW

62. Liz's high score in a video game is 1200 points less than three times her friend's high score. Let x represent her friend's high score. Which expression can be used to determine Liz's high score? **D**

(A) $1200 - 3x$ (B) $\frac{x - 1200}{3}$ (C) $\frac{x}{3} - 1200$ (D) $3x - 1200$

63. The total cost, c, of a school banquet is given by $c = 25n + 1400$, where n is the total number of students attending the banquet. The total cost of the banquet was \$9900. How many students attended the banquet? **B**

(A) 177 (B) 340 (C) 396 (D) 452

5 ASSESS AND RETEACH

Daily Homework Quiz
Transparency Available

1. Graph $y = -\frac{2}{3}x^2 + 6$. Compare it with the graph of $y = x^2$.

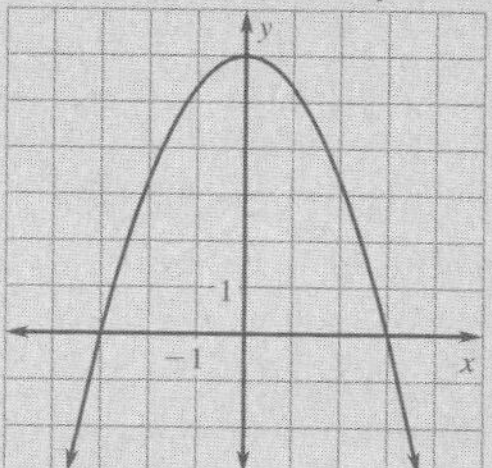

Both graphs have the same axis of symmetry. This graph opens down, is wider than the graph of $y = x^2$, and has a vertex that is 6 units higher.

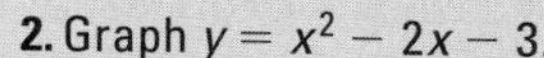

2. Graph $y = x^2 - 2x - 3$.

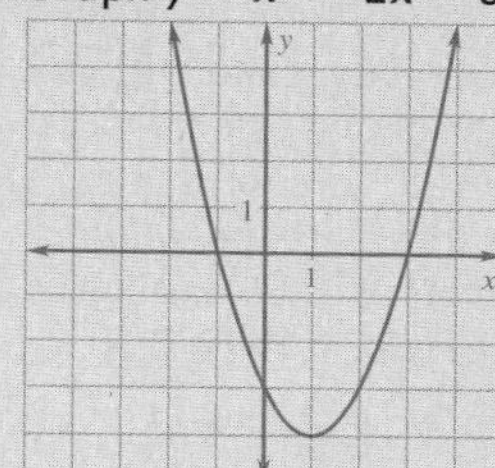

3. Tell whether the function $y = x^2 - 6x + 4$ has a *minimum* or a *maximum* value. Then find the minimum or maximum value. **minimum value, $y = -5$**

Available at **classzone.com**

Diagnosis/Remediation
- Practice A, B, C in Chapter 4 Resource Book, pp. 6–11
- Study Guide in Chapter 4 Resource Book, pp. 12–13
- Practice Workbook, pp. 54–56
- @HomeTutor

Challenge
Additional challenge is available in the Chapter 4 Resource Book, p. 16.

1 PLAN AND PREPARE

Learn the Method

- Students will learn to use a graphing calculator to find the maximum or minimum value of a function.

Keystroke Help

Keystrokes for several models of calculators are available in blackline format in the *Chapter 4 Resource Book*.

2 TEACH

Tips for Success

For the example shown on this page, students may actually get a display that shows the maximum at X = −2.499999, Y = 7.5. Explain that this is just a rounding problem and that this really means that the maximum value of $y = 7.5$ occurs when $x = -2.5$. To confirm this, have students select the *value* feature and enter −2.5 or use the *table* feature with ΔTbl = 0.5.

Alternative Strategy

Show students that they can sometimes use the *table* feature to find a maximum or minimum value. However, unless this occurs at an integral value of x, the maximum or minimum value will not show up unless the ΔTbl setting is adjusted.

Extra Example

Find the minimum value of $y = \frac{1}{2}x^2 + 6x - 4$ and the value of x where it occurs. $y = -22$ at $x = -6$

3 ASSESS AND RETEACH

Which graph has a minimum value? Which graph has a maximum value? Find the two values.
$f(x) = -x^2 + 5x - 1$ max.; 5.25
$g(x) = 2x^2 - 7x - 3$ min.; −9.125

@HomeTutor
classzone.com
Keystrokes

4.1 Find Maximum and Minimum Values

QUESTION How can you use a graphing calculator to find the maximum or minimum value of a function?

EXAMPLE Find the maximum value of a function

Find the maximum value of $y = -2x^2 - 10x - 5$ and the value of x where it occurs.

STEP 1 *Graph function*

Graph the given function and select the *maximum* feature.

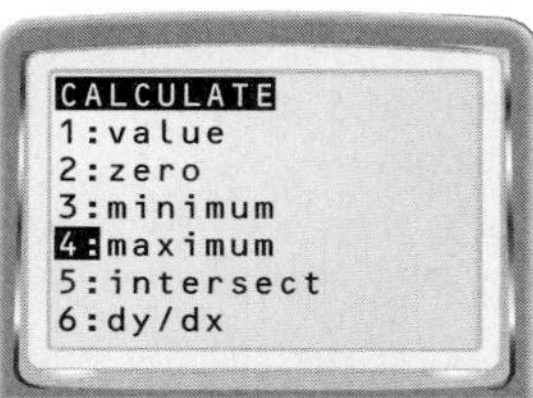

STEP 2 *Choose left bound*

Move the cursor to the left of the maximum point. Press ENTER.

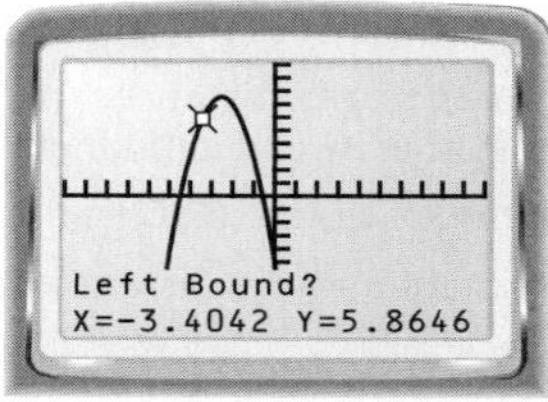

STEP 3 *Choose right bound*

Move the cursor to the right of the maximum point. Press ENTER.

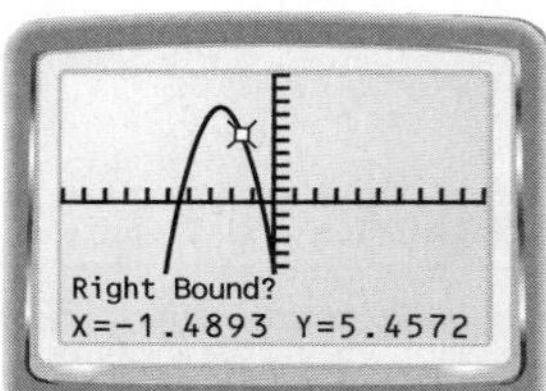

STEP 4 *Find maximum*

Put the cursor approximately on the maximum point. Press ENTER.

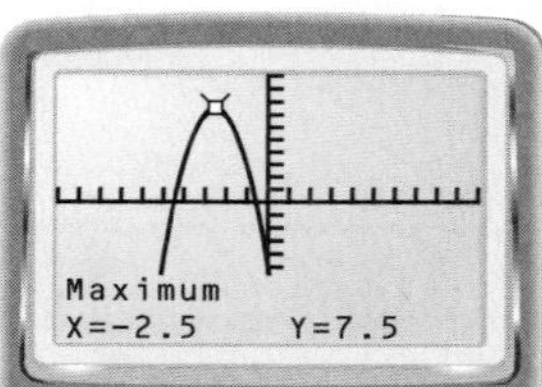

▶ The maximum value of the function is $y = 7.5$ and occurs at $x = -2.5$.

PRACTICE

Tell whether the function has a *maximum value* or a *minimum value*. Then find the maximum or minimum value and the value of x where it occurs.

1. $y = x^2 - 6x + 4$
2. $f(x) = x^2 - 3x + 3$
3. $y = -3x^2 + 9x + 2$
4. $y = 0.5x^2 + 0.8x - 2$ minimum value; −2.32 at $x = -0.8$
5. $h(x) = \frac{1}{2}x^2 - 3x + 2$ minimum value; −2.5 at $x = 3$
6. $y = -\frac{3}{8}x^2 + 6x - 5$ maximum value; 19 at $x = 8$

1. minimum value; −5 at $x = 3$
2. minimum value; 0.75 at $x = 1.5$
3. maximum value; 8.75 at $x = 1.5$

4.2 Graph Quadratic Functions in Vertex or Intercept Form

MA-HS-5.3.6 Students will model, solve and graph quadratic equations in real-world and mathematical problems. DOK 2

Before You graphed quadratic functions in standard form.

Now You will graph quadratic functions in vertex form or intercept form.

Why? So you can find the height of a jump, as in Ex. 51.

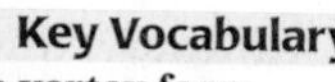

Key Vocabulary
- vertex form
- intercept form

In Lesson 4.1, you learned that the standard form of a quadratic function is $y = ax^2 + bx + c$ where $a \neq 0$. Another useful form of a quadratic function is the **vertex form**, $y = a(x - h)^2 + k$.

KEY CONCEPT *For Your Notebook*

Graph of Vertex Form $y = a(x - h)^2 + k$

The graph of $y = a(x - h)^2 + k$ is the parabola $y = ax^2$ translated horizontally h units and vertically k units.

Characteristics of the graph of $y = a(x - h)^2 + k$:

- The vertex is (h, k).
- The axis of symmetry is $x = h$.
- The graph opens up if $a > 0$ and down if $a < 0$.

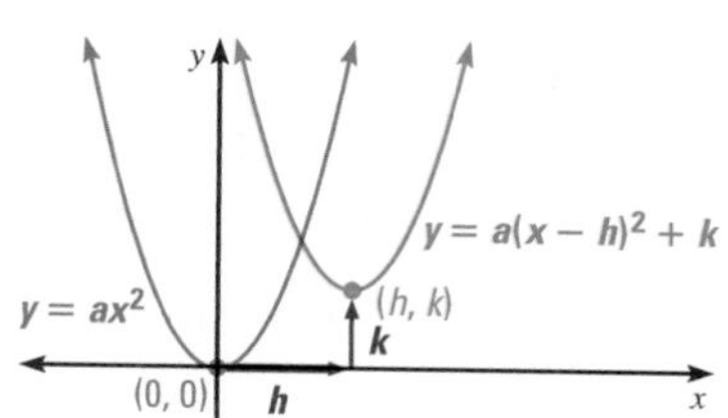

EXAMPLE 1 Graph a quadratic function in vertex form

Graph $y = -\frac{1}{4}(x + 2)^2 + 5$.

Solution

STEP 1 **Identify** the constants $a = -\frac{1}{4}$, $h = -2$, and $k = 5$. Because $a < 0$, the parabola opens down.

STEP 2 **Plot** the vertex $(h, k) = (-2, 5)$ and draw the axis of symmetry $x = -2$.

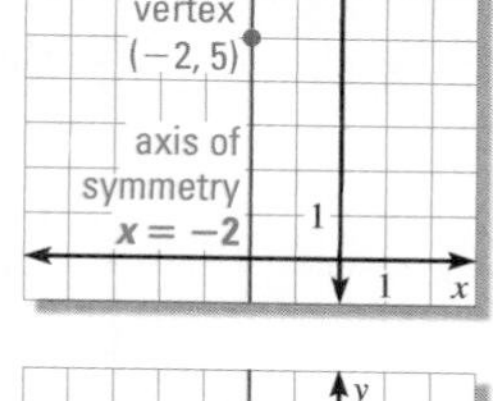

STEP 3 **Evaluate** the function for two values of x.

$$x = 0: \; y = -\frac{1}{4}(0 + 2)^2 + 5 = 4$$

$$x = 2: \; y = -\frac{1}{4}(2 + 2)^2 + 5 = 1$$

Plot the points (0, 4) and (2, 1) and their reflections in the axis of symmetry.

STEP 4 **Draw** a parabola through the plotted points.

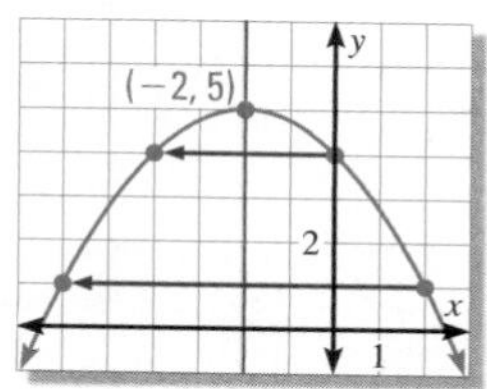

1 PLAN AND PREPARE

Warm-Up Exercises

Transparency Available

Find the product.

1. $(x + 6)(x + 3)$ $x^2 + 9x + 18$
2. $(x - 5)^2$ $x^2 - 10x + 25$
3. $4(x + 5)(x - 5)$ $4x^2 - 100$
4. A projectile, shot from the ground, reaches its highest point of 225 meters after 3.2 seconds. For how many seconds is the projectile in the air? 6.4 sec

Notetaking Guide

Transparency Available

Promotes interactive learning and notetaking skills, pp. 96–98.

Pacing

Basic: 1 day
Average: 1 day
Advanced: 1 day
Block: 0.5 block with 4.1
- See *Teaching Guide/Lesson Plan.*

2 FOCUS AND MOTIVATE

Essential Question

Big Idea 1, p. 235

To graph a quadratic function, what are the advantages in having it written in vertex form or intercept form? **Tell students they will learn how to answer this question by comparing functions written in these forms to their graphs.**

Resource Planning Guide

Chapter Resource Book
- Teaching Guide/Lesson Plan (pp. 17–18)
- Activity Master (p. 19)
- Practice levels A, B, C (pp. 22–27)
- Study Guide (pp. 28–29)
- Catch-up for Absent Students (p. 30)
- Problem Solving Workshop (p. 31)
- Challenge (p. 32)

Workbooks
- Notetaking Guide (pp. 96–98)
- Practice Workbook (pp. 57–59)

Teaching Options
- **Power Presentations CD-ROM** provides dynamic electronic teaching resources for the classroom.
- **Activity Generator CD-ROM** provides editable activities for all ability levels.

Interactive Technology
- Easy Planner
- Power Presentations CD-ROM
- Activity Generator CD-ROM
- Animated Algebra
- Test Generator CD-ROM
- Online Quiz
- eWorkbook
- eEdition
- @HomeTutor

Resources for English Learners
- Quick Reference for English Learners
- Spanish Study Guide
- Multi-Language Visual Glossary
- Student Resources in Spanish

See also the *Algebra 2 Toolkit* for more strategies for meeting individual needs.

Motivating the Lesson

You are working in a recreation program for children. You decide to see who can throw a ball the highest. If you can measure how fast the children threw the balls and the height of their hands, you can use a quadratic function to determine how high each ball went.

TEACH

Extra Example 1

Graph $y = \frac{1}{2}(x - 3)^2 - 5$.

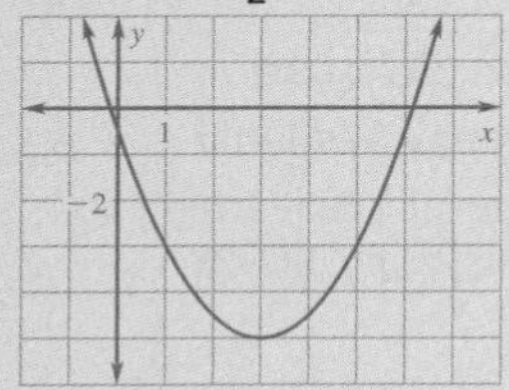

Key Question to Ask for Example 1

- When you see an equation of a quadratic function in vertex form, how do you know if the vertex is a maximum or minimum point? **If $a > 0$ the vertex is a minimum point, and if $a < 0$ the vertex is a maximum point.**

Extra Example 2

On the Tacoma Narrows Bridge, what are the minimum and maximum distances between the suspension cables and the roadway? (Use the model given in Example 2.) **27 ft; 307 ft**

1–3. See Additional Answers beginning on p. AA1.

EXAMPLE 2 Use a quadratic model in vertex form

CIVIL ENGINEERING The Tacoma Narrows Bridge in Washington has two towers that each rise 307 feet above the roadway and are connected by suspension cables as shown. Each cable can be modeled by the function

$$y = \frac{1}{7000}(x - 1400)^2 + 27$$

where x and y are measured in feet. What is the distance d between the two towers?

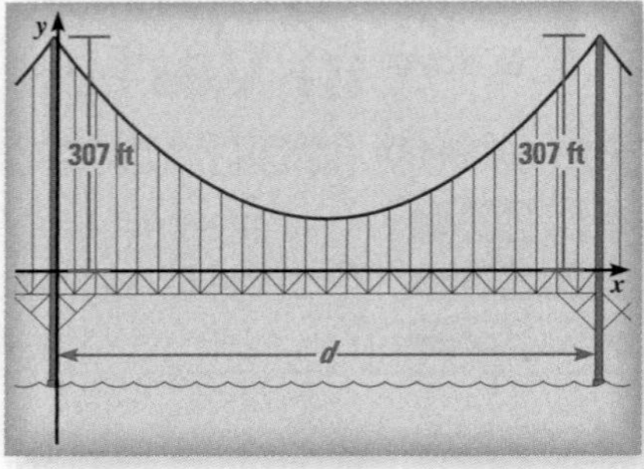

Not drawn to scale

Solution

The vertex of the parabola is (1400, 27). So, a cable's lowest point is 1400 feet from the left tower shown above. Because the heights of the two towers are the same, the symmetry of the parabola implies that the vertex is also 1400 feet from the right tower. So, the distance between the two towers is $d = 2(1400) = 2800$ feet.

GUIDED PRACTICE for Examples 1 and 2

Graph the function. Label the vertex and axis of symmetry. **1–3. See margin.**

1. $y = (x + 2)^2 - 3$
2. $y = -(x - 1)^2 + 5$
3. $f(x) = \frac{1}{2}(x - 3)^2 - 4$
4. **WHAT IF?** Suppose an architect designs a bridge with cables that can be modeled by $y = \frac{1}{6500}(x - 1400)^2 + 27$ where x and y are measured in feet. Compare this function's graph to the graph of the function in Example 2. **This graph is slightly steeper than the graph in Example 2. They both have the same vertex and axis of symmetry, and both open up.**

INTERCEPT FORM If the graph of a quadratic function has at least one x-intercept, then the function can be represented in **intercept form**, $y = a(x - p)(x - q)$.

KEY CONCEPT *For Your Notebook*

Graph of Intercept Form $y = a(x - p)(x - q)$

Characteristics of the graph of $y = a(x - p)(x - q)$:

- The x-intercepts are p and q.
- The axis of symmetry is halfway between $(p, 0)$ and $(q, 0)$. It has equation $x = \frac{p + q}{2}$.
- The graph opens up if $a > 0$ and opens down if $a < 0$.

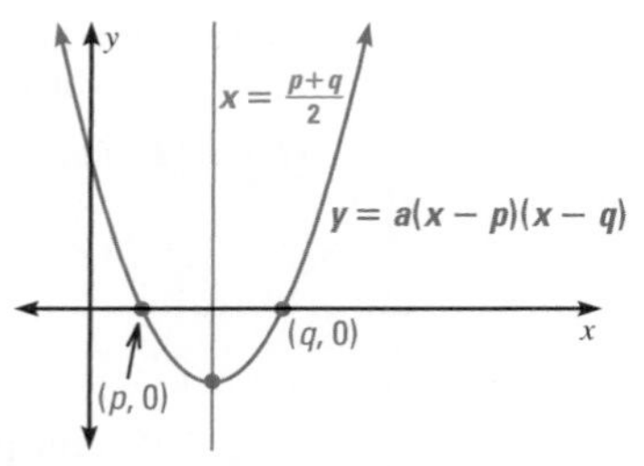

Differentiated Instruction

Inclusion Students have now been shown three forms of a quadratic function (standard form, vertex form, and intercept form), along with how to graph and identify characteristics of each. For students with memory and organizational difficulties, this can be overwhelming. Take the time to work through an example of a quadratic function using all three forms. In **Example 3**, show how the graph is the same for $y = 2x^2 + 4x - 6$ and $y = 2(x + 1)^2 - 8$.

See also the *Algebra 2 Toolkit* for more strategies.

EXAMPLE 3 Graph a quadratic function in intercept form

Graph $y = 2(x + 3)(x - 1)$.

Solution

AVOID ERRORS
Remember that the x-intercepts for a quadratic function written in the form $y = a(x - p)(x - q)$ are p and q, not $-p$ and $-q$.

STEP 1 **Identify** the x-intercepts. Because $p = -3$ and $q = 1$, the x-intercepts occur at the points $(-3, 0)$ and $(1, 0)$.

STEP 2 **Find** the coordinates of the vertex.

$$x = \frac{p + q}{2} = \frac{-3 + 1}{2} = -1$$

$$y = 2(-1 + 3)(-1 - 1) = -8$$

So, the vertex is $(-1, -8)$.

STEP 3 **Draw** a parabola through the vertex and the points where the x-intercepts occur.

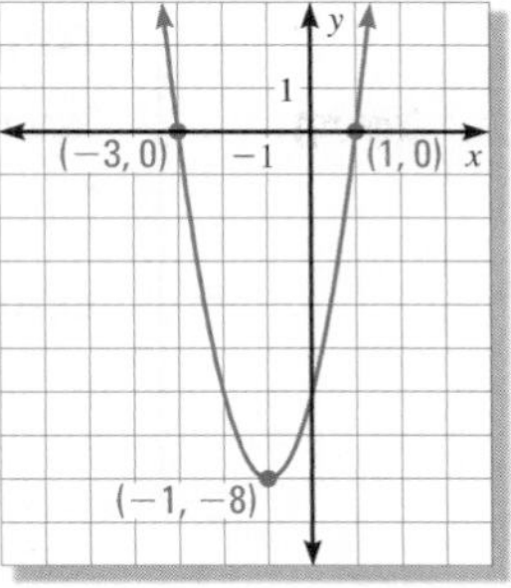

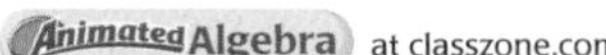 at classzone.com

EXAMPLE 4 Use a quadratic function in intercept form

FOOTBALL The path of a placekicked football can be modeled by the function $y = -0.026x(x - 46)$ where x is the horizontal distance (in yards) and y is the corresponding height (in yards).

a. How far is the football kicked?

b. What is the football's maximum height?

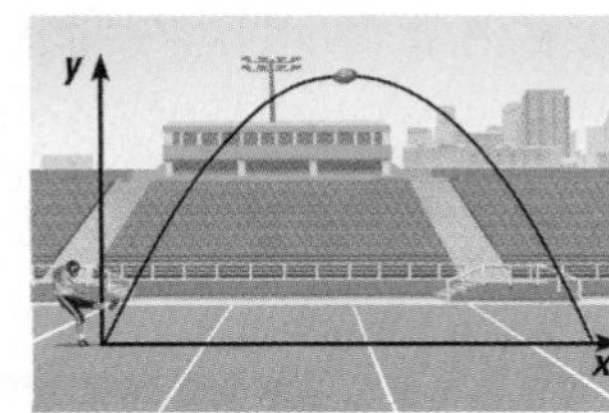

Solution

a. Rewrite the function as $y = -0.026(x - 0)(x - 46)$. Because $p = 0$ and $q = 46$, you know the x-intercepts are 0 and 46. So, you can conclude that the football is kicked a distance of 46 yards.

b. To find the football's maximum height, calculate the coordinates of the vertex.

$$x = \frac{p + q}{2} = \frac{0 + 46}{2} = 23$$

$$y = -0.026(23)(23 - 46) \approx 13.8$$

The maximum height is the y-coordinate of the vertex, or about 13.8 yards.

GUIDED PRACTICE for Examples 3 and 4

Graph the function. Label the vertex, axis of symmetry, and x-intercepts. 5–7. See margin.

5. $y = (x - 3)(x - 7)$ **6.** $f(x) = 2(x - 4)(x + 1)$ **7.** $y = -(x + 1)(x - 5)$

8. WHAT IF? In Example 4, what is the maximum height of the football if the football's path can be modeled by the function $y = -0.025x(x - 50)$? 15.625 yd

5.
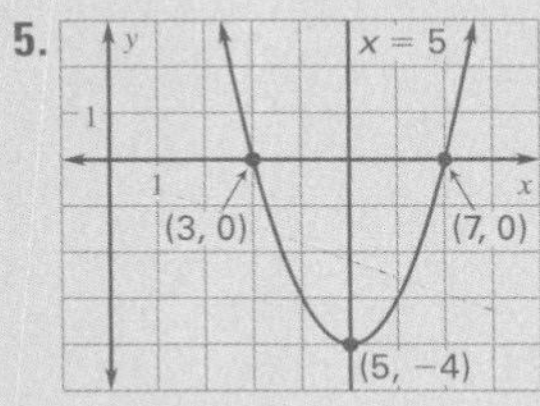

6.
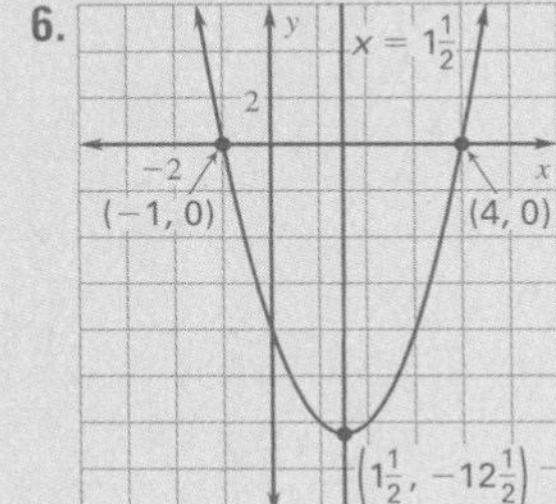

7.
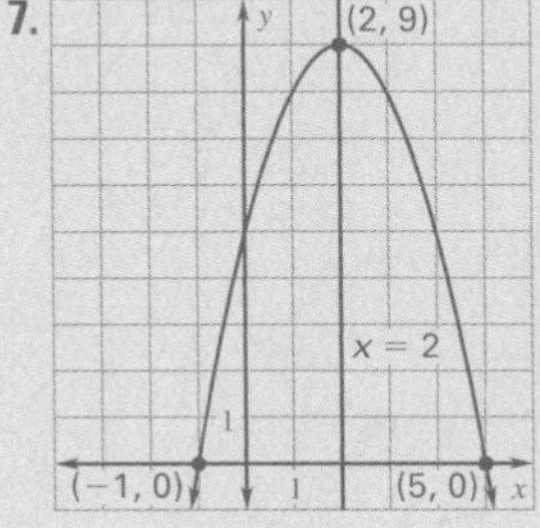

Reading Strategy

Some students may overlook the part of the sentence above the Key Concept box on page 246 that says, "If the graph of a quadratic function has at least one x-intercept, . . .". Ask students why they think this is included. Ask them to sketch some parabolas that have no x-intercepts.

Extra Example 3

Graph $y = -x(x - 4)$.

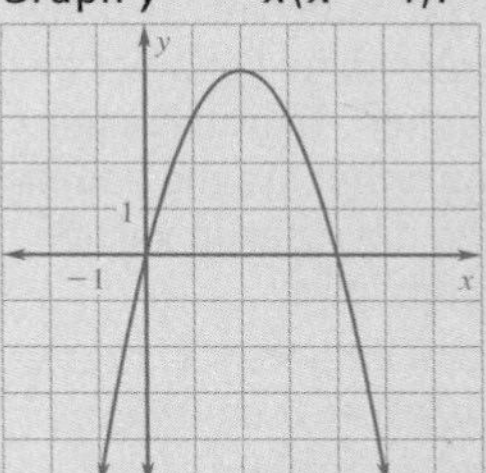

Key Question to Ask for Example 3

- When a quadratic function is written in intercept form $y = a(x - p)(x - q)$, how can you find the x-values of the intercepts and the vertex? **The x-values of the intercepts are p and q; the x-value of the vertex is $\frac{1}{2}(p + q)$.**

An **Animated Algebra** activity is available on-line for **Example 3**. This activity is also available on the **Power Presentations CD-ROM**.

Extra Example 4

If an object is propelled straight upward from Earth at an initial velocity of 80 feet per second, its height after t seconds is given by the function $h(t) = -16t(t - 5)$, where t is the time in seconds after the object is propelled and h is the object's height in feet.

a. How many seconds after it is propelled will the object hit the ground? **5 sec**

b. What is the object's maximum height? **100 ft**

Key Question to Ask for Example 4

- How can you find the x-value of the vertex? **It is the mean of the x-intercepts.**

Extra Example 5

Write $y = 3(x - 4)(x + 6)$ in standard form. $y = 3x^2 + 6x - 72$

Extra Example 6

Write $f(x) = -\frac{1}{2}(x + 8)^2 + 35$ in standard form.

$f(x) = -\frac{1}{2}x^2 - 8x + 3$

Closing the Lesson

Have students summarize the major points of the lesson and answer the Essential Question: To graph a quadratic function, what are the advantages in having it written in vertex form or intercept form?

- **You can graph a quadratic function that is written in standard, vertex, or intercept form.**
- **You can use algebra to change a quadratic function from one form to another.**

When a quadratic function is written in vertex form, you can read the coordinates of the vertex directly from the equation. When a quadratic function is written in intercept form, you can read the x-intercepts directly from the equation.

p. 249

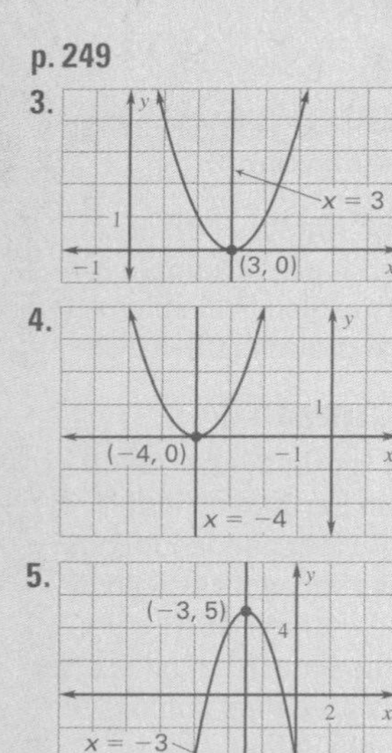

FOIL METHOD You can change quadratic functions from intercept form or vertex form to standard form by multiplying algebraic expressions. One method for multiplying two expressions each containing two terms is *FOIL.*

KEY CONCEPT *For Your Notebook*

FOIL Method

Words To multiply two expressions that each contain two terms, add the products of the First terms, the Outer terms, the Inner terms, and the Last terms.

Example F O I L

$(x + 4)(x + 7) = x^2 + 7x + 4x + \mathbf{28} = x^2 + 11x + 28$

EXAMPLE 5 Change from intercept form to standard form

REVIEW FOIL
For help with using the FOIL method, see p. 985.

Write $y = -2(x + 5)(x - 8)$ in standard form.

$y = -2(x + 5)(x - 8)$	Write original function.
$= -2(x^2 - 8x + 5x - 40)$	Multiply using FOIL.
$= -2(x^2 - 3x - 40)$	Combine like terms.
$= -2x^2 + 6x + 80$	Distributive property

EXAMPLE 6 Change from vertex form to standard form

Write $f(x) = 4(x - 1)^2 + 9$ in standard form.

$f(x) = 4(x - 1)^2 + 9$	Write original function.
$= 4(x - 1)(x - 1) + 9$	Rewrite $(x - 1)^2$.
$= 4(x^2 - x - x + 1) + 9$	Multiply using FOIL.
$= 4(x^2 - 2x + 1) + 9$	Combine like terms.
$= 4x^2 - 8x + 4 + 9$	Distributive property
$= 4x^2 - 8x + 13$	Combine like terms.

GUIDED PRACTICE for Examples 5 and 6

Write the quadratic function in standard form.

9. $y = -(x - 2)(x - 7)$ $y = -x^2 + 9x - 14$
10. $y = -4(x - 1)(x + 3)$ $y = -4x^2 - 8x + 12$
11. $f(x) = 2(x + 5)(x + 4)$ $f(x) = 2x^2 + 18x + 40$
12. $y = -7(x - 6)(x + 1)$ $y = -7x^2 + 35x + 42$
13. $y = -3(x + 5)^2 - 1$ $y = -3x^2 - 30x - 76$
14. $g(x) = 6(x - 4)^2 - 10$ $g(x) = 6x^2 - 48x + 86$
15. $f(x) = -(x + 2)^2 + 4$ $f(x) = -x^2 - 4x$
16. $y = 2(x - 3)^2 + 9$ $y = 2x^2 - 12x + 27$

p. 249

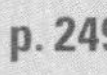

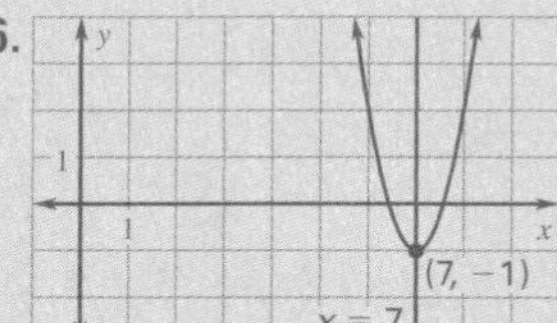

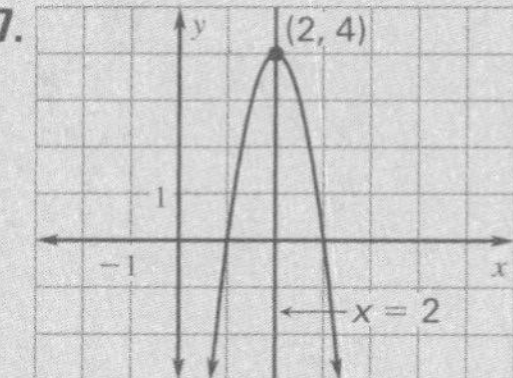

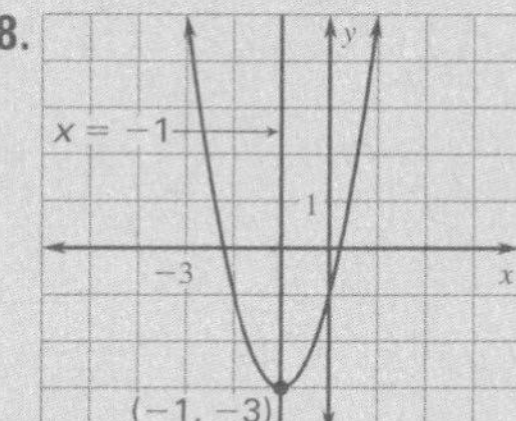

4.2 EXERCISES

HOMEWORK KEY ○ = **WORKED-OUT SOLUTIONS** on p. WS8 for Exs. 19, 29, and 53
★ = **STANDARDIZED TEST PRACTICE** Exs. 2, 12, 22, 49, 54, and 55

SKILL PRACTICE

A

1. **VOCABULARY** Copy and complete: A quadratic function in the form $y = a(x - h)^2 + k$ is in __?__ form. vertex

2. ★ **WRITING** *Explain* how to find a quadratic function's maximum value or minimum value when the function is given in intercept form.

XAMPLE 1
n p. 245
or Exs. 3–12

The maximum minimum found by bstituting the coordinate, $\frac{+q}{2}$, of the rtex into the uation for x.

GRAPHING WITH VERTEX FORM Graph the function. Label the vertex and axis of symmetry. 3–11. See margin.

3. $y = (x - 3)^2$
4. $y = (x + 4)^2$
5. $f(x) = -(x + 3)^2 + 5$
6. $y = 3(x - 7)^2 - 1$
7. $g(x) = -4(x - 2)^2 + 4$
8. $y = 2(x + 1)^2 - 3$
9. $f(x) = -2(x - 1)^2 - 5$
10. $y = -\frac{1}{4}(x + 2)^2 + 1$
11. $y = \frac{1}{2}(x - 3)^2 + 2$

12. ★ **MULTIPLE CHOICE** What is the vertex of the graph of the function $y = 3(x + 2)^2 - 5$? B

Ⓐ (2, −5) Ⓑ (−2, −5) Ⓒ (−5, 2) Ⓓ (5, −2)

XAMPLE 3
n p. 247
or Exs. 13–23

GRAPHING WITH INTERCEPT FORM Graph the function. Label the vertex, axis of symmetry, and x-intercepts. 13–21. See margin.

13. $y = (x + 3)(x - 3)$
14. $y = (x + 1)(x - 3)$
15. $y = 3(x + 2)(x + 6)$
16. $f(x) = 2(x - 5)(x - 1)$
17. $y = -(x - 4)(x + 6)$
18. $g(x) = -4(x + 3)(x + 7)$
19. $y = (x + 1)(x + 2)$
20. $f(x) = -2(x - 3)(x + 4)$
21. $y = 4(x - 7)(x + 2)$

22. ★ **MULTIPLE CHOICE** What is the vertex of the graph of the function $y = -(x - 6)(x + 4)$? A

Ⓐ (1, 25) Ⓑ (−1, 21) Ⓒ (−6, 4) Ⓓ (6, −4)

23. **ERROR ANALYSIS** *Describe* and correct the error in analyzing the graph of the function $y = 5(x - 2)(x + 3)$.
$p = 2$ and $q = -3$; the x-intercepts of the graph are 2 and −3.

The x-intercepts of the graph are −2 and 3.

XAMPLES
and 6
n p. 248
or Exs. 24–32

WRITING IN STANDARD FORM Write the quadratic function in standard form.

24. $y = (x + 4)(x + 3)$
$y = x^2 + 7x + 12$
25. $y = (x - 5)(x + 3)$
$y = x^2 - 2x - 15$
26. $h(x) = 4(x + 1)(x - 6)$
$h(x) = 4x^2 - 20x - 24$
27. $y = -3(x - 2)(x - 4)$
$y = -3x^2 + 18x - 24$
28. $f(x) = (x + 5)^2 - 2$
$f(x) = x^2 + 10x + 23$
29. $y = (x - 3)^2 + 6$
$y = x^2 - 6x + 15$
30. $g(x) = -(x + 6)^2 + 10$
$g(x) = -x^2 - 12x - 26$
31. $y = 5(x + 3)^2 - 4$
$y = 5x^2 + 30x + 41$
32. $f(x) = 12(x - 1)^2 + 4$
$f(x) = 12x^2 - 24x + 16$

MINIMUM OR MAXIMUM VALUES Find the minimum value or the maximum value of the function.

33. $y = 3(x - 3)^2 - 4$
minimum: −4
34. $g(x) = -4(x + 6)^2 - 12$
maximum: −12
35. $y = 15(x - 25)^2 + 130$
minimum: 130
36. $f(x) = 3(x + 10)(x - 8)$
minimum: −243
37. $y = -(x - 36)(x + 18)$
maximum: 729
38. $y = -12x(x - 9)$
maximum: 243
39. $y = 8x(x + 15)$
minimum: −450
40. $y = 2(x - 3)(x - 6)$
minimum: −4.5
41. $g(x) = -5(x + 9)(x - 4)$
maximum: 211.25

4 PRACTICE AND APPLY

Assignment Guide

Answer Transparencies available for all exercises

Basic:
Day 1: EP p. 1010 Exs. 10–15
pp. 249–251
Exs. 1, 2, 4–12 even, 13–21 odd, 22–29, 33–35, 42–44, 51–54, 57

Average:
Day 1: pp. 249–251
Exs. 1, 2, 3–11 odd, 12–22 even, 23, 27–29, 36–38, 42, 45–48, 51–55

Advanced:
Day 1: pp. 249–251
Exs. 1, 2, 9–12, 19–22, 30–32, 39–50*, 52–56*

Block:
pp. 249–251
Exs. 1, 2, 3–11 odd, 12–22 even, 23, 27–29, 36–38, 42, 45–48, 51–55 (with 4.1)

Differentiated Instruction

See *Algebra 2 Best Practices Toolkit* for suggestions on addressing the needs of a diverse classroom.

Homework Check

For a quick check of student understanding of key concepts, go over the following exercises:

Basic: 4, 15, 26, 51, 52
Average: 7, 18, 28, 52, 53
Advanced: 10, 20, 32, 53, 54

Extra Practice

- Student Edition, p. 1013
- Chapter 4 Resource Book: Practice levels A, B, C, pp. 22–27

Practice Worksheet

An easily-readable reduced practice page (with answers) for this lesson can be found on p. 234C.

9.

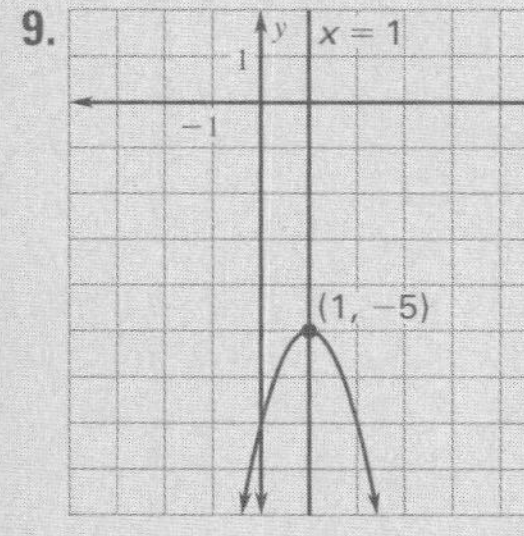

10.

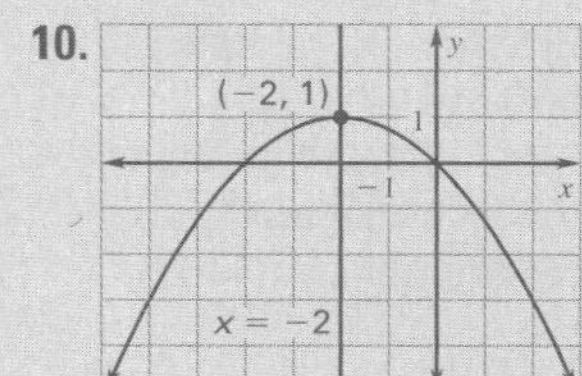

11.

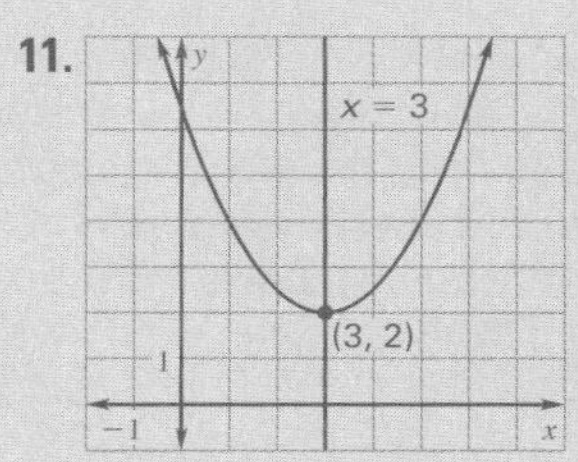

13–21. See Additional Answers beginning on p. AA1.

Avoiding Common Errors

Exercise 12 Some students may think that the vertex is (2, −5) because they see the numbers 2 and −5 in the equation. Others may think the vertex is (−2, 5) because they have picked up the "take the opposite" idea that applies to the *x*-coordinate and have incorrectly applied this to the *y*-coordinate also. Remind them that in vertex form $y = a(x - h)^2 + k$, the vertex is (h, k). So for $y = 3(x + 2)^2 - 5$, $h = -2$ and $k = -5$.

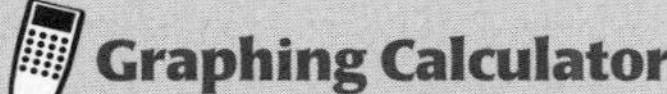

Graphing Calculator

Exercise 42 To explore the roles of *a*, *h*, and *k*, encourage students to experiment by looking at many different graphs, which can be done quickly and easily with a graphing calculator. For example, in part (b), they can try several different values of *h*, not just the value suggested in the exercise. To see the effects of changing these three variables, students should change one of them at a time, while keeping the other values fixed. Make sure that students know that when $h = 3$ they should enter (X − 3)^2, and when $h = -1$ they should enter (X − (−1))^2 or (X + 1)^2.

Internet Reference

Exercise 52 Additional information about Gateshead Millennium Bridge can be found at www.gateshead.gov.uk/bridge/background.htm

43–48. See Additional Answers beginning on p. AA1.

50. $y = a(x - h)^2 + k = a(x^2 - 2xh + h^2) + k = ax^2 - 2ahx + ah^2 + k$, $x = -\frac{b}{2a} = \frac{2ah}{2a} = h$; $y = a(x - p)(x - q) = a(x^2 - (p + q)x + pq) = ax^2 - a(p + q)x + apq$, $x = -\frac{b}{2a} = \frac{a(p + q)}{2a} = \frac{p + q}{2}$.

42a. The graph opens down and is narrower.

42b. The vertex is shifted 4 units left.

42c. The vertex is shifted 4 units up.

B

42. GRAPHING CALCULATOR Consider the function $y = a(x - h)^2 + k$ where $a = 1$, $h = 3$, and $k = -2$. Predict the effect of each change in *a*, *h*, or *k* described in parts (a)–(c). Use a graphing calculator to check your prediction by graphing the original and revised functions in the same coordinate plane.

a. *a* changes to −3 **b.** *h* changes to −1 **c.** *k* changes to 2

MAKING A GRAPH **Graph the function. Label the vertex and axis of symmetry.** 43–48. See margin.

43. $y = 5(x - 2.25)^2 - 2.75$ **44.** $g(x) = -8(x + 3.2)^2 + 6.4$ **45.** $y = -0.25(x - 5.2)^2 + 8.5$

46. $y = -\frac{2}{3}\left(x - \frac{1}{2}\right)^2 + \frac{4}{5}$ **47.** $f(x) = -\frac{3}{4}(x + 5)(x + 8)$ **48.** $g(x) = \frac{5}{2}\left(x - \frac{4}{3}\right)\left(x - \frac{2}{5}\right)$

C

49. ★ **OPEN-ENDED MATH** Write two different quadratic functions in intercept form whose graphs have axis of symmetry $x = 3$. *Sample answer:* $y = (x - 8)(x + 2)$, $y = (x - 4)(x - 2)$, $y = (x + 3)(x - 9)$

50. CHALLENGE Write $y = a(x - h)^2 + k$ and $y = a(x - p)(x - q)$ in standard form. Knowing the vertex of the graph of $y = ax^2 + bx + c$ occurs at $x = -\frac{b}{2a}$, show that the vertex of the graph of $y = a(x - h)^2 + k$ occurs at $x = h$ and that the vertex of the graph of $y = a(x - p)(x - q)$ occurs at $x = \frac{p + q}{2}$. See margin.

PROBLEM SOLVING

EXAMPLES 2 and 4 on pp. 246–247 for Exs. 51–54

A

51. BIOLOGY The function $y = -0.03(x - 14)^2 + 6$ models the jump of a red kangaroo where *x* is the horizontal distance (in feet) and *y* is the corresponding height (in feet). What is the kangaroo's maximum height? How long is the kangaroo's jump? 6 ft; about 28 ft

52. CIVIL ENGINEERING The arch of the Gateshead Millennium Bridge forms a parabola with equation $y = -0.016(x - 52.5)^2 + 45$ where *x* is the horizontal distance (in meters) from the arch's left end and *y* is the distance (in meters) from the base of the arch. What is the width of the arch? about 105 m

53. MULTI-STEP PROBLEM Although a football field appears to be flat, its surface is actually shaped like a parabola so that rain runs off to both sides. The cross section of a field with synthetic turf can be modeled by

$$y = -0.000234x(x - 160)$$

where *x* and *y* are measured in feet.

a. What is the field's width? 160 ft

b. What is the maximum height of the field's surface? about 1.5 ft

y surface of football field

x

Not drawn to scale

○ = WORKED-OUT SOLUTIONS on p. WS1 ★ = STANDARDIZED TEST PRACTICE

55c. hot-air: domain: $5.52 < x < 22.6$, range: $0 < y < 55.5$; hot oil: domain: $5.35 < x < 21.8$, range: $0 < y < 44.1$; since moisture content and popping volume cannot be negative, the domain and range must each be positive numbers. A positive domain occurs between the *x*-intercepts and the greatest number in the range occurs at the maximum point, which is the vertex.

4. *Sample answer:* The conventional spring pogo stick reaches a height of 18 inches and the bow spring pogo stick reaches a height of 42 inches; *a* and *h*.

B

54. ★ **SHORT RESPONSE** A jump on a pogo stick with a conventional spring can be modeled by $y = -0.5(x - 6)^2 + 18$, and a jump on a pogo stick with a bow spring can be modeled by $y = -1.17(x - 6)^2 + 42$, where x and y are measured in inches. *Compare* the maximum heights of the jumps on the two pogo sticks. Which constants in the functions affect the maximum heights of the jumps? Which do not?

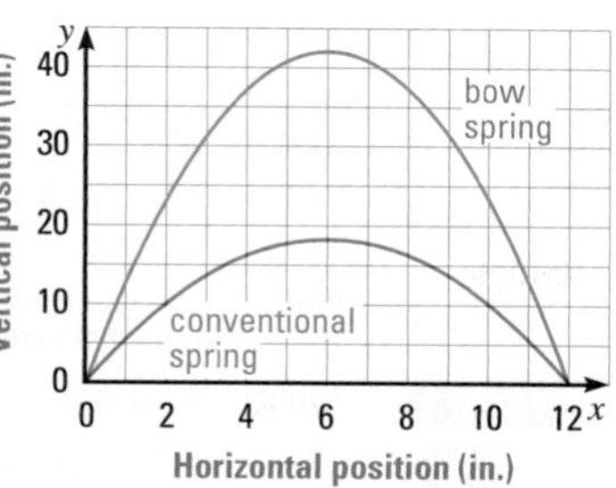

55. ★ **EXTENDED RESPONSE** A kernel of popcorn contains water that expands when the kernel is heated, causing it to pop. The equations below give the "popping volume" y (in cubic centimeters per gram) of popcorn with moisture content x (as a percent of the popcorn's weight).

Hot-air popping: $y = -0.761(x - 5.52)(x - 22.6)$

Hot-oil popping: $y = -0.652(x - 5.35)(x - 21.8)$

a. **Interpret** For hot-air popping, what moisture content maximizes popping volume? What is the maximum volume? **about 14%; about 55.5 cm^3**

b. **Interpret** For hot-oil popping, what moisture content maximizes popping volume? What is the maximum volume? **about 13.6%; about 44.1 cm^3**

c. **Graphing Calculator** Graph the functions in the same coordinate plane. What are the domain and range of each function in this situation? *Explain* how you determined the domain and range. **See margin.**

C

56. **CHALLENGE** Flying fish use their pectoral fins like airplane wings to glide through the air. Suppose a flying fish reaches a maximum height of 5 feet after flying a horizontal distance of 33 feet. Write a quadratic function $y = a(x - h)^2 + k$ that models the flight path, assuming the fish leaves the water at (0, 0). *Describe* how changing the value of a, h, or k affects the flight path. **See margin.**

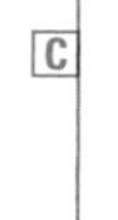

KENTUCKY MIXED REVIEW

TEST PRACTICE at classzone.com

57. A salesperson wants to analyze the time he spends driving to visit clients. In a typical week, the salesperson drives 870 miles during a period of 22 hours. His average speed is 65 miles per hour on the highway and 30 miles per hour in the city. About how many hours a week does the salesperson spend driving in the city? **D**

Ⓐ 6 h Ⓑ 8.2 h Ⓒ 13.9 h Ⓓ 16 h

58. What is the approximate area of the shaded region? **B**

Ⓐ 21.5 cm^2

Ⓑ 42.9 cm^2

Ⓒ 121.4 cm^2

Ⓓ 150 cm^2

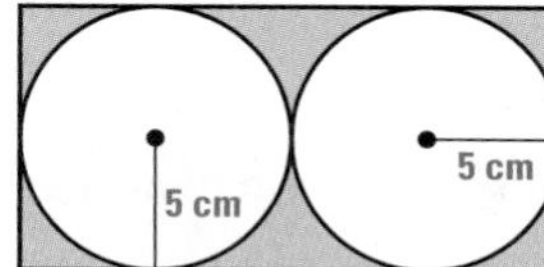

5 ASSESS AND RETEACH

Daily Homework Quiz

Transparency Available

1. Graph each function on the same coordinate plane.

a. $f(x) = -2(x + 2)^2 + 6$

b. $g(x) = \frac{1}{3}(x - 1)(x + 5)$

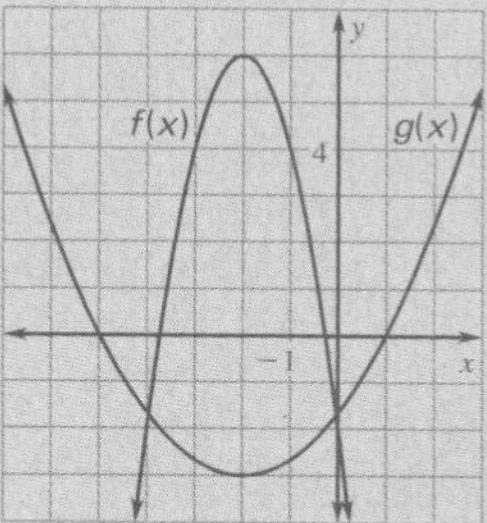

Write the quadratic function in standard form.

2. $f(x) = -4(x - 1)(x - 6)$
$f(x) = -4x^2 + 28x - 24$

3. $y = 2(x - 7)^2 - 90$
$y = 2x^2 - 28x + 8$

4. Find the maximum value of $g(x) = -2(x + 5)(x - 3)$. **32**

Available at **classzone.com**

Diagnosis/Remediation

- Practice A, B, C in Chapter 4 Resource Book, pp. 22–27
- Study Guide in Chapter 4 Resource Book, pp. 28–29
- Practice Workbook, pp. 57–59
- @HomeTutor

Challenge

Additional challenge is available in the Chapter 4 Resource Book, p. 32.

56. $y = -\frac{5}{1089}(x - 33)^2 + 5$; changing the value of *a* makes the path wider or narrower, changing the value of *h* affects the horizontal distance, and changing the value of *k* affects the vertical distance of the flight path.

4.3 Solve $x^2 + bx + c = 0$ by Factoring

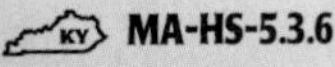

MA-HS-5.3.6 Students will model, solve and graph quadratic equations in real-world and mathematical problems. DOK 2

Before You graphed quadratic functions.

Now You will solve quadratic equations.

Why? So you can double the area of a picnic site, as in Ex. 42.

1 PLAN AND PREPARE

Warm-Up Exercises

Transparency Available

Find the product.

1. $(m - 8)(m - 9)$ $m^2 - 17m + 72$
2. $(z + 6)(z - 10)$ $z^2 - 4z - 60$
3. $(y + 20)(y - 20)$ $y^2 - 400$
4. $(d + 9)^2$ $d^2 + 18d + 81$
5. $(x - 14)^2$ $x^2 - 28x + 196$
6. A car travels at an average speed of $(m + 7)$ miles per hour for $(m + 2)$ hours. What distance does it travel? $(m^2 + 9m + 14)$ mi

Notetaking Guide

Transparency Available

Promotes interactive learning and notetaking skills, pp. 99–101.

Pacing

Basic: 1 day
Average: 1 day
Advanced: 1 day
Block: 0.5 block with 4.4
• See *Teaching Guide/Lesson Plan.*

2 FOCUS AND MOTIVATE

Essential Question

Big Idea 2, p. 235

How can factoring be used to solve quadratic equations when $a = 1$? **Tell students they will learn how to answer this question by learning how to apply the zero product property.**

Key Vocabulary
- **monomial**
- **binomial**
- **trinomial**
- **quadratic equation**
- **root of an equation**
- **zero of a function**

A **monomial** is an expression that is either a number, a variable, or the product of a number and one or more variables. A **binomial**, such as $x + 4$, is the sum of two monomials. A **trinomial**, such as $x^2 + 11x + 28$, is the sum of three monomials.

You know how to use FOIL to write $(x + 4)(x + 7)$ as $x^2 + 11x + 28$. You can use factoring to write a trinomial as a product of binomials. To factor $x^2 + bx + c$, find integers m and n such that:

$$x^2 + bx + c = (x + m)(x + n)$$
$$= x^2 + (m + n)x + mn$$

So, the *sum* of m and n must equal b and the *product* of m and n must equal c.

EXAMPLE 1 Factor trinomials of the form $x^2 + bx + c$

Factor the expression.

a. $x^2 - 9x + 20$ **b.** $x^2 + 3x - 12$

Solution

a. You want $x^2 - 9x + 20 = (x + m)(x + n)$ where $mn = 20$ and $m + n = -9$.

AVOID ERRORS
When factoring $x^2 + bx + c$ where $c > 0$, you must choose factors $x + m$ and $x + n$ such that m and n have the same sign.

Factors of 20: m, n	1, 20	−1, −20	2, 10	−2, −10	4, 5	−4, −5
Sum of factors: $m + n$	21	−21	12	−12	9	−9

▶ Notice that $m = -4$ and $n = -5$. So, $x^2 - 9x + 20 = (x - 4)(x - 5)$.

b. You want $x^2 + 3x - 12 = (x + m)(x + n)$ where $mn = -12$ and $m + n = 3$.

Factors of −12: m, n	−1, 12	1, −12	−2, 6	2, −6	−3, 4	3, −4
Sum of factors: $m + n$	11	−11	4	−4	1	−1

▶ Notice that there are no factors m and n such that $m + n = 3$. So, $x^2 + 3x - 12$ cannot be factored.

GUIDED PRACTICE for Example 1

Factor the expression. If the expression cannot be factored, say so.

1. $x^2 - 3x - 18$ $(x - 6)(x + 3)$
2. $n^2 - 3n + 9$ cannot be factored
3. $r^2 + 2r - 63$ $(r + 9)(r - 7)$

Resource Planning Guide

Chapter Resource Book
- Teaching Guide/Lesson Plan (pp. 33–34)
- Activity Master (p. 35)
- Practice levels A, B, C (pp. 36–38)
- Study Guide (pp. 39–40)
- Catch-up for Absent Students (p. 41)
- Problem Solving Workshop (p. 42)
- Challenge (p. 43)

Workbooks
- Notetaking Guide (pp. 99–101)
- Practice Workbook (pp. 60–61)

Teaching Options
- **Power Presentations CD-ROM** provides dynamic electronic teaching resources for the classroom.
- **Activity Generator CD-ROM** provides editable activities for all ability levels.

Interactive Technology
- Easy Planner
- Power Presentations CD-ROM
- Activity Generator CD-ROM
- Animated Algebra
- Test Generator CD-ROM
- Online Quiz
- eWorkbook
- eEdition
- @HomeTutor

Resources for English Learners
- Quick Reference for English Learners
- Spanish Study Guide
- Multi-Language Visual Glossary
- Student Resources in Spanish

See also the *Algebra 2 Toolkit* for more strategies for meeting individual needs.

FACTORING SPECIAL PRODUCTS Factoring quadratic expressions often involves trial and error. However, some expressions are easy to factor because they follow special patterns.

KEY CONCEPT *For Your Notebook*

Special Factoring Patterns

Pattern Name	Pattern	Example
Difference of Two Squares	$a^2 - b^2 = (a + b)(a - b)$	$x^2 - 4 = (x + 2)(x - 2)$
Perfect Square Trinomial	$a^2 + 2ab + b^2 = (a + b)^2$	$x^2 + 6x + 9 = (x + 3)^2$
	$a^2 - 2ab + b^2 = (a - b)^2$	$x^2 - 4x + 4 = (x - 2)^2$

EXAMPLE 2 Factor with special patterns

Factor the expression.

a. $x^2 - 49 = x^2 - 7^2$ — Difference of two squares
$= (x + 7)(x - 7)$

b. $d^2 + 12d + 36 = d^2 + 2(d)(6) + 6^2$ — Perfect square trinomial
$= (d + 6)^2$

c. $z^2 - 26z + 169 = z^2 - 2(z)(13) + 13^2$ — Perfect square trinomial
$= (z - 13)^2$

GUIDED PRACTICE for Example 2

Factor the expression.

4. $x^2 - 9$ $(x - 3)(x + 3)$

5. $q^2 - 100$ $(q - 10)(q + 10)$

6. $y^2 + 16y + 64$ $(y + 8)^2$

7. $w^2 - 18w + 81$ $(w - 9)^2$

SOLVING QUADRATIC EQUATIONS You can use factoring to solve certain *quadratic equations*. A **quadratic equation** in one variable can be written in the form $ax^2 + bx + c = 0$ where $a \neq 0$. This is called the **standard form** of the equation. The solutions of a quadratic equation are called the **roots** of the equation. If the left side of $ax^2 + bx + c = 0$ can be factored, then the equation can be solved using the *zero product property.*

KEY CONCEPT *For Your Notebook*

Zero Product Property

Words If the product of two expressions is zero, then one or both of the expressions equal zero.

Algebra If A and B are expressions and $AB = 0$, then $A = 0$ or $B = 0$.

Example If $(x + 5)(x + 2) = 0$, then $x + 5 = 0$ or $x + 2 = 0$. That is, $x = -5$ or $x = -2$.

Motivating the Lesson

You want to double the area of a garden in your backyard by adding the same amount to its length and width. You can figure out how to do this by writing a quadratic equation and solving it by factoring.

3 TEACH

Extra Example 1

Factor the expression.

a. $x^2 + 14x + 48$ $(x + 6)(x + 8)$

b. $x^2 - 9x - 5$ cannot be factored

Key Questions to Ask for Example 1

- If a trinomial of the form $x^2 + bx + c$ can be factored with b and c both positive, what will be the signs in the binomial factors? both positive
- If a trinomial of the form $x^2 + bx + c$ can be factored with b negative and c positive, what will be the signs in the binomial factors? both negative
- If a trinomial of the form $x^2 + bx + c$ can be factored with c negative, what will be the signs in the binomial factors? one positive, one negative

Extra Example 2

Factor the expression.

a. $m^2 - 121$ $(m + 11)(m - 11)$

b. $r^2 + 14r + 49$ $(r + 7)^2$

c. $p^2 - 24p + 144$ $(p - 12)^2$

Key Question to Ask for Example 2

- How can you recognize when a trinomial of the form $x^2 + bx + c$ is a perfect square trinomial? c is a perfect square and $|b|$ is twice the square root of c.

Differentiated Instruction

Advanced Challenge students to use properties of real numbers to prove the zero product property. If they need a hint in getting started, tell them to assume that $ab = 0$, but $a \neq 0$. By applying the multiplicative inverse, associative, and multiplicative identity properties, they should then be able to prove that under these assumptions, $b = 0$. Have these students write up their proofs carefully, showing a reason for each step.

See also the *Algebra 2 Toolkit* for more strategies.

Extra Example 3

What are the roots of the equation $x^2 - x - 42 = 0$? **B**

Ⓐ $-7, 6$ Ⓑ $-6, 7$

Ⓒ $-7, -6$ Ⓓ $6, 7$

Key Questions to Ask for Example 3

- If an equation of the form $x^2 + bx + c = 0$ with $c < 0$ can be solved by factoring, what do you know about the signs of the roots? **one positive, one negative**
- If an equation of the form $x^2 + bx + c = 0$ has only one root, what kind of trinomial is $x^2 + bx + c$? **a perfect square trinomial**

Avoiding Common Errors

When you are discussing Example 3, some students may look at the equation $(x - 9)(x + 4) = 0$ and say that the roots are -9 and 4. Emphasize that the next step after factoring the trinomial is to set each factor equal to 0 and solve each equation.

Extra Example 4

You have a rectangular vegetable garden in your backyard that measures 15 feet by 10 feet. You want to double the area of the garden by adding the same distance x to the length and width of the garden. Find the value of x and the new dimensions of the garden. **$x = 5$; 20 ft by 15 ft**

Key Question to Ask for Example 4

- In Example 4, why is the negative root of the quadratic equation rejected? **The variable x represents a length, and length cannot be negative.**

EXAMPLE 3 Standardized Test Practice

UNDERSTAND ANSWER CHOICES
Sometimes a standardized test question may ask for the *solution set* of an equation. The answer choices will be given in the format $\{a, b\}$.

What are the roots of the equation $x^2 - 5x - 36 = 0$?

Ⓐ $-4, -9$ Ⓑ $4, -9$ Ⓒ $-4, 9$ Ⓓ $4, 9$

Solution

$x^2 - 5x - 36 = 0$	**Write original equation.**
$(x - 9)(x + 4) = 0$	**Factor.**
$x - 9 = 0$ or $x + 4 = 0$	**Zero product property**
$x = 9$ or $x = -4$	**Solve for x.**

▸ The correct answer is C. Ⓐ Ⓑ Ⓒ Ⓓ

EXAMPLE 4 Use a quadratic equation as a model

NATURE PRESERVE A town has a nature preserve with a rectangular field that measures 600 meters by 400 meters. The town wants to double the area of the field by adding land as shown. Find the new dimensions of the field.

Solution

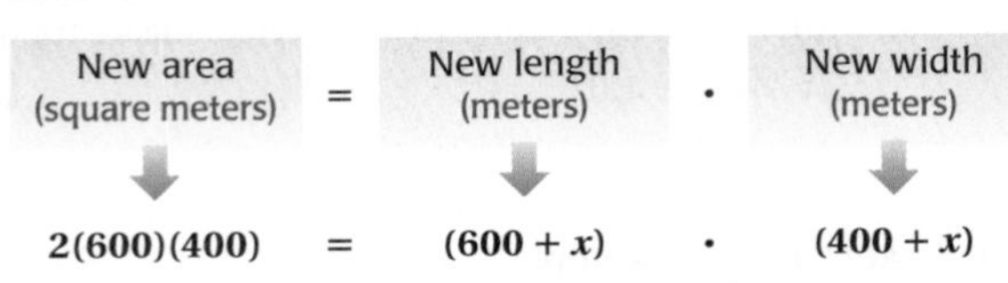

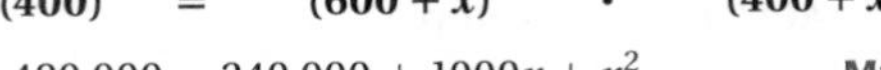

$$2(600)(400) = (600 + x) \cdot (400 + x)$$

$480{,}000 = 240{,}000 + 1000x + x^2$	**Multiply using FOIL.**
$0 = x^2 + 1000x - 240{,}000$	**Write in standard form.**
$0 = (x - 200)(x + 1200)$	**Factor.**
$x - 200 = 0$ or $x + 1200 = 0$	**Zero product property**
$x = 200$ or $x = -1200$	**Solve for x.**

▸ Reject the negative value, -1200. The field's length and width should each be increased by 200 meters. The new dimensions are 800 meters by 600 meters.

GUIDED PRACTICE for Examples 3 and 4

8. Solve the equation $x^2 - x - 42 = 0$. **$-6, 7$**

9. **WHAT IF?** In Example 4, suppose the field initially measures 1000 meters by 300 meters. Find the new dimensions of the field. **1200 m by 500 m**

ZEROS OF A FUNCTION In Lesson 4.2, you learned that the x-intercepts of the graph of $y = a(x - p)(x - q)$ are p and q. Because the function's value is zero when $x = p$ and when $x = q$, the numbers p and q are also called **zeros** of the function.

 **EXAMPLE 5** Find the zeros of quadratic functions

UNDERSTAND REPRESENTATIONS
f a real number k is
zero of the function
$= ax^2 + bx + c$, then
is an x-intercept
of this function's
graph and k is also a
root of the equation
$x^2 + bx + c = 0$.

Find the zeros of the function by rewriting the function in intercept form.

a. $y = x^2 - x - 12$ **b.** $y = x^2 + 12x + 36$

Solution

a. $y = x^2 - x - 12$ **Write original function.**

$= (x + 3)(x - 4)$ **Factor.**

The zeros of the function are -3 and 4.

CHECK Graph $y = x^2 - x - 12$. The graph passes through $(-3, 0)$ and $(4, 0)$.

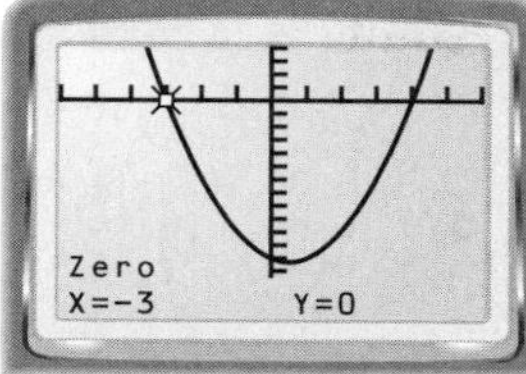

b. $y = x^2 + 12x + 36$ **Write original function.**

$= (x + 6)(x + 6)$ **Factor.**

The zero of the function is -6.

CHECK Graph $y = x^2 + 12x + 36$. The graph passes through $(-6, 0)$.

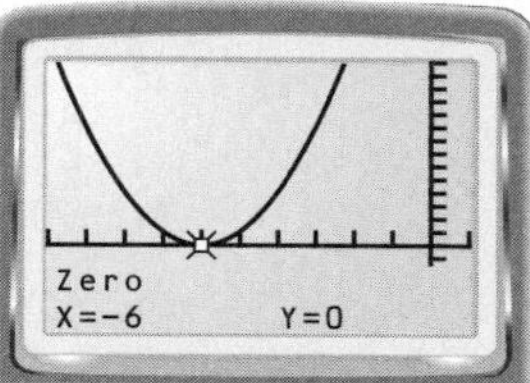

 **GUIDED PRACTICE** for Example 5

Find the zeros of the function by rewriting the function in intercept form.

10. $y = x^2 + 5x - 14$ $-7, 2$ **11.** $y = x^2 - 7x - 30$ $-3, 10$ **12.** $f(x) = x^2 - 10x + 25$ 5

4.3 EXERCISES

HOMEWORK KEY

○ = **WORKED-OUT SOLUTIONS** on p. WS8 for Exs. 33, 47, and 67

★ = **STANDARDIZED TEST PRACTICE** Exs. 2, 41, 56, 58, 63, and 71

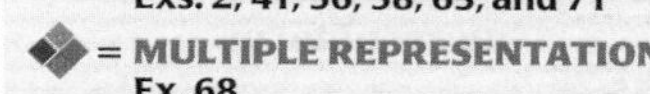

◆ = **MULTIPLE REPRESENTATIONS** Ex. 68

SKILL PRACTICE

A

1. **VOCABULARY** What is a zero of a function $y = f(x)$? an x-value that makes the function equal to zero

2. ★ **WRITING** *Explain* the difference between a monomial, a binomial, and a trinomial. Give an example of each type of expression. See margin.

EXAMPLE 1
on p. 252
for Exs. 3–14

FACTORING **Factor the expression. If the expression cannot be factored, say so.**

3. $x^2 + 6x + 5$ $(x + 1)(x + 5)$
4. $x^2 - 7x + 10$ $(x - 5)(x - 2)$
5. $a^2 - 13a + 22$ $(a - 11)(a - 2)$
6. $r^2 + 15r + 56$ $(r + 8)(r + 7)$
7. $p^2 + 2p + 4$ cannot be factored
8. $q^2 - 11q + 28$ $(q - 7)(q - 4)$
9. $b^2 + 3b - 40$ $(b + 8)(b - 5)$
10. $x^2 - 4x - 12$ $(x - 6)(x + 2)$
11. $x^2 - 7x - 18$ $(x - 9)(x + 2)$
12. $c^2 - 9c - 18$ cannot be factored
13. $x^2 + 9x - 36$ $(x + 12)(x - 3)$
14. $m^2 + 8m - 65$ $(m + 13)(m - 5)$

Extra Example 5

Find the zeros of the function by rewriting the function in intercept form.

a. $y = x^2 + 3x - 28$ $y = (x + 7)(x - 4)$; -7 and 4

b. $y = x^2 - 4x + 4$ $y = (x - 2)^2$; 2

Graphing Calculator

When you are discussing Example 5, use the calculator screens on the page or a graphing calculator demonstration to show students that the zeros of a function are the x-coordinates of where the graph crosses the x-axis.

Closing the Lesson

Have students summarize the major points of the lesson and answer the Essential Question: How can factoring be used to solve quadratic equations when $a = 1$?

- A trinomial of the form $x^2 + bx + c$ can be factored if there are two integers whose product is c and whose sum is b.
- A difference of two squares and a perfect square trinomial are two special factoring patterns.

If the left side of $ax^2 + bx + c = 0$ can be factored, factor the trinomial, use the zero product property to set each factor equal to 0, and solve the resulting linear equations.

2. A monomial is a number, variable, or product of a number and one or more variables, while a binomial is the sum of two monomials and a trinomial is the sum of three monomials. *Sample answer:* $3xy^4$, $2x - 8$, $6y^2z - 2y^2 + 12$

4 PRACTICE AND APPLY

Assignment Guide

Answer Transparencies available for all exercises

Basic:
Day 1: pp. 255–258
Exs. 1–6, 15–18, 25–37 odd, 39–47, 56–59, 65–69, 73

Average:
Day 1: pp. 255–258
Exs. 1, 2, 7–11, 18–20, 24–32 even, 39–43, 48–52, 56–62, 65–71, 74

Advanced:
Day 1: pp. 255–258
Exs. 1, 2, 12–14, 21–23, 34–38 even, 41–43, 53–64*, 66–72*

Block:
pp. 255–258
Exs. 1, 2, 7–11, 18–20, 24–32 even, 39–43, 48–52, 56–62, 65–71, 74 (with 4.4)

Differentiated Instruction

See *Algebra 2 Best Practices Toolkit* for suggestions on addressing the needs of a diverse classroom.

Homework Check

For a quick check of student understanding of key concepts, go over the following exercises:

Basic: 6, 16, 29, 46, 65
Average: 8, 18, 30, 50, 66
Advanced: 12, 22, 34, 54, 67

Extra Practice

- Student Edition, p. 1013
- Chapter 4 Resource Book: Practice levels A, B, C, pp. 36–38

Practice Worksheet

An easily-readable reduced practice page (with answers) for this lesson can be found on p. 234C.

EXAMPLE 2 on p. 253 for Exs. 15–23

FACTORING WITH SPECIAL PATTERNS **Factor the expression.**

15. $x^2 - 36$ $(x+6)(x-6)$
16. $b^2 - 81$ $(b-9)(b+9)$
17. $x^2 - 24x + 144$ $(x-12)^2$
18. $t^2 - 16t + 64$ $(t-8)^2$
19. $x^2 + 8x + 16$ $(x+4)^2$
20. $c^2 + 28c + 196$ $(c+14)^2$
21. $n^2 + 14n + 49$ $(n+7)^2$
22. $s^2 - 26s + 169$ $(s-13)^2$
23. $z^2 - 121$ $(z-11)(z+11)$

EXAMPLE 3 on p. 254 for Exs. 24–41

SOLVING EQUATIONS **Solve the equation.**

24. $x^2 - 8x + 12 = 0$ 2, 6
25. $x^2 - 11x + 30 = 0$ 5, 6
26. $x^2 + 2x - 35 = 0$ −7, 5
27. $a^2 - 49 = 0$ −7, 7
28. $b^2 - 6b + 9 = 0$ 3
29. $c^2 + 5c + 4 = 0$ −4, −1
30. $n^2 - 6n = 0$ 0, 6
31. $t^2 + 10t + 25 = 0$ −5
32. $w^2 - 16w + 48 = 0$ 4, 12
(33.) $z^2 - 3z = 54$ −6, 9
34. $r^2 + 2r = 80$ −10, 8
35. $u^2 = -9u$ 0, −9
36. $m^2 = 7m$ 0, 7
37. $14x - 49 = x^2$ 7
38. $-3y + 28 = y^2$ −7, 4

ERROR ANALYSIS ***Describe*** **and correct the error in solving the equation.** 39, 40. See margin.

39.

$x^2 - x - 6 = 0$
$(x-2)(x+3) = 0$
$x - 2 = 0$ or $x + 3 = 0$
$x = 2$ or $x = -3$

40.

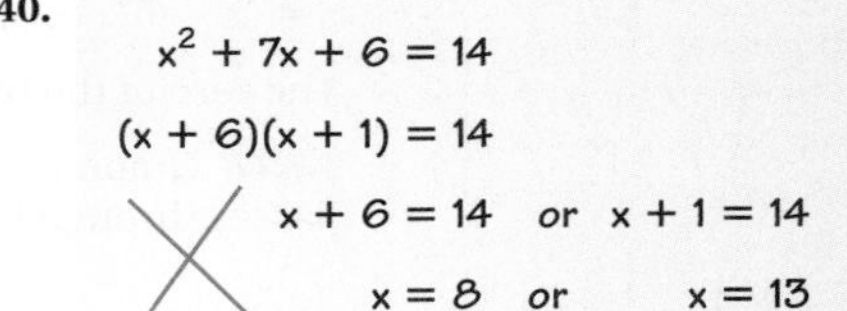

41. ★ **MULTIPLE CHOICE** What are the roots of the equation $x^2 + 2x - 63 = 0$? A

Ⓐ 7, −9 Ⓑ −7, −9 Ⓒ −7, 9 Ⓓ 7, 9

EXAMPLE 4 on p. 254 for Exs. 42–43

WRITING EQUATIONS **Write an equation that you can solve to find the value of *x*.**

42. A rectangular picnic site measures 24 feet by 10 feet. You want to double the site's area by adding the same distance x to the length and the width. $2(24)(10) = (24 + x)(10 + x)$

43. A rectangular performing platform in a park measures 10 feet by 12 feet. You want to triple the platform's area by adding the same distance x to the length and the width. $3(10)(12) = (10 + x)(12 + x)$

EXAMPLE 5 on p. 255 for Exs. 44–55

FINDING ZEROS **Find the zeros of the function by rewriting the function in intercept form.**

44. $y = x^2 + 6x + 8$ −4, −2
45. $y = x^2 - 8x + 16$ 4
46. $y = x^2 - 4x - 32$ −4, 8
(47.) $y = x^2 + 7x - 30$ −10, 3
48. $f(x) = x^2 + 11x$ −11, 0
49. $g(x) = x^2 - 8x$ 0, 8
50. $y = x^2 - 64$ −8, 8
51. $y = x^2 - 25$ −5, 5
52. $f(x) = x^2 - 12x - 45$ −3, 1
53. $g(x) = x^2 + 19x + 84$ −12, −7
54. $y = x^2 + 22x + 121$ −11
55. $y = x^2 + 2x + 1$ −1

56. ★ **MULTIPLE CHOICE** What are the zeros of $f(x) = x^2 + 6x - 55$? B

Ⓐ −11, −5 Ⓑ −11, 5 Ⓒ −5, 11 Ⓓ 5, 11

B

57. **REASONING** Write a quadratic equation of the form $x^2 + bx + c = 0$ that has roots 8 and 11. $x^2 - 19x + 88 = 0$

58. ★ **SHORT RESPONSE** For what integers b can the expression $x^2 + bx + 7$ be factored? *Explain.* −8 or 8; the only factors of 7 are ±1 and ±7. To make the constant term positive, the only factorizations can be $(x-1)(x-7)$ or $(x+1)(x+7)$, which will give a b-term of −8 or 8, respectively.

○ = WORKED-OUT SOLUTIONS on p. WS1 ★ = STANDARDIZED TEST PRACTICE

---

39. The equation was not factored correctly; $x^2 - x - 6 = 0$, $(x-3)(x+2) = 0$, $x = 3$ or $x = -2$.

40. The equation must be written in the form $ax^2 + bx + c = 0$ before factoring; $x^2 + 7x + 6 = 14$, $x^2 + 7x - 8 = 0$, $(x+8)(x-1) = 0$, $x = -8$ or $x = 1$.

GEOMETRY Find the value of x.

59. Area of rectangle = 36 4

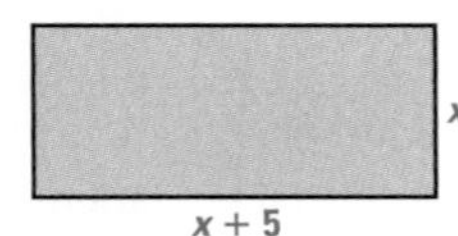

60. Area of rectangle = 84 5

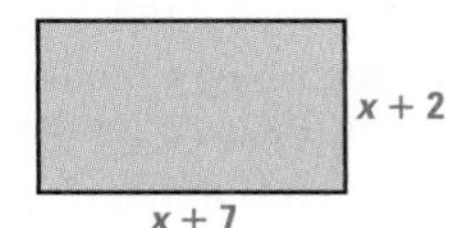

61. Area of triangle = 42 3

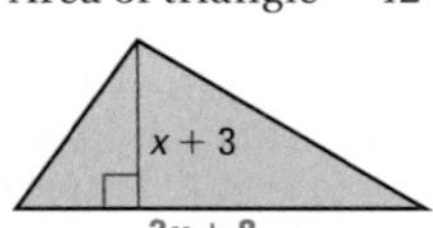

62. Area of trapezoid = 32 4

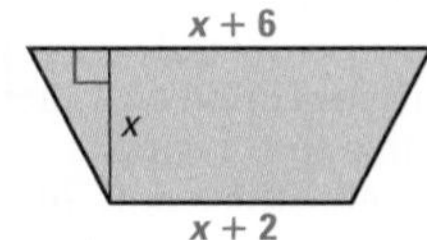

63. ★ **OPEN-ENDED MATH** Write a quadratic function with zeros that are equidistant from 10 on a number line. *Sample answer:* $x^2 - 20x + 91 = 0$

64. CHALLENGE Is there a formula for factoring the *sum* of two squares? You will investigate this question in parts (a) and (b).

a. Consider the sum of two squares $x^2 + 16$. If this sum can be factored, then there are integers m and n such that $x^2 + 16 = (x + m)(x + n)$. Write two equations that m and n must satisfy. $m \cdot n = 16, m + n = 0$

b. Show that there are no integers m and n that satisfy both equations you wrote in part (a). What can you conclude?

…b. *Sample …swer:* For …$+ n = 0$, m …d n must …opposites. They are …posites, …n their …duct would …a negative …mber; there …not a formula …factoring …sum of two …uares. C

PROBLEM SOLVING

…XAMPLE 4 A …n p. 254 …or Exs. 65–67

65. SKATE PARK A city's skate park is a rectangle 100 feet long by 50 feet wide. The city wants to triple the area of the skate park by adding the same distance x to the length and the width. Write and solve an equation to find the value of x. What are the new dimensions of the skate park? $3(50)(100) = (50 + x)(100 + x)$, -200, 50; 100 ft by 150 ft

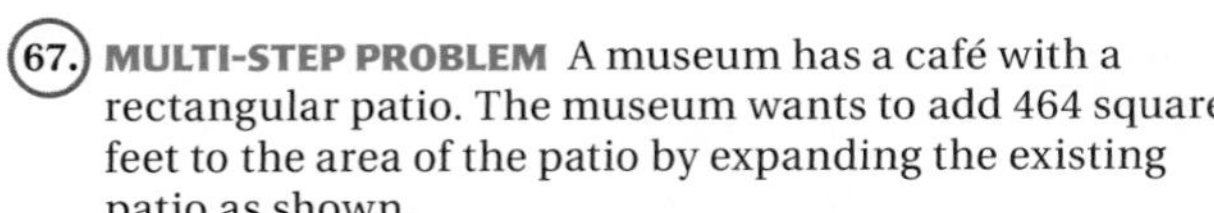

66. ZOO A rectangular enclosure at a zoo is 35 feet long by 18 feet wide. The zoo wants to double the area of the enclosure by adding the same distance x to the length and the width. Write and solve an equation to find the value of x. What are the new dimensions of the enclosure? $2(35)(18) = (35 + x)(18 + x)$, -63, 10; 45 ft by 28 ft

@HomeTutor for problem solving help at classzone.com

67. MULTI-STEP PROBLEM A museum has a café with a rectangular patio. The museum wants to add 464 square feet to the area of the patio by expanding the existing patio as shown.

a. Find the area of the existing patio. 600 ft^2

b. Write a verbal model and an equation that you can use to find the value of x. See margin.

c. Solve your equation. By what distance x should the length and the width of the patio be expanded? -58, 8; 8 ft

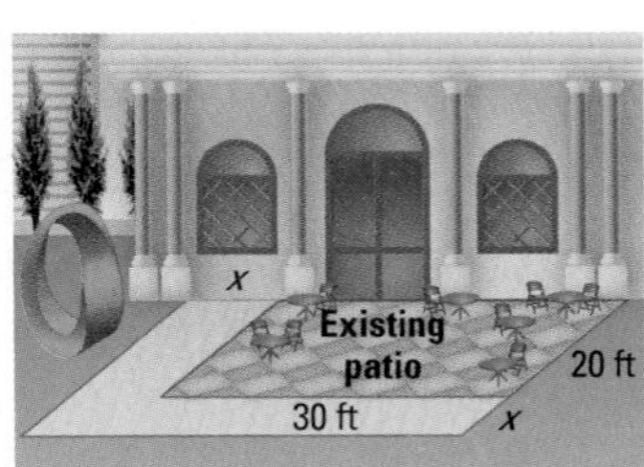

Avoiding Common Errors

Exercises 30, 35, 36 Students often miss zeros of functions (or roots of equations) that are 0. For example, in Exercise 30 when students use factoring to rewrite $n^2 - 6n = 0$ as $n(n - 6) = 0$, make sure they understand that there are two factors that must be set equal to 0, not just one. They should see that they should write "$n = 0$ or $n - 6 = 0$" and then "$n = 0$ or $n = 6$."

Study Strategy

Exercises 59–62 While most students will remember the formula for the area of a rectangle, which was used in Example 4, some students may not remember the formula for the area of a triangle or the area of a trapezoid. You may want to supply students with a list of geometry formulas to use as a reference throughout this course, or you could require students to develop their own lists in their notebooks of all the formulas they encounter.

67b. area of new patio = area of existing patio + area of expansion, $(30 + x)(20 + x) = 600 + 464$

Differentiated Instruction

Kinesthetic Learners Students can model the diagram in **Exercise 68** on page 258 using algebra tiles. For part (c), students may find it helpful to rearrange one x^2-tile, eight x-tiles, and fifteen 1-tiles to construct the diagram. Then have students work through other factorizations in a similar manner.

See also the *Algebra 2 Toolkit* for more strategies.

5 ASSESS AND RETEACH

Daily Homework Quiz

Transparency Available

Factor the expression.

1. $y^2 + 5y - 24$ $(y + 8)(y - 3)$
2. $z^2 - 225$ $(z + 15)(z - 15)$
3. $4w^2 - 20w + 25$ $(2w - 5)^2$
4. Solve $x^2 - 9x + 8 = 0$. 1, 8
5. Find the zeros of $f(x) = x^2 + 14x + 49$. -7
6. The dimensions of a playground are 50 feet by 75 feet. You want to double its area by adding the same distance x to the length and width. Find x and the new dimensions of the playground. $x = 25$; 75 ft by 100 ft

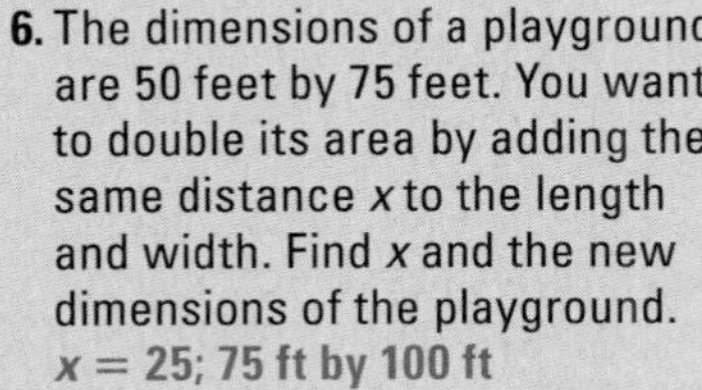

Online Quiz

Available at **classzone.com**

Diagnosis/Remediation

- Practice A, B, C in Chapter 4 Resource Book, pp. 36–38
- Study Guide in Chapter 4 Resource Book, pp. 39–40
- Practice Workbook, pp. 60–61
- @HomeTutor

Challenge

Additional challenge is available in the Chapter 4 Resource Book, p. 43.

68b. $(x + 3)(x + 2)$; each factor represents the length of a side of the rectangle

68c.

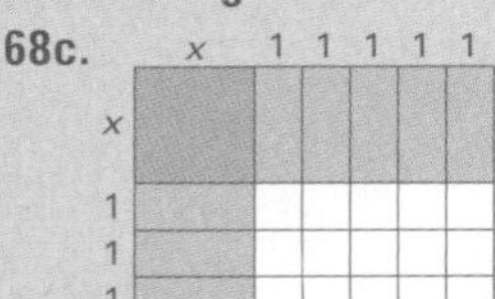

B

68. **MULTIPLE REPRESENTATIONS** Use the diagram shown.

a. **Writing an Expression** Write a quadratic trinomial that represents the area of the diagram. $x^2 + 5x + 6$

b. **Describing a Model** Factor the expression from part (a). *Explain* how the diagram models the factorization. b, c. See margin.

c. **Drawing a Diagram** Draw a diagram that models the factorization $x^2 + 8x + 15 = (x + 5)(x + 3)$.

69. **SCHOOL FAIR** At last year's school fair, an 18 foot by 15 foot rectangular section of land was roped off for a dunking booth. The length and width of the section will each be increased by x feet for this year's fair in order to triple the original area. Write and solve an equation to find the value of x. What is the length of rope needed to enclose the new section?
$3(18)(15) = (18 + x)(15 + x)$, $-45, 12$; 114 ft

70. **RECREATION CENTER** A rectangular deck for a recreation center is 21 feet long by 20 feet wide. Its area is to be halved by subtracting the same distance x from the length and the width. Write and solve an equation to find the value of x. What are the deck's new dimensions?
$0.5(21)(20) = (21 - x)(20 - x)$, 6, 35; 15 ft by 14 ft

71. ★ **SHORT RESPONSE** A square garden has sides that are 10 feet long. A gardener wants to double the area of the garden by adding the same distance x to the length and the width. Write an equation that x must satisfy. Can you solve the equation you wrote by factoring? *Explain* why or why not.
$2(100) = (10 + x)(10 + x)$; no; there are no real numbers a and b such that $ab = -100$ and $a + b = 20$.

C

72. **CHALLENGE** A grocery store wants to double the area of its parking lot by expanding the existing lot as shown. By what distance x should the lot be expanded? 60 ft

KENTUCKY MIXED REVIEW

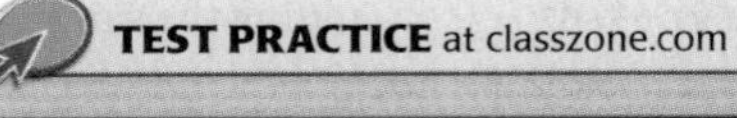

73. What is the slope of the line shown? D

Ⓐ $-\frac{5}{4}$ Ⓑ $-\frac{4}{5}$

Ⓒ $\frac{4}{5}$ Ⓓ $\frac{5}{4}$

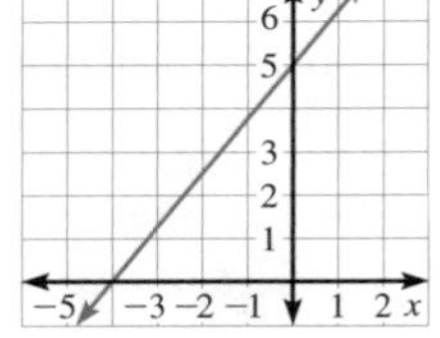

74. Which of the following best describes the graphs of the equations below? B

$$y = 3x - 2$$

$$-4y = x + 8$$

Ⓐ The lines have the same x-intercept.

Ⓑ The lines have the same y-intercept.

Ⓒ The lines are perpendicular to each other.

Ⓓ The lines are parallel to each other.

4.4 Solve $ax^2 + bx + c = 0$ by Factoring

MA-HS-5.3.6 **Students will model, solve and graph quadratic equations in real-world and mathematical problems. DOK 2**

Before You used factoring to solve equations of the form $x^2 + bx + c = 0$.

Now You will use factoring to solve equations of the form $ax^2 + bx + c = 0$.

Why? So you can maximize a shop's revenue, as in Ex. 64.

Key Vocabulary
monomial, *p. 252*

To factor $ax^2 + bx + c$ when $a \neq 1$, find integers k, l, m, and n such that:

$$ax^2 + bx + c = (kx + m)(lx + n) = klx^2 + (kn + lm)x + mn$$

So, k and l must be factors of a, and m and n must be factors of c.

EXAMPLE 1 Factor $ax^2 + bx + c$ where $c > 0$

Factor $5x^2 - 17x + 6$.

Solution

You want $5x^2 - 17x + 6 = (kx + m)(lx + n)$ where k and l are factors of 5 and m and n are factors of 6. You can assume that k and l are positive and $k \geq l$. Because $mn > 0$, m and n have the same sign. So, m and n must both be negative because the coefficient of x, -17, is negative.

FACTOR EXPRESSIONS
When factoring $ax^2 + bx + c$ where $a > 0$, it is customary to choose factors $kx + m$ and $lx + n$ such that k and l are positive.

k, l	5, 1	5, 1	5, 1	5, 1
m, n	$-6, -1$	$-1, -6$	$-3, -2$	$-2, -3$
$(kx + m)(lx + n)$	$(5x - 6)(x - 1)$	$(5x - 1)(x - 6)$	$(5x - 3)(x - 2)$	$(5x - 2)(x - 3)$
$ax^2 + bx + c$	$5x^2 - 11x + 6$	$5x^2 - 31x + 6$	$5x^2 - 13x + 6$	$5x^2 - 17x + 6$

▶ The correct factorization is $5x^2 - 17x + 6 = (5x - 2)(x - 3)$.

EXAMPLE 2 Factor $ax^2 + bx + c$ where $c < 0$

Factor $3x^2 + 20x - 7$.

Solution

You want $3x^2 + 20x - 7 = (kx + m)(lx + n)$ where k and l are factors of 3 and m and n are factors of -7. Because $mn < 0$, m and n have opposite signs.

k, l	3, 1	3, 1	3, 1	3, 1
m, n	$7, -1$	$-1, 7$	$-7, 1$	$1, -7$
$(kx + m)(lx + n)$	$(3x + 7)(x - 1)$	$(3x - 1)(x + 7)$	$(3x - 7)(x + 1)$	$(3x + 1)(x - 7)$
$ax^2 + bx + c$	$3x^2 + 4x - 7$	$3x^2 + 20x - 7$	$3x^2 - 4x - 7$	$3x^2 - 20x - 7$

▶ The correct factorization is $3x^2 + 20x - 7 = (3x - 1)(x + 7)$.

1 PLAN AND PREPARE

Warm-Up Exercises

Transparency Available

Find the product.

1. $(4y - 3)(3y + 8)$ $12y^2 + 23y - 24$
2. $(5m + 6)(5m - 6)$ $25m^2 - 36$
3. $(4q - 5)^2$ $16q^2 - 40q + 25$
4. Solve $x^2 - x - 30 = 0$. $-5, 6$
5. The side of a square is $(2n - 3)$ inches long. Find its area. $(4n^2 - 12n + 9)$ in.^{2}

Notetaking Guide

Transparency Available

Promotes interactive learning and notetaking skills, pp. 102–104.

Pacing

Basic: 2 days
Average: 2 days
Advanced: 2 days
Block: 0.5 block with 4.3
0.5 block with 4.5

- See *Teaching Guide/Lesson Plan.*

2 FOCUS AND MOTIVATE

Essential Question

Big Idea 2, p. 235

How can factoring be used to solve quadratic equations when $a \neq 1$? **Tell students they will learn how to answer this question by expanding the factoring process they learned in Lesson 4.3.**

Resource Planning Guide

Chapter Resource Book
- Teaching Guide/Lesson Plan (pp. 44–45)
- Practice levels A, B, C (pp. 46–48)
- Study Guide (pp. 49–50)
- Catch-up for Absent Students (p. 51)
- Application (p. 52)
- Challenge (p. 53)

Workbooks
- Notetaking Guide (pp. 102–104)
- Practice Workbook (pp. 62–63)

Teaching Options
- **Power Presentations CD-ROM** provides dynamic electronic teaching resources for the classroom.
- **Activity Generator CD-ROM** provides editable activities for all ability levels.

Interactive Technology
- Easy Planner
- Power Presentations CD-ROM
- Activity Generator CD-ROM
- Animated Algebra
- Test Generator CD-ROM
- Online Quiz
- eWorkbook
- eEdition
- @HomeTutor

Resources for English Learners
- Quick Reference for English Learners
- Spanish Study Guide
- Multi-Language Visual Glossary
- Student Resources in Spanish

See also the *Algebra 2 Toolkit* for more strategies for meeting individual needs.

Motivating the Lesson

Ask students if any of them have jobs or hobbies that involve art, crafts, or gardening. Ask them to describe situations where they had to surround a rectangular object by a border. Tell them that solving quadratic equations can help to find the optimal width of the border.

3 TEACH

Extra Example 1

Factor $3x^2 - 10x + 8$.
$(3x - 4)(x - 2)$

Extra Example 2

Factor $6x^2 + x - 15$.
$(2x - 3)(3x + 5)$

Key Question to Ask for Examples 1 and 2

- When you factor $ax^2 + bx + c$, how can you check that you have the correct factors? **Multiply the binomials and compare the product to the original trinomial.**

Extra Example 3

Factor the expression.

a. $81x^2 - 25$ $(9x + 5)(9x - 5)$
b. $49z^2 + 112z + 64$ $(7z + 8)^2$
c. $9r^2 - 66r + 121$ $(3r - 11)^2$

Extra Example 4

Factor the expression.

a. $3x^2 - 300$ $3(x + 10)(x - 10)$
b. $8m^2 + 28m - 120$
$4(2m - 5)(m + 6)$
c. $-7t^2 - 63t$ $-7t(t + 9)$
d. $-25y^2 + 60y - 35$
$-5(5y - 7)(y - 1)$

Key Question to Ask for Example 4

- What should always be your first step when you are asked to factor a polynomial? **Check for a common monomial factor.**

✓ **GUIDED PRACTICE** for Examples 1 and 2

Factor the expression. If the expression cannot be factored, say so.

1. $7x^2 - 20x - 3$ $(7x + 1)(x - 3)$
2. $5z^2 + 16z + 3$ $(5z + 1)(z + 3)$
3. $2w^2 + w + 3$ cannot be factored
4. $3x^2 + 5x - 12$ $(3x - 4)(x + 3)$
5. $4u^2 + 12u + 5$ $(2u + 1)(2u + 5)$
6. $4x^2 - 9x + 2$ $(4x - 1)(x - 2)$

FACTORING SPECIAL PRODUCTS If the values of a and c in $ax^2 + bx + c$ are perfect squares, check to see whether you can use one of the special factoring patterns from Lesson 4.3 to factor the expression.

EXAMPLE 3 Factor with special patterns

Factor the expression.

a. $9x^2 - 64 = (3x)^2 - 8^2$ **Difference of two squares**
$= (3x + 8)(3x - 8)$

b. $4y^2 + 20y + 25 = (2y)^2 + 2(2y)(5) + 5^2$ **Perfect square trinomial**
$= (2y + 5)^2$

c. $36w^2 - 12w + 1 = (6w)^2 - 2(6w)(1) + 1^2$ **Perfect square trinomial**
$= (6w - 1)^2$

✓ **GUIDED PRACTICE** for Example 3

Factor the expression.

7. $16x^2 - 1$ $(4x + 1)(4x - 1)$
8. $9y^2 + 12y + 4$ $(3y + 2)^2$
9. $4r^2 - 28r + 49$ $(2r - 7)^2$
10. $25s^2 - 80s + 64$ $(5s - 8)^2$
11. $49z^2 + 42z + 9$ $(7z + 3)^2$
12. $36n^2 - 9$ $(6n - 3)(6n + 3)$

FACTORING OUT MONOMIALS When factoring an expression, first check to see whether the terms have a common monomial factor.

EXAMPLE 4 Factor out monomials first

Factor the expression.

AVOID ERRORS
Be sure to factor out the common monomial from all of the terms of the expression, not just the first term.

a. $5x^2 - 45 = 5(x^2 - 9)$
$= 5(x + 3)(x - 3)$

b. $6q^2 - 14q + 8 = 2(3q^2 - 7q + 4)$
$= 2(3q - 4)(q - 1)$

c. $-5z^2 + 20z = -5z(z - 4)$

d. $12p^2 - 21p + 3 = 3(4p^2 - 7p + 1)$

 **GUIDED PRACTICE** for Example 4

Factor the expression.

13. $3s^2 - 24$ $3(s^2 - 8)$
14. $8t^2 + 38t - 10$ $2(4t - 1)(t + 5)$
15. $6x^2 + 24x + 15$ $3(2x^2 + 8x + 5)$
16. $12x^2 - 28x - 24$ $4(3x + 2)(x - 3)$
17. $-16n^2 + 12n$ $-4n(4n - 3)$
18. $6z^2 + 33z + 36$ $3(2z + 3)(z + 4)$

Differentiated Instruction

Visual Learners Students who have difficulty working with a table may find it more convenient to write a partial solution, and then fill in the blanks with possible factors. For $3x^2 + 20x - 7$ in **Example 2**, begin with ($x +$)($x -$). Try factors of 3 as the coefficient of the first term of each binomial, and try factors of 7 as the second term of each binomial. Students can then find the product in each test case using the FOIL method, and compare it to the given trinomial.

See also the *Algebra 2 Toolkit* for more strategies.

SOLVING QUADRATIC EQUATIONS As you saw in Lesson 4.3, if the left side of the quadratic equation $ax^2 + bx + c = 0$ can be factored, then the equation can be solved using the zero product property.

EXAMPLE 5 Solve quadratic equations

Solve (a) $3x^2 + 10x - 8 = 0$ and (b) $5p^2 - 16p + 15 = 4p - 5$.

a. $3x^2 + 10x - 8 = 0$ **Write original equation.**

$(3x - 2)(x + 4) = 0$ **Factor.**

$3x - 2 = 0$ or $x + 4 = 0$ **Zero product property**

$x = \frac{2}{3}$ or $x = -4$ **Solve for *x*.**

b. $5p^2 - 16p + 15 = 4p - 5$ **Write original equation.**

$5p^2 - 20p + 20 = 0$ **Write in standard form.**

$p^2 - 4p + 4 = 0$ **Divide each side by 5.**

$(p - 2)^2 = 0$ **Factor.**

$p - 2 = 0$ **Zero product property**

$p = 2$ **Solve for *p*.**

INTERPRET EQUATIONS
If the square of an expression is zero, then the expression itself must be zero.

EXAMPLE 6 Use a quadratic equation as a model

QUILTS You have made a rectangular quilt that is 5 feet by 4 feet. You want to use the remaining 10 square feet of fabric to add a decorative border of uniform width to the quilt. What should the width of the quilt's border be?

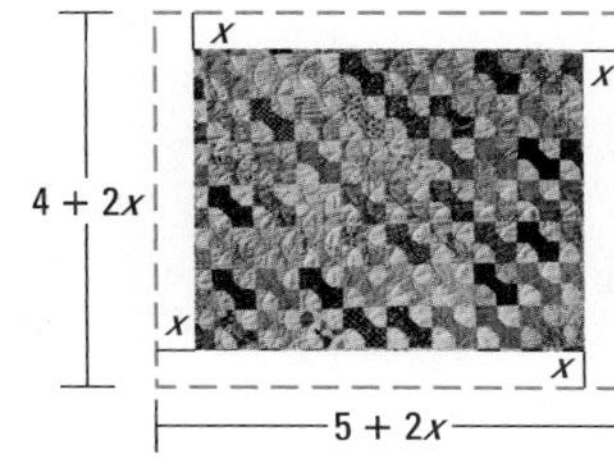

Solution

Write a verbal model. Then write an equation.

Area of border (square feet)	=	Area of quilt and border (square feet)	–	Area of quilt (square feet)
10	=	**(5 + 2x)(4 + 2x)**	–	**(5)(4)**

$10 = 20 + 18x + 4x^2 - 20$ **Multiply using FOIL.**

$0 = 4x^2 + 18x - 10$ **Write in standard form.**

$0 = 2x^2 + 9x - 5$ **Divide each side by 2.**

$0 = (2x - 1)(x + 5)$ **Factor.**

$2x - 1 = 0$ or $x + 5 = 0$ **Zero product property**

$x = \frac{1}{2}$ or $x = -5$ **Solve for *x*.**

▶ Reject the negative value, −5. The border's width should be $\frac{1}{2}$ ft, or 6 in.

Extra Example 5

Solve the equation.

a. $4x^2 - 17x - 15 = 0$ $-\frac{3}{4}, 5$

b. $3y^2 + 22y + 60 = -14y - 48$ -6

Extra Example 6

You are designing a garden for the grounds of your high school. You want the garden to be made up of a rectangular flower bed surrounded by a border of uniform width to be covered with decorative stones. You have decided that the flower bed will be 22 feet by 15 feet, and your budget will allow for enough stone to cover 120 square feet. What should be the width of the border? **$1\frac{1}{2}$ ft or 18 in.**

Key Questions to Ask for Examples 5 and 6

- Why is the negative solution part of the final answer in Example 5a, but not in Example 6? **In both cases, the quadratic equation has both a positive and a negative solution. However, Example 6 is an applied problem where a negative solution does not make sense.**
- In Example 6, why do the expressions for the length and width of the quilt contain the term $2x$, rather than x? **Each dimension, length and width, consists of the original measurement plus the widths of two borders.**

Teaching Strategy

Have students work individually or in small groups to develop a flow chart that shows questions to ask themselves whenever they are factoring an expression. Work to develop a consensus among all students about the steps to include and how the flowchart should be organized.

Extra Example 7

An Internet service provider sells high-speed internet service for $30 per month to 1500 customers. For each $1 increase in price, the number of customers will decrease by 25. How much should the company charge in order to maximize monthly revenue? What is the maximum monthly revenue? **$45/month; $50,625**

Key Question to Ask for Example 7

- In Example 7, once you have written the revenue function in Step 2, how can you tell that the function will have a maximum value, rather than a minimum value? **$a < 0$, so the graph will be a parabola opening down; the y-coordinate of the vertex will be a maximum value.**

Closing the Lesson

Have students summarize the major points of the lesson and answer the Essential Question: How can factoring be used to solve quadratic equations when $a \neq 1$?

- **When factoring an algebraic expression, look first for a common monomial factor.**
- **To solve a quadratic equation by factoring, write the equation in standard form, factor, and then apply the zero product property.**

First write the equation in standard form. Then factor out any common monomial. Next, factor the expression either using a special pattern or by finding integers k, ℓ, m, and n such that k and ℓ are factors of a, m and n are factors of c, and $kn + \ell m = b$. Finally, use the zero product property to solve the equation.

FACTORING AND ZEROS To find the maximum or minimum value of a quadratic function, you can first use factoring to write the function in intercept form $y = a(x - p)(x - q)$. Because the function's vertex lies on the axis of symmetry $x = \frac{p+q}{2}$, the maximum or minimum occurs at the *average* of the zeros p and q.

EXAMPLE 7 Solve a multi-step problem

MAGAZINES A monthly teen magazine has 28,000 subscribers when it charges $10 per annual subscription. For each $1 increase in price, the magazine loses about 2000 subscribers. How much should the magazine charge to maximize annual revenue? What is the maximum annual revenue?

Solution

STEP 1 **Define** the variables. Let x represent the price increase and $R(x)$ represent the annual revenue.

STEP 2 **Write** a verbal model. Then write and simplify a quadratic function.

Annual revenue (dollars)	=	Number of subscribers (people)	·	Subscription price (dollars/person)

$$\mathbf{R(x) = (28{,}000 - 2000x) \cdot (10 + x)}$$

$$R(x) = (-2000x + 28{,}000)(x + 10)$$

$$R(x) = -2000(x - 14)(x + 10)$$

STEP 3 **Identify** the zeros and find their average. Find how much each subscription should cost to maximize annual revenue.

The zeros of the revenue function are 14 and −10. The average of the zeros is $\frac{14 + (-10)}{2} = 2$. To maximize revenue, each subscription should cost $10 + $2 = $12.

STEP 4 **Find** the maximum annual revenue.

$R(2) = -2000(2 - 14)(2 + 10) = \$288{,}000$

▶ The magazine should charge $12 per subscription to maximize annual revenue. The maximum annual revenue is $288,000.

GUIDED PRACTICE for Examples 5, 6, and 7

Solve the equation.

19. $6x^2 - 3x - 63 = 0$ **$-3, 3\frac{1}{2}$**
20. $12x^2 + 7x + 2 = x + 8$ **$-1, \frac{1}{2}$**
21. $7x^2 + 70x + 175 = 0$ **−5**
22. **WHAT IF?** In Example 7, suppose the magazine initially charges $11 per annual subscription. How much should the magazine charge to maximize annual revenue? What is the maximum annual revenue? **$12.50; $312,500**

4.4 EXERCISES

HOMEWORK KEY
○ = WORKED-OUT SOLUTIONS on p. WS8 for Exs. 27, 39, and 63
★ = STANDARDIZED TEST PRACTICE Exs. 2, 12, 64, 65, and 67

SKILL PRACTICE

A

1. **VOCABULARY** What is the greatest common monomial factor of the terms of the expression $12x^2 + 8x + 20$? 4

2. ★ **WRITING** *Explain* how the values of a and c in $ax^2 + bx + c$ help you determine whether you can use a perfect square trinomial factoring pattern. *a* and *c* must be perfect squares.

EXAMPLES 1 and 2 on p. 259 for Exs. 3–12

FACTORING **Factor the expression. If the expression cannot be factored, say so.**

3. $2x^2 + 5x + 3$ $(2x + 3)(x + 1)$
4. $3n^2 + 7n + 4$ $(3n + 4)(n + 1)$
5. $4r^2 + 5r + 1$ $(4r + 1)(r + 1)$
6. $6p^2 + 5p + 1$ $(3p + 1)(2p + 1)$
7. $11z^2 + 2z - 9$ $(11z - 9)(z + 1)$
8. $15x^2 - 2x - 8$ $(5x - 4)(3x + 2)$
9. $4y^2 - 5y - 4$ cannot be factored
10. $14m^2 + m - 3$ $(7m - 3)(2m + 1)$
11. $9d^2 - 13d - 10$ $(9d + 5)(d - 2)$
12. ★ **MULTIPLE CHOICE** Which factorization of $5x^2 + 14x - 3$ is correct? D

  Ⓐ $(5x - 3)(x + 1)$ Ⓑ $(5x + 1)(x - 3)$
  Ⓒ $5(x - 1)(x + 3)$ Ⓓ $(5x - 1)(x + 3)$

EXAMPLE 3 on p. 260 for Exs. 13–21

FACTORING WITH SPECIAL PATTERNS **Factor the expression.**

13. $9x^2 - 1$ $(3x + 1)(3x - 1)$
14. $4r^2 - 25$ $(2r + 5)(2r - 5)$
15. $49n^2 - 16$ $(7n - 4)(7n + 4)$
16. $16s^2 + 8s + 1$ $(4s + 1)^2$
17. $49x^2 + 70x + 25$ $(7x + 5)^2$
18. $64w^2 + 144w + 81$ $(8w + 9)^2$
19. $9p^2 - 12p + 4$ $(3p - 2)^2$
20. $25t^2 - 30t + 9$ $(5t - 3)^2$
21. $36x^2 - 84x + 49$ $(6x - 7)^2$

EXAMPLE 4 on p. 260 for Exs. 22–31

FACTORING MONOMIALS FIRST **Factor the expression.**

22. $12x^2 - 4x - 40$ $4(3x + 5)(x - 2)$
23. $18z^2 + 36z + 16$ $2(3z + 4)(3z + 2)$
24. $32v^2 - 2$ $2(4v + 1)(4v - 1)$
25. $6u^2 - 24u$ $6u(u - 4)$
26. $12m^2 - 36m + 27$ $3(2m - 3)^2$
27. $20x^2 + 124x + 24$ $4(5x + 1)(x + 6)$
28. $21x^2 - 77x - 28$ $7(3x + 1)(x - 4)$
29. $-36n^2 + 48n - 15$ $-3(6n - 5)(2n - 1)$
30. $-8y^2 + 28y - 60$ $-4(2y^2 - 7y + 15)$
31. **ERROR ANALYSIS** *Describe* and correct the error in factoring the expression. 4 should be factored out of each term in the binomial; $4x^2 - 36 = 4(x^2 - 9) = 4(x + 3)(x - 3)$.

$$4x^2 - 36 = 4(x^2 - 36) = 4(x + 6)(x - 6)$$ ✗

EXAMPLE 5 on p. 261 for Exs. 32–40

SOLVING EQUATIONS **Solve the equation.**

32. $16x^2 - 1 = 0$ $-\frac{1}{4}, \frac{1}{4}$
33. $11q^2 - 44 = 0$ $-2, 2$
34. $14s^2 - 21s = 0$ $0, 1\frac{1}{2}$
35. $45n^2 + 10n = 0$ $0, -\frac{2}{9}$
36. $4x^2 - 20x + 25 = 0$ $2\frac{1}{2}$
37. $4p^2 + 12p + 9 = 0$ $-1\frac{1}{2}$
38. $15x^2 + 7x - 2 = 0$ $\frac{1}{5}, -\frac{2}{3}$
39. $6r^2 - 7r - 5 = 0$ $-\frac{1}{2}, 1\frac{2}{3}$
40. $36z^2 + 96z + 15 = 0$ $-2\frac{1}{2}, -\frac{1}{6}$

EXAMPLE 7 on p. 262 for Exs. 41–49

FINDING ZEROS **Find the zeros of the function by rewriting the function in intercept form.**

41. $y = 4x^2 - 19x - 5$ $-\frac{1}{4}, 5$
42. $g(x) = 3x^2 - 8x + 5$ $1\frac{2}{3}, 1$
43. $y = 5x^2 - 27x - 18$ $-\frac{3}{5}, 6$
44. $f(x) = 3x^2 - 3x$ $0, 1$
45. $y = 11x^2 - 19x - 6$
46. $y = 16x^2 - 2x - 5$
47. $y = 15x^2 - 5x - 20$ $-1, 1\frac{1}{3}$
48. $y = 18x^2 - 6x - 4$ $-\frac{1}{3}, \frac{2}{3}$
49. $g(x) = 12x^2 + 5x - 7$ $-1, \frac{7}{12}$

45. $-\frac{3}{11}, 2$
46. $-\frac{1}{2}, \frac{5}{8}$

4 PRACTICE AND APPLY

Assignment Guide

Answer Transparencies available for all exercises

Basic:
Day 1: pp. 263–265
Exs. 1–18
Day 2: pp. 263–265
Exs. 23–39 odd, 41–43, 50–52, 62–65, 69–70

Average:
Day 1: pp. 263–265
Exs. 1–12, 16–21
Day 2: pp. 263–265
Exs. 22–28 even, 31, 32–36 even, 44–46, 50–58, 62–67, 70

Advanced:
Day 1: pp. 263–265
Exs. 1, 2, 5–12, 15–21
Day 2: pp. 263–265
Exs. 28–30, 38–40, 47–61*, 63–68*

Block:
pp. 263–265
Exs. 1–12, 16–21 (with 4.3)
pp. 263–265
Exs. 22–28 even, 31, 32–36 even, 44–46, 50–58, 62–67, 70 (with 4.5)

Differentiated Instruction

See *Algebra 2 Best Practices Toolkit* for suggestions on addressing the needs of a diverse classroom.

Homework Check

For a quick check of student understanding of key concepts, go over the following exercises:

Basic: 4, 14, 25, 35, 62
Average: 8, 18, 28, 36, 63
Advanced: 10, 20, 30, 38, 66

Extra Practice

- Student Edition, p. 1013
- Chapter 4 Resource Book: Practice levels A, B, C, pp. 46–48

Practice Worksheet

An easily-readable reduced practice page (with answers) for this lesson can be found on p. 234C.

Avoiding Common Errors

Exercise 22 Students who factor out the common factor 2 rather than the *greatest* common factor, 4, are unlikely to end up with the completely factored form of the expression, $4(3x + 5)(x - 2)$. Emphasize that factoring monomials first means to factor out the *greatest common factor* (GCF) of all the terms.

Exercises 22–30 Some students may factor out a common monomial factor and think they are done. In all of these exercises except Exercise 25, once the greatest common monomial factor has been factored out, the other factor can be factored further. Explain that factoring out a common monomial factor is often just the first step, and emphasize the concept of factoring an expression *completely*.

65. \$5.75; letting x represent the number of \$.25 decreases in the sandwich price, the revenue R is given by the function $R = (330 + 15x)(6 - 0.25x)$. The zeros of this function are −22 and 24, and their average is 1. So, to maximize the daily revenue, each sandwich should be sold for $6 - 0.25(1)$, or \$5.75. The maximum daily revenue is then $(330 + 15(1))(5.75) = (345)(5.75) = \$1983.75$.

B **GEOMETRY Find the value of x.**

50. Area of square = 36 **3**

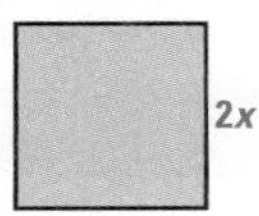

51. Area of rectangle = 30 **3**

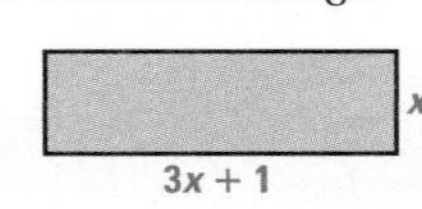

52. Area of triangle = 115 **5**

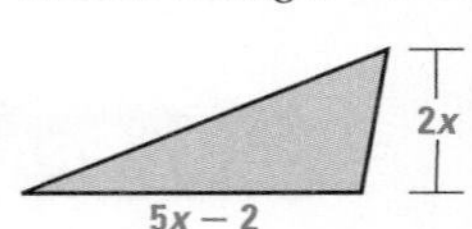

SOLVING EQUATIONS Solve the equation.

53. $2x^2 - 4x - 8 = -x^2 + x$ **$-1, 2\frac{2}{3}$**

54. $24x^2 + 8x + 2 = 5 - 6x$ **$-\frac{3}{4}, \frac{1}{6}$**

55. $18x^2 - 22x = 28$ **$-\frac{7}{9}, 2$**

56. $13x^2 + 21x = -5x^2 + 22$ **$-1\frac{5}{6}, \frac{2}{3}$**

57. $x = 4x^2 - 15x$ **0, 4**

58. $(x + 8)^2 = 16 - x^2 + 9x$ **no solution**

C **CHALLENGE Factor the expression.**

59. $2x^3 - 5x^2 + 3x$ **$x(2x - 3)(x - 1)$**

60. $8x^4 - 8x^3 - 6x^2$ **$2x^2(2x + 1)(2x - 3)$**

61. $9x^3 - 4x$ **$x(3x - 2)(3x + 2)$**

PROBLEM SOLVING

EXAMPLE 6 on p. 261 for Exs. 62–63

A 62. **ARTS AND CRAFTS** You have a rectangular stained glass window that measures 2 feet by 1 foot. You have 4 square feet of glass with which to make a border of uniform width around the window. What should the width of the border be? **6 in.**

@HomeTutor for problem solving help at classzone.com

63. **URBAN PLANNING** You have just planted a rectangular flower bed of red roses in a city park. You want to plant a border of yellow roses around the flower bed as shown. Because you bought the same number of red and yellow roses, the areas of the border and flower bed will be equal. What should the width of the border of yellow roses be? **2 ft**

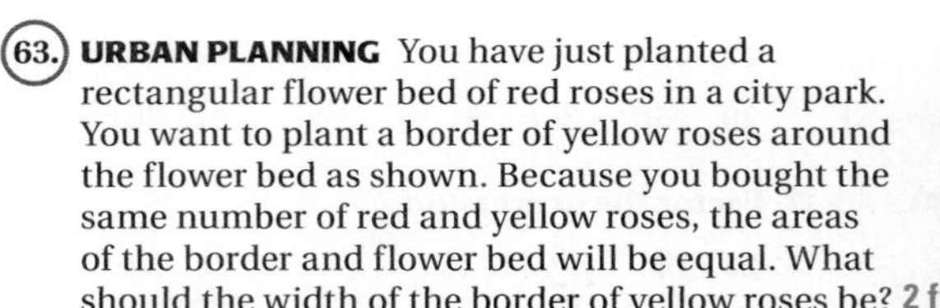

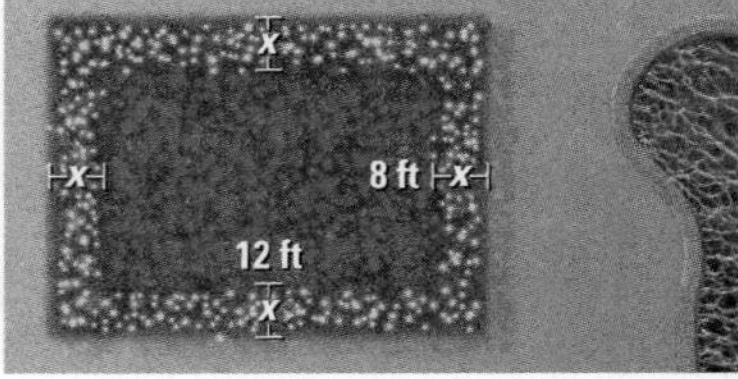

@HomeTutor for problem solving help at classzone.com

EXAMPLE 7 on p. 262 for Exs. 64–65

64. ★ **MULTIPLE CHOICE** A surfboard shop sells 45 surfboards per month when it charges \$500 per surfboard. For each \$20 decrease in price, the store sells 5 more surfboards per month. How much should the shop charge per surfboard in order to maximize monthly revenue? **A**

(A) \$340 (B) \$492 (C) \$508 (D) \$660

B 65. ★ **SHORT RESPONSE** A restaurant sells about 330 sandwiches each day at a price of \$6 each. For each \$.25 decrease in price, 15 more sandwiches are sold per day. How much should the restaurant charge to maximize daily revenue? *Explain* each step of your solution. What is the maximum daily revenue? **See margin.**

66. **PAINTINGS** You place a mat around a 25 inch by 21 inch painting as shown. The mat is twice as wide at the left and right of the painting as it is at the top and bottom of the painting. The area of the mat is 714 square inches. How wide is the mat at the left and right of the painting? at the top and bottom of the painting? **8.5 in.; 4.25 in.**

○ = WORKED-OUT SOLUTIONS on p. WS1 ★ = STANDARDIZED TEST PRACTICE

Quiz, p. 265

1.

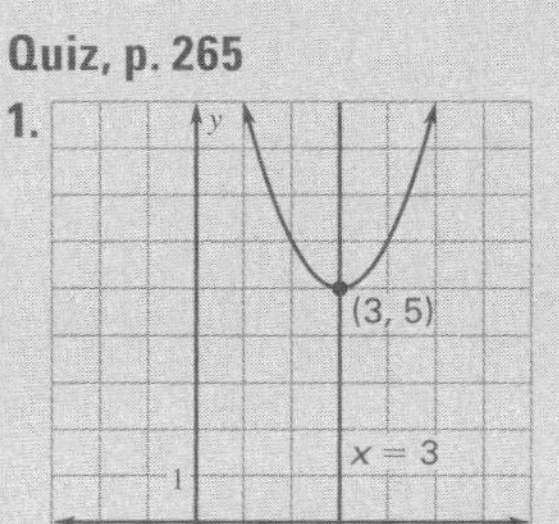

2.

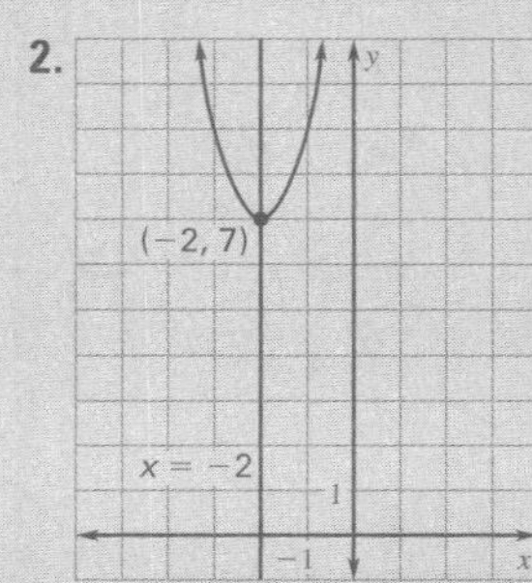

3.

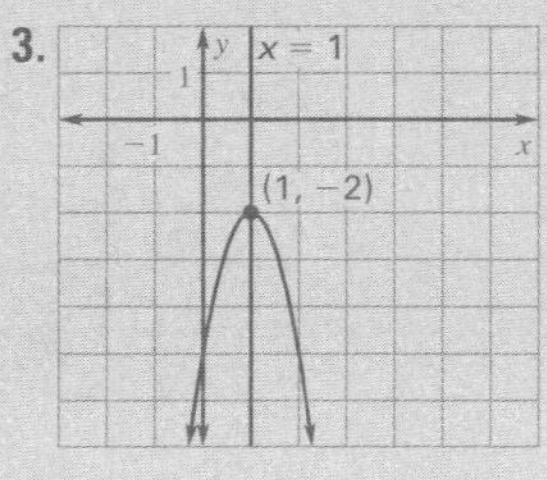

. 18 in., n.; 11,664 . *Sample* *swer*: I found vertex of volume ation from t (b).

67. ★ **EXTENDED RESPONSE** A U.S. Postal Service guideline states that for a rectangular package like the one shown, the sum of the length and the girth cannot exceed 108 inches. Suppose that for one such package, the length is 36 inches and the girth is as large as possible.

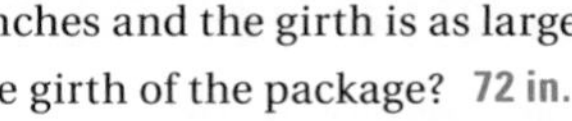

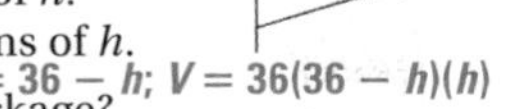

a. What is the girth of the package? 72 in.

b. Write an expression for the package's width w in terms of h. Write an equation giving the package's volume V in terms of h. $w = 36 - h$; $V = 36(36 - h)(h)$

c. What height and width maximize the volume of the package? What is the maximum volume? *Explain* how you found it.

C 68. **CHALLENGE** Recall from geometry the theorem about the products of the lengths of segments of two chords that intersect in the interior of a circle. Use this theorem to find the value of x in the diagram. 2

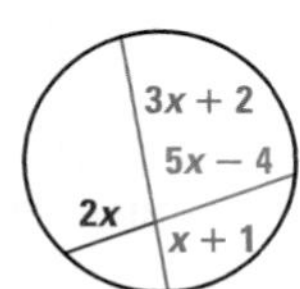

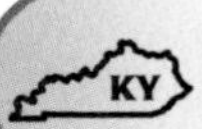

KENTUCKY MIXED REVIEW

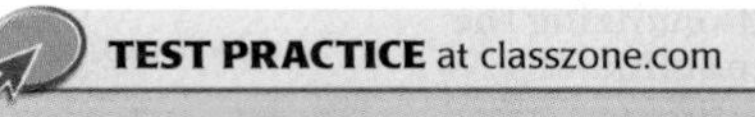

TEST PRACTICE at classzone.com

69. A pizza is divided into 12 equal slices as shown. The diameter of the pizza is 16 inches. What is the approximate area of one slice of pizza? **B**

(A) 15.47 in.^{2} (B) 16.76 in.^{2}

(C) 21.21 in.^{2} (D) 67.02 in.^{2}

70. While shopping at Store A, Sam finds a television on sale for \$210. His friend tells him that the same television at Store B is on sale for \$161. About what percent of the cost of the television at Store A does Sam save by buying the television at Store B? **B**

(A) 20% (B) 23% (C) 30% (D) 77%

QUIZ for Lessons 4.1–4.4

Graph the function. Label the vertex and axis of symmetry. *(p. 236)* 1–3. See margin.

1. $y = x^2 - 6x + 14$
2. $y = 2x^2 + 8x + 15$
3. $f(x) = -3x^2 + 6x - 5$

Write the quadratic function in standard form. *(p. 245)*

4. $y = (x - 4)(x - 8)$ $y = x^2 - 12x + 32$
5. $g(x) = -2(x + 3)(x - 7)$ $y = -2x^2 + 8x + 42$
6. $y = 5(x + 6)^2 - 2$ $y = 5x^2 + 60x + 178$

Solve the equation.

7. $x^2 + 9x + 20 = 0$ *(p. 252)* $-5, -4$
8. $n^2 - 11n + 24 = 0$ *(p. 252)* 3, 8
9. $z^2 - 3z - 40 = 0$ *(p. 252)* $-5, 8$
10. $5s^2 - 14s - 3 = 0$ *(p. 259)* $-\frac{1}{5}, 3$
11. $7a^2 - 30a + 8 = 0$ *(p. 259)* $\frac{2}{7}, 4$
12. $4x^2 + 20x + 25 = 0$ *(p. 259)* $-2\frac{1}{2}$

13. **DVD PLAYERS** A store sells about 50 of a new model of DVD player per month at a price of \$140 each. For each \$10 decrease in price, about 5 more DVD players per month are sold. How much should the store charge in order to maximize monthly revenue? What is the maximum monthly revenue? *(p. 259)* \$120; \$7200

5 ASSESS AND RETEACH

Daily Homework Quiz

Transparency Available

Factor the expression.

1. $8r^2 + 6r - 5$ $(2r - 1)(4r + 5)$
2. $3p^2 - 7p + 4$ $(p - 1)(3p - 4)$
3. $5z^2 - 80$ $5(z + 4)(z - 4)$
4. $9m^2 + 30mn + 25n^2$ $(3m + 5n)^2$
5. Solve $5x^2 + x - 4 = 0$. $-1, \frac{4}{5}$
6. A mat of uniform width and area 115 square inches surrounds an 8×10-inch photograph. What is the width of the mat? $2\frac{1}{2}$ in.

Online Quiz

Available at **classzone.com**

Diagnosis/Remediation

- Practice A, B, C in Chapter 4 Resource Book, pp. 46–48
- Study Guide in Chapter 4 Resource Book, pp. 49–50
- Practice Workbook, pp. 62–63
- @HomeTutor

Challenge

Additional challenge is available in the Chapter 4 Resource Book, p. 53.

Quiz

An easily-readable reduced copy of the quiz (with answers) on Lessons 4.1–4.4 from the Assessment Book can be found on p. 234G.

1 PLAN AND PREPARE

Warm-Up Exercises

Transparency Available

Find the exact value.

1. $\sqrt{49}$ 7
2. $-\sqrt{144}$ −12
3. Use a calculator to approximate the value of $\sqrt{\frac{82}{16}}$ to the nearest tenth. 2.3
4. The area of half of a square mural is $60\frac{1}{2}$ square feet. What is the length of a side of the mural? 11 ft

Notetaking Guide

Transparency Available

Promotes interactive learning and notetaking skills, pp. 105–107.

Pacing

Basic: 1 day
Average: 1 day
Advanced: 1 day
Block: 0.5 block with 4.4

- See *Teaching Guide/Lesson Plan.*

2 FOCUS AND MOTIVATE

Essential Question

Big Ideas 2 and 3, p. 235

How can you use square roots to solve a quadratic equation? Tell students they will learn how to answer this question by solving quadratic equations of the form $x^2 = s$ when $s > 0$.

4.5 Solve Quadratic Equations by Finding Square Roots

MA-HS-5.3.6 Students will model, solve and graph quadratic equations in real-world and mathematical problems. DOK 2

Before You solved quadratic equations by factoring.

Now You will solve quadratic equations by finding square roots.

Why? So you can solve problems about astronomy, as in Ex. 39.

Key Vocabulary
- square root
- radical
- radicand
- rationalizing the denominator
- conjugates

A number r is a **square root** of a number s if $r^2 = s$. A positive number s has two square roots, written as $\sqrt{s}$ and $-\sqrt{s}$. For example, because $3^2 = 9$ and $(-3)^2 = 9$, the two square roots of 9 are $\sqrt{9} = 3$ and $-\sqrt{9} = -3$. The positive square root of a number is also called the *principal* square root.

The expression $\sqrt{s}$ is called a **radical**. The symbol $\sqrt{\ }$ is a *radical sign*, and the number s beneath the radical sign is the **radicand** of the expression.

KEY CONCEPT *For Your Notebook*

Properties of Square Roots ($a > 0$, $b > 0$)

Product Property $\sqrt{ab} = \sqrt{a} \cdot \sqrt{b}$ **Example** $\sqrt{18} = \sqrt{9} \cdot \sqrt{2} = 3\sqrt{2}$

Quotient Property $\sqrt{\frac{a}{b}} = \frac{\sqrt{a}}{\sqrt{b}}$ **Example** $\sqrt{\frac{2}{25}} = \frac{\sqrt{2}}{\sqrt{25}} = \frac{\sqrt{2}}{5}$

SIMPLIFYING SQUARE ROOTS You can use the properties above to simplify expressions containing square roots. A square-root expression is simplified if:

- no radicand has a perfect-square factor other than 1, and
- there is no radical in a denominator

EXAMPLE 1 Use properties of square roots

USE A CALCULATOR
You can use a calculator to approximate $\sqrt{s}$ when s is not a perfect square. For example, $\sqrt{80} \approx 8.944$.

Simplify the expression.

a. $\sqrt{80} = \sqrt{16} \cdot \sqrt{5} = 4\sqrt{5}$

b. $\sqrt{6} \cdot \sqrt{21} = \sqrt{126} = \sqrt{9} \cdot \sqrt{14} = 3\sqrt{14}$

c. $\sqrt{\frac{4}{81}} = \frac{\sqrt{4}}{\sqrt{81}} = \frac{2}{9}$

d. $\sqrt{\frac{7}{16}} = \frac{\sqrt{7}}{\sqrt{16}} = \frac{\sqrt{7}}{4}$

GUIDED PRACTICE for Example 1

Simplify the expression.

1. $\sqrt{27}$ $3\sqrt{3}$
2. $\sqrt{98}$ $7\sqrt{2}$
3. $\sqrt{10} \cdot \sqrt{15}$ $5\sqrt{6}$
4. $\sqrt{8} \cdot \sqrt{28}$ $4\sqrt{14}$
5. $\sqrt{\frac{9}{64}}$ $\frac{3}{8}$
6. $\sqrt{\frac{15}{4}}$ $\frac{\sqrt{15}}{2}$
7. $\sqrt{\frac{11}{25}}$ $\frac{\sqrt{11}}{5}$
8. $\sqrt{\frac{36}{49}}$ $\frac{6}{7}$

Resource Planning Guide

Chapter Resource Book
- Teaching Guide/Lesson Plan (pp. 54–55)
- Practice levels A, B, C (pp. 56–58)
- Study Guide (pp. 59–60)
- Catch-up for Absent Students (p. 61)
- Problem Solving Workshop (p. 62)
- Challenge (p. 64)

Workbooks
- Notetaking Guide (pp. 105–107)
- Practice Workbook (pp. 64–65)

Teaching Options
- **Power Presentations CD-ROM** provides dynamic electronic teaching resources for the classroom.
- **Activity Generator CD-ROM** provides editable activities for all ability levels.

Interactive Technology
- Easy Planner
- Power Presentations CD-ROM
- Activity Generator CD-ROM
- Animated Algebra
- Test Generator CD-ROM
- Online Quiz
- eWorkbook
- eEdition
- @HomeTutor

Resources for English Learners
- Quick Reference for English Learners
- Spanish Study Guide
- Multi-Language Visual Glossary
- Student Resources in Spanish

See also the *Algebra 2 Toolkit* for more strategies for meeting individual needs.

RATIONALIZING THE DENOMINATOR Suppose the denominator of a fraction has the form $\sqrt{b}$, $a + \sqrt{b}$, or $a - \sqrt{b}$ where a and b are rational numbers. The table shows how to eliminate the radical from the denominator. This is called **rationalizing the denominator**.

Form of the denominator	Multiply numerator and denominator by:
$\sqrt{b}$	$\sqrt{b}$
$a + \sqrt{b}$	$a - \sqrt{b}$
$a - \sqrt{b}$	$a + \sqrt{b}$

The expressions $a + \sqrt{b}$ and $a - \sqrt{b}$ are called **conjugates** of each other. Their product is always a rational number.

EXAMPLE 2 Rationalize denominators of fractions

Simplify (a) $\sqrt{\frac{5}{2}}$ and (b) $\frac{3}{7+\sqrt{2}}$.

Solution

a. $\sqrt{\frac{5}{2}} = \frac{\sqrt{5}}{\sqrt{2}}$

$= \frac{\sqrt{5}}{\sqrt{2}} \cdot \frac{\sqrt{2}}{\sqrt{2}}$

$= \frac{\sqrt{10}}{2}$

b. $\frac{3}{7+\sqrt{2}} = \frac{3}{7+\sqrt{2}} \cdot \frac{7-\sqrt{2}}{7-\sqrt{2}}$

$= \frac{21 - 3\sqrt{2}}{49 - 7\sqrt{2} + 7\sqrt{2} - 2}$

$= \frac{21 - 3\sqrt{2}}{47}$

SOLVING QUADRATIC EQUATIONS You can use square roots to solve some types of quadratic equations. For example, if $s > 0$, then the equation $x^2 = s$ has two real-number solutions: $x = \sqrt{s}$ and $x = -\sqrt{s}$. These solutions are often written in condensed form as $x = \pm\sqrt{s}$ (read as "plus or minus the square root of s").

EXAMPLE 3 Solve a quadratic equation

Solve $3x^2 + 5 = 41$.

$3x^2 + 5 = 41$	**Write original equation.**
$3x^2 = 36$	**Subtract 5 from each side.**
$x^2 = 12$	**Divide each side by 3.**
$x = \pm\sqrt{12}$	**Take square roots of each side.**
$x = \pm\sqrt{4} \cdot \sqrt{3}$	**Product property**
$x = \pm 2\sqrt{3}$	**Simplify.**

AVOID ERRORS
When solving an equation of the form $x^2 = s$ where $s > 0$, make sure to find both the positive and negative solutions.

▶ The solutions are $2\sqrt{3}$ and $-2\sqrt{3}$.

CHECK Check the solutions by substituting them into the original equation.

$3x^2 + 5 = 41$ | $3x^2 + 5 = 41$

$3(2\sqrt{3})^2 + 5 \stackrel{?}{=} 41$ | $3(-2\sqrt{3})^2 + 5 \stackrel{?}{=} 41$

$3(12) + 5 \stackrel{?}{=} 41$ | $3(12) + 5 \stackrel{?}{=} 41$

$41 = 41$ ✓ | $41 = 41$ ✓

Differentiated Instruction

English Learners The word *rationalize*, which means to make something appear to be reasonable, may confuse some students. Explain that, in mathematics, words such as *rationalize* and *rational* are always associated with *ratio.* To *rationalize the denominator* means to make it rational; that is, to free the denominator of irrational radicals which cannot be expressed as a ratio of integers.

See also the *Algebra 2 Toolkit* for more strategies.

Motivating the Lesson

Ask students to think about what would happen if they simultaneously drop two objects of slightly different weights from the roof of the school. In this lesson, students will use a formula to calculate the time it takes a dropped object to reach the ground. Students will see that the duration of a fall depends only on the object's initial height, and not on its weight.

3 TEACH

Extra Example 1

Simplify the expression.

a. $\sqrt{75}$ $5\sqrt{3}$

b. $\sqrt{7} \cdot \sqrt{35}$ $7\sqrt{5}$

c. $\sqrt{\frac{100}{169}}$ $\frac{10}{13}$

d. $\sqrt{\frac{11}{144}}$ $\frac{\sqrt{11}}{12}$

Extra Example 2

Simplify the expression.

a. $\sqrt{\frac{2}{15}}$ $\frac{\sqrt{30}}{15}$

b. $\frac{4}{5-\sqrt{2}}$ $\frac{20+4\sqrt{2}}{23}$

Key Question to Ask for Example 2

- In Example 2b, can you think of a shortcut for multiplying the conjugates $7 + \sqrt{2}$ and $7 - \sqrt{2}$? Use the pattern, in reverse, for factoring a difference of two squares: $(7 + \sqrt{2})(7 - \sqrt{2}) = 7^2 - (\sqrt{2})^2 = 49 - 2 = 47$.

Extra Example 3

Solve $2x^2 - 15 = 65$. $2\sqrt{10}, -2\sqrt{10}$

Extra Example 4

What are the solutions of the equation $\frac{1}{3}(x-4)^2 = 11$? **D**

Ⓐ $4 - \sqrt{11}, 4 + \sqrt{11}$

Ⓑ $4 - \frac{\sqrt{11}}{3}, 4 + \frac{\sqrt{11}}{3}$

Ⓒ $-4 - \sqrt{33}, -4 + \sqrt{33}$

Ⓓ $4 - \sqrt{33}, 4 + \sqrt{33}$

Key Question to Ask for Example 4

- What do you know about the solutions of the equation in Example 4 before you actually start solving it? **The solutions are conjugates.**

Avoiding Common Errors

Some students may misinterpret the graph at the bottom of page 268 and think that the horizontal axis shows the horizontal distance the object has traveled. Students should be able to use the graph title, "Height of Dropped Object," and to show how that title helps describe the vertical axis. Emphasize that when drawing graphs for applied problems, it is important to label the axes appropriately and include a caption that explains the graph.

Study Strategy

In their science classes, students probably will be working with measurements in the metric system. Tell them that the formula given on page 268 applies for measurements in feet and seconds. For measurements in meters and seconds, the appropriate formula is $h = -4.9t^2 + h_0$.

EXAMPLE 4 Standardized Test Practice

What are the solutions of the equation $\frac{1}{5}(z+3)^2 = 7$?

Ⓐ $-38, 32$

Ⓑ $-3 - 5\sqrt{7}, -3 + 5\sqrt{7}$

Ⓒ $-3 - \sqrt{35}, -3 + \sqrt{35}$

Ⓓ $-3 - \frac{\sqrt{35}}{5}, -3 + \frac{\sqrt{35}}{5}$

Solution

$\frac{1}{5}(z+3)^2 = 7$ — **Write original equation.**

$(z+3)^2 = 35$ — **Multiply each side by 5.**

$z + 3 = \pm\sqrt{35}$ — **Take square roots of each side.**

$z = -3 \pm \sqrt{35}$ — **Subtract 3 from each side.**

The solutions are $-3 + \sqrt{35}$ and $-3 - \sqrt{35}$.

▶ The correct answer is C. Ⓐ Ⓑ Ⓒ Ⓓ

GUIDED PRACTICE for Examples 2, 3, and 4

Simplify the expression.

9. $\sqrt{\frac{6}{5}}$ $\frac{\sqrt{30}}{5}$ **10.** $\sqrt{\frac{9}{8}}$ $\frac{3\sqrt{2}}{4}$ **11.** $\sqrt{\frac{17}{12}}$ $\frac{\sqrt{51}}{6}$ **12.** $\sqrt{\frac{19}{21}}$ $\frac{\sqrt{399}}{21}$

13. $\frac{-6}{7-\sqrt{5}}$ $\frac{-3\sqrt{5}-21}{22}$ **14.** $\frac{2}{4+\sqrt{11}}$ $\frac{-2\sqrt{11}+8}{5}$ **15.** $\frac{-1}{9+\sqrt{7}}$ $\frac{\sqrt{7}-9}{74}$ **16.** $\frac{4}{8-\sqrt{3}}$ $\frac{4\sqrt{3}+32}{61}$

Solve the equation.

17. $5x^2 = 80$ ± 4 **18.** $z^2 - 7 = 29$ ± 6 **19.** $3(x-2)^2 = 40$ $2 \pm \frac{2\sqrt{30}}{3}$

MODELING DROPPED OBJECTS When an object is dropped, its height h (in feet) above the ground after t seconds can be modeled by the function

$$h = -16t^2 + h_0$$

where h_0 is the object's initial height (in feet). The graph of $h = -16t^2 + 200$, representing the height of an object dropped from an initial height of 200 feet, is shown at the right.

The model $h = -16t^2 + h_0$ assumes that the force of air resistance on the object is negligible. Also, this model works only on Earth. For planets with stronger or weaker gravity, different models are used (see Exercise 39).

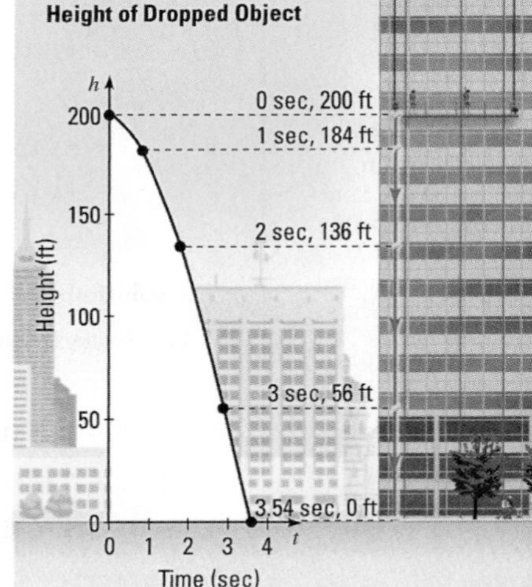

EXAMPLE 5 Model a dropped object with a quadratic function

SCIENCE COMPETITION For a science competition, students must design a container that prevents an egg from breaking when dropped from a height of 50 feet. How long does the container take to hit the ground?

After a successful egg drop

ANOTHER WAY

For alternative methods for solving the problem in Example 5, turn to page 272 for the Problem Solving Workshop.

Solution

$h = -16t^2 + h_0$	**Write height function.**
$0 = -16t^2 + 50$	**Substitute 0 for h and 50 for h_0.**
$-50 = -16t^2$	**Subtract 50 from each side.**
$\frac{50}{16} = t^2$	**Divide each side by −16.**
$\pm\sqrt{\frac{50}{16}} = t$	**Take square roots of each side.**
$\pm 1.8 \approx t$	**Use a calculator.**

▶ Reject the negative solution, −1.8, because time must be positive. The container will fall for about 1.8 seconds before it hits the ground.

 at classzone.com

 **GUIDED PRACTICE** for Example 5

20. **WHAT IF?** In Example 5, suppose the egg container is dropped from a height of 30 feet. How long does the container take to hit the ground? about 1.4 sec

4.5 EXERCISES

HOMEWORK KEY

○ = **WORKED-OUT SOLUTIONS** on p. WS8 for Exs. 17, 27, and 41

★ = **STANDARDIZED TEST PRACTICE** Exs. 2, 19, 34, 35, 36, 40, and 41

SKILL PRACTICE

1. **VOCABULARY** In the expression $\sqrt{72}$, what is 72 called? radicand

2. ★ **WRITING** *Explain* what it means to "rationalize the denominator" of a quotient containing square roots. eliminating the radical from the denominator

EXAMPLES 1 and 2 on pp. 266–267 for Exs. 3–20

SIMPLIFYING RADICAL EXPRESSIONS **Simplify the expression.**

3. $\sqrt{28}$ $2\sqrt{7}$

4. $\sqrt{192}$ $8\sqrt{3}$

5. $\sqrt{150}$ $5\sqrt{6}$

6. $\sqrt{3} \cdot \sqrt{27}$ 9

7. $4\sqrt{6} \cdot \sqrt{6}$ 24

8. $5\sqrt{24} \cdot 3\sqrt{10}$ $60\sqrt{15}$

9. $\sqrt{\frac{5}{16}}$ $\frac{\sqrt{5}}{4}$

10. $\sqrt{\frac{35}{36}}$ $\frac{\sqrt{35}}{6}$

11. $\frac{8}{\sqrt{3}}$ $\frac{8\sqrt{3}}{3}$

12. $\frac{7}{\sqrt{12}}$ $\frac{7\sqrt{3}}{6}$

13. $\sqrt{\frac{18}{11}}$ $\frac{3\sqrt{22}}{11}$

14. $\sqrt{\frac{13}{28}}$ $\frac{\sqrt{91}}{14}$

15. $\frac{2}{1-\sqrt{3}}$ $-\sqrt{3}-1$

16. $\frac{1}{5+\sqrt{6}}$ $\frac{-\sqrt{6}+5}{19}$

(17.) $\frac{\sqrt{2}}{4+\sqrt{5}}$ $\frac{4\sqrt{2}-\sqrt{10}}{11}$

18. $\frac{3+\sqrt{7}}{2-\sqrt{10}}$ $-\frac{\sqrt{70}+3\sqrt{10}+2\sqrt{7}+6}{6}$

Extra Example 5

If you drop an object off the roof of an apartment building that is 240 feet tall, about how long will it take the object to hit the ground? 3.9 sec

Key Question to Ask for Example 5

- How would a graph of time versus height compare to the one on page 268? The graph would have a similar shape, but the *h*-intercept would be 50 and the *t*-intercept would be about 1.8.

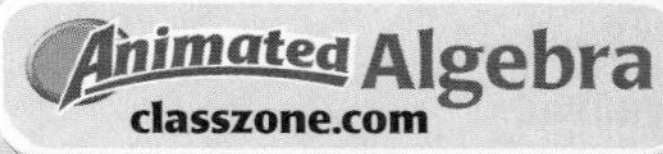

An **Animated Algebra** activity is available on-line for **Example 5**. This activity is also available on the **Power Presentations CD-ROM**.

Closing the Lesson

Have students summarize the major points of the lesson and answer the Essential Question: How can you use square roots to solve a quadratic equation?

- A square root expression is simplified if no radicand has a perfect square factor other than 1 and if there is no radical in the denominator.
- When an object is dropped from a height of h_0 feet, its height h (in feet) above the ground after t seconds is given by the function $h = -16t^2 + h_0$.

If a quadratic equation is written in the form $x^2 = s$ or $(x - a)^2 = s$, where $s > 0$, then you can solve it by taking the square roots of both sides and simplifying the results.

4 PRACTICE AND APPLY

Assignment Guide

Answer Transparencies available for all exercises

Basic:
Day 1: SRH p. 979 Exs. 1–10
pp. 269–271
Exs. 1, 2, 3–19 odd, 20, 21–31 odd, 38–41, 45

Average:
Day 1: pp. 269–271
Exs. 1, 2–18 even, 19–21, 25–30, 34, 35, 38–42, 44

Advanced:
Day 1: pp. 269–271
Exs. 1, 2, 7–10, 15–19, 25–43*

Block:
pp. 269–271
Exs. 1, 2–18 even, 19–21, 25–30, 34, 35, 38–42, 44 (with 4.4)

Differentiated Instruction

See *Algebra 2 Best Practices Toolkit* for suggestions on addressing the needs of a diverse classroom.

Homework Check

For a quick check of student understanding of key concepts, go over the following exercises:

Basic: 5, 13, 23, 29, 38
Average: 6, 14, 25, 28, 39
Advanced: 8, 16, 26, 32, 39

Extra Practice

- Student Edition, p. 1013
- Chapter 4 Resource Book: Practice levels A, B, C, pp. 56–58

Practice Worksheet

An easily-readable reduced practice page (with answers) for this lesson can be found on p. 234C.

35. Factor: $x^2 - 4 = 0$, $(x + 2)(x - 2) = 0$, $x = -2$ or $x = 2$; solve the equation: $x^2 - 4 = 0$, $x^2 = 4$, $x = \pm 2$.

---

19. ★ **MULTIPLE CHOICE** What is a completely simplified expression for $\sqrt{108}$? C

 (A) $2\sqrt{27}$ (B) $3\sqrt{12}$ (C) $6\sqrt{3}$ (D) $10\sqrt{8}$

ERROR ANALYSIS ***Describe*** **and correct the error in simplifying the expression or solving the equation.**

20. $\sqrt{96} = \sqrt{4} \cdot \sqrt{24}$
 $= 2\sqrt{24}$

 4 is not the largest perfect square to divide evenly into 96; $\sqrt{96} = \sqrt{16} \cdot \sqrt{6} = 4\sqrt{6}$.

21. $5x^2 = 405$
 $x^2 = 81$
 $x = 9$

 The equation has two solutions; $x^2 = 81$, $x = \pm 9$.

EXAMPLES 3 and 4 on pp. 267–268 for Exs. 21–34

B **SOLVING QUADRATIC EQUATIONS** **Solve the equation.**

22. $s^2 = 169$ ± 13
23. $a^2 = 50$ $\pm 5\sqrt{2}$
24. $x^2 = 84$ $\pm 2\sqrt{21}$
25. $6z^2 = 150$ ± 5
26. $4p^2 = 448$ $\pm 4\sqrt{7}$
27. $-3w^2 = -213$ $\pm\sqrt{71}$
28. $7r^2 - 10 = 25$ $\pm\sqrt{5}$
29. $\frac{x^2}{25} - 6 = -2$ ± 10
30. $\frac{t^2}{20} + 8 = 15$ $\pm 2\sqrt{35}$
31. $4(x - 1)^2 = 8$ $1 \pm \sqrt{2}$
32. $7(x - 4)^2 - 18 = 10$ 2, 6
33. $2(x + 2)^2 - 5 = 8$ $-2 \pm \frac{\sqrt{26}}{2}$

34. ★ **MULTIPLE CHOICE** What are the solutions of $3(x + 2)^2 + 4 = 13$? C

 (A) $-5, 1$ (B) $-1, 5$ (C) $-2 \pm \sqrt{3}$ (D) $2 \pm \sqrt{3}$

35. ★ **SHORT RESPONSE** *Describe* two different methods for solving the equation $x^2 - 4 = 0$. Include the steps for each method. See margin.

C 36. ★ **OPEN-ENDED MATH** Write an equation of the form $x^2 = s$ that has **(a)** two real solutions, **(b)** exactly one real solution, and **(c)** no real solutions.
 (a) *Sample answer:* $x^2 = 31$, (b) $x^2 = 0$, (c) *Sample answer:* $x^2 = -12$

37. **CHALLENGE** Solve the equation $a(x + b)^2 = c$ in terms of a, b, and c. $-b \pm \sqrt{\frac{c}{a}}$

PROBLEM SOLVING

EXAMPLE 5 on p. 269 for Exs. 38–39

A 38. **CLIFF DIVING** A cliff diver dives off a cliff 40 feet above water. Write an equation giving the diver's height h (in feet) above the water after t seconds. How long is the diver in the air?

 $h = -16t^2 + 40$; about 1.6 sec

39. **ASTRONOMY** On any planet, the height h (in feet) of a falling object t seconds after it is dropped can be modeled by $h = -\frac{g}{2}t^2 + h_0$ where h_0 is the object's initial height (in feet) and g is the acceleration (in feet per second squared) due to the planet's gravity. For each planet in the table, find the time it takes for a rock dropped from a height of 150 feet to hit the surface. Earth: about 3.1 sec, Mars: 5 sec, Jupiter: about 2.0 sec, Saturn: about 3.2 sec, Pluto: about 12.2 sec

Planet	Earth	Mars	Jupiter	Saturn	Pluto
g (ft/sec^2)	32	12	76	30	2

@HomeTutor for problem solving help at classzone.com

○ = WORKED-OUT SOLUTIONS on p. WS1 ★ = STANDARDIZED TEST PRACTICE

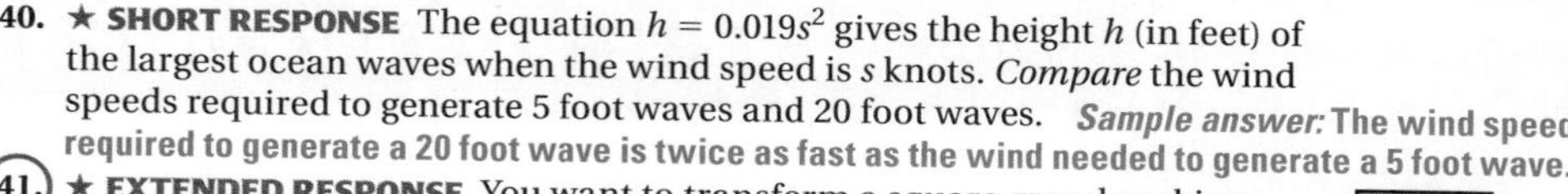

40. ★ **SHORT RESPONSE** The equation $h = 0.019s^2$ gives the height h (in feet) of the largest ocean waves when the wind speed is s knots. *Compare* the wind speeds required to generate 5 foot waves and 20 foot waves. ***Sample answer:*** **The wind speed required to generate a 20 foot wave is twice as fast as the wind needed to generate a 5 foot wave.**

B **41.** ★ **EXTENDED RESPONSE** You want to transform a square gravel parking lot with 10 foot sides into a circular lot. You want the circle to have the same area as the square so that you do not have to buy any additional gravel.

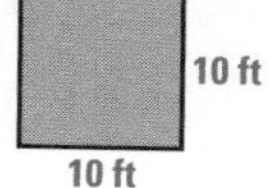

a. **Model** Write an equation you can use to find the radius r of the circular lot. $\pi r^2 = 100$

b. **Solve** What should the radius of the circular lot be? **about 5.6 ft**

c. **Generalize** In general, if a square has sides of length s, what is the radius r of a circle with the same area? *Justify* your answer algebraically. **See margin.**

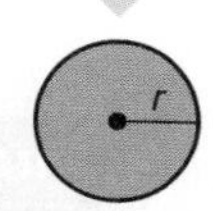

42. BICYCLING The air resistance R (in pounds) on a racing cyclist is given by the equation $R = 0.00829s^2$ where s is the bicycle's speed (in miles per hour).

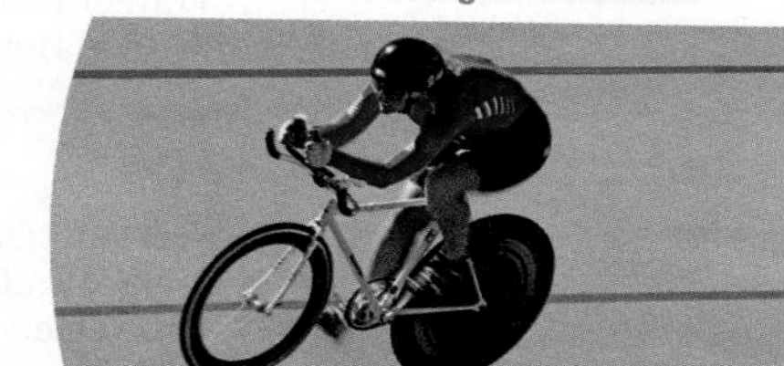

a. What is the speed of a racing cyclist who experiences 5 pounds of air resistance?

b. What happens to the air resistance if the cyclist's speed doubles? *Justify* your answer algebraically. **See margin.**

42a. about 24.6 mi/h

C **43. CHALLENGE** For a swimming pool with a rectangular base, Torricelli's law implies that the height h of water in the pool t seconds after it begins draining is given by $h = \left(\sqrt{h_0} - \frac{2\pi d^2\sqrt{3}}{lw}t\right)^2$ where l and w are the pool's length and width, d is the diameter of the drain, and h_0 is the water's initial height. (All measurements are in inches.) In terms of l, w, d, and h_0, what is the time required to drain the pool when it is completely filled? $\left(-\sqrt{h_0} \pm \sqrt{h}\right)\left(\frac{-\ell w}{2\pi d^2\sqrt{3}}\right)$

KENTUCKY MIXED REVIEW

TEST PRACTICE at classzone.com

44. The graph of which inequality is shown? **B**

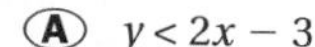

Ⓐ $y < 2x - 3$

Ⓑ $y > 2x - 3$

Ⓒ $y \le 2x - 3$

Ⓓ $y \ge 2x - 3$

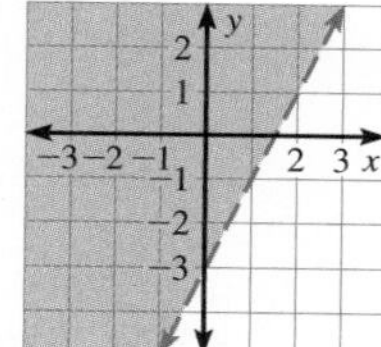

45. Which two lines are perpendicular? **C**

Ⓐ $3x + y = -1$ and $x + 3y = -24$

Ⓑ $3x - y = 12$ and $3x + y = 15$

Ⓒ $3x + y = -1$ and $-x + 3y = 6$

Ⓓ $3x - y = 12$ and $x - 3y = 9$

EXTRA PRACTICE for Lesson 4.5, p. 1013

ONLINE QUIZ at classzone.com

5 ASSESS AND RETEACH

Daily Homework Quiz

Transparency Available

Simplify the expression.

1. $3\sqrt{20} \cdot \sqrt{40}$ **$60\sqrt{2}$**

2. $\frac{5}{6 + \sqrt{3}}$ **$\frac{30 - 5\sqrt{3}}{33}$**

3. Solve $3n^2 - 5 = 49$. **$3\sqrt{2}, -3\sqrt{2}$**

4. If a ball is dropped from a height of 100 feet, how long will it take for the ball to hit the ground? **2.5 sec**

Online Quiz

Available at **classzone.com**

Diagnosis/Remediation

- Practice A, B, C in Chapter 4 Resource Book, pp. 56–58
- Study Guide in Chapter 4 Resource Book, pp. 59–60
- Practice Workbook, pp. 64–65
- @HomeTutor

Challenge

Additional challenge is available in the Chapter 4 Resource Book, p. 64.

41c. $\sqrt{\frac{s^2}{\pi}}$; $s^2 = \pi r^2$, $\frac{s^2}{\pi} = r^2$, $\sqrt{\frac{s^2}{\pi}} = r$

42b. The air resistance quadruples. Replace s with $2s$ (double the cyclist's speed): $R = 0.00829(2s)^2 = 0.00829(4s^2) = 4(0.00829s^2)$.

Alternative Strategy

Method 1 Example 5 on page 269 can be solved by using a calculator table. Enter the height function for this problem, $y = -16t^2 + 50$, use the *table* feature with TblStart = 0 and ΔTbl = .1, and look for an entry where the value of *y* is 0. If 0 does not appear in the Y_1 column, look for entries where the value changes from positive to negative. This method allows students to see how the height gets closer to 0 as time increases.

Graphing Calculator

Some students may not feel that they have solved the problem because they have not found the exact *x*-value that gives $y = 0$. If they want to refine the table to use a smaller value of ΔTbl, they will get closer to 0. Have these students try this and report what happens. They should see that they will never hit 0 exactly. Ask them why. If necessary, refer them back to the algebra solution for this example on page 269 so that they can see that the exact value is an irrational number, which can only be approximated by a decimal.

Another Way to Solve Example 5, page 269

MULTIPLE REPRESENTATIONS In Example 5 on page 269, you solved a quadratic equation by finding square roots. You can also solve a quadratic equation using a table or a graph.

PROBLEM

SCIENCE COMPETITION For a science competition, students must design a container that prevents an egg from breaking when dropped from a height of 50 feet. How long does the container take to hit the ground?

METHOD 1

Using a Table One alternative approach is to write a quadratic equation and then use a table of values to solve the equation. You can use a graphing calculator to make the table.

STEP 1 **Write** an equation that models the situation using the height function $h = -16t^2 + h_0$.

$h = -16t^2 + h_0$ **Write height function.**

$0 = -16t^2 + 50$ **Substitute 0 for *h* and 50 for h_0.**

STEP 2 **Enter** the function $y = -16x^2 + 50$ into a graphing calculator. Note that time is now represented by *x* and height is now represented by *y*.

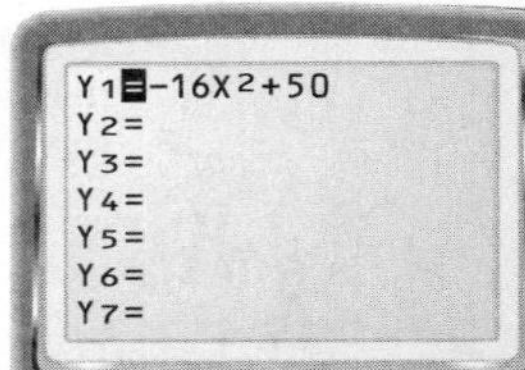

STEP 3 **Make** a table of values for the function. Set the table so that the *x*-values start at 0 and increase in increments of 0.1.

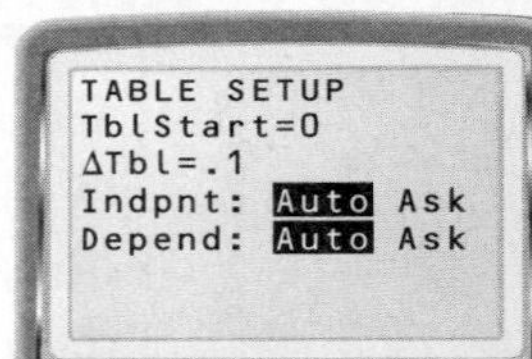

STEP 4 **Scroll** through the table to find the time *x* at which the height *y* of the container is 0 feet.

The table shows that $y = 0$ between $x = 1.7$ and $x = 1.8$ because *y* has a change of sign.

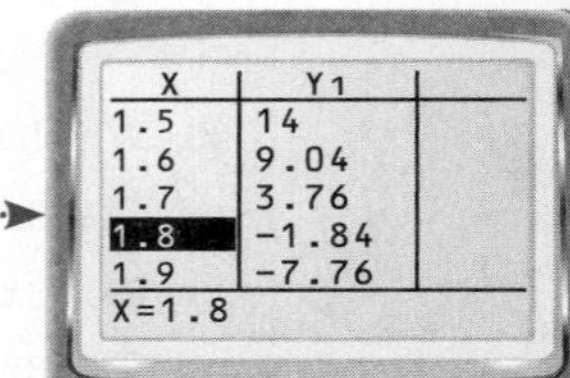

X	Y1
1.5	14
1.6	9.04
1.7	3.76
1.8	-1.84
1.9	-7.76

X=1.8

▸ The container hits the ground between 1.7 and 1.8 seconds after it is dropped.

METHOD 2

Using a Graph Another approach is to write a quadratic equation and then use a graph to solve the equation. You can use a graphing calculator to make the graph.

STEP 1 **Write** an equation that models the situation using the height function $h = -16t^2 + h_0$.

$h = -16t^2 + h_0$ **Write height function.**

$0 = -16t^2 + 50$ **Substitute 0 for *h* and 50 for h_0.**

STEP 2 **Enter** the function $y = -16x^2 + 50$ into a graphing calculator. Note that time is now represented by x and height is now represented by y.

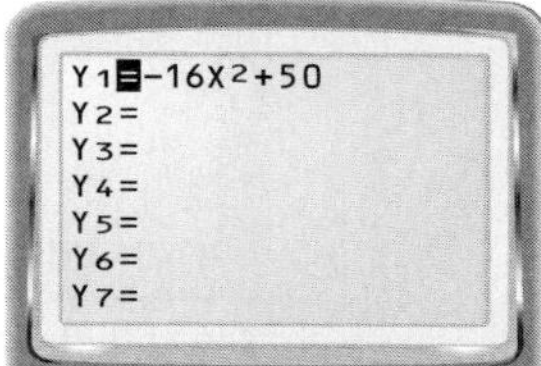

STEP 3 **Graph** the height function. Adjust the viewing window so that you can see the point where the graph crosses the positive x-axis. Find the positive x-value for which $y = 0$ using the *zero* feature. The graph shows that $y = 0$ when $x \approx 1.8$.

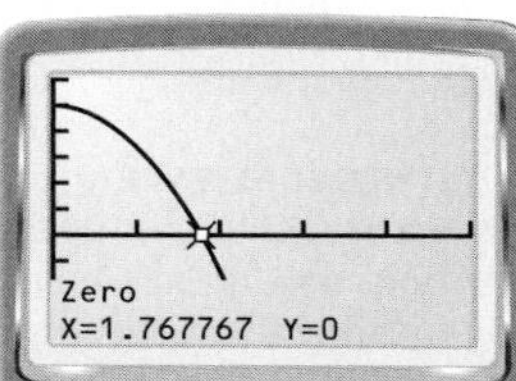

▶ The container hits the ground about 1.8 seconds after it is dropped.

PRACTICE

SOLVING EQUATIONS Solve the quadratic equation using a table and using a graph.

1. $2x^2 - 12x + 10 = 0$ **1, 5**
2. $x^2 + 7x + 12 = 0$ **−4, −3**
3. $9x^2 - 30x + 25 = 0$ $1\frac{2}{3}$
4. $7x^2 - 3 = 0$ **about −0.65, about 0.65**
5. $x^2 + 3x - 6 = 0$ **about −4.4, about 1.4**

6. **WHAT IF?** How long does it take for an egg container to hit the ground when dropped from a height of 100 feet? Find the answer using a table and using a graph. **2.5 sec**

7. **WIND PRESSURE** The pressure P (in pounds per square foot) from wind blowing at s miles per hour is given by $P = 0.00256s^2$. What wind speed produces a pressure of 30 lb/ft^2? Solve this problem using a table and using a graph. **about 108 mph**

8. **BIRDS** A bird flying at a height of 30 feet carries a shellfish. The bird drops the shellfish to break it and get the food inside. How long does it take for the shellfish to hit the ground? Find the answer using a table and using a graph. **about 1.4 sec**

9. **DROPPED OBJECT** You are dropping a ball from a window 29 feet above the ground to your friend who will catch it 4 feet above the ground. How long is the ball in the air before your friend catches it? Solve this problem using a table and using a graph. **1.25 sec**

10. **REASONING** *Explain* how to use the *table* feature of a graphing calculator to approximate the solution of the problem on page 272 to the nearest hundredth of a second. Use this procedure to find the approximate solution. **Set the increments to 0.01; about 1.77 sec**

Alternative Strategy

Method 2 Example 5 on page 269 can be also solved by using a calculator graph. Start by entering the height function, $y = -16t^2 + 50$, then make a calculator graph and use the *zero* feature to approximate the time, to the nearest tenth of a second, when the container hits the ground. This method allows students to visualize how the height of the container decreases over time until it hits the ground.

Avoiding Common Errors

Some students may use all digits shown on the calculator screen and write 1.767767 seconds as their answer, thinking that the more digits they give, the better the answer. First, ask them how you would ever measure a time that precisely. Then, ask how precisely the height was measured. Point out that the height given in the example, 50 feet, has two significant digits. So the answer should also have two significant digits, and should be written to the nearest tenth of a second.

Mathematical Reasoning

Multiple Representations There are three representations of the solution to Example 5: an algebraic one on page 269, a numerical one on page 272, and a graphical one on page 273. Ask students which of these best helps them understand the problem. Make sure that they understand that the graph on page 273 shows how the container's vertical position changes with time, and is *not* a graph of the container's path.

Kentucky Mixed Review

1. B
2. A
3. C
4. B
5. A
6. A
7. a. Slices sold $= 80 - 5x$; Price $= 2 + 0.25x$
   b. $R = (80 - 5x)(2 + 0.25x)$
   c. $x = 4$; increasing the price by $4 \bullet 0.25 = \$1$ will maximize revenue.

Lessons 4.1–4.5

1. **CRAFTS** You are creating a metal border of uniform width for a rectangular wall mirror that is 20 inches by 24 inches. You have 416 square inches of metal to use. What is the greatest possible width x of the border?

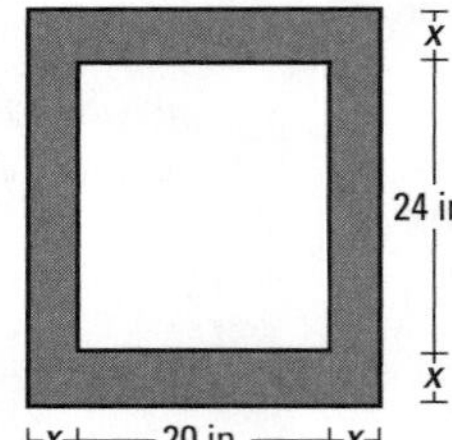

A. 2 inches B. 4 inches
C. 16 inches D. 26 inches

2. **PHYSICAL SCIENCE** A pinecone falls from a tree branch that is 20 feet above the ground. About how many seconds does it take for the pinecone to hit the ground?

A. 0.80 second
B. 0.89 second
C. 1.12 seconds
D. 1.25 seconds

3. **FIREFIGHTING** Some harbor police departments have firefighting boats with water cannons. The boats are used to fight fires that occur within the harbor. The function $y = -0.0035x(x - 143.9)$ models the path of water shot by a water cannon where x is the horizontal distance (in feet) and y is the corresponding height (in feet). How far does the water cannon shoot?

A. 12.0 feet
B. 71.9 feet
C. 143.9 feet
D. 287.8 feet

4. **COMPUTERS** The diagonal of the screen on a laptop computer measures 15 inches. The ratio of the screen's width w to its height h is 4 : 3. What is the height of the laptop screen?

A. 3 inches B. 9 inches
C. 12 inches D. 81 inches

5. **QUADRATIC FUNCTION** Which function's graph has a vertex of $(-3, 2)$?

A. $y = -3x^2 - 18x - 25$
B. $y = -\frac{1}{2}x^2 + 2x + 5$
C. $y = x^2 + x - 6$
D. $y = x^2 - 4x - 25$

6. **VEGETABLE GARDEN** You have a rectangular vegetable garden that measures 42 feet by 8 feet. You want to double the area of the garden by expanding the length and width as shown. What is the value of x?

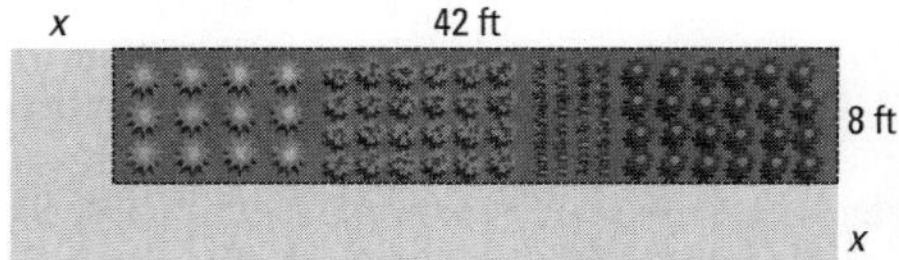

A. 6 feet
B. 11 feet
C. 15 feet
D. 57 feet

7. **OPEN-RESPONSE** When Lou's Pizza Shop charges \$2 per slice, they sell about 80 slices of pizza each day. For each \$.25 increase in price, the shop sells 5 fewer slices each day.

   a. Write the number of slices and the price per slice in terms of x, the number of price increases.
   b. Write a function that gives the shop's total revenue R if there are x price increases.
   c. What value of x maximizes R? *Explain* the meaning of your answer in this situation.

4.6 Perform Operations with Complex Numbers

MA-HS-5.3.6 **Students will model, solve and graph quadratic equations in real-world and mathematical problems. DOK 2**

Before You performed operations with real numbers.

Now You will perform operations with complex numbers.

Why? So you can solve problems involving fractals, as in Exs. 70–73.

Key Vocabulary
- imaginary unit i
- complex number
- imaginary number
- complex conjugates
- complex plane
- absolute value of a complex number

Not all quadratic equations have real-number solutions. For example, $x^2 = -1$ has no real-number solutions because the square of any real number x is never a negative number.

To overcome this problem, mathematicians created an expanded system of numbers using the **imaginary unit i**, defined as $i = \sqrt{-1}$. Note that $i^2 = -1$. The imaginary unit i can be used to write the square root of *any* negative number.

KEY CONCEPT *For Your Notebook*

The Square Root of a Negative Number

Property	Example
1. If r is a positive real number, then $\sqrt{-r} = i\sqrt{r}$.	$\sqrt{-3} = i\sqrt{3}$
2. By Property (1), it follows that $(i\sqrt{r})^2 = -r$.	$(i\sqrt{3})^2 = i^2 \cdot 3 = -3$

EXAMPLE 1 Solve a quadratic equation

Solve $2x^2 + 11 = -37$.

$2x^2 + 11 = -37$ — **Write original equation.**

$2x^2 = -48$ — **Subtract 11 from each side.**

$x^2 = -24$ — **Divide each side by 2.**

$x = \pm\sqrt{-24}$ — **Take square roots of each side.**

$x = \pm i\sqrt{24}$ — **Write in terms of *i*.**

$x = \pm 2i\sqrt{6}$ — **Simplify radical.**

▶ The solutions are $2i\sqrt{6}$ and $-2i\sqrt{6}$.

GUIDED PRACTICE for Example 1

Solve the equation.

1. $x^2 = -13$ $\pm i\sqrt{13}$
2. $x^2 = -38$ $\pm i\sqrt{38}$
3. $x^2 + 11 = 3$ $\pm 2i\sqrt{2}$
4. $x^2 - 8 = -36$ $\pm 2i\sqrt{7}$
5. $3x^2 - 7 = -31$ $\pm 2i\sqrt{2}$
6. $5x^2 + 33 = 3$ $\pm i\sqrt{6}$

1 PLAN AND PREPARE

Warm-Up Exercises
Transparency Available

1. Simplify $\frac{3}{4 - \sqrt{5}}$. $\frac{12 + 3\sqrt{5}}{11}$

Solve the equation.

2. $3x^2 + 8 = 23$ $\sqrt{5}, -\sqrt{5}$
3. $2(x + 7)^2 = 16$ $-7 + 2\sqrt{2}, -7 - 2\sqrt{2}$
4. Three times the square of a number is 15. What is the number? $-\sqrt{5}, \sqrt{5}$

Notetaking Guide
Transparency Available

Promotes interactive learning and notetaking skills, pp. 108–111.

Pacing
Basic: 2 days
Average: 2 days
Advanced: 2 days
Block: 1 block
- See *Teaching Guide/Lesson Plan.*

2 FOCUS AND MOTIVATE

Essential Question
Big Idea 3, p. 235

How do you perform operations on complex numbers? **Tell students they will learn how to answer this question by learning how to add, subtract, multiply, and divide with the imaginary unit *i* and with complex numbers.**

Resource Planning Guide

Chapter Resource Book
- Teaching Guide/Lesson Plan (pp. 65–66)
- Practice levels A, B, C (pp. 67–69)
- Study Guide (pp. 70–71)
- Catch-up for Absent Students (p. 72)
- Application (p. 73)
- Challenge (p. 74)

Workbooks
- Notetaking Guide (pp. 108–111)
- Practice Workbook (pp. 66–67)

Teaching Options
- **Power Presentations CD-ROM** provides dynamic electronic teaching resources for the classroom.
- **Activity Generator CD-ROM** provides editable activities for all ability levels.

Interactive Technology
- Easy Planner
- Power Presentations CD-ROM
- Activity Generator CD-ROM
- Animated Algebra
- Test Generator CD-ROM
- Online Quiz
- eWorkbook
- eEdition
- @HomeTutor

Resources for English Learners
- Quick Reference for English Learners
- Spanish Study Guide
- Multi-Language Visual Glossary
- Student Resources in Spanish

See also the *Algebra 2 Toolkit* for more strategies for meeting individual needs.

COMPLEX NUMBERS A **complex number** written in **standard form** is a number $a + bi$ where a and b are real numbers. The number a is the *real part* of the complex number, and the number bi is the *imaginary part.*

If $b \neq 0$, then $a + bi$ is an **imaginary number**. If $a = 0$ and $b \neq 0$, then $a + bi$ is a **pure imaginary number**. The diagram shows how different types of complex numbers are related.

Two complex numbers $a + bi$ and $c + di$ are equal if and only if $a = c$ and $b = d$. For example, if $x + yi = 5 - 3i$, then $x = 5$ and $y = -3$.

Complex Numbers ($a + bi$)

Real Numbers ($a + 0i$)	Imaginary Numbers ($a + bi, b \neq 0$)
-1 $\frac{5}{2}$	$2 + 3i$ $5 - 5i$
π $\sqrt{2}$	Pure Imaginary Numbers ($0 + bi, b \neq 0$): $-4i$ $6i$

KEY CONCEPT *For Your Notebook*

Sums and Differences of Complex Numbers

To add (or subtract) two complex numbers, add (or subtract) their real parts and their imaginary parts separately.

Sum of complex numbers: $(a + bi) + (c + di) = (a + c) + (b + d)i$

Difference of complex numbers: $(a + bi) - (c + di) = (a - c) + (b - d)i$

EXAMPLE 2 Add and subtract complex numbers

Write the expression as a complex number in standard form.

a. $(8 - i) + (5 + 4i)$ **b.** $(7 - 6i) - (3 - 6i)$ **c.** $10 - (6 + 7i) + 4i$

Solution

a. $(8 - i) + (5 + 4i) = (8 + 5) + (-1 + 4)i$ **Definition of complex addition**

$= 13 + 3i$ **Write in standard form.**

b. $(7 - 6i) - (3 - 6i) = (7 - 3) + (-6 + 6)i$ **Definition of complex subtraction**

$= 4 + 0i$ **Simplify.**

$= 4$ **Write in standard form.**

c. $10 - (6 + 7i) + 4i = [(10 - 6) - 7i] + 4i$ **Definition of complex subtraction**

$= (4 - 7i) + 4i$ **Simplify.**

$= 4 + (-7 + 4)i$ **Definition of complex addition**

$= 4 - 3i$ **Write in standard form.**

GUIDED PRACTICE for Example 2

Write the expression as a complex number in standard form.

7. $(9 - i) + (-6 + 7i)$ **$3 + 6i$** **8.** $(3 + 7i) - (8 - 2i)$ **$-5 + 9i$** **9.** $-4 - (1 + i) - (5 + 9i)$ **$-10 - 10i$**

Motivating the Lesson

Ask students what kinds of numbers they used when they were young children, and what new kinds of numbers they learned to use as they moved through school. Explain that each time they learned about new kinds of numbers, such as fractions, negative numbers, and irrational numbers, they were able to solve equations they could not solve before. Complex numbers are just one more step in that process.

3 TEACH

Extra Example 1

Solve $2x^2 + 18 = -72$.
$-3i\sqrt{5}, 3i\sqrt{5}$

Key Question to Ask for Example 1

- In Lesson 4.5, you learned to solve equations such as $2x^2 - 11 = 37$ by finding square roots. What one additional step is needed to solve the equation in Example 1? **Rewrite $\sqrt{-24}$ as $i\sqrt{24}$.**

Extra Example 2

Write the expression as a complex number in standard form.

a. $(12 - 11i) + (-8 + 3i)$ **$4 - 8i$**

b. $(15 - 9i) - (24 - 9i)$ **-9**

c. $35 - (13 + 4i) + i$ **$22 - 3i$**

Teaching Strategy

Have students extend the diagram of the complex number system shown on this page by including the subsets of the real numbers shown on page 2 of Lesson 1.1.

Differentiated Instruction

Inclusion The imaginary number i can often be a difficult concept to process. It may be helpful when working through examples to show the simplification steps explicitly. For **Example 1** on page 275, show the additional steps $x = \pm\sqrt{-24} = \pm\sqrt{(-1)(24)} = \pm\sqrt{-1} \cdot \sqrt{24} = \pm i\sqrt{24}$ to help solidify that i represents $\sqrt{-1}$.

See also the *Algebra 2 Toolkit* for more strategies.

EXAMPLE 3 Use addition of complex numbers in real life

ELECTRICITY Circuit components such as resistors, inductors, and capacitors all oppose the flow of current. This opposition is called *resistance* for resistors and *reactance* for inductors and capacitors. A circuit's total opposition to current flow is *impedance*. All of these quantities are measured in ohms (Ω).

EADING
Jote that while a omponent's resistance r reactance is a real umber, its impedance s a complex number.

Component and symbol	Resistor	Inductor	Capacitor
Resistance or reactance	R	L	C
Impedance	R	Li	$-Ci$

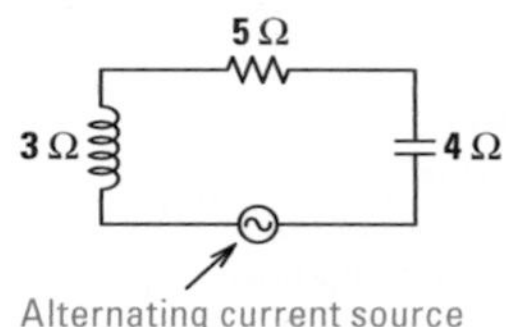

Alternating current source

The table shows the relationship between a component's resistance or reactance and its contribution to impedance. A *series circuit* is also shown with the resistance or reactance of each component labeled.

The impedance for a series circuit is the sum of the impedances for the individual components. Find the impedance of the circuit shown above.

Solution

The resistor has a resistance of 5 ohms, so its impedance is 5 ohms. The inductor has a reactance of 3 ohms, so its impedance is $3i$ ohms. The capacitor has a reactance of 4 ohms, so its impedance is $-4i$ ohms.

Impedance of circuit $= 5 + 3i + (-4i)$ **Add the individual impedances.**

$= 5 - i$ **Simplify.**

▶ The impedance of the circuit is $5 - i$ ohms.

MULTIPLYING COMPLEX NUMBERS To multiply two complex numbers, use the distributive property or the FOIL method just as you do when multiplying real numbers or algebraic expressions.

EXAMPLE 4 Multiply complex numbers

Write the expression as a complex number in standard form.

a. $4i(-6 + i)$ **b.** $(9 - 2i)(-4 + 7i)$

Solution

a. $4i(-6 + i) = -24i + 4i^2$ **Distributive property**

$= -24i + 4(-1)$ **Use $i^2 = -1$.**

$= -24i - 4$ **Simplify.**

$= -4 - 24i$ **Write in standard form.**

AVOID ERRORS
When simplifying an expression that involves complex numbers, be sure to simplify i^2 to -1.

b. $(9 - 2i)(-4 + 7i) = -36 + 63i + 8i - 14i^2$ **Multiply using FOIL.**

$= -36 + 71i - 14(-1)$ **Simplify and use $i^2 = -1$.**

$= -36 + 71i + 14$ **Simplify.**

$= -22 + 71i$ **Write in standard form.**

Extra Example 3

Each component of the circuit has been labeled with its resistance or reactance. Find the impedance of the circuit. **12 + 2*i* ohms**

7 Ω 9 Ω 12 Ω

Extra Example 4

Write the expression as a complex number in standard form.

a. $-5i(8 - 9i)$ **$-45 - 40i$**

b. $(-8 + 2i)(4 - 7i)$ **$-18 + 64i$**

Key Question to Ask for Example 4

- If you use the FOIL method to multiply two complex numbers of the form $a + bi$ and $c + di$, which of the products F, O, I, and L contribute to the real part of the product, and which products contribute to the imaginary part? **real part: F and L; imaginary part: O and I**

Extra Example 5

Write the quotient $\frac{3 + 4i}{5 - i}$ in standard form. $\frac{11}{26} + \frac{23}{26}i$

Key Question to Ask for Example 5

- How are complex conjugates similar to the conjugates that you used in Lesson 4.5 to rationalize denominators? **In both cases the conjugates are the sum and the difference of the same two terms.**

Extra Example 6

Plot the complex numbers in the same complex plane.

a. $4 + 2i$ **b.** $-1 + 3i$

c. $-4i$ **d.** $2 - 2i$

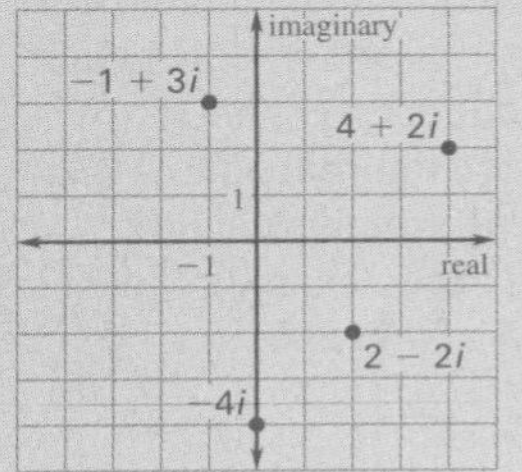

Key Question to Ask for Example 6

- When complex numbers are plotted in the complex plane, what kind of numbers appear on the imaginary axis? **pure imaginary numbers**

Teaching Strategy

Relate the real and imaginary parts of a complex number to the real (horizontal) and imaginary (vertical) axes. Students should realize that points on the horizontal axis represent real numbers, points on the vertical axis represent pure imaginary numbers, and points in the quadrants represent complex numbers.

COMPLEX CONJUGATES Two complex numbers of the form $a + bi$ and $a - bi$ are called **complex conjugates**. The product of complex conjugates is always a real number. For example, $(2 + 4i)(2 - 4i) = 4 - 8i + 8i + 16 = 20$. You can use this fact to write the quotient of two complex numbers in standard form.

EXAMPLE 5 Divide complex numbers

Write the quotient $\frac{7 + 5i}{1 - 4i}$ in standard form.

REWRITE QUOTIENTS
When a quotient has an imaginary number in the denominator, rewrite the denominator as a real number so you can express the quotient in standard form.

$$\frac{7 + 5i}{1 - 4i} = \frac{7 + 5i}{1 - 4i} \cdot \frac{1 + 4i}{1 + 4i}$$ **Multiply numerator and denominator by $1 + 4i$, the complex conjugate of $1 - 4i$.**

$$= \frac{7 + 28i + 5i + 20i^2}{1 + 4i - 4i - 16i^2}$$ **Multiply using FOIL.**

$$= \frac{7 + 33i + 20(-1)}{1 - 16(-1)}$$ **Simplify and use $i^2 = 1$.**

$$= \frac{-13 + 33i}{17}$$ **Simplify.**

$$= -\frac{13}{17} + \frac{33}{17}i$$ **Write in standard form.**

✓ GUIDED PRACTICE for Examples 3, 4, and 5

10. **WHAT IF?** In Example 3, what is the impedance of the circuit if the given capacitor is replaced with one having a reactance of 7 ohms? **$5 - 4i$**

Write the expression as a complex number in standard form.

11. $i(9 - i)$ **$1 + 9i$**
12. $(3 + i)(5 - i)$ **$16 + 2i$**
13. $\frac{5}{1 + i}$ **$\frac{5}{2} - \frac{5}{2}i$**
14. $\frac{5 + 2i}{3 - 2i}$ **$\frac{11}{13} + \frac{16}{13}i$**

COMPLEX PLANE Just as every real number corresponds to a point on the real number line, every complex number corresponds to a point in the **complex plane**. As shown in the next example, the complex plane has a horizontal axis called the *real axis* and a vertical axis called the *imaginary axis*.

EXAMPLE 6 Plot complex numbers

Plot the complex numbers in the same complex plane.

a. $3 - 2i$ **b.** $-2 + 4i$ **c.** $3i$ **d.** $-4 - 3i$

Solution

a. To plot $3 - 2i$, start at the origin, move 3 units to the right, and then move 2 units down.

b. To plot $-2 + 4i$, start at the origin, move 2 units to the left, and then move 4 units up.

c. To plot $3i$, start at the origin and move 3 units up.

d. To plot $-4 - 3i$, start at the origin, move 4 units to the left, and then move 3 units down.

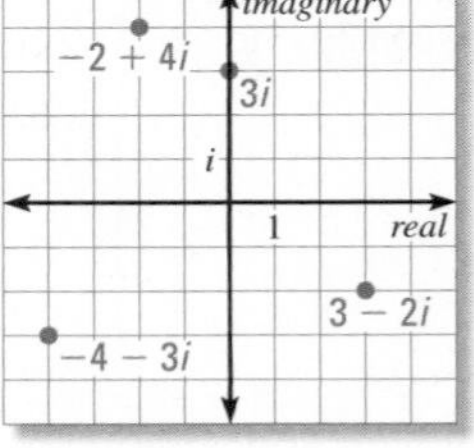

Differentiated Instruction

Advanced Select students to work in a small group to develop a mini-lesson on how to use complex conjugates to divide complex numbers. The lesson should include several examples and a general proof of why the product of two complex conjugates must be a real number. Have the group present and discuss their mini-lesson with their classmates. Teaching their classmates will help reinforce students' understanding of the concepts involved.

See also the *Algebra 2 Toolkit* for more strategies.

KEY CONCEPT — *For Your Notebook*

Absolute Value of a Complex Number

The **absolute value** of a complex number $z = a + bi$, denoted $|z|$, is a nonnegative real number defined as $|z| = \sqrt{a^2 + b^2}$. This is the distance between z and the the origin in the complex plane.

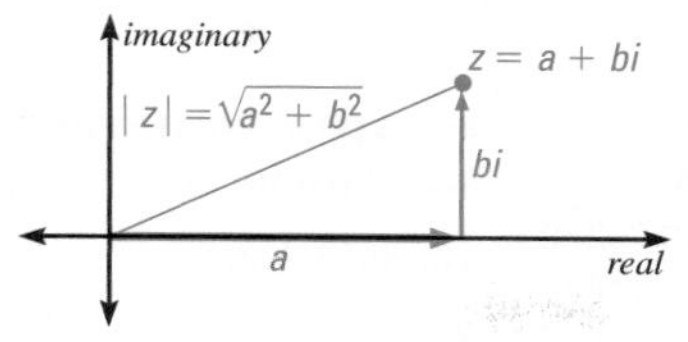

EXAMPLE 7 Find absolute values of complex numbers

Find the absolute value of (a) $-4 + 3i$ and (b) $-3i$.

a. $|-4 + 3i| = \sqrt{(-4)^2 + 3^2} = \sqrt{25} = 5$

b. $|-3i| = |0 + (-3i)| = \sqrt{0^2 + (-3)^2} = \sqrt{9} = 3$

 Animated Algebra at classzone.com

✓ GUIDED PRACTICE for Examples 6 and 7

Plot the complex numbers in the same complex plane. Then find the absolute value of each complex number. 15–18. See margin for art.

15. $4 - i$ $\sqrt{17}$ **16.** $-3 - 4i$ 5 **17.** $2 + 5i$ $\sqrt{29}$ **18.** $-4i$ 4

4.6 EXERCISES

HOMEWORK KEY
○ = WORKED-OUT SOLUTIONS on p. WS8 for Exs. 11, 29, and 67
★ = STANDARDIZED TEST PRACTICE Exs. 2, 21, 50, 60, 69, and 74

SKILL PRACTICE

A

1. VOCABULARY What is the complex conjugate of $a - bi$? $a + bi$

2. ★ WRITING Is every complex number an imaginary number? *Explain.* No. *Sample answer:* 7 is a complex number because it can be written as $7 + 0i$, but it is not an imaginary number.

EXAMPLE 1 on p. 275 for Exs. 3–11

SOLVING QUADRATIC EQUATIONS Solve the equation.

3. $x^2 = -28$ $\pm 2i\sqrt{7}$ **4.** $r^2 = -624$ $\pm 4i\sqrt{39}$ **5.** $z^2 + 8 = 4$ $\pm 2i$

6. $s^2 - 22 = -112$ $\pm 3i\sqrt{10}$ **7.** $2x^2 + 31 = 9$ $\pm i\sqrt{11}$ **8.** $9 - 4y^2 = 57$ $\pm 2i\sqrt{3}$

9. $6t^2 + 5 = 2t^2 + 1$ $\pm i$ **10.** $3p^2 + 7 = -9p^2 + 4$ $\pm \frac{1}{2}i$ **(11.)** $-5(n - 3)^2 = 10$ $3 \pm i\sqrt{2}$

EXAMPLE 2 on p. 276 for Exs. 12–21

ADDING AND SUBTRACTING Write the expression as a complex number in standard form.

12. $(6 - 3i) + (5 + 4i)$ $11 + i$ **13.** $(9 + 8i) + (8 - 9i)$ $17 - i$ **14.** $(-2 - 6i) - (4 - 6i)$ -6

15. $(-1 + i) - (7 - 5i)$ $-8 + 6i$ **16.** $(8 + 20i) - (-8 + 12i)$ $16 + 8i$ **17.** $(8 - 5i) - (-11 + 4i)$ $19 - 9i$

18. $(10 - 2i) + (-11 - 7i)$ $-1 - 9i$ **19.** $(14 + 3i) + (7 + 6i)$ $21 + 9i$ **20.** $(-1 + 4i) + (-9 - 2i)$ $-10 + 2i$

Extra Example 7

Find the absolute value of $5 - 12i$ and $17i$. 13, 17

Key Question to Ask for Example 7

- What is the same for the distance definitions of absolute value for real and complex numbers? In both cases, the absolute value is the distance of the number from a zero point, which is 0 for real numbers and the origin (0, 0) for complex numbers.

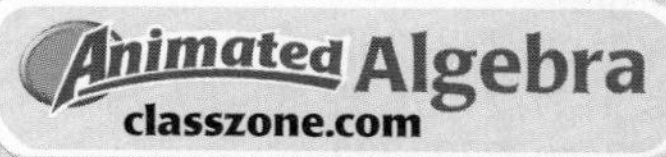

An **Animated Algebra** activity is available on-line for **Example 7**. This activity is also available on the **Power Presentations CD-ROM**.

Closing the Lesson

Have students summarize the major points of the lesson and answer the Essential Question: How do you perform operations on complex numbers?

- The imaginary unit i is defined as $i = \sqrt{-1}$.
- The standard form of a complex number is $a + bi$, where a and b are real numbers.
- When working with complex numbers, replace i^2 with -1.

To add or subtract complex numbers, add or subtract their real parts and their imaginary parts separately. To multiply complex numbers, use the distributive property or the FOIL method. To divide complex numbers, multiply the numerator and denominator by the complex conjugate of the denominator.

15–18.

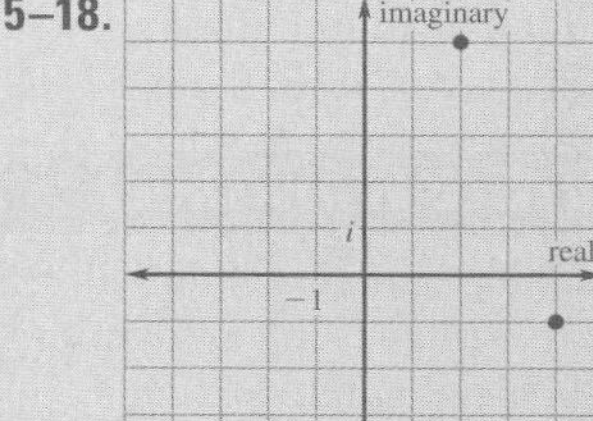

4 PRACTICE AND APPLY

Assignment Guide

Answer Transparencies available for all exercises

Basic:
Day 1: SRH p. 987 Exs. 11–19 odd pp. 279–282
Exs. 1–21, 65–67, 77
Day 2: pp. 279–282
Exs. 23–33 odd, 34–37, 42–45, 50–53, 68–71

Average:
Day 1: pp. 279–282
Exs. 1–17, 21, 51, 52, 65–67, 78
Day 2: pp. 279–282
Exs. 22–32 even, 37–39, 45–47, 50, 53–55, 57–60, 68–75

Advanced:
Day 1: pp. 279–282
Exs. 1, 2, 5–11, 14–21, 51, 52, 65–67, 78
Day 2: pp. 279–282
Exs. 26, 27, 31–33, 39–41, 47–50, 54–64*, 68–76*

Block:
pp. 279–282
Exs. 1–17, 21, 22–32 even, 37–39, 45–47, 50–55, 57–60, 65–75, 78

Differentiated Instruction

See *Algebra 2 Best Practices Toolkit* for suggestions on addressing the needs of a diverse classroom.

Homework Check

For a quick check of student understanding of key concepts, go over the following exercises:
Basic: 6, 14, 25, 36, 65
Average: 8, 16, 30, 38, 66
Advanced: 10, 20, 32, 40, 67

Extra Practice

- Student Edition, p. 1013
- Chapter 4 Resource Book: Practice levels A, B, C, pp. 67–69

Practice Worksheet

An easily-readable reduced practice page (with answers) for this lesson can be found on p. 234C.

---

21. ★ **MULTIPLE CHOICE** What is the standard form of the expression $(2 + 3i) - (7 + 4i)$? **C**

Ⓐ -4 Ⓑ $-5 + 7i$ Ⓒ $-5 - i$ Ⓓ $5 + i$

EXAMPLES 4 and 5 on pp. 277–278 for Exs. 22–33

MULTIPLYING AND DIVIDING Write the expression as a complex number in standard form.

22. $6i(3 + 2i)$ $-12 + 18i$ **23.** $-i(4 - 8i)$ $-8 - 4i$ **24.** $(5 - 7i)(-4 - 3i)$ $-41 + 13$

25. $(-2 + 5i)(-1 + 4i)$ $-18 - 13i$ **26.** $(-1 - 5i)(-1 + 5i)$ 26 **27.** $(8 - 3i)(8 + 3i)$ 73

28. $\frac{7i}{8 + i}$ $\frac{7}{65} + \frac{56}{65}i$ **(29.)** $\frac{6i}{3 - i}$ $-\frac{3}{5} + \frac{9}{5}i$ **30.** $\frac{-2 - 5i}{3i}$ $-\frac{5}{3} + \frac{2}{3}i$

31. $\frac{4 + 9i}{12i}$ $\frac{3}{4} - \frac{1}{3}i$ **32.** $\frac{7 + 4i}{2 - 3i}$ $\frac{2}{13} + \frac{29}{13}i$ **33.** $\frac{-1 - 6i}{5 + 9i}$ $-\frac{59}{106} - \frac{21}{106}i$

EXAMPLE 6 on p. 278 for Exs. 34–41

PLOTTING COMPLEX NUMBERS Plot the numbers in the same complex plane. **34–41. See margin.**

34. $1 + 2i$ **35.** $-5 + 3i$ **36.** $-6i$ **37.** $4i$

38. $-7 - i$ **39.** $5 - 5i$ **40.** 7 **41.** -2

EXAMPLE 7 on p. 279 for Exs. 42–50

FINDING ABSOLUTE VALUE Find the absolute value of the complex number.

42. $4 + 3i$ 5 **43.** $-3 + 10i$ $\sqrt{109}$ **44.** $10 - 7i$ $\sqrt{149}$ **45.** $-1 - 6i$ $\sqrt{37}$

46. $-8i$ 8 **47.** $4i$ 4 **48.** $-4 + i$ $\sqrt{17}$ **49.** $7 + 7i$ $7\sqrt{2}$

50. ★ **MULTIPLE CHOICE** What is the absolute value of $9 + 12i$? **B**

Ⓐ 7 Ⓑ 15 Ⓒ 108 Ⓓ 225

B **STANDARD FORM** Write the expression as a complex number in standard form.

51. $-8 - (3 + 2i) - (9 - 4i)$ $-20 + 2i$ **52.** $(3 + 2i) + (5 - i) + 6i$ $8 + 7i$ **53.** $5i(3 + 2i)(8 + 3i)$ $-125 + 90i$

54. $(1 - 9i)(1 - 4i)(4 - 3i)$ $-179 + 53i$ **55.** $\frac{(5 - 2i) + (5 + 3i)}{(1 + i) - (2 - 4i)}$ $-\frac{5}{26} - \frac{51}{26}i$ **56.** $\frac{(10 + 4i) - (3 - 2i)}{(6 - 7i)(1 - 2i)}$ $-\frac{2}{5} + \frac{1}{5}i$

ERROR ANALYSIS *Describe* and correct the error in simplifying the expression.

57.
$(1 + 2i)(4 - i)$
$= 4 - i + 8i - 2i^2$
$= -2i^2 + 7i + 4$
✗

58.
$|2 - 3i| = \sqrt{2^2 - 3^2}$
$= \sqrt{-5}$
$= i\sqrt{5}$
✗

57. $i^2 = -1$, so $-2i^2 = 2$; $4 - i + 8i - 2i^2 = 6 + 7i$.

58. The absolute value formula is $\sqrt{a^2 + b^2}$; $\sqrt{2^2 + (-3)^2} = \sqrt{13}$.

59. **ADDITIVE AND MULTIPLICATIVE INVERSES** The additive inverse of a complex number z is a complex number z_a such that $z + z_a = 0$. The multiplicative inverse of z is a complex number z_m such that $z \cdot z_m = 1$. Find the additive and multiplicative inverses of each complex number. **See margin.**

a. $z = 2 + i$ **b.** $z = 5 - i$ **c.** $z = -1 + 3i$

C **60.** ★ **OPEN-ENDED MATH** Find two imaginary numbers whose sum is a real number. How are the imaginary numbers related? *Sample answer:* $3 + 2i$ and $6 - 2i$; the imaginary parts are opposites.

CHALLENGE Write the expression as a complex number in standard form. **61–64. See margin.**

61. $\frac{a + bi}{c + di}$ **62.** $\frac{a - bi}{c - di}$ **63.** $\frac{a + bi}{c - di}$ **64.** $\frac{a - bi}{c + di}$

◯ = WORKED-OUT SOLUTIONS on p. WS1 ★ = STANDARDIZED TEST PRACTICE

34–41.

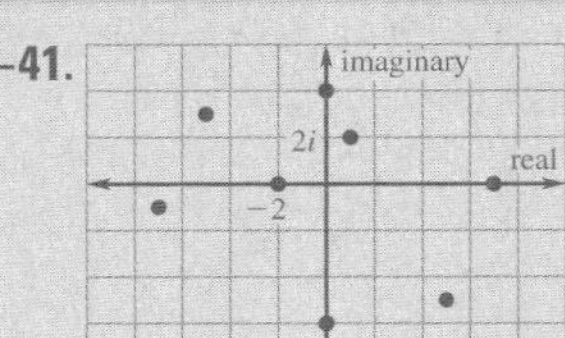

59a. additive: $-2 - i$, multiplicative: $\frac{2}{5} - \frac{1}{5}i$

59b. additive: $-5 + i$, multiplicative: $\frac{5}{26} + \frac{1}{26}i$

59c. additive: $1 - 3i$, multiplicative: $-\frac{1}{10} - \frac{3}{10}i$

61. $\frac{ac + bd + (bc - ad)i}{c^2 + d^2}$

62. $\frac{ac + bd + (ad - bc)i}{c^2 + d^2}$

63. $\frac{ac - bd + (bc + ad)i}{c^2 + d^2}$

64. $\frac{ac - bd - (bc + ad)i}{c^2 + d^2}$

PROBLEM SOLVING

EXAMPLE 3 A on p. 277 for Exs. 65–67

CIRCUITS **In Exercises 65–67, each component of the circuit has been labeled with its resistance or reactance. Find the impedance of the circuit.**

65. 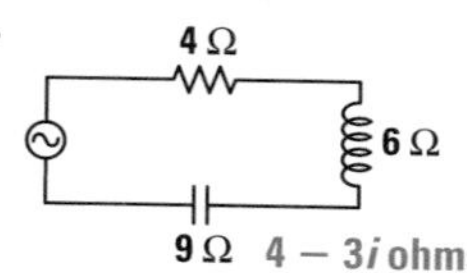

$4 - 3i$ ohms

66. 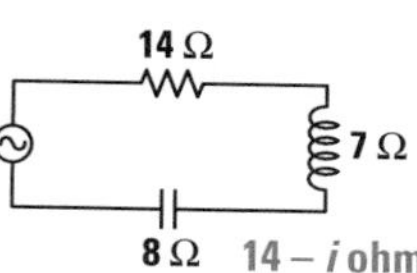

$14 - i$ ohms

67. 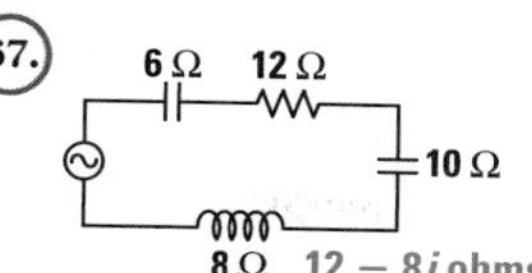

$12 - 8i$ ohms

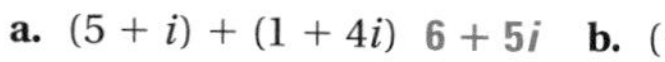

for problem solving help at classzone.com

68. VISUAL THINKING The graph shows how you can geometrically add two complex numbers (in this case, $4 + i$ and $2 + 5i$) to find their sum (in this case, $6 + 6i$). Find each of the following sums by drawing a graph.

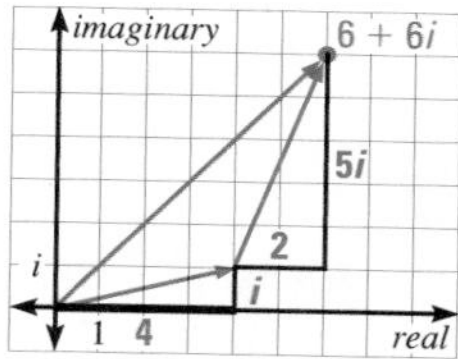

a. $(5 + i) + (1 + 4i)$ $6 + 5i$ b. $(-7 + 3i) + (2 - 2i)$ $-5 + i$

c. $(3 - 2i) + (-1 - i)$ $2 - 3i$ d. $(4 + 2i) + (-5 - 3i)$ $-1 - i$

B **69.** ★ **SHORT RESPONSE** Make a table that shows the powers of i from i^1 to i^8 in the first row and the simplified forms of these powers in the second row. *Describe* the pattern you observe in the table. Verify that the pattern continues by evaluating the next four powers of i.
See margin for table; the pattern repeats every four powers of i; $i^9 = i$, $i^{10} = -1$, $i^{11} = -i$, $i^{12} = 1$.

In Exercises 70–73, use the example below to determine whether the complex number c belongs to the Mandelbrot set. *Justify* your answer.

EXAMPLE Investigate the Mandelbrot set

Consider the function $f(z) = z^2 + c$ and this infinite list of complex numbers: $z_0 = 0$, $z_1 = f(z_0)$, $z_2 = f(z_1)$, $z_3 = f(z_2)$, ... If the absolute values of $z_0, z_1, z_2, z_3, \ldots$ are all less than some fixed number N, then c belongs to the *Mandelbrot set*. If the absolute values become infinitely large, then c does not belong to the Mandelbrot set.

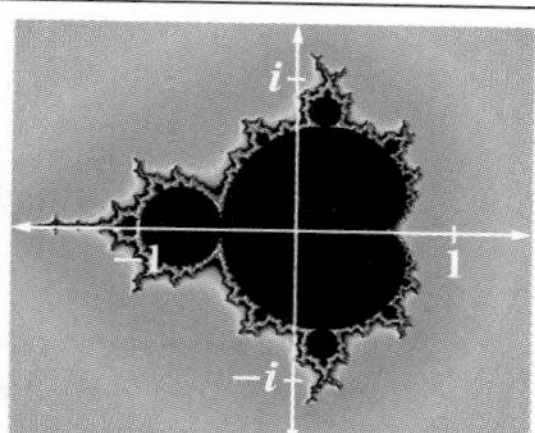

The Mandelbrot set is the black region in the complex plane above.

Tell whether $c = 1 + i$ belongs to the Mandelbrot set.

Solution

Let $f(z) = z^2 + (1 + i)$.

$z_0 = 0$ $\quad |z_0| = 0$

$z_1 = f(0) = 0^2 + (1 + i) = 1 + i$ $\quad |z_1| \approx 1.41$

$z_2 = f(1 + i) = (1 + i)^2 + (1 + i) = 1 + 3i$ $\quad |z_2| \approx 3.16$

$z_3 = f(1 + 3i) = (1 + 3i)^2 + (1 + i) = -7 + 7i$ $\quad |z_3| \approx 9.90$

$z_4 = f(-7 + 7i) = (-7 + 7i)^2 + (1 + i) = 1 - 97i$ $\quad |z_4| \approx 97.0$

▶ Because the absolute values are becoming infinitely large, $c = 1 + i$ does not belong to the Mandelbrot set.

70. $c = i$ does not belong to the Mandelbrot set

71. $c = -1 + i$ does not belong to the Mandelbrot set

72. $c = -1$ belongs to the Mandelbrot set

73. $c = -0.5i$ belongs to the Mandelbrot set

Teaching Strategy

Exercises 30–31 Some students may be confused when the denominator is a pure imaginary number. Tell them to write the denominators as $0 + 3i$ and $0 + 12i$ to help clear up the confusion.

Exercises 53–54 If students wonder which multiplication should be done first, have them perform the multiplications in different orders and compare the results. Students should conclude that the associative property of multiplication (Lesson 1.1) also holds in the complex number system.

Avoiding Common Errors

Exercises 53, 54, 56 In these multi-step calculations, some students may make the error of not using standard form to write the result of one procedure before going on to the next one. Remind them to replace i^2 with -1 *immediately* whenever they obtain it in a calculation and to combine "like terms" (real or imaginary) whenever possible.

Internet Reference

Exercises 70–73, 76 For more information about Mandelbrot and Julia sets, visit aleph0.clarku.edu/~djoyce/julia/julia.html

69.

Powers of i	i^1	i^2	i^3	i^4	i^5	i^6	i^7	i^8
Simplified	i	-1	$-i$	1	i	-1	$-i$	1

5 ASSESS AND RETEACH

Daily Homework Quiz

Transparency Available

1. Solve $3x^2 + 8 = -76$. $2i\sqrt{7}, -2i\sqrt{7}$

Evaluate each expression if $X = 5 - 8i$ and $Y = -9 + 3i$. Write your answer as a complex number in standard form.

2. $X - Y$ $14 - 11i$
3. $\frac{X}{Y}$ $-\frac{23}{30} + \frac{19}{30}i$
4. $X + Y$ $-4 - 5i$
5. $X \cdot Y$ $-21 + 87i$
6. $6Y$ $-54 + 18i$
7. $|Y|$ $3\sqrt{10}$
8. Plot X and Y in the same complex plane.

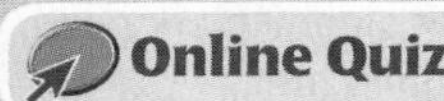

9. A line segment connects $-2 + 3i$ and $-1 - i$. Which axis does the segment cross? the real axis

Online Quiz

Available at **classzone.com**

Diagnosis/Remediation

- Practice A, B, C in Chapter 4 Resource Book, pp. 67–69
- Study Guide in Chapter 4 Resource Book, pp. 70–71
- Practice Workbook, pp. 66–67
- @HomeTutor

Challenge

Additional challenge is available in the Chapter 4 Resource Book, p. 74.

74. ★ **SHORT RESPONSE** Evaluate $\sqrt{-4} \cdot \sqrt{-25}$ and $\sqrt{100}$. Does the rule $\sqrt{a} \cdot \sqrt{b} = \sqrt{ab}$ on page 266 hold when a and b are negative numbers? $-10, 10$; no

75. **PARALLEL CIRCUITS** In a *parallel circuit*, there is more than one pathway through which current can flow. To find the impedance Z of a parallel circuit with two pathways, first calculate the impedances Z_1 and Z_2 of the pathways separately by treating each pathway as a series circuit. Then apply this formula:

$$Z = \frac{Z_1 Z_2}{Z_1 + Z_2}$$

What is the impedance of each parallel circuit shown below?

a. 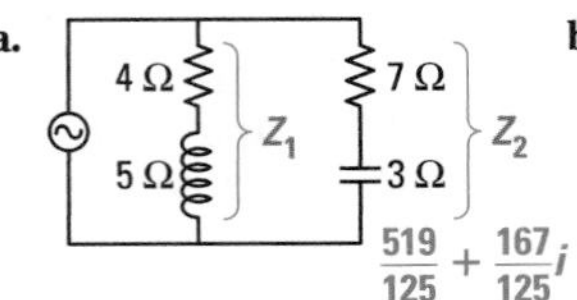

$\frac{519}{125} + \frac{167}{125}i$

b. 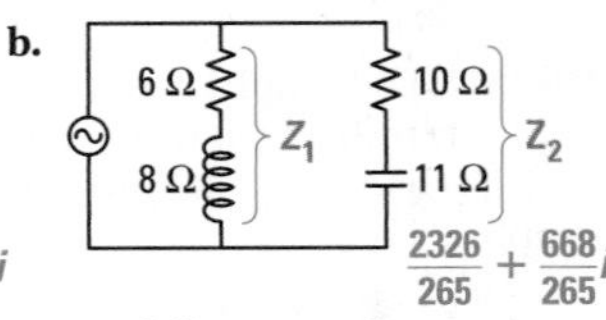

$\frac{2326}{265} + \frac{668}{265}i$

c. 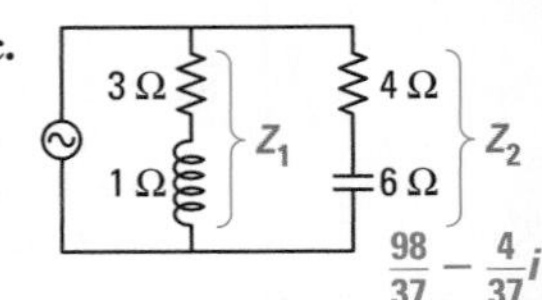

$\frac{98}{37} - \frac{4}{37}i$

C 76. **CHALLENGE** *Julia sets*, like the Mandelbrot set shown on page 281, are fractals defined on the complex plane. For every complex number c, there is an associated Julia set determined by the function $f(z) = z^2 + c$.

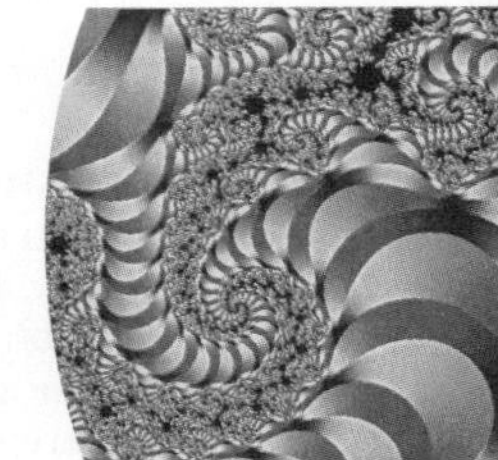

A Julia set

For example, the Julia set corresponding to $c = 1 + i$ is determined by the function $f(z) = z^2 + 1 + i$. A number z_0 is a member of this Julia set if the absolute values of the numbers $z_1 = f(z_0)$, $z_2 = f(z_1)$, $z_3 = f(z_2)$, . . . are all less than some fixed number N, and z_0 is not a member if these absolute values grow infinitely large.

Tell whether the given number z_0 belongs to the Julia set associated with the function $f(z) = z^2 + 1 + i$.

a. $z_0 = i$ belongs to the Julia set
b. $z_0 = 1$ does not belong to the Julia set
c. $z_0 = 2i$ does not belong to the Julia set
d. $z_0 = 2 + 3i$ does not belong to the Julia set

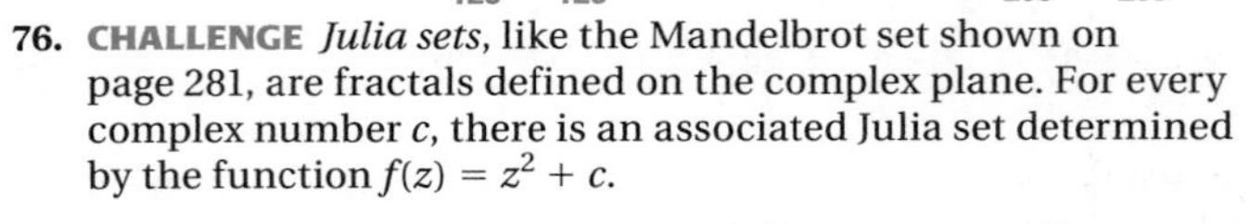

KENTUCKY MIXED REVIEW

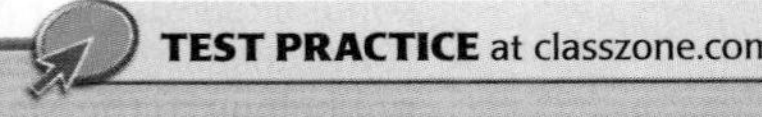

TEST PRACTICE at classzone.com

77. There are 185 students in this year's freshman class. What additional information is needed to predict the number of students in next year's freshman class? **A**

Ⓐ The rate of change in the number of students in the freshman class
Ⓑ The number of females in this year's freshman class
Ⓒ The number of students in this year's senior class
Ⓓ The maximum number of students in the school

78. What are the slope m and y-intercept b of the line that contains the point $(-4, 1)$ and has the same y-intercept as $3x - 2y = 10$? **A**

Ⓐ $m = -\frac{3}{2}, b = -5$ Ⓑ $m = 1, b = 5$
Ⓒ $m = \frac{3}{2}, b = 7$ Ⓓ $m = \frac{9}{4}, b = 10$

4.7 Using Algebra Tiles to Complete the Square

MATERIALS • algebra tiles

QUESTION How can you use algebra tiles to complete the square for a quadratic expression?

If you are given an expression of the form $x^2 + bx$, you can add a constant c to the expression so that the result $x^2 + bx + c$ is a perfect square trinomial. This process is called *completing the square.*

EXPLORE Complete the square for the expression $x^2 + 6x$

STEP 1

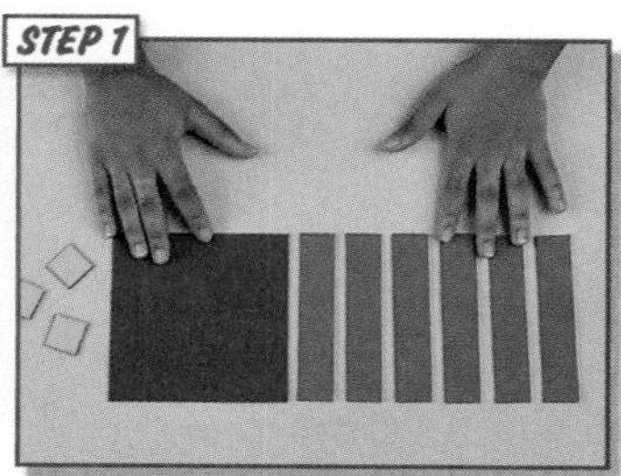

Model the expression

Use algebra tiles to model the expression $x^2 + 6x$. You will need to use one x^2-tile and six x-tiles for this expression.

STEP 2

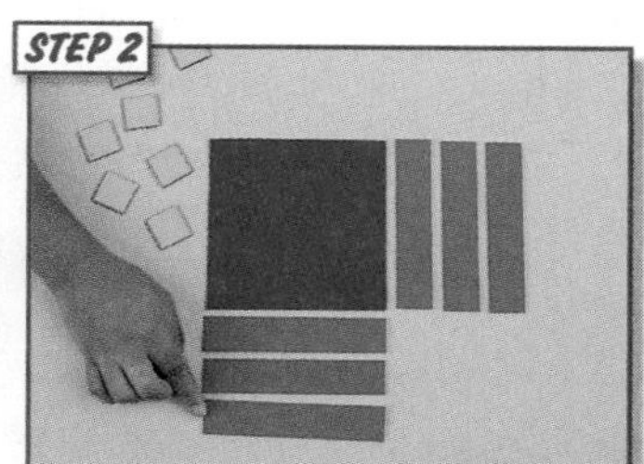

Make a square

Arrange the tiles in a square. You want the length and width of the square to be equal. Your arrangement will be incomplete in one of the corners.

STEP 3

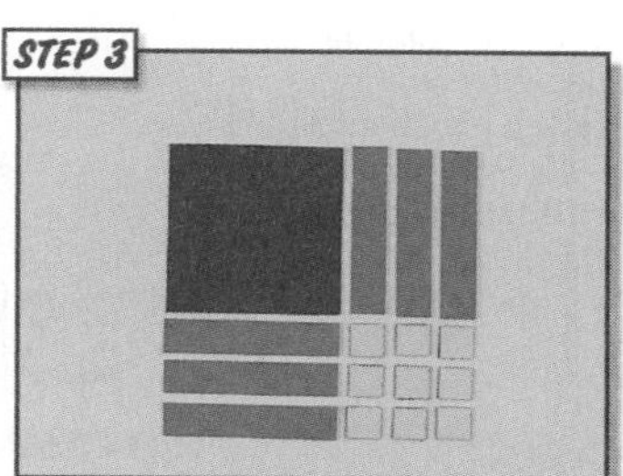

Complete the square

Find the number of 1-tiles needed to complete the square. By adding nine 1-tiles, you can see that $x^2 + 6x + 9$ is equal to $(x + 3)^2$.

DRAW CONCLUSIONS Use your observations to complete these exercises

1. Copy and complete the table at the right by following the steps above. See margin.
2. Look for patterns in the last column of your table. Consider the general statement $x^2 + bx + c = (x + d)^2$.
   a. How is d related to b in each case? d is $\frac{1}{2}$ of b.
   b. How is c related to d in each case? c is equal to d^2.
   c. How can you obtain the numbers in the table's second column directly from the coefficients of x in the expressions from the first column? Divide the coefficient by 2 and then square it.

Completing the Square		
Expression	Number of 1-tiles needed to complete the square	Expression written as a square
$x^2 + 2x + \underline{?}$	?	?
$x^2 + 4x + \underline{?}$	?	?
$x^2 + 6x + \underline{?}$	9	$x^2 + 6x + 9 = (x + 3)^2$
$x^2 + 8x + \underline{?}$	?	?
$x^2 + 10x + \underline{?}$	?	?

1. row 1: 1, $(x + 1)^2$; row 2: 4, $(x + 2)^2$; row 4: 16, $(x + 4)^2$; row 5: 25, $(x + 5)^2$

1 PLAN AND PREPARE

Explore the Concept

- Students will use algebra tiles to model the process of completing the square.
- This activity leads into the study of finding the constant c that needs to be added to $x^2 + bx$ to form a perfect square trinomial in Example 2 in Lesson 4.7.

Materials

Each student will need:

- a set of algebra tiles
- Activity Support Master (*Chapter 4 Resource Book*, p. 77)

Recommended Time

Work activity: 10 min
Discuss results: 5 min

Grouping

Students should work individually.

2 TEACH

Tips for Success

Make sure that students are correctly distinguishing between x^2-tiles, x-tiles, and 1-tiles.

Key Question

- How should you split up the 6 x-tiles and arrange them in order to end up with a square? Split them in half, placing 3 of them to the right of the x^2-tile and 3 of them below it.

Key Discovery

The constant that can be added to form a perfect square is found by taking half the coefficient of x and squaring it.

3 ASSESS AND RETEACH

Complete the square.

1. $x^2 + 18x$ $x^2 + 18x + 81$
2. $x^2 + 24x$ $x^2 + 24x + 144$

1 PLAN AND PREPARE

Warm-Up Exercises

Transparency Available

Solve the equation.

1. $(x-5)^2 = 49$ 12, −2
2. $(x+6)^2 = 20$ $-6 + 2\sqrt{5}$, $-6 - 2\sqrt{5}$

Factor the expression.

3. $x^2 + 18x + 81$ $(x+9)^2$
4. $x^2 - 22x + 121$ $(x-11)^2$
5. 27 plus some number is 6^2. What is that number? 9

Notetaking Guide

Transparency Available

Promotes interactive learning and notetaking skills, pp. 112–115.

Pacing

Basic: 2 days

Average: 2 days

Advanced: 2 days

Block: 1 block

- See *Teaching Guide/Lesson Plan.*

2 FOCUS AND MOTIVATE

Essential Question

Big Idea 2, p. 235

How is the process of completing the square used to solve quadratic equations? **Tell students they will learn how to answer this question by learning the process of completing the square.**

4.7 Complete the Square

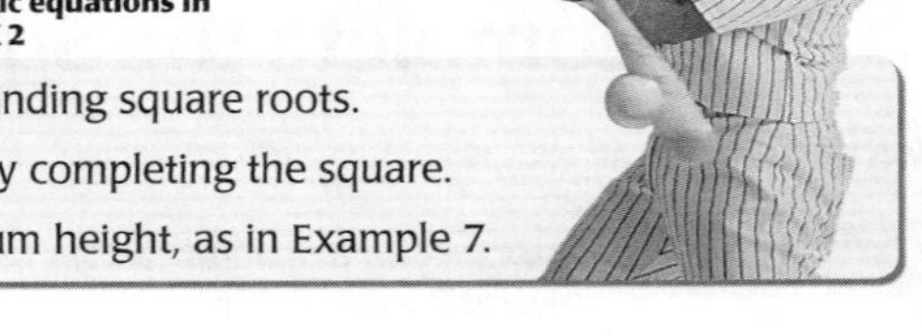

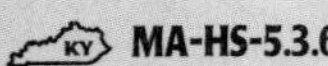

MA-HS-5.3.6 **Students will model, solve and graph quadratic equations in real-world and mathematical problems. DOK 2**

Before You solved quadratic equations by finding square roots.

Now You will solve quadratic equations by completing the square.

Why? So you can find a baseball's maximum height, as in Example 7.

Key Vocabulary
- **completing the square**

In Lesson 4.5, you solved equations of the form $x^2 = k$ by finding square roots. This method also works if one side of an equation is a perfect square trinomial.

EXAMPLE 1 Solve a quadratic equation by finding square roots

ANOTHER WAY
You can also find the solutions by writing the given equation as $x^2 - 8x - 9 = 0$ and solving this equation by factoring.

Solve $x^2 - 8x + 16 = 25$.

$x^2 - 8x + 16 = 25$ **Write original equation.**

$(x-4)^2 = 25$ **Write left side as a binomial squared.**

$x - 4 = \pm 5$ **Take square roots of each side.**

$x = 4 \pm 5$ **Solve for x.**

▶ The solutions are $4 + 5 = 9$ and $4 - 5 = -1$.

PERFECT SQUARES In Example 1, the trinomial $x^2 - 8x + 16$ is a perfect square because it equals $(x-4)^2$. Sometimes you need to add a term to an expression $x^2 + bx$ to make it a square. This process is called **completing the square**.

KEY CONCEPT *For Your Notebook*

Completing the Square

Words To complete the square for the expression $x^2 + bx$, add $\left(\frac{b}{2}\right)^2$.

Diagrams In each diagram, the combined area of the shaded regions is $x^2 + bx$. Adding $\left(\frac{b}{2}\right)^2$ completes the square in the second diagram.

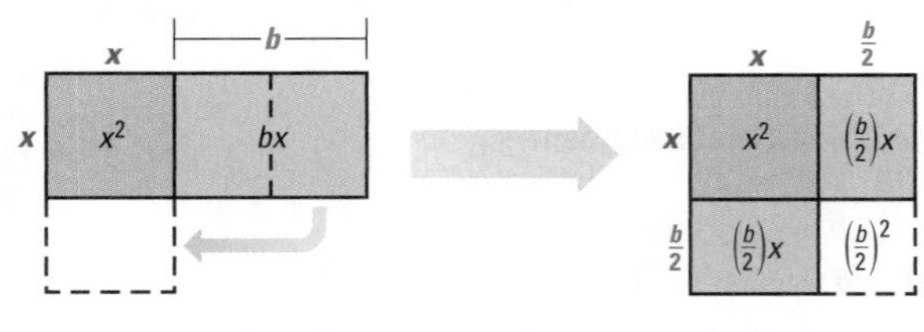

Algebra $x^2 + bx + \left(\frac{b}{2}\right)^2 = \left(x + \frac{b}{2}\right)\left(x + \frac{b}{2}\right) = \left(x + \frac{b}{2}\right)^2$

Resource Planning Guide

Chapter Resource Book
- Teaching Guide/Lesson Plan (pp. 75–76)
- Practice levels A, B, C (pp. 78–80)
- Study Guide (pp. 81–82)
- Catch-up for Absent Students (p. 83)
- Problem Solving Workshop (p. 84)
- Challenge (p. 85)

Workbooks
- Notetaking Guide (pp. 112–115)
- Practice Workbook (pp. 68–69)

Teaching Options
- **Power Presentations CD-ROM** provides dynamic electronic teaching resources for the classroom.
- **Activity Generator CD-ROM** provides editable activities for all ability levels.

Interactive Technology
- Easy Planner
- Power Presentations CD-ROM
- Activity Generator CD-ROM
- Animated Algebra
- Test Generator CD-ROM
- Online Quiz
- eWorkbook
- eEdition
- @HomeTutor

Resources for English Learners
- Quick Reference for English Learners
- Spanish Study Guide
- Multi-Language Visual Glossary
- Student Resources in Spanish

See also the *Algebra 2 Toolkit* for more strategies for meeting individual needs.

EXAMPLE 2 Make a perfect square trinomial

Find the value of c that makes $x^2 + 16x + c$ a perfect square trinomial. Then write the expression as the square of a binomial.

Solution

STEP 1 **Find** half the coefficient of x. $\frac{16}{2} = 8$

STEP 2 **Square** the result of Step 1. $8^2 = 64$

STEP 3 **Replace** c with the result of Step 2. $x^2 + 16x + 64$

	x	8
x	x^2	$8x$
8	$8x$	64

▶ The trinomial $x^2 + 16x + c$ is a perfect square when $c = 64$. Then $x^2 + 16x + 64 = (x + 8)(x + 8) = (x + 8)^2$.

GUIDED PRACTICE for Examples 1 and 2

Solve the equation by finding square roots.

1. $x^2 + 6x + 9 = 36$ **−9, 3**
2. $x^2 - 10x + 25 = 1$ **4, 6**
3. $x^2 - 24x + 144 = 100$ **2, 22**

Find the value of c that makes the expression a perfect square trinomial. Then write the expression as the square of a binomial.

4. $x^2 + 14x + c$ **49; $(x + 7)^2$**
5. $x^2 + 22x + c$ **121; $(x + 11)^2$**
6. $x^2 - 9x + c$ **$\frac{81}{4}$; $\left(x - \frac{9}{2}\right)^2$**

SOLVING EQUATIONS The method of completing the square can be used to solve *any* quadratic equation. When you complete a square as part of solving an equation, you must add the same number to *both* sides of the equation.

EXAMPLE 3 Solve $ax^2 + bx + c = 0$ when $a = 1$

Solve $x^2 - 12x + 4 = 0$ by completing the square.

$x^2 - 12x + 4 = 0$	**Write original equation.**
$x^2 - 12x = -4$	**Write left side in the form $x^2 + bx$.**
$x^2 - 12x + 36 = -4 + 36$	**Add $\left(\frac{-12}{2}\right)^2 = (-6)^2 = 36$ to each side.**
$(x - 6)^2 = 32$	**Write left side as a binomial squared.**
$x - 6 = \pm\sqrt{32}$	**Take square roots of each side.**
$x = 6 \pm \sqrt{32}$	**Solve for x.**
$x = 6 \pm 4\sqrt{2}$	**Simplify: $\sqrt{32} = \sqrt{16} \cdot \sqrt{2} = 4\sqrt{2}$**

EVIEW RADICALS
or help with mplifying square oots, see p. 266.

▶ The solutions are $6 + 4\sqrt{2}$ and $6 - 4\sqrt{2}$.

CHECK You can use algebra or a graph.

Algebra Substitute each solution in the original equation to verify that it is correct.

Graph Use a graphing calculator to graph $y = x^2 - 12x + 4$. The x-intercepts are about $0.34 \approx 6 - 4\sqrt{2}$ and $11.66 \approx 6 + 4\sqrt{2}$.

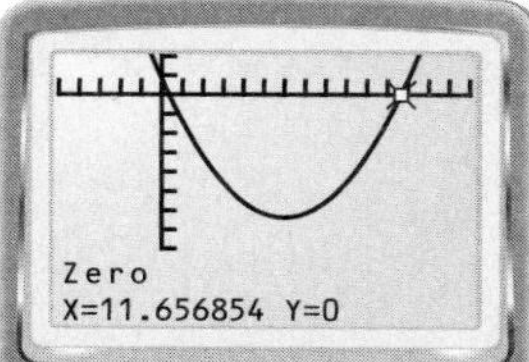

Motivating the Lesson

Ask students what sports they like to play or watch that involve hitting or throwing a ball. Ask them how they think how hard the ball is hit or thrown affects how high the ball will go. Tell them that a quadratic equation can be used to find the ball's maximum height if the initial height and speed are known.

3 TEACH

Extra Example 1

Solve $x^2 + 20x + 100 = 81$. **−19, −1**

Extra Example 2

Find the value of c that makes $x^2 - 26x + c$ a perfect square trinomial. Then write the expression as the square of a trinomial. **169; $(x - 13)^2$**

Key Question to Ask for Example 2

- If $x^2 + bx + c = 0$ is a perfect square trinomial and b is an odd integer, what do you know about the value of c? **It will be a fraction.**

Extra Example 3

Solve $x^2 - 10x + 1 = 0$ by completing the square. **$5 + 2\sqrt{6}$, $5 - 2\sqrt{6}$**

Differentiated Instruction

Below Level Some students have trouble completing the square because there are so many steps. Show them how to break the process into three parts: (1) Get the equation into the form needed for completing the square. (2) Complete the square. (3) Finish the solution by taking square roots of both sides and simplifying the results. If students are making errors, analyze their work carefully to see what part of the process is giving them trouble and give them extra practice on that part of the process. See also the *Algebra 2 Toolkit* for more strategies.

Extra Example 4

Solve $3x^2 - 36x + 150 = 0$ by completing the square. $6 + i\sqrt{14}$, $6 - i\sqrt{14}$

Key Question to Ask for Example 4

- What can you conclude about the solutions after you write the step "$(x + 2)^2 = -3$"? **The solutions will be complex numbers because they include the square root of −3.**

Extra Example 5

The area of the triangle shown is 144 square units. What is the value of x? C

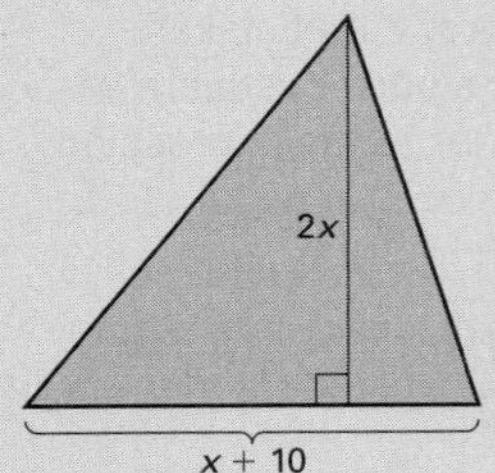

Ⓐ −18 Ⓑ −18 or 8

Ⓒ 8 Ⓓ 16

Teaching Strategy

After you discussed Examples 3 and 4, ask students to write a list of steps to follow in solving *any* quadratic equation by completing the square. Work to develop a consensus among all students about the list of steps.

EXAMPLE 4 Solve $ax^2 + bx + c = 0$ when $a \neq 1$

Solve $2x^2 + 8x + 14 = 0$ by completing the square.

$2x^2 + 8x + 14 = 0$	**Write original equation.**
$x^2 + 4x + 7 = 0$	**Divide each side by the coefficient of x^2.**
$x^2 + 4x = -7$	**Write left side in the form $x^2 + bx$.**
$x^2 + 4x + 4 = -7 + 4$	**Add $\left(\frac{4}{2}\right)^2 = 2^2 = 4$ to each side.**
$(x + 2)^2 = -3$	**Write left side as a binomial squared.**
$x + 2 = \pm\sqrt{-3}$	**Take square roots of each side.**
$x = -2 \pm \sqrt{-3}$	**Solve for x.**
$x = -2 \pm i\sqrt{3}$	**Write in terms of the imaginary unit i.**

▸ The solutions are $-2 + i\sqrt{3}$ and $-2 - i\sqrt{3}$.

EXAMPLE 5 Standardized Test Practice

The area of the rectangle shown is 72 square units. What is the value of x?

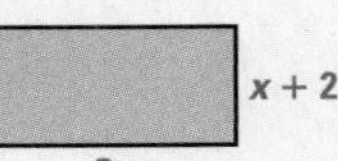

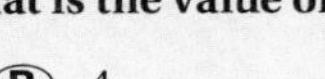

Ⓐ −6 Ⓑ 4

Ⓒ 8.48 Ⓓ −6 or 4

ELIMINATE CHOICES

You can eliminate choices A and D because the side lengths are negative when $x = -6$.

Solution

Use the formula for the area of a rectangle to write an equation.

$3x(x + 2) = 72$	**Length × Width = Area**
$3x^2 + 6x = 72$	**Distributive property**
$x^2 + 2x = 24$	**Divide each side by the coefficient of x^2.**
$x^2 + 2x + 1 = 24 + 1$	**Add $\left(\frac{2}{2}\right)^2 = 1^2 = 1$ to each side.**
$(x + 1)^2 = 25$	**Write left side as a binomial squared.**
$x + 1 = \pm 5$	**Take square roots of each side.**
$x = -1 \pm 5$	**Solve for x.**

So, $x = -1 + 5 = 4$ or $x = -1 - 5 = -6$. You can reject $x = -6$ because the side lengths would be −18 and −4, and side lengths cannot be negative.

▸ The value of x is 4. The correct answer is B. Ⓐ Ⓑ Ⓒ Ⓓ

GUIDED PRACTICE for Examples 3, 4, and 5

Solve the equation by completing the square.

7. $x^2 + 6x + 4 = 0$ $-3 \pm \sqrt{5}$ **8.** $x^2 - 10x + 8 = 0$ $5 \pm \sqrt{17}$ **9.** $2n^2 - 4n - 14 = 0$ $1 \pm 2\sqrt{2}$

10. $3x^2 + 12x - 18 = 0$ $-2 \pm \sqrt{10}$ **11.** $6x(x + 8) = 12$ $-4 \pm 3\sqrt{2}$ **12.** $4p(p - 2) = 100$ $1 \pm \sqrt{26}$

VERTEX FORM Recall from Lesson 4.2 that the vertex form of a quadratic function is $y = a(x - h)^2 + k$ where (h, k) is the vertex of the function's graph. To write a quadratic function in vertex form, use completing the square.

EXAMPLE 6 Write a quadratic function in vertex form

Write $y = x^2 - 10x + 22$ in vertex form. Then identify the vertex.

$y = x^2 - 10x + 22$	**Write original function.**
$y + ? = (x^2 - 10x + ?) + 22$	**Prepare to complete the square.**
$y + 25 = (x^2 - 10x + 25) + 22$	**Add $\left(\frac{-10}{2}\right)^2 = (-5)^2 = 25$ to each side.**
$y + 25 = (x - 5)^2 + 22$	**Write $x^2 - 10x + 25$ as a binomial squared.**
$y = (x - 5)^2 - 3$	**Solve for y.**

▶ The vertex form of the function is $y = (x - 5)^2 - 3$. The vertex is $(5, -3)$.

EXAMPLE 7 Find the maximum value of a quadratic function

BASEBALL The height y (in feet) of a baseball t seconds after it is hit is given by this function:

$$y = -16t^2 + 96t + 3$$

Find the maximum height of the baseball.

Solution

The maximum height of the baseball is the y-coordinate of the vertex of the parabola with the given equation.

$y = -16t^2 + 96t + 3$	**Write original function.**
$y = -16(t^2 - 6t) + 3$	**Factor −16 from first two terms.**
$y + (-16)(?) = -16(t^2 - 6t + ?) + 3$	**Prepare to complete the square.**
$y + (-16)(9) = -16(t^2 - 6t + 9) + 3$	**Add (−16)(9) to each side.**
$y - 144 = -16(t - 3)^2 + 3$	**Write $t^2 - 6t + 9$ as a binomial squared.**
$y = -16(t - 3)^2 + 147$	**Solve for y.**

AVOID ERRORS
When you complete the square, be sure to add (−16)(9) = −144 to each side, not just 9.

▶ The vertex is (3, 147), so the maximum height of the baseball is 147 feet.

 at classzone.com

✓ **GUIDED PRACTICE** for Examples 6 and 7

Write the quadratic function in vertex form. Then identify the vertex.

13. $y = x^2 - 8x + 17$
$y = (x - 4)^2 + 1$; $(4, 1)$

14. $y = x^2 + 6x + 3$
$y = (x + 3)^2 - 6$; $(-3, -6)$

15. $f(x) = x^2 - 4x - 4$
$y = (x - 2)^2 - 8$; $(2, -8)$

16. WHAT IF? In Example 7, suppose the height of the baseball is given by $y = -16t^2 + 80t + 2$. Find the maximum height of the baseball. 102 ft

Extra Example 6

Write $y = x^2 + 18x + 95$ in vertex form. Then identify the vertex.
$y = (x + 9)^2 + 14$; vertex: $(-9, 14)$

Extra Example 7

The height y (in feet) of a ball that was thrown up in the air from the roof of a building after t seconds is given by the function $y = -16t^2 + 64t + 50$. Find the maximum height of the ball. 114 ft

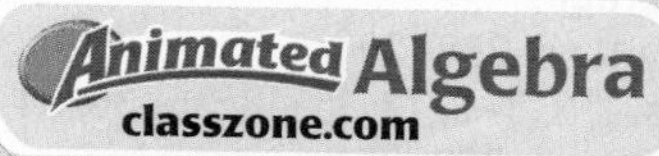

An **Animated Algebra** activity is available on-line for **Example 7**. This activity is also available on the **Power Presentations CD-ROM**.

Closing the Lesson

Have students summarize the major points of the lesson and answer the Essential Question: How is the process of completing the square used to solve quadratic equations?

- **To find the value of c that makes an expression of the form $x^2 + bx + c$ a perfect square, take half the coefficient of x and square it.**
- **The method of completing the square can be used to solve any quadratic equation, whether the solutions are real or imaginary.**

You complete the square so that one side of the equation can be written as the square of a binomial. Then you take square roots of both sides and simplify the results.

4.7 EXERCISES

HOMEWORK KEY
○ = **WORKED-OUT SOLUTIONS** on p. WS8 for Exs. 27, 45, and 65
★ = **STANDARDIZED TEST PRACTICE** Exs. 2, 12, 34, 58, 59, and 67
◆ = **MULTIPLE REPRESENTATIONS** Ex. 66

4 PRACTICE AND APPLY

Assignment Guide

Answer Transparencies available for all exercises

Basic:
Day 1: pp. 288–291
Exs. 1–6, 12–16, 22–27, 34
Day 2: pp. 288–291
Exs. 35–46, 50–55, 62–66, 69–70

Average:
Day 1: pp. 288–291
Exs. 1, 2, 5–8, 12, 15–18, 25–30, 34
Day 2: pp. 288–291
Exs. 35–40, 43–47, 50, 51, 55–59, 62–67, 69–70

Advanced:
Day 1: pp. 288–291
Exs. 1, 2, 9–12, 18–21, 28–34, 61*
Day 2: pp. 288–291
Exs. 35–40, 45–49, 55–60, 62–68*, 69–70

Block:
pp. 288–291
Exs. 1, 2, 5–8, 12, 15–18, 25–30, 34–40, 43–47, 50, 51, 55–59, 62–67, 69–84

Differentiated Instruction

See *Algebra 2 Best Practices Toolkit* for suggestions on addressing the needs of a diverse classroom.

Homework Check

For a quick check of student understanding of key concepts, go over the following exercises:

Basic: 4, 14, 24, 36, 62
Average: 8, 18, 28, 37, 64
Advanced: 10, 20, 32, 38, 65

Extra Practice

- Student Edition, p. 1013
- Chapter 4 Resource Book: Practice levels A, B, C, pp. 78–80

Practice Worksheet

An easily-readable reduced practice page (with answers) for this lesson can be found on p. 234C.

SKILL PRACTICE

A

1. **VOCABULARY** What is the difference between a binomial and a trinomial?
A binomial is the sum of two monomials and a trinomial is the sum of three monomials.

2. ★ **WRITING** *Describe* what completing the square means for an expression of the form $x^2 + bx$.
To complete the square, add $\left(\frac{b}{2}\right)^2$ so that the expression becomes the square of a binomial, $\left(x + \frac{b}{2}\right)^2$

EXAMPLE 1 on p. 284 for Exs. 3–12

SOLVING BY SQUARE ROOTS **Solve the equation by finding square roots.**

3. $x^2 + 4x + 4 = 9$ $-5, 1$
4. $x^2 + 10x + 25 = 64$ $-13, 3$
5. $n^2 + 16n + 64 = 36$ $-14, -$
6. $m^2 - 2m + 1 = 144$ $-11, 13$
7. $x^2 - 22x + 121 = 13$ $11 \pm \sqrt{13}$
8. $x^2 - 18x + 81 = 5$ $9 \pm \sqrt{5}$
9. $t^2 + 8t + 16 = 45$ $-4 \pm 3\sqrt{5}$
10. $4u^2 + 4u + 1 = 75$ $\frac{-1 \pm 5\sqrt{3}}{2}$
11. $9x^2 - 12x + 4 = -3$ $\frac{2 \pm i}{3}$

12. ★ **MULTIPLE CHOICE** What are the solutions of $x^2 - 4x + 4 = -1$? A

Ⓐ $2 \pm i$ Ⓑ $-2 \pm i$ Ⓒ $-3, -1$ Ⓓ $1, 3$

EXAMPLE 2 on p. 285 for Exs. 13–21

FINDING C **Find the value of *c* that makes the expression a perfect square trinomial. Then write the expression as the square of a binomial.**

13. $x^2 + 6x + c$ $9; (x + 3)^2$
14. $x^2 + 12x + c$ $36; (x + 6)^2$
15. $x^2 - 24x + c$ $144; (x - 12)$
16. $x^2 - 30x + c$ $225; (x - 15)^2$
17. $x^2 - 2x + c$ $1; (x - 1)^2$
18. $x^2 + 50x + c$ $625; (x + 25)$
19. $x^2 + 7x + c$ $\frac{49}{4}; \left(x + \frac{7}{2}\right)^2$
20. $x^2 - 13x + c$ $\frac{169}{4}; \left(x - \frac{13}{2}\right)^2$
21. $x^2 - x + c$ $\frac{1}{4}; \left(x - \frac{1}{2}\right)^2$

EXAMPLES 3 and 4 on pp. 285–286 for Exs. 22–34

COMPLETING THE SQUARE **Solve the equation by completing the square.**

22. $x^2 + 4x = 10$ $-2 \pm \sqrt{14}$
23. $x^2 + 8x = -1$ $-4 \pm \sqrt{15}$
24. $x^2 + 6x - 3 = 0$ $-3 \pm 2\sqrt{3}$
25. $x^2 + 12x + 18 = 0$ $-6 \pm 3\sqrt{2}$
26. $x^2 - 18x + 86 = 0$ $9 \pm i\sqrt{5}$
27. $x^2 - 2x + 25 = 0$ $1 \pm 2i\sqrt{}$
28. $2k^2 + 16k = -12$ $-4 \pm \sqrt{10}$
29. $3x^2 + 42x = -24$ $-7 \pm \sqrt{41}$
30. $4x^2 - 40x - 12 = 0$ $5 \pm 2\sqrt{}$
31. $3s^2 + 6s + 9 = 0$ $-1 \pm i\sqrt{2}$
32. $7t^2 + 28t + 56 = 0$ $-2 \pm 2i$
33. $6r^2 + 6r + 12 = 0$ $-\frac{1}{2} \pm \frac{i\sqrt{}}{}$

34. ★ **MULTIPLE CHOICE** What are the solutions of $x^2 + 10x + 8 = -5$? C

Ⓐ $5 \pm 2\sqrt{3}$ Ⓑ $5 \pm 4\sqrt{3}$ Ⓒ $-5 \pm 2\sqrt{3}$ Ⓓ $-5 \pm 4\sqrt{3}$

EXAMPLE 5 on p. 286 for Exs. 35–38

GEOMETRY **Find the value of *x*.**

35. Area of rectangle = 50 $-5 + 5\sqrt{3}$

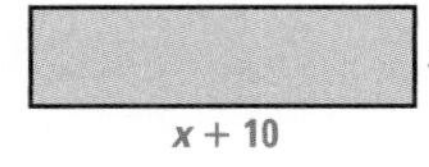

36. Area of parallelogram = 48 $-3 + \sqrt{57}$

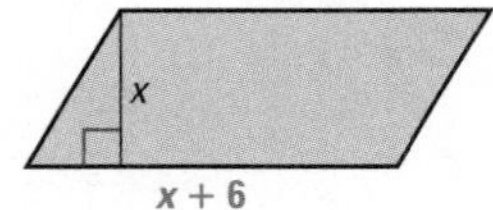

37. Area of triangle = 40 $-2 + 2\sqrt{21}$

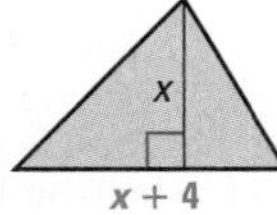

38. Area of trapezoid = 20 $-1 + \sqrt{11}$

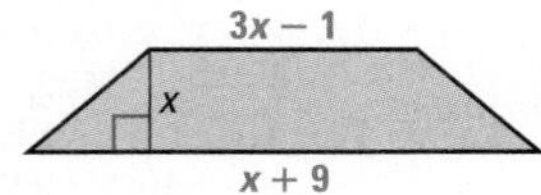

39. (2.8, 125.44); at 2.8 seconds the water will reach a maximum height of 125.44 feet.

FINDING THE VERTEX **In Exercises 39 and 40, use completing the square to find the vertex of the given function's graph. Then tell what the vertex represents.**

Buckingham Fountain

39. At Buckingham Fountain in Chicago, the water's height h (in feet) above the main nozzle can be modeled by $h = -16t^2 + 89.6t$ where t is the time (in seconds) since the water has left the nozzle.

40. When you walk x meters per minute, your rate y of energy use (in calories per minute) can be modeled by $y = 0.0085x^2 - 1.5x + 120$. (88.2, 53.8); walking 88.2 meters per minute uses 53.8 calories per minute

EXAMPLES 6 and 7 on p. 287 for Exs. 41–49

WRITING IN VERTEX FORM **Write the quadratic function in vertex form. Then identify the vertex.** 41–49. See margin.

41. $y = x^2 - 8x + 19$ 42. $y = x^2 - 4x - 1$ 43. $y = x^2 + 12x + 37$

44. $y = x^2 + 20x + 90$ (45.) $f(x) = x^2 - 3x + 4$ 46. $g(x) = x^2 + 7x + 2$

47. $y = 2x^2 + 24x + 25$ 48. $y = 5x^2 + 10x + 7$ 49. $y = 2x^2 - 28x + 99$

ERROR ANALYSIS ***Describe*** **and correct the error in solving the equation.**

50.
$$x^2 + 10x + 13 = 0$$
$$x^2 + 10x = -13$$
$$x^2 + 10x + 25 = -13 + 25$$
$$(x + 5)^2 = 12$$
$$x + 5 = \pm\sqrt{12}$$
$$x = -5 \pm \sqrt{12}$$
$$x = -5 \pm 4\sqrt{3}$$

$\sqrt{12} = 2\sqrt{3}$; $x = -5 \pm 2\sqrt{3}$

51.
$$4x^2 + 24x - 11 = 0$$
$$4(x^2 + 6x) = 11$$
$$4(x^2 + 6x + 9) = 11 + 9$$
$$4(x + 3)^2 = 20$$
$$(x + 3)^2 = 5$$
$$x + 3 = \pm\sqrt{5}$$
$$x = -3 \pm \sqrt{5}$$

51. 36 should be added to each side instead of 9; $4(x^2 + 6x + 9) = 11 + 36$; $4(x + 3)^2 = 47$; $(x + 3)^2 = \frac{47}{4}$; $x + 3 = \pm\frac{\sqrt{47}}{2}$; $x = -3 \pm \frac{\sqrt{47}}{2}$.

B **COMPLETING THE SQUARE** **Solve the equation by completing the square.**

52. $x^2 + 9x + 20 = 0$ $-5, -4$
53. $x^2 + 3x + 14 = 0$ $-\frac{3}{2} \pm \frac{i\sqrt{47}}{2}$
54. $7q^2 + 10q = 2q^2 + 155$ $-1 \pm 4\sqrt{2}$
55. $3x^2 + x = 2x - 6$ $\frac{1}{6} \pm \frac{i\sqrt{71}}{6}$
56. $0.1x^2 - x + 9 = 0.2x$ $6 \pm 3i\sqrt{6}$
57. $0.4v^2 + 0.7v = 0.3v - 2$ $-0.5 \pm 0.5i\sqrt{19}$

58. ★ **OPEN-ENDED MATH** Write a quadratic equation with real-number solutions that can be solved by completing the square but not by factoring. *Sample answer:* $x^2 + 6x + 4 = 0$

59. ★ **SHORT RESPONSE** In this exercise, you will investigate the graphical effect of completing the square.

a. Graph each pair of functions in the same coordinate plane. See margin.

$y = x^2 + 2x$ $y = x^2 + 4x$ $y = x^2 - 6x$

$y = (x + 1)^2$ $y = (x + 2)^2$ $y = (x - 3)^2$

b. *Compare* the graphs of $y = x^2 + bx$ and $y = \left(x + \frac{b}{2}\right)^2$. What happens to the graph of $y = x^2 + bx$ when you complete the square?
The graphs have the same shape and open the same direction; the vertex is shifted up $\frac{b^2}{4}$ units.

C 60. **REASONING** For what value(s) of k does $x^2 + bx + \left(\frac{b}{2}\right)^2 = k$ have exactly 1 real solution? 2 real solutions? 2 imaginary solutions? 0; $k > 0$; $k < 0$

61. **CHALLENGE** Solve $x^2 + bx + c = 0$ by completing the square. Your answer will be an expression for x in terms of b and c. $\frac{-b \pm \sqrt{b^2 - 4c}}{2}$

Avoiding Common Errors

Exercises 52–53 Many students have trouble completing the square to solve quadratic equations when the coefficient of x is odd because it involves fractions. These students can benefit from extra practice with expressions such as those in Exercises 19–21.

41. $y = (x - 4)^2 + 3$; $(4, 3)$
42. $y = (x - 2)^2 - 5$; $(2, -5)$
43. $y = (x + 6)^2 + 1$; $(-6, 1)$
44. $y = (x + 10)^2 - 10$; $(-10, -10)$
45. $y = \left(x - \frac{3}{2}\right)^2 + \frac{7}{4}$; $\left(\frac{3}{2}, \frac{7}{4}\right)$
46. $y = \left(x + \frac{7}{2}\right)^2 - \frac{41}{4}$; $\left(-\frac{7}{2}, -\frac{41}{4}\right)$
47. $y = 2(x + 6)^2 - 47$; $(-6, -47)$
48. $y = 5(x + 1)^2 + 2$; $(-1, 2)$
49. $y = 2(x - 7)^2 + 1$; $(7, 1)$

59a.

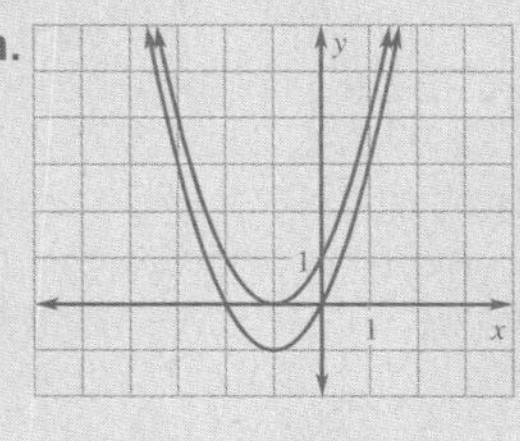

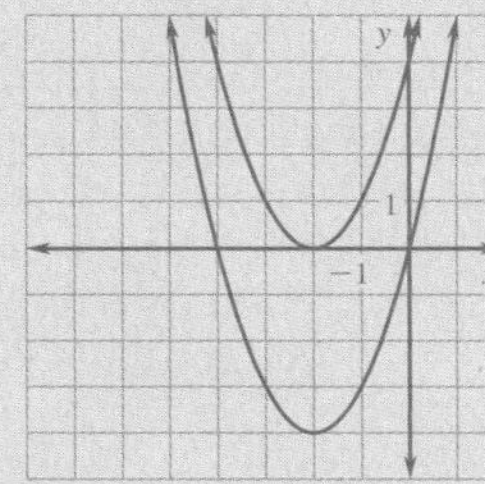

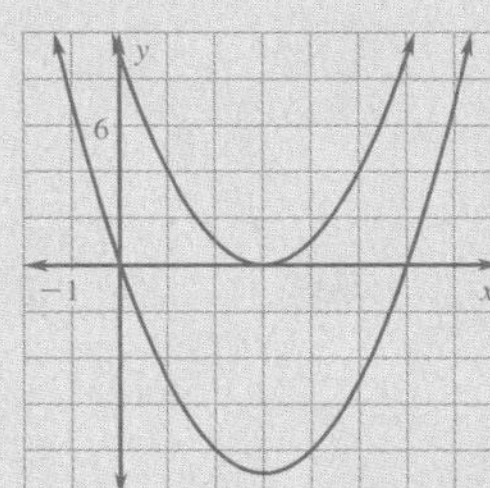

Graphing Calculator

Exercises 62–66 If your class completed the Graphing Calculator Activity for Lesson 4.1, refer them to page 244 to review how to use a graphing calculator to find a maximum or minimum value of a quadratic function. Students can solve these applied problems algebraically and then use their graphing calculators as a check.

66c.

Height (ft)
Horizontal position (ft)

PROBLEM SOLVING

EXAMPLE 7 A on p. 287 for Exs. 62–65

62. DRUM MAJOR While marching, a drum major tosses a baton into the air and catches it. The height h (in feet) of the baton after t seconds can be modeled by $h = -16t^2 + 32t + 6$. Find the maximum height of the baton. 22 ft

@HomeTutor for problem solving help at classzone.com

63. VOLLEYBALL The height h (in feet) of a volleyball t seconds after it is hit can be modeled by $h = -16t^2 + 48t + 4$. Find the volleyball's maximum height. 40 ft

@HomeTutor for problem solving help at classzone.com

64. Selling the skateboards for $60 would maximize weekly revenue at $3600.

64. SKATEBOARD REVENUE A skateboard shop sells about 50 skateboards per week for the price advertised. For each $1 decrease in price, about 1 more skateboard per week is sold. The shop's revenue can be modeled by $y = (70 - x)(50 + x)$. Use vertex form to find how the shop can maximize weekly revenue.

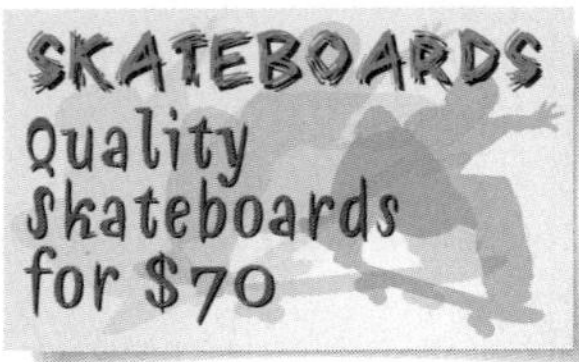

65. VIDEO GAME REVENUE A store sells about 40 video game systems each month when it charges $200 per system. For each $10 increase in price, about 1 less system per month is sold. The store's revenue can be modeled by $y = (200 + 10x)(40 - x)$. Use vertex form to find how the store can maximize monthly revenue.
Selling systems for $300 would maximize monthly revenue at $9000.

B

66. MULTIPLE REPRESENTATIONS The path of a ball thrown by a softball player can be modeled by the function

$$y = -0.0110x^2 + 1.23x + 5.50$$

where x is the softball's horizontal position (in feet) and y is the corresponding height (in feet).

a. **Rewriting a Function** Write the given function in vertex form. $y = -0.011(x - 55.9)^2 + 39.9$

b. **Making a Table** Make a table of values for the function. Include values of x from 0 to 120 in increments of 10. See margin.

c. **Drawing a Graph** Use your table to graph the function. What is the maximum height of the softball? How far does it travel? See margin for art; about 40 ft; about 116 ft.

67. ★ EXTENDED RESPONSE Your school is adding a rectangular outdoor eating section along part of a 70 foot side of the school. The eating section will be enclosed by a fence along its three open sides. The school has 120 feet of fencing and plans to use 1500 square feet of land for the eating section.

a. Write an equation for the area of the eating section. $1500 = (120 - 2x)(x)$

b. Solve the equation. *Explain* why you must reject one of the solutions.

c. What are the dimensions of the eating section? about 42.25 ft by 35.5 ft

67b. about 17.75, about 42.25; 17.25 must be rejected because it gives a length for the garden that is greater than the length of the side of the school.

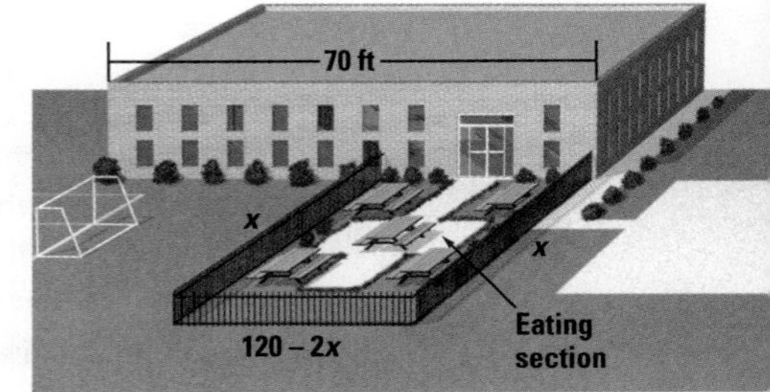

○ = WORKED-OUT SOLUTIONS on p. WS1 ★ = STANDARDIZED TEST PRACTICE ◆ = MULTIPLE REPRESENTATION

66b.

x	0	10	20	30	40	50	60	70	80	90	100	110	120
y	5.5	16.7	25.7	32.5	37.1	39.5	39.7	37.7	33.5	27.1	18.5	7.7	−5.3

GEOMETRY C REVIEW

The volume of clay equals the difference of the volumes of two cylinders.

68. CHALLENGE In your pottery class, you are given a lump of clay with a volume of 200 cubic centimeters and are asked to make a cylindrical pencil holder. The pencil holder should be 9 centimeters high and have an inner radius of 3 centimeters. What thickness x should your pencil holder have if you want to use all of the clay? **about 0.90 cm**

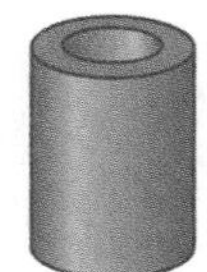

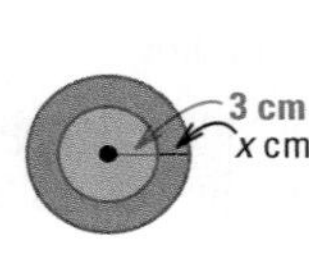

Top view

Side view

KENTUCKY MIXED REVIEW

TEST PRACTICE at classzone.com

69. If quadrilateral $MNPQ$ is reflected in the line $y = 3$, in which quadrant will the image of point N appear? **A**

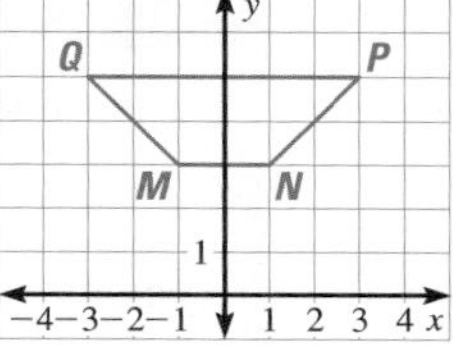

Ⓐ Quadrant I Ⓑ Quadrant II

Ⓒ Quadrant III Ⓓ Quadrant IV

70. A hose adds 120 gallons of water to a swimming pool in 1.5 hours. How many hours will it take for the hose to fill a different swimming pool that holds 600 gallons of water? **C**

Ⓐ 5 h Ⓑ 6.25 h Ⓒ 7.5 h Ⓓ 8 h

QUIZ for Lessons 4.5–4.7

Solve the equation.

1. $4x^2 = 64$ *(p. 266)* ± 4
2. $3(p - 1)^2 = 15$ *(p. 266)* $1 \pm \sqrt{5}$
3. $16(m + 5)^2 = 8$ *(p. 266)* $\frac{-5 \pm \sqrt{2}}{2}$
4. $-2z^2 = 424$ *(p. 275)* $2i\sqrt{53}$
5. $s^2 + 12 = 9$ *(p. 275)* $\pm i\sqrt{3}$
6. $7x^2 - 4 = -6$ *(p. 275)* $\pm\frac{\sqrt{14}}{7}i$

Write the expression as a complex number in standard form. *(p. 275)*

7. $(5 - 3i) + (-2 + 5i)$ $3 + 2i$
8. $(-2 + 9i) - (7 + 8i)$ $-9 + i$
9. $3i(7 - 9i)$ $27 + 21i$
10. $(8 - 3i)(-6 - 10i)$ $-78 - 62i$
11. $\frac{4i}{-6 - 11i}$ $-\frac{44}{157} - \frac{24}{157}i$
12. $\frac{3 - 2i}{-8 + 5i}$ $-\frac{34}{89} + \frac{1}{89}i$

Write the quadratic function in vertex form. Then identify the vertex. *(p. 284)* 13–18. See margin.

13. $y = x^2 - 4x + 9$
14. $y = x^2 + 14x + 45$
15. $f(x) = x^2 - 10x + 17$
16. $g(x) = x^2 - 2x - 7$
17. $y = x^2 + x + 1$
18. $y = x^2 + 9x + 19$

19. **FALLING OBJECT** A student drops a ball from a school roof 45 feet above ground. How long is the ball in the air? *(p. 266)* about 1.7 sec

5 ASSESS AND RETEACH

Daily Homework Quiz

Transparency Available

1. What value of c makes $x^2 - 5x + c$ a perfect square trinomial? Write the trinomial as the square of a binomial. $\frac{25}{4}; \left(x - \frac{5}{2}\right)^2$
2. Solve $x^2 - 14x + 9 = 0$ by completing the square. $7 + 2\sqrt{10}, 7 - 2\sqrt{10}$
3. Solve $3x^2 - 24x = -48$ by completing the square. 4
4. Write $y = 3x^2 + 24x + 40$ in vertex form. Then identify the vertex. $y = 3(x + 4)^2 - 8; (-4, -8)$

Online Quiz

Available at **classzone.com**

Diagnosis/Remediation

- Practice A, B, C in Chapter 4 Resource Book, pp. 78–80
- Study Guide in Chapter 4 Resource Book, pp. 81–82
- Practice Workbook, pp. 68–69
- @HomeTutor

Challenge

Additional challenge is available in the Chapter 4 Resource Book, p. 85.

Quiz

An easily-readable reduced copy of the quiz (with answers) on Lessons 4.5–4.7 from the Assessment Book can be found on p. 234G.

Quiz

13. $y = (x - 2)^2 + 5; (2, 5)$
14. $y = (x + 7)^2 - 4; (-7, -4)$
15. $y = (x - 5)^2 - 8; (5, -8)$
16. $y = (x - 1)^2 - 8; (1, -8)$
17. $y = \left(x + \frac{1}{2}\right)^2 + \frac{3}{4}; \left(-\frac{1}{2}, \frac{3}{4}\right)$
18. $y = \left(x + \frac{9}{2}\right)^2 - \frac{5}{4}; \left(-\frac{9}{2}, -\frac{5}{4}\right)$

1 PLAN AND PREPARE

Warm-Up Exercises

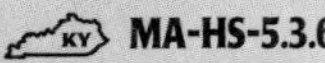

Transparency Available

1. Write $15x^2 + 6x = 14x^2 - 12$ in standard form. $x^2 + 6x + 12 = 0$
2. Evaluate $b^2 - 4ac$ when $a = 3$, $b = -6$, and $c = 5$. -24
3. A student is solving an equation by completing the square. Write the step in the solution that appears just before "$(x - 3) = \pm 5$". $(x - 3)^2 = 25$

Notetaking Guide

Transparency Available

Promotes interactive learning and notetaking skills, pp. 116–119.

Pacing

Basic: 1 day
Average: 1 day
Advanced: 1 day
Block: 0.5 block with 4.9
• See *Teaching Guide/Lesson Plan.*

2 FOCUS AND MOTIVATE

Essential Question

Big Idea 2, p. 235

How do you use the quadratic formula and the discriminant? **Tell students they will learn how to answer this question by using the quadratic formula and the discriminant to solve quadratic equations.**

4.8 Use the Quadratic Formula and the Discriminant

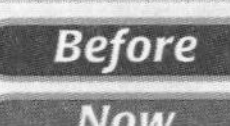

MA-HS-5.3.6 **Students will model, solve and graph quadratic equations in real-world and mathematical problems. DOK 2**

Before You solved quadratic equations by completing the square.

Now You will solve quadratic equations using the quadratic formula.

Why? So you can model the heights of thrown objects, as in Example 5.

Key Vocabulary
• quadratic formula
• discriminant

In Lesson 4.7, you solved quadratic equations by completing the square for *each equation separately.* By completing the square *once* for the general equation $ax^2 + bx + c = 0$, you can develop a formula that gives the solutions of *any* quadratic equation. (See Exercise 67.) The formula for the solutions is called the **quadratic formula**.

KEY CONCEPT *For Your Notebook*

The Quadratic Formula

Let a, b, and c be real numbers such that $a \neq 0$. The solutions of the quadratic equation $ax^2 + bx + c = 0$ are $x = \frac{-b \pm \sqrt{b^2 - 4ac}}{2a}$.

EXAMPLE 1 Solve an equation with two real solutions

Solve $x^2 + 3x = 2$.

AVOID ERRORS
Remember to write the quadratic equation in standard form before applying the quadratic formula.

$x^2 + 3x = 2$	**Write original equation.**
$x^2 + 3x - 2 = 0$	**Write in standard form.**
$x = \frac{-b \pm \sqrt{b^2 - 4ac}}{2a}$	**Quadratic formula**
$x = \frac{-3 \pm \sqrt{3^2 - 4(1)(-2)}}{2(1)}$	$a = 1, b = 3, c = -2$
$x = \frac{-3 \pm \sqrt{17}}{2}$	**Simplify.**

▶ The solutions are $x = \frac{-3 + \sqrt{17}}{2} \approx 0.56$ and $x = \frac{-3 - \sqrt{17}}{2} \approx -3.56$.

CHECK Graph $y = x^2 + 3x - 2$ and note that the x-intercepts are about 0.56 and about -3.56. ✓

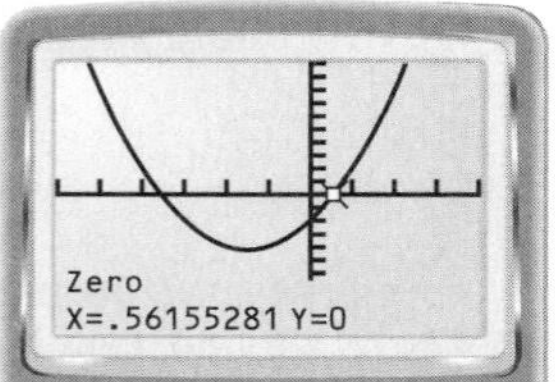

Resource Planning Guide

Chapter Resource Book
• Teaching Guide/Lesson Plan (pp. 86–87)
• Activity Master (p. 88)
• Practice levels A, B, C (pp. 90–92)
• Study Guide (pp. 93–94)
• Catch-up for Absent Students (p. 95)
• Application (p. 96)
• Challenge (p. 97)

Workbooks
• Notetaking Guide (pp. 116–119)
• Practice Workbook (pp. 70–71)

Teaching Options
• **Power Presentations CD-ROM** provides dynamic electronic teaching resources for the classroom.
• **Activity Generator CD-ROM** provides editable activities for all ability levels.

Interactive Technology
• Easy Planner
• Power Presentations CD-ROM
• Activity Generator CD-ROM
• Animated Algebra
• Test Generator CD-ROM
• Online Quiz
• eWorkbook
• eEdition
• @HomeTutor

Resources for English Learners
• Quick Reference for English Learners
• Spanish Study Guide
• Multi-Language Visual Glossary
• Student Resources in Spanish

See also the *Algebra 2 Toolkit* for more strategies for meeting individual needs.

EXAMPLE 2 Solve an equation with one real solution

Solve $25x^2 - 18x = 12x - 9$.

$25x^2 - 18x = 12x - 9$	Write original equation.
$25x^2 - 30x + 9 = 0$	Write in standard form.
$x = \frac{30 \pm \sqrt{(-30)^2 - 4(25)(9)}}{2(25)}$	$a = 25, b = -30, c = 9$
$x = \frac{30 \pm \sqrt{0}}{50}$	Simplify.
$x = \frac{3}{5}$	Simplify.

NOTHER WAY
u can also use
:toring to solve this
uation because the
t side factors as
$x - 3)^2$.

▸ The solution is $\frac{3}{5}$.

CHECK Graph $y = 25x^2 - 30x + 9$ and note that the only x-intercept is $0.6 = \frac{3}{5}$. ✓

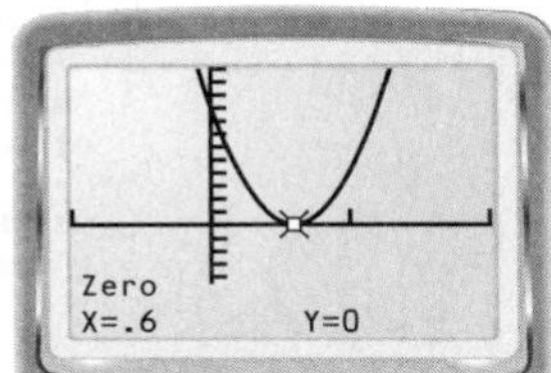

EXAMPLE 3 Solve an equation with imaginary solutions

Solve $-x^2 + 4x = 5$.

$-x^2 + 4x = 5$	Write original equation.
$-x^2 + 4x - 5 = 0$	Write in standard form.
$x = \frac{-4 \pm \sqrt{4^2 - 4(-1)(-5)}}{2(-1)}$	$a = -1, b = 4, c = -5$
$x = \frac{-4 \pm \sqrt{-4}}{-2}$	Simplify.
$x = \frac{-4 \pm 2i}{-2}$	Rewrite using the imaginary unit i.
$x = 2 \pm i$	Simplify.

▸ The solutions are $2 + i$ and $2 - i$.

CHECK Graph $y = -x^2 + 4x - 5$. There are no x-intercepts. So, the original equation has no real solutions. The algebraic check for the imaginary solution $2 + i$ is shown.

$$-(2 + i)^2 + 4(2 + i) \stackrel{?}{=} 5$$
$$-3 - 4i + 8 + 4i \stackrel{?}{=} 5$$
$$5 = 5 ✓$$

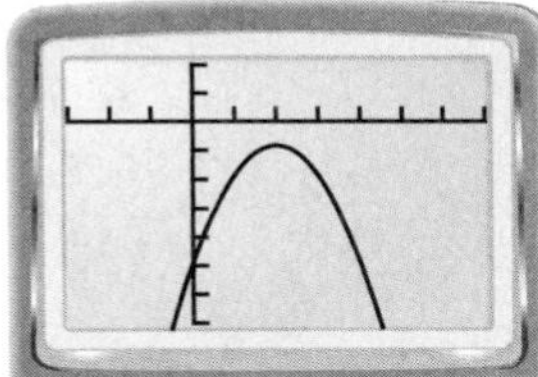

GUIDED PRACTICE for Examples 1, 2, and 3

Use the quadratic formula to solve the equation.

1. $x^2 = 6x - 4$ $3 \pm \sqrt{5}$
2. $4x^2 - 10x = 2x - 9$ $1\frac{1}{2}$
3. $7x - 5x^2 - 4 = 2x + 3$ $\frac{5 \pm i\sqrt{115}}{10}$

Motivating the Lesson

You are practicing soccer penalty kicks. You are trying to figure out how hard to kick the ball to make sure that it does not go above the goal. You can use a quadratic function to help you figure this out.

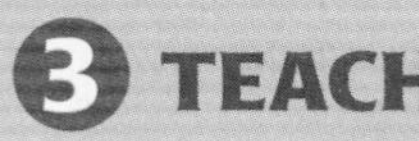

3 TEACH

Extra Example 1

Solve $x^2 - 5x = 7$. $\frac{5 + \sqrt{53}}{2}, \frac{5 - \sqrt{53}}{2}$

Extra Example 2

Solve $16x^2 - 23x = 17x - 25$. $\frac{5}{4}$

Extra Example 3

Solve $x^2 - 6x + 10 = 0$. $3 + i$, $3 - i$

Key Questions to Ask for Examples 1, 2, and 3

- How can you tell if a quadratic equation has one or two solutions? **If the number under the square root symbol is 0, the equation has one solution, otherwise it has two solutions.**
- How are the two solutions in Example 3 related? **They are complex conjugates.**

Avoiding Common Errors

In **Example 3**, students often make errors in the last step of the solution. They may think they can "cancel" the 2's and write $\frac{-4 \pm 2i}{-2}$ as $-4 \pm i$. Remind them to divide all the terms in the numerator by -2, so $\frac{-4 \pm 2i}{-2} = \frac{-4}{-2} \pm \frac{2i}{-2} = 2 \pm i$.

Extra Example 4

Find the discriminant of the quadratic equation and give the number and type of solutions of the equation.

a. $x^2 + 10x + 23 = 0$ **8; two real solutions**

b. $x^2 + 10x + 25 = 0$ **0; one real solution**

c. $x^2 + 10x + 27 = 0$ **−8; two imaginary solutions**

Key Question to Ask for Example 4

- Does the discriminant give the solution of a quadratic equation? **No, it gives the number and type of solutions, but it does not give the actual solution.**

Mathematical Reasoning

The use of the discriminant can be refined to distinguish between rational and irrational solutions. Give students several quadratic equations for which $b^2 - 4ac$ is positive, some with rational solutions and some with irrational solutions. Ask them to come up with a conjecture about how the value of the discriminant is related to whether the solutions are rational or irrational. Students should be able to explain why the solutions will be rational whenever the value of the discriminant is a perfect square.

DISCRIMINANT In the quadratic formula, the expression $b^2 - 4ac$ is called the **discriminant** of the associated equation $ax^2 + bx + c = 0$.

$$x = \frac{-b \pm \sqrt{b^2 - 4ac}}{2a} \quad \leftarrow \text{discriminant}$$

You can use the discriminant of a quadratic equation to determine the equation's number and type of solutions.

KEY CONCEPT *For Your Notebook*

Using the Discriminant of $ax^2 + bx + c = 0$

Value of discriminant	$b^2 - 4ac > 0$	$b^2 - 4ac = 0$	$b^2 - 4ac < 0$
Number and type of solutions	Two real solutions	One real solution	Two imaginary solutions
Graph of $y = ax^2 + bx + c$	Two x-intercepts	One x-intercept	No x-intercept

EXAMPLE 4 Use the discriminant

Find the discriminant of the quadratic equation and give the number and type of solutions of the equation.

a. $x^2 - 8x + 17 = 0$ **b.** $x^2 - 8x + 16 = 0$ **c.** $x^2 - 8x + 15 = 0$

Solution

Equation	**Discriminant**	**Solution(s)**
$ax^2 + bx + c = 0$	$b^2 - 4ac$	$x = \frac{-b \pm \sqrt{b^2 - 4ac}}{2a}$
a. $x^2 - 8x + 17 = 0$	$(-8)^2 - 4(1)(17) = -4$	Two imaginary: $4 \pm i$
b. $x^2 - 8x + 16 = 0$	$(-8)^2 - 4(1)(16) = 0$	One real: 4
c. $x^2 - 8x + 15 = 0$	$(-8)^2 - 4(1)(15) = 4$	Two real: 3, 5

GUIDED PRACTICE for Example 4

Find the discriminant of the quadratic equation and give the number and type of solutions of the equation.

4. $2x^2 + 4x - 4 = 0$ **5.** $3x^2 + 12x + 12 = 0$ **6.** $8x^2 = 9x - 11$

7. $7x^2 - 2x = 5$ **144; two real solutions** **8.** $4x^2 + 3x + 12 = 3 - 3x$ **−108; two imaginary solutions** **9.** $3x - 5x^2 + 1 = 6 - 7x$ **0; one real solution**

4. 48; two real solutions

5. 0; one real solution

6. −271; two imaginary solutions

Differentiated Instruction

Inclusion When using the quadratic formula and the discriminant, there is a lot of information to be processed and organized. Using a table as shown may be helpful to students when writing solutions.

a	b	c	$b^2 - 4ac$	Number of solutions	$\frac{-b + \sqrt{b^2 - 4ac}}{2a}$	$\frac{-b - \sqrt{b^2 - 4ac}}{2a}$

See also the *Algebra 2 Toolkit* for more strategies.

MODELING LAUNCHED OBJECTS In Lesson 4.5, the function $h = -16t^2 + h_0$ was used to model the height of a *dropped* object. For an object that is *launched or thrown*, an extra term v_0t must be added to the model to account for the object's initial vertical velocity v_0 (in feet per second). Recall that h is the height (in feet), t is the time in motion (in seconds), and h_0 is the initial height (in feet).

$h = -16t^2 + h_0$ **Object is dropped.**

$h = -16t^2 + v_0t + h_0$ **Object is launched or thrown.**

As shown below, the value of v_0 can be positive, negative, or zero depending on whether the object is launched upward, downward, or parallel to the ground.

$v_0 > 0$

$v_0 < 0$

$v_0 = 0$

EXAMPLE 5 Solve a vertical motion problem

JUGGLING A juggler tosses a ball into the air. The ball leaves the juggler's hand 4 feet above the ground and has an initial vertical velocity of 40 feet per second. The juggler catches the ball when it falls back to a height of 3 feet. How long is the ball in the air?

Solution

Because the ball is thrown, use the model $h = -16t^2 + v_0t + h_0$. To find how long the ball is in the air, solve for t when $h = 3$.

$h = -16t^2 + v_0t + h_0$ **Write height model.**

$3 = -16t^2 + 40t + 4$ **Substitute 3 for h, 40 for v_0, and 4 for h_0.**

$0 = -16t^2 + 40t + 1$ **Write in standard form.**

$t = \frac{-40 \pm \sqrt{40^2 - 4(-16)(1)}}{2(-16)}$ **Quadratic formula**

$t = \frac{-40 \pm \sqrt{1664}}{-32}$ **Simplify.**

$t \approx -0.025$ or $t \approx 2.5$ **Use a calculator.**

▶ Reject the solution -0.025 because the ball's time in the air cannot be negative. So, the ball is in the air for about 2.5 seconds.

GUIDED PRACTICE for Example 5

10. **WHAT IF?** In Example 5, suppose the ball leaves the juggler's hand with an initial vertical velocity of 50 feet per second. How long is the ball in the air? about 3.1 sec

Extra Example 5

A basketball player passes the ball to a teammate. The ball leaves the player's hand 5 feet above the ground and has an initial vertical velocity of 55 feet per second. The teammate catches the ball when it returns to a height of 5 feet. How long is the ball in the air? about 3.4 sec

Graphing Calculator

You can use a graphing calculator demonstration to enhance students' understanding of Example 5. Simulate the motion of the ball by graphing this pair of parametric equations: $X_{1T} = T$, $Y_{1T} = -16T^2 + 40T + 4$. A good choice of window settings is Tmin = 0, Tmax = 5, Tstep = .01, Xmin = 0, Xmax = 5, Xscl = 1, Ymin = −5, Ymax = 30, Yscl = 5.

Closing the Lesson

Have students summarize the major points of the lesson and answer the Essential Question: How do you use the quadratic formula and the discriminant?

- The quadratic formula can be used to solve any quadratic equation.
- For a quadratic function in standard form, the discriminant $b^2 - 4ac$ can be used to determine the number and type of solutions.

The quadratic formula can be used to solve any quadratic equation, whether the roots are real or imaginary, by substituting the three coefficients from the standard form into the formula and simplifying the result. The discriminant gives the number and type of solutions of a quadratic equation.

4.8 EXERCISES

HOMEWORK KEY
○ = **WORKED-OUT SOLUTIONS** on p. WS9 for Exs. 19, 39, and 71
★ = **STANDARDIZED TEST PRACTICE** Exs. 2, 12, 51, 55, 62, 69, 72, and 73

4 PRACTICE AND APPLY

Assignment Guide

Answer Transparencies available for all exercises

Basic:
Day 1: EP p. 1010 Exs. 7–9
pp. 296–299
Exs. 1, 2, 4–12 even, 13–21 odd, 22–24, 31–33, 40–42, 49–51, 68–72, 75

Average:
Day 1: pp. 296–299
Exs. 1, 2, 6–8, 12, 16–18, 25–27, 34–36, 43–45, 49–58, 62, 68–73, 76

Advanced:
Day 1: pp. 296–299
Exs. 1, 2, 9–12, 19–21, 28–30, 37–39, 46–48, 51–67*, 69–74*

Block:
pp. 296–299
Exs. 1, 2, 6–8, 12, 16–18, 25–27, 34–36, 43–45, 49–58, 62, 68–73, 76 (with 4.9)

Differentiated Instruction

See *Algebra 2 Best Practices Toolkit* for suggestions on addressing the needs of a diverse classroom.

Homework Check

For a quick check of student understanding of key concepts, go over the following exercises:
Basic: 6, 14, 24, 32, 68
Average: 8, 18, 26, 36, 68
Advanced: 10, 20, 30, 38, 69

Extra Practice

- Student Edition, p. 1013
- Chapter 4 Resource Book: Practice levels A, B, C, pp. 90–92

Practice Worksheet

An easily-readable reduced practice page (with answers) for this lesson can be found on p. 234C.

SKILL PRACTICE

A

1. **VOCABULARY** Copy and complete: You can use the _?_ of a quadratic equation to determine the equation's number and type of solutions. discriminant

2. ★ **WRITING** *Describe* a real-life situation in which you can use the model $h = -16t^2 + v_0t + h_0$ but not the model $h = -16t^2 + h_0$.

2. *Sample answer:* A volleyball player jumps to hit a ball 7 feet above the ground. The ball leaves the player's hand with a vertical velocity of −45 feet per second. How long is the ball in the air?

EXAMPLES 1, 2, and 3 on pp. 292–293 for Exs. 3–30

EQUATIONS IN STANDARD FORM Use the quadratic formula to solve the equation.

3. $x^2 - 4x - 5 = 0$ −1, 5
4. $x^2 - 6x + 7 = 0$ $3 \pm \sqrt{2}$
5. $t^2 + 8t + 19 = 0$ $-4 \pm i\sqrt{3}$
6. $x^2 - 16x + 7 = 0$ $8 \pm \sqrt{57}$
7. $8w^2 - 8w + 2 = 0$ $\frac{1}{2}$
8. $5p^2 - 10p + 24 = 0$ $\frac{5 \pm i\sqrt{95}}{5}$
9. $4x^2 - 8x + 1 = 0$ $\frac{2 \pm \sqrt{3}}{2}$
10. $6u^2 + 4u + 11 = 0$ $\frac{-2 \pm i\sqrt{62}}{6}$
11. $3r^2 - 8r - 9 = 0$ $\frac{4 \pm \sqrt{43}}{3}$

12. ★ **MULTIPLE CHOICE** What are the complex solutions of the equation $2x^2 - 16x + 50 = 0$? A

Ⓐ $4 + 3i, 4 - 3i$ Ⓑ $4 + 12i, 4 - 12i$
Ⓒ $16 + 3i, 16 - 3i$ Ⓓ $16 + 12i, 16 - 12i$

EQUATIONS NOT IN STANDARD FORM Use the quadratic formula to solve the equation.

13. $3w^2 - 12w = -12$ 2
14. $x^2 + 6x = -15$ $-3 \pm i\sqrt{6}$
15. $s^2 = -14 - 3s$ $\frac{-3 \pm i\sqrt{47}}{2}$
16. $-3y^2 = 6y - 10$ $-\frac{3 \pm \sqrt{39}}{3}$
17. $3 - 8v - 5v^2 = 2v$ $-\frac{5 \pm 2\sqrt{10}}{5}$
18. $7x - 5 + 12x^2 = -3x$ $\frac{-5 \pm \sqrt{85}}{12}$
19. $4x^2 + 3 = x^2 - 7x$ $\frac{-7 \pm \sqrt{13}}{6}$
20. $6 - 2t^2 = 9t + 15$ $-3, -\frac{3}{2}$
21. $4 + 9n - 3n^2 = 2 - n$ $\frac{5 \pm \sqrt{31}}{3}$

SOLVING USING TWO METHODS Solve the equation using the quadratic formula. Then solve the equation by factoring to check your solution(s).

22. $z^2 + 15z + 24 = -32$ −7, −8
23. $x^2 - 5x + 10 = 4$ 2, 3
24. $m^2 + 5m - 99 = 3m$ −11, 9
25. $s^2 - s - 3 = s$ −1, 3
26. $r^2 - 4r + 8 = 5r$ 1, 8
27. $3x^2 + 7x - 24 = 13x$ −2, 4
28. $45x^2 + 57x + 1 = 5$ $-1\frac{1}{3}, \frac{1}{15}$
29. $5p^2 + 40p + 100 = 25$ −5, −3
30. $9n^2 - 42n - 162 = 21n$ −2, 9

EXAMPLE 4 on p. 294 for Exs. 31–39

USING THE DISCRIMINANT Find the discriminant of the quadratic equation and give the number and type of solutions of the equation.

31. $x^2 - 8x + 16 = 0$ 0; one real solution
32. $s^2 + 7s + 11 = 0$ 5; two real solutions
33. $8p^2 + 8p + 3 = 0$ −32; two imaginary solutions
34. $-4w^2 + w - 14 = 0$ −223; two imaginary solutions
35. $5x^2 + 20x + 21 = 0$ −20; two imaginary solutions
36. $8z - 10 = z^2 - 7z + 3$ 173; two real solutions
37. $8n^2 - 4n + 2 = 5n - 11$ −335; two imaginary solutions
38. $5x^2 + 16x = 11x - 3x^2$ 25; two real solutions
39. $7r^2 - 5 = 2r + 9r^2$ −36; two imaginary solutions

B

SOLVING QUADRATIC EQUATIONS Solve the equation using any method.

41. $\frac{1 \pm i\sqrt{67}}{2}$

45. $\frac{1 \pm \sqrt{229}}{12}$

40. $16t^2 - 7t = 17t - 9$ $\frac{3}{4}$
41. $7x - 3x^2 = 85 + 2x^2 + 2x$
42. $4(x - 1)^2 = 6x + 2$ $\frac{7 \pm \sqrt{41}}{4}$
43. $25 - 16v^2 = 12v(v + 5)$ $-2\frac{1}{2}, \frac{5}{14}$
44. $\frac{3}{2}y^2 - 6y = \frac{3}{4}y - 9$ $\frac{9 \pm i\sqrt{15}}{4}$
45. $3x^2 + \frac{9}{2}x - 4 = 5x + \frac{3}{4}$
46. $1.1(3.4x - 2.3)^2 = 15.5$ −0.43, 1.78
47. $19.25 = -8.5(2r - 1.75)^2$ $0.875 \pm 0.752i$
48. $4.5 = 1.5(3.25 - s)^2$ 1.52, 4.98

ERROR ANALYSIS ***Describe*** **and correct the error in solving the equation.** 49, 50. See margin.

49.

$$3x^2 + 6x + 15 = 0$$
$$x = \frac{-6 \pm \sqrt{6^2 - 4(3)(15)}}{2(3)}$$
$$= \frac{-6 \pm \sqrt{-144}}{6}$$
$$= \frac{-6 \pm 12}{6}$$
$$= 1 \text{ or } -3$$

50.

$$x^2 + 6x + 8 = 2$$
$$x = \frac{-6 \pm \sqrt{6^2 - 4(1)(8)}}{2(1)}$$
$$= \frac{-6 \pm \sqrt{4}}{2}$$
$$= \frac{-6 \pm 2}{2}$$
$$= -2 \text{ or } -4$$

51. ★ **SHORT RESPONSE** For a quadratic equation $ax^2 + bx + c = 0$ with two real solutions, show that the mean of the solutions is $-\frac{b}{2a}$. How is this fact related to the symmetry of the graph of $y = ax^2 + bx + c$? See margin.

VISUAL THINKING **In Exercises 52–54, the graph of a quadratic function $y = ax^2 + bx + c$ is shown. Tell whether the discriminant of $ax^2 + bx + c = 0$ is** ***positive, negative,*** **or** ***zero.***

52.
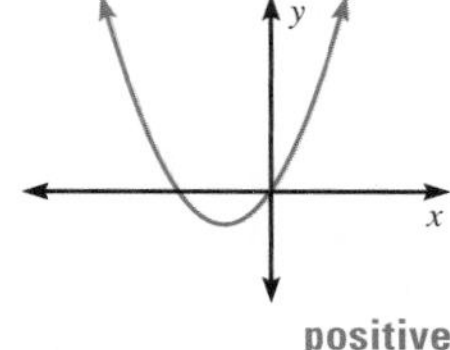
positive

53.
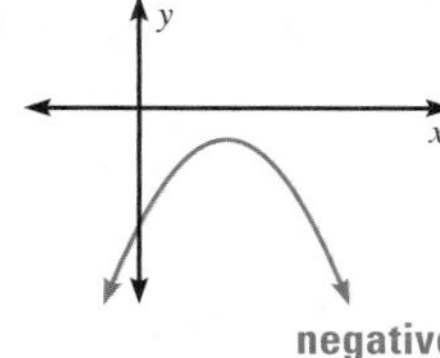
negative

54.
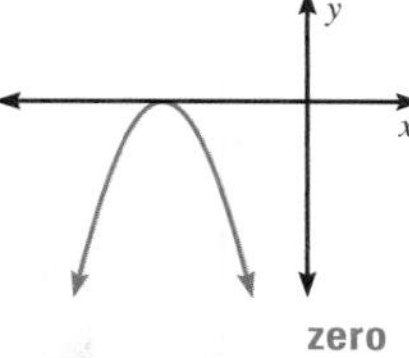
zero

55. ★ **MULTIPLE CHOICE** What is the value of c if the discriminant of $2x^2 + 5x + c = 0$ is -23? C

Ⓐ -23 Ⓑ -6 Ⓒ 6 Ⓓ 14

THE CONSTANT TERM **Use the discriminant to find all values of c for which the equation has (a) two real solutions, (b) one real solution, and (c) two imaginary solutions.**

56. $x^2 - 4x + c = 0$ a. $c < 4$ b. $c = 4$ c. $c > 4$

57. $x^2 + 8x + c = 0$ a. $c < 16$ b. $c = 16$ c. $c > 16$

58. $-x^2 + 16x + c = 0$

59. $3x^2 + 24x + c = 0$

60. $-4x^2 - 10x + c = 0$

61. $x^2 - x + c = 0$

62. ★ **OPEN-ENDED MATH** Write a quadratic equation in standard form that has a discriminant of -10. *Sample answer:* $0.5x^2 + 2x + 7 = 0$

C **WRITING EQUATIONS** **Write a quadratic equation in the form $ax^2 + bx + c = 0$ such that $c = 4$ and the equation has the given solutions.**

63. -4 and 3 $-\frac{1}{3}x^2 - \frac{1}{3}x + 4 = 0$

64. $-\frac{4}{3}$ and -1 $3x^2 + 7x + 4 = 0$

65. $-1 + i$ and $-1 - i$ $2x^2 + 4x + 4 = 0$

66. **REASONING** Show that there is no quadratic equation $ax^2 + bx + c = 0$ such that a, b, and c are real numbers and $3i$ and $-2i$ are solutions.

67. **CHALLENGE** Derive the quadratic formula by completing the square to solve the general quadratic equation $ax^2 + bx + c = 0$. See margin.

8a. $c > -64$
8b. $c = -64$
8c. $c < -64$
9a. $c < 48$
9b. $c = 48$
9c. $c > 48$
0a. $c > -6.25$
0b. $c = -6.25$
0c. $c < -6.25$
1a. $c < 0.25$
1b. $c = 0.25$
1c. $c > 0.25$

6. *Sample nswer:* If $3i$ is solution en $-3i$ ust also be solution and if $-2i$ is a solution en $2i$ is also solution. quadratic quation can nly have two olutions, not ur.

Avoiding Common Errors

Exercises 3–21 Students learning to use the quadratic formula may sometimes remember the formula incorrectly, or they may substitute into the formula incorrectly. Until they memorize the formula, encourage students to copy the formula from their textbook each time they need to use it. Then caution them about the need for the equation to be written in standard form before identifying the values of *a*, *b*, and *c* which are to be used in the formula.

Study Strategy

Exercises 40–48 After students have completed these exercises, ask them how they decided which method to use for each one that you assigned. Have them make a chart showing the advantages and disadvantages of each of the methods they have learned, and a sample equation that they think will be most easily solved by each of these methods. Students should keep this chart in their notebooks for reference.

49. $\sqrt{-144} = 12i$;
$$x = \frac{-6 \pm \sqrt{-144}}{6} = \frac{-6 \pm 12i}{6} = -1 \pm 2i$$

50. The equation must first be rewritten in the form $ax^2 + bx + c = 0$.
$$x^2 + 6x + 6 = 0$$
$$x = \frac{-6 \pm \sqrt{6^2 - 4(1)(6)}}{2(1)} = \frac{-6 \pm \sqrt{12}}{2} = \frac{-6 \pm 2\sqrt{3}}{2} = -3 \pm \sqrt{3}$$

51. $$\frac{\frac{-b + \sqrt{b^2 - 4ac}}{2a} + \frac{-b - \sqrt{b^2 - 4ac}}{2a}}{2} = \frac{\frac{-2b}{2a}}{2} = \frac{-b}{2a},$$ which is the formula for the axis of symmetry.

67. See Additional Answers beginning on p. AA1.

Reading Strategy

Exercise 68 If students have trouble translating the information given in this problem into an equation or knowing what to do with the equation once it is written, ask them to read each sentence separately and tell you what information in the sentence is important. Remind them that sometimes a sentence that contains no numbers still includes information that is needed to solve the problem. For example, in this exercise, the first sentence tells the reader that this is a problem about a thrown object, which should lead students to use the model for a thrown object given on page 295.

PROBLEM SOLVING

EXAMPLE 5 A on p. 295 for Exs. 68–69

68. FOOTBALL In a football game, a defensive player jumps up to block a pass by the opposing team's quarterback. The player bats the ball downward with his hand at an initial vertical velocity of −50 feet per second when the ball is 7 feet above the ground. How long do the defensive player's teammates have to intercept the ball before it hits the ground? **about 0.13 sec**

@HomeTutor for problem solving help at classzone.com

69. ★ MULTIPLE CHOICE For the period 1990–2002, the number S (in thousands) of cellular telephone subscribers in the United States can be modeled by $S = 858t^2 + 1412t + 4982$ where t is the number of years since 1990. In what year did the number of subscribers reach 50 million? **C**

Ⓐ 1991 Ⓑ 1992 Ⓒ 1996 Ⓓ 2000

@HomeTutor for problem solving help at classzone.com

70. MULTI-STEP PROBLEM A stunt motorcyclist makes a jump from one ramp 20 feet off the ground to another ramp 20 feet off the ground. The jump between the ramps can be modeled by $y = -\frac{1}{640}x^2 + \frac{1}{4}x + 20$ where x is the horizontal distance (in feet) and y is the height above the ground (in feet).

a. What is the motorcycle's height r when it lands on the ramp? **20 ft**

b. What is the distance d between the ramps? **160 ft**

c. What is the horizontal distance h the motorcycle has traveled when it reaches its maximum height? **80 ft**

d. What is the motorcycle's maximum height k above the ground? **30 ft**

(71.) BIOLOGY The number S of ant species in Kyle Canyon, Nevada, can be modeled by the function $S = -0.000013E^2 + 0.042E - 21$ where E is the elevation (in meters). Predict the elevation(s) at which you would expect to find 10 species of ants. **1141 m, 2090 m**

B

72. ★ SHORT RESPONSE A city planner wants to create adjacent sections for athletics and picnics in the yard of a youth center. The sections will be rectangular and will be surrounded by fencing as shown. There is 900 feet of fencing available. Each section should have an area of 12,000 square feet.

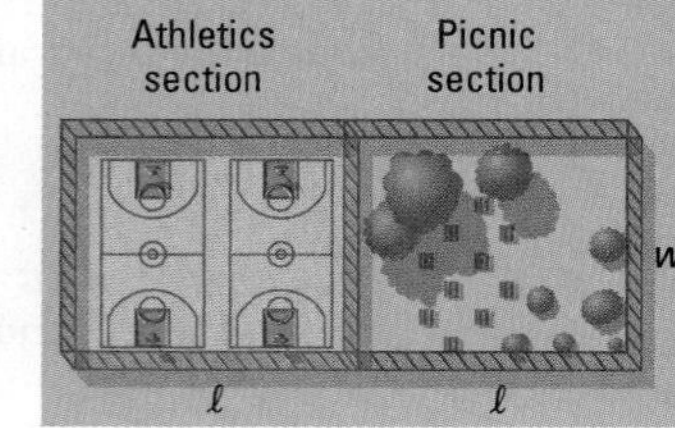

a. Show that $w = 300 - \frac{4}{3}\ell$. **$4\ell + 3w = 900$, $3w = 900 - 4\ell$, $w = 300 - \frac{4}{3}\ell$**

b. Find the possible dimensions of each section. **69.37 ft by 172.97 ft or 230.63 ft by 52.03 ft**

○ = WORKED-OUT SOLUTIONS on p. WS1 ★ = STANDARDIZED TEST PRACTICE

73a.

t	0	0.25	0.5	0.75	1
(x, y)	(0, 6)	(5, 10.25)	(10, 12.5)	(15, 12.75)	(20, 11)

73. ★ **EXTENDED RESPONSE** You can model the position (x, y) of a moving object using a pair of *parametric equations*. Such equations give x and y in terms of a third variable t that represents time. For example, suppose that when a basketball player attempts a free throw, the path of the basketball can be modeled by the parametric equations

$$x = 20t$$

$$y = -16t^2 + 21t + 6$$

where x and y are measured in feet, t is measured in seconds, and the player's feet are at $(0, 0)$.

a. **Evaluate** Make a table of values giving the position (x, y) of the basketball after 0, 0.25, 0.5, 0.75, and 1 second. **a, b. See margin.**

b. **Graph** Use your table from part (a) to graph the parametric equations.

c. **Solve** The position of the basketball rim is (15, 10). The top of the backboard is (15, 12). Does the player make the free throw? *Explain.* **No; the height of the ball when $x = 15$ is 12.75 feet, which is above the backboard, so the free throw would not be made.**

C 74. **CHALLENGE** The Stratosphere Tower in Las Vegas is 921 feet tall and has a "needle" at its top that extends even higher into the air. A thrill ride called the Big Shot catapults riders 160 feet up the needle and then lets them fall back to the launching pad.

a. The height h (in feet) of a rider on the Big Shot can be modeled by $h = -16t^2 + v_0t + 921$ where t is the elapsed time (in seconds) after launch and v_0 is the initial vertical velocity (in feet per second). Find v_0 using the fact that the maximum value of h is $921 + 160 = 1081$ feet. **about 101.2 ft/sec**

b. A brochure for the Big Shot states that the ride up the needle takes two seconds. *Compare* this time with the time given by the model $h = -16t^2 + v_0t + 921$ where v_0 is the value you found in part (a). Discuss the model's accuracy. **According to the model, it would take about 3.2 seconds to travel up the ride. The model's accuracy is slightly off what the brochure states.**

KENTUCKY MIXED REVIEW

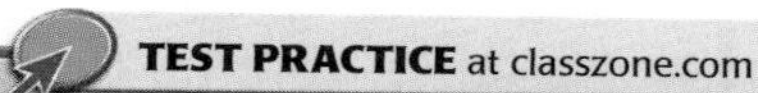

75. In the figure shown, $\overline{AB}$ is parallel to $\overline{ED}$. Which equation can be used to find the value of x? **D**

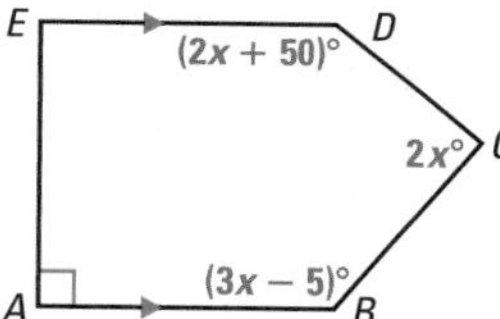

Ⓐ $5x + 225 = 360$ Ⓑ $5x + 235 = 540$

Ⓒ $7x + 235 = 360$ Ⓓ $7x + 225 = 540$

76. Music recital tickets are \$4 for students and \$6 for adults. A total of 725 tickets are sold and \$3650 is collected. Which pair of equations can be used to determine the number of students, s, and the number of adults, a, who attended the music recital? **A**

Ⓐ $s + a = 725$, $4s + 6a = 3650$

Ⓑ $s + a = 725$, $6s + 4a = 3650$

Ⓒ $s - a = 725$, $4s - 6a = 3650$

Ⓓ $4s + 6a = 725$, $s + a = 3650$

5 ASSESS AND RETEACH

Daily Homework Quiz

Transparency Available

Use the quadratic formula to solve the equation.

1. $4x^2 - 4x + 1 = 0$ $\frac{1}{2}$
2. $-x^2 + 8x = 20$ $4 + 2i, 4 - 2i$
3. $-x^2 = 6x - 2$ $-3 \pm \sqrt{11}$
4. Find the discriminant of $2x^2 + 3x - 6 = 0$ and give the number and type of solutions of the equation. **57; two real solutions**
5. An object is thrown upward from a height of 15 feet at an initial velocity of 35 feet per second. How long will it take for the object to hit the ground? **about 2.6 sec**

Available at **classzone.com**

Diagnosis/Remediation

- Practice A, B, C in Chapter 4 Resource Book, pp. 90–92
- Study Guide in Chapter 4 Resource Book, pp. 93–94
- Practice Workbook, pp. 70–71
- @HomeTutor

Challenge

Additional challenge is available in the Chapter 4 Resource Book, p. 97.

73b.

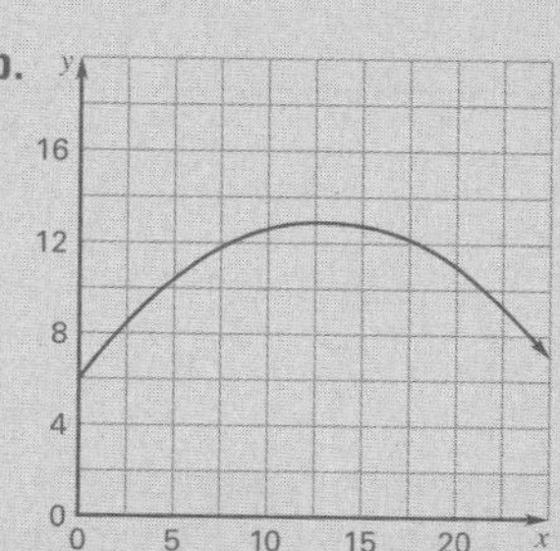

4.9 Graph and Solve Quadratic Inequalities

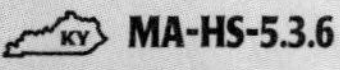 MA-HS-5.3.6 **Students will model, solve and graph quadratic equations in real-world and mathematical problems. DOK 2**

Before You graphed and solved linear inequalities.

Now You will graph and solve quadratic inequalities.

Why? So you can model the strength of a rope, as in Example 2.

1 PLAN AND PREPARE

Warm-Up Exercises

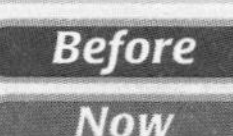 **Transparency Available**

1. Solve $x^2 - 2x - 24 = 0$. **−4, 6**
2. Solve $-8 < 3x - 5 < 7$. $-1 < x < 4$
3. A point on a graph moves so that the function $y = 2x^2 - 3x - 20$ describes how the vertical position y is related to its horizontal position x. What is the vertical position when the horizontal position is −3? **7**

Notetaking Guide

Transparency Available

Promotes interactive learning and notetaking skills, pp. 120–124.

Pacing

Basic: 2 days
Average: 2 days
Advanced: 2 days
Block: 0.5 block with 4.8
0.5 block with 4.10

- See *Teaching Guide/Lesson Plan.*

2 FOCUS AND MOTIVATE

Essential Question

Big Idea 2, p. 235

How do you solve quadratic inequalities in one variable? **Tell students they will learn how to answer this question by learning three methods for solving quadratic inequalities.**

Key Vocabulary
- quadratic inequality in two variables
- quadratic inequality in one variable

A **quadratic inequality in two variables** can be written in one of the following forms:

$y < ax^2 + bx + c$ $\quad y \le ax^2 + bx + c$ $\quad y > ax^2 + bx + c$ $\quad y \ge ax^2 + bx + c$

The graph of any such inequality consists of all solutions (x, y) of the inequality.

KEY CONCEPT *For Your Notebook*

Graphing a Quadratic Inequality in Two Variables

To graph a quadratic inequality in one of the forms above, follow these steps:

STEP 1 **Graph** the parabola with equation $y = ax^2 + bx + c$. Make the parabola *dashed* for inequalities with < or > and *solid* for inequalities with ≤ or ≥.

STEP 2 **Test** a point (x, y) inside the parabola to determine whether the point is a solution of the inequality.

STEP 3 **Shade** the region inside the parabola if the point from Step 2 is a solution. Shade the region outside the parabola if it is not a solution.

EXAMPLE 1 Graph a quadratic inequality

Graph $y > x^2 + 3x - 4$.

Solution

AVOID ERRORS
Be sure to use a dashed parabola if the symbol is > or < and a solid parabola if the symbol is ≥ or ≤.

STEP 1 **Graph** $y = x^2 + 3x - 4$. Because the inequality symbol is >, make the parabola dashed.

STEP 2 **Test** a point inside the parabola, such as (0, 0).

$$y > x^2 + 3x - 4$$
$$0 \overset{?}{>} 0^2 + 3(0) - 4$$
$$0 > -4 \checkmark$$

So, (0, 0) is a solution of the inequality.

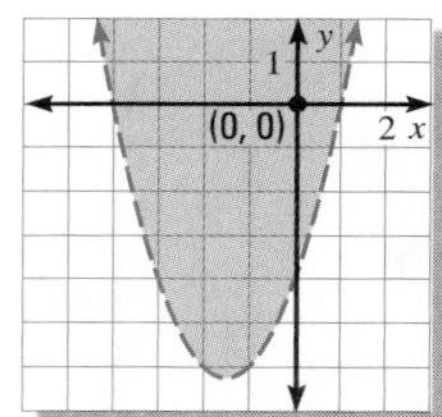

STEP 3 **Shade** the region inside the parabola.

Animated Algebra at classzone.com

Resource Planning Guide

Chapter Resource Book
- Teaching Guide/Lesson Plan (pp. 98–99)
- Activity Master (p. 100)
- Practice levels A, B, C (pp. 103–108)
- Study Guide (pp. 109–110)
- Catch-up for Absent Students (p. 111)
- Application (p. 112)
- Challenge (p. 113)

Workbooks
- Notetaking Guide (pp. 120–124)
- Practice Workbook (pp. 72–74)

Teaching Options
- **Power Presentations CD-ROM** provides dynamic electronic teaching resources for the classroom.
- **Activity Generator CD-ROM** provides editable activities for all ability levels.

Interactive Technology
- Easy Planner
- Power Presentations CD-ROM
- Activity Generator CD-ROM
- Animated Algebra
- Test Generator CD-ROM
- Online Quiz
- eWorkbook
- eEdition
- @HomeTutor

Resources for English Learners
- Quick Reference for English Learners
- Spanish Study Guide
- Multi-Language Visual Glossary
- Student Resources in Spanish

See also the *Algebra 2 Toolkit* for more strategies for meeting individual needs.

EXAMPLE 2 Use a quadratic inequality in real life

RAPPELLING A manila rope used for rappelling down a cliff can safely support a weight W (in pounds) provided

$$W \leq 1480d^2$$

where d is the rope's diameter (in inches). Graph the inequality.

Solution

Graph $W = 1480d^2$ for nonnegative values of d. Because the inequality symbol is $\leq$, make the parabola solid. Test a point inside the parabola, such as (1, 2000).

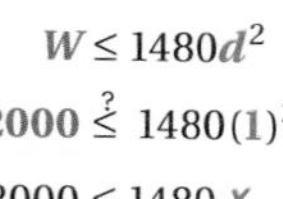

$$W \leq 1480d^2$$

$$2000 \overset{?}{\leq} 1480(1)^2$$

$$2000 \leq 1480 \text{ ✗}$$

Because (1, 2000) is not a solution, shade the region below the parabola.

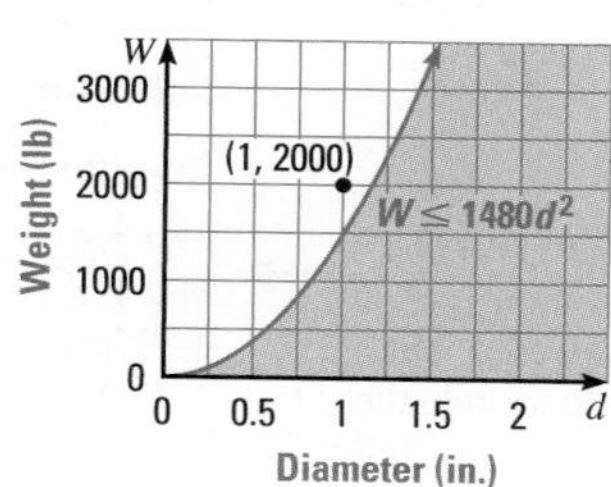

SYSTEMS OF QUADRATIC INEQUALITIES Graphing a *system* of quadratic inequalities is similar to graphing a system of linear inequalities. First graph each inequality in the system. Then identify the region in the coordinate plane common to all of the graphs. This region is called the *graph of the system.*

EXAMPLE 3 Graph a system of quadratic inequalities

Graph the system of quadratic inequalities.

$y \leq -x^2 + 4$ **Inequality 1**

$y > x^2 - 2x - 3$ **Inequality 2**

Solution

STEP 1 **Graph** $y \leq -x^2 + 4$. The graph is the red region inside and including the parabola $y = -x^2 + 4$.

STEP 2 **Graph** $y > x^2 - 2x - 3$. The graph is the blue region inside (but not including) the parabola $y = x^2 - 2x - 3$.

STEP 3 **Identify** the **purple region** where the two graphs overlap. This region is the graph of the system.

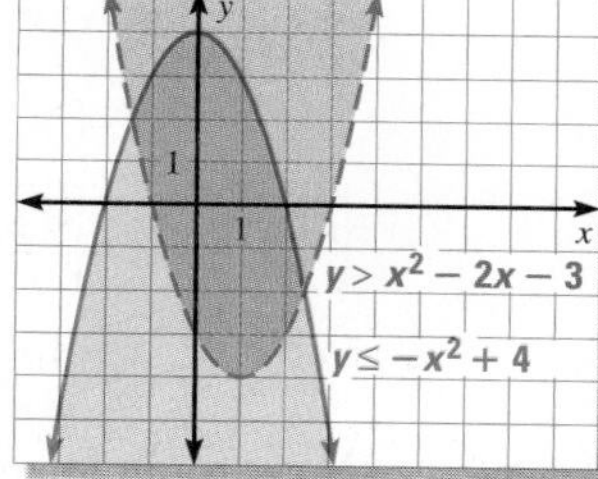

✓ **GUIDED PRACTICE** for Examples 1, 2, and 3

Graph the inequality. 1–4. See margin.

1. $y > x^2 + 2x - 8$
2. $y \leq 2x^2 - 3x + 1$
3. $y < -x^2 + 4x + 2$
4. Graph the system of inequalities consisting of $y \geq x^2$ and $y < -x^2 + 5$.

Motivating the Lesson

Ask if any students enjoy rock climbing and, if so, what factors they think are important in making sure a rope will safely support their weight. Tell them that a quadratic inequality can be used to determine if a rope is strong enough to support them.

3 TEACH

Extra Example 1

Graph $y < -x^2 - 4x$.

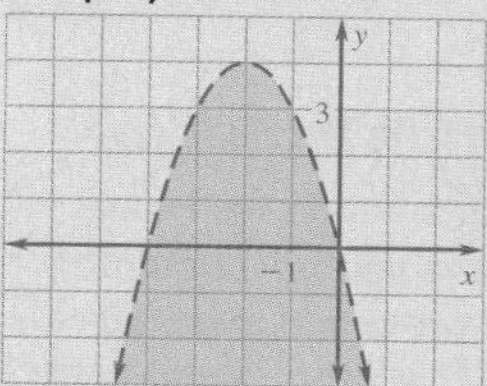

An **Animated Algebra** activity is available on-line for **Example 1**. This activity is also available on the **Power Presentations CD-ROM**.

Extra Example 2

A computer desk with a solid glass top can safely support a weight W (in pounds) provided $W \leq 250x^2$, where x is the thickness of the desktop (in inches). Graph the inequality.

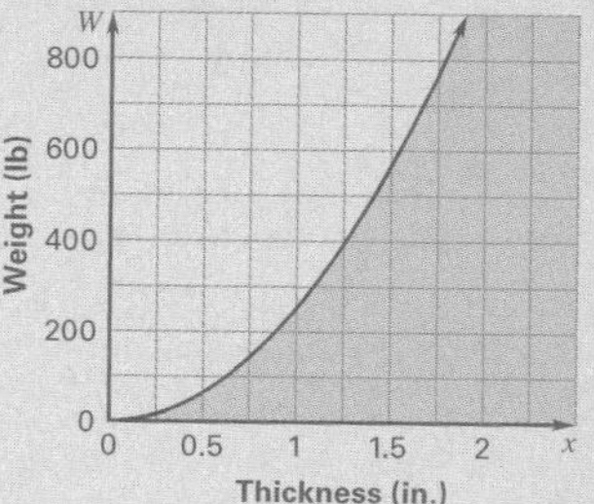

1–4. See Additional Answers beginning on p. AA1.

Extra Example 3

Graph the system of inequalities.
$y > x^2 - 3$
$y \le -2x^2 + 4x + 2$

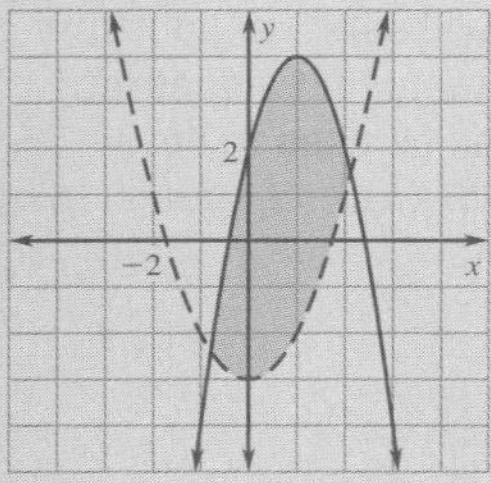

Extra Example 4

Solve $x^2 + 2x \ge 8$ by using a table. **$x \le -4$ or $x \ge 2$**

Key Question to Ask for Example 4

- If you use a graphing calculator to create a table and the table does not include the x-values for which the value of the quadratic expression is 0, what can you do that might still allow you to solve the inequality by making a table? **Adjust the ΔTbl setting on your calculator and see if you now get 0 for any values of the quadratic expression.**

Extra Example 5

Solve $\frac{1}{2}x^2 + 3x - 2 < 0$ by graphing. **approximately $-6.61 < x < 0.61$**

ONE-VARIABLE INEQUALITIES A **quadratic inequality in one variable** can be written in one of the following forms:

$ax^2 + bx + c < 0$ $\quad ax^2 + bx + c \le 0$ $\quad ax^2 + bx + c > 0$ $\quad ax^2 + bx + c \ge 0$

You can solve quadratic inequalities using tables, graphs, or algebraic methods.

EXAMPLE 4 Solve a quadratic inequality using a table

Solve $x^2 + x \le 6$ using a table.

Solution

Rewrite the inequality as $x^2 + x - 6 \le 0$. Then make a table of values.

MAKE A TABLE
To give the exact solution, your table needs to include the x-values for which the value of the quadratic expression is 0.

x	−5	−4	−3	−2	−1	0	1	2	3	4
$x^2 + x - 6$	14	6	0	−4	−6	−6	−4	0	6	14

Notice that $x^2 + x - 6 \le 0$ when the values of x are between −3 and 2, inclusive.

▸ The solution of the inequality is $-3 \le x \le 2$.

GRAPHING TO SOLVE INEQUALITIES Another way to solve $ax^2 + bx + c < 0$ is to first graph the related function $y = ax^2 + bx + c$. Then, because the inequality symbol is <, identify the x-values for which the graph lies *below* the x-axis. You can use a similar procedure to solve quadratic inequalities that involve ≤, >, or ≥.

EXAMPLE 5 Solve a quadratic inequality by graphing

Solve $2x^2 + x - 4 \ge 0$ by graphing.

Solution

The solution consists of the x-values for which the graph of $y = 2x^2 + x - 4$ lies on or above the x-axis. Find the graph's x-intercepts by letting $y = 0$ and using the quadratic formula to solve for x.

$$0 = 2x^2 + x - 4$$

$$x = \frac{-1 \pm \sqrt{1^2 - 4(2)(-4)}}{2(2)}$$

$$x = \frac{-1 \pm \sqrt{33}}{4}$$

$$x \approx 1.19 \text{ or } x \approx -1.69$$

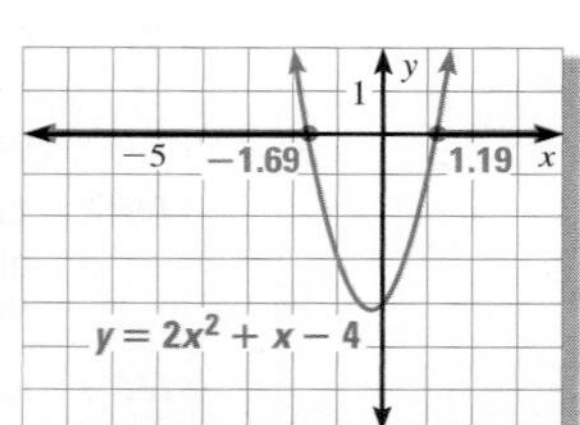

Sketch a parabola that opens up and has 1.19 and −1.69 as x-intercepts. The graph lies on or above the x-axis to the left of (and including) $x = -1.69$ and to the right of (and including) $x = 1.19$.

▸ The solution of the inequality is approximately $x \le -1.69$ or $x \ge 1.19$.

✓ **GUIDED PRACTICE** for Examples 4 and 5

5. Solve the inequality $2x^2 + 2x \le 3$ using a table and using a graph. **$-1.8 \le x \le 0.82$**

EXAMPLE 6 Use a quadratic inequality as a model

ROBOTICS The number T of teams that have participated in a robot-building competition for high school students can be modeled by

$$T(x) = 7.51x^2 - 16.4x + 35.0,\ 0 \le x \le 9$$

where x is the number of years since 1992. For what years was the number of teams greater than 100?

Solution

You want to find the values of x for which:

$$T(x) > 100$$

$$7.51x^2 - 16.4x + 35.0 > 100$$

$$7.51x^2 - 16.4x - 65 > 0$$

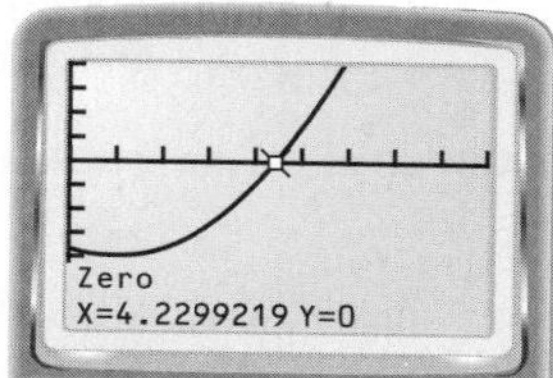

Graph $y = 7.51x^2 - 16.4x - 65$ on the domain $0 \le x \le 9$. The graph's x-intercept is about 4.2. The graph lies above the x-axis when $4.2 < x \le 9$.

▶ There were more than 100 teams participating in the years 1997–2001.

EXAMPLE 7 Solve a quadratic inequality algebraically

Solve $x^2 - 2x > 15$ algebraically.

Solution

First, write and solve the equation obtained by replacing > with =.

$x^2 - 2x = 15$	**Write equation that corresponds to original inequality.**
$x^2 - 2x - 15 = 0$	**Write in standard form.**
$(x + 3)(x - 5) = 0$	**Factor.**
$x = -3$ or $x = 5$	**Zero product property**

The numbers -3 and 5 are the *critical x-values* of the inequality $x^2 - 2x > 15$. Plot -3 and 5 on a number line, using open dots because the values do not satisfy the inequality. The critical x-values partition the number line into three intervals. Test an x-value in each interval to see if it satisfies the inequality.

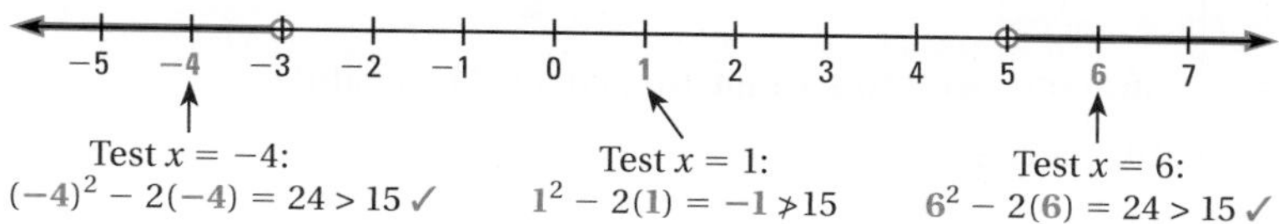

Test $x = -4$: $(-4)^2 - 2(-4) = 24 > 15$ ✓

Test $x = 1$: $1^2 - 2(1) = -1 \ngtr 15$

Test $x = 6$: $6^2 - 2(6) = 24 > 15$ ✓

▶ The solution is $x < -3$ or $x > 5$.

✓ GUIDED PRACTICE for Examples 6 and 7

6. **ROBOTICS** Use the information in Example 6 to determine in what years at least 200 teams participated in the robot-building competition. **1998–2001**

7. Solve the inequality $2x^2 - 7x > 4$ algebraically. **$x < -0.5$ or $x > 4$**

Extra Example 6

Use the information in Example 6 to determine the first year that at least 300 teams participated in the robot-building competition. **2000**

Extra Example 7

Solve $3x^2 - 9x - 12 < 0$ algebraically. **$-1 < x < 4$**

Key Question to Ask for Example 7

- Could the algebraic method shown in Example 7 be used if the quadratic equation corresponding to the given inequality had irrational roots? **You would not be able to solve the quadratic equation by factoring. However, you could still apply this method by solving the equation by the quadratic formula and using approximate values for the roots as the critical x-values.**

Closing the Lesson

Have students summarize the major points of the lesson and answer the Essential Question: How do you solve quadratic inequalities in one variable?

- **The graph of a quadratic inequality in two variables is the region inside or outside a parabola.**
- **The solutions of a quadratic inequality in one variable can be represented by intervals on a number line.**

Quadratic inequalities can be solved by using a table, by graphing, or algebraically by finding critical values and testing a number in each interval into which the critical numbers partition the number line.

Differentiated Instruction

Inclusion For solving quadratic inequalities in one variable, three methods are introduced: using a table, graphing, and algebraically. It will be helpful to the student to demonstrate each method using the same example. Show students how **Example 7** can be solved using tables and by graphing.

See also the *Algebra 2 Toolkit* for more strategies.

4.9 EXERCISES

HOMEWORK KEY

○ = **WORKED-OUT SOLUTIONS** on p. WS9 for Exs. 17, 39, and 73

★ = **STANDARDIZED TEST PRACTICE** Exs. 2, 44, 45, 68, and 73

◆ = **MULTIPLE REPRESENTATIONS** Ex. 74

4 PRACTICE AND APPLY

Assignment Guide

Answer Transparencies available for all exercises

Basic:
Day 1: pp. 304–307
Exs. 1–5, 7–17 odd, 18–25, 70, 71, 78–79
Day 2: pp. 304–307
Exs. 26–29, 35–38, 44–51, 58–61, 72–74

Average:
Day 1: pp. 304–307
Exs. 1–5, 6–16 even, 18–25, 70, 71, 78–79
Day 2: pp. 304–307
Exs. 29–31, 38–40, 44, 45, 50–54, 58–67, 72–76

Advanced:
Day 1: pp. 304–307
Exs. 1–5, 12–17, 20–25, 70, 71, 78–79
Day 2: pp. 304–307
Exs. 32–34, 41–45, 54–69*, 72–77*

Block:
pp. 304–307
Exs. 1–5, 6–16 even, 18–25, 70, 71, 78–79 (with 4.8)
pp. 304–307
Exs. 29–31, 38–40, 44, 45, 50–54, 58–67, 72–76 (with 4.10)

Differentiated Instruction

See *Algebra 2 Best Practices Toolkit* for suggestions on addressing the needs of a diverse classroom.

Homework Check

For a quick check of student understanding of key concepts, go over the following exercises:

Basic: 9, 20, 28, 48, 70
Average: 12, 22, 30, 52, 72
Advanced: 16, 24, 32, 56, 74

Extra Practice

- Student Edition, p. 1013
- Chapter 4 Resource Book: Practice levels A, B, C, pp. 103–108

Practice Worksheet

An easily-readable reduced practice page (with answers) for this lesson can be found on p. 234C.

SKILL PRACTICE

A

1. **VOCABULARY** Give an example of a quadratic inequality in one variable and an example of a quadratic inequality in two variables. *Sample answer:* $3x^2 - 2x + 5 > 0$, $y \geq x^2 + 4x - 8$

2. ★ **WRITING** *Explain* how to solve $x^2 + 6x - 8 < 0$ using a table, by graphing, and algebraically. See margin.

EXAMPLE 1 on p. 300 for Exs. 3–19

MATCHING INEQUALITIES WITH GRAPHS Match the inequality with its graph.

3. $y \leq x^2 + 4x + 3$ C
4. $y > -x^2 + 4x - 3$ A
5. $y < x^2 - 4x + 3$ B

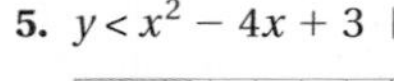

A. 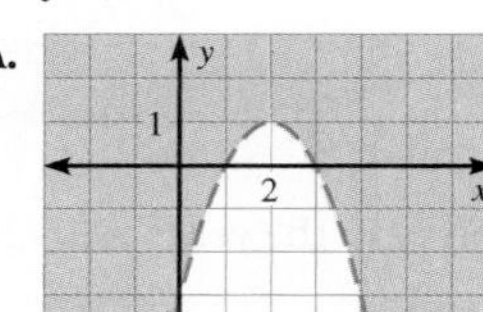

B. 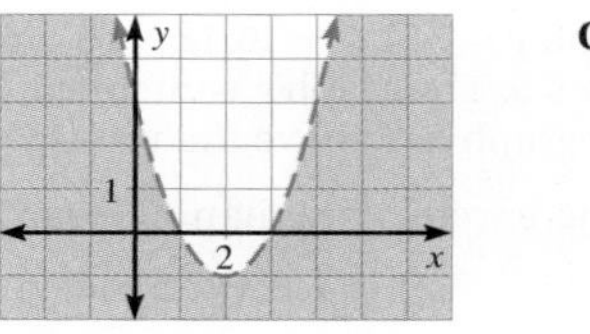

C. 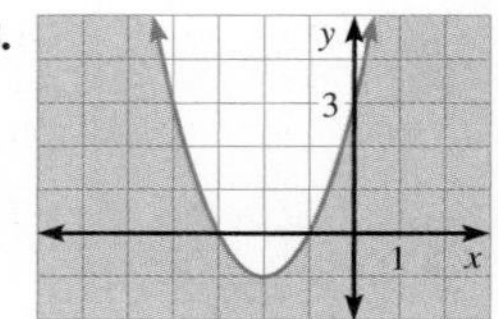

GRAPHING QUADRATIC INEQUALITIES Graph the inequality. 6–17. See margin.

6. $y < -x^2$
7. $y \geq 4x^2$
8. $y > x^2 - 9$
9. $y \leq x^2 + 5x$
10. $y < x^2 + 4x - 5$
11. $y > x^2 + 7x + 12$
12. $y \leq -x^2 + 3x + 10$
13. $y \geq 2x^2 + 5x - 7$
14. $y \geq -2x^2 + 9x - 4$
15. $y < 4x^2 - 3x - 5$
16. $y > 0.1x^2 - x + 1.2$
17. $y \leq -\frac{2}{3}x^2 + 3x + 1$

ERROR ANALYSIS Describe and correct the error in graphing $y \geq x^2 + 2$. 18, 19. See margin for art.

18. 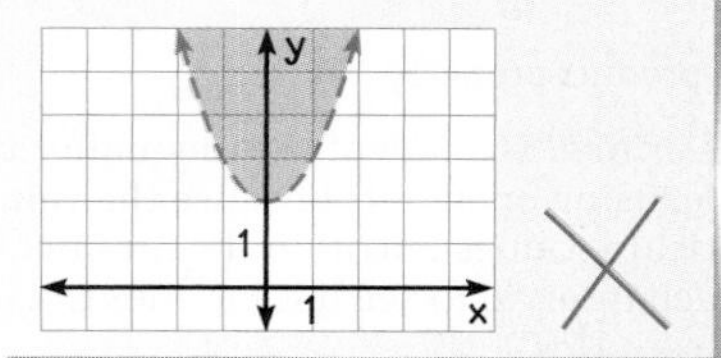

The parabola should be a solid line.

19. 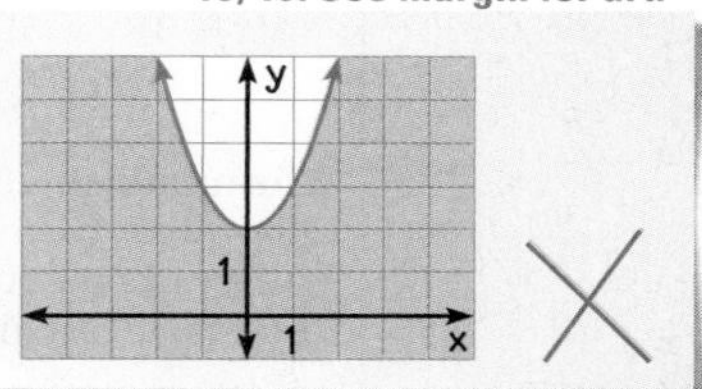

The inside of the parabola should be shaded.

EXAMPLE 3 on p. 301 for Exs. 20–25

GRAPHING SYSTEMS Graph the system of inequalities. 20–25. See margin.

20. $y \geq 2x^2$, $y < -x^2 + 1$
21. $y > -5x^2$, $y > 3x^2 - 2$
22. $y \geq x^2 - 4$, $y \leq -2x^2 + 7x + 4$
23. $y \leq -x^2 + 4x - 4$, $y < 2x^2 + x - 8$
24. $y > 3x^2 + 3x - 5$, $y < -x^2 + 5x + 10$
25. $y \geq x^2 - 3x - 6$, $y \geq 2x^2 + 7x + 6$

EXAMPLE 4 on p. 302 for Exs. 26–34

SOLVING USING A TABLE Solve the inequality using a table.

26. $x^2 - 5x < 0$ $0 < x < 5$
27. $x^2 + 2x - 3 > 0$ $x < -3$ or $x > 1$
28. $x^2 + 3x \leq 10$ $-5 \leq x \leq 2$
29. $x^2 - 2x \geq 8$ $x \leq -2$ or $x \geq 4$
30. $-x^2 + 15x - 50 > 0$ $5 < x < 10$
31. $x^2 - 10x < -16$ $2 < x < 8$
32. $x^2 - 4x > 12$ $x < -2$ or $x > 6$
33. $3x^2 - 6x - 2 \leq 7$ $-1 \leq x \leq 3$
34. $2x^2 - 6x - 9 \geq 11$ $x \leq -2$ or $x \geq 5$

2. Table: make a table of values and find where the outputs are less than 0; graph: draw the graph of the function and find where the graph is below the x-axis; algebraically: factor the expression and test points on a number line between the critical x-values to find where the x-values satisfy the inequality.

6–17. See Additional Answers beginning on p. AA1.

18–19. 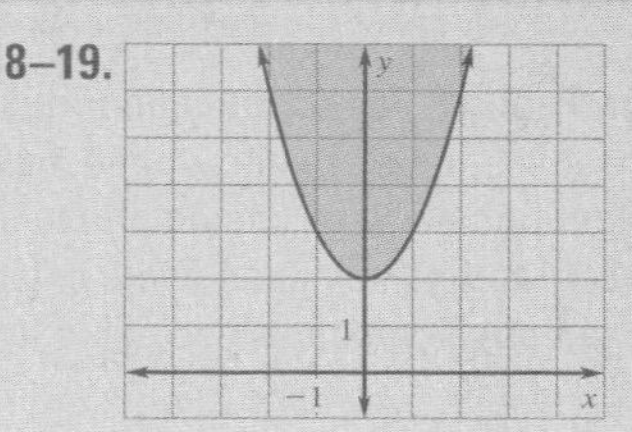

EXAMPLE 5 on p. 302 for Exs. 35–43

SOLVING BY GRAPHING **Solve the inequality by graphing.**

35. $x^2 - 6x < 0$ $0 < x < 6$

36. $x^2 + 8x \le -7$ $-7 \le x \le -1$

37. $x^2 - 4x + 2 > 0$ $x < 0.59$ or $x > 3.4$

38. $x^2 + 6x + 3 > 0$ $x < -5.4$ or $x > -0.55$

39. $3x^2 + 2x - 8 \le 0$ $-2 \le x \le 1.3$

40. $3x^2 + 5x - 3 < 1$ $-2.3 < x < 0.59$

41. $-6x^2 + 19x \ge 10$ $0.67 \le x \le 2.5$

42. $-\frac{1}{2}x^2 + 4x \ge 1$ $0.26 \le x \le 7.7$

43. $4x^2 - 10x - 7 < 10$ $-1.2 < x < 3.7$

44. ★ **MULTIPLE CHOICE** What is the solution of $3x^2 - x - 4 > 0$? A

Ⓐ $x < -1$ or $x > \frac{4}{3}$ Ⓑ $-1 < x < \frac{4}{3}$

Ⓒ $x < -\frac{4}{3}$ or $x > 1$ Ⓓ $1 < x < \frac{4}{3}$

45. ★ **MULTIPLE CHOICE** What is the solution of $2x^2 + 9x \le 56$? B

Ⓐ $x \le -8$ or $x \ge 3.5$ Ⓑ $-8 \le x \le 3.5$

Ⓒ $x \le 0$ or $x \ge 4.5$ Ⓓ $0 \le x \le 4.5$

EXAMPLE 7 on p. 303 for Exs. 46–57

SOLVING ALGEBRAICALLY **Solve the inequality algebraically.**

46. $4x^2 < 25$ $-2.5 < x < 2.5$

47. $x^2 + 10x + 9 < 0$ $-9 < x < -1$

48. $x^2 - 11x \ge -28$ $x \le 4$ or $x \ge 7$

49. $3x^2 - 13x > 10$ (49. $x < -\frac{2}{3}$ or $x > 5$)

50. $2x^2 - 5x - 3 \le 0$ $-\frac{1}{2} \le x \le 3$

51. $4x^2 + 8x - 21 \ge 0$ $x \le -3.5$ or $x \ge 1.5$

52. $-4x^2 - x + 3 \le 0$ $x \le -1$ or $x \ge 0.75$

53. $5x^2 - 6x - 2 \le 0$ $-0.27 \le x \le 1.5$

54. $-3x^2 + 10x > -2$ $-0.19 < x < 3.5$

55. $-2x^2 - 7x \ge 4$ $-2.8 \le x \le -0.72$

56. $3x^2 + 1 < 15x$ $0.07 < x < 4.9$

57. $6x^2 - 5 > 8x$ $x < -0.46$ or $x > 1.8$

B

58. **GRAPHING CALCULATOR** In this exercise, you will use a different graphical method to solve Example 6 on page 303. a–d. Check students work.

a. Enter the equations $y = 7.51x^2 - 16.4x + 35.0$ and $y = 100$ into a graphing calculator.

b. Graph the equations from part (a) for $0 \le x \le 9$ and $0 \le y \le 300$.

c. Use the *intersect* feature to find the point where the graphs intersect.

d. During what years was the number of participating teams greater than 100? *Explain* your reasoning.

CHOOSING A METHOD **Solve the inequality using any method.**

59. $8x^2 - 3x + 1 < 10$ $-0.89 < x < 1.3$

60. $4x^2 + 11x + 3 \ge -3$ $x \le -2$ or $x \ge -0.75$

61. $-x^2 - 2x - 1 > 2$ no solution

62. $-3x^2 + 4x - 5 \le 2$ all reals

63. $x^2 - 7x + 4 > 5x - 2$ $x < 0.52$ or $x > 11.5$

64. $2x^2 + 9x - 1 \ge -3x + 1$ $x \le -6.2$ or $x \ge 0.16$

65. $3x^2 - 2x + 1 \le -x^2 + 1$ $0 \le x \le 0.5$

66. $5x^2 + x - 7 < 3x^2 - 4x$ $-3.5 < x < 1$

67. $6x^2 - 5x + 2 < -3x^2 + x$ no solution

C

68. ★ **OPEN-ENDED MATH** Write a quadratic inequality in one variable that has a solution of $x < -2$ or $x > 5$. *Sample answer:* $x^2 - 3x - 10 > 0$

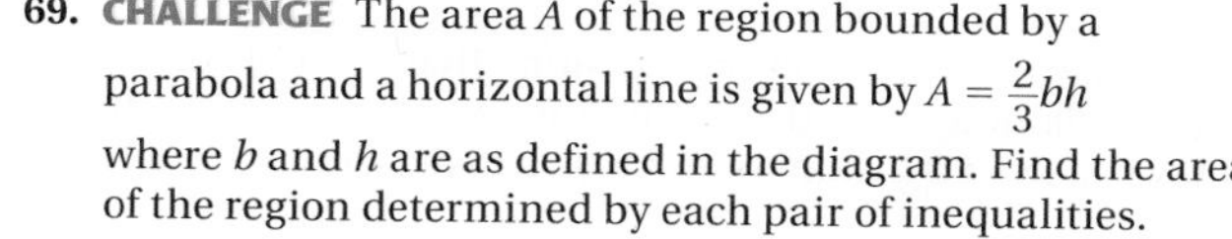

69. **CHALLENGE** The area A of the region bounded by a parabola and a horizontal line is given by $A = \frac{2}{3}bh$ where b and h are as defined in the diagram. Find the area of the region determined by each pair of inequalities.

a. $y \le -x^2 + 4x$, $y \ge 0$ $10\frac{2}{3}$

b. $y \ge x^2 - 4x - 5$, $y \le 3$ $32\sqrt{3}$

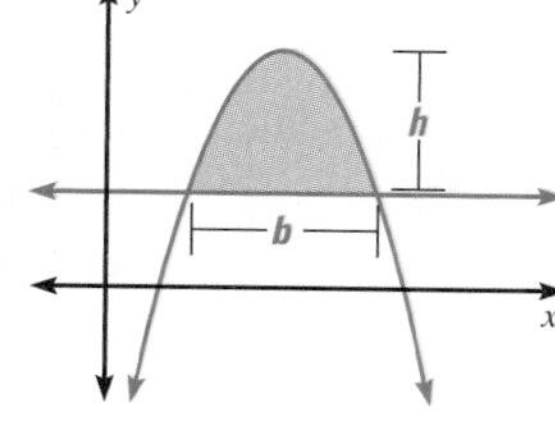

20.

21.

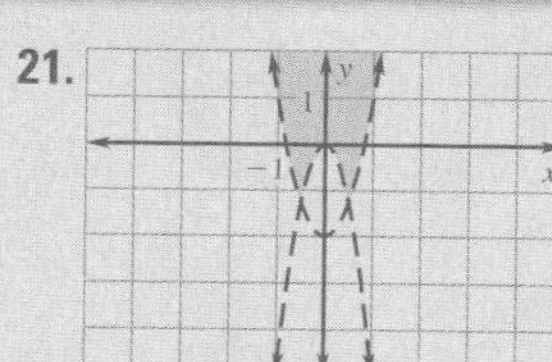

22.

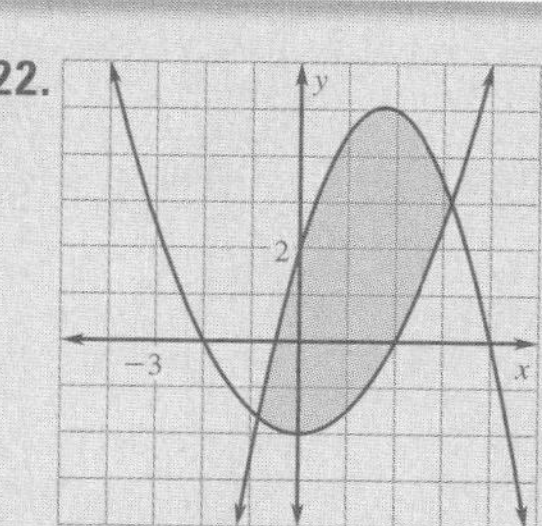

Graphing Calculator

Exercises 6–17 Demonstrate how to graph an inequality in two variables with a graphing calculator by using the graph style that shades the region either above or below the graph of the equation that is entered. First demonstrate the process with a linear inequality in two variables, and then move on to a quadratic inequality in two variables. You can extend your demonstration to show graphing systems of linear and quadratic inequalities in two variables. Stress that the calculator does not distinguish between solid and dashed boundary lines or curves.

Avoiding Common Errors

Exercises 35–43 Some students may confuse what they are trying to do here with what they did in Exercises 6–17. Point out that Exercises 6–17 involve quadratic inequalities in *two* variables, while those in Exercises 35–43 involve quadratic inequalities in *one* variable. Emphasize that while the method used in these exercises involves an *x-y* graph, the answers involve only *x*-values.

23.

24.

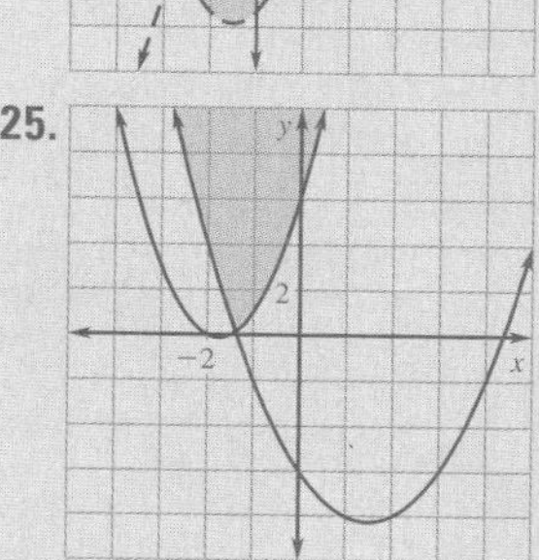

25.

PROBLEM SOLVING

Reading Strategy

Exercises 70–72, 75–77 In these exercises the domain is not specified, so students will need to figure out for themselves that the graph is restricted to the first quadrant. Ask a student to read one of these exercises aloud and then tell you what the variables represent. Then ask if it would make sense in the context of the problem for either of the variables to have a negative value. Encourage students to follow this line of thinking whenever they are solving applied problems modeled by equations or inequalities.

70.

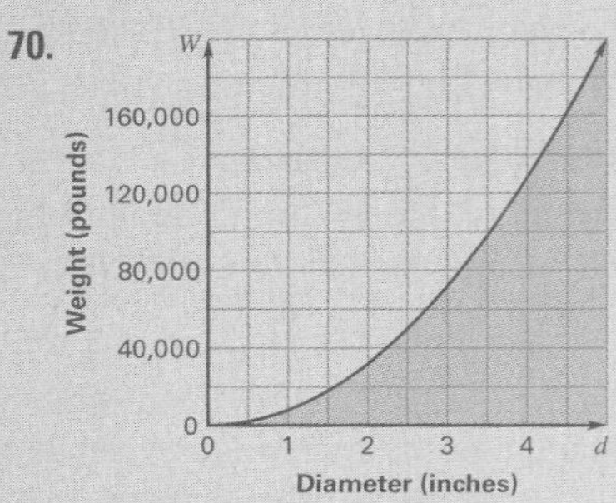

71.

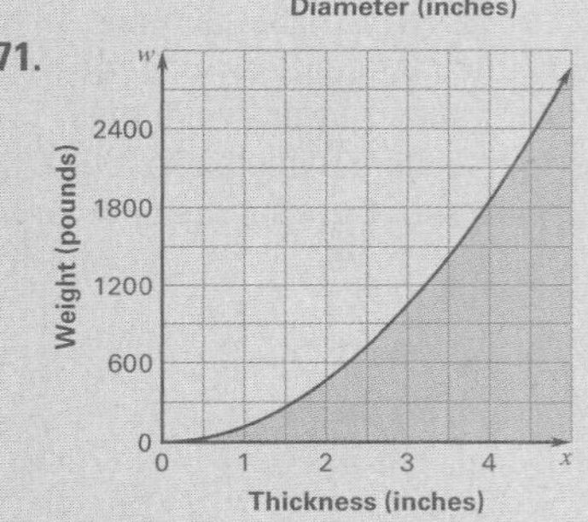

74b. See below.

74c. *Sample answer:* Restricting the domain to ages ranging from 16 to 70 includes the majority of people who drive.

74d. Traffic light. *Sample answer:* The values where audio stimuli is faster than visual stimuli gives negative reaction times. So, a visual stimulus typically creates a faster reaction time than an audio stimulus.

EXAMPLE 2 on p. 301 for Exs. 70–71

A

70. ENGINEERING A wire rope can safely support a weight W (in pounds) provided $W \le 8000d^2$ where d is the rope's diameter (in inches). Graph the inequality. **See margin.**

@HomeTutor for problem solving help at classzone.com

71. WOODWORKING A hardwood shelf in a wooden bookcase can safely support a weight W (in pounds) provided $W \le 115x^2$ where x is the shelf's thickness (in inches). Graph the inequality. **See margin.**

@HomeTutor for problem solving help at classzone.com

EXAMPLE 6 on p. 303 for Exs. 72–74

72. ARCHITECTURE The arch of the Sydney Harbor Bridge in Sydney, Australia, can be modeled by $y = -0.00211x^2 + 1.06x$ where x is the distance (in meters) from the left pylons and y is the height (in meters) of the arch above the water. For what distances x is the arch above the road? **$55 < x < 447$**

73. ★ **SHORT RESPONSE** The length L (in millimeters) of the larvae of the black porgy fish can be modeled by

$$L(x) = 0.00170x^2 + 0.145x + 2.35,\ 0 \le x \le 40$$

where x is the age (in days) of the larvae. Write and solve an inequality to find at what ages a larvae's length tends to be greater than 10 millimeters. *Explain* how the given domain affects the solution. **$37 \le x \le 40$; the domain restricts the number of days to less than or equal to 40.**

B

74. ◆ **MULTIPLE REPRESENTATIONS** A study found that a driver's reaction time $A(x)$ to audio stimuli and his or her reaction time $V(x)$ to visual stimuli (both in milliseconds) can be modeled by

$$A(x) = 0.0051x^2 - 0.319x + 15,\ 16 \le x \le 70$$

$$V(x) = 0.005x^2 - 0.23x + 22,\ 16 \le x \le 70$$

where x is the driver's age (in years).

a. Writing an Inequality Write an inequality that you can use to find the x-values for which $A(x)$ is less than $V(x)$. **$0.0001x^2 - 0.089x - 7 < 0$**

b. Making a Table Use a table to find the solution of the inequality from part (a). Your table should contain x-values from 16 to 70 in increments of 6. **b–d. See margin.**

c. Drawing a Graph Check the solution you found in part (b) by using a graphing calculator to solve the inequality $A(x) < V(x)$ graphically. *Describe* how you used the domain $16 \le x \le 70$ to determine a reasonable solution.

d. Interpret Based on your results from parts (b) and (c), do you think a driver would react more quickly to a traffic light changing from green to yellow or to the siren of an approaching ambulance? *Explain.*

○ = WORKED-OUT SOLUTIONS on p. WS1 ★ = STANDARDIZED TEST PRACTICE ◆ = MULTIPLE REPRESENTATIONS

74b.

x	16	22	28	34	40	46	52	58	64	70
y	−8.3984	−8.9096	−9.4136	−9.9104	−10.4	−10.8824	−11.3576	−11.8256	−12.2864	−12.74

75. **SOCCER** The path of a soccer ball kicked from the ground can be modeled by

$$y = -0.0540x^2 + 1.43x$$

where x is the horizontal distance (in feet) from where the ball was kicked and y is the corresponding height (in feet).

a. A soccer goal is 8 feet high. Write and solve an inequality to find at what values of x the ball is low enough to go into the goal. **$-0.054x^2 + 1.43x - 8 < 0$; $x \leq 8.0$ or $x \geq 18.5$**

b. A soccer player kicks the ball toward the goal from a distance of 15 feet away. No one is blocking the goal. Will the player score a goal? *Explain* your reasoning. **No; the ball will go over the goal by 1.3 feet.**

C 76. **MULTI-STEP PROBLEM** A truck that is 11 feet tall and 7 feet wide is traveling under an arch. The arch can be modeled by

$$y = -0.0625x^2 + 1.25x + 5.75$$

where x and y are measured in feet.

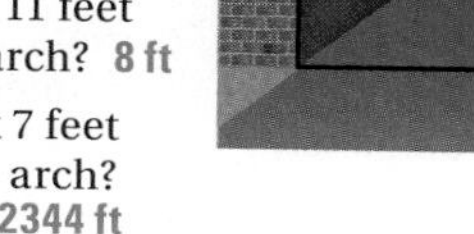

a. Will the truck fit under the arch? *Explain* your reasoning.

76a. Yes; a truck 7 feet wide will have an extra 2.81 inches of clearance.

b. What is the maximum width that a truck 11 feet tall can have and still make it under the arch? **8 ft**

c. What is the maximum height that a truck 7 feet wide can have and still make it under the arch? **11.2344 ft**

77. **CHALLENGE** For clear blue ice on lakes and ponds, the maximum weight w (in tons) that the ice can support is given by

$$w(x) = 0.1x^2 - 0.5x - 5$$

where x is the thickness of the ice (in inches).

a. Calculate What thicknesses of ice can support a weight of 20 tons? **about 18.5 in.**

b. Interpret *Explain* how you can use the graph of $w(x)$ to determine the minimum x-value in the domain for which the function gives meaningful results. **Ice cannot hold a negative number of tons, so where the graph is above the x-axis is the x-values where the function gives meaningful results.**

KENTUCKY MIXED REVIEW

TEST PRACTICE at classzone.com

78. Rachel is a cross-country runner. Her coach recorded the data shown at the right during a timed practice run. If Rachel continues to run at the same rate, what is the approximate distance she will run in 25 minutes? **B**

Time (minutes)	Distance (kilometers)
6	1.2
12	2.4
15	3

Ⓐ 4.2 km Ⓑ 5 km
Ⓒ 6 km Ⓓ 10 km

79. Which set of dimensions corresponds to a pyramid similar to the one shown? **C**

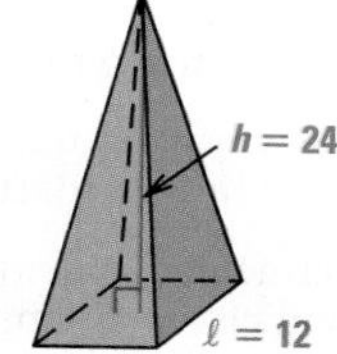

Ⓐ $w = 1$ unit, $\ell = 2$ units, $h = 4$ units

Ⓑ $w = 2$ units, $\ell = 3$ units, $h = 6$ units

Ⓒ $w = 3$ units, $\ell = 4$ units, $h = 8$ units

Ⓓ $w = 4$ units, $\ell = 6$ units, $h = 12$ units

5 ASSESS AND RETEACH

Daily Homework Quiz

Transparency Available

1. Solve $3x^2 + 2x - 1 < 0$ by graphing. **$-1 < x < \frac{1}{3}$**

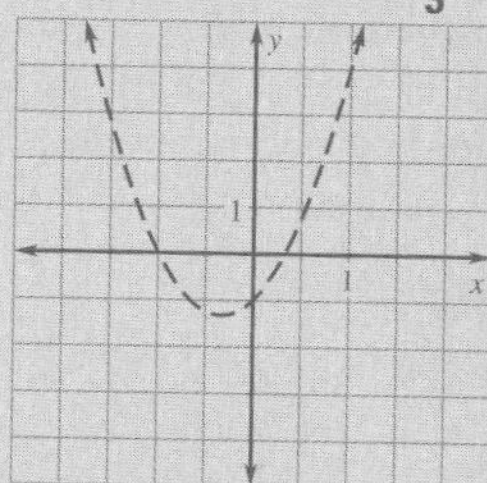

2. Graph $y \geq 2x^2 - 4$ and $y < -x^2 + 3$ as a system of inequalities.

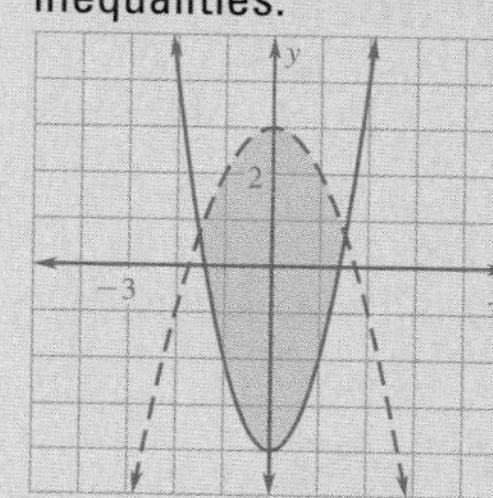

Solve the inequality.

3. $x^2 + 4x \leq 5$ **$-5 \leq x \leq 1$**

4. $2x^2 + x - 15 > 0$ **$x < -3$ or $x > \frac{5}{2}$**

Online Quiz

Available at **classzone.com**

Diagnosis/Remediation

- Practice A, B, C in Chapter 4 Resource Book, pp. 103–108
- Study Guide in Chapter 4 Resource Book, pp. 109–110
- Practice Workbook, pp. 72–74
- @HomeTutor

Challenge

Additional challenge is available in the Chapter 4 Resource Book, p. 113.

1 PLAN AND PREPARE

- Students will collect data from a simple experiment and use the *quadratic regression* feature on their graphing calculators to find a quadratic model for the data.
- This activity leads into the study of finding the best-fitting quadratic model for given data in Example 4 in Lesson 4.10.

Materials

Each student will need:
- compass
- 50 pennies
- graphing calculator

Recommended Time

Work activity: 15 min
Discuss results: 5 min

Grouping

Students should work individually.

2 TEACH

Tips for Success

Make sure that students know how to use the *stat plot* menu and how to set up an appropriate viewing window.

Key Discovery

If the points on a scatter plot appear to lie on a parabola or approximately on a parabola, you can use the *quadratic regression* feature on your calculator to find a quadratic model for the data.

3 ASSESS AND RETEACH

How do you know whether to use the *linear regression* or *quadratic regression* feature of your calculator when you want to find a model for a set of data? **Look at the scatter plot and see whether the points seem to lie on or close to a line, or on or close to a parabola.**

Investigating Algebra ACTIVITY *Use before Lesson 4.10*

@HomeTutor
classzone.com
Keystrokes

4.10 Modeling Data with a Quadratic Function

MATERIALS • compass • 50 pennies • graphing calculator

QUESTION **How can you fit a quadratic function to a set of data?**

EXPLORE **Collect and model quadratic data**

STEP 1 ***Collect data***
Draw five circles using a compass. Use diameters of 1 inch, 2 inches, 3 inches, 4 inches, and 5 inches. Place as many pennies as you can in each circle, making sure that each penny is completely within the circle.

STEP 2 ***Record data***
Record your results from Step 1 in a table like the one shown at the right. Also, record the number of pennies that would fit in a circle with a diameter of 0 inch.

Diameter of circle (in.), x	Number of pennies, y
0	?
1	?
2	?
3	?
4	?
5	?

STEP 3 ***Enter data***
Enter the data you collected into two lists of a graphing calculator.

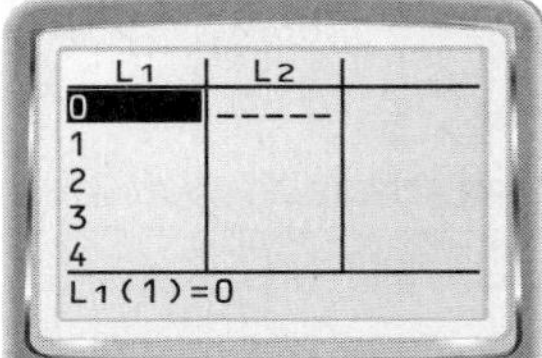

STEP 4 ***Display data***
Display the data in a scatter plot. Notice that the points appear to lie on a parabola.

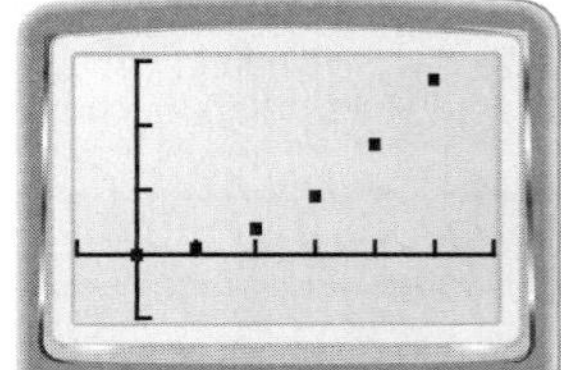

STEP 5 ***Find model***
Use the *quadratic regression* feature to find a quadratic model for the data.

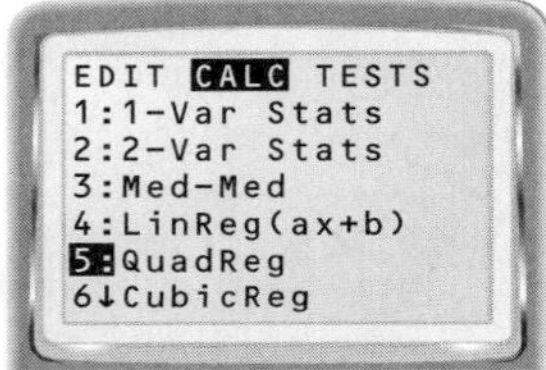

DRAW CONCLUSIONS **Use your observations to complete these exercises**
1–4. Check students' work.

1. Graph your model from Step 5 on the same screen as the scatter plot. *Describe* how well the model fits the data.
2. Use your model from Step 5 to predict the number of pennies that will fit in a circle with a diameter of 6 inches. Check your prediction by drawing a circle with a diameter of 6 inches and filling it with pennies.
3. *Explain* why you would expect the number of pennies that fit inside a circle to be a quadratic function of the circle's diameter.
4. The diameter of a penny is 0.75 inch. Use this fact to write a quadratic function giving an upper limit L on the number of pennies that can fit inside a circle with diameter x inches.

4.10 Write Quadratic Functions and Models

MA-HS-5.3.6 **Students will model, solve and graph quadratic equations in real-world and mathematical problems. DOK 2**

Before You wrote linear functions and models.

Now You will write quadratic functions and models.

Why? So you can model the cross section of parabolic dishes, as in Ex. 46.

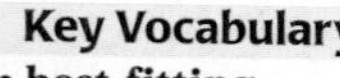

Key Vocabulary
- **best-fitting quadratic model**

In Lessons 4.1 and 4.2, you learned how to graph quadratic functions. In this lesson, you will write quadratic functions given information about their graphs.

EXAMPLE 1 Write a quadratic function in vertex form

Write a quadratic function for the parabola shown.

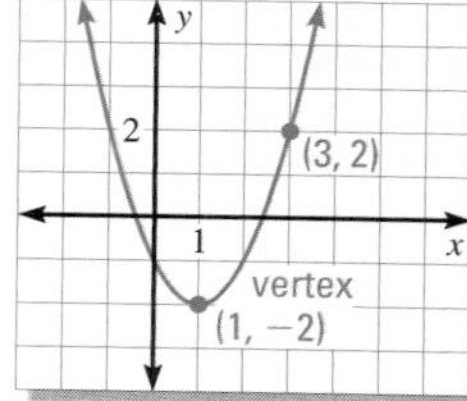

Solution

Use vertex form because the vertex is given.

$y = a(x - h)^2 + k$ **Vertex form**

$y = a(x - 1)^2 - 2$ **Substitute 1 for h and −2 for k.**

Use the other given point, (3, 2), to find a.

$2 = a(3 - 1)^2 - 2$ **Substitute 3 for x and 2 for y.**

$2 = 4a - 2$ **Simplify coefficient of a.**

$1 = a$ **Solve for a.**

▶ A quadratic function for the parabola is $y = (x - 1)^2 - 2$.

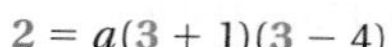

EXAMPLE 2 Write a quadratic function in intercept form

Write a quadratic function for the parabola shown.

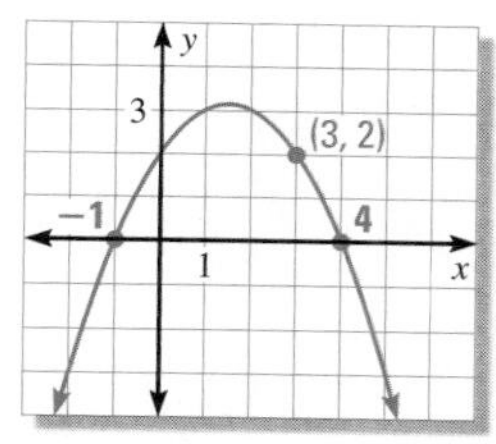

Solution

Use intercept form because the x-intercepts are given.

$y = a(x - p)(x - q)$ **Intercept form**

$y = a(x + 1)(x - 4)$ **Substitute −1 for p and 4 for q.**

Use the other given point, (3, 2), to find a.

$2 = a(3 + 1)(3 - 4)$ **Substitute 3 for x and 2 for y.**

$2 = -4a$ **Simplify coefficient of a.**

$-\frac{1}{2} = a$ **Solve for a.**

▶ A quadratic function for the parabola is $y = -\frac{1}{2}(x + 1)(x - 4)$.

AVOID ERRORS
Be sure to substitute the x-intercepts and the coordinates of the given point for the correct letters in $y = a(x - p)(x - q)$.

1 PLAN AND PREPARE

Warm-Up Exercises

Transparency Available

Solve the system of equations.

1. $2x + y = 5$
   $6x + 4y = 22$ **(−1, 7)**
2. $x + z = -3$
   $y + z = 2$
   $x + y = 1$ **(−2, 3, −1)**
3. $a - b + c = 3$
   $a + b + c = 7$
   $4a - 2b + c = 4$ **(1, 2, 4)**
4. Find two numbers with sum 50 and difference 10. **30, 20**

Notetaking Guide

Transparency Available

Promotes interactive learning and notetaking skills, pp. 125–128.

Pacing

Basic: 1 day
Average: 1 day
Advanced: 1 day
Block: 0.5 block with 4.9
- See *Teaching Guide/Lesson Plan.*

2 FOCUS AND MOTIVATE

Essential Question

Big Idea 1, p. 235

If you know three points on the graph of a quadratic function, how can you find an equation for the function? **Tell students they will learn how to answer this question by setting up and solving a system of equations in three variables.**

Resource Planning Guide

Chapter Resource Book
- Teaching Guide/Lesson Plan (pp. 114–115)
- Practice levels A, B, C (pp. 117–119)
- Study Guide (pp. 120–121)
- Catch-up for Absent Students (p. 122)
- Problem Solving Workshop (p. 123)
- Challenge (p. 124)

Workbooks
- Notetaking Guide (pp. 125–128)
- Practice Workbook (pp. 75–76)

Teaching Options
- **Power Presentations CD-ROM** provides dynamic electronic teaching resources for the classroom.
- **Activity Generator CD-ROM** provides editable activities for all ability levels.

Interactive Technology
- Easy Planner
- Power Presentations CD-ROM
- Activity Generator CD-ROM
- Animated Algebra
- Test Generator CD-ROM
- Online Quiz
- eWorkbook
- eEdition
- @HomeTutor

Resources for English Learners
- Quick Reference for English Learners
- Spanish Study Guide
- Multi-Language Visual Glossary
- Student Resources in Spanish

See also the *Algebra 2 Toolkit* for more strategies for meeting individual needs.

Motivating the Lesson

You run a business producing albums from digital photos. You have kept track of the number of albums sold and monthly revenue over the past year. You can use a graphing calculator to find a quadratic model that will predict revenue for any number of albums sold in the future.

3 TEACH

Extra Example 1

Write a quadratic function for the parabola shown.

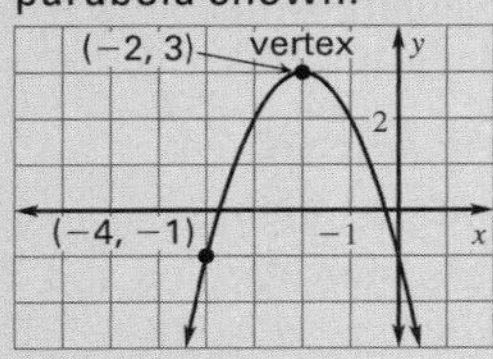

in vertex form: $y = -(x + 2)^2 + 3$

Extra Example 2

Write a quadratic function for the parabola shown.

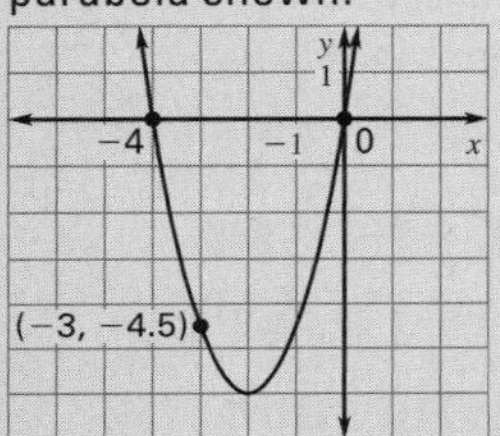

in intercept form: $y = \frac{3}{2}x(x + 4)$

Extra Example 3

Write a quadratic function in standard form for the parabola that passes through the points (−2, 30), (1, 6), and (4, 36). $y = 3x^2 - 5x + 8$

Key Question to Ask for Example 3

- What equation do you start with, and what values do you substitute? **Start with $y = ax^2 + bx + c$ and substitute values of x and y from the ordered pairs.**

EXAMPLE 3 Write a quadratic function in standard form

Write a quadratic function in standard form for the parabola that passes through the points (−1, −3), (0, −4), and (2, 6).

Solution

STEP 1 **Substitute** the coordinates of each point into $y = ax^2 + bx + c$ to obtain the system of three linear equations shown below.

$-3 = a(-1)^2 + b(-1) + c$	Substitute −1 for x and −3 for y.
$-3 = a - b + c$	Equation 1
$-4 = a(0)^2 + b(0) + c$	Substitute 0 for x and −4 for y.
$-4 = c$	Equation 2
$6 = a(2)^2 + b(2) + c$	Substitute 2 for x and 6 for y.
$6 = 4a + 2b + c$	Equation 3

REVIEW SYSTEMS OF EQUATIONS

For help with solving systems of linear equations in three variables, see p. 178.

STEP 2 **Rewrite** the system of three equations in Step 1 as a system of two equations by substituting −4 for c in Equations 1 and 3.

$a - b + c = -3$	Equation 1
$a - b - 4 = -3$	Substitute −4 for c.
$a - b = 1$	Revised Equation 1
$4a + 2b + c = 6$	Equation 3
$4a + 2b - 4 = 6$	Substitute −4 for c.
$4a + 2b = 10$	Revised Equation 3

STEP 3 **Solve** the system consisting of revised Equations 1 and 3. Use the elimination method.

$a - b = 1$  × 2 → $2a - 2b = 2$

$4a + 2b = 10$ → $4a + 2b = 10$

$$6a = 12$$
$$a = 2$$

So $2 - b = 1$, which means $b = 1$.

The solution is $a = 2$, $b = 1$, and $c = -4$.

▶ A quadratic function for the parabola is $y = 2x^2 + x - 4$.

✓ GUIDED PRACTICE for Examples 1, 2, and 3

3. $y = \frac{1}{4}(x + 2)(x - 5)$

Write a quadratic function whose graph has the given characteristics.

1. vertex: (4, −5) passes through: (2, −1) $y = (x - 4)^2 - 5$
2. vertex: (−3, 1) passes through: (0, −8) $y = -(x + 3)^2 + 1$
3. x-intercepts: −2, 5 passes through: (6, 2)

Write a quadratic function in standard form for the parabola that passes through the given points.

4. (−1, 5), (0, −1), (2, 11) $y = 4x^2 - 2x - 1$
5. (−2, −1), (0, 3), (4, 1) $y = -\frac{5}{12}x^2 + \frac{7}{6}x + 3$
6. (−1, 0), (1, −2), (2, −15) $y = -4x^2 - x + 3$

QUADRATIC REGRESSION In Chapter 2, you used a graphing calculator to perform linear regression on a data set in order to find a linear model for the data. A graphing calculator can also be used to perform *quadratic regression*. The model given by quadratic regression is called the **best-fitting quadratic model**.

EXAMPLE 4 Solve a multi-step problem

PUMPKIN TOSSING A pumpkin tossing contest is held each year in Morton, Illinois, where people compete to see whose catapult will send pumpkins the farthest. One catapult launches pumpkins from 25 feet above the ground at a speed of 125 feet per second. The table shows the horizontal distances (in feet) the pumpkins travel when launched at different angles. Use a graphing calculator to find the best-fitting quadratic model for the data.

Angle (degrees)	20	30	40	50	60	70
Distance (feet)	372	462	509	501	437	323

Solution

STEP 1 **Enter** the data into two lists of a graphing calculator.

```
L1   L2
30   462
40   509
50   501
60   437
70   323
L2(6)=323
```

STEP 2 **Make** a scatter plot of the data. Note that the points show a parabolic trend.

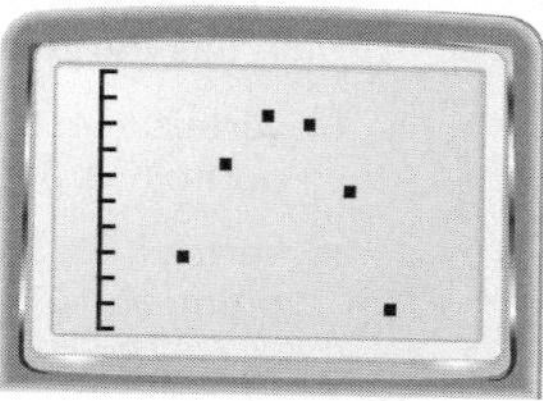

STEP 3 **Use** the quadratic regression feature to find the best-fitting quadratic model for the data.

STEP 4 **Check** how well the model fits the data by graphing the model and the data in the same viewing window.

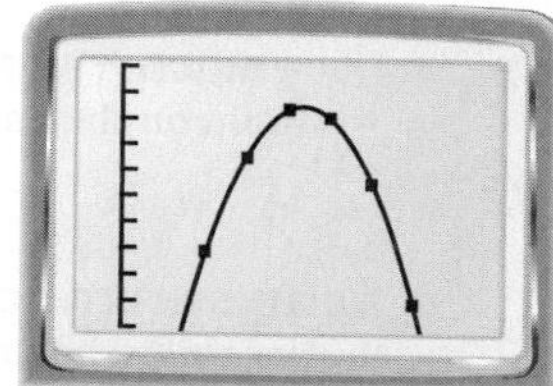

▶ The best-fitting quadratic model is $y = -0.261x^2 + 22.6x + 23.0$.

✓ GUIDED PRACTICE for Example 4

7. **PUMPKIN TOSSING** In Example 4, at what angle does the pumpkin travel the farthest? *Explain* how you found your answer. **About 43°; the vertex of the graph gives what angle measure produces the greatest distance.**

Extra Example 4

The drama club at your high school sells T-shirts as a fundraiser. The table shows data from the last four years for the price charged for a T-shirt, *x*, and the total revenue earned from selling them, *y*. Use a graphing calculator to find the best-fitting quadratic model for the data.

x	8	10	12	14
y	1180	1450	1675	1550

$y = -24.69x^2 + 609.9x - 2134$

Closing the Lesson

Have students summarize the major points of the lesson and answer the Essential Question: If you know three points on the graph of a quadratic function, how can you find an equation for the function?

- **If you know the coordinates of the vertex and one other point on a parabola, or two *x*-intercepts and the coordinates of another point, you can write an equation for the quadratic function.**
- **If you know any three points on the graph of a parabola, you can find an equation of the quadratic function.**

Use the equation $y = ax^2 + bx + c$ and the *x*- and *y*-coordinates of the three points to write three equations in the variables *a*, *b*, and *c*. Solve that system of equations to determine *a*, *b*, and *c*. Then substitute those values to obtain the equation for the function.

4.10 EXERCISES

HOMEWORK KEY
○ = WORKED-OUT SOLUTIONS on p. WS9 for Exs. 19, 35, and 49
★ = STANDARDIZED TEST PRACTICE Exs. 2, 15, 16, 43, 44, and 51
◆ = MULTIPLE REPRESENTATIONS Ex. 50

4 PRACTICE AND APPLY

Assignment Guide

Answer Transparencies available for all exercises

Basic:
Day 1: pp. 312–315
Exs. 1–8, 15–22, 26–29, 31–33, 40, 41, 46–50, 53

Average:
Day 1: pp. 312–315
Exs. 1–3, 9–11, 15–17, 23–27, 34–36, 40–44, 46–51, 54

Advanced:
Day 1: pp. 312–315
Exs. 1, 2, 5, 12–16, 19, 23–25, 37–52*, 54

Block:
pp. 312–315
Exs. 1–3, 9–11, 15–17, 23–27, 34–36, 40–44, 46–51, 54 (with 4.9)

Differentiated Instruction

See *Algebra 2 Best Practices Toolkit* for suggestions on addressing the needs of a diverse classroom.

Homework Check

For a quick check of student understanding of key concepts, go over the following exercises:
Basic: 8, 20, 32, 46, 48
Average: 10, 22, 34, 47, 49
Advanced: 14, 24, 38, 47, 50

Extra Practice

- Student Edition, p. 1013
- Chapter 4 Resource Book: Practice levels A, B, C, pp. 117–119

Practice Worksheet

An easily-readable reduced practice page (with answers) for this lesson can be found on p. 234C.

SKILL PRACTICE

A

1. **VOCABULARY** Copy and complete: When you perform quadratic regression on a set of data, the quadratic model obtained is called the _?_. **best-fitting quadratic mode**

2. ★ **WRITING** *Describe* how to write an equation of a parabola if you know three points on the parabola that are not the vertex or x-intercepts.

2. Substitute the coordinates of each point into $y = ax^2 + bx + c$ to obtain a system of equations. Solve the system of equations for a, b, and c.

EXAMPLE 1 on p. 309 for Exs. 3–15

WRITING IN VERTEX FORM Write a quadratic function in vertex form for the parabola shown.

3. 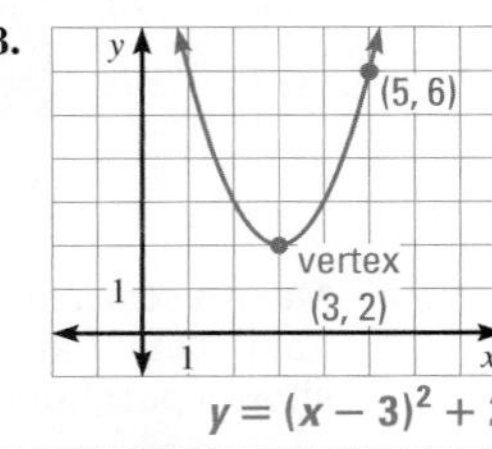

$y = (x - 3)^2 + 2$

4. 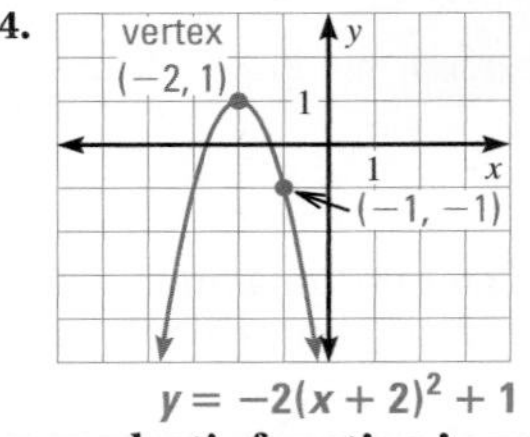

$y = -2(x + 2)^2 + 1$

5. 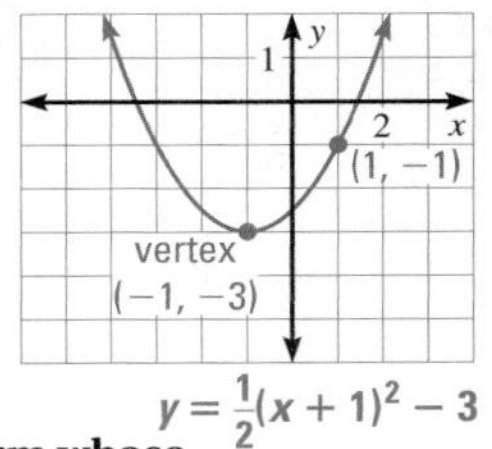

$y = \frac{1}{2}(x + 1)^2 - 3$

WRITING IN VERTEX FORM Write a quadratic function in vertex form whose graph has the given vertex and passes through the given point.

6. vertex: (−4, 1) point: (−2, 5) $y = (x + 4)^2 + 1$
7. vertex: (1, 6) point: (−1, 2) $y = -(x - 1)^2 + 6$
8. vertex: (5, −4) point: (1, 20) $y = \frac{3}{2}(x - 5)^2 -$
9. vertex: (−3, 3) point: (1, −1) $y = -\frac{1}{4}(x + 3)^2 + 3$
10. vertex: (5, 0) point: (2, −27) $y = -3(x - 5)^2$
11. vertex: (−4, −2) point: (0, 30) $y = 2(x + 4)^2 - 2$
12. vertex: (2, 1) point: (4, −2) $y = -\frac{3}{4}(x - 2)^2 + 1$
13. vertex: (−1, −4) point: (2, −1) $y = \frac{1}{3}(x + 1)^2 - 4$
14. vertex: (3, 5) point: (7, −3) $y = -\frac{1}{2}(x - 3)^2 +$

15. ★ **MULTIPLE CHOICE** The vertex of a parabola is (5, −3) and another point on the parabola is (1, 5). Which point is also on the parabola? **C**

Ⓐ (0, 3) Ⓑ (−1, 9) Ⓒ (−1, 15) Ⓓ (7, 7)

EXAMPLE 2 on p. 309 for Exs. 16–26

16. ★ **MULTIPLE CHOICE** The x-intercepts of a parabola are 4 and 7 and another point on the parabola is (2, −20). Which point is also on the parabola? **D**

Ⓐ (1, 21) Ⓑ (8, −4) Ⓒ (5, −40) Ⓓ (5, 4)

WRITING IN INTERCEPT FORM Write a quadratic function in intercept form for the parabola shown.

17. 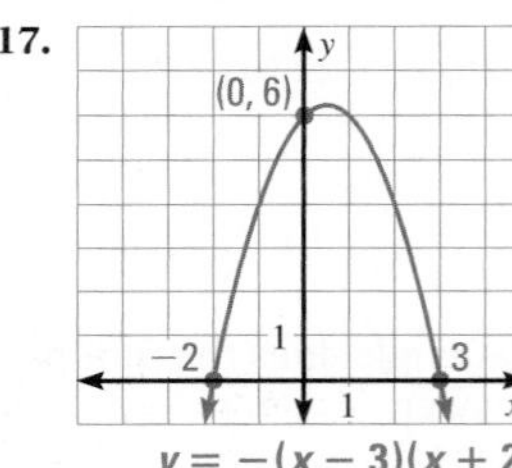

$y = -(x - 3)(x + 2)$

18. 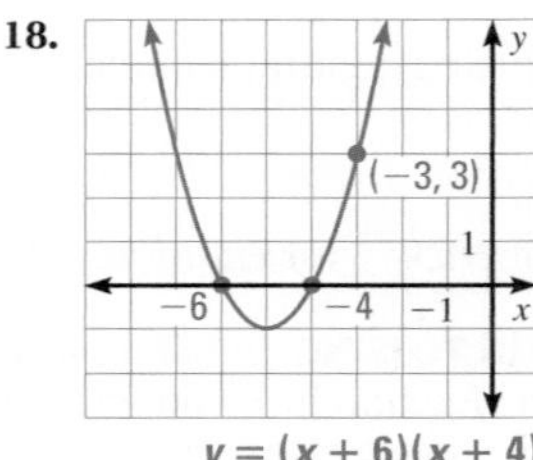

$y = (x + 6)(x + 4)$

19. 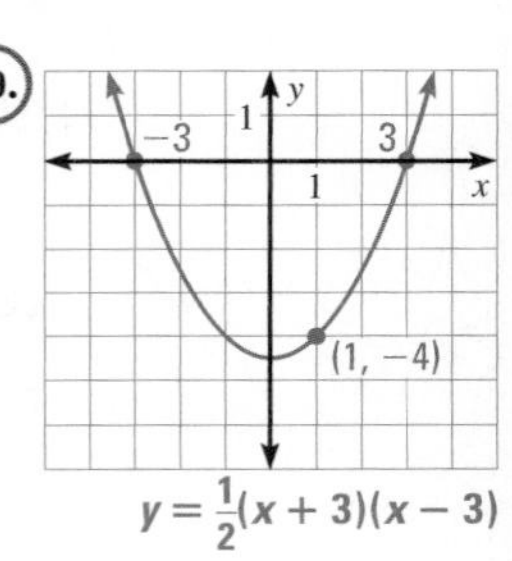

$y = \frac{1}{2}(x + 3)(x - 3)$

WRITING IN INTERCEPT FORM Write a quadratic function in intercept form whose graph has the given x-intercepts and passes through the given point.

20. x-intercepts: 2, 5; point: (4, −2) $y = (x-2)(x-5)$
21. x-intercepts: −3, 0; point: (2, 10) $y = x(x+3)$
22. x-intercepts: −1, 4; point: (2, 4) $y = -\frac{2}{3}(x+1)(x-4)$
23. x-intercepts: 3, 7; point: (6, −9) $y = 3(x-3)(x-7)$
24. x-intercepts: −5, −1; point: (−7, −24) $y = -2(x+5)(x+1)$
25. x-intercepts: −6, 3; point: (0, −9) $y = \frac{1}{2}(x+6)(x-3)$

ERROR ANALYSIS *Describe* and correct the error in writing a quadratic function whose graph has the given x-intercepts or vertex and passes through the given point. 26, 27. See margin.

26. x-intercepts: 4, −3; point: (5, −5)

$y = a(x-5)(x+5)$
$-3 = a(4-5)(4+5)$
$-3 = -9a$
$\frac{1}{3} = a$, so $y = \frac{1}{3}(x-5)(x+5)$ ✗

27. vertex: (2, 3); point: (1, 5)

$y = a(x-2)(x-3)$
$5 = a(1-2)(1-3)$
$5 = 2a$
$\frac{5}{2} = a$, so $y = \frac{5}{2}(x-2)(x-3)$ ✗

EXAMPLE 3 on p. 310 for Exs. 28–39

WRITING IN STANDARD FORM Write a quadratic function in standard form for the parabola shown.

28. 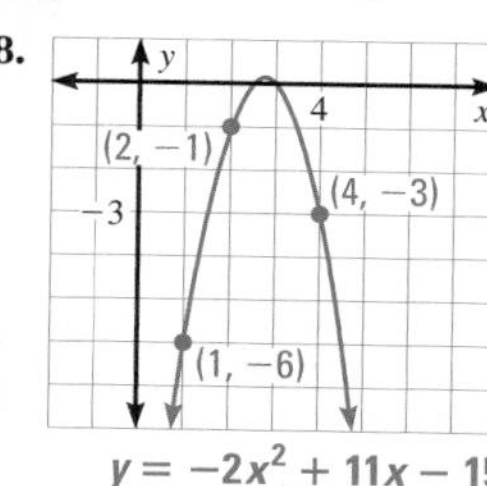

$y = -2x^2 + 11x - 15$

29. 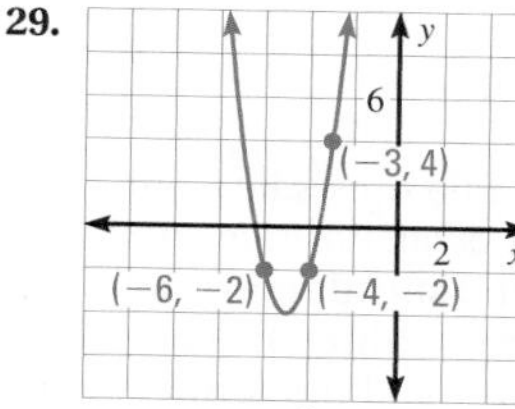

$y = 2x^2 + 20x + 46$

30. 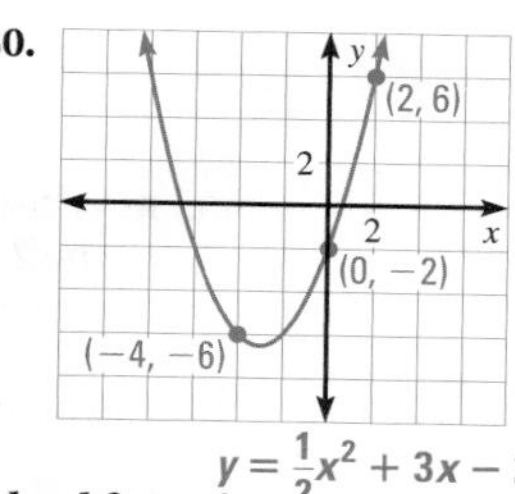

$y = \frac{1}{2}x^2 + 3x - 2$

WRITING IN STANDARD FORM Write a quadratic function in standard form for the parabola that passes through the given points. 31–39. See margin.

31. (−4, −3), (0, −2), (1, 7)
32. (−2, −4), (0, −10), (3, −7)
33. (−2, 4), (0, 5), (1, −11)
34. (−1, −1), (1, 11), (3, 7)
35. (−1, 9), (1, 1), (3, 17)
36. (−6, −1), (−3, −4), (3, 8)
37. (−2, −13), (2, 3), (4, 5)
38. (−6, 29), (−4, 12), (2, −3)
39. (−3, −2), (3, 10), (6, −2)

B **WRITING QUADRATIC FUNCTIONS** Write a quadratic function whose graph has the given characteristics.

40. passes through: (−0.5, −1), (2, 8), (11, 25) $y = -0.15x^2 + 3.82x + 0.95$
41. x-intercepts: −11, 3; passes through: (1, −192) $y = 8x^2 + 64x - 264$
42. vertex: (4.5, 7.25); passes through: (7, −3) $y = -1.64(x-4.5)^2 + 7.25$

43. ★ **OPEN-ENDED MATH** Draw a parabola that passes through (−2, 3). Write a function for the parabola in standard form, intercept form, and vertex form. *Sample answer:* $y = \frac{3}{4}x^2$

C 44. ★ **SHORT RESPONSE** Suppose you are given a set of data pairs (x, y). *Describe* how you can use ratios to determine whether the data can be modeled by a quadratic function of the form $y = ax^2$. Set up the ordered pairs in the ratio $\frac{x^2}{y}$, and if they are all equal, then they have the form $y = ax^2$.

45. **CHALLENGE** Find a function of the form $y = ax^2 + bx + c$ whose graph passes through (1, −4), (−3, −16), and (7, 14). *Explain* what the model tells you about the points. $y = 3x - 7$; the points are linear, not quadratic.

Avoiding Common Errors

Exercises 31–39 Some students do not realize that after they have eliminated a variable from a pair of equations, they must eliminate the *same* variable from another pair of equations to obtain two equations in the same two variables. Show students the procedure to follow by working Extra Example 3 or one of Exercises 34–39 in class, or by giving students a handout that shows a complete step-by-step solution.

Graphing Calculator

Exercises 31–39 Because the process of solving three equations and three variables can be quite time-consuming, some students may ask if there is an easier way to find a quadratic function whose graph passes through three given points. Challenge these students to see if they can find a way to do this with their graphing calculators. If you have discussed Example 4, they should see that they can enter the three ordered pairs into a list and then use *quadratic regression* to find the standard equation of the function.

31. $y = \frac{7}{4}x^2 + \frac{29}{4}x - 2$
32. $y = \frac{4}{5}x^2 - \frac{7}{5}x - 10$
33. $y = -\frac{11}{2}x^2 - \frac{21}{2}x + 5$
34. $y = -2x^2 + 6x + 7$
35. $y = 3x^2 - 4x + 2$
36. $y = \frac{1}{3}x^2 + 2x - 1$
37. $y = -\frac{1}{2}x^2 + 4x - 3$
38. $y = \frac{3}{4}x^2 - x - 4$
39. $y = -\frac{2}{3}x^2 + 2x + 10$

26. The intercepts and point were substituted in for the wrong variables; $y = a(x-4)(x+3)$; $-5 = a(5-4)(5+3)$; $-5 = 8a$; $a = -\frac{5}{8}$, so $y = -\frac{5}{8}(x-4)(x+3)$.

27. The vertex form of the equation should be used instead of the intercept form; $y = a(x-2)^2 + 3$; $5 = a(1-2)^2 + 3$; $5 = a + 3$; $a = 2$, so $y = 2(x-2)^2 + 3$.

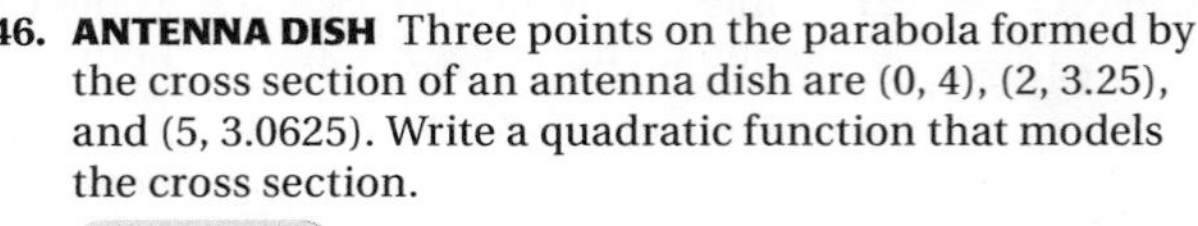

Vocabulary

Exercise 52 Some students may not remember the meaning of a *chord* of a circle. Remind them that a chord is simply any segment that connects two points on a circle, and that a diameter is the longest chord in a circle. Encourage students to experiment with several different ways to place the chords to find the maximum number of regions for a given number of chords.

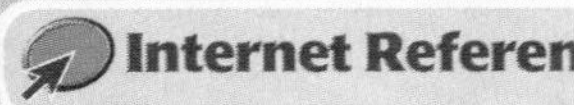

Exercise 51 Additional information about the Garabit Viaduct can be found at www.pbs.org/wgbh/buildingbig/wonder/structure/garabit_viaduct.html

48a.

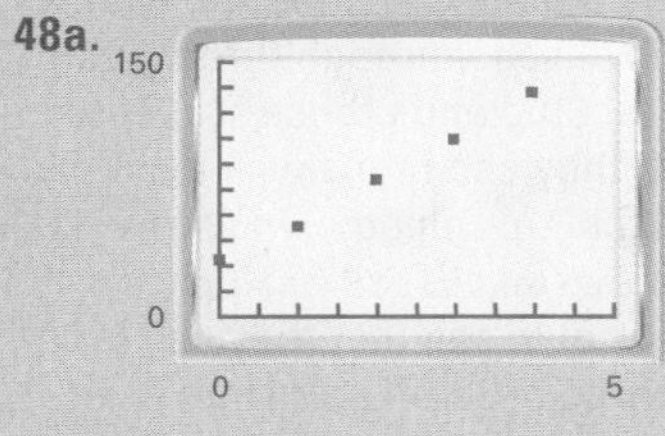

50a.

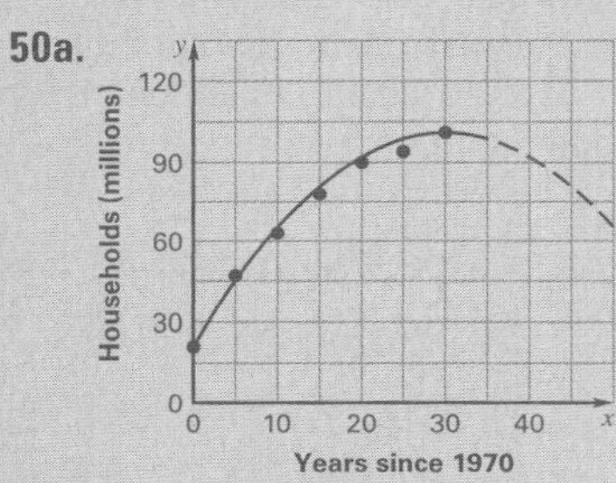

50c. *Sample answer:*

x	y
0	22.3
5	44.8
10	63.3
15	77.8
20	88.3
25	94.8
30	97.3

The numbers in the original table are close to the numbers in the table in part (b).

EXAMPLES 1 and 3 on pp. 309–310 for Exs. 46–47

A

46. $y = \frac{1}{16}x^2 - \frac{1}{2}x + 4$

46. ANTENNA DISH Three points on the parabola formed by the cross section of an antenna dish are (0, 4), (2, 3.25), and (5, 3.0625). Write a quadratic function that models the cross section.

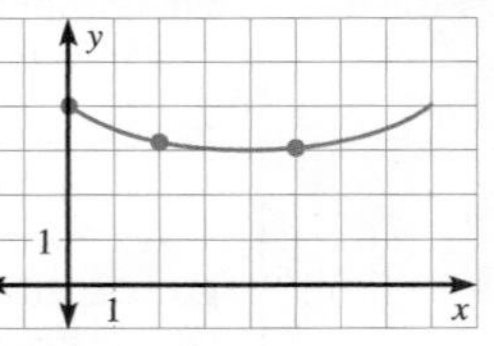

@HomeTutor for problem solving help at classzone.com

47. FOOTBALL Two points on the parabolic path of a kicked football are (0, 0) and the vertex (20, 15). Write a quadratic function that models the path. $y = -\frac{3}{80}(x - 20)^2 + 15$

@HomeTutor for problem solving help at classzone.com

EXAMPLE 4 on p. 311 for Exs. 48–50

48. MULTI-STEP PROBLEM The bar graph shows the average number of hours per person per year spent on the Internet in the United States for the years 1997–2001.

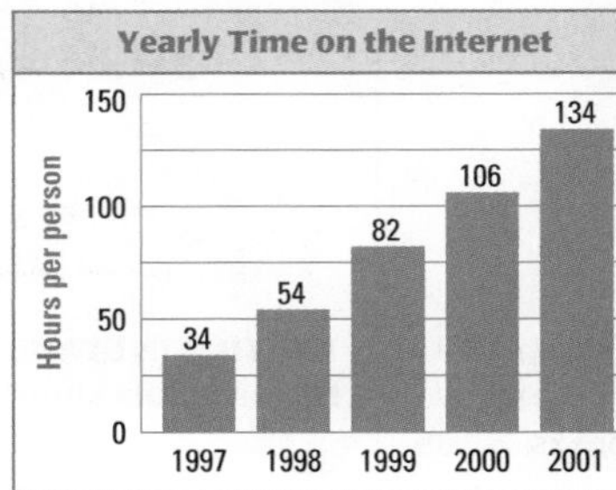

a. Use a graphing calculator to create a scatter plot. See margin.

b. Use the quadratic regression feature of the calculator to find the best-fitting quadratic model for the data. $y = 0.86x^2 + 21.8x + 33.3$

c. Use your model from part (b) to predict the average number of hours a person will spend on the Internet in 2010. about 462

49. RUNNING The table shows how wind affects a runner's performance in the 200 meter dash. Positive wind speeds correspond to tailwinds, and negative wind speeds correspond to headwinds. The change t in finishing time is the difference beween the runner's time when the wind speed is s and the runner's time when there is no wind.

Wind speed (m/sec), s	−6	−4	−2	0	2	4	6
Change in finishing time (sec), t	2.28	1.42	0.67	0	−0.57	−1.05	−1.42

a. Use a graphing calculator to find the best-fitting quadratic model. $y = 0.012x^2 - 0.309x - 4.76$

b. Predict the change in finishing time when the wind speed is 10 m/sec. about −6.65 sec

B

50. MULTIPLE REPRESENTATIONS The table shows the number of U.S. households (in millions) with color televisions from 1970 through 2000.

Years since 1970	0	5	10	15	20	25	30
Households with color TVs (millions)	21	47	63	78	90	94	101

a. **Drawing a Graph** Make a scatter plot of the data. Draw the parabola that you think best fits the data. See margin.

b. **Writing a Function** Estimate the coordinates of three points on the parabola. Use the points to write a quadratic function for the data. *Sample answer:* $y = -0.08x^2 + 4.9x + 22$

c. **Making a Table** Use your function from part (b) to make a table of data for the years listed in the original table above. *Compare* the numbers of households given by your function with the numbers in the original table. See margin.

= WORKED-OUT SOLUTIONS on p. WS1 ★ = STANDARDIZED TEST PRACTICE

Quiz, p. 315

4.

5.

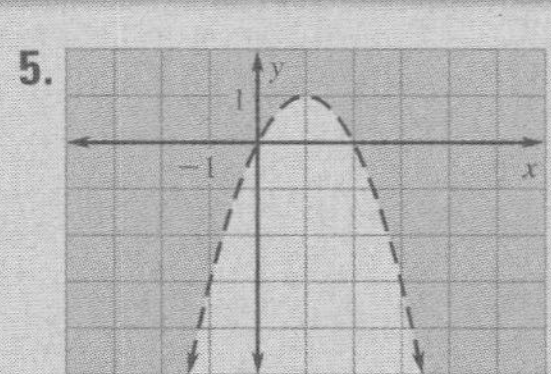

6.

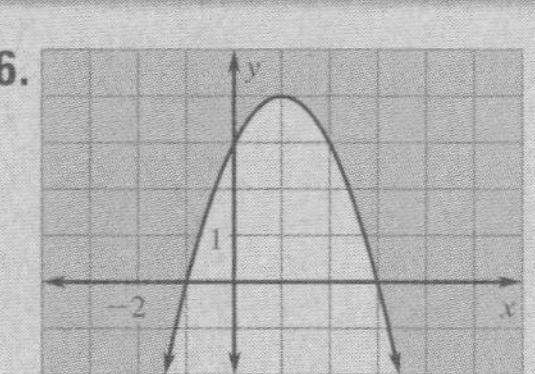

51. ★ **MULTIPLE CHOICE** The Garabit Viaduct in France has a parabolic arch as part of its support. Three points on the parabola that models the arch are (0, 0), (40, 38.2), and (165, 0) where x and y are measured in meters. Which point is also on the parabola? C

Ⓐ (10, −11.84) Ⓑ (26.74, 25) Ⓒ (80, 51.95) Ⓓ (125, 45)

C 52. **CHALLENGE** Let R be the maximum number of regions into which a circle can be divided using n chords. For example, the diagram shows that $R = 4$ when $n = 2$. Copy and complete the table. Then write a quadratic model giving R as a function of n.
$y = 0.5x^2 + 0.5x + 1$

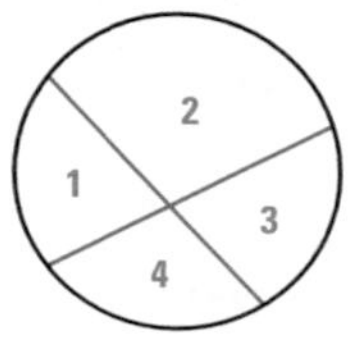

n	0	1	2	3	4	5	6
R	?	?	4	?	?	?	?
	1	2		7	11	16	22

KENTUCKY MIXED REVIEW

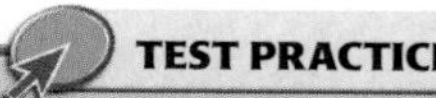

53. Charlie receives some money for his birthday. He deposits one third of the money in the bank. He purchases a concert ticket for \$45. Then he spends half of the remaining money on dinner. Charlie has \$8.50 left. How much money did he receive for his birthday? **B**

Ⓐ \$80 Ⓑ \$93 Ⓒ \$118 Ⓓ \$124

54. Which equation represents a line that is parallel to the line that passes through (−4, 9) and (5, −3)? **C**

Ⓐ $-4x + 3y = 29$ Ⓑ $2x + 3y = 9$

Ⓒ $4x + 3y = -12$ Ⓓ $2x - 3y = 11$

QUIZ *for Lessons 4.8–4.10*

Use the quadratic formula to solve the equation. *(p. 292)*

1. $x^2 - 4x + 5 = 0$ $2 \pm i$
2. $2x^2 - 8x + 1 = 0$ $\frac{4 \pm \sqrt{14}}{2}$
3. $3x^2 + 5x + 4 = 0$ $\frac{-5 \pm i\sqrt{23}}{6}$

Graph the inequality. *(p. 300)* 4–6. See margin.

4. $y < -3x^2$
5. $y > -x^2 + 2x$
6. $y \geq -x^2 + 2x + 3$

Solve the inequality. *(p. 300)*

7. $0 \geq x^2 + 5$ no solution
8. $12 \leq x^2 - 7x$ $x \leq -1.4$ or $x \geq 8.4$
9. $2x^2 + 2 > -5x$ $x \leq -2$ or $x \geq -0.5$

Write a quadratic function whose graph has the given characteristics. *(p. 309)*

10. vertex: (5, 7)
passes through: (3, 11)
$y = (x - 5)^2 + 7$
11. x-intercepts: −3, 5
passes through: (7, −40)
$y = -2(x + 3)(x - 5)$
12. passes through:
(−1, 2), (4, −23), (2, −7)
$y = -x^2 - 2x + 1$

13. **SPORTS** A person throws a baseball into the air with an initial vertical velocity of 30 feet per second and then lets the ball hit the ground. The ball is released 5 feet above the ground. How long is the ball in the air? *(p. 292)* about 2 sec

5 ASSESS AND RETEACH

Daily Homework Quiz

Transparency Available

1. Write a quadratic function in vertex form for this parabola.

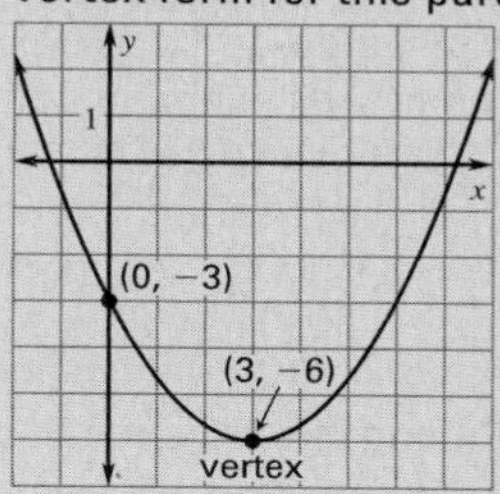

$y = \frac{1}{3}(x - 3)^2 - 6$

2. Write a quadratic function in standard form for the parabola that passes through (−5, 2), (−1, 10), and (2, −5).
$y = -x^2 - 4x + 7$

Available at **classzone.com**

Diagnosis/Remediation

- Practice A, B, C in Chapter 4 Resource Book, pp. 117–119
- Study Guide in Chapter 4 Resource Book, pp. 120–121
- Practice Workbook, pp. 75–76
- @HomeTutor

Challenge

Additional challenge is available in the Chapter 4 Resource Book, p. 124.

Quiz

An easily-readable reduced copy of the quiz (with answers) on Lessons 4.8–4.10 from the Assessment Book can be found on p. 234G.

Kentucky Mixed Review

1. B
2. D
3. C
4. C
5. C
6. D
7. a. $(8 - x)(5 - x) = \frac{2}{3}(8 \cdot 5)$
   b. $x = 1.12, 11.9$
   c. About 1.12 inches; the other solution is greater than 5, and would therefore exceed the width of the paper.

Lessons 4.6–4.10

1. **GAMES** You are playing a lawn version of tic-tac-toe in which you toss bean bags onto a large board. One of your tosses can be modeled by the function $y = -0.12x^2 + 1.2x + 2$ where x is the bean bag's horizontal position (in feet) and y is the corresponding height (in feet). What is the bean bag's maximum height?

   A. 2.5 feet
   B. 5 feet
   C. 6 feet
   D. 10 feet

2. **MUSICAL INSTRUMENTS** A music store sells about 50 of a new model of drum per month at a price of $120 each. For each $5 decrease in price, about 4 more drums per month are sold. Which inequality can you use to find the prices that result in monthly revenues over $6500?

   A. $(50 + 5x)(120 - 4x) > 6500$
   B. $(50 - 5x)(120 + 4x) > 6500$
   C. $(50 - 4x)(120 + 5x) > 6500$
   D. $(50 + 4x)(120 - 5x) > 6500$

3. **SPORTS** You throw a ball to your friend. The ball leaves your hand 5 feet above the ground and has an initial vertical velocity of 50 feet per second. Your friend catches the ball when it falls to a height of 3 feet. About how long is the ball in the air?

   A. 0.04 second
   B. 0.1 second
   C. 3.16 seconds
   D. 3.22 seconds

4. **ABSOLUTE VALUE** What is the absolute value of $-4 + 5i$?

   A. 3
   B. $2\sqrt{10}$
   C. $\sqrt{41}$
   D. $3\sqrt{5}$

5. **LIGHTING** The diagram shows a design for a hanging glass lamp. Which equation models the parabolic cross section of the lamp?

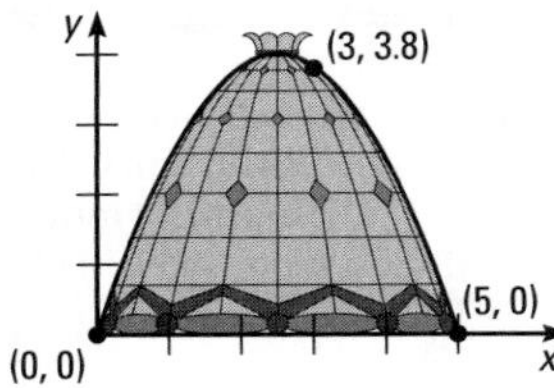

   A. $y = x(x - 5)$
   B. $y = -x(x + 5)$
   C. $y = -0.63x(x - 5)$
   D. $y = 0.63x(x + 5)$

6. **COMPLEX CONJUGATES** What is the product of $5 - 9i$ and its complex conjugate?

   A. -56 B. -11
   C. 56 D. 106

7. **OPEN-RESPONSE** Jill is designing notepaper with solid stripes along the paper's top and left sides as shown. The stripes will take up one third of the area of the paper. The paper measures 5 inches by 8 inches.

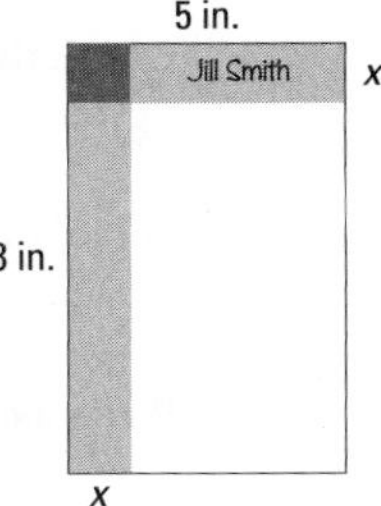

   a. Write an equation that you can use to solve for x.
   b. Find all values of x that are solutions to the equation.
   c. What is the width of the stripes? Why must you reject one of the solutions?

CHAPTER SUMMARY

Animated Algebra
classzone.com
Electronic Function Library

BIG IDEAS
For Your Notebook

Graphing and Writing Quadratic Functions in Several Forms

You can graph or write a quadratic function in standard form, vertex form, or intercept form.

Form	Equation	Information about quadratic function
Standard form	$y = ax^2 + bx + c$	• The x-coordinate of the vertex is $-\frac{b}{2a}$. • The axis of symmetry is $x = -\frac{b}{2a}$.
Vertex form	$y = a(x - h)^2 + k$	• The vertex is (h, k). • The axis of symmetry is $x = h$.
Intercept form	$y = a(x - p)(x - q)$	• The x-intercepts are p and q. • The axis of the symmetry is $x = \frac{p + q}{2}$.

Solving Quadratic Equations Using a Variety of Methods

There are several different methods you can use to solve a quadratic equation.

Equation contains:	Example	Method
Binomial without x-term	$5x^2 - 45 = 0$	Isolate the x^2-term. Then take square roots of each side.
Factorable trinomial	$x^2 - 5x + 6 = 0$	Factor the trinomial. Then use the zero product property.
Unfactorable trinomial	$x^2 - 8x + 35 = 0$	Complete the square, *or* use the quadratic formula.

Performing Operations with Square Roots and Complex Numbers

You can use the following properties to simplify expressions involving square roots or complex numbers.

Square roots	If $a > 0$ and $b > 0$, then $\sqrt{ab} = \sqrt{a} \cdot \sqrt{b}$ and $\sqrt{\frac{a}{b}} = \frac{\sqrt{a}}{\sqrt{b}}$.
Complex numbers	• The imaginary unit i is defined as $i = \sqrt{-1}$, so that $i^2 = -1$. • If r is a positive real number, then $\sqrt{-r} = i\sqrt{r}$ and $(i\sqrt{r})^2 = -r$. • $(a + bi) + (c + di) = (a + c) + (b + d)i$ • $(a + bi) - (c + di) = (a - c) + (b - d)i$ • $\lvert a + bi \rvert = \sqrt{a^2 + b^2}$

Additional Resources

The following resources are available to help review the materials in this chapter.

Chapter 4 Resource Book
- Chapter Review Games and Activities, p. 125
- Cumulative Practice, Chs. 1–4, pp. 127–128

Student Resources in Spanish

eWorkbook

@HomeTutor

Vocabulary Practice

Vocabulary practice is available at **classzone.com**

Extra Example 4.1

Graph $y = x^2 - 2x - 5$.

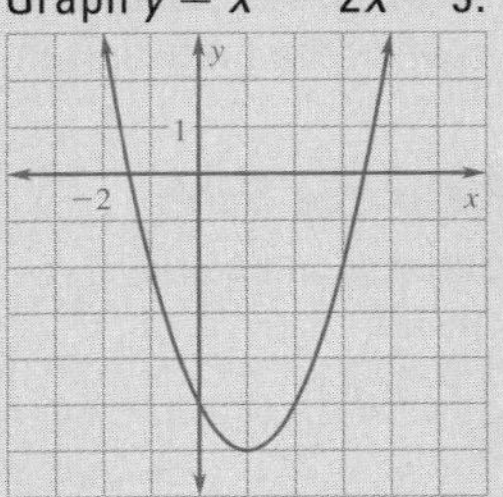

5. 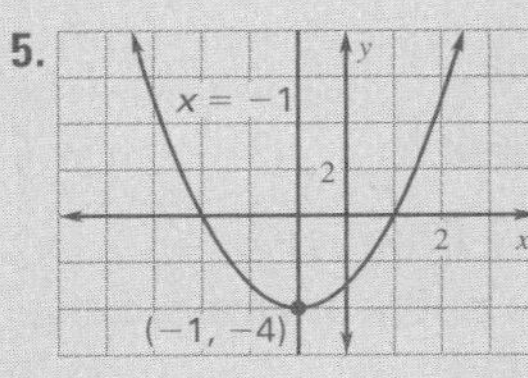

6. 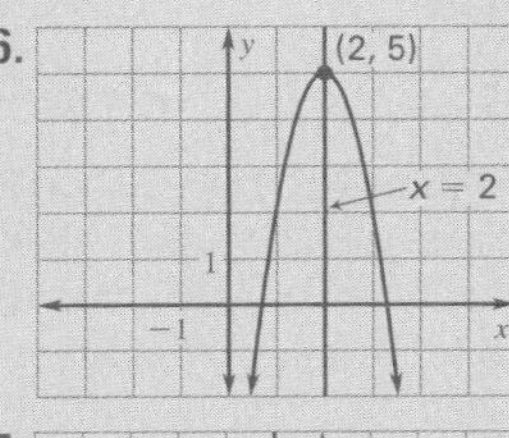

7. 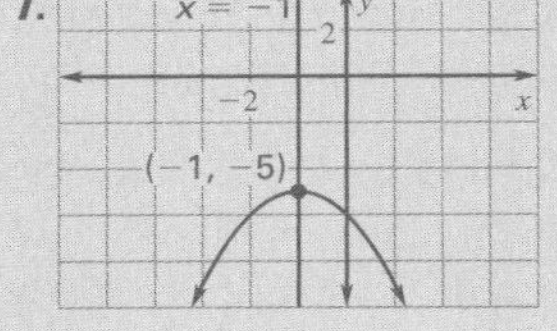

4 CHAPTER REVIEW

@HomeTutor
classzone.com
• Multi-Language Glossary
• Vocabulary practice

REVIEW KEY VOCABULARY

- quadratic function, *p. 236*
- standard form of a quadratic function, *p. 236*
- parabola, *p. 236*
- vertex, *p. 236*
- axis of symmetry, *p. 236*
- minimum, maximum value, *p. 238*
- vertex form, *p. 245*
- intercept form, *p. 246*
- monomial, binomial, trinomial, *p. 252*
- quadratic equation, *p. 253*
- standard form of a quadratic equation, *p. 253*
- root of an equation, *p. 253*
- zero of a function, *p. 254*
- square root, *p. 266*
- radical, radicand, *p. 266*
- rationalizing the denominator, *p. 267*
- conjugates, *p. 267*
- imaginary unit *i*, *p. 275*
- complex number, *p. 276*
- standard form of a complex number, *p. 276*
- imaginary number, *p. 276*
- pure imaginary number, *p. 276*
- complex conjugates, *p. 278*
- complex plane, *p. 278*
- absolute value of a complex number, *p. 279*
- completing the square, *p. 284*
- quadratic formula, *p. 292*
- discriminant, *p. 294*
- quadratic inequality in two variables, *p. 300*
- quadratic inequality in one variable, *p. 302*
- best-fitting quadratic model, *p. 31*

VOCABULARY EXERCISES

1. **WRITING** Given a quadratic function in standard form, explain how to determine whether the function has a maximum value or a minimum value.
If $a < 0$, the function has a maximum value and if $a > 0$, then the function has a minimum value.
2. Copy and complete: A(n) ___?___ is a complex number $a + bi$ where $a = 0$ and $b \neq 0$. **pure imaginary number**
3. Copy and complete: A function of the form $y = a(x - h)^2 + k$ is written in ___?___. **vertex form**
4. Give an example of a quadratic equation that has a negative discriminant.
Sample answer: $y = 3x^2 + 5x + 12$

REVIEW EXAMPLES AND EXERCISES

Use the review examples and exercises below to check your understanding of the concepts you have learned in each lesson of Chapter 4.

4.1 Graph Quadratic Functions in Standard Form *pp. 236–243*

EXAMPLE

Graph $y = -x^2 - 4x - 5$.

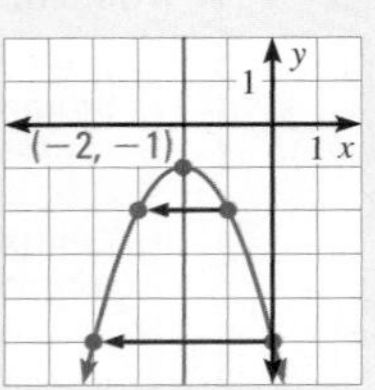

Because $a < 0$, the parabola opens down. Find and plot the vertex $(-2, -1)$. Draw the axis of symmetry $x = -2$. Plot the y-intercept at $(0, -5)$, and plot its reflection $(-4, -5)$ in the axis of symmetry. Plot two other points: $(-1, -2)$ and its reflection $(-3, -2)$ in the axis of symmetry. Draw a parabola through the plotted points.

EXERCISES

EXAMPLE 3 on p. 238 for Exs. 5–7

Graph the function. Label the vertex and axis of symmetry. **5–7. See margin.**

5. $y = x^2 + 2x - 3$
6. $y = -3x^2 + 12x - 7$
7. $f(x) = -x^2 - 2x - 6$

@HomeTutor
classzone.com
Chapter Review Practice

4.2 Graph Quadratic Functions in Vertex or Intercept Form pp. 245–251

EXAMPLE

Graph $y = (x - 4)(x + 2)$.

Identify the x-intercepts. The quadratic function is in intercept form $y = a(x - p)(x - q)$ where $a = 1$, $p = 4$, and $q = -2$. Plot the x-intercepts at $(4, 0)$ and $(-2, 0)$.

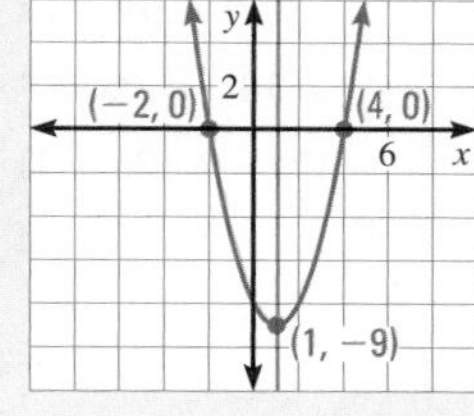

Find the coordinates of the vertex.

$$x = \frac{p + q}{2} = \frac{4 + (-2)}{2} = 1$$

$$y = (1 - 4)(1 + 2) = -9$$

Plot the vertex at $(1, -9)$. Draw a parabola through the plotted points as shown.

EXERCISES

EXAMPLES 1, 3, and 4
on pp. 245–247
for Exs. 8–14

Graph the function. Label the vertex and axis of symmetry. 8–13. See margin.

8. $y = (x - 1)(x + 5)$
9. $g(x) = (x + 3)(x - 2)$
10. $y = -3(x + 1)(x - 6)$
11. $y = (x - 2)^2 + 3$
12. $f(x) = (x + 6)^2 + 8$
13. $y = -2(x + 8)^2 - 3$

14. **BIOLOGY** A flea's jump can be modeled by the function $y = -0.073x(x - 33)$ where x is the horizontal distance (in centimeters) and y is the corresponding height (in centimeters). How far did the flea jump? What was the flea's maximum height? 33 cm; about 20 cm

4.3 Solve $x^2 + bx + c = 0$ by Factoring pp. 252–258

EXAMPLE

Solve $x^2 - 13x - 48 = 0$.

Use factoring to solve for x.

$x^2 - 13x - 48 = 0$	**Write original equation.**
$(x - 16)(x + 3) = 0$	**Factor.**
$x - 16 = 0$ or $x + 3 = 0$	**Zero product property**
$x = 16$ or $x = -3$	**Solve for x.**

EXERCISES

EXAMPLE 3
on p. 254
for Exs. 15–21

Solve the equation.

15. $x^2 + 5x = 0$ −5, 0
16. $z^2 = 63z$ 0, 63
17. $s^2 - 6s - 27 = 0$ −3, 9
18. $k^2 + 12k - 45 = 0$ −15, 3
19. $x^2 + 18x = -81$ −9
20. $n^2 + 5n = 24$ −8, 3

21. **URBAN PLANNING** A city wants to double the area of a rectangular playground that is 72 feet by 48 feet by adding the same distance x to the length and the width. Write and solve an equation to find the value of x. $(72 + x)(48 + x) = 2(72)(48)$; 24 ft

Extra Example 4.2

Graph $y = -(x + 1)^2 + 4$

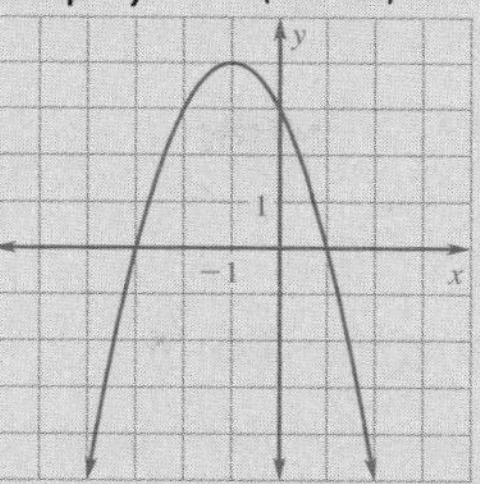

Extra Example 4.3

Solve $x^2 + 11x - 42 = 0$. −14, 3

11.
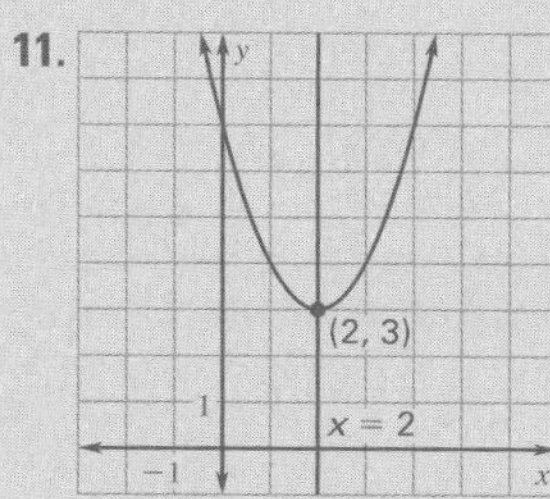

12.
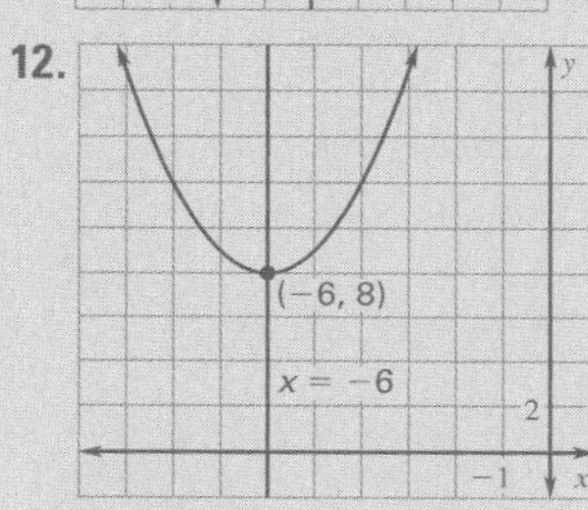

13.
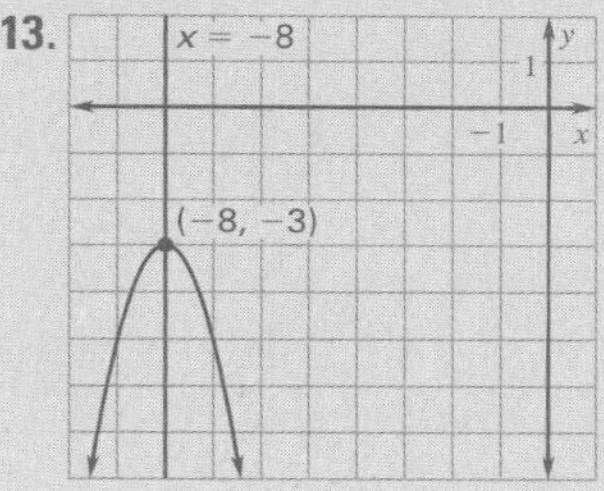

8.
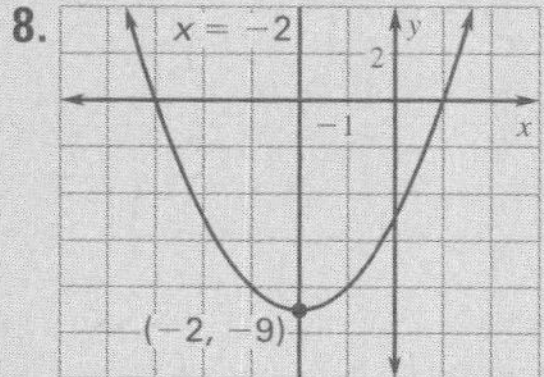

9.
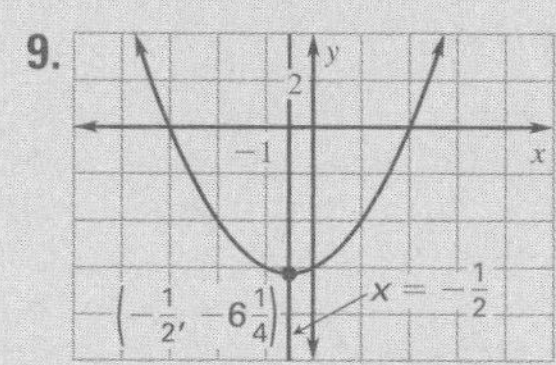

10.
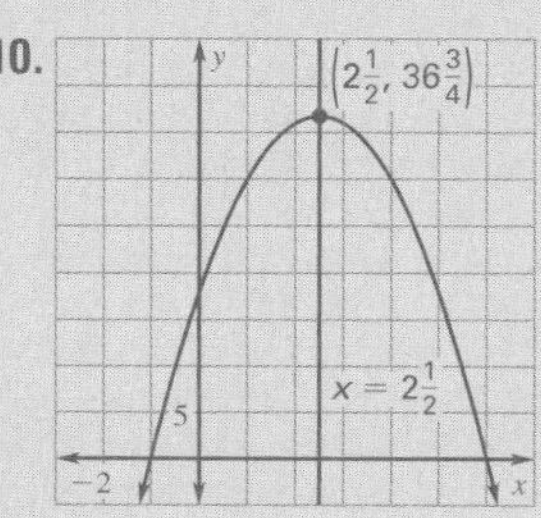

Extra Example 4.4

Solve $12z^2 + 7z = 10$. $-\frac{5}{4}, \frac{2}{3}$

Extra Example 4.5

Solve $2(x + 8)^2 = 108$.
$-8 + 3\sqrt{6}, -8 - 3\sqrt{6}$

Extra Example 4.6

Write $\frac{5 + i}{2 - 3i}$ as a complex number in standard form. $\frac{7}{13} + \frac{17}{13}i$

4 CHAPTER REVIEW

4.4 Solve $ax^2 + bx + c = 0$ by Factoring

pp. 259–264

EXAMPLE

Solve $-30x^2 + 9x + 12 = 0$.

$-30x^2 + 9x + 12 = 0$	**Write original equation.**
$10x^2 - 3x - 4 = 0$	**Divide each side by −3.**
$(5x - 4)(2x + 1) = 0$	**Factor.**
$5x - 4 = 0$ or $2x + 1 = 0$	**Zero product property**
$x = \frac{4}{5}$ or $x = -\frac{1}{2}$	**Solve for *x*.**

EXERCISES

EXAMPLE 5 on p. 261 for Exs. 22–24

Solve the equation.

22. $16 = 38r - 12r^2$ $\frac{1}{2}, 2\frac{2}{3}$

23. $3x^2 - 24x - 48 = 0$ $4 \pm 4\sqrt{2}$

24. $20a^2 - 13a - 21 = 0$ $-\frac{3}{4}, 1\frac{2}{5}$

4.5 Solve Quadratic Equations by Finding Square Roots

pp. 266–271

EXAMPLE

Solve $4(x - 7)^2 = 80$.

$4(x - 7)^2 = 80$	**Write original equation.**
$(x - 7)^2 = 20$	**Divide each side by 4.**
$x - 7 = \pm\sqrt{20}$	**Take square roots of each side.**
$x = 7 \pm 2\sqrt{5}$	**Add 7 to each side and simplify.**

EXERCISES

EXAMPLES 3 and 4 on pp. 267–268 for Exs. 25–28

Solve the equation.

25. $3x^2 = 108$ ± 6

26. $5y^2 + 4 = 14$ $\pm\sqrt{2}$

27. $3(p + 1)^2 = 81$ $-1 \pm 3\sqrt{3}$

28. GEOGRAPHY The total surface area of Earth is 510,000,000 square kilometers. Use the formula $S = 4\pi r^2$, which gives the surface area of a sphere with radius r, to find the radius of Earth. about 6371 km

4.6 Perform Operations with Complex Numbers

pp. 275–282

EXAMPLE

Write $(6 - 4i)(1 - 3i)$ as a complex number in standard form.

$(6 - 4i)(1 - 3i) = 6 - 18i - 4i + 12i^2$	**Multiply using FOIL.**
$= 6 - 22i + 12(-1)$	**Simplify and use $i^2 = -1$.**
$= -6 - 22i$	**Write in standard form.**

@HomeTutor
classzone.com
Chapter Review Practice

EXAMPLES 2, 4, and 5 on pp. 276–278 for Exs. 29–34

EXERCISES

Write the expression as a complex number in standard form.

29. $-9i(2 - i)$ $-9 - 18i$
30. $(5 + i)(4 - 2i)$ $22 - 6i$
31. $(2 - 5i)(2 + 5i)$ 29
32. $(8 - 6i) + (7 + 4i)$ $15 - 2i$
33. $(2 - 3i) - (6 - 5i)$ $-4 + 2i$
34. $\frac{4i}{-3 + 6i}$ $\frac{8}{15} - \frac{4}{15}i$

4.7 Complete the Square

pp. 284–291

EXAMPLE

Solve $x^2 - 8x + 13 = 0$ by completing the square.

$x^2 - 8x + 13 = 0$	Write original equation.
$x^2 - 8x = -13$	Write left side in the form $x^2 + bx$.
$x^2 - 8x + 16 = -13 + 16$	Add $\left(\frac{-8}{2}\right)^2 = (-4)^2 = 16$ to each side.
$(x - 4)^2 = 3$	Write left side as a binomial squared.
$x - 4 = \pm\sqrt{3}$	Take square roots of each side.
$x = 4 \pm \sqrt{3}$	Solve for x.

EXAMPLES 3 and 4 on pp. 285–286 for Exs. 35–37

EXERCISES

Solve the equation by completing the square.

35. $x^2 - 6x - 15 = 0$ $3 \pm 2\sqrt{6}$
36. $3x^2 - 12x + 1 = 0$ $2 \pm \frac{\sqrt{33}}{3}$
37. $x^2 + 3x - 1 = 0$ $\frac{-3 \pm \sqrt{13}}{2}$

4.8 Use the Quadratic Formula and the Discriminant

pp. 292–299

EXAMPLE

Solve $3x^2 + 6x = -2$.

$3x^2 + 6x = -2$	Write original equation.
$3x^2 + 6x + 2 = 0$	Write in standard form.
$x = \frac{-6 \pm \sqrt{6^2 - 4(3)(2)}}{2(3)}$	Use $a = 3$, $b = 6$, and $c = 2$ in quadratic formula.
$x = \frac{-3 \pm \sqrt{3}}{3}$	Simplify.

EXAMPLES 1, 2, 3, and 5 on pp. 292–295 for Exs. 38–41

EXERCISES

Use the quadratic formula to solve the equation.

38. $x^2 + 4x - 3 = 0$ $-2 \pm \sqrt{7}$
39. $9x^2 = -6x - 1$ $-\frac{1}{3}$
40. $6x^2 - 8x = -3$ $\frac{4 \pm i\sqrt{2}}{6}$

41. **VOLLEYBALL** A person spikes a volleyball over a net when the ball is 9 feet above the ground. The volleyball has an initial vertical velocity of −40 feet per second. The volleyball is allowed to fall to the ground. How long is the ball in the air after it is spiked? about 0.2 sec

Extra Example 4.7

Solve $x^2 + 10x + 17 = 0$ by completing the square. $-5 + 2\sqrt{2}$, $-5 - 2\sqrt{2}$

Extra Example 4.8

Solve $2x^2 - 5x + 8 = 0$. $\frac{5 + i\sqrt{39}}{4}$, $\frac{5 - i\sqrt{39}}{4}$

4 CHAPTER REVIEW

Extra Example 4.9
Solve $x^2 + 3x - 6 < 0$.
approximately $-4.37 < x < 1.37$

Extra Example 4.10
Write a quadratic function for the parabola shown.

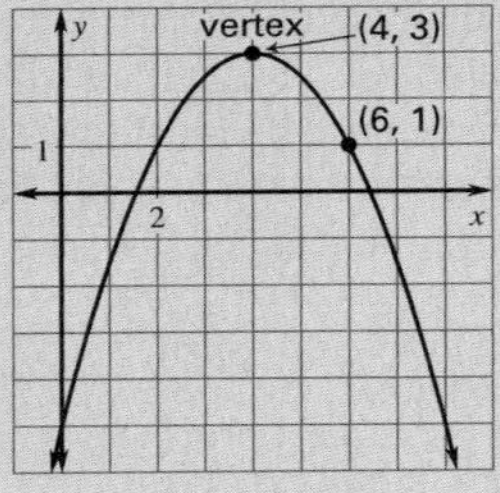

$y = -\frac{1}{2}(x - 4)^2 + 3$

48. $y = -\frac{7}{144}(x - 12)^2 + 7$

4.9 Graph and Solve Quadratic Inequalities

pp. 300–307

EXAMPLE

Solve $-2x^2 + 2x + 5 \le 0$.

The solution consists of the x-values for which the graph of $y = -2x^2 + 2x + 5$ lies on or below the x-axis. Find the graph's x-intercepts by letting $y = 0$ and using the quadratic formula to solve for x.

$$x = \frac{-2 \pm \sqrt{2^2 - 4(-2)(5)}}{2(-2)}$$

$$= \frac{-2 \pm \sqrt{44}}{-4} = \frac{-1 \pm \sqrt{11}}{-2}$$

$$x \approx -1.16 \text{ or } x \approx 2.16$$

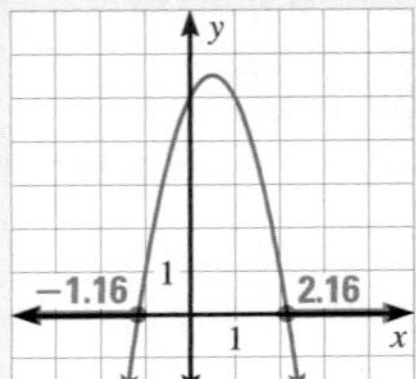

Sketch a parabola that opens down and has -1.16 and 2.16 as x-intercepts. The solution of the inequality is approximately $x \le -1.16$ or $x \ge 2.16$.

EXAMPLE 5 on p. 302 for Exs. 42–44

EXERCISES

Solve the inequality by graphing.

42. $2x^2 - 11x + 5 < 0$ $0.5 < x < 5$

43. $-x^2 + 4x + 3 \ge 0$ $-0.65 \le x \le 4.6$

44. $\frac{1}{2}x^2 + 3x - 6 > 0$ $x < -7.6$ or $x > 1.6$

4.10 Write Quadratic Functions and Models

pp. 309–315

EXAMPLE

Write a quadratic function for the parabola shown.

Because you are given the x-intercepts $p = -3$ and $q = 2$, use the intercept form $y = a(x - p)(x - q) = a(x + 3)(x - 2)$.

Use the other given point, $(1, -2)$, to find a.

$-2 = a(1 + 3)(1 - 2)$	**Substitute 1 for x and −2 for y.**
$-2 = -4a$	**Simplify coefficient of a.**
$\frac{1}{2} = a$	**Solve for a.**

▶ A quadratic function for the parabola is $y = \frac{1}{2}(x + 3)(x - 2)$.

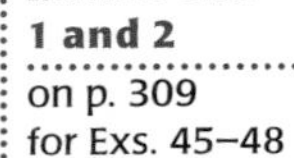

EXAMPLES 1 and 2 on p. 309 for Exs. 45–48

EXERCISES

Write a quadratic function whose graph has the given characteristics.

45. x-intercepts: $-3, 2$
passes through: $(3, 12)$
$y = 2(x + 3)(x - 2)$

46. passes through:
$(5, 2), (0, 2), (8, -6)$
$y = -\frac{1}{3}(x + 1)(x - 6)$

47. vertex: $(2, 7)$
passes through: $(4, 2)$
$y = -\frac{5}{4}(x - 2)^2 + 7$

48. **SOCCER** The parabolic path of a soccer ball that is kicked from the ground passes through the point $(0, 0)$ and has vertex $(12, 7)$ where the coordinates are in feet. Write a quadratic function that models the soccer ball's path. See margin.

4 CHAPTER TEST

Graph the function. Label the vertex and axis of symmetry. 1–3. See margin.

1. $y = x^2 - 8x - 20$ **2.** $y = -(x + 3)^2 + 5$ **3.** $f(x) = 2(x + 4)(x - 2)$

Factor the expression.

4. $x^2 - 11x + 30$ $(x - 6)(x - 5)$ **5.** $z^2 + 2z - 15$ $(z + 5)(z - 3)$ **6.** $n^2 - 64$ $(n - 8)(n + 8)$

7. $2s^2 + 7s - 15$ $(2s - 3)(s + 5)$ **8.** $9x^2 + 30x + 25$ $(3x + 5)^2$ **9.** $6t^2 + 23t + 20$ $(3t + 4)(2t + 5)$

Solve the equation.

10. $x^2 - 3x - 40 = 0$ $-5, 8$ **11.** $r^2 - 13r + 42 = 0$ $6, 7$ **12.** $2w^2 + 13w - 7 = 0$ $-7, 0.5$

13. $10y^2 + 11y - 6 = 0$ $-1.5, 0.4$ **14.** $2(m - 7)^2 = 16$ $7 \pm 2\sqrt{2}$ **15.** $(x + 2)^2 - 12 = 36$ $-2 \pm 4\sqrt{3}$

Write the expression as a complex number in standard form.

16. $(3 + 4i) - (2 - 5i)$ $1 + 9i$ **17.** $(2 - 7i)(1 + 2i)$ $16 - 3i$ **18.** $\frac{3 + i}{2 - 3i}$ $\frac{3}{13} + \frac{11}{13}i$

Solve the equation by completing the square.

19. $x^2 + 4x - 14 = 0$ $-2 \pm 3\sqrt{2}$ **20.** $x^2 - 10x - 7 = 0$ $5 \pm 4\sqrt{2}$ **21.** $4x^2 + 8x + 3 = 0$ $-1\frac{1}{2}, -\frac{1}{2}$

Use the quadratic formula to solve the equation.

22. $3x^2 + 10x - 5 = 0$ $\frac{-5 \pm 2\sqrt{10}}{3}$ **23.** $2x^2 - x + 6 = 0$ $\frac{1 \pm i\sqrt{47}}{4}$ **24.** $5x^2 + 2x + 5 = 0$ $\frac{-1 \pm 2i\sqrt{6}}{5}$

Graph the inequality. 25–27. See margin.

25. $y \ge x^2 - 8$ **26.** $y < x^2 + 4x - 21$ **27.** $y > -x^2 + 5x + 50$

Write a quadratic function whose graph has the given characteristics.

28. x-intercepts: $-7, -3$; passes through: $(-1, 12)$ $y = (x + 7)(x + 3)$

29. vertex: $(-3, -2)$; passes through: $(1, -10)$

29. $y = -\frac{1}{2}(x + 3)^2 - 2$

30. passes through: $(4, 8), (7, -4), (8, 0)$ $y = 2x^2 - 26x + 80$

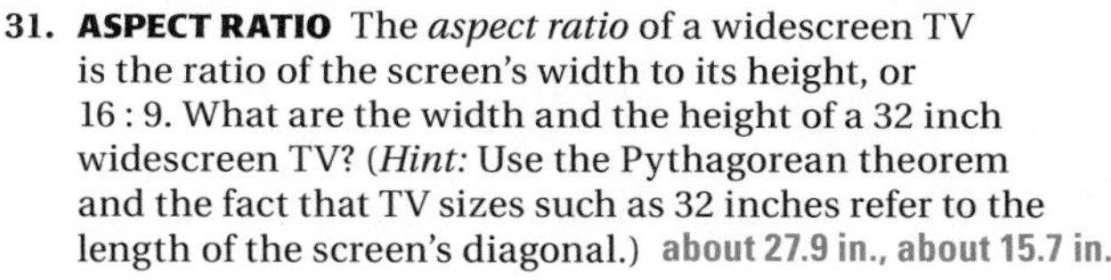

31. ASPECT RATIO The *aspect ratio* of a widescreen TV is the ratio of the screen's width to its height, or 16 : 9. What are the width and the height of a 32 inch widescreen TV? (*Hint:* Use the Pythagorean theorem and the fact that TV sizes such as 32 inches refer to the length of the screen's diagonal.) about 27.9 in., about 15.7 in.

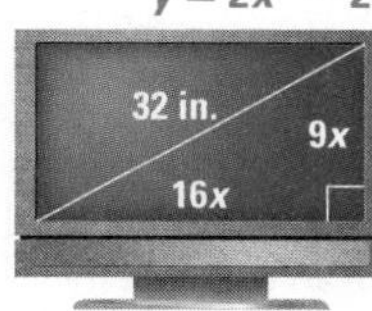

32. WOOD STRENGTH The data show how the strength of Douglas fir wood is related to the percent moisture in the wood. The strength value for wood with 2% moisture is defined to be 1. All other strength values are relative to this value. (For example, wood with 4% moisture is 97.9% as strong as wood with 2% moisture.) Use the quadratic regression feature of a graphing calculator to find the best-fitting quadratic model for the data. $y = 0.00075x^2 - 0.048x + 1.1$

Percent moisture, m	2	4	6	8	10
Strength, s	1	0.979	0.850	0.774	0.714
Percent moisture, m	12	14	16	18	20
Strength, s	0.643	0.589	0.535	0.494	0.458

Additional Resources

Assessment Book

- Chapter Test, Levels A, B, C, pp. 49–54
- Standardized Chapter Test, pp. 55–56
- SAT/ACT Chapter Test, pp. 57–58
- Alternative Assessment, pp. 59–60

Test Generator CD-ROM

Chapter Test

Easily-readable reduced copies (with answers) of Chapter Test B, the Standardized Chapter Test, and the Alternative Assessment from the Assessment Book can be found on pp. 234G–234H.

25.

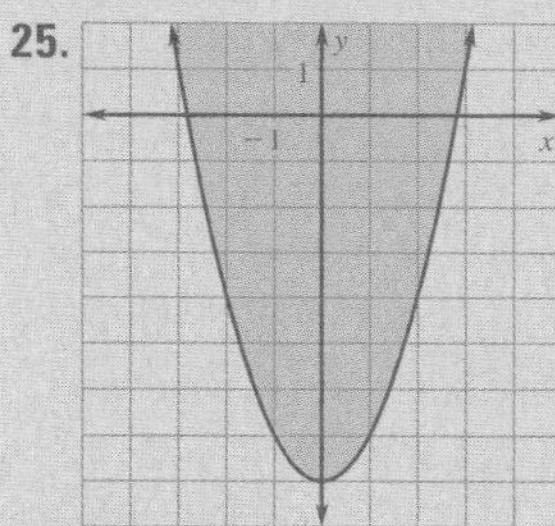

26.

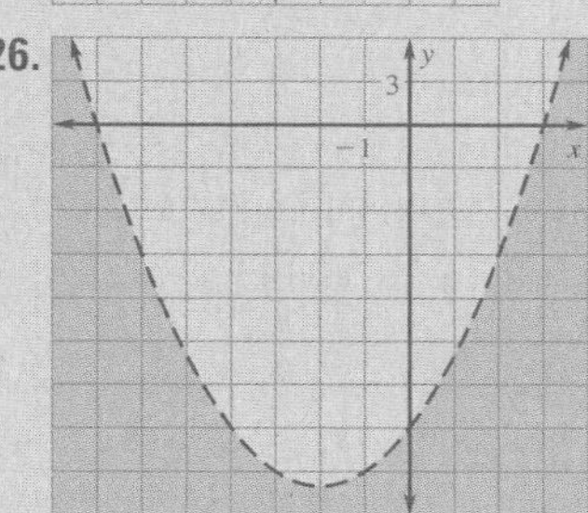

27.

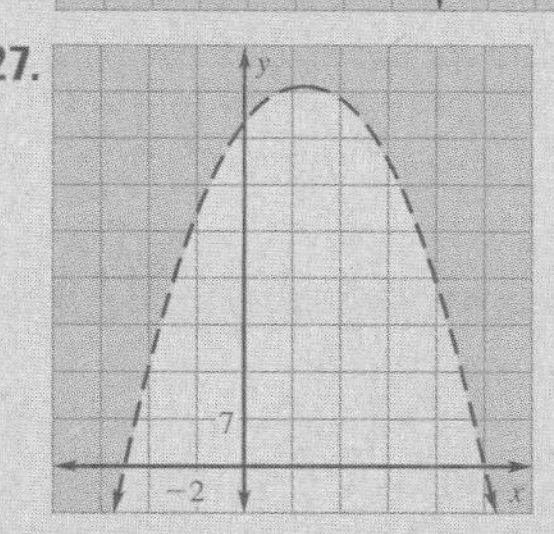

1.

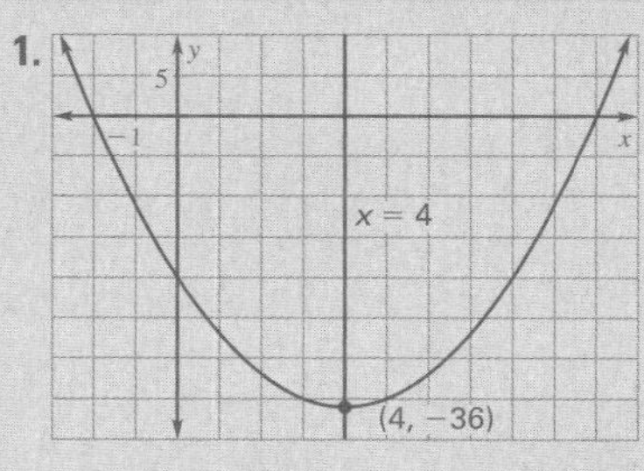

2.

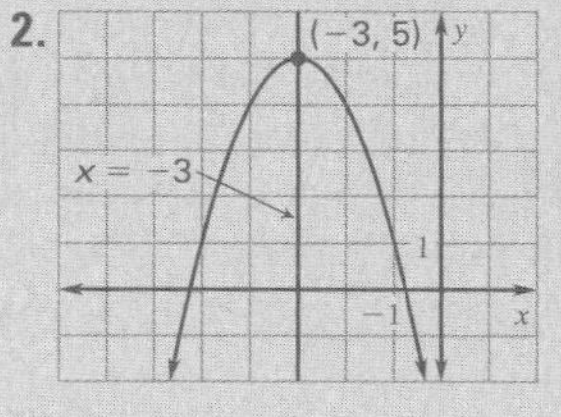

3.

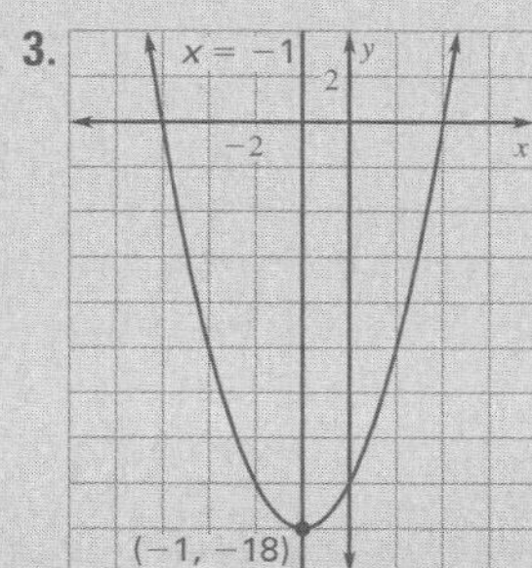

MULTIPLE-CHOICE QUESTIONS

Some of the information you need to solve a multiple-choice question may appear in a table, a diagram, or a graph.

PROBLEM 1

The area of the shaded region is 56 square meters. What is the height of the trapezoid?

A. 3 meters B. 4 meters

C. 6 meters D. 7.5 meters

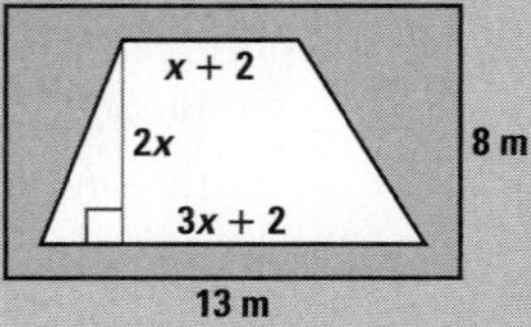

Plan

INTERPRET THE DIAGRAM You know the area of the shaded region. Use the diagram to find the area of the rectangle, and write an expression for the area the trapezoid. The difference of these two areas is the area of the shaded regi

Solution

STEP 1 Find expressions for the two areas.

Area of rectangle:

$A = \ell w$

$= 13(8)$

$= 104 \text{ m}^2$

Area of trapezoid:

$A = \frac{1}{2}(b_1 + b_2)h$

$= \frac{1}{2}[(x + 2) + (3x + 2)](2x)$

$= \frac{1}{2}(2x)(4x + 4)$

$= x(4x + 4)$

$= 4x^2 + 4x$

STEP 2 Write an equation for the area of the shaded region and solve by factoring.

Area of shaded region = Area of rectangle − Area of trapezoid

$56 = 104 - (4x^2 + 4x)$ **Substitute.**

$-48 = -4x^2 - 4x$ **Subtract 104 from each side.**

$4x^2 + 4x - 48 = 0$ **Write in standard form.**

$x^2 + x - 12 = 0$ **Divide each side by 4.**

$(x - 3)(x + 4) = 0$ **Factor.**

$x = 3$ or $x = -4$ **Zero product property**

STEP 3 Find the possible heights.

The height of the trapezoid is given by the expression $2x$. Therefore, the possil heights are $2(3) = 6$ meters and $2(-4) = -8$ meters.

STEP 4 Reject the negative height.

Because height cannot be negative, the height of the trapezoid is 6 meters.

▶ The correct answer is C.

PROBLEM 2

The height h (in feet) of a lobbed tennis ball after t seconds is shown by the graph. What is the initial vertical velocity of the tennis ball?

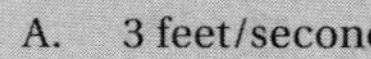
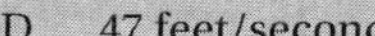

A. 3 feet/second B. 16 feet/second

C. 37.5 feet/second D. 47 feet/second

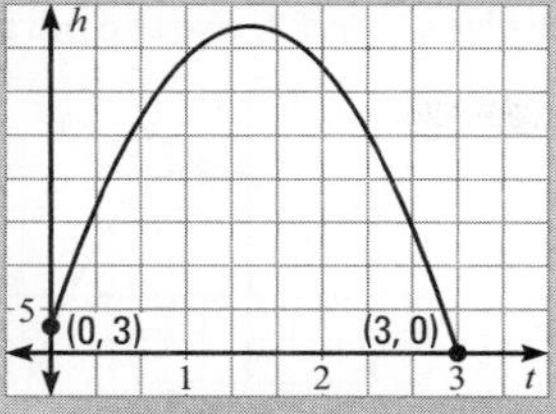

Plan

INTERPRET THE GRAPH The graph is a parabola passing through the points (0, 3) and (3, 0). In order to find the initial vertical velocity of the tennis ball, you must write an equation of the parabola.

Solution

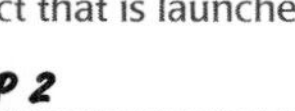

Because the tennis ball is launched, the parabola has an equation of the form $h = -16t^2 + v_0t + h_0$ where v_0 is the initial vertical velocity and h_0 is the initial height of the tennis ball.

P 2
the initial height in
model.

The graph passes through (0, 3), so the initial height of the tennis ball is 3 feet. When you substitute 3 for h_0 in the model, you obtain $h = -16t^2 + v_0t + 3$.

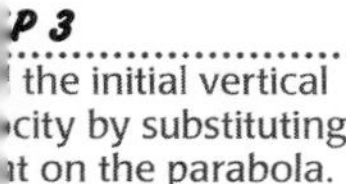

Use the fact that the graph of $h = -16t^2 + v_0t + 3$ passes through (3, 0) to find the initial vertical velocity v_0.

$0 = -16(\mathbf{3})^2 + v_0(\mathbf{3}) + 3$ **Substitute 0 for *h* and 3 for *t*.**

$0 = -141 + 3v_0$ **Simplify.**

$47 = v_0$ **Solve for v_0.**

The initial vertical velocity is 47 feet per second.

▶ The correct answer is D.

PRACTICE

In Exercises 1 and 2, use the graph in Problem 2.

1. What is the maximum height of the tennis ball to the nearest tenth of a foot?

   A. 36.3 feet B. 36.8 feet C. 37.5 feet D. 38.0 feet

2. What does the x-coordinate of the vertex of the graph represent?

   A. The maximum height of the tennis ball

   B. The number of seconds the ball is in the air

   C. The number of seconds it takes the ball to reach its maximum height

   D. The initial height of the tennis ball

TEST PREPARATION

Kentucky Test Preparation

1. C
2. C

Kentucky Test Practice

1. B
2. B
3. B
4. C
5. B
6. B
7. B
8. D

TEST PREPARATION

MULTIPLE-CHOICE

In Exercises 1 and 2, use the parabola below.

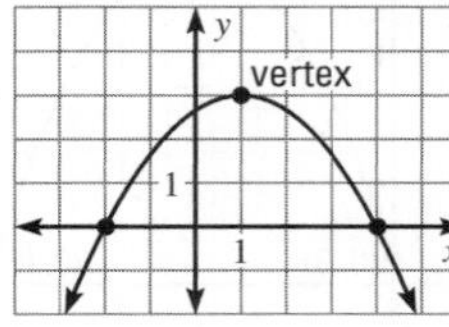

1. Which statement is *not* true about the parabola?

   A. The x-intercepts are -2 and 4.

   B. The y-intercept is -2.

   C. The maximum value is 3.

   D. The axis of symmetry is $x = 1$.

2. What is an equation of the parabola?

   A. $y = (x - 2)(x + 4)$

   B. $y = -\frac{1}{3}(x + 2)(x - 4)$

   C. $y = -(x + 2)(x - 4)$

   D. $y = -3(x + 2)(x - 4)$

3. You are using glass tiles to make a picture frame for a square photograph with sides 10 inches long. You want the frame to form a uniform border around the photograph. You have enough tiles to cover 300 square inches. What is the largest possible frame width x?

   A. 3.6 inches

   B. 5 inches

   C. 7.3 inches

   D. 15 inches

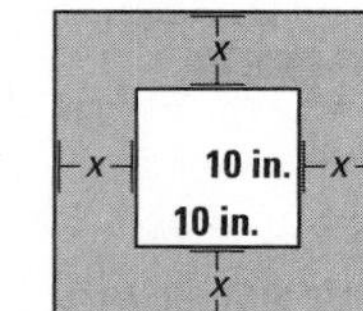

4. At a flea market held each weekend, an artist sells handmade earrings. The table below shows the average number of pairs of earrings sold for several prices. Given the pattern in the table, how much should the artist charge to maximize revenue?

Price	\$15	\$14	\$13	\$12
Pairs sold	50	60	70	80

   A. \$5 B. \$7.50 C. \$10 D. \$15

5. The graph of which inequality is shown?

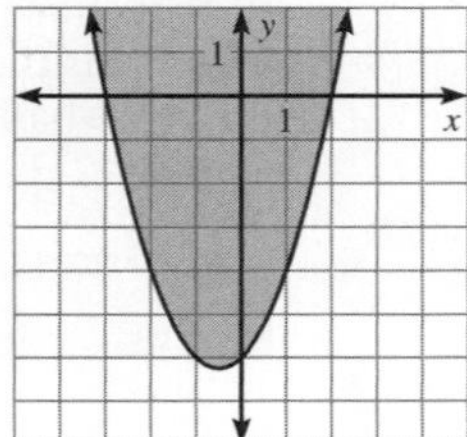

   A. $y \geq -x^2 - x + 6$ B. $y \geq x^2 + x - 6$

   C. $y > 2x^2 + 2x - 12$ D. $y \geq -2x^2 - 2x + 12$

In Exercises 6 and 7, use the information below.

The graph shows the height h (in feet) after t seconds of a horseshoe tossed during a game of horseshoes. The initial vertical velocity of the horseshoe is 30 feet per second.

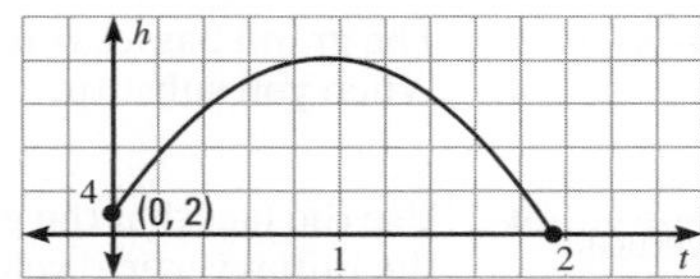

6. To the nearest tenth of a second, how long is the horseshoe in the air?

   A. 0.1 second B. 1.9 seconds

   C. 2.1 seconds D. 3.9 seconds

7. To the nearest tenth of a foot, what is the maximum height of the horseshoe?

   A. 1.9 feet B. 8.1 feet

   C. 16.1 feet D. 32.2 feet

8. The diagram shows a circle inscribed in a square. The area of the shaded region is 21.5 square inches. To the nearest tenth of an inch, how long is a side of the square?

   A. 4.6 inches

   B. 8.7 inches

   C. 9.7 inches

   D. 10.0 inches

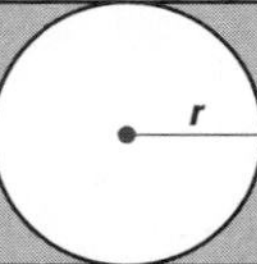

MULTIPLE-CHOICE

9. What is the value of k in the equation $6x^2 - 11x - 10 = (3x + 2)(2x - k)$?
   A. -8 B. -5
   C. 5 D. 8

10. What is the real part of the standard form of the expression $(5 + i)(10 - i)$?
   A. 49
   B. 50
   C. 51
   D. 54

11. For what value of c is $x^2 - 7x + c$ a perfect square trinomial?
   A. $\frac{7}{2}$
   B. $\frac{49}{4}$
   C. $\frac{49}{2}$
   D. 49

12. What is the maximum value of the function $y = -3(x - 2)^2 + 6$?
   A. -6 B. 2
   C. 6 D. There is no maximum value.

13. What is the greatest zero of the function $y = x^2 - 25x + 66$?
   A. -22
   B. -3
   C. 3
   D. 22

14. What is the absolute value of $-5 + 12i$?
   A. 5
   B. 7
   C. 13
   D. 17

OPEN-RESPONSE

15. A parabola passes through the following points: $(0, -22), (2, -6), (5, -12)$
   a. What is the x-coordinate of the vertex of the parabola?
   b. Use your calculator to write a quadratic equation that models the given data.

16. Given the function $f(x) = 4x^2 + 24x + 39$ —
   a. Find the y-intercept of the function.
   b. Find the minimum value of the function.

17. A volleyball is hit upward by a player in a game. The height h (in feet) of the volleyball after t seconds is given by the function $h = -16t^2 + 30t + 6$.
   a. What is the maximum height of the volleyball? *Explain* your reasoning.
   b. After how many seconds does the volleyball reach its maximum height?
   c. After how many seconds does the volleyball hit the ground?

TEST PREPARATION

9. A
10. C
11. B
12. C
13. D
14. C
15. a. 3
b. $y = -2x^2 + 12x - 22$
16. a. 39
b. 3
17. a. About 20 feet; find the x-coordinate of the vertex to be $\frac{15}{16}$, then substitute that value into the equation to find the maximum height.
b. about 0.9 sec
c. about 2 sec

5 Pacing and Assignment Guide

REGULAR SCHEDULE

Pre-AP For pacing and assignments for a Pre-AP course, see the *Algebra 2 Toolkit*.

Lesson	Les. Day	BASIC	AVERAGE	ADVANCED
5.1 MA-HS-5.2.1	Day 1	SRH p. 982 Exs. 1–4, 21–24; pp. 333–335 Exs. 1–6, 15–17, 25–35 odd, 36–43, 49–52, 56	pp. 333–335 Exs. 1, 2, 7–10, 18–20, 24–34 even, 36–46, 49–53, 56	pp. 333–335 Exs. 1, 2, 11–14, 21–23, 24–36 even, 40–48*, 50–54*
5.2 MA-HS-5.1.5	Day 1	pp. 341–344 Exs. 1–5, 9–12, 15–23 odd, 61–62	pp. 341–344 Exs. 1, 2, 5–7, 10–13, 16–22 even, 23, 61–62	pp. 341–344 Exs. 1, 2, 6–8, 11–14, 18–22, 61–62
	Day 2	pp. 341–344 Exs. 24–32, 37–43, 54–58	pp. 341–344 Exs. 24–27, 30–34, 37, 43–46, 50, 54–59	pp. 341–344 Exs. 24–26, 34–37, 44–53*, 56–60*
5.3 MA-HS-5.2.3	Day 1	SRH p. 983 Exs. 1–15 odd; pp. 349–352 Exs. 1, 2, 3–13 odd, 15–19, 26–31, 38–40, 47–50, 59–62, 66	pp. 349–352 Exs. 1, 2, 4–14 even, 15, 20–23, 26, 27, 32–35, 41–43, 47–55 odd, 59–63, 65	pp. 349–352 Exs. 1, 2, 10–15, 23–25, 34–37, 44–47, 50–64*, 66
5.4 MA-HS-5.2.3	Day 1	EP p. 1013 Exs. 13–16; pp. 356–359 Exs. 1, 2, 3–29 odd, 30–34, 41–44, 58–62, 66	pp. 356–359 Exs. 1, 2, 4–8 even, 9, 10–28 even, 30, 31, 35–37, 41, 45–47, 51–53, 60–63, 67	pp. 356–359 Exs. 1, 2, 7–9, 15–17, 21–23, 27–29, 38–41, 47–57*, 60–65*
5.5 MA-HS-5.2.3	Day 1	pp. 366–368 Exs. 1–20, 47–48	pp. 366–368 Exs. 1, 2, 4–10, 12–20, 36, 37, 47–48	pp. 366–368 Exs. 1–18, 36, 37, 47–48
	Day 2	pp. 366–368 Exs. 21–35, 41–44	pp. 366–368 Exs. 23–28, 31–35, 38, 39, 41–45	pp. 366–368 Exs. 24–28, 32–35, 38–46*
5.6 MA-HS-5.1.5	Day 1	EP p. 1013 Exs. 45–48; pp. 374–377 Exs. 1–18, 52–53	pp. 374–377 Exs. 1, 2, 4–10, 12–18, 36–38, 52–53	pp. 374–377 Exs. 1, 2, 5–10, 13–18, 36–39, 52–53
	Day 2	pp. 374–377 Exs. 19–29, 45–49	pp. 374–377 Exs. 21–23, 27–32, 39, 40, 45–50	pp. 374–377 Exs. 23, 30–44*, 46–51*
5.7 MA-HS-5.1.5	Day 1	pp. 383–386 Exs. 1–6, 9–15, 20–27, 32, 33, 66–67	pp. 383–386 Exs. 1, 2, 4–7, 9, 12–17, 22–29, 32, 33, 66–67	pp. 383–386 Exs. 1, 2, 5–9, 14–19, 24–31, 33, 66–67
	Day 2	pp. 383–386 Exs. 35–49 odd, 59–63	pp. 383–386 Exs. 34–50 even, 51–55, 61–64	pp. 383–386 Exs. 38–41, 44–58*, 61–65*
5.8 MA-HS-5.1.5	Day 1	pp. 390–392 Exs. 1–8, 13–17, 21–26, 30, 39–42, 45	pp. 390–392 Exs. 1, 2, 6–10, 13, 14, 18–21, 25–33, 39–43, 46	pp. 390–392 Exs. 1, 2, 11, 12, 21–44*
5.9 MA-HS-5.1.1	Day 1	EP p. 1012 Exs. 35–38; pp. 397–399 Exs. 1–17	pp. 397–399 Exs. 1–5, 7–17, 22	pp. 397–399 Exs. 1, 2, 4, 5, 7–17, 22, 23
	Day 2	pp. 397–399 Exs. 18, 19, 25–28, 31–32	pp. 397–399 Exs. 18–21, 25–29, 31–32	pp. 397–399 Exs. 18–21, 24–32*
Review	Day 1	pp. 402–406 Exs. 1–41	pp. 402–406 Exs. 1–41	pp. 402–406 Exs. 1–41
Assess	Day 1	Chapter 5 Test	Chapter 5 Test	Chapter 5 Test
Yearly Pacing		Chapter 5 Total – 16 days	Chapters 1–5 Total – 70 days	Remaining – 90 days

*Challenge Exercises EP = Extra Practice SRH = Skills Review Handbook

BLOCK SCHEDULE

DAY 1	DAY 2	DAY 3	DAY 4	DAY 5	DAY 6	DAY 7	DAY 8
5.1	**5.2 (CONT.)**	**5.4**	**5.5 (CONT.)**	**5.6 (CONT.)**	**5.7 (CONT.)**	**5.9**	**REVIEW**
pp. 333–335 Exs. 1, 2, 7–10, 18–20, 24–34 even, 36–46, 49–53, 56	pp. 341–344 Exs. 24–27, 30–34, 37, 43–46, 50, 54–59	pp. 356–359 Exs. 1, 2, 4–8 even, 9, 10–28 even, 30, 31, 35–37, 41, 45–47, 51–53, 60–63, 67	pp. 366–368 Exs. 23–28, 31–35, 38, 39, 41–45	pp. 374–377 Exs. 21–23, 27–32, 39, 40, 45–50	pp. 383–386 Exs. 34–50 even, 51–55, 61–64	pp. 397–399 Exs. 1–5, 7–22, 25–29, 31–32	pp. 402–406 Exs. 1–41
5.2	**5.3**	**5.5**	**5.6**	**5.7**	**5.8**		**ASSESS**
pp. 341–344 Exs. 1, 2, 5–7, 10–13, 16–22 even, 23, 61–62	pp. 349–352 Exs. 1, 2, 4–14 even, 15, 20–23, 26, 27, 32–35, 41–43, 47–55 odd, 59–63, 65	pp. 366–368 Exs. 1, 2, 4–10, 12–20, 36, 37, 47–48	pp. 374–377 Exs. 1, 2, 4–10, 12–18, 36–38, 52–53	pp. 383–386 Exs. 1, 2, 4–7, 9, 12–17, 22–29, 32, 33, 66–67	pp. 390–392 Exs. 1, 2, 6–10, 13, 14, 18–21, 25–33, 39–43, 46		Chapter 5 Test

Yearly Pacing Chapter 5 Total – 8 days Chapters 1–5 Total – 35 days Remaining – 45 days

Chapter Resource Guide 5

RESOURCE MANAGER

Chapter Resource Book

CHAPTER SUPPORT									
Parents as Partners (Chapter Overview with home involvement exercises and activity)								p. 1	
LESSON SUPPORT **Standards**	**5.1** MA-HS-5.2.1	**5.2** MA-HS-5.1.5	**5.3** MA-HS-5.2.3	**5.4** MA-HS-5.2.3	**5.5** MA-HS-5.2.3	**5.6** MA-HS-5.1.5	**5.7** MA-HS-5.1.5	**5.8** MA-HS-5.1.5	**5.9** MA-HS-5.1.1
Teaching Guide/Lesson Plan	p. 3	p. 14	p. 26	p. 37	p. 47	p. 58	p. 69	p. 82	p. 98
Activity Masters	p. 5		p. 28				p. 71		
Technology Activities & Keystrokes		p. 16				p. 60	p. 73	p. 84	p. 100
Activity Support Masters									
Practice (3 levels)	p. 6	p. 18	p. 29	p. 39	p. 49	p. 61	p. 74	p. 87	p. 102
Study Guide	p. 9	p. 21	p. 32	p. 42	p. 52	p. 64	p. 77	p. 93	p. 105
Catch-Up for Absent Students	p. 11	p. 23	p. 34	p. 44	p. 54	p. 66	p. 79	p. 95	p. 107
Problem Solving/Application	p. 12	p. 24	p. 35	p. 45	p. 55	p. 67	p. 80	p. 96	p. 108
Challenge Practice	p. 13	p. 25	p. 36	p. 46	p. 57	p. 68	p. 81	p. 97	p. 109

REVIEW			
Chapter Review Games and Activities	p. 110	Cumulative Practice	p. 112
Project with Rubric	p. 111	Resource Book Answers	A1

Transparencies	5.1	5.2	5.3	5.4	5.5	5.6	5.7	5.8	5.9
Warm-Up/Daily Homework Quiz	✔	✔	✔	✔	✔	✔	✔	✔	✔
Notetaking Guide	✔	✔	✔	✔	✔	✔	✔	✔	✔
Teacher Support		✔						✔	✔
Answer Transparencies	✔	✔	✔	✔	✔	✔	✔	✔	✔

ASSESSMENT BOOK

Quizzes	p. 61	SAT/ACT Chapter Test	p. 72
Chapter Tests (3 levels)	p. 64	Alternative Assessment with Rubric	p. 74
Standardized Chapter Test	p. 70		

TECHNOLOGY

- Easy Planner
- Test and Practice Generator
- Power Presentations
- @HomeTutor
- Activity Generator
- Animated Algebra
- Classzone.com
- eEdition Plus Online
- eWorkbook Plus Online
- ML Assessment System

ADDITIONAL RESOURCES

Kentucky

- Worked-Out Solution Key
- Notetaking Guide
- Practice Workbook
- Algebra 2 Toolkit
- Benchmark Tests
- Remediation Workbook

- Spanish Study Guide
- Spanish Assessment Book
- Spanish Resources in Spanish
- Multi-Language Visual Glossary

5 Lesson Practice Level B

LESSON 5.1 Practice B
For use with pages 330–335

Evaluate the expression. Tell which properties of exponents you used.

1. $2^5 \cdot 2^3$ 256
2. $(-7)^2(-7)$ -343 **1–8.** Check properties.
3. $4^{-6} \cdot 4^{-1}$ $\frac{1}{16,384}$
4. $(5^{-2})^2$ $\frac{1}{625}$
5. $\frac{4^{-7}}{4^{-3}}$ $\frac{1}{256}$
6. $\frac{8^{-4}}{8^2}$ $\frac{1}{262,144}$
7. $\left(\frac{2}{3}\right)^3$ $\frac{8}{27}$
8. $\left(\frac{4}{5}\right)^{-3}$ $\frac{125}{64}$

Write the answer in scientific notation. **9.** 1.342×10^{12} **10.** 3.38×10^{-5} **11.** 1.054×10^{-2}

9. $(6.1 \times 10^5)(2.2 \times 10^6)$
10. $(2.6 \times 10^{-7})(1.3 \times 10^2)$
11. $(3.4 \times 10^{-1})(3.1 \times 10^{-2})$
12. $(5.8 \times 10^{-7})(8.1 \times 10^{12})$ 4.698×10^6
13. $(4.5 \times 10^4)^2$ 2.025×10^9
14. $(3.7 \times 10^{-5})^2$ 1.369×10^{-9}
15. $(7.2 \times 10^{-3})^3$ 3.73248×10^{-7}
16. $\frac{9.9 \times 10^9}{1.5 \times 10^8}$ 6.6×10^1
17. $\frac{8.4 \times 10^{-6}}{2.4 \times 10^9}$ 3.5×10^{-15}

Simplify the expression. Tell which properties of exponents you used. **18–29.** Check properties.

18. $\frac{x^8}{x^4}$ x^4
19. $\frac{y^4}{y^{-7}}$ y^{11}
20. $(3^2s^3)^6$ $531,441s^{18}$
21. $(4^0w^2)^{-5}$ $\frac{1}{w^{10}}$
22. $(y^4z^2)(y^{-3}z^{-5})$ $\frac{y}{z^3}$
23. $(2m^3n^{-1})(8m^4n^{-2})$ $\frac{16m^7}{n^3}$
24. $(7c^7d^2)^{-2}$ $\frac{1}{49c^{14}d^4}$
25. $(5g^4h^{-3})^{-3}$ $\frac{h^9}{125g^{12}}$
26. $\frac{x^5y^{-8}}{x^5y^{-6}}$ $\frac{1}{y^2}$
27. $\frac{16q^0r^{-6}}{4q^{-3}r^{-7}}$ $4q^3r$
28. $\frac{12a^{-3}b^9}{21a^2b^{-5}}$ $\frac{4b^{14}}{7a^5}$
29. $\frac{8e^{-4}f^{-2}}{18ef^{-5}}$ $\frac{4f^3}{9e^5}$

Write an expression for the surface area or volume in terms of *x*.

30. $S = 4\pi r^2$ $S = \frac{4}{9}\pi x^2$
31. $V = \frac{1}{3}\pi r^2 h$ $V = \frac{4}{3}\pi x^4$
32. $V = \frac{4}{3}\pi r^3$ $V = \frac{32}{3}\pi x^6$

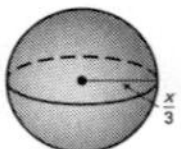

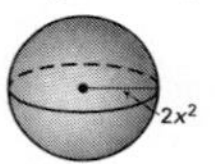

33. **Birds** Some scientists estimate that there are about 8600 species of birds in the world. The mean number of birds per species is approximately 12,000,000. About how many birds are there in the world? Write your answer in scientific notation. about 1.03×10^{11}

34. **Biology** A red blood cell has a diameter of approximately 0.00075 centimeter. If one of the arteries in your body has a diameter of 0.0456 centimeter, how many red blood cells could fit across the artery? Write your answer in scientific notation. about 6.1×10^1

LESSON 5.1

LESSON 5.2 Practice B
For use with pages 337–344

1. yes; $f(x) = -2x + 7$; 1; linear; -2
2. yes; $g(x) = -x^3 + 2x + 8$; 3; cubic; -1

Decide whether the function is a polynomial function. If it is, write the function in standard form and state the degree, type, and leading coefficient.

1. $f(x) = 7 - 2x$ See above.
2. $g(x) = 2x - x^3 + 8$ See above.
3. $h(x) = x^4 - x^{-3}$ no

Use direct substitution to evaluate the polynomial function for the given value of *x*.

4. $f(x) = 6x^4 - x^3 + 3x^2 - 5x + 9; x = -1$ 24
5. $g(x) = 7x - x^4 + 1; x = -4$ -283

Use synthetic substitution to evaluate the polynomial function for the given value of *x*.

6. $f(x) = 7x^4 - 3x^3 + x^2 + 5x - 9; x = 2$ 93
7. $g(x) = x^3 - 8x + 6; x = -3$ 3

Describe the end behavior of the graph of the polynomial function by completing these statements: $f(x) \to$ __?__ as $x \to -\infty$ and $f(x) \to$ __?__ as $x \to +\infty$.

8. $f(x) = -5x^3$ $+\infty, -\infty$
9. $f(x) = 2x^5 - 7x^2 - 4x$ $-\infty, +\infty$
10. $f(x) = 2x^8 + 9x^7 + 10$ $+\infty, +\infty$
11. $f(x) = -12x^6 - 2x + 5$ $-\infty, -\infty$

Graph the polynomial function.

12. $f(x) = -x^3 - 2$
13. $g(x) = x^4 + 2x$
14. $h(x) = -x^4 + 2x^3 - 5x + 1$

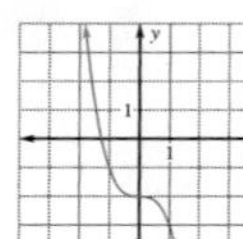
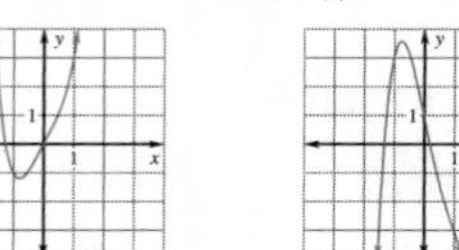

15. **Shopping** The retail space in shopping centers in the United States from 1986 to 2003 can be modeled by
$S = -0.0388t^4 + 1.723t^3 - 28t^2 + 309t + 3481$
where *S* is the amount of retail space (in millions of square feet) and *t* is the number of years since 1986.
 a. Describe the end behavior of the graph of the function.
 b. Graph the function on the domain $0 \le t \le 17$.
 c. Use the graph to estimate the first year that the amount of retail space was greater than 5000 million square feet.
 d. Use the model to predict the amount of retail space in the year 2010. Is it appropriate to use the model to make this prediction? Explain.

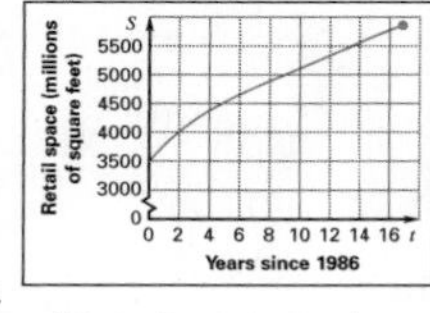

15. a. $S(t) \to -\infty$ as $t \to -\infty$ and $S(t) \to -\infty$ as $t \to +\infty$ **c.** 1996 **d.** about 5715 million ft^2; *Sample answer:* No. The function starts to decrease after 2007, and the amount of retail space will probably continue to increase over time.

LESSON 5.2

LESSON 5.3 Practice B
For use with pages 346–352

Find the sum or difference.

1. $(2y^2 - 5y + 1) + (y^2 - y - 4)$ $3y^2 - 6y - 3$
2. $(12x^2 + 8x - 3) - (11x^2 - x + 5)$ $x^2 + 9x - 8$
3. $(6m^3 - 5) - (m^3 + 4m^2 - 9m - 2)$ $5m^3 - 4m^2 + 9m - 3$
4. $(5s^4 - 2s^3 + 9) - (-2s^4 + 8s^2 - s + 2)$ $7s^4 - 2s^3 - 8s^2 + s + 7$
5. $(7q - 3q^3) + (16 - 8q^3 + 5q^2 - q)$ $-11q^3 + 5q^2 + 6q + 16$
6. $(-4z^4 + 6z - 9) + (11 - z^3 + 3z^2 + z^4)$ $-3z^4 - z^3 + 3z^2 + 6z + 2$
7. $(10v^4 - 2v^2 + 6v^3 - 7) - (9 - v + 2v^4)$ $8v^4 + 6v^3 - 2v^2 + v - 16$
8. $(4x^5 + 3x^4 - 5x + 1) - (x^3 + 2x^4 - x^5 + 1)$ $5x^5 + x^4 - x^3 - 5x$

Find the product.

9. $2x^3(5x - 1)$ $10x^4 - 2x^3$
10. $(w - 8)(w - 1)$ $w^2 - 9w + 8$
11. $(c + 4)(c + 10)$ $c^2 + 14c + 40$
12. $(g + 9)(g - 2)$ $g^2 + 7g - 18$
13. $(y - 1)(y^2 + 6y - 2)$ $y^3 + 5y^2 - 8y + 2$
14. $(n + 5)(2n^2 - n - 7)$ $2n^3 + 9n^2 - 12n - 35$
15. $(x - 3)^2$ $x^2 - 6x + 9$
16. $(4t + 1)^2$ $16t^2 + 8t + 1$
17. $(z - 5)^3$ $z^3 - 15z^2 + 75z - 125$
18. $(2f + 1)^3$ $8f^3 + 12f^2 + 6f + 1$

Write the volume of the figure as a polynomial in standard form.

19. $V = \ell wh$

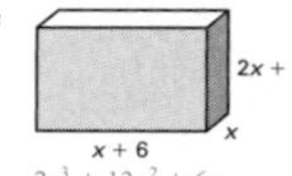

$2x^3 + 13x^2 + 6x$

20. $V = \frac{1}{3}\pi r^2 h$ $\frac{1}{3}\pi x^3 - \pi x^2 - 3\pi x + 9\pi$

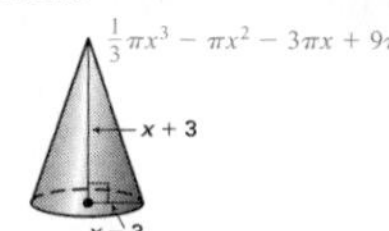

21. **Bottled Water** From 1990 to 1999, the per capita consumption *B* of bottled water (in gallons) and the population *P* of the United States (in thousands) can be modeled by
$B = 0.0977t^2 + 0.186t + 7.86$ and
$P = 3226t + 250,359$
where *t* is the number of years since 1990. Write a model for the total consumption *C* of bottled water (in thousands of gallons). What was the total consumption of bottled water in 1998? $C = 315t^3 + 25,060t^2 - 71,923t + 1,967,822$; about 4,308,326 thousand gallons

LESSON 5.3

LESSON 5.4 Practice B
For use with pages 353–359

Factor the sum or difference of cubes.

1. $x^3 + 125$ $(x + 5)(x^2 - 5x + 25)$
2. $y^3 - 8$ $(y - 2)(y^2 + 2y + 4)$
3. $64n^3 - 27$ $(4n - 3)(16n^2 + 12n + 9)$
4. $27g^3 + 343$ $(3g + 7)(9g^2 - 21g + 49)$
5. $2w^3 + 54$ $2(w + 3)(w^2 - 3w + 9)$
6. $40v^3 - 625$ $5(2v - 5)(4v^2 + 10v + 25)$

Factor the polynomial by grouping.

7. $r^3 - 3r^2 + 6r - 18$ $(r^2 + 6)(r - 3)$
8. $x^3 + 6x^2 + 7x + 42$ $(x^2 + 7)(x + 6)$
9. $c^3 + 4c^2 - 9c - 36$ $(c + 3)(c - 3)(c + 4)$
10. $z^3 - 2z^2 - 16z + 32$ $(z + 4)(z - 4)(z - 2)$
11. $25p^3 - 25p^2 - p + 1$ $(5p + 1)(5p - 1)(p - 1)$
12. $9m^3 + 18m^2 - 4m - 8$ $(3m + 2)(3m - 2)(m + 2)$

Factor the polynomial in quadratic form.

13. $x^4 - 36$ $(x^2 - 6)(x^2 + 6)$
14. $c^4 - 81$ $(c + 3)(c - 3)(c^2 + 9)$
15. $x^4 + x^2 - 20$ $(x + 2)(x - 2)(x^2 + 5)$
16. $6y^6 - 5y^3 - 4$ $(2y^3 + 1)(3y^3 - 4)$

Factor the polynomial completely.

17. $x^6 - 4$ $(x^3 + 2)(x^3 - 2)$
18. $d^4 - 7d^2 + 10$ $(d^2 - 5)(d^2 - 2)$
19. $24q^3 - 81$ $3(2q - 3)(4q^2 + 6q + 9)$
20. $a^6 + 7a^3 + 6$ $(a^3 + 6)(a + 1)(a^2 - a + 1)$
21. $-4x^4 + 26x^2 - 30$ $-2(2x^2 - 3)(x^2 - 5)$
22. $2b^4 + 14b^3 - 16b - 112$ $2(b + 7)(b - 2)(b^2 + 2b + 4)$

Find the real-number solutions of the equation.

23. $n^4 + 6n^3 = 0$ $-6, 0$
24. $4k^3 = 9k^2$ $0, \frac{9}{4}$
25. $x^3 + 2x^2 - 25x - 50 = 0$ $-5, -2, 5$
26. $6w^3 + 30w^2 - 18w - 90 = 0$ $-5, -\sqrt{3}, \sqrt{3}$
27. $y^4 - 14y^2 + 45 = 0$ $-3, -\sqrt{5}, \sqrt{5}, 3$
28. $3r^5 + 15r^3 - 18r = 0$ $-1, 0, 1$

29. Write a binomial that can be factored either as the difference of two squares or as the difference of two cubes. Show the complete factorization of your binomial. *Sample answer:* $x^6 - 1$; $(x + 1)(x - 1)(x^2 + x + 1)(x^2 - x + 1)$

30. **City Park** You are designing a marble planter for a city park. You want the length of the planter to be six times the height, and the width to be three times the height. The sides should be one foot thick. Because the planter will be on the sidewalk, it does not need a bottom. What should the outer dimensions of the planter be if it is to hold 4 cubic feet of dirt? 6 ft by 3 ft by 1 ft

LESSON 5.4

LESSON 5.5

Practice B

For use with pages 362–368

Divide using polynomial long division.

1. $(x^2 + 5x - 14) \div (x - 2)$ $x + 7$
2. $(x^2 - 2x - 48) \div (x + 5)$ $x - 7 - \frac{13}{x + 5}$
3. $(x^3 + x + 30) \div (x + 3)$ $x^2 - 3x + 10$
4. $(6x^2 - 5x + 9) \div (2x - 1)$ $3x - 1 + \frac{8}{2x - 1}$
5. $(8x^3 + 5x^2 - 12x + 10) \div (x^2 - 3)$ $8x + 5 + \frac{12x + 25}{x^2 - 3}$
6. $(5x^4 + 2x^3 - 9x + 12) \div (x^2 - 3x + 4)$ $5x^2 + 17x + 31 + \frac{16x - 112}{x^2 - 3x + 4}$

Divide using synthetic division.

7. $(x^2 + 7x + 12) \div (x + 4)$ $x + 3$
8. $(x^3 - 3x^2 + 8x - 5) \div (x - 1)$ $x^2 - 2x + 6 + \frac{1}{x - 1}$
9. $(x^4 - 7x^2 + 9x - 10) \div (x - 2)$ $x^2 - 5x - 1 - \frac{12}{x - 2}$
10. $(2x^4 - x^3 + 4) \div (x + 1)$ $2x^3 - 3x^2 + 3x - 3 + \frac{7}{x + 1}$
11. $(2x^4 - 11x^3 + 15x^2 + 6x - 18) \div (x - 3)$ $2x^3 - 5x^2 + 6$
12. $(x^4 - 6x^3 - 40x + 33) \div (x - 7)$ $x^3 + x^2 + 7x + 9 + \frac{96}{x - 7}$

A polynomial *f* and a factor of *f* are given. Factor *f* completely. 13. $(x - 6)(x + 1)(x + 2)$ 14. $(x - 10)(x - 4)(x + 2)$

13. $f(x) = x^3 - 3x^2 - 16x - 12; x - 6$
14. $f(x) = x^3 - 12x^2 + 12x + 80; x - 10$
15. $f(x) = x^3 - 18x^2 + 95x - 126; x - 9$ $(x - 9)(x - 2)(x - 7)$
16. $f(x) = x^3 - x^2 - 21x + 45; x + 5$ $(x + 5)(x - 3)^2$
17. $f(x) = 4x^3 - 4x^2 - 9x + 9; x - 1$ $(x - 1)(2x + 3)(2x - 3)$
18. $f(x) = 3x^3 - 16x^2 - 103x + 36; x + 4$ $(x + 4)(3x - 1)(x - 9)$

A polynomial *f* and one zero of *f* are given. Find the other zeros of *f*.

19. $f(x) = x^3 + 2x^2 - 20x + 24; -6$ 2
20. $f(x) = x^3 + 11x^2 - 150x - 1512; -14$ $-9, 12$
21. $f(x) = 2x^3 + 3x^2 - 39x - 20; 4$ $-5, -\frac{1}{2}$
22. $f(x) = 15x^3 - 119x^2 - 10x + 16; 8$ $-\frac{2}{5}, \frac{1}{3}$
23. $f(x) = x^3 - 3x^2 - 45x + 175; -7$ 5
24. $f(x) = x^3 - 9x^2 - 5x + 45; 9$ $-\sqrt{5}, \sqrt{5}$
25. **Geometry** The volume of the box shown at the right is given by $V = 2x^3 - 11x^2 + 10x + 8$. Find an expression for the missing dimension. $x - 2$

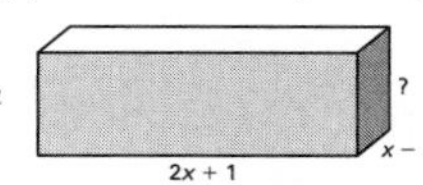

26. **Fuel Consumption** From 1995 to 2002, the total fuel consumption T (in billions of gallons) by cars in the United States and the U.S. population P (in millions) can be modeled by

$T = -0.003x^3 - 0.02x^2 + 1.3x + 68$ and $P = 3x + 267$

where x is the number of years since 1995. Write a function for the average amount of fuel consumed by each person from 1995 to 2002. Answers may vary depending on rounding. $A = -0.001x^2 + 0.0823x - 6.8943 + \frac{1909}{3x + 267}$

LESSON 5.6

Practice B

For use with pages 370–377

1. $\pm1, \pm3, \pm7, \pm21$
2. $\pm1, \pm2, \pm3, \pm5, \pm6, \pm10, \pm15, \pm30, \pm\frac{1}{2}, \pm\frac{3}{2}, \pm\frac{5}{2}, \pm\frac{15}{2}$

List the possible rational zeros of the function using the rational zero theorem.

1. $f(x) = x^4 - 6x^3 + 8x^2 - 21$ See above.
2. $h(x) = 2x^3 + 7x^2 - 7x + 30$ See above.
3. $h(x) = 5x^4 + 12x^3 - 16x^2 + 10$ See below.
4. $g(x) = 9x^5 + 3x^3 + 7x - 4$ $\pm1, \pm2, \pm4, \pm\frac{1}{9}, \pm\frac{2}{9}, \pm\frac{1}{3}, \pm\frac{4}{9}, \pm\frac{2}{3}, \pm\frac{4}{3}$

Find all real zeros of the function.

5. $f(x) = x^3 - 3x^2 - 6x + 8$ $-2, 1, 4$
6. $g(x) = x^3 + 4x^2 - x - 4$ $-4, -1, 1$
7. $h(x) = x^3 + 4x^2 + x - 6$ $-3, -2, 1$
8. $g(x) = x^3 + 5x^2 - x - 5$ $-5, -1, 1$
9. $f(x) = x^3 + 72 - 5x^2 - 18x$ $-4, 3, 6$
10. $f(x) = x^3 + x^2 - 2x - 2$ $-\sqrt{2}, -1, \sqrt{2}$

Use the graph to shorten the list of possible rational zeros of the function. Then find all real zeros of the function.

11. $f(x) = 4x^3 - 8x^2 - 15x + 9$ $-\frac{3}{2}, \frac{1}{2}, 3$
12. $f(x) = 2x^3 - 5x^2 - 4x + 10$ $-\sqrt{2}, \sqrt{2}, \frac{5}{2}$

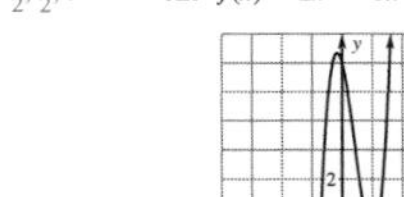

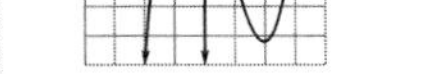

3. $\pm1, \pm2, \pm5, \pm10, \pm\frac{1}{5}, \pm\frac{2}{5}$

Find all real zeros of the function.

13. $g(x) = 2x^3 + 4x^2 - 2x - 4$ $-2, -1, 1$
14. $f(x) = 2x^3 - 5x^2 - 14x + 8$ $-2, \frac{1}{2}, 4$
15. $h(x) = 8x^3 - 6x^2 - 23x + 6$ $-\frac{3}{2}, \frac{1}{4}, 2$
16. $g(x) = 2x^4 + x^3 - x^2 - x - 1$ $-1, 1$
17. $h(x) = 2x^4 + 5x^3 - 5x^2 - 5x + 3$ $-3, -1, \frac{1}{2}, 1$
18. $f(x) = 2x^4 + 3x^3 - 6x^2 - 6x + 4$ $-2, -\sqrt{2}, \sqrt{2}, \frac{1}{2}$
19. **Mail** From 1995 to 2003, the amount of mail M (in billions of pieces) handled by the U.S. Postal Service can be modeled by

$M = 0.05(t^4 - 18t^3 + 89t^2 - 32t + 3680)$

where t is the number of years since 1995. In which year was there about 204,000,000,000 pieces of mail handled?

a. Write a polynomial equation that can be used to answer the question. $t^4 - 18t^3 + 89t^2 - 32t - 400$

b. List the possible whole-number solutions of the equation in part (a) that are less than or equal to 8. $\pm1, \pm2, \pm4, \pm8$

c. Use synthetic division to determine which of the possible solutions in part (b) is an actual solution. Then answer the question in the problem statement. 4; 1999

d. Use a graphing calculator to graph and identify any additional real solutions of the equation that are reasonable. about 6.4 or 2001

LESSON 5.7

Practice B

For use with pages 379–386

Identify the number of solutions or zeros.

1. $f(x) = 5x^3 - 6x^2 + 2x - 3$ 3
2. $g(s) = 8s^6 - 3s^4 - 11s^3 - 2s^2 + 4$ 6
3. $-3y^7 + 5y^5 - 12y + 2 = 6$ 7
4. $4 - 7x = x^2 - 3x^5$ 5

Find all the zeros of the polynomial function. 8. $2, 7, -3i, 3i$ 9. $-3, 2 + \sqrt{3}, 2 - \sqrt{3}$

5. $h(x) = x^3 - 3x^2 - x + 3$ $-1, 1, 3$
6. $f(x) = x^4 - 4x^3 - 20x^2 + 48x$ $-4, 0, 2, 6$
7. $g(x) = x^3 + 5x^2 + x + 5$ $-5, -i, i$
8. $g(x) = x^4 - 9x^3 + 23x^2 - 81x + 126$
9. $f(x) = x^3 - x^2 - 11x + 3$
10. $h(x) = 2x^4 + x^3 + x^2 + x - 1$ $-1, \frac{1}{2}, -i, i$

Write a polynomial function *f* of least degree that has rational coefficients, a leading coefficient of 1, and the given zeros.

11. $-7, -4$ $f(x) = x^2 + 11x + 28$
12. $1, 2, 5$ $f(x) = x^3 - 8x^2 + 17x - 10$
13. $-3, 0, 1$ $f(x) = x^3 + 2x^2 - 3x$
14. $4, i, -i$ $f(x) = x^3 - 4x^2 + x - 4$
15. $-5, 0, -2i, 2i$ $f(x) = x^4 + 5x^3 + 4x^2 + 20x$
16. $8, 2 + i$ $f(x) = x^3 - 12x^2 + 37x - 40$
17. **Multiple Choice** Which is *not* a possible classification of the zeros of $f(x) = x^4 + 2x^3 - 7x^2 - 7x + 3$ according to Descartes' rule of signs? D

   A. 2 positive real zeros, 2 negative real zeros, and 0 imaginary zeros
   B. 0 positive real zeros, 2 negative real zeros, and 2 imaginary zeros
   C. 0 positive real zeros, 0, negative real zeros, and 4 imaginary zeros
   D. 1 positive real zero, 1 negative real zero, and 2 imaginary zeros

Use a graphing calculator to graph the function. Then use the *zero* (or *root*) feature to approximate the real zeros of the function.

18. $g(x) = x^3 - x^2 - 5x + 3$ $-2.09, 0.57, 2.51$
19. $h(x) = 2x^3 - x^2 - 3x - 1$ $-0.62, -0.50, 1.62$
20. $f(x) = x^4 - 2x - 1$ $-0.47, 1.40$
21. $g(x) = x^4 - x^3 - 20x^2 + 10x + 27$ $-4.09, -0.98, 1.47, 4.60$
22. **Sporting Goods** For 1998 through 2005, the sales S (in billions of dollars) of sporting goods can be modeled by

$S = 0.007t^3 + 0.1t^2 + 1.4x + 70$

where t is the number of years since 1998. In which year were sales about \$78 billion? 2002

23. **Grocery Store Revenue** For the 25 years that a grocery store has been open, its annual revenue R (in millions of dollars) can be modeled by

$R = \frac{1}{10{,}000}(-t^4 + 12t^3 - 77t^2 + 600t + 13,650)$

where t is the number of years the store has been open. In what year(s) was the revenue \$1.5 million? 3 and 9 years after opening

5 Lesson Practice Level B

LESSON 5.8 **Practice B** *For use with pages 387–392*

1. The error is in calling -6 a factor. The correct statement is *If -6 is a solution of the polynomial equation $f(x) = 0$, then $(x + 6)$ is a factor of $f(x)$.*

1. Describe and correct the error in the following statement.

If -6 is a solution of the polynomial equation $f(x) = 0$, then -6 *is a factor of $f(x)$*.

State the maximum number of turns in the graph of the function.

2. $f(x) = x^4 + 2x^2 + 4$ 3 **3.** $f(x) = -3x^3 + x^2 - x + 5$ 2 **4.** $g(x) = 2x^6 + 1$ 5

5. $g(x) = 4x^2 - 5x + 3$ 1 **6.** $h(x) = 3x^7 - 6x^2 + 7$ 6 **7.** $h(x) = 2x^9 - 8x^7 + 7x^5$ 8

Determine the *x*-intercepts of the function.

8. $g(x) = (x + 3)(x - 2)(x - 5)$ $-3, 2, 5$ **9.** $h(x) = (x + 4)(x - 6)(x - 8)$ $-4, 6, 8$

10. $f(x) = (x + 3)^2(x - 2)$ $-3, 2$ **11.** $f(x) = (x + 5)(x + 1)(x - 7)$ $-5, -1, 7$

12. $g(x) = (x + 6)^3(x + 2)$ $-6, -2$ **13.** $h(x) = (x - 8)^5$ 8

Graph the function.

14. $f(x) = (x - 3)(x + 2)(x + 1)$

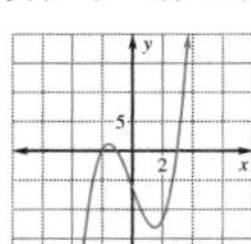

15. $g(x) = (x - 3)^2(x + 2)$

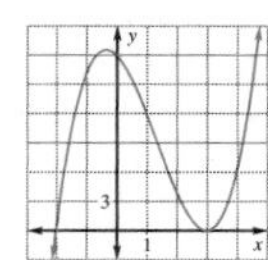

16. $h(x) = 0.3(x + 6)(x - 1)(x - 4)$

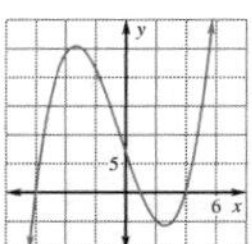

17. $g(x) = \frac{5}{6}(x + 1)^2(x - 1)(x - 4)$

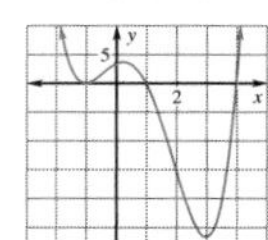

18. $h(x) = (x - 1)(x^2 + x + 1)$

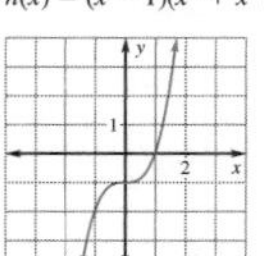

19. $f(x) = (x + 2)(x^2 + 2x + 2)$

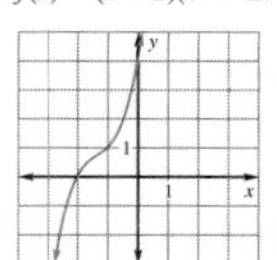

LESSON 5.8

LESSON 5.8 **Practice B** *continued* *For use with pages 387–392*

20. $(-0.5, 0.5)$: max, $(0.5, -0.3)$: min; $-0.9, 0, 0.6$; 3
21. $(-2, 0)$: min, $(-0.5, 5)$: max, $(1, 0)$: min; $-2, 1$; 4
22. $(-2.8, 1.9)$: max, $(0, 0.25)$: min, $(2, 1)$: max; $-3.8, 2.8$; 4

Estimate the coordinates of each turning point and state whether each corresponds to a local maximum or a local minimum. Then estimate all real zeros and determine the least degree the function can have. See above.

20.

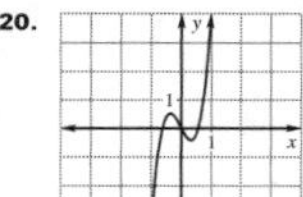

21.

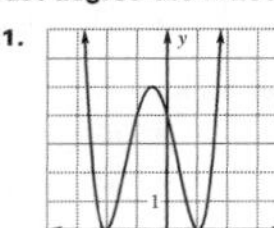

22.

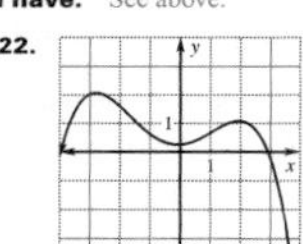

Use a graphing calculator to graph the function. Identify the *x*-intercepts and points where local maximums or local minimums occur.

23. $f(x) = 3x^3 - 9x + 1$ x-int: $-1.79, 0.11, 1.67$; max: $(-1, 7)$; min: $(1, -5)$

24. $h(x) = -\frac{1}{3}x^3 + x - \frac{2}{3}$ x-int: $-2, 1$; max: $(1, 0)$; min: $\left(-1, -\frac{4}{3}\right)$

25. $g(x) = -\frac{1}{4}x^4 + 2x^2$ x-int: $-2.83, 0, 2.83$; max: $(-2, 4), (2, 4)$; min: $(0, 0)$

26. $f(x) = x^5 - 6x^3 + 9x$ See below.

27. $h(x) = x^5 - 5x^3 + 4x$

28. $g(x) = x^4 - 2x^3 - 3x^2 + 5x + 2$ See below.

27. x-int: $-2, -1, 0, 1, 2$; max: $(-1.64, 3.63), (0.54, 1.42)$; min: $(-0.54, -1.42), (1.64, -3.63)$

29. Food The average number E of eggs eaten per person each year in the United States from 1970 to 2000 can be modeled by

$E = 0.000944t^4 - 0.052t^3 + 0.95t^2 - 9.4t + 308$

where t is the number of years since 1970. Graph the function and identify any turning points on the function on the interval $0 \le t \le 30$. What real-life meaning do these points have? $(25.33, 222.93)$; *Sample answer:* From 1970 to 1995, per capita egg consumption decreased to about 223 eggs, then began to increase again.

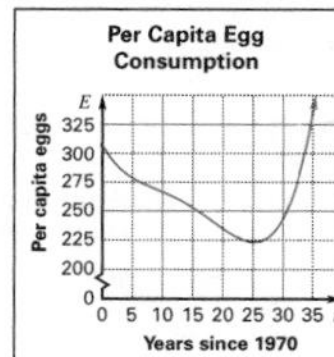

30. Quonset Huts A Quonset hut is a dwelling shaped like half a cylinder. You have 600 square feet of material with which to build a Quonset hut.

a. The formula for surface area is $S = \pi r^2 + \pi r\ell$ where r is the radius of the semicircle and ℓ is the length of the hut. Substitute 600 for S and solve for ℓ. $\ell = \frac{600}{\pi r} - r$

b. The formula for the volume of the hut is $V = \frac{1}{2}\pi r^2\ell$. Write an equation for the volume V of the Quonset hut as a polynomial function of r by substituting the expression for ℓ from part (a) into the volume formula. $V = 300r - 0.5\pi r^3$

c. Use the function from part (b) to find the maximum volume of a Quonset hut with a surface area of 600 square feet. What are the hut's dimensions? 1596 ft^3; $r \approx 7.98$ ft, $\ell \approx 15.95$ ft

26. x-int: $-1.73, 0, 1.73$; max: $(-1.73, 0), (0.77, 4.46)$; min: $(-0.77, -4.46), (1.73, 0)$
28. x-int: $-1.53, -0.35, 1.88, 2$; max: $(0.61, 3.62)$; min: $(-1.05, -3.03), (1.94, -0.03)$

LESSON 5.8

LESSON 5.9 **Practice B** *For use with pages 393–399*

1. $f(x) = (x + 2)(x + 1)(x - 2)$
2. $f(x) = 2(x + 1)(x - 1)(x - 3)$
3. $f(x) = \frac{1}{2}(x - 2)(x - 3)(x - 4)$

Write the cubic function whose graph is shown. See above.

1.

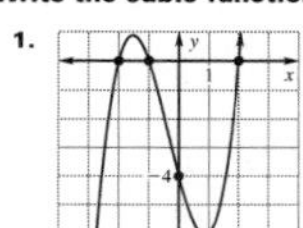

2.

3.

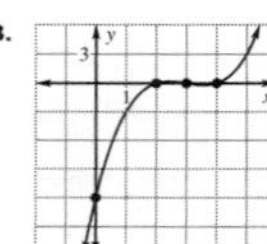

Write a cubic function whose graph passes through the points.

4. $(-2, 0), (0, 0), (1, 0), (2, 1)$ $f(x) = \frac{1}{8}x(x + 2)(x - 1)$

5. $(-4, 0), (-1, 0), (3, 0), (2, -2)$ $f(x) = \frac{1}{9}(x + 4)(x + 1)(x - 3)$

6. $(-5, 0), (3, 0), (4, 0), (-1, -1)$ $f(x) = -\frac{1}{80}(x + 5)(x - 3)(x - 4)$

7. $(-3, 0), (0, 0), (1, 0), (-2, 4)$ $f(x) = \frac{2}{3}x(x + 3)(x - 1)$

Show that the *n*th-order differences for the given function of degree *n* are nonzero and constant. See below.

8. $f(x) = -x^3 + 2x^2 - 1$ **9.** $f(x) = x^4 - 5x^3 + 3$

Use finite differences and a system of equations to find a polynomial function that fits the data.

10.

x	1	2	3	4	5	6
f(x)	5	19	49	101	181	295

$f(x) = x^3 + 2x^2 + x + 1$

11.

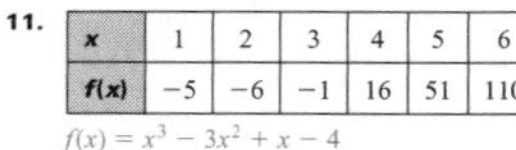

x	1	2	3	4	5	6
f(x)	-5	-6	-1	16	51	110

$f(x) = x^3 - 3x^2 + x - 4$

12. Space Exploration The table shows the average speed y (in feet per second) of a space shuttle for different times t (in seconds) after launch.

t	10	20	30	40	50	60	70	80
y	202.4	463.4	748.2	979.3	1186.3	1421.3	1795.4	2283.5

a. Use a graphing calculator to find a polynomial model for the data. $y = 0.007t^3 - 0.74t^2 + 49t - 236$

b. When the space shuttle reaches a speed of approximately 4400 feet per second, its booster rockets fall off. Use the model from part (a) to determine how long after launch this happens. about 101 sec

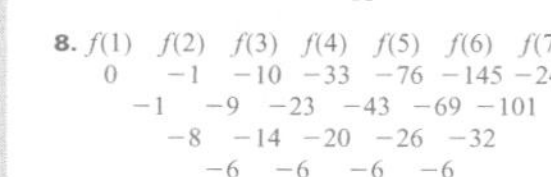

8. $f(1)$ $f(2)$ $f(3)$ $f(4)$ $f(5)$ $f(6)$ $f(7)$
0 -1 -10 -33 -76 -145 -246
-1 -9 -23 -43 -69 -101
-8 -14 -20 -26 -32
-6 -6 -6 -6

9. $f(1)$ $f(2)$ $f(3)$ $f(4)$ $f(5)$ $f(6)$ $f(7)$
-1 -21 -51 -61 3 219 689
-20 -30 -10 64 216 470
-10 20 74 152 254
30 54 78 102
24 24 24

LESSON 5.9

CHAPTER 5

Quiz 1

For use after Lessons 5.1–5.3

Evaluate the expression.

1. $5^5 \cdot 5^{-2}$
2. $(7^4)^2$
3. $\left(\frac{2^{-2}}{3}\right)^2$
4. $\left(\frac{3}{4}\right)^{-3}$

Simplify the expression.

5. $(a^5b^{-7})(a^{-4}b^9)$
6. $(r^{-3}s^4)^{-4}$

Graph the polynomial function.

7. $f(x) = x^3 - 5x + 1$

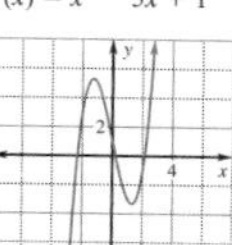

8. $f(x) = -3x^3 - 2x + 4$

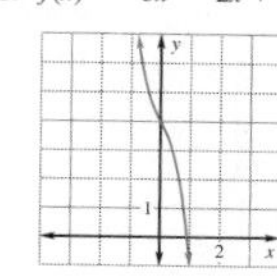

Perform the indicated operation.

9. $(2x^4 + 9x - 7) - (x^4 + 6x + 5)$
10. $(x - 6)(x^2 - 8x + 9)$
11. $(x - 2)(x + 3)(x - 5)$
12. $(7x - 3)^2$

13. **Brain Cells** An ant brain has approximately 300,000 brain cells. If an army ant colony consists of 75,000 members, how many brain cells do they share all together? Write your answer in scientific notation.

Answers

1. 125
2. 5,764,801
3. $\frac{1}{144}$
4. $\frac{64}{27}$
5. ab^2
6. $\frac{r^{12}}{s^{16}}$
7. See left.
8. See left.
9. $x^4 + 3x - 12$
10. $x^3 - 14x^2 + 57x - 54$
11. $x^3 - 4x^2 - 11x + 30$
12. $49x^2 - 42x + 9$
13. 2.25×10^{10}

CHAPTER 5

Quiz 2

For use after Lessons 5.4–5.6

Factor the polynomial completely.

1. $3x^3 - 81$
2. $3x^3 + 6x^2 + x + 2$
3. $4x^7 - 64x^3$
4. $5x^2 - 20x - 25$

Divide using polynomial long division or synthetic division.

5. $(x^4 + 10x^3 + 8x^2 - 59x + 40) \div (x^2 + 3x - 5)$
6. $(2x^3 - 25x^2 + 83x - 88) \div (x - 8)$

Find all real zeros of the function.

7. $f(x) = x^3 - 3x^2 - x + 3$
8. $f(x) = x^3 - 6x^2 + 4x - 24$
9. $f(x) = x^4 - 2x^3 - 8x^2 + 8x + 16$

10. **Construction** You have 432 cubic inches of concrete to make a rectangular prism for a small bench. You want the width and the height to be 6 inches less than the length. What should the dimensions of the bench be?

Answers

1. $3(x - 3)(x^2 + 3x + 9)$
2. $(3x^2 + 1)(x + 2)$
3. $4x^3(x^2 + 4)(x - 2)(x + 2)$
4. $5(x - 5)(x + 1)$
5. $x^2 + 7x - 8$
6. $2x^2 - 9x + 11$
7. $-1, 1, 3$
8. $6, 2i, -2i$
9. $-2, 2, 1 + \sqrt{5}, 1 - \sqrt{5}$
10. 6 in. by 6 in. by 12 in.

CHAPTER 5

Quiz 3

For use after Lessons 5.7–5.9

Find all zeros of the polynomial function.

1. $g(x) = x^3 - 2x^2 - x + 2$
2. $h(x) = 2x^4 - 3x^3 - 27x^2 + 62x - 24$

Write a polynomial function *f* of least degree that has rational coefficients, a leading coefficient of 1, and the given zeros.

3. $-2, 5, 3$
4. $2, i, -i$
5. $-3, \sqrt{2}, -\sqrt{2}$

Graph the function.

6. $f(x) = (x - 5)(x + 5)(x - 1)$

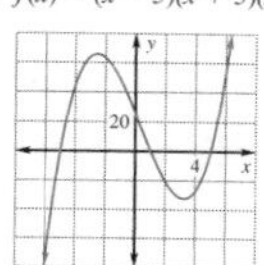

7. $f(x) = x(x - 1)(x + 2)(x - 3)$

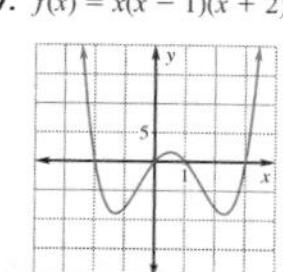

Write a cubic function whose graph passes through the given points.

8. $(-3, 0), (3, 0), (-4, 0), (-5, 8)$
9. $(2, 0), (-5, 0), (-1, 0), (0, 10)$

10. Use finite differences and a system of equations to find a polynomial function that fits the data in the table.

x	1	2	3	4	5	6
$f(x)$	9	21	43	75	117	169

Answers

1. $-1, 1, 2$
2. $-4, \frac{1}{2}, 2, 3$
3. $f(x) = x^3 - 6x^2 - x + 30$
4. $f(x) = x^3 - 2x^2 + x - 2$
5. $f(x) = x^3 + 3x^2 - 2x - 6$
6. See left.
7. See left.
8. $f(x) = -\frac{1}{2}(x + 3)(x - 3)(x + 4)$
9. $f(x) = -(x - 2)(x + 5)(x + 1)$
10. $f(x) = 5x^2 - 3x + 7$

5 Assessment

CHAPTER 5 Chapter Test B
For use after Chapter 5

1. Write $(4.3 \times 10^4)^{-2}$ in scientific notation.
2. Simplify $(q^2u^4)^{-2}$.
3. Use direct substitution to evaluate $-2x^3 + 2x^2 + 6x - 4$ for $x = -1$.
4. Use synthetic substitution to evaluate $2x^4 - 4x^2 + x - 20$ for $x = 2$.
5. Graph $f(x) = 4x^3 - 4x - 2$.

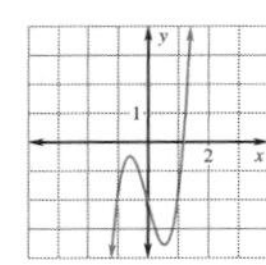

Perform the indicated operation.

6. $(y^5 - 2y^2 - y^4) + (3y^2 - y^4)$
7. $(x^2 - 2x + 4)(3 - x)^2$

Factor the polynomial completely using any method.

8. $\frac{1}{4}x^4 - 4$
9. $y^3 + 6y^2 - 3y - 18$
10. **Shipping** A shipping box is shaped like a rectangular prism. It has a total volume of 96 cubic inches. The height is two inches less than the width and the length is eight inches longer than the width. What are the dimensions of the box?

Divide using polynomial long division or synthetic division.

11. $(x^3 - 13x - 12) \div (x - 4)$
12. $(x^3 + 6x^2 - 9x - 54) \div (x - 3)$
13. Find the other zeros of $f(x) = x^3 + 5x^2 - 18x - 72$ given that one zero is 4.

Answers

1. 5.408×10^{-10}
2. $q^{-4}u^{-8}$
3. -6
4. -2
5. See left.
6. $y^5 - 2y^4 + y^2$
7. $x^4 - 8x^3 + 25x^2 - 42x + 36$
8. $\left(\frac{1}{2}x^2 - 2\right)\left(\frac{1}{2}x^2 + 2\right)$
9. $(y + 6)(y^2 - 3)$
10. 4 in. × 2 in. × 12 in.
11. $x^2 + 4x + 3$
12. $x^2 + 9x + 18$
13. -6 and -3

CHAPTER 5 Chapter Test B *continued*
For use after Chapter 5

14. List the possible rational zeros of $f(x) = 2x^3 + 4x^2 - 6x - 6$ using the rational zero theorem.
15. Find all real zeros of $f(x) = x^3 + 4x^2 - 5x - 20$.
16. Write a polynomial function f of least degree that has rational coefficients, a leading coefficient of 1, and the zeros 2, -3, and $-3i$.
17. Determine the possible numbers of positive real zeros, negative real zeros, and imaginary zeros for $f(x) = x^5 - x^4 + 3x^3 - 2x^2 - 4x + 5$.

Graph the function.

18. $f(x) = x(x + 1)(x - 2)$

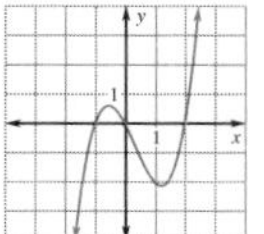

19. $f(x) = -(x + 1)(x - 2)^2$

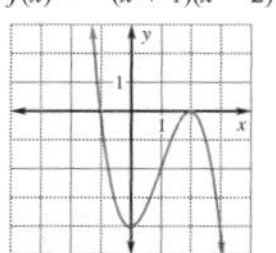

20. Use a graphing calculator to graph $f(x) = (x^2 - 1)(x^2 - 5)$. Identify the x-intercepts and points where local maximums or local minimums occur.
21. Write a cubic function whose graph passes through the points $(-3, 0)$, $(0, -6)$, $(-2, 0)$, and $(1, 0)$.
22. Show that the third-order differences for $f(x) = x^3 - 5x^2 + 3x - 5$ are nonzero and constant.

$f(-1)$ $f(0)$ $f(1)$ $f(2)$ $f(3)$ $f(4)$ $f(5)$

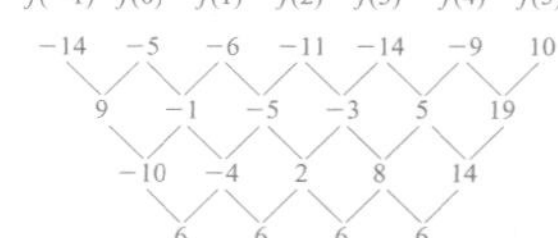

Answers

14. $\pm\frac{1}{2}, \pm 1, \pm\frac{3}{2}, \pm 2, \pm 3, \pm 6$
15. $x = -4, \pm\sqrt{5}$
16. $x^4 + x^3 + 3x^2 + 9x - 54$
17. positive zeros: 0, 2, or 4; negative zeros: 1; imaginary zeros: 0, 2, or 4
18. See left.
19. See left.
20. x-intercepts: -1, 1, $\pm\sqrt{5}$; minima at $x \approx -1.732$ and $x \approx 1.732$; maximum at $x = 0$
21. $f(x) = (x + 3)(x + 2)(x - 1)$
22. See left.

CHAPTER 5 Standardized Test
For use after Chapter 9

Multiple Choice

1. What is the simplified form of $\frac{8a^2bc^{-1}}{12ab^3c}$? B
   - Ⓐ $\frac{2ab^2c^2}{3}$
   - Ⓑ $\frac{2a}{3b^2c^2}$
   - Ⓒ $\frac{2a}{3b^2}$
   - Ⓓ $\frac{2a}{3bc}$
2. What is $(3.2 \times 10^5)(1.4 \times 10^{-2})$ written in scientific notation? A
   - Ⓐ 4.48×10^3
   - Ⓑ 4.48×10^7
   - Ⓒ 44.8×10^3
   - Ⓓ 44.8×10^7
3. Which equation is the graph of the polynomial function shown? A

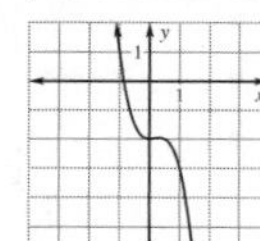

   - Ⓐ $f(x) = -2x^3 + x^2 - 2$
   - Ⓑ $f(x) = 3x^4 - x^2 + 1$
   - Ⓒ $f(x) = x^3 - x + 7$
   - Ⓓ $f(x) = -2x^4 + x^2 - 1$
4. What is the degree of the polynomial $h(t) = -8t^2 + 5 - 3t^3$? C
   - Ⓐ 1 Ⓑ 2 Ⓒ 3 Ⓓ 4
5. What is the greatest common monomial factor of $9x^3y^2 + 15x^2y - 6xy^2$? C
   - Ⓐ $3x^2$
   - Ⓑ $3y^2$
   - Ⓒ $3xy$
   - Ⓓ $3x^2y^2$
6. Which polynomial represents the volume of the cone shown? A

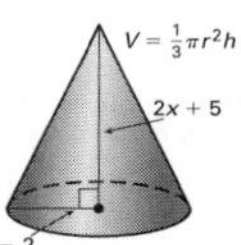

   - Ⓐ $\frac{2\pi}{3}x^3 - \pi x^2 - 4\pi x + \frac{20\pi}{3}$
   - Ⓑ $\frac{2\pi}{3}x^2 + \frac{\pi x}{3} - \frac{10\pi}{3}$
   - Ⓒ $\frac{-\pi x^2}{3} - 4\pi x + \frac{20\pi}{3}$
   - Ⓓ $\frac{4\pi x^3}{3} + 4\pi x^2 - 5\pi x - \frac{50\pi}{3}$
7. What is the *complete* factorization of $3x^4 - 3x^2$? B
   - Ⓐ $3x^2(x^2 - 1)$
   - Ⓑ $3x^2(x - 1)(x + 1)$
   - Ⓒ $3x(x - 1)(x + 1)$
   - Ⓓ $3(x^4 - x^2)$
8. If $x + 3$ is a factor of $x^3 - x^2 - 17x - 15$, what is another factor? A
   - Ⓐ $x + 1$
   - Ⓑ $x - 1$
   - Ⓒ $x + 5$
   - Ⓓ $x - 3$
9. If $x - 2$ is a factor of a polynomial $f(x)$, which of the following statements does *not* have to be true? B
   - Ⓐ $f(2) = 0$
   - Ⓑ $f(-2) = 0$
   - Ⓒ 2 is a root of $f(x)$.
   - Ⓓ 2 is a zero of $f(x)$.

CHAPTER 5 Standardized Test *continued*
For use after Chapter 5

14. a. $V = w^3 - 2w^2 - 120w$ **b.** width: 20 in., length: 30 in., height: 8 in.

10. Which is *not* a possible rational solution of $f(x) = 3x^3 - 11x^2 + 5x - 6$? A
    - Ⓐ $\pm\frac{1}{2}$
    - Ⓑ $\pm\frac{2}{3}$
    - Ⓒ ± 2
    - Ⓓ ± 6
11. Based upon Descartes' Rule of Signs, which of the following is *the only* possible classification of the roots of the function $u(k) = -3k^3 + 5k^2 - k + 4$? A
    - Ⓐ 3 positives, 0 negatives, 0 imaginary
    - Ⓑ 0 positives, 3 negatives, 0 imaginary
    - Ⓒ 1 positive, 1 negative, 1 imaginary
    - Ⓓ 2 positives, 1 negative, 0 imaginary
12. What is (are) the local minimum value(s) for $v(x) = 2x^3 - x^2 + 1$? B
    - Ⓐ 0
    - Ⓑ $\frac{1}{3}$
    - Ⓒ 0 and $\frac{1}{3}$
    - Ⓓ There are none.

Gridded Answer

13. How many solutions does $j(m) = -7m^3 - m^4 + 1$ have?

4

15. a. quadratic; $y = -20.17x^2 + 262.56x + 1144.91$ **b.** 182 **c.** There are two intersection points at $x \approx -2$ and $x \approx 15$. This means that the number of students was 500 in about 1988 and 2005.

Short Response

14. A package has a length 10 inches greater than its width and a height 12 inches less than its width.
    - **a.** Determine the polynomial function which will calculate the volume of a package with width w. See above.
    - **b.** To carry this package onto an airplane, it cannot be larger than 4800 cubic inches. What should its dimensions be if you want to have the maximum allowable volume? See above.

Extended Response

15. The number of students that use a college math lab is tracked for several academic years. The results are summarized in the table below. See left.

Year	1990	1991	1992	1993
Students	1287	1365	1402	1693

Year	1994	1995	1996	1997
Students	1952	1874	2021	2111

Year	1998	1999	2000	2001
Students	1994	1878	1763	1524

   - **a.** Let 1990 correspond to year $x = 0$, 1991 to year $x = 1$, and so on. Enter the data into your graphing calculator and make a scatter plot. Which polynomial function does it seem to model? Use polynomial regression to obtain a model. Round to two decimal places. What is the regression equation you obtained?
   - **b.** Graph the model and predict what the number of students will be in 2006.
   - **c.** Graph $y = 500$ in the same viewing window. Find the intersection point(s). Explain the significance of your results.

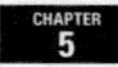

Alternative Assessment and Math Journal

For use after Chapter 5

Journal **1.** If you are asked to write a polynomial function of least degree with zeros of 2 and $\sqrt{7}$, what would be the degree of the polynomial? Explain.

Because 2 is a zero of the polynomial function, you know that $x - 2$ is a factor of the polynomial. Why is the zero (2) related to the factor $x - 2$ instead of the factor $x + 2$?

Multi-Step Problem **2.** You are designing a cylindrical, plastic glass with an outside layer of water that, when frozen, keeps the contents of the glass cold. The outer height of the glass should be four times its outer radius, and the thickness of the sides and bottom of the glass should be 1 centimeter. The glass is to hold 140π cubic centimeters of liquid.

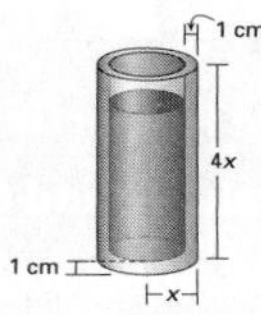

a. Critical Thinking Why might you have chosen 140π cubic centimeters for the capacity of the glass? (*Hint:* 1 fl oz = 29.573 cm^3)

b. Write a function $V_1(x)$ for the volume of liquid the glass can hold. Substitute 140π for $V_1(x)$ and rewrite the resulting equation in standard form.

c. Use the rational zero theorem to list the rational possiblities for the outer radius. Use a graphing calculator to determine which rational possibilities for the outer radius are reasonable.

d. Use the *zero* (or *root*) feature of a graphing calculator and the equation from part (b) to approximate the outer radius of the glass to the nearest whole number.

e. The thickness of the glass (1 cm) includes the thickness of the plastic and the space for the water. Write a function $V_2(x)$ for the volume of the sides and bottom of the glass. Use your answer from part (d) to approximate this volume to the nearest whole number.

f. Challenge If the thickness of the plastic is 0.25 centimeter, approximate the volume of water that can be enclosed in the outer layer of the glass. Explain your answer.

1. Complete answers should include: that the degree must be 3. If $\sqrt{7}$ is a zero, $-\sqrt{7}$ is a zero (irrational conjugates theorem). As implied by the corollary to the fundamental theorem of algebra, a polynomial with three zeros has degree 3; that evaluating the expression when $x = 2$ results in the value of 0, while evaluating when $x = 2$ results in a value of 4. **2. a.** *Sample answer:* The capacity of the glass is a little less than 15 fluid ounces which is ideal for drinks that come in 12-ounce cans. It allows for the entire can of liquid, maybe some ice, and some extra space to avoid spilling. **b.** $V_1(x) = \pi(x - 1)^2(4x - 1)$; $4x^3 - 9x^2 + 6x - 141 = 0$ **c.** $\pm1, \pm\frac{1}{2}, \pm\frac{1}{4}, \pm3, \pm\frac{3}{2}, \pm\frac{3}{4}, \pm47, \pm\frac{47}{2}, \pm\frac{47}{4}, \pm141, \pm\frac{141}{2}, \pm\frac{141}{4}$; None are reasonable. **d.** about 4 cm **e.** $V_2(x) = 4\pi x^3 - \pi(x - 1)^2(4x - 1)$; $V_2(4) \approx 380\ \text{cm}^3$ **f.** 190 cm^3; *Sample answer:* Because the plastic accounts for half of the thickness of the outer layer, it takes up half of the volume of the outer layer.

Alternative Assessment Rubric *continued*

For use after Chapter 5

Journal Solution **1.** Complete answers should include:

- an explanation that the polynomial must be of degree 3. If $\sqrt{7}$ is a zero, then $-\sqrt{7}$ must also be a zero (irrational conjugates theorem). As implied by the corollary to the fundamental theorem of algebra, a polynomial with three zeros has degree 3.
- an explanation that evaluating the expression $x - 2$ when $x = 2$ results in the desired value of 0, while evaluating the expression $x + 2$ when $x = 2$ results in a value of 4.

Multi-Step Problem Solution **2. a.** *Sample answer:* The capacity of the glass is a little less than 15 fluid ounces. This capacity is ideal for carbonated drinks that often come in 12-ounce cans. It allows for the entire can of liquid, maybe some ice, and some extra space to avoid spilling.

b. $V_1(x) = \pi(x - 1)^2(4x - 1)$; $4x^3 - 9x^2 + 6x - 141 = 0$

c. $\pm1, \pm\frac{1}{2}, \pm\frac{1}{4}, \pm3, \pm\frac{3}{2}, \pm\frac{3}{4}, \pm47, \pm\frac{47}{2}, \pm\frac{47}{4}, \pm141, \pm\frac{141}{2}, \pm\frac{141}{4}$;
None of the rational possibilities are reasonable.

d. about 4 cm

e. $V_2(x) = 4\pi x^3 - \pi(x - 1)^2(4x - 1)$; $V_2(4) \approx 380\ \text{cm}^3$

f. 190 cm^3; *Sample answer:* Because the plastic accounts for half of the thickness of the outer layer, it takes up half of the volume of the outer layer.

Multi-Step Problem Rubric

4 The student answers all parts of the problem correctly and completely. The student shows all work. The student's work is neat.

3 The student answers all parts of the problem. The student's work may contain one or two errors in the calculations, functions, or explanations. The student shows most work. The student's work is neat.

2 The student answers all parts of the problem. The student's work contains more than two errors in the calculations, functions, or explanations. The student shows some work. The student's work is sloppy.

1 The student does not complete all parts of the problem. The student's work has several errors in the calculations, functions, or explanations. The student's work is sloppy, or no work is shown.

PLAN AND PREPARE

Main Ideas

Students learn and apply properties of exponents as they simplify expressions involving powers and add, subtract, and multiply polynomials. They learn methods to factor and solve polynomial equations, including the Remainder and Factor Theorems. Using intercepts and other methods, they graph polynomial functions, classify the zeros of the functions, and find all real zeros. Finally, students write higher degree polynomial functions using intercepts and finite differences.

Prerequisite Skills

- Graphing quadratic functions and identifying the vertex and axis of symmetry for the graph
- Factoring quadratic polynomials
- Solving quadratic equations

Additional resources for reviewing prerequisite skills are:

- Skills Review Handbook, pp. 975–1009
- @HomeTutor

5 Polynomials and Polynomial Functions

KY

Before

In previous chapters, you learned the following skills, which you'll use in Chapter 5: graphing functions, factoring, and solving equations.

Prerequisite Skills

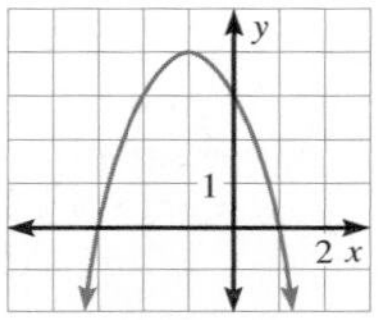

VOCABULARY CHECK

Copy and complete the statement.

1. The **zeros** of the function graphed are _?_. −3 and 1
2. The **maximum value** of the function graphed is _?_. 4
3. The **standard form** of a quadratic equation in one variable is _?_ where $a \neq 0$. $y = ax^2 + bx + c$

SKILLS CHECK

Graph the function. Label the vertex and the axis of symmetry. *(Review pp. 236, 245 for 5.2.)* 4–6. See margin.

4. $y = -2(x-1)^2 + 4$
5. $y = 3(x-2)(x+3)$
6. $y = -x^2 - 4x + 4$

Factor the expression. *(Review pp. 252, 259 for 5.4.)*

7. $x^2 + 9x + 20$ $(x+4)(x+5)$
8. $2x^2 + 5x - 3$ $(2x-1)(x+3)$
9. $9x^2 - 64$ $(3x-8)(3x+8)$

Solve the equation. *(Review pp. 252, 259 for 5.4–5.7.)*

10. $2x^2 + x + 6 = 0$ See margin.
11. $10x^2 + 13x = 3$ −1.5, 0.2
12. $x^2 + 6x + 2 = 20$ $-3 \pm 3\sqrt{3}$

@HomeTutor Prerequisite skills practice at classzone.com

328

Chapter Planning Guide

Chapter 5 Resource Book
- Teaching Guide/Lesson Plan (pp. 3, 14, 26, 37, 47, 58, 69, 82, 98)
- Project with Rubric (p. 111)

Assessment and Intervention
- Assessment Book (pp. 61–75)
- Benchmark Tests
- Remediation Book

Interactive Technology
- Easy Planner
- Power Presentations CD-ROM
- Activity Generator CD-ROM
- Animated Algebra
- Test Generator CD-ROM
- Online Quizzes
- eWorkbook
- eEdition
- @HomeTutor

Resources for English Learners
- Quick Reference for English Learners
- Spanish Study Guide
- Multi-Language Visual Glossary
- Student Resources in Spanish

Now

In Chapter 5, you will apply the big ideas listed below and reviewed in the Chapter Summary on page 401. You will also use the key vocabulary listed below.

Big Ideas

1. **Graphing polynomial functions**
2. **Performing operations with polynomials**
3. **Solving polynomial equations and finding zeros**

KEY VOCABULARY

- polynomial, *p. 337*
- polynomial function, *p. 337*
- synthetic substitution, *p. 338*
- end behavior, *p. 339*
- factored completely, *p. 353*
- factor by grouping, *p. 354*
- quadratic form, *p. 355*
- polynomial long division, *p. 362*
- synthetic division, *p. 363*
- repeated solution, *p. 379*
- local maximum, *p. 388*
- local minimum, *p. 388*
- finite differences, *p. 393*

Why?

You can use polynomial functions to model real-life situations. For example, you can use a polynomial function to model the relationship between the speed of an object and the power needed to maintain that speed.

Animated Algebra

The animation illustrated below for Exercise 61 on page 351 helps you answer this question: How does the power needed to keep a bicycle moving at a constant speed change as the conditions change?

The power exerted by a bicyclist depends on speed and resistance.

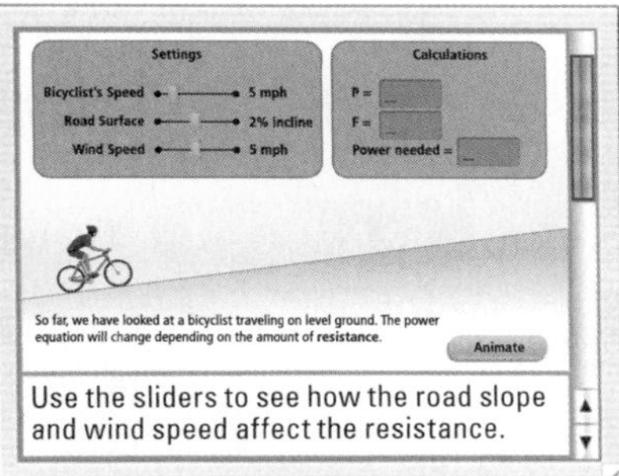

Use the sliders to see how the road slope and wind speed affect the resistance.

Animated Algebra at classzone.com

Other animations for Chapter 5: pages 331, 340, 371, 388, 396, and 401

Algebra 2 Toolkit

- Reading Strategies for Chapter 5, pp. 17–18
- Differentiated Instruction Notes, pp. 59–62
- English Learners Notes, pp. 109–110
- Inclusion Notes, pp. 143–144
- Teaching Strategies with Sample Worksheets, pp. 163–186
- Using Technology in the Classroom, pp. 187–192
- Tips for New Teachers, pp. 201–202
- Math Background Notes, pp. 235–238
- Pre-AP Strategies and Copymasters, pp. 319–320, 377–388
- Teacher Survival Activities, pp. 477–478, 505–506
- Bulletin Board Idea, p. 529
- Teacher Tool Transparencies, following p. 538

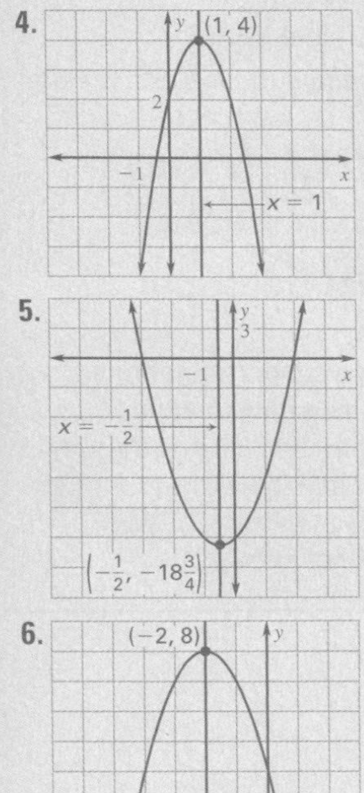

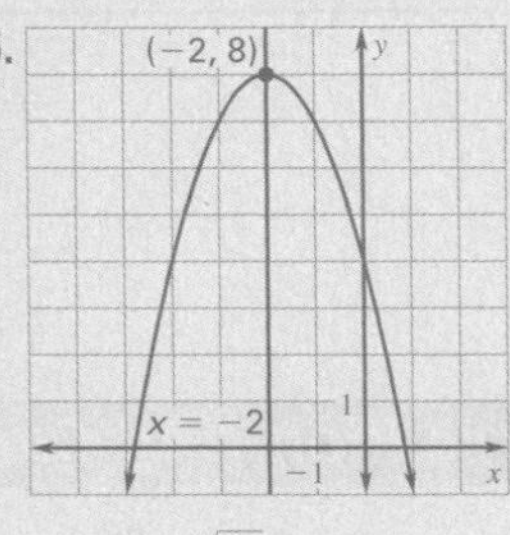

10. $\frac{-1 \pm i\sqrt{47}}{4}$

1 PLAN AND PREPARE

Warm-Up Exercises

Transparency Available

Simplify each expression.

1. $(-2)^3$ -8
2. $5^2 - 3^4$ -56
3. Evaluate $-5xy^2$ when $x = 4$ and $y = -3$. -180
4. A gigabyte is about 10^3 megabytes. A music player has 4 gigabytes of memory. About how many megabytes is this? 4000 megabytes

Notetaking Guide

Transparency Available

Promotes interactive learning and notetaking skills, pp. 132–134.

Pacing

Basic: 1 day
Average: 1 day
Advanced: 1 day
Block: 0.5 block with 5.2
- See *Teaching Guide/Lesson Plan.*

2 FOCUS AND MOTIVATE

Essential Question

Big Idea 2, p. 329

How do you simplify algebraic expressions with exponents?
Tell students they will learn how to answer this question by applying rules for positive, zero, and negative exponents.

5.1 Use Properties of Exponents

MA-HS-5.2.1

Before	You evaluated powers.
Now	You will simplify expressions involving powers.
Why?	So you can compare the volumes of two stars, as in Example 5.

Key Vocabulary
- scientific notation

MA-HS-5.2.1
Students will apply order of operations, real number properties (identity, inverse, commutative, associative, distributive, closure) and rules of exponents (integer) to simplify algebraic expressions. DOK 1

AVOID ERRORS
When you multiply powers, do not multiply the bases. For example, $3^2 \cdot 3^5 \neq 9^7$.

Consider what happens when you multiply two powers that have the same base:

$$2^3 \cdot 2^5 = (2 \cdot 2 \cdot 2) \cdot (2 \cdot 2 \cdot 2 \cdot 2 \cdot 2) = 2^8$$

Note that the exponent 8 in the product is the sum of the exponents 3 and 5 in the factors. This property is one of several properties of exponents shown below.

KEY CONCEPT *For Your Notebook*

Properties of Exponents

Let a and b be real numbers and let m and n be integers.

Property Name	Definition	Example
Product of Powers	$a^m \cdot a^n = a^{m+n}$	$5^3 \cdot 5^{-1} = 5^{3+(-1)} = 5^2 = 25$
Power of a Power	$(a^m)^n = a^{mn}$	$(3^3)^2 = 3^{3 \cdot 2} = 3^6 = 729$
Power of a Product	$(ab)^m = a^m b^m$	$(2 \cdot 3)^4 = 2^4 \cdot 3^4 = 1296$
Negative Exponent	$a^{-m} = \frac{1}{a^m}, a \neq 0$	$7^{-2} = \frac{1}{7^2} = \frac{1}{49}$
Zero Exponent	$a^0 = 1, a \neq 0$	$(-89)^0 = 1$
Quotient of Powers	$\frac{a^m}{a^n} = a^{m-n}, a \neq 0$	$\frac{6^{-3}}{6^{-6}} = 6^{-3-(-6)} = 6^3 = 216$
Power of a Quotient	$\left(\frac{a}{b}\right)^m = \frac{a^m}{b^m}, b \neq 0$	$\left(\frac{4}{7}\right)^2 = \frac{4^2}{7^2} = \frac{16}{49}$

EXAMPLE 1 Evaluate numerical expressions

a. $(-4 \cdot 2^5)^2 = (-4)^2 \cdot (2^5)^2$ **Power of a product property**
$= 16 \cdot 2^{5 \cdot 2}$ **Power of a power property**
$= 16 \cdot 2^{10} = 16{,}384$ **Simplify and evaluate power.**

b. $\left(\frac{11^5}{11^8}\right)^{-1} = \frac{11^8}{11^5}$ **Negative exponent property**
$= 11^{8-5}$ **Quotient of powers property**
$= 11^3 = 1331$ **Simplify and evaluate power.**

Resource Planning Guide

Chapter Resource Book
- Teaching Guide/Lesson Plan (pp. 3–4)
- Activity Master (p. 5)
- Practice levels A, B, C (pp. 6–8)
- Study Guide (pp. 9–10)
- Catch-up for Absent Students (p. 11)
- Application (p. 12)
- Challenge (p. 13)

Workbooks
- Notetaking Guide (pp. 132–134)
- Practice Workbook (pp. 77–78)

Teaching Options
- **Power Presentations CD-ROM** provides dynamic electronic teaching resources for the classroom.
- **Activity Generator CD-ROM** provides editable activities for all ability levels.

Interactive Technology
- Easy Planner
- Power Presentations CD-ROM
- Activity Generator CD-ROM
- Animated Algebra
- Test Generator CD-ROM
- Online Quiz
- eWorkbook
- eEdition
- @HomeTutor

Resources for English Learners
- Quick Reference for English Learners
- Spanish Study Guide
- Multi-Language Visual Glossary
- Student Resources in Spanish

See also the *Algebra 2 Toolkit* for more strategies for meeting individual needs.

SCIENTIFIC NOTATION A number is expressed in **scientific notation** if it is in the form $c \times 10^n$ where $1 \le c < 10$ and n is an integer. When you work with numbers in scientific notation, the properties of exponents can make calculations easier.

EXAMPLE 2 Use scientific notation in real life

LOCUSTS A swarm of locusts may contain as many as 85 million locusts per square kilometer and cover an area of 1200 square kilometers. About how many locusts are in such a swarm?

Solution

Number of locusts	=	Locusts per square kilometer	×	Number of square kilometers

$= 85{,}000{,}000 \times 1200$ **Substitute values.**

$= (8.5 \times 10^7)(1.2 \times 10^3)$ **Write in scientific notation.**

$= (8.5 \times 1.2)(10^7 \times 10^3)$ **Use multiplication properties.**

$= 10.2 \times 10^{10}$ **Product of powers property**

$= 1.02 \times 10^1 \times 10^{10}$ **Write 10.2 in scientific notation.**

$= 1.02 \times 10^{11}$ **Product of powers property**

▶ The number of locusts is about 1.02×10^{11}, or about 102,000,000,000.

VIEW SCIENTIFIC TATION
help with scientific ation, see p. 982.

✓ GUIDED PRACTICE for Examples 1 and 2

Evaluate the expression. Tell which properties of exponents you used.

1. $(4^2)^3$ 4096; power of a power property
2. $(-8)(-8)^3$ 4096; product of powers property
3. $\left(\frac{2}{9}\right)^3$ $\frac{8}{729}$; power of a quotient property
4. $\frac{6 \cdot 10^{-4}}{9 \cdot 10^7}$

$\frac{2}{\times 10^{11}}$; quotient owers property, ative exponent erty

SIMPLIFYING EXPRESSIONS You can use the properties of exponents to simplify algebraic expressions. A simplified expression contains only positive exponents.

EXAMPLE 3 Simplify expressions

a. $b^{-4}b^6b^7 = b^{-4+6+7} = b^9$ **Product of powers property**

b. $\left(\frac{r^{-2}}{s^3}\right)^{-3} = \frac{(r^{-2})^{-3}}{(s^3)^{-3}}$ **Power of a quotient property**

$= \frac{r^6}{s^{-9}}$ **Power of a power property**

$= r^6s^9$ **Negative exponent property**

c. $\frac{16m^4n^{-5}}{2n^{-5}} = 8m^4n^{-5-(-5)}$ **Quotient of powers property**

$= 8m^4n^0 = 8m^4$ **Zero exponent property**

Animated Algebra at classzone.com

TERPRET BASES
this book, it is sumed that any base h a zero or negative ponent is nonzero.

Motivating the Lesson

Ask students if they have grown any cultures in their laboratory courses. Scientists use exponents to model the growth of bacteria in a laboratory. In this lesson students will learn several rules for simplifying expressions involving exponents.

3 TEACH

Extra Example 1

Evaluate the expression.

a. $(-3^2 \cdot 5)^3$ −91,125

b. $\left(\frac{1^4}{3^2}\right)^{-2}$ 81

Key Question to Ask for Example 1

- What is the value of the expression in part (b) if you apply the quotient of powers property first and then the negative exponent property? 1331

Extra Example 2

A Federal Reserve gold bar weighs 400 troy ounces. What is the weight of 250,000 of the gold bars? 10^8 troy oz

Extra Example 3

Simplify the expression.

a. $w^5w^{-8}w^6$ w^3

b. $\left(\frac{c}{d^{-4}}\right)^{-2}$ $\frac{1}{c^2d^8}$

c. $\frac{a^{-3}b^2}{a^5}$ $\frac{b^2}{a^8}$

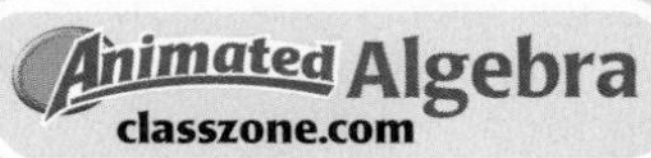

An **Animated Algebra** activity is available on-line for **Example 3**. This activity is also available on the **Power Presentations CD-ROM**.

Differentiated Instruction

Inclusion Students may be overwhelmed by the long list of properties of exponents shown on page 330. Show them with numerical examples how all of these rules can be justified by explicitly writing out the products. For example, it can be shown that $(3^3)^2 = (3 \cdot 3 \cdot 3)(3 \cdot 3 \cdot 3) = 3^6$ without memorizing any of the properties.

See also the *Algebra 2 Toolkit* for more strategies.

Extra Example 4

What is the simplified form of $\left(\frac{a^2b^{-1}}{2a^3b^2}\right)^3$? D

(A) $8a^3b^6$ (B) $\frac{b^9}{6a^3}$

(C) $\frac{1}{8a^3b^6}$ (D) $\frac{1}{8a^3b^9}$

Key Questions to Ask for Example 4

- How is answer B different from answer A? $\frac{1}{x^{11}} = x^{-11}$
- Why is answer D incorrect? **The expression y^0 simplifies to 1, not to y.**

Extra Example 5

The radius of Jupiter is about 11 times greater than the radius of Earth. How many times as great as Earth's volume is Jupiter's volume? **about 1331 times**

Key Question to Ask for Example 5

- Why does $1500r$ represent the radius of Betelgeuse? **The radius of Betelgeuse is 1500 times the radius r of the sun.**

Closing the Lesson

Have students summarize the major points of the lesson and answer the Essential Question: How do you simplify algebraic expressions with exponents?

- **The properties of exponents can be used to evaluate numerical expressions.**
- **Numbers in the form $c \times 10^n$ where $1 \le c < 10$ and n is an integer are in scientific notation.**
- **An algebraic expression is simplified when it contains only positive exponents.**

You simplify an algebraic expression by using the properties of exponents to rewrite it with only positive exponents.

EXAMPLE 4 Standardized Test Practice

What is the simplified form of $\frac{(x^{-3}y^3)^2}{x^5y^6}$?

(A) x^{11} (B) $\frac{1}{x^{11}}$ (C) $\frac{1}{x^6y}$ (D) $\frac{1}{x^{11}y}$

Solution

$\frac{(x^{-3}y^3)^2}{x^5y^6} = \frac{(x^{-3})^2(y^3)^2}{x^5y^6}$	**Power of a product property**
$= \frac{x^{-6}y^6}{x^5y^6}$	**Power of a power property**
$= x^{-6-5}y^{6-6}$	**Quotient of powers property**
$= x^{-11}y^0$	**Simplify exponents.**
$= x^{-11} \cdot 1$	**Zero exponent property**
$= \frac{1}{x^{11}}$	**Negative exponent property**

▶ The correct answer is B. (A) (B) (C) (D)

EXAMPLE 5 Compare real-life volumes

ASTRONOMY Betelgeuse is one of the stars found in the constellation Orion. Its radius is about 1500 times the radius of the sun. How many times as great as the sun's volume is Betelgeuse's volume?

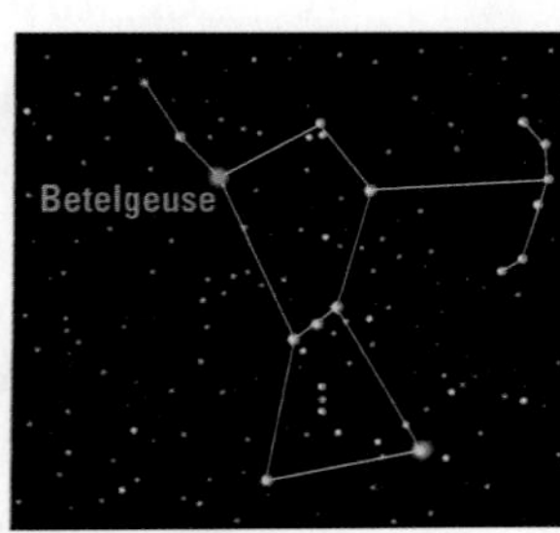

Solution

Let r represent the sun's radius. Then $1500r$ represents Betelgeuse's radius.

$\frac{\text{Betelgeuse's volume}}{\text{Sun's volume}} = \frac{\frac{4}{3}\pi(1500r)^3}{\frac{4}{3}\pi r^3}$	**The volume of a sphere is $\frac{4}{3}\pi r^3$.**
$= \frac{\frac{4}{3}\pi 1500^3 r^3}{\frac{4}{3}\pi r^3}$	**Power of a product property**
$= 1500^3 r^0$	**Quotient of powers property**
$= 1500^3 \cdot 1$	**Zero exponent property**
$= 3{,}375{,}000{,}000$	**Evaluate power.**

▶ Betelgeuse's volume is about 3.4 billion times as great as the sun's volume.

GUIDED PRACTICE for Examples 3, 4, and 5

$\frac{x^3}{y^{24}}$; quotient of powers property, power of a quotient property, negative exponent property

Simplify the expression. Tell which properties of exponents you used.

5. $x^{-6}x^5x^3$ x^2; product of powers property
6. $(7y^2z^5)(y^{-4}z^{-1})$ $\frac{7z^4}{y^2}$; product of powers property, negative exponent property
7. $\left(\frac{s^3}{t^{-4}}\right)^2$ s^6t^8; power of a power property, negative exponent property
8. $\left(\frac{x^4y^{-2}}{x^3y^6}\right)^3$

5.1 EXERCISES

HOMEWORK KEY
○ = WORKED-OUT SOLUTIONS on p. WS9 for Exs. 17, 31, and 51
★ = STANDARDIZED TEST PRACTICE Exs. 2, 36, 46, 51, and 53

SKILL PRACTICE

4. $\frac{1}{4096}$; power of a power property, negative exponent property

A

1. **VOCABULARY** State the name of the property illustrated.

   a. $a^m \cdot a^n = a^{m+n}$ Product of powers property
   b. $a^{-m} = \frac{1}{a^m}, a \neq 0$ Negative exponent property
   c. $(ab)^m = a^m b^m$ Power of a product property

2. ★ **WRITING** Is the number 25.2×10^{-3} in scientific notation? *Explain.* No; 25.2 is not between 1 and 10.

EXAMPLE 1 on p. 330 for Exs. 3–14

9. $\frac{343}{8}$; power of a quotient property, negative exponent property

EVALUATING NUMERICAL EXPRESSIONS Evaluate the expression. Tell which properties of exponents you used.

3. $3^3 \cdot 3^2$ 243; product of powers property
4. $(4^{-2})^3$ See margin.
5. $(-5)(-5)^4$ -3125; product of powers property
6. $(2^4)^2$ 256; power of a power property
7. $\frac{5^2}{5^5}$ $\frac{1}{125}$; quotient of powers property
8. $\left(\frac{3}{5}\right)^4$ $\frac{81}{625}$; power of a quotient property
9. $\left(\frac{2}{7}\right)^{-3}$
10. $9^3 \cdot 9^{-1}$ 81; product of powers property
11. $\frac{3^4}{3^{-2}}$ 729; quotient of powers property
12. $\left(\frac{2}{3}\right)^{-5}\left(\frac{2}{3}\right)^4$ See margin.
13. $6^3 \cdot 6^0 \cdot 6^{-5}$ $\frac{1}{36}$; product of powers prop., negative exponent prop.
14. $\left(\left(\frac{1}{2}\right)^{-5}\right)^2$ See margin.

EXAMPLE 2 on p. 331 for Exs. 15–23

SCIENTIFIC NOTATION Write the answer in scientific notation.

15. $(4.2 \times 10^3)(1.5 \times 10^6)$ 6.3×10^9
16. $(1.2 \times 10^{-3})(6.7 \times 10^{-7})$ 8.04×10^{-10}
17. $(6.3 \times 10^5)(8.9 \times 10^{-12})$ 5.607×10^{-6}
18. $(7.2 \times 10^9)(9.4 \times 10^8)$ 6.768×10^{18}
19. $(2.1 \times 10^{-4})^3$ 9.261×10^{-12}
20. $(4.0 \times 10^3)^4$ 2.56×10^{14}
21. $\frac{8.1 \times 10^{12}}{5.4 \times 10^9}$ 1.5×10^3
22. $\frac{1.1 \times 10^{-3}}{5.5 \times 10^{-8}}$ 2×10^4
23. $\frac{(7.5 \times 10^8)(4.5 \times 10^{-4})}{1.5 \times 10^7}$ 2.25×10^{-2}

EXAMPLES 3 and 4 on pp. 331–332 for Exs. 24–39

2. $\frac{3}{2}$; power of a quotient property, product of powers property, negative exponent property

SIMPLIFYING ALGEBRAIC EXPRESSIONS Simplify the expression. Tell which properties of exponents you used. 24–35. See margin.

24. $\frac{w^{-2}}{w^6}$
25. $(2^2y^3)^5$
26. $(p^3q^2)^{-1}$
27. $(w^3x^{-2})(w^6x^{-1})$
28. $(5s^{-2}t^4)^{-3}$
29. $(3a^3b^5)^{-3}$
30. $\frac{x^{-1}y^2}{x^2y^{-1}}$
31. $\frac{3c^3d}{9cd^{-1}}$
32. $\frac{4r^4s^5}{24r^4s^{-5}}$
33. $\frac{2a^3b^{-4}}{3a^5b^{-2}}$
34. $\frac{y^{11}}{4z^3} \cdot \frac{8z^7}{y^7}$
35. $\frac{x^2y^{-3}}{3y^2} \cdot \frac{y^2}{x^{-4}}$

36. ★ **MULTIPLE CHOICE** What is the simplified form of $\frac{2x^2y}{6xy^{-1}}$? B

Ⓐ $\frac{y^2}{3}$ Ⓑ $\frac{xy^2}{3}$ Ⓒ $\frac{x}{3}$ Ⓓ $\frac{1}{3}$

4 PRACTICE AND APPLY

Assignment Guide

Answer Transparencies available for all exercises

Basic:
Day 1: SRH p. 982 Exs. 1–4, 21–24
pp. 333–335
Exs. 1–6, 15–17, 25–35 odd, 36–43, 49–52, 56

Average:
Day 1: pp. 333–335
Exs. 1, 2, 7–10, 18–20, 24–34 even, 36–46, 49–53, 56

Advanced:
Day 1: pp. 333–335
Exs. 1, 2, 11–14, 21–23, 24–36 even, 40–48*, 50–54*

Block:
pp. 333–335
Exs. 1, 2, 7–10, 18–20, 24–34 even, 36–46, 49–53, 56

Differentiated Instruction

See *Algebra 2 Best Practices Toolkit* for suggestions on addressing the needs of a diverse classroom.

Homework Check

For a quick check of student understanding of key concepts, go over the following exercises:

Basic: 4, 16, 27, 33, 49
Average: 8, 20, 28, 34, 49
Advanced: 12, 22, 29, 35, 50

Extra Practice

- Student Edition, p. 1014
- Chapter 5 Resource Book: Practice levels A, B, C, pp. 6–8

Practice Worksheet

An easily-readable reduced practice page (with answers) for this lesson can be found on p. 328C.

14. 1024; power of a power property, power of a quotient property, negative exponent property

24–35. See Additional Answers beginning on p. AA1.

Mathematical Reasoning

Exercise 13 To demonstrate why $6^0 = 1$, use the sequence $6^5 = 7776$, $6^4 = 1296$, $6^3 = 216$, $6^2 = 36$, and $6^1 = 6$. Since each power of 6 is one-sixth of the previous power, it follows that $\frac{6^1}{6} = \frac{6}{6} = 1$.

Avoiding Common Errors

Exercises 40–42 Remind students that since area is measured in square units and volume is measured in cubic units, their expressions for area and volume should have x^2-terms and x^3-terms, respectively.

Exercise 54 More information about the layers of Earth can be found at www.seismo.unr.edu/ftp/pub/louie/class/100/interior.html

37. The exponents should be subtracted, not divided; x^8.

ERROR ANALYSIS *Describe* and correct the error in simplifying the expression.

37. $\frac{x^{10}}{x^2} = x^5$ ✗

38. 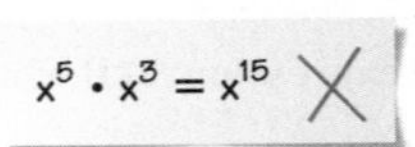
$x^5 \cdot x^3 = x^{15}$ ✗

The exponents should be added, not multiplied; x^8.

39. $(-3)^2(-3)^4 = 9^6$ ✗

The base should not change; $(-3)^6$.

B

GEOMETRY Write an expression for the figure's area or volume in terms of x.

40. $A = \frac{\sqrt{3}}{4}s^2$ $\frac{x^2\sqrt{3}}{36}$

41. $V = \pi r^2 h$ $\frac{\pi x^3}{2}$

42. $V = \ell wh$ $\frac{10x^3}{3}$

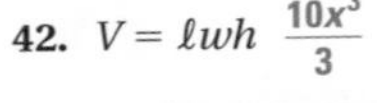

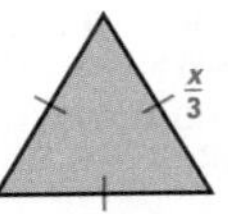

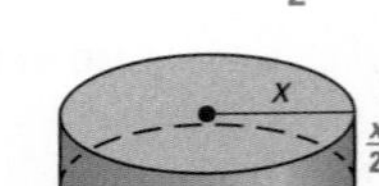

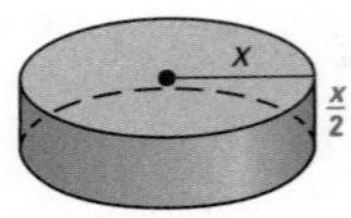

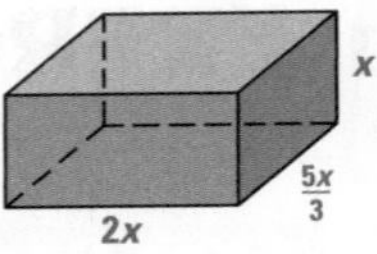

REASONING Write an expression that makes the statement true.

43. $x^{15}y^{12}z^8 = x^4y^7z^{11} \cdot ?$ $x^{11}y^5z^{-3}$

44. $3x^3y^2 = \frac{12x^2y^5}{?}$ $4x^{-1}y^3$

45. $(a^5b^4)^2 = a^{14}b^{-1} \cdot ?$ $a^{-4}b^9$

46. ★ **OPEN-ENDED MATH** Find three different ways to complete the following statement so that it is true: $x^{12}y^{16} = (x^?y^?)(x^?y^?)$.
Sample answer: $(x^6y^4)(x^6y^{12})$, $(x^{10}y^{10})(x^2y^6)$, $(x^8y^7)(x^4y^9)$

CHALLENGE Refer to the properties of exponents on page 330.

C

47. Show how the negative exponent property can be derived from the quotient of powers property and the zero exponent property. $\frac{1}{a^m} = \frac{a^0}{a^m} = a^{0-m} = a^{-m}$

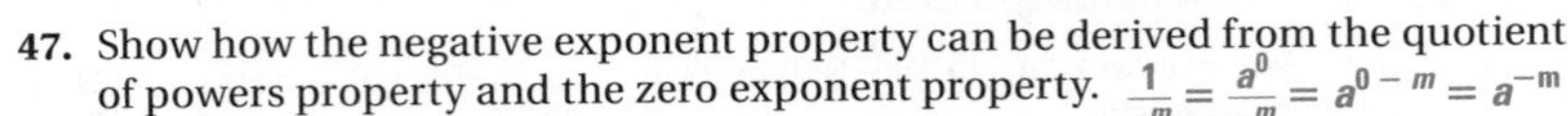

48. Show how the quotient of powers property can be derived from the product of powers property and the negative exponent property. $\frac{a^m}{a^n} = a^m \cdot \left(\frac{1}{a^n}\right) = a^m \cdot a^{-n} = a^{m-n}$

PROBLEM SOLVING

EXAMPLE 2 A on p. 331 for Exs. 49–50

49. OCEAN VOLUME The table shows the surface areas and average depths of four oceans. Calculate the volume of each ocean by multiplying the surface area of each ocean by its average depth. Write your answers in scientific notation. Pacific: 6.2868×10^{17} m³, Atlantic: 3.01824×10^{17} m³, Indian: 2.71656×10^{17} m³, Arctic: 1.7061×10^{16} m³

Ocean	Surface area (square meters)	Average depth (meters)
Pacific	1.56×10^{14}	4.03×10^3
Atlantic	7.68×10^{13}	3.93×10^3
Indian	6.86×10^{13}	3.96×10^3
Arctic	1.41×10^{13}	1.21×10^3

@HomeTutor for problem solving help at classzone.com

50. EARTH SCIENCE The continents of Earth move at a very slow rate. The South American continent has been moving about 0.000022 mile per year for the past 125,000,000 years. How far has the continent moved in that time? Write your answer in scientific notation. 2.75×10^3 mi

@HomeTutor for problem solving help at classzone.com

○ = WORKED-OUT SOLUTIONS on p. WS1 ★ = STANDARDIZED TEST PRACTICE

334

XAMPLE 5
p. 332
Exs. 51–52

51. ★ **SHORT RESPONSE** A typical cultured black pearl is made by placing a bead with a diameter of 6 millimeters inside an oyster. The resulting pearl has a diameter of about 9 millimeters. *Compare* the volume of the resulting pearl with the volume of the bead. *Sample answer:* The volume of the pearl is $\frac{27}{8}$ times as large as the volume of the bead.

B

52. **MULTI-STEP PROBLEM** A can of tennis balls consists of three spheres of radius r stacked vertically inside a cylinder of radius r and height h.

a. Write an expression for the total volume of the three tennis balls in terms of r. $4\pi r^3$

b. Write an expression for the volume of the cylinder in terms of r and h. $\pi r^2 h$

c. Write an expression for h in terms of r using the fact that the height of the cylinder is the sum of the diameters of the three tennis balls. $6r$

d. What fraction of the can's volume is taken up by the tennis balls? $\frac{2}{3}$

53. ★ **EXTENDED RESPONSE** You can think of a penny as a cylinder with a radius of about 9.53 millimeters and a height of about 1.55 millimeters.

a. **Calculate** Approximate the volume of a penny. Give your answer in cubic meters. about 4.4225×10^{-7} m^3

b. **Estimate** Approximate the volume of your classroom in cubic meters. *Explain* how you obtained your answer. Check student's work.

c. **Interpret** Use your results from parts (a) and (b) to estimate how many pennies it would take to fill your classroom. Do you think your answer is an overestimate or an underestimate? *Explain.* Check student's work.

C

54. **CHALLENGE** Earth's core is approximately spherical in shape and is divided into a solid inner core (the yellow region in the diagram shown) and a liquid outer core (the dark orange region in the diagram).

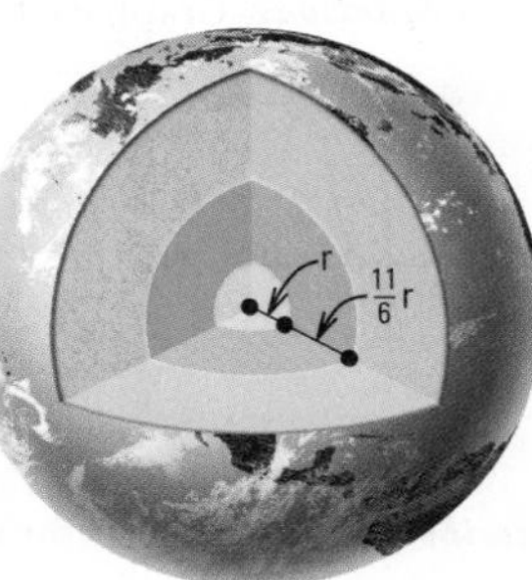

a. Earth's radius is about 5 times as great as the radius of Earth's inner core. Find the ratio of Earth's total volume to the volume of Earth's inner core. $\frac{125}{1}$

b. Find the ratio of the volume of Earth's outer core to the volume of Earth's inner core. $\frac{4697}{216}$

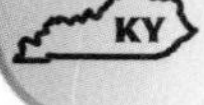

KENTUCKY MIXED REVIEW

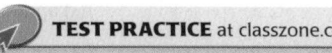

TEST PRACTICE at classzone.com

55. What are the zeros of the function $y = 2x^2 + 5x - 12$? C

Ⓐ $-\frac{3}{2}, -4$ Ⓑ $-\frac{3}{2}, 4$ Ⓒ $\frac{3}{2}, -4$ Ⓓ $\frac{3}{2}, 4$

56. In the diagram, $\overrightarrow{NP}$ bisects $\angle MNQ$ and $m\angle MNP$ is $x°$. Which equation can be used to find y, which represents $m\angle MNQ$? C

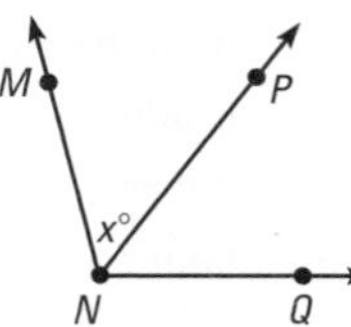

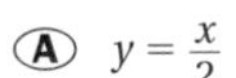

Ⓐ $y = \frac{x}{2}$ Ⓑ $y = x$

Ⓒ $y = 2x$ Ⓓ $y = 180 - x$

5 ASSESS AND RETEACH

Daily Homework Quiz

Transparency Available

1. Multiply $(5.4 \times 10^4)(2.5 \times 10^{-7})$. Write the answer in scientific notation. 1.35×10^{-2}

Simplify the expression. Tell which properties of exponents you used.

2. $\frac{a^2b^{-5}}{3a^5} \cdot \frac{b}{a^{-4}}$ $\frac{a}{3b^4}$; Product of powers, quotient of powers, negative exponent properties

3. The mass of Saturn is about 5.7×10^{26} kilograms. The mass of Jupiter is about 3.7×10^{27} kilograms. About how many times greater is Jupiter's mass? about 6.5 times

Online Quiz

Available at **classzone.com**

Diagnosis/Remediation

- Practice A, B, C in Chapter 5 Resource Book, pp. 6–8
- Study Guide in Chapter 5 Resource Book, pp. 9–10
- Practice Workbook, pp. 77–78
- @HomeTutor

Challenge

Additional challenge is available in the Chapter 5 Resource Book, p. 13.

@HomeTutor classzone.com Keystrokes

1 PLAN AND PREPARE

Explore the Concept

- Students use graphing calculators to investigate the end behavior of the graph of a polynomial function.
- This activity leads into the study of graphs of polynomial functions in Lesson 5.2, Example 4.

Materials

Each student or group of students will need a graphing calculator.

Recommended Time

Work activity: 10 min
Discuss results: 5 min

Grouping

Students can work individually or in pairs. If students work in pairs, they can take turns graphing and explaining end behavior.

2 TEACH

Tips for Success

If students have trouble determining the end behavior from the graph, tell them to examine the table of values on their calculator to examine the behavior of the y-values as the x-values increase or decrease.

Key Discovery

The end behavior of the graphs of $f(x) = x^n$ and $f(x) = -x^n$ is determined by the sign of x and whether n is even or odd.

3 ASSESS AND RETEACH

Compare the end behaviors of the graphs of $f(x) = x^7$ and $f(x) = -x^7$.
For the graph of $f(x) = x^7$: as $x \to +\infty$, $f(x) \to +\infty$; and as $x \to -\infty$, $f(x) \to -\infty$. For the graph of $f(x) = -x^7$: as $x \to +\infty$, $f(x) \to -\infty$; and as $x \to -\infty$, $f(x) \to +\infty$.

5.2 End Behavior of Polynomial Functions

MATERIALS • graphing calculator

QUESTION **How is the end behavior of a polynomial function related to the function's equation?**

Functions of the form $f(x) = \pm x^n$, where n is a positive integer, are examples of *polynomial functions*. The *end behavior* of a polynomial function's graph is its behavior as x approaches positive infinity ($+\infty$) or as x approaches negative infinity ($-\infty$).

EXPLORE **Investigate the end behavior of $f(x) = \pm x^n$ where n is even**

Graph the function. Describe the end behavior of the graph.

a. $f(x) = x^4$ **b.** $f(x) = -x^4$

STEP 1 ***Graph functions*** Graph each function on a graphing calculator.

a.

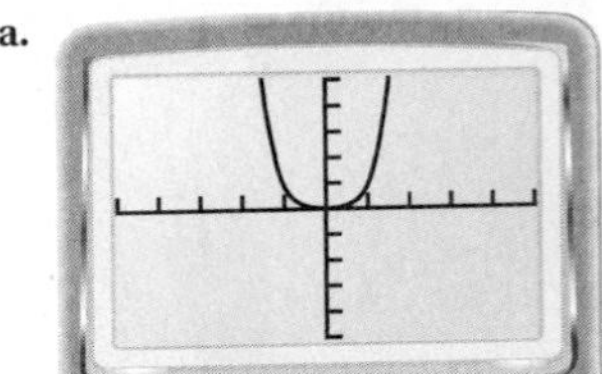

b.

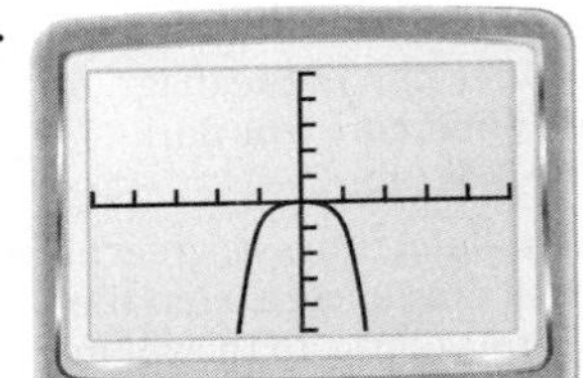

STEP 2 ***Describe end behavior*** Summarize the end behavior of each function.

Function	As x approaches $-\infty$	As x approaches $+\infty$
a. $f(x) = x^4$	$f(x)$ approaches $+\infty$	$f(x)$ approaches $+\infty$
b. $f(x) = -x^4$	$f(x)$ approaches $-\infty$	$f(x)$ approaches $-\infty$

DRAW CONCLUSIONS **Use your observations to complete these exercises**

Graph the function. Then describe its end behavior as shown above. **1–4. See margin.**

1. $f(x) = x^5$ 2. $f(x) = -x^5$ 3. $f(x) = x^6$ 4. $f(x) = -x^6$
5. Make a conjecture about the end behavior of each family of functions. **See margin.**
   a. $f(x) = x^n$ where n is odd b. $f(x) = -x^n$ where n is odd
   c. $f(x) = x^n$ where n is even d. $f(x) = -x^n$ where n is even
6. Make a conjecture about the end behavior of the function $f(x) = x^6 - x$. *Explain* your reasoning.

6. $f(x)$ approaches $+\infty$ as x approaches $-\infty$ and $f(x)$ approaches $+\infty$ as x approaches $+\infty$. *Sample answer:* n is an even power and the end behavior is not affected by subtracting x.

1–4. Check students' graphs.
1. $f(x)$ approaches $-\infty$ as x approaches $-\infty$ and $f(x)$ approaches $+\infty$ as x approaches $+\infty$.
2. $f(x)$ approaches $+\infty$ as x approaches $-\infty$ and $f(x)$ approaches $-\infty$ as x approaches $+\infty$.
3. $f(x)$ approaches $+\infty$ as x approaches $-\infty$ and $f(x)$ approaches $+\infty$ as x approaches $+\infty$.
4. $f(x)$ approaches $-\infty$ as x approaches $-\infty$ and $f(x)$ approaches $-\infty$ as x approaches $+\infty$.
5a–d. See Additional Answers beginning on p. AA1.

5.2 Evaluate and Graph Polynomial Functions

MA-HS-5.1.5

Before	You evaluated and graphed linear and quadratic functions.
Now	You will evaluate and graph other polynomial functions.
Why?	So you can model skateboarding participation, as in Ex. 55.

Key Vocabulary
- polynomial
- polynomial function
- synthetic substitution
- end behavior

MA-HS-5.1.5
tudents will:
etermine if a relation
s a function; determine
he domain and range
f a function (linear and
uadratic); determine
he slope and intercepts
f a linear function;
etermine the
aximum, minimum,
nd intercepts (roots/
eros) of a quadratic
unction and evaluate
function written in
unction notation for
specified rational
umber. DOK 2

Recall that a monomial is a number, a variable, or a product of numbers and variables. A **polynomial** is a monomial or a sum of monomials. A **polynomial function** is a function of the form

$$f(x) = a_nx^n + a_{n-1}x^{n-1} + \cdots + a_1x + a_0$$

where $a_n \neq 0$, the exponents are all whole numbers, and the coefficients are all real numbers. For this function, a_n is the **leading coefficient**, n is the **degree**, and a_0 is the **constant term**. A polynomial function is in **standard form** if its terms are written in descending order of exponents from left to right.

Common Polynomial Functions

Degree	Type	Standard form	Example
0	Constant	$f(x) = a_0$	$f(x) = -14$
1	Linear	$f(x) = a_1x + a_0$	$f(x) = 5x - 7$
2	Quadratic	$f(x) = a_2x^2 + a_1x + a_0$	$f(x) = 2x^2 + x - 9$
3	Cubic	$f(x) = a_3x^3 + a_2x^2 + a_1x + a_0$	$f(x) = x^3 - x^2 + 3x$
4	Quartic	$f(x) = a_4x^4 + a_3x^3 + a_2x^2 + a_1x + a_0$	$f(x) = x^4 + 2x - 1$

EXAMPLE 1 Identify polynomial functions

Decide whether the function is a polynomial function. If so, write it in standard form and state its degree, type, and leading coefficient.

a. $h(x) = x^4 - \frac{1}{4}x^2 + 3$

b. $g(x) = 7x - \sqrt{3} + \pi x^2$

c. $f(x) = 5x^2 + 3x^{-1} - x$

d. $k(x) = x + 2^x - 0.6x^5$

Solution

a. The function is a polynomial function that is already written in standard form. It has degree 4 (quartic) and a leading coefficient of 1.

b. The function is a polynomial function written as $g(x) = \pi x^2 + 7x - \sqrt{3}$ in standard form. It has degree 2 (quadratic) and a leading coefficient of π.

c. The function is not a polynomial function because the term $3x^{-1}$ has an exponent that is not a whole number.

d. The function is not a polynomial function because the term 2^x does not have a variable base and an exponent that is a whole number.

1 PLAN AND PREPARE

Warm-Up Exercises

Transparency Available

Evaluate the expression when $x = -4$.

1. $x^2 + 5x$ -4
2. $-3x^3 - 2x^2 + 10$ 170
3. The expression $x^2 - 4$ represents the amount of matting in square inches that is needed to mat a picture. How much matting is needed if $x = 6$? 32 in.^{2}

Notetaking Guide

Transparency Available

Promotes interactive learning and notetaking skills, pp. 135–137.

Pacing

Basic: 2 days
Average: 2 days
Advanced: 2 days
Block: 0.5 block with 5.1
0.5 block with 5.3

- See *Teaching Guide/Lesson Plan.*

2 FOCUS AND MOTIVATE

Essential Question

Big Idea 1, p. 329

How can you graph a polynomial function? **Tell students they will learn how to answer this question by using a table of values and the characteristics of the graph's end behavior.**

Resource Planning Guide

Chapter Resource Book
- Teaching Guide/Lesson Plan (pp. 14–15)
- Practice levels A, B, C (pp. 18–20)
- Study Guide (pp. 21–22)
- Catch-up for Absent Students (p. 23)
- Problem Solving Workshop (p. 24)
- Challenge (p. 25)

Workbooks
- Notetaking Guide (pp. 135–137)
- Practice Workbook (pp. 79–80)

Teaching Options
- **Power Presentations CD-ROM** provides dynamic electronic teaching resources for the classroom.
- **Activity Generator CD-ROM** provides editable activities for all ability levels.

Interactive Technology
- Easy Planner
- Power Presentations CD-ROM
- Activity Generator CD-ROM
- Animated Algebra
- Test Generator CD-ROM
- Online Quiz
- eWorkbook
- eEdition
- @HomeTutor

Resources for English Learners
- Quick Reference for English Learners
- Spanish Study Guide
- Multi-Language Visual Glossary
- Student Resources in Spanish

See also the *Algebra 2 Toolkit* for more strategies for meeting individual needs.

Motivating the Lesson

Students have used linear equations to model real world situations. Some situations, such as a graph of games won by the school's varsity teams over the last ten years, may not be linear. In this lesson students will examine and use the graphs of nonlinear polynomial functions.

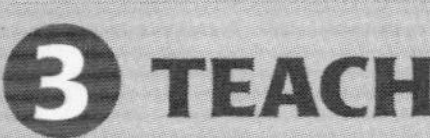

Extra Example 1

Decide whether the function is a polynomial function. If so, write it in standard form and state its degree, type, and leading coefficient.

a. $f(x) = 6x^{1/2} - 5x$ no

b. $g(x) = -8x^5 - 4x^2 + \sqrt{10} + x^4$ yes; $g(x) = -8x^5 + x^4 - 4x^2 + \sqrt{10}$; 5; degree 5; -8

c. $f(x) = x^3 - \frac{4}{5}x^2 - 1$ yes; $f(x) = x^3 - \frac{4}{5}x^2 - 1$; cubic; 1

d. $h(x) = -3x^4 - 9x^{-2} - 4 + x^4$ no

Key Questions to Ask for Example 1

- How do you determine the leading coefficient of a polynomial function? It is the coefficient of the term with the greatest exponent.
- How do you determine the degree of a polynomial function? It is the greatest exponent.

Extra Example 2

Use direct substitution to evaluate $f(x) = -3x^3 + x^2 - 12x - 5$ when $x = 2$. -49

Key Question to Ask for Example 2

- How do you determine the value of 162 in step 3? You evaluate 3^4 and multiply by 2.

EXAMPLE 2 Evaluate by direct substitution

Use direct substitution to evaluate $f(x) = 2x^4 - 5x^3 - 4x + 8$ when $x = 3$.

$f(x) = 2x^4 - 5x^3 - 4x + 8$	**Write original function.**
$f(3) = 2(3)^4 - 5(3)^3 - 4(3) + 8$	**Substitute 3 for *x*.**
$= 162 - 135 - 12 + 8$	**Evaluate powers and multiply.**
$= 23$	**Simplify.**

✓ GUIDED PRACTICE for Examples 1 and 2

Decide whether the function is a polynomial function. If so, write it in standard form and state its degree, type, and leading coefficient.

1. $f(x) = 13 - 2x$
2. $p(x) = 9x^4 - 5x^{-2} + 4$ not a polynomial function
3. $h(x) = 6x^2 + \pi - 3x$

1. polynomial function; $f(x) = -2x + 13$, degree: 1, type: linear, leading coefficient: -2

3. polynomial function; $h(x) = 6x^2 - 3x + \pi$, degree: 2, type: quadratic, leading coefficient: 6

Use direct substitution to evaluate the polynomial function for the given value of *x*.

4. $f(x) = x^4 + 2x^3 + 3x^2 - 7;\ x = -2$ 5
5. $g(x) = x^3 - 5x^2 + 6x + 1;\ x = 4$ 9

SYNTHETIC SUBSTITUTION Another way to evaluate a polynomial function is to use **synthetic substitution**. This method, shown in the next example, involves fewer operations than direct substitution.

EXAMPLE 3 Evaluate by synthetic substitution

Use synthetic substitution to evaluate $f(x)$ from Example 2 when $x = 3$.

Solution

AVOID ERRORS
The row of coefficients for $f(x)$ must include a coefficient of 0 for the "missing" x^2-term.

STEP 1 **Write** the coefficients of $f(x)$ in order of descending exponents. Write the value at which $f(x)$ is being evaluated to the left.

x-value → 3 | 2 −5 0 −4 8 **← coefficients**

STEP 2 **Bring down** the leading coefficient. **Multiply** the leading coefficient by the *x*-value. Write the product under the second coefficient. **Add.**

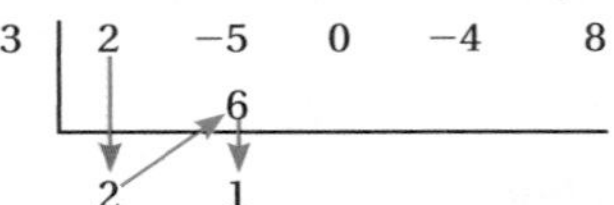

STEP 3 **Multiply** the previous sum by the *x*-value. Write the product under the third coefficient. **Add.** Repeat for all of the remaining coefficients. The final sum is the value of $f(x)$ at the given *x*-value.

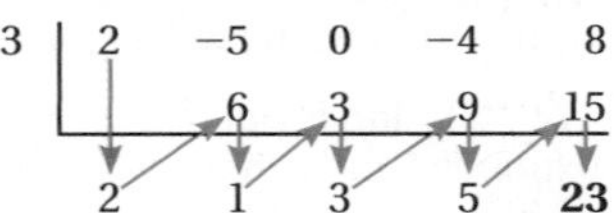

▸ Synthetic substitution gives $f(3) = 23$, which matches the result in Example 2.

Differentiated Instruction

Visual Learners It might be helpful to show students that the synthetic substitution in **Example 3** comes from rewriting the polynomial function as $f(x) = ((((2x - 5)x + 0)x - 4)x + 8)$ and evaluating this function for $x = 3$. Have students rewrite the polynomial functions in **Guided Practice Exercises 4 and 5** to help reinforce why synthetic substitution works.

See also the *Algebra 2 Toolkit* for more strategies.

END BEHAVIOR The **end behavior** of a function's graph is the behavior of the graph as x approaches positive infinity ($+\infty$) or negative infinity ($-\infty$). For the graph of a polynomial function, the end behavior is determined by the function's degree and the sign of its leading coefficient.

EADING
e expression "$\to +\infty$" is read as approaches positive finity."

KEY CONCEPT — *For Your Notebook*

End Behavior of Polynomial Functions

Degree: odd
Leading coefficient: positive

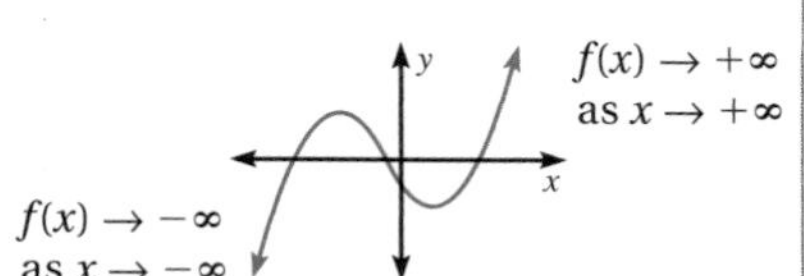

Degree: odd
Leading coefficient: negative

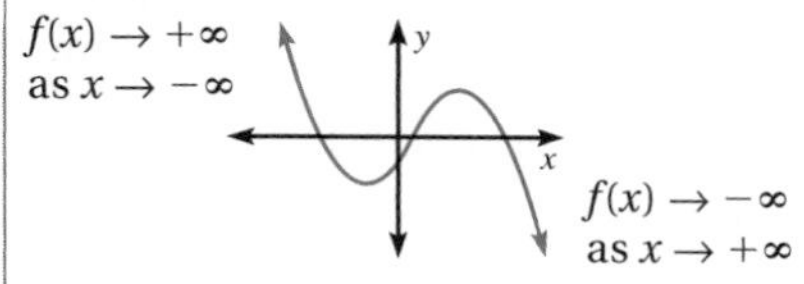

Degree: even
Leading coefficient: positive

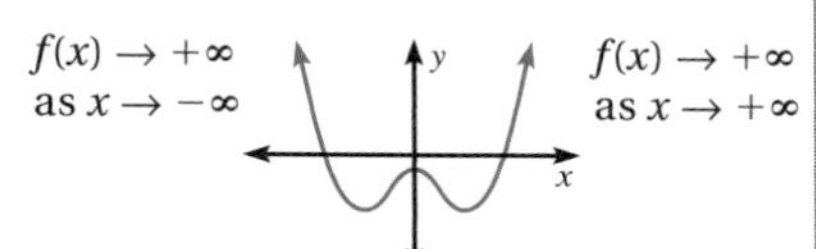

Degree: even
Leading coefficient: negative

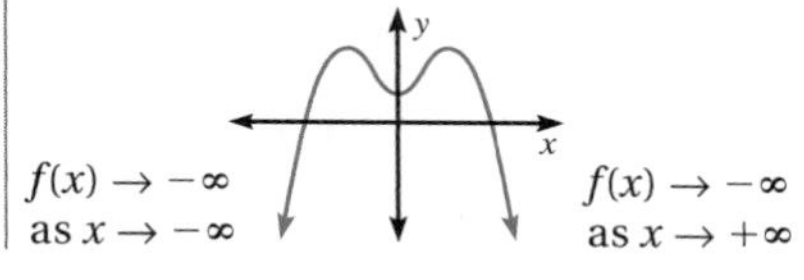

EXAMPLE 4 Standardized Test Practice

What is true about the degree and leading coefficient of the polynomial function whose graph is shown?

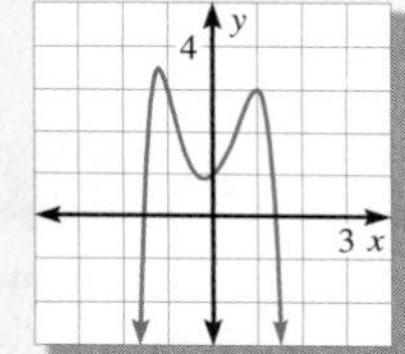

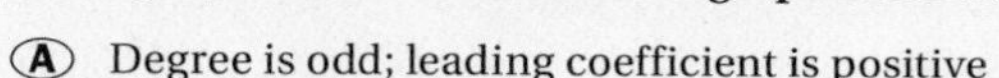

Ⓐ Degree is odd; leading coefficient is positive

Ⓑ Degree is odd; leading coefficient is negative

Ⓒ Degree is even; leading coefficient is positive

Ⓓ Degree is even; leading coefficient is negative

From the graph, $f(x) \to -\infty$ as $x \to -\infty$ and $f(x) \to -\infty$ as $x \to +\infty$. So, the degree is even and the leading coefficient is negative.

▶ The correct answer is D. Ⓐ Ⓑ Ⓒ Ⓓ

GUIDED PRACTICE for Examples 3 and 4

Use synthetic substitution to evaluate the polynomial function for the given value of x.

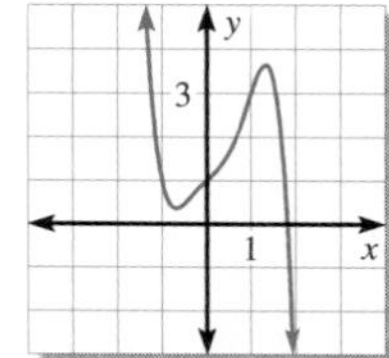

6. $f(x) = 5x^3 + 3x^2 - x + 7;\ x = 2$ **57**
7. $g(x) = -2x^4 - x^3 + 4x - 5;\ x = -1$ **−10**
8. *Describe* the degree and leading coefficient of the polynomial function whose graph is shown.

legree: odd, leading efficient: negative

Extra Example 3

Use synthetic substitution to evaluate $f(x)$ from Extra Example 2 when $x = 2$. **−49**

Key Question to Ask for Example 3

- How do you get "5" in the fourth column of Step 3? **Multiply the previous value in the third column, 3, by the x-value, 3. Write the product 9 in the second line. Add −4 and 9 to get 5.**

Extra Example 4

What is true about the degree and leading coefficient of the polynomial function whose graph is shown? **A**

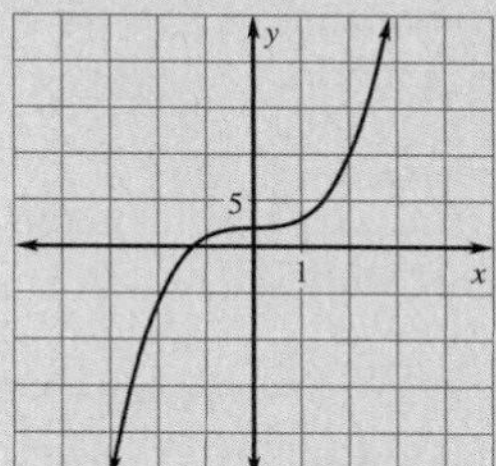

Ⓐ Degree is odd; leading coefficient is positive

Ⓑ Degree is odd; leading coefficient is negative

Ⓒ Degree is even; leading coefficient is positive

Ⓓ Degree is even; leading coefficient is negative.

Key Question to Ask for Example 4

- How can you eliminate answers A and B immediately? **The end behavior shows that the degree must be even.**

Differentiated Instruction

Auditory Learners As an alternative to the Reading tip, students should also learn to read the expression "$x \to +\infty$" as "x increases without bound" and the expression "$x \to -\infty$" as "x decreases without bound." Verbalizing in this manner may be easier for some students to comprehend compared to the more abstract "approaches infinity."

See also the *Algebra 2 Toolkit* for more strategies.

GRAPHING POLYNOMIAL FUNCTIONS To graph a polynomial function, first plot points to determine the shape of the graph's middle portion. Then use what you know about end behavior to sketch the ends of the graph.

EXAMPLE 5 Graph polynomial functions

Graph (a) $f(x) = -x^3 + x^2 + 3x - 3$ and (b) $f(x) = x^4 - x^3 - 4x^2 + 4$.

Solution

a. To graph the function, make a table of values and plot the corresponding points. Connect the points with a smooth curve and check the end behavior.

x	−3	−2	−1	0	1	2	3
y	24	3	−4	−3	0	−1	−12

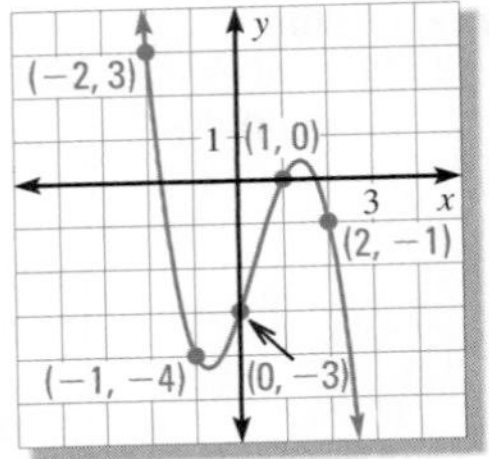

The degree is odd and leading coefficient is negative. So, $f(x) \to +\infty$ as $x \to -\infty$ and $f(x) \to -\infty$ as $x \to +\infty$.

b. To graph the function, make a table of values and plot the corresponding points. Connect the points with a smooth curve and check the end behavior.

x	−3	−2	−1	0	1	2	3
y	76	12	2	4	0	−4	22

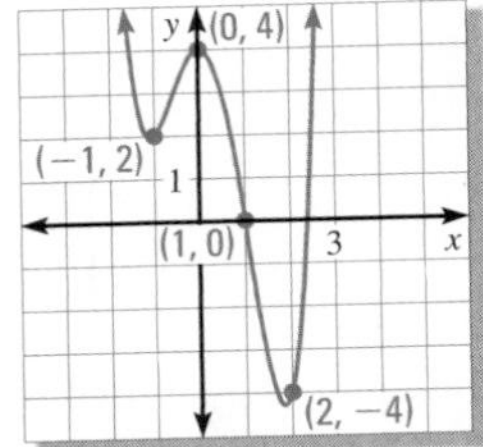

The degree is even and leading coefficient is positive. So, $f(x) \to +\infty$ as $x \to -\infty$ and $f(x) \to +\infty$ as $x \to +\infty$.

Animated Algebra at classzone.com

EXAMPLE 6 Solve a multi-step problem

PHYSICAL SCIENCE The energy E (in foot-pounds) in each square foot of a wave is given by the model $E = 0.0029s^4$ where s is the wind speed (in knots). Graph the model. Use the graph to estimate the wind speed needed to generate a wave with 1000 foot-pounds of energy per square foot.

Solution

STEP 1 **Make** a table of values. The model only deals with positive values of s.

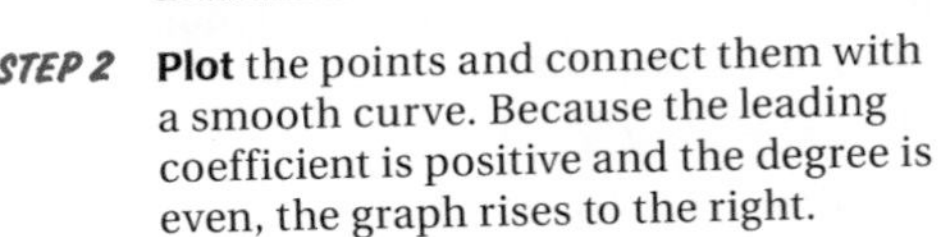

s	0	10	20	30	40
E	0	29	464	2349	7424

STEP 2 **Plot** the points and connect them with a smooth curve. Because the leading coefficient is positive and the degree is even, the graph rises to the right.

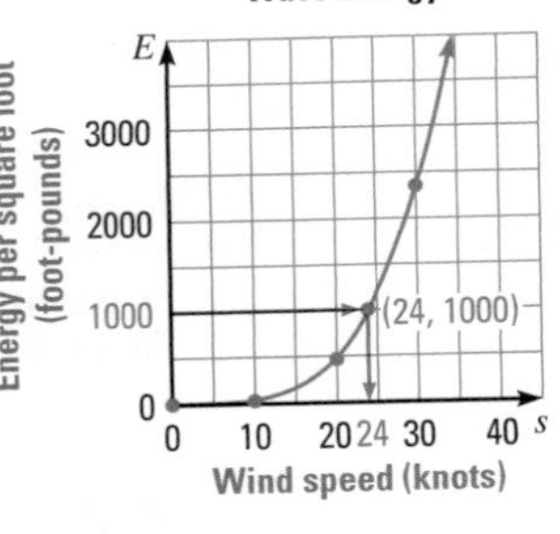

STEP 3 **Examine** the graph to see that $s \approx 24$ when $E = 1000$.

▸ The wind speed needed to generate the wave is about 24 knots.

Extra Example 5

Graph (a) $f(x) = -x^4 + 4x^3 - x^2 + 6$ and (b) $f(x) = x^3 - 3x^2 + x + 1$.

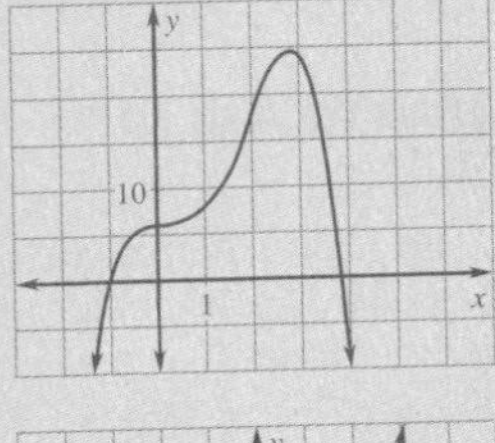

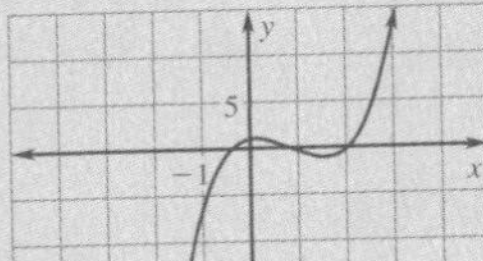

Animated Algebra classzone.com

An **Animated Algebra** activity is available on-line for **Example 5**. This activity is also available on the **Power Presentations CD-ROM**.

Extra Example 6

The length in feet L of each vertical support cable of a suspension bridge can be modeled by the equation $L = 0.0001x^2 + 5$, where x is the distance in feet of each cable from the bridge's vertical axis of symmetry. Graph the model. Use the model to estimate the length of a cable that is 500 feet from the center of the bridge. **30 ft**

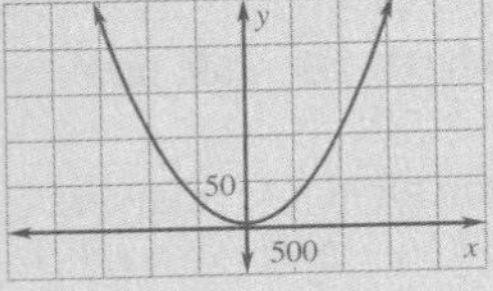

Closing the Lesson

Have students summarize the major points of the lesson and answer the Essential Question: How can you graph a polynomial function?

- **Use direct substitution or synthetic substitution to evaluate a polynomial function.**
- **The end behavior is determined by the degree and the sign of its leading coefficient.**

To graph a polynomial function, plot points to determine the shape of the graph's middle section. Use the end behavior to sketch the ends of the graph.

Guided Practice, p. 341

9.

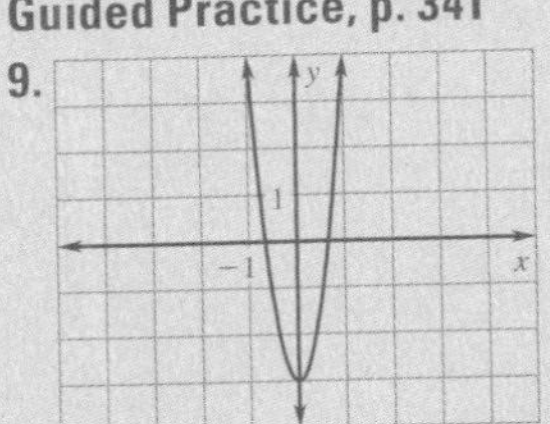

10.

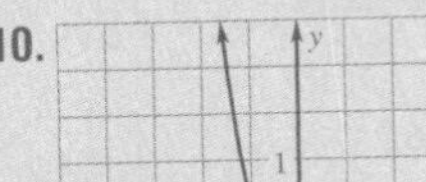

11.

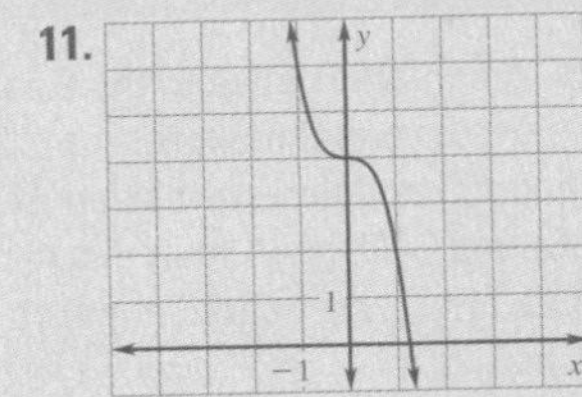

✓ **GUIDED PRACTICE** for Examples 5 and 6

Graph the polynomial function. 9–11. See margin.

9. $f(x) = x^4 + 6x^2 - 3$
10. $f(x) = -x^3 + x^2 + x - 1$
11. $f(x) = 4 - 2x^3$

12. **WHAT IF?** If wind speed is measured in miles per hour, the model in Example 6 becomes $E = 0.0051s^4$. Graph this model. What wind speed is needed to generate a wave with 2000 foot-pounds of energy per square foot? See margin for art; about 25 mi/h.

5.2 EXERCISES

HOMEWORK KEY
- ◯ = **WORKED-OUT SOLUTIONS** on p. WS10 for Exs. 21, 27, and 57
- ★ = **STANDARDIZED TEST PRACTICE** Exs. 2, 24, 37, 50, 52, and 59
- ◆ = **MULTIPLE REPRESENTATIONS** Ex. 56

SKILL PRACTICE

A

1. **VOCABULARY** Identify the degree, type, leading coefficient, and constant term of the polynomial function $f(x) = 6 + 2x^2 - 5x^4$. degree: 4, type: quartic, leading coefficient: −5, constant term: 6
2. ★ **WRITING** *Explain* what is meant by the end behavior of a polynomial function. The behavior of the function as x approaches $+\infty$ and as x approaches $-\infty$.

EXAMPLE 1 on p. 337 for Exs. 3–8

POLYNOMIAL FUNCTIONS Decide whether the function is a polynomial function. If so, write it in standard form and state its degree, type, and leading coefficient. 3–8. See margin.

3. $f(x) = 8 - x^2$
4. $f(x) = 6x + 8x^4 - 3$
5. $g(x) = \pi x^4 + \sqrt{6}$
6. $h(x) = x^3\sqrt{10} + 5x^{-2} + 1$
7. $h(x) = -\frac{5}{2}x^3 + 3x - 10$
8. $g(x) = 8x^3 - 4x^2 + \frac{2}{x}$

EXAMPLE 2 on p. 338 for Exs. 9–14

DIRECT SUBSTITUTION Use direct substitution to evaluate the polynomial function for the given value of x.

9. $f(x) = 5x^3 - 2x^2 + 10x - 15;\ x = -1$ −32
10. $f(x) = 8x + 5x^4 - 3x^2 - x^3;\ x = 2$ 76
11. $g(x) = 4x^3 - 2x^5;\ x = -3$ 378
12. $h(x) = 6x^3 - 25x + 20;\ x = 5$ 645
13. $h(x) = x + \frac{1}{2}x^4 - \frac{3}{4}x^3 + 10;\ x = -4$ 182
14. $g(x) = 4x^5 + 6x^3 + x^2 - 10x + 5;\ x = -2$ −147

EXAMPLE 3 on p. 338 for Exs. 15–23

SYNTHETIC SUBSTITUTION Use synthetic substitution to evaluate the polynomial function for the given value of x.

15. $f(x) = 5x^3 - 2x^2 - 8x + 16;\ x = 3$ 109
16. $f(x) = 8x^4 + 12x^3 + 6x^2 - 5x + 9;\ x = -2$ 75
17. $g(x) = x^3 + 8x^2 - 7x + 35;\ x = -6$ 149
18. $h(x) = -8x^3 + 14x - 35;\ x = 4$ −491
19. $f(x) = -2x^4 + 3x^3 - 8x + 13;\ x = 2$ −11
20. $g(x) = 6x^5 + 10x^3 - 27;\ x = -3$ −1755
21. $h(x) = -7x^3 + 11x^2 + 4x;\ x = 3$ −78
22. $f(x) = x^4 + 3x - 20;\ x = 4$ 248

23. **ERROR ANALYSIS** *Describe* and correct the error in evaluating the polynomial function $f(x) = -4x^4 + 9x^2 - 21x + 7$ when $x = -2$. The coefficient of x^3 was left out; See margin for art.

−2	−4	9	−21	7
		8	−34	110
	−4	17	−55	117

✗

4 PRACTICE AND APPLY

Assignment Guide

Answer Transparencies available for all exercises

Basic:
Day 1: pp. 341–344
Exs. 1–5, 9–12, 15–23 odd, 61–62
Day 2: pp. 341–344
Exs. 24–32, 37–43, 54–58

Average:
Day 1: pp. 341–344
Exs. 1, 2, 5–7, 10–13, 16–22 even, 23, 61–62
Day 2: pp. 341–344
Exs. 24–27, 30–34, 37, 43–46, 50, 54–59

Advanced:
Day 1: pp. 341–344
Exs. 1, 2, 6–8, 11–14, 18–22, 61–62
Day 2: pp. 341–344
Exs. 24–26, 34–37, 44–53*, 56–60*

Block:
pp. 341–344
Exs. 1, 2, 5–7, 10–13, 16–22 even, 23, 61–62 (with 5.1)
pp. 341–344
Exs. 24–27, 30–34, 37, 43–46, 50, 54–59 (with 5.3)

Differentiated Instruction

See *Algebra 2 Best Practices Toolkit* for suggestions on addressing the needs of a diverse classroom.

Homework Check

For a quick check of student understanding of key concepts, go over the following exercises:
Basic: 4, 10, 17, 26, 54
Average: 6, 12, 18, 44, 56
Advanced: 8, 14, 20, 48, 58

Extra Practice

- Student Edition, p. 1014
- Chapter 5 Resource Book: Practice levels A, B, C, pp. 18–20

Practice Worksheet

An easily-readable reduced practice page (with answers) for this lesson can be found on p. 328C.

Guided Practice

12.

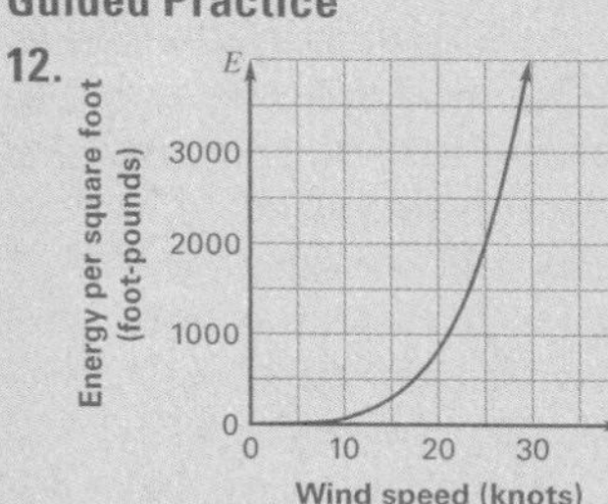

Skill Practice

3–8. See Additional Answers beginning on p. AA1.

23.

−2	−4	0	9	−21	7
		8	−16	14	14
	−4	8	−7	−7	21

38. 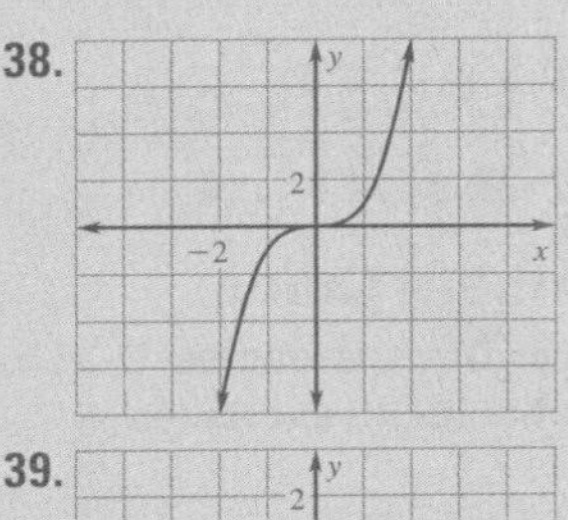

39. 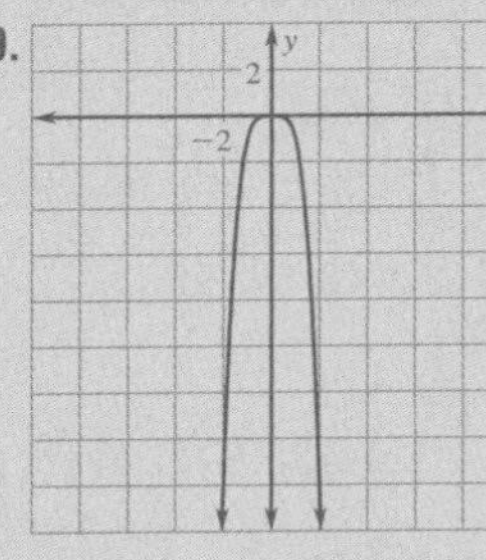

40. 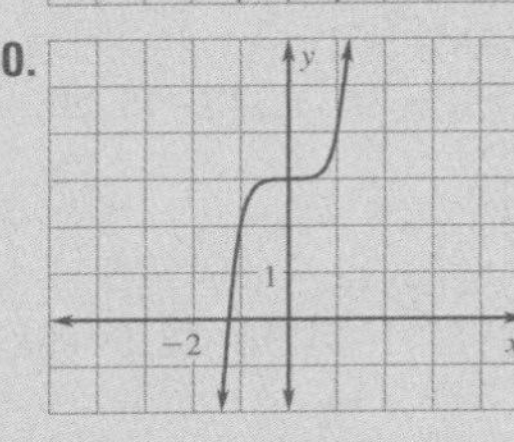

41. 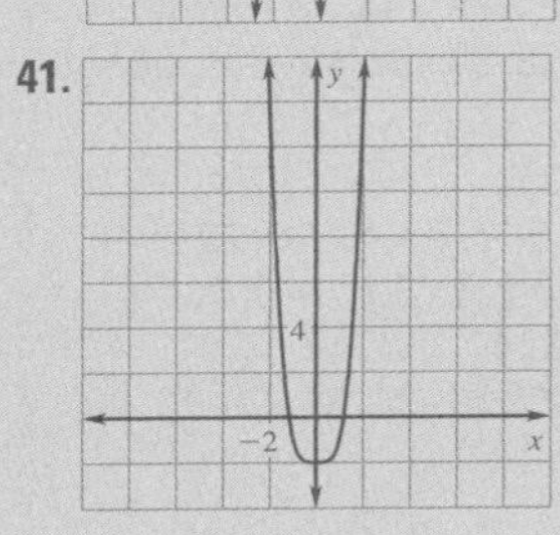

42. 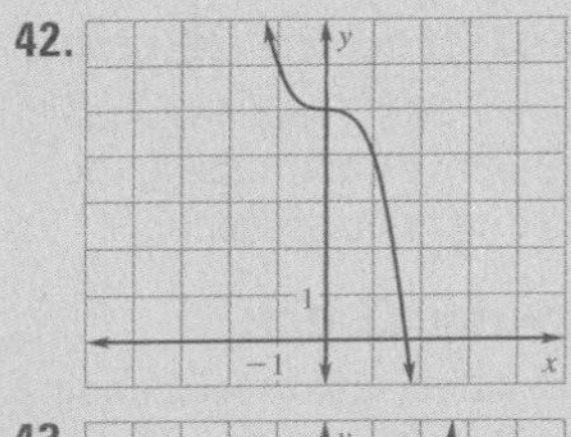

43. 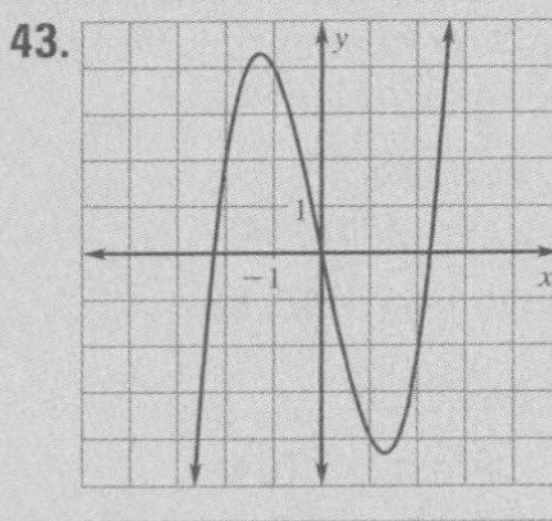

44. 45. 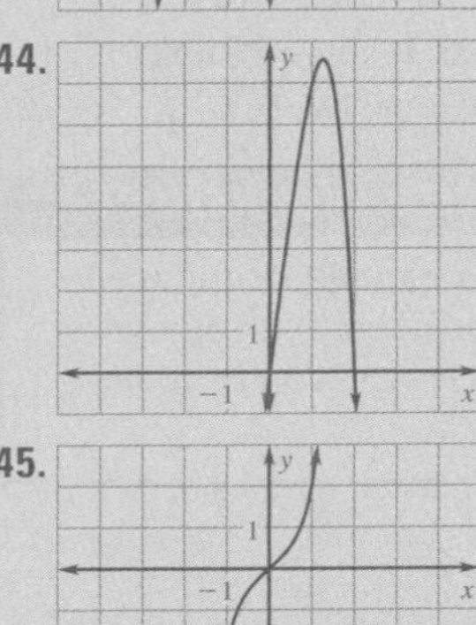

EXAMPLE 4
on p. 339
for Exs. 24–27

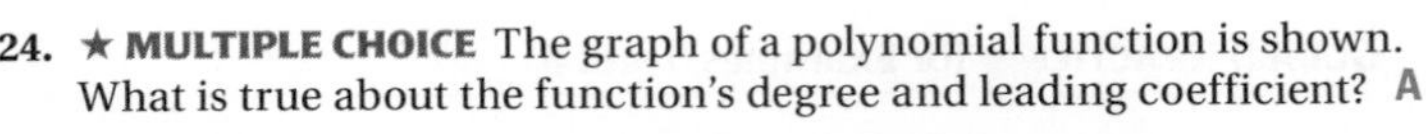

24. ★ **MULTIPLE CHOICE** The graph of a polynomial function is shown. What is true about the function's degree and leading coefficient? **A**

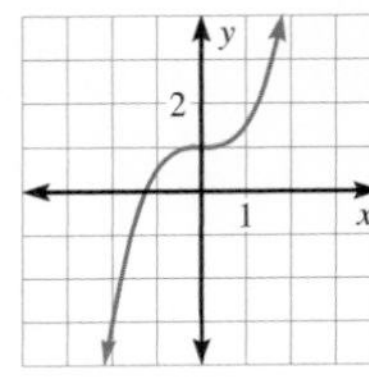

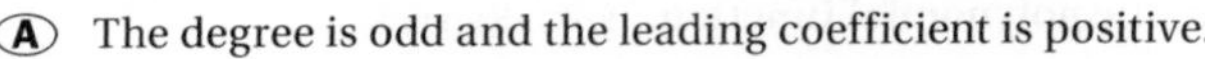

(A) The degree is odd and the leading coefficient is positive.

(B) The degree is odd and the leading coefficient is negative.

(C) The degree is even and the leading coefficient is positive.

(D) The degree is even and the leading coefficient is negative.

USING END BEHAVIOR ***Describe*** **the degree and leading coefficient of the polynomial function whose graph is shown.**

25. degree: even, leading coefficient: positive
26. degree: odd, leading coefficient: negative
27. degree: even, leading coefficient: negative

25. 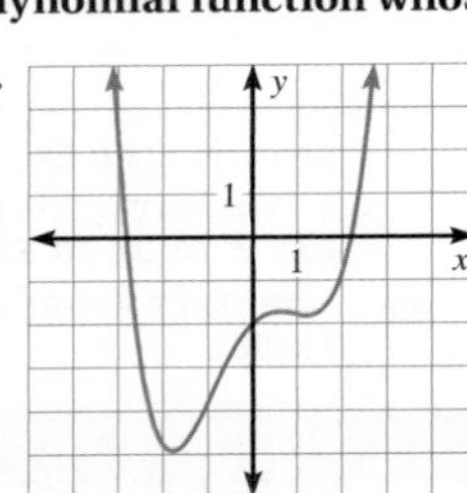

26. 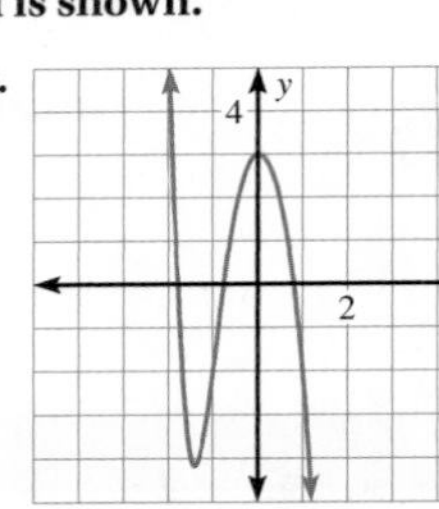

(27.) 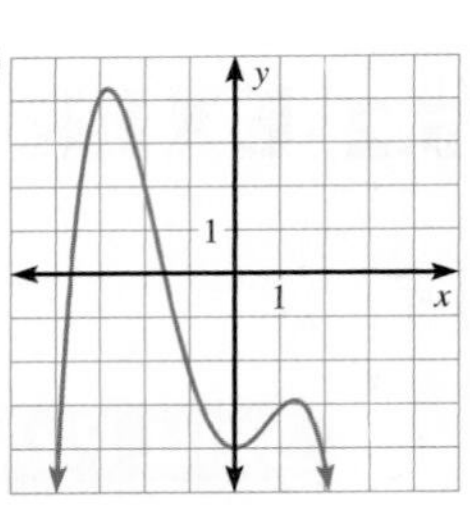

B

DESCRIBING END BEHAVIOR ***Describe*** **the end behavior of the graph of the polynomial function by completing these statements: $f(x) \to$ _?_ as $x \to -\infty$ and $f(x) \to$ _?_ as $x \to +\infty$.**

28. $f(x) = 10x^4$ $+\infty, +\infty$
29. $f(x) = -x^6 + 4x^3 - 3x$ $-\infty, -\infty$
30. $f(x) = -2x^3 + 7x - 4$ $+\infty, -\infty$
31. $f(x) = x^7 + 3x^4 - x^2$ $-\infty, +\infty$
32. $f(x) = 3x^{10} - 16x$ $+\infty, +\infty$
33. $f(x) = -6x^5 + 14x^2 + 20$ $+\infty, -\infty$
34. $f(x) = 0.2x^3 - x + 45$ $-\infty, +\infty$
35. $f(x) = 5x^8 + 8x^7$ $+\infty, +\infty$
36. $f(x) = -x^{273} + 500x^{271}$ $+\infty, -\infty$

37. ★ **OPEN-ENDED MATH** Write a polynomial function f of degree 5 such that the end behavior of the graph of f is given by $f(x) \to +\infty$ as $x \to -\infty$ and $f(x) \to -\infty$ as $x \to +\infty$. Then graph the function to verify your answer. *Sample answer:* $f(x) = -x^5 - 2x^4 + 1$

EXAMPLE 5
on p. 340
for Exs. 38–50

GRAPHING POLYNOMIALS **Graph the polynomial function.** 38–49. See margin.

38. $f(x) = x^3$
39. $f(x) = -x^4$
40. $f(x) = x^5 + 3$
41. $f(x) = x^4 - 2$
42. $f(x) = -x^3 + 5$
43. $f(x) = x^3 - 5x$
44. $f(x) = -x^4 + 8x$
45. $f(x) = x^5 + x$
46. $f(x) = -x^3 + 3x^2 - 2x + 5$
47. $f(x) = x^5 + x^2 - 4$
48. $f(x) = x^4 - 5x^2 + 6$
49. $f(x) = -x^4 + 3x^3 - x + 1$

50. ★ **MULTIPLE CHOICE** Which function is represented by the graph shown? **B**

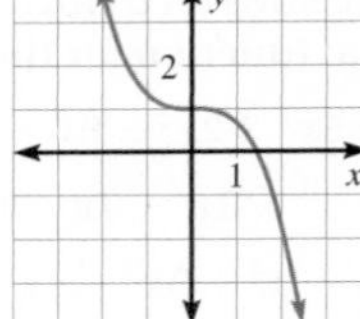

(A) $f(x) = \frac{1}{3}x^3 + 1$ (B) $f(x) = -\frac{1}{3}x^3 + 1$

(C) $f(x) = \frac{1}{3}x^3 - 1$ (D) $f(x) = -\frac{1}{3}x^3 - 1$

C

51. **VISUAL THINKING** Suppose $f(x) \to +\infty$ as $x \to -\infty$ and $f(x) \to -\infty$ as $x \to +\infty$. *Describe* the end behavior of $g(x) = -f(x)$. $g(x) \to -\infty$ as $x \to -\infty$ and $g(x) \to +\infty$ as $x \to +$

52. ★ **SHORT RESPONSE** A cubic polynomial function f has leading coefficient 2 and constant term −5. If $f(1) = 0$ and $f(2) = 3$, what is $f(-5)$? *Explain* how you found your answer. See margin.

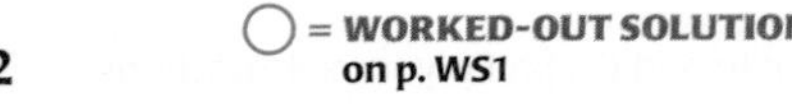

○ = WORKED-OUT SOLUTIONS on p. WS1 ★ = STANDARDIZED TEST PRACTICE ◆ = MULTIPLE REPRESENTATI

46. 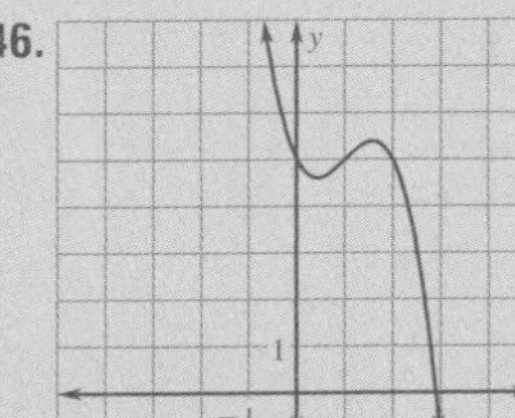

47. 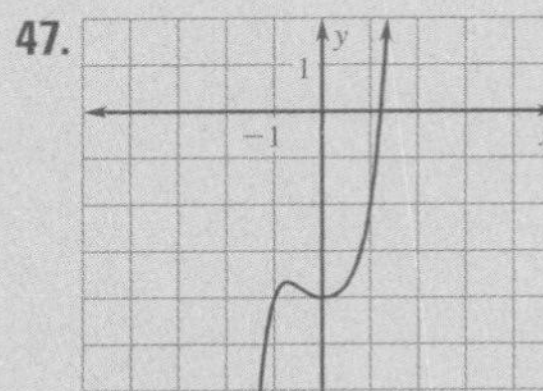

48. 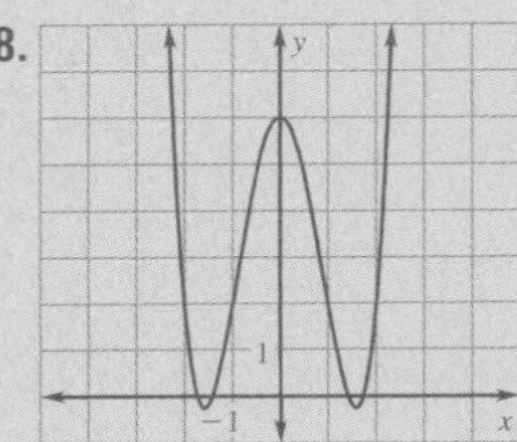

53. **CHALLENGE** Let $f(x) = x^3$ and $g(x) = x^3 - 2x^2 + 4x$.

a. Copy and complete the table. **See margin.**

x	$f(x)$	$g(x)$	$\frac{f(x)}{g(x)}$
10	?	?	?
20	?	?	?
50	?	?	?
100	?	?	?
200	?	?	?

b. Use the numbers in the table to complete this statement: As $x \to +\infty$, $\frac{f(x)}{g(x)} \to$ _?_. **1**

c. *Explain* how the result from part (b) shows that the functions f and g have the same end behavior as $x \to +\infty$.

Sample answer: **As $x \to +\infty$, $\frac{f(x)}{g(x)} \to 1$ and therefore $f(x) \approx g(x)$. So, f and g have the same end behavior.**

PROBLEM SOLVING

AMPLE 6 A
p. 340
Exs. 54–59

54. **DIAMONDS** The weight of an ideal round-cut diamond can be modeled by

$$w = 0.0071d^3 - 0.090d^2 + 0.48d$$

where w is the diamond's weight (in carats) and d is its diameter (in millimeters). According to the model, what is the weight of a diamond with a diameter of 15 millimeters? **about 11 carats**

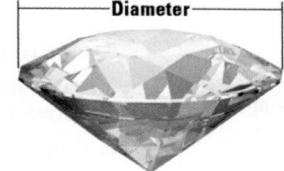

Diameter

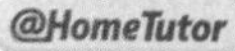

for problem solving help at classzone.com

55. **SKATEBOARDING** From 1992 to 2003, the number of people in the United States who participated in skateboarding can be modeled by

$$S = -0.0076t^4 + 0.14t^3 - 0.62t^2 + 0.52t + 5.5$$

where S is the number of participants (in millions) and t is the number of years since 1992. Graph the model. Then use the graph to estimate the first year that the number of skateboarding participants was greater than 8 million. **See margin for art; 1998.**

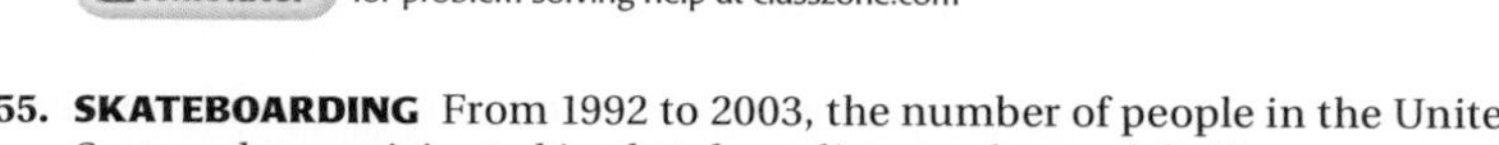
@HomeTutor for problem solving help at classzone.com

56. **MULTIPLE REPRESENTATIONS** From 1987 to 2003, the number of indoor movie screens M in the United States can be modeled by

$$M = -11.0t^3 + 267t^2 - 592t + 21{,}600$$

where t is the number of years since 1987.

a. **Classifying a Function** State the degree and type of the function. **3, cubic**

b. **Making a Table** Make a table of values for the function. **b, c. See margin.**

c. **Sketching a Graph** Use your table to graph the function.

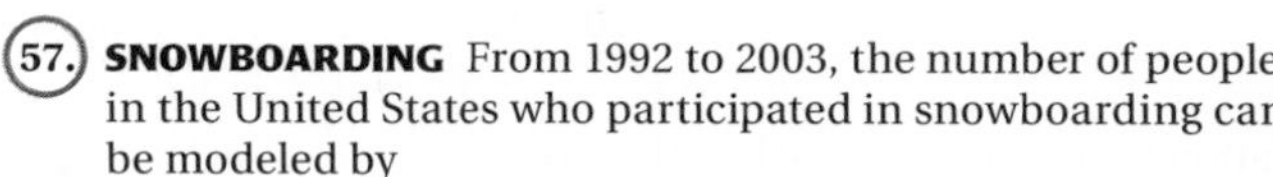

57. **SNOWBOARDING** From 1992 to 2003, the number of people in the United States who participated in snowboarding can be modeled by

$$S = 0.0013t^4 - 0.021t^3 + 0.084t^2 + 0.037t + 1.2$$

where S is the number of participants (in millions) and t is the number of years since 1992. Graph the model. Use the graph to estimate the first year that the number of snowboarding participants was greater than 2 million. **See margin for art; 2002.**

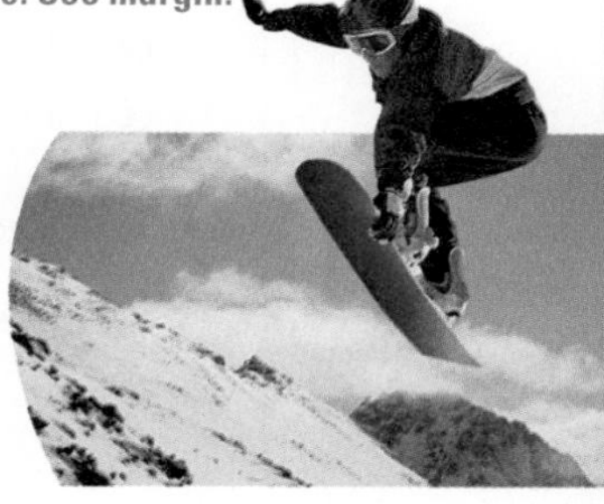

Study Strategy

Exercises 28–36 Students may find it helpful to put the information in the Key Concept box on page 339, into a table, with column headings identifying whether the degree of the function is even or odd and whether the leading coefficient is positive or negative. Then they can use their table to identify the end behavior of each function.

Avoiding Common Errors

Exercises 38–49 Students should be careful when building their table of values that they do not incorrectly evaluate $-x^n$ as $(-x)^n$.

Teaching Strategy

Exercises 55–57 Suggest that students label the year underneath each x-axis. That will help them identify where to place a vertical line to find the y-value.

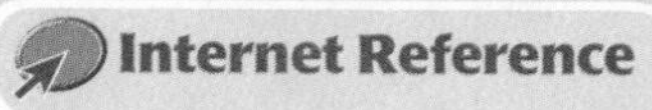

Exercise 59 For more information about the Sarus crane, visit the International Crane Foundation's website www.savingcranes.org/species/sarus.cfm

53a. See Additional Answers beginning on p. AA1.

55.

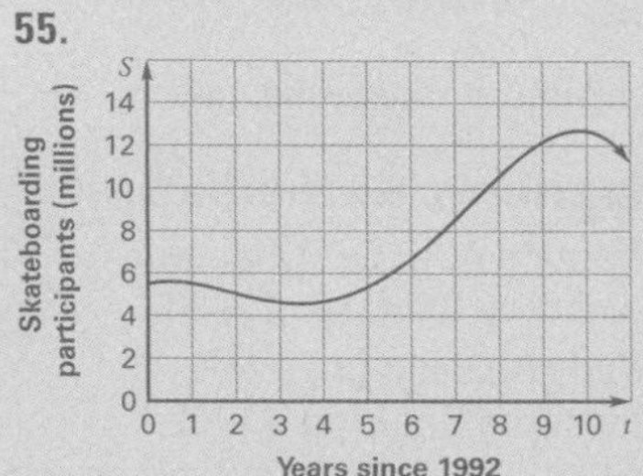

56b–c. See Additional Answers beginning on p. AA1.

57.

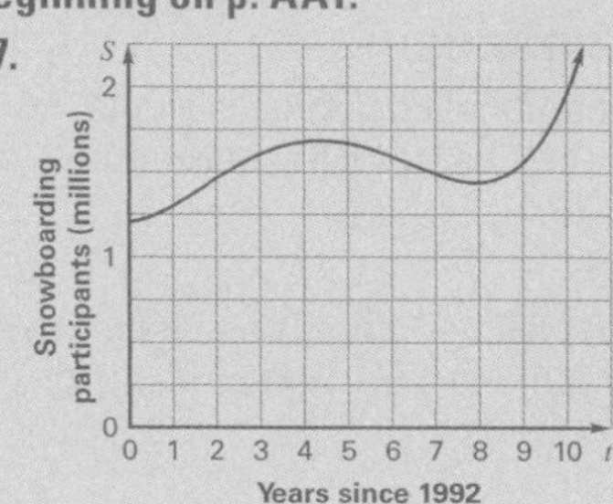

49.

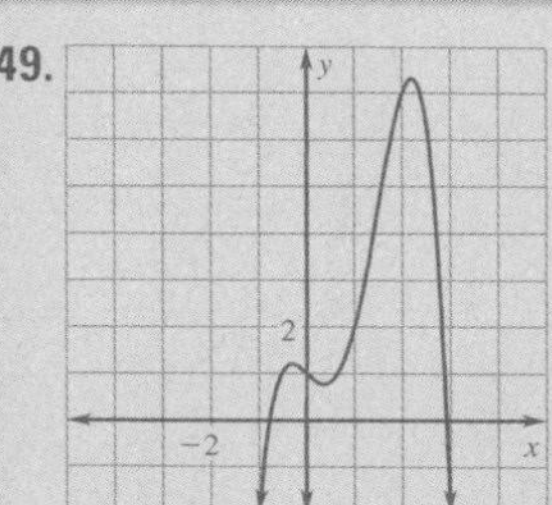

52. −480. *Sample answer:* I used the standard form of a cubic equation, $f(x) = ax^3 + bx^2 + cx + d$, and substituted 2 for a and −5 for d. Then I put in 1 for x and set $f(x)$ equal to 0, and 2 for x and set $f(x)$ equal to 3. This left me with two equations with two variables, b and c. I used substitution to solve for the variables, which gave me the function $f(x) = 2x^3 - 7x^2 + 10x - 5$. Finally, I substituted −5 for x to get −480.

5 ASSESS AND RETEACH

Daily Homework Quiz

Transparency Available

1. Tell whether the function $f(x) = -3x^3 - 5x^{-1} + 8$ is a polynomial function. If so, write it in standard form and state its degree, type, and leading coefficient. **no**
2. Use synthetic substitution to evaluate $f(x) = 4x^4 - x^3 + 3x^2 + 5x - 3$ when $x = -2$. **71**
3. The estimated number of electric vehicles V in the United States from 1995 to 2004 is given by the equation $V = 10x^4 + 200x + 3000$, where x is the number of years since 1995. Graph the model. Use it to estimate the number of electric vehicles in 2003. **45,560**

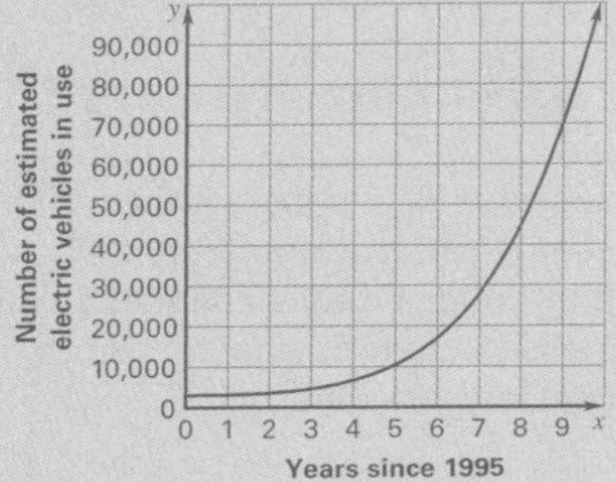

Available at **classzone.com**

Diagnosis/Remediation

- Practice A, B, C in Chapter 5 Resource Book, pp. 18–20
- Study Guide in Chapter 5 Resource Book, pp. 21–22
- Practice Workbook, pp. 79–80
- @HomeTutor

Challenge

Additional challenge is available in the Chapter 5 Resource Book, p. 25.

58b, 59b. See Additional Answers beginning on p. AA1.

58c. 15,700 periodicals; no; *Sample answer:* It seems unreasonable for the number of periodicals to go from 4100 in 2002 to 15,700 in 2010.

59c. Sarus. *Sample answer:* Substituting 3 into each equation gives the Sarus chick weighing about 120 grams and the Hooded chick weighing about 92 grams. The weight of the Sarus is closer to 130 than the weight of the Hooded chick is.

B

58. MULTI-STEP PROBLEM From 1980 to 2002, the number of quarterly periodicals P published in the United States can be modeled by

$$P = 0.138t^4 - 6.24t^3 + 86.8t^2 - 239t + 1450$$

where t is the number of years since 1980.

a. *Describe* the end behavior of the graph of the model. **$P \to +\infty$ as $t \to -\infty$ and $P \to +\infty$ as $t \to +\infty$**

b. Graph the model on the domain $0 \le t \le 22$. **See margin.**

c. Use the model to predict the number of quarterly periodicals in the year 2010. Is it appropriate to use the model to make this prediction? *Explain.*

59. ★ EXTENDED RESPONSE The weight of Sarus crane chicks S and hooded crane chicks H (both in grams) during the 10 days following hatching can be modeled by the functions

$$S = -0.122t^3 + 3.49t^2 - 14.6t + 136$$

$$H = -0.115t^3 + 3.71t^2 - 20.6t + 124$$

where t is the number of days after hatching.

a. **Calculate** According to the models, what is the difference in weight between 5-day-old Sarus crane chicks and hooded crane chicks? **35.625 g**

b. **Graph** Sketch the graphs of the two models. **See margin.**

c. **Apply** A biologist finds that the weight of a crane chick after 3 days is 130 grams. What species of crane is the chick more likely to be? *Explain* how you found your answer.

C

60. CHALLENGE The weight y (in pounds) of a rainbow trout can be modeled by $y = 0.000304x^3$ where x is the length of the trout (in inches).

a. Write a function that relates the weight y and length x of a rainbow trout if y is measured in kilograms and x is measured in centimeters. Use the fact that 1 kilogram ≈ 2.20 pounds and 1 centimeter ≈ 0.394 inch. **$y = 0.0109x^3$**

b. Graph the original function and the function from part (a) in the same coordinate plane. What type of transformation can you apply to the graph of $y = 0.000304x^3$ to produce the graph from part (a)? **Stretch it by a factor of about 36.**

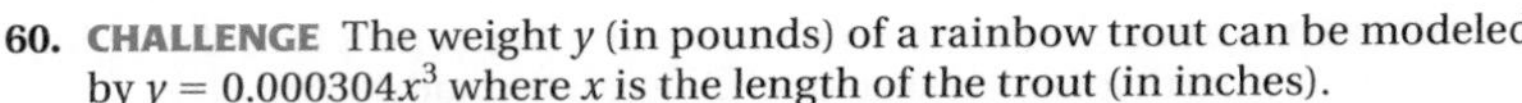

KY KENTUCKY MIXED REVIEW

TEST PRACTICE at classzone.com

61. Amanda starts a business that sells silk-screened shirts. Her overhead costs are \$500, and then she pays an additional \$4.25 per shirt in material costs. If Amanda sells the silk-screened shirts for \$10.50 each, how many shirts must she sell before she can make a profit? **C**

Ⓐ 34 Ⓑ 48

Ⓒ 80 Ⓓ 118

62. Which equation best represents the line that passes through the point $(-4, -3)$ and is perpendicular to the line shown? **B**

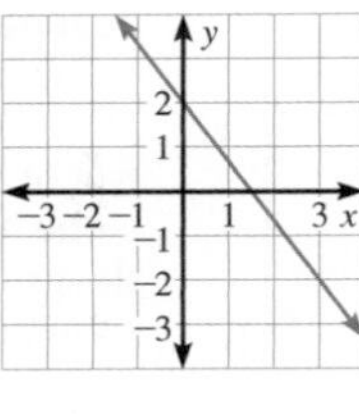

Ⓐ $y = -\frac{4}{3}x$ Ⓑ $y = \frac{3}{4}x$

Ⓒ $y = -\frac{4}{3}x - \frac{25}{3}$ Ⓓ $y = \frac{3}{4}x + 1$

Graphing Calculator ACTIVITY *Use after Lesson 5.2*

@HomeTutor
classzone.com
Keystrokes

5.2 Set a Good Viewing Window

QUESTION **What is a good viewing window for a polynomial function?**

When you graph a function with a graphing calculator, you should choose a viewing window that displays the important characteristics of the graph.

EXAMPLE **Graph a polynomial function**

Graph $f(x) = 0.2x^3 - 5x^2 + 38x - 97$.

STEP 1 ***Graph the function***

Graph the function in the standard viewing window.

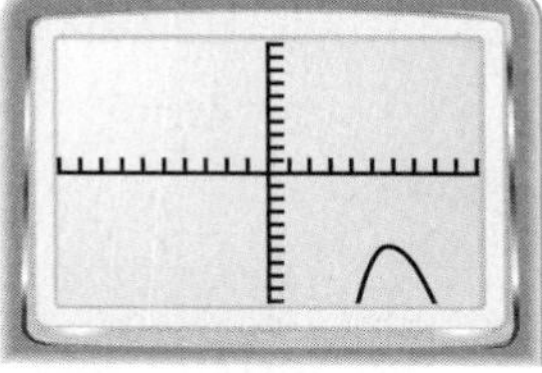

$-10 \le x \le 10$, $-10 \le y \le 10$

STEP 2 ***Adjust horizontally***

Adjust the horizontal scale so that the end behavior of the graph as $x \to +\infty$ is visible.

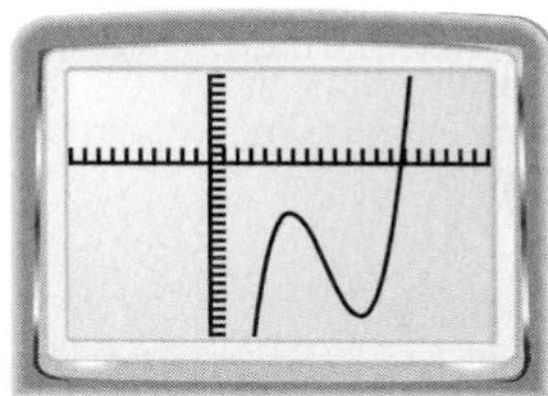

$-10 \le x \le 20$, $-10 \le y \le 10$

STEP 3 ***Adjust vertically***

Adjust the vertical scale so that the turning points and end behavior of the graph as $x \to -\infty$ are visible.

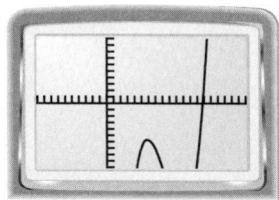

$-10 \le x \le 20$, $-20 \le y \le 10$

PRACTICE

Find intervals for x and y that describe a good viewing window for the graph of the polynomial function. 1–8. See margin.

1. $f(x) = x^3 + 4x^2 - 8x + 11$
2. $f(x) = -x^3 + 36x^2 - 10$
3. $f(x) = x^4 - 4x^2 + 2$
4. $f(x) = -x^4 - 2x^3 + 3x^2 - 4x + 5$
5. $f(x) = -x^4 + 3x^3 + 15x$
6. $f(x) = 2x^4 - 7x^3 + x - 8$
7. $f(x) = -x^5 + 9x^3 - 12x + 18$
8. $f(x) = x^5 - 7x^4 + 25x^3 - 40x^2 + 13x$
9. **REASONING** Let $g(x) = f(x) + c$ where $f(x)$ and $g(x)$ are polynomial functions and c is a positive constant. How is a good viewing window for the graph of $f(x)$ related to a good viewing window for the graph of $g(x)$? *Sample answer:* The window for $g(x)$ should be the same x-interval, but the y-interval will be shifted by c units.
10. **BASEBALL** From 1994 to 2003, the average salary S (in thousands of dollars) for major league baseball players can be modeled by

$$S(x) = -4.10x^3 + 67.4x^2 - 121x + 1170$$

where x is the number of years since 1994. Find intervals for the horizontal and vertical axes that describe a good viewing window for the graph of S. *Sample answer:* $-5 \le x \le 25$, $500 \le y \le 4000$

1–8. Sample answers are given.
1. $-10 \le x \le 10$, $-10 \le y \le 50$
2. $-25 \le x \le 50$, $-500 \le y \le 7500$
3. $-5 \le x \le 5$, $-10 \le y \le 10$
4. $-5 \le x \le 5$, $-10 \le y \le 30$
5. $-5 \le x \le 5$, $-40 \le y \le 30$
6. $-5 \le x \le 5$, $-40 \le y \le 30$
7. $-5 \le x \le 5$, $-50 \le y \le 50$
8. $-5 \le x \le 10$, $-20 \le y \le 20$

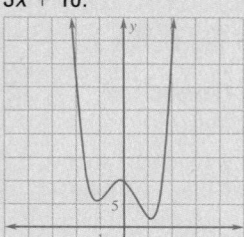

1 PLAN AND PREPARE

Learn the Method

- Students will learn how to set a good viewing window for a polynomial function.
- Students can apply the concepts they learn in this activity to the graphing exercises in the rest of the chapter.

Keystroke Help

Keystrokes for several models of calculators are available in blackline format in the *Chapter 5 Resource Book*.

2 TEACH

Tips for Success

Tell student to record the values they assign to XMIN, XMAX, YMIN, and YMAX in a chart. That way, if they incorrectly adjust a window, they can reset the previous values and try again.

Extra Example

Graph $f(x) = 4x^4 + x^3 - 10x^2 - 3x + 10$.

3 ASSESS AND RETEACH

1. What are the characteristics of a good viewing window for a polynomial function? The viewing window should show the general pattern of the middle of the graph as well as the end behavior of the graph.
2. Find intervals for x and y that describe a good viewing window for the graph of $f(x) = x^3 - 4x^2 + 2x + 1$. Sample: $-5 \le x \le 5$, $-10 \le y \le 10$

1 PLAN AND PREPARE

Warm-Up Exercises

Transparency Available

Simplify the expression.

1. $(-3x^3)(5x)$ $-15x^4$
2. $9x - 18x$ $-9x$
3. $10y^2 + 7y - 8y^2 - 1$
   $2y^2 + 7y - 1$
4. $4(-5a + 6) - 2(a - 8)$
   $-22a + 40$
5. Each side of a square is $(2x + 5)$ inches long. Write an expression for the perimeter of the square $(8x + 20)$ in.

Notetaking Guide

Transparency Available

Promotes interactive learning and notetaking skills, pp. 138–140.

Pacing

Basic: 1 day
Average: 1 day
Advanced: 1 day
Block: 0.5 block with 5.2
- See *Teaching Guide/Lesson Plan.*

2 FOCUS AND MOTIVATE

Essential Question

Big Idea 2, p. 329

What are the special product patterns? **Tell students they will learn how to answer this question by studying how to multiply polynomials.**

5.3 Add, Subtract, and Multiply Polynomials

MA-HS-5.2.3

Before You evaluated and graphed polynomial functions.
Now You will add, subtract, and multiply polynomials.
Why? So you can model collegiate sports participation, as in Ex. 63.

Key Vocabulary
- **like terms,** *p. 12*

To add or subtract polynomials, add or subtract the coefficients of like terms. You can use a vertical or horizontal format.

EXAMPLE 1 Add polynomials vertically and horizontally

a. Add $2x^3 - 5x^2 + 3x - 9$ and $x^3 + 6x^2 + 11$ in a vertical format.

b. Add $3y^3 - 2y^2 - 7y$ and $-4y^2 + 2y - 5$ in a horizontal format.

REVIEW SIMPLIFYING
For help with simplifying expressions, see p. 10.

Solution

a.
$$\begin{array}{r} 2x^3 - 5x^2 + 3x - 9 \\ +\quad x^3 + 6x^2 \quad\quad + 11 \\ \hline 3x^3 + x^2 + 3x + 2 \end{array}$$

b. $(3y^3 - 2y^2 - 7y) + (-4y^2 + 2y - 5)$
$= 3y^3 - 2y^2 - 4y^2 - 7y + 2y - 5$
$= 3y^3 - 6y^2 - 5y - 5$

MA-HS-5.2.3
Students will: add, subtract and multiply polynomial expressions; factor polynomial expressions using the greatest common monomial factor and factor quadratic polynomials of the form $ax^2 + bx + c$, when $a = 1$ and b and c are integers. DOK 2

EXAMPLE 2 Subtract polynomials vertically and horizontally

a. Subtract $3x^3 + 2x^2 - x + 7$ from $8x^3 - x^2 - 5x + 1$ in a vertical format.

b. Subtract $5z^2 - z + 3$ from $4z^2 + 9z - 12$ in a horizontal format.

Solution

a. Align like terms, then add the opposite of the subtracted polynomial.

$$\begin{array}{r} 8x^3 - x^2 - 5x + 1 \\ -\ (3x^3 + 2x^2 - x + 7) \\ \hline \end{array} \quad\longrightarrow\quad \begin{array}{r} 8x^3 - x^2 - 5x + 1 \\ +\ -3x^3 - 2x^2 + x - 7 \\ \hline 5x^3 - 3x^2 - 4x - 6 \end{array}$$

b. Write the opposite of the subtracted polynomial, then add like terms.

$(4z^2 + 9z - 12) - (5z^2 - z + 3) = 4z^2 + 9z - 12 - 5z^2 + z - 3$
$= 4z^2 - 5z^2 + 9z + z - 12 - 3$
$= -z^2 + 10z - 15$

GUIDED PRACTICE for Examples 1 and 2

Find the sum or difference.

1. $(t^2 - 6t + 2) + (5t^2 - t - 8)$ $6t^2 - 7t - 6$
2. $(8d - 3 + 9d^3) - (d^3 - 13d^2 - 4)$ $8d^3 + 13d^2 + 8d + 1$

Resource Planning Guide

Chapter Resource Book
- Teaching Guide/Lesson Plan (pp. 26–27)
- Activity Master (p. 28)
- Practice levels A, B, C (pp. 29–31)
- Study Guide (pp. 32–33)
- Catch-up for Absent Students (p. 34)
- Application (p. 35)
- Challenge (p. 36)

Workbooks
- Notetaking Guide (pp. 138–140)
- Practice Workbook (pp. 81–82)

Teaching Options
- **Power Presentations CD-ROM** provides dynamic electronic teaching resources for the classroom.
- **Activity Generator CD-ROM** provides editable activities for all ability levels.

Interactive Technology
- Easy Planner
- Power Presentations CD-ROM
- Activity Generator CD-ROM
- Animated Algebra
- Test Generator CD-ROM
- Online Quiz
- eWorkbook
- eEdition
- @HomeTutor

Resources for English Learners
- Quick Reference for English Learners
- Spanish Study Guide
- Multi-Language Visual Glossary
- Student Resources in Spanish

See also the *Algebra 2 Toolkit* for more strategies for meeting individual needs.

MULTIPLYING POLYNOMIALS To multiply two polynomials, you multiply each term of the first polynomial by each term of the second polynomial.

EXAMPLE 3 Multiply polynomials vertically and horizontally

a. Multiply $-2y^2 + 3y - 6$ and $y - 2$ in a vertical format.

b. Multiply $x + 3$ and $3x^2 - 2x + 4$ in a horizontal format.

Solution

a.

$$\begin{array}{r} -2y^2 + 3y - 6 \\ \times \qquad\quad y - 2 \\ \hline 4y^2 - 6y + 12 \\ -2y^3 + 3y^2 - 6y \quad \\ \hline -2y^3 + 7y^2 - 12y + 12 \end{array}$$

Multiply $-2y^2 + 3y - 6$ by -2.

Multiply $-2y^2 + 3y - 6$ by y.

Combine like terms.

b. $(x + 3)(3x^2 - 2x + 4) = (x + 3)3x^2 - (x + 3)2x + (x + 3)4$

$= 3x^3 + 9x^2 - 2x^2 - 6x + 4x + 12$

$= 3x^3 + 7x^2 - 2x + 12$

EXAMPLE 4 Multiply three binomials

Multiply $x - 5$, $x + 1$, and $x + 3$ in a horizontal format.

$(x - 5)(x + 1)(x + 3) = (x^2 - 4x - 5)(x + 3)$

$= (x^2 - 4x - 5)x + (x^2 - 4x - 5)3$

$= x^3 - 4x^2 - 5x + 3x^2 - 12x - 15$

$= x^3 - x^2 - 17x - 15$

PRODUCT PATTERNS Some binomial products occur so frequently that it is worth memorizing their patterns. You can verify these product patterns by multiplying.

KEY CONCEPT *For Your Notebook*

Special Product Patterns

Sum and Difference	Example
$(a + b)(a - b) = a^2 - b^2$	$(x + 4)(x - 4) = x^2 - 16$
Square of a Binomial	**Example**
$(a + b)^2 = a^2 + 2ab + b^2$	$(y + 3)^2 = y^2 + 6y + 9$
$(a - b)^2 = a^2 - 2ab + b^2$	$(3z^2 - 5)^2 = 9z^4 - 30z^2 + 25$
Cube of a Binomial	**Example**
$(a + b)^3 = a^3 + 3a^2b + 3ab^2 + b^3$	$(x + 2)^3 = x^3 + 6x^2 + 12x + 8$
$(a - b)^3 = a^3 - 3a^2b + 3ab^2 - b^3$	$(p - 3)^3 = p^3 - 9p^2 + 27p - 27$

VOID ERRORS
general,
$\pm b)^2 \neq a^2 \pm b^2$
nd
$\pm b)^3 \neq a^3 \pm b^3$.

Differentiated Instruction

Inclusion When multiplying polynomials vertically as in **Example 3a**, have students use grid paper to properly align the multiplied terms so that like terms are added together. Students should make sure that the terms in each vertical column have the same degree.

See also the *Algebra 2 Toolkit* for more strategies.

Motivating the Lesson

Distribute index cards to your students so that eight cards have x^2 written on them, seven cards have x written on them, and three have 1 written on them. Write the expression $(5x^2 + 7x + 1) + (3x^2 - 4x + 2)$. Ask groups of students who have the appropriate cards to come to the front of the room to model the first polynomial. Then add or subtract students who represent the second polynomial. The final group of students represents the sum of the two polynomials.

3 TEACH

Extra Example 1

a. Add $4x^3 + 4x^2 - 3x + 10$ and $-5x^3 - 2x^2 - 4x - 4$ in a vertical format. $-x^3 + 2x^2 - 7x + 6$

b. Add $2x^3 + 2x^2 - 3x + 5$ and $3x^3 - 4x^2 - 1x - 7$ in a horizontal format. $5x^3 - 2x^2 - 4x - 2$

Extra Example 2

a. Subtract $-4x^3 + 6x^2 + 9x - 3$ from $3x^3 + 4x^2 + 7x + 12$ in a vertical format. $7x^3 - 2x^2 - 2x + 15$

b. Subtract $6y^2 - 6y - 13$ from $3y^2 - 4y + 7$ in a horizontal format. $-3y^2 + 2y + 20$

Extra Example 3

a. Multiply $3x^2 + 3x + 5$ and $2x + 3$ in a vertical format. $6x^3 + 15x^2 + 19x + 15$

b. Multiply $x^2 - 2x + 3$ and $x - 5$ in a horizontal format. $x^3 - 7x^2 + 13x - 15$

Key Question to Ask for Example 3

- Which property was used twice in part (b)? Distributive property

EXAMPLE 5 Use special product patterns

a. $(3t + 4)(3t - 4) = (3t)^2 - 4^2$ **Sum and difference**

$= 9t^2 - 16$

b. $(8x - 3)^2 = (8x)^2 - 2(8x)(3) + 3^2$ **Square of a binomial**

$= 64x^2 - 48x + 9$

c. $(pq + 5)^3 = (pq)^3 + 3(pq)^2(5) + 3(pq)(5)^2 + 5^3$ **Cube of a binomial**

$= p^3q^3 + 15p^2q^2 + 75pq + 125$

✓ **GUIDED PRACTICE** for Examples 3, 4, and 5

Find the product.

3. $(x + 2)(3x^2 - x - 5)$
$3x^3 + 5x^2 - 7x - 10$

4. $(a - 5)(a + 2)(a + 6)$
$a^3 + 3a^2 - 28a - 60$

5. $(xy - 4)^3$
$x^3y^3 - 12x^2y^2 + 48xy -$

EXAMPLE 6 Use polynomial models

PETROLEUM Since 1980, the number W (in thousands) of United States wells producing crude oil and the average daily oil output per well O (in barrels) can be modeled by

$$W = -0.575t^2 + 10.9t + 548 \quad \text{and} \quad O = -0.249t + 15.4$$

where t is the number of years since 1980. Write a model for the average *total* amount T of crude oil produced per day. What was the average total amount of crude oil produced per day in 2000?

Oil refinery in Long Beach, Californi

DETERMINE SIGNIFICANT DIGITS

When multiplying models, round your result so that its terms have the same number of significant digits as the model with the fewest number of significant digits.

Solution

To find a model for T, multiply the two given models.

$$\begin{array}{rrrrr} & & -0.575t^2 + & 10.9t + & 548 \\ \times & & - & 0.249t + & 15.4 \\ \hline & & -8.855t^2 + & 167.86t + & 8439.2 \\ 0.143175t^3 - & & 2.7141t^2 - & 136.452t & \\ \hline 0.143175t^3 - & & 11.5691t^2 + & 31.408t + & 8439.2 \end{array}$$

▶ Total daily oil output can be modeled by $T = 0.143t^3 - 11.6t^2 + 31.4t + 8440$ where T is measured in thousands of barrels. By substituting $t = 20$ into the model, you can estimate that the average total amount of crude oil produced per day in 2000 was about 5570 thousand barrels, or 5,570,000 barrels.

 **GUIDED PRACTICE** for Example 6

6. INDUSTRY The models below give the average depth D (in feet) of new wells drilled and the average cost per foot C (in dollars) of drilling a new well. In both models, t represents the number of years since 1980. Write a model for the average *total* cost T of drilling a new well.
$T = 59.078t^3 + 1392.98t^2 - 20,057t + 318,394$

$$D = 109t + 4010 \quad \text{and} \quad C = 0.542t^2 - 7.16t + 79.4$$

Extra Example 4

Multiply $x - 1$, $x - 1$, and $x + 2$ in a horizontal format. $x^3 - 3x + 2$

Key Question to Ask for Example 4

- What does $(x^2 - 4x - 5)$ represent? **It is the product of $x - 5$ and $x + 1$.**

Extra Example 5

Find the product of the binomials.

a. $(5y - 3)(5y + 3)$ $25y^2 - 9$

b. $(4a + 7)^2$ $16a^2 + 56a + 49$

c. $(mn - 6)^3$ $m^3n^3 + 18m^2n^2 + 108mn - 216$

Key Question to Ask for Example 5

- Is the product of two binomials always a trinomial? **no**

Extra Example 6

New highway markers are placed every $(6x - 6)$ feet along a stretch of highway. The total number of markers is represented by $x^2 - 3x + 1$. Write a model for the distance along the highway where the markers are placed. If the markers are placed every 528 feet, what length of highway received new markers? $6x^3 - 24x^2 + 24x - 6$; **765.5 mi**

Closing the Lesson

Have students summarize the major points of the lesson and answer the Essential Question: What are the special product patterns?

- **You can add or subtract polynomials horizontally or vertically by adding or subtracting like terms.**
- **You multiply two polynomials by multiplying each term of the first polynomial by each term of the second.**

The special product patterns are:

- $(a + b)(a - b) = a^2 - b^2$
- $(a + b)^2 = a^2 + 2ab + b^2$ and $(a - b)^2 = a^2 - 2ab + b^2$
- $(a + b)^3 = a^3 + 3a^2b + 3ab^2 + b^3$ and $(a - b)^3 = a^3 - 3a^2b + 3ab^2 - b^3$

Differentiated Instruction

Below Level When students use the special product patterns, encourage them to write the general pattern, list the values of the variables in the general pattern, and then rewrite the values for that pattern. For example,
$(2x^2 - 1)^2$:
Using $(a - b)^2 = a^2 - 2ab + b^2$ with $a = 2x^2$ and $b = 1$, then $(2x^2 - 1)^2 = (2x^2)^2 - 2(2x^2)(1) + (1)^2 = 4x^4 - 4x^2 + 1$.
See also the *Algebra 2 Toolkit* for more strategies.

5.3 EXERCISES

HOMEWORK KEY

○ = **WORKED-OUT SOLUTIONS** on p. WS10 for Exs. 11, 21, and 61

★ = **STANDARDIZED TEST PRACTICE** Exs. 2, 15, 47, 56, and 63

SKILL PRACTICE

A

1. **VOCABULARY** When you add or subtract polynomials, you add or subtract the coefficients of _?_. like terms

2. ★ **WRITING** *Explain* how a polynomial subtraction problem is equivalent to a polynomial addition problem. *Sample answer:* To subtract a polynomial, add the opposite of each term that is being subtracted.

XAMPLES and 2 | n p. 346 | r Exs. 3–15

ADDING AND SUBTRACTING POLYNOMIALS Find the sum or difference.

3. $(3x^2 - 5) + (7x^2 - 3)$ $10x^2 - 8$
4. $(x^2 - 3x + 5) - (-4x^2 + 8x + 9)$ $5x^2 - 11x - 4$
5. $(4y^2 + 9y - 5) - (4y^2 - 5y + 3)$ $14y - 8$
6. $(z^2 + 5z - 7) + (5z^2 - 11z - 6)$ $6z^2 - 6z - 13$
7. $(3s^3 + s) + (4s^3 - 2s^2 + 7s + 10)$ $7s^3 - 2s^2 + 8s + 10$
8. $(2a^2 - 8) - (a^3 + 4a^2 - 12a + 4)$ $-a^3 - 2a^2 + 12a - 12$
9. $(5c^2 + 7c + 1) + (2c^3 - 6c + 8)$ $2c^3 + 5c^2 + c + 9$
10. $(4t^3 - 11t^2 + 4t) - (-7t^2 - 5t + 8)$ $4t^3 - 4t^2 + 9t - 8$
11. $(5b - 6b^3 + 2b^4) - (9b^3 + 4b^4 - 7)$ $-2b^4 - 15b^3 + 5b + 7$
12. $(3y^2 - 6y^4 + 5 - 6y) + (5y^4 - 6y^3 + 4y)$ $-y^4 - 6y^3 + 3y^2 - 2y + 5$
13. $(x^4 - x^3 + x^2 - x + 1) + (x + x^4 - 1 - x^2)$ $2x^4 - x^3$
14. $(8v^4 - 2v^2 + v - 4) - (3v^3 - 12v^2 + 8v)$ $8v^4 - 3v^3 + 10v^2 - 7v - 4$

15. ★ **MULTIPLE CHOICE** What is the result when $2x^4 - 8x^2 - x + 10$ is subtracted from $8x^4 - 4x^3 - x + 2$? B

Ⓐ $-6x^4 + 4x^3 - 8x^2 + 8$ Ⓑ $6x^4 - 4x^3 + 8x^2 - 8$

Ⓒ $10x^4 - 8x^3 - 4x^2 + 12$ Ⓓ $6x^4 + 4x^3 - 2x - 8$

XAMPLE 3 | n p. 347 | r Exs. 16–25

MULTIPLYING POLYNOMIALS Find the product of the polynomials.

16. $x(2x^2 - 5x + 7)$ $2x^3 - 5x^2 + 7x$
17. $5x^2(6x + 2)$ $30x^3 + 10x^2$
18. $(y - 7)(y + 6)$ $y^2 - y - 42$
19. $(3z + 1)(z - 3)$ $3z^2 - 8z - 3$
20. $(w + 4)(w^2 + 6w - 11)$ $w^3 + 10w^2 + 13w - 44$
21. $(2a - 3)(a^2 - 10a - 2)$ $2a^3 - 23a^2 + 26a + 6$
22. $(5c^2 - 4)(2c^2 + c - 3)$ $10c^4 + 5c^3 - 23c^2 - 4c + 12$
23. $(-x^2 + 4x + 1)(x^2 - 8x + 3)$ $-x^4 + 12x^3 - 34x^2 + 4x + 3$
24. $(-d^2 + 4d + 3)(3d^2 - 7d + 6)$ $-3d^4 + 19d^3 - 25d^2 + 3d + 18$
25. $(3y^2 + 6y - 1)(4y^2 - 11y - 5)$ $12y^4 - 9y^3 - 85y^2 - 19y + 5$

ERROR ANALYSIS *Describe* and correct the error in simplifying the expression.

26.
$$(x^2 - 3x + 4) - (x^3 + 7x - 2)$$
$$= x^2 - 3x + 4 - x^3 + 7x - 2$$
$$= -x^3 + x^2 + 4x + 2$$

When subtracting polynomials, write the opposite of the subtracted polynomial, then add like terms; $(x^2 - 3x + 4) - (x^3 + 7x - 2) = x^2 - 3x + 4 - x^3 - 7x + 2 = -x^3 + x^2 - 10x + 6$.

27.
$$(2x - 7)^3 = (2x)^3 - 7^3$$
$$= 8x^3 - 343$$

The cube of a binomial $(a - b)^3$ is found by $a^3 - 3a^2b + 3ab^2 - b^3$; $(2x - 7)^3 = (2x)^3 - 3(2x)^2(7) + 3(2x)(7)^2 - (7)^3, = 8x^3 - 84x^2 + 294x + 343$.

XAMPLE 4 | n p. 347 | r Exs. 28–37

MULTIPLYING THREE BINOMIALS Find the product of the binomials.

28. $(x + 4)(x - 6)(x - 5)$ $x^3 - 7x^2 - 14x + 120$
29. $(x + 1)(x - 7)(x + 3)$ $x^3 - 3x^2 - 25x - 21$
30. $(z - 4)(-z + 2)(z + 8)$ $-z^3 - 2z^2 + 40z - 64$
31. $(a - 6)(2a + 5)(a + 1)$ $2a^3 - 5a^2 - 37a - 30$
32. $(3p + 1)(p + 3)(p + 1)$ $3p^3 + 13p^2 + 13p + 3$
33. $(b - 2)(2b - 1)(-b + 1)$ $-2b^3 + 7b^2 - 7b + 2$
34. $(2s + 1)(3s - 2)(4s - 3)$ $24s^3 - 22s^2 - 5s + 6$
35. $(w - 6)(4w - 1)(-3w + 5)$ $-12w^3 + 95w^2 - 83w + 30$
36. $(4x - 1)(-2x - 7)(-5x - 4)$ $40x^3 + 162x^2 + 69x - 28$
37. $(3q - 8)(-9q + 2)(q - 2)$ $-27q^3 + 132q^2 - 172q + 32$

4 PRACTICE AND APPLY

Assignment Guide

Answer Transparencies available for all exercises

Basic:
Day 1: SRH p. 983 Exs. 1–15 odd
pp. 349–352
Exs. 1, 2, 3–13 odd, 15–19, 26–31, 38–40, 47–50, 59–62, 66

Average:
Day 1: pp. 349–352
Exs. 1, 2, 4–14 even, 15, 20–23, 26, 27, 32–35, 41–43, 47–55 odd, 59–63, 65

Advanced:
Day 1: pp. 349–352
Exs. 1, 2, 10–15, 23–25, 34–37, 44–47, 50–64*, 66

Block:
pp. 349–352
Exs. 1, 2, 4–14 even, 15, 20–23, 26, 27, 32–35, 41–43, 47–55 odd, 59–63, 65 (with 5.2)

Differentiated Instruction

See *Algebra 2 Best Practices Toolkit* for suggestions on addressing the needs of a diverse classroom.

Homework Check

For a quick check of student understanding of key concepts, go over the following exercises:

Basic: 6, 19, 30, 38, 59
Average: 8, 22, 34, 42, 60
Advanced: 12, 24, 36, 46, 61

Extra Practice

- Student Edition, p. 1014
- Chapter 5 Resource Book: Practice levels A, B, C, pp. 29–31

Practice Worksheet

An easily-readable reduced practice page (with answers) for this lesson can be found on p. 328C.

Mathematical Reasoning

Exercises 3–14 Point out that students can apply the distributive property when subtracting polynomials. The terms in the polynomial being subtracted can be multiplied by −1 before combining like terms. This may help students avoid the common error of applying the subtraction sign to only the first term of the polynomial being subtracted.

Avoiding Common Errors

Exercises 39–42, 44, 46 Some students mistakenly simplify $(a + b)^2$ as $a^2 + b^2$ and simplify $(a - b)^3$ as $a^3 - b^3$. To help them avoid these errors, ask them to identify the separate terms and exponent for each expression. Then have them write the appropriate pattern from the Key Concept on p. 347, substitute the terms and exponents into the pattern, and simplify.

Study Strategy

Exercise 58 One problem solving technique is to solve a similar but easier problem and then apply its solution strategy to the original problem. In this exercise, students can first substitute values for *a*, *b*, *c*, and *d* and see how the coefficient of x^3 and the constant term are related to those values.

52. $(a + b)(a - b) = a^2 - ab + ab - b^2 = a^2 - b^2$

53. $(a + b)^2 = (a + b)(a + b) = a^2 + ab + ab + b^2 = a^2 + 2ab + b^2$

54. $(a + b)^3 = (a + b)(a + b)(a + b) = (a + b)(a^2 + 2ab + b^2) = a^3 + 2a^2b + ab^2 + a^2b + 2ab^2 + b^3 = a^3 + 3a^2b + 3ab^2 + b^3$

55. $(a - b)^3 = (a - b)(a - b)(a - b) = (a - b)(a^2 - 2ab + b^2) = a^3 - 2a^2b + ab^2 - a^2b + 2ab^2 - b^3 = a^3 - 3a^2b + 3ab^2 - b^3$

57a. $(x - 1)(x^4 + x^3 + x^2 + x + 1)$; $(x - 1)(x^5 + x^4 + x^3 + x^2 + x + 1)$

EXAMPLE 5 on p. 348 for Exs. 38–47

SPECIAL PRODUCTS **Find the product.**

38. $(x + 5)(x - 5)$ $x^2 - 25$

39. $(w - 9)^2$ $w^2 - 18w + 81$

40. $(y + 4)^3$ $y^3 + 12y^2 + 48y +$

41. $(2c + 5)^2$ $4c^2 + 20c + 25$

42. $(3t - 4)^3$ $27x^3 - 108x^2 + 144x - 64$

43. $(5p - 3)(5p + 3)$ $25p^2 - 9$

44. $(7x - y)^3$ $343x^3 - 147x^2y + 21xy^2 - y^3$

45. $(2a + 9b)(2a - 9b)$ $4a^2 - 81b^2$

46. $(3z + 7y)^3$ $343y^3 + 441y^2z + 189yz^2 + 27z^3$

47. ★ **MULTIPLE CHOICE** Which expression is equivalent to $(3x - 2y)^2$? D

Ⓐ $9x^2 - 4y^2$ Ⓑ $9x^2 + 4y^2$

Ⓒ $9x^2 + 12xy + 4y^2$ Ⓓ $9x^2 - 12xy + 4y^2$

B

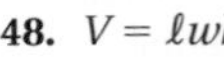 **GEOMETRY** **Write the figure's volume as a polynomial in standard form.**

48. $V = \ell wh$

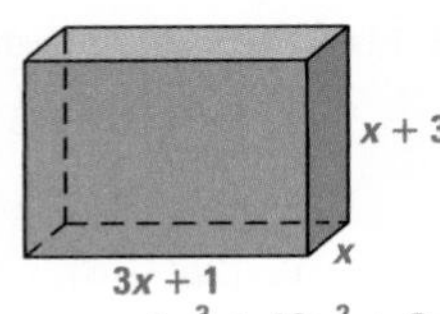

$3x^3 + 10x^2 + 3x$

49. $V = \pi r^2 h$

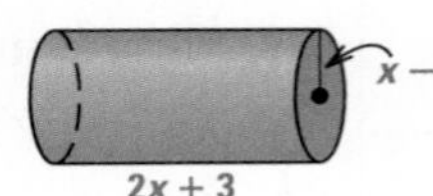

$2\pi x^3 - 13\pi x^2 + 8\pi x + 48\pi$

50. $V = s^3$

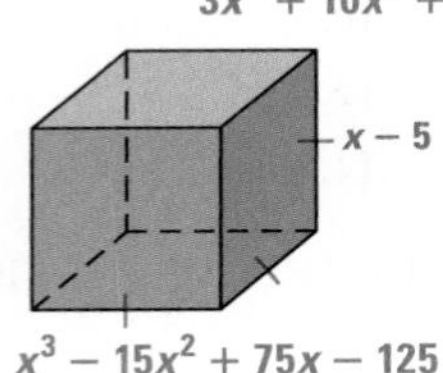

$x^3 - 15x^2 + 75x - 125$

51. $V = \frac{1}{3}Bh$

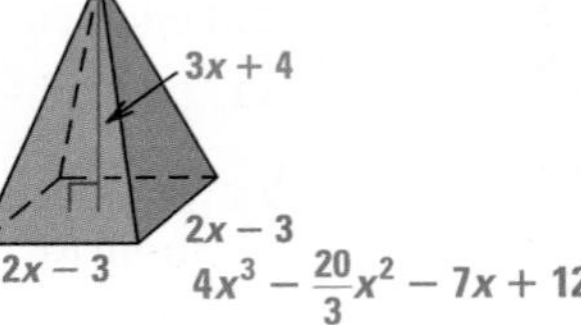

$4x^3 - \frac{20}{3}x^2 - 7x + 12$

SPECIAL PRODUCTS **Verify the special product pattern by multiplying.** 52–55. See margin.

52. $(a + b)(a - b) = a^2 - b^2$

53. $(a + b)^2 = a^2 + 2ab + b^2$

54. $(a + b)^3 = a^3 + 3a^2b + 3ab^2 + b^3$

55. $(a - b)^3 = a^3 - 3a^2b + 3ab^2 - b^3$

C

56. ★ **EXTENDED RESPONSE** Let $p(x) = x^4 - 7x + 14$ and $q(x) = x^2 - 5$.

a. What is the degree of the polynomial $p(x) + q(x)$? 4

b. What is the degree of the polynomial $p(x) - q(x)$? 4

c. What is the degree of the polynomial $p(x) \cdot q(x)$? 6

d. In general, if $p(x)$ and $q(x)$ are polynomials such that $p(x)$ has degree m, $q(x)$ has degree n, and $m > n$, what are the degrees of $p(x) + q(x)$, $p(x) - q(x)$, and $p(x) \cdot q(x)$? m, m, $m + n$

57. **FINDING A PATTERN** Look at the following polynomial factorizations.

$x^2 - 1 = (x - 1)(x + 1)$

$x^3 - 1 = (x - 1)(x^2 + x + 1)$

$x^4 - 1 = (x - 1)(x^3 + x^2 + x + 1)$

a. Factor $x^5 - 1$ and $x^6 - 1$ into the product of $x - 1$ and another polynomial. Check your answers by multiplying. See margin.

b. In general, how can $x^n - 1$ be factored? Show that this factorization works by multiplying the factors. $(x - 1)(x^{n-1} + x^{n-2} + x^{n-3} + \cdots + 1)$

58. **CHALLENGE** Suppose $f(x) = (x + a)(x + b)(x + c)(x + d)$. If $f(x)$ is written in standard form, show that the coefficient of x^3 is the sum of a, b, c, and d, and the constant term is the product of a, b, c, and d. See margin.

○ = WORKED-OUT SOLUTIONS on p. WS1 ★ = STANDARDIZED TEST PRACTICE

58. $(x + a)(x + b)(x + c)(x + d) = (x^2 + ax + bx + ab)(x^2 + cx + dx + cd) = x^4 + cx^3 + dx^3 + cdx^2 + ax^3 + acx^2 + adx^2 + acdx + bx^3 + bcx^2 + bdx^2 + bcdx + abx^2 + abcx + abdx + abcd = x^4 + (a + b + c + d)x^3 + (cd + ac + ad + bc + bd + ab)x^2 + (acd + bcd + abc + abd)x + abcd$, so the coefficient of x^3 is the sum of *a*, *b*, *c*, and *d* and the constant term is the product of *a*, *b*, *c*, and *d*.

PROBLEM SOLVING

EXAMPLE 6 A on p. 348 for Exs. 59–61

59. HIGHER EDUCATION Since 1970, the number (in thousands) of males M and females F attending institutes of higher education can be modeled by

$$M = 0.091t^3 - 4.8t^2 + 110t + 5000 \quad \text{and} \quad F = 0.19t^3 - 12t^2 + 350t + 3600$$

where t is the number of years since 1970. Write a model for the total number of people attending institutes of higher education. $0.281t^3 - 16.8t^2 + 460t + 8600$

@HomeTutor for problem solving help at classzone.com

60. ELECTRONICS From 1999 to 2004, the number of DVD players D (in millions) sold in the United States and the average price per DVD player P (in dollars) can be modeled by

$$D = 4.11t + 4.44 \quad \text{and} \quad P = 6.82t^2 - 61.7t + 265$$

where t is the number of years since 1999. Write a model for the total revenue R from DVD sales. According to the model, what was the total revenue in 2002? $28.0302t^3 - 223.3062t^2 + 815.202t + 1176.6$; about \$2369.3 million

@HomeTutor for problem solving help at classzone.com

61. BICYCLING The equation $P = 0.00267sF$ gives the power P (in horsepower) needed to keep a certain bicycle moving at speed s (in miles per hour), where F is the force (in pounds) of road and air resistance. On level ground, the equation

$$F = 0.0116s^2 + 0.789$$

models the force F. Write a model (in terms of s only) for the power needed to keep the bicycle moving at speed s on level ground. How much power is needed to keep the bicycle moving at 10 miles per hour? $F = 0.000031s^3 + 0.002107s$; about 0.05 horsepower

Animated Algebra at classzone.com

B **62. MULTI-STEP PROBLEM** A dessert is made by taking a hemispherical mound of marshmallow on a 0.5 centimeter thick cookie and covering it with a chocolate shell 1 centimeter thick. Use the diagrams to write two polynomial functions in standard form: $M(r)$ for the combined volume of the marshmallow plus cookie, and $D(r)$ for the volume of the entire dessert. Then use $M(r)$ and $D(r)$ to write a function $C(r)$ for the volume of the chocolate. See margin.

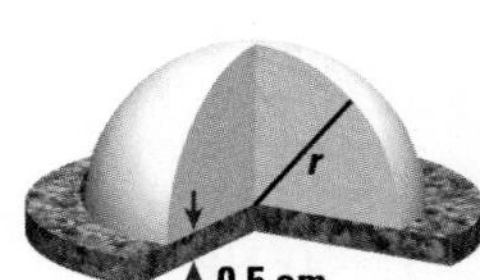

Marshmallow on cookie

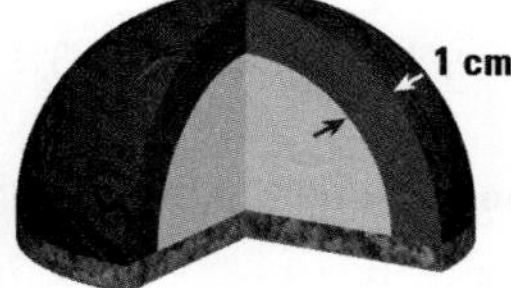

Chocolate layer added

63. ★ SHORT RESPONSE From 1997 to 2002, the number of NCAA lacrosse teams for men L_m and women L_w, as well as the average size of a men's team S_m and a women's team S_w, can be modeled by

$$L_m = 5.57t + 182 \quad \text{and} \quad S_m = -0.127t^3 + 0.822t^2 - 1.02t + 31.5$$

$$L_w = 12.2t + 185 \quad \text{and} \quad S_w = -0.0662t^3 + 0.437t^2 - 0.725t + 22.3$$

where t is the number of years since 1997. Write a model for the *total* number of people N on NCAA lacrosse teams. *Explain* how you obtained your model.

$N = $ .51503t^4 − .45106t^3 + 5.9226t^2 + 7.75t + 9858.5; calculate $L_m \cdot S_m + L_w \cdot S_w$.

Graphing Calculator

Exercise 61 Students can graph the model on their graphing calculators and use the graph to determine how much power is necessary at 10 miles per hour.

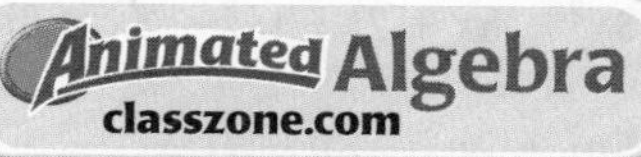

An **Animated Algebra** activity is available on-line for **Exercise 61**. This activity is also available on the **Power Presentations CD-ROM**.

Internet Reference

Exercise 63 Additional information about the NCAA lacrosse teams can be found at www.ncaa.org/sports/lacrosse/mens and www.ncaa.org/sports/lacrosse/womens

62. $M(r) = \frac{2}{3}\pi r^3 + \frac{1}{2}\pi r^2 + \pi r + \frac{1}{2}\pi$, $D(r) = \frac{2}{3}\pi r^3 + \frac{5}{2}\pi r^2 + 3\pi r + \frac{7}{6}\pi$, $C(r) = 2\pi r^2 + 2\pi r + \frac{2}{3}\pi$

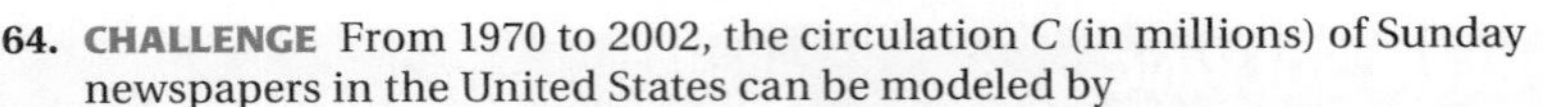

C 64. **CHALLENGE** From 1970 to 2002, the circulation C (in millions) of Sunday newspapers in the United States can be modeled by

$$C = -0.00105t^3 + 0.0281t^2 + 0.465t + 48.8$$

where t is the number of years since 1970. Rewrite C as a function of s, where s is the number of years since 1975. $C = -0.00105s^3 + 0.01235s^2 + 0.66725s + 51.6962$

KENTUCKY MIXED REVIEW

TEST PRACTICE at classzone.com

65. The table shows the total cost y of heating oil. Which equation best represents the total cost of the heating oil as a function of the number of gallons x? **D**

Ⓐ $x = 0.67y$ Ⓑ $y = 0.67x$

Ⓒ $x = 1.5y$ Ⓓ $y = 1.5x$

Number of gallons (x)	Total cost (y)
50	\$75
200	\$300
500	\$750

66. A student is making a circle graph of the results of a survey that asked what people's favorite sport is. What central angle should be used for the section representing basketball? **C**

Ⓐ 35° Ⓑ 105°

Ⓒ 126° Ⓓ 234°

Activity	Number of people
Basketball	350
Soccer	210
Softball or Baseball	200
Other	240

QUIZ for Lessons 5.1–5.3

Evaluate the expression. *(p. 330)*

1. $3^5 \cdot 3^{-1}$ **81**
2. $(2^4)^2$ **256**
3. $\left(\frac{2}{3^{-2}}\right)^2$ **324**
4. $\left(\frac{3}{5}\right)^{-2}$ $\frac{25}{9}$

Simplify the expression. *(p. 330)*

5. $(x^4y^{-2})(x^{-3}y^8)$ xy^6
6. $(a^2b^{-5})^{-3}$ $\frac{b^{15}}{a^6}$
7. $\frac{x^3y^7}{x^{-4}y^0}$ x^7y^7
8. $\frac{c^3d^{-2}}{c^5d^{-1}}$ $\frac{1}{c^2d}$

Graph the polynomial function. *(p. 337)* **9–11. See margin.**

9. $g(x) = 2x^3 - 3x + 1$
10. $h(x) = x^4 - 4x + 2$
11. $f(x) = -2x^3 + x^2 - 5$

Perform the indicated operation. *(p. 346)*

12. $(x^3 + x^2 - 6) - (2x^2 + 4x - 8)$ $x^3 - x^2 - 4x + 2$
13. $(-3x^2 + 4x - 10) + (x^2 - 9x + 15)$ $-2x^2 - 5x + 5$
14. $(x - 5)(x^2 - 5x + 7)$ $x^3 - 10x^2 + 32x - 35$
15. $(x + 3)(x - 6)(3x - 1)$ $3x^3 - 10x^2 - 51x + 18$
16. **NATIONAL DEBT** On July 21, 2004, the national debt of the United States was about \$7,282,000,000,000. The population of the United States at that time was about 294,000,000. Suppose the national debt was divided evenly among everyone in the United States. How much would each person owe? *(p. 330)* **\$24,768.71 per person**

EXTRA PRACTICE for Lesson 5.3, p. 1014

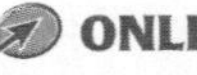

ONLINE QUIZ at classzone.com

5 ASSESS AND RETEACH

Daily Homework Quiz

Transparency Available

Find the sum, difference, or product.

1. $(3x^2 + 5x + 2) + (x^2 - 3x + 6)$ $4x^2 + 2x + 8$
2. $(5p^3 + 2p^2 - 3p - 7) - (2p^3 - 4p^2 - 5p + 6)$ $3p^3 + 6p^2 + 2p - 13$
3. $(4a^2 + 6a + 9)(2a - 3)$ $8a^3 - 27$
4. $6(x - 1)(x + 1)$ $6x^2 - 6$
5. The floor space in square feet of retail stores A, B, and C can be modeled by $A = x^2 + 4x - 7$, $B = 2x^2 - 7x + 1$, and $C = -4x^2 + 250x - 1$. Write a model for the total amount of floor space T for all three stores. What is the total floor space of the three stores if $x = 50$? $-x^2 + 247x - 7$; 9843 ft^2

Online Quiz

Available at **classzone.com**

Diagnosis/Remediation

- Practice A, B, C in Chapter 5 Resource Book, pp. 29–31
- Study Guide in Chapter 5 Resource Book, pp. 32–33
- Practice Workbook, pp. 81–82
- @HomeTutor

Challenge

Additional challenge is available in the Chapter 5 Resource Book, p. 36.

Quiz

An easily-readable reduced copy of the quiz (with answers) on Lessons 5.1–5.3 from the Assessment Book can be found on p. 328F.

Quiz 9–11. See Additional Answers beginning on p. AA1.

5.4 Factor and Solve Polynomial Equations

MA-HS-5.2.3

Before	You factored and solved quadratic equations.
Now	You will factor and solve other polynomial equations.
Why?	So you can find dimensions of archaeological ruins, as in Ex. 58.

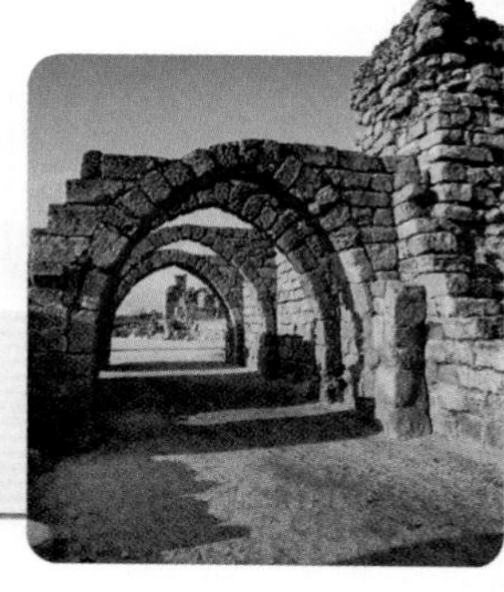

Key Vocabulary
- factored completely
- factor by grouping
- quadratic form

MA-HS-5.2.3
Students will: add, subtract and multiply polynomial expressions; factor polynomial expressions using the greatest common monomial factor and factor quadratic polynomials of the form $ax^2 + bx + c$, when $a = 1$ and b and c are integers. DOK 2

In Chapter 4, you learned how to factor the following types of quadratic expressions.

Type	Example
General trinomial	$2x^2 - 3x - 20 = (2x + 5)(x - 4)$
Perfect square trinomial	$x^2 + 8x + 16 = (x + 4)^2$
Difference of two squares	$9x^2 - 1 = (3x + 1)(3x - 1)$
Common monomial factor	$8x^2 + 20x = 4x(2x + 5)$

You can also factor polynomials with degree greater than 2. Some of these polynomials can be *factored completely* using techniques learned in Chapter 4.

KEY CONCEPT *For Your Notebook*

Factoring Polynomials

Definition

A factorable polynomial with integer coefficients is **factored completely** if it is written as a product of unfactorable polynomials with integer coefficients.

Examples

$2(x + 1)(x - 4)$ and $5x^2(x^2 - 3)$ are factored completely.

$3x(x^2 - 4)$ is *not* factored completely because $x^2 - 4$ can be factored as $(x + 2)(x - 2)$.

EXAMPLE 1 Find a common monomial factor

Factor the polynomial completely.

a. $x^3 + 2x^2 - 15x = x(x^2 + 2x - 15)$ **Factor common monomial.**

$= x(x + 5)(x - 3)$ **Factor trinomial.**

b. $2y^5 - 18y^3 = 2y^3(y^2 - 9)$ **Factor common monomial.**

$= 2y^3(y + 3)(y - 3)$ **Difference of two squares**

c. $4z^4 - 16z^3 + 16z^2 = 4z^2(z^2 - 4z + 4)$ **Factor common monomial.**

$= 4z^2(z - 2)^2$ **Perfect square trinomial**

1 PLAN AND PREPARE

Warm-Up Exercises
Transparency Available

Multiply the polynomials.

1. $(x + 2)(x + 3)$ $x^2 + 5x + 6$

2. $(2x - 1)(2x + 1)$ $4x^2 - 1$

3. $(x - 7)^2$ $x^2 - 14x + 49$

4. $3x^2(x + 5)$ $3x^3 + 15x^2$

5. The dimensions of a box are modeled by $(x + 4)$, $(x + 2)$, and $(x + 6)$. Write a polynomial that models the volume of the box. $x^3 + 12x^2 + 44x + 48$

Notetaking Guide
Transparency Available

Promotes interactive learning and notetaking skills, pp. 141–143.

Pacing
Basic: 1 day
Average: 1 day
Advanced: 1 day
Block: 0.5 block with 5.5
- See *Teaching Guide/Lesson Plan.*

2 FOCUS AND MOTIVATE

Essential Question
Big Idea 3, p. 329

How can you solve a higher-degree polynomial equation? **Tell students they will learn how to answer this question by factoring the polynomial and using the zero product property.**

Resource Planning Guide

Chapter Resource Book
- Teaching Guide/Lesson Plan (pp. 37–38)
- Practice levels A, B, C (pp. 39–41)
- Study Guide (pp. 42–43)
- Catch-up for Absent Students (p. 44)
- Application (p. 45)
- Challenge (p. 46)

Workbooks
- Notetaking Guide (pp. 141–143)
- Practice Workbook (pp. 83–84)

Teaching Options
- **Power Presentations CD-ROM** provides dynamic electronic teaching resources for the classroom.
- **Activity Generator CD-ROM** provides editable activities for all ability levels.

Interactive Technology
- Easy Planner
- Power Presentations CD-ROM
- Activity Generator CD-ROM
- Animated Algebra
- Test Generator CD-ROM
- Online Quiz
- eWorkbook
- eEdition
- @HomeTutor

Resources for English Learners
- Quick Reference for English Learners
- Spanish Study Guide
- Multi-Language Visual Glossary
- Student Resources in Spanish

See also the *Algebra 2 Toolkit* for more strategies for meeting individual needs.

Motivating the Lesson

Have students work in groups to research two-variable data (such as time and cost) from various sources. Have them then plot the data to see if a polynomial equation might be a reasonable model for the data. In this lesson they will learn how to solve polynomial equations.

3 TEACH

Extra Example 1

Factor the polynomial completely.

a. $y^3 - 4y^2 - 12y$ $y(y-6)(y+2)$

b. $3x^3 + 30x^2 + 75x$ $3x(x+5)^2$

c. $5g^5 - 80g^3$ $5g^3(g-4)(g+4)$

Key Question to Ask for Example 1

- How can you check that your factors are correct? **Compare the product of the factors to the original polynomial.**

Extra Example 2

Factor the polynomial completely.

a. $27x^3 + 125$
$(3x+5)(9x^2 - 15x + 25)$

b. $-2d^5 + 250d^2$
$-2d^2(d-5)(d^2+5d+25)$

Key Question to Ask for Example 2

- How do the factors for the sum of two cubes differ from the factors for the difference of two cubes? **The binomial factors have opposite operation signs, as do the middle terms of the trinomial factors.**

Extra Example 3

Factor the polynomial $27t^3 + 45t^2 - 3t - 5$ completely.
$(3t+1)(3t-1)(3t+5)$

FACTORING PATTERNS In part (b) of Example 1, the special factoring pattern for the difference of two squares is used to factor the expression completely. There are also factoring patterns that you can use to factor the sum or difference of two *cubes.*

KEY CONCEPT *For Your Notebook*

Special Factoring Patterns

Sum of Two Cubes

$a^3 + b^3 = (a+b)(a^2 - ab + b^2)$

Example

$8x^3 + 27 = (2x)^3 + 3^3$
$= (2x+3)(4x^2 - 6x + 9)$

Difference of Two Cubes

$a^3 - b^3 = (a-b)(a^2 + ab + b^2)$

Example

$64x^3 - 1 = (4x)^3 - 1^3$
$= (4x-1)(16x^2 + 4x + 1)$

EXAMPLE 2 Factor the sum or difference of two cubes

Factor the polynomial completely.

a. $x^3 + 64 = x^3 + 4^3$ — Sum of two cubes
$= (x+4)(x^2 - 4x + 16)$

b. $16z^5 - 250z^2 = 2z^2(8z^3 - 125)$ — Factor common monomial.
$= 2z^2[(2z)^3 - 5^3]$ — Difference of two cubes
$= 2z^2(2z-5)(4z^2 + 10z + 25)$

✓ **GUIDED PRACTICE** for Examples 1 and 2

Factor the polynomial completely.

1. $x^3 - 7x^2 + 10x$ $x(x-5)(x-2)$
2. $3y^5 - 75y^3$ $3y^3(y-5)(y+5)$
3. $16b^5 + 686b^2$ $2b^2(2b+7)(4b^2 - 14b + 49)$
4. $w^3 - 27$ $(w-3)(w^2 + 3w + 9)$

FACTORING BY GROUPING For some polynomials, you can **factor by grouping** pairs of terms that have a common monomial factor. The pattern for factoring by grouping is shown below.

$$ra + rb + sa + sb = r(a+b) + s(a+b)$$
$$= (r+s)(a+b)$$

EXAMPLE 3 Factor by grouping

AVOID ERRORS
An expression is not factored completely until *all* factors, such as $x^2 - 16$, cannot be factored further.

Factor the polynomial $x^3 - 3x^2 - 16x + 48$ completely.

$x^3 - 3x^2 - 16x + 48 = x^2(x-3) - 16(x-3)$ — Factor by grouping.
$= (x^2 - 16)(x-3)$ — Distributive property
$= (x+4)(x-4)(x-3)$ — Difference of two squares

Differentiated Instruction

Visual Learners When discussing factoring by grouping, point out that students may also see the following pattern:

$$ra + rb + sa + sb = ra + sa + rb + sb$$
$$= (r+s)a + (r+s)b$$
$$= (r+s)(a+b)$$

Stress that this pattern gives the same result as shown above **Example 3.**

See also the *Algebra 2 Toolkit* for more strategies.

QUADRATIC FORM An expression of the form $au^2 + bu + c$, where u is any expression in x, is said to be in **quadratic form**. The factoring techniques you studied in Chapter 4 can sometimes be used to factor such expressions.

EXAMPLE 4 Factor polynomials in quadratic form

Factor completely: (a) $16x^4 - 81$ and (b) $2p^8 + 10p^5 + 12p^2$.

a. $16x^4 - 81 = (4x^2)^2 - 9^2$ — **Write as difference of two squares.**

$= (4x^2 + 9)(4x^2 - 9)$ — **Difference of two squares**

$= (4x^2 + 9)(2x + 3)(2x - 3)$ — **Difference of two squares**

b. $2p^8 + 10p^5 + 12p^2 = 2p^2(p^6 + 5p^3 + 6)$ — **Factor common monomial.**

$= 2p^2(p^3 + 3)(p^3 + 2)$ — **Factor trinomial in quadratic form.**

DENTIFY UADRATIC FORM
he expression $6x^4 - 81$ is in uadratic form because can be written as $^2 - 81$ where $u = 4x^2$.

GUIDED PRACTICE for Examples 3 and 4

Factor the polynomial completely.

5. $x^3 + 7x^2 - 9x - 63$
$(x - 3)(x + 3)(x + 7)$

6. $16g^4 - 625$
$(2g + 5)(2g - 5)(4g^2 + 25)$

7. $4t^6 - 20t^4 + 24t^2$
$4t^2(t^2 - 3)(t^2 - 2)$

SOLVING POLYNOMIAL EQUATIONS In Chapter 4, you learned how to use the zero product property to solve factorable quadratic equations. You can extend this technique to solve some higher-degree polynomial equations.

EXAMPLE 5 Standardized Test Practice

What are the real-number solutions of the equation $3x^5 + 15x = 18x^3$?

(A) 0, 1, 3, 5
(B) −1, 0, 1
(C) 0, 1, $\sqrt{5}$
(D) $-\sqrt{5}$, −1, 0, 1, $\sqrt{5}$

Solution

$3x^5 + 15x = 18x^3$ — **Write original equation.**

$3x^5 - 18x^3 + 15x = 0$ — **Write in standard form.**

$3x(x^4 - 6x^2 + 5) = 0$ — **Factor common monomial.**

$3x(x^2 - 1)(x^2 - 5) = 0$ — **Factor trinomial.**

$3x(x + 1)(x - 1)(x^2 - 5) = 0$ — **Difference of two squares**

$x = 0, x = -1, x = 1, x = \sqrt{5}$, or $x = -\sqrt{5}$ — **Zero product property**

▶ The correct answer is D. (A) (B) (C) (D)

VOID ERRORS
o not divide each side f an equation by a ariable or a variable xpression, such as $3x$. oing so will result in he loss of solutions.

GUIDED PRACTICE for Example 5

Find the real-number solutions of the equation.

8. $4x^5 - 40x^3 + 36x = 0$
−3, 3, −1, 1, 0

9. $2x^5 + 24x = 14x^3$
$-\sqrt{3}, \sqrt{3}$, 2, 0, −2

10. $-27x^3 + 15x^2 = -6x^4$
$0, \frac{9 \pm \sqrt{41}}{4}$

Extra Example 4

Factor completely (a) $10x^4 - 10$ and (b) $3m^{12} + 54m^7 + 51m^2$.
(a) $10(x^2 + 1)(x + 1)(x - 1)$,
(b) $3m^2(m^5 + 17)(m^5 + 1)$

Key Question to Ask for Example 4

- The factor $(p^6 + 5p^3 + 6)$ has quadratic form because it can be written as $au^2 + bu + c$. Which expression is equal to u? p^3

Extra Example 5

What are the real number solutions of $2x^5 = 12x^3 - 16x$? C

(A) $\frac{1}{2}, 1, \sqrt{3}$
(B) $-1, 1, \sqrt{3}$
(C) $0, 2, -2, \sqrt{2}, -\sqrt{2}$
(D) $-3, \frac{1}{2}, 1$

Key Questions to Ask for Example 5

- How were the roots $\sqrt{5}$ and $-\sqrt{5}$ derived? Since $x^2 - 5 = 0$, $x^2 = 5$, and $x = \pm\sqrt{5}$.
- Which solution will be lost if you first divide both sides of the equation by x? 0

Avoiding Common Errors

Students may have difficulty recognizing that a polynomial is in quadratic form when the degree of the polynomial is an even number greater than 2. Review the power of a power property of exponents to help students rewrite the power x^{2n} as $(x^n)^2$.

Teaching Strategy

You may want to review that if a factor is of the form $x^2 + a$ where $a > 0$, then x^2 has a negative value and x is not a real number.

Extra Example 6

You are making a metal tray by cutting equal squares from each corner of a rectangular sheet of metal as shown. What should the dimension of each cut-out square be for the volume of the tray to be 60 cubic inches? 5 in.

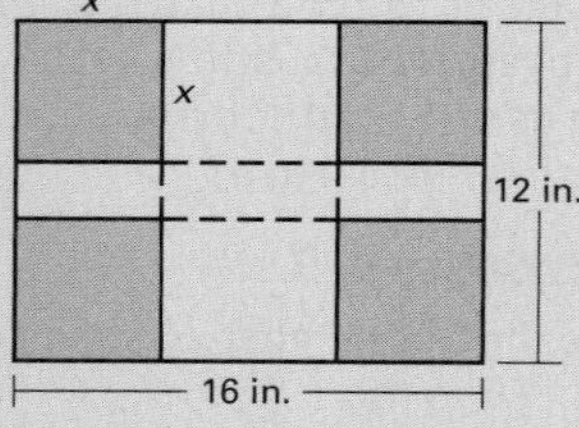

Key Questions to Ask for Example 6

- How do you determine the expression for the interior length of the basin? Because each side of the form is 1 foot thick, the interior length is 2 feet shorter than the exterior length.
- Why can't you solve the equation when it is in the form $36 = (2x - 2)(x - 2)(x - 1)$? One side is not zero, so you cannot apply the zero product property.

Closing the Lesson

Have students summarize the major points of the lesson and answer the Essential Question: How can you solve a higher-degree polynomial equation?

- To factor a polynomial completely, look for common monomial factors, use the factoring patterns, or factor by grouping.
- To find the real number solutions of a factorable quadratic equation, factor it and use the zero product property.

Factor the polynomial completely and use the zero product property.

EXAMPLE 6 Solve a polynomial equation

CITY PARK You are designing a marble basin that will hold a fountain for a city park. The basin's sides and bottom should be 1 foot thick. Its outer length should be twice its outer width and outer height.

What should the outer dimensions of the basin be if it is to hold 36 cubic feet of water?

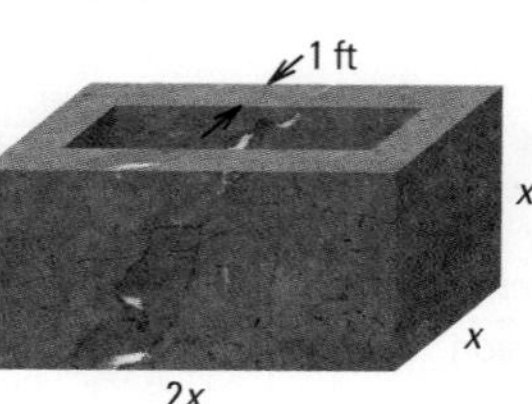

ANOTHER WAY
For alternative methods to solving the problem in Example 6, turn to page 360 for the **Problem Solving Workshop**.

Solution

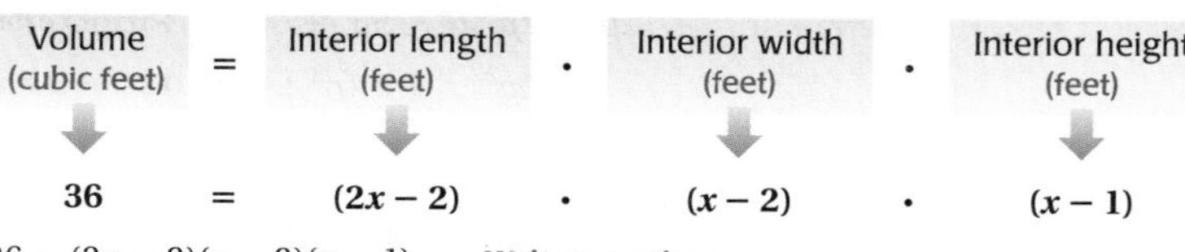

$36 = (2x - 2) \cdot (x - 2) \cdot (x - 1)$

$36 = (2x - 2)(x - 2)(x - 1)$	Write equation.
$0 = 2x^3 - 8x^2 + 10x - 40$	Write in standard form.
$0 = 2x^2(x - 4) + 10(x - 4)$	Factor by grouping.
$0 = (2x^2 + 10)(x - 4)$	Distributive property

▶ The only real solution is $x = 4$. The basin is 8 ft long, 4 ft wide, and 4 ft high.

GUIDED PRACTICE for Example 6

11. **WHAT IF?** In Example 6, what should the basin's dimensions be if it is to hold 40 cubic feet of water and have outer length $6x$, width $3x$, and height x? length: 12 ft, width: 6 ft, height: 2 ft

5.4 EXERCISES

HOMEWORK KEY
○ = **WORKED-OUT SOLUTIONS** on p. WS10 for Exs. 7, 23, and 61
★ = **STANDARDIZED TEST PRACTICE** Exs. 2, 9, 41, 63, and 64

SKILL PRACTICE

A

1. **VOCABULARY** The expression $8x^6 + 10x^3 - 3$ is in __?__ form because it can be written as $2u^2 + 5u - 3$ where $u = 2x^3$. quadratic

2. ★ **WRITING** What condition must the factorization of a polynomial satisfy in order for the polynomial to be factored completely?
It must be written as the product of a monomial and one or more prime polynomials.

EXAMPLE 1 on p. 353 for Exs. 3–9

MONOMIAL FACTORS **Factor the polynomial completely.**

3. $14x^2 - 21x$ $7x(2x - 3)$
4. $30b^3 - 54b^2$ $6b^2(5b - 9)$
5. $c^3 + 9c^2 + 18c$ $c(c + 3)(c + 6)$
6. $z^3 - 6z^2 - 72z$ $z(z - 12)(z + 6)$
7. $3y^5 - 48y^3$ $3y^3(y - 4)(y + 4)$
8. $54m^5 + 18m^4 + 9m^3$ $9m^3(6m^2 + 2m + 1)$

9. ★ **MULTIPLE CHOICE** What is the complete factorization of $2x^7 - 32x^3$? A

Ⓐ $2x^3(x + 2)(x - 2)(x^2 + 4)$
Ⓑ $2x^3(x^2 + 2)(x^2 - 2)$
Ⓒ $2x^3(x^2 + 4)^2$
Ⓓ $2x^3(x + 2)^2(x - 2)^2$

XAMPLE 2
n p. 354
r Exs. 10–17

SUM OR DIFFERENCE OF CUBES Factor the polynomial completely. 10–17. See margin.

10. $x^3 + 8$ 11. $y^3 - 64$ 12. $27m^3 + 1$ 13. $125n^3 + 216$

14. $27a^3 - 1000$ 15. $8c^3 + 343$ 16. $192w^3 - 3$ 17. $-5z^3 + 320$

XAMPLE 3
n p. 354
r Exs. 18–23

FACTORING BY GROUPING Factor the polynomial completely.

18. $x^3 + x^2 + x + 1$ $(x + 1)(x^2 + 1)$
19. $y^3 - 7y^2 + 4y - 28$ $(y - 7)(y^2 + 4)$
20. $n^3 + 5n^2 - 9n - 45$ $(n - 3)(n + 3)(n + 5)$
21. $3m^3 - m^2 + 9m - 3$ $(3m - 1)(m^2 + 3)$
22. $25s^3 - 100s^2 - s + 4$ $(s - 4)(5s - 1)(5s + 1)$
23. $4c^3 + 8c^2 - 9c - 18$ $(c + 2)(2c - 3)(2c + 3)$

XAMPLE 4
n p. 355
r Exs. 24–29

QUADRATIC FORM Factor the polynomial completely.

24. $x^4 - 25$ $(x^2 + 5)(x^2 - 5)$
25. $a^4 + 7a^2 + 6$ $(a^2 + 1)(a^2 + 6)$
26. $3s^4 - s^2 - 24$ $(s^2 - 3)(3s^2 + 8)$
27. $32z^5 - 2z$ $2z(2z - 1)(2z + 1)(4z^2 + 1)$
28. $36m^6 + 12m^4 + m^2$ $m^2(6m^2 + 1)^2$
29. $15x^5 - 72x^3 - 108x$ $3x(x^2 - 6)(5x^2 + 6)$

XAMPLE 5
n p. 355
r Exs. 30–41

ERROR ANALYSIS *Describe* and correct the error in finding all real-number solutions.

30.

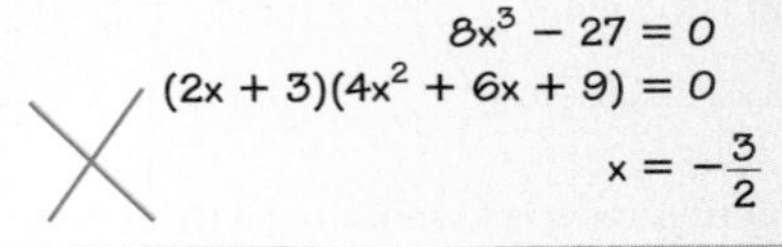

31.

$3x^3 - 48x = 0$
$3x(x^2 - 16) = 0$
$x^2 - 16 = 0$
$x = -4$ or $x = 4$

30. The equation is not factored correctly, $(a^3 - b^3) = (a - b)(a^2 + ab + b^2)$; $(2x - 3)(4x^2 + 6x + 9) = 0$, $x = \frac{3}{2}$.

31. The factor $3x$ should also be set equal to 0; $x = 0$, or $x = -4$, $x = 4$.

SOLVING EQUATIONS Find the real-number solutions of the equation.

32. $y^3 - 5y^2 = 0$ 0, 5
33. $18s^3 = 50s$ $0, -1\frac{2}{3}, 1\frac{2}{3}$
34. $g^3 + 3g^2 - g - 3 = 0$ −3, −1, 1
35. $m^3 + 6m^2 - 4m - 24 = 0$ 2, −2, −6
36. $4w^4 + 40w^2 - 44 = 0$ −1, 1
37. $4z^5 = 84z^3$ $0, -\sqrt{21}, \sqrt{21}$
38. $5b^3 + 15b^2 + 12b = -36$ −3
39. $x^6 - 4x^4 - 9x^2 + 36 = 0$ $-\sqrt{3}, \sqrt{3}, 2, -2$
40. $48p^5 = 27p^3$ $0, -\frac{3}{4}, \frac{3}{4}$

41. ★ **MULTIPLE CHOICE** What are the real-number solutions of the equation $3x^4 - 27x^2 + 9x = x^3$? C

Ⓐ −1, 0, 3 Ⓑ −3, 0, 3 Ⓒ $-3, 0, \frac{1}{3}, 3$ Ⓓ $-3, -\frac{1}{3}, 0, 3$

B **CHOOSING A METHOD** Factor the polynomial completely using any method.

42. $16x^3 - 44x^2 - 42x$ $2x(2x - 7)(4x + 3)$
43. $n^4 - 4n^2 - 60$ $(n^2 - 10)(n^2 + 6)$
44. $-4b^4 - 500b$ $-4b(b + 5)(b^2 - 5b + 25)$
45. $36a^3 - 15a^2 + 84a - 35$ $(12a - 5)(3a^2 + 7)$
46. $18c^4 + 57c^3 - 10c^2$ $c^2(3c + 10)(6c - 1)$
47. $2d^4 - 13d^2 - 45$ $(d + 3)(d - 3)(2d^2 + 5)$
48. $32x^5 - 108x^2$ $4x^2(2x - 3)(4x^2 + 6x + 9)$
49. $8y^6 - 38y^4 - 10y^2$ $2y^2(y^2 - 5)(4y^2 + 1)$
50. $z^5 - 3z^4 - 16z + 48$ $(z - 2)(z + 2)(z - 3)(z^2 + 4)$

GEOMETRY Find the possible value(s) of x.

51. Area = 48 2

$x + 4$, $3x + 2$

52. Volume = 40 5

$x - 4$, $2x$, $x - 1$

53. Volume = 125π 5

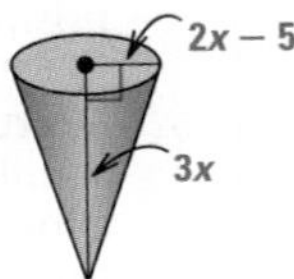

C **CHOOSING A METHOD** Factor the polynomial completely using any method.

54. $x^3y^6 - 27$ $(xy^2 - 3)(x^2y^4 + 3xy^2 + 9)$
55. $7ac^2 + bc^2 - 7ad^2 - bd^2$ $(c + d)(c - d)(7a + b)$
56. $x^{2n} - 2x^n + 1$ $(x^n - 1)^2$

57. **CHALLENGE** Factor $a^5b^2 - a^2b^4 + 2a^4b - 2ab^3 + a^3 - b^2$ completely. $(a^3 - b^2)(ab + 1)^2$

4 PRACTICE AND APPLY

Assignment Guide

Answer Transparencies available for all exercises

Basic:
Day 1: EP p. 1013 Exs. 13–16
pp. 356–359
Exs. 1, 2, 3–29 odd, 30–34, 41–44, 58–62, 66

Average:
Day 1: pp. 356–359
Exs. 1, 2, 4–8 even, 9, 10–28 even, 30, 31, 35–37, 41, 45–47, 51–53, 60–63, 67

Advanced:
Day 1: pp. 356–359
Exs. 1, 2, 7–9, 15–17, 21–23, 27–29, 38–41, 47–57*, 60–65*

Block:
pp. 356–359
Exs. 1, 2, 4–8 even, 9, 10–28 even, 30, 31, 35–37, 41, 45–47, 51–53, 60–63, 67 (with 5.5)

Differentiated Instruction

See *Algebra 2 Best Practices Toolkit* for suggestions on addressing the needs of a diverse classroom.

Homework Check

For a quick check of student understanding of key concepts, go over the following exercises:

Basic: 5, 11, 19, 32, 58
Average: 6, 14, 20, 36, 60
Advanced: 8, 16, 22, 38, 62

Extra Practice

- Student Edition, p. 1014
- Chapter 5 Resource Book: Practice levels A, B, C, pp. 39–41

Practice Worksheet

An easily-readable reduced practice page (with answers) for this lesson can be found on p. 328C.

10. $(x + 2)(x^2 - 2x + 4)$
11. $(y - 4)(y^2 + 4y + 16)$
12. $(3m + 1)(9m^2 - 3m + 1)$
13. $(5n + 6)(25n^2 - 30n + 36)$
14. $(3a - 10)(9a^2 + 30a + 100)$
15. $(2c + 7)(4c^2 + 14c + 49)$
16. $3(4w - 1)(16w^2 + 4w + 1)$
17. $-5(z - 4)(z^2 + 4z + 16)$

PROBLEM SOLVING

Reading Strategy

Exercise 62 Word problems often contain extraneous information. This problem involves the volume of a rectangular solid, so determine which measurements in the problem are needed to calculate volume.

EXAMPLE 6 A on p. 356 for Exs. 58–63

58. **ARCHAEOLOGY** At the ruins of Caesarea, archaeologists discovered a huge hydraulic concrete block with a volume of 945 cubic meters. The block's dimensions are x meters high by $12x - 15$ meters long by $12x - 21$ meters wide. What is the height of the block? **3 m**

 for problem solving help at classzone.com

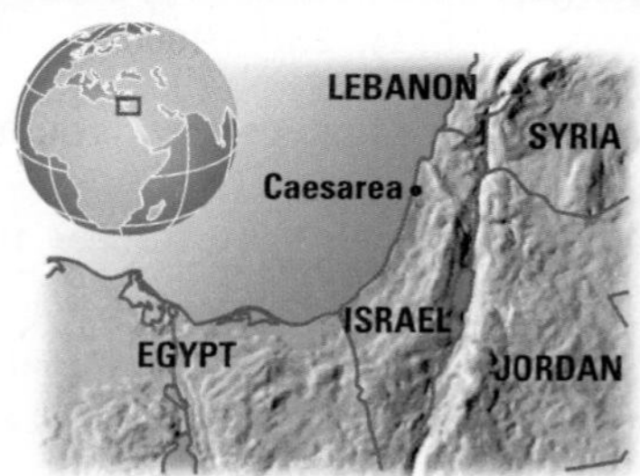

59. **CHOCOLATE MOLD** You are designing a chocolate mold shaped like a hollow rectangular prism for a candy manufacturer. The mold must have a thickness of 1 centimeter in all dimensions. The mold's outer dimensions should also be in the ratio 1:3:6. What should the outer dimensions of the mold be if it is to hold 112 cubic centimeters of chocolate? **3 cm by 9 cm by 18 cm**

@HomeTutor for problem solving help at classzone.com

60c. 2.5; bottom: length: 20 ft, width: 15 ft, height: 2.5 ft; middle: length: 15 ft, width: 10 ft, height: 2.5 ft; top: length: 10 ft, width: 5 ft, height: 2.5 ft

60. **MULTI-STEP PROBLEM** A production crew is assembling a three-level platform inside a stadium for a performance. The platform has the dimensions shown in the diagrams, and has a total volume of 1250 cubic feet.

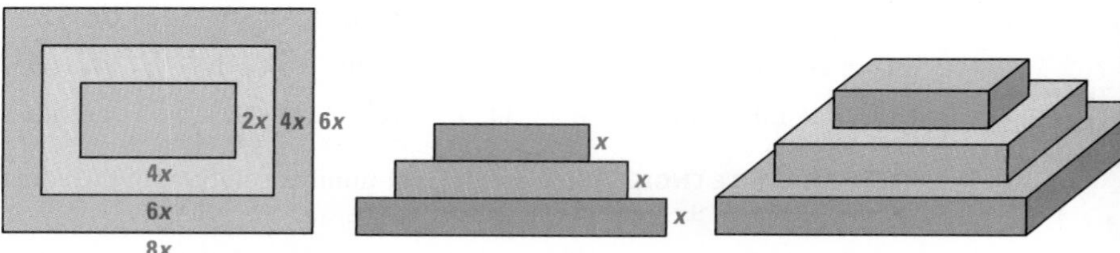

a. **Write Expressions** What is the volume, in terms of x, of each of the three levels of the platform? **bottom: $48x^3$, middle: $24x^3$ top: $8x^3$**

b. **Write an Equation** Use what you know about the total volume to write an equation involving x. **$1250 = 80x^3$**

c. **Solve** Solve the equation from part (b). Use your solution to calculate the dimensions of each of the three levels of the platform.

(61.) **SCULPTURE** Suppose you have 250 cubic inches of clay with which to make a sculpture shaped as a rectangular prism. You want the height and width each to be 5 inches less than the length. What should the dimensions of the prism be? **length: 10 in., width: 5 in., height: 5 in.**

B

62. length: 4 ft, width: 2 ft, height 12 ft

62. **MANUFACTURING** A manufacturer wants to build a rectangular stainless steel tank with a holding capacity of 670 gallons, or about 89.58 cubic feet. The tank's walls will be one half inch thick, and about 6.42 cubic feet of steel will be used for the tank. The manufacturer wants the outer dimensions of the tank to be related as follows:

- The width should be 2 feet less than the length.
- The height should be 8 feet more than the length.

What should the outer dimensions of the tank be?

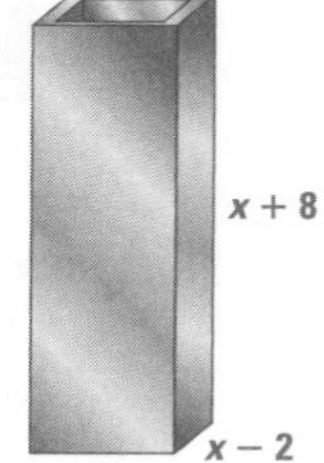

◯ = WORKED-OUT SOLUTIONS on p. WS1 ★ = STANDARDIZED TEST PRACTICE

64a.

y	1	2	3	4	5	6	7	8	9	10
$y^3 + y^2$	2	12	36	80	150	252	392	576	810	1100

The volume cannot be $\frac{7}{3}$ because the only x-value that corresponds to that volume is about -1.37, which would yield a negative edge length.

63. ★ **SHORT RESPONSE** A platform shaped like a rectangular prism has dimensions $x - 2$ feet by $3 - 2x$ feet by $3x + 4$ feet. *Explain* why the volume of the platform cannot be $\frac{7}{3}$ cubic feet.

64. ★ **EXTENDED RESPONSE** In 2000 B.C., the Babylonians solved polynomial equations using tables of values. One such table gave values of $y^3 + y^2$. To be able to use this table, the Babylonians sometimes had to manipulate the equation, as shown below.

$ax^3 + bx^2 = c$	**Original equation**
$\frac{a^3x^3}{b^3} + \frac{a^2x^2}{b^2} = \frac{a^2c}{b^3}$	**Multiply each side by $\frac{a^2}{b^3}$.**
$\left(\frac{ax}{b}\right)^3 + \left(\frac{ax}{b}\right)^2 = \frac{a^2c}{b^3}$	**Rewrite cubes and squares.**

They then found $\frac{a^2c}{b^3}$ in the $y^3 + y^2$ column of the table. Because the corresponding y-value was $y = \frac{ax}{b}$, they could conclude that $x = \frac{by}{a}$.

a. Calculate $y^3 + y^2$ for $y = 1, 2, 3, \ldots, 10$. Record the values in a table. **See margin.**

b. Use your table and the method described above to solve $x^3 + 2x^2 = 96$. **4**

c. Use your table and the method described above to solve $3x^3 + 2x^2 = 512$. $5\frac{1}{3}$

d. How can you modify the method described above for equations of the form $ax^4 + bx^3 = c$? **In the first step, multiply by $\frac{a^3}{b^4}$.**

a. If there was not a piece of the solid missing, the volume would be a^3. The volume of the piece missing is b^3. So, the volume of the solid is $a^3 - b^3$.

b. solid I: $(a)(a - b)$, solid II: $(b)(a - b)$, solid III: $(b)(a - b)$

65. **CHALLENGE** Use the diagram to complete parts (a)–(c).

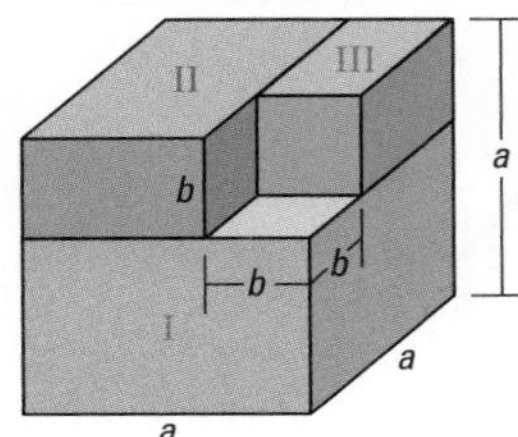

a. *Explain* why $a^3 - b^3$ is equal to the sum of the volumes of solid I, solid II, and solid III.

b. Write an algebraic expression for the volume of each of the three solids. Leave your expressions in factored form.

c. Use the results from parts (a) and (b) to derive the factoring pattern for $a^3 - b^3$ given on page 354.
$a^3 - b^3 = (a)(a)(a - b) + (a)(b)(a - b) + (b)(b)(a - b), = (a - b)(a^2 + ab + b^2)$

KENTUCKY MIXED REVIEW

KY

TEST PRACTICE at classzone.com

66. Which inequality best describes the range of the function represented by the graph shown? **A**

Ⓐ $y \le 3$ Ⓑ $y \ge 3$

Ⓒ $-3 \le y \le 3$ Ⓓ $-4 \le y \le 4$

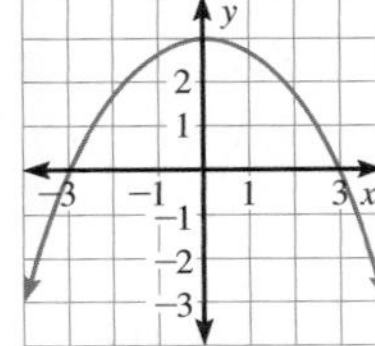

67. A poster is shaped like an equilateral triangle with a side length of 30 inches. What is the approximate area of the poster? **C**

Ⓐ 195 in.^{2} Ⓑ 318 in.^{2}

Ⓒ 390 in.^{2} Ⓓ 780 in.^{2}

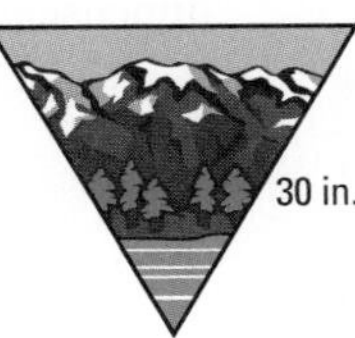

5 ASSESS AND RETEACH

Daily Homework Quiz

Transparency Available

Factor the polynomial completely.

1. $27 - y^3$ $(3 - y)(9 + 3y + y^2)$
2. $28x^3 - 7x^2 + 36x - 9$ $(7x^2 + 9)(4x - 1)$
3. What are the real number solutions of the equation $2x = x^2 + x^3$? $-2, 0, 1$
4. The width of a rug is 3 feet shorter than its length. If the area of the rug is 108 square feet, what are the dimensions of the rug? 9 ft × 12 ft

Available at **classzone.com**

Diagnosis/Remediation

- Practice A, B, C in Chapter 5 Resource Book, pp. 39–41
- Study Guide in Chapter 5 Resource Book, pp. 42–43
- Practice Workbook, pp. 83–84
- @HomeTutor

Challenge

Additional challenge is available in the Chapter 5 Resource Book, p. 46.

Alternative Strategy

Example 6 on page 356 can be solved by using a table or a graph. Both methods allow students to visualize the solution and will help students to better understand the algebraic solution given in Lesson 5.4.

Another Way to Solve Example 6, page 356

MULTIPLE REPRESENTATIONS In Example 6 on page 356, you solved a polynomial equation by factoring. You can also solve a polynomial equation using a table or a graph.

PROBLEM

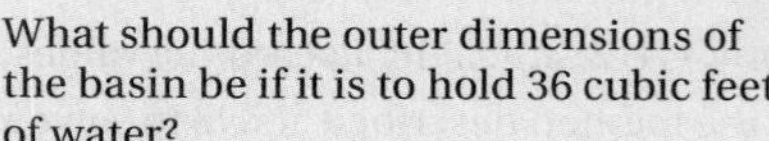

CITY PARK You are designing a marble basin that will hold a fountain for a city park. The basin's sides and bottom should be 1 foot thick. Its outer length should be twice its outer width and outer height.

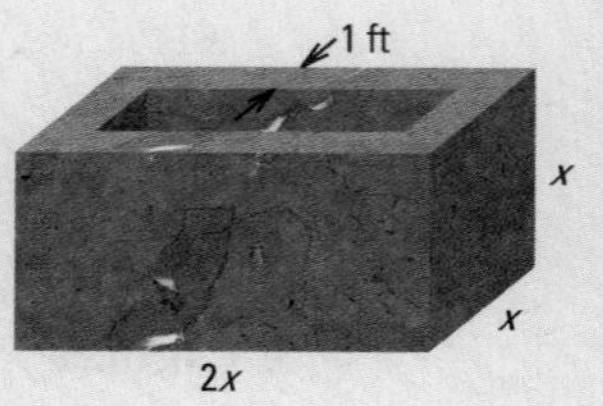

What should the outer dimensions of the basin be if it is to hold 36 cubic feet of water?

METHOD 1

Using a Table One alternative approach is to write a function for the volume of the basin and make a table of values for the function. Using the table, you can find the value of x that makes the volume of the basin 36 cubic feet.

STEP 1 **Write** the function. From the diagram, you can see that the volume y of water the basin can hold is given by this function:

$$y = (2x - 2)(x - 2)(x - 1)$$

STEP 2 **Make** a table of values for the function. Use only positive values of x because the basin's dimensions must be positive.

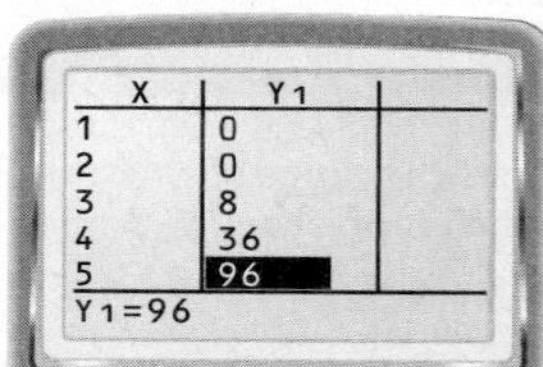

STEP 3 **Identify** the value of x for which $y = 36$. The table shows that $y = 36$ when $x = 4$.

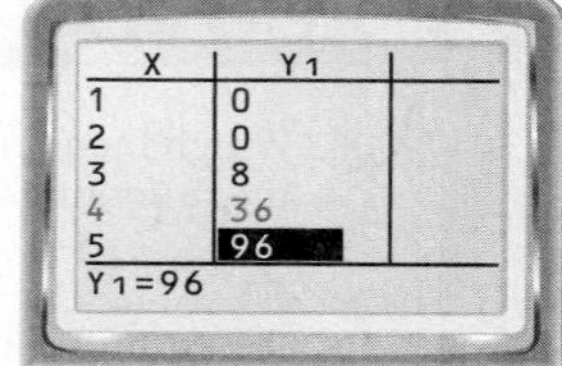

▸ The volume of the basin is 36 cubic feet when x is 4 feet. So, the outer dimensions of the basin should be as follows:

Length $= 2x = 8$ feet

Width $= x = 4$ feet

Height $= x = 4$ feet

METHOD 2 **Using a Graph** Another approach is to make a graph. You can use the graph to find the value of x that makes the volume of the basin 36 cubic feet.

STEP 1 **Write** the function. From the diagram, you can see that the volume y of water the basin can hold is given by this function:

$$y = (2x - 2)(x - 2)(x - 1)$$

STEP 2 **Graph** the equations $y = 36$ and $y = (x - 1)(2x - 2)(x - 2)$. Choose a viewing window that shows the intersection of the graphs.

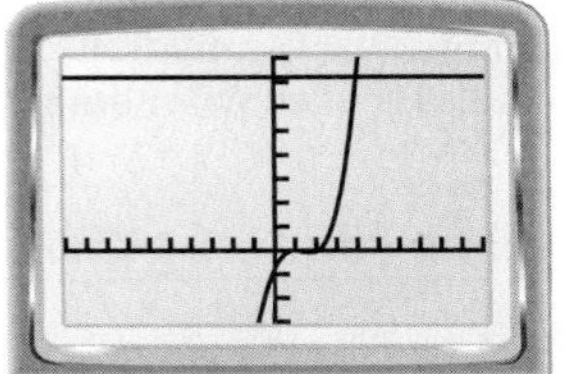

STEP 3 **Identify** the coordinates of the intersection point. On a graphing calculator, you can use the *intersect* feature. The intersection point is (4, 36).

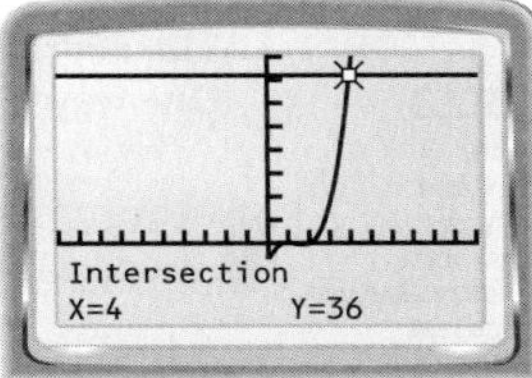

▶ The volume of the basin is 36 cubic feet when x is 4 feet. So, the outer dimensions of the basin should be as follows:

Length $= 2x = 8$ feet

Width $= x = 4$ feet

Height $= x = 4$ feet

PRACTICE

SOLVING EQUATIONS Solve the polynomial equation using a table or using a graph.

1. $x^3 + 4x^2 - 8x = 96$ **4**
2. $x^3 - 9x^2 - 14x + 7 = -33$ **about −2.6, about 1.6, 10**
3. $2x^3 - 11x^2 + 3x + 5 = 59$ **6**
4. $x^4 + x^3 - 15x^2 - 8x + 6 = -45$ **about −3.4, about −2.5, about 2.0, 3**
5. $-x^4 + 2x^3 + 6x^2 + 17x - 4 = 32$ **about 1.4, 4**
6. $-3x^4 + 4x^3 + 8x^2 + 4x - 11 = 13$ **about 1.6, 2**
7. $4x^4 - 16x^3 + 29x^2 - 95x = -150$ **2.5**
8. **WHAT IF?** In the problem on page 360, suppose the basin is to hold 200 cubic feet of water. Find the outer dimensions of the basin using a table and using a graph. **height: 6 ft, width: 6 ft, length: 12 ft**
9. **PACKAGING** A factory needs a box that has a volume of 1728 cubic inches. The width should be 4 inches less than the height, and the length should be 6 inches greater than the height. Find the dimensions of the box using a table and using a graph. **height: 12 in., width: 8 in., length: 18 in.**
10. **AGRICULTURE** From 1970 to 2002, the average yearly pineapple consumption P (in pounds) per person in the United States can be modeled by the function

$$P(x) = 0.0000984x^4 - 0.00712x^3 + 0.162x^2 - 1.11x + 12.3$$

where x is the number of years since 1970. In what year was the pineapple consumption about 9.97 pounds per person? Solve the problem using a table and a graph. **1975**

Graphing Calculator

Students should realize that to work with tables or graphs, they can enter a polynomial in any form, including standard form or factored form.

Avoiding Common Errors

Exercises 1–7 Some students may not rewrite these exercises in function form before entering them into their calculators. Remind students that all terms, including the constant, must be on the same side of the equal sign for the equation to be in function form.

1 PLAN AND PREPARE

Warm-Up Exercises

Transparency Available

1. Use the quadratic formula to solve $2x^2 - 3x - 1 = 0$. Round to the nearest hundredth. **1.78, −0.28**
2. Use synthetic substitution to evaluate $f(x) = x^3 + x^2 - 3x - 10$ when $x = 2$. **−4**
3. A company's income is modeled by the function $P = 22x^2 - 571x$. What is the value of P when $x = 200$? **765,800**

Notetaking Guide

Transparency Available

Promotes interactive learning and notetaking skills, pp. 144–146.

Pacing

Basic: 2 days
Average: 2 days
Advanced: 2 days
Block: 0.5 block with 5.4
0.5 block with 5.6

• See *Teaching Guide/Lesson Plan.*

2 FOCUS AND MOTIVATE

Essential Question

Big Idea 3, p. 329

If you know one zero of a polynomial function, how can you determine another zero? **Tell students they will learn how to answer this question by using synthetic division.**

5.5 Apply the Remainder and Factor Theorems

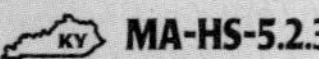

MA-HS-5.2.3

Before You used special patterns to factor polynomials.
Now You will use theorems to factor polynomials.
Why? So you can determine attendance at sports games, as in Ex. 43.

Key Vocabulary
- **polynomial long division**
- **synthetic division**

MA-HS-5.2.3
Students will: add, subtract and multiply polynomial expressions; factor polynomial expressions using the greatest common monomial factor and factor quadratic polynomials of the form $ax^2 + bx + c$, when $a = 1$ and b and c are integers. DOK 2

When you divide a polynomial $f(x)$ by a divisor $d(x)$, you get a quotient polynomial $q(x)$ and a remainder polynomial $r(x)$.

$$\frac{f(x)}{d(x)} = q(x) + \frac{r(x)}{d(x)}$$

The degree of the remainder must be less than the degree of the divisor. One way to divide polynomials is called **polynomial long division**.

EXAMPLE 1 Use polynomial long division

Divide $f(x) = 3x^4 - 5x^3 + 4x - 6$ by $x^2 - 3x + 5$.

Solution

Write polynomial division in the same format you use when dividing numbers. Include a "0" as the coefficient of x^2 in the dividend. At each stage, divide the term with the highest power in what is left of the dividend by the first term of the divisor. This gives the next term of the quotient.

$$x^2 - 3x + 5\,\overline{)\,3x^4 - 5x^3 + 0x^2 + 4x - 6}$$

$3x^2 + 4x - 3$	← quotient
$3x^4 - 9x^3 + 15x^2$	**Multiply divisor by $3x^4/x^2 = 3x^2$.**
$4x^3 - 15x^2 + 4x$	**Subtract. Bring down next term.**
$4x^3 - 12x^2 + 20x$	**Multiply divisor by $4x^3/x^2 = 4x$.**
$-3x^2 - 16x - 6$	**Subtract. Bring down next term.**
$-3x^2 + 9x - 15$	**Multiply divisor by $-3x^2/x^2 = -3$.**
$-25x + 9$	← **remainder**

AVOID ERRORS
The expression added to the quotient in the result of the long division problem is $\frac{r(x)}{d(x)}$, not $r(x)$.

$$\frac{3x^4 - 5x^3 + 4x - 6}{x^2 - 3x + 5} = 3x^2 + 4x - 3 + \frac{-25x + 9}{x^2 - 3x + 5}$$

CHECK You can check the result of a division problem by multiplying the quotient by the divisor and adding the remainder. The result should be the dividend.

$(3x^2 + 4x - 3)(x^2 - 3x + 5) + (-25x + 9)$

$= 3x^2(x^2 - 3x + 5) + 4x(x^2 - 3x + 5) - 3(x^2 - 3x + 5) - 25x + 9$

$= 3x^4 - 9x^3 + 15x^2 + 4x^3 - 12x^2 + 20x - 3x^2 + 9x - 15 - 25x + 9$

$= 3x^4 - 5x^3 + 4x - 6$ ✓

Resource Planning Guide

Chapter Resource Book
- Teaching Guide/Lesson Plan (pp. 47–48)
- Practice levels A, B, C (pp. 49–51)
- Study Guide (pp. 52–53)
- Catch-up for Absent Students (p. 54)
- Problem Solving Workshop (p. 55)
- Challenge (p. 57)

Workbooks
- Notetaking Guide (pp. 144–146)
- Practice Workbook (pp. 85–86)

Teaching Options
- **Power Presentations CD-ROM** provides dynamic electronic teaching resources for the classroom.
- **Activity Generator CD-ROM** provides editable activities for all ability levels.

Interactive Technology
- Easy Planner
- Power Presentations CD-ROM
- Activity Generator CD-ROM
- Animated Algebra
- Test Generator CD-ROM
- Online Quiz
- eWorkbook
- eEdition
- @HomeTutor

Resources for English Learners
- Quick Reference for English Learners
- Spanish Study Guide
- Multi-Language Visual Glossary
- Student Resources in Spanish

See also the *Algebra 2 Toolkit* for more strategies for meeting individual needs.

EXAMPLE 2 Use polynomial long division with a linear divisor

Divide $f(x) = x^3 + 5x^2 - 7x + 2$ by $x - 2$.

$$\begin{array}{r l}
x^2 + 7x + 7 & \leftarrow \text{quotient} \\
x - 2\,\overline{)\,x^3 + 5x^2 - 7x + 2} & \\
\underline{x^3 - 2x^2} & \text{Multiply divisor by } x^3/x = x^2. \\
7x^2 - 7x & \text{Subtract.} \\
\underline{7x^2 - 14x} & \text{Multiply divisor by } 7x^2/x = 7x. \\
7x + 2 & \text{Subtract.} \\
\underline{7x - 14} & \text{Multiply divisor by } 7x/x = 7. \\
16 & \leftarrow \text{remainder}
\end{array}$$

▶ $\dfrac{x^3 + 5x^2 - 7x + 2}{x - 2} = x^2 + 7x + 7 + \dfrac{16}{x - 2}$

✓ **GUIDED PRACTICE** for Examples 1 and 2

Divide using polynomial long division.

1. $(2x^4 + x^3 + x - 1) \div (x^2 + 2x - 1)$ $2x^2 - 3x + 8 + \dfrac{-18x + 7}{x^2 + 2x - 1}$

2. $(x^3 - x^2 + 4x - 10) \div (x + 2)$ $x^2 - 3x + 10 + \dfrac{-30}{x + 2}$

SYNTHETIC DIVISION If you use synthetic substitution to evaluate $f(x)$ in Example 2 when $x = 2$, as shown below, you can see that $f(2)$ equals the remainder when $f(x)$ is divided by $x - 2$. Also, the other values below the line match the coefficients of the quotient. For this reason, synthetic substitution is sometimes called **synthetic division**. Synthetic division can be used to divide any polynomial by a divisor of the form $x - k$.

$$\begin{array}{r|rrrr}
2 & 1 & 5 & -7 & 2 \\
 & & 2 & 14 & 14 \\ \hline
 & 1 & 7 & 7 & 16
\end{array}$$

coefficients of quotient → 1 7 7 | 16 ← remainder

KEY CONCEPT *For Your Notebook*

Remainder Theorem

If a polynomial $f(x)$ is divided by $x - k$, then the remainder is $r = f(k)$.

EXAMPLE 3 Use synthetic division

Divide $f(x) = 2x^3 + x^2 - 8x + 5$ by $x + 3$ using synthetic division.

DIVIDE POLYNOMIALS Because the divisor is $x + 3 = x - (-3)$, evaluate the dividend when $x = -3$.

$$\begin{array}{r|rrrr}
-3 & 2 & 1 & -8 & 5 \\
 & & -6 & 15 & -21 \\ \hline
 & 2 & -5 & 7 & -16
\end{array}$$

▶ $\dfrac{2x^3 + x^2 - 8x + 5}{x + 3} = 2x^2 - 5x + 7 - \dfrac{16}{x + 3}$

Differentiated Instruction

Inclusion Students may lose track of the degree of the terms of the coefficients when using synthetic division. It may be helpful to show the degree of the terms above their work. The following shows how this can be done to start **Example 3**.

$$\begin{array}{r|rrrr}
 & x^3 & x^2 & x & 1 \\
-3 & 2 & 1 & -8 & 5 \\ \hline
 & x^2 & x & 1 &
\end{array}$$

See also the *Algebra 2 Toolkit* for more strategies.

Motivating the Lesson

In this lesson students will learn two methods for dividing polynomials, the long division method and synthetic division. Tell students both methods should look familiar: the long division algorithm for polynomials because it is similar to the long division algorithm for whole numbers; and synthetic division because it is related to synthetic substitution, studied in Lesson 5.2. For polynomials, synthetic division shortens the procedure because only the coefficients of the terms are used.

3 TEACH

Extra Example 1

Divide $f(x) = x^3 + 3x^2 - 7$ by $x^2 - x - 2$. $x + 4 + \dfrac{6x + 1}{x^2 - x - 2}$

Key Questions to Ask for Example 1

- In the dividend, why is there a 0 for the coeffcient of the x^2-term? The dividend has no actual x^2-term but an x^2-term is needed as a placeholder in the long division algorithm.

Extra Example 2

Divide $f(x) = 3x^3 + 17x^2 + 21x - 11$ by $x + 3$. $3x^2 + 8x - 3 + \dfrac{-2}{x + 3}$

Extra Example 3

Divide $f(x) = 2x^3 + 9x^2 + 14x + 5$ by $x - 3$. $2x^2 + 15x + 59 + \dfrac{182}{x - 3}$

Key Question to Ask for Example 3

- To divide a polynomial $f(x)$ by $x + a$, for which value will you evaluate the polynomial using synthetic division? $-a$

Extra Example 4

Factor $f(x) = 2x^3 - 11x^2 + 3x + 36$ completely given that $x - 3$ is a factor. $(x - 3)(x - 4)(2x + 3)$

Key Questions to Ask for Example 4

- What is $f(4)$? What is $f(-2)$? 0, 0
- If you use synthetic division to divide the polynomial by $-\frac{2}{3}$, what will be the remainder? 0

Reading Strategy

The phrase if and only if in the Factor Theorem means that if a polynomial $f(x)$ has a factor $x - k$ then $f(k) = 0$, and if $f(k) = 0$ then $f(x)$ has a factor $x - k$.

Avoiding Common Errors

Point out the Avoid Errors note next to Example 4. Some students tend to overlook the fact that the last number generated by synthetic division when dividing by a factor should be zero. This leads to incorrect factoring.

FACTOR THEOREM Suppose the remainder is 0 when a polynomial $f(x)$ is divided by $x - k$. Then

$$\frac{f(x)}{x-k} = q(x) + \frac{0}{x-k} = q(x)$$

where $q(x)$ is the quotient polynomial. Therefore, $f(x) = (x - k) \cdot q(x)$, so that $x - k$ is a factor of $f(x)$. This result is summarized by the *factor theorem.*

KEY CONCEPT *For Your Notebook*

Factor Theorem

A polynomial $f(x)$ has a factor $x - k$ if and only if $f(k) = 0$.

The factor theorem can be used to solve a variety of problems.

Problem	Example
Given one *factor* of a polynomial, find the other *factors.*	See Example 4 below.
Given one *zero* of a polynomial function, find the other *zeros.*	See Example 5 on page 365.
Given one *solution* of a polynomial equation, find the other *solutions.*	See Example 6 on page 365.

EXAMPLE 4 Factor a polynomial

Factor $f(x) = 3x^3 - 4x^2 - 28x - 16$ completely given that $x + 2$ is a factor.

Solution

AVOID ERRORS
The remainder after using synthetic division should always be zero when you are dividing a polynomial by one of its factors.

Because $x + 2$ is a factor of $f(x)$, you know that $f(-2) = 0$. Use synthetic division to find the other factors.

−2	3	−4	−28	−16
		−6	20	16
	3	−10	−8	0

Use the result to write $f(x)$ as a product of two factors and then factor completely.

$f(x) = 3x^3 - 4x^2 - 28x - 16$ **Write original polynomial.**

$= (x + 2)(3x^2 - 10x - 8)$ **Write as a product of two factors.**

$= (x + 2)(3x + 2)(x - 4)$ **Factor trinomial.**

GUIDED PRACTICE for Examples 3 and 4

Divide using synthetic division.

3. $(x^3 + 4x^2 - x - 1) \div (x + 3)$ $x^2 + x - 4 + \frac{11}{x+3}$

4. $(4x^3 + x^2 - 3x + 7) \div (x - 1)$ $4x^2 + 5x + 2 + \frac{9}{x-1}$

Factor the polynomial completely given that $x - 4$ is a factor.

5. $f(x) = x^3 - 6x^2 + 5x + 12$ $(x - 4)(x - 3)(x + 1)$

6. $f(x) = x^3 - x^2 - 22x + 40$ $(x - 4)(x - 2)(x + 5)$

EXAMPLE 5 Standardized Test Practice

One zero of $f(x) = x^3 - 2x^2 - 23x + 60$ is $x = 3$. What is another zero of f?

Ⓐ -5 Ⓑ -4 Ⓒ 2 Ⓓ 5

Solution

Because $f(3) = 0$, $x - 3$ is a factor of $f(x)$. Use synthetic division.

3	1	−2	−23	60
		3	3	−60
	1	1	−20	0

Use the result to write $f(x)$ as a product of two factors. Then factor completely.

$$f(x) = x^3 - 2x^2 - 23x + 60 = (x - 3)(x^2 + x - 20) = (x - 3)(x + 5)(x - 4)$$

The zeros are 3, −5, and 4.

▶ The correct answer is A. Ⓐ Ⓑ Ⓒ Ⓓ

EXAMPLE 6 Use a polynomial model

BUSINESS The profit P (in millions of dollars) for a shoe manufacturer can be modeled by $P = -21x^3 + 46x$ where x is the number of shoes produced (in millions). The company now produces 1 million shoes and makes a profit of \$25,000,000, but would like to cut back production. What lesser number of shoes could the company produce and still make the same profit?

Solution

$25 = -21x^3 + 46x$ **Substitute 25 for P in $P = -21x^3 + 46x$.**

$0 = 21x^3 - 46x + 25$ **Write in standard form.**

You know that $x = 1$ is one solution of the equation. This implies that $x - 1$ is a factor of $21x^3 - 46x + 25$. Use synthetic division to find the other factors.

1	21	0	−46	25
		21	21	−25
	21	21	−25	0

So, $(x - 1)(21x^2 + 21x - 25) = 0$. Use the quadratic formula to find that $x \approx 0.7$ is the other positive solution.

▶ The company could still make the same profit producing about 700,000 shoes.

GUIDED PRACTICE for Examples 5 and 6

Find the other zeros of f given that $f(-2) = 0$.

7. $f(x) = x^3 + 2x^2 - 9x - 18$ −3, 3

8. $f(x) = x^3 + 8x^2 + 5x - 14$ −7, 1

9. **WHAT IF?** In Example 6, how does the answer change if the profit for the shoe manufacturer is modeled by $P = -15x^3 + 40x$?

The company could ...ake the same profit ...roducing about 900,000 ...hoes.

Extra Example 5

One zero of $f(x) = x^3 + x^2 - 16x - 16$ is 4. What is another zero of $f(x)$? B

Ⓐ −2 Ⓑ −1

Ⓒ 1 Ⓓ 2

Key Question to Ask for Example 5

- What is the value of $f(-5)$? 0

Extra Example 6

A company's profit C (in thousands of dollars) can be modeled by $C = -5x^3 + 6x^2 + 15x$, where x is the number of items produced in thousands. The profit is \$14,000 for producing 2000 items. What other number of items would produce about the same profit? about 850 items

Key Question to Ask for Example 6

- What does the synthetic divisor represent? the 1 million shoes the manufacturer now produces

Closing the Lesson

Have students summarize the major points of the lesson and answer the Essential Question: If you know one zero of a polynomial function, how can you determine another zero?

- The Factor Theorem states that a polynomial $f(x)$ has a factor $x - k$ if and only if $f(k) = 0$.
- You can divide a polynomial by a factor by using long division or synthetic division.

If you know one zero of a polynomial function, you can use synthetic division and factor the results to find the other zeros.

5.5 EXERCISES

HOMEWORK KEY
- ◯ = **WORKED-OUT SOLUTIONS** on p. WS10 for Exs. 17, 25, and 43
- ★ = **STANDARDIZED TEST PRACTICE** Exs. 2, 35, 39, 44, and 45
- ◆ = **MULTIPLE REPRESENTATIONS** Ex. 38

4 PRACTICE AND APPLY

Assignment Guide

Answer Transparencies available for all exercises

Basic:
Day 1: pp. 366–368
Exs. 1–20, 47–48
Day 2: pp. 366–368
Exs. 21–35, 41–44

Average:
Day 1: pp. 366–368
Exs. 1, 2, 4–10, 12–20, 36, 37, 47–48
Day 2: pp. 366–368
Exs. 23–28, 31–35, 38, 39, 41–45

Advanced:
Day 1: pp. 366–368
Exs. 1–18, 36, 37, 47–48
Day 2: pp. 366–368
Exs. 24–28, 32–35, 38–46*

Block:
pp. 366–368
Exs. 1, 2, 4–10, 12–20, 36, 37, 47–48, (with 5.4)
pp. 366–368
Exs. 23–28, 31–35, 38, 39, 41–45 (with 5.6)

Differentiated Instruction

See *Algebra 2 Best Practices Toolkit* for suggestions on addressing the needs of a diverse classroom.

Homework Check

For a quick check of student understanding of key concepts, go over the following exercises:
Basic: 4, 14, 22, 30, 43
Average: 6, 16, 24, 32, 44
Advanced: 8, 18, 26, 34, 45

Extra Practice

- Student Edition, p. 1014
- Chapter 5 Resource Book: Practice levels A, B, C, pp. 49–51

Practice Worksheet

An easily-readable reduced practice page (with answers) for this lesson can be found on p. 328C.

SKILL PRACTICE

A

2. The red numbers are the coefficients of the quotient and the blue number is the remainder.

1. **VOCABULARY** State the remainder theorem.
If a polynomial $f(x)$ is divided by $x - k$, then the remainder is $r = f(k)$.

2. ★ **WRITING** Synthetic division has been used to divide $f(x) = x^4 - 5x^2 + 8x - 2$ by $x + 3$. *Explain* what the colored numbers represent in the division problem.

−3	1	0	−5	8	−
		−3	9	−12	1
	1	−3	4	−4	1

EXAMPLES 1 and 2 on pp. 362–363 for Exs. 3–10

USING LONG DIVISION Divide using polynomial long division.

3. $(x^2 + x - 17) \div (x - 4)$ $x + 5 + \frac{3}{x-4}$
4. $(3x^2 - 11x - 26) \div (x - 5)$ $3x + 4 + \frac{-6}{x-5}$
5. $(x^3 + 3x^2 + 3x + 2) \div (x - 1)$ $x^2 + 4x + 7 + \frac{9}{x-1}$
6. $(8x^2 + 34x - 1) \div (4x - 1)$ $2x + 9 + \frac{8}{4x-1}$
7. $(3x^3 + 11x^2 + 4x + 1) \div (x^2 + x)$
8. $(7x^3 + 11x^2 + 7x + 5) \div (x^2 + 1)$
9. $(5x^4 - 2x^3 - 7x^2 - 39) \div (x^2 + 2x - 4)$
10. $(4x^4 + 5x - 4) \div (x^2 - 3x - 2)$

7–10. See margin.

EXAMPLE 3 on p. 363 for Exs. 11–20

USING SYNTHETIC DIVISION Divide using synthetic division.

11. $(2x^2 - 7x + 10) \div (x - 5)$ $2x + 3 + \frac{25}{x-5}$
12. $(4x^2 - 13x - 5) \div (x - 2)$ $4x - 5 + \frac{-15}{x-2}$
13. $(x^2 + 8x + 1) \div (x + 4)$ $x + 4 + \frac{-15}{x+4}$
14. $(x^2 + 9) \div (x - 3)$ $x + 3 + \frac{18}{x-3}$
15. $(x^3 - 5x^2 - 2) \div (x - 4)$ $x^2 - x - 4 + \frac{-18}{x-4}$
16. $(x^3 - 4x + 6) \div (x + 3)$ $x^2 - 3x + 5 + \frac{-9}{x+3}$
17. $(x^4 - 5x^3 - 8x^2 + 13x - 12) \div (x - 6)$ $x^3 + x^2 - 2x + 1 + \frac{-6}{x-6}$
18. $(x^4 + 4x^3 + 16x - 35) \div (x + 5)$ $x^3 - x^2 + 5x - 9 + \frac{10}{x+5}$

ERROR ANALYSIS *Describe* and correct the error in using synthetic division to divide $x^3 - 5x + 3$ by $x - 2$.

19. The degree of the answer should be reduced by 1; $x^2 + 2x - 1 + \frac{1}{x-2}$.

20. The coefficient of x^2 was not included; $x^2 + 2x - 1 + \frac{1}{x-2}$; See margin for art.

19. 

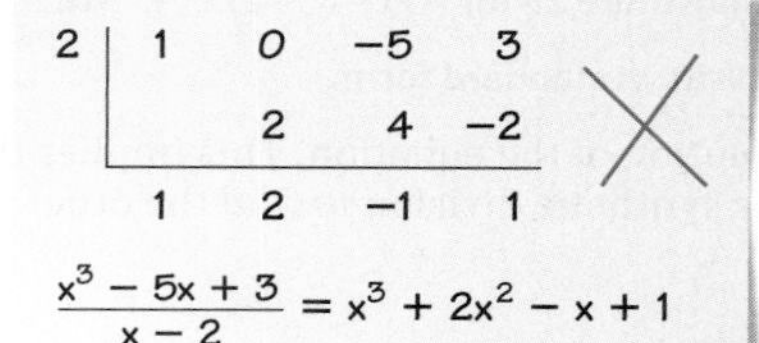

20.

2	1	−5	3
		2	−6
	1	−3	−3

$\frac{x^3 - 5x + 3}{x - 2} = x^2 - 3x - \frac{3}{x-2}$

B

EXAMPLE 4 on p. 364 for Exs. 21–28

FACTOR Given polynomial $f(x)$ and a factor of $f(x)$, factor $f(x)$ completely.

21. $f(x) = x^3 - 10x^2 + 19x + 30;\ x - 6$ $(x - 6)(x - 5)(x + 1)$
22. $f(x) = x^3 + 6x^2 + 5x - 12;\ x + 4$ $(x - 1)(x + 3)(x + 4)$
23. $f(x) = x^3 - 2x^2 - 40x - 64;\ x - 8$ $(x - 8)(x + 2)(x + 4)$
24. $f(x) = x^3 + 18x^2 + 95x + 150;\ x + 10$ $(x + 3)(x + 5)(x + 10)$
25. $f(x) = x^3 + 2x^2 - 51x + 108;\ x + 9$ $(x - 4)(x - 3)(x + 9)$
26. $f(x) = x^3 - 9x^2 + 8x + 60;\ x + 2$ $(x - 6)(x - 5)(x + 2)$
27. $f(x) = 2x^3 - 15x^2 + 34x - 21;\ x - 1$ $(2x - 7)(x - 3)(x - 1)$
28. $f(x) = 3x^3 - 2x^2 - 61x - 20;\ x - 5$ $(x - 5)(3x + 1)(x + 4)$

EXAMPLE 5 on p. 365 for Exs. 29–35

FIND ZEROS Given polynomial function f and a zero of f, find the other zeros.

29. $f(x) = x^3 - 2x^2 - 21x - 18;\ -3$ $-1, 6$
30. $f(x) = 4x^3 - 25x^2 - 154x + 40;\ 10$ $-4, \frac{1}{4}$
31. $f(x) = 10x^3 - 81x^2 + 71x + 42;\ 7$ $-\frac{2}{5}, \frac{3}{2}$
32. $f(x) = 3x^3 + 34x^2 + 72x - 64;\ -4$ $-8, \frac{2}{3}$
33. $f(x) = 2x^3 - 10x^2 - 71x - 9;\ 9$
34. $f(x) = 5x^3 - x^2 - 18x + 8;\ -2$

33, 34. See margin

7. $3x + 8 + \frac{-4x + 1}{x^2 + x}$

8. $7x + 11 + \frac{-6}{x^2 + 1}$

9. $5x^2 - 12x + 37 + \frac{-122x + 109}{x^2 + 2x - 4}$

10. $4x^2 + 12x + 44 + \frac{161x + 84}{x^2 - 3x - 2}$

20.

2	1	0	−5	3
		2	4	−2
	1	2	−1	1

33. $\frac{-4 \pm \sqrt{14}}{2}$

34. $\frac{11 \pm \sqrt{41}}{10}$

35. ★ **MULTIPLE CHOICE** One zero of $f(x) = 4x^3 + 15x^2 - 63x - 54$ is $x = -6$. What is another zero of f? **D**

Ⓐ -9 Ⓑ -3 Ⓒ -1 Ⓓ 3

GEOMETRY You are given an expression for the volume of the rectangular prism. Find an expression for the missing dimension.

36. $V = 2x^3 + 17x^2 + 46x + 40$ **2x + 5**

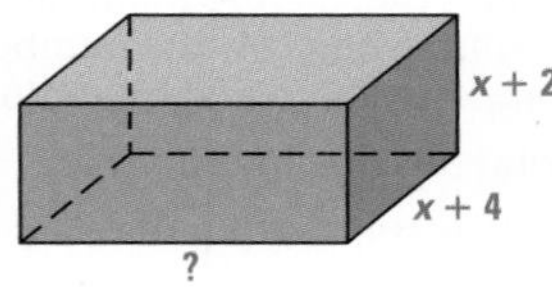

37. $V = x^3 + 13x^2 + 34x - 48$ **x + 8**

x − 1

?

x + 6

38. **MULTIPLE REPRESENTATIONS** Consider the polynomial function $f(x) = x^3 - 5x^2 - 12x + 36$.

a. **Zeros of a Function** Given that $f(2) = 0$, find the other zeros of f. **−3, 6**

b. **Factors of an Expression** Based on your results from part (a), what are the factors of the polynomial $x^3 - 5x^2 - 12x + 36$? **$(x - 6)(x - 2)(x + 3)$**

c. **Solutions of an Equation** What are the solutions of the polynomial equation $x^3 - 5x^2 - 12x + 36 = 0$? **−3, 2, 6**

39. ★ **MULTIPLE CHOICE** What is the value of k such that $x - 5$ is a factor of $x^3 - x^2 + kx - 30$? **A**

Ⓐ -14 Ⓑ -2 Ⓒ 26 Ⓓ 32

C 40. **CHALLENGE** It can be shown that $2x - 1$ is a factor of the polynomial function $f(x) = 30x^3 + 7x^2 - 39x + 14$.

a. What can you conclude is a zero of f? **0.5**

b. Use synthetic division to write $f(x)$ in the form $(x - k) \cdot q(x)$. **$(x - 0.5)(15x^2 + 11x - 14)$**

c. Write $f(x)$ as the product of linear factors with integer coefficients. **$(2x - 1)(3x - 2)(5x + 7)$**

PROBLEM SOLVING

EXAMPLE 6 on p. 365 for Exs. 41–43

A 41. **CLOTHING** The profit P (in millions of dollars) for a T-shirt manufacturer can be modeled by $P = -x^3 + 4x^2 + x$ where x is the number of T-shirts produced (in millions). Currently, the company produces 4 million T-shirts and makes a profit of \$4,000,000. What lesser number of T-shirts could the company produce and still make the same profit? **1 million T-shirts**

@HomeTutor for problem solving help at classzone.com

42. **MP3 PLAYERS** The profit P (in millions of dollars) for a manufacturer of MP3 players can be modeled by $P = -4x^3 + 12x^2 + 16x$ where x is the number of MP3 players produced (in millions). Currently, the company produces 3 million MP3 players and makes a profit of \$48,000,000. What lesser number of MP3 players could the company produce and still make the same profit? **2 million MP3 players**

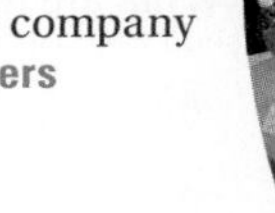

@HomeTutor for problem solving help at classzone.com

Teaching Strategy

Exercises 3–18 Choose one of these exercises and use both polynomial long division and synthetic division to show how the two processes are related.

Avoiding Common Errors

Exercises 11–18 Based on their experiences using long division to divide polynomials, it is common for students to subtract the two numbers above the synthetic division line. Explain that because the synthetic divisor for the factor $x - a$ is a and not $-a$, the numbers above the line should be added.

5 ASSESS AND RETEACH

Daily Homework Quiz

 Transparency Available

1. Divide $6x^4 - x^3 - x^2 + 11x - 18$ by $2x^2 + x - 3$. $3x^2 - 2x + 5 + \frac{-3}{2x^2 + x - 3}$
2. Use synthetic division to divide $f(x) = x^3 - 3x^2 - 5x - 25$ by $x - 5$. $x^2 + 2x + 5$
3. One zero of $f(x) = x^3 - x^2 - 17x - 15$ is $x = -1$. What is another zero of $f(x)$? 5 or −3
4. One of the costs C (in thousands of dollars) to print a novel can be modeled by $C = x^3 - 10x^2 + 28x$, where x is the number of novels printed in thousands. The company now prints 5000 novels at a cost of \$15,000. What other numbers of novels would cost about the same amount? about 4300 or about 700

 Online Quiz

Available at classzone.com

Diagnosis/Remediation

- Practice A, B, C in Chapter 5 Resource Book, pp. 49–51
- Study Guide in Chapter 5 Resource Book, pp. 52–53
- Practice Workbook, pp. 85–86
- @HomeTutor

Challenge

Additional challenge is available in the Chapter 5 Resource Book, p. 57.

45. $-0.00233x^3 + 0.249x^2 - 21.0x + 1740 + \frac{-445{,}000}{3.10x + 256}$; divided the overnight stays function by the total visits function

43. **WOMEN'S BASKETBALL** From 1985 to 2003, the total attendance A (in thousands) at NCAA women's basketball games and the number T of NCAA women's basketball teams can be modeled by

$$A = -1.95x^3 + 70.1x^2 - 188x + 2150 \quad \text{and} \quad T = 14.8x + 725$$

where x is the number of years since 1985. Write a function for the average attendance per team from 1985 to 2003. $f(x) = -0.132x^2 + 11.2x - 560.9 + \frac{408{,}803}{14.8x + 725}$

B

44. ★ **EXTENDED RESPONSE** The price p (in dollars) that a radio manufacturer is able to charge for a radio is given by $p = 40 - 4x^2$ where x is the number (in millions) of radios produced. It costs the company \$15 to make a radio.

   a. Write an expression for the company's total revenue in terms of x. $40x - 4x^3$

   b. Write a function for the company's profit P by subtracting the total cost to make x radios from the expression in part (a). $P = 25x - 4x^3$

   c. Currently, the company produces 1.5 million radios and makes a profit of \$24,000,000. Write and solve an equation to find a lesser number of radios that the company could produce and still make the same profit. $24 = 25x - 4x^3$, 1.386, −2.886; 1,386,000 radios

   d. Do all the solutions in part (c) make sense in this situation? *Explain.* No; the negative solution does not make sense because the company cannot produce a negative number of radios.

45. ★ **SHORT RESPONSE** Since 1990, overnight stays S and total visits V (both in millions) to national parks can be modeled by

$$S = -0.00722x^4 + 0.176x^3 - 1.40x^2 + 3.39x + 17.6$$

$$V = 3.10x + 256$$

where x is the number of years since 1990. Write a function for the percent of visits to national parks that were overnight stays. *Explain* how you constructed your function. See margin.

Joshua Tree National Park, Californ

C

46. **CHALLENGE** The profit P (in millions of dollars) for a DVD manufacturer can be modeled by $P = -6x^3 + 72x$ where x is the number of DVDs produced (in millions). Show that 2 million DVDs is the only production level for the company that yields a profit of \$96,000,000. The only other solution is −4. The company cannot produce a negative number of DVDs.

KENTUCKY MIXED REVIEW

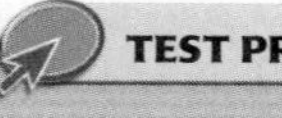 TEST PRACTICE at classzone.com

47. James leaves his home to walk to school. Four minutes later, his friend leaves her home to ride her bike to school. James averages 3 miles per hour and his friend averages 10 miles per hour. James and his friend travel a combined total of 8 miles and arrive at school at the same time. How long did it take James to walk to school? C

   Ⓐ 34 min Ⓑ 38 min

   Ⓒ 40 min Ⓓ 44 min

48. What are the coordinates of the x-intercept of the graph of $2x + 3y = 15$? B

   Ⓐ $\left(-\frac{15}{2}, 0\right)$ Ⓑ $\left(\frac{15}{2}, 0\right)$

   Ⓒ $(0, 5)$ Ⓓ $(13, 0)$

Lessons 5.1–5.5

1. **ASTRONOMY** The average distance between Earth and the sun is 1.64×10^{11} yards. The length of a football field, including the end zones, is 1.20×10^2 yards. About how many football fields stretched end-to-end would it take to reach from Earth to the sun?

   A. 1.37×10^7

   B. 1.37×10^9

   C. 1.37×10^{10}

   D. 1.37×10^{13}

2. **PRODUCT DESIGN** You are designing a rectangular picnic cooler with length 4 times its width and height 2 times its width. The cooler has insulation that is 1 inch thick on each of the four sides and 2 inches thick on the top and bottom. Let x represent the width of the cooler. What is a polynomial function $C(x)$ in standard form for the volume of the inside of the cooler?

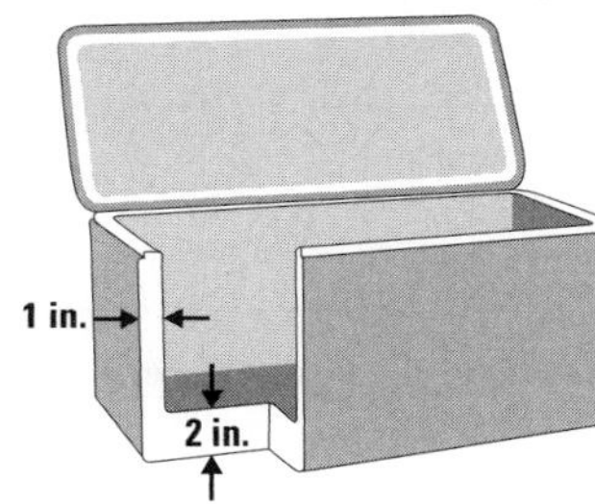

   A. $C(x) = 8x^3 - 18x^2 + 12x - 2$

   B. $C(x) = 8x^3 - 28x^2 + 28x - 8$

   C. $C(x) = 8x^3 - 36x^2 + 48x - 16$

   D. $C(x) = 8x^3 + 36x^2 + 48x + 16$

3. **END BEHAVIOR** Which polynomial function has degree 4 and end behavior given by $f(x) \to -\infty$ as $x \to -\infty$ and $f(x) \to -\infty$ as $x \to +\infty$?

   A. $f(x) = 4x^3 - 4x^2 + x + 5$

   B. $f(x) = x^4 - x^3 + 2x^2 - 5x + 2$

   C. $f(x) = -x^4 + 5x^2 - x + 20$

   D. $f(x) = -4x^6 + x^4 + 4$

4. **PACKAGING DESIGN** A floral shop has a rectangular gift box with a volume of 540 cubic inches. The width of the gift box is 3 inches less than the height, and the length is 15 inches greater than the height. What is the height of the gift box to the nearest tenth of an inch?

   A. 3.7 inches

   B. 6.7 inches

   C. 12.0 inches

   D. 21.7 inches

5. **MANUFACTURING** The price p (in dollars) that a camera manufacturer is able to charge for a camera is given by $p = 100 - 10x^2$ where x is the number (in millions) of cameras produced. It costs the company $30 to make a camera. Currently, the company produces 2 million cameras and makes a profit of $60,000,000. What other number of cameras could the company produce and still make the same profit?

   A. 1 million

   B. 3 million

   C. 4 million

   D. 5 million

6. **OPEN-RESPONSE** From 1995 to 2003, the average monthly cell phone bill C (in dollars) for subscribers in the United States can be modeled by the function

   $$C = -0.027t^4 + 0.32t^3 - 0.25t^2 - 4.9t + 51$$

   where t is the number of years since 1995.

   a. According to this model, what was the average monthly cell phone bill in 2001?

   b. Do you think the model will accurately predict cell phone bills for years beyond 2006? Justify your answer.

Kentucky Mixed Review

1. B
2. C
3. C
4. B
5. A
6. a. $46.73

   b. No; cell phone bills cannot be a negative amount as the function shows after 2006.

1 PLAN AND PREPARE

Warm-Up Exercises

Transparency Available

Factor completely.

1. $x^2 - x - 12$ $(x - 4)(x + 3)$
2. $2x^2 - 5x - 3$ $(x - 3)(2x + 1)$
3. Use synthetic division to divide $2x^3 - 3x^2 - 18x - 8$ by $x - 4$. $2x^2 + 5x + 2$
4. The volume of a box is modeled by $f(x) = x(x - 1)(x - 2)$, where x is the length in meters. What is the volume when the length is 3 meters? 6 m^3

Notetaking Guide

Transparency Available

Promotes interactive learning and notetaking skills, pp. 147–149.

Pacing

Basic: 2 days
Average: 2 days
Advanced: 2 days
Block: 0.5 block with 5.5
0.5 block with 5.7

- See *Teaching Guide/Lesson Plan.*

2 FOCUS AND MOTIVATE

Essential Question

Big Idea 3, p. 329

How can you find all the real zeros of $f(x)$ when the leading coefficient is 1? Tell students they will learn how to answer this question by using synthetic division.

5.6 Find Rational Zeros

MA-HS-5.1.5

Before You found the zeros of a polynomial function given one zero.

Now You will find all real zeros of a polynomial function.

Why? So you can model manufacturing processes, as in Ex. 45.

Key Vocabulary
- **zero of a function,** *p. 254*
- **constant term,** *p. 337*
- **leading coefficient,** *p. 337*

MA-HS-5.1.5
Students will: determine if a relation is a function; determine the domain and range of a function (linear and quadratic); determine the slope and intercepts of a linear function; determine the maximum, minimum, and intercepts (roots/zeros) of a quadratic function and evaluate a function written in function notation for a specified rational number. DOK 2

The polynomial function $f(x) = 64x^3 + 152x^2 - 62x - 105$ has $-\frac{5}{2}$, $-\frac{3}{4}$, and $\frac{7}{8}$ as its zeros. Notice that the numerators of these zeros (−5, −3, and 7) are factors of the constant term, −105. Also notice that the denominators (2, 4, and 8) are factors of the leading coefficient, 64. These observations are generalized by the *rational zero theorem.*

KEY CONCEPT *For Your Notebook*

The Rational Zero Theorem

If $f(x) = a_nx^n + \cdots + a_1x + a_0$ has *integer* coefficients, then every rational zero of f has the following form:

$$\frac{p}{q} = \frac{\text{factor of constant term } a_0}{\text{factor of leading coefficient } a_n}$$

EXAMPLE 1 List possible rational zeros

List the possible rational zeros of f using the rational zero theorem.

a. $f(x) = x^3 + 2x^2 - 11x + 12$

Factors of the constant term: ±1, ±2, ±3, ±4, ±6, ±12

Factors of the leading coefficient: ±1

Possible rational zeros: $\pm\frac{1}{1}, \pm\frac{2}{1}, \pm\frac{3}{1}, \pm\frac{4}{1}, \pm\frac{6}{1}, \pm\frac{12}{1}$

Simplified list of possible zeros: ±1, ±2, ±3, ±4, ±6, ±12

AVOID ERRORS
Be sure your lists include both the positive and negative factors of the constant term and the leading coefficient.

b. $f(x) = 4x^4 - x^3 - 3x^2 + 9x - 10$

Factors of the constant term: ±1, ±2, ±5, ±10

Factors of the leading coefficient: ±1, ±2, ±4

Possible rational zeros:

$$\pm\frac{1}{1}, \pm\frac{2}{1}, \pm\frac{5}{1}, \pm\frac{10}{1}, \pm\frac{1}{2}, \pm\frac{2}{2}, \pm\frac{5}{2}, \pm\frac{10}{2}, \pm\frac{1}{4}, \pm\frac{2}{4}, \pm\frac{5}{4}, \pm\frac{10}{4}$$

Simplified list of possible zeros: ±1, ±2, ±5, ±10, $\pm\frac{1}{2}, \pm\frac{5}{2}, \pm\frac{1}{4}, \pm\frac{5}{4}$

Resource Planning Guide

Chapter Resource Book
- Teaching Guide/Lesson Plan (pp. 58–59)
- Practice levels A, B, C (pp. 61–63)
- Study Guide (pp. 64–65)
- Catch-up for Absent Students (p. 66)
- Problem Solving Workshop (p. 67)
- Challenge (p. 68)

Workbooks
- Notetaking Guide (pp. 147–149)
- Practice Workbook (pp. 87–88)

Teaching Options
- **Power Presentations CD-ROM** provides dynamic electronic teaching resources for the classroom.
- **Activity Generator CD-ROM** provides editable activities for all ability levels.

Interactive Technology
- Easy Planner
- Power Presentations CD-ROM
- Activity Generator CD-ROM
- Animated Algebra
- Test Generator CD-ROM
- Online Quiz
- eWorkbook
- eEdition
- @HomeTutor

Resources for English Learners
- Quick Reference for English Learners
- Spanish Study Guide
- Multi-Language Visual Glossary
- Student Resources in Spanish

See also the *Algebra 2 Toolkit* for more strategies for meeting individual needs.

✓ GUIDED PRACTICE for Example 1

List the possible rational zeros of f using the rational zero theorem.

1. $f(x) = x^3 + 9x^2 + 23x + 15$ $\pm1, \pm3, \pm5, \pm15$

2. $f(x) = 2x^3 + 3x^2 - 11x - 6$ $\pm1, \pm2, \pm3, \pm6, \pm\frac{1}{2}, \pm\frac{3}{2}$

VERIFYING ZEROS In Lesson 5.5, you found zeros of polynomial functions when one zero was known. The rational zero theorem is a starting point for finding zeros when no zeros are known.

However, the rational zero theorem lists only *possible* zeros. In order to find the *actual* zeros of a polynomial function f, you must test values from the list of possible zeros. You can test a value by evaluating $f(x)$ using the test value as x.

EXAMPLE 2 Find zeros when the leading coefficient is 1

Find all real zeros of $f(x) = x^3 - 8x^2 + 11x + 20$.

Solution

STEP 1 **List** the possible rational zeros. The leading coefficient is 1 and the constant term is 20. So, the possible rational zeros are:

$$x = \pm\frac{1}{1}, \pm\frac{2}{1}, \pm\frac{4}{1}, \pm\frac{5}{1}, \pm\frac{10}{1}, \pm\frac{20}{1}$$

AVOID ERRORS
Notice that not every *possible* zero generated by the rational zero theorem is an *actual* zero of f.

STEP 2 **Test** these zeros using synthetic division.

Test $x = 1$:

1	1	−8	11	20
		1	−7	4
	1	−7	4	24

↑ 1 is not a zero.

Test $x = -1$:

−1	1	−8	11	20
		−1	9	−20
	1	−9	20	0

↑ −1 is a zero.

Because −1 is a zero of f, you can write $f(x) = (x + 1)(x^2 - 9x + 20)$.

STEP 3 **Factor** the trinomial in $f(x)$ and use the factor theorem.

$$f(x) = (x + 1)(x^2 - 9x + 20) = (x + 1)(x - 4)(x - 5)$$

▶ The zeros of f are −1, 4, and 5.

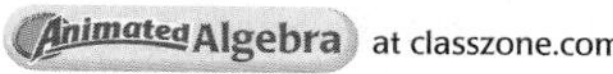 at classzone.com

✓ GUIDED PRACTICE for Example 2

Find all real zeros of the function.

3. $f(x) = x^3 - 4x^2 - 15x + 18$ −3, 1, 6

4. $f(x) = x^3 - 8x^2 + 5x + 14$ −1, 2, 7

LIMITING THE SEARCH FOR ZEROS In Example 2, the leading coefficient of the polynomial function is 1. When the leading coefficient is not 1, the list of possible rational zeros can increase dramatically. In such cases, the search can be shortened by sketching the function's graph.

Motivating the Lesson

If you know the linear factors for a polynomial function, then each linear factor can be used to identify a zero of the function. In this lesson students will learn a way to list all possible rational zeros of a polynomial function. By using the actual rational zeros to write linear factors of the function, they can identify the polynomial whose roots are the non-rational zeros of the original polynomial function.

3 TEACH

Extra Example 1

List the possible rational zeros of f using the rational zero theorem.

a. $f(x) = x^3 + x^2 - 3x - 6$ $\pm1, \pm2, \pm3, \pm6$

b. $f(x) = 2x^3 + 7x^2 - 4x + 8$ $\pm\frac{1}{2}, \pm1, \pm2, \pm4, \pm8$

Key Question to Ask for Example 1

- In part (b), why are $\pm\frac{4}{5}$ not possible zeros of the polynomial? The possible zeros are factors of the constant term, 10, divided by factors of the leading coefficient, 4. So $\pm\frac{5}{4}$ are possible zeros, not $\pm\frac{4}{5}$.

Extra Example 2

Find all real zeros of $f(x) = x^3 - 5x^2 + 7x - 35$. 5

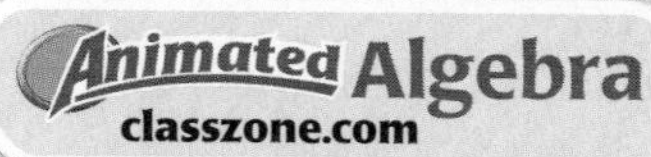

An **Animated Algebra** activity is available on-line for **Example 2**. This activity is also available on the **Power Presentations CD-ROM**.

Differentiated Instruction

Inclusion Take the time to review how to find all factors of a number. A common error in listing the possible rational zeros of a polynomial function arises from not properly listing the factors of the constant term and leading coefficient.

See also the *Algebra 2 Toolkit* for more strategies.

Extra Example 3

Find all real zeros of $f(x) = 9x^4 + 3x^3 - 30x^2 + 6x + 12$.
$1, -2, \frac{1+\sqrt{7}}{3}, \frac{1-\sqrt{7}}{3}$

Key Questions to Ask for Example 3

- What is the maximum possible number of real zeros that the function can have? 4
- Why are $-\frac{3}{2}, -\frac{1}{2}, \frac{3}{5}$, and $\frac{12}{5}$ reasonable values to check? The graph appears to cross the x-axis at these points.
- Why are ± 12 not reasonable values to check? The end behavior shows that the values of the function at ± 12 are quite large.

Avoiding Common Errors

Stress that a graph shows only *reasonable* values to check for rational zeros and that these values *may not be* actual zeros. Use the case of $-\frac{3}{2}$ in Step 3 of Example 3 as a case in point. The value of f at $-\frac{3}{2}$ is $-\frac{21}{4}$, not 0.

EXAMPLE 3 Find zeros when the leading coefficient is not 1

Find all real zeros of $f(x) = 10x^4 - 11x^3 - 42x^2 + 7x + 12$.

Solution

STEP 1 **List** the possible rational zeros of f: $\pm\frac{1}{1}, \pm\frac{2}{1}, \pm\frac{3}{1}, \pm\frac{4}{1}, \pm\frac{6}{1}, \pm\frac{12}{1}, \pm\frac{1}{2}, \pm\frac{3}{2}, \pm\frac{1}{5}, \pm\frac{2}{5}, \pm\frac{3}{5}, \pm\frac{4}{5}, \pm\frac{6}{5}, \pm\frac{12}{5}, \pm\frac{1}{10}, \pm\frac{3}{10}$

STEP 2 **Choose** reasonable values from the list above to check using the graph of the function. For f, the values

$$x = -\frac{3}{2}, x = -\frac{1}{2}, x = \frac{3}{5}, \text{ and } x = \frac{12}{5}$$

are reasonable based on the graph shown at the right.

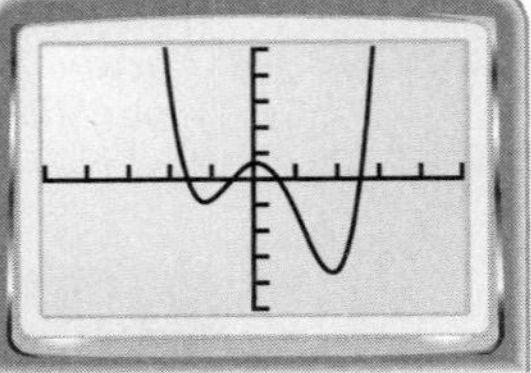

STEP 3 **Check** the values using synthetic division until a zero is found.

$-\frac{3}{2}$	10	−11	−42	7	12
		−15	39	$\frac{9}{2}$	$-\frac{69}{4}$
	10	−26	−3	$\frac{23}{2}$	$-\frac{21}{4}$

$-\frac{1}{2}$	10	−11	−42	7	12
		−5	8	17	−12
	10	−16	−34	24	0

$-\frac{1}{2}$ is a zero.

STEP 4 **Factor** out a binomial using the result of the synthetic division.

$f(x) = \left(x + \frac{1}{2}\right)(10x^3 - 16x^2 - 34x + 24)$ **Write as a product of factors.**

$= \left(x + \frac{1}{2}\right)(2)(5x^3 - 8x^2 - 17x + 12)$ **Factor 2 out of the second factor.**

$= (2x + 1)(5x^3 - 8x^2 - 17x + 12)$ **Multiply the first factor by 2.**

STEP 5 **Repeat** the steps above for $g(x) = 5x^3 - 8x^2 - 17x + 12$. Any zero of g will also be a zero of f. The possible rational zeros of g are:

$$x = \pm 1, \pm 2, \pm 3, \pm 4, \pm 6, \pm 12, \pm\frac{1}{5}, \pm\frac{2}{5}, \pm\frac{3}{5}, \pm\frac{4}{5}, \pm\frac{6}{5}, \pm\frac{12}{5}$$

The graph of g shows that $\frac{3}{5}$ may be a zero. Synthetic division shows that $\frac{3}{5}$ *is* a zero and $g(x) = \left(x - \frac{3}{5}\right)(5x^2 - 5x - 20) = (5x - 3)(x^2 - x - 4)$. It follows that:

$$f(x) = (2x + 1) \cdot g(x) = (2x + 1)(5x - 3)(x^2 - x - 4)$$

STEP 6 **Find** the remaining zeros of f by solving $x^2 - x - 4 = 0$.

$x = \frac{-(-1) \pm \sqrt{(-1)^2 - 4(1)(-4)}}{2(1)}$ **Substitute 1 for a, −1 for b, and −4 for c in the quadratic formula.**

$x = \frac{1 \pm \sqrt{17}}{2}$ **Simplify.**

▶ The real zeros of f are $-\frac{1}{2}, \frac{3}{5}, \frac{1+\sqrt{17}}{2}$, and $\frac{1-\sqrt{17}}{2}$.

GUIDED PRACTICE for Example 3

Find all real zeros of the function.

5. $f(x) = 48x^3 + 4x^2 - 20x + 3$ $-\frac{3}{4}, \frac{1}{6}, \frac{1}{2}$

6. $f(x) = 2x^4 + 5x^3 - 18x^2 - 19x + 42$ $-2, \frac{3}{2}, -1 \pm 2\sqrt{2}$

EXAMPLE 4 Solve a multi-step problem

ICE SCULPTURES Some ice sculptures are made by filling a mold with water and then freezing it. You are making such an ice sculpture for a school dance. It is to be shaped like a pyramid with a height that is 1 foot greater than the length of each side of its square base. The volume of the ice sculpture is 4 cubic feet. What are the dimensions of the mold?

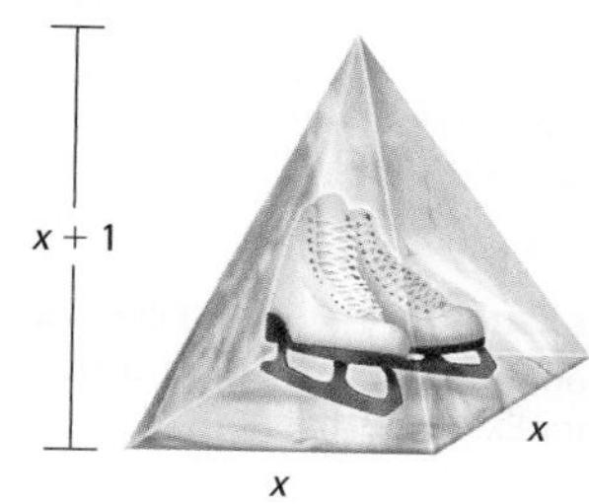

Solution

STEP 1 **Write** an equation for the volume of the ice sculpture.

Volume (cubic feet)	=	$\frac{1}{3}$ ·	Area of base (square feet)	·	Height (feet)
4	=	$\frac{1}{3}$ ·	x^2	·	$(x + 1)$

$4 = \frac{1}{3}x^2(x + 1)$ **Write equation.**

$12 = x^3 + x^2$ **Multiply each side by 3 and simplify.**

$0 = x^3 + x^2 - 12$ **Subtract 12 from each side.**

STEP 2 **List** the possible rational solutions: $\pm\frac{1}{1}, \pm\frac{2}{1}, \pm\frac{3}{1}, \pm\frac{4}{1}, \pm\frac{6}{1}, \pm\frac{12}{1}$

STEP 3 **Test** possible solutions. Only positive x-values make sense.

$$\begin{array}{r|rrrr} 1 & 1 & 1 & 0 & -12 \\ & & 1 & 2 & 2 \\ \hline & 1 & 2 & 2 & -10 \end{array} \qquad \begin{array}{r|rrrr} 2 & 1 & 1 & 0 & -12 \\ & & 2 & 6 & 12 \\ \hline & 1 & 3 & 6 & 0 \end{array}$$

2 is a solution.

STEP 4 **Check** for other solutions. The other two solutions, which satisfy $x^2 + 3x + 6 = 0$, are $x = \frac{-3 \pm i\sqrt{15}}{2}$ and can be discarded because they are imaginary numbers.

▶ The only reasonable solution is $x = 2$. The base of the mold is 2 feet by 2 feet. The height of the mold is $2 + 1 = 3$ feet.

GUIDED PRACTICE for Example 4

7. **WHAT IF?** In Example 4, suppose the base of the ice sculpture has sides that are 1 foot longer than the height. The volume of the ice sculpture is 6 cubic feet. What are the dimensions of the mold? base side: 3 ft, height: 2 ft

Extra Example 4

A prism has a square base with a height that is 5 feet longer than each side of the base. The volume of the prism is 28 cubic feet. What is the height of the prism? 7 ft

Key Questions to Ask for Example 4

- Why does the top row of the synthetic division have a zero? There is no x-term.
- What method can you use to determine the solutions of $x^2 + 3x + 6 = 0$? quadratic formula or complete the square

Closing the Lesson

Have students summarize the major points of the lesson and answer the Essential Question: How can you find all real zeros of $f(x)$ when the leading coefficient is 1?

- Use the Rational Zero Theorem to make a list of all possible rational zeros. Use a graph to narrow down the list.
- If the polynomial has a nonfactorable quadratic factor, use the quadratic formula to find the real zeros.

Make a list of all possible rational zeros, then identify which ones are actual zeros by using synthetic division. Use the quadratic formula to find any irrational zeros.

5.6 EXERCISES

HOMEWORK KEY
○ = **WORKED-OUT SOLUTIONS** on p. WS11 for Exs. 7, 21, and 47
★ = **STANDARDIZED TEST PRACTICE** Exs. 2, 23, 38, 39, 40, and 50

SKILL PRACTICE

A

1. **VOCABULARY** Copy and complete: If a polynomial function has integer coefficients, then every rational zero of the function has the form $\frac{p}{q}$, where p is a factor of the _?_ and q is a factor of the _?_. constant, leading coefficient

2. ★ **WRITING** *Describe* a method you can use to shorten the list of possible rational zeros when using the rational zero theorem.
Sample answer: Draw a graph of the function so you can see approximately where the zeros are.

EXAMPLE 1 on p. 370 for Exs. 3–10

LISTING RATIONAL ZEROS List the possible rational zeros of the function using the rational zero theorem.

3. $f(x) = x^3 - 3x + 28$ ±1, ±2, ±4, ±7, ±14, ±28
4. $g(x) = x^3 - 4x^2 + x - 10$ ±1, ±2, ±5, ±10
5. $f(x) = 2x^4 + 6x^3 - 7x + 9$ $\pm1, \pm3, \pm9, \pm\frac{1}{2}, \pm\frac{3}{2}, \pm\frac{9}{2}$
6. $h(x) = 2x^3 + x^2 - x - 18$ $\pm1, \pm2, \pm3, \pm6, \pm9, \pm18, \pm\frac{1}{2}, \pm\frac{3}{2}, \pm\frac{9}{2}$
7. $g(x) = 4x^5 + 3x^3 - 2x - 14$
8. $f(x) = 3x^4 + 5x^3 - 3x + 42$
9. $h(x) = 8x^4 + 4x^3 - 10x + 15$
10. $h(x) = 6x^3 - 3x^2 + 12$

7–10. See margin.

EXAMPLE 2 on p. 371 for Exs. 11–18

FINDING REAL ZEROS Find all real zeros of the function.

11. $f(x) = x^3 - 12x^2 + 35x - 24$ 1, 3, 8
12. $f(x) = x^3 - 5x^2 - 22x + 56$ −4, 2, 7
13. $g(x) = x^3 - 31x - 30$ −5, −1, 6
14. $h(x) = x^3 + 8x^2 - 9x - 72$ −8, −3, 3
15. $h(x) = x^4 + 7x^3 + 26x^2 + 44x + 24$ −2, −1
16. $f(x) = x^4 - 2x^3 - 9x^2 + 10x - 24$ −3, 4
17. $f(x) = x^4 + 2x^3 - 9x^2 - 2x + 8$ −4, −1, 1, 2
18. $g(x) = x^4 - 16x^2 - 40x - 25$ −1, 5

EXAMPLE 3 on p. 372 for Exs. 19–35

ELIMINATING POSSIBLE ZEROS Use the graph to shorten the list of possible rational zeros of the function. Then find all real zeros of the function.

19. $f(x) = 4x^3 - 20x + 16$ $1, \frac{-1 \pm \sqrt{17}}{2}$

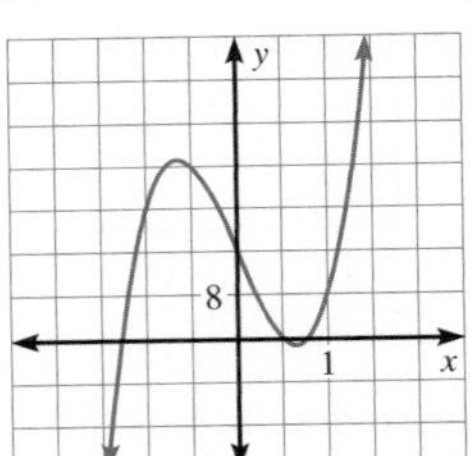

20. $f(x) = 4x^3 - 12x^2 - x + 15$ $-1, \frac{3}{2}, \frac{5}{2}$

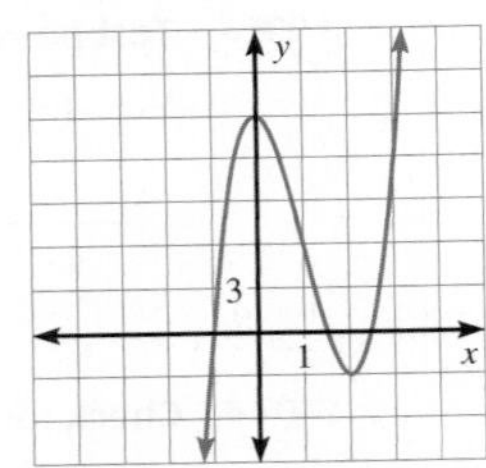

21. $f(x) = 6x^3 + 25x^2 + 16x - 15$ $-3, -\frac{5}{3}, \frac{1}{2}$

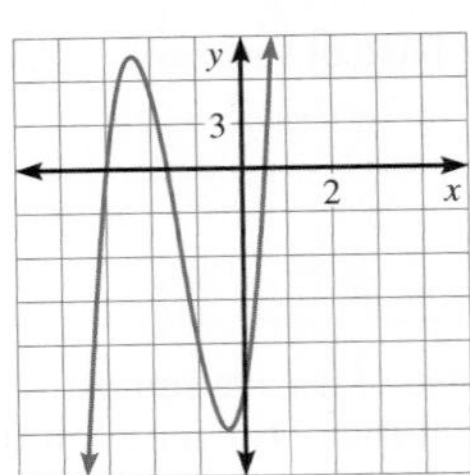

22. $f(x) = -3x^3 + 20x^2 - 36x + 16$ $\frac{2}{3}, 2, 4$

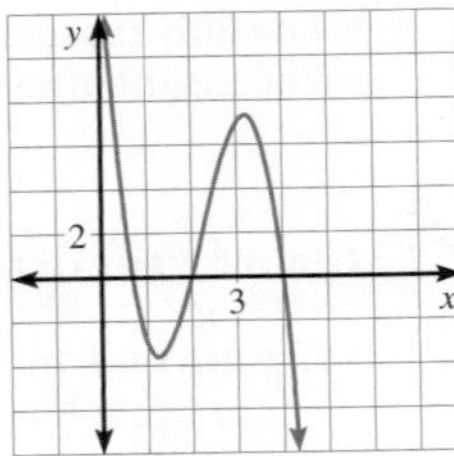

4 PRACTICE AND APPLY

Assignment Guide

Answer Transparencies available for all exercises

Basic:
Day 1: EP p. 1013 Exs. 45–48
pp. 374–377
Exs. 1–18, 52–53
Day 2: pp. 374–377
Exs. 19–29, 45–49

Average:
Day 1: pp. 374–377
Exs. 1, 2, 4–10, 12–18, 36–38, 52–53
Day 2: pp. 374–377
Exs. 21–23, 27–32, 39, 40, 45–50

Advanced:
Day 1: pp. 374–377
Exs. 1, 2, 5–10, 13–18, 36–39, 52–53
Day 2: pp. 374–377
Exs. 23, 30–44*, 46–51*

Block:
pp. 374–377
Exs. 1, 2, 4–10, 12–18, 36–38, 52–53 (with 5.5)
pp. 374–377
Exs. 21–23, 27–32, 39, 40, 45–50 (with 5.7)

Differentiated Instruction

See *Algebra 2 Best Practices Toolkit* for suggestions on addressing the needs of a diverse classroom.

Homework Check

For a quick check of student understanding of key concepts, go over the following exercises:
Basic: 6, 12, 20, 45, 46
Average: 8, 14, 28, 46, 47
Advanced: 10, 16, 32, 47, 48

Extra Practice

- Student Edition, p. 1014
- Chapter 5 Resource Book: Practice levels A, B, C, pp. 61–63

Practice Worksheet

An easily-readable reduced practice page (with answers) for this lesson can be found on p. 328C.

7. $\pm1, \pm2, \pm7, \pm14, \pm\frac{1}{2}, \pm\frac{7}{2}, \pm\frac{1}{4}, \pm\frac{7}{4}$
8. $\pm1, \pm2, \pm3, \pm6, \pm7, \pm14, \pm21, \pm42, \pm\frac{1}{3}, \pm\frac{2}{3}, \pm\frac{7}{3}, \pm\frac{14}{3}$
9. $\pm1, \pm3, \pm5, \pm15, \pm\frac{1}{2}, \pm\frac{3}{2}, \pm\frac{5}{2}, \pm\frac{15}{2}, \pm\frac{1}{4}, \pm\frac{3}{4}, \pm\frac{5}{4}, \pm\frac{15}{4}, \pm\frac{1}{8}, \pm\frac{3}{8}, \pm\frac{5}{8}, \pm\frac{15}{8}$
10. $\pm1, \pm2, \pm3, \pm4, \pm6, \pm12, \pm\frac{1}{2}, \pm\frac{3}{2}, \pm\frac{1}{3}, \pm\frac{2}{3}, \pm\frac{4}{3}, \pm\frac{1}{6}$

23. ★ **MULTIPLE CHOICE** According to the rational zero theorem, which is *not* a possible zero of the function $f(x) = 2x^4 - 5x^3 + 10x^2 - 9$? **C**

Ⓐ -9 Ⓑ $-\frac{1}{2}$ Ⓒ $\frac{5}{2}$ Ⓓ 3

B **FINDING REAL ZEROS** **Find all real zeros of the function.**

24. $f(x) = 2x^3 + 2x^2 - 8x - 8$ **−2, −1, 2**
25. $g(x) = 2x^3 - 7x^2 + 9$ **$-1, \frac{3}{2}, 3$**
26. $h(x) = 2x^3 - 3x^2 - 14x + 15$ **$-\frac{5}{2}, 1, 3$**
27. $f(x) = 3x^3 + 4x^2 - 35x - 12$ **$-4, -\frac{1}{3}, 3$**
28. $f(x) = 3x^3 + 19x^2 + 4x - 12$ **$-6, -1, \frac{2}{3}$**
29. $g(x) = 2x^3 + 5x^2 - 11x - 14$ **$-\frac{7}{2}, -1, 2$**
30. $g(x) = 2x^4 + 9x^3 + 5x^2 + 3x - 4$ **$-4, \frac{1}{2}$**
31. $h(x) = 2x^4 - x^3 - 7x^2 + 4x - 4$ **−2, 2**
32. $h(x) = 3x^4 - 6x^3 - 32x^2 + 35x - 12$ **−3, 4**
33. $f(x) = 2x^4 - 9x^3 + 37x - 30$ **$-2, 1, \frac{5}{2}, 3$**
34. $f(x) = x^5 - 3x^4 - 5x^3 + 15x^2 + 4x - 12$ **−2, −1, 1, 2, 3**
35. $h(x) = 2x^5 + 5x^4 - 3x^3 - 2x^2 - 5x + 3$ **$-3, \frac{1}{2}, 1$**

ERROR ANALYSIS ***Describe*** **and correct the error in listing the possible rational zeros of the function.**

36.
$f(x) = x^3 + 7x^2 + 2x + 14$
Possible zeros: ✗
1, 2, 7, 14

37.
$f(x) = 6x^3 - 3x^2 + 12x + 5$
Possible zeros: ✗
$\pm1, \pm2, \pm3, \pm6, \pm\frac{1}{5}, \pm\frac{2}{5}, \pm\frac{3}{5}, \pm\frac{6}{5}$

38. ★ **OPEN-ENDED MATH** Write a polynomial function f that has a leading coefficient of 4 and has 12 possible rational zeros according to the rational zero theorem. ***Sample answer:*** **$f(x) = 4x^3 - 2x^2 + 8x - 7$**

39. ★ **MULTIPLE CHOICE** Which of the following is *not* a zero of the function $f(x) = 40x^5 - 42x^4 - 107x^3 + 107x^2 + 33x - 36$? **B**

Ⓐ $-\frac{3}{2}$ Ⓑ $-\frac{3}{8}$ Ⓒ $\frac{3}{4}$ Ⓓ $\frac{4}{5}$

40. ★ **SHORT RESPONSE** Let a_n be the leading coefficient of a polynomial function f and a_0 be the constant term. If a_n has r factors and a_0 has s factors, what is the largest number of possible rational zeros of f that can be generated by the rational zero theorem? *Explain* your reasoning.

C **MATCHING** **Find all real zeros of the function. Then match each function with its graph.**

41. $f(x) = x^3 - 2x^2 - x + 2$ **−1, 1, 2; B**
42. $g(x) = x^3 - 3x^2 + 2$ **$1, 1 \pm \sqrt{3}$; C**
43. $h(x) = x^3 + x^2 - x + 2$ **−2; A**

A.
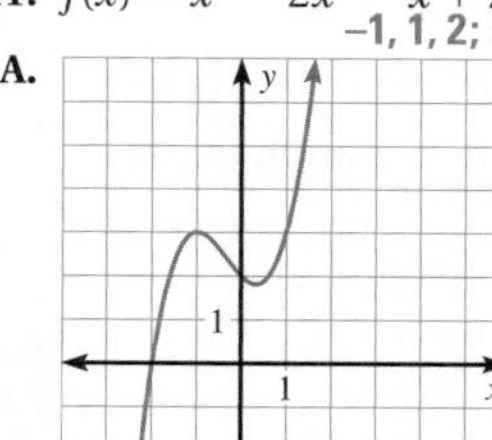

B.
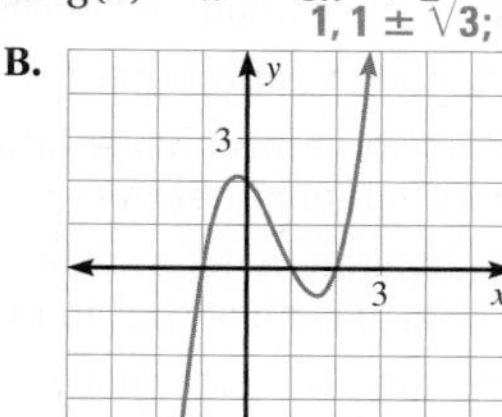

C.
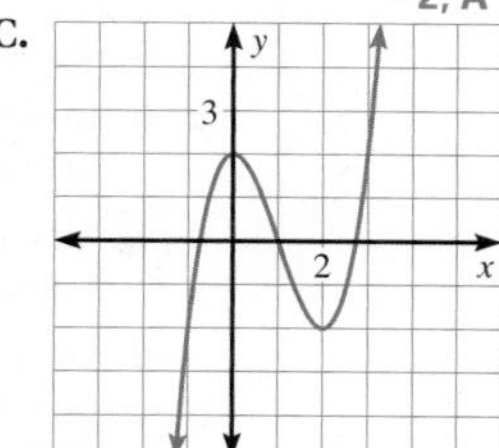

44. **CHALLENGE** Is it possible for a cubic function to have more than three real zeros? Is it possible for a cubic function to have no real zeros? *Explain.*

. The possible ros should clude both sitive and gative factors; ssible zeros: 1, ±2, ±7, ±14.

. p should factors of 5 d q should factors of 6; ssible zeros: 1, ±5, $\pm\frac{1}{2}$, $\pm\frac{5}{2}$, $\frac{1}{3}$, $\pm\frac{5}{3}$, $\pm\frac{1}{6}$, $\pm\frac{5}{6}$.

. rs; each of e factors of a_n n be paired th each of the ctors of a_0. If ere are r ctors of a_n and actors of , then the al number of ctors is rs.

. No; no; a nction cannot ve more zeros at its degree d a cubic nction must ve at least e real zero cause the aphs of the nctions cross x-axis at st once.

Avoiding Common Errors

Exercises 24–35 If students are using a graphing calculator to choose reasonable values to check, they should make sure that the graphing window is set to show the end behavior of the graph. Otherwise, they may miss some possible zeros. For a review of how to set a good viewing window for a polynomial function, refer students to the graphing calculator activity on page 345.

Study Strategy

Exercise 38 Have students set up a chart of the possible values of $\frac{p}{q}$ for their choices of q, and cross out any duplicate values so they don't miscount possible rational zeros.

Teaching Strategy

Exercises 45–48 Students will need to recall various volume formulas from geometry to work these exercises. You may wish to review the necessary formulas with them.

PROBLEM SOLVING

EXAMPLE 4 on p. 373 for Exs. 45–48

A

45. MANUFACTURING At a factory, molten glass is poured into molds to make paperweights. Each mold is a rectangular prism with a height 4 inches greater than the length of each side of its square base. Each mold holds 63 cubic inches of molten glass. What are the dimensions of the mold? **length: 3 in., width: 3 in., height: 7 in.**

@HomeTutor for problem solving help at classzone.com

46. SWIMMING POOL You are designing a rectangular swimming pool that is to be set into the ground. The width of the pool is 5 feet more than the depth, and the length is 35 feet more than the depth. The pool holds 2000 cubic feet of water. What are the dimensions of the pool? **length: 40 ft, width: 10 ft, depth: 5 ft**

@HomeTutor for problem solving help at classzone.com

GEOMETRY In Exercises 47 and 48, write a polynomial equation to model the situation. Then list the possible rational solutions of the equation.

47. A rectangular prism has edges of lengths x, $x - 1$, and $x - 2$ and a volume of 24. $x^3 - 3x^2 + 2x - 24 = 0$; $\pm1, \pm2, \pm3, \pm4, \pm6, \pm8, \pm12, \pm24$

48. A pyramid has a square base with sides of length x, a height of $2x - 5$, and a volume of 3. $2x^3 - 5x^2 - 9 = 0$; $\pm1, \pm3, \pm9, \pm\frac{1}{2}, \pm\frac{3}{2}, \pm\frac{9}{2}$

B

49. MULTI-STEP PROBLEM From 1994 to 2003, the amount of athletic equipment E (in millions of dollars) sold domestically can be modeled by

$$E(t) = -10t^3 + 140t^2 - 20t + 18{,}150$$

where t is the number of years since 1994. Use the following steps to find the year when about \$20,300,000,000 of athletic equipment was sold.

a. Write a polynomial equation that can be used to find the answer. $-10t^3 + 140t^2 - 20t - 2150 = 0$

b. List the possible whole-number solutions of the equation in part (a) that are less than 10. **1, 2, 5**

c. Use synthetic division to determine which of the possible solutions in part (b) is an actual solution. Then calculate the year which corresponds to the solution. **5; 1999**

50. ★ EXTENDED RESPONSE Since 1990, the number of U.S. travelers to foreign countries F (in thousands) can be modeled by

$$F(t) = 12t^4 - 264t^3 + 2028t^2 - 3924t + 43{,}916$$

where t is the number of years since 1990. Use the following steps to find the year when there were about 56,300,000 travelers.

a. Write a polynomial equation that can be used to find the answer.

50a. $12t^4 - 264t^3 + 2028t^2 - 3924t - 12{,}384 = 0$

b. List the possible whole-number solutions of the equation in part (a) that are less than or equal to 10. **1, 2, 3, 4, 6, 8, 9**

c. Use synthetic division to determine which of the possible solutions in part (b) is an actual solution. **8**

d. Graph the function $F(t)$ and explain why there are no other reasonable solutions. Then calculate the year which corresponds to the solution. **The only other solution is negative and therefore does not correspond to a year since 1990; 1998**

○ = WORKED-OUT SOLUTIONS on p. WS1

★ = STANDARDIZED TEST PRACTICE

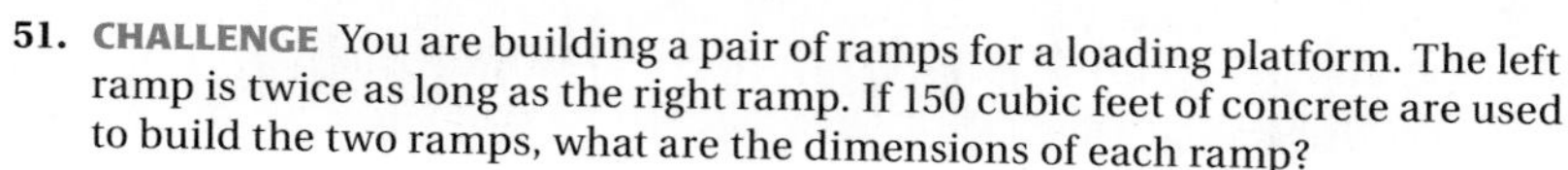

C **51. CHALLENGE** You are building a pair of ramps for a loading platform. The left ramp is twice as long as the right ramp. If 150 cubic feet of concrete are used to build the two ramps, what are the dimensions of each ramp?

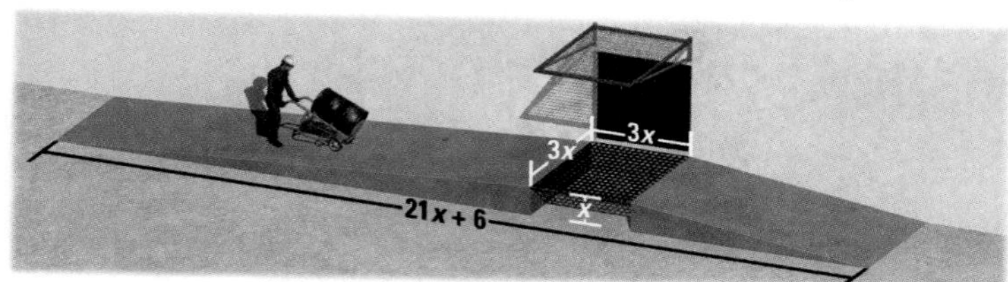

left ramp: length: 24 ft, width: 5 ft, height: $1\frac{2}{3}$ ft; right ramp: length: 12 ft, width: 5 ft, height: $1\frac{2}{3}$

KENTUCKY MIXED REVIEW

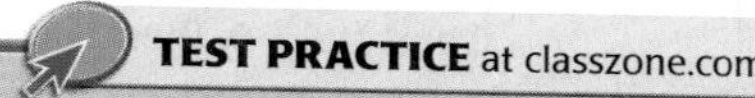

TEST PRACTICE at classzone.com

52. An electronics store has a 30%-off sale on all DVD players. Which statement best represents the functional relationship between the sale price of a DVD player and the original price? **B**

Ⓐ The original price is dependent on the sale price.

Ⓑ The sale price is dependent on the original price.

Ⓒ The sale price and the original price are independent of each other.

Ⓓ The relationship cannot be determined.

53. The area of a rectangle is $132s^8t^{17}$ square units. The length of the rectangle is $12s^5t^9$ units. What is the width of the rectangle? **A**

Ⓐ $11s^3t^8$ units　　Ⓑ $120s^3t^8$ units

Ⓒ $144s^{13}t^{26}$ units　　Ⓓ $1584s^{13}t^{26}$ units

QUIZ for Lessons 5.4–5.6

Factor the polynomial completely. *(p. 353)*

1. $2x^3 - 54$　$2(x-3)(x^2+3x+9)$

2. $x^3 - 3x^2 + 2x - 6$　$(x-3)(x^2+2)$

3. $x^3 + x^2 + x + 1$　$(x+1)(x^2+1)$

4. $6x^5 - 150x$　$6x(x^2-5)(x^2+5)$

5. $3x^4 - 24x^2 + 48$　$3(x-2)^2(x+2)^2$

6. $2x^3 - 3x^2 - 12x + 18$　$(2x-3)(x^2-6)$

Divide using polynomial long division or synthetic division. *(p. 362)*

7. $(x^4 + x^3 - 8x^2 + 5x + 5) \div (x^2 + 5x - 2)$　$x^2 - 4x + 14 + \frac{-73x+33}{x^2+5x-2}$

8. $(4x^3 + 27x^2 + 3x + 64) \div (x + 7)$　$4x^2 - x + 10 + \frac{-6}{x+7}$

Find all real zeros of the function. *(p. 370)*

9. $f(x) = 2x^3 - 19x^2 + 50x + 30$　$-\frac{1}{2}$

10. $f(x) = x^3 - 4x^2 - 25x - 56$　8

11. $f(x) = x^4 + 4x^3 - 13x^2 - 4x + 12$　$-6, -1, 1, 2$

12. $f(x) = 4x^4 - 5x^2 + 42x - 20$　$-\frac{5}{2}, \frac{1}{2}$

13. LANDSCAPING You are a landscape artist designing a square patio that is to be made from 128 cubic feet of concrete. The thickness of the patio is 15.5 feet less than each side length. What are the dimensions of the patio? *(p. 370)*
length: 16 ft, width: 16 ft, thickness: 0.5 ft

EXTRA PRACTICE for Lesson 5.6, p. 1014

ONLINE QUIZ at classzone.com

5 ASSESS AND RETEACH

Daily Homework Quiz

Transparency Available

1. List the possible rational zeros of $f(x) = x^3 + 8x^2 - x + 4$.
$\pm1, \pm2, \pm4$

Find all real zeros of the function.

2. $f(x) = x^3 - 3x^2 - 6x + 8$
$-2, 1, 4$

3. $f(x) = 2x^3 - 3x^2 - 17x + 30$
$-3, 2, \frac{5}{2}$

4. The volume V of a storage shed with a triangular roof can be modeled by $V = x^3 + \frac{1}{2}x^2(6 - x)$. If the volume of the shed is 80 cubic feet, find x. 4

Online Quiz

Available at **classzone.com**

Diagnosis/Remediation

- Practice A, B, C in Chapter 5 Resource Book, pp. 61–63
- Study Guide in Chapter 5 Resource Book, pp. 64–65
- Practice Workbook, pp. 87–88
- @HomeTutor

Challenge

Additional challenge is available in the Chapter 5 Resource Book, p. 68.

Quiz

An easily-readable reduced copy of the quiz (with answers) on Lessons 5.4–5.6 from the Assessment Book can be found on p. 328F.

1 PLAN AND PREPARE

Learn the Method

- Students will use a spreadsheet to help locate the positions of zeros of polynomial functions. They can use this method to find the zeros in Example 3 of Lesson 5.6, and in Exercises 24–35 of the same lesson.

2 TEACH

Tips for Success

Discuss the values in columns A and B to make sure that students understand that the function is being evaluated for values of x in increments of 1 beginning with $x = 0$.

Extra Example

Find all real zeros of $f(x) = 3x^3 + 13x^2 - 10x - 56$. $-4, -\frac{7}{3}, 2$

3 ASSESS AND RETEACH

1. What does the expression in cell B2 represent? **the polynomial expression, replacing x with A2**
2. Suppose the possible rational zeros of a polynomial function are $\pm\frac{1}{3}, \pm1, \pm\frac{7}{3}$, and ±7. Which zero corresponds to a zero located between 2.3 and 2.4? $\frac{7}{3}$

Spreadsheet ACTIVITY Use after Lesson 5.6

@HomeTutor classzone.com Keystrokes

5.6 Use the Location Principle

QUESTION How can you use the Location Principle to identify zeros of a polynomial function?

You can use the following result, called the *Location Principle*, to help you find zeros of polynomial functions:

> If f is a polynomial function and a and b are two numbers such that $f(a) < 0$ and $f(b) > 0$, then f has at least one real zero between a and b.

EXAMPLE Find zeros of a polynomial function

Find all real zeros of $f(x) = 6x^3 + 5x^2 - 17x - 6$.

STEP 1 *Enter values for x*

Enter "x" into cell A1. Enter "0" into cell A2. Type "=A2+1" into cell A3. Select cells A3 through A7, and use the *fill down* command to fill in values of x.

	A	B
1	x	
2	0	
3	1	
4	2	
5	3	
6	4	
7	5	

STEP 2 *Enter values for f(x)*

Enter "$f(x)$" into cell B1. Enter "=6*A2^3+5*A2^2–17*A2–6" into cell B2. Select cells B2 through B7, and use the *fill down* command to fill in the values of $f(x)$.

	A	B
1	x	$f(x)$
2	0	−6
3	1	−12
4	2	28
5	3	150
6	4	390
7	5	784

STEP 3 *Use Location Principle*

The spreadsheet in Step 2 shows that $f(1) < 0$ and $f(2) > 0$. So, by the Location Principle, f has a zero between 1 and 2. The rational zero theorem shows that the only possible *rational* zero between 1 and 2 is $\frac{3}{2}$. Synthetic division confirms that $\frac{3}{2}$ is a zero and that f can be factored as:

$$f(x) = \left(x - \frac{3}{2}\right)(6x^2 + 14x + 4) = (2x - 3)(3x^2 + 7x + 2) = (2x - 3)(3x + 1)(x + 2)$$

▶ The zeros of f are $\frac{3}{2}, -\frac{1}{3}$, and -2.

PRACTICE

Find all real zeros of the function.

1. $f(x) = 6x^3 - 10x^2 - 6x + 10$ $-1, 1, \frac{5}{3}$
2. $f(x) = 24x^4 - 38x^3 - 191x^2 - 157x - 28$ $-\frac{7}{6}, -1, -\frac{1}{4}, 4$
3. $f(x) = 36x^3 + 109x^2 - 341x + 70$ 3. $-5, \frac{2}{9}, 1\frac{3}{4}$
4. $f(x) = 12x^4 + 25x^3 - 160x^2 - 305x - 132$ $-4, -1, -\frac{3}{4}, \frac{11}{3}$

5.7 Apply the Fundamental Theorem of Algebra

MA-HS-5.1.5

Before You found zeros using the rational zero theorem.

Now You will classify the zeros of polynomial functions.

Why? So you can determine boat speed, as in Example 6.

Key Vocabulary
- **repeated solution**
- **irrational conjugates,** *p. 267*
- **complex conjugates,** *p. 278*

MA-HS-5.1.5
Students will: determine if a relation is a function; determine the domain and range of a function (linear and quadratic); determine the slope and intercepts of a linear function; determine the maximum, minimum, and intercepts (roots/zeros) of a quadratic function and evaluate a function written in function notation for a specified rational number. DOK 2

The equation $x^3 - 5x^2 - 8x + 48 = 0$, which becomes $(x + 3)(x - 4)^2 = 0$ when factored, has only two distinct solutions: -3 and 4. Because the factor $x - 4$ appears twice, however, you can count the solution 4 twice. So, with 4 counted as a **repeated solution**, this *third*-degree equation has *three* solutions: -3, 4, and 4.

The previous result is generalized by the *fundamental theorem of algebra*, first proved by the German mathematician Karl Friedrich Gauss (1777–1855).

KEY CONCEPT *For Your Notebook*

The Fundamental Theorem of Algebra

Theorem: If $f(x)$ is a polynomial of degree n where $n > 0$, then the equation $f(x) = 0$ has at least one solution in the set of complex numbers.

Corollary: If $f(x)$ is a polynomial of degree n where $n > 0$, then the equation $f(x) = 0$ has exactly n solutions provided each solution repeated twice is counted as 2 solutions, each solution repeated three times is counted as 3 solutions, and so on.

The corollary to the fundamental theorem of algebra also implies that an nth-degree polynomial function f has exactly n zeros.

EXAMPLE 1 **Find the number of solutions or zeros**

a. How many solutions does the equation $x^3 + 5x^2 + 4x + 20 = 0$ have?

b. How many zeros does the function $f(x) = x^4 - 8x^3 + 18x^2 - 27$ have?

Solution

a. Because $x^3 + 5x^2 + 4x + 20 = 0$ is a polynomial equation of degree 3, it has three solutions. (The solutions are -5, $-2i$, and $2i$.)

b. Because $f(x) = x^4 - 8x^3 + 18x^2 - 27$ is a polynomial function of degree 4, it has four zeros. (The zeros are -1, 3, 3, and 3.)

✓ **GUIDED PRACTICE** for Example 1

1. How many solutions does the equation $x^4 + 5x^2 - 36 = 0$ have? 4
2. How many zeros does the function $f(x) = x^3 + 7x^2 + 8x - 16$ have? 3

1 PLAN AND PREPARE

Warm-Up Exercises
Transparency Available

1. What is the degree of $f(x) = 8x^6 - 4x^5 + 3x^2 + 2$? 6
2. Solve $x^2 - 2x + 3 = 0$. $1 \pm i\sqrt{2}$
3. The function $P = x^4 + 3x^3 - 30x^2 - 6x + 56$ models the profits of a company. What are the real solutions of the function? $-7, \pm\sqrt{2}, 4$

Notetaking Guide
Transparency Available
Promotes interactive learning and notetaking skills, pp. 150–153.

Pacing
Basic: 2 days
Average: 2 days
Advanced: 2 days
Block: 0.5 block with 5.6
0.5 block with 5.8
- See *Teaching Guide/Lesson Plan.*

2 FOCUS AND MOTIVATE

Essential Question
Big Idea 3, p. 329
How can you determine the possible number of positive, negative, and imaginary zeros of a polynomial function? Tell students they will learn how to answer this question by using a property called Descartes' rule of signs.

Resource Planning Guide

Chapter Resource Book
- Teaching Guide/Lesson Plan (pp. 69–70)
- Activity Master (p. 71)
- Practice levels A, B, C (pp. 74–76)
- Study Guide (pp. 77–78)
- Catch-up for Absent Students (p. 79)
- Application (p. 80)
- Challenge (p. 81)

Workbooks
- Notetaking Guide (pp. 150–153)
- Practice Workbook (pp. 89–90)

Teaching Options
- **Power Presentations CD-ROM** provides dynamic electronic teaching resources for the classroom.
- **Activity Generator CD-ROM** provides editable activities for all ability levels.

Interactive Technology
- Easy Planner
- Power Presentations CD-ROM
- Activity Generator CD-ROM
- Animated Algebra
- Test Generator CD-ROM
- Online Quiz
- eWorkbook
- eEdition
- @HomeTutor

Resources for English Learners
- Quick Reference for English Learners
- Spanish Study Guide
- Multi-Language Visual Glossary
- Student Resources in Spanish

See also the *Algebra 2 Toolkit* for more strategies for meeting individual needs.

Motivating the Lesson

Discuss with students how they could determine the number of real zeros of a polynomial function. Tell them that in this lesson they will learn a formula that will tell them the number of real zeros.

3 TEACH

Extra Example 1

a. How many solutions does the equation $x^4 + 8x^2 - 5x + 2$ have? 4

b. How many zeros does the function $f(x) = x^3 + x^2 - 3x - 3$ have? 3 (the zeros are -1, $\sqrt{3}$, $-\sqrt{3}$)

Key Questions to Ask for Example 1

- Which solutions in part (a) are real? Which are imaginary? -5 is real, $-2i$ and $2i$ are imaginary
- If $f(x)$ is a fifth degree function, how many zeros does it have? 5

Extra Example 2

Find all the zeros of $f(x) = x^5 - 4x^3 + x^2 - 4$. $-1, \pm 2, \frac{1 \pm i\sqrt{3}}{2}$

Key Question to Ask for Example 2

- How do you know that -1 could be a repeated zero? After using -1 as a zero, the resulting function that you need to factor still has -1 as a possible zero.

Study Strategy

Suggest that students complete the synthetic division to make sure that they see how the repeated zero is identified.

EXAMPLE 2 Find the zeros of a polynomial function

Find all zeros of $f(x) = x^5 - 4x^4 + 4x^3 + 10x^2 - 13x - 14$.

Solution

STEP 1 **Find** the rational zeros of f. Because f is a polynomial function of degree 5, it has 5 zeros. The possible rational zeros are ± 1, ± 2, ± 7, and ± 14. Using synthetic division, you can determine that -1 is a zero repeated twice and 2 is also a zero.

STEP 2 **Write** $f(x)$ in factored form. Dividing $f(x)$ by its known factors $x + 1$, $x + 1$, and $x - 2$ gives a quotient of $x^2 - 4x + 7$. Therefore:

$$f(x) = (x + 1)^2(x - 2)(x^2 - 4x + 7)$$

STEP 3 **Find** the complex zeros of f. Use the quadratic formula to factor the trinomial into linear factors.

$$f(x) = (x + 1)^2(x - 2)\left[x - (2 + i\sqrt{3})\right]\left[x - (2 - i\sqrt{3})\right]$$

▶ The zeros of f are -1, -1, 2, $2 + i\sqrt{3}$, and $2 - i\sqrt{3}$.

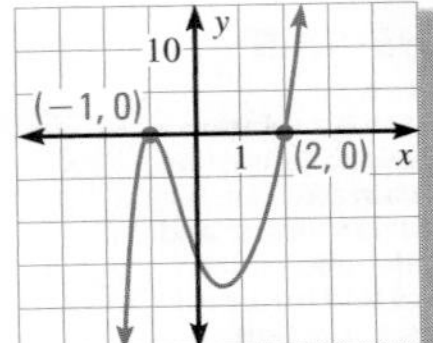

BEHAVIOR NEAR ZEROS The graph of f in Example 2 is shown at the right. Note that only the *real* zeros appear as x-intercepts. Also note that the graph is tangent to the x-axis at the repeated zero $x = -1$, but crosses the x-axis at the zero $x = 2$. This concept can be generalized as follows:

- When a factor $x - k$ of a function f is raised to an odd power, the graph of f crosses the x-axis at $x = k$.
- When a factor $x - k$ of a function f is raised to an even power, the graph of f is tangent to the x-axis at $x = k$.

GUIDED PRACTICE for Example 2

Find all zeros of the polynomial function.

3. $f(x) = x^3 + 7x^2 + 15x + 9$ $-3, -1$

4. $f(x) = x^5 - 2x^4 + 8x^2 - 13x + 6$ $1, -2, 1 + i\sqrt{2}, 1 - i\sqrt{2}$

REVIEW COMPLEX NUMBERS
For help with complex conjugates, see p. 278.

COMPLEX CONJUGATES Also in Example 2, notice that the zeros $2 + i\sqrt{3}$ and $2 - i\sqrt{3}$ are complex conjugates. This illustrates the first theorem given below. A similar result applies to irrational zeros of polynomial functions, as shown in the second theorem below.

KEY CONCEPT *For Your Notebook*

Complex Conjugates Theorem

If f is a polynomial function with real coefficients, and $a + bi$ is an imaginary zero of f, then $a - bi$ is also a zero of f.

Irrational Conjugates Theorem

Suppose f is a polynomial function with rational coefficients, and a and b are rational numbers such that $\sqrt{b}$ is irrational. If $a + \sqrt{b}$ is a zero of f, then $a - \sqrt{b}$ is also a zero of f.

EXAMPLE 3 Use zeros to write a polynomial function

Write a polynomial function f of least degree that has rational coefficients, a leading coefficient of 1, and 3 and $2 + \sqrt{5}$ as zeros.

Solution

Because the coefficients are rational and $2 + \sqrt{5}$ is a zero, $2 - \sqrt{5}$ must also be a zero by the irrational conjugates theorem. Use the three zeros and the factor theorem to write $f(x)$ as a product of three factors.

$$f(x) = (x - 3)[x - (2 + \sqrt{5})][x - (2 - \sqrt{5})] \quad \textbf{Write } f(x) \textbf{ in factored form.}$$
$$= (x - 3)[(x - 2) - \sqrt{5}][(x - 2) + \sqrt{5}] \quad \textbf{Regroup terms.}$$
$$= (x - 3)[(x - 2)^2 - 5] \quad \textbf{Multiply.}$$
$$= (x - 3)[(x^2 - 4x + 4) - 5] \quad \textbf{Expand binomial.}$$
$$= (x - 3)(x^2 - 4x - 1) \quad \textbf{Simplify.}$$
$$= x^3 - 4x^2 - x - 3x^2 + 12x + 3 \quad \textbf{Multiply.}$$
$$= x^3 - 7x^2 + 11x + 3 \quad \textbf{Combine like terms.}$$

CHECK You can check this result by evaluating $f(x)$ at each of its three zeros.

$$f(3) = 3^3 - 7(3)^2 + 11(3) + 3 = 27 - 63 + 33 + 3 = 0 \checkmark$$
$$f(2 + \sqrt{5}) = (2 + \sqrt{5})^3 - 7(2 + \sqrt{5})^2 + 11(2 + \sqrt{5}) + 3$$
$$= 38 + 17\sqrt{5} - 63 - 28\sqrt{5} + 22 + 11\sqrt{5} + 3$$
$$= 0 \checkmark$$

Since $f(2 + \sqrt{5}) = 0$, by the irrational conjugates theorem $f(2 - \sqrt{5}) = 0$. ✓

GUIDED PRACTICE for Example 3

Write a polynomial function f of least degree that has rational coefficients, a leading coefficient of 1, and the given zeros.

. $f(x) = x^5 - 10x^4 +$
$0x^3 - 60x^2 + 104x -$
0

5. $-1, 2, 4$ **$f(x) = x^3 - 5x^2 + 2x + 8$**

6. $4, 1 + \sqrt{5}$ **$f(x) = x^3 - 6x^2 + 4x + 16$**

7. $2, 2i, 4 - \sqrt{6}$

8. $3, 3 - i$ **$f(x) = x^3 - 9x^2 + 28x - 30$**

DESCARTES' RULE OF SIGNS French mathematician René Descartes (1596–1650) found the following relationship between the coefficients of a polynomial function and the number of positive and negative zeros of the function.

KEY CONCEPT *For Your Notebook*

Descartes' Rule of Signs

Let $f(x) = a_n x^n + a_{n-1}x^{n-1} + \cdots + a_2x^2 + a_1x + a_0$ be a polynomial function with real coefficients.

- The number of *positive real zeros* of f is equal to the number of changes in sign of the coefficients of $f(x)$ or is less than this by an even number.
- The number of *negative real zeros* of f is equal to the number of changes in sign of the coefficients of $f(-x)$ or is less than this by an even number.

Extra Example 3

Write a polynomial function f of least degree that has rational coefficients, a leading coefficient of 1, and 2 and $-2 - 5i$ as zeros.
$f(x) = x^3 + 2x^2 + 21x - 58$

Key Questions to Ask for Example 3

- Which theorem, the Complex Conjugates Theorem or the Irrational Conjugates Theorem, tells you that $2 - \sqrt{5}$ is also a zero of the function? **$2 + \sqrt{5}$ is not an imaginary number, so $2 - \sqrt{5}$ is a zero by the Irrational Conjugates Theorem.**
- Which special binomial product pattern is applied when the expression in brackets is multiplied in Step 3? **$(a - b)(a + b) = a^2 - b^2$**

Mathematical Reasoning

Multiple Representations Have students graph the function in Example 3 to check the zeros. Since $2 + \sqrt{5} \approx 4.2$ and $2 - \sqrt{5} \approx -0.2$, the graph should cross the x-axis at 3, at about 4.2, and about -0.2.

Extra Example 4

Determine the possible number of positive real zeros, negative real zeros, and imaginary zeros for $f(x) = 2x^6 - 3x^2 - x + 1$. **0 or 2 positive real zeros; 0 or 2 negative real zeros; 2, 4, or 6 imaginary zeros**

Key Questions to Ask for Example 4

- Where does the first sign change in $f(x)$ occur? **It occurs between the first two terms.**
- Will $f(x)$ and $f(-x)$ always have the same number of sign changes? **no**

Extra Example 5

Approximate the real zeros of $f(x) = 4x^5 + 12x^4 - x - 3$
$x = -3, x \approx 0.71, x \approx -0.71$

Key Questions to Ask for Example 5

- How are the x-intercepts of the graph related to the zeros of the function? **They are the same values.**
- Must the graph of a function always cross the x-axis at its real zeros? Explain. **No; a graph may be tangent to the x-axis without crossing it. When this happens, the graph changes direction at the axis.**

Avoiding Common Errors

When students apply Descartes' rule of signs, remind them that $f(-x)$ is not necessary equal to $-f(x)$. Specifically, $(-x)^n = x^n$ if n is even and $(-x)^n = -x^n$ if n is odd.

Teaching Strategy

Students may be frustrated if they try to reproduce the graph in Example 5 because the scales of the axes are not obvious. To see the graph, tell students to set the XMIN and XMAX values in their graphing window to -3 and 3 and to set their YMIN and YMAX values -100 and 20.

EXAMPLE 4 Use Descartes' rule of signs

Determine the possible numbers of positive real zeros, negative real zeros, and imaginary zeros for $f(x) = x^6 - 2x^5 + 3x^4 - 10x^3 - 6x^2 - 8x - 8$.

Solution

$$f(x) = x^6 - 2x^5 + 3x^4 - 10x^3 - 6x^2 - 8x - 8$$

The coefficients in $f(x)$ have **3 sign changes**, so f has 3 or 1 positive real zero(s).

$$f(-x) = (-x)^6 - 2(-x)^5 + 3(-x)^4 - 10(-x)^3 - 6(-x)^2 - 8(-x) - 8$$
$$= x^6 + 2x^5 + 3x^4 + 10x^3 - 6x^2 + 8x - 8$$

The coefficients in $f(-x)$ have **3 sign changes**, so f has 3 or 1 negative real zero(s).

The possible numbers of zeros for f are summarized in the table below.

Positive real zeros	Negative real zeros	Imaginary zeros	Total zeros
3	3	0	6
3	1	2	6
1	3	2	6
1	1	4	6

✓ **GUIDED PRACTICE** for Example 4

Determine the possible numbers of positive real zeros, negative real zeros, and imaginary zeros for the function.

9. $f(x) = x^3 + 2x - 11$ **positive: 1, negative: 0, imaginary: 2**

10. $g(x) = 2x^4 - 8x^3 + 6x^2 - 3x + 1$ **positive: 4, 2, or 0, negative: 0, imaginary: 4, 2, or 0**

APPROXIMATING ZEROS All of the zeros of the function in Example 4 are irrational or imaginary. Irrational zeros can be approximated using technology.

EXAMPLE 5 Approximate real zeros

Approximate the real zeros of $f(x) = x^6 - 2x^5 + 3x^4 - 10x^3 - 6x^2 - 8x - 8$.

Solution

ANOTHER WAY In Example 5, you can also approximate the zeros of f using the calculator's *trace* feature. However, this generally gives less precise results than the *zero* (or *root*) feature.

Use the *zero* (or *root*) feature of a graphing calculator, as shown below.

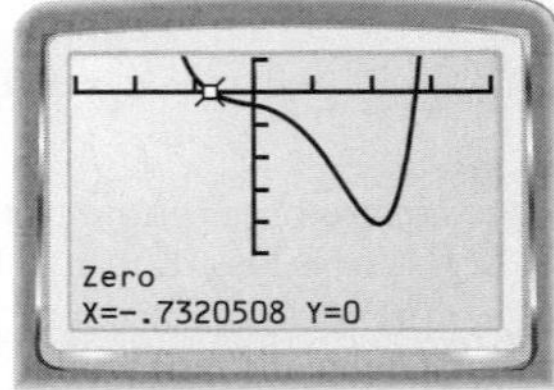

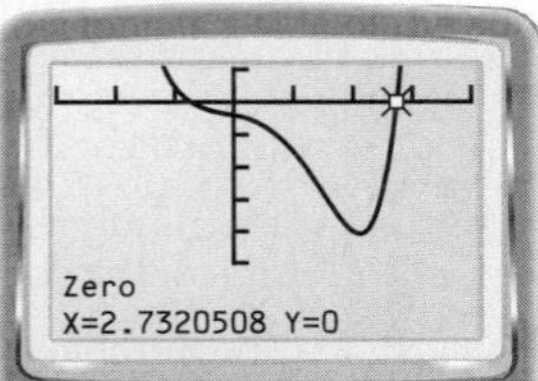

▸ From these screens, you can see that the zeros are $x \approx -0.73$ and $x \approx 2.73$.

Differentiated Instruction

Visual Learners To use Descartes' rule of signs, it may be easier to write a list of the signs of the terms of the polynomial below it in order to see the number of sign changes. For **Example 4**, you would write the following.

$f(x) = x^6 - 2x^5 + 3x^4 - 10x^3 - 6x^2 - 8x - 8$
+ − + − − − − 3 sign changes

$f(-x) = x^6 + 2x^5 + 3x^4 + 10x^3 - 6x^2 + 8x - 8$
+ + + + − + − 3 sign changes

See also the *Algebra 2 Toolkit* for more strategies.

EXAMPLE 6 Approximate real zeros of a polynomial model

TACHOMETER A tachometer measures the speed (in revolutions per minute, or RPMs) at which an engine shaft rotates. For a certain boat, the speed x of the engine shaft (in 100s of RPMs) and the speed s of the boat (in miles per hour) are modeled by

$$s(x) = 0.00547x^3 - 0.225x^2 + 3.62x - 11.0$$

What is the tachometer reading when the boat travels 15 miles per hour?

Solution

Substitute 15 for $s(x)$ in the given function. You can rewrite the resulting equation as:

$$0 = 0.00547x^3 - 0.225x^2 + 3.62x - 26.0$$

Then, use a graphing calculator to approximate the real zeros of $f(x) = 0.00547x^3 - 0.225x^2 + 3.62x - 26.0$.

From the graph, there is one real zero: $x \approx 19.9$.

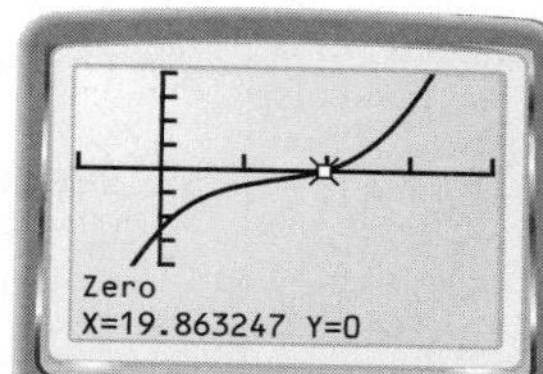

▶ The tachometer reading is about 1990 RPMs.

✓ **GUIDED PRACTICE** for Examples 5 and 6

11. Approximate the real zeros of $f(x) = 3x^5 + 2x^4 - 8x^3 + 4x^2 - x - 1$. $x \approx -2.2, x \approx -0.3, x \approx 1.1$

12. **WHAT IF?** In Example 6, what is the tachometer reading when the boat travels 20 miles per hour? about 2310 RPMs

5.7 EXERCISES

HOMEWORK KEY

○ = **WORKED-OUT SOLUTIONS** on p. WS11 for Exs. 15, 37, and 61

★ = **STANDARDIZED TEST PRACTICE** Exs. 2, 9, 33, 51, 52, 63, and 64

SKILL PRACTICE

1. **VOCABULARY** Copy and complete: For the equation $(x - 1)^2(x + 2) = 0$, a(n) __?__ solution is 1 because the factor $x - 1$ appears twice. repeated

2. ★ **WRITING** *Explain* the difference between complex conjugates and irrational conjugates. Complex conjugates include imaginary numbers and irrational conjugates include irrational numbers.

EXAMPLE 1 on p. 379 for Exs. 3–9

NUMBER OF SOLUTIONS OR ZEROS Identify the number of solutions or zeros.

3. $x^4 + 2x^3 - 4x^2 + x - 10 = 0$ 4
4. $5y^3 - 3y^2 + 8y = 0$ 3
5. $9t^6 - 14t^3 + 4t - 1 = 0$ 6
6. $f(z) = -7z^4 + z^2 - 25$ 4
7. $g(s) = 12s^7 - 9s^6 + 4s^5 - s^3 - 20s + 50$ 7
8. $h(x) = -x^{12} + 7x^8 + 5x^4 - 8x + 6$ 12

9. ★ **MULTIPLE CHOICE** How many zeros does the function $f(x) = 16x - 22x^3 + 6x^6 + 19x^5 - 3$ have? D

Ⓐ 1 Ⓑ 3 Ⓒ 5 Ⓓ 6

Extra Example 6

In Example 6, what is the tachometer reading when the boat travels 10 miles per hour? about 1290 RPMs

Key Questions to Ask for Example 6

- Why is the tachometer reading 1990 RPMs and not 19.9 RPMs? The variable x represents the speed in 100s of RPMs.
- How many imaginary zeros does the function have? 2
- Why does only the real zero represent a solution to the problem? Speed is expressed as a real number.

Closing the Lesson

Have students summarize the major points of the lesson and answer the Essential Question: How do you determine the possible number of positive, negative, and imaginary zeros of a polynomial function?

- If $f(x)$ is a polynomial of degree n, then $f(x) = 0$ has exactly n solutions.
- If a polynomial function with real coefficients has an imaginary zero, then the complex conjugate of that zero is also a zero of the function.
- If $a + \sqrt{b}$ is a zero of a polynomial function with rational roots, a and b are rational, and $\sqrt{b}$ is irrational, then $a - \sqrt{b}$ is also a zero of the function.
- You can use Descartes' rule of signs to determine the number of positive real zeros, negative real zeros, and imaginary zeros that a polynomial function with real coefficients has.
- You can use the root or zero feature on a graphing calculator to approximate the real zeros of a polynomial function.

Descartes' rule of signs states that the number of positive real zeros of a polynomial function f is equal to the number of sign changes of $f(x)$ or is less than this by an even number, and that the number of negative zeros is determined similarly by using $f(-x)$.

4 PRACTICE AND APPLY

Assignment Guide

Answer Transparencies available for all exercises

Basic:
Day 1: pp. 383–386
Exs. 1–6, 9–15, 20–27, 32, 33, 66–67
Day 2: pp. 383–386
Exs. 35–49 odd, 59–63

Average:
Day 1: pp. 383–386
Exs. 1, 2, 4–7, 9, 12–17, 22–29, 32, 33, 66–67
Day 2: pp. 383–386
Exs. 34–50 even, 51–55, 61–64

Advanced:
Day 1: pp. 383–386
Exs. 1, 2, 5–9, 14–19, 24–31, 33, 66–67
Day 2: pp. 383–386
Exs. 38–41, 44–58*, 61–65*

Block:
pp. 383–386
Exs. 1, 2, 4–7, 9, 12–17, 22–29, 32, 33, 66–67 (with 5.6)
pp. 383–386
Exs. 34–50 even, 51–55, 61–64 (with 5.8)

Differentiated Instruction

See *Algebra 2 Best Practices Toolkit* for suggestions on addressing the needs of a diverse classroom.

Homework Check

For a quick check of student understanding of key concepts, go over the following exercises:

Basic: 4, 12, 22, 34, 59

Average: 6, 14, 26, 36, 60

Advanced: 16, 30, 38, 46, 62

Extra Practice

- Student Edition, p. 1014
- Chapter 5 Resource Book: Practice levels A, B, C, pp. 74–76

Practice Worksheet

An easily-readable reduced practice page (with answers) for this lesson can be found on p. 328C.

EXAMPLE 2 on p. 380 for Exs. 10–19

FINDING ZEROS Find all zeros of the polynomial function.

10. $f(x) = x^4 - 6x^3 + 7x^2 + 6x - 8$ **$-1, 1, 2, 4$**
11. $f(x) = x^4 + 5x^3 - 7x^2 - 29x + 30$ **$-5, -3, 1, 2$**
12. $g(x) = x^4 - 9x^2 - 4x + 12$ **$-2, 1, 3$**
13. $h(x) = x^3 + 5x^2 - 4x - 20$ **$-5, -2, 2$**
14. $f(x) = x^4 + 15x^2 - 16$ **$-1, 1, 4i, -4i$**
15. $f(x) = x^4 + x^3 + 2x^2 + 4x - 8$ **$-2, 1, 2i, -2i$**
16. $h(x) = x^4 + 4x^3 + 7x^2 + 16x + 12$ **$-3, -1, 2i, -2i$**
17. $g(x) = x^4 - 2x^3 - 3x^2 + 2x + 2$ **$1, -1, 1 + \sqrt{3}, 1 - \sqrt{3}$**
18. $g(x) = 4x^4 + 4x^3 - 11x^2 - 12x - 3$ **$-\sqrt{3}, -\frac{1}{2}, \sqrt{3}$**
19. $h(x) = 2x^4 + 13x^3 + 19x^2 - 10x - 24$ **$-4, -2, -\frac{3}{2}, 1$**

EXAMPLE 3 on p. 381 for Exs. 20–32

WRITING POLYNOMIAL FUNCTIONS Write a polynomial function f of least degree that has rational coefficients, a leading coefficient of 1, and the given zeros. **20–31. See margin.**

20. $1, 2, 3$
21. $-2, 1, 3$
22. $-5, -1, 2$
23. $-3, 1, 6$
24. $2, -i, i$
25. $3i, 2 - i$
26. $-1, 2, -3i$
27. $5, 5, 4 + i$
28. $4, -\sqrt{5}, \sqrt{5}$
29. $-4, 1, 2 - \sqrt{6}$
30. $-2, -1, 2, 3, \sqrt{11}$
31. $3, 4 + 2i, 1 + \sqrt{7}$

32. **ERROR ANALYSIS** *Describe* and correct the error in writing a polynomial function with rational coefficients and zeros 2 and $1 + i$.

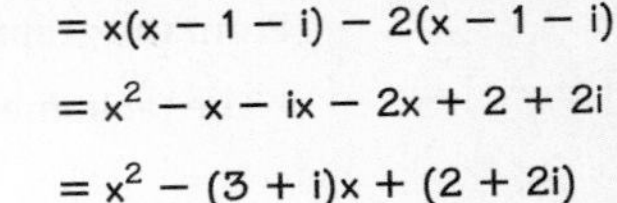

32. The conjugate of $1 + i$, $1 - i$, must also be a zero; $f(x) = (x - 2)[x - (1 + i)][x - (1 - i)]$, $= (x - 2)(x^2 - 2x + 2)$, $= x^3 - 4x^2 + 6x - 4$.

33. ★ **OPEN-ENDED MATH** Write a polynomial function of degree 5 with zeros 1, 2, and $-i$. ***Sample answer:*** **$f(x) = x^5 - 4x^4 + 6x^3 - 6x^2 + 5x - 2$**

EXAMPLE 4 B on p. 382 for Exs. 34–41

CLASSIFYING ZEROS Determine the possible numbers of positive real zeros, negative real zeros, and imaginary zeros for the function. **34–41. See margin.**

34. $f(x) = x^4 - x^2 - 6$
35. $g(x) = -x^3 + 5x^2 + 12$
36. $g(x) = x^3 - 4x^2 + 8x + 7$
37. $h(x) = x^5 - 2x^3 - x^2 + 6x + 5$
38. $h(x) = x^5 - 3x^3 + 8x - 10$
39. $f(x) = x^5 + 7x^4 - 4x^3 - 3x^2 + 9x - 15$
40. $g(x) = x^6 + x^5 - 3x^4 + x^3 + 5x^2 + 9x - 18$
41. $f(x) = x^7 + 4x^4 - 10x + 25$

EXAMPLE 5 on p. 382 for Exs. 42–49

APPROXIMATING ZEROS Use a graphing calculator to graph the function. Then use the *zero* (or *root*) feature to approximate the real zeros of the function.

42. $f(x) = x^3 - x^2 - 8x + 5$ **$x \approx -2.7, x \approx 0.61, x \approx 3.1$**
43. $f(x) = -x^4 - 4x^2 + x + 8$ **$x \approx -1.1, x \approx 1.3$**
44. $g(x) = x^3 - 3x^2 + x + 6$ **$x \approx -1.1$**
45. $h(x) = x^4 - 5x - 3$ **$x \approx -0.58, x \approx 1.9$**
46. $h(x) = 3x^3 - x^2 - 5x + 3$ **$x \approx -1.4, x \approx 0.72, x = 1$**
47. $g(x) = x^4 - x^3 + 2x^2 - 6x - 3$ **$x \approx -0.42, x \approx 2.0$**
48. $f(x) = 2x^6 + x^4 + 31x^2 - 35$ **$x \approx -1.0, x \approx 1.0$**
49. $g(x) = x^5 - 16x^3 - 3x^2 + 42x + 30$ **$x \approx -3.5, x \approx -1.1, x = -1, x \approx 2.1, x \approx 3.6$**

50. **REASONING** Two zeros of $f(x) = x^3 - 6x^2 - 16x + 96$ are 4 and -4. *Explain* why the third zero must also be a real number.

50. It cannot be imaginary because there are three total zeros and if one is imaginary, its conjugate also has to be a zero.

51. ★ **SHORT RESPONSE** *Describe* the possible numbers of positive real, negative real, and imaginary zeros for a cubic function with rational coefficients. **There could be 3, 2, 1, or 0 positive zeros, 3, 2, 1, or 0 negative zeros, and 2 or 0 imaginary zeros.**

52. ★ **MULTIPLE CHOICE** Which is *not* a possible classification of the zeros of $f(x) = x^5 - 4x^3 + 6x^2 + 12x - 6$ according to Descartes' rule of signs? **C**

    (A) 3 positive real zeros, 2 negative real zeros, and 0 imaginary zeros
    (B) 3 positive real zeros, 0 negative real zeros, and 2 imaginary zeros
    (C) 1 positive real zero, 4 negative real zeros, and 0 imaginary zeros
    (D) 1 positive real zero, 2 negative real zeros, and 2 imaginary zeros

○ = WORKED-OUT SOLUTIONS on p. WS1 ★ = STANDARDIZED TEST PRACTICE

20. $f(x) = x^3 - 6x^2 + 11x - 6$
21. $f(x) = x^3 - 2x^2 - 5x + 6$
22. $f(x) = x^3 + 4x^2 - 7x - 10$
23. $f(x) = x^3 - 4x^2 - 15x + 18$
24. $f(x) = x^3 - 2x^2 + x - 2$
25. $f(x) = x^4 - 4x^3 + 14x^2 - 36x + 45$
26. $f(x) = x^4 - x^3 + 7x^2 - 9x - 18$
27. $f(x) = x^4 - 18x^3 + 122x^2 - 370x + 425$
28. $f(x) = x^3 - 4x^2 - 5x + 20$
29. $f(x) = x^4 - x^3 - 18x^2 + 10x + 8$
30. $f(x) = x^6 - 2x^5 - 18x^4 + 30x^3 + 89x^2 - 88x - 132$
31. $f(x) = x^5 - 13x^4 + 60x^3 - 82x^2 - 144x + 360$

CLASSIFYING ZEROS **Determine the numbers of positive real zeros, negative real zeros, and imaginary zeros for the function with the given degree and graph. *Explain* your reasoning.** 53–55. See margin.

53. Degree: 3

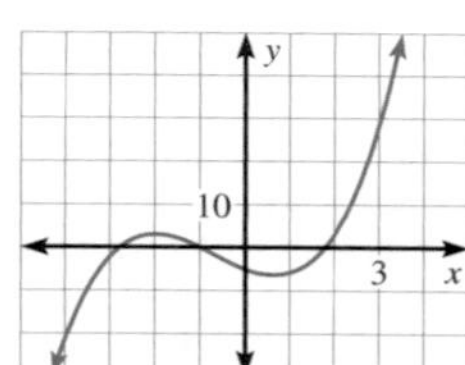

54. Degree: 4

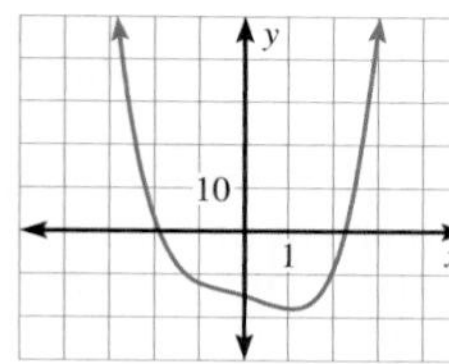

55. Degree: 5

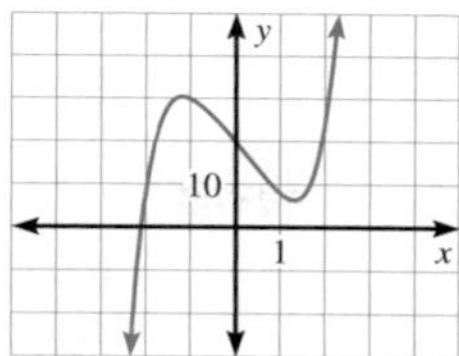

C **CHALLENGE** **Show that the given number is a zero of the given function but that the conjugate of the number is *not* a zero.** 56, 57. See margin.

56. $f(x) = x^3 - 2x^2 + 2x + 5i;\ 2 - i$

57. $g(x) = x^3 + 2x^2 + 2i - 2;\ -1 + i$

58. *Explain* why the results of Exercises 56 and 57 do not contradict the complex conjugate theorem on page 380. The function is not a polynomial with real coefficients.

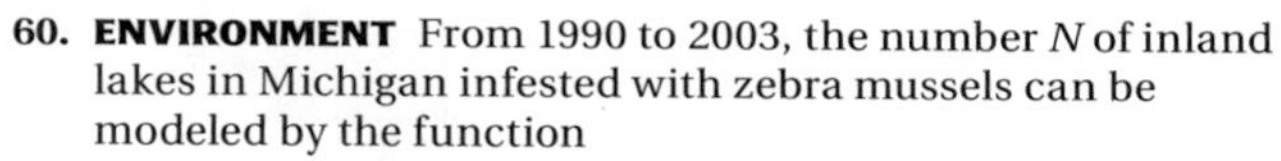

PROBLEM SOLVING

EXAMPLE 6 A on p. 383 for Exs. 59–62

59. BUSINESS For the 12 years that a grocery store has been open, its annual revenue R (in millions of dollars) can be modeled by the function

$$R = 0.0001(-t^4 + 12t^3 - 77t^2 + 600t + 13{,}650)$$

where t is the number of years since the store opened. In which year(s) was the revenue \$1.5 million? year 3 and year 9

@HomeTutor for problem solving help at classzone.com

60. ENVIRONMENT From 1990 to 2003, the number N of inland lakes in Michigan infested with zebra mussels can be modeled by the function

$$N = -0.028t^4 + 0.59t^3 - 2.5t^2 + 8.3t - 2.5$$

where t is the number of years since 1990. In which year did the number of infested inland lakes first reach 120? 1999

Pipe clogged with zebra mussels

@HomeTutor for problem solving help at classzone.com

(61.) PHYSIOLOGY A study group found that a person's score S on a step-climbing exercise test was related to his or her amount of hemoglobin x (in grams per 100 milliliters of blood) by this function:

$$S = -0.015x^3 + 0.6x^2 - 2.4x + 19$$

Given that the normal range of hemoglobin is 12–18 grams per 100 milliliters of blood, what is the most likely amount of hemoglobin for a person who scores 75? about 16.4 g per 100 mL

62. POPULATION From 1890 to 2000, the American Indian, Eskimo, and Aleut population P (in thousands) can be modeled by the function

$$P = 0.0035t^3 - 0.235t^2 + 4.87t + 243$$

where t is the number of years since 1890. In which year did the population first reach 722,000? 1963

Teaching Strategy

Exercises 25–27, 29–31 The error analysis shown in Exercise 32 highlights the most likely error students will make while working these exercises. It may be worthwhile doing Exercise 32 before students attempt Exercises 25–27 and 29–31.

Mathematical Reasoning

Exercise 50 Lead students to the generalization that a polynomial of odd degree must have an odd number of real zeros and, in particular, must have at least one real zero.

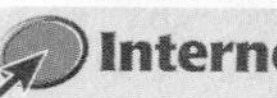

Internet Reference

Exercise 60 For more information about zebra mussels infestation, visit nas.er.usgs.gov/queries/FactSheet.asp?speciesID=5

53. Positive real zeros: 1, negative real zeros: 2, imaginary zeros: 0; the graph crosses the positive x-axis once and the negative x-axis twice.

54. Positive real zeros: 1, negative real zeros: 1, imaginary zeros: 2; the graph crosses the positive x-axis once and the negative x-axis once. Since the function has degree 4, the remaining 2 zeros must be imaginary.

55. Positive real zeros: 0, negative real zeros: 1, imaginary zeros: 4; the graph does not cross the positive x-axis and it crosses the negative x-axis once. Since the function has degree 5, the remaining 4 zeros must be imaginary.

56. $f(2 - i) = (2 - i)^3 - 2(2 - i)^2 + 2(2 - i) + 5i = 2 - 11i - 6 + 8i + 4 - 2i + 5i = 0$, so $2 - i$ is a zero; $f(2 + i) = (2 + i)^3 - 2(2 + i)^2 + 2(2 + i) + 5i = 2 + 11i - 6 - 8i + 4 + 2i + 5i = 10i$, so $2 + i$ is not a zero.

57. $f(-1 + i) = (-1 + i)^3 + 2(-1 + i)^2 + 2i - 2 = 2 + 2i - 4i + 2i - 2 = 0$, so $-1 + i$ is a zero; $f(-1 - i) = (-1 - i)^3 + 2(-1 - i)^2 + 2i - 2 = 2 - 2i + 4i + 2i - 2 = 4i$, so $-1 - i$ is not a zero.

34. positive: 1, negative: 1, imaginary: 2

35. positive: 1, negative: 0, imaginary: 2

36. positive: 2 or 0, negative: 1, imaginary: 2 or 0

37. positive: 2 or 0, negative: 3 or 1, imaginary: 4, 2, or 0

38. positive: 3 or 1, negative: 2 or 0, imaginary: 4, 2, or 0

39. positive: 3 or 1, negative: 2 or 0, imaginary: 4, 2, or 0

40. positive: 3 or 1, negative: 3 or 1, imaginary: 4, 2, or 0

41. positive: 2 or 0, negative: 1, imaginary: 6 or 4

5 ASSESS AND RETEACH

Daily Homework Quiz

Transparency Available

1. Find all the zeros of $f(x) = x^4 - x^2 - 20$. $\pm\sqrt{5}, \pm 2i$
2. Write a polynomial function of least degree that has rational coefficients, a leading coefficient of 1, and -3 and $1 - 7i$ as zeros. $x^3 + x^2 + 44x + 150$
3. Determine the possible numbers of positive real zeros, negative real zeros, and imaginary zeros for $f(x) = 2x^5 - 3x^4 - 5x^3 + 10x^2 + 3x - 5$. 3 positive, 2 negative, 0 imaginary; 3 positive, 0 negative, 2 imaginary; 1 positive, 2 negative, 2 imaginary; or 1 positive, 0 negative, 4 imaginary
4. The profit P for printing envelopes is modeled by $P = -0.001x^3 - 0.06x^2 + 30.5x$, where x is the number of envelopes printed in thousands. What is the least number of envelopes that can be printed for a profit of \$1500? about 70,000 envelopes

Available at **classzone.com**

Diagnosis/Remediation

- Practice A, B, C in Chapter 5 Resource Book, pp. 74–76
- Study Guide in Chapter 5 Resource Book, pp. 77–78
- Practice Workbook, pp. 89–90
- @HomeTutor

Challenge

Additional challenge is available in the Chapter 5 Resource Book, p. 81.

63. 0 in., about 59 in.; the bookshelf would have nearly 0 inches of deflection near each end because of the supports holding the bookshelf, so the answers make sense because they represent each end of a 60 inch bookshelf.

64b. $v = 1000g^3 + 1000g^2 + 1000g + 1000$

64c. About 1.048; about 4.8%; first I substituted \$4300 for v into the function in part (b) to get about 1.048. Then, I subtracted 1 from the growth rate and changed it to a percent to find the interest rate.

63. ★ **SHORT RESPONSE** A 60-inch-long bookshelf is warped under 180 pounds of books. The deflection d of the bookshelf (in inches) is given by

$$d = (2.724 \times 10^{-7})x^4 - (3.269 \times 10^{-5})x^3 + (9.806 \times 10^{-4})x^2$$

where x is the distance (in inches) from the bookshelf's left end. Approximate the real zeros of the function on the domain $0 \le x \le 60$. *Explain* why all your answers make sense in this situation.

64. ★ **EXTENDED RESPONSE** You plan to save \$1000 each year towards buying a used car in four years. At the end of each summer, you deposit \$1000 earned from summer jobs into your bank account. The table shows the value of your deposits over the four year period. In the table, g is the growth factor $1 + r$ where r is the annual interest rate expressed as a decimal.

	Year 1	Year 2	Year 3	Year 4
Value of 1st deposit	1000	$1000g$	$1000g^2$	$1000g^3$
Value of 2nd deposit	–	1000	?	?
Value of 3rd deposit	–	–	1000	?
Value of 4th deposit	–	–	–	1000

a. **Apply** Copy and complete the table. row 2: $1000g$, $1000g^2$; row 3: $1000g$

b. **Model** Write a polynomial function that gives the value v of your account at the end of the fourth summer in terms of g.

c. **Reasoning** You want to buy a car that costs about \$4300. What growth factor do you need to obtain this amount? What annual interest rate do you need? *Explain* how you found your answers.

65. CHALLENGE A monument with the dimensions shown is to be built using 1000 cubic feet of marble. What is the value of x? about 4.3 ft

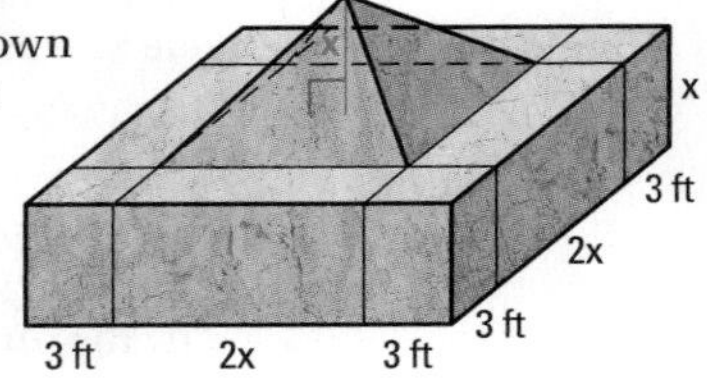

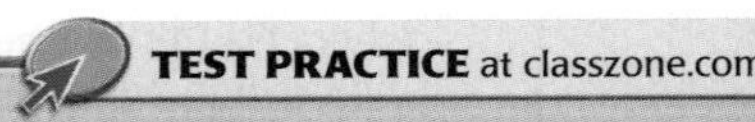

KENTUCKY MIXED REVIEW

66. Which of the following is the solution of this system of linear equations? **A**

$$-2x + 3y = 20$$
$$4x + 4y = -15$$

Ⓐ $\left(-\frac{25}{4}, \frac{5}{2}\right)$ Ⓑ $\left(\frac{5}{2}, -\frac{25}{4}\right)$ Ⓒ $\left(\frac{25}{2}, \frac{35}{4}\right)$ Ⓓ No solution

67. What is the approximate volume of the bird feeder shown? **C**

Ⓐ 156 in.^{3} Ⓑ 184 in.^{3}
Ⓒ 212 in.^{3} Ⓓ 269 in.^{3}

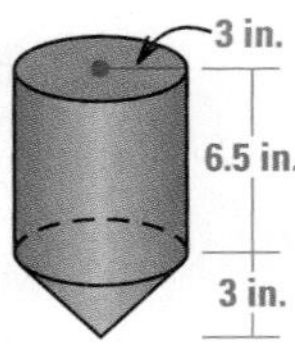

5.8 Analyze Graphs of Polynomial Functions

MA-HS-5.1.5

Before You graphed polynomial functions by making tables.

Now You will use intercepts to graph polynomial functions.

Why? So you can maximize the volume of structures, as in Ex. 42.

Key Vocabulary
- local maximum
- local minimum

MA-HS-5.1.5
Students will: determine if a relation is a function; determine the domain and range of a function (linear and quadratic); determine the slope and intercepts of a linear function; determine the maximum, minimum, and intercepts (roots/zeros) of a quadratic function and evaluate a function written in function notation for a specified rational number. DOK 2

In this chapter you have learned that zeros, factors, solutions, and x-intercepts are closely related concepts. The relationships are summarized below.

CONCEPT SUMMARY *For Your Notebook*

Zeros, Factors, Solutions, and Intercepts

Let $f(x) = a_nx^n + a_{n-1}x^{n-1} + \cdots + a_1x + a_0$ be a polynomial function. The following statements are equivalent.

Zero: k is a zero of the polynomial function f.

Factor: $x - k$ is a factor of the polynomial $f(x)$.

Solution: k is a solution of the polynomial equation $f(x) = 0$.

x-intercept: If k is a real number, k is an x-intercept of the graph of the polynomial function f. The graph of f passes through $(k, 0)$.

EXAMPLE 1 Use x-intercepts to graph a polynomial function

Graph the function $f(x) = \frac{1}{6}(x + 3)(x - 2)^2$.

Solution

STEP 1 **Plot** the intercepts. Because -3 and 2 are zeros of f, plot $(-3, 0)$ and $(2, 0)$.

STEP 2 **Plot** points between and beyond the x-intercepts.

x	-2	-1	0	1	3
y	$\frac{8}{3}$	3	2	$\frac{2}{3}$	1

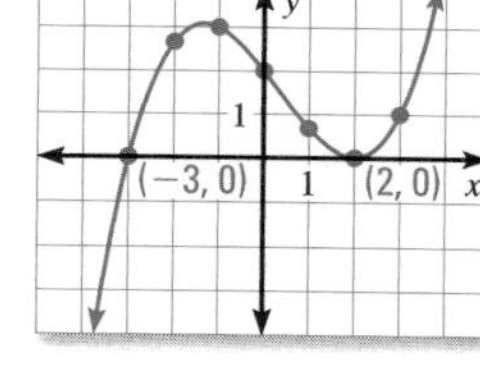

STEP 3 **Determine** end behavior. Because f has three factors of the form $x - k$ and a constant factor of $\frac{1}{6}$, it is a cubic function with a positive leading coefficient. So, $f(x) \to -\infty$ as $x \to -\infty$ and $f(x) \to +\infty$ as $x \to +\infty$.

STEP 4 **Draw** the graph so that it passes through the plotted points and has the appropriate end behavior.

1 PLAN AND PREPARE

Warm-Up Exercises

Transparency Available

1. Multiply $(x + 2)(3x + 1)$. $3x^2 + 7x + 2$
2. Find the x-intercepts of $y = (x + 6)(x - 5)$. -6 and 5
3. An object is projected vertically upward. Its distance D in feet above the ground after t seconds is given by $D = -16t^2 + 144t + 100$. Find its maximum distance above the ground. 424 ft

Notetaking Guide

Transparency Available

Promotes interactive learning and notetaking skills, pp. 154–156.

Pacing

Basic: 1 day
Average: 1 day
Advanced: 1 day
Block: 0.5 block with 5.7
- See *Teaching Guide/Lesson Plan.*

2 FOCUS AND MOTIVATE

Essential Question

Big Idea 1, p. 329

When does a graph have a local maximum or local minimum? **Tell students they will learn how to answer this question by examining the turning points of the graph.**

Resource Planning Guide

Chapter Resource Book
- Teaching Guide/Lesson Plan (pp. 82–83)
- Activity Master (p. 84)
- Practice levels A, B, C (pp. 87–92)
- Study Guide (pp. 93–94)
- Catch-up for Absent Students (p. 95)
- Application (p. 96)
- Challenge (p. 97)

Workbooks
- Notetaking Guide (pp. 154–156)
- Practice Workbook (pp. 91–93)

Teaching Options
- **Power Presentations CD-ROM** provides dynamic electronic teaching resources for the classroom.
- **Activity Generator CD-ROM** provides editable activities for all ability levels.

Interactive Technology
- Easy Planner
- Power Presentations CD-ROM
- Activity Generator CD-ROM
- Animated Algebra
- Test Generator CD-ROM
- Online Quiz
- eWorkbook
- eEdition
- @HomeTutor

Resources for English Learners
- Quick Reference for English Learners
- Spanish Study Guide
- Multi-Language Visual Glossary
- Student Resources in Spanish

See also the *Algebra 2 Toolkit* for more strategies for meeting individual needs.

Motivating the Lesson

Have students work in groups to create a box. Each group should start with the same sized piece of poster board and cut a square out of each corner to make the box. Ask students to compare the volumes of their boxes to see which group created the box with the greatest volume. In this lesson the students will learn a technique for determining how large the cut out squares should be to insure the greatest possible volume.

3 TEACH

Extra Example 1

Graph the function $f(x) = -(x + 2)(x - 1)^2$.

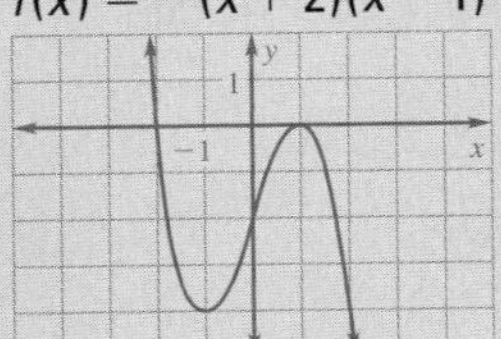

Extra Example 2

Graph the function $f(x) = x^4 + 4x^3 + 3x^2 - 4x - 4$. Identify the x-intercepts and the points where the local maximums and local minimums occur.

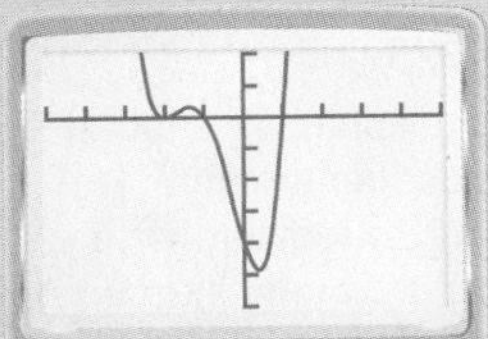

x-intercepts: $-2, -1, 1$; min: $(-2, 0)$ and $(0.4, -4.8)$; max: $(-1.4, 0.3)$

An **Animated Algebra** activity is available on-line for **Example 2**. This activity is also available on the **Power Presentations CD-ROM**.

TURNING POINTS Another important characteristic of graphs of polynomial functions is that they have *turning points* corresponding to local maximum and minimum values.

- The y-coordinate of a turning point is a **local maximum** of the function if the point is higher than all nearby points.
- The y-coordinate of a turning point is a **local minimum** of the function if the point is lower than all nearby points.

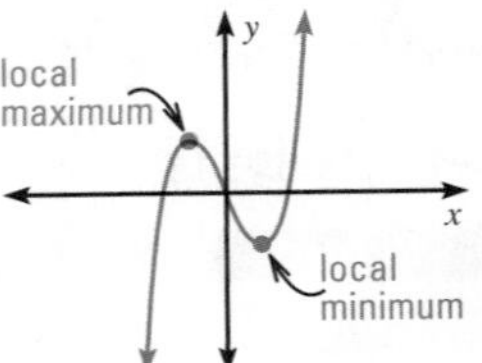

KEY CONCEPT *For Your Notebook*

Turning Points of Polynomial Functions

1. The graph of every polynomial function of degree n has *at most* $n - 1$ turning points.
2. If a polynomial function has n distinct real zeros, then its graph has *exactly* $n - 1$ turning points.

EXAMPLE 2 Find turning points

Graph the function. Identify the x-intercepts and the points where the local maximums and local minimums occur.

a. $f(x) = x^3 - 3x^2 + 6$ **b.** $g(x) = x^4 - 6x^3 + 3x^2 + 10x - 3$

Solution

a. Use a graphing calculator to graph the function.

Notice that the graph of f has one x-intercept and two turning points.

You can use the graphing calculator's *zero, maximum,* and *minimum* features to approximate the coordinates of the points.

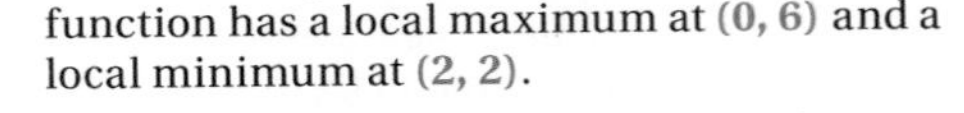

▶ The x-intercept of the graph is $x \approx -1.20$. The function has a local maximum at $(0, 6)$ and a local minimum at $(2, 2)$.

FIND MAXIMUMS AND MINIMUMS
For help with using the *maximum* and *minimum* features of a graphing calculator, see p. 244.

b. Use a graphing calculator to graph the function.

Notice that the graph of g has four x-intercepts and three turning points.

You can use the graphing calculator's *zero, maximum,* and *minimum* features to approximate the coordinates of the points.

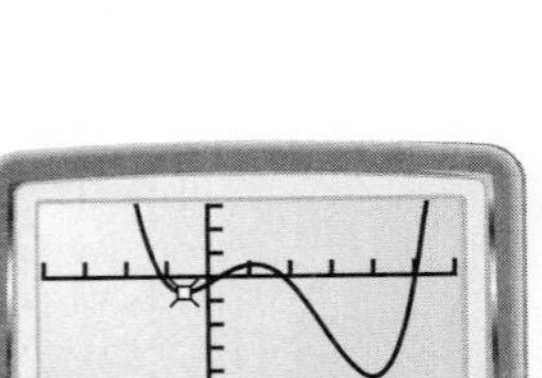

▶ The x-intercepts of the graph are $x \approx -1.14$, $x \approx 0.29$, $x \approx 1.82$, and $x \approx 5.03$. The function has a local maximum at $(1.11, 5.11)$ and local minimums at $(-0.57, -6.51)$ and $(3.96, -43.04)$.

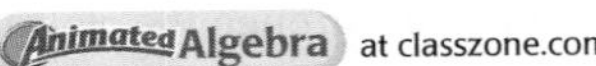 at classzone.com

Differentiated Instruction

English Learners Since it can be argued that all points on curves are turning to some degree, the description *turning point* may be unclear to some students. Explain that a turning point is where a curve completely changes direction from up to down or from down to up.

See also the *Algebra 2 Toolkit* for more strategies.

EXAMPLE 3 Maximize a polynomial model

ARTS AND CRAFTS You are making a rectangular box out of a 16-inch-by-20-inch piece of cardboard. The box will be formed by making the cuts shown in the diagram and folding up the sides. You want the box to have the greatest volume possible.

- How long should you make the cuts?
- What is the maximum volume?
- What will the dimensions of the finished box be?

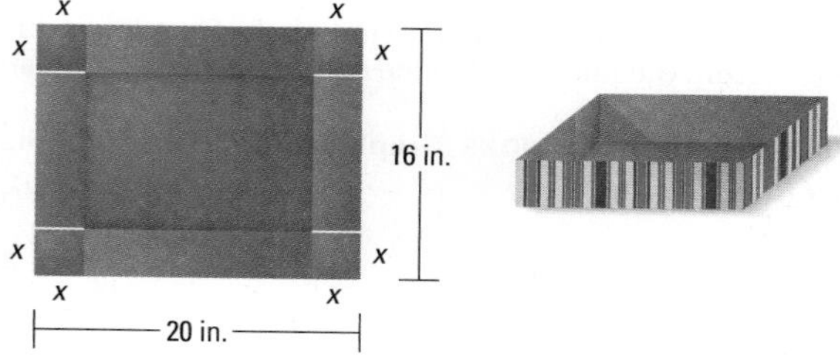

Solution

Write a verbal model for the volume. Then write a function.

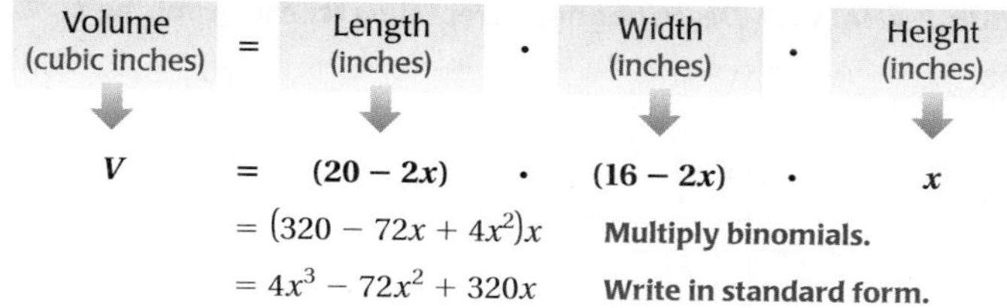

$$V = (20 - 2x) \cdot (16 - 2x) \cdot x$$

$= (320 - 72x + 4x^2)x$ **Multiply binomials.**

$= 4x^3 - 72x^2 + 320x$ **Write in standard form.**

To find the maximum volume, graph the volume function on a graphing calculator, as shown at the right. Consider only the interval $0 < x < 8$ because this describes the physical restrictions on the size of the flaps.

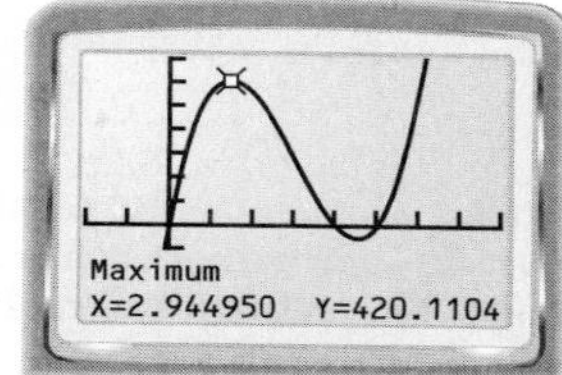

From the graph, you can see that the maximum volume is about 420 and occurs when $x \approx 2.94$.

▶ You should make the cuts about 3 inches long. The maximum volume is about 420 cubic inches. The dimensions of the box with this volume will be about $x = 3$ inches by $x = 10$ inches by $x = 14$ inches.

GUIDED PRACTICE for Examples 1, 2, and 3

Graph the function. Identify the x-intercepts and the points where the local maximums and local minimums occur. 1–4. See margin.

1. $f(x) = 0.25(x + 2)(x - 1)(x - 3)$
2. $g(x) = 2(x - 1)^2(x - 4)$
3. $h(x) = 0.5x^3 + x^2 - x + 2$
4. $f(x) = x^4 + 3x^3 - x^2 - 4x - 5$
5. **WHAT IF?** In Example 3, how do the answers change if the piece of cardboard is 10 inches by 15 inches? See margin.

Extra Example 3

In Example 3, what is the maximum volume and what are the dimensions if you start with a piece of cardboard that is 12 inches by 15 inches? **The maximum volume is about 177 in.^{3} and occurs when the dimensions are about 7.6 in., 10.6 in., and 2.2 in.**

Key Question to Ask for Example 3

- Why does the interval $0 < x < 8$ describe the physical restrictions on the size of the flaps? **The flaps cannot have a zero or negative length and must be less than half the width of the cardboard in length.**

Closing the Lesson

Have students summarize the major points of the lesson and answer the Essential Question: When does a graph have a local maximum or local minimum?

- **If k is a real zero of the polynomial function f, then $x - k$ is a factor of the polynomial $f(x)$, k is a solution of $f(x) = 0$, and k is an x-intercept of the graph of f.**
- **The graph of a polynomial function of degree n has at most $n - 1$ turning points. Also, if the function has n distinct real zeros, then its graph has exactly $n - 1$ turning points.**
- **Turning points of a polynomial function are called local maximums or local minimums.**

A graph has a local maximum (minimum) when the y-coordinate of a point is greater than (less than) the y-coordinates of all nearby points.

1. x-intercepts: −2, 1, 3; local minimum: (2.1, −1.0); local maximum: (−0.79, 2.1)
2. x-intercepts: 1, 4; local minimum: (3, −8); local maximum: (−1, 0)
3. x-intercept: −3.1; local minimum: (0.39, 1.8); local maximum: (−1.7, 4.1)
4. x-intercepts: −3.1, 1.4; local minimums: (−2.3, −9.6), (0.68, −7.0); local maximum: (−0.65, −3.5)
5. The cuts should be about 2 inches long. The maximum volume is about 132 cubic inches. The dimensions of the box would be 6 inches by 11 inches by 2 inches.

5.8 EXERCISES

HOMEWORK KEY

○ = **WORKED-OUT SOLUTIONS** on p. WS11 for Exs. 3, 19, and 41
★ = **STANDARDIZED TEST PRACTICE** Exs. 2, 21, 30, 32, 33, and 43
◆ = **MULTIPLE REPRESENTATIONS** Ex. 42

SKILL PRACTICE

A

1. **VOCABULARY** Copy and complete: A local maximum or local minimum of a polynomial function occurs at a __?__ point of the function's graph. **turning**

2. ★ **WRITING** *Explain* what a local maximum of a function is and how it may be different from the maximum value of the function. **See margin.**

EXAMPLE 1 on p. 387 for Exs. 3–14

2. ***Sample answer:*** **A local maximum occurs at a turning point on the graph of a function and is higher than any nearby point, but it may not be the highest point on the graph.**

GRAPHING POLYNOMIAL FUNCTIONS **Graph the function.** **3–12. See margin.**

(3.) $f(x) = (x - 2)^2(x + 1)$

4. $f(x) = (x + 1)^2(x - 1)(x - 3)$

5. $g(x) = \frac{1}{3}(x - 5)(x + 2)(x - 3)$

6. $h(x) = \frac{1}{12}(x + 4)(x + 8)(x - 1)$

7. $h(x) = 4(x + 1)(x + 2)(x - 1)$

8. $f(x) = 0.2(x - 4)^2(x + 1)^2$

9. $f(x) = 2(x + 2)^2(x + 4)^2$

10. $h(x) = 5(x - 1)(x - 2)(x - 3)$

11. $g(x) = (x - 3)(x^2 + x + 1)$

12. $h(x) = (x - 4)(2x^2 - 2x + 1)$

ERROR ANALYSIS ***Describe*** **and correct the error in graphing *f*.** **13–14. See margin.**

13. $f(x) = (x + 2)(x - 1)^2$

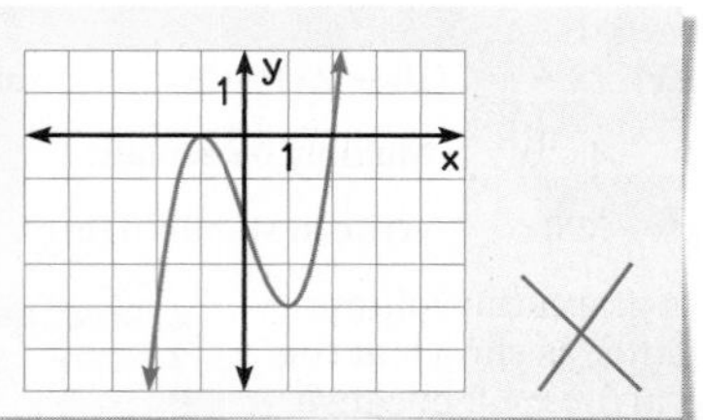

14. $f(x) = x(x - 3)^3$

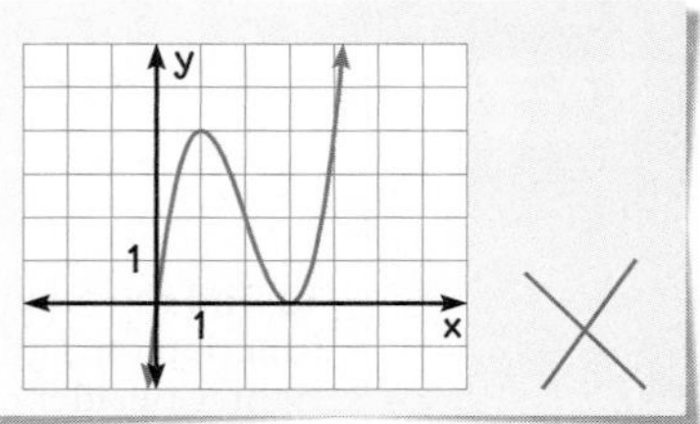

EXAMPLE 2 on p. 388 for Exs. 15–30

ANALYZING GRAPHS **Estimate the coordinates of each turning point and state whether each corresponds to a local maximum or a local minimum. Then estimate all real zeros and determine the least degree the function can have.** **15–20. See margin.**

15.

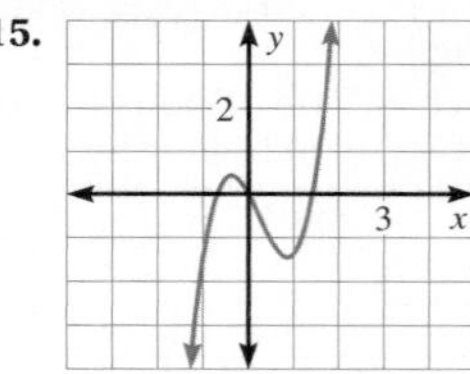

16.

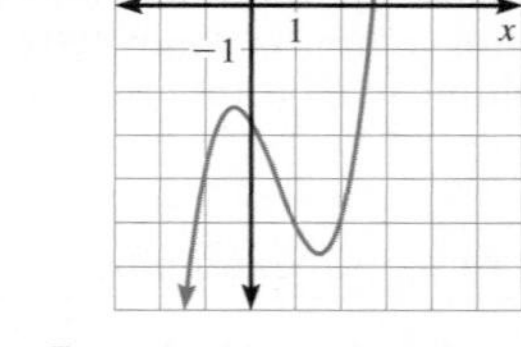

17.

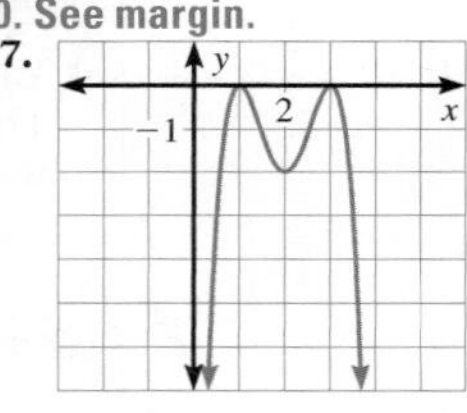

18.

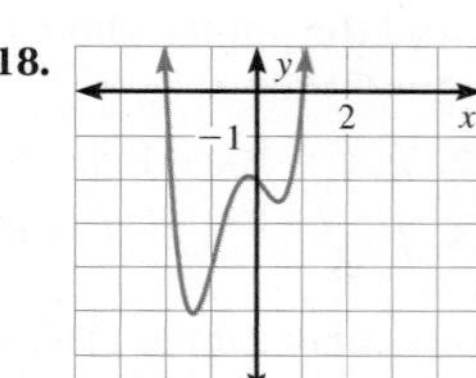

(19.)

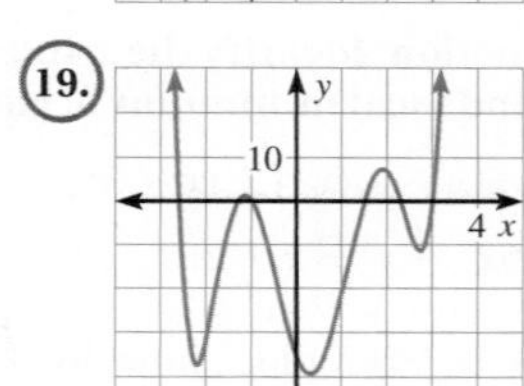

20.

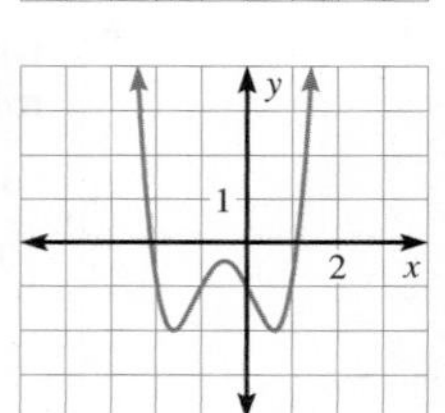

4 PRACTICE AND APPLY

Assignment Guide

Answer Transparencies available for all exercises

Basic:
Day 1: pp. 390–392
Exs. 1–8, 13–17, 21–26, 30, 39–42, 45

Average:
Day 1: pp. 390–392
Exs. 1, 2, 6–10, 13, 14, 18–21, 25–33, 39–43, 46

Advanced:
Day 1: pp. 390–392
Exs. 1, 2, 11, 12, 21–44*

Block:
pp. 390–392
Exs. 1, 2, 6–10, 13, 14, 18–21, 25–33, 39–43, 46 (with 5.7)

Differentiated Instruction

See *Algebra 2 Best Practices Toolkit* for suggestions on addressing the needs of a diverse classroom.

Homework Check

For a quick check of student understanding of key concepts, go over the following exercises:

Basic: 4, 8, 16, 24, 39
Average: 8, 10, 18, 26, 40
Advanced: 10, 12, 26, 28, 40

Extra Practice

- Student Edition, p. 1014
- Chapter 5 Resource Book: Practice levels A, B, C, pp. 87–92

Practice Worksheet

An easily-readable reduced practice page (with answers) for this lesson can be found on p. 328C.

3–14. See Additional Answers beginning on p. AA1.

15–20. Sample answers are given.

15. local maximum: (−0.3, 0.3), local minimum: (0.9, −1.3); zeros: −0.75, 0, 1.4, least degree: 3

16. local maximum: (−0.5, −2.4), local minimum: (1.5, −5.7); zero: 2.7, least degree: 3

17. local maximums: (1, 0), (3, 0), local minimum: (2, −2); zeros: 1, 3, least degree: 4

18. local maximum: (−0.25, −2), local minimums: (−1.5, −5), (0.5, −2.4); zeros: −2, 1, least degree: 4

19. local maximums: (−1.1, 0.8), (1.9, 8), local minimums: (−2.2, −38), (0.3, −41), (2.8, −13); zeros: −2.6, −1.2, 1.5, 2.2, 3, least degree: 6

20. local maximum: (−0.5, −0.5), local minimums: (−1.7, −2), (0.6, −2); zeros: −2.1, −1, 1.1, least degree: 4

31. *Sample answer:* Quadratic functions only have one turning point, therefore one maximum or minimum value. Cubic functions can have two turning points, therefore one maximum and one minimum, and the end behavior is to infinity, so there is no real maximum or minimum value.

32. Sometimes. *Sample answer:* The graph of $y = x^3 + 10x$ does not have a turning point, but more of a bend in the graph.

21. ★ **MULTIPLE CHOICE** Which point is a local maximum of the function $f(x) = 0.25(x + 2)(x - 1)^2$? B

Ⓐ $(-2, 0)$ Ⓑ $(-1, 1)$ Ⓒ $(1, 0)$ Ⓓ $(2, 1)$

B **GRAPHING CALCULATOR** **Use a graphing calculator to graph the polynomial function. Identify the x-intercepts and the points where the local maximums and local minimums occur.** 22–29. See margin.

22. $f(x) = 2x^3 + 8x^2 - 3$

23. $g(x) = 0.5x^3 - 2x + 2.5$

24. $h(x) = -x^4 + 3x$

25. $f(x) = x^5 - 4x^3 + x^2 + 2$

26. $g(x) = x^4 - 3x^2 + x$

27. $h(x) = x^4 - 5x^3 + 2x^2 + x - 3$

28. $h(x) = x^5 + 2x^2 - 17x - 4$

29. $g(x) = 0.7x^4 - 8x^3 + 5x$

30. ★ **MULTIPLE CHOICE** What is a turning point of the graph of the function $g(x) = x^4 - 9x^2 + 4x + 12$? D

Ⓐ $(-3, 0)$ Ⓑ $(-1, 0)$ Ⓒ $(0, 12)$ Ⓓ $(2, 0)$

31. **REASONING** Why is the adjective *local* used to describe the maximums and minimums of cubic functions but not quadratic functions?

32. ★ **SHORT RESPONSE** Does a cubic function *always, sometimes,* or *never* have a turning point? *Justify* your answer.

33. ★ **OPEN-ENDED MATH** Write a cubic function, a quartic function, and a fifth-degree function whose graphs have x-intercepts only at $x = -2$, 0, and 4.
Sample answer: $y = x(x + 2)(x - 4)$, $y = x(x + 2)(x - 4)^2$, $y = x^3(x + 2)(x - 4)$

C **DOMAIN AND RANGE** **Graph the function. Then identify its domain and range.** 34–37. See margin.

34. $f(x) = x(x - 3)^2$

35. $f(x) = x^2(x - 2)(x - 4)(x - 5)$

36. $f(x) = (x + 1)^3(x - 1)$

37. $f(x) = (x + 2)(x + 1)(x - 1)^2(x - 2)^2$

38. **CHALLENGE** In general, what can you say about the domain and range of odd-degree polynomial functions? What can you say about the domain and range of even-degree polynomial functions? Odd-degree: domain and range will always be all real numbers; even-degree: domain will always be all real numbers, range will either be all numbers greater than or equal to the minimum value or all numbers less than or equal to the maximum value.

PROBLEM SOLVING

EXAMPLE 3 A
on p. 389
for Exs. 39–40

In Exercises 39 and 40, assume that the box is constructed using the method illustrated in Example 3 on page 389.

39. **POSTCARDS** Marcie wants to make a box to hold her postcard collection from a piece of cardboard that is 10 inches by 18 inches. What are the dimensions of the box with the maximum volume? What is the maximum volume of the box? maximum: about 5.8 in. by 13.8 in. by 2.1 in.; about 168 in.^{3}

@HomeTutor for problem solving help at classzone.com

40. **COIN COLLECTION** Jorge is making a box for his coin collection from a piece of cardboard that is 30 centimeters by 40 centimeters. What are the dimensions of the box with the maximum volume? What is the maximum volume of the box? maximum: about 18.6 cm by 28.6 cm by 5.7 cm; about 3032 cm^3

@HomeTutor for problem solving help at classzone.com

Study Strategy

Exercises 15–20 Point out that a local maximum occurs where the graph has a peak and a local minimum occurs where the graph has a valley.

Teaching Strategy

Exercises 22–29, 39–40 Students may need to review the graphing calculator activity on setting a good viewing window before attempting these exercises.

Avoiding Common Errors

Exercises 39–40 Students may incorrectly subtract the width of the cutout x from each dimension of the cardboard only once. Having them draw sketches may help them see that $2x$ should be subtracted from each dimension of the cardboard.

22. x-intercepts: −3.9, −0.67, 0.57; local maximum: (−2.7, 16); local minimum: (0, −3)

23. x-intercept: −2.5; local maximum: (−1.2, 4.0); local minimum: (1.2, 0.96)

24. x-intercepts: 0, 1.4; local maximum: (0.91, 2.0); local minimum: none

25. x-intercepts: −2.2, 1, 1.7; local maximums: (−1.6, 10.5), (0.17, 2.0); local minimums: (0, 2), (1.5, −1.7)

26. x-intercepts: −1.9, 0, 1.5; local maximum: (0.17, 0.08); local minimums: (−1.3, −3.5), (1.1, −1.1)

27. x-intercepts: −0.77, 4.5; local maximum: (0.47, −2.6); local minimums: (−0.16, −3.1), (3.4, −39.4)

28. x-intercepts: −2.1, −0.23, 2.0; local maximum: (−1.5, 18.4) local minimum: (1.2, −19.1)

29. x-intercepts: −0.77, 0, 0.82; local maximum: (0.47, 1.6); local minimum: (−0.46, −1.5)

34–37. See Additional Answers beginning on p. AA1.

5 ASSESS AND RETEACH

Daily Homework Quiz

Transparency Available

1. Graph the function $f(x) = 2(x - 1)(x + 3)^2$. Identify the x-intercepts and the points where the local maximums and minimums occur.

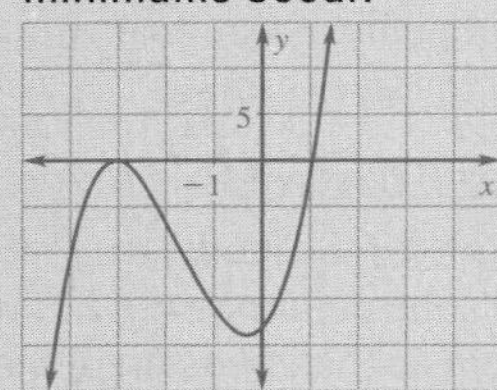

x-intercepts: $x = -3, 1$; local maximum: $(-3, 0)$; local minimum: $(-0.34, -19.0)$

2. You are making a rectangular box out of a 22-inch by 30-inch piece of cardboard as shown in the diagram. You want the box to have the greatest possible volume. How long should you make the cuts? What is the maximum volume?

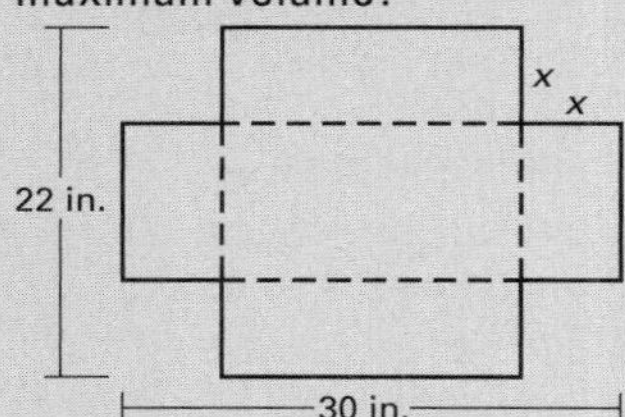

A square about 4.2 inches on a side should be cut from each corner to produce a box with a maximum volume of about 1234 in.^{3}

Available at **classzone.com**

Diagnosis/Remediation

- Practice A, B, C in Chapter 5 Resource Book, pp. 87–92
- Study Guide in Chapter 5 Resource Book, pp. 93–94
- Practice Workbook, pp. 91–93
- @HomeTutor

Challenge

Additional challenge is available in the Chapter 5 Resource Book, p. 97.

41, 42c, 43a. See Additional Answers beginning on p. AA1.

41. **SWIMMING** For a swimmer doing the breaststroke, the function

$$S = -241t^7 + 1060t^6 - 1870t^5 + 1650t^4 - 737t^3 + 144t^2 - 2.43t$$

models the swimmer's speed S (in meters per second) during one complete stroke, where t is the number of seconds since the start of the stroke. Graph the function. According to the model, at what time during the stroke is the swimmer going the fastest? **See margin for art; after about 0.95 sec.**

B

42.  **MULTIPLE REPRESENTATIONS** You have 600 square feet of material for building a greenhouse that is shaped like half a cylinder.

a. **Writing an Expression** The surface area S of the greenhouse is given by $S = \pi r^2 + \pi r\ell$. Substitute 600 for S and then write an expression for ℓ in terms of r. $\frac{600 - \pi r^2}{\pi r}$

b. **Writing a Function** The volume V of the greenhouse is given by $V = \frac{1}{2}\pi r^2\ell$. Write an equation that gives V as a polynomial function of r alone. $V = \frac{1}{2}r(600 - \pi r^2)$

c. **Graphing a Function** Graph the volume function from part (b). What are the dimensions r and ℓ that maximize the volume of the greenhouse? What is the maximum volume? **See margin for art; r = about 8 ft, ℓ = about 15.9 ft; about 1595.77 ft^3**

43b. Maximum: (11.7, 44,970.9), minimum: (29.8, 40,078.2). *Sample answer:* The maximum indicates that in 1971 the number of students enrolled was about 44,971. The minimum indicates that in 1990 there were about 40,078 students enrolled.

43. ★ **EXTENDED RESPONSE** From 1960 to 2001, the number of students S (in thousands) enrolled in public schools in the United States can be modeled by $S = 1.64x^3 - 102x^2 + 1710x + 36{,}300$ where x is the number of years since 1960.

a. Graph the function. **See margin.**

b. Identify any turning points on the domain $0 \le x \le 41$. What real-life meaning do these points have?

c. What is the range of the function? **$36{,}300 \le y \le 47{,}978$**

C

44. **CHALLENGE** A cylinder is inscribed in a sphere of radius 8. Write an equation for the volume of the cylinder as a function of h. Find the value of h that maximizes the volume of the inscribed cylinder. What is the maximum volume of the cylinder?

$V(h) = h\pi\left(64 - \frac{h^2}{4}\right)$; about 9.2; about 1238

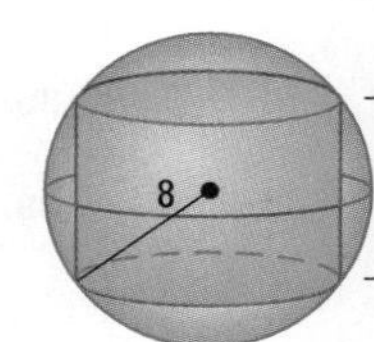

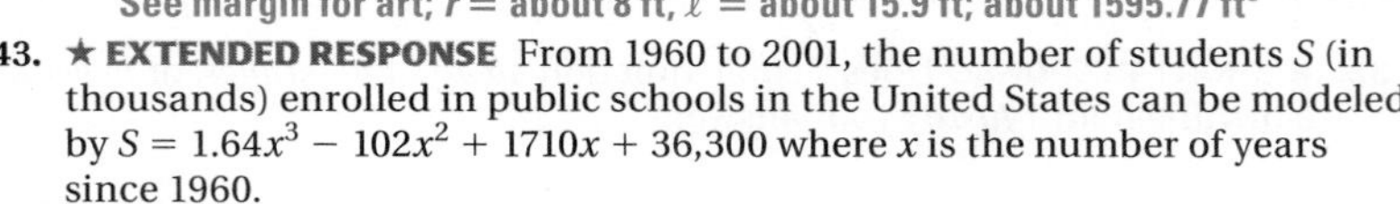

KENTUCKY MIXED REVIEW

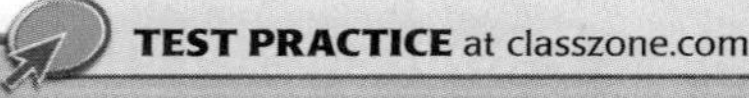

45. A painter is repainting a spherical section of a sculpture. Which measure would be most useful in determining the amount of paint the painter needs to buy? **D**

Ⓐ Radius Ⓑ Circumference

Ⓒ Volume Ⓓ Surface area

46. Which equation is the parent function of the graph represented? **C**

Ⓐ $y = x$ Ⓑ $y = |x|$

Ⓒ $y = x^2$ Ⓓ $y = x^3$

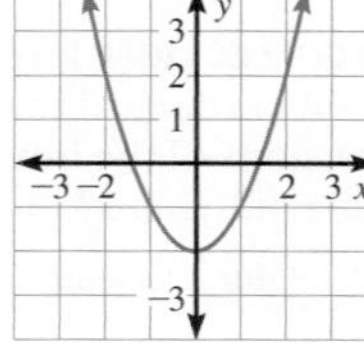

5.9 Write Polynomial Functions and Models

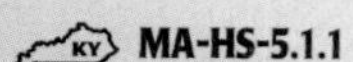

MA-HS-5.1.1

Before You wrote linear and quadratic functions.

Now You will write higher-degree polynomial functions.

Why? So you can model launch speed, as in Example 4.

1 PLAN AND PREPARE

Warm-Up Exercises

Transparency Available

1. What are the zeros of $f(x) = (2x - 1)(x + 5)(x - 8)$? $-5, \frac{1}{2}, 8$
2. What is the next number in the pattern 20, 14, 8, 2, ...? -4
3. A store's profit is modeled by $P = 0.89x^4 - 2.55x^3 + 22.48x^2 - 59.68x + 19$, where x is the number of years after 1990. What was the profit in 1999? about \$5283

Notetaking Guide

Transparency Available

Promotes interactive learning and notetaking skills, pp. 157–159.

Pacing

Basic: 2 days

Average: 2 days

Advanced: 2 days

Block: 1 block

- See *Teaching Guide/Lesson Plan.*

2 FOCUS AND MOTIVATE

Essential Question

Big Idea 3, p. 329

How can you write a polynomial function that models a set of equally-spaced data? **Tell students they will learn how to answer this question by using finite differences.**

ey Vocabulary
nite differences

IA-HS-5.1.1
udents will entify multiple presentations (tables, aphs, equations) functions (linear, adratic, absolute lue, exponential) real-world or athematical oblems. DOK 2

You know that two points determine a line and that three points determine a parabola. In Example 1, you will see that four points determine the graph of a cubic function.

EXAMPLE 1 Write a cubic function

Write the cubic function whose graph is shown.

(−4, 0) (3, 0) (1, 0) (0, −6) 2 4 x y

Solution

STEP 1 **Use** the three given x-intercepts to write the function in factored form.

$$f(x) = a(x + 4)(x - 1)(x - 3)$$

STEP 2 **Find** the value of a by substituting the coordinates of the fourth point.

$$-6 = a(0 + 4)(0 - 1)(0 - 3)$$

$$-6 = 12a$$

$$-\frac{1}{2} = a$$

▶ The function is $f(x) = -\frac{1}{2}(x + 4)(x - 1)(x - 3)$.

CHECK Check the end behavior of f. The degree of f is odd and $a < 0$. So $f(x) \to +\infty$ as $x \to -\infty$ and $f(x) \to -\infty$ as $x \to +\infty$, which matches the graph. ✓

FINITE DIFFERENCES In Example 1, you found a function given its graph. Functions can also be written from a set of data using *finite differences.*

When the x-values in a data set are equally spaced, the differences of consecutive y-values are called **finite differences**. For example, some finite differences for the function $f(x) = x^2$ are shown below.

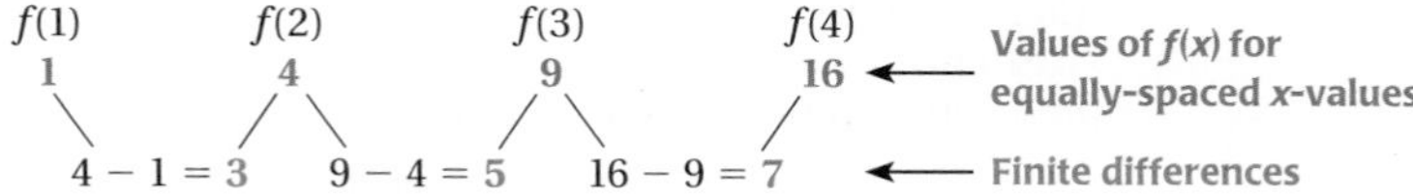

The finite differences above are called *first-order differences.* You can also calculate higher-order differences, as shown in the next example.

Resource Planning Guide

Chapter Resource Book
- Teaching Guide/Lesson Plan (pp. 98–99)
- Practice levels A, B, C (pp. 102–104)
- Study Guide (pp. 105–106)
- Catch-up for Absent Students (p. 107)
- Problem Solving Workshop (p. 108)
- Challenge (p. 109)

Workbooks
- Notetaking Guide (pp. 157–159)
- Practice Workbook (pp. 94–95)

Teaching Options
- **Power Presentations CD-ROM** provides dynamic electronic teaching resources for the classroom.
- **Activity Generator CD-ROM** provides editable activities for all ability levels.

Interactive Technology
- Easy Planner
- Power Presentations CD-ROM
- Activity Generator CD-ROM
- Animated Algebra
- Test Generator CD-ROM
- Online Quiz
- eWorkbook
- eEdition
- @HomeTutor

Resources for English Learners
- Quick Reference for English Learners
- Spanish Study Guide
- Multi-Language Visual Glossary
- Student Resources in Spanish

See also the *Algebra 2 Toolkit* for more strategies for meeting individual needs.

Motivating the Lesson

Present the sequence 2, 5, 10, 17, 26, ... to your students. After they see that the differences are 3, 5, 7, 9, ..., ask them to verify that each term can be expressed as $n^2 + 1$, where n is a positive integer. In this lesson, students will study some patterns of numbers and learn how they can determine rules for generating the patterns.

3 TEACH

Extra Example 1

Write the cubic function whose graph is shown.

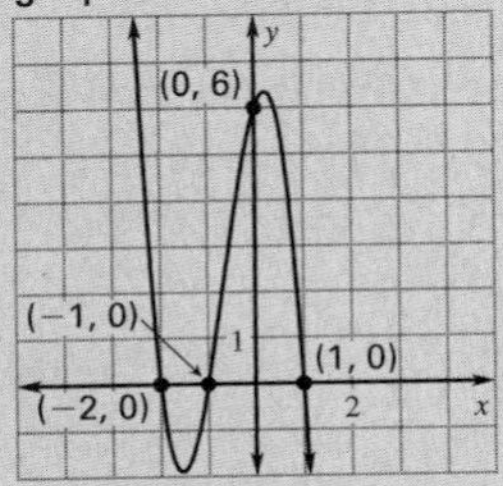

$f(x) = -3(x + 2)(x + 1)(x - 1)$

Key Questions to Ask for Example 1

- How do you know the factored form is $f(x) = a(x + 4)(x - 1)(x - 3)$ in Step 1? If m is an x-intercept of $f(x)$, then $(x - m)$ is a factor of $f(x)$.
- If you were given a point other than the y-intercept in Step 2, could you substitute its coordinates for x and $f(x)$? yes

Key Questions to Ask for Example 2

- What is $f(6)$? 21
- What is the first-order difference between $f(11)$ and $f(10)$? 11
- What is the first-order difference between $f(n + 1)$ and $f(n)$? $f(n + 1)$

EXAMPLE 2 Find finite differences

The first five triangular numbers are shown below. A formula for the nth triangular number is $f(n) = \frac{1}{2}(n^2 + n)$. Show that this function has constant second-order differences.

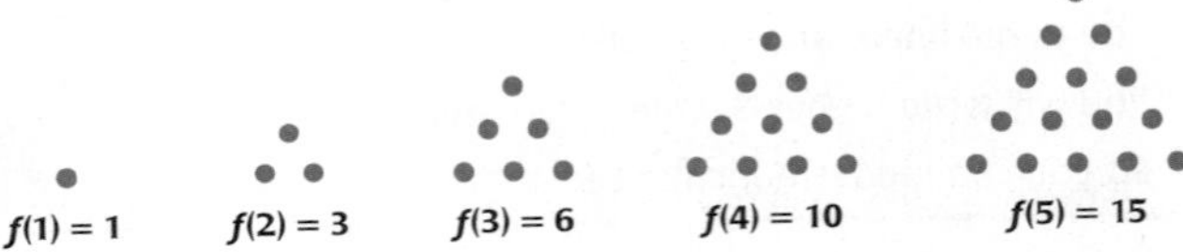

Solution

Write the first several triangular numbers. Find the first-order differences by subtracting consecutive triangular numbers. Then find the second-order differences by subtracting consecutive first-order differences.

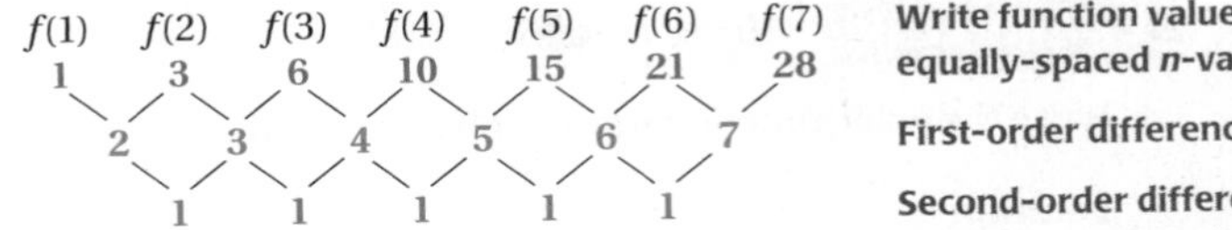

▶ Each second-order difference is 1, so the second-order differences are constant.

✓ GUIDED PRACTICE for Examples 1 and 2

Write a cubic function whose graph passes through the given points.

1. $(-4, 0), (0, 10), (2, 0), (5, 0)$
   $y = 0.25x^3 - 0.75x^2 - 4.5x + 10$
2. $(-1, 0), (0, -12), (2, 0), (3, 0)$
   $y = -2x^3 + 8x^2 - 2x - 12$
3. GEOMETRY Show that $f(n) = \frac{1}{2}n(3n - 1)$, a formula for the nth pentagonal number, has constant second-order differences. See margin.

PROPERTIES OF FINITE DIFFERENCES In Example 2, notice that the function has degree two and that the second-order differences are constant. This illustrates the first of the following two properties of finite differences.

KEY CONCEPT *For Your Notebook*

Properties of Finite Differences

1. If a polynomial function $f(x)$ has degree n, then the nth-order differences of function values for equally-spaced x-values are nonzero and constant.
2. Conversely, if the nth-order differences of equally-spaced data are nonzero and constant, then the data can be represented by a polynomial function of degree n.

The second property of finite differences allows you to write a polynomial function that models a set of equally-spaced data.

Differentiated Instruction

Inclusion Some students may find a table of differences difficult to write because the alignment of the columns must be precise. One helpful technique is to rotate a sheet of ruled notebook paper so that the lines are vertical. Each functional value is then written in every other column.
See also the *Algebra 2 Toolkit* for more strategies.

EXAMPLE 3 Model with finite differences

The first seven triangular pyramidal numbers are shown below. Find a polynomial function that gives the *n*th triangular pyramidal number.

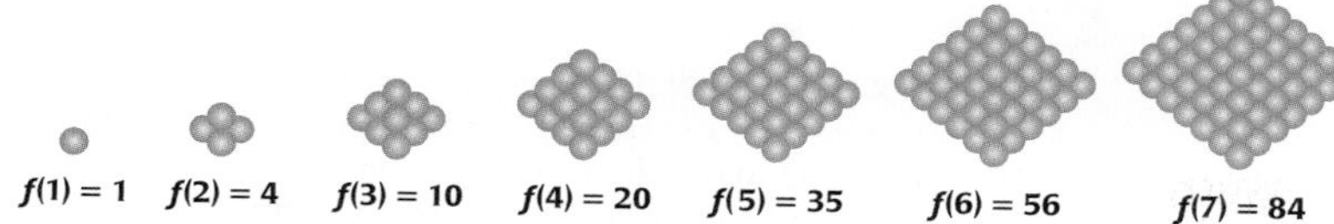

$f(1) = 1$ $f(2) = 4$ $f(3) = 10$ $f(4) = 20$ $f(5) = 35$ $f(6) = 56$ $f(7) = 84$

Solution

Begin by finding the finite differences.

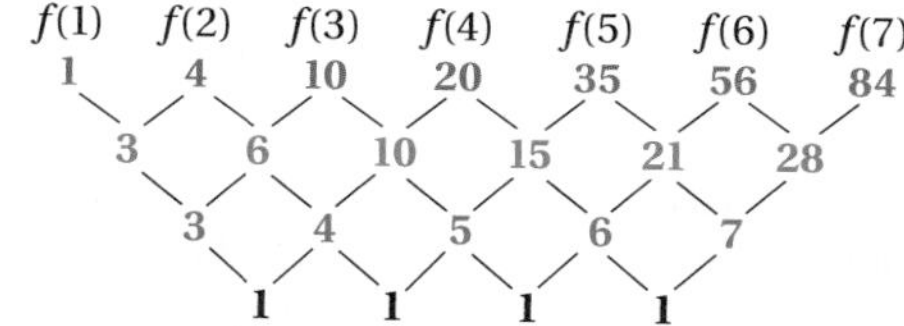

Write function values for equally-spaced *n*-values.

First-order differences

Second-order differences

Third-order differences

Because the third-order differences are constant, you know that the numbers can be represented by a cubic function of the form $f(n) = an^3 + bn^2 + cn + d$.

By substituting the first four triangular pyramidal numbers into the function, you obtain a system of four linear equations in four variables.

$a(1)^3 + b(1)^2 + c(1) + d = 1 \rightarrow a + b + c + d = 1$

$a(2)^3 + b(2)^2 + c(2) + d = 4 \rightarrow 8a + 4b + 2c + d = 4$

$a(3)^3 + b(3)^2 + c(3) + d = 10 \rightarrow 27a + 9b + 3c + d = 10$

$a(4)^3 + b(4)^2 + c(4) + d = 20 \rightarrow 64a + 16b + 4c + d = 20$

REVIEW SYSTEMS
For help with using matrices to solve linear systems, see p. 210.

Write the linear system as a matrix equation $AX = B$. Enter the matrices A and B into a graphing calculator, and then calculate the solution $X = A^{-1}B$.

$$\underbrace{\begin{bmatrix} 1 & 1 & 1 & 1 \\ 8 & 4 & 2 & 1 \\ 27 & 9 & 3 & 1 \\ 64 & 16 & 4 & 1 \end{bmatrix}}_{A} \underbrace{\begin{bmatrix} a \\ b \\ c \\ d \end{bmatrix}}_{X} = \underbrace{\begin{bmatrix} 1 \\ 4 \\ 10 \\ 20 \end{bmatrix}}_{B}$$

Calculate $X = A^{-1}B$.

▶ The solution is $a = \frac{1}{6}$, $b = \frac{1}{2}$, $c = \frac{1}{3}$, and $d = 0$. So, the *n*th triangular pyramidal number is given by $f(n) = \frac{1}{6}n^3 + \frac{1}{2}n^2 + \frac{1}{3}n$.

GUIDED PRACTICE for Example 3

4. Use finite differences to find a polynomial function that fits the data in the table. $f(x) = -x^3 + 5x^2 + x + 1$

x	1	2	3	4	5	6
$f(x)$	6	15	22	21	6	−29

3.

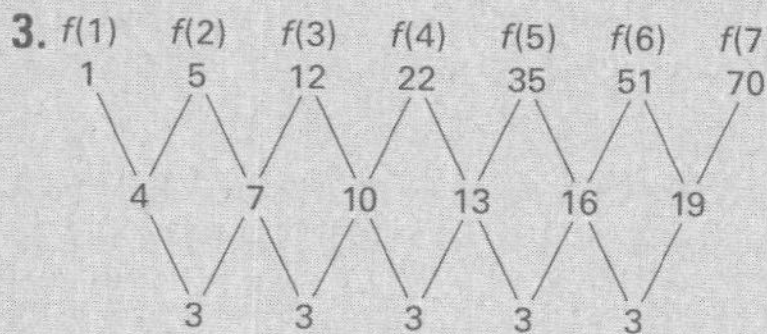

Extra Example 2

The first five pentagonal numbers are 1, 5, 12, 22, 35, as shown below. A formula for the *n*th pentagonal number is $f(n) = \frac{n(3n-1)}{2}$. Show that this function has constant second-order differences.

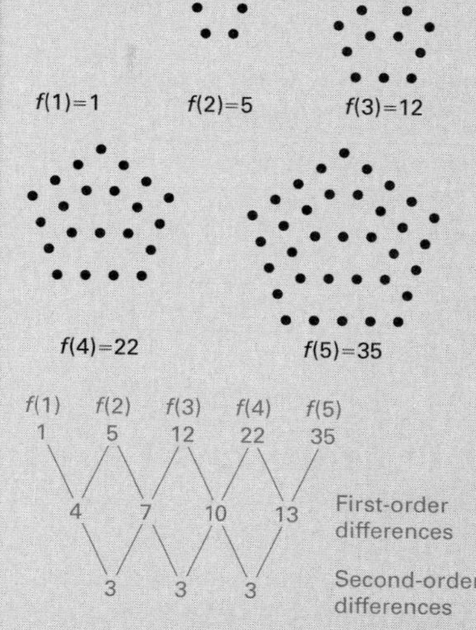

Each second-order difference is 3, so the second-order differences are constant.

Extra Example 3

The first five centered square numbers are shown below. Find a polynomial function that gives the *n*th centered square number.

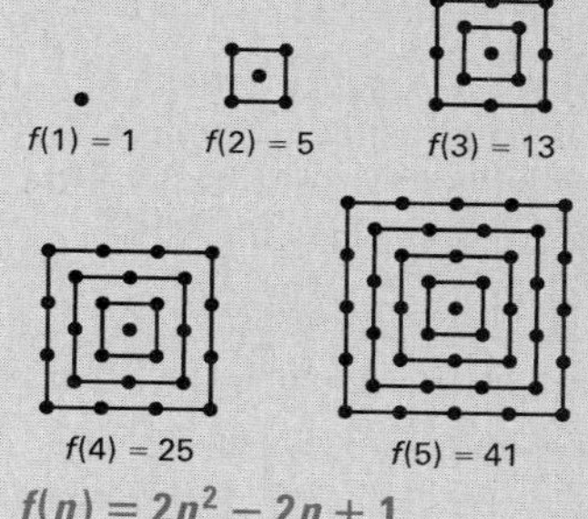

$f(n) = 2n^2 - 2n + 1$

Key Questions to Ask for Example 3

- Why are the values of $f(n)$ in the system of linear equations 1, 4, 10, and 20? **These are the first four triangular pyramidal numbers.**
- If the fourth order differences of a set of equally spaced data are constant, what is the degree of the polynomial that represents the data? **4**

Extra Example 4

The table shows the number of vehicles y in thousands fueled by Ethanol 85 each year x from 1999 to 2004. Find a polynomial model for the data. Use the model to predict the number of vehicles that will be fueled by Ethanol 85 in 2005.

Year	Number of Vehicles
0	24.604
1	87.570
2	100.303
3	120.951
4	133.776
5	146.195

$y = 1.87x^3 - 18.53x^2 + 70.07x + 26.80$; about 184,000 vehicles

Key Question to Ask for Example 4

- Why is a cubic model more reasonable than a linear model for the data? **Using linear regression, some data points are above or below the linear model. Using cubic regression, most data points are very close to the model. So, cubic regression is a more reasonable model.**

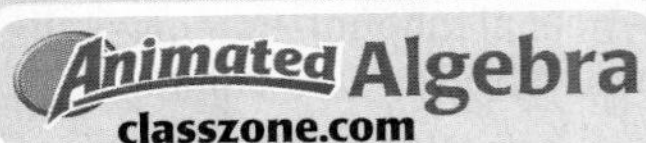

An **Animated Algebra** activity is available on-line for **Example 4**. This activity is also available on the **Power Presentations CD-ROM**.

Closing the Lesson

Have students summarize the major points of the lesson and answer the Essential Question: How can you write a polynomial function that models a set of equally-spaced data?

- **A polynomial function $f(x)$ has degree n, if and only if the nth-order differences of function values for equally-spaced x-values are nonzero constants.**
- **You can write a polynomial function that models equally-spaced data.**

First, determine which order differences are constant to determine the degree n. Then solve a system of $n + 1$ equations in $n + 1$ unknowns to find the coefficients for the model.

CUBIC REGRESSION In Examples 1 and 3, you found a cubic model that *exactly* fits a set of data points. In many real-life situations, you cannot find a simple model to fit data points exactly. Instead, you can use the *regression* feature of a graphing calculator to find an nth-degree polynomial model that best fits the data.

EXAMPLE 4 Solve a multi-step problem

SPACE EXPLORATION The table shows the typical speed y (in feet per second) of a space shuttle x seconds after launch. Find a polynomial model for the data. Use the model to predict the time when the shuttle's speed reaches 4400 feet per second, at which point its booster rockets detach.

x	10	20	30	40	50	60	70	80
y	202.4	463.3	748.2	979.3	1186.3	1421.3	1795.4	2283.5

Solution

STEP 1 **Enter** the data into a graphing calculator and make a scatter plot. The points suggest a cubic model.

STEP 2 **Use** cubic regression to obtain this polynomial model:

$y = 0.00650x^3 - 0.739x^2 + 49.0x - 236$

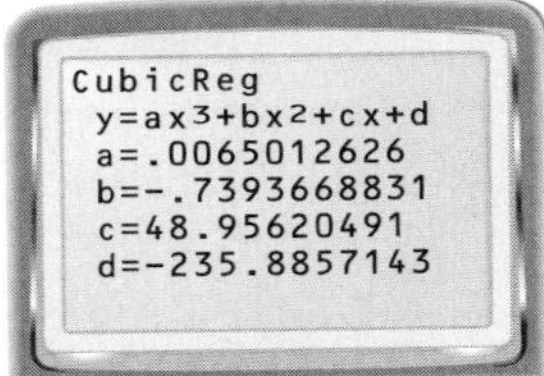

STEP 3 **Check** the model by graphing it and the data in the same viewing window.

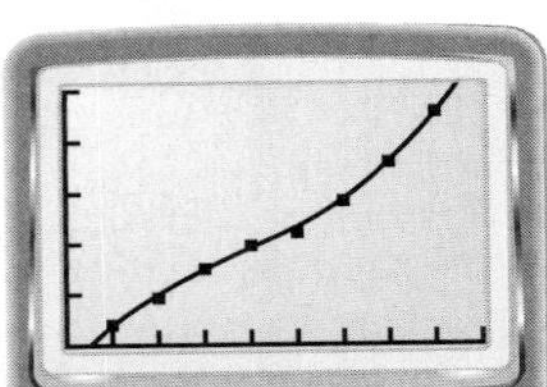

STEP 4 **Graph** the model and $y = 4400$ in the same viewing window. Use the *intersect* feature.

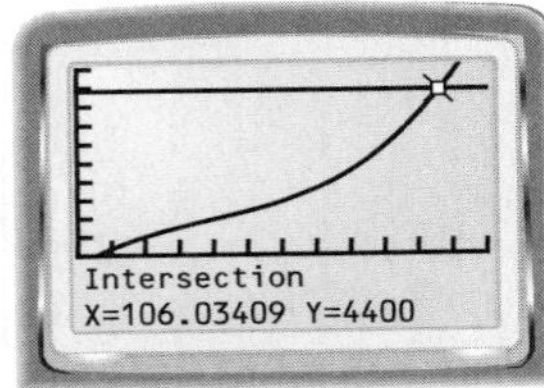

ANOTHER WAY

You can also find the value of x for which $y = 4400$ by subtracting 4400 from the right side of the cubic model, graphing the resulting function, and using the *zero* feature to find the graph's x-intercept.

▶ The booster rockets detach about 106 seconds after launch.

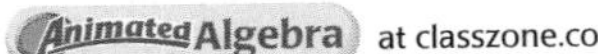
Animated Algebra at classzone.com

GUIDED PRACTICE for Example 4

Use a graphing calculator to find a polynomial function that fits the data.

5.

x	1	2	3	4	5	6
$f(x)$	5	13	17	11	11	56

6.

x	0	2	4	6	8	10
$f(x)$	8	0	15	69	98	87

5. $y = 2.71x^3 - 25.5x^2 + 71.8x - 45.7$

6. $y = -0.587x^3 + 8.99x^2 - 23.4x + 9.62$

5.9 EXERCISES

HOMEWORK KEY
○ = **WORKED-OUT SOLUTIONS** on p. WS11 for Exs. 9, 15, and 27
★ = **STANDARDIZED TEST PRACTICE** Exs. 2, 10, 22, 23, and 28

SKILL PRACTICE

A

1. **VOCABULARY** Copy and complete: When the x-values in a data set are equally spaced, the differences of consecutive y-values are called _?_. finite differences

2. ★ **WRITING** *Describe* first-order differences and second-order differences. See margin.

EXAMPLE 1
on p. 393
for Exs. 3–11

WRITING CUBIC FUNCTIONS **Write the cubic function whose graph is shown.**

3.
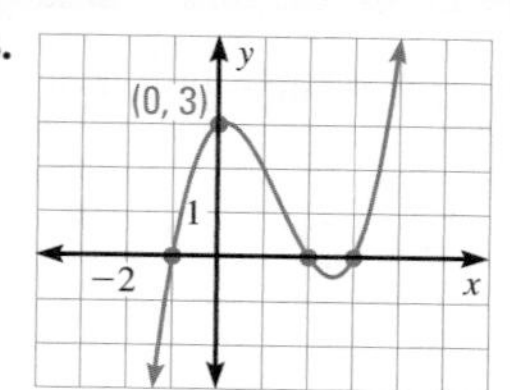
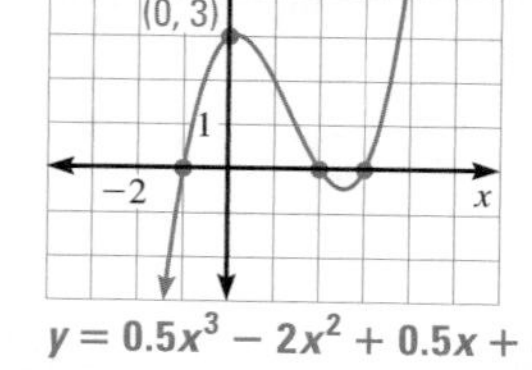

$y = 0.5x^3 - 2x^2 + 0.5x + 3$

4.
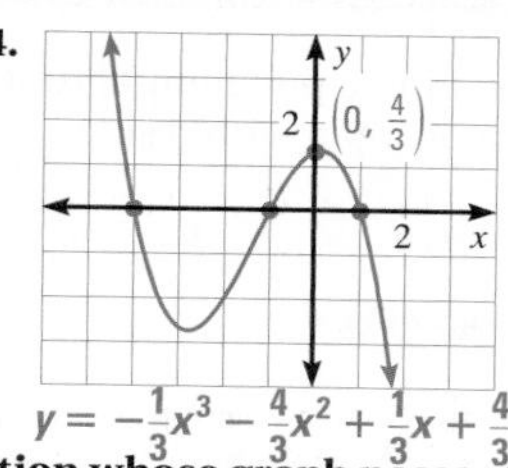

$y = -\frac{1}{3}x^3 - \frac{4}{3}x^2 + \frac{1}{3}x + \frac{4}{3}$

5.
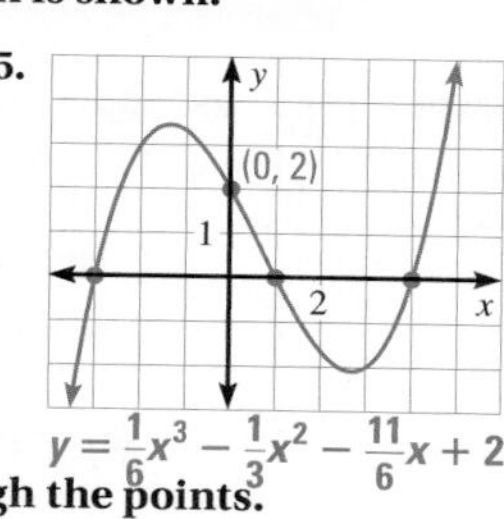

$y = \frac{1}{6}x^3 - \frac{1}{3}x^2 - \frac{11}{6}x + 2$

CUBIC MODELS **Write a cubic function whose graph passes through the points.**

6. (−3, 0), (−1, 10), (0, 0), (4, 0) $y = x^3 - x^2 - 12x$

7. (−2, 0), (−1, 0), (0, −8), (2, 0) $y = 2x^3 + 2x^2 - 8x - 8$

8. (−3, 0), (1, 0), (3, 2), (4, 0) See margin.

9. (−5, 0), (0, 0), (1, −12), (6, 0) $y = \frac{2}{5}x^3 - \frac{2}{5}x^2 - 12x$

10. ★ **MULTIPLE CHOICE** Which cubic function's graph passes through the points (−3, 0), (−1, 0), (3, 0), and (0, 3)? B

Ⓐ $f(x) = (x - 3)(x + 3)(x - 1)$

Ⓑ $f(x) = -\frac{1}{3}(x - 3)(x + 3)(x + 1)$

Ⓒ $f(x) = -2(x - 3)(x + 3)(x - 1)$

Ⓓ $f(x) = (x - 3)(x + 3)(x + 1)$

11. **ERROR ANALYSIS** A student tried to write a cubic function whose graph has x-intercepts −1, 2, and 5, and passes through (1, 3). *Describe* and correct the error in the student's calculation of the leading coefficient a. See margin.

$1 = a(3 + 1)(3 - 2)(3 - 5)$
$1 = -8a$
$-\frac{1}{8} = a$

EXAMPLE 2 B
on p. 394
for Exs. 12–17

FINDING FINITE DIFFERENCES **Show that the nth-order differences for the given function of degree n are nonzero and constant.** 12–17. See margin.

12. $f(x) = 5x^3 - 10$
13. $f(x) = -2x^2 + 5x$
14. $f(x) = x^4 - 3x^2 + 2$
15. $f(x) = 4x^2 - 9x + 2$
16. $f(x) = x^3 - 4x^2 - x + 1$
17. $f(x) = 2x^5 - 3x^2 + x$

EXAMPLE 3
on p. 395
for Exs. 18–21

FINDING A MODEL **Use finite differences and a system of equations to find a polynomial function that fits the data in the table.** 18–21. See margin.

18.

x	1	2	3	4	5	6
$f(x)$	0	−3	−8	−15	−24	−35

19.

x	1	2	3	4	5	6
$f(x)$	11	14	9	−4	−25	−54

20.

x	1	2	3	4	5	6
$f(x)$	−12	−14	−10	6	40	98

21.

x	1	2	3	4	5	6
$f(x)$	5	14	27	41	53	60

2. First-order differences are the differences between consecutive output values of a function when the input values are equally spaced. Second-order differences are the differences between consecutive first-order differences.

8. $y = -\frac{1}{6}x^3 + x^2 + \frac{11}{6}x - 2$

11. 1 should have been substituted for x and 3 for y; $3 = a(1 + 1)(1 - 2)(1 - 5)$, $3 = 8a$, $a = \frac{3}{8}$.

12–17. See Additional Answers beginning on p. AA1.
18. $f(x) = -x^2 + 1$
19. $f(x) = -4x^2 + 15x$
20. $f(x) = x^3 - 3x^2 - 10$
21. $f(x) = -0.5x^3 + 5x^2 - 2.5x + 3$

4 PRACTICE AND APPLY

Assignment Guide

Answer Transparencies available for all exercises

Basic:
Day 1: EP p. 1012 Exs. pp. 397–399 Exs. 1–17
Day 2: pp. 397–399 Exs. 18, 19, 25–28, 31–32

Average:
Day 1: pp. 397–399 Exs. 1–5, 7–17, 22
Day 2: pp. 397–399 Exs. 18–21, 25–29, 31–32

Advanced:
Day 1: pp. 397–399 Exs. 1, 2, 4, 5, 7–17, 22, 23
Day 2: pp. 397–399 Exs. 18–21, 24–32*

Block:
pp. 397–399 Exs. 1–5, 7–22, 25–29, 31–32

Differentiated Instruction

See *Algebra 2 Best Practices Toolkit* for suggestions on addressing the needs of a diverse classroom.

Homework Check

For a quick check of student understanding of key concepts, go over the following exercises:
Basic: 4, 12, 18, 25, 26
Average: 6, 14, 20, 25, 27
Advanced: 8, 16, 21, 25, 28

Extra Practice

- Student Edition, p. 1014
- Chapter 5 Resource Book: Practice levels A, B, C, pp. 102–104

Practice Worksheet

An easily-readable reduced practice page (with answers) for this lesson can be found on p. 328C.

Mathematical Reasoning

Exercises 6, 8, 9 These exercises do not have the y-intercept as the given fourth point. Students should reason that they need to use the x-intercepts to first write $f(x) = a(x - m)(x - n)(x - p)$ as before and then substitute the non-intercept point to determine a.

Study Strategy

Exercises 18–21, 25–28 To check their answers, students can plot the data points and their functions on a graphing calculator to see if the points lie on the graph of the function.

Graphing Calculator

Exercise 27 Students can also use their calculator's trace function to estimate the answers to parts (b) and (c).

24. Check students' work. The third order differences are all $6a$.

C

22. ★ **OPEN-ENDED MATH** Write two different cubic functions whose graphs pass through the points $(-3, 0)$, $(-1, 0)$, and $(2, 6)$.
Sample answer: $f(x) = 0.35x^3 + 1.1x^2 - 0.15x - 0.9$, $f(x) = 0.2x^3 + 0.8x^2 + 0.6x$

23. ★ **SHORT RESPONSE** How many points do you need to determine a quartic function? a quintic (fifth-degree) function? *Justify* your answers.
5; 6; there must be one more data point than the degree of the equation.

24. CHALLENGE Substitute the expressions $k, k + 1, k + 2, \ldots, k + 5$ for x in the function $f(x) = ax^3 + bx^2 + cx + d$ to generate six equally-spaced ordered pairs. Then show that third-order differences are constant. **See margin.**

PROBLEM SOLVING

EXAMPLE 3 A on p. 395 for Ex. 25

25. **GEOMETRY** Find a polynomial function that gives the number of diagonals d of a polygon with n sides. $d = 0.5n^2 - 1.5n$

Number of sides, n	3	4	5	6	7	8
Number of diagonals, d	0	2	5	9	14	20

@HomeTutor for problem solving help at classzone.com

EXAMPLE 4 on p. 396 for Exs. 26–28

26. AVIATION The table shows the number of active pilots (in thousands) with airline transport licenses in the United States for the years 1997 to 2004. Use a graphing calculator to find a polynomial model for the data.
$p = -0.013t^3 - 0.302t^2 + 4.68t + 131$

Years since 1997, t	0	1	2	3	4	5	6	7
Transport pilots, p	131	135	138	142	145	145	144	145

@HomeTutor for problem solving help at classzone.com

(27.) **MULTI-STEP PROBLEM** The table shows the average U.S. movie ticket price (in dollars) for various years from 1983 to 2003.

Years since 1983, t	0	4	8	12	16	20
Movie ticket price, m	3.15	3.91	4.21	4.35	5.08	6.03

$m = 0.000817t^3 - 0.0215t^2 + 0.249t + 3.17$

a. Use a graphing calculator to find a polynomial model for the data.

b. Estimate the average U.S. movie ticket price in 2010. **about $10.30**

c. In which year was the average U.S. movie ticket price about $4.50? **1995**

B

28. yard work: $p = 47.5t^2 - 22.5t + 30$, pet care: $p = 75t^2 - 205t + 160$; pet care; it is increasing at a faster rate.

28. ★ **SHORT RESPONSE** Based on data collected from friends, you estimate the cumulative profits (in dollars) after each of six months for two potential businesses. Find a polynomial function that models the profit for each business. Which business will yield the greatest long-term profit? Why?

Yard work	Month, t	1	2	3	4	5	6
	Profit, p	30	210	410	680	1070	1630
Pet care	Month, t	1	2	3	4	5	6
	Profit, p	30	50	220	540	1010	1630

○ = WORKED-OUT SOLUTIONS on p. WS1 ★ = STANDARDIZED TEST PRACTICE

29.

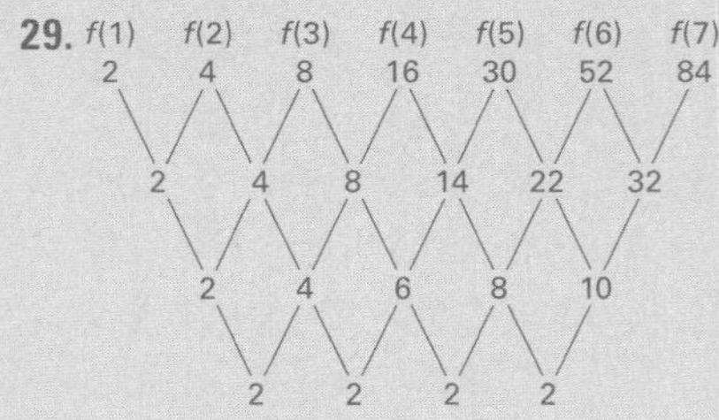

29. GEOMETRY The maximum number of regions R into which space can be divided by n intersecting spheres is given by $R(n) = \frac{1}{3}n^3 - n^2 + \frac{8}{3}n$. Show that this function has constant third-order differences. See margin.

C 30. **CHALLENGE** A cylindrical cake is divided into the maximum number of pieces p by c planes. When $c = 1, 2, 3, 4, 5,$ and 6 the values of $p(c)$ are 2, 4, 8, 15, 26, and 42 respectively. What is the maximum number of pieces into which the cake can be divided when it is cut by 8 planes?
$f(1) = 2, f(2) = 4, f(3) = 7, f(4) = 11, f(5) = 16, f(6) = 22, f(7) = 29; p = 0.5c^2 + 0.5c + 1$

KENTUCKY MIXED REVIEW

TEST PRACTICE at classzone.com

31. Graph the linear system. What is the solution of the system? **B**

$$-3x - 2y = -8$$
$$2x - y = 10$$

(A) (−4, −18) (B) (4, −2) (C) (12, 14) (D) No solution

32. The height h above the ground (in feet) of a stuntman falling from a window is given by $h = -16t^2 + 90$ where t is the time (in seconds). An air cushion that is 9 feet high is positioned on the ground below the window. About how many seconds will the stuntman fall before he hits the air cushion? **A**

(A) 2.25 sec (B) 2.37 sec (C) 8.66 sec (D) 9.48 sec

QUIZ for Lessons 5.7–5.9

Find all zeros of the polynomial function. *(p. 379)*

1. $f(x) = x^3 - 4x^2 - 11x + 30$ $-3, 2, 5$
2. $f(x) = 2x^4 - 2x^3 - 49x^2 + 9x + 180$ $-4, -\frac{3\sqrt{2}}{2}, \frac{3\sqrt{2}}{2}, 5$

Write a polynomial function f of least degree that has rational coefficients, a leading coefficient of 1, and the given zeros. *(p. 379)*

3. $-4, -1, 2$ $x^3 + 3x^2 - 6x - 8$
4. $4, 1 + i$ $x^3 - 6x^2 + 10x - 8$
5. $-3, 5, 7 + \sqrt{2}$ $x^4 - 16x^3 + 60x^2 + 116x - 705$
6. $1, -2i, 3 - \sqrt{6}$ $x^5 - 7x^4 + 13x^3 - 31x^2 + 36x - 12$

Graph the function. *(p. 387)* 7–10. See margin.

7. $f(x) = -(x - 3)(x - 2)(x + 2)$
8. $f(x) = 3(x - 1)(x + 1)(x - 4)$
9. $f(x) = x(x - 4)(x - 1)(x + 2)$
10. $f(x) = (x - 3)(x + 2)^2(x + 3)^2$

Write a cubic function whose graph passes through the given points. *(p. 393)*

11. (−5, 0), (−2, 0), (1, 9), (2, 0) $y = -0.5x^3 - 2.5x^2 + 2x + 10$
12. (−1, 0), (0, 16), (2, 0), (4, 0) $y = 2x^3 - 10x^2 + 4x + 16$

13. **DRIVE-INS** The table shows the number of U.S. drive-in movie theaters for the years 1995 to 2002. Find a polynomial model that fits the data. *(p. 393)* $y = x^3 - 10.5x^2 - 5x + 847$

Years since 1995, t	0	1	2	3	4	5	6	7
Drive-in movie theaters, D	848	826	815	750	737	667	663	634

5 ASSESS AND RETEACH

Daily Homework Quiz

Transparency Available

1. Write the cubic function that passes through the points $\left(0, -\frac{3}{2}\right)$, (−3, 0), (−1, 0), and (2, 0). $f(x) = \frac{1}{4}(x + 3)(x - 2)(x + 1)$
2. What are the second-order differences for $f(x) = \frac{1}{2}(3n^2 + 3n + 2)$? 3
3. The first five square pyramidal numbers are 1, 5, 14, 30, and 55. Find a polynomial function that gives the nth square pyramidal number. $f(n) = \frac{n^3}{3} + \frac{n^2}{2} + \frac{n}{6}$

Online Quiz

Available at **classzone.com**

Diagnosis/Remediation

- Practice A, B, C in Chapter 5 Resource Book, pp. 102–104
- Study Guide in Chapter 5 Resource Book, pp. 105–106
- Practice Workbook, pp. 94–95
- @HomeTutor

Challenge

Additional challenge is available in the Chapter 5 Resource Book, p. 109.

Quiz

An easily-readable reduced copy of the quiz (with answers) on Lessons 5.7–5.9 from the Assessment Book can be found on p. 328F.

Quiz 7–10. See Additional Answers beginning on p. AA1.

Kentucky Mixed Review

1. B
2. B
3. A
4. A
5. C
6. C
7. a. $-0.000324x^3 + 0.0542x^2 - 1.71x + 13.9$
   b. 54 pounds

Lessons 5.6–5.9

1. **POLYNOMIAL FUNCTIONS** Which polynomial function has zeros -2, 1, and $4 - i$?
   A $f(x) = x^4 - 7x^3 + 2x^2 + 28x - 24$
   B $f(x) = x^4 - 7x^3 + 7x^2 + 33x - 34$
   C $f(x) = x^4 - 9x^3 + 18x^2 + 4x - 24$
   D $f(x) = x^4 - 9x^3 + 23x^2 - x - 34$

2. **GEOMETRY** The volume of the rectangular prism shown is 180 cubic inches. What is the height of the rectangular prism?

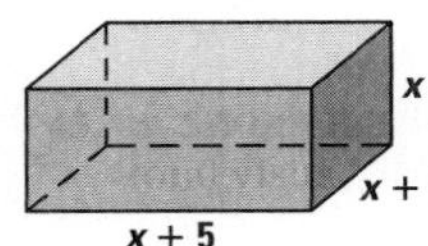

   A 3 inches
   B 4 inches
   C 5 inches
   D 8 inches

3. **MAXIMUM VOLUME** You want to make an open box (four sides and a bottom) from a piece of cardboard that is 20 inches by 30 inches. You will cut an x-by-x square from each corner. What value of x will maximize the volume of the box?
   A 3.9 inches
   B 7.8 inches
   C 10 inches
   D 12.2 inches

4. **DESCARTES' RULE OF SIGNS** How many positive real zeros does the following function have?

$$f(x) = 2x^5 + 5x^4 + 5x^3 + 25x^2 + 7x - 10$$

   A 1
   B 2
   C 4
   D 5

5. **SCULPTURE** You are making a sculpture that is a pyramid with a square base. You want the height of the pyramid to be 4 inches less than the length of a side of the base. You want the volume of the sculpture to be 200 cubic inches. What is the approximate length of a side of the sculpture's base?
   A 6.3 inches
   B 7.5 inches
   C 10 inches
   D 11.3 inches

6. **REVENUE** For the period 1985–2005, the annual revenue R (in millions of dollars) of a department store can be modeled by

$$R = 0.0014t^3 - 0.0305t^2 + 0.232t + 3.19$$

   where t is the number of years since 1985. According to the model, in which year was the revenue \$3.86 million?
   A 1990 B 1994
   C 1995 D 2000

7. **OPEN-RESPONSE** The table below shows the average relationship between length (in inches) and weight (in pounds) for an alligator as it grows.

Length	Weight
12	0.2
24	0.7
36	8.6
48	17.7
54	28.0
60	39.6
66	45.4
72	49.6

   a. Use a calculator to find a 3rd degree polynomial model for this data.
   b. Use your model to find the average weight of alligators 75 inches long.

5 CHAPTER SUMMARY

classzone.com
Electronic Function Library

BIG IDEAS

For Your Notebook

Big Idea 1

Graphing Polynomial Functions

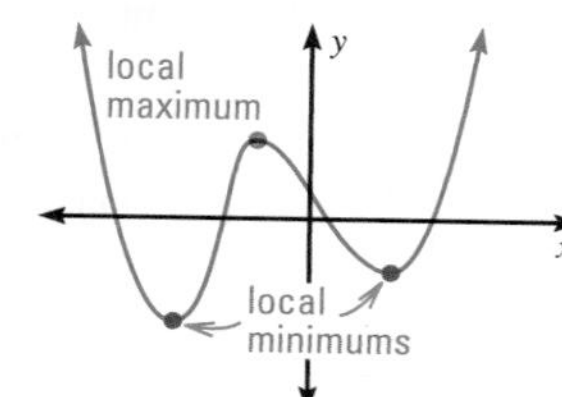

The end behavior of the graph of $f(x)$ is

$f(x) \to +\infty$ as $x \to -\infty$ and $f(x) \to +\infty$ as $x \to +\infty$

so $f(x)$ is of even degree and has a positive leading coefficient.

The graph has 3 turning points, so the degree of $f(x)$ is *at least* 4 and $f(x)$ has *at least* 4 zeros.

Big Idea 2

Performing Operations with Polynomials

You can add, subtract, multiply, and divide polynomials. You can also factor polynomials using any combination of the methods below.

Factoring method	Example
General trinomial	$6x^2 - 7x - 3 = (3x + 1)(2x - 3)$
Perfect square trinomial	$x^2 + 10x + 25 = (x + 5)^2$
Difference of two squares	$x^2 - 49 = (x + 7)(x - 7)$
Common monomial factor	$15x^3 + 9x^2 = 3x^2(5x + 3)$
Sum or difference of two cubes	$8x^3 - 27 = (2x - 3)(4x^2 + 6x + 9)$
Factor by grouping	$x^3 - 5x^2 + 9x - 45 = x^2(x - 5) + 9(x - 5) = (x^2 + 9)(x - 5)$

Big Idea 3

Solving Polynomial Equations and Finding Zeros

The terms *zero*, *factor*, *solution*, and *x-intercept* are closely related. Consider the function $f(x) = 2x^3 - x^2 - 13x - 6$.

-2 is a **zero** of f.	$f(-2) = 2(-2)^3 - (-2)^2 - 13(-2) - 6 = 0$
$x + 2$ is a **factor** of $f(x)$.	$2x^3 - x^2 - 13x - 6 = (x + 2)(x - 3)(2x + 1)$
$x = -2$ is a **solution** of the equation $f(x) = 0$.	$2(-2)^3 - (-2)^2 - 13(-2) - 6 = 0$
-2 is an ***x*-intercept** of the graph of f.	

Additional Resources

The following resources are available to help review the materials in this chapter.

Chapter 5 Resource Book

- Chapter Review Games and Activities, p. 110
- Cumulative Practice, Chs. 1–5, pp. 112–113

Student Resources in Spanish

eWorkbook

@HomeTutor

Vocabulary Practice

Vocabulary practice is available at **classzone.com**

Extra Example 5.1
Simplify $(2x^4y^2)^3y^{-5}$. $8x^{12}y$

5. 128; product of powers property
6. $\frac{1}{27}$; power of a power property, product of powers property, negative exponent property
7. $\frac{y^{10}}{x^4}$; power of a power property, negative exponent property
8. $\frac{y^6}{27x^{12}}$; power of a power property, negative exponent property
9. $\frac{16}{9}$; quotient of powers property, negative exponent property
10. 4×10^4; quotient of powers property
11. $\frac{1}{x^8y^8}$; power of a quotient property, negative exponent property
12. $\frac{y^7}{8x^9}$; quotient of powers property, negative exponent property

5 CHAPTER REVIEW

@HomeTutor
classzone.com
• Multi-Language Glossary
• Vocabulary practice

REVIEW KEY VOCABULARY

- scientific notation, *p. 331*
- polynomial, *p. 337*
- polynomial function, *p. 337*
- leading coefficient, *p. 337*
- degree, *p. 337*
- constant term, *p. 337*
- standard form of a polynomial function, *p. 337*
- synthetic substitution, *p. 338*
- end behavior, *p. 339*
- factored completely, *p. 353*
- factor by grouping, *p. 354*
- quadratic form, *p. 355*
- polynomial long division, *p. 362*
- synthetic division, *p. 363*
- repeated solution, *p. 379*
- local maximum, *p. 388*
- local minimum, *p. 388*
- finite differences, *p. 393*

VOCABULARY EXERCISES

1. Copy and complete: At each of its turning points, the graph of a polynomial function has a(n) _?_ or a(n) _?_. **local maximum, local minimum**

2. **WRITING** *Explain* how you can tell whether a solution of a polynomial equation is a repeated solution when the equation is written in factored form. **If there is a power on the factor or the factor appears more than once.**

3. **WRITING** *Explain* how you can tell whether a number is expressed in scientific notation. **If it is in the form $c \times 10^n$ where $1 \le c < 10$ and n is an integer.**

4. Let f be a fourth-degree polynomial function with four distinct real zeros. How many turning points does the graph of f have? **3 turning points**

REVIEW EXAMPLES AND EXERCISES

Use the review examples and exercises below to check your understanding of the concepts you have learned in each lesson of Chapter 5.

5.1 Use Properties of Exponents

pp. 330–335

EXAMPLE

Simplify the expression.

$(x^2y^3)^3x^4 = (x^2)^3(y^3)^3x^4$ **Power of a product property**

$= x^6y^9x^4$ **Power of a power property**

$= x^{6+4}y^9$ **Product of powers property**

$= x^{10}y^9$ **Simplify exponent.**

EXERCISES

EXAMPLES 1, 2, 3, and 4 on pp. 330–332 for Exs. 5–12

Evaluate or simplify the expression. Tell which properties of exponents you used. **5–12. See margin.**

5. $2^2 \cdot 2^5$
6. $(3^2)^{-3}(3^3)$
7. $(x^{-2}y^5)^2$
8. $(3x^4y^{-2})^{-3}$
9. $\left(\frac{3}{4}\right)^{-2}$
10. $\frac{8 \times 10^7}{2 \times 10^3}$
11. $\left(\frac{x^2}{y^{-2}}\right)^{-4}$
12. $\frac{2x^{-6}y^5}{16x^3y^{-2}}$

@HomeTutor
classzone.com
Chapter Review Practice

5.2 Evaluate and Graph Polynomial Functions

pp. 337–344

EXAMPLE

Graph the polynomial function $f(x) = x^3 - 2x^2 + 3$.

Make a table of values.

x	−2	−1	0	1	2	3
$f(x)$	−13	0	3	2	3	12

Plot the points, connect the points with a smooth curve, and check the end behavior.

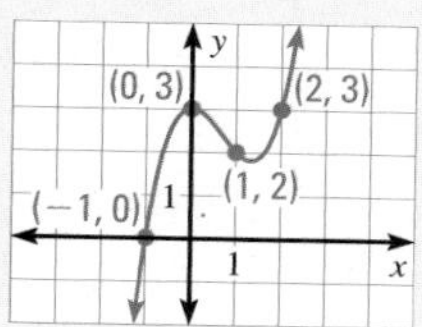

The degree is odd and the leading coefficient is positive, so $f(x) \to -\infty$ as $x \to -\infty$ and $f(x) \to +\infty$ as $x \to +\infty$.

EXERCISES

EXAMPLES 5 and 6 on p. 340 for Exs. 13–16

Graph the polynomial function. 13–15. See margin.

13. $f(x) = -x^4$ 14. $f(x) = x^3 - 4$ 15. $f(x) = x^3 + 2x + 3$

16. **FISH CONSUMPTION** From 1990 to 2002, the amount of fish F (in millions of pounds) caught for human consumption in the United States can be modeled by

$$F = -0.907t^4 + 28.0t^3 - 258t^2 + 902t + 12{,}700$$

where t is the number of years since 1990. Graph the function. Use the graph to estimate the year when the amount of fish caught first was greater than 14.5 *billion* pounds. See margin for art; 1999

5.3 Add, Subtract, and Multiply Polynomials

pp. 346–352

EXAMPLE

Perform the indicated operation.

a. $(3x^3 - 6x^2 - 7x + 5) + (x^3 + 8x + 3) = 3x^3 + x^3 - 6x^2 - 7x + 8x + 5 + 3$
$= 4x^3 - 6x^2 + x + 8$

b. $(x - 4)(2x^2 - 7x + 5) = (x - 4)2x^2 - (x - 4)7x + (x - 4)5$
$= 2x^3 - 8x^2 - 7x^2 + 28x + 5x - 20$
$= 2x^3 - 15x^2 + 33x - 20$

EXERCISES

EXAMPLES 1, 2, 4, and 5 on pp. 346–348 for Exs. 17–20

Perform the indicated operation.

17. $(5x^3 - x + 3) + (x^3 - 9x^2 + 4x)$ $6x^3 - 9x^2 + 3x + 3$
18. $(x^3 + 4x^2 - 5x) - (4x^3 + x^2 - 7)$ $-3x^3 + 3x^2 - 5x + 7$
19. $(x - 6)(5x^2 + x - 8)$ $5x^3 - 29x^2 - 14x + 48$
20. $(x - 4)(x + 7)(5x - 1)$ $5x^3 + 14x^2 - 143x + 28$

Extra Example 5.2

Graph the polynomial function $f(x) = x^3 + x^2 - 3x + 5$.

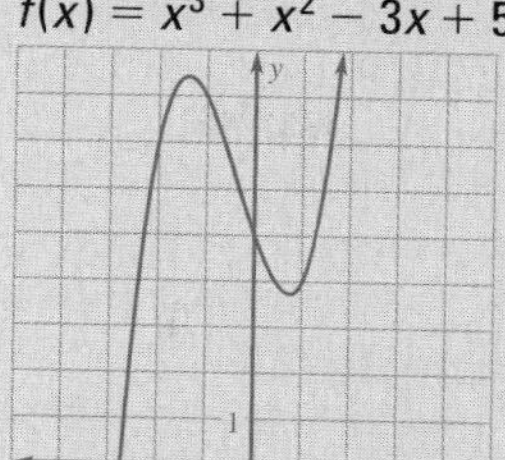

Extra Example 5.3

Perform the indicated operation.

a. $(x^3 + 2x^2 - 5x + 7) - (4x^3 - 5x^2 + 3)$
$-3x^3 + 7x^2 - 5x + 4$

b. $(7x - 4) \cdot (x^3 - x^2 + 6)$
$7x^4 - 11x^3 + 4x^2 + 42x - 24$

13.
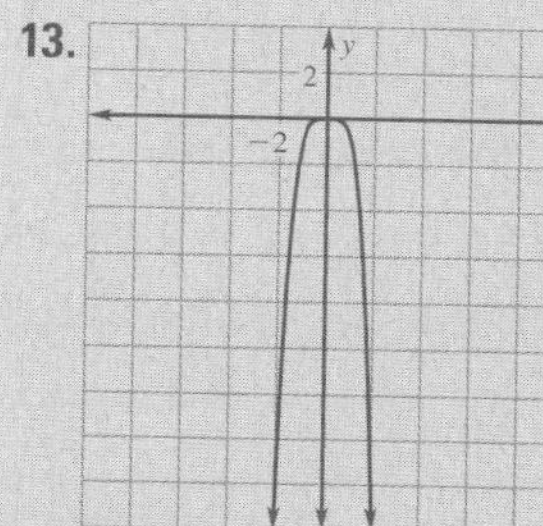

14.
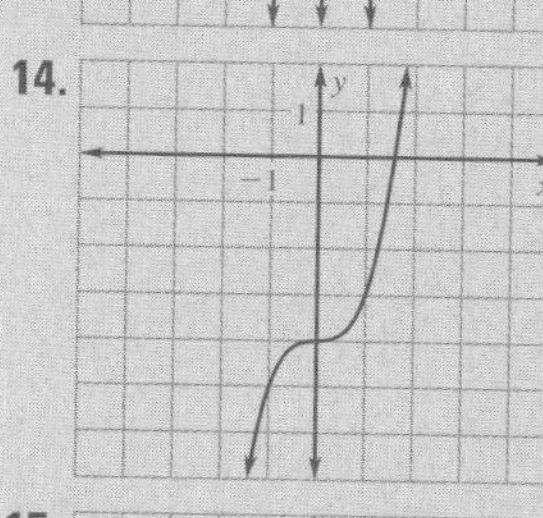

15.
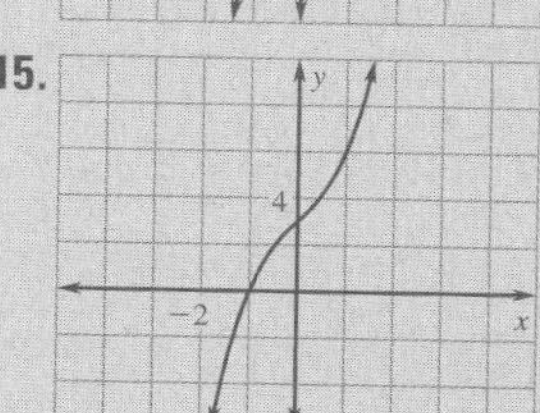

16.
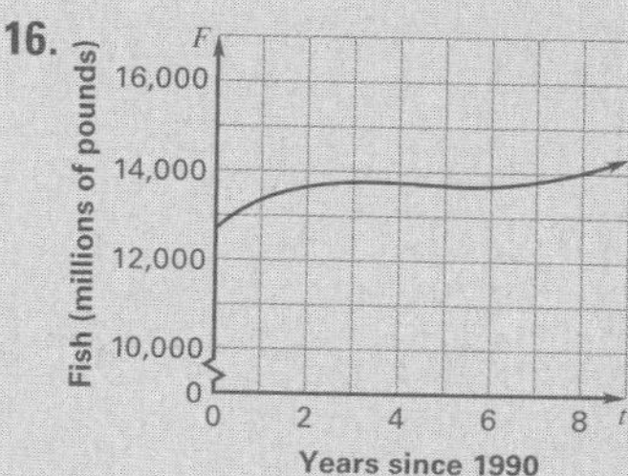

Extra Example 5.4

Factor the polynomial completely.

a. $3x^3 + 2x^2 - 12x - 8$ $(x - 2)(x + 2)(3x + 2)$

b. $4x^4y - 11x^3y^2 + 6x^2y^3$ $x^2y(4x - 3y)(x - 2y)$

c. $a^4 - 64b^2$ $(a^2 + 8b)(a^2 - 8b)$

Extra Example 5.5

Divide $15x^3 - 53x^2 - 102x - 40$ by $x - 5$. $15x^2 + 22x + 8$

5 CHAPTER REVIEW

5.4 Factor and Solve Polynomial Equations

pp. 353–359

EXAMPLE

Factor the polynomial completely.

a. $x^3 + 125 = x^3 + 5^3 = (x + 5)(x^2 - 5x + 25)$ — **Sum of two cubes**

b. $x^3 + 5x^2 - 9x - 45 = x^2(x + 5) - 9(x + 5)$ — **Factor by grouping.**

$= (x^2 - 9)(x + 5)$ — **Distributive property**

$= (x + 3)(x - 3)(x + 5)$ — **Difference of two squares**

c. $3x^6 + 12x^4 - 96x^2 = 3x^2(x^4 + 4x^2 - 32)$ — **Factor common monomial.**

$= 3x^2(x^2 - 4)(x^2 + 8)$ — **Factor trinomial in quadratic form.**

$= 3x^2(x + 2)(x - 2)(x^2 + 8)$ — **Difference of two squares**

EXERCISES

EXAMPLES 2, 3, 4, and 6 on pp. 354–356 for Exs. 21–24

Factor the polynomial completely.

21. $64x^3 - 8$ $8(2x - 1)(4x^2 + 2x + 1)$

22. $2x^5 - 12x^3 + 10x$ $2x(x - 1)(x + 1)(x^2 - 5)$

23. $2x^3 - 7x^2 - 8x + 28$ $(x - 2)(x + 2)(2x - 7)$

24. SCULPTURE You have 240 cubic inches of clay with which to make a sculpture shaped as a rectangular prism. You want the width to be 4 inches less than the length and the height to be 2 inches more than 3 times the length. What should the dimensions of the sculpture be? **length: 6 in., width: 2 in., height: 20 in.**

5.5 Apply the Remainder and Factor Theorems

pp. 362–368

EXAMPLE

Divide $f(x) = 4x^4 + 29x^3 + 4x^2 - 14x + 37$ by $x + 7$.

Rewrite the divisor in the form $x - k$. Because $x + 7 = x - (-7)$, $k = -7$.

−7	4	29	4	−14	37
		−28	−7	21	−49
	4	1	−3	7	−12

So, $\frac{4x^4 + 29x^3 + 4x^2 - 14x + 37}{x + 7} = 4x^3 + x^2 - 3x + 7 - \frac{12}{x + 7}$.

EXERCISES

EXAMPLES 1, 3, and 4 on pp. 362–364 for Exs. 25–32

Divide.

25. $(x^3 - 3x^2 - x - 10) \div (x^2 + 3x - 1)$ $x - 6 + \frac{18x - 16}{x^2 + 3x - 1}$

26. $(4x^4 - 17x^2 + 9x - 18) \div (2x^2 - 2)$ $2x^2 - \frac{13}{2} + \frac{9x - 31}{2x^2 - 2}$

27. $(2x^3 - 11x^2 + 13x - 44) \div (x - 5)$ $2x^2 - x + 8 + \frac{-4}{x - 5}$

28. $(5x^4 + 2x^2 - 15x + 10) \div (x + 2)$ $5x^3 - 10x^2 + 22x - 59 + \frac{128}{x + 2}$

Given polynomial $f(x)$ and a factor of $f(x)$, factor $f(x)$ completely.

29. $f(x) = x^3 - 5x^2 - 2x + 24$; $x + 2$ $(x + 2)(x - 3)(x - 4)$

30. $f(x) = x^3 - 11x^2 + 14x + 80$; $x - 8$ $(x - 8)(x - 5)(x + 2)$

31. $f(x) = 9x^3 - 9x^2 - 4x + 4$; $x - 1$ $(x - 1)(3x - 2)(3x + 2)$

32. $f(x) = 2x^3 + 7x^2 - 33x - 18$; $x + 6$ $(x + 6)(x - 3)(2x + 1)$

@HomeTutor
classzone.com
Chapter Review Practice

5.6 Find Rational Zeros

pp. 370–377

EXAMPLE

Find all real zeros of $f(x) = x^3 + 6x^2 + 5x - 12$.

The leading coefficient is 1 and the constant term is -12.

Possible rational zeros: $x = \pm\frac{1}{1}, \pm\frac{2}{1}, \pm\frac{3}{1}, \pm\frac{4}{1}, \pm\frac{6}{1}, \pm\frac{12}{1}$

Test these zeros using synthetic division. Test $x = 1$:

$$\begin{array}{r|rrrr} 1 & 1 & 6 & 5 & -12 \\ & & 1 & 7 & 12 \\ \hline & 1 & 7 & 12 & 0 \end{array} \leftarrow \textbf{1 is a zero.}$$

You can write $f(x) = (x - 1)(x^2 + 7x + 12)$. Factor the trinomial.

$$f(x) = (x - 1)(x^2 + 7x + 12) = (x - 1)(x + 3)(x + 4)$$

The zeros of f are 1, -3, and -4.

EXAMPLES 2 and 3
on pp. 371–372
for Exs. 33–34

EXERCISES

Find all real zeros of the function.

33. $f(x) = x^3 - 4x^2 - 11x + 30$ **$-3, 2, 5$**

34. $f(x) = 2x^4 - x^3 - 42x^2 + 16x + 160$ **$-4, -2, \frac{5}{2}, 4$**

5.7 Apply the Fundamental Theorem of Algebra

pp. 379–386

EXAMPLE

Write a polynomial function f of least degree that has rational coefficients, a leading coefficient of 1, and -4 and $5 + \sqrt{2}$ as zeros.

Because $5 + \sqrt{2}$ is a zero, $5 - \sqrt{2}$ must also be a zero.

$f(x) = (x + 4)[x - (5 + \sqrt{2})][x - (5 - \sqrt{2})]$ **Write $f(x)$ in factored form.**

$= (x + 4)[(x - 5) - \sqrt{2}][(x - 5) + \sqrt{2}]$ **Regroup terms.**

$= (x + 4)[(x - 5)^2 - 2]$ **Multiply.**

$= x^3 - 6x^2 - 17x + 92$ **Multiply.**

XAMPLES
and 6
n pp. 381–383
or Exs. 35–38

EXERCISES

Write a polynomial function f of least degree that has rational coefficients, a leading coefficient of 1, and the given zeros.

35. $-4, 1, 5$ **$x^3 - 2x^2 - 19x + 20$**

36. $-1, -1, 6, 3i$

37. $2, 7, 3 - \sqrt{5}$

$x^5 - 4x^4 -$
$^3 - 42x^2 -$
$x - 54$

$x^4 - 15x^3 +$
$x^2 - 120x +$

38. ECONOMICS For the 15 years that a computer store has been open, its annual revenue R (in millions of dollars) can be modeled by

$$R = -0.0040t^4 + 0.088t^3 - 0.36t^2 - 0.55t + 5.8$$

where t is the number of years since the store opened. In what year was the revenue first greater than \$7 million? **near the end of the 7th year**

Extra Example 5.6

Find all real zeros of $f(x) = x^3 + x^2 - 9x - 9$. **$-3, -1, 3$**

Extra Example 5.7

Write a polynomial function of least degree that has rational coefficients, a leading coefficient of 1, and -5 and $2i$ as zeros.
$f(x) = x^3 + 5x^2 + 4x + 20$

Extra Example 5.8

Graph the function $f(x) = x^3 + 2x^2 - 5x - 6$. Identify the x-intercepts and the points where the local maximum and local minimums occur.

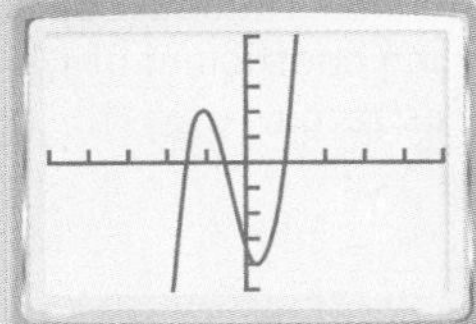

x-intercepts: $x = -3, -1, 2$; local maximum: $x \approx -2.12$, local minimum: $x \approx 0.79$

Extra Example 5.9

Use finite differences and a system of equations to find a polynomial function that fits the data.

x	1	2	3	4	5	6
$f(x)$	6	12	21	33	48	66

$f(x) = \frac{3}{2}x^2 + \frac{3}{2}x + 3$

39. x-intercept: -1.7; local maximum: $(0, -1)$; local minimum: $(-1, -2)$

40. x-intercepts: 0.25, 1.3; local maximum: $(-1.1, 7.1)$; local minimums: $(-2, 6)$, $(0.88, -3.2)$

5 CHAPTER REVIEW

5.8 Analyze Graphs of Polynomial Functions

pp. 387–392

EXAMPLE

Graph the function $f(x) = x^3 - 4x + 2$. Identify the x-intercepts and the points where the local maximums and local minimums occur.

Use a graphing calculator to graph the function.

Notice that the graph has three x-intercepts and two turning points. You can use the graphing calculator's *zero*, *maximum*, and *minimum* features to approximate the coordinates of the points.

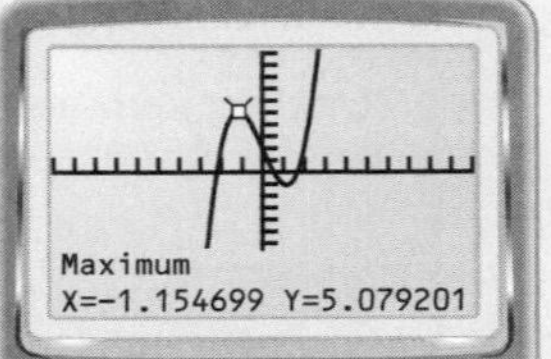

The x-intercepts of the graph are about -2.21, 0.54, and 1.68. The function has a local maximum at $(-1.15, 5.08)$ and a local minimum at $(1.15, -1.08)$.

EXERCISES

EXAMPLE 2 on p. 388 for Exs. 39–40

Use a graphing calculator to graph the function. Identify the x-intercepts and the points where the local maximums and local minimums occur. 39, 40. See margin.

39. $f(x) = -2x^3 - 3x^2 - 1$

40. $f(x) = x^4 + 3x^3 - x^2 - 8x + 2$

5.9 Write Polynomial Functions and Models

pp. 393–399

EXAMPLE

Use finite differences and a system of equations to find a polynomial function that fits the data.

x	1	2	3	4	5	6
$f(x)$	1	9	23	43	69	101

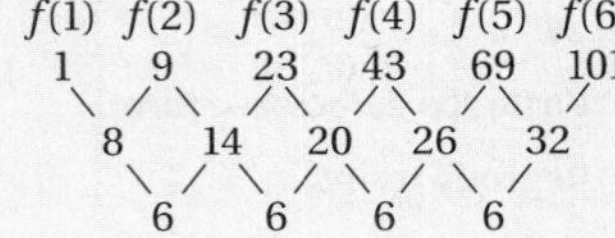

Write function values for equally-spaced x-values.

First-order differences

Second-order differences

Because the second-order differences are constant, the data can be represented by a function of the form $f(x) = ax^2 + bx + c$. By substituting the first 3 data points into the function, you obtain a system of 3 linear equations in 3 variables.

$a(1)^2 + b(1) + c = 1 \longrightarrow a + b + c = 1$

$a(2)^2 + b(2) + c = 9 \longrightarrow 4a + 2b + c = 9$

$a(3)^2 + b(3) + c = 23 \longrightarrow 9a + 3b + c = 23$

Solve the system. The solution is $(3, -1, -1)$, so $f(x) = 3x^2 - x - 1$.

EXERCISES

EXAMPLE 3 on p. 395 for Ex. 41

41. Use finite differences to find a polynomial function that fits the data. $y = x^3 - 8x^2 + 2x - 1$

x	1	2	3	4	5	6
$f(x)$	-6	-21	-40	-57	-66	-61

5 CHAPTER TEST

1. x; product of powers property

2. $\frac{x^{10}}{32y^{15}}$; power of a product property, negative exponent property

3. x^8y^4; power of a quotient property, negative exponent property

4. $\frac{3x^3y^3}{27x - 5y^3}$; power of a product property

21. $x^4 + 2x^3 - x^2 - 22x - 12$

22. $x^4 - 10x^3 + 2x^2 - 92x + 60$

23. *x*-intercepts: 0.62, 1.6, 4; local maximum: (0.33, 4.5); local minimum: (3, −5)

24. *x*-intercepts: 0.34, 1.1; local maximum: (−0.88, 5.1); local minimums: (−2.2, 1.8), (0.79, 1.5)

Simplify the expression. Tell which properties of exponents you used.

1. $x^3 \cdot x^2 \cdot x^{-4}$
2. $(2x^{-2}y^3)^{-5}$
3. $\left(\frac{x^{-4}}{y^2}\right)^{-2}$
4. $\frac{3(xy)^3}{27x - 5y^3}$

Graph the polynomial function. 5–7. See margin.

5. $f(x) = -x^3$
6. $f(x) = x^4 - 2x^2 - 5x + 1$
7. $f(x) = x^5 - x^4 - 9$

Perform the indicated operation.

8. $(2x^3 + 5x^2 - 7x + 4) + (x^3 - 3x^2 - 4x)$ $3x^3 + 2x^2 - 11x + 4$
9. $(3x^3 - 4x^2 + 3x - 5) - (x^2 + 4x - 8)$ $3x^3 - 5x^2 - x + 3$
10. $(3x - 2)(x^2 + 4x - 7)$ $3x^3 + 10x^2 - 29x + 14$
11. $(3x - 5)^3$ $27x^3 - 135x^2 + 225x - 125$
12. $(3x^3 - 14x^2 + 16x - 22) \div (x - 4)$ $3x^2 - 2x + 8 + \frac{10}{x - 4}$
13. $(6x^4 + 7x^2 + 4x - 17) \div (3x^2 - 3x + 2)$ $2x^2 + 2x + 3 + \frac{9x - 23}{2x^2 - 3x + 3}$

Factor the polynomial completely.

14. $8x^3 + 27$ $(2x + 3)(4x^2 - 6x + 9)$
15. $x^4 + 5x^2 - 6$ $(x - 1)(x + 1)(x^2 + 6)$
16. $x^3 - 3x^2 - 4x + 12$ $(x - 3)(x - 2)(x + 2)$

Find all real zeros of the function.

17. $f(x) = x^3 + x^2 - 22x - 40$ −4, −2, 5
18. $f(x) = 4x^4 - 8x^3 - 19x^2 + 23x - 6$ $-2, \frac{1}{2}, 3$

Write a polynomial function *f* of least degree that has rational coefficients, a leading coefficient of 1, and the given zeros.

19. −1, 3, 4 $x^3 - 6x^2 + 5x + 12$
20. 6, $2i$ $x^3 - 6x^2 + 4x - 24$
21. −3, −1, $1 - \sqrt{5}$
22. $1 + 3i$, $4 + \sqrt{10}$

Use a graphing calculator to graph the function. Identify the *x*-intercepts and the points where the local maximums and local minimums occur.

23. $f(x) = x^3 - 5x^2 + 3x + 4$
24. $f(x) = x^4 + 3x^3 - x^2 - 6x + 2$

Use finite differences and a system of equations to find a polynomial function that fits the data in the table.

25.

x	1	2	3	4	5	6
$f(x)$	3	1	1	3	7	13

$f(x) = x^2 - 5x + 7$

26.

x	1	2	3	4	5	6
$f(x)$	0	−7	−4	21	80	185

$f(x) = 2x^3 - 7x^2 + 5$

27. **GROSS DOMESTIC PRODUCT** In 2003, the gross domestic product (GDP) of the United States was about 1.099×10^{13} dollars. The population of the U.S. in 2003 was about 2.91×10^8. What was the per capita GDP in 2003? about $37,766

28. **TELEVISION** From 1980 to 2002, the number T (in millions) of households in the United States with televisions and the percent P of those households with VCRs can be modeled by

$$T = 1.22x + 76.9 \quad \text{and} \quad P = -0.205x^2 + 8.36x + 1.98$$

where x is the number of years since 1980. Write a polynomial model for the total number of U.S. households with both televisions and VCRs. $y = -0.2501x^3 - 5.5653x^2 + 645.3x + 152.262$

29. **GEOMETRY** A rectangular prism has edges of lengths x, $x + 2$, and $2x - 3$ inches. The volume of the prism is 1040 cubic inches. Write a polynomial equation that models the prism's volume. What are the prism's dimensions? $1040 = 2x^3 + x^2 - 6x$; 8 in. by 10 in. by 13 in.

Additional Resources

Assessment Book

- Chapter Test, Levels A, B, C, pp. 64–69
- Standardized Chapter Test, pp. 70–71
- SAT/ACT Chapter Test, pp. 72–73
- Alternative Assessment, pp. 74–75

Test Generator CD-ROM

Chapter Test

Easily-readable reduced copies (with answers) of Chapter Test B, the Standardized Chapter Test, and the Alternative Assessment from the Assessment Book can be found on pp. 328G–328H.

5.
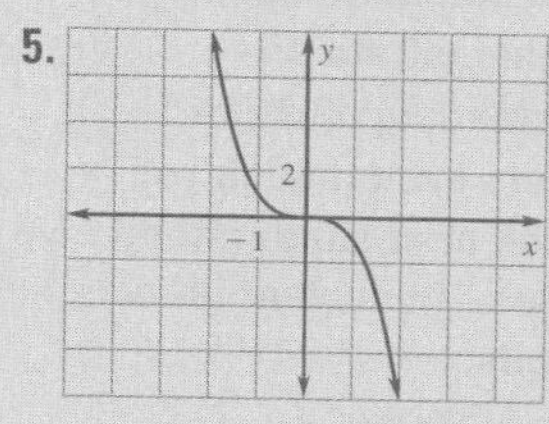

6.
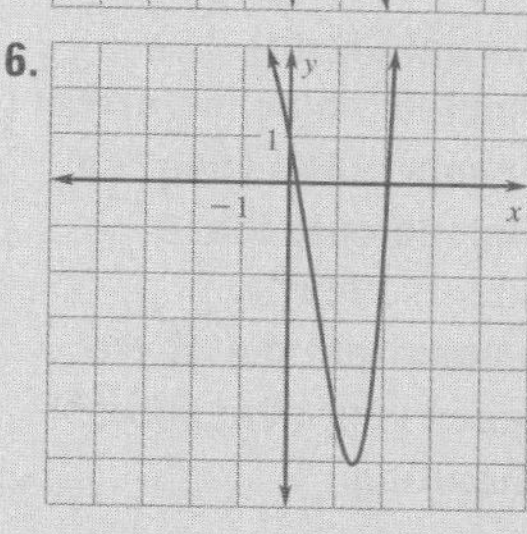

7.
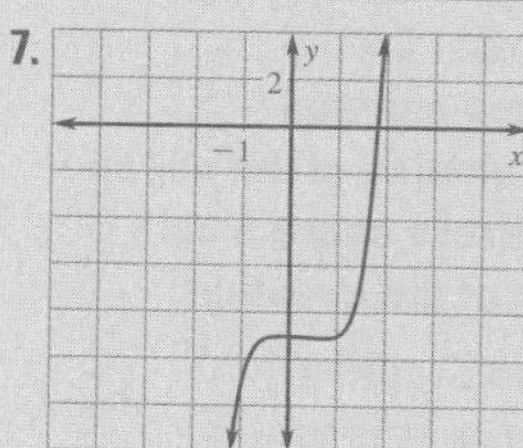

Kentucky General Scoring Rubric

4 Points (Full credit)
- You complete all important components of the question and communicate ideas clearly.
- You demonstrate in-depth understanding of the relevant concepts and/or processes.
- Where appropriate, you choose more efficient and/or sophisticated processes.
- Where appropriate, you offer insightful interpretations or extensions (generalizations, applications, analogies).

3 Points (Full or Partial Credit)
- You complete most important components of the question and communicate clearly.
- You demonstrate an understanding of major concepts even though you overlook or misunderstand some less-important ideas or details.

2 Points (Partial Credit)
- You complete some important components of the question and communicate those components clearly.
- You demonstrate that there are gaps in your conceptual understanding.

1 Point (Partial Credit)
- You show minimal understanding of the question.
- You address only a small portion of the question.

0 Points (No Credit)
- Your answer is totally incorrect or irrelevant.

BLANK (No Credit)
- You did not give any answer at all.

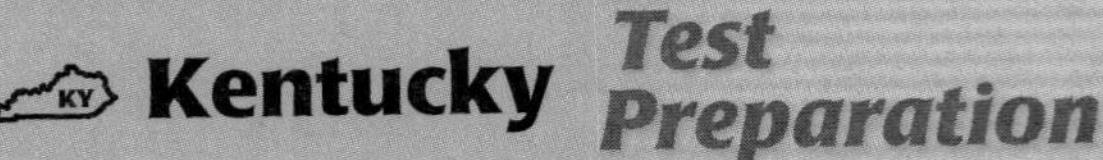

TEST PREPARATION

Scoring Rubric

Full Credit
- solution is complete and correct

Partial Credit
- solution is complete but has errors,
or
- solution is without error but incomplete

No Credit
- no solution is given,
or
- solution makes no sense

OPEN-RESPONSE QUESTIONS

PROBLEM

The width of a rectangular prism is 2 meters less than its length, and the height is 1 meter less than its width. The volume of the prism is 30 cubic meters.

a. Write an expression for the length, height, and width of the prism.

b. The volume of the prism is 300 cubic meters. Find the dimensions of the prism.

Below are sample solutions to the problem. Read each solution and the comments on the left to see why the sample represents *full credit, partial credit,* or *no credit.*

SAMPLE 1: Full credit solution

The expressions for the dimensions are clearly explained.

a. Let the length of the prism be x.
The width is 2 meters less than the length, so width $= x - 2$.
The height is 1 meter less than the width, so height $= (x - 2) - 1 = x - 3$.

The equation is correct and all steps are clearly shown.

b. The volume of a rectangular prism is the product of its length, width, and height.

$30 = x(x - 2)(x - 3)$ **Write equation.**

$30 = x(x^2 - 5x + 6)$ **Multiply binomials.**

$0 = x^3 - 5x^2 + 6x - 30$ **Write in standard form.**

$0 = x^2(x - 5) + 6(x - 5)$ **Factor by grouping.**

$0 = (x^2 + 6)(x - 5)$ **Distributive property**

The solution of the equation is correct.

The only real solution is $x = 5$. The factor $x^2 + 6$ does not produce any real solutions.

Use substitution to find the dimensions: length $= \mathbf{x} = \mathbf{5}$ meters

width $= \mathbf{x} - 2 = \mathbf{5} - 2 = 3$ meters

height $= \mathbf{x} - 3 = \mathbf{5} - 3 = 2$ meters

The dimensions are correct.

The prism is 5 meters long, 3 meters wide, and 2 meters high.

SAMPLE 2: Partial credit solution

a. Let length $= x$, width $= x - 2$, and height $= x - 3$.

The equation is correct.

b. $30 = x(x - 2)(x - 3)$

$0 = x^3 - 5x^2 + 6x - 30$

$0 = (x^2 + 6)(x - 5)$

$x = \pm i\sqrt{6}$ or $x = 5$

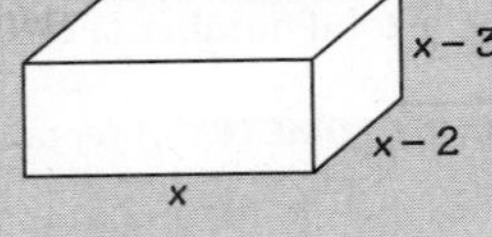

Imaginary solutions should be discarded. Dimensions are not given.

TEST PRACTICE
classzone.com

SAMPLE 3: No credit solution

The volume of a prism is the length cubed.

$x^3 = 30$

$x \approx 3.11$

The length of the prism is 3.11 meters.

he equation is incorrect.

he answer is incorrect.

PRACTICE Apply the Scoring Rubric

Use the rubric on page 408 to score the solution to the problem below as *full credit, partial credit,* or *no credit. Explain* your reasoning.

PROBLEM The volume of a sphere with radius r is given by the function $V = \frac{4}{3}\pi r^3$.

a. Graph the function.

b. Use the graph to estimate the radius of a sphere with a volume of 750 cubic feet.

1. The table shows the volumes of spheres with radii from 0 to 7 feet. Only positive r-values make sense.

r	0	1	2	3	4	5	6	7
V	0	4.189	33.51	113.1	268.1	523.6	904.8	1437

From the graph, you can see that the r-coordinate that corresponds to a V-coordinate of 750 is about 5.6.

A sphere with a volume of 750 cubic feet has a radius of about 5.6 feet.

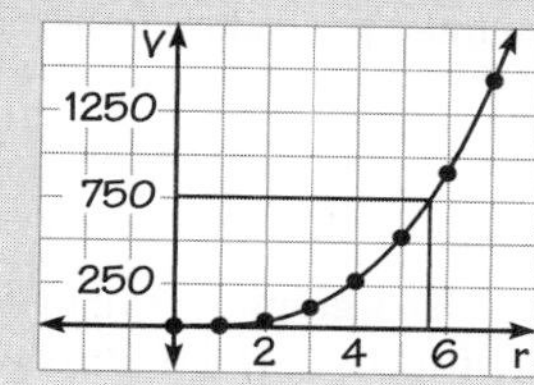

2. The table shows the volume V of a sphere with radius r.

r	0	2	4	6	8	10
V	0	10.67	85.33	288.0	682.7	1333

The r-coordinate that corresponds to a V-coordinate of 750 is 8.2, so the radius of a sphere with a volume of 750 cubic feet is about 8.2 feet.

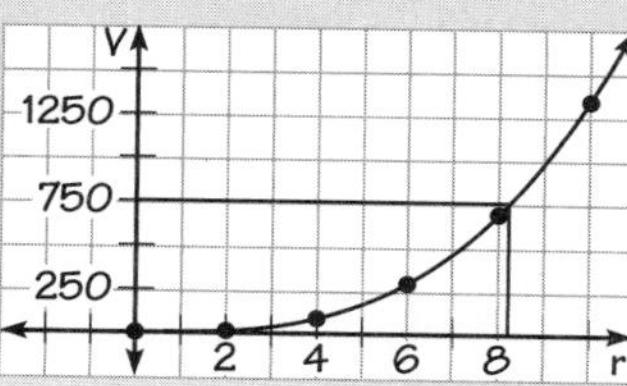

TEST PREPARATION

Kentucky Test Preparation

KY

1. Full credit; the expressions for the dimensions are clearly explained, the table and graph are correct, and the solution is correct.
2. No credit; the table and graph are incorrect, and the solution is incorrect.

Kentucky Test Practice

1. a. About 18.18 million; in 1960, about 68.6 million people voted and in 1980, about 86.78 million people voted.
   b. 2000; In 1980, 86.78 million people voted. In 2000, 106.8 million people voted.
2. a. Negative, odd
   b. 5; The leading coefficient is negative because the function decreases as x approaches infinity. The number of real zeroes is 5 because the graph crosses the x-axis 5 times. The degree is at least 5 (possibly greater) because there are 5 real zeroes.
3. a. (1.6, 11.9), (24.9, 16.3)
   b. the fuel efficiency increased steadily after 1971 and then began to decrease after 1995.
4. a. Yes
   b. $\pm\sqrt{5}, + -i$
5. a. 2003
   b. No; CD sales will not continue to increase indefinitely.
6. a. $f(x) = \frac{1}{3}x^3 + 4x^2 - \frac{28}{3}x + 9$; $g(x) = 2x^3 - 5x^2 + x$;
   b. $f(x) + g(x) = \frac{7}{3}x^3 - x^2 - \frac{25}{3}x + 9$

TEST PREPARATION

Kentucky Test Practice

OPEN-RESPONSE

1. Since 1960, the number of voters y (in millions) in United States federal elections can be modeled by the function

$$y = -0.0006x^3 + 0.0383x^2 + 0.383x + 68.6$$

where x is the number of years since 1960.

a. According to the model, how many more people voted in 1980 than in 1960?

b. Did more people vote in 1980 or in 2000?

2. Consider the graph below.

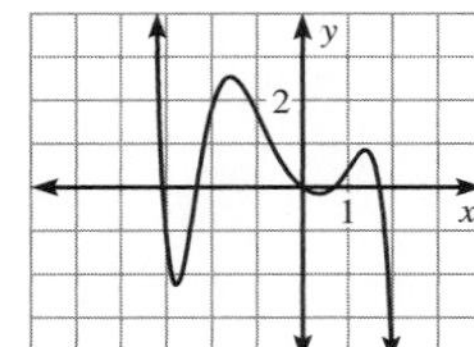

a. What does the graph of the polynomial function tell you about the sign of the leading coefficient?

b. What does the graph tell you about the degree of function and the number of real zeroes?

3. Since 1970, the average fuel efficiency E (in miles per gallon) for all vehicles in the United States can be modeled by the function

$$E = -0.0007t^3 + 0.0278t^2 - 0.0843t + 12.0$$

where t is the number of years since 1970.

a. Use a graphing calculator to graph the function, and identify any turning points on the interval $0 \le t \le 30$.

b. What real-life meaning does a turning point have in this situation?

4. Consider the function below.

$$f(x) = x^4 - 4x^2 - 5$$

a. Can you use the rational zero theorem to find the zeros of the function?

b. Find all roots of the function.

5. From 1990 to 2003, the number of CD singles (in millions) sold in the United States can be modeled by the polynomial function

$$y = 0.014x^5 - 0.40x^4 + 3.8x^3 - 13x^2 + 15x + 1.2$$

where x is the number of years since 1990.

a. Use a graphing calculator to graph the function on the domain $0 \le x \le 13$. According to the model, in which year were the most CD singles sold?

b. Do you think that sales will continue to follow the model indefinitely? *Explain* your reasoning.

6. Consider the following tables.

x	1	2	3	4	5	6
$f(x)$	4	9	26	57	104	169

x	1	2	3	4	5	6
$g(x)$	−2	−2	12	52	130	258

a. Use finite differences and a system of equations to find a polynomial function that fits the data in each table.

b. Find $f(x) + g(x)$. Show your procedure.

TEST PRACTICE
classzone.com

OPEN-RESPONSE

7. You are making an open box to hold paper clips out of a piece of cardboard that is 5 inches by 8 inches. The box will be formed by making the cuts shown in the diagram and folding up the sides. You want the box to have the greatest volume possible.

a. Use a graphing calculator to find how long you should make the cuts. *Explain* your reasoning.

b. What is the maximum volume of the box?

c. What will the dimensions of the finished box be?

8. From 1980 to 2002, the number of hospitals H in the United States and the average number of hospital beds B in each hospital can be modeled by

$H = -58.7t + 7070$ and $B = 0.0066t^3 - 0.192t^2 - 0.174t + 196$

where t is the number of years since 1980.

a. Write a model for the total number of hospital beds in U.S. hospitals.

b. According to the model, how many beds were in U.S. hospitals in 1995?

c. How does the model change if you want to find the number of hospital beds *in thousands*? *Explain* your reasoning.

MULTIPLE-CHOICE

9. Which expression is equivalent to $\frac{x^2y}{z^4}$?

A. $\frac{z^{-4}y^0}{x^{-2}}$

B. $xyz \cdot \frac{x}{z^{-3}}$

C. $(x^{-1}y^2z^2)^2(x^{-1}y^1z^2)^{-4}$

D. $\frac{(x^2yz)^3}{x^4y^2z^7}$

10. What are all the real solutions of the equation $x^4 = 125x$?

A. 0 B 0, 5, −5

C. 0, 5 D 0, $5i$, $-5i$

11. Which polynomial function has −1, 3, and $-4i$ as zeros?

A. $f(x) = x^4 - 2x^3 + 13x^2 - 32x - 48$

B. $f(x) = x^4 + 2x^3 + 13x^2 + 32x - 48$

C. $f(x) = x^4 - 2x^3 - 19x^2 + 32x + 48$

D. $f(x) = x^4 + 2x^3 + 19x^2 - 32x + 48$

12. How many *real* zeros does the function $f(x) = 2x^4 + 3x^2 - 1$ have?

A. 0 real zeros B. 1 real zero

C. 2 real zeros D. 4 real zeros

13. Evaluate the expression $\left(\frac{3}{2}\right)^{-2}$.

A. $\frac{4}{9}$ B. $\frac{9}{4}$

C. $\sqrt{\frac{2}{3}}$ D. $\sqrt{\frac{3}{2}}$

14. The graph of a quartic function is shown. How many imaginary zeros does the function have?

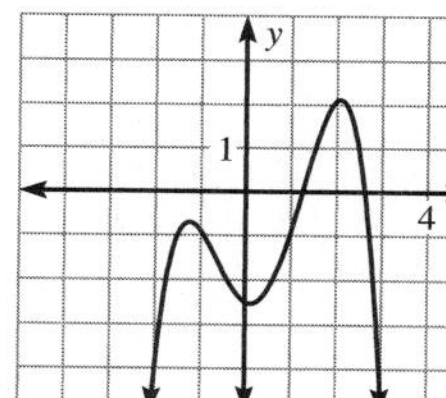

A. 0 imaginary zeros B. 1 imaginary zero

C. 2 imaginary zeros D. 4 imaginary zeros

TEST PREPARATION

7. a. 1 inch; the local maximum of the graph of the volume occurs at (1, 18).
b. 18 in.^{3}
c. 6 in. by 3 in. by 1 in.
8. a. $y = -0.387t^4 + 57.9t^3 - 1347t^2 - 12{,}735t + 1{,}385{,}720$
b. about 1,070,000 hospital beds
c. Each term would be divided by 1000; when representing a number *in thousands*, it must be divided by 1000, so each term must be divided by 1000.
9. D
10. C
11. A
12. C
13. A
14. C

6 Pacing and Assignment Guide

REGULAR SCHEDULE

Pre-AP For pacing and assignments for a Pre-AP course, see the *Algebra 2 Toolkit*.

Lesson	Les. Day	BASIC	AVERAGE	ADVANCED
6.1 MA-HS-1.3.1	Day 1	EP p. 1013 Exs. 33–36; pp. 417–419 Exs. 1–6, 7–19 odd, 21–25, 33–37, 46–51, 60–64, 67	pp. 417–419 Exs. 1, 2, 8–20 even, 25–28, 33, 38–41, 46–49, 50–58 even, 60–65, 68	pp. 417–419 Exs. 1, 2, 10, 14, 19, 20, 29–33, 42–47, 50–66*
6.2 MA-HS-5.2.1	Day 1	EP p. 1014 Exs. 4–7; pp. 424–427 Exs. 1–7, 15–19, 23–27, 32–35, 41–46, 52–55, 60–62, 83–87, 91	pp. 424–427 Exs. 1, 2, 8–11, 19–21, 23, 28–30, 35–37, 41, 42, 46–48, 55–57, 62–64, 67–77 odd, 83–89, 92	pp. 424–427 Exs. 1, 2, 12–14, 21–23, 30, 31, 38–40, 49–51, 57–59, 64–69, 75–82*, 84–90*
6.3 MA-HS-5.1.5	Day 1	pp. 432–434 Exs. 1–8, 11–15, 20–23, 28–31, 43–46, 48	pp. 432–434 Exs. 1, 2, 6–8, 11, 15–17, 23–25, 31–39, 43–46, 49	pp. 432–434 Exs. 1, 2, 9–11, 18, 19, 26, 27, 33–42*, 44–47*
6.4 MA-HS-5.1.5	Day 1	EP p. 1014 Exs. 8–11; pp. 442–445 Exs. 1–8, 12–18, 21, 46–48	pp. 442–445 Exs. 1, 2, 5–10, 12–14, 16–19, 21, 46–48	pp. 442–445 Exs. 1, 2, 6–11, 14–21, 46–48
	Day 2	pp. 442–445 Exs. 22–34, 49, 52–53	pp. 442–445 Exs. 25–28, 31–43, 49, 50, 52–53	pp. 442–445 Exs. 26–28, 34–45*, 49–53*
6.5	Day 1	pp. 449–451 Exs. 1–5, 9–12, 16–20, 35–38, 41	pp. 449–451 Exs. 1, 2, 5–7, 9, 12–14, 19–21, 25–27, 35–39, 42	pp. 449–451 Exs. 1, 2, 7–9, 14, 15, 22–34*, 36–40*, 42–50
6.6	Day 1	EP p. 1013 Exs. 17–20; pp. 456–459 Exs. 1–9, 12–19, 22, 56, 57	pp. 456–459 Exs. 1, 2, 5–12, 14–20, 22, 56, 57	pp. 456–459 Exs. 1, 2, 5–12, 15–22, 56, 57
	Day 2	pp. 456–459 Exs. 23–39, 43–46, 58–60, 63–64	pp. 456–459 Exs. 26–30, 32, 33, 36–40, 43, 44, 45–53 odd, 58–61, 63–64	pp. 456–459 Exs. 28–31, 39–44, 46–52 even, 53–55*, 58–64*
Review	Day 1	pp. 466–468 Exs. 1–32	pp. 466–468 Exs. 1–32	pp. 466–468 Exs. 1–32
Assess	Day 1	Chapter 6 Test	Chapter 6 Test	Chapter 6 Test
Yearly Pacing		Chapter 6 Total – 10 days	Chapters 1–6 Total – 80 days	Remaining – 80 days

*Challenge Exercises EP = Extra Practice SRH = Skills Review Handbook

BLOCK SCHEDULE

DAY 1	DAY 2	DAY 3	DAY 4	DAY 5
6.1	**6.3**	**6.4 (CONT.)**	**6.6**	**REVIEW**
pp. 417–419 Exs. 1, 2, 8–20 even, 25–28, 33, 38–41, 46–49, 50–58 even, 60–65, 68	pp. 432–434 Exs. 1, 2, 6–8, 11, 15–17, 23–25, 31–39, 43–46, 49	pp. 442–445 Exs. 25–28, 31–43, 49, 50, 52–53	pp. 456–459 Exs. 1, 2, 5–12, 14–20, 22, 26–30, 32, 33, 36–40, 43, 44, 45–53 odd, 56–61, 63–64	pp. 466–468 Exs. 1–32
6.2	**6.4**	**6.5**		**ASSESS**
pp. 424–427 Exs. 1, 2, 8–11, 19–21, 23, 28–30, 35–37, 41, 42, 46–48, 55–57, 62–64, 67–77 odd, 83–89, 92	pp. 442–445 Exs. 1, 2, 5–10, 12–14, 16–19, 21, 46–48	pp. 449–451 Exs. 1, 2, 5–7, 9, 12–14, 19–21, 25–27, 35–39, 42		Chapter 6 Test
Yearly Pacing	Chapter 6 Total – 5 days	Chapters 1–6 Total – 40 days	Remaining – 40 days	

Chapter Resource Guide 6

RESOURCE MANAGER

Chapter Resource Book						
CHAPTER SUPPORT						
Parents as Partners (Chapter Overview with home involvement exercises and activity)					p. 1	
LESSON SUPPORT **Standards**	**6.1** **MA-HS-1.3.1**	**6.2** **MA-HS-5.2.1**	**6.3** **MA-HS-5.1.5**	**6.4** **MA-HS-5.1.5**	**6.5**	**6.6**
Teaching Guide/Lesson Plan	p. 3	p. 16	p. 27	p. 40	p. 51	p. 64
Activity Masters	p. 5	p. 18			p. 53	
Technology Activities & Keystrokes	p. 7		p. 29	p. 42	p. 55	p. 66
Activity Support Masters						
Practice (3 levels)	p. 8	p. 19	p. 31	p. 43	p. 56	p. 69
Study Guide	p. 11	p. 22	p. 34	p. 46	p. 59	p. 72
Catch-Up for Absent Students	p. 13	p. 24	p. 36	p. 48	p. 61	p. 74
Problem Solving/Application	p. 14	p. 25	p. 37	p. 49	p. 62	p. 75
Challenge Practice	p. 15	p. 26	p. 39	p. 50	p. 63	p. 76
REVIEW						
Chapter Review Games and Activities		p. 77	Cumulative Practice			p. 79
Project with Rubric		p. 78	Resource Book Answers			A1

Transparencies	*6.1*	*6.2*	*6.3*	*6.4*	*6.5*	*6.6*
Warm-Up/Daily Homework Quiz	✔	✔	✔	✔	✔	✔
Notetaking Guide	✔	✔	✔	✔	✔	✔
Teacher Support				✔	✔	
Answer Transparencies	✔	✔	✔	✔	✔	✔

ASSESSMENT BOOK

Quizzes	p. 76	SAT/ACT Chapter Test	p. 87
Chapter Tests (3 levels)	p. 79	Alternative Assessment with Rubric	p. 89
Standardized Chapter Test	p. 85	Cumulative Test	p. 91

TECHNOLOGY

- Easy Planner
- Test and Practice Generator
- Power Presentations
- @HomeTutor
- Activity Generator
- Animated Algebra
- Classzone.com
- eEdition Plus Online
- eWorkbook Plus Online
- ML Assessment System

ADDITIONAL RESOURCES

Kentucky

- Worked-Out Solution Key
- Notetaking Guide
- Practice Workbook
- Algebra 2 Toolkit
- Benchmark Tests
- Remediation Workbook
- Spanish Study Guide
- Spanish Assessment Book
- Spanish Resources in Spanish
- Multi-Language Visual Glossary

6 Lesson Practice Level B

LESSON 6.1

Practice B

For use with pages 414–419

Rewrite the expression using rational exponent notation.

1. $\sqrt[3]{7}$ $7^{1/3}$ **2.** $(\sqrt[3]{6})^2$ $6^{2/3}$ **3.** $(\sqrt[5]{14})^4$ $14^{4/5}$

4. $(\sqrt[7]{-21})^3$ $-21^{3/7}$ **5.** $(\sqrt[8]{11})^7$ $11^{7/8}$ **6.** $(\sqrt[9]{-2})^4$ $-2^{4/9}$

Rewrite the expression using radical notation.

7. $17^{1/3}$ $\sqrt[3]{17}$ **8.** $44^{1/6}$ $\sqrt[6]{44}$ **9.** $33^{2/3}$ $(\sqrt[3]{33})^2$

10. $9^{5/3}$ $(\sqrt[3]{9})^5$ **11.** $(-28)^{7/5}$ $(\sqrt[5]{-28})^7$ **12.** $39^{4/7}$ $(\sqrt[7]{39})^4$

Evaluate the expression without using a calculator.

13. $(\sqrt[3]{8})^2$ 4 **14.** $(\sqrt[4]{16})^3$ 8 **15.** $(\sqrt[4]{81})^4$ 81

16. $36^{3/2}$ 216 **17.** $4^{5/2}$ 32 **18.** $27^{2/3}$ 9

19. $125^{4/3}$ 625 **20.** $(-8)^{1/3}$ -2 **21.** $(-32)^{3/5}$ -8

Evaluate the expression using a calculator. Round the result to two decimal places when appropriate.

22. $\sqrt[3]{38}$ 3.36 **23.** $\sqrt[6]{112}$ 2.20 **24.** $\sqrt[7]{-215}$ -2.15

25. $(241)^{1/5}$ 3.00 **26.** $(-133)^{1/3}$ -5.10 **27.** $(69)^{1/4}$ 2.88

28. $(96)^{2/3}$ 20.97 **29.** $(356)^{5/9}$ 26.15 **30.** $(-2427)^{4/7}$ -85.97

31. **Geometry** Find the radius of a sphere with a volume of 589 cubic centimeters. 5.2 cm

Solve the equation. Round the result to two decimal places when appropriate.

32. $x^3 + 17 = 132$ 4.86 **33.** $2x^5 + 73 = 53$ -1.58 **34.** $(x + 3)^4 = 362$ $-7.36, 1.36$

In Exercises 35–38, use the following information.

Water and Ice Water, in its liquid state, has a density of 0.9971 grams per cubic centimeter. Ice has a density of 0.9168 grams per cubic centimeter. A cubic container is filled with 600 grams of liquid water. A different cubic container is filled with 600 grams of ice. Round the answers to two decimal places when appropriate.

35. Find the volume of the container filled with liquid water. 601.75 cm^3

36. Find the length of the edges of the cubic container that is filled with liquid water. 8.44 cm

37. Find the volume of the container filled with ice. 654.45 cm^3

38. Find the length of the edges of the cubic container that is filled with ice. 8.68 cm

LESSON 6.1

LESSON 6.2

Practice B

For use with pages 420–427

Simplify the expression using the properties of radicals and rational exponents.

1. $7^{1/3} \cdot 7^{4/3}$ $7^{5/3}$ **2.** $\frac{4^{2/3}}{4^{1/3}}$ $4^{1/3}$ **3.** $(6^{2/3})^{3/4}$ $6^{1/2}$

4. $5^{1/4} \cdot 3^{1/4}$ $15^{1/4}$ **5.** $\sqrt[4]{2} \cdot \sqrt[4]{8}$ 2 **6.** $\frac{\sqrt[4]{192}}{\sqrt[4]{6}}$ $2\sqrt[4]{2}$

7. $\frac{11}{\sqrt[4]{11}}$ $11^{3/4}$ **8.** $\sqrt[3]{7} \cdot \sqrt[3]{49}$ 7 **9.** $(3^{3/2})^2$ 27

10. $\left(\frac{54}{64}\right)^{1/3}$ $\frac{3\sqrt[3]{2}}{4}$ **11.** $\frac{\sqrt[4]{32}}{\sqrt[4]{2}}$ 2 **12.** $\frac{\sqrt[5]{5}}{\sqrt[5]{27}}$ $\frac{\sqrt[5]{45}}{3}$

Simplify the expression. Assume all variables are positive.

13. $x^{5/3} \cdot x^{4/3}$ x^3 **14.** $\sqrt{x^{2/5}}$ $x^{1/5}$ **15.** $(x^{1/2})^{2/7}$ $x^{1/7}$

16. $\left(\frac{x^2}{27}\right)^{1/3}$ $\frac{x^{2/3}}{3}$ **17.** $\sqrt[3]{16x^4}$ $2x\sqrt[3]{2x}$ **18.** $(x^{-3})^{2/5}$ $\frac{1}{x^{6/5}}$

19. $\frac{x^{7/5}}{x^{4/5}}$ $x^{3/5}$ **20.** $\frac{\sqrt[3]{64x^3y}}{4x^{-3}y}$ $\frac{x^4\sqrt[3]{y}}{y}$ **21.** $x^5 \cdot x^{\sqrt{3}}$ $x^{5+\sqrt{3}}$

22. $(x^{\sqrt{2}})^{3\sqrt{2}}$ x^6 **23.** $\frac{x^{4\sqrt{3}}}{2x^{2\sqrt{3}}}$ $\frac{x^{2\sqrt{3}}}{2}$ **24.** $(\sqrt[3]{x^4} \cdot \sqrt{x^5})^{-2}$ $\frac{1}{x^{23/3}}$

Perform the indicated operation. Assume all variables are positive.

25. $6\sqrt[3]{5} + 2\sqrt[3]{5}$ $8\sqrt[3]{5}$ **26.** $5\sqrt{5} - \sqrt{45}$ $2\sqrt{5}$

27. $2\sqrt{27} - 3\sqrt{48}$ $-6\sqrt{3}$ **28.** $2\sqrt{x} + 7\sqrt{x}$ $9\sqrt{x}$

29. $3(x^{1/2}y^3)^2 - (x^3y^{18})^{1/3}$ $2xy^6$ **30.** $4x^{\sqrt{3}} + x^{\sqrt{3}}$ $5x^{\sqrt{3}}$

Write the expression in simplest form. Assume all variables are positive.

31. $\sqrt[4]{3x^7y^9z^3}$ $xy^2\sqrt[4]{3x^3yz^3}$ **32.** $\sqrt{x^3y^4z} \cdot \sqrt{xyz^4}$ $x^2y^2z^2\sqrt{yz}$ **33.** $\sqrt[3]{\frac{81x^2y^3}{8xy^4z}}$ $\frac{3\sqrt[3]{3xy^2z^2}}{2yz}$

34. **Circumference** The equatorial circumference of Earth is 4.01×10^4 kilometers. One kilometer is equivalent to 3.94×10^4 inches. What is the equatorial circumference of Earth in inches? 1.58×10^9 in.

35. **Swimming Pool** A wooden deck and a circular swimming pool cover an area of 514.16 square feet of the lawn. The rectangular deck is 20 feet wide and 10 feet long. What is the radius of the pool? 10 ft

LESSON 6.2

LESSON 6.3

Practice B

For use with pages 428–434

Let $f(x) = 7x^{1/2} - 2$, $g(x) = -x^{1/2} + 4$ and $h(x) = -4x^{1/2} + 1$. Perform the indicated operation.

1. $f(x) + g(x)$ $6x^{1/2} + 2$ **2.** $f(x) + h(x)$ $3x^{1/2} - 1$ **3.** $h(x) + g(x)$ $-5x^{1/2} + 5$

4. $f(x) - g(x)$ $8x^{1/2} - 6$ **5.** $h(x) - f(x)$ $-11x^{1/2} + 3$ **6.** $g(x) - h(x)$ $3x^{1/2} + 3$

Let $f(x) = 4x^2$, $g(x) = -3x^{4/3}$ and $h(x) = x^{1/2}$. Perform the indicated operation.

7. $f(x) \cdot g(x)$ $-12x^{10/3}$ **8.** $f(x) \cdot h(x)$ $4x^{5/2}$ **9.** $h(x) \cdot g(x)$ $-3x^{11/6}$

10. $\frac{f(x)}{g(x)}$ $-\frac{4x^{2/3}}{3}$ **11.** $\frac{h(x)}{f(x)}$ $\frac{1}{4x^{3/2}}$ **12.** $\frac{h(x)}{g(x)}$ $-\frac{1}{3x^{5/6}}$

Let $f(x) = 2x + 3$, $g(x) = \frac{3}{x+1}$ and $h(x) = \frac{x+5}{2}$. Perform the indicated operation.

13. $f(g(x))$ $\frac{3x+9}{x+1}$ **14.** $g(h(x))$ $\frac{6}{x+7}$

15. $f(h(x))$ $x + 8$ **16.** $g(f(x))$ $\frac{3}{2x+4}$

17. $h(f(x))$ $x + 4$ **18.** $g(g(x))$ $\frac{3x+3}{x+4}$

Let $f(x) = 3x + 2$, $g(x) = 2x^2$ and $h(x) = \frac{-4}{x+3}$. State the domain of the operation.

19. $f(x) + g(x)$ all real numbers **20.** $h(x) - f(x)$ all real numbers except $x = -3$

21. $h(x) \cdot g(x)$ all real numbers except $x = -3$ **22.** $\frac{g(x)}{f(x)}$ all real numbers except $x = -\frac{2}{3}$

23. $h(g(x))$ all real numbers **24.** $f(g(x))$ all real numbers

In Exercises 25–29, use the following information.

Computer Sale You have a coupon for \$200 off the price of a personal computer. When you arrive at the store, you find that the computers are on sale for 20% off. Let x represent the original price of the computer.

25. Use a function notation to describe your cost, $f(x)$, using only the coupon. $f(x) = x - 200$

26. Use a function notation to describe your cost, $g(x)$, with only the 20% discount. $g(x) = 0.8x$

27. Form the composition of the functions f and g that represents your cost if you use the coupon first, then take the 20% discount. $g(f(x)) = 0.8x - 160$

28. Form the composition of the functions f and g that represents your cost if you use the discount first, then use the coupon. $f(g(x)) = 0.8x - 200$

29. Would you pay less for the computer if you used the coupon first or took the 20% discount first? pay less with discount first

LESSON 6.3

LESSON 6.4 Practice B
For use with pages 438–445

Find an equation for the inverse relation.

1. $y = 2x + 1$ $y = \frac{1}{2}x - \frac{1}{2}$
2. $y = \frac{1}{3}x$ $y = 3x$
3. $y = 6x - 3$ $y = \frac{1}{6}x + \frac{1}{2}$
4. $y = -4x + 6$ $y = \frac{3}{2} - \frac{1}{4}x$
5. $y = \frac{1}{2} - \frac{2}{3}x$ $y = \frac{3}{4} - \frac{3}{2}x$
6. $y = x^2 + 2$ $y = \pm\sqrt{x - 2}$

Verify that *f* and *g* are inverse functions. **7–12.** Show that $f(g(x)) = x$ and $g(f(x)) = x$.

7. $f(x) = x + 4;\ g(x) = x - 4$
8. $f(x) = 7x;\ g(x) = \frac{1}{7}x$
9. $f(x) = x^5;\ g(x) = \sqrt[5]{x}$
10. $f(x) = 2x - 4;\ g(x) = \frac{1}{2}x + 2$
11. $f(x) = 3 - x;\ g(x) = 3 - x$
12. $f(x) = x^2 + 5, x \geq 0;\ g(x) = \sqrt{x - 5}$

Graph the function *f*. Then use the horizontal line test to determine whether the inverse of *f* is a function.

13. $f(x) = 2x + 1$ function

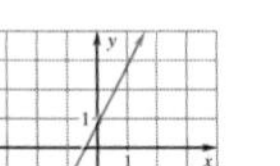

14. $f(x) = -x - 2$ function

15. $f(x) = \frac{1}{2}x^2 - 1$ not a function

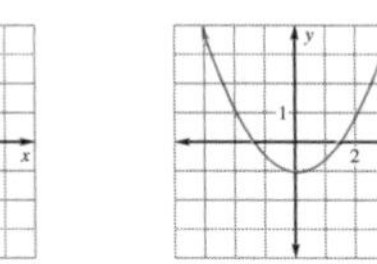

16. $f(x) = -x^2 + 3, x \geq 0$ function

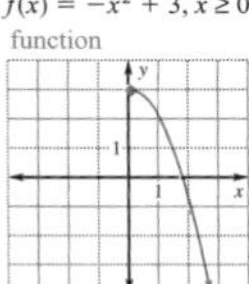

17. $f(x) = \frac{1}{4}x^3$ function

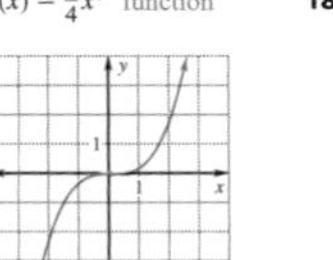

18. $f(x) = |x| + 1$ not a function

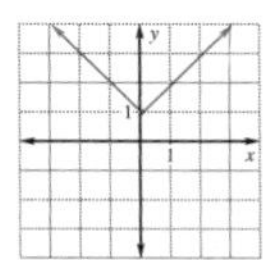

19. **Temperature Conversion** The formula to convert temperatures from degrees Celsius to Fahrenheit is $F = \frac{9}{5}C + 32$. Write the inverse function, which converts temperatures from Fahrenheit to Celsius. What is the Celsius temperature that is equal to 94 degrees Fahrenheit? $C = \frac{5}{9}(F - 32)$; 34.4°C

20. **Sale Price** A department store is having a storewide 20% discount sale. The sale price S of an item that has a regular price of R is $S = R - 0.2R$. Write the inverse function. What is the regular price for an item that is on sale for \$38.40? $R = \frac{S}{0.8}$; \$48.00

LESSON 6.5 Practice B
For use with pages 446–451

Graph the square root function. Then state the domain and range.

1. $f(x) = \sqrt{x} - 2$

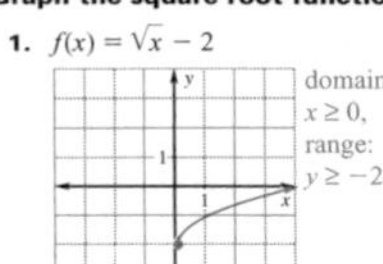

domain: $x \geq 0$, range: $y \geq -2$

2. $f(x) = \sqrt{x - 2}$

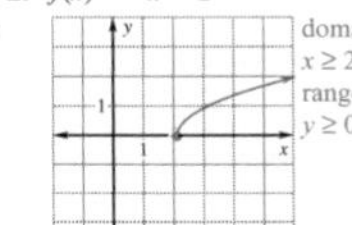

domain: $x \geq 2$, range: $y \geq 0$

3. $f(x) = 3\sqrt{x + 1}$

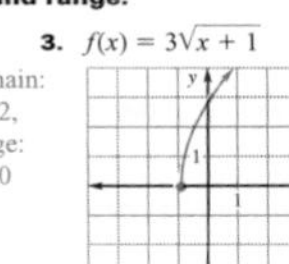

domain: $x \geq -1$, range: $y \geq 0$

4. $f(x) = \sqrt{x + 2} - 2$

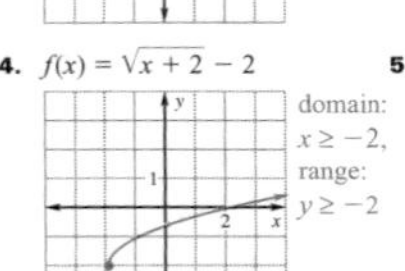

domain: $x \geq -2$, range: $y \geq -2$

5. $f(x) = \sqrt{x - 1} + 1$

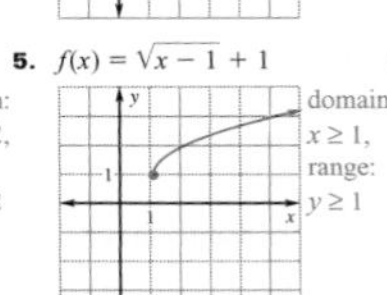

domain: $x \geq 1$, range: $y \geq 1$

6. $f(x) = -\sqrt{x - 3}$

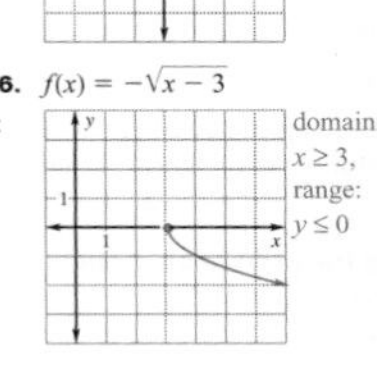

domain: $x \geq 3$, range: $y \leq 0$

Graph the cube root function. Then state the domain and range.

7. $f(x) = \sqrt[3]{x} + 1$

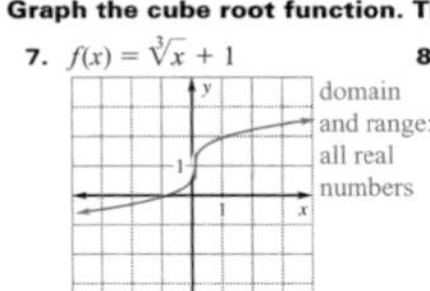

domain and range: all real numbers

8. $f(x) = \sqrt[3]{x - 4}$

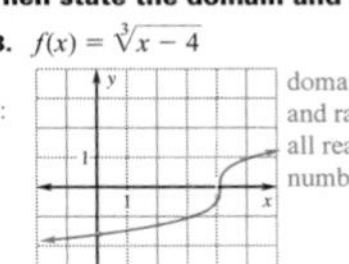

domain and range: all real numbers

9. $f(x) = 3\sqrt[3]{x}$ domain and range: all real numbers

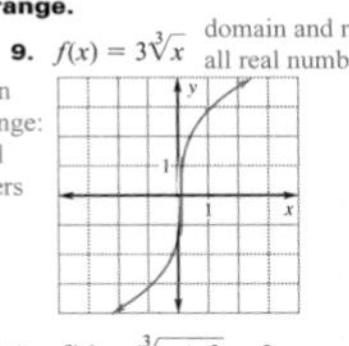

10. $f(x) = \sqrt[3]{x + 2}$

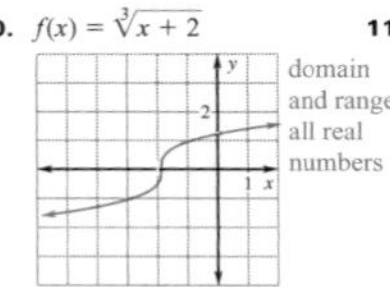

domain and range: all real numbers

11. $f(x) = -\sqrt[3]{x} - 1$

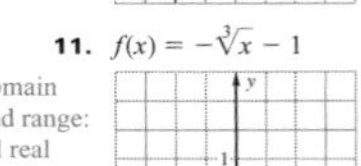

domain and range: all real numbers

12. $f(x) = \sqrt[3]{x + 2} - 2$

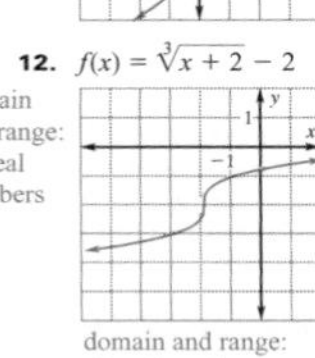

domain and range: all real numbers

In Exercises 13 and 14, use the following information.

Speed of Sound The speed of sound in feet per second through air of any temperature measured in Celsius is given by $V = \frac{1087\sqrt{t + 273}}{16.52}$, where t is the temperature.

13. Identify the domain and range of the function. domain: $t \geq -273$, range: $V \geq 0$
14. What is the temperature of the air if the speed of sound is 1250 feet per second? 87.9°C

LESSON 6.6 Practice B
For use with pages 452–459

Solve the equation. Check your solution.

1. $\sqrt{x} + 3 = 12$ 81
2. $x^{1/2} - 4 = 1$ 25
3. $3\sqrt{x + 2} = 6$ 2
4. $(2x - 3)^{1/2} + 2 = 2$ $\frac{3}{2}$
5. $5\sqrt{3x} = 15$ 3
6. $3\sqrt{4 - 3x} = 21$ -15
7. $7 - \sqrt{x - 4} = -6$ 173
8. $\sqrt{3x + 4} + \frac{3}{2} = 3$ $-\frac{7}{12}$
9. $2(x - 1)^{1/2} - 3 = 7$ 26

Solve the equation. Check your solution.

10. $\sqrt[3]{x} + 1 = -2$ -27
11. $4\sqrt[3]{x} + 2 = 0$ $-\frac{1}{8}$
12. $\sqrt[3]{2x + 7} = 5$ 59
13. $(x + 4)^{1/3} - 2 = -6$ -68
14. $8\sqrt[3]{x} + 3 = 11$ 1
15. $3x^{1/3} - 2 = -4$ $-\frac{8}{27}$
16. $-2\sqrt[3]{2x + 5} + 7 = 15$ $-\frac{69}{2}$
17. $\frac{1}{2}(5x + 1)^{1/3} + \frac{5}{2} = 4$ $\frac{26}{5}$
18. $6\sqrt[3]{x - 3} + 2 = \frac{1}{2}$ $\frac{191}{64}$

Solve the equation. Check for extraneous solutions.

19. $x^{5/3} = 243$ 27
20. $x^{3/2} + 3 = 11$ 4
21. $2x^{5/3} = -64$ -8
22. $(x - 2)^{3/4} = 8$ 18
23. $(2x + 12)^{2/3} - 3 = 13$ 26
24. $(3x + 21)^{4/3} + 9 = 90$ 2

Solve the equation. Check for extraneous solutions.

25. $\sqrt{x - 3} = \sqrt{2x - 7}$ 4
26. $\sqrt{x + 3} = \sqrt{4x - 8}$ $\frac{11}{3}$
27. $\sqrt[3]{4x - 9} = \sqrt[3]{2x - 4}$ $\frac{5}{2}$
28. $\sqrt[4]{3x + 3} = \sqrt[4]{2x - 7}$ no solution
29. $\sqrt{x} + 1 = \sqrt{3x - 3}$ 4
30. $\sqrt[3]{3x + 9} = \sqrt[3]{x + 6}$ $-\frac{3}{2}$
31. $x + 2 = \sqrt{2x + 7}$ 1
32. $\sqrt{2x + 3} = 1 + \sqrt{x + 1}$ $-1, 3$

In Exercises 33–35, use the following information.

Velocity The velocity of a free falling object is given by $V = \sqrt{2gh}$, where V is velocity (in meters per second), g is acceleration due to gravity (in meters per second squared) and h is the distance (in meters) the object has fallen. The value of g depends on which body/planet is attracting the object. If an object hits the surface with a velocity of 30 meters per second, from what height was it dropped in each of the following situations?

33. You are on Earth where $g = 9.81\ m/s^2$. 45.87 m
34. You are on the Moon where $g = 1.57\ m/s^2$. 286.62 m
35. You are on Mars where $g = 3.72\ m/s^2$. 120.97 m

6 Assessment

CHAPTER 6 Quiz 1
For use after Lessons 6.1–6.2

Evaluate the expression without using a calculator.

1. $8^{2/3}$
2. $81^{-3/2}$
3. $-125^{4/3}$
4. $(-32)^{3/5}$

Solve the equation. Round your answer to two decimal places when appropriate.

5. $x^5 = 25$
6. $x^3 = -21$
7. $x^4 + 11 = 29$
8. $(x + 4)^3 = -33$

Simplify the expression. Assume all variables are positive.

9. $\sqrt[3]{27} \cdot \sqrt[3]{64}$
10. $(\sqrt{6} \cdot \sqrt[3]{6})^6$
11. $(x^8y^4)^{1/10} + 3(x^{1/5}y^{1/10})^4$
12. $\dfrac{2\sqrt{9^5} + 7\sqrt{9^5}}{\sqrt{9^7}}$
13. $\dfrac{6\sqrt{x^2}\sqrt{x^2}}{81\sqrt{x^{16}}}$
14. $y^3\sqrt[5]{32x^4} - 7\sqrt[5]{x^4y^{15}}$
15. Find a radical expression for the perimeter of the shaded triangle. Simplify the expression.

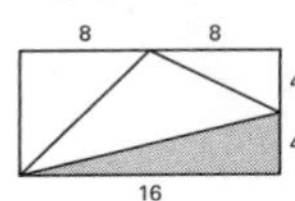

Answers

1. 4
2. $\frac{1}{729}$
3. -625
4. -8
5. 1.90
6. -2.76
7. 2.06
8. -7.21
9. 12
10. $6^5 = 7776$
11. $4x^{4/5}y^{2/5}$
12. 1
13. $\frac{2}{27x^6}$
14. $-5x^{4/5}y^3$
15. $16 + 4 + \sqrt{16^2 + 4^2}$; $20 + 4\sqrt{17}$

CHAPTER 6 Quiz 2
For use after Lessons 6.3–6.4

Let $f(x) = 5x^3 - 2x$ and $g(x) = 3x^3$. Perform the indicated operation and state the domain.

1. $f(x) + g(x)$
2. $f(x) - g(x)$
3. $f(x) \cdot g(x)$
4. $\dfrac{f(x)}{g(x)}$
5. $f(g(x))$
6. $g(f(x))$

Verify that f and g are inverse functions.

7. $f(x) = x - 7, g(x) = x + 7$
8. $f(x) = \frac{2}{5}x + \frac{1}{3}, g(x) = \frac{5}{2}x - \frac{5}{6}$
9. $f(x) = 6x^3, g(x) = \sqrt[3]{\frac{x}{6}}$

Find the inverse of the function.

10. $f(x) = 3x + 10$
11. $f(x) = -\frac{3}{8}x^7$
12. $f(x) = x^2 - 9, x \geq -9$
13. The cost (in dollars) of g gallons of gasoline can be modeled by $C(g) = 2.25g$. The amount of gasoline used by a SUV can be modeled by $g(d) = 0.025d^{1.24}$ where d is the distance (in miles). Find $C(g(d))$. Evaluate $C(g(500))$. What does $C(g(500))$ represent?

Answers

1. $8x^3 - 2x$; all real numbers
2. $2x^3 - 2x$; all real numbers
3. $15x^6 - 6x^4$; all real numbers
4. $\frac{5x^2 - 2}{3x^2}$; all real numbers except 0
5. $135x^9 - 6x^3$; all real numbers
6. $3(5x^3 - 2x)^3$; all real numbers
7. $f(g(x)) = x$, $g(f(x)) = x$
8. $f(g(x)) = x$, $g(f(x)) = x$
9. $f(g(x)) = x$, $g(f(x)) = x$
10. $f^{-1}(x) = \frac{1}{3}x - \frac{10}{3}$
11. $f^{-1}(x) = \sqrt[7]{-\frac{8}{3}x}$
12. $f^{-1}(x) = \sqrt{x + 9}$; $x \geq -9$
13. $C(g(d)) = 0.05625d^{1.24}$; \$124.99; cost of gas for 500 mi

CHAPTER 6 Quiz 3
For use after Lessons 6.5–6.6

Graph the function. Then state the domain and range.

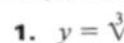

1. $y = \sqrt[3]{x}$

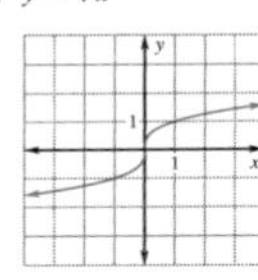

2. $y = \sqrt{x} + 5$

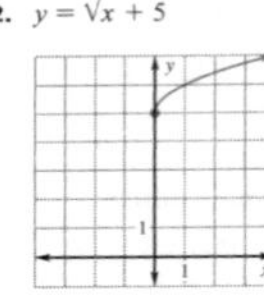

3. $y = \sqrt{x - 4} + 6$

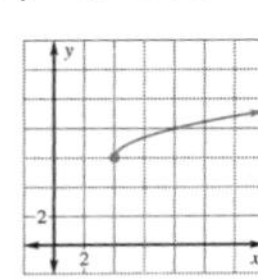

4. $y = -\frac{2}{3}\sqrt[3]{x}$

5. $y = \sqrt[3]{x} + 8$

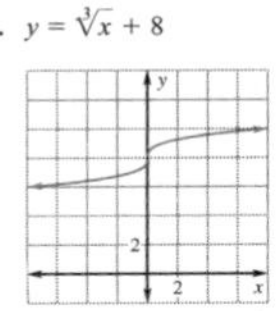

6. $y = \sqrt[3]{x + 6} - 7$

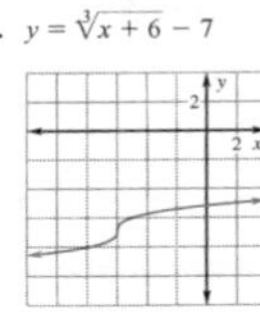

Solve the equation.

7. $\sqrt{3x + 12} = 6$
8. $\frac{1}{2}(5x + 7)^{2/3} = \frac{9}{2}$
9. $\sqrt{8x + 9} + 3 = 6$
10. $x - 4 = \sqrt{8x - 48}$
11. $\sqrt{7x - 7} = \sqrt{3x - 2}$
12. $\sqrt[3]{\frac{1}{8}x - 11} = \sqrt[3]{x - 4}$
13. The period T (in seconds) of a pendulum can be modeled by $T = 1.11\sqrt{\ell}$ where ℓ is the pendulum's length (in feet). How long is a pendulum with a period of 5 seconds?

Answers

1. See left. domain: all reals; range: all reals
2. See left. domain: $x \geq 0$; range: $y \geq 5$
3. See left. domain: $x \geq 4$; range: $y \geq 6$
4. See left. domain: all reals; range: all reals
5. See left. domain: all reals; range: all reals
6. See left. domain: all reals; range: all reals
7. 8
8. 4
9. 0
10. 8
11. $\frac{5}{4}$
12. -8
13. 20.29 ft

CHAPTER 6 Chapter Test B
For use after Chapter 6

Find the indicated real nth root(s) of a.

1. $n = 5, a = -32$

Evaluate the expression without using a calculator.

2. $\sqrt[3]{729}$
3. $\sqrt[3]{343}$
4. Evaluate $\sqrt[5]{-748}$ using a calculator. Round the result to two decimal places if appropriate.
5. In physics, transitional kinetic energy E (in Joules) is given by the equation $E = \frac{1}{2}mv^2$, where m represents the mass (in kilograms), and v the velocity (in meters per second). Find the velocity of a thrown baseball at time of release whose mass is 0.148 kg, and whose transitional kinetic energy is equal to 90.65 Joules.

Simplify the expression. Assume all variables are positive.

6. $\dfrac{27^{-1/3}}{27^{-4/3}}$
7. $\sqrt{80} - \sqrt{245}$
8. $\sqrt[3]{-125x^3}$
9. $\dfrac{4y^{2.7}}{y^{1.35}}$

Let $f(x) = x^2 - 4$, and $g(x) = -x^3$. Perform the indicated operation and state the domain.

10. $f(x) - g(x)$
11. $g(x) \cdot g(x)$
12. $g(f(x))$
13. A rental car costs \$35 for a 1-day rental, plus \$.05 per mile. The total cost (in dollars) is given by the equation $C(m) = 35 + 0.05m$, where m represents the mileage. The car averages 32 miles per gallon, and so the total mileage is given by the equation $m(g) = 32g$. Find $C(m(g))$, and find the total cost after using 8 gallons of gas.

Verify that f and g are inverse functions.

14. $f(x) = 3x - 4, g(x) = \dfrac{x + 4}{3}$
15. $f(x) = 2x^5, g(x) = \sqrt[5]{\frac{x}{2}}$

Answers

1. -2
2. 9
3. 7
4. -3.76
5. 35 m/s
6. 27
7. $-3\sqrt{5}$
8. $-5x$
9. $4y^{1.35}$
10. $x^3 + x^2 - 4$; all real numbers
11. x^6; all real numbers
12. $-x^6 + 12x^4 - 48x^2 + 64$; all real numbers
13. $C(m(g)) = 35 + 1.6g$; \$47.80
14. $f(g(x)) = x$, $g(f(x)) = x$
15. $f(g(x)) = x$, $g(f(x)) = x$

CHAPTER 6

Chapter Test B *continued*

For use after Chapter 6

Find the inverse of the function.

16. $f(x) = 3x^8, x \le 0$

17. $g(x) = \frac{3}{2}x^3 + 4$

Graph the function. Then state the domain and range.

18. $y = \frac{2}{3}\sqrt{x}$

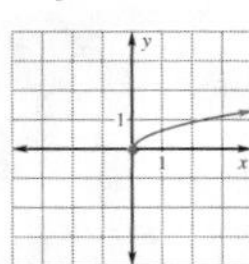

19. $y = -\frac{3}{4}\sqrt[3]{x}$

20. $y = \frac{3}{5}\sqrt{x+4} - 1$

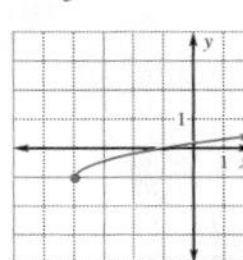

21. $y = -\frac{1}{2}\sqrt[3]{x-2} + 2$

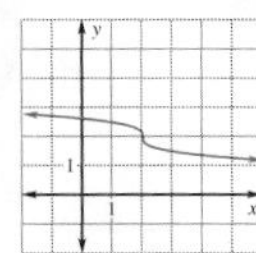

Solve the equation.

22. $\sqrt[5]{4x - 8} = 2$

23. $60 - \frac{1}{20}(x + 75)^{3/2} = 10$

24. $x + 1 = \sqrt{19 - x}$

25. $4\sqrt{x} - 2 = \sqrt{5 - x}$

Answers

16. $f^{-1}(x) = -\sqrt[8]{\frac{x}{3}}$

17. $f^{-1}(x) = \sqrt[3]{\frac{2x - 8}{3}}$

18. See left. domain: $x \ge 0$; range $y \ge 0$

19. See left. domain: all real numbers; range: all real numbers

20. See left. domain: $x \ge -4$; range $y \ge -1$

21. See left. domain: all real numbers; range: all real numbers

22. 10

23. 25

24. 3

25. 1

CHAPTER 6

Standardized Test

For use after Chapter 6

Multiple Choice

1. What is the value of $(-243)^{3/5}$? A

Ⓐ -27 Ⓑ -3
Ⓒ 3 Ⓓ 27

2. What is the solution to $3x^5 + 350 = -379$? B

Ⓐ $-\frac{729}{\sqrt[5]{3}}$ Ⓑ -3
Ⓒ 3 Ⓓ $\frac{729}{\sqrt[5]{3}}$

3. Which expression is the simplest form of $4\sqrt[3]{32} - \sqrt[3]{32}$? B

Ⓐ $3\sqrt[3]{4}$ Ⓑ $6\sqrt[3]{4}$
Ⓒ 6 Ⓓ $16\sqrt[3]{2} - 4$

4. What is the simplified expression of the length of the triangle's hypotenuse? C

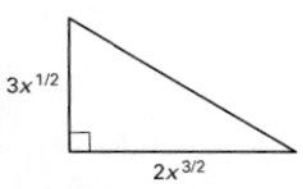

Ⓐ $\sqrt{2x^{3/2} + 3x^{1/2}}$ Ⓑ $2x^{3/2} + 3x^{1/2}$
Ⓒ $\sqrt{4x^3 + 9x}$ Ⓓ $4x^3 + 9x^2$

5. Assuming all variables are positive, what is the simplified form of $-z^2\sqrt{16z^3} + 3\sqrt{36z^7}$? B

Ⓐ $-z^3\sqrt{z}$ Ⓑ $14z^3\sqrt{z}$
Ⓒ $14z^4\sqrt{z}$ Ⓓ $92z^3\sqrt{z}$

6. If $h(t) = t^{2/3} - 9$ and $j(t) = 3t + 5t^{2/3}$, what is $h(t) - j(t)$? A

Ⓐ $-4t^{2/3} - 3t - 9$ Ⓑ $4t^{2/3} + 3t + 9$
Ⓒ $3t + 6t^{4/3}$ Ⓓ $-7t^{7/3} - 9$

7. What is $g(f(x))$ if $f(x) = 3x^2$ and $g(x) = 2x^{1/2}$? B

Ⓐ $x\sqrt{6}$ Ⓑ $2x\sqrt{3}$
Ⓒ $6\sqrt{x}$ Ⓓ $6x$

8. Given $u(x) = \sqrt{4x - 1}$ and, $v(x) = x - 5$ what is the domain of $u(v(x))$? D

Ⓐ All real numbers Ⓑ $x \ge 0$
Ⓒ $x \ge \frac{1}{4}$ Ⓓ $x \ge \frac{21}{4}$

9. Which function represents the inverse of the graph shown? C

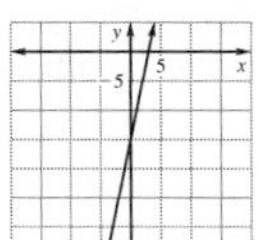

Ⓐ $y = -5x + 3$ Ⓑ $y = \frac{1}{5}x - 3$
Ⓒ $y = \frac{1}{5}x + 3$ Ⓓ $y = 5x + 3$

10. What is the inverse of the power function $g(t) = -\frac{8}{27}t^3$? C

Ⓐ $h(t) = -\frac{2}{3}\sqrt[3]{t}$ Ⓑ $h(t) = -\frac{8}{27}\sqrt[3]{t}$
Ⓒ $h(t) = -\frac{3}{2}\sqrt[3]{t}$ Ⓓ $h(t) = -\frac{3}{2}t$

11. Which of the following pairs of functions are *not* inverses of one another? C

Ⓐ $u(x) = x - 2$; $v(x) = x + 2$
Ⓑ $u(x) = 5x - 1$; $v(x) = \frac{1}{5}x + \frac{1}{5}$
Ⓒ $u(x) = x^3 + 1$; $v(x) = \sqrt[3]{x} - 1$
Ⓓ $u(x) = \sqrt{x - 2}$; $v(x) = x^2 + 2$

CHAPTER 6

Standardized Test *continued*

For use after Chapter 6

12. The graph of $y = \sqrt{x}$ is shifted 2 units up and 3 units to the left. Which is the equation of the translated function? D

Ⓐ $y = \sqrt{x - 2} - 3$
Ⓑ $y = \sqrt{x + 2} - 3$
Ⓒ $y = \sqrt{x + 2} + 3$
Ⓓ $y = \sqrt{x + 3} + 2$

13. What are the domain and range of the function $y = 5\sqrt{x - 2}$? D

Ⓐ Domain: all real numbers; range: all real numbers
Ⓑ Domain: $x \ge 2$; range: all real numbers
Ⓒ Domain: all real numbers; range: $y \ge 0$
Ⓓ Domain: $x \ge 2$; range: $y \ge 0$

14. What is(are) the solution(s) to $x - 2 = \sqrt{2x - 1}$? B

Ⓐ $x = 1$ Ⓑ $x = 5$
Ⓒ $x = 1$ and 5 Ⓓ No solution

Gridded Answer

15. What is the solution of $(x - 5)^{2/3} - 2 = 2$?

		1	3

Short Response

16. You are digging a garden in your backyard. You would like the length to be 5 feet greater than the width. Determine the function $A(x)$ to calculate the area of the garden. What should the dimensions of the garden be if you would like your garden to cover 104 square feet of ground?
$A(x) = x(x - 5)$; 13 ft by 8 ft

Extended Response

17. The XYZ Widget Company determines that it costs them $4 to produce each widget plus an initial fixed cost of $2250. See below.

a. Determine the cost function $C(x)$ for producing x number of widgets.

b. Unfortunately, the sharp increase in fuel prices have led the company's pricing analysts to believe that costs will increase overall by 10%. Determine the function $f(x)$ which represents a 10% increase.

c. Which composition of functions makes sense to calculate the total cost with the 10% increase, $C(f(x))$ or $f(C(x))$? Why?

d. How much will it cost the company to produce 100,000 widgets before and after the increase?

17. a. $C(x) = 4x + 2250$ **b.** $f(x) = 1.10x$
c. $f(C(x))$, because the 10% increase will not affect the $2250 otherwise.
d. before: $402,250; after: $442,475

CHAPTER 6

Alternative Assessment and Math Journal

For use after Chapter 6

Journal **1.** Why do students often think it is not possible to multiply or divide two radicals with different indices ($\sqrt[m]{a} \cdot \sqrt[n]{a}$ or $\frac{\sqrt[m]{a}}{\sqrt[n]{a}}$, when $m \ne n$)? How do rational exponents help you to multiply or divide two radicals with different indices? Write two examples to support your answer.

Multi-Step Problem **2.** Your school is putting on a prom fashion show, and you are in charge of building a platform to serve as a stage. The main part of the stage is a rectangle, and the "runway" is a square. The length and width of the main part of the stage are 3 times and 2 times the side length of the runway, respectively.

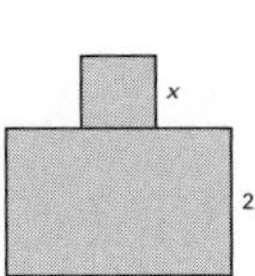

a. Write a function $A_1(x)$ for the area of the main part of the stage and a function $A_2(x)$ for the area of the runway.

b. Write a function $A(x)$ for the area of the entire stage.

c. Graph the function A. How can you use the graph to explain why the inverse of A is not a function?

d. **Writing** How can you restrict the domain of A so that A^{-1} is a function? Why does this restriction make sense in the context of the problem?

e. Find the inverse of A, assuming that its domain is restricted as described in part (d). What information can you obtain from the inverse function?

f. You have 700 square feet of plywood to make the stage floor. Use the inverse from part (e) to find the dimensions of the runway and the main part of the stage.

1. Complete answers should include: an explanation that because the properties of radicals require two radicals to have the same index, students often think that it is not possible to multiply or divide two radicals with different indices; an explanation that rewriting both radicals in rational exponent form allows for the application of the product or quotient property; two examples that illustrate how to use rational exponents to multiply and divide two radicals with different indices.

2. a. $A_1(x) = 6x^2$; $A_2(x) = x^2$ **b.** $A(x) = 7x^2$

c.

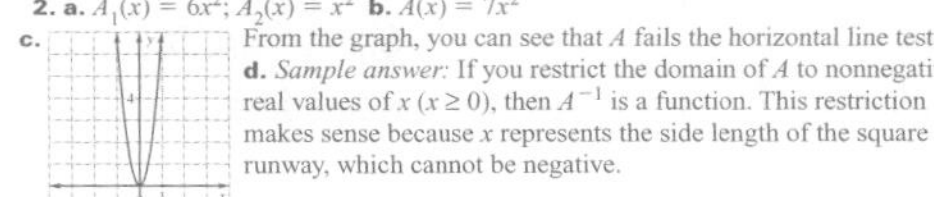

From the graph, you can see that A fails the horizontal line test. **d.** *Sample answer:* If you restrict the domain of A to nonnegative real values of x ($x \ge 0$), then A^{-1} is a function. This restriction makes sense because x represents the side length of the square runway, which cannot be negative.

e. $x = \sqrt{\frac{1}{7}A}$; The inverse function gives the side length of the runway in terms of the area of the entire stage. **f.** Runway: 10 ft by 10 ft, Main part of stage: 30 ft by 20 ft

PLAN AND PREPARE

Main Ideas

First, students will learn the meaning of *n*th roots and rational exponents, how to interchange rational exponent notation and radical notation, and how to apply the properties of rational exponents. Next, they will learn to perform function operations, including composition. Then, they will learn how to determine whether a given function has an inverse that is also a function. Finally, students will learn to graph square root and cube root functions and to solve radical equations.

Prerequisite Skills

- Simplifying expressions involving exponents
- Solving equations for the dependent variable
- Graphing polynomial functions

Additional resources for reviewing prerequisite skills are:

- Skills Review Handbook, pp. 975–1009
- @HomeTutor

6 Rational Exponents and Radical Functions

MA-HS-1.3.1
MA-HS-5.2.1
MA-HS-5.1.5
MA-HS-5.1.5

Before

In previous chapters, you learned the following skills, which you'll use in Chapter 6: simplifying expressions involving exponents, rewriting equations, and graphing polynomial functions.

Prerequisite Skills

VOCABULARY CHECK

Copy and complete the statement.

1. The **square roots** of 81 are _?_ and _?_. −9, 9
2. In the expression 2^5, the **exponent** is _?_. 5
3. For the polynomial function whose graph is shown, the sign of the **leading coefficient** is _?_. positive

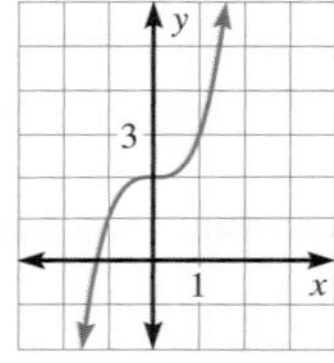

SKILLS CHECK

Simplify the expression. *(Review p. 330 for 6.2.)*

4. $\dfrac{5x^2y}{15x^3y^{-1}}$ $\dfrac{y^2}{3x}$
5. $\dfrac{32x^{-3}y^4}{24x^{-3}y^{-2}} \cdot \dfrac{3x}{9y}$ $\dfrac{4xy^5}{9}$
6. $(2x^5y^{-3})^{-3}$ $\dfrac{y^9}{8x^{15}}$

Solve the equation for *y*. *(Review p. 26 for 6.4.)*

7. $-2x - 5y = 10$ $y = -\frac{2}{5}x - 2$
8. $x - \frac{1}{3}y = -1$ $y = 3x + 3$
9. $8x - 4xy = 3$ $y = -\frac{3}{4x} + 2$

Graph the polynomial function. *(Review p. 337 for 6.5.)* 10–12. See margin.

10. $f(x) = x^3 - 4x + 6$
11. $f(x) = -x^5 + 7x^2 + 2$
12. $f(x) = x^4 - 4x^2 + x$

412

Chapter Planning Guide

Chapter 6 Resource Book
- Teaching Guide/Lesson Plan (pp. 3, 16, 27, 40, 51, 64)
- Project with Rubric (p. 78)

Assessment and Intervention
- Assessment Book (pp. 76–90)
- Benchmark Tests
- Remediation Book

Interactive Technology
- Easy Planner
- Power Presentations CD-ROM
- Activity Generator CD-ROM
- Animated Algebra
- Test Generator CD-ROM
- Online Quizzes
- eWorkbook
- eEdition
- @HomeTutor

Resources for English Learners
- Quick Reference for English Learners
- Spanish Study Guide
- Multi-Language Visual Glossary
- Student Resources in Spanish

Now

In Chapter 6, you will apply the big ideas listed below and reviewed in the Chapter Summary on page 465. You will also use the key vocabulary listed below.

Big Ideas

1. **Using rational exponents**
2. **Performing function operations and finding inverse functions**
3. **Graphing radical functions and solving radical equations**

KEY VOCABULARY

- *n*th root of *a*, *p. 414*
- index of a radical, *p. 414*
- simplest form of a radical, *p. 422*
- like radicals, *p. 422*
- power function, *p. 428*
- composition, *p. 430*
- inverse relation, *p. 438*
- inverse function, *p. 438*
- radical function, *p. 446*
- radical equation, *p. 452*

Why?

You can use a radical function to model the time you are suspended in the air during a jump. For example, the hang time of a basketball player can be modeled by a radical function.

Animated Algebra

The animation illustrated below for Exercise 60 on page 458 helps you answer this question: What is the relationship between the height of a jump and the time the jumper is suspended in air?

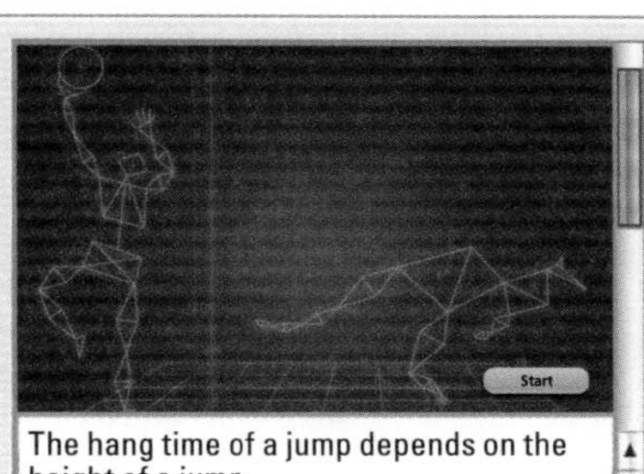

The hang time of a jump depends on the height of a jump.

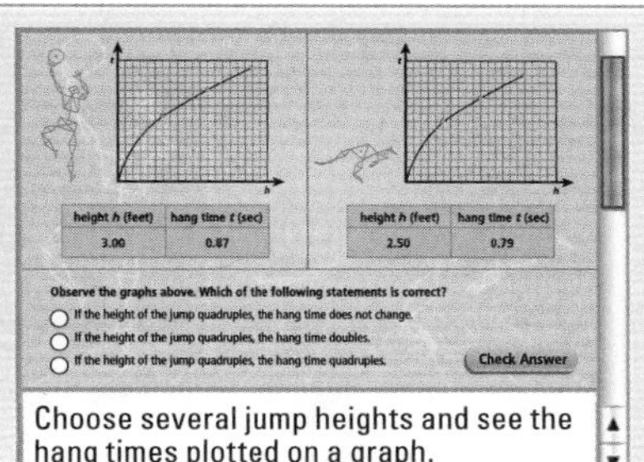

Choose several jump heights and see the hang times plotted on a graph.

Animated Algebra at classzone.com

Other animations for Chapter 6: pages 431, 444, 448, and 465

Algebra 2 Toolkit

- Reading Strategies for Chapter 6, pp. 19–20
- Differentiated Instruction Notes, pp. 63–66
- English Learners Notes, pp. 111–112
- Inclusion Notes, pp. 145–146
- Teaching Strategies with Sample Worksheets, pp. 163–186
- Using Technology in the Classroom, pp. 187–192
- Tips for New Teachers, pp. 203–204
- Math Background Notes, pp. 239–241
- Pre-AP Strategies and Copymasters, pp. 321–322, 389–398
- Teacher Survival Activities, pp. 479–480, 507–508
- Bulletin Board Idea, p. 530
- Teacher Tool Transparencies, following p. 538

10. 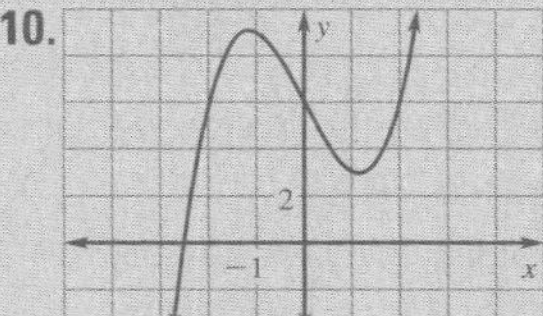

11. 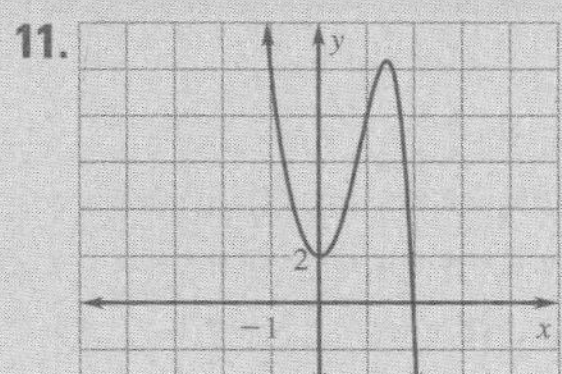

12. 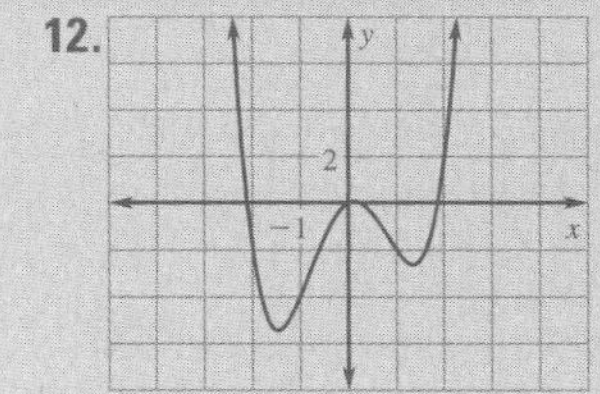

1 PLAN AND PREPARE

Warm-Up Exercises

Transparency Available

Evaluate without using a calculator.

1. $\sqrt{121}$ 11
2. 5^{-2} $\frac{1}{25}$
3. Solve $(x + 7)^2 = 24$. Write answers with radicals in simplified form. $-7 \pm 2\sqrt{6}$
4. A ball has a surface area s of 1253 square inches. Use the formula $r = \frac{1}{3.54}\sqrt{s}$ to find the radius r of the ball. about 10 in.

Notetaking Guide

Transparency Available

Promotes interactive learning and notetaking skills, pp. 162–164.

Pacing

Basic: 1 day

Average: 1 day

Advanced: 1 day

Block: 0.5 block with 6.2

- See *Teaching Guide/Lesson Plan.*

2 FOCUS AND MOTIVATE

Essential Question

Big Idea 1, p. 413

What is the relationship between nth roots and rational exponents? **Tell students they will learn how to answer this question by rewriting radical and exponential expressions.**

6.1 Evaluate nth Roots and Use Rational Exponents

 MA-HS-1.3.1

Before You evaluated square roots and used properties of exponents.

Now You will evaluate nth roots and study rational exponents.

Why? So you can find the radius of a spherical object, as in Ex. 60.

Key Vocabulary
- ***n*th root of *a***
- **index of a radical**

MA-HS-1.3.1
Students will solve real-world and mathematical problems to specified accuracy levels by simplifying expressions with real numbers involving addition, subtraction, multiplication, division, absolute value, integer exponents, roots (square, cube) and factorials. DOK 2

You can extend the concept of a square root to other types of roots. For example, 2 is a cube root of 8 because $2^3 = 8$. In general, for an integer n greater than 1, if $b^n = a$, then b is an ***n*th root of *a***. An nth root of a is written as $\sqrt[n]{a}$ where n is the **index** of the radical.

You can also write an nth root of a as a power of a. If you assume the power of a power property applies to rational exponents, then the following is true:

$$(a^{1/2})^2 = a^{(1/2)\cdot 2} = a^1 = a$$
$$(a^{1/3})^3 = a^{(1/3)\cdot 3} = a^1 = a$$
$$(a^{1/4})^4 = a^{(1/4)\cdot 4} = a^1 = a$$

Because $a^{1/2}$ is a number whose square is a, you can write $\sqrt{a} = a^{1/2}$. Similarly, $\sqrt[3]{a} = a^{1/3}$ and $\sqrt[4]{a} = a^{1/4}$. In general, $\sqrt[n]{a} = a^{1/n}$ for any integer n greater than 1.

KEY CONCEPT *For Your Notebook*

Real nth Roots of a

Let n be an integer $(n > 1)$ and let a be a real number.

	***n* is an even integer.**		***n* is an odd integer.**
$a < 0$	No real nth roots.	$a < 0$	One real nth root: $\sqrt[n]{a} = a^{1/n}$
$a = 0$	One real nth root: $\sqrt[n]{0} = 0$	$a = 0$	One real nth root: $\sqrt[n]{0} = 0$
$a > 0$	Two real nth roots: $\pm\sqrt[n]{a} = \pm a^{1/n}$	$a > 0$	One real nth root: $\sqrt[n]{a} = a^{1/n}$

EXAMPLE 1 Find nth roots

Find the indicated real nth root(s) of a.

a. $n = 3, a = -216$ **b.** $n = 4, a = 81$

Solution

a. Because $n = 3$ is odd and $a = -216 < 0$, -216 has one real cube root. Because $(-6)^3 = -216$, you can write $\sqrt[3]{-216} = -6$ or $(-216)^{1/3} = -6$.

b. Because $n = 4$ is even and $a = 81 > 0$, 81 has two real fourth roots. Because $3^4 = 81$ and $(-3)^4 = 81$, you can write $\pm\sqrt[4]{81} = \pm 3$ or $\pm 81^{1/4} = \pm 3$.

Resource Planning Guide

Chapter Resource Book
- Teaching Guide/Lesson Plan (pp. 3–4)
- Activity Master (p. 5)
- Practice levels A, B, C (pp. 8–10)
- Study Guide (pp. 11–12)
- Catch-up for Absent Students (p. 13)
- Problem Solving Workshop (p. 14)
- Challenge (p. 15)

Workbooks
- Notetaking Guide (pp. 162–164)
- Practice Workbook (pp. 96–97)

Teaching Options
- **Power Presentations CD-ROM** provides dynamic electronic teaching resources for the classroom.
- **Activity Generator CD-ROM** provides editable activities for all ability levels.

Interactive Technology
- Easy Planner
- Power Presentations CD-ROM
- Activity Generator CD-ROM
- Animated Algebra
- Test Generator CD-ROM
- Online Quiz
- eWorkbook
- eEdition
- @HomeTutor

Resources for English Learners
- Quick Reference for English Learners
- Spanish Study Guide
- Multi-Language Visual Glossary
- Student Resources in Spanish

See also the *Algebra 2 Toolkit* for more strategies for meeting individual needs.

RATIONAL EXPONENTS A rational exponent does not have to be of the form $\frac{1}{n}$. Other rational numbers such as $\frac{3}{2}$ and $-\frac{1}{2}$ can also be used as exponents. Two properties of rational exponents are shown below.

KEY CONCEPT *For Your Notebook*

Rational Exponents

Let $a^{1/n}$ be an nth root of a, and let m be a positive integer.

$$a^{m/n} = (a^{1/n})^m = (\sqrt[n]{a})^m$$

$$a^{-m/n} = \frac{1}{a^{m/n}} = \frac{1}{(a^{1/n})^m} = \frac{1}{(\sqrt[n]{a})^m}, a \neq 0$$

EXAMPLE 2 Evaluate expressions with rational exponents

Evaluate (a) $16^{3/2}$ and (b) $32^{-3/5}$.

Solution

	Rational Exponent Form	Radical Form
a.	$16^{3/2} = (16^{1/2})^3 = 4^3 = 64$	$16^{3/2} = (\sqrt{16})^3 = 4^3 = 64$
b.	$32^{-3/5} = \frac{1}{32^{3/5}} = \frac{1}{(32^{1/5})^3} = \frac{1}{2^3} = \frac{1}{8}$	$32^{-3/5} = \frac{1}{32^{3/5}} = \frac{1}{(\sqrt[5]{32})^3} = \frac{1}{2^3} = \frac{1}{8}$

EXAMPLE 3 Approximate roots with a calculator

	Expression	Keystrokes	Display
a.	$9^{1/5}$	9  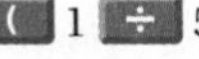 1  5) ENTER	1.551845574
b.	$12^{3/8}$	12  3  8 	2.539176951
c.	$(\sqrt[4]{7})^3 = 7^{3/4}$	7  3  4) ENTER	4.303517071

AVOID ERRORS
Be sure to use parentheses to enclose a rational exponent: 9^(1/5) ≈ 1.552. Without them, the calculator evaluates a power and then divides: 9^1/5 = 1.8.

GUIDED PRACTICE for Examples 1, 2, and 3

Find the indicated real nth root(s) of a.

1. $n = 4, a = 625$ ± 5
2. $n = 6, a = 64$ ± 2
3. $n = 3, a = -64$ -4
4. $n = 5, a = 243$ 3

Evaluate the expression without using a calculator.

5. $4^{5/2}$ 32
6. $9^{-1/2}$ $\frac{1}{3}$
7. $81^{3/4}$ 27
8. $1^{7/8}$ 1

Evaluate the expression using a calculator. Round the result to two decimal places when appropriate.

9. $4^{2/5}$ 1.74
10. $64^{-2/3}$ 0.06
11. $(\sqrt[4]{16})^5$ 32
12. $(\sqrt[3]{-30})^2$ 9.65

Motivating the Lesson

If you are a skier, you want to make sure that you will be safe from frostbite. The Wind Chill Temperature Index adopted by the National Weather Service in 2001 uses a formula that contains rational exponents to calculate the wind chill temperature for a given temperature and wind speed, and to find frostbite dangers.

3 TEACH

Extra Example 1

Find the indicated real nth root(s) of a.

a. $n = 5, a = -32$ -2

b. $n = 6, a = 1$ ± 1

Extra Example 2

Evaluate.

a. $125^{2/3}$ 25

b. $8^{-4/3}$ $\frac{1}{16}$

Key Questions to Ask for Example 2

- In part (a) of Example 2, can you also evaluate $16^{3/2}$ as $(16^3)^{1/2}$? Yes; $(16^3)^{1/2} = 4096^{1/2} = \sqrt{4096} = 64$.
- Why do you think $16^{3/2}$ is calculated as $(16^{1/2})^3$, rather than as $(16^3)^{1/2}$, in this example? Possible answer: It is easier to work with smaller numbers.

Extra Example 3

Evaluate the expression using a calculator. Round the result to two decimal places when appropriate.

a. $22^{1/4}$ 2.17

b. $35^{5/6}$ 19.35

c. $(\sqrt[5]{11})^4$ 6.81

Differentiated Instruction

Inclusion Students may attempt to memorize these rules for rational exponents and, without realizing, interchange the variables m and n in their calculations. Have students use other variables or symbols, or have them create examples by replacing a, m, and n with positive integers until they are comfortable with the values they represent.

See also the *Algebra 2 Toolkit* for more strategies.

Extra Example 4

Solve the equation.

a. $6x^3 = 384$ $x = 4$

b. $(x - 8)^5 = 100$ $x \approx 10.51$

Key Questions to Ask for Example 4

- Under what conditions will an equation of the form $(x - k)^n = a$ have no real solutions? if n is even and a is negative
- Under what conditions will an equation of the form $(x - k)^n = a$ have exactly one real solution? if n is odd, or if n is even and $a = 0$

Extra Example 5

An exercise ball is made from 7854 square centimeters of material. Find the diameter of the ball. (Use the formula $S = 4\pi r^2$ for the surface area of a sphere.) about 50 cm

Closing the Lesson

Have students summarize the major points of the lesson and answer the Essential Question: What is the relationship between nth roots and rational exponents?

- The concept of square roots can be extended to cube roots, fourth roots, and so on.
- Radical expressions can be written in exponential form by using rational exponents.

The nth root of a real number a can also be written as a to the $\frac{1}{n}$ power.

EXAMPLE 4 Solve equations using *n*th roots

Solve the equation.

a. $4x^5 = 128$

$x^5 = 32$ **Divide each side by 4.**

$x = \sqrt[5]{32}$ **Take fifth root of each side.**

$x = 2$ **Simplify.**

b. $(x - 3)^4 = 21$

$x - 3 = \pm\sqrt[4]{21}$ **Take fourth roots of each side.**

$x = \pm\sqrt[4]{21} + 3$ **Add 3 to each side.**

$x = \sqrt[4]{21} + 3$ or $x = -\sqrt[4]{21} + 3$ **Write solutions separately.**

$x \approx 5.14$ or $x \approx 0.86$ **Use a calculator.**

AVOID ERRORS
When n is even and $a > 0$, be sure to consider both the positive and negative nth roots of a.

EXAMPLE 5 Use *n*th roots in problem solving

BIOLOGY A study determined that the weight w (in grams) of coral cod near Palawan Island, Philippines, can be approximated using the model

$$w = 0.0167\ell^3$$

where ℓ is the coral cod's length (in centimeters). Estimate the length of a coral cod that weighs 200 grams.

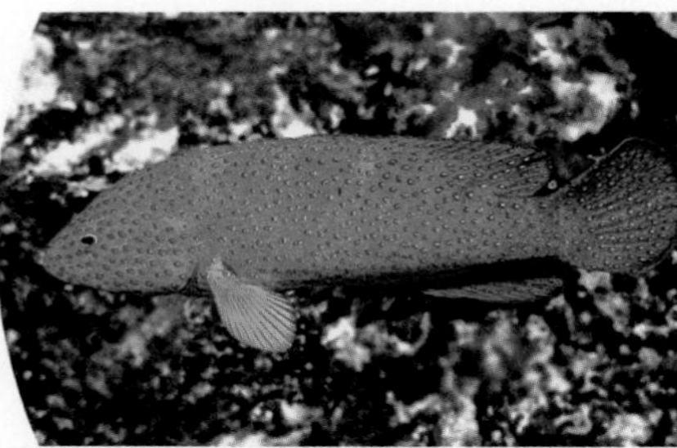

Solution

$w = 0.0167\ell^3$ **Write model for weight.**

$200 = 0.0167\ell^3$ **Substitute 200 for w.**

$11{,}976 \approx \ell^3$ **Divide each side by 0.0167.**

$\sqrt[3]{11{,}976} \approx \ell$ **Take cube root of each side.**

$22.9 \approx \ell$ **Use a calculator.**

▶ A coral cod that weighs 200 grams is about 23 centimeters long.

GUIDED PRACTICE for Examples 4 and 5

Solve the equation. Round the result to two decimal places when appropriate.

13. $x^3 = 64$ 4

14. $\frac{1}{2}x^5 = 512$ 4

15. $3x^2 = 108$ ± 6

16. $\frac{1}{4}x^3 = 2$ 2

17. $(x - 2)^3 = -14$ -0.41

18. $(x + 5)^4 = 16$ $-7, -3$

19. WHAT IF? Use the information from Example 5 to estimate the length of a coral cod that has the given weight.

a. 275 grams about 25 cm **b.** 340 grams about 27 cm **c.** 450 grams about 30 cm

6.1 EXERCISES

HOMEWORK KEY

○ = **WORKED-OUT SOLUTIONS** on p. WS12 for Exs. 9, 25, and 63

★ = **STANDARDIZED TEST PRACTICE** Exs. 2, 33, 46, 47, and 65

SKILL PRACTICE

A

1. **VOCABULARY** Copy and complete: In the expression $\sqrt[4]{10{,}000}$, the number 4 is called the _?_. index

2. ★ **WRITING** *Explain* how the sign of a determines the number of real fourth roots of a and the number of real fifth roots of a. See margin.

EXAMPLE 1 on p. 414 for Exs. 3–20

Fourth roots: if $a < 0$, no real roots; if $a = 0$, one real root = 0; if $a > 0$, two real roots; fifth roots: if $a < 0$, one real root; if $a = 0$, one real root = 0; if $a > 0$, one real root.

MATCHING EXPRESSIONS Match the expression in rational exponent notation with the equivalent expression in radical notation.

3. $2^{1/3}$ C
4. $2^{3/2}$ A
5. $2^{2/3}$ D
6. $2^{1/2}$ B

A. $(\sqrt{2})^3$
B. $\sqrt{2}$
C. $\sqrt[3]{2}$
D. $(\sqrt[3]{2})^2$

USING RATIONAL EXPONENT NOTATION Rewrite the expression using rational exponent notation.

7. $\sqrt[3]{12}$ $12^{1/3}$
8. $\sqrt[5]{8}$ $8^{1/5}$
9. $(\sqrt[3]{10})^7$ $10^{7/3}$
10. $(\sqrt[8]{15})^3$ $15^{3/8}$

USING RADICAL NOTATION Rewrite the expression using radical notation.

11. $5^{1/4}$ $\sqrt[4]{5}$
12. $7^{1/3}$ $\sqrt[3]{7}$
13. $14^{2/5}$ $(\sqrt[5]{14})^2$
14. $21^{9/4}$ $(\sqrt[4]{21})^9$

FINDING *N*TH ROOTS Find the indicated real *n*th root(s) of *a*.

15. $n = 2, a = 64$ ± 8
16. $n = 3, a = -27$ -3
17. $n = 4, a = 0$ 0
18. $n = 3, a = 343$ 7
19. $n = 4, a = -16$ no real roots
20. $n = 5, a = -32$ -2

EXAMPLE 2 on p. 415 for Exs. 21–33

EVALUATING EXPRESSIONS Evaluate the expression without using a calculator.

21. $\sqrt[6]{64}$ 2
22. $8^{1/3}$ 2
23. $16^{3/2}$ 64
24. $\sqrt[3]{-125}$ -5
25. $27^{2/3}$ 9
26. $(-243)^{1/5}$ -3
27. $(\sqrt[3]{8})^{-2}$ $\frac{1}{4}$
28. $(\sqrt[3]{-64})^4$ 256
29. $(\sqrt[4]{16})^{-7}$ $\frac{1}{128}$
30. $25^{3/2}$ 125
31. $64^{-2/3}$ $\frac{1}{16}$
32. $\frac{1}{81^{-3/4}}$ 27

33. ★ **MULTIPLE CHOICE** What is the value of $128^{5/7}$? C

Ⓐ 8 Ⓑ 16 Ⓒ 32 Ⓓ 64

EXAMPLE 3 on p. 415 for Exs. 34–46

APPROXIMATING ROOTS Evaluate the expression using a calculator. Round the result to two decimals places when appropriate.

34. $\sqrt[5]{32{,}768}$ 8
35. $\sqrt[7]{1695}$ 2.89
36. $\sqrt[9]{-230}$ -1.83
37. $85^{1/6}$ 2.10
38. $25^{-1/3}$ 0.34
39. $20{,}736^{1/4}$ 12
40. $(\sqrt[4]{187})^3$ 50.57
41. $(\sqrt{6})^{-5}$ 0.01
42. $(\sqrt[5]{-8})^8$ 27.86
43. $86^{-5/6}$ 0.02
44. $1974^{2/7}$ 8.74
45. $\frac{1}{(-17)^{3/5}}$ -0.18

46. ★ **MULTIPLE CHOICE** Which expression has the greatest value? B

Ⓐ $27^{3/5}$ Ⓑ $5^{3/2}$ Ⓒ $\sqrt[3]{81}$ Ⓓ $(\sqrt[3]{2})^8$

B

47. ★ **OPEN-ENDED MATH** Write two different expressions of the form $a^{1/n}$ that equal 3, where a is a real number and n is an integer greater than 1. *Sample answer:* $27^{1/3}$, $81^{1/4}$

4 PRACTICE AND APPLY

Assignment Guide

Answer Transparencies available for all exercises

Basic:
Day 1: EP p. 1013 Exs. 33–36
pp. 417–419
Exs. 1–6, 7–19 odd, 21–25, 33–37, 46–51, 60–64, 67

Average:
Day 1: pp. 417–419
Exs. 1, 2, 8–20 even, 25–28, 33, 38–41, 46–49, 50–58 even, 60–65, 68

Advanced:
Day 1: pp. 417–419
Exs. 1, 2, 10, 14, 19, 20, 29–33, 42–47, 50–66*

Block:
pp. 417–419
Exs. 1, 2, 8–20 even, 25–28, 33, 38–41, 46–49, 50–58 even, 60–65, 68 (with 6.2)

Differentiated Instruction

See *Algebra 2 Best Practices Toolkit* for suggestions on addressing the needs of a diverse classroom.

Homework Check

For a quick check of student understanding of key concepts, go over the following exercises:

Basic: 8, 22, 36, 50, 60
Average: 12, 26, 40, 54, 61
Advanced: 18, 30, 44, 56, 61

Extra Practice

- Student Edition, p. 1015
- Chapter 6 Resource Book: Practice levels A, B, C, pp. 8–10

Practice Worksheet

An easily-readable reduced practice page (with answers) for this lesson can be found on p. 412C.

Avoiding Common Errors

Exercises 13–14 Some students may incorrectly rewrite $14^{2/5}$ as $(\sqrt{14})^5$ and $21^{9/4}$ as $(\sqrt[9]{21})^4$. If they have trouble remembering which number in a rational exponent is the power and which is the root, tell them to look at square roots, which are more familiar than other roots. Have them compare $9^{2/1} = 9^2 = 81$ with $9^{1/2} = \sqrt{9} = 3$. This should help them master the idea that a rational exponent represents "power over root."

Mathematical Reasoning

Exercises 15–20 Some students may ask why, since a positive number has 2 square roots, it doesn't have 3 cube roots, 4 fourth roots, and so on. Tell them that this is an excellent question and shows they are really thinking. Explain that in this lesson, we are finding only *real* roots. Explain to your students that although they learned to find square roots of negative numbers in Chapter 4, methods for finding imaginary third and higher roots require trigonometry, and that this is something they will learn to do in a more advanced course.

59b.

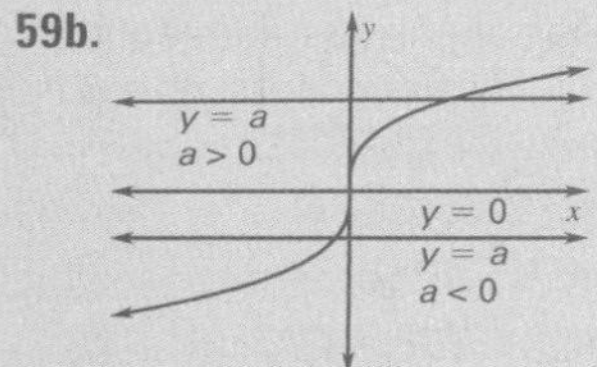

EXAMPLE 4 on p. 416 for Exs. 48–58

ERROR ANALYSIS ***Describe*** **and correct the error in solving the equation.**

48.

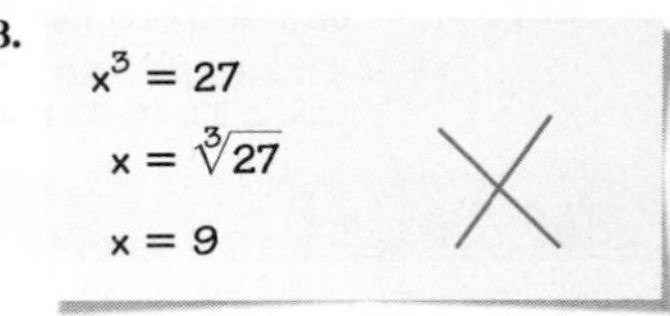

The cube root of 27 is 3, not 9; $x = 3$.

49.

$x^4 = 81$

$x = \sqrt[4]{81}$

$x = 3$

There are two real solutions; $x = \pm 3$.

SOLVING EQUATIONS **Solve the equation. Round the result to two decimal places when appropriate.**

50. $x^3 = 125$ 5	**51.** $5x^3 = 1080$ 6	**52.** $x^6 + 36 = 100$ ±2
53. $(x - 5)^4 = 256$ 1, 9	**54.** $x^5 = -48$ −2.17	**55.** $7x^4 = 56$ ±1.68
56. $x^3 + 40 = 25$ −2.47	**57.** $(x + 10)^5 = 70$ −7.66	**58.** $x^6 - 34 = 181$ ±2.45

59a. For $a > 0$, the line $y = a$ intersects the graph of $y = x^n$ twice giving two real solutions. For $a = 0$, the line $y = a$ intersects the graph of $y = x^n$ once giving one real solution. For $a < 0$, the line $y = a$ does not intersect the graph of $y = x^n$ giving no real solutions.

C **59.** **CHALLENGE** The general shape of the graph of $y = x^n$, where n is a positive *even* integer, is shown in red.

a. *Explain* how the graph justifies the results in the Key Concept box on page 414 when n is a positive *even* integer.

b. Draw a similar graph that justifies the results in the Key Concept box when n is a positive *odd* integer. See margin.

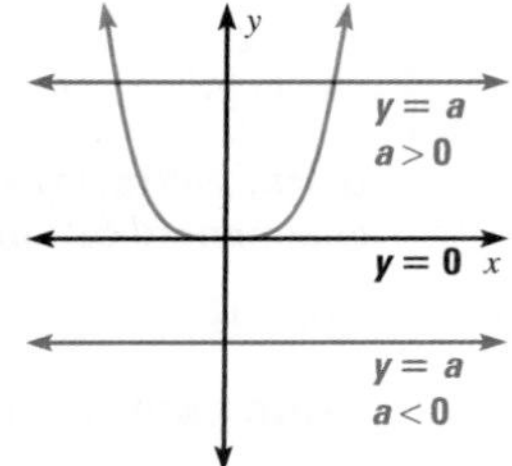

PROBLEM SOLVING

EXAMPLE 5 A on p. 416 for Exs. 60–65

60. SHOT PUT The shot used in men's shot put has a volume of about 905 cubic centimeters. Find the radius of the shot. (*Hint:* Use the formula $V = \frac{4}{3}\pi r^3$ for the volume of a sphere.) about 6 cm

@HomeTutor for problem solving help at classzone.com

61. BOWLING A bowling ball has a surface area of about 232 square inches. Find the radius of the bowling ball. (*Hint:* Use the formula $S = 4\pi r^2$ for the surface area of a sphere.) about 4.30 in.

@HomeTutor for problem solving help at classzone.com

62. INFLATION If the average price of an item increases from p_1 to p_2 over a period of n years, the annual rate of inflation r (expressed as a decimal) is given by $r = \left(\frac{p_2}{p_1}\right)^{1/n} - 1$. Find the rate of inflation for each item in the table. Write each answer as a percent rounded to the nearest tenth. butter: 2.7%, chicken: 2.3%, eggs: 1.8%, sugar: 4.0%

Item	Price in 1950	Price in 1990
Butter (lb)	\$.7420	\$2.195
Chicken (lb)	\$.4430	\$1.087
Eggs (dozen)	\$.6710	\$1.356
Sugar (lb)	\$.0936	\$.4560

(63.) MULTI-STEP PROBLEM The power p (in horsepower) used by a fan with rotational speed s (in revolutions per minute) can be modeled by the formula $p = ks^3$ for some constant k. A certain fan uses 1.2 horsepower when its speed is 1700 revolutions per minute. First find the value of k for this fan. Then find the speed of the fan if it uses 1.5 horsepower. $\frac{3}{12,282,500,000}$; about 1800 RPM

○ = WORKED-OUT SOLUTIONS on p. WS1   ★ = STANDARDIZED TEST PRACTICE

64. **WATER RATE** A *weir* is a dam that is built across a river to regulate the flow of water. The flow rate Q (in cubic feet per second) can be calculated using the formula $Q = 3.367\ell h^{3/2}$ where ℓ is the length (in feet) of the bottom of the spillway and h is the depth (in feet) of the water on the spillway. Determine the flow rate of a weir with a spillway that is 20 feet long and has a water depth of 5 feet. **about 753 ft^3 per sec**

B 65. ★ **EXTENDED RESPONSE** Some games use dice in the shape of regular polyhedra. You are designing dice and want them all to have the same volume as a cube with an edge length of 16 millimeters.

Name	Tetrahedron	Octahedron	Dodecahedron	Icosahedron
Number of faces	4	8	12	20
Volume formula	$V = 0.118x^3$	$V = 0.471x^3$	$V = 7.663x^3$	$V = 2.182x^3$

a. Find the volume of a cube with an edge length of 16 millimeters. **4096 mm^3**

b. Find the edge length x for each of the polyhedra shown in the table.

tetrahedron:
t 32.6 mm,
hedron:
t 20.6 mm,
ecahedron:
t 8.12 mm,
ahedron:
t 12.3 mm

c. Does the polyhedron with the greatest number of faces have the smallest edge length? *Explain.* **It decreases.**

C 66. **CHALLENGE** The mass of the particles that a river can transport is proportional to the sixth power of the speed of the river. A certain river normally flows at a speed of 1 meter per second. What must its speed be in order to transport particles that are twice as massive as usual? 10 times as massive? 100 times as massive? **2^6, 10^6, 100^6**

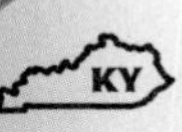
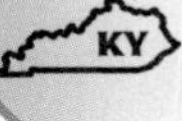

TEST PRACTICE at classzone.com

KENTUCKY MIXED REVIEW

67. Which expression is equivalent to $2x(4x + 1) - (7x + 3)(x - 4)$? **D**

Ⓐ $x^2 - 23x - 12$ Ⓑ $15x^2 - 23x - 12$

Ⓒ $-x^2 + 27x + 12$ Ⓓ $x^2 + 27x + 12$

68. Frank digs a trench around the triangular garden shown. What is the approximate length of the trench that he digs? **A**

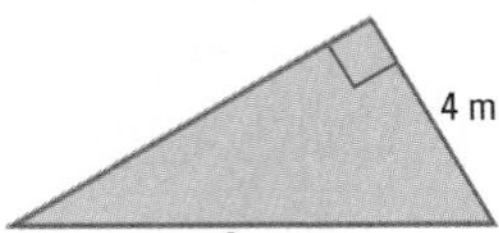

Ⓐ 18.9 m

Ⓑ 19.3 m

Ⓒ 25.9 m

Ⓓ 37.9 m

5 ASSESS AND RETEACH

Daily Homework Quiz

Transparency Available

1. Find the nth roots of a if $n = 4$ and $a = 10{,}000$. **±10**

Evaluate the expression without using a calculator.

2. $49^{-3/2}$ **$\frac{1}{343}$**

3. $(\sqrt[4]{81})^{-1}$ **$\frac{1}{3}$**

Solve the equation. Round the result to two decimal places when appropriate.

4. $6x^5 = -192$ **−2**

5. $(x + 7)^4 = 50$ **−9.66, −4.34**

Available at **classzone.com**

Diagnosis/Remediation

- Practice A, B, C in Chapter 6 Resource Book, pp. 8–10
- Study Guide in Chapter 6 Resource Book, pp. 11–12
- Practice Workbook, pp. 96–97
- @HomeTutor

Challenge

Additional challenge is available in the Chapter 6 Resource Book, p. 15.

1 PLAN AND PREPARE

Warm-Up Exercises

Transparency Available

Simplify the expression.

1. $4^3 \cdot 4^8$ 4^{11}
2. $\frac{8^5}{8^{-4}}$ 8^9
3. $\sqrt{48}$ $4\sqrt{3}$
4. $\sqrt{30} \cdot \sqrt{15}$ $15\sqrt{2}$
5. $\sqrt{80} - \sqrt{20}$ $2\sqrt{5}$

Notetaking Guide

Transparency Available

Promotes interactive learning and notetaking skills, pp. 165–168.

Pacing

Basic: 1 day
Average: 1 day
Advanced: 1 day
Block: 0.5 block with 6.1
- See *Teaching Guide/Lesson Plan.*

2 FOCUS AND MOTIVATE

Essential Question

Big Idea 1, p. 413

How are the properties of rational exponents related to the properties of integer exponents? **Tell students they will learn how to answer this question by using the properties of rational exponents to simplify expressions.**

6.2 Apply Properties of Rational Exponents

KY MA-HS-5.2.1

Before You simplified expressions involving integer exponents.
Now You will simplify expressions involving rational exponents.
Why? So you can find velocities, as in Ex. 84.

Key Vocabulary
- simplest form of a radical
- like radicals

MA-HS-5.2.1
Students will apply order of operations, real number properties (identity, inverse, commutative, associative, distributive, closure) and rules of exponents (integer) to simplify algebraic expressions. DOK 1

The properties of integer exponents you learned in Lesson 5.1 can also be applied to rational exponents.

KEY CONCEPT *For Your Notebook*

Properties of Rational Exponents

Let a and b be real numbers and let m and n be rational numbers. The following properties have the same names as those listed on page 330, but now apply to rational exponents as illustrated.

	Property	Example
1.	$a^m \cdot a^n = a^{m+n}$	$5^{1/2} \cdot 5^{3/2} = 5^{(1/2+3/2)} = 5^2 = 25$
2.	$(a^m)^n = a^{mn}$	$(3^{5/2})^2 = 3^{(5/2 \cdot 2)} = 3^5 = 243$
3.	$(ab)^m = a^m b^m$	$(16 \cdot 9)^{1/2} = 16^{1/2} \cdot 9^{1/2} = 4 \cdot 3 = 12$
4.	$a^{-m} = \frac{1}{a^m}, a \neq 0$	$36^{-1/2} = \frac{1}{36^{1/2}} = \frac{1}{6}$
5.	$\frac{a^m}{a^n} = a^{m-n}, a \neq 0$	$\frac{4^{5/2}}{4^{1/2}} = 4^{(5/2-1/2)} = 4^2 = 16$
6.	$\left(\frac{a}{b}\right)^m = \frac{a^m}{b^m}, b \neq 0$	$\left(\frac{27}{64}\right)^{1/3} = \frac{27^{1/3}}{64^{1/3}} = \frac{3}{4}$

EXAMPLE 1 Use properties of exponents

Use the properties of rational exponents to simplify the expression.

a. $7^{1/4} \cdot 7^{1/2} = 7^{(1/4+1/2)} = 7^{3/4}$

b. $(6^{1/2} \cdot 4^{1/3})^2 = (6^{1/2})^2 \cdot (4^{1/3})^2 = 6^{(1/2 \cdot 2)} \cdot 4^{(1/3 \cdot 2)} = 6^1 \cdot 4^{2/3} = 6 \cdot 4^{2/3}$

c. $(4^5 \cdot 3^5)^{-1/5} = [(4 \cdot 3)^5]^{-1/5} = (12^5)^{-1/5} = 12^{[5 \cdot (-1/5)]} = 12^{-1} = \frac{1}{12}$

d. $\frac{5}{5^{1/3}} = \frac{5^1}{5^{1/3}} = 5^{(1-1/3)} = 5^{2/3}$

e. $\left(\frac{42^{1/3}}{6^{1/3}}\right)^2 = \left[\left(\frac{42}{6}\right)^{1/3}\right]^2 = (7^{1/3})^2 = 7^{(1/3 \cdot 2)} = 7^{2/3}$

Resource Planning Guide

Chapter Resource Book
- Teaching Guide/Lesson Plan (pp. 16–17)
- Activity Master (p. 18)
- Practice levels A, B, C (pp. 19–21)
- Study Guide (pp. 22–23)
- Catch-up for Absent Students (p. 24)
- Problem Solving Workshop (p. 25)
- Challenge (p. 26)

Workbooks
- Notetaking Guide (pp. 165–168)
- Practice Workbook (pp. 98–99)

Teaching Options
- **Power Presentations CD-ROM** provides dynamic electronic teaching resources for the classroom.
- **Activity Generator CD-ROM** provides editable activities for all ability levels.

Interactive Technology
- Easy Planner
- Power Presentations CD-ROM
- Activity Generator CD-ROM
- Animated Algebra
- Test Generator CD-ROM
- Online Quiz
- eWorkbook
- eEdition
- @HomeTutor

Resources for English Learners
- Quick Reference for English Learners
- Spanish Study Guide
- Multi-Language Visual Glossary
- Student Resources in Spanish

See also the *Algebra 2 Toolkit* for more strategies for meeting individual needs.

EXAMPLE 2 Apply properties of exponents

BIOLOGY A mammal's surface area S (in square centimeters) can be approximated by the model $S = km^{2/3}$ where m is the mass (in grams) of the mammal and k is a constant. The values of k for some mammals are shown below. Approximate the surface area of a rabbit that has a mass of 3.4 kilograms (3.4×10^3 grams).

Mammal	Sheep	Rabbit	Horse	Human	Monkey	Bat
k	8.4	9.75	10.0	11.0	11.8	57.5

Solution

$S = km^{2/3}$ — **Write model.**

$= 9.75(3.4 \times 10^3)^{2/3}$ — **Substitute 9.75 for k and 3.4×10^3 for m.**

$= 9.75(3.4)^{2/3}(10^3)^{2/3}$ — **Power of a product property**

$\approx 9.75(2.26)(10^2)$ — **Power of a power property**

≈ 2200 — **Simplify.**

▶ The rabbit's surface area is about 2200 square centimeters.

GUIDED PRACTICE for Examples 1 and 2

Simplify the expression.

1. $(5^{1/3} \cdot 7^{1/4})^3$ $5 \cdot 7^{3/4}$
2. $2^{3/4} \cdot 2^{1/2}$ $2^{5/4}$
3. $\dfrac{3}{3^{1/4}}$ $3^{3/4}$
4. $\left(\dfrac{20^{1/2}}{5^{1/2}}\right)^3$ 8
5. **BIOLOGY** Use the information in Example 2 to approximate the surface area of a sheep that has a mass of 95 kilograms (9.5×10^4 grams). about 17,500 cm^2

PROPERTIES OF RADICALS The third and sixth properties on page 420 can be expressed using radical notation when $m = \frac{1}{n}$ for some integer n greater than 1.

KEY CONCEPT *For Your Notebook*

Properties of Radicals

Product property of radicals

$$\sqrt[n]{a \cdot b} = \sqrt[n]{a} \cdot \sqrt[n]{b}$$

Quotient property of radicals

$$\sqrt[n]{\frac{a}{b}} = \frac{\sqrt[n]{a}}{\sqrt[n]{b}},\ b \neq 0$$

EXAMPLE 3 Use properties of radicals

Use the properties of radicals to simplify the expression.

a. $\sqrt[3]{12} \cdot \sqrt[3]{18} = \sqrt[3]{12 \cdot 18} = \sqrt[3]{216} = 6$ **Product property**

b. $\dfrac{\sqrt[4]{80}}{\sqrt[4]{5}} = \sqrt[4]{\dfrac{80}{5}} = \sqrt[4]{16} = 2$ **Quotient property**

Motivating the Lesson

Discuss how seismographs measure earthquakes, using the Richter scale. Explain that properties of rational exponents can be used to compare the magnitudes of earthquakes.

3 TEACH

Extra Example 1

Use the properties of rational exponents to simplify the expression.

a. $12^{1/8} \cdot 12^{5/6}$ $12^{23/24}$

b. $(5^{1/3} \cdot 7^{1/4})^3$ $5 \cdot 7^{3/4}$

c. $(2^6 \cdot 4^6)^{-1/6}$ $\frac{1}{8}$

d. $\dfrac{10}{10^{2/5}}$ $10^{3/5}$

e. $\left(\dfrac{56^{1/4}}{7^{1/4}}\right)^5$ $8^{5/4}$

Extra Example 2

The ratio of the magnitudes of two earthquakes with magnitudes m_1 and m_2 (as measured on the Richter scale) is given by the equation $r = \frac{10^{m_1}}{10^{m_2}}$. The table gives the magnitudes of some of the largest earthquakes that have occurred in the U.S. How many times stronger was the 1964 quake in Alaska than the 1812 quake in Missouri?

Year	State	Magnitude
1812	MO	7.9
1906	CA	7.7
1958	AK	8.3
1964	AK	9.2

about 20 times

Extra Example 3

Use the properties of radicals to simplify the expression.

a. $\sqrt[3]{125} \cdot \sqrt[3]{8}$ 10

b. $\dfrac{\sqrt[5]{96}}{\sqrt[5]{3}}$ 2

Differentiated Instruction

Kinesthetic Learners The properties of radicals may seem straightforward, yet many students will erroneously apply them over addition and subtraction as well. Choose values for a, b, and n. Have students create a table of values and draw conclusions about the expressions $\sqrt[n]{a+b}$, $\sqrt[n]{a} + \sqrt[n]{b}$, $\sqrt[n]{a-b}$, and $\sqrt[n]{a} - \sqrt[n]{b}$. Then have them relate their results to the properties of radicals.

See also the *Algebra 2 Toolkit* for more strategies.

Extra Example 4

Write the expression in simplest form.

a. $\sqrt[3]{104}$ $2\sqrt[3]{13}$

b. $\dfrac{\sqrt[4]{10}}{\sqrt[4]{27}}$ $\dfrac{\sqrt[4]{30}}{3}$

Key Questions to Ask for Example 4

- In part (a) of Example 4, why is 135 factored as 27 • 5, rather than as 9 • 15 or as 3 • 45? **Because 27 is a perfect cube**
- In part (b) of Example 4, why are the numerator and denominator of the given expression multiplied by $\sqrt[5]{4}$, rather than $\sqrt[5]{8}$? **Because $8 \cdot 4 = 32$, which is 2^5.**

Extra Example 5

Simplify the expression.

a. $7\sqrt[5]{12} - \sqrt[5]{12}$ $6\sqrt[5]{12}$

b. $4(9^{2/3}) + 8(9^{2/3})$ $12(9^{2/3})$

c. $\sqrt[3]{81} - \sqrt[3]{24}$ $\sqrt[3]{3}$

Key Question to Ask for Example 5

- In part (c) of Example 5, $\sqrt[3]{54}$ and $\sqrt[3]{2}$ are unlike radicals, so how can the final answer be the single radical $2\sqrt[3]{2}$? **$\sqrt[3]{54}$ can be simplified to $3\sqrt[3]{2}$. Once this has been done, you have two like radicals that can be combined by subtraction.**

SIMPLEST FORM A radical with index n is in **simplest form** if the radicand has no perfect nth powers as factors and any denominator has been rationalized.

EXAMPLE 4 Write radicals in simplest form

Write the expression in simplest form.

a. $\sqrt[3]{135} = \sqrt[3]{27 \cdot 5}$ — Factor out perfect cube.

$= \sqrt[3]{27} \cdot \sqrt[3]{5}$ — Product property

$= 3\sqrt[3]{5}$ — Simplify.

REVIEW RADICALS
For help with rationalizing denominators of radical expressions, see p. 266.

b. $\dfrac{\sqrt[5]{7}}{\sqrt[5]{8}} = \dfrac{\sqrt[5]{7}}{\sqrt[5]{8}} \cdot \dfrac{\sqrt[5]{4}}{\sqrt[5]{4}}$ — Make denominator a perfect fifth power.

$= \dfrac{\sqrt[5]{28}}{\sqrt[5]{32}}$ — Product property

$= \dfrac{\sqrt[5]{28}}{2}$ — Simplify.

LIKE RADICALS Radical expressions with the same index and radicand are **like radicals**. To add or subtract like radicals, use the distributive property.

EXAMPLE 5 Add and subtract like radicals and roots

Simplify the expression.

a. $\sqrt[4]{10} + 7\sqrt[4]{10} = (1 + 7)\sqrt[4]{10} = 8\sqrt[4]{10}$

b. $2(8^{1/5}) + 10(8^{1/5}) = (2 + 10)(8^{1/5}) = 12(8^{1/5})$

c. $\sqrt[3]{54} - \sqrt[3]{2} = \sqrt[3]{27} \cdot \sqrt[3]{2} - \sqrt[3]{2} = 3\sqrt[3]{2} - \sqrt[3]{2} = (3 - 1)\sqrt[3]{2} = 2\sqrt[3]{2}$

GUIDED PRACTICE for Examples 3, 4, and 5

Simplify the expression.

6. $\sqrt[4]{27} \cdot \sqrt[4]{3}$ 3

7. $\dfrac{\sqrt[3]{250}}{\sqrt[3]{2}}$ 5

8. $\sqrt[5]{\dfrac{3}{4}}$ $\dfrac{\sqrt[5]{24}}{2}$

9. $\sqrt[3]{5} + \sqrt[3]{40}$ $3\sqrt[3]{5}$

VARIABLE EXPRESSIONS The properties of rational exponents and radicals can also be applied to expressions involving variables. Because a variable can be positive, negative, or zero, sometimes absolute value is needed when simplifying a variable expression.

	Rule	Example
When n is odd	$\sqrt[n]{x^n} = x$	$\sqrt[7]{5^7} = 5$ and $\sqrt[7]{(-5)^7} = -5$
When n is even	$\sqrt[n]{x^n} = \lvert x \rvert$	$\sqrt[4]{3^4} = 3$ and $\sqrt[4]{(-3)^4} = 3$

Absolute value is not needed when all variables are assumed to be positive.

Differentiated Instruction

Auditory Learners Students may struggle with determining the like factors in an expression. Have students read the expression aloud, listening for repeated words or phrases. Those words or phrases that are heard more than once for an expression likely indicate what to factor out of the expression using the distributive property.

See also the *Algebra 2 Toolkit* for more strategies.

EXAMPLE 6 Simplify expressions involving variables

Simplify the expression. Assume all variables are positive.

a. $\sqrt[3]{64y^6} = \sqrt[3]{4^3(y^2)^3} = \sqrt[3]{4^3} \cdot \sqrt[3]{(y^2)^3} = 4y^2$

b. $(27p^3q^{12})^{1/3} = 27^{1/3}(p^3)^{1/3}(q^{12})^{1/3} = 3p^{(3 \cdot 1/3)}q^{(12 \cdot 1/3)} = 3pq^4$

c. $\sqrt[4]{\dfrac{m^4}{n^8}} = \dfrac{\sqrt[4]{m^4}}{\sqrt[4]{n^8}} = \dfrac{\sqrt[4]{m^4}}{\sqrt[4]{(n^2)^4}} = \dfrac{m}{n^2}$

d. $\dfrac{14xy^{1/3}}{2x^{3/4}z^{-6}} = 7x^{(1-3/4)}y^{1/3}z^{-(-6)} = 7x^{1/4}y^{1/3}z^6$

EXAMPLE 7 Write variable expressions in simplest form

Write the expression in simplest form. Assume all variables are positive.

a. $\sqrt[5]{4a^8b^{14}c^5} = \sqrt[5]{4a^5a^3b^{10}b^4c^5}$ **Factor out perfect fifth powers.**

$= \sqrt[5]{a^5b^{10}c^5} \cdot \sqrt[5]{4a^3b^4}$ **Product property**

$= ab^2c\sqrt[5]{4a^3b^4}$ **Simplify.**

b. $\sqrt[3]{\dfrac{x}{y^8}} = \sqrt[3]{\dfrac{x \cdot y}{y^8 \cdot y}}$ **Make denominator a perfect cube.**

$= \sqrt[3]{\dfrac{xy}{y^9}}$ **Simplify.**

$= \dfrac{\sqrt[3]{xy}}{\sqrt[3]{y^9}}$ **Quotient property**

$= \dfrac{\sqrt[3]{xy}}{y^3}$ **Simplify.**

VOID ERRORS
ou must multiply both e numerator *and* enominator of the action by *y* so that the alue of the fraction oes not change.

EXAMPLE 8 Add and subtract expressions involving variables

Perform the indicated operation. Assume all variables are positive.

a. $\frac{1}{5}\sqrt{w} + \frac{3}{5}\sqrt{w} = \left(\frac{1}{5} + \frac{3}{5}\right)\sqrt{w} = \frac{4}{5}\sqrt{w}$

b. $3xy^{1/4} - 8xy^{1/4} = (3 - 8)xy^{1/4} = -5xy^{1/4}$

c. $12\sqrt[3]{2z^5} - z\sqrt[3]{54z^2} = 12z\sqrt[3]{2z^2} - 3z\sqrt[3]{2z^2} = (12z - 3z)\sqrt[3]{2z^2} = 9z\sqrt[3]{2z^2}$

✓ **GUIDED PRACTICE** for Examples 6, 7, and 8

Simplify the expression. Assume all variables are positive.

10. $\sqrt[3]{27q^9}$ $3q^3$ **11.** $\sqrt[5]{\dfrac{x^{10}}{y^5}}$ $\dfrac{x^2}{y}$ **12.** $\dfrac{6xy^{3/4}}{3x^{1/2}y^{1/2}}$ $2x^{1/2}y^{1/4}$ **13.** $\sqrt{9w^5} - w\sqrt{w^3}$ $2w^2\sqrt{w}$

Extra Example 6

Simplify the expression. Assume all variables are positive.

a. $\sqrt[4]{625z^{12}}$ $5z^3$
b. $(32m^5n^{30})^{1/5}$ $2mn^6$
c. $\sqrt[6]{\dfrac{r^6}{s^{18}}}$ $\dfrac{r}{s^3}$
d. $\dfrac{56ab^{3/4}}{7a^{5/6}c^{-3}}$ $8a^{1/6}b^{3/4}c^3$

Extra Example 7

Write the expression in simplest form. Assume all variables are positive.

a. $\sqrt[3]{6x^4y^9z^{14}}$ $xy^3z^4\sqrt[3]{6xz^2}$
b. $\sqrt[7]{\dfrac{p^8}{q^5}}$ $\dfrac{p\sqrt[7]{pq^2}}{q}$

Extra Example 8

Perform the indicated operation. Assume all variables are positive.

a. $18\sqrt[3]{u} - 11\sqrt[3]{u}$ $7\sqrt[3]{u}$
b. $15a^4b^{2/3} + 8a^4b^{2/3}$ $23a^4b^{2/3}$
c. $10\sqrt[4]{5s^7} - s\sqrt[4]{80s^3}$ $8s\sqrt[4]{5s^3}$

Closing the Lesson

Have students summarize the major points of the lesson and answer the Essential Question: How are the properties of rational exponents related to the properties of integer exponents?

- **Expressions involving rational exponents can be simplified by using the properties of exponents.**
- **Expressions involving radicals can be simplified by using the properties of radicals and by rationalizing the denominator.**

All the properties of integer exponents also apply to rational exponents.

6.2 EXERCISES

HOMEWORK KEY ○ = **WORKED-OUT SOLUTIONS** on p. WS12 for Exs. 5, 27, and 85
★ = **STANDARDIZED TEST PRACTICE** Exs. 2, 23, 51, 69, 86, and 89

4 PRACTICE AND APPLY

Assignment Guide

Answer Transparencies available for all exercises

Basic:
Day 1: EP p. 1014 Exs. 4–7
pp. 424–427
Exs. 1–7, 15–19, 23–27, 32–35, 41–46, 52–55, 60–62, 83–87, 91

Average:
Day 1: pp. 424–427
Exs. 1, 2, 8–11, 19–21, 23, 28–30, 35–37, 41, 42, 46–48, 55–57, 62–64, 67–77 odd, 83–89, 92

Advanced:
Day 1: pp. 424–427
Exs. 1, 2, 12–14, 21–23, 30, 31, 38–40, 49–51, 57–59, 64–69, 75–82*, 84–90*

Block:
pp. 424–427
Exs. 1, 2, 8–11, 19–21, 23, 28–30, 35–37, 41, 42, 46–48, 55–57, 62–64, 67–77 odd, 83–89, 92 (with 6.1)

Differentiated Instruction

See *Algebra 2 Best Practices Toolkit* for suggestions on addressing the needs of a diverse classroom.

Homework Check

For a quick check of student understanding of key concepts, go over the following exercises:

Basic: 4, 26, 44, 52, 83
Average: 18, 28, 36, 60, 84
Advanced: 38, 50, 58, 64, 84

Extra Practice

- Student Edition, p. 1015
- Chapter 6 Resource Book: Practice levels A, B, C, pp. 19–21

Practice Worksheet

An easily-readable reduced practice page (with answers) for this lesson can be found on p. 412C.

SKILL PRACTICE

A

1. **VOCABULARY** Are $2\sqrt{5}$ and $2\sqrt[3]{5}$ like radicals? *Explain* why or why not.
No; they do not have the same index.

2. ★ **WRITING** Under what conditions is a radical expression in simplest form?
If the radicand has no perfect *n*th powers as factors and any denominator has been rationalized.

EXAMPLE 1 on p. 420 for Exs. 3–14

PROPERTIES OF RATIONAL EXPONENTS Simplify the expression.

3. $5^{3/2} \cdot 5^{1/2}$ **25**
4. $(6^{2/3})^{1/2}$ **$6^{1/3}$**
5. $3^{1/4} \cdot 27^{1/4}$ **3**
6. $\dfrac{9}{9^{-4/5}}$ **$9^{9/5}$**
7. $\dfrac{80^{1/4}}{5^{-1/4}}$ **$2 \cdot 5^{1/2}$**
8. $\left(\dfrac{7^3}{4^3}\right)^{-1/3}$ **$\dfrac{4}{7}$**
9. $\dfrac{11^{2/5}}{11^{4/5}}$ **$\dfrac{\sqrt[5]{1331}}{11}$**
10. $(12^{3/5} \cdot 8^{3/5})^5$ **884,736**
11. $\dfrac{120^{-2/5} \cdot 120^{2/5}}{7^{-3/4}}$ **$7^{3/4}$**
12. $\dfrac{64^{5/9} \cdot 64^{2/9}}{4^{3/4}}$ **$8 \cdot 2^{1/6}$**
13. $(16^{5/9} \cdot 5^{7/9})^{-3}$ **$\dfrac{\sqrt[3]{50}}{16,000}$**
14. $\dfrac{13^{3/7}}{13^{5/7}}$ **$\dfrac{\sqrt[7]{371,293}}{13}$**

EXAMPLE 3 on p. 421 for Exs. 15–22

PROPERTIES OF RADICALS Simplify the expression.

15. $\sqrt{20} \cdot \sqrt{5}$ **10**
16. $\sqrt[3]{16} \cdot \sqrt[3]{4}$ **4**
17. $\sqrt[4]{8} \cdot \sqrt[4]{8}$ **$2\sqrt{2}$**
18. $(\sqrt[3]{3} \cdot \sqrt[4]{3})^{12}$ **2187**
19. $\dfrac{\sqrt[5]{64}}{\sqrt[5]{2}}$ **2**
20. $\dfrac{\sqrt{3}}{\sqrt{75}}$ **$\dfrac{1}{5}$**
21. $\dfrac{\sqrt[4]{36} \cdot \sqrt[4]{9}}{\sqrt[4]{4}}$ **3**
22. $\dfrac{\sqrt[4]{8} \cdot \sqrt[4]{16}}{\sqrt[8]{2} \cdot \sqrt[8]{3}}$ **$\dfrac{2\sqrt[8]{69,984}}{3}$**

EXAMPLE 4 on p. 422 for Exs. 23–31

23. ★ **MULTIPLE CHOICE** What is the simplest form of the expression $3\sqrt[4]{32} \cdot (-6\sqrt[4]{5})$? **C**

Ⓐ $\sqrt[4]{10}$ Ⓑ $-18\sqrt[4]{10}$ Ⓒ $-36\sqrt[4]{10}$ Ⓓ $36\sqrt[8]{10}$

SIMPLEST FORM Write the expression in simplest form.

24. $\sqrt{72}$ **$6\sqrt{2}$**
25. $\sqrt[6]{256}$ **$2\sqrt[3]{2}$**
26. $\sqrt[3]{108} \cdot \sqrt[3]{4}$ **$6\sqrt[3]{2}$**
27. $5\sqrt[4]{64} \cdot 2\sqrt[4]{8}$ **$40\sqrt[4]{2}$**
28. $\sqrt[3]{\dfrac{1}{6}}$ **$\dfrac{\sqrt[3]{36}}{6}$**
29. $\dfrac{3}{\sqrt[4]{144}}$ **$\dfrac{\sqrt{3}}{2}$**
30. $\sqrt[6]{\dfrac{81}{4}}$ **$\dfrac{\sqrt[3]{36}}{2}$**
31. $\dfrac{\sqrt[3]{9}}{\sqrt[5]{27}}$ **$\sqrt[15]{3}$**

EXAMPLE 5 on p. 422 for Exs. 32–41

COMBINING RADICALS AND ROOTS Simplify the expression.

32. $2\sqrt[6]{3} + 7\sqrt[6]{3}$ **$9\sqrt[6]{3}$**
33. $\frac{3}{5}\sqrt[3]{5} - \frac{1}{5}\sqrt[3]{5}$ **$\frac{2}{5}\sqrt[3]{5}$**
34. $25\sqrt[5]{2} - 15\sqrt[5]{2}$ **$10\sqrt[5]{2}$**
35. $\frac{1}{8}\sqrt[4]{7} + \frac{3}{8}\sqrt[4]{7}$ **$\frac{1}{2}\sqrt[4]{7}$**
36. $6\sqrt[3]{5} + 4\sqrt[3]{625}$ **$26\sqrt[3]{5}$**
37. $-6\sqrt[7]{2} + 2\sqrt[7]{256}$ **$-2\sqrt[7]{2}$**
38. $12\sqrt[4]{2} - 7\sqrt[4]{512}$ **$-16\sqrt[4]{2}$**
39. $2\sqrt[4]{1250} - 8\sqrt[4]{32}$ **$-6\sqrt[4]{2}$**
40. $5\sqrt[3]{48} - \sqrt[3]{750}$ **$5\sqrt[3]{6}$**

ERROR ANALYSIS *Describe* and correct the error in simplifying the expression. **41, 42. See margin.**

41. $2\sqrt[3]{10} + 6\sqrt[3]{5} = (2 + 6)\sqrt[3]{15}$
$= 8\sqrt[3]{15}$ ✗

42. $\sqrt[3]{\dfrac{x}{y^2}} = \sqrt[3]{\dfrac{x}{y^2 \cdot y}} = \sqrt[3]{\dfrac{x}{y^3}}$
$= \dfrac{\sqrt[3]{x}}{y}$ ✗

41. The radicands are not the same, so they cannot be combined; $2\sqrt[3]{10} + 6\sqrt[3]{5}$.

42. The numerator must also be multiplied by *y*; $\sqrt[3]{\dfrac{x \cdot y}{y^2 \cdot y}} = \sqrt[3]{\dfrac{xy}{y^3}} = \dfrac{\sqrt[3]{xy}}{y}$.

AMPLE 6 B
p. 423
Exs. 43–51

VARIABLE EXPRESSIONS **Simplify the expression. Assume all variables are positive.**

43. $x^{1/4} \cdot x^{1/3}$ $x^{7/12}$
44. $(y^4)^{1/6}$ $y^{2/3}$
45. $\sqrt[4]{81x^4}$ $3x$
46. $\frac{2}{x^{-3/2}}$ $2x^{3/2}$
47. $\frac{x^{2/5}y}{xy^{-1/3}}$ $\frac{y^{4/3}}{x^{3/5}}$
48. $\sqrt[3]{\frac{x^{15}}{y^6}}$ $\frac{x^5}{y^2}$
49. $(\sqrt[3]{x^2} \cdot \sqrt[6]{x^4})^{-3}$ $\frac{1}{x^4}$
50. $\frac{\sqrt[3]{x} \cdot \sqrt{x^5}}{\sqrt{25x^{16}}}$ $\frac{\sqrt[6]{x^5}}{5x^6}$

51. ★ **OPEN-ENDED MATH** Write two variable expressions with noninteger exponents whose quotient is $x^{3/4}$. ***Sample answer:*** $x^{5/4}$ **and** $x^{1/2}$

AMPLE 7
p. 423
Exs. 52–59

SIMPLEST FORM **Write the expression in simplest form. Assume all variables are positive.**

52. $\sqrt{49x^5}$ $7x^2\sqrt{x}$
53. $\sqrt[4]{12x^2y^6z^{12}}$ $yz^3\sqrt[4]{12x^2y^2}$
54. $\sqrt[3]{4x^3y^5} \cdot \sqrt[3]{12y^2}$ $2xy^2\sqrt[3]{6y}$
55. $\sqrt{x^2yz^3} \cdot \sqrt{x^3z^5}$ $x^2z^4\sqrt{xy}$
56. $\frac{-3}{\sqrt[5]{x^6}}$ $\frac{-3\sqrt[5]{x^4}}{x^2}$
57. $\sqrt[3]{\frac{x^3}{y^4}}$ $\frac{x\sqrt[3]{y^2}}{y^2}$
58. $\sqrt{\frac{20x^3y^2}{9xz^3}}$ $\frac{2xy\sqrt{5z}}{3z^2}$
59. $\frac{\sqrt[4]{x^6}}{\sqrt[7]{x^5}}$ $\sqrt[14]{x^{11}}$

AMPLE 8
p. 423
Exs. 60–65

COMBINING VARIABLE EXPRESSIONS **Perform the indicated operation. Assume all variables are positive.**

60. $3\sqrt[5]{x} + 9\sqrt[5]{x}$ $12\sqrt[5]{x}$
61. $\frac{3}{4}y^{3/2} - \frac{1}{4}y^{3/2}$ $\frac{1}{2}y^{3/2}$
62. $-7\sqrt[3]{y} + 16\sqrt[3]{y}$ $9\sqrt[3]{y}$
63. $(x^4y)^{1/2} + (xy^{1/4})^2$ $2x^2y^{1/2}$
64. $x\sqrt{9x^3} - 2\sqrt{x^5}$ $x^2\sqrt{x}$
65. $y\sqrt[4]{32x^6} + \sqrt[4]{162x^2y^4}$ $(2xy + 3y)\sqrt[4]{2x^2}$

GEOMETRY **Find simplified expressions for the perimeter and area of the given figure.**

66. 

perimeter: $2x^3 + 4x^{2/3}$, area: $2x^{11/3}$

67. 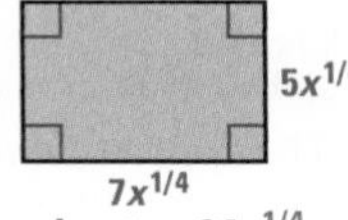

perimeter: $24x^{1/4}$, area: $35x^{1/2}$

68. 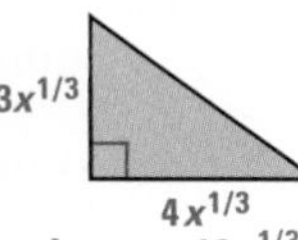

perimeter: $12x^{1/3}$, area: $6x^{2/3}$

69. ★ **MULTIPLE CHOICE** What is the simplified form of $-\frac{1}{6}\sqrt{4x} - \frac{1}{6}\sqrt{9x}$? C

(A) $-\frac{1}{3}\sqrt{x}$ (B) $-\frac{1}{3}\sqrt{36x}$ (C) $-\frac{5}{6}\sqrt{x}$ (D) $-\frac{5}{6}\sqrt{36x}$

DECIMAL EXPONENTS **Simplify the expression. Assume all variables are positive.**

70. $x^{0.5} \cdot x^2$ $x^{2.5}$
71. $y^{-0.6} \cdot y^{-6}$ $\frac{1}{y^{6.6}}$
72. $(x^6y^2)^{-0.75}$ $\frac{1}{x^{4.5}y^{1.5}}$
73. $\frac{x^{0.3}}{x^{1.5}}$ $\frac{1}{x^{1.2}}$
74. $(x^5y^{-3})^{-0.25}$ $\frac{y^{0.75}}{x^{1.25}}$
75. $\frac{y^{-0.5}}{y^{0.8}}$ $\frac{1}{y^{1.3}}$
76. $10x^{0.6} + (4x^{0.3})^2$ $26x^{0.6}$
77. $15z^{0.3} - (2z^{0.1})^3$ $7z^{0.3}$

C **IRRATIONAL EXPONENTS** **The properties in this lesson can also be applied to irrational exponents. Simplify the expression. Assume all variables are positive.**

78. $\frac{x^{5\sqrt{3}}}{x^{2\sqrt{3}}}$ $x^{3\sqrt{3}}$
79. $(x^{\sqrt{2}})^{\sqrt{3}}$ $x^{\sqrt{6}}$
80. $\left(\frac{x^{\pi}}{x^{\pi/3}}\right)^2$ $x^{4\pi/3}$
81. $x^2y^{\sqrt{2}} + 3x^2y^{\sqrt{2}}$ $4x^2y^{\sqrt{2}}$

82. **CHALLENGE** Solve the equation using the properties of rational exponents.

a. $\frac{3}{9^x} = 243$ -2
b. $2^x \cdot 2^{x+1} = \frac{1}{16}$ -2.5
c. $(4^x)^{x+2} = 64$ $-3, 1$

Study Strategy

Exercises 24–27 Emphasize that to simplify a square root, you look for perfect square factors, to simplify a cube root, you look for perfect cube factors, and so on. If students are having difficulty with this, help them to make a list of perfect squares, perfect cubes, perfect fourth powers, and so on, and to use this list as a reference while working exercises like these. If you expect students to memorize perfect powers, tell them how high they need to go for each power.

Avoiding Common Errors

Exercises 28, 29 Students often make errors in rationalizing denominators when the index is higher than 2. For example, in Exercise 28, they may multiply numerator and denominator by $\sqrt[3]{6}$ rather than by $\sqrt[3]{36}$. This error comes from an incorrect understanding of the process of rationalizing denominators. When they simplify $\frac{1}{\sqrt{6}}$ by multiplying by 1 in the form $\frac{\sqrt{6}}{\sqrt{6}}$, these students may think that they should multiply by whatever they see in the denominator, rather than realizing that the goal is to make the radicand in the denominator a perfect square. To help these students, review rationalizing the denominator for square roots by forming perfect squares, and then show them that the same idea is used to form perfect cubes when working with cube roots, and likewise when the index of the radical is higher than 3.

Mathematical Reasoning

Exercises 78–81 While students may be able to work these exercises mechanically, perceptive students may ask what irrational exponents *mean*. You can explain to curious students the basic idea of exponential functions. Using a calculator graph of $f(x) = 2^x$, you can demonstrate that there is a point on the graph that represents $(\sqrt{2}, 2^{\sqrt{2}})$. Tell these students that they will study exponential functions in Chapter 7.

Internet Reference

Exercise 87 Additional information about the apparent magnitude of stars can be found at curious.astro.cornell.edu/question.php?number=569

PROBLEM SOLVING

EXAMPLE 2 on p. 421 for Exs. 83–84

A

83. BIOLOGY Look back at Example 2 on page 421. Use the model $S = km^{2/3}$ to approximate the surface area of the mammal given its mass.

a. Bat: 32 grams **about 580 cm^2**

b. Human: 59 kilograms **about 16,671 cm^2**

@HomeTutor for problem solving help at classzone.com

84. AIRPLANE VELOCITY The velocity v (in feet per second) of a jet can be approximated by the model

$$v = 8.8\sqrt{\frac{L}{A}}$$

where A is the area of the wings (in square feet) and L is the lift (in Newtons). Find the velocity of a jet with a wing area of 5.5×10^3 square feet and a lift of 1.4×10^7 Newtons. **about 444 ft/sec**

@HomeTutor for problem solving help at classzone.com

85. PINHOLE CAMERA The optimum diameter d (in millimeters) of the pinhole in a pinhole camera can be modeled by

$$d = 1.9\left[(5.5 \times 10^{-4})\ell\right]^{1/2}$$

where ℓ is the length of the camera box (in millimeters). Find the optimum pinhole diameter for a camera box with a length of 10 centimeters. **about 0.45 mm**

86. ★ SHORT RESPONSE Show that the hypotenuse of an isosceles right triangle with legs of length x is $x\sqrt{2}$.
If h is the hypotenuse, then $x^2 + x^2 = h^2$, $2x^2 = h^2$, $h = \sqrt{2x^2}$, $h = x\sqrt{2}$.

B

87. STAR MAGNITUDE The *apparent magnitude* of a star is a number that indicates how faint the star is in relation to other stars. The expression $\frac{2.512^{m_1}}{2.512^{m_2}}$ tells how many times fainter a star with magnitude m_1 is than a star with magnitude m_2.

a. How many times fainter is Altair than Vega? **about 2 times fainter**

b. How many times fainter is Deneb than Altair? **about 1.6 times fainter**

c. How many times fainter is Deneb than Vega? **about 3 times fainter**

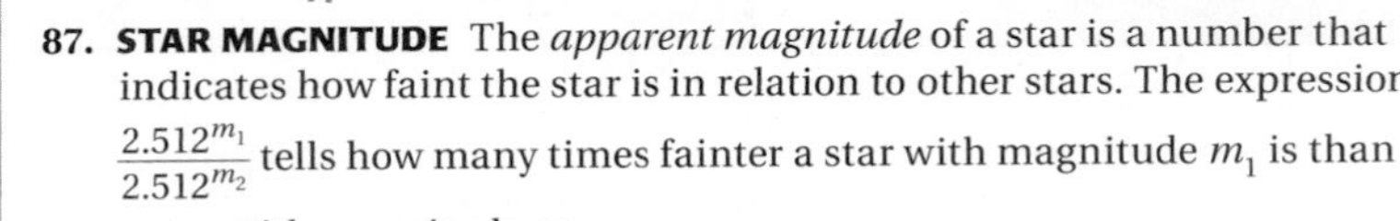

Star	Apparent magnitude	Constellation
Vega	0.03	Lyra
Altair	0.77	Aquila
Deneb	1.25	Cygnus

88. PHYSICAL SCIENCE The maximum horizontal distance d that an object can travel when launched at an optimum angle of projection is given by

$$d = \frac{v_0\sqrt{(v_0)^2 + 2gh_0}}{g}$$

where h_0 is the object's initial height, v_0 is its initial speed, and g is the acceleration due to gravity. Simplify the model when $h_0 = 0$. $d = \frac{v_0^2}{g}$

○ = WORKED-OUT SOLUTIONS on p. WS1 ★ = STANDARDIZED TEST PRACTICE

89b. $S = 4\pi\left(\sqrt[3]{\frac{3V}{4\pi}}\right)^2 = 4\pi\left(\frac{3V}{4\pi}\right)^{2/3} = \frac{4\pi(3V)^{2/3}}{(4\pi)^{2/3}} = (4\pi)^{1/3}(3V)^{2/3}$

89. ★ **EXTENDED RESPONSE** You have filled two round balloons with water. One balloon contains twice as much water as the other balloon.

a. Solve the formula for the volume of a sphere, $V = \frac{4}{3}\pi r^3$, for r. $r = \sqrt[3]{\frac{3V}{4\pi}}$

b. Substitute the expression for r from part (a) into the formula for the surface area of a sphere, $S = 4\pi r^2$. Simplify to show that $S = (4\pi)^{1/3}(3V)^{2/3}$. See margin.

c. *Compare* the surface areas of the two water balloons using the formula from part (b). The balloon with twice as much water will have $\sqrt[3]{4}$, or about 1.59, times the surface area of the balloon with less water.

C 90. **CHALLENGE** Substitute different combinations of odd and even positive integers for m and n in the expression $\sqrt[n]{x^m}$. If x is not always positive, when is absolute value needed in simplifying the expression? If m is odd and n is even.

KENTUCKY MIXED REVIEW

TEST PRACTICE at classzone.com

91. Which equation best represents a line parallel to the line shown? **A**

Ⓐ $-5x + 8y = 14$ Ⓑ $-2x + 4y = -3$

Ⓒ $-x - 4y = 14$ Ⓓ $8x + 5y = 20$

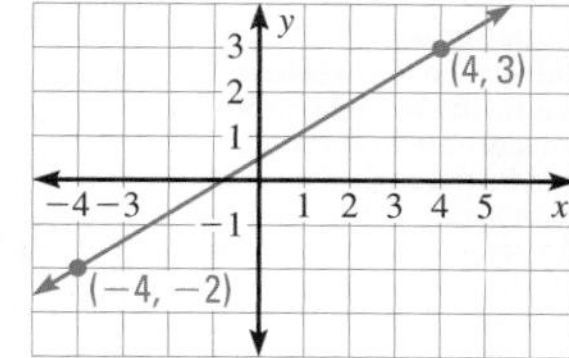

92. What is the solution of the inequality $-5 \le -6x + 3 \le 15$? **B**

Ⓐ $-3 \le x \le \frac{1}{3}$ Ⓑ $-2 \le x \le \frac{4}{3}$ Ⓒ $\frac{1}{3} \le x \le -3$ Ⓓ $\frac{4}{3} \le x \le -2$

QUIZ for Lessons 6.1–6.2

Evaluate the expression without using a calculator. *(p. 414)*

1. $36^{3/2}$ 216
2. $64^{-2/3}$ $\frac{1}{16}$
3. $-(625^{3/4})$ -125
4. $(-32)^{2/5}$ 4

Solve the equation. Round your answer to two decimal places when appropriate. *(p. 414)*

5. $x^4 = 20$ ± 2.11
6. $x^5 = -10$ -1.58
7. $x^6 + 5 = 26$ ± 1.66
8. $(x + 3)^3 = -16$ -5.52

Simplify the expression. Assume all variables are positive. *(p. 420)*

9. $\sqrt[4]{32} \cdot \sqrt[4]{8}$ 4
10. $(\sqrt{10} \cdot \sqrt[3]{10})^8$ $1{,}000{,}000\sqrt[3]{100}$
11. $(x^6y^4)^{1/8} + 2(x^{1/3}y^{1/4})^2$ $x^{3/4}y^{1/2} + 2x^{2/3}y^{1/2}$
12. $\frac{3\sqrt{7^3} + 4\sqrt{7^3}}{\sqrt{7^5}}$ 1
13. $\frac{2\sqrt{x} \cdot \sqrt{x^3}}{\sqrt{64x^{15}}}$ $\frac{\sqrt{x}}{4x^6}$
14. $y^2\sqrt[5]{64x^6} - 6\sqrt[5]{2x^6y^{10}}$ $-4xy^2\sqrt[5]{2x}$

15. **GEOMETRY** Find a radical expression for the perimeter of the red triangle inscribed in the square shown to the right. Simplify the expression. *(p. 420)* $10 + 6\sqrt{5}$

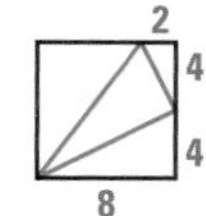

5 ASSESS AND RETEACH

Daily Homework Quiz

Transparency Available

Simplify the expression. Assume all variables are positive.

1. $7^{5/6} \cdot 7^{7/6}$ 49
2. $\frac{\sqrt[3]{375}}{\sqrt[3]{3}}$ 5
3. $\sqrt[4]{243} - \sqrt[4]{48}$ $\sqrt[4]{3}$
4. $(243a^{-10}b^{15})^{-1/5}$ $\frac{a^2}{3b^3}$
5. $\sqrt[4]{\frac{x^3}{y^6}}$ $\frac{\sqrt[4]{x^3y^2}}{y^2}$
6. $\frac{1}{5}a^2b + \frac{3}{10}a^2b$ $\frac{1}{2}a^2b$
7. What is the length of the hypotenuse of a right triangle if the legs have lengths x and $2x$? $\sqrt{5}x$

Online Quiz

Available at **classzone.com**

Diagnosis/Remediation

- Practice A, B, C in Chapter 6 Resource Book, pp. 19–21
- Study Guide in Chapter 6 Resource Book, pp. 22–23
- Practice Workbook, pp. 98–99
- @HomeTutor

Challenge

Additional challenge is available in the Chapter 6 Resource Book, p. 26.

Quiz

An easily-readable reduced copy of the quiz (with answers) on Lessons 6.1–6.2 from the Assessment Book can be found on p. 412E.

1 PLAN AND PREPARE

Warm-Up Exercises

Transparency Available

Perform the indicated operation. Assume all variables are positive.

1. $9x^{2/3} - 2x^{2/3}$ $7x^{2/3}$

2. $\frac{28x}{4x^{1/5}}$ $7x^{4/5}$

Let $f(x) = 3x + 5$ and $g(x) = 2x^2 - 7$. Find the following.

3. $f(-6)$ -13

4. $g(-4)$ 25

Notetaking Guide

Transparency Available

Promotes interactive learning and notetaking skills, pp. 169–172.

Pacing

Basic: 1 day

Average: 1 day

Advanced: 1 day

Block: 0.5 block with 6.4

• See *Teaching Guide/Lesson Plan.*

2 FOCUS AND MOTIVATE

Essential Question

Big Idea 2, p. 413

What operations can be performed on a pair of functions to obtain a third function? **Tell students they will learn how to answer this question by learning to perform operations on functions.**

6.3 Perform Function Operations and Composition

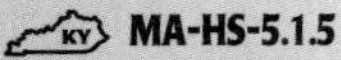

MA-HS-5.1.5

Before	You performed operations with algebraic expressions.
Now	You will perform operations with functions.
Why?	So you can model biological processes, as in Example 3.

Key Vocabulary
- power function
- composition

MA-HS-5.1.5
Students will: determine if a relation is a function; determine the domain and range of a function (linear and quadratic); determine the slope and intercepts of a linear function; determine the maximum, minimum, and intercepts (roots/zeros) of a quadratic function and evaluate a function written in function notation for a specified rational number. DOK 2

In Chapter 5 you learned how to add, subtract, multiply, and divide polynomial functions. These operations can be defined for any number of functions.

KEY CONCEPT — *For Your Notebook*

Operations on Functions

Let f and g be any two functions. A new function h can be defined by performing any of the four basic operations on f and g.

Operation	Definition	Example: $f(x) = 5x$, $g(x) = x + 2$
Addition	$h(x) = f(x) + g(x)$	$h(x) = 5x + (x + 2) = 6x + 2$
Subtraction	$h(x) = f(x) - g(x)$	$h(x) = 5x - (x + 2) = 4x - 2$
Multiplication	$h(x) = f(x) \cdot g(x)$	$h(x) = 5x(x + 2) = 5x^2 + 10x$
Division	$h(x) = \frac{f(x)}{g(x)}$	$h(x) = \frac{5x}{x + 2}$

The domain of h consists of the x-values that are in the domains of both f and g. Additionally, the domain of the quotient does not include x-values for which $g(x) = 0$.

POWER FUNCTIONS So far you have studied several types of functions, including linear functions, quadratic functions, and polynomial functions of higher degree. Another common type of function is a **power function**, which has the form $y = ax^b$ where a is a real number and b is a rational number.

EXAMPLE 1 Add and subtract functions

Let $f(x) = 4x^{1/2}$ and $g(x) = -9x^{1/2}$. Find the following.

a. $f(x) + g(x)$ **b.** $f(x) - g(x)$ **c.** the domains of $f + g$ and $f - g$

Solution

a. $f(x) + g(x) = 4x^{1/2} + (-9x^{1/2}) = [4 + (-9)]x^{1/2} = -5x^{1/2}$

b. $f(x) - g(x) = 4x^{1/2} - (-9x^{1/2}) = [4 - (-9)]x^{1/2} = 13x^{1/2}$

c. The functions f and g each have the same domain: all nonnegative real numbers. So, the domains of $f + g$ and $f - g$ also consist of all nonnegative real numbers.

REVIEW DOMAIN
For help with domains of functions, see p. 72.

Resource Planning Guide

Chapter Resource Book
- Teaching Guide/Lesson Plan (pp. 27–28)
- Practice levels A, B, C (pp. 31–33)
- Study Guide (pp. 34–35)
- Catch-up for Absent Students (p. 36)
- Problem Solving Workshop (p. 37)
- Challenge (p. 39)

Workbooks
- Notetaking Guide (pp. 169–172)
- Practice Workbook (pp. 100–101)

Teaching Options
- **Power Presentations CD-ROM** provides dynamic electronic teaching resources for the classroom.
- **Activity Generator CD-ROM** provides editable activities for all ability levels.

Interactive Technology
- Easy Planner
- Power Presentations CD-ROM
- Activity Generator CD-ROM
- Animated Algebra
- Test Generator CD-ROM
- Online Quiz
- eWorkbook
- eEdition
- @HomeTutor

Resources for English Learners
- Quick Reference for English Learners
- Spanish Study Guide
- Multi-Language Visual Glossary
- Student Resources in Spanish

See also the *Algebra 2 Toolkit* for more strategies for meeting individual needs.

EXAMPLE 2 Multiply and divide functions

Let $f(x) = 6x$ and $g(x) = x^{3/4}$. Find the following.

a. $f(x) \cdot g(x)$ **b.** $\frac{f(x)}{g(x)}$ **c.** the domains of $f \cdot g$ and $\frac{f}{g}$

Solution

a. $f(x) \cdot g(x) = (6x)(x^{3/4}) = 6x^{(1+3/4)} = 6x^{7/4}$

b. $\frac{f(x)}{g(x)} = \frac{6x}{x^{3/4}} = 6x^{(1-3/4)} = 6x^{1/4}$

c. The domain of f consists of all real numbers, and the domain of g consists of all nonnegative real numbers. So, the domain of $f \cdot g$ consists of all nonnegative real numbers. Because $g(0) = 0$, the domain of $\frac{f}{g}$ is restricted to all *positive* real numbers.

EXAMPLE 3 Solve a multi-step problem

RHINOS For a white rhino, heart rate r (in beats per minute) and life span s (in minutes) are related to body mass m (in kilograms) by these functions:

$$r(m) = 241m^{-0.25} \qquad s(m) = (6 \times 10^6)m^{0.2}$$

- Find $r(m) \cdot s(m)$.
- Explain what this product represents.

Solution

STEP 1 **Find** and simplify $r(m) \cdot s(m)$.

$r(m) \cdot s(m) = 241m^{-0.25}[(6 \times 10^6)m^{0.2}]$	**Write product of $r(m)$ and $s(m)$.**
$= 241(6 \times 10^6)m^{(-0.25+0.2)}$	**Product of powers property**
$= (1446 \times 10^6)m^{-0.05}$	**Simplify.**
$= (1.446 \times 10^9)m^{-0.05}$	**Use scientific notation.**

STEP 2 **Interpret** $r(m) \cdot s(m)$.

Multiplying heart rate by life span gives the total number of heartbeats for a white rhino over its entire lifetime.

✓ GUIDED PRACTICE for Examples 1, 2, and 3

Let $f(x) = -2x^{2/3}$ and $g(x) = 7x^{2/3}$. Find the following.

1. $f(x) + g(x)$ $5x^{2/3}$
2. $f(x) - g(x)$ $-9x^{2/3}$
3. the domains of $f + g$ and $f - g$ all real numbers; all real numbers

Let $f(x) = 3x$ and $g(x) = x^{1/5}$. Find the following.

4. $f(x) \cdot g(x)$ $3x^{6/5}$
5. $\frac{f(x)}{g(x)}$ $3x^{4/5}$
6. the domains of $f \cdot g$ and $\frac{f}{g}$ all real numbers; all real numbers except $x = 0$
7. **RHINOS** Use the result of Example 3 to find a white rhino's number of heartbeats over its lifetime if its body mass is 1.7×10^5 kilograms. about 7.92×10^8 heartbeats

Motivating the Lesson

In a sale at your favorite clothing store, everything is 30% off. When you get to the store, you find a sweater you like on a rack that has a sign saying "Additional 25% off given at register." You can use composition of functions to figure out the price you will pay for the sweater.

3 TEACH

Extra Example 1

Let $f(x) = 5x^{1/3}$ and $g(x) = -11x^{1/3}$. Find the following.

a. $f(x) + g(x)$ $-6x^{1/3}$

b. $f(x) - g(x)$ $16x^{1/3}$

c. the domains of $f + g$ and $f - g$ **domains of $f + g$ and $f - g$: all real numbers**

Extra Example 2

Let $f(x) = 8x$ and $g(x) = 2x^{5/6}$. Find the following.

a. $f(x) \cdot g(x)$ $16x^{11/6}$

b. $\frac{f(x)}{g(x)}$ $4x^{1/6}$

c. the domains of $f \cdot g$ and $\frac{f}{g}$ **domain of $f \cdot g$: all nonnegative real numbers; domain of $\frac{f}{g}$: all positive real numbers**

Extra Example 3

A small company sells computer printers over the Internet. The company's total monthly revenue (R) and costs (C) are modeled by the functions $R(x) = 120x$ and $C(x) = 2500 + 75x$, where x is the number of printers sold.

- Find $R(x) - C(x)$. $45x - 2500$
- Explain what this difference means. **Subtracting costs from revenue gives the company's monthly profit.**

COMPOSITION OF FUNCTIONS Another operation that can be performed with two functions is *composition.*

KEY CONCEPT *For Your Notebook*

Composition of Functions

The **composition** of a function g with a function f is:

$$h(x) = g(f(x))$$

The domain of h is the set of all x-values such that x is in the domain of f and $f(x)$ is in the domain of g.

Domain of f | Range of f

Input of f — x → Output of f — $f(x)$ → Input of g → Output of g — $g(f(x))$

Domain of g | Range of g

READING
As with subtraction and division of functions, you need to be alert to the order of functions when they are composed. In general, $f(g(x))$ is not equal to $g(f(x))$.

EXAMPLE 4 Standardized Test Practice

Let $f(x) = 2x - 7$ and $g(x) = x^2 + 4$. What is the value of $g(f(3))$?

Ⓐ -5 Ⓑ -3 Ⓒ 3 Ⓓ 5

Solution

To evaluate $g(f(3))$, you first must find $f(3)$.

$$f(3) = 2(3) - 7 = -1$$

Then $g(f(3)) = g(-1) = (-1)^2 + 4 = 1 + 4 = 5$.

So, the value of $g(f(3))$ is 5.

▶ The correct answer is D. Ⓐ Ⓑ Ⓒ Ⓓ

EXAMPLE 5 Find compositions of functions

Let $f(x) = 4x^{-1}$ and $g(x) = 5x - 2$. Find the following.

a. $f(g(x))$ **b.** $g(f(x))$

c. $f(f(x))$ **d.** the domain of each composition

Solution

a. $f(g(x)) = f(5x - 2) = 4(5x - 2)^{-1} = \frac{4}{5x - 2}$

b. $g(f(x)) = g(4x^{-1}) = 5(4x^{-1}) - 2 = 20x^{-1} - 2 = \frac{20}{x} - 2$

c. $f(f(x)) = f(4x^{-1}) = 4(4x^{-1})^{-1} = 4(4^{-1}x) = 4^0x = x$

d. The domain of $f(g(x))$ consists of all real numbers except $x = \frac{2}{5}$ because $g\left(\frac{2}{5}\right) = 0$ is not in the domain of f. (Note that $f(0) = \frac{4}{0}$, which is undefined.) The domains of $g(f(x))$ and $f(f(x))$ consist of all real numbers except $x = 0$, again because 0 is not in the domain of f.

AVOID ERRORS
You cannot always determine the domain of a composition from its equation. For instance, the domain of $f(f(x)) = x$ appears to be all real numbers, but it is actually all real numbers except zero.

Extra Example 4

Let $f(x) = 3x - 4$ and $g(x) = x^2 - 1$. What is the value of $f(g(-3))$? C

Ⓐ -34 Ⓑ 8

Ⓒ 20 Ⓓ 168

Key Questions to Ask for Example 4

- In Example 4, how do you know which function to apply first? **Apply *f* first because you should evauate inside the parentheses first.**
- In this example, should you evaluate both of the given functions by substituting 3 for x? Explain. **No; substitute 3 for x in function f, and then substitute the resulting value, $f(x)$, for x in function g.**

Extra Example 5

Let $f(x) = 6x^{-2}$ and $g(x) = 4x + 5$. Find the following.

a. $f(g(x))$ $\frac{6}{(4x + 5)^2}$

b. $g(f(x))$ $\frac{24}{x^2} + 5$

c. $g(g(x))$ $16x + 25$

d. the domain of each composition **domain of $f(g(x))$: all real numbers except $x = -\frac{5}{4}$; domain of $g(f(x))$: all real numbers except $x = 0$; domain of $g(g(x))$: all real numbers**

Reading Strategy

Because we read and do most mathematical operations from left to right, students may be confused when they are introduced to composition of functions, which requires working from right to left. Compare the procedure to that of working from the innermost parentheses outward in evaluating expressions.

Differentiated Instruction

Below Level To help students build a concrete understanding of the concept of composition of functions, have them work in pairs to build "function machines" using cardboard boxes or other materials. By hooking up two of these boxes in tandem, they can simulate the idea of composite function. Reversing the order of the two boxes can be used to demonstrate that, in general, $f(g(x)) \neq g(f(x))$.

See also the *Algebra 2 Toolkit* for more strategies.

EXAMPLE 6 Solve a multi-step problem

PAINT STORE You have a \$10 gift certificate to a paint store. The store is offering 15% off your entire purchase of any paints and painting supplies. You decide to purchase a \$30 can of paint and \$25 worth of painting supplies.

Use composition of functions to do the following:

- Find the sale price of your purchase when the \$10 gift certificate is applied before the 15% discount.
- Find the sale price of your purchase when the 15% discount is applied before the \$10 gift certificate.

Solution

STEP 1 **Find** the total amount of your purchase. The total amount for the paint and painting supplies is \$30 + \$25 = \$55.

STEP 2 **Write** functions for the discounts. Let x be the regular price, $f(x)$ be the price after the \$10 gift certificate is applied, and $g(x)$ be the price after the 15% discount is applied.

Function for \$10 gift certificate: $f(x) = x - 10$

Function for 15% discount: $g(x) = x - 0.15x = 0.85x$

STEP 3 **Compose** the functions.

The composition $g(f(x))$ represents the sale price when the \$10 gift certificate is applied before the 15% discount.

$g(f(x)) = g(x - 10) = 0.85(x - 10)$

The composition $f(g(x))$ represents the sale price when the 15% discount is applied before the \$10 gift certificate.

$f(g(x)) = f(0.85x) = 0.85x - 10$

STEP 4 **Evaluate** the functions $g(f(x))$ and $f(g(x))$ when $x = 55$.

$g(f(55)) = 0.85(55 - 10) = 0.85(45) = \$38.25$

$f(g(55)) = 0.85(55) - 10 = 46.75 - 10 = \$36.75$

▶ The sale price is \$38.25 when the \$10 gift certificate is applied before the 15% discount. The sale price is \$36.75 when the 15% discount is applied before the \$10 gift certificate.

Animated Algebra at classzone.com

$\frac{2}{2x+7}$, all real
nbers except
−3.5; $\frac{4}{x} + 7$, all real
nbers except
0; x, all real
nbers except $x = 0$.

Sample answer:
sale price is \$32
en the gift certificate
pplied before the
% discount. The sale
ce is \$29 when the
certificate is applied
er the 20% discount.

✓ GUIDED PRACTICE for Examples 4, 5, and 6

Let $f(x) = 3x - 8$ and $g(x) = 2x^2$. Find the following.

8. $g(f(5))$ 98
9. $f(g(5))$ 142
10. $f(f(5))$ 13
11. $g(g(5))$ 5000
12. Let $f(x) = 2x^{-1}$ and $g(x) = 2x + 7$. Find $f(g(x))$, $g(f(x))$, and $f(f(x))$. Then state the domain of each composition.
13. **WHAT IF?** In Example 6, how do your answers change if the gift certificate to the paint store is \$15 and the store discount is 20%?

Extra Example 6

Your starting wage for your part-time job was \$6 an hour. All employees get a 5% raise after 6 months. You are given an additional raise of \$.75 per hour as a reward for your outstanding work.

- Find your new hourly wage if the 5% raise is applied before the 75-cent raise. **\$7.05**
- Find your new hourly wage if the 75-cent raise is applied before the 5% raise. **about \$7.09**

Key Question to Ask for Example 6

- Explain why the two results in Example 6 are different. **If the discount is applied after the gift certificate is applied, the 15% will be taken off a smaller amount.**

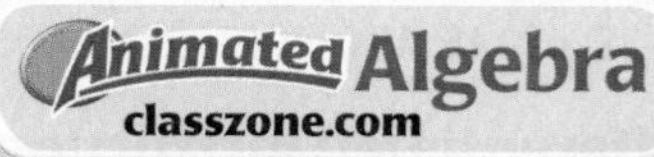

An **Animated Algebra** activity is available on-line for **Example 6**. This activity is also available on the **Power Presentations CD-ROM**.

Closing the Lesson

Have students summarize the major points of the lesson and answer the Essential Question: What operations can be performed on a pair of functions to obtain a third function?

- **Composition of functions involves applying two functions in succession.**
- **For subtraction, division, and composition of functions, changing the order in which the two functions are written affects the result.**

Two functions can be combined by the operations of addition, subtraction, multiplication, division, and composition.

Differentiated Instruction

Auditory Learners Encourage students to verbalize the composition of functions and then state what the notation represents. For **Example 6**, have students say, "The composition *g* of *f* of *x* represents the sale price of your purchase, calculated by first deducting the \$10 gift certificate, and then applying the 15% discount." Stress that the order in which the functions are applied is extremely important in composition of functions.

See also the *Algebra 2 Toolkit* for more strategies.

4 PRACTICE AND APPLY

Assignment Guide

Answer Transparencies available for all exercises

Basic:
Day 1: pp. 432–434
Exs. 1–8, 11–15, 20–23, 28–31, 43–46, 48

Average:
Day 1: pp. 432–434
Exs. 1, 2, 6–8, 11, 15–17, 23–25, 31–39, 43–46, 49

Advanced:
Day 1: pp. 432–434
Exs. 1, 2, 9–11, 18, 19, 26, 27, 33–42*, 44–47*

Block:
pp. 432–434
Exs. 1, 2, 6–8, 11, 15–17, 23–25, 31–39, 43–46, 49 (with 6.4)

Differentiated Instruction

See *Algebra 2 Best Practices Toolkit* for suggestions on addressing the needs of a diverse classroom.

Homework Check

For a quick check of student understanding of key concepts, go over the following exercises:

Basic: 4, 14, 22, 28, 43
Average: 6, 16, 24, 32, 44
Advanced: 8, 18, 26, 34, 45

Extra Practice

- Student Edition, p. 1015
- Chapter 6 Resource Book: Practice levels A, B, C, pp. 31–33

Practice Worksheet

An easily-readable reduced practice page (with answers) for this lesson can be found on p. 412C.

6.3 EXERCISES

HOMEWORK KEY
○ = WORKED-OUT SOLUTIONS on p. WS12 for Exs. 3, 13, and 45
★ = STANDARDIZED TEST PRACTICE Exs. 2, 11, 38, 39, and 44
◆ = MULTIPLE REPRESENTATIONS Ex. 46

SKILL PRACTICE

A

1. **VOCABULARY** Copy and complete: The function $h(x) = g(f(x))$ is called the __?__ of the function g with the function f. composition

2. ★ **WRITING** Tell whether the sum of two power functions is *sometimes*, *always*, or *never* a power function. *Explain* your reasoning. Sometimes. *Sample answer:* $3x^2 + 2x^2 = 5x^2$ is a power function, but, $2x^3 + (-2x^3) = 0$ is not a power function.

EXAMPLE 1 on p. 428 for Exs. 3–11

ADD AND SUBTRACT FUNCTIONS Let $f(x) = -3x^{1/3} + 4x^{1/2}$ and $g(x) = 5x^{1/3} + 4x^{1/2}$. Perform the indicated operation and state the domain. 3–10. See margin.

3. $f(x) + g(x)$
4. $g(x) + f(x)$
5. $f(x) + f(x)$
6. $g(x) + g(x)$
7. $f(x) - g(x)$
8. $g(x) - f(x)$
9. $f(x) - f(x)$
10. $g(x) - g(x)$

11. ★ **MULTIPLE CHOICE** What is $f(x) + g(x)$ if $f(x) = -7x^{2/3} - 1$ and $g(x) = 2x^{2/3} + 6$? B

(A) $5x^{2/3} - 5$ (B) $-5x^{2/3} + 5$ (C) $9x^{2/3} + 7$ (D) $-9x^{2/3} - 7$

EXAMPLE 2 on p. 429 for Exs. 12–19

MULTIPLY AND DIVIDE FUNCTIONS Let $f(x) = 4x^{2/3}$ and $g(x) = 5x^{1/2}$. Perform the indicated operation and state the domain. 12–19. See margin.

12. $f(x) \cdot g(x)$
13. $g(x) \cdot f(x)$
14. $f(x) \cdot f(x)$
15. $g(x) \cdot g(x)$
16. $\frac{f(x)}{g(x)}$
17. $\frac{g(x)}{f(x)}$
18. $\frac{f(x)}{f(x)}$
19. $\frac{g(x)}{g(x)}$

EXAMPLE 4 on p. 430 for Exs. 20–27

EVALUATE COMPOSITIONS OF FUNCTIONS Let $f(x) = 3x + 2$, $g(x) = -x^2$, and $h(x) = \frac{x-2}{5}$. Find the indicated value.

20. $f(g(-3))$ -25
21. $g(f(2))$ -64
22. $h(f(-9))$ $-\frac{27}{5}$
23. $g(h(8))$ $-\frac{36}{25}$
24. $h(g(5))$ $-\frac{27}{5}$
25. $f(f(7))$ 71
26. $h(h(-4))$ $-\frac{16}{25}$
27. $g(g(-5))$ -625

EXAMPLE 5 on p. 430 for Exs. 28–38

B

FIND COMPOSITIONS OF FUNCTIONS Let $f(x) = 3x^{-1}$, $g(x) = 2x - 7$, and $h(x) = \frac{x+4}{3}$. Perform the indicated operation and state the domain. 28–35. See margin.

28. $f(g(x))$
29. $g(f(x))$
30. $h(f(x))$
31. $g(h(x))$
32. $h(g(x))$
33. $f(f(x))$
34. $h(h(x))$
35. $g(g(x))$

ERROR ANALYSIS Let $f(x) = x^2 - 3$ and $g(x) = 4x$. *Describe* and correct the error in the composition.

36.
$f(g(x)) = f(4x)$
$= (x^2 - 3)(4x)$
$= 4x^3 - 12x$

$4x$ should have been substituted for x in the equation instead of multiplying by it; $= (4x)^2 - 3$, $= 16x^2 - 3$.

37.
$g(f(x)) = g(x^2 - 3)$
$= 4x^2 - 3$

4 should b[e] distribute[d] to each term, not just the fir[st] term; $= 4x^2 - 1$[2]

3. $2x^{1/3} + 8x^{1/2}$, all nonnegative real numbers
4. $2x^{1/3} + 8x^{1/2}$, all nonnegative real numbers
5. $-6x^{1/3} + 8x^{1/2}$, all nonnegative real numbers
6. $10x^{1/3} + 8x^{1/2}$, all nonnegative real numbers
7. $-8x^{1/3}$, all nonnegative real numbers
8. $8x^{1/3}$, all nonnegative real numbers
9. 0, all nonnegative real numbers
10. 0, all nonnegative real numbers
12. $20x^{7/6}$, nonnegative real numbers
13. $20x^{7/6}$, nonnegative real numbers
14. $16x^{4/3}$, all real numbers
15. $25x$, all nonnegative real numbers
16. $\frac{4}{5}x^{1/6}$, positive real numbers
17. $\frac{5}{4x^{1/6}}$, positive real numbers
18. 1, all real numbers except 0
19. 1, positive real numbers

38. ★ **MULTIPLE CHOICE** What is $g(f(x))$ if $f(x) = 7x^2$ and $g(x) = 3x^{-2}$? A

Ⓐ $\frac{3}{49x^4}$ Ⓑ 21 Ⓒ $21x^4$ Ⓓ $\frac{7}{9x^4}$

C 39. ★ **OPEN-ENDED MATH** Find two different functions f and g such that $f(g(x)) = g(f(x))$. *Sample answer:* $f(x) = 3x$, $g(x) = 2x$

CHALLENGE **Find functions f and g such that $f(g(x)) = h(x)$, $g(x) \neq x$, and $f(x) \neq x$.** 40–42. Sample answers are given.

40. $h(x) = \sqrt[3]{x + 2}$
$f(x) = \sqrt[3]{x}$, $g(x) = x + 2$

41. $h(x) = \frac{4}{3x^2 + 7}$
$f(x) = \frac{4}{x + 7}$, $g(x) = 3x^2$

42. $h(x) = |2x + 9|$
$f(x) = |x + 9|$, $g(x) = 2x$

PROBLEM SOLVING

EXAMPLE 3 A on p. 429 for Exs. 43, 46

43. **BIOLOGY** For a mammal that weighs w grams, the volume b (in milliliters) of air breathed in and the volume d (in milliliters) of "dead space" (the portion of the lungs not filled with air) can be modeled by:

$$b(w) = 0.007w \qquad d(w) = 0.002w$$

The breathing rate r (in breaths per minute) of a mammal that weighs w grams can be modeled by:

$$r(w) = \frac{1.1w^{0.734}}{b(w) - d(w)}$$

Simplify $r(w)$ and calculate the breathing rate for body weights of 6.5 grams, 300 grams, and 70,000 grams. $r(w) = 220w^{-0.266}$; about 134 breaths per minute, about 48.3 breaths per minute, about 11.3 breaths per minute

@HomeTutor for problem solving help at classzone.com

EXAMPLE 6 on p. 431 for Exs. 44–45

44. ★ **SHORT RESPONSE** The cost (in dollars) of producing x sneakers in a factory is given by $C(x) = 60x + 750$. The number of sneakers produced in t hours is given by $x(t) = 50t$. Find $C(x(t))$. Evaluate $C(x(5))$ and explain what this number represents. $C(x(t)) = 3000t + 750$; 15,750, in 5 hours 250 sneakers were produced at a cost of $15,750.

@HomeTutor for problem solving help at classzone.com

45. **MULTI-STEP PROBLEM** An online movie store is having a sale. You decide to open a charge account and buy four DVDs.

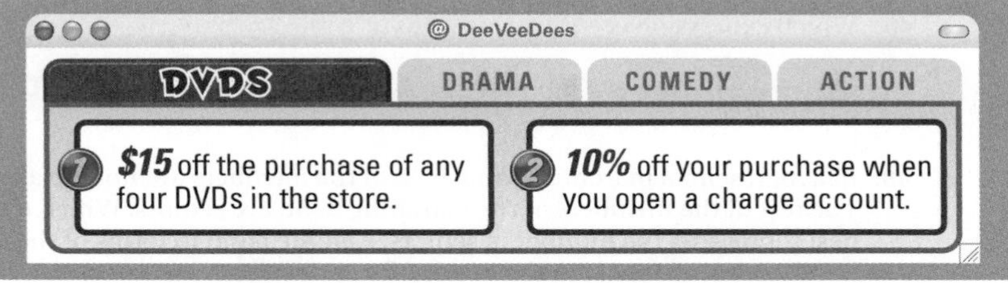

DeeVeeDees
DVDS
DRAMA
COMEDY
ACTION
1 $15 off the purchase of any four DVDs in the store.
2 10% off your purchase when you open a charge account.

a. Use composition of functions to find the sale price of $85 worth of DVDs when the $15 discount is applied before the 10% discount. $63

b. Use composition of functions to find the sale price of $85 worth of DVDs when the 10% discount is applied before the $15 discount. $61.50

c. Which order of discounts gives you a better deal? *Explain.* Apply the 10% discount before the $15 discount; you pay $61.50 using this method and $63 using the other method.

Avoiding Common Errors

Exercises 20, 21, 23, 24, 27 If students do not give correct answers for these exercises, check how they are evaluating $g(x) = -x^2$ for a numerical value of x. If you find that they are getting positive values rather than negative ones, they may be confusing $-x^2$ with $(-x)^2$. Remind them of the difference in meaning between these two expressions.

Teaching Strategy

Exercises 28–35 Finding the domains of composite functions requires care. Go back to the Key Concept box on page 430 and discuss exactly what it is saying about domains and ranges. For this group of exercises, have students start by writing down the domain and range of each of the three given functions and then applying the diagram on page 430 to the various compositions of these functions. By observing that g and h are both linear functions, they should be able to see that any composition that involves one or both of these two functions will have all real numbers as its domain, so it is only the compositions that involve f that require careful attention.

28. $\frac{3}{2x - 7}$, all real numbers except $x = 3.5$

29. $\frac{6}{x} - 7$, all real numbers except $x = 0$

30. $\frac{1}{x} + \frac{4}{3}$, all real numbers except $x = 0$

31. $\frac{2x - 13}{3}$, all real numbers

32. $\frac{2x - 3}{3}$, all real numbers

33. x, all real numbers except $x = 0$

34. $\frac{x + 16}{9}$, all real numbers

35. $4x - 21$, all real numbers

5 ASSESS AND RETEACH

Daily Homework Quiz

Transparency Available

Let $f(x) = -2x^{1/4}$ and $g(x) = 6x^{1/4}$. Find the following.

1. $f(x) + g(x)$ **$4x^{1/4}$**
2. $g(x) - f(x)$ **$8x^{1/4}$**
3. $f(x) \cdot g(x)$ **$-12x^{1/2}$**
4. the domain of $f \cdot g$ **all nonnegative real numbers (or $x \geq 0$)**
5. $\frac{g(x)}{f(x)}$ **-3**
6. the domain of $\frac{f}{g}$ **all positive real numbers**

Let $f(x) = 5x - 3$ and $g(x) = -x^2 + 2$. Find the following.

7. $g(f(-2))$ **-167**
8. $f(g(x))$ **$-5x^2 + 7$**
9. You have a \$25 gift certificate for a book store. The store is offering 10% off all books. When should you use the certificate, *before* or *after* the 10% discount? **after**

Online Quiz

Available at **classzone.com**

Diagnosis/Remediation

- Practice A, B, C in Chapter 6 Resource Book, pp. 31–33
- Study Guide in Chapter 6 Resource Book, pp. 34–35
- Practice Workbook, pp. 100–101
- @HomeTutor

Challenge

Additional challenge is available in the Chapter 6 Resource Book, p. 39.

46a. $r(x) = \frac{20 - x}{6.4}$; $s(x) = \frac{\sqrt{144 + x^2}}{0.9}$

46b. $t(x) = \frac{20 - x}{6.4} + \frac{\sqrt{144 + x^2}}{0.9}$

46c. 1.7; to minimize the time spent fetching the ball, Elvis should run for $20 - 1.7 = 18.3$ meters before he swims to the ball.

B **46.** **MULTIPLE REPRESENTATIONS** A mathematician at a lake throws a tennis ball from point A along the water's edge to point B in the water, as shown. His dog, Elvis, first runs along the beach from point A to point D and then swims to fetch the ball at point B.

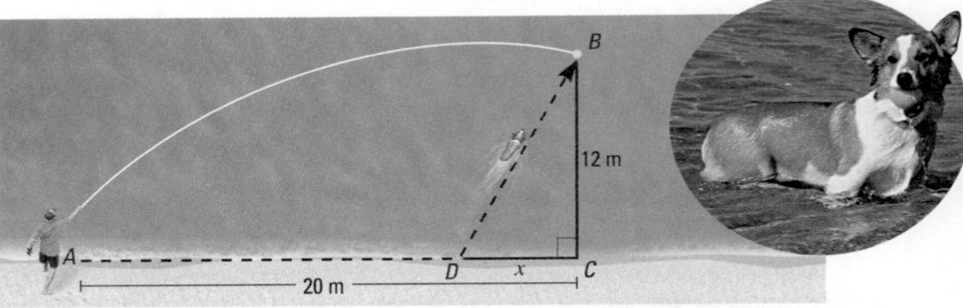

a–c. See margin.

a. **Using a Diagram** Elvis's running speed is about 6.4 meters per second. Write a function $r(x)$ for the time he spends running from point A to point D. Elvis's swimming speed is about 0.9 meter per second. Write a function $s(x)$ for the time he spends swimming from point D to point B.

b. **Writing a Function** Write a function $t(x)$ that represents the total time Elvis spends traveling from point A to point D to point B.

c. **Using a Graph** Use a graphing calculator to graph $t(x)$. Find the value of x that minimizes $t(x)$. *Explain* the meaning of this value.

C **47.** **CHALLENGE** To approximate the square root of a number n, the Babylonians used a method that involves starting with an initial guess x and calculating a sequence of values that approaches the exact answer. Their method was based on the function shown at the right.

$$f(x) = \frac{x + \frac{n}{x}}{2}$$

a. Let $n = 2$, and choose $x = 1$ as an initial guess for $\sqrt{n} = \sqrt{2}$. Calculate $f(x)$, $f(f(x))$, $f(f(f(x)))$, and $f(f(f(f(x))))$.

47a. 1.5, about 1.4166667, about 1.4142157, about 1.4142136

b. How many times do you need to compose the function in order for the result to approximate $\sqrt{2}$ to three decimal places? six decimal places? **3 times; 4 times**

KY KENTUCKY MIXED REVIEW

TEST PRACTICE at classzone.com

48. Which expression is equivalent to $(6x^3y^5z^{-1})(-3x^{-4}y^2)$? **C**

Ⓐ $-\frac{18y^{10}}{x^{12}z}$ Ⓑ $-\frac{18z}{x^7y^3}$ Ⓒ $-\frac{18y^7}{xz}$ Ⓓ $-\frac{y^7}{18xz}$

49. In a high school marching band, 68% of the members are underclassmen. The rest of the members of the marching band are seniors. Which equation best represents the number of seniors, s, in the band in terms of the total number of students, t, in the band? **B**

Ⓐ $s = \frac{8}{17}t$ Ⓑ $s = \frac{8}{25}t$

Ⓒ $s = \frac{17}{8}t$ Ⓓ $s = \frac{25}{8}t$

@HomeTutor
classzone.com
Keystrokes

6.3 Use Operations with Functions

QUESTION How can you use a graphing calculator to perform operations with functions?

EXAMPLE Perform function operations

Let $f(x) = x^2 - 3x + 6$ and $g(x) = x - 4$. Find $f(4) + g(4)$ and $f(g(-2))$.

STEP 1 *Form sum*

Enter $y_1 = x^2 - 3x + 6$ and $y_2 = x - 4$. The sum can be entered as $y_3 = y_1 + y_2$. To do so, press VARS, choose the Y-Vars menu, and select Function.

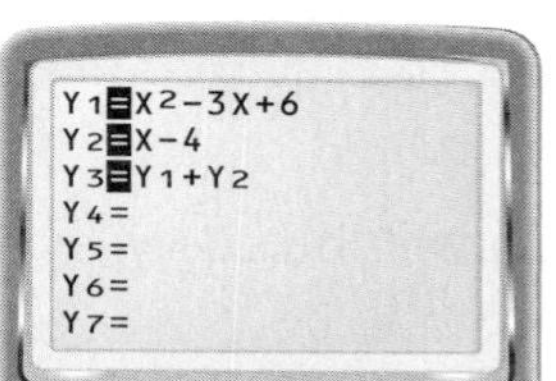

STEP 2 *Evaluate sum*

On the home screen, enter $y_3(4)$ and press ENTER. The screen shows that $y_3(4) = 10$, so $f(4) + g(4) = 10$.

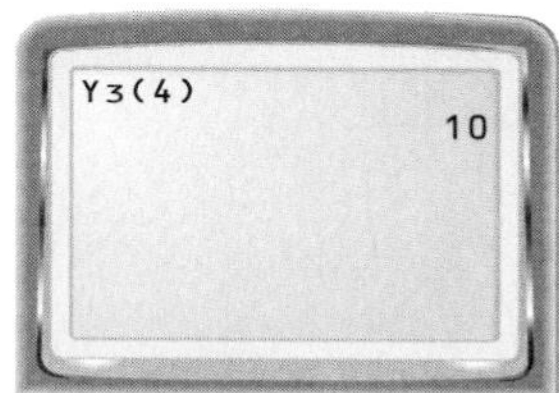

STEP 3 *Form composition*

The composition $f(g(x))$ can be entered as $y_3 = y_1(y_2)$.

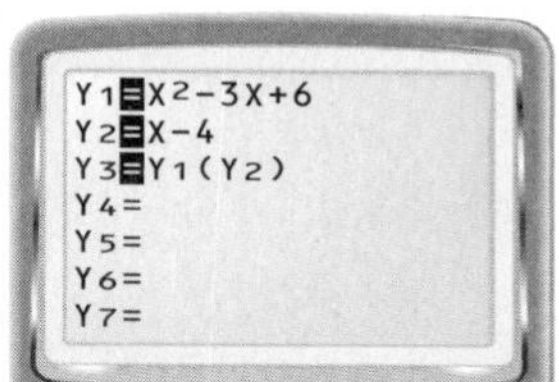

STEP 4 *Evaluate composition*

On the home screen, enter $y_3(-2)$ and press ENTER. The screen shows that $y_3(-2) = 60$, so $f(g(-2)) = 60$.

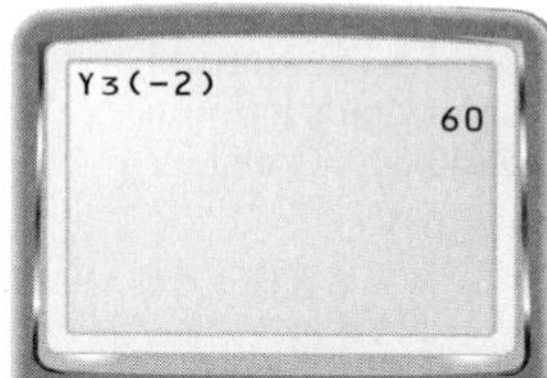

PRACTICE

Use a graphing calculator and the functions f and g to find the indicated value.

1. $f(x) = x^3 + 5x - 3$, $g(x) = -3x^2 - x$: $g(7) + f(7)$ **221**
2. $f(x) = x^{1/3}$, $g(x) = 9x$: $\frac{f(-8)}{g(-8)}$ **$\frac{1}{36}$**
3. $f(x) = 5x^3 - 3x^2$, $g(x) = -2x^2 - 5$: $g(2) - f(2)$ **−41**
4. $f(x) = 2x^2 + 7x - 2$, $g(x) = x - 6$: $f(g(5))$ **−7**

1 PLAN AND PREPARE

Learn the Method

- Students will learn how to use a graphing calculator to perform operations with functions. Students can use the method to check many of the Skill Practice exercises in Lesson 6.3.

Keystroke Help

Keystrokes for several models of calculators are available in blackline format in the *Chapter 6 Resource Book*.

2 TEACH

Tips for Success

In Steps 2 and 4, be sure students understand that they need to press VARS to access y_3 again to enter it on the home screen.

Alternative Strategy

Show students how to find the required function values by using the *table* feature of a graphing calculator, rather than the home screen.

Extra Example

Let $f(x) = 4x - 5$ and $g(x) = x^2 + 2x - 7$. Find $f(3) - g(3)$ and $g(f(-4))$. **−1; 392**

3 ASSESS AND RETEACH

If you try to evaluate a composite function with your calculator and get an ERROR message, what would this mean? **It would mean that the value you chose is not in the domain of the composite function.**

Kentucky Mixed Review

1. A
2. C
3. D
4. C
5. C
6. B
7. a. 5.99 inches
   b. The volume will rise by a factor of 8

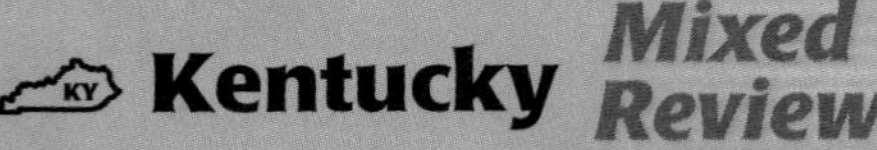

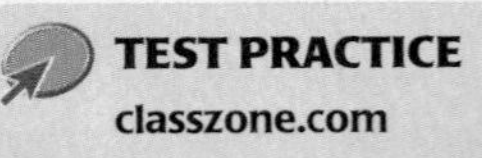

Lessons 6.1–6.3

1. **BOWLING** The formula for the volume V of a sphere in terms of its surface area S is $V = 3^{-1}(4\pi)^{-1/2}(S^3)^{1/2}$. A candlepin bowling ball has a surface area of about 79 square inches. What is its volume to the nearest cubic inch?

   A. 66 in.^{3} B. 184 in.^{3}
   C. 368 in.^{3} D. 594 in.^{3}

2. **AREA OF SHADED REGION** A triangle is inscribed in a square, as shown. Which function $r(x)$ represents the area of the shaded region?

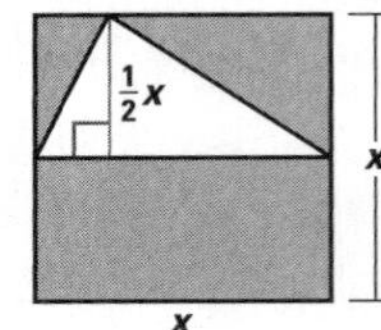

   A. $r(x) = \frac{3}{4}x$
   B. $r(x) = \frac{1}{4}x^2$
   C. $r(x) = \frac{3}{4}x^2$
   D. $r(x) = \frac{1}{2}x^4$

3. **SALARY** You are working as a sales representative for a clothing manufacturer. You are paid an annual salary plus a bonus of 3% of your sales over \$100,000. Consider these two functions:

   $f(x) = x - 100{,}000$ $g(x) = 0.03x$

   Which expression represents your bonus when $x > 100{,}000$?

   A. $f(x) \cdot g(x)$
   B. $\frac{f(x)}{g(x)}$
   C. $f(g(x))$
   D. $g(f(x))$

4. **SWIMMING POOL** A cylindrical above-ground pool has a height of 5 feet and a radius of x feet. You use a hose to fill the pool with water. Water flows from the hose at a rate of 128 cubic feet per hour. After 8.8 hours, the pool is half full. What is the radius of the pool to the nearest foot? Use 3.14 for π.

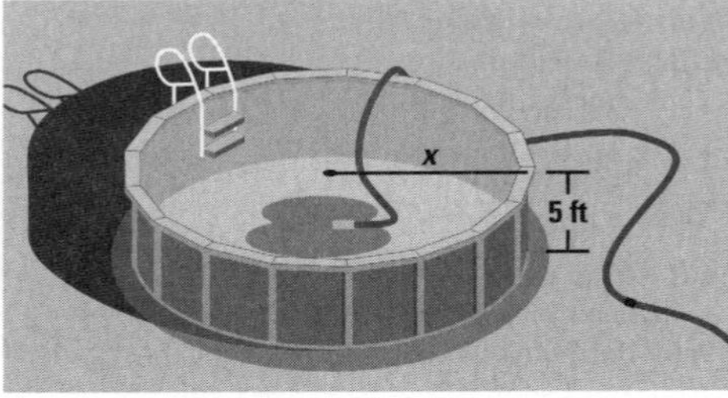

   A. 6 feet B. 7 feet
   C. 12 feet D. 24 feet

5. **FUNCTION COMPOSITION** Which function $f(x)$ satisfies the condition that $f(f(x)) = x$?

   A. $f(x) = 3x^{-2}$
   B. $f(x) = x + 3$
   C. $f(x) = 5 - x$
   D. $f(x) = x^{1/2}$

6. **SIMPLIFYING AN EXPRESSION** What is the simplified form of the expression $\left(\frac{16^{1/2}}{4^{1/2}}\right)^5$?

   A. 2
   B. 32
   C. 512
   D. 1024

7. **OPEN-RESPONSE** The volume of a sphere is 900 cubic inches.

   a. Use the formula for the volume of a sphere, $V = \frac{4}{3}\pi r^3$, to find the radius r of the sphere to the nearest hundredth of an inch. Use 3.14 for π.

   b. What happens to the volume when the radius is doubled?

6.4 Exploring Inverse Functions

MATERIALS • graph paper • straightedge

QUESTION How are a function and its *inverse* related?

EXPLORE Find the inverse of $f(x) = \frac{x-3}{2}$

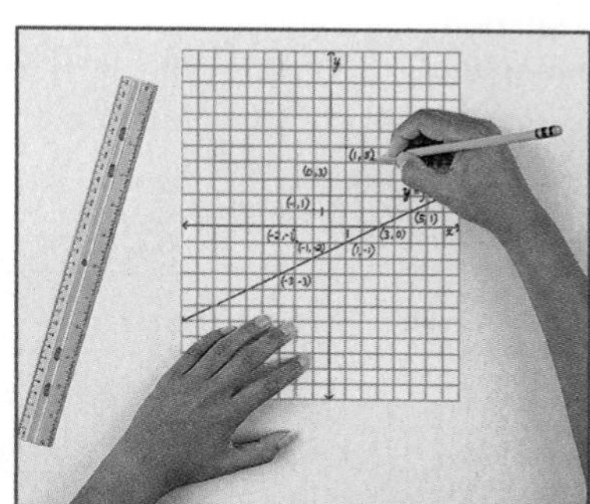

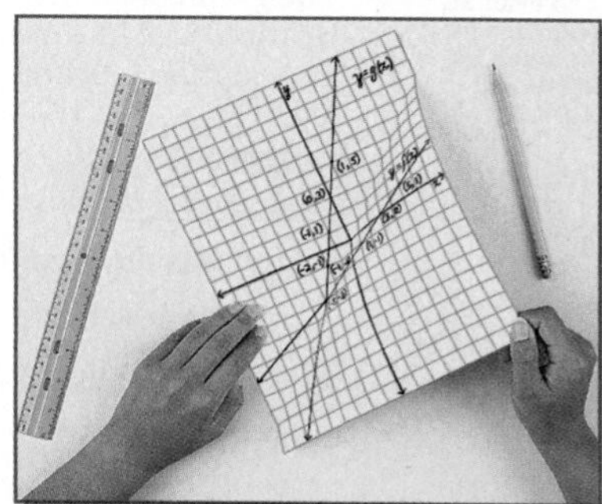

STEP 1 ***Graph function*** Choose values of x and find the corresponding values of $y = f(x)$. Plot the points and draw the line that passes through them.

STEP 2 ***Interchange coordinates*** Interchange the x- and y-coordinates of the ordered pairs found in Step 1. Plot the new points and draw the line that passes through them.

STEP 3 ***Write equation*** Write an equation of the line from Step 2. Call this function g.

STEP 4 ***Compare graphs*** Fold your graph paper so that the graphs of f and g coincide. How are the graphs geometrically related?

STEP 5 ***Describe functions*** In words, f is the function that subtracts 3 from x and then divides the result by 2. Describe the function g in words.

STEP 6 ***Find compositions*** Predict what the compositions $f(g(x))$ and $g(f(x))$ will be. Confirm your predictions by finding $f(g(x))$ and $g(f(x))$.

The functions f and g are called *inverses* of each other.

DRAW CONCLUSIONS Use your observations to complete these exercises

Complete Exercises 1–3 for each function below.

$f(x) = 3x + 2$ $\qquad f(x) = \frac{x-1}{6}$ $\qquad f(x) = 4 - \frac{3}{2}x$

1. Complete Steps 1–3 above to find the inverse of the function. $g(x) = \frac{x-2}{3}$, $g(x) = 6x + 1$, $g(x) = -\frac{2}{3}(x - 4)$
2. Complete Step 4. How can you graph the inverse of a function without first finding ordered pairs (x, y)? **Reflect the graph of $f(x)$ over the line $y = x$.**
3. Complete Steps 5 and 6. How can you test to see if the function you found in Exercise 1 is indeed the inverse of the original function? **Find the compositions $f(g(x))$ and $g(f(x))$ and if they both equal x, then $f(x)$ and $g(x)$ are inverses of each other.**

1 PLAN AND PREPARE

Explore the Concept

- Students will plot points to graph a linear equation and then graph the points found by interchanging coordinates to explore the concept of inverse functions.
- This activity leads into the study of finding inverse relations in Example 1 in Lesson 6.4.

Materials

Each student will need:

- graph paper
- a straightedge

Recommended Time

Work activity: 15 min
Discuss results: 5 min

Grouping

Students should work individually.

2 TEACH

Tips for Success

To avoid careless errors, have students list the points they used to graph the given equation and then list the points obtained by interchanging coordinates.

Key Discovery

The graphs of inverse linear functions are reflections of each other in the line $y = x$.

3 ASSESS AND RETEACH

If linear functions f and g are inverses, what is the result of finding $f(g(x))$ and $g(f(x))$? x

1 PLAN AND PREPARE

Warm-Up Exercises

Transparency Available

1. Solve $x = 4y^3$ for y. $y = \sqrt[3]{\frac{x}{4}}$
2. If $f(x) = 4x + 1$ and $g(x) = \sqrt{x - 1} + 1$, find $f(g(x))$ and $g(f(x))$. $f(g(x)) = 4\sqrt{x - 1} + 5$; $g(f(x)) = \sqrt{4x} + 1$
3. The formula for the area of a square is $A = s^2$. What is a formula for finding s when A is known? $s = \sqrt{A}$

Notetaking Guide

Transparency Available

notetaking skills, pp. 173–175.

Pacing

Basic: 2 days

Average: 2 days

Advanced: 2 days

Block: 0.5 block with 6.3
0.5 block with 6.5

- See *Teaching Guide/Lesson Plan.*

2 FOCUS AND MOTIVATE

Essential Question

Big Idea 2, p. 413

How do you find the inverse relation of a given function? **Tell students they will learn how to answer this question by learning the steps for finding the inverse of a function.**

6.4 Use Inverse Functions

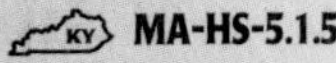 **MA-HS-5.1.5**

Before	You performed operations with functions.
Now	You will find inverse functions.
Why?	So you can convert temperatures, as in Ex. 48.

Key Vocabulary
- **inverse relation**
- **inverse function**

MA-HS-5.1.5
Students will: determine if a relation is a function; determine the domain and range of a function (linear and quadratic); determine the slope and intercepts of a linear function; determine the maximum, minimum, and intercepts (roots/zeros) of a quadratic function and evaluate a function written in function notation for a specified rational number. DOK 2

In Lesson 2.1, you learned that a relation is a pairing of input values with output values. An **inverse relation** interchanges the input and output values of the original relation. This means that the domain and range are also interchanged.

Original relation

x	0	1	2	3	4
y	6	4	2	0	−2

Inverse relation

x	6	4	2	0	−2
y	0	1	2	3	4

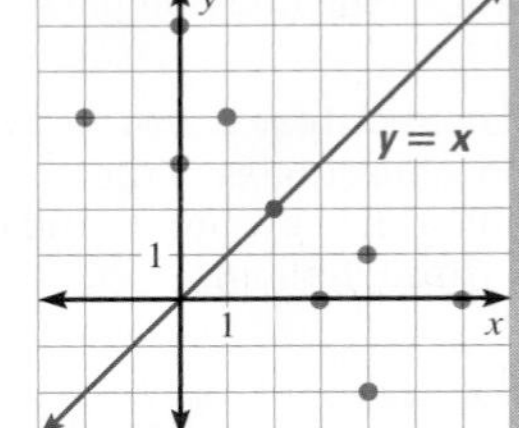

The graph of an inverse relation is a *reflection* of the graph of the original relation. The line of reflection is $y = x$. To find the inverse of a relation given by an equation in x and y, switch the roles of x and y and solve for y.

EXAMPLE 1 Find an inverse relation

Find an equation for the inverse of the relation $y = 3x - 5$.

$y = 3x - 5$	Write original relation.
$x = 3y - 5$	Switch x and y.
$x + 5 = 3y$	Add 5 to each side.
$\frac{1}{3}x + \frac{5}{3} = y$	Solve for y. This is the inverse relation.

In Example 1, both the original relation and the inverse relation happen to be functions. In such cases, the two functions are called **inverse functions**.

READING
The symbol −1 in f^{-1} is not to be interpreted as an exponent. In other words, $f^{-1}(x) \neq \frac{1}{f(x)}$.

KEY CONCEPT *For Your Notebook*

Inverse Functions

Functions f and g are inverses of each other provided:

$$f(g(x)) = x \quad \text{and} \quad g(f(x)) = x$$

The function g is denoted by f^{-1}, read as "f inverse."

Resource Planning Guide

Chapter Resource Book
- Teaching Guide/Lesson Plan (pp. 40–41)
- Practice levels A, B, C (pp. 43–45)
- Study Guide (pp. 46–47)
- Catch-up for Absent Students (p. 48)
- Application (p. 49)
- Challenge (p. 50)

Workbooks
- Notetaking Guide (pp. 173–175)
- Practice Workbook (pp. 102–103)

Teaching Options
- **Power Presentations CD-ROM** provides dynamic electronic teaching resources for the classroom.
- **Activity Generator CD-ROM** provides editable activities for all ability levels.

Interactive Technology
- Easy Planner
- Power Presentations CD-ROM
- Activity Generator CD-ROM
- Animated Algebra
- Test Generator CD-ROM
- Online Quiz
- eWorkbook
- eEdition
- @HomeTutor

Resources for English Learners
- Quick Reference for English Learners
- Spanish Study Guide
- Multi-Language Visual Glossary
- Student Resources in Spanish

See also the *Algebra 2 Toolkit* for more strategies for meeting individual needs.

EXAMPLE 2 Verify that functions are inverses

Verify that $f(x) = 3x - 5$ and $f^{-1}(x) = \frac{1}{3}x + \frac{5}{3}$ are inverse functions.

Solution

STEP 1 **Show** that $f(f^{-1}(x)) = x$.

$$f(f^{-1}(x)) = f\left(\frac{1}{3}x + \frac{5}{3}\right)$$
$$= 3\left(\frac{1}{3}x + \frac{5}{3}\right) - 5$$
$$= x + 5 - 5$$
$$= x ✓$$

STEP 2 **Show** that $f^{-1}(f(x)) = x$.

$$f^{-1}(f(x)) = f^{-1}(3x - 5)$$
$$= \frac{1}{3}(3x - 5) + \frac{5}{3}$$
$$= x - \frac{5}{3} + \frac{5}{3}$$
$$= x ✓$$

EXAMPLE 3 Solve a multi-step problem

FITNESS Elastic bands can be used in exercising to provide a range of resistance. A band's resistance R (in pounds) can be modeled by $R = \frac{3}{8}L - 5$ where L is the total length of the stretched band (in inches).

- Find the inverse of the model.
- Use the inverse function to find the length at which the band provides 19 pounds of resistance.

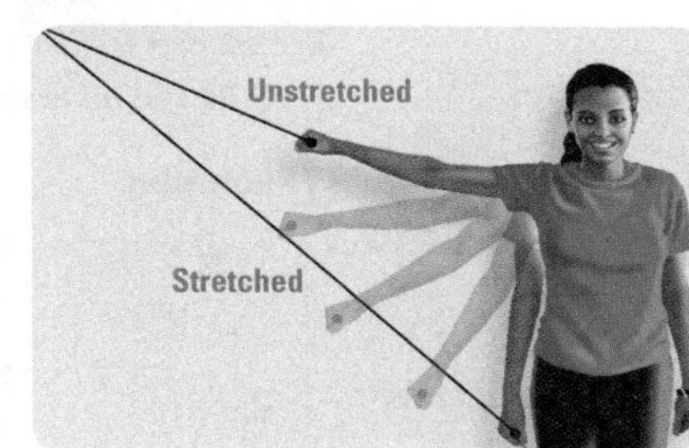

Solution

STEP 1 **Find** the inverse function.

$R = \frac{3}{8}L - 5$	**Write original model.**
$R + 5 = \frac{3}{8}L$	**Add 5 to each side.**
$\frac{8}{3}R + \frac{40}{3} = L$	**Multiply each side by $\frac{8}{3}$.**

STEP 2 **Evaluate** the inverse function when $R = 19$.

$$L = \frac{8}{3}R + \frac{40}{3} = \frac{8}{3}(19) + \frac{40}{3} = \frac{152}{3} + \frac{40}{3} = \frac{192}{3} = 64$$

▶ The band provides 19 pounds of resistance when it is stretched to 64 inches.

FIND INVERSES
Notice that you do not switch the variables when you are finding inverses of models. This would be confusing because the letters are chosen to remind you of the real-life quantities they represent.

GUIDED PRACTICE for Examples 1, 2, and 3

Find the inverse of the given function. Then verify that your result and the original function are inverses. 1–3. See margin.

1. $f(x) = x + 4$
2. $f(x) = 2x - 1$
3. $f(x) = -3x + 1$
4. **FITNESS** Use the inverse function in Example 3 to find the length at which the band provides 13 pounds of resistance. 48 in.

Motivating the Lesson

You are on a family vacation in Canada, where the metric system is used. All road distances are given in kilometers, but you want to know the distances in miles. If you know the formula for converting from miles to kilometers, you can use an inverse function to convert from kilometers to miles.

3 TEACH

Extra Example 1

Find an equation for the inverse of the relation $y = 4x + 2$. $y = \frac{1}{4}x - \frac{1}{2}$

Extra Example 2

Verify that $f(x) = 4x + 2$ and $f^{-1}(x) = \frac{1}{4}x - \frac{1}{2}$ are inverse functions.

Step 1
$f(f^{-1}(x)) = f\left(\frac{1}{4}x - \frac{1}{2}\right) =$
$4\left(\frac{1}{4}x - \frac{1}{2}\right) + 2 = x - 2 + 2 = x$

Step 2
$f^{-1}(f(x)) = f^{-1}(4x + 2) =$
$\frac{1}{4}(4x + 2) - \frac{1}{2} = x + \frac{1}{2} - \frac{1}{2} = x$

Extra Example 3

A small company produces greeting cards. The cost C (in dollars) of producing n greeting cards per month can be modeled by the function $C = 360 + 0.60n$.

- Find the inverse of the model. $n = \frac{C}{0.60} - 600$
- Use the inverse function to find the number of greeting cards produced in a month in which the company's total cost to produce the cards was \$615. 425 cards

1–3. See Additional Answers beginning on p. AA1.

Differentiated Instruction

Below Level Some students may have trouble following the steps used to find inverse functions. As an alternative, talk about an inverse function as a function that "undoes" a function. Ask students how you undo adding a number, multiplying by a number, cubing a number, and so on. Then show them that they can find the inverse of a function by undoing the operations that have been done to x, but in the reverse order. In **Example 1**, the original function multiplies a number by 3 and subtracts 5, so the inverse will add 5 and then divide by 3.

See also the *Algebra 2 Toolkit* for more strategies.

Extra Example 4

Find the inverse of $f(x) = x^2 + 2$, $x \le 0$ Then graph f and f^{-1}.

$f^{-1}(x) = -\sqrt{x-2}$

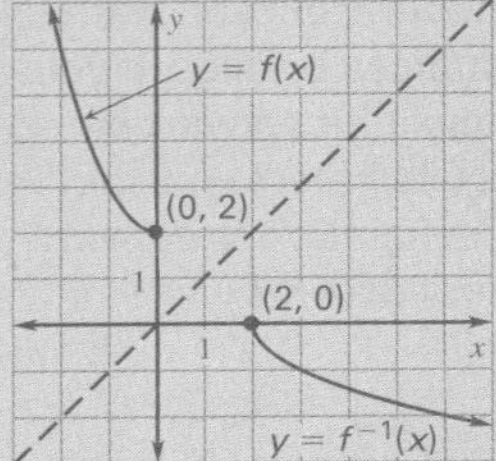

Key Question to Ask for Example 4

- Example 4 shows that you must restrict the domain of the function $f(x) = x^2$ in order to have a function whose inverse is also a function. Is the same true of the function $f(x) = x^3$? Explain. **No; the graph of $f(x) = x^3$ on its entire domain, which is all real numbers, passes the horizontal line test, so its inverse is also a function.**

Teaching Strategy

When introducing the horizontal line test, review the vertical line test. Be sure that students understand that the vertical line test is used to determine whether a graph represents a function, while the horizontal line test is used to determine whether the inverse of a given function is also a function.

Vocabulary

Tell students that functions that pass the horizontal line test are called "one-to-one" functions. Ask them why they think this name is used.

INVERSES OF NONLINEAR FUNCTIONS The graphs of the power functions $f(x) = x^2$ and $g(x) = x^3$ are shown below along with their reflections in the line $y = x$. Notice that the inverse of $g(x) = x^3$ is a function, but that the inverse of $f(x) = x^2$ is *not* a function.

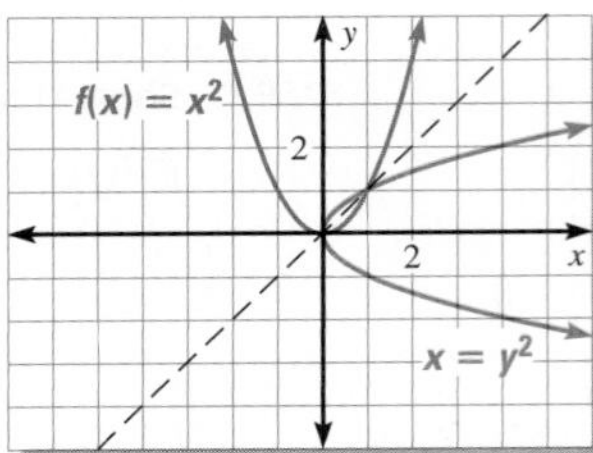

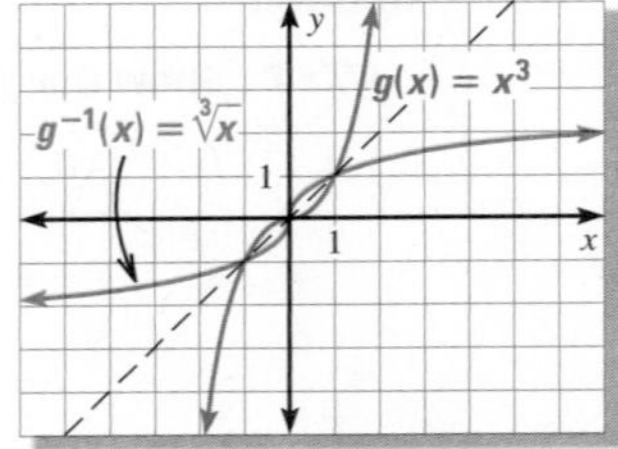

If the domain of $f(x) = x^2$ is *restricted* to only nonnegative real numbers, then the inverse of f is a function.

EXAMPLE 4 Find the inverse of a power function

Find the inverse of $f(x) = x^2, x \ge 0$. Then graph f and f^{-1}.

Solution

$f(x) = x^2$	**Write original function.**
$y = x^2$	**Replace $f(x)$ with y.**
$x = y^2$	**Switch x and y.**
$\pm\sqrt{x} = y$	**Take square roots of each side.**

The domain of f is restricted to nonnegative values of x. So, the range of f^{-1} must also be restricted to nonnegative values, and therefore the inverse is $f^{-1}(x) = \sqrt{x}$. (If the domain was restricted to $x \le 0$, you would choose $f^{-1}(x) = -\sqrt{x}$.)

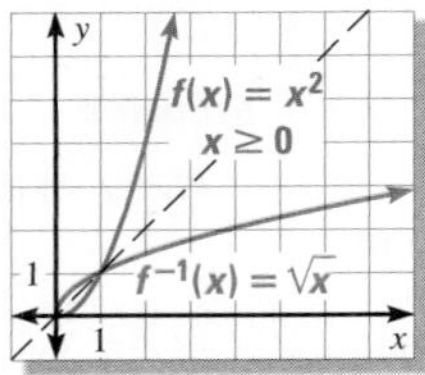

CHECK SOLUTION

You can check the solution of Example 4 by noting that the graph of $f^{-1}(x) = \sqrt{x}$ is the reflection of the graph of $f(x) = x^2, x \ge 0$, in the line $y = x$.

HORIZONTAL LINE TEST You can use the graph of a function f to determine whether the inverse of f is a function by applying the *horizontal line test.*

KEY CONCEPT *For Your Notebook*

Horizontal Line Test

The inverse of a function f is also a function if and only if no horizontal line intersects the graph of f more than once.

Inverse is a function

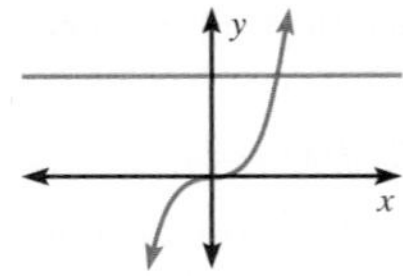

Inverse is not a function

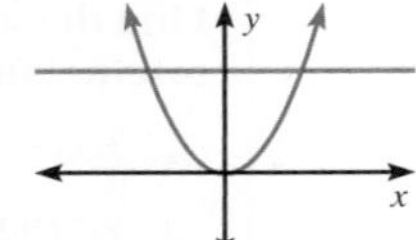

Differentiated Instruction

Visual Learners While the algebraic method of verifying that two functions are inverse functions is the most accurate method, it may not help to solidify the concepts for some students. In **Example 5**, provide groups of students with grid paper and have them graph $f(x)$ and the line $y = x$ on the same coordinate plane. Have them graph the inverse of f by reflecting its graph over the line $y = x$, and then verify that the image is the graph of $f^{-1} = \sqrt[3]{\frac{x-1}{2}}$.

See also the *Algebra 2 Toolkit* for more strategies.

EXAMPLE 5 Find the inverse of a cubic function

Consider the function $f(x) = 2x^3 + 1$. Determine whether the inverse of f is a function. Then find the inverse.

Solution

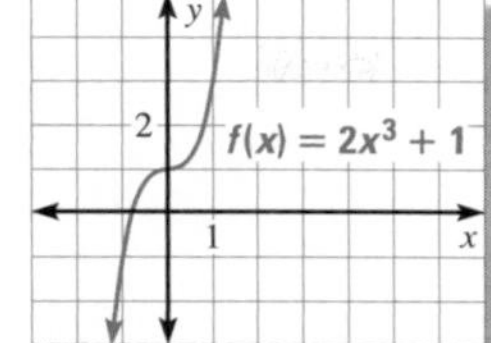

Graph the function f. Notice that no horizontal line intersects the graph more than once. So, the inverse of f is itself a function. To find an equation for f^{-1}, complete the following steps:

$f(x) = 2x^3 + 1$	**Write original function.**
$y = 2x^3 + 1$	**Replace $f(x)$ with y.**
$x = 2y^3 + 1$	**Switch x and y.**
$x - 1 = 2y^3$	**Subtract 1 from each side.**
$\frac{x-1}{2} = y^3$	**Divide each side by 2.**
$\sqrt[3]{\frac{x-1}{2}} = y$	**Take cube root of each side.**

▶ The inverse of f is $f^{-1}(x) = \sqrt[3]{\frac{x-1}{2}}$.

GUIDED PRACTICE for Examples 4 and 5

Find the inverse of the function. Then graph the function and its inverse.

5–10. See margin for art.

5. $f(x) = x^6, x \geq 0$ $f^{-1}(x) = \sqrt[6]{x}$
6. $g(x) = \frac{1}{27}x^3$ $g^{-1}(x) = 3\sqrt[3]{x}$
7. $f(x) = -\frac{64}{125}x^3$ $f^{-1}(x) = -\frac{5}{4}\sqrt[3]{x}$
8. $f(x) = -x^3 + 4$ $f^{-1}(x) = \sqrt[3]{4 - x}$
9. $f(x) = 2x^5 + 3$ $f^{-1}(x) = \sqrt[5]{\frac{x-3}{2}}$
10. $g(x) = -7x^5 + 7$ $g^{-1}(x) = \sqrt[5]{\frac{x-7}{-7}}$

EXAMPLE 6 Find the inverse of a power model

TICKET PRICES The average price P (in dollars) for a National Football League ticket can be modeled by

$$P = 35t^{0.192}$$

where t is the number of years since 1995. Find the inverse model that gives time as a function of the average ticket price.

Solution

$P = 35t^{0.192}$	**Write original model.**
$\frac{P}{35} = t^{0.192}$	**Divide each side by 35.**
$\left(\frac{P}{35}\right)^{1/0.192} = (t^{0.192})^{1/0.192}$	**Raise each side to the power $\frac{1}{0.192}$.**
$\left(\frac{P}{35}\right)^{5.2} \approx t$	**Simplify. This is the inverse model.**

Extra Example 5

Consider the function $f(x) = 3x^5 - 2$. Determine whether the inverse of f is a function. Then find the inverse.
Yes; $f^{-1}(x) = \sqrt[5]{\frac{x+2}{3}}$

Key Question to Ask for Example 5

- Three operations are done to x to obtain the expression $2x^3 + 1$: Raise x to the third power (cube it), multiply by 2, and add 1. What three operations can be done to get back to x, and in what order? Subtract 1, divide by 2, and take the cube root.

Extra Example 6

The population of a town can be modeled by $P = 16{,}500t^{0.15}$, where t is the number of years since 1998. Find the inverse model that gives the number of years as a function of the population. $t = \left(\frac{P}{16{,}500}\right)^{6.67}$

8.
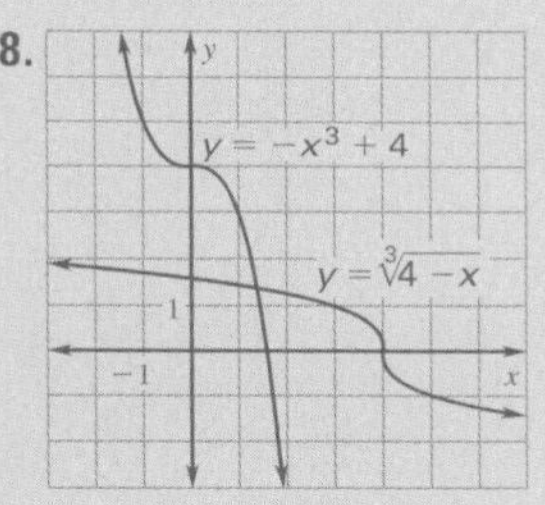

9.
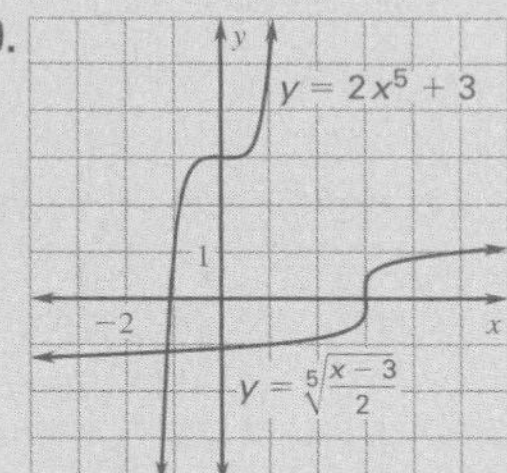

10.
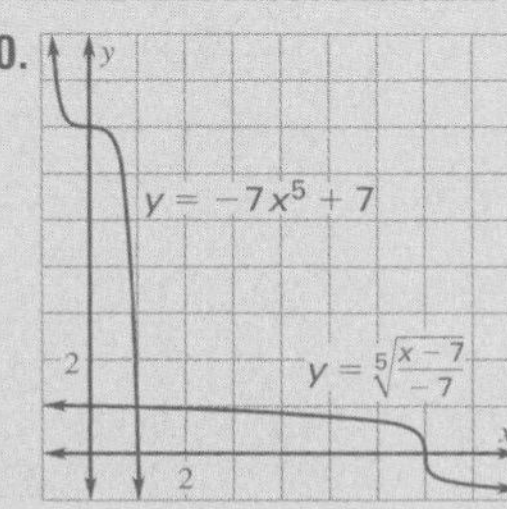
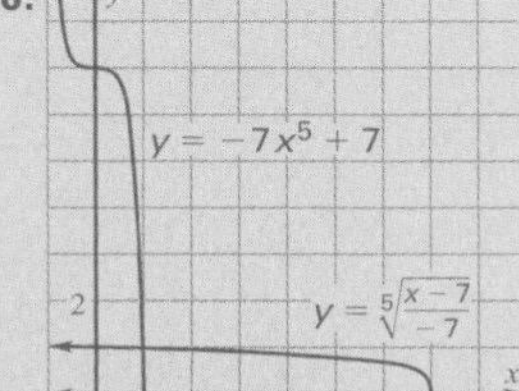

5.
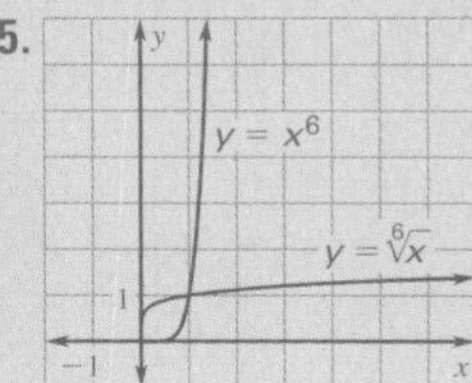

6.
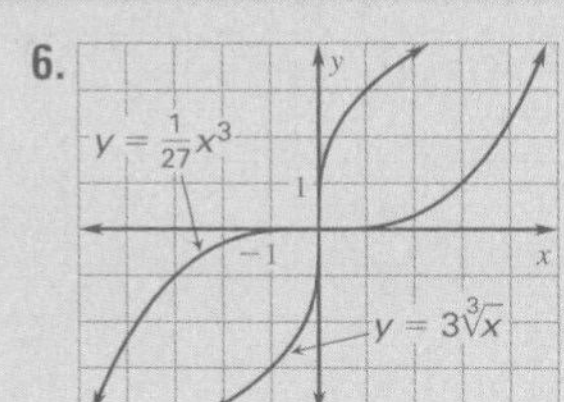

7.
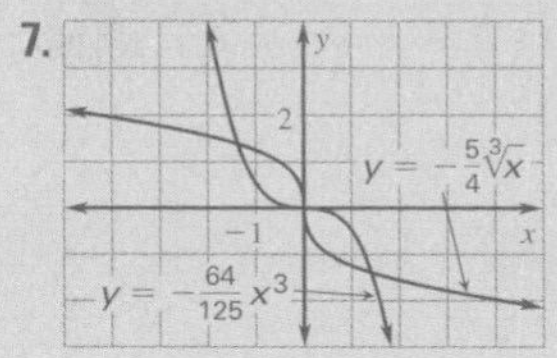

Extra Example 7

Use the inverse model from Extra Example 6 to predict the year in which the population of the town will reach 25,000. 2014

Closing the Lesson

Have students summarize the major points of the lesson and answer the Essential Question: How do you find the inverse relation of a given function?

- An inverse relation interchanges the input and output values of any relation.
- If the graph of a function passes the horizontal line test, then the inverse of the function is also a function.

To find an equation of the inverse of a given function involving x and y, write the original equation, switch x and y, and solve for y.

EXAMPLE 7 Use an inverse power model to make a prediction

Use the inverse power model from Example 6 to predict the year when the average ticket price will reach \$58.

Solution

$t = \left(\frac{P}{35}\right)^{5.2}$ **Write inverse power model.**

$= \left(\frac{58}{35}\right)^{5.2}$ **Substitute 58 for *P*.**

≈ 14 **Use a calculator.**

▶ You can predict that the average ticket price will reach \$58 about 14 years after 1995, or in 2009.

✓ GUIDED PRACTICE for Examples 6 and 7

11. **TICKET PRICES** The average price P (in dollars) for a Major League Baseball ticket can be modeled by $P = 10.7t^{0.272}$ where t is the number of years since 1995. Write the inverse model. Then use the inverse to predict the year when the average ticket price will reach \$25. $t = \left(\frac{P}{10.7}\right)^{3.68}$; 2018

6.4 EXERCISES

HOMEWORK KEY
○ = WORKED-OUT SOLUTIONS on p. WS12 for Exs. 7, 15, and 49
★ = STANDARDIZED TEST PRACTICE Exs. 2, 14, 21, 28, and 48

SKILL PRACTICE

1. **VOCABULARY** State the definition of an inverse relation.
An inverse relation interchanges the input and output values of the original relation.
2. ★ **WRITING** *Explain* how to determine whether a function g is an inverse of f.
If $f(g(x)) = x$ and $g(f(x)) = x$, then f and g are inverses.

EXAMPLE 1 on p. 438 for Exs. 3–13

INVERSE RELATIONS **Find an equation for the inverse relation.**

3. $y = 4x - 1$ $y = \frac{x+1}{4}$
4. $y = -2x + 5$ $y = \frac{5-x}{2}$
5. $y = 7x - 6$ $y = \frac{x+6}{7}$
6. $y = 10x - 28$ $y = \frac{x+28}{10}$
7. $y = 12x + 7$ $y = \frac{x-7}{12}$
8. $y = -18x - 5$ $y = \frac{x+5}{-18}$
9. $y = 5x + \frac{1}{3}$ $y = \frac{1}{5}x - \frac{1}{15}$
10. $y = -\frac{2}{3}x + 2$ $y = \frac{6-3x}{2}$
11. $y = -\frac{3}{5}x + \frac{7}{5}$ $y = \frac{7-5x}{3}$

ERROR ANALYSIS ***Describe*** **and correct the error in finding the inverse of the relation.**

12.
$y = 6x - 11$
$x = 6y - 11$
$x + 11 = 6y$
$\frac{x}{6} + 11 = y$

13.
$y = -x + 3$
$-x = y + 3$
$-x - 3 = y$

12. Each term must be divided by 6; $x + 11 = 6y$, $\frac{x+11}{6} = y$.

13. Switching the roles of x and y does not include switching the sign of the variables; $x = -y + 3$, $x - 3 = -y$, $3 - x = y$.

15. $f(g(x)) = x - 4 + 4 = x$, $g(f(x)) = x + 4 - 4 = x$

16. $f(g(x)) = 2\left(\frac{1}{2}x - \frac{3}{2}\right) + 3 = x - 3 + 3 = x$, $g(f(x)) = \frac{1}{2}(2x + 3) - \frac{3}{2} = x + \frac{3}{2} - \frac{3}{2} = x$

17. $f(g(x)) = \frac{1}{4}[(4x)^{1/3}]^3 = \frac{1}{4}(4x) = x$, $g(f(x)) = \left(4\left(\frac{1}{4}x^3\right)\right)^{1/3} = (x^3)^{1/3} = x$

18. $f(g(x)) = \frac{1}{5}(5x + 5) - 1 = x + 1 - 1 = x$, $g(f(x)) = 5\left(\frac{1}{5}x - 1\right) + 5 = x - 5 + 5 = x$

14. ★ **OPEN-ENDED MATH** Write a function f such that the graph of f^{-1} is a line with a slope of 3. *Sample answer:* $f(x) = \frac{x-2}{3}$

XAMPLE 2
n p. 439
or Exs. 15–21

VERIFYING INVERSE FUNCTIONS Verify that f and g are inverse functions. 15–20. See margin.

(15.) $f(x) = x + 4,\ g(x) = x - 4$

16. $f(x) = 2x + 3,\ g(x) = \frac{1}{2}x - \frac{3}{2}$

17. $f(x) = \frac{1}{4}x^3,\ g(x) = (4x)^{1/3}$

18. $f(x) = \frac{1}{5}x - 1,\ g(x) = 5x + 5$

19. $f(x) = 4x + 9,\ g(x) = \frac{1}{4}x - \frac{9}{4}$

20. $f(x) = 5x^2 - 2,\ x \ge 0;\ g(x) = \left(\frac{x+2}{5}\right)^{1/2}$

21. ★ **MULTIPLE CHOICE** What is the inverse of the function whose graph is shown? B

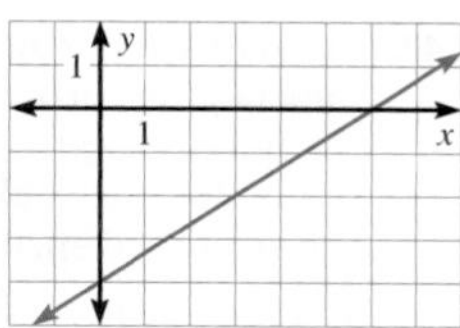

Ⓐ $g(x) = \frac{3}{2}x - 6$ Ⓑ $g(x) = \frac{3}{2}x + 6$

Ⓒ $g(x) = \frac{2}{3}x - 6$ Ⓓ $g(x) = \frac{3}{2}x + 12$

XAMPLE 4 B
n p. 440
or Exs. 22–28

INVERSES OF POWER FUNCTIONS Find the inverse of the power function.

22. $f(x) = x^7$ $f^{-1}(x) = \sqrt[7]{x}$

23. $f(x) = 4x^4,\ x \ge 0$ $f^{-1}(x) = \sqrt[4]{\frac{x}{4}}$

24. $f(x) = -10x^6,\ x \le 0$ $f^{-1}(x) = -\sqrt[6]{\frac{x}{-10}}$

25. $f(x) = 32x^5$ $f^{-1}(x) = \frac{\sqrt[5]{x}}{2}$

26. $f(x) = -\frac{2}{5}x^3$ $f^{-1}(x) = \sqrt[3]{\frac{-5x}{2}}$

27. $f(x) = \frac{16}{25}x^2,\ x \le 0$ $f^{-1}(x) = -\frac{5}{4}\sqrt{x}$

28. ★ **MULTIPLE CHOICE** What is the inverse of $f(x) = -\frac{1}{64}x^3$? C

Ⓐ $g(x) = -4x^3$ Ⓑ $g(x) = 4\sqrt[3]{x}$ Ⓒ $g(x) = -4\sqrt[3]{x}$ Ⓓ $g(x) = \sqrt[3]{-4x}$

XAMPLE 5
n p. 441
or Exs. 29–43

HORIZONTAL LINE TEST Graph the function f. Then use the graph to determine whether the inverse of f is a function. 29–37. See Additional Answers beginning on p. AA1 for art.

29. $f(x) = 3x + 1$ function

30. $f(x) = -x - 5$ function

31. $f(x) = \frac{1}{4}x^2 - 1$ not a function

32. $f(x) = -6x^2,\ x \ge 0$ function

33. $f(x) = \frac{1}{3}x^3$ function

34. $f(x) = x^3 - 2$ function

35. $f(x) = (x - 4)(x + 1)$ not a function

36. $f(x) = |x| + 4$ not a function

37. $f(x) = 4x^4 - 5x^2 - 6$ not a function

INVERSES OF NONLINEAR FUNCTIONS Find the inverse of the function.

38. $f(x) = \frac{3}{2}x^4,\ x \ge 0$ $f^{-1}(x) = \sqrt[4]{\frac{2x}{3}}$

39. $f(x) = x^3 - 2$ $f^{-1}(x) = \sqrt[3]{x + 2}$

40. $f(x) = \frac{3}{4}x^5 + 5$ $f^{-1}(x) = \sqrt[5]{\frac{4x - 20}{3}}$

41. $f(x) = -\frac{2}{5}x^6 + 8,\ x \le 0$ $f^{-1}(x) = -\sqrt[6]{\frac{40 - 5x}{2}}$

42. $f(x) = \frac{2x^3 - 6}{9}$ $f^{-1}(x) = \sqrt[3]{\frac{9x + 6}{2}}$

43. $f(x) = x^4 - 9,\ x \ge 0$ $f^{-1}(x) = \sqrt[4]{x + 9}$

C

44. **REASONING** Determine whether the statement is *true* or *false*. *Explain* your reasoning.

a. If $f(x) = x^n$ where n is a positive even integer, then the inverse of f is a function. False. *Sample answer:* The graph of the inverse will not pass the vertical line test.

b. If $f(x) = x^n$ where n is a positive odd integer, then the inverse of f is a function. True. *Sample answer:* The graph of the inverse will pass the vertical line test.

45. **CHALLENGE** Show that the inverse of any linear function $f(x) = mx + b$, where $m \ne 0$, is also a linear function. Give the slope and y-intercept of the graph of f^{-1} in terms of m and b.

$f^{-1}(x) =$
$x - \frac{b}{m}$, this
the graph of
ine and the
aphs of lines
e always
ictions if
$\ne 0$; slope: $\frac{1}{m}$,
intercept: $-\frac{b}{m}$.

4 PRACTICE AND APPLY

Assignment Guide

Answer Transparencies available for all exercises

Basic:
Day 1: EP p. 1014 Exs. 8–11
pp. 442–445
Exs. 1–8, 12–18, 21, 46–48, 58–66
Day 2: pp. 442–445
Exs. 22–34, 49, 52–53

Average:
Day 1: pp. 442–445
Exs. 1, 2, 5–10, 12–14, 16–19, 21, 46–48
Day 2: pp. 442–445
Exs. 25–28, 31–43, 49, 50, 52–53

Advanced:
Day 1: pp. 442–445
Exs. 1, 2, 6–11, 14–21, 46–48
Day 2: pp. 442–445
Exs. 26–28, 34–45*, 49–53*

Block:
pp. 442–445
Exs. 1, 2, 5–10, 12–14, 16–19, 21, 46–48 (with 6.3)
pp. 442–445
Exs. 25–28, 31–43, 49, 50, 52–53 (with 6.5)

Differentiated Instruction

See *Algebra 2 Best Practices Toolkit* for suggestions on addressing the needs of a diverse classroom.

Homework Check

For a quick check of student understanding of key concepts, go over the following exercises:
Basic: 4, 16, 22, 30, 46
Average: 8, 18, 26, 34, 47
Advanced: 10, 27, 36, 48, 50

Extra Practice

- Student Edition, p. 1015
- Chapter 6 Resource Book: Practice levels A, B, C, pp. 43–45

Practice Worksheet

An easily-readable reduced practice page (with answers) for this lesson can be found on p. 412C.

19. $f(g(x)) = 4\left(\frac{1}{4}x - \frac{9}{4}\right) + 9 = x - 9 + 9 = x$, $g(f(x)) = \frac{1}{4}(4x + 9) - \frac{9}{4} = x + \frac{9}{4} - \frac{9}{4} = x$

20. $f(g(x)) = \left(5\left(\frac{x+2}{5}\right)^{1/2}\right)^2 - 2 = 5\left(\frac{x+2}{5}\right) - 2 = x + 2 - 2 = x$,

$g(f(x)) = \left(\frac{5x^2 + 2 - 2}{5}\right)^{1/2} = \left(\frac{5x^2}{5}\right)^{1/2} = (x^2)^{1/2} = x$

Avoiding Common Errors

Exercises 15–20 Some students have trouble with these exercises because they do not understand what they are trying to do and why. They may multiply the functions rather than forming the composite functions or make errors in the algebraic steps needed to find $f(g(x))$ and $g(f(x))$. Review the process of finding compositions of functions from Lesson 6.3 and give these students extra practice in this skill as needed.

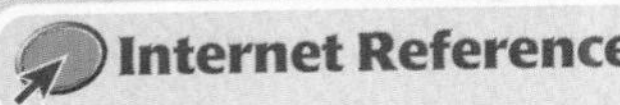

Exercise 48 For more information about Anchorage, Alaska, visit www.anchoragechamber.org and click on "Visitor Info".

An **Animated Algebra** activity is available on-line for **Exercise 49**. This activity is also available on the **Power Presentations CD-ROM**.

Mathematical Reasoning

Exercise 51 Ask students if they can think of a nonlinear function that is its own inverse. If they need a hint, say, "The opposite of the opposite of a number is the original number. What about the reciprocal of the reciprocal of a number?" If they are able to come up with the function $f(x) = \frac{1}{x}$, ask them if they can find any related functions that are also their own inverses.

51a. The reflection of the graph $g(x) = -x$ in the line $y = x$ is the graph itself. When the x- and y-coordinates of the original function are switched around, it is the same as the original function. If $g(x) = -x$, then $g^{-1}(x)$ is found by solving $x = -y$, which is $-x = y$, the original function.

PROBLEM SOLVING

EXAMPLE 3 A on p. 439 for Exs. 46–48

46. EXCHANGE RATES The *euro* is the unit of currency for the European Union. On a certain day, the number E of euros that could be obtained for D dollars was given by this function:

$$E = 0.81419D$$

Find the inverse of the function. Then use the inverse to find the number of dollars that could be obtained for 250 euros on that day. **$D = \frac{E}{0.81419}$; about \$307**

@HomeTutor for problem solving help at classzone.com

47. MULTI-STEP PROBLEM When calibrating a spring scale, you need to know how far the spring stretches for various weights. Hooke's law states that the length a spring stretches is proportional to the weight attached to it. A model for one scale is $\ell = 0.5w + 3$ where ℓ is the total length (in inches) of the stretched spring and w is the weight (in pounds) of the object.

a. Find the inverse of the given model. **$w = 2\ell - 6$**

b. If you place a weight on the scale and the spring stretches to a total length of 6.5 inches, how heavy is the weight? **7 lb**

@HomeTutor for problem solving help at classzone.com

B

48. ★ EXTENDED RESPONSE At the start of a dog sled race in Anchorage, Alaska, the temperature was 5°C. By the end of the race, the temperature was −10°C. The formula for converting temperatures from degrees Fahrenheit F to degrees Celsius C is $C = \frac{5}{9}(F - 32)$.

a. Find the inverse of the given model. *Describe* what information you can obtain from the inverse.

b. Find the Fahrenheit temperatures at the start and end of the race. **41°F, 14°F**

c. Use a graphing calculator to graph the original function and its inverse. Find the temperature that is the same on both temperature scales. **−40°**

48a. $F = \frac{9}{5}C + 32$; this will convert degrees Celsius to degrees Fahrenheit.

EXAMPLES 6 and 7 on pp. 441–442 for Exs. 49–50

49. BOAT SPEED The maximum hull speed v (in knots) of a boat with a displacement hull can be approximated by

$$v = 1.34\sqrt{\ell}$$

where ℓ is the length (in feet) of the boat's waterline. Find the inverse of the model. Then find the waterline length needed to achieve a maximum speed of 7.5 knots.

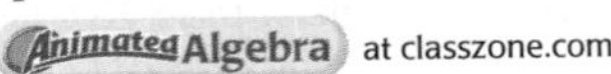

at classzone.com

49. $\ell = \left(\frac{v}{1.34}\right)^2$; about 31.3 ft

50. BIOLOGY The body surface area A (in square meters) of a person with a mass of 60 kilograms can be approximated by the model

$$A = 0.2195h^{0.3964}$$

where h is the person's height (in centimeters). Find the inverse of the model. Then estimate the height of a 60 kilogram person who has a body surface area of 1.6 square meters. **$h = \left(\frac{A}{0.2195}\right)^{2.523}$; about 150 cm**

○ = WORKED-OUT SOLUTIONS on p. WS1 ★ = STANDARDIZED TEST PRACTICE

Quiz, p. 445

9. $f(g(x)) = x + 9 - 9 = x$, $g(f(x)) = x - 9 + 9 = x$

10. $f(g(x)) = 5\left(\sqrt[3]{\frac{x}{5}}\right)^3 = 5\left(\frac{x}{5}\right) = x$, $g(f(x)) = \sqrt[3]{\frac{5x^3}{5}} = \sqrt[3]{x^3} = x$

11. $f(g(x)) = -\frac{3}{2}\left(-\frac{2}{3}x + \frac{1}{6}\right) + \frac{1}{4} = x - \frac{1}{4} + \frac{1}{4} = x$, $g(f(x)) = -\frac{2}{3}\left(-\frac{3}{2}x + \frac{1}{4}\right) + \frac{1}{6} = x - \frac{1}{6} + \frac{1}{6} = x$

12. $f(g(x)) = 6\left(\left(\frac{x-1}{6}\right)^{1/2}\right)^2 + 1 = 6\left(\frac{x-1}{6}\right) + 1 = x - 1 + 1 = x$, $g(f(x)) = \left(\frac{6x^2 + 1 - 1}{6}\right)^{1/2} = \left(\frac{6x^2}{6}\right)^{1/2} = (x^2)^{1/2} = x$

. Sample swer: $f(x) =$ $+ 2$, $f(x) =$ $- 7$, $) = -x + 4$

51. **CHALLENGE** Consider the function $g(x) = -x$.

a. Graph $g(x) = -x$ and explain why it is its own inverse. Also verify that $g(x) = g^{-1}(x)$ algebraically. **See margin.**

b. Graph other linear functions that are their own inverses. Write equations of the lines you graphed.

c. Use your results from part (b) to write a general equation describing the family of linear functions that are their own inverses. **$f(x) = -x + b$**

KENTUCKY MIXED REVIEW

TEST PRACTICE at classzone.com

52. What is the value of $f(x) = -5x^4 + 3x^3 + 10x^2 - x - 8$ when $x = -1$? **A**

Ⓐ -5 Ⓑ -1 Ⓒ 1 Ⓓ 3

53. At a school's annual choir competition, there are a total of 750 adults and students in the audience. The number of students, s, is 30 more than three times the number of adults, a. Which system of linear equations could be used to determine the numbers of students and adults in the audience? **B**

Ⓐ $s + a = 30$, $s = 750 - 3a$

Ⓑ $s + a = 750$, $s = 30 + 3a$

Ⓒ $s + a = 750$, $a = 30 + 3s$

Ⓓ $s + a = 30$, $a = 750 - 3s$

QUIZ for Lessons 6.3–6.4

Let $f(x) = 4x^2 - x$ and $g(x) = 2x^2$. Perform the indicated operation and state the domain. *(p. 428)*

1. $f(x) + g(x)$ **$6x^2 - x$, all real numbers**
2. $g(x) - f(x)$ **$-2x^2 + x$, all real numbers**
3. $f(x) \cdot g(x)$ **$8x^4 - 2x^3$, all real numbers**
4. $\frac{f(x)}{g(x)}$ **$2 - \frac{1}{2x}$, all real numbers except $x = 0$**
5. $f(g(x))$ **$16x^4 - 2x^2$**
6. $g(f(x))$ **$32x^4 - 16x^3 + 2x^2$**
7. $f(f(x))$ **$64x^4 - 32x^3 + x$**
8. $g(g(x))$ **$8x^4$**

Verify that f and g are inverse functions. *(p. 438)* **9–12. See margin.**

9. $f(x) = x - 9$, $g(x) = x + 9$
10. $f(x) = 5x^3$, $g(x) = \sqrt[3]{\frac{x}{5}}$
11. $f(x) = -\frac{3}{2}x + \frac{1}{4}$, $g(x) = -\frac{2}{3}x + \frac{1}{6}$
12. $f(x) = 6x^2 + 1, x \geq 0$; $g(x) = \left(\frac{x-1}{6}\right)^{1/2}$

Find the inverse of the function. *(p. 438)*

13. $f(x) = -\frac{1}{3}x + 5$ **$f^{-1}(x) = -3x + 15$**
14. $f(x) = x^2 - 16, x \geq 0$ **$f^{-1}(x) = \sqrt{x + 16}$**
15. $f(x) = -\frac{2}{9}x^5$ **$f^{-1}(x) = \sqrt[5]{\frac{-9x}{2}}$**
16. $f(x) = 5x + 12$ **$f^{-1}(x) = \frac{x - 12}{5}$**
17. $f(x) = -3x^3 - 4$ **$f^{-1}(x) = \sqrt[3]{\frac{x + 4}{-3}}$**
18. $f(x) = 9x^4 - 49, x \leq 0$ **$f^{-1}(x) = -\sqrt[4]{\frac{x + 49}{9}}$**
19. **GASOLINE COSTS** The cost (in dollars) of g gallons of gasoline can be modeled by $C(g) = 2.15g$. The amount of gasoline used by a car can be modeled by $g(d) = 0.02d$ where d is the distance (in miles) that the car has been driven. Find $C(g(d))$ and $C(g(400))$. What does $C(g(400))$ represent? *(p. 428)* **$0.043d$, 17.2; it will cost \$17.20 to drive the sports car 400 miles.**

5 ASSESS AND RETEACH

Daily Homework Quiz

Transparency Available

1. Find an equation for the inverse of the relation $y = -2x + 7$. $y = -\frac{1}{2}x + \frac{7}{2}$
2. Find the inverse of $f(x) = -x^2 + 4$, $x \geq 0$. Then graph f and f^{-1}. $f^{-1}(x) = \sqrt{4 - x}$

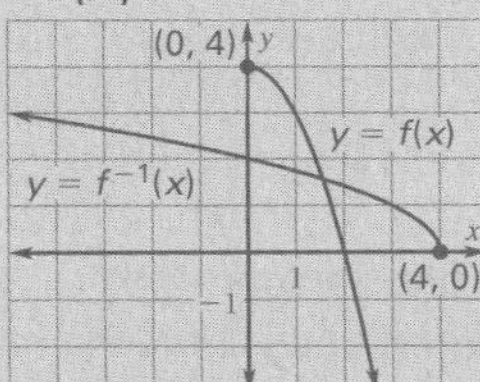

3. Consider the function $f(x) = 4x^3 + 5$. Determine whether the inverse of f is a function. Then find the inverse. Yes; $f^{-1}(x) = \sqrt[3]{\frac{x - 5}{4}}$
4. What formula can you use to find the Fahrenheit temperature when you know the Celsius temperature? $F = 1.8C + 32$

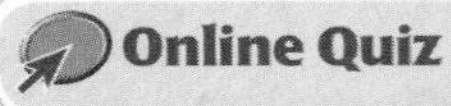

Available at **classzone.com**

Diagnosis/Remediation

- Practice A, B, C in Chapter 6 Resource Book, pp. 43–45
- Study Guide in Chapter 6 Resource Book, pp. 46–47
- Practice Workbook, pp. 102–103
- @HomeTutor

Challenge

Additional challenge is available in the Chapter 6 Resource Book, p. 50.

Quiz

An easily-readable reduced copy of the quiz (with answers) on Lessons 6.3–6.4 from the Assessment Book can be found on p. 412E.

1 PLAN AND PREPARE

Warm-Up Exercises

Transparency Available

State the domain and range of the function.

1. $f(x) = 2x - 5$ **domain and range: all real numbers**
2. $g(x) = -x^2 + 6$ **domain: all real numbers; range: $y \le 6$**
3. $y = \frac{1}{2}(x + 4)^2 - 8$ **domain: all real numbers; range: $y \ge -8$**

Notetaking Guide

Transparency Available

Promotes interactive learning and notetaking skills, pp. 176–179.

Pacing

Basic: 1 day
Average: 1 day
Advanced: 1 day
Block: 0.5 block with 6.4

- See *Teaching Guide/Lesson Plan.*

2 FOCUS AND MOTIVATE

Essential Question

Big Idea 3, p. 413

What do the graphs of square root and cube root functions look like? **Tell students they will learn how to answer this question by graphing a variety of square root and cube root functions.**

6.5 Graph Square Root and Cube Root Functions

Before You graphed polynomial functions.
Now You will graph square root and cube root functions.
Why? So you can graph the speed of a racing car, as in Ex. 38.

Key Vocabulary
- **radical function**
- **parent function,** *p. 89*

In Lesson 6.4, you saw the graphs of $y = \sqrt{x}$ and $y = \sqrt[3]{x}$. These are examples of **radical functions**. In this lesson, you will learn to graph functions of the form $y = a\sqrt{x - h} + k$ and $y = a\sqrt[3]{x - h} + k$.

KEY CONCEPT — *For Your Notebook*

Parent Functions for Square Root and Cube Root Functions

The parent function for the family of square root functions is $f(x) = \sqrt{x}$.

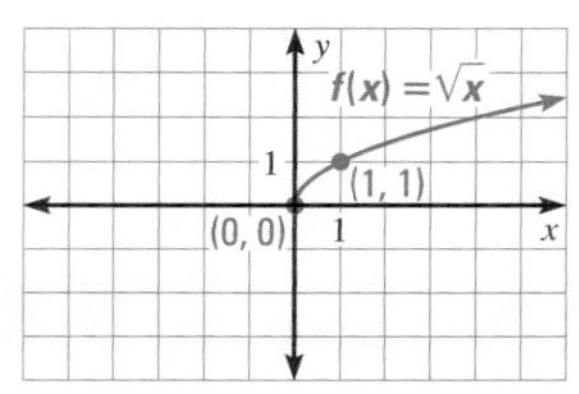

Domain: $x \ge 0$, Range: $y \ge 0$

The parent function for the family of cube root functions is $g(x) = \sqrt[3]{x}$.

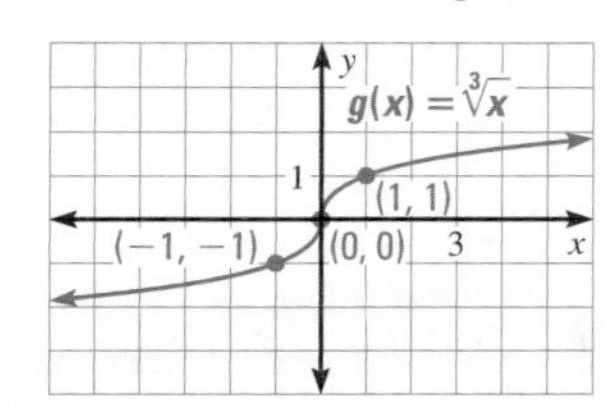

Domain and range: all real numbers

EXAMPLE 1 Graph a square root function

Graph $y = \frac{1}{2}\sqrt{x}$, and state the domain and range. Compare the graph with the graph of $y = \sqrt{x}$.

Solution

Make a table of values and sketch the graph.

x	0	1	2	3	4
y	0	0.5	0.71	0.87	1

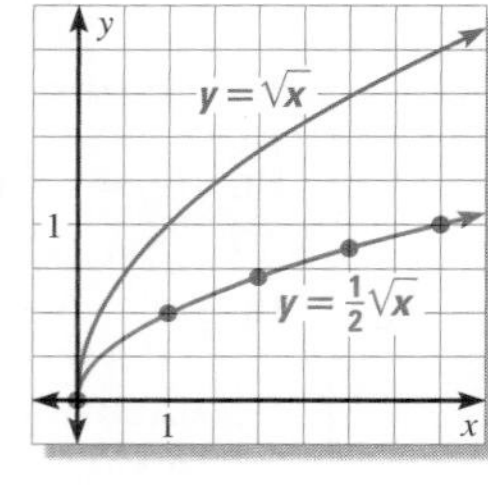

REVIEW DOMAIN AND RANGE
For help with the domain and range of a function, see p. 72.

The radicand of a square root must be nonnegative. So, the domain is $x \ge 0$. The range is $y \ge 0$.

The graph of $y = \frac{1}{2}\sqrt{x}$ is a vertical shrink of the graph of $y = \sqrt{x}$ by a factor of $\frac{1}{2}$.

Resource Planning Guide

Chapter Resource Book
- Teaching Guide/Lesson Plan (pp. 51–52)
- Activity Master (p. 53)
- Practice levels A, B, C (pp. 56–58)
- Study Guide (pp. 59–60)
- Catch-up for Absent Students (p. 61)
- Application (p. 62)
- Challenge (p. 63)

Workbooks
- Notetaking Guide (pp. 176–179)
- Practice Workbook (pp. 104–105)

Teaching Options
- **Power Presentations CD-ROM** provides dynamic electronic teaching resources for the classroom.
- **Activity Generator CD-ROM** provides editable activities for all ability levels.

Interactive Technology
- Easy Planner
- Power Presentations CD-ROM
- Activity Generator CD-ROM
- Animated Algebra
- Test Generator CD-ROM
- Online Quiz
- eWorkbook
- eEdition
- @HomeTutor

Resources for English Learners
- Quick Reference for English Learners
- Spanish Study Guide
- Multi-Language Visual Glossary
- Student Resources in Spanish

See also the *Algebra 2 Toolkit* for more strategies for meeting individual needs.

EXAMPLE 2 Graph a cube root function

Graph $y = -3\sqrt[3]{x}$, and state the domain and range. Compare the graph with the graph of $y = \sqrt[3]{x}$.

Solution

Make a table of values and sketch the graph.

x	−2	−1	0	1	2
y	3.78	3	0	−3	−3.78

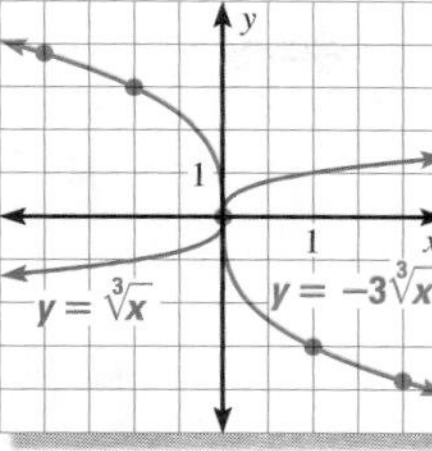

The domain and range are all real numbers.

The graph of $y = -3\sqrt[3]{x}$ is a vertical stretch of the graph of $y = \sqrt[3]{x}$ by a factor of 3 followed by a reflection in the x-axis.

REVIEW STRETCHES AND SHRINKS
For help with vertical stretches and shrinks, see p. 123.

EXAMPLE 3 Solve a multi-step problem

PENDULUMS The *period* of a pendulum is the time the pendulum takes to complete one back-and-forth swing. The period T (in seconds) can be modeled by $T = 1.11\sqrt{\ell}$ where ℓ is the pendulum's length (in feet).

- Use a graphing calculator to graph the model.
- How long is a pendulum with a period of 3 seconds?

Solution

STEP 1 **Graph** the model. Enter the equation $y = 1.11\sqrt{x}$. The graph is shown below.

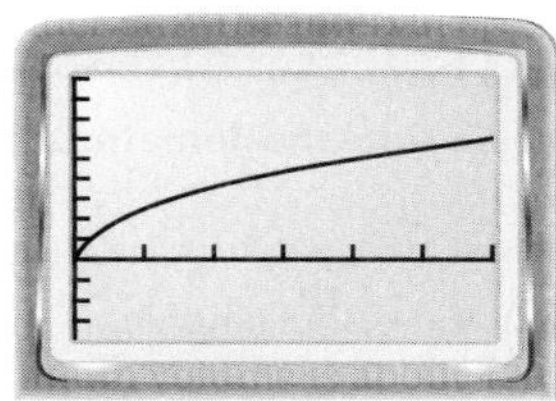

STEP 2 **Use** the *trace* feature to find the value of x when $y = 3$. The graph shows $x \approx 7.3$.

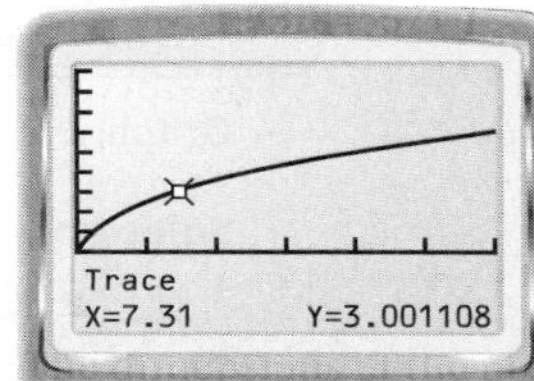

▶ A pendulum with a period of 3 seconds is about 7.3 feet long.

✓ GUIDED PRACTICE for Examples 1, 2, and 3

Graph the function. Then state the domain and range. 1–4. See margin for art.

1. $y = -3\sqrt{x}$ domain: $x \ge 0$, range: $y \le 0$
2. $f(x) = \frac{1}{4}\sqrt{x}$ domain: $x \ge 0$, range: $y \ge 0$
3. $y = -\frac{1}{2}\sqrt[3]{x}$ domain: all real numbers, range: all real numbers
4. $g(x) = 4\sqrt[3]{x}$ domain: all real numbers, range: all real numbers

5. **WHAT IF?** Use the model in Example 3 to find the length of a pendulum with a period of 1 second. about 0.8 ft

Motivating the Lesson

By measuring the skid marks of a vehicle and taking into account information about the efficiency of the brakes and the surface on which the car was traveling, a police officer can use a formula involving a square root function to estimate how fast a car was traveling at the time of an accident.

3 TEACH

Extra Example 1

Graph $y = -2\sqrt{x}$, and state the domain and range. Compare the graph with the graph of $y = \sqrt{x}$.

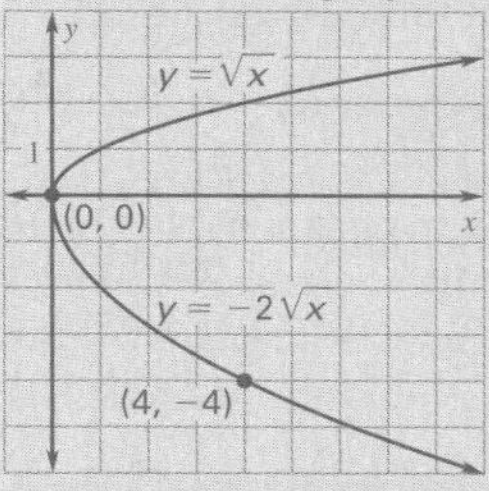

domain: $x \ge 0$; range: $y \le 0$; vertical stretch of the graph of $y = \sqrt{x}$ and reflection in the x-axis

Extra Example 2

Graph $y = \frac{3}{2}\sqrt[3]{x}$, and state the domain and range. Compare the graph with the graph of $y = \sqrt[3]{x}$.

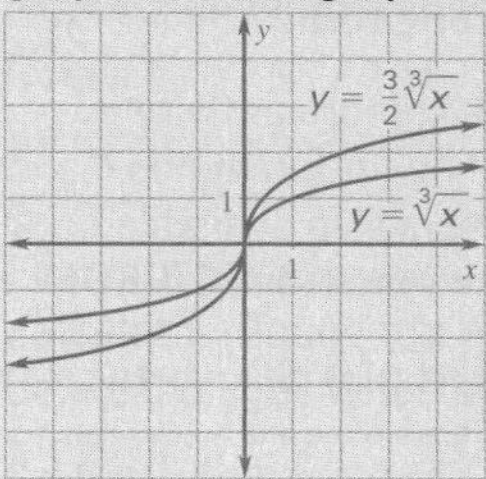

domain and range: all real numbers; vertical stretch of the graph of $y = \sqrt[3]{x}$

1–4. See Additional Answers beginning on p. AA1.

Extra Example 3

Biologists have found that the shoulder height h (in centimeters) of a male African elephant can be modeled by $h = 62.5\sqrt[3]{t} + 75.8$, where t is the elephant's age (in years).

- Use a graphing calculator to graph the model.

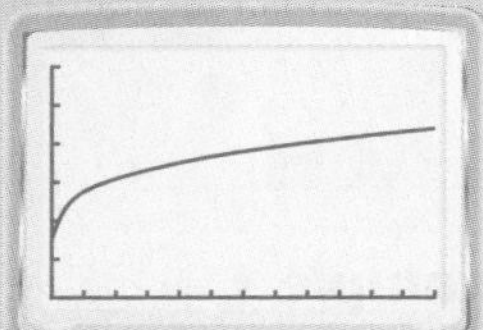

- Estimate the age of an elephant whose shoulder height is 200 centimeters. **about 7.8 yr**

Extra Example 4

Graph $y = 3\sqrt{x + 2} - 4$. Then state the domain the range.

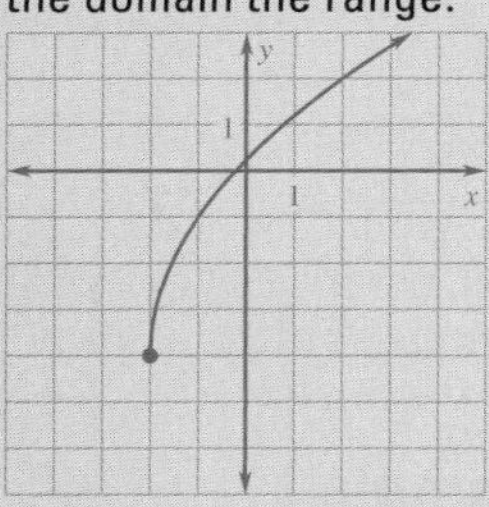

domain: $x \geq -2$; range: $y \geq -4$

An **Animated Algebra** activity is available on-line for **Examples 4** and **5**. This activity is also available on the **Power Presentations CD-ROM**.

Extra Example 5

Graph $y = -\frac{5}{2}\sqrt[3]{x - 2} + 3$. Then state the domain the range.

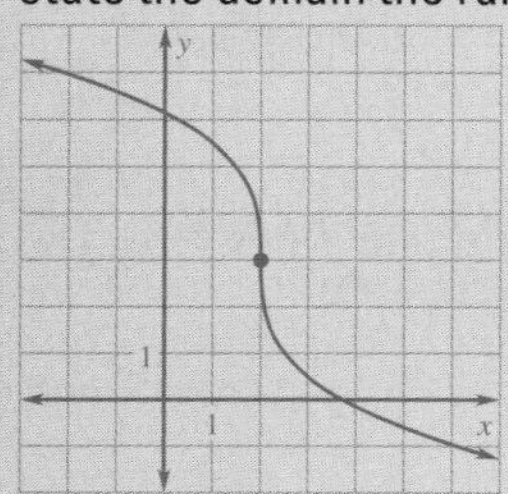

domain: all real numbers; range: all real numbers

TRANSLATIONS OF RADICAL FUNCTIONS The procedure for graphing functions of the form $y = a\sqrt{x - h} + k$ and $y = a\sqrt[3]{x - h} + k$ is described below.

KEY CONCEPT *For Your Notebook*

Graphs of Radical Functions

To graph $y = a\sqrt{x - h} + k$ or $y = a\sqrt[3]{x - h} + k$, follow these steps:

STEP 1 **Sketch** the graph of $y = a\sqrt{x}$ or $y = a\sqrt[3]{x}$.

STEP 2 **Translate** the graph horizontally h units and vertically k units.

EXAMPLE 4 Graph a translated square root function

Graph $y = -2\sqrt{x - 3} + 2$. Then state the domain and range.

Solution

STEP 1 **Sketch** the graph of $y = -2\sqrt{x}$ (shown in blue). Notice that it begins at the origin and passes through the point $(1, -2)$.

REVIEW TRANSLATIONS
For help with translating graphs, see p. 123.

STEP 2 **Translate** the graph. For $y = -2\sqrt{x - 3} + 2$, $h = 3$ and $k = 2$. So, shift the graph of $y = -2\sqrt{x}$ right 3 units and up 2 units. The resulting graph starts at $(3, 2)$ and passes through $(4, 0)$.

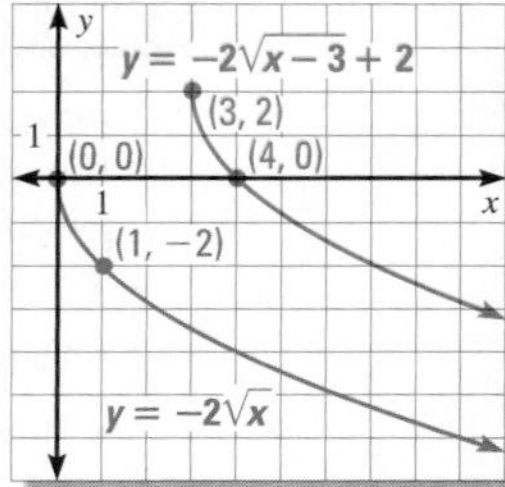

From the graph, you can see that the domain of the function is $x \geq 3$ and the range of the function is $y \leq 2$.

Animated Algebra at classzone.com

EXAMPLE 5 Graph a translated cube root function

Graph $y = 3\sqrt[3]{x + 4} - 1$. Then state the domain and range.

Solution

STEP 1 **Sketch** the graph of $y = 3\sqrt[3]{x}$ (shown in blue). Notice that it passes through the origin and the points $(-1, -3)$ and $(1, 3)$.

STEP 2 **Translate** the graph. Note that for $y = 3\sqrt[3]{x + 4} - 1$, $h = -4$ and $k = -1$. So, shift the graph of $y = 3\sqrt[3]{x}$ left 4 units and down 1 unit. The resulting graph passes through the points $(-5, -4)$, $(-4, -1)$, and $(-3, 2)$.

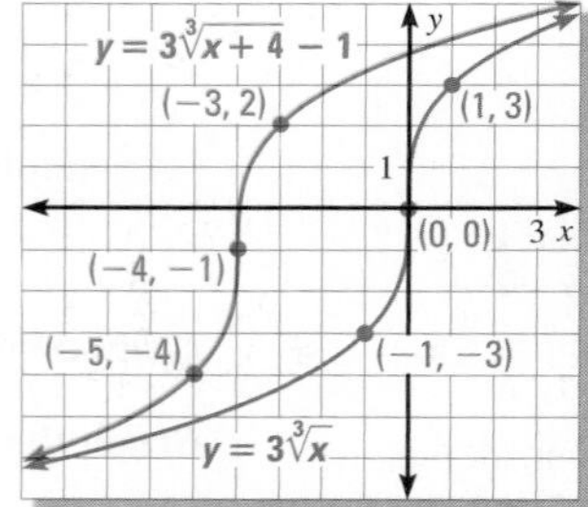

From the graph, you can see that the domain and range of the function are both all real numbers.

Animated Algebra at classzone.com

Differentiated Instruction

Inclusion For radical functions not written in the form shown at the top of this page, many students may have difficulty drawing a graph based on an unfamiliar form. Remind students that the x-axis, for example, is horizontal, so the horizontal change is determined by the constant next to the x. Write radical functions in other forms—for instance, $y - k = a(x - h)^{1/2}$—and have students practice identifying h and k.

See also the *Algebra 2 Toolkit* for more strategies.

✓ **GUIDED PRACTICE** for Examples 4 and 5

Graph the function. Then state the domain and range. 6–11. See margin for art.

6. $y = -4\sqrt{x} + 2$
domain: $x \ge 0$, range: $y \le 2$

7. $y = 2\sqrt{x + 1}$
domain: $x \ge -1$, range: $y \ge 0$

8. $f(x) = \frac{1}{2}\sqrt{x - 3} - 1$
domain: $x \ge 3$, range: $y \ge -1$

9. $y = 2\sqrt[3]{x - 4}$
domain: all real numbers, range: all real numbers

10. $y = \sqrt[3]{x} - 5$
domain: all real numbers, range: all real numbers

11. $g(x) = -\sqrt[3]{x + 2} - 3$
domain: all real numbers, range: all real numbers

6.5 EXERCISES

HOMEWORK KEY

○ = WORKED-OUT SOLUTIONS on p. WS12 for Exs. 11, 17, and 37

★ = STANDARDIZED TEST PRACTICE Exs. 2, 9, 25, 27, and 37

◆ = MULTIPLE REPRESENTATIONS Ex. 39

SKILL PRACTICE

A

1. **VOCABULARY** Copy and complete: Square root functions and cube root functions are examples of _?_ functions. radical

2. ★ **WRITING** The graph of $y = \sqrt{x}$ is the graph of $y = a\sqrt{x - h} + k$ with $a = 1$, $h = 0$, and $k = 0$. Predict how the graph of $y = \sqrt{x}$ will change if:
a. $a = -3$ ... The graph will be reflected over the x-axis and will rise faster.
b. $h = 2$ The graph will be translated 2 units right.
c. $k = 4$ The graph will be translated 4 units up.

EXAMPLE 1 on p. 446 for Exs. 3–9

SQUARE ROOT FUNCTIONS Graph the function. Then state the domain and range. 3–8. See margin for art.

3. $y = -4\sqrt{x}$
domain: $x \ge 0$, range: $y \le 0$

4. $f(x) = \frac{1}{2}\sqrt{x}$
domain: $x \ge 0$, range: $y \ge 0$

5. $y = -\frac{4}{5}\sqrt{x}$
domain: $x \ge 0$, range: $y \le 0$

6. $y = -6\sqrt{x}$
domain: $x \ge 0$, range: $y \le 0$

7. $y = 5\sqrt{x}$
domain: $x \ge 0$, range: $y \ge 0$

8. $g(x) = 9\sqrt{x}$
domain: $x \ge 0$, range: $y \ge 0$

9. ★ **MULTIPLE CHOICE** The graph of which function is shown? D

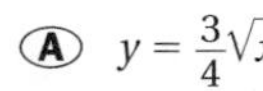

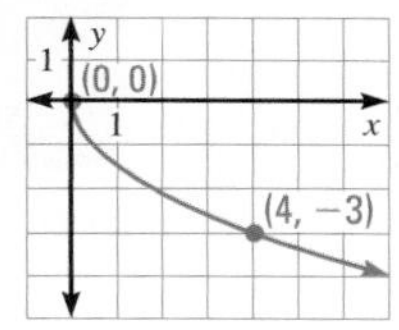

Ⓐ $y = \frac{3}{4}\sqrt{x}$ Ⓑ $y = -\frac{3}{4}\sqrt{x}$

Ⓒ $y = \frac{3}{2}\sqrt{x}$ Ⓓ $y = -\frac{3}{2}\sqrt{x}$

EXAMPLE 2 on p. 447 for Exs. 10–15

CUBE ROOT FUNCTIONS Graph the function. Then state the domain and range. 10–15. See margin.

10. $y = \frac{1}{4}\sqrt[3]{x}$

11. $y = 2\sqrt[3]{x}$

12. $f(x) = -5\sqrt[3]{x}$

13. $h(x) = -\frac{1}{7}\sqrt[3]{x}$

14. $g(x) = 6\sqrt[3]{x}$

15. $y = \frac{7}{9}\sqrt[3]{x}$

B

EXAMPLES 4 and 5 on p. 448 for Exs. 16–24

RADICAL FUNCTIONS Graph the function. Then state the domain and range. 16–24. See margin.

16. $f(x) = 2\sqrt{x - 1} + 3$

17. $y = (x + 1)^{1/2} + 8$

18. $y = -4\sqrt{x - 5} + 1$

19. $y = \frac{3}{4}x^{1/3} - 1$

20. $y = -2\sqrt[3]{x + 5} + 5$

21. $h(x) = -3\sqrt[3]{x + 7} - 6$

22. $y = -\sqrt{x - 4} - 7$

23. $g(x) = -\frac{1}{3}\sqrt[3]{x} - 6$

24. $y = 4\sqrt[3]{x - 4} + 5$

25. ★ **SHORT RESPONSE** *Explain* why there are limitations on the domain and range of the function $y = \sqrt{x - 5} + 4$. The domain is limited because the square root of a negative number is not a real number. Since the domain is restricted, the range is also affected.

Closing the Lesson

Have students summarize the major points of the lesson and answer the Essential Question: What do the graphs of square root and cube root functions look like?

- The graphs of square root and cube root functions can be obtained by using tables of values or by using transformations of the graphs of $y = \sqrt{x}$ and $y = \sqrt[3]{x}$.

The graph of a square root function is half of a parabola with its axis of symmetry along a horizontal line. The graph of a cube root function is the graph of a cubing function reflected in the line $y = x$.

Guided Practice

9.
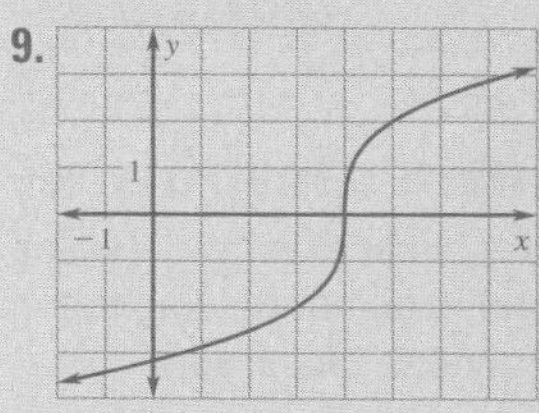

10.
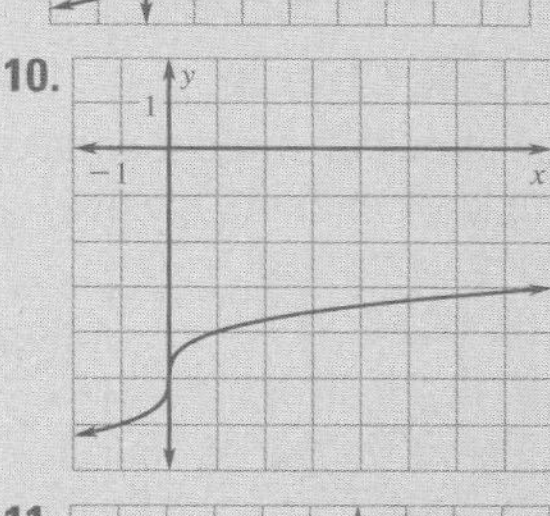

11.
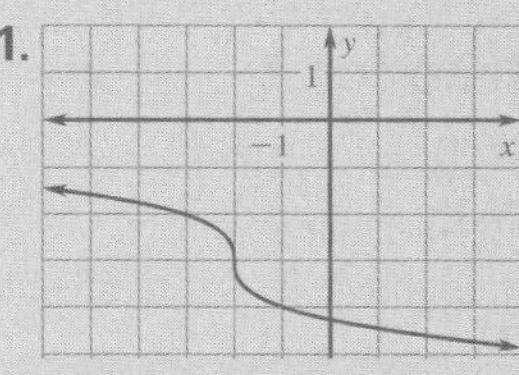

Skill Practice

3–8, 10–24. See Additional Answers beginning on p. AA1.

Guided Practice

6.
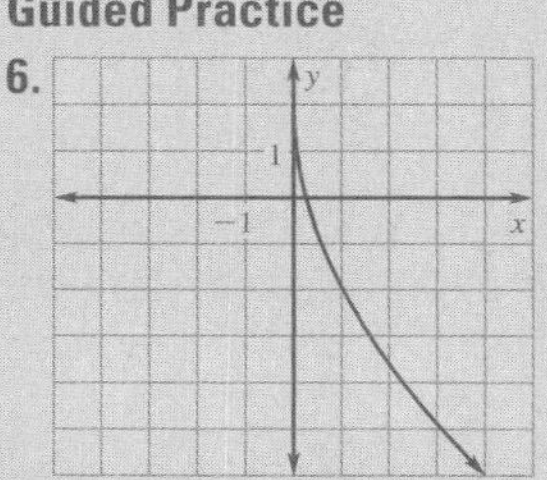

7.
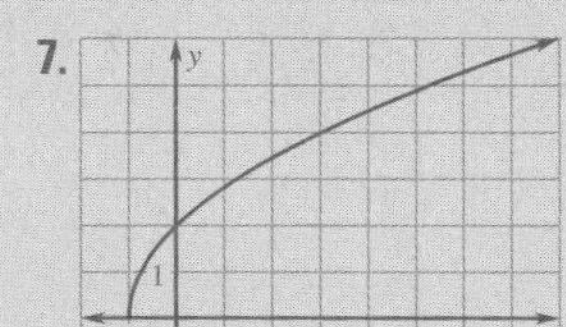

8.
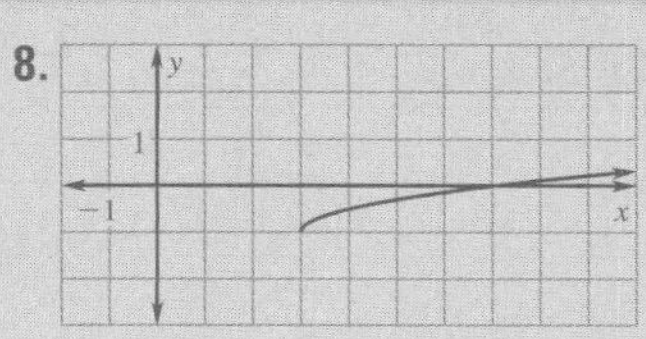

4 PRACTICE AND APPLY

Assignment Guide

Answer Transparencies available for all exercises

Basic:
Day 1: pp. 449–451
Exs. 1–5, 9–12, 16–20, 35–38, 41

Average:
Day 1: pp. 449–451
Exs. 1, 2, 5–7, 9, 12–14, 19–21, 25–27, 35–39, 42

Advanced:
Day 1: pp. 449–451
Exs. 1, 2, 7–9, 14, 15, 22–34*, 36–40*, 42–50

Block:
pp. 449–451
Exs. 1, 2, 5–7, 9, 12–14, 19–21, 25–27, 35–39, 42

Differentiated Instruction

See *Algebra 2 Best Practices Toolkit* for suggestions on addressing the needs of a diverse classroom.

Homework Check

For a quick check of student understanding of key concepts, go over the following exercises:

Basic: 4, 10, 12, 18, 35
Average: 6, 12, 20, 21, 35
Advanced: 8, 14, 22, 24, 36

Extra Practice

- Student Edition, p. 1015
- Chapter 6 Resource Book: Practice levels A, B, C, pp. 56–58

Practice Worksheet

An easily-readable reduced practice page (with answers) for this lesson can be found on p. 412C.

28–33. See Additional Answers beginning on p. AA1.

---

26. The graph was translated horizontally in the wrong direction; the graph of $y = -2\sqrt[3]{x+1} - 3$ is the graph of $y = -2\sqrt[3]{x}$ translated left 1 unit and down 3 units.

26. ERROR ANALYSIS A student tried to explain how the graphs of $y = -2\sqrt[3]{x}$ and $y = -2\sqrt[3]{x+1} - 3$ are related. *Describe* and correct the error.

> The graph of $y = -2\sqrt[3]{x+1} - 3$ is the graph of $y = -2\sqrt[3]{x}$ translated right 1 unit and down 3 units.

27. ★ MULTIPLE CHOICE If the graph of $y = 3\sqrt[3]{x}$ is shifted left 2 units, what is the equation of the translated graph? C

(A) $y = 3\sqrt[3]{x-2}$ (B) $y = 3\sqrt[3]{x} - 2$ (C) $y = 3\sqrt[3]{x+2}$ (D) $y = 3\sqrt[3]{x} + 2$

C

REASONING Find the domain and range of the function without graphing. *Explain* how you found your answers. 28–33. See margin.

28. $y = \sqrt{x+5}$ **29.** $y = \sqrt{x-12}$ **30.** $y = \frac{1}{3}\sqrt{x} - 4$

31. $y = \frac{1}{2}\sqrt[3]{x+7}$ **32.** $g(x) = \sqrt[3]{x+7}$ **33.** $f(x) = \frac{1}{4}\sqrt{x-3} + 6$

34. CHALLENGE Graph $y = \sqrt[4]{x}$, $y = \sqrt[5]{x}$, $y = \sqrt[6]{x}$, and $y = \sqrt[7]{x}$ on a graphing calculator. Make generalizations about the graph of $y = \sqrt[n]{x}$ when n is even and when n is odd. *Sample answer:* If n is even, the graph will have a restricted domain and range. If n is odd, the domain and range will be all real numbers.

PROBLEM SOLVING

EXAMPLE 3 (A) on p. 447 for Exs. 35–36

35. INDIRECT MEASUREMENT The distance d (in miles) that a pilot can see to the horizon can be modeled by $d = 1.22\sqrt{a}$ where a is the plane's altitude (in feet above sea level). Graph the model on a graphing calculator. Then determine at what altitude the pilot can see 8 miles. about 43 ft above sea level

@HomeTutor for problem solving help at classzone.com

36. PENDULUMS Use the model $T = 1.11\sqrt{\ell}$ for the period of a pendulum from Example 3 on page 447.

a. Find the period of a pendulum with a length of 2 feet. about 1.6 sec

b. Find the length of a pendulum with a period of 2 seconds. about 3.25 ft

@HomeTutor for problem solving help at classzone.com

37. ★ SHORT RESPONSE The speed v (in meters per second) of sound waves in air depends on the temperature K (in kelvins) and can be modeled by:

$$v = 331.5\sqrt{\frac{K}{273.15}}, K \geq 0$$

a. Kelvin temperature K is related to Celsius temperature C by the formula $K = 273.15 + C$. Write an equation that gives the speed v of sound waves in air as a function of the temperature C in degrees Celsius.

$v = 331.5\sqrt{1 + \frac{C}{273.15}}$

b. What are a reasonable domain and range for the function from part (a)? domain: $C \geq -273.15$, range: $v \geq 0$

○ = WORKED-OUT SOLUTIONS on p. WS1 ★ = STANDARDIZED TEST PRACTICE ◆ = MULTIPLE REPRESENTATIO

39b. *Sample:*

A	2	4	6	8	10
v_t	306.1	216.44	176.72	153.05	136.89

39c.

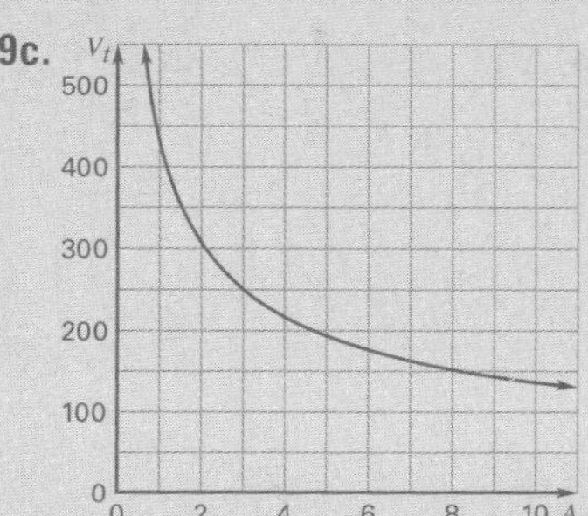

 **38. DRAG RACING** For a given total weight, the speed of a car at the end of a drag race is a function of the car's power. For a car with a total weight of 3500 pounds, the speed s (in miles per hour) can be modeled by $s = 14.8\sqrt[3]{p}$ where p is the power (in horsepower). Graph the model. Then determine the power of a 3500 pound car that reaches a speed of 200 miles per hour. **about 308 horsepower**

39. MULTIPLE REPRESENTATIONS Under certain conditions, a skydiver's terminal velocity v_t (in feet per second) is given by

$$v_t = 33.7\sqrt{\frac{W}{A}}$$

where W is the weight of the skydiver (in pounds) and A is the skydiver's cross-sectional surface area (in square feet). Note that skydivers can vary their cross-sectional surface area by changing positions as they fall.

a. **Writing an Equation** Write an equation that gives v_t as a function of A for a skydiver who weighs 165 pounds. $v_t = 33.7\sqrt{\frac{165}{A}}$

b. **Making a Table** Make a table of values for the equation from part (a). **See margin.**

c. **Drawing a Graph** Use your table to graph the equation. **See margin.**

 **40. CHALLENGE** The surface area S of a right circular cone with a slant height of 1 unit is given by $S = \pi r + \pi r^2$ where r is the cone's radius.

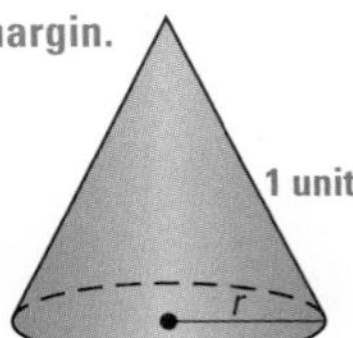

a. Use completing the square to show the following: **See margin.**

$$r = \frac{1}{\sqrt{\pi}}\sqrt{S + \frac{\pi}{4}} - \frac{1}{2}$$

b. Graph the equation from part (a) using a graphing calculator. **See margin.**

c. Find the radius of a right circular cone with a slant height of 1 unit and a surface area of $\frac{3\pi}{4}$ square units. **0.5 unit**

KENTUCKY MIXED REVIEW

 **TEST PRACTICE** at classzone.com

41. Which equation best represents the relationship between x and y shown in the table? **B**

Ⓐ $y = 25x + 12$

Ⓑ $y = 45x - 8x^2$

Ⓒ $y = 8x^2 - 45x$

Ⓓ $y = 70 - 33x^3$

x	y
0	0
1	37
2	58
3	63

42. The two polygons are similar. What is the value of y? **C**

Ⓐ 24 Ⓑ 134

Ⓒ 168 Ⓓ 204

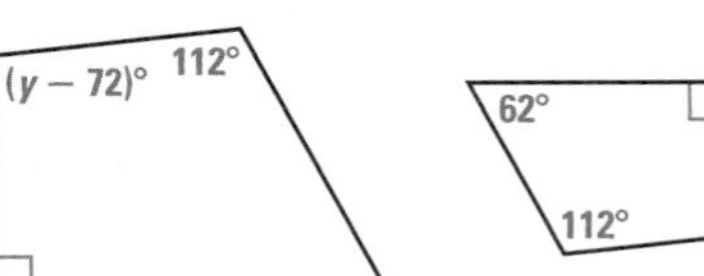

5 ASSESS AND RETEACH

Daily Homework Quiz

Transparency Available

Graph the function. Then state the domain and range.

1. $y = -2\sqrt[3]{x}$

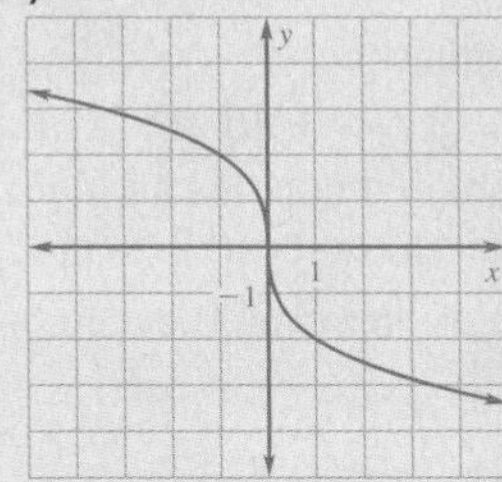

domain: all real numbers; range: all real numbers

2. $f(x) = -\sqrt{x+3} + 1$

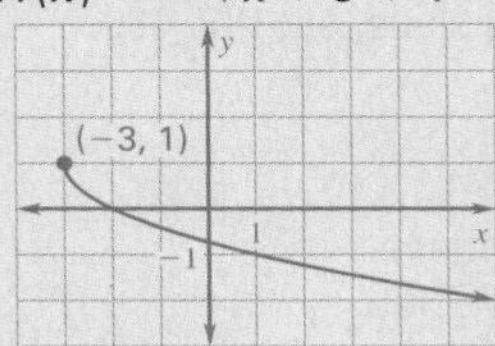

domain: $x \geq -3$; range: $y \leq 1$

3. A pendulum has a period of 1.8 seconds. Use the formula $T = 1.11\sqrt{\ell}$ to find the length of the pendulum. **about 2.6 ft**

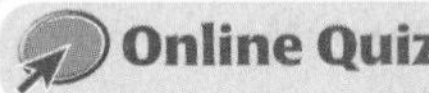

Available at **classzone.com**

Diagnosis/Remediation

- Practice A, B, C in Chapter 6 Resource Book, pp. 56–58
- Study Guide in Chapter 6 Resource Book, pp. 59–60
- Practice Workbook, pp. 104–105
- @HomeTutor

Challenge

Additional challenge is available in the Chapter 6 Resource Book, p. 63.

40a–b. See Additional Answers beginning on p. AA1.

1 PLAN AND PREPARE

Warm-Up Exercises

Transparency Available

Evaluate the expression.

1. $64^{2/3}$ **16** **2.** $(-32)^{3/5}$ **−8**

3. Expand $(x - 5)^2$. $x^2 - 10x + 25$

Solve the equation.

4. $x^2 + 6x + 9 = x + 45$ **−9, 4**

5. A cone-shaped cup has a height of 7 cm and a radius of 2.5 cm. Use $V = \frac{1}{3}\pi r^2 h$ to find the volume of the cup. **about 45.8 cm³**

Notetaking Guide

Transparency Available

Promotes interactive learning and notetaking skills, pp. 180–183.

Pacing

Basic: 2 days
Average: 2 days
Advanced: 2 days
Block: 1 block
• See *Teaching Guide/Lesson Plan.*

2 FOCUS AND MOTIVATE

Essential Question

Big Idea 3, p. 413

Why is it necessary to check every apparent solution of a radical equation in the original equation? **Tell students they will learn how to answer this question by solving radical equations and checking their solutions.**

6.6 Solve Radical Equations

Before	You solved polynomial equations.
Now	You will solve radical equations.
Why?	So you can calculate hang time, as in Ex. 60.

Key Vocabulary
- **radical equation**
- **extraneous solution,** *p. 52*

Equations with radicals that have variables in their radicands are called **radical equations**. An example of a radical equation is $\sqrt[3]{2x+7} = 3$.

KEY CONCEPT *For Your Notebook*

Solving Radical Equations

To solve a radical equation, follow these steps:

STEP 1 **Isolate** the radical on one side of the equation, if necessary.

STEP 2 **Raise** each side of the equation to the same power to eliminate the radical and obtain a linear, quadratic, or other polynomial equation.

STEP 3 **Solve** the polynomial equation using techniques you learned in previous chapters. Check your solution.

EXAMPLE 1 Solve a radical equation

Solve $\sqrt[3]{2x+7} = 3$.

$\sqrt[3]{2x+7} = 3$	**Write original equation.**
$(\sqrt[3]{2x+7})^3 = 3^3$	**Cube each side to eliminate the radical.**
$2x + 7 = 27$	**Simplify.**
$2x = 20$	**Subtract 7 from each side.**
$x = 10$	**Divide each side by 2.**

CHECK Check $x = 10$ in the original equation.

$\sqrt[3]{2(10)+7} \stackrel{?}{=} 3$	**Substitute 10 for *x*.**
$\sqrt[3]{27} \stackrel{?}{=} 3$	**Simplify.**
$3 = 3$ ✓	**Solution checks.**

GUIDED PRACTICE for Example 1

Solve the equation. Check your solution.

1. $\sqrt[3]{x} - 9 = -1$ **512** **2.** $\sqrt{x+25} = 4$ **−9** **3.** $2\sqrt[3]{x-3} = 4$ **11**

Resource Planning Guide

Chapter Resource Book
- Teaching Guide/Lesson Plan (pp. 64–65)
- Activity Master (p. 66)
- Practice levels A, B, C (pp. 69–71)
- Study Guide (pp. 72–73)
- Catch-up for Absent Students (p. 74)
- Problem Solving Workshop (p. 75)
- Challenge (p. 76)

Workbooks
- Notetaking Guide (pp. 180–183)
- Practice Workbook (pp. 106–107)

Teaching Options
- **Power Presentations CD-ROM** provides dynamic electronic teaching resources for the classroom.
- **Activity Generator CD-ROM** provides editable activities for all ability levels.

Interactive Technology
- Easy Planner
- Power Presentations CD-ROM
- Activity Generator CD-ROM
- Animated Algebra
- Test Generator CD-ROM
- Online Quiz
- eWorkbook
- eEdition
- @HomeTutor

Resources for English Learners
- Quick Reference for English Learners
- Spanish Study Guide
- Multi-Language Visual Glossary
- Student Resources in Spanish

See also the *Algebra 2 Toolkit* for more strategies for meeting individual needs.

EXAMPLE 2 Solve a radical equation given a function

WIND VELOCITY In a hurricane, the mean sustained wind velocity v (in meters per second) is given by

$$v(p) = 6.3\sqrt{1013 - p}$$

where p is the air pressure (in millibars) at the center of the hurricane. Estimate the air pressure at the center of a hurricane when the mean sustained wind velocity is 54.5 meters per second.

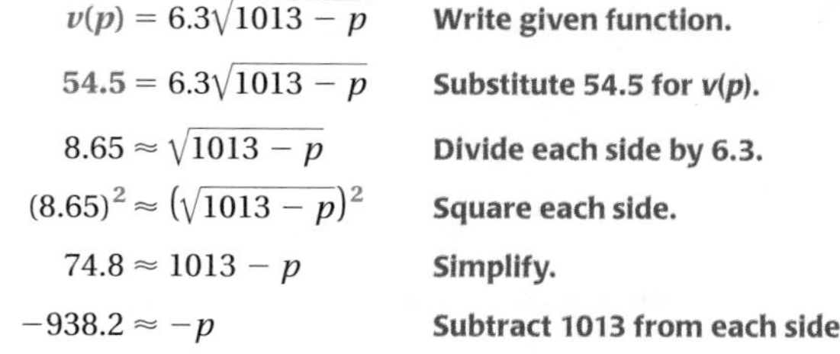

ANOTHER WAY
For alternative methods for solving the problem in Example 2, turn to page 460 for the **Problem Solving Workshop**.

Solution

$v(p) = 6.3\sqrt{1013 - p}$	**Write given function.**
$54.5 = 6.3\sqrt{1013 - p}$	**Substitute 54.5 for $v(p)$.**
$8.65 \approx \sqrt{1013 - p}$	**Divide each side by 6.3.**
$(8.65)^2 \approx (\sqrt{1013 - p})^2$	**Square each side.**
$74.8 \approx 1013 - p$	**Simplify.**
$-938.2 \approx -p$	**Subtract 1013 from each side.**
$938.2 \approx p$	**Divide each side by −1.**

▶ The air pressure at the center of the hurricane is about 938 millibars.

GUIDED PRACTICE for Example 2

4. **WHAT IF?** Use the function in Example 2 to estimate the air pressure at the center of a hurricane when the mean sustained wind velocity is 48.3 meters per second. about 954 millibars

RATIONAL EXPONENTS When an equation contains a power with a rational exponent, you can solve the equation using a procedure similar to the one for solving radical equations. In this case, you first isolate the power and then raise each side of the equation to the reciprocal of the rational exponent.

EXAMPLE 3 Standardized Test Practice

What is the solution of the equation $4x^{3/2} = 108$?

Ⓐ 3 Ⓑ 6 Ⓒ 9 Ⓓ 27

Solution

$4x^{3/2} = 108$	**Write original equation.**
$x^{3/2} = 27$	**Divide each side by 4.**
$(x^{3/2})^{2/3} = 27^{2/3}$	**Raise each side to the power $\frac{2}{3}$.**
$x = 9$	**Simplify.**

▶ The correct answer is C. Ⓐ Ⓑ Ⓒ Ⓓ

Motivating the Lesson

Many formulas used in physics and electronics involve radicals. Ask students who are taking or have taken these courses to bring in some of these formulas and explain to the class how the formulas are used.

3 TEACH

Extra Example 1

Solve $\sqrt{5x - 9} = 11$. 26

Extra Example 2

If an 8-foot ladder is leaned against a wall, the height of the ladder along wall is given by $h(x) = \sqrt{64 - x^2}$, where x is the distance along the floor from the base of the ladder to the wall. Estimate the distance that the ladder should be placed from the wall in order for the ladder to reach 7 feet off the floor. about 3.9 ft

Extra Example 3

Solve $7x^{3/5} = 56$. D

Ⓐ 4.8 Ⓑ 8
Ⓒ 12.8 Ⓓ 32

Key Question to Ask for Example 3

- Of the answer choices for Example 3, 27 is the only one that is a perfect cube. How can this observation help you to see that 27 is the only possible solution of the equation among the choices given? In order for $x^{2/3}$ to be an integer, $x^{1/3}$ must be an integer, which means that x must be a perfect cube.

Extra Example 4

Solve $(x - 4)^{2/3} - 9 = 16$. **129**

Key Question to Ask for Example 4

- In an equation with a rational exponent, why should you raise both sides to the power that is the reciprocal of the exponent in the given equation? **The power of a power property says that to raise a power to a power, you multiply the exponents. The product of a number and its reciprocal is 1, so the expression $(x + 2)^1 = x + 2$, which makes it easy to solve for x.**

Extra Example 5

Solve $\sqrt{x - 6} = x - 8$. **10 (The apparent solution 7 is extraneous.)**

Key Question to Ask for Example 5

- Look at the original equation in Example 5. How can you tell, without working through the check, that -2 cannot be a solution of this equation? **If -2 is substituted for x, the value of the left side will be -1, but the value of the right side cannot be negative because it is a principal square root.**

EXAMPLE 4 Solve an equation with a rational exponent

Solve $(x + 2)^{3/4} - 1 = 7$.

$(x + 2)^{3/4} - 1 = 7$	Write original equation.
$(x + 2)^{3/4} = 8$	Add 1 to each side.
$\left[(x + 2)^{3/4}\right]^{4/3} = 8^{4/3}$	Raise each side to the power $\frac{4}{3}$.
$x + 2 = (8^{1/3})^4$	Apply properties of exponents.
$x + 2 = 2^4$	Simplify.
$x + 2 = 16$	Simplify.
$x = 14$	Subtract 2 from each side.

▶ The solution is 14. Check this in the original equation.

✓ GUIDED PRACTICE for Examples 3 and 4

Solve the equation. Check your solution.

5. $3x^{3/2} = 375$ **25**

6. $-2x^{3/4} = -16$ **16**

7. $-\frac{2}{3}x^{1/5} = -2$ **243**

8. $(x + 3)^{5/2} = 32$ **1**

9. $(x - 5)^{5/3} = 243$ **32**

10. $(x + 2)^{1/3} + 3 = 7$ **62**

EXTRANEOUS SOLUTIONS Raising each side of an equation to the same power may introduce extraneous solutions. When you use this procedure, you should always check each apparent solution in the *original* equation.

EXAMPLE 5 Solve an equation with an extraneous solution

Solve $x + 1 = \sqrt{7x + 15}$.

$x + 1 = \sqrt{7x + 15}$	Write original equation.
$(x + 1)^2 = (\sqrt{7x + 15})^2$	Square each side.
$x^2 + 2x + 1 = 7x + 15$	Expand left side and simplify right side.
$x^2 - 5x - 14 = 0$	Write in standard form.
$(x - 7)(x + 2) = 0$	Factor.
$x - 7 = 0$ or $x + 2 = 0$	Zero-product property
$x = 7$ or $x = -2$	Solve for x.

REVIEW FACTORING
For help with factoring, see p. 252.

CHECK

Check $x = 7$ in the original equation.

$x + 1 = \sqrt{7x + 15}$

$7 + 1 \stackrel{?}{=} \sqrt{7(7) + 15}$

$8 \stackrel{?}{=} \sqrt{64}$

$8 = 8$ ✓

Check $x = -2$ in the original equation.

$x + 1 = \sqrt{7x + 15}$

$-2 + 1 \stackrel{?}{=} \sqrt{7(-2) + 15}$

$-1 \stackrel{?}{=} \sqrt{1}$

$-1 \neq 1$

▶ The only solution is 7. (The apparent solution -2 is extraneous.)

Differentiated Instruction

Advanced Challenge students to explore whether it is possible to obtain extraneous solutions when you solve an equation by cubing both sides, as it is when you square both sides. Then ask them to extend their findings to raising both sides to any odd and any even power. Ask students who are able to work through this investigation successfully to explain what they have discovered to the class.

See also the *Algebra 2 Toolkit* for more strategies.

SQUARING TWICE When an equation contains two radicals, you may need to square each side twice in order to eliminate both radicals.

EXAMPLE 6 Solve an equation with two radicals

Solve $\sqrt{x+2} + 1 = \sqrt{3-x}$.

Solution

METHOD 1 Solve using algebra.

$\sqrt{x+2} + 1 = \sqrt{3-x}$	Write original equation.
$(\sqrt{x+2} + 1)^2 = (\sqrt{3-x})^2$	Square each side.
$x + 2 + 2\sqrt{x+2} + 1 = 3 - x$	Expand left side and simplify right side.
$2\sqrt{x+2} = -2x$	Isolate radical expression.
$\sqrt{x+2} = -x$	Divide each side by 2.
$(\sqrt{x+2})^2 = (-x)^2$	Square each side again.
$x + 2 = x^2$	Simplify.
$0 = x^2 - x - 2$	Write in standard form.
$0 = (x-2)(x+1)$	Factor.
$x - 2 = 0$ or $x + 1 = 0$	Zero-product property
$x = 2$ or $x = -1$	Solve for x.

REVIEW FOIL METHOD
For help with multiplying algebraic expressions using the FOIL method, see p. 245.

Check $x = 2$ in the original equation.	Check $x = -1$ in the original equation.
$\sqrt{x+2} + 1 = \sqrt{3-x}$	$\sqrt{x+2} + 1 = \sqrt{3-x}$
$\sqrt{2+2} + 1 \stackrel{?}{=} \sqrt{3-2}$	$\sqrt{-1+2} + 1 \stackrel{?}{=} \sqrt{3-(-1)}$
$\sqrt{4} + 1 \stackrel{?}{=} \sqrt{1}$	$\sqrt{1} + 1 \stackrel{?}{=} \sqrt{4}$
$3 \neq 1$	$2 = 2$ ✓

▶ The only solution is −1. (The apparent solution 2 is extraneous.)

METHOD 2 Use a graph to solve the equation.

Use a graphing calculator to graph $y_1 = \sqrt{x+2} + 1$ and $y_2 = \sqrt{3-x}$. Then find the intersection points of the two graphs by using the *intersect* feature. You will find that the only point of intersection is (−1, 2). Therefore, −1 is the only solution of the equation $\sqrt{x+2} + 1 = \sqrt{3-x}$.

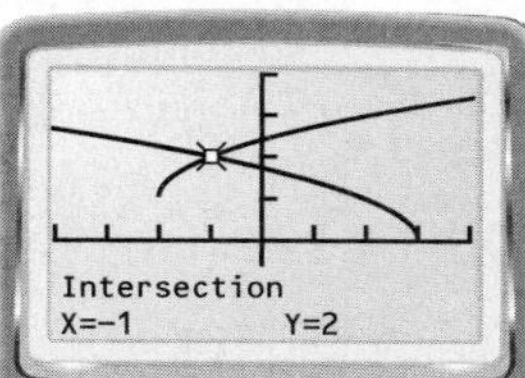

GUIDED PRACTICE for Examples 5 and 6

Solve the equation. Check for extraneous solutions.

11. $x - \frac{1}{2} = \sqrt{\frac{1}{4}x}$ **1**

12. $\sqrt{10x + 9} = x + 3$ **0, 4**

13. $\sqrt{2x+5} = \sqrt{x+7}$ **2**

14. $\sqrt{x+6} - 2 = \sqrt{x-2}$ **3**

Extra Example 6

Solve $\sqrt{x+6} = \sqrt{11-x} - 3$.
−5 (The apparent solution 10 is extraneous.)

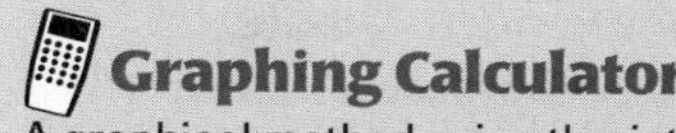

Graphing Calculator

A graphical method using the *intersect* feature is shown for solving the equation given in **Example 6**. This can be used as either a check for the algebraic solution or as an alternate method for solving the equation. Also ask students to use their calculators to solve the equation numerically using the *table* feature. Then ask which of the three methods they prefer, and what they think are the advantages and disadvantages of each method. Make sure that students observe that the graphical and numerical methods do *not* show extraneous solutions.

Closing the Lesson

Have students summarize the major points of the lesson and answer the Essential Question: Why is it necessary to check every apparent solution of a radical equation in the original equation?

- **To solve a radical equation, isolate the radical, raise both sides to the same power to eliminate the radical, and then solve the resulting equation.**
- **Always check every apparent solution in the *original* equation.**

Raising both sides of an equation to the same power sometimes introduces extraneous solutions.

Differentiated Instruction

English Learners Extraneous solutions are "extra," as their name suggests—they are not vital or necessary—so they should be discarded. Show students that it is in squaring both sides of the equation in the initial step of the solution in **Example 5** that an extraneous solution is introduced.

See also the *Algebra 2 Toolkit* for more strategies.

4 PRACTICE AND APPLY

Assignment Guide

Answer Transparencies available for all exercises

Basic:
Day 1: EP p. 1013 Exs. 17–20
pp. 456–459
Exs. 1–9, 12–19, 22, 56, 57
Day 2: pp. 456–459
Exs. 23–39, 43–46, 58–60, 63–64

Average:
Day 1: pp. 456–459
Exs. 1, 2, 5–12, 14–20, 22, 56, 57
Day 2: pp. 456–459
Exs. 26–30, 32, 33, 36–40, 43, 44, 45–53 odd, 58–61, 63–64

Advanced:
Day 1: pp. 456–459
Exs. 1, 2, 5–12, 15–22, 56, 57
Day 2: pp. 456–459
Exs. 28–31, 39–44, 46–52 even, 53–55*, 58–64*

Block:
pp. 456–459
Exs. 1, 2, 5–12, 14–20, 22, 26–30, 32, 33, 36–40, 43, 44, 45–53 odd, 56–61, 63–64

Differentiated Instruction

See *Algebra 2 Best Practices Toolkit* for suggestions on addressing the needs of a diverse classroom.

Homework Check

For a quick check of student understanding of key concepts, go over the following exercises:

Basic: 4, 24, 36, 45, 56

Average: 16, 26, 38, 47, 56

Advanced: 20, 30, 42, 48, 57

Extra Practice

- Student Edition, p. 1015
- Chapter 6 Resource Book: Practice levels A, B, C, pp. 69–71

Practice Worksheet

An easily-readable reduced practice page (with answers) for this lesson can be found on p. 412C.

6.6 EXERCISES

HOMEWORK KEY
○ = **WORKED-OUT SOLUTIONS** on p. WS12 for Exs. 5, 13, and 59
★ = **STANDARDIZED TEST PRACTICE** Exs. 2, 12, 22, 43, 44, 59, and 60

SKILL PRACTICE

A

1. **VOCABULARY** Copy and complete: When you solve an equation algebraically, an apparent solution that must be rejected because it does not satisfy the original equation is called a(n) _?_ solution. **extraneous**

2. ★ **WRITING** A student was asked to solve $\sqrt{3x-1} - \sqrt{9x-5} = 0$. His first step was to square each side. While trying to isolate x, he gave up in frustration. What could the student have done to avoid this situation? **Add $\sqrt{9x-5}$ to each side of the equation before squaring each side.**

EXAMPLE 1 on p. 452 for Exs. 3–21

EQUATIONS WITH SQUARE ROOTS Solve the equation. Check your solution.

3. $\sqrt{5x+1} = 6$ **7**
4. $\sqrt{3x+10} = 8$ **18**
5. $\sqrt{9x} + 11 = 14$ **1**
6. $\sqrt{2x} - \frac{2}{3} = 0$ **$\frac{2}{9}$**
7. $-2\sqrt{24x} + 13 = -11$ **6**
8. $8\sqrt{10x} - 7 = 9$ **$\frac{2}{5}$**
9. $\sqrt{x-25} + 3 = 5$ **29**
10. $-4\sqrt{x} - 6 = -20$ **$12\frac{1}{4}$**
11. $\sqrt{-2x+3} - 2 = 10$ **$-70\frac{1}{2}$**

12. ★ **MULTIPLE CHOICE** What is the solution of $\sqrt{8x+3} = 3$? **C**

Ⓐ $-\frac{3}{4}$ Ⓑ 0 Ⓒ $\frac{3}{4}$ Ⓓ $\frac{9}{8}$

EQUATIONS WITH CUBE ROOTS Solve the equation. Check your solution.

13. $\sqrt[3]{x} - 10 = -3$ **343**
14. $\sqrt[3]{x-16} = 2$ **24**
15. $\sqrt[3]{12x} - 13 = -7$ **18**
16. $3\sqrt[3]{16x} - 7 = 17$ **32**
17. $-5\sqrt[3]{8x} + 12 = -8$ **8**
18. $\sqrt[3]{4x+5} = \frac{1}{2}$ **$-1\frac{7}{32}$**
19. $\sqrt[3]{x-3} + 2 = 4$ **11**
20. $\sqrt[3]{4x+2} - 6 = -10$ **$-16\frac{1}{2}$**
21. $-4\sqrt[3]{x+10} + 3 = 15$ **−37**

22. ★ **OPEN-ENDED MATH** Write a radical equation of the form $\sqrt[3]{ax+b} = c$ that has −3 as a solution. *Explain* the method you used to find your equation. ***Sample answer:*** **$\sqrt[3]{9x-37} = -4$; I substituted values in for *a* and *c* and −3 in for *x* and then solved for *b*.**

EXAMPLES 3 and 4 on pp. 453–454 for Exs. 23–33

EQUATIONS WITH RATIONAL EXPONENTS Solve the equation. Check your solution.

23. $2x^{3/2} = 16$ **4**
24. $\frac{1}{2}x^{5/2} = 16$ **4**
25. $9x^{3/5} = 72$ **32**
26. $(16x)^{3/4} + 44 = 556$ **256**
27. $\frac{1}{7}(x+9)^{3/2} = 49$ **40**
28. $(x-5)^{5/3} - 73 = 170$ **32**
29. $\left(\frac{1}{3}x - 11\right)^{1/2} = 5$ **108**
30. $(5x-19)^{5/6} = 32$ **$16\frac{3}{5}$**
31. $(3x+5)^{7/3} + 22 = 150$ **1**

ERROR ANALYSIS *Describe* and correct the error in solving the equation.

32.
$$\sqrt[3]{x} + 2 = 4$$
$$(\sqrt[3]{x} + 2)^3 = 4^3$$
$$x + 8 = 64$$
$$x = 56$$

33.
$$(x+7)^{1/2} = 5$$
$$[(x+7)^{1/2}]^2 = 5$$
$$x + 7 = 5$$
$$x = -2$$

32. 2 should be subtracted from both sides first; $(\sqrt[3]{x})^3 = 2^3$, $x = 8$.

33. Both sides must be raised to the power; $[(x+7)^{1/2}]^2 = 5^2$, $x + 7 = 25$, $x = 18$.

XAMPLE 5 B
n p. 454
or Exs. 34–44

SOLVING RADICAL EQUATIONS **Solve the equation. Check for extraneous solutions.**

34. $x - 6 = \sqrt{3x}$ 12

35. $x - 10 = \sqrt{9x}$ 25

36. $x = \sqrt{16x + 225}$ 25

37. $\sqrt{21x + 1} = x + 5$ 3, 8

38. $\sqrt{44 - 2x} = x - 10$ 14

39. $\sqrt{x^2 + 4} = x + 5$ $-2\frac{1}{10}$

40. $x - 2 = \sqrt{\frac{3}{2}x - 2}$ 4

41. $\sqrt[4]{3 - 8x^2} = 2x$ $\frac{1}{2}$

42. $\sqrt[3]{8x^3 - 1} = 2x - 1$ 0, $\frac{1}{2}$

43. ★ **MULTIPLE CHOICE** What is (are) the solution(s) of $\sqrt{32x - 64} = 2x$? A

Ⓐ 4 Ⓑ −16 Ⓒ 4, −16 Ⓓ 1, 3

44. ★ **SHORT RESPONSE** *Explain* how you can tell that $\sqrt{x + 4} = -5$ has no solution without solving it. It is not possible to take the square root of a number and get a negative answer.

XAMPLE 6
n p. 455
or Exs. 45–52

EQUATIONS WITH TWO RADICALS **Solve the equation. Check for extraneous solutions.**

45. $\sqrt{4x + 1} = \sqrt{x + 10}$ 3

46. $\sqrt[3]{12x - 5} - \sqrt[3]{8x + 15} = 0$ 5

47. $\sqrt{3x - 8} + 1 = \sqrt{x + 5}$ 4

48. $\sqrt{\frac{2}{3}x - 4} = \sqrt{\frac{2}{5}x - 7}$ $-11\frac{1}{4}$

49. $\sqrt{x + 2} = 2 - \sqrt{x}$ $\frac{1}{4}$

50. $\sqrt{2x + 3} + 2 = \sqrt{6x + 7}$ 3

51. $\sqrt{2x + 5} = \sqrt{x + 2} + 1$ −2, 2

52. $\sqrt{5x + 6} + 3 = \sqrt{3x + 3} + 4$ −1, 2

C

SOLVING SYSTEMS **Solve the system of equations.**

53. $3\sqrt{x} + 5\sqrt{y} = 31$
$5\sqrt{x} - 5\sqrt{y} = -15$ (4, 25)

54. $5\sqrt{x} - 2\sqrt{y} = 4\sqrt{2}$
$2\sqrt{x} + 3\sqrt{y} = 13\sqrt{2}$ (8, 18)

55. **CHALLENGE** Give an example of a radical equation that has two extraneous solutions. *Sample answer:* $\sqrt{4x - 3} = -x$

PROBLEM SOLVING

XAMPLE 2 A
n p. 453
or Exs. 56–57

56. **MAXIMUM SPEED** In an amusement park ride called the Sky Flyer, a rider suspended by a cable swings back and forth like a pendulum from a tall tower. A rider's maximum speed v (in meters per second) occurs at the bottom of each swing and can be approximated by $v = \sqrt{2gh}$ where h is the height (in meters) at the top of each swing and g is the acceleration due to gravity ($g \approx 9.8$ m/sec^2). If a rider's maximum speed was 15 meters per second, what was the rider's height at the top of the swing? about 11.5 m

@HomeTutor for problem solving help at classzone.com

Teaching Strategy

Exercise 37 Based on Examples 5 and 6, some students think that when a radical equation has two apparent solutions, one of them will always be extraneous. Use this exercise to show that a radical equation can in fact have two solutions. After having students work this exercise algebraically, including verifying that 3 and 8 are both solutions by substituting into the original equation, ask them to solve the equation graphically. Seeing the two curves intersect twice on the calculator screen will reinforce this result.

Avoiding Common Errors

Exercises 47, 49–52 Many students make errors in expanding a binomial square containing a radical, such as $(\sqrt{3x - 8} + 1)^2$ in Exercise 47. Although they may know the patterns for a square of a binomial and be able to apply them to simpler expressions such as $(x + 3)^2$, they may not see that the same rules apply here and just square the expression term-by-term, which conveniently "gets rid of" the radical. Have these students write down the rules $(a + b)^2 = a^2 + 2ab + b^2$ and $(a - b)^2 = a^2 - 2ab + b^2$. Then, for each of these exercises, they should write down the expressions to be substituted for a and b and substitute carefully into the appropriate pattern.

An **Animated Algebra** activity is available on-line for **Exercise 60**. This activity is also available on the **Power Presentations CD-ROM**.

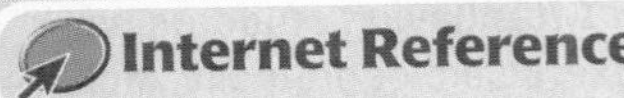

Exercise 61 More information about the Beaufort wind scale can be found at the National Weather Service's website www.crh.noaa.gov/lot/webpage/beaufort

57. BURNING RATE A burning candle has a radius of r inches and was initially h_0 inches tall. After t minutes, the height of the candle has been reduced to h inches. These quantities are related by the formula

$$r = \sqrt{\frac{kt}{\pi(h_0 - h)}}$$

where k is a constant. How long will it take for the entire candle to burn if its radius is 0.875 inch, its initial height is 6.5 inches, and $k = 0.04$? **about 391 min**

@HomeTutor for problem solving help at classzone.com

58. CONSTRUCTION The length ℓ (in inches) of a standard nail can be modeled by $\ell = 54d^{3/2}$ where d is the diameter (in inches) of the nail. What is the diameter of a standard nail that is 3 inches long? **about 0.15 in.**

59. *Sample answer:* The elephant with a shoulder height of 250 centimeters is about 20 years older than the elephant with a shoulder height of 150 centimeters.

B

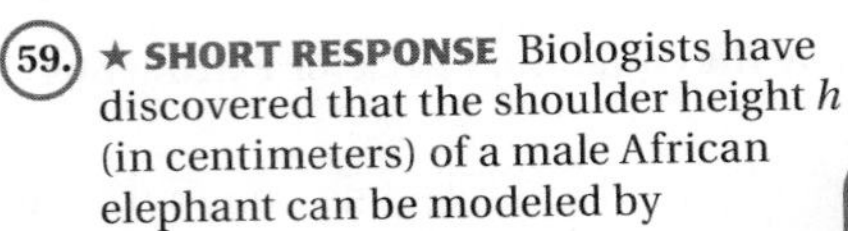

59. ★ **SHORT RESPONSE** Biologists have discovered that the shoulder height h (in centimeters) of a male African elephant can be modeled by

$$h = 62.5\sqrt[3]{t} + 75.8$$

where t is the age (in years) of the elephant. *Compare* the ages of two elephants, one with a shoulder height of 150 centimeters and the other with a shoulder height of 250 centimeters.

60. ★ **EXTENDED RESPONSE** "Hang time" is the time you are suspended in the air during a jump. Your hang time t (in seconds) is given by the function $t = 0.5\sqrt{h}$ where h is the height of the jump (in feet). A basketball player jumps and has a hang time of 0.81 second. A kangaroo jumps and has a hang time of 1.12 seconds.

a. **Solve** Find the heights that the basketball player and the kangaroo jumped. **about 2.6 ft, about 5 ft**

b. **Calculate** Double the hang times of the basketball player and the kangaroo and calculate the corresponding heights of each jump. **about 10.5 ft, about 20 ft**

c. **Interpret** If the hang time doubles, does the height of the jump double? *Explain.* **No; the height is quadrupled.**

Animated Algebra at classzone.com

61. MULTI-STEP PROBLEM The Beaufort wind scale was devised to measure wind speed. The Beaufort numbers B, which range from 0 to 12, can be modeled by

$$B = 1.69\sqrt{s + 4.25} - 3.55$$

where s is the speed (in miles per hour) of the wind.

Beaufort Wind Scale	
Beaufort number	**Force of wind**
0	Calm
3	Gentle breeze
6	Strong breeze
9	Strong gale
12	Hurricane

a. Find the wind speed that corresponds to the Beaufort number $B = 0$. **about 0.162 mi/h**

b. Find the wind speed that corresponds to the Beaufort number $B = 12$. **about 80.4 mi/h**

c. Write an inequality that describes the range of wind speeds represented by the Beaufort model. **$0.162 \le s \le 80.4$**

○ = WORKED-OUT SOLUTIONS on p. WS1 ★ = STANDARDIZED TEST PRACTICE

Quiz, p. 459

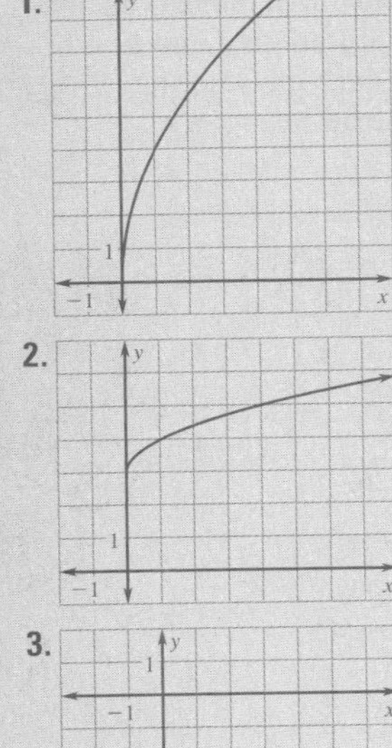

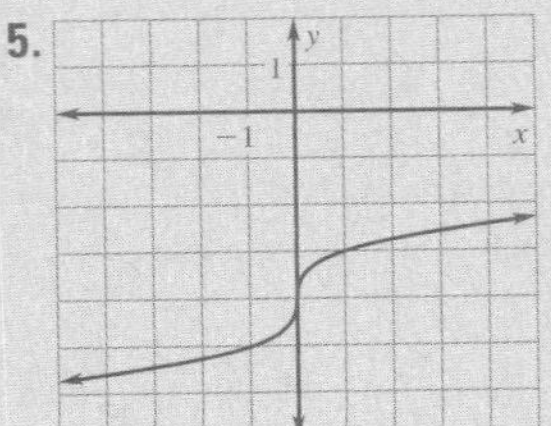

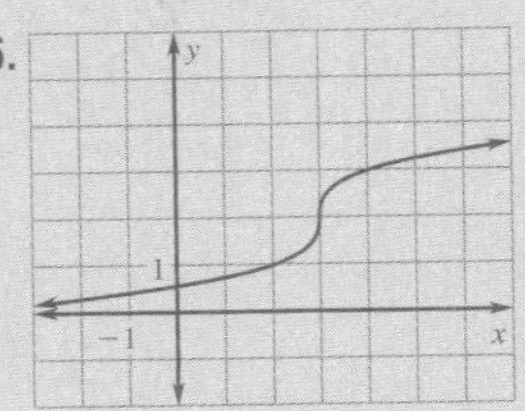

C **62. CHALLENGE** You are trying to determine a truncated pyramid's height, which cannot be measured directly. The height h and slant height ℓ of the truncated pyramid are related by the formula shown below.

$$\ell = \sqrt{h^2 + \frac{1}{4}(b_2 - b_1)^2}$$

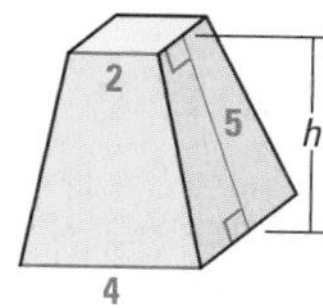

In the given formula, b_1 and b_2 are the side lengths of the upper and lower bases of the pyramid, respectively. If $\ell = 5$, $b_1 = 2$, and $b_2 = 4$, what is the height of the pyramid? **about 4.9**

KENTUCKY MIXED REVIEW

TEST PRACTICE at classzone.com

63. What are the zeros of the function $y = 12x^2 + 11x - 15$? **A**

Ⓐ $-\frac{5}{3}, \frac{3}{4}$ Ⓑ $\frac{5}{3}, -\frac{3}{4}$ Ⓒ $-1, \frac{5}{4}$ Ⓓ $2, \frac{5}{2}$

64. Which equation represents the line that contains the point $(-4, 2)$ and has slope $-\frac{5}{2}$? **D**

Ⓐ $-5x - 2y = 1$ Ⓑ $-2x + 5y = 18$

Ⓒ $2x - 5y = -16$ Ⓓ $5x + 2y = -16$

QUIZ *for Lessons 6.5–6.6*

Graph the function. Then state the domain and range. *(p. 446)* **1–6. See margin for art.**

1. $y = 4\sqrt{x}$ **domain: $x \geq 0$, range: $y \geq 0$**
2. $y = \sqrt{x} + 3$ **domain: $x \geq 0$, range: $y \geq 3$**
3. $g(x) = \sqrt{x + 2} - 5$ **domain: $x \geq -2$, range: $y \geq -5$**
4. $y = -\frac{1}{2}\sqrt[3]{x}$ **domain: all real numbers, range: all real numbers**
5. $f(x) = \sqrt[3]{x} - 4$ **domain: all real numbers, range: all real numbers**
6. $y = \sqrt[3]{x - 3} + 2$ **domain: all real numbers, range: all real numbers**

Solve the equation. Check for extraneous solutions. *(p. 452)*

7. $\sqrt{6x + 15} = 9$ **11**
8. $\frac{1}{4}(7x + 8)^{3/2} = 54$ **4**
9. $\sqrt[3]{3x + 5} + 2 = 5$ **$7\frac{1}{3}$**
10. $x - 3 = \sqrt{10x - 54}$ **7, 9**
11. $\sqrt{4x - 4} = \sqrt{5x - 1} - 1$ **2, 10**
12. $\sqrt[3]{\frac{4}{5}x - 9} = \sqrt[3]{x - 6}$ **−15**

13. **ASTRONOMY** According to Kepler's third law of planetary motion, the function $P = 0.199a^{3/2}$ relates a planet's orbital period P (in days) to the length a (in millions of kilometers) of the orbit's minor axis. The orbital period of Mars is about 1.88 years. What is the length of the orbit's minor axis? *(p. 452)* **about 228,000,000 km**

5 ASSESS AND RETEACH

Daily Homework Quiz

Transparency Available

Solve the equation.

1. $\sqrt[3]{6 - 2x} = -2$ **7**
2. $6x^{2/5} = 24$ **32**
3. $(x - 1)^{2/3} - 13 = 3$ **65**
4. $x - 4 = \sqrt{9x}$ **16 (The apparent solution 1 is extraneous.)**
5. $\sqrt{x + 6} - \sqrt{x - 5} = 1$ **30**

Online Quiz

Available at **classzone.com**

Diagnosis/Remediation

- Practice A, B, C in Chapter 6 Resource Book, pp. 69–71
- Study Guide in Chapter 6 Resource Book, pp. 72–73
- Practice Workbook, pp. 106–107
- @HomeTutor

Challenge

Additional challenge is available in the Chapter 6 Resource Book, p. 76.

Quiz

An easily-readable reduced copy of the quiz (with answers) on Lessons 6.5–6.6 from the Assessment Book can be found on p. 412E.

Alternative Strategy

Method 1 Example 2 on page 453 can be solved by using a calculator table to find an approximate solution for the radical equation $6.3\sqrt{1013 - p} = 54.5$. This method allows students to see numerically how the wind velocity decreases as the air pressure at the center of the hurricane increases.

Avoiding Common Errors

Some students may make errors in entering the function into their graphing calculators. Remind these students that parentheses are needed around $(1013 - x)$ to show that this complete expression is under the radical sign.

PROBLEM SOLVING WORKSHOP LESSON 6.6

Using ALTERNATIVE METHODS

Another Way to Solve Example 2, page 453

MULTIPLE REPRESENTATIONS In Example 2 on page 453, you solved a radical equation algebraically. You can also solve a radical equation using a table or a graph.

PROBLEM

WIND VELOCITY In a hurricane, the mean sustained wind velocity v (in meters per second) is given by

$$v(p) = 6.3\sqrt{1013 - p}$$

where p is the air pressure (in millibars) at the center of the hurricane. Estimate the air pressure at the center of a hurricane when the mean sustained wind velocity is 54.5 meters per second.

METHOD 1

Using a Table The problem requires solving the radical equation $6.3\sqrt{1013 - p} = 54.5$. One way to solve this equation is to make a table of values. You can use a graphing calculator to make the table.

STEP 1 **Enter** the function $y = 6.3\sqrt{1013 - x}$ into a graphing calculator. Note that x represents air pressure and y represents wind velocity. Set up a table to display x-values starting at 900 and increasing in increments of 10.

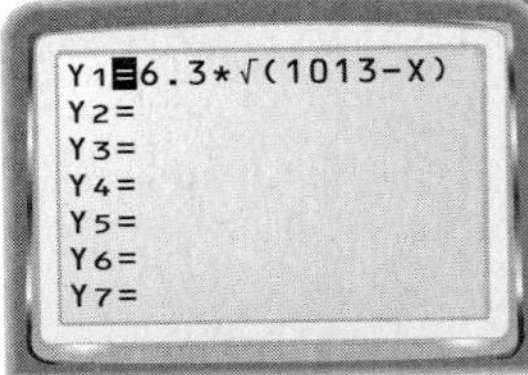

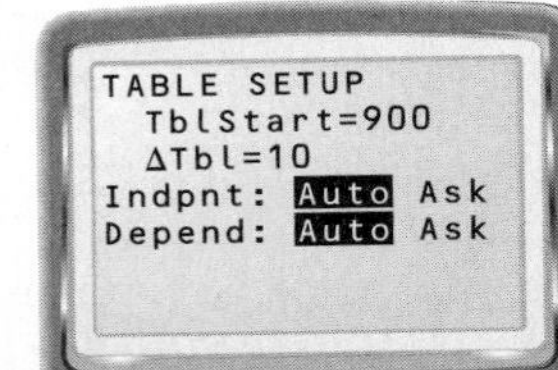

STEP 2 **Make** a table of values for the function. The first table below shows that $y = 54.5$ between $x = 930$ and $x = 940$. To approximate x more precisely, set up the table to display x-values starting at 930 and increasing in increments of 1. The second table below shows that $y = 54.5$ between $x = 938$ and $x = 939$.

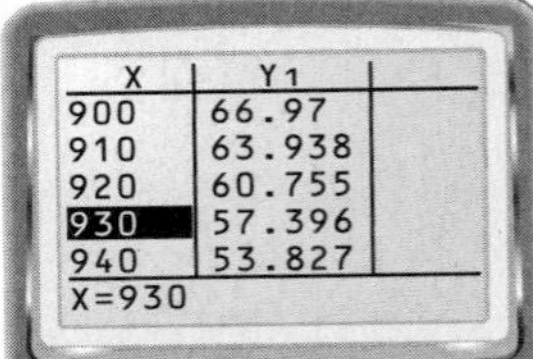

X	Y1
900	66.97
910	63.938
920	60.755
930	57.396
940	53.827

X=930

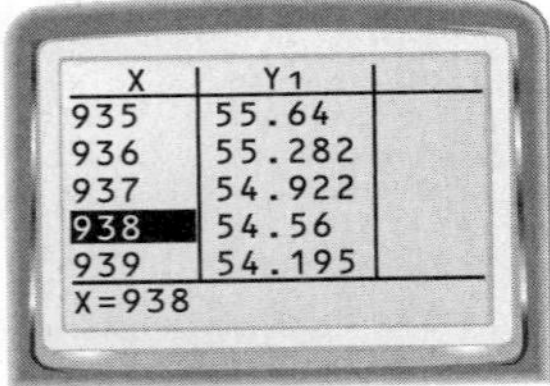

X	Y1
935	55.64
936	55.282
937	54.922
938	54.56
939	54.195

X=938

▶ The mean sustained wind velocity is 54.5 meters per second when the air pressure is between 938 and 939 millibars.

METHOD 2 **Using a Graph** You can also use a graph to solve the equation $6.3\sqrt{1013 - p} = 54.5$.

STEP 1 **Enter** the functions $y = 6.3\sqrt{1013 - x}$ and $y = 54.5$ into a graphing calculator.

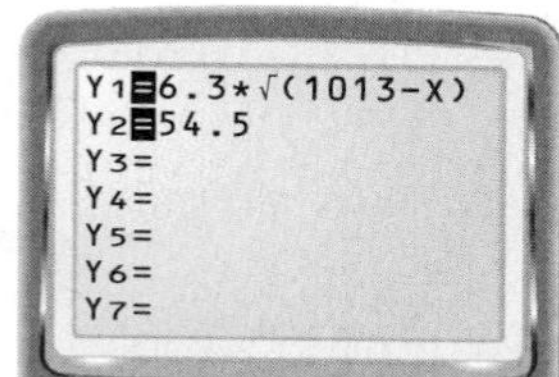

STEP 2 **Graph** the functions from Step 1. Adjust the viewing window so that it shows the interval $800 \le x \le 1100$ with a scale of 50 and the interval $25 \le y \le 75$ with a scale of 5.

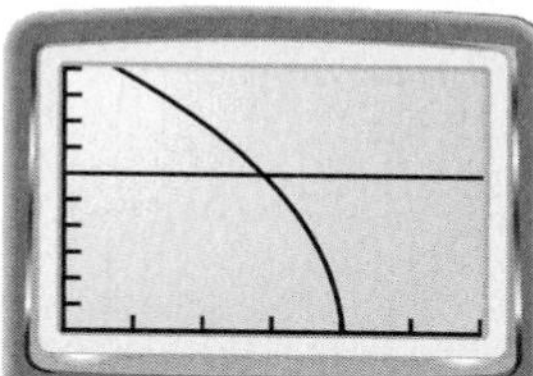

STEP 3 **Find** the intersection point of the two graphs using the *intersect* feature. The graphs intersect at about (938, 54.5).

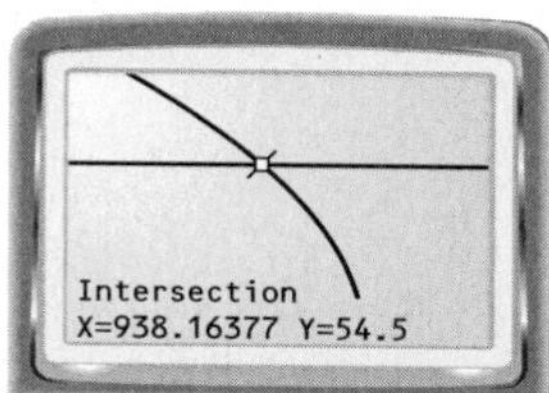

▶ The mean sustained wind velocity is 54.5 meters per second when the air pressure is about 938 millibars.

PRACTICE

SOLVING EQUATIONS Solve the radical equation using a table and using a graph.

1. $\sqrt{25 - x} = 8$ **−39**
2. $2.3\sqrt{x - 1} = 11.5$ **26**
3. $4.3\sqrt{x - 7} = 30$ **about 55.7**
4. $6\sqrt{2 - 7x} - 1.2 = 22.8$ **−2**
5. **ROCKETS** A model rocket is launched 25 feet from you. When the rocket is at height h, the distance d between you and the rocket is given by $d = \sqrt{625 + h^2}$ where h and d are measured in feet. What is the rocket's height when the distance between you and the rocket is 100 feet? **about 97 ft**
6. **WHAT IF?** In the problem on page 460, what is the air pressure at the center of a hurricane when the mean sustained wind velocity is 25 meters per second? **about 997 millibars**
7. **GEOMETRY** The lateral surface area L of a right circular cone is given by

$$L = \pi r\sqrt{r^2 + h^2}$$

where r is the radius and h is the height. Find the height of a right circular cone with a radius of 7.5 centimeters and a lateral surface area of 900 square centimeters. **about 37.5 cm**

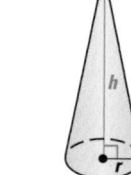

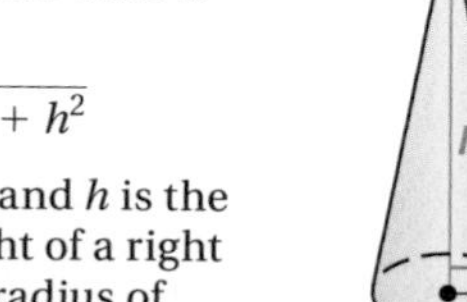

Alternative Strategy

Method 2 Example 2 on page 453 can also be solved by using a calculator graph. Use the *intersect* method to find the intersection point of the curve $y_1 = 6.3\sqrt{1013 - p}$ and the line $y_2 = 54.5$. This method also allows students to see graphically how the wind velocity decreases as the air pressure at the center of the hurricane increases.

Mathematical Reasoning

Multiple Representations Putting together the solution in the lesson and the two alternative solutions in this workshop gives three methods of solving the same problem: algebraic (page 453), numerical (Method 1), and graphical (Method 2). Ask students which of these methods they prefer and why. Your class discussion could also include these questions: "Which method do you think is easiest?" "Which method gives the most accurate answer?" "Which method helps you understand the problem best?"

1 PLAN AND PREPARE

Warm-Up Exercises

Find the domain and range of the function.

1. $y = 2\sqrt{x}$ **domain: $x \geq 0$; range: $y \geq 0$**
2. $y = -\sqrt{x} + 1$ **domain: $x \geq 0$; range: $y \leq 1$**
3. $y = \sqrt{-x}$ **domain: $x \leq 0$; range: $y \geq 0$**
4. $y = \sqrt{x + 6}$ **domain: $x \geq -6$; range: $y \geq 0$**
5. $y = 3\sqrt{x - 4} - 2$ **domain: $x \geq 4$; range: $y \geq -2$**

2 FOCUS AND MOTIVATE

Essential Question

Big Idea 3, p. 413

How is the domain of a radical function used in finding the solution of a radical inequality with a graphing calculator? **Tell students they will learn how to answer this question by using tables and graphs to solve radical inequalities and by writing the solutions for these inequalities.**

3 TEACH

Extra Example 1

Use a table to solve $-2\sqrt{x} + 8 \leq 2$. **$x \geq 9$**

NCTM STANDARDS

Standard 6: Apply/adapt strategies to solve problems

Standard 9: Apply math in contexts outside of mathematics

Solve Radical Inequalities

GOAL Solve radical inequalities by using tables and graphs.

In Chapter 4, you learned how to use tables and graphs to solve quadratic inequalities. You can also use tables and graphs to solve radical inequalities.

EXAMPLE 1 Solve a radical inequality using a table

Use a table to solve $3\sqrt{x} - 1 \leq 11$.

Solution

STEP 1 **Enter** the function $y = 3\sqrt{x} - 1$ into a graphing calculator.

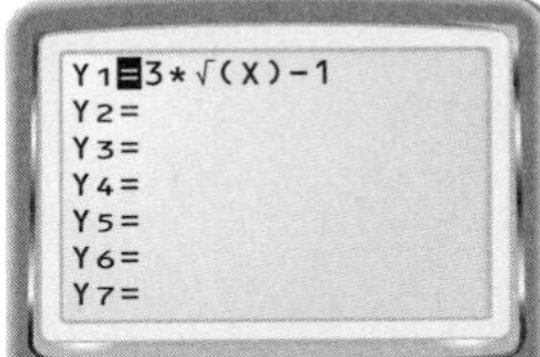

STEP 2 **Set up** the table to display x-values starting at 0 and increasing in increments of 1.

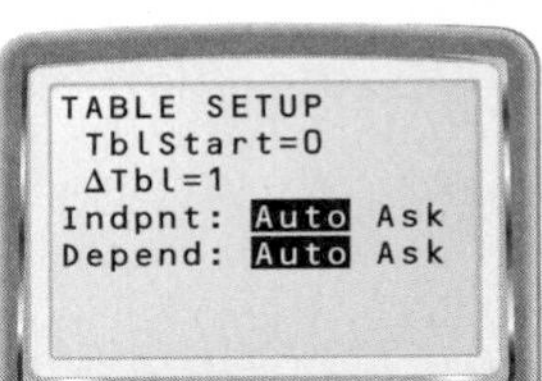

STEP 3 **Make** the table of values for $y = 3\sqrt{x} - 1$. Scroll through the table to find the x-value for which $y = 11$. This x-value is 16. It appears that $3\sqrt{x} - 1 \leq 11$ when $x \leq 16$.

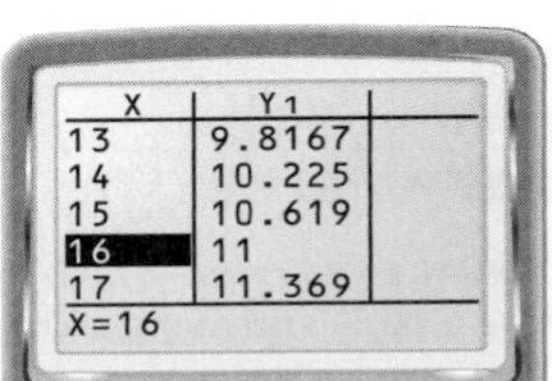

STEP 4 **Check** the domain of $y = 3\sqrt{x} - 1$. The domain is $x \geq 0$, so the solutions of $3\sqrt{x} - 1 \leq 11$ cannot be negative. (This is indicated by the word ERROR next to the negative x-values.)

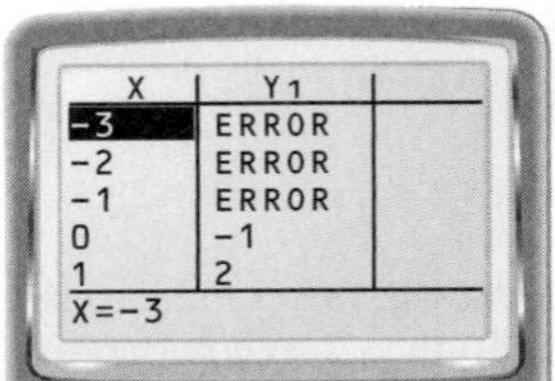

▸ The solution of the inequality is $x \leq 16$ *and* $x \geq 0$, which you can write as $0 \leq x \leq 16$.

EXAMPLE 2 Solve a radical inequality using a graph

Use a graph to solve $\sqrt{x-5} > 3$.

Solution

STEP 1 **Enter** the functions $y = \sqrt{x-5}$ and $y = 3$ into a graphing calculator.

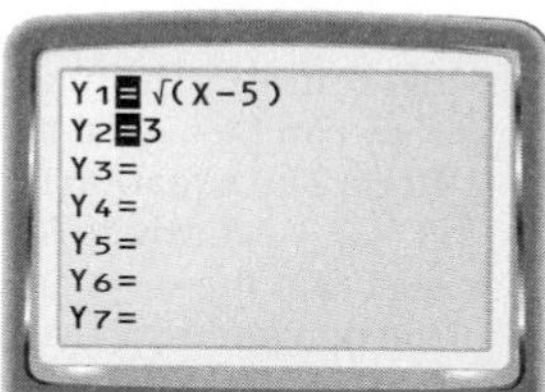

STEP 2 **Graph** the functions from Step 1. Adjust the viewing window so that the x-axis shows $0 \le x \le 30$ with a scale of 5 and the y-axis shows $-3 \le y \le 8$ with a scale of 1.

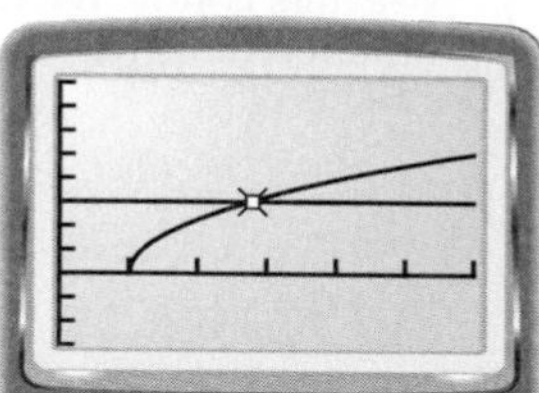

STEP 3 **Identity** the x-values for which the graph of $y = \sqrt{x-5}$ lies above the graph of $y = 3$. You can use the *intersect* feature to show that the graphs intersect when $x = 14$. The graph of $y = \sqrt{x-5}$ lies above the graph of $y = 3$ when $x > 14$.

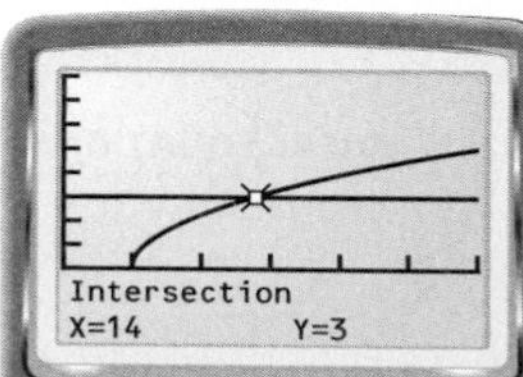

NTERPRET DOMAIN
a Example 2, note
hat the domain of
= $\sqrt{x-5}$ is $x \ge 5$.
herefore, the domain
oes not affect the
olution.

▶ The solution of the inequality is $x > 14$.

PRACTICE

XAMPLE 1
n p. 462
or Exs. 1–6

Use a table to solve the inequality.

1. $2\sqrt{x} - 5 \ge 3$ $x \ge 16$ **2.** $\sqrt{x-4} \le 5$ $4 \le x \le 29$ **3.** $4\sqrt{x} + 1 \le 9$ $0 \le x \le 4$

4. $\sqrt{x+7} \ge 3$ $x \ge 2$ **5.** $\sqrt{x} + \sqrt{x+3} \ge 3$ $x \ge 1$ **6.** $\sqrt{x} + \sqrt{x-5} \le 5$ $5 \le x \le 9$

XAMPLE 2
n p. 463
or Exs. 7–12

Use a graph to solve the inequality.

7. $2\sqrt{x} + 3 \le 8$ $0 \le x \le 6.25$ **8.** $\sqrt{x+3} \ge 2.6$ $x \ge 3.76$ **9.** $7\sqrt{x} + 1 < 9$ $0 \le x < 1.3$

10. $4\sqrt{3x-7} > 7.8$ $x > 3.6$ **11.** $\sqrt{x} - \sqrt{x+5} < -1$ $0 \le x < 4$ **12.** $\sqrt{x+2} + \sqrt{x-1} \le 9$ $1 \le x \le 19.8$

13. SAILBOAT RACE In order to compete in the America's Cup sailboat race, a boat must satisfy the rule

$$\ell + 1.25\sqrt{s} - 9.8\sqrt[3]{d} \le 16$$

where ℓ is the length (in meters) of the boat, s is the area (in square meters) of the sails, and d is the volume (in cubic meters) of water displaced by the boat. A boat has a length of 20 meters and displaces 27 cubic meters of water. What is the maximum allowable value for s? about 413 m^2

Extra Example 2

Use a graph to solve $\sqrt{x+4} > 6$. $x > 32$

Key Question to Ask for Example 2

- If your graph does not show any intersection of the radical function and the constant function, does that mean that the radical inequality has no solution? Explain. **No; you may need to adjust your viewing window to see the intersection, or the inequality may be true for all real numbers in the domain of the radical function.**

Closing the Lesson

Have students summarize the major points of the lesson and answer the Essential Question: How is the domain of a rational function used in finding the solution of a rational inequality with a graphing calculator?

- **A radical inequality can be solved with a graphing calculator by either making a table or by graphing a radical function and a constant function on the same screen.**

The solution can include only x-values that fall within the domain of the radical function, so you must take this into account in writing the solution.

4 PRACTICE AND APPLY

Teaching Strategy

After students have completed the exercises, ask them which method they prefer, and what they think are the advantages and disadvantages of each method. Discuss the limitations of using a table in finding exact solutions.

Kentucky Mixed Review

1. A
2. C
3. D
4. D
5. C
6. a. The Pythagorean Theorem relates the sides of a right triangle. Here, $d^2 = 50^2 + h^2$. Solving for d yields the given equation
   b. 87 feet
   c. When $h = 0$, the distance d is $\sqrt{2500 + 0} = \sqrt{2500} = 50$ feet.

Kentucky Mixed Review

Lessons 6.4–6.6

1. **BUSINESS** A manager at a clothing store is determining the retail prices of items so that they can be tagged and placed on the sales floor. The equation that the manager uses is $R = C + MC$ where R is the retail price, C is the cost that the store pays for the item, and M is the percent (expressed as a decimal) that the item is marked up. The markup for women's sweaters is 40%. What is the inverse of the function that gives the retail price of women's sweaters?

   A. $C = \frac{R}{1.4}$

   B. $C = \frac{R}{0.6}$

   C. $C = 1.4R$

   D. $C = 0.6R$

2. **RADICAL EQUATIONS** What is the solution of the equation $\sqrt{3x - 5} = 4$?

   A. 4 B. 5

   C. 7 D. 10

3. **MONETARY EXCHANGE** On a certain day, the function that gives Swedish kronor in terms of U.S. dollars is $k = 0.134d$ where k represents kronor and d represents U.S. dollars. How many dollars do you receive for 25 kronor?

   A. \$3.35 B. \$21.65

   C. \$28.35 D. \$186.57

4. **RADICAL FUNCTIONS** Which radical function has a domain of $x \geq 4$?

   A. $y = -5\sqrt{x + 4}$

   B. $y = -\sqrt{x} - 4$

   C. $y = 4\sqrt{x}$

   D. $y = 2\sqrt{x - 4} + 8$

5. **VERTICAL MOTION** An object is launched upward from ground level and reaches a maximum height of h feet. The initial velocity v (in feet per second) of the object is given by the function $v = 8\sqrt{h}$. What is the approximate maximum height of an object that is launched upward with an initial velocity of 110 feet per second?

   A. 83.9 feet B. 156.3 feet

   C. 189.1 feet D. 311.1 feet

6. **OPEN-RESPONSE** Your friend releases a weather balloon 50 feet from you. When the balloon is at height h, the distance d between you and the balloon is given by

$$d = \sqrt{2500 + h^2}$$

where h and d are measured in feet, as shown in the diagram below.

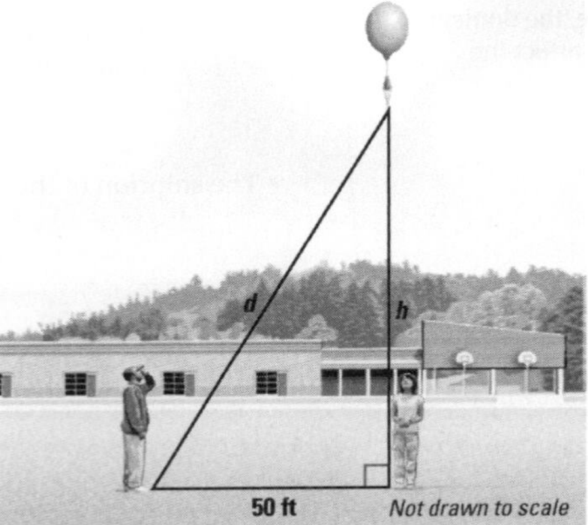

   a. *Explain* why this equation is correct.

   b. To the nearest foot, what is the height of the balloon when the distance d between you and the balloon is 100 feet?

   c. The distance d will never be less than 50 feet, which is the horizontal distance along the ground. *Explain* how the equation models this fact.

Animated Algebra
classzone.com
Electronic Function Library

BIG IDEAS

For Your Notebook

Big Idea 1

Using Rational Exponents

The following are properties of rational exponents. Let a and b be real numbers and let m and n be rational numbers.

Property	Example
$a^m \cdot a^n = a^{m+n}$	$4^{5/2} \cdot 4^{1/2} = 4^3 = 64$
$(a^m)^n = a^{mn}$	$(2^8)^{1/4} = 2^2 = 4$
$(ab)^m = a^m b^m$	$(25 \cdot 4)^{1/2} = 25^{1/2} \cdot 4^{1/2} = 5 \cdot 2 = 10$
$a^{-m} = \frac{1}{a^m}, a \neq 0$	$8^{-1/3} = \frac{1}{8^{1/3}} = \frac{1}{2}$
$\frac{a^m}{a^n} = a^{m-n}, a \neq 0$	$\frac{9^{5/8}}{9^{1/8}} = 9^{4/8} = 9^{1/2} = 3$
$\left(\frac{a}{b}\right)^m = \frac{a^m}{b^m}, b \neq 0$	$\left(\frac{16}{81}\right)^{1/4} = \frac{16^{1/4}}{81^{1/4}} = \frac{2}{3}$

Big Idea 2

Performing Function Operations and Finding Inverse Functions

Operation	Definition	Example: $f(x) = 2x, g(x) = x - 5$
Addition	$h(x) = f(x) + g(x)$	$h(x) = 2x + (x - 5) = 3x - 5$
Subtraction	$h(x) = f(x) - g(x)$	$h(x) = 2x - (x - 5) = x + 5$
Multiplication	$h(x) = f(x) \cdot g(x)$	$h(x) = 2x(x - 5) = 2x^2 - 10x$
Division	$h(x) = \frac{f(x)}{g(x)}$	$h(x) = \frac{2x}{x - 5}$
Composition	$h(x) = g(f(x))$	$h(x) = 2x - 5$
Inverse	$h(x) = g^{-1}(x)$	$h(x) = x + 5$

Big Idea 3

Graphing Radical Functions and Solving Radical Equations

To **graph** radical functions, use the graph of the parent functions. For example, to graph $y = \sqrt{x+1} - 2$, translate the graph of $y = \sqrt{x}$ left 1 unit and down 2 units.

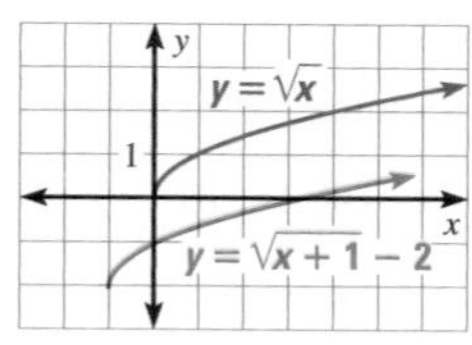

To **solve** a radical equation, first isolate the radical. Then raise each side of the equation to the same power and solve the polynomial equation.

$\sqrt{2x-5} - 3 = 2$	**Write equation.**
$\sqrt{2x-5} = 5$	**Isolate radical.**
$(\sqrt{2x-5})^2 = 5^2$	**Square each side.**
$2x - 5 = 25$	**Simplify.**
$x = 15$	**Solve.**

Additional Resources

The following resources are available to help review the materials in this chapter.

Chapter 6 Resource Book

- Chapter Review Games and Activities, p. 77
- Cumulative Practice, Chs. 1–6, pp. 79–80

Student Resources in Spanish

eWorkbook

@HomeTutor

Vocabulary Practice

Vocabulary practice is available at **classzone.com**

Extra Example 6.1

Evaluate the expression.

a. $(\sqrt[5]{-32})^2$ 4

b. $64^{5/3}$ 1024

6 CHAPTER REVIEW

@HomeTutor
classzone.com
• Multi-Language Glossary
• Vocabulary practice

REVIEW KEY VOCABULARY

- *n*th root of *a*, *p. 414*
- index of a radical, *p. 414*
- simplest form of a radical, *p. 422*
- like radicals, *p. 422*
- power function, *p. 428*
- composition, *p. 430*
- inverse relation, *p. 438*
- inverse function, *p. 438*
- radical function, *p. 446*
- radical equation, *p. 452*

VOCABULARY EXERCISES

1. Copy and complete: The index of the radical $\sqrt[4]{7}$ is __?__. 4
2. List two different pairs of like radicals. *Sample answer:* $2\sqrt[3]{x}$ and $-3\sqrt[3]{x}$, $\sqrt{xy}+1$ and $3\sqrt{xy}$
3. Copy and complete: A(n) __?__ function has the form $y = ax^b$ where a is a real number and b is a rational number. power
4. **WRITING** *Explain* how the graph of a function and the graph of its inverse are related. They are reflections of each other in the line $y = x$.
5. **WRITING** *Explain* how to use the horizontal line test to determine whether the inverse of a function f is also a function. If a horizontal line crosses the graph of the function more than once, the inverse is not a function.
6. **WRITING** *Describe* how the graph of $y = \sqrt[3]{x-4} + 5$ is related to the graph of the parent function $y = \sqrt[3]{x}$. It is translated 4 units right and 5 units up.
7. **REASONING** A student began solving the equation $x^{2/3} = 5$ by cubing each side. What will the student have to do next? What could the student have done to solve the equation in just one step? Take the square root of each side; raise each side to the $\frac{3}{2}$ power.

REVIEW EXAMPLES AND EXERCISES

Use the review examples and exercises below to check your understanding of the concepts you have learned in each lesson of Chapter 6.

6.1 Evaluate *n*th Roots and Use Rational Exponents *pp. 414–419*

EXAMPLE

Evaluate the expression.

a. $(\sqrt[4]{16})^5 = 2^5 = 32$

b. $27^{-4/3} = \frac{1}{27^{4/3}} = \frac{1}{(27^{1/3})^4} = \frac{1}{3^4} = \frac{1}{81}$

EXERCISES

EXAMPLE 2 on p. 415 for Exs. 8–15

Evaluate the expression without using a calculator.

8. $81^{1/4}$ 3
9. $0^{1/3}$ 0
10. $\sqrt[3]{-64}$ −4
11. $\sqrt[3]{125}$ 5
12. $256^{3/4}$ 64
13. $27^{-2/3}$ $\frac{1}{9}$
14. $(\sqrt[3]{8})^7$ 128
15. $\frac{1}{(\sqrt[5]{-32})^{-3}}$ −8

@HomeTutor
classzone.com
Chapter Review Practice

6.2 Apply Properties of Rational Exponents

pp. 420–427

EXAMPLE

Write the expression in simplest form. Assume all variables are positive.

a. $\sqrt[3]{48} = \sqrt[3]{8 \cdot 6} = \sqrt[3]{8} \cdot \sqrt[3]{6} = 2\sqrt[3]{6}$

b. $\left(\frac{x^4}{y^8}\right)^{1/2} = \frac{(x^4)^{1/2}}{(y^8)^{1/2}} = \frac{x^{4 \cdot 1/2}}{y^{8 \cdot 1/2}} = \frac{x^2}{y^4}$

XAMPLES
, 6, and 7
n pp. 422–423
or Exs. 16–19

EXERCISES

Write the expression in simplest form. Assume all variables are positive.

16. $\sqrt[3]{80}$ $2\sqrt[3]{10}$
17. $(3^4 \cdot 5^4)^{-1/4}$ $\frac{1}{15}$
18. $(25a^{10}b^{16})^{1/2}$ $5a^5b^8$
19. $\sqrt{\frac{18x^5y^4}{49xz^3}}$ $\frac{3x^2y^2\sqrt{2z}}{7z^2}$

6.3 Perform Function Operations and Composition

pp. 428–434

EXAMPLE

Let $f(x) = 3x^2 + 1$ and $g(x) = x + 4$. Perform the indicated operation.

a. $f(x) + g(x) = (3x^2 + 1) + (x + 4) = 3x^2 + x + 5$

b. $f(x) \cdot g(x) = (3x^2 + 1)(x + 4) = 3x^3 + 12x^2 + x + 4$

c. $f(g(x)) = f(x + 4) = 3(x + 4)^2 + 1 = 3(x^2 + 8x + 16) + 1 = 3x^2 + 24x + 49$

XAMPLES
, 2, and 5
n pp. 428–430
or Exs. 20–23

EXERCISES

Let $f(x) = 4x - 6$ and $g(x) = x + 8$. Perform the indicated operation.

20. $f(x) + g(x)$ $5x + 2$
21. $f(x) - g(x)$ $3x - 14$
22. $f(x) \cdot g(x)$ $4x^2 + 26x - 48$
23. $f(g(x))$ $4x + 26$

6.4 Use Inverse Functions

pp. 438–445

EXAMPLE

Find the inverse of the function $y = 3x + 7$.

$y = 3x + 7$	**Write original function.**
$x = 3y + 7$	**Switch x and y.**
$x - 7 = 3y$	**Subtract 7 from each side.**
$\frac{1}{3}x - \frac{7}{3} = y$	**Divide each side by 3.**

XAMPLES
, 4, and 5
n pp. 438–441
or Exs. 24–26

EXERCISES

Find the inverse of the function.

24. $y = \frac{1}{3}x + 4$ $y = 3x - 12$
25. $y = 4x^2 + 9, x \geq 0$ $y = \frac{\sqrt{x-9}}{2}$
26. $f(x) = x^3 - 4$ $f^{-1}(x) = \sqrt[3]{x + 4}$

Extra Example 6.2

Write the expression in simplest form. Assume all variables are positive.

a. $\sqrt[3]{250}$ $5\sqrt[3]{2}$

b. $\sqrt[5]{\frac{c}{d^8}}$ $\frac{\sqrt[5]{cd^2}}{d^2}$

Extra Example 6.3

Let $f(x) = x^2 - 1$ and $g(x) = 2x + 5$. Perform the indicated operation.

a. $f(x) - g(x)$ $x^2 - 2x - 6$

b. $f(x) \cdot g(x)$ $2x^3 + 5x^2 - 2x - 5$

c. $g(f(x))$ $2x^2 + 3$

Extra Example 6.4

Find the inverse of the function $f(x) = 2x^3 + 5$. $f^{-1}(x) = \sqrt[3]{\frac{x-5}{2}}$

Extra Examples 6.5

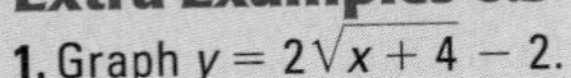
1. Graph $y = 2\sqrt{x+4} - 2$.

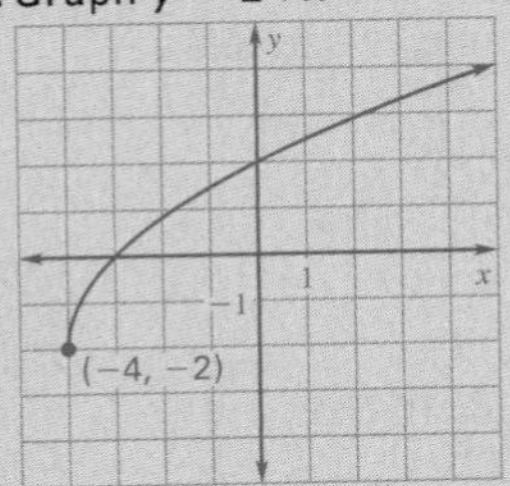

2. Graph $y = -\sqrt[3]{x-2} + 3$.

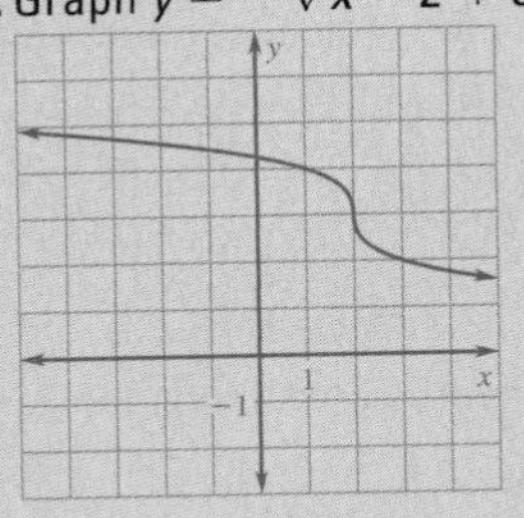

Extra Example 6.6

Solve $\sqrt[3]{5x - 14} = -4$. -10

27.
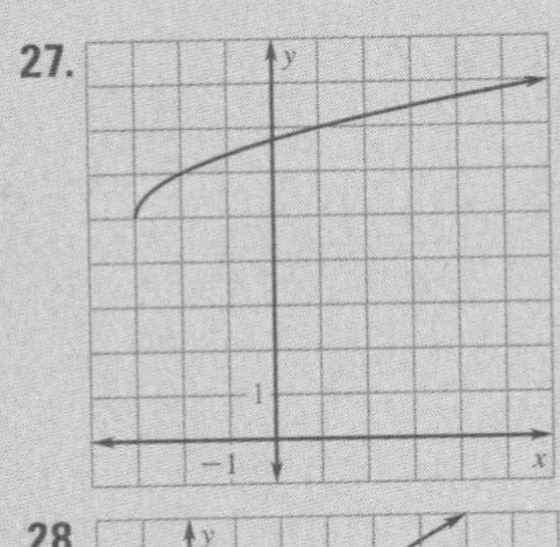

28.
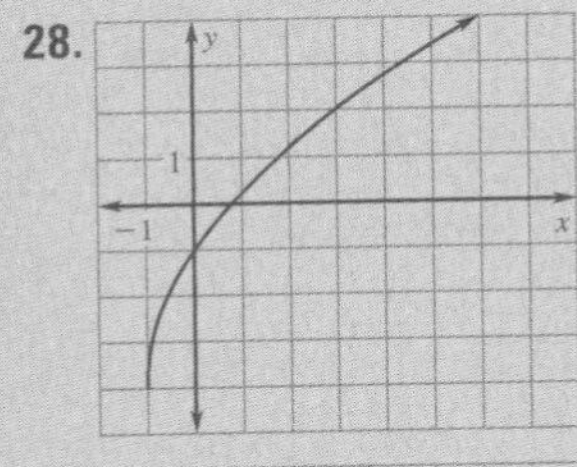

29.
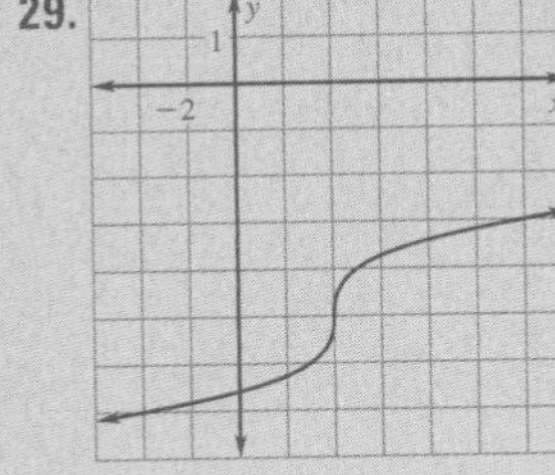

6 CHAPTER REVIEW

6.5 Graph Square Root and Cube Root Functions *pp. 446–451*

EXAMPLE

Graph $y = -\sqrt{x-3} + 2$.

Sketch the graph of $y = -\sqrt{x}$. Notice that it begins at the origin and passes through the point $(1, -1)$.

For $y = -\sqrt{x-3} + 2$, $h = 3$, and $k = 2$. So, shift the graph of $y = -\sqrt{x}$ right 3 units and up 2 units. The resulting graph begins at the point $(3, 2)$ and passes through the point $(4, 1)$.

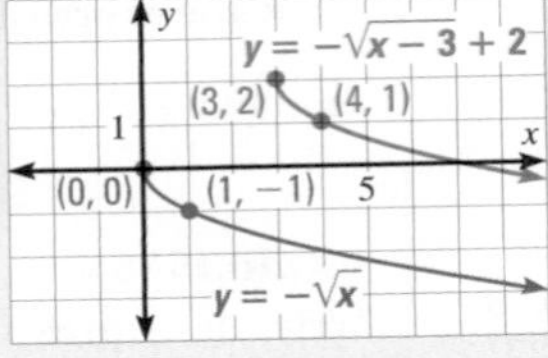

EXAMPLE

Graph $y = \sqrt[3]{x+2} - 4$.

Sketch the graph of $y = \sqrt[3]{x}$. Notice that it passes through the points $(-1, -1)$, $(0, 0)$, and $(1, 1)$.

For $y = \sqrt[3]{x+2} - 4$, $h = -2$ and $k = -4$. So, shift the graph of $y = \sqrt[3]{x}$ left 2 units and down 4 units. The resulting graph passes through the points $(-3, -5)$, $(-2, -4)$, and $(-1, -3)$.

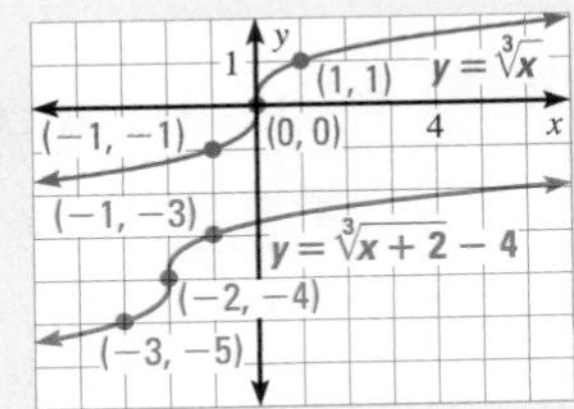

EXAMPLES 4 and 5 on p. 448 for Exs. 27–29

EXERCISES

Graph the function. Then state the domain and range. 27–29. See margin for art.

27. $y = \sqrt{x+3} + 5$
domain: $x \geq -3$, range: $y \geq 5$

28. $y = 3\sqrt{x+1} - 4$
domain: $x \geq -1$, range: $y \geq -4$

29. $y = \sqrt[3]{x-4} - 5$
domain: all real numbers, range: all real numbers

6.6 Solve Radical Equations *pp. 452–459*

EXAMPLE

Solve $\sqrt{4x+9} = 5$.

$\sqrt{4x+9} = 5$	**Write original equation.**
$(\sqrt{4x+9})^2 = 5^2$	**Square each side to eliminate the radical.**
$4x + 9 = 25$	**Simplify.**
$4x = 16$	**Subtract 9 from each side.**
$x = 4$	**Divide each side by 4.**

CHECK Check $x = 4$ in the original equation.

$\sqrt{4x+9} = \sqrt{4(4)+9} = \sqrt{25} = 5$ ✓

EXAMPLES 1, 3, and 5 on pp. 452–454 for Exs. 30–32

EXERCISES

Solve the equation. Check for extraneous solutions.

30. $\sqrt[3]{5x - 4} = 2$ $2\frac{2}{5}$

31. $3x^{3/4} = 24$ 16

32. $\sqrt{x^2 - 10} = \sqrt{3x}$ $-2, 5$

CHAPTER TEST

Evaluate the expression without using a calculator.

1. $-125^{1/3}$ -5
2. $32^{1/5}$ 2
3. $\sqrt[4]{81}$ 3
4. $\sqrt[3]{27}$ 3
5. $8^{5/3}$ 32
6. $16^{-3/2}$ $\frac{1}{64}$
7. $(\sqrt[3]{-27})^2$ 9
8. $(\sqrt[3]{64})^{-4}$ $\frac{1}{256}$

Write the expression in simplest form. Assume all variables are positive.

9. $\sqrt[3]{88}$ $2\sqrt[3]{11}$
10. $\sqrt[5]{16} \cdot \sqrt[5]{8}$ $2\sqrt[5]{4}$
11. $\sqrt{\frac{12}{49}}$ $\frac{2\sqrt{3}}{7}$
12. $\frac{\sqrt[3]{24}}{\sqrt[3]{9}}$ $\frac{2\sqrt[3]{9}}{3}$
13. $\sqrt[3]{64x^4y^2}$ $4x\sqrt[3]{xy^2}$
14. $\sqrt[4]{2x^6y^8z}$ $xy^2\sqrt[4]{2x^2z}$
15. $\sqrt[5]{\frac{x^6}{y^4}}$ $\frac{x\sqrt[5]{xy}}{y}$
16. $\sqrt{\frac{75x^5y^6}{36xz^5}}$ $\frac{5x^2y^3\sqrt{3z}}{6z^3}$

Let $f(x) = 2x + 9$ and $g(x) = 3x - 1$. Perform the indicated operation and state the domain.

17. $f(x) + g(x)$
18. $f(x) - g(x)$
19. $f(x) \cdot g(x)$
20. $\frac{f(x)}{g(x)}$
21. $f(g(x))$ $6x + 7$, all real numbers
22. $g(f(x))$ $6x + 26$, all real numbers
23. $f(f(x))$ $4x + 27$, all real numbers
24. $g(g(x))$ $9x - 4$, all real numbers

Find the inverse of the function.

25. $y = -2x + 5$ $y = \frac{5 - x}{2}$
26. $y = \frac{1}{3}x + 4$ $y = 3x - 12$
27. $f(x) = 5x - 12$ $f^{-1}(x) = \frac{x + 12}{5}$
28. $y = \frac{1}{2}x^4, x \geq 0$ $y = \sqrt[4]{2x}$
29. $f(x) = x^3 + 5$ $f^{-1}(x) = \sqrt[3]{x - 5}$
30. $f(x) = -2x^3 + 1$ $f^{-1}(x) = \sqrt[3]{\frac{1 - x}{2}}$

Graph the function. Then state the domain and range. 31–33. See margin for art.

31. $y = -6\sqrt[3]{x}$
32. $y = \sqrt{x - 4} - 2$
33. $f(x) = -\sqrt[3]{x + 3} + 4$

Solve the equation. Check for extraneous solutions.

34. $\sqrt{3x + 7} = 4$ 3
35. $\sqrt{3x} - \sqrt{x + 6} = 0$ 3
36. $x - 3 = \sqrt{x - 1}$ 5

37. **KINETIC ENERGY** The kinetic energy E (in joules) of a 1250 kilogram compact car is given by the equation $E = 625s^2$ where s is the speed of the car (in meters per second).
    a. Write an inverse model that gives the speed of the car as a function of its kinetic energy. $s = \frac{\sqrt{E}}{25}$
    b. Use the inverse model to find the speed of the car if its kinetic energy is 120,000 joules. Give the speed in kilometers per hour. about 49.9 km/h
    c. If the kinetic energy doubles, will the speed double? *Explain* why or why not. No. *Sample answer:* Doubling the kinetic energy will increase the speed to about 70.5 kilometers per hour, which is not double the answer in part (b).

38. **BOWLING SCORES** In bowling, a *handicap* is a change in score to adjust for differences in players' abilities. You belong to a bowling league in which each bowler's handicap h is determined by his or her average a using this formula:

$$h = 0.9(200 - a)$$

If a bowler's average is over 200, the handicap is 0. Find the inverse of the model. Then find your average if your handicap is 36. $a = -\frac{h}{0.9} + 200$; 160

17. $5x + 8$; all real numbers
18. $-x + 10$; all real numbers
19. $6x^2 + 25x - 9$; all real numbers
20. $\frac{2x + 9}{3x - 1}$; all real numbers except $x = \frac{1}{3}$

31. domain: all real numbers, range: all real numbers
32. domain: $x \geq 4$, range: $y \geq -2$
33. domain: all real numbers, range: all real numbers

Additional Resources

Assessment Book

- Chapter Test, Levels A, B, C, pp. 79–84
- Standardized Chapter Test, pp. 85–86
- SAT/ACT Chapter Test, pp. 87–88
- Alternative Assessment, pp. 89–90

Test Generator CD-ROM

Chapter Test

Easily-readable reduced copies (with answers) of Chapter Test B, the Standardized Chapter Test, and the Alternative Assessment from the Assessment Book can be found on pp. 412E–412F.

31.

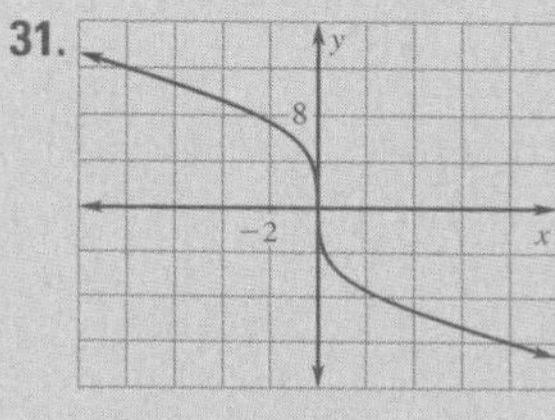

32.

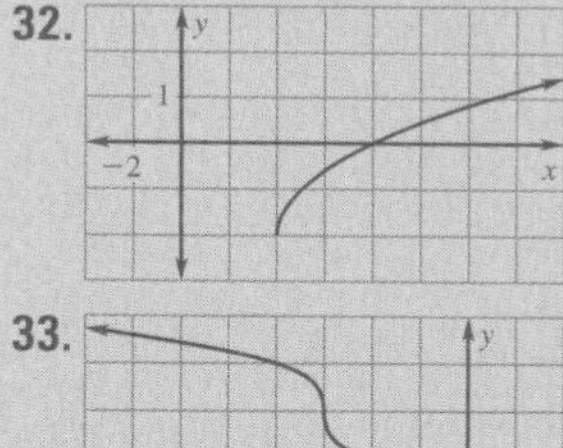

33.

MULTIPLE-CHOICE QUESTIONS

If you have difficulty solving a multiple-choice problem directly, you may be able to use another approach to eliminate incorrect answer choices and obtain the correct answer.

PROBLEM 1

The volume of a sphere is given by $V = \frac{4}{3}\pi r^3$. The surface area of a sphere is given by $S = 4\pi r^2$. Which choice correctly expresses S as a function of V?

A. $4\pi V^2$ B. $\sqrt[3]{\frac{9V^2}{4\pi}}$ C. $\sqrt[3]{36\pi V^2}$ D. $\sqrt[3]{\frac{3V^2}{4\pi}}$

METHOD 1

SOLVE DIRECTLY Solve for r in terms of V and substitute this expression in the formula for S.

STEP 1 Solve for r in terms of V.

$$V = \frac{4}{3}\pi r^3$$

$$\frac{3}{4\pi}V = r^3$$

$$r = \sqrt[3]{\frac{3}{4\pi}V}$$

STEP 2 Substitute the above expression for r in the formula for S.

$$S = 4\pi r^2$$

$$= 4\pi\left(\sqrt[3]{\frac{3}{4\pi}V}\right)^2$$

STEP 3 Simplify the expression into a form similar to the answer choices.

$$S = 4\pi\left(\sqrt[3]{\frac{3}{4\pi}V}\right)^2 = 4\pi\sqrt[3]{\frac{9V^2}{4^2\pi^2}}$$

$$= \sqrt[3]{\frac{4^3\pi^3 9V^2}{4^2\pi^2}} = \sqrt[3]{36\pi V^2}$$

▸ The correct answer is C.

METHOD 2

ELIMINATE CHOICES Choose a value of r that will produce associated values of V and S. Then check the answer choices.

STEP 1 Compute the volume and surface area for a single value of r, such as $r = 2$.

Volume: $V = \frac{4}{3}\pi r^3 = \frac{4}{3}\pi(2)^3 \approx 33.51$

Surface Area: $S = 4\pi r^2 = 4\pi(2)^2 \approx 50.27$

STEP 2 Substitute $V \approx 33.51$ into the answer choices. The correct choice will yield a surface area of 50.27.

Choice A: $4\pi V^2 = 4\pi(33.51)^2 \approx 14{,}111 \neq 50.27$

Choice B: $\sqrt[3]{\frac{9V^2}{4\pi}} = \sqrt[3]{\frac{9(33.51)^2}{4\pi}} \approx 9.30 \neq 50.27$

Choice C: $\sqrt[3]{36\pi V^2} = \sqrt[3]{36\pi(50.27)} \approx 50.27$

Choice D: $\sqrt[3]{\frac{3V^2}{4\pi}} = \sqrt[3]{\frac{3(33.51)^2}{4\pi}} \approx 6.45 \neq 50.27$

▸ The correct answer is C.

TEST PREPARATION

470

PROBLEM 2

Find all solutions of the equation $\sqrt{2x-1}+3=6$.

A. 1 B. 2 C. 4 D. 5.

METHOD 1

SOLVE DIRECTLY Solve the equation for x.

STEP 1 Isolate x.

$$\sqrt{2x-1}+3=6$$
$$\sqrt{2x-1}=3$$
$$2x-1=9$$
$$2x=10$$
$$x=5$$

STEP 2 **Check,** in order to avoid including an extraneous root.

$$\sqrt{2x-1}+3=\sqrt{2(5)-1}+3$$
$$=\sqrt{9}+3$$
$$=3+3$$
$$=6$$

The correct answer is D.

METHOD 2

ELIMINATE CHOICES Another method is to test which value of x satisfies the equation.

Choice A: $\sqrt{2x-1}+3=\sqrt{2(1)-1}+3$
$=\sqrt{1}+3$
$=1+3$
$\neq 6$

Choice B: $\sqrt{2x-1}+3=\sqrt{2(2)-1}+3$
$=\sqrt{3}+3$
$\neq 6$

Choice C: $\sqrt{2x-1}+3=\sqrt{2(4)-1}+3$
$=\sqrt{7}+3$
$\neq 6$

Choice D: $\sqrt{2x-1}+3=\sqrt{2(5)-1}+3$
$=\sqrt{9}+3$
$=3+3$
$=6$

▶ The correct answer is D.

PRACTICE

Explain **why you can eliminate the highlighted answer choice.**

What is the solution of the equation $\sqrt{2x-3}-3=6$?

A. 0 B. ✗ 6 C. 39 D. 42

Which expression is equivalent to $(9x^{3/2})^{-1/2}$?

A. $\frac{9}{2x^{3/4}}$ B. $\frac{1}{3x^{3/4}}$ C. ✗ $9x^3$ D. $3x^{3/4}$

TEST PREPARATION

Kentucky Test Preparation

1. **Substituting $x = 6$ yields $\sqrt{2(6)-3}-3=\sqrt{3}-3=0\neq 6$.**
2. **Substituting $x = 1$ yields 9 , which is equal to $\frac{1}{3}$. However, substituting $x = 1$ in $9x^3$ yields $9(1) = 9$.**

Kentucky Test Practice

1. C
2. D
3. D
4. D
5. B
6. A
7. C
8. C
9. B
10. C
11. C
12. D
13. B

Kentucky Test Practice

TEST PREPARATION

MULTIPLE-CHOICE

1. Simplify the expression $4^{1/2} \bullet 2^4$.

A. 16 B. $8^{4^{1/2}}$

C. 32 D. 64

2. If $f(x) = 2x^{-3/2}$, then $f(0.25)$ equals what?

A. -8 B. -4

C. -0.25 D. 16

3. What is the solution of the equation $(8x)^{3/5} = 8$?

A. $8^{-2/5}$ B. 1

C. $8^{2/5}$ D. 4

4. Most carnivorous dinosaurs, called theropods, walked on 2 legs. The height at the hip of a theropod can be modeled by the function $h(\ell) = 3.49\ell^{1.14}$, where ℓ is the length (in centimeters) of the dinosaur's instep.

The length of the instep can be modeled by $\ell(p) = 1.2p$, where p is the footprint length (in centimeters). Which expression represents h in terms of p?

A. $4.188p$ B. $4.188p^{1.14}$

C. $4.30p$ D. $4.30p^{1.14}$

5. In the equation $\sqrt[4]{16x^3y^4z} = 2x^ayz^b$, what is the sum of a and b? Assume all variables are positive.

A. $\frac{1}{2}$ B. 1

C. $\frac{7}{4}$ D. 4

6. The expression $\frac{5y^2 - 15y}{3y^2 - y^3}$ is equivalent to:

A. $-\frac{5}{y}$ B. $\frac{5}{y}$

C. $\frac{10}{3}$ D. $\frac{5}{3} - \frac{15}{y^2}$

7. What is the value of $\frac{1}{(\sqrt[4]{625})^{-2}}$?

A. $\frac{1}{25}$ B. $\frac{1}{5}$

C. 25 D. 78,125

8. Let $f(x) = \frac{2}{5}x^{-0.25}$ and $g(x) = 5x^{3.25}$. Approximated to three decimal places, what is the value of $f(x) \cdot g(x)$ when $x = 3$?

A. 0.054 B. 0.110

C. 54.00 D. 93.531

9. What is the y-intercept of the graph of the function $y = \sqrt[3]{x - 8}$?

A. -8 B. -2

C. 2 D. 8

10. Let $f(x) = \sqrt{x - 2} + 3$ and $g(x) = \sqrt{x + 13}$. For what value of x does $f(x) = g(x)$?

A. -4 B. -3

C. 3 D. 9

11. Consider the function $y = 3x + 9$. What is the slope of the graph of the inverse function?

A. -3 B. $-\frac{1}{3}$

C. $\frac{1}{3}$ D. 3

12. The expression $(k^{-1/2})\sqrt[3]{k^4}$ is equivalent to:

A. $k^{-2/3}$ B. k^3

C. $k^{3/5}$ D. $k^{5/6}$

13. Simplify $(-4x^3)(5x^4)$.

A. $-20x^{12}$ B. $-2x^{12}$

C. $-20x^7$ D. $-2x^7$

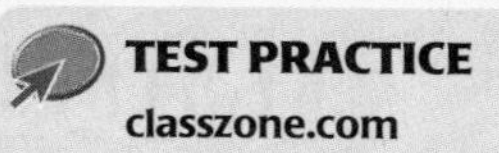

MULTIPLE-CHOICE

14. What is the solution of the equation $\sqrt{2x+3} = 5$?

A. -14 B. -4

C. 1 D. 11

15. The graph of which function is shown?

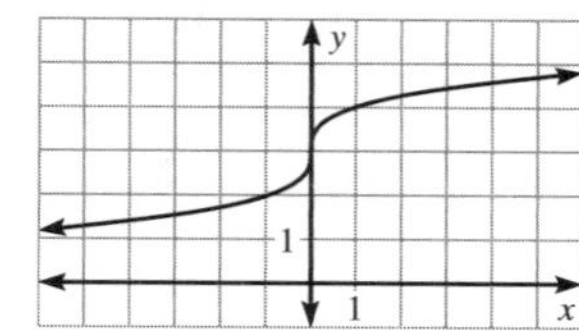

A. $y = \sqrt[3]{x+3}$ B. $y = \sqrt[3]{x-3}$

C. $y = \sqrt[3]{x} + 3$ D. $y = \sqrt[3]{x} - 3$

16. What is the inverse of $y = -2x^5 + 10$?

A. $y = \sqrt[5]{5 - \frac{1}{2}x}$ B. $y = 20 - \sqrt[5]{2x}$

C. $y = \sqrt[5]{2x} - 20$ D. $y = \sqrt[5]{\frac{1}{2}x - 5}$

17. Let $f(x) = 2x^{1/2}$ and $g(x) = 4x^2$. What is the value of $g(f(9))$?

A. -144 B. -36

C. 36 D. 144

18. What is the value of $\left(\frac{5^5}{2^5}\right)^{-1/5}$?

A. $\frac{1}{160}$ B. $\frac{1}{10}$

C. $\frac{2}{5}$ D. $\frac{5}{2}$

19. Which expression is equivalent to $\sqrt{9x^2y^3}$ for *all* real numbers x and y?

A. $3xy^{3/2}$

B. $3|x|y^{3/2}$

C. $3|x|(|y|)^{3/2}$

D. all of the above

OPEN-RESPONSE

20. Consider the following equation:

$$-\sqrt{x+4} = \sqrt{x-1} + 1$$

a. Solve the equation algebraically.

b. Solve the equation by graphing.

c. Are the results the same? *Explain* why or why not.

21. You have a $10 gift card to spend at a local toy store. The store has a sale offering 15% off all board games.

a. Use composition of functions to find the final price of a board game that originally costs $27 when the $10 is subtracted before the 15% discount is applied.

b. Use composition of functions to find the final price of the board game when the 15% discount is applied before the $10 is subtracted.

c. How much more money can you save if the store applies the 15% discount first?

TEST PREPARATION

14. D
15. C
16. A
17. D
18. C
19. B
20. a. $-\sqrt{x+4} = \sqrt{x-1} + 1$
$(-\sqrt{x+4})^2 = (\sqrt{x-1} + 1)^2$
$x + 4 = x - 1 + 2\sqrt{x-1} + 1$
$4 = 2\sqrt{(x-1)}$
$2 = \sqrt{(x-1)}$
$2^2 = (\sqrt{(x-1)})^2$
$4 = x - 1$
$5 = x$
Check:
$-\sqrt{(5+4)} = \sqrt{(5-1)} + 1$
$-\sqrt{9} = \sqrt{4} + 1$
$-3 \neq 3$
b.

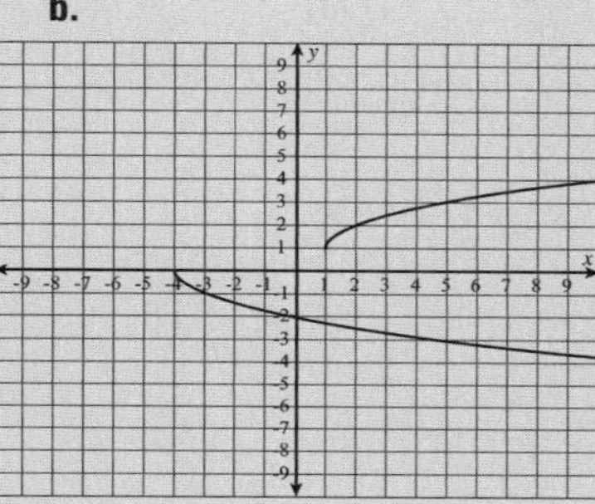

c. Yes; both methods yield no solution.
21. a. $14.45
b. $12.95
c. $1.50

Additional Resources

The following resources are available to help review the materials in Chapters 1–6.

Chapter Resource Books

- Chapter 4 CRB, Cumulative Review, pp. 127–128
- Chapter 5 CRB, Cumulative Review, pp. 112–113
- Chapter 6 CRB, Cumulative Review, pp. 79–80

Assessment Book

- Cumulative Test, Chapters 1–6, pp. 91–94

13. 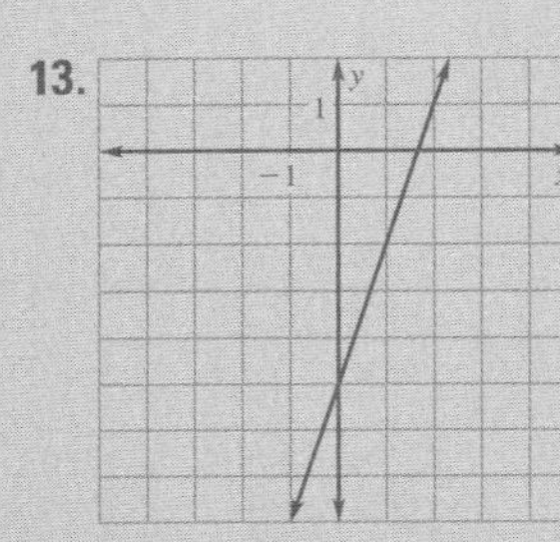

14. 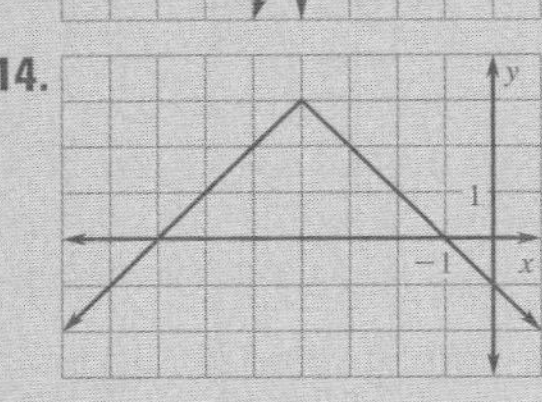

15. 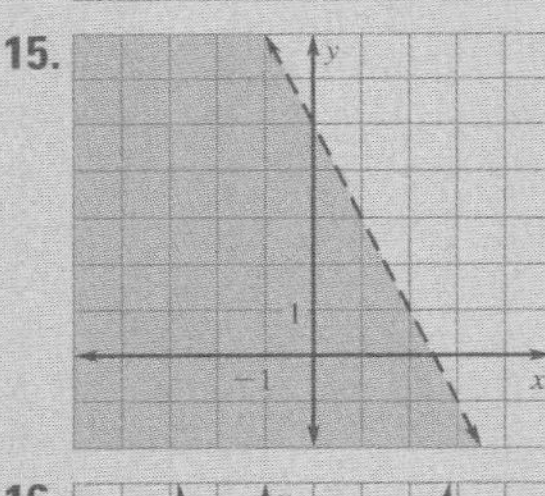

16. 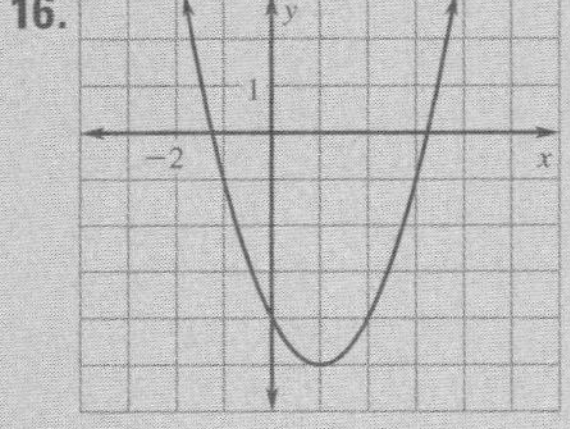

43. $10x^2 - 28x - 6$, all real numbers

50. $f^{-1}(x) = \frac{3x^3 - 7}{2}$

51. $f^{-1}(x) = \sqrt[5]{\frac{-9x + 18}{8}}$

Write an equation of the line that passes through the given point and has the given slope. *(p. 98)*

1. $(3, 1), m = 4$ $y = 4x - 11$
2. $(4, 6), m = 7$ $y = 7x - 22$
3. $(-3, 2), m = -8$ $y = -8x - 22$
4. $(1, -5), m = 9$ $y = 9x - 14$
5. $(-5, 8), m = \frac{4}{5}$ $y = \frac{4}{5}x + 12$
6. $(2, -10), m = -\frac{3}{4}$ $y = -\frac{3}{4}x - \frac{17}{2}$

Solve the equation. Check your solution(s).

7. $-2x + 7 = 15$ *(p. 18)* -4
8. $|4x - 6| = 14$ *(p. 51)* $-2, 5$
9. $x^2 - 9x + 14 = 0$ *(p. 252)* $2, 7$
10. $4x^2 - 6x + 9 = 0$ *(p. 292)* $\frac{3 \pm 3i\sqrt{3}}{4}$
11. $x^3 + 3x^2 - 10x = 0$ *(p. 353)* $2, 0, -5$
12. $\sqrt{8x + 1} = 7$ *(p. 452)* 6

Graph the equation or inequality in a coordinate plane. 13–21. See margin.

13. $y = 3x - 5$ *(p. 89)*
14. $y = -|x + 4| + 3$ *(p. 123)*
15. $y < -2x + 5$ *(p. 132)*
16. $y = x^2 - 2x - 4$ *(p. 236)*
17. $y = 2(x - 6)^2 - 5$ *(p. 245)*
18. $y > x^2 + 2x + 1$ *(p. 300)*
19. $y = x^3 - 2$ *(p. 337)*
20. $y = 3(x + 2)(x - 1)^2$ *(p. 387)*
21. $y = -\sqrt{x - 2} + 4$ *(p. 446)*

Solve the system of linear equations using any method.

22. $2x + 5y = 1$ *(p. 160)*
$3x - 2y = 30$
$(8, -3)$
23. $3x - y = -9$ *(p. 160)*
$4x + 3y = 14$
$(-1, 6)$
24. $2x + 3y = 47$ *(p. 178)*
$7x - 8y = -2$
$2x - y + 3z = -19$
$(10, 9, -10)$

Write the expression as a complex number in standard form. *(p. 275)*

25. $(4 - 2i) + (5 + i)$ $9 - i$
26. $(3 + 4i) - (7 + 2i)$ $-4 + 2i$
27. $(4 - 2i)(6 + 5i)$ $34 + 8i$

Write the quadratic function in vertex form by completing the square. *(p. 284)*

28. $y = x^2 + 6x + 16$ $y = (x + 3)^2 + 7$
29. $y = -x^2 + 12x - 46$ $y = -(x - 6)^2 - 10$
30. $y = 2x^2 - 4x + 7$ $y = 2(x - 1)^2 + 5$

Simplify the expression. Assume all variables are positive.

31. $(2x^3y^2)^3$ *(p. 330)* $8x^9y^6$
32. $(x^8)^{-3/4}$ *(p. 420)* $\frac{1}{x^6}$
33. $\frac{x^3y^{-4}}{x^{-4}y^{-5}}$ *(p. 330)* x^7y
34. $\left(\frac{x^2y^{1/3}}{x^{1/4}y}\right)^2$ *(p. 420)* $\frac{x^{7/2}}{y^{4/3}}$

Perform the indicated operation.

35. $(x^2 + 11x - 9) + (4x^2 - 5x - 7)$ *(p. 346)* $5x^2 + 6x - 16$
36. $(x^3 + 3x - 10) - (2x^3 + 3x^2 + 8x)$ *(p. 346)* $-x^3 - 3x^2 - 5x - 10$
37. $(2x - 5)(x^2 + 4x - 7)$ *(p. 346)* $2x^3 + 3x^2 - 34x + 35$
38. $(x^3 - 10x^2 + 33x - 28) \div (x - 5)$ *(p. 362)* $x^2 - 5x + 8 + \frac{12}{x - 5}$

Factor the polynomial completely. *(p. 353)*

39. $x^4 - 3x^2 - 40$ $(x^2 - 8)(x^2 + 5)$
40. $x^3 - 125$ $(x - 5)(x^2 + 5x + 25)$
41. $x^3 - 6x^2 - 9x + 54$ $(x - 6)(x - 3)(x + 3)$

Let $f(x) = 2x - 6$ and $g(x) = 5x + 1$. Perform the indicated operation and state the domain. *(p. 428)*

42. $f(x) + g(x)$ $7x - 5$, all real numbers
43. $f(x) \cdot g(x)$
44. $f(g(x))$ $10x - 4$, all real numbers
45. $g(f(x))$ $10x - 29$, all real numbers

Find the inverse of the function. *(p. 438)*

46. $f(x) = 4x + 6$ $f^{-1}(x) = \frac{x - 6}{4}$
47. $f(x) = \frac{3}{7}x + 7$ $f^{-1}(x) = \frac{7x - 49}{3}$
48. $f(x) = \frac{1}{3}x - \frac{2}{3}$ $f^{-1}(x) = 3x + 2$
49. $f(x) = \frac{x^3 - 5}{6}$ $f^{-1}(x) = \sqrt[3]{6x + 5}$
50. $f(x) = \sqrt[3]{\frac{2x + 7}{3}}$
51. $f(x) = -\frac{8}{9}x^5 + 2$

17. 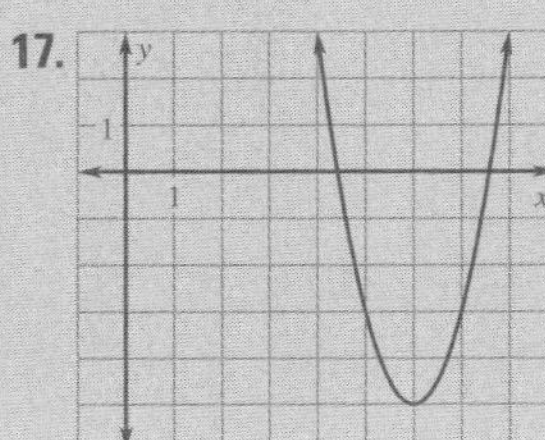

18. 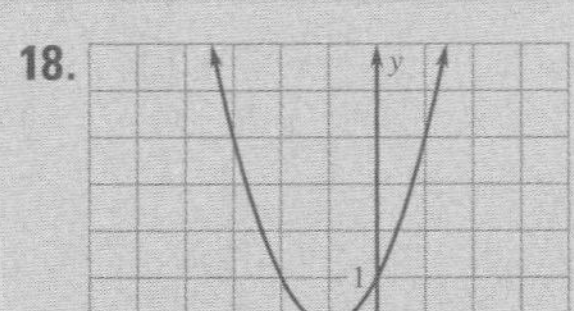

19. 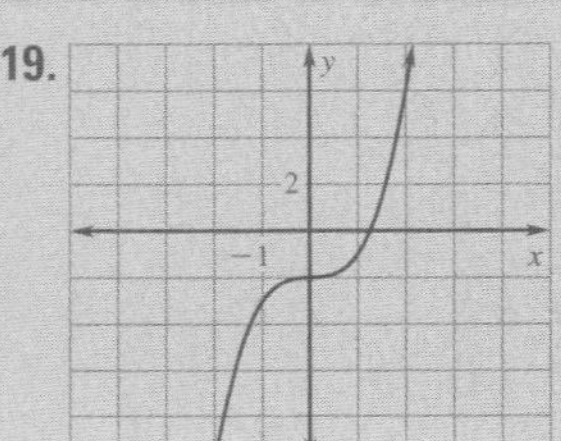

52. **BICYCLE COSTS** You want to buy a bicycle that costs $360. In order to pay for the bicycle, you save $30 per week. How many weeks will it take to save enough money to buy the bicycle? *(p. 34)* 12 wk

53. **CHARITABLE DONATIONS** The table below shows the amounts of money (in millions of dollars) received by a charitable organization during the first 6 years of its existence. Approximate the best-fitting line for the data. Then use the best-fitting line to predict the amount of money the organization will receive in the eighth year of its existence. *(p. 113)* $y = 0.499x + 1.25$; about $5,240,000

Year	1	2	3	4	5	6
Donations (millions of dollars)	1.71	2.3	2.78	3.22	3.69	4.28

54. **ICE SHOW** The attendance at an ice show was 9800 people. The tickets for the ice show were $35 for lower-level seats and $25 for upper-level seats. The total income from ticket sales was $280,000. Use a linear system to find the numbers of lower-level and upper-level tickets sold for the ice show. *(p. 160)* 3500 lower-level, 6300 upper-level

55. **CONCERT TICKETS** Tickets to a school's band concert are $4 for students, $8 for adults, and $6 for senior citizens. At Friday night's concert, there were 140 students, 170 adults, and 55 senior citizens in attendance. At Saturday night's concert, there were 126 students, 188 adults, and 64 senior citizens in attendance. Organize this information using matrices. Then use matrix multiplication to find the income from ticket sales for Friday and Saturday nights' concerts. *(p. 195)* $4642

56. **PHYSICAL SCIENCE** While standing at the edge of a cliff, you drop a rock from a height of 85 feet above the ground. Write an equation giving the height h (in feet) of the rock above the ground after t seconds. How long does it take for the rock to hit the ground? *(p. 266)* $h = -16t^2 + 85$; about 2.3 sec

57. **BASEBALL** Three points on the parabola formed by throwing a baseball are (0, 6), (20, 56), and (36, 24). Write a quadratic function that models the baseball's path. *(p. 309)* $y = -\frac{1}{8}x^2 + 5x + 6$

58. **MANUFACTURING** At a factory, molten plastic is poured into molds to make toy blocks. Each mold is a rectangular prism with a height that is 3 inches greater than the length of each side of the square base. A machine pours 200 cubic inches of liquid plastic into each mold. What are the dimensions of a mold? *(p. 370)* 5 in. by 5 in. by 8 in.

59. **PROFIT** Your friend starts a housekeeping business. The table below shows the profit (in dollars) of the business during the first 6 months of its existence. Use a graphing calculator to find a polynomial model for the data. Predict the profit in the ninth month. *(p. 393)* $y = x^3 - 5x + 6$; $690

Month	1	2	3	4	5	6
Profit (dollars)	2	4	18	50	106	192

60. **GEOMETRY** You have a beach ball that has a volume of approximately 7240 cubic inches. Find the radius of the beach ball. (*Hint:* Use the formula $V = \frac{4}{3}\pi r^3$ for the volume of a sphere.) *(p. 414)* about 12 in.

20.

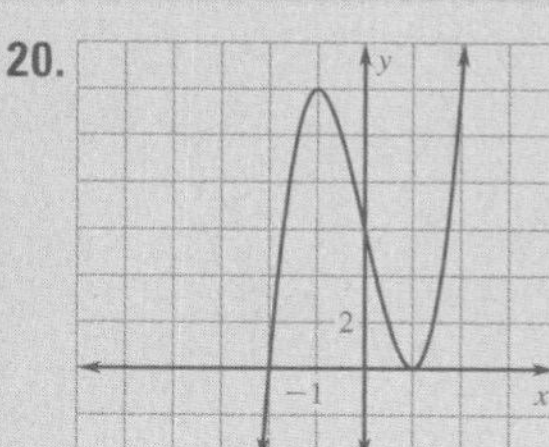

21.

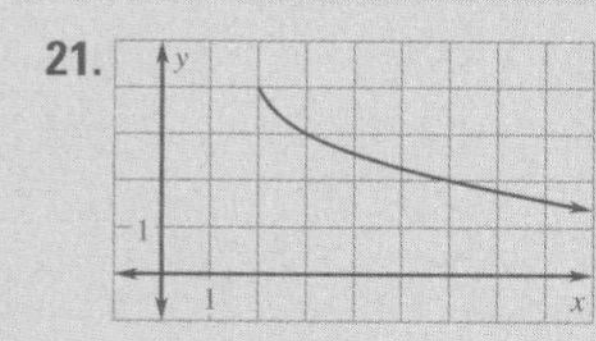

7 Pacing and Assignment Guide

REGULAR SCHEDULE

Pre-AP For pacing and assignments for a Pre-AP course, see the *Algebra 2 Toolkit*.

Lesson	Les. Day	BASIC	AVERAGE	ADVANCED
7.1 MA-HS-5.1.4	Day 1	pp. 482–485 Exs. 1–10, 15–19, 24–30, 35–39, 45	pp. 482–485 Exs. 1–5, 9–12, 17–20, 24–33, 35–42, 46	pp. 482–485 Exs. 1, 2, 12–14, 21–44*
7.2 MA-HS-5.1.4	Day 1	pp. 489–491 Exs. 1–10, 15–19, 30–34, 37	pp. 489–491 Exs. 1–6, 9–12, 15, 19–27, 30–35, 38	pp. 489–491 Exs. 1, 2, 10–15, 20–36*
7.3 MA-HS-5.1.4	Day 1	EP p. 1015 Exs. 12–15; pp. 495–498 Exs. 1–8, 15–22, 31–35 odd, 39–44, 55–59, 63	pp. 495–498 Exs. 1, 2, 7–11, 15–18, 23–26, 34–36, 39–45, 51–53, 55–61, 64	pp. 495–498 Exs. 1, 2, 11–16, 27–30, 36–38, 44–62*
7.4	Day 1	EP p. 1015 Exs. 34–36; pp. 503–505 Exs. 1–15, 20–23, 58, 59	pp. 503–505 Exs. 1–7, 10–17, 22–25, 58, 59	pp. 503–505 Exs. 1–6, 14–19, 24–27, 54–59*
	Day 2	pp. 503–505 Exs. 28–40, 45–47, 60, 61, 64–65	pp. 503–505 Exs. 32–42, 48–52, 60–62, 64–65	pp. 503–505 Exs. 33–36, 41–44, 48–53, 60–65*
7.5	Day 1	pp. 510–513 Exs. 1–11, 15–20, 31–36, 43–48, 69–72, 75	pp. 510–513 Exs. 1, 2, 10–12, 21–26, 31, 32, 37–40, 43, 44, 49–54, 61–64, 69–73, 76	pp. 510–513 Exs. 1, 2, 12–14, 26–30, 39–44, 53–68*, 71–74*
7.6 MA-HS-5.1.4	Day 1	EP p. 1010 Exs. 16–21; pp. 519–522 Exs. 1–8, 12–20, 54–58	pp. 519–522 Exs. 1, 2, 5–10, 14–21, 54–58	pp. 519–522 Exs. 1, 2, 6–11, 15–23, 54–58
	Day 2	pp. 519–522 Exs. 24–39, 59, 62–63	pp. 519–522 Exs. 27–31, 36–47, 59, 60, 62–63	pp. 519–522 Exs. 28–31, 38–53*, 59–61*
7.7 MA-HS-5.1.4	Day 1	pp. 533–536 Exs. 1–12	pp. 533–536 Exs. 1, 2, 4–13	pp. 533–536 Exs. 1, 2, 5–14
	Day 2	pp. 533–536 Exs. 15–24, 31–34, 37–38	pp. 533–536 Exs. 17–20, 24–29, 31–35, 37–38	pp. 533–536 Exs. 19–22, 24–38*
Review	Day 1	pp. 539–542 Exs. 1–38	pp. 539–542 Exs. 1–38	pp. 539–542 Exs. 1–38
Assess	Day 1	Chapter 7 Test	Chapter 7 Test	Chapter 7 Test
Yearly Pacing		Chapter 7 Total – 12 days	Chapters 1–7 Total – 92 days	Remaining – 68 days

*Challenge Exercises EP = Extra Practice SRH = Skills Review Handbook

BLOCK SCHEDULE

DAY 1	DAY 2	DAY 3	DAY 4	DAY 5	DAY 6
7.1	**7.3**	**7.4 (CONT.)**	**7.6**	**7.7**	**Review**
pp. 482–485 Exs. 1–5, 9–12, 17–20, 24–33, 35–42, 46	pp. 495–498 Exs. 1, 2, 7–11, 15–18, 23–26, 34–36, 39–45, 51–53, 55–61, 64	pp. 503–505 Exs. 32–42, 48–52, 60–62, 64–65	pp. 519–522 Exs. 1, 2, 5–10, 14–21, 27–31, 36–47, 54–60, 62–63	pp. 533–536 Exs. 1, 2, 4–13, 17–20, 24–29, 31–35, 37–55	pp. 539–542 Exs. 1–38
7.2	**7.4**	**7.5**			**ASSESS**
pp. 489–491 Exs. 1–6, 9–12, 15, 19–27, 30–35, 38	pp. 503–505 Exs. 1–7, 10–17, 22–25, 58, 59	pp. 510–513 Exs. 1, 2, 10–12, 21–26, 31, 32, 37–40, 43, 44, 49–54, 61–64, 69–73, 76			Chapter 7 Test
Yearly Pacing	Chapter 7 Total – 6 days		Chapters 1–7 Total – 46 days		Remaining – 34 days

RESOURCE MANAGER

Chapter Resource Book

CHAPTER SUPPORT							
Parents as Partners (Chapter Overview with home involvement exercises and activity)						p. 1	
LESSON SUPPORT	**7.1**	**7.2**	**7.3**	**7.4**	**7.5**	**7.6**	**7.7**
Standards	MA-HS-5.1.4	MA-HS-5.1.4	MA-HS-5.1.4			MA-HS-5.1.4	MA-HS-5.1.4
Teaching Guide/Lesson Plan	p. 3	p. 14	p. 27	p. 38	p. 51	p. 62	p. 73
Activity Masters				p. 40			
Technology Activities & Keystrokes	p. 5	p. 16	p. 29	p. 41	p. 53	p. 64	p. 75
Activity Support Masters							
Practice (3 levels)	p. 6	p. 19	p. 30	p. 42	p. 54	p. 65	p. 76
Study Guide	p. 9	p. 22	p. 33	p. 45	p. 57	p. 68	p. 79
Catch-Up for Absent Students	p. 11	p. 24	p. 35	p. 47	p. 59	p. 70	p. 81
Problem Solving/Application	p. 12	p. 25	p. 36	p. 48	p. 60	p. 71	p. 82
Challenge Practice	p. 13	p. 26	p. 37	p. 50	p. 61	p. 72	p. 83
REVIEW							
Chapter Review Games and Activities		p. 84		Cumulative Practice		pp. 87–88	
Project with Rubric		p. 85		Resource Book Answers		A1	

Transparencies	7.1	7.2	7.3	7.4	7.5	7.6	7.7
Warm-Up/Daily Homework Quiz	✔	✔	✔	✔	✔	✔	✔
Notetaking Guide	✔	✔	✔	✔	✔	✔	✔
Teacher Support	✔	✔	✔	✔		✔	
Answer Transparencies	✔	✔	✔	✔	✔	✔	✔

ASSESSMENT BOOK

Quizzes	p. 95	SAT/ACT Chapter Test	p. 106
Chapter Tests (3 levels)	p. 98	Alternative Assessment with Rubric	p. 108
Standardized Chapter Test	p. 104		

TECHNOLOGY

- Easy Planner
- Test and Practice Generator
- Power Presentations
- @HomeTutor
- Activity Generator
- Animated Algebra
- Classzone.com
- eEdition Plus Online
- eWorkbook Plus Online
- ML Assessment System

ADDITIONAL RESOURCES

Kentucky

- Worked-Out Solution Key
- Notetaking Guide
- Practice Workbook
- Algebra 2 Toolkit
- Benchmark Tests
- Remediation Workbook
- Spanish Study Guide
- Spanish Assessment Book
- Spanish Resources in Spanish
- Multi-Language Visual Glossary

Lesson Practice Level B

LESSON 7.1 Practice B

For use with pages 478–485

Match the function with its graph.

1. $f(x) = \left(\frac{4}{3}\right)^x - 3$ C

2. $f(x) = 3^x + 2$ A

3. $f(x) = -4^{x+1} + 1$ B

A. 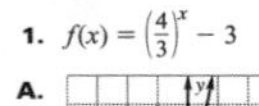

B. 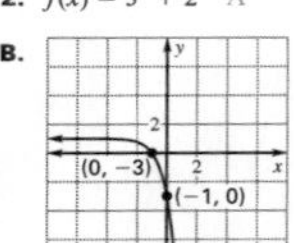

C. 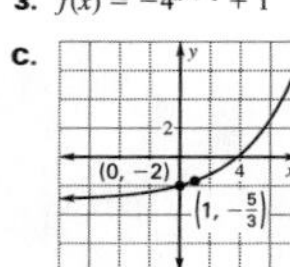

Graph the function. State the domain and range.

4. $f(x) = 4^{x-2}$

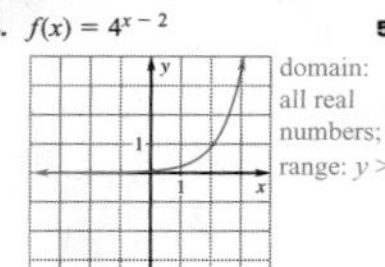

domain: all real numbers; range: $y > 0$

5. $f(x) = 2^x + 1$

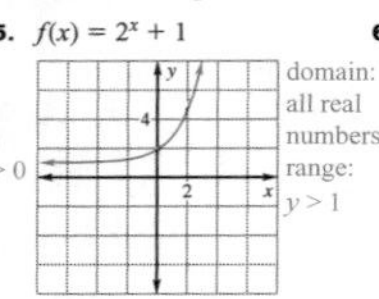

domain: all real numbers; range: $y > 1$

6. $f(x) = -3^{x+1}$

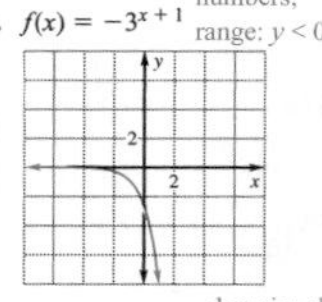

domain: all real numbers; range: $y < 0$

7. $f(x) = 2^{x-2} - 3$

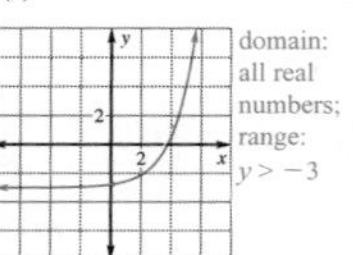

domain: all real numbers; range: $y > -3$

8. $f(x) = -2(3^{x+1}) + 2$

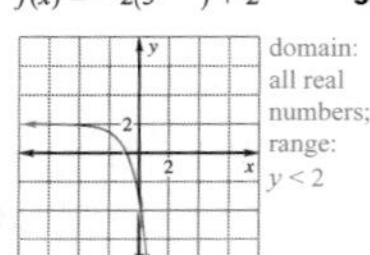

domain: all real numbers; range: $y < 2$

9. $f(x) = \left(\frac{3}{2}\right)^x - 2$

domain: all real numbers; range: $y > -2$

In Exercises 10–12, use the following information.

Account Balance You deposit $3500 in an account that earns 2.5% annual interest. Find the balance after one year if the interest is compounded with the given frequency.

10. annually $3587.50 **11.** quarterly $3588.32 **12.** monthly $3588.51

In Exercises 13–15, use the following information.

Population From 1990 to 2000, the population of California can be modeled by $P = 29{,}816{,}591(1.0128)^t$ where t is the number of years since 1990.

13. What was the population in 1990? 29,816,591

14. What is the growth factor and annual percent increase? 1.0128; 1.28%

15. Estimate the population in 2007. 37,013,552

LESSON 7.2 Practice B

For use with pages 486–491

Tell whether the function represents *exponential growth* or *exponential decay*.

1. $f(x) = \frac{5}{3}\left(\frac{4}{5}\right)^x$ exponential decay

2. $f(x) = \frac{3}{5}\left(\frac{5}{4}\right)^x$ exponential growth

3. $f(x) = 5(2)^{-x}$ exponential decay

Match the function with its graph.

4. $f(x) = \left(\frac{2}{3}\right)^{x+2}$ B

5. $f(x) = -\left(\frac{1}{2}\right)^x + 3$ C

6. $f(x) = 2\left(\frac{2}{3}\right)^{x-1} - 2$ A

A. 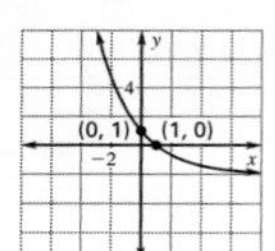

B. 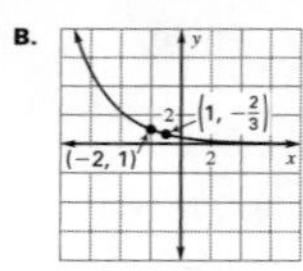

C. 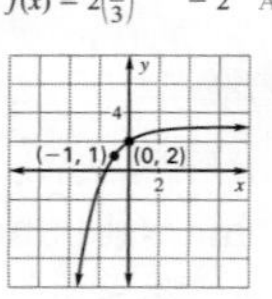

Graph the function. State the domain and range.

7. $f(x) = \left(\frac{1}{3}\right)^{x+1} + 2$

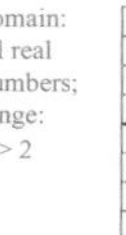
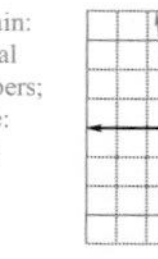

domain: all real numbers; range: $y > 2$

8. $f(x) = \left(\frac{1}{2}\right)^x - 3$

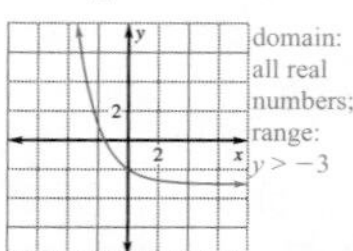

domain: all real numbers; range: $y > -3$

9. $f(x) = 3\left(\frac{1}{4}\right)^{x-2} + 1$

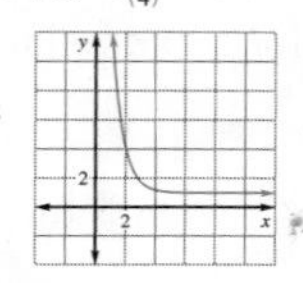

domain: all real numbers; range: $y > 1$

10. $f(x) = -\left(\frac{2}{3}\right)^x + 3$

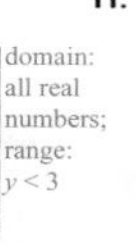

domain: all real numbers; range: $y < 3$

11. $f(x) = 4\left(\frac{3}{4}\right)^{x+1} - 5$

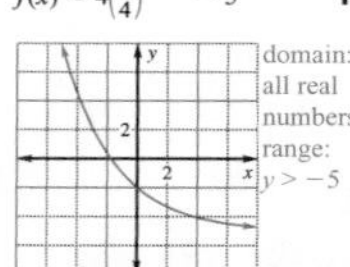

domain: all real numbers; range: $y > -5$

12. $f(x) = -2\left(\frac{1}{6}\right)^{x-4} + 6$

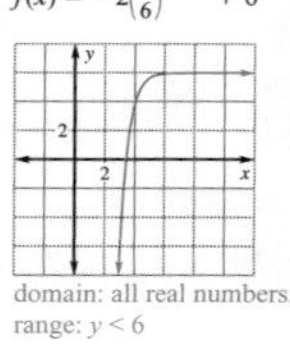

domain: all real numbers; range: $y < 6$

In Exercises 13–15, use the following information.

Depreciation You buy a new car for $22,500. The value of the car decreases by 25% each year.

13. Write an exponential decay model giving the car's value V (in dollars) after t years. $V = 22{,}500(0.75)^t$

14. What is the value of the car after three years? $9492.19

15. In approximately how many years is the car worth $5300? 5

LESSON 7.3 Practice B

For use with pages 492–498

Simplify the expression.

1. $e^{-5} \cdot e^2$ $\frac{1}{e^3}$

2. $e^3 \cdot e^{-3}$ 1

3. $(e^4)^{-3}$ $\frac{1}{e^{12}}$

4. $(2e^3)^2$ $4e^6$

5. $\left(\frac{3e^3}{6e^2}\right)^2$ $\frac{e^2}{4}$

6. $\left(\frac{8e^2}{2e^5}\right)^{-1}$ $\frac{e^3}{4}$

7. $3e^x \cdot 2e^{4x}$ $6e^{5x}$

8. $\sqrt{9e^4} \cdot 2e^{-3}$ $\frac{6}{e}$

9. $\frac{e^3}{e^{x+3}}$ $\frac{1}{e^x}$

Use a calculator to evaluate the expression. Round the result to three decimal places.

10. e^7 1096.633 **11.** $e^{-3/2}$ 0.223 **12.** $e^{0.6}$ 1.822 **13.** $e^{\sqrt{3}}$ 5.652

Tell whether the function is an example of *exponential growth* or *exponential decay*. **14.** exponential growth **15.** exponential decay **16.** exponential decay

14. $f(x) = 4e^{2x}$

15. $f(x) = e^{-5x}$

16. $f(x) = 6e^{-x}$

17. $f(x) = \frac{1}{4}e^{4x}$ exponential growth

18. $f(x) = \frac{1}{8}e^{-x}$ exponential decay

19. $f(x) = -e^{-x/2}$ exponential growth

Graph the function. State the domain and range.

20. $f(x) = 3e^x$

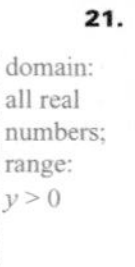

domain: all real numbers; range: $y > 0$

21. $f(x) = 3e^{-x}$

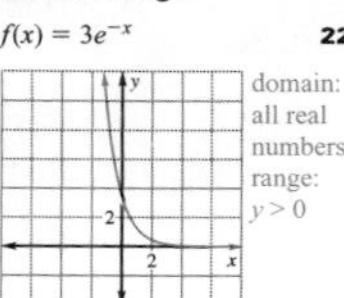

domain: all real numbers; range: $y > 0$

22. $f(x) = -e^x + 3$

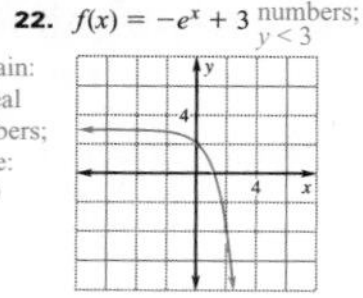

domain: all real numbers; range: $y < 3$

23. $f(x) = 2e^{x-1} + 1$

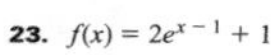
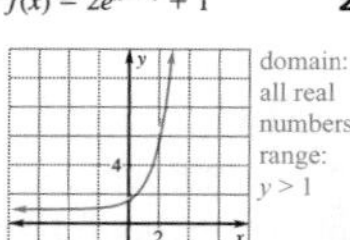

domain: all real numbers; range: $y > 1$

24. $f(x) = \frac{1}{2}e^{x-2} - 3$

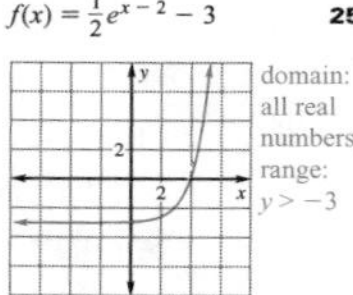

domain: all real numbers; range: $y > -3$

25. $f(x) = e^{2x+1} + 2$

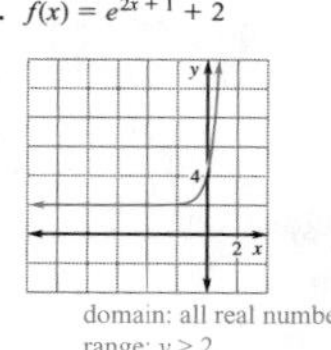

domain: all real numbers; range: $y > 2$

In Exercises 26 and 27, use the following information.

Finance You deposit $2200 in an account that pays 3% annual interest. After 15 years, you withdraw the money.

26. What is the balance if the interest is compounded quarterly? $3444.50

27. What is the balance if the interest is compounded continuously? $3450.29

LESSON 7.4 Practice B

For use with pages 499–505

Rewrite the equation in exponential form.

1. $\log_7 49 = 2$ $7^2 = 49$

2. $\log_2 16 = 4$ $2^4 = 16$

3. $\log_5 125 = 3$ $5^3 = 125$

4. $\log_{16} 4 = \frac{1}{2}$ $16^{1/2} = 4$

5. $\log_4 \frac{1}{4} = -1$ $4^{-1} = \frac{1}{4}$

6. $\log_3 \frac{1}{9} = -2$ $3^{-2} = \frac{1}{9}$

Evaluate the logarithm without using a calculator.

7. $\log_9 81$ 2

8. $\log_8 1$ 0

9. $\log_3 \frac{1}{3}$ −1

10. $\log_4 2$ $\frac{1}{2}$

11. $\log_{27} 3$ $\frac{1}{3}$

12. $\log_4 4^{2/3}$ $\frac{2}{3}$

Use a calculator to evaluate the logarithm. Round the result to three decimal places.

13. $\ln \sqrt{5}$ 0.805

14. $\log 110$ 2.041

15. $\ln \frac{1}{2}$ −0.693

Find the inverse of the function.

16. $y = \log_5 x$ $f^{-1}(x) = 5^x$

17. $y = \ln x$ $f^{-1}(x) = e^x$

18. $y = \log_{1/5} x$ $f^{-1}(x) = \left(\frac{1}{5}\right)^x$

19. $y = \log \frac{x}{2}$ $f^{-1}(x) = 2(10^x)$

20. $y = \log_6(x + 2)$ $f^{-1}(x) = 6^x - 2$

21. $y = \log_3 9x$ $f^{-1}(x) = 3^{x-2}$

Graph the function. State the domain and range.

22. $f(x) = \log_3 x$

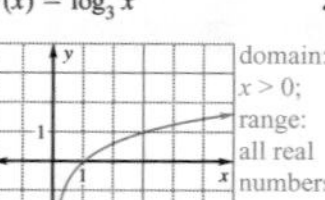

domain: $x > 0$; range: all real numbers

23. $f(x) = \log_3(x + 2)$

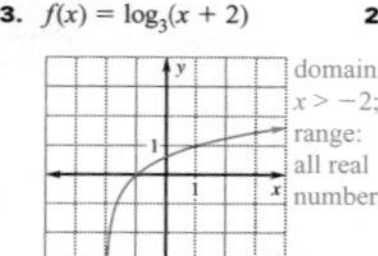

domain: $x > -2$; range: all real numbers

24. $f(x) = -\log_3 x - 1$

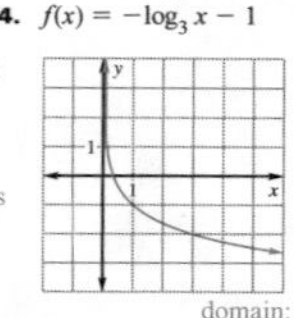

domain: $x > 0$; range: all real numbers

25. Galloping Speed Four-legged animals run with two different types of motion: trotting and galloping. An animal that is trotting has at least one foot on the ground at all times. An animal that is galloping has all four feet off the ground at times. The number S of strides per minute at which an animal breaks from a trot to a gallop is related to the animal's weight w (in pounds) by the model $S = 256.2 - 47.9 \log w$. Approximate the number of strides per minute for a 450 pound horse when it breaks from a trot to a gallop. 129

26. Tornadoes The wind speed S (in miles per hour) near the center of a tornado is related to the distance d (in miles) the tornado travels by the model $S = 93 \log d + 65$. Approximate the wind speed of a tornado that traveled 75 miles. 239.4 mi/h

LESSON 7.5 Practice B
For use with pages 507–513

Match the expression with the logarithm that has the same value.

1. $\log \sqrt{2} + \log \sqrt{8}$ C
2. $\log 4 - \log 10$ A
3. $2 \log 4 - \log 2$ D
4. $-3 \log \frac{1}{3}$ B

A. $\log \frac{2}{5}$
B. $\log 27$
C. $\log 4$
D. $\log 8$

Use $\log 4 \approx 0.602$ and $\log 7 \approx 0.845$ to evaluate the logarithm.

5. $\log 28$ 1.447
6. $\log \frac{7}{4}$ 0.243
7. $\log 16$ 1.204
8. $\log 49$ 1.690
9. $\log \frac{1}{4}$ −0.602
10. $\log \frac{49}{64}$ −0.116

Expand the expression.

11. $\log_3 3x$ $\log_3 3 + \log_3 x$
12. $\log \frac{2x}{5}$ $\log 2 + \log x - \log 5$
13. $\log_7 x^2y$ $2 \log_7 x + \log_7 y$
14. $\log_2 \frac{x^2}{4}$ $2 \log_2 x - \log_2 4$
15. $\ln \sqrt{xy}$ $\frac{1}{2} \ln x + \frac{1}{2} \ln y$
16. $\log 5\sqrt[3]{x}$ $\log 5 + \frac{1}{3} \log x$
17. $\ln \frac{1}{2x^2}$ $-\ln 2 - 2 \ln x$
18. $\log_9 \frac{2x^3}{3}$ $\log_9 2 + 3 \log_9 x - \frac{1}{2}$
19. $\log_6 \frac{xy^2}{\sqrt{z}}$ $\log_6 x + 2 \log_6 y - \frac{1}{2} \log_6 z$

Condense the expression.

20. $\log_3 4 + \log_3 2 + \log_3 2$ $\log_3 16$
21. $\log 4 + 3 \log x + \log y$ $\log 4x^3y$
22. $\log 3 + \frac{1}{2} \log x - \log 5$ $\log \frac{3\sqrt{x}}{5}$
23. $2 \ln x - \ln 3 + \ln 6$ $\ln 2x^2$
24. $3 \log x + \log 4 - \log x - \log 6$ $\log \frac{2x^2}{3}$
25. $3 \ln(x + 1) - 2 \ln y + \ln y + \ln 2$ $\ln \frac{2(x+1)^3}{y}$

Use the change-of-base formula to evaluate the logarithm. Round your result to three decimal places.

26. $\log_7 12$ 1.277
27. $\log_4 112$ 3.404
28. $\log_5 1.25$ 0.139
29. $\log_{2.2} 22$ 3.920
30. $\log_{4.2} 18.1$ 2.018
31. $\log_{1/3} 0.0005$ 6.919

In Exercises 32–34, use the following information.

Henderson-Hasselbach Formula The pH of a patient's blood can be calculated using the Henderson-Hasselbach Formula, $\text{pH} = 6.1 + \log \frac{B}{C}$, where B is the concentration of bicarbonate and C is the concentration of carbonic acid. The normal pH of blood is approximately 7.4.

32. Expand the right side of the formula. $\text{pH} = 6.1 + \log B - \log C$
33. Find the pH of blood that has bicarbonate concentration of 38 and carbonic acid concentration of 2.0? 7.38
34. Is the pH in Exercise 33 above normal or below normal? just below normal

LESSON 7.6 Practice B
For use with pages 515–522

Solve the exponential equation. Check for extraneous solutions. Round the result to three decimal places if necessary.

1. $e^x = 1$ 0
2. $e^x = 4$ 1.386
3. $e^x + 1 = 7$ 1.792
4. $5^x = 12$ 1.544
5. $4^x - 6 = 4$ 1.661
6. $3^{4x} = 27$ 0.750
7. $e^{2x} = 4$ 0.693
8. $3e^{3x} = 12$ 0.462
9. $10^{2x-3} + 3 = 19$ 2.102
10. $3e^x + 7 = 9$ −0.405
11. $10^{x+2} - 12 = 22$ −0.469
12. $10^{-x+4} + 7 = 5$ no solution
13. $3^{-3x+1} = 3^{x-9}$ $\frac{5}{2}$
14. $8^{2x} = 8^{x+7}$ 7
15. $7^{2x-3} - 4 = 14$ 2.243
16. $4e^{3x} = 1$ −0.462
17. $e^{5x+2} = e^{3x+12}$ 5
18. $3e^{3-x} = 15$ 1.391
19. $9^{2x} = 3^{2x+4}$ 2
20. $25^{x-4} = 5^{3x+1}$ −9
21. $8^{x-1} = \left(\frac{1}{2}\right)^{2x-1}$ $\frac{4}{5}$
22. $3(2^{x+6}) = 17$ −3.497
23. $5^{0.5x} + 12 = 21$ 2.730
24. $-5e^x - 3 = 24$ no solution
25. $\frac{3}{4}e^{3x} - 8 = -6$ 0.327
26. $\frac{2}{3}(4^{3x}) - 5 = -2$ 0.362
27. $10^{2x+1} + 2 = 2$ no solution

Solve the logarithmic equation. Check for extraneous solutions. Round the result to three decimal places if necessary. 32. no solution 37. −58,824 41. 29.333

28. $\log x = 3$ 1000
29. $\ln x = 4$ 54.598
30. $\log_3 x = 5$ 243
31. $\log_7(2 - x) = \log_7 5x$ $\frac{1}{3}$
32. $\ln(3x - 3) = \ln(x - 6)$
33. $\ln(5 - 2x) = \ln(5x + 3)$ $\frac{2}{7}$
34. $\log_4 3x = 6$ 1365.333
35. $\log_2(3x - 1) = 8$ 85.667
36. $7 - \log_3 8x = 2$ 30.375
37. $2 \log_7(1 - 2x) = 12$
38. $3 \ln x - 7 = 4$ 39.121
39. $\ln(1 - 3x) + 3 = 9$ −134.143
40. $\log 7x + 4 = 5$ $\frac{10}{7}$
41. $4 + \log_9(3x - 7) = 6$
42. $\log_2 2x + \log_2 x = 5$ 4
43. $\log_6(2x - 6) + \log_6 x = 2$ 6
44. $\ln 3x - \ln 2 = 4$ 36.399
45. $\ln(-5x + 3) = \ln 2x + 2$ 0.152

46. **Multiple Choice** You deposit \$500 in an account that pays 3.25% annual interest compounded monthly. About how long does it take for the balance to quadruple? B

    A. 36.3 years B. 42.7 years C. 45.1 years

In Exercises 47–49, use the following information.

Compounding Interest You deposit \$700 in an account that pays 2.75% annual interest. How long does it take the balance to reach the following amounts?

47. \$1000 when interested is compounded quarterly 13.0 yr
48. \$1500 when interested is compounded yearly 28.1 yr
49. \$2000 when interested is compounded continuously 38.2 yr

50. **Rocket Velocity** Disregarding the force of gravity, the maximum velocity v of a rocket is given by $v = t \ln M$, where t is the velocity of the exhaust and M is the ratio of the mass of the rocket with fuel to its mass without fuel. A solid propellant rocket has an exhaust velocity of 2.3 kilometers per second. Its maximum velocity is 7.2 kilometers per second. Find its mass ratio M. 22.88

LESSON 7.7 Practice B
For use with pages 529–536

Write an exponential function $y = ab^x$ whose graph passes through the given points.

1. $\left(0, \frac{1}{2}\right), \left(2, \frac{9}{2}\right)$ $y = \frac{1}{2}(3)^x$
2. $\left(1, \frac{2}{5}\right), \left(3, \frac{8}{5}\right)$ $y = \frac{1}{5}(2)^x$
3. $(1, 12), \left(-1, \frac{3}{4}\right)$ $y = 3(4)^x$
4. $(2, 2), (3, 1)$ $y = 8\left(\frac{1}{2}\right)^x$
5. $(0, 5), \left(2, \frac{20}{9}\right)$ $y = 5\left(\frac{2}{3}\right)^x$
6. $\left(0, \frac{3}{4}\right), \left(1, \frac{1}{4}\right)$ $y = \left(\frac{3}{4}\right)\left(\frac{1}{3}\right)^x$

Find an exponential model by solving for y.

7. $\ln y = 1.924x + 3.634$ $y = 37.86(6.85)^x$
8. $\ln y = 0.283x - 6.275$ $y = 0.0019(1.33)^x$
9. $\ln y = -3.5x + 4.129$ $y = 62.12(0.03)^x$

Use the points (x, y) to draw a scatter plot of the points $(x, \ln y)$. Then find an exponential model for the data.

10.

x	1	2	3	4	5	6
y	3.36	9.41	26.34	73.76	206.52	578.27

$y = 1.2(2.8)^x$

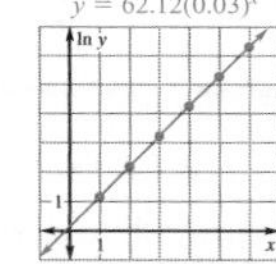

Write a power function $y = ax^b$ whose graph passes through the given points.

11. $(1, 3), (2, 24)$ $y = 3x^3$
12. $(1, 0.5), (4, 8)$ $y = \frac{1}{2}x^2$
13. $(1, 2), (4, 16)$ $y = 2x^{1.5}$
14. $(1, -4), (4, -64)$ $y = -4x^2$
15. $(4, 0.5), (9, 0.75)$ $y = \frac{1}{4}x^{0.5}$
16. $(3, -7.794), (7, -64.82)$ $y = -\frac{1}{2}x^{2.5}$

Find a power model by solving for y.

17. $\ln y = 3.3 \ln x + 2.56$ $y = 12.94x^{3.3}$
18. $\ln y = 1.05 \ln x - 4.28$ $y = 0.014x^{1.05}$
19. $\ln y = 2 \ln 2x + 3.15$ $y = 93.34x^2$

Use the points (x, y) to draw a scatter plot of the points $(\ln x, \ln y)$. Then find a power model for the data.

20.

x	1	2	3	4	5	6
y	2.1	7.313	15.172	25.464	38.051	52.831

$y = 2.1x^{1.8}$

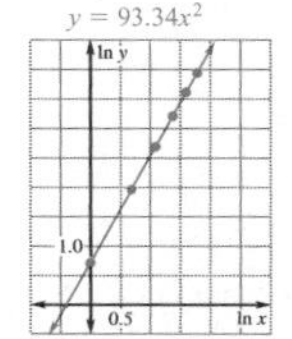

21. **Minimum Wage** The table shows the minimum hourly wage in the United States since 1960. Let $x = 1$ represent the year 1960, $x = 2$ represent the year 1965 and so on. Let y represent the minimum hourly wage. Use a graphing calculator to find a power model for the data. Use the model to estimate the minimum hourly wage in 2020.

Year	1960	1965	1970	1975	1980	1985	1990	1995	2000	2005
Wage	\$1.00	\$1.25	\$1.60	\$2.10	\$3.10	\$3.35	\$3.80	\$4.25	\$5.15	\$5.15

$y = 0.81x^{0.79}$; \$6.14

7 Assessment

CHAPTER 7 Quiz 1
For use after Lessons 7.1–7.3

Graph the function. State the domain and range.

1. $y = 3 \cdot 2^{x-3}$

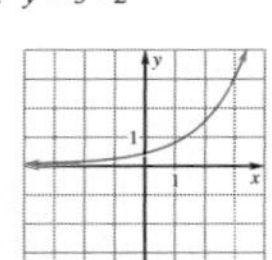

2. $y = \left(\frac{3}{4}\right)^x$

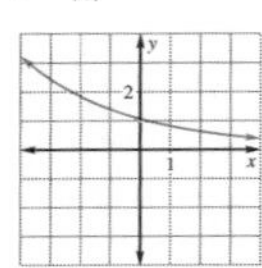

3. $y = \left(\frac{4}{5}\right)^x + 3$

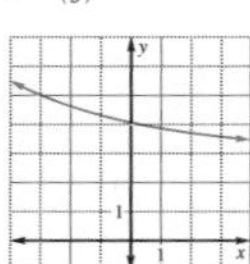

Simplify the expression.

4. $4e^3 \cdot e^5$ **5.** $(-4e^{2x})^3$

6. $\frac{e^{5x}}{4e^2}$ **7.** $\frac{9e^{6x}}{3e^{4x}}$

Graph the function. State the domain and range.

8. $y = 3e^x$

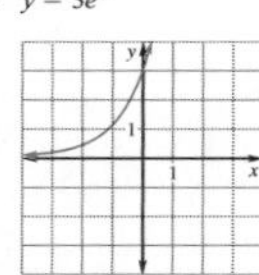

9. $y = 2e^{-4x}$

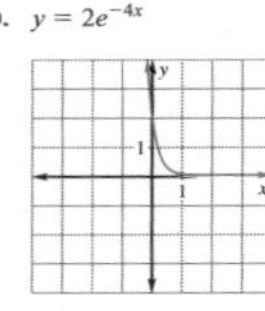

10. Compound Interest You deposit $3000 in an account that pays 5% annual interest compounded continuously. What is the balance after 2 years?

Answers

1. See left.; domain: all reals, range: $y > 0$
2. See left.; domain: all reals, range: $y > 0$
3. See left.; domain: all reals, range: $y > 3$
4. $4e^8$
5. $-64e^{6x}$
6. $\frac{1}{4}e^{5x-2}$
7. $3e^{2x}$
8. See left.; domain: all reals, range: $y > 0$
9. See left.; domain: all reals, range: $y > 0$
10. $3315.51

CHAPTER 7 Quiz 2
For use after Lessons 7.4–7.5

Evaluate the logarithm without using a calculator.

1. $\log_2 8$ **2.** $\log_6 1$

3. $\log_5 5$ **4.** $\log_{1/3} 27$

Graph the function. State the domain and range.

5. $y = \log_5 x$

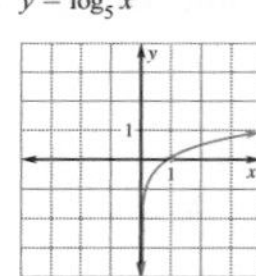

6. $y = \ln x + 3$

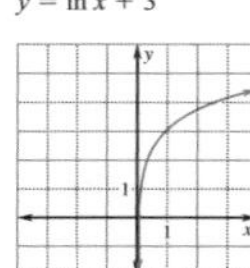

Expand the expression.

7. $\log_3 4x$ **8.** $\ln 4x^2y^5$

Condense the expression.

9. $\log_5 24 - \log_5 6$ **10.** $\log_8 6 + 2\log_8 3$

Use the change-of-base formula to evaluate the logarithm.

11. $\log_4 12$ **12.** $\log_9 18$

13. Sound Intensity The sound of a barking dog has an intensity of $I = 10^{-4}$ watts per square meter. Use the model $L(I) = 10\log\frac{I}{I_o}$ where $I_o = 10^{-12}$ watts per square meter, to find the barking dog's loudness $L(I)$.

Answers

1. 3
2. 0
3. 1
4. −3
5. See left.; domain: $x > 0$, range: all reals
6. See left.; domain: $x > 0$, range: all reals
7. $\log_3 4 + \log_3 x$
8. $\ln 4 + 2\ln x + 5\ln y$
9. $\log_5 4$
10. $\log_8 54$
11. 1.792
12. 1.315
13. 80

CHAPTER 7 Quiz 3
For use after Lessons 7.6–7.7

Solve the equation.

1. $3^{x+1} = 27^{x+3}$ **2.** $e^x = 5$

3. $2^{3x} + 9 = 25$ **4.** $4^{x+1} - 7 = 14$

5. $\log_6(5x + 8) = \log_6(13x)$ **6.** $\ln(4x - 2) = \ln(8x)$

7. $9\ln x = 54$ **8.** $\log_3(x + 7) = 3$

Write an exponential function $y = ab^x$ whose graph passes through the given points.

9. (1, 6), (2, 36) **10.** (2, 16), (3, 64)

Write a power function $y = ax^b$ whose graph passes through the given points.

11. (2, 2), (4, 16) **12.** (3, 3), (6, 12)

13. Shoes A store begins selling a new type of baseball shoe. The table shows the number y of pairs sold during week x. Find a power model for the following data.

Week, x	1	2
Pairs sold, y	10	80

Answers

1. −4
2. $\ln 5 \approx 1.609$
3. $\frac{4}{3}$
4. 1.196
5. 1
6. no solution
7. $e^6 \approx 403.429$
8. 20
9. $y = 6^x$
10. $y = 4^x$
11. $y = \frac{1}{4}x^3$
12. $y = \frac{1}{3}x^2$
13. $y = 10x^3$

CHAPTER 7 Chapter Test B
For use after Chapter 7

Graph the function. State the domain and range.

1. $y = \frac{1}{2} \cdot 2^x$

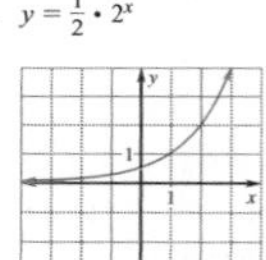

2. $y = -2 \cdot 3^{x+1} + 2$

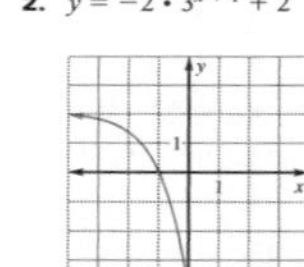

Graph the function. State the domain and range.

3. $y = 2\left(\frac{2}{3}\right)^x$

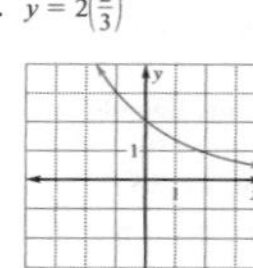

4. $y = \frac{1}{2}\left(\frac{3}{4}\right)^{x+1} - 2$

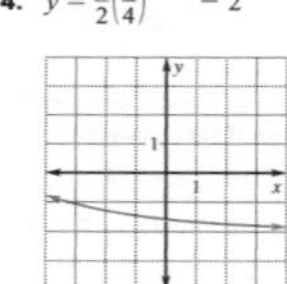

5. On your birthday you receive a PDA for $300. The value of the PDA decreases by 20% each year. What will its value be 4 years from now?

Graph the function. State the domain and range.

6. $y = 0.4e^{-2x}$

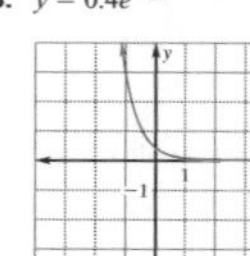

7. $y = -3e^{0.5x}$

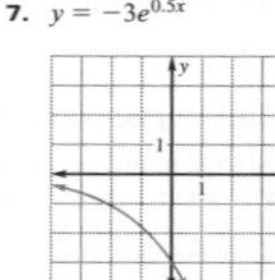

Find the inverse of the function.

8. $y = \log_4(x + 3)$ **9.** $y = 2e^{x-2}$

Answers

1. See left.; domain: all reals, range: $y > 0$
2. See left.; domain: all reals, range: $y < 2$
3. See left.; domain: all reals, range: $y > 0$
4. See left.; domain: all reals, range: $y > -2$
5. $122.88
6. See left.; domain: all reals, range: $y > 0$
7. See left.; domain: all reals, range: $y < 0$
8. $4^x - 3$
9. $\ln\frac{x}{2} + 2$

CHAPTER 7 Chapter Test B *continued*
For use after Chapter 7

Simplify the expression.

10. $(2e^{-2x}) \cdot e^{2x}$ **11.** $\sqrt[3]{16e^{12}}$

12. $\log_5 625^x$ **13.** $4^{\log_2 8x}$

Graph the function. State the domain and range.

14. $y = \log_7 x$ **15.** $y = \log_3 (x + 2) - 2$

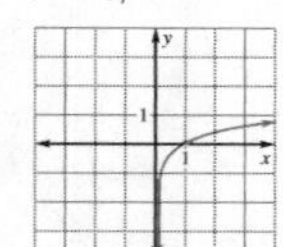

Expand the expression.

16. $\log_{1/2} \sqrt{xy}$ **17.** $\ln xy$

Condense the expression.

18. $\ln 4xy^2 - 2 \ln x^2y$ **19.** $\log_5 \sqrt[3]{x^2y} + \log_5 \sqrt[3]{xy^5}$

Solve the equation by equating exponents.

20. $4^{(2x+4)} = 16^{(3x-6)}$

21. $(0.25)^{x+8} = (0.5)^{x^2+1}$

Solve the equation.

22. $\log_2 (x^2 + 2x) = 3$

23. $\log_3 x + \log_3 (x - 6) = 3$

24. You deposit $300 into a savings account that pays 5% annual interest. If the account compounds daily, how long will it take for the account to reach $3000? If necessary, round your answer to two decimal places.

25. Write an exponential function whose graph passes through the points (2, 16) and (5, 128).

26. Write a power function whose graph passes through the points (2, 5) and (6, 9).

Answers

10. 2
11. $2 \cdot \sqrt[3]{2}e^4$
12. $4x$
13. $64x^2$
14. See left. domain: $x > 0$ range: $y < 1$
15. See left. domain: $x > -2$ range: $y < 0$
16. $\log_{1/2} \sqrt{x} + \log_{1/2} \sqrt{y}$
17. $\ln x + \ln y$
18. $\ln \frac{4}{x^3}$
19. $\log_5 (xy^2)$
20. 4
21. 5, −3
22. 2, −4
23. 9
24. 46.05 years
25. $y = 4 \cdot 2^x$
26. $y = 3.45 \cdot x^{0.54}$

CHAPTER 7 Standardized Test
For use after Chapter 7

Multiple Choice

1. Which function is shown in the graph? C

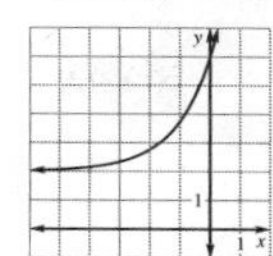

Ⓐ $f(x) = 2(2.3)^x - 2$
Ⓑ $f(x) = 4(2.3)^x$
Ⓒ $f(x) = 4(2.3)^x + 2$
Ⓓ $f(x) = 5(2.3)^x - 3$

2. Gasoline costs $1.99 per gallon. If the price per gallon increases an average of 6% per month, which function models the exponential growth of the pricing? B

Ⓐ $f(x) = 1.06(1.99)^x$
Ⓑ $f(x) = 1.99(1.06)^x$
Ⓒ $f(x) = [1.06(1.99)]^x$
Ⓓ $f(x) = \frac{1.99}{1.06^x}$

3. Which function represents exponential growth? D

Ⓐ $u(t) = -7.0\left(\frac{2}{3}\right)^t$
Ⓑ $u(t) = -7.0\left(\frac{3}{2}\right)^t$
Ⓒ $u(t) = 7.0(0.8)^t$
Ⓓ $u(t) = 7.0\left(\frac{9}{10}\right)^t$

4. What is the horizontal asymptote of the function $y = 2(0.3)^{x-1} - 4$? A

Ⓐ $y = -4$ Ⓑ $y = 0.3$
Ⓒ $y = 2$ Ⓓ $y = 4$

5. What is the simplified expression of $\frac{7(e^{3x})^2}{14e^x}$? A

Ⓐ $\frac{1}{2}e^{5x}$ Ⓑ $\frac{1}{2}e^{8x}$
Ⓒ $\frac{1}{2}e^{9x^2-x}$ Ⓓ $\frac{7}{2}e^{8x}$

6. Which function does *not* model exponential decay? D

Ⓐ $r(x) = \frac{3}{4}e^{-3x}$
Ⓑ $r(x) = \frac{4}{3}e^{-3x}$
Ⓒ $r(x) = 4e^{-3x}$
Ⓓ $r(x) = \frac{3}{4}e^{3x}$

7. What is the value of $-2e^{3.2}$, rounded to the nearest thousandth? B

Ⓐ −77.967 Ⓑ −49.065
Ⓒ −0.082 Ⓓ −0.081

8. Which expression is equivalent to x? C

Ⓐ $\log x$ Ⓑ $\log 2^x$
Ⓒ $\log 10^x$ Ⓓ $\log 100^x$

9. What is an equivalent expression for $2 \log_4 3 + \log_4 2$? D

Ⓐ $2 \log_4 6$ Ⓑ $\log_4 6$
Ⓒ $\log_4 12$ Ⓓ $\log_4 18$

10. Which of the following is *not* equivalent to $\log_5 8$? B

Ⓐ $\frac{\ln 8}{\ln 5}$ Ⓑ $2 \log_5 4$
Ⓒ $3 \log_5 2$ Ⓓ $\log_5 4 + \log_5 2$

CHAPTER 7 Standardized Test *continued*
For use after Chapter 7

11. What is the inverse of the function $y = 8^{2x}$? A

Ⓐ $y = \frac{\ln x}{2\ln 8}$ Ⓑ $y = \frac{2\ln x}{\ln 8}$
Ⓒ $y = \frac{\ln 8}{2\ln x}$ Ⓓ $y = \frac{2\ln 8}{\ln x}$

12. What is the solution to the equation $\log_4 4x + 2\log_4 x = 4$? D

Ⓐ 1 Ⓑ 2
Ⓒ 3 Ⓓ 4

13. A pheasant farmer started her farm with 120 pheasants. An analysis of her records shows that her pheasant population has increased by 15% each year. The farmer wants to determine a model of pheasant population growth using an exponential function. According to her model, what will the pheasant population be in 10 years? B

Ⓐ 311 Ⓑ 485
Ⓒ 501 Ⓓ 1380

Gridded Answer

14. What is the value of x in the equation $3^x = \left(\frac{1}{9}\right)^{(2x-10)}$? 4

Short Response

15. You invest an amount of money in a mutual fund. After four years, the balance of your account is $1,669.34 and after ten years, it is $2,576.29.

a. If you were to graph this trend, what would the coordinates of your points be? (4, 1669.34), (10, 2576.29)

b. Assuming the interest rate is constant from year to year and compounded annually, what is the initial amount you invested? The interest rate? Explain how you determined these values. principal: $1250, interest rate: 7.5%

Extended Response

16. In the spring, you decide to start cleaning your room on a weekly basis. The first cleaning takes you 135 minutes. You notice that for each cleaning after that, you decrease the time it takes from the week before by one-fifth. See below.

a. Complete the table below showing the time it takes each week to clean. Round to the nearest minute.

Week	1	2	3	4
Minutes	135	?	?	?
Week	5	6	7	8
Minutes	?	?	?	?

b. Determine the exponential function which models this trend. Explain how you determined the function.

c. In which week will it take you less than 15 minutes to clean your room?

d. How long will it take you in the 20th week to clean your room?

16. a. 108, 86, 69, 55, 44, 35, 28
b. $y = 135(0.8)^x$; answers will vary.
c. the ninth week **d.** 2 min

CHAPTER 7 Alternative Assessment and Math Journal
For use after Chapter 7

Journal

1. In the definition of a logarithm ($\log_b y = x$ if and only if $b^x = y$), b can be any positive number except 1. Explain why this constraint means y must be positive ($y > 0$). Give two examples to support your answer, one where x is negative and one where x is a fraction between 0 and 1.

Multi-Step Problem

2. In 1995, a home builder builds the exact same model of house in two different cities in two different states. The table shows the value of each house, v_1 and v_2, for t years after 1995.

Time, t	2	4	6	8	10
Value, v_1 (in thousands of dollars)	260	275	279	285	287
Value, v_2 (in thousands of dollars)	210	250	300	361	420

a. Use a graphing calculator to draw two scatter plots, one of $\ln v_1$ versus t and another of $\ln v_1$ versus $\ln t$, in the same viewing window.

b. Use a graphing calculator to draw two scatter plots, one of $\ln v_2$ versus t and another of $\ln v_2$ versus $\ln t$, in the same viewing window.

c. Based on your scatter plots from parts (a) and (b), does an exponential function or a power function better fit each set of original data?

d. Writing Describe how to verify your answer for part (c) using a graphing calculator.

e. Find a model for the value of each house.

f. Estimate the value of each house in 2002 to the nearest thousand.

g. Approximately how many years would it take the value of the first house, v_1, to reach $300,000? Determine the solution algebraically.

h. Critical Thinking Determine the year when the values of the two houses were equal. Describe how you can find the solution graphically and algebraically. Explain why using an algebraic method would be more difficult than in part (g).

i. Critical Thinking Describe the rate of change in the value of each house. What factors may have affected the values of the two houses?

1. Because $\log_b y = x$ is equivalent to $b^x = y$ and there is no power x that will make b^x negative, y must be a positive; two examples that support the claim

2. a. **b.**

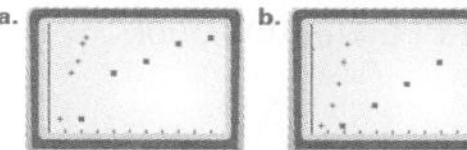

c. $v_1(t)$: power function; $v_2(t)$: exponential function **d.** use a graphing calculator to compare correlation coefficients **e.** $v_1(t) = 250t^{0.06}$; $v_2(t) = 177(1.09)^t$ **f.** v_1: $281,000; v_2: $324,000 **g.** 21 yr **h.** 2000; find the intersection of the graphs and set $v_1(t) = v_2(t)$; difficult to isolate ts **i.** first house: increased less over time, second house: increased more over time; location, population growth/decline, economic development, reassessment, and surrounding development

PLAN AND PREPARE

Main Ideas

Students will learn to graph and use exponential growth and decay functions, including functions involving the natural base *e*. Next, they will learn to evaluate and graph logarithmic functions and to use the properties of logarithms to rewrite logarithmic expressions. Then, students will learn to solve exponential and logarithmic equations. Finally, students will learn to write and apply exponential and power functions.

Prerequisite Skills

- Graphing functions
- Finding inverse functions
- Using given data to write functions

Additional resources for reviewing prerequisite skills are:

- Skills Review Handbook, pp. 975–1009
- @HomeTutor

7 Exponential and Logarithmic Functions

KY

Before

In previous chapters, you learned the following skills, which you'll use in Chapter 7: graphing functions, finding inverse functions, and writing functions.

Prerequisite Skills

VOCABULARY CHECK

Copy and complete the statement using the graph at the right.

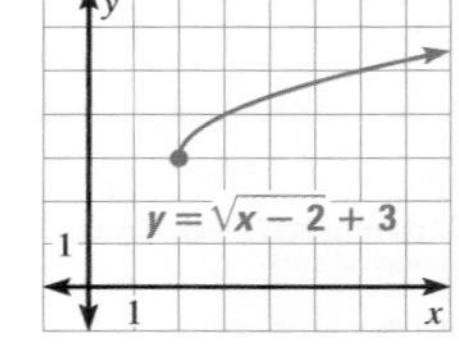

1. The **domain** of the function is __?__. $x \geq 2$
2. The **range** of the function is __?__. $y \geq 3$
3. The **inverse** of the function is __?__. $y = (x-3)^2 + 2$

SKILLS CHECK

Graph the function. State the domain and range. *(Review p. 446 for 7.1–7.3.)* 4–6. See margin.

4. $y = -2\sqrt{x} - 1$
5. $y = \sqrt{x+3}$
6. $y = \sqrt[3]{x-2} + 5$

Find the inverse of the function. *(Review p. 438 for 7.4.)*

7. $y = 3x + 5$ $\quad y = \frac{x-5}{3}$
8. $y = -2x^3 + 1$ $\quad y = \sqrt[3]{\frac{x-1}{-2}}$
9. $y = \frac{1}{2}x^2, x \geq 0$ $\quad y = \sqrt{2x}$

Write a quadratic function in standard form for the parabola that passes through the given points. *(Review p. 309 for 7.7.)*

10. $(0, -1), (1, 2), (3, 14)$
11. $(3, 8), (4, 17), (7, 56)$
12. $(-3, 9), (1, -7), (5, -55)$ $\quad y = -x^2 - 6x$

10, 11. See margin.

476

Chapter Planning Guide

Chapter 7 Resource Book
- Teaching Guide/Lesson Plan (pp. 3, 14, 27, 38, 51, 62, 73)
- Project with Rubric (p. 85)

Assessment and Intervention
- Assessment Book (pp. 95–109)
- Benchmark Tests
- Remediation Book

Interactive Technology
- Easy Planner
- Power Presentations CD-ROM
- Activity Generator CD-ROM
- Animated Algebra
- Test Generator CD-ROM
- Online Quizzes
- eWorkbook
- eEdition
- @HomeTutor

Resources for English Learners
- Quick Reference for English Learners
- Spanish Study Guide
- Multi-Language Visual Glossary
- Student Resources in Spanish

Now

In Chapter 7, you will apply the big ideas listed below and reviewed in the Chapter Summary on page 538. You will also use the key vocabulary listed below.

Big Ideas

1. **Graphing exponential and logarithmic functions**
2. **Solving exponential and logarithmic equations**
3. **Writing and applying exponential and power functions**

KEY VOCABULARY

- exponential function, *p. 478*
- exponential growth function, *p. 478*
- growth factor, *p. 478*
- asymptote, *p. 478*
- exponential decay function, *p. 486*
- decay factor, *p. 486*
- natural base *e*, *p. 492*
- logarithm of *y* with base *b*, *p. 499*
- common logarithm, *p. 500*
- natural logarithm, *p. 500*
- exponential equation, *p. 515*
- logarithmic equation, *p. 517*

Why?

You can use exponential and logarithmic functions to model many scientific relationships. For example, you can use a logarithmic function to relate the size of a telescope lens and the ability of the telescope to see certain stars.

Animated Algebra

The animation illustrated below for Example 7 on page 519 helps you answer this question: How is the diameter of a telescope's objective lens related to the apparent magnitude of the dimmest star that can be seen with the telescope?

The magnitude of stars is a measure of their brightness as viewed from Earth.

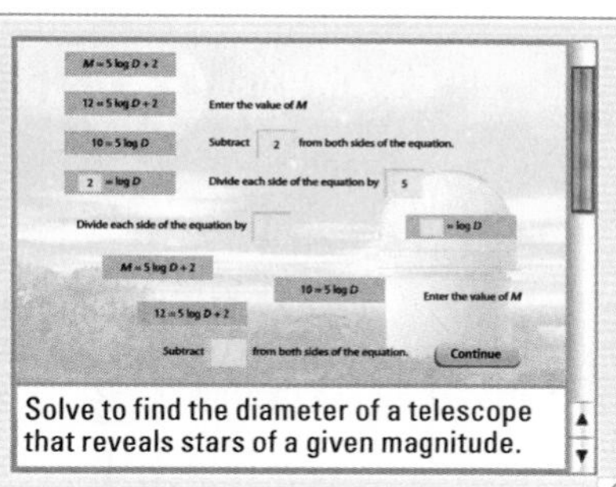

Solve to find the diameter of a telescope that reveals stars of a given magnitude.

Animated Algebra at classzone.com

Other animations for Chapter 7: pages 480, 487, 502, and 538

Algebra 2 Toolkit

- Reading Strategies for Chapter 7, pp. 21–22
- Differentiated Instruction Notes, pp. 67–70
- English Learners Notes, pp. 113–114
- Inclusion Notes, pp. 147–148
- Teaching Strategies with Sample Worksheets, pp. 163–186
- Using Technology in the Classroom, pp. 187–192
- Tips for New Teachers, pp. 205–206
- Math Background Notes, pp. 242–244
- Pre-AP Strategies and Copymasters, pp. 323–324, 399–408
- Teacher Survival Activities, pp. 481–482, 509–510
- Bulletin Board Idea, p. 531
- Teacher Tool Transparencies, following p. 538

4.

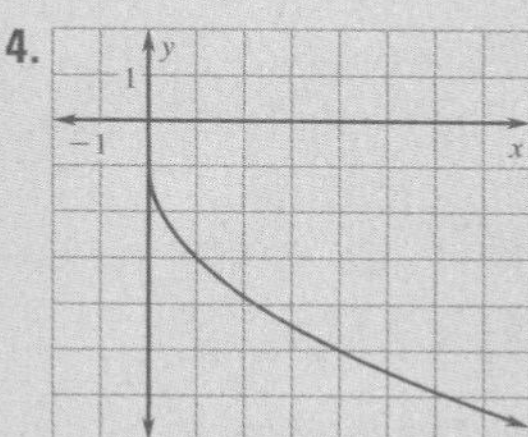

domain: $x \geq 0$, range: $y \leq -1$

5.

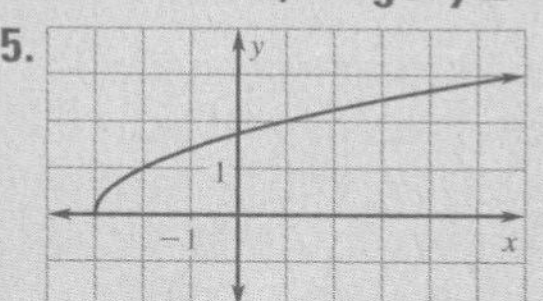

domain: $x \geq -3$, range: $y \geq 0$

6.

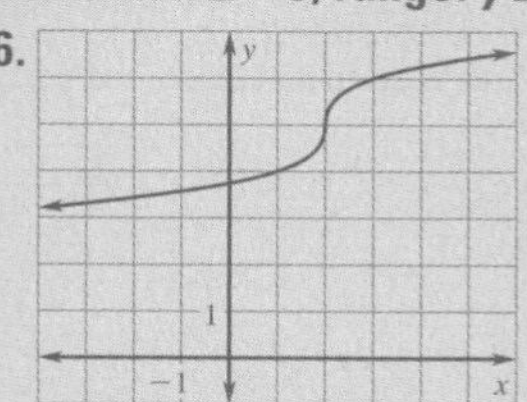

domain: all real numbers, range: all real numbers

10. $y = x^2 + 2x - 1$

11. $y = x^2 + 2x - 7$

1 PLAN AND PREPARE

Warm-Up Exercises

Transparency Available

Evaluate the expression without using a calculator.

1. 5^{-2} $\frac{1}{25}$
2. $8^{2/3}$ 4
3. $-3 \cdot 4^{3/2}$ -24
4. State the domain and range of the function $y = -(x-2)^2 + 3$. **domain: all real numbers; range: $y \le 3$**

Notetaking Guide

Transparency Available

Promotes interactive learning and notetaking skills, pp. 185–188.

Pacing

Basic: 1 day

Average: 1 day

Advanced: 1 day

Block: 0.5 block with 7.2

• See *Teaching Guide/Lesson Plan.*

2 FOCUS AND MOTIVATE

Essential Question

Big Idea 1, p. 477

What does the graph of an exponential growth function look like? **Tell students they will learn how to answer this question by graphing a variety of exponential growth functions.**

7.1 Graph Exponential Growth Functions

MA-HS-5.1.4 Students will recognize and solve problems that can be modeled using an exponential function, such as compound interest problems.

Before You graphed polynomial and radical functions.

Now You will graph and use exponential growth functions.

Why? So you can model sports equipment costs, as in Ex. 40.

Key Vocabulary
- exponential function
- exponential growth function
- growth factor
- asymptote

An **exponential function** has the form $y = ab^x$ where $a \neq 0$ and the base b is a positive number other than 1. If $a > 0$ and $b > 1$, then the function $y = ab^x$ is an **exponential growth function**, and b is called the **growth factor**. The simplest type of exponential growth function has the form $y = b^x$.

KEY CONCEPT *For Your Notebook*

Parent Function for Exponential Growth Functions

The function $f(x) = b^x$, where $b > 1$, is the parent function for the family of exponential growth functions with base b. The general shape of the graph of $f(x) = b^x$ is shown below.

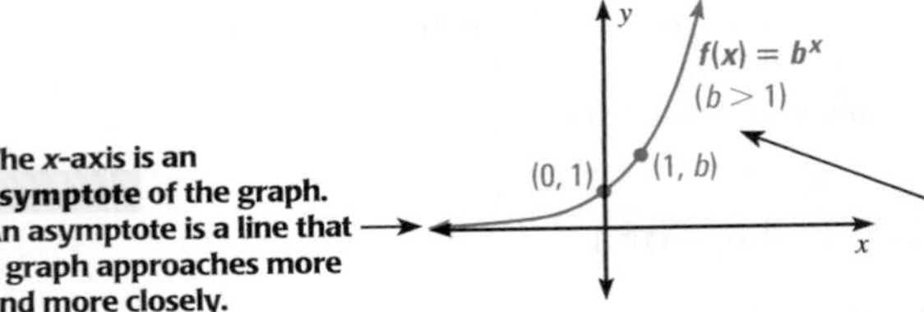

The x-axis is an asymptote of the graph. An asymptote is a line that a graph approaches more and more closely.

The graph rises from left to right, passing through the points (0, 1) and (1, b).

The domain of $f(x) = b^x$ is all real numbers. The range is $y > 0$.

EXAMPLE 1 Graph $y = b^x$ for $b > 1$

Graph $y = 2^x$.

Solution

STEP 1 **Make** a table of values.

x	-2	-1	0	1	2	3
y	$\frac{1}{4}$	$\frac{1}{2}$	1	2	4	8

STEP 2 **Plot** the points from the table.

STEP 3 **Draw,** from *left* to *right*, a smooth curve that begins just above the x-axis, passes through the plotted points, and moves up to the right.

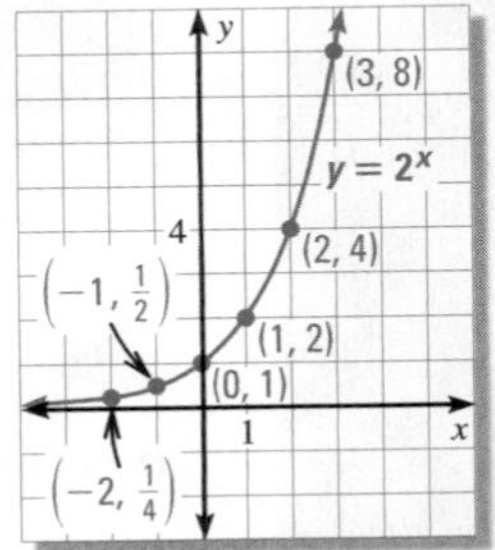

Resource Planning Guide

Chapter Resource Book
- Teaching Guide/Lesson Plan (pp. 3–4)
- Practice levels A, B, C (pp. 6–8)
- Study Guide (p. 9–10)
- Catch-up for Absent Students (p. 11)
- Problem Solving Workshop (p. 12)
- Challenge (p. 13)

Workbooks
- Notetaking Guide (pp. 185–188)
- Practice Workbook (pp. 108–109)

Teaching Options
- **Power Presentations CD-ROM** provides dynamic electronic teaching resources for the classroom.
- **Activity Generator CD-ROM** provides editable activities for all ability levels.

Interactive Technology
- Easy Planner
- Power Presentations CD-ROM
- Activity Generator CD-ROM
- Animated Algebra
- Test Generator CD-ROM
- Online Quiz
- eWorkbook
- eEdition
- @HomeTutor

Resources for English Learners
- Quick Reference for English Learners
- Spanish Study Guide
- Multi-Language Visual Glossary
- Student Resources in Spanish

See also the *Algebra 2 Toolkit* for more strategies for meeting individual needs.

The graph of a function $y = ab^x$ is a vertical stretch or shrink of the graph of $y = b^x$. The y-intercept of the graph of $y = ab^x$ occurs at $(0, a)$ rather than $(0, 1)$.

EXAMPLE 2 Graph $y = ab^x$ for $b > 1$

Graph the function.

a. $y = \frac{1}{2} \cdot 4^x$

b. $y = -\left(\frac{5}{2}\right)^x$

Solution

a. Plot $\left(0, \frac{1}{2}\right)$ and $(1, 2)$. Then, from *left* to *right*, draw a curve that begins just above the x-axis, passes through the two points, and moves up to the right.

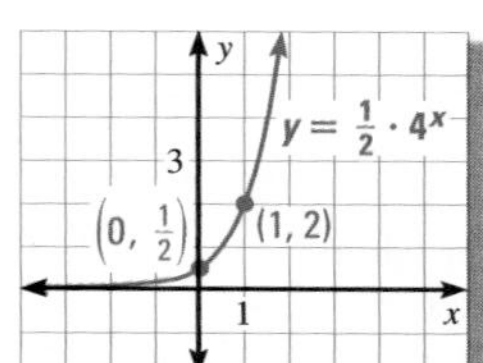

b. Plot $(0, -1)$ and $\left(1, -\frac{5}{2}\right)$. Then, from *left* to *right*, draw a curve that begins just below the x-axis, passes through the two points, and moves down to the right.

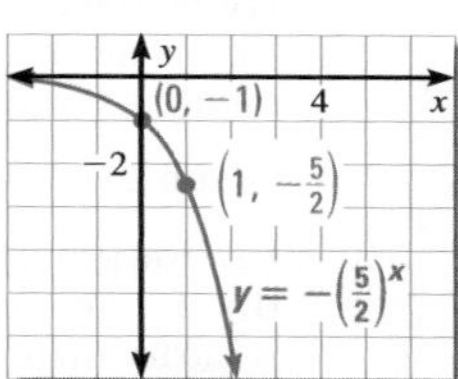

LASSIFY UNCTIONS
ote that the nction in part (b) of xample 2 is not an xponential growth nction because $= -1 < 0$.

TRANSLATIONS To graph a function of the form $y = ab^{x-h} + k$, begin by sketching the graph of $y = ab^x$. Then translate the graph horizontally by h units and vertically by k units.

EXAMPLE 3 Graph $y = ab^{x-h} + k$ for $b > 1$

Graph $y = 4 \cdot 2^{x-1} - 3$. State the domain and range.

Solution

Begin by sketching the graph of $y = 4 \cdot 2^x$, which passes through $(0, 4)$ and $(1, 8)$. Then translate the graph right 1 unit and down 3 units to obtain the graph of $y = 4 \cdot 2^{x-1} - 3$.

The graph's asymptote is the line $y = -3$. The domain is all real numbers, and the range is $y > -3$.

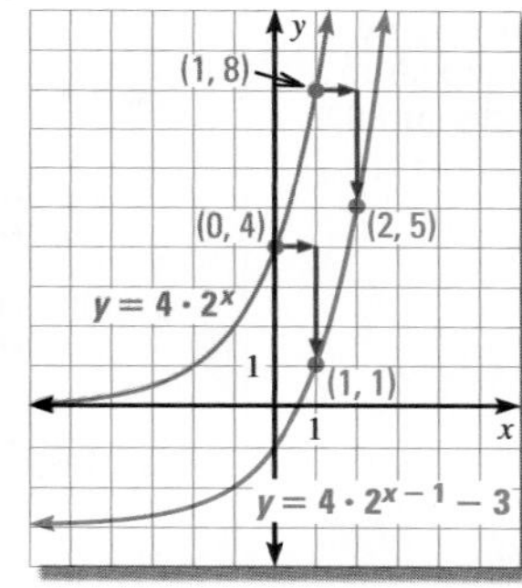

GUIDED PRACTICE for Examples 1, 2, and 3

Graph the function. State the domain and range. 1–3. See margin.

1. $y = 4^x$
2. $y = \frac{1}{2} \cdot 3^x$
3. $f(x) = 3^{x+1} + 2$

Motivating the Lesson

If you know the current tuition at the college you want to attend and the percent by which tuition has been increasing annually, you can use an exponential growth model to estimate the tuition for the year in which you will start college.

3 TEACH

Extra Example 1

Graph $y = 5^x$.

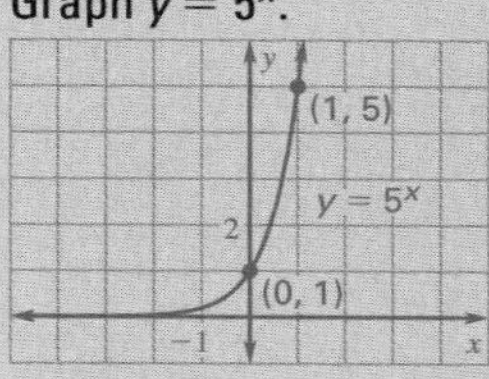

Extra Example 2

Graph the function.

a. $y = \left(\frac{1}{3}\right) \cdot 3^x$

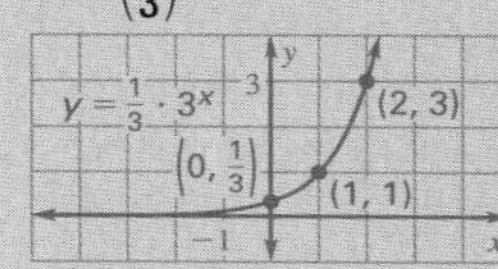

b. $y = -\left(\frac{7}{2}\right)^x$

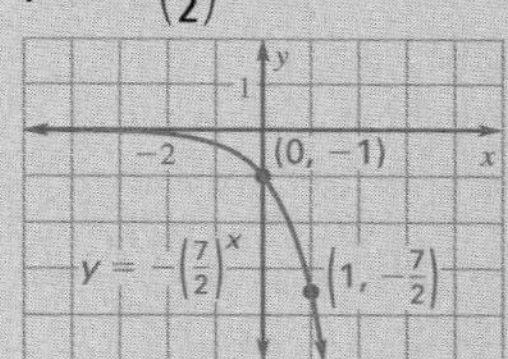

Extra Example 3

Graph $y = 2 \cdot 4^{x+2} + 1$. State the domain and range.

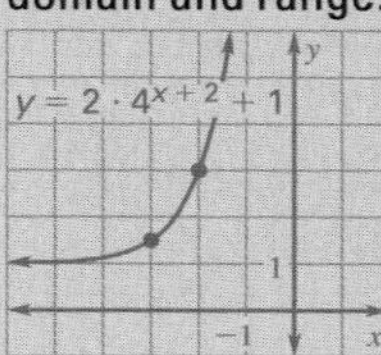

domain: all real numbers; range: $y > 1$

1–3. See Additional Answers beginning on p. AA1.

Extra Example 4

In 1970, the population of Kern County, California, where Bakersfield is located, was about 330,000. From 1970 to 2000, the county population grew at an average annual rate of about 2.4%.

- Write an exponential growth model giving the population P of Kern County t years after 1970. About how many people lived in Kern County in 1990? $P = 330{,}000(1.024)^t$; about 530,000 people
- Graph the model.

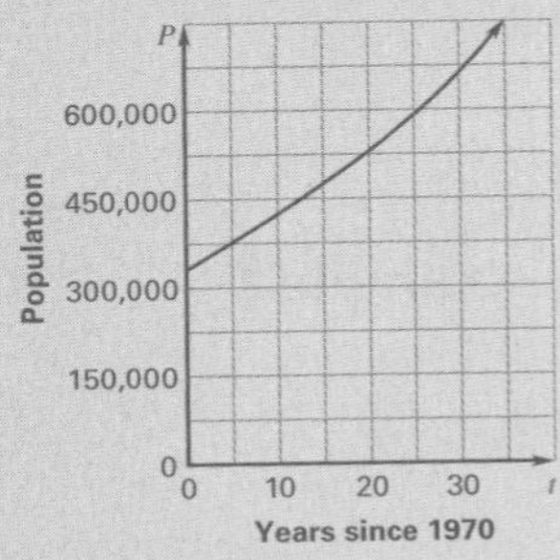

- Use the graph to estimate the year when the population of Kern County was about 400,000. 1978

Key Questions to Ask for Example 4

- Will the number of computer security incidents continue to grow at 92% a year? Explain. Possible answer: No; the rate of growth will probably slow down considerably as protection against viruses is developed.

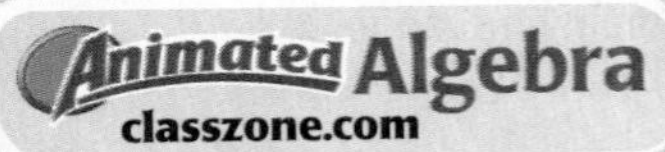

An **Animated Algebra** activity is available on-line for **Example 4**. This activity is also available on the **Power Presentations CD-ROM**.

Vocabulary

If students are having trouble remembering the difference between the growth factor and the percent increase, have them write "growth factor = 1 + percent increase" in their notebooks for reference.

EXPONENTIAL GROWTH MODELS When a real-life quantity increases by a fixed percent each year (or other time period), the amount y of the quantity after t years can be modeled by the equation

$$y = a(1 + r)^t$$

where a is the initial amount and r is the percent increase expressed as a decimal. Note that the quantity $1 + r$ is the growth factor.

EXAMPLE 4 Solve a multi-step problem

COMPUTERS In 1996, there were 2573 computer viruses and other computer security incidents. During the next 7 years, the number of incidents increased by about 92% each year.

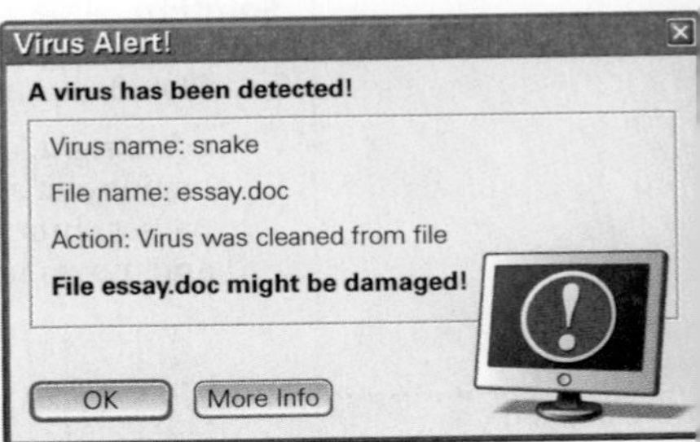

- Write an exponential growth model giving the number n of incidents t years after 1996. About how many incidents were there in 2003?
- Graph the model.
- Use the graph to estimate the year when there were about 125,000 computer security incidents.

Solution

STEP 1 The initial amount is $a = 2573$ and the percent increase is $r = 0.92$. So, the exponential growth model is:

$n = a(1 + r)^t$ **Write exponential growth model.**

$= 2573(1 + 0.92)^t$ **Substitute 2573 for *a* and 0.92 for *r*.**

$= 2573(1.92)^t$ **Simplify.**

AVOID ERRORS
Notice that the percent increase and the growth factor are two different values. An increase of 92% corresponds to a growth factor of 1.92.

Using this model, you can estimate the number of incidents in 2003 ($t = 7$) to be $n = 2573(1.92)^7 \approx 247{,}485$.

STEP 2 The graph passes through the points (0, 2573) and (1, 4940.16). Plot a few other points. Then draw a smooth curve through the points.

STEP 3 Using the graph, you can estimate that the number of incidents was about 125,000 during 2002 ($t \approx 6$).

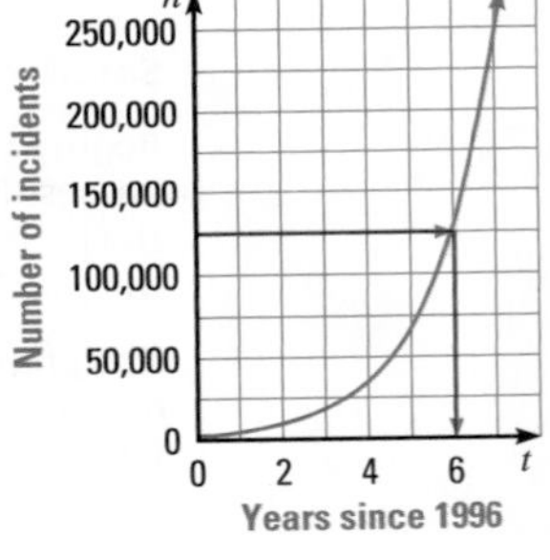

 at classzone.com

✓ **GUIDED PRACTICE** for Example 4

4. **WHAT IF?** In Example 4, estimate the year in which there were about 250,000 computer security incidents. 2003

5. In the exponential growth model $y = 527(1.39)^x$, identify the initial amount, the growth factor, and the percent increase. 527, 1.39, 39%

COMPOUND INTEREST Exponential growth functions are used in real-life situations involving *compound interest.* Compound interest is interest paid on the initial investment, called the *principal*, and on previously earned interest. Interest paid only on the principal is called *simple interest.*

KEY CONCEPT *For Your Notebook*

Compound Interest

Consider an initial principal P deposited in an account that pays interest at an annual rate r (expressed as a decimal), compounded n times per year. The amount A in the account after t years is given by this equation:

$$A = P\left(1 + \frac{r}{n}\right)^{nt}$$

EXAMPLE 5 Find the balance in an account

FINANCE You deposit \$4000 in an account that pays 2.92% annual interest. Find the balance after 1 year if the interest is compounded with the given frequency.

a. Quarterly

b. Daily

Solution

a. With interest compounded quarterly, the balance after 1 year is:

$A = P\left(1 + \frac{r}{n}\right)^{nt}$	Write compound interest formula.
$= 4000\left(1 + \frac{0.0292}{4}\right)^{4 \cdot 1}$	$P = 4000, r = 0.0292, n = 4, t = 1$
$= 4000(1.0073)^4$	Simplify.
≈ 4118.09	Use a calculator.

▸ The balance at the end of 1 year is \$4118.09.

b. With interest compounded daily, the balance after 1 year is:

$A = P\left(1 + \frac{r}{n}\right)^{nt}$	Write compound interest formula.
$= 4000\left(1 + \frac{0.0292}{365}\right)^{365 \cdot 1}$	$P = 4000, r = 0.0292, n = 365, t = 1$
$= 4000(1.00008)^{365}$	Simplify.
≈ 4118.52	Use a calculator.

▸ The balance at the end of 1 year is \$4118.52.

GUIDED PRACTICE for Example 5

6. FINANCE You deposit \$2000 in an account that pays 4% annual interest. Find the balance after 3 years if the interest is compounded daily. \$2254.98

Extra Example 5

You deposit \$5500 in an account that pays 3.6% annual interest. Find the balance after 2 years if interest is compounded with the given frequency.

a. semiannually \$5906.82

b. monthly \$5909.97

Key Questions to Ask for Example 5

- Without doing any calculations, what do you know about what the balance would be in Example 5 if interest were compounded monthly? **It would be greater than \$4118.09 and less than \$4118.52.**
- In compound interest, why does the amount of interest earned increase as the frequency of compounding increases? **The more often interest is compounded, the sooner the new interest is added to the balance on which interest is earned.**

Closing the Lesson

Have students summarize the major points of the lesson and answer the Essential Question: What does the graph of an exponential growth function look like?

- **An exponential growth function is a function of the form $y = ab^x$ with $a > 0$ and $b > 1$.**
- **Exponential growth models, such as the compound interest formula, describe situations in which a quantity increases by a fixed percent each time period.**

The graph of an exponential growth function of the form $y = ab^x$ is a curve that rises from left to right and gets steeper as x increases. The x-axis is a horizontal asymptote of the graph.

Differentiated Instruction

Kinesthetic Learners The concept of compound interest will be new to some students. Before presenting them with the formula for calculating the amount in an interest-earning account over time, choose simple values for P, r, and n. Have groups of students explore how to calculate the interest earned for various values of t. Then, after they have learned the formula, have them verify their results.

See also the *Algebra 2 Toolkit* for more strategies.

7.1 EXERCISES

HOMEWORK KEY
○ = **WORKED-OUT SOLUTIONS** on p. WS13 for Exs. 17, 29, and 37
★ = **STANDARDIZED TEST PRACTICE** Exs. 2, 24, 25, 32, 40, and 41
◆ = **MULTIPLE REPRESENTATIONS** Ex. 42

4 PRACTICE AND APPLY

Assignment Guide

Answer Transparencies available for all exercises

Basic:
Day 1: pp. 482–485
Exs. 1–10, 15–19, 24–30, 35–39, 45

Average:
Day 1: pp. 482–485
Exs. 1–5, 9–12, 17–20, 24–33, 35–42, 46

Advanced:
Day 1: pp. 482–485
Exs. 1, 2, 12–14, 21–44*

Block:
pp. 482–485
Exs. 1–5, 9–12, 17–20, 24–33, 35–42, 46 (with 7.2)

Differentiated Instruction

See *Algebra 2 Best Practices Toolkit* for suggestions on addressing the needs of a diverse classroom.

Homework Check

For a quick check of student understanding of key concepts, go over the following exercises:
Basic: 6, 8, 18, 35, 37
Average: 9, 11, 20, 35, 38
Advanced: 12, 14, 22, 36, 38

Extra Practice

- Student Edition, p. 1016
- Chapter 7 Resource Book: Practice levels A, B, C, pp. 6–8

Practice Worksheet

An easily-readable reduced practice page (with answers) for this lesson can be found on p. 476C.

SKILL PRACTICE

A

1. **VOCABULARY** In the exponential growth model $y = 2.4(1.5)^x$, identify the initial amount, the growth factor, and the percent increase. **2.4, 1.5, 50%**

2. ★ **WRITING** What is an asymptote? **An asymptote is a line that a graph approaches very closely but never meets.**

EXAMPLES 1 and 2 on pp. 478–479 for Exs. 3–14

MATCHING GRAPHS **Match the function with its graph.**

3. $y = 3 \cdot 2^x$ **C**
4. $y = -3 \cdot 2^x$ **A**
5. $y = 2 \cdot 3^x$ **B**

A. (0, −3), (1, −6)

B.
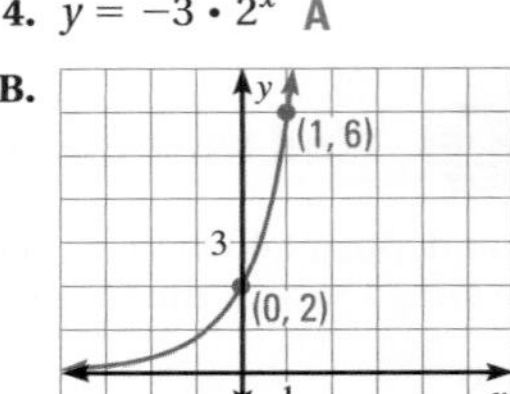

C.
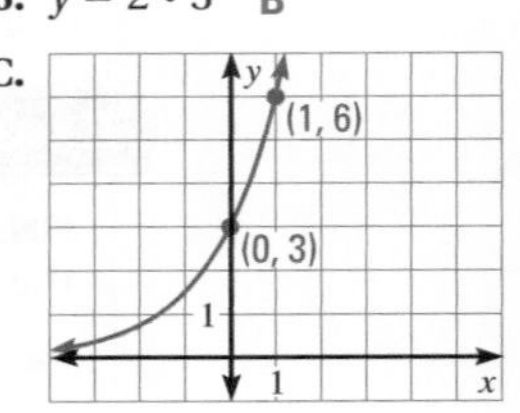

GRAPHING FUNCTIONS **Graph the function.** **6–14. See margin.**

6. $y = 3^x$
7. $y = -2^x$
8. $f(x) = 5 \cdot 2^x$
9. $y = 5^x$
10. $y = 2 \cdot 4^x$
11. $g(x) = -(1.5)^x$
12. $y = 3\left(\frac{4}{3}\right)^x$
13. $y = \frac{1}{2} \cdot 3^x$
14. $h(x) = -2(2.5)^x$

EXAMPLE 3 on p. 479 for Exs. 15–24

TRANSLATING GRAPHS **Graph the function. State the domain and range.** **15–23. See margin.**

15. $y = -3 \cdot 2^{x+2}$
16. $y = 5 \cdot 4^x + 2$
17. $y = 2^{x+1} + 3$
18. $y = 3^{x-2} - 1$
19. $y = 2 \cdot 3^{x-2} - 1$
20. $y = -3 \cdot 4^{x-1} - 2$
21. $f(x) = 6 \cdot 2^{x-3} + 3$
22. $g(x) = 5 \cdot 3^{x+2} - 4$
23. $h(x) = -2 \cdot 5^{x-1} + 1$

24. ★ **MULTIPLE CHOICE** The graph of which function is shown? **B**

    (A) $f(x) = 2(1.5)^x - 1$
    (B) $f(x) = 2(1.5)^x + 1$
    (C) $f(x) = 3(1.5)^x - 1$
    (D) $f(x) = 3(1.5)^x + 1$

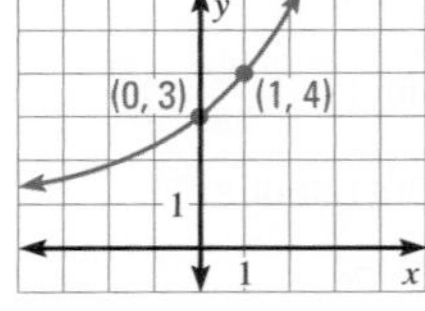

25. ★ **MULTIPLE CHOICE** The student enrollment E of a high school was 1310 in 1998 and has increased by 10% per year since then. Which exponential growth model gives the school's student enrollment in terms of t, where t is the number of years since 1998? **D**

    (A) $E = 0.1(1310)^t$
    (B) $E = 1310(0.1)^t$
    (C) $E = 1.1(1310)^t$
    (D) $E = 1310(1.1)^t$

6.
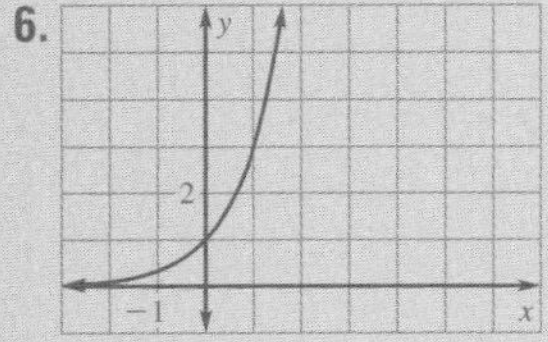

7.
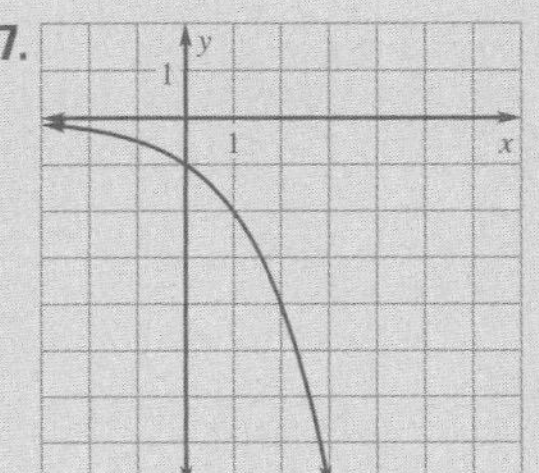

8.
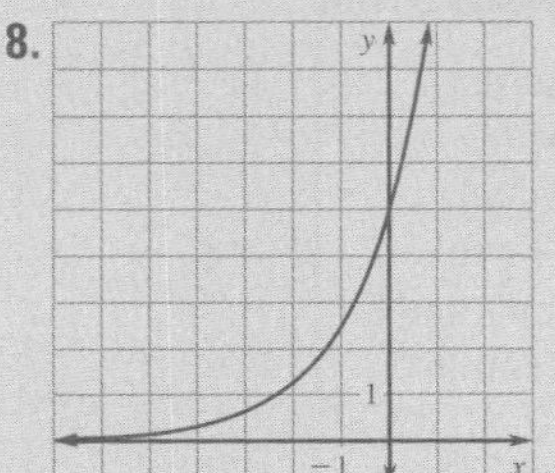

9.
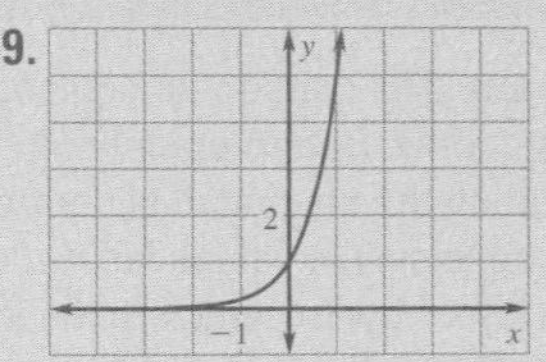

27. The power of $(x - 3)$ translates the parent graph 3 units to the right, not to the left.

ERROR ANALYSIS ***Describe*** **and correct the error in graphing the function.**

26. $y = 2 \cdot 4^x$ The y-intercept should be (0, 2), not (0, 1).

27. $y = 2^{x-3} + 3$ 26, 27. See margin for art.

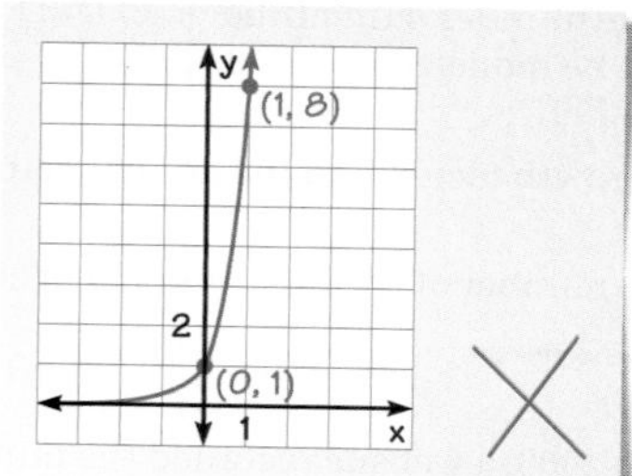

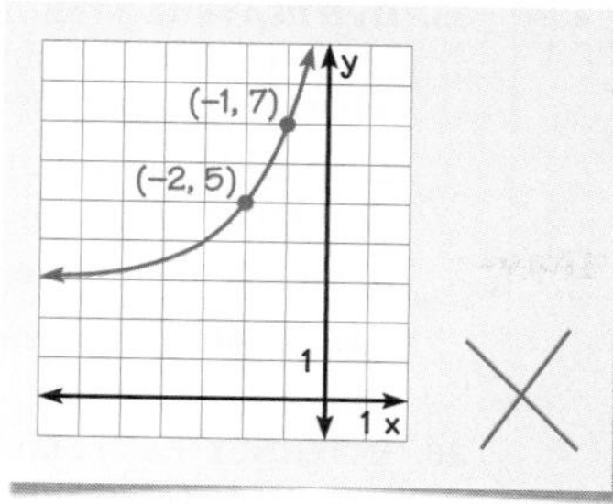

B **WRITING MODELS** **In Exercises 28–30, write an exponential growth model that describes the situation.**

28. In 1992, 1219 monk parakeets were observed in the United States. For the next 11 years, about 12% more parakeets were observed each year. $y = 1219(1.12)^t$, where y represents the number of monk parakeets and t represents the number of years since 1992.

29. You deposit \$800 in an account that pays 2% annual interest compounded daily. $A = 800\left(1 + \frac{.02}{365}\right)^{365t}$, where A represents the amount in the account after t years.

30. You purchase an antique table for \$450. The value of the table increases by 6% per year. $y = 450(1.06)^t$, where y represents the value of the table after t years.

3a. The graph o longer has a ertical stretch f 2.

3b. The graph vill increase lower.

3c. The raph will be 'anslated 3 nits to the right stead of 4 nits to the left.

3d. The raph will be anslated 1 unit own instead of units up.

31. GRAPHING CALCULATOR You deposit \$1500 in a bank account that pays 3% annual interest compounded yearly.

a. Type 1500 into a graphing calculator and press ENTER. Then enter the formula ANS * 1.03, as shown at the right. Press ENTER seven times to find your balance after 7 years. \$1844.81

b. Find the number of years it takes for your balance to exceed \$2500. 18 yr

```
1500
                1500
Ans*1.03
                1545
             1591.35
           1639.0905
         1688.263215
```

32. ★ **OPEN-ENDED MATH** Write an exponential function of the form $y = ab^{x-h} + k$ whose graph has a y-intercept of 5 and an asymptote of $y = 2$. *Sample answer:* $y = 9 \cdot 3^{x-1} + 2$

33. GRAPHING CALCULATOR Consider the exponential growth function $y = ab^{x-h} + k$ where $a = 2$, $b = 5$, $h = -4$, and $k = 3$. Predict the effect on the function's graph of each change in a, b, h, or k described in parts (a)–(d). Use a graphing calculator to check your prediction.

a. a changes to 1 **b.** b changes to 4 **c.** h changes to 3 **d.** k changes to −1

C **34. CHALLENGE** Consider the exponential function $f(x) = ab^x$.

a. Show that $\frac{f(x+1)}{f(x)} = b$. $\frac{ab^{x+1}}{ab^x} = \frac{b^x b^1}{b^x} = b$

b. Use the result from part (a) to explain why there is no exponential function of the form $f(x) = ab^x$ whose graph passes through the points in the table below.

x	0	1	2	3	4
y	4	4	8	24	72

Sample answer: Since the points (0, 4) and (1, 4) are of the form $f(x)$ and $f(x + 1)$, when $f(x)$ and $f(x + 1)$ are substituted into the equation from part (a), $b = 1$ and therefore the function is no longer exponential.

Avoiding Common Errors

Exercises 15, 17–23 When graphing translations of exponential functions, some students may do the horizontal shifts in the wrong direction. For example, in Exercise 17 they would translate the graph of $y = 2^x$ right 1 unit and up 3 units, rather than left 1 unit and up 3 units because they associate + with movement from left to right and from bottom to top. To help these students, review graphing quadratic functions of the form $y = a(x - h)^2 + k$, where the vertex is (h, k).

13.

14.

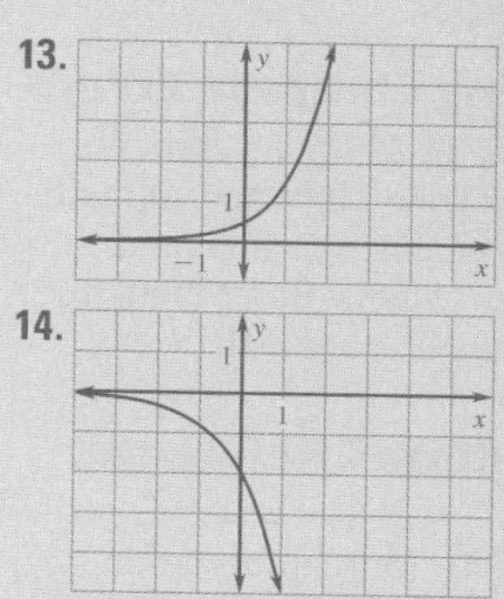

15–23. See Additional Answers beginning on p. AA1.

26.

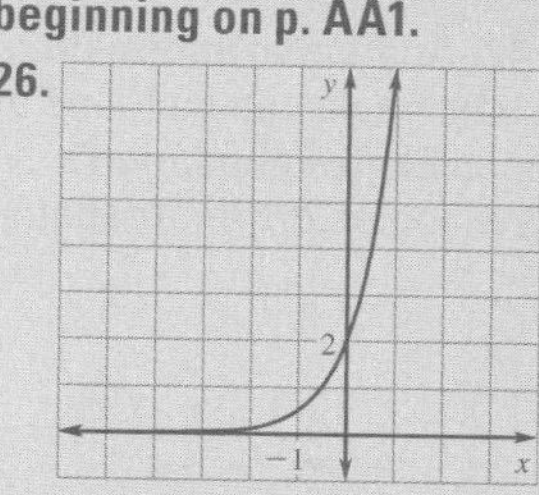

27.

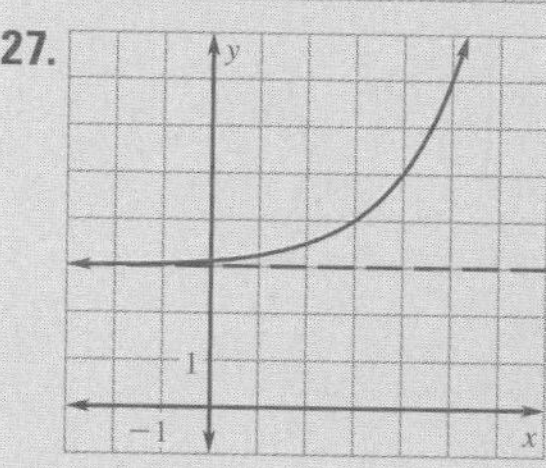

10.

11.

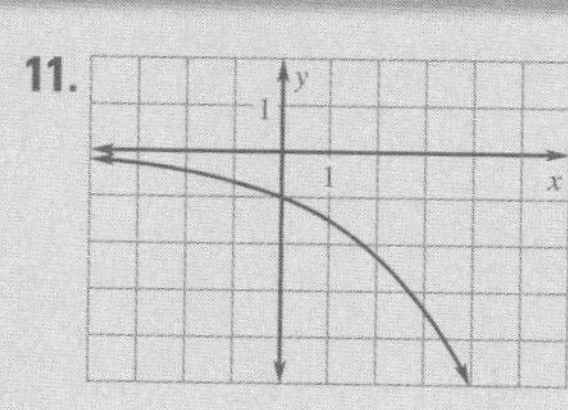

12.

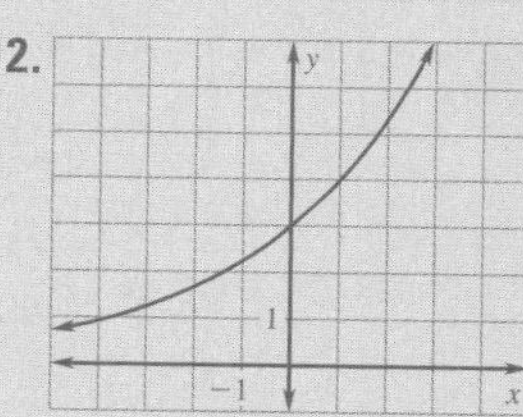

Study Strategy

Exercises 35, 36 If students have trouble identifying the initial amount, the growth factor, and the annual percent increase for these models, have them rewrite the given equations by replacing 2.47 in Exercise 35 with $1 + 1.47$, and replacing 1.50 in Exercise 36 with $1 + 0.50$. Then tell them to write the general exponential growth model equation $y = a(1 + r)^t$ directly below the rewritten equations and match up the values of a, the initial amount, r, the annual percent increase, and $1 + r$, the growth factor.

Avoiding Common Errors

Exercises 37, 38 Many students forget to divide r by n and/or multiply t by n in solving compound interest problems. Refer them to the formula on page 481.

Internet Reference

Exercise 41 More information about the Minnesota Vikings can be found at www.vikings.com

Exercise 42 Additional information about the bald eagle can be found at the American Eagle Foundation's site at www.eagles.org/moreabout.html

35b.

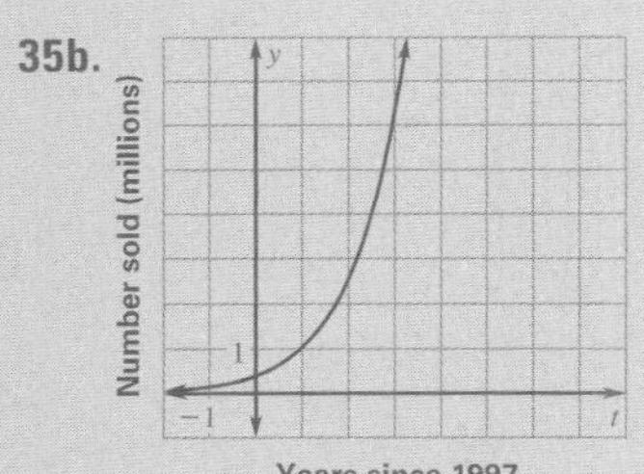

36b.

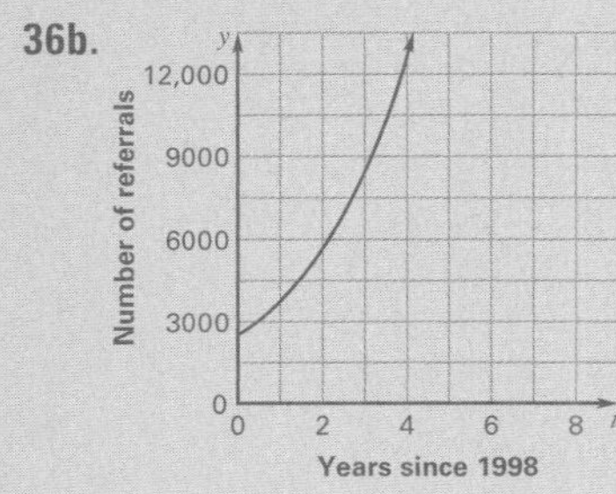

PROBLEM SOLVING

EXAMPLE 4 on p. 480 for Exs. 35–36

A

35. DVD PLAYERS From 1997 to 2002, the number n (in millions) of DVD players sold in the United States can be modeled by $n = 0.42(2.47)^t$ where t is the number of years since 1997.

a. Identify the initial amount, the growth factor, and the annual percent increase. **0.42 million, 2.47, 147%**

b. Graph the function. Estimate the number of DVD players sold in 2001. **See margin for art; about 16 million DVD players.**

@HomeTutor for problem solving help at classzone.com

36. INTERNET Each March from 1998 to 2003, a website recorded the number y of referrals it received from Internet search engines. The results can be modeled by $y = 2500(1.50)^t$ where t is the number of years since 1998.

a. Identify the initial amount, the growth factor, and the annual percent increase. **2500, 1.50, 50%**

b. Graph the function and state the domain and range. Estimate the number of referrals the website received from Internet search engines in March of 2002. **See margin for art; domain: $t \geq 0$, range: $y \geq 2500$; about 13,000 referrals.**

@HomeTutor for problem solving help at classzone.com

EXAMPLE 5 on p. 481 for Exs. 37–38

37. ACCOUNT BALANCE You deposit \$2200 in a bank account. Find the balance after 4 years for each of the situations described below.

a. The account pays 3% annual interest compounded quarterly. **\$2479.38**

b. The account pays 2.25% annual interest compounded monthly. **\$2406.98**

c. The account pays 2% annual interest compounded daily. **\$2383.23**

B

38. DEPOSITING FUNDS You want to have \$3000 in your savings account after 3 years. Find the amount you should deposit for each of the situations described below.

a. The account pays 2.25% annual interest compounded quarterly. **\$2804.71**

b. The account pays 3.5% annual interest compounded monthly. **\$2701.39**

c. The account pays 4% annual interest compounded yearly. **\$2666.99**

39. MULTI-STEP PROBLEM In 1990, the population of Austin, Texas, was 494,290. During the next 10 years, the population increased by about 3% each year.

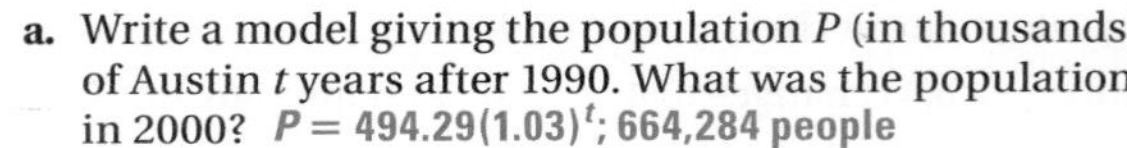

a. Write a model giving the population P (in thousands) of Austin t years after 1990. What was the population in 2000? **$P = 494.29(1.03)^t$; 664,284 people**

b. Graph the model and state the domain and range. **See margin for art; domain: $t \geq 0$, range: $P \geq 494.29$.**

c. Estimate the year when the population was about 590,000. **1996**

Austin, Texas

40. ★ SHORT RESPONSE At an online auction, the opening bid for a pair of in-line skates is \$50. The price of the skates increases by 10.5% per bid during the next 6 bids.

a. Write a model giving the price p (in dollars) of the skates after n bids. **$p = 50(1.105)^n$**

b. What was the price after 5 bids? According to the model, what will the price be after 100 bids? Is this predicted price reasonable? *Explain.*

40b. \$82.37; \$1,084,420.72; no. ***Sample answer:*** **This amount is unreasonable because the model is only defined for 6 bids and 100 is out of this domain.**

○ = WORKED-OUT SOLUTIONS on p. WS1 ★ = STANDARDIZED TEST PRACTICE ◆ = MULTIPLE REPRESENTATIONS

39b.

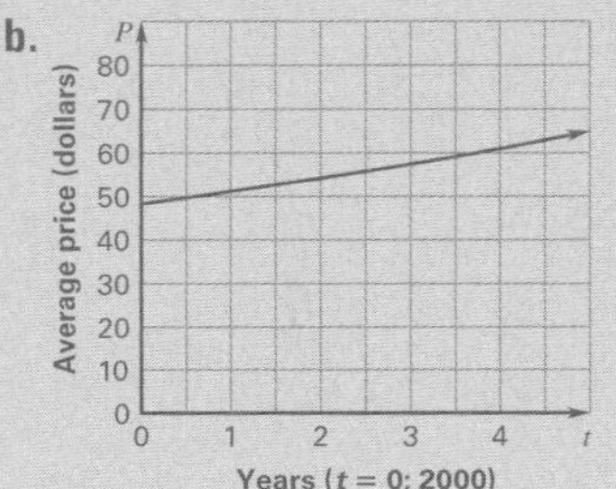

41b.

P: 0, 10, 20, 30, 40, 50, 60, 70, 80 — Average price (dollars); t: 0, 1, 2, 3, 4 — Years (t = 0; 2000)

42b.

t	n
0	41
8	81.097
24	317.29

41c. *Sample answer:* Since he function is only defined when t is between 0 and 4, you can look at the graph between these values to determine the minimum or maximum that gives meaningful results.

41. ★ **EXTENDED RESPONSE** In 2000, the average price of a football ticket for a Minnesota Viking's game was $48.28. During the next 4 years, the price increased an average of 6% each year.

a. Write a model giving the average price p (in dollars) of a ticket t years after 2000. $p = 48.28(1.06)^t$

b. Graph the model. Estimate the year when the average price of a ticket was about $60. See margin for art; 2003.

c. *Explain* how you can use the graph of $p(t)$ to determine the minimum and maximum t-values in the domain for which the function gives meaningful results.

42. ◆ **MULTIPLE REPRESENTATIONS** In 1977, there were 41 breeding pairs of bald eagles in Maryland. Over the next 24 years, the number of breeding pairs increased by about 8.9% each year.

a. Writing an Equation Write a model giving the number n of breeding pairs of bald eagles in Maryland t years after 1977. $n = 41(1.089)^t$

b. Making a Table Make a table of values for the model. See margin.

c. Drawing a Graph Graph the model. See margin.

d. Using a Graph About how many breeding pairs of bald eagles were in Maryland in 2001? about 317 breeding pairs

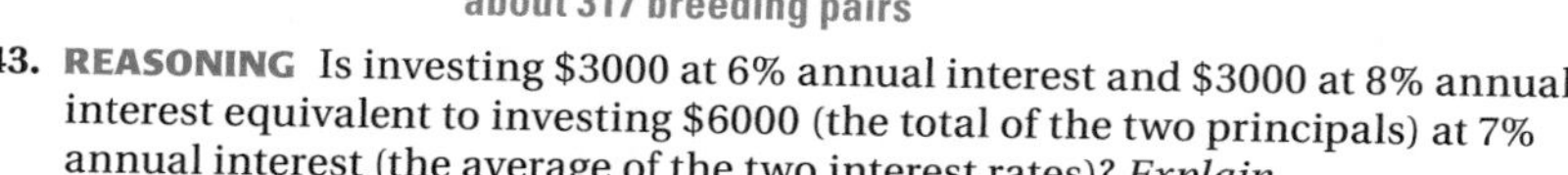

43. No. *Sample answer:* The initial amount is all that is equivalent. The first $6000 amount grows at a faster rate. C

43. **REASONING** Is investing $3000 at 6% annual interest and $3000 at 8% annual interest equivalent to investing $6000 (the total of the two principals) at 7% annual interest (the average of the two interest rates)? *Explain.*

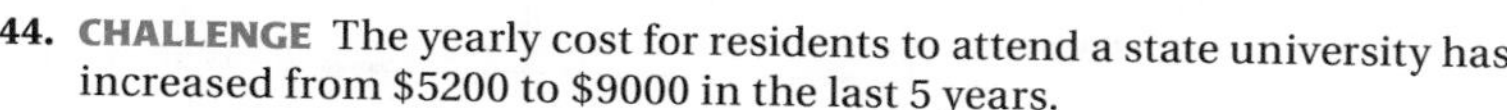

44. **CHALLENGE** The yearly cost for residents to attend a state university has increased from $5200 to $9000 in the last 5 years.

a. To the nearest tenth of a percent, what has been the average annual growth rate in cost? 11.6%

b. If this growth rate continues, what will the cost be in 5 more years? $15,582.79

KENTUCKY MIXED REVIEW

45. What is the effect on the graph of the equation $y = x^2 - 2$ when it is changed to $y = x^2 + 8$? **A**

Ⓐ The graph is translated 10 units up.

Ⓑ The graph is translated 10 units down.

Ⓒ The graph is translated 10 units to the right.

Ⓓ The graph is translated 10 units to the left.

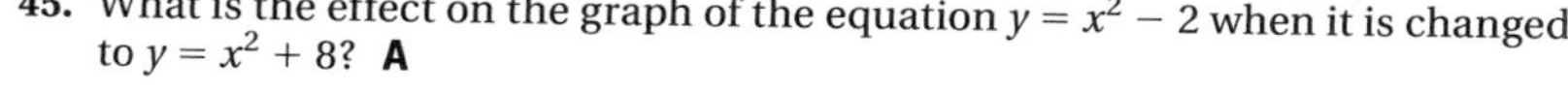

46. What is the approximate length of arc AB? **C**

Ⓐ 5.3 cm Ⓑ 8.4 cm

Ⓒ 16.8 cm Ⓓ 33.5 cm

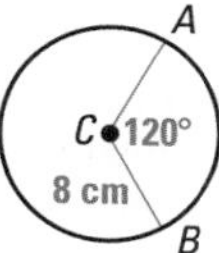

EXTRA PRACTICE for Lesson 7.1, p. 1016   **ONLINE QUIZ** at classzone.com

5 ASSESS AND RETEACH

Daily Homework Quiz

Transparency Available

1. Graph $y = \left(\frac{3}{2}\right) \cdot 2^x$. State the domain and range. domain: all real numbers; range: $y > 0$

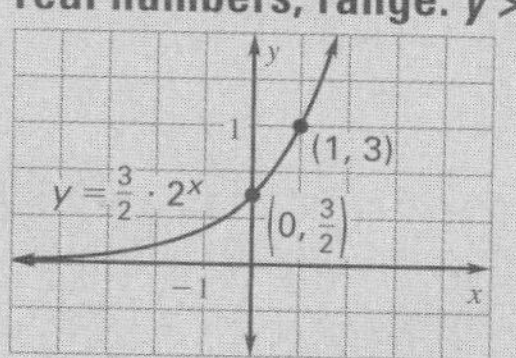

2. Graph $y = 3 \cdot 2^{x-2} - 1$. State the domain and range.

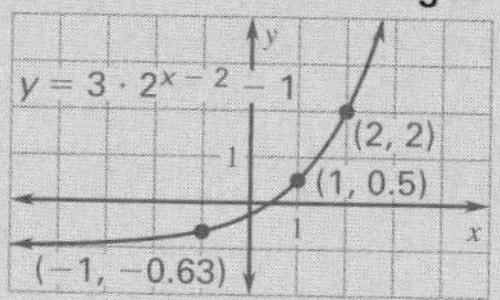

domain: all real numbers; range: $y > -1$

3. You deposit $1500 in an account that pays 3% annual interest compounded daily. What will be the balance in your account after 1 year? $1545.68

Available at **classzone.com**

Diagnosis/Remediation

- Practice A, B, C in Chapter 7 Resource Book, pp. 6–8
- Study Guide in Chapter 7 Resource Book, pp. 9–10
- Practice Workbook, pp. 108–109
- @HomeTutor

Challenge

Additional challenge is available in the Chapter 7 Resource Book, p. 13.

42c.

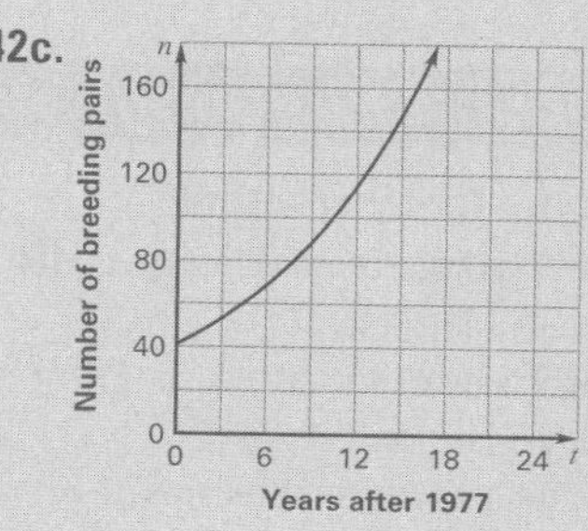

7.2 Graph Exponential Decay Functions

MA-HS-5.1.4 Students will recognize and solve problems that can be modeled using an exponential function, such as compound interest problems.

Before You graphed and used exponential growth functions.

Now You will graph and use exponential decay functions.

Why? So you can model depreciation, as in Ex. 31.

1 PLAN AND PREPARE

Warm-Up Exercises

Transparency Available

Evaluate the expression without using a calculator.

1. $\left(\frac{1}{3}\right)^{-3}$ 27

2. $-\left(\frac{2}{5}\right)^{0}$ −1

3. $4\left(\frac{2}{3}\right)^{-2} + 1$ 10

4. A savings account pays 3% interest compounded monthly. What is the growth factor for this account? 1.0025

Notetaking Guide

Transparency Available

Promotes interactive learning and notetaking skills, pp. 189–191.

Pacing

Basic: 1 day

Average: 1 day

Advanced: 1 day

Block: 0.5 block with 7.1

• See *Teaching Guide/Lesson Plan.*

2 FOCUS AND MOTIVATE

Essential Question

Big Idea 1, p. 477

What does the graph of an exponential decay function look like? Tell students they will learn how to answer this question by graphing a variety of exponential decay functions.

Key Vocabulary
- exponential decay function
- decay factor

In Lesson 7.1 you studied exponential growth functions. In this lesson, you will study **exponential decay functions**, which have the form $y = ab^x$ where $a > 0$ and $0 < b < 1$. The base b of an exponential decay function is called the **decay factor**.

KEY CONCEPT *For Your Notebook*

Parent Function for Exponential Decay Functions

The function $f(x) = b^x$, where $0 < b < 1$, is the parent function for the family of exponential decay functions with base b. The general shape of the graph of $f(x) = b^x$ is shown below.

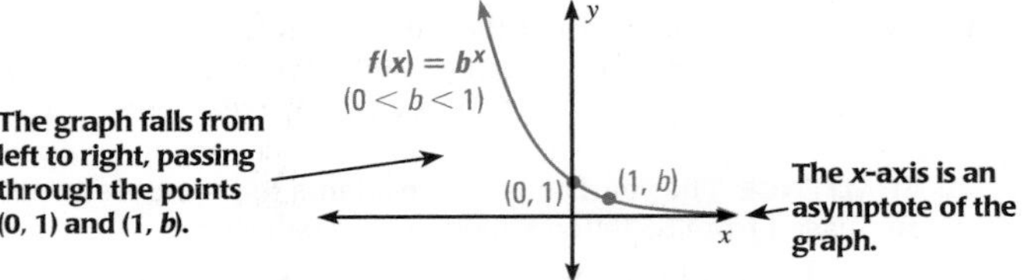

The domain of $f(x) = b^x$ is all real numbers. The range is $y > 0$.

EXAMPLE 1 Graph $y = b^x$ for $0 < b < 1$

Graph $y = \left(\frac{1}{2}\right)^x$.

Solution

STEP 1 **Make** a table of values.

x	−3	−2	−1	0	1	2
y	8	4	2	1	$\frac{1}{2}$	$\frac{1}{4}$

STEP 2 **Plot** the points from the table.

STEP 3 **Draw,** from *right* to *left*, a smooth curve that begins just above the x-axis, passes through the plotted points, and moves up to the left.

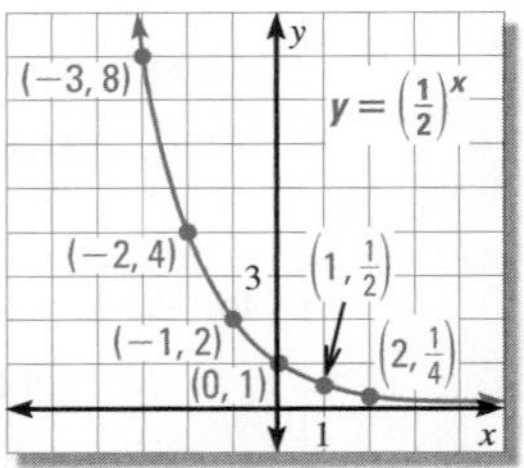

Resource Planning Guide

Chapter Resource Book
- Teaching Guide/Lesson Plan (pp. 14–15)
- Activity Master (p. 16)
- Practice levels A, B, C (pp. 19–21)
- Study Guide (pp. 22–23)
- Catch-up for Absent Students (p. 24)
- Problem Solving Workshop (p. 25)
- Challenge (p. 26)

Workbooks
- Notetaking Guide (pp. 189–191)
- Practice Workbook (pp. 110–111)

Teaching Options
- **Power Presentations CD-ROM** provides dynamic electronic teaching resources for the classroom.
- **Activity Generator CD-ROM** provides editable activities for all ability levels.

Interactive Technology
- Easy Planner
- Power Presentations CD-ROM
- Activity Generator CD-ROM
- Animated Algebra
- Test Generator CD-ROM
- Online Quiz
- eWorkbook
- eEdition
- @HomeTutor

Resources for English Learners
- Quick Reference for English Learners
- Spanish Study Guide
- Multi-Language Visual Glossary
- Student Resources in Spanish

See also the *Algebra 2 Toolkit* for more strategies for meeting individual needs.

TRANSFORMATIONS Recall from Lesson 7.1 that the graph of a function $y = ab^x$ is a vertical stretch or shrink of the graph of $y = b^x$, and the graph of $y = ab^{x-h} + k$ is a translation of the graph of $y = ab^x$.

EXAMPLE 2 Graph $y = ab^x$ for $0 < b < 1$

LASSIFY UNCTIONS
ote that the function part (b) of Example 2 not an exponential ecay function because $= -3 < 0$.

Graph the function.

a. $y = 2\left(\frac{1}{4}\right)^x$ **b.** $y = -3\left(\frac{2}{5}\right)^x$

Solution

a. Plot (0, 2) and $\left(1, \frac{1}{2}\right)$. Then, from *right* to *left*, draw a curve that begins just above the x-axis, passes through the two points, and moves up to the left.

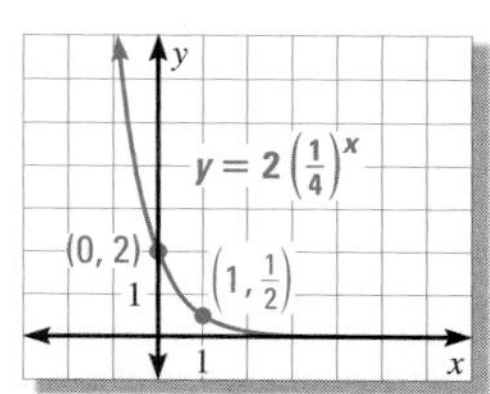

b. Plot (0, −3) and $\left(1, -\frac{6}{5}\right)$. Then, from *right* to *left*, draw a curve that begins just below the x-axis, passes through the two points, and moves down to the left.

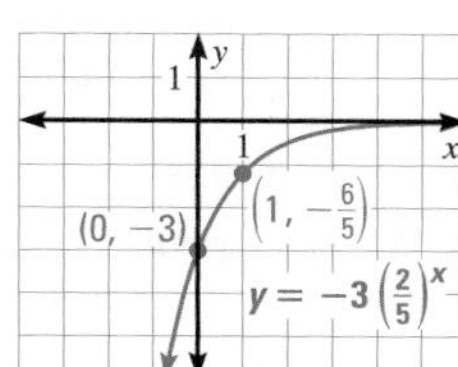

Animated Algebra at classzone.com

✓ GUIDED PRACTICE for Examples 1 and 2

Graph the function. 1–3. See margin.

1. $y = \left(\frac{2}{3}\right)^x$ **2.** $y = -2\left(\frac{3}{4}\right)^x$ **3.** $f(x) = 4\left(\frac{1}{5}\right)^x$

EXAMPLE 3 Graph $y = ab^{x-h} + k$ for $0 < b < 1$

Graph $y = 3\left(\frac{1}{2}\right)^{x+1} - 2$. State the domain and range.

Solution

Begin by sketching the graph of $y = 3\left(\frac{1}{2}\right)^x$, which passes through (0, 3) and $\left(1, \frac{3}{2}\right)$.

Then translate the graph left 1 unit and down 2 units. Notice that the translated graph passes through (−1, 1) and $\left(0, -\frac{1}{2}\right)$.

The graph's asymptote is the line $y = -2$. The domain is all real numbers, and the range is $y > -2$.

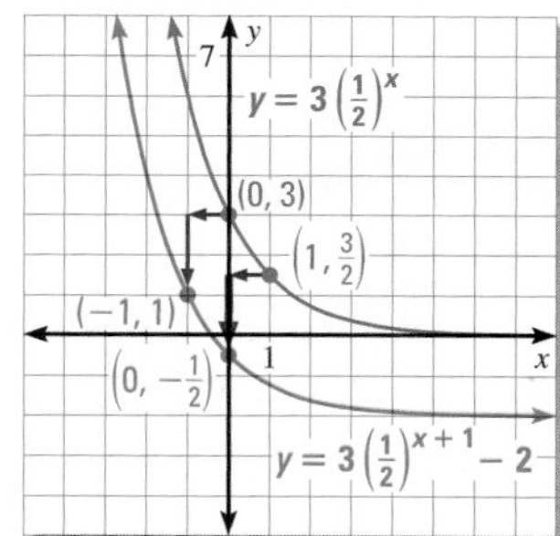

Motivating the Lesson

Your new computer cost $2600. The value of the computer decreases by about 15% each year. You can use an exponential decay function to estimate how much the computer will be worth in two years.

3 TEACH

Extra Example 1

Graph $y = \left(\frac{1}{5}\right)^x$.

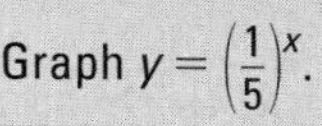

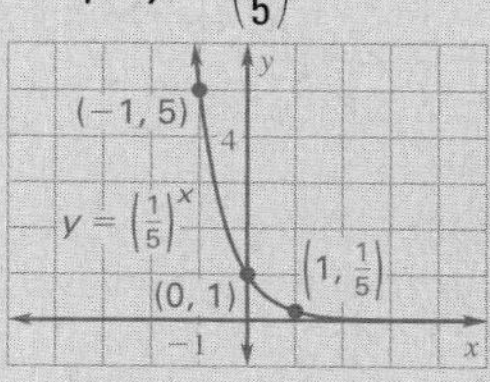

Extra Example 2

Graph the function.

a. $y = 3\left(\frac{2}{3}\right)^x$

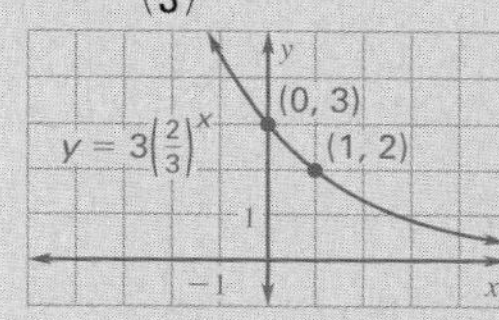

b. $y = -2\left(\frac{3}{4}\right)^x$

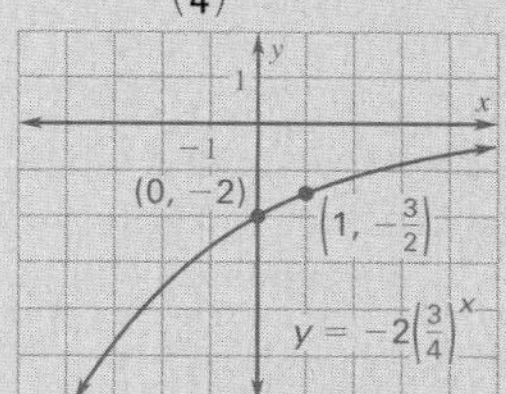

Animated Algebra
classzone.com

An **Animated Algebra** activity is available on-line for **Example 2**. This activity is also available on the **Power Presentations CD-ROM**.

1–3. See Additional Answers beginning on p. AA1.

Differentiated Instruction

Auditory Learners Have students talk with each other about the transformations of the graph of the form $y = ab^x$ that occur in the function in **Example 3** where $b = \frac{1}{2}$. Have students make up their own functions of the form $y = ab^{x-h} + k$ for different a, h, and k, and then have them discuss the transformations with each other.

See also the *Algebra 2 Toolkit* for more strategies.

Extra Example 3

Graph $y = 2\left(\frac{1}{3}\right)^{x-2} + 1$. State the domain and range. **domain: all real numbers; range: $y > 1$**

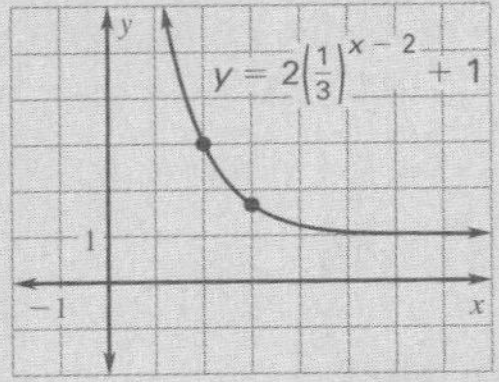

Extra Example 4

A new car costs \$25,000. The value of the car decreases by 15% each year.

- Write an exponential decay model giving the car's value y (in dollars) after t years. Estimate the value after 4 years. **$y = 25{,}000(0.85)^t$; about \$13,050**
- Graph the model.

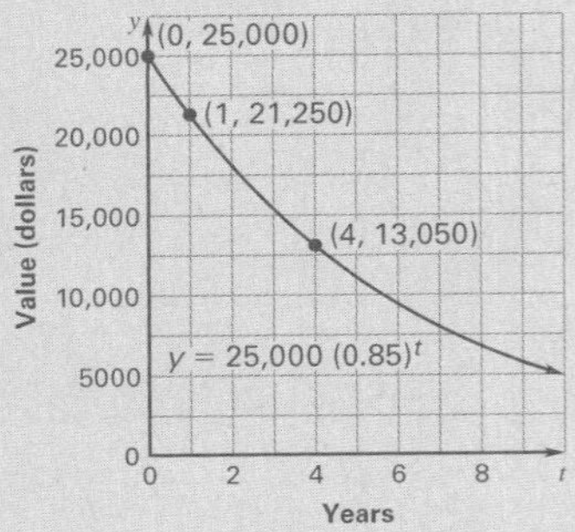

- Use the graph to estimate when the value of the car will be \$8000. **after about 7 yr**

Closing the Lesson

Have students summarize the major points of the lesson and answer the Essential Question: What does the graph of an exponential decay function look like?

- **An exponential decay function is a function of the form $y = ab^x$ with $a > 0$ and $0 < b < 1$.**
- **Exponential decay models describe situations in which a quantity decreases by a fixed percent each time period.**

The graph of an exponential decay function is a curve that falls from left to right and gets less and less steep as x increases. The x-axis or a line parallel to it is a horizontal asymptote of the graph.

EXPONENTIAL DECAY MODELS When a real-life quantity decreases by a fixed percent each year (or other time period), the amount y of the quantity after t years can be modeled by the equation

$$y = a(1 - r)^t$$

where a is the initial amount and r is the percent decrease expressed as a decimal. Note that the quantity $1 - r$ is the decay factor.

EXAMPLE 4 Solve a multi-step problem

SNOWMOBILES A new snowmobile costs \$4200. The value of the snowmobile decreases by 10% each year.

- Write an exponential decay model giving the snowmobile's value y (in dollars) after t years. Estimate the value after 3 years.
- Graph the model.
- Use the graph to estimate when the value of the snowmobile will be \$2500.

Solution

AVOID ERRORS
Notice that the percent decrease, 10%, tells you how much value the snowmobile *loses* each year. The decay factor, 0.90, tells you what fraction of the snowmobile's value *remains* each year.

STEP 1 The initial amount is $a = 4200$ and the percent decrease is $r = 0.10$. So, the exponential decay model is:

$y = a(1 - r)^t$ — **Write exponential decay model.**

$= 4200(1 - 0.10)^t$ — **Substitute 4200 for a and 0.10 for r.**

$= 4200(0.90)^t$ — **Simplify.**

When $t = 3$, the snowmobile's value is $y = 4200(0.90)^3 = \$3061.80$.

STEP 2 The graph passes through the points (0, 4200) and (1, 3780). It has the t-axis as an asymptote. Plot a few other points. Then draw a smooth curve through the points.

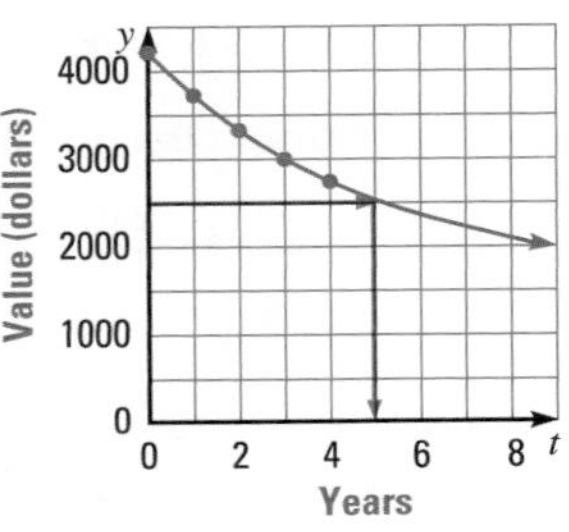

STEP 3 Using the graph, you can estimate that the value of the snowmobile will be \$2500 after about 5 years.

GUIDED PRACTICE for Examples 3 and 4

Graph the function. State the domain and range. **4–6. See margin.**

4. $y = \left(\frac{1}{4}\right)^{x-1} + 1$
5. $y = 5\left(\frac{2}{3}\right)^{x+1} - 2$
6. $g(x) = -3\left(\frac{3}{4}\right)^{x-5} + 4$
7. **WHAT IF?** In Example 4, suppose the value of the snowmobile decreases by 20% each year. Write and graph an equation to model this situation. Use the graph to estimate when the value of the snowmobile will be \$2500. **$y = 4200(0.8)^t$, see margin for art; after about 2 yr.**
8. **SNOWMOBILE** The value of a snowmobile has been decreasing by 7% each year since it was new. After 3 years, the value is \$3000. Find the original cost of the snowmobile. **\$3729.69**

4–6. See Additional Answers beginning on p. AA1.

7.

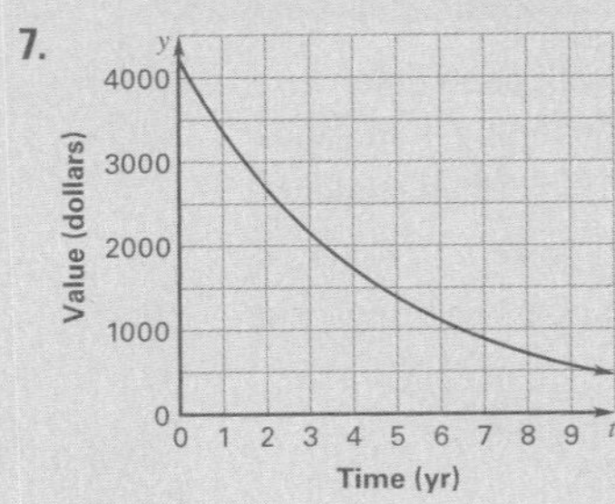

7.2 EXERCISES

HOMEWORK KEY

○ = WORKED-OUT SOLUTIONS on p. WS13 for Exs. 9, 19, and 33

★ = STANDARDIZED TEST PRACTICE Exs. 2, 15, 27, 28, 33, and 35

SKILL PRACTICE

A

1. **VOCABULARY** In the exponential decay model $y = 1250(0.85)^t$, identify the initial amount, the decay factor, and the percent decrease. 1250, 0.85, 15%

2. ★ **WRITING** *Explain* how to tell whether the function $y = b^x$ represents exponential growth or exponential decay. If b is greater than 1, then the function represents exponential growth. If b is greater than 0 and less than 1, the function represents exponential decay.

CLASSIFYING FUNCTIONS **Tell whether the function represents *exponential growth* or *exponential decay*.**

3. $f(x) = 3\left(\frac{3}{4}\right)^x$ exponential decay
4. $f(x) = 4\left(\frac{5}{2}\right)^x$ exponential growth
5. $f(x) = \frac{2}{7} \cdot 4^x$ exponential growth
6. $f(x) = 25(0.25)^x$ exponential decay

EXAMPLES 1 and 2 on pp. 486–487 for Exs. 7–15

GRAPHING FUNCTIONS **Graph the function.** 7–14. See margin.

7. $y = \left(\frac{1}{4}\right)^x$
8. $y = \left(\frac{1}{3}\right)^x$
9. $f(x) = 2\left(\frac{1}{5}\right)^x$
10. $y = -(0.2)^x$
11. $y = -4\left(\frac{1}{3}\right)^x$
12. $g(x) = 2(0.75)^x$
13. $y = \left(\frac{3}{5}\right)^x$
14. $h(x) = -3\left(\frac{3}{8}\right)^x$

15. ★ **MULTIPLE CHOICE** The graph of which function is shown? B

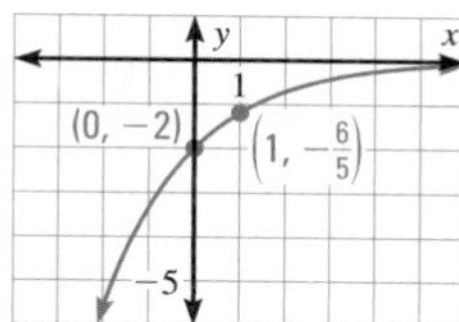

Ⓐ $y = 2\left(-\frac{3}{5}\right)^x$ Ⓑ $y = -2\left(\frac{3}{5}\right)^x$

Ⓒ $y = -2\left(\frac{2}{5}\right)^x$ Ⓓ $y = 2\left(-\frac{2}{5}\right)^x$

EXAMPLE 3 on p. 487 for Exs. 16–25

B

TRANSLATING GRAPHS **Graph the function. State the domain and range.** 16–24. See margin.

16. $y = \left(\frac{1}{3}\right)^x + 1$
17. $y = -\left(\frac{1}{2}\right)^{x-1}$
18. $y = 2\left(\frac{1}{3}\right)^{x+1} - 3$
19. $y = \left(\frac{2}{3}\right)^{x-4} - 1$
20. $y = 3(0.25)^x + 3$
21. $y = \left(\frac{1}{3}\right)^{x-2} + 2$
22. $f(x) = -3\left(\frac{1}{4}\right)^{x-1}$
23. $g(x) = 6\left(\frac{1}{2}\right)^{x+5} - 2$
24. $h(x) = 4\left(\frac{1}{2}\right)^{x+1}$

25. **GRAPHING CALCULATOR** Consider the exponential decay function $y = ab^{x-h} + k$ where $a = 3$, $b = 0.4$, $h = 2$, and $k = -1$. Predict the effect on the function's graph of each change in a, b, h, or k described in parts (a)–(d). Use a graphing calculator to check your prediction.

   a. a changes to 4 b. b changes to 0.2

   c. h changes to 5 d. k changes to 3

...The graph is ...rtical stretch ...factor of $\frac{4}{3}$. ...The graph ...be steeper ...ause the ...ay factor is ...ller. ...The graph ...es 5 units to ...ight instead ...units to the ... .The ...zontal ...nptote moves ...= 3.

26. **ERROR ANALYSIS** You invest $500 in the stock of a company. The value of the stock decreases 2% each year. *Describe* and correct the error in writing a model for the value of the stock after t years. The decay factor is $1 - r$, not r; $y = 500(0.98)^t$.

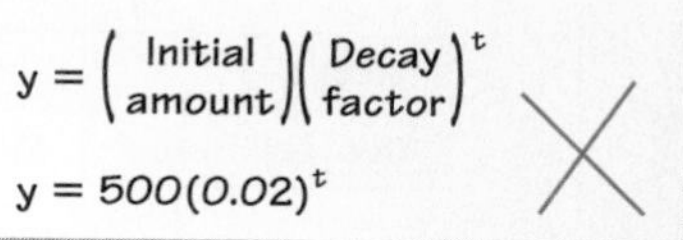

4 PRACTICE AND APPLY

Assignment Guide

Answer Transparencies available for all exercises

Basic:
Day 1: pp. 489–491
Exs. 1–10, 15–19, 30–34, 37–49 odd

Average:
Day 1: pp. 489–491
Exs. 1–6, 9–12, 15, 19–27, 30–35, 38

Advanced:
Day 1: pp. 489–491
Exs. 1, 2, 10–15, 20–36*

Block:
pp. 489–491
Exs. 1–6, 9–12, 15, 19–27, 30–35, 38 (with 7.1)

Differentiated Instruction

See *Algebra 2 Best Practices Toolkit* for suggestions on addressing the needs of a diverse classroom.

Homework Check

For a quick check of student understanding of key concepts, go over the following exercises:

Basic: 8, 10, 16, 18, 30
Average: 9, 12, 20, 22, 30
Advanced: 10, 14, 21, 24, 31

Extra Practice

- Student Edition, p. 1016
- Chapter 7 Resource Book: Practice levels A, B, C, pp. 19–21

Practice Worksheet

An easily-readable reduced practice page (with answers) for this lesson can be found on p. 476C.

7–24. See Additional Answers beginning on p. AA1.

Avoiding Common Errors

Exercises 17–19, 21–24 Some students may think that a horizontal shift in the graph of an exponential function affects the domain. Demonstrate that the domain of all exponential functions and their translations is the set of all real numbers, just as with quadratic functions. Go back to the definition of domain and point out that the value of x can be any real number in any exponential growth or decay function or any translation of these functions. You can use a graphing calculator demonstration to reinforce this idea visually.

Teaching Strategy

Exercises 31–33 Explain the concept of depreciation and how it is used in the business world. Discuss the difference between an item losing the same *dollar amount* of value each year, or "straight-line" depreciation, versus losing the same *percent* of its value each year, which is based on an exponential decay model.

31b.

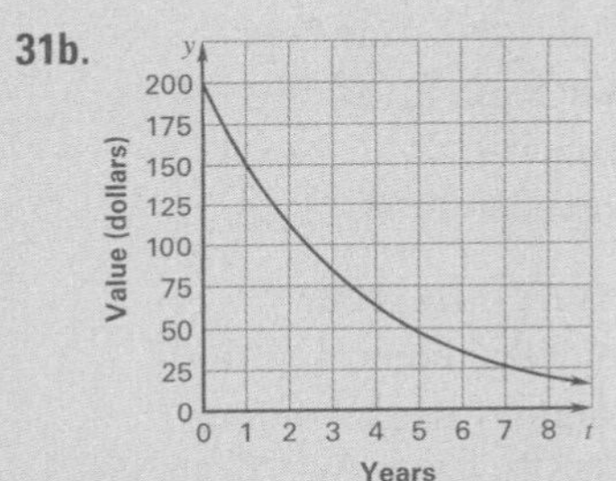

33a.

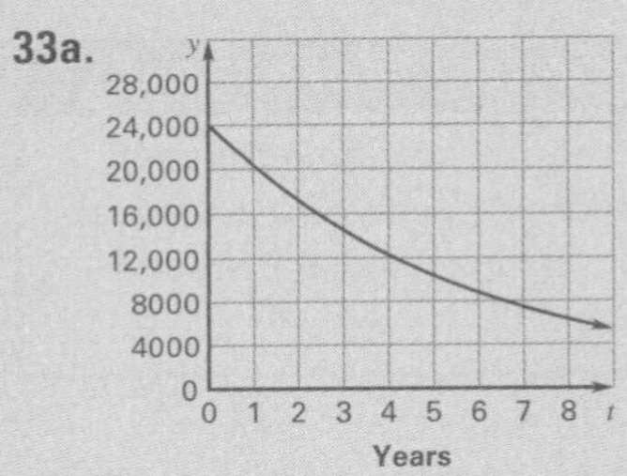

34b.

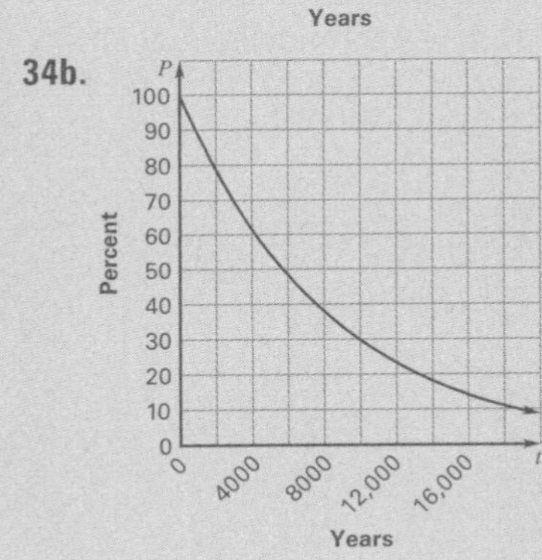

27. ★ **MULTIPLE CHOICE** What is the asymptote of the graph of $y = \left(\frac{1}{2}\right)^{x-2} + 3$? **D**

Ⓐ $y = -3$ Ⓑ $y = -2$ Ⓒ $y = 2$ Ⓓ $y = 3$

C

28. ★ **OPEN-ENDED MATH** Write an exponential function whose graph lies between the graphs of $y = (0.5)^x$ and $y = (0.25)^x + 3$. ***Sample answer:*** $(0.3)^x + 1$

29. **CHALLENGE** Do $f(x) = 5(4)^{-x}$ and $g(x) = 5(0.25)^x$ represent the same function? *Justify* your answer. **Yes;** $5(4)^{-x} = 5\left(\frac{1}{4}\right)^x$ **and 0.25 is the decimal equivalent to** $\frac{1}{4}$.

PROBLEM SOLVING

EXAMPLE 4 A on p. 488 for Exs. 30–31

30. **MEDICINE** When a person takes a dosage of I milligrams of ibuprofen, the amount A (in milligrams) of medication remaining in the person's bloodstream after t hours can be modeled by the equation $A = I(0.71)^t$.

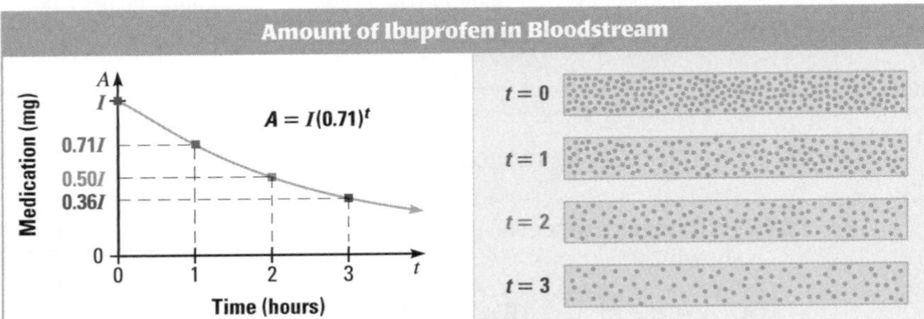

Find the amount of ibuprofen remaining in a person's bloodstream for the given dosage and elapsed time since the medication was taken.

a. Dosage: 200 mg
Time: 1.5 hours

b. Dosage: 325 mg
Time: 3.5 hours

c. Dosage: 400 mg
Time: 5 hours

30a. about 119.65 mg
30b. about 98.01 mg
30c. about 72.17 mg

@HomeTutor for problem solving help at classzone.com

31. **BIKE COSTS** You buy a new mountain bike for \$200. The value of the bike decreases by 25% each year.

a. Write a model giving the mountain bike's value y (in dollars) after t years. Use the model to estimate the value of the bike after 3 years. $y = 200(0.75)^t$**; about \$84.3**

b. Graph the model. **See margin.**

c. Estimate when the value of the bike will be \$100. **after about 2.5 yr**

@HomeTutor for problem solving help at classzone.com

32. **DEPRECIATION** The table shows the amount d that a boat depreciates during each year t since it was new. Show that the ratio of depreciation amounts for consecutive years is constant. Then write an equation that gives d as a function of t. $\frac{1832}{1906} \approx 0.96$; $\frac{1762}{1832} \approx 0.96$; $\frac{1692}{1762} \approx 0.96$; $\frac{1627}{1692} \approx 0.96$; $d = 1985(0.96)^t$

Year, t	1	2	3	4	5
Depreciation, d	\$1906	\$1832	\$1762	\$1692	\$1627

○ = WORKED-OUT SOLUTIONS on p. WS1 ★ = STANDARDIZED TEST PRACTICE

35b.

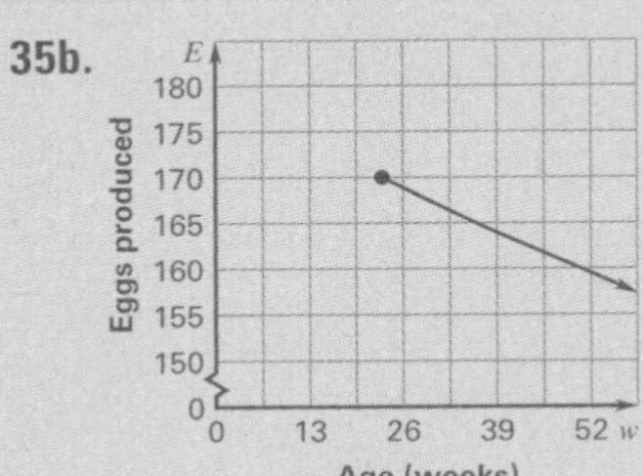

33. ★ **SHORT RESPONSE** The value of a car can be modeled by the equation $y = 24{,}000(0.845)^t$ where t is the number of years since the car was purchased.

a. Graph the model. Estimate when the value of the car will be \$10,000. **See margin for art; after 5 yr.**

b. Use the model to predict the value of the car after 50 years. Is this a reasonable value? *Explain.* **\$5.29; no. *Sample answer:* A car does not normally last 50 years.**

B 34. **MULTI-STEP PROBLEM** When a plant or animal dies, it stops acquiring carbon-14 from the atmosphere. Carbon-14 decays over time with a half-life of about 5730 years. The percent P of the original amount of carbon-14 that remains in a sample after t years is given by this equation:

$$P = 100\left(\frac{1}{2}\right)^{t/5730}$$

a. What percent of the original carbon-14 remains in a sample after 2500 years? 5000 years? 10,000 years? **about 73.9%; about 54.6%; about 29.8%**

b. Graph the model. **See margin.**

c. An archaeologist found a bison bone that contained about 37% of the carbon-14 present when the bison died. Use the graph to estimate the age of the bone when it was found. **about 8000 yr**

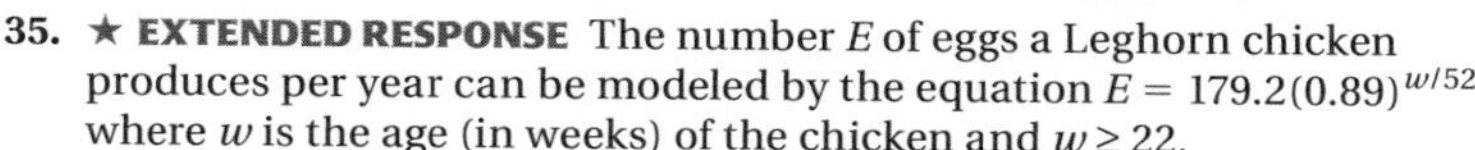

35. ★ **EXTENDED RESPONSE** The number E of eggs a Leghorn chicken produces per year can be modeled by the equation $E = 179.2(0.89)^{w/52}$ where w is the age (in weeks) of the chicken and $w \geq 22$.

a. **Interpret** Identify the decay factor and the percent decrease. **0.89, 11%**

b. **Graph** Graph the model. **See margin.**

c. **Estimate** Estimate the egg production of a chicken that is 2.5 years old. **about 134 eggs per yr**

d. **Reasoning** *Explain* how you can rewrite the given equation so that time is measured in years rather than in weeks. **Change the exponent to just w.**

C 36. **CHALLENGE** You buy a new stereo for \$1300 and are able to sell it 4 years later for \$275. Assume that the resale value of the stereo decays exponentially with time. Write an equation giving the stereo's resale value V (in dollars) as a function of the time t (in years) since you bought it. **$V = 1300(0.678)^t$**

KENTUCKY MIXED REVIEW

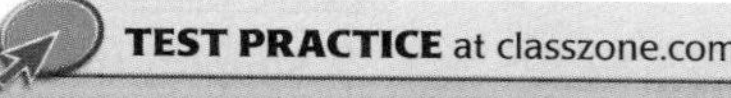

37. If $\triangle PQR$ is translated to the left 3 units and down 2 units, in which quadrant will the image of point Q appear? **C**

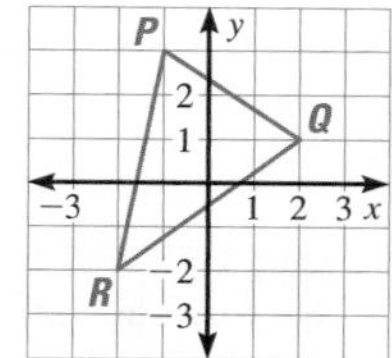

Ⓐ Quadrant I Ⓑ Quadrant II
Ⓒ Quadrant III Ⓓ Quadrant IV

38. This year's price for a certain laptop computer is 16.7% lower than last year's price of \$960. Approximately what percent of this year's price for the computer is last year's price? **D**

Ⓐ 83.3% Ⓑ 85.0% Ⓒ 116.7% Ⓓ 120.0%

5 ASSESS AND RETEACH

Daily Homework Quiz

Transparency Available

1. Graph $y = 4\left(\frac{1}{2}\right)^x$. State the domain and range.

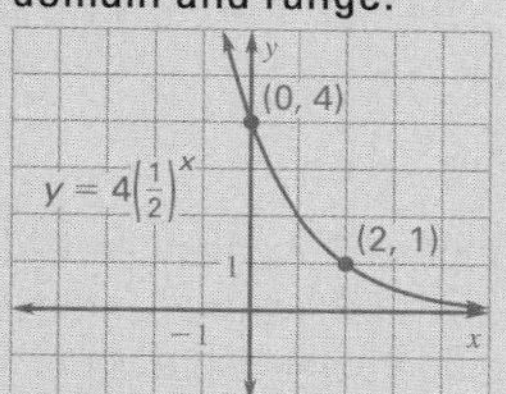

domain: all real numbers; range: $y > 0$

2. Graph $y = 3\left(\frac{1}{4}\right)^{x+2} + 2$. State the domain and range.

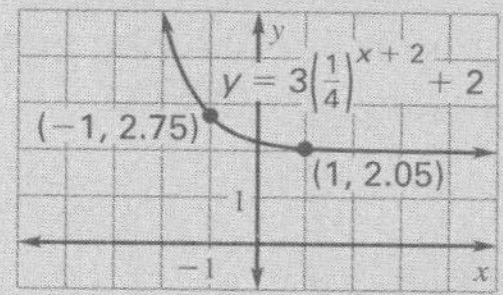

domain: all real numbers; range: $y > 2$

3. A new laptop computer costs \$1500. The value of the computer decreases by 22% each year.

a. Estimate the value of the computer after 2 years. **about \$913**

b. Estimate when the computer will be worth \$550. **after about 4 yr**

Available at **classzone.com**

Diagnosis/Remediation

- Practice A, B, C in Chapter 7 Resource Book, pp. 19–21
- Study Guide in Chapter 7 Resource Book, pp. 22–23
- Practice Workbook, pp. 110–111
- @HomeTutor

Challenge

Additional challenge is available in the Chapter 7 Resource Book, p. 26.

1 PLAN AND PREPARE

Warm-Up Exercises

Transparency Available

Simplify the expression.

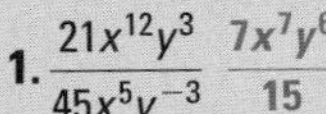

1. $\dfrac{21x^{12}y^3}{45x^5y^{-3}}$ $\dfrac{7x^7y^6}{15}$
2. $(-2a^3b^2)^4$ $16a^{12}b^8$
3. $\sqrt[3]{64r^9s^6t^3}$ $4r^3s^2t$
4. An account with a balance of \$1000 pays 3.65% annual interest, compounded daily. What is the balance at the end of 1 year if no money is added to the principal? **\$1037.17**

Notetaking Guide

Transparency Available

Promotes interactive learning and notetaking skills, pp. 192–194.

Pacing

Basic: 1 day
Average: 1 day
Advanced: 1 day
Block: 0.5 block with 7.4
- See *Teaching Guide/Lesson Plan.*

2 FOCUS AND MOTIVATE

Essential Question

Big Idea 1, p. 477

When is the natural base *e* useful? **Tell students they will learn how to answer this question by studying exponential functions related to continuous change.**

7.3 Use Functions Involving *e*

MA-HS-5.1.4 Students will recognize and solve problems that can be modeled using an exponential function, such as compound interest problems.

Before You studied exponential growth and decay functions.
Now You will study functions involving the natural base *e*.
Why? So you can model visibility underwater, as in Ex. 59.

Key Vocabulary
- natural base *e*

The history of mathematics is marked by the discovery of special numbers such as π and *i*. Another special number is denoted by the letter *e*. The number is called the **natural base *e*** or the *Euler number* after its discoverer, Leonhard Euler (1707–1783). The expression $\left(1+\frac{1}{n}\right)^n$ approaches *e* as *n* increases.

n	10^1	10^2	10^3	10^4	10^5	10^6
$\left(1+\frac{1}{n}\right)^n$	2.59374	2.70481	2.71692	2.71815	2.71827	2.71828

KEY CONCEPT *For Your Notebook*

The Natural Base *e*

The natural base *e* is irrational. It is defined as follows:

As n approaches $+\infty$, $\left(1+\frac{1}{n}\right)^n$ approaches $e \approx 2.718281828$.

EXAMPLE 1 Simplify natural base expressions

Simplify the expression.

REVIEW EXPONENTS
For help with properties of exponents, see p. 330.

a. $e^2 \cdot e^5 = e^{2+5}$
$= e^7$

b. $\dfrac{12e^4}{3e^3} = 4e^{4-3}$
$= 4e$

c. $(5e^{-3x})^2 = 5^2(e^{-3x})^2$
$= 25e^{-6x} = \dfrac{25}{e^{6x}}$

EXAMPLE 2 Evaluate natural base expressions

Use a calculator to evaluate the expression.

	Expression	Keystrokes	Display
a.	e^4	2nd [e^x] 4) ENTER	54.59815003
b.	$e^{-0.09}$	2nd [e^x] (–) .09) ENTER	0.9139311853

Resource Planning Guide

Chapter Resource Book
- Teaching Guide/Lesson Plan (pp. 27–28)
- Practice levels A, B, C (pp. 30–32)
- Study Guide (pp. 33–34)
- Catch-up for Absent Students (p. 35)
- Application (p. 36)
- Challenge (p. 37)

Workbooks
- Notetaking Guide (pp. 192–194)
- Practice Workbook (pp. 112–113)

Teaching Options
- **Power Presentations CD-ROM** provides dynamic electronic teaching resources for the classroom.
- **Activity Generator CD-ROM** provides editable activities for all ability levels.

Interactive Technology
- Easy Planner
- Power Presentations CD-ROM
- Activity Generator CD-ROM
- Animated Algebra
- Test Generator CD-ROM
- Online Quiz
- eWorkbook
- eEdition
- @HomeTutor

Resources for English Learners
- Quick Reference for English Learners
- Spanish Study Guide
- Multi-Language Visual Glossary
- Student Resources in Spanish

See also the *Algebra 2 Toolkit* for more strategies for meeting individual needs.

✓ **GUIDED PRACTICE** for Examples 1 and 2

Simplify the expression.

1. $e^7 \cdot e^4$ e^{11}
2. $2e^{-3} \cdot 6e^5$ $12e^2$
3. $\frac{24e^8}{4e^5}$ $6e^3$
4. $(10e^{-4x})^3$ $\frac{1000}{e^{12x}}$
5. Use a calculator to evaluate $e^{3/4}$. about 2.117

KEY CONCEPT — *For Your Notebook*

Natural Base Functions

A function of the form $y = ae^{rx}$ is called a *natural base exponential function.*

- If $a > 0$ and $r > 0$, the function is an exponential growth function.
- If $a > 0$ and $r < 0$, the function is an exponential decay function.

The graphs of the basic functions $y = e^x$ and $y = e^{-x}$ are shown below.

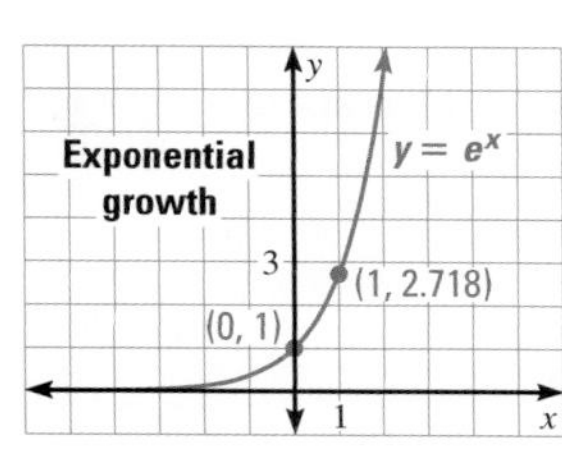

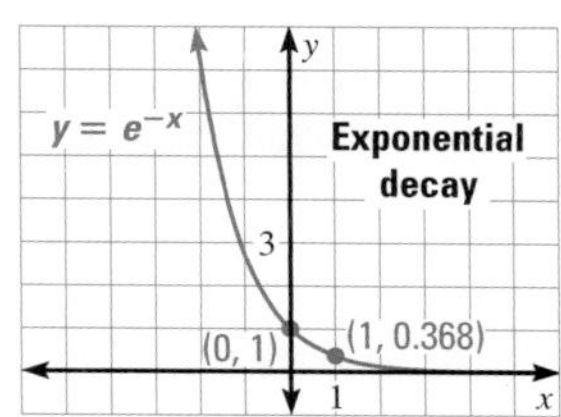

EXAMPLE 3 Graph natural base functions

Graph the function. State the domain and range.

a. $y = 3e^{0.25x}$

b. $y = e^{-0.75(x-2)} + 1$

Solution

ANOTHER WAY
You can also write the function from part (a) in the form $y = ab^x$ in order to graph it:
$y = 3e^{0.25x}$
$y = 3(e^{0.25})^x$
$y \approx 3(1.28)^x$

a. Because $a = 3$ is positive and $r = 0.25$ is positive, the function is an exponential growth function. Plot the points (0, 3) and (1, 3.85) and draw the curve.

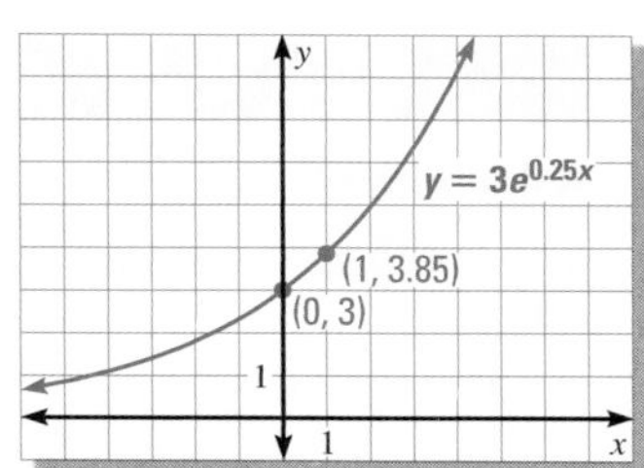

The domain is all real numbers, and the range is $y > 0$.

b. $a = 1$ is positive and $r = -0.75$ is negative, so the function is an exponential decay function. Translate the graph of $y = e^{-0.75x}$ right 2 units and up 1 unit.

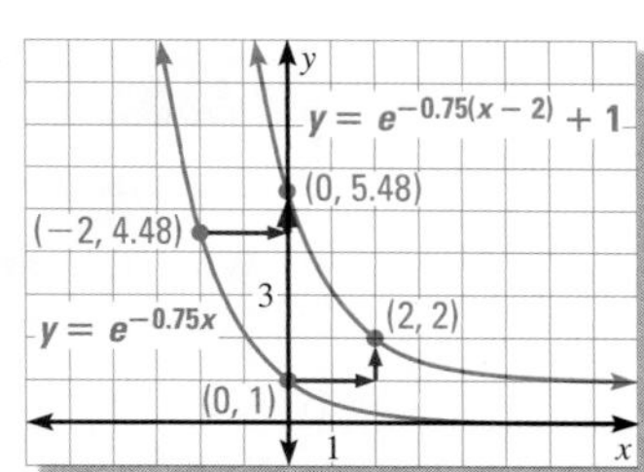

The domain is all real numbers, and the range is $y > 1$.

Motivating the Lesson

You and your parents are saving money for your education in an account. You can use a formula with the natural base *e* to estimate how much money will be in your account when the money is needed.

3 TEACH

Extra Example 1

Simplify the expression.

a. $e^9 \cdot e^6$ e^{15}

b. $\frac{60e^8}{12e^3}$ $5e^5$

c. $(-10e^{-5x})^3$ $\frac{-1000}{e^{15x}}$

Extra Example 2

Use a calculator to evaluate the expression.

a. e^6 403.429

b. $e^{-0.28}$ 0.756

Extra Example 3

Graph the function. State the domain and range.

a. $y = 4e^{0.5x}$ domain: all real numbers; range: $y > 0$

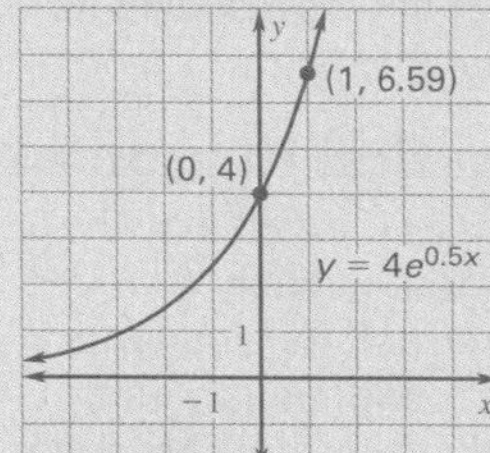

b. $y = e^{-1.5(x+2)} - 4$ domain: all real numbers; range: $y > -4$

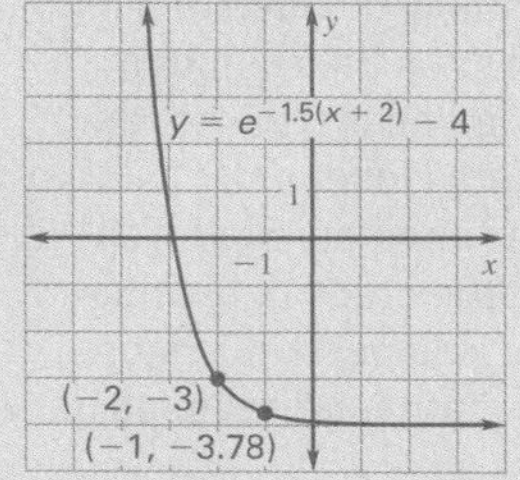

Differentiated Instruction

Advanced Encourage students to do Internet and/or library research on the history and significance of the number *e*. You could ask these students to work individually or in a small group and to either write reports on their findings or do a presentation for their classmates. Either a written report or oral presentation should include graphics.

See also the *Algebra 2 Toolkit* for more strategies.

Extra Example 4

Annual sales of a certain product can be modeled by the function $S = 60{,}000e^{-0.15t}$, where S is the number of units sold and t is the number of years since the product went on the market.

- Graph the model.

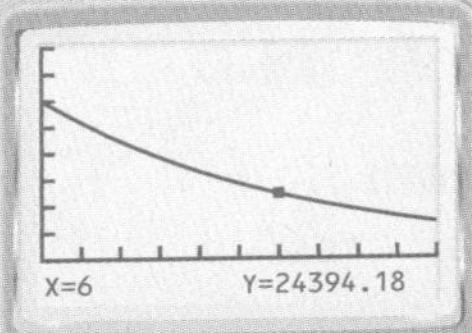

- Use the graph to estimate the annual sales 6 years after the product went on the market. **about 24,400 units**

Avoiding Common Errors

When students see the equation $y = ae^{rx}$ that defines the natural base exponential function in the Key Concept box on page 493, they may think that e is a variable because they are used to letters representing variables and because there are several other variables in the equation. Make sure that they understand that e is in fact a constant—a specific irrational number like π.

Mathematical Reasoning

Students may be puzzled by the concept of continuously compounded interest. Ask students if the result of continuously compounding of interest will be much different from daily compounding. Use this as an opportunity to discuss informally the idea of a limiting process: As the frequency of compounding increases, the process gets closer and closer to continuous compounding. Tell students that the study of limiting processes is important in more advanced mathematics, especially calculus.

EXAMPLE 4 Solve a multi-step problem

BIOLOGY The length ℓ (in centimeters) of a tiger shark can be modeled by the function

$$\ell = 337 - 276e^{-0.178t}$$

where t is the shark's age (in years).

- Graph the model.
- Use the graph to estimate the length of a tiger shark that is 3 years old.

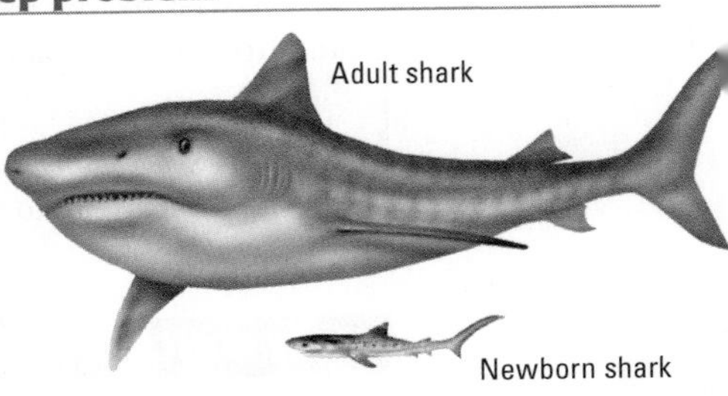

INTERPRET VARIABLES

On a graphing calculator, enter the function $\ell = 337 - 276e^{-0.178t}$ using the variables x and y, as shown below: $y = 337 - 276e^{-0.178x}$

Solution

STEP 1 **Graph** the model, as shown.

STEP 2 **Use** the *trace* feature to determine that $\ell \approx 175$ when $t = 3$.

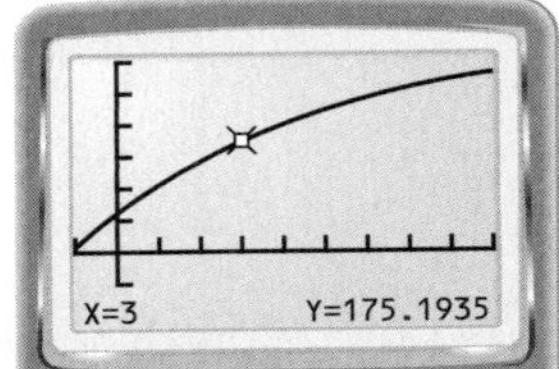

▶ The length of a 3-year-old tiger shark is about 175 centimeters.

✓ GUIDED PRACTICE for Examples 3 and 4

Graph the function. State the domain and range. 6–8. See margin.

6. $y = 2e^{0.5x}$
7. $f(x) = \frac{1}{2}e^{-x} + 1$
8. $y = 1.5e^{0.25(x-1)} - 2$
9. **WHAT IF?** In Example 4, use the given function to estimate the length of a tiger shark that is 5 years old. **about 224 cm**

CONTINUOUSLY COMPOUNDED INTEREST In Lesson 7.1, you learned that the balance of an account earning compound interest is given by this formula:

$$A = P\left(1 + \frac{r}{n}\right)^{nt}$$

As the frequency n of compounding approaches positive infinity, the compound interest formula approximates the following formula.

KEY CONCEPT — *For Your Notebook*

Continuously Compounded Interest

When interest is compounded *continuously*, the amount A in an account after t years is given by the formula

$$A = Pe^{rt}$$

where P is the principal and r is the annual interest rate expressed as a decimal.

6.
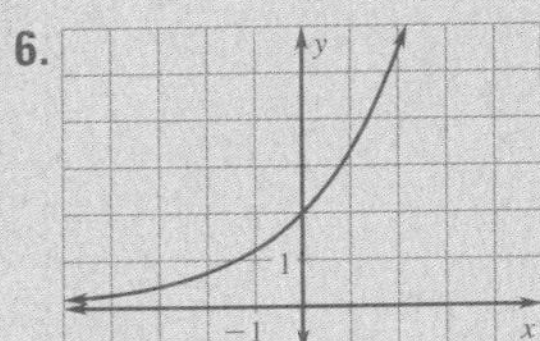

domain: all real numbers, range: $y > 0$

7.
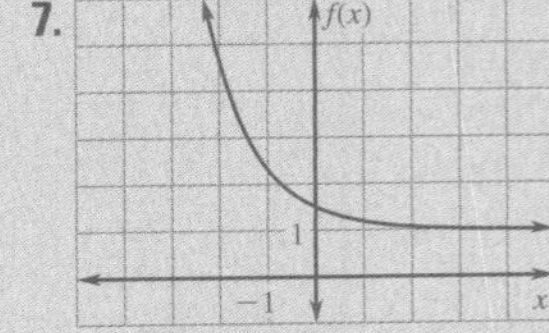

domain: all real numbers, range: $y > 1$

8.
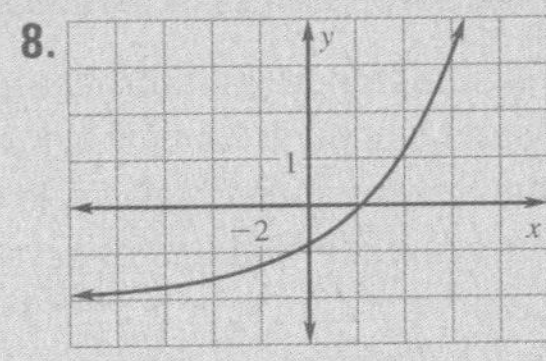

domain: all real numbers, range: $y > -2$

EXAMPLE 5 Model continuously compounded interest

FINANCE You deposit \$4000 in an account that pays 6% annual interest compounded continuously. What is the balance after 1 year?

Solution

Use the formula for continuously compounded interest.

$A = Pe^{rt}$	Write formula.
$= 4000e^{0.06(1)}$	Substitute 4000 for P, 0.06 for r, and 1 for t.
≈ 4247.35	Use a calculator.

▶ The balance at the end of 1 year is \$4247.35.

✓ GUIDED PRACTICE for Example 5

10. **FINANCE** You deposit \$2500 in an account that pays 5% annual interest compounded continuously. Find the balance after each amount of time.

    a. 2 years \$2762.93 b. 5 years \$3210.06 c. 7.5 years \$3637.48

11. **FINANCE** Find the amount of interest earned in parts (a)–(c) of Exercise 10. \$262.93; \$710.06; \$1137.48

7.3 EXERCISES

HOMEWORK KEY

○ = **WORKED-OUT SOLUTIONS** on p. WS13 for Exs. 5, 35, and 57

★ = **STANDARDIZED TEST PRACTICE** Exs. 2, 15, 16, 52, 53, and 60

SKILL PRACTICE

1. **VOCABULARY** Copy and complete: The number __?__ is an irrational number approximately equal to 2.71828. *e*

2. ★ **WRITING** Tell whether the function $f(x) = \frac{1}{3}e^{4x}$ is an example of *exponential growth* or *exponential decay. Explain.* Exponential growth; the exponent is $4x$ and 4 is greater than 0, so the function is an exponential growth function.

XAMPLE 1
p. 492
Exs. 3–18

SIMPLIFYING EXPRESSIONS Simplify the expression.

3. $e^3 \cdot e^4$ e^7
4. $e^{-2} \cdot e^6$ e^4
5. $(2e^{3x})^3$ $8e^{9x}$
6. $(2e^{-2})^{-4}$ $\frac{e^8}{16}$
7. $(3e^{5x})^{-1}$ $\frac{1}{3e^{5x}}$
8. $e^x \cdot e^{-3x} \cdot e^4$ e^{-2x+4}
9. $\sqrt{9e^6}$ $3e^3$
10. $e^x \cdot 5e^{x+3}$ $5e^{2x+3}$
11. $\frac{3e}{e^x}$ $3e^{1-x}$
12. $\frac{4e^x}{e^{4x}}$ $\frac{4}{e^{3x}}$
13. $\sqrt[3]{8e^{9x}}$ $2e^{3x}$
14. $\frac{6e^{4x}}{8e}$ $\frac{3e^{4x-1}}{4}$

15. ★ **MULTIPLE CHOICE** What is the simplified form of $(4e^{2x})^3$? C

    Ⓐ $4e^{6x}$ Ⓑ $4e^{8x}$ Ⓒ $64e^{6x}$ Ⓓ $64e^{8x}$

16. ★ **MULTIPLE CHOICE** What is the simplified form of $\sqrt{\frac{4(27e^{13}x)}{3e^7x^{-3}}}$? D

    Ⓐ $6e^{10}x$ Ⓑ $6e^6x^4$ Ⓒ $\frac{6e^3}{x^2}$ Ⓓ $6e^3x^2$

Extra Example 5

You deposit \$3000 in an account that pays 3.5% annual interest compounded continuously. What is the balance after 3 years? \$3332.13

Key Question to Ask for Example 5

- What formula could you use to calculate just the amount of interest earned on an account in which interest is compounded continuously? $I = Pe^{rt} - P$

Closing the Lesson

Have students summarize the major points of the lesson and answer the Essential Question: When is the natural base *e* useful?

- As n approaches $+\infty$, $\left(1 + \frac{1}{n}\right)^n$ approaches the irrational number e, which is approximately 2.718.
- The formula for the amount A in an account when interest is compounded continuously is $A = Pe^{rt}$, where P is the principal, r is the annual interest rate expressed as a decimal, and t is the time in years.

The natural base *e* is a special irrational number. This base is used in many applications of exponential functions, including continuously increasing or decreasing biological phenomena and continuously compounded interest.

4 PRACTICE AND APPLY

Assignment Guide

Answer Transparencies available for all exercises

Basic:
Day 1: EP p. 1015 Exs. 12–15
pp. 495–498
Exs. 1–8, 15–22, 31–35 odd, 39–44, 55–59, 63

Average:
Day 1: pp. 495–498
Exs. 1, 2, 7–11, 15–18, 23–26, 34–36, 39–45, 51–53, 55–61, 64

Advanced:
Day 1: pp. 495–498
Exs. 1, 2, 11–16, 27–30, 36–38, 44–62*

Block:
pp. 495–498
Exs. 1, 2, 7–11, 15–18, 23–26, 34–36, 39–45, 51–53, 55–61, 64 (with 7.4)

Differentiated Instruction

See *Algebra 2 Best Practices Toolkit* for suggestions on addressing the needs of a diverse classroom.

Homework Check

For a quick check of student understanding of key concepts, go over the following exercises:

Basic: 6, 20, 42, 55, 57
Average: 10, 24, 45, 56, 57
Advanced: 14, 28, 48, 56, 58

Extra Practice

- Student Edition, p. 1016
- Chapter 7 Resource Book: Practice levels A, B, C, pp. 30–32

Practice Worksheet

An easily-readable reduced practice page (with answers) for this lesson can be found on p. 476C.

ERROR ANALYSIS *Describe* and correct the error in simplifying the expression.

17. $(3e^{5x})^2 = 3e^{(5x)(2)}$
$= 3e^{10x}$

The 3 should be raised to the second power also; $(3e^{5x})^2 = 3^2e^{(5x)(2)} = 9e^{10x}$.

18. $\frac{e^{6x}}{e^{-2x}} = e^{6x-2x}$
$= e^{4x}$

$-2x$ should be subtracted; $e^{6x-(-2x)} = e^{8x}$.

EXAMPLE 2 on p. 492 for Exs. 19–30

EVALUATING EXPRESSIONS Use a calculator to evaluate the expression.

19. e^3 about 20.086
20. $e^{-3/4}$ about 0.472
21. $e^{2.2}$ about 9.025
22. $e^{1/2}$ about 1.649
23. $e^{-2/5}$ about 0.670
24. $e^{4.3}$ about 73.700
25. e^7 about 1096.633
26. e^{-4} about 0.018
27. $2e^{-0.3}$ about 1.482
28. $5e^{2/3}$ about 9.739
29. $-6e^{2.4}$ about -66.139
30. $0.4e^{4.1}$ about 24.136

GROWTH OR DECAY Tell whether the function is an example of *exponential growth* or *exponential decay.*

31. $f(x) = 3e^{-x}$ exponential decay
32. $f(x) = \frac{1}{3}e^{4x}$ exponential growth
33. $f(x) = e^{-4x}$ exponential decay
34. $f(x) = \frac{3}{5}e^{x}$ exponential growth
35. $f(x) = \frac{1}{4}e^{-5x}$ exponential decay
36. $f(x) = e^{3x}$ exponential growth
37. $f(x) = 2e^{4x}$ exponential growth
38. $f(x) = 4e^{-2x}$ exponential decay

EXAMPLE 3 on p. 493 for Exs. 39–50

MATCHING GRAPHS Match the function with its graph.

39. $y = 0.5e^{0.5x}$ B
40. $y = 2e^{0.5x}$ C
41. $y = e^{0.5x} + 2$ A

A.

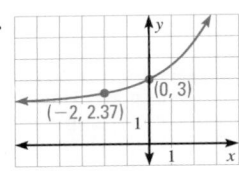

B.
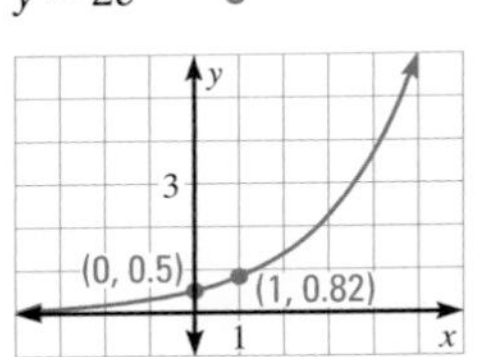

C.
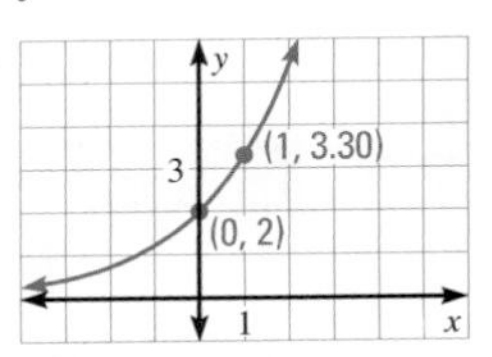

GRAPHING FUNCTIONS Graph the function. State the domain and range. 42–50. See margin.

42. $y = e^{-2x}$
43. $y = 3e^{x}$
44. $y = 0.5e^{x}$
45. $y = 2e^{-3x} - 1$
46. $y = 2.5e^{-0.5x} + 2$
47. $y = 0.6e^{x-2}$
48. $f(x) = \frac{1}{2}e^{x+3} - 2$
49. $g(x) = \frac{4}{3}e^{x-1} + 1$
50. $h(x) = e^{-2(x+1)} - 3$

51. **GRAPHING CALCULATOR** Use the *table* feature of a graphing calculator to find the value of n for which $\left(1 + \frac{1}{n}\right)^n$ gives the value of e correct to 9 decimal places. *Explain* the process you used to find your answer.

51. 10,000,000,000. *Sample answer:* Since small values of n were increasing the function very slowly, I checked larger intervals. I noticed that every power of 10 gave an answer one digit closer to the actual value of e.

52. ★ **SHORT RESPONSE** Can e be expressed as a ratio of two integers? *Explain* your reasoning. No; e is an irrational number which is defined to be a number that cannot be expressed as a ratio of 2 integers.

53. ★ **OPEN-ENDED MATH** Find values of a, b, r, and q such that $f(x) = ae^{rx}$ and $g(x) = be^{qx}$ are exponential *decay* functions and $\frac{f(x)}{g(x)}$ is an exponential *growth* function. *Sample answer:* $f(x) = \frac{1}{2}e^{-3x}$, $g(x) = \frac{2}{3}e^{-5x}$

C 54. **CHALLENGE** *Explain* why $A = P\left(1 + \frac{r}{n}\right)^{nt}$ approximates $A = Pe^{rt}$ as n approaches positive infinity. (*Hint:* Let $m = \frac{n}{r}$.) See margin.

○ = WORKED-OUT SOLUTIONS on p. WS1 ★ = STANDARDIZED TEST PRACTICE

42–50. See Additional Answers beginning on p. AA1.

54. Let $m = \frac{n}{r}$, so $n = mr$ and $\frac{r}{n} = \frac{1}{m}$. Substituting into $A = P\left(1 + \frac{r}{n}\right)^{nt}$ gives $A = P\left(1 + \frac{1}{m}\right)^{mrt}$ which can be written as $A = P\left(\left(1 + \frac{1}{m}\right)^m\right)^{rt}$. By definition, $\left(1 + \frac{1}{m}\right)^m$ approaches e as m approaches $\pm\infty$. Thus the equation becomes $A = Pe^{rt}$.

PROBLEM SOLVING

XAMPLE 4 A
n p. 494
or Exs. 55–56

55. CAMERA PHONES The number of camera phones shipped globally can be modeled by the function $y = 1.28e^{1.31x}$ where x is the number of years since 1997 and y is the number of camera phones shipped (in millions). How many camera phones were shipped in 2002? **about 895 million camera phones**

@HomeTutor for problem solving help at classzone.com

56. BIOLOGY Scientists used traps to study the Formosan subterranean termite population in New Orleans. The mean number y of termites collected annually can be modeled by $y = 738e^{0.345t}$ where t is the number of years since 1989. What was the mean number of termites collected in 1999? **about 23,247 termites**

@HomeTutor for problem solving help at classzone.com

XAMPLE 5
n p. 495
or Exs. 57–58

57. FINANCE You deposit \$2000 in an account that pays 4% annual interest compounded continuously. What is the balance after 5 years? **\$2442.81**

58. FINANCE You deposit \$800 in an account that pays 2.65% annual interest compounded continuously. What is the balance after 12.5 years? **\$1114.17**

B

59. MULTI-STEP PROBLEM The percent L of surface light that filters down through bodies of water can be modeled by the exponential function $L(x) = 100e^{kx}$ where k is a measure of the murkiness of the water and x is the depth below the surface (in meters).

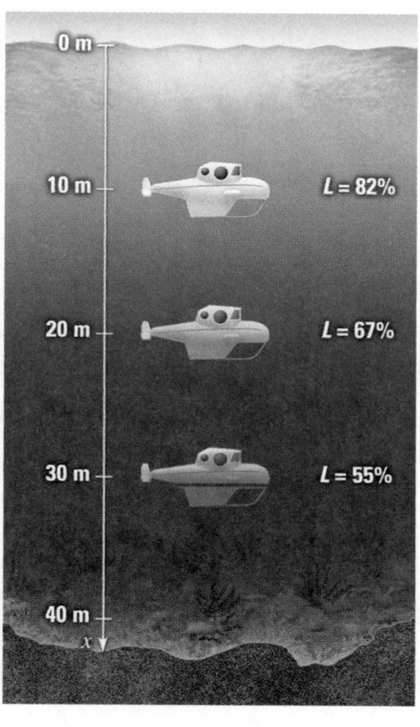

a. A recreational submersible is traveling in clear water with a k-value of about -0.02. Write and graph an equation giving the percent of surface light that filters down through clear water as a function of depth. $L(x) = 100e^{-0.02x}$, **see margin for art.**

b. Use your graph to estimate the percent of surface light available at a depth of 40 meters. **about 45%**

c. Use your graph to estimate how deep the submersible can descend in clear water before only 50% of surface light is available. **about 35 m**

60. ★ EXTENDED RESPONSE The growth of the bacteria *mycobacterium tuberculosis* can be modeled by the function $P(t) = P_0e^{0.116t}$ where $P(t)$ is the population after t hours and P_0 is the population when $t = 0$.

a. **Model** At 1:00 P.M., there are 30 *mycobacterium tuberculosis* bacteria in a sample. Write a function for the number of bacteria after 1:00 P.M. $P(t) = 30e^{0.116t}$

b. **Graph** Graph the function from part (a). **See margin.**

c. **Estimate** What is the population at 5:00 P.M.? **about 48 bacteria**

d. **Reasoning** *Describe* how to find the population at 3:45 P.M. **Let $t = 2.75$ and evaluate $P(2.75)$.**

Internet Reference

Exercise 62 For more information about the Gateway Arch, visit the National Park Service's website at www.nps.gov/jeff/arch.html

Graphing Calculator

Exercises 42–50 Use a graphing calculator demonstration or guide students in a calculator investigation to help them see both graphically and numerically that the domain of all exponential functions is the set of all real numbers, and that the range is directly related to the equation of the horizontal asymptote. Use the *table* feature to show that the *y*-values get closer and closer to a fixed value, but never get there, either as *x* decreases or increases, depending on whether you are looking at an increasing or decreasing function.

59a.

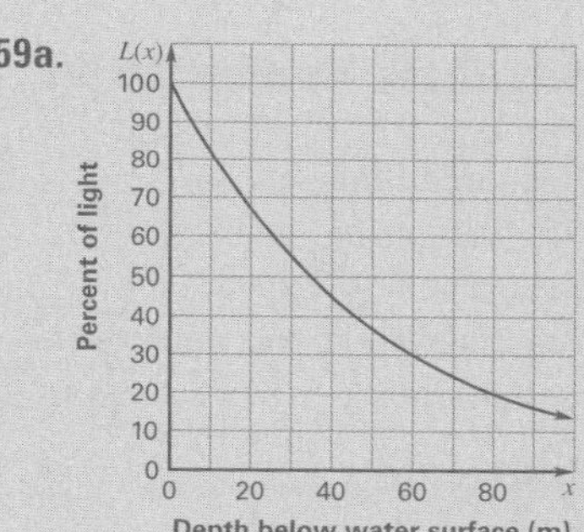

60b.

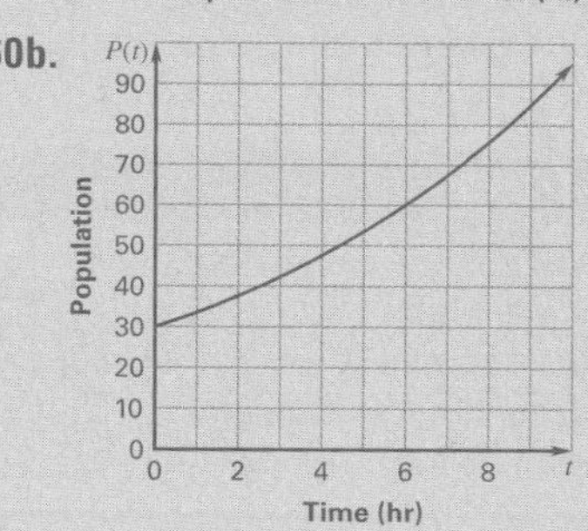

5 ASSESS AND RETEACH

Daily Homework Quiz

Transparency Available

1. Simplify $(e^x \cdot e^{-3x})^2$. $\frac{1}{e^{4x}}$
2. Use a calculator to evaluate $e^{-0.35}$. (Round to three decimal places.) 0.705
3. State the domain and range of the function $y = 2e^{0.3(x-5)} + 3$. domain: all real numbers; range: $y > 3$
4. You deposit $1200 in an account that pays 4.8% annual interest compounded continuously. What is the balance after 4 years? $1454.00

Available at **classzone.com**

Diagnosis/Remediation

- Practice A, B, C in Chapter 7 Resource Book, pp. 30–32
- Study Guide in Chapter 7 Resource Book, pp. 33–34
- Practice Workbook, pp. 112–113
- @HomeTutor

Challenge

Additional challenge is available in the Chapter 7 Resource Book, p. 37.

Quiz

An easily-readable reduced copy of the quiz (with answers) on Lessons 7.1–7.3 from the Assessment Book can be found on p. 476E.

Quiz 1–3, 8–11. See Additional Answers beginning on p. AA1.

12.

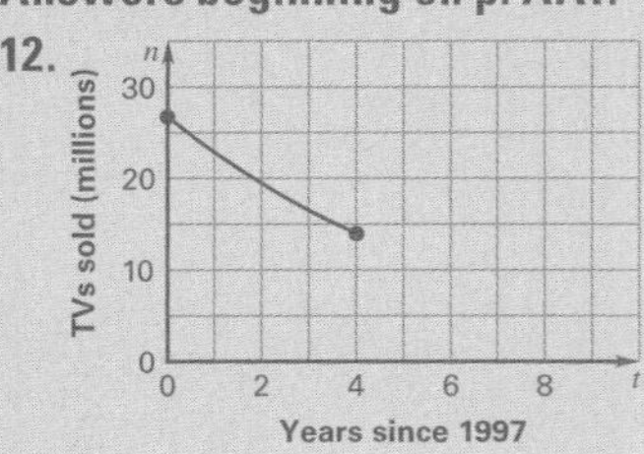

61. **RATE OF HEALING** The area of a wound decreases exponentially with time. The area A of a wound after t days can be modeled by $A = A_0 e^{-0.05t}$ where A_0 is the initial wound area. If the initial wound area is 4 square centimeters, what is the area after 14 days? about 1.986 cm^2

C 62. **CHALLENGE** The height y (in feet) of the Gateway Arch in St. Louis, Missouri, can be modeled by the function $y = 757.7 - 63.85(e^{x/127.7} + e^{-x/127.7})$ where x is the horizontal distance (in feet) from the center of the arch.

a. Use a graphing calculator to graph the function. How tall is the arch at its highest point? 630 ft

b. About how far apart are the ends of the arch? about 630 ft

KY KENTUCKY MIXED REVIEW

TEST PRACTICE at classzone.com

63. Which of the following shows that the conjecture is false? "The square root of a number x is always less than x." **A**

Ⓐ $x = \frac{1}{4}$ Ⓑ $x = 4$ Ⓒ $x = 48$ Ⓓ $x = 900$

64. Quadrilateral $MNPQ$ is a rhombus. $\angle P$ measures 55°. What are the measures of $\angle M$, $\angle N$, and $\angle Q$? **D**

Ⓐ 55°, 35°, and 35° Ⓑ 55°, 55°, and 55°
Ⓒ 55°, 110°, and 110° Ⓓ 55°, 125°, and 125°

QUIZ for Lessons 7.1–7.3

Graph the function. State the domain and range. 1–3. See margin for art.

1. $y = 2 \cdot 3^{x-2}$ *(p. 478)* domain: all real numbers, range: $y > 0$
2. $y = \left(\frac{2}{5}\right)^x$ *(p. 486)* domain: all real numbers, range: $y > 0$
3. $f(x) = \left(\frac{3}{8}\right)^x + 2$ *(p. 486)* domain: all real numbers, range: $y > 2$

Simplify the expression. *(p. 492)*

4. $3e^4 \cdot e^3$ $3e^7$
5. $(-5e^{3x})^3$ $-125e^{9x}$
6. $\frac{e^{4x}}{5e}$ $\frac{1}{5}e^{4x-1}$
7. $\frac{8e^{5x}}{6e^{2x}}$ $\frac{4}{3}e^{3x}$

Graph the function. State the domain and range. *(p. 492)* 8–11. See margin.

8. $y = 2e^x$
9. $y = 3e^{-2x}$
10. $y = e^{x+1} - 2$
11. $g(x) = 4e^{-3x} + 1$

12. **TV SALES** From 1997 to 2001, the number n (in millions) of black-and-white TVs sold in the United States can be modeled by $n = 26.8(0.85)^t$ where t is the number of years since 1997. Identify the decay factor and the percent decrease. Graph the model and state the domain and range. Estimate the number of black-and-white TVs sold in 1999. *(p. 478)* 0.85, 15%; see margin for art, domain: $t \ge 0$, range: $n > 0$; 19,363,000 TVs.

13. **FINANCE** You deposit $1200 in an account that pays 4.5% annual interest compounded continuously. What is the balance after 5 years? *(p. 492)* $1502.79

EXTRA PRACTICE for Lesson 7.3, p. 1016  **ONLINE QUIZ** at classzone.com

7.4 Evaluate Logarithms and Graph Logarithmic Functions

Before You evaluated and graphed exponential functions.
Now You will evaluate logarithms and graph logarithmic functions.
Why? So you can model the wind speed of a tornado, as in Example 4.

Key Vocabulary
- logarithm of *y* with base *b*
- common logarithm
- natural logarithm

You know that $2^2 = 4$ and $2^3 = 8$. However, for what value of x does $2^x = 6$? Mathematicians define this x-value using a *logarithm* and write $x = \log_2 6$. The definition of a logarithm can be generalized as follows.

KEY CONCEPT *For Your Notebook*

Definition of Logarithm with Base *b*

Let b and y be positive numbers with $b \neq 1$. The **logarithm of *y* with base *b*** is denoted by $\log_b y$ and is defined as follows:

$$\log_b y = x \quad \text{if and only if} \quad b^x = y$$

The expression $\log_b y$ is read as "log base b of y."

This definition tells you that the equations $\log_b y = x$ and $b^x = y$ are equivalent. The first is in *logarithmic form* and the second is in *exponential form*.

EXAMPLE 1 **Rewrite logarithmic equations**

	Logarithmic Form	Exponential Form
a.	$\log_2 8 = 3$	$2^3 = 8$
b.	$\log_4 1 = 0$	$4^0 = 1$
c.	$\log_{12} 12 = 1$	$12^1 = 12$
d.	$\log_{1/4} 4 = -1$	$\left(\frac{1}{4}\right)^{-1} = 4$

Parts (b) and (c) of Example 1 illustrate two special logarithm values that you should learn to recognize. Let b be a positive real number such that $b \neq 1$.

Logarithm of 1

$\log_b 1 = 0$ because $b^0 = 1$.

Logarithm of *b* with Base *b*

$\log_b b = 1$ because $b^1 = b$.

 **GUIDED PRACTICE** for Example 1

Rewrite the equation in exponential form.

1. $\log_3 81 = 4$ $3^4 = 81$ 2. $\log_7 7 = 1$ $7^1 = 7$ 3. $\log_{14} 1 = 0$ $14^0 = 1$ 4. $\log_{1/2} 32 = -5$ $\left(\frac{1}{2}\right)^{-5} = 32$

1 PLAN AND PREPARE

Warm-Up Exercises
Transparency Available

1. Find the inverse of the function $y = 3x - 5$. $y = \frac{1}{3}x + \frac{5}{3}$
2. An account that pays 3% annual interest compounded continuously has a balance of \$10,000 on June 1, 2008. If no money is added, what is the balance on June 1, 2010? **about \$10,618.37**

Notetaking Guide
Transparency Available
Promotes interactive learning and notetaking skills, pp. 195–198.

Pacing
Basic: 2 days
Average: 2 days
Advanced: 2 days
Block: 0.5 block with 7.3
0.5 block with 7.5
- See *Teaching Guide/Lesson Plan*.

2 FOCUS AND MOTIVATE

Essential Question
Big Idea 1, p. 477
What is the relationship between exponential and logarithmic functions? **Tell students they will learn how to answer this question by graphing logarithmic functions and comparing their graphs to those of exponential functions.**

Resource Planning Guide

Chapter Resource Book
- Teaching Guide/Lesson Plan (pp. 38–39)
- Activity Master (p. 40)
- Practice levels A, B, C (pp. 42–44)
- Study Guide (pp. 45–46)
- Catch-up for Absent Students (p. 47)
- Problem Solving Workshop (p. 48)
- Challenge (p. 50)

Workbooks
- Notetaking Guide (pp. 195–198)
- Practice Workbook (pp. 114–115)

Teaching Options
- **Power Presentations CD-ROM** provides dynamic electronic teaching resources for the classroom.
- **Activity Generator CD-ROM** provides editable activities for all ability levels.

Interactive Technology
- Easy Planner
- Power Presentations CD-ROM
- Activity Generator CD-ROM
- Animated Algebra
- Test Generator CD-ROM
- Online Quiz
- eWorkbook
- eEdition
- @HomeTutor

Resources for English Learners
- Quick Reference for English Learners
- Spanish Study Guide
- Multi-Language Visual Glossary
- Student Resources in Spanish

See also the *Algebra 2 Toolkit* for more strategies for meeting individual needs.

Motivating the Lesson

Ask students who have studied chemistry to explain the meaning and importance of pH value. Explain that the pH formula uses common logarithms, which students will study in this lesson.

3 TEACH

Extra Example 1

Rewrite the equation in exponential form.

a. $\log_2 32 = 5$ $2^5 = 32$

b. $\log_{10} 1 = 0$ $10^0 = 1$

c. $\log_9 9 = 1$ $9^1 = 9$

d. $\log_{1/5} 25 = -2$ $\left(\frac{1}{5}\right)^{-2} = 25$

Extra Example 2

Evaluate the logarithm.

a. $\log_3 81$ 4

b. $\log_{1/4} 256$ -4

c. $\log_{10} 0.001$ -3

d. $\log_{64} 2$ $\frac{1}{6}$

Extra Example 3

Use a calculator to evaluate the logarithm.

a. $\log 0.85$ -0.071

b. $\ln 22$ 3.091

Extra Example 4

The sales of a certain video game can be modeled by $y = 20 \ln(x - 1) + 35$, where y is the monthly number (in thousands) of games sold during the xth month after the game is released for sale ($x > 1$). Estimate the number of video games sold during the 10th month after the game is released. about 79,000 games

EXAMPLE 2 Evaluate logarithms

Evaluate the logarithm.

a. $\log_4 64$ b. $\log_5 0.2$ c. $\log_{1/5} 125$ d. $\log_{36} 6$

Solution

To help you find the value of $\log_b y$, ask yourself what power of b gives you y.

a. 4 to what power gives 64? $4^3 = 64$, so $\log_4 64 = 3$.

b. 5 to what power gives 0.2? $5^{-1} = 0.2$, so $\log_5 0.2 = -1$.

c. $\frac{1}{5}$ to what power gives 125? $\left(\frac{1}{5}\right)^{-3} = 125$, so $\log_{1/5} 125 = -3$.

d. 36 to what power gives 6? $36^{1/2} = 6$, so $\log_{36} 6 = \frac{1}{2}$.

SPECIAL LOGARITHMS A **common logarithm** is a logarithm with base 10. It is denoted by $\log_{10}$ or simply by log. A **natural logarithm** is a logarithm with base e. It can be denoted by $\log_e$, but is more often denoted by ln.

Common Logarithm	Natural Logarithm
$\log_{10} x = \log x$	$\log_e x = \ln x$

Most calculators have keys for evaluating common and natural logarithms.

EXAMPLE 3 Evaluate common and natural logarithms

Expression	Keystrokes	Display	Check
a. $\log 8$	LOG 8) ENTER	0.903089987	$10^{0.903} \approx 8$ ✓
b. $\ln 0.3$	LN .3) ENTER	−1.203972804	$e^{-1.204} \approx 0.3$ ✓

EXAMPLE 4 Evaluate a logarithmic model

TORNADOES The wind speed s (in miles per hour) near the center of a tornado can be modeled by

$$s = 93 \log d + 65$$

where d is the distance (in miles) that the tornado travels. In 1925, a tornado traveled 220 miles through three states. Estimate the wind speed near the tornado's center.

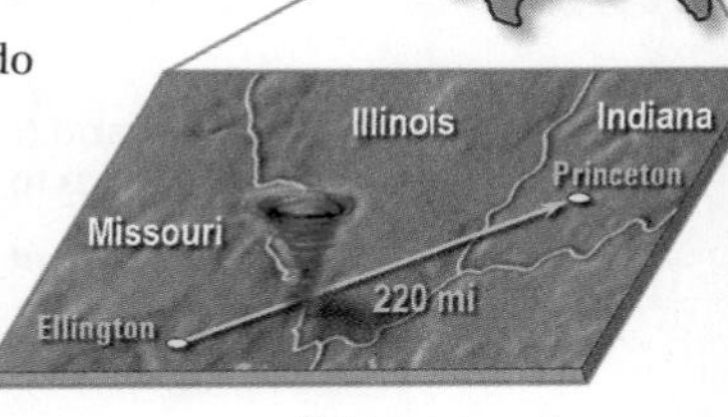

Not drawn to scale

Solution

$s = 93 \log d + 65$ Write function.

$= 93 \log 220 + 65$ Substitute 220 for d.

$\approx 93(2.342) + 65$ Use a calculator.

$= 282.806$ Simplify.

▶ The wind speed near the tornado's center was about 283 miles per hour.

Differentiated Instruction

Below Level The concept of logarithms may cause confusion. After discussing **Example 1**, give students practice in rewriting a given exponential equation in logarithmic form. Prepare a diagram to show students how the three numbers involved move when you change from logarithmic to exponential form, and vice versa. Stress that the *base* is the same in both forms, just written in a different position, and that the *logarithm* is the *exponent*. Students may also benefit from a worksheet of mixed practice in changing between the two forms.

See also the *Algebra 2 Toolkit* for more strategies.

✓ GUIDED PRACTICE for Examples 2, 3, and 4

Evaluate the logarithm. Use a calculator if necessary.

5. $\log_2 32$ 5 **6.** $\log_{27} 3$ $\frac{1}{3}$ **7.** $\log 12$ about 1.079 **8.** $\ln 0.75$ about −0.288

9. **WHAT IF?** Use the function in Example 4 to estimate the wind speed near a tornado's center if its path is 150 miles long. about 267 mi/h

INVERSE FUNCTIONS By the definition of a logarithm, it follows that the logarithmic function $g(x) = \log_b x$ is the inverse of the exponential function $f(x) = b^x$. This means that:

$$g(f(x)) = \log_b b^x = x \quad \text{and} \quad f(g(x)) = b^{\log_b x} = x$$

EXAMPLE 5 Use inverse properties

Simplify the expression.

a. $10^{\log 4}$ **b.** $\log_5 25^x$

Solution

a. $10^{\log 4} = 4$ $\quad b^{\log_b x} = x$

b. $\log_5 25^x = \log_5 (5^2)^x$ **Express 25 as a power with base 5.**

$= \log_5 5^{2x}$ **Power of a power property**

$= 2x$ $\quad \log_b b^x = x$

EXAMPLE 6 Find inverse functions

Find the inverse of the function.

a. $y = 6^x$ **b.** $y = \ln (x + 3)$

REVIEW INVERSES
For help with finding inverses of functions, see p. 437.

Solution

a. From the definition of logarithm, the inverse of $y = 6^x$ is $y = \log_6 x$.

b. $y = \ln (x + 3)$ **Write original function.**

$x = \ln (y + 3)$ **Switch *x* and *y*.**

$e^x = y + 3$ **Write in exponential form.**

$e^x - 3 = y$ **Solve for *y*.**

▶ The inverse of $y = \ln (x + 3)$ is $y = e^x - 3$.

✓ GUIDED PRACTICE for Examples 5 and 6

Simplify the expression.

10. $8^{\log_8 x}$ x **11.** $\log_7 7^{-3x}$ $-3x$ **12.** $\log_2 64^x$ $6x$ **13.** $e^{\ln 20}$ 20

14. Find the inverse of $y = 4^x$. $y = \log_4 x$

15. Find the inverse of $y = \ln (x - 5)$. $y = e^x + 5$

Extra Example 5

Simplify the expression.

a. $e^{\ln 9}$ 9

b. $\log_3 27^x$ $3x$

Key Questions to Ask for Example 5

- In Example 5a, what is the base of the exponential form? 10; log 4 means $\log_{10} 4$.
- In Example 5b, why is 25 rewritten as 5^2? To match the base of 25^x to the logarithmic base.

Extra Example 6

Find the inverse of the function.

a. $y = 8^x$ $y = \log_8 x$

b. $y = \ln (x - 4)$ $y = e^x + 4$

Key Question to Ask for Example 6

- For an exponential function and a logarithmic function to be inverses, what must the two functions have in common? They must have the same base.

Mathematical Reasoning

Both $y = b^x$ and $y = \log_b x$, where $b > 0$, $b \neq 1$ have inverses. What must be true of their graphs? Their graphs pass the horizontal line test.

GRAPHING LOGARITHMIC FUNCTIONS You can use the inverse relationship between exponential and logarithmic functions to graph logarithmic functions.

KEY CONCEPT *For Your Notebook*

Parent Graphs for Logarithmic Functions

The graph of $f(x) = \log_b x$ is shown below for $b > 1$ and for $0 < b < 1$. Because $f(x) = \log_b x$ and $g(x) = b^x$ are inverse functions, the graph of $f(x) = \log_b x$ is the reflection of the graph of $g(x) = b^x$ in the line $y = x$.

Graph of $f(x) = \log_b x$ for $b > 1$

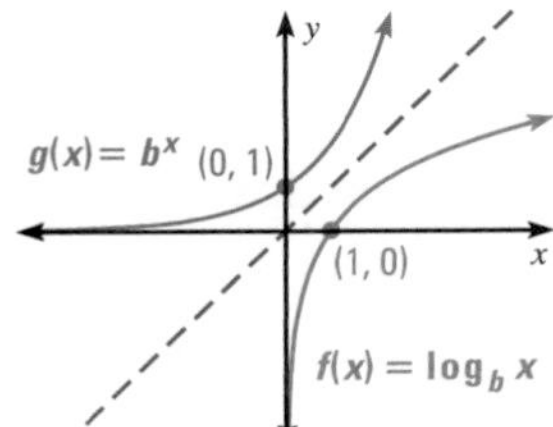

Graph of $f(x) = \log_b x$ for $0 < b < 1$

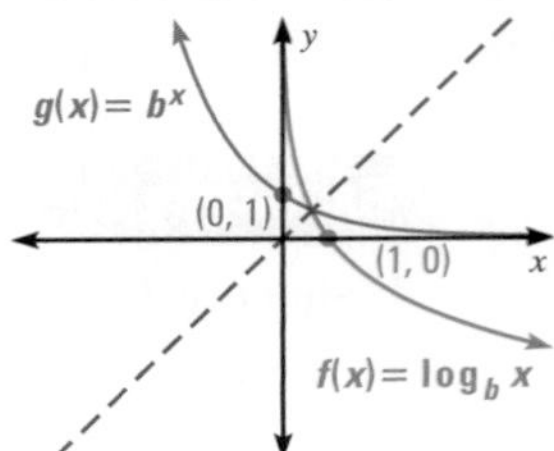

Note that the *y*-axis is a vertical asymptote of the graph of $f(x) = \log_b x$. The domain of $f(x) = \log_b x$ is $x > 0$, and the range is all real numbers.

EXAMPLE 7 Graph logarithmic functions

Graph the function.

a. $y = \log_3 x$

b. $y = \log_{1/2} x$

Solution

a. Plot several convenient points, such as (1, 0), (3, 1), and (9, 2). The *y*-axis is a vertical asymptote.

From *left* to *right*, draw a curve that starts just to the right of the *y*-axis and moves up through the plotted points, as shown below.

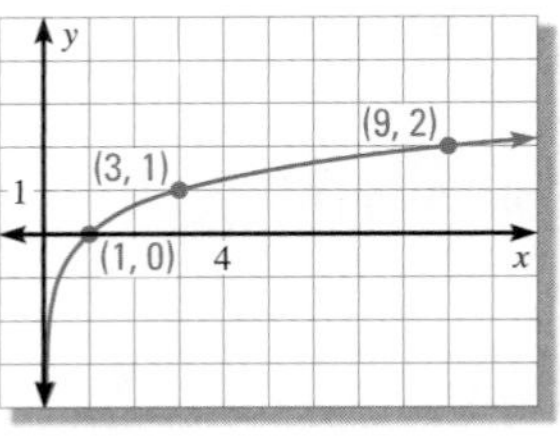

b. Plot several convenient points, such as (1, 0), (2, −1), (4, −2), and (8, −3). The *y*-axis is a vertical asymptote.

From *left* to *right*, draw a curve that starts just to the right of the *y*-axis and moves down through the plotted points, as shown below.

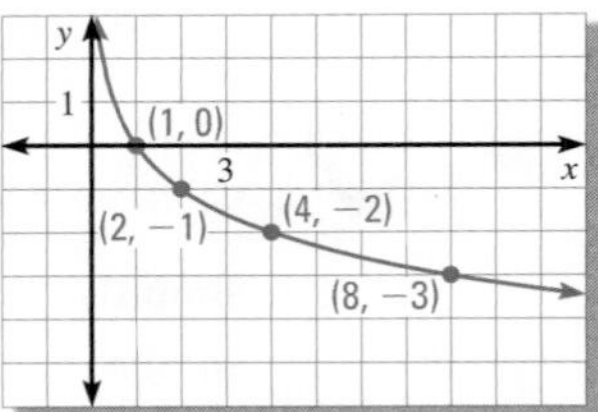

Animated Algebra at classzone.com

Extra Example 7

Graph the function.

a. $\log_2 x$

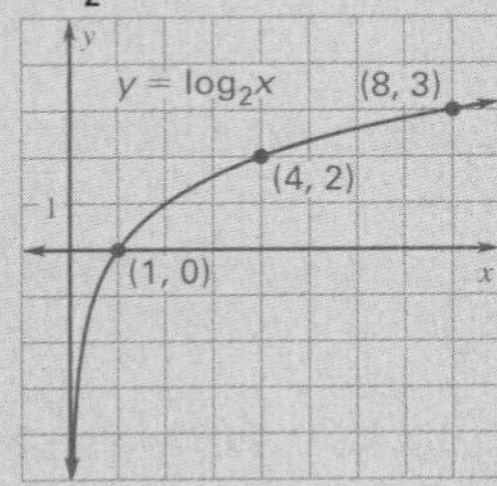

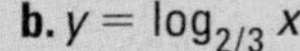
b. $y = \log_{2/3} x$

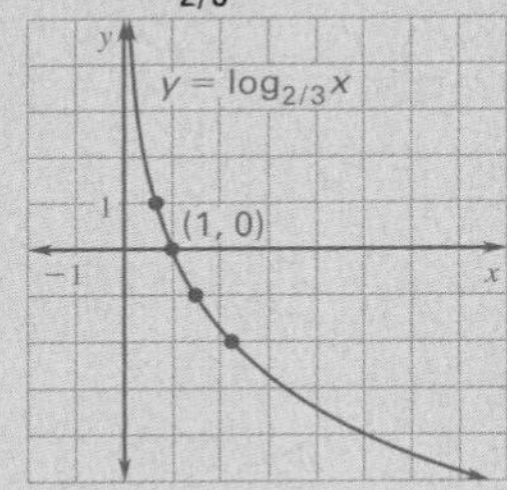

Key Question to Ask for Example 7

- What two points are on the graph of any logarithmic function of the form $y = \log_b x$? (1, 0) and $(b, 1)$

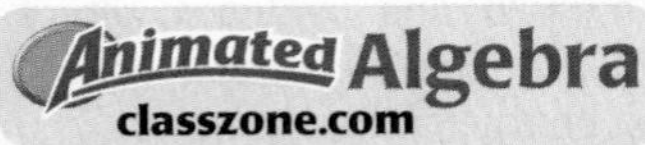

An **Animated Algebra** activity is available on-line for **Example 7**. This activity is also available on the **Power Presentations CD-ROM**.

Avoiding Common Errors

Some students may have trouble making a table of values to use for graphing a logarithmic function. Because students at this point are more familiar and comfortable with exponential functions than logarithmic ones, show them how they can use what they already know. Suggest making a table of values by choosing the *y*-values first, using consecutive integers, and then finding the corresponding *x*-values to form the ordered pairs. A similar approach is to construct a table for the corresponding exponential function and then to reverse *x* and *y* in each pair to find ordered pairs for the logarithmic function.

Differentiated Instruction

Visual Learners Reinforce the inverse relationship between $y = \log_b x$ and $y = b^x$ by having students graph the reflection in the line $y = x$ of each of the graphs in **Example 7**. Have students write and graph each inverse function and compare each graph to the graph of the reflection.

See also the *Algebra 2 Toolkit* for more strategies.

TRANSLATIONS You can graph a logarithmic function of the form $y = \log_b (x - h) + k$ by translating the graph of the parent function $y = \log_b x$.

EXAMPLE 8 Translate a logarithmic graph

Graph $y = \log_2 (x + 3) + 1$. State the domain and range.

Solution

STEP 1 **Sketch** the graph of the parent function $y = \log_2 x$, which passes through (1, 0), (2, 1), and (4, 2).

STEP 2 **Translate** the parent graph left 3 units and up 1 unit. The translated graph passes through (−2, 1), (−1, 2), and (1, 3). The graph's asymptote is $x = -3$. The domain is $x > -3$, and the range is all real numbers.

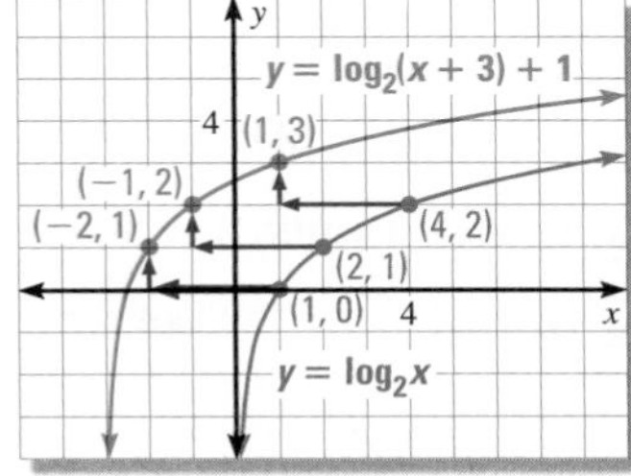

Extra Example 8

Graph $y = \log_3 (x - 2) + 4$. State the domain and range. domain: $x > 2$; range: all real numbers

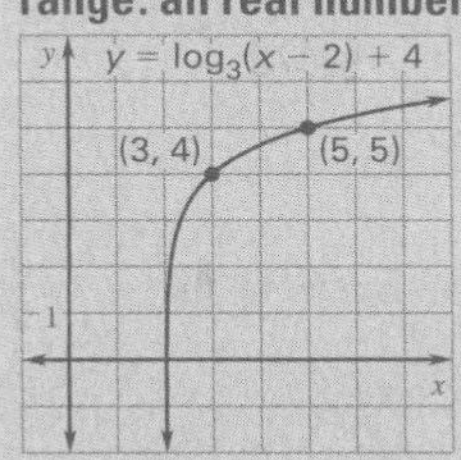

Key Question to Ask for Example 8

- Do translations of a logarithmic graph affect the domain and/or the range? Explain. A horizontal translation affects the domain, but not the range. A vertical translation does not affect the domain or range, since the range is always all real numbers.

GUIDED PRACTICE for Examples 7 and 8

Graph the function. State the domain and range. 16–18. See margin for art.

16. $y = \log_5 x$
domain: $x > 0$,
range: all real numbers

17. $y = \log_{1/3} (x - 3)$
domain: $x > 3$,
range: all real numbers

18. $f(x) = \log_4 (x + 1) - 2$
domain: $x > -1$,
range: all real numbers

Closing the Lesson

Have students summarize the major points of the lesson and answer the Essential Question: What is the relationship between exponential and logarithmic functions?

- The equations $\log_b y = x$ (logarithmic form) and $b^x = y$ (exponential form) are equivalent.
- The graph of a logarithmic function rises from left to right if $b > 1$ and falls from left to right if $0 < b < 1$. The graph has a vertical asymptote.

Exponential and logarithmic functions with the same base are inverses.

7.4 EXERCISES

HOMEWORK KEY

○ = **WORKED-OUT SOLUTIONS** on p. WS13 for Exs. 13, 33, and 61

★ = **STANDARDIZED TEST PRACTICE** Exs. 2, 36, 61, and 62

SKILL PRACTICE

A

1. **VOCABULARY** Copy and complete: A logarithm with base 10 is called a(n) _?_ logarithm. common

2. ★ **WRITING** *Describe* the relationship between $y = 5^x$ and $y = \log_5 x$. The functions are inverses of each other.

EXAMPLE 1 on p. 499 for Exs. 3–7

EXPONENTIAL FORM **Rewrite the equation in exponential form.**

3. $\log_4 16 = 2$ $4^2 = 16$
4. $\log_7 343 = 3$ $7^3 = 343$
5. $\log_6 \frac{1}{36} = -2$ $6^{-2} = \frac{1}{36}$
6. $\log_{64} 1 = 0$ $64^0 = 1$

7. **ERROR ANALYSIS** *Describe* and correct the error in rewriting the equation $2^{-3} = \frac{1}{8}$ in logarithmic form. See margin.

$\log_2 -3 = \frac{1}{8}$ ✗

EXAMPLE 2 on p. 500 for Exs. 8–19

EVALUATING LOGARITHMS **Evaluate the logarithm without using a calculator.**

8. $\log_{15} 15$ 1
9. $\log_7 49$ 2
10. $\log_6 216$ 3
11. $\log_2 64$ 6
12. $\log_9 1$ 0
13. $\log_{1/2} 8$ −3
14. $\log_3 \frac{1}{27}$ −3
15. $\log_{16} \frac{1}{4}$ $-\frac{1}{2}$
16. $\log_{1/4} 16$ −2
17. $\log_8 512$ 3
18. $\log_5 625$ 4
19. $\log_{11} 121$ 2

7. *Sample answer:* The −3 and $\frac{1}{8}$ are switched around; $\log_2 \frac{1}{8} = -3$.

Guided Practice

16.

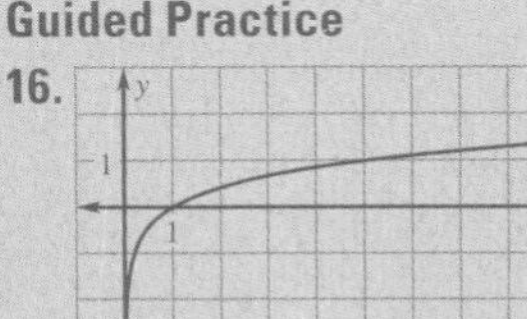

17.

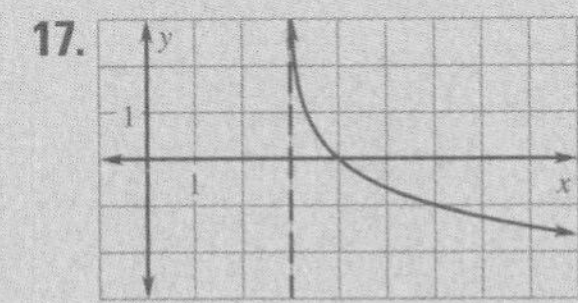

18.

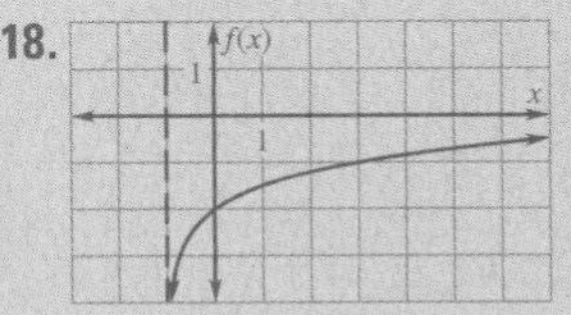

4 PRACTICE AND APPLY

Assignment Guide

Answer Transparencies available for all exercises

Basic:
Day 1: EP p. 1015 Exs. 34–36
pp. 503–505
Exs. 1–15, 20–23, 58, 59
Day 2: pp. 503–505
Exs. 28–40, 45–47, 60, 61, 64–65

Average:
Day 1: pp. 503–505
Exs. 1–7, 10–17, 22–25, 58, 59
Day 2: pp. 503–505
Exs. 32–42, 48–52, 60–62, 64–65

Advanced:
Day 1: pp. 503–505
Exs. 1–6, 14–19, 24–27, 54–59*
Day 2: pp. 503–505
Exs. 33–36, 41–44, 48–53, 60–65*

Block:
pp. 503–505
Exs. 1–7, 10–17, 22–25, 58, 59
(with 7.3)
pp. 503–505
Exs. 32–42, 48–52, 60–62, 64–65
(with 7.5)

Differentiated Instruction

See *Algebra 2 Best Practices Toolkit* for suggestions on addressing the needs of a diverse classroom.

Homework Check

For a quick check of student understanding of key concepts, go over the following exercises:

Basic: 4, 10, 22, 38, 58
Average: 5, 14, 24, 40, 58
Advanced: 6, 18, 26, 42, 59

Extra Practice

- Student Edition, p. 1016
- Chapter 7 Resource Book: Practice levels A, B, C, pp. 42–44

Practice Worksheet

An easily-readable reduced practice page (with answers) for this lesson can be found on p. 476C.

EXAMPLE 3 on p. 500 for Exs. 20–27

CALCULATING LOGARITHMS **Use a calculator to evaluate the logarithm.**

20. $\log 14$ about 1.146
21. $\ln 6$ about 1.792
22. $\ln 0.43$ about −0.844
23. $\log 6.213$ about 0.793
24. $\log 27$ about 1.431
25. $\ln 5.38$ about 1.683
26. $\log 0.746$ about −0.127
27. $\ln 110$ about 4.70

EXAMPLE 5 on p. 501 for Exs. 28–36

USING INVERSE PROPERTIES **Simplify the expression.**

28. $7^{\log_7 x}$ x
29. $\log_5 5^x$ x
30. $30^{\log_{30} 4}$ 4
31. $10^{\log 8}$ 8
32. $\log_6 36^x$ $2x$
33. $\log_3 81^x$ $4x$
34. $\log_5 125^x$ $3x$
35. $\log_2 32^x$ $5x$

36. ★ **MULTIPLE CHOICE** Which expression is equivalent to $\log 100^x$? B

(A) x (B) $2x$ (C) $10x$ (D) $100x$

EXAMPLE 6 on p. 501 for Exs. 37–44

FINDING INVERSES **Find the inverse of the function.**

37. $y = \log_8 x$ $y = 8^x$
38. $y = 7^x$ $y = \log_7 x$
39. $y = (0.4)^x$ $y = \log_{0.4} x$
40. $y = \log_{1/2} x$ $y = \left(\frac{1}{2}\right)^x$
41. $y = e^{x+2}$ $y = \ln x - 2$
42. $y = 2^x - 3$ $y = \log_2(x + 3)$
43. $y = \ln(x + 1)$ $y = e^x - 1$
44. $y = 6 + \log x$ $y = 10^{x-6}$

EXAMPLES 7 and 8 on pp. 502–503 for Exs. 45–53

GRAPHING FUNCTIONS **Graph the function. State the domain and range.** 45–53. See margin.

45. $y = \log_4 x$
46. $y = \log_6 x$
47. $y = \log_{1/3} x$
48. $y = \log_{1/5} x$
49. $y = \log_2(x - 3)$
50. $y = \log_3 x + 4$
51. $f(x) = \log_4(x + 2) - 1$
52. $g(x) = \log_6(x - 4) + 2$
53. $h(x) = \log_5(x + 1) - 3$

CHALLENGE **Evaluate the logarithm. (*Hint:* For each logarithm $\log_b x$, rewrite b and x as powers of the same number.)**

54. $\log_{27} 9$ $\frac{2}{3}$
55. $\log_8 32$ $\frac{5}{3}$
56. $\log_{125} 625$ $\frac{4}{3}$
57. $\log_4 128$ $\frac{7}{2}$

PROBLEM SOLVING

EXAMPLE 4 on p. 500 for Exs. 58–59

58. **ALTIMETER** Skydivers use an instrument called an altimeter to track their altitude as they fall. The altimeter determines altitude by measuring air pressure. The altitude h (in meters) above sea level is related to the air pressure P (in pascals) by the function in the diagram below.

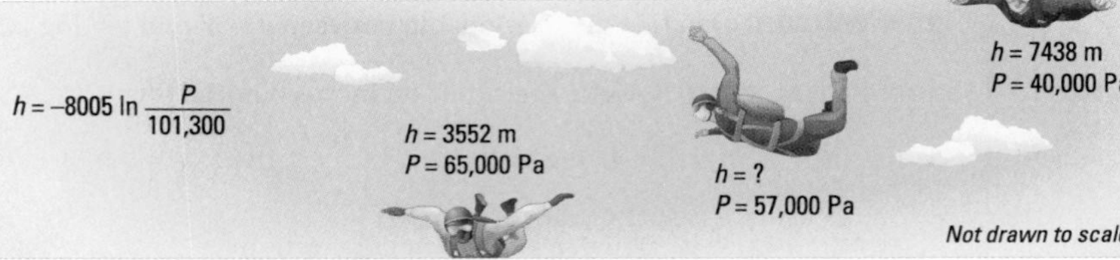

What is the altitude above sea level when the air pressure is 57,000 pascals? about 4603 m

@HomeTutor for problem solving help at classzone.com

59. **CHEMISTRY** The pH value for a substance measures how acidic or alkaline the substance is. It is given by the formula $\text{pH} = -\log[H^+]$ where H^+ is the hydrogen ion concentration (in moles per liter). Lemon juice has a hydrogen ion concentration of $10^{-2.3}$ moles per liter. What is its pH value? 2.3

@HomeTutor for problem solving help at classzone.com

○ = WORKED-OUT SOLUTIONS on p. WS1 ★ = STANDARDIZED TEST PRACTICE

45–53. See Additional Answers beginning on p. AA1.

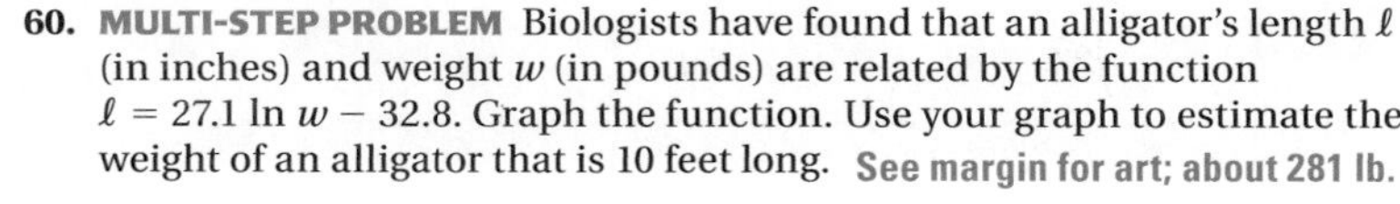

60. **MULTI-STEP PROBLEM** Biologists have found that an alligator's length ℓ (in inches) and weight w (in pounds) are related by the function $\ell = 27.1 \ln w - 32.8$. Graph the function. Use your graph to estimate the weight of an alligator that is 10 feet long. See margin for art; about 281 lb.

B (61.) ★ **SHORT RESPONSE** The energy magnitude M of an earthquake can be modeled by

$$M = 0.29(\ln E) - 9.9$$

where E is the amount of energy released (in ergs).

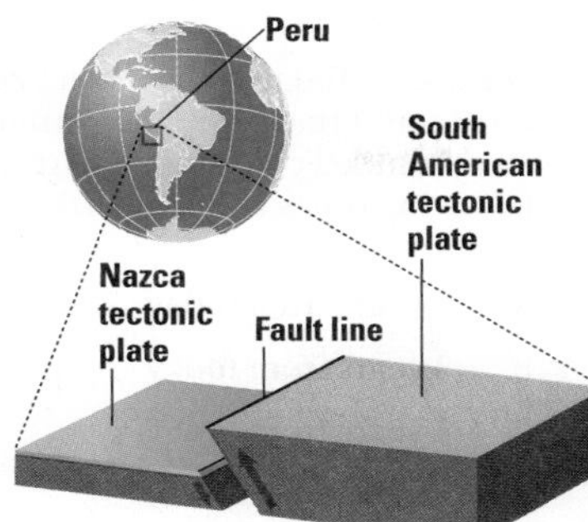

a. In 2001, a powerful earthquake in Peru, caused by the slippage of two tectonic plates along a fault, released 2.5×10^{24} ergs. What was the energy magnitude of the earthquake? about 8.4

b. Find the inverse of the given function. *Describe* what it represents.

b. $= e^{(M - 1.17)/0.291}$; e inverse presents e amount of ergy released, ergs, as a nction of e moment agnitude.

62. ★ **EXTENDED RESPONSE** A study in Florida found that the number of fish species s in a pool or lake can be modeled by the function

$$s = 30.6 - 20.5(\log A) + 3.8(\log A)^2$$

where A is the area (in square meters) of the pool or lake.

a. **Graph** Use a graphing calculator to graph the function on the domain $200 \le A \le 35{,}000$. See margin.

b. **Estimate** Use your graph to estimate the number of fish species in a lake with an area of 30,000 square meters. about 15 species

c. **Estimate** Use your graph to estimate the area of a lake that contains 6 species of fish. about 4000 m^2

d. **Reasoning** *Describe* what happens to the number of fish species as the area of a pool or lake increases. *Explain* why your answer makes sense.

d. The number fish species creases; the rger the area a pool lake, the ore room ere is for more rieties of fish thrive.

C 63. **CHALLENGE** The function $s = 0.159 + 0.118(\log d)$ gives the slope s of a beach in terms of the average diameter d (in millimeters) of sand particles on the beach. Find the inverse of this function. Then use the inverse to estimate the average diameter of the sand particles on a beach with a slope of 0.2.

$d = 10^{(s - 0.159)/0.118}$; about 2.23 mm

KENTUCKY MIXED REVIEW

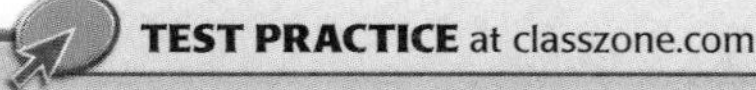

TEST PRACTICE at classzone.com

64. Which statement best describes the graph of a person's distance traveled over time? C

Ⓐ The person first runs, then walks.

Ⓑ The person travels at a constant speed.

Ⓒ The person first walks, then runs.

Ⓓ The person's speed decreases over time.

Distance / Time

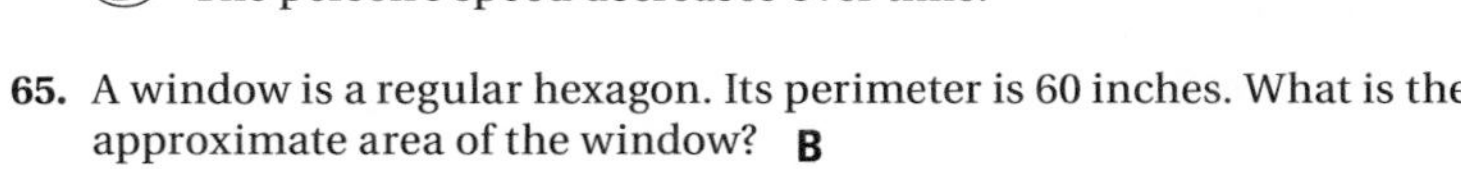

65. A window is a regular hexagon. Its perimeter is 60 inches. What is the approximate area of the window? B

Ⓐ 155.9 in.^{2} Ⓑ 259.8 in.^{2} Ⓒ 300.0 in.^{2} Ⓓ 519.6 in.^{2}

5 ASSESS AND RETEACH

Daily Homework Quiz

Transparency Available

1. Rewrite the equation $\log_7 343 = 3$ in exponential form. $7^3 = 343$
2. Evaluate $\log_2 \frac{1}{64}$. -6
3. Find the inverse of the function $y = \log(x - 2)$. $y = 10^x + 2$
4. Graph $y = \log_5(x + 4) - 3$. State the domain and range. domain: $x > -4$; range: all real numbers

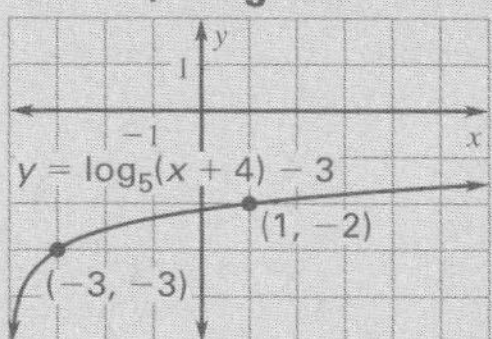

Available at **classzone.com**

Diagnosis/Remediation

- Practice A, B, C in Chapter 7 Resource Book, pp. 42–44
- Study Guide in Chapter 7 Resource Book, pp. 45–46
- Practice Workbook, pp. 114–115
- @HomeTutor

Challenge

Additional challenge is available in the Chapter 7 Resource Book, p. 50.

60.

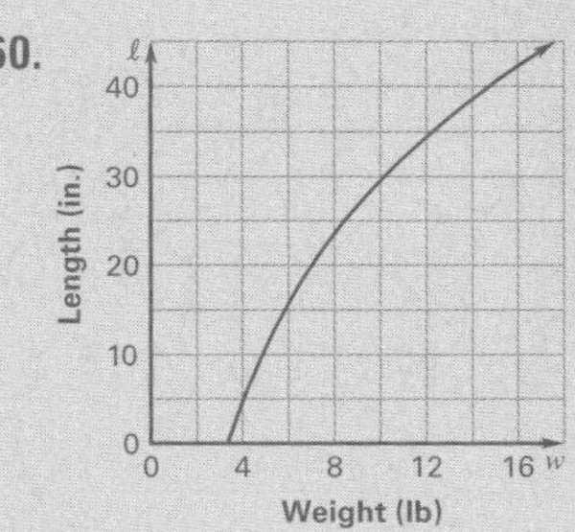

62a.

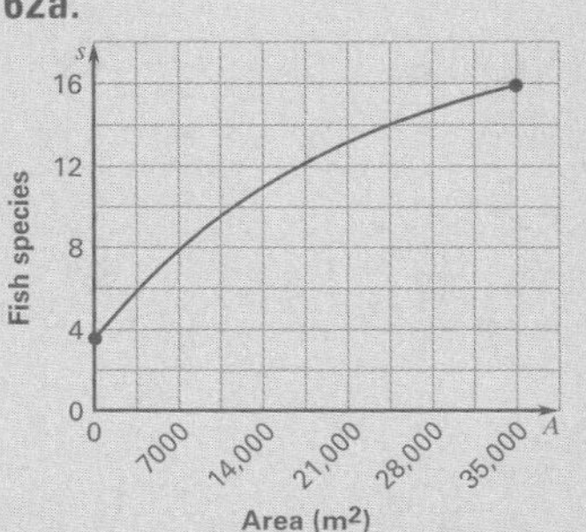

1. C
2. A
3. C
4. C
5. B
6. a. 5.69 mg
   b. 12 years, 3 months

Kentucky Mixed Review

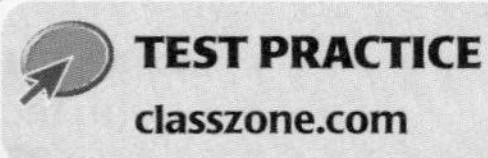

Lessons 7.1–7.4

1. **INTEREST** Today you deposit \$2000 into an account that pays 5.6% annual interest, compounded continuously. At which of the following times will it have first reached at least \$2,500?

   A. 2 years from today

   B. 3 years from today

   C. 4 years from today

   D. 5 years from today

2. **GEOMETRIC PATTERNS** When a piece of paper is folded in half, the paper is divided into two regions, each of which has half the area of the paper. If this process is repeated, the number of regions increases while the area of each region decreases. The table below shows the number of regions and the fractional area of each region after each successive fold. Which function can be used to find the fractional area $A(n)$ of each region after n folds?

Fold number	0	1	2	3	4
Number of regions	1	2	4	8	16
Fractional area of each region	1	$\frac{1}{2}$	$\frac{1}{4}$	$\frac{1}{8}$	$\frac{1}{16}$

   A. $A(n) = \frac{1}{2^n}$

   B. $A(n) = \frac{1}{(n+1)^n}$

   C. $A(n) = \frac{1}{n+1}$

   D. $A(n) = 2^n$

3. **CERTIFICATES OF DEPOSIT** A local bank offers certificate of deposit (CD) accounts that you can use to save money and earn interest. You deposit \$1500 into a three year CD that pays 2% annual interest. The interest for the CD is compounded monthly. How much interest will the CD earn by the end of its term?

   A. \$87.42 B. \$90.83

   C. \$92.68 D. \$124.50

4. **PETROLEUM** The amount y (in billions of barrels) of oil collected by a petroleum company drilling on the U.S. continental shelf can be modeled by $y = 12.263 \ln x - 45.381$ where x is the number of wells drilled. About how many barrels of oil would you expect to be collected if 1000 wells are drilled?

   A. 11.1 billion

   B. 30.5 billion

   C. 39.3 billion

   D. 84.7 billion

5. **TRANSLATIONS** The graph shown below is a translation of the graph of $y = \log_3 x$. What is the equation of the graph?

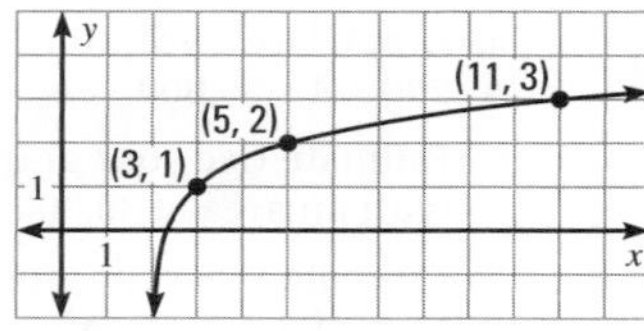

   A. $y = \log_3 (x - 2) - 1$

   B. $y = \log_3 (x - 2) + 1$

   C. $y = \log_3 (x - 1) + 2$

   D. $y = \log_3 (x + 2) - 1$

6. **OPEN-RESPONSE** Tritium is a radioactive substance used to illuminate signs. The amount of tritium disappears over time, a process called radioactive decay. If you start with a 10 milligram sample of tritium, the number y of milligrams left after t years is given by $y = 10e^{-0.0564t}$.

   a. Find the number of milligrams of tritium left after 10 years. Round your answer to the nearest hundredth of a milligram.

   b. After how long will the amount be exactly 5 milligrams? Round your answer to the nearest number of *months.*

7.5 Apply Properties of Logarithms

Before You evaluated logarithms.

Now You will rewrite logarithmic expressions.

Why? So you can model the loudness of sounds, as in Ex. 63.

Key Vocabulary
- **base,** *p. 10*

KEY CONCEPT *For Your Notebook*

Properties of Logarithms

Let b, m, and n be positive numbers such that $b \neq 1$.

Product Property	$\log_b mn = \log_b m + \log_b n$
Quotient Property	$\log_b \frac{m}{n} = \log_b m - \log_b n$
Power Property	$\log_b m^n = n \log_b m$

EXAMPLE 1 Use properties of logarithms

Use $\log_4 3 \approx 0.792$ and $\log_4 7 \approx 1.404$ to evaluate the logarithm.

AVOID ERRORS
Note that in general $\log_b \frac{m}{n} \neq \frac{\log_b m}{\log_b n}$ and $\log_b mn \neq (\log_b m)(\log_b n)$.

a. $\log_4 \frac{3}{7} = \log_4 3 - \log_4 7$ — **Quotient property**

$\approx 0.792 - 1.404$ — **Use the given values of $\log_4 3$ and $\log_4 7$.**

$= -0.612$ — **Simplify.**

b. $\log_4 21 = \log_4 (3 \cdot 7)$ — **Write 21 as $3 \cdot 7$.**

$= \log_4 3 + \log_4 7$ — **Product property**

$\approx 0.792 + 1.404$ — **Use the given values of $\log_4 3$ and $\log_4 7$.**

$= 2.196$ — **Simplify.**

c. $\log_4 49 = \log_4 7^2$ — **Write 49 as 7^2.**

$= 2 \log_4 7$ — **Power property**

$\approx 2(1.404)$ — **Use the given value of $\log_4 7$.**

$= 2.808$ — **Simplify.**

GUIDED PRACTICE for Example 1

Use $\log_6 5 \approx 0.898$ and $\log_6 8 \approx 1.161$ to evaluate the logarithm.

1. $\log_6 \frac{5}{8}$ **−0.263** **2.** $\log_6 40$ **2.059** **3.** $\log_6 64$ **2.322** **4.** $\log_6 125$ **2.694**

1 PLAN AND PREPARE

Warm-Up Exercises

Transparency Available

Evaluate the logarithm.

1. $\log_5 625$ 4

2. $\log 0.00001$ −5

3. $\log_{32} 2$ $\frac{1}{5}$

4. $\log_{36} \frac{1}{6}$ $-\frac{1}{2}$

5. $\log_8 4$ $\frac{2}{3}$

Notetaking Guide

Transparency Available

Promotes interactive learning and notetaking skills, pp. 199–201.

Pacing

Basic: 1 day
Average: 1 day
Advanced: 1 day
Block: 0.5 block with 7.4
- See *Teaching Guide/Lesson Plan.*

2 FOCUS AND MOTIVATE

Essential Question

Big Idea 2, p. 477

How can you use a calculator to evaluate a logarithm when the base is not 10 or *e*? **Tell students they will learn how to answer this question by learning to use the change-of-base formula.**

Resource Planning Guide

Chapter Resource Book
- Teaching Guide/Lesson Plan (pp. 51–52)
- Practice levels A, B, C (pp. 54–56)
- Study Guide (pp. 57–58)
- Catch-up for Absent Students (p. 59)
- Application (p. 60)
- Challenge (p. 61)

Workbooks
- Notetaking Guide (pp. 199–201)
- Practice Workbook (pp. 116–117)

Teaching Options
- **Power Presentations CD-ROM** provides dynamic electronic teaching resources for the classroom.
- **Activity Generator CD-ROM** provides editable activities for all ability levels.

Interactive Technology
- Easy Planner
- Power Presentations CD-ROM
- Activity Generator CD-ROM
- Animated Algebra
- Test Generator CD-ROM
- Online Quiz
- eWorkbook
- eEdition
- @HomeTutor

Resources for English Learners
- Quick Reference for English Learners
- Spanish Study Guide
- Multi-Language Visual Glossary
- Student Resources in Spanish

See also the *Algebra 2 Toolkit* for more strategies for meeting individual needs.

Motivating the Lesson

You can use properties of logarithms to decide how many times as great the noise level is at a rock concert as the noise level at a string quartet concert.

3 TEACH

Extra Example 1

Use $\log_3 12 \approx 2.262$ and $\log_3 2 \approx 0.631$ to evaluate the logarithm.

a. $\log_3 6$ 1.631

b. $\log_3 24$ 2.893

c. $\log_3 32$ 3.155

Extra Example 2

Expand $\log_7 \frac{3x^2}{5y^3}$.

$\log_7 3 + 2 \log_7 x - \log_7 5 - 3 \log_7 y$

Extra Example 3

Which of the following is equivalent to $\ln 8 + 2 \ln 5 - \ln 10$? D

(A) ln 4

(B) ln 8

(C) ln 18

(D) ln 20

Key Question to Ask for Examples 2 and 3

- What does it mean to "expand" or "condense" a logarithmic expression? Expanding a logarithmic expression means to break down a single logarithm into the sum and/or difference of two or more logarithms with the same base as the original expression. Condensing a logarithmic expression is the reverse of expanding, so the result is a single logarithm.

REWRITING EXPRESSIONS You can use the properties of logarithms to expand and condense logarithmic expressions.

EXAMPLE 2 Expand a logarithmic expression

REWRITE EXPRESSIONS When you are expanding or condensing an expression involving logarithms, you may assume any variables are positive.

Expand $\log_6 \frac{5x^3}{y}$.

$\log_6 \frac{5x^3}{y} = \log_6 5x^3 - \log_6 y$ **Quotient property**

$= \log_6 5 + \log_6 x^3 - \log_6 y$ **Product property**

$= \log_6 5 + 3 \log_6 x - \log_6 y$ **Power property**

EXAMPLE 3 Standardized Test Practice

Which of the following is equivalent to $\log 9 + 3 \log 2 - \log 3$?

(A) log 8 (B) log 14 (C) log 18 (D) log 24

Solution

$\log 9 + 3 \log 2 - \log 3 = \log 9 + \log 2^3 - \log 3$ **Power property**

$= \log (9 \cdot 2^3) - \log 3$ **Product property**

$= \log \frac{9 \cdot 2^3}{3}$ **Quotient property**

$= \log 24$ **Simplify.**

▶ The correct answer is D. (A) (B) (C) (D)

GUIDED PRACTICE for Examples 2 and 3

5. Expand $\log 3x^4$. $\log 3 + 4 \log x$

6. Condense $\ln 4 + 3 \ln 3 - \ln 12$. ln 9

CHANGE-OF-BASE FORMULA Logarithms with any base other than 10 or e can be written in terms of common or natural logarithms using the *change-of-base formula*. This allows you to evaluate any logarithm using a calculator.

KEY CONCEPT *For Your Notebook*

Change-of-Base Formula

If a, b, and c are positive numbers with $b \neq 1$ and $c \neq 1$, then:

$$\log_c a = \frac{\log_b a}{\log_b c}$$

In particular, $\log_c a = \frac{\log a}{\log c}$ and $\log_c a = \frac{\ln a}{\ln c}$.

Differentiated Instruction

Inclusion Instead of having to apply the properties of logarithms shown on page 507 strictly from memory, highlight the division bar and the subtraction sign in the quotient property. Ask students to notice that this short horizontal line is used twice here, so it will help them keep the operations used separate from those in the product property.

See also the *Algebra 2 Toolkit* for more strategies.

EXAMPLE 4 Use the change-of-base formula

Evaluate $\log_3 8$ using common logarithms and natural logarithms.

Solution

Using common logarithms: $\log_3 8 = \frac{\log 8}{\log 3} \approx \frac{0.9031}{0.4771} \approx 1.893$

Using natural logarithms: $\log_3 8 = \frac{\ln 8}{\ln 3} \approx \frac{2.0794}{1.0986} \approx 1.893$

EXAMPLE 5 Use properties of logarithms in real life

SOUND INTENSITY For a sound with intensity I (in watts per square meter), the loudness $L(I)$ of the sound (in decibels) is given by the function

$$L(I) = 10 \log \frac{I}{I_0}$$

where I_0 is the intensity of a barely audible sound (about 10^{-12} watts per square meter). An artist in a recording studio turns up the volume of a track so that the sound's intensity doubles. By how many decibels does the loudness increase?

Solution

Let I be the original intensity, so that $2I$ is the doubled intensity.

Increase in loudness $= L(2I) - L(I)$	**Write an expression.**
$= 10 \log \frac{2I}{I_0} - 10 \log \frac{I}{I_0}$	**Substitute.**
$= 10\left(\log \frac{2I}{I_0} - \log \frac{I}{I_0}\right)$	**Distributive property**
$= 10\left(\log 2 + \log \frac{I}{I_0} - \log \frac{I}{I_0}\right)$	**Product property**
$= 10 \log 2$	**Simplify.**
≈ 3.01	**Use a calculator.**

▶ The loudness increases by about 3 decibels.

GUIDED PRACTICE for Examples 4 and 5

Use the change-of-base formula to evaluate the logarithm.

7. $\log_5 8$ about 1.292
8. $\log_8 14$ about 1.269
9. $\log_{26} 9$ about 0.674
10. $\log_{12} 30$ about 1.369
11. **WHAT IF?** In Example 5, suppose the artist turns up the volume so that the sound's intensity triples. By how many decibels does the loudness increase? about 4.771 decibels

Extra Example 4

Evaluate $\log_6 24$ using common logarithms and natural logarithms. approximately 1.774; approximately 1.774

Teaching Strategy

Before discussing Example 4, give students specific examples of using the change-of-base formula to rewrite logarithms in bases other than 10 or e as quotients of common or natural logarithms.

Extra Example 5

The Richter scale is used to measure the magnitude of earthquakes. If an earthquake has intensity I, then its magnitude on the Richter scale, R, is given by the function $R(I) = \log \frac{I}{I_0}$, where I_0 is the intensity of a barely felt earthquake. If the intensity of one earthquake is 50 times that of another, how many points greater is the bigger earthquake on the Richter scale? about 1.7 points

Closing the Lesson

Have students summarize the major points of the lesson and answer the Essential Question: How can you use a calculator to evaluate a logarithm when the base is not 10 or e?

- The product, quotient, and power properties of logarithms are directly related to the corresponding properties of exponents.
- The properties of logarithms can be used to expand or condense logarithmic expressions.

The change-of-base formula allows you to evaluate a logarithm with any base by finding the quotient of two common logarithms or of two natural logarithms. Thus, you can rewrite the logarithm using the change-of-base formula and then evaluate the resulting expression using a calculator.

7.5 EXERCISES

HOMEWORK KEY
○ = **WORKED-OUT SOLUTIONS** on p. WS13 for Exs. 11, 17, and 71
★ = **STANDARDIZED TEST PRACTICE** Exs. 2, 43, 44, 64, 71, and 73

4 PRACTICE AND APPLY

Assignment Guide

Answer Transparencies available for all exercises

Basic:
Day 1: pp. 510–513
Exs. 1–11, 15–20, 31–36, 43–48, 69–72, 75

Average:
Day 1: pp. 510–513
Exs. 1, 2, 10–12, 21–26, 31, 32, 37–40, 43, 44, 49–54, 61–64, 69–73, 76

Advanced:
Day 1: pp. 510–513
Exs. 1, 2, 12–14, 26–30, 39–44, 53–68*, 71–74*

Block:
pp. 510–513
Exs. 1, 2, 10–12, 21–26, 31, 32, 37–40, 43, 44, 49–54, 61–64, 69–73, 76 (with 7.4)

Differentiated Instruction

See *Algebra 2 Best Practices Toolkit* for suggestions on addressing the needs of a diverse classroom.

Homework Check

For a quick check of student understanding of key concepts, go over the following exercises:

Basic: 8, 18, 34, 46, 69
Average: 10, 22, 38, 52, 70
Advanced: 12, 28, 42, 54, 71

Extra Practice

- Student Edition, p. 1016
- Chapter 7 Resource Book: Practice levels A, B, C, pp. 54–56

Practice Worksheet

An easily-readable reduced practice page (with answers) for this lesson can be found on p. 476D.

2. Use common logarithms in the change of base formula, or use natural logarithms in the change of base formula.

SKILL PRACTICE

A

1. **VOCABULARY** Copy and complete: To condense the expression $\log_3 2x + \log_3 y$, you need to use the _?_ property of logarithms. product

2. ★ **WRITING** *Describe* two ways to evaluate $\log_7 12$ using a calculator. See margin.

EXAMPLE 1 on p. 507 for Exs. 3–14

MATCHING EXPRESSIONS **Match the expression with the logarithm that has the same value.**

3. $\ln 6 - \ln 2$ B
4. $2 \ln 6$ D
5. $6 \ln 2$ A
6. $\ln 6 + \ln 2$ C

A. $\ln 64$ **B.** $\ln 3$ **C.** $\ln 12$ **D.** $\ln 36$

APPROXIMATING EXPRESSIONS **Use $\log 4 \approx 0.602$ and $\log 12 \approx 1.079$ to evaluate the logarithm.**

7. $\log 3$ 0.477
8. $\log 48$ 1.681
9. $\log 16$ 1.204
10. $\log 64$ 1.806
11. $\log 144$ 2.158
12. $\log \frac{1}{3}$ -0.477
13. $\log \frac{1}{4}$ -0.602
14. $\log \frac{1}{12}$ -1.079

EXAMPLE 2 on p. 508 for Exs. 15–32

EXPANDING EXPRESSIONS **Expand the expression.**

15. $\log_3 4x$ $\log_3 4 + \log_3 x$
16. $\ln 15x$ $\ln 15 + \ln x$
17. $\log 3x^4$ $\log 3 + 4 \log x$
18. $\log_5 x^5$ $5 \log_5 x$
19. $\log_2 \frac{2}{5}$ $\log_2 2 - \log_2 5$
20. $\ln \frac{12}{5}$ $\ln 12 - \ln 5$
21. $\log_4 \frac{x}{3y}$ $\log_4 x - \log_4 3 - \log_4 y$
22. $\ln 4x^2y$ $\ln 4 + 2 \ln x + \ln y$
23. $\log_7 5x^3yz^2$
24. $\log_6 36x^2$ $\log_6 36 + 2 \log_6 x$
25. $\ln x^2y^{1/3}$ $2 \ln x + \frac{1}{3} \ln y$
26. $\log 10x^3$ $\log 10 + 3 \log x$
27. $\log_2 \sqrt{x}$ $\frac{1}{2} \log_2 x$
28. $\ln \frac{6x^2}{y^4}$ $\ln 6 + 2 \ln x - 4 \ln y$
29. $\ln \sqrt[4]{x^3}$ $\frac{3}{4} \ln x$
30. $\log_3 \sqrt{9x}$ $\frac{1}{2}(\log_3 9 + \log_3 x)$

21. $\log_4 x - (\log_4 3 + \log_4 y)$

23. $\log_7 5 + 3\log_7 x + \log_7 y + 2\log_7 z$

ERROR ANALYSIS *Describe* **and correct the error in expanding the logarithmic expression.**

31. $\log_2 5x = (\log_2 5)(\log_2 x)$ ✗

32. $\ln 8x^3 = 3 \ln 8 + \ln x$

31. The two parts should be added, not multiplied; $\log_2 5 + \log_2 x$.

32. The power of 3 is attached to the x, not the 8; $\ln 8 + 3 \ln x$.

EXAMPLE 3 on p. 508 for Exs. 33–43

CONDENSING EXPRESSIONS **Condense the expression.**

33. $\log_4 7 - \log_4 10$ $\log_4 \frac{7}{10}$
34. $\ln 12 - \ln 4$ $\ln 3$
35. $2 \log x + \log 11$ $\log 11x^2$
36. $6 \ln x + 4 \ln y$ $\ln x^6y^4$
37. $5 \log x - 4 \log y$ $\log \frac{x^5}{y^4}$
38. $5 \log_4 2 + 7 \log_4 x + 4 \log_4 y$ $\log_4 32x^7y^4$
39. $\ln 40 + 2 \ln \frac{1}{2} + \ln x$ $\ln 10x$
40. $\log_5 4 + \frac{1}{3} \log_5 x$ $\log_5 4\sqrt[3]{x}$
41. $6 \ln 2 - 4 \ln y$ $\ln \frac{64}{y^4}$
42. $2(\log_3 20 - \log_3 4) + 0.5 \log_3 4$ $\log_3 50$

43. ★ **MULTIPLE CHOICE** Which of the following is equivalent to $3 \log_4 6$? C

Ⓐ $\log_4 18$ Ⓑ $\log_4 72$ Ⓒ $\log_4 216$ Ⓓ $\log_4 256$

44. ★ **MULTIPLE CHOICE** Which of the following statements is *not* correct? D

Ⓐ $\log_3 48 = \log_3 16 + \log_3 3$ Ⓑ $\log_3 48 = 3\log_3 2 + \log_3 6$

Ⓒ $\log_3 48 = 2\log_3 4 + \log_3 3$ Ⓓ $\log_3 48 = \log_3 8 + 2\log_3 3$

EXAMPLE 4 on p. 509 for Exs. 45–61

B **CHANGE-OF-BASE FORMULA Use the change-of-base formula to evaluate the logarithm.**

45. $\log_4 7$ about 1.404 46. $\log_5 13$ about 1.594 47. $\log_3 15$ about 2.465 48. $\log_8 22$ about 1.486

49. $\log_3 6$ about 1.631 50. $\log_5 14$ about 1.640 51. $\log_6 17$ about 1.581 52. $\log_2 28$ about 4.807

53. $\log_7 19$ about 1.513 54. $\log_4 48$ about 2.792 55. $\log_9 27$ 1.5 56. $\log_8 32$ about 1.667

57. $\log_6 \frac{24}{5}$ about 0.875 58. $\log_2 \frac{15}{7}$ about 1.100 59. $\log_3 \frac{9}{40}$ about −1.358 60. $\log_7 \frac{3}{16}$ about −0.860

61. **ERROR ANALYSIS** *Describe* and correct the error in using the change-of-base formula. When using the change of base formula, the base goes in the denominator; $\frac{\log 7}{\log 3}$.

$\log_3 7 = \frac{\log 3}{\log 7}$ ✗

EXAMPLE 5 on p. 509 for Exs. 62–63

SOUND INTENSITY In Exercises 62 and 63, use the function in Example 5.

62. Find the decibel level of the sound made by each object shown below.

a.

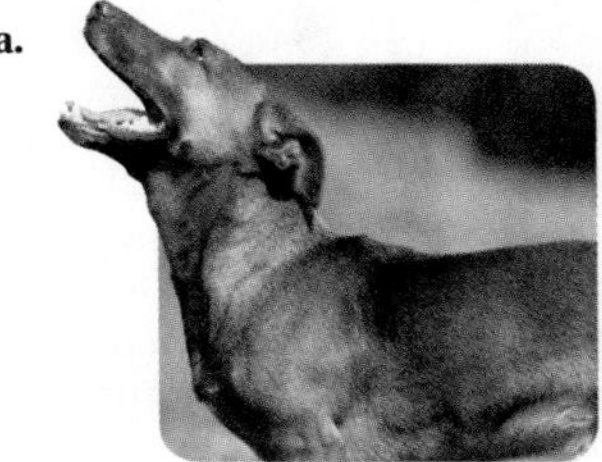

b.

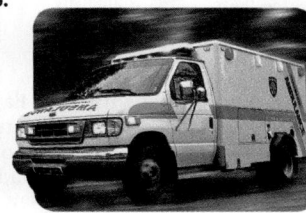

c.

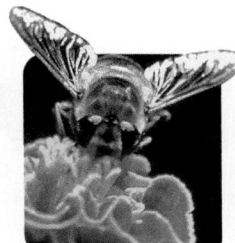

Barking dog: $I = 10^{-4}$ W/m² 80 decibels

Ambulance siren: $I = 10^{0}$ W/m² 120 decibels

Bee: $I = 10^{-6.5}$ W/m² 55 decibels

63. The intensity of the sound of a trumpet is 10^3 watts per square meter. Find the decibel level of a trumpet. 150 decibels

64. ★ **OPEN-ENDED MATH** For each statement, find positive numbers M, N, and b (with $b \neq 1$) that show the statement is false in general. a–b. Sample answers are given.

a. $\log_b (M + N) = \log_b M + \log_b N$ $M = 5, N = 6, b = 3, 2.183 \neq 1.465 + 1.631$

b. $\log_b (M - N) = \log_b M - \log_b N$ $M = 6, N = 5, b = 3, 0 \neq 1.631 - 1.465$

C **CHALLENGE In Exercises 65–68, use the given hint and properties of exponents to prove the property of logarithms.** 65–68. See margin.

65. **Product property** $\log_b mn = \log_b m + \log_b n$
(*Hint:* Let $x = \log_b m$ and let $y = \log_b n$. Then $m = b^x$ and $n = b^y$.)

66. **Quotient property** $\log_b \frac{m}{n} = \log_b m - \log_b n$
(*Hint:* Let $x = \log_b m$ and let $y = \log_b n$. Then $m = b^x$ and $n = b^y$.)

67. **Power property** $\log_b m^n = n \log_b m$
(*Hint:* Let $x = \log_b m$. Then $m = b^x$ and $m^n = b^{nx}$.)

68. **Change-of-base formula** $\log_c a = \frac{\log_b a}{\log_b c}$
(*Hint:* Let $x = \log_b a$, $y = \log_b c$, and $z = \log_c a$. Then $a = b^x$, $c = b^y$, and $a = c^z$, so that $b^x = c^z$.)

65. Let $x = \log_b m$ and $y = \log_b n$, convert these to exponential form to get $m = b^x$ and $n = b^y$. Then $mn = b^x b^y$; $mn = b^{x+y}$. Convert this to logarithmic form to get $\log_b (mn) = x + y$. Using substitution, to get $\log_b (mn) = \log_b m + \log_b n$.

Avoiding Common Errors

Exercise 21 Some students may write the answer as $\log_4 x - \log_4 3 + \log_4 y$, rather than $\log_4 x - \log_4 3 - \log_4 y$ because they see the product $3y$. Show these students how to expand the given logarithmic expression step-by-step so that the denominator is first treated as a unit: $\log_4 \frac{x}{3y} = \log_4 x - \log_4 3y = \log_4 x - (\log_4 3 + \log_4 y) = \log_4 x - \log_4 3 - \log_4 y$.

Study Strategy

Exercises 45–60 Students may have trouble remembering whether $\log_4 7$ is equal to $\frac{\log 7}{\log 4}$ or $\frac{\log 4}{\log 7}$, and similarly in the other exercises in this group. These students may find it easier to remember that the base in the logarithmic expression is in the denominator (as the "base") of the fraction.

66. Let $x = \log_b m$ and $y = \log_b n$. Convert these to exponential form and you get $m = b^x$ and $n = b^y$. Then $\frac{m}{n} = \frac{b^x}{b^y}$ which simplifies to b^{x-y}. Convert this to logarithmic form and you get $\log_b \left(\frac{m}{n}\right) = x - y$. Use substitution to get $\log_b \left(\frac{m}{n}\right) = \log_b m - \log_b n$.

67. Let $x = \log_b m$, convert this to exponential form, and you have $m = b^x$ and then $m^n = b^{nx}$. When you convert this to logarithmic form, you have $\log_b m^n = nx$. Use substitution to get $\log_b m^n = n \log_b m$.

68. Let $x = \log_b a$, $y = \log_b c$, and $z = \log_c a$. Convert these to exponential form to get $a = b^x$, $c = b^y$, $a = c^z$. Since $a = b^x$ and $a = c^z$, then $b^x = c^z$. Then take the log of both sides, to end up with $\log_b b^x = \log_b c^z$. This simplifies to $x \log_b b = z \log_b c$. Since $\log_b b = 1$ and $\log_b c = y$, use substitution to get $x = yz$. Then solve for z and the result is $z = \frac{x}{y}$, and by substitution, $\log_c a = \frac{\log_b a}{\log_b c}$.

71. 10;
$L(10I) - L(I)$
$= 10 \log \frac{10I}{I_0} - 10 \log \frac{I}{I_0}$
$= 10\left(\log \frac{10I}{I_0} - \log \frac{I}{I_0}\right)$
$= 10\left(\log 10 + \log \frac{I}{I_0} - \log \frac{I}{I_0}\right)$
$= 10 \log 10$
$= 10(1) = 10$

74b.
$s(h) = 2 \ln (100h)$
$= 2 \log_e (100h)$
$= 2 \log_e 100 + 2 \log_e h$
$= 2 \frac{\log 100}{\log e} + 2 \frac{\log h}{\log e}$
$= 2 \frac{2}{\log e} + 2 \frac{\log h}{\log e}$
$= \frac{2}{\log e}(2 + \log h)$

PROBLEM SOLVING

EXAMPLE 5 [A] on p. 509 for Exs. 69–72

69. **CONVERSATION** Three groups of people are having separate conversations in a room. The sound of each conversation has an intensity of 1.4×10^{-5} watts per square meter. What is the decibel level of the combined conversations in the room? **about 76 decibels**

@HomeTutor for problem solving help at classzone.com

70. **PARKING GARAGE** The sound made by each of five cars in a parking garage has an intensity of 3.2×10^{-4} watts per square meter. What is the decibel level of the sound made by all five cars in the parking garage? **about 92 decibels**

@HomeTutor for problem solving help at classzone.com

[B] 71. ★ **SHORT RESPONSE** The intensity of the sound TV ads make is ten times as great as the intensity for an average TV show. How many decibels louder is a TV ad? *Justify* your answer using properties of logarithms. **See margin.**

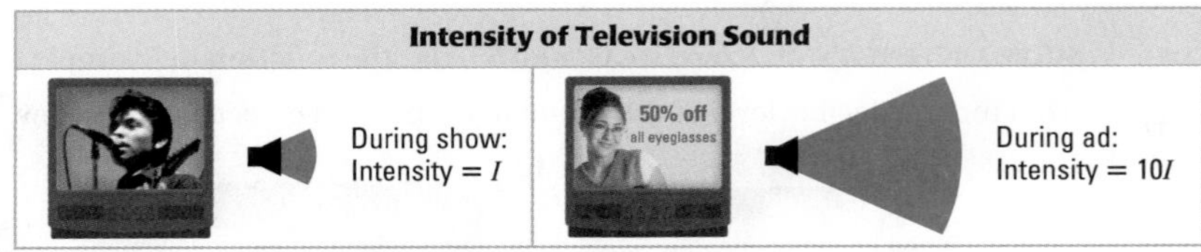

72. **BIOLOGY** The loudest animal on Earth is the blue whale. It can produce a sound with an intensity of $10^{6.8}$ watts per square meter. The loudest sound a human can make has an intensity of $10^{0.8}$ watts per square meter. *Compare* the decibel levels of the sounds made by a blue whale and a human.
***Sample answer:* A blue whale can create sounds that are 60 decibels louder than that of a human.**

73. ★ **EXTENDED RESPONSE** The f-stops on a 35 millimeter camera control the amount of light that enters the camera. Let s be a measure of the amount of light that strikes the film and let f be the f-stop. Then s and f are related by the equation:

$$s = \log_2 f^2$$

a. **Use Properties** Expand the expression for s. $s = 2 \log_2 f$

b. **Calculate** The table shows the first eight f-stops on a 35 millimeter camera. Copy and complete the table. *Describe* the pattern you observe.
***Sample answer:* The amount of light increases by about 1 each time.**

f	1.414	2.000	2.828	4.000	5.657	8.000	11.314	16.000
s	?	?	?	?	?	?	?	?
	about 1	2	about 3	4	about 5	6	about 7	8

c. **Reasoning** Many 35 millimeter cameras have nine f-stops. What do you think the ninth f-stop is? *Explain* your reasoning.
About 22.627; if you set up the equation $9 = 2 \log_2 f$ and solve for f, the result is $2^{9/2}$.

○ = WORKED-OUT SOLUTIONS on p. WS1
★ = STANDARDIZED TEST PRACTICE

Quiz, p. 513

5.
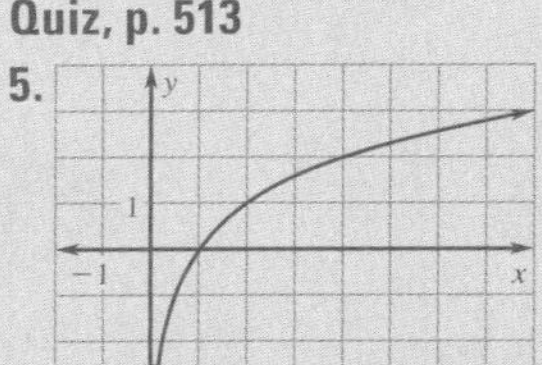

6.
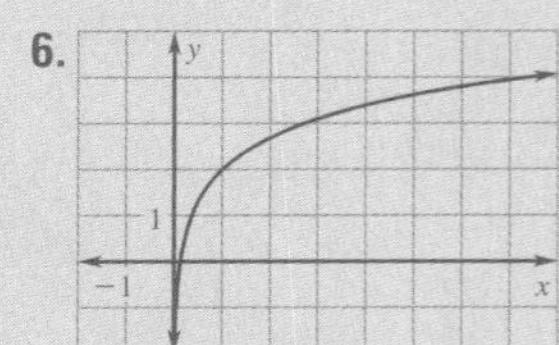

7.
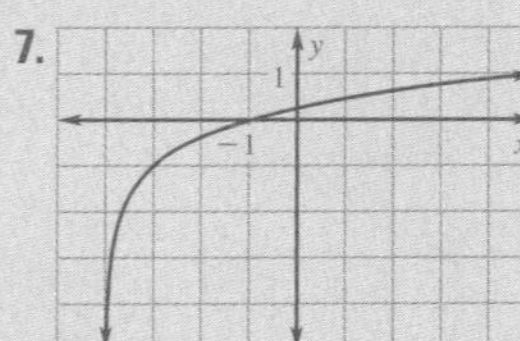

C **74. CHALLENGE** Under certain conditions, the wind speed s (in knots) at an altitude of h meters above a grassy plain can be modeled by this function:

$$s(h) = 2 \ln (100h)$$

a. By what factor does the wind speed increase when the altitude doubles? **about 1.386 knots**

b. Show that the given function can be written in terms of common logarithms as $s(h) = \frac{2}{\log e}(\log h + 2)$. **See margin.**

KENTUCKY MIXED REVIEW

KY

TEST PRACTICE at classzone.com

75. Which of the following is *not* an example of a Pythagorean triple? **C**

Ⓐ 8, 15, 17 Ⓑ 48, 64, 80 Ⓒ 7, 23, 25 Ⓓ 11, 60, 61

76. Which inequality best describes the range of the function whose graph is shown? **B**

Ⓐ $y \le -1$ Ⓑ $y \le 3$

Ⓒ $y \ge -1$ Ⓓ $y \ge 3$

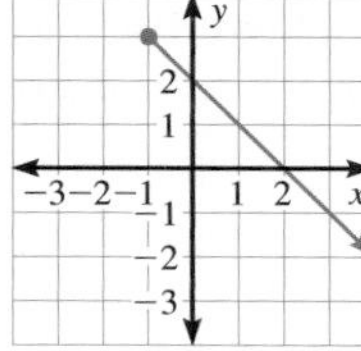

QUIZ for Lessons 7.4–7.5

Evaluate the logarithm without using a calculator. *(p. 499)*

1. $\log_4 16$ **2** **2.** $\log_5 1$ **0** **3.** $\log_8 8$ **1** **4.** $\log_{1/2} 32$ **−5**

Graph the function. State the domain and range. *(p. 499)* **5–7. See margin for art.**

5. $y = \log_2 x$ **domain: $x > 0$, range: all real numbers**

6. $y = \ln x + 2$ **domain: $x > 0$, range: all real numbers**

7. $y = \log_3 (x + 4) - 1$ **domain: $x > -4$, range: all real numbers**

Expand the expression. *(p. 507)*

8. $\log_2 5x$ **$\log_2 5 + \log_2 x$**

9. $\log_5 x^7$ **$7 \log_5 x$**

10. $\ln 5xy^3$ **$\ln 5 + \ln x + 3 \ln y$**

11. $\log_3 \frac{6y^4}{x^8}$ **$\log_3 6 + 4 \log_3 y - 8 \log_3 x$**

Condense the expression. *(p. 507)*

12. $\log_3 5 - \log_3 20$ **$\log_3 \frac{1}{4}$**

13. $\ln 6 + \ln 4x$ **$\ln 24x$**

14. $\log_6 5 + 3 \log_6 2$ **$\log_6 40$**

15. $4 \ln x - 5 \ln x$ **$\ln \frac{1}{x}$**

Use the change-of-base formula to evaluate the logarithm. *(p. 507)*

16. $\log_3 10$ **about 2.096** **17.** $\log_7 14$ **about 1.356** **18.** $\log_5 24$ **about 1.975** **19.** $\log_8 40$ **about 1.774**

20. SOUND INTENSITY The sound of an alarm clock has an intensity of $I = 10^{-4}$ watts per square meter. Use the model $L(I) = 10 \log \frac{I}{I_0}$, where $I_0 = 10^{-12}$ watts per square meter, to find the alarm clock's loudness $L(I)$. *(p. 507)* **80 decibels**

5 ASSESS AND RETEACH

Daily Homework Quiz

Transparency Available

Use $\log_5 20 \approx 1.861$ and $\log_5 8 \approx 1.292$ to evaluate the logarithm.

1. $\log_5 160$ **3.153**
2. $\log_5 8000$ **5.583**
3. Expand $\ln \frac{\sqrt[3]{x}}{y^2}$. **$\frac{1}{3} \ln x - 2 \ln y$**
4. Condense $5 \log_2 x - 4 \log_2 y$. **$\log_2 \frac{x^5}{y^4}$**
5. Use the change-of-base formula to evaluate $\log_4 50$. **2.822**
6. The intensity level of an electric guitar is $10^{2.8}$ watts per square meter. Use the formula $L(I) = 10 \log \frac{I}{I_0}$, where $I_0 \approx 10^{-12}$ watts per square meter, to find the decibel level of the guitar. **about 148 decibels**

Online Quiz

Available at **classzone.com**

Diagnosis/Remediation

- Practice A, B, C in Chapter 7 Resource Book, pp. 54–56
- Study Guide in Chapter 7 Resource Book, pp. 57–58
- Practice Workbook, pp. 116–117
- @HomeTutor

Challenge

Additional challenge is available in the Chapter 7 Resource Book, p. 61.

Quiz

An easily-readable reduced copy of the quiz (with answers) on Lessons 7.4–7.5 from the Assessment Book can be found on p. 476E.

@HomeTutor
classzone.com
Keystrokes

1 PLAN AND PREPARE

Learn the Method

- Students will learn how to use a graphing calculator to graph logarithmic functions. This gives an alternative to graphing these functions by hand, as described in Lesson 7.4.

Keystroke Help

Keystrokes for several models of calculators are available in blackline format in the *Chapter 7 Resource Book*.

2 TEACH

Tips for Success

Students who do not get the correct graphs are probably entering the functions incorrectly. Check the keystrokes that they have used. They may have made errors with parentheses. Have these students follow the keystrokes in Step 2 of the Example and adapt these as needed.

Extra Example

Use a graphing calculator to graph $y = \log_3 x$ and $y = \log_3 (x + 4) - 2$.

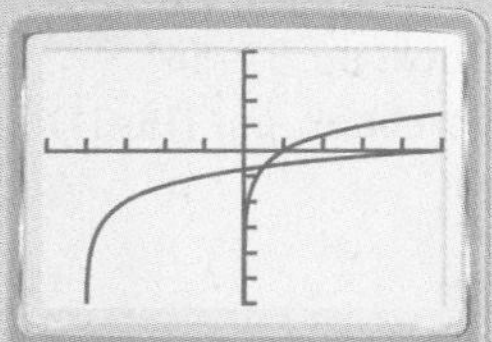

3 ASSESS AND RETEACH

Why must the change-of-base formula be used if the base is not 10 or e? **A graphing calculator has logarithm keys only for base 10 and for base e.**

1–12. See Additional Answers beginning on p. AA1.

7.5 Graph Logarithmic Functions

QUESTION **How can you graph logarithmic functions on a graphing calculator?**

You can use a graphing calculator to graph logarithmic functions simply by using the LOG or LN key. To graph a logarithmic function having a base other than 10 or e, you need to use the change-of-base formula to rewrite the function in terms of common or natural logarithms.

EXAMPLE **Graph logarithmic functions**

Use a graphing calculator to graph $y = \log_2 x$ and $y = \log_2 (x - 3) + 1$.

STEP 1 ***Rewrite functions*** Use the change-of-base formula to rewrite each function in terms of common logarithms.

$$y = \log_2 x = \frac{\log x}{\log 2} \qquad y = \log_2 (x - 3) + 1 = \frac{\log (x - 3)}{\log 2} + 1$$

STEP 2 ***Enter functions***

Enter each function into a graphing calculator.

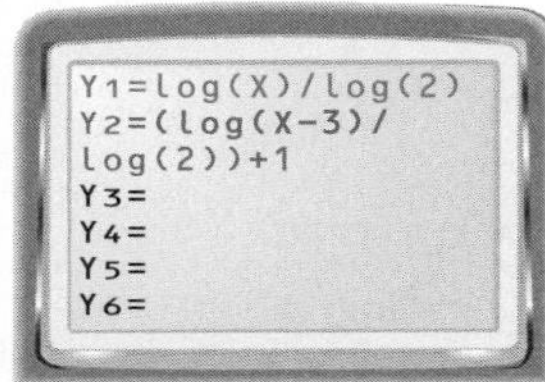

STEP 3 ***Graph functions***

Graph the functions.

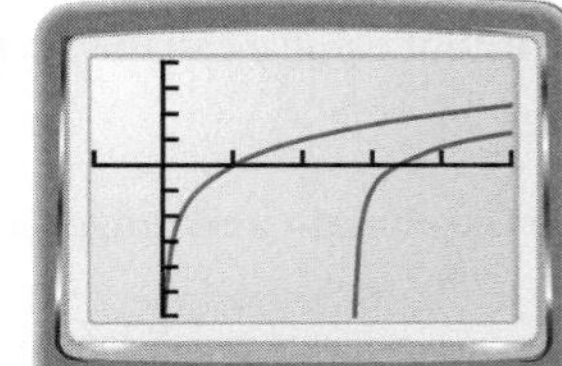

PRACTICE

Use a graphing calculator to graph the function. **1–12. See margin.**

1. $y = \log_4 x$
2. $y = \log_8 x$
3. $f(x) = \log_3 x$
4. $y = \log_5 x$
5. $y = \log_{12} x$
6. $g(x) = \log_9 x$
7. $y = \log_3 (x + 2)$
8. $y = \log_5 x - 1$
9. $f(x) = \log_4 (x - 5) - 2$
10. $y = \log_2 (x + 4) - 7$
11. $y = \log_7 (x - 5) + 3$
12. $g(x) = \log_3 (x + 6) - 6$

13. **REASONING** Graph $y = \ln x$. If your calculator did not have a natural logarithm key, explain how you could graph $y = \ln x$ using the LOG key. **See margin for art; $\ln x = \log_e x = \frac{\log x}{\log e}$.**

13.
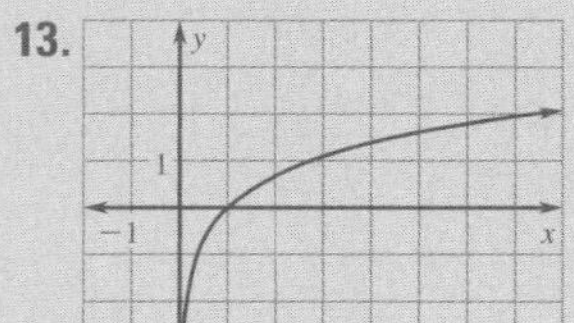

7.6 Solve Exponential and Logarithmic Equations

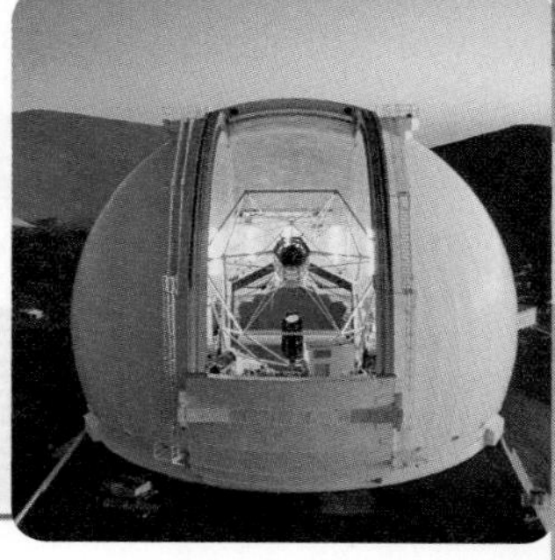

MA-HS-5.1.4 Students will recognize and solve problems that can be modeled using an exponential function, such as compound interest problems.

Before You studied exponential and logarithmic functions.

Now You will solve exponential and logarithmic equations.

Why? So you can solve problems about astronomy, as in Example 7.

Key Vocabulary
- exponential equation
- logarithmic equation
- extraneous solution, *p. 52*

Exponential equations are equations in which variable expressions occur as exponents. The result below is useful for solving certain exponential equations.

KEY CONCEPT *For Your Notebook*

Property of Equality for Exponential Equations

Algebra If b is a positive number other than 1, then $b^x = b^y$ if and only if $x = y$.

Example If $3^x = 3^5$, then $x = 5$. If $x = 5$, then $3^x = 3^5$.

EXAMPLE 1 Solve by equating exponents

Solve $4^x = \left(\frac{1}{2}\right)^{x-3}$.

$4^x = \left(\frac{1}{2}\right)^{x-3}$ Write original equation.

$(2^2)^x = (2^{-1})^{x-3}$ Rewrite 4 and $\frac{1}{2}$ as powers with base 2.

$2^{2x} = 2^{-x+3}$ Power of a power property

$2x = -x + 3$ Property of equality for exponential equations

$x = 1$ Solve for x.

▶ The solution is 1.

CHECK Check the solution by substituting it into the original equation.

$4^1 \stackrel{?}{=} \left(\frac{1}{2}\right)^{1-3}$ Substitute 1 for x.

$4 \stackrel{?}{=} \left(\frac{1}{2}\right)^{-2}$ Simplify.

$4 = 4$ ✓ Solution checks.

✓ GUIDED PRACTICE for Example 1

Solve the equation.

1. $9^{2x} = 27^{x-1}$ -3
2. $100^{7x+1} = 1000^{3x-2}$ $-\frac{8}{5}$
3. $81^{3-x} = \left(\frac{1}{3}\right)^{5x-6}$ -6

1 PLAN AND PREPARE

Warm-Up Exercises

Transparency Available

1. Write $\log_3(2x - 7) = 4$ in exponential form. $3^4 = 2x - 7$
2. Write $8^x = 30$ in logarithmic form. $\log_8 30 = x$

Solve the equation.

3. $100^x = 1000$ $\frac{3}{2}$
4. $\log_5 x = -3$ $\frac{1}{125}$
5. $x^2 - 7x - 60 = 0$ $-5, 12$

Notetaking Guide

Transparency Available

Promotes interactive learning and notetaking skills, pp. 202–205.

Pacing

Basic: 2 days
Average: 2 days
Advanced: 2 days
Block: 1 block
- See *Teaching Guide/Lesson Plan.*

2 FOCUS AND MOTIVATE

Essential Question

Big Idea 2, p. 477

Why do logarithmic equations sometimes have extraneous solutions? **Tell students they will learn how to answer this question by solving logarithmic equations and checking the apparent solutions.**

Resource Planning Guide

Chapter Resource Book
- Teaching Guide/Lesson Plan (pp. 62–63)
- Practice levels A, B, C (pp. 65–67)
- Study Guide (pp. 68–69)
- Catch-up for Absent Students (p. 70)
- Application (p. 71)
- Challenge (p. 72)

Workbooks
- Notetaking Guide (pp. 202–205)
- Practice Workbook (pp. 118–119)

Teaching Options
- **Power Presentations CD-ROM** provides dynamic electronic teaching resources for the classroom.
- **Activity Generator CD-ROM** provides editable activities for all ability levels.

Interactive Technology
- Easy Planner
- Power Presentations CD-ROM
- Activity Generator CD-ROM
- Animated Algebra
- Test Generator CD-ROM
- Online Quiz
- eWorkbook
- eEdition
- @HomeTutor

Resources for English Learners
- Quick Reference for English Learners
- Spanish Study Guide
- Multi-Language Visual Glossary
- Student Resources in Spanish

See also the *Algebra 2 Toolkit* for more strategies for meeting individual needs.

When it is not convenient to write each side of an exponential equation using the same base, you can solve the equation by taking a logarithm of each side.

EXAMPLE 2 Take a logarithm of each side

ANOTHER WAY
For an alternative method for solving the problem in Example 2, turn to page 523 for the **Problem Solving Workshop**.

Solve $4^x = 11$.

$4^x = 11$	**Write original equation.**
$\log_4 4^x = \log_4 11$	**Take $\log_4$ of each side.**
$x = \log_4 11$	**$\log_b b^x = x$**
$x = \dfrac{\log 11}{\log 4}$	**Change-of-base formula**
$x \approx 1.73$	**Use a calculator.**

▶ The solution is about 1.73. Check this in the original equation.

NEWTON'S LAW OF COOLING An important application of exponential equations is *Newton's law of cooling.* This law states that for a cooling substance with initial temperature T_0, the temperature T after t minutes can be modeled by

$$T = (T_0 - T_R)e^{-rt} + T_R$$

where T_R is the surrounding temperature and r is the substance's cooling rate.

EXAMPLE 3 Use an exponential model

CARS You are driving on a hot day when your car overheats and stops running. It overheats at 280°F and can be driven again at 230°F. If $r = 0.0048$ and it is 80°F outside, how long (in minutes) do you have to wait until you can continue driving?

Solution

$T = (T_0 - T_R)e^{-rt} + T_R$	**Newton's law of cooling**
$230 = (280 - 80)e^{-0.0048t} + 80$	**Substitute for T, T_0, T_R, and r.**
$150 = 200e^{-0.0048t}$	**Subtract 80 from each side.**
$0.75 = e^{-0.0048t}$	**Divide each side by 200.**
$\ln 0.75 = \ln e^{-0.0048t}$	**Take natural log of each side.**
$-0.2877 \approx -0.0048t$	**$\ln e^x = \log_e e^x = x$**
$60 \approx t$	**Divide each side by -0.0048.**

▶ You have to wait about 60 minutes until you can continue driving.

GUIDED PRACTICE for Examples 2 and 3

Solve the equation.

4. $2^x = 5$ **about 2.32**

5. $7^{9x} = 15$ **about 0.155**

6. $4e^{-0.3x} - 7 = 13$ **about −5.365**

Motivating the Lesson

Ask students who have studied radioactive decay in their science classes to explain the concept of half-life. Point out that the half-life of a radioactive substance can be found by using an exponential model with the natural base e.

3 TEACH

Extra Example 1

Solve $3^x = \left(\frac{1}{9}\right)^{x+3}$. **−2**

Key Question to Ask for Example 1

- For the method used to solve the equation to work, what must be true? **You must be able to write both sides as powers of the same base.**

Extra Example 2

Solve $9^x = 35$. **about 1.62**

Key Question to Ask for Example 2

- Why is it not possible to use the method of Example 1 in Example 2? **It is impossible to write 4 and 11 as powers of the same base.**

Extra Example 3

Hot chocolate that has been heated to 90°C is poured into a mug and placed on a table in a room with a temperature of 20°C. If $r = 0.145$ when the time t is measured in minutes, how long will it take for the hot chocolate to cool to a temperature of 30°C? **about 13 min**

SOLVING LOGARITHMIC EQUATIONS **Logarithmic equations** are equations that involve logarithms of variable expressions. You can use the following property to solve some types of logarithmic equations.

KEY CONCEPT *For Your Notebook*

Property of Equality for Logarithmic Equations

Algebra If b, x, and y are positive numbers with $b \neq 1$, then $\log_b x = \log_b y$ if and only if $x = y$.

Example If $\log_2 x = \log_2 7$, then $x = 7$. If $x = 7$, then $\log_2 x = \log_2 7$.

EXAMPLE 4 Solve a logarithmic equation

Solve $\log_5 (4x - 7) = \log_5 (x + 5)$.

$\log_5 (4x - 7) = \log_5 (x + 5)$ **Write original equation.**

$4x - 7 = x + 5$ **Property of equality for logarithmic equations**

$3x - 7 = 5$ **Subtract x from each side.**

$3x = 12$ **Add 7 to each side.**

$x = 4$ **Divide each side by 3.**

▶ The solution is 4.

CHECK Check the solution by substituting it into the original equation.

$\log_5 (4x - 7) = \log_5 (x + 5)$ **Write original equation.**

$\log_5 (4 \cdot 4 - 7) \stackrel{?}{=} \log_5 (4 + 5)$ **Substitute 4 for x.**

$\log_5 9 = \log_5 9$ ✓ **Solution checks.**

EXPONENTIATING TO SOLVE EQUATIONS The property of equality for exponential equations on page 515 implies that if you are given an equation $x = y$, then you can *exponentiate* each side to obtain an equation of the form $b^x = b^y$. This technique is useful for solving some logarithmic equations.

EXAMPLE 5 Exponentiate each side of an equation

Solve $\log_4 (5x - 1) = 3$.

$\log_4 (5x - 1) = 3$ **Write original equation.**

$4^{\log_4 (5x - 1)} = 4^3$ **Exponentiate each side using base 4.**

$5x - 1 = 64$ $b^{\log_b x} = x$

$5x = 65$ **Add 1 to each side.**

$x = 13$ **Divide each side by 5.**

▶ The solution is 13.

CHECK $\log_4 (5x - 1) = \log_4 (5 \cdot 13 - 1) = \log_4 64$

Because $4^3 = 64$, $\log_4 64 = 3$. ✓

Extra Example 4

Solve $\log_4 (2x + 8) = \log_4 (6x - 12)$. 5

Key Question to Ask for Example 4

- If each side of an equation contains a single logarithm and there are no other terms, what must be true in order for you to be able to solve the equation by the method used in Example 4? **Both logarithms must have the same base.**

Extra Example 5

Solve $\log_7 (3x - 2) = 2$. 17

Mathematical Reasoning

Multiple Representations The Key Concept box states the property of equality for logarithmic equations algebraically and gives an example. Ask students to state this property in words, using vocabulary such as *logarithm* and *base*, but without using any mathematical symbols. Then ask them to demonstrate this property graphically, using either a hand-drawn or calculator-generated graph.

Differentiated Instruction

Advanced Have students work in a small group to research *one-to-one* functions. Ask these students to present a mini-lesson on this topic to the class. The presentation should discuss the connection between one-to-one functions and relevant concepts that have been discussed in Chapters 6 and 7: inverse functions, the horizontal line test, the relationship between exponential and logarithmic functions with the same base, the property of equality for exponential functions, and the property of equality for logarithmic functions.

See also the *Algebra 2 Toolkit* for more strategies.

Extra Example 6

What is (are) the solution(s) of $\log_6 3x + \log_6 (x - 4) = 2$? D

Ⓐ $-6, 2$

Ⓑ $-2, 6$

Ⓒ 2

Ⓓ 6

Key Question to Ask for Example 6

- Before starting, how can you tell that the given equation cannot have any solutions that are less than or equal to 5? **Because the domain of $y = \log_b x$ is $x > 0$, in this equation, you must have $2x > 0$ and $x - 5 > 0$, which means that $x > 5$.**

EXTRANEOUS SOLUTIONS Because the domain of a logarithmic function generally does not include all real numbers, be sure to check for extraneous solutions of logarithmic equations. You can do this algebraically or graphically.

EXAMPLE 6 Standardized Test Practice

ELIMINATE CHOICES
Instead of solving the equation in Example 6 directly, you can substitute each possible answer into the equation to see whether it is a solution.

What is (are) the solution(s) of $\log 2x + \log (x - 5) = 2$?

Ⓐ $-5, 10$ Ⓑ 5 Ⓒ 10 Ⓓ 5, 10

Solution

$\log 2x + \log (x - 5) = 2$	**Write original equation.**
$\log [2x(x - 5)] = 2$	**Product property of logarithms**
$10^{\log [2x(x - 5)]} = 10^2$	**Exponentiate each side using base 10.**
$2x(x - 5) = 100$	$b^{\log_b x} = x$
$2x^2 - 10x = 100$	**Distributive property**
$2x^2 - 10x - 100 = 0$	**Write in standard form.**
$x^2 - 5x - 50 = 0$	**Divide each side by 2.**
$(x - 10)(x + 5) = 0$	**Factor.**
$x = 10$ or $x = -5$	**Zero product property**

CHECK Check the apparent solutions 10 and -5 using algebra or a graph.

Algebra Substitute 10 and -5 for x in the original equation.

$$\log 2x + \log (x - 5) = 2$$
$$\log (2 \cdot 10) + \log (10 - 5) \stackrel{?}{=} 2$$
$$\log 20 + \log 5 \stackrel{?}{=} 2$$
$$\log 100 \stackrel{?}{=} 2$$
$$2 = 2 \checkmark$$

So, 10 is a solution.

$$\log 2x + \log (x - 5) = 2$$
$$\log [2(-5)] + \log (-5 - 5) \stackrel{?}{=} 2$$
$$\log (-10) + \log (-10) \stackrel{?}{=} 2$$

Because $\log (-10)$ is not defined, -5 is *not* a solution.

Graph Graph $y = \log 2x + \log (x - 5)$ and $y = 2$ in the same coordinate plane. The graphs intersect only once, when $x = 10$. So, 10 is the only solution.

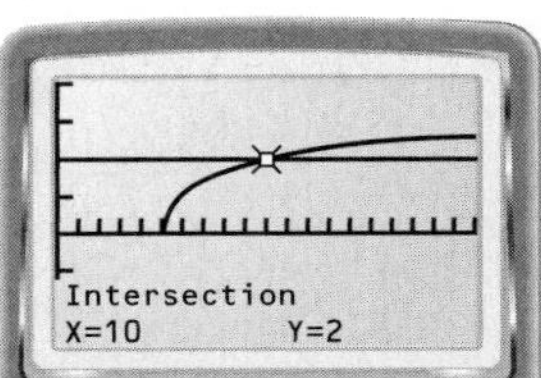

▸ The correct answer is C. Ⓐ Ⓑ Ⓒ Ⓓ

GUIDED PRACTICE for Examples 4, 5, and 6

Solve the equation. Check for extraneous solutions.

7. $\ln (7x - 4) = \ln (2x + 11)$ 3
8. $\log_2 (x - 6) = 5$ 38
9. $\log 5x + \log (x - 1) = 2$ 5
10. $\log_4 (x + 12) + \log_4 x = 3$ 4

EXAMPLE 7 Use a logarithmic model

ASTRONOMY The *apparent magnitude* of a star is a measure of the brightness of the star as it appears to observers on Earth. The apparent magnitude M of the dimmest star that can be seen with a telescope is given by the function

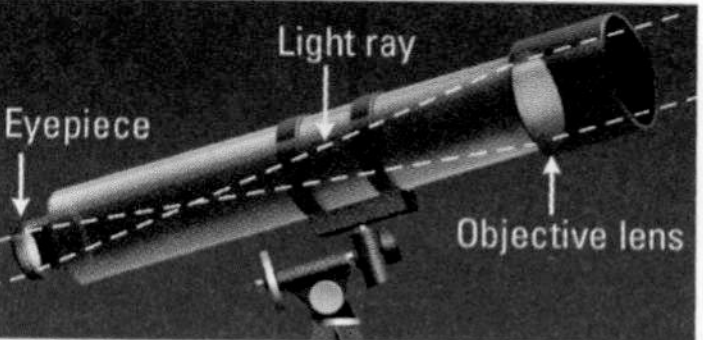

$$M = 5 \log D + 2$$

where D is the diameter (in millimeters) of the telescope's objective lens. If a telescope can reveal stars with a magnitude of 12, what is the diameter of its objective lens?

ANOTHER WAY
For an alternative method for solving the problem in Example 7, turn to page 523 for the **Problem Solving Workshop**.

Solution

$M = 5 \log D + 2$	Write original equation.
$12 = 5 \log D + 2$	Substitute 12 for M.
$10 = 5 \log D$	Subtract 2 from each side.
$2 = \log D$	Divide each side by 5.
$10^2 = 10^{\log D}$	Exponentiate each side using base 10.
$100 = D$	Simplify.

▸ The diameter is 100 millimeters.

 at classzone.com

GUIDED PRACTICE for Example 7

11. **WHAT IF?** Use the information from Example 7 to find the diameter of the objective lens of a telescope that can reveal stars with a magnitude of 7. 10 mm

7.6 EXERCISES

HOMEWORK KEY
○ = **WORKED-OUT SOLUTIONS** on p. WS14 for Exs. 15, 35, and 57
★ = **STANDARDIZED TEST PRACTICE** Exs. 2, 44, 47, 58, and 60
 = **MULTIPLE REPRESENTATIONS** Ex. 59

SKILL PRACTICE

A

1. **VOCABULARY** Copy and complete: The equation $5^x = 8$ is an example of a(n) _?_ equation. exponential

2. ★ **WRITING** When do logarithmic equations have extraneous solutions? *Sample answer:* When you have to factor to solve.

EXAMPLE 1 on p. 515 for Exs. 3–11

SOLVING EXPONENTIAL EQUATIONS Solve the equation.

3. $5^{x-4} = 25^{x-6}$ 8
4. $7^{3x+4} = 49^{2x+1}$ 2
5. $8^{x-1} = 32^{3x-2}$ $\frac{7}{12}$
6. $27^{4x-1} = 9^{3x+8}$ $\frac{19}{6}$
7. $4^{2x-5} = 64^{3x}$ $-\frac{5}{7}$
8. $3^{3x-7} = 81^{12-3x}$ $\frac{11}{3}$
9. $36^{5x+2} = \left(\frac{1}{6}\right)^{11-x}$ $-\frac{5}{3}$
10. $10^{3x-10} = \left(\frac{1}{100}\right)^{6x-1}$ $\frac{4}{5}$
11. $25^{10x+8} = \left(\frac{1}{125}\right)^{4-2x}$ -2

Extra Example 7

The population of deer in a forest preserve can be modeled by the equation $P = 50 + 200 \ln (t + 1)$, where t is the time in years from the present. In how many years will be deer population reach 500? about 8.5 yr

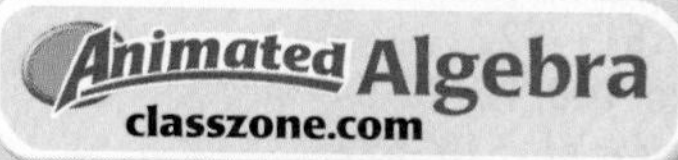

An **Animated Algebra** activity is available on-line for **Example 7**. This activity is also available on the **Power Presentations CD-ROM**.

Closing the Lesson

Have students summarize the major points of the lesson and answer the Essential Question: Why do logarithmic equations sometimes have extraneous solutions?

- Exponential equations can be solved either by equating exponents or by taking the logarithm of each side.
- Logarithmic equations can be solved either by applying the property of equality for logarithmic equations or by exponentiating each side.

Logarithmic equations sometimes have extraneous solutions because the domain of a logarithmic function generally does not include all real numbers, so any apparent solution that would lead to the logarithm of a nonpositive number must be rejected.

4 PRACTICE AND APPLY

Assignment Guide

Answer Transparencies available for all exercises

Basic:
Day 1: EP p. 1010 Exs. 16–21
pp. 519–522
Exs. 1–8, 12–20, 54–58
Day 2: pp. 519–522
Exs. 24–39, 59, 62–63

Average:
Day 1: pp. 519–522
Exs. 1, 2, 5–10, 14–21, 54–58
Day 2: pp. 519–522
Exs. 27–31, 36–47, 59, 60, 62–63

Advanced:
Day 1: pp. 519–522
Exs. 1, 2, 6–11, 15–23, 54–58
Day 2: pp. 519–522
Exs. 28–31, 38–53*, 59–61*

Block:
pp. 519–522
Exs. 1, 2, 5–10, 14–21, 27–31, 36–47, 54–60, 62–63

Differentiated Instruction

See *Algebra 2 Best Practices Toolkit* for suggestions on addressing the needs of a diverse classroom.

Homework Check

For a quick check of student understanding of key concepts, go over the following exercises:

Basic: 4, 14, 26, 32, 54
Average: 8, 18, 28, 36, 56
Advanced: 10, 22, 30, 40, 59

Extra Practice

- Student Edition, p. 1016
- Chapter 7 Resource Book: Practice levels A, B, C, pp. 65–67

Practice Worksheet

An easily-readable reduced practice page (with answers) for this lesson can be found on p. 476D.

EXAMPLE 2 on p. 516 for Exs. 12–23

SOLVING EXPONENTIAL EQUATIONS Solve the equation.

12. $8^x = 20$ about 1.441
13. $e^{-x} = 5$ about −1.609
14. $7^{3x} = 18$ about 0.495
15. $11^{5x} = 33$ about 0.292
16. $7^{6x} = 12$ about 0.213
17. $4e^{-2x} = 17$ about −0.723
18. $10^{3x} + 4 = 9$ about 0.233
19. $-3e^{2x} + 16 = 5$ about 0.650
20. $0.5^x - 0.25 = 4$ about −2.087
21. $\frac{1}{3}(6)^{-4x} + 1 = 6$ about −0.378
22. $2^{0.1x} - 5 = 7$ about 35.850
23. $\frac{3}{4}e^{2x} + \frac{7}{2} = 4$ about −0.203

EXAMPLE 4 on p. 517 for Exs. 24–31

SOLVING LOGARITHMIC EQUATIONS Solve the equation. Check for extraneous solutions.

24. $\log_5 (5x + 9) = \log_5 6x$ 9
25. $\ln (4x - 7) = \ln (x + 11)$ 6
26. $\ln (x + 19) = \ln (7x - 8)$ $\frac{9}{2}$
27. $\log_5 (2x - 7) = \log_5 (3x - 9)$ no solution
28. $\log (12x - 11) = \log (3x + 13)$ $\frac{8}{3}$
29. $\log_3 (18x + 7) = \log_3 (3x + 38)$ $\frac{31}{15}$
30. $\log_6 (3x - 10) = \log_6 (14 - 5x)$ no solution
31. $\log_8 (5 - 12x) = \log_8 (6x - 1)$ $\frac{1}{3}$

EXAMPLES 5 and 6 on pp. 517–518 for Exs. 32–44 [B]

EXPONENTIATING TO SOLVE EQUATIONS Solve the equation. Check for extraneous solutions.

32. $\log_4 x = -1$ $\frac{1}{4}$
33. $5 \ln x = 35$ e^7 or about 1096.633
34. $\frac{1}{3} \log_5 12x = 2$ $\frac{15{,}625}{12}$
35. $5.2 \log_4 2x = 16$ about 35.601
36. $\log_2 (x - 4) = 6$ 68
37. $\log_2 x + \log_2 (x - 2) = 3$ 4
38. $\log_4 (-x) + \log_4 (x + 10) = 2$ −8, −2
39. $\ln (x + 3) + \ln x = 1$ about 0.729
40. $4 \ln (-x) + 3 = 21$ about −90.017
41. $\log_5 (x + 4) + \log_5 (x + 1) = 2$ about 2.720
42. $\log_6 3x + \log_6 (x - 1) = 3$ 9
43. $\log_3 (x - 9) + \log_3 (x - 3) = 2$ about 10.243

44. ★ **MULTIPLE CHOICE** What is the solution of $3 \log_8 (2x + 7) + 8 = 10$? A

Ⓐ −1.5 Ⓑ −1.179 Ⓒ 4 Ⓓ 4.642

ERROR ANALYSIS *Describe* and correct the error in solving the equation.

45.
$$3^{x+1} = 6^x$$
$$\log_3 3^{x+1} = \log_3 6^x$$
$$x + 1 = x \log_3 6$$
$$x + 1 = 2x$$
$$1 = x$$

46.
$$\log_3 10x = 5$$
$$e^{\log_3 10x} = e^5$$
$$10x = e^5$$
$$x = \frac{e^5}{10}$$

45. The log was not simplified correctly, $x\log_3 6 \neq 2x$; $\log_3 6 \approx 1.631$, $x = 1.585$.

46. *Sample answer:* When converting the log to exponential form, 3 should have been used instead of *e*; $3^{\log_3 10x} = 3^5$, $10x = 243$, $x = 24.3$.

47. ★ **OPEN-ENDED MATH** Give an example of an exponential equation whose only solution is 4 and an example of a logarithmic equation whose only solution is −3. *Sample answer:* $3^x = 81$, $\log_5 (x + 4) = 0$

[C] **CHALLENGE** Solve the equation.

48. $3^{x+4} = 6^{2x-5}$ about 5.374
49. $10^{3x-8} = 2^{5-x}$ about 2.879
50. $\log_2 (x + 1) = \log_8 3x$ no solution
51. $\log_3 x = \log_9 6x$ 6
52. $2^{2x} - 12 \cdot 2^x + 32 = 0$ 2, 3
53. $5^{2x} + 20 \cdot 5^x - 125 = 0$ 1

○ = WORKED-OUT SOLUTIONS on p. WS1 ★ = STANDARDIZED TEST PRACTICE  = MULTIPLE REPRESENTATIONS

PROBLEM SOLVING

EXAMPLE 3 A
p. 516
Exs. 54–58

54. **COOKING** You are cooking beef stew. When you take the beef stew off the stove, it has a temperature of 200°F. The room temperature is 75°F and the cooling rate of the beef stew is $r = 0.054$. How long (in minutes) will it take to cool the beef stew to a serving temperature of 100°F? **about 30 min**

@HomeTutor for problem solving help at classzone.com

55. **THERMOMETER** As you are hanging an outdoor thermometer, its reading drops from the indoor temperature of 75°F to 37°F in one minute. If the cooling rate is $r = 1.37$, what is the outdoor temperature? **about 24°F**

@HomeTutor for problem solving help at classzone.com

56. **COMPOUND INTEREST** You deposit $100 in an account that pays 6% annual interest. How long will it take for the balance to reach $1000 for each given frequency of compounding?

a. Annual **40 yr** b. Quarterly **38.75 yr** c. Daily **38.38 yr**

57. **RADIOACTIVE DECAY** One hundred grams of radium are stored in a container. The amount R (in grams) of radium present after t years can be modeled by $R = 100e^{-0.00043t}$. After how many years will only 5 grams of radium be present? **about 6967 yr**

58. ★ **MULTIPLE CHOICE** You deposit $800 in an account that pays 2.25% annual interest compounded continuously. About how long will it take for the balance to triple? **C**

Ⓐ 24 years Ⓑ 36 years

Ⓒ 48.8 years Ⓓ 52.6 years

EXAMPLE 7 B
p. 519
Ex. 59

59. **MULTIPLE REPRESENTATIONS** The Richter scale is used for measuring the magnitude of an earthquake. The Richter magnitude R is given by the function

$$R = 0.67 \log (0.37E) + 1.46$$

where E is the energy (in kilowatt-hours) released by the earthquake. **a, b. See margin.**

a. **Making a Graph** Graph the function using a graphing calculator. Use your graph to approximate the amount of energy released by each earthquake indicated in the diagram above. **See margin for art.**

b. **Solving Equations** Write and solve a logarithmic equation to find the amount of energy released by each earthquake in the diagram.

(margin, partially cut off:) Japan: ut 000,000 watt-hours, ece: about 00,000 watt-hours, : ut 23,500 watt-hours. Japan: 6.6 = log(0.37E) + , 126,893,702 watt-hours; ece: 5.9 = log(0.37E) + , 11,446,269 watt-hours; ; 4.1 = 0.67 0.37E) + , 23,556 watt-hours

Avoiding Common Errors

Exercises 5, 6 Because they could write both sides as powers of 5 in Exercise 3 and powers of 7 in Exercise 4, some students may think the idea is to write both sides as powers of the smaller base in the given equation. They then find that this does not work in these exercises. If this happens, review the property of equality for exponential equations and emphasize that they must write both sides as *powers* of the same base, not *multiples* of the same base. Remind them that the common base does not have to be one of the bases that appear in the original equation.

Teaching Strategy

Exercises 24–43 Be sure students are able to distinguish the type of equations in 24–31 that are solved by applying the property of equality for logarithmic equations, from the type in Exercises 32–43 that are solved by exponentiating both sides. The first type can be called "log = log" equations, and the second type, "log = number" equations. Give students additional mixed practice including both types of equations so that they will learn to distinguish between them and to choose the appropriate method of solution for each logarithmic equation they encounter.

Internet Reference

Exercise 59 More information about the Richter scale can be found at www. www.seismo.unr.edu/ftp/pub/louie/class/100/magnitude.html

59a.

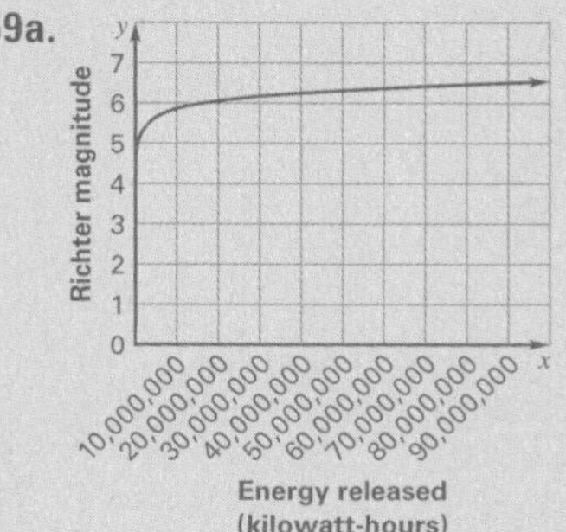

5 ASSESS AND RETEACH

Daily Homework Quiz

 **Transparency Available**

Solve the equation.

1. $25^x = 125^{-x+2}$ $\frac{6}{5}$
2. $8^x = 5$ about 0.77
3. $\log_7(5x - 8) = \log_7(2x + 19)$ 9
4. $\log_3(5x + 1) = 4$ 16
5. $\log_5 5x + \log_5(x - 4) = 2$ 5
6. Boiling water has a temperature of 212°F. Water has a cooling rate of $r = 0.042$. Use the formula $T = (T_0 - T_R)e^{-rt} + T_R$ to find the number of minutes t it will take for boiling water to cool to a temperature of 80°F if the room temperature is 72°F. about 68 min

Online Quiz

Available at **classzone.com**

Diagnosis/Remediation

- Practice A, B, C in Chapter 7 Resource Book, pp. 65–67
- Study Guide in Chapter 7 Resource Book, pp. 68–69
- Practice Workbook, pp. 118–119
- @HomeTutor

Challenge

Additional challenge is available in the Chapter 7 Resource Book, p. 72.

60. ★ **EXTENDED RESPONSE** If X-rays of a fixed wavelength strike a material x centimeters thick, then the intensity $I(x)$ of the X-rays transmitted through the material is given by $I(x) = I_0e^{-\mu x}$, where I_0 is the initial intensity and μ is a number that depends on the type of material and the wavelength of the X-rays. The table shows the values of μ for various materials. These μ-values apply to X-rays of medium wavelength.

Material	Aluminum	Copper	Lead
Value of μ	0.43	3.2	43

a. Find the thickness of aluminum shielding that reduces the intensity of X-rays to 30% of their initial intensity. (*Hint:* Find the value of x for which $I(x) = 0.3I_0$.) about 2.8 cm

b. Repeat part (a) for copper shielding. about 0.38 cm

c. Repeat part (a) for lead shielding. about 0.03 cm

d. Reasoning Your dentist puts a lead apron on you before taking X-rays of your teeth to protect you from harmful radiation. Based on your results from parts (a)–(c), explain why lead is a better material to use than aluminum or copper. The lead apron does not have to be as thick as aluminum or copper to result in the same intensity.

C **61. CHALLENGE** You plant a sunflower seedling in your garden. The seedling's height h (in centimeters) after t weeks can be modeled by the function below, which is called a *logistic function*.

$$h(t) = \frac{256}{1 + 13e^{-0.65t}}$$

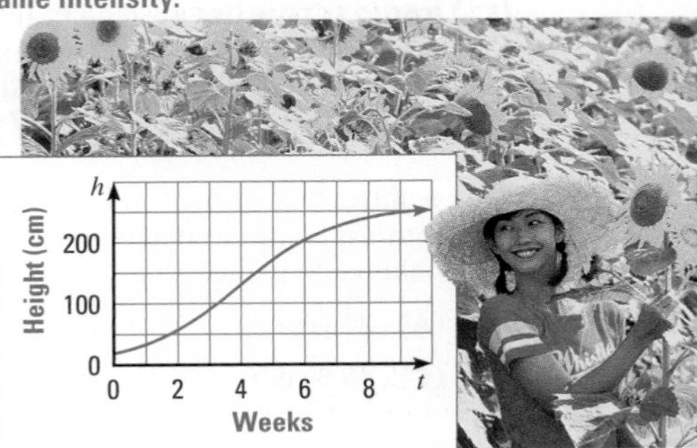

Find the time it takes the sunflower seedling to reach a height of 200 centimeters. about 5.9 wk

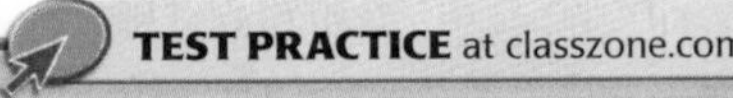

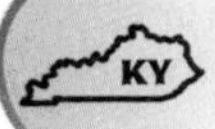

KENTUCKY MIXED REVIEW

TEST PRACTICE at classzone.com

62. Which list shows the functions in order from the widest graph to the narrowest graph? **B**

Ⓐ $y = -5x^2, y = -\frac{2}{3}x^2, y = \frac{5}{6}x^2, y = 8x^2$

Ⓑ $y = -\frac{2}{3}x^2, y = \frac{5}{6}x^2, y = -5x^2, y = 8x^2$

Ⓒ $y = \frac{5}{6}x^2, y = -\frac{2}{3}x^2, y = 8x^2, y = -5x^2$

Ⓓ $y = 8x^2, y = \frac{5}{6}x^2, y = -\frac{2}{3}x^2, y = -5x^2$

63. In the diagram, $m\angle 2 = m\angle 3$. What is $m\angle 1$? **B**

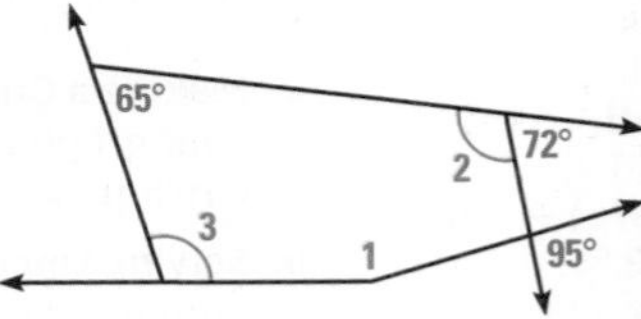

Ⓐ 136° Ⓑ 164°

Ⓒ 174° Ⓓ 194°

EXTRA PRACTICE for Lesson 7.6, p. 1016

 **ONLINE QUIZ** at classzone.com

Using ALTERNATIVE METHODS

Another Way to Solve Examples 2 and 7, pp. 516 and 519

MULTIPLE REPRESENTATIONS In Examples 2 and 7 on pages 516 and 519, respectively, you solved exponential and logarithmic equations algebraically. You can also solve such equations using tables and graphs.

PROBLEM 1

Solve the following exponential equation: $4^x = 11$.

METHOD 1

Using a Table One way to solve the equation is to make a table of values.

STEP 1 **Enter** the function $y = 4^x$ into a graphing calculator.

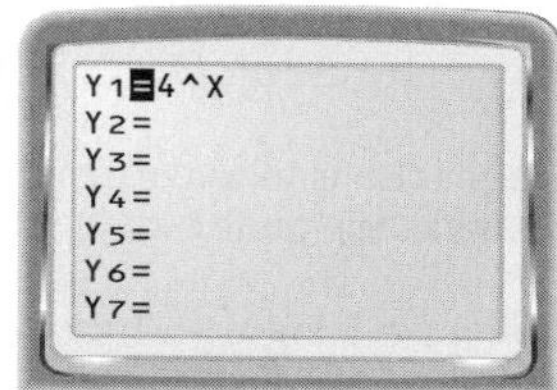

STEP 2 **Create** a table of values for the function.

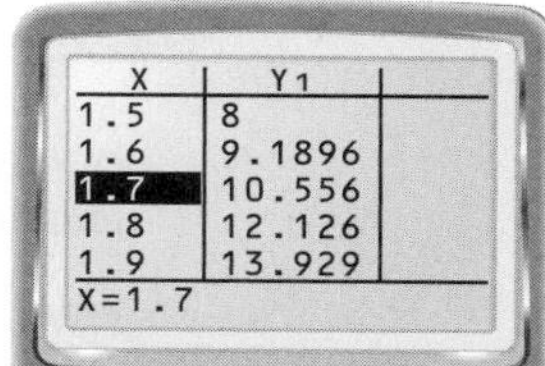

X	Y1
1.5	8
1.6	9.1896
1.7	10.556
1.8	12.126
1.9	13.929

X=1.7

STEP 3 **Scroll** through the table to find when $y = 11$. The table in Step 2 shows that $y = 11$ between $x = 1.7$ and $x = 1.8$.

▶ The solution of $4^x = 11$ is between 1.7 and 1.8.

METHOD 2

Using a Graph You can also use a graph to solve the equation.

STEP 1 **Enter** the functions $y = 4^x$ and $y = 11$ into a graphing calculator.

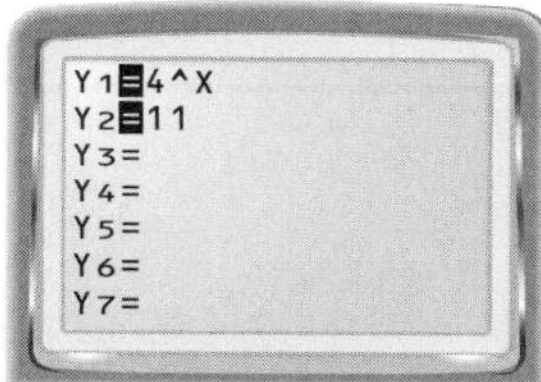

STEP 2 **Graph** the functions. Use the *intersect* feature to find the intersection point of the graphs. The graphs intersect at about (1.73, 11).

Use a viewing window of $0 \le x \le 5$ and $0 \le y \le 20$.

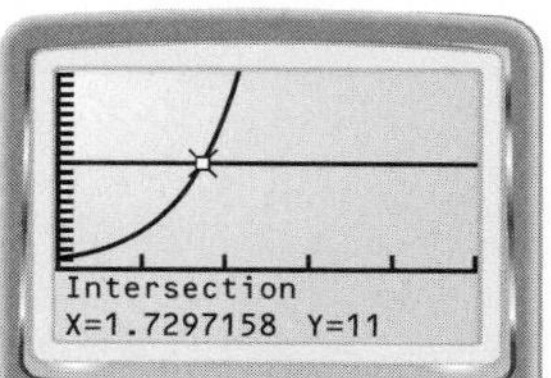

▶ The solution of $4^x = 11$ is about 1.73.

Alternative Strategy

Method 1 Example 2 on page 516 can be solved by using a table. This method allows students to see how the value of 4^x gets closer and closer to 11 as the value of x approaches the solution of the equation. This allows students to approach solving the equation entirely in terms of exponents, rather than working with logarithms, as in the algebraic solution in Lesson 7.6.

Method 2 Example 2 on page 516 can also be solved by using a graph. This method allows students to visualize the solution as the x-coordinate of the intersection point of the two functions $y_1 = 4^x$ and $y_2 = 11$. Again, the emphasis is on the exponential function, and there is no need to use logarithms.

Avoiding Common Errors

Method 1 Some students may have trouble approximating the solution because they are looking at the wrong portion of the table. To avoid this, ask students to estimate the value by mental math before working with their calculators. Since $4^1 = 4$ and $4^2 = 16$, they should immediately see that they should concentrate on values of x between $x = 1$ and $x = 2$.

Graphing Calculator

Method 1 Students may feel that "between 1.7 and 1.8" is not a really a solution, and notice that the table displayed on this page shows y-values of 10.556 and 12.126, which are not very close to 11. Ask them how they might change the table to get a more accurate solution. They should see that to get another decimal place of accuracy, they will need to change ΔTbl to 0.01 and look between $x = 1.71$ and $x = 1.80$. The y-value at $x = 1.73$ is 11.004, giving 1.73 as a solution that is a good approximation to the actual irrational solution.

Alternative Strategy

Method 1 Example 7 on page 519 can be solved by using a table. This method allows students to see how the value of M increases as the value of D increases in the application and does not require the series of steps used in the algebraic solution given in Lesson 7.6. The table works well in this case because the answer is exact.

Teaching Strategy

It can take a long time to scroll through the table up to $x = 100$ if you start at $x = 1$ and use ΔTbl = 1, as shown in Step 2. Ask students for suggestions on how to do this more efficiently. Good suggestions would be to estimate the solution mentally before using the table and starting with a larger ΔTbl value, such as ΔTbl = 10.

PROBLEM 2

ASTRONOMY The *apparent magnitude* of a star is a measure of the brightness of the star as it appears to observers on Earth. The apparent magnitude M of the dimmest star that can be seen with a telescope is given by the function

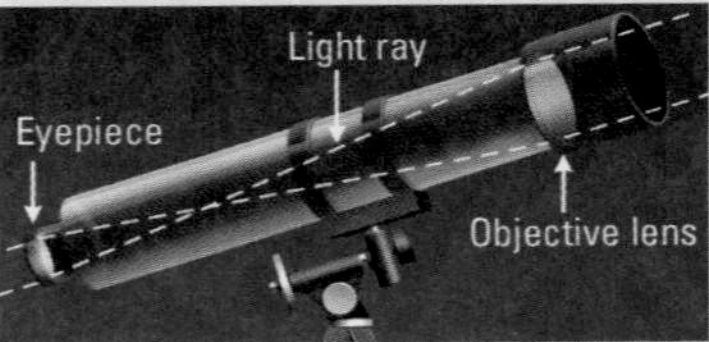

$$M = 5 \log D + 2$$

where D is the diameter (in millimeters) of the telescope's objective lens. If a telescope can reveal stars with a magnitude of 12, what is the diameter of its objective lens?

METHOD 1

Using a Table Notice that the problem requires solving the following logarithmic equation:

$$5 \log D + 2 = 12$$

One way to solve this equation is to make a table of values. You can use a graphing calculator to make the table.

STEP 1 **Enter** the function $y = 5 \log x + 2$ into a graphing calculator.

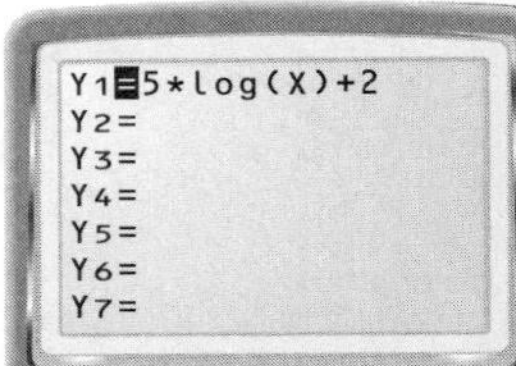

STEP 2 **Create** a table of values for the function. Make sure that the x-values are in the domain of the function ($x > 0$).

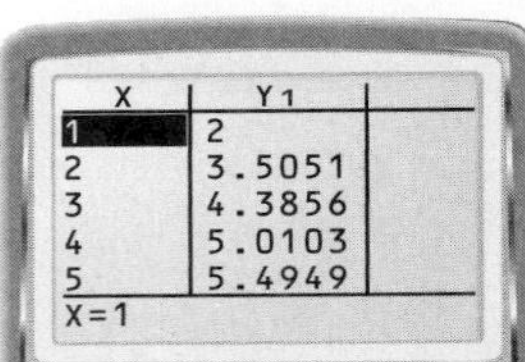

STEP 3 **Scroll** through the table of values to find when $y = 12$.

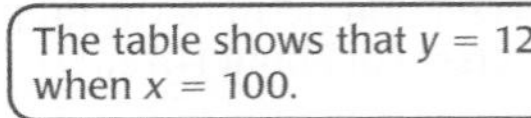

The table shows that $y = 12$ when $x = 100$.

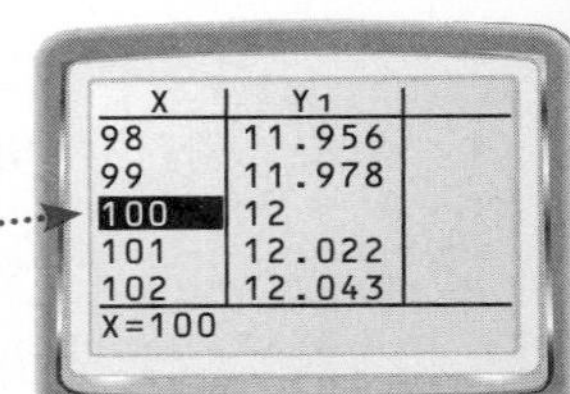

▸ To reveal stars with a magnitude of 12, a telescope must have an objective lens with a diameter of 100 millimeters.

METHOD 2 **Using a Graph** You can also use a graph to solve the equation $5 \log D + 2 = 12$.

STEP 1 **Enter** the functions $y = 5 \log x + 2$ and $y = 12$ into a graphing calculator.

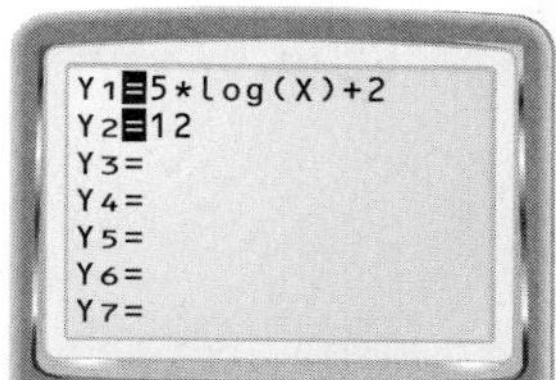

STEP 2 **Graph** the functions. Use the *intersect* feature to find the intersection point of the graphs. The graphs intersect at (100, 12).

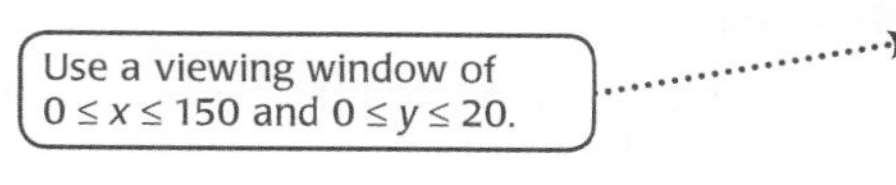

Use a viewing window of $0 \le x \le 150$ and $0 \le y \le 20$.

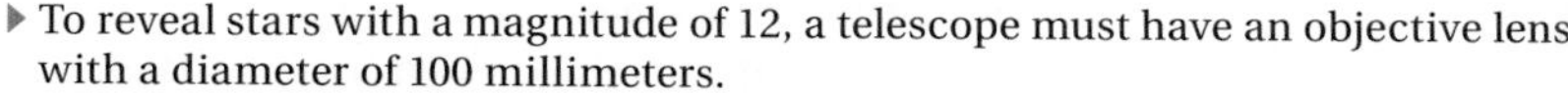

▶ To reveal stars with a magnitude of 12, a telescope must have an objective lens with a diameter of 100 millimeters.

PRACTICE

EXPONENTIAL EQUATIONS **Solve the equation using a table and using a graph.** 1–4. Sample viewing windows are given.

1. $8 - 2e^{3x} = -14$
   about 0.799 (viewing window: $0 \le x \le 2$, $-16 \le y \le 6$)
2. $7 - 10^{5-x} = -9$
   about 3.80 (viewing window: $0 \le x \le 10$, $-16 \le y \le 6$)
3. $e^{5x-8} + 3 = 15$
   about 2.10 (viewing window: $0 \le x \le 5$, $-1 \le y \le 17$)
4. $1.6(3)^{-4x} + 5.6 = 6$
   about 0.315 (viewing window: $0 \le x \le 5$, $-1 \le y \le 12$)

LOGARITHMIC EQUATIONS **Solve the equation using a table and using a graph.** 5–8. Sample viewing windows are given.

5. $\log_2 5x = 2$
   0.8 (viewing window: $0 \le x \le 5$, $-3 \le y \le 5$)
6. $\log(-3x + 7) = 1$
   -1 (viewing window: $-5 \le x \le 5$, $-1 \le y \le 2$)
7. $4 \ln x + 6 = 12$
   about 4.48 (viewing window: $0 \le x \le 6$, $-5 \le y \le 14$)
8. $11 \log(x + 9) - 5 = 8$
   about 6.20 (viewing window: $0 \le x \le 10$, $-1 \le y \le 10$)
9. **ECONOMICS** From 1998 to 2003, the United States gross national product y (in billions of dollars) can be modeled by $y = 8882(1.04)^x$ where x is the number of years since 1998. Use a table and a graph to find the year when the gross national product was \$10 trillion. 2001
10. **WRITING** In Method 1 of Problem 1 on page 523, explain how you could use a table to find the solution of $4^x = 11$ more precisely. See margin.
11. **WHAT IF?** In Problem 2 on page 524, suppose the telescope can reveal stars of magnitude 14. Find the diameter of the telescope's objective lens using a table and using a graph. about 251.19 mm
12. **FINANCE** You deposit \$5000 in an account that pays 3% annual interest compounded quarterly. How long will it take for the balance to reach \$6000? Solve the problem using a table and using a graph. 6.25 yr
13. **OCEANOGRAPHY** The density d (in grams per cubic centimeter) of seawater with a salinity of 30 parts per thousand is related to the water temperature T (in degrees Celsius) by the following equation:

$$d = 1.0245 - e^{0.1226T - 7.828}$$

For deep water in the South Atlantic Ocean off Antarctica, $d = 1.0241$ g/cm^3. Use a table and a graph to find the water's temperature. about 0.03225°C

Alternative Strategy

Method 2 Example 7 on page 519 can also be solved by using a graph. This method allows students to visualize how the value of M increases as the value of D increases in the application. It shows students how a logarithmic graph first increases rapidly and then at a slower and slower rate.

10. *Sample answer:* Once you find a range of values, keep adjusting ΔTbl on the calculator to find values to a smaller decimal place.

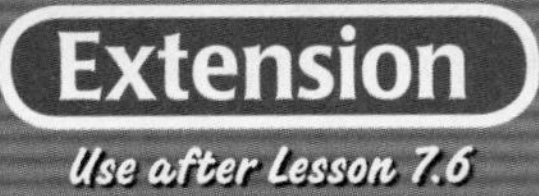

Solve Exponential and Logarithmic Inequalities

GOAL Solve exponential and logarithmic inequalities using tables and graphs.

In the Problem Solving Workshop on pages 523–525, you learned how to solve exponential and logarithmic equations using tables and graphs. You can use these same methods to solve exponential and logarithmic inequalities.

EXAMPLE 1 Solve an exponential inequality

CARS Your family purchases a new car for \$20,000. Its value decreases by 15% each year. During what interval of time does the car's value exceed \$10,000?

Solution

Let y represent the value of the car (in dollars) x years after it is purchased. A function relating x and y is $y = 20{,}000(1 - 0.15)^x$, or $y = 20{,}000(0.85)^x$. To find the values of x for which $y > 10{,}000$, solve the inequality $20{,}000(0.85)^x > 10{,}000$.

METHOD 1 Use a table

STEP 1 **Enter** the function $y = 20{,}000(0.85)^x$ into a graphing calculator. Set the starting x-value of the table to 0 and the step value to 0.1.

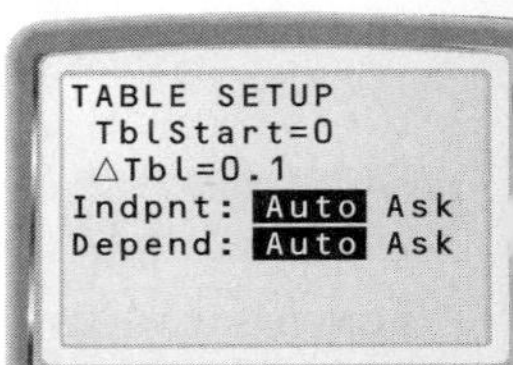

STEP 2 **Use** the *table* feature to create a table of values. Scrolling through the table shows that $y > 10{,}000$ when $0 \le x \le 4.2$.

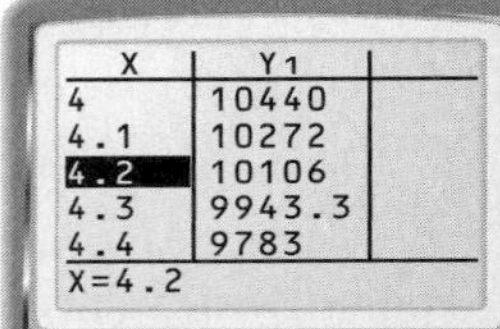

▶ The car value exceeds \$10,000 for about the first 4.2 years after it is purchased.

To check the solution's reasonableness, note that $y \approx 10{,}440$ when $x = 4$ and $y \approx 8874$ when $x = 5$. So, $4 < x < 5$, which agrees with the solution obtained above.

METHOD 2 Use a graph

Graph $y = 20{,}000(0.85)^x$ and $y = 10{,}000$ in the same viewing window. Set the viewing window to show $0 \le x \le 8$ and $0 \le y \le 25{,}000$. Using the *intersect* feature, you can determine that the graphs intersect when $x \approx 4.27$.

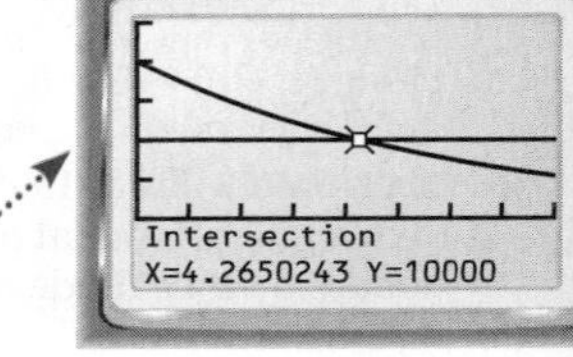

The graph of $y = 20{,}000(0.85)^x$ is above the graph of $y = 10{,}000$ when $0 \le x < 4.27$.

▶ The car value exceeds \$10,000 for about the first 4.27 years after it is purchased.

1 PLAN AND PREPARE

Warm-Up Exercises

Use a table or graph to solve each equation. Round to the nearest hundredth when necessary.

1. $8^x = 80$ 2.11
2. $e^{2x} + 5 = 32$ 1.65
3. $2000(1 - 0.25)^x = 500$ 4.82
4. $\log 3x = 1.5$ 10.54
5. $\log_4 x = 3.5$ 128

2 FOCUS AND MOTIVATE

Essential Question

Big Idea 2, p. 477

How can a graphing calculator be used to solve an exponential or logarithmic inequality? Tell students they will learn how to answer this question by solving exponential and logarithmic inequalities using both tables and graphs.

3 TEACH

Extra Example 1

A townhouse was purchased for \$125,000. The value of the townhouse increases by 6% each year. During what interval of time will the townhouse be less than \$175,000? during about the first 5.77 yr (or 5 yr 9 months) after the townhouse is purchased

NCTM STANDARDS

Standard 2: Understand functions; Represent situations using algebraic symbols

EXAMPLE 2 Solve a logarithmic inequality

Solve $\log_2 x \le 2$.

Solution

METHOD 1 Use a table

STEP 1 **Enter** the function $y = \log_2 x$ into a graphing calculator as $y = \frac{\log x}{\log 2}$.

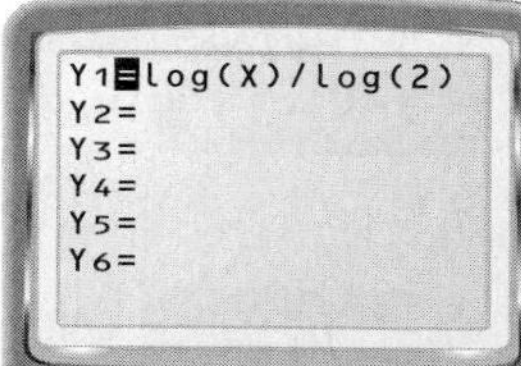

STEP 2 **Use** the *table* feature to create a table of values. Identify the x-values for which $y \le 2$. These x-values are given by $0 < x \le 4$.

Make sure that the x-values are reasonable and in the domain of the function ($x > 0$).

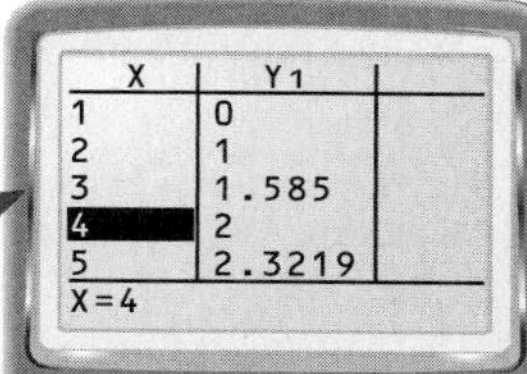

▶ The solution is $0 < x \le 4$.

METHOD 2 Use a graph

Graph $y = \log_2 x$ and $y = 2$ in the same viewing window. Using the *intersect* feature, you can determine that the graphs intersect when $x = 4$.

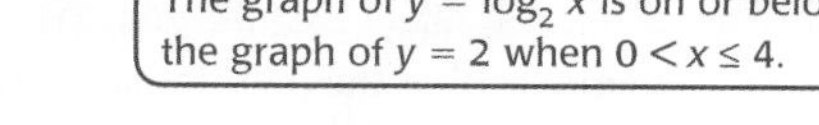

The graph of $y = \log_2 x$ is on or below the graph of $y = 2$ when $0 < x \le 4$.

Intersection
X=4 Y=2

▶ The solution is $0 < x \le 4$.

PRACTICE

XAMPLE 1
n p. 526
or Exs. 1–6

Solve the exponential inequality using a table and using a graph.

1. $3^x \le 20$ $x \le 2.727$
2. $28\left(\frac{2}{3}\right)^x > 9$ $x < 2.799$
3. $244(0.35)^x \ge 50$ $x \le 1.51$
4. $-63(0.96)^x < -27$ $x < 20.76$
5. $95(1.6)^x \le 1620$ $x \le 6.03$
6. $-284\left(\frac{9}{7}\right)^x > -135$ $x < -2.96$

XAMPLE 2
n p. 527
or Exs. 7–12

Solve the logarithmic inequality using a table and using a graph.

7. $\log_3 x \ge 3$ $x \ge 27$
8. $\log_5 x < 2$ $0 < x < 25$
9. $\log_6 x + 9 \le 11$ $0 < x \le 36$
10. $2 \log_4 x - 1 > 4$ $x > 32$
11. $-4 \log_2 x > -20$ $0 < x < 32$
12. $0 \le \log_7 x \le 1$ $1 \le x \le 7$

13. **FINANCE** You deposit \$1000 in an account that pays 3.5% annual interest compounded monthly. When is your balance at least \$1200? after 5.25 yr

14. **RATES OF RETURN** An investment that earns a rate of return r doubles in value in t years, where $t = \frac{\ln 2}{\ln (1 + r)}$ and r is expressed as a decimal. What rates of return will double the value of an investment in less than 10 years? $r > 7.18\%$

Extra Example 2

Solve $\log_3 (x + 2) > 3$. $x > 25$

Key Question to Ask for Example 2

- In Example 2, why is the solution $0 < x \le 4$, rather than just $x \le 4$? The domain of the function $y = \log_2 x$ is $x > 0$, so only positive numbers can be solutions of the given inequality.

Closing the Lesson

Have students summarize the major points of the lesson and answer the Essential Question: How can a graphing calculator be used to solve an exponential or logarithmic inequality?

- To solve an exponential or logarithmic inequality by using a table or graph, use the same basic methods as you would use for solving the equation that would be obtained by replacing the inequality symbol with an equal sign. Then, depending on the inequality symbol, observe the interval of x-values that gives the solution of the inequality.

A graphing calculator can be used to solve any exponential or logarithmic inequality either by using a table or a graph.

4 PRACTICE AND APPLY

Teaching Strategy

After students have completed the practice exercises, ask them which method they prefer and why. Lead a discussion of the advantages and disadvantages of each method.

1 PLAN AND PREPARE

Explore the Concept

- Students will collect data and model their data with an exponential function.
- This activity leads into the study of finding exponential models in Example 2 in Lesson 7.7.

Materials

Each student or group of students will need:

- 100 pennies
- a cup
- graphing calculator

Recommended Time

Work activity: 10 min
Discuss results: 10 min

Grouping

Students can work individually or in pairs. If students work in pairs, they can alternate between shaking the pennies and removing and counting the "heads."

2 TEACH

Key Discovery

Approximately half the pennies will be removed each time, so that the function $y = 100 \cdot \left(\frac{1}{2}\right)^x$, or, equivalently, $y = 100 \cdot 2^{-x}$ will theoretically model the data. The actual result with real data may vary somewhat from this.

3 ASSESS AND RETEACH

If you repeated this experiment 10 times and combined your results, what would you expect to find? The result would probably be closer to the theoretical model.

Investigating Algebra ACTIVITY Use before Lesson 7.7

@HomeTutor classzone.com Keystrokes

7.7 Model Data with an Exponential Function

MATERIALS • 100 pennies • cup • graphing calculator

QUESTION How can you model data with an exponential function?

EXPLORE Collect and record data

STEP 1 ***Make a table***

Make a table like the one shown to record your results. Check students' work.

Number of toss, x	0	1	2	3	4	5	6	7
Number of pennies remaining, y	?	?	?	?	?	?	?	?

STEP 2 ***Perform an experiment***

Record the initial number of pennies in the table, and place the pennies in a cup. Shake the pennies, and then spill them onto a flat surface.

Remove all of the pennies showing "heads." Count the number of pennies remaining, and record this number in the table.

STEP 3 ***Continue collecting data***

Repeat Step 2 with the remaining pennies until there are no pennies left to return to the cup.

DRAW CONCLUSIONS Use your observations to complete these exercises

1. What is the initial number of pennies? By what percent would you expect the number of pennies remaining to decrease after each toss? 100; 50%
2. Use your answers from Exercise 1 to write an exponential function that should model the data in the table. $y = 100(0.5)^x$
3. Use a graphing calculator to make a scatter plot of the data pairs (x, y). In the same viewing window, graph your function from Exercise 2. Is the function a good model for the data? *Explain.* Yes; the curve is very close to the data points.
4. Use the calculator's *exponential regression* feature to find an exponential function that models the data. *Compare* this function with the function you wrote in Exercise 2. Check students' work.

7.7 Write and Apply Exponential and Power Functions

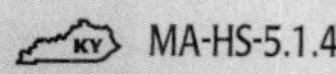 MA-HS-5.1.4 Students will recognize and solve problems that can be modeled using an exponential function, such as compound interest problems.

Before You wrote linear, quadratic, and other polynomial functions.

Now You will write exponential and power functions.

Why? So you can model biology problems, as in Example 5.

ey Vocabulary
- **ower function,** *428*
- **xponential unction,** *p. 478*

In Chapter 2, you learned that two points determine a line. Similarly, two points determine an exponential curve.

EXAMPLE 1 Write an exponential function

Write an exponential function $y = ab^x$ whose graph passes through (1, 12) and (3, 108).

Solution

STEP 1 **Substitute** the coordinates of the two given points into $y = ab^x$.

$12 = ab^1$ **Substitute 12 for *y* and 1 for *x*.**

$108 = ab^3$ **Substitute 108 for *y* and 3 for *x*.**

STEP 2 **Solve** for a in the first equation to obtain $a = \frac{12}{b}$, and substitute this expression for a in the second equation.

$108 = \left(\frac{12}{b}\right)b^3$ **Substitute $\frac{12}{b}$ for *a* in second equation.**

$108 = 12b^2$ **Simplify.**

$9 = b^2$ **Divide each side by 12.**

$3 = b$ **Take the positive square root because $b > 0$.**

STEP 3 **Determine** that $a = \frac{12}{b} = \frac{12}{3} = 4$. So, $y = 4 \cdot 3^x$.

TRANSFORMING EXPONENTIAL DATA A set of more than two points (x, y) fits an exponential pattern if and only if the set of transformed points $(x, \ln y)$ fits a linear pattern.

Graph of points (x, y)

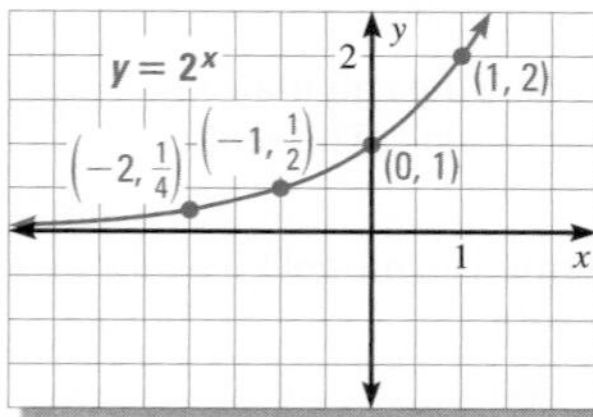

The graph is an exponential curve.

Graph of points $(x, \ln y)$

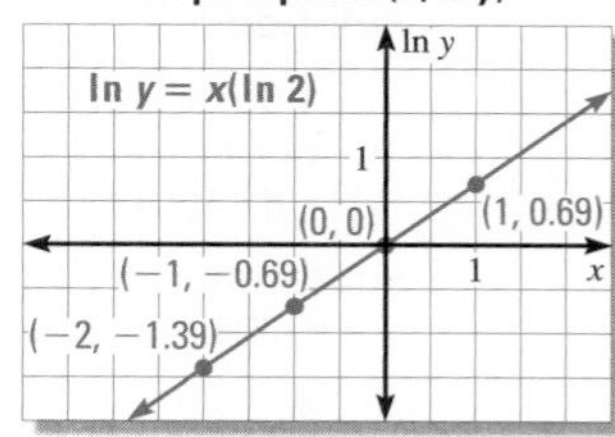

The graph is a line.

1 PLAN AND PREPARE

Warm-Up Exercises

Transparency Available

1. Write an equation in slope-intercept form for the line through (2, 5) and (6, −3). $y = -2x + 9$
2. Write an equation in point-slope form for the line through (2, 4.53) and (5, 5.22). $y - 4.53 = 0.23(x - 2)$ or $y - 5.22 = 0.23(x - 5)$
3. What is the value of y if the point (10, y) is on the line $y = 5.8x + 2.4$? 60.4

Notetaking Guide

Transparency Available

Promotes interactive learning and notetaking skills, pp. 206–209.

Pacing

Basic: 2 days
Average: 2 days
Advanced: 2 days
Block: 1 block
- See *Teaching Guide/Lesson Plan.*

2 FOCUS AND MOTIVATE

Essential Question

Big Idea 3, p. 477

How do you determine whether a set of data fits an exponential pattern or a power pattern? **Tell students they will learn how to answer this question by using natural logarithms.**

Resource Planning Guide

Chapter Resource Book
- Teaching Guide/Lesson Plan (pp. 73–74)
- Practice levels A, B, C (pp. 76–78)
- Study Guide (pp. 79–80)
- Catch-up for Absent Students (p. 81)
- Problem Solving Workshop (p. 82)
- Challenge (p. 83)

Workbooks
- Notetaking Guide (pp. 206–209)
- Practice Workbook (pp. 120–121)

Teaching Options
- **Power Presentations CD-ROM** provides dynamic electronic teaching resources for the classroom.
- **Activity Generator CD-ROM** provides editable activities for all ability levels.

Interactive Technology
- Easy Planner
- Power Presentations CD-ROM
- Activity Generator CD-ROM
- Animated Algebra
- Test Generator CD-ROM
- Online Quiz
- eWorkbook
- eEdition
- @HomeTutor

Resources for English Learners
- Quick Reference for English Learners
- Spanish Study Guide
- Multi-Language Visual Glossary
- Student Resources in Spanish

See also the *Algebra 2 Toolkit* for more strategies for meeting individual needs.

Motivating the Lesson

Your family owns a small company. The company's revenue has been steadily increasing from year to year. You can use modeling techniques to determine whether a linear, exponential, or power function best models the relationship between years and revenue to predict future revenue.

Extra Example 1

Write an exponential function $y = ab^x$ whose graph passes through (1, 10) and (4, 80). $y = 5 \cdot 2^x$

Extra Example 2

The table shows the number y of students enrolled in an elementary school during the xth year that the school has been open.

x	1	2	3	4	5
y	370	417	460	523	598

- Draw a scatter plot of the data pairs $(x, \ln y)$. Is an exponential model a good fit for the original data pairs (x, y)? **yes**

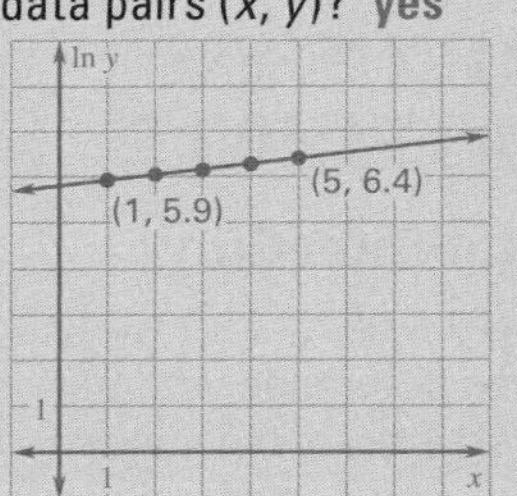

- Find an exponential model for the original data. $y = 322(1.13)^x$ **(Answers may vary slightly depending on the points used.)**

Extra Example 3

Use a graphing calculator to find an exponential model for the data in Extra Example 2. Predict the enrollment for the sixth year. $y = 327(1.13)^x$; **about 680 students**

EXAMPLE 2 Find an exponential model

SCOOTERS A store sells motor scooters. The table shows the number y of scooters sold during the xth year that the store has been open.

Year, x	1	2	3	4	5	6	7
Number of scooters sold, y	12	16	25	36	50	67	96

- Draw a scatter plot of the data pairs $(x, \ln y)$. Is an exponential model a good fit for the original data pairs (x, y)?
- Find an exponential model for the original data.

Solution

STEP 1 **Use** a calculator to create a table of data pairs $(x, \ln y)$.

x	1	2	3	4	5	6	7
$\ln y$	2.48	2.77	3.22	3.58	3.91	4.20	4.56

STEP 2 **Plot** the new points as shown. The points lie close to a line, so an exponential model should be a good fit for the original data.

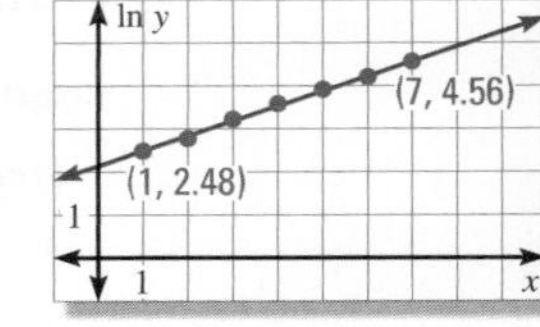

STEP 3 **Find** an exponential model $y = ab^x$ by choosing two points on the line, such as (1, 2.48) and (7, 4.56). Use these points to write an equation of the line. Then solve for y.

$\ln y - 2.48 = 0.35(x - 1)$ **Equation of line**

$\ln y = 0.35x + 2.13$ **Simplify.**

$y = e^{0.35x + 2.13}$ **Exponentiate each side using base *e*.**

$y = e^{2.13}(e^{0.35})^x$ **Use properties of exponents.**

$y = 8.41(1.42)^x$ **Exponential model**

USE POINT-SLOPE FORM
Because the axes are x and $\ln y$, the point-slope form is rewritten as $\ln y - y_1 = m(x - x_1)$. The slope of the line through (1, 2.48) and (7, 4.56) is:

$$\frac{4.56 - 2.48}{7 - 1} \approx 0.35$$

EXPONENTIAL REGRESSION A graphing calculator that performs exponential regression uses all of the original data to find the best-fitting model.

EXAMPLE 3 Use exponential regression

SCOOTERS Use a graphing calculator to find an exponential model for the data in Example 2. Predict the number of scooters sold in the eighth year.

Solution

Enter the original data into a graphing calculator and perform an exponential regression. The model is $y = 8.46(1.42)^x$.

Substituting $x = 8$ (for year 8) into the model gives $y = 8.46(1.42)^8 \approx 140$ scooters sold.

GUIDED PRACTICE for Examples 1, 2, and 3

Write an exponential function $y = ab^x$ whose graph passes through the given points.

1. (1, 6), (3, 24) $y = 3 \cdot 2^x$
2. (2, 8), (3, 32) $y = \frac{1}{2} \cdot 4^x$
3. (3, 8), (6, 64) $y = 2^x$
4. **WHAT IF?** In Examples 2 and 3, how would the exponential models change if the scooter sales were as shown in the table below?
   The initial amount would change to 11.39 and the growth rate to 1.45.

Year, x	1	2	3	4	5	6	7
Number of scooters sold, y	15	23	40	52	80	105	140

WRITING POWER FUNCTIONS Recall from Lesson 6.3 that a power function has the form $y = ax^b$. Because there are only two constants (a and b), only two points are needed to determine a power curve through the points.

EXAMPLE 4 Write a power function

Write a power function $y = ax^b$ whose graph passes through (3, 2) and (6, 9).

Solution

STEP 1 **Substitute** the coordinates of the two given points into $y = ax^b$.

$2 = a \cdot 3^b$ Substitute 2 for y and 3 for x.

$9 = a \cdot 6^b$ Substitute 9 for y and 6 for x.

STEP 2 **Solve** for a in the first equation to obtain $a = \frac{2}{3^b}$, and substitute this expression for a in the second equation.

$9 = \left(\frac{2}{3^b}\right)6^b$ Substitute $\frac{2}{3^b}$ for a in second equation.

$9 = 2 \cdot 2^b$ Simplify.

$4.5 = 2^b$ Divide each side by 2.

$\log_2 4.5 = b$ Take $\log_2$ of each side.

$\frac{\log 4.5}{\log 2} = b$ Change-of-base formula

$2.17 \approx b$ Use a calculator.

STEP 3 **Determine** that $a = \frac{2}{3^{2.17}} \approx 0.184$. So, $y = 0.184x^{2.17}$.

GUIDED PRACTICE for Example 4

Write a power function $y = ax^b$ whose graph passes through the given points.

5. (2, 1), (7, 6) $y = 0.371x^{1.43}$
6. (3, 4), (6, 15) $y = 0.492x^{1.91}$
7. (5, 8), (10, 34) $y = 0.278x^{2.09}$
8. **REASONING** Try using the method of Example 4 to find a power function whose graph passes through (3, 5) and (3, 7). What can you conclude?
   Sample answer: The points cannot form a power function.

Extra Example 4

Write a power function $y = ax^b$ whose graph passes through (4, 6) and (8, 15). $y = 0.96x^{1.32}$

Key Questions to Ask for Example 4

- How does the method shown in the solution for Example 4 involve a system of equations? The two given points are used in Step 1 to write a nonlinear system of two equations. In Steps 2 and 3, this system is solved by the substitution method.
- Why is the change-of-base formula needed in Step 2 of the solution? A calculator does not have a key for base 2 logarithms, so the change-of-base formula must be used to convert to either common or natural logarithms.

Graphing Calculator

Students can also create the scatter plots for Examples 2 and 5 with their graphing calculators. If students are not familiar with this process, demonstrate how to enter the data into lists, use the STAT PLOT menu, select appropriate window settings, and plot the data points. Then demonstrate how to graph the equation of the model obtained in Step 3 of the solutions for these examples on the same screen as the scatter plot. When you discuss Examples 3 and 6, ask students to graph the equations obtained by exponential or power regression on the same screen as the scatter plot and observe if this gives a better fit than the equations obtained in Examples 2 and 5.

Extra Example 5

The period of a planet is the length of time it takes for the planet to make one complete revolution around the Sun. The table shows the mean distance R, in astronomical units, of each of several planets from the Sun and the period P, in years, of each of these planets.

Planet	R	P
Mercury	0.39	0.24
Venus	0.72	0.62
Earth	1.00	1.00
Mars	1.52	1.88
Jupiter	5.20	11.9

- Draw a scatter plot of the data pairs ($\ln R$, $\ln P$). Is an exponential model a good fit for the original data pairs (R, P)? **Yes**

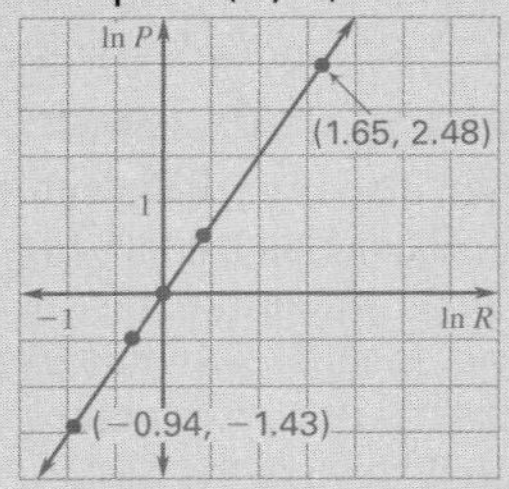

- Find a power model for the original data. $P = 0.99R^{1.51}$ **(Answers may vary slightly depending on the points used.)**

Key Question to Ask for Example 5

- What is the difference, in terms of constants and variables, between an exponential model and a power model? **In an exponential model, the base is a constant and the exponent is a variable, while in a power model, the base is a variable and the exponent is a constant.**

TRANSFORMING POWER DATA A set of more than two points (x, y) fits a power pattern if and only if the set of transformed points $(\ln x, \ln y)$ fits a linear pattern.

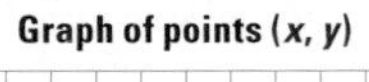
Graph of points (x, y)

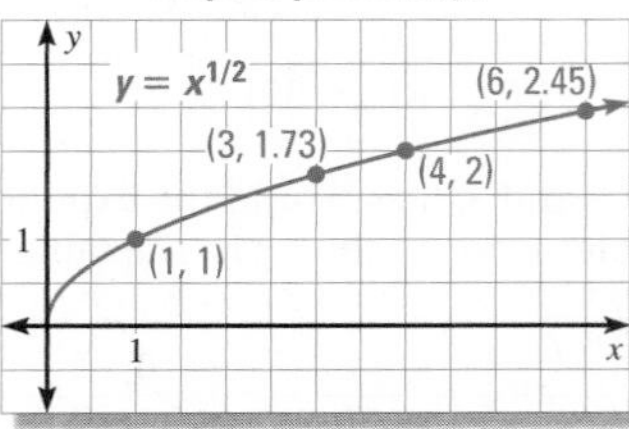

The graph is a power curve.

Graph of points $(\ln x, \ln y)$

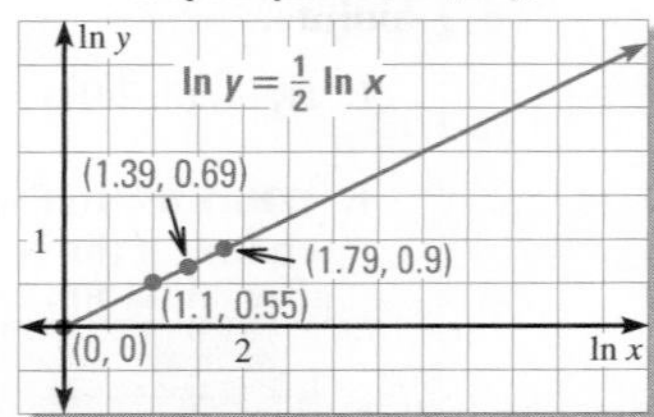

The graph is a line.

EXAMPLE 5 Find a power model

BIOLOGY The table at the right shows the typical wingspans x (in feet) and the typical weights y (in pounds) for several types of birds.

- Draw a scatter plot of the data pairs $(\ln x, \ln y)$. Is a power model a good fit for the original data pairs (x, y)?
- Find a power model for the original data.

Bird	Wingspan (ft), x	Weight (lb),
Cuckoo	1.90	0.23
Crow	2.92	1.04
Curlew	3.41	1.69
Goose	5.35	6.76
Vulture	8.40	16.03

Solution

STEP 1 **Use** a calculator to create a table of data pairs $(\ln x, \ln y)$.

$\ln x$	0.642	1.072	1.227	1.677	2.128
$\ln y$	−1.470	0.039	0.525	1.911	2.774

STEP 2 **Plot** the new points as shown. The points lie close to a line, so a power model should be a good fit for the original data.

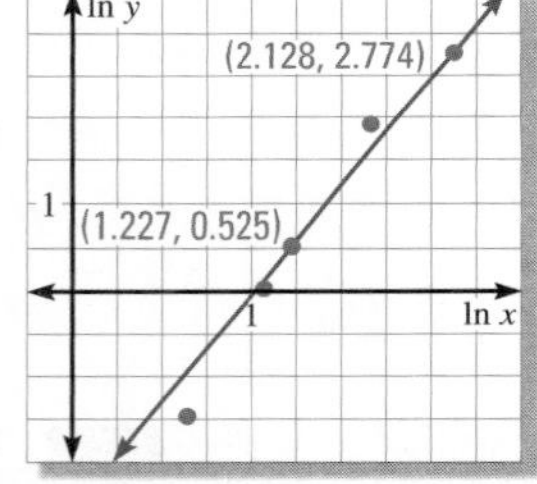

STEP 3 **Find** a power model $y = ax^b$ by choosing two points on the line, such as (1.227, 0.525) and (2.128, 2.774). Use these points to write an equation of the line. Then solve for y.

$\ln y - y_1 = m(\ln x - x_1)$ **Equation when axes are ln x and ln y**

$\ln y - 2.774 = 2.5(\ln x - 2.128)$ **Substitute.**

$\ln y = 2.5 \ln x - 2.546$ **Simplify.**

$\ln y = \ln x^{2.5} - 2.546$ **Power property of logarithms**

$y = e^{\ln x^{2.5} - 2.546}$ **Exponentiate each side using base *e*.**

$y = e^{-2.546} \cdot e^{\ln x^{2.5}}$ **Product of powers property**

$y = 0.0784x^{2.5}$ **Simplify.**

USE POINT-SLOPE FORM
The slope of the line is $\frac{2.774 - 0.525}{2.128 - 1.227} \approx 2.50$.

Differentiated Instruction

Inclusion For real-world problems like the one in **Example 5**, suggest that students write the data from a graphing calculator in a table to organize their work. They can create either rows or columns, with headers x, $\ln x$, y, and $\ln y$. This will help them see relationships and facilitate their comparison of the values in order to properly determine whether a set of points fits a power model. See also the *Algebra 2 Toolkit* for more strategies.

POWER REGRESSION A graphing calculator that performs power regression uses all of the original data to find the best-fitting model.

EXAMPLE 6 Use power regression

BIOLOGY Use a graphing calculator to find a power model for the data in Example 5. Estimate the weight of a bird with a wingspan of 4.5 feet.

Solution

Enter the original data into a graphing calculator and perform a power regression. The model is $y = 0.0442x^{2.87}$.

Substituting $x = 4.5$ into the model gives $y = 0.0442(4.5)^{2.87} \approx 3.31$ pounds.

✓ GUIDED PRACTICE for Examples 5 and 6

9. The table below shows the atomic number x and the melting point y (in degrees Celsius) for the alkali metals. Find a power model for the data. $y = 397.61x^{-0.639}$

Alkali metal	Lithium	Sodium	Potassium	Rubidium	Cesium
Atomic number, x	3	11	19	37	55
Melting point, y	180.5	97.8	63.7	38.9	28.5

7.7 EXERCISES

HOMEWORK KEY
○ = **WORKED-OUT SOLUTIONS** on p. WS14 for Exs. 11, 23, and 33
★ = **STANDARDIZED TEST PRACTICE** Exs. 2, 27, 33, and 35

SKILL PRACTICE

A

1. **VOCABULARY** Copy and complete: Given a set of more than two data pairs (x, y), you can decide whether a(n) _?_ function fits the data well by making a scatter plot of the points $(x, \ln y)$. exponential

2. ★ **WRITING** *Explain* how you can determine whether a power function is a good model for a set of data pairs (x, y). Create a table of the points $(\ln x, \ln y)$. Plot the points. If the points lie close to a line, a power model is a good fit.

XAMPLE 1
n p. 529
r Exs. 3–10

WRITING EXPONENTIAL FUNCTIONS Write an exponential function $y = ab^x$ whose graph passes through the given points.

3. (1, 3), (2, 12) $y = \frac{3}{4} \cdot 4^x$
4. (2, 24), (3, 144) $y = \frac{2}{3} \cdot 6^x$
5. (3, 1), (5, 4) $y = \frac{1}{8} \cdot 2^x$
6. (3, 27), (5, 243) $y = 3^x$
7. (1, 2), (3, 50) $y = \frac{2}{5} \cdot 5^x$
8. (1, 40), (3, 640) $y = 10 \cdot 4^x$
9. (−1, 10), (4, 0.31) $y = 4.99 \cdot 0.499^x$
10. (2, 6.4), (5, 409.6) $y = 0.4 \cdot 4^x$

XAMPLE 2
n p. 530
r Exs. 11–14

FINDING EXPONENTIAL MODELS Use the points (x, y) to draw a scatter plot of the points $(x, \ln y)$. Then find an exponential model for the data. 11–14. See margin for art.

11. (1, 18), (2, 36), (3, 72), (4, 144), (5, 288) $y = 9(2)^x$
12. (1, 3.3), (2, 10.1), (3, 30.6), (4, 92.7), (5, 280.9) $y = 1.09(3.04)^x$
13. (1, 9.8), (2, 12.2), (3, 15.2), (4, 19), (5, 23.8) $y = 7.83(1.25)^x$
14. (1, 1.4), (2, 6.7), (3, 32.9), (4. 161.4), (5, 790.9) $y = 0.284(4.88)^x$

Extra Example 6

Use a graphing calculator to find a power model for the data in Extra Example 5. Estimate the period of Saturn, whose mean distance from the Sun is 9.54 astronomical units. $P = R^{1.5}$; about 29.5 yr

Key Question to Ask for Example 6

- If the methods illustrated in Examples 5 and 6 for finding the equation of the best-fitting power model give different results, which equation do you think would be more accurate? Explain. The power regression method in Example 6 is generally more accurate because it uses all of the original data points, rather than just two points.

Closing the Lesson

Have students summarize the major points of the lesson and answer the Essential Question: How do you determine whether a set of data fits an exponential pattern or a power pattern?

- Two points determine an exponential model or a power model.
- The equation of an exponential or power model can be found from two points on the graph by solving a nonlinear system of equations.

If the set of transformed points $(x, \ln y)$ fits a linear pattern, then the set of original points (x, y) fits an exponential pattern. If the set of transformed points $(\ln x, \ln y)$ fits a linear pattern, then the set of original points (x, y) fits a power pattern.

14.
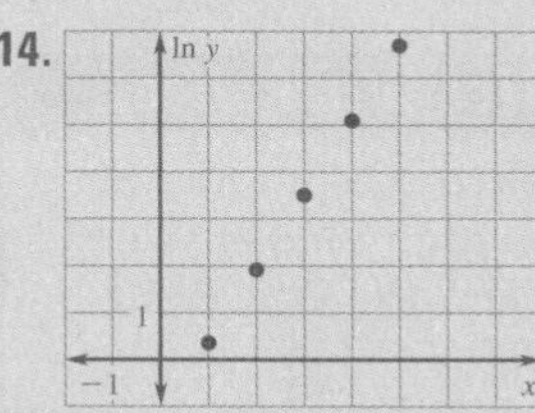

11.
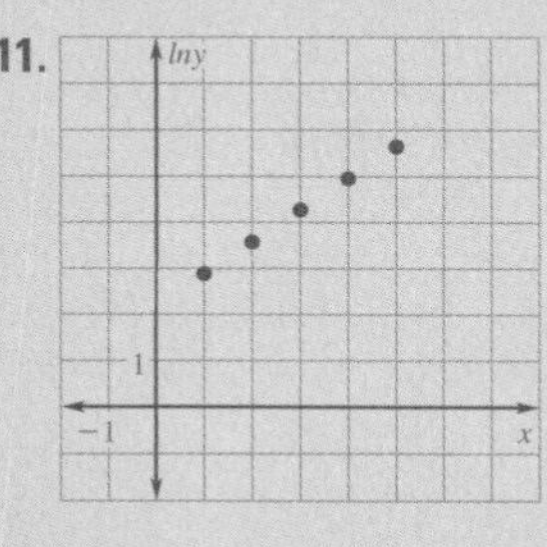

12.
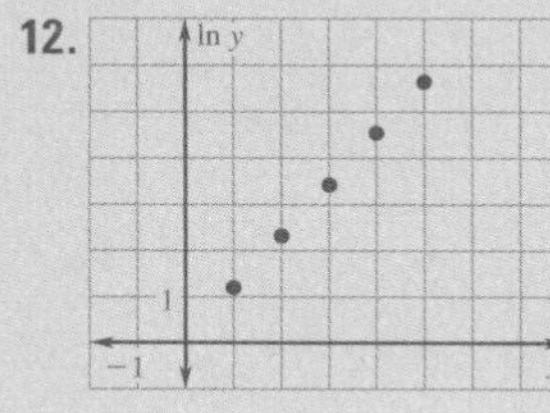

13.
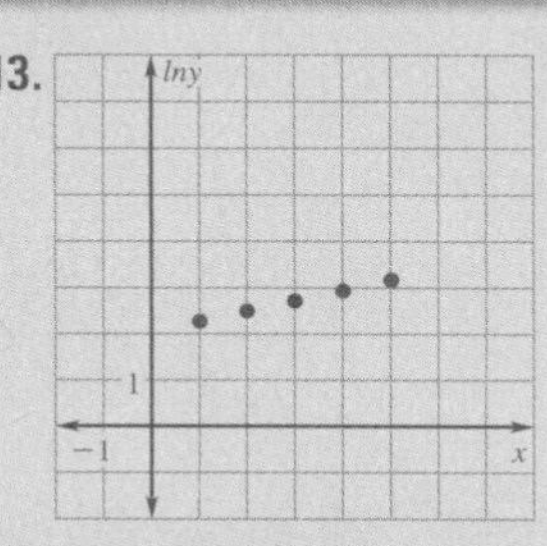

4 PRACTICE AND APPLY

Assignment Guide

Answer Transparencies available for all exercises

Basic:
Day 1: pp. 533–536
Exs. 1–12
Day 2: pp. 533–536
Exs. 15–24, 31–34, 37–38

Average:
Day 1: pp. 533–536
Exs. 1, 2, 4–13
Day 2: pp. 533–536
Exs. 17–20, 24–29, 31–35, 37–38

Advanced:
Day 1: pp. 533–536
Exs. 1, 2, 5–14
Day 2: pp. 533–536
Exs. 19–22, 24–38*

Block:
pp. 533–536
Exs. 1, 2, 4–13, 17–20, 24–29, 31–35, 37–38

Differentiated Instruction

See *Algebra 2 Best Practices Toolkit* for suggestions on addressing the needs of a diverse classroom.

Homework Check

For a quick check of student understanding of key concepts, go over the following exercises:
Basic: 4, 12, 16, 24, 31
Average: 6, 13, 18, 25, 32
Advanced: 8, 14, 20, 26, 33

Extra Practice

- Student Edition, p. 1016
- Chapter 7 Resource Book: Practice levels A, B, C, pp. 76–78

Practice Worksheet

An easily-readable reduced practice page (with answers) for this lesson can be found on p. 476D.

EXAMPLE 4 B on p. 531 for Exs. 15–22

WRITING POWER FUNCTIONS Write a power function $y = ax^b$ whose graph passes through the given points.

15. (4, 3), (8, 15) $y = 0.12x^{2.32}$
16. (5, 9), (8, 34) $y = 0.0950x^{2.83}$
17. (2, 3), (6, 12) $y = 1.25x^{1.26}$
18. (3, 14), (9, 44) $y = 4.45x^{1.04}$
19. (4, 8), (8, 30) $y = 0.569x^{1.91}$
20. (5, 10), (12, 81) $y = 0.214x^{2.39}$
21. (4, 6.2), (7, 23) $y = 0.241x^{2.34}$
22. (3.1, 5), (6.8, 9.7) $y = 1.93x^{0.8}$

EXAMPLE 5 on p. 532 for Exs. 23–26

FINDING POWER MODELS Use the given points (x, y) to draw a scatter plot of the points $(\ln x, \ln y)$. Then find a power model for the data. 23–26. See margin for art.

23. (1, 0.6), (2, 4.1), (3, 12.4), (4, 27), (5, 49.5) $y = 0.606x^{2.74}$
24. (1, 1.5), (2, 4.8), (3, 9.5), (4, 15.4), (5, 22.3) $y = 1.50x^{1.}$
25. (1, 2.5), (2, 3.7), (3, 4.7), (4, 5.5), (5, 6.2) $y = 2.50x^{0.567}$
26. (1, 0.81), (2, 0.99), (3, 1.11), (4, 1.21), (5, 1.2 $y = 0.810x^{0.2}$

27. ★ **MULTIPLE CHOICE** Which equation is equivalent to $\log y = 2x + 1$? A

Ⓐ $y = 10(100)^x$ Ⓑ $y = 10^x$ Ⓒ $y = e^{2x+1}$ Ⓓ $y = e^2$

ERROR ANALYSIS *Describe* and correct the error in writing y as a function of x.

28.
$\ln y = 2x + 1$
$y = e^{2x+1}$
$y = e^{2x} + e^1$
$y = (e^2)^x + e$
$y = 7.39^x + 2.72$

28. The third step should be multiplication, not addition; $y = e^{2x} \cdot e^1 = (e^2)^x \cdot e$, $y = 2.72(7.39)^x$.

29.
$\ln y = 3 \ln x - 2$
$\ln y = \ln 3x - 2$
$y = e^{\ln 3x - 2}$
$y = e^{\ln 3x} \cdot e^{-2}$
$y = (3x)(0.135) = 0.405x$

29. The x should be raised to the 3, not multiplied by it; $\ln y = \ln x^3 - 2$, $y = e^{\ln x^3 - 2}$, $y = e^{\ln x^3} \cdot e^{-2}$, $y = 0.135x^3$

C 30. **CHALLENGE** Take the natural logarithm of both sides of the equations $y = ab^x$ and $y = ax^b$. What are the slope and y-intercept of the line relating x and $\ln y$ for $y = ab^x$? of the line relating $\ln x$ and $\ln y$ for $y = ax^b$? $\ln b$, $\ln a$; b, $\ln a$

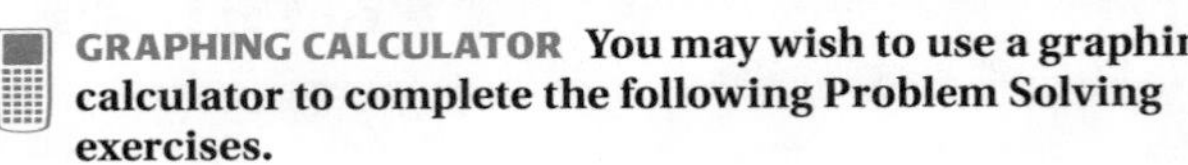

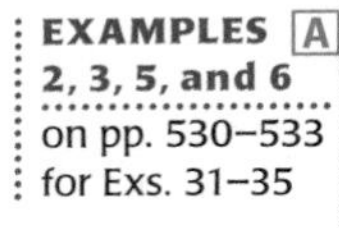

GRAPHING CALCULATOR You may wish to use a graphing calculator to complete the following Problem Solving exercises.

EXAMPLES A 2, 3, 5, and 6 on pp. 530–533 for Exs. 31–35

31. **BIOLOGY** Scientists use the circumference of an animal's femur to estimate the animal's weight. The table shows the femur circumference C (in millimeters) and the weight W (in kilograms) for several animals.

Animal	Giraffe	Polar bear	Lion	Squirrel	Otter
C (mm)	173	135	93.5	13	28
W (kg)	710	448	143	0.399	9.68

a. Draw a scatter plot of the data pairs $(\ln C, \ln W)$. See margin.

b. Find a power model for the original data. $y = 0.000466x^{2.80}$

c. Predict the weight of a cheetah if the circumference of its femur is 68.7 millimeters. about 64.8 kg

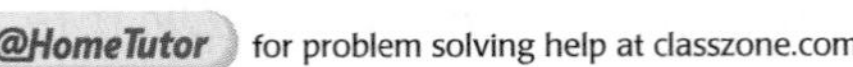

◯ = WORKED-OUT SOLUTIONS on p. WS1 ★ = STANDARDIZED TEST PRACTICE

534

23.
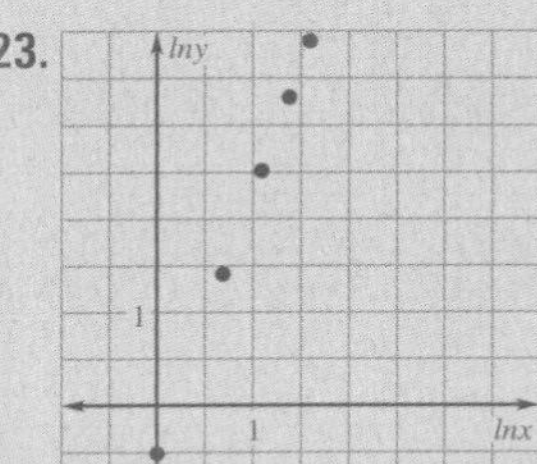

24.
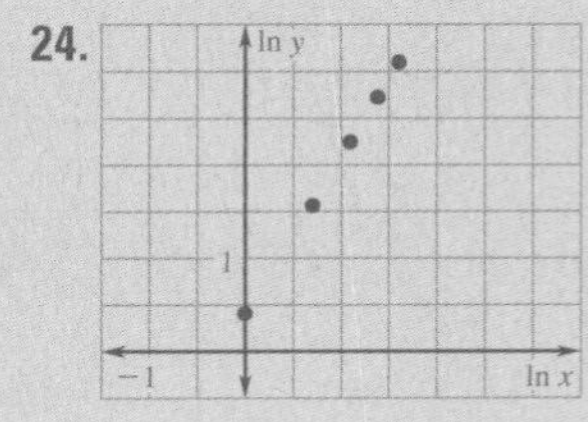

25.
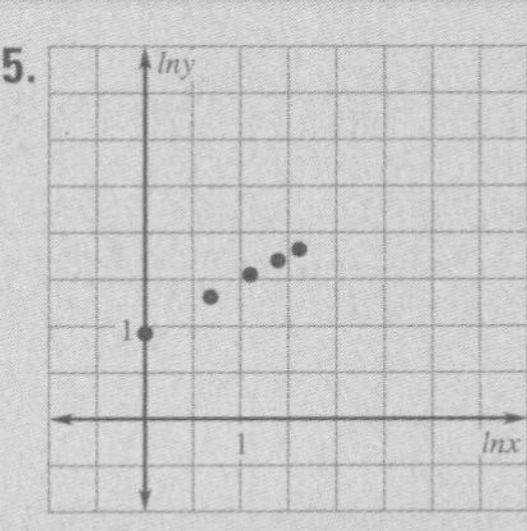

b. Graph the ints (x, y) hey appear ear, then a e is the best If not, graph points (x, y), if these ints appear ear, then an ponential del is the best for the data. not, graph the ints $(\ln x, \ln$ if these points pear linear, n a power del is the best for the data; $= 33.8x + 28$.

32. **ASTRONOMY** The table shows the mean distance x from the sun (in astronomical units) and the period y (in years) of six planets. Draw a scatter plot of the data pairs $(\ln x, \ln y)$. Find a power model for the original data. **See margin for art; $y = x^{1.50}$.**

Planet	Mercury	Venus	Earth	Mars	Jupiter	Saturn
x	0.387	0.723	1.000	1.524	5.203	9.539
y	0.241	0.615	1.000	1.881	11.862	29.458

@HomeTutor for problem solving help at classzone.com

33. ★ **SHORT RESPONSE** The table shows the numbers of business and non-business users of instant messaging for the years 1998–2004.

Years since 1997	1	2	3	4	5	6	7
Business users (in millions)	1	2	5	7	20	40	80
Non-business users (in millions)	55	97	140	160	195	235	260

a. Find an exponential model for the number of business users over time. **$y = 0.475(2.08)^x$**

b. *Explain* how to tell whether a linear, exponential, or power function best models the number of non-business users over time. Then find the best-fitting model.

B

34. **MULTI-STEP PROBLEM** The boiling point of water increases with atmospheric pressure. At sea level, where the atmospheric pressure is about 760 millimeters of mercury, water boils at 100°C. The table shows the boiling point T of water (in degrees Celsius) for several different values of atmospheric pressure P (in millimeters of mercury).

P	T
149	60
234	70
355	80
526	90
760	100
1075	110

a. **Graph** Draw a scatter plot of the data pairs $(\ln P, \ln T)$. **See margin.**

b. **Model** Find a power model for the original data. **$T = 13.1(P)^{0.306}$**

c. **Predict** When the atmospheric pressure is 620 millimeters of mercury, at what temperature does water boil? **about 93.7°C**

c. Exponential ction; the ints for (x, y) appear re linear n the points $(x, \ln y)$, so exponential del appears to the best fit for data.

35. ★ **EXTENDED RESPONSE** Your visual *near point* is the closest point at which your eyes can see an object distinctly. Your near point moves farther away from you as you grow older. The diagram shows the near point y (in centimeters) at age x (in years).

Visual Near Point Distances

Age 10	10 cm
Age 20	12 cm
Age 30	15 cm
Age 40	25 cm
Age 50	40 cm
Age 60	100 cm

a. **Graph** Draw a scatter plot of the data pairs $(x, \ln y)$. **See margin.**

b. **Graph** Draw a scatter plot of the data pairs $(\ln x, \ln y)$. **See margin.**

c. **Interpret** Based on your scatter plots, does an exponential function or a power function best fit the original data? *Explain* your reasoning.

d. **Model** Based on your answer for part (c), write a model for the original data. Use your model to predict the near point for an 80-year-old person. **$y = 4.98(1.05)^x$; about 247 cm**

Avoiding Common Errors

Exercises 5–8 In each of these exercises, students should obtain an equation of the form "a number" $= b^2$ in one of the steps of the solution. For example, in Exercise 7 this equation is $25 = b^2$. The next step is to find the value of b, the base for the exponential model. Some students may write both square roots, for example, $b = \pm 5$ in Exercise 7. Explain to these students that, although they are correct that the quadratic equation has two solutions, only the positive square root applies here because the base of an exponential function must be a positive number other than 1. (If necessary, refer students back to the definition of an exponential function at the beginning of Lesson 7.1 on page 478.)

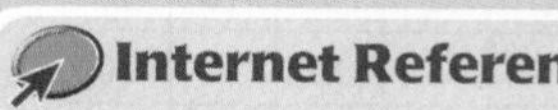

Exercise 32 Additional information about the planets in our solar system can be found at the website solarsystem.nasa.gov/planets/index.cfm

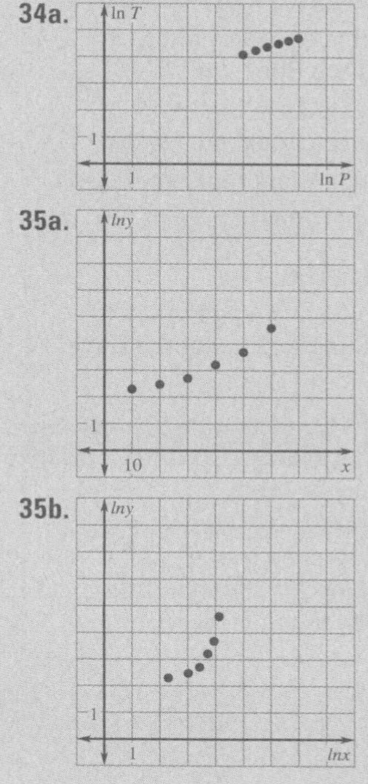

26.
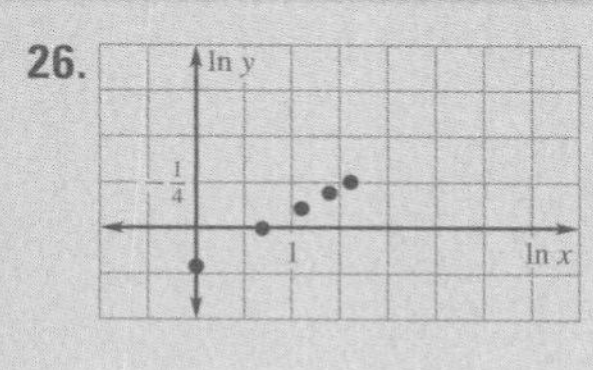

31a.
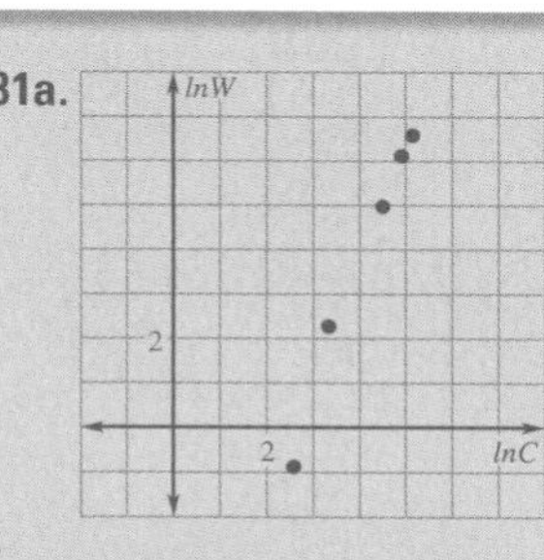

32.
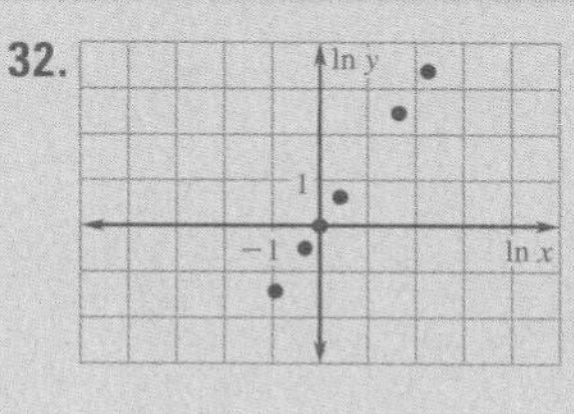

5 ASSESS AND RETEACH

Daily Homework Quiz

 Transparency Available

1. Write an exponential function $y = ab^x$ whose graph passes through (2, 48) and (4,768). $y = 3 \cdot 4^x$.
2. Find an exponential model for the data in the table.

x	1	2	3	4	5
y	35	64	112	205	376

$y = 19.4(1.81)^x$

3. Write a power function $y = ax^b$ whose graph passes through (3, 8) and (6, 35). $y = 0.77x^{2.13}$
4. Find a power model for the data in the table.

x	3	6	10	15	19
y	1	5	15	41	70

$y = 0.08x^{2.3}$

Online Quiz

Available at **classzone.com**

Diagnosis/Remediation

- Practice A, B, C in Chapter 7 Resource Book, pp. 76–78
- Study Guide in Chapter 7 Resource Book, pp. 79–80
- Practice Workbook, pp. 120–121
- @HomeTutor

Challenge

Additional challenge is available in the Chapter 7 Resource Book, p. 83.

Quiz

An easily-readable reduced copy of the quiz (with answers) on Lessons 7.6–7.7 from the Assessment Book can be found on p. 476E.

C **36. CHALLENGE** A doctor measures an astronaut's pulse rate y (in beats per minute) at various times x (in minutes) after the astronaut has finished exercising. The results are shown in the table. The astronaut's resting pulse rate is 70 beats per minute. Write an exponential model for the data. $y = 148(0.94)^x$

x	0	2	4	6	8	10	12	14
y	172	132	110	92	84	78	75	72

KENTUCKY MIXED REVIEW

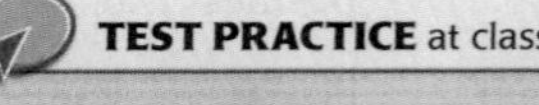

37. A poster is 8 inches taller than it is wide. The area of the poster is 384 square inches. Which equation can be used to find the width of the poster? **B**

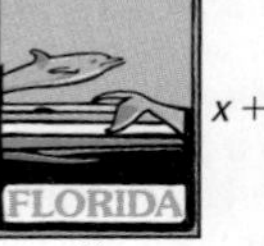

Ⓐ $x + 8 = 384$ Ⓑ $x(x + 8) = 384$

Ⓒ $x^2 + (x + 8)^2 = 384^2$ Ⓓ $x + (x + 8) = 384$

38. Use the graph of $y = -\frac{3}{4}x + 1$ to solve the equation for x when $y = -2$. **B**

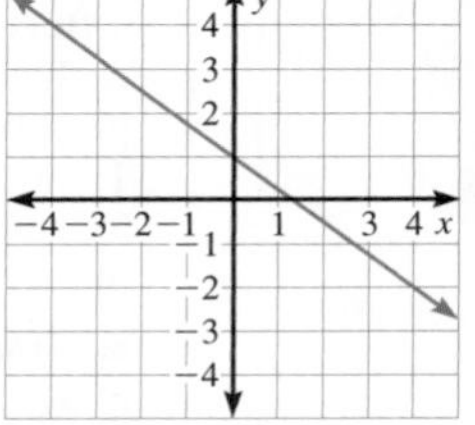

Ⓐ $x = 3$ Ⓑ $x = 4$

Ⓒ $x = 8$ Ⓓ $x = 11$

QUIZ for Lessons 7.6–7.7

Solve the equation. Check for extraneous solutions. *(p. 515)*

1. $2^{x+1} = 16^{x+2}$ $-\frac{7}{3}$
2. $e^{-x} = 4$ about −1.386
3. $3^{2x} + 5 = 13$ about 0.946
4. $3^{x+1} - 5 = 10$ about 1.465
5. $\log_4 (4x + 7) = \log_4 11x$ 1
6. $\ln (3x - 2) = \ln 6x$ no solution
7. $\log_3 x = -1$ $\frac{1}{3}$
8. $6 \ln x = 30$ about 148.41
9. $\log_2 (x + 4) = 5$ 28

Write an exponential function $y = ab^x$ whose graph passes through the given points. *(p. 529)*

10. (1, 5), (2, 30) $y = \frac{5}{6}(6)^x$
11. (1, 4), (2, 32) $y = \frac{1}{2}(8)^x$
12. (2, 15), (3, 45) $y = \frac{5}{3}(3)^x$

Write a power function $y = ax^b$ whose graph passes through the given points. *(p. 529)*

13. (4, 8), (9, 23) $y = 1.32x^{1.30}$
14. (3, 12), (10, 36) $y = 4.40x^{0.912}$
15. (5, 4), (11, 51) $y = 0.0222x^{3.23}$
16. **BIOLOGY** The average weight y (in kilograms) of an Atlantic cod from the Gulf of Maine can be modeled by $y = 0.51(1.46)^x$ where x is the age of the cod (in years). Estimate the age of a cod that weighs 15 kilograms. *(p. 515)* about 9 yr

Lessons 7.5–7.7

1. **MUSIC** In music, a *cent* is a unit that is used to express a small step up or down in pitch. The number c of cents by which two notes differ in pitch is given by

$$c = 1200 \log_2 \frac{a}{b}$$

where a and b are the frequencies of the notes a and b.

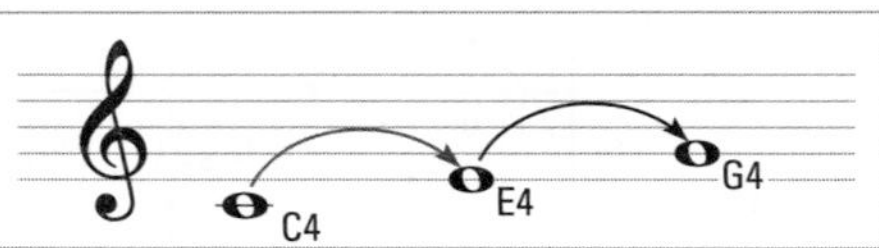

Three notes on the standard scale are C4, E4, and G4. You can compare the difference in the number of cents from C4 to E4 with the difference in the number of cents from E4 to G4 by evaluating this expression:

$$1200 \log_2 \frac{E4}{C4} - 1200 \log_2 \frac{G4}{E4}$$

Which of the following is the expression written as a single logarithm?

A. $1200 \log_2 \frac{C4}{G4}$

B. $1200 \log_2 \frac{G4}{C4}$

C. $1200 \log_2 \frac{E4}{C4 \cdot G4}$

D. $1200 \log_2 \frac{(E4)^2}{C4 \cdot G4}$

2. **EXPONENTIAL FUNCTIONS** Which exponential function of the form $y = ab^x$ has a graph that passes through the points (2, 7) and (5, 56)?

A. $y = 0.28(5)^x$

B. $y = 1.75(2)^x$

C. $y = 2(1.75)^x$

D. $y = 18.35(1.25)^x$

3. **INTEREST RATES** The *effective interest rate* is a rate associated with the formula for continuously compounded interest. The effective interest rate takes into account the effects of compounding on the *nominal interest rate* (the interest rate in the formula for continuous compounding). The relationship between the effective interest rate E and the nominal interest rate N is given by the equation $N = \ln(E + 1)$ where E and N are expressed as decimals. Which of the following is the approximate effective interest rate for an account that has a nominal interest rate of 10%?

A. 1.0% B. 9.5%

C. 10.5% D. 11.5%

4. **TRANSPORTATION** The table below shows the total number of miles traveled in the United States each year during 1997–2001. Which power function best models the data pairs (x, y)?

Years since 1990, x	Miles (billions), y
7	2562
8	2632
9	2691
10	2747
11	2782

A. $y = x^{0.185}$

B. $y = x^{1.791}$

C. $y = 0.185x^{1.791}$

D. $y = 1791x^{0.185}$

5. **OPEN-RESPONSE** The total expenditures y (in billions of dollars) for U.S. elementary and secondary schools can be modeled by $y = 385(1.04)^x$ where x is the number of years since 1996.

a. *Explain* the real-world meaning of the values 385 and 1.04 in this model.

b. During which year did the total expenditures first surpass $550 billion? *Explain* how you found your answer.

Kentucky Mixed Review

1. D
2. B
3. C
4. D
5. a. 385 represents $385 billion, the expenditures in year 0, 1996. The value 1.04 indicates that the rate of growth is 4% each year.
b. 2006. *Sample answer:* First, solve the equation $550 = 385(1.04)^x$ using logarithms. The value of $x = 9.09$ indicates that after 9 years, the expenditures had not reached $550 billion. However, 10 years from 1996, or 2006, the expenditures will surpass $550 billion.

Additional Resources

The following resources are available to help review the materials in this chapter.

Chapter 7 Resource Book

- Chapter Review Games and Activities, p. 84
- Cumulative Practice, Chs. 1–7, pp. 86–87

Student Resources in Spanish

eWorkbook

@HomeTutor

Vocabulary Practice

Vocabulary practice is available at **classzone.com**

7 CHAPTER SUMMARY

Animated Algebra
classzone.com
Electronic Function Library

BIG IDEAS

For Your Notebook

Big Idea 1 Graphing Exponential and Logarithmic Functions

Parent functions for exponential functions have the form $y = b^x$. Parent functions for logarithmic functions have the form $y = \log_b x$.

Exponential Growth	Exponential Decay	Logarithmic Functions	
(0, 1), $y = b^x$	$y = b^x$, (0, 1)	$y = \log_b x$, (1, 0)	(1, 0), $y = \log_b x$
$b > 1$	$0 < b < 1$	$b > 1$	$0 < b < 1$

Big Idea 2 Solving Exponential and Logarithmic Equations

Solving an Exponential Equation	Solving a Logarithmic Equation
If each side can be written using the same base, equate exponents. $3^{x+1} = 9^x$ $3^{x+1} = (3^2)^x$ $x + 1 = 2x$ $1 = x$	If the equation has the form $\log_b x = \log_b y$, use the fact that $x = y$. $\log_2 (4x - 2) = \log_2 3x$ $4x - 2 = 3x$ $x = 2$
If each side cannot be written using the same base, take a logarithm of each side. $6^x = 15$ $\log_6 6^x = \log_6 15$ $x = \frac{\log 15}{\log 6} \approx 1.511$	If a logarithm is set equal to a constant, exponentiate each side. $\log_5 (x + 1) = 2$ $x + 1 = 5^2$ $x = 24$

Big Idea 3 Writing and Applying Exponential and Power Functions

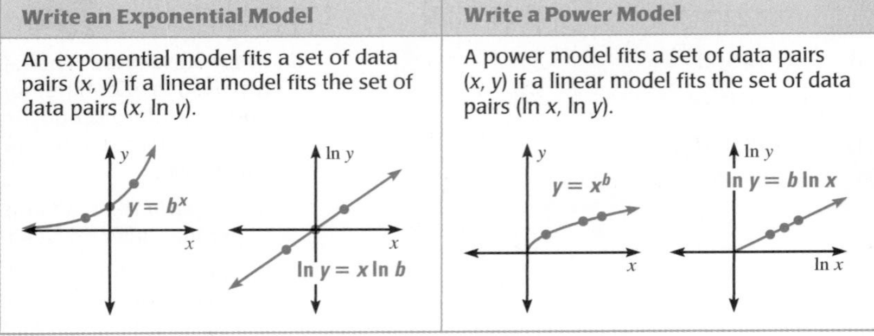

Write an Exponential Model	Write a Power Model
An exponential model fits a set of data pairs (x, y) if a linear model fits the set of data pairs $(x, \ln y)$.	A power model fits a set of data pairs (x, y) if a linear model fits the set of data pairs $(\ln x, \ln y)$.

7 CHAPTER REVIEW

@HomeTutor
classzone.com
• Multi-Language Glossary
• Vocabulary practice

REVIEW KEY VOCABULARY

- exponential function, *p. 478*
- exponential growth function, *p. 478*
- growth factor, *p. 478*
- asymptote, *p. 478*
- exponential decay function, *p. 486*
- decay factor, *p. 486*
- natural base *e*, *p. 492*
- logarithm of *y* with base *b*, *p. 499*
- common logarithm, *p. 500*
- natural logarithm, *p. 500*
- exponential equation, *p. 515*
- logarithmic equation, *p. 517*

VOCABULARY EXERCISES

1. What is the asymptote of the graph of the function $y = -2\left(\frac{1}{4}\right)^{x+1} + 5$? $y = 5$
2. Identify the decay factor in the model $y = 7.2(0.89)^x$. **0.89**
3. **WRITING** *Explain* the meaning of $\log_b y$. ***Sample answer:*** **$\log_b y = x$ if and only if $b^x = y$.**
4. Copy and complete: A logarithm with base *e* is called a(n) __?__ logarithm. **natural**
5. Is $y = (1.4)^x$ an *exponential function* or a *power function*? *Explain.*
Exponential function. *Sample answer:* The variable is in the exponent.

REVIEW EXAMPLES AND EXERCISES

Use the review examples and exercises below to check your understanding of the concepts you have learned in each lesson of Chapter 7.

7.1 Graph Exponential Growth Functions

pp. 478–485

EXAMPLE

Graph $y = 2 \cdot 3^{x-2} + 3$. State the domain and range.

Begin by sketching the graph of $y = 2 \cdot 3^x$, which passes through (0, 2) and (1, 6). Then translate the graph right 2 units and up 3 units. Notice that the translated graph passes through (2, 5) and (3, 9).

The graph's asymptote is the line $y = 3$. The domain is all real numbers, and the range is $y > 3$.

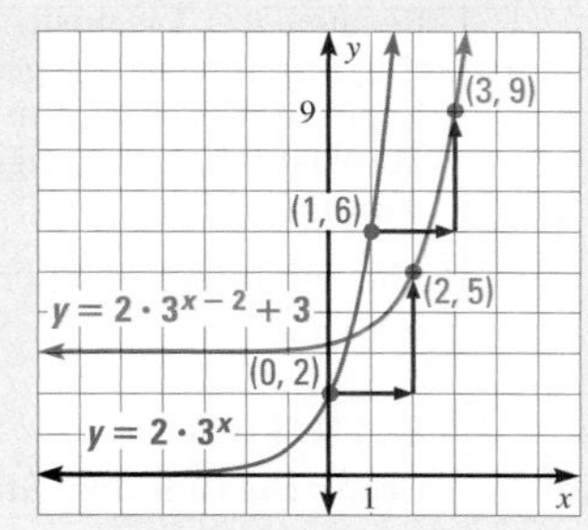

EXERCISES

EXAMPLES 1, 2, 3, and 5 on pp. 478–481 for Exs. 6–9

Graph the function. State the domain and range. 6–8. See margin.

6. $y = 5^x$
7. $y = 3(2.5)^x$
8. $f(x) = -3 \cdot 4^{x+1} - 2$
9. **FINANCE** You deposit \$1500 in an account that pays 7% annual interest compounded daily. Find the balance after 2 years. **\$1725.39**

Extra Example 7.1

Graph $y = \frac{1}{2} \cdot 2^{x+4} - 3$. State the domain and range. **domain: all real numbers; range: $y > -3$**

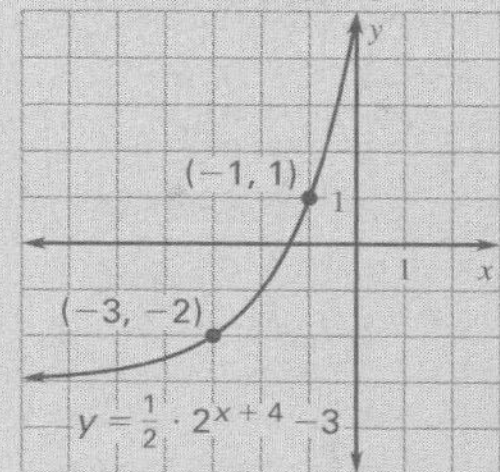

6.

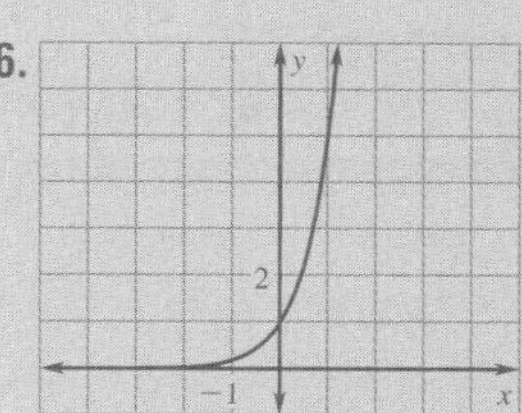

domain: all real numbers, range: $y > 0$

7.

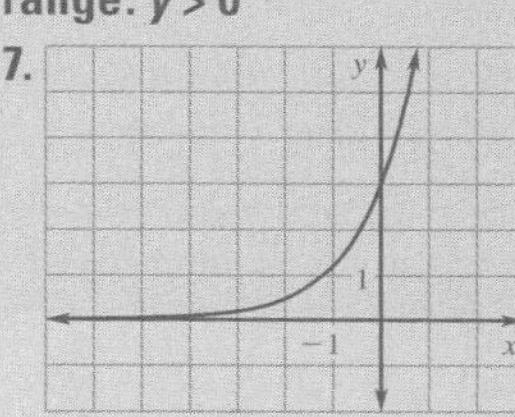

domain: all real numbers, range: $y > 0$

8.

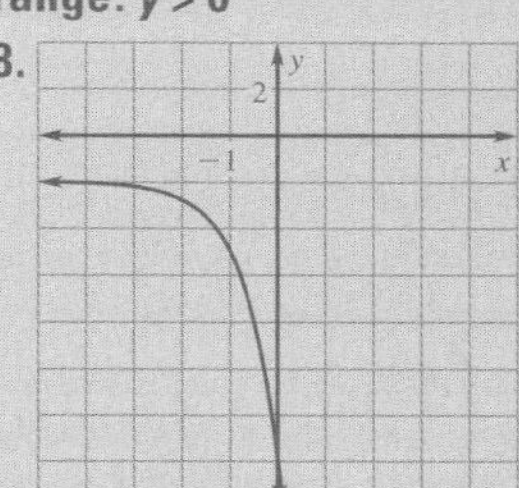

domain: all real numbers, range: $y < -2$

7 CHAPTER REVIEW

Extra Example 7.2

Graph $y = 3\left(\frac{1}{3}\right)^{x-3} + 2$. State the domain and range. **domain: all real numbers; range: $y > 2$**

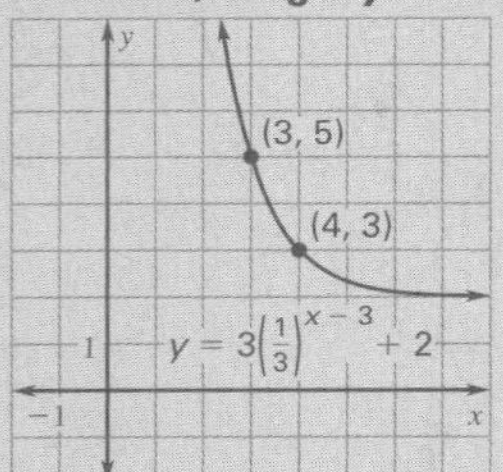

Extra Example 7.3

Graph $y = e^{-2(x+1)} - 4$. State the domain and range. **domain: all real numbers; range: $y > -4$**

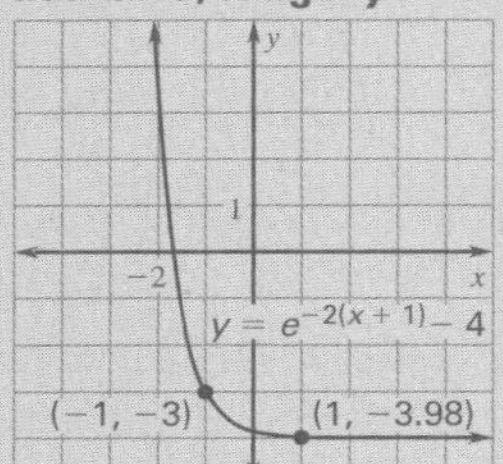

10.

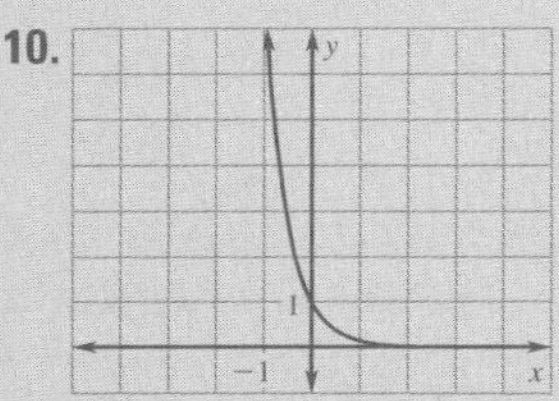

domain: all real numbers, range: $y > 0$

11.

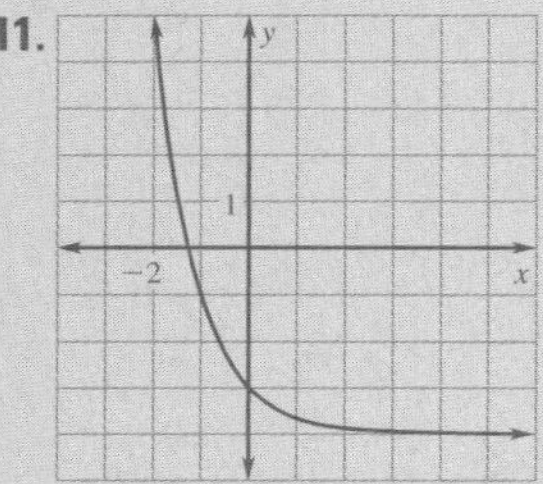

domain: all real numbers, range: $y > -4$

12.

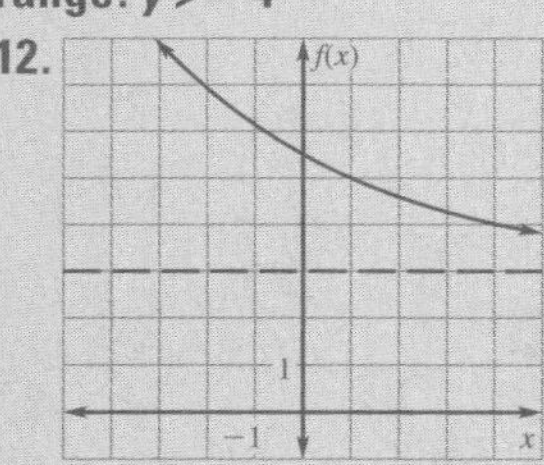

domain: all real numbers, range: $y > 3$

7.2 Graph Exponential Decay Functions

pp. 486–491

EXAMPLE

Graph $y = 2\left(\frac{1}{4}\right)^{x+2} - 2$. State the domain and range.

Begin by sketching the graph of $y = 2\left(\frac{1}{4}\right)^x$, which passes through (0, 2) and $\left(1, \frac{1}{2}\right)$. Then translate the graph left 2 units and down 2 units. Notice that the translated graph passes through (−2, 0) and $\left(-1, -\frac{3}{2}\right)$.

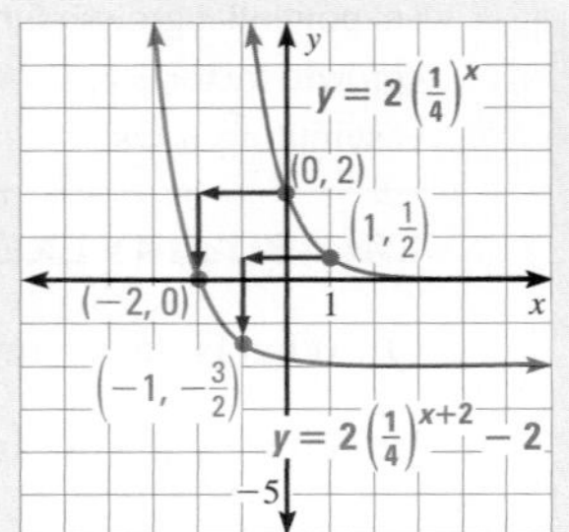

The graph's asymptote is the line $y = -2$. The domain is all real numbers, and the range is $y > -2$.

EXERCISES

EXAMPLES 1, 2, and 3 on pp. 486–487 for Exs. 10–12

Graph the function. State the domain and range. **10–12. See margin.**

10. $y = \left(\frac{1}{8}\right)^x$

11. $y = \left(\frac{1}{3}\right)^x - 4$

12. $f(x) = 2(0.8)^{x-1} + 3$

7.3 Use Functions Involving *e*

pp. 492–498

EXAMPLE

Graph $y = e^{0.25(x-1)} - 5$. State the domain and range.

Because $a = 1$ is positive and $r = 0.25$ is positive, the function is an exponential growth function. Begin by sketching the graph of $y = e^{0.25x}$. Translate the graph right 1 unit and down 5 units.

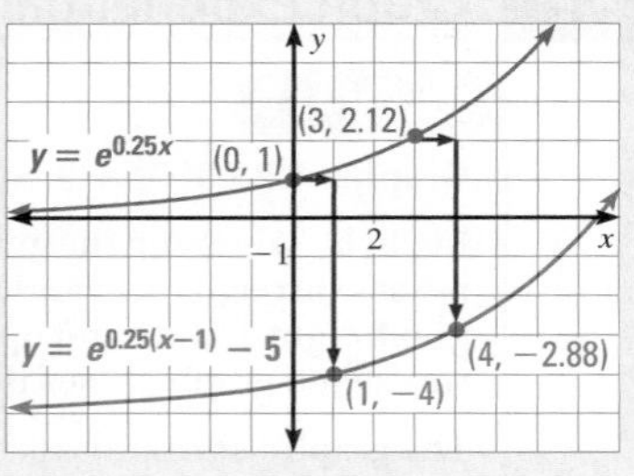

The domain is all real numbers, and the range is $y > -5$.

EXERCISES

EXAMPLES 3 and 5 on pp. 493–495 for Exs. 13–16

Graph the function. State the domain and range. **13–15. See margin.**

13. $y = 2e^{-x}$

14. $y = e^{x-2}$

15. $f(x) = e^{-0.4(x+2)} + 6$

16. **PHYSIOLOGY** Nitrogen-13 is a radioactive isotope of nitrogen used in a physiological test called positron emission tomograph (PET). A typical PET scan begins with 6.9 picograms of nitrogen-13 (1 picogram = 10^{-12} grams). The number N of picograms of nitrogen-13 remaining after t minutes can be modeled by $N = 6.9e^{-0.0695t}$. How many picograms of nitrogen-13 remain after 10 minutes? **about 3.44 picograms**

13.

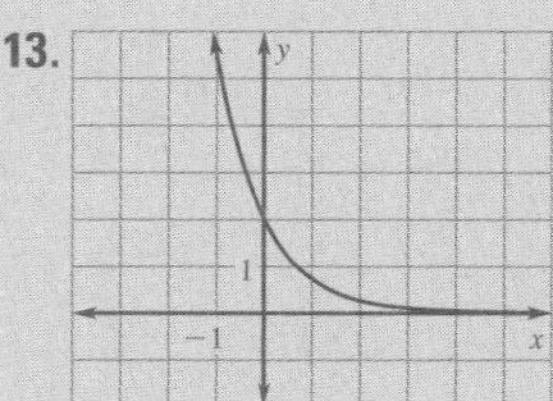

domain: all real numbers, range: $y > 0$

14.

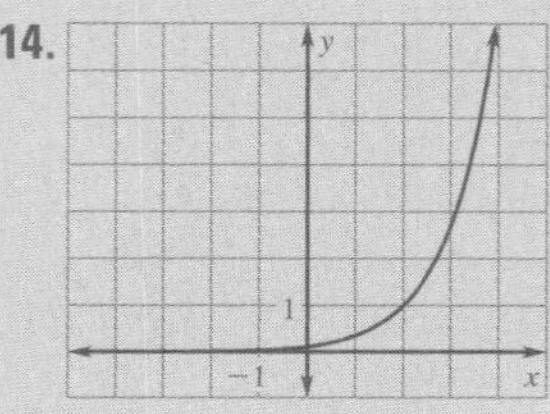

domain: all real numbers, range: $y > 0$

15.

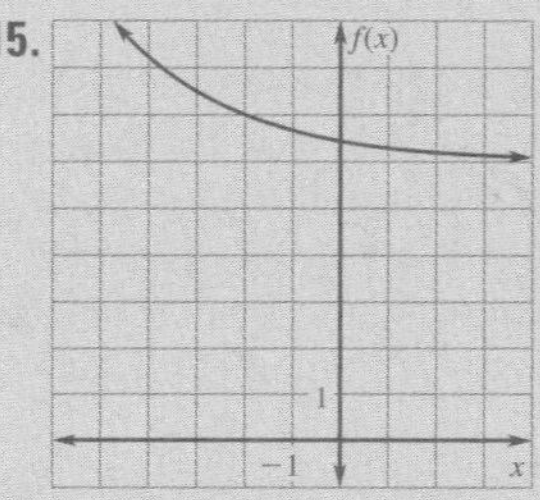

domain: all real numbers, range: $y > 6$

@HomeTutor classzone.com Chapter Review Practice

7.4 Find Logarithms and Graph Logarithmic Functions *pp. 499–505*

EXAMPLE

Evaluate the logarithm.

a. $\log_5 625$ b. $\log 0.001$ c. $\log_{125} 5$ d. $\log_2 \frac{1}{64}$

To help you find the value of $\log_b y$, ask yourself what power of b gives you y.

a. 5 to what power gives 625?
$5^4 = 625$, so $\log_5 625 = 4$.

b. 10 to what power gives 0.001?
$10^{-3} = 0.001$, so $\log 0.001 = -3$.

c. 125 to what power gives 5?
$125^{1/3} = 5$, so $\log_{125} 5 = \frac{1}{3}$.

d. 2 to what power gives $\frac{1}{64}$?
$2^{-6} = \frac{1}{64}$, so $\log_2 \frac{1}{64} = -6$.

EXERCISES

EXAMPLES 4, 7, and 8
pp. 500–503
Exs. 17–24

Evaluate the logarithm without using a calculator.

17. $\log_3 243$ 5
18. $\log_7 1$ 0
19. $\log_{1/6} 216$ −3
20. $\log_{125} \frac{1}{5}$ $-\frac{1}{3}$

Graph the function. State the domain and range. 21–23. See margin.

21. $y = \log_{1/6} x$
22. $y = \log_3 x - 4$
23. $f(x) = \ln (x - 1) + 3$

24. **BIOLOGY** Researchers have found that after 25 years of age, the average size of the pupil in a person's eye decreases. The relationship between pupil diameter d (in millimeters) and age a (in years) can be modeled by $d = -2.1158 \ln a + 13.669$. What is the average diameter of a pupil for a person 25 years old? 50 years old? about 6.86 mm; about 5.39 mm

7.5 Apply Properties of Logarithms *pp. 507–513*

EXAMPLES

Expand the expression.

$$\log_5 \frac{6x}{y^3} = \log_5 6x - \log_5 y^3$$
$$= \log_5 6 + \log_5 x - \log_5 y^3$$
$$= \log_5 6 + \log_5 x - 3 \log_5 y$$

Condense the expression.

$$3 \log_3 8 - \log_3 16 = \log_3 8^3 - \log_3 16$$
$$= \log_3 \frac{8^3}{16}$$
$$= \log_3 32$$

EXERCISES

EXAMPLES 1 and 3
on p. 508
for Exs. 25–31

Expand the expression.

25. $\log_8 3xy$ $\log_8 3 + \log_8 x + \log_8 y$
26. $\ln 10x^3y$ $\ln 10 + 3 \ln x + \ln y$
27. $\log \frac{8}{y^4}$ $\log 8 - 4 \log y$
28. $\ln \frac{3y}{x^5}$ $\ln 3 + \ln y - 5 \ln x$

Condense the expression.

29. $3 \log_7 4 + \log_7 6$ $\log_7 384$
30. $\ln 12 - 2 \ln x$ $\ln \frac{12}{x^2}$
31. $2 \ln 3 + 5 \ln 2 - \ln 8$ $\ln 36$

Extra Example 7.4

Evaluate the logarithm.

a. $\log_2 128$ 7
b. $\log 100{,}000$ 5
c. $\log_{1024} 4$ $\frac{1}{5}$
d. $\log_5 \frac{1}{625}$ −4

Extra Examples 7.5

1. Expand $\log_6 \frac{5\sqrt[3]{x}}{y^4}$.
$\log_6 5 + \frac{1}{3} \log_6 x - 4 \log_6 y$

2. Condense $3 \ln 4 + \ln 9 - \ln 3$.
$\ln 192$

21.
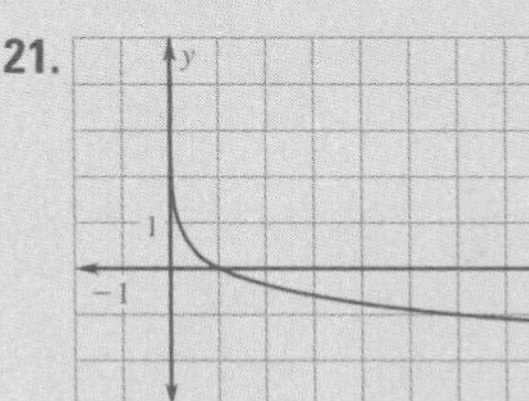
domain: $x > 0$, range: all real numbers

22.
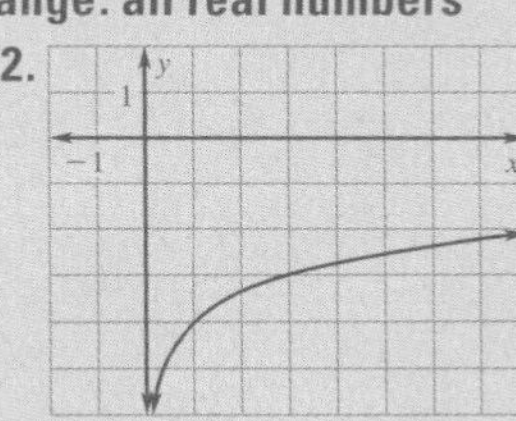
domain: $x > 0$, range: all real numbers

23.
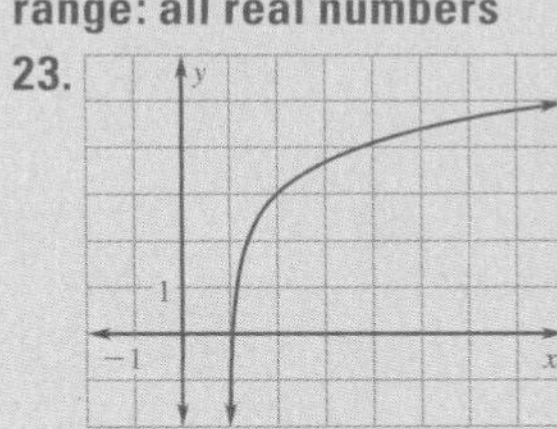
domain: $x > 0$, range: all real numbers

7 CHAPTER REVIEW

Extra Example 7.6

Solve the equation.

a. $18^x = 10$ about 0.797

b. $\log_2 2x + \log_2 (x + 4) = 6$ 4

Extra Example 7.7

Write an exponential function $y = ab^x$ whose graph passes through (2, 45) and (4, 405). $y = 5 \cdot 3^x$

7.6 Solve Exponential and Logarithmic Equations

pp. 515–522

EXAMPLE

Solve the equation.

a. $7^x = 12$

$\log_7 7^x = \log_7 12$

$x = \log_7 12$

$x = \frac{\log 12}{\log 7} \approx 1.277$

b. $\log_2 (3x - 7) = 5$

$2^{\log_2 (3x - 7)} = 2^5$

$3x - 7 = 32$

$x = 13$

EXAMPLES 2, 5, and 6 on pp. 516–518 for Exs. 32–34

EXERCISES

Solve the equation. Check for extraneous solutions.

32. $5^x = 32$ about 2.153

33. $\log_3 (2x - 5) = 2$ 7

34. $\ln x + \ln (x + 2) = 3$ about 3.592

7.7 Write and Apply Exponential and Power Functions

pp. 529–536

EXAMPLE

Write an exponential function $y = ab^x$ whose graph passes through (−1, 2) and (3, 32).

Substitute the coordinates of the two given points into $y = ab^x$.

$2 = ab^{-1}$ **Substitute 2 for y and −1 for x.**

$32 = ab^3$ **Substitute 32 for y and 3 for x.**

Solve for a in the first equation to obtain $a = 2b$, and substitute this expression for a in the second equation.

$32 = (2b)b^3$ **Substitute 2b for a in second equation.**

$32 = 2b^4$ **Product of powers property**

$16 = b^4$ **Divide each side by 2.**

$2 = b$ **Take the positive fourth root because $b > 0$.**

Because $b = 2$, it follows that $a = 2(2) = 4$. So, $y = 4 \cdot 2^x$.

EXAMPLES 1 and 5 on pp. 529–532 for Exs. 35–38

EXERCISES

Write an exponential function $y = ab^x$ whose graph passes through the points.

35. (3, 8), (5, 2) $y = 64\left(\frac{1}{2}\right)^x$

36. (−2, 2), (1, 0.25) $y = \frac{1}{2}\left(\frac{1}{2}\right)^x$

37. (2, 9), (4, 324) $y = \frac{1}{4} \cdot 6^x$

38. SPORTING GOODS A store begins selling a new type of basketball shoe. The table shows sales of the shoe over time. Find a power model for the data. $y = 28.0x^{0.750}$

Week, x	1	2	3	4	5	6
Pairs sold, y	28	47	64	79	94	107

Chapter Test, p. 543

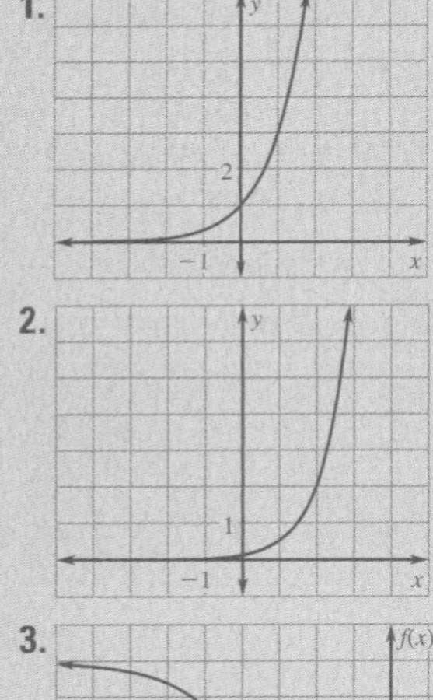

1.

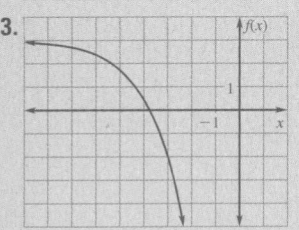

2.

3.

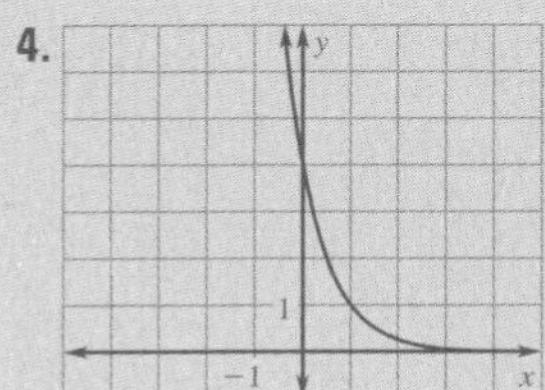

4.

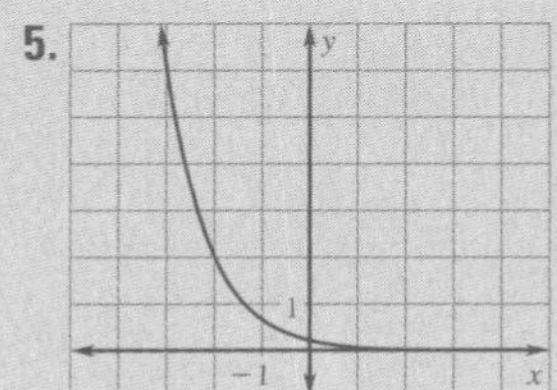

5.

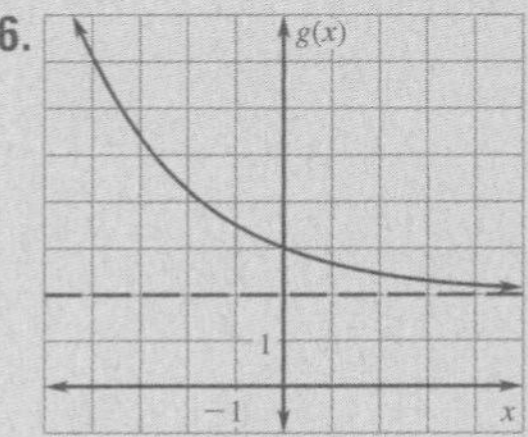

6.

domain: all
al numbers,
nge: $y < 3$

Graph the function. State the domain and range. 1–9. See margin for art.

1. $y = 3^x$ domain: all real numbers, range: $y > 0$
2. $y = 2 \cdot 4^{x-2}$ domain: all real numbers, range: $y > 0$
3. $f(x) = -5 \cdot 2^{x+3} + 3$
4. $y = 4(0.25)^x$ domain: all real numbers, range: $y > 0$
5. $y = 2\left(\frac{1}{3}\right)^{x+2}$ domain: all real numbers, range: $y > 0$
6. $g(x) = \left(\frac{2}{3}\right)^x + 2$ domain: all real numbers, range: $y > 2$
7. $y = \frac{1}{2}e^{-x}$ domain: all real numbers, range: $y > 0$
8. $y = 2.5e^{-0.5x} + 1$ domain: all real numbers, range: $y > 1$
9. $h(x) = \frac{1}{3}e^{x-1} - 2$ domain: all real numbers, range: $y > -2$

Evaluate the logarithm without using a calculator.

10. $\log_5 25$ 2
11. $\log_2 \frac{1}{32}$ −5
12. $\log_6 1$ 0

Graph the function. State the domain and range. 13–15. See margin for art.

13. $y = \log_2 x$ domain: $x > 0$, range: all real numbers
14. $y = \ln x - 3$ domain: $x > 0$, range: all real numbers
15. $f(x) = \log(x + 3) + 2$ domain: $x > -3$, range: all real numbers

Condense the expression.

16. $2 \ln 7 - 3 \ln 4$ $\ln \frac{49}{64}$
17. $\log_4 3 + 5 \log_4 2$ $\log_4 96$
18. $\log 5 + \log x - 2 \log 3$ $\log \frac{5x}{9}$

Use the change-of-base formula to evaluate the logarithm.

19. $\log_5 50$ about 2.431
20. $\log_6 23$ about 1.750
21. $\log_9 45$ about 1.732

Solve the equation. Check for extraneous solutions.

22. $7^{2x} = 30$ about 0.874
23. $3 \log(x - 4) = 6$ 104
24. $\log_4 x + \log_4(x + 6) = 2$ 2

25. Write an exponential function $y = ab^x$ whose graph passes through $(-1, 48)$ and $(2, 6)$. $y = 24\left(\frac{1}{2}\right)^x$

26. Write a power function $y = ax^b$ whose graph passes through $(3, 8)$ and $(6, 15)$. $y = 2.95x^{0.907}$

27. **LANDSCAPING** From 1996 to 2001, the number of households that purchased lawn and garden products at home gardening centers increased by about 4.85% per year. In 1996, about 62 million households purchased lawn and garden products. Write a function giving the number of households H (in millions) that purchased lawn and garden products t years after 1996. $H = 62(1.0485)^t$

28. **FINANCE** You deposit $2500 in an account that pays 3.5% annual interest compounded continuously. What is the balance after 8 years? $3307.82

29. **EARTH SCIENCE** Rivers and streams carry small particles of sediment downstream. The table shows the diameter x (in millimeters) of several particles of sediment and the speed y (in meters per second) of the current needed to carry each particle downstream.

Type of sediment	x	y
Mud	0.2	0.10
Gravel	5	0.50
Coarse gravel	11	0.75
Pebbles	20	1.00
Small stones	45	1.50

a. Draw a scatter plot of the data pairs $(\ln x, \ln y)$. See margin.

b. Find a power model for the original data. Estimate the speed of the current needed to carry a particle with a diameter of 120 millimeters downstream. $y = 0.224x^{0.500}$; about 2.45 m/s

Additional Resources

Assessment Book

- Chapter Test, Levels A, B, C, pp. 98–103
- Standardized Chapter Test, pp. 104–105
- SAT/ACT Chapter Test, pp. 106–107
- Alternative Assessment, pp. 108–109

Test Generator CD-ROM

Chapter Test

Easily-readable reduced copies (with answers) of Chapter Test B, the Standardized Chapter Test, and the Alternative Assessment from the Assessment Book can be found on pp. 476E–476F.

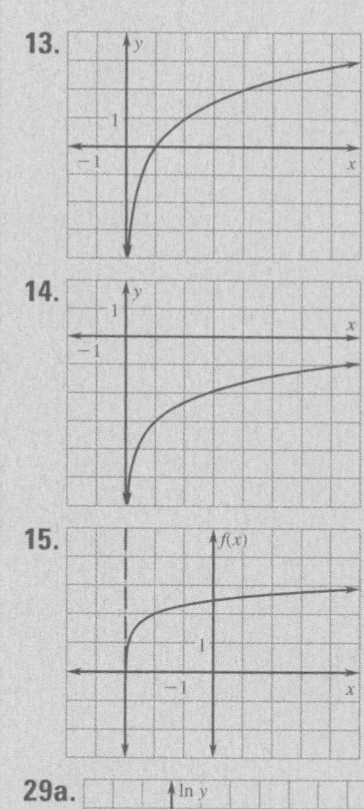

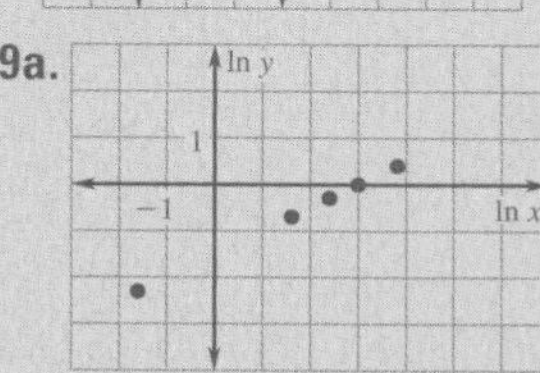

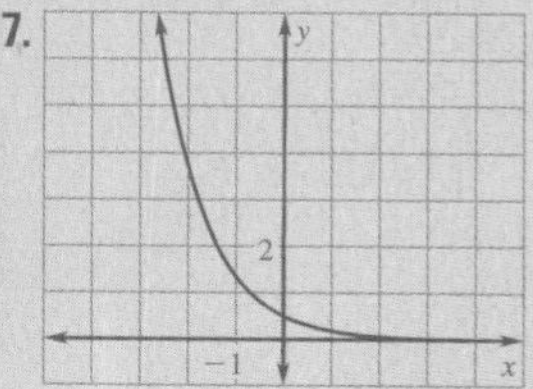

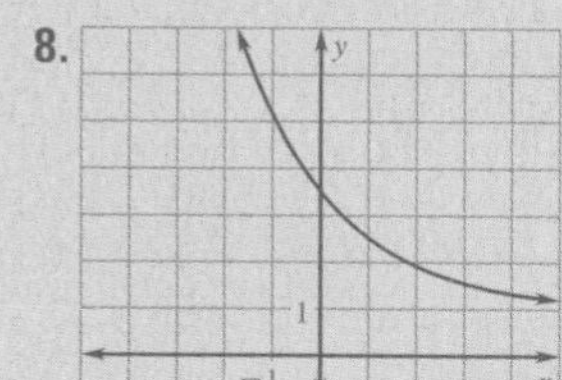

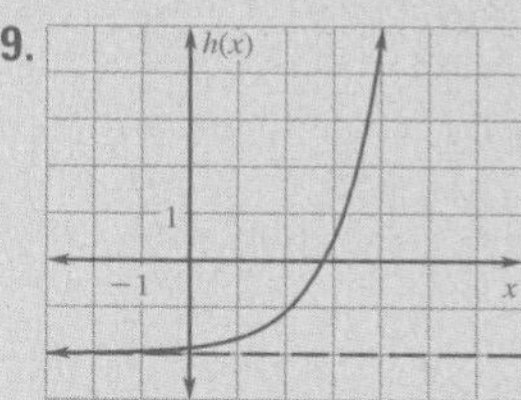

TEST PREPARATION

MULTIPLE-CHOICE QUESTIONS

If you have difficulty solving a multiple-choice problem directly, you may be able to use another approach. First, eliminate as many wrong answers as you can. Then, make an educated guess from among the remaining choices.

PROBLEM 1

Which exponential function has a graph that passes through the points (2, −12) and (4, −48)?

A. $y = 3 \cdot 2^x$ B. $y = -\sqrt{3} \cdot 2^x$ C. $y = -\frac{4}{3} \cdot 3^x$ D. $y = -3 \cdot 2^x$

METHOD 1

SOLVE DIRECTLY Substitute the coordinates of the two points into $y = ab^x$ and solve the resulting system.

STEP 1 **Substitute** the coordinates of the points into $y = ab^x$.

$-12 = ab^2$ Substitute (2, −12).

$-48 = ab^4$ Substitute (4, −48).

STEP 2 **Solve** the first equation for a.

$\frac{-12}{b^2} = a$ Divide each side by b^2.

STEP 3 **Substitute** $\frac{-12}{b^2}$ for a in the second equation and solve for b.

$-48 = \left(\frac{-12}{b^2}\right)b^4$ Substitute.

$-48 = -12b^2$ Simplify.

$4 = b^2$ Divide each side by −12.

$2 = b$ Take the positive square root because $b > 0$.

STEP 4 **Substitute** the value of b into $a = \frac{-12}{b^2}$ to find the value of a.

$$a = \frac{-12}{b^2} = \frac{-12}{2^2} = \frac{-12}{4} = -3$$

The equation is $y = -3 \cdot 2^x$.

▸ The correct answer is D.

METHOD 2

ELIMINATE CHOICES Another method is to chec whether both of the points are solutions of the equations given in the answer choices.

Substitute the coordinates of the points into th equation in each answer choice. You can stop a soon as you realize that one of the points is not solution.

Choice A: $y = 3 \cdot 2^x$

$-12 \stackrel{?}{=} 3 \cdot 2^2$

$-12 \neq 12$

Choice B: $y = -\sqrt{3} \cdot 2^x$

$-12 \stackrel{?}{=} -\sqrt{3} \cdot 2^2$

$-12 \neq -4\sqrt{3}$

Choice C: $y = -\frac{4}{3} \cdot 3^x$ $y = -\frac{4}{3} \cdot 3^x$

$-12 \stackrel{?}{=} -\frac{4}{3} \cdot 3^2$ $-48 \stackrel{?}{=} -\frac{4}{3} \cdot 3^4$

$-12 = -12$ ✓ $-48 \neq -108$

Choice D: $y = -3 \cdot 2^x$ $y = -3 \cdot 2^x$

$-12 \stackrel{?}{=} -3 \cdot 2^2$ $-48 \stackrel{?}{=} -3 \cdot 2^4$

$-12 = -12$ ✓ $-48 = -48$ ✓

▸ The correct answer is D.

PROBLEM 2

You buy a new personal computer for \$1600. It is estimated that the computer's value will decrease by 50% each year. After about how many years will the computer be worth \$250?

A. $1\frac{1}{3}$ years B. 2 years C. $2\frac{2}{3}$ years D. 3 years

METHOD 1

SOLVE DIRECTLY Write and solve an equation to find the time it takes for the computer to depreciate to \$250.

Let y be the value (in dollars) of the computer t years after the purchase. An exponential decay model for the value is:

$$y = a(1 - r)^t$$
$$250 = 1600(1 - 0.5)^t$$
$$0.156 \approx (0.5)^t$$
$$\log_{0.5} 0.156 = \log_{0.5} (0.5)^t$$
$$t \approx \frac{\log 0.156}{\log 0.5} \approx 2.68 \text{ years}$$

The computer will be worth \$250 after about $2.68 \approx 2\frac{2}{3}$ years.

▶ The correct answer is C.

METHOD 2

ELIMINATE CHOICES Use estimation to find how long it will take for the computer to depreciate to \$250.

The computer depreciates by 50% each year.

After 0 years, it is worth \$1600.

After 1 year, it will be worth 0.5(\$1600) = \$800.

After 2 years, it will be worth 0.5(\$800) = \$400.

After 3 years, it will be worth 0.5(\$400) = \$200.

The computer will be worth \$250 at some time *between* 2 and 3 years after purchase. So, you can eliminate choices A, B, and D.

▶ The correct answer is C.

PRACTICE

Explain **why you can eliminate the highlighted answer choice.**

1. Which power function has a graph that passes through the points (−2, −16) and (1, 2)?

   A. $y = \frac{1}{2}x^5$ B. $y = 2x^5$ C. ✗ $y = 2x^{1/2}$ D. $y = 2x^3$

2. For which equation is 4 a solution?

   A. ✗ $e^{2x} + 1 = 17$ B. $\log_2 (x + 2) = \log_2 2x$
   C. $3^{x-2} + 1 = 10$ D. $\ln (x + 2) + \ln x = 1$

3. What is the domain of the function $y = -5 \cdot 2^{x+2}$?

   A. All real numbers B. ✗ All real numbers except −2
   C. All real numbers less than 0 D. All real numbers greater than −5

TEST PREPARATION

Kentucky Test Preparation

1. ***Sample answer:*** **$(-16)^{1/2}$ is not defined.**
2. ***Sample answer:*** **e^8 is much greater than 17.**
3. ***Sample answer:*** **If $x = -2$, $y = 2^0 = 1$.**

Kentucky Test Practice

KY

1. C
2. A
3. B
4. D
5. C
6. B
7. A
8. D
9. C
10. A
11. B

MULTIPLE-CHOICE

1. In 1999, the tuition for one year at Harvard University was \$22,054. During the next 4 years, the tuition increased by 4.25% each year. Which model represents the situation?

A. $y = 22{,}054(0.0425)^t$

B. $y = 22{,}054(0.425)^t$

C. $y = 22{,}054(1.0425)^t$

D. $y = 22{,}054(1.425)^t$

2. You deposit \$1000 in an account that pays 3% annual interest. How much more interest is earned after 2 years if the interest is compounded daily than if the interest is compounded monthly?

A. \$.07 B. \$1.27

C. \$61.76 D. \$1061.76

3. The graph of which function is shown?

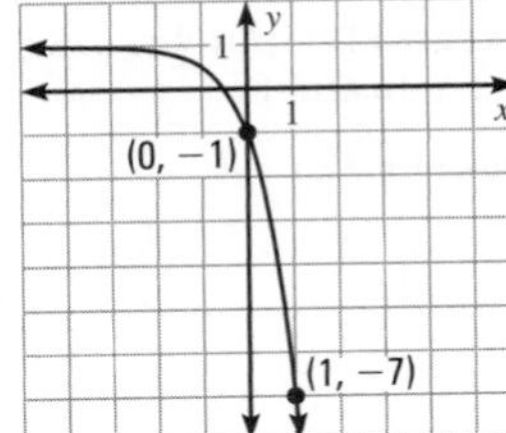

A. $y = 2 \cdot 4^x + 1$ B. $y = -2 \cdot 4^x + 1$

C. $y = 2 \cdot 4^x - 1$ D. $y = -2 \cdot 4^x - 1$

4. Which function can be obtained by translating the graph of $y = \log_3 (x + 2) - 4$ left 1 unit?

A. $y = \log_3 (x + 2) - 5$

B. $y = \log_3 (x + 2) - 3$

C. $y = \log_3 (x + 1) - 4$

D. $y = \log_3 (x + 3) - 4$

5. Which expression is equivalent to $3 \log x + \log 3$?

A. $\log 9x$ B. $4 \log 3x$

C. $\log 3x^3$ D. $\log (x^3 + 3)$

6. The population of the United States is expected to increase by 0.9% each year from 2003 to 2014. The U.S. population was about 290 million in 2003. To the nearest million, what is the projected population for 2010?

A. 295 million

B. 309 million

C. 574 million

D. 4891 million

7. Which expression is equivalent to $\sqrt{100e^{6x}}$?

A. $10e^{3x}$ B. $7e^x + 3e^{2x}$

C. $(2e^x)^3$ D. $10e^{\sqrt{6x}}$

8. Which function is an exponential decay function?

A. $y = 2 \cdot 5^x$ B. $y = -2 \cdot 5^x$

C. $y = 2e^x$ D. $y = 2(0.5)^x$

9. Which function is the inverse of $y = e^{2x} - 3$?

A. $y = 2 \ln (x + 3)$ B. $y = 2 \ln (x - 3)$

C. $y = \dfrac{\ln (x + 3)}{2}$ D. $y = \dfrac{\ln (x - 3)}{2}$

10. The graph of $f(x) = ab^x$ passes through the points (0, 8) and (2, 2). What is the value of $f(5)$?

A. $\frac{1}{4}$ B. 2

C. 8 D. 40

11. The graph of which function is shown?

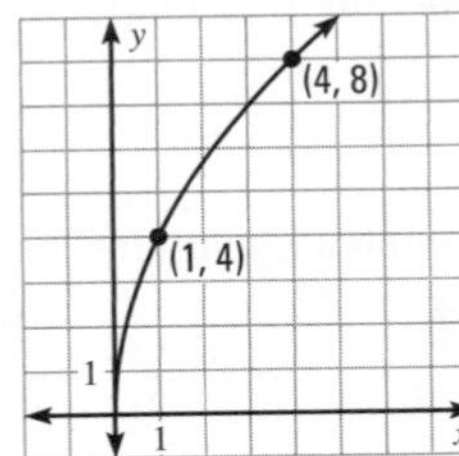

A. $y = 4x^{0.25}$ B. $y = 4x^{0.5}$

C. $y = \frac{1}{2}x^2$ D. $y = 2x^{1/3}$

TEST PREPARATION

MULTIPLE-CHOICE

12. What is the solution of the equation $\log_3 (5x + 3) = 5$?

A. $\frac{2}{5}$ B. $\frac{4}{15}$ C. $\frac{12}{5}$ D. 48

13. What is the solution set of the equation $\log(x + 3) + \log x = 1$?

A. {2, −5} B. {2} C. {5} D. {2, 5}

14. The model $y = 7.7e^{0.14x}$ gives the number y (in thousands per cubic centimeter) of bacteria in a liquid culture after x hours. To the nearest tenth of an hour, after how many hours will there be 50,000 bacteria per cubic centimeter?

A. 1.87 hr B. 13.4 hr

C. 46.4 hr D. 62.7 hr

15. What is the solution to the equation $9^{2x+1} = 3^{5x-1}$?

A. $\frac{3}{8}$ B. $\frac{2}{3}$ C. 2 D. 3

16. The diagram below shows the first three stages of a sequence. What fraction of the circle is shaded in the nth stage?

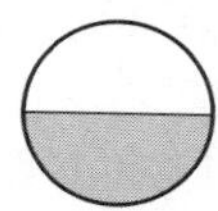
Stage 1

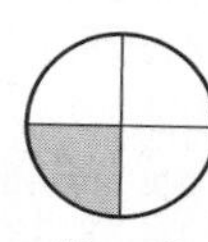
Stage 2

Stage 3

A. $\frac{1}{2n}$ B. $2n$ C. 2^n D. 2^{-n}

OPEN-RESPONSE

17. A movie grosses $37 million in its first week of release. The weekly gross y decreases by 30% each week.

a. Write an exponential decay model for the weekly gross in week x.

b. What is a reasonable domain for this situation? *Explain.*

18. The table shows the number of transistors per integrated circuit for computers introduced in various years.

a. Find an exponential model for the original data.

b. Use your model to predict the number of transistors per integrated circuit in 2008.

c. In 1965, Gordon Moore made an observation that became known as Moore's law. Moore's law states that the number of transistors per integrated circuit would double about every 18 months. According to your model, does Moore's law hold? Justify your answer.

Year	Transistors
1974	6,000
1979	29,000
1982	134,000
1985	275,000
1989	1,200,000
1993	3,100,000
1997	7,500,000
1999	9,500,000
2000	42,000,000
2004	125,000,000

19. For a temperature of 60°F and a height of h feet above sea level, the air pressure P (in pounds per square inch) can be modeled by the equation $P = 14.7e^{-0.0004h}$, and the air density D (in pounds per cubic foot) can be modeled by the equation $D = 0.0761e^{-0.0004h}$.

a. What is the air density at 10,000 feet above sea level?

b. To the nearest foot, at what height is the air pressure 12 pounds per square inch?

c. What is the relationship between air pressure and air density at 60°F? *Explain* your reasoning.

d. One rule of thumb states that air pressure decreases by about 1% for every 80 meter increase in altitude. Do you agree with this? *Explain.*

12. D
13. B
14. B
15. D
16. D
17. a. $y = 37(0.7)^x; 0 \le x \le 11$.
b. ***Sample answer:*** **This domain is how long it takes the movie to gross less than a million dollars per week.**
18. a. $y = 7370(1.37)^x$
b. about 328 million transistors
c. No. *Sample answer:* The factor of change for 18 months (1.5 years) is $1.37^{1.5} \approx 1.6$**, which is a little less than doubling.**
19. a. about 0.00139 lb/ft³
b. 507 ft
c. *Sample answer:* Both have the same parent graph with a different vertical stretch.
d. No. *Sample answer:* Computing the air pressure for 80 meter increments creates a decrease in air pressure that is greater than 1% for each increment.

8 Pacing and Assignment Guide

REGULAR SCHEDULE

Pre-AP For pacing and assignments for a Pre-AP course, see the *Algebra 2 Toolkit.*

Lesson	Les. Day	BASIC	AVERAGE	ADVANCED
8.1 *MA-HS-5.1.7*	Day 1	pp. 555–557 Exs. 1–8, 11–16, 20–26, 31, 37–40, 43	pp. 555–557 Exs. 1, 2, 6–9, 11, 14–17, 22, 23, 26–34, 37–41, 44	pp. 555–557 Exs. 1, 2, 8–11, 17–19, 22, 23, 27–42*
8.2 *MA-HS-5.1.3*	Day 1	EP p. 1016 Exs. 5–8; pp. 561–563 Exs. 1–6, 11–23 odd, 24–30, 37–40, 43	pp. 561–563 Exs. 1, 2, 6–8, 13–20, 23–26, 29–35, 37–41, 44	pp. 561–563 Exs. 1, 2, 7–10, 17–24, 29–42*
8.3 *MA-HS-5.1.3*	Day 1	SRH p. 993 Exs. 2, 5, 6; pp. 568–571 Exs. 1–9, 13–20, 31–33, 37	pp. 568–571 Exs. 1–6, 9–14, 18–27, 31–35, 38	pp. 568–571 Exs. 1, 2, 6, 10–14, 18–36*
8.4 **MA-HS-5.2.5**	Day 1	EP p. 1013 Exs. 21–24; pp. 577–580 Exs. 1–13, 18–22, 48	pp. 577–580 Exs. 1–5, 9–13, 18–27, 48	pp. 577–580 Exs. 1–5, 10–17, 20–27, 48
	Day 2	pp. 577–580 Exs. 23–29, 49–51, 54–55	pp. 577–580 Exs. 28–41, 49–52, 54	pp. 577–580 Exs. 30–47*, 49–53*
8.5 **MA-HS-5.2.5**	Day 1	SRH p. 986 Exs. 23–26; pp. 586–588 Exs. 1–5, 9–11, 15–19, 25–29, 31, 32, 41–43, 46	pp. 586–588 Exs. 1, 2, 4–6, 11–13, 15, 19–21, 25, 26, 27–37 odd, 41–44, 47	pp. 586–588 Exs. 1, 2, 7, 8, 13–15, 22–26, 29–45*
8.6	Day 1	SRH p. 980 Exs. 13–20; pp. 592–595 Exs. 1–13, 33, 34, 39–40	pp. 592–595 Exs. 1–3, 6–13, 28, 29, 33, 34, 39–40	pp. 592–595 Exs. 1–3, 8–13, 28–34*, 39–40
	Day 2	pp. 592–595 Exs. 14–22, 26, 27, 35, 36	pp. 592–595 Exs. 16–23, 26, 27, 35–37	pp. 592–595 Exs. 18–27, 35–38*
Review	Day 1	pp. 603–606 Exs. 1–36	pp. 603–606 Exs. 1–36	pp. 603–606 Exs. 1–36
Assess	Day 1	Chapter 8 Test	Chapter 8 Test	Chapter 8 Test
Yearly Pacing		Chapter 8 Total – 10 days	Chapters 1–8 Total – 102 days	Remaining – 58 days

*Challenge Exercises EP = Extra Practice SRH = Skills Review Handbook

BLOCK SCHEDULE

DAY 1	DAY 2	DAY 3	DAY 4	DAY 5
8.1	**8.3**	**8.4 (CONT.)**	**8.6**	**REVIEW**
pp. 555–557 Exs. 1, 2, 6–9, 11, 14–17, 22, 23, 26–34, 37–41, 44	pp. 568–571 Exs. 1–6, 9–14, 18–27, 31–35, 38	pp. 577–580 Exs. 28–41, 49–52, 54	pp. 592–595 Exs. 1–3, 6–13, 16–23, 26–29, 33–37, 39–40	pp. 603–606 Exs. 1–36
8.2	**8.4**	**8.5**		**ASSESS**
pp. 561–563 Exs. 1, 2, 6–8, 13–20, 23–26, 29–35, 37–41, 44	pp. 577–580 Exs. 1–5, 9–13, 18–27, 48	pp. 586–588 Exs. 1, 2, 4–6, 11–13, 15, 19–21, 25, 26, 27–37 odd, 41–44, 47		Chapter 8 Test

Yearly Pacing Chapter 8 Total – 5 days Chapters 1–8 Total – 51 days Remaining – 29 days

Chapter Resource Guide 8

RESOURCE MANAGER

Chapter Resource Book						
CHAPTER SUPPORT						
Parents as Partners (Chapter Overview with home involvement exercises and activity)					p. 1	
LESSON SUPPORT	**8.1**	**8.2**	**8.3**	**8.4**	**8.5**	**8.6**
Standards	*MA-HS-5.1.7*	*MA-HS-5.1.3*	*MA-HS-5.1.3*	**MA-HS-5.2.5**	**MA-HS-5.2.5**	
Teaching Guide/Lesson Plan	p. 3	p. 13	p. 24	p. 38	p. 49	p. 59
Activity Masters			p. 26			
Technology Activities & Keystrokes		p. 15	p. 28	p. 40		p. 61
Activity Support Masters						
Practice (3 levels)	p. 5	p. 16	p. 29	p. 41	p. 51	p. 63
Study Guide	p. 8	p. 19	p. 32	p. 44	p. 54	p. 66
Catch-Up for Absent Students	p. 10	p. 21	p. 34	p. 46	p. 56	p. 68
Problem Solving/Application	p. 11	p. 22	p. 35	p. 47	p. 57	p. 69
Challenge Practice	p. 12	p. 23	p. 37	p. 48	p. 58	p. 70
REVIEW						
Chapter Review Games and Activities		p. 71	Cumulative Practice			pp. 74–75
Project with Rubric		p. 72	Resource Book Answers			A1

Transparencies	*8.1*	*8.2*	*8.3*	*8.4*	*8.5*	*8.6*
Warm-Up/Daily Homework Quiz	✔	✔	✔	✔	✔	✔
Notetaking Guide	✔	✔	✔	✔	✔	✔
Teacher Support		✔	✔			
Answer Transparencies	✔	✔	✔	✔	✔	✔

ASSESSMENT BOOK

Quizzes	p. 110	SAT/ACT Chapter Test	p. 120
Chapter Tests (3 levels)	p. 112	Alternative Assessment with Rubric	p. 122
Standardized Chapter Test	p. 118		

TECHNOLOGY

- Easy Planner
- Test and Practice Generator
- Power Presentations
- @HomeTutor
- Activity Generator
- Animated Algebra
- Classzone.com
- eEdition Plus Online
- eWorkbook Plus Online
- ML Assessment System

ADDITIONAL RESOURCES

Kentucky

- Worked-Out Solution Key
- Notetaking Guide
- Practice Workbook
- Algebra 2 Toolkit
- Benchmark Tests
- Remediation Workbook
- Spanish Study Guide
- Spanish Assessment Book
- Spanish Resources in Spanish
- Multi-Language Visual Glossary

LESSON 8.1 Practice B
For use with pages 551–557

Tell whether *x* and *y* show *direct variation, inverse variation,* or *neither.*

1. $y = 2x + 3$ neither
2. $y = \frac{x}{3}$ direct variation
3. $x = \frac{3}{y}$ inverse variation
4. $\frac{1}{2}xy = 2$ inverse variation

The variables *x* and *y* vary inversely. Use the given values to write an equation relating *x* and *y*. Then find *y* when *x* = 0.5.

5. $x = 4, y = 6$ $y = \frac{24}{x}$; 48
6. $x = 2, y = \frac{5}{2}$ $y = \frac{5}{x}$; 10
7. $x = 48, y = \frac{1}{12}$ $y = \frac{4}{x}$; 8
8. $x = -3, y = 2$ $y = \frac{-6}{x}$; -12
9. $x = \frac{4}{3}, y = \frac{3}{2}$ $y = \frac{2}{x}$; 4
10. $x = \frac{1}{2}, y = \frac{1}{3}$ $y = \frac{1}{6x}$; $\frac{1}{3}$

Determine whether *x* and *y* show *direct variation, inverse variation,* or *neither.*

11.

x	1	2	3	4
y	1	4	9	16

neither

12.

x	2	5	8	15
y	60	24	15	8

inverse variation

13.

x	1	4	7	10
y	7.5	30	52.5	75

direct variation

The variable *z* varies jointly with *x* and *y*. Use the given values to write an equation relating *x, y,* and *z*. Then find *z* when *x* = 4 and *y* = 7.

14. $x = 3, y = 5, z = 30$ $z = 2xy$; 56
15. $x = 6, y = \frac{1}{2}, z = 24$ $z = 8xy$; 224
16. $x = \frac{3}{2}, y = 18, z = 9$ $z = \frac{1}{3}xy$; $\frac{28}{3}$

In Exercises 17–20, use the following information.

Simple Interest The simple interest I (in dollars) for a savings account is jointly proportional to the product of the time t (in years) and the principal P (in dollars). After fifteen months, the interest on a principal of \$2500 is \$78.13.

17. Find the constant of variation k. 0.025
18. Write an equation that relates I, t and P. $I = 0.025tP$
19. What will the interest I be after ten years? \$625
20. What does the constant of variation k represent? The interest rate of the savings account

In Exercises 21–23, use the following information.

Boyle's Law Boyle's Law states that for a constant temperature, the pressure p of a gas varies inversely with its volume V. A sample of oxygen gas has a volume of 50.25 cubic milliliters at a pressure of 20.6 atmospheres.

21. Find the constant of variation k. 1035.15
22. Write an equation that relates p and V. $V = \frac{1035.15}{p}$
23. Find the volume of the oxygen gas if the pressure changes to 15.2 atmospheres. 68.1 mL^3

LESSON 8.1

LESSON 8.2 Practice B
For use with pages 558–563

1. $x = 2; y = 1$ 2. $x = \frac{4}{3}; y = \frac{2}{3}$ 3. $x = \frac{3}{2}; y = \frac{1}{2}$
4. $x = -\frac{3}{2}; y = 2$ 5. $x = 2; y = 2$ 6. $x = -2; y = 2$

Find the vertical and horizontal asymptotes of the graph of the function. See above.

1. $f(x) = \frac{4}{x-2} + 1$
2. $f(x) = \frac{2x+2}{3x-4}$
3. $f(x) = \frac{x+1}{2x-3}$
4. $f(x) = \frac{4x}{2x+3}$
5. $f(x) = \frac{2x-1}{x-2}$
6. $f(x) = \frac{6x-1}{3x+6}$

Graph the function. State the domain and range. See below.

7. $f(x) = \frac{2}{x+3}$

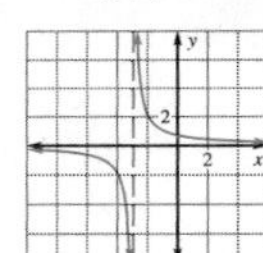

8. $f(x) = \frac{x+1}{x-3}$

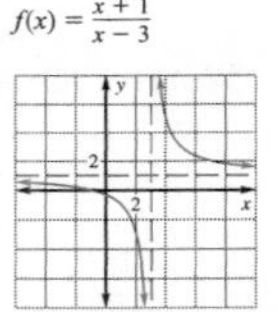

9. $f(x) = \frac{4x}{2x-1}$

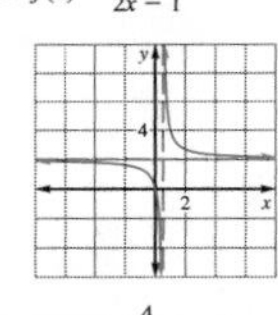

10. $f(x) = \frac{-3}{x+2}$

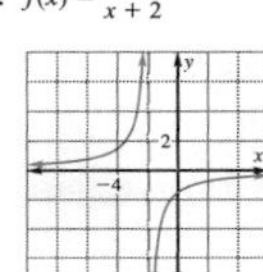

11. $f(x) = \frac{3x-2}{2x+1}$

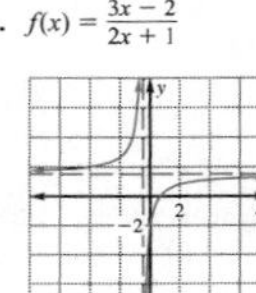

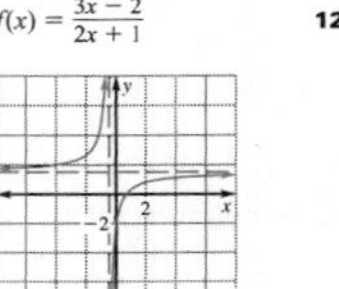

12. $f(x) = \frac{4}{3x-2} - 1$

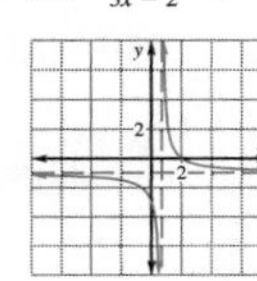

In Exercises 13–16, use the following information.

Phone Bill Your local phone company charges a \$65 installation fee and a monthly fee of \$32. Let x represent the number of months of phone service.

13. Write an equation that represents the total cost C. $C = 32x + 65$
14. Write an equation that represents the average cost A per month. $A = \frac{32x + 65}{x}$
15. Graph the model in Exercise 14.
16. How many months until the average cost per month is \$33.25? 52 months

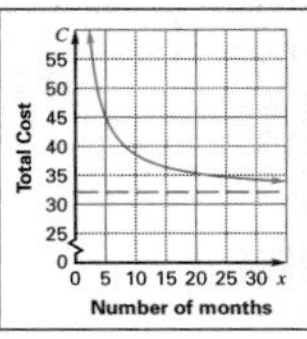

7. domain: all reals except -3; range: all reals except 0
8. domain: all reals except 3; range: all reals except 1
9. domain: all reals except $\frac{1}{2}$; range: all reals except 2
10. domain: all reals except -2; range: all reals except 0
11. domain: all reals except $-\frac{1}{2}$; range: all reals except $\frac{3}{2}$
12. domain: all reals except $\frac{2}{3}$; range: all reals except -1

LESSON 8.2

LESSON 8.3 Practice B
For use with pages 565–571

1. x-intercepts: $-5, 3$; vertical asymptotes: $x = -6, x = 6$
2. x-intercept: 1; vertical asymptotes: $x = -\sqrt{2}, x = \sqrt{2}$
3. x-intercept: $\frac{1}{2}$; vertical asymptote: none

Identify the *x*-intercept(s) and vertical asymptote(s) of the graph of the function. See above.

1. $y = \frac{x^2 + 2x - 15}{x^2 - 36}$
2. $y = \frac{x^2 - 2x + 1}{x^2 - 2}$
3. $y = \frac{2x - 1}{x^2 + 7}$

Graph the function.

4. $f(x) = \frac{2x + 4}{x^2 - 16}$

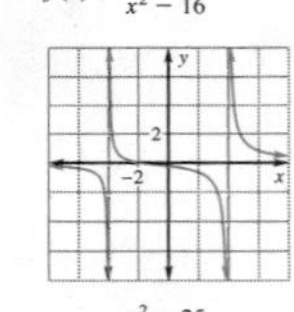

5. $f(x) = \frac{2x^2}{x^2 + 5x + 4}$

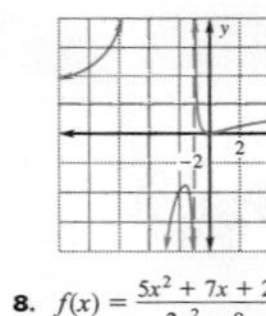

6. $f(x) = \frac{x^2 - 3}{2x^2 + 5x - 12}$

7. $f(x) = \frac{x^2 - 25}{x - 4}$

8. $f(x) = \frac{5x^2 + 7x + 2}{2x^2 - 8}$

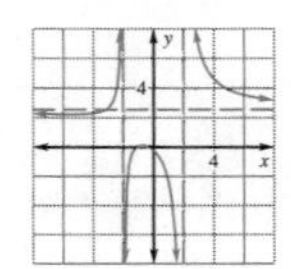

9. $f(x) = \frac{2x^2 + 3}{x^3}$

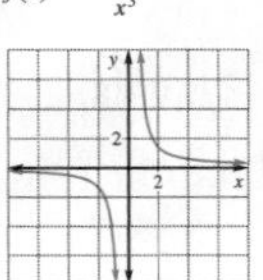

10. **Critical Thinking** Give an example of a rational function whose graph has two vertical asymptotes: $x = 6$ and $x = 0$, and does not have any x-intercepts. *Sample answer:* $y = \frac{3}{x^2 - 6x}$

In Exercises 11–13, use the following information.

Pollution Suppose organic waste was dumped into a pond. Part of the decomposition process includes oxidation, whereby oxygen that is dissolved in the pond water is combined with decomposing material. The oxygen level L in the pond can be modeled by $L = \frac{t^2 - t + 1}{t^2 + 1}$ where t represents the number of weeks after the waste is dumped. The normal oxygen level in the pond is $L = 1$.

11. Graph the model for $0 \leq t \leq 20$.
12. Explain how the oxygen level changed during the 20 weeks after the waste was dumped. The oxygen level dropped to 50% of normal and then slowly increased to 95% of normal.

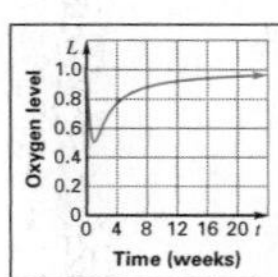

LESSON 8.3

LESSON 8.4

Practice B

For use with pages 573–580

LESSON 8.4

Simplify the rational expression, if possible.

1. $\frac{3x-3}{6}$ $\frac{x-1}{2}$

2. $\frac{(x+7)(x+9)}{(x-9)(x+7)}$ $\frac{x+9}{x-9}$

3. $\frac{x+2}{x^2-4x+4}$ not possible

4. $\frac{x^2+4x-5}{x^2-25}$ $\frac{x-1}{x-5}$

5. $\frac{x^2+4x}{x^2-2x-24}$ $\frac{x}{x-6}$

6. $\frac{x^2+10x-11}{x^2+7x-8}$ $\frac{x+11}{x+8}$

Multiply the expressions. Simplify the result.

9. $\frac{x}{2(x-6)(x-1)}$

7. $\frac{6x^3y}{xy^2} \cdot \frac{3x^2y}{8x^3}$ $\frac{9x}{4}$

8. $\frac{44x^7y^4}{5xy^2} \cdot \frac{12xy^5}{22x^5y^3}$ $\frac{24x^2y^4}{5}$

9. $\frac{5x(x-2)}{(x+1)(x-6)} \cdot \frac{(x+1)}{10(x-2)(x-1)}$ See above.

10. $\frac{x^2+4x+3}{x^2+5x+6} \cdot \frac{x^2-3x-10}{x^2+x}$ $\frac{x-5}{x}$

11. $\frac{x^2-9x+20}{x^2+9x+14} \cdot \frac{x^2+6x+8}{x^2-x-20}$ $\frac{x-4}{x+7}$

12. $\frac{x^3-9x}{x^2+6x+9} \cdot \frac{x^3+3x^2}{x-3}$ x^3

Divide the expressions. Simplify the result.

13. $\frac{10x^4}{3xy^2} \div \frac{6x^2y}{xy^4}$ $\frac{5x^2y}{9}$

14. $\frac{16x^2y}{81xy^2} \div \frac{24x^2y}{54x^3y^3}$ $\frac{4x^2y}{9}$

15. $\frac{2x^2+4x}{x^2-4} \div \frac{x^2-3x+2}{3x-6}$ $\frac{6x}{(x-2)(x-1)}$

16. $\frac{9x^2}{6x-3} \div \frac{3x^2-12x}{2x^2-x}$ $\frac{x^2}{x-4}$

17. $(x^2+9x+18) \div \frac{x^2-3x-18}{x^2-9x+18}$ $(x+6)(x-3)$

18. $\frac{3x^2+4x+1}{x^2-4} \div \frac{x+1}{x^2+8x+12}$ $\frac{(3x+1)(x+6)}{x-2}$

19. **Geometry** In the diagrams below, the length of the edge of the square is twice as long as the radius of the circle. Find the ratio of the area of the circle to the area of the square. Write your answer in simplified form. $\frac{\pi}{4}$

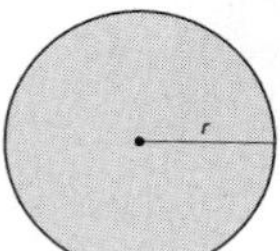

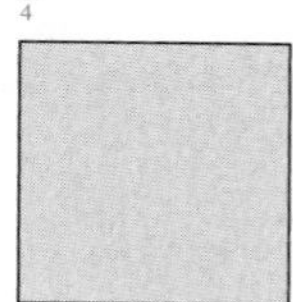

LESSON 8.5

Practice B

For use with pages 582–588

LESSON 8.5

Find the least common denominator.

1. $\frac{2}{x-3}, \frac{3}{2x+3}$ $(x-3)(2x+3)$

2. $\frac{8}{x+2}, \frac{2x}{x-1}$ $(x+2)(x-1)$

3. $\frac{3x}{x-2}, \frac{2}{x^2-4}$ $(x-2)(x+2)$

4. $\frac{x}{3x(x+3)}, \frac{1}{x^2-9}, \frac{4}{x(x-3)}$ $3x(x-3)(x+3)$

Perform the indicated operation and simplify.

5. $\frac{2}{3x+1} + \frac{x}{3x+1}$ $\frac{x+2}{3x+1}$

6. $\frac{x}{x^2-4x+3} + \frac{5}{x-3}$ $\frac{6x-5}{(x-3)(x-1)}$

7. $\frac{3x}{x-5} - \frac{2}{x^2-25}$ $\frac{3x^2+15x-2}{(x-5)(x+5)}$

8. $\frac{3}{x} + \frac{2}{x-2} - \frac{2}{x^2}$ $\frac{5x^2-8x+4}{x^2(x-2)}$

9. $\frac{x}{x+3} - \frac{3}{x+2} - \frac{1}{x^2+5x+6}$ $\frac{x^2-x-10}{(x+3)(x+2)}$

10. $\frac{2x}{x^2+4x+4} + \frac{x-1}{x(x+2)}$ $\frac{(3x-2)(x+1)}{x(x+2)^2}$

11. $2 + \frac{x}{x^2-2}$ $\frac{2x^2+x-4}{x^2-2}$

12. $\frac{x-2}{x^2+x-12} + \frac{x}{x^2-2x-3}$ $\frac{(2x-1)(x+2)}{(x+4)(x-3)(x+1)}$

Simplify the complex fraction.

13. $\frac{\frac{2}{x}+\frac{3}{x-1}}{\frac{1}{2x-2}}$ $\frac{2(5x-2)}{x}$

14. $\frac{\frac{3}{x+2}+\frac{2}{3}}{\frac{2x}{x+2}-\frac{1}{x}}$ $\frac{x(2x+13)}{3(2x^2-x-2)}$

15. $\frac{\frac{3x}{2x-1}-2}{\frac{5}{4x}-\frac{x}{2x-1}}$ $\frac{4x(x-2)}{4x^2-10x+5}$

In Exercises 16 and 17, use the following information.

Doctors Over a twenty year period the number of doctors of medicine M (in thousands) in the United States can be approximated by $M = \frac{28{,}390 + 693t}{85 - t}$ where $t = 0$ represents 1980. The number of doctors of osteopathy B (in thousands) can be approximated by $B = \frac{776 - 12t}{55 - 2t}$.

$T = \frac{-1374t^2 - 20{,}461t + 1{,}627{,}410}{(85-t)(55-2t)}$

16. Write an expression for the total number T of doctors of medicine (MD) and doctors of osteopathy (DO). Simplify the result.

17. How many MDs did the United States have in 1990? how many DOs? about 470,933 MDs; about 18,743 DOs

LESSON 8.6

Practice B

For use with pages 589–595

Determine whether the given *x*-value is a solution of the equation.

1. $\frac{4}{2x-3} + \frac{2}{x+4} = \frac{2x}{x^2-8}; x = \frac{3}{2}$ no

2. $\frac{x}{x+4} - \frac{2}{x} = \frac{2x-8}{x^2}; x = 4$ yes

Solve the equation by cross multiplying. Check for extraneous solutions.

3. $2 = \frac{x+2}{x-3}$ 8

4. $\frac{1}{x+5} = \frac{2}{7x}$ 2

5. $\frac{x}{3} = \frac{-2}{x+7}$ −6, −1

6. $\frac{2x+4}{5x} = \frac{2}{x}$ 3

7. $\frac{x+1}{x-2} = \frac{x-3}{x}$ 1

8. $\frac{2x+3}{3x} = \frac{x}{2x-3}$ −3, 3

9. $\frac{x-5}{-3} = \frac{4}{x+2}$ 1, 2

10. $\frac{2x-6}{x-6} = \frac{x}{x+2}$ −6, 2

Solve the equation by using the LCD. Check for extraneous solutions.

11. $\frac{3}{2} + \frac{1}{x} = 1 + \frac{4}{x}$ 6

12. $\frac{-x+1}{x-1} + 2 = \frac{1}{x}$ no solution

13. $1 + \frac{6}{x} = \frac{2x-4}{x} - 3$ −5

14. $\frac{6}{x-3} - 4 = \frac{2}{x-3}$ 4

15. $\frac{4}{x-3} + \frac{2}{x+3} = \frac{2x+2}{x^2-9}$ −1

16. $\frac{x^2}{3x-1} + 2 = \frac{2(x-3)}{3x-1}$ −2

17. $\frac{x}{2x-1} - \frac{2}{2x+1} = \frac{x^2+20}{4x^2-1}$ −3, 6

18. $x + \frac{5}{x+6} = \frac{6x-1}{x+6}$ no solution

LESSON 8.6

19. **Average Cost** It costs a manufacturing company \$8.00 to produce one can of paint. If the initial investment in the production line was \$50,000, how many cans of paint must be produced before the average cost per can falls to \$10.00? 25,000 cans

20. **Brakes** The braking distance of a car can be modeled by $d = s + \frac{s^2}{20}$ where d is the distance (in feet) that the car travels before coming to a stop, and s is the speed at which the car is traveling (in miles per hour). Find the speed that results in a braking distance of 240 feet. 60 mi/h

In Exercises 21 and 22, use the following information.

Fuel Efficiency The cost of fueling your car for one year can be calculated using this equation: Fuel cost for one year $= \frac{\text{(Miles driven} \times \text{Price per gallon)}}{\text{Fuel efficiency rate}}$

21. Last year you drove 22,500 miles, paid \$2.25 per gallon of gasoline and spent a total of \$2025 on gasoline. What is the fuel efficiency rate of your car? 25 mi/gal

22. How much would you have saved if your car's fuel efficiency rate were 35 miles per gallon? \$578.57

8 Assessment

CHAPTER 8 Quiz 1
For use after Lessons 8.1–8.3

The variables x and y vary inversely. Use the given values to write an equation relating x and y. Then, find y when $x = -2$.

1. $x = 7, y = 2$
2. $x = 3, y = -8$
3. $x = -4, y = \frac{3}{2}$
4. $x = -\frac{1}{3}, y = -27$

Graph the function.

5. $y = \frac{5}{4x}$ 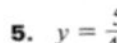

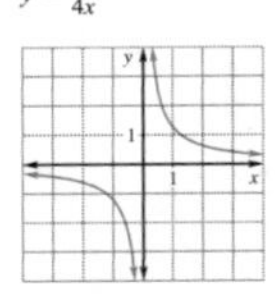

6. $y = \frac{5}{x-3} + 1$

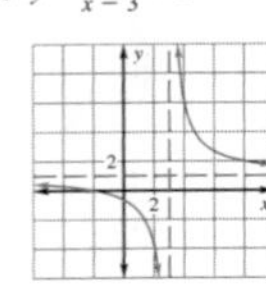

7. $y = \frac{-3x}{4x-8}$

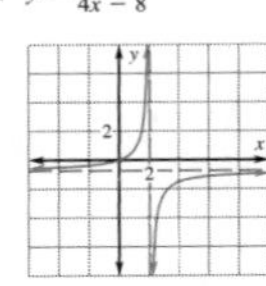

8. $y = \frac{-3}{x^2-4}$

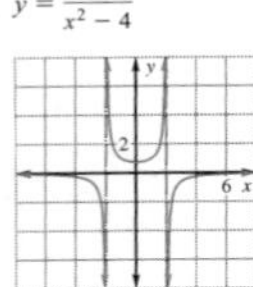

9. $y = \frac{x^2-4}{x^2+3}$

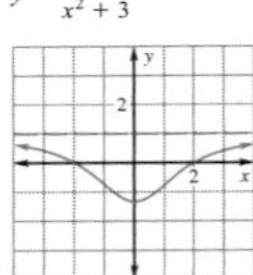

10. The variable z varies jointly with x and y. Also, $z = -60$ when $x = 3$ and $y = -5$. Write an equation that relates x, y, and z. Find z when $x = 6$ and $y = 8$.

Answers

1. $y = \frac{14}{x}$; -7
2. $y = -\frac{24}{x}$; 12
3. $y = -\frac{6}{x}$; 3
4. $y = \frac{9}{x}$; -4.5
5. See left.
6. See left.
7. See left.
8. See left.
9. See left.
10. $z = 4xy$; 192 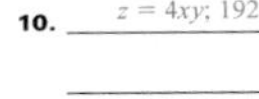

CHAPTER 8 Quiz 2
For use after Lessons 8.4–8.6

Perform the indicated operation and simplify.

1. $\frac{x^2-2x-15}{x^2+x-12} \cdot \frac{2x^2-6x}{x^3+3x^2}$
2. $\frac{x^2-10x+21}{x^2-4} \cdot \frac{x-2}{x-7}$
3. $\frac{x^2+8x+12}{x^2-7x+10} \div \frac{x^2+10x+24}{x^2+x-6}$

Perform the indicated operation and simplify.

4. $\frac{1}{x+3} + \frac{1}{x-3}$
5. $\frac{4}{x-4} - \frac{3}{x+2}$
6. $\frac{5x+4}{x^2-64} + \frac{3}{x-8}$

Solve the equation.

7. $\frac{x-3}{x-2} = \frac{9}{x+6}$
8. $\frac{x-6}{x-4} - \frac{3x-2}{x-4} = 4$
9. $\frac{3x+9}{x^2-9} = \frac{2x+7}{x-3}$
10. **Garden Fence** A farmer wants to fence in the garden shown below. Write a simplified rational expression for the ratio of the garden's perimeter to its area.

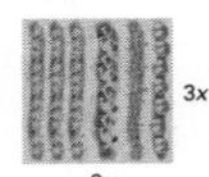

Answers

1. $\frac{2(x-5)}{x(x+4)}$
2. $\frac{x-3}{x+2}$
3. $\frac{(x+2)(x+3)}{(x-5)(x+4)}$
4. $\frac{2x}{x^2-9}$
5. $\frac{x+20}{x^2-2x-8}$
6. $\frac{8x+28}{x^2-64}$
7. 0, 6
8. 2
9. -2
10. $\frac{4}{3x}$

CHAPTER 8 Chapter Test B
For use after Chapter 8

The variables x and y vary inversely. Use the given values to write an equation relating x and y. Then find y when $x = 2$.

1. $x = 3, y = 4$
2. $x = 4, y = -2$

Write an equation relating x, y, and z given that z varies jointly with x and y. Then find z when $x = 2$ and $y = 3$.

3. $x = 5, y = -3, z = 15$
4. $x = -2, y = -2, z = -16$

Graph the function. State the domain and range.

5. $y = \frac{-2}{x}$

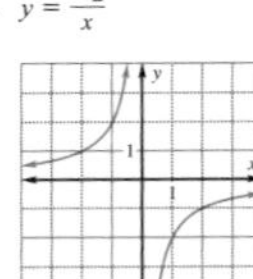

6. $y = \frac{2}{x+1} - 1$

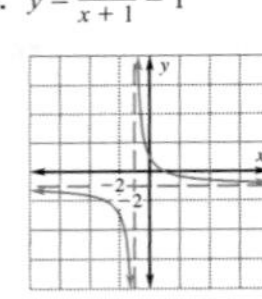

7. A used car can be purchased by paying \$1000 down at the time of purchase, and then paying \$200 per month for 25 months. Write and graph an equation that gives the average cost per month as a function of the number of months of service. After how many months will the average cost be \$325?

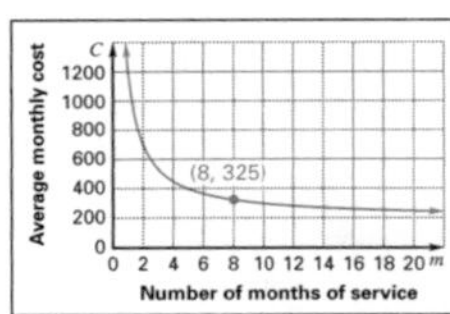

8. The value M (in dollars) of a watercraft t years after it was purchased new can be estimated using the function $M(t) = \frac{5000}{t} + 600$ where $t \geq 1$. Estimate the watercraft's value 4 years after purchase. What does the value of the watercraft approach as time passes?

Answers

1. $y = \frac{12}{x}$; 6
2. $y = -\frac{8}{x}$; -4
3. $z = -xy$; -6
4. $z = -4xy$; -24
5. See left. domain: all real numbers except 0, range: all real numbers except 0
6. See left. domain: all real numbers except -1, range: all real numbers except -1
7. $C(m) = \frac{1000}{m} + 200$, $1 \leq m \leq 25$; See left. 8 months
8. \$1850; \$600

CHAPTER 8 Chapter Test B *continued*
For use after Chapter 8

Graph the function.

9. $y = \frac{3x^2}{2x+1}$

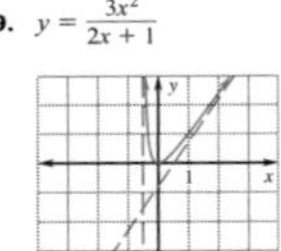

10. $y = \frac{4x+1}{8x-3}$

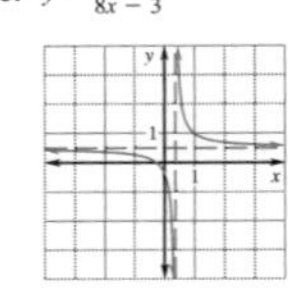

Simplify the rational expression, if possible.

11. $\frac{x^2+7x+12}{x^2-7x+12}$
12. $\frac{x^2+5x}{x^2+6x+5}$

Perform the indicated operation and simplify.

13. $\frac{5x^2y}{4y^3} \cdot \frac{12x^2y^2}{30x^3}$
14. $\frac{2x^3}{7xy^2} \div \frac{6xy^2}{14y^3}$

Find the least common multiple of the polynomials.

15. $x^2 + 4x + 3$ and $x^2 - 9$
16. $x^2 - 4x$ and $x^3 - 8x^2 + 16x$

Perform the indicated operation and simplify.

17. $\frac{7}{5x} - \frac{4}{3x}$
18. $\frac{2x}{x^2-1} + \frac{2x-3}{x^2+5x+4}$

Solve the equation by cross multiplying.

19. $\frac{x+4}{3x+5} = \frac{2x-1}{3x+1}$
20. $\frac{x^2+1}{3-3x} = \frac{x+2}{3}$

Solve the equation by using the LCD.

21. $\frac{3+x}{2} + 2x = \frac{6x+1}{4-x}$
22. $\frac{x+5}{2x+3} + \frac{x+1}{-2x} = -1$

Answers

9. See left.
10. See left.
11. not possible
12. $\frac{x}{x+1}$
13. $\frac{x}{2}$
14. $\frac{2x}{3y}$
15. $(x+1)(x+3)(x-3)$
16. $x(x-4)^2$
17. $\frac{1}{15x}$
18. $\frac{4x^2+3x+3}{(x^2-1)(x+4)}$
19. $-1, 3$
20. $-1, \frac{1}{2}$
21. $-1, 2$
22. $-3, \frac{1}{4}$

CHAPTER 8 Standardized Test

For use after Chapter 8

Multiple Choice

1. Which equation represents inverse variation? A

Ⓐ $y = \frac{5}{x}$ Ⓑ $y = x + 5$

Ⓒ $\frac{y}{5} = x$ Ⓓ $y = 5x$

2. If x varies directly with y and $y = -12$ when $x = 4$, what is the value of y when $x = -3$? C

Ⓐ -16 Ⓑ -9

Ⓒ 9 Ⓓ 16

3. Let r vary directly with s and inversely with t. Which equation represents this relationship? B

Ⓐ $r = ast$ Ⓑ $r = \frac{as}{t}$

Ⓒ $r = \frac{at}{s}$ Ⓓ $r = \frac{a}{st}$

4. Which function represents the graph shown? C

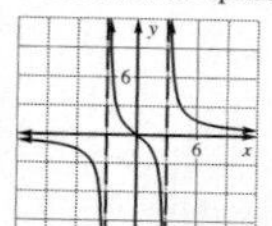

Ⓐ $y = \frac{7}{x^2 - 9}$ Ⓑ $y = \frac{x^2 - 9}{7x^3}$

Ⓒ $y = \frac{7x}{x^2 - 9}$ Ⓓ $y = \frac{x^2 - 9}{7x}$

5. What is (are) the vertical asymptote(s) of the function in Exercise 4? C

Ⓐ $x = -3$ Ⓑ $x = 3$

Ⓒ $x = \pm 3$ Ⓓ There are none.

6. Which function has the domain of all real numbers except -2? A

Ⓐ $y = \frac{x-2}{x+2}$ Ⓑ $y = \frac{x}{x-2}$

Ⓒ $y = \frac{x}{x-2}$ Ⓓ $y = \frac{x+2}{x-2}$

7. What are the asymptotes of the function $y = \frac{4x^2 + 3x + 1}{x^2 - 1}$? D

Ⓐ $x = 0, y = 0$

Ⓑ $x = 1, y = \frac{1}{4}$

Ⓒ $x = 0, x = 1, y = 4$

Ⓓ $x = -1, x = 1, y = 4$

8. What is the simplified form of $\frac{2x^2 - 9x + 10}{x^2 + x - 6}$? B

Ⓐ $\frac{2x - 5}{x - 3}$ Ⓑ $\frac{2x - 5}{x + 3}$

Ⓒ $\frac{2x + 5}{x - 3}$ Ⓓ $\frac{2x + 5}{x + 3}$

9. Which expression is the product of $\frac{24a^2b}{13abc} \cdot \frac{39a^2c^3}{8b^2c^2}$? A

Ⓐ $\frac{9a^3}{b^2}$ Ⓑ $9a^3b^2$

Ⓒ $\frac{117a^3b^2}{13b^2}$ Ⓓ $\frac{117a^3b^2}{13}$

10. The least common multiple of which pair of expressions is $3x(x + 2)(x + 1)$? C

Ⓐ $x^2 + 3x + 2; x + 2$

Ⓑ $x^2 + 3x + 2; 3x + 6$

Ⓒ $x^2 + 3x + 2; 3x^2 + 6x$

Ⓓ $x^2 + 3x + 2; 3x^3 + 6x^2$

CHAPTER 8 Standardized Test *continued*

For use after Chapter 8

11. The legs of a right triangle have lengths x and $x\sqrt{3}$. What is the simplified ratio of the area of the triangle to the hypotenuse? B

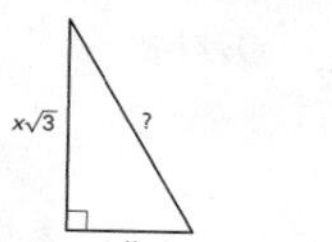

Ⓐ $\frac{\sqrt{3}}{4x}$ Ⓑ $\frac{\sqrt{3}}{4}x$

Ⓒ $\frac{\sqrt{3}}{2}x$ Ⓓ $\frac{4\sqrt{3}}{3x}$

12. Which expression represents the simplified form of $\frac{3x - 2}{\frac{1}{x-2} + \frac{5}{x}}$? D

Ⓐ $\frac{x}{x - 2}$ Ⓑ $\frac{3x - 2}{2(3x - 5)}$

Ⓒ $\frac{(3x - 2)(x - 2)}{3x - 5}$ Ⓓ $\frac{x(3x - 2)(x - 2)}{2(3x - 5)}$

Gridded Answer

13. What is the solution of $\frac{2}{x - 1} = \frac{-1}{x - 4}$?

(Grid answer: 3)

Short Response

14. You join a health club which charges you a \$175 registration fee plus a \$25 per month charge.

a. Determine the equation which calculates the total amount y you have paid in fees for your membership through month x. $y = 175 + 25x$

b. Determine the equation which calculates the average monthly payment y you have made through month x. Which is the first month you average less than \$40 per month for membership? $y = \frac{175}{x} + 25$; month 12

Extended Response

15. A packaging engineer for the Bubble Beverage Company is given the task of designing a new can. The company would like to minimize the surface area of the can in order to minimize overall packaging cost.

a. What is the surface area of a can with radius r and height h? What is the volume of a can with radius r and height h?

b. If the can must hold 355 ml of soda, determine the formula for the surface area of the can in terms of radius r. (*Hint:* Use the fact that the volume is 355 ml and solve for h in terms of r.)

c. For what value of r is the surface area a minimum? Round to one decimal place. (*Hint:* 1 cu cm = 1 ml)

d. If aluminum costs the company \$.001 per cubic centimeter, how much will it cost the company to supply the aluminum for the can?

15. a. surface area $= 2\pi r^2 + 2\pi rh$, volume $= \pi r^2 h$
b. surface area $= 2\pi r^2 + \frac{710}{r}$
c. 3.8 cm **d.** about \$.28/can

CHAPTER 8 Alternative Assessment and Math Journal

For use after Chapter 8

Journal

1. Consider the rational function $f(x) = \frac{2x^2 - 9x - 5}{3x^3 + 3x^2 - 6x}$. Without graphing, identify the x-intercept(s), the vertical asymptote(s), and the horizontal asymptote. Explain your answers. Write a rational function $g(x)$ so that g has zeros 4 and -2, a vertical asymptote $x = 1$, and no horizontal asymptote.

Multi-Step Problem

2. A standard beverage can has a volume of 21.7 cubic inches.

a. Use the formula for the volume of a cylinder, $V = \pi r^2 h$, to write an equation that gives the height h of a can in terms of its radius r.

b. Write an equation that gives the can's surface area S in terms of its radius r by substituting the expression for h from part (a) into the formula for the surface area of a cylinder, $S = 2\pi r^2 + 2\pi rh$.

c. Rewrite your equation from part (b) as a quotient of two polynomials. Do you expect the graph of $S(r)$ to have a horizontal asymptote? Explain.

d. Use a graphing calculator and its *minimum* feature to find the minimum value of S. What are the dimensions r and h of the can that uses the least material?

e. Compare your result from part (d) with the dimensions of an actual beverage can, which has a radius of 1.25 inches and a height of 4.42 inches.

f. Writing Why might a manufacturer choose not to make the beverage can with the least amount of material possible?

g. Critical Thinking Is it possible to make the beverage container shaped like a prism with a square base using less material than it takes to make the cylindrical can with minimal surface area? Explain.

1. Complete answers should include: identification of the x-intercepts $\left(-\frac{1}{2} \text{ and } 5\right)$, the vertical asymptotes ($x = -2$, $x = 0$, and $x = 1$), and the horizontal asymptote ($y = 0$); an explanation that the x-intercepts are the real zeros of the polynomial in the numerator; an explanation that the vertical asymptotes exist at the real zeros of the polynomial in the denominator; an explanation that because the degree of the numerator is less than the degree of the denominator, the horizontal asymptote is $y = 0$; an example of a rational function where the numerator has the factors $(x - 4)$ and $(x + 2)$, the denominator has the factor $(x - 1)$, and the degree of the numerator is greater than the degree of the denominator.
2. a. $h = \frac{21.7}{\pi r^2}$ **b.** $S = 2\pi r^2 + \frac{43.4}{r}$ **c.** $S = \frac{2\pi r^3 + 43.4}{r}$; No. Because the degree of the numerator is greater than the degree of the denominator, $S(r)$ has no horizontal asymptote. **d.** Minimum: $S \approx 43.1$ in.^{2}; $r \approx 1.51$ in., $h \approx 3.03$ in. **e.** *Sample answer:* An actual beverage can is taller and narrower than the can with minimal surface area. **f.** *Sample answer:* The taller, narrower can is probably easier to hold in one hand. **g.** No. The minimum surface area of the beverage container shaped like a prism with a square base is 46.7 in.^{2}. It requires more material than the cylinder with the least surface area (43.1 in.^{2}).

CHAPTER 8 Alternative Assessment Rubric *continued*

For use after Chapter 8

Journal Solution

1. Complete answers should include:

- identification of the x-intercepts $\left(-\frac{1}{2} \text{ and } 5\right)$, the vertical asymptotes ($x = -2$, $x = 0$, and $x = 1$), and the horizontal asymptote ($y = 0$).
- an explanation that the x-intercepts are the real zeros of the polynomial in the numerator.
- an explanation that the vertical asymptotes exist at the real zeros of the polynomial in the denominator.
- an explanation that because the degree of the numerator is less than the degree of the denominator, the horizontal asymptote is $y = 0$.
- an example of a rational function where the numerator has the factors $(x - 4)$ and $(x + 2)$, the denominator has the factor $(x - 1)$, and the degree of the numerator is greater than the degree of the denominator.

Multi-Step Problem Solution

2. a. $h = \frac{21.7}{\pi r^2}$

b. $S = 2\pi r^2 + \frac{43.4}{r}$

c. $S = \frac{2\pi r^3 + 43.4}{r}$; No. Because the degree of the numerator is greater than the degree of the denominator, $S(r)$ has no horizontal asymptote.

d. Minimum: $S \approx 43.1$ in.^{2}; $r \approx 1.51$ in., $h \approx 3.03$ in.

e. *Sample answer:* An actual beverage can is taller and narrower than the can with minimal surface area.

f. *Sample answer:* The taller, narrower can is probably easier to hold in one hand.

g. No. The minimum surface area of the beverage container shaped like a prism with a square base is 46.7 in.^{2}. It requires more material than the cylinder with the least surface area (43.1 in.^{2}).

Multi-Step Problem Rubric

4 The student answers all parts of the problem correctly and completely. The student shows all work. The student's work is neat.

3 The student answers all parts of the problem. The student's work may contain one or two errors in the calculations, equations, or explanations. The student shows most work. The student's work is neat.

2 The student answers all parts of the problem. The student's work contains more than two errors in the calculations, equations, or explanations. The student shows some work. The student's work is sloppy.

1 The student does not complete all parts of the problem. The student's work has several errors in the calculations, equations, or explanations. The student's work is sloppy, or no work is shown.

PLAN AND PREPARE

Main Ideas

Students learn to write and use models for inverse variation and joint variation. They learn to graph rational functions, to multiply, divide, add, and subtract rational expressions, and to simplify complex fractions. Finally, students learn to solve rational equations.

Prerequisite Skills

- Writing direct variation equations
- Factoring polynomials
- Performing polynomial operations

Additional resources for reviewing prerequisite skills are:

- Skills Review Handbook, pp. 975–1009
- @HomeTutor

8 Rational Functions

Before

In previous chapters, you learned the following skills, which you'll use in Chapter 8: writing direct variation equations, factoring polynomials, and performing polynomial operations.

Prerequisite Skills

VOCABULARY CHECK

1. The **asymptote** of the graph at the right is __?__. $y = 0$
2. Two variables x and y show **direct variation** provided __?__ where a is a nonzero constant. $y = ax$
3. An **extraneous solution** of a transformed equation is not an actual __?__ of the original equation. solution

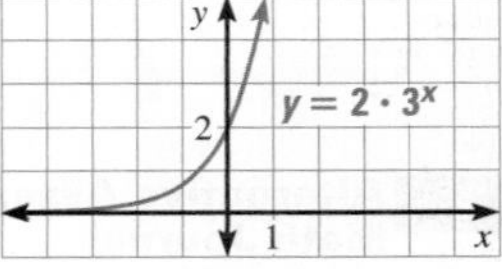

SKILLS CHECK

The variables x and y vary directly. Write an equation that relates x and y. Then find the value of y when $x = -2$. *(Review p. 107 for 8.1.)*

4. $x = 2, y = 8$ $y = 4x; -8$
5. $x = -1, y = 4$ $y = -4x; 8$
6. $x = 12, y = 2$ $y = \frac{1}{6}x; -\frac{1}{3}$

Factor the polynomial completely. *(Review pp. 252, 353 for 8.4, 8.5.)*

7. $x^2 - 11x - 26$ $(x - 13)(x + 2)$
8. $2x^3 - 4x^2 + 2x$ $2x(x - 1)^2$
9. $6x^4 - 4x^3 - 24x + 16$ $2(3x - 2)(x^3 - 4)$

Perform the indicated operation. *(Review p. 346 for 8.4, 8.5.)*

10. $(3x^2 - 6) + (7x^2 - x)$ $10x^2 - x - 6$
11. $(-2x^2 + 6) - (x^2 - x)$ $-3x^2 + x + 6$
12. $(x + 2)(x - 9)^2$ $x^3 - 16x^2 + 45x + 162$

548

Chapter Planning Guide

Chapter 8 Resource Book
- Teaching Guide/Lesson Plan (pp. 3, 13, 24, 38, 49, 59)
- Project with Rubric (p. 72)

Assessment and Intervention
- Assessment Book (pp. 110–123)
- Benchmark Tests
- Remediation Book

Interactive Technology
- Easy Planner
- Power Presentations CD-ROM
- Activity Generator CD-ROM
- Animated Algebra
- Test Generator CD-ROM
- Online Quizzes
- eWorkbook
- eEdition
- @HomeTutor

Resources for English Learners
- Quick Reference for English Learners
- Spanish Study Guide
- Multi-Language Visual Glossary
- Student Resources in Spanish

Now

In Chapter 8, you will apply the big ideas listed below and reviewed in the Chapter Summary on page 602. You will also use the key vocabulary listed below.

Big Ideas

1. **Graphing rational functions**
2. **Performing operations with rational expressions**
3. **Solving rational equations**

KEY VOCABULARY

- inverse variation, *p. 551*
- constant of variation, *p. 551*
- joint variation, *p. 553*
- rational function, *p. 558*
- simplified form of a rational expression, *p. 573*
- complex fraction, *p. 584*
- cross multiplying, *p. 589*

Why?

You can use rational functions to model real-life situations. For example, you can model the time it takes to travel across the United States and back in an airplane.

Animated Algebra

The animation illustrated below for Exercise 41 on page 587 helps you answer this question: How does the time required to fly from New York to Los Angeles and back depend on the speeds of the airplane and the jet stream?

The winds of the jet stream affect the overall speed of an airplane.

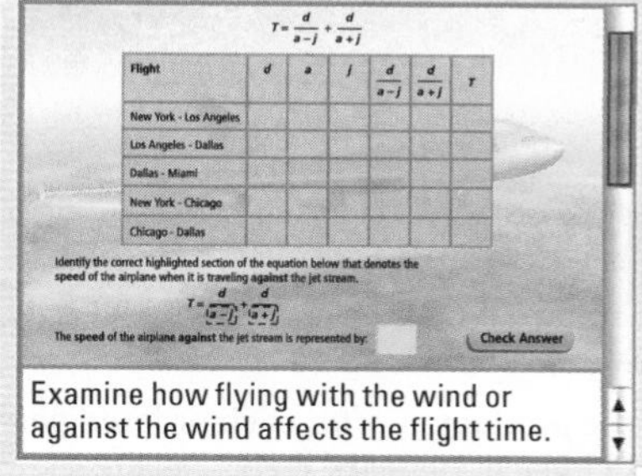

Examine how flying with the wind or against the wind affects the flight time.

Animated Algebra at classzone.com

Other animations for Chapter 8: pages 554, 559, 568, and 602

Algebra 2 Toolkit

- Reading Strategies for Chapter 8, pp. 23–24
- Differentiated Instruction Notes, pp. 71–74
- English Learners Notes, pp. 115–116
- Inclusion Notes, pp. 149–150
- Teaching Strategies with Sample Worksheets, pp. 163–186
- Using Technology in the Classroom, pp. 187–192
- Tips for New Teachers, pp. 207–208
- Math Background Notes, pp. 245–246
- Pre-AP Strategies and Copymasters, pp. 325–326, 409–420
- Teacher Survival Activities, pp. 483–484, 511–512
- Bulletin Board Idea, p. 532
- Teacher Tool Transparencies, following p. 538

1 PLAN AND PREPARE

Explore the Concept

- Students will collect and record data and then model their data with an inverse variation equation.
- This activity leads into the study of modeling data with an inverse variation equation in Lesson 8.1, Example 4.

Materials

Each group of students will need:

- tape measure or meter stick
- centimeter ruler
- masking tape

Recommended Time

Work activity: 10 min

Discuss results: 5 min

Grouping

Students should work in groups of two to collect the data.

2 TEACH

Key Discovery

The product of the distance x (in meters) and the apparent height y (in centimeters) is approximately the same for each x-y pair.

3 ASSESS AND RETEACH

Why might there be some small differences in the products $x \cdot y$ that you calculated? **Errors in measurement or the limitations of the measuring instruments can produce variations in the x and y measurements.**

8.1 Investigating Inverse Variation

MATERIALS • tape measure or meter stick • centimeter ruler • masking tape

QUESTION How can you model data that show inverse variation?

EXPLORE Collect and record data

STEP 1 ***Mark distances***

Work with a partner. Have your partner stand against a wall. Place the end of the tape measure against the wall between your partner's feet. Use tape to mark off distances from 3 meters to 9 meters away from the wall.

STEP 2 ***Measure apparent height***

Face your partner, with your toes touching the 3 meter mark. Hold a centimeter ruler at arm's length and line up the "0" end of the ruler with the top of your partner's head. Measure the apparent height of your partner to the nearest centimeter.

STEP 3 ***Repeat for other distances***

Repeat Step 2 for each marked distance and record your results in a table like the one shown. **Check students' work.**

Distance (m), x	3	4	5	6	7	8	9
Apparent height (cm), y	?	?	?	?	?	?	?

DRAW CONCLUSIONS Use your observations to complete these exercises

1. Does apparent height vary directly with distance? *Justify* your answer mathematically. **No. *Sample answer:* When you divi[de] the distance and the apparent heig[ht] you do not get a constant value.**
2. Find the product $x \cdot y$ for each ordered pair in the table. What do you notice? **Check students' work. *Sample answer:* The product values are very similar.**
3. Based on your results from Exercise 2, write an equation relating distance and apparent height. **Check students' work**
4. Use your equation to predict your partner's apparent height at an unmeasured distance. Then test your prediction by measuring your partner's apparent height at that distance. How close was your prediction? **Check students' work.**

8.1 Model Inverse and Joint Variation

MA-HS-5.1.7 *Students will apply and use direct and inverse variation to solve real-world and mathematical problems.*

Before You wrote and used direct variation models.

Now You will use inverse variation and joint variation models.

Why? So you can model music frequencies, as in Ex. 40.

Key Vocabulary
- inverse variation
- constant of variation
- joint variation

You have learned that two variables x and y show direct variation if $y = ax$ for some nonzero constant a. Another type of variation is called *inverse variation.*

KEY CONCEPT *For Your Notebook*

Inverse Variation

Two variables x and y show **inverse variation** if they are related as follows:

$$y = \frac{a}{x},\ a \neq 0$$

The constant a is the **constant of variation**, and y is said to *vary inversely* with x.

EXAMPLE 1 Classify direct and inverse variation

Tell whether x and y show *direct variation, inverse variation,* or *neither.*

	Given Equation	Rewritten Equation	Type of Variation
a.	$xy = 7$	$y = \frac{7}{x}$	Inverse
b.	$y = x + 3$		Neither
c.	$\frac{y}{4} = x$	$y = 4x$	Direct

REVIEW DIRECT VARIATION
The equation in part (b) does not show direct variation because $y = x + 3$ is not of the form $y = ax$.

EXAMPLE 2 Write an inverse variation equation

The variables x and y vary inversely, and $y = 7$ when $x = 4$. Write an equation that relates x and y. Then find y when $x = -2$.

$y = \frac{a}{x}$ Write general equation for inverse variation.

$7 = \frac{a}{4}$ Substitute 7 for y and 4 for x.

$28 = a$ Solve for a.

▶ The inverse variation equation is $y = \frac{28}{x}$. When $x = -2$, $y = \frac{28}{-2} = -14$.

1 PLAN AND PREPARE

Warm-Up Exercises
Transparency Available

1. y varies directly with x. If $y = 36$ when $x = 8$, find y when $x = 5$. $y = 22.5$
2. If you travel at a constant speed, the distance you travel varies directly with time. If you travel 182 miles in 3.5 hours, how far will you travel at the same constant speed in 5 hours? 260 mi

Notetaking Guide
Transparency Available

Promotes interactive learning and notetaking skills, pp. 211–214.

Pacing
Basic: 1 day
Average: 1 day
Advanced: 1 day
Block: 0.5 block with 8.2
- See *Teaching Guide/Lesson Plan.*

2 FOCUS AND MOTIVATE

Essential Question
Big Idea 3, p. 549

What are the differences between direct, inverse, and joint variation? Tell students they will learn how to answer this question by solving and categorizing different kinds of variation problems.

Resource Planning Guide

Chapter Resource Book
- Teaching Guide/Lesson Plan (pp. 3–4)
- Practice levels A, B, C (pp. 5–7)
- Study Guide (pp. 8–9)
- Catch-up for Absent Students (p. 10)
- Problem Solving Workshop (p. 11)
- Challenge (p. 12)

Workbooks
- Notetaking Guide (pp. 211–214)
- Practice Workbook (pp. 122–123)

Teaching Options
- **Power Presentations CD-ROM** provides dynamic electronic teaching resources for the classroom.
- **Activity Generator CD-ROM** provides editable activities for all ability levels.

Interactive Technology
- Easy Planner
- Power Presentations CD-ROM
- Activity Generator CD-ROM
- Animated Algebra
- Test Generator CD-ROM
- Online Quiz
- eWorkbook
- eEdition
- @HomeTutor

Resources for English Learners
- Quick Reference for English Learners
- Spanish Study Guide
- Multi-Language Visual Glossary
- Student Resources in Spanish

See also the *Algebra 2 Toolkit* for more strategies for meeting individual needs.

Motivating the Lesson

Discuss the physics principle that the force F between two objects of masses m_1 and m_2, at a distance of d meters apart, is $F = \frac{gm_1m_2}{d^2}$, where g is the constant of gravity. Tell students that this equation describes how the force depends on the other variables. In this lesson students will learn several different ways to classify how variables can depend on each other.

3 TEACH

Extra Example 1

Tell whether x and y show *direct variation, inverse variation,* or *neither.*

a. $y - 3x = 0$ **direct**

b. $x = \frac{3}{y}$ **inverse**

c. $x + y = 5$ **neither**

Key Question to Ask for Example 1

- Why is $y = \frac{a}{x}$ called inverse variation? **As the value of x increases, the value of y decreases.**

Extra Example 2

The variables x and y vary inversely, and $y = 15$ when $x = \frac{1}{3}$. Write an equation that relates x and y. Then find y when $x = -10$.

$y = \frac{5}{x}$; $y = -\frac{1}{2}$

EXAMPLE 3 Write an inverse variation model

MP3 PLAYERS The number of songs that can be stored on an MP3 player varies inversely with the average size of a song. A certain MP3 player can store 2500 songs when the average size of a song is 4 megabytes (MB).

- Write a model that gives the number n of songs that will fit on the MP3 player as a function of the average song size s (in megabytes).
- Make a table showing the number of songs that will fit on the MP3 player if the average size of a song is 2 MB, 2.5 MB, 3 MB, and 5 MB as shown below. What happens to the number of songs as the average song size increases?

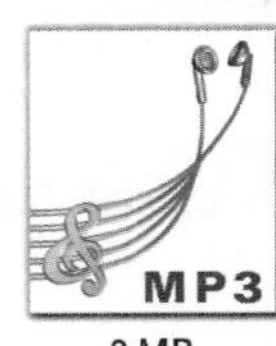

2 MB

2.5 MB

3 MB

5 MB

Solution

STEP 1 **Write** an inverse variation model.

$n = \frac{a}{s}$ **Write general equation for inverse variation.**

$2500 = \frac{a}{4}$ **Substitute 2500 for n and 4 for s.**

$10{,}000 = a$ **Solve for a.**

▸ A model is $n = \frac{10{,}000}{s}$.

STEP 2 **Make** a table of values.

Average size of song (MB), s	2	2.5	3	5
Number of songs, n	5000	4000	3333	2000

▸ From the table, you can see that the number of songs that will fit on the MP3 player decreases as the average song size increases.

GUIDED PRACTICE for Examples 1, 2, and 3

Tell whether x and y show *direct variation, inverse variation,* or *neither.*

1. $3x = y$ **direct variation**
2. $xy = 0.75$ **inverse variation**
3. $y = x - 5$ **neither**

The variables x and y vary inversely. Use the given values to write an equation relating x and y. Then find y when $x = 2$.

4. $x = 4, y = 3$ **$y = \frac{12}{x}$; 6**
5. $x = 8, y = -1$ **$y = \frac{-8}{x}$; -4**
6. $x = \frac{1}{2}, y = 12$ **$y = \frac{6}{x}$; 3**
7. **WHAT IF?** In Example 3, what is a model for the MP3 player if it stores 3000 songs when the average song size is 5 MB? **$n = \frac{15{,}000}{s}$**

Differentiated Instruction

Below Level Some students may be confused by the term *constant of variation.* Is it a constant or is it a variable? When it is written as a, it looks like a variable, just like x and y. To emphasize the idea that this value is constant for a *particular* problem, have students write tables with an extra row at the bottom showing the value of a. This will reinforce the idea that a always has the same value in a particular problem, while the values of x and y (or whatever variables are involved) vary.

See also the *Algebra 2 Toolkit* for more strategies.

CHECKING FOR INVERSE VARIATION The general equation $y = \frac{a}{x}$ for inverse variation can be rewritten as $xy = a$. This tells you that a set of data pairs (x, y) shows inverse variation if the products xy are constant or approximately constant.

EXAMPLE 4 Check data for inverse variation

COMPUTER CHIPS The table compares the area A (in square millimeters) of a computer chip with the number c of chips that can be obtained from a silicon wafer.

- Write a model that gives c as a function of A.
- Predict the number of chips per wafer when the area of a chip is 81 square millimeters.

Area (mm²), A	58	62	66	70
Number of chips, c	448	424	392	376

Solution

AVOID ERRORS
To check data pairs (x, y) for *direct* variation, you find the *quotients* $\frac{y}{x}$. However, to check data pairs for *inverse* variation, you find the *products xy*.

STEP 1 **Calculate** the product $A \cdot c$ for each data pair in the table.

$58(448) = 25{,}984$

$62(424) = 26{,}288$

$66(392) = 25{,}872$

$70(376) = 26{,}320$

Each product is approximately equal to 26,000. So, the data show inverse variation. A model relating A and c is:

$$A \cdot c = 26{,}000, \text{ or } c = \frac{26{,}000}{A}$$

STEP 2 **Make** a prediction. The number of chips per wafer for a chip with an area of 81 square millimeters is $c = \frac{26{,}000}{81} \approx 321$.

✓ **GUIDED PRACTICE** for Example 4

8. **WHAT IF?** In Example 4, predict the number of chips per wafer when the area of each chip is 79 square millimeters. **about 329 chips**

KEY CONCEPT *For Your Notebook*

Joint Variation

Joint variation occurs when a quantity varies directly with *the product of two or more* other quantities. In the equations below, a is a nonzero constant.

$z = axy$ **z varies jointly with x and y.**

$p = aqrs$ **p varies jointly with q, r, and s.**

Differentiated Instruction

Inclusion Because there are several different types of variation (direct, inverse, joint), students may reverse the sense of the variation when translating from a sentence to an equation, or from an equation to sentence form. Have students work in pairs and practice translating sentences into equations of variation, and vice versa. Have them make a list of key words that help them determine each of the different types of variation. See also the *Algebra 2 Toolkit* for more strategies.

Extra Example 3

The driving time between two specific locations varies inversely with the average driving speed. The driving distance between Chicago and Minneapolis is about 400 miles.

- Write a model that gives the driving time t in hours (not including stops) between Chicago and Minneapolis as a function of average driving speed r in miles per hour. $t = \frac{400}{r}$
- Make a table showing the driving time for average driving speeds of 32 miles per hour, 40 miles per hour, 50 miles per hour, and 60 miles per hour.

r	32	40	50	60
t	$12\frac{1}{2}$	10	8	$6\frac{2}{3}$

Extra Example 4

Moving cartons are manufactured in a variety of sizes and shapes to accommodate the variety of objects that need to be packed. The table compares the area A of the bottom of a rectangular carton (in square inches) with the height h for four available cartons that have the same volume. Write a model that gives h as a function of A. Then predict the height of a carton with the same volume as those in the table that has a base area of 75 square inches.

A	50	100	120	150
h	24	12	10	8

$h = \frac{1200}{A}$; 16 in.

Key Question to Ask for Example 4

- Without testing the given data pairs in Example 4 for either direct or inverse variation, how can you tell by looking at the table that the data do *not* show direct variation? **As the value of A increases, the value of c decreases. With positive data values, this cannot happen in direct variation.**

Extra Example 5

The variable z varies jointly with x and y. Also, $z = 60$ when $x = -4$ and $y = 5$. Find z when $x = 7$ and $y = 2$. -42

Extra Example 6

Write an equation for the given relationship.

a. r varies inversely with s. $r = \frac{a}{s}$

b. z varies jointly with x and the square root of y. $z = ax\sqrt{y}$

c. p varies inversely with the cube of q. $p = \frac{a}{q^3}$

d. m varies directly with the square of n and inversely with p. $m = \frac{an^2}{p}$

e. z varies jointly with u and v and inversely with the square of w. $z = \frac{auv}{w^2}$

Key Question to Ask for Example 6

- If you are writing a variation equation that involves both direct and inverse variation, do you need two constants of variation? No; only one constant is needed for all variation equations.

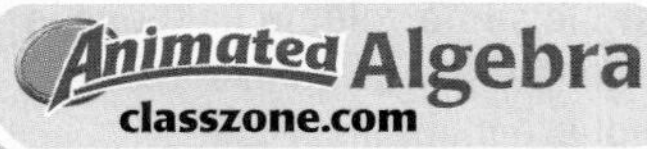

An **Animated Algebra** activity is available on-line for **Example 6**. This activity is also available on the **Power Presentations CD-ROM**.

Closing the Lesson

Have students summarize the major points of the lesson and answer the Essential Question: What are the differences between direct, inverse, and joint variation?

- y varies directly with x if $y = ax$ for a nonzero constant a.
- y varies inversely with x if $xy = a$ for a nonzero constant a.
- z varies jointly with x and y if $z = axy$ for a nonzero constant a.

In direct variation, the ratio of two variables has a constant value, while in inverse variation, the product of two variables has a constant value. In joint variation, one variable depends on the product of other variables.

EXAMPLE 5 Write a joint variation equation

The variable z varies jointly with x and y. Also, $z = -75$ when $x = 3$ and $y = -5$. Write an equation that relates x, y, and z. Then find z when $x = 2$ and $y = 6$.

Solution

STEP 1 **Write** a general joint variation equation.

$z = axy$

STEP 2 **Use** the given values of z, x, and y to find the constant of variation a.

$-75 = a(3)(-5)$	Substitute -75 for z, 3 for x, and -5 for y.
$-75 = -15a$	Simplify.
$5 = a$	Solve for a.

STEP 3 **Rewrite** the joint variation equation with the value of a from Step 2.

$z = 5xy$

STEP 4 **Calculate** z when $x = 2$ and $y = 6$ using substitution.

$z = 5xy = 5(2)(6) = 60$

EXAMPLE 6 Compare different types of variation

Write an equation for the given relationship.

	Relationship	Equation
a.	y varies inversely with x.	$y = \frac{a}{x}$
b.	z varies jointly with x, y, and r.	$z = axyr$
c.	y varies inversely with the square of x.	$y = \frac{a}{x^2}$
d.	z varies directly with y and inversely with x.	$z = \frac{ay}{x}$
e.	x varies jointly with t and r and inversely with s.	$x = \frac{atr}{s}$

Animated Algebra at classzone.com

GUIDED PRACTICE for Examples 5 and 6

The variable z varies jointly with x and y. Use the given values to write an equation relating x, y, and z. Then find z when $x = -2$ and $y = 5$.

9. $x = 1, y = 2, z = 7$ $z = \frac{7}{2}xy$; -35

10. $x = 4, y = -3, z = 24$ $z = -2xy$; 20

11. $x = -2, y = 6, z = 18$ $z = \frac{-3}{2}xy$; 15

12. $x = -6, y = -4, z = 56$ $z = \frac{7}{3}xy$; $-\frac{70}{3}$

Write an equation for the given relationship.

13. x varies inversely with y and directly with w. $x = \frac{a}{y}w$

14. p varies jointly with q and r and inversely with s. $p = \frac{aqr}{s}$

8.1 EXERCISES

HOMEWORK KEY
○ = **WORKED-OUT SOLUTIONS** on p. WS14 for Exs. 15, 21, and 39
★ = **STANDARDIZED TEST PRACTICE** Exs. 2, 11, 30, 35, and 41

SKILL PRACTICE

A

1. **VOCABULARY** Copy and complete: If z varies directly with the product of x and y, then z is said to vary __?__ with x and y. jointly

2. ★ **WRITING** *Describe* how to tell whether a set of data pairs (x, y) shows inverse variation. If the product of the x-values and the corresponding y-values are the same.

EXAMPLE 1 on p. 551 for Exs. 3–11

DETERMINING VARIATION **Tell whether x and y show *direct variation, inverse variation,* or *neither.***

3. $xy = \frac{1}{5}$ inverse variation
4. $y = x + 4$ neither
5. $\frac{y}{x} = 8$ direct variation
6. $4x = y$ direct variation
7. $y = \frac{2}{x}$ inverse variation
8. $x + y = 6$ neither
9. $8y = x$ direct variation
10. $xy = 12$ inverse variation

11. ★ **MULTIPLE CHOICE** Which equation represents inverse variation? C

Ⓐ $y = 4x$ Ⓑ $y = x - 1$ Ⓒ $xy = 5$ Ⓓ $\frac{y}{7} = x$

EXAMPLE 2 on p. 551 for Exs. 12–19

USING INVERSE VARIATION **The variables x and y vary inversely. Use the given values to write an equation relating x and y. Then find y when $x = 3$.**

12. $x = 5, y = -4$ $y = \frac{-20}{x}; -\frac{20}{3}$
13. $x = 1, y = 9$ $y = \frac{9}{x}; 3$
14. $x = -3, y = 8$ $y = \frac{-24}{x}; -8$
15. $x = 7, y = 2$ $y = \frac{14}{x}; \frac{14}{3}$
16. $x = \frac{3}{4}, y = 28$ $y = \frac{21}{x}; 7$
17. $x = -4, y = -\frac{5}{4}$ $y = \frac{5}{x}; \frac{5}{3}$
18. $x = -12, y = -\frac{1}{6}$ $y = \frac{2}{x}; \frac{2}{3}$
19. $x = \frac{5}{3}, y = -7$ $y = \frac{-35}{3x}; -\frac{35}{9}$

EXAMPLE 4 on p. 553 for Exs. 20–23

INTERPRETING DATA **Determine whether x and y show *direct variation, inverse variation,* or *neither.***

20.

x	y
1.5	40
2.5	24
4	15
7.5	8
10	6

inverse variation

21.

x	y
12	132
18	198
23	253
29	319
34	374

direct variation

22.

x	y
4	16
5	11
6.2	10
7	9
11	6

neither

23.

x	y
4	21
6	14
8	10.5
8.4	10
12	7

inverse variation

EXAMPLE 5 B on p. 554 for Exs. 24–30

USING JOINT VARIATION **Write an equation relating x, y, and z given that z varies jointly with x and y. Then find z when $x = -4$ and $y = 5$.**

24. $x = 2, y = -6, z = 24$ $z = -2xy; 40$
25. $x = 8, y = 6, z = 12$ $z = \frac{1}{4}xy; -5$
26. $x = -\frac{1}{4}, y = -3, z = 15$ $z = 20xy; -400$
27. $x = 6, y = -7, z = -3$ $z = \frac{1}{14}xy; \frac{-10}{7}$
28. $x = 9, y = -2, z = 6$ $z = -\frac{1}{3}xy; \frac{20}{3}$
29. $x = 5, y = -3, z = 75$ $z = -5xy; 100$

30. ★ **MULTIPLE CHOICE** Suppose z varies jointly with x and y, and $z = -36$ when $x = -3$ and $y = -4$. What is the constant of variation? A

Ⓐ -3 Ⓑ -2 Ⓒ 3 Ⓓ 12

4 PRACTICE AND APPLY

Assignment Guide

Answer Transparencies available for all exercises

Basic:
Day 1: pp. 555–557
Exs. 1–8, 11–16, 20–26, 31, 37–40, 43

Average:
Day 1: pp. 555–557
Exs. 1, 2, 6–9, 11, 14–17, 22, 23, 26–34, 37–41, 44

Advanced:
Day 1: pp. 555–557
Exs. 1, 2, 8–11, 17–19, 22, 23, 27–42*

Block:
pp. 555–557
Exs. 1, 2, 6–9, 11, 14–17, 22, 23, 26–34, 37–41, 44 (with 8.2)

Differentiated Instruction

See *Algebra 2 Best Practices Toolkit* for suggestions on addressing the needs of a diverse classroom.

Homework Check

For a quick check of student understanding of key concepts, go over the following exercises:

Basic: 4, 14, 24, 31, 37
Average: 8, 16, 26, 32, 38
Advanced: 10, 18, 28, 33, 39

Extra Practice

- Student Edition, p. 1017
- Chapter 8 Resource Book: Practice levels A, B, C, pp. 5–7

Practice Worksheet

An easily-readable reduced practice page (with answers) for this lesson can be found on p. 548C.

Teaching Strategy

Exercises 12–19, 24–29 Students may have trouble with exercises like these if they think that solving direct, inverse, and joint variation problems are three separate skills to learn. Guide the class in developing a list of steps that can be followed in solving *any* variation problem. Make sure that students understand the importance of finding, and then using, the constant of variation.

Avoiding Common Errors

Exercises 24–29 Some students may be confused that they are asked to *find z* when they are *given z*, and just repeat the given values as their answers. Explain to these students that they have been given the value of *z* that goes with particular values of *x* and *y*, and that they need to find the value of *z* that goes with a *different* pair of values for *x* and *y*.

EXAMPLE 6 on p. 554 for Exs. 31–33

WRITING EQUATIONS **Write an equation for the given relationship.**

31. x varies directly with y and inversely with z. $x = \frac{ay}{z}$

32. y varies jointly with x and the square of z. $y = axz^2$

33. w varies inversely with y and jointly with x and z. $w = \frac{axz}{y}$

34. **ERROR ANALYSIS** A variable z varies jointly with x and the cube of y and inversely with the square root of w. *Describe* and correct the error in writing an equation relating the variables.

$z = \frac{a\sqrt{w}}{xy^3}$ ✗

The inverse and direct variation pieces are reversed; $z = \frac{axy^3}{\sqrt{w}}$.

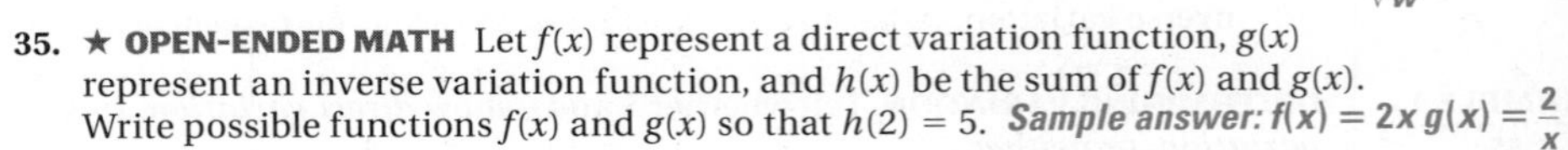

C

35. ★ **OPEN-ENDED MATH** Let $f(x)$ represent a direct variation function, $g(x)$ represent an inverse variation function, and $h(x)$ be the sum of $f(x)$ and $g(x)$. Write possible functions $f(x)$ and $g(x)$ so that $h(2) = 5$. *Sample answer:* $f(x) = 2x$ $g(x) = \frac{2}{x}$

36. **CHALLENGE** Suppose x varies inversely with y and y varies inversely with z. How does x vary with z? *Justify* your answer algebraically. directly; $x = \frac{a}{y}$, $y = \frac{b}{z}$, $x = \frac{a}{\left(\frac{b}{z}\right)} \rightarrow x = \left(\frac{a}{b}\right)z$

PROBLEM SOLVING

EXAMPLES 3 and 4 on pp. 552–553 for Exs. 37–39

A

37. **DIGITAL CAMERAS** The number n of photos your digital camera can store varies inversely with the average size s (in megapixels) of the photos. Your digital camera can store 54 photos when the average photo size is 1.92 megapixels. Write a model that gives n as a function of s. How many photos can your camera store when the average photo size is 3.87 megapixels? $n = \frac{103.68}{s}$; 26 photos

@HomeTutor for problem solving help at classzone.com

38. **ELECTRONICS** The table below compares the current I (in milliamps) with the resistance R (in ohms) for several electrical circuits. Write a model that gives R as a function of I. Then predict R when $I = 34$ milliamps. *Sample answer:* $R = \frac{9000}{I}$; about 265 ohms

Current (milliamps), I	7.4	8.9	12.1	17.9
Resistance (ohms), R	1200	1000	750	500

@HomeTutor for problem solving help at classzone.com

39. **SNOWSHOES** When you stand on snow, the average pressure P (in pounds per square inch) that you exert on the snow varies inversely with the total area A (in square inches) of the soles of your footwear. Suppose the pressure is 0.43 pound per square inch when you wear the snowshoes shown. Write an equation that gives P as a function of A. Then find the pressure if you wear the boots shown. $P = \frac{172}{A}$; about 2.87 lb/in.^{2}

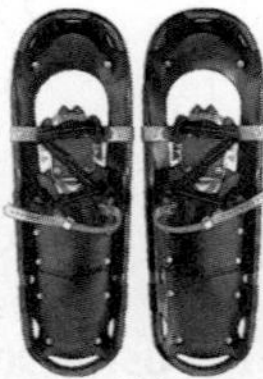

$A = 400$ in.^{2}

$A = 60$ in.^{2}

B

40. **MULTI-STEP PROBLEM** A piano string's frequency f (in hertz) varies directly with the square root of the string's tension T (in Newtons) and inversely with both the string's length L and diameter d (each in centimeters).

    a. The middle C note has a frequency of 262 Hz. The string producing this note has a tension of 670 N, a length of 62 cm, and a diameter of 0.1025 cm. Write an equation relating f, T, L, and d. $f = \frac{64.3\sqrt{T}}{Ld}$

    b. Find the frequency of the note produced by a string with a tension of 1629 N, a length of 201.6 cm, and a diameter of 0.49 cm. about 26.27 Hz

◯ = WORKED-OUT SOLUTIONS on p. WS1

★ = STANDARDIZED TEST PRACTICE

41. ★ **EXTENDED RESPONSE** The *law of universal gravitation* states that the gravitational force F (in Newtons) between two objects varies jointly with their masses m_1 and m_2 (in kilograms) and inversely with the square of the distance d (in meters) between the two objects. The constant of variation is denoted by G and is called the *universal gravitational constant.*

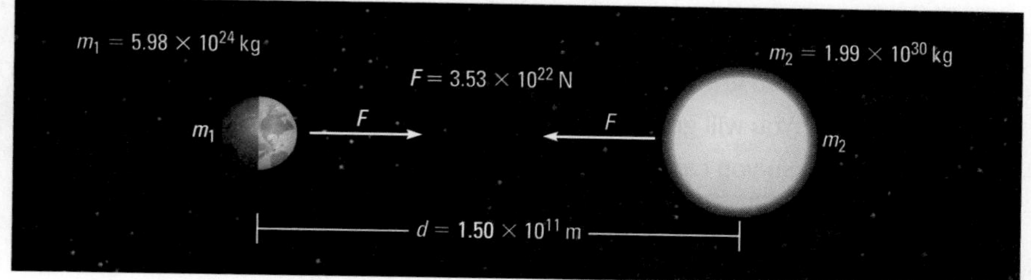

a. **Model** Write an equation that gives F in terms of m_1, m_2, d and G. $F = \frac{Gm_1m_2}{d^2}$

b. **Approximate** Use the information above about Earth and the Sun to approximate the universal gravitational constant G. 6.7×10^{-11}

c. **Reasoning** *Explain* what happens to the gravitational force as the masses of the two objects increase and the distance between them is held constant. *Explain* what happens to the gravitational force as the masses of the two objects are held constant and the distance between them increases. **It decreases; it increases.**

C 42. **CHALLENGE** The load P (in pounds) that can be safely supported by a horizontal beam varies jointly with the beam's width W and the square of its depth D, and inversely with its unsupported length L.

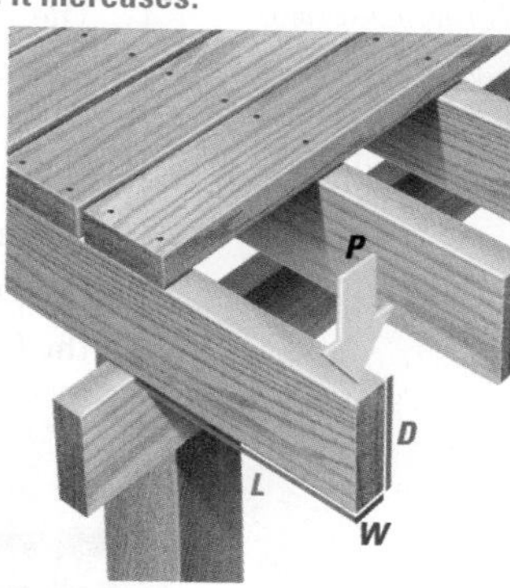

a. How does P change when the width and length of the beam are doubled? **It remains the same.**

b. How does P change when the width and depth of the beam are doubled? **8 times greater**

c. How does P change when all three dimensions are doubled? **4 times greater**

d. *Describe* several ways a beam can be modified if the safe load it is required to support is increased by a factor of 4. ***Sample answer:*** **Double the depth, 4 times the width, or 8 times the width and twice the length**

KENTUCKY MIXED REVIEW

43. What is the approximate area of $\triangle MNP$? **C**

Ⓐ 40.5 cm^2 Ⓑ 57.3 cm^2

Ⓒ 70.1 cm^2 Ⓓ 114.6 cm^2

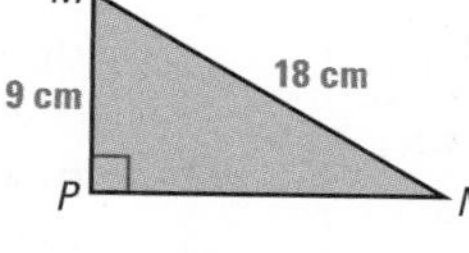

44. The solid at the right has 14 faces: 8 hexagons and 6 squares. How many vertices does the solid have? **A**

Ⓐ 24 Ⓑ 32

Ⓒ 44 Ⓓ 88

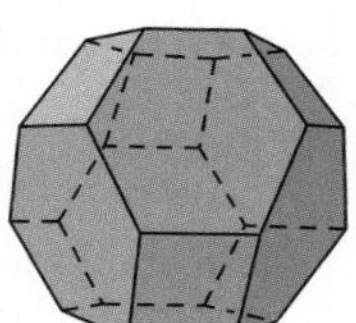

EXTRA PRACTICE for Lesson 8.1, p. 1017

5 ASSESS AND RETEACH

Daily Homework Quiz

Transparency Available

1. p and q vary inversely, and $q = -15$ when $p = -3$. Write an equation that relates p and q. Then find q when $p = 45$. $q = \frac{45}{p}$; $q = 1$
2. Write an equation for the following relationship: z varies jointly with the square of x and the cube root of y. $z = ax^2\sqrt[3]{y}$
3. The current in a simple electrical circuit varies inversely with the resistance. If the current is 40 amps when the resistance is 2.5 ohms, find the current when the resistance is 4 ohms. **25 amps**

Online Quiz

Available at **classzone.com**

Diagnosis/Remediation

- Practice A, B, C in Chapter 8 Resource Book, pp. 5–7
- Study Guide in Chapter 8 Resource Book, pp. 8–9
- Practice Workbook, pp. 122–123
- @HomeTutor

Challenge

Additional challenge is available in the Chapter 8 Resource Book, p. 12.

1 PLAN AND PREPARE

Warm-Up Exercises

Transparency Available

State the domain and range.

1. $y = (x + 4)^2 - 2$ **domain: all real numbers; range: $y \geq -2$**
2. $y = -2(x - 3)^2 + 5$ **domain: all real numbers; range: $y \leq 5$**
3. Explain how the graph of $y = (x + 2)^2 - 6$ can be obtained from the graph of $y = x^2$. **Translate the graph of $y = x^2$ left 2 units and down 6 units.**

Notetaking Guide

Transparency Available

Promotes interactive learning and notetaking skills, pp. 215–217.

Pacing

Basic: 1 day

Average: 1 day

Advanced: 1 day

Block: 0.5 block with 8.1

- See *Teaching Guide/Lesson Plan.*

2 FOCUS AND MOTIVATE

Essential Question

Big Idea 1, p. 549

What does the graph of the rational function $y = \frac{a}{x-h} + k$ look like?

Tell students they will learn how to answer this question by translating graphs of the function $y = \frac{a}{x}$.

8.2 Graph Simple Rational Functions

MA-HS-5.1.3

Before You graphed polynomial functions.

Now You will graph rational functions.

Why? So you can find average monthly costs, as in Ex. 38.

Key Vocabulary
- **rational function**
- **domain,** *p. 72*
- **range,** *p. 72*
- **asymptote,** *p. 478*

MA-HS-5.1.3
Students will demonstrate how equations and graphs are models of the relationship between two real-world quantities (e.g., the relationship between degrees Celsius and degrees Fahrenheit).

A **rational function** has the form $f(x) = \frac{p(x)}{q(x)}$ where $p(x)$ and $q(x)$ are polynomials and $q(x) \neq 0$. The inverse variation function $f(x) = \frac{a}{x}$ is a rational function. The graph of this function when $a = 1$ is shown below.

KEY CONCEPT *For Your Notebook*

Parent Function for Simple Rational Functions

The graph of the parent function $f(x) = \frac{1}{x}$ is a *hyperbola*, which consists of two symmetrical parts called *branches*. The domain and range are all nonzero real numbers.

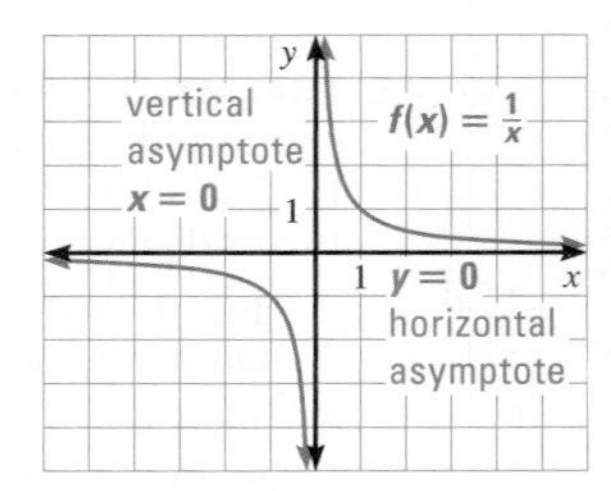

Any function of the form $g(x) = \frac{a}{x}$ $(a \neq 0)$ has the same asymptotes, domain, and range as the function $f(x) = \frac{1}{x}$.

EXAMPLE 1 **Graph a rational function of the form $y = \frac{a}{x}$**

Graph the function $y = \frac{6}{x}$. Compare the graph with the graph of $y = \frac{1}{x}$.

Solution

INTERPRET TRANSFORMATIONS

The graph of $y = \frac{6}{x}$ is a vertical stretch of the graph of $y = \frac{1}{x}$ by a factor of 6.

STEP 1 **Draw** the asymptotes $x = 0$ and $y = 0$.

STEP 2 **Plot** points to the left and to the right of the vertical asymptote, such as $(-3, -2)$, $(-2, -3)$, $(2, 3)$, and $(3, 2)$.

STEP 3 **Draw** the branches of the hyperbola so that they pass through the plotted points and approach the asymptotes.

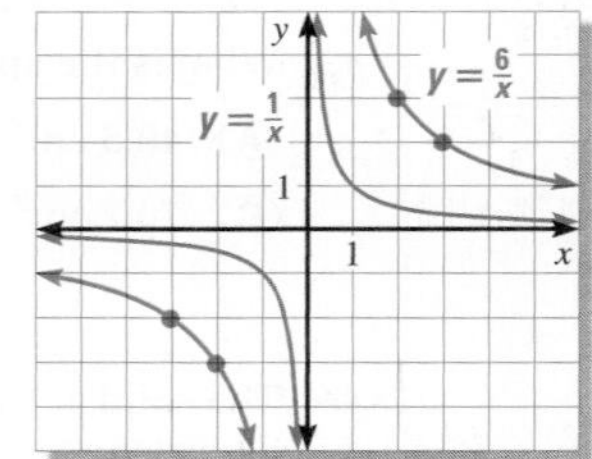

The graph of $y = \frac{6}{x}$ lies farther from the axes than the graph of $y = \frac{1}{x}$. Both graphs lie in the first and third quadrants and have the same asymptotes, domain, and range.

Resource Planning Guide

Chapter Resource Book
- Teaching Guide/Lesson Plan (pp. 13–14)
- Practice levels A, B, C (pp. 16–18)
- Study Guide (pp. 19–20)
- Catch-up for Absent Students (p. 21)
- Application (p. 22)
- Challenge (p. 23)

Workbooks
- Notetaking Guide (pp. 215–217)
- Practice Workbook (pp. 124–125)

Teaching Options
- **Power Presentations CD-ROM** provides dynamic electronic teaching resources for the classroom.
- **Activity Generator CD-ROM** provides editable activities for all ability levels.

Interactive Technology
- Easy Planner
- Power Presentations CD-ROM
- Activity Generator CD-ROM
- Animated Algebra
- Test Generator CD-ROM
- Online Quiz
- eWorkbook
- eEdition
- @HomeTutor

Resources for English Learners
- Quick Reference for English Learners
- Spanish Study Guide
- Multi-Language Visual Glossary
- Student Resources in Spanish

See also the *Algebra 2 Toolkit* for more strategies for meeting individual needs.

KEY CONCEPT *For Your Notebook*

Graphing Translations of Simple Rational Functions

To graph a rational function of the form $y = \frac{a}{x-h} + k$, follow these steps:

STEP 1 **Draw** the asymptotes $x = h$ and $y = k$.

STEP 2 **Plot** points to the left and to the right of the vertical asymptote.

STEP 3 **Draw** the two branches of the hyperbola so that they pass through the plotted points and approach the asymptotes.

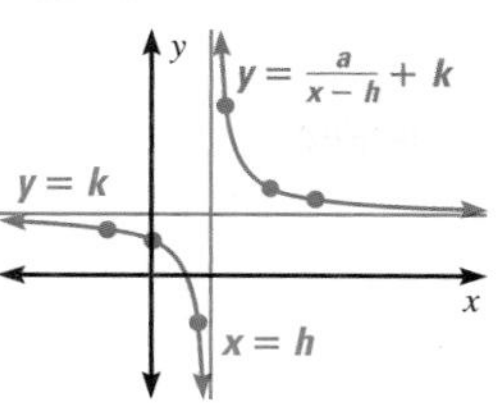

EXAMPLE 2 Graph a rational function of the form $y = \frac{a}{x-h} + k$

Graph $y = \frac{-4}{x+2} - 1$. State the domain and range.

Solution

STEP 1 **Draw** the asymptotes $x = -2$ and $y = -1$.

STEP 2 **Plot** points to the left of the vertical asymptote, such as $(-3, 3)$ and $(-4, 1)$, and points to the right, such as $(-1, -5)$ and $(0, -3)$.

STEP 3 **Draw** the two branches of the hyperbola so that they pass through the plotted points and approach the asymptotes.

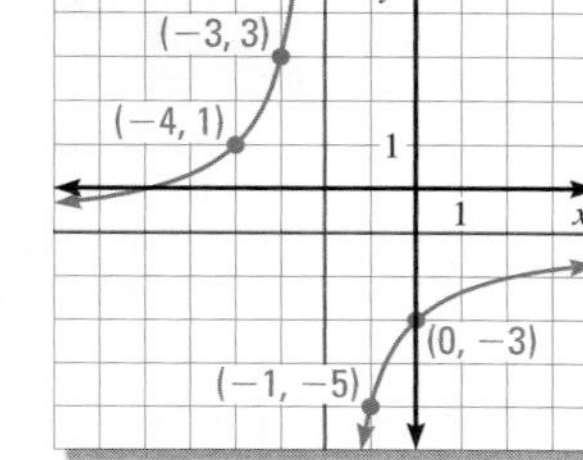

The domain is all real numbers except −2, and the range is all real numbers except −1.

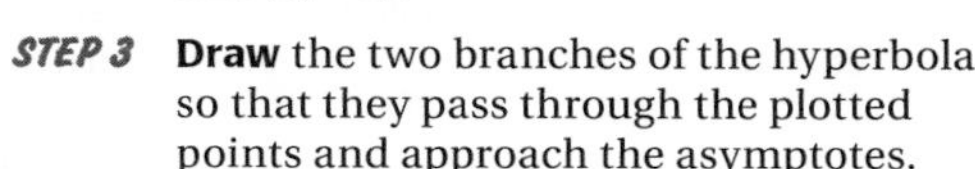
Animated Algebra at classzone.com

NTERPRET RANSFORMATIONS

he graph of $= \frac{-4}{x+2} - 1$ is the raph of $y = \frac{-4}{x}$ anslated left 2 units nd down 1 unit.

GUIDED PRACTICE for Examples 1 and 2

Graph the function. State the domain and range. 1–3. See margin on p. 560.

1. $f(x) = \frac{-4}{x}$
2. $y = \frac{8}{x} - 5$
3. $y = \frac{1}{x-3} + 2$

OTHER RATIONAL FUNCTIONS All rational functions of the form $y = \frac{ax+b}{cx+d}$ also have graphs that are hyperbolas.

- The vertical asymptote of the graph is the line $x = -\frac{d}{c}$, because the function is undefined when the denominator $cx + d$ is zero.
- The horizontal asymptote is the line $y = \frac{a}{c}$.

Differentiated Instruction

Kinesthetic Learners When students are first learning how to graph a rational function, have them follow the first two steps listed in the Key Concept box at the top of this page. Before connecting the points with lines, have students cut or carefully tear off the two "quarters" of the coordinate plane in which there are no points plotted. This will help them visualize the graph of a rational function as being restricted by its asymptotes.

See also the *Algebra 2 Toolkit* for more strategies.

Motivating the Lesson

You are comparing two health club plans. One plan has a higher initiation fee but a lower monthly fee than the other. You can use rational functions to model the average monthly cost of the plans.

3 TEACH

Extra Example 1

Graph the function $y = \frac{4}{x}$. Compare the graph with the graph of $y = \frac{1}{x}$.

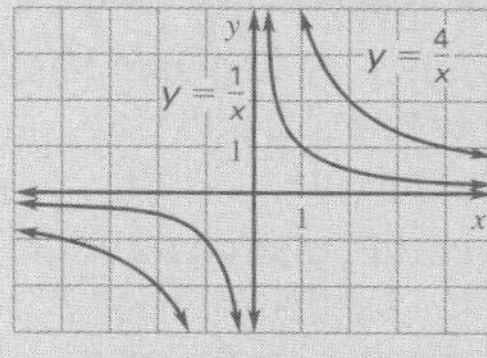

The graph of $y = \frac{4}{x}$ is farther from the axes than the graph of $y = \frac{1}{x}$. Both graphs lie in the first and third quadrants and have the same asymptotes, domain, and range.

Extra Example 2

Graph $y = \frac{-3}{x-1} + 2$. State the domain and range.

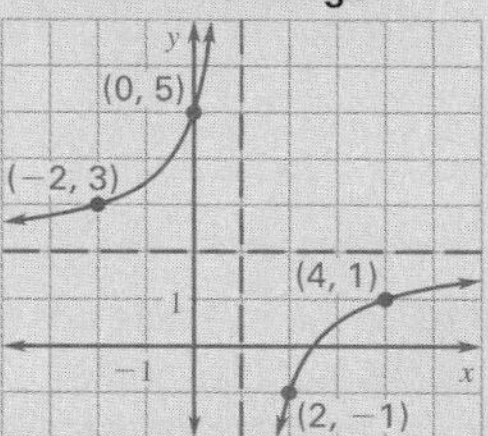

domain: all real numbers except 1; range: all real numbers except 2

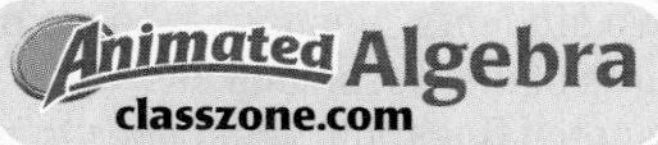

An **Animated Algebra** activity is available on-line for **Example 2**. This activity is also available on the **Power Presentations CD-ROM**.

Extra Example 3

Graph $y = \frac{3x - 6}{x + 2}$. State the domain and range.

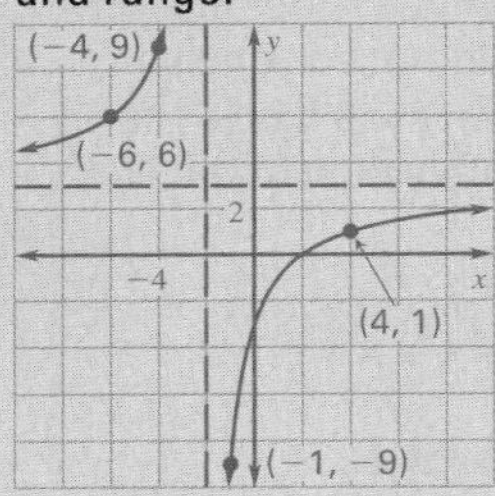

domain: all real numbers except −2; range: all real numbers except 3

Extra Example 4

Your long-distance calling plan has a fixed monthly fee of $4.95 and costs 5 cents a minute.

- Write an equation that gives your average cost C (in dollars) per minute m during a given month. $C = \frac{4.95 + 0.05m}{m}$
- Graph the function. Use the graph to estimate when the average cost is $.14 per minute. **55 min**

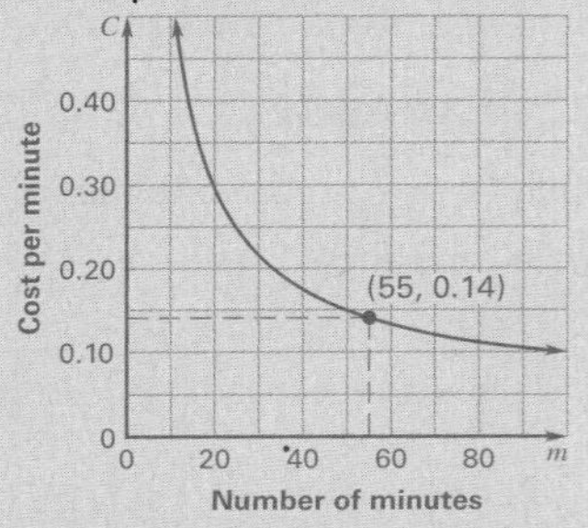

- What happens to the average cost per minute as the number of minutes increases? **It approaches 5 cents.**

Closing the Lesson

Have students summarize the major points of the lesson and answer the Essential Question: What does the graph of the function $y = \frac{a}{x-h} + k$ look like?

- **The graph of the function $y = \frac{1}{x}$ is a hyperbola.**
- **The graph of the function $y = \frac{a}{x-h} + k$ has asymptotes $x = h$ and $y = k$.**

The graph of a simple rational function is a hyperbola, which is a curve made up of two branches. The graph has one vertical and one horizontal asymptote.

EXAMPLE 3 Graph a rational function of the form $y = \frac{ax + b}{cx + d}$

Graph $y = \frac{2x + 1}{x - 3}$. State the domain and range.

Solution

STEP 1 **Draw** the asymptotes. Solve $x - 3 = 0$ for x to find the vertical asymptote $x = 3$. The horizontal asymptote is the line $y = \frac{a}{c} = \frac{2}{1} = 2$.

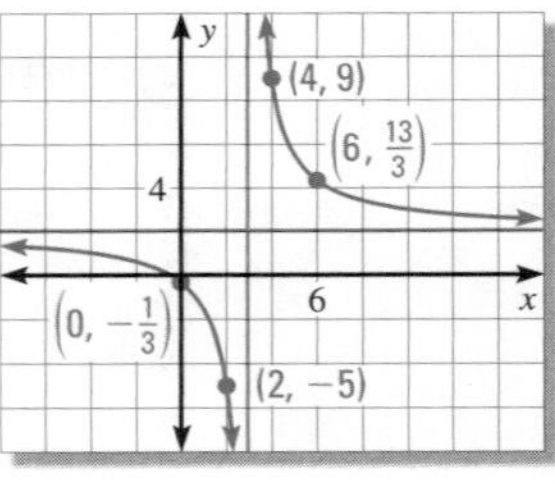

STEP 2 **Plot** points to the left of the vertical asymptote, such as $(2, -5)$ and $\left(0, -\frac{1}{3}\right)$, and points to the right, such as $(4, 9)$ and $\left(6, \frac{13}{3}\right)$.

STEP 3 **Draw** the two branches of the hyperbola so that they pass through the plotted points and approach the asymptotes.

▶ The domain is all real numbers except 3. The range is all real numbers except 2.

EXAMPLE 4 Solve a multi-step problem

3-D MODELING A 3-D printer builds up layers of material to make three-dimensional models. Each deposited layer bonds to the layer below it. A company decides to make small display models of engine components using a 3-D printer. The printer costs $24,000. The material for each model costs $300.

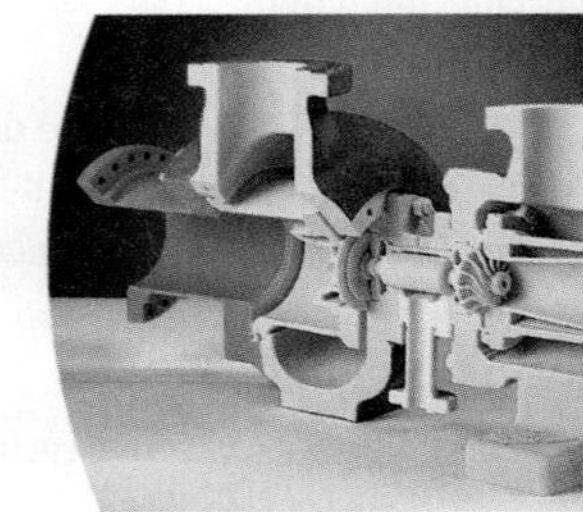

- Write an equation that gives the average cost per model as a function of the number of models printed.
- Graph the function. Use the graph to estimate how many models must be printed for the average cost per model to fall to $700.
- What happens to the average cost as more models are printed?

Solution

STEP 1 **Write** a function. Let c be the average cost and m be the number of models printed.

$$c = \frac{\text{Unit cost} \cdot \text{Number printed} + \text{Cost of printer}}{\text{Number printed}} = \frac{300m + 24{,}000}{m}$$

DRAW GRAPHS
Because the number of models and average cost cannot be negative, graph only the branch of the hyperbola that lies in the first quadrant.

STEP 2 **Graph** the function. The asymptotes are the lines $m = 0$ and $c = 300$. The average cost falls to $700 per model after 60 models are printed.

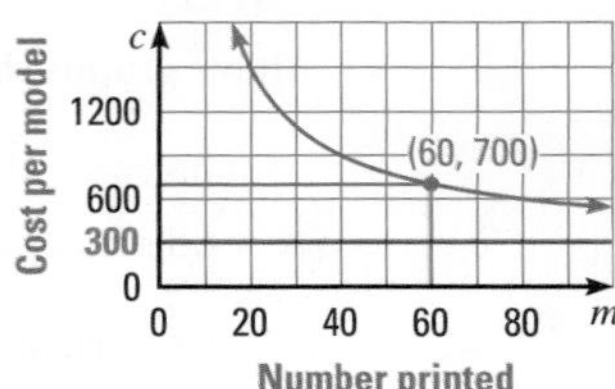

STEP 3 **Interpret** the graph. As more models are printed, the average cost per model approaches $300.

1. 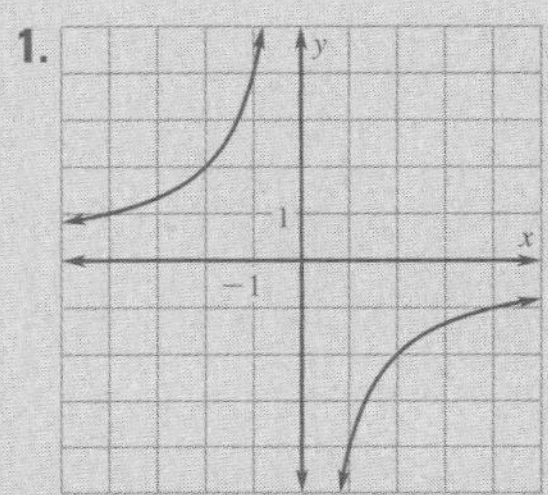

domain: all real numbers except 0, range: all real numbers except 0

2. 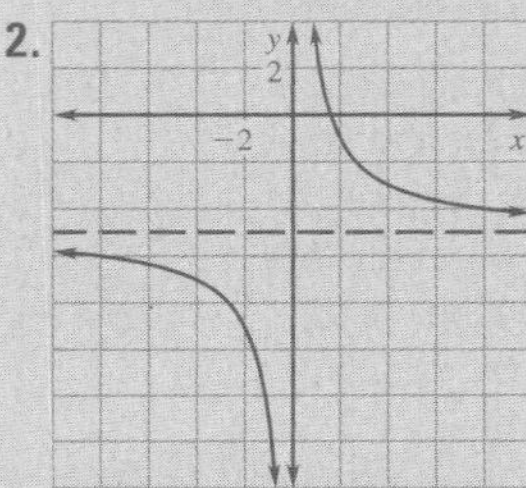

domain: all real numbers except 0, range: all real numbers except −5

3. 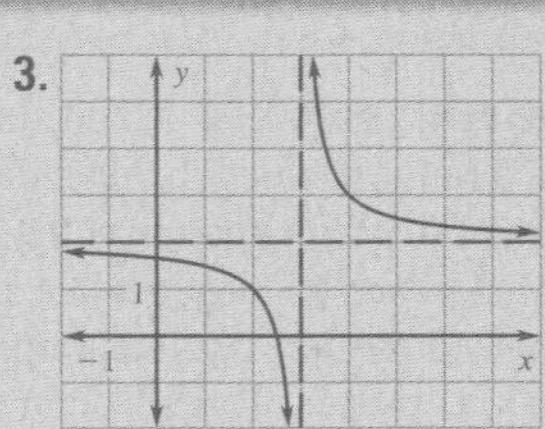

domain: all real numbers except 3 range: all real numbers except 2

✓ GUIDED PRACTICE for Examples 3 and 4

Graph the function. State the domain and range. 4–6. See margin.

4. $y = \frac{x-1}{x+3}$ **5.** $y = \frac{2x+1}{4x-2}$ **6.** $f(x) = \frac{-3x+2}{-x-1}$

7. WHAT IF? In Example 4, how do the function and graph change if the cost of the 3-D printer is \$21,000? *Sample answer:* In the function, 24,000 is replaced by 21,000. On the graph, the asymptotes remain at $m = 0$ and $c = 300$, but the values decrease from a smaller starting point.

8.2 EXERCISES

HOMEWORK KEY
- ○ = WORKED-OUT SOLUTIONS on p. WS14 for Exs. 5, 21, and 39
- ★ = STANDARDIZED TEST PRACTICE Exs. 2, 23, 35, 40, and 41
- ◆ = MULTIPLE REPRESENTATIONS Ex. 39

SKILL PRACTICE

1. VOCABULARY Copy and complete: The function $y = \frac{7}{x+4} + 3$ has a(n) __?__ of all real numbers except 3 and a(n) __?__ of all real numbers except −4. range; domain

2. ★ WRITING Is $f(x) = \frac{-3x+5}{2^x+1}$ a rational function? *Explain* your answer.
No; the denominator is an exponential function, not a polynomial function.

EXAMPLE 1 on p. 558 for Exs. 3–10

GRAPHING FUNCTIONS **Graph the function. Compare the graph with the graph of $y = \frac{1}{x}$.** 3–10. See margin.

3. $y = \frac{3}{x}$ **4.** $y = \frac{10}{x}$ **(5.)** $y = \frac{-5}{x}$ **6.** $y = \frac{-0.5}{x}$

7. $y = \frac{0.1}{x}$ **8.** $f(x) = \frac{15}{x}$ **9.** $g(x) = \frac{-6}{x}$ **10.** $h(x) = \frac{-3}{x}$

EXAMPLE 2 on p. 559 for Exs. 11–23

GRAPHING FUNCTIONS **Graph the function. State the domain and range.** 11–22. See margin.

11. $y = \frac{4}{x} + 3$ **12.** $y = \frac{3}{x} - 2$ **13.** $y = \frac{6}{x-1}$ **14.** $f(x) = \frac{1}{x+2}$

15. $y = \frac{-5}{x} - 7$ **16.** $y = \frac{-6}{x} + 4$ **17.** $y = \frac{-3}{x+2}$ **18.** $g(x) = \frac{-2}{x-7}$

19. $y = \frac{-4}{x+4} + 3$ **20.** $y = \frac{10}{x+7} - 5$ **(21.)** $y = \frac{-3}{x-4} - 1$ **22.** $h(x) = \frac{11}{x-9} + 9$

23. ★ MULTIPLE CHOICE What are the asymptotes of the graph of $y = \frac{3}{x+8} - 3$? D

Ⓐ $x = 8, y = 3$ Ⓑ $x = 8, y = -3$ Ⓒ $x = -8, y = 3$ Ⓓ $x = -8, y = -3$

24. GRAPHING CALCULATOR Consider the function $y = \frac{a}{x-h} + k$ where $a = 1$, $h = 3$, and $k = -2$. Predict the effect on the functions graph of each change in a, h, or k described in parts (a)–(c). Use a graphing calculator to check your prediction by graphing the original and revised functions in the same coordinate plane. a–c. See margin.

a. a changes to −3 **b.** h changes to −1 **c.** k changes to 2

4 PRACTICE AND APPLY

Assignment Guide

Answer Transparencies available for all exercises

Basic:
Day 1: EP p. 1016 Exs. 5–8
pp. 561–563
Exs. 1–6, 11–23 odd, 24–30, 37–40, 43

Average:
Day 1: pp. 561–563
Exs. 1, 2, 6–8, 13–20, 23–26, 29–35, 37–41, 44

Advanced:
Day 1: pp. 561–563
Exs. 1, 2, 7–10, 17–24, 29–42*

Block:
pp. 561–563
Exs. 1, 2, 6–8, 13–20, 23–26, 29–35, 37–41, 44 (with 8.1)

Differentiated Instruction

See *Algebra 2 Best Practices Toolkit* for suggestions on addressing the needs of a diverse classroom.

Homework Check

For a quick check of student understanding of key concepts, go over the following exercises:
Basic: 4, 11, 13, 24, 30
Average: 6, 14, 15, 26, 33
Advanced: 8, 17, 18, 29, 34

Extra Practice

- Student Edition, p. 1017
- Chapter 8 Resource Book: Practice levels A, B, C, pp. 16–18

Practice Worksheet

An easily-readable reduced practice page (with answers) for this lesson can be found on p. 548C.

Guided Practice

4.

domain: all real numbers except −3, range: all real numbers except 1

5.

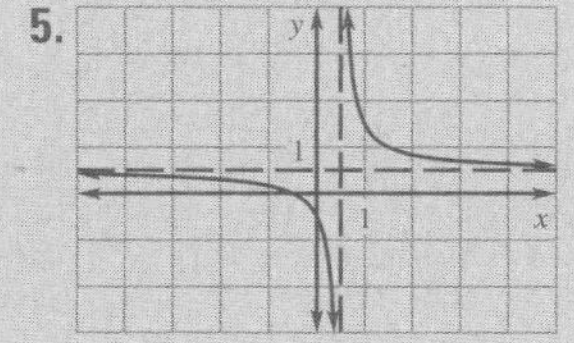

domain: all real numbers except $\frac{1}{2}$, range: all real numbers except $\frac{1}{2}$

6.

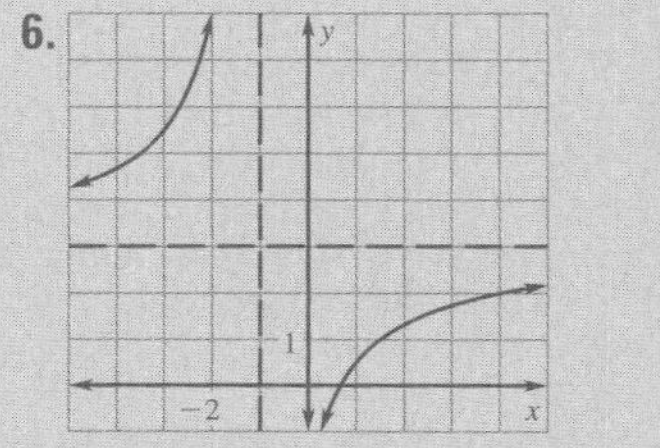

domain: all real numbers except −1, range: all real numbers except 3

Skill Practice

3–22. See Additional Answers beginning on p. AA1.

24a. The graph will lie farther from the asymptotes and is a reflection in either asymptote.

24b. The vertical asymptote is shifted left 4 units.

24c. The horizontal asymptote is shifted up 4 units.

Study Strategy

Exercises 11–22 A good way to remember the roles of the constants in an equation of the form $y = \frac{a}{x-h} + k$ is to compare it to the vertex form of the equation of a quadratic function, $y = a(x-h)^2 + k$. Have students make a chart in their notebooks with one column for each of these equations and listing how the constants affect the graph in each case.

Teaching Strategy

Exercises 11–22, 27–34 Students may notice that the graphs of the functions in these two sets of exercises look alike, and wonder why the equations look so different. Show them that the equations in the second group can be rewritten to look like those in the first group by polynomial long division. For example, using the function in Exercise 32, $\frac{6x-1}{3x-1} = 2 + \frac{1}{3x-1}$, so the function in this exercise is rewritten as $f(x) = \frac{1}{3x-1} + 2$.

Internet Reference

Exercise 41 Additional information about the Doppler effect can be found at www.kettering.edu/~drussell/Demos/doppler/doppler.html

25. The graph should be $y = \frac{-8}{x}$, not $y = \frac{8}{x}$.

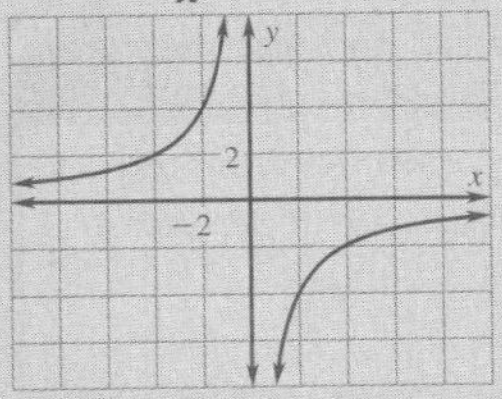

26. The vertical asymptote should be $x = 1$, not $x = -1$.

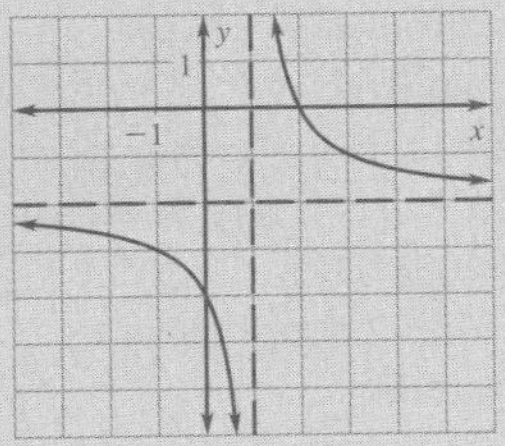

27–34. See Additional Answers beginning on p. AA1.

ERROR ANALYSIS ***Describe*** **and correct the error in the graph.** 25, 26. See margin.

25. $y = \frac{-8}{x}$

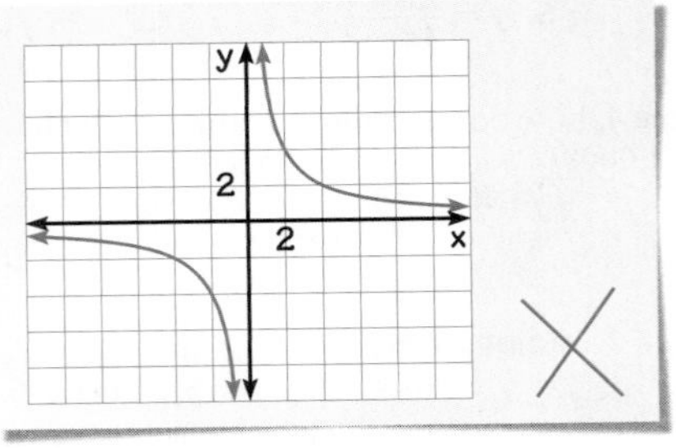

26. $y = \frac{2}{x-1} - 2$

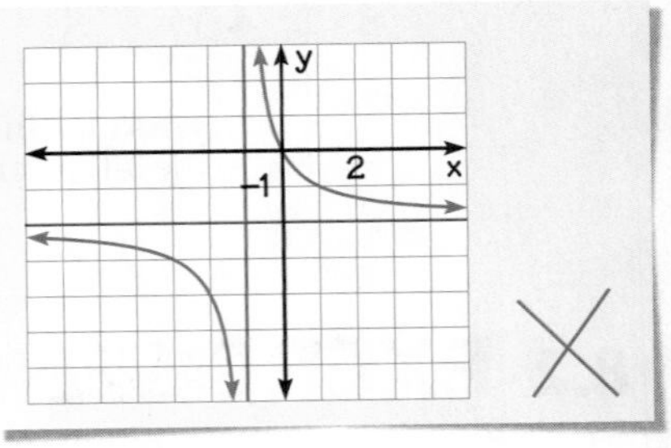

EXAMPLE 3 B on p. 560 for Exs. 27–34

GRAPHING FUNCTIONS **Graph the function. State the domain and range.** 27–34. See margin.

27. $y = \frac{x+4}{x-3}$ **28.** $y = \frac{x-1}{x+5}$ **29.** $y = \frac{x+6}{4x-8}$ **30.** $y = \frac{8x+3}{2x-6}$

31. $y = \frac{-5x+2}{4x+5}$ **32.** $f(x) = \frac{6x-1}{3x-1}$ **33.** $g(x) = \frac{5x}{2x+3}$ **34.** $h(x) = \frac{5x+3}{-x+10}$

35. ★ **OPEN-ENDED MATH** Write a rational function such that the domain is all real numbers except −8 and the range is all real numbers except 3. *Sample answer:* $y = \frac{3x+1}{x+8}$

C **36. CHALLENGE** Show that the equation $f(x) = \frac{a}{x-h} + k$ represents a rational function by writing the right side as a quotient of polynomials.
$f(x) = \frac{a}{x-h} + \frac{k(x-h)}{(x-h)} \rightarrow \frac{a+kx-kh}{x-h}$

Problem Solving

EXAMPLE 4 A on p. 560 for Exs. 37–38

37. INTERNET SERVICE An Internet service provider charges a $50 installation fee and a monthly fee of $43. Write and graph an equation that gives the average cost per month as a function of the number of months of service. After how many months will the average cost be $53? $c = \frac{43m+50}{m}$, see margin for art; 5 mo.

@HomeTutor for problem solving help at classzone.com

38. ROCK CLIMBING GYM To join a rock climbing gym, you must pay an initial fee of $100 and a monthly fee of $59. Write and graph an equation that gives the average cost per month as a function of the number of months of membership. After how many months will the average cost be $69? $c = \frac{59m+100}{m}$, see margin for art; 10 mo.

@HomeTutor for problem solving help at classzone.com

(39.) ◆ **MULTIPLE REPRESENTATIONS** The time t (in seconds) it takes for sound to travel 1 kilometer can be modeled by $t = \frac{1000}{0.6T + 331}$ where T is the air temperature (in degrees Celsius).

a. **Evaluating a Function** How long does it take for sound to travel 5 kilometers when the air temperature is 25°C? *Explain.*

b. **Drawing a Graph** Suppose you are 1 kilometer from a lightning strike, and it takes 3 seconds to hear the thunder. Graph the given function, and use the graph to estimate the air temperature. See margin for art; about 3.9°C.

39a. About 14.5 sec. *Sample answer:* Substitute 25 for T to find $t \approx 2.89$. Since you are 5 kilometers away, multiply t by 5 to get $5(2.89) \approx 14.5$ seconds.

◯ = WORKED-OUT SOLUTIONS on p. WS1 ★ = STANDARDIZED TEST PRACTICE ◆ = MULTIPLE REPRESENTATIONS

37.

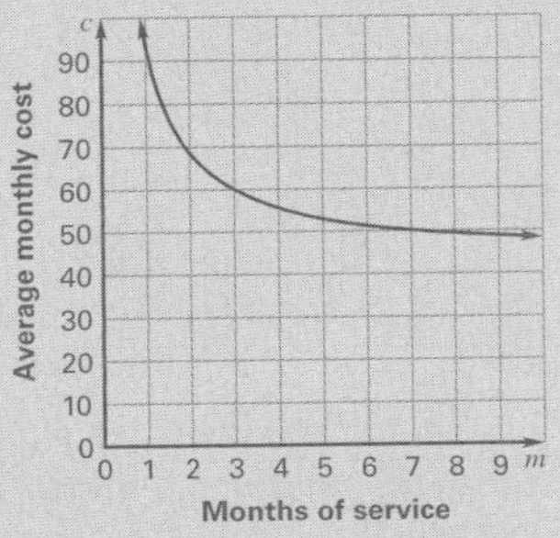

38.

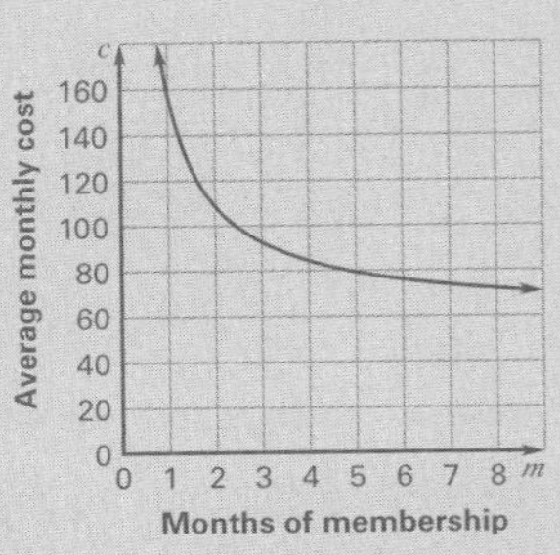

39b.

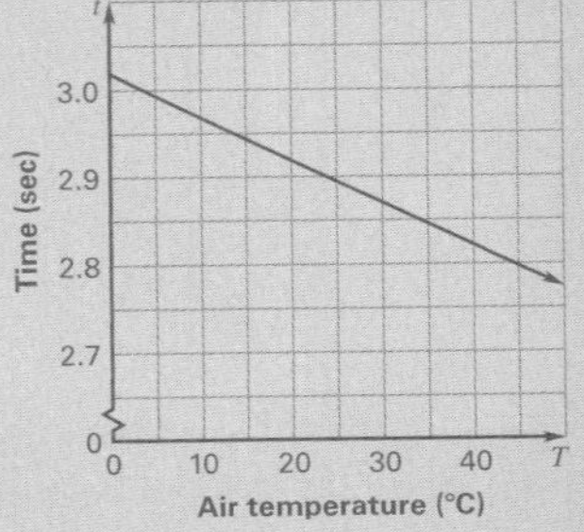

B **40.** ★ **SHORT RESPONSE** A business is studying the cost to remove a pollutant from the ground at its site. The function $y = \frac{15x}{1.1 - x}$ models the estimated cost y (in thousands of dollars) to remove x percent (expressed as a decimal) of the pollutant.

a. Graph the function. *Describe* a reasonable domain and range. **See margin.**

b. How much does it cost to remove 20% of the pollutant? 40% of the pollutant? 80% of the pollutant? Does doubling the percent of the pollutant removed double the cost? *Explain.*

40b. \$3333.33; \$8571.43; \$40,000; no. *Sample answer:* The values are not increasing at a constant rate.

41. ★ **EXTENDED RESPONSE** The *Doppler effect* occurs when the source of a sound is moving relative to a listener, so that the frequency f_l (in hertz) heard by the listener is different from the frequency f_s (in hertz) at the source. The frequency heard depends on whether the sound source is approaching or moving away from the listener. In both equations below, r is the speed (in miles per hour) of the sound source.

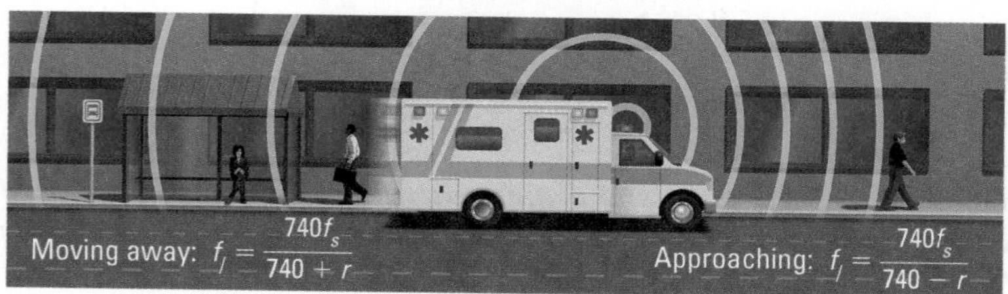

a. An ambulance siren has a frequency of 2000 hertz. Write two equations modeling the frequencies you hear when the ambulance is approaching and when the ambulance is moving away.

41a. Approaching: $f_l = \frac{1,480,000}{740 - r}$, moving away: $f_l = \frac{1,480,000}{740 + r}$

b. Graph the equations from part (a) using the domain $0 \le r \le 60$. **See margin.**

c. For any speed r, how does the frequency heard for an approaching sound source compare with the frequency heard when the source moves away? **The frequency of a sound that is approaching is greater than that of a sound moving away.**

C **42. CHALLENGE** A sailboat travels at a speed of 10 knots for 3 hours. It then uses a motor for power, which increases its speed to 15 knots. Write and graph an equation giving the boat's average speed s (in knots) for the entire trip as a function of the time t (in hours) that it uses the motor for power. **$s = \frac{30 + 15(t - 3)}{t}$, see margin for art.**

KENTUCKY MIXED REVIEW

43. On Monday, Anna reads one quarter of a novel. On Tuesday, she reads one third of the remaining pages. On Wednesday, she reads one quarter of the remaining pages. On Thursday, she reads the remaining 105 pages. How many pages does the novel have? **B**

Ⓐ 219 Ⓑ 280 Ⓒ 340 Ⓓ 420

44. Which equation best describes the relationship between x and y shown in the table? **D**

x	0.2	0.5	0.8	1.1
y	0.16	1	2.56	4.84

Ⓐ $y = 4x$ Ⓑ $x = 4y$ Ⓒ $x = 4y^2$ Ⓓ $y = 4x^2$

5 ASSESS AND RETEACH

Daily Homework Quiz

Transparency Available

Graph the function. State the domain and range.

1. $y = \frac{-1}{x + 4} + 3$

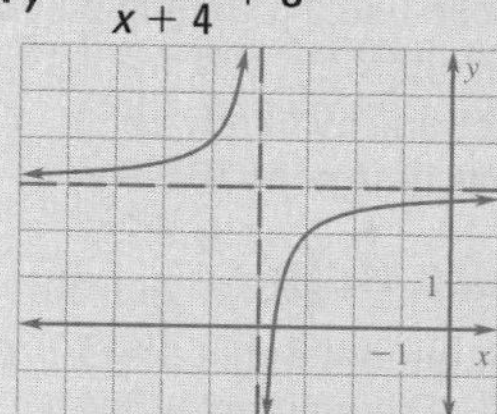

domain: all real numbers except −4; range: all real numbers except 3

2. $y = \frac{x + 3}{x - 1}$

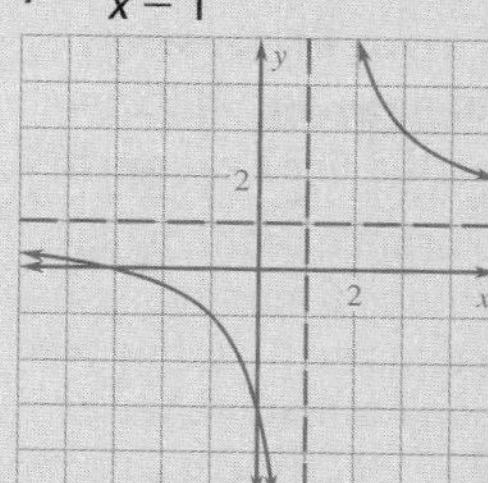

domain: all real numbers except 1; range: all real numbers except 1

3. The average income at a fruit stand is \$12 times the number of customers n, minus \$75, all divided by n. Use a graph of the average income to estimate the number of customers that makes the average income \$8 per customer. **19 customers**

Available at **classzone.com**

Diagnosis/Remediation

- Practice A, B, C in Chapter 8 Resource Book, pp. 16–18
- Study Guide in Chapter 8 Resource Book, pp. 19–20
- Practice Workbook, pp. 124–125
- @HomeTutor

Challenge

Additional challenge is available in the Chapter 8 Resource Book, p. 23.

40a, 41b, 42. See Additional Answers beginning on p. AA1.

Graphing Calculator ACTIVITY *Use after Lesson 8.2*

@HomeTutor classzone.com Keystrokes

8.2 Graph Rational Functions

QUESTION **How can you use a graphing calculator to graph rational functions?**

Most graphing calculators have two graphing modes: *connected* mode and *dot* mode. *Connected* mode displays the graph of a rational function as a smooth curve, while *dot* mode displays the graph as a series of dots.

EXAMPLE **Graph a rational function**

Graph $y = \frac{x+3}{x-3}$.

STEP 1 ***Enter function***
Enter the rational function, using parentheses.

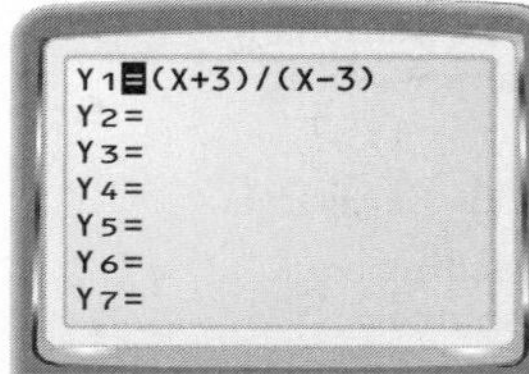

STEP 2 ***Use connected mode***
Graph the function in *connected* mode.

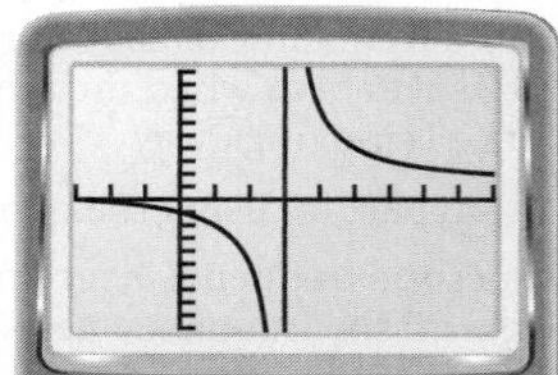

STEP 3 ***Use dot mode***
Graph the function in *dot* mode.

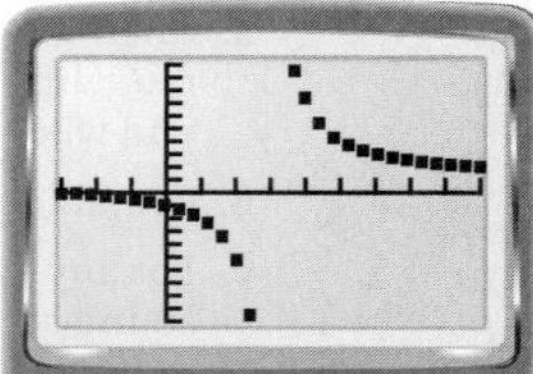

The graph in Step 2 includes a vertical line at approximately $x = 3$. This line is *not* part of the graph. It is simply the graphing calculator's attempt at connecting the two branches of the graph.

PRACTICE

Use a graphing calculator to graph the rational function. Choose a viewing window that displays the important characteristics of the graph. 1–8. See margin.

1. $y = \frac{5}{x} + 2$
2. $y = 7 - \frac{3}{x}$
3. $y = 4 + \frac{2}{x-5}$
4. $y = \frac{6}{x+1} + 2$
5. $y = \frac{7}{2x+8}$
6. $y = \frac{9-2x}{x-3}$
7. $f(x) = \frac{x-4}{x+2}$
8. $g(x) = \frac{5x-2}{3x+9}$
9. **SKATEBOARDING** You are trying to decide whether it is worth joining a skate park. It costs \$100 to join and then \$4 for each visit. Write a function that gives the average cost y per visit after x visits. Graph the function. What happens to the average cost as the number of visits increases? What are a reasonable domain and range for the function? See margin.

1 PLAN AND PREPARE

Learn the Method

- Students learn how to use a graphing calculator to graph rational functions in both connected mode and dot mode. After this activity, students can use a graphing calculator as an alternative to graphing these functions by hand, using asymptotes, and point plotting.

Keystroke Help

Keystrokes for several models of calculators are available in blackline format in the *Chapter 8 Resource Book*.

2 TEACH

Tips for Success

If students obtain graphs that only include one branch of the hyperbola, guide them in modifying their window settings so that they will be able to see both branches.

Extra Example

Graph $y = \frac{2x+6}{x-3}$ in connected mode and dot mode.

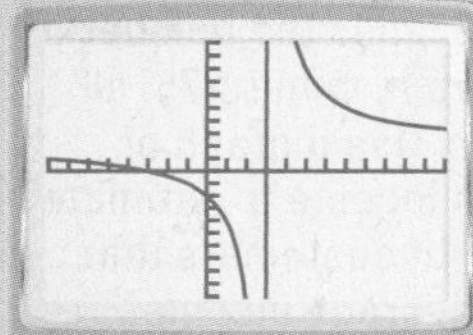

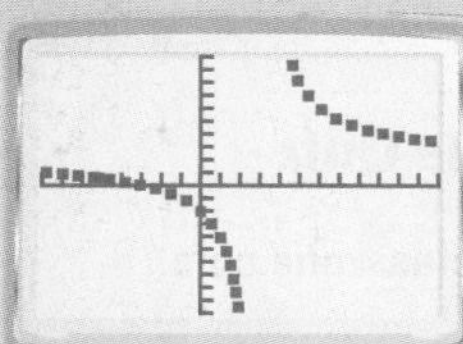

3 ASSESS AND RETEACH

What does the vertical line that appears in connected mode represent? The line is the vertical asymptote of the graph.

1–8. See Additional Answers beginning on p. AA1.

9. $y = \frac{100 + 4x}{x}$;

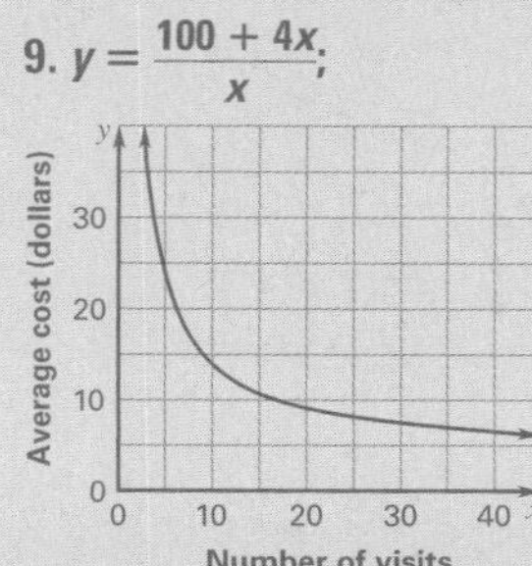

The average cost gets closer to \$4. *Sample answer:* domain: $0 \le x \le 50$, range: $0 \le y \le 6$

8.3 Graph General Rational Functions

MA-HS-5.1.3

Before You graphed rational functions involving linear polynomials.

Now You will graph rational functions with higher-degree polynomials.

Why? So you can solve problems about altitude, as in Ex. 35.

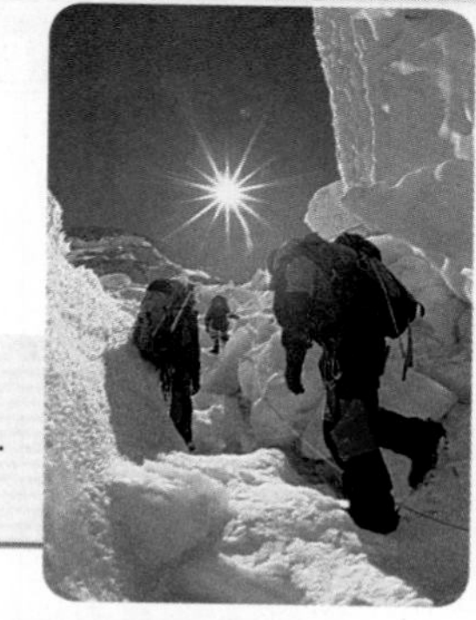

Key Vocabulary
- **end behavior,** *p. 339*
- **asymptote,** *p. 478*
- **rational function,** *p. 558*

MA-HS-5.1.3
Students will demonstrate how equations and graphs are models of the relationship between two real-world quantities (e.g., the relationship between degrees Celsius and degrees Fahrenheit).

KEY CONCEPT *For Your Notebook*

Graphs of Rational Functions

Let $p(x)$ and $q(x)$ be polynomials with no common factors other than ± 1. The graph of the following rational function has the characteristics listed below.

$$f(x) = \frac{p(x)}{q(x)} = \frac{a_m x^m + a_{m-1}x^{m-1} + \cdots + a_1 x + a_0}{b_n x^n + b_{n-1}x^{n-1} + \cdots + b_1 x + b_0}$$

1. The x-intercepts of the graph of f are the real zeros of $p(x)$.
2. The graph of f has a vertical asymptote at each real zero of $q(x)$.
3. The graph of f has at most one horizontal asymptote, which is determined by the degrees m and n of $p(x)$ and $q(x)$.

$m < n$	The line $y = 0$ is a horizontal asymptote.
$m = n$	The line $y = \frac{a_m}{b_n}$ is a horizontal asymptote.
$m > n$	The graph has no horizontal asymptote. The graph's end behavior is the same as the graph of $y = \frac{a_m}{b_n}x^{m-n}$.

EXAMPLE 1 **Graph a rational function ($m < n$)**

Graph $y = \frac{6}{x^2 + 1}$. State the domain and range.

Solution

The numerator has no zeros, so there is no x-intercept. The denominator has no real zeros, so there is no vertical asymptote.

The degree of the numerator, 0, is less than the degree of the denominator, 2. So, the line $y = 0$ (the x-axis) is a horizontal asymptote.

The graph passes through the points $(-3, 0.6)$, $(-1, 3)$, $(0, 6)$, $(1, 3)$, and $(3, 0.6)$. The domain is all real numbers, and the range is $0 < y \le 6$.

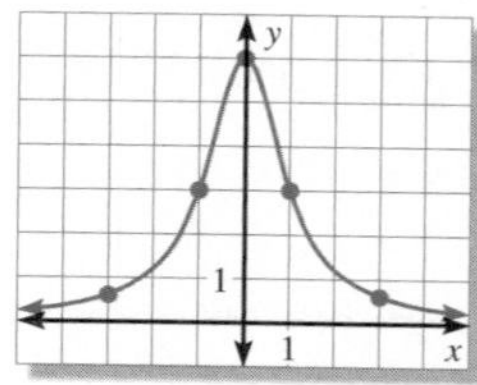

1 PLAN AND PREPARE

Warm-Up Exercises
Transparency Available

1. Graph $y = \frac{2}{x}$.

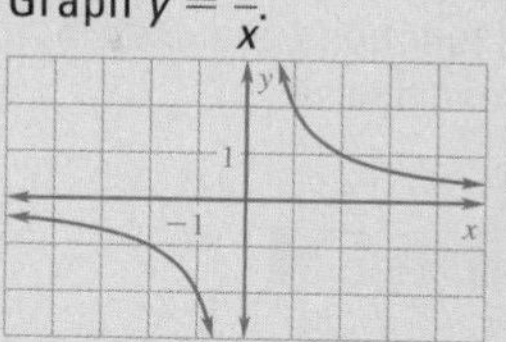

2. Find the vertical and horizontal asymptotes of $y = \frac{4x + 5}{x - 1}$. **vertical: $x = 1$; horizontal: $y = 4$**

Notetaking Guide
Transparency Available
Promotes interactive learning and notetaking skills, pp. 218–220.

Pacing
Basic: 1 day
Average: 1 day
Advanced: 1 day
Block: 0.5 block with 8.4
- See *Teaching Guide/Lesson Plan.*

2 FOCUS AND MOTIVATE

Essential Question
Big Idea 1, p. 549
What are the steps for graphing a general rational function? **Tell students they will learn how to answer this question by identifying the intercepts, asymptotes, and end behavior of a rational function.**

Resource Planning Guide

Chapter Resource Book
- Teaching Guide/Lesson Plan (pp. 24–25)
- Activity Master (p. 26)
- Practice levels A, B, C (pp. 29–31)
- Study Guide (pp. 32–33)
- Catch-up for Absent Students (p. 34)
- Problem Solving Workshop (p. 35)
- Challenge (p. 37)

Workbooks
- Notetaking Guide (pp. 218–220)
- Practice Workbook (pp. 126–127)

Teaching Options
- **Power Presentations CD-ROM** provides dynamic electronic teaching resources for the classroom.
- **Activity Generator CD-ROM** provides editable activities for all ability levels.

Interactive Technology
- Easy Planner
- Power Presentations CD-ROM
- Activity Generator CD-ROM
- Animated Algebra
- Test Generator CD-ROM
- Online Quiz
- eWorkbook
- eEdition
- @HomeTutor

Resources for English Learners
- Quick Reference for English Learners
- Spanish Study Guide
- Multi-Language Visual Glossary
- Student Resources in Spanish

See also the *Algebra 2 Toolkit* for more strategies for meeting individual needs.

Motivating the Lesson

Ask which students are interested in careers in business. Explain that many decisions in business involve figuring out how to minimize costs and maximize profits. Mathematical models and graphs, including graphs of rational functions, are used in making these decisions.

3 TEACH

Extra Example 1

Graph $y = \frac{-2}{x^2 + 2}$. State the domain and range.

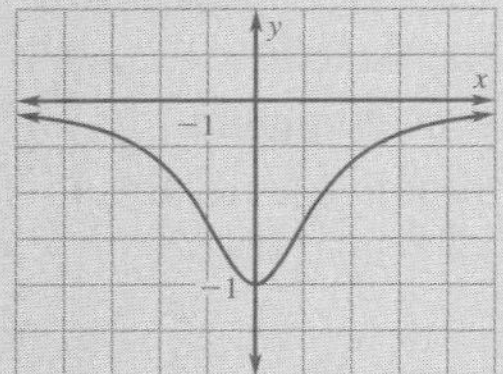

domain: all real numbers; range: $-1 \le y < 0$

Extra Example 2

Graph $y = \frac{-x^2}{x^2 - 4}$.

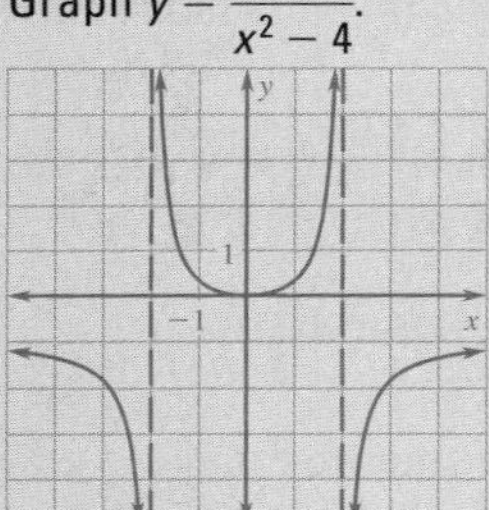

Extra Example 3

Graph $y = \frac{x^2 - 2x + 1}{x + 2}$.

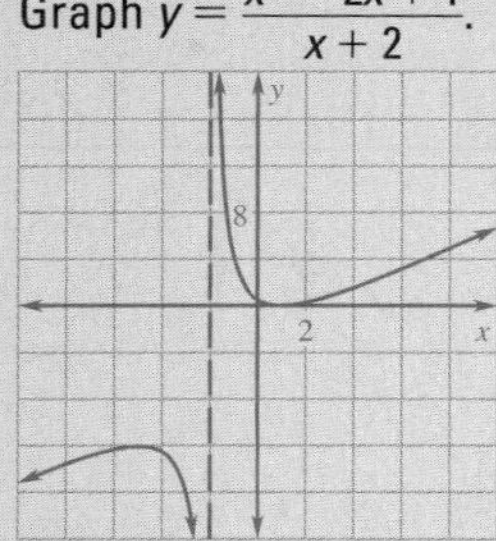

EXAMPLE 2 Graph a rational function ($m = n$)

Graph $y = \frac{2x^2}{x^2 - 9}$.

REVIEW ZEROS OF FUNCTIONS
For help with finding zeros of functions, see p. 252.

Solution

The zero of the numerator $2x^2$ is 0, so 0 is an x-intercept. The zeros of the denominator $x^2 - 9$ are ± 3, so $x = 3$ and $x = -3$ are vertical asymptotes.

The numerator and denominator have the same degree, so the horizontal asymptote is $y = \frac{a_m}{b_n} = \frac{2}{1} = 2$.

Plot points between and beyond the vertical asymptotes.

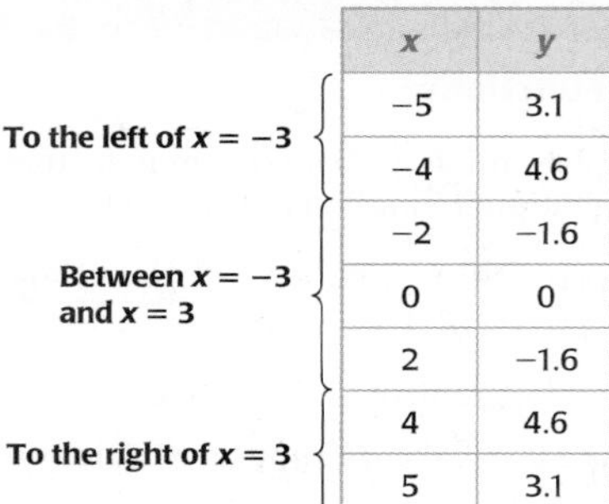

	x	y
To the left of $x = -3$	−5	3.1
	−4	4.6
Between $x = -3$ and $x = 3$	−2	−1.6
	0	0
	2	−1.6
To the right of $x = 3$	4	4.6
	5	3.1

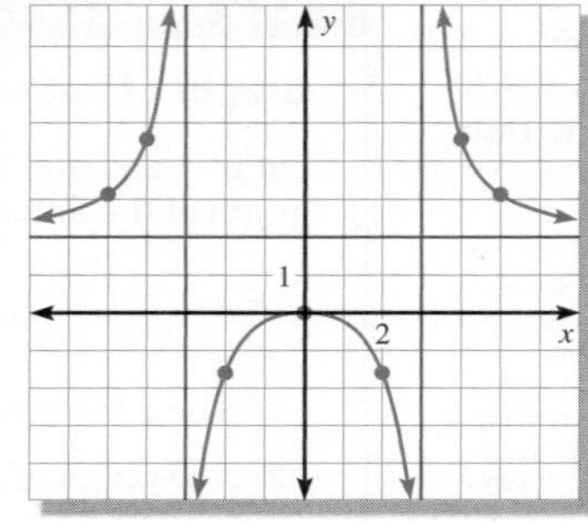

EXAMPLE 3 Graph a rational function ($m > n$)

Graph $y = \frac{x^2 + 3x - 4}{x - 2}$.

Solution

The numerator factors as $(x + 4)(x - 1)$, so the x-intercepts are -4 and 1. The zero of the denominator $x - 2$ is 2, so $x = 2$ is a vertical asymptote.

The degree of the numerator, 2, is greater than the degree of the denominator, 1, so the graph has no horizontal asymptote. The graph has the same end behavior as the graph of $y = x^{2-1} = x$. Plot points on each side of the vertical asymptote.

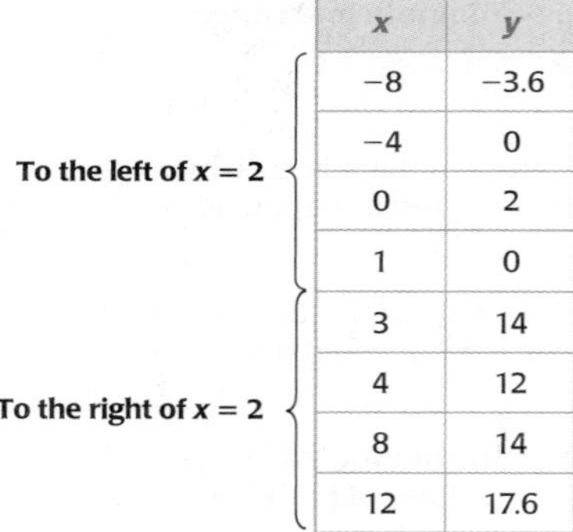

	x	y
To the left of $x = 2$	−8	−3.6
	−4	0
	0	2
	1	0
To the right of $x = 2$	3	14
	4	12
	8	14
	12	17.6

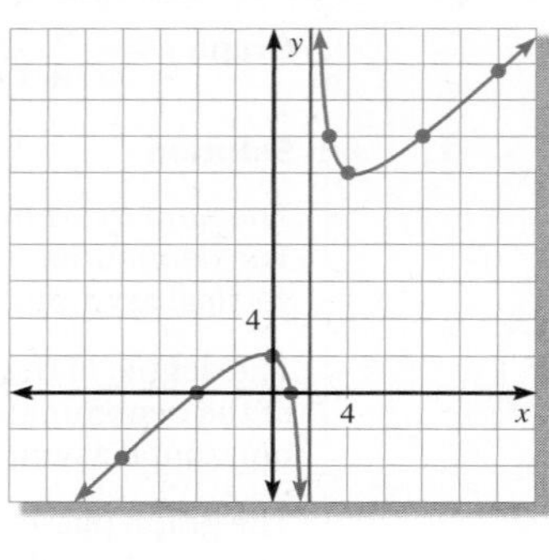

Differentiated Instruction

Visual Learners Students may struggle to select points between or beyond the vertical asymptotes. To help them visualize these locations, have students draw just the x-axis as a number line, and pick one point in each of the three regions to test.

See also the *Algebra 2 Toolkit* for more strategies.

GUIDED PRACTICE for Examples 1, 2, and 3

Graph the function. 1–4. See margin.

1. $y = \frac{4}{x^2 + 2}$ **2.** $y = \frac{3x^2}{x^2 - 1}$ **3.** $f(x) = \frac{x^2 - 5}{x^2 + 1}$ **4.** $y = \frac{x^2 - 2x - 3}{x - 4}$

EXAMPLE 4 Solve a multi-step problem

MANUFACTURING A food manufacturer wants to find the most efficient packaging for a can of soup with a volume of 342 cubic centimeters. Find the dimensions of the can that has this volume and uses the least amount of material possible.

Solution

STEP 1 **Write** an equation that gives the height h of the soup can in terms of its radius r. Use the formula for the volume of a cylinder and the fact that the soup can's volume is 342 cubic centimeters.

$V = \pi r^2 h$ **Formula for volume of cylinder**

$342 = \pi r^2 h$ **Substitute 342 for V.**

$\frac{342}{\pi r^2} = h$ **Solve for h.**

STEP 2 **Write** a function that gives the surface area S of the soup can in terms of only its radius r.

$S = 2\pi r^2 + 2\pi rh$ **Formula for surface area of cylinder**

$= 2\pi r^2 + 2\pi r\left(\frac{342}{\pi r^2}\right)$ **Substitute $\frac{342}{\pi r^2}$ for h.**

$= 2\pi r^2 + \frac{684}{r}$ **Simplify.**

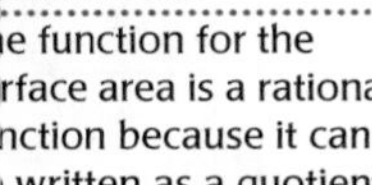

ITERPRET
JNCTIONS
e function for the rface area is a rational nction because it can written as a quotient polynomials:

$S = \frac{2\pi r^3 + 684}{r}$

STEP 3 **Graph** the function for the surface area S using a graphing calculator. Then use the *minimum* feature to find the minimum value of S.

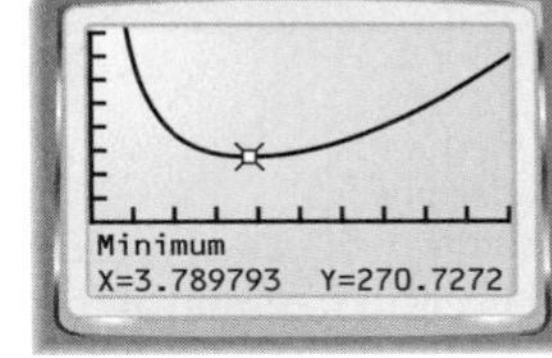

You get a minimum value of about 271, which occurs when $r \approx 3.79$ and $h \approx \frac{342}{\pi(3.79)^2} \approx 7.58$.

▶ So, the soup can using the least amount of material has a radius of about 3.79 centimeters and a height of about 7.58 centimeters. Notice that the height and the diameter are equal for this can.

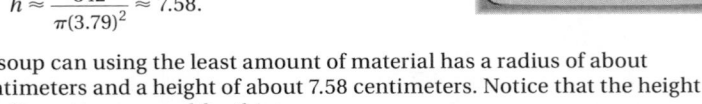

GUIDED PRACTICE for Example 4

5. WHAT IF? In Example 4, suppose the manufacturer wants to find the most efficient packaging for a soup can with a volume of 544 cubic centimeters. Find the dimensions of this can. $r \approx 4.42$ cm, $h \approx 8.86$ cm

An **Animated Algebra** activity is available on-line for **Example 3**. This activity is also available on the **Power Presentations CD-ROM**.

Extra Example 4

A carton manufacturer has a large order for rectangular cartons with square bottoms that have a volume of 6000 cubic inches. Find the dimensions of the carton with that volume that uses the least amount of material. **The carton is a cube with all edges about 18.17 in.**

Key Question to Ask for Example 4

- Why does the graph in Example 4 show only one branch of a hyperbola? **The dimensions of the can must be positive, so it is only necessary to look at the graph in Quadrant I.**

Closing the Lesson

Have students summarize the major points of the lesson and answer the Essential Question: What are the steps for graphing a general rational function?

- **The number of vertical asymptotes is the number of real zeros of the denominator. The number of horizontal asymptotes depends on the degrees of the numerator and denominator.**
- **If the leading terms of the numerator and denominator are $a_m x^m$ and $b_n x^n$ and $m > n$, the end behavior of the graph is the same as the end behavior of $y = \frac{a_m}{b_n} x^{m-n}$.**

Locate the x-intercepts, if any, and all vertical and horizontal asymptotes. Identify the end behavior of the graph, then make a table of values, including x-values in each of the sections into which any vertical asymptotes divide the graph. Connect the points you find with smooth curves.

1–4. See Additional Answers beginning on p. AA1.

Differentiated Instruction

Advanced The graph in Example 3 has an oblique (or "slant") asymptote, which is the line $y = x + 5$. Have students work individually or in a small group to research this topic and prepare a written report or present a mini-lesson to their classmates. The report or presentation should answer these questions: (1) What type of rational function has an oblique asymptote? (2) How can polynomial long division be used to find the equation of an oblique asymptote? (3) How can an oblique asymptote and vertical asymptote be used together as "guide lines" in graphing a rational function?

See also the *Algebra 2 Toolkit* for more strategies.

8.3 EXERCISES

HOMEWORK KEY
○ = **WORKED-OUT SOLUTIONS** on p. WS15 for Exs. 7, 15, and 33
★ = **STANDARDIZED TEST PRACTICE** Exs. 2, 6, 14, 24, and 35
◆ = **MULTIPLE REPRESENTATIONS** Ex. 33

4 PRACTICE AND APPLY

Assignment Guide

Answer Transparencies available for all exercises

Basic:
Day 1: SRH p. 993 Exs. 2, 5, 6
pp. 568–571
Exs. 1–9, 13–20, 31–33, 37

Average:
Day 1: pp. 568–571
Exs. 1–6, 9–14, 18–27, 31–35, 38

Advanced:
Day 1: pp. 568–571
Exs. 1, 2, 6, 10–14, 18–36*

Block:
pp. 568–571
Exs. 1–6, 9–14, 18–27, 31–35, 38 (with 8.4)

Differentiated Instruction

See *Algebra 2 Best Practices Toolkit* for suggestions on addressing the needs of a diverse classroom.

Homework Check

For a quick check of student understanding of key concepts, go over the following exercises:
Basic: 8, 9, 16, 18, 31
Average: 10, 11, 19, 20, 32
Advanced: 11, 12, 22, 24, 32

Extra Practice

- Student Edition, p. 1017
- Chapter 8 Resource Book: Practice levels A, B, C, pp. 29–31

Practice Worksheet

An easily-readable reduced practice page (with answers) for this lesson can be found on p. 548C.

SKILL PRACTICE

A

1. VOCABULARY Copy and complete: The graph of a rational function f has no __?__ when the degree of the function's numerator is greater than the degree of its denominator. horizontal asymptote

2. ★ WRITING Let $f(x) = \frac{p(x)}{q(x)}$ where $p(x)$ and $q(x)$ are polynomials with no common factors other than ±1. *Describe* how to find the x-intercepts and the vertical asymptotes of the graph of f. To find the x-intercepts, find the real zeros of the numerator $p(x)$. To find the vertical asymptotes, find the real zeros of the denominator $q(x)$.

EXAMPLES 1, 2, and 3 on pp. 565–566 for Exs. 3–23

MATCHING GRAPHS Match the function with its graph.

3. $y = \frac{-10}{x^2 - 9}$ C

4. $y = \frac{x^2 - 10}{x^2 + 3}$ A

5. $y = \frac{x^3}{x^2 - 4}$ B

A. 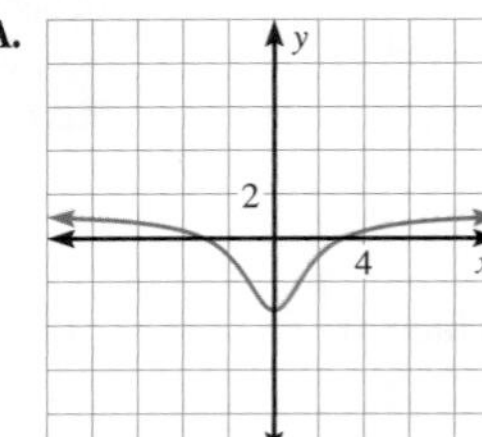

B. 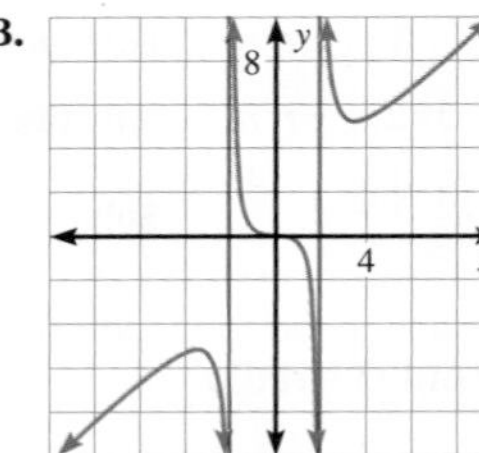

C. 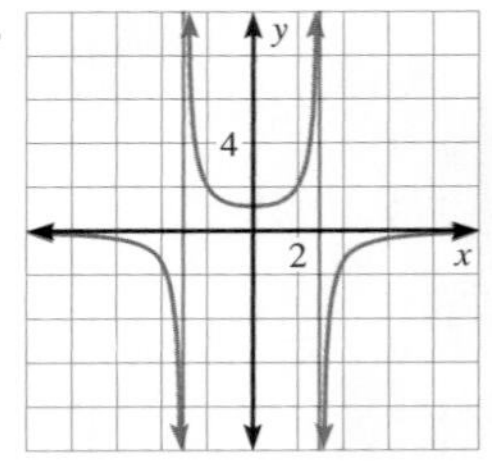

6. ★ MULTIPLE CHOICE The graph of which function is shown? A

Ⓐ $y = \frac{3}{x^2 - 4}$ Ⓑ $y = \frac{3x^2}{x^2 - 4}$

Ⓒ $y = \frac{x^2 - 4}{3x^2}$ Ⓓ $y = \frac{x^3}{x^2 - 4}$

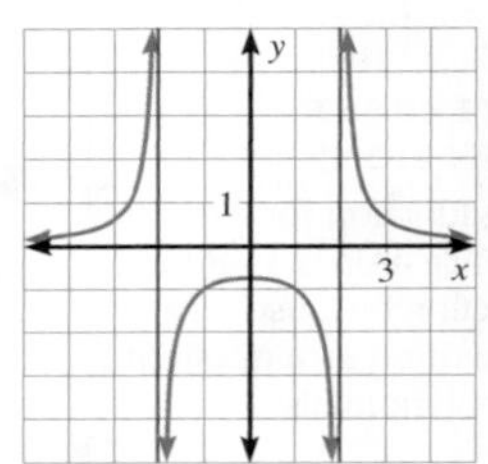

Animated Algebra at classzone.com

ANALYZING GRAPHS Identify the x-intercept(s) and vertical asymptote(s) of the graph of the function.

7. $y = \frac{5}{x^2 - 1}$ none; $x = 1$, $x = -1$

8. $y = \frac{x + 1}{x^2 + 5}$ -1; none

9. $f(x) = \frac{x^2 + 9}{x^2 - 2x - 15}$ none; $x = 5$, $x = -3$

10. $y = \frac{x^2 - 7x - 60}{x + 3}$ 12, -5; $x = -3$

11. $y = \frac{x^3 + 27}{3x^2 + x}$ -3; $x = 0$, $x = -\frac{1}{3}$

12. $g(x) = \frac{2x^2 - 3x - 20}{x^2 + 1}$ $-\frac{5}{2}$, 4; none

13. ERROR ANALYSIS *Describe* and correct the error in finding the vertical asymptote(s) of $f(x) = \frac{x - 2}{x^2 - 8x + 7}$.

The vertical asymptote occurs at the zero of the numerator $x - 2$. So, the vertical asymptote is $x = 2$.

13. The vertical asymptote occurs at the zeros of the denominator not the numerator; the vertical asymptotes occur at the zeros of the denominator $x^2 - 8x + 7$. So, the vertical asymptotes are at $x = 7$ and $x = 1$.

15. 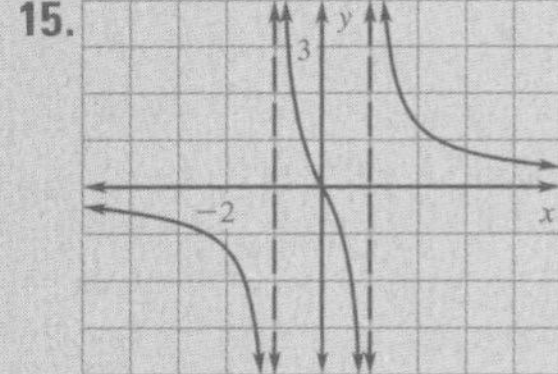

16. 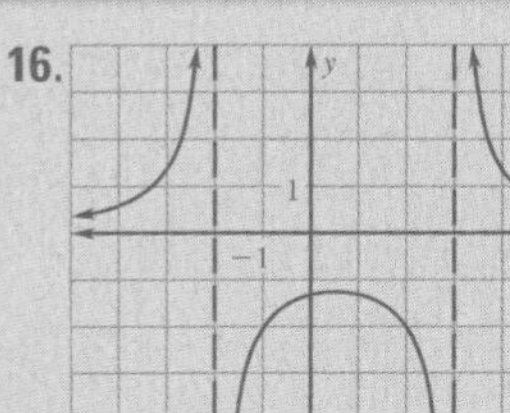

17. 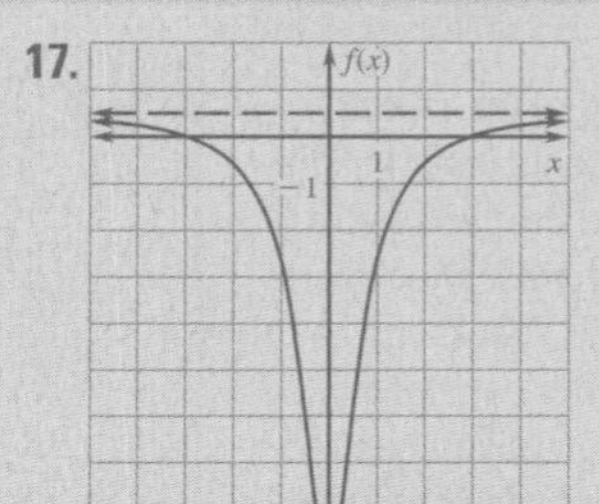

18. 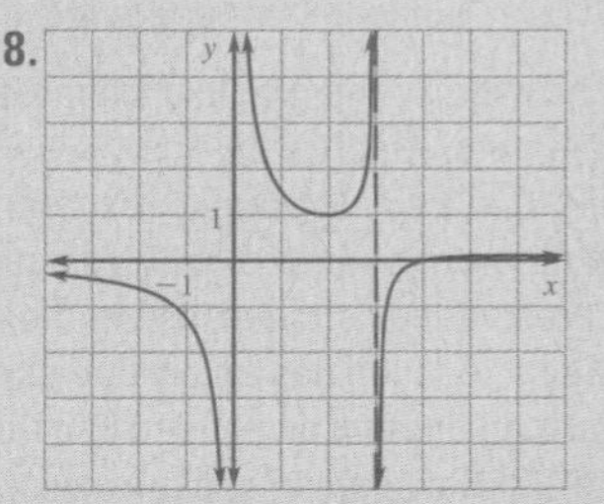

14. ★ **MULTIPLE CHOICE** What is the horizontal asymptote of the graph of the function $y = \frac{4x^2 - 21x + 5}{x^2 - 12}$? C

Ⓐ $y = 0$ Ⓑ $y = \frac{1}{4}$ Ⓒ $y = 4$ Ⓓ $y = 4x$

B **GRAPHING FUNCTIONS** **Graph the function.** 15–23. See margin.

15. $y = \frac{2x}{x^2 - 1}$ **16.** $y = \frac{8}{x^2 - x - 6}$ **17.** $f(x) = \frac{x^2 - 9}{2x^2 + 1}$

18. $y = \frac{x - 4}{x^2 - 3x}$ **19.** $y = \frac{x^2 + 11x + 18}{2x + 1}$ **20.** $g(x) = \frac{x^3 - 8}{6 - x^2}$

21. $y = \frac{x^2 + 3}{2x^3}$ **22.** $y = \frac{x^2 - 5x - 36}{3x}$ **23.** $h(x) = \frac{3x^2 + 10x - 8}{x^2 + 4}$

Sample answer: $y = \frac{6x^4 + 5x - 1}{2x^2 - 3x + 2}$ and $y = \frac{3x^3 - 7}{x + 5}$

24. ★ **OPEN-ENDED MATH** Write two different rational functions whose graphs have the same end behavior as the graph of $y = 3x^2$.

GRAPHING CALCULATOR **Use a graphing calculator to find the range of the rational function.**

25. $y = \frac{15}{x^2 + 2}$ $0 < y \le 7.5$ **26.** $y = \frac{3x^2}{x^2 - 9}$ all real numbers except $0 < y \le 3$ **27.** $y = \frac{x^2 - 2x}{2x + 3}$ all real numbers except $-0.209 < y < -4.791$

C **CHALLENGE** **The graph of a function of the form $f(x) = \frac{a}{x^2 + b}$ is shown. Find the values of a and b.**

28.

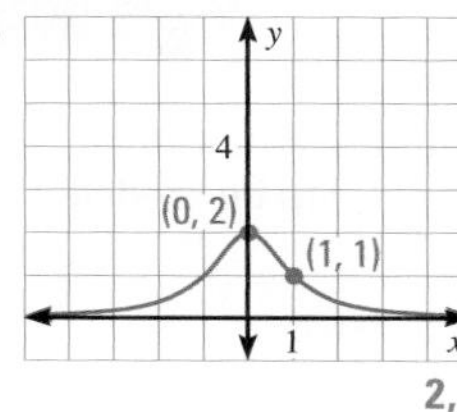

2, 1

29.

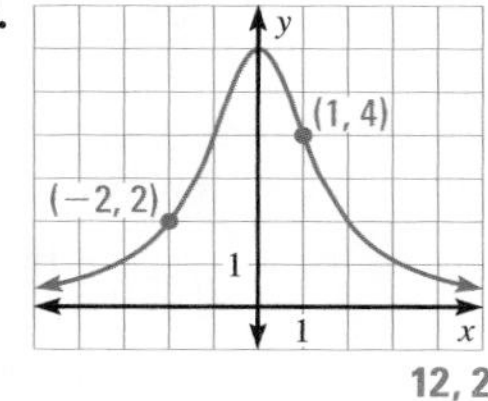

12, 2

30.

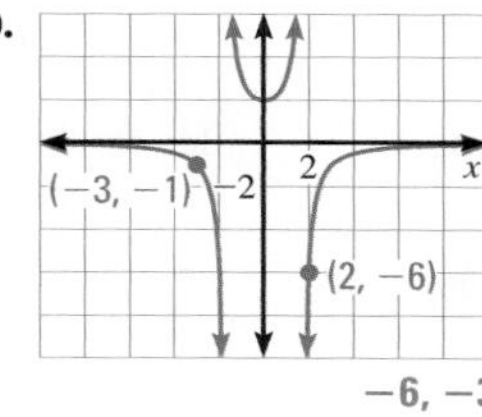

−6, −3

PROBLEM SOLVING

EXAMPLE 4 A on p. 567 for Exs. 31–32

GRAPHING CALCULATOR **You may wish to use a graphing calculator to complete the following Problem Solving exercises.**

31. **AGRICULTURE** A farmer makes cylindrical bales of hay that have a volume of 100 cubic feet. Each bale is to be wrapped in plastic to keep the hay dry.

a. Using the formula for the volume of a cylinder, write an equation that gives the length ℓ of a bale in terms of the radius r. a. $\ell = \frac{100}{\pi r^2}$

b. Write a function that gives the surface area of a bale in terms of only the radius r. b. $S = 2\pi r^2 +$

c. Find the dimensions of a bale that has the given volume and uses the least amount of plastic possible when the bale is wrapped. $r \approx 2.515$ ft, $\ell \approx 5.032$ ft

@HomeTutor for problem solving help at classzone.com

Mathematical Reasoning

Exercises 3–5 These exercises provide a good opportunity to talk about symmetry and its importance in graphing parabolas. Point out that graphs A and C have line symmetry with respect to the *y*-axis, while graph B has point symmetry with respect to the origin.

An **Animated Algebra** activity is available on-line for **Exercise 6**. This activity is also available on the **Power Presentations CD-ROM**.

Avoiding Common Errors

Exercises 7–12 Some students may confuse the roles of the numerator and denominator in determining *x*-intercepts and vertical asymptotes. Remind them that an *x*-intercept occurs when $y = 0$, and a fraction is 0 when its numerator (but not its denominator) is 0. A vertical asymptote occurs where a function is undefined, which corresponds to the denominator being 0. Also, remind students that an asymptote is a line, so it must be written as an equation, not as a value.

22.

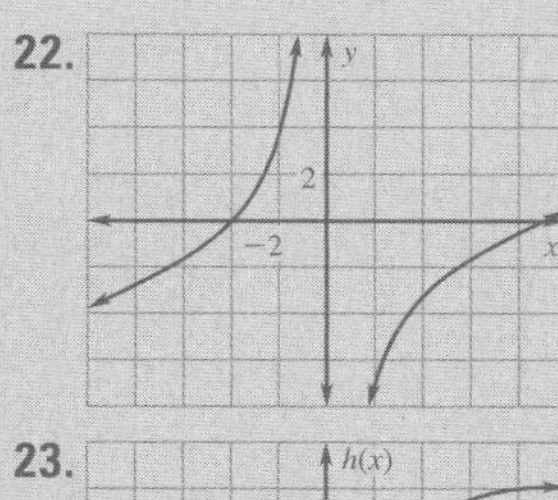

23.

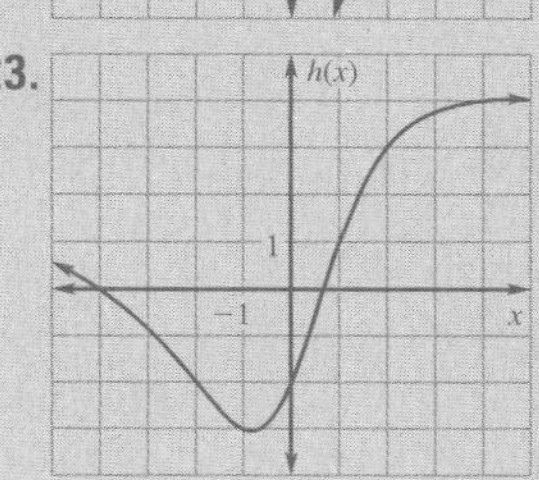

19.

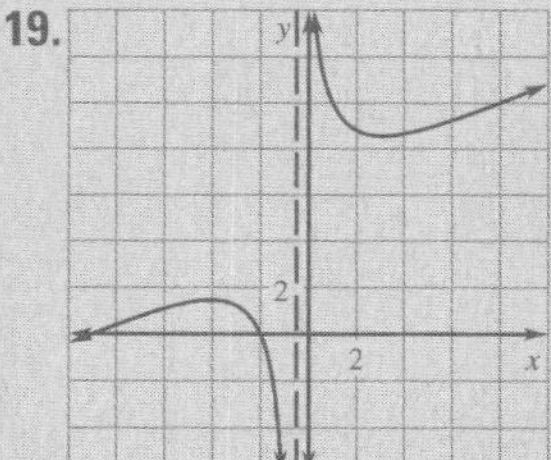

20.

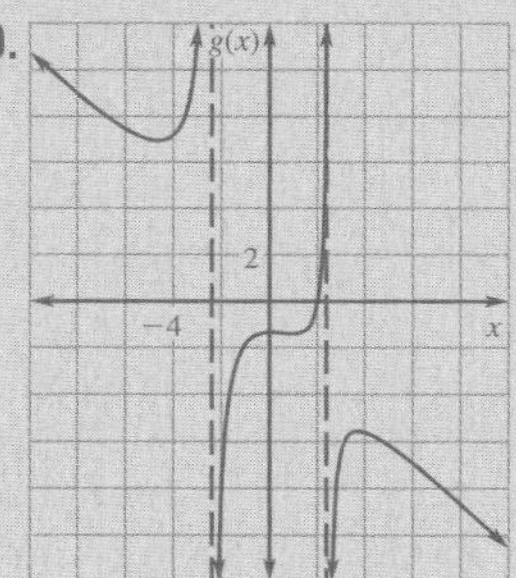

21.

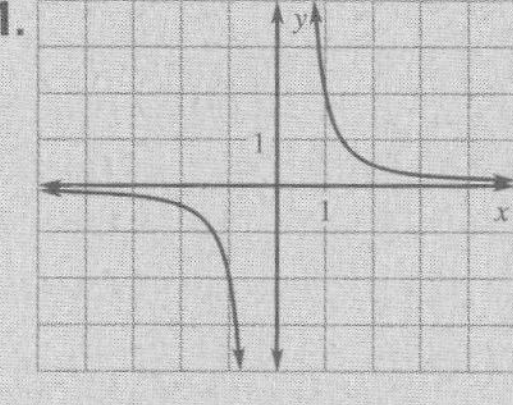

Study Strategy

Exercise 32 Provide students will a hand-out that summarizes the formulas for the volume and surface area of the common solids. Tell students to keep this in their notebooks for future reference in geometric applications.

Exercise 34 For more information about the New York Stock Exchange, visit www.nyse.com

33a.

Depth (m)	Mean Temperature (°C)
1000	4.763
1050	4.580
1100	4.409
1150	4.251
1200	4.104
1250	3.967
1300	3.839

33b.

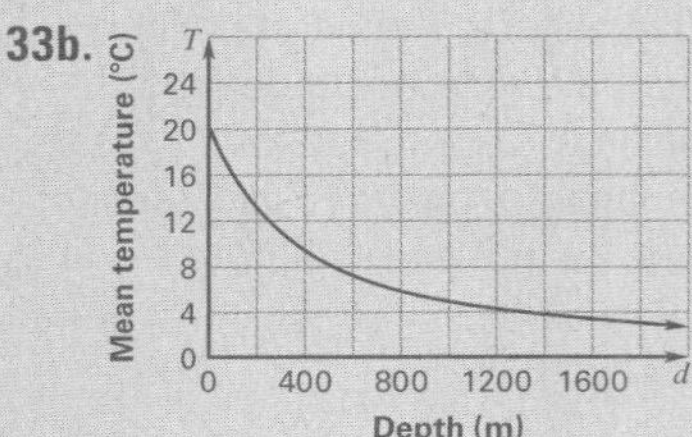

34a.

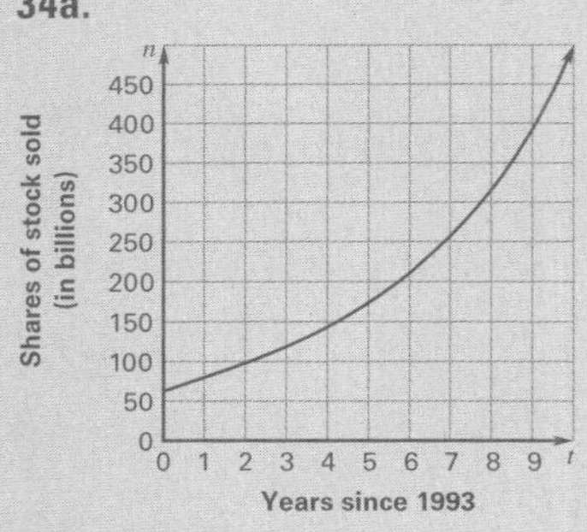

35a.

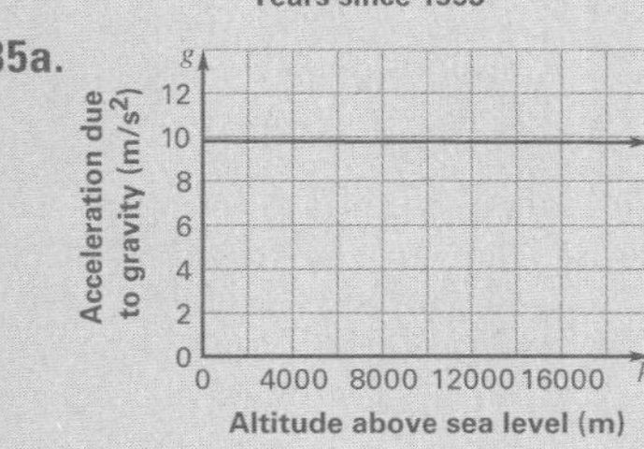

32. AQUARIUM DESIGN A manufacturer is designing an aquarium whose base is a regular hexagon. The aquarium should have a volume of 24 cubic feet and use the least amount of material possible. Let s be the length (in feet) of a side of the base, and let h be the height (in feet).

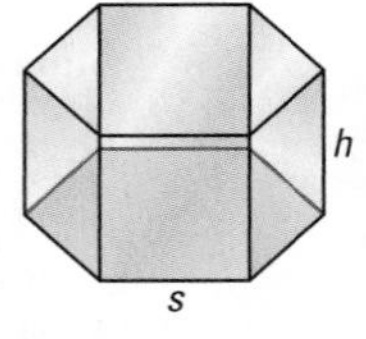

a. Write an equation that gives h in terms of s. (*Hint:* The volume of the aquarium is given by $V = \frac{3\sqrt{3}}{2}s^2h$.) $h = \frac{16\sqrt{3}}{3s^2}$

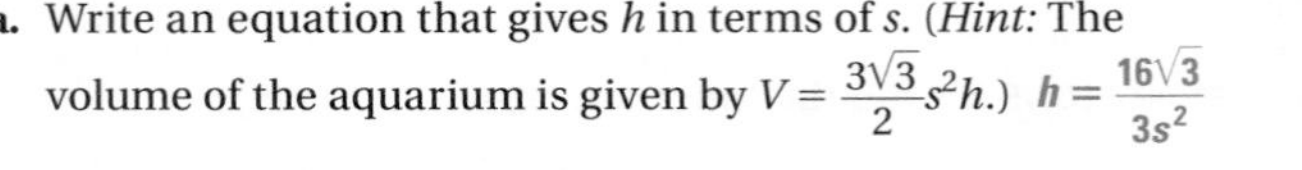

b. Find the dimensions s and h that minimize the amount of material used. (*Hint:* The surface area of the aquarium is given by $S = \frac{3\sqrt{3}}{2}s^2 + 6sh$.) $s \approx 2.201$ ft, $h \approx 1.907$ ft

@HomeTutor for problem solving help at classzone.com

B **33.** ◆ **MULTIPLE REPRESENTATIONS** The mean temperature T (in degrees Celsius) of the Atlantic Ocean between latitudes 40°N and 40°S can be modeled by

$$T = \frac{17{,}800d + 20{,}000}{3d^2 + 740d + 1000}$$

where d is the depth (in meters).

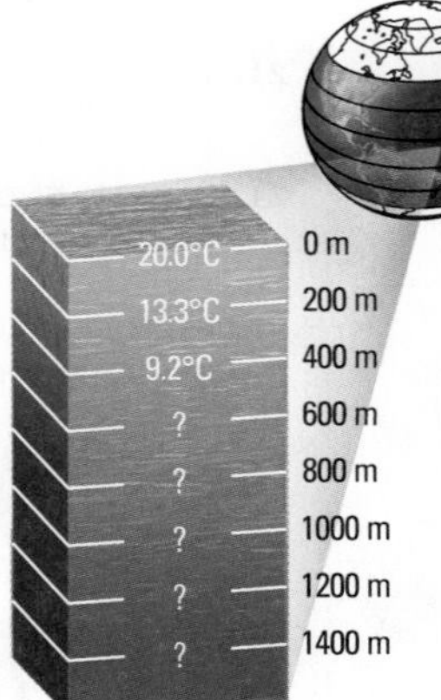

a. Making a Table Make a table of values showing the mean temperature for depths from 1000 meters to 1300 meters in 50 meter intervals. See margin.

b. Using a Graph Graph the model. Use your graph to estimate the depth at which the mean temperature is 4°C. See margin for art; about 1238 m.

34. MULTI-STEP PROBLEM From 1993 to 2002, the number n (in billions) of shares of stock sold on the New York Stock Exchange can be modeled by

$$n = \frac{1054t + 6204}{-6.62t + 100}$$

where t is the number of years since 1993.

a. Graph the model. See margin.

b. *Describe* the general trends shown by the graph.

c. Estimate the year when the number of shares of stock sold was first greater than 100 billion. 1996

34b. *Sample answer:* As the year increases the number of shares sold increases.

35. ★ EXTENDED RESPONSE The acceleration due to gravity g (in meters per second squared) changes as altitude changes and is given by the function

$$g = \frac{3.99 \times 10^{14}}{h^2 + (1.28 \times 10^7)h + (4.07 \times 10^{13})}$$

where h is the altitude (in meters) above sea level.

This spacecraft reached an altitude of 112 km in 2004.

a. Graph Graph the function. See margin.

b. Apply A mountaineer is climbing to a height of 8000 meters. What is the value of g at this altitude? about 9.78 m/sec²

c. Apply A spacecraft reaches an altitude of 112 kilometers above Earth. What is the value of g at this altitude? about 9.47 m/sec²

d. Explain *Describe* what happens to the value of g as altitude increases.

35d. *Sample answer:* g decreases, but at a very small rate.

○ = WORKED-OUT SOLUTIONS on p. WS1 ★ = STANDARDIZED TEST PRACTICE ◆ = MULTIPLE REPRESENTATIONS

36b. $V = \pi r^2\left(\frac{\frac{100}{\pi} - r^2 - 2r - 1}{2r + 1}\right)$

36c.

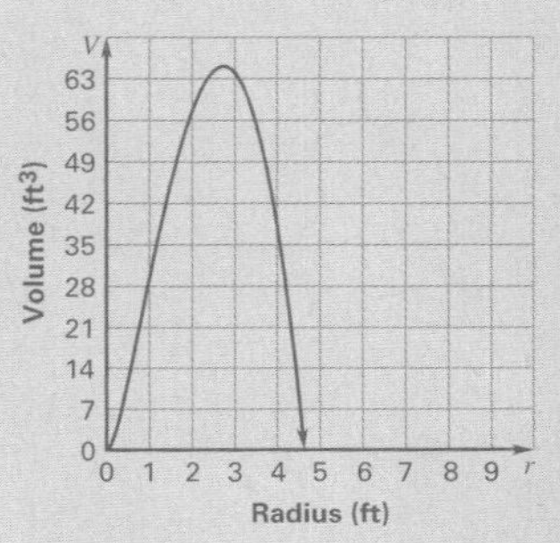

36a. $h = \dfrac{\frac{100}{\pi} - r^2 - 2r - 1}{2r + 1}$

C **36. CHALLENGE** You need to build a cylindrical water tank using 100 cubic feet of concrete. The sides and the base of the tank must be 1 foot thick.

a. Write an equation that gives the tank's inner height h in terms of its inner radius r.

b. Write an equation that gives the volume V of water that the tank can hold as a function of r. **See margin.**

c. Graph the equation from part (b). What values of r and h maximize the tank's capacity? **See margin for art; $r \approx 2.74$ ft, $h \approx 2.75$ ft.**

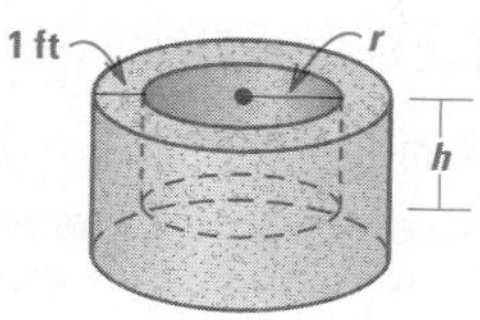

KENTUCKY MIXED REVIEW

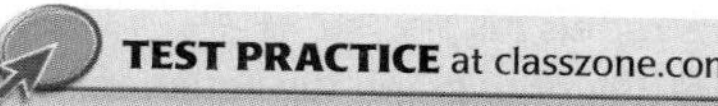

37. Doris plants a 75 square foot rectangular garden. She uses 36 feet of fencing to enclose the garden. What are the approximate dimensions of the garden? **D**

Ⓐ 5.6 ft by 13.4 ft Ⓑ 5.7 ft by 12.3 ft Ⓒ 6.0 ft by 12.0 ft Ⓓ 6.6 ft by 11.4 ft

38. The circle graph represents 840 students. The red section of the circle graph represents the number of students who ride a bus to school everyday. How many students ride a bus to school everyday? **C**

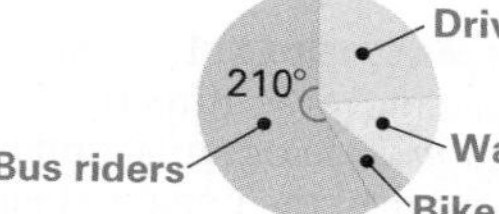

Ⓐ 176 Ⓑ 350

Ⓒ 490 Ⓓ 513

QUIZ *for Lessons 8.1–8.3*

The variables x and y vary inversely. Use the given values to write an equation relating x and y. Then find y when $x = -4$. *(p. 551)*

1. $x = 8, y = 3$ $\quad y = \frac{24}{x}; -6$

2. $x = 2, y = -9$ $\quad y = \frac{-18}{x}; \frac{9}{2}$

3. $x = -5, y = \frac{8}{3}$ $\quad y = \frac{-40}{3x}; \frac{10}{3}$

4. $x = -\frac{1}{4}, y = -32$ $\quad y = \frac{8}{x}; -2$

Graph the function. **5–10. See margin.**

5. $y = \dfrac{3}{2x}$ *(p. 558)*

6. $y = \dfrac{4}{x - 2} + 1$ *(p. 558)*

7. $f(x) = \dfrac{-2x}{3x - 6}$ *(p. 558)*

8. $y = \dfrac{-8}{x^2 - 1}$ *(p. 565)*

9. $y = \dfrac{x^2 - 6}{x^2 + 2}$ *(p. 565)*

10. $g(x) = \dfrac{x^3 - 8}{2x^2}$ *(p. 565)*

11. SOFTBALL A pitcher throws 16 strikes in her first 38 pitches. The table shows how the pitcher's strike percentage changes if she throws x consecutive strikes after the first 38 pitches. Write a rational function for the strike percentage in terms of x. Graph the function. How many consecutive strikes must the pitcher throw to reach a strike percentage of 0.60? *(p. 558)*
See margin for art; $y = \frac{x + 16}{x + 38}$; 17 strikes.

x	Total strikes	Total pitches	Strike percentage
0	16	38	0.42
5	21	43	0.49
10	26	48	0.54
x	$x + 16$	$x + 38$	?

46–53. See Additional Answers beginning on p. AA1.

5 ASSESS AND RETEACH

Daily Homework Quiz

Transparency Available

1. Graph the function $y = \dfrac{8}{x^2 + 4}$. State the domain and range.

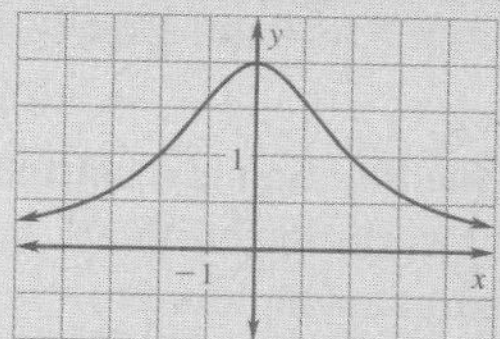

domain: all real numbers; range: $0 < y \le 2$

2. Graph the function $y = \dfrac{x^2 + 3}{x^2 - 1}$. Identify the asymptotes.

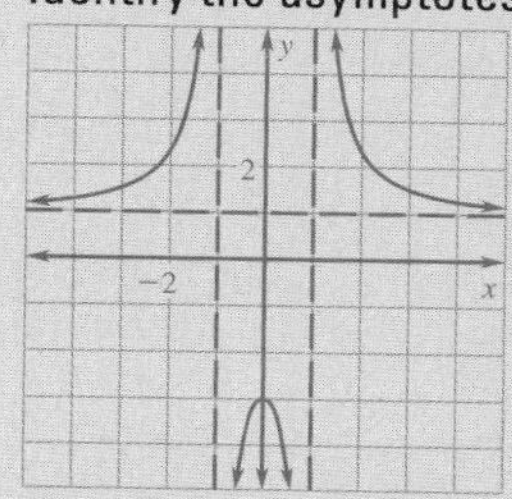

vertical: $x = -1$, $x = 1$; horizontal: $y = 1$

Available at **classzone.com**

Diagnosis/Remediation

- Practice A, B, C in Chapter 8 Resource Book, pp. 29–31
- Study Guide in Chapter 8 Resource Book, pp. 32–33
- Practice Workbook, pp. 126–127
- @HomeTutor

Challenge

Additional challenge is available in the Chapter 8 Resource Book, p. 37.

Quiz

An easily-readable reduced copy of the quiz (with answers) on Lessons 8.1–8.3 from the Assessment Book can be found on p. 548E.

Quiz 5–11. See Additional Answers beginning on p. AA1.

Kentucky Mixed Review

1. B
2. C
3. B
4. D
5. B
6. B
7. a. \$1200
   b. \$500; the function is a shifted inverse variation, with a horizontal asymptote at $M = 500$
   c. No, because $M(0)$ is undefined.

Kentucky Mixed Review

Lessons 8.1–8.3

1. **EFFICIENT PACKAGING** A food manufacturer wants to find the most efficient packaging for a cylindrical canister of oatmeal with a volume of 1663 cubic centimeters. An equation that gives the canister's surface area S in terms of its radius r is $S = 2\pi r^2 + \frac{3326}{r}$. Use a graphing calculator to graph the equation. What is the approximate radius r of the canister that uses the least material possible?
   - A. 5.1 inches
   - B. 6.4 inches
   - C. 6.6 inches
   - D. 8.1 inches

2. **BODY MASS INDEX** The body mass index b of a person varies directly with the person's weight w (in kilograms) and inversely with the square of the person's height h (in meters). A person who is 1.6 meters tall and weighs 51.2 kilograms has a body mass index of 20. What is the approximate height of a person who weighs 45 kilograms and has a body mass index of 20?
   - A. 1.2 meters
   - B. 1.4 meters
   - C. 1.5 meters
   - D. 2.3 meters

3. **CANDY SALES** The number y of boxes of candy a manufacturer sells each month varies inversely with the price x (in dollars). In one month, the manufacturer sells 800 boxes of candy at a price of \$5 per box. About how many boxes of candy will the manufacturer sell at a price of \$7 per box?
   - A. 457 boxes
   - B. 571 boxes
   - C. 643 boxes
   - D. 686 boxes

4. **INVERSE VARIATION** Which equation represents inverse variation?
   - A. $y = x + 3$
   - B. $y = 2x$
   - C. $y = \frac{x}{3}$
   - D. $xy = 11$

5. **PLAYGROUND AREA** You are designing a rectangular playground that has an area of 200 square yards. A building borders the length of the playground. You use fencing for the other three sides. Which length ℓ and width w minimize the amount of fencing needed?
   - A. $\ell = 14$ yards; $w = 14$ yards
   - B. $\ell = 20$ yards; $w = 10$ yards
   - C. $\ell = 25$ yards; $w = 8$ yards
   - D. $\ell = 28$ yards; $w = 7$ yards

6. **PHOTO PRINTING** Your family buys a photo printer. The printer costs \$200. The ink and paper cost about \$.60 for each photo you print. Which equation gives the average cost C of a printed photo as a function of the number x of photos printed?
   - A. $C = \frac{200 - 0.6x}{x}$
   - B. $C = \frac{200 + 0.6x}{x}$
   - C. $C = 200 + 0.6x$
   - D. $C = 200.6x$

7. **OPEN-RESPONSE** The value M (in dollars) of a motorcycle t years after it was purchased new can be estimated using the function $M(t) = \frac{3500}{t} + 500$, where $t \geq 1$.
   a. Estimate the motorcycle's value 5 years after it was purchased.
   b. What does the value of the motorcycle approach as time passes? *Explain.*
   c. Can you use this particular model to determine the initial price of the motorcycle? *Explain.*

8.4 Multiply and Divide Rational Expressions

MA-HS-5.2.5

Before You graphed rational functions.

Now You will multiply and divide rational expressions.

Why? So you can compare the efficiencies of two designs, as in Ex. 51.

Key Vocabulary
- **simplified form of a rational expression**
- **reciprocal,** *p. 4*

MA-HS-5.2.5
Students will add, subtract, multiply and divide simple rational expressions with monomial first-degree denominators and integer numerators (e.g., $\frac{3}{5x}+\frac{4}{3y}$; $\frac{9}{2a}-\frac{-7}{4b}$; $\frac{3}{-5x}\times\frac{-4}{7y}$; $\frac{5}{2c}\div\frac{9}{-11d}$), and will express the results in simplified form. DOK 1

A rational expression is in **simplified form** if its numerator and denominator have no common factors (other than ± 1). To simplify a rational expression, apply the following property.

KEY CONCEPT *For Your Notebook*

Simplifying Rational Expressions

Let a, b, and c be expressions with $b \neq 0$ and $c \neq 0$. Then the following property applies.

Property	$\frac{a\not{c}}{b\not{c}} = \frac{a}{b}$	**Divide out the common factor c.**
Examples	$\frac{15}{65} = \frac{3 \cdot \not{5}}{13 \cdot \not{5}} = \frac{3}{13}$	**Divide out the common factor 5.**
	$\frac{4\cancel{(x+3)}}{(x-5)\cancel{(x+3)}} = \frac{4}{x-5}$	**Divide out the common factor $x + 3$.**

Simplifying a rational expression usually requires two steps. First, factor the numerator and denominator. Then, divide out any factors that are common to both the numerator and denominator. Here is an example:

$$\frac{x^2+7x}{x^2} = \frac{\cancel{x}(x+7)}{\cancel{x} \cdot x} = \frac{x+7}{x}$$

Notice that you can divide out common factors in the second expression above. However, you cannot divide out like terms in the third expression.

AVOID ERRORS
Do not divide out variable terms that are not factors.

$$\frac{x-5}{x-3} \neq \frac{-5}{-3}$$

EXAMPLE 1 Simplify a rational expression

Simplify: $\frac{x^2-2x-15}{x^2-9}$

$\frac{x^2-2x-15}{x^2-9} = \frac{(x+3)(x-5)}{(x+3)(x-3)}$ **Factor numerator and denominator.**

$= \frac{\cancel{(x+3)}(x-5)}{\cancel{(x+3)}(x-3)}$ **Divide out common factor.**

$= \frac{x-5}{x-3}$ **Simplified form**

1 PLAN AND PREPARE

Warm-Up Exercises
Transparency Available

Factor the expression.

1. $10x - 5x^2$ $5x(2 - x)$
2. $x^2 - 2x - 48$ $(x + 6)(x - 8)$
3. $x^3 - 125$ $(x - 5)(x^2 + 5x + 25)$
4. What is the volume and surface area of a cardboard shipping carton that measures 15 inches by 18 inches by 20 inches? 5400 in.^3, 1860 in.^2

Notetaking Guide
Transparency Available

Promotes interactive learning and notetaking skills, pp. 221–223.

Pacing
Basic: 2 days
Average: 2 days
Advanced: 2 days
Block: 0.5 block with 8.3
0.5 block with 8.5
- See *Teaching Guide/Lesson Plan.*

2 FOCUS AND MOTIVATE

Essential Question
Big Idea 2, p. 549

What are the steps for multiplying and dividing rational expressions? **Tell students they will learn how to answer this question by using operations similar to multiplication and division of rational numbers.**

Resource Planning Guide

Chapter Resource Book
- Teaching Guide/Lesson Plan (pp. 38–39)
- Practice levels A, B, C (pp. 41–43)
- Study Guide (pp. 44–45)
- Catch-up for Absent Students (p. 46)
- Application (p. 47)
- Challenge (p. 48)

Workbooks
- Notetaking Guide (pp. 221–223)
- Practice Workbook (pp. 128–129)

Teaching Options
- **Power Presentations CD-ROM** provides dynamic electronic teaching resources for the classroom.
- **Activity Generator CD-ROM** provides editable activities for all ability levels.

Interactive Technology
- Easy Planner
- Power Presentations CD-ROM
- Activity Generator CD-ROM
- Animated Algebra
- Test Generator CD-ROM
- Online Quiz
- eWorkbook
- eEdition
- @HomeTutor

Resources for English Learners
- Quick Reference for English Learners
- Spanish Study Guide
- Multi-Language Visual Glossary
- Student Resources in Spanish

See also the *Algebra 2 Toolkit* for more strategies for meeting individual needs.

Motivating the Lesson

You are interested in a career in industrial design. People in this field need to have the ability to design products that are attractive, practical, and reasonably priced. Using the minimum amount of material necessary for a product is desirable for keeping down the weight and the cost of production. Finding ratios of rational expressions is useful in making choices in this kind of work.

3 TEACH

Extra Example 1

Simplify: $\frac{x^2 - 8x + 16}{x + 2x - 24}$ $\frac{x - 4}{x + 6}$

Key Question to Ask for Example 1

- What special factoring pattern is used to factor the denominator? **the difference of two squares: $a^2 - b^2 = (a + b)(a - b)$**

Extra Example 2

A company makes kitchen canisters with the same base. Style 1 is a cylinder whose height is equal to its radius. Style 2 is a cylinder whose height is twice its radius.

- Find the surface area and volume of each canister. **Style 1: $SA = 4\pi r^2$; $V = \pi r^3$; Style 2: $SA = 6\pi r^2$; $V = 2\pi r^3$**
- Calculate the ratio of surface area to volume for each canister. **Style 1: $\frac{4}{r}$; Style 2: $\frac{3}{r}$**
- What do the ratios tell you about the efficiencies of the two canisters? **$\frac{4}{r} > \frac{3}{r}$ for all positive numbers r, so Style 1 is less efficient than Style 2.**

EFFICIENCY Manufacturers often package their products in a way that uses the least amount of packaging material. One measure of the efficiency of a package is the ratio of its surface area to its volume. The smaller the ratio, the more efficient the packaging.

EXAMPLE 2 Solve a multi-step problem

PACKAGING A company makes a tin to hold flavored popcorn. The tin is a rectangular prism with a square base. The company is designing a new tin with the same base and twice the height of the old tin.

- Find the surface area and volume of each tin.
- Calculate the ratio of surface area to volume for each tin.
- What do the ratios tell you about the efficiencies of the two tins?

Solution

	Old tin	New tin	
STEP 1	$S = 2s^2 + 4sh$	$S = 2s^2 + 4s(2h)$	**Find surface area, S.**
		$= 2s^2 + 8sh$	
	$V = s^2h$	$V = s^2(2h)$	**Find volume, V.**
		$= 2s^2h$	
STEP 2	$\frac{S}{V} = \frac{2s^2 + 4sh}{s^2h}$	$\frac{S}{V} = \frac{2s^2 + 8sh}{2s^2h}$	**Write ratio of S to V.**
	$= \frac{\cancel{s}(2s + 4h)}{\cancel{s}(sh)}$	$= \frac{\cancel{2s}(s + 4h)}{\cancel{2s}(sh)}$	**Divide out common factor.**
	$= \frac{2s + 4h}{sh}$	$= \frac{s + 4h}{sh}$	**Simplified form**

STEP 3 $\frac{2s + 4h}{sh} > \frac{s + 4h}{sh}$ because the left side of the inequality has a greater numerator than the right side and both have the same (positive) denominator. The ratio of surface area to volume is *greater* for the old tin than for the new tin. So, the old tin is *less* efficient than the new tin.

GUIDED PRACTICE for Examples 1 and 2

Simplify the expression, if possible.

1. $\frac{2(x + 1)}{(x + 1)(x + 3)}$ $\frac{2}{x + 3}$
2. $\frac{40x + 20}{10x + 30}$ $\frac{2(2x + 1)}{x + 3}$
3. $\frac{4}{x(x + 2)}$ simplified form
4. $\frac{x + 4}{x^2 - 16}$ $\frac{1}{x - 4}$
5. $\frac{x^2 - 2x - 3}{x^2 - x - 6}$ $\frac{x + 1}{x + 2}$
6. $\frac{2x^2 + 10x}{3x^2 + 16x + 5}$ $\frac{2x}{3x + 1}$
7. **WHAT IF?** In Example 2, suppose the new popcorn tin is the same height as the old tin but has a base with sides twice as long. What is the ratio of surface area to volume for this tin? $\frac{2s + 2h}{sh}$

KEY CONCEPT *For Your Notebook*

Multiplying Rational Expressions

The rule for multiplying rational expressions is the same as the rule for multiplying numerical fractions: multiply numerators, multiply denominators, and write the new fraction in simplified form.

Let a, b, c, and d be expressions with $b \neq 0$ and $d \neq 0$.

Property $\frac{a}{b} \cdot \frac{c}{d} = \frac{ac}{bd}$ **Simplify $\frac{ac}{bd}$ if possible.**

Example $\frac{5x^2}{2xy^2} \cdot \frac{6xy^3}{10y} = \frac{30x^3y^3}{20xy^3} = \frac{\cancel{10} \cdot 3 \cdot \cancel{x} \cdot x^2 \cdot \cancel{y^3}}{\cancel{10} \cdot 2 \cdot \cancel{x} \cdot \cancel{y^3}} = \frac{3x^2}{2}$

EXAMPLE 3 Standardized Test Practice

What is a simplified form of $\frac{8x^3y}{2xy^2} \cdot \frac{7x^4y^3}{4y}$?

Ⓐ $\frac{5}{2}x^6y$ Ⓑ $7x^6y$ Ⓒ $7x^{11}y$ Ⓓ $7x^7y^{4/3}$

ANOTHER WAY

In Example 3, you can also first simplify each fraction, then multiply, and finally simplify the result:

$\frac{8x^3y}{2xy^2} \cdot \frac{7x^4y^3}{4y}$

$= \frac{4x^2}{y} \cdot \frac{7x^4y^2}{4}$

$= \frac{\cancel{4} \cdot 7 \cdot x^6 \cdot \cancel{y} \cdot y}{\cancel{4} \cdot \cancel{y}}$

$= 7x^6y$

Solution

$\frac{8x^3y}{2xy^2} \cdot \frac{7x^4y^3}{4y} = \frac{56x^7y^4}{8xy^3}$ **Multiply numerators and denominators.**

$= \frac{\cancel{8} \cdot 7 \cdot \cancel{x} \cdot x^6 \cdot \cancel{y^3} \cdot y}{\cancel{8} \cdot \cancel{x} \cdot \cancel{y^3}}$ **Factor and divide out common factors.**

$= 7x^6y$ **Simplified form**

▶ The correct answer is B. Ⓐ Ⓑ Ⓒ Ⓓ

EXAMPLE 4 Multiply rational expressions

Multiply: $\frac{3x - 3x^2}{x^2 + 4x - 5} \cdot \frac{x^2 + x - 20}{3x}$

$\frac{3x - 3x^2}{x^2 + 4x - 5} \cdot \frac{x^2 + x - 20}{3x} = \frac{3x(1 - x)}{(x - 1)(x + 5)} \cdot \frac{(x + 5)(x - 4)}{3x}$ **Factor numerators and denominators.**

$= \frac{3x(1 - x)(x + 5)(x - 4)}{(x - 1)(x + 5)(3x)}$ **Multiply numerators and denominators.**

$= \frac{3x(-1)(x - 1)(x + 5)(x - 4)}{(x - 1)(x + 5)(3x)}$ **Rewrite $1 - x$ as $(-1)(x - 1)$.**

$= \frac{\cancel{3x}(-1)\cancel{(x - 1)}\cancel{(x + 5)}(x - 4)}{\cancel{(x - 1)}\cancel{(x + 5)}\cancel{(3x)}}$ **Divide out common factors.**

$= (-1)(x - 4)$ **Simplify.**

$= -x + 4$ **Multiply.**

Extra Example 3

What is a simplified form of $\frac{5x^2y^3}{3xy^4} \cdot \frac{27x^5}{15x^4y}$? C

Ⓐ $\frac{x^2}{3y^2}$ Ⓑ $3x^2y^2$

Ⓒ $\frac{3x^2}{y^2}$ Ⓓ $3x^{12}y^8$

Key Questions to Ask for Example 3

- Is $7x^6y$ a rational expression? **Yes, it can be written with a denominator of 1.**
- What is an alternative to dividing out the common factors x and y^3? **Use the quotient property of exponents.**

Extra Example 4

Multiply: $\frac{20x - 5x^2}{x^2 - x} \cdot \frac{x^2 + 3x - 4}{x^2 - 16}$ −5

Key Question to Ask for Example 4

- What happened to the denominator in the final simplified form in Example 4? **After all the common factors were divided out, the denominator became 1, so it does not need to be written.**

Extra Example 5

Multiply: $\frac{x-4}{x^3+8} \cdot (x^2 - 2x + 4)$

$\frac{x-4}{x+2}$

Key Question to Ask for Example 5

- What special factoring pattern must be used in Example 5? the difference of two cubes: $a^3 - b^3 = (a - b)(a^2 + ab + b^2)$

Extra Example 6

Divide:

$\frac{x^2 - 4x - 21}{5x + 15} \div \frac{x^2 + 3x - 70}{x^2 - 100}$ $\frac{x-10}{5}$

Key Questions to Ask for Example 6

- Why is there no variable in the final expression? All of the factors involving x are common to the numerator and denominator, so they were divided out.
- Does the solution show that the quotient of the two given rational expressions is equal to $\frac{7}{2}$ for *every* possible value of x? Explain. No. The first rational expression is undefined when $x = 5$. The second is undefined when $x = 5$ or $x = 6$, and dividing by the second expression is undefined when $x = 0$ or $x = 6$. The quotient is undefined $\left(\text{and so is not equal to } \frac{7}{2}\right)$ for x-values of 0, 5, or 6.

EXAMPLE 5 Multiply a rational expression by a polynomial

Multiply: $\frac{x+2}{x^3 - 27} \cdot (x^2 + 3x + 9)$

$\frac{x+2}{x^3-27} \cdot (x^2 + 3x + 9) = \frac{x+2}{x^3-27} \cdot \frac{x^2+3x+9}{1}$ — **Write polynomial as a rational expression.**

$= \frac{(x+2)(x^2+3x+9)}{(x-3)(x^2+3x+9)}$ — **Factor denominator.**

$= \frac{(x+2)\cancel{(x^2+3x+9)}}{(x-3)\cancel{(x^2+3x+9)}}$ — **Divide out common factors.**

$= \frac{x+2}{x-3}$ — **Simplified form**

✓ GUIDED PRACTICE for Examples 3, 4, and 5

Multiply the expressions. Simplify the result.

8. $\frac{3x^5y^2}{8xy} \cdot \frac{6xy^2}{9x^3y}$ $\frac{x^2y^2}{4}$

9. $\frac{2x^2 - 10x}{x^2 - 25} \cdot \frac{x+3}{2x^2}$ $\frac{x+3}{x(x+5)}$

10. $\frac{x+5}{x^3 - 1} \cdot (x^2 + x + 1)$ $\frac{x+5}{x-1}$

KEY CONCEPT *For Your Notebook*

Dividing Rational Expressions

To divide one rational expression by another, multiply the first rational expression by the reciprocal of the second rational expression.

Let a, b, c, and d be expressions with $b \neq 0$, $c \neq 0$ and $d \neq 0$.

Property $\frac{a}{b} \div \frac{c}{d} = \frac{a}{b} \cdot \frac{d}{c} = \frac{ad}{bc}$ **Simplify $\frac{ad}{bc}$ if possible.**

Examples $\frac{2}{5} \div \frac{7}{3} = \frac{2}{5} \cdot \frac{3}{7} = \frac{6}{35}$

$\frac{7}{x+1} \div \frac{x+2}{2x-3} = \frac{7}{x+1} \cdot \frac{2x-3}{x+2} = \frac{7(2x-3)}{(x+1)(x+2)}$

EXAMPLE 6 Divide rational expressions

Divide: $\frac{7x}{2x-10} \div \frac{x^2 - 6x}{x^2 - 11x + 30}$

$\frac{7x}{2x-10} \div \frac{x^2-6x}{x^2-11x+30} = \frac{7x}{2x-10} \cdot \frac{x^2-11x+30}{x^2-6x}$ — **Multiply by reciprocal.**

$= \frac{7x}{2(x-5)} \cdot \frac{(x-5)(x-6)}{x(x-6)}$ — **Factor.**

$= \frac{7\cancel{x}\cancel{(x-5)}\cancel{(x-6)}}{2\cancel{(x-5)}\cancel{(x)}\cancel{(x-6)}}$ — **Divide out common factors.**

$= \frac{7}{2}$ — **Simplified form**

Differentiated Instruction

Visual Learners Help students organize their thought process when multiplying and dividing two rational expressions. When multiplying, have students connect the two fraction bars with their pencil as a guide to remind them to multiply across numerators and across denominators. If they try to do the same when the operation is division, they will trace over the division sign, and that should be a reminder to change to multiplication by the reciprocal of the divisor.

See also the *Algebra 2 Toolkit* for more strategies.

EXAMPLE 7 Divide a rational expression by a polynomial

Divide: $\frac{6x^2 + x - 15}{4x^2} \div (3x^2 + 5x)$

$$\frac{6x^2 + x - 15}{4x^2} \div (3x^2 + 5x) = \frac{6x^2 + x - 15}{4x^2} \cdot \frac{1}{3x^2 + 5x}$$ **Multiply by reciprocal.**

$$= \frac{(3x + 5)(2x - 3)}{4x^2} \cdot \frac{1}{x(3x + 5)}$$ **Factor.**

$$= \frac{\cancel{(3x + 5)}(2x - 3)}{4x^2(x)\cancel{(3x + 5)}}$$ **Divide out common factors.**

$$= \frac{2x - 3}{4x^3}$$ **Simplified form**

✓ GUIDED PRACTICE for Examples 6 and 7

Divide the expressions. Simplify the result.

11. $\frac{4x}{5x - 20} \div \frac{x^2 - 2x}{x^2 - 6x + 8}$ $\frac{4}{5}$

12. $\frac{2x^2 + 3x - 5}{6x} \div (2x^2 + 5x)$ $\frac{x - 1}{6x^2}$

8.4 EXERCISES

HOMEWORK KEY
◯ = **WORKED-OUT SOLUTIONS** on p. WS15 for Exs. 7, 25, and 49
★ = **STANDARDIZED TEST PRACTICE** Exs. 2, 20, 23, 50, and 52

SKILL PRACTICE

1. VOCABULARY Copy and complete: To divide one rational expression by another, multiply the first rational expression by the _?_ of the second rational expression. reciprocal

2. ★ WRITING How do you know when a rational expression is simplified? When there are no common factors between the numerator and the denominator.

KAMPLE 1
p. 573
r Exs. 3–20

REASONING **Match the rational expression with its simplified form.**

3. $\frac{x^2 - 9x + 14}{x^2 - 5x - 14}$ B

4. $\frac{x^2 - 4}{x^2 + 9x + 14}$ A

5. $\frac{x^2 + 5x - 14}{x^2 - 4x + 4}$ C

A. $\frac{x - 2}{x + 7}$

B. $\frac{x - 2}{x + 2}$

C. $\frac{x + 7}{x - 2}$

SIMPLIFYING **Simplify the rational expression, if possible.**

implified form

simplified
n

6. $\frac{4x^2}{20x^2 - 12x}$ $\frac{x}{5x - 3}$

(7.) $\frac{x^2 - x - 20}{x^2 + 2x - 15}$

8. $\frac{x^2 + 2x - 24}{x^2 + 7x + 6}$ $\frac{x - 4}{x + 1}$

9. $\frac{x^2 - 11x + 24}{x^2 - 3x - 40}$ $\frac{x - 3}{x + 5}$

10. $\frac{x^2 + 4x + 4}{x^2 - 5x + 4}$

11. $\frac{2x^2 + 2x - 4}{x^2 - 5x - 14}$ $\frac{2(x - 1)}{x - 7}$

12. $\frac{x - 4}{x^3 - 64}$ $\frac{1}{x^2 + 4x + 16}$

13. $\frac{x^2 - 36}{x^2 + 12x + 36}$ $\frac{x - 6}{x + 6}$

14. $\frac{3x^3 + 6x^2 + 12x}{x^3 - 8}$ $\frac{3x}{x - 2}$

15. $\frac{8x^2 + 10x - 3}{6x^2 + 13x + 6}$ $\frac{4x - 1}{3x + 2}$

16. $\frac{5x^2 + 18x - 8}{10x^2 - x - 2}$ simplified form

17. $\frac{x^3 - 5x^2 - 3x + 15}{x^2 - 8x + 15}$ $\frac{x^2 - 3}{x - 3}$

Extra Example 7

Divide: $\frac{3x^2 + 13x - 10}{6x^2} \div (3x^2 - 2x)$ $\frac{x + 5}{6x^3}$

Key Question to Ask for Example 7

- In the first step of the solution, where does the 1 in the numerator come from? To divide by a rational expression, you multiply by the reciprocal of that expression.

Closing the Lesson

Have students summarize the major points of the lesson and answer the Essential Question: What are the steps for multiplying and dividing rational expressions?

- The rules for multiplying and dividing with rational expressions are the same as the rules for those operations with rational numbers.

To multiply rational expressions you multiply the numerators, multiply the denominators, and simplify the resulting fraction. To divide rational expressions, you multiply the first expression by the reciprocal of the second expression.

4 PRACTICE AND APPLY

Assignment Guide

Answer Transparencies available for all exercises

Basic:
Day 1: EP p. 1013 Exs. 21–24
pp. 577–580
Exs. 1–13, 18–22, 48
Day 2: pp. 577–580
Exs. 23–29, 49–51, 54–55

Average:
Day 1: pp. 577–580
Exs. 1–5, 9–13, 18–27, 48
Day 2: pp. 577–580
Exs. 28–41, 49–52, 54

Advanced:
Day 1: pp. 577–580
Exs. 1–5, 10–17, 20–27, 48
Day 2: pp. 577–580
Exs. 30–47*, 49–53*

Block:
pp. 577–580
Exs. 1–5, 9–13, 18–27, 48 (with 8.3)
pp. 577–580
Exs. 28–41, 49–52, 54 (with 8.5)

Differentiated Instruction

See *Algebra 2 Best Practices Toolkit* for suggestions on addressing the needs of a diverse classroom.

Homework Check

For a quick check of student understanding of key concepts, go over the following exercises:

Basic: 8, 12, 21, 24, 48
Average: 10, 22, 26, 34, 50
Advanced: 14, 23, 30, 38, 51

Extra Practice

- Student Edition, p. 1017
- Chapter 8 Resource Book: Practice levels A, B, C, pp. 41–43

Practice Worksheet

An easily-readable reduced practice page (with answers) for this lesson can be found on p. 548D.

ERROR ANALYSIS ***Describe*** **and correct the error in simplifying the rational expression.** 18, 19. See margin.

18. $\frac{\cancel{x^2} + 16x - 80}{\cancel{x^2} - 16} = \frac{16x - 80}{-16} = -x + 5$ ✗

19. $\frac{x^2 + 16x + 48}{x^2 + 8x + 16} = \frac{x^2 + 2x + 3}{x^2 + x + 1}$ ✗ (16x and 48 crossed out to 2 and 3; 8x and 16 crossed out to 1 and 1)

20. ★ **MULTIPLE CHOICE** Which rational expression is in simplified form? B

(A) $\frac{x^2 - x - 6}{x^2 + 3x + 2}$ (B) $\frac{x^2 + 6x + 8}{x^2 + 2x - 3}$ (C) $\frac{x^2 - 6x + 9}{x^2 - 2x - 3}$ (D) $\frac{x^2 + 3x - 4}{x^2 + x - 2}$

EXAMPLE 2 B on p. 574 for Exs. 21–23

GEOMETRY **A farmer wants to fence in the field shown. Write a simplified rational expression for the ratio of the field's perimeter to its area.**

21. 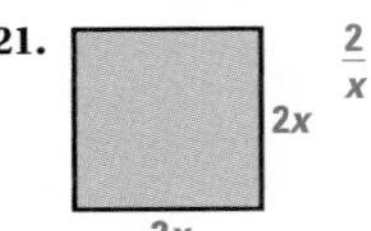

$\frac{2}{x}$

22. 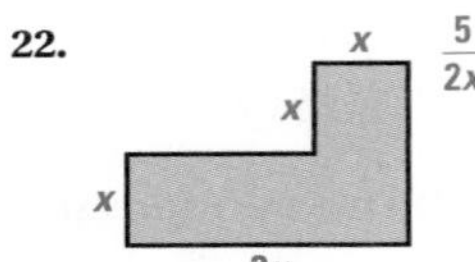

$\frac{5}{2x}$

23. ★ **SHORT RESPONSE** Which of the fields in Exercises 21 and 22 has the lower fencing cost per unit of area? *Explain.* Exercise 21. *Sample answer:* The perimeter of Exercise 21 is smaller and the areas are the same.

EXAMPLES 3, 4, and 5 on pp. 575–576 for Exs. 24–33

MULTIPLYING **Multiply the expressions. Simplify the result.**

24. $\frac{5x^3y}{x^2y^2} \cdot \frac{y^3}{15x^2}$ $\frac{y^2}{3x}$

25. $\frac{48x^5y^3}{y^4} \cdot \frac{x^2y}{6x^3y^2}$ $\frac{8x^4}{y^2}$

26. $\frac{x(x-3)}{x-2} \cdot \frac{(x+3)(x-2)}{x}$ $x^2 - 9$

27. $\frac{4(x+5)}{x^2} \cdot \frac{x(x+1)}{2(x+5)}$ $\frac{2(x+1)}{x}$

28. $\frac{3x-12}{x+5} \cdot \frac{x+6}{2x-8}$ $\frac{3(x+6)}{2(x+5)}$

29. $\frac{x+5}{4x-16} \cdot \frac{2x^2-32}{x^2-25}$ $\frac{x+4}{2(x-5)}$

30. $\frac{x^2+3x-4}{x^2+4x+4} \cdot \frac{2x^2+4x}{x^2-4x+3}$ $\frac{2x(x+4)}{(x+2)(x-3)}$

31. $\frac{x^2-3x-10}{x^2-2x-15} \cdot (x^2+10x+21)$ $(x+2)(x+$

32. $\frac{x^2+5x-36}{x^2-49} \cdot (x^2-11x+28)$ $\frac{(x+9)(x-4)^2}{x+7}$

33. $\frac{4x^2+20x}{x^3+4x^2} \cdot (x^2+8x+16)$ $\frac{4(x+5)(x+4)}{x}$

EXAMPLES C 6 and 7 on pp. 576–577 for Exs. 34–43

DIVIDING **Divide the expressions. Simplify the result.**

34. $\frac{5x^2y^3}{x^7} \div \frac{30xy^4}{y^3}$ $\frac{y^2}{6x^6}$

35. $\frac{8x^2y^2z}{xz^3} \div \frac{10xy}{x^4z}$ $\frac{4x^4y}{5z}$

36. $\frac{(x+3)(x-2)}{x(x+1)} \div \frac{x+3}{x}$ $\frac{x-2}{x+1}$

37. $\frac{8x^2}{x+4} \div \frac{x}{2(x-4)}$ $\frac{16x(x-4)}{(x+4)}$

38. $\frac{x^2-6x-27}{2x^2+2x} \div \frac{x^2-14x+45}{x^2}$ $\frac{x(x+3)}{2(x-5)(x+1)}$

39. $\frac{x^2-4x-5}{x+5} \div (x^2+6x+5)$ $\frac{x-5}{(x+5)^2}$

40. $\frac{3x^2+13x+4}{x^2-4} \div \frac{4x+16}{x+2}$ $\frac{3x+1}{4(x-2)}$

41. $\frac{x^2-x-2}{x^2+4x-5} \div \frac{x-2}{5x+25}$ $\frac{5(x+1)}{x-1}$

42. $\frac{x^2-8x+15}{x^2+4x} \div (x^2-x-20)$ $\frac{x-3}{x(x+4)^2}$

43. $\frac{x^2+12x+32}{6x+42} \div \frac{x^2+4x}{x^2-49}$ $\frac{(x+8)(x-7)}{6x}$

○ = WORKED-OUT SOLUTIONS on p. WS1 ★ = STANDARDIZED TEST PRACTICE

---

18. *Sample answer:* You can only divide out common factors. The x^2-terms are attached by addition so you cannot divide them out; $\frac{x^2 + 16x - 80}{x^2 - 16} = \frac{(x-4)(x+20)}{(x-4)(x+4)} = \frac{x+20}{x+4}$.

19. *Sample answer:* You can only divide out common factors. Since the factors that are divided out are not common factors of the entire numerator and denominator, you cannot divide them out; $\frac{x^2 + 16x + 48}{x^2 + 8x + 16} = \frac{(x+4)(x+12)}{(x+4)(x+4)} = \frac{x+12}{x+4}$.

POINT DISCONTINUITY **In Exercises 44–46, use the following information.**

The graph of a rational function can have a hole in it, called a *point discontinuity*, where the function is undefined. An example is shown below.

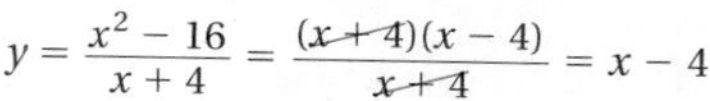

$$y = \frac{x^2 - 16}{x + 4} = \frac{(x+4)(x-4)}{x+4} = x - 4$$

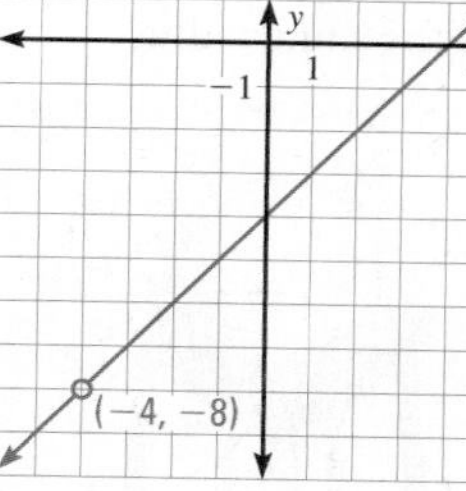

The graph of $y = \frac{x^2 - 16}{x + 4}$ is the same as the graph of $y = x - 4$ except that there is a hole at $(-4, -8)$ because the rational function is not defined when $x = -4$.

Graph the rational function. Use an open circle for a point discontinuity. **44–46. See margin.**

44. $y = \frac{x^2 + 10x + 21}{x + 3}$ **45.** $y = \frac{x^2 - 36}{x - 6}$ **46.** $y = \frac{2x^2 - x - 10}{x + 2}$

47. **CHALLENGE** Find the ratio of the perimeter to the area of the triangle shown at the right. $\frac{4}{7x}$

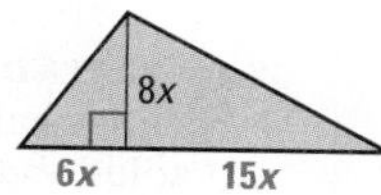

PROBLEM SOLVING

EXAMPLE 2 A on p. 574 for Exs. 48, 50–52

48. **GEOMETRY** Find the ratio of the volume of the square pyramid to the volume of the inscribed cone. Write your answer in simplified form. $\frac{4}{\pi}$

@HomeTutor for problem solving help at classzone.com

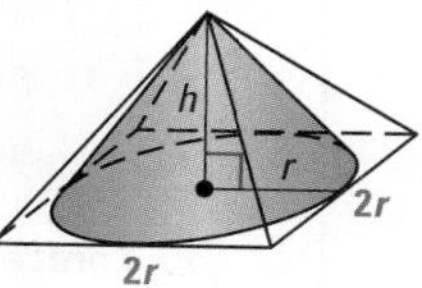

(49.) **ENTERTAINMENT** From 1992 to 2002, the gross ticket sales S (in millions of dollars) to Broadway shows and the total attendance A (in millions) at the shows can be modeled by

$$S = \frac{-6420t + 292{,}000}{6.02t^2 - 125t + 1000} \quad \text{and} \quad A = \frac{-407t + 7220}{5.92t^2 - 131t + 1000}$$

where t is the number of years since 1992. Write a model for the *average* dollar amount a person paid per ticket as a function of the year. What was the average amount a person paid per ticket in 1999? **See margin.**

@HomeTutor for problem solving help at classzone.com

50. ★ **SHORT RESPONSE** Almost all of the energy generated by a long-distance runner is released in the form of heat. For a runner with height H and speed V, the rate h_g of heat generated and the rate h_r of heat released can be modeled by $h_g = k_1H^3V^2$ and $h_r = k_2H^2$ where k_1 and k_2 are constants.

a. Write the ratio of heat generated to heat released. Simplify the expression.

b. When the ratio of heat generated to heat released equals 1, how is speed related to height? Does a taller or shorter runner have the advantage? *Explain.*

Thermogram of runner

a. $\frac{k_1H^3V^2}{k_2H^2} = \frac{HV^2}{k_2}$ b. $V^2 = \frac{k_2}{k_1H}$; e shorter nner has the vantage. mple answer: e larger e height e smaller e fraction presenting locity.

49. $\frac{S}{A} = \frac{(-6420t + 292{,}000)(5.92t^2 - 131t + 1000)}{(6.02t^2 - 125t + 1000)(-407t + 7220)}$; $50.21

Avoiding Common Errors

Exercises 12, 14 Many students have trouble remembering how to factor a difference of two cubes. Have students write the correct pattern in their notebooks for factoring both the difference of two cubes and the sum of two cubes.

44.

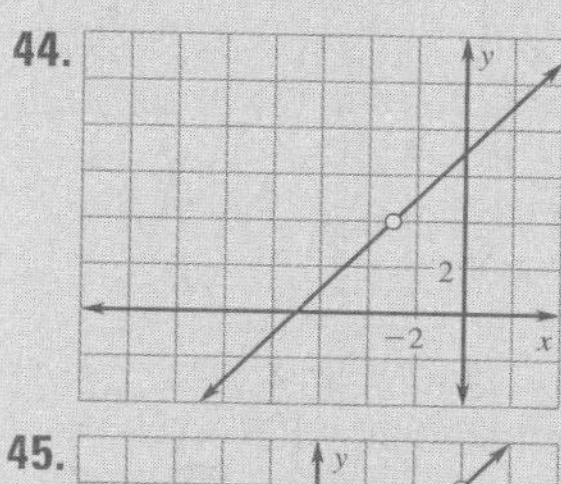

45.

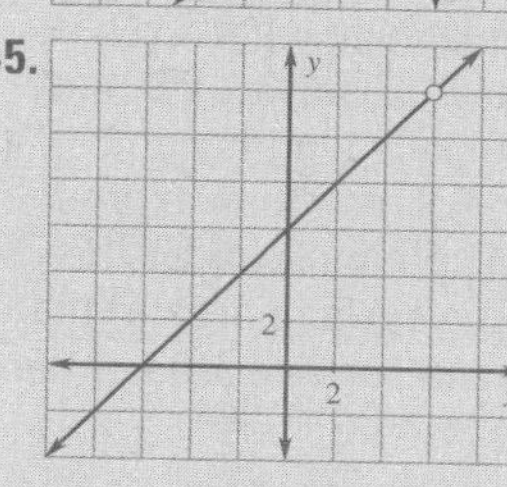

46.

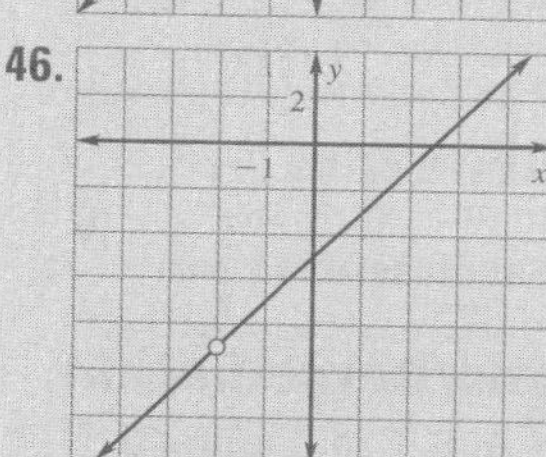

5 ASSESS AND RETEACH

Daily Homework Quiz

Transparency Available

Perform the operation.

1. $\frac{x^2 + 15x + 36}{x^2 - 144}$ $\frac{x + 3}{x - 12}$

2. $\frac{5x}{x^2 - 6x + 9} \cdot \frac{x^2 + 4x - 21}{x^2 + 7x}$ $\frac{5}{x - 3}$

3. $\frac{x^3 - 1}{2x^2 + x - 3} \div (x^2 + x + 1)$ $\frac{1}{2x + 3}$

4. A cube has edge length x. A rectangular prism has a square base with side length x and height $x + 2$. Write an expression in simplified form for the ratio of the surface area of the prism to the surface area of the cube. $\frac{3x + 4}{3x}$

Online Quiz

Available at **classzone.com**

Diagnosis/Remediation

- Practice A, B, C in Chapter 8 Resource Book, pp. 41–43
- Study Guide in Chapter 8 Resource Book, pp. 44–45
- Practice Workbook, pp. 128–129
- @HomeTutor

Challenge

Additional challenge is available in the Chapter 8 Resource Book, p. 48.

51a. $V_{sphere} = \frac{4}{3}\pi r^3$, $V_{cylinder} = \pi r^2 h$, since the volumes are the same, set the equations equal to each other resulting in $h = \frac{4}{3}r$.

51b. $SA_{sphere} = 4\pi r^2$, $SA_{cylinder} = \frac{14}{3}\pi r^2$

51c. $\frac{6}{7}$. *Sample answer:* The spherical tank uses less material.

B

51. MULTI-STEP PROBLEM A manufacturer is comparing two designs for a water tower: a sphere and a cylinder. Both designs have the same volume and the same radius.

a. Show that the height h of the cylindrical tank is $\frac{4}{3}r$.

b. Write an expression for the surface area of each tank in terms of r.

c. Find the ratio of the surface area of the spherical tank to the surface area of the cylindrical tank. *Explain* what the ratio tells you about which water tower would take less material to build.

52. ★ EXTENDED RESPONSE The surface area S and the volume V of a cylindrical can are given by $S = 2\pi r^2 + 2\pi rh$ and $V = \pi r^2 h$ where r is the radius and h is the height.

a. **Model** Write and simplify an expression for the efficiency ratio $\frac{S}{V}$. $\frac{2(r + h)}{rh}$

b. **Calculate** Find the efficiency ratio for each can listed in the table. **soup can: about 0.784, coffee can: about 0.382, paint can: about 0.341**

	Soup can	Coffee can	Paint can
Height, h	10.2 cm	15.9 cm	19.4 cm
Radius, r	3.4 cm	7.8 cm	8.4 cm

c. **Compare** Rank the three cans in part (b) according to efficiency. *Explain* your ranking. **Soup can, coffee can, paint can. *Sample answer:* The closer the efficiency is to 1, the more efficient the space is being used.**

C

53. CHALLENGE A fuel storage container is shaped like a cylinder with a hemisphere on each end, as shown. The length of the cylinder is ℓ and the radius of each hemisphere is r. Show that the ratio of the surface area to the volume of the container is $\frac{6(2r + \ell)}{r(4r + 3\ell)}$.

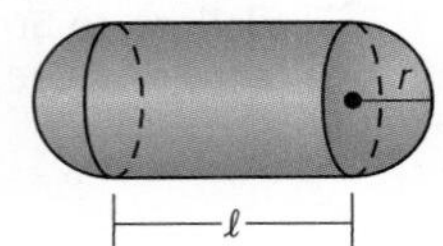

$$\frac{SA}{V} = \frac{2\pi r\ell + 4\pi r^2}{\frac{4}{3}\pi r^3 + \pi r^2 \ell} = \frac{2\pi r(2r + \ell)}{\pi r^2\left(\frac{4}{3}r + \ell\right)} = \frac{2(2r + \ell)}{r\left(\frac{4}{3}r + \ell\right)} = \left(\frac{3}{3}\right) \cdot \frac{2(2r + \ell)}{r\left(\frac{4}{3}r + \ell\right)} = \frac{6(2r + \ell)}{r(4r + 3\ell)}$$

KENTUCKY MIXED REVIEW

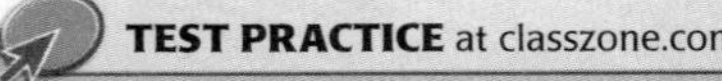

TEST PRACTICE at classzone.com

54. Which expression is equivalent to $3y[4 - (y + 2)] + 5y(y - 3)$? **A**

Ⓐ $2y^2 - 9y$ Ⓑ $2y^2 - 3y$ Ⓒ $2y - 9$ Ⓓ $2y^2 - 6y + 15$

55. Each year about 6800 freshmen attend the University of Texas. This is about 16% of the total enrollment. About how many students attend the University of Texas? **C**

Ⓐ 17,700 Ⓑ 41,300 Ⓒ 42,500 Ⓓ 46,000

EXTRA PRACTICE for Lesson 8.4, p. 1017

ONLINE QUIZ at classzone.com

@HomeTutor classzone.com Keystrokes

8.4 Verify Operations with Rational Expressions

QUESTION How can you use a graphing calculator to verify the results of operations on rational expressions?

EXAMPLE Check a simplified rational expression in two ways

Simplify $\frac{x^2 - x - 12}{x^2 - 9x + 20}$. Then verify the result numerically and graphically.

STEP 1 ***Simplify expression***

Simplify the rational expression by factoring the numerator and denominator, then dividing out common factors.

$$\frac{x^2 - x - 12}{x^2 - 9x + 20} = \frac{\cancel{(x-4)}(x+3)}{\cancel{(x-4)}(x-5)} = \frac{x+3}{x-5}$$

STEP 2 ***Enter expressions***

Enter the original expression as y_1 and the simplified result as y_2. Use the *thick* graph style for y_2.

```
\Y1■(X²-X-12)/
  (X²-9X+20)
\Y2■(X+3)/(X-5)
\Y3=
\Y4=
\Y5=
\Y6=
```

Remember to use parentheses correctly.

STEP 3 ***Display table***

Use the *table* feature to examine corresponding values of the two expressions.

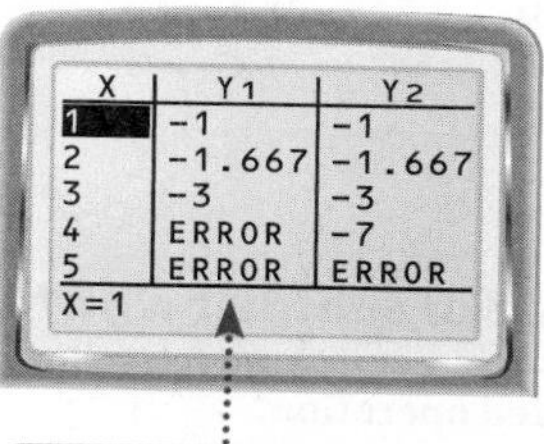

X	Y1	Y2
1	-1	-1
2	-1.667	-1.667
3	-3	-3
4	ERROR	-7
5	ERROR	ERROR

X=1

The values of y_1 and y_2 are the same, except that y_1 is undefined when $x = 4$ and $x = 5$, and y_2 is undefined only when $x = 5$.

STEP 4 ***Display graphs***

Put your calculator in *connected* mode. Display the graphs in an appropriate viewing window.

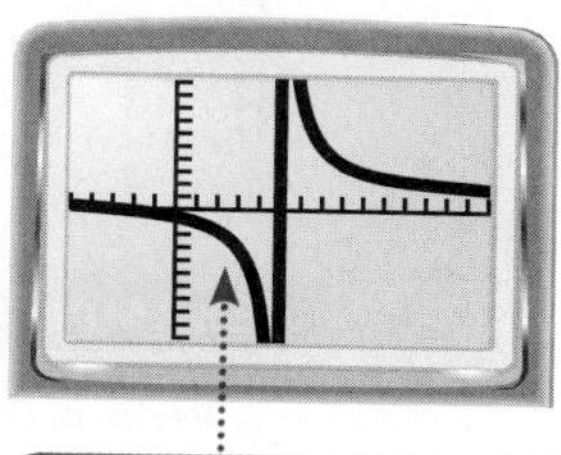

By using the *thick* graph style for y_2, you can see the graph of y_2 being drawn over the graph of y_1. So, the graphs coincide.

PRACTICE

Simplify the expression. Verify your result numerically and graphically.

1. $\frac{x^2 - 5x}{x^2 - 7x + 10}$ $\frac{x}{x-2}$
2. $\frac{3x^2 + 6x}{x^2 - 2x - 8}$ $\frac{3x}{x-4}$
3. $\frac{x^2 + 5x + 4}{x^2 + x - 12}$ $\frac{x+1}{x-3}$

Perform the indicated operation and simplify. Verify your result numerically and graphically.

4. $\frac{x+3}{5x^2} \cdot \frac{x-1}{x+3}$ $\frac{x-1}{5x^2}$
5. $\frac{4x^2 - 8x}{5x + 15} \div \frac{x-2}{x+3}$ $\frac{4x}{5}$
6. $\frac{x^2 - 3x - 10}{x^2 + 3x + 3} \cdot \frac{x^2 + 2x - 3}{x^2 + x - 2}$ $\frac{(x-5)(x+3)}{x^2 + 3x + 3}$

1 PLAN AND PREPARE

Learn the Method

- Students learn how to use the table and graph feature of a graphing calculator to verify the results of operations on rational expressions.
- Students can use a graphing calculator to check their answers to the exercises in Lesson 8.4.

Keystroke Help

Keystrokes for several models of calculators are available in blackline format in the *Chapter 8 Resource Book*.

2 TEACH

Extra Example

Simplify $\frac{x^2 + 2x - 3}{x^2 - 9}$. Verify the result numerically and algebraically. $\frac{x-1}{x-3}$

X	Y1	Y2
-3	ERROR	.66667
-2	.6	.6
-1	.5	.5
0	-.33333	.33333
1	0	0
2	-1	-1
3	ERROR	ERROR

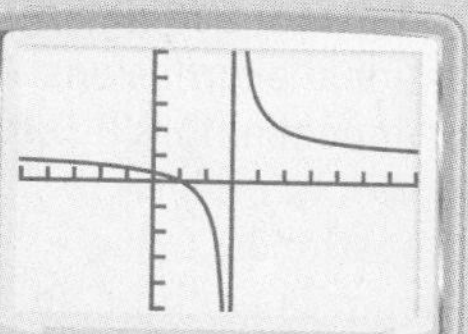

3 ASSESS AND RETEACH

For $x = 4$, why do you see ERROR in your table under Y1 but not under Y2? **$x = 4$ results in a 0 denominator for Y1, the original expression, but not for Y2, the reduced expression.**

8.5 Add and Subtract Rational Expressions

MA-HS-5.2.5

Before	You multiplied and divided rational expressions.
Now	You will add and subtract rational expressions.
Why?	So you can determine monthly car loan payments, as in Ex. 43.

1 PLAN AND PREPARE

Warm-Up Exercises

Transparency Available

1. Add $\frac{7}{20} + \frac{9}{20}$. $\frac{4}{5}$
2. Find the least common multiple of 20 and 45. 180
3. Add $\frac{5}{18} + \frac{31}{72}$. $\frac{17}{24}$
4. Simplify $\dfrac{\frac{1}{2} - \frac{2}{5}}{\frac{1}{3} + \frac{3}{4}}$. $\frac{6}{65}$

Notetaking Guide

Transparency Available

Promotes interactive learning and notetaking skills, pp. 224–227.

Pacing

Basic: 1 day

Average: 1 day

Advanced: 1 day

Block: 0.5 block with 8.4

- See *Teaching Guide/Lesson Plan.*

2 FOCUS AND MOTIVATE

Essential Question

Big Idea 2, p. 549

What are the steps for adding or subtracting rational expressions with different denominators? **Tell students they will learn how to answer this question by using operations similar to addition and subtraction of rational numbers.**

Key Vocabulary
- complex fraction

MA-HS-5.2.5

Students will add, subtract, multiply and divide simple rational expressions with monomial first-degree denominators and integer numerators (e.g., $\frac{3}{5x} + \frac{4}{3y}$; $\frac{9}{2a} - \frac{-7}{4b}$; $\frac{3}{-5x} \times \frac{-4}{7y}$; $\frac{5}{2c} \div \frac{9}{-11d}$), and will express the results in simplified form. DOK 1

As with numerical fractions, the procedure used to add (or subtract) two rational expressions depends upon whether the expressions have *like* or *unlike* denominators.

KEY CONCEPT — *For Your Notebook*

Adding or Subtracting with Like Denominators

To add (or subtract) rational expressions with *like* denominators, simply add (or subtract) their numerators. Then place the result over the common denominator.

Let a, b, and c be expressions with $c \neq 0$.

	Addition	Subtraction
Properties	$\frac{a}{c} + \frac{b}{c} = \frac{a+b}{c}$	$\frac{a}{c} - \frac{b}{c} = \frac{a-b}{c}$
Examples	$\frac{3x}{5x^2} + \frac{7}{5x^2} = \frac{3x+7}{5x^2}$	$\frac{9x^3}{x+1} - \frac{x^2}{x+1} = \frac{9x^3 - x^2}{x+1}$

EXAMPLE 1 Add or subtract with like denominators

Perform the indicated operation.

a. $\frac{7}{4x} + \frac{3}{4x}$

b. $\frac{2x}{x+6} - \frac{5}{x+6}$

Solution

a. $\frac{7}{4x} + \frac{3}{4x} = \frac{7+3}{4x} = \frac{10}{4x} = \frac{5}{2x}$ **Add numerators and simplify result.**

b. $\frac{2x}{x+6} - \frac{5}{x+6} = \frac{2x-5}{x+6}$ **Subtract numerators.**

GUIDED PRACTICE for Example 1

Perform the indicated operation and simplify.

1. $\frac{7}{12x} - \frac{5}{12x}$ $\frac{1}{6x}$

2. $\frac{2}{3x^2} + \frac{1}{3x^2}$ $\frac{1}{x^2}$

3. $\frac{4x}{x-2} - \frac{x}{x-2}$ $\frac{3x}{x-2}$

4. $\frac{2x^2}{x^2+1} + \frac{2}{x^2+1}$ 2

Resource Planning Guide

Chapter Resource Book
- Teaching Guide/Lesson Plan (pp. 49–50)
- Practice levels A, B, C (pp. 51–53)
- Study Guide (pp. 54–55)
- Catch-up for Absent Students (p. 56)
- Problem Solving Workshop (p. 57)
- Challenge (p. 58)

Workbooks
- Notetaking Guide (pp. 224–227)
- Practice Workbook (pp. 130–131)

Teaching Options
- **Power Presentations CD-ROM** provides dynamic electronic teaching resources for the classroom.
- **Activity Generator CD-ROM** provides editable activities for all ability levels.

Interactive Technology
- Easy Planner
- Power Presentations CD-ROM
- Activity Generator CD-ROM
- Animated Algebra
- Test Generator CD-ROM
- Online Quiz
- eWorkbook
- eEdition
- @HomeTutor

Resources for English Learners
- Quick Reference for English Learners
- Spanish Study Guide
- Multi-Language Visual Glossary
- Student Resources in Spanish

See also the *Algebra 2 Toolkit* for more strategies for meeting individual needs.

KEY CONCEPT *For Your Notebook*

Adding or Subtracting with Unlike Denominators

To add (or subtract) two rational expressions with *unlike* denominators, find a common denominator. Rewrite each rational expression using the common denominator. Then add (or subtract).

Let a, b, c, and d be expressions with $c \neq 0$ and $d \neq 0$.

Addition

$$\frac{a}{c} + \frac{b}{d} = \frac{ad}{cd} + \frac{bc}{cd} = \frac{ad + bc}{cd}$$

Subtraction

$$\frac{a}{c} - \frac{b}{d} = \frac{ad}{cd} - \frac{bc}{cd} = \frac{ad - bc}{cd}$$

You can always find a common denominator of two rational expressions by multiplying their denominators, as shown above. However, if you use the least common denominator (LCD), which is the least common multiple (LCM) of the denominators, you may have less simplifying to do.

EXAMPLE 2 Find a least common multiple (LCM)

Find the least common multiple of $4x^2 - 16$ and $6x^2 - 24x + 24$.

Solution

STEP 1 **Factor** each polynomial. Write numerical factors as products of primes.

$$4x^2 - 16 = 4(x^2 - 4) = (2^2)(x + 2)(x - 2)$$

$$6x^2 - 24x + 24 = 6(x^2 - 4x + 4) = (2)(3)(x - 2)^2$$

STEP 2 **Form** the LCM by writing each factor to the highest power it occurs in either polynomial.

$$\text{LCM} = (2^2)(3)(x + 2)(x - 2)^2 = 12(x + 2)(x - 2)^2$$

EXAMPLE 3 Add with unlike denominators

Add: $\frac{7}{9x^2} + \frac{x}{3x^2 + 3x}$

Solution

To find the LCD, factor each denominator and write each factor to the highest power it occurs. Note that $9x^2 = 3^2x^2$ and $3x^2 + 3x = 3x(x + 1)$, so the LCD is $3^2x^2(x + 1) = 9x^2(x + 1)$.

$$\frac{7}{9x^2} + \frac{x}{3x^2 + 3x} = \frac{7}{9x^2} + \frac{x}{3x(x + 1)}$$ **Factor second denominator.**

$$= \frac{7}{9x^2} \cdot \frac{x + 1}{x + 1} + \frac{x}{3x(x + 1)} \cdot \frac{3x}{3x}$$ **LCD is $9x^2(x + 1)$.**

$$= \frac{7x + 7}{9x^2(x + 1)} + \frac{3x^2}{9x^2(x + 1)}$$ **Multiply.**

$$= \frac{3x^2 + 7x + 7}{9x^2(x + 1)}$$ **Add numerators.**

REVIEW LCDS
For help with finding least common denominators, see p. 986.

Motivating the Lesson

If you ride your bike at two different speeds on two parts of a trip, then your total distance divided by your total time can be represented by a complex fraction.

3 TEACH

Extra Example 1

Perform the indicated operation.

a. $\frac{12}{5x} - \frac{2}{5x}$ $\frac{2}{x}$

b. $\frac{3x}{2x + 5} + \frac{1}{2x + 5}$ $\frac{3x + 1}{2x + 5}$

Extra Example 2

Find the least common multiple of $5x^2 - 45$ and $4x^2 + 24x + 36$. $20(x + 3)^2(x - 3)$

Key Questions to Ask for Example 2

- What is the first step in factoring each of the given polynomials? **Factor out the greatest common factor.**
- What special factoring patterns are used in factoring the two given polynomials? **difference of two squares: $a^2 - b^2 = (a + b)(a - b)$; perfect square trinomial: $a^2 - 2ab + b^2 = (a - b)^2$**

Extra Example 3

Add: $\frac{3}{10x^2} + \frac{2x}{5x^2 - 10x}$ $\frac{4x^2 + 3x - 6}{10x^2(x - 2)}$

Key Question to Ask for Example 3

- Why is the first rational expression multiplied by $\frac{x + 1}{x + 1}$ while the second expression is multiplied by $\frac{3x}{3x}$? **By comparing each of the original denominators to the LCD, you can see that the first one is missing the factor $(x + 1)$ and the second is missing the factor $3x$.**

Differentiated Instruction

English Learners Before introducing *unlike* denominators, have students come up with a list of paired items that are unlike. Have students discuss in small groups the difference between "like" and "unlike." Then give them a list of fractions, and have them practice writing pairs of fractions that have like denominators and pairs of fractions that have unlike denominators, all from the given list.

See also the *Algebra 2 Toolkit* for more strategies.

Extra Example 4

Subtract: $\frac{x}{3x-15} - \frac{2x+2}{x^2-4x-5}$

$\frac{x-6}{3(x-5)}$

Avoiding Common Errors

Example 4 Many students make sign errors in subtraction problems like this one, where the rational expression being subtracted contains one or more negative signs. Have students write parentheses around the numerator being subtracted, to help emphasize the need to subtract each term inside the parentheses.

EXAMPLE 4 Subtract with unlike denominators

Subtract: $\frac{x+2}{2x-2} - \frac{-2x-1}{x^2-4x+3}$

Solution

$\frac{x+2}{2x-2} - \frac{-2x-1}{x^2-4x+3}$

$= \frac{x+2}{2(x-1)} - \frac{-2x-1}{(x-1)(x-3)}$ Factor denominators.

$= \frac{x+2}{2(x-1)} \cdot \frac{x-3}{x-3} - \frac{-2x-1}{(x-1)(x-3)} \cdot \frac{2}{2}$ LCD is $2(x-1)(x-3)$.

$= \frac{x^2-x-6}{2(x-1)(x-3)} - \frac{-4x-2}{2(x-1)(x-3)}$ Multiply.

$= \frac{x^2-x-6-(-4x-2)}{2(x-1)(x-3)}$ Subtract numerators.

$= \frac{x^2+3x-4}{2(x-1)(x-3)}$ Simplify numerator.

$= \frac{\cancel{(x-1)}(x+4)}{2\cancel{(x-1)}(x-3)}$ Factor numerator. Divide out common factor.

$= \frac{x+4}{2(x-3)}$ Simplify.

AVOID ERRORS
After you simplify the numerator, check to see if the numerator has a factor in common with the denominator. If so, the expression can be simplified further.

✓ GUIDED PRACTICE for Examples 2, 3, and 4

Find the least common multiple of the polynomials.

5. $5x^3$ and $10x^2 - 15x$ $5x^3(2x-3)$

6. $8x - 16$ and $12x^2 + 12x - 72$ $24(x-2)(x+3)$

Perform the indicated operation and simplify.

7. $\frac{3}{4x} - \frac{1}{7}$ $\frac{21-4x}{28x}$

8. $\frac{1}{3x^2} + \frac{x}{9x^2-12x}$ $\frac{x^2+3x-4}{3x^2(3x-4)}$

9. $\frac{x}{x^2-x-12} + \frac{5}{12x-48}$ $\frac{17x+15}{12(x-4)(x+3)}$

10. $\frac{x+1}{x^2+4x+4} - \frac{6}{x^2-4}$ $\frac{x^2-7x-14}{(x-2)(x+2)^2}$

KEY CONCEPT *For Your Notebook*

Simplifying Complex Fractions

A **complex fraction** is a fraction that contains a fraction in its numerator or denominator. A complex fraction can be simplified using either of the methods below.

Method 1: If necessary, simplify the numerator and denominator by writing each as a single fraction. Then divide the numerator by the denominator.

Method 2: Multiply the numerator and the denominator by the least common denominator (LCD) of *every* fraction in the numerator and denominator. Then simplify.

Differentiated Instruction

Advanced Pair advanced students with classmates who are struggling with adding and subtracting rational expressions with unlike denominators. Encourage the advanced students to start by trying to diagnose which part of the process is causing the most trouble and to focus on helping with the appropriate skills. By explaining the process, advanced students will develop a deeper understanding of the concepts and struggling students will benefit from peer instruction.

See also the *Algebra 2 Toolkit* for more strategies.

EXAMPLE 5 Simplify a complex fraction (Method 1)

PHYSICS Let f be the focal length of a thin camera lens, p be the distance between an object being photographed and the lens, and q be the distance between the lens and the film. For the photograph to be in focus, the variables should satisfy the *lens equation* below. Simplify the complex fraction.

$$\textbf{Lens equation: } f = \frac{1}{\frac{1}{p} + \frac{1}{q}}$$

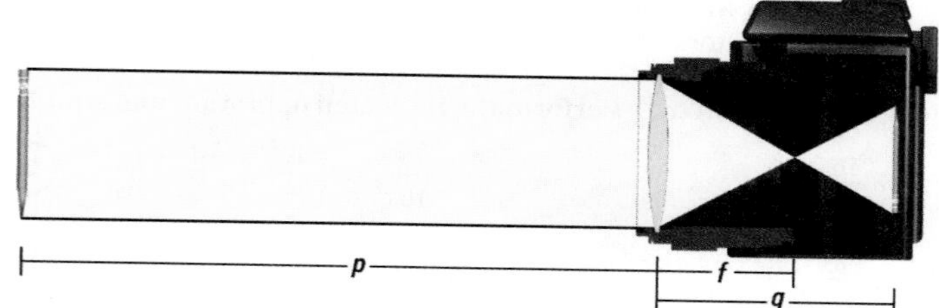

Solution

$$f = \frac{1}{\frac{1}{p} + \frac{1}{q}} = \frac{1}{\frac{q}{pq} + \frac{p}{pq}} = \frac{1}{\frac{q + p}{pq}}$$ **Write denominator as a single fraction.**

$$= \frac{pq}{q + p}$$ **Divide numerator by denominator.**

EXAMPLE 6 Simplify a complex fraction (Method 2)

Simplify: $\dfrac{\frac{5}{x+4}}{\frac{1}{x+4} + \frac{2}{x}}$

Solution

The LCD of all the fractions in the numerator and denominator is $x(x + 4)$.

$$\frac{\frac{5}{x+4}}{\frac{1}{x+4} + \frac{2}{x}} = \frac{\frac{5}{x+4}}{\frac{1}{x+4} + \frac{2}{x}} \cdot \frac{x(x+4)}{x(x+4)}$$ **Multiply numerator and denominator by the LCD.**

$$= \frac{5x}{x + 2(x + 4)}$$ **Simplify.**

$$= \frac{5x}{3x + 8}$$ **Simplify.**

GUIDED PRACTICE for Examples 5 and 6

Simplify the complex fraction.

11. $\dfrac{\frac{x}{6} - \frac{x}{3}}{\frac{x}{5} - \frac{7}{10}}$ $\dfrac{-5x}{3(2x-7)}$

12. $\dfrac{\frac{2}{x} - 4}{\frac{2}{x} + 3}$ $\dfrac{2(1-2x)}{2+3x}$

13. $\dfrac{\frac{3}{x+5}}{\frac{2}{x-3} + \frac{1}{x+5}}$ $\dfrac{3(x-3)}{3x+7}$

Extra Example 5

A college student drives home for a weekend. The distance between her home and her dormitory is d miles, her average speed coming home is r_1, and her average speed driving back to college is r_2. So her average driving trip for the round trip is given by the complex fraction $\dfrac{2d}{\frac{d}{r_1} + \frac{d}{r_2}}$. Simplify the complex fraction. $\dfrac{2r_1r_2}{r_1 + r_2}$

Extra Example 6

Simplify: $\dfrac{\frac{6}{x-5} + \frac{1}{x}}{\frac{3}{x} - \frac{2}{x-5}}$ $\dfrac{7x-5}{x-15}$

Closing the Lesson

Have students summarize the major points of the lesson and answer the Essential Question: What are the steps for adding or subtracting rational expressions with different denominators?

- **The rules for adding and subtracting rational expressions are the same as the rules for these operations with rational numbers.**
- **Complex fractions can be simplified by two methods: simplifying numerator and denominator and then dividing the denominator by the numerator; or multiplying the numerator and denominator by the least common denominator of all fractions, and then simplifying the result.**

To add or subtract rational expressions, find the least common denominator, rewrite each fraction with the common denominator, add or subtract, and simplify the result if necessary.

4 PRACTICE AND APPLY

Assignment Guide

Answer Transparencies available for all exercises

Basic:
Day 1: SRH p. 986 Exs. 23–26
pp. 586–588
Exs. 1–5, 9–11, 15–19, 25–29, 31, 32, 41–43, 46

Average:
Day 1: pp. 586–588
Exs. 1, 2, 4–6, 11–13, 15, 19–21, 25, 26, 27–37 odd, 41–44, 47

Advanced:
Day 1: pp. 586–588
Exs. 1, 2, 7, 8, 13–15, 22–26, 29–45*

Block:
pp. 586–588
Exs. 1, 2, 4–6, 11–13, 15, 19–21, 25, 26, 27–37 odd, 41–44, 47 (with 8.4)

Differentiated Instruction

See *Algebra 2 Best Practices Toolkit* for suggestions on addressing the needs of a diverse classroom.

Homework Check

For a quick check of student understanding of key concepts, go over the following exercises:

Basic: 4, 10, 18, 41, 42
Average: 6, 12, 20, 31, 42
Advanced: 8, 14, 24, 34, 43

Extra Practice

- Student Edition, p. 1017
- Chapter 8 Resource Book: Practice levels A, B, C, pp. 51–53

Practice Worksheet

An easily-readable reduced practice page (with answers) for this lesson can be found on p. 548D.

8.5 EXERCISES

HOMEWORK KEY
○ = **WORKED-OUT SOLUTIONS** on p. WS15 for Exs. 5, 17, and 43
★ = **STANDARDIZED TEST PRACTICE** Exs. 2, 15, 26, 37, and 44

SKILL PRACTICE

A

1. **VOCABULARY** Copy and complete: A fraction that contains a fraction in its numerator or denominator is called a(n) __?__. complex fraction

2. ★ **WRITING** *Explain* how to add rational expressions with unlike denominators. See margin.

EXAMPLE 1 on p. 582 for Exs. 3–8

LIKE DENOMINATORS **Perform the indicated operation and simplify.**

3. $\frac{15}{4x} + \frac{5}{4x}$ $\frac{5}{x}$

4. $\frac{x}{16x^2} - \frac{4}{16x^2}$ $\frac{x-4}{16x^2}$

5. $\frac{9}{x+1} - \frac{2x}{x+1}$ $\frac{9-2x}{x+1}$

6. $\frac{3x^2}{x-8} + \frac{6x}{x-8}$ $\frac{3x(x+2)}{x-8}$

7. $\frac{5x}{x+3} + \frac{15}{x+3}$ 5

8. $\frac{4x^2}{2x-1} - \frac{1}{2x-1}$ $2x+1$

EXAMPLE 2 on p. 583 for Exs. 9–15

FINDING LCMS **Find the least common multiple of the polynomials.**

9. $3x$ and $3(x-2)$ $3x(x-2)$

10. $2x^2$ and $4x+12$ $4x^2(x+3)$

11. $2x$ and $2x(x-5)$ $2x(x-5)$

12. $24x^2$ and $8x^2-16x$ $24x^2(x-2)$

13. x^2-25, x, and $x-5$ $x(x-5)(x+5)$

14. $9x^2-16$ and $3x^2-2x-8$ $(x-2)(3x+4)(3x-4)$

15. ★ **MULTIPLE CHOICE** What is the least common multiple of the polynomials $3x^2-9x$ and $6x^2$? D

Ⓐ $3x(x-3)$ Ⓑ $6x^2$ Ⓒ $6x(x-3)$ Ⓓ $6x^2(x-3)$

EXAMPLES 3 and 4 on pp. 583–584 for Exs. 16–26

UNLIKE DENOMINATORS **Perform the indicated operation and simplify.**

16. $\frac{12}{5x} + \frac{7}{6x}$ $\frac{107}{30x}$

17. $\frac{8}{3x^2} - \frac{5}{4x}$ $\frac{32-15x}{12x^2}$

18. $\frac{x-4}{5x} - \frac{12}{5(x-4)}$ $\frac{x^2-20x+16}{5x(x-4)}$

19. $\frac{12}{x^2+5x-24} + \frac{3}{x-3}$

20. $\frac{3}{x+4} - \frac{1}{x+6}$ $\frac{2(x+7)}{(x+6)(x+4)}$

21. $\frac{9}{x-3} + \frac{2x}{x+1}$ $\frac{2x^2+3x+9}{(x+1)(x-3)}$

22. $\frac{x+4}{x^2-4} - \frac{15}{x-2}$

23. $\frac{-15x}{x^2-8x+16} + \frac{12}{x-4}$

24. $\frac{x^2-5}{x^2+5x-14} - \frac{x+3}{x+7}$

19. $\frac{3(x+12)}{(x+8)(x-3)}$
22. $\frac{-2(7x+13)}{(x+2)(x-2)}$
23. $\frac{-3(x+16)}{(x-4)^2}$
24. $\frac{-x+1}{(x+7)(x-2)}$

25. **ERROR ANALYSIS** *Describe* and correct the error in adding the rational expressions. See margin.

$$\frac{x}{x+2} + \frac{4}{x-5} = \frac{x+4}{(x+2)(x-5)}$$ ✗

26. ★ **MULTIPLE CHOICE** Which expression is equivalent to $\frac{2x}{x+4} - \frac{x^2+4}{x^2-16}$? C

Ⓐ $\frac{1}{x+4}$ Ⓑ $\frac{(x+2)(x-2)}{(x+4)(x-4)}$ Ⓒ $\frac{x^2-8x-4}{(x+4)(x-4)}$ Ⓓ $\frac{3x^2-8x+4}{(x+4)(x-4)}$

B

UNLIKE DENOMINATORS **Perform the indicated operation(s) and simplify.**

27. $\frac{x}{x^2-9} + \frac{x+1}{x^2+6x+9}$ $\frac{(2x+3)(x-1)}{(x-3)(x+3)^2}$

28. $\frac{x+3}{x^2-2x-8} - \frac{x-5}{x^2-12x+32}$ $\frac{-2(x+7)}{(x-4)(x+2)(x-8)}$

29. $\frac{x+2}{x-4} + \frac{2}{x} + \frac{5x}{3x-1}$ $\frac{8x^3-9x^2-28x+8}{x(x-4)(3x-1)}$

30. $\frac{x+3}{x^2-25} - \frac{x-1}{x-5} + \frac{3}{x+3}$ $\frac{-x^3-3x^2-x-51}{(x-5)(x+5)(x+3)}$

2. *Sample answer:* Factor the denominators, find the least common denominator, multiply each fraction by the missing part(s) of the least common denominator, add the numerators and place over the least common denominator.

25. You must have a common denominator before you can add values in the numerator; $\frac{x(x-5)+4(x+2)}{(x+2)(x-5)} = \frac{x^2-x+8}{(x+2)(x-5)}$.

KAMPLES and 6
p. 585
r Exs. 31–36

SIMPLIFYING COMPLEX FRACTIONS **Simplify the complex fraction.**

31. $\dfrac{\frac{x}{3}-6}{10+\frac{4}{x}}$ $\dfrac{x(x-18)}{6(5x+2)}$

32. $\dfrac{15-\frac{2}{x}}{\frac{x}{5}+4}$ $\dfrac{5(15x-2)}{x(x+20)}$

33. $\dfrac{\frac{16}{x-2}}{\frac{4}{x+1}+\frac{6}{x}}$ $\dfrac{8x(x+1)}{(x-2)(5x+3)}$

34. $\dfrac{\frac{1}{2x-5}-\frac{7}{8x-20}}{\frac{x}{2x-5}}$ $\dfrac{-3}{4x}$

35. $\dfrac{\frac{3}{x-2}-\frac{6}{x^2-4}}{\frac{3}{x+2}+\frac{1}{x-2}}$ $\dfrac{3x}{4(x-1)}$

36. $\dfrac{\frac{1}{3x^2-3}}{\frac{5}{x+1}-\frac{x+4}{x^2-3x-4}}$ $\dfrac{x-4}{12(x-1)(x-6)}$

37. ★ **OPEN-ENDED MATH** Write two different complex fractions that each simplify to $\frac{x-3}{x+4}$. *Sample answer:* $\dfrac{\frac{x^2-x-6}{x^2+4x}}{\frac{x+2}{x}}$, $\dfrac{\frac{x^2+3x-18}{4}}{\frac{x^2+10x+24}{4}}$

C **CHALLENGE** **Simplify the complex fraction.**

38. $\dfrac{\frac{1}{x}-\frac{x}{x^{-1}+1}}{\frac{5}{x}}$ $\dfrac{-(x^3-x-1)}{5(x+1)}$

39. $\dfrac{\frac{3-2x}{x^3}}{\frac{2}{x^2}-\frac{1}{x^3+x^2}}$ $\dfrac{(3-2x)(x+1)}{x(2x+1)}$

40. $\dfrac{3x^{-2}+(2x-1)^{-1}}{\frac{6}{x^{-1}+2}+3x^{-1}}$ $\dfrac{(1+2x)(x^2+6x-3)}{3x(2x-1)(2x^2+2x+1)}$

PROBLEM SOLVING

KAMPLE 3 A
p. 583
r Ex. 41

41. JET STREAM The total time T (in hours) needed to fly from New York to Los Angeles and back (ignoring layovers) can be modeled by the equation in the diagram, where d is the distance each way (in miles), a is the average airplane speed (in miles per hour), and j is the average speed of the jet stream (in miles per hour).

$$T=\frac{d}{a-j}+\frac{d}{a+j}$$

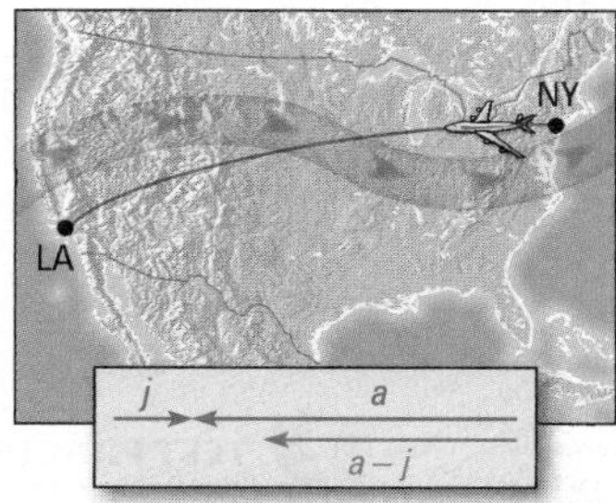

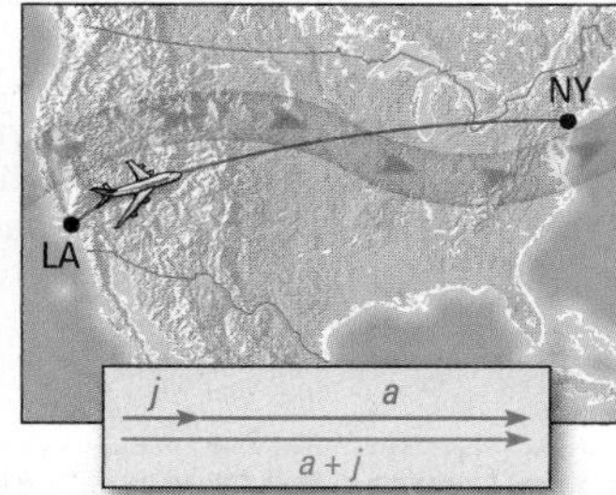

Rewrite the equation so that the right side is simplified. Then find the total time if $d = 2468$ miles, $a = 510$ mi/h, and $j = 115$ mi/h. $T=\dfrac{2da}{(a-j)(a+j)}$; about 10.2 h

Animated Algebra at classzone.com

KAMPLES and 6
p. 585
r Exs. 42–43
$\dfrac{R_1R_2}{R_2+R_1}$; about
4 ohms

42. ELECTRONICS If two resistors in a parallel circuit have resistances R_1 and R_2 (both in ohms), then the total resistance R_t (in ohms) is given by the equation shown. Simplify the complex fraction. Then find the total resistance if $R_1 = 2000$ ohms and $R_2 = 5600$ ohms.

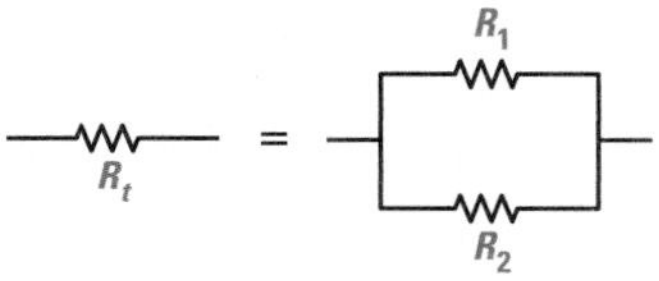

R_t = [parallel circuit with R_1 and R_2]

$$R_t=\frac{1}{\frac{1}{R_1}+\frac{1}{R_2}}$$

@HomeTutor for problem solving help at classzone.com

Avoiding Common Errors

Exercises 16–24 Some students may always choose the product of the two denominators as the common denominator. Explain that this will always give a common denominator, but much of the time it will not give the *least* common denominator. Use a simple example, such as Exercise 16 or 17, to show that using the product of the denominators results in having to do more simplification.

Study Strategy

Exercises 31–36 Some students may be unsure what it means to "simplify" a complex fraction and how to know when they are done. Have them write this reminder in their notebooks: "A complex fraction is simplified when it has no more than one fraction bar."

Exercise 41 More information about the jet stream can be found at www.pbs.org/wgbh/nova/balloon/science/jetstream.html

An **Animated Algebra** activity is available on-line for **Exercise 41**. This activity is also available on the **Power Presentations CD-ROM**.

5 ASSESS AND RETEACH

Daily Homework Quiz

Transparency Available

1. Find the least common multiple of $3x^2 - 6x - 45$ and $2x^2 - 20x + 50$. $6(x-5)^2(x+3)$

2. Add: $\frac{5}{x^2-1} + \frac{2x}{x^2+5x-6}$ $\frac{2x^2+7x+30}{(x+1)(x-1)(x+6)}$

3. Subtract: $\frac{x-4}{3x-15} - \frac{x+1}{x^2-3x-10}$ $\frac{x^2-5x-11}{3(x-5)(x+2)}$

4. Simplify: $\frac{\frac{6}{x-3}}{\frac{4}{x-3} - \frac{5}{x^2}}$ $\frac{6x^2}{4x^2-5x+15}$

Available at **classzone.com**

Diagnosis/Remediation

- Practice A, B, C in Chapter 8 Resource Book, pp. 51–53
- Study Guide in Chapter 8 Resource Book, pp. 54–55
- Practice Workbook, pp. 130–131
- @HomeTutor

Challenge

Additional challenge is available in the Chapter 8 Resource Book, p. 58.

44a–d. See Additional Answers beginning on p. AA1.

45. $1 + \cfrac{1}{2 + \cfrac{1}{2 + \cfrac{1}{2 + \cfrac{1}{2 + \frac{1}{2}}}}}$, $1 + \cfrac{1}{2 + \cfrac{1}{2 + \cfrac{1}{2 + \cfrac{1}{2 + \cfrac{1}{2 + \frac{1}{2}}}}}}$; $\frac{7}{5}, \frac{17}{12}, \frac{41}{29}, \frac{99}{70}, \frac{239}{169}$; $\sqrt{2}$

43a. $M = \frac{Pi}{1 - \left(\frac{1}{1+i}\right)^{12t}} = \frac{Pi}{1 - \frac{1}{(1+i)^{12t}}} = \frac{Pi}{\frac{(1+i)^{12t} - 1}{(1+i)^{12t}}} = \frac{Pi(1+i)^{12t}}{(1+i)^{12t} - 1}$

B

43. CAR LOANS If you borrow P dollars to buy a car and agree to repay the loan over t years at an annual interest rate of i (expressed as a decimal), then your monthly payment M is given by either formula below.

Formula 1: $M = \frac{Pi}{1 - \left(\frac{1}{1+i}\right)^{12t}}$ **Formula 2:** $M = \frac{Pi(1+i)^{12t}}{(1+i)^{12t} - 1}$

a. Show that the formulas are equivalent by simplifying the first formula.

b. Find your monthly payment if you borrow \$15,500 at an annual interest rate of 6% and repay the loan over 4 years. **\$990.41**

44. ★ EXTENDED RESPONSE The amount A (in milligrams) of aspirin in a person's bloodstream can be modeled by

$$A = \frac{391t^2 + 0.112}{0.218t^4 + 0.991t^2 + 1}$$

where t is the time (in hours) after one dose is taken.

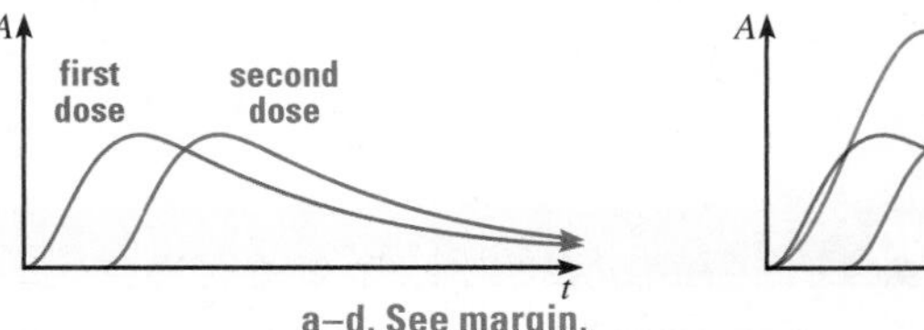

a–d. See margin.

a. Graph the equation using a graphing calculator.

b. A second dose of the drug is taken 1 hour after the first dose. Write an equation to model the amount of the second dose in the bloodstream.

c. Write and graph a model for the *total* amount of aspirin in the bloodstream after the second dose is taken.

d. About how long after the second dose has been taken is the greatest amount of aspirin in the bloodstream?

C

45. CHALLENGE Find the next two expressions in the pattern shown. Then simplify all five expressions. What value do the expressions approach? **See margin.**

$1 + \cfrac{1}{2 + \frac{1}{2}}, 1 + \cfrac{1}{2 + \cfrac{1}{2 + \frac{1}{2}}}, 1 + \cfrac{1}{2 + \cfrac{1}{2 + \cfrac{1}{2 + \frac{1}{2}}}}, \ldots$

KENTUCKY MIXED REVIEW

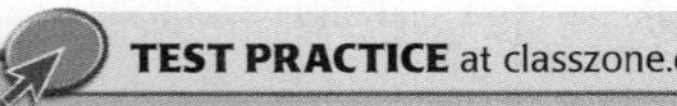

46. One leg of a right triangle is 4 centimeters longer than the other leg. The hypotenuse is 20 centimeters. About how long is the shorter leg? **B**

Ⓐ 10.4 cm Ⓑ 12.0 cm Ⓒ 12.6 cm Ⓓ 16.0 cm

47. Which of the following is the solution of this system of linear equations? **B**

$$3x - 4y = -18$$
$$5x + 2y = -4$$

Ⓐ $(-2, -3)$ Ⓑ $(-2, 3)$ Ⓒ $(2, -3)$ Ⓓ $(3, -2)$

8.6 Solve Rational Equations

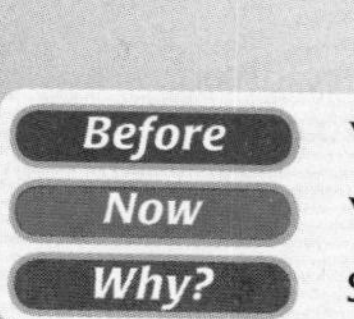

Before	You solved polynomial equations.
Now	You will solve rational equations.
Why?	So you can model mobile phone costs, as in Ex. 38.

Key Vocabulary
cross multiplying
extraneous solution, *p. 52*

You can use **cross multiplying** to solve a rational equation when each side of the equation is a single rational expression.

EXAMPLE 1 Solve a rational equation by cross multiplying

Solve: $\frac{3}{x+1} = \frac{9}{4x+5}$

$\frac{3}{x+1} = \frac{9}{4x+5}$ **Write original equation.**

$3(4x+5) = 9(x+1)$ **Cross multiply.**

$12x + 15 = 9x + 9$ **Distributive property**

$3x + 15 = 9$ **Subtract 9*x* from each side.**

$3x = -6$ **Subtract 15 from each side.**

$x = -2$ **Divide each side by 3.**

▸ The solution is −2. Check this in the original equation.

EXAMPLE 2 Write and use a rational model

ALLOYS An *alloy* is formed by mixing two or more metals. Sterling silver is an alloy composed of 92.5% silver and 7.5% copper by weight. Jewelry silver is composed of 80% silver and 20% copper by weight. How much pure silver should you mix with 15 ounces of jewelry silver to make sterling silver?

Solution

$$\text{Percent of copper in mixture} = \frac{\text{Weight of copper in mixture}}{\text{Total weight of mixture}}$$

$\frac{7.5}{100} = \frac{0.2(15)}{15+x}$ ***x* is the amount of silver added.**

$7.5(15 + x) = 100(0.2)(15)$ **Cross multiply.**

$112.5 + 7.5x = 300$ **Simplify.**

$7.5x = 187.5$ **Subtract 112.5 from each side.**

$x = 25$ **Divide each side by 7.5.**

▸ You should mix 25 ounces of pure silver with the jewelry silver.

1 PLAN AND PREPARE

Warm-Up Exercises

Transparency Available

Solve the equation.

1. $\frac{4}{x} = \frac{6}{15}$ **10**

2. $5(3x - 2) = 4(4x - 1)$ **−6**

3. $x(x - 4) = 3(x - 4) + x$ **2, 6**

4. $2x^2 + 5x - 12 = 0$ **$-4, \frac{3}{2}$**

5. How much alcohol is there in 30 liters of a 45% alcohol solution? **13.5 L**

Notetaking Guide

Transparency Available

Promotes interactive learning and notetaking skills, pp. 228–230.

Pacing

Basic: 2 days
Average: 2 days
Advanced: 2 days
Block: 1 block
- See *Teaching Guide/Lesson Plan.*

2 FOCUS AND MOTIVATE

Essential Question

Big Idea 3, p. 549

What are the steps for solving rational equations? **Tell students they will learn how to answer this question by isolating the variable on one side of the equation.**

Resource Planning Guide

Chapter Resource Book
- Teaching Guide/Lesson Plan (pp. 59–60)
- Activity Master (p. 61)
- Practice levels A, B, C (pp. 63–65)
- Study Guide (pp. 66–67)
- Catch-up for Absent Students (p. 68)
- Problem Solving Workshop (p. 69)
- Challenge (p. 70)

Workbooks
- Notetaking Guide (pp. 228–230)
- Practice Workbook (pp. 132–133)

Teaching Options
- **Power Presentations CD-ROM** provides dynamic electronic teaching resources for the classroom.
- **Activity Generator CD-ROM** provides editable activities for all ability levels.

Interactive Technology
- Easy Planner
- Power Presentations CD-ROM
- Activity Generator CD-ROM
- Animated Algebra
- Test Generator CD-ROM
- Online Quiz
- eWorkbook
- eEdition
- @HomeTutor

Resources for English Learners
- Quick Reference for English Learners
- Spanish Study Guide
- Multi-Language Visual Glossary
- Student Resources in Spanish

See also the *Algebra 2 Toolkit* for more strategies for meeting individual needs.

Motivating the Lesson

So far this year Mikhala has taken 5 algebra tests. She wants to know what score she will need on the next test so that her overall average is 88%. Tell students Mikhala can write and solve a rational equation to find out what score she needs.

3 TEACH

Extra Example 1

Solve: $\frac{7}{x-2} = \frac{11}{2x-10}$ **16**

Extra Example 2

The coolant in a car radiator is a mixture of antifreeze and water. The recommended mixture for your car is 50% antifreeze. If you have a mixture of 7 liters of coolant that is 40% antifreeze, how much antifreeze should you add to bring the mixture up to the recommended level? **1.4 L**

Extra Example 3

What is the solution of $\frac{15}{x} + \frac{4}{5} = \frac{7}{x}$? **D**

Ⓐ 27.5 Ⓑ 10

Ⓒ −5 Ⓓ −10

Extra Example 4

Solve: $\frac{12}{x+7} = 1 - \frac{12}{x}$ **−4, 21**

GUIDED PRACTICE for Examples 1 and 2

Solve the equation by cross multiplying. Check your solution(s).

1. $\frac{3}{5x} = \frac{2}{x-7}$ **−3**

2. $\frac{-4}{x+3} = \frac{5}{x-3}$ **$-\frac{1}{3}$**

3. $\frac{1}{2x+5} = \frac{x}{11x+8}$ **−1, 4**

4. WHAT IF? In Example 2, suppose you have 10 ounces of jewelry silver. How much pure silver must be mixed with the jewelry silver to make sterling silver? **$16\frac{2}{3}$ oz**

USING LCDS When a rational equation is not expressed as a proportion, you can solve it by multiplying each side of the equation by the least common denominator of each rational expression.

EXAMPLE 3 Standardized Test Practice

What is the solution of $\frac{5}{x} + \frac{7}{4} = -\frac{9}{x}$?

Ⓐ −10 Ⓑ −8 Ⓒ −4 Ⓓ 6

ELIMINATE CHOICES
You can eliminate choice D because it yields a positive value on the left side of the equation and a negative value on the right side.

Solution

$\frac{5}{x} + \frac{7}{4} = -\frac{9}{x}$	**Write original equation.**
$4x\left(\frac{5}{x} + \frac{7}{4}\right) = 4x\left(-\frac{9}{x}\right)$	**Multiply each side by the LCD, 4x.**
$20 + 7x = -36$	**Simplify.**
$7x = -56$	**Subtract 20 from each side.**
$x = -8$	**Divide each side by 7.**

▸ The correct answer is B. Ⓐ Ⓑ Ⓒ Ⓓ

EXAMPLE 4 Solve a rational equation with two solutions

Solve: $1 - \frac{8}{x-5} = \frac{3}{x}$

$1 - \frac{8}{x-5} = \frac{3}{x}$	**Write original equation.**
$x(x-5)\left(1 - \frac{8}{x-5}\right) = x(x-5) \cdot \frac{3}{x}$	**Multiply each side by the LCD, $x(x-5)$.**
$x(x-5) - 8x = 3(x-5)$	**Simplify.**
$x^2 - 5x - 8x = 3x - 15$	**Simplify.**
$x^2 - 16x + 15 = 0$	**Write in standard form.**
$(x-1)(x-15) = 0$	**Factor.**
$x = 1$ or $x = 15$	**Zero product property**

▸ The solutions are 1 and 15. Check these in the original equation.

EXTRANEOUS SOLUTIONS When solving a rational equation, you may obtain solutions that are extraneous. Be sure to check for extraneous solutions by substituting back into the original equation.

EXAMPLE 5 Check for extraneous solutions

Solve: $\frac{6}{x-3} = \frac{8x^2}{x^2-9} - \frac{4x}{x+3}$

Solution

Write each denominator in factored form. The LCD is $(x+3)(x-3)$.

$$\frac{6}{x-3} = \frac{8x^2}{(x+3)(x-3)} - \frac{4x}{x+3}$$

$$(x+3)(x-3) \cdot \frac{6}{x-3} = (x+3)(x-3) \cdot \frac{8x^2}{(x+3)(x-3)} - (x+3)(x-3) \cdot \frac{4x}{x+3}$$

$$6(x+3) = 8x^2 - 4x(x-3)$$

$$6x + 18 = 8x^2 - 4x^2 + 12x$$

$$0 = 4x^2 + 6x - 18$$

$$0 = 2x^2 + 3x - 9$$

$$0 = (2x-3)(x+3)$$

$$2x - 3 = 0 \quad \text{or} \quad x + 3 = 0$$

$$x = \frac{3}{2} \quad \text{or} \quad x = -3$$

REVIEW EXTRANEOUS SOLUTIONS
For help with extraneous solutions, see p. 51.

You can use algebra or a graph to check whether either of the two solutions is extraneous.

Algebra The solution $\frac{3}{2}$ checks, but the apparent solution -3 is extraneous, because substituting it in the equation results in division by zero, which is undefined.

$$\frac{6}{-3-3} \neq \frac{8(-3)^2}{(-3)^2-9} - \frac{4(-3)}{-3+3}$$

Division by zero is undefined

Graph Graph $y = \frac{6}{x-3}$ and $y = \frac{8x^2}{x^2-9} - \frac{4x}{x+3}$.

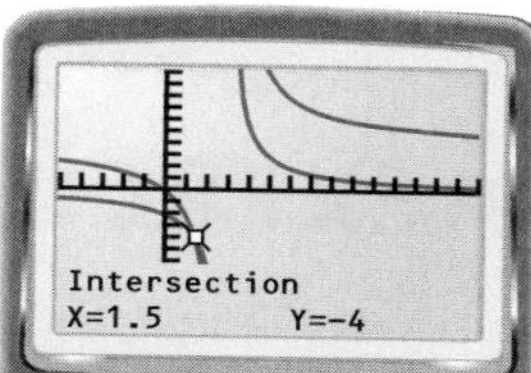

The graphs intersect when $x = \frac{3}{2}$, but not when $x = -3$.

▶ The solution is $\frac{3}{2}$.

GUIDED PRACTICE for Examples 3, 4, and 5

Solve the equation by using the LCD. Check for extraneous solutions.

5. $\frac{7}{2} + \frac{3}{x} = 3$ -6

6. $\frac{2}{x} + \frac{4}{3} = 2$ 3

7. $\frac{3}{7} + \frac{8}{x} = 1$ 14

8. $\frac{3}{2} + \frac{4}{x-1} = \frac{x+1}{x-1}$ -3

9. $\frac{3x}{x+1} - \frac{5}{2x} = \frac{3}{2x}$ $-\frac{2}{3}, 2$

10. $\frac{5x}{x-2} = 7 + \frac{10}{x-2}$ no solution

Extra Example 5

Solve and check for extraneous solutions: $\frac{7}{x-1} - 5 = \frac{6}{x^2-1}$ $-\frac{3}{5}, 2$; neither is extraneous.

Key Questions to Ask for Example 5

- Before you start solving the equation, you can determine which numbers can *possibly* be extraneous solutions. What are they? 3 and -3
- In general, before you start solving a rational equation, how can you determine which numbers might possibly be extraneous solutions? Find all numbers that make one or more of the denominators equal to 0.

Vocabulary

In Example 5, make sure that students understand the meaning of *extraneous*. Discuss the difference between an extraneous solution and a wrong answer that might be obtained by making algebraic or arithmetic errors.

Mathematical Reasoning

Multiple Representations The textbook shows how the apparent solutions for Example 5 can be checked algebraically or by using a graphing calculator. Ask students whether they think a calculator table could also be used for this purpose. If so, what modification might need to be made to the table settings? Ask students which method for checking they prefer and why.

Extra Example 6

A company produces computer desks. The average cost to produce x desks can be modeled by the function $C(x) = \frac{4000 + 50x}{x}$. How many desks should the company produce each month in order to achieve an average cost of $85 per desk? **about 114 desks**

Key Question to Ask for Example 6

- Suppose that the model continues to be an accurate predictor of sales of entertainment software for years beyond 2003. Without drawing a graph, how can you determine a value which the total sales of entertainment software would never exceed? **In this rational function, the degrees of the numerator and denominator are equal, so the graph has a horizontal asymptote at $\frac{848}{115} \approx 7.4$. This means the total sales would never exceed about $7.4 billion.**

Closing the Lesson

Have students summarize the major points of the lesson and answer the Essential Question: What are the steps for solving rational equations?

- **A rational equation can be solved by finding cross products if there is a single rational expression on each side of the equation.**
- **Rational equations sometimes have extraneous solutions.**

If the equation is written as a proportion, find the cross products. If not, multiply each side of the equation by the LCD for all the rational expressions. Simplify, then solve the resulting equation. Check the possible solutions in the original equation.

3. Graph both sides of the equation. If the graphs intersect at a possible solution, then it is a solution. If the graphs do not intersect at a possible solution, then it is an extraneous solution.

EXAMPLE 6 Solve a rational equation given a function

VIDEO GAME SALES From 1995 through 2003, the annual sales S (in billions of dollars) of entertainment software can be modeled by

$$S(t) = \frac{848t^2 + 3220}{115t^2 + 1000}, \quad 0 \le t \le 8$$

where t is the number of years since 1995. For which year were the total sales of entertainment software about $5.3 billion?

ANOTHER WAY
For alternative methods for solving the problem in Example 6, turn to page 596 for the **Problem Solving Workshop**.

Solution

$S(t) = \frac{848t^2 + 3220}{115t^2 + 1000}$	Write given function.
$5.3 = \frac{848t^2 + 3220}{115t^2 + 1000}$	Substitute 5.3 for $S(t)$.
$5.3(115t^2 + 1000) = 848t^2 + 3220$	Multiply each side by $115t^2 + 1000$.
$609.5t^2 + 5300 = 848t^2 + 3220$	Simplify.
$5300 = 238.5t^2 + 3220$	Subtract $609.5t^2$ from each side.
$2080 = 238.5t^2$	Subtract 3220 from each side.
$8.72 \approx t^2$	Divide each side by 238.5.
$\pm 2.95 \approx t$	Take square roots of each side.

Because -2.95 is not in the domain ($0 \le t \le 8$), the only solution is 2.95.

▶ So, the total sales of entertainment software were about $5.3 billion about 3 years after 1995, or in 1998.

GUIDED PRACTICE for Example 6

11. **WHAT IF?** Use the information in Example 6 to determine in which year the total sales of entertainment software were about $4.5 billion. **1997**

8.6 EXERCISES

HOMEWORK KEY
○ = **WORKED-OUT SOLUTIONS** on p. WS15 for Exs. 5, 15, and 35
★ = **STANDARDIZED TEST PRACTICE** Exs. 2, 13, 28, 29, 34, and 36

SKILL PRACTICE

1. **VOCABULARY** Copy and complete: When you write $\frac{x}{3} = \frac{x+2}{5}$ as $5x = 3(x + 2)$, you are __?__. **cross multiplying**

2. ★ **WRITING** A student solved the equation $\frac{5}{x-4} = \frac{x}{x-4}$ and got the solutions 4 and 5. Which, if either, of these is extraneous? *Explain.*
4; 4 is not in the domain of the equation because you cannot divide by zero.

3. **REASONING** *Describe* how you can use a graph to determine if an apparent solution of a rational equation is extraneous. **See margin.**

Differentiated Instruction

Auditory Learners Have students work in pairs or small groups to discuss the extraneous solution in **Example 6**. Have them hypothesize why the inputs are restricted to $0 \le t \le 8$, and then ask them to extend their discussion to what values may or may not be viable in similar real-world situations and why.

See also the *Algebra 2 Toolkit* for more strategies.

EXAMPLE 1 on p. 589 for Exs. 4–13

CROSS MULTIPLYING Solve the equation by cross multiplying. Check for extraneous solutions.

4. $\frac{4}{2x} = \frac{5}{x+6}$ 4

5. $\frac{9}{3x} = \frac{4}{x+2}$ 6

6. $\frac{6}{x-1} = \frac{9}{x+1}$ 5

7. $\frac{8}{3x-2} = \frac{2}{x-1}$ 2

8. $\frac{x}{x+1} = \frac{3}{x+1}$ 3

9. $\frac{x-3}{x+5} = \frac{x}{x+2}$ −1

10. $\frac{x}{x^2-2} = \frac{-1}{x}$ ±1

11. $\frac{4(x-4)}{x^2+2x-8} = \frac{4}{x+4}$ no solution

12. $\frac{9}{x^2-6x+9} = \frac{3x}{x^2-3x}$ 6

13. ★ **MULTIPLE CHOICE** What is the solution of $\frac{3}{x+2} = \frac{6}{x-1}$? A

Ⓐ −5 Ⓑ −4 Ⓒ −1 Ⓓ 4

EXAMPLES 3, 4, and 5 on pp. 590–591 for Exs. 14–27

LEAST COMMON DENOMINATOR Solve the equation by using the LCD. Check for extraneous solutions.

14. $\frac{4}{x} + x = 5$ 1, 4

15. $\frac{2}{3x} + \frac{1}{6} = \frac{4}{3x}$ 4

16. $\frac{5}{x} - 2 = \frac{2}{x+3}$ $\frac{-3 \pm \sqrt{129}}{4}$

17. $\frac{1}{2x} + \frac{3}{x+7} = \frac{-1}{x}$ $-\frac{7}{3}$

18. $\frac{1}{x-2} + 2 = \frac{3x}{x+2}$ 1, 6

19. $\frac{5}{x^2+x-6} = 2 + \frac{x-3}{x-2}$ 19. $\frac{-1 \pm \sqrt{79}}{3}$

20. $\frac{x+1}{x+6} + \frac{1}{x} = \frac{2x+1}{x+6}$ −2, 3

21. $\frac{2}{x-3} + \frac{1}{x} = \frac{x-1}{x-3}$ 1

22. $\frac{6x}{x+4} + 4 = \frac{2x+2}{x-1}$ $-\frac{3}{2}$, 2

23. $\frac{10}{x} + 3 = \frac{x+9}{x-4}$ $-\frac{5}{2}$, 8

24. $\frac{18}{x^2-3x} - \frac{6}{x-3} = \frac{5}{x}$ no solution

25. $\frac{x+3}{x-3} + \frac{x}{x-5} = \frac{x+5}{x-5}$ 0, 7

B **ERROR ANALYSIS** *Describe* and correct the error in the first step of solving the equation. 26, 27. See margin.

26. $\frac{3}{2x} + \frac{4}{x^2} = 1$

$3x^2 + 8x = 1$ ✗

27. $\frac{5}{x} + \frac{23}{6} = \frac{45}{x}$

$\frac{28}{x+6} = \frac{45}{x}$ ✗

28. ★ **MULTIPLE CHOICE** What is (are) the solution(s) of $\frac{2}{x-3} = \frac{1}{x^2-2x-3}$? C

Ⓐ $-3, -\frac{1}{2}$ Ⓑ $-\frac{1}{2}, 3$ Ⓒ $-\frac{1}{2}$ Ⓓ 3

29. ★ **OPEN-ENDED MATH** Give an example of a rational equation that you would solve using cross multiplication. Then give an example of a rational equation that you would solve by multiplying each side by the LCD of the fractions.
Sample answer: $\frac{6}{x+5} = \frac{2x}{x-1}$; $\frac{4}{x} + \frac{5}{3} = \frac{12}{x}$

C **CHALLENGE In Exercises 30–32, *a* is a nonzero real number. Tell whether the algebraic statement is *always true, sometimes true,* or *never true. Explain* your answer.**

30. For the equation $\frac{1}{x-a} = \frac{x}{x-a}$, $x = a$ is an extraneous solution.
Always true; when $x = a$, the denominators of the fractions are zero.

31. The equation $\frac{3}{x-a} = \frac{x}{x-a}$ has exactly one solution.
Sometimes true; the equation will have exactly one solution except when $x = a$.

32. The equation $\frac{1}{x-a} = \frac{2}{x+a} + \frac{2a}{x^2-a^2}$ has no solution.
Always true; the only apparent solution is an extraneous solution.

26. The student "cross multiplied" the fractions on the left side of the equation. Both sides of the equation should have been multiplied by the LCD, $2x^2$; $2x^2\left(\frac{3}{2x} + \frac{4}{x^2}\right) = 2x^2(1)$, $3x + 8 = 2x^2$.

27. The student simply added numerators and denominators on the left side of the equation. Both sides of the equation should have been multiplied by the LCD, $6x$; $6x\left(\frac{5}{x} + \frac{23}{6}\right) = 6x\left(\frac{45}{x}\right)$, $30 + 23x = 270$.

4 PRACTICE AND APPLY

Assignment Guide

Answer Transparencies available for all exercises

Basic:
Day 1: SRH p. 980 Exs. 13–20 pp. 592–595 Exs. 1–13, 33, 34, 39–40
Day 2: pp. 592–595 Exs. 14–22, 26, 27, 35, 36

Average:
Day 1: pp. 592–595 Exs. 1–3, 6–13, 28, 29, 33, 34, 39–40
Day 2: pp. 592–595 Exs. 16–23, 26, 27, 35–37

Advanced:
Day 1: pp. 592–595 Exs. 1–3, 8–13, 28–34*, 39–40
Day 2: pp. 592–595 Exs. 18–27, 35–38*

Block:
pp. 592–595 Exs. 1–3, 6–13, 16–23, 26–29, 33–37, 39–40

Differentiated Instruction

See *Algebra 2 Best Practices Toolkit* for suggestions on addressing the needs of a diverse classroom.

Homework Check

For a quick check of student understanding of key concepts, go over the following exercises:

Basic: 6, 14, 18, 33, 35
Average: 8, 20, 21, 34, 35
Advanced: 10, 22, 24, 34, 35

Extra Practice

- Student Edition, p. 1017
- Chapter 8 Resource Book: Practice levels A, B, C, pp. 63–65

Practice Worksheet

An easily-readable reduced practice page (with answers) for this lesson can be found on p. 548D.

Avoiding Common Errors

Exercises 14, 16, 22, 23 Because both sides of a rational equation are multiplied by the LCD in order to "clear fractions," some students think they do not have to "do anything" to terms that are not fractions, and so fail to multiply these terms by the LCD. Remind students that they must multiply each *side* of the equation by the LCD. Have them write out the step that shows the multiplication of both sides by the LCD (as in the solutions for Examples 3 and 4) every time this method is used.

36b. $\frac{5t+40}{8t}$; the expression represents the amount of work done by you and your friend while working together for 5 hours.

36c. $\frac{5}{t} = \frac{3}{8} \rightarrow t = 13\frac{1}{3}$ h; when working together, you and your friend can complete one room.

PROBLEM SOLVING

EXAMPLE 2 on p. 589 for Exs. 33–34

A

33. VOLLEYBALL So far in your volleyball match, you have put into play 37 of the 44 serves you have attempted. Solve the equation $\frac{90}{100} = \frac{37 + x}{44 + x}$ to find the number of consecutive serves you need to put into play in order to raise your service percentage to 90%. 26 serves

@HomeTutor for problem solving help at classzone.com

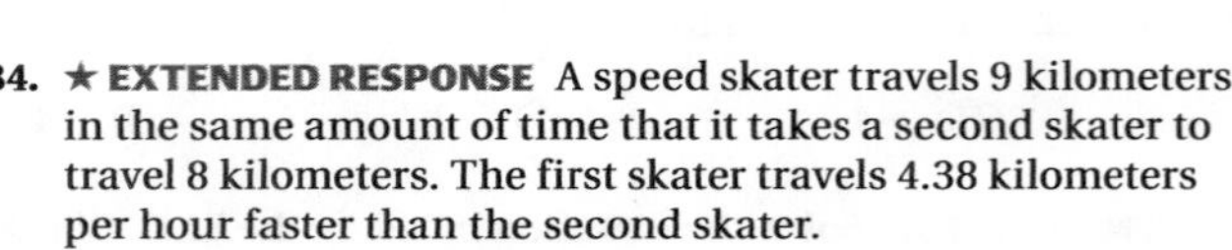

34. ★ EXTENDED RESPONSE A speed skater travels 9 kilometers in the same amount of time that it takes a second skater to travel 8 kilometers. The first skater travels 4.38 kilometers per hour faster than the second skater.

a. Use the verbal model below to write an equation that relates the skating times of the skaters. $\frac{9}{4.38 + x} = \frac{8}{x}$

$$\frac{\text{Distance for skater 1}}{\text{Skater 1 speed}} = \frac{\text{Distance for skater 2}}{\text{Skater 2 speed}}$$

b. Solve the equation in part (a) to find the speeds of both skaters. Skater 1: 39.42 km/h, Skater 2: 35.04 km/h

c. How long did the skaters skate? *Explain* your answer. About 0.23 h. *Sample answer:* Divide the distance, 9 kilometers, by the rate, 39.42 kilometers per hour, to find the time.

@HomeTutor for problem solving help at classzone.com

EXAMPLE 6 on p. 592 for Ex. 35

35. MUSIC INDUSTRY From 1994 through 2003, the number n (in millions) of CDs shipped can be modeled by

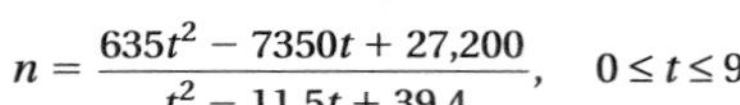

$$n = \frac{635t^2 - 7350t + 27{,}200}{t^2 - 11.5t + 39.4}, \quad 0 \le t \le 9$$

where t is the number of years since 1994. During which year was the total number of CDs shipped about 720 million? 1995

B

36. ★ EXTENDED RESPONSE You can paint a room in 8 hours. Working together, you and your friend can paint the room in just 5 hours.

a. Let t be the time (in hours) your friend would take to paint the room when working alone. Copy and complete the table.

	Work Rate	·	Time	=	Work Done
You	$\frac{1 \text{ room}}{8 \text{ hours}}$		5 hours		? $\frac{5}{8}$
Friend	? $\frac{1 \text{ room}}{t \text{ hours}}$		5 hours		? $\frac{5}{t}$

b. What is the sum of the expressions in the table's last column? *Explain.*

c. Write and solve an equation to find how long your friend would take to paint the room when working alone. *Explain* your answer.

b, c. See margin.

37. GEOMETRY *Golden rectangles* are rectangles for which the ratio of the width w to the length ℓ is equal to the ratio of ℓ to $\ell + w$. The ratio of the length to the width for these rectangles is called the *golden ratio*. Find the value of the golden ratio using a rectangle with a width of 1 unit. $\frac{1 + \sqrt{5}}{2}$

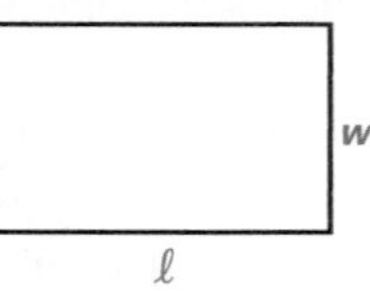

○ = WORKED-OUT SOLUTIONS on p. WS1 ★ = STANDARDIZED TEST PRACTICE

38a. $f(x) = \frac{-0.27x^3 + 1.4x^2 + 1.05x + 39.4}{-8.25x^3 + 53.1x^2 - 7.82x + 138}$

C **38. CHALLENGE** Let x be the number of years since 1998, let $g(x)$ be the average monthly bill (in dollars) for mobile phone users in the United States, and let $h(x)$ be the average number of minutes used by U.S. mobile phone users. Then $g(x)$ and $h(x)$ are as given below.

$$g(x) = -0.27x^3 + 1.40x^2 + 1.05x + 39.4$$

$$h(x) = -8.25x^3 + 53.1x^2 - 7.82x + 138$$

a. Write a rational function $f(x)$ that gives the average price per minute x years after 1998. **See margin.**

b. Find the average price per minute in 1998. **about $0.29 per min**

c. In what year did the average price per minute fall to 11 cents? **2002**

KENTUCKY MIXED REVIEW

TEST PRACTICE at classzone.com

39. What are the coordinates of the y-intercept of the line $-2x - \frac{1}{3}y = 12$? **B**

(A) $(-6, 0)$ (B) $(0, -36)$ (C) $(0, 4)$ (D) $(12, 0)$

40. What is the value of x? **B**

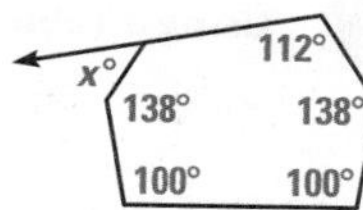

(A) 38 (B) 48 (C) 58 (D) 68

QUIZ for Lessons 8.4–8.6

Perform the indicated operation and simplify. *(p. 573)*

1. $\frac{x^2 - 2x - 24}{x^2 + 3x - 10} \cdot \frac{3x^2 - 6x}{x^3 + 4x^2}$ $\frac{3(x-6)}{x(x+5)}$

2. $\frac{x^2 - 10x + 16}{x^2 - 1} \cdot (x - 1)$ $\frac{(x-8)(x-2)}{x+1}$

3. $\frac{x^2 + 9x + 20}{x^2 - 11x + 28} \div \frac{x^2 + 8x + 15}{x^2 - 3x - 4}$ $\frac{(x+4)(x+1)}{(x-7)(x+3)}$

4. $\frac{x^2 + 12x + 36}{x^2 - 8x + 12} \div (x^2 - 36)$ $\frac{(x+6)}{(x-6)^2(x-2)}$

Perform the indicated operation and simplify. *(p. 582)*

5. $\frac{1}{x+4} + \frac{1}{x-4}$ $\frac{2x}{(x-4)(x+4)}$

6. $\frac{4x+3}{x^2-16} + \frac{2}{x-4}$ $\frac{6x+11}{(x-4)(x+4)}$

7. $\frac{4}{x+5} - \frac{6x-1}{x^2+10x+25}$ $\frac{-2x+21}{(x+5)^2}$

Solve the equation. Check for extraneous solutions. *(p. 589)*

8. $\frac{x-4}{x-1} = \frac{10}{x+7}$ $-2, 9$

9. $\frac{x-4}{x-2} - \frac{2x-1}{x-2} = 2$ $\frac{1}{3}$

10. $\frac{3x+6}{x^2-4} = \frac{x+1}{x-2}$ **no solution**

11. $\frac{5}{x} + \frac{x+1}{x+2} = \frac{2x+9}{x+2}$ $-5, 2$

12. $\frac{x-3}{x+2} = \frac{x-1}{3x-1}$ $\frac{1}{2}, 5$

13. $\frac{x-1}{x} + \frac{2x-1}{x+3} = \frac{x+6}{x+3}$ $-\frac{1}{2}, 3$

14. **BATTING AVERAGE** So far this baseball season, you have gotten a hit 12 times out of 60 at-bats. Solve the equation $0.360 = \frac{12+x}{60+x}$ to find the number of consecutive hits you have to get to raise your batting average to 0.360. *(p. 589)* **15 hits**

5 ASSESS AND RETEACH

Daily Homework Quiz

Transparency Available

Solve the equation.

1. $\frac{5}{2x+3} = \frac{6}{x-2}$ -4

2. $5 - \frac{6}{x+3} = \frac{12}{x}$ $-\frac{12}{5}, 3$

3. $\frac{1}{x} + \frac{2}{x^2} = \frac{3}{x^3}$ $-3, 1$

4. $\frac{x-2}{x-1} + \frac{x}{x+1} = \frac{38}{x^2-1}$ $-4, 5$

5. So far this season, a baseball team has won 36 of its first 64 games. How many consecutive games does the team need to win to raise its winning percentage to 60%? **6 games**

Online Quiz

Available at **classzone.com**

Diagnosis/Remediation

- Practice A, B, C in Chapter 8 Resource Book, pp. 63–65
- Study Guide in Chapter 8 Resource Book, pp. 66–67
- Practice Workbook, pp. 132–133
- @HomeTutor

Challenge

Additional challenge is available in the Chapter 8 Resource Book, p. 70.

Quiz

An easily-readable reduced copy of the quiz (with answers) on Lessons 8.4–8.6 from the Assessment Book can be found on p. 548E.

Alternative Strategy

Method 1 Example 6 on page 592 can be solved by using a table. This method allows students to see how the total sales of entertainment software increased year by year over the period 1995–2003. This method is much faster than the algebraic solution on page 592 (which also requires a calculator in the final step).

PROBLEM SOLVING WORKSHOP LESSON 8.6

Using ALTERNATIVE METHODS

Another Way to Solve Example 6, page 592

MULTIPLE REPRESENTATIONS In Example 6 on page 592, you solved a rational equation algebraically. You can also solve rational equations using tables and graphs.

PROBLEM

VIDEO GAME SALES From 1995 through 2003, the annual sales S (in billions of dollars) of entertainment software can be modeled by

$$S(t) = \frac{848t^2 + 3220}{115t^2 + 1000}, \quad 0 \le t \le 8$$

where t is the number of years since 1995. For which year were the total sales of entertainment software about \$5.3 billion?

METHOD 1

Using a Table The problem requires solving the following rational equation:

$$5.3 = \frac{848t^2 + 3220}{115t^2 + 1000}$$

One way to solve this equation is to make a table of values. You can use a graphing calculator to make the table.

STEP 1 **Enter** the function $y = \frac{848x^2 + 3220}{115x^2 + 1000}$ into a graphing calculator.

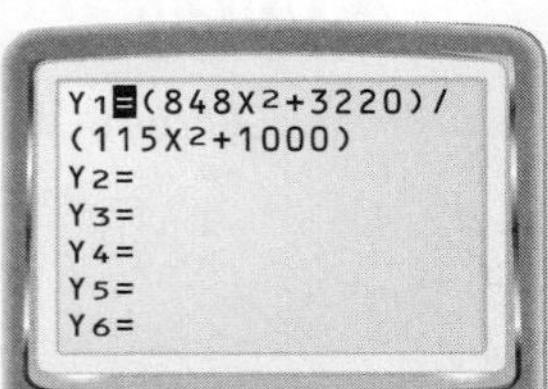

STEP 2 **Set up** a table of values for the function. Start the table at zero so that the first several x-values in the table are in the domain of the function. The step value ($\triangle$Tbl) should represent one entire year.

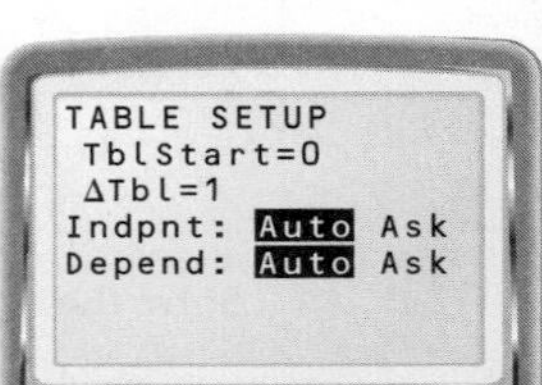

STEP 3 **Create** the table of values. You can see that $y \approx 5.3$ when $x = 3$.

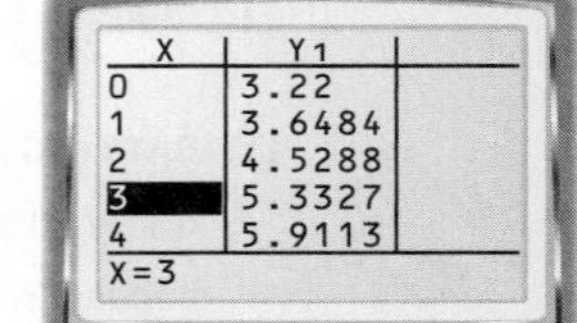

X	Y1
0	3.22
1	3.6484
2	4.5288
3	5.3327
4	5.9113

X=3

▶ Because $x = 3$ represents the number of years after 1995, total sales of entertainment software were about \$5.3 billion in 1998.

METHOD 2 **Using a Graph** You can also use a graph to solve $5.3 = \frac{848t^2 + 3220}{115t^2 + 1000}$.

STEP 1 **Enter** the functions $y = \frac{848x^2 + 3220}{115x^2 + 1000}$ and $y = 5.3$ into a graphing calculator.

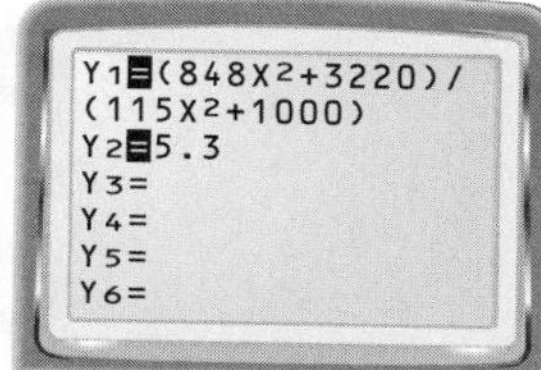

STEP 2 **Graph** the functions. Adjust the viewing window so that it shows the point in the first quadrant where the graphs intersect.

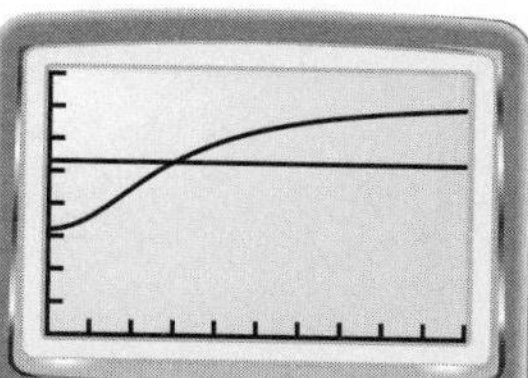

STEP 3 **Find** the intersection point of the graphs using the calculator's *intersect* feature. The graphs intersect at about (3.0, 5.3).

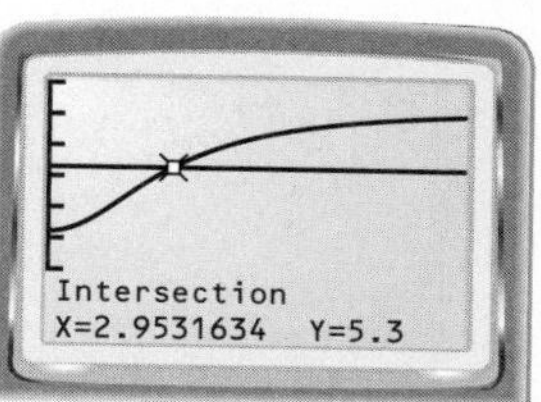

▶ Total sales of entertainment software were about \$5.3 billion 3 years after 1995, or in the year 1998.

PRACTICE

RATIONAL EQUATIONS **Solve the equation using a table and using a graph.**

1. $\frac{80x^2 + 300}{15x^2 + 200} = 4.2$ **about ±5.6**

2. $\frac{5x + 5}{x^2 + 4} = 2$ **1.5, 1**

3. $\frac{9x + 2}{x - 5} = 20.75$ **9**

4. $\frac{6x^2}{2x - 3} = 18$ **3**

5. $\frac{14x^2 + 60}{5x^2 + 7} = 3.5$ **about ±3.2**

6. **WHAT IF?** In the problem on page 596, suppose you want to find the year when total sales of entertainment software were \$4.5 billion. Find this year using a table and using a graph. **1997**

7. **DIVING** The recommended percent p of oxygen (by volume) in the air that a diver breathes is given by $p = \frac{660}{d + 33}$ where d is the depth (in feet) of the diver.
   a. At what depth is air containing 5% oxygen recommended? Use a table to find the answer. **99 ft**
   b. At what depth is air containing 10% oxygen recommended? Use a graph to find the answer. **33 ft**

Alternative Strategy

Method 2 Example 6 on page 592 can also be solved by using a graph. This method allows students to visualize the pattern of how the total sales of entertainment software increased over the period 1995–2003. The graph not only provides a convenient way to solve the equation, but also shows that the growth in sales was rapid during the first few years of this time period and then started to level off.

Avoiding Common Errors

If students do not obtain an appropriate graph, they may either have made errors in entering the two functions or in choosing an appropriate viewing window. The most common error in entering a rational function is to omit the parentheses around the complete numerator and the complete denominator. Check students' calculators to catch errors and guide them in correcting any errors.

1 PLAN AND PREPARE

Warm-Up Exercises

Solve the inequality.

1. $5 - 2x > -7$ $x < 6$
2. $3(2x + 5) \le 4x + 1$ $x \le -7$
3. $x^2 + 3x - 18 < 0$ $-6 < x < 3$
4. $2x^2 - 9x - 5 \ge 0$ $x \le -\frac{1}{2}$ or $x \ge 5$

2 FOCUS AND MOTIVATE

Essential Question

Big Idea 3, p. 549

What methods can be used to solve quadratic inequalities? Tell students they will learn how to answer this question by using tables, graphs, and algebraic methods to solve quadratic inequalities.

3 TEACH

Extra Example 1

Use a table to solve $\frac{x^2 - x - 6}{x - 1} < 0$.

$x < -2$ or $1 < x < 3$

Extra Example 2

You join a video rental club. There is a monthly fee of $10, and the rental fee for members is $1.25 for each DVD. Use a graph to determine how many DVDs you have to rent per month for your average cost to fall below $2 per rental.

14 or more DVDs

NCTM STANDARDS

Standard 2: Analyze situations using algebraic symbols

Standard 10: Create representations to communicate mathematical ideas

Extension — Solve Rational Inequalities

Use after Lesson 8.6

GOAL Find solutions of rational inequalities.

In Lesson 8.6, you solved rational equations. You can also solve rational inequalities using tables, graphs, or algebraic methods.

EXAMPLE 1 Solve a rational inequality using a table

Use a table to solve $\frac{x^2 - 2x + 1}{x - 2} > x$.

Solution

Subtract x from each side of the inequality so that 0 is on one side.

$$\frac{x^2 - 2x + 1}{x - 2} - x > 0 \quad \textbf{Subtract } x \textbf{ from each side.}$$

Enter $y = \frac{x^2 - 2x + 1}{x - 2} - x$ into a graphing calculator.

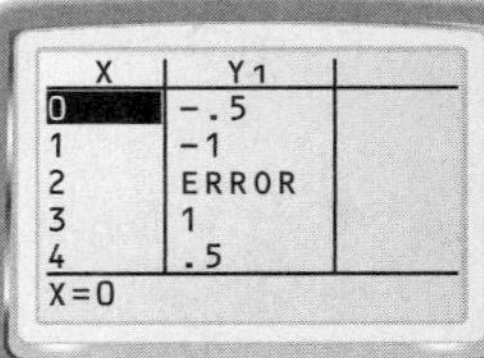

X	Y1
0	-.5
1	-1
2	ERROR
3	1
4	.5

X=0

Use the *table* feature to find values of x for which y is positive.

The value of y is undefined when $x = 2$ and appears to be positive when $x > 2$. Use a smaller step value for x to convince yourself of this.

▶ The solution is $x > 2$.

EXAMPLE 2 Solve a rational inequality by graphing

From 1990 to 2001, the number d (in thousands) of doctors in the United States can be modeled by the function $d = \frac{966t^2 + 50{,}300}{t^2 + 79.7}$ where t is the number of years since 1990. When were there fewer than 800,000 doctors?

Solution

The problem requires solving this inequality:

$$\frac{966t^2 + 50{,}300}{t^2 + 79.7} < 800$$

Enter $y_1 = \frac{966x^2 + 50{,}300}{x^2 + 79.7}$ and $y_2 = 800$ into a graphing calculator.

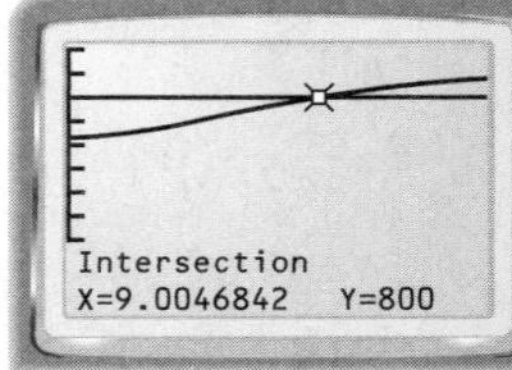

Graph the functions and use the *intersect* feature. The graph of y_1 lies below the graph of y_2 when $0 \le x \le 9$.

▶ In the years 1990–1999, there were fewer than 800,000 doctors.

EXAMPLE 3 Solve a rational inequality algebraically

Solve $\frac{6}{x-2} \geq -4$ algebraically.

Solution

STEP 1 **Rewrite** the inequality so that one side is 0. Then write the other side as a simplified rational expression.

$\frac{6}{x-2} \geq -4$	**Write original inequality.**
$\frac{6}{x-2} + 4 \geq 0$	**Add 4 to each side.**
$\frac{6 + 4(x-2)}{x-2} \geq 0$	**Write left side as a single fraction.**
$\frac{4x-2}{x-2} \geq 0$	**Simplify.**

STEP 2 **Identify** the *critical x-values,* which are the x-values that make the numerator or denominator equal to 0.

Numerator equal to 0:	**Denominator equal to 0:**
$4x - 2 = 0$	$x - 2 = 0$
$x = \frac{1}{2}$	$x = 2$

So, the critical x-values are $x = \frac{1}{2}$ and $x = 2$.

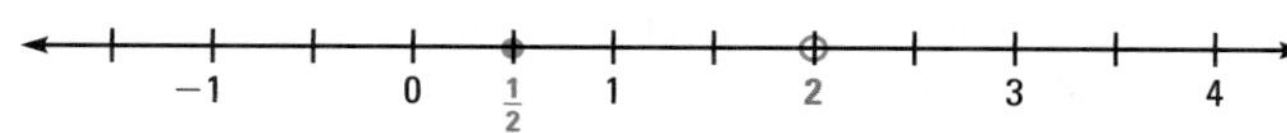

The critical x-values divide the number line into three intervals. Note that $x = \frac{1}{2}$ will be included in the solution, but $x = 2$ will not because it results in division by zero.

STEP 3 **Test** an x-value in each interval to see if it satisfies the original inequality. If it does, *every* x-value in the interval will satisfy the inequality. If it does not, *no* x-value in the interval will satisfy the inequality.

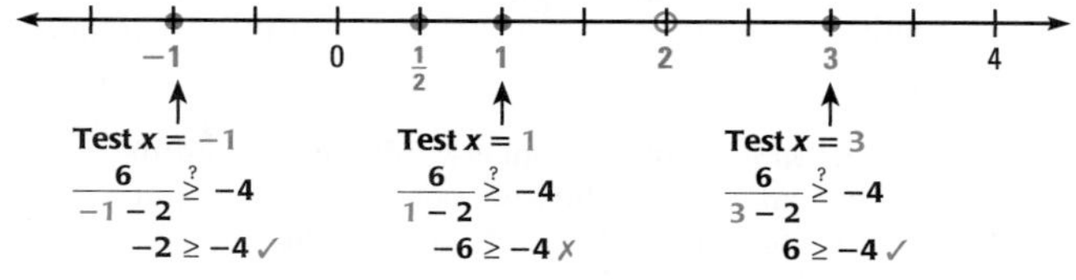

STEP 4 **Graph** the intervals where the tested x-values produce true statements.

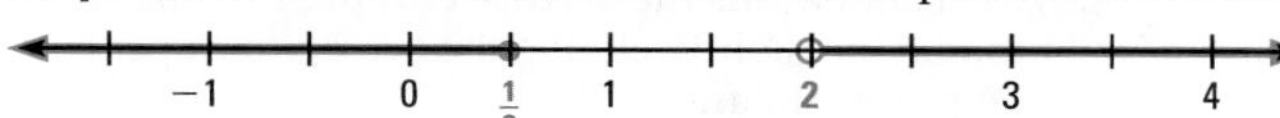

STEP 5 **Write** inequalities to describe the solution.

▶ The solution is $x \leq \frac{1}{2}$ or $x > 2$.

AVOID ERRORS

Do not multiply each side of an inequality by an expression involving x if the expression can take on both positive and negative values.

Extra Example 3

Solve $\frac{x+1}{x-3} \leq 3$ algebraically.
$x < 3$ or $x \geq 5$

Key Question to Ask for Example 3

- The given inequality contains the symbol ≥, so why does the second part of the solution contain the symbol > rather than ≥? **The number 2 cannot be part of the solution because $x = 2$ would produce a zero denominator.**

Closing the Lesson

Have students summarize the major points of the lesson and answer the Essential Question: What methods can be used to solve quadratic inequalities?

- **To solve a quadratic inequality with a table, rewrite the inequality so that 0 is on one side. Enter the inequality into a graphing calculator and use the table feature to determine when the inequality is positive or negative.**
- **To solve a quadratic inequality graphically, graph each side of the inequality. Use the graph to decide which side of the point of intersection satisfies the original inequality.**
- **To solve a quadratic inequality using algebraic methods, rewrite the inequality so that 0 is on one side and a single rational expression on the other side. Identify the critical x-values that make the numerator or denominator 0, test an x-value in each interval, and graph the intervals where the tested x-values produce true statements.**

Quadratic inequalities can be solved by using a table, a graph, or algebraic methods.

4 PRACTICE AND APPLY

Graphing Calculator

Exercises 1–6 Show students how finding an entry of 0 or ERROR in the Y_1 column of their calculator table can guide them toward the solution. Show them a variety of graphs of rational functions to demonstrate that either of these two situations *may* indicate that the function is changing signs, but that this is not always the case. Also make sure that they understand that ERROR indicates a vertical asymptote, so the corresponding x-value can *never* be part of the solution. This can be important in deciding which inequality symbols to write in the solution.

PRACTICE

EXAMPLE 1 on p. 598 for Exs. 1–6

Use a table to solve the inequality.

1. $\frac{5}{x-2} < 0$ $x < 2$
2. $\frac{x-5}{x+3} > 1$ $x < -3$
3. $\frac{x^2 - 3x + 2}{x - 3} < x$ $x < 3$
4. $\frac{10}{x+2} > 0$ $x > -2$
5. $\frac{-2x-3}{x-4} > 0$ $-1.5 < x < 4$
6. $\frac{x^2 - 4x + 8}{x - 1} < x$ $x < 1$ or $x > 2\frac{2}{3}$

EXAMPLE 2 on p. 598 for Exs. 7–12

Use a graph to solve the inequality.

7. $-\frac{4}{x+5} < 0$ $x > -5$
8. $\frac{4}{x-3} < 0$ $x < 3$
9. $\frac{8}{x^2+1} \geq 4$ $-1 \leq x \leq 1$
10. $\frac{20}{x^2+1} < 2$ $x < -3$ or $x > 3$
11. $\frac{3x+2}{x-1} < -2$ $0 < x < 1$
12. $\frac{3x+2}{x-1} > x$ $x < -0.449$ or $1 < x < 4.449$

EXAMPLE 3 on p. 599 for Exs. 13–18

Solve the inequality algebraically.

13. $\frac{3}{x+2} > 0$ $x > -2$
14. $-\frac{1}{x+5} \leq -2$ $-5 < x \leq -4.5$
15. $\frac{2}{x+2} > \frac{1}{x+3}$ $-4 < x < -3$ or $x > -2$
16. $\frac{5}{x-4} < \frac{1}{x+4}$ $x < -6$ or $-4 < x < 4$
17. $\frac{5}{x+3} \geq \frac{4}{x+2}$ $-3 < x < -2$ or $x \geq 2$
18. $\frac{2}{x+6} > \frac{-3}{x-3}$ $x > 3$ or $-6 < x < -2.$

19. **EGG PRODUCTION** From 1994 to 2002, the total number E (in billions) of eggs produced in the United States can be modeled by

$$E = \frac{-3680}{t - 50}, \quad 0 \leq t \leq 8$$

where t is the number of years since 1994. For what years was the number of eggs produced greater than 80 billion? 1999 to 2002

20. **PHONE COSTS** One phone company advertises a flat rate of \$.07 per minute for long-distance calls. Your long-distance plan charges \$5.00 per month plus a rate of \$.05 per minute. How many minutes do you have to talk each month so that your average cost is less than \$.07 per minute? more than 250 min

21. **SATELLITE TV** You subscribe to a satellite television service. The monthly cost for programming is \$43, and there is a one-time installation fee of \$50. The average monthly cost c of the service is given by $c = \frac{43t + 50}{t}$ where t is the time (in months) that you have subscribed to the service. For what subscription times is the average monthly cost at most \$47? Solve the problem using a table and using a graph. at least 13 mo

22. **FUNDRAISER** Your school is publishing a wildlife calendar to raise money for a local charity. The total cost of using the photos in the calendar is \$710. In addition to this one-time charge, the unit cost of printing each calendar is \$4.50.
    a. The school wants the average cost per calendar to be below \$10. Write a rational inequality relating the average cost per calendar to the desired cost per calendar. $\frac{710 + 4.5c}{c} < 10$
    b. Solve the inequality from part (a) by graphing. How many calendars need to be printed to bring the average cost per calendar below \$10? at least 130 calendars
    c. Suppose the school wanted to have the average cost per calendar be below \$6. How many calendars would then need to be printed? at least 474 calendars

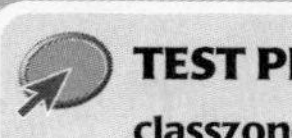
TEST PRACTICE
classzone.com

Lessons 8.4–8.6

1. **TRAVEL** A car travels 120 miles in the same amount of time that it takes a truck to travel 100 miles. The car travels 10 miles per hour faster than the truck. Use the verbal model to find the speed of the truck.

$$\frac{\text{Distance for car}}{\text{Speed of car}} = \frac{\text{Distance for truck}}{\text{Speed of truck}}$$

   A. 40 miles/hour
   B. 50 miles/hour
   C. 55 miles/hour
   D. 60 miles/hour

2. **RIVER CURRENT** The speed of a river's current is 3 miles per hour. You travel 2 miles with the current and then return to where you started in a total time of 1.25 hours. What is your approximate speed in still water?

   A. 3.0 miles/hour
   B. 3.9 miles/hour
   C. 5.0 miles/hour
   D. 5.5 miles/hour

3. **CYCLING** A cyclist travels 50 miles from her home to a state park at a speed of s miles per hour. On the return trip, she increases her speed by 5 miles per hour. Which expression represents the *total* time of the cyclist's round trip?

   A. $100s + 250$
   B. $\frac{2s + 5}{50}$
   C. $\frac{250}{s^2 - 5s}$
   D. $\frac{100s + 250}{s^2 + 5s}$

4. **ALLOYS** Brass is an alloy composed of 55% copper and 45% zinc by weight. You have 25 ounces of copper. About how many ounces of zinc do you need to make brass?

   A. 20.45 ounces
   B. 22.73 ounces
   C. 25.45 ounces
   D. 30.56 ounces

5. **GEOMETRY** In simplest form, what is the ratio of the volume of the rectangular prism to the volume of the inscribed cylinder?

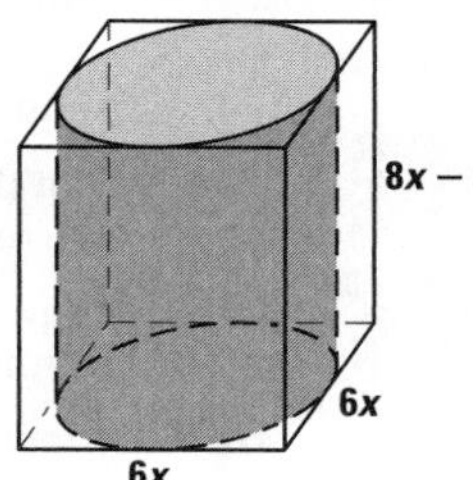

   A. $\frac{\pi}{4}$
   B. $\frac{4}{\pi}$
   C. π
   D. $\frac{12}{\pi}$

6. **OPEN-RESPONSE** Consider the following sphere and cube.

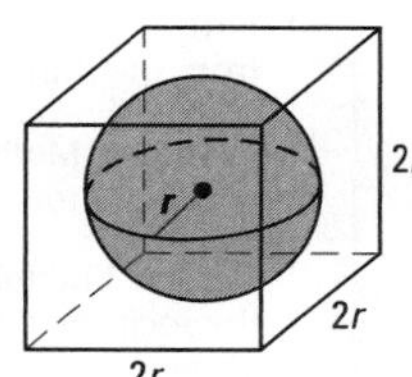

   a. Find the ratio of the volume of the sphere to the volume of the cube. Use the formula $V = \frac{4}{3}\pi r^3$ for the volume of a sphere and the formula $V = s^3$ for the volume of a cube where r is the radius of the sphere and s is the side length of the cube. Write your answer as a decimal rounded to the nearest hundredth.

   b. Show your procedure.

Kentucky Mixed Review

1. B
2. C
3. D
4. A
5. B
6. a. 0.52

b. $\frac{\text{Volume of sphere}}{\text{Volume of cube}} = \frac{\frac{4\pi r^3}{3}}{s^3} = \frac{\frac{4\pi r^3}{3}}{s^3} \cdot \frac{3}{3} = \frac{4\pi r^3}{3s^3}$

The side length of the cube is $2r$, so the ratio is

$\frac{4\pi r^3}{3s^3} = \frac{4\pi r^3}{3(2r)^3} = \frac{4\pi r^3}{24r^3} = \frac{\pi}{6} \approx 0.52$

8 CHAPTER SUMMARY

Animated Algebra
classzone.com
Electronic Function Library

Additional Resources

The following resources are available to help review the materials in this chapter.

Chapter 8 Resource Book

- Chapter Review Games and Activities, p. 71
- Cumulative Practice, Chs. 1–8, pp. 73–74

Student Resources in Spanish

eWorkbook

@HomeTutor

Vocabulary Practice

Vocabulary practice is available at **classzone.com**

BIG IDEAS

For Your Notebook

Big Idea 1

Graphing Rational Functions

Use the following steps to graph $f(x) = \frac{p(x)}{q(x)} = \frac{a_m x^m + a_{m-1}x^{m-1} + \cdots + a_1 x + a_0}{b_n x^n + b_{n-1}x^{n-1} + \cdots + b_1 x + b_0}$

where $p(x)$ and $q(x)$ have no common factors other than ± 1.

STEP 1 **Plot** the x-intercepts. The x-intercepts are the real zeros of $p(x)$.

STEP 2 **Draw** the vertical asymptote(s). A vertical asymptote occurs at each real zero of $q(x)$.

STEP 3 **Draw** the horizontal asymptote, if it exists.

If $m < n$, $y = 0$ is a horizontal asymptote.

If $m = n$, $y = \frac{a_m}{b_n}$ is a horizontal asymptote.

If $m > n$, there is no horizontal asymptote.

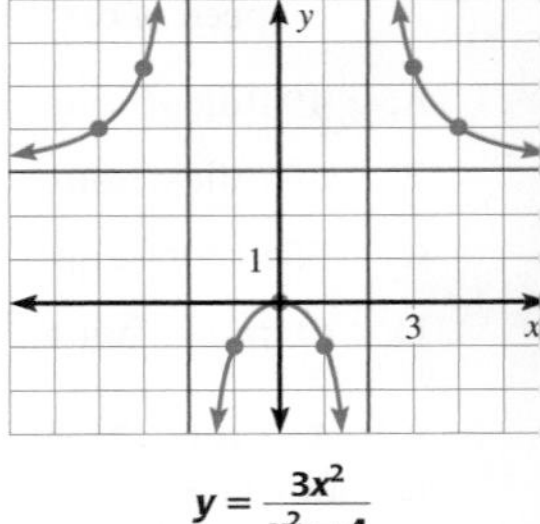

$y = \frac{3x^2}{x^2 - 4}$

STEP 4 **Plot** several points on both sides of each vertical asymptote.

Big Idea 2

Performing Operations with Rational Expressions

Operation	Example
Simplify Divide out common factors from the numerator and denominator.	$\frac{x^2 + 3x}{x^2 + 8x + 15} = \frac{x(x+3)}{(x+5)(x+3)} = \frac{x}{x+5}$
Multiply Multiply numerators and denominators. Then simplify.	$\frac{x}{15} \cdot \frac{3}{x^2 + 7x} = \frac{3x}{15x(x+7)} = \frac{1}{5(x+7)}$
Divide Multiply the first expression by the reciprocal of the second expression. Then simplify.	$\frac{x^2}{3x+1} \div \frac{1}{6x+2} = \frac{x^2}{3x+1} \cdot \frac{2(3x+1)}{1} = 2x^2$
Add or Subtract Write the expressions with like denominators. Then add or subtract the numerators over the common denominator. Lastly, simplify.	$\frac{5}{x} + \frac{x}{x+2} = \frac{5(x+2)}{x(x+2)} + \frac{x^2}{x(x+2)} = \frac{x^2 + 5x + 10}{x(x+2)}$

Big Idea 3

Solving Rational Equations

Solve $\frac{x}{x+1} + \frac{2}{x+4} = 1.$

STEP 1 **Find** the LCD. LCD is $(x + 1)(x + 4)$.

STEP 2 **Multiply** each side of the equation by the LCD. $x(x + 4) + 2(x + 1) = (x + 1)(x + 4)$

STEP 3 **Solve** the resulting equation.

$$x^2 + 4x + 2x + 2 = x^2 + 5x + 4$$
$$6x + 2 = 5x + 4$$
$$x = 2$$

@HomeTutor
classzone.com
• Multi-Language Glossary
• Vocabulary practice

REVIEW KEY VOCABULARY

- inverse variation, *p. 551*
- constant of variation, *p. 551*
- joint variation, *p. 553*
- rational function, *p. 558*
- simplified form of a rational expression, *p. 573*
- complex fraction, *p. 584*
- cross multiplying, *p. 589*

VOCABULARY EXERCISES

1. Copy and complete: If two variables x and y are related by an equation of the form $y = \frac{a}{x}$ where $a \neq 0$, then x and y show __?__. **inverse variation**
2. Suppose z varies jointly with x and y. What can you say about $\frac{z}{xy}$? **It is the constant of variation.**
3. Copy and complete: A function of the form $f(x) = \frac{p(x)}{q(x)}$ where $p(x)$ and $q(x)$ are polynomials and $q(x) \neq 0$ is called a(n) __?__. **rational function**
4. Give two examples of a complex fraction. **See margin.**
5. Copy and complete: When you rewrite the equation $\frac{3}{x} = \frac{2}{x-1}$ as $3(x - 1) = 2x$, you are __?__. **cross multiplying**

REVIEW EXAMPLES AND EXERCISES

Use the review examples and exercises below to check your understanding of the concepts you have learned in each lesson of Chapter 8.

8.1 Model Inverse and Joint Variation

pp. 551–557

EXAMPLE

The variables x and y vary inversely, and $y = 12$ when $x = 3$. Write an equation that relates x and y. Then find y when $x = -4$.

$y = \frac{a}{x}$ **Write general equation for inverse variation.**

$12 = \frac{a}{3}$ **Substitute 12 for y and 3 for x.**

$36 = a$ **Solve for a.**

▸ The inverse variation equation is $y = \frac{36}{x}$. When $x = -4$, $y = \frac{36}{-4} = -9$.

EXERCISES

EXAMPLE 2 on p. 551 for Exs. 6–9

The variables x and y vary inversely. Use the given values to write an equation relating x and y. Then find y when $x = -3$.

6. $x = 1, y = 5$ $\quad y = \frac{5}{x}; -\frac{5}{3}$
7. $x = -4, y = -6$ $\quad y = \frac{24}{x}; -8$
8. $x = \frac{5}{2}, y = 18$ $\quad y = \frac{45}{x}; -15$
9. $x = -12, y = \frac{2}{3}$ $\quad y = \frac{-8}{x}; \frac{8}{3}$

Extra Example 8.1

The variables x and y vary inversely, and $y = 18$ when $x = -4$. Write an equation that relates x and y. Then find y when $x = 12$. $y = -\frac{72}{x}$; $y = -6$

4. *Sample answer:*

$$\frac{\frac{2}{x+3}}{\frac{1}{x+1} - \frac{5}{x-1}} \text{ and } \frac{\frac{2x}{3x+5}}{1 + \frac{4x-2}{x+2}}$$

8 CHAPTER REVIEW

Extra Example 8.2

Graph $y = \frac{-2}{x - 4} + 3$. State the domain and range.

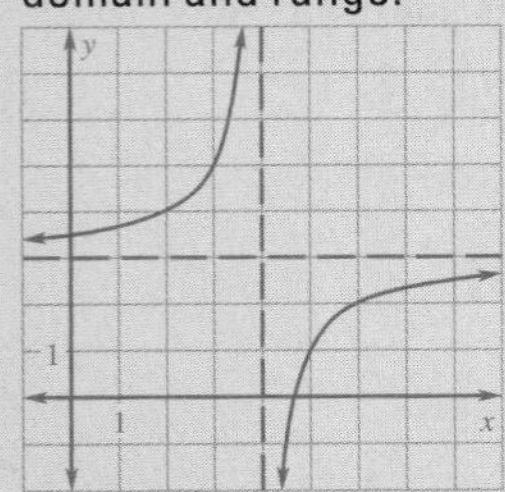

domain: all real numbers except 4; range: all real numbers except 3

Extra Example 8.3

Graph $y = \frac{x^2 + 4}{x^2 - 4}$.

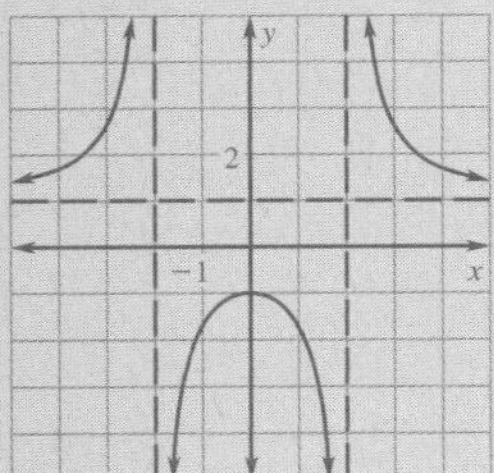

8.2 Graph Simple Rational Functions *pp. 558–563*

EXAMPLE

Graph $y = \frac{2x + 5}{x - 1}$. State the domain and range.

STEP 1 **Draw** the asymptotes. Solve $x - 1 = 0$ for x to find the vertical asymptote $x = 1$. The horizontal asymptote is the line $y = \frac{2}{1} = 2$.

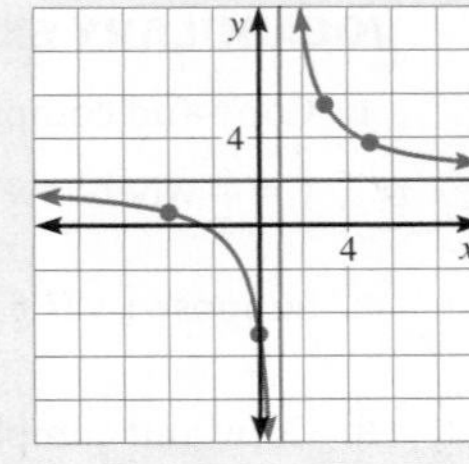

STEP 2 **Plot** points to the left and to the right of the vertical asymptote.

STEP 3 **Draw** the two branches of the hyperbola so that they pass through the plotted points and approach the asymptotes.

▶ The domain is all real numbers except 1. The range is all real numbers except 2.

EXERCISES

EXAMPLES 2 and 3 on pp. 559–560 for Exs. 10–12

Graph the function. State the domain and range. **10–12. See margin.**

10. $y = \frac{4}{x - 3}$ **11.** $y = \frac{1}{x + 5} + 2$ **12.** $f(x) = \frac{3x - 2}{x - 4}$

10.

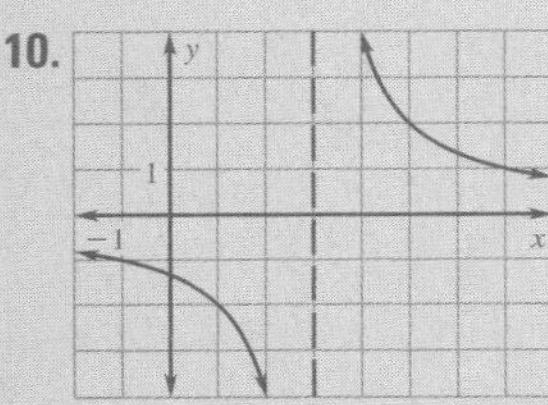

domain: all real numbers except 3, range: all real numbers except 0

11.

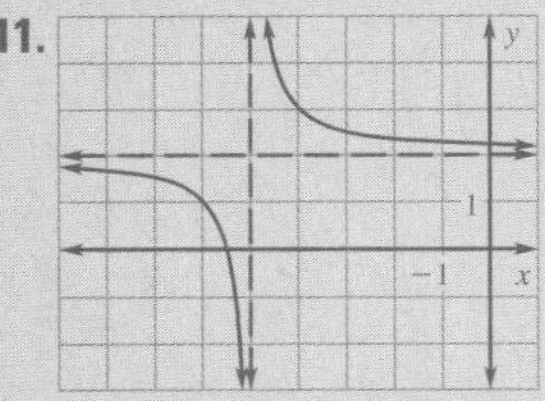

domain: all real numbers except −5, range: all real numbers except 2

12.

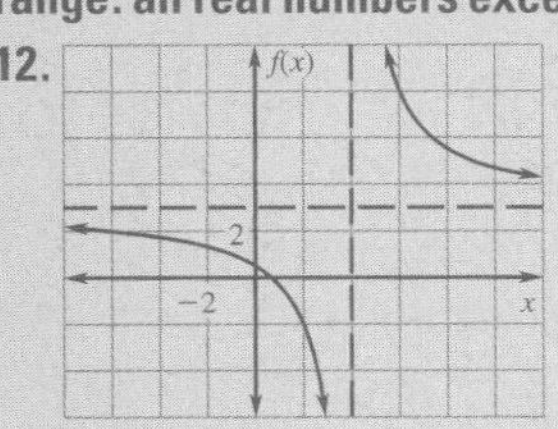

domain: all real numbers except 4, range: all real numbers except 3

8.3 Graph General Rational Functions *pp. 565–571*

EXAMPLE

Graph $y = \frac{2x^2}{x + 2}$.

- The numerator has 0 as its only zero, so the graph has an x-intercept at $(0, 0)$.
- The denominator has -2 as its only zero, so the graph has a vertical asymptote at $x = -2$.
- The degree of the numerator (2) is greater than the degree of the denominator (1). So, there is no horizontal asymptote. The graph has the same end behavior as the graph of $y = \frac{2}{1}x^{2-1} = 2x$.

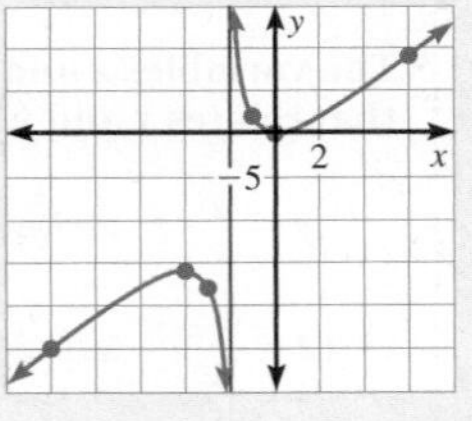

EXERCISES

EXAMPLES 1, 2, and 3 on pp. 565–566 for Exs. 13–18

Graph the function. **13–18. See margin.**

13. $y = \frac{5}{x^2 + 1}$ **14.** $y = \frac{4x^2}{x - 1}$ **15.** $h(x) = \frac{6x^2}{x - 2}$

16. $y = \frac{-8}{x^2 + 3}$ **17.** $y = \frac{x^2 + 6}{x^2 - 3x - 40}$ **18.** $g(x) = \frac{x^2 - 1}{x + 4}$

13.

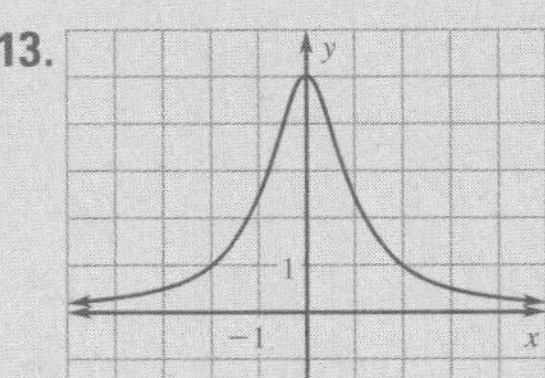

14.

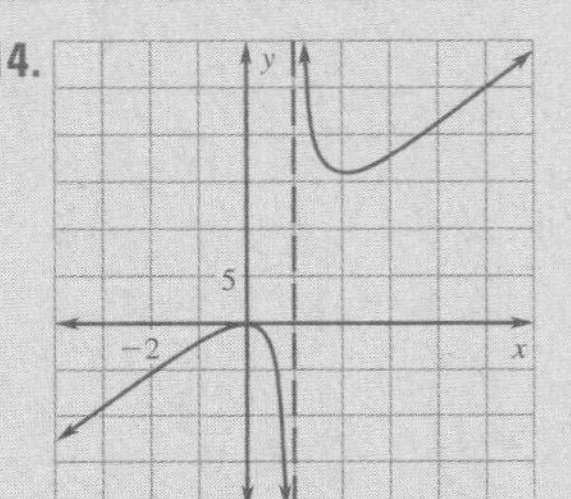

15.

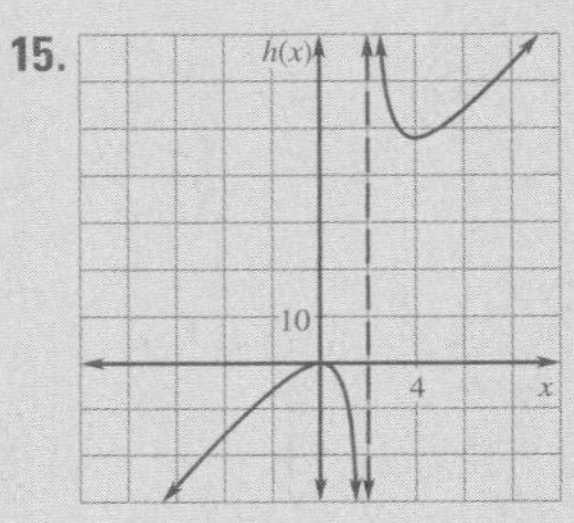

@HomeTutor
classzone.com
Chapter Review Practice

8.4 Multiply and Divide Rational Expressions *pp. 573–580*

EXAMPLE

Divide: $\frac{3x + 27}{6x - 48} \div \frac{x^2 + 9x}{x^2 - 4x - 32}$

$$\frac{3x + 27}{6x - 48} \div \frac{x^2 + 9x}{x^2 - 4x - 32} = \frac{3x + 27}{6x - 48} \cdot \frac{x^2 - 4x - 32}{x^2 + 9x}$$ **Multiply by reciprocal.**

$$= \frac{3(x + 9)}{6(x - 8)} \cdot \frac{(x + 4)(x - 8)}{x(x + 9)}$$ **Factor.**

$$= \frac{\cancel{3}\cancel{(x + 9)}(x + 4)\cancel{(x - 8)}}{2\cancel{(3)}\cancel{(x - 8)}(x)\cancel{(x + 9)}}$$ **Divide out common factors.**

$$= \frac{x + 4}{2x}$$ **Simplified form**

EXERCISES

XAMPLES
, 4, 6, and 7
n pp. 575–577
r Exs. 19–22

Perform the indicated operation. Simplify the result.

19. $\frac{80x^4}{y^3} \cdot \frac{xy}{5x^2}$ $\frac{16x^3}{y^2}$

20. $\frac{x - 3}{2x - 8} \cdot \frac{6x^2 - 96}{x^2 - 9}$ $\frac{3(x + 4)}{x + 3}$

21. $\frac{16x^2 - 8x + 1}{x^3 - 7x^2 + 12x} \div \frac{20x^2 - 5x}{15x^3}$ $\frac{3x(4x - 1)}{(x - 4)(x - 3)}$

22. $\frac{x^2 - 13x + 40}{x^2 - 2x - 15} \div (x^2 - 5x - 24)$ $\frac{1}{(x + 3)^2}$

8.5 Add and Subtract Rational Expressions *pp. 582–588*

EXAMPLE

Add: $\frac{x}{6x + 24} + \frac{x + 2}{x^2 + 9x + 20}$

The denominators factor as $6(x + 4)$ and $(x + 4)(x + 5)$, so the LCD is $6(x + 4)(x + 5)$. Use this result to rewrite each expression with a common denominator, and then add.

$$\frac{x}{6x + 24} + \frac{x + 2}{x^2 + 9x + 20} = \frac{x}{6(x + 4)} + \frac{x + 2}{(x + 4)(x + 5)}$$

$$= \frac{x}{6(x + 4)} \cdot \frac{x + 5}{x + 5} + \frac{x + 2}{(x + 4)(x + 5)} \cdot \frac{6}{6}$$

$$= \frac{x^2 + 5x}{6(x + 4)(x + 5)} + \frac{6x + 12}{6(x + 4)(x + 5)}$$

$$= \frac{x^2 + 11x + 12}{6(x + 4)(x + 5)}$$

EXERCISES

XAMPLES
and 4
n pp. 583–584
r Exs. 23–25

Perform the indicated operation and simplify. 23–25. See margin.

23. $\frac{5}{6(x + 3)} + \frac{x + 4}{2x}$

24. $\frac{5x}{x + 8} + \frac{4x - 9}{x^2 + 5x - 24}$

25. $\frac{x + 2}{x^2 + 4x + 3} - \frac{5x}{x^2 - 9}$

Extra Example 8.4

Multiply:

$\frac{6x^2 - 18x}{x^2 - 10x + 21} \cdot \frac{x^2 - 14x + 49}{3x^2}$

$\frac{2(x - 7)}{x}$

Extra Example 8.5

Subtract: $\frac{3x}{4x - 12} - \frac{x - 5}{(x - 3)(x + 6)}$

$\frac{3x^2 + 14x + 20}{4(x - 3)(x - 6)}$

23. $\frac{3x^2 + 26x + 36}{6x(x + 3)}$

24. $\frac{5x^2 - 11x - 9}{(x + 8)(x - 3)}$

25. $\frac{-2(2x^2 + 3x + 3)}{(x - 3)(x + 3)(x + 1)}$

16.

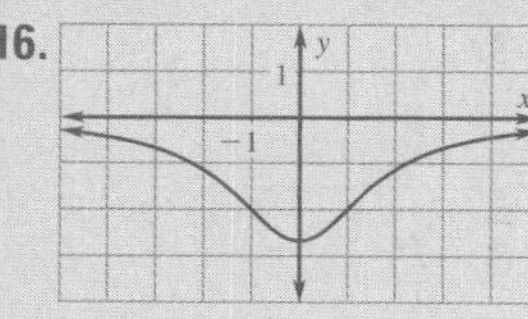

17.

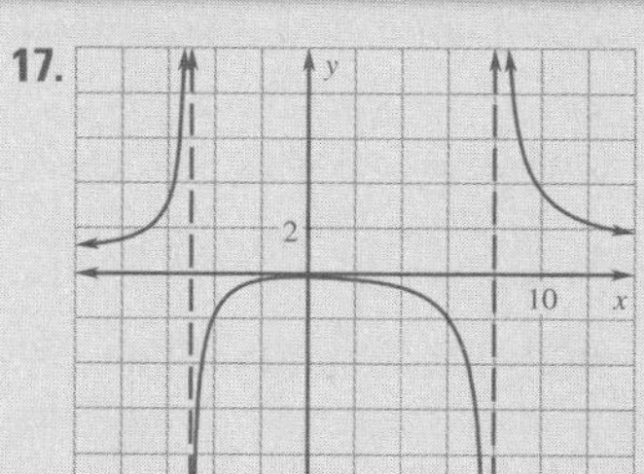

18.

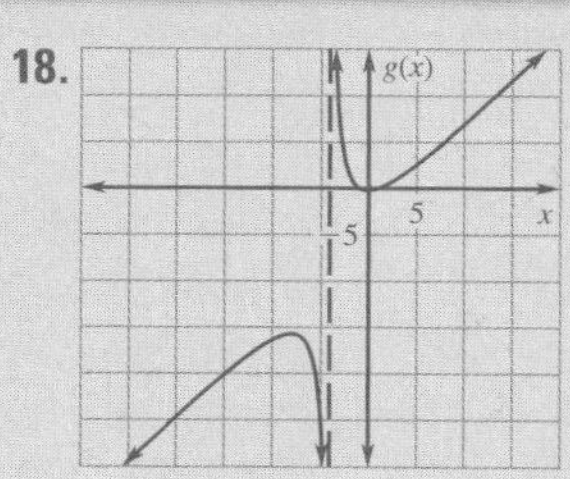

8 CHAPTER REVIEW

Extra Example 8.6

Solve $\frac{5(x-1)}{x^2-9} = \frac{15}{x+3}$. 4

8.6 Solve Rational Equations

pp. 589–595

EXAMPLE

Solve: $\frac{3x}{x+1} + \frac{6}{2x} = \frac{7}{x}$

The least common denominator is $2x(x + 1)$.

$\frac{3x}{x+1} + \frac{6}{2x} = \frac{7}{x}$	**Write original equation.**
$2x(x+1)\left(\frac{3x}{x+1} + \frac{6}{2x}\right) = 2x(x+1) \cdot \frac{7}{x}$	**Multiply each side by the LCD, $2x(x + 1)$.**
$2x(3x) + 6(x + 1) = 2(x + 1)(7)$	**Simplify.**
$6x^2 + 6x + 6 = 14x + 14$	**Simplify.**
$6x^2 - 8x - 8 = 0$	**Write in standard form.**
$3x^2 - 4x - 4 = 0$	**Divide each side by 2.**
$(3x + 2)(x - 2) = 0$	**Factor.**
$3x + 2 = 0$ or $x - 2 = 0$	**Zero product property**
$x = -\frac{2}{3}$ or $x = 2$	**Solve for x.**

▶ The solutions are $-\frac{2}{3}$ and 2. Check these in the original equation to make sure neither solution is extraneous.

EXERCISES

EXAMPLES 1, 4, and 5 on pp. 589–591 for Exs. 26–36

Solve the equation by cross multiplying. Check your solution(s).

26. $\frac{2x}{9} = \frac{2}{x}$ ± 3

27. $\frac{5}{x} = \frac{7}{x+2}$ 5

28. $\frac{x-1}{4} = \frac{3x}{9}$ -3

29. $\frac{2}{x+2} = \frac{6}{2x+5}$ -1

30. $\frac{x+12}{3} = \frac{2x+3}{x+2}$ $-5, -3$

31. $\frac{2x}{x+4} = \frac{-3x}{4x-3}$ $-\frac{6}{11}, 0$

Solve the equation by using the LCD. Check for extraneous solutions.

32. $\frac{5}{2} + \frac{3}{x} = 3$ 6

33. $\frac{8(x-1)}{x^2-4} = \frac{4}{x+2}$ 0

34. $\frac{3x}{x+1} = \frac{12}{x^2-1} + 2$ $-2, 5$

35. $\frac{2(x+7)}{x+4} - 2 = \frac{2x+20}{2x+8}$ no solution

36. BASKETBALL So far this season, a basketball player has made 60 of 75 free-throw attempts.

a. Write a rational expression that represents the player's free-throw percentage (expressed as a decimal) if she makes her next x free throws. $p = \frac{60+x}{75+x}$

b. How many consecutive free throws must the player make in order to raise her free-throw percentage to at least 82%? at least 9 free throws

Chapter Test, p. 607

7.

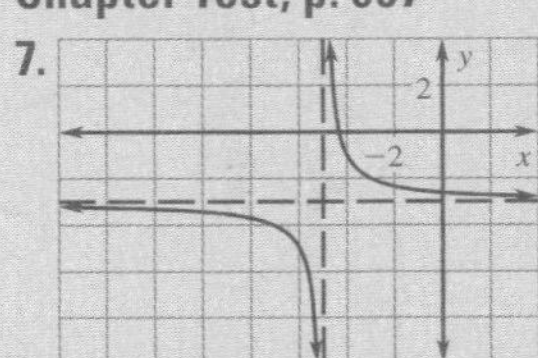

domain: all real numbers except −5, range: all real numbers except −3

8 CHAPTER TEST

The variables x and y vary inversely. Use the given values to write an equation relating x and y. Then find y when $x = 4$.

1. $x = 5, y = 2$ $y = \frac{10}{x}; \frac{5}{2}$
2. $x = -2, y = 8$ $y = \frac{-16}{x}; -4$
3. $x = \frac{3}{2}, y = 10$ $y = \frac{15}{x}; \frac{15}{4}$
4. $x = 3, y = 6$ $y = \frac{18}{x}; \frac{9}{2}$
5. $x = -4, y = \frac{7}{2}$ $y = \frac{-14}{x}; -\frac{7}{2}$
6. $x = \frac{3}{4}, y = \frac{5}{8}$ $y = \frac{15}{32x}; \frac{15}{128}$

Graph the function. State the domain and range. 7–9. See margin.

7. $y = \frac{2}{x+5} - 3$
8. $y = \frac{-1}{x-4} - 1$
9. $f(x) = \frac{6-x}{2x+1}$

Graph the function. 10–12. See margin.

10. $y = \frac{4}{x^2+2}$
11. $y = \frac{x^2-4}{x^2+8x+15}$
12. $g(x) = \frac{x^2+3}{2x-1}$

Find the least common multiple of the polynomials.

13. $(x-3)(x+5)$ and $x(x+5)$ $x(x-3)(x+5)$
14. $4x^2(x-2)$ and $8x(x+2)$ $8x^2(x-2)(x+2)$
15. $x^2 - 4x$ and $x^2 - 2x - 8$ $x(x-4)(x+2)$
16. $2x + 6$ and $x^3 + 10x^2 + 21x$ $2x(x+7)(x+3)$

Perform the indicated operation and simplify.

17. $\frac{3x^2y}{4x^3y^5} \div \frac{6y^2}{2xy^3}$ $\frac{1}{4y^3}$
18. $\frac{x^2-3x-4}{x^2-3x-18} \cdot \frac{x-6}{x+1}$ $\frac{x-4}{x+3}$
19. $\frac{x^2-8x+15}{x^2+12x+32} \cdot \frac{x+4}{x^2-25}$ $\frac{x-3}{(x+5)(x+8)}$
20. $\frac{x^2-11x+28}{x^2+5x+4} \div (x^2-16)$ $\frac{x-7}{(x+4)^2(x+1)}$
21. $\frac{3x}{x+5} - \frac{4x+1}{x+5}$ $\frac{-x-1}{x+5}$
22. $\frac{4}{x-3} + \frac{2}{x+6}$ $\frac{6(x+3)}{(x-3)(x+6)}$
23. $\frac{3x}{x^2+x-12} - \frac{6}{x+4}$ $\frac{-3(x-6)}{(x+4)(x-3)}$
24. $\frac{4}{x+5} + \frac{2x}{x^2-25}$ $\frac{2(3x-10)}{(x+5)(x-5)}$

Solve the equation. Check for extraneous solutions.

25. $\frac{3}{x+2} = \frac{x-3}{2x+4}$ 9
26. $\frac{1}{x+6} + \frac{x+1}{x} = \frac{13}{x+6}$ 2, 3
27. $\frac{x-2}{x-1} = \frac{x+2}{x+4}$ 6

28. **SOUND INTENSITY** The intensity I of a sound varies inversely with the square of the distance r from the source of the sound. Write an equation relating I, r, and a constant a. $I = \frac{a}{r^2}$

29. **CABLE TV** You have subscribed to a cable television service. The cable company charges you a one-time installation fee of \$30 and a monthly fee of \$50. Write and graph a model that gives the average cost per month as a function of the number of months you have subscribed to the service. After how many months will the average cost be \$56? $C = \frac{30 + 50m}{m}$, see margin for art; 5 mo.

30. **WEB HOSTING** You are building a new website for your school. A company that hosts websites offers a dedicated server for a \$50 setup fee plus a monthly fee of \$99. How many months would you need to use this service in order for your average monthly cost to fall to \$100? 50 mo

Additional Resources

Assessment Book

- Chapter Test, Levels A, B, C, pp. 112–117
- Standardized Chapter Test, pp. 118–119
- SAT/ACT Chapter Test, pp. 120–121
- Alternative Assessment, pp. 122–123

Test Generator CD-ROM

Chapter Test

Easily-readable reduced copies (with answers) of Chapter Test B, the Standardized Chapter Test, and the Alternative Assessment from the Assessment Book can be found on pp. 548E–548F.

10.
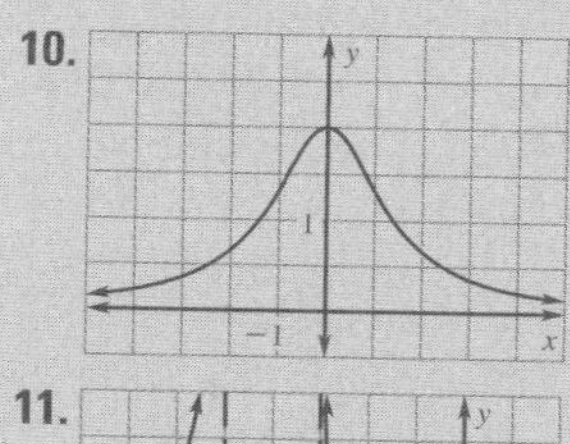

11.
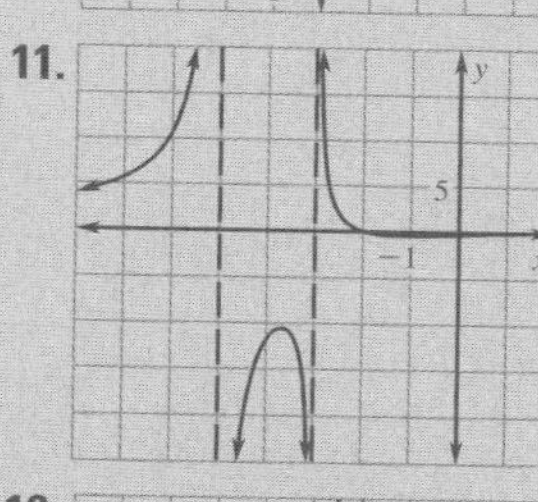

12.
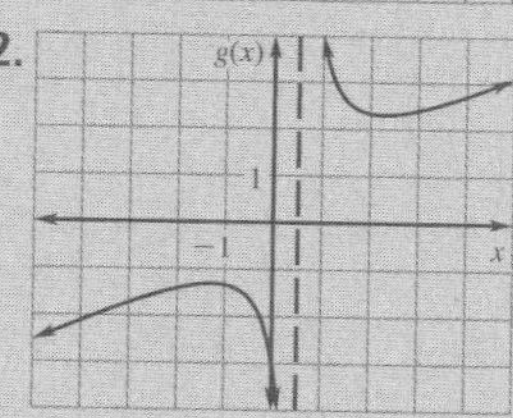

29.
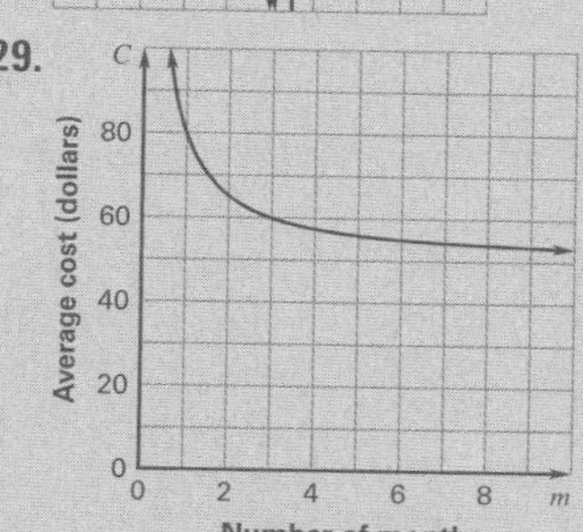

8.
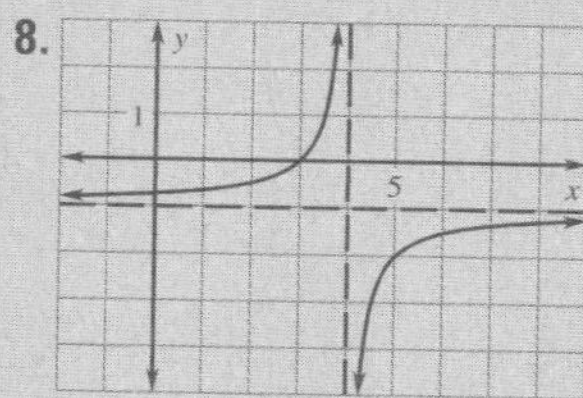

domain: all real numbers except 4,
range: all real numbers except −1

9.
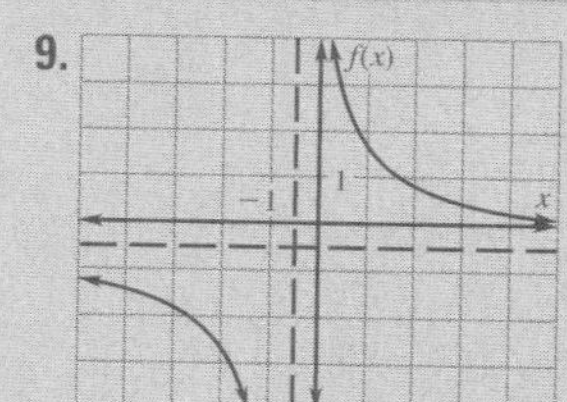

domain: all real numbers except $-\frac{1}{2}$,
range: all real numbers except $-\frac{1}{2}$

MULTIPLE-CHOICE QUESTIONS

Some of the information you need to solve a multiple-choice question may appear in a table, a diagram, or a graph.

PROBLEM 1

Which rational expression represents the ratio of the perimeter to the area of the playground shown in the diagram?

A. $\frac{9}{7x}$ B. $\frac{1}{x}$

C. $\frac{11}{14x}$ D. $\frac{1}{2x}$

Plan

INTERPRET THE DIAGRAM Determine the missing dimensions on the diagram. Then use them to write expressions for the perimeter and area of the playground.

Solution

STEP 1 Find the missing dimensions and write an expression for the perimeter.

Copy the diagram. Then find and label the missing dimensions.

Use subtraction and addition to find the dimensions that are not labeled on the diagram. The missing dimensions are $\mathbf{4x}$ and $\mathbf{3x}$.

$$\text{Perimeter} = \mathbf{4x} + x + 2x + \mathbf{3x} + 6x + 2x$$
$$= 18x$$

STEP 2 Write an expression for the area.

The playground consists of two rectangles, one with dimensions $\mathbf{x}$ **by** $\mathbf{2x}$ and the other with dimensions $\mathbf{2x}$ **by** $\mathbf{6x}$.

To find the area of the playground, add the areas of the two rectangles.

$$\text{Area} = \mathbf{x(2x)} + \mathbf{2x(6x)}$$
$$= 2x^2 + 12x^2$$
$$= 14x^2$$

STEP 3 Find the ratio of the perimeter to the area.

The ratio of the perimeter to the area is:

$$\frac{\text{Perimeter}}{\text{Area}} = \frac{18x}{14x^2} = \frac{2x(9)}{2x(7x)} = \frac{9}{7x}$$

▸ The correct answer is A.

TEST PRACTICE
classzone.com

PROBLEM 2

The table shows how the force F (in pounds) needed to loosen a certain bolt with a wrench depends on the length ℓ (in inches) of the wrench's handle. Which equation relates ℓ and F?

ℓ (in.)	F (lb)
4	375
6	250
10	150
12	125

A. $F = 1500\ell$ B. $F = 93.75\ell$

C. $F = \frac{1500}{\ell}$ D. $F = \frac{93.75}{\ell}$

Plan

INTERPRET THE TABLE The table shows four data pairs (ℓ, F). To write an equation relating ℓ and F, you need to find a pattern in the data. As ℓ increases, the value of F decreases, but not in a linear pattern. So the relationship *may* be an inverse variation.

Solution

P 1 tify a pattern in the pairs (ℓ, F).

Find the product $\ell \cdot F$ for each data pair.

$4(375) = 1500$ $6(250) = 1500$

$10(150) = 1500$ $12(125) = 1500$

P 2 e an equation that tes ℓ and F.

Each product equals 1500, so the data show inverse variation.

An equation relating ℓ and F is the following:

$\ell \cdot F = 1500$ **Use the result from Step 1.**

$F = \frac{1500}{\ell}$ **Solve for F.**

▶ The correct answer is C.

PRACTICE

1. Which rational expression represents the ratio of the perimeter to the area of the figure shown?

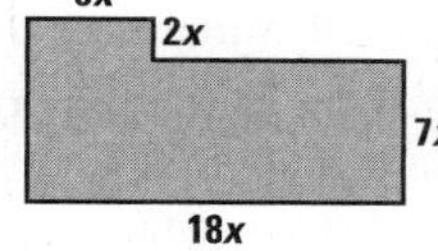

A. $\frac{29}{67x}$ B. $\frac{3}{10x^2}$

C. $\frac{11x}{18x^2}$ D. $\frac{9}{23x}$

2. Which equation represents the ordered pairs in the table?

x	2	4	6	8	10
y	180	90	60	45	36

A. $y = \frac{360}{x}$ B. $y = \frac{x}{360}$ C. $y = \frac{90}{x}$ D. $y = \frac{x}{90}$

TEST PREPARATION

Kentucky Test Preparation

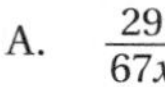

1. D
2. A

Kentucky Test Practice

1. B
2. C
3. A
4. C
5. D
6. D
7. B
8. A

Kentucky Test Practice

TEST PREPARATION

MULTIPLE-CHOICE

In Exercises 1 and 2, use the given graph of a rational function.

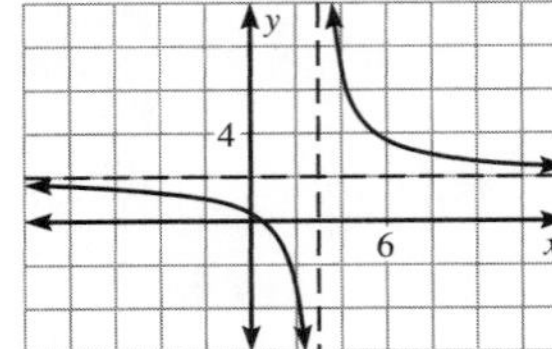

1. What is the range of the function?
   - A. All real numbers
   - B. All real numbers except 2
   - C. All real numbers except 3
   - D. All real numbers except 5

2. Which statement is false?
   - A. The line $x = 3$ is an asymptote.
   - B. The line $y = 2$ is an asymptote.
   - C. The function is undefined for $x = 2$.
   - D. The value of y is unbounded.

In Exercises 3 and 4, use the given table.

p	−12	3	30	−1.5
q	2	1	−5	−0.5
r	−2	1	−2	1

3. What is the relationship among the variables?
   - A. The variable p varies jointly with q and r.
   - B. The variable p varies jointly with q and the square of r.
   - C. The variable r varies inversely with the sum of p and q.
   - D. The variable q varies inversely with the sum of p and r.

4. What is the value of r when $p = 20$ and $q = -4$?
   - A. -5
   - B. $-\frac{10}{3}$
   - C. $-\frac{5}{3}$
   - D. $-\frac{1}{5}$

In Exercises 5 and 6, use the given graph of a rational function.

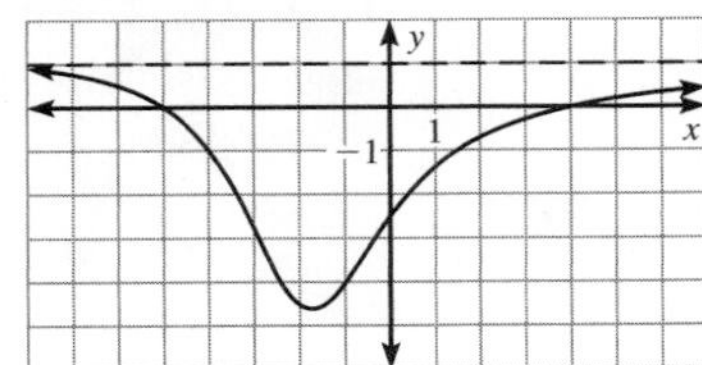

5. What are the x-intercepts of the graph?
   - A. -5 and -2.5
   - B. -2.5 and 4
   - C. -4 and 5
   - D. -5 and 4

6. What is the horizontal asymptote of the graph?
   - A. $x = -2$
   - B. $y = 0$
   - C. $x = 1$
   - D. $y = 1$

7. Consider a rectangle whose dimensions change but whose area remains constant. The rectangle's length ℓ varies inversely with its width w. The diagram below shows the rectangle at one moment in time. Which equation relates ℓ and w?

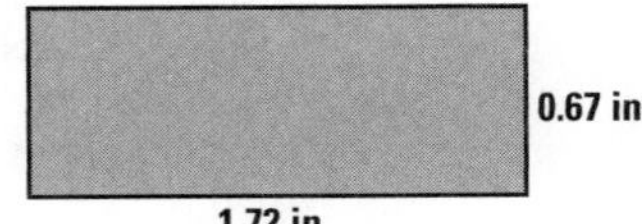

   - A. $w = 0.67\ell$
   - B. $\ell w = 1.1524$
   - C. $w = 1.72\ell$
   - D. $\ell = 1.1524w$

8. What is the approximate radius of a cylinder that has the same volume as the rectangular prism below and has the least surface area possible?

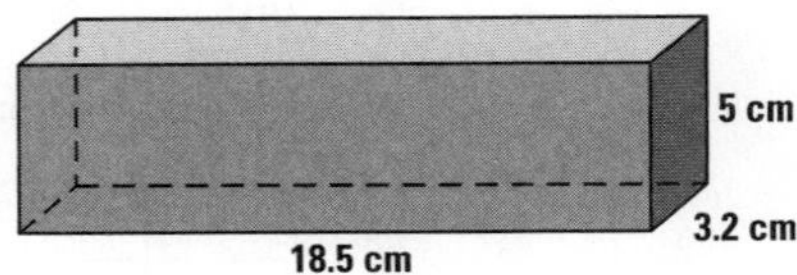

   - A. 3.61 cm
   - B. 3.84 cm
   - C. 6.00 cm
   - D. 7.66 cm

TEST PRACTICE
classzone.com

MULTIPLE-CHOICE

9. What is the solution to the equation below?

$$\frac{4}{x+1} - \frac{1}{x} = 1$$

A. -1

B. 0

C. $\frac{2}{3}$

D. 1

10. What is the domain of the function below?

$$f(x) = \frac{x-3}{2x^2 - 4x + 2}$$

A. all real numbers except 3

B. all real numbers except 1

C. all real numbers except 1 and 3

D. all real numbers

11. The variables m and n vary inversely, and $m = -2$ when $n = -8$. What is the value of n when $m = 5$?

A. -4

B. -3.2

C. 3.2

D. 4

12. So far, Luis has turned in 15 of 17 homework assignments. However, Luis plans to do every future assignment. What is the *total* number of assignments that Luis must turn in to have a homework percentage of exactly 95%? Find out by solving the equation $\frac{15+x}{17+x} = 0.95$.

A. 3 assignments

B. 23 assignments

C. 38 assignments

D. 40 assignments

OPEN-RESPONSE

13. From 1980 to 2001, the number n (in millions) of males enrolled in high school in the United States can be modeled by

$$n = \frac{0.0441x^2 - 1.08x + 7.25}{0.00565x^2 - 0.142x + 1.00}$$

where x is the number of years since 1980.

a. Make a table of values showing the enrollment at 2 year intervals for the years 1980 to 2000.

b. Graph the model.

c. Use your graph to estimate the year in which 7.7 million males were enrolled in high school.

d. Analyze the graph's trend. Do you think it will it continue indefinitely? Justify your answer.

14. A digital video recorder costs \$99.99, and a programming service for the digital video recorder costs \$12.95 per month.

a. Write a model that gives the average cost per month C as a function of the number of months m you have subscribed to the service.

b. Graph the model. Use the graph to estimate the number of months that you need to subscribe before the average cost drops to \$14 per month.

c. What is the equation of the horizontal asymptote? What does the asymptote represent?

TEST PREPARATION

9. D

10. B

11. C

12. B

13. a.

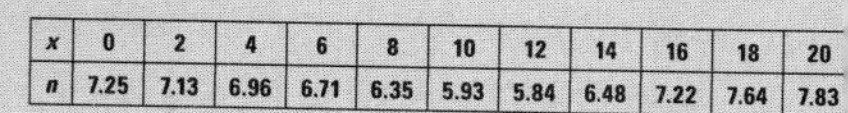

x	0	2	4	6	8	10	12	14	16	18	20
n	7.25	7.13	6.96	6.71	6.35	5.93	5.84	6.48	7.22	7.64	7.83

b.

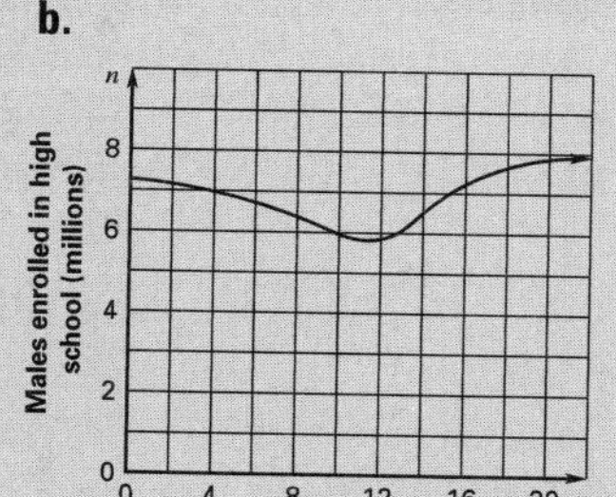

c. 1998

d. Yes. *Sample answer:* This data set is for a 20-year period and about halfway through that period the number of males in high school drops to 5.8 million. I think another drop will occur in about 2010.

14. a.

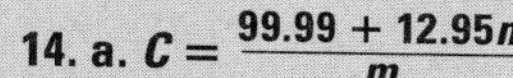

$$C = \frac{99.99 + 12.95m}{m}$$

b.

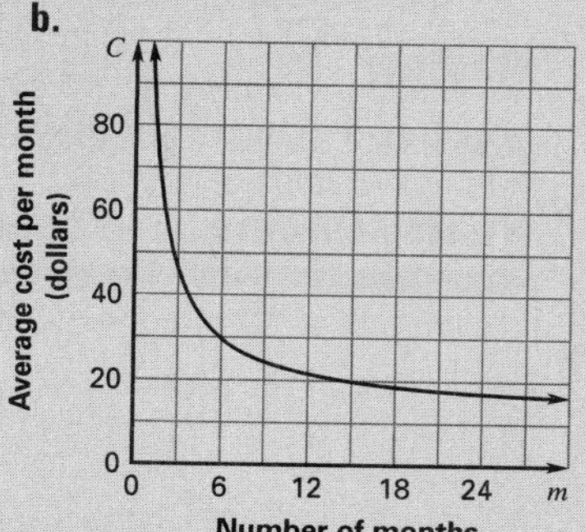

96 mo.

c. $C = 12.95$; the value that the average cost per month approaches as time goes on.

9 Pacing and Assignment Guide

REGULAR SCHEDULE

Pre-AP For pacing and assignments for a Pre-AP course, see the *Algebra 2 Toolkit*.

Lesson	Les. Day	BASIC	AVERAGE	ADVANCED
9.1 MA-HS-3.3.1	Day 1	EP p. 1011 Exs. 5–8; pp. 617–619 Exs. 1–8, 18–21, 23–27 odd, 31–33, 47–54, 58	pp. 617–619 Exs. 1, 2, 9–13, 18–21, 22–26 even, 34–42, 47–56, 59	pp. 617–619 Exs. 1, 2, 15–19, 28–30, 34–46*, 48–57*
9.2 MA-HS-5.3.6	Day 1	pp. 623–625 Exs. 1, 2, 3–17 odd, 23–30, 38, 55–58, 61	pp. 623–625 Exs. 1, 2, 4–18 even, 23–25, 30–33, 38–42, 51, 52, 56–59, 62	pp. 623–625 Exs. 1, 2, 19–22, 25, 34–54*, 57–60*
9.3 MA-HS-3.1.6	Day 1	pp. 629–632 Exs. 1–8, 9–21 odd, 22–30 even, 31–43 odd, 44–46, 53, 62–66, 70	pp. 629–632 Exs. 1, 2, 10–20 even, 23–29 odd, 30–38 even, 43–59 odd, 63–68	pp. 629–632 Exs. 1, 2, 18–21, 26–29, 39–43, 48–69*
9.4 MA-HS-3.1.5	Day 1	pp. 637–639 Exs. 1, 2, 3–13 odd, 15–22, 35–38, 48–51, 54	pp. 637–639 Exs. 1, 2, 4–10 even, 15, 16, 23–28, 35, 39–45, 48–52, 55	pp. 637–639 Exs. 1, 2, 12–14, 29–47*, 49–53*
9.5 MA-HS-3.1.5	Day 1	pp. 645–648 Exs. 1, 2, 3–15 odd, 16–23, 26–29, 38–42, 45	pp. 645–648 Exs. 1, 2, 4–14 even, 15–17, 20–23, 26, 30–35, 38–43, 46	pp. 645–648 Exs. 1, 2, 12–15, 22–37*, 39–44*, 46
9.6 MA-HS-3.1.5	Day 1	EP p. 1013 Exs. 41–44; pp. 655–657 Exs. 1–8, 12, 13–21 odd, 48	pp. 655–657 Exs. 1, 2, 5–9, 12, 14–20 even, 21, 48	pp. 655–657 Exs. 1, 2, 6–12, 14–20 even, 21, 48
	Day 2	pp. 655–657 Exs. 22–36 even, 37–39, 49–51, 54–55	pp. 655–657 Exs. 23–35 odd, 36–44 even, 45, 49–52, 54–55	pp. 655–657 Exs. 25–27, 32–36, 41–47*, 49–53*, 54
9.7 MA-HS-5.3.6	Day 1	EP p. 1012 Exs. 5–8; pp. 661–664 Exs. 1–5, 9–15, 21–25, 39–42, 46	pp. 661–664 Exs. 1, 2, 4–6, 14–17, 21, 26–29, 34–36, 39–44, 47	pp. 661–664 Exs. 1, 2, 7, 8, 17–21, 30–38*, 40–45*
Review	Day 1	pp. 669–672 Exs. 1–37	pp. 669–672 Exs. 1–37	pp. 669–672 Exs. 1–37
Assess	Day 1	Chapter 9 Test	Chapter 9 Test	Chapter 9 Test

Yearly Pacing Chapter 9 Total – 10 days Chapters 1–9 Total – 112 days Remaining – 48 days

*Challenge Exercises EP = Extra Practice SRH = Skills Review Handbook

BLOCK SCHEDULE

DAY 1	DAY 2	DAY 3	DAY 4	DAY 5
9.1	**9.3**	**9.5**	**9.6 (CONT.)**	**REVIEW**
pp. 617–619 Exs. 1, 2, 9–13, 18–21, 22–26 even, 34–42, 47–56, 59	pp. 629–632 Exs. 1, 2, 10–20 even, 23–29 odd, 30–38 even, 43–59 odd, 63–68	pp. 645–648 Exs. 1, 2, 4–14 even, 15–17, 20–23, 26, 30–35, 38–43, 46	pp. 655–657 Exs. 23–35 odd, 36–44 even, 45, 49–52, 54–55	pp. 669–672 Exs. 1–37
9.2	**9.4**	**9.6**	**9.7**	**ASSESS**
pp. 623–625 Exs. 1, 2, 4–18 even, 23–25, 30–33, 38–42, 51, 52, 56–59, 62	pp. 637–639 Exs. 1, 2, 4–10 even, 15, 16, 23–28, 35, 39–45, 48–52, 55	pp. 655–657 Exs. 1, 2, 5–9, 12, 14–20 even, 21, 48	pp. 661–664 Exs. 1, 2, 4–6, 14–17, 21, 26–29, 34–36, 39–44, 47	Chapter 9 Test

Yearly Pacing Chapter 9 Total – 5 days Chapters 1–9 Total – 56 days Remaining – 24 days

Chapter Resource Guide 9

RESOURCE MANAGER

Chapter Resource Book

CHAPTER SUPPORT							
Parents as Partners (Chapter Overview with home involvement exercises and activity)						p. 1	
LESSON SUPPORT	**9.1**	**9.2**	**9.3**	**9.4**	**9.5**	**9.6**	**9.7**
Standards	**MA-HS-3.3.1**	**MA-HS-5.3.6**	MA-HS-3.1.6	**MA-HS-3.1.5**	**MA-HS-3.1.5**	**MA-HS-3.1.5**	**MA-HS-5.3.6**
Teaching Guide/Lesson Plan	p. 3	p. 14	p. 24	p. 35	p. 47	p. 58	p. 71
Activity Masters	p. 5			p. 37			
Technology Activities & Keystrokes			p. 26		p. 49		p. 73
Activity Support Masters							
Practice (3 levels)	p. 6	p. 16	p. 27	p. 38	p. 50	p. 60	p. 76
Study Guide	p. 9	p. 19	p. 30	p. 41	p. 53	p. 66	p. 79
Catch-Up for Absent Students	p. 11	p. 21	p. 32	p. 43	p. 55	p. 68	p. 81
Problem Solving/Application	p. 12	p. 22	p. 33	p. 44	p. 56	p. 69	p. 82
Challenge Practice	p. 13	p. 23	p. 34	p. 46	p. 57	p. 70	p. 83
REVIEW							
Chapter Review Games and Activities		p. 84		Cumulative Practice		pp. 87–88	
Project with Rubric		p. 85		Resource Book Answers		A1	

Transparencies	***9.1***	***9.2***	***9.3***	***9.4***	***9.5***	***9.6***	***9.7***
Warm-Up/Daily Homework Quiz	✔	✔	✔	✔	✔	✔	✔
Notetaking Guide	✔	✔	✔	✔	✔	✔	✔
Teacher Support	✔	✔	✔	✔	✔	✔	✔
Answer Transparencies	✔	✔	✔	✔	✔	✔	✔

ASSESSMENT BOOK

Quizzes	p. 124	SAT/ACT Chapter Test	p. 135
Chapter Tests (3 levels)	p. 127	Alternative Assessment with Rubric	p. 137
Standardized Chapter Test	p. 133		

TECHNOLOGY

- Easy Planner
- Test and Practice Generator
- Power Presentations
- @HomeTutor
- Activity Generator
- Animated Algebra
- Classzone.com
- eEdition Plus Online
- eWorkbook Plus Online
- ML Assessment System

ADDITIONAL RESOURCES

Kentucky

- Worked-Out Solution Key
- Notetaking Guide
- Practice Workbook
- Algebra 2 Toolkit
- Benchmark Tests
- Remediation Workbook

- Spanish Study Guide
- Spanish Assessment Book
- Spanish Resources in Spanish
- Multi-Language Visual Glossary

9 Lesson Practice Level B

LESSON 9.1 Practice B
For use with pages 614–619

7. $\sqrt{97}$; $\left(-\frac{5}{2}, -6\right)$ 8. $\sqrt{13}$; (1.8, 2.9) 9. $\sqrt{38.65}$; (1.35, 3.6)

Find the distance between the two points. Then find the midpoint of the line segment joining the two points.

1. (5, 2), (4, 3) $\sqrt{2}$; $\left(\frac{9}{2}, \frac{5}{2}\right)$
2. (−2, 2), (4, 6) $2\sqrt{13}$; (1, 4)
3. (−3, 5), (2, 0) $5\sqrt{2}$; $\left(-\frac{1}{2}, \frac{5}{2}\right)$
4. (7, 1), (2, 7) $\sqrt{61}$; $\left(\frac{9}{2}, 4\right)$
5. (5, 5), (−5, 1) $2\sqrt{29}$; (0, 3)
6. (9, 3), (1, 1) $2\sqrt{17}$; (5, 2)
7. (−7, −8), (2, −4)
8. (2.4, 1.2), (1.2, 4.6)
9. (0, 6.4), (2.7, 0.8)
10. (−3.9, 2.1), (2.7, −2.2) $\sqrt{62.05}$; (−0.6, −0.05)
11. $\left(\frac{1}{2}, 3\right)$, $\left(\frac{7}{2}, 1\right)$ $\sqrt{13}$; (2, 2)
12. $\left(\frac{2}{3}, -\frac{3}{2}\right)$, $\left(4, \frac{3}{2}\right)$ $\frac{\sqrt{181}}{3}$; $\left(\frac{7}{3}, 0\right)$

The vertices of a triangle are given. Classify the triangle as *scalene, isosceles,* or *equilateral.*

13. (2, 7), (4, 4), (−1, −1) scalene
14. (−2, 5), (−1, −4), (7, 4) isosceles
15. (1, 6), (2, 5), (2, 7) isosceles

Write an equation for the perpendicular bisector of the line segment joining the two points.

16. (3, 5), (1, 7) $y = x + 4$
17. (7, 5), (1, 2) $y = -2x + \frac{23}{2}$
18. (2, 4), (−3, −6) $y = -\frac{1}{2}x - \frac{5}{4}$
19. (−2, 1), (−4, −5) $y = -\frac{1}{3}x - 3$
20. (8, −4), (6, 4) $y = \frac{1}{4}x - \frac{7}{4}$
21. (−1, 3), (4, 1) $y = \frac{5}{2}x - \frac{7}{4}$

Use the given distance *d* between the two points to find the value of *x* or *y*.

22. (3, 6), (7, *y*); $d = 4\sqrt{2}$ 2; 10
23. (*x*, −4), (3, 2); $d = 2\sqrt{10}$ 1; 5
24. (−2, −7), (*x*, −12); $d = \sqrt{89}$ −10; 6
25. (1, *y*), (−1, 3); $d = 2\sqrt{10}$ −3; 9

In Exercises 26–31, use the following information.

Rival School The center of your hometown is at the origin of the coordinate plane shown. The location of your home, high school and rival school are also displayed on the coordinate plane. Each unit on the coordinate plane represents two miles. Round your answers to two decimal places.

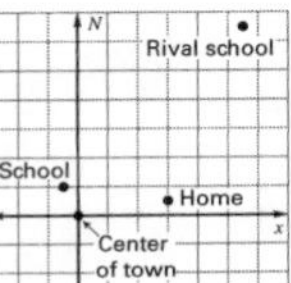

26. Determine the coordinates of your home. (6, 1)
27. Determine the coordinates of your high school. (−1, 2)
28. Determine the coordinates of your rival school. (11, 13)
29. Approximate the distance from home to the high school. 7.07 mi
30. Approximate the distance from your high school to the rival school. 16.28 mi
31. On Friday night, you decide to attend the football game because your school is playing the rival school. It's an away game so you have to drive to the game from home. How long (in minutes) will it take to drive to the rival school if you average 35 miles per hour? about 22 min

LESSON 9.1

LESSON 9.2 Practice B
For use with pages 620–625

Tell whether the parabola opens *up, down, left,* or *right.*

1. $x^2 = -4y$ down
2. $y^2 = 7x$ right
3. $y^2 = -2x$ left

Graph the equation. Identify the focus and directrix of the parabola.

4. $x^2 = 12y$ (0, 3); $y = -3$
5. $y^2 = -4x$ (−1, 0); $x = 1$
6. $x^2 = -y$ $\left(0, -\frac{1}{4}\right)$; $y = \frac{1}{4}$

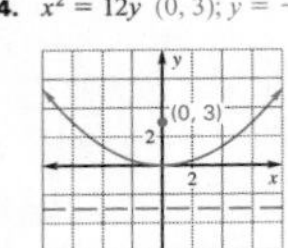
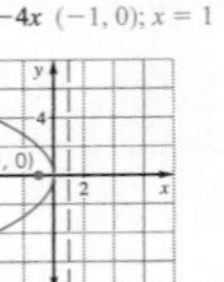
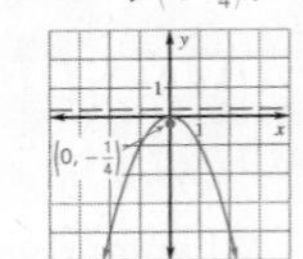

7. $y^2 - 6x = 0$ $\left(\frac{3}{2}, 0\right)$; $x = -\frac{3}{2}$
8. $x^2 + 8y = 0$ (0, −2); $y = 2$
9. $2x^2 - y = 0$ $\left(0, \frac{1}{8}\right)$; $y = -\frac{1}{8}$

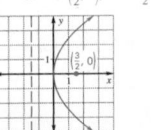

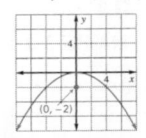

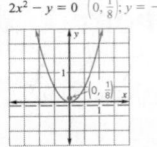

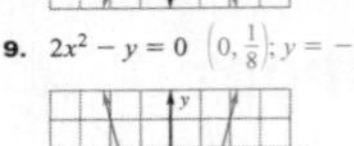

Write the standard form of the equation of the parabola with the given focus and vertex at (0, 0).

10. (2, 0) $y^2 = 8x$
11. (0, 1) $x^2 = 4y$
12. (−1, 0) $y^2 = -4x$
13. $\left(0, \frac{1}{2}\right)$ $x^2 = 2y$
14. (3, 0) $y^2 = 12x$
15. (0, −6) $x^2 = -24y$

Write the standard form of the equation of the parabola with the given directrix and vertex at (0, 0).

16. $x = 3$ $y^2 = -12x$
17. $y = -2$ $x^2 = 8y$
18. $x = -1$ $y^2 = 4x$
19. $y = 4$ $x^2 = -16y$
20. $x = \frac{1}{4}$ $y^2 = -x$
21. $y = -\frac{1}{2}$ $x^2 = 2y$

22. **Television Antenna Dish** The cross section of a television antenna dish is a parabola. The receiver is located at the focus, 2.5 feet above the vertex. Assume the vertex is at the origin. Write an equation for the cross section of the dish. $x^2 = 10y$

23. **Headlight** The filament of a light bulb is a thin wire that glows when electricity passes through it. The filament of a car headlight is at the focus of a parabolic reflector, which sends light out in a straight beam. Given that the filament is 1.5 inches from the vertex, write an equation for the cross section of the reflector. $y^2 = 6x$

LESSON 9.2

LESSON 9.3 Practice B
For use with pages 626–632

Graph the equation. Identify the radius of the circle.

1. $x^2 + y^2 = 9$ 3
2. $x^2 + y^2 = 20$ $2\sqrt{5}$
3. $x^2 + y^2 = 64$ 8

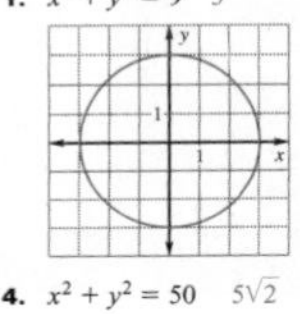
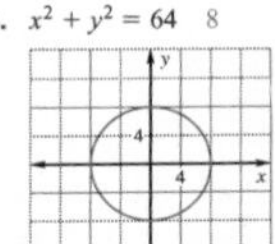

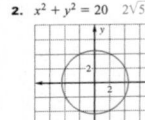

4. $x^2 + y^2 = 50$ $5\sqrt{2}$
5. $5x^2 + 5y^2 = 80$ 4
6. $3x^2 + 3y^2 = 120$ $2\sqrt{10}$

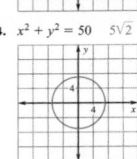

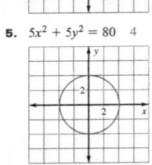

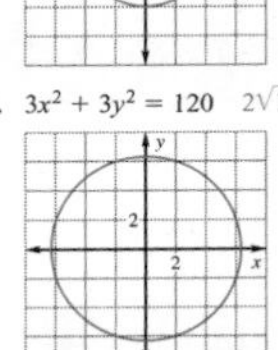

Write the standard form of the equation of the circle with the given radius and whose center is the origin.

7. $\sqrt{7}$ $x^2 + y^2 = 7$
8. $2\sqrt{5}$ $x^2 + y^2 = 20$
9. $3\sqrt{10}$ $x^2 + y^2 = 90$

Write the standard form of the equation of the circle that passes through the given point and whose center is the origin.

10. (2, 3) $x^2 + y^2 = 13$
11. (−3, 5) $x^2 + y^2 = 34$
12. (4, −6) $x^2 + y^2 = 52$

The equations of both circles and parabolas are given. Graph the equation.

13. $x^2 + 3y = 0$
14. $2x^2 + 2y^2 = 8$
15. $x^2 - 8y = 0$

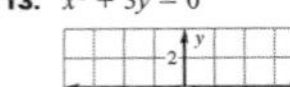
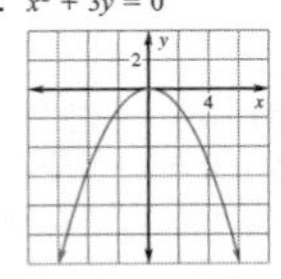
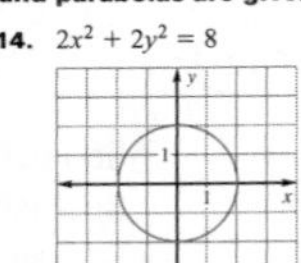
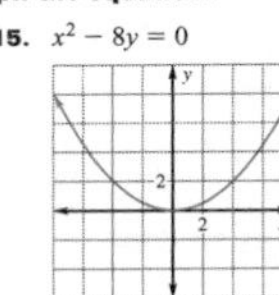

Write an equation of the line tangent to the given circle at the given point.

16. $x^2 + y^2 = 17$; (1, 4) $y = -\frac{1}{4}x + \frac{17}{4}$
17. $x^2 + y^2 = 52$; (−4, 6) $y = \frac{2}{3}x + \frac{26}{3}$

18. **Capitol Dome** The Capitol Dome sits atop the Capitol Building in Washington, D.C. The base of the dome is circular with a diameter of 96 feet. Suppose a coordinate plane was placed over the base of the dome with the origin at the center of the dome. Write an equation in standard form for the outside boundary of the dome. $x^2 + y^2 = 2304$

LESSON 9.3

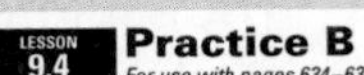

LESSON 9.4 Practice B
For use with pages 634–639

3. vertices: (0, ±10); co-vertices: (±8, 0); foci: (0, ±6)
6. vertices: (±9, 0); co-vertices: (0, ±2); foci: $(0, \pm\sqrt{77})$

Graph the equation. Identify the vertices, co-vertices and foci of the ellipse.

1. $\frac{x^2}{16} + \frac{y^2}{36} = 1$ vertices: (0, ±6); co-vertices: (±4, 0); foci: $(0, \pm 2\sqrt{5})$
2. $\frac{x^2}{49} + \frac{y^2}{4} = 1$ vertices: (±7, 0); co-vertices: (0, ±2); foci: $(\pm 3\sqrt{5}, 0)$
3. $\frac{x^2}{64} + \frac{y^2}{100} = 1$ See above.

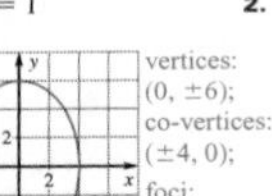
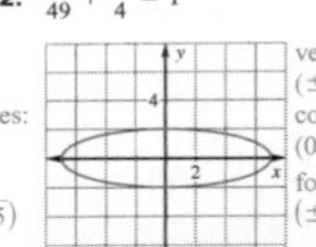
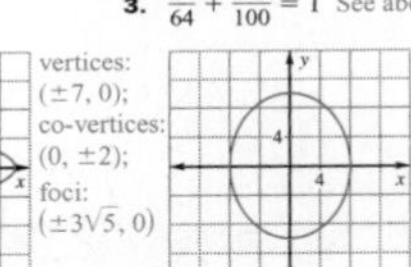

4. $9x^2 + 4y^2 = 36$ vertices: (0, ±3); co-vertices: (±2, 0); foci: $(0, \pm\sqrt{5})$
5. $16x^2 + 25y^2 = 400$ vertices: (±5, 0); co-vertices: (0, ±4); foci: (±3, 0)
6. $4x^2 + 81y^2 = 324$ See above.

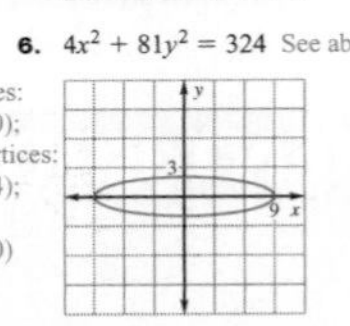

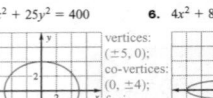

Write an equation of the ellipse with the given characteristics and center at (0, 0).

7. Vertex: (3, 0) Co-vertex: (0, 2) $\frac{x^2}{9} + \frac{y^2}{4} = 1$
8. Vertex: (0, 5) Co-vertex: (1, 0) $\frac{x^2}{1} + \frac{y^2}{25} = 1$
9. Vertex: (−6, 0) Co-vertex: (0, −3) $\frac{x^2}{36} + \frac{y^2}{9} = 1$
10. Vertex: (0, 4) Focus: $(0, 2\sqrt{3})$ $\frac{x^2}{4} + \frac{y^2}{16} = 1$
11. Vertex: (−7, 0) Focus: $(2\sqrt{6}, 0)$ $\frac{x^2}{49} + \frac{y^2}{25} = 1$
12. Co-vertex: (0, 6) Focus: $(-2\sqrt{7}, 0)$ $\frac{x^2}{64} + \frac{y^2}{36} = 1$

The equations of parabolas, circles and ellipses are given. Graph the equation.

13. $x^2 + 12y = 0$
14. $3x^2 + 3y^2 = 48$
15. $6x^2 + 8y^2 = 96$

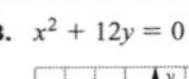
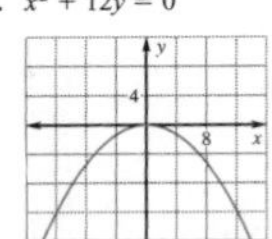
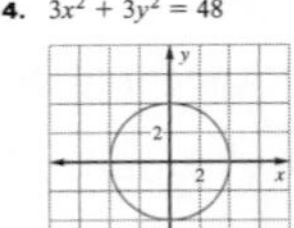
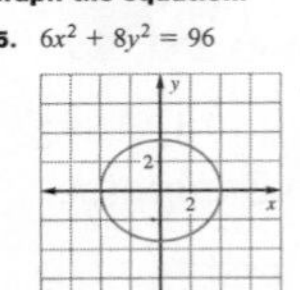

16. **Swimming Pool** An elliptical pool is 20 feet long and 16 feet wide. Write an equation for the perimeter of the swimming pool. Assume the major axis of the pool is vertical. $\frac{x^2}{64} + \frac{y^2}{100} = 1$

17. **Race Track** The shape of a dirt race track for car racing is approximately an ellipse. The track is 400 feet long and 250 feet wide. Write an equation for the perimeter of the race track. Assume the major axis of the track is horizontal. $\frac{x^2}{200^2} + \frac{y^2}{125^2} = 1$

LESSON 9.4

LESSON 9.5 Practice B
For use with pages 642–648

3. vertices: $(0, \pm 5)$; foci: $(0, \pm\sqrt{29})$; asymptotes: $y = \pm\frac{5}{2}x$
6. vertices: $(0, \pm 2)$; foci: $(0, \pm 2\sqrt{5})$; asymptotes: $y = \pm\frac{1}{2}x$

Graph the equation. Identify the vertices, foci, and asymptotes of the hyperbola.

1. $\frac{x^2}{16} - \frac{y^2}{4} = 1$

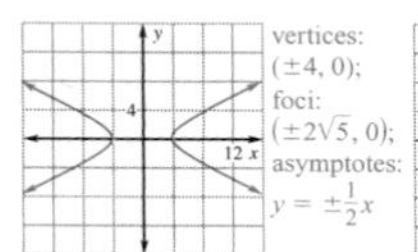

vertices: $(\pm 4, 0)$; foci: $(\pm 2\sqrt{5}, 0)$; asymptotes: $y = \pm\frac{1}{2}x$

2. $\frac{x^2}{9} - \frac{y^2}{36} = 1$

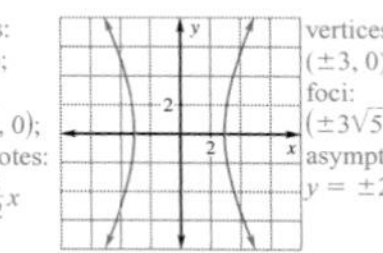

vertices: $(\pm 3, 0)$; foci: $(\pm 3\sqrt{5}, 0)$; asymptotes: $y = \pm 2x$

3. $\frac{y^2}{25} - \frac{x^2}{4} = 1$ See above.

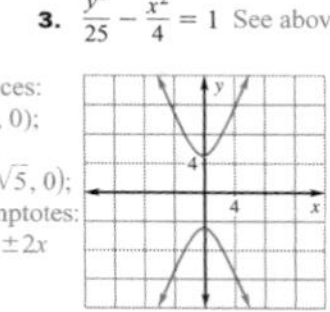

4. $x^2 - 4y^2 = 4$ **5.** $2y^2 - 10x^2 = 40$ **6.** $16y^2 - 4x^2 = 64$ See above.

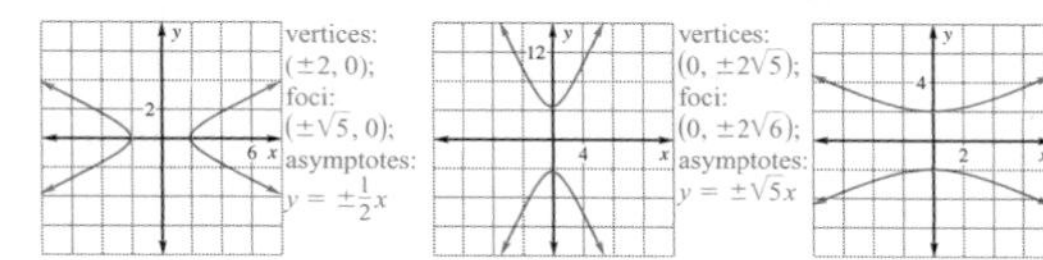

4. vertices: $(\pm 2, 0)$; foci: $(\pm\sqrt{5}, 0)$; asymptotes: $y = \pm\frac{1}{2}x$

5. vertices: $(0, \pm 2\sqrt{5})$; foci: $(0, \pm 2\sqrt{6})$; asymptotes: $y = \pm\sqrt{5}x$

Write an equation of the hyperbola with the given foci and vertices.

7. Foci: $(6, 0), (-6, 0)$ $\frac{x^2}{16} - \frac{y^2}{20} = 1$
Vertices: $(4, 0), (-4, 0)$

8. Foci: $(0, 8), (0, -8)$ $\frac{y^2}{49} - \frac{x^2}{15} = 1$
Vertices: $(0, 7), (0, -7)$

9. Foci: $(\sqrt{13}, 0), (-\sqrt{13}, 0)$ $\frac{x^2}{4} - \frac{y^2}{9} = 1$
Vertices: $(2, 0), (-2, 0)$

10. Foci: $(0, \sqrt{61}), (0, -\sqrt{61})$ $\frac{y^2}{36} - \frac{x^2}{25} = 1$
Vertices: $(0, 6), (0, -6)$

The equations of a parabola, an ellipse, and a hyperbola are given. Graph the equation.

11. $25x^2 + 4y^2 = 100$

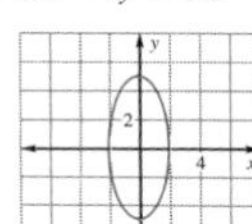

12. $25x^2 + 4y = 0$

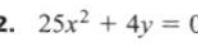

13. $25x^2 - 4y^2 = 100$

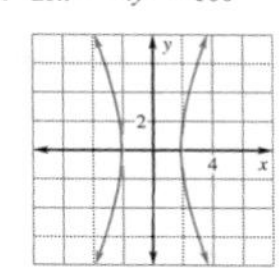

14. Machine Shop A machine shop needs to make a small automotive part by drilling four holes of radius r from a flat circular piece of radius R. The area of the resulting part is eight square inches. Write an equation that relates r and R. $\frac{R^2}{\left(\frac{8}{\pi}\right)} - \frac{r^2}{\left(\frac{2}{\pi}\right)} = 1$

LESSON 9.5

LESSON 9.6 Practice B
For use with pages 650–657

Graph the equation. Identify the important characteristics of the graph.

1. $x^2 + (y - 3)^2 = 9$

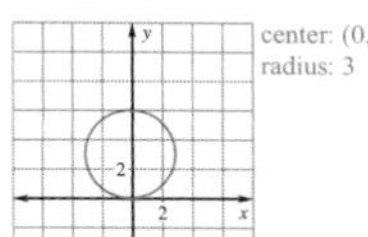

center: $(0, 3)$; radius: 3

2. $\frac{(x-4)^2}{16} + \frac{(y-2)^2}{4} = 1$

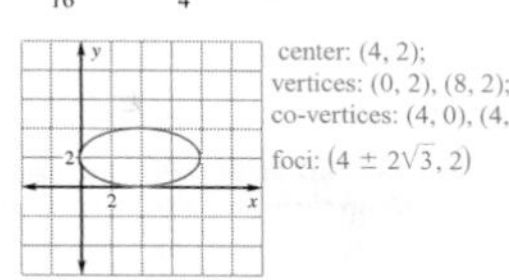

center: $(4, 2)$; vertices: $(0, 2), (8, 2)$; co-vertices: $(4, 0), (4, 4)$; foci: $(4 \pm 2\sqrt{3}, 2)$

3. $(x - 3)^2 = 8(y + 4)$

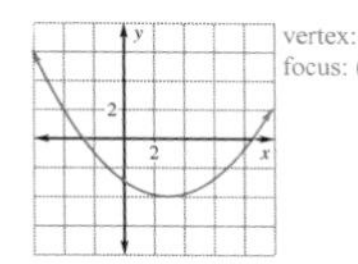

vertex: $(3, -4)$; focus: $(3, -1)$

4. $\frac{(y+2)^2}{18} - \frac{(x+1)^2}{25} = 1$

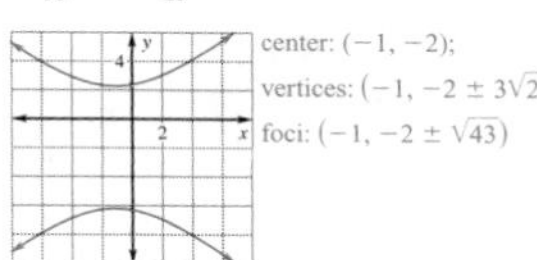

center: $(-1, -2)$; vertices: $(-1, -2 \pm 3\sqrt{2})$; foci: $(-1, -2 \pm \sqrt{43})$

5. $\frac{(x+3)^2}{32} + \frac{(y-4)^2}{36} = 1$

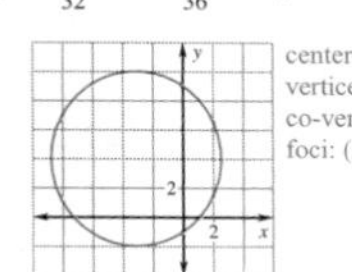

center: $(-3, 4)$; vertices: $(-3, 10), (-3, -2)$; co-vertices $(-3 \pm 4\sqrt{2}, 4)$; foci: $(-3, 2), (-3, 6)$

6. $(x - 5)^2 + (y + 2)^2 = 28$

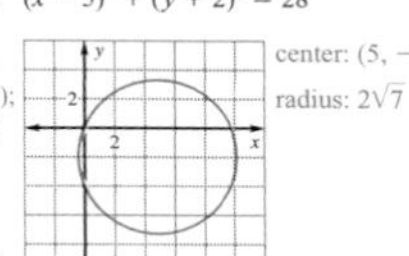

center: $(5, -2)$; radius: $2\sqrt{7}$

LESSON 9.6

Write an equation of the conic section.

7. Circle with a center at $(2, -6)$ and a radius of 4 $(x - 2)^2 + (y + 6)^2 = 16$

8. Parabola with vertex $(3, 3)$ and focus at $(3, 0)$ $(x - 3)^2 = -12(y - 3)$

9. Ellipse with vertices at $(-2, -1)$ and $(-2, 7)$ and co-vertices at $(-4, 3)$ and $(0, 3)$ $\frac{(x+2)^2}{4} + \frac{(y-3)^2}{16} = 1$

10. Hyperbola with vertices at $(2, 4)$ and $(8, 4)$ and foci at $(-2, 4)$ and $(12, 4)$ $\frac{(x-5)^2}{9} - \frac{(y-4)^2}{40} = 1$

Identify the line(s) of symmetry for the conic section.

11. $(y - 2)^2 = 16(x - 6)$ $y = 2$

12. $(x - 3)^2 + (y + 4)^2 = 48$ any line that passes through the point $(3, -4)$

13. $\frac{(x-7)^2}{81} + \frac{y^2}{62} = 1$ $x = 7, y = 0$

14. $\frac{(y+5)^2}{24} - (x - 3)^2 = 1$ $x = 3, y = -5$

LESSON 9.6 Practice B *continued*
For use with pages 650–657

Use the discriminant to classify the conic section.

15. $2x^2 + 5x + y + 14 = 0$ parabola

16. $4x^2 + 4y^2 - 6x + 8y - 10 = 0$ circle

17. $5x^2 - 5y^2 + 4x - 3y + 4 = 0$ hyperbola

18. $x^2 + 4y^2 - 8x - 12y - 2 = 0$ ellipse

Classify the conic section and write its equation in standard form. Then graph the equation.

19. $y^2 + 8x - 2y - 15 = 0$

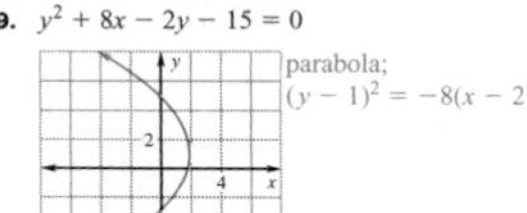

parabola; $(y - 1)^2 = -8(x - 2)$

20. $x^2 + y^2 - 12x + 2y + 15 = 0$

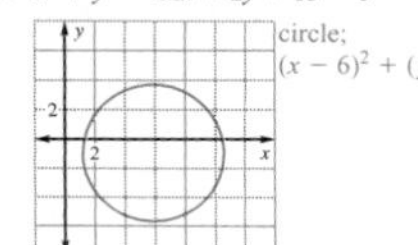

circle; $(x - 6)^2 + (y + 1)^2 = 22$

21. $x^2 - 9y^2 + 54y - 90 = 0$

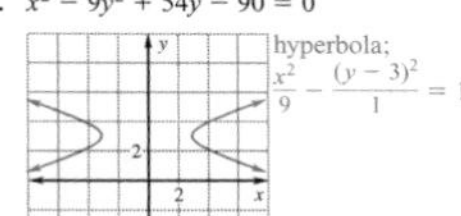

hyperbola; $\frac{x^2}{9} - \frac{(y-3)^2}{1} = 1$

22. $9x^2 + 36y^2 + 54x - 144y - 99 = 0$

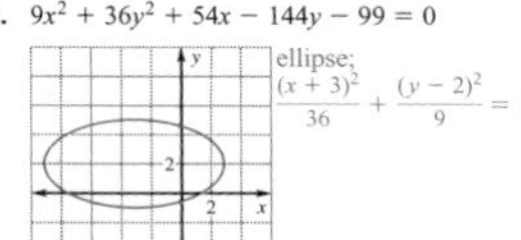

ellipse; $\frac{(x+3)^2}{36} + \frac{(y-2)^2}{9} = 1$

23. $x^2 + 10x - 6y + 7 = 0$

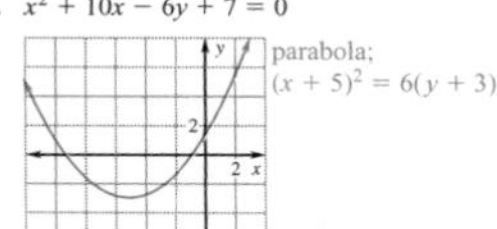

parabola; $(x + 5)^2 = 6(y + 3)$

24. $-2x^2 + 5y^2 + 24x - 20y - 102 = 0$

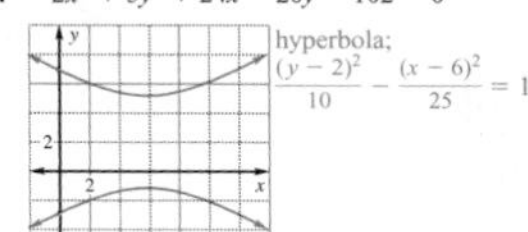

hyperbola; $\frac{(y-2)^2}{10} - \frac{(x-6)^2}{25} = 1$

25. Designing a Menu As part of the graphics art department, your job is to create various art pieces and graphical models for your documents. Your newest project is to design a menu that incorporates the picture of a tree. The equation used to model the tree trunk is $9x^2 - y^2 + 8y - 52 = 0$. Write this equation in standard form and then graph the equation. $\frac{x^2}{4} - \frac{(y-4)^2}{36} = 1$

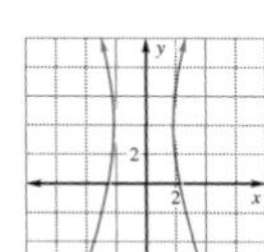

26. Long Jump A competitor's first long jump can be modeled by $x^2 - 20x + 20y = 0$ where x and y are measured in feet and the origin marks the start of the jump. Write the equation in standard form. How far was the first jump? $(x - 10)^2 = -20(y - 5)$; 20 ft

LESSON 9.6

LESSON 9.7 Practice B
For use with pages 658–664

1. $(-2.87, 3.87), (0.87, 0.13)$ 3. $(0, 2), (4.5, 4.25)$
4. $(-0.68, 3.04), (1.08, -2.24)$ 6. $(-1.41, -2.13), (1.67, -1.64)$

Solve the system using a graphing calculator.

1. $x^2 + (y - 3)^2 - 9 = 0$
$x + y - 1 = 0$ See above.

2. $2x^2 - y^2 + 4x - 6 = 0$
$2x + y + 4 = 0$ no solution

3. $x^2 - y - 4x + 2 = 0$
$x - 2y + 4 = 0$ See above.

4. $6x^2 + y^2 = 12$
$3x + y = 1$ See above.

5. $(x - 2)^2 + y^2 = 16$
$x = 6$ $(6, 0)$

6. $x - 2x^2 - 3y = 1$
$9x^2 + 4y^2 = 36$ See above.

7. Multiple Choice Which ordered pair is a solution of the linear quadratic system below? C
$x^2 - 4x + 4y^2 - 8y = 8$
$2x + y = 7$

A. $(1, 5)$ **B.** $(5, -1)$ **C.** $(2, 3)$ **D.** $(-3, 2)$

Solve the system using substitution.

8. $x^2 + y^2 = 45$
$y = 2x$ $(-3, -6), (3, 6)$

9. $x^2 - 3y - 3 = 0$
$x - y = 1$ $(0, -1), (3, 2)$

10. $x^2 - 2x + y^2 - 2y = 2$
$x + y = 4$ $(1, 3), (3, 1)$

11. $-x^2 + 2y^2 = 16$
$x - y = 0$ $(-4, -4), (4, 4)$

12. $3x + y^2 + 2 = 0$
$3x = y - 2$ $(-1, -1), \left(-\frac{2}{3}, 0\right)$

13. $2x^2 + 6y^2 = 18$ no solution
$x + 4y + 8 = 0$

14. $2x^2 + y - 3 = 0$
$3x + y = -6$ $\left(-\frac{3}{2}, -\frac{3}{2}\right), (3, -15)$

15. $4x^2 - x - y^2 + 6 = 0$
$2x - y = 3$ $\left(\frac{3}{11}, -\frac{27}{11}\right)$

16. $2x + y^2 - 4y + 4 = 0$
$-x + y = 2$ $(-2, 0), (0, 2)$

Solve the system.

17. $x^2 - y^2 + 4x - 4 = 0$ $(1, 1), (1, -1)$
$-x^2 + y^2 - 3x + 3 = 0$

18. $x^2 + 2y^2 - 3y = 0$ $(-1, 1), (1, 1)$
$x^2 + y^2 - 2 = 0$

19. $2x^2 - y^2 - x - 4 = 0$ $(-4, \pm 4\sqrt{2}), (2, \pm\sqrt{2})$
$-x^2 + y^2 + 3x - 4 = 0$

20. $2x^2 + 3y^2 = 1$ no solution
$x^2 + y^2 + 4 = 0$

21. Farming A farmer has 1400 feet of fence to enclose a rectangular area that borders a river. No fence is needed along the river. Is it possible for the farmer to enclose five acres? (1 acre = 43,560 square feet) If possible, find the dimensions of the enclosure. 466.6 ft by 466.8 ft; or 233.4 ft by 933.2 ft

22. Radio The range of a radio station is bounded by a circle given by the equation $x^2 + y^2 = 920$ where x and y are measured in miles. A straight highway that passes through the area can be modeled by the equation $y = \frac{1}{2}x + 20$. Find the length of the highway that lies within the range of the radio station. about 49 mi

LESSON 9.7

9 Assessment

CHAPTER 9 Quiz 1
For use after Lessons 9.1–9.3

Find the distance between the two points. Then find the midpoint of the line segment joining the two points.

1. $(3, -2), (7, -6)$
2. $(5, 7), (11, 5)$
3. $(2, -2), (5, 4)$

Write the standard form of the equation of the parabola with the given focus and vertex at (0, 0).

4. $(0, 4)$
5. $(-5, 0)$
6. $(0, -6)$

Graph the equation. Identify the radius of the circle.

7. $x^2 + y^2 = 50$

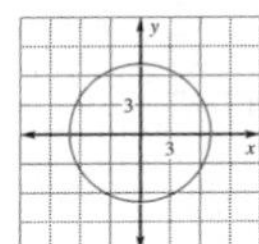

8. $x^2 + y^2 = 81$

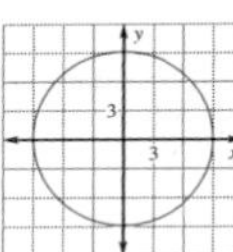

9. $2x^2 + 2y^2 = 72$

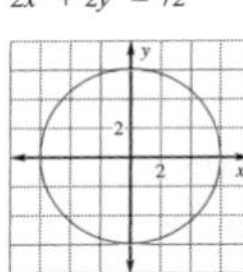

10. **Phone Service** A cellular phone tower services a 12 mile radius. You get a flat tire 5 miles east and 10 miles south of the tower. Are you in the tower's range? Explain.

Answers

1. distance: $4\sqrt{2}$, midpoint: $(5, -4)$
2. distance: $2\sqrt{10}$, midpoint: $(8, 6)$
3. distance: $3\sqrt{5}$, midpoint: $\left(\frac{7}{2}, 1\right)$
4. $x^2 = 16y$
5. $y^2 = -20x$
6. $x^2 = -24y$
7. See left. $5\sqrt{2}$
8. See left. 9
9. See left. 6
10. yes; $5^2 + 10^2 < 12^2$

CHAPTER 9 Quiz 2
For use after Lessons 9.4–9.5

Graph the equation. Identify the vertices, co-vertices, and foci of the ellipse.

1. $\frac{x^2}{36} + \frac{y^2}{9} = 1$

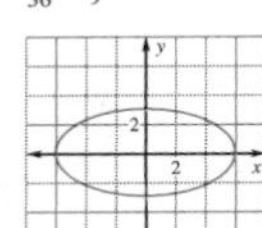

2. $64x^2 + 16y^2 = 1024$

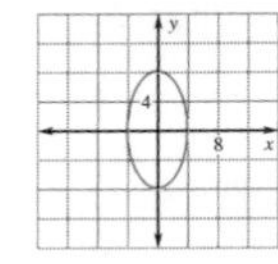

Write an equation of the ellipse with the given characteristics and center at (0, 0).

3. Vertex: $(0, 6)$
   Co-vertex: $(-5, 0)$
4. Vertex: $(9, 0)$
   Focus: $(-6, 0)$
5. Co-vertex: $(-\sqrt{13}, 0)$
   Focus: $(0, -4)$

Graph the equation. Identify the vertices, foci, and asymptotes of the hyperbola.

6. $\frac{y^2}{16} - \frac{x^2}{36} = 1$

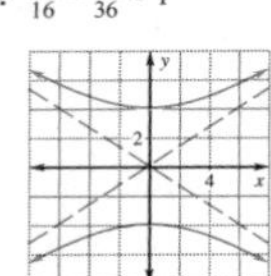

7. $9x^2 - 25y^2 = 225$

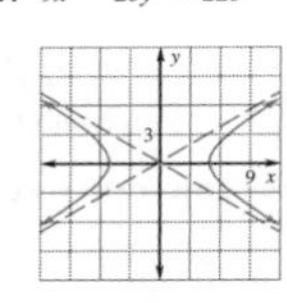

Write an equation of the hyperbola with the given foci and vertices.

8. Foci: $(-6, 0), (6, 0)$
   Vertices: $(-3, 0), (3, 0)$
9. Foci: $(0, -4), (0, 4)$
   Vertices: $(0, -2), (0, 2)$

10. **Gardens** An elliptical garden is 13 feet long and 7 feet wide. Write an equation for the garden. Then find the area of the garden.

Answers

1. See left. vertices: $(\pm 6, 0)$, co-vertices: $(0, \pm 3)$, foci: $(\pm 3\sqrt{3}, 0)$
2. See left. vertices: $(0, \pm 8)$, co-vertices: $(\pm 4, 0)$, foci: $(0, \pm 4\sqrt{3})$
3. $\frac{x^2}{25} + \frac{y^2}{36} = 1$
4. $\frac{x^2}{81} + \frac{y^2}{45} = 1$
5. $\frac{x^2}{13} + \frac{y^2}{29} = 1$
6. See left. vertices: $(0, \pm 4)$, foci: $(0, \pm 2\sqrt{13})$, asymptotes: $y = \pm\frac{2}{3}x$
7. See left. vertices: $(\pm 5, 0)$, foci: $(\pm\sqrt{34}, 0)$, asymptotes: $y = \pm\frac{3}{5}x$
8. $\frac{x^2}{9} - \frac{y^2}{27} = 1$
9. $\frac{y^2}{4} - \frac{x^2}{12} = 1$
10. $\frac{x^2}{169} + \frac{y^2}{49} = 1$, 285.88 ft^2

CHAPTER 9 Quiz 3
For use after Lessons 9.6–9.7

Write an equation of the conic section.

1. Ellipse with vertices at $(4, -9)$ and $(4, 7)$ and foci at $(4, -6)$ and $(4, 4)$
2. Parabola with vertex at $(-4, 3)$ and focus at $(-4, -2)$

Classify the conic section and write its equation in standard form. Then graph the equation.

3. $x^2 + y^2 - 6x - 8y = 0$

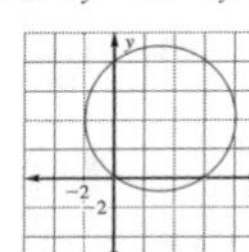

4. $x^2 - 4y^2 - 4x - 8y = 36$

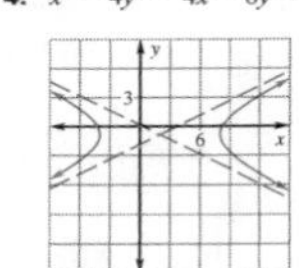

Solve the system.

5. $-6x^2 + y^2 - 5y = 0$
   $3x^2 + y^2 - 9x - 5y = 18$
6. $y^2 - 5x - 3y - 4 = 0$
   $3y^2 - 9y + x - 12 = 0$

7. **Lab Experiment** In a lab experiment, you record images of a steel ball rolling past a magnet. The equation $25x^2 - 9y^2 - 100x + 72y - 269 = 0$ models the ball's path. Write the equation for the path in standard form.

Answers

1. $\frac{(x-4)^2}{39} + \frac{(y+1)^2}{64} = 1$
2. $(x + 4)^2 = -20(y - 3)$
3. circle; $(x - 3)^2 + (y - 4)^2 = 25$ See left.
4. hyperbola; $\frac{(x-2)^2}{35} - \frac{(y+1)^2}{9} = 1$ See left.
5. $(2, 8), (2, -3), (-1, 6), (-1, -1)$
6. $(0, 4), (0, -1)$
7. $\frac{(x-2)^2}{9} - \frac{(y-4)^2}{25} = 1$

CHAPTER 9 Chapter Test B
For use after Chapter 9

1. Find the distance between the points $(-2, 2)$ and $(2, -4)$. What is the midpoint of the line segment joining the two points?
2. The vertices of a triangle are $(3, 1)$, $(5, -2)$, and $(1, 3)$. Classify the triangle as *scalene*, *isosceles*, or *equilateral*.
3. Write an equation for the perpendicular bisector of the line segment joining the points $(3, -2)$ and $(-1, 4)$.

Graph the equation. Identify the focus, directrix, and axis of symmetry of the parabola.

4. $y = \frac{1}{2}x^2$
5. $\frac{5}{6}y^2 = \frac{2}{3}x$

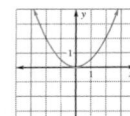

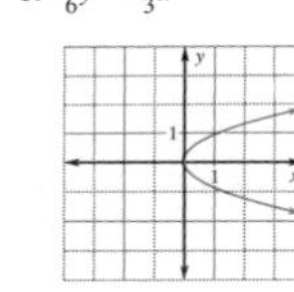

6. Write the standard form of the equation of the parabola with focus at $(2, 0)$ and vertex at $(0, 0)$.

Graph the equation. Identify the radius of the circle.

7. $x^2 + y^2 = 4$

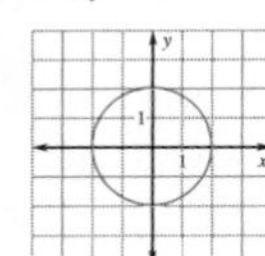

8. $x^2 = -y^2 + 16$

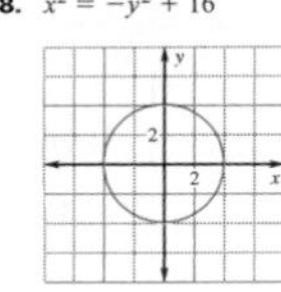

9. Write an equation of the line tangent to the circle $x^2 + y^2 = 29$ at the point $(-2, 5)$.

Answers

1. $2\sqrt{13}$, $(0, -1)$
2. scalene
3. $y = \frac{2}{3}x + \frac{1}{3}$
4. See left. focus: $\left(0, \frac{1}{2}\right)$, directrix: $y = -\frac{1}{2}$, axis of symmetry: x-axis
5. See left. focus: $\left(\frac{1}{5}, 0\right)$, directrix: $x = -\frac{1}{5}$, axis of symmetry: y-axis
6. $y^2 = 8x$
7. See left. $r = 2$
8. See left. $r = 4$
9. $y = \frac{2}{5}x + \frac{29}{5}$

CHAPTER 9

Chapter Test B *continued*

For use after Chapter 9

10. Graph the equation $x^2 + \frac{y^2}{9} = 4$. Identify the vertices, co-vertices, and foci of the ellipse.

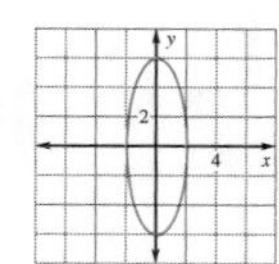

11. Write an equation of the ellipse with center at (0, 0), a focus at (−3, 0), and a vertex at (−4, 0).

12. Art Project You are drawing an elliptical eye for an art project. The eye should be 3 centimeters long and 2 centimeters wide. Using the x-axis as the major axis, write an equation of this ellipse.

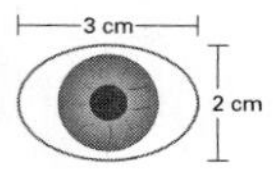

13. Graph the equation $\frac{y^2}{16} - \frac{x^2}{4} = 1$. Identify the vertices, foci, and asymptotes of the hyperbola.

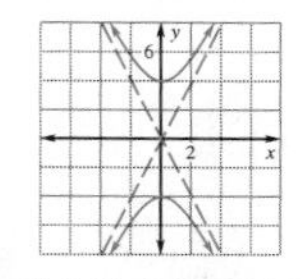

14. Write an equation of the hyperbola with foci (−3, 0) and (3, 0) and vertices of (−2, 0) and (2, 0).

15. Write an equation of the ellipse with vertices at (−2, 4) and (−2, −2) and co-vertices at (−3, 1) and (−1, 1).

16. Identify the line(s) of symmetry for the conic section $4(x - 2)^2 + 9(y + 3)^2 = 36$.

17. Use the discriminant to classify the conic section $2x^2 - xy - 2y^2 + 3x - 1 = 0$.

Solve the system.

18. $\frac{x^2}{4} - y^2 - 1 = 0$
$x = 4y$

19. $25x^2 + 4y^2 - 100 = 0$
$y = 2x$

Answers

10. See left.
vertices: $(0, \pm 6)$,
co-vertices: $(\pm 2, 0)$,
foci $(0, \pm 4\sqrt{2})$

11. $\frac{x^2}{16} + \frac{y^2}{7} = 1$

12. $\frac{4x^2}{9} + y^2 = 1$

13. See left.
vertices: $(0, \pm 4)$,
foci: $(0, \pm 2\sqrt{5})$,
asymptotes: $y = \pm 2x$

14. $\frac{x^2}{4} - \frac{y^2}{5} = 1$

15. $\frac{(x+2)^2}{1} + \frac{(y-1)^2}{9} = 1$

16. $x = 2, y = -3$

17. hyperbola

18. $\left(-\frac{4\sqrt{3}}{3}, -\frac{\sqrt{3}}{3}\right)$, $\left(\frac{4\sqrt{3}}{3}, \frac{\sqrt{3}}{3}\right)$

19. $\left(-\frac{10\sqrt{41}}{41}, -\frac{20\sqrt{41}}{41}\right)$, $\left(\frac{10\sqrt{41}}{41}, \frac{20\sqrt{41}}{41}\right)$

CHAPTER 9

Standardized Test

For use after Chapter 9

Multiple Choice

1. What is the distance between (−2, 1) and (7, −3)? D

Ⓐ $\sqrt{13}$ Ⓑ $\sqrt{29}$
Ⓒ $\sqrt{65}$ Ⓓ $\sqrt{97}$

2. If the endpoints of the diameter of a circle are (3, 10) and (−1, 6), what are the coordinates of its center? C

Ⓐ (−2, −2) Ⓑ (2, 2)
Ⓒ (1, 8) Ⓓ (2, 16)

3. What is the focus of the graph shown? D

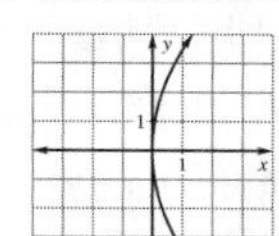

Ⓐ (0, −3) Ⓑ (0, 3)
Ⓒ (−3, 0) Ⓓ (3, 0)

4. What is the standard form of the parabola with directrix $x = -2$ and vertex (0, 0)? D

Ⓐ $y^2 = -8x$ Ⓑ $x^2 = -2y$
Ⓒ $x^2 = 2y$ Ⓓ $y^2 = 8x$

5. What is the equation of the tangent line through the point (−3, −4) on a circle centered at the origin? B

Ⓐ $y = -\frac{3}{4}x + \frac{25}{4}$

Ⓑ $y = -\frac{3}{4}x - \frac{25}{4}$

Ⓒ $y = \frac{3}{4}x - \frac{25}{4}$

Ⓓ $y = \frac{3}{4}x + \frac{25}{4}$

6. The pizzeria in your town delivers anywhere within a 4 mile radius. If you consider that the pizzeria is located at the origin, at which of your friends' houses, with coordinates in miles listed below, can the pizza be delivered? D

Ⓐ (0.82, 3.92) Ⓑ (1, 3.90)
Ⓒ (1.5, 3.8) Ⓓ (2, 3.4)

7. What is the equation of an ellipse with a vertex of (0, 3) and a co-vertex of (−2, 0)? A

Ⓐ $\frac{x^2}{4} + \frac{y^2}{9} = 1$

Ⓑ $\frac{x^2}{3} + \frac{y^2}{2} = 1$

Ⓒ $4x^2 + 9y^2 = 36$

Ⓓ $9x^2 - 4y^2 = 36$

8. Which elliptical equation is represented in the graph shown? B

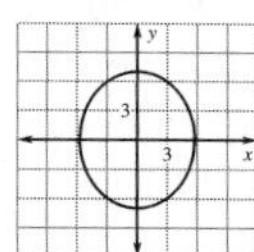

Ⓐ $\frac{x^2}{49} + \frac{y^2}{33} = 1$ Ⓑ $\frac{x^2}{33} + \frac{y^2}{49} = 1$

Ⓒ $\frac{x^2}{7} + \frac{y^2}{4} = 1$ Ⓓ $\frac{x^2}{4} + \frac{y^2}{7} = 1$

9. What are the foci of the ellipse given by $3x^2 + 4y^2 = 48$? A

Ⓐ (−2, 0) and (2, 0)
Ⓑ (0, −2) and (0, 2)
Ⓒ (−4, 0) and (4, 0)
Ⓓ (0, −4) and (0, 4)

CHAPTER 9

Standardized Test *continued*

For use after Chapter 9

10. Which is the equation of a hyperbola with vertices at (0, −6) and (0, 6) and foci at (0, −8) and (0, 8)? D

Ⓐ $\frac{x^2}{64} - \frac{y^2}{36} = 1$ Ⓑ $\frac{y^2}{64} - \frac{x^2}{36} = 1$

Ⓒ $\frac{x^2}{36} - \frac{y^2}{28} = 1$ Ⓓ $\frac{y^2}{36} - \frac{x^2}{28} = 1$

11. What are the asymptotes of the hyperbola $y^2 - 16x^2 - 256 = 0$? C

Ⓐ $y = \pm\frac{1}{16}x$ Ⓑ $y = \pm\frac{1}{4}x$
Ⓒ $y = \pm 4x$ Ⓓ $y = \pm 16x$

12. What is the equation of the parabola with vertex at (1, −5) and directrix $y = -3$? C

Ⓐ $x - 1 = 12(y + 5)^2$
Ⓑ $x + 1 = 12(y - 5)^2$
Ⓒ $(x - 1)^2 = 12(y + 5)$
Ⓓ $(x + 1)^2 = 12(y - 5)$

13. The equation $4x^2 - 9y^2 - 18x + 3y - 12 = 0$ represents which conic section? C

Ⓐ Circle Ⓑ Ellipse
Ⓒ Hyperbola Ⓓ Parabola

14. Which ordered pair is a solution of the system of equations shown? D

$2x^2 - 12x + y^2 - 54 = 0$

$y - 3x = 5$

Ⓐ (0, 5) Ⓑ (0, 54)
Ⓒ (1, −8) Ⓓ (1, 8)

17. b. $\frac{x^2}{22.73^2} + \frac{y^2}{11.37^2} = 1$ or $\frac{x^2}{11.37^2} + \frac{y^2}{22.73^2} = 1$

Gridded Answer

15. What is the radius of the circle $x^2 - 10x + y^2 + 4y - 20 = 0$?

7

Short Response at least 53; $x^2 + y^2 = 53^2$; $(x + 3)^2 + (y - 10)^2 = 50^2$

16. A saleswoman uses a map to mark her sales territory. If she considers her office to be located at (0, 0) and her three favorite clients at (24, 15), (−52, 3), and (10, −27), how large should her sales radius be? Determine the equation for the circle with that radius. If she decides to open an office in her home located at (−3, 10), what should the equation be?

Extended Response

17. A cowboy is practicing his lassoing technique by lassoing the fence posts at his ranch. Consider that his lariat forms a perfectly elliptical shape centered at the origin while he twirls it.

a. If the fence posts are 20 inches in circumference and the cowboy would like to add 5 inches extra "cushion" to the minimum dimension in setting his lariat, what should the length of the minor axis be? 11.37 in.

b. If the cowboy likes to set his lasso so that the major axis is twice that of the minor axis, determine the equation of the ellipse which models the twirling path of his lariat. See left.

CHAPTER 9

Alternative Assessment and Math Journal

For use after Chapter 9

Journal

1. Determine values for A, B, and C such that the equation below represents the conic with a horizontal axis and a vertical axis. Then rewrite your equation for each conic in standard form, identify (h, k), and describe the translation.

$Ax^2 + Bxy + Cy^2 + 2x - 4y + 5 = 0$

a. Circle **b.** Ellipse **c.** Parabola **d.** Hyperbola

Multi-Step Problem

2. Your aunt is a mail carrier for a post office that receives mail for all addresses within a 5-mile radius. Her route covers the portions of Main Street, Carson Road, and Eagle Drive that pass through this region.

a. If the post office is located at the point (0, 0), write and graph an inequality that represents the area where the mail is delivered.

b. Carson Road follows one branch of a hyperbolic path given by $y^2 - x^2 - 4y - 23 = 0$. Graph the portion of Carson Road that is on your aunt's route in the same coordinate plane as part (a).

c. If your aunt begins delivery on Carson Road at the point (−3, −4), where on Carson Road does she end delivery? How do you know? Support your answer algebraically.

d. After Carson Road, your aunt continues on Eagle Drive. Eagle Drive follows a path given by $y^2 + 16x - 64 = 0$. Graph the portion of Eagle Drive that is on your aunt's route in the same coordinate plane as part (a).

e. Does Eagle Drive follow a *parabolic*, *elliptical*, or *hyperbolic* path? Justify your answer.

f. Where on Eagle Drive does your aunt end delivery? Support your answer algebraically.

g. After Eagle Drive, your aunt turns on Main Street. Main Street is a straight road that cuts through the center of the circular region past the post office. Find the equation that represents Main Street. Then graph the portion of Main Street that is on your aunt's route in the same coordinate plane as part (a).

h. Critical Thinking Estimate the length of your aunt's route using the sides of the triangle formed by the intersections of the roads on her route. Does your answer overestimate or underestimate the length of her route? Explain.

1. a–d. Complete answers should include: values for A, B, and C such that the discriminant $(B^2 - 4AC)$ is negative for the circle $(A = C)$ and the ellipse $(A \neq C)$, is equal to zero for the parabola, and is postive for the hyperbola. B must be equal to zero to ensure horizontal or vertical axes.; a standard form equation for each conic, obtained by completing the square; identification of (h, k), and a description of each translation. **2. a.** $x^2 + y^2 \leq 25$; See graph. **b.** See graph. **c.** (3, −4); intersection of the circle and hyperbola. **d.** See graph. **e.** parabolic; $B^2 - 4AC = 0$ **f.** (3, 4) **g.** $y = \frac{4}{3}x$; See graph. **h.** 24 mi; underestimates; *Sample answer:* The straight-line distance is shorter than the curved path.

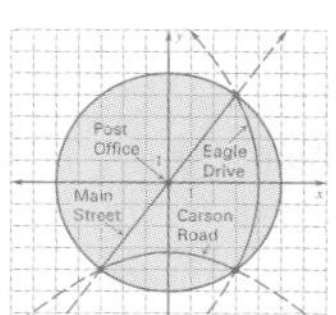

PLAN AND PREPARE

Main Ideas

This chapter introduces students to properties and characteristics of conic sections. Students start by applying the distance and midpoint formulas, then learn how to graph and write equations for parabolas, circles, ellipses, and hyperbolas. They investigate translations of conic sections and methods for classifying conic sections based on equations. Finally, students use graphing, substitution, and elimination to solve quadratic systems.

Prerequisite Skills

- Graphing quadratic functions and identifying the vertex and axis of symmetry
- Solving quadratic equations by completing the square
- Solving systems of linear equations in two variables using algebraic methods

Additional resources for reviewing prerequisite skills are:

- Skills Review Handbook, pp. 975–1009
- @HomeTutor

9 Quadratic Relations and Conic Sections

Before

In previous chapters, you learned the following skills, which you'll use in Chapter 9: graphing quadratic functions, completing the square, and solving linear systems.

Prerequisite Skills

VOCABULARY CHECK

Copy and complete the statement.

1. The graph of a(n) _?_ function is a **parabola**. quadratic
2. The graph of the **rational function** $y = \frac{2}{x}$, shown at the right, is a _?_. hyperbola
3. Two equations of the form $Ax + By = C$ and $Dx + Ey = F$ form a _?_ **system of equations**. linear

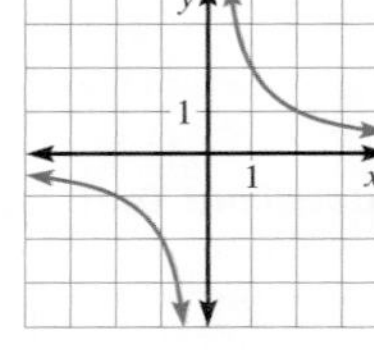

SKILLS CHECK

Graph. Label the vertex and axis of symmetry. *(Review pp. 236, 245 for 9.2.)* 4–7. See margin.

4. $y = x^2 - 3$
5. $y = -0.25x^2$
6. $y = 3(x + 1)^2$
7. $y = 0.5(x - 2)^2 + 4$

Solve the equation by completing the square. *(Review p. 284 for 9.6.)*

8. $x^2 - 4x + 7 = 0$ $2 \pm i\sqrt{3}$
9. $x^2 - 8x - 15 = 0$ $4 \pm \sqrt{31}$
10. $3x^2 + 9x - 12 = 0$ $-4, 1$

Solve the system using any algebraic method. *(Review p. 160 for 9.7.)*

11. $2x - y = 11$, $-x - 2y = -3$ $(5, -1)$
12. $x + 5y = -17$, $-2x - 3y = 13$ $(-2, -3)$
13. $-4x + 7y = -14$, $2x - 6y = 12$ $(0, -2)$

@HomeTutor Prerequisite skills practice at classzone.com

612

Chapter Planning Guide

Chapter 9 Resource Book
- Teaching Guide/Lesson Plan (pp. 3, 14, 24, 35, 47, 58, 71)
- Project with Rubric (p. 85)

Assessment and Intervention
- Assessment Book (pp. 124–138)
- Benchmark Tests
- Remediation Book

Interactive Technology
- Easy Planner
- Power Presentations CD-ROM
- Activity Generator CD-ROM
- Animated Algebra
- Test Generator CD-ROM
- Online Quizzes
- eWorkbook
- eEdition
- @HomeTutor

Resources for English Learners
- Quick Reference for English Learners
- Spanish Study Guide
- Multi-Language Visual Glossary
- Student Resources in Spanish

In Chapter 9, you will apply the big ideas listed below and reviewed in the Chapter Summary on page 668. You will also use the key vocabulary listed below.

Big Ideas

1. Writing equations of conic sections
2. Graphing equations of conic sections
3. Solving quadratic systems

KEY VOCABULARY

- distance formula, *p. 614*
- focus, foci, *pp. 620, 634, 642*
- directrix, *p. 620*
- circle, *p. 626*
- ellipse, *p. 634*
- vertices, *pp. 634, 642*
- major axis, *p. 634*
- co-vertices, *p. 634*
- minor axis, *p. 634*
- hyperbola, *p. 642*
- transverse axis, *p. 642*
- conic sections, *p. 650*
- general second-degree equation, *p. 653*
- quadratic system, *p. 658*

Why?

You can use conic sections to describe the shapes of real-world objects. For example, you can use a parabola to model the cross section of a radio telescope.

Animated Algebra

The animation illustrated below for Exercise 58 on page 625 helps you answer this question: How do the dimensions of a radio telescope determine the equation that models its cross section?

Radio telescopes have a parabolic cross section that concentrates radio waves.

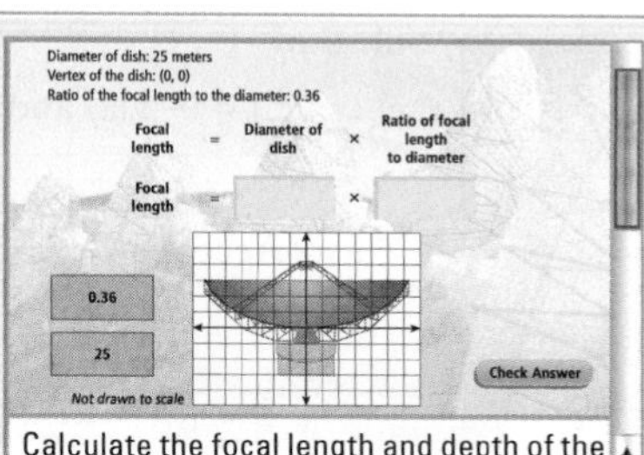

Calculate the focal length and depth of the telescope dish.

Animated Algebra at classzone.com

Other animations for Chapter 9: pages 615, 621, 635, 643, 649, and 651

Algebra 2 Toolkit

- Reading Strategies for Chapter 9, pp. 25–26
- Differentiated Instruction Notes, pp. 75–78
- English Learners Notes, pp. 117–118
- Inclusion Notes, pp. 151–152
- Teaching Strategies with Sample Worksheets, pp. 163–186
- Using Technology in the Classroom, pp. 187–192
- Tips for New Teachers, pp. 209–210
- Math Background Notes, pp. 247–249
- Pre-AP Strategies and Copymasters, pp. 327–328, 421–424
- Teacher Survival Activities, pp. 485–486, 513–514
- Bulletin Board Idea, p. 533
- Teacher Tool Transparencies, following p. 538

4. 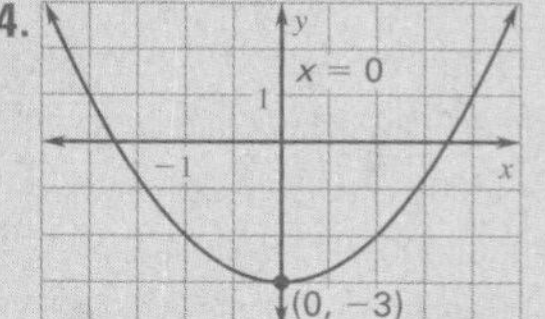

5. 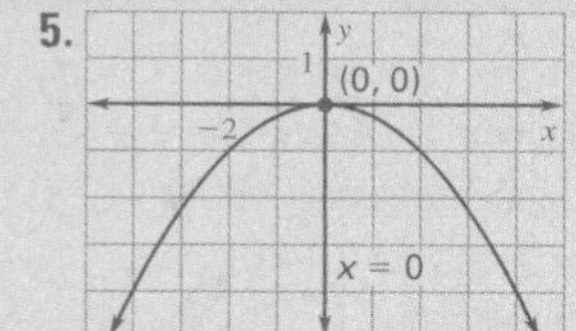

6. 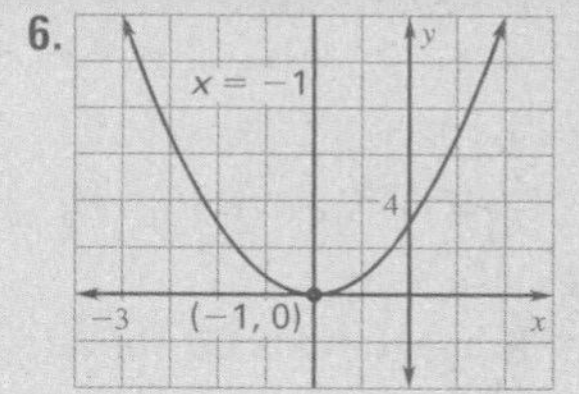

7. 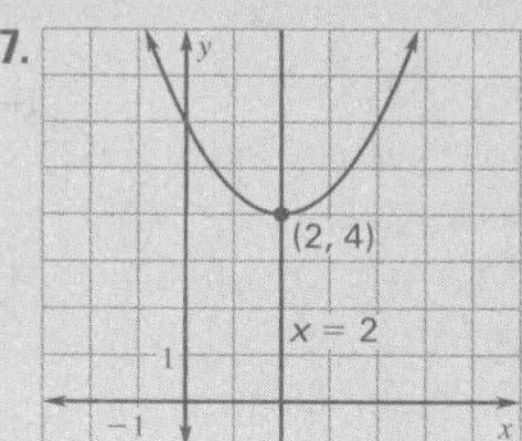

9.1 Apply the Distance and Midpoint Formulas

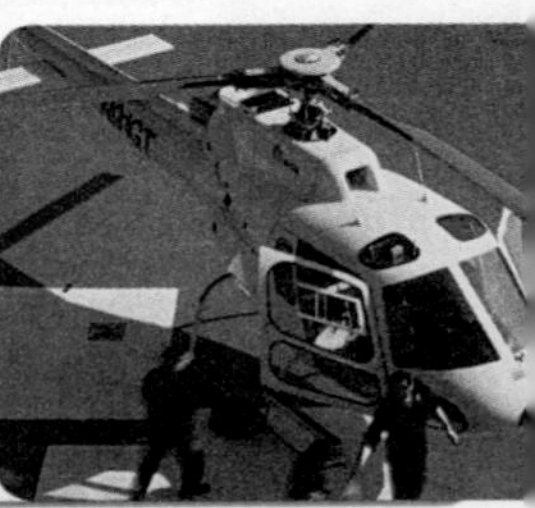

MA-HS-3.3.1

Before You found the slope of a line passing through two points.

Now You will find the length and midpoint of a line segment.

Why? So you can find real-world distances, as in Exs. 48–51.

Key Vocabulary
- distance formula
- midpoint formula

MA-HS-3.3.1
Students will apply algebraic concepts and graphing in the coordinate plane to analyze and solve problems (e.g., finding the final coordinates for a specified polygon, midpoints, betweenness of points, parallel and perpendicular lines, the distance between two points, the slope of a segment). DOK 2

To find the distance d between $A(x_1, y_1)$ and $B(x_2, y_2)$, apply the Pythagorean theorem to right triangle ABC.

$$(AB)^2 = (AC)^2 + (BC)^2$$
$$d^2 = (x_2 - x_1)^2 + (y_2 - y_1)^2$$
$$d = \sqrt{(x_2 - x_1)^2 + (y_2 - y_1)^2}$$

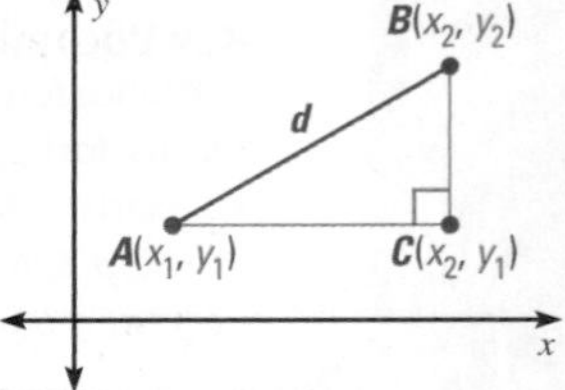

The final equation is the **distance formula**.

KEY CONCEPT *For Your Notebook*

The Distance Formula

The distance d between (x_1, y_1) and (x_2, y_2) is $d = \sqrt{(x_2 - x_1)^2 + (y_2 - y_1)^2}$.

★ **EXAMPLE 1 Standardized Test Practice**

What is the distance between (−3, 5) and (4, −1)?

Ⓐ $\sqrt{13}$ Ⓑ $\sqrt{65}$ Ⓒ $\sqrt{85}$ Ⓓ 13

Solution

Let $(x_1, y_1) = (-3, 5)$ and $(x_2, y_2) = (4, -1)$.

$$d = \sqrt{(x_2 - x_1)^2 + (y_2 - y_1)^2} = \sqrt{(4 - (-3))^2 + (-1 - 5)^2} = \sqrt{49 + 36} = \sqrt{85}$$

▸ The correct answer is C. Ⓐ Ⓑ Ⓒ Ⓓ

EXAMPLE 2 Classify a triangle using the distance formula

Classify $\triangle ABC$ as *scalene, isosceles,* or *equilateral*.

$$AB = \sqrt{(7-4)^2 + (3-6)^2} = \sqrt{18} = 3\sqrt{2}$$
$$BC = \sqrt{(2-7)^2 + (1-3)^2} = \sqrt{29}$$
$$AC = \sqrt{(2-4)^2 + (1-6)^2} = \sqrt{29}$$

▸ Because $BC = AC$, $\triangle ABC$ is isosceles.

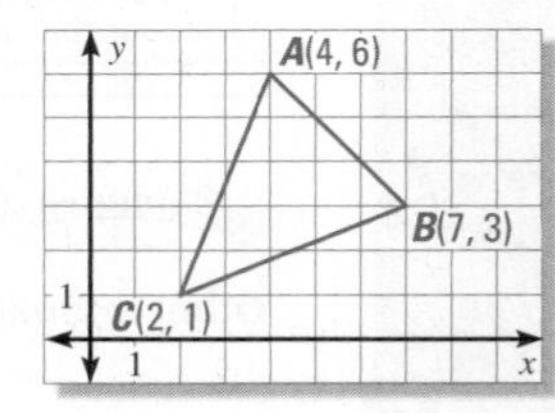

1 PLAN AND PREPARE

Warm-Up Exercises
Transparency Available

Simplify the expression.

1. $\sqrt{(5-2)^2 + (10-6)^2}$ 5
2. $\sqrt{(-1-1)^2 + (8+4)^2}$ $2\sqrt{37}$
3. You made \$36 in tips waiting tables on Friday night. On Saturday night you made \$48 in tips. How much did you average in tips for the two nights? **\$42**

Notetaking Guide
Transparency Available

Promotes interactive learning and notetaking skills, pp. 232–234.

Pacing
Basic: 1 day
Average: 1 day
Advanced: 1 day
Block: 0.5 block with 9.2
- See *Teaching Guide/Lesson Plan.*

2 FOCUS AND MOTIVATE

Essential Question
Big Idea 2, p. 613

If you are given the coordinates of the endpoints of the diameter of a circle, how can you find the center and radius of the circle? **Tell students they will learn how to answer this question by applying the distance and midpoint formulas.**

Resource Planning Guide

Chapter Resource Book
- Teaching Guide/Lesson Plan (pp. 3–4)
- Activity Master (p. 5)
- Practice levels A, B, C (pp. 6–8)
- Study Guide (pp. 9–10)
- Catch-up for Absent Students (p. 11)
- Problem Solving Workshop (p. 12)
- Challenge (p. 13)

Workbooks
- Notetaking Guide (pp. 232–234)
- Practice Workbook (pp. 134–135)

Teaching Options
- **Power Presentations CD-ROM** provides dynamic electronic teaching resources for the classroom.
- **Activity Generator CD-ROM** provides editable activities for all ability levels.

Interactive Technology
- Easy Planner
- Power Presentations CD-ROM
- Activity Generator CD-ROM
- Animated Algebra
- Test Generator CD-ROM
- Online Quiz
- eWorkbook
- eEdition
- @HomeTutor

Resources for English Learners
- Quick Reference for English Learners
- Spanish Study Guide
- Multi-Language Visual Glossary
- Student Resources in Spanish

See also the *Algebra 2 Toolkit* for more strategies for meeting individual needs.

✓ GUIDED PRACTICE for Examples 1 and 2

1. What is the distance between (3, −3) and (−1, 5)? $4\sqrt{5}$
2. The vertices of a triangle are $R(-1, 3)$, $S(5, 2)$, and $T(3, 6)$. Classify $\triangle RST$ as *scalene, isosceles,* or *equilateral.* scalene

KEY CONCEPT — *For Your Notebook*

The Midpoint Formula

A line segment's *midpoint* is equidistant from the segment's endpoints. The **midpoint formula,** shown below, gives the midpoint of the line segment joining $A(x_1, y_1)$ and $B(x_2, y_2)$.

$$M\left(\frac{x_1 + x_2}{2}, \frac{y_1 + y_2}{2}\right)$$

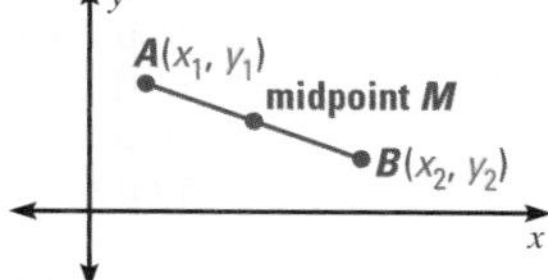

In words, each coordinate of M is the mean of the corresponding coordinates of A and B.

EXAMPLE 3 Find the midpoint of a line segment

Find the midpoint of the line segment joining (−5, 1) and (−1, 6).

Solution

Let $(x_1, y_1) = (-5, 1)$ and $(x_2, y_2) = (-1, 6)$.

$$\left(\frac{x_1 + x_2}{2}, \frac{y_1 + y_2}{2}\right) = \left(\frac{-5 + (-1)}{2}, \frac{1 + 6}{2}\right) = \left(-3, \frac{7}{2}\right)$$

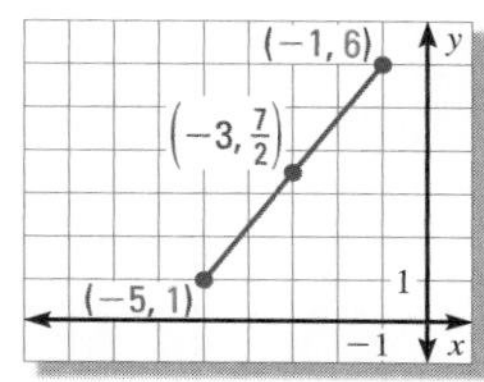

Animated Algebra at classzone.com

EXAMPLE 4 Find a perpendicular bisector

REVIEW EQUATIONS
For help with writing equations of perpendicular lines, see p. 98.

Write an equation for the perpendicular bisector of the line segment joining $A(-3, 4)$ and $B(5, 6)$.

Solution

STEP 1 **Find** the midpoint of the line segment.

$$\left(\frac{x_1 + x_2}{2}, \frac{y_1 + y_2}{2}\right) = \left(\frac{-3 + 5}{2}, \frac{4 + 6}{2}\right) = (1, 5)$$

STEP 2 **Calculate** the slope of $\overline{AB}$.

$$m = \frac{y_2 - y_1}{x_2 - x_1} = \frac{6 - 4}{5 - (-3)} = \frac{2}{8} = \frac{1}{4}$$

STEP 3 **Find** the slope of the perpendicular bisector: $-\frac{1}{m} = -\frac{1}{1/4} = -4$.

STEP 4 **Use** point-slope form: $y - 5 = -4(x - 1)$, or $y = -4x + 9$.

▸ An equation for the perpendicular bisector of $\overline{AB}$ is $y = -4x + 9$.

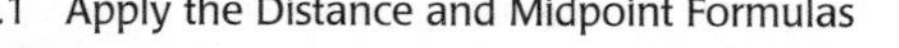

Differentiated Instruction

English Learners Before introducing the term *midpoint,* have students work in pairs to define the word themselves, using the parts of the term as hints. Then have them draw a few line segments and locate their respective midpoints.

See also the *Algebra 2 Toolkit* for more strategies.

Motivating the Lesson

Place a transparent coordinate system over a map of your town. Choose two locations. Ask students how they can use the Pythagorean Theorem to find the straight line distance between the two locations. In this lesson they will learn a formula for finding the distance between two points in the coordinate plane.

3 TEACH

Extra Example 1

What is the distance between (−5, 1) and (−3, 2)? B

Ⓐ $\sqrt{3}$ Ⓑ $\sqrt{5}$
Ⓒ $\sqrt{61}$ Ⓓ $\sqrt{65}$

Extra Example 2

Classify $\triangle DEF$ as *scalene, isosceles,* or *equilateral.*

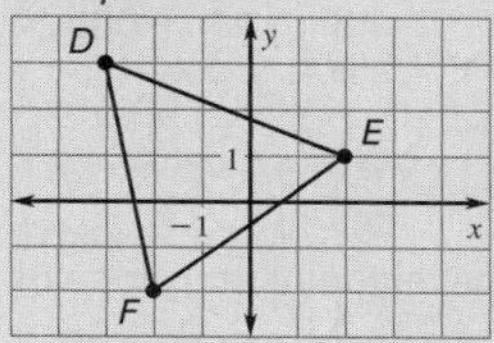

scalene ($DE = \sqrt{29}$, $DF = \sqrt{26}$, $EF = \sqrt{25}$)

Extra Example 3

Find the midpoint of the segment joining (−2, 3) and (4, −2). $\left(1, \frac{1}{2}\right)$

An **Animated Algebra** activity is available on-line for **Example 3.** This activity is also available on the **Power Presentations CD-ROM.**

Extra Example 4

Write an equation for the perpendicular bisector of the line segment joining $A(5, 4)$ and $B(-1, 6)$. $y = 3x - 1$

Extra Example 5

A circular swimming pool has a slide at B and stairs at A and C. Use the three labeled points to estimate the diameter of the pool. (Each unit in the coordinate plane represents 1 meter.)

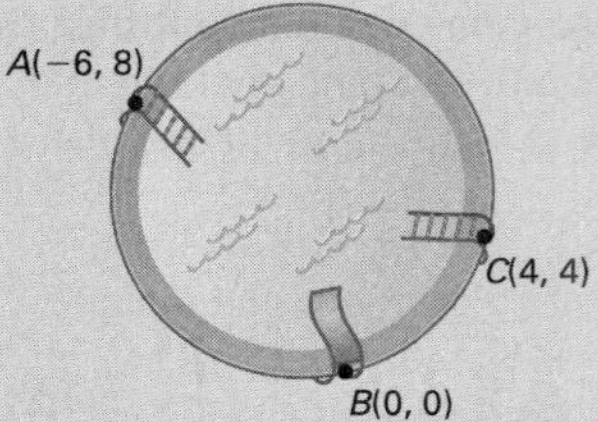

The three perpendicular bisectors are $y = -x + 4$, $y = \frac{3}{4}x + \frac{25}{4}$, and $y = \frac{5}{2}x + 17$. They meet at $\left(-\frac{9}{7}, \frac{37}{7}\right)$ so $r \approx 5.44$ meters.

Key Questions to Ask for Example 5

- What are the midpoint and slope of $\overline{AO}$? **midpoint: $\left(\frac{34+0}{2}, \frac{34+0}{2}\right) = (17, 17)$; slope: $\frac{34-0}{34-0} = 1$**
- What are the midpoint and slope of $\overline{OB}$? **midpoint: $\left(\frac{-66+0}{2}, \frac{22+0}{2}\right) = (-33, 11)$; slope: $\frac{22-0}{-66-0} = \frac{22}{-66} = -\frac{1}{3}$**

Closing the Lesson

Have students summarize the major points of the lesson and answer the Essential Question: If you are given the coordinates of the endpoints of the diameter of a circle, how can you find the center and radius of the circle?

- **The distance between (x_1, y_1) and (x_2, y_2) is $d = \sqrt{(x_2 - x_1)^2 + (y_2 - y_1)^2}$.**
- **The midpoint of the line segment joining (x_1, y_1) and (x_2, y_2) is $\left(\frac{x_1 + x_2}{2}, \frac{y_1 + y_2}{2}\right)$.**

Use the midpoint formula to find the midpoint of the diameter; that point is the center of the circle. Then use the distance formula to find the distance between the center and either endpoint; that distance is the radius of the circle.

FINDING A CIRCLE'S CENTER Recall from geometry that the perpendicular bisector of any chord of a circle passes through the circle's center. You can use this theorem to find the center of a circle given three points on the circle.

EXAMPLE 5 Solve a multi-step problem

ASTEROID CRATER Many scientists believe that an asteroid slammed into Earth about 65 million years ago on what is now Mexico's Yucatan peninsula, creating an enormous crater that is now deeply buried by sediment. Use the labeled points on the outline of the circular crater to estimate its diameter. (Each unit in the coordinate plane represents 1 mile.)

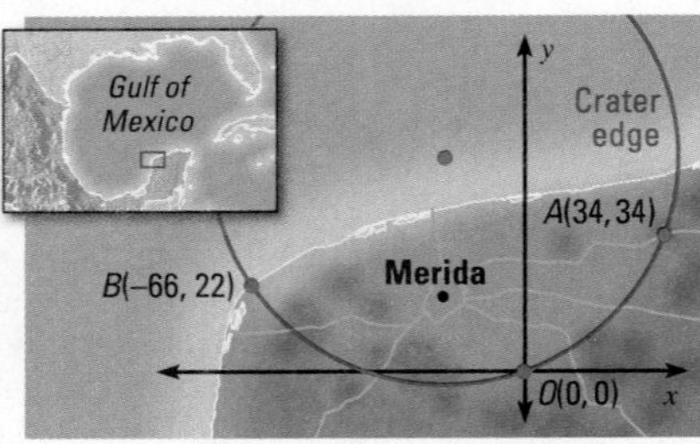

Solution

STEP 1 **Write** equations for the perpendicular bisectors of $\overline{AO}$ and $\overline{OB}$ using the method of Example 4.

$y = -x + 34$ — **Perpendicular bisector of $\overline{AO}$**

$y = 3x + 110$ — **Perpendicular bisector of $\overline{OB}$**

REVIEW SYSTEMS
For help with solving systems of equations, see p. 160.

STEP 2 **Find** the coordinates of the center of the circle, where $\overline{AO}$ and $\overline{OB}$ intersect, by solving the system formed by the two equations in Step 1.

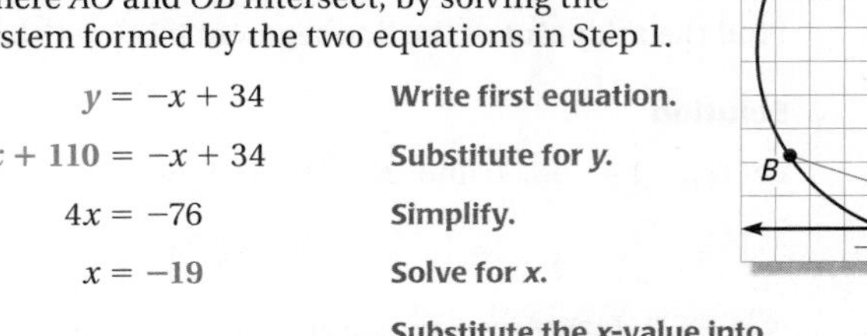

$y = -x + 34$	**Write first equation.**
$3x + 110 = -x + 34$	**Substitute for y.**
$4x = -76$	**Simplify.**
$x = -19$	**Solve for x.**
$y = -(-19) + 34$	**Substitute the x-value into the first equation.**
$y = 53$	**Solve for y.**

The center of the circle is $C(-19, 53)$.

STEP 3 **Calculate** the radius of the circle using the distance formula. The radius is the distance between C and any of the three given points.

$$OC = \sqrt{(-19 - 0)^2 + (53 - 0)^2} = \sqrt{3170} \approx 56.3$$

Use $(x_1, y_1) = (0, 0)$ and $(x_2, y_2) = (-19, 53)$.

▶ The crater has a diameter of about $2(56.3) = 112.6$ miles.

GUIDED PRACTICE for Examples 3, 4, and 5

For the line segment joining the two given points, (a) find the midpoint and (b) write an equation for the perpendicular bisector.

3. (0, 0), (−4, 12) **a. (−2, 6)** **4.** (−2, 1), (4, −7) **a. (1, −3)** **5.** (3, 8), (−5, −10) **a. (−1, −1)**

6. The points (0, 0), (6, −2), and (16, 8) lie on a circle. Use the method given in Example 5 to find the diameter of the circle. **20**

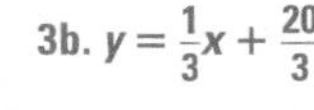

3b. $y = \frac{1}{3}x + \frac{20}{3}$

4b. $y = \frac{3}{4}x - \frac{15}{4}$

5b. $y = -\frac{4}{9}x - \frac{13}{9}$

Differentiated Instruction

Advanced Draw a sketch so that two lines through P_1 and P_2 are parallel to the y-axis and intersect the x-axis at $A_1(x_1, 0)$ and $A_2(x_2, 0)$. Explain that the line through the midpoint M parallel to the y-axis bisects $\overline{A_1A_2}$ at M_1. If $x_1 < x_2$, then $x_2 - x_1 > 0$, and $A_1A_2 = x_2 - x_1$. Therefore, the x-coordinate of $M_1 = x_1 + \frac{1}{2}(x_2 - x_1) = \frac{x_1 + x_2}{2}$ = the x-coordinate of M. Ask students to use a similar proof to show that the y-coordinate of M is $\frac{y_1 + y_2}{2}$. See also the *Algebra 2 Toolkit* for more strategies.

9.1 EXERCISES

HOMEWORK KEY

○ = WORKED-OUT SOLUTIONS on p. WS15 for Exs. 7, 27, and 53

★ = STANDARDIZED TEST PRACTICE Exs. 2, 18, 19, 37, and 56

SKILL PRACTICE

A

1. **VOCABULARY** State the distance and midpoint formulas. See margin.

2. ★ **WRITING** When finding the midpoint of a line segment joining two points, does it matter which point you choose as (x_1, y_1)? *Explain.* No; addition is a commutative operation.

EXAMPLES 1 and 3 on pp. 614–615 for Exs. 3–21

USING THE FORMULAS Find the distance between the two points. Then find the midpoint of the line segment joining the two points.

3. (0, 0), (8, 15) $17; \left(4, \frac{15}{2}\right)$
4. (0, 0), (4, 2) $2\sqrt{5}; (2, 1)$
5. (0, 6), (5, −4) $5\sqrt{5}; \left(\frac{5}{2}, 1\right)$
6. (−7, 0), (5, 3) $3\sqrt{17}; \left(-1, \frac{3}{2}\right)$
7. (2, −1), (6, −5) $4\sqrt{2}; (4, -3)$
8. (−1, −2), (8, 4) $3\sqrt{13}; \left(\frac{7}{2}, 1\right)$
9. (−4, 8), (8, −4) $12\sqrt{2}; (2, 2)$
10. (6, −3), (10, −9) $2\sqrt{13}; (8, -6)$
11. (−4, 4), (5, −4) $\sqrt{145}; \left(\frac{1}{2}, 0\right)$
12. (11, −12), (18, 12) $25; \left(\frac{29}{2}, 0\right)$
13. (−5, 1), (15, 8)
14. (9, 9), (−16, −16)
15. (−3.8, 15), (6.2, −11) $2\sqrt{194}; (1.2, 2)$
16. (1.5, 4), (2.3, 9)
17. (−2.4, −6.7), (3.1, −5.3)

13. $\sqrt{449}; \left(5, \frac{9}{2}\right)$

14. $25\sqrt{2}; \left(-\frac{7}{2}, -\frac{7}{2}\right)$

16. $\frac{\sqrt{641}}{5}$ or about 5.06; (1.9, 6.5)

17. $\frac{\sqrt{3221}}{10}$ or about 5.68; (0.35, −6)

18. ★ **MULTIPLE CHOICE** What is the distance between (−4, 3) and (6, 6)? C

Ⓐ $\sqrt{13}$ Ⓑ $\sqrt{85}$ Ⓒ $\sqrt{109}$ Ⓓ $\sqrt{181}$

19. ★ **MULTIPLE CHOICE** What is the midpoint of the line segment joining (−3, 7) and (5, −2)? A

Ⓐ $\left(1, \frac{5}{2}\right)$ Ⓑ $\left(-4, \frac{5}{2}\right)$ Ⓒ $\left(1, \frac{9}{2}\right)$ Ⓓ $\left(-4, \frac{9}{2}\right)$

ERROR ANALYSIS ***Describe*** **and correct the error in finding the distance between the two points.** 20, 21, See margin.

20. (5, −1), (2, 6)

$$d = \sqrt{(2-5)^2 + (6-1)^2} = \sqrt{9 + 25} = \sqrt{34}$$

21. (−4, 3), (2, 8)

$$d = \sqrt{(2-(-4))^2 - (8-3)^2} = \sqrt{36 - 25} = \sqrt{11}$$

EXAMPLE 2 on p. 614 for Exs. 22–30

CLASSIFYING TRIANGLES The vertices of a triangle are given. Classify the triangle as *scalene, isosceles,* or *equilateral.*

22. (−5, 0), (0, 6), (5, 0) isosceles
23. (0, −3), (0, 3), (3, 0) isosceles
24. (3, 5), (5, −3), (7, −3) scalene
25. (−2, 5), (1, −1), (4, 6) scalene
26. (1, 4), (4, 1), (7, 4) isosceles
27. (−4, 1), (−2, 6), (0, −1) scalene
28. (−1, −6), (1, 1), (4, −5) scalene
29. (−4, 3), (2, −1), (8, −1) scalene
30. (3, 5), (6, 9), (11, 9) isosceles

EXAMPLE 4 on p. 615 for Exs. 31–36

B

WRITING EQUATIONS Write an equation for the perpendicular bisector of the line segment joining the two points.

31. (3, 8), (7, 14) $y = -\frac{2}{3}x + \frac{43}{3}$
32. (−5, 6), (1, 8) $y = -3x + 1$
33. (−3, −6), (−1, 2) $y = -\frac{1}{4}x - \frac{5}{2}$
34. (1, 4), (6, −6) $y = \frac{1}{2}x - \frac{11}{4}$
35. (−3, −5), (9, −2) $y = -4x + \frac{17}{2}$
36. (5, 10), (10, 7) $y = \frac{5}{3}x - 4$

37. ★ **OPEN-ENDED MATH** Find two points not on the lines $x = 4$ or $y = 2$ such that the midpoint of the line segment joining the points is (4, 2). *Sample answer:* (6, 4), (2, 0)

4 PRACTICE AND APPLY

Assignment Guide

Answer Transparencies available for all exercises

Basic:
Day 1: EP p. 1011 Exs. 5–8
pp. 617–619
Exs. 1–8, 18–21, 23–27 odd, 31–33, 47–54, 58

Average:
Day 1: pp. 617–619
Exs. 1, 2, 9–13, 18–21, 22–26 even, 34–42, 47–56, 59

Advanced:
Day 1: pp. 617–619
Exs. 1, 2, 15–19, 28–30, 34–46*, 48–57*

Block:
pp. 617–619
Exs. 1, 2, 9–13, 18–21, 22–26 even, 34–42, 47–56, 59 (with 9.2)

Differentiated Instruction

See *Algebra 2 Best Practices Toolkit* for suggestions on addressing the needs of a diverse classroom.

Homework Check

For a quick check of student understanding of key concepts, go over the following exercises:

Basic: 4, 7, 25, 32, 47

Average: 10, 12, 26, 34, 50

Advanced: 16, 30, 36, 51, 52

Extra Practice

- Student Edition, p. 1018
- Chapter 9 Resource Book: Practice levels A, B, C, pp. 6–8

Practice Worksheet

An easily-readable reduced practice page (with answers) for this lesson can be found on p. 612C.

1. The distance d between (x_1, y_1) and (x_2, y_2) is $d = \sqrt{(x_2 - x_1)^2 + (y_2 - y_1)^2}$; the midpoint of the line segment joining $A(x_1, y_1)$ and $B(x_2, y_2)$ is $M\left(\frac{x_1 + x_2}{2}, \frac{y_1 + y_2}{2}\right)$.

20. −1 should be subtracted from 6 not 1; $d = \sqrt{(2-5)^2 + (6-(-1))^2} = \sqrt{9 + 49} = \sqrt{58}$.

21. The difference of the squares should be added not subtracted; $d = \sqrt{(2-(-4))^2 + (8-3)^2} = \sqrt{36 + 25} = \sqrt{61}$.

Avoiding Common Errors

Exercises 3–17 After applying the distance formula, some students may calculate the midpoint by subtracting the x- and y-coordinates. To help them avoid this error, suggest that when they calculate the midpoint it is sufficient to remember that the x-coordinate of the midpoint is the average of the x-coordinates and the y-coordinate of the midpoint is the average of the y-coordinates.

Teaching Strategy

Exercise 37 Suggest that students start by graphing $x = 4$, $y = 2$, and (4, 2). Then students can explore how to find two points that have (4, 2) as their midpoint.

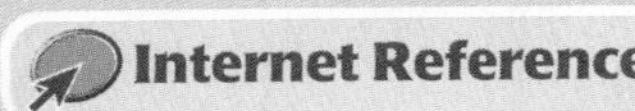

Internet Reference

Exercise 55 For more information about the meteor craters near Odessa, Texas, visit www.utpb.edu/ceed/GeologicalResources/West_Texas_Geology/Links/odessa_meteor.htm

GEOMETRY A *median* of a triangle is a line segment joining a vertex and the midpoint of the opposite side. The ordered pairs represent vertices of a triangle. Write an equation of the line containing the median that joins the first vertex to the side opposite it.

38. (8, 4), (0, 0), (10, 0) $y = \frac{4}{3}x - \frac{20}{3}$

39. (3, 10), (4, 2), (10, 8) $y = -\frac{5}{4}x + \frac{55}{4}$

40. (2, 6), (3, 1), (7, 5) $y = -x + 8$

FINDING A COORDINATE Use the given distance d between the two points to find the value of x or y.

41. (0, 3), (x, 5); $d = 2\sqrt{10}$ ± 6

42. (−3, −1), (2, y); $d = \sqrt{41}$ −5, 3

43. (x, 7), (−4, 1); $d = 6\sqrt{2}$ −10, 2

44. (1, y), (8, 13); $d = \sqrt{74}$ 8, 18

C **45. REASONING** Let (x, y) be any point on the line $y = 2x$. Write and simplify an equation that gives the distance d between (x, y) and (2, 3) as a function of x alone. Then find the coordinates of two points on the line $y = 2x$ that are each $\sqrt{10}$ units from (2, 3). $d(x) = \sqrt{5x^2 - 16x + 13}$; $\left(\frac{1}{5}, \frac{2}{5}\right)$, (3, 6)

46. CHALLENGE Show that $M\left(\frac{x_1 + x_2}{2}, \frac{y_1 + y_2}{2}\right)$ is the midpoint of the line segment with endpoints (x_1, y_1) and (x_2, y_2). To do this, show that M is equidistant from each endpoint and that M lies on the line containing (x_1, y_1) and (x_2, y_2). See margin.

PROBLEM SOLVING

EXAMPLE 1 A on p. 614 for Exs. 47–52

47. ROBOTS A remote-controlled robot can be instructed to move by entering coordinates on a control panel. If the robot is instructed to move from (6, 11) straight to (−2, 26), how far does the robot move? Assume the coordinates are in meters. 17 m

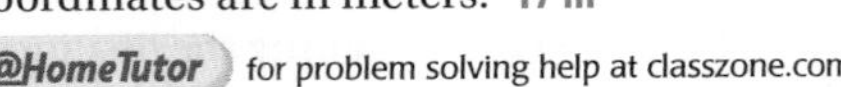

@HomeTutor for problem solving help at classzone.com

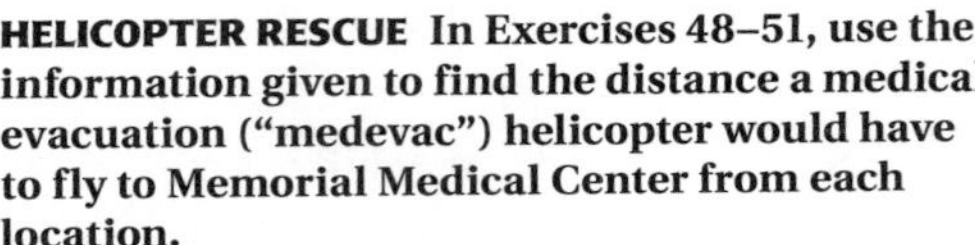

HELICOPTER RESCUE In Exercises 48–51, use the information given to find the distance a medical evacuation ("medevac") helicopter would have to fly to Memorial Medical Center from each location.

The Highway Department in Sangamon County, Illinois, uses a map that has its origin in central Springfield. Each unit on the map represents 1 mile, and the letters N, S, E, and W indicate direction. For example, 4W 5.6N is 4 miles west and 5.6 miles north of the origin. On a coordinate plane, 4W 5.6N corresponds to the point (−4, 5.6). Memorial Medical is at 0 0.5N, or (0, 0.5).

Capital Airport 1.1W 2.8N
Memorial Medical 0 0.5N
Washington Park 1.4W 0.8S
Spaulding Dam 2.9E 3.0S
University of Illinois 2.2E 5.1S

48. Capital Airport about 2.55 mi

49. University of Illinois about 6.02 mi

50. Washington Park about 1.91 mi

51. Spaulding Dam about 4.55 mi

@HomeTutor for problem solving help at classzone.com

52. COMMUTING To get from her home to her office, Li must drive around a lake. If she drives 2 miles north, then 5 miles east, and then 4 miles south, what is the straight-line distance between Li's home and her office? about 5.39 mi

○ = WORKED-OUT SOLUTIONS on p. WS1 ★ = STANDARDIZED TEST PRACTICE

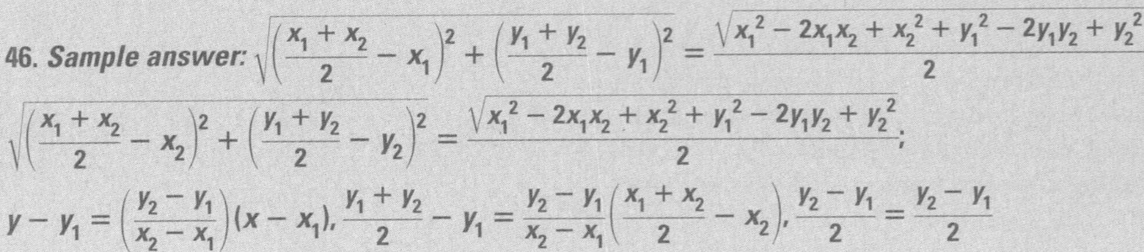

46. Sample answer: $\sqrt{\left(\frac{x_1 + x_2}{2} - x_1\right)^2 + \left(\frac{y_1 + y_2}{2} - y_1\right)^2} = \frac{\sqrt{x_1^2 - 2x_1x_2 + x_2^2 + y_1^2 - 2y_1y_2 + y_2^2}}{2}$,

$\sqrt{\left(\frac{x_1 + x_2}{2} - x_2\right)^2 + \left(\frac{y_1 + y_2}{2} - y_2\right)^2} = \frac{\sqrt{x_1^2 - 2x_1x_2 + x_2^2 + y_1^2 - 2y_1y_2 + y_2^2}}{2}$;

$y - y_1 = \left(\frac{y_2 - y_1}{x_2 - x_1}\right)(x - x_1)$, $\frac{y_1 + y_2}{2} - y_1 = \frac{y_2 - y_1}{x_2 - x_1}\left(\frac{x_1 + x_2}{2} - x_2\right)$, $\frac{y_2 - y_1}{2} = \frac{y_2 - y_1}{2}$

AMPLE 3
p. 615
Ex. 53

53. **MULTI-STEP PROBLEM** The diagram shows part of a trail system at a nature preserve. Each unit represents 0.1 mile. Suppose that you go from the visitor center *V* to the observation stand *S*, and then take a break at *M*, halfway between the observation stand and the picnic area *P*.

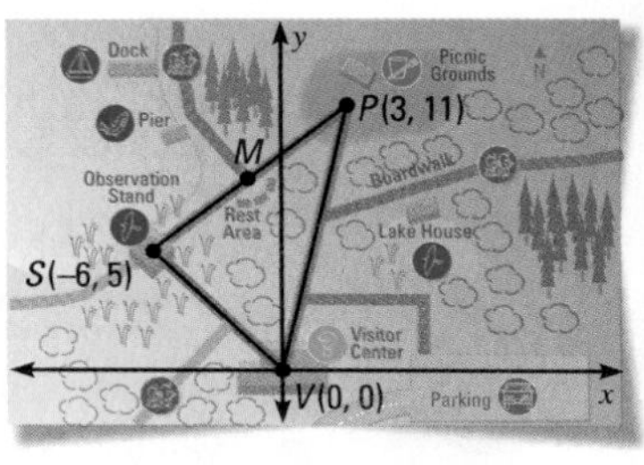

a. What are the coordinates of *M*? **(−1.5, 8)**

b. What is the total distance traveled from *V* to *M*? **about 1.32 mi**

c. What is the distance from *M* back to *V* through *P*? **about 1.68 mi**

AMPLE 5 B
p. 616
Exs. 54–55

54. **ARCHAEOLOGY** While on an archaeological dig, you uncover a piece of a circular dish. You lay the piece on a coordinate plane and mark three points on the dish's edge at (−4, 2), (0, 0), and (6, 4) where each unit represents 1 inch. What was the original diameter of the dish? **about 11.75 in.**

55. **METEOR CRATERS** Five meteor craters are clustered together near Odessa, Texas. Three points on the edge of the circular main crater can be represented by (−220, 220), (0, 0), and (200, 40) where each unit represents 1 foot. What is the diameter of the crater to the nearest 10 feet? **about 550 ft**

56. ★ **EXTENDED RESPONSE** You are ordering a triangular sail for your sailboat. When you get the sail, you plan to sew a thin decorative strip connecting the midpoints M_1 and M_2 of two sides of the sail, as shown in the diagram.

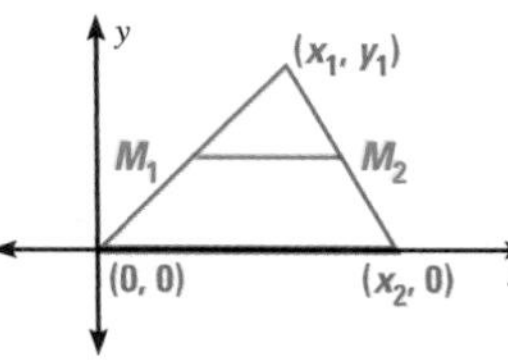

a. Write expressions for the coordinates of M_1 and M_2.

$\left(\frac{x_1}{2}, \frac{y_1}{2}\right)$, $\left(\frac{x_1 + x_2}{2}, \frac{y_1}{2}\right)$

b. Write a simplified expression for the length of the strip. *Compare* this length with the length of the sail's base.

$\frac{x_2}{2}$; the strip is one-half the length of the base.

c. Do your results from part (b) depend upon the shape of the triangular sail? *Explain.* **No; the length of the strip will always be $\frac{x_2}{2}$.**

C

57. **CHALLENGE** At time $t = 0$, a car begins traveling east at 60 miles per hour from a point 100 miles west and 40 miles north of a radio tower. The tower has a transmission range of 50 miles. Use the distance formula to find the times *t* during which the car is in range of the tower. $\frac{7}{6} \le t \le \frac{13}{6}$

KY KENTUCKY MIXED REVIEW

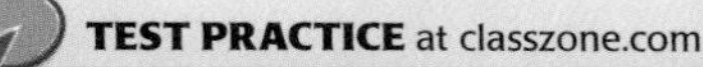

TEST PRACTICE at classzone.com

58. What are the *x*-intercepts of the graph of the function $y = 3x^2 - 12x - 15$? **A**

Ⓐ $x = -1, x = 5$　　Ⓑ $x = -5, x = 1$

Ⓒ $x = -5, x = \frac{1}{3}$　　Ⓓ $x = -1, x = \frac{5}{3}$

59. What is the approximate surface area of the three-dimensional figure represented by the net shown? **A**

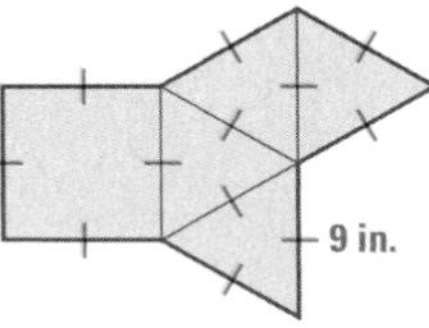

Ⓐ 221 in.^{2}　　Ⓑ 243 in.^{2}

Ⓒ 324 in.^{2}　　Ⓓ 405 in.^{2}

5 ASSESS AND RETEACH

Daily Homework Quiz

Transparency Available

The vertices of a triangle are $A(8, 5)$, $B(1, -2)$, and $C(-3, -2)$.

1. Classify $\triangle ABC$ as *scalene*, *isosceles*, or *equilateral*. **scalene**

2. Write an equation of the perpendicular bisector of $\overline{BC}$. $x = -1$

The entryway to an office building has a circular mosaic tile with a scalene triangle inscribed in a circle. The vertices of the triangle are $A(0, 0)$, $B(8, 2)$ and $C(4, 6)$.

3. What is the center of the circumscribed circle? **(3.8, 1.8)**

4. What is the area of the circle? **about 55.5 square feet**

Online Quiz

Available at **classzone.com**

Diagnosis/Remediation

- Practice A, B, C in Chapter 9 Resource Book, pp. 6–8
- Study Guide in Chapter 9 Resource Book, pp. 9–10
- Practice Workbook, pp. 134–135
- @HomeTutor

Challenge

Additional challenge is available in the Chapter 9 Resource Book, p. 13.

1 PLAN AND PREPARE

Warm-Up Exercises

Transparency Available

1. Solve $x = \frac{1}{2}y^2$ for y^2. $y^2 = 2x$
2. Solve $y = -\frac{1}{6}x^2$ for x^2. $x^2 = -6y$
3. Identify the axis of symmetry for the graph of $y = 3x^2$. $x = 0$
4. Identify the vertex of the graph of $y = 3x^2$. (0, 0)
5. The equation $y = -0.016x^2 + 16x$ models the path of a rocket. What is the vertex of the graph of the function? (500, 4000)

Notetaking Guide

Transparency Available

Promotes interactive learning and notetaking skills, pp. 235–237.

Pacing

Basic: 1 day
Average: 1 day
Advanced: 1 day
Block: 0.5 block with 9.1
• See *Teaching Guide/Lesson Plan.*

2 FOCUS AND MOTIVATE

Essential Question

Big Idea 2, p. 613

Which two features of a parabola are equidistant from its vertex? Tell students they will learn how to answer this question by identifying the focus and directrix.

9.2 Graph and Write Equations of Parabolas

KY **MA-HS-5.3.6** Students will model, solve and graph quadratic equations in real-world and mathematical problems. DOK 2

Before You graphed and wrote equations of parabolas that open up or down.
Now You will graph and write equations of parabolas that open left or right.
Why? So you can model sound projection, as in Ex. 56.

Key Vocabulary
- **focus**
- **directrix**
- **parabola,** *p. 236*
- **vertex,** *p. 236*

You know that the graph of $y = ax^2$ is a parabola that opens up or down with vertex (0, 0) and axis of symmetry $x = 0$. On any parabola, each point is equidistant from a point called the **focus** and a line called the **directrix**.

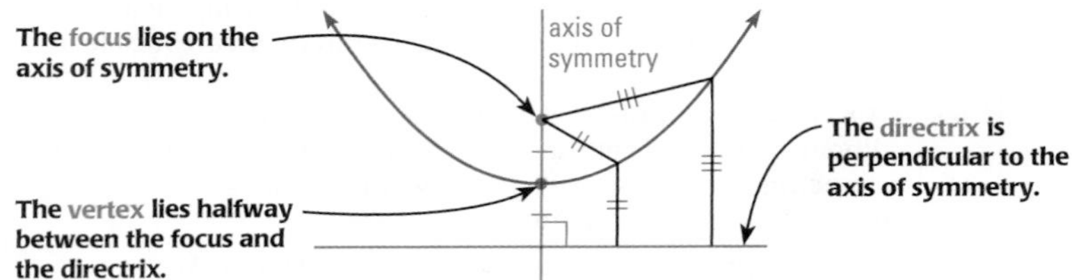

The equation of a parabola that opens up or down and has vertex (0, 0) can also be written in the form $x^2 = 4py$. Parabolas can open left or right as well, in which case the equation has the form $y^2 = 4px$ when the vertex is (0, 0). Note below that for any parabola, the focus and directrix each lie $|p|$ units from the vertex.

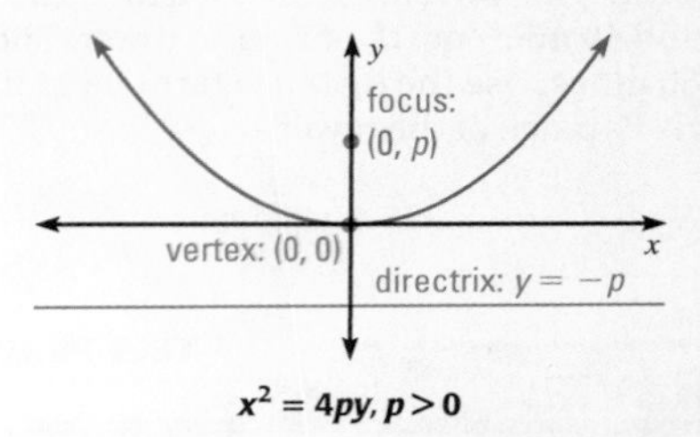

$x^2 = 4py, p > 0$

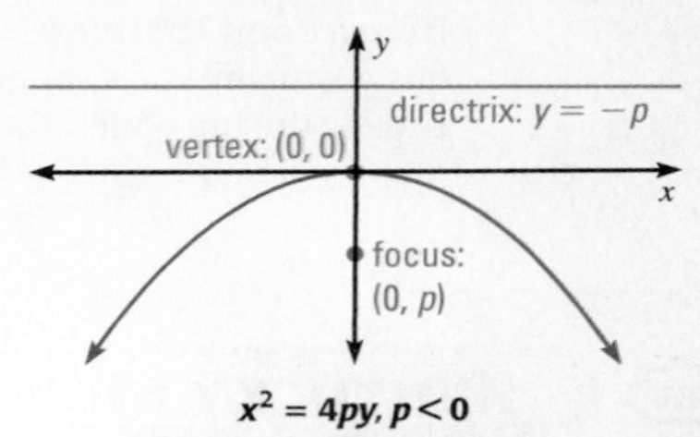

$x^2 = 4py, p < 0$

IDENTIFY FUNCTIONS
Notice that parabolas that open left or right do *not* represent functions.

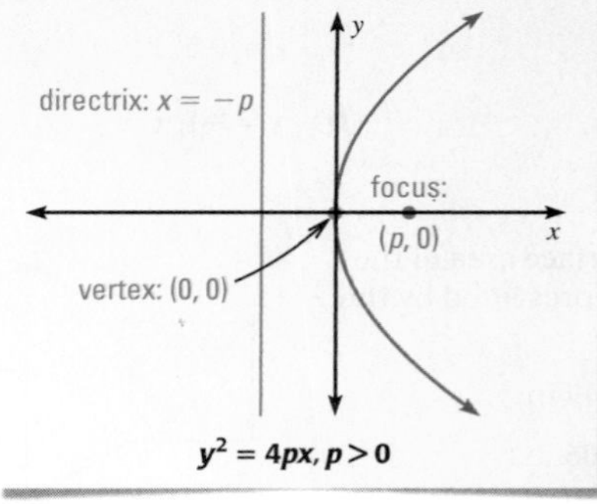

$y^2 = 4px, p > 0$

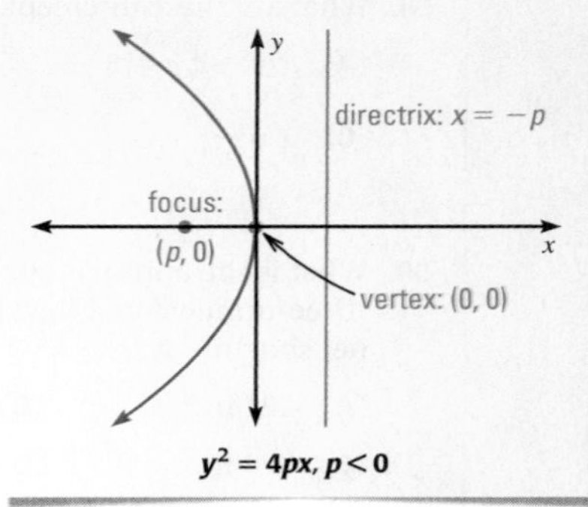

$y^2 = 4px, p < 0$

Resource Planning Guide

Chapter Resource Book
- Teaching Guide/Lesson Plan (pp. 14–15)
- Practice levels A, B, C (pp. 16–18)
- Study Guide (pp. 19–20)
- Catch-up for Absent Students (p. 21)
- Application (p. 22)
- Challenge (p. 23)

Workbooks
- Notetaking Guide (pp. 235–237)
- Practice Workbook (pp. 136–137)

Teaching Options
- **Power Presentations CD-ROM** provides dynamic electronic teaching resources for the classroom.
- **Activity Generator CD-ROM** provides editable activities for all ability levels.

Interactive Technology
- Easy Planner
- Power Presentations CD-ROM
- Activity Generator CD-ROM
- Animated Algebra
- Test Generator CD-ROM
- Online Quiz
- eWorkbook
- eEdition
- @HomeTutor

Resources for English Learners
- Quick Reference for English Learners
- Spanish Study Guide
- Multi-Language Visual Glossary
- Student Resources in Spanish

See also the *Algebra 2 Toolkit* for more strategies for meeting individual needs.

KEY CONCEPT — *For Your Notebook*

Standard Equation of a Parabola with Vertex at the Origin

The standard form of the equation of a parabola with vertex at (0, 0) is as follows:

Equation	Focus	Directrix	Axis of Symmetry
$x^2 = 4py$	$(0, p)$	$y = -p$	Vertical ($x = 0$)
$y^2 = 4px$	$(p, 0)$	$x = -p$	Horizontal ($y = 0$)

EXAMPLE 1 Graph an equation of a parabola

Graph $x = -\frac{1}{8}y^2$. Identify the focus, directrix, and axis of symmetry.

Solution

STEP 1 **Rewrite** the equation in standard form.

$x = -\frac{1}{8}y^2$ **Write original equation.**

$-8x = y^2$ **Multiply each side by −8.**

STEP 2 **Identify** the focus, directrix, and axis of symmetry. The equation has the form $y^2 = 4px$ where $p = -2$. The focus is $(p, 0)$, or $(-2, 0)$. The directrix is $x = -p$, or $x = 2$. Because y is squared, the axis of symmetry is the x-axis.

STEP 3 **Draw** the parabola by making a table of values and plotting points. Because $p < 0$, the parabola opens to the left. So, use only negative x-values.

x	−1	−2	−3	−4	−5
y	±2.83	±4	±4.90	±5.66	±6.32

Animated Algebra at classzone.com

...LVE FOR *Y*

... fill in the table, note ...at because $-8x = y^2$, ... $= \pm\sqrt{-8x}$. The value ... y will be a real ...mber only when ... ≤ 0.

EXAMPLE 2 Write an equation of a parabola

Write an equation of the parabola shown.

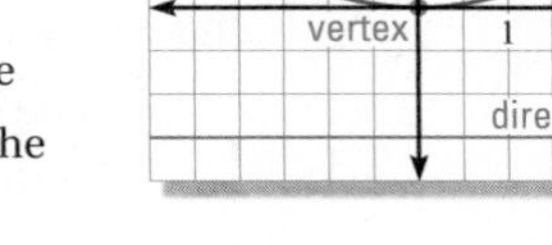

Solution

The graph shows that the vertex is (0, 0) and the directrix is $y = -p = -\frac{3}{2}$. Substitute $\frac{3}{2}$ for p in the standard form of the equation of a parabola.

$x^2 = 4py$ **Standard form, vertical axis of symmetry**

$x^2 = 4\left(\frac{3}{2}\right)y$ **Substitute $\frac{3}{2}$ for p.**

$x^2 = 6y$ **Simplify.**

Motivating the Lesson

Show students a picture of a searchlight. The shape of the mirror in the searchlight is obtained by revolving a parabola about its axis. In a searchlight, a source of light at the focus is reflected out in parallel rays. In this lesson students will learn about the focus of a parabola, which is also important in the construction of mirrors for telescopes and the shape of TV satellite antennas.

3 TEACH

Extra Example 1

Graph $y^2 = 20x$. Identify the focus, directrix, and axis of symmetry.

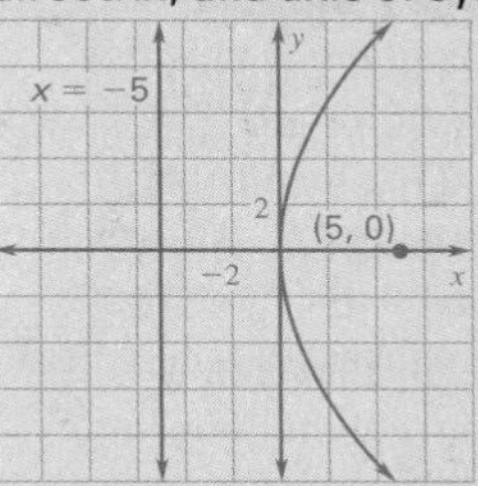

focus: (5, 0), directrix: $x = -5$, axis of symmetry: $y = 0$

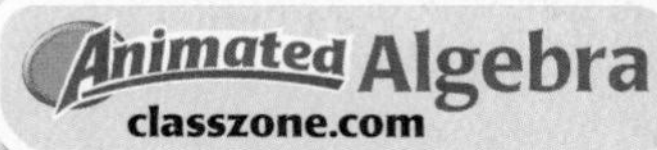

An **Animated Algebra** activity is available on-line for **Example 1**. This activity is also available on the **Power Presentations CD-ROM**.

Extra Example 2

Write an equation of the parabola shown. $y^2 = -12x$

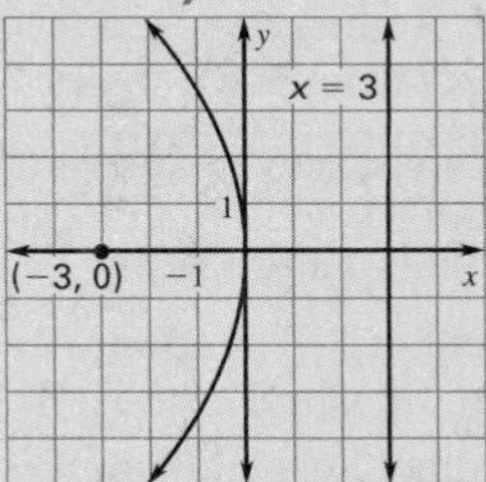

Differentiated Instruction

Advanced Point out that set-builder notation (as previously discussed in the Differentiated Instruction notes on pages 43 and 170) can be used to represent non-linear equations like those for the parabolas in this lesson. For example, the set of points that lie on the parabola graphed in **Example 1** can be given in set-builder notation as $\{(x, y) \mid -8x = y^2\}$, which is read "the set of all ordered pairs (x, y) such that $-8x$ is equal to y^2." Inform students that set-builder notation can be used in a similar manner for the other conic sections discussed in the next three lessons.

See also the *Algebra 2 Toolkit* for more strategies.

Extra Example 3

A flashlight uses a parabolic mirror and a light source. Write an equation for the mirror's cross section. How deep is the mirror?

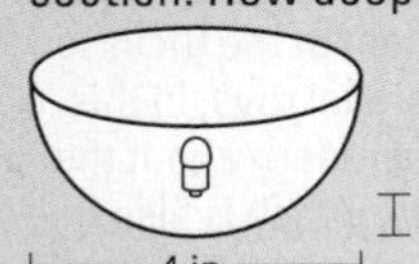

$x^2 = 2y$; 2 in.

Study Strategy

If the squared term is y, then the parabola has a horizontal axis of symmetry and the equation is not a function. If the squared term is x, the parabola has a vertical axis of symmetry and the equation is a function.

Closing the Lesson

Have students summarize the major points of the lesson and answer the Essential Question: Which two features of a parabola are equidistant from its vertex?

- **Every point on a parabola is equidistant from the focus and the directrix.**
- **The focus of a parabola lies on the axis of symmetry.**
- **The directrix of a parabola is perpendicular to the axis of symmetry.**
- **The vertex of a parabola lies halfway between its focus and directrix.**
- **For a parabola with vertex (0, 0), focus (0, p), directrix $y = -p$, and axis of symmetry $x = 0$, the standard equation is $x^2 = 4py$. For a parabola with vertex (0, 0), focus (p, 0), directrix $x = -p$, and axis of symmetry $y = 0$, the standard equation is $y^2 = 4px$.**

For a parabola, the directrix and focus are equidistant from the vertex.

GUIDED PRACTICE for Examples 1 and 2

Graph the equation. Identify the focus, directrix, and axis of symmetry of the parabola. 1–4. See margin for art.

1. $y^2 = -6x$ $\left(-\frac{3}{2}, 0\right)$, $x = \frac{3}{2}$, $y = 0$
2. $x^2 = 2y$ $\left(0, \frac{1}{2}\right)$, $y = -\frac{1}{2}$, $x = 0$
3. $y = -\frac{1}{4}x^2$ $(0, -1)$, $y = 1$, $x = 0$
4. $x = \frac{1}{3}y^2$ $\left(\frac{3}{4}, 0\right)$, $x = -\frac{3}{4}$, $y =$

Write the standard form of the equation of the parabola with vertex at (0, 0) and the given directrix or focus.

5. Directrix: $y = 2$ $x^2 = -8y$
6. Directrix: $x = 4$ $y^2 = -16x$
7. Focus: $(-2, 0)$ $y^2 = -8x$
8. Focus: $(0, 3)$ $x^2 = 12y$

PARABOLIC REFLECTORS *Parabolic reflectors* have cross sections that are parabolas. Incoming sound, light, or other energy that arrives at a parabolic reflector parallel to the axis of symmetry is directed to the focus (Diagram 1). Similarly, energy that is emitted from the focus of a parabolic reflector and then strikes the reflector is directed parallel to the axis of symmetry (Diagram 2).

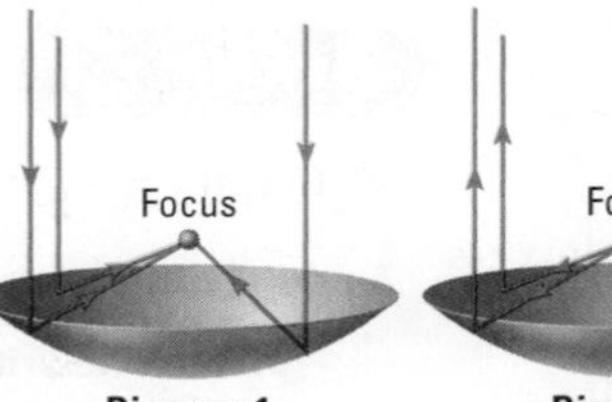

EXAMPLE 3 Solve a multi-step problem

SOLAR ENERGY The EuroDish, developed to provide electricity in remote areas, uses a parabolic reflector to concentrate sunlight onto a high-efficiency engine located at the reflector's focus. The sunlight heats helium to 650°C to power the engine.

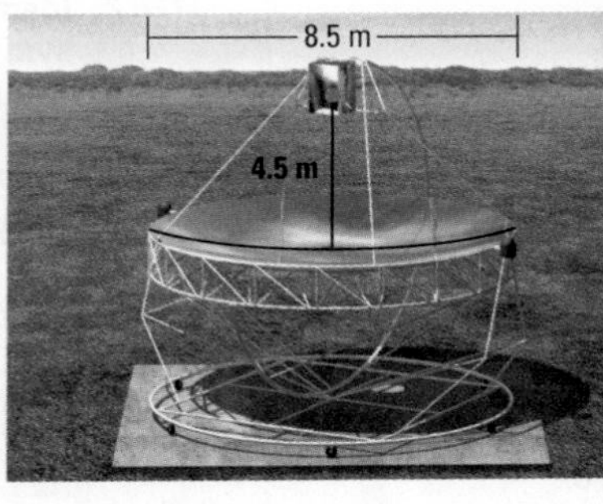

- Write an equation for the EuroDish's cross section with its vertex at (0, 0).
- How deep is the dish?

Solution

STEP 1 **Write** an equation for the cross section. The engine is at the focus, which is $|p| = 4.5$ meters from the vertex. Because the focus is above the vertex, p is positive, so $p = 4.5$. An equation for the cross section of the EuroDish with its vertex at the origin is as follows:

$x^2 = 4py$ **Standard form, vertical axis of symmetry**

$x^2 = 4(4.5)y$ **Substitute 4.5 for *p*.**

$x^2 = 18y$ **Simplify.**

STEP 2 **Find** the depth of the EuroDish. The depth is the y-value at the dish's outside edge. The dish extends $\frac{8.5}{2} = 4.25$ meters to either side of the vertex (0, 0), so substitute 4.25 for x in the equation from Step 1.

$x^2 = 18y$ **Equation for the cross section**

$(4.25)^2 = 18y$ **Substitute 4.25 for *x*.**

$1.0 \approx y$ **Solve for *y*.**

▶ The dish is about 1 meter deep.

1. 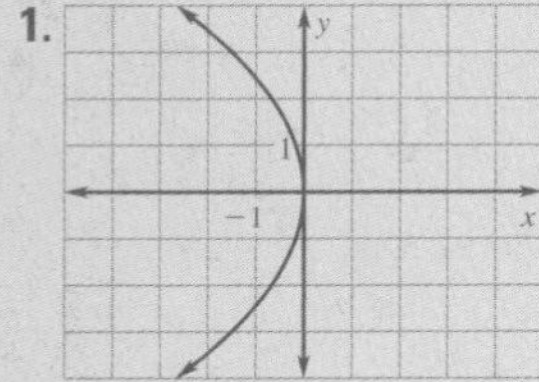
2. 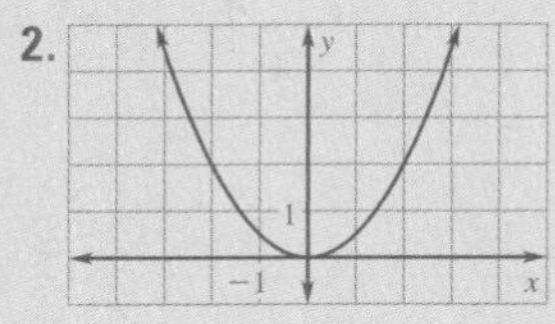
3. 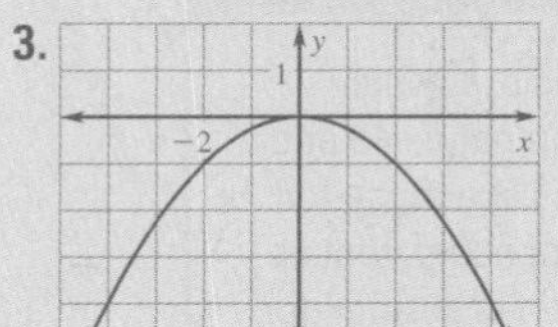
4. 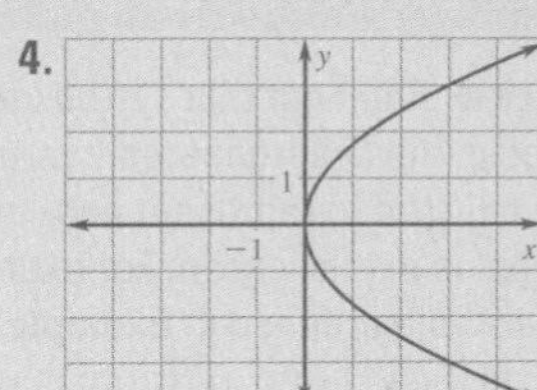

GUIDED PRACTICE for Example 3

9. **MICROWAVES** A parabolic microwave antenna is 16 feet in diameter. Find an equation for the cross section of the antenna with its vertex at the origin and its focus 10 feet to the right of its vertex. Then find the antenna's depth. $y^2 = 40x$; 1.6 ft

9.2 EXERCISES

HOMEWORK KEY
○ = **WORKED-OUT SOLUTIONS** on p. WS16 for Exs. 15, 27, and 57
★ = **STANDARDIZED TEST PRACTICE** Exs. 2, 25, 38, 51, 52, and 59

SKILL PRACTICE

A

1. **VOCABULARY** Copy and complete: A parabola is the set of all points in a plane equidistant from a point called the _?_ and a line called the _?_. focus, directrix

2. ★ **WRITING** *Compare* the graphs of $x^2 = 4py$ and $y^2 = 4px$. *Sample answer:* $x^2 = 4py$ opens up/down depending on the value of p while $y^2 = 4px$ opens left/right depending on the value of p.

EXAMPLE 1 on p. 621 for Exs. 3–25

GRAPHING **Graph the equation. Identify the focus, directrix, and axis of symmetry of the parabola.** 3–22. See margin.

3. $y^2 = 16x$	4. $x^2 = -6y$	5. $x^2 = 20y$	6. $y^2 = 28x$
7. $y^2 = -10x$	8. $x^2 = 30y$	9. $y^2 = -2x$	10. $x^2 = -36y$
11. $x^2 = 12y$	12. $-2y = x^2$	13. $x = 4y^2$	14. $-x^2 = 48y$
15. $5x^2 = -15y$	16. $-y^2 = 18x$	17. $-24x = 3y^2$	18. $14x = 6y^2$
19. $\frac{1}{8}x^2 - y = 0$	20. $4x - 11y^2 = 0$	21. $5x^2 + 12y = 0$	22. $-5x + \frac{1}{3}y^2 = 0$

ERROR ANALYSIS ***Describe*** **and correct the error in graphing the parabola.** 23, 24. See margin for art.

23.

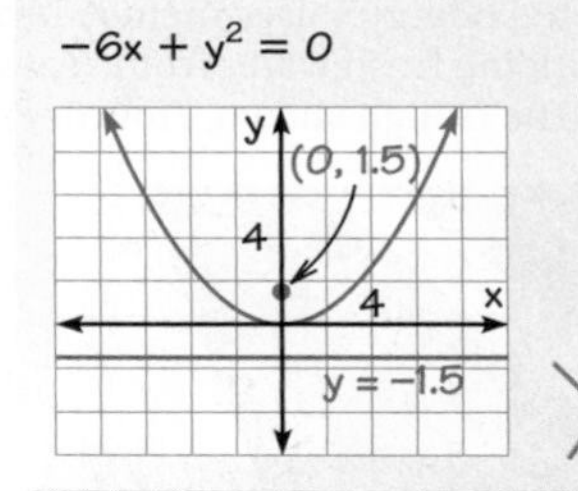

The parabola should open to the left rather than to the right.

24.

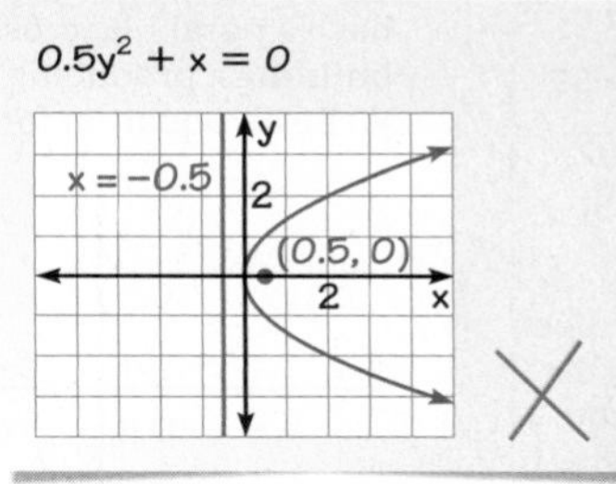

The parabola should open to the right rather than up.

25. ★ **MULTIPLE CHOICE** What is the directrix of the parabola $15y + 3x^2 = 0$? D

Ⓐ $x = -5$ Ⓑ $x = -1.25$ Ⓒ $y = -1.25$ Ⓓ $y = 1.25$

EXAMPLE 2 on p. 621 for Exs. 26–50

B

WRITING EQUATIONS **Write the standard form of the equation of the parabola with the given focus and vertex at (0, 0).**

26. $(2, 0)$ $y^2 = 8x$	27. $(-5, 0)$ $y^2 = -20x$	28. $(3, 0)$ $y^2 = 12x$	29. $(0, -4)$ $x^2 = -16y$
30. $(0, 8)$ $x^2 = 32y$	31. $(0, -10)$ $x^2 = -40y$	32. $(0, -6)$ $x^2 = -24y$	33. $(-9, 0)$ $y^2 = -36x$
34. $\left(0, \frac{7}{4}\right)$ $x^2 = 7y$	35. $\left(0, -\frac{3}{8}\right)$ $x^2 = -\frac{3}{2}y$	36. $\left(\frac{5}{2}, 0\right)$ $y^2 = 10x$	37. $\left(-\frac{9}{16}, 0\right)$ $y^2 = -\frac{9}{4}x$

4 PRACTICE AND APPLY

Assignment Guide

Answer Transparencies available for all exercises

Basic:
Day 1: pp. 623–625
Exs. 1, 2, 3–17 odd, 23–30, 38, 55–58, 61

Average:
Day 1: pp. 623–625
Exs. 1, 2, 4–18 even, 23–25, 30–33, 38–42, 51, 52, 56–59, 62

Advanced:
Day 1: pp. 623–625
Exs. 1, 2, 19–22, 25, 34–54*, 57–60*

Block:
pp. 623–625
Exs. 1, 2, 4–18 even, 23–25, 30–33, 38–42, 51, 52, 56–59, 62 (with 9.1)

Differentiated Instruction

See *Algebra 2 Best Practices Toolkit* for suggestions on addressing the needs of a diverse classroom.

Homework Check

For a quick check of student understanding of key concepts, go over the following exercises:
Basic: 9, 13, 28, 55, 56
Average: 12, 16, 32, 56, 58
Advanced: 20, 22, 36, 58, 59

Extra Practice

- Student Edition, p. 1018
- Chapter 9 Resource Book: Practice levels A, B, C, pp. 16–18

Practice Worksheet

An easily-readable reduced practice page (with answers) for this lesson can be found on p. 612C.

3–22. See Additional Answers beginning on p. AA1.

23.

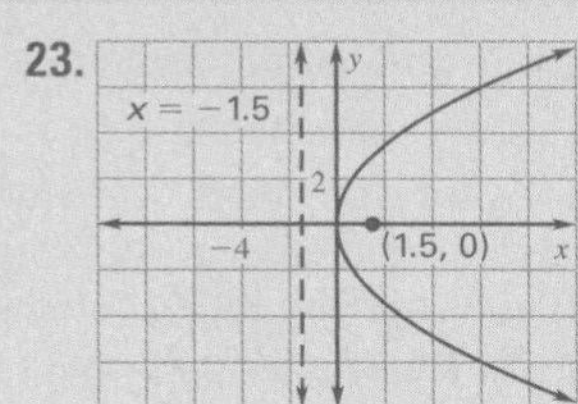

24.

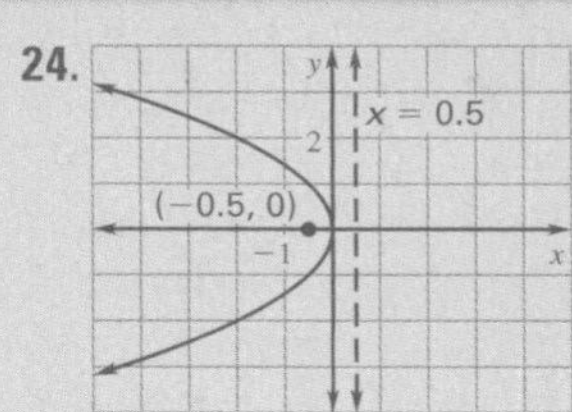

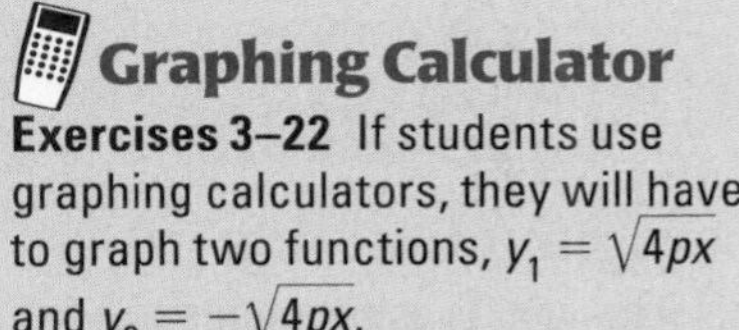

Graphing Calculator

Exercises 3–22 If students use graphing calculators, they will have to graph two functions, $y_1 = \sqrt{4px}$ and $y_2 = -\sqrt{4px}$.

Mathematical Reasoning

Exercises 3–22 Students are asked to compare the algebraic representation of a parabola with its geometric representation. The exercises prepare students to differentiate between the algebraic and geometric properties of parabolas. They will make similar comparisons later in the chapter for the other conic sections.

Avoiding Common Errors

Exercises 3–22, 26–37 Some students may have trouble remembering where the focus is relative to the graph. Remind them that p is the directed distance from the vertex to the focus. Thus, if $p > 0$ the focus is p units in a positive direction from the vertex (to the right or above), and if $p < 0$ the focus is p units in a negative direction from the vertex (to the left or below).

Internet Reference

Exercise 56 Additional information about dolphin echolocation can be found at people.cornellcollege.edu/d-wilson/geo105/echolocation.htm

Animated Algebra
classzone.com

An **Animated Algebra** activity is available on-line for **Exercise 58.** This activity is also available on the **Power Presentations CD-ROM**.

51a. The new focus will be located at (0, 1) rather than $\left(0, \frac{1}{4}\right)$. The new directrix will be $y = -1$ rather than $y = -\frac{1}{4}$. The parabola will be wider.

51b. The new focus will be located at $\left(-\frac{1}{8}, 0\right)$ rather than $\left(\frac{3}{2}, 0\right)$. The new directrix will be at $x = \frac{1}{8}$ rather than $x = -\frac{3}{2}$. The parabola will open left rather than right and be narrower.

52. *Sample answer:* Both equations describe the family of vertical parabolas with vertices at the origin. Dividing both sides of $x^2 = 4py$ by $4p$ gives $y = \frac{1}{4p}x^2$, which can be written as $y = ax^2$ where $a = \frac{1}{4p}$.

38. ★ **MULTIPLE CHOICE** What is an equation of the parabola with focus at $(-8, 0)$ and vertex at $(0, 0)$? **A**

Ⓐ $y^2 = -32x$ Ⓑ $y^2 = -0.5x$ Ⓒ $x^2 = -8y$ Ⓓ $x^2 = -32y$

WRITING EQUATIONS Write the standard form of the equation of the parabola with the given directrix and vertex at (0, 0).

39. $x = 3$ $y^2 = -12x$
40. $y = -7$ $x^2 = 28y$
41. $x = -5$ $y^2 = 20x$
42. $y = 12$ $x^2 = -48y$
43. $y = -4$ $x^2 = 16y$
44. $x = -2$ $y^2 = 8x$
45. $y = 6$ $x^2 = -24y$
46. $x = 11$ $y^2 = -44x$
47. $x = -\frac{3}{2}$ $y^2 = 6x$
48. $y = \frac{5}{12}$ $x^2 = -\frac{5}{3}y$
49. $y = -\frac{11}{6}$ $x^2 = \frac{22}{3}y$
50. $x = -\frac{1}{18}$ $y^2 = \frac{2}{9}x$

51. ★ **SHORT RESPONSE** Predict how the indicated change in a will affect the focus, directrix, and shape of the given equation's graph. Then graph both the original and revised equations in the same coordinate plane. **a–b. See margin for art.**
 a. $x^2 = ay$; a changes from 1 to 4
 b. $y^2 = ax$; a changes from 6 to $-\frac{1}{2}$

52. ★ **WRITING** Suppose that $x^2 = 4py$ and $y = ax^2$ represent the same parabola. *Explain* how a and p are related. **See margin.**

C

53. **VISUAL THINKING** As $|p|$ increases, how does the width of the graph of $x^2 = 4py$ change? *Explain.* **See margin.**

54. **CHALLENGE** Consider the parabola with focus $(0, p)$ and directrix $y = -p$. Let (x, y) be any point on the parabola. Use the fact that (x, y) is equidistant from the focus and directrix to show that $x^2 = 4py$. **See margin.**

PROBLEM SOLVING

EXAMPLE 3 **A**
on p. 622
for Exs. 55–59

55. **SOLAR ENERGY** Solar energy can be concentrated using long troughs that have a parabolic cross section. The collected energy's uses include heating buildings, producing electricity, and producing fresh water from seawater. Write an equation for the cross section of the trough shown. How deep is it? **$x^2 = 24y$; about 3 ft**

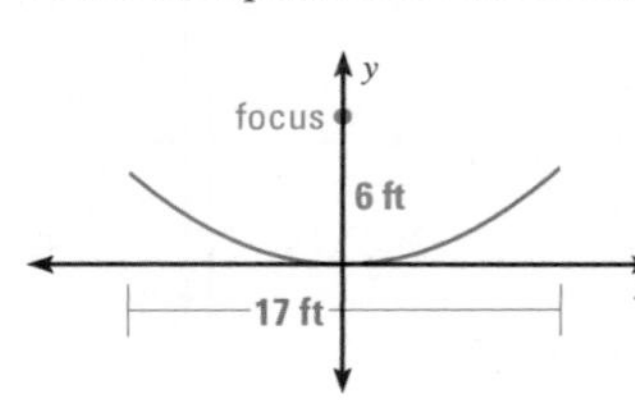

@HomeTutor for problem solving help at classzone.com

56. **BIOLOGY** Scientists studying dolphin *echolocation* can simulate the projection of a dolphin's clicking sounds using computer models. The models originate the sounds at the focus of a parabolic reflector. The parabola in the graph models the cross section (with units in inches) of the reflector used to simulate sound projection for a bottlenose dolphin. What is the *focal length* (the distance from the vertex to the focus)? **$\frac{4}{3}$ in.**

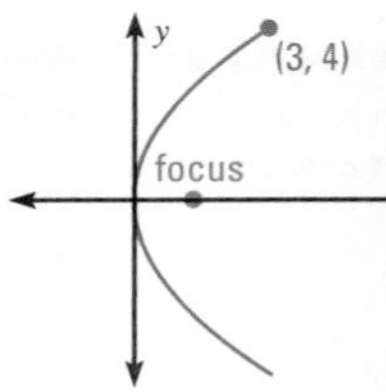

@HomeTutor for problem solving help at classzone.com

○ = WORKED-OUT SOLUTIONS on p. WS1 ★ = STANDARDIZED TEST PRACTICE

51a.

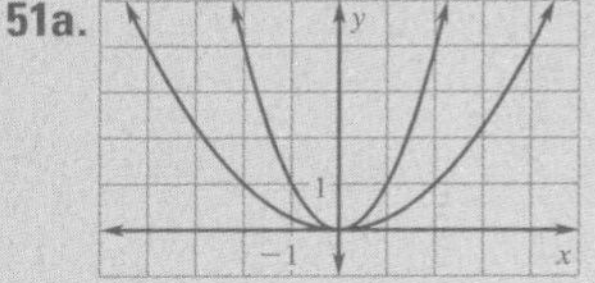

51b.

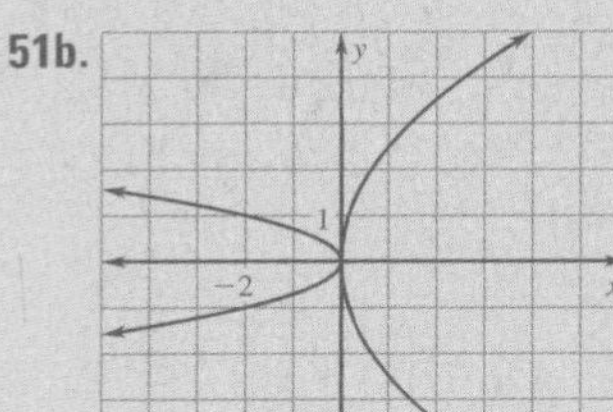

53. The graph gets wider. *Sample answer:* As the value of $|p|$ increases, then the focus and directrix (each of which lie $|p|$ units from the vertex) get further and further away from the vertex and from each other. Since each point on a parabola is equidistant from the focus and the directrix, this has the effect of making the parabola wider and wider as $|p|$ increases.

54. See Additional Answers beginning on p. AA1.

57. **MULTI-STEP PROBLEM** The parabolic antenna used by a television station to transmit is 146 inches in diameter. Its focus is 48 inches from the vertex.

a. Sketch the antenna twice: once opening upward and once opening left. **See margin.**

b. Use your sketches from part (a) to write two equations for the antenna's cross section: one of the form $x^2 = 4py$ and one of the form $y^2 = 4px$. **$x^2 = 192y$, $y^2 = -192x$**

c. How deep is the antenna's dish? Does it matter which equation from part (b) you use to find your answer? *Explain.* **About 27.8 in.; no. *Sample answer:* Except for the direction they open, they are identical.**

B **58.** **RADIO TELESCOPES** The Very Large Array in New Mexico consists of 27 radio telescopes. For each parabolic telescope dish, the diameter is 25 meters and the distance between the vertex and focus is 0.36 times the diameter. Write an equation for the cross section of a dish opening upward with its vertex at the origin. How deep is each dish? **$x^2 = 36y$; about 4.3 m**

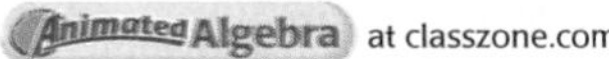
Animated Algebra at classzone.com

59. ★ **EXTENDED RESPONSE** Searchlights use parabolic reflectors to project their beams. The cross section of a 9.5-inch-deep searchlight reflector has equation $x^2 = 10.5y$.

a. How wide is the beam of light projected from the searchlight's reflector? **about 20 in.**

b. Write an equation for the cross section of a reflector that has the same depth as the original reflector, but which projects a wider beam. *Explain* how you found your answer. How wide is the new reflector's beam?

Sample ...*wer:* $= 50y$; ...ose a value ... such that ... 10.5; about ... in.

c. Repeat part (b) for a beam narrower than the original. ***Sample answer:* $x^2 = 8y$; choose a value for $4p$ such that $4p < 10.5$; about 17.4 in.**

C **60.** **CHALLENGE** The *latus rectum* of a parabola is the line segment that is parallel to the directrix, passes through the focus, and has endpoints that lie on the parabola. Find the length in terms of p of the latus rectum of a parabola with equation $x^2 = 4py$. **$4p$**

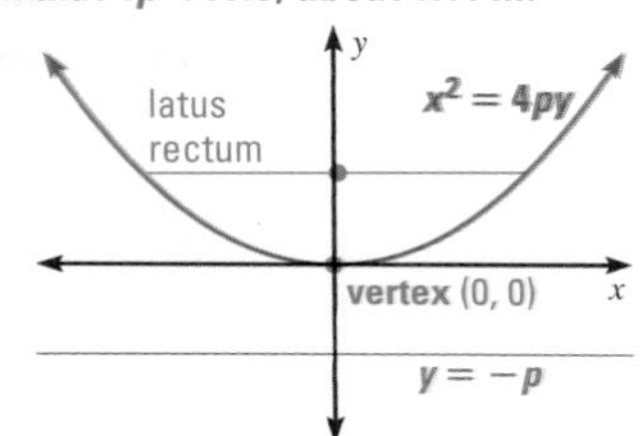

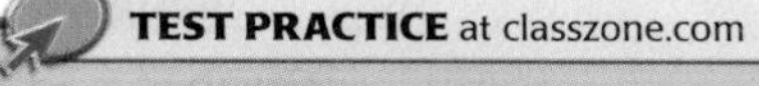

KENTUCKY MIXED REVIEW

61. The figure shows a triangular city park. What is the perimeter of the park? **C**

Ⓐ 170 yd Ⓑ 190 yd Ⓒ 200 yd Ⓓ 273 yd

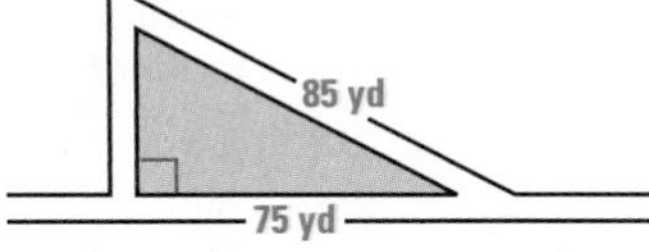

62. Sarah has 9 points less than she needs to make a grade of A in her mathematics course. Her point total for the course is 423 points. How many points are possible in the course? (Assume she needs 90% of the total possible points for an A.) **C**

Ⓐ 460 Ⓑ 470 Ⓒ 480 Ⓓ 490

5 ASSESS AND RETEACH

Daily Homework Quiz

Transparency Available

1. Graph $x^2 = -8y$. Identify the focus, directrix, and axis of symmetry.

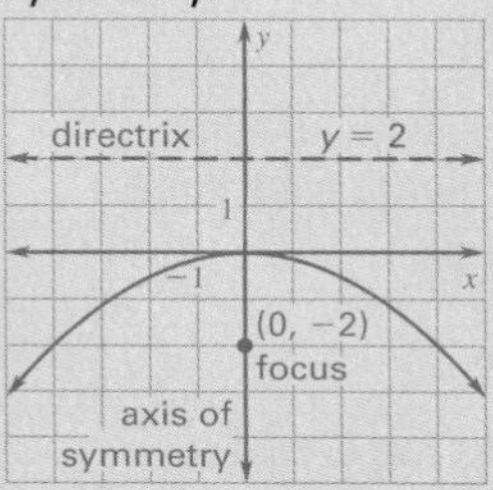

2. Write an equation of the parabola shown. **$y^2 = 12x$**

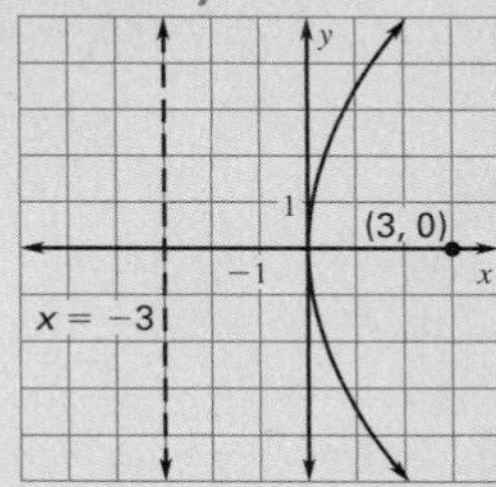

The cross section of a portable searchlight reflector is a parabola. The axis of symmetry is vertical, the widest part of the parabola is 8 inches across, and the light bulb is 1 inch from the vertex.

3. Write an equation for the cross section. **$x^2 = 4y$**
4. How deep is the reflector? **4 in.**

Available at **classzone.com**

Diagnosis/Remediation

- Practice A, B, C in Chapter 9 Resource Book, pp. 16–18
- Study Guide in Chapter 9 Resource Book, pp. 19–20
- Practice Workbook, pp. 136–137
- @HomeTutor

Challenge

Additional challenge is available in the Chapter 9 Resource Book, p. 23.

57a. See Additional Answers beginning on p. AA1.

1 PLAN AND PREPARE

Warm-Up Exercises

Transparency Available

Find the distance between (0, 0) and the given point.

1. (3, 4) 5
2. (5, 12) 13

What is the slope of a line perpendicular to each line?

3. $y = \frac{1}{3}x - 5$ -3
4. $y = -4x - 7$ $\frac{1}{4}$

Notetaking Guide

Transparency Available

Promotes interactive learning and notetaking skills, pp. 238–240.

Pacing

Basic: 1 day
Average: 1 day
Advanced: 1 day
Block: 0.5 block with 9.4
- See *Teaching Guide/Lesson Plan.*

2 FOCUS AND MOTIVATE

Essential Question

Big Idea 1, p. 613

What information do you need to write the equation of a circle with center (0, 0)? Tell students they will learn how to answer this question by learning the standard form of an equation with center (0, 0).

9.3 Graph and Write Equations of Circles

MA-HS-3.1.6 Students will know the definitions and basic properties of a circle and will use them to prove basic theorems and solve problems.

Before You graphed and wrote equations of parabolas.
Now You will graph and write equations of circles.
Why? So you can model transmission ranges, as in Ex. 62.

Key Vocabulary
- circle
- center
- radius

A **circle** is the set of all points (x, y) in a plane that are equidistant from a fixed point, called the **center** of the circle. The distance r between the center and any point (x, y) on the circle is the **radius**.

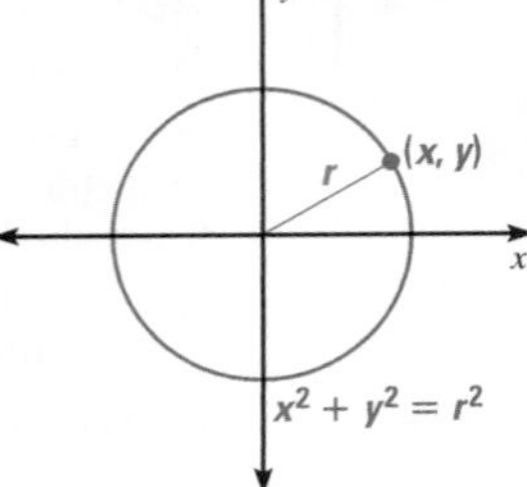

For a circle with center at the origin and radius r, the distance between any point (x, y) on the circle and the center $(0, 0)$ is r, so the following is true:

$\sqrt{(x-0)^2 + (y-0)^2} = r$ **Distance formula**

$(x-0)^2 + (y-0)^2 = r^2$ **Square each side.**

$x^2 + y^2 = r^2$ **Simplify.**

KEY CONCEPT — *For Your Notebook*

Standard Equation of a Circle with Center at the Origin

The standard form of the equation of a circle with center at (0, 0) and radius r is as follows:

$$x^2 + y^2 = r^2$$

EXAMPLE 1 Graph an equation of a circle

Graph $y^2 = -x^2 + 36$. Identify the radius of the circle.

Solution

STEP 1 **Rewrite** the equation $y^2 = -x^2 + 36$ in standard form as $x^2 + y^2 = 36$.

STEP 2 **Identify** the center and radius. From the equation, the graph is a circle centered at the origin with radius $r = \sqrt{36} = 6$.

STEP 3 **Draw** the circle. First plot several convenient points that are 6 units from the origin, such as (0, 6), (6, 0), (0, −6), and (−6, 0). Then draw the circle that passes through the points.

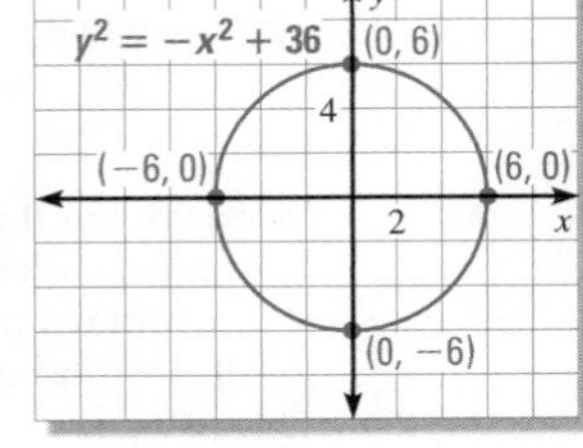

Animated Algebra at classzone.com

Resource Planning Guide

Chapter Resource Book
- Teaching Guide/Lesson Plan (pp. 24–25)
- Practice levels A, B, C (pp. 27–29)
- Study Guide (pp. 30–31)
- Catch-up for Absent Students (p. 32)
- Problem Solving Workshop (p. 33)
- Challenge (p. 34)

Workbooks
- Notetaking Guide (pp. 238–240)
- Practice Workbook (pp. 138–139)

Teaching Options
- **Power Presentations CD-ROM** provides dynamic electronic teaching resources for the classroom.
- **Activity Generator CD-ROM** provides editable activities for all ability levels.

Interactive Technology
- Easy Planner
- Power Presentations CD-ROM
- Activity Generator CD-ROM
- Animated Algebra
- Test Generator CD-ROM
- Online Quiz
- eWorkbook
- eEdition
- @HomeTutor

Resources for English Learners
- Quick Reference for English Learners
- Spanish Study Guide
- Multi-Language Visual Glossary
- Student Resources in Spanish

See also the *Algebra 2 Toolkit* for more strategies for meeting individual needs.

EXAMPLE 2 Write an equation of a circle

The point (2, −5) lies on a circle whose center is the origin. Write the standard form of the equation of the circle.

Solution

Because the point (2, −5) lies on the circle, the circle's radius r must be the distance between the center (0, 0) and (2, −5). Use the distance formula.

$r = \sqrt{(2-0)^2 + (-5-0)^2} = \sqrt{4+25} = \sqrt{29}$ **The radius is $\sqrt{29}$.**

Use the standard form with $r = \sqrt{29}$ to write an equation of the circle.

$x^2 + y^2 = r^2$ **Standard form**

$x^2 + y^2 = (\sqrt{29})^2$ **Substitute $\sqrt{29}$ for r.**

$x^2 + y^2 = 29$ **Simplify.**

EXAMPLE 3 Standardized Test Practice

What is an equation of the line tangent to the circle $x^2 + y^2 = 13$ at (−3, 2)?

Ⓐ $y = \frac{2}{3}x + 4$ Ⓑ $y = \frac{3}{2}x - \frac{5}{2}$ Ⓒ $y = \frac{3}{2}x + \frac{13}{2}$ Ⓓ $y = -\frac{3}{2}x + \frac{13}{3}$

IMINATE CHOICES
Example 3, you can ninate choice D cause a quick sketch the circle shows that slope of the tangent e at (−3, 2) must be sitive.

Solution

A line tangent to a circle is perpendicular to the radius at the point of tangency. Because the radius to the point (−3, 2) has slope $m = \frac{2-0}{-3-0} = -\frac{2}{3}$, the slope of the tangent line at (−3, 2) is the negative reciprocal of $-\frac{2}{3}$, or $\frac{3}{2}$. An equation of the tangent line is as follows:

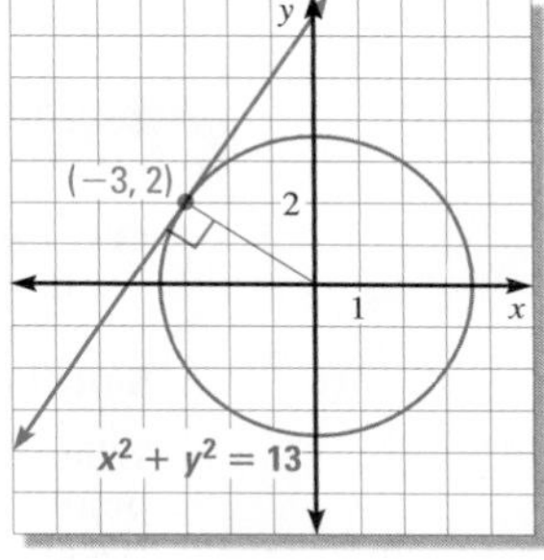

$y - 2 = \frac{3}{2}(x - (-3))$ **Point-slope form**

$y - 2 = \frac{3}{2}x + \frac{9}{2}$ **Distributive property**

$y = \frac{3}{2}x + \frac{13}{2}$ **Solve for y.**

▶ The correct answer is C. Ⓐ Ⓑ Ⓒ Ⓓ

✓ GUIDED PRACTICE for Examples 1, 2, and 3

Graph the equation. Identify the radius of the circle. 1–3. See margin on p. 628 for art.

1. $x^2 + y^2 = 9$ 3
2. $y^2 = -x^2 + 49$ 7
3. $x^2 - 18 = -y^2$ $3\sqrt{2}$
4. Write the standard form of the equation of the circle that passes through (5, −1) and whose center is the origin. $x^2 + y^2 = 26$
5. Write an equation of the line tangent to the circle $x^2 + y^2 = 37$ at (6, 1). $y = -6x + 37$

Motivating the Lesson

Show students a picture of the two Mars Exploration Rovers. Each rover has two pairs of hazard avoidance cameras. Each pair of cameras can see about one third of the interior of a 10-foot-radius circle. In this lesson students will learn of other applications that deal with circles with known centers and radii.

3 TEACH

Extra Example 1

Graph $x^2 - 4 = -y^2$. Identify the radius of the circle. $r = 2$

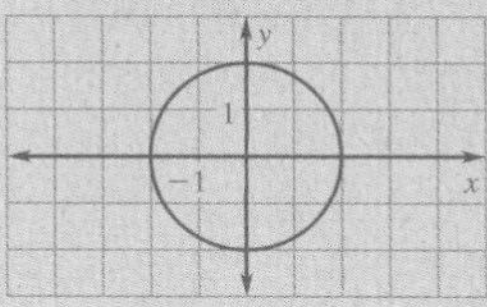

An **Animated Algebra** activity is available on-line for **Example 1**. This activity is also available on the **Power Presentations CD-ROM**.

Extra Example 2

The point (−4, 7) lies on a circle whose center is the origin. Write the standard form of the equation of the circle. $x^2 + y^2 = 65$

Extra Example 3

What is an equation of the line tangent to the circle $x^2 + y^2 = 61$ at (5, −6)? B

Ⓐ $y = -\frac{5}{6}x - \frac{11}{6}$

Ⓑ $y = \frac{5}{6}x - \frac{61}{6}$

Ⓒ $y = \frac{5}{6}x - \frac{11}{6}$

Ⓓ $y = \frac{6}{5}x$

Differentiated Instruction

Below Level Have students graph the points (3, 4) and (0, 0) and draw the segment between them. Then ask them to use the distance formula to find the length of the segment. Have them use a compass to demonstrate that the segment is a radius of the circle with center (0, 0) and through the point (3, 4). Show them that $x^2 + y^2 = r^2$ for all points on the circle.

See also the *Algebra 2 Toolkit* for more strategies.

Extra Example 4

A business owner wants to buy a property within a 30 mile radius of the airport. She finds a property 10 miles west and 24 miles south of the airport. Is the property within a 30 mile radius of the airport? yes

Extra Example 5

In Extra Example 4, suppose that the owner drives due east of the property to another property. For how many miles will she be within 30 miles of the airport? 28 mi

Key Question to Ask for Example 5

- Why does the expression $|9 - (-9.2)|$ represent how far you will be in the tower's range? The distance between (4, 9) and (4, −9.2) is $\sqrt{(4-4)^2 + (9-(-9.2))^2}$ or $|9 - (-9.2)| = 18.2$.

Closing the Lesson

Have students summarize the major points of the lesson and answer the Essential Question: What information do you need to write the equation of a circle with center (0, 0)?

- The standard form of the equation of a circle with center (0, 0) and radius r is $x^2 + y^2 = r^2$.
- The inequality $x^2 + y^2 < r^2$ represents the region inside the circle $x^2 + y^2 = r^2$.
- The inequality $x^2 + y^2 > r^2$ represents the region outside the circle $x^2 + y^2 = r^2$.

You need to know the radius.

CIRCLES AND INEQUALITIES The regions inside and outside the circle $x^2 + y^2 = r^2$ can be described by inequalities, with $x^2 + y^2 < r^2$ representing the region inside the circle and $x^2 + y^2 > r^2$ representing the region outside the circle.

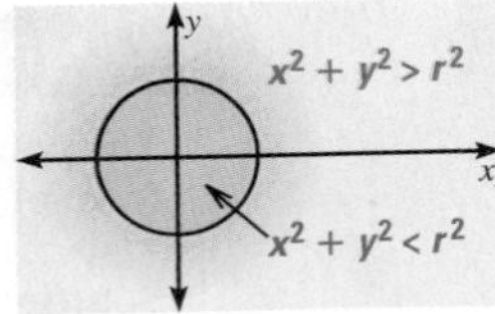

EXAMPLE 4 Write a circular model

CELL PHONES A cellular phone tower services a 10 mile radius. You get a flat tire 4 miles east and 9 miles north of the tower. Are you in the tower's range?

Solution

STEP 1 **Write** an inequality for the region covered by the tower. From the diagram, this region is all points that satisfy the following inequality:

$$x^2 + y^2 < 10^2$$

STEP 2 **Substitute** the coordinates (4, 9) into the inequality from Step 1.

$x^2 + y^2 < 10^2$	**Inequality from Step 1**
$4^2 + 9^2 \overset{?}{<} 10^2$	**Substitute for x and y.**
$97 < 100$ ✓	**The inequality is true.**

▶ So, you are in the tower's range.

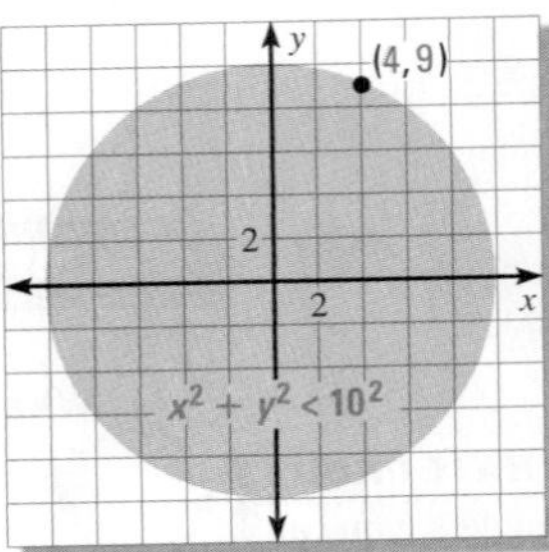

In the diagram above, the origin represents the tower and the positive *y*-axis represents north.

EXAMPLE 5 Apply a circular model

CELL PHONES In Example 4, suppose that you fix your tire and then drive south. For how many more miles will you be in range of the tower?

Solution

When you leave the tower's range, you will be at a point on the circle $x^2 + y^2 = 10^2$ whose x-coordinate is 4 and whose y-coordinate is negative. Find the point $(4, y)$ where $y < 0$ on the circle $x^2 + y^2 = 10^2$.

$x^2 + y^2 = 10^2$	**Equation of the circle**
$4^2 + y^2 = 10^2$	**Substitute 4 for x.**
$y = \pm\sqrt{84}$	**Solve for y.**
$y \approx \pm 9.2$	**Use a calculator.**

y
(4, 9)
2
2
x
(4, y)

▶ Because $y < 0$, $y \approx -9.2$. You will be in the tower's range from (4, 9) to (4, −9.2), a distance of $|9 - (-9.2)| = 18.2$ miles.

GUIDED PRACTICE for Examples 4 and 5

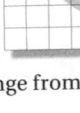

6. **WHAT IF?** In Examples 4 and 5, suppose you drive west after fixing your tire. For how many more miles will you be in range of the tower? about 8.4 mi

Guided Practice, p. 627

1.

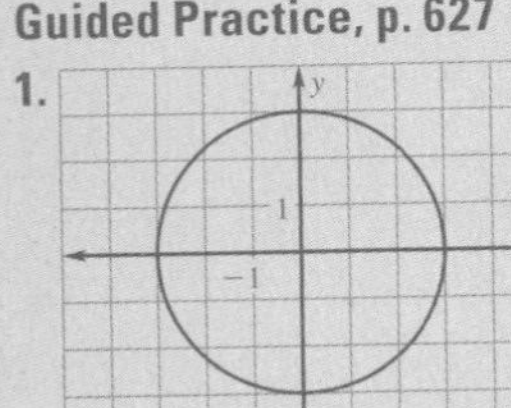

2.

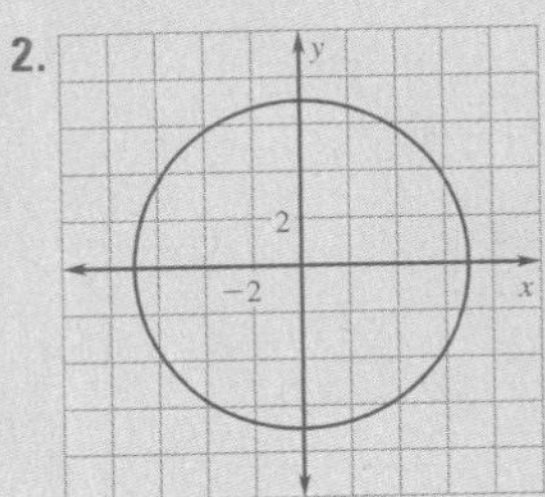

3.

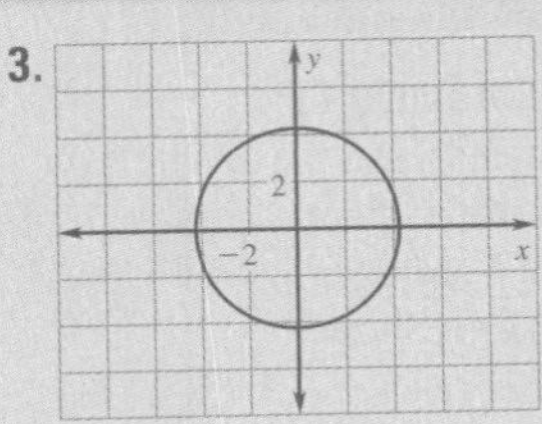

9.3 EXERCISES

HOMEWORK KEY
○ = **WORKED-OUT SOLUTIONS** on p. WS16 for Exs. 17, 39, and 65
★ = **STANDARDIZED TEST PRACTICE** Exs. 2, 21, 43, 59, 64, and 66
◆ = **MULTIPLE REPRESENTATIONS** Ex. 68

SKILL PRACTICE

A

1. **VOCABULARY** The radius of a circle is the distance from any point on the circle to a fixed point called the circle's _?_. center

2. ★ **WRITING** How are the slope of a line tangent to a circle and the slope of the radius at the point of tangency related? They are opposite reciprocals of one another.

XAMPLE 1
p. 626
r Exs. 3–21

MATCHING GRAPHS **Match the equation with its graph.**

3. $x^2 + y^2 = 9$ C
4. $x^2 + y^2 = 36$ E
5. $x^2 + y^2 = 4$ A
6. $x^2 + y^2 = 6$ D
7. $x^2 + y^2 = 16$ F
8. $x^2 + y^2 = 3$ B

A. 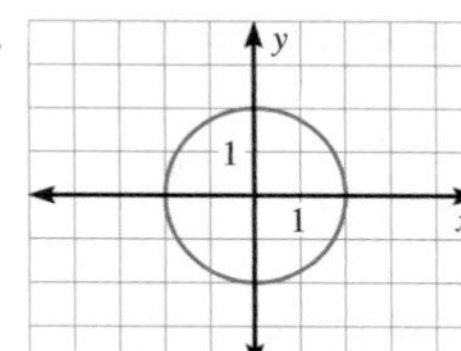

B. 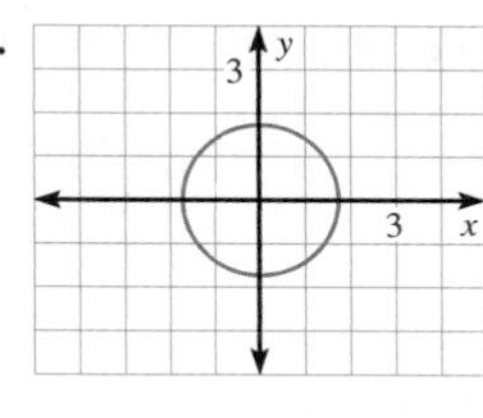

C. 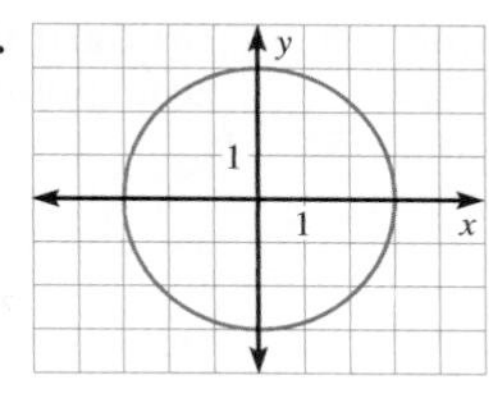

D. 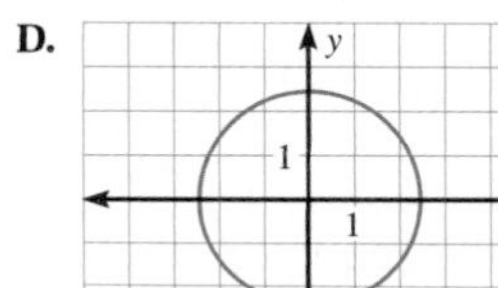

E. 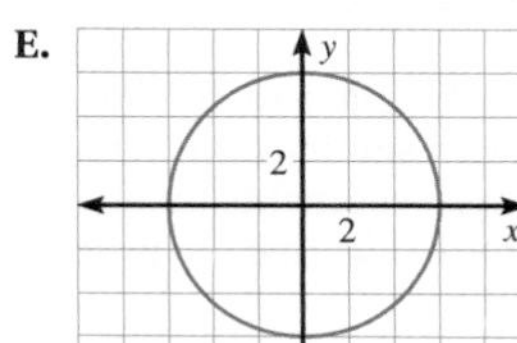

F. 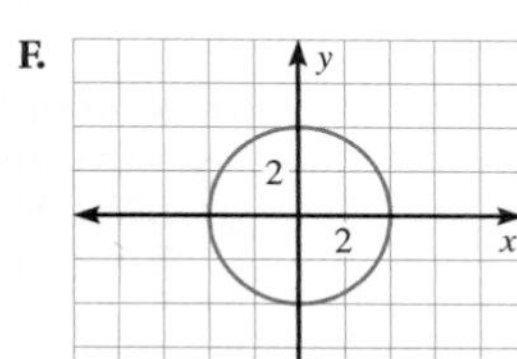

GRAPHING **Graph the equation. Identify the radius of the circle.** 9–20. See margin for art.

9. $x^2 + y^2 = 1$ 1
10. $x^2 + y^2 = 81$ 9
11. $x^2 + y^2 = 25$ 5
12. $x^2 + y^2 = 12$ $2\sqrt{3}$
13. $y^2 = 27 - x^2$ $3\sqrt{3}$
14. $x^2 = -y^2 + 40$ $2\sqrt{10}$
15. $x^2 = 15 - y^2$ $\sqrt{15}$
16. $y^2 = -x^2 + 9$ 3
17. $15x^2 + 15y^2 = 60$ 2
18. $7x^2 + 7y^2 = 112$ 4
19. $4x^2 + 4y^2 = 128$ $4\sqrt{2}$
20. $8x^2 + 8y^2 = 192$ $2\sqrt{6}$

21. ★ **MULTIPLE CHOICE** What is the radius of the circle $3x^2 + 3y^2 = 54$? A

(A) $3\sqrt{2}$ (B) $3\sqrt{6}$ (C) 18 (D) 54

XAMPLE 2
n p. 627
r Exs. 22–43

WRITING EQUATIONS **Write the standard form of the equation of the circle with the given radius and whose center is the origin.**

22. 12 $x^2 + y^2 = 144$
23. 8 $x^2 + y^2 = 64$
24. 2 $x^2 + y^2 = 4$
25. 16 $x^2 + y^2 = 256$
26. $\sqrt{2}$ $x^2 + y^2 = 2$
27. $\sqrt{15}$ $x^2 + y^2 = 15$
28. $5\sqrt{2}$ $x^2 + y^2 = 50$
29. $4\sqrt{6}$ $x^2 + y^2 = 96$

30. **ERROR ANALYSIS** *Describe* and correct the error in writing an equation of the circle with the given center and radius.
The radius should be squared; $x^2 + y^2 = 144$.

Center: (0, 0); Radius: 12
Equation: $x^2 + y^2 = 12$

4 PRACTICE AND APPLY

Assignment Guide

Answer Transparencies available for all exercises

Basic:
Day 1: pp. 629–632
Exs. 1–8, 9–21 odd, 22–30 even, 31–43 odd, 44–46, 53, 62–66, 70

Average:
Day 1: pp. 629–632
Exs. 1, 2, 10–20 even, 23–29 odd, 30–38 even, 43–59 odd, 63–68

Advanced:
Day 1: pp. 629–632
Exs. 1, 2, 18–21, 26–29, 39–43, 48–69*, 72

Block:
pp. 629–632
Exs. 1, 2, 10–20 even, 23–29 odd, 30–38 even, 43–59 odd, 63–68 (with 9.4)

Differentiated Instruction

See *Algebra 2 Best Practices Toolkit* for suggestions on addressing the needs of a diverse classroom.

Homework Check

For a quick check of student understanding of key concepts, go over the following exercises:

Basic: 11, 24, 53, 62, 65
Average: 14, 34, 55, 63, 66
Advanced: 18, 40, 56, 64, 67

Extra Practice

- Student Edition, p. 1018
- Chapter 9 Resource Book: Practice levels A, B, C, pp. 27–29

Practice Worksheet

An easily-readable reduced practice page (with answers) for this lesson can be found on p. 612C.

9–20. See Additional Answers beginning on p. AA1.

Mathematical Reasoning

Exercises 3–20 These exercises ask students to translate between a circle's geometric definition and its equation. They prepare students to differentiate between the equations and graphs of circles and parabolas in Exercises 44–52.

Avoiding Common Errors

Exercises 22–29, 31–42 Watch for students who neglect to square the length of the radius when they write the equation. Point out to students that this error is highlighted in Exercise 30.

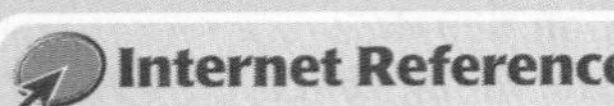

Internet Reference

Exercise 63 For more information about the Mexican free-tailed bats, visit www.nps.gov/cave/bat-bft.html

WRITING EQUATIONS **Write the standard form of the equation of the circle that passes through the given point and whose center is the origin.**

31. $(-6, 0)$ $x^2 + y^2 = 36$
32. $(0, 5)$ $x^2 + y^2 = 25$
33. $(-4, 3)$ $x^2 + y^2 = 25$
34. $(2, -4)$ $x^2 + y^2 = 2$
35. $(-6, 8)$ $x^2 + y^2 = 100$
36. $(-9, 2)$ $x^2 + y^2 = 85$
37. $(4, -10)$ $x^2 + y^2 = 116$
38. $(-8, -5)$ $x^2 + y^2 = 8$
39. $(-8, 14)$ $x^2 + y^2 = 260$
40. $(5, -12)$ $x^2 + y^2 = 169$
41. $(-11, -11)$ $x^2 + y^2 = 242$
42. $(9, 40)$ $x^2 + y^2 = 1681$
43. ★ **MULTIPLE CHOICE** What is the equation in standard form of the circle that passes through the point $(4, -6)$ and whose center is the origin? C

    (A) $x^2 + y^2 = 5$ (B) $x^2 + y^2 = 10$ (C) $x^2 + y^2 = 52$ (D) $x^2 + y^2 = 2\sqrt{13}$

B

GRAPHING **In Exercises 44–52, equations of both circles and parabolas are given. Graph the equation.** 44–52. See margin.

44. $y^2 + x^2 = 49$
45. $4x^2 + y = 0$
46. $7x^2 + 7y^2 = 63$
47. $y^2 - 121 = -x^2$
48. $x^2 + 16y = 0$
49. $3x = -y^2$
50. $12x^2 + 12y^2 = 192$
51. $2x^2 + 2y^2 = 16$
52. $6x + 6y^2 = 0$

EXAMPLE 3 on p. 627 for Exs. 53–58

TANGENT LINES **Write an equation of the line tangent to the given circle at the given point.**

53. $x^2 + y^2 = 17$; $(1, 4)$
54. $x^2 + y^2 = 13$; $(2, -3)$
55. $x^2 + y^2 = 34$; $(-5, 3)$
56. $x^2 + y^2 = 40$; $(-6, -2)$
57. $x^2 + y^2 = 106$; $(-5, 9)$
58. $x^2 + y^2 = 250$; $(15, 5)$

53. $y = -\frac{1}{4}x + \frac{17}{4}$
54. $y = \frac{2}{3}x - \frac{13}{3}$
55. $y = \frac{5}{3}x + \frac{34}{3}$
56. $y = -3x - 20$
57. $y = \frac{5}{9}x + \frac{106}{9}$
58. $y = -3x + 50$

59. ★ **OPEN-ENDED MATH** Write equations in standard form for three circles centered at the origin so that each circle passes between $(-3, 5)$ and $(-6, 2)$. *Sample answer:* $x^2 + y^2 = 35$, $x^2 + y^2 = 36$, $x^2 + y^2 = 38$

C

60. **REASONING** Use the diagram to show that an angle inscribed in a semicircle is a right angle. (*Hint:* Show that the segments meeting at (x, y) have slopes that are negative reciprocals.)

    Sample answer: $m_1 = \frac{\sqrt{r^2 - x^2}}{x + r}$, $m_2 = \frac{\sqrt{r^2 - x^2}}{x - r}$, $m_1 m_2 = -1$

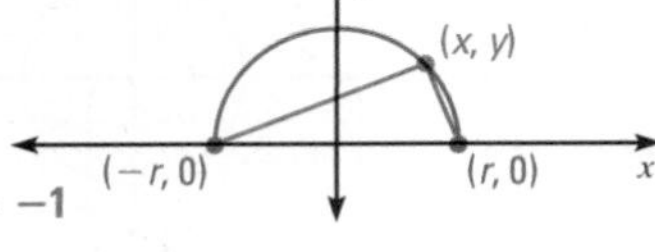

61. **CHALLENGE** Suppose two congruent circles intersect so that each passes through the other's center, as shown. Write an equation that gives the length ℓ of the chord formed by joining the intersection points in terms of the radius r of each circle. $\ell = r\sqrt{3}$

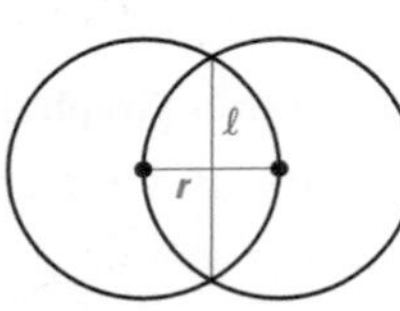

PROBLEM SOLVING

EXAMPLE 4 on p. 628 for Exs. 62–64

A

62. **CELL PHONES** A cellular phone tower services a 15 mile radius. On a hiking trip, you are 9 miles east and 11 miles north of the cell tower. Are you in the region served by the tower? yes

    @HomeTutor for problem solving help at classzone.com

63. **BATS** During the warmer months, more than 1 million Mexican free-tailed bats live under the Congress Avenue Bridge in Austin, Texas. The bats have an estimated feeding range of 50 miles. Is a location 40 miles north and 25 miles west of the bridge located within this range? yes

    @HomeTutor for problem solving help at classzone.com

○ = WORKED-OUT SOLUTIONS on p. WS1 ★ = STANDARDIZED TEST PRACTICE ◆ = MULTIPLE REPRESENTATIONS

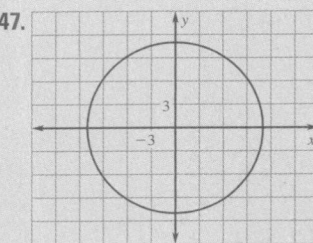

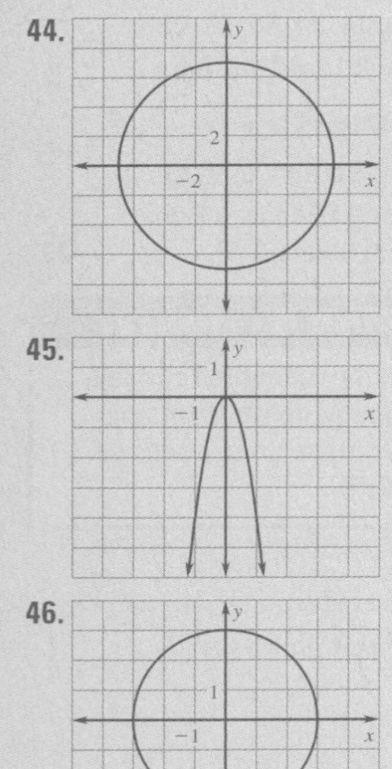

46.

47.

48.

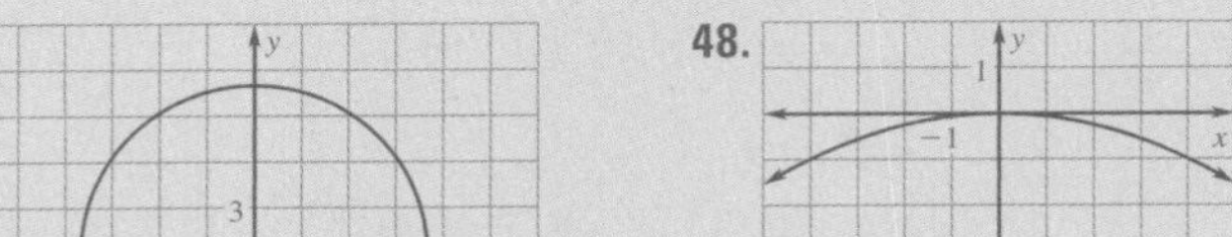

49.

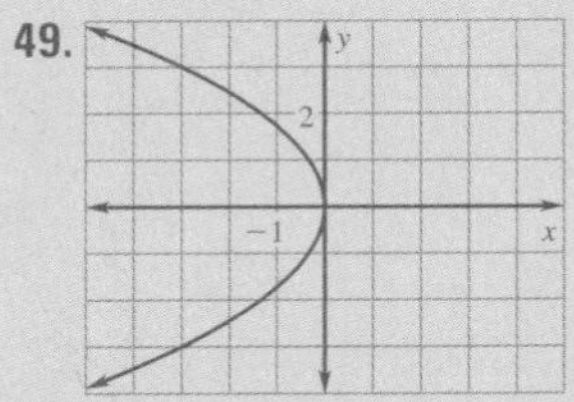

64. ★ **MULTIPLE CHOICE** An appliance store claims to provide free delivery up to 100 miles from the store. The following points represent the locations of houses, with the origin representing the store. (All coordinates are in miles.) Which house is located outside the free delivery area? **D**

Ⓐ (95, 30) Ⓑ (90, 35) Ⓒ (80, 55) Ⓓ (75, 70)

XAMPLE 5
n p. 628
r Exs. 65–67

65. **MULTI-STEP PROBLEM** "Class B" airspace sometimes consists of a stack of cylindrical layers as shown. Seen from above, the airspace forms circles whose origin is the control tower. A plane in straight and level flight flies through the top layer along the line $y = -4$, as shown.

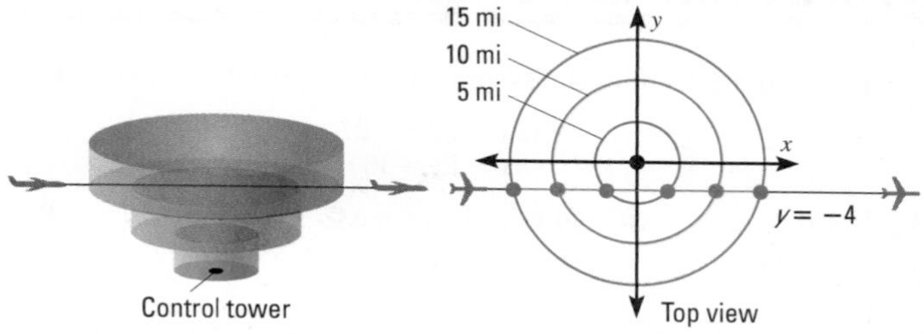

a. For how many miles will the plane be in the top-most layer of Class B airspace? **about 28.9 mi**

b. For how many miles will the plane be above the middle layer of Class B airspace? **about 18.3 mi**

c. For how many miles will the plane be above the lowest layer of Class B airspace? **6 mi**

B

Yes. *Sample* *wer:* The ght of the nel at the ter of the lkway is ut 79.7 inches the worker nly 74 inches .

66. ★ **SHORT RESPONSE** A circular utility tunnel 8 feet in diameter has a 6-foot-wide walkway across its bottom. Could a worker who is 6 feet 2 inches tall walk down the center of the walkway without ducking? *Explain.* (*Hint:* Write an equation of the tunnel's cross section. Find the x-coordinate of an endpoint of the walkway and substitute to find the y-coordinate.)

67. **GROUNDSKEEPING** A row of sprinklers is to be installed parallel to and 4.5 feet away from the back edge of a flower bed. Each sprinkler waters a region with a 6 foot radius. How far apart should the sprinklers be placed to water the entire flower bed with the least possible overlap in coverage, as shown? **about 7.94 ft**

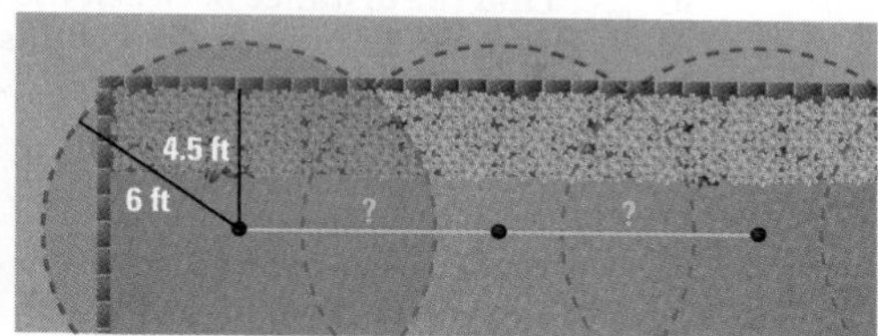

. $x^2 + y^2 \le 0$,
$+ y^2 \le 225$,
$+ y^2 \le 625$,
$+ y^2 \le 1225$

. It will be at st 5.4; 400 < so it will be east a rating.

68. ◆ **MULTIPLE REPRESENTATIONS** The Modified Mercalli Intensity Scale rates an earthquake's "shaking strength." In general, the rating decreases as distance from the earthquake's epicenter increases. Suppose an earthquake has a Mercalli rating of 6.0 at its epicenter, a 5.7 rating 15 miles away from the epicenter, a 5.4 rating 25 miles away, and a 5.1 rating 35 miles away.

a. **Drawing Graphs** Represent the situation described above using circles in a coordinate plane. **See margin.**

b. **Writing Inequalities** For each circle from part (a), write an inequality describing the coordinates of locations with a Mercalli rating *at least* as great as the Mercalli rating represented by the circle.

c. **Making a Prediction** What can you predict about the Mercalli rating 12 miles west and 16 miles south of the epicenter? *Explain.*

Reading Strategy

Exercise 59 Before students begin the exercise, make sure they understand what the circles will look like if they pass *between* the two points. Ask them to sketch possible solutions.

Teaching Strategy

Exercise 61 Before students write an equation, suggest that they draw the segments between the centers of the circles and the endpoints of ℓ.

68a.

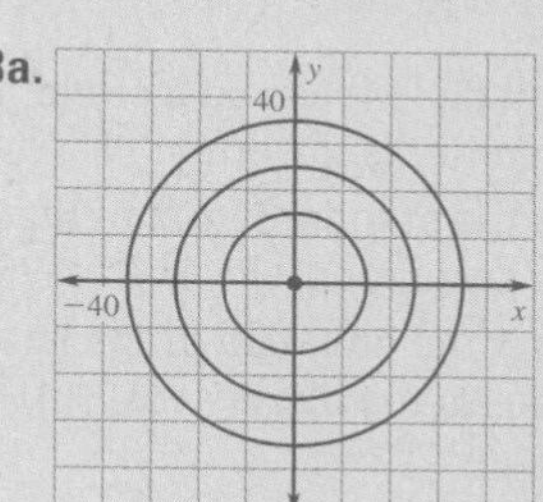

50.

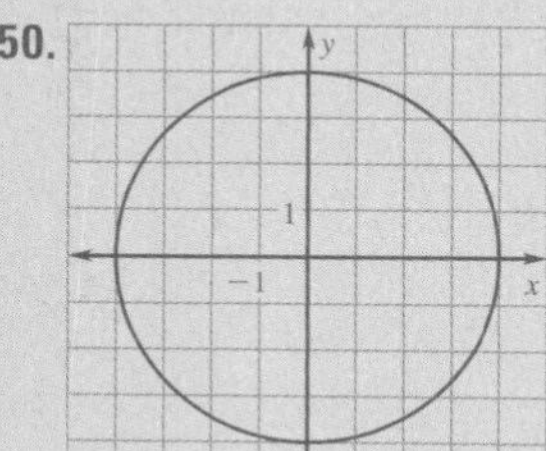

51.

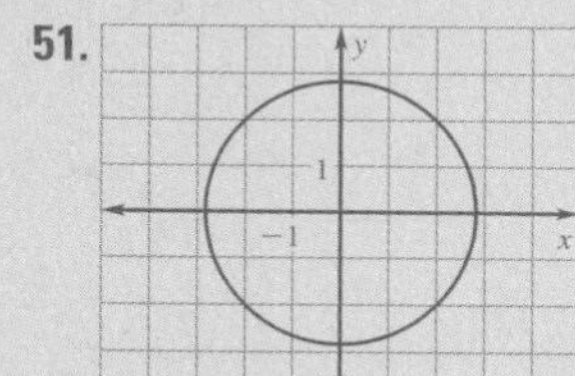

52.

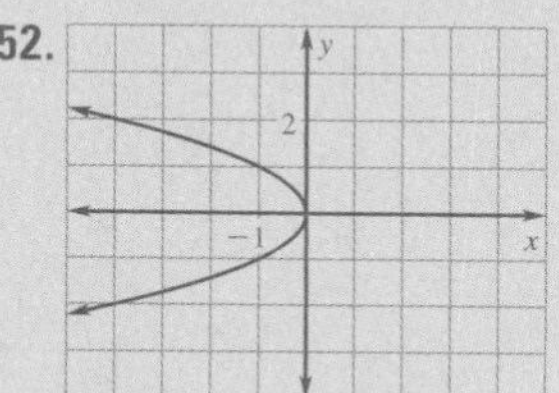

5 ASSESS AND RETEACH

Daily Homework Quiz

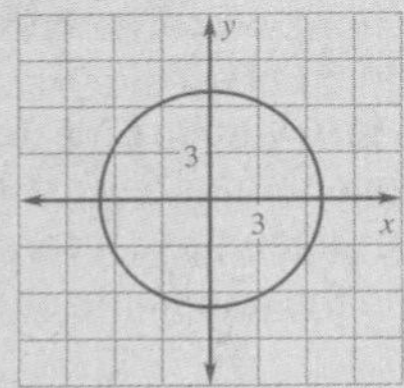
Transparency Available

1. Graph $y^2 - 49 = -x^2$.

The point (3, −4) lies on a circle whose center is the origin.

2. Write the standard form of the circle's equation. $x^2 + y^2 = 25$
3. What is the equation of the line tangent to the circle at (3, −4)? $y = \frac{3}{4}x - \frac{25}{4}$

A signal from a radio station has a circular range of 50 miles. A DJ drives 25 miles north and 42 miles east of the station.

4. Is he still in the station's range? yes
5. If he begins driving west, for how many miles will he be in the station's range? about 85.3 mi

Online Quiz

Available at **classzone.com**

Diagnosis/Remediation

- Practice A, B, C in Chapter 9 Resource Book, pp. 27–29
- Study Guide in Chapter 9 Resource Book, pp. 30–31
- Practice Workbook, pp. 138–139
- @HomeTutor

Challenge

Additional challenge is available in the Chapter 9 Resource Book, p. 34.

Quiz

An easily-readable reduced copy of the quiz (with answers) on Lessons 9.1–9.3 from the Assessment Book can be found on p. 612E.

Quiz 13–18. See Additional Answers beginning on p. AA1.

C **69. CHALLENGE** Two radio transmitters, one with a 40 mile range and one with a 60 mile range, stand 80 miles apart. You are driving 60 miles per hour on a highway parallel to the line segment connecting the two towers. How long will you be within range of *both* transmitters simultaneously? **about 18 min**

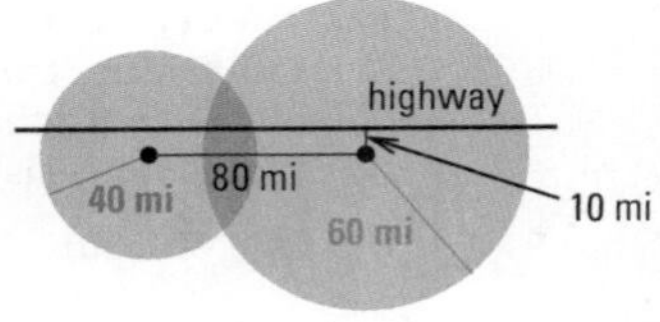

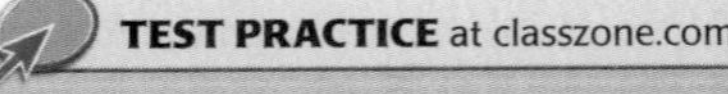

KENTUCKY MIXED REVIEW

70. How many solutions does the system of equations below have? **D**

$$-12x + 3y = -27$$
$$8x - 2y = 18$$

(A) None (B) One (C) Two (D) Infinitely many

71. What is the approximate perimeter of quadrilateral *PQRS*? **C**

(A) 11.7 units
(B) 16.4 units
(C) 20.8 units
(D) 21.5 units

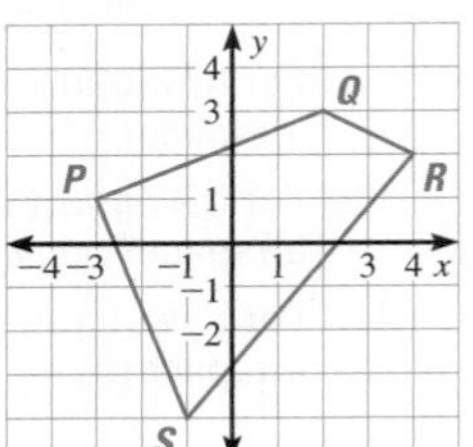

QUIZ for Lessons 9.1–9.3

Find the distance between the two points. Then find the midpoint of the line segment joining the two points. *(p. 614)*

1. (4, −3), (8, −7) $4\sqrt{2}$; (6, −5)
2. (−2, 5), (4, 9) $2\sqrt{13}$; (1, 7)
3. (−5, 1), (−4, 8) $5\sqrt{2}$; (−4.5, 4
4. (1, 2), (7, 1) $\sqrt{37}$; (4, 1.5)
5. (−6, −5), (−1, 8) $\sqrt{194}$; (−3.5, 1.5)
6. (3, −2), (6, 5) $\sqrt{58}$; (4.5, 1.5)

Write the standard form of the equation of the parabola with the given focus and vertex at (0, 0). *(p. 620)*

7. (0, 3) $x^2 = 12y$
8. (−2, 0) $y^2 = -8x$
9. (6, 0) $y^2 = 24x$
10. (0, −4) $x^2 = -16y$
11. (0, 5) $x^2 = 20y$
12. (−1, 0) $y^2 = -4x$

Graph the equation. Identify the radius of the circle. *(p. 626)* 13–18. See margin for art.

13. $x^2 + y^2 = 4$ 2
14. $x^2 + y^2 = 64$ 8
15. $x^2 + y^2 = 20$ $2\sqrt{5}$
16. $x^2 + y^2 = 75$ $5\sqrt{3}$
17. $3x^2 + 3y^2 = 48$ 4
18. $6x^2 + 6y^2 = 108$ $3\sqrt{2}$

19. **ASTRONOMY** If the plane in which Jupiter orbits the sun is a coordinate plane with its origin at the sun and coordinates in millions of miles, then a circle through the point (350, 370) just encloses Jupiter's orbit. Imagine replacing the sun with the star KY Cygni, whose radius is about 650 million miles. Would KY Cygni contain Jupiter's orbit? *Explain.* *(p. 626)* Yes; the radius of Jupiter's orbit is about 509 million miles. Since 509 < 650, KY Cygni would contain Jupiter's orbit.

EXTRA PRACTICE for Lesson 9.3, p. 1018

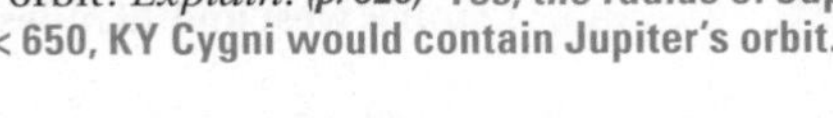

@HomeTutor
classzone.com
Keystrokes

9.3 Graph Equations of Circles

QUESTION How can you use a graphing calculator to graph a circle?

To graph a circle on most graphing calculators, you must first rewrite the circle's equation as two functions that taken together represent the circle.

EXAMPLE Graph a circle

Use a graphing calculator to graph $x^2 + y^2 = 25$.

STEP 1* Solve for *y

Begin by solving the equation for y.

$$x^2 + y^2 = 25$$
$$y^2 = 25 - x^2$$
$$y = \pm\sqrt{25 - x^2}$$

Together, the functions $y = \sqrt{25 - x^2}$ and $y = -\sqrt{25 - x^2}$ represent the circle.

***STEP 2* Enter functions**

Enter the two functions as y_1 and y_2. You can enter y_2 as $-y_1$.

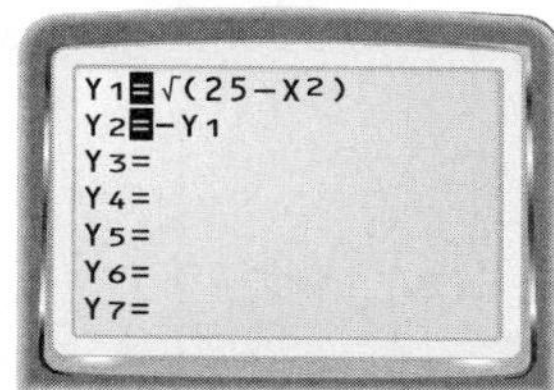

***STEP 3* Graph functions**

The graphs are shown in the standard window ($-10 \le x \le 10$ and $-10 \le y \le 10$). Because the calculator screen is not square, a horizontal distance of 1 unit is longer than a vertical distance of 1 unit, and the circle is stretched into an oval.

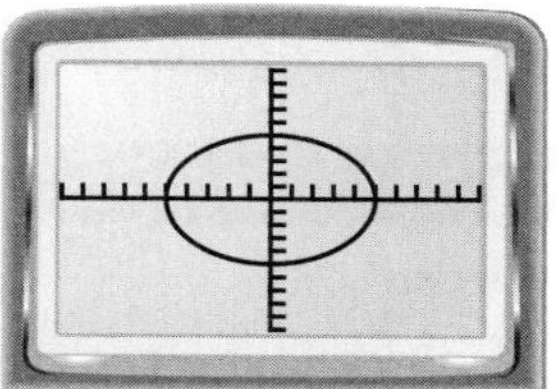

***STEP 4* Adjust graph**

To show the circle in true proportion, set a window so that the ratio of (Xmax − Xmin) to (Ymax − Ymin) is 3 : 2. Such a "square window" can also be obtained by pressing ZOOM and selecting ZSquare.

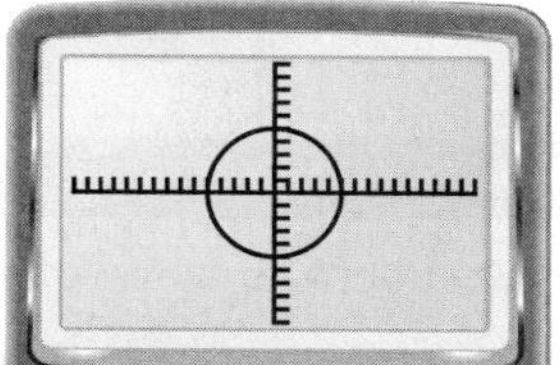

PRACTICE

Use a graphing calculator to graph the equation. Give the viewing window that you used and verify that it is a "square window." **1–6. See margin.**

1. $x^2 + y^2 = 144$ **2.** $x^2 + y^2 = 80$ **3.** $x^2 + y^2 = 576$

4. $0.5x^2 + 0.5y^2 = 12$ **5.** $7x^2 + 7y^2 = 105$ **6.** $16x^2 + 16y^2 = 9$

1–6. Check students' graphs. Sample viewing windows are given.

1. $-22.5 \le x \le 22.5$, $-15 \le y \le 15$; $\frac{45}{30} = \frac{3}{2}$
2. $-15.16 \le x \le 15.16$, $-10 \le y \le 10$; $\frac{30.32}{20} \approx \frac{3}{2}$
3. $-37.5 \le x \le 37.5$, $-25 \le y \le 25$; $\frac{75}{50} = \frac{3}{2}$
4. $-15 \le x \le 15$, $-10 \le y \le 10$; $\frac{30}{20} = \frac{3}{2}$
5. $-6 \le x \le 6$, $-4 \le y \le 4$; $\frac{12}{8} = \frac{3}{2}$
6. $-3 \le x \le 3$, $-2 \le y \le 2$; $\frac{6}{4} = \frac{3}{2}$

1 PLAN AND PREPARE

Learn the Method

- Students will use a graphing calculator to graph a circle.
- Students can go back to Lesson 9.3 and use their graphing calculators to graph many of the equations.

Keystroke Help

Keystrokes for several models of calculators are available in blackline format in the *Chapter 9 Resource Book*.

2 TEACH

Tips for Success

Make sure students use the *negation* key, not the subtraction key, when they enter $-y_1$ as the second function.

Extra Example

Use a graphing calculator to graph $x^2 + y^2 = 64$.

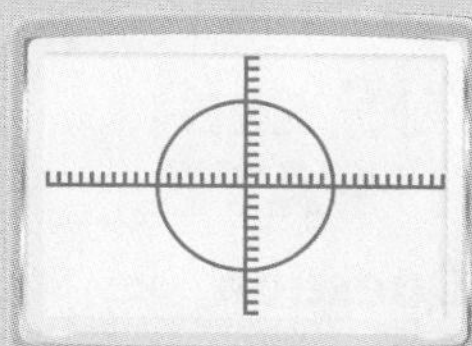

Key Question to Ask for Example

- On the screen of your graphing calculator, why might you see gaps between the top half and bottom half of the circle? **The screen shows the graphs of two different functions, so the calculator may not connect the points as it would for a single function.**

3 ASSESS AND RETEACH

Explain how to graph $x^2 + y^2 = 54$ on your graphing calculator. How should you set your viewing window so the graph appears as a circle? **Solve the equation for y and enter the two functions as Y1 and Y2. Make sure $\frac{\text{XMAX} - \text{XMIN}}{\text{YMAX} - \text{YMIN}} = \frac{3}{2}$.**

1 PLAN AND PREPARE

Warm-Up Exercises

Transparency Available

Solve $a^2 + b^2 = c^2$ for the missing value.

1. $a = 9$, $b = 3$ $c = 3\sqrt{10}$

2. $a = 2$, $c = 12$ $b = 2\sqrt{35}$

3. $b = 6$, $c = 10$ $a = 8$

4. If $9x^2 + 4y^2 = 36$ is rewritten in the form $\frac{x^2}{a^2} + \frac{y^2}{b^2} = 1$, what are the values of a and b? $a = \pm 2$, $b = \pm 3$

Notetaking Guide

Transparency Available

Promotes interactive learning and notetaking skills, pp. 241–243.

Pacing

Basic: 1 day

Average: 1 day

Advanced: 1 day

Block: 0.5 block with 9.3

- See *Teaching Guide/Lesson Plan.*

2 FOCUS AND MOTIVATE

Essential Question

Big Idea 1, p. 613

What points do you need to write an equation of an ellipse? **Tell students they will learn how to answer this question by exploring how the vertices, co-vertices, and foci of an ellipse are related to an equation for the ellipse.**

9.4 Graph and Write Equations of Ellipses

MA-HS-3.1.5

Before	You graphed and wrote equations of parabolas and circles.
Now	You will graph and write equations of ellipses.
Why?	So you can model an elliptical region, as in Example 3.

Key Vocabulary
- ellipse
- foci
- vertices
- major axis
- center
- co-vertices
- minor axis

An **ellipse** is the set of all points P in a plane such that the sum of the distances between P and two fixed points, called the **foci**, is a constant.

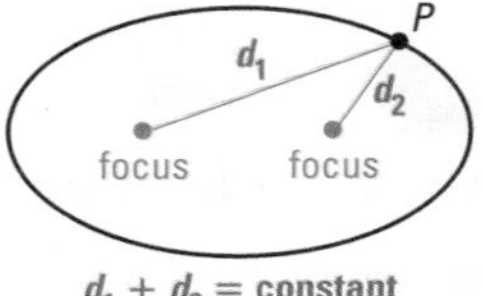

$d_1 + d_2 =$ constant

The line through the foci intersects the ellipse at the two **vertices**. The **major axis** joins the vertices. Its midpoint is the ellipse's **center**. The line perpendicular to the major axis at the center intersects the ellipse at the two **co-vertices**, which are joined by the **minor axis**. In this chapter, ellipses have a horizontal or a vertical major axis.

IDENTIFY AXES

Observe that the major axis of an ellipse contains the foci and is always longer than the minor axis.

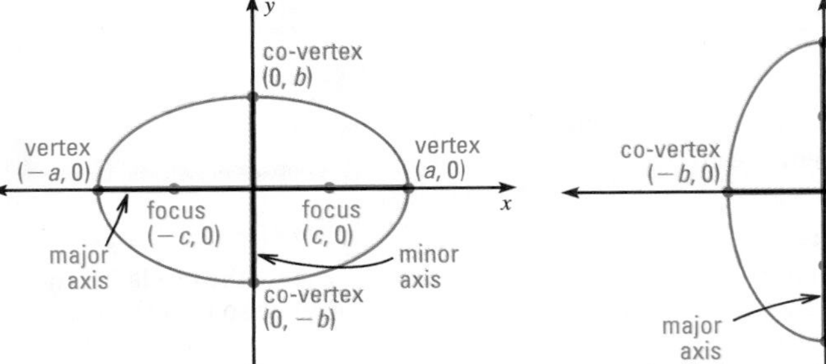

Ellipse with horizontal major axis

$$\frac{x^2}{a^2} + \frac{y^2}{b^2} = 1$$

Ellipse with vertical major axis

$$\frac{x^2}{b^2} + \frac{y^2}{a^2} = 1$$

MA-HS-3.1.5

Students will classify and apply properties of two-dimensional geometric figures (e.g., number of sides, vertices, length of sides, sum of interior and exterior angle measures). DOK 2

KEY CONCEPT *For Your Notebook*

Standard Equation of an Ellipse with Center at the Origin

Equation	Major Axis	Vertices	Co-Vertices
$\frac{x^2}{a^2} + \frac{y^2}{b^2} = 1$	Horizontal	$(\pm a, 0)$	$(0, \pm b)$
$\frac{x^2}{b^2} + \frac{y^2}{a^2} = 1$	Vertical	$(0, \pm a)$	$(\pm b, 0)$

The major and minor axes are of lengths $2a$ and $2b$, respectively, where $a > b > 0$. The foci of the ellipse lie on the major axis at a distance of c units from the center, where $c^2 = a^2 - b^2$.

Resource Planning Guide

Chapter Resource Book
- Teaching Guide/Lesson Plan (pp. 35–36)
- Activity Master (p. 37)
- Practice levels A, B, C (pp. 38–40)
- Study Guide (pp. 41–42)
- Catch-up for Absent Students (p. 43)
- Problem Solving Workshop (p. 44)
- Challenge (p. 46)

Workbooks
- Notetaking Guide (pp. 241–243)
- Practice Workbook (pp. 140–141)

Teaching Options
- **Power Presentations CD-ROM** provides dynamic electronic teaching resources for the classroom.
- **Activity Generator CD-ROM** provides editable activities for all ability levels.

Interactive Technology
- Easy Planner
- Power Presentations CD-ROM
- Activity Generator CD-ROM
- Animated Algebra
- Test Generator CD-ROM
- Online Quiz
- eWorkbook
- eEdition
- @HomeTutor

Resources for English Learners
- Quick Reference for English Learners
- Spanish Study Guide
- Multi-Language Visual Glossary
- Student Resources in Spanish

See also the *Algebra 2 Toolkit* for more strategies for meeting individual needs.

EXAMPLE 1 Graph an equation of an ellipse

Graph the equation $4x^2 + 25y^2 = 100$. Identify the vertices, co-vertices, and foci of the ellipse.

Solution

STEP 1 **Rewrite** the equation in standard form.

$4x^2 + 25y^2 = 100$ **Write original equation.**

$\frac{4x^2}{100} + \frac{25y^2}{100} = \frac{100}{100}$ **Divide each side by 100.**

$\frac{x^2}{25} + \frac{y^2}{4} = 1$ **Simplify.**

STEP 2 **Identify** the vertices, co-vertices, and foci. Note that $a^2 = 25$ and $b^2 = 4$, so $a = 5$ and $b = 2$. The denominator of the x^2-term is greater than that of the y^2-term, so the major axis is horizontal.

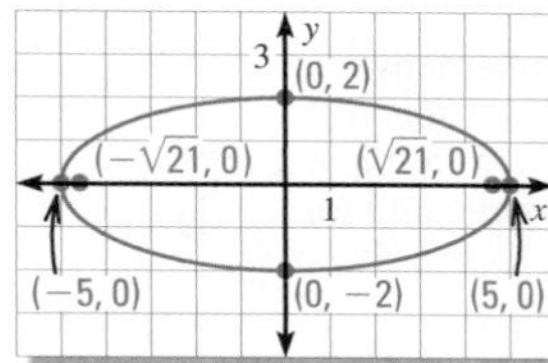

The vertices of the ellipse are at $(\pm a, 0) = (\pm 5, 0)$. The co-vertices are at $(0, \pm b) = (0, \pm 2)$. Find the foci.

$c^2 = a^2 - b^2 = 5^2 - 2^2 = 21$, so $c = \sqrt{21}$

The foci are at $(\pm\sqrt{21}, 0)$, or about $(\pm 4.6, 0)$.

STEP 3 **Draw** the ellipse that passes through each vertex and co-vertex.

Animated Algebra at classzone.com

ANOTHER WAY
...u can graph the ...pse using a graphing ...culator by solving for ...o obtain

$\pm 2\sqrt{1 - \frac{x^2}{25}}$

...d then entering ...s equation as two ...parate functions.

GUIDED PRACTICE for Example 1

Graph the equation. Identify the vertices, co-vertices, and foci of the ellipse.

1–3. See margin for art.

1. $\frac{x^2}{16} + \frac{y^2}{9} = 1$
   $(\pm 4, 0), (0, \pm 3), (\pm\sqrt{7}, 0)$

2. $\frac{x^2}{36} + \frac{y^2}{49} = 1$
   $(0, \pm 7), (\pm 6, 0), (0, \pm\sqrt{13})$

3. $25x^2 + 9y^2 = 225$
   $(0, \pm 5), (\pm 3, 0), (0, \pm 4)$

EXAMPLE 2 Write an equation given a vertex and a co-vertex

Write an equation of the ellipse that has a vertex at (0, 4), a co-vertex at (−3, 0), and center at (0, 0).

Solution

Sketch the ellipse as a check for your final equation. By symmetry, the ellipse must also have a vertex at (0, −4) and a co-vertex at (3, 0).

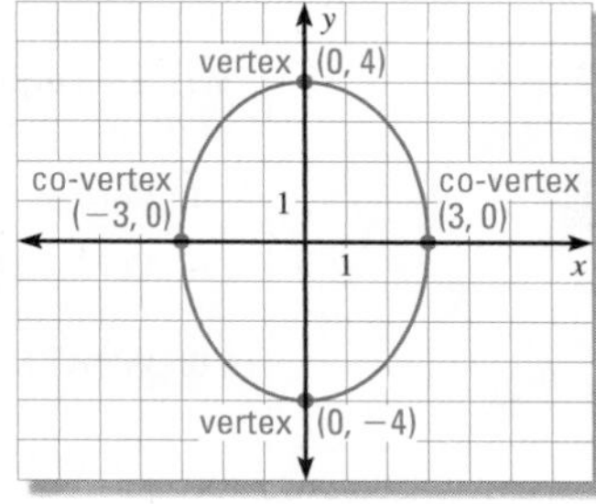

Because the vertex is on the y-axis and the co-vertex is on the x-axis, the major axis is vertical with $a = 4$, and the minor axis is horizontal with $b = 3$.

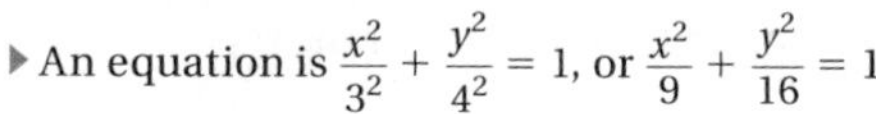

▶ An equation is $\frac{x^2}{3^2} + \frac{y^2}{4^2} = 1$, or $\frac{x^2}{9} + \frac{y^2}{16} = 1$.

Motivating the Lesson

To help students visualize an ellipse, fill a glass about halfway with water. Have students look directly down into the glass and then tilt it. The resulting surface is an ellipse, and its shape will vary with increased or decreased tilt.

3 TEACH

Extra Example 1

Graph the equation $25x^2 + 4y^2 = 100$. Identify the vertices, co-vertices, and foci of the ellipse.

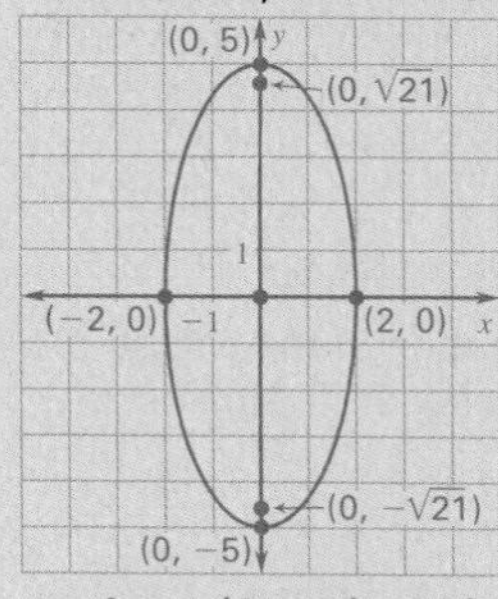

vertices: (0, −5) and (0, 5); co-vertices: (2, 0) and (−2, 0); foci: $(0, \sqrt{21})$ and $(0, -\sqrt{21})$

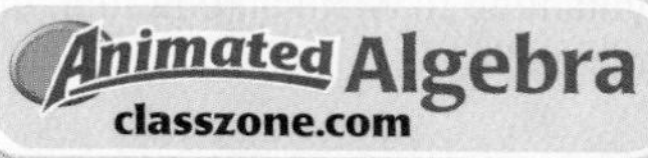

An **Animated Algebra** activity is available on-line for **Example 1**. This activity is also available on the **Power Presentations CD-ROM**.

Extra Example 2

Write an equation of the ellipse that has a vertex at (0, −7), a co-vertex at (4, 0), and center at (0, 0).

$\frac{x^2}{16} + \frac{y^2}{49} = 1$

1–3. See Additional Answers beginning on p. AA1.

Differentiated Instruction

Kinesthetic Learners Show students that they can draw the ellipse in **Example 1** using the definition. On a large coordinate grid, attach tacks at the foci. Then measure a piece of string that is 10 units long and attach the ends to the tacks. Place a pencil against the string, pull tight, and trace the shape of an ellipse. Show that the length of the string is $10 = 2a = d_1 + d_2$.

See also the *Algebra 2 Toolkit* for more strategies.

Extra Example 3

Marketing research shows that a hand lotion bottle with an elliptical base is easier to hold than a similar-sized bottle with a circular base. Write an equation of the ellipse. Find the area of the elliptical base. $\frac{x^2}{16} + \frac{y^2}{9} = 1$; $A \approx 37.7 \text{ cm}^2$

Extra Example 4

Write an equation of the ellipse that has a vertex at (0, 10) and a focus at (0, 8). $\frac{x^2}{36} + \frac{y^2}{100} = 1$

Closing the Lesson

Have students summarize the major points of the lesson and answer the Essential Question: What points do you need to write an equation of an ellipse?

- **In an ellipse, the sum of the distances between any point on the ellipse and two points called the foci is a constant.**
- **The equation $\frac{x^2}{a^2} + \frac{y^2}{b^2} = 1$ defines an ellipse with a horizontal major axis, vertices $(\pm a, 0)$, and co-vertices $(0, \pm b)$. The equation $\frac{x^2}{b^2} + \frac{y^2}{a^2} = 1$ defines an ellipse with a vertical major axis, vertices $(0, \pm a)$, and co-vertices $(\pm b, 0)$.**
- **The foci of an ellipse lie on the major axis at at distance of c units from the center, where $c^2 = a^2 - b^2$.**

For an ellipse with center at the origin, if you are given a vertex and a co-vertex, use these points to find values of a and b. If you are given a focus and either a vertex or a co-vertex, use the equation $c^2 = a^2 - b^2$ to solve for a or b. Then use the values of a and b to write the standard equation of the ellipse.

EXAMPLE 3 Solve a multi-step problem

LIGHTNING When lightning strikes, an elliptical region where the strike most likely hit can often be identified. Suppose it is determined that there is a 50% chance that a lightning strike hit within the elliptical region shown in the diagram.

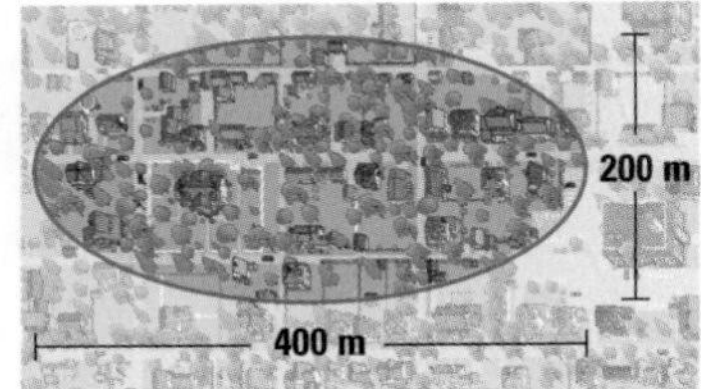

- Write an equation of the ellipse.
- The area A of an ellipse is $A = \pi ab$. Find the area of the elliptical region.

ANOTHER WAY
For an alternative method for solving the problem in Example 3, turn to page 640 for the **Problem Solving Workshop**.

Solution

STEP 1 The major axis is horizontal, with $a = \frac{400}{2} = 200$ and $b = \frac{200}{2} = 100$.

An equation is $\frac{x^2}{200^2} + \frac{y^2}{100^2} = 1$, or $\frac{x^2}{40{,}000} + \frac{y^2}{10{,}000} = 1$.

STEP 2 The area is $A = \pi(200)(100) \approx 62{,}800$ square meters.

EXAMPLE 4 Write an equation given a vertex and a focus

Write an equation of the ellipse that has a vertex at (−8, 0), a focus at (4, 0), and center at (0, 0).

Solution

Make a sketch of the ellipse. Because the given vertex and focus lie on the x-axis, the major axis is horizontal, with $a = 8$ and $c = 4$. To find b, use the equation $c^2 = a^2 - b^2$.

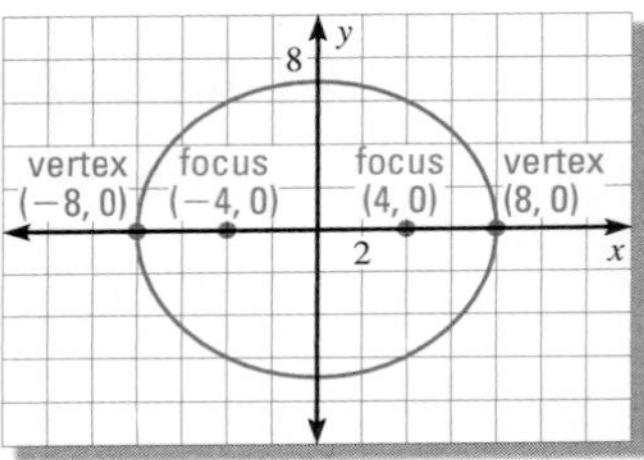

$4^2 = 8^2 - b^2$

$b^2 = 8^2 - 4^2 = 48$

$b = \sqrt{48}$, or $4\sqrt{3}$

▶ An equation is $\frac{x^2}{8^2} + \frac{y^2}{(4\sqrt{3})^2} = 1$, or $\frac{x^2}{64} + \frac{y^2}{48} = 1$.

✓ **GUIDED PRACTICE** for Examples 2, 3, and 4

Write an equation of the ellipse with the given characteristics and center at (0, 0).

4. Vertex: (7, 0); co-vertex: (0, 2) $\frac{x^2}{49} + \frac{y^2}{4} = 1$
5. Vertex: (0, 6); co-vertex: (−5, 0) $\frac{x^2}{25} + \frac{y^2}{36} = 1$
6. Vertex: (0, 8); focus: (0, −3) $\frac{x^2}{55} + \frac{y^2}{64} = 1$
7. Vertex: (−5, 0); focus: (3, 0) $\frac{x^2}{25} + \frac{y^2}{16} = 1$
8. **WHAT IF?** In Example 3, suppose that the elliptical region is 250 meters from east to west and 350 meters from north to south. Write an equation of the elliptical boundary and find the area of the region. $\frac{x^2}{15{,}625} + \frac{y^2}{30{,}625} = 1$, about $68{,}700 \text{ m}^2$

Differentiated Instruction

Below Level Have students investigate the definition of an ellipse. Place two pushpins in a piece of cardboard. Tie the ends of a piece of string to the pins. Using a pencil and keeping the string taut, move the pencil and draw the ellipse.

See also the *Algebra 2 Toolkit* for more strategies.

9.4 EXERCISES

HOMEWORK KEY ○ = WORKED-OUT SOLUTIONS on p. WS16 for Exs. 11, 29, and 49
★ = STANDARDIZED TEST PRACTICE Exs. 2, 35, 45, 46, 51, and 52

SKILL PRACTICE

A

1. **VOCABULARY** Copy and complete: An ellipse is the set of all points P such that the sum of the distances between P and two fixed points, called the _?_, is a constant. foci

2. ★ **WRITING** *Describe* how to find the foci of an ellipse given the coordinates of its vertices and co-vertices. Given vertices $(\pm a, 0)$ or $(0, \pm a)$, co-vertices $(0, \pm b)$ or $(\pm b, 0)$, then the foci are located at $(\pm c, 0)$ or $(0, \pm c)$ where $c^2 = a^2 - b^2$.

AMPLE 1 p. 635 Exs. 3–16

GRAPHING **Graph the equation. Identify the vertices, co-vertices, and foci of the ellipse.** 3–14. See margin.

3. $\frac{x^2}{16} + \frac{y^2}{4} = 1$
4. $\frac{x^2}{4} + y^2 = 25$
5. $\frac{x^2}{9} + \frac{y^2}{49} = 1$
6. $\frac{x^2}{144} + \frac{y^2}{64} = 1$
7. $\frac{x^2}{400} + \frac{y^2}{81} = 1$
8. $\frac{x^2}{36} + \frac{y^2}{225} = 1$
9. $4x^2 + y^2 = 36$
10. $9x^2 + y^2 = 9$
11. $16x^2 + 9y^2 = 144$
12. $25x^2 + 49y^2 = 1225$
13. $16x^2 + 25y^2 = 1600$
14. $72x^2 + 8y^2 = 648$

ERROR ANALYSIS ***Describe*** **and correct the error in graphing the ellipse.** 15, 16. See margin for art.

15.

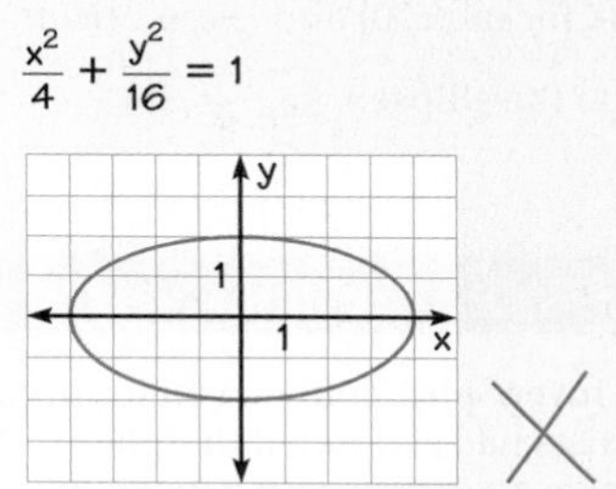

he major should be y-axis, not x-axis.

16.

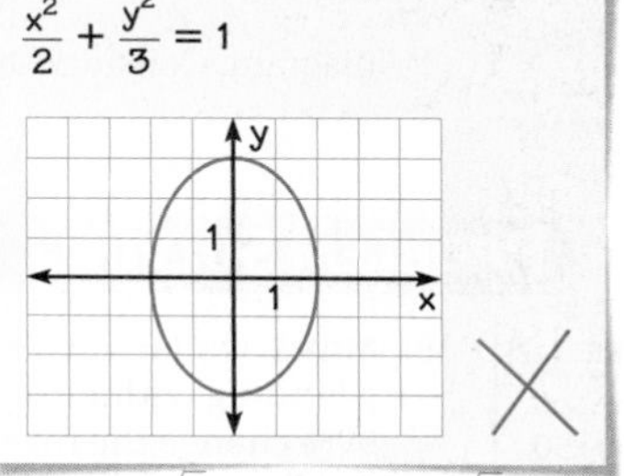

$a = \sqrt{3}$ not 3 and $b = \sqrt{2}$ not 2.

AMPLES nd 4 pp. 635–636 Exs. 17–35

WRITING EQUATIONS **Write an equation of the ellipse with the given characteristics and center at (0, 0).**

17. Vertex: (5, 0) Co-vertex: (0, −3) $\frac{x^2}{25} + \frac{y^2}{9} = 1$
18. Vertex: (0, −10) Co-vertex: (6, 0) $\frac{x^2}{36} + \frac{y^2}{100} = 1$
19. Vertex: (14, 0) Co-vertex: (0, −9) $\frac{x^2}{196} + \frac{y^2}{81} = 1$
20. Vertex: (0, −6) Co-vertex: (4, 0) $\frac{x^2}{16} + \frac{y^2}{36} = 1$
21. Vertex: (0, 12) Co-vertex: (11, 0) $\frac{x^2}{121} + \frac{y^2}{144} = 1$
22. Vertex: (20, 0) Co-vertex: (0, −16) $\frac{x^2}{400} + \frac{y^2}{256} = 1$
23. Vertex: (0, 8) Focus: (0, 6) $\frac{x^2}{28} + \frac{y^2}{64} = 1$
24. Vertex: (4, 0) Focus: $(\sqrt{7}, 0)$ $\frac{x^2}{16} + \frac{y^2}{9} = 1$
25. Vertex: (0, 9) Focus: $(0, -4\sqrt{2})$ $\frac{x^2}{49} + \frac{y^2}{81} = 1$
26. Vertex: (−5, 0) Focus: (3, 0) $\frac{x^2}{25} + \frac{y^2}{16} = 1$
27. Vertex: (0, −4) Focus: $(0, -2\sqrt{3})$ $\frac{x^2}{4} + \frac{y^2}{16} = 1$
28. Vertex: (13, 0) Focus: $(-4\sqrt{3}, 0)$ $\frac{x^2}{169} + \frac{y^2}{121} = 1$
29. Co-vertex: $(0, \sqrt{7})$ Focus: (−3, 0) $\frac{x^2}{16} + \frac{y^2}{7} = 1$
30. Co-vertex: $(-3\sqrt{5}, 0)$ Focus: (0, 6) $\frac{x^2}{45} + \frac{y^2}{81} = 1$
31. Co-vertex: $(0, -5\sqrt{7})$ Focus: (−15, 0) $\frac{x^2}{400} + \frac{y^2}{175} = 1$
32. Co-vertex: (0, 15) Focus: (−8, 0) $\frac{x^2}{289} + \frac{y^2}{225} = 1$
33. Co-vertex: $(2\sqrt{15}, 0)$ Focus: (0, 14) $\frac{x^2}{60} + \frac{y^2}{256} = 1$
34. Co-vertex: (−32, 0) Focus: (0, 24) $\frac{x^2}{1024} + \frac{y^2}{1600} = 1$

4 PRACTICE AND APPLY

Assignment Guide

Answer Transparencies available for all exercises

Basic:
Day 1: pp. 637–639
Exs. 1, 2, 3–13 odd, 15–22, 35–38, 48–51, 54

Average:
Day 1: pp. 637–639
Exs. 1, 2, 4–10 even, 15, 16, 23–28, 35, 39–45, 48–52, 55

Advanced:
Day 1: pp. 637–639
Exs. 1, 2, 12–14, 29–47*, 49–53*

Block:
pp. 637–639
Exs. 1, 2, 4–10 even, 15, 16, 23–28, 35, 39–45, 48–52, 55 (with 9.3)

Differentiated Instruction

See *Algebra 2 Best Practices Toolkit* for suggestions on addressing the needs of a diverse classroom.

Homework Check

For a quick check of student understanding of key concepts, go over the following exercises:
Basic: 7, 18, 22, 48, 49
Average: 10, 24, 28, 48, 50
Advanced: 12, 30, 34, 49, 50

Extra Practice

- Student Edition, p. 1018
- Chapter 9 Resource Book: Practice levels A, B, C, pp. 38–40

Practice Worksheet

An easily-readable reduced practice page (with answers) for this lesson can be found on p. 612C.

3–14. See Additional Answers beginning on p. AA1.

15.

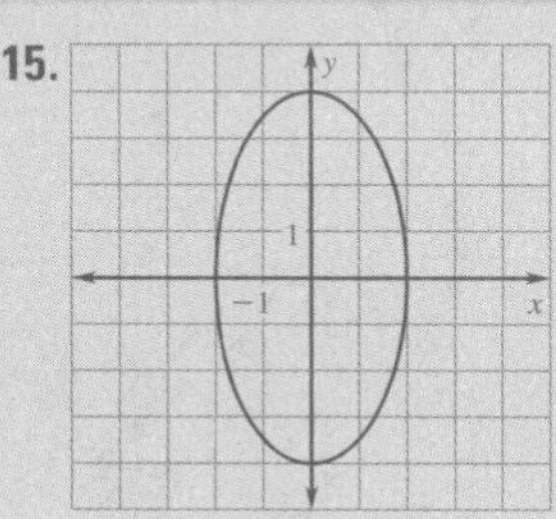

16.

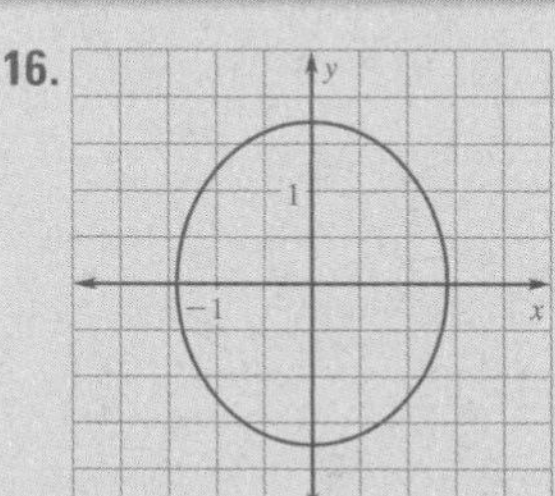

Avoiding Common Errors

Exercises 3–14 Because of their familiarity with the Pythagorean theorem, some students are likely to find the foci of an ellipse by solving $c^2 = a^2 + b^2$. Refer to the diagrams on page 634 to point out that, in this context, $|c| < |a|$.

Reading Strategy

Exercise 49 If students get the incorrect answer, it may be that they were unaware that they were given the lengths of the axes and not the values of *a* and *b* directly. Tell them to always draw and label a diagram with the given information to help them decipher the information in an application problem.

36–44. See Additional Answers beginning on p. AA1.

45.

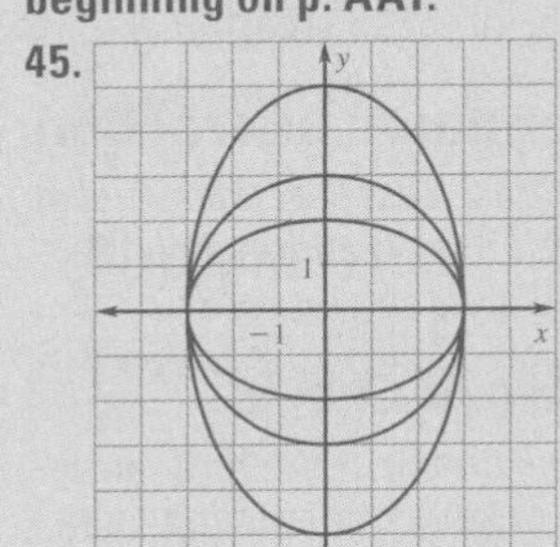

47. ***Sample answer:*** **By definition, the value of $d_1 + d_2$ for the point $P(a, 0)$ is the constant $\sqrt{(a-(-c))^2 + (0-0)^2} + \sqrt{(a-c)^2 + (0-0)^2} = \sqrt{(a+c)^2} + \sqrt{(a-c)^2} = a + c + a - c = 2a$. Similarly, for the point $(0, b)$, this value is also $2a$. Since $d_1 = d_2$ for this point, the distance from $(0, b)$ to the point $(c, 0)$ is $\frac{1}{2}(2a) = a$. A right triangle can be formed with right angle at the origin and the two points $(0, b)$ and $(c, 0)$ as the other two vertices. The legs of this triangle have lengths b and c, and the length of the hypotenuse is the distance from $(0, b)$ to the point $(c, 0)$ which was shown to be a. Therefore, by the Pythagorean Theorem, $c^2 + b^2 = a^2$ or $c^2 = a^2 - b^2$.**

35. ★ **MULTIPLE CHOICE** What is an equation of the ellipse with center at the origin, a vertex at $(0, -12)$, and a co-vertex at $(-8, 0)$? **B**

Ⓐ $\frac{x^2}{144} + \frac{y^2}{64} = 1$ Ⓑ $\frac{x^2}{64} + \frac{y^2}{144} = 1$ Ⓒ $\frac{x^2}{12} + \frac{y^2}{8} = 1$ Ⓓ $\frac{x^2}{8} + \frac{y^2}{12} = 1$

B

GRAPHING In Exercises 36–44, the equations of parabolas, circles, and ellipses are given. Graph the equation. **36–44. See margin.**

36. $x^2 + y^2 = 64$ **37.** $25x^2 + 81y^2 = 2025$ **38.** $36y + x^2 = 0$

39. $65y^2 = 130x$ **40.** $30x^2 + 30y^2 = 480$ **41.** $\frac{x^2}{75} + \frac{4y}{25} = 0$

42. $\frac{3x^2}{48} + \frac{4y^2}{400} = 1$ **43.** $\frac{x^2}{64} + \frac{y^2}{64} = 4$ **44.** $16x^2 + 10y^2 = 160$

45. ★ **SHORT RESPONSE** Consider the graph of $\frac{x^2}{9} + \frac{y^2}{25} = 1$. *Describe* the effects on the graph of changing the denominator of the y^2-term first from 25 to 9 and then from 9 to 4. Graph the original equation and the two revised equations in the same coordinate plane. **The conic changes from an ellipse elongated along the y-axis to a circle to an ellipse elongated along the x-axis; see margin for art.**

C

46. ★ **OPEN-ENDED MATH** Write an equation of an ellipse in standard form. Graph the equation on a graphing calculator by rewriting it as two functions. Give a viewing window that does not distort the shape of the ellipse, and explain how you found your viewing window.

46. ***Sample answer:*** $\frac{x^2}{64} + \frac{y^2}{49} = 1$; $-15 \le x \le 15$, $-10 \le y \le 10$, **the vertices are $(\pm 8, 0)$ and the co-vertices are $(0, \pm 7)$, which can be found in the window.**

47. **CHALLENGE** Use the definition of an ellipse to show that $c^2 = a^2 - b^2$ for any ellipse with equation $\frac{x^2}{a^2} + \frac{y^2}{b^2} = 1$ and foci at $(c, 0)$ and $(-c, 0)$. (*Hint:* Draw a diagram. Consider the point $P(a, 0)$ on the ellipse.) **See margin.**

PROBLEM SOLVING

EXAMPLE 3 A on p. 636 for Exs. 48–50

48. **MARS** On January 3, 2004, the Mars rover Spirit bounced on its airbags to a landing within Gusev crater. Scientists had estimated that there was a 99% chance the rover would land inside an ellipse with a major axis 81 kilometers long and a minor axis 12 kilometers long. Write an equation of the ellipse. Then find its area.

48. $\frac{x^2}{(40.5)^2} + \frac{y^2}{6^2} = 1$; **about 763 km²**

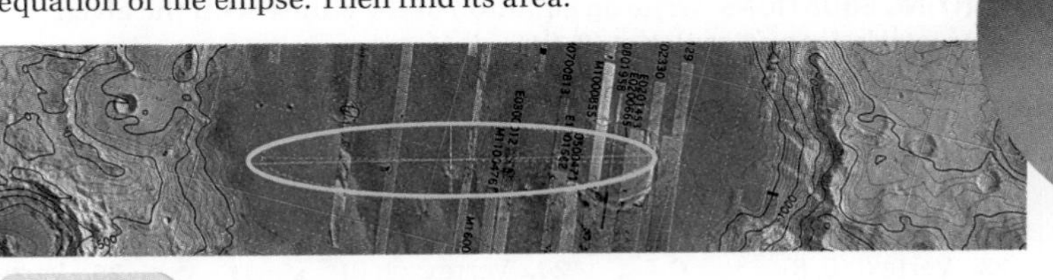

Artist's render of landing

@HomeTutor for problem solving help at classzone.com

49. **AUSTRALIAN FOOTBALL** The playing field for Australian football is an ellipse that is between 135 and 185 meters long and between 110 and 155 meters wide. Write equations of ellipses with vertical major axes that model the largest and smallest fields described. Then write an inequality that describes the possible areas of these fields. $\frac{x^2}{(77.5)^2} + \frac{y^2}{(92.5)^2} = 1$, $\frac{x^2}{(55)^2} + \frac{y^2}{(67.5)^2} = 1$; **about $11{,}700 \le A \le 22{,}500$**

@HomeTutor for problem solving help at classzone.com

○ = WORKED-OUT SOLUTIONS on p. WS1 ★ = STANDARDIZED TEST PRACTICE

51.

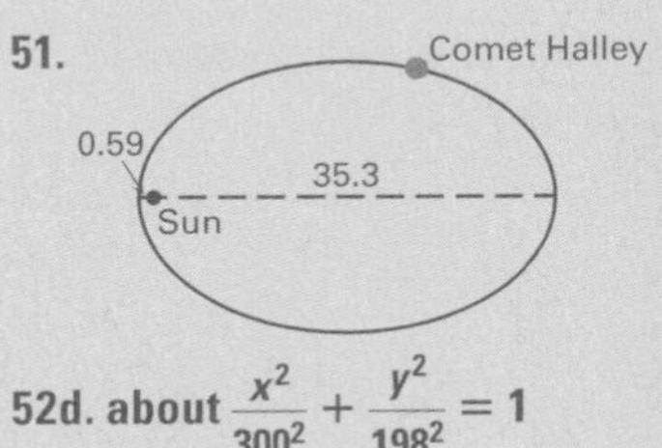

52d. about $\frac{x^2}{300^2} + \frac{y^2}{198^2} = 1$

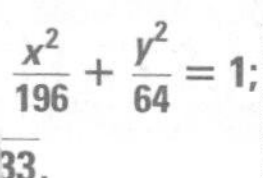
$\frac{x^2}{196} + \frac{y^2}{64} = 1;$
33.

50. **HEALTH CARE** A *lithotripter* uses shock waves to break apart kidney stones or gallstones inside the body. Shock waves generated at one focus of an *ellipsoid* (a three-dimensional shape with an elliptical cross section) reflect to the stone positioned at the second focus. Write an equation for the cross section of the ellipsoid with the dimensions shown. How far apart are the foci?

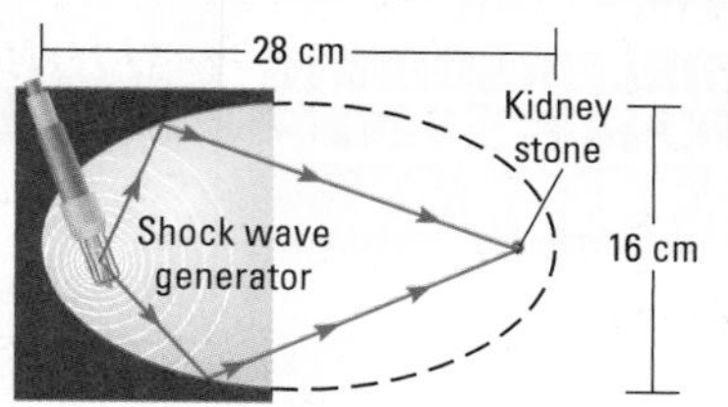

B

51. ★ **SHORT RESPONSE** Halley's comet ranges from 0.59 to 35.3 astronomical units from the sun, which is at one focus of the comet's elliptical orbit. (An *astronomical unit* is Earth's mean distance from the sun.) *Explain* using a sketch how to find a and c. Then write an equation for the orbit. **See margin for art. *Sample answer:* $\frac{x^2}{21.1} + \frac{y^2}{320.4}$**

52. ★ **EXTENDED RESPONSE** A small airplane with enough fuel to fly 600 miles safely will take off from airport A and land at airport B, 450 miles away.

a. **Reason** The region in which the airplane can fly is bounded by an ellipse. *Explain* why this is so.

b. **Calculate** Let (0, 0) represent the center of the ellipse. Find the coordinates of each airport. **(±225, 0)**

c. **Apply** Suppose the plane flies from airport A straight past airport B to a vertex of the ellipse and then straight back to airport B. How far does the plane fly? Use your answer to find the coordinates of the vertex. **600 mi; (±300, 0)**

d. **Model** Write an equation of the ellipse. **See margin.**

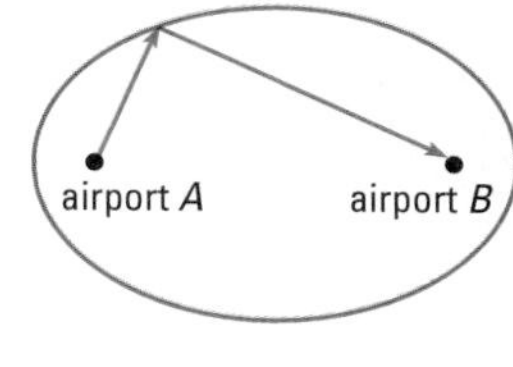

. *Sample* *wer:* The n of the tances from point on the pse to each port remains stant, in this e 600 miles.

C

53. **CHALLENGE** An art museum worker leaves an 8-foot-tall painting leaning against a wall. Later, the top of the painting slides down the wall, and the painting falls to the floor. Use the diagram to find an equation of the path of the point (x, y) as the painting falls. $\frac{x^2}{4} + \frac{y^2}{36} = 1$

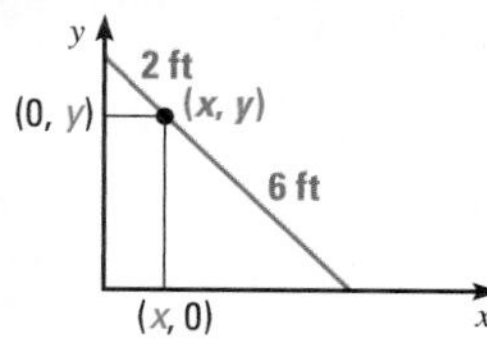

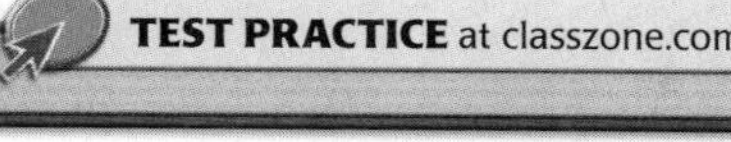

KENTUCKY MIXED REVIEW

TEST PRACTICE at classzone.com

54. Iris wants to make candles shaped like rectangular prisms that measure 3 inches long, 2 inches wide, and 5 inches high. To make the candles, she melts the cylindrical block of wax shown. How many candles can she make? **C**

Ⓐ 113 Ⓑ 126
Ⓒ 136 Ⓓ 288

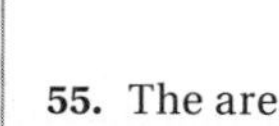

55. The area of a triangle is $45m^7n^{13}$ square units and its height is $15m^{10}n^9$ units. What is the length of the triangle's base? **B**

Ⓐ $\frac{3m^3}{n^4}$ units Ⓑ $\frac{6n^4}{m^3}$ units
Ⓒ $3m^3n^4$ units Ⓓ $6m^{17}n^{22}$ units

5 ASSESS AND RETEACH

Daily Homework Quiz

Transparency Available

1. Graph the equation $\frac{x^2}{36} + \frac{y^2}{225} = 1$. Identify the vertices, co-vertices, and foci of the ellipse.

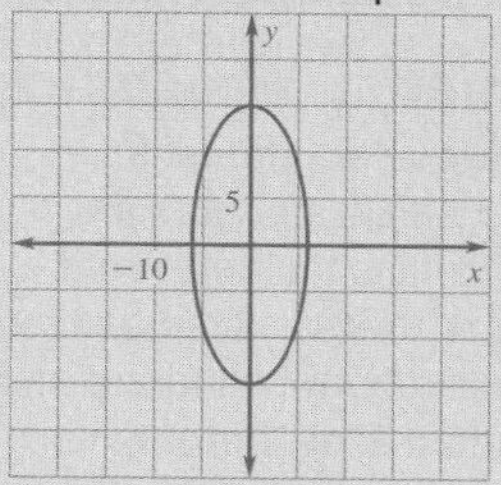

vertices: (0, ±15), co-vertices: (±6, 0), foci: (0, $\pm 3\sqrt{21}$)

Write the equation of the ellipse with center at (0, 0) and the given characteristics.

2. Vertex (0, −7), co-vertex (4, 0) **$\frac{x^2}{16} + \frac{y^2}{49} = 1$**

3. Vertex (−9, 0), focus ($\sqrt{65}$, 0) **$\frac{x^2}{81} + \frac{y^2}{16} = 1$**

4. An elliptical swimming pool is 40 feet long and 30 feet wide. What is the surface area of the pool? **about 942.5 ft^2**

Online Quiz

Available at **classzone.com**

Diagnosis/Remediation

- Practice A, B, C in Chapter 9 Resource Book, pp. 38–40
- Study Guide in Chapter 9 Resource Book, pp. 41–42
- Practice Workbook, pp. 140–141
- @HomeTutor

Challenge

Additional challenge is available in the Chapter 9 Resource Book, p. 46.

PROBLEM SOLVING WORKSHOP LESSON 9.4

Using ALTERNATIVE METHODS

Alternative Strategy

Example 3 on page 636 can be solved by approximating the area under the ellipse. This method allows students to visualize the area measure and will help them better understand the algebraic formula given on page 636. It will also prepare them to explore the area under a curve in calculus.

Mathematical Reasoning

Multiple Representations In Exercises 1 and 2, students are asked to examine multiple representations of the area bounded by the ellipse in the first quadrant and the coordinate axes. Determining closer and closer approximations of the area suggest the idea of a limiting sum. Students will investigate such sums when they study sums of infinite series in Chapter 12.

1. About 66,100 m^2; better. *Sample answer:* More rectangles means there is less area of the ellipse not included.

3a. $\frac{x^2}{125^2} + \frac{y^2}{100^2} = 1$

Another Way to Solve Example 3, page 636

MULTIPLE REPRESENTATIONS In the second part of Example 3 on page 636, you found the area of an ellipse using a formula. You can also approximate the area of an ellipse by summing the areas of rectangles.

PROBLEM

LIGHTNING When lightning strikes, an elliptical region where the strike most likely hit can often be identified. Suppose it is determined that there is a 50% chance that a lightning strike hit within the elliptical region shown in the diagram.

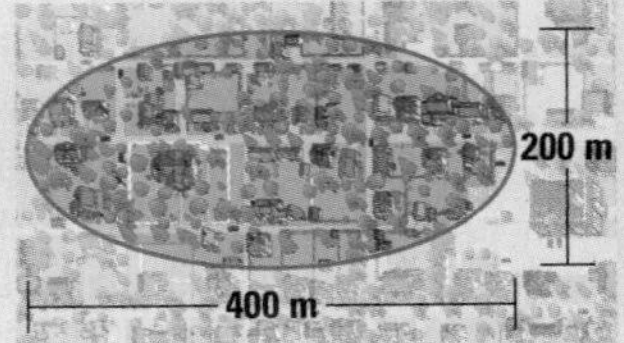

- Write an equation of the ellipse.
- Find the area of the elliptical region.

METHOD

Summing Rectangles As you saw on page 636, the ellipse has the equation $\frac{x^2}{200^2} + \frac{y^2}{100^2} = 1$. Approximate the area of the ellipse as follows.

STEP 1 **Graph** the first-quadrant portion of the ellipse. Then draw rectangles of width 40 and height equal to the y-value of the ellipse at the rectangle's left edge. The first rectangle's height is $y_1 = 100$. To find the other y-values, solve for y to obtain $y = \sqrt{100^2 - \frac{x^2}{4}}$. Use a calculator to get $y_2 \approx 98.0$, $y_3 \approx 91.7$, $y_4 = 80$, and $y_5 = 60$.

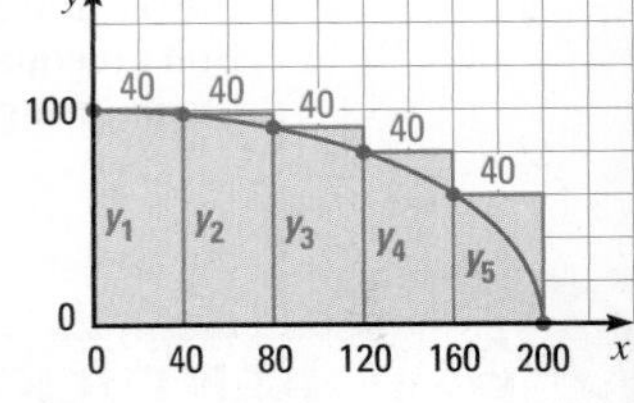

STEP 2 **Calculate** the total area A of the rectangles.

$$A \approx 40(100) + 40(98.0) + 40(91.7) + 40(80) + 40(60) = 17{,}188 \text{ m}^2$$

STEP 3 **Multiply** the total area of the rectangles by 4 to obtain an estimate of $4(17{,}188) \approx 68{,}800$ square meters for the area of the ellipse.

PRACTICE

1. Solve the problem above using rectangles of width 20. Is this estimate better or worse than the estimate above? *Explain.* **See margin.**

2. **REASONING** *Explain* using your results from Exercise 1 how to obtain a closer and closer approximation of the ellipse's area. **Use rectangles whose widths are smaller than the previous set of rectangles.**

3. **WHAT IF?** Suppose that the ellipse in the problem had a horizontal major axis of 250 meters and a minor axis of 200 meters.
   a. Write an equation of the ellipse. **See marg**
   b. Use the method above to approximate the area of the ellipse. **about 39,000 m^2**

Lessons 9.1–9.4

1. **PARABOLIC REFLECTORS** Parabolic reflectors with a microphone at the focus allow the operator to listen to sounds from far away. A certain parabolic microphone has a reflector that is 22.4 inches in diameter and 6 inches deep. Approximately how far is the focus from the vertex?

   A. 5.2 inches B. 6 inches
   C. 11.2 inches D. 24.8 inches

2. **RADAR** An anchored fishing boat's radar has a range of 16 miles. A second boat 6 miles north and 4 miles east of the fishing boat begins moving westward. For approximately what distance will the second boat be in radar range of the first boat?

   A. 14.8 miles
   B. 18.8 miles
   C. 21.5 miles
   D. 29.6 miles

3. **PLANETARY ORBIT** In its elliptical orbit, Mercury ranges from 29 million miles to 44 million miles from the sun. The sun is at one focus of the orbit. Which equation could represent Mercury's orbit?

   A. $\frac{x^2}{(36.5)^2} + \frac{y^2}{(7.5)^2} = 1$
   B. $\frac{x^2}{(44)^2} + \frac{y^2}{(29)^2} = 1$
   C. $\frac{x^2}{(36.5)^2} + \frac{y^2}{(29)^2} = 1$
   D. $\frac{x^2}{(36.5)^2} + \frac{y^2}{(35.7)^2} = 1$

4. **DRIVING DISTANCE** To get from your home to the beach, you drive 8 miles south, then 16 miles east, and then 4 miles south. What is the straight-line distance from your home to the beach?

   A. 16.5 miles B. 20 miles
   C. 21.5 miles D. 28 miles

5. **ACCIDENT INVESTIGATION** A car skids while turning to avoid an accident. The circular skid mark is shown below. The car's speed v (in meters per second) can be approximated by $v = \sqrt{9.8\mu r}$ where r is the radius (in meters) of the skid mark and μ is a constant that depends on the road surface and weather conditions $(0 \le \mu \le 1)$. About how fast was the car traveling if it is determined that $\mu = 0.7$?

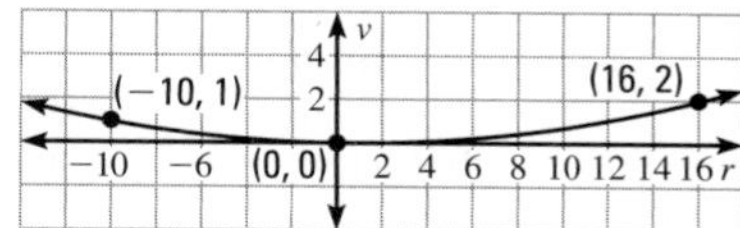

   A. 9.4 m/s
   B. 19.8 m/s
   C. 20.0 m/s
   D. 28.3 m/s

6. **TANGENT LINES** Two lines are tangent to the circle $x^2 + y^2 = 13$, one at $(-2, -3)$ and one at $(3, -2)$. What is the relationship between the two lines?

   A. The two lines are parallel.
   B. The two lines are perpendicular.
   C. The two lines intersect at the origin.
   D. The two lines intersect at $\left(0, \frac{13}{2}\right)$.

7. **OPEN-RESPONSE** You can make a solar hot dog cooker by shaping foil-lined cardboard into a parabolic trough and passing a wire through the focus of each end piece.

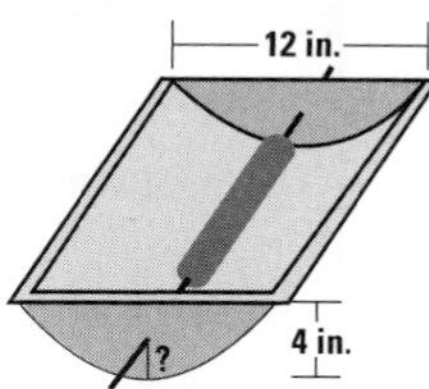

   a. For the trough shown, how far from the bottom, to the nearest tenth of an inch, should you place the wire?

   b. *Explain* how you found your answer.

Kentucky Mixed Review

1. A
2. B
3. D
4. B
5. C
6. B
7. a. 2.3 inches
   b. $x^2 = 4py$
   $4^2 = 4p(4)$
   $\frac{36}{16} = p$
   $\frac{9}{4} = 2.3 = p$

1 PLAN AND PREPARE

Warm-Up Exercises

Transparency Available

Identify the foci of each ellipse.

1. $\frac{x^2}{15} + \frac{y^2}{16} = 1$ (0, −1) and (0, 1)

2. $\frac{x^2}{49} + \frac{y^2}{45} = 1$ (2, 0) and (−2, 0)

3. You sail 5 miles due north from your mooring. Then you sail 3 miles due east. How far are you from your mooring? about 5.8 mi

Notetaking Guide

Transparency Available

Promotes interactive learning and notetaking skills, pp. 244–247.

Pacing

Basic: 1 day

Average: 1 day

Advanced: 1 day

Block: 0.5 block with 9.6

• See *Teaching Guide/Lesson Plan*.

2 FOCUS AND MOTIVATE

Essential Question

Big Idea 1, p. 613

What kind of figure can be used to locate the vertices and asymptotes of a hyperbola? Tell students they will learn how to answer this question by identifying the vertices and asymptotes of a hyperbola.

9.5 Graph and Write Equations of Hyperbolas

MA-HS-3.1.5

Before	You graphed and wrote equations of parabolas, circles, and ellipses.
Now	You will graph and write equations of hyperbolas.
Why?	So you can model curved mirrors, as in Example 3.

Key Vocabulary
- hyperbola
- foci
- vertices
- transverse axis
- center

Recall that an ellipse is the set of all points P in a plane such that the *sum* of the distances between P and two fixed points (the foci) is a constant.

A **hyperbola** is the set of all points P such that the *difference* of the distances between P and two fixed points, again called the **foci**, is a constant.

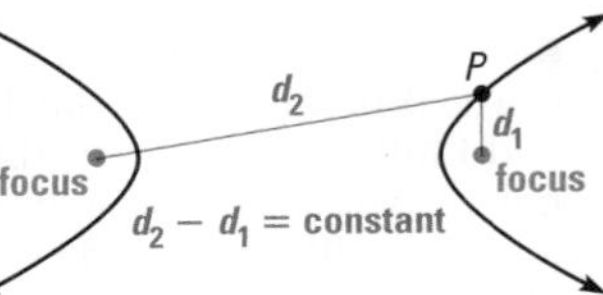

The line through the foci intersects the hyperbola at the two **vertices**. The **transverse axis** joins the vertices. Its midpoint is the hyperbola's **center**. A hyperbola has two *branches*, and has two asymptotes that contain the diagonals of a rectangle centered at the hyperbola's center, as shown.

IDENTIFY AXES

If the x^2-term in the equation of a hyperbola is positive, the transverse axis lies on the x-axis. If the y^2-term is positive, the transverse axis lies on the y-axis.

MA-HS-3.1.5
Students will classify and apply properties of two-dimensional geometric figures (e.g., number of sides, vertices, length of sides, sum of interior and exterior angle measures). DOK 2

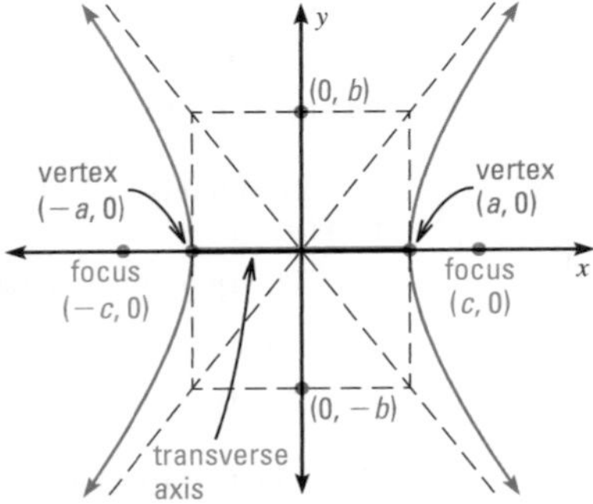

Hyperbola with horizontal transverse axis

$$\frac{x^2}{a^2} - \frac{y^2}{b^2} = 1$$

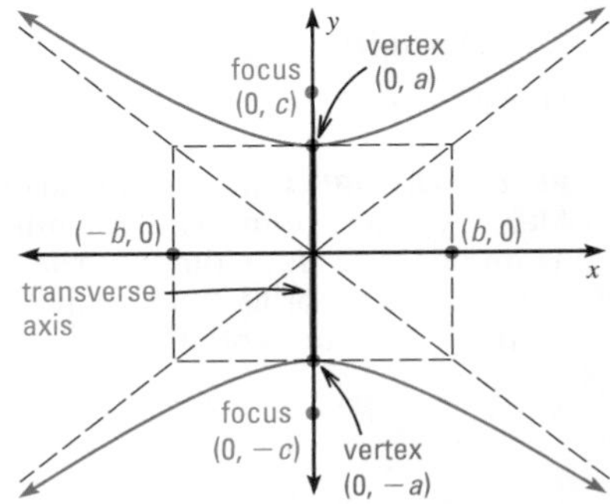

Hyperbola with vertical transverse axis

$$\frac{y^2}{a^2} - \frac{x^2}{b^2} = 1$$

KEY CONCEPT *For Your Notebook*

Standard Equation of a Hyperbola with Center at the Origin

Equation	Transverse Axis	Asymptotes	Vertices
$\frac{x^2}{a^2} - \frac{y^2}{b^2} = 1$	Horizontal	$y = \pm\frac{b}{a}x$	$(\pm a, 0)$
$\frac{y^2}{a^2} - \frac{x^2}{b^2} = 1$	Vertical	$y = \pm\frac{a}{b}x$	$(0, \pm a)$

The foci lie on the transverse axis, c units from the center, where $c^2 = a^2 + b^2$.

Resource Planning Guide

Chapter Resource Book
- Teaching Guide/Lesson Plan (pp. 47–48)
- Practice levels A, B, C (pp. 50–52)
- Study Guide (pp. 53–54)
- Catch-up for Absent Students (p. 55)
- Application (p. 56)
- Challenge (p. 57)

Workbooks
- Notetaking Guide (pp. 244–247)
- Practice Workbook (pp. 142–143)

Teaching Options
- **Power Presentations CD-ROM** provides dynamic electronic teaching resources for the classroom.
- **Activity Generator CD-ROM** provides editable activities for all ability levels.

Interactive Technology
- Easy Planner
- Power Presentations CD-ROM
- Activity Generator CD-ROM
- Animated Algebra
- Test Generator CD-ROM
- Online Quiz
- eWorkbook
- eEdition
- @HomeTutor

Resources for English Learners
- Quick Reference for English Learners
- Spanish Study Guide
- Multi-Language Visual Glossary
- Student Resources in Spanish

See also the *Algebra 2 Toolkit* for more strategies for meeting individual needs.

EXAMPLE 1 Graph an equation of a hyperbola

Graph $25y^2 - 4x^2 = 100$. Identify the vertices, foci, and asymptotes of the hyperbola.

Solution

STEP 1 **Rewrite** the equation in standard form.

$$25y^2 - 4x^2 = 100 \quad \textbf{Write original equation.}$$

$$\frac{25y^2}{100} - \frac{4x^2}{100} = \frac{100}{100} \quad \textbf{Divide each side by 100.}$$

$$\frac{y^2}{4} - \frac{x^2}{25} = 1 \quad \textbf{Simplify.}$$

STEP 2 **Identify** the vertices, foci, and asymptotes. Note that $a^2 = 4$ and $b^2 = 25$, so $a = 2$ and $b = 5$. The y^2-term is positive, so the transverse axis is vertical and the vertices are at $(0, \pm 2)$. Find the foci.

$$c^2 = a^2 + b^2 = 2^2 + 5^2 = 29, \text{ so } c = \sqrt{29}$$

The foci are at $(0, \pm\sqrt{29}) \approx (0, \pm 5.4)$.

The asymptotes are $y = \pm\frac{a}{b}x$, or $y = \pm\frac{2}{5}x$.

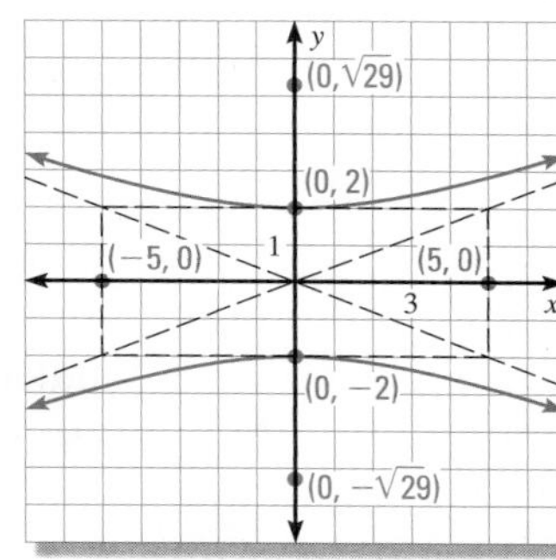

SOLVE FOR *Y*

To plot points on the hyperbola, solve its equation for y to obtain $y = \pm 2\sqrt{1 + \frac{x^2}{25}}$. Then make a table of values.

STEP 3 **Draw** the hyperbola. First draw a rectangle centered at the origin that is $2a = 4$ units high and $2b = 10$ units wide. The asymptotes pass through opposite corners of the rectangle. Then, draw the hyperbola passing through the vertices and approaching the asymptotes.

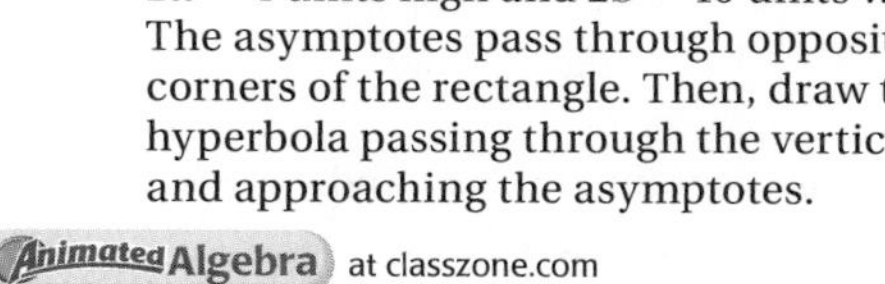

Animated Algebra at classzone.com

EXAMPLE 2 Write an equation of a hyperbola

Write an equation of the hyperbola with foci at $(-4, 0)$ and $(4, 0)$ and vertices at $(-3, 0)$ and $(3, 0)$.

Solution

The foci and vertices lie on the x-axis equidistant from the origin, so the transverse axis is horizontal and the center is the origin. The foci are each 4 units from the center, so $c = 4$. The vertices are each 3 units from the center, so $a = 3$.

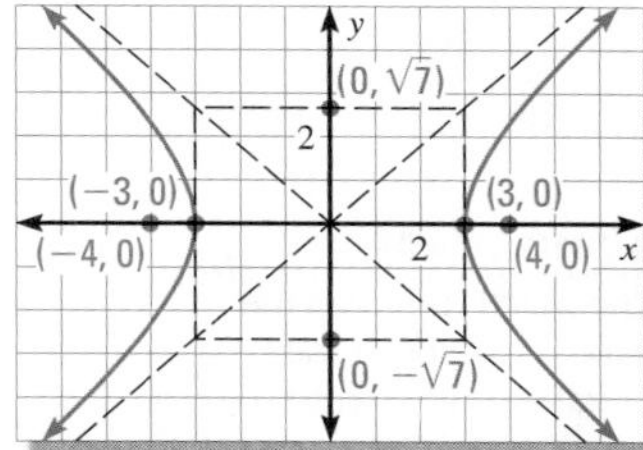

Because $c^2 = a^2 + b^2$, you have $b^2 = c^2 - a^2$. Find b^2.

$$b^2 = c^2 - a^2 = 4^2 - 3^2 = 7$$

Because the transverse axis is horizontal, the standard form of the equation is as follows:

$$\frac{x^2}{3^2} - \frac{y^2}{7} = 1 \quad \textbf{Substitute 3 for } a \textbf{ and 7 for } b^2.$$

$$\frac{x^2}{9} - \frac{y^2}{7} = 1 \quad \textbf{Simplify.}$$

Differentiated Instruction

Inclusion Before completing **Example 1**, students should be familiar with the properties of the hyperbola. Give students graphs of several different hyperbolas on a sheet of paper. In an organized table, have students identify the transverse axis, asymptotes, and vertices of the graph. Then have them write an equation for each graph.

See also the *Algebra 2 Toolkit* for more strategies.

Motivating the Lesson

Tell students they already have seen one form of a hyperbola when they graphed equations such as $y = \frac{1}{x}$. In this lesson they will study another form of hyperbola, represented by the equations $\frac{x^2}{a^2} - \frac{y^2}{b^2} = 1$ or $\frac{y^2}{a^2} - \frac{x^2}{b^2} = 1$.

3 TEACH

Extra Example 1

Graph $x^2 - 4y^2 = 9$. Identify the vertices, foci, and asymptotes of the hyperbola.

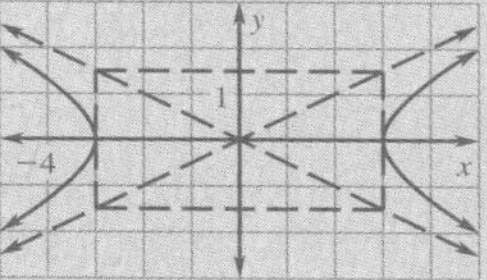

Vertices: $(\pm 3, 0)$; foci: $\left(\pm\frac{3\sqrt{5}}{2}, 0\right)$; asymptotes: $y = \pm\frac{1}{2}x$

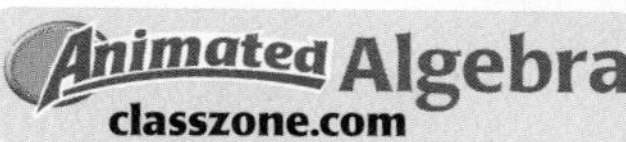

An **Animated Algebra** activity is available on-line for **Example 1**. This activity is also available on the **Power Presentations CD-ROM**.

Extra Example 2

Write an equation of the hyperbola with foci at $(-8, 0)$ and $(8, 0)$ and vertices at $(-5, 0)$ and $(5, 0)$.

$\frac{x^2}{25} - \frac{y^2}{39} = 1$

Vocabulary

The transverse axis, which joins the vertices, has a length of $2a$ units. The segment through the center of the transverse axis and perpendicular to it, is called the *conjugate axis*. Its length is $2b$ units.

GUIDED PRACTICE for Examples 1 and 2

Graph the equation. Identify the vertices, foci, and asymptotes of the hyperbola. 1–3. See margin for art.

1. $\frac{x^2}{16} - \frac{y^2}{49} = 1$ $(\pm 4, 0), (\pm\sqrt{65}, 0), y = \pm\frac{7}{4}x$
2. $\frac{y^2}{36} - x^2 = 1$ $(0, \pm 6), (0, \pm\sqrt{37}), y = \pm 6x$
3. $4y^2 - 9x^2 = 36$ $(0, \pm 3), (0, \pm\sqrt{13}), y = \pm\frac{3}{2}x$

Write an equation of the hyperbola with the given foci and vertices.

4. Foci: $(-3, 0), (3, 0)$
   Vertices: $(-1, 0), (1, 0)$ $x^2 - \frac{y^2}{8} = 1$
5. Foci: $(0, -10), (0, 10)$
   Vertices: $(0, -6), (0, 6)$ $\frac{y^2}{36} - \frac{x^2}{64} = 1$

EXAMPLE 3 Solve a multi-step problem

PHOTOGRAPHY You can take panoramic photographs using a hyperbolic mirror. Light rays heading toward the focus behind the mirror are reflected to a camera positioned at the other focus as shown. After a photograph is taken, computers can "unwarp" the distorted image into a 360° view.

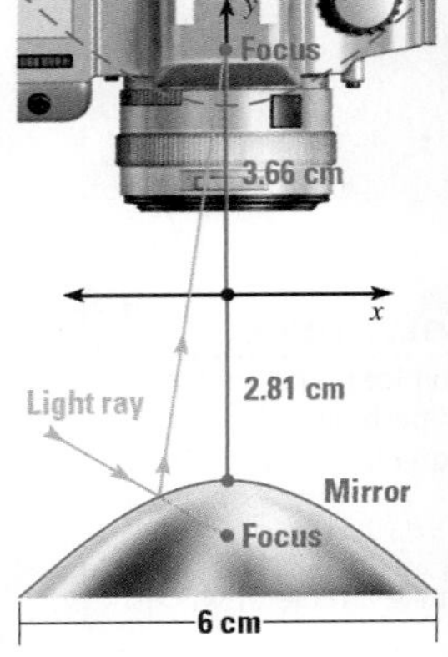

- Write an equation for the cross section of the mirror.
- The mirror is 6 centimeters wide. How tall is it?

Solution

STEP 1 From the diagram, $a = 2.81$ and $c = 3.66$.

To write an equation, find b^2.

$$b^2 = c^2 - a^2 = 3.66^2 - 2.81^2 \approx 5.50$$

▶ Because the transverse axis is vertical, the standard form of the equation for the cross section of the mirror is as follows:

$$\frac{y^2}{2.81^2} - \frac{x^2}{5.50} = 1, \quad \text{or} \quad \frac{y^2}{7.90} - \frac{x^2}{5.50} = 1$$

STEP 2 Find the y-coordinate at the mirror's bottom edge. Because the mirror is 6 centimeters wide, substitute $x = 3$ into the equation and solve.

$$\frac{y^2}{7.90} - \frac{3^2}{5.50} = 1 \quad \text{Substitute 3 for } x.$$

$$y^2 \approx 20.83 \quad \text{Solve for } y^2.$$

$$y \approx -4.56 \quad \text{Solve for } y.$$

▶ So, the mirror has a height of $-2.81 - (-4.56) = 1.75$ centimeters.

AVOID ERRORS
The mirror is below the x-axis, so choose the negative square root.

GUIDED PRACTICE for Example 3

6. **WHAT IF?** In Example 3, suppose that the mirror remains 6 centimeters wide, but that $a = 3$ centimeters and $c = 5$ centimeters. How tall is the mirror? **0.75 cm**

Extra Example 3

A military plane is flying along a hyperbolic path with focus $(0, 2\sqrt{3})$ and will go through the point $(0, 2)$. The center of a town below the flight path is located at X. Write an equation for the path of the plane. How high is the plane when it is directly above the center of the town?

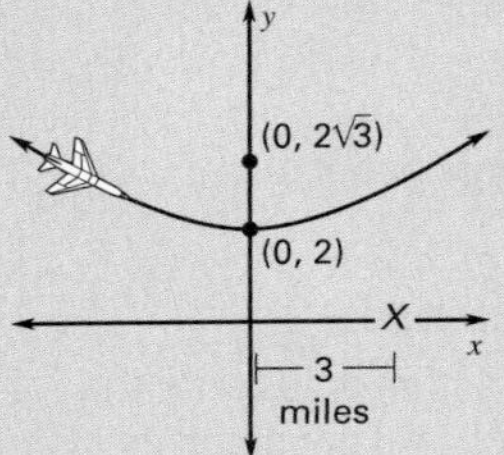

$\frac{y^2}{4} - \frac{x^2}{8} = 1$; about 2.9 mi

Closing the Lesson

Have students summarize the major points of the lesson and answer the Essential Question: What kind of figure can be used to locate the vertices and asymptotes of a hyperbola?

- **For each point on a hyperbola, the difference of the distances from any point to the foci is a constant.**
- **For a hyperbola with center at the origin, if the transverse axis is horizontal, the vertex is $(\pm a, 0)$, and the foci are $(\pm c, 0)$, the general form of the equation is $\frac{x^2}{a^2} \frac{y^2}{b^2} = 1$ and the asymptotes are $y = \pm\frac{b}{a}x$. If the transverse axis is vertical, the vertices are $(0, \pm a)$, and the foci are $(0, \pm c)$, the general form of the equation is $\frac{y^2}{a^2} - \frac{x^2}{b^2} = 1$ and the asymptotes are $y = \pm\frac{a}{b}x$.**
- **The foci lie on the transverse axis, c units from the center, where $c^2 = a^2 + b^2$.**

The figure that is centered at the origin, has dimensions $2a$ and $2b$, and whose diagonals contain the asymptotes of the hyperbola, is a rectangle.

1–3. See Additional Answers beginning on p. AA1.

Differentiated Instruction

Advanced Have students graph several inverse variation functions where $xy = c$. This is a special case of the hyperbola, called the "rectangular" hyperbola. From their graphs, students should see that the asymptotes are perpendicular.

See also the *Algebra 2 Toolkit* for more strategies.

9.5 EXERCISES

HOMEWORK KEY
○ = **WORKED-OUT SOLUTIONS** on p. WS17 for Exs. 13, 23, and 41
★ = **STANDARDIZED TEST PRACTICE** Exs. 2, 15, 26, 33, 35, and 43
◆ = **MULTIPLE REPRESENTATIONS** Ex. 42

SKILL PRACTICE

A

1. **VOCABULARY** Copy and complete: The points $(-2, 0)$ and $(2, 0)$ in the graph at the right are the _?_ of the hyperbola. The line segment joining these two points is the _?_.
vertices, transverse axis

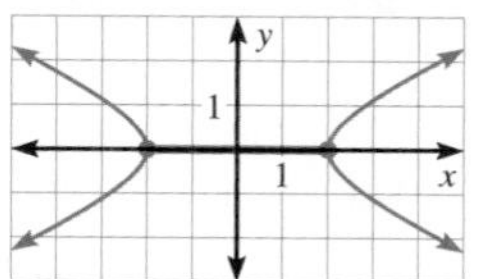

2. ★ **WRITING** *Compare* the definitions of an ellipse and a hyperbola. In an ellipse the sum of the distances remains constant while in a hyperbola the difference of the distances remains constant.

EXAMPLE 1
on p. 643
for Exs. 3–17

GRAPHING **Graph the equation. Identify the vertices, foci, and asymptotes of the hyperbola.** 3–14. See margin.

3. $\frac{x^2}{25} - \frac{y^2}{4} = 1$
4. $\frac{x^2}{9} - \frac{y^2}{36} = 1$
5. $\frac{y^2}{81} - \frac{x^2}{25} = 1$
6. $\frac{x^2}{144} - \frac{y^2}{36} = 1$
7. $\frac{y^2}{196} - \frac{x^2}{100} = 1$
8. $\frac{y^2}{49} - \frac{x^2}{121} = 1$
9. $4x^2 - y^2 = 256$
10. $49x^2 - 4y^2 = 196$
11. $9y^2 - 25x^2 = 225$
12. $25y^2 - 64x^2 = 1600$
13. $81x^2 - 16y^2 = 1296$
14. $49y^2 - 100x^2 = 4900$

15. ★ **MULTIPLE CHOICE** What are the foci of the hyperbola with equation $45y^2 - 200x^2 = 1800$? D

Ⓐ $(\pm 2\sqrt{10}, 0)$ Ⓑ $(0, \pm 2\sqrt{10})$ Ⓒ $(\pm 7, 0)$ Ⓓ $(0, \pm 7)$

ERROR ANALYSIS *Describe* **and correct the error in graphing the equation.** 16, 17. See margin for art.

16. The hyperbola should open up and down with vertices $(0, \pm 6)$.

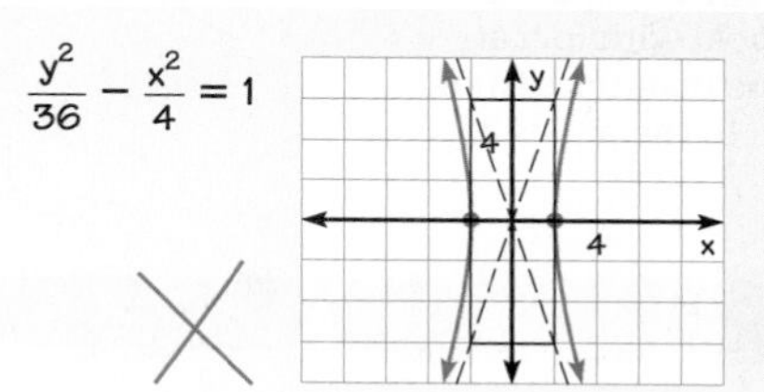

17. The equation of a hyperbola must equal 1, so the hyperbola's vertices should be located at $(\pm 4, 0)$.

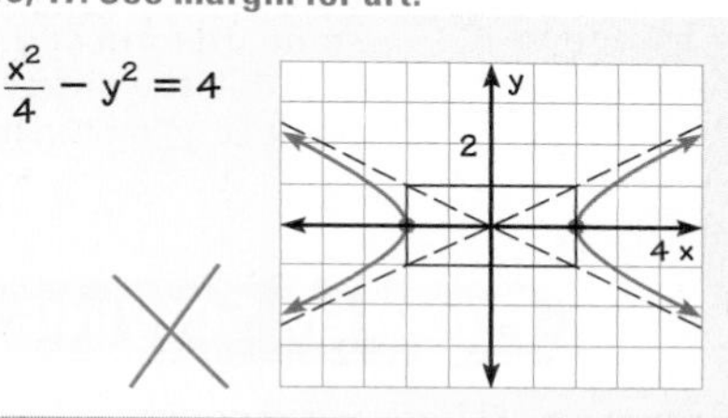

EXAMPLE 2
on p. 643
for Exs. 18–26

WRITING EQUATIONS **Write an equation of the hyperbola with the given foci and vertices.**

18. Foci: $(0, -4), (0, 4)$
Vertices: $(0, -2), (0, 2)$ $\frac{y^2}{4} - \frac{x^2}{12} = 1$

19. Foci: $(-6, 0), (6, 0)$
Vertices: $(-2, 0), (2, 0)$ $\frac{x^2}{4} - \frac{y^2}{32} = 1$

20. Foci: $(-5, 0), (5, 0)$
Vertices: $(-1, 0), (1, 0)$ $x^2 - \frac{y^2}{24} = 1$

21. Foci: $(0, -12), (0, 12)$
Vertices: $(0, -7), (0, 7)$ $\frac{y^2}{49} - \frac{x^2}{95} = 1$

22. Foci: $(-10, 0), (10, 0)$
Vertices: $(-5\sqrt{3}, 0), (5\sqrt{3}, 0)$ $\frac{x^2}{75} - \frac{y^2}{25} = 1$

23. Foci: $(0, -4\sqrt{5}), (0, 4\sqrt{5})$
Vertices: $(0, -4), (0, 4)$ $\frac{y^2}{16} - \frac{x^2}{64} = 1$

24. Foci: $(0, -3), (0, 3)$
Vertices: $(0, -2\sqrt{2}), (0, 2\sqrt{2})$ $\frac{y^2}{8} - x^2 = 1$

25. Foci: $(-3\sqrt{6}, 0), (3\sqrt{6}, 0)$
Vertices: $(-2, 0), (2, 0)$ $\frac{x^2}{4} - \frac{y^2}{50} = 1$

4 PRACTICE AND APPLY

Assignment Guide

Answer Transparencies available for all exercises

Basic:
Day 1: pp. 645–648
Exs. 1, 2, 3–15 odd, 16–23, 26–29, 38–42, 45

Average:
Day 1: pp. 645–648
Exs. 1, 2, 4–14 even, 15–17, 20–23, 26, 30–35, 38–43, 46

Advanced:
Day 1: pp. 645–648
Exs. 1, 2, 12–15, 22–37*, 39–44*, 46

Block:
pp. 645–648
Exs. 1, 2, 4–14 even, 15–17, 20–23, 26, 30–35, 38–43, 46 (with 9.6)

Differentiated Instruction

See *Algebra 2 Best Practices Toolkit* for suggestions on addressing the needs of a diverse classroom.

Homework Check

For a quick check of student understanding of key concepts, go over the following exercises:
Basic: 5, 9, 18, 20, 38
Average: 6, 10, 20, 22, 39
Advanced: 12, 14, 22, 24, 40

Extra Practice

- Student Edition, p. 1018
- Chapter 9 Resource Book: Practice levels A, B, C, pp. 50–52

Practice Worksheet

An easily-readable reduced practice page (with answers) for this lesson can be found on p. 612D.

3–14. See Additional Answers beginning on p. AA1.

16.

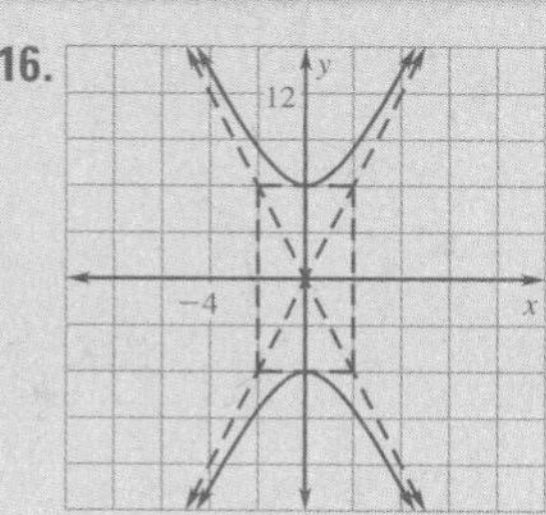

17.

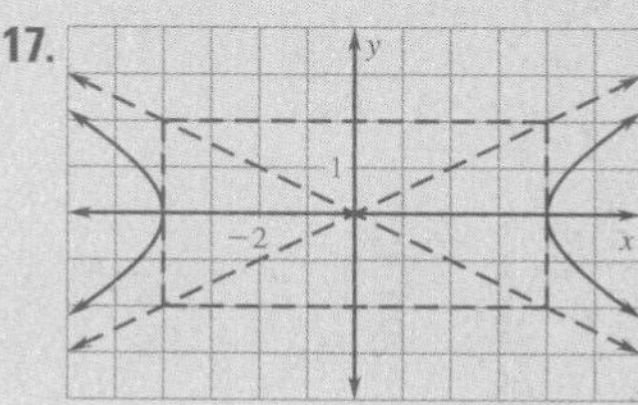

Avoiding Common Errors

Exercises 3–14 Make sure that students understand that the rectangle is not part of the graph of a hyperbola, but only a visual aid to draw the asymptotes, which in turn are a visual aid to draw the branches of the hyperbola.

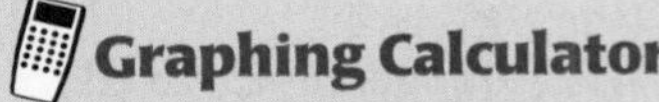

Graphing Calculator

Exercises 18–25, 33 Students can use a graphing calculator to check their answers to these exercises.

Vocabulary

Exercise 35 Remind students that a transverse axis cuts across a hyperbola and divides it into four parts at the vertices. A transverse axis can be either horizontal or vertical.

27.
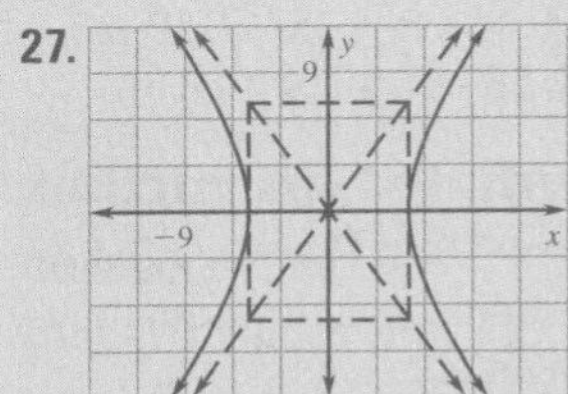

28.
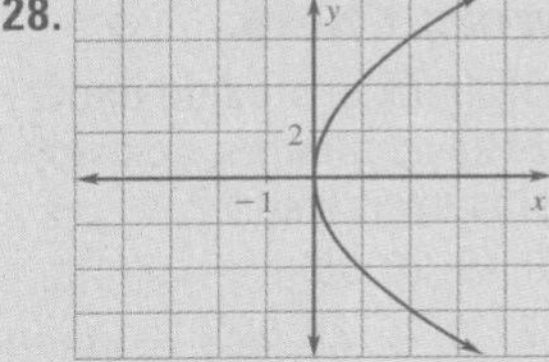

29.
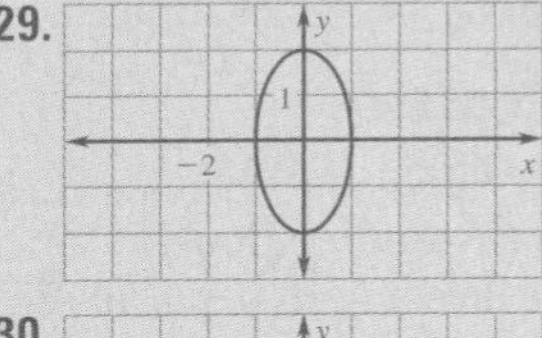

30.
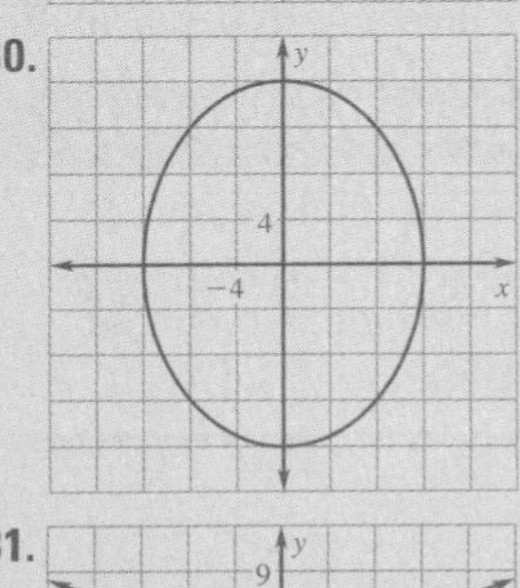

31.
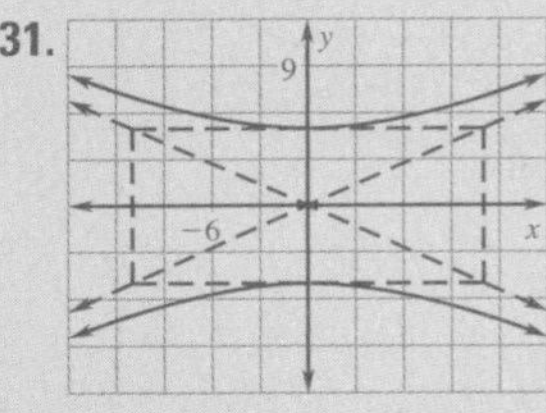

32.
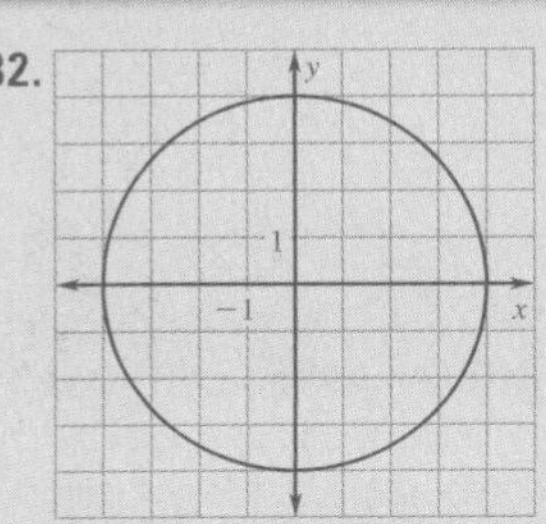

33a. The hyperbola will be narrower, the vertices are the same, but the foci move to $(\pm\sqrt{13}, 0)$.

33b. The hyperbola will be wider, the vertices are the same, but the foci move to $(0, \pm\sqrt{41})$.

35. *Sample answer:* $x^2 - \frac{y^2}{4} = 1$, $\frac{x^2}{4} - \frac{y^2}{16} = 1$, $\frac{x^2}{9} - \frac{y^2}{36} = 1$; as the value of a gets larger the hyperbola is stretched vertically.

36. *Sample answer:* Choose (x, y) to be $(-a, 0)$. $d_1 = 2a + c$ and $d_2 = c$ therefore $|d_2 - d_1| = 2a$.

39. $\frac{x^2}{\frac{1}{2}} - \frac{y^2}{\frac{1}{4}} = 1$

26. ★ **MULTIPLE CHOICE** What is an equation of the hyperbola with foci at $(0, -6\sqrt{3})$ and $(0, 6\sqrt{3})$ and with vertices at $(0, -8)$ and $(0, 8)$? **C**

Ⓐ $\frac{x^2}{64} - \frac{y^2}{108} = 1$ Ⓑ $\frac{x^2}{44} - \frac{y^2}{68} = 1$ Ⓒ $\frac{y^2}{64} - \frac{x^2}{44} = 1$ Ⓓ $\frac{y^2}{108} - \frac{x^2}{64} = 1$

B

GRAPHING In Exercises 27–32, the equations of parabolas, circles, ellipses, and hyperbolas are given. Graph the equation. **27–32. See margin.**

27. $\frac{x^2}{25} - \frac{y^2}{49} = 1$

28. $y^2 = 18x$

29. $48x^2 + 12y^2 = 48$

30. $\frac{x^2}{144} + \frac{y^2}{256} = 1$

31. $\frac{y^2}{25} - \frac{x^2}{121} = 1$

32. $18x^2 + 18y^2 = 288$

33. ★ **SHORT RESPONSE** *Describe* the effects of the indicated change on the shape of the hyperbola and on the locations of the vertices and foci.

a. $\frac{x^2}{9} - \frac{y^2}{36} = 1$; change 36 to 4

b. $\frac{y^2}{16} - \frac{x^2}{4} = 1$; change 4 to 25

34. **GRAPHING CALCULATOR** Graph each hyperbola using a graphing calculator. Tell what two functions you entered into the calculator.

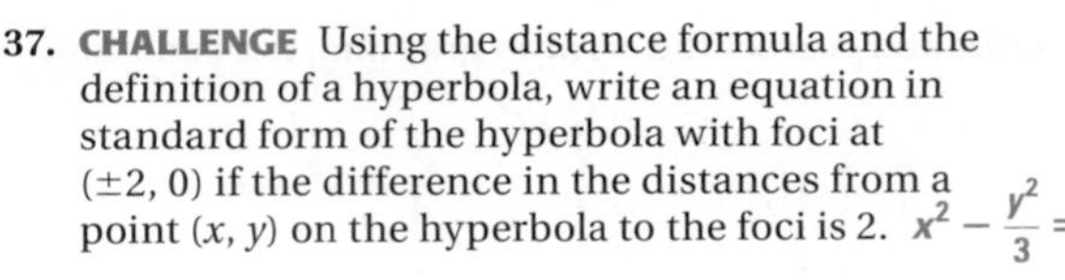

a. $\frac{y^2}{15} - \frac{x^2}{30} = 1$ $y = \pm\sqrt{15 + \frac{x^2}{2}}$

b. $\frac{x^2}{8.4} - \frac{y^2}{5.5} = 1$ $y = \pm\sqrt{\frac{5.5x^2}{8.4} - 5.5}$

c. $5x^2 - 7.5y^2 = 12$ $y = \pm\sqrt{\frac{5x^2 - 12}{7.5}}$

35. ★ **OPEN-ENDED MATH** Give equations of three hyperbolas with horizontal transverse axes and asymptotes $y = \pm 2x$. *Compare* the hyperbolas.

C

36. **REASONING** Use the diagram at the right to show that $|d_2 - d_1| = 2a$. (*Hint:* $|d_2 - d_1|$ is constant, so choose a convenient location for (x, y).)

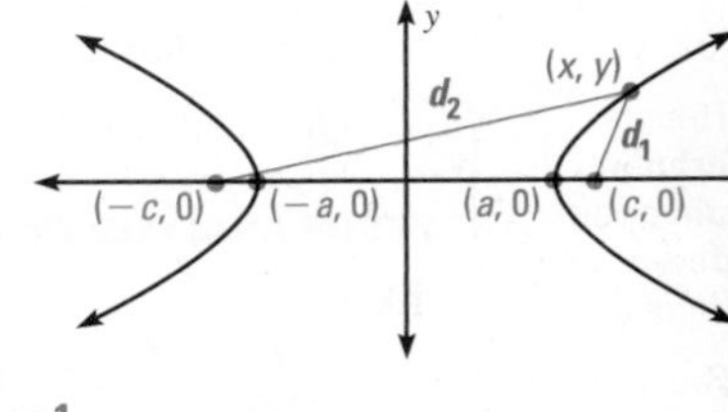

37. **CHALLENGE** Using the distance formula and the definition of a hyperbola, write an equation in standard form of the hyperbola with foci at $(\pm 2, 0)$ if the difference in the distances from a point (x, y) on the hyperbola to the foci is 2. $x^2 - \frac{y^2}{3} = 1$

PROBLEM SOLVING

EXAMPLE 3 A on p. 644 for Exs. 38–40

38. **TELESCOPES** A satellite is carrying a telescope that has a hyperbolic mirror for which $a = 33$ and $c = 56$ (in centimeters). Write an equation for the cross section of the mirror if the transverse axis is horizontal. $\frac{x^2}{1089} - \frac{y^2}{2047} = 1$

@HomeTutor for problem solving help at classzone.com

39. **SPINNING CUBE** The outline of a cube spinning around an axis through a pair of opposite corners contains a portion of a hyperbola, as shown. The coordinates given represent a vertex and a focus of the hyperbola for a cube that measures 1 unit on each edge. Write an equation that models this hyperbola.

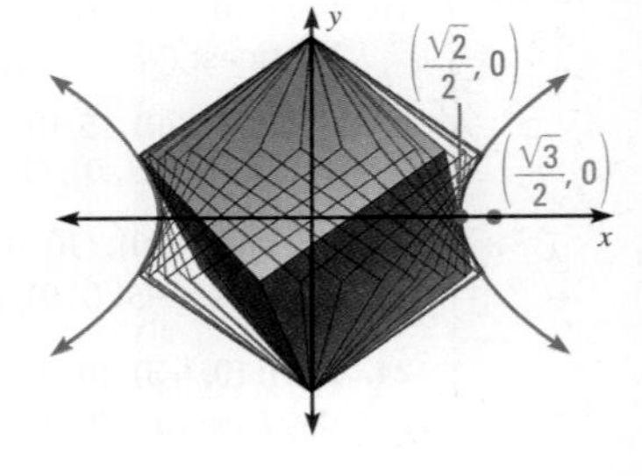

@HomeTutor for problem solving help at classzone.com

○ = WORKED-OUT SOLUTIONS on p. WS1 ★ = STANDARDIZED TEST PRACTICE ◆ = MULTIPLE REPRESENTATIONS

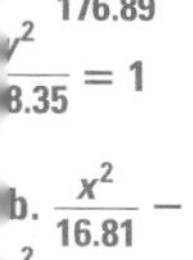

a. $\frac{x^2}{176.89} - \frac{y^2}{618.35} = 1$

b. $\frac{x^2}{16.81} - \frac{y^2}{608.19} = 1$

40. SUN'S SHADOW Each day, except at the fall and spring equinoxes, the tip of the shadow of a vertical pole traces a branch of a hyperbola across the ground. The diagram shows shadow paths for a 20 meter tall flagpole in Dallas, Texas.

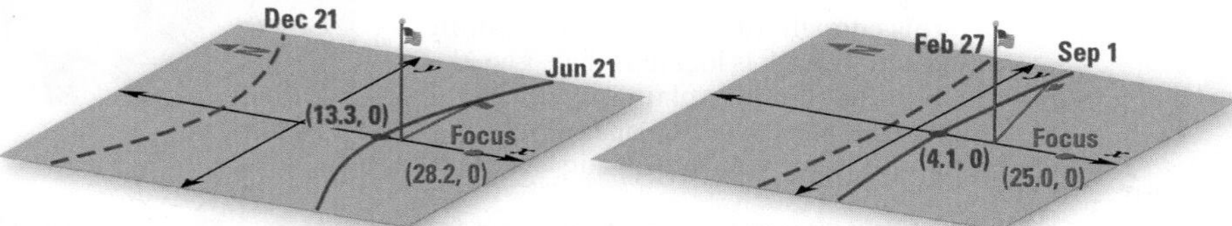

a. Write an equation of the hyperbola with center at the origin that models the June 21 path, given that $a = 13.3$ meters and $c = 28.2$ meters.

b. Write an equation of the hyperbola with center at the origin that models the September 1 path, given that $a = 4.1$ meters and $c = 25.0$ meters.

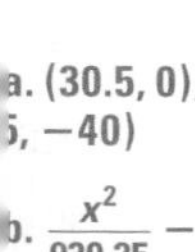

a. (30.5, 0), (85, −40)

b. $\frac{x^2}{930.25} - \frac{y^2}{1125.45} = 1$

c. about 54.6 ft

41. MULTI-STEP PROBLEM The roof of the St. Louis Science Center has a hyperbolic cross section with the dimensions shown.

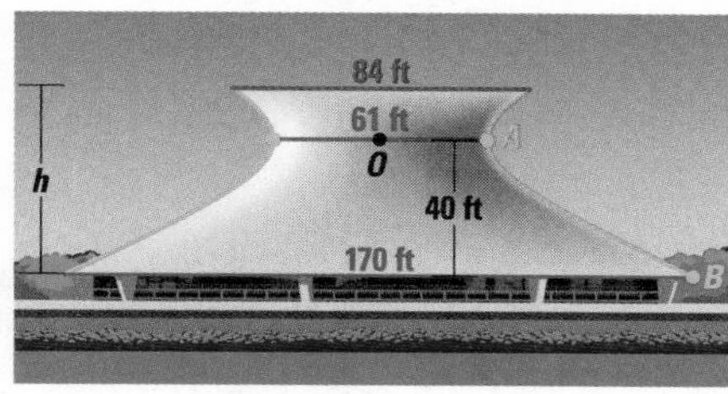

a. Suppose a coordinate grid is overlaid on the diagram with its origin at O, the center of the narrowest part of the roof. What are the coordinates of the points at A and B?

b. Use your answers from part (a) to write an equation that models the cross section.

c. Find the total height h of the roof.

B

42. MULTIPLE REPRESENTATIONS A circular walkway is to be built around a statue in a park. There is enough concrete available for the walkway to have an area of 600 square feet.

a. **Writing an Equation** Let the inside and outside radii of the walkway be x feet and y feet, respectively. Draw a diagram of the situation. Then write an equation relating x and y. $\pi y^2 - \pi x^2 = 600$

b. **Making a Table** Give four possible pairs of dimensions x and y that satisfy the equation from part (a). *Sample answer:* About (1, 13.9), (3, 14.1), (6, 15.1), (9, 16.5)

c. **Drawing a Graph** Graph the equation from part (a). What portion of the graph represents solutions that make sense in this situation?

c. See margin for c; the part of the hyperbola found in the first quadrant.

d. **Reasoning** How does the width of the walkway, $y - x$, change as both x and y increase? *Explain* why this makes sense. It gets smaller; since the area of concrete remains constant as the radii increases, the width decreases.

43. ★ SHORT RESPONSE Two stones dropped at the same time into still water produce circular ripples whose intersection points form hyperbolas with foci where the stones hit the water. The graph shows one hyperbola formed by stones dropped 12 feet apart with ripples at 1 foot intervals.

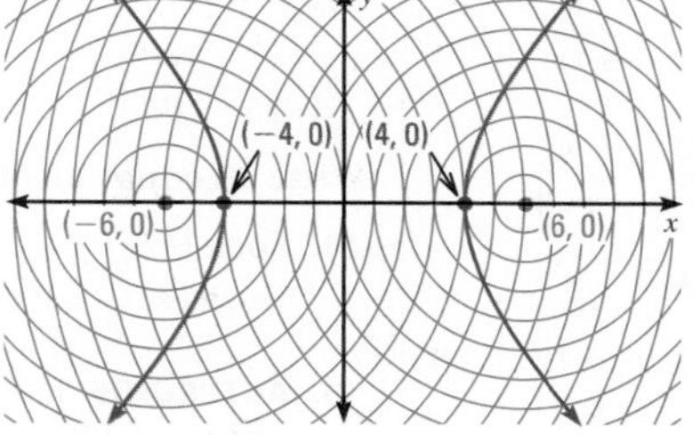

a. Write an equation of this hyperbola. $\frac{x^2}{16} - \frac{y^2}{20} = 1$

b. Use the definition of a hyperbola to explain why the graph shown is a hyperbola. (*Hint:* Examine the distances from each intersection point to the foci.) *Sample answer:* Choose any point on the graph and observe that the difference of the distances from that point and the foci remain constant.

Internet Reference

Exercise 41 More information about the St. Louis Science Center can be found at www.slsc.org

42c.

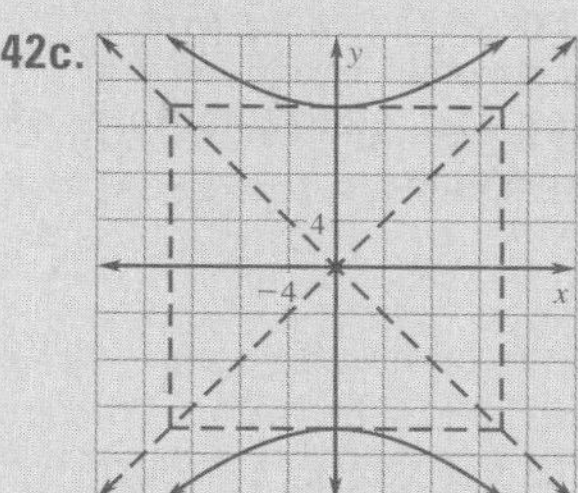

5 ASSESS AND RETEACH

Daily Homework Quiz

Transparency Available

1. Graph $\frac{x^2}{4} - \frac{y^2}{9} = 1$. Identify the vertices, foci, and asymptotes of the hyperbola.

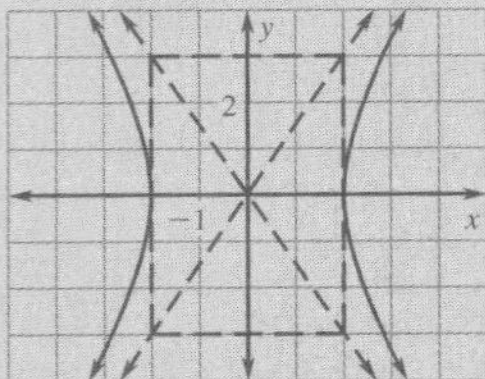

vertices: $(\pm 2, 0)$, foci: $(\pm\sqrt{13}, 0)$, asymptotes: $y = \pm\frac{3}{2}x$

A cylindrical lampshade casts two shadows on a wall. The outline of the shadows can be modeled by the region between the branches of a hyperbola for which $c = \pm 2$ and $a = \pm 1$ (in feet).

2. Write an equation for the hyperbola if the transverse axis is vertical. **$y^2 - \frac{x^2}{3} = 1$**
3. How wide is the shadow at the foci? **2 ft**

Online Quiz

Available at **classzone.com**

Diagnosis/Remediation

- Practice A, B, C in Chapter 9 Resource Book, pp. 50–52
- Study Guide in Chapter 9 Resource Book, pp. 53–54
- Practice Workbook, pp. 142–143
- @HomeTutor

Challenge

Additional challenge is available in the Chapter 9 Resource Book, p. 57.

Quiz

An easily-readable reduced copy of the quiz (with answers) on Lessons 9.4–9.5 from the Assessment Book can be found on p. 612E.

Quiz 1–3, 7–9. See Additional Answers beginning on p. AA1.

C **44. CHALLENGE** Two microphones placed 1 mile apart record the bugling of a bull elk. Microphone A receives the sound 2 seconds after microphone B. Sound travels at 1100 feet per second. Is this enough information to determine where the elk is located? If so, give the location. If not, explain why not.

No. *Sample answer:* Using microphones A and B as the foci, there is more than one location for the elk to be located.

KENTUCKY MIXED REVIEW

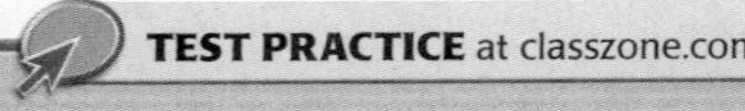

TEST PRACTICE at classzone.com

45. Which equation does the graph represent? **A**

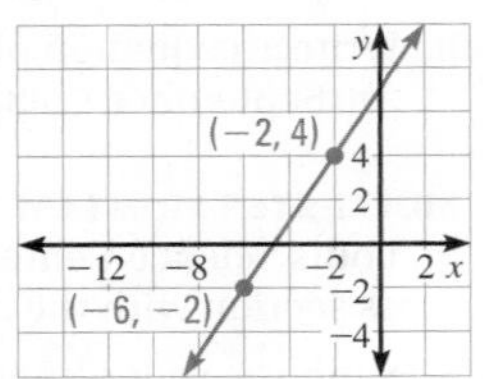

Ⓐ $-3x + 2y = 14$

Ⓑ $-2x + 3y = 6$

Ⓒ $2x + 3y = -18$

Ⓓ $3x + 2y = 1$

46. The endpoints of a diameter of a circle are $(-5, 8)$ and $(9, -3)$. What is the center of the circle? **C**

Ⓐ $\left(-8, \frac{17}{2}\right)$ Ⓑ $(2, 3)$ Ⓒ $\left(2, \frac{5}{2}\right)$ Ⓓ $\left(7, -\frac{11}{2}\right)$

QUIZ for Lessons 9.4–9.5

Graph the equation. Identify the vertices, co-vertices, and foci of the ellipse. *(p. 634)* **1–3. See margin for art.**

1. $\frac{x^2}{25} + \frac{y^2}{4} = 1$ **$(\pm 5, 0)$, $(0, \pm 2)$, $(\pm\sqrt{21}, 0)$**
2. $\frac{x^2}{16} + \frac{y^2}{49} = 1$ **$(0, \pm 7)$, $(\pm 4, 0)$, $(0, \pm\sqrt{33})$**
3. $36x^2 + 9y^2 = 324$ **$(0, \pm 6)$, $(\pm 3, 0)$, $(0, \pm 3\sqrt{3})$**

Write an equation of the ellipse with the given characteristics and center at (0, 0). *(p. 634)*

4. Vertex: $(0, 5)$ Co-vertex: $(-4, 0)$ **$\frac{x^2}{16} + \frac{y^2}{25} = 1$**
5. Vertex: $(10, 0)$ Focus: $(-8, 0)$ **$\frac{x^2}{100} + \frac{y^2}{36} = 1$**
6. Co-vertex: $(-\sqrt{15}, 0)$ Focus: $(0, -5)$ **$\frac{x^2}{15} + \frac{y^2}{40} = 1$**

Graph the equation. Identify the vertices, foci, and asymptotes of the hyperbola. *(p. 642)* **7–9. See margin for art.**

7. $\frac{y^2}{25} - \frac{x^2}{64} = 1$
8. $4x^2 - 16y^2 = 64$
9. $12y^2 - 20x^2 = 240$

7. $(0, \pm 5)$, $(0, \pm\sqrt{89})$; $y = \pm\frac{5}{8}x$

8. $(\pm 4, 0)$, $(\pm 2\sqrt{5}, 0)$; $y = \pm\frac{1}{2}x$

9. $(0, \pm 2\sqrt{5})$, $(0, \pm 4\sqrt{2})$; $y = \pm\frac{\sqrt{15}}{3}x$

Write an equation of the hyperbola with the given foci and vertices. *(p. 642)*

10. Foci: $(-5, 0)$, $(5, 0)$ Vertices: $(-2, 0)$, $(2, 0)$ **$\frac{x^2}{4} - \frac{y^2}{21} = 1$**
11. Foci: $(0, -3)$, $(0, 3)$ Vertices: $(0, -1)$, $(0, 1)$ **$y^2 - \frac{x^2}{8} = 1$**
12. Foci: $(-3\sqrt{6}, 0)$, $(3\sqrt{6}, 0)$ Vertices: $(-3, 0)$, $(3, 0)$ **$\frac{x^2}{9} - \frac{y^2}{45} =$**
13. **ASTEROIDS** The largest asteroid, 1 Ceres, ranges from 2.55 astronomical units to 2.98 astronomical units from the sun, which is located at one focus of the asteroid's elliptical orbit. Find a and c. Then write an equation of the orbit of 1 Ceres. *(p. 634)* **2.765, 0.215; $\frac{x^2}{7.645} + \frac{y^2}{7.599} = 1$**

EXTRA PRACTICE for Lesson 9.5, p. 1018

ONLINE QUIZ at classzone.com

9.6 Exploring Intersections of Planes and Cones

MATERIALS • flashlight • graph paper

How do a plane and a double-napped cone intersect to form different conic sections?

The reason that parabolas, circles, ellipses, and hyperbolas are called *conics* or *conic sections* is that each can be formed by the intersection of a plane and a double-napped cone, as shown below.

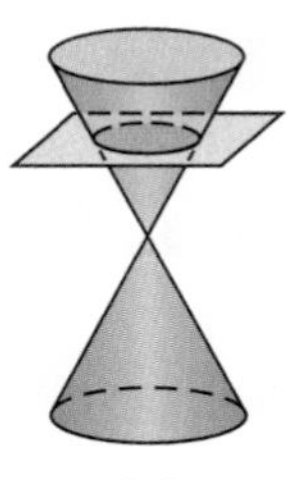
Circle

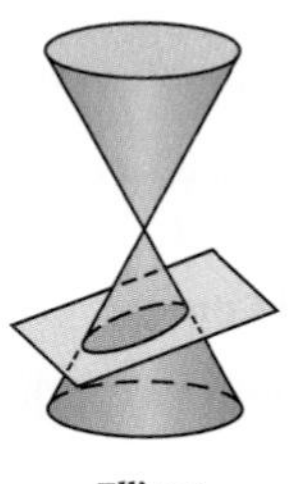
Ellipse

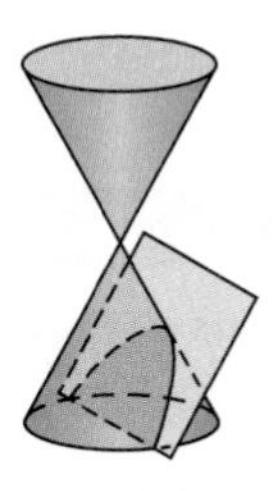
Parabola

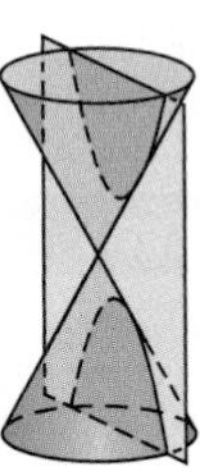
Hyperbola

EXPLORE **Find an equation of a conic**

***STEP 1* Draw axes**
Work in a group. On a piece of graph paper, draw x- and y-axes to make a coordinate plane. Then tape the paper to a wall.

***STEP 2* Model a circle**
Aim a flashlight perpendicular to the paper so that the light forms a circle centered on the origin of the coordinate plane. Trace the circle on the graph paper. Find the circle's radius, and use it to write the standard form of the circle's equation.

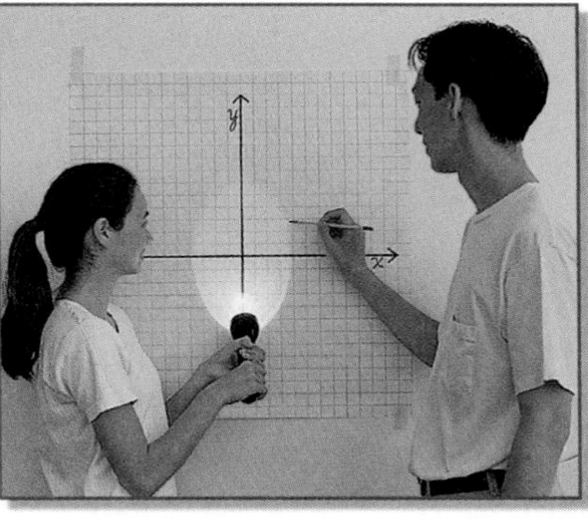

***STEP 3* Model an ellipse**
Tilt the flashlight, and aim it at the paper to form an ellipse with a vertical major axis and center at the origin. Trace the ellipse and write the standard form of its equation.

DRAW CONCLUSIONS **Use your observations to complete these exercises**

1. *Compare* the equations for your circle and for your ellipse with the equations of other groups. Are your equations all the same? Why or why not? **See margin.**
2. Refer to the diagram of a hyperbola to explain how you can orient the flashlight beam to form a branch of a hyperbola on the wall. ***Sample answer:* Hold the flashlight parallel to and against the wall.**

1 PLAN AND PREPARE

Explore the Concept
- Students will use a flashlight and graph paper to explore conics.
- This activity leads into the study of describing conic sections in Lesson 9.6.

Materials
Each group of students will need:
- a flashlight
- graph paper

Recommended Time
Work activity: 10 min
Discuss results: 5 min

Grouping
Students can work in groups of two, taking turns holding the flashlight and drawing the conic section. They should discuss how to write the equations.

2 TEACH

Alternative Strategy
Tape a large piece of graph paper to a wall and draw coordinates axes on it. Ask two students to hold the flashlight and draw the figures. Lead the class in a discussion of the equations. Then ask students to work in groups of two or three to answer the *Draw Conclusions* questions.

Key Discovery
The size and shape of a conic can be described in terms of how and where a plane intersects a cone.

3 ASSESS AND RETEACH

Suppose you slice a cone with a plane to produce a circle. How could you produce an ellipse with the same cone and plane? **Tilt the plane.**

1. No. *Sample answer:* The dimensions of the ellipse and circle depend on how far from the wall the flashlight was held.

1 PLAN AND PREPARE

Warm-Up Exercises

Transparency Available

Tell which conic section the equation describes.

1. $y = \frac{1}{4}x^2$ parabola
2. $x^2 + y^2 = 25$ circle
3. $\frac{x^2}{9} - \frac{y^2}{25} = 1$ hyperbola
4. $\frac{x^2}{25} + \frac{y^2}{9} = 1$ ellipse

Notetaking Guide

Transparency Available

Promotes interactive learning and notetaking skills, pp. 248–252.

Pacing

Basic: 2 days

Average: 2 days

Advanced: 2 days

Block: 0.5 block with 9.5
0.5 block with 9.7

- See *Teaching Guide/Lesson Plan.*

2 FOCUS AND MOTIVATE

Essential Question

Big Idea 1, p. 613

How do you identify and graph a conic if it is translated from the general equation for that conic?

Tell students they will learn how to answer this question by writing and analyzing equations of translated conics.

9.6 Translate and Classify Conic Sections

MA-HS-3.1.5

Before You graphed and wrote equations of conic sections.

Now You will translate conic sections.

Why? So you can model motion, as in Ex. 49.

Key Vocabulary
- conic sections (conics)
- general second-degree equation
- discriminant

MA-HS-3.1.5
Students will classify and apply properties of two-dimensional geometric figures (e.g., number of sides, vertices, length of sides, sum of interior and exterior angle measures). DOK 2

Because parabolas, circles, ellipses, and hyperbolas are formed when a plane intersects a double-napped cone, they are called **conic sections** or **conics**.

Previously, you studied equations of parabolas with vertices at the origin and equations of circles, ellipses, and hyperbolas with centers at the origin. Now you will study how translating conics in the coordinate plane affects their equations.

KEY CONCEPT *For Your Notebook*

Standard Form of Equations of Translated Conics

In the following equations, the point (h, k) is the *vertex* of the parabola and the *center* of the other conics.

Circle $(x - h)^2 + (y - k)^2 = r^2$

	Horizontal axis	Vertical axis
Parabola	$(y - k)^2 = 4p(x - h)$	$(x - h)^2 = 4p(y - k)$
Ellipse	$\frac{(x-h)^2}{a^2} + \frac{(y-k)^2}{b^2} = 1$	$\frac{(x-h)^2}{b^2} + \frac{(y-k)^2}{a^2} = 1$
Hyperbola	$\frac{(x-h)^2}{a^2} - \frac{(y-k)^2}{b^2} = 1$	$\frac{(y-k)^2}{a^2} - \frac{(x-h)^2}{b^2} = 1$

EXAMPLE 1 Graph the equation of a translated circle

Graph $(x - 2)^2 + (y + 3)^2 = 9$.

Solution

STEP 1 **Compare** the given equation to the standard form of an equation of a circle. You can see that the graph is a circle with center at $(h, k) = (2, -3)$ and radius $r = \sqrt{9} = 3$.

STEP 2 **Plot** the center. Then plot several points that are each 3 units from the center:

$(2 + 3, -3) = (5, -3)$ $\quad$ $(2 - 3, -3) = (-1, -3)$

$(2, -3 + 3) = (2, 0)$ $\quad$ $(2, -3 - 3) = (2, -6)$

STEP 3 **Draw** a circle through the points.

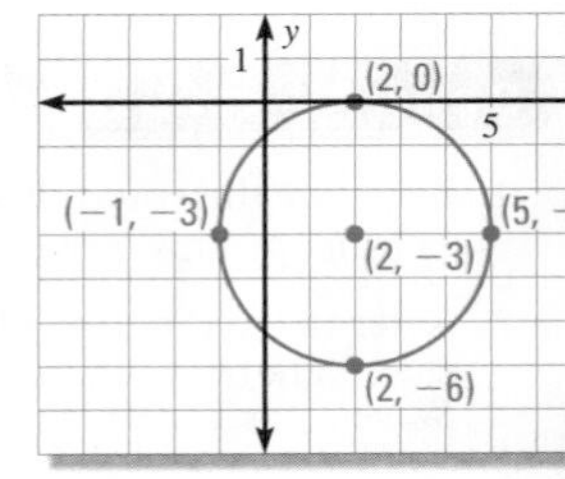

Resource Planning Guide

Chapter Resource Book
- Teaching Guide/Lesson Plan (pp. 58–59)
- Practice levels A, B, C (pp. 60–65)
- Study Guide (pp. 66–67)
- Catch-up for Absent Students (p. 68)
- Application (p. 69)
- Challenge (p. 70)

Workbooks
- Notetaking Guide (pp. 248–252)
- Practice Workbook (pp. 144–146)

Teaching Options
- **Power Presentations CD-ROM** provides dynamic electronic teaching resources for the classroom.
- **Activity Generator CD-ROM** provides editable activities for all ability levels.

Interactive Technology
- Easy Planner
- Power Presentations CD-ROM
- Activity Generator CD-ROM
- Animated Algebra
- Test Generator CD-ROM
- Online Quiz
- eWorkbook
- eEdition
- @HomeTutor

Resources for English Learners
- Quick Reference for English Learners
- Spanish Study Guide
- Multi-Language Visual Glossary
- Student Resources in Spanish

See also the *Algebra 2 Toolkit* for more strategies for meeting individual needs.

EXAMPLE 2 Graph the equation of a translated hyperbola

Graph $\frac{(y-3)^2}{4} - \frac{(x+1)^2}{9} = 1$.

Solution

STEP 1 **Compare** the given equation to the standard forms of equations of hyperbolas. The equation's form tells you that the graph is a hyperbola with a vertical transverse axis. The center is at $(h, k) = (-1, 3)$. Because $a^2 = 4$ and $b^2 = 9$, you know that $a = 2$ and $b = 3$.

STEP 2 **Plot** the center, vertices, and foci. The vertices lie $a = 2$ units above and below the center, at $(-1, 5)$ and $(-1, 1)$. Because $c^2 = a^2 + b^2 = 13$, the foci lie $c = \sqrt{13} \approx 3.6$ units above and below the center, at $(-1, 6.6)$ and $(-1, -0.6)$.

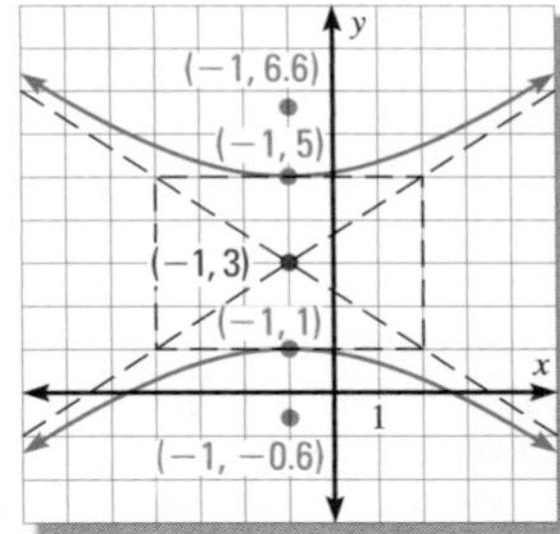

STEP 3 **Draw** the hyperbola. Draw a rectangle centered at $(-1, 3)$ that is $2a = 4$ units high and $2b = 6$ units wide. Draw the asymptotes through the opposite corners of the rectangle. Then draw the hyperbola passing through the vertices and approaching the asymptotes.

LVE FOR Y
plot additional points the hyperbola, solve y to obtain
$= 3 \pm 2\sqrt{1 + \frac{(x+1)^2}{9}}$.
en make a table of ues.

Animated Algebra at classzone.com

✓ GUIDED PRACTICE for Examples 1 and 2

Graph the equation. Identify the important characteristics of the graph.

1–4. See margin for art.

1. $(x + 1)^2 + (y - 3)^2 = 4$
2. $(x - 2)^2 = 8(y + 3)$
3. $(x + 3)^2 - \frac{(y-4)^2}{4} = 1$
4. $\frac{(x-2)^2}{16} + \frac{(y-1)^2}{9} = 1$

ircle with center , 3) and radius 2
arabola with vertex −3), focus (2, −1), ctrix $y = -5$
yperbola with tices (−4, 4) and , 4), asymptotes $2x + 10$ $y = -2x - 2$
llipse with center), vertices (6, 1) and , 1) and co-vertices) and (2, −2)

EXAMPLE 3 Write an equation of a translated parabola

Write an equation of the parabola whose vertex is at $(-2, 3)$ and whose focus is at $(-4, 3)$.

Solution

STEP 1 **Determine** the form of the equation. Begin by making a rough sketch of the parabola. Because the focus is to the left of the vertex, the parabola opens to the left, and its equation has the form $(y - k)^2 = 4p(x - h)$ where $p < 0$.

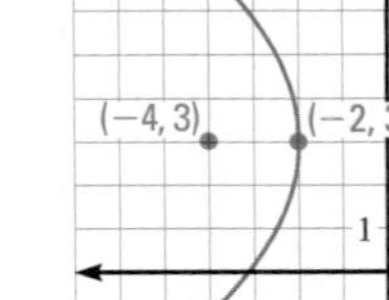

STEP 2 **Identify** h and k. The vertex is at $(-2, 3)$, so $h = -2$ and $k = 3$.

STEP 3 **Find** p. The vertex $(-2, 3)$ and focus $(-4, 3)$ both lie on the line $y = 3$, so the distance between them is $|p| = |-4 - (-2)| = 2$, and thus $p = \pm 2$. Because $p < 0$, it follows that $p = -2$, so $4p = -8$.

▶ The standard form of the equation is $(y - 3)^2 = -8(x + 2)$.

Motivating the Lesson

Have students write the equation of a circle with vertex (0, 0) and radius 3 and then graph the equation on graph paper. Then ask them to translate the graph 2 units up and 3 units right. Have them discuss the relationship between the two circles and determine the center and radius of the translated circle.

3 TEACH

Extra Example 1

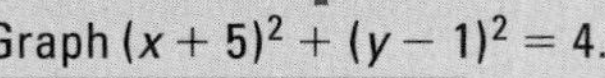

Graph $(x + 5)^2 + (y - 1)^2 = 4$.

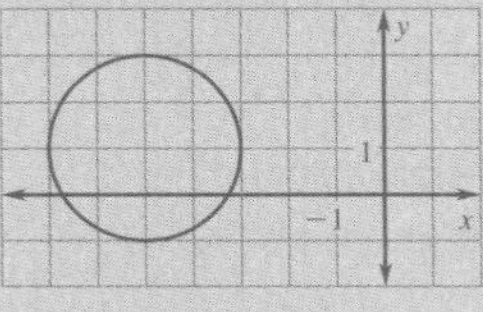

Extra Example 2

Graph $\frac{(x+2)^2}{9} - \frac{(y-1)^2}{16} = 1$.

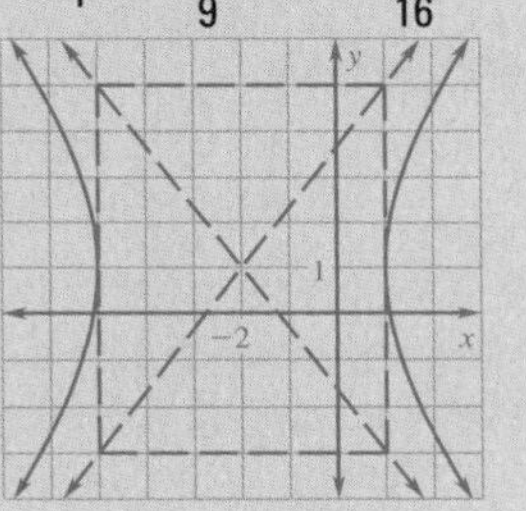

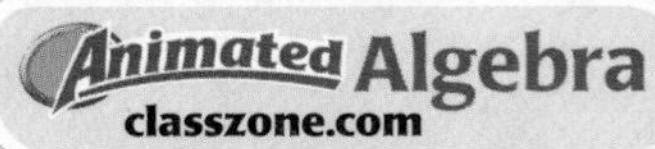

An **Animated Algebra** activity is available on-line for **Example 2**. This activity is also available on the **Power Presentations CD-ROM**.

Extra Example 3

Write the equation of a parabola whose vertex is at (4, −2) and whose focus is at (4, 1).
$(x - 4)^2 = 12(y + 2)$

1–4. See Additional Answers beginning on p. AA1.

Extra Example 4

Write the equation of an ellipse with foci at (3, 5) and (3, −1) and co-vertices at (1, 2) and (5, 2). $\frac{(x-3)^2}{4}+\frac{(y-2)^2}{13}=1$

Extra Example 5

Identify the line(s) of symmetry for each conic section in Extra Examples 1 through 4. **Extra Example 1 involves a circle, so any line through the center (−5, 1) is a line of symmetry. Extra Example 2 involves a hyperbola. The center is (−2, 1), so $x = -2$ and $y = 1$ are lines of symmetry. Extra Example 3 involves a parabola with a vertical axis, so that axis, $x = 4$, is a line of symmetry. Extra Example 4 involves an ellipse with center (3, 2), so $x = 3$ and $y = 2$ are lines of symmetry.**

Key Questions to Ask for Example 5

- What are the general forms of the lines of symmetry for a hyperbola? **$x = h$ and $y = k$**
- What are the general forms of the lines of symmetry for a parabola? **If the parabola opens up or down, $x = h$ is a line of symmetry. If the parabola opens left or right, $y = k$ is a line of symmetry.**
- What are the general forms of the lines of symmetry for an ellipse? **$x = h$ and $y = k$**

EXAMPLE 4 Write an equation of a translated ellipse

Write an equation of the ellipse with foci at (1, 2) and (7, 2) and co-vertices at (4, 0) and (4, 4).

Solution

STEP 1 **Determine** the form of the equation. First sketch the ellipse. The foci lie on the major axis, so the axis is horizontal. The equation has this form:

$$\frac{(x-h)^2}{a^2}+\frac{(y-k)^2}{b^2}=1$$

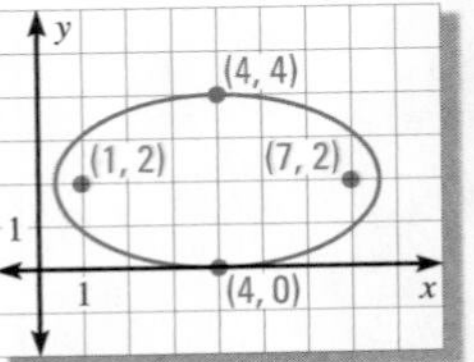

STEP 2 **Identify** h and k by finding the center, which is halfway between the foci (or the co-vertices).

$$(h, k)=\left(\frac{1+7}{2}, \frac{2+2}{2}\right)=(4, 2)$$

FIND DISTANCE
The co-vertices lie on a vertical line through the center and the foci lie on a horizontal line through the center, so you do not have to use the distance formula.

STEP 3 **Find** b, the distance between a co-vertex and the center (4, 2), and c, the distance between a focus and the center. Choose the co-vertex (4, 4) and the focus (1, 2): $b = |4-2| = 2$ and $c = |1-4| = 3$.

STEP 4 **Find** a. For an ellipse, $a^2 = b^2 + c^2 = 2^2 + 3^2 = 13$, so $a = \sqrt{13}$.

▶ The standard form of the equation is $\frac{(x-4)^2}{13}+\frac{(y-2)^2}{4}=1$.

EXAMPLE 5 Identify symmetries of conic sections

Identify the line(s) of symmetry for each conic section in Examples 1–4.

Solution

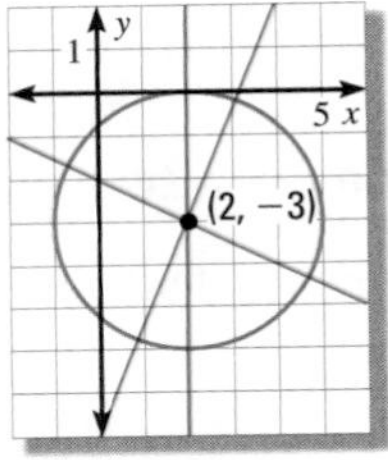

For the circle in Example 1, any line through the center (2, −3) is a line of symmetry.

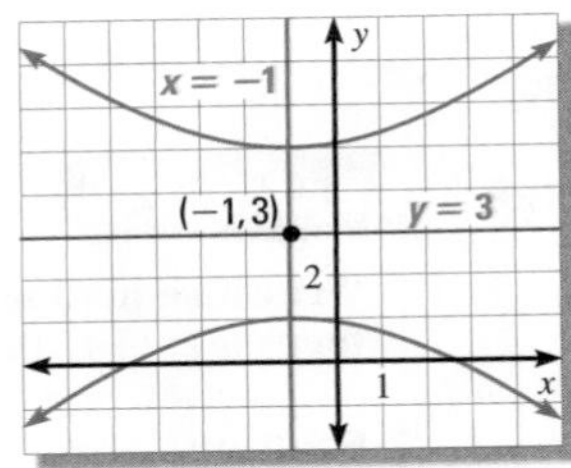

For the hyperbola in Example 2, $x = -1$ and $y = 3$ are lines of symmetry.

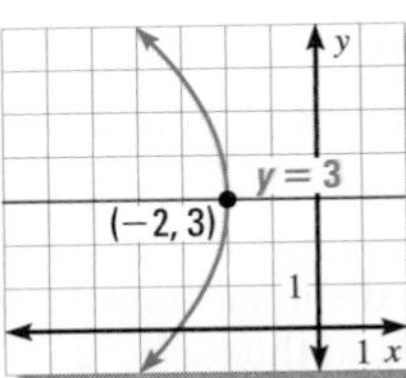

For the parabola in Example 3, $y = 3$ is a line of symmetry.

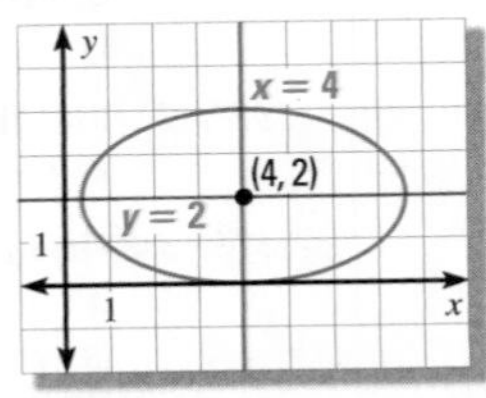

For the ellipse in Example 4, $x = 4$ and $y = 2$ are lines of symmetry.

✓ **GUIDED PRACTICE** for Examples 3, 4, and 5

Write an equation of the conic section.

5. Parabola with vertex at (3, −1) and focus at (3, 2) $(x-3)^2 = 12(y+1)$
6. Hyperbola with vertices at (−7, 3) and (−1, 3) and foci at (−9, 3) and (1, 3) $\frac{(x+4)^2}{9} - \frac{(y-3)^2}{16} = 1$

Identify the line(s) of symmetry for the conic section.

7. $\frac{(x-5)^2}{64} + \frac{y^2}{16} = 1$ $x = 5, y = 0$
8. $(x+5)^2 = 8(y-2)$ $x = -5$
9. $\frac{(x-1)^2}{49} - \frac{(y-2)^2}{121} = 1$ $x = 1, y = 2$

KEY CONCEPT *For Your Notebook*

Classifying Conics Using Their Equations

Any conic can be described by a **general second-degree equation** in x and y: $Ax^2 + Bxy + Cy^2 + Dx + Ey + F = 0$. The expression $B^2 - 4AC$ is the **discriminant** of the equation and can be used to identify the type of conic.

Discriminant	Type of Conic
$B^2 - 4AC < 0$, $B = 0$, and $A = C$	Circle
$B^2 - 4AC < 0$ and either $B \neq 0$ or $A \neq C$	Ellipse
$B^2 - 4AC = 0$	Parabola
$B^2 - 4AC > 0$	Hyperbola

If $B = 0$, each axis of the conic is horizontal or vertical.

EXAMPLE 6 Classify a conic

Classify the conic given by $4x^2 + y^2 - 8x - 8 = 0$. Then graph the equation.

Solution

Note that $A = 4$, $B = 0$, and $C = 1$, so the value of the discriminant is:

$$B^2 - 4AC = 0^2 - 4(4)(1) = -16$$

Because $B^2 - 4AC < 0$ and $A \neq C$, the conic is an ellipse.

COMPLETE THE SQUARE For help with completing the square, see p. 284.

To graph the ellipse, first complete the square in x.

$$4x^2 + y^2 - 8x - 8 = 0$$
$$(4x^2 - 8x) + y^2 = 8$$
$$4(x^2 - 2x) + y^2 = 8$$
$$4(x^2 - 2x + ?) + y^2 = 8 + 4(?)$$
$$4(x^2 - 2x + 1) + y^2 = 8 + 4(1)$$
$$4(x-1)^2 + y^2 = 12$$
$$\frac{(x-1)^2}{3} + \frac{y^2}{12} = 1$$

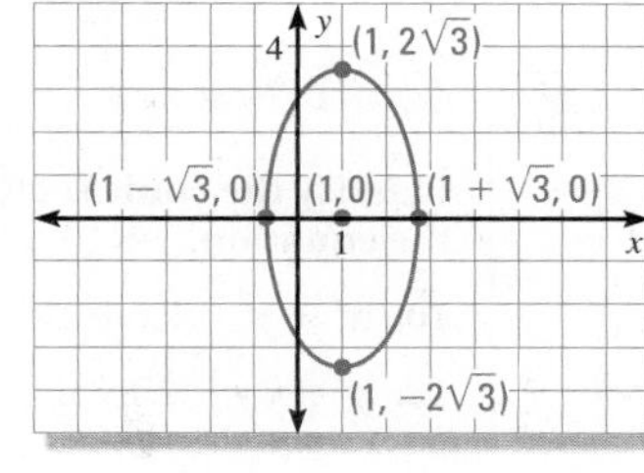

From the equation, you can see that $(h, k) = (1, 0)$, $a = \sqrt{12} = 2\sqrt{3}$, and $b = \sqrt{3}$. Use these facts to draw the ellipse.

Extra Example 6

Classify the conic given by $x - 3 = \frac{1}{2}(y-2)^2$. Then graph the equation.

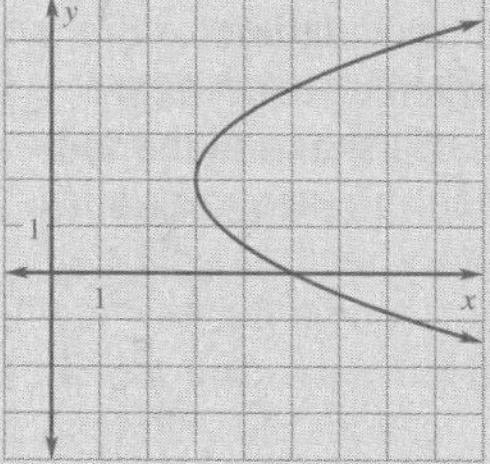

parabola

Avoiding Common Errors

In Example 6, students may forget that the coefficients of the x^2 and y^2 terms must be 1 before they can complete the squares in x and y.

Differentiated Instruction

Inclusion Some students learn better by seeing concrete examples in organized tables. Have students expand on the information given in the Key Concept box by choosing values for A, B, and C and creating a table listing each equation, discriminant, and type of conic. Suggest that students also include a sketch with each entry.

See also the *Algebra 2 Toolkit* for more strategies.

Extra Example 7

You are walking into a tunnel whose opening can be modeled by the equation $9x^2 + 16y^2 - 18x + 64y - 71 = 0$. Write an equation for the curve of the opening in standard form. What is the shape of the tunnel opening? Graph the equation.

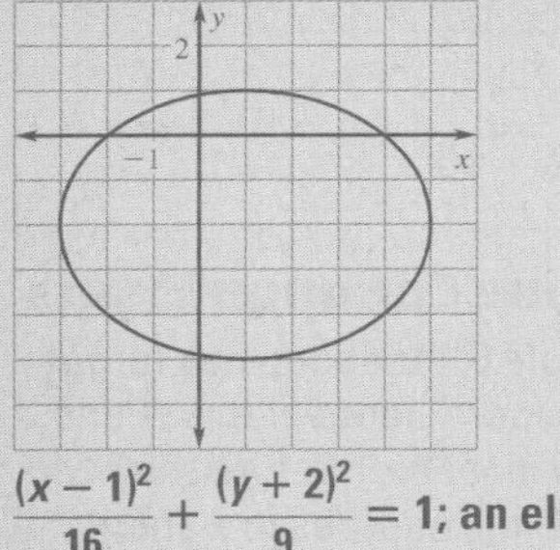

$\frac{(x-1)^2}{16} + \frac{(y+2)^2}{9} = 1$; an ellipse

Closing the Lesson

Have students summarize the major points of the lesson and answer the Essential Question: How do you identify and graph a conic if it is translated from the general equation for that conic?

- **Let (h, k) be the center of a translated circle, ellipse, or hyperbola. To write the standard form of the equations of the translated conics, use the standard form of equations for the conics with center $(0, 0)$. Replace every occurrence of x with $(x - h)$ and every occurrence of y with $(y - k)$.**
- **A circle has an infinite number of lines of symmetry through its center. A parabola has one line of symmetry, which is its axis of symmetry. An ellipse has two perpendicular lines of symmetry, one through its vertices and the other through its co-vertices. A hyperbola has two perpendicular lines of symmetry that intersect in the center of the hyperbola.**
- **You can identify a conic section by its discriminant.**

Classify the conic by its discriminant. Complete the square if necessary to write the general equation in standard form. Use the values of h and k to translate the center and other points of the conic.

EXAMPLE 7 Solve a multi-step problem

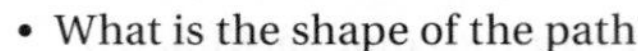

PHYSICAL SCIENCE In a lab experiment, you record images of a steel ball rolling past a magnet. The equation $16x^2 - 9y^2 - 96x + 36y - 36 = 0$ models the ball's path.

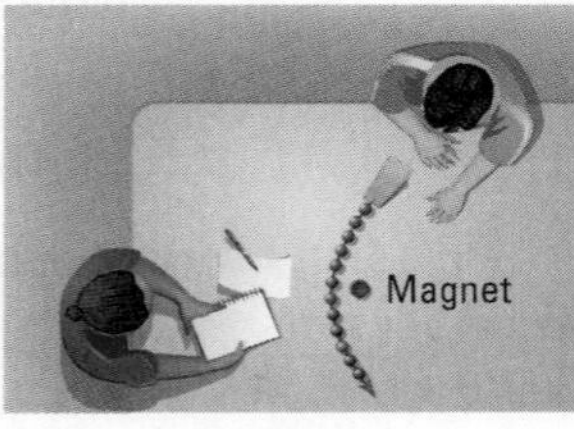

- What is the shape of the path?
- Write an equation for the path in standard form.
- Graph the equation of the path.

Solution

STEP 1 **Identify** the shape. The equation is a general second-degree equation with $A = 16$, $B = 0$, and $C = -9$. Find the value of the discriminant.

$$B^2 - 4AC = 0^2 - 4(16)(-9) = 576$$

Because $B^2 - 4AC > 0$, the shape of the path is a hyperbola.

STEP 2 **Write** an equation. To write an equation of the hyperbola, complete the square in both x and y simultaneously.

AVOID ERRORS
To complete the square in two variables, you must add a quantity to or subtract a quantity from each side for *each* variable.

$$16x^2 - 9y^2 - 96x + 36y - 36 = 0$$
$$(16x^2 - 96x) - (9y^2 - 36y) = 36$$
$$16(x^2 - 6x + ?) - 9(y^2 - 4y + ?) = 36 + 16(?) - 9(?)$$
$$16(x^2 - 6x + 9) - 9(y^2 - 4y + 4) = 36 + 16(9) - 9(4)$$
$$16(x - 3)^2 - 9(y - 2)^2 = 144$$
$$\frac{(x-3)^2}{9} - \frac{(y-2)^2}{16} = 1$$

STEP 3 **Graph** the equation. From the equation, the transverse axis is horizontal, $(h, k) = (3, 2)$, $a = \sqrt{9} = 3$, and $b = \sqrt{16} = 4$. The vertices are at $(3 \pm a, 2)$, or $(6, 2)$ and $(0, 2)$.

Plot the center and vertices. Then draw a rectangle $2a = 6$ units wide and $2b = 8$ units high centered at $(3, 2)$, draw the asymptotes, and draw the hyperbola.

Notice that the path of the ball is modeled by just the right-hand branch of the hyperbola.

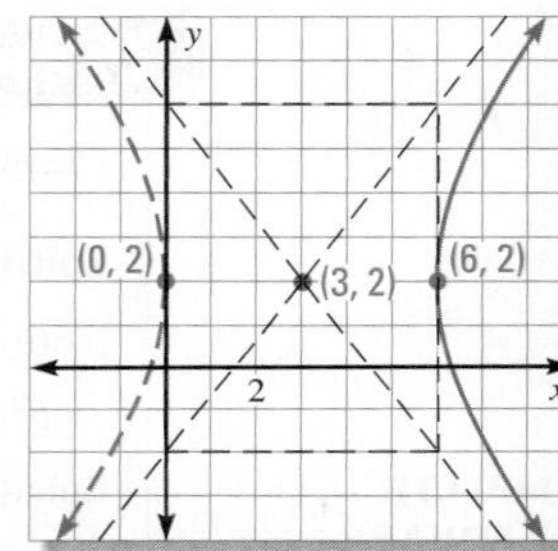

10. circle, $(x - 1)^2 + (y + 2)^2 = 4$

11. ellipse, $\frac{(x-1)^2}{3} + \frac{y^2}{6} = 1$

12. parabola, $(y - 2)^2 = 2(x - 1)$

13. hyperbola, $\frac{(x-2)^2}{4} - \frac{(y+2)^2}{16} = 1$

14. ellipse, $\frac{(x-1.5)^2}{6.25} + \frac{y^2}{4} = 1$; see margin for art.

✓ GUIDED PRACTICE for Examples 6 and 7

Classify the conic section and write its equation in standard form. Then graph the equation. 10–13. See margin for art.

10. $x^2 + y^2 - 2x + 4y + 1 = 0$

11. $2x^2 + y^2 - 4x - 4 = 0$

12. $y^2 - 4y - 2x + 6 = 0$

13. $4x^2 - y^2 - 16x - 4y - 4 = 0$

14. ASTRONOMY An asteroid's path is modeled by $4x^2 + 6.25y^2 - 12x - 16 = 0$ where x and y are in astronomical units from the sun. Classify the path and write its equation in standard form. Then graph the equation.

10–13. See Additional Answers beginning on p. AA1.

14.

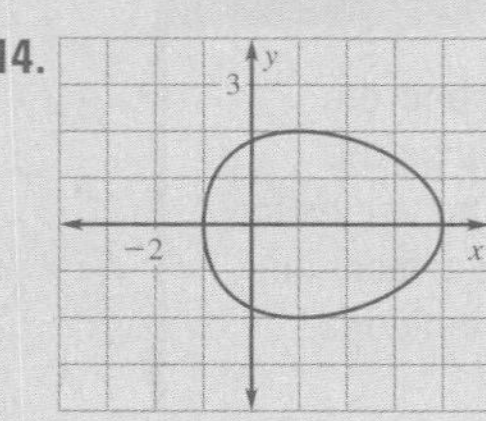

9.6 EXERCISES

HOMEWORK KEY
○ = **WORKED-OUT SOLUTIONS** on p. WS17 for Exs. 3, 19, and 49
★ = **STANDARDIZED TEST PRACTICE** Exs. 2, 12, 36, 45, 51, and 52

SKILL PRACTICE

A

1. **VOCABULARY** *Explain* why circles, ellipses, parabolas, and hyperbolas are called conic sections. **The intersection of a plane and a double-napped cone form them.**
2. ★ **WRITING** *Explain* how the discriminant of a general second-degree equation can be used to identify what conic the equation represents. **See margin.**

EXAMPLES 1 and 2 on pp. 650–651 for Exs. 3–12

GRAPHING **Graph the equation. Identify the important characteristics of the graph.** **3–11. See margin.**

3. $(x + 4)^2 = -8(y - 2)$
4. $(x - 2)^2 + (y - 7)^2 = 9$
5. $\frac{(x - 6)^2}{25} - (y + 1)^2 = 1$
6. $\frac{(y + 4)^2}{49} - \frac{(x + 8)^2}{9} = 1$
7. $\frac{(x + 2)^2}{16} + \frac{(y - 2)^2}{36} = 1$
8. $(x - 5)^2 + (y + 1)^2 = 64$
9. $(y - 1)^2 = 4(x + 6)$
10. $\frac{x^2}{25} + \frac{(y - 2)^2}{4} = 1$
11. $\frac{(x + 3)^2}{9} - \frac{(y - 4)^2}{16} = 1$

12. ★ **MULTIPLE CHOICE** What are the coordinates of the co-vertices of the ellipse with equation $\frac{(x - 4)^2}{16} + \frac{(y - 1)^2}{4} = 1$? **C**

Ⓐ (0, 1), (8, 1) Ⓑ (−8, 1), (0, 1) Ⓒ (4, 3), (4, −1) Ⓓ (−4, 3), (−4, −1)

EXAMPLES 3 and 4 on pp. 651–652 for Exs. 13–21

WRITING EQUATIONS **Write an equation of the conic section.**

13. Circle with center at (−5, 1) and radius 6 $(x + 5)^2 + (y - 1)^2 = 36$
14. Circle with center at (9, −1) and radius 2 $(x - 9)^2 + (y + 1)^2 = 4$
15. Parabola with vertex at (−4, −3) and focus at (1, −3) $(y + 3)^2 = 20(x + 4)$
16. Parabola with vertex at (5, 3) and directrix $y = 6$ $(x - 5)^2 = -12(y - 3)$
17. Ellipse with vertices at (−3, 4) and (5, 4) and foci at (−1, 4) and (3, 4) $\frac{(x - 1)^2}{16} + \frac{(y - 4)^2}{12} = 1$
18. Ellipse with vertices at (−2, 1) and (−2, 9) and co-vertices at (−4, 5) and (0, 5)
19. Hyperbola with vertices at (6, −3) and (6, 1) and foci at (6, −6) and (6, 4) **18, 19. See margin.**
20. Hyperbola with vertices at (1, 7) and (7, 7) and foci at (−1, 7) and (9, 7) $\frac{(x - 4)^2}{9} - \frac{(y - 7)^2}{16} = 1$

21. **ERROR ANALYSIS** *Describe* and correct the error in writing an equation of the ellipse with vertices at (−7, 3) and (3, 3) and co-vertices at (−2, 6) and (−2, 0). **The center is at (−2, 3), not (2, −3);** $\frac{(x + 2)^2}{25} + \frac{(y - 3)^2}{9} = 1.$

> Axis is horizontal; (h, k) = (−2, 3);
> $a = |-7 - (-2)| = 5$; $b = |6 - 3| = 3$;
> Equation: $\frac{(x - 2)^2}{25} + \frac{(y + 3)^2}{9} = 1$ ✗

EXAMPLE 5 on p. 652 for Exs. 22–27

LINES OF SYMMETRY **Identify the line(s) of symmetry for the conic section.**

22. $\frac{(x + 5)^2}{49} + \frac{(y - 2)^2}{16} = 1$ $x = -5, y = 2$
23. $(y - 4)^2 = 6(x + 6)$ $y = 4$
24. $\frac{(x - 1)^2}{36} - \frac{(y - 2)^2}{9} = 1$ $x = 1, y = 2$
25. $(y - 5)^2 - \frac{(x - 3)^2}{9} = 1$ $x = 3, y = 5$
26. $(x + 3)^2 = 10(y - 1)$ $x = -3$
27. $(x + 2)^2 + (y + 1)^2 = 121$ **any line passing through the point (−2, −1)**

If $B^2 - 4AC < 0$ where $B = 0$ and $A = C$, then it is a circle. If $B^2 - 4AC < 0$ and $B \neq 0$ or $A \neq C$, then it is an ellipse. If $B^2 - 4AC = 0$, then it is a parabola. If $B^2 - 4AC > 0$, then it is a hyperbola.

3–11. See Additional Answers beginning on p. AA1.

18. $\frac{(x + 2)^2}{4} + \frac{(y - 5)^2}{16} = 1$

19. $\frac{(y + 1)^2}{4} - \frac{(x - 6)^2}{21} = 1$

4 PRACTICE AND APPLY

Assignment Guide

Answer Transparencies available for all exercises

Basic:
Day 1: EP p. 1013 Exs. 41–44
pp. 655–657
Exs. 1–8, 12, 13–21 odd, 48
Day 2: pp. 655–657
Exs. 22–36 even, 37–39, 49–51, 54–55

Average:
Day 1: pp. 655–657
Exs. 1, 2, 5–9, 12, 14–20 even, 21, 48
Day 2: pp. 655–657
Exs. 23–35 odd, 36–44 even, 45, 49–52, 54–55

Advanced:
Day 1: pp. 655–657
Exs. 1, 2, 6–12, 14–20 even, 21, 48
Day 2: pp. 655–657
Exs. 25–27, 32–36, 41–47*, 49–53*, 54

Block:
pp. 655–657
Exs. 1, 2, 5–9, 12, 14–20 even, 21, 48 (with 9.5)
pp. 655–657
Exs. 23–35 odd, 36–44 even, 45, 49–52, 54–55 (with 9.7)

Differentiated Instruction

See *Algebra 2 Best Practices Toolkit* for suggestions on addressing the needs of a diverse classroom.

Homework Check

For a quick check of student understanding of key concepts, go over the following exercises:
Basic: 6, 15, 22, 30, 49
Average: 8, 16, 25, 33, 50
Advanced: 10, 18, 26, 41, 50

Extra Practice

- Student Edition, p. 1018
- Chapter 9 Resource Book: Practice levels A, B, C, pp. 60–65

Practice Worksheet

An easily-readable reduced practice page (with answers) for this lesson can be found on p. 612D.

Mathematical Reasoning

Exercise 53 For each diagram, ask students to describe how the degenerate conic is related to each of the other conics that are formed. For example, in Diagram 1 the degenerate conic is a point, and that point (when viewed from above) is the center of each circle. In Diagram 2 the degenerate conic (viewed from the front), which appears to be an X, forms the asymptotes of the hyperbolas. In Diagram 3, the degenerate conic is an "element" of the cone, or a line on the cone that contains the point where the two cones touch.

37–44. See Additional Answers beginning on p. AA1.

45. If the non-zero coefficients of x^2 and y^2 are the same, it's a circle. If the non-zero coefficients of x^2 and y^2 are both positive and different, it's an ellipse. If one of the non-zero coefficients of x^2 or y^2 is negative and the other one is positive, it's a hyperbola. If one of the coefficients of x^2 or y^2 is zero, it's a parabola.

50.

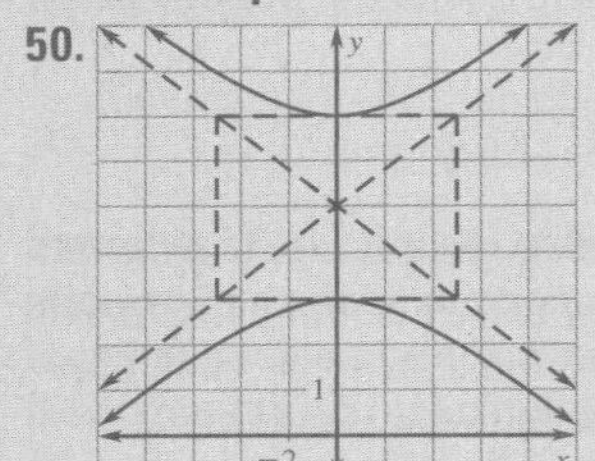

EXAMPLE 6 B
on p. 653
for Exs. 28–36

CLASSIFYING CONICS **Use the discriminant to classify the conic section.**

28. $6x^2 - 2y^2 + 24x + 2y - 1 = 0$ **hyperbola**

29. $x^2 + y^2 - 10x - 6y + 18 = 0$ **circle**

30. $y^2 - 10y - 5x + 57 = 0$ **parabola**

31. $4x^2 + y^2 - 48x - 14y + 189 = 0$ **ellipse**

32. $9x^2 + 4y^2 + 8y + 18x - 41 = 0$ **ellipse**

33. $x^2 - 18x + 6y + 99 = 0$ **parabola**

34. $x^2 + y^2 - 6x + 8y - 24 = 0$ **circle**

35. $8x^2 - 9y^2 - 40x + 4y + 145 = 0$ **hyperbola**

36. ★ **MULTIPLE CHOICE** The equation $4x^2 + y^2 + 32x - 10y + 85 = 0$ represents what conic section? **B**

Ⓐ Circle Ⓑ Ellipse Ⓒ Hyperbola Ⓓ Parabola

EXAMPLES 6 and 7
on pp. 653–654
for Exs. 37–44

CLASSIFYING AND GRAPHING **Classify the conic section and write its equation in standard form. Then graph the equation.** **37–44. See margin.**

37. $x^2 + y^2 - 14x + 4y - 11 = 0$

38. $x^2 + 4y^2 - 10x + 16y + 37 = 0$

39. $x^2 - 16x - 8y + 80 = 0$

40. $9y^2 - x^2 - 54y + 8x + 56 = 0$

41. $9x^2 + 4y^2 - 36x - 24y + 36 = 0$

42. $y^2 + 14y + 16x + 33 = 0$

43. $x^2 + y^2 + 16x - 8y + 16 = 0$

44. $x^2 - 4y^2 + 8x - 24y - 24 = 0$

45. ★ **SHORT RESPONSE** Consider a general second-degree equation where $B = 0$. *Explain* how you can classify the equation's graph without graphing or using the discriminant. **See margin.**

C

46. **REASONING** In Chapter 8, you graphed hyperbolas with equations of the form $y = \frac{a}{x}$. Write $y = \frac{a}{x}$ as a general second-degree equation, and use the discriminant to show that the graph is a hyperbola. **$xy = a$, $B^2 - 4AC = 1^2 - 4(0)(0) = 1$**

47. **CHALLENGE** Find expressions in terms of c, h, and k for the coordinates of the foci of a hyperbola with a vertical transverse axis and center (h, k). Then find equations of the asymptotes in terms of a, b, h, and k.
$(h, k \pm c)$; $y = \frac{a}{b}x + \left(\frac{bk - ah}{b}\right)$, $y = -\frac{a}{b}x + \left(\frac{bk + ah}{b}\right)$

PROBLEM SOLVING

EXAMPLES A **3 and 4**
on pp. 651–652
for Ex. 48

48. **ICE SKATING** A figure skater practices skating figure eights, which are formed by etching two externally tangent circles in the ice. Write equations for the circles in a figure eight if each is 8 feet in diameter, the circles intersect at the origin, and the centers of the circles are on the y-axis.

@HomeTutor for problem solving help at classzone.com

EXAMPLES 6 and 7
on pp. 653–654
for Exs. 49–50

49. **JUMPING STILTS** The leap of a person wearing "jumping stilts" is modeled by $x^2 - 10x + 4y = 0$ where x and y are in feet and the origin marks the start of the leap. Write an equation in standard form for the path of the leap. How high and how far does the person jump? **$(x - 5)^2 = -4\left(y - \frac{25}{4}\right)$; $6\frac{1}{4}$ ft, 10 ft**

@HomeTutor for problem solving help at classzone.com

50. **SPACECRAFT** A spacecraft uses Saturn's gravitational force to "slingshot" around the planet on the path $21y^2 - 210y - 4x^2 = -441$, where the origin represents Saturn's center and x and y are in hundreds of thousands of kilometers. What is the shape of the path? Write an equation in standard form for the path. Then graph the equation. **Hyperbola; $\frac{(y - 5)^2}{4} - \frac{x^2}{21} = 1$; see margin for art.**

○ = **WORKED-OUT SOLUTIONS on p. WS1** ★ = **STANDARDIZED TEST PRACTICE**

$- 100)^2 +$
$- 60)^2 \le 150^2$,
$- 80)^2 +$
$- 70)^2 \le 100^2$

. See margin art; one; the tance from r position to hotel is less n the radius he hotel's smitter, but are about feet from café's smitter ich is out ange.

. *Sample wer:* Find distance n the hotel he café. If greater than yards they not overlap. 's less than equal to yards they rlap.

B **51.** ★ **EXTENDED RESPONSE** You are in a park surfing the Internet on a wireless connection. A hotel's wireless transmitter is located 100 yards east and 60 yards south of you. It has a range of 150 yards. A café's transmitter is located 80 yards west and 70 yards south of you. It has a range of 100 yards.

a. With your location as the origin, write inequalities for circular regions around the hotel and café in which you can get wireless Internet access.

b. Graph the inequalities. Are you in only one region or in both? *Explain.*

c. *Explain* how to determine whether the regions overlap without graphing.

52. ★ **SHORT RESPONSE** Tell what conic section is formed in the situation described. *Explain* your reasoning.

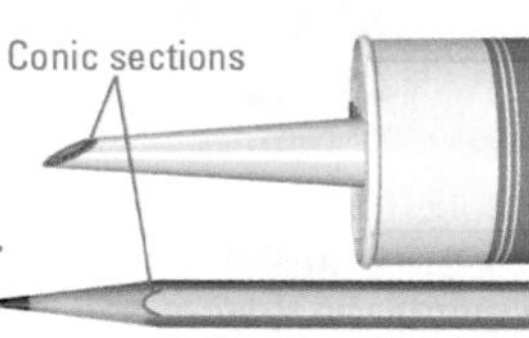

a. To use a new tube of caulk for the first time, you cut the cone-shaped tip diagonally as shown. **Ellipse; the cut enters the cone diagonally and exits the other side.**

b. When you sharpen a pencil with flat sides, each side intersects the cone-shaped tip as shown. **parabola**

C **53.** **CHALLENGE** A *degenerate* conic results when the intersection of a plane with a double-napped cone is not a parabola, circle, ellipse, or hyperbola.

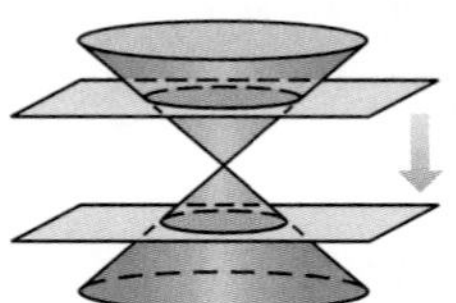
Diagram 1

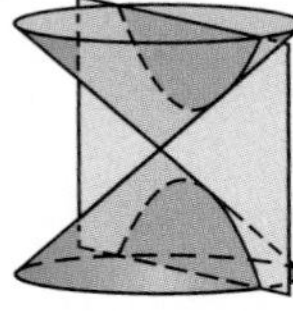
Diagram 2

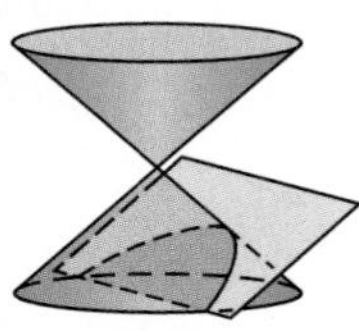
Diagram 3

a. In Diagram 1, a plane perpendicular to the cone's axis passes through the cone, intersecting it in a circle whose radius decreases and then increases. When is the intersection not a circle? What is it? **when the plane crosses the point where the cones meet; point**

b. In Diagram 2, a plane parallel to the cone's axis passes through the cone, intersecting it in a hyperbola whose vertices get closer together and then farther apart. When is the intersection not a hyperbola? What is it? **when the plane crosses the point where the cones meet; two triangles**

c. In Diagram 3, a plane parallel to the cone's nappe passes through the cone, intersecting it in a parabola that first gets narrower, then flips and gets wider. When is the intersection not a parabola? What is it? **when the plane is on the parallel edge of the cone; line**

KENTUCKY MIXED REVIEW

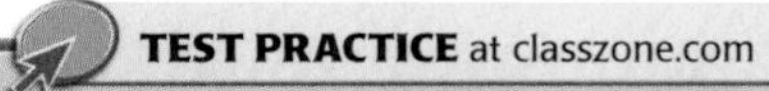

54. In 2003, the population of Texas was about 39,000 less than 3 times the population of Virginia. Let x represent the population of Virginia. Which expression represents the population of Texas? **D**

Ⓐ $39{,}000 - 3x$ Ⓑ $\frac{x - 39{,}000}{3}$

Ⓒ $\frac{x}{3} - 39{,}000$ Ⓓ $3x - 39{,}000$

55. The measure of each interior angle of a regular polygon is 135°. How many sides does the polygon have? **C**

Ⓐ 6 Ⓑ 7 Ⓒ 8 Ⓓ 9

5 ASSESS AND RETEACH

Daily Homework Quiz

Transparency Available

1. Write an equation of the hyperbola with vertices at (0, −2) and (0, 4) and foci at (0, 6) and (0, −4). Identify the line(s) of symmetry.
   $\frac{(y-1)^2}{9} - \frac{x^2}{16} = 1$; **lines of symmetry at $y = 1$ and $x = 0$**

You are biking along a path modeled by the equation $x^2 - 6x - 8y + 1 = 0$.

2. Use the discriminant to identify the conic section. **parabola**
3. Write the equation in standard form. $(x - 3)^2 = 8(y + 1)$
4. Graph the equation of the path. Identify the vertex and any lines of symmetry.

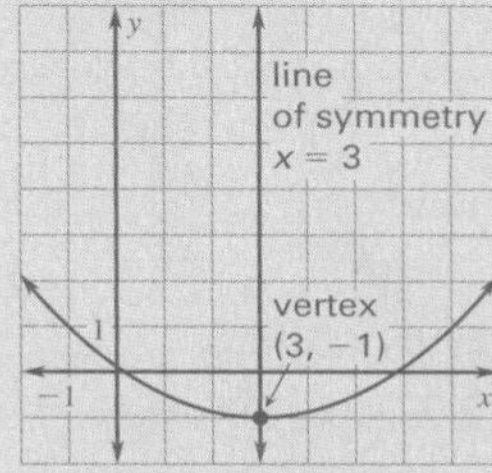

Available at **classzone.com**

Diagnosis/Remediation

- Practice A, B, C in Chapter 9 Resource Book, pp. 60–65
- Study Guide in Chapter 9 Resource Book, pp. 66–67
- Practice Workbook, pp. 144–146
- @HomeTutor

Challenge

Additional challenge is available in the Chapter 9 Resource Book, p. 70.

51b.

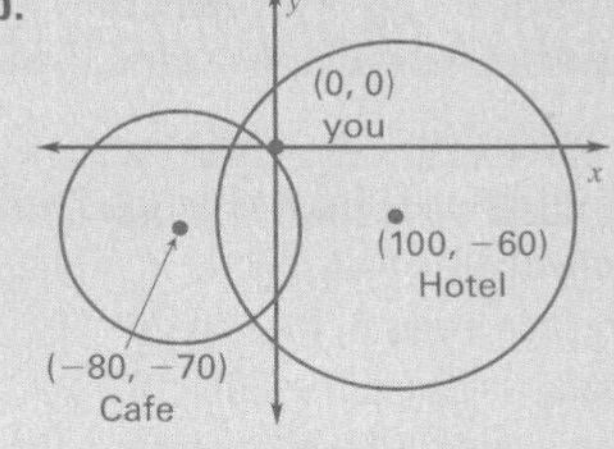

9.7 Solve Quadratic Systems

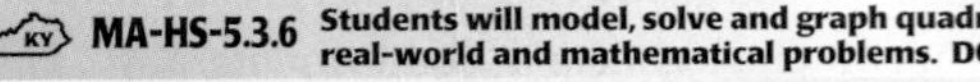
MA-HS-5.3.6 **Students will model, solve and graph quadratic equations in real-world and mathematical problems. DOK 2**

Before You solved linear systems.

Now You will solve quadratic systems.

Why? So you can find intersections involving conics, as in Ex. 40.

1 PLAN AND PREPARE

Warm-Up Exercises

Transparency Available

Solve the system by substitution.

1. $y = x + 1$ and $4x + 5y = 23$ (2, 3)
2. $x + 3y = -1$ and $2x - y = 5$ (2, − 1)
3. The admission price to a show was \$3 for students and \$4.50 for nonstudents. The sales from 200 tickets totaled \$720. How many of each kind of ticket were sold? **120 students and 80 nonstudents**

Notetaking Guide

Transparency Available

Promotes interactive learning and notetaking skills, pp. 253–256.

Pacing

Basic: 1 day
Average: 1 day
Advanced: 1 day
Block: 0.5 block with 9.6
- See *Teaching Guide/Lesson Plan*.

2 FOCUS AND MOTIVATE

Essential Question

Big Idea 3, p. 613

How can you identify the points of intersection of two distinct conics? **Tell students they will learn how to answer this question by solving quadratic systems.**

Key Vocabulary
- quadratic system

In Chapter 3, you solved systems of linear equations by graphing, substitution, and elimination. You can use the same techniques to solve systems that include one or more equations of conics. These systems are called **quadratic systems**.

If the graphs of the equations in a system are a line and a conic section, the graphs can intersect in zero, one, or two points, and so the system can have zero, one, or two solutions. Three possible scenarios are shown below.

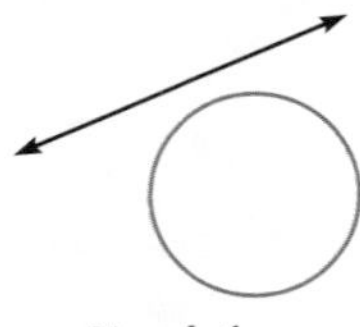
No solution

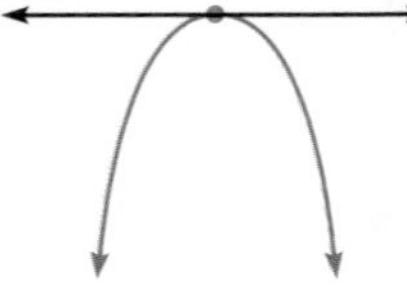
One solution

Two solutions

EXAMPLE 1 Solve a linear-quadratic system by graphing

Solve the system using a graphing calculator.

$y^2 - 7x + 3 = 0$ **Equation 1**
$2x - y = 3$ **Equation 2**

Solution

STEP 1 **Solve** each equation for y.

$y^2 - 7x + 3 = 0$
$y^2 = 7x - 3$
$y = \pm\sqrt{7x - 3}$ **Equation 1**

$2x - y = 3$
$-y = -2x + 3$
$y = 2x - 3$ **Equation 2**

AVOID ERRORS
To graph Equation 1, be sure to enter both $y = \sqrt{7x - 3}$ and $y = -\sqrt{7x - 3}$ into the graphing calculator.

STEP 2 **Graph** the equations $y = \sqrt{7x - 3}$, $y = -\sqrt{7x - 3}$, and $y = 2x - 3$.

Use the calculator's *intersect* feature to find the coordinates of the intersection points. The graphs of $y = -\sqrt{7x - 3}$ and $y = 2x - 3$ intersect at (0.75, −1.5). The graphs of $y = \sqrt{7x - 3}$ and $y = 2x - 3$ intersect at (4, 5).

Intersection
X=.75 Y=-1.5

▶ The solutions are (0.75, −1.5) and (4, 5). Check the solutions by substituting the coordinates of the points into each of the original equations.

Resource Planning Guide

Chapter Resource Book
- Teaching Guide/Lesson Plan (pp. 71–72)
- Activity Master (p. 73)
- Practice levels A, B, C (pp. 76–78)
- Study Guide (pp. 79–80)
- Catch-up for Absent Students (p. 81)
- Problem Solving Workshop (p. 82)
- Challenge (p. 83)

Workbooks
- Notetaking Guide (pp. 253–256)
- Practice Workbook (pp. 147–148)

Teaching Options
- **Power Presentations CD-ROM** provides dynamic electronic teaching resources for the classroom.
- **Activity Generator CD-ROM** provides editable activities for all ability levels.

Interactive Technology
- Easy Planner
- Power Presentations CD-ROM
- Activity Generator CD-ROM
- Animated Algebra
- Test Generator CD-ROM
- Online Quiz
- eWorkbook
- eEdition
- @HomeTutor

Resources for English Learners
- Quick Reference for English Learners
- Spanish Study Guide
- Multi-Language Visual Glossary
- Student Resources in Spanish

See also the *Algebra 2 Toolkit* for more strategies for meeting individual needs.

 **EXAMPLE 2** **Solve a linear-quadratic system by substitution**

Solve the system using substitution.

$x^2 + y^2 = 10$ **Equation 1**
$y = -3x + 10$ **Equation 2**

Solution

Substitute $-3x + 10$ for y in Equation 1 and solve for x.

$x^2 + y^2 = 10$ **Equation 1**

$x^2 + (-3x + 10)^2 = 10$ **Substitute for *y*.**

$x^2 + 9x^2 - 60x + 100 = 10$ **Expand the power.**

$10x^2 - 60x + 90 = 0$ **Combine like terms.**

$x^2 - 6x + 9 = 0$ **Divide each side by 10.**

$(x - 3)^2 = 0$ **Perfect square trinomial**

$x = 3$ **Zero product property**

AVOID ERRORS
You can also substitute $x = 3$ in Equation 1 to find y. This yields *two* apparent solutions, (3, 1) and (3, −1). However, (3, −1) is extraneous because it does not satisfy Equation 2.

To find the y-coordinate of the solution, substitute $x = 3$ in Equation 2.

$y = -3(3) + 10 = 1$

▸ The solution is (3, 1).

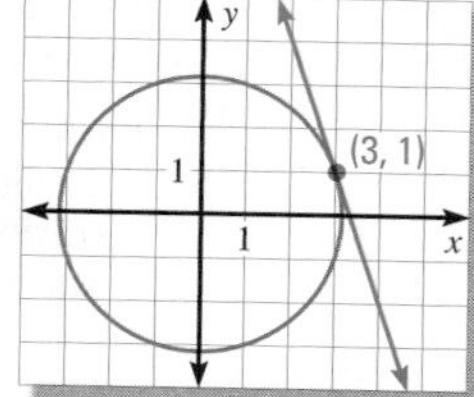

CHECK You can check the solution by graphing the equations in the system. You can see from the graph shown that the line and the circle intersect only at the point (3, 1).

 **GUIDED PRACTICE** for Examples 1 and 2

Solve the system using a graphing calculator.

1. $x^2 + y^2 = 13$
   $y = x - 1$ **(−2, −3), (3, 2)**
2. $x^2 + 8y^2 - 4 = 0$
   $y = 2x + 7$ **no solution**
3. $y^2 + 6x - 1 = 0$
   $y = -0.4x + 2.6$
   (−1.57, 3.23), (−22.9, 11.8)

Solve the system using substitution.

4. $y = 0.5x - 3$
   $x^2 + 4y^2 - 4 = 0$ **no solution**
5. $y^2 - 2x - 10 = 0$
   $y = -x - 1$ **(−3, 2), (3, −4)**
6. $y = 4x - 8$
   $9x^2 - y^2 - 36 = 0$
   (2, 0), $\left(\frac{50}{7}, \frac{144}{7}\right)$

QUADRATIC SYSTEMS Two distinct conic sections can have from zero to four points of intersection. Several possible scenarios are shown below.

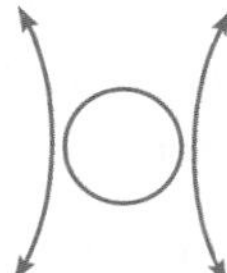
No solution

One solution

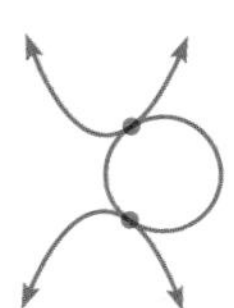
Two solutions

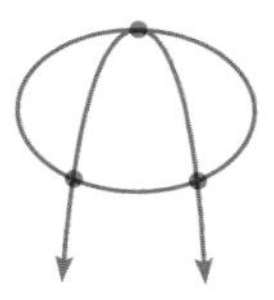
Three solutions

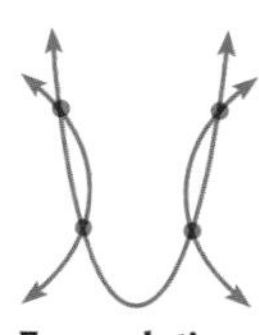
Four solutions

In the examples on the next page, you will use elimination to solve systems of two second-degree equations.

Differentiated Instruction

Visual Learners Students will often write down the coordinates of one point, and forget to check for other solutions to a system of equations. After graphing the systems of equations in **Guided Practice Exercises 1–3**, have students look at each graph and write down the number of solutions of the system indicated by their graph. This will help students to remember to find all of the solutions to the system of equations.

See also the *Algebra 2 Toolkit* for more strategies.

Motivating the Lesson

The signal from a radio station has a range of 50 miles. Another radio station is located 80 miles north and 100 miles east of the first radio station. This second station transmits in a range of 100 miles. Have students graph two circles that represent the ranges of the two stations. Ask them what will happen when they are driving in their car and reach the overlapping regions of the two circles. The equations of the two circles represent a quadratic system and in this lesson they will investigate some characteristics of the solutions of quadratic systems.

3 TEACH

Extra Example 1

Solve the system using a graphing calculator.
$-3x + 5y = 49$, $y^2 + 10x = 34$
(−3, 8)

Key Question to Ask for Example 1

- Before graphing, how could you determine the possible number of solutions? **The first equation is a parabola and the second equation is a line. The line might not intersect the parabola, the line might be tangent to the parabola, or the line might cut through the parabola and intersect it in two points. Thus, the system has no solutions, one solution, or two solutions.**

Extra Example 2

Solve the system using substitution.
$2x + y = -5$
$y = x^2 + 6x + 7$
(−6, 7) and (−2, −1)

Extra Example 3

Solve the system by elimination.
$x^2 - y + 3 = 0$
$x^2 + y^2 = 9$ (0, 3)

Key Question to Ask for Example 3

- Why do the conics in the system have only one value of y for $x = 4$? **(4, 0) is a vertex of the hyperbola and a co-vertex of the ellipse.**

Teaching Strategy

Emphasize the importance of the "Another Way" note next to Example 3. Whenever students have a system of equations to solve, they should examine the system and use the easiest method to solve that system.

Extra Example 4

In a science fiction movie script, scientists report that their planet's orbit follows a path modeled by the equation $16x^2 + 4y^2 = 64$ and that a comet follows a parabolic path modeled by the equation $y = x^2 - 4$. Where can the scientists report that the comet might intersect the planet's orbit? **(0, −4), (−2, 0), or (2, 0)**

Closing the Lesson

Have students summarize the major points of the lesson and answer the Essential Question: How can you identify the points of intersection of two distinct conic sections?

- **Systems of equations that include one or more equations of conics are called quadratic systems.**
- **You can use graphing, substitution, or elimination to solve a quadratic system.**
- **A quadratic system can have zero through four solutions.**

Write an equation to model each conic. Then solve the quadratic system by graphing, substitution, or elimination. The number of solutions may be 0, 1, 2, 3, or 4.

EXAMPLE 3 Solve a quadratic system by elimination

Solve the system by elimination. $9x^2 + y^2 - 90x + 216 = 0$ **Equation 1**
$x^2 - y^2 - 16 = 0$ **Equation 2**

Solution

ANOTHER WAY
You can also solve by substitution: Solve Equation 2 for y^2, then substitute the result in Equation 1.

Add the equations to eliminate the y^2-term and obtain a quadratic equation in x.

$$9x^2 + y^2 - 90x + 216 = 0$$
$$x^2 - y^2 \qquad - 16 = 0$$
$$10x^2 \quad - 90x + 200 = 0 \quad \textbf{Add.}$$
$$x^2 - 9x + 20 = 0 \quad \textbf{Divide each side by 10.}$$
$$(x - 4)(x - 5) = 0 \quad \textbf{Factor.}$$
$$x = 4 \text{ or } x = 5 \quad \textbf{Zero product property}$$

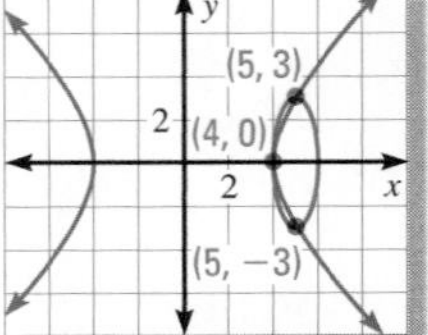

When $x = 4$, $y = 0$. When $x = 5$, $y = \pm 3$.

▶ The solutions are (4, 0), (5, 3), and (5, −3), as shown.

EXAMPLE 4 Solve a real-life quadratic system

NAVIGATION A ship uses LORAN (long-distance radio navigation) to find its position. Radio signals from stations A and B locate the ship on the blue hyperbola, and signals from stations B and C locate the ship on the red hyperbola. The equations of the hyperbolas are given below. Find the ship's position if it is east of the y-axis.

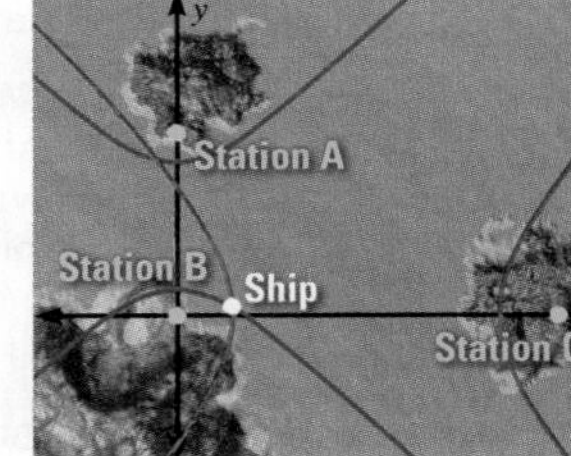

$x^2 - y^2 - 16x + 32 = 0$ **Equation 1**
$-x^2 + y^2 - 8y + 8 = 0$ **Equation 2**

Solution

STEP 1 **Add** the equations to eliminate the x^2- and y^2-terms.

$$x^2 - y^2 - 16x \qquad + 32 = 0$$
$$-x^2 + y^2 \qquad - 8y + 8 = 0$$
$$-16x - 8y + 40 = 0 \quad \textbf{Add.}$$
$$y = -2x + 5 \quad \textbf{Solve for } y.$$

STEP 2 **Substitute** $-2x + 5$ for y in Equation 1 and solve for x.

$$x^2 - y^2 - 16x + 32 = 0 \quad \textbf{Equation 1}$$
$$x^2 - (-2x + 5)^2 - 16x + 32 = 0 \quad \textbf{Substitute for } y.$$
$$3x^2 - 4x - 7 = 0 \quad \textbf{Simplify.}$$
$$(x + 1)(3x - 7) = 0 \quad \textbf{Factor.}$$
$$x = -1 \text{ or } x = \frac{7}{3} \quad \textbf{Zero product property}$$

STEP 3 **Substitute** for x in $y = -2x + 5$ to find the solutions $(-1, 7)$ and $\left(\frac{7}{3}, \frac{1}{3}\right)$.

▶ Because the ship is east of the y-axis, it is at $\left(\frac{7}{3}, \frac{1}{3}\right)$.

✓ GUIDED PRACTICE for Examples 3 and 4

Solve the system.

7. $-2y^2 + x + 2 = 0$
   $x^2 + y^2 - 1 = 0$ **$(0, \pm1), \left(-\frac{1}{2}, \pm\frac{\sqrt{3}}{2}\right)$**

8. $x^2 + y^2 - 16x + 39 = 0$
   $x^2 - y^2 - 9 = 0$ **(3, 0) (5, ±4)**

9. $x^2 + 4y^2 + 4x + 8y = 8$
   $y^2 - x + 2y = 5$
   (−6, −1), (−2, −3), (−2, 1)

10. **WHAT IF?** In Example 4, suppose that a ship's LORAN system locates the ship on the two hyperbolas whose equations are given below. Find the ship's location if it is south of the x-axis. **$\left(\frac{7}{4}, -\frac{1}{4}\right)$**

$x^2 - y^2 - 12x + 18 = 0$ Equation 1
$y^2 - x^2 - 4y + 2 = 0$ Equation 2

9.7 EXERCISES

HOMEWORK KEY
○ = **WORKED-OUT SOLUTIONS** on p. WS17 for Exs. 5, 15, and 41
★ = **STANDARDIZED TEST PRACTICE** Exs. 2, 21, 34, 42, and 44

SKILL PRACTICE

1. **VOCABULARY** Copy and complete: The equations $x^2 + 5x + 3y^2 = 9$ and $4x^2 - 12y + 16 = 0$ form a(n) __?__ system of equations. **quadratic**

2. ★ **WRITING** *Explain* what method you would use to solve the following system. Do not solve the system. ***Sample answer:*** **Elimination could be used because the coefficient of each y^2 is 1.**

$3x^2 + y^2 - 5x = 0$ Equation 1
$2x^2 + y^2 - 15 = 0$ Equation 2

EXAMPLE 1 on p. 658 for Exs. 3–8

SOLVING BY GRAPHING **Solve the system using a graphing calculator.**

3. $x^2 + y^2 - 32 = 0$
   $y - x = 0$ **(−4, −4), (4, 4)**

4. $y + 2x^2 - 9 = 0$
   $y + 4x + 1 = 0$ **(−1.45, 4.80), (3.45, −14.8)**

5. $y - 3x + 4 = 0$
   $-3x^2 + y^2 - 6 = 0$ **(0.472, −2.58), (3.53, 6.58)**

6. $y + 2x = 6$
   $3x^2 + y^2 = 12$ **no solution**

7. $x^2 + y^2 = 16$
   $y - 2x = 1$ **(−2.18, −3.36), (1.38, 3.76)**

8. $3(y + 3)^2 + 4x = 0$
   $y - 2x = 11$ **(−8.70, −6.41), (−5.63, −0.260)**

EXAMPLE 2 on p. 659 for Exs. 9–21

SOLVING BY SUBSTITUTION **Solve the system using substitution.**

9. $y^2 - x - 6 = 0$
   $y + x = 0$ **(3, −3), (−2, 2)**

10. $x^2 + y^2 - 25 = 0$
    $y = 2x - 10$ **(3, −4), (5, 0)**

11. $-2x + y - 8 = 0$
    $x^2 + 4y^2 - 40 = 0$ **See margin.**

12. $-x^2 + 2y^2 = 8$
    $-x + y = -2$ **(0, −2), (8, 6)**

13. $6x^2 + 3y^2 = 12$
    $y = -x + 2$ **$(0, 2), \left(\frac{4}{3}, \frac{2}{3}\right)$**

14. $-3x + y = 6$
    $8x + y^2 + 24 = 0$ **no solution**

15. $4x^2 - 5y^2 = -76$
    $2x + y = -6$ **$(-1, -4), \left(-\frac{13}{2}, 7\right)$**

16. $x^2 + y^2 = 20$
    $y = x - 4$ **See margin.**

17. $9x^2 + 4y^2 = 36$
    $-x + y = -4$ **no solution**

18. $x^2 + 6x + 4y - 3 = 0$
    $y + 3x + 1 = 0$ **(−1, 2), (7, −22)**

19. $4x^2 + 2y^2 - x - y = 6$
    $3x - y = 2$ **See margin.**

20. $4x^2 - y^2 - 32x - 2y = -59$
    $2x + y - 7 = 0$ **no solution**

21. ★ **MULTIPLE CHOICE** Which ordered pair is a solution of the linear-quadratic system below? **B**

$6x^2 - 5x + 8y^2 + y = 23$
$-x + y = -1$

Ⓐ (−1, −2) Ⓑ (2, 1) Ⓒ (3, 2) Ⓓ (−2, −3)

4 PRACTICE AND APPLY

Assignment Guide

Answer Transparencies available for all exercises

Basic:
Day 1: EP p. 1012 Exs. 5–8
pp. 661–664
Exs. 1–5, 9–15, 21–25, 39–42, 46

Average:
Day 1: pp. 661–664
Exs. 1, 2, 4–6, 14–17, 21, 26–29, 34–36, 39–44, 47

Advanced:
Day 1: pp. 661–664
Exs. 1, 2, 7, 8, 17–21, 30–38*, 40–45*

Block:
pp. 661–664
Exs. 1, 2, 4–6, 14–17, 21, 26–29, 34–36, 39–44, 47 (with 9.6)

Differentiated Instruction

See *Algebra 2 Best Practices Toolkit* for suggestions on addressing the needs of a diverse classroom.

Homework Check

For a quick check of student understanding of key concepts, go over the following exercises:

Basic: 4, 10, 22, 39, 42
Average: 6, 14, 26, 40, 43
Advanced: 8, 18, 30, 41, 43

Extra Practice

- Student Edition, p. 1018
- Chapter 9 Resource Book: Practice levels A, B, C, pp. 76–78

Practice Worksheet

An easily-readable reduced practice page (with answers) for this lesson can be found on p. 612C.

11. $\left(\frac{-64 - 2\sqrt{106}}{17}, \frac{8 - 4\sqrt{106}}{17}\right), \left(\frac{-64 + 2\sqrt{106}}{17}, \frac{4 + 2\sqrt{106}}{17}\right)$

16. $(2 - \sqrt{6}, -2 - \sqrt{6}), (2 + \sqrt{6}, -2 + \sqrt{6})$

19. $\left(\frac{7 + 3\sqrt{3}}{11}, \frac{-1 + 9\sqrt{3}}{11}\right), \left(\frac{7 - 3\sqrt{3}}{11}, \frac{-1 - 9\sqrt{3}}{11}\right)$

Study Strategy

Exercises 3–33 Suggest that students check their solutions by solving each system by at least one other method.

Avoiding Common Errors

Exercises 22–33 When elimination requires subtracting the equations, students may subtract only the terms they want to eliminate. Encourage them to multiply all the terms of one equation by −1, then add.

EXAMPLES 3 and 4 on p. 660 for Exs. 22–35

B

SOLVING QUADRATIC SYSTEMS Solve the system.

22. $6x^2 - y^2 - 15 = 0$
$x^2 + y^2 - 13 = 0$ $(-2, \pm 3), (2, \pm 3)$

23. $5x^2 + 25y^2 - 125 = 0$
$-x + y^2 - 5 = 0$ $(0, \pm\sqrt{5}), (-5, 0)$

24. $10y = x^2$
$x^2 - 6 = -2$ $\left(\pm 2, \frac{2}{5}\right)$

25. $x^2 - y^2 - 4x + 2 = 0$
$-x^2 + y^2 - 4y + 2 = 0$ $\left(\frac{1}{2}, \frac{1}{2}\right)$

26. $x^2 - 2y = 6$
$x^2 - y^2 = -27$ $(-4.43, 6.83), (4.43, 6.83)$

27. $x^2 + 2y^2 - 10 = 0$
$4y^2 + x + 4 = 0$ no solution

28. $x^2 + y^2 - 16x + 39 = 0$
$x^2 - y^2 - 9 = 0$ $(3, 0), (5, \pm 4)$

29. $x^2 - y^2 - 8x + 8y = 24$
$x^2 + y^2 - 8x - 8y = -24$ no solution

30. $16x^2 - y^2 + 16y - 128 = 0$
$y^2 - 48x - 16y - 32 = 0$

30. $(-2, 8), (5, 8 \pm 4\sqrt{21})$

31. $4x^2 - 56x + 9y^2 = -160$
$4x^2 + y^2 - 64 = 0$ $(4, 0)$

32. $x^2 - y^2 - 32x + 128 = 0$
$y^2 - x^2 - 8y + 8 = 0$

32. $\left(\frac{7}{3}, \frac{23}{3}\right), \left(\frac{23}{5}, -\frac{7}{5}\right)$

33. $y^2 + x - 3 = 0$
$x^2 - 4x + 3y + 1 = 0$ $(-1, -2), (2, 1)$

34. ★ **MULTIPLE CHOICE** How many solutions does the system consisting of the equations $x^2 + y^2 + 6x = 0$ and $y^2 + x - 6 = 0$ have? D

Ⓐ 0　Ⓑ 1　Ⓒ 2　Ⓓ 4

35. **ERROR ANALYSIS** *Describe* and correct the error in using substitution to begin solving the system below. Then solve the system.

$x^2 + y^2 - 2x - 2y = -1$ **Equation 1**
$y^2 + x = 1$ **Equation 2**

Solve Equation 2 for x: $x = 1 - y^2$

Substitute for x in Equation 1:

$(1 - y^2)^2 + y^2 - 2(1 - y^2) - 2y = -1$

$1 - 2y^2 + y^2 + y^2 - 2 + 2y^2 - 2y = -1$

$2y^2 - 2y = 0$ ✗

When $(1 - y^2)^2$ was expanded, the last term should have been y^4; $1 - 2y^2 + y^4 + y^2 - 2 + 2y^2 - 2y = -1$, $y^4 + y^2 - 2y = 0$; $(0, 1), (1, 0)$.

36. **REASONING** Solve the system consisting of the equations $\frac{x^2}{2} + \frac{y^2}{4} = 1$ and $4y^2 = 16 - 8x^2$. What do you notice? They are the same equation.

C

37. **GRAPHING CALCULATOR** Consider the system consisting of the equations $3y^2 + x^2 + 4x + 18y = -28$ and $9y^2 - 4x^2 + 8x + 90y = -185$. Solve each equation for y. Then use a graphing calculator to solve the system. about $(-2.32, -2.02), (-0.296, -2.82)$

38. **CHALLENGE** Solve the system of three equations shown. $(0, 1), (1, 0)$

$x^2 + y^2 = 1$ **Equation 1**
$x^2 + y^2 + 4x + 4y - 5 = 0$ **Equation 2**
$x + y - 1 = 0$ **Equation 3**

PROBLEM SOLVING

EXAMPLE 2 on p. 659 for Exs. 39–41

A

39. **TRAFFIC SAFETY** A car passes a parked police car and continues at a constant speed r. The police car begins accelerating at a constant rate when it is passed. The diagram indicates the distance d (in miles) the police car travels as a function of time t (in minutes) after being passed. Write and solve a system of equations to find how long it takes the police car to catch up to the other car.

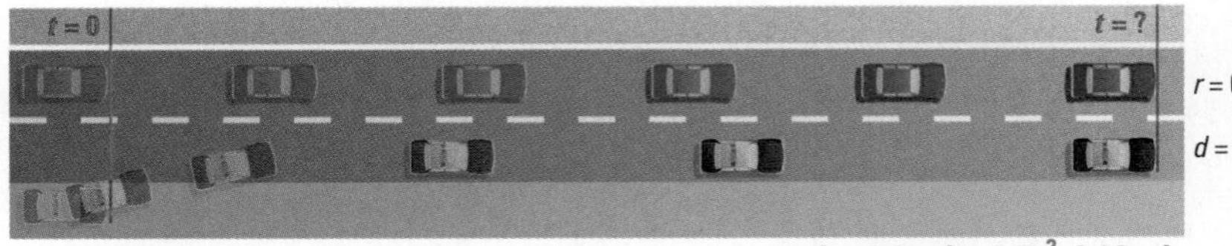

$d = 0.8t$, $d = 2.5t^2$, 0.32 min

@HomeTutor for problem solving help at classzone.com

○ = WORKED-OUT SOLUTIONS on p. WS1　★ = STANDARDIZED TEST PRACTICE

40. BASEBALL The path of a baseball hit for a home run can be modeled by $y = -\frac{x^2}{484} + x + 3$ where x and y are in feet and home plate is the origin. The ball lands in the stands, which are modeled by $4y - x = -352$ for $x \geq 400$. How far horizontally and vertically from home plate does the ball land? **about 459 ft, about 26.7 ft**

@HomeTutor for problem solving help at classzone.com

41. MULTI-STEP PROBLEM To be eligible for a parking pass on a college campus, a student must live at least 1 mile from the campus center.

campus center; Oak Lane; College Drive; 1 mi; (0, 0); 1 mi; Main Street; 2 mi; 5 mi; x; y

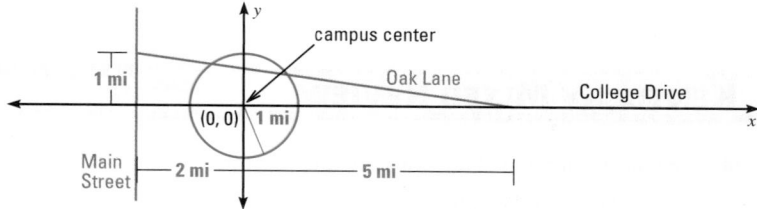

a. Write equations that represent the circle and Oak Lane. **$x^2 + y^2 = 1$, $y = -\frac{1}{7}x + \frac{5}{7}$**

b. Solve the system that consists of the equations from part (a). **$\left(-\frac{3}{5}, \frac{4}{5}\right), \left(\frac{4}{5}, \frac{3}{5}\right)$**

c. For what length of Oak Lane are students *not* eligible for a parking pass? **about 1.41 mi**

EXAMPLES 3 and 4 on p. 660 for Exs. 42–43

42. ★ SHORT RESPONSE A high school gym has a dome-shaped ceiling modeled by $x^2 + y^2 + 60y - 3456 = 0$ where x and y are in feet. A tennis player in the gym hits a shot modeled by $x^2 + y = 36$ where the origin is located at the base of the net. Solve the system of equations by both elimination and substitution. Do any solutions represent the ball hitting the ceiling? *Explain.* **Yes; when the ball reaches 36 feet, it hits the ceiling.**

43. NAVIGATION A ship's LORAN system locates the ship on hyperbolas with the given equations. Find the ship's location for each pair of hyperbolas. In part (b), assume the ship is west of the y-axis.

a. $x^2 - y^2 - 8x + 8 = 0$
$y^2 - x^2 - 8y + 8 = 0$ **(1, 1)**

b. $xy - 24 = 0$
$x^2 - 25y^2 + 100 = 0$ **about (−8.94, −2.68)**

44. ★ EXTENDED RESPONSE A *seismograph* measures the intensity of an earthquake. A seismograph can determine distance to an earthquake's epicenter, but not direction. On January 22, 2003, a powerful earthquake struck Mexico's state of Colima. The diagram shows approximate distances from three seismic stations to the epicenter. The relative positions of the seismic stations are described below.

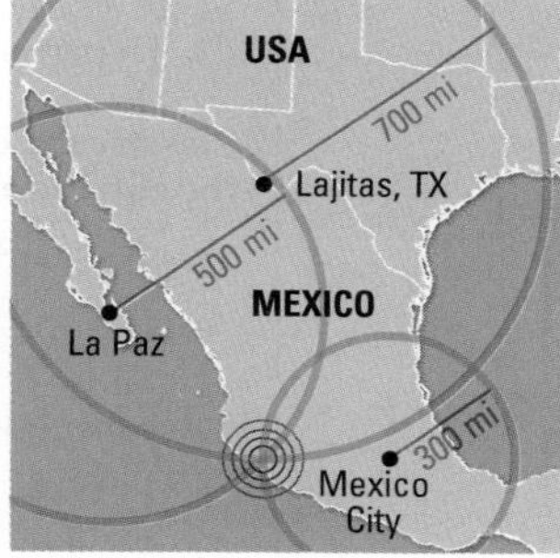

Mexico City: 700 miles south and 300 miles east of Lajitas

La Paz: 400 miles south and 400 miles west of Lajitas

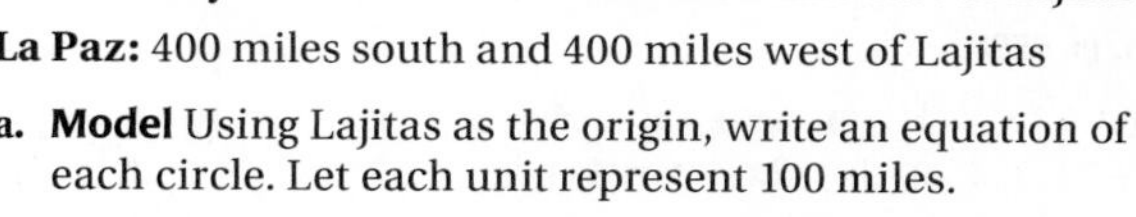

a. **Model** Using Lajitas as the origin, write an equation of each circle. Let each unit represent 100 miles.

a. Lajitas: $x^2 + y^2 = 49$, La Paz: $(x + 4)^2 + (y + 4)^2 = 25$, Mexico City: $(x - 3)^2 + (y + 7)^2 = 9$

b. **Eliminate** Use the equation for the circle centered at Lajitas with each of the other two equations from part (a) to eliminate the x^2- and y^2-terms and find two new equations. **$8x + 8y = -56$, $-6x + 14y = -98$**

c. **Solve** Solve the system of linear equations that results from part (b) to find the coordinates of the epicenter. **(0, −7)**

d. **Reasoning** *Explain* why three stations are required to locate the epicenter. **Three equations generate a system of two linear equations which can be solved to find the epicenter.**

5 ASSESS AND RETEACH

Daily Homework Quiz

Transparency Available

1. Solve the system using a graphing calculator.
   $y^2 = x^2 - 9$
   $2y = x - 3$ **(−5, −4) and (3, 0)**
2. Solve the system using substitution.
   $x - y = -1$
   $y = x^2 + 1$ **(0, 1) and (1, 2)**
3. A system for tracking ships has just located a ship on a path modeled by $2x^2 - y^2 = 1$. Earlier the ship was located on a path modeled by $2y^2 - x^2 = 1$. If the ship is in the first quadrant of a coordinate system, what is the ship's location in the coordinate system now? **(1, 1)**

Available at **classzone.com**

Diagnosis/Remediation

- Practice A, B, C in Chapter 9 Resource Book, pp. 76–78
- Study Guide in Chapter 9 Resource Book, pp. 79–80
- Practice Workbook, pp. 147–148
- @HomeTutor

Challenge

Additional challenge is available in the Chapter 9 Resource Book, p. 83.

Quiz

An easily-readable reduced copy of the quiz (with answers) on Lessons 9.6–9.7 from the Assessment Book can be found on p. 612E.

Quiz 3–7, 14. See Additional Answers beginning on p. AA1.

C **45. CHALLENGE** What is the width w of the thickest box that will fit in a mailbox with the dimensions shown? (*Hint:* Use the Pythagorean theorem and the fact that $\triangle ABC \sim \triangle CDE$ to write a system of two second-degree equations.) **about 0.831 in.**

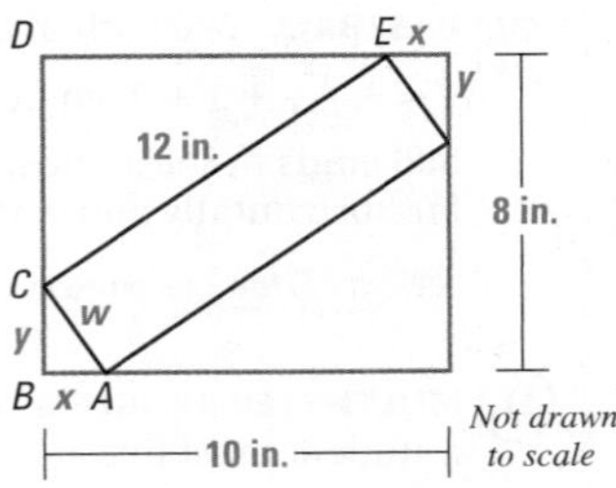

KENTUCKY MIXED REVIEW

TEST PRACTICE at classzone.com

46. What is an equation of the line that contains the point $(-5, 2)$ and has a slope of $-\frac{4}{3}$? **D**

Ⓐ $-4x + 3y = 26$ Ⓑ $-3x + 4y = 23$

Ⓒ $4x + 3y = 7$ Ⓓ $4x + 3y = -14$

47. Which inequality is the solution of $14 - 5x \le 7x + 5$? **D**

Ⓐ $x \le -\frac{3}{4}$ Ⓑ $x \le \frac{3}{4}$

Ⓒ $x \ge -\frac{3}{4}$ Ⓓ $x \ge \frac{3}{4}$

QUIZ *for Lessons 9.6–9.7*

Write an equation of the conic section. *(p. 650)*

1. Ellipse with vertices at $(3, -10)$ and $(3, 6)$ and foci at $(3, -7)$ and $(3, 3)$ $\frac{(x-3)^2}{64} + \frac{(y+2)^2}{39} = 1$
2. Parabola with vertex at $(-5, 2)$ and focus at $(-5, -1)$ $(x + 5)^2 = -12(y - 2)$
3. Hyperbola with foci at $(-3, 1)$ and $(6, 1)$ and vertices at $(0, 1)$ and $(3, 1)$ **See margin.**

Classify the conic section and write its equation in standard form. Then graph the equation. *(p. 650)* **4–7. See margin.**

4. $9x^2 - 4y^2 - 36x - 32y - 64 = 0$
5. $-x^2 - y^2 - 4x + 12y + 129 = 0$
6. $x^2 + 6x - y + 16 = 0$
7. $12x^2 + 45y^2 + 120x + 90y - 150 = 0$

Solve the system. *(p. 658)*

8. $x + 2y^2 = -6$
   $x + 8y = 0$ **(−24, 3), (−8, 1)**
9. $x^2 + 4x + y^2 + 6y = 12$
   $2x - y = 4$ **(−2, −8), (2, 0)**
10. $x^2 - y - 4 = 0$
    $x^2 + 3y^2 - 4y - 10 = 0$ **$(\pm\sqrt{6}, 2)$, $(\pm\sqrt{3}, -1)$**
11. $y^2 - 6x - 2y - 3 = 0$
    $2y^2 - 4y + x + 6 = 0$ **no solution**
12. $y^2 - 4x^2 - 4y = 0$
    $2x^2 + y^2 - 8x - 4y = -8$ **no solution**
13. $16x^2 + 9y^2 + 32x - 18y = 119$
    $x^2 + y^2 + 2x + 6y = 15$ **(−4, 1), (2, 1)**
14. **RADAR** A radar station reports that a ship is 10 miles away. At the same time, a second station 20 miles east and 15 miles north of the first one reports that the ship is 15 miles away. Write and solve a system of equations to locate the ship relative to the first station. Is only one location possible? *Explain.* *(p. 658)* **See margin.**

EXTRA PRACTICE for Lesson 9.7, p. 1018

Extension

Use after Lesson 9.7

Determine Eccentricity of Conic Sections

GOAL Find and apply the eccentricity of a conic section.

Key Vocabulary
eccentricity

In an ellipse that is nearly circular, the ratio $c:a$ is close to 0. In a more oval ellipse, $c:a$ is close to 1. This ratio is the **eccentricity** of the ellipse. Every conic has an eccentricity e associated with it.

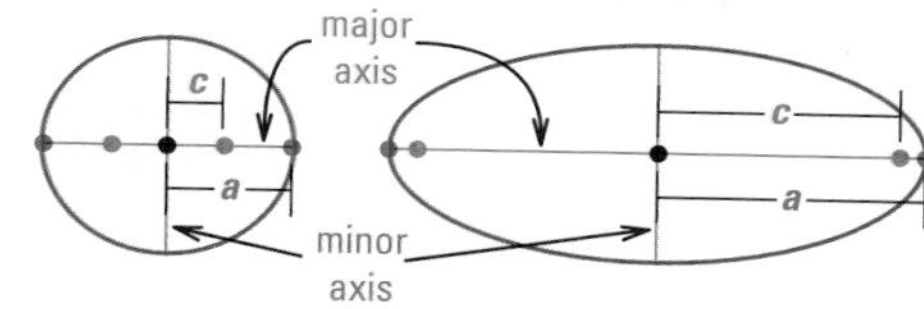

KEY CONCEPT *For Your Notebook*

Eccentricity of Conic Sections

The eccentricity of each conic section is defined below. For an ellipse or hyperbola, c is the distance from each focus to the center, and a is the distance from each vertex to the center.

Circle: $e = 0$

Parabola: $e = 1$

Ellipse: $e = \frac{c}{a}$, and $0 < e < 1$

Hyperbola: $e = \frac{c}{a}$, and $e > 1$

EXAMPLE 1 Find eccentricity

Find the eccentricity of the conic section represented by the equation.

a. $(x + 3)^2 + (y - 1)^2 = 25$

b. $\frac{(x + 4)^2}{36} + \frac{(y - 2)}{16} = 1$

Solution

a. Because this equation represents a circle, the eccentricity is $e = 0$.

b. This equation represents an ellipse with $a = \sqrt{36} = 6$, $b = \sqrt{16} = 4$, and $c = \sqrt{a^2 - b^2} = 2\sqrt{5}$. The eccentricity is $e = \frac{c}{a} = \frac{2\sqrt{5}}{6} \approx 0.745$.

EXAMPLE 2 Use eccentricity to write an equation

Write an equation of a hyperbola with center $(-2, 6)$, vertex $(6, 6)$, and $e = 2$.

Solution

Use the form $\frac{(x - h)^2}{a^2} - \frac{(y - k)^2}{b^2} = 1$. The vertex lies $6 - (-2) = 8$ units from the center, so $a = 8$. Because $e = \frac{c}{a} = 2$, you know that $\frac{c}{8} = 2$, or $c = 16$.

So, $b^2 = c^2 - a^2 = 256 - 64 = 192$. The equation is $\frac{(x + 2)^2}{64} - \frac{(y - 6)^2}{192} = 1$.

1 PLAN AND PREPARE

Warm-Up Exercises

Find the value of a for the given equations or for the standard equation of a conic.

1. $c^2 = a^2 + b^2$, $c = 9$, and $b = 5$ $2\sqrt{14}$
2. $c^2 = a^2 - b^2$, $c = 12$, and $b = 4$ $4\sqrt{10}$
3. ellipse with center $(3, 2)$, vertices $(9, 2)$ and $(-3, 2)$, and co-vertices $(3, 5)$ and $(3, -1)$ 6

2 FOCUS AND MOTIVATE

Essential Question

Big Idea 1, p. 613

For which conics is the ratio $\frac{c}{a}$ a fixed value, and for which conics does that ratio have different values? **Tell students they will learn how to answer this question by calculating the eccentricity of a conic.**

3 TEACH

Extra Example 1

Identify the conic represented by the equation and find its eccentricity.

a. $(y + 2)^2 - (x + 2)^2 = 1$ **hyperbola, $c \approx 1.4$ and $a = 1$; $e \approx 1.4$**

b. $y^2 = \frac{1}{3}(x + 2)$ **parabola; $e = 1$**

NCTM STANDARDS

Standard 2: Use models to understand relationships

Standard 9: Grasp how mathematical ideas interconnect

Extra Example 2

Write an equation of an ellipse with foci $(-2 + \sqrt{21}, 3)$ and $(-2 - \sqrt{21}, 3)$ and $e = \frac{\sqrt{21}}{5}$.
$\frac{(x+2)^2}{25} + \frac{(y-3)^2}{4} = 1$

Extra Example 3

A star system 41 light years from Earth, known as 55 Cancri, has a planet that orbits its sun in an elliptical path. The eccentricity of its orbit is $e = 0.24$ and the length of the vertical major axis is about 5.8 astronomical units. Find an equation of the planet's orbit. $\frac{x^2}{8.41} + \frac{y^2}{7.9} = 1$

Key Question to Ask for Example 3

- The eccentricity of the elliptical orbit of Venus is about 0.007. Which planet has an ellipse that is closer to a circle, Pluto or Venus? **Venus**

Closing the Lesson

Have students summarize the major points of the lesson and answer the Essential Question: For which conics is the ratio $\frac{c}{a}$ a fixed value, and for which conics does that ratio have different values?

- **For a circle $c = 0$, so $\frac{c}{a} = 0$, and for a parabola $c = a$, so $\frac{c}{a} = 1$.**
- **For an ellipse $0 < \frac{c}{a} < 1$. For a hyperbola $\frac{c}{a} > 1$.**

The ratio $\frac{c}{a}$ is the eccentricity of a conic. The eccentricity of circles and parabolas are 0 and 1, respectively. The eccentricity of an ellipse and a hyperbola depend on the values of a and b in the equations.

4 PRACTICE AND APPLY

Avoiding Common Errors

Exercises 7–12 If students mix up the relationship among a^2, b^2, and c^2 in ellipses and hyperbolas, they will evaluate e incorrectly. Remind them that $0 < e < 1$ for an ellipse and that $e > 1$ for a hyperbola.

EXAMPLE 3 Use eccentricity to write a model

ASTRONOMY Pluto orbits the sun in an elliptical path with the center of the sun at one focus. The eccentricity of the orbit is $e = 0.249$ and the length of the major axis is about 79.0 astronomical units. Find an equation of Pluto's orbit. (Assume that the major axis is horizontal.)

Solution

The equation of the orbit has the form $\frac{x^2}{a^2} + \frac{y^2}{b^2} = 1$. Using the length of the major axis, you know that $2a = 79.0$, or $a = 39.5$. You can use the eccentricity and the value of a to find the value of c, and then use the values of a and c to find b.

$$e = \frac{c}{a}, \text{ so } 0.249 = \frac{c}{39.5}, \text{ or } c \approx 9.84$$

$$c^2 = a^2 - b^2, \text{ so } b = \sqrt{a^2 - c^2} = \sqrt{(39.5)^2 - (9.84)^2} \approx 38.3$$

So, an equation for Pluto's orbit is $\frac{x^2}{(39.5)^2} + \frac{y^2}{(38.3)^2} = 1$, or $\frac{x^2}{1560} + \frac{y^2}{1470} = 1$,

where x and y are measured in astronomical units.

PRACTICE

EXAMPLE 1 on p. 665 for Exs. 1–6

Find the eccentricity of the conic section.

1. $7(x-3)^2 + 7(y+7)^2 = 56$ **0**
2. $16(x+1)^2 - 9(y-5)^2 = 144$ $\frac{5}{3}$
3. $\frac{(x-6)^2}{49} + \frac{(y-5)^2}{64} = 1$ $\frac{\sqrt{15}}{8} \approx 0.484$
4. $\frac{(y-4)^2}{100} - \frac{(x+2)^2}{9} = 1$ $\frac{\sqrt{109}}{10} \approx 1.04$
5. $(x-5)^2 = 10y$ **1**
6. $81(x+4)^2 + (y-9)^2 = 81$ $\frac{4\sqrt{5}}{9} \approx 0.994$

EXAMPLE 2 on p. 665 for Exs. 7–12

8. $\frac{(x+4)^2}{12} + \frac{y^2}{16} = 1$

Write an equation of the conic section.

7. Ellipse with vertices at $(-6, 4)$ and $(6, 4)$, and $e = 0.4$ $\frac{x^2}{36} + \frac{24(y-4)^2}{756} = 1$
8. Ellipse with foci at $(-4, 2)$ and $(-4, -2)$, and $e = 0.5$
9. Ellipse with center at $(0, 5)$, vertex at $(7, 5)$, and $e = 0.2$ $\frac{x^2}{49} + \frac{25(y-5)^2}{1176} = 1$
10. Hyperbola with foci at $(4, -5)$ and $(4, 3)$, and $e = 2.5$ **See margin.**
11. Hyperbola with vertices at $(1, -4)$ and $(7, -4)$, and $e = 1.8$ $\frac{(x-4)^2}{9} - \frac{25(x+4)^2}{504} = 1$
12. Hyperbola with center at $(-2, 3)$, focus at $(-5, 3)$, and $e = 4$ $\frac{16(x+2)^2}{9} - \frac{16(y-3)^2}{135} = 1$

EXAMPLE 3 on p. 666 for Exs. 13–14

13. **ASTRONOMY** Nereid, a moon of Neptune, has the most eccentric orbit of any moon in the solar system. The eccentricity of the orbit is $e = 0.751$ and the length of the major axis is about 11.0 million kilometers. Find an equation of Nereid's orbit. *Sample answer:* $\frac{x^2}{30.25} + \frac{y^2}{13.19} = 1$
14. **SATELLITES** A communications satellite is in an elliptical orbit around Earth, whose center is one focus of the orbit. The eccentricity of the orbit is $e = 0.394$, and the satellite is 14,300 kilometers from Earth's center at the closest point in its orbit. What is the satellite's distance from Earth's center at the farthest point in its orbit? **about 32,900 km**
15. **REASONING** *Explain* why the definition of eccentricity for ellipses and hyperbolas implies that $0 < e < 1$ for an ellipse and $e > 1$ for a hyperbola. **In the ellipse $0 < c < a$, therefore $0 < \frac{c}{a} < 1$. In the hyperbola $0 < a < c$, therefore $\frac{c}{a} > 1$.**

10. $\frac{(y+1)^2}{16} - \frac{(x-4)^2}{84} = 1$

Lessons 9.5–9.7

1. **WHISPER DISHES** A person at the focus of one of two facing parabolic dishes can hear a soft sound made at the focus of the other dish. The California Science Center in Los Angeles has two such "whisper dishes" whose vertices are about 47 feet apart. Each dish's focus is about 1.5 feet from its vertex. What are equations for the cross sections of the dishes if one dish's vertex is at the origin and the other dish's vertex is on the positive x-axis?

   A. $y^2 = 1.5x; y^2 = 1.5(x - 47)$
   B. $y^2 = 6x; y^2 = 6(x - 47)$
   C. $y^2 = 1.5x; y^2 = -1.5(x - 47)$
   D. $y^2 = 6x; y^2 = -6(x - 47)$

2. **MODELING AREA** The shaded region shown below is formed by two squares centered at the origin. The area of the shaded region is 28 square units. Which equation describes the possible values of x and y?

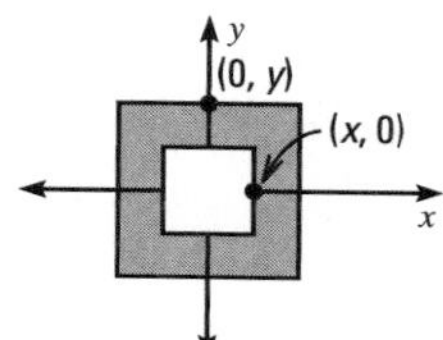

   A. $\frac{x^2}{7} - \frac{y^2}{7} = 1$ B. $\frac{y^2}{7} - \frac{x^2}{7} = 1$
   C. $\frac{x^2}{28} - \frac{y^2}{80} = 1$ D. $\frac{y^2}{28} - \frac{x^2}{28} = 1$

3. **HYPERBOLIC MIRROR** A hyperbolic mirror reflects light rays directed toward one focus to the other focus. A certain hyperbolic mirror can be represented by the right branch of the hyperbola with this equation:

$$\frac{x^2}{64} - \frac{y^2}{80} = 1$$

   If light from point (0, 9) is directed at the focus at (12, 0), at approximately what point on the mirror will the light be reflected to the focus at (−12, 0)?

   A. (4.8, 5.4) B. (5.1, 5.2)
   C. (7.5, 3.4) D. (8.4, 2.7)

4. **AVIATION** When a jet breaks the sound barrier, sound waves form a "Mach cone" behind the jet, and a sonic boom is heard as the cone passes. The Mach cone for a jet in level flight meets the ground in a hyperbola with the jet directly above the hyperbola's center. Suppose a jet makes a sonic boom heard along the hyperbola $\frac{x^2}{36} - \frac{y^2}{100} = 1$ where x and y are in miles. What is the shortest possible horizontal distance you could be from the jet when you first hear the boom?

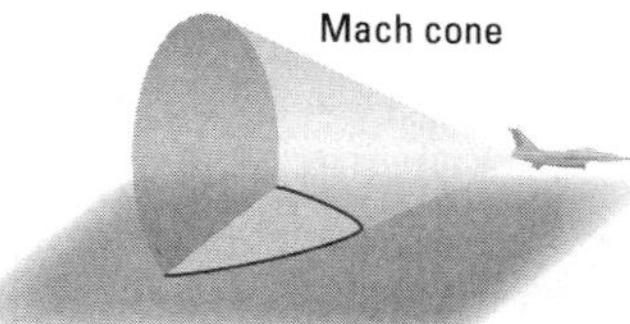

   A. 4 miles B. 6 miles
   C. 10 miles D. 11.7 miles

5. **CASSEGRAIN TELESCOPE** The diagram shows the mirrors in a Cassegrain telescope. The equations of the mirrors are given below. Which type of conic section does the surface of mirror B represent?

   Mirror A: $y^2 - 72x - 450 = 0$

   Mirror B: $88.4x^2 - 49.7y^2 - 4390 = 0$

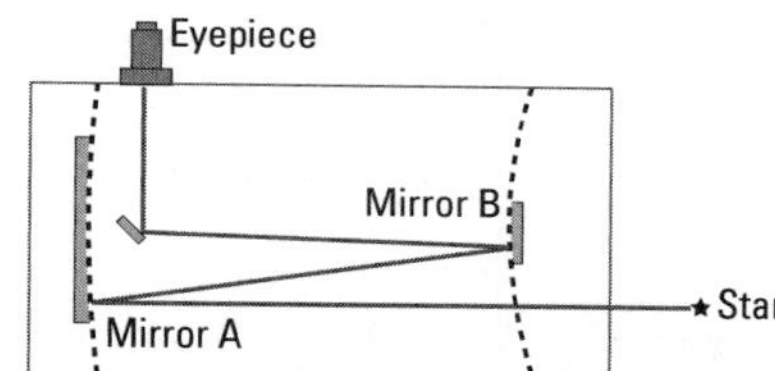

   A. Circle B. Parabola
   C. Ellipse D. Hyperbola

6. **OPEN-RESPONSE** Consider the equations $9x^2 + y^2 + 8y = 20$ and $x^2 + 4y^2 = 16$.

   a. Graph both equations on the same coordinate axes.

   b. Find all points of intersection.

Kentucky Mixed Review

1. D
2. B
3. D
4. B
5. D
6. a.

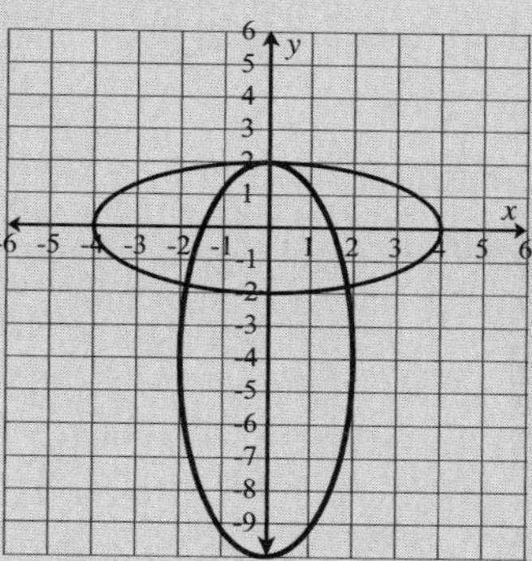

b. $(0, 2), \left(\pm\frac{8\sqrt{66}}{35}, -\frac{62}{35}\right) \approx (\pm 1.86, -1.77)$

9 CHAPTER SUMMARY

Additional Resources

The following resources are available to help review the materials in this chapter.

Chapter 9 Resource Book
- Chapter Review Games and Activities, p. 84
- Cumulative Practice, Chs. 1–9, pp. 86–87

Student Resources in Spanish

eWorkbook

@HomeTutor

Vocabulary Practice

Vocabulary practice is available at **classzone.com**

BIG IDEAS — *For Your Notebook*

Big Idea 1 — Writing Equations of Conic Sections

Conic	Equation	Key facts		
Circle	$x^2 + y^2 = r^2$	radius r		
Parabola	$x^2 = 4py$	*Axis of symmetry* vertical	*Focus* $(0, p)$	*Directrix* $y = -p$
	$y^2 = 4px$	*Axis of symmetry* horizontal	*Focus* $(p, 0)$	*Directrix* $x = -p$
Ellipse	$\frac{x^2}{a^2} + \frac{y^2}{b^2} = 1$	*Major axis* horizontal	*Vertices* $(\pm a, 0)$	*Co-vertices* $(0, \pm b)$
	$\frac{x^2}{b^2} + \frac{y^2}{a^2} = 1$	*Major axis* vertical	*Vertices* $(0, \pm a)$	*Co-vertices* $(\pm b, 0)$
Hyperbola	$\frac{x^2}{a^2} - \frac{y^2}{b^2} = 1$	*Transverse axis* horizontal	*Asymptotes* $y = \pm\frac{b}{a}x$	*Vertices* $(\pm a, 0)$
	$\frac{y^2}{a^2} - \frac{x^2}{b^2} = 1$	*Transverse axis* vertical	*Asymptotes* $y = \pm\frac{a}{b}x$	*Vertices* $(0, \pm a)$

Big Idea 2 — Graphing Equations of Conic Sections

Circle

$(x - h)^2 + (y - k)^2 = r^2$

Parabola

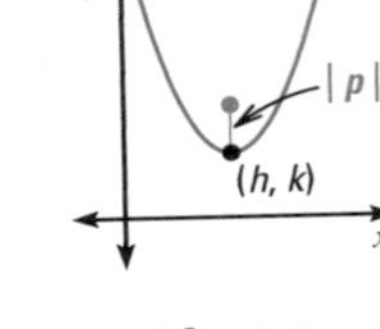

$(x - h)^2 = 4p(y - k)$

Ellipse

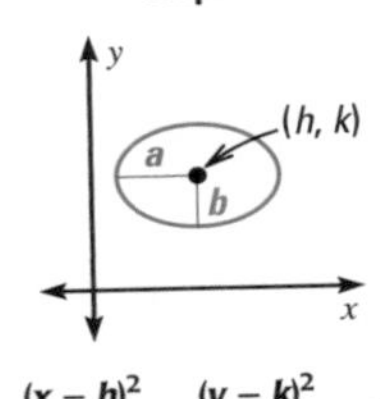

$\frac{(x - h)^2}{a^2} + \frac{(y - k)^2}{b^2} = 1$

Hyperbola

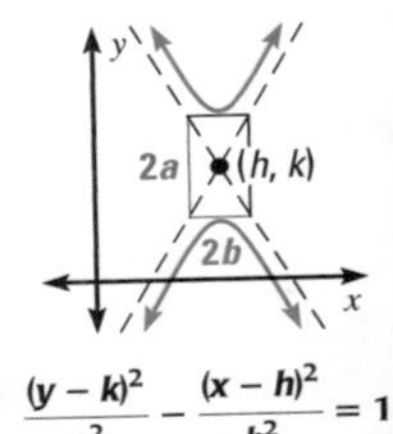

$\frac{(y - k)^2}{a^2} - \frac{(x - h)^2}{b^2} = 1$

Big Idea 3 — Solving Quadratic Systems

Method	Description	When to use
Graphing	Graph the equations. Identify any points of intersection.	When graphing is easy or when using a graphing calculator
Substitution	Solve one equation for one of the variables and substitute it into the other equation.	When you can easily solve for one variable (or its square) in terms of the other variable
Elimination	Multiply one or both equations by a constant as needed, and add.	When you can eliminate one or more of the variable terms

CHAPTER REVIEW

@HomeTutor
classzone.com
- Multi-Language Glossary
- Vocabulary practice

REVIEW KEY VOCABULARY

- distance formula, *p. 614*
- midpoint formula, *p. 615*
- focus, foci, *pp. 620, 634, 642*
- directrix, *p. 620*
- circle, *p. 626*
- center, *pp. 626, 634, 642*
- radius, *p. 626*
- ellipse, *p. 634*
- vertices, *pp. 634, 642*
- major axis, *p. 634*
- co-vertices, *p. 634*
- minor axis, *p. 634*
- hyperbola, *p. 642*
- transverse axis, *p. 642*
- conic sections, *p. 650*
- general second-degree equation, *p. 653*
- discriminant, *p. 653*
- quadratic system, *p. 658*

VOCABULARY EXERCISES

1. Copy and complete: A(n) __?__ is the set of all points in a plane equidistant from a point called the focus and a line called the directrix. **parabola**
2. Copy and complete: The line segment joining the two co-vertices of an ellipse is the __?__. **minor axis**
3. Copy and complete: The line segment joining the two vertices of a hyperbola is the __?__. **transverse axis**
4. **WRITING** *Describe* how the asymptotes of a hyperbola help you draw the hyperbola. **The asymptotes indicate how wide or narrow the hyperbola is.**

REVIEW EXAMPLES AND EXERCISES

Use the review examples and exercises below to check your understanding of the concepts you have learned in each lesson of Chapter 9.

9.1 Apply the Distance and Midpoint Formulas

pp. 614–619

EXAMPLE

Find the distance between (−5, 3) and (1, −3). Then find the midpoint of the line segment joining the two points.

$$d = \sqrt{(x_2 - x_1)^2 + (y_2 - y_1)^2} = \sqrt{(1 - (-5))^2 + (-3 - 3)^2} = \sqrt{72} = 6\sqrt{2} \approx 8.49$$

$$M\left(\frac{x_1 + x_2}{2}, \frac{y_1 + y_2}{2}\right) = \left(\frac{-5 + 1}{2}, \frac{3 + (-3)}{2}\right) = (-2, 0)$$

EXERCISES

EXAMPLES 1 and 3
on pp. 614–615
for Exs. 5–8

Find the distance between the two points. Then find the midpoint of the line segment joining the two points.

5. (−6, −5), (2, −3) **$2\sqrt{17}$; (−2, −4)**
6. (−2, 5), (1, 9) **5; $\left(-\frac{1}{2}, 7\right)$**
7. (−3, −4), (2, 5) **$\sqrt{106}$; $\left(-\frac{1}{2}, \frac{1}{2}\right)$**
8. **SKYDIVING** A skydiver lands 200 yards west and 40 yards north of a target. A second skydiver lands 30 yards east and 140 yards south of the same target. How far from each other do the two skydivers land? **about 292 yd**

Extra Example 9.1

Find the distance between (−4, 1) and (5, −7). Then find the midpoint of the line segment joining the two points. **distance: $\sqrt{145}$; midpoint: $\left(\frac{1}{2}, -3\right)$**

9 CHAPTER REVIEW

Extra Example 9.2

Graph $x^2 = -20y$. Identify the focus, directrix, and axis of symmetry.

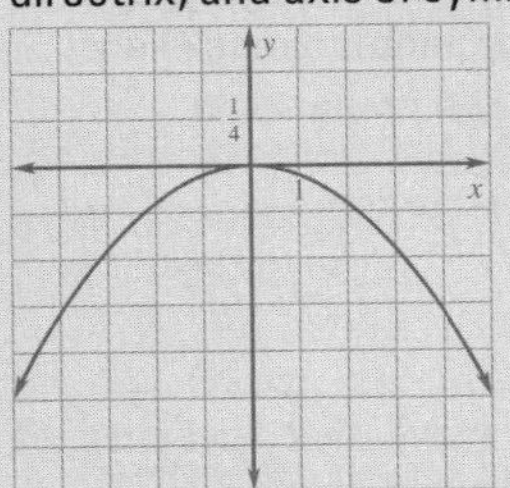

focus: $(0, -5)$, directrix: $y = 5$, axis of symmetry: $x = 0$

Extra Example 9.3

Graph $y^2 = 625 - x^2$. Identify the radius. $r = 25$

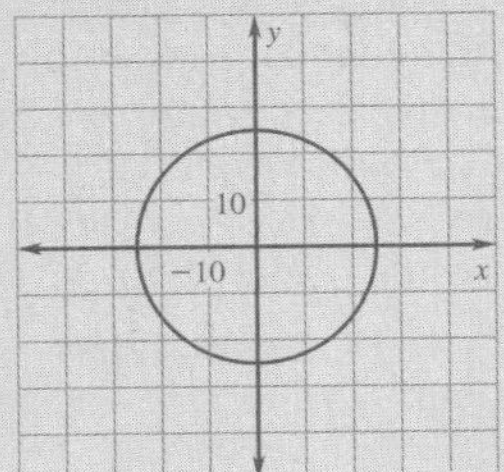

9.

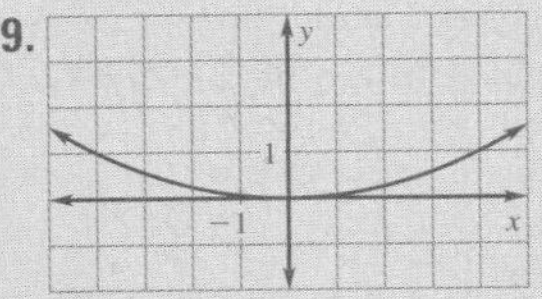

10.

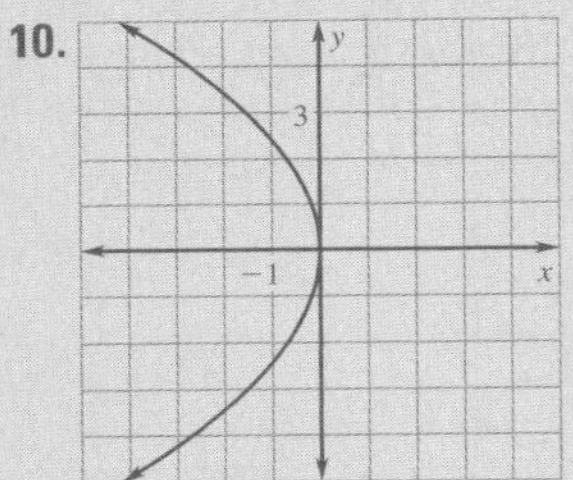

11.

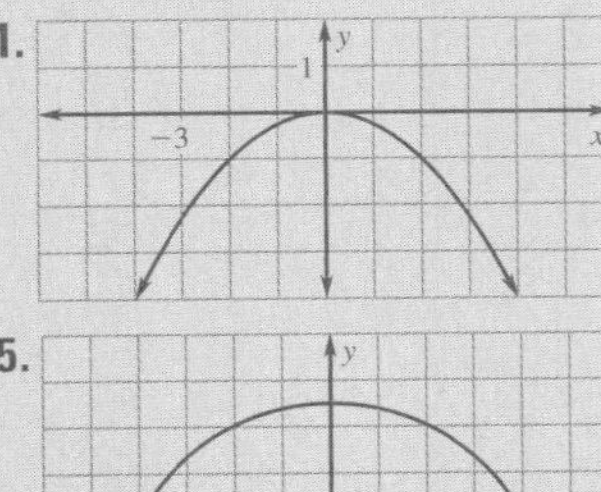

15.

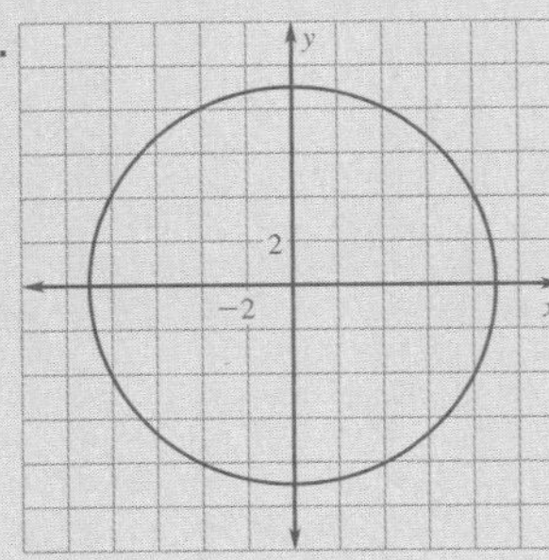

9.2 Graph and Write Equations of Parabolas

pp. 620–625

EXAMPLE

Graph $x = \frac{1}{12}y^2$. Identify the focus, directrix, and axis of symmetry.

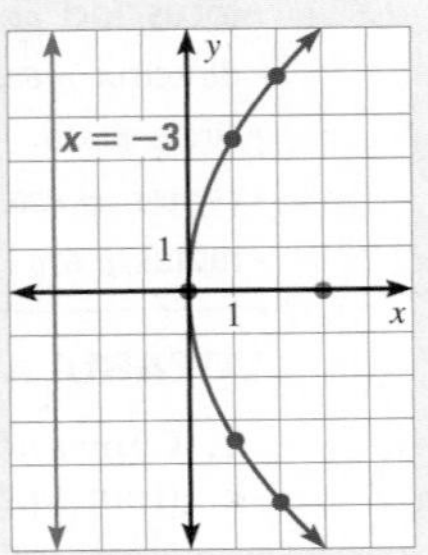

STEP 1 **Rewrite** $x = \frac{1}{12}y^2$ in standard form as $y^2 = 12x$.

STEP 2 **Identify** the focus, directrix, and axis of symmetry. The equation has the form $y^2 = 4px$ with $4p = 12$, so $p = 3$. The focus is $(p, 0)$, or $(3, 0)$, and the directrix is $x = -p$, or $x = -3$. Because y is squared, the axis of symmetry is the x-axis.

STEP 3 **Draw** the parabola. Because $p > 0$, the parabola opens to the right. Some points on the parabola are $(0, 0)$, $(1, \pm 3.46)$, and $(2, \pm 4.90)$.

EXERCISES

EXAMPLES 1 and 2 on p. 621 for Exs. 9–14

Graph the equation. Identify the focus, directrix, and axis of symmetry of the parabola. 9–11. See margin for art.

9. $x^2 = 16y$ $(0, 4)$, $y = -4$, $x = 0$
10. $y^2 = -6x$ $\left(-\frac{3}{2}, 0\right)$, $x = \frac{3}{2}$, $y = 0$
11. $x^2 + 4y = 0$ $(0, -1)$, $y = 1$, $x = 0$

Write the standard form of the equation of the parabola with the given focus or directrix and vertex at (0, 0).

12. Focus: $(-5, 0)$ $y^2 = -20x$
13. Focus: $(0, 3)$ $x^2 = 12y$
14. Directrix: $x = -6$ $y^2 = 24x$

9.3 Graph and Write Equations of Circles

pp. 626–632

EXAMPLE

Graph $x^2 = 64 - y^2$. Identify the radius of the circle.

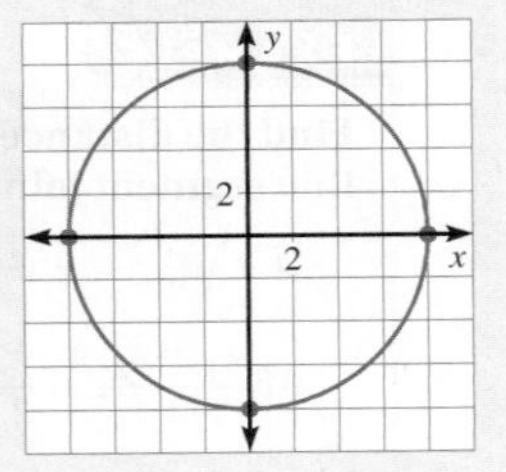

STEP 1 **Rewrite** $x^2 = 64 - y^2$ in standard form as $x^2 + y^2 = 64$.

STEP 2 **Identify** the radius. The graph is a circle with center at the origin and radius $r = \sqrt{64} = 8$.

STEP 3 **Draw** a circle passing through points that are 8 units from the origin, such as $(8, 0)$, $(0, 8)$, $(-8, 0)$, and $(0, -8)$.

EXERCISES

EXAMPLES 1 and 2 on pp. 626–627 for Exs. 15–20

Graph the equation. Identify the radius of the circle. 15–17. See margin for art.

15. $x^2 + y^2 = 81$ 9
16. $x^2 = 40 - y^2$ $2\sqrt{10}$
17. $3x^2 + 3y^2 = 147$ 7

Write the standard form of the equation of the circle that passes through the given point and whose center is the origin.

18. $(5, 9)$ $x^2 + y^2 = 106$
19. $(-8, 2)$ $x^2 + y^2 = 68$
20. $(-7, -4)$ $x^2 + y^2 = 65$

16.

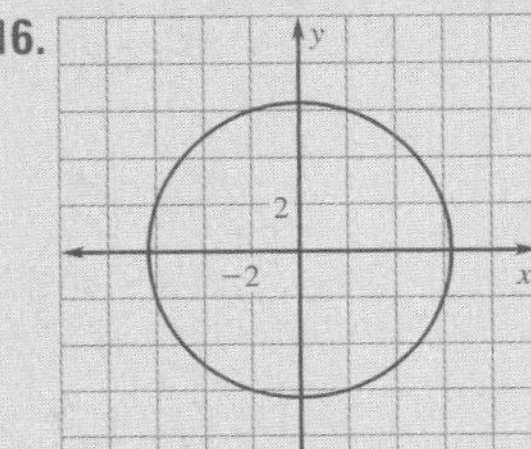

17.

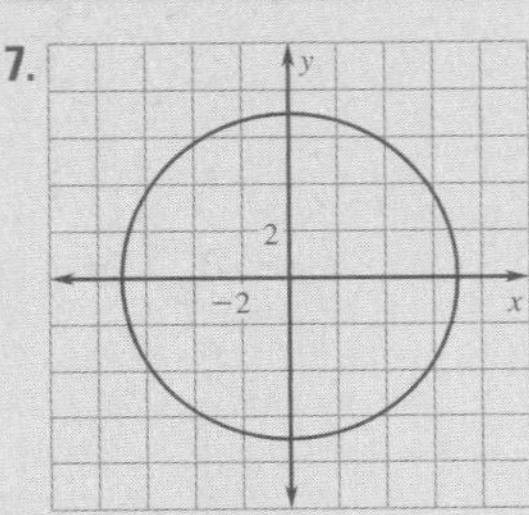

@HomeTutor
classzone.com
Chapter Review Practice

9.4 Graph and Write Equations of Ellipses

pp. 634–639

EXAMPLE

Graph $4x^2 + y^2 = 16$. Identify the vertices, co-vertices, and foci.

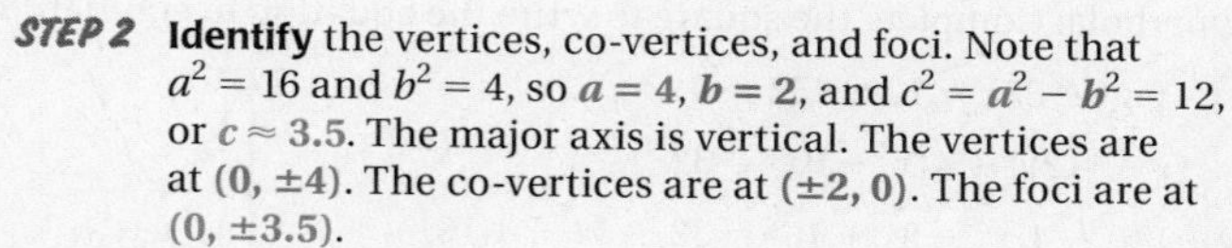

STEP 1 **Rewrite** $4x^2 + y^2 = 16$ in standard form as $\frac{x^2}{4} + \frac{y^2}{16} = 1$.

STEP 2 **Identify** the vertices, co-vertices, and foci. Note that $a^2 = 16$ and $b^2 = 4$, so $a = 4$, $b = 2$, and $c^2 = a^2 - b^2 = 12$, or $c \approx 3.5$. The major axis is vertical. The vertices are at $(0, \pm 4)$. The co-vertices are at $(\pm 2, 0)$. The foci are at $(0, \pm 3.5)$.

STEP 3 **Draw** the ellipse.

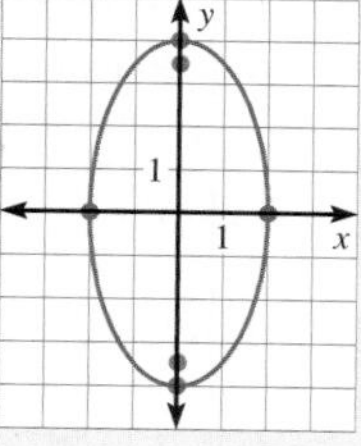

EXERCISES

XAMPLES
, 2, and 4
n pp. 635–636
or Exs. 21–25

21–23. See margin for art.

Graph the equation. Identify the vertices, co-vertices, and foci of the ellipse.

21. $16x^2 + 25y^2 = 400$
$(\pm 5, 0), (0, \pm 4), (\pm 3, 0)$

22. $81x^2 + 9y^2 = 729$
$(0, \pm 9), (\pm 3, 0), (0, \pm 6\sqrt{2})$

23. $64x^2 + 36y^2 = 2304$
$(0, \pm 8), (\pm 6, 0), (0, \pm 2\sqrt{7})$

Write an equation of the ellipse with the given characteristics and center at (0, 0).

24. Vertex: $(-6, 0)$; co-vertex: $(0, -3)$
$\frac{x^2}{36} + \frac{y^2}{9} = 1$

25. Vertex: $(0, -8)$; focus: $(0, 5)$
$\frac{y^2}{64} + \frac{x^2}{39} = 1$

9.5 Graph and Write Equations of Hyperbolas

pp. 642–648

EXAMPLE

Graph $4x^2 - 9y^2 = 36$. Identify the vertices, foci, and asymptotes.

STEP 1 **Rewrite** $4x^2 - 9y^2 = 36$ in standard form as $\frac{x^2}{9} - \frac{y^2}{4} = 1$.

STEP 2 **Identify** the vertices, foci, and asymptotes. Note that $a^2 = 9$ and $b^2 = 4$, so $a = 3$, $b = 2$, and $c^2 = a^2 + b^2 = 13$, or $c \approx 3.6$. The transverse axis is horizontal. The vertices are at $(\pm 3, 0)$. The foci are at $(\pm 3.6, 0)$. The asymptotes are $y = \pm\frac{b}{a}x = \pm\frac{2}{3}x$.

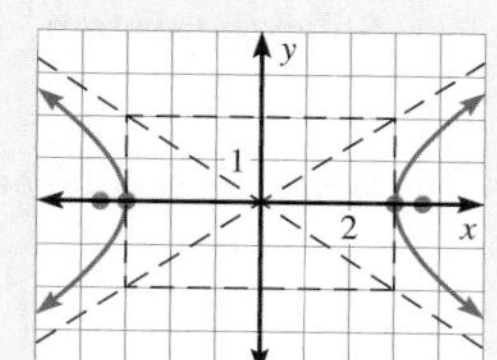

STEP 3 **Draw** asymptotes through opposite corners of a rectangle centered at (0, 0) that is $2a = 6$ units wide and $2b = 4$ units high. Draw the hyperbola.

EXERCISES

XAMPLES
and 2
p. 643
Exs. 26–30

Graph the equation. Identify the vertices, foci, and asymptotes. 26–28. See margin for art.

26. $9x^2 - y^2 = 9$
$(\pm 1, 0), (\pm\sqrt{10}, 0), y = \pm 3x$

27. $4x^2 - 16y^2 = 64$
$(\pm 4, 0), (\pm 2\sqrt{5}, 0), y = \pm\frac{1}{2}x$

28. $100y^2 - 36x^2 = 3600$
$(0, \pm 6), (0, \pm 2\sqrt{34}), y = \pm\frac{3}{5}x$

Write an equation of the hyperbola with the given foci and vertices.

29. Foci: $(0, \pm 5)$; vertices: $(0, \pm 2)$ $\frac{y^2}{4} - \frac{x^2}{21} = 1$

30. Foci: $(\pm 9, 0)$; vertices: $(\pm 4, 0)$ $\frac{x^2}{16} - \frac{y^2}{65} = 1$

21.

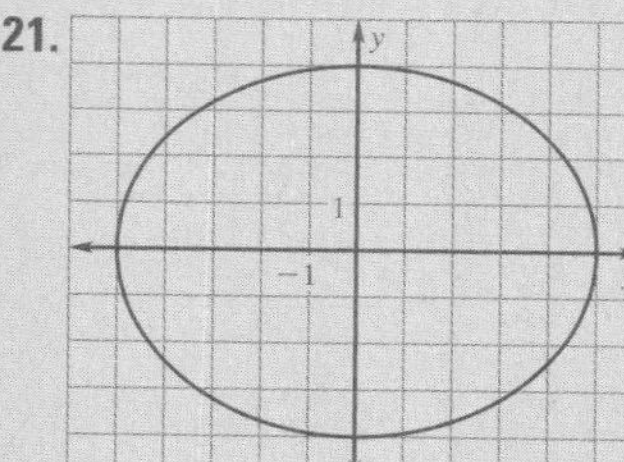

22.

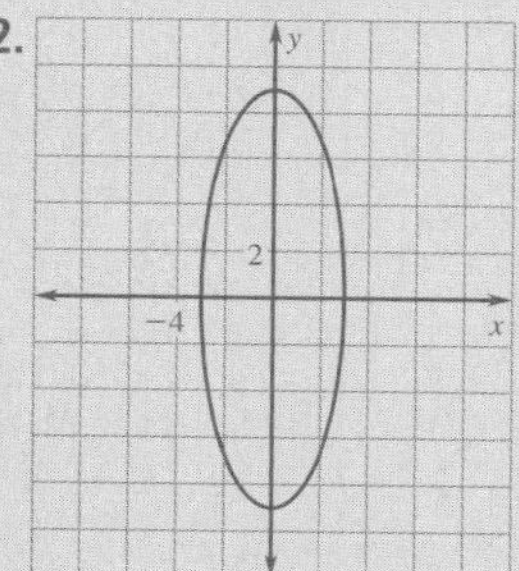

23.

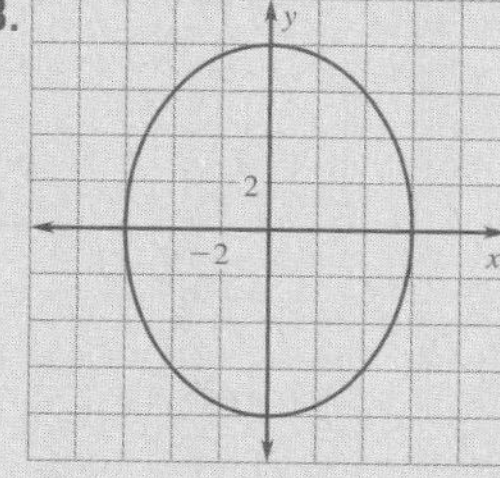

Extra Example 9.4

Graph $9x^2 + y^2 = 9$. Identify the vertices, co-vertices, and foci.

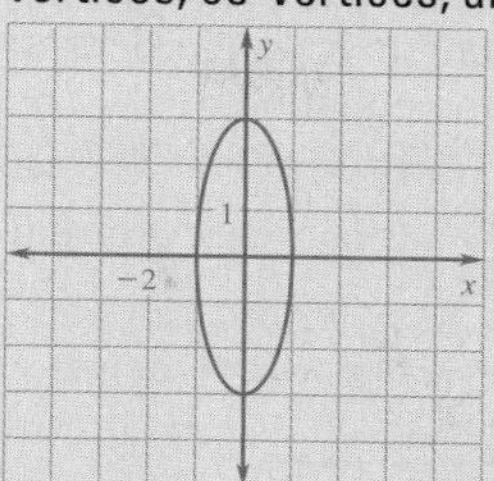

vertices: $(0, -3)$ and $(0, 3)$,
co-vertices: $(-1, 0)$ and $(1, 0)$,
foci: $(0, -2\sqrt{2})$ and $(0, 2\sqrt{2})$

Extra Example 9.5

Graph $9x^2 - y^2 = 225$. Identify the vertices, foci, and asymptotes.

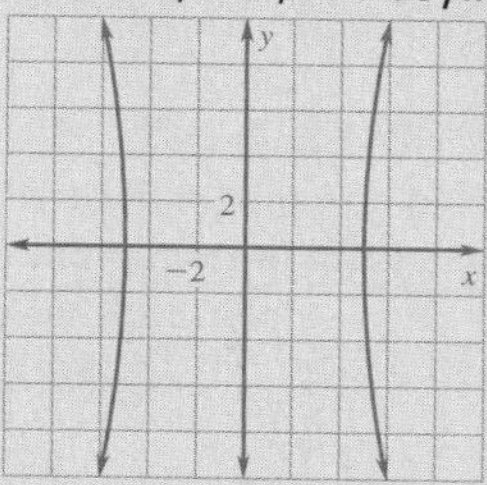

vertices: $(-5, 0)$ and $(5, 0)$;
foci: $(-5\sqrt{10}, 0)$ and $(5\sqrt{10}, 0)$,
asymptotes: $y = \pm 3x$

26.

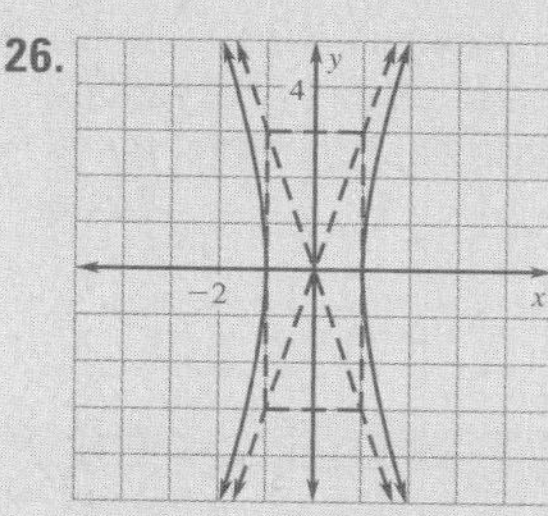

27.

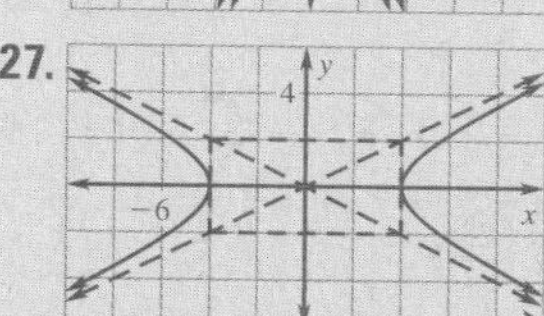

28.

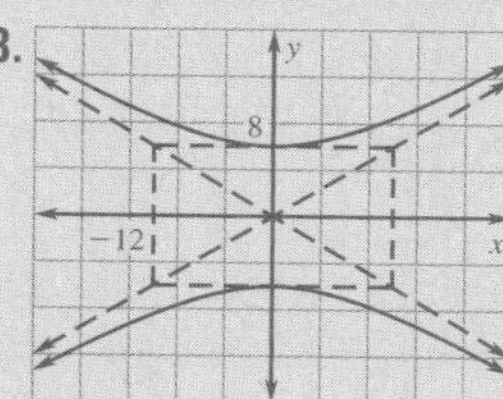

9 CHAPTER REVIEW

Extra Example 9.6

Classify the conic section $x^2 + 16y^2 + 4x - 96y + 132 = 0$ and write its equation in standard form. Then graph the equation.

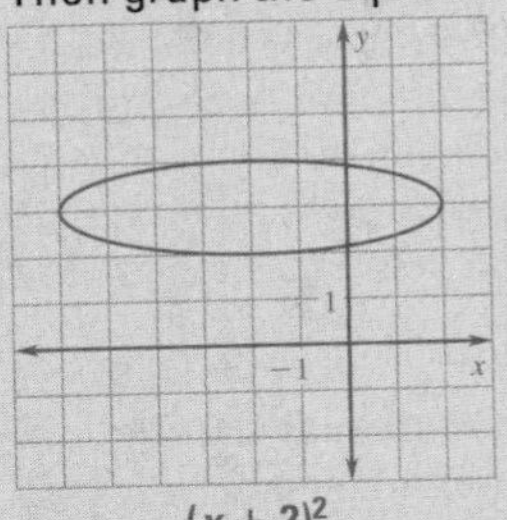

ellipse; $\frac{(x+2)^2}{16} + (y-3)^2 = 1$

Extra Example 9.7

Solve the system.
$x^2 + y^2 = 36$
$3x^2 - y^2 - 28 = 0$ $(-4, -2\sqrt{5})$, $(-4, 2\sqrt{5})$, $(4, -2\sqrt{5})$, $(4, 2\sqrt{5})$

31. ellipse, $\frac{(x+5)^2}{9} + \frac{(y+4)^2}{4} = 1$

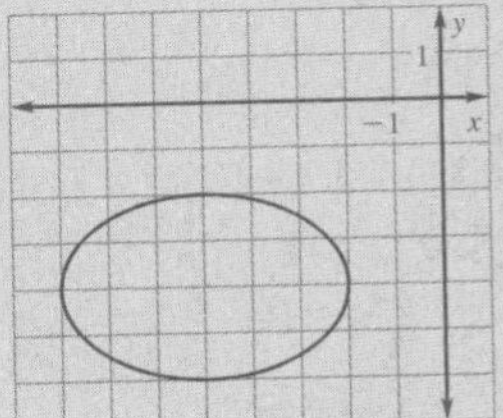

32.

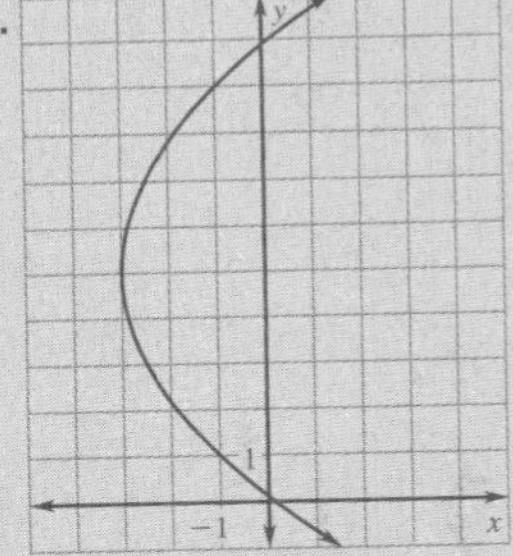

33.

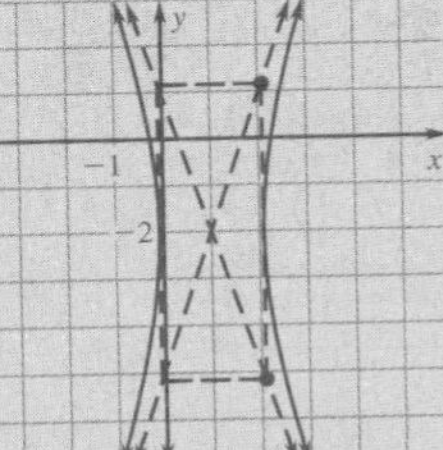

34.

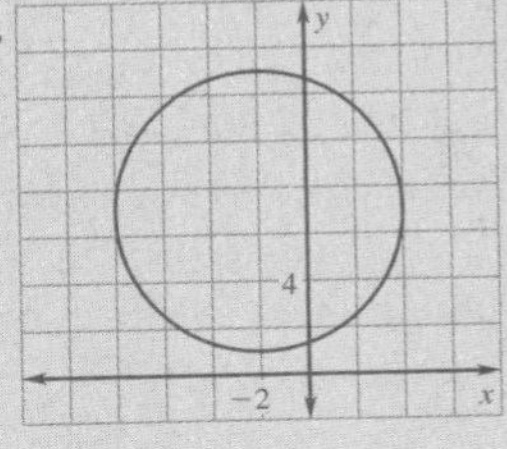

9.6 Translate and Classify Conic Sections — pp. 650–657

EXAMPLE

Classify the conic section $-4x^2 + y^2 + 32x - 12y - 32 = 0$ and write its equation in standard form. Then graph the equation.

Because $A = -4$, $B = 0$, and $C = 1$, the discriminant is $B^2 - 4AC = 16 > 0$, so the conic is a hyperbola. Complete the square to write the equation in standard form.

$$-4x^2 + y^2 + 32x - 12y - 32 = 0$$
$$(y^2 - 12y) - 4(x^2 - 8x) = 32$$
$$(y^2 - 12y + 36) - 4(x^2 - 8x + 16) = 32 + 36 - 4(16)$$
$$(y-6)^2 - 4(x-4)^2 = 4$$
$$\frac{(y-6)^2}{4} - (x-4)^2 = 1$$

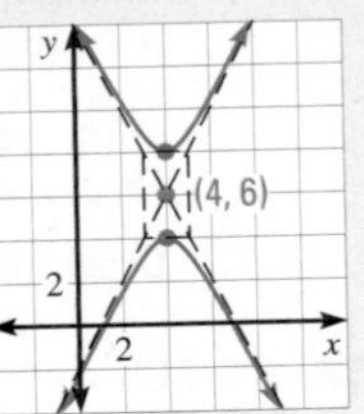

From the equation, $(h, k) = (4, 6)$, $a = \sqrt{4} = 2$, and $b = 1$. The vertices are $(4, 6 + 2) = (4, 8)$ and $(4, 6 - 2) = (4, 4)$. The graph is shown above.

EXERCISES

EXAMPLE 6 on p. 653 for Exs. 31–34

Classify the conic section and write its equation in standard form. Then graph the equation. 31–34. See margin for art.

31. $4x^2 + 9y^2 + 40x + 72y + 208 = 0$ See margin.

32. $y^2 - 10y - 8x + 1 = 0$ parabola, $(y-5)^2 = 8(x+3)$

33. $9x^2 - y^2 - 18x - 4y - 5 = 0$ hyperbola, $\frac{(x-1)^2}{\frac{10}{9}} - \frac{(y+2)^2}{10} = 1$

34. $x^2 + y^2 + 4x - 14y + 17 = 0$ circle, $(x+2)^2 + (y-7)^2 = 36$

9.7 Solve Quadratic Systems — pp. 658–664

EXAMPLE

Solve the system. $\quad 12x^2 - 81y^2 + 16 = 0$
$\quad 2x^2 + 9y = 0$

Write the second equation as $y = -\frac{2}{9}x^2$. Then substitute in the first equation.

$12x^2 - 81\left(-\frac{2}{9}x^2\right)^2 + 16 = 0$ **Substitute for y in first equation.**

$12x^2 - 4x^4 + 16 = 0$ **Simplify.**

$x^4 - 3x^2 - 4 = 0$ **Divide each side by −4.**

$(x^2 - 4)(x^2 + 1) = 0$ **Factor.**

By the zero product property, $x = \pm 2$. The solutions are $\left(2, -\frac{8}{9}\right)$ and $\left(-2, -\frac{8}{9}\right)$.

EXERCISES

EXAMPLES 2 and 3 on pp. 659–660 for Exs. 35–37

Solve the system.

35. $y^2 = 4x$
$2x - 5y = -8$ (16, 8), (1, 2)

36. $x^2 + y^2 - 100 = 0$
$x + y - 14 = 0$ (8, 6), (6, 8)

37. $16x^2 - 4y^2 = 64$
$4x^2 + 9y^2 - 40x = -64$ (2, 0)

Chapter Test, p. 673

7.

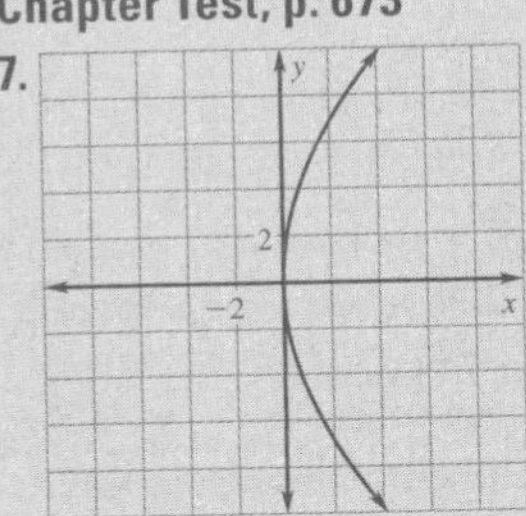

8.

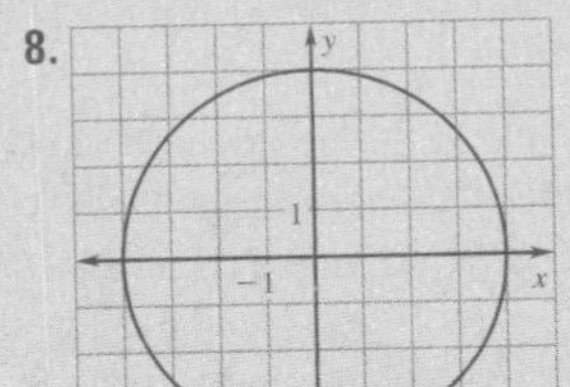

9.

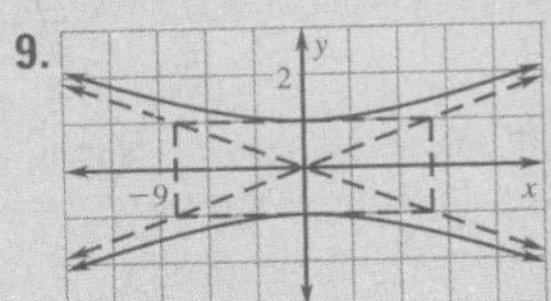

9 CHAPTER TEST

Find the distance between the two points. Then find the midpoint of the line segment joining the two points.

1. $(-1, 5), (7, 3)$ $2\sqrt{17}; (3, 4)$
2. $(4, 2), (8, 8)$ $2\sqrt{13}; (6, 5)$
3. $(-1, -6), (1, 5)$ $5\sqrt{5}; \left(0, -\frac{1}{2}\right)$
4. $(2, -5), (3, 1)$ $\sqrt{37}; \left(\frac{5}{2}, -2\right)$
5. $(-6, -2), (-3, 5)$ $\sqrt{58}; \left(-\frac{9}{2}, \frac{3}{2}\right)$
6. $(1, 9), (10, -2)$ $\sqrt{202}; \left(\frac{11}{2}, \frac{7}{2}\right)$

Graph the equation. 7–15. See margin.

7. $y^2 - 24x = 0$
8. $x^2 + y^2 = 16$
9. $64y^2 - x^2 = 64$
10. $18x^2 + 2y^2 = 18$
11. $(x - 6)^2 + (y + 1)^2 = 36$
12. $(x + 4)^2 = 6(y - 2)$
13. $\frac{(x + 4)^2}{9} - \frac{(y - 7)^2}{49} = 1$
14. $\frac{(x - 8)^2}{81} + \frac{(y - 2)^2}{100} = 1$
15. $\frac{(y - 5)^2}{9} - (x + 3)^2 = 1$

Write the standard form of the equation of the conic section with the given characteristics.

16. Parabola with vertex at (0, 0) and directrix at $x = -6$ $y^2 = 24x$
17. Parabola with vertex at (−2, −1) and focus at (−2, 5) $(x + 2)^2 = 24(y + 1)$
18. Circle with center at (0, 0) and passing through (−5, 2) $x^2 + y^2 = 29$
19. Circle with center at (1, −4) and radius 6 $(x - 1)^2 + (y + 4)^2 = 36$
20. Ellipse with center at (0, 0), vertex at (0, 6), and co-vertex at (−3, 0) $\frac{x^2}{9} + \frac{y^2}{36} = 1$
21. Ellipse with vertices at (−1, 4) and (7, 4) and foci at (1, 4) and (5, 4) $\frac{(x - 3)^2}{16} + \frac{(y - 4)^2}{12} = 1$
22. Hyperbola with vertices at (0, −6) and (0, 6) and foci at (0, −9) and (0, 9) $\frac{y^2}{36} - \frac{x^2}{45} = 1$
23. Hyperbola with vertex at (2, −5), focus at (−1, −5), and center at (5, −5) $\frac{(x - 5)^2}{9} - \frac{(y + 5)^2}{27} = 1$

Classify the conic section and write its equation in standard form. 24–29. See margin.

24. $x^2 + 4y^2 - 6x - 16y + 21 = 0$
25. $x^2 + y^2 + 8x + 12y + 3 = 0$
26. $4x^2 - 9y^2 - 40x + 64 = 0$
27. $y^2 - 16y - 12x + 40 = 0$
28. $25x^2 + 4y^2 + 50x - 24y - 39 = 0$
29. $y^2 - 16x^2 + 14y + 64x - 31 = 0$

Solve the system.

30. $4x^2 + y^2 = 16$; $x + y = 2$ $\left(-\frac{6}{5}, \frac{16}{5}\right), (2, 0)$
31. $x^2 + 4y^2 - 8y = 4$; $y^2 - 2y - 8x - 16 = 0$ $(-2, 0), (-2, 2)$
32. $y^2 - x^2 + 2x - 5 = 0$; $x^2 + y^2 - 2x - 3 = 0$ $(1, -2), (1, 2)$

33. **WATER SURFACE** A cylindrical glass of water has a 1.5 inch radius. If the glass is tilted 60°, the water's surface meets the glass in an ellipse with minor axis 3 inches long and major axis 6 inches long. Write equations that model the water's surface with the glass upright and after the glass is tilted. Use the center of the water's surface as the origin. $x^2 + y^2 = 2.25, \frac{x^2}{9} + \frac{y^2}{36} = 1$

34. **ASTRONOMY** The Green Bank Telescope in West Virginia has a main reflector whose cross section is a portion of a "parent" parabola. A diagram of the reflector's cross section and the parent parabola is shown. Write an equation that models the parent parabola if its vertex is at (0, 0). What is the distance from the vertex to the focus? $x^2 = \frac{10{,}816}{45}y$; about 60.1 m

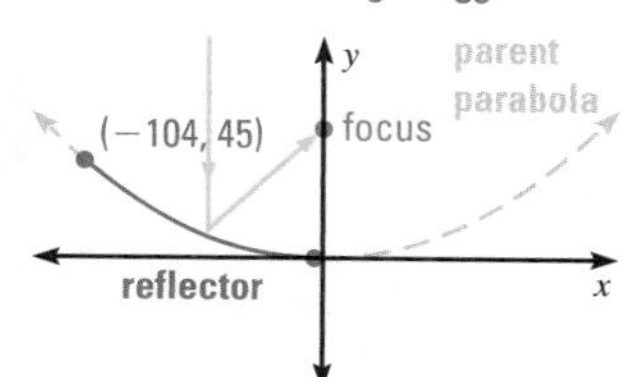

10.
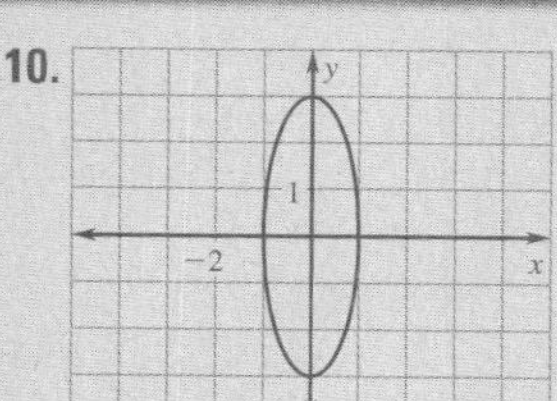

11.
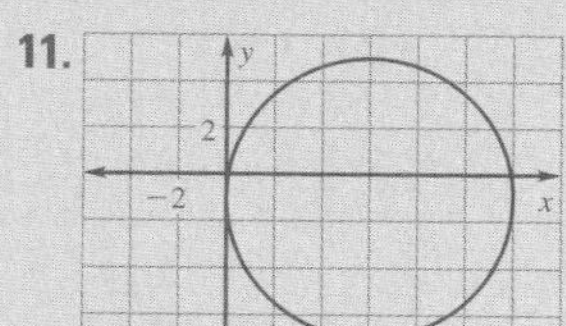

12.
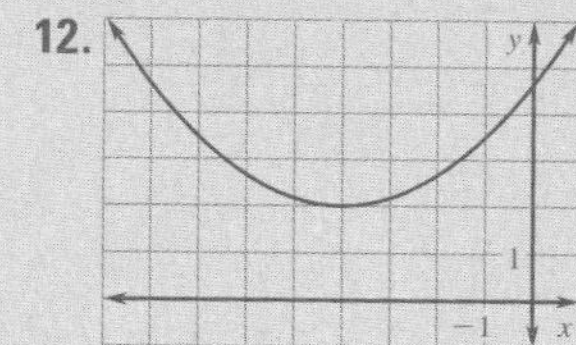

Additional Resources

Assessment Book

- Chapter Test, Levels A, B, C, pp. 127–132
- Standardized Chapter Test, pp. 133–134
- SAT/ACT Chapter Test, pp. 135–136
- Alternative Assessment, pp. 137–138

Test Generator CD-ROM

Chapter Test

Easily-readable reduced copies (with answers) of Chapter Test B, the Standardized Chapter Test, and the Alternative Assessment from the Assessment Book can be found on pp. 612E–612F.

13.
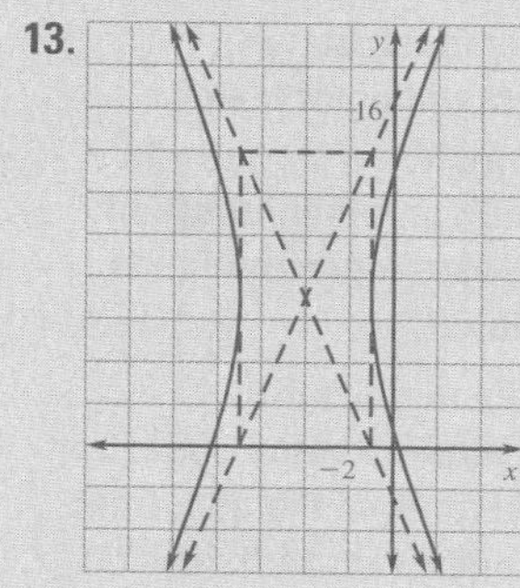

14.
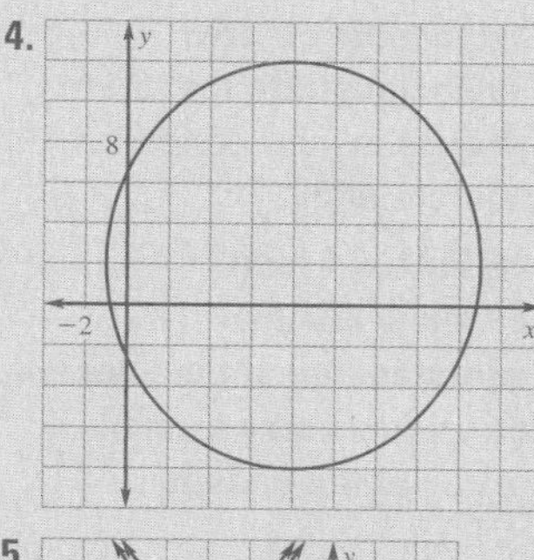

15.
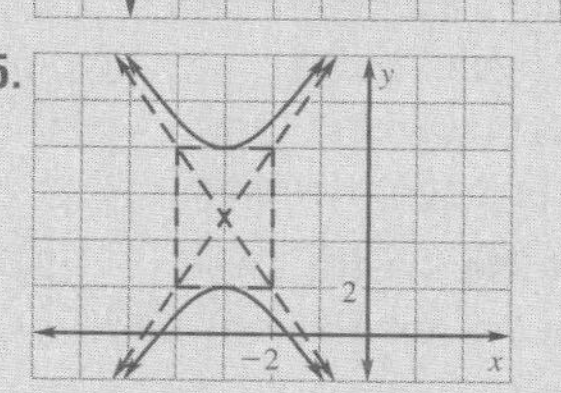

24–29. See Additional Answers beginning on p. AA1.

Kentucky General Scoring Rubric

4 Points (Full credit)

- You complete all important components of the question and communicate ideas clearly.
- You demonstrate in-depth understanding of the relevant concepts and/or processes.
- Where appropriate, you choose more efficient and/or sophisticated processes.
- Where appropriate, you offer insightful interpretations or extensions (generalizations, applications, analogies).

3 Points (Full or Partial Credit)

- You complete most important components of the question and communicate clearly.
- You demonstrate an understanding of major concepts even though you overlook or misunderstand some less-important ideas or details.

2 Points (Partial Credit)

- You complete some important components of the question and communicate those components clearly.
- You demonstrate that there are gaps in your conceptual understanding.

1 Point (Partial Credit)

- You show minimal understanding of the question.
- You address only a small portion of the question.

0 Points (No Credit)

- Your answer is totally incorrect or irrelevant.

BLANK (No Credit)

- You did not give any answer at all.

Kentucky Test Preparation

TEST PREPARATION

Scoring Rubric

Full Credit
- solution is complete and correct

Partial Credit
- solution is complete but has errors,

or
- solution is without error but incomplete

No Credit
- no solution is given,

or
- solution makes no sense

OPEN-RESPONSE QUESTIONS

PROBLEM

Two vertices of an equilateral triangle are $A(0, 0)$ and $B(6, 0)$.

a. Write and solve a system of equations to find the coordinates of the third vertex C of $\triangle ABC$.

b. Is there only one possible position for the third vertex? *Explain.*

Below are sample solutions to the problem. Read each solution and the comments on the left to see why the sample represents *full credit, partial credit*, or *no credit*.

SAMPLE 1: Full credit solution

The solution is set up logically and thoroughly.

a. Because $AB = 6 - 0 = 6$ and $\triangle ABC$ is equilateral, $AC = BC = 6$. Let (x, y) represent the coordinates of vertex C. Use the distance formula.

For AC: $\sqrt{(x-0)^2 + (y-0)^2} = 6$ $x^2 + y^2 = 36$

For BC: $\sqrt{(x-6)^2 + (y-0)^2} = 6$

$$(x-6)^2 + y^2 = 36$$
$$x^2 - 12x + 36 + y^2 = 36$$
$$x^2 + y^2 - 12x = 0$$

The correct equations are obtained, and a valid method is used to solve the system.

Solve the system by adding -1 times the second equation to the first.

$$x^2 + y^2 = 36$$
$$-x^2 - y^2 + 12x = 0$$
$$12x = 36 \Rightarrow x = 3$$

Substitute **3** for x in the first equation: $\mathbf{3}^2 + y^2 = 36$, so $y^2 = 27$, or $y = \pm 3\sqrt{3}$

The system is solved correctly. A correct conclusion is drawn.

b. The solutions of the system are $(3, \pm 3\sqrt{3})$. So, the third vertex is at $C(3, 3\sqrt{3})$ or $C(3, -3\sqrt{3})$. There are two solutions, because C can be above or below $\overline{AB}$

SAMPLE 2: Partial credit solution

The equations are correct, but what they express is not explained.

The distance between A and B is 6.

$AC = 6 \Rightarrow x^2 + y^2 = 36$ $BC = 6 \Rightarrow x^2 + y^2 - 12x = 0$

Solve the system by substituting **36** for $\mathbf{x^2 + y^2}$ in the second equation.

$$\mathbf{x^2 + y^2} - 12x = 0$$
$$\mathbf{36} - 12x = 0$$
$$x = 3$$

The additional vertex is omitted. An incorrect conclusion is drawn.

Find y when $x = 3$: $x^2 + y^2 = 36$, so $y^2 = 27$, and $y = \pm 3\sqrt{3}$. The coordinates of the third vertex are $C(3, 3\sqrt{3})$. This is the only possible position of the vertex, because the dimensions of a triangle must be positive.

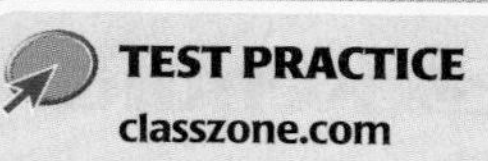

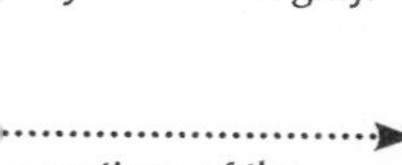

…alid approach is used, the solution is set up …cally and thoroughly.

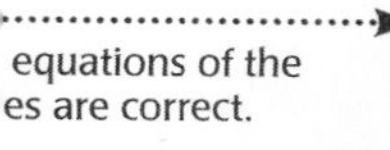

…equations of the …es are correct.

…answer is correct, but …k is not shown.

…answer shows a …c misunderstanding.

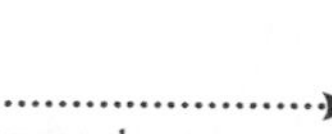

SAMPLE 3: Partial credit solution

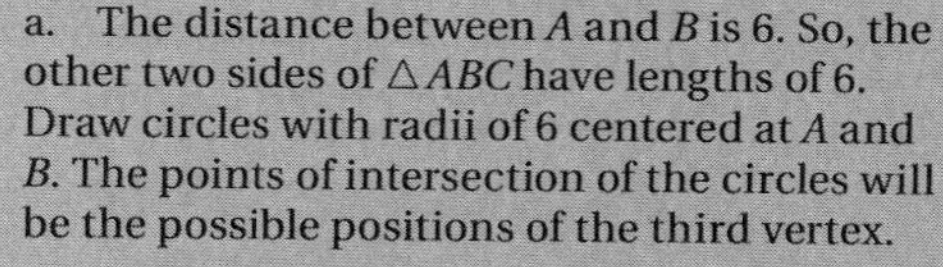

a. The distance between A and B is 6. So, the other two sides of $\triangle ABC$ have lengths of 6. Draw circles with radii of 6 centered at A and B. The points of intersection of the circles will be the possible positions of the third vertex.

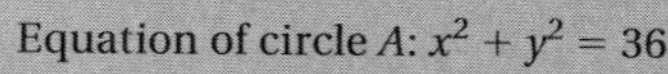

Equation of circle A: $x^2 + y^2 = 36$

Equation of circle B: $(x - 6)^2 + y^2 = 36$

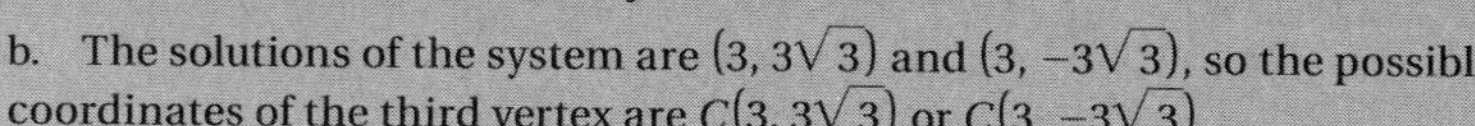

b. The solutions of the system are $(3, 3\sqrt{3})$ and $(3, -3\sqrt{3})$, so the possible coordinates of the third vertex are $C(3, 3\sqrt{3})$ or $C(3, -3\sqrt{3})$.

SAMPLE 4: No credit solution

Because $AB = 6$ and $\overline{AB}$ is horizontal, the vertex at C is 6 units above or below either A or B. The possible coordinates of C are $(0, 6)$, $(0, -6)$, $(6, 6)$, or $(6, -6)$.

PRACTICE Apply the Scoring Rubric

Use the rubric on page 674 to score the solution to the problem below as *full credit, partial credit,* or *no credit. Explain* your reasoning.

PROBLEM $\triangle RST$ is isosceles with $RT = ST$ and has vertices at $R(-2, 2)$, $S(4, -1)$, and $T(2, y)$.

a. Find y.

b. Is there only one possible value of y? *Explain.*

1. a. If $\triangle RST$ is isosceles with $RT = ST$, then T lies on the perpendicular bisector of $\overline{RS}$.

Midpoint of $\overline{RS} = \left(\frac{-2+4}{2}, \frac{2+(-1)}{2}\right) = (1, 0.5)$

Slope of $\overline{RS} = \frac{-1-2}{4-(-2)} = \frac{-3}{6} = -0.5$

The perpendicular bisector of $\overline{RS}$ has a slope of 2, the negative reciprocal of -0.5. Its equation is $y - 0.5 = 2(x - 1)$, or $y = 2x - 1.5$. Substituting 2 for x gives $y = 2.5$.

b. Since $y = 2x - 1.5$ is a function, this is the only value of y for $x = 2$.

TEST PREPARATION

Kentucky Test Preparation

1. Full credit; a valid approach was used and the work shown is correct. The student has clearly answered all of the questions.

Kentucky Test Practice

1. a. Yes
   b. Find the intersection of the two circles with centers (6, 3) and (−5, −4) and radii $\sqrt{85}$.
2. a. Above
   b. The focus is at (−11.52, 0), which is above the bottom edge of the reflector at (−12.5, 0)
3. a. *Sample answer:* The sum of the distances from any point to each of the foci remains constant
   b. $\frac{x^2}{30.25} + \frac{y^2}{18} = 1$.
4. The distance d is 16 yards. *Sample answer:* Set the center of the circle as (0, 0). Then the equation of the circle is $x^2 + y^2 = 100$. The part of the edge of the penalty area cut off by the penalty arc is 18 − 12, or 6 yards from the center of the circle. Therefore, the y-coordinate of each endpoint of the segment with length d is −6. Substituting −6 for y in the equation of the circle gives $x^2 + 36 = 100$, or $x = \pm 8$. So the endpoints of the segment are (±8, −6). The distance d between the points is 16 yards.
5. a. $\frac{x^2}{2.6^2} - \frac{y^2}{18.2^2} = 1$
   b. Change the equation so the center will be located at (6.3, 18.2)
6. a. They are the same.
   b. The only difference is that they have different centers.

Kentucky Test Practice

TEST PREPARATION

OPEN-RESPONSE

1. A rhombus is a quadrilateral with four congruent sides. The vertices of figure $ABCD$ are $A(6, 3)$, $B(-3, 5)$, $C(-5, -4)$, and $D(4, -5)$.
   a. Can you change the coordinates of one vertex of $ABCD$ to make it a rhombus?
   b. If so, explain how and find the coordinates. If not, explain why not.

2. A lamp for indoor gardening uses a parabolic reflector with the height and width shown to concentrate light on plants.
   a. Is the focus of the reflector above or below the reflector's bottom edge?
   b. *Explain* your reasoning.

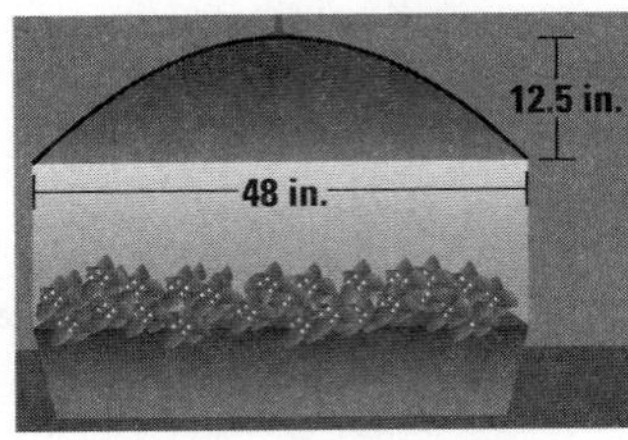

3. For each set of concentric circles shown below, the measures of the radii are the consecutive integers from 1 to 9.

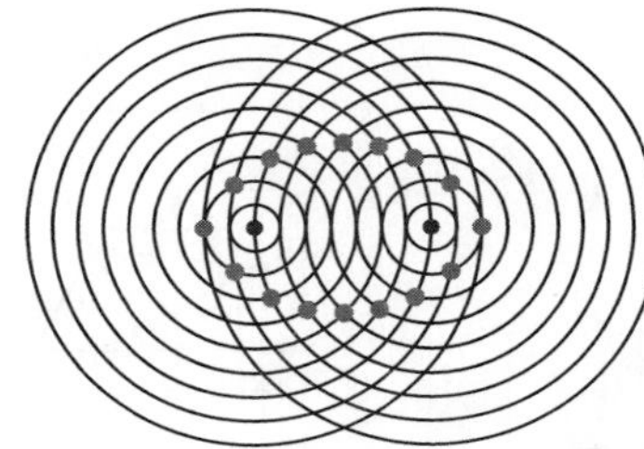

   a. *Explain* how you can use this information to demonstrate that the highlighted points lie on an ellipse whose foci are the centers of the circles.
   b. Write an equation of the ellipse.

4. A soccer field has a penalty-kick mark 12 yards from the goal. From the mark's center, an arc with a radius of 10 yards is drawn outside the penalty area as shown in the diagram.

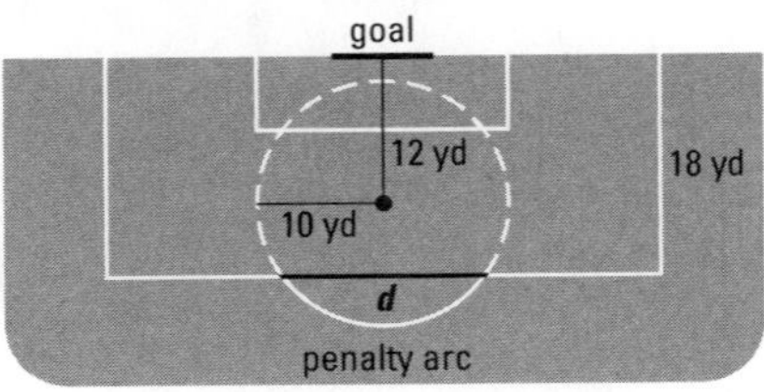

   a. *Explain* how to use an equation of a circle to find the distance d along the edge of the penalty area between the endpoints of the arc.
   b. Find the distance d.

5. The *Tractricious* sculpture at the Fermi National Accelerator Laboratory in Batavia, Illinois, has a hyperbolic cross section as shown below.

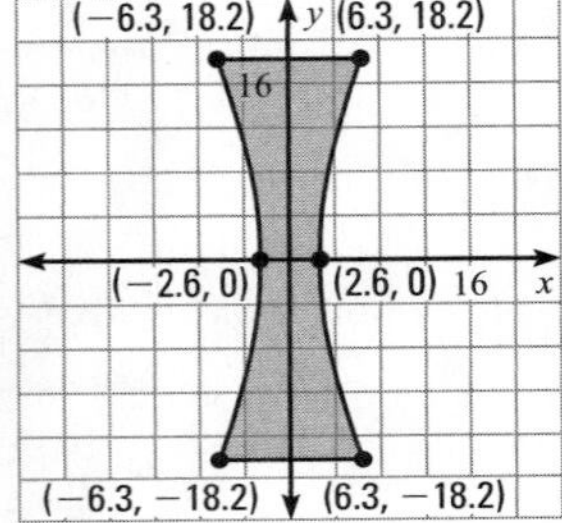

   a. Use the graph to write an equation of the hyperbola that models the cross section of the sculpture. (Each unit represents 1 foot.)
   b. *Explain* how to modify your equation so the origin is at the bottom left of the sculpture.

6. Consider the ellipses represented by $4x^2 + 6y^2 = 48$ and $\frac{(x-5)^2}{12} + \frac{(y+7)^2}{8} = 1$.
   a. Without applying area formulas, compare the areas.
   b. *Explain* how you made your comparison.

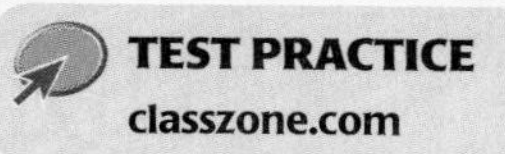

OPEN-RESPONSE

7. A satellite in a *geostationary* orbit appears to stay above a single place on Earth's surface. A satellite originally in a low orbit can be boosted using an elliptical *Hohmann transfer orbit* to a higher geostationary orbit. A satellite originally in a circular orbit 4200 miles from Earth's center is boosted to a circular geostationary orbit 22,240 miles from Earth's center.

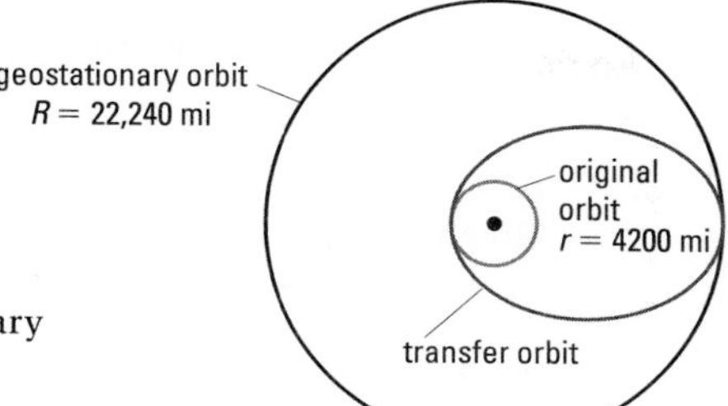

a. Write equations that model the original and geostationary orbits. Use Earth's center as the origin.

b. Earth's center is at one focus of the transfer orbit. Write an equation that models the transfer orbit. Use Earth's center as the origin, and choose a horizontal major axis as shown in the diagram.

8. Points one quarter of the way along the sides of a square are connected to form a second square. The pattern continues.

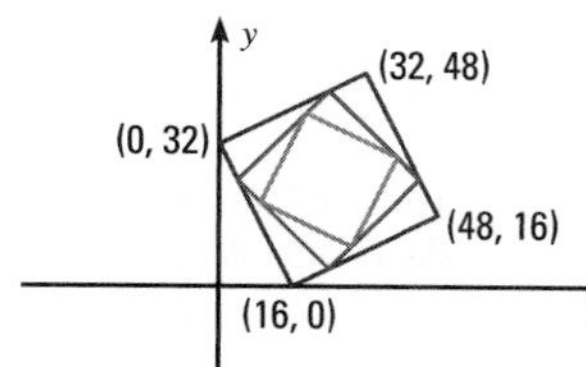

a. *Explain* how to use the midpoint formula to find the coordinates of the vertices for each new square in the pattern.

b. Find the coordinates of the vertices of the second and third squares.

c. Find the ratio of the areas of successive squares.

MULTIPLE-CHOICE

9. Which equation represents a hyperbola?

A. $x^2 - 3y + 4x - 15 = 0$

B. $x^2 + y^2 + 4x - 18y - 15 = 0$

C. $x^2 - y^2 + 4x - 18y - 15 = 0$

D. $-2x^2 - y^2 + 4x - 18y - 15 = 0$

10. At what point(s) do the graphs represented by $x^2 + y^2 = 36$ and $-y^2 + x = 6$ intersect?

A. (6, 0) B. (−6, 0)

C. $(-7, -\sqrt{13})$ D. (6, 0) and (−6, 0)

11. Which statement about the graph of the equation $12(x - 6) = -(y + 4)^2$ is *not* true?

A. The vertex is at (6, −4).

B. The axis of symmetry is $y = -4$.

C. The focus is at (6, −7).

D. The graph represents a function.

12. The conic section represented by the equation $\frac{(x-2)^2}{81} - \frac{(y-5)^2}{4} = 1$ has the line of symmetry $x = s$. What is the value of s?

A. 2 B. 5

C. 7 D. 9

13. To the nearest tenth, what is the distance between (−10, 2) and (7, 7)?

A. 5.8 B. 8.0

C. 17.7 D. 22.0

14. What is the radius of the circle represented by the equation $8x^2 + 8y^2 = 720$? Round your answer to the nearest tenth.

A. 3.4 B. 9.5

C. 26.8 D. 90.0

TEST PREPARATION

7. a. $x^2 + y^2 = 4200^2$; $x^2 + y^2 = 22{,}240^2$
b. $\frac{(x - 9090)^2}{13{,}220^2} + \frac{y^2}{9665^2} = 1$. (To find a and c, solve the system of equations $c = a - 4200$ and $a + c = 22{,}240$.)
8. a. Find the midpoint of each side and then find the midpoint from that point to the vertex.
b. (4, 24), (24, 44), (44, 24), (24, 4); (9, 19), (19, 39), (39, 29), (29, 9)
c. Each square has an area that is $\frac{5}{8}$ of the area of the previous square.
9. C
10. A
11. D
12. A
13. C
14. B

Additional Resources

The following resources are available to help review the materials in Chapters 7–9.

Chapter Resource Books

- Chapter 7 CRB, Cumulative Review, pp. 86–87
- Chapter 8 CRB, Cumulative Review, pp. 73–74
- Chapter 9 CRB, Cumulative Review, pp. 86–87

10. 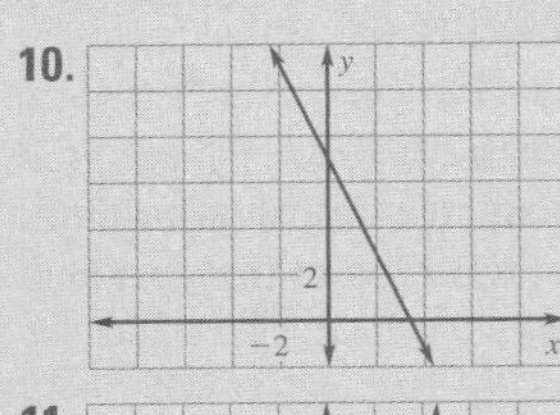

11. 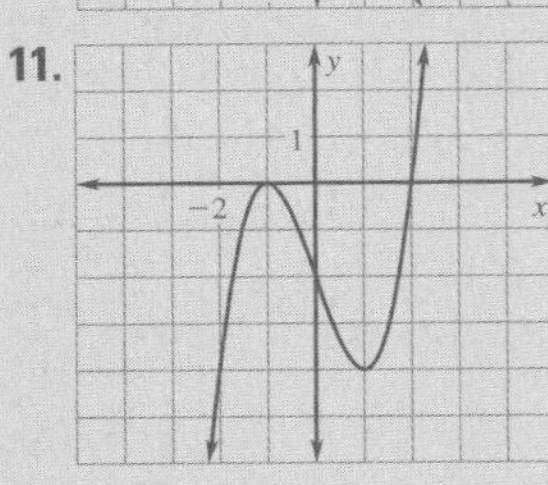

12. 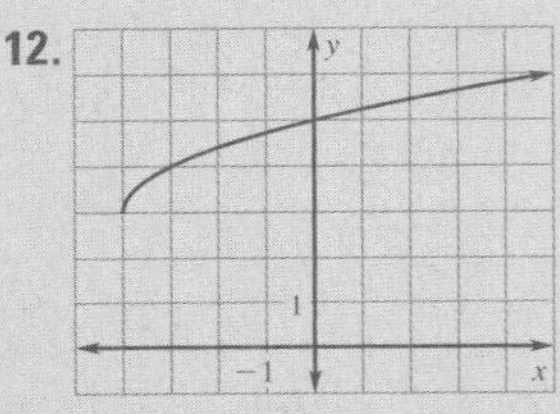

13. 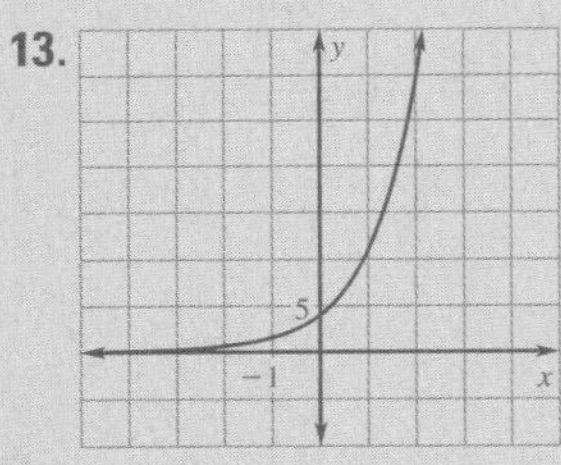

14. 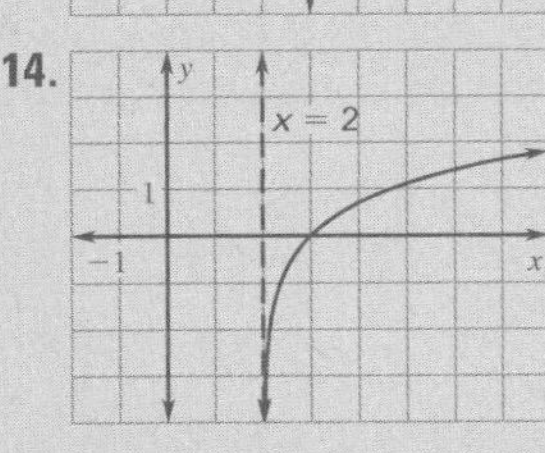

15. 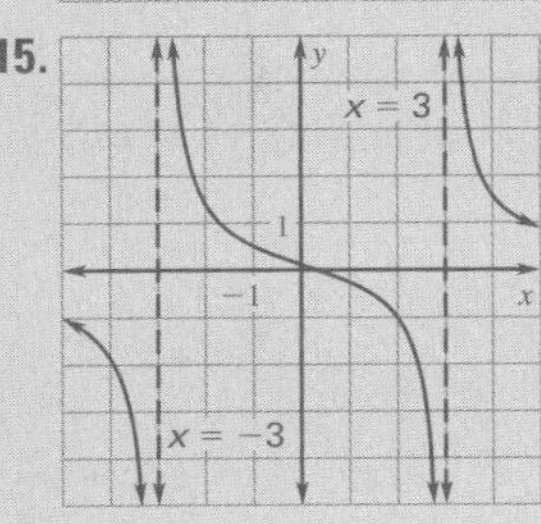

Solve the equation. Check your solution(s).

1. $5x + 24 = 11 - 2x$ *(p. 18)* $-\frac{13}{7}$
2. $|4x - 7| = 13$ *(p. 51)* $-\frac{3}{2}, 5$
3. $x^2 - 12x + 35 = 0$ *(p. 252)* 5, 7
4. $2x^2 - 5x + 5 = 0$ *(p. 292)* 4. $\frac{5 \pm i\sqrt{15}}{4}$
5. $x^3 + 3x^2 - 18x = 40$ *(p. 370)* −2, −5, 4
6. $\sqrt{x - 2} = x - 4$ *(p. 452)* 6
7. $4^x - 5 = 3$ *(p. 515)* $\frac{3}{2}$
8. $\frac{x + 3}{3x + 1} = \frac{x}{x + 2}$ *(p. 589)* −1, 3
9. $\frac{x - 4}{x - 3} + 2 = \frac{2x - 3}{x - 3}$ *(p. 58*

Graph the equation. 10–15. See margin.

10. $y = -2x + 7$ *(p. 89)*
11. $y = (x + 1)^2(x - 2)$ *(p. 387)*
12. $y = \sqrt{x + 4} + 3$ *(p. 446)*
13. $y = 4e^x$ *(p. 492)*
14. $y = \ln(x - 2)$ *(p. 499)*
15. $y = \frac{3x - 1}{x^2 - 9}$ *(p. 565)*

Factor the expression.

16. $2x^2 - 20x - 48$ *(p. 259)* $2(x - 12)(x + 2)$
17. $6x^2 + 7x - 20$ *(p. 259)* $(3x - 4)(2x + 5)$
18. $x^3 + 8x^2 - 4x - 32$ *(p. 35* $(x + 8)(x - 2)(x +$

Find the inverse of the function. *(p. 438)*

19. $f(x) = 6x - 1$ $f^{-1}(x) = \frac{x + 1}{6}$
20. $f(x) = x^3 - 5$ $f^{-1}(x) = \sqrt[3]{x + 5}$
21. $f(x) = x^5$ $f^{-1}(x) = x^{1/5}$

Tell whether the function is an example of *exponential growth* or *exponential decay*. *(pp. 486, 492)*

22. $f(x) = 5(1.4^x)$ growth
23. $f(x) = 3(0.6)^x$ decay
24. $f(x) = 8e^{-2x}$ decay

Condense the expression. *(p. 507)*

25. $3 \ln x - \ln 5$ $\ln \frac{x^3}{5}$
26. $\log_3 4 + 2 \log_3 7$ $\log_3 196$
27. $5 \log x + \log y - 3 \log z$ $\log \frac{x^5 y}{z^3}$

The variables *x* and *y* vary inversely. Use the given values to write an equation relating *x* and *y*. *(p. 551)*

28. $x = 18, y = 6$ $y = \frac{108}{x}$
29. $x = 5, y = -15$ $y = \frac{-75}{x}$
30. $x = 6, y = 9$ $y = \frac{54}{x}$

Perform the indicated operation and simplify.

31. $\frac{x - 5}{x + 7} \cdot \frac{3x + 21}{x^2 - 25}$ *(p. 573)* $\frac{3}{x + 5}$
32. $\frac{2x + 8}{x - 3} \div \frac{x + 4}{x^2 - x - 6}$ *(p. 573)* $2x + 4$ or $2(x + 2)$
33. $\frac{x - 3}{x + 5} + \frac{7}{x - 2}$ *(p. 582)* $\frac{x^2 + 2x + \ldots}{x^2 + 3x - \ldots}$

Find the distance between the two points. Then find the midpoint of the line segment joining the two points. *(p. 614)*

34. $(-8, 5), (-4, -1)$ $2\sqrt{13}$; $(-6, 2)$
35. $(3, 5), (8, 7)$ $\sqrt{29}$; $\left(\frac{11}{2}, 6\right)$
36. $(-2, 7), (1, 14)$ $\sqrt{58}$; $\left(-\frac{1}{2}, \frac{21}{2}\right)$

Classify the conic section and write its equation in standard form. Then graph the equation. *(p. 650)* 37–40. See margin for art.

37. $x^2 + y^2 + 12x - 4y + 15 = 0$ circle, $(x + 6)^2 + (y - 2)^2 = 25$
38. $4x^2 - 16y^2 - 56x + 160y - 268 = 0$ See margin.
39. $y^2 + 6x + 4y + 16 = 0$ parabola, $(y + 2)^2 = -6(x + 2)$
40. $2x^2 + 3y^2 + 4x + 12y - 14 = 0$ ellipse, $\frac{(x + 1)^2}{14} + \frac{(y + 2)^2}{\frac{28}{3}} =$
41. **FENCING** You have 380 feet of fencing to enclose a rectangular garden. You want the length of the garden to be 40 feet greater than the width. Find the length and width of the garden if you use all of the fencing. *(p. 34)* 115 ft, 75 ft

37. 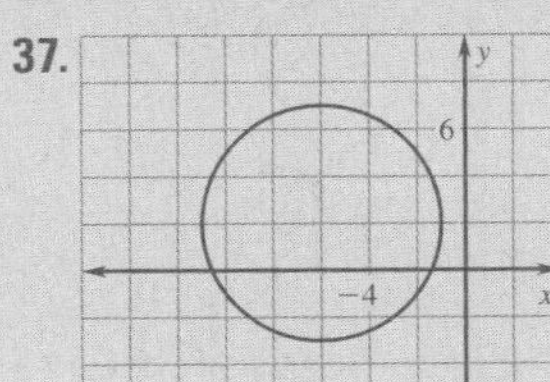

38. hyperbola, $\frac{(x - 7)^2}{16} - \frac{(y - 5)^2}{4} = 1$

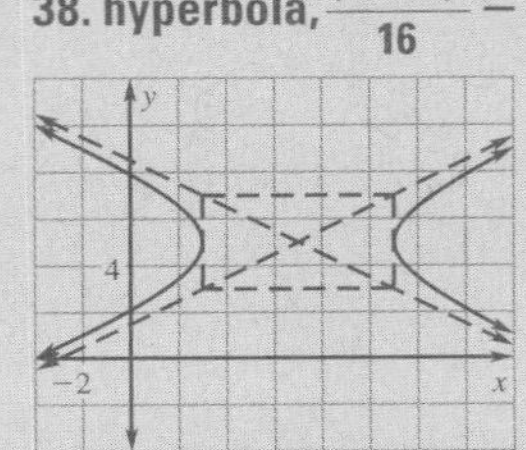

39. 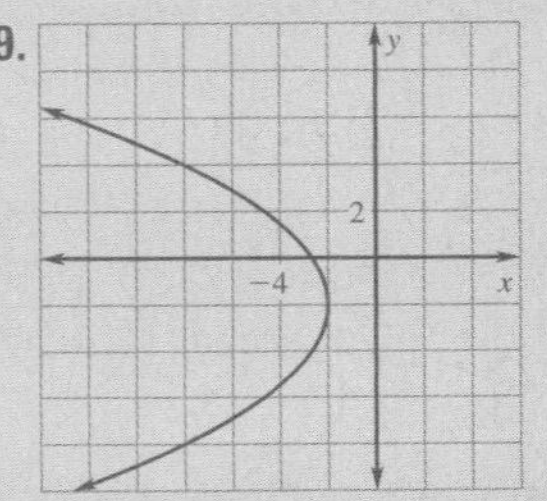

42. **RECREATION** You have \$30 to spend at a carnival. It costs \$2.50 to take one ride and \$1.50 to play one game. Write and graph an inequality that represents the possible numbers of rides you can take and games you can play. Then list all ordered pairs (rides, games) that use all \$30. *(p. 132)* **$2.5r + 1.5g \leq 30$, see margin for art; (0, 20), (3, 15), (6, 10), (9, 5), (12, 0).**

43. **BASKETBALL** The price of admission to a high school basketball game is \$5 for adults and \$2 for students. At a game that had a total attendance of 650 people, the total income from ticket sales was \$2500. Write and solve a linear system to find the numbers of adults and students who attended the basketball game. *(p. 160)* **400 adults, 250 students**

44. **BUSINESS** Two telephone companies compete for customers in a town. Initially, each company has 700 customers. Every month, 5% of company A's customers switch to company B, and 2% of company B's customers switch to company A. The transition matrix T and population matrix M_0 model this situation.

$$T = \begin{bmatrix} 0.95 & 0.02 \\ 0.05 & 0.98 \end{bmatrix} \qquad M_0 = \begin{bmatrix} 700 \\ 700 \end{bmatrix}$$

Find $M_1 = TM_0$, $M_2 = TM_1$, and $M_3 = TM_2$. *Explain* what these matrices represent. *Describe* what happens to the distribution of customers over time if this pattern continues. *(p. 195)* **See margin.**

45. **MAPS** A county map uses a coordinate grid for which one unit represents a quarter of a mile. A lake on the map has an approximately triangular shape with vertices near (2, 2), (12, 19), and (18, 7). Estimate the area of the surface of the lake. *(p. 203)* **about 7 mi^2**

46. **TENNIS** While serving, a tennis player strikes the ball at a height of 9 feet above the court. The initial downward velocity of the ball is 16 feet per second. How long does it take the ball to strike the court on the opponent's side? (*Hint:* Use the function $h = -16t^2 + v_0t + h_0$.) *(p. 292)* **about 1.4 sec**

47. **DISCOUNTS** A store is having a sale in which you can take \$50 off the cost of any television in the store. The store also offers 15% off your purchase if you open a charge account. Use composition of functions to write a new function that gives the sale price of a television that originally costs t dollars if \$50 is subtracted before the 15% discount is applied. Then find the sale price of a television that originally cost \$480. *(p. 428)* **$0.85(t - 50)$, \$365.50**

48. **ACCOUNT BALANCE** You deposit \$4500 in a savings account that pays 2.75% annual interest compounded monthly. Find the account balance after 5 years. *(p. 478)* **\$5162.50**

49. **STAMPS** The table shows the cumulative number s of different designs of stamps produced in the United States during the period 1904–2004. The variable t represents the number of years since 1904. Find an exponential model for the data. *(p. 529)* **$s = 348(1.02)^t$**

t	0	10	20	30	40	50	60	70	80	90	100
s	313	459	616	751	926	1063	1260	1552	2109	2887	3894

42.

Number of games (g): 0, 6, 12, 18
Number of rides (r): 0, 4, 8, 12

44. $\begin{bmatrix} 679 \\ 721 \end{bmatrix}, \begin{bmatrix} 659 \\ 741 \end{bmatrix}, \begin{bmatrix} 641 \\ 759 \end{bmatrix}$; the matrices represent the number of customers for companies A and B in successive months; company A will continue to have a decreasing customer base while company B will continue to grow.

40.

y: 4
x: −2

10 Pacing and Assignment Guide

REGULAR SCHEDULE

Pre-AP For pacing and assignments for a Pre-AP course, see the *Algebra 2 Toolkit*.

Lesson	Les. Day	BASIC	AVERAGE	ADVANCED
10.1 *MA-HS-4.4.2*	Day 1	pp. 686–689 Exs. 1–4, 7, 8, 11–13, 17–21, 30–33, 42–46, 62–68, 72	pp. 686–689 Exs. 1, 2, 4, 5, 8, 9, 13, 14, 17, 22–25, 34–37, 42, 47–50, 55, 56, 62–70, 73	pp. 686–689 Exs. 1, 2, 6, 10, 15–17, 26–29, 38–42, 51–61*, 63, 65–71*
10.2 *MA-HS-4.4.2*	Day 1	pp. 694–697 Exs. 1–5, 11–14, 19–21, 24–26, 32–37, 48–51, 54	pp. 694–697 Exs. 1, 2, 6–8, 11, 12, 15, 16, 19, 21, 22, 27–29, 32–41, 48–52, 55	pp. 694–697 Exs. 1, 2, 9, 10, 17–19, 22, 23, 30–47*, 49–53*
10.3 **MA-HS-4.4.1**	Day 1	SRH p. 992 Exs. 1–4; pp. 701–704 Exs. 1, 2, 3–9 odd, 11–13, 17–21, 24–28, 35–41, 44	pp. 701–704 Exs. 1, 2, 4–8 even, 13, 14, 17–19, 22–32, 35–42, 45	pp. 701–704 Exs. 1, 2, 9, 10, 15, 16, 18, 19, 22, 23, 26–34*, 36–43*
10.4 **MA-HS-4.4.1**	Day 1	SRH p. 1004 Exs. 1–9; pp. 710–713 Exs. 1–5, 9–11, 15–22, 26–30, 42–47, 51	pp. 710–713 Exs. 1, 2, 5–7, 11–13, 15–17, 22–24, 26, 27, 30–39, 42–49, 52	pp. 710–713 Exs. 1, 2, 7, 8, 13–15, 18, 19, 24, 25, 31–50*
10.5 **MA-HS-4.4.1**	Day 1	pp. 721–723 Exs. 1–7, 9–13, 15, 37	pp. 721–723 Exs. 1, 2, 4–7, 10–15, 33, 37	pp. 721–723 Exs. 1, 2, 5–15, 33, 37
	Day 2	pp. 721–723 Exs. 16–19, 22–28, 38–40, 43–44	pp. 721–723 Exs. 17–20, 23–31 odd, 32, 34, 38–41, 43–44	pp. 721–723 Exs. 19–21, 24–32, 34–42*, 44
10.6 **MA-HS-4.2.1**	Day 1	SRH p. 799 Exs. 46, 50, 63, 64; pp. 727–730 Exs. 1–9, 47	pp. 727–730 Exs. 1–9, 39, 47	pp. 727–730 Exs. 1–9, 39, 47
	Day 2	pp. 727–730 Exs. 10–13, 18–21, 26–34, 43–46, 50–51	pp. 727–730 Exs. 13–15, 21–23, 26, 27, 30–38, 43–46, 48, 50–51	pp. 727–730 Exs. 15–17, 23–25, 30–38, 40–51*
Review	Day 1	pp. 734–736 Exs. 1–29	pp. 734–736 Exs. 1–29	pp. 734–736 Exs. 1–29
Assess	Day 1	Chapter 10 Test	Chapter 10 Test	Chapter 10 Test
Yearly Pacing		Chapter 10 Total – 10 days	Chapters 1–10 Total – 122 days	Remaining – 38 days

*Challenge Exercises EP = Extra Practice SRH = Skills Review Handbook

BLOCK SCHEDULE

DAY 1	DAY 2	DAY 3	DAY 4	DAY 5
10.1	**10.3**	**10.5**	**10.6**	**REVIEW**
pp. 686–689 Exs. 1, 2, 4, 5, 8, 9, 13, 14, 17, 22–25, 34–37, 42, 47–50, 55, 56, 62–70, 73	pp. 701–704 Exs. 1, 2, 4–8 even, 13, 14, 17–19, 22–32, 35–42, 45	pp. 721–723 Exs. 1, 2, 4–7, 10–15, 17–20, 23–31 odd, 32–34, 37–41, 43–44	pp. 727–730 Exs. 1–9, 13–15, 21–23, 26, 27, 30–39, 43–48, 50–51	pp. 734–736 Exs. 1–29
10.2	**10.4**			**ASSESS**
pp. 694–697 Exs. 1, 2, 6–8, 11, 12, 15, 16, 19, 21, 22, 27–29, 32–41, 48–52, 55	pp. 710–713 Exs. 1, 2, 5–7, 11–13, 15–17, 22–24, 26, 27, 30–39, 42–49, 52			Chapter 10 Test
Yearly Pacing	Chapter 10 Total – 5 days	Chapters 1–10 Total – 61 days	Remaining – 19 days	

RESOURCE MANAGER

Chapter Resource Book

CHAPTER SUPPORT						
Parents as Partners (Chapter Overview with home involvement exercises and activity)					p. 1	
LESSON SUPPORT **Standards**	10.1 *MA-HS-4.4.2*	10.2 *MA-HS-4.4.2*	10.3 **MA-HS-4.4.1**	10.4 **MA-HS-4.4.1**	10.5 **MA-HS-4.4.1**	10.6 **MA-HS-4.2.1**
Teaching Guide/Lesson Plan	p. 3	p. 14	p. 26	p. 37	p. 49	p. 59
Activity Masters	p. 5					
Technology Activities & Keystrokes		p. 16		p. 39		p. 61
Activity Support Masters				p. 40		
Practice (3 levels)	p. 6	p. 18	p. 28	p. 41	p. 51	p. 62
Study Guide	p. 9	p. 21	p. 31	p. 44	p. 54	p. 65
Catch-Up for Absent Students	p. 11	p. 23	p. 33	p. 46	p. 56	p. 67
Problem Solving/Application	p. 12	p. 24	p. 34	p. 47	p. 57	p. 68
Challenge Practice	p. 13	p. 25	p. 36	p. 48	p. 58	p. 69
REVIEW						
Chapter Review Games and Activities		p. 70	Cumulative Practice			p. 72
Project with Rubric		p. 71	Resource Book Answers			A1

Transparencies	10.1	10.2	10.3	10.4	10.5	10.6
Warm-Up/Daily Homework Quiz	✔	✔	✔	✔	✔	✔
Notetaking Guide	✔	✔	✔	✔	✔	✔
Teacher Support						
Answer Transparencies	✔	✔	✔	✔	✔	✔

ASSESSMENT BOOK

Quizzes	p. 139	SAT/ACT Chapter Test	p. 150
Chapter Tests (3 levels)	p. 142	Alternative Assessment with Rubric	p. 152
Standardized Chapter Test	p. 148		

TECHNOLOGY

- Easy Planner
- Test and Practice Generator
- Power Presentations
- @HomeTutor
- Activity Generator
- Animated Algebra
- Classzone.com
- eEdition Plus Online
- eWorkbook Plus Online
- ML Assessment System

ADDITIONAL RESOURCES

Kentucky

- Additional Lesson F Simulations and Sampling Distributions
- Additional Lesson G Law of Large Numbers
- Additional Lesson I Expected Value
- Worked-Out Solution Key
- Notetaking Guide
- Practice Workbook
- Algebra 2 Toolkit
- Benchmark Tests
- Remediation Workbook
- Spanish Study Guide
- Spanish Assessment Book
- Spanish Resources in Spanish
- Multi-Language Visual Glossary

10 Lesson Practice Level B

LESSON 10.1 Practice B
For use with pages 692–689

Each event can occur in the given number of ways. Find the number of ways all of the events can occur.

1. Event 1: 3 ways; Event 2: 7 ways   21 ways
2. Event 1: 8 ways; Event 2: 5 ways   40 ways
3. Event 1: 4 ways; Event 2: 2 ways; Event 3: 9 ways   72 ways
4. Event 1: 6 ways; Event 2: 7 ways; Event 3: 4 ways   168 ways

For the given configuration, determine how many different computer passwords are possible if (a) digits and letters can be repeated, and (b) digits and letters cannot be repeated. See below.

5. 3 digits followed by 4 letters
6. 2 digits followed by 5 letters
7. 1 letter followed by 6 digits
8. 4 letters followed by 4 digits

Evaluate the expression.

9. 5!   120
10. 10!   3,628,800
11. 9!   362,880
12. 14!   87,178,291,200
13. 5(3!)   30
14. 4! • 6!   17,280
15. $\frac{7!}{3! \cdot 2!}$ 420
16. $\frac{11!}{(6+2)!}$ 990

Find the number of permutations.

17. ${}_4P_3$ 24
18. ${}_7P_5$ 2520
19. ${}_8P_4$ 1680
20. ${}_9P_0$ 1
21. ${}_{10}P_3$ 720
22. ${}_9P_6$ 60,480
23. ${}_{14}P_7$ 17,297,280
24. ${}_{12}P_{12}$ 479,001,600

Find the number of distinguishable permutations of the letters in the word.

25. MATH   24
26. SOUTH   120
27. BALL   12
28. ODD   3
29. SPANISH   2520
30. MINNESOTA   181,440
31. DELAWARE   10,080
32. LETTERS   1260

33. **Men's Suits** A men's department store sells 3 different suit jackets, 6 different shirts, 8 different ties, and 4 different pairs of pants. How many different suits consisting of a jacket, shirt, tie, and pants are possible?   576

34. **Batting Order** A baseball manager is determining the batting order for the team. The team has 9 members, but the manager definitely wants the pitcher to bat last. How many batting orders are possible?   40,320

35. **Chore** Your chores for the week are to cut the grass, wash the car, clean your room, clean the garage, and shine your shoes. You are to do 1 chore each day from Monday through Friday. You can do each chore on whatever day you want, except that you must wash the car either Thursday or Friday. In how many different orders can you perform your chores?   48

5. a. 456,976,000 **b.** 258,336,000   **6. a.** 1,188,137,600 **b.** 710,424,000
7. a. 26,000,000 **b.** 3,931,200   **8. a.** 4,569,760,000 **b.** 1,808,352,000

LESSON 10.1

LESSON 10.2 Practice B
For use with pages 690–697

Find the number of combinations.

1. ${}_6C_4$ 15
2. ${}_8C_5$ 56
3. ${}_7C_3$ 35
4. ${}_9C_7$ 36
5. ${}_{13}C_9$ 715
6. ${}_{10}C_6$ 210
7. ${}_{12}C_8$ 495
8. ${}_{14}C_{10}$ 1001

Find the number of possible 5-card hands that contain the cards specified. The cards are taken from a standard 52-card deck.

9. 5 red cards   65,780
10. 4 spades and 1 card that is not a spade   27,885
11. 3 face cards (kings, queens, or jacks) and 2 cards that are not face cards   171,600
12. 2 aces and 3 cards that are not aces   103,776
13. At most 1 diamond   1,645,020
14. At least 1 king   886,656

Use the binomial theorem to write the binomial expansion. See below.

15. $(x - 2)^4$
16. $(x + 3)^3$
17. $(2x + 5)^5$
18. $(4x - 1)^6$
19. $(x + 6y)^3$
20. $(x - 5y)^5$
21. $(3x - y)^6$
22. $(8x + y)^4$

23. Find the coefficient of x^6 in the expansion of $(2x + 3)^{10}$.   1,088,640
24. Find the coefficient of x^4 in the expansion of $(3x - 1)^{11}$.   −26,730
25. Find the coefficient of x^7 in the expansion of $(2x - 5)^9$.   115,200
26. Find the coefficient of x^3 in the expansion of $(3x + 2)^{12}$.   3,041,280

27. **School Play** A teacher is holding tryouts for the school play. There are 15 students trying out for 7 parts in the play. Each student can play each part. In how many ways can the teacher select the students?   6435

28. **Soccer Starters** A youth indoor soccer team has 6 starting players. The starting players must consist of 3 boys and 3 girls. There are 7 boys and 6 girls on the team. Each player can play each position. In how many ways can the coach select players to start the game?   700

29. **Football Cards** You have a plastic sheet that holds 9 trading cards. You want to fill the sheet with football cards consisting of 4 quarterbacks, 3 running backs, and 2 wide receivers. In your collection of cards, you have 10 quarterbacks, 7 running backs, and 8 wide receivers. In how many different ways can you select the cards?   205,800

15. $x^4 - 8x^3 + 24x^2 - 32x + 16$ **16.** $x^3 + 9x^2 + 27x + 27$
17. $32x^5 + 400x^4 + 2000x^3 + 5000x^2 + 6250x + 3125$
18. $4096x^6 - 6144x^5 + 3840x^4 - 1280x^3 + 240x^2 - 24x + 1$
19. $x^3 + 18x^2y + 108xy^2 + 216y^3$ **20.** $x^5 - 25x^4y + 250x^3y^2 - 1250x^2y^3 + 3125xy^4 - 3125y^5$
21. $729x^6 - 1458x^5y + 1215x^4y^2 - 540x^3y^3 + 135x^2y^4 - 18xy^5 + y^6$
22. $4096x^4 + 2048x^3y + 384x^2y^2 + 32xy^3 + y^4$

LESSON 10.2

LESSON 10.3 Practice B
For use with pages 698–704

You have an equally likely chance of choosing any integer from 1 through 80. Find the probability of the given event.

1. An odd number is chosen. $\frac{1}{2}$
2. A number greater than 50 is chosen. $\frac{3}{8}$
3. A perfect square is chosen. $\frac{1}{10}$
4. A perfect cube is chosen. $\frac{1}{20}$
5. A multiple of 3 is chosen. $\frac{13}{40}$
6. A factor of 200 is chosen. $\frac{1}{8}$
7. An even number greater than 30 is chosen. $\frac{5}{16}$
8. An odd number less than 70 is chosen. $\frac{7}{16}$

You are rolling a 20-sided die where the sides are numbered 1 through 20. Find the indicated odds.

9. In favor of rolling a 10 $\frac{1}{19}$
10. In favor of rolling a number less than 6 $\frac{1}{3}$
11. Against rolling a 1, 3, or 5 $\frac{17}{3}$
12. Against rolling a number greater than 13 $\frac{13}{7}$
13. In favor of rolling an even number less than 10 $\frac{1}{4}$
14. Against rolling an odd number greater than 10 $\frac{3}{1}$

Find the probability that a dart thrown at the square target shown will hit the given region. Assume the dart is equally likely to hit any point inside the target. Round your answer to three decimal places.

15. The center *a*   0.022
16. The border *f*   0.455
17. The center *a* or the ring *b*   0.087
18. The four rings (*b*, *c*, *d*, and *e*) or the center *a*   0.545
19. The ring *d* or *e*   0.349

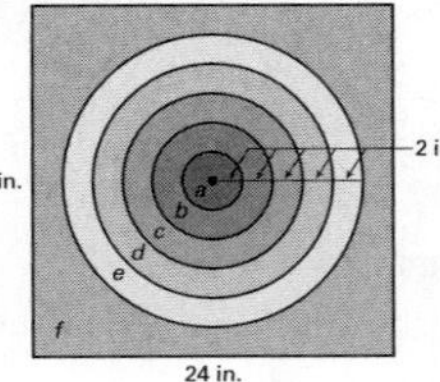

20. **Flag Carriers** Six students of different heights are going to march in single file in a parade carrying flags. The order in which they march is to be randomly selected. What is the probability that they will march in order of height from shortest to tallest? Round your answer to six decimal places.   0.001389

LESSON 10.3

LESSON 10.4

LESSON 10.4 Practice B
For use with pages 707–713

Events *A* and *B* are disjoint. Find *P*(*A* or *B*).

1. $P(A) = 0.1, P(B) = 0.45$ 0.55

2. $P(A) = 0.85, P(B) = 0.05$ 0.90

3. $P(A) = \frac{1}{2}, P(B) = \frac{1}{5}$ $\frac{7}{10}$

Find the indicated probability.

4. $P(A) = \frac{1}{6}, P(B) = \frac{5}{6}$ $\frac{2}{3}$
$P(A \text{ or } B) = \frac{1}{3}$
$P(A \text{ and } B) = \underline{\ ?\ }$

5. $P(A) = 0.23, P(B) = 0.36$
$P(A \text{ or } B) = 0.25$
$P(A \text{ and } B) = \underline{\ ?\ }$
0.34

6. $P(A) = \frac{5}{8}, P(B) = \frac{1}{4}$ $\frac{3}{8}$
$P(A \text{ or } B) = \frac{1}{2}$
$P(A \text{ and } B) = \underline{\ ?\ }$

Find $P(\overline{A})$.

7. $P(A) = 1$ 0

8. $P(A) = 0.25$ 0.75

9. $P(A) = \frac{9}{16}$ $\frac{7}{16}$

Find the indicated probability. State whether *A* and *B* are disjoint events.

10. $P(A) = \frac{2}{13}, P(B) = \underline{\ ?\ }$
$P(A \text{ or } B) = \frac{8}{13}$
$P(A \text{ and } B) = \frac{4}{13}$
$\frac{10}{13}$; not disjoint

11. $P(A) = 17\%, P(B) = 35\%$
$P(A \text{ or } B) = 52\%$
$P(A \text{ and } B) = \underline{\ ?\ }$
0%; disjoint

12. $P(A) = \frac{5}{6}, P(B) = \frac{2}{5}$
$P(A \text{ or } B) = \underline{\ ?\ }$
$P(A \text{ and } B) = \frac{2}{3}$
$\frac{17}{30}$; not disjoint

Two six-sided dice are rolled. Find the probability of the given event. (Refer to Example 4 on page 709 of the textbook for the possible outcomes.)

13. The sum is greater than 4. $\frac{1}{6}$

14. The sum is 6 or 11. $\frac{7}{36}$

15. The sum is neither 5 nor 9. $\frac{7}{9}$

16. The sum is greater than 7 and less than 11. $\frac{1}{3}$

17. Honors Banquet Of the 120 students honored at an academic banquet, 40% won awards for mathematics and 55% for English. Fourteen of these students won awards for both mathematics and English. One of the 120 students is chosen at random to be interviewed for a newspaper article. What is the probability that the student won an award in mathematics or English? $\frac{5}{6}$

18. Parakeets A pet store has 18 light green parakeets (5 females and 13 males) and 25 sky blue parakeets (15 females and 10 males). You randomly choose one of the parakeets. What is the probability that it is a male or a sky blue parakeet? $\frac{38}{43}$

19. Potluck Dinner The organizer of a potluck dinner sends 6 people a list of 10 different recipes and asks each person to bring one of the items on the list. If all 6 people randomly choose a recipe from the list, what is the probability that at least 2 will bring the same thing? 0.8488

LESSON 10.5

LESSON 10.5 Practice B
For use with pages 717–723

Events *A* and *B* are independent. Find the indicated probability.

1. $P(A) = \frac{5}{8}$ $\frac{1}{2}$
$P(B) = \frac{4}{5}$
$P(A \text{ and } B) = \underline{\ ?\ }$

2. $P(A) = \underline{\ ?\ }$ 1
$P(B) = 0.3$
$P(A \text{ and } B) = 0.3$

3. $P(A) = 0.9$ 0.6
$P(B) = \underline{\ ?\ }$
$P(A \text{ and } B) = 0.54$

Events *A* and *B* are dependent. Find the indicated probability.

4. $P(A) = 0.4$ 0.16
$P(B \mid A) = 0.4$
$P(A \text{ and } B) = \underline{\ ?\ }$

5. $P(A) = \underline{\ ?\ }$ 0.25
$P(B \mid A) = 0.6$
$P(A \text{ and } B) = 0.15$

6. $P(A) = 0.3$ 0.9
$P(B \mid A) = \underline{\ ?\ }$
$P(A \text{ and } B) = 0.27$

Let *n* be a randomly selected integer from 1 to 40. Find the indicated probability.

7. *n* is prime given that it is even. $\frac{1}{20}$

8. *n* is 15 given that it is a multiple of 3. $\frac{1}{13}$

9. *n* is 32 given that it is greater than 25. $\frac{1}{15}$

10. *n* is 13 given that it is odd. $\frac{1}{20}$

Find the probability of drawing the given cards from a standard deck of 52 cards (a) with replacement and (b) without replacement.

11. A club, then a diamond **a.** $\frac{1}{16}$ **b.** $\frac{13}{204}$

12. A jack, then a 7 **a.** $\frac{1}{169}$ **b.** $\frac{4}{663}$

13. A 5, then a face card, then an ace **a.** $\frac{3}{2197}$ **b.** $\frac{8}{5525}$

14. A king, then another king, then a third king **a.** $\frac{1}{2197}$ **b.** $\frac{1}{5525}$

In Exercises 15–17, use the following information.

File Cabinet Each drawer in a 5-drawer file cabinet has 50 folders. You are searching for some information that is in one of the folders, but you do not know which folder has the information.

15. What is the probability that the information is in the first drawer you choose? 0.2

16. What is the probability that the information is not in the first folder you choose? 0.996

17. What is the probability that the information is not in the first six folders you choose? 0.976

18. Apples The probability of selecting a rotten apple from a basket is 14%. What is the probability of selecting 3 good apples when selecting 1 from each of 3 different baskets? 0.636

LESSON 10.6 Practice B
For use with pages 724–730

Calculate the probability of tossing a coin 25 times and getting the given number of heads.

1. 2 0.00000894 **2.** 10 0.0974 **3.** 18 0.0143 **4.** 25 0.00000003

Calculate the probability of randomly guessing the given number of correct answers on a 20-question multiple choice exam that has choices A, B, C, and D for each question.

5. 10 0.00992 **6.** 8 0.0609 **7.** 18 0.000000002 **8.** 5 0.202

Calculate the probability of *k* successes for a binomial experiment consisting of *n* trials with probability *p* of success on each trial.

9. $k \geq 4, n = 8, p = 0.16$ 0.02667

10. $k \leq 5, n = 10, p = 0.45$ 0.738

11. $k \geq 3, n = 5, p = 0.34$ 0.2199

12. $k \leq 8, n = 12, p = 0.60$ 0.775

A binomial experiment consists of *n* trials with probability *p* of success on each trial. Draw a histogram of the binomial distribution that shows the probability of exactly *k* successes. *Describe* the distribution as either *symmetric* or *skewed*. Then find the most likely number of successes.

13. $n = 4, p = 0.45$

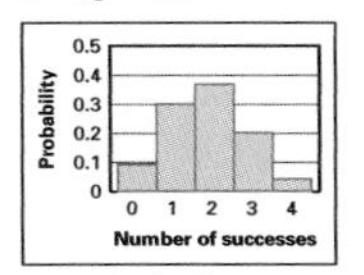

symmetric; $k = 2$

14. $n = 5, p = 0.75$

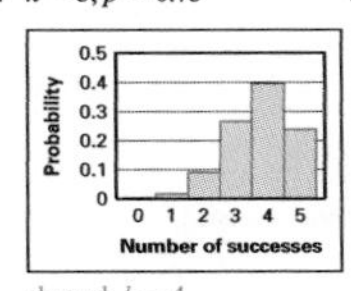

skewed; $k = 4$

15. $n = 6, p = 0.83$

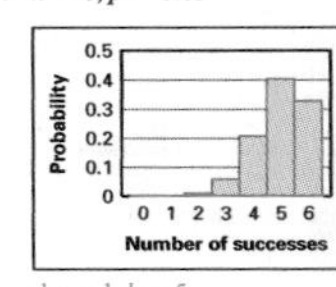

skewed; $k = 5$

In Exercises 16 and 17, use the following information.

Puppies A registered golden retriever gives birth to a litter of 11 puppies. Assume that the probability of a puppy being male is 0.5.

16. Because the owner of the dog can expect to get more money for a male puppy, what is the most likely number of males in the litter? 5 or 6

17. What is the probability at least 7 of the puppies will be male? 0.2744

LESSON 10.6

10 Assessment

CHAPTER 10 Quiz 1
For use after Lessons 10.1–10.2

For the given license plate configuration, determine how many different plates are possible if letters and digits (a) can be repeated (b) can not be repeated.

1. 3 letters followed by 2 digits
2. 2 digits followed by 2 letters

Find the number of distinguishable permutations in the word.

3. NINE
4. POPCORN

Find the number of combinations.

5. ${}_9C_7$
6. ${}_{13}C_{12}$

Use the binomial theorem to write the binomial expansion.

7. $(x + 3)^3$
8. $(2s - 1)^4$

9. **Menu Choices** A sub shop runs a lunch special where you can buy a large sub with one bun, two cheeses, two meats, and three vegetables for $6.00. You have a choice of 3 different buns, 6 cheeses, 7 meats, and 8 vegetables. How many different variations of the sub special are possible?

Answers

1. a. 1,757,600
   b. 1,404,000
2. a. 67,600
   b. 58,500
3. 12
4. 1260
5. 36
6. 13
7. $x^3 + 9x^2 + 27x + 27$
8. $16s^4 - 32s^3 + 24s^2 - 8s + 1$
9. 52,920

CHAPTER 10 Quiz 2
For use after Lessons 10.3–10.4

A card is randomly drawn from a standard deck of 52 cards. Find the probability of drawing the given card.

1. The king of clubs
2. A heart
3. A black card
4. A card other than a 9

You randomly select a marble from a bag. The bag contains 7 black, 14 red, 6 white, and 13 blue marbles. Find the indicated odds.

5. In favor of choosing black
6. In favor of choosing red or blue
7. Against choosing white
8. Against choosing blue or white

Find the indicated probability.

9. $P(A) = 0.5$
   $P(B) = 0.45$
   $P(A \text{ or } B) = \underline{\ ?\ }$
   $P(A \text{ and } B) = 0.2$
10. $P(A) = \underline{\ ?\ }$
    $P(B) = 0.54$
    $P(A \text{ or } B) = 0.66$
    $P(A \text{ and } B) = 0.22$
11. $P(A) = 18\%$
    $P(B) = 43\%$
    $P(A \text{ or } B) = 61\ \%$
    $P(A \text{ and } B) = \underline{\ ?\ }$

12. **Cards** A card is randomly selected from a standard deck of 52 cards. What is the probability that it is a heart or a jack?

Answers

1. $\frac{1}{52}$
2. $\frac{1}{4}$
3. $\frac{1}{2}$
4. $\frac{12}{13}$
5. 7 : 33
6. 27 : 13
7. 17 : 3
8. 21 : 19
9. 0.75
10. 0.34
11. 0
12. $\frac{4}{13} \approx 0.308$

CHAPTER 10 Quiz 3
For use after Lessons 10.5–10.6

Find the probability of randomly drawing the given marbles from a bag of 4 red, 7 green, and 2 blue marbles without replacement.

1. green, then red
2. red, then blue
3. red, then red

Calculate the probability of tossing a coin 6 times and getting the given number of tails.

4. 0
5. 1
6. 3
7. 5

A binomial experiment consists of *n* trials with probability *p* of success on each trial. Draw a histogram of the binomial distribution that shows the probability of exactly *k* successes.

8. $n = 3, p = 0.5$

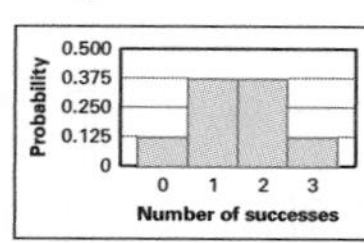

9. Describe the histogram as either symmetric or skewed.

Answers

1. $\frac{7}{39}$
2. $\frac{2}{39}$
3. $\frac{1}{13}$
4. 0.016
5. 0.094
6. 0.313
7. 0.094
8. See left.
9. symmetric

CHAPTER 10 Chapter Test B
For use after Chapter 10

1. Each event can occur in the given number of ways. Find the number of ways all the events can occur.

   Event A: 3 ways; Event B: 3 ways; Event C: 4 ways
2. Evaluate 8!.
3. Find ${}_8P_4$.
4. Find the number of distinguishable permutations of the letters in the word SENSES.
5. **Elevator** There are 5 people waiting on an elevator to get to the bottom floor, and they are all equally likely to exit first. How many different ways can they exit the elevator?

Find the number of combinations.

6. ${}_8C_3$
7. ${}_7C_4$
8. Find the coefficient of x^4 in the expansion of $(x + 3)^8$.
9. **Zoo Exhibits** You are visiting a zoo, and have 7 exhibits left to see. You have time to see 3 more. How many different combinations of exhibits can you see?

A card is randomly drawn from a standard deck of 52 cards. Find the probability of drawing the given card.

10. The ace of spades
11. A heart
12. **Car Lot** At a car lot, there are 16 white, 7 red, 8 blue, and 9 black cars. You randomly pick a set of keys to one of the cars. What are the odds against choosing a set of keys to a blue car?

Events *A* and *B* are mutually exclusive. Find *P*(*A* or *B*).

13. $P(A) = \frac{1}{5}, P(B) = \frac{3}{4}$
14. $P(A) = 0.4, P(B) = 0.5$

Answers

1. 36
2. 40,320
3. 1680
4. 60
5. 120
6. 56
7. 35
8. 5670
9. 35
10. $\frac{1}{52}$
11. $\frac{1}{4}$
12. 4 : 1
13. $\frac{19}{20}$
14. 0.9

Find the indicated probability.

15. $P(A) = 0.35$

$P(B) = 0.5$

$P(A \text{ or } B) = 0.85$

$P(A \text{ and } B) = \underline{\ ?\ }$

16. $P(A) = 0.4$

$P(\overline{A}) = \underline{\ ?\ }$

17. Events A and B are independent. Find the indicated probability.

$P(A) = 0.2$

$P(B) = 0.3$

$P(A \text{ and } B) = \underline{\ ?\ }$

18. Events A and B are dependent. Find the indicated probability.

$P(A) = 0.5$

$P(B \mid A) = 0.7$

$P(A \text{ and } B) = \underline{\ ?\ }$

19. What is the probability of rolling a die three times, and getting outcomes of 1, 2, and 3, in this order?

There are 5 sprinters in each race, and all are equally likely to win. There are 10 races run. You randomly guess the winner of each race. Calculate the probability that you will guess the given number of correct winners.

20. 3

21. 5

22. **Fishing** When you go fishing, you are successful in catching at least one fish 73% of the time. What is the probability that you do not catch a fish on 3 of your next 5 fishing trips?

Answers

15. 0
16. 0.6
17. 0.06
18. 0.35
19. $\frac{1}{216}$
20. 0.20
21. 0.03
22. 0.10

Multiple Choice

1. You have 10 shirts and 5 pairs of pants. How many different outfits can you make from them? C

Ⓐ 0.5 Ⓑ 2
Ⓒ 50 Ⓓ 2500

2. How many different license plates with 2 vowels followed by 4 digits are possible if letters and digits cannot be repeated? B

Ⓐ 60,480 Ⓑ 100,800
Ⓒ 164,025 Ⓓ 250,000

3. How many distinguishable permutations of the letters in PROBABILITY are there? A

Ⓐ $\frac{11!}{(2!)(2!)}$ Ⓑ $\frac{11!}{2!}$
Ⓒ $11!$ Ⓓ $(11!)(2!)$

4. On his long trip to Washington D.C., Dan decides to take along 5 magazines from the 12 he has recently purchased. How many different ways can Dan make his selection? A

Ⓐ 792 Ⓑ 33,264
Ⓒ 95,040 Ⓓ 3,991,680

5. What is the probability of drawing a red face card from a standard deck of 52 cards? B

Ⓐ $\frac{3}{52}$ Ⓑ $\frac{3}{26}$ Ⓒ $\frac{3}{13}$ Ⓓ $\frac{1}{2}$

6. Your book club will choose 12 books from 6 biographies, 8 historical novels, 12 romance novels, and 10 science fiction novels. How many different sets of exactly 3 biographies, 3 historical novels, 3 romance novels, and 3 science fiction novels can be chosen? C

Ⓐ 81 Ⓑ 5760
Ⓒ 29,568,000 Ⓓ 38,320,128,000

7. Which is the coefficient of x^5 in the expansion of $(2x - 3)^8$? A

Ⓐ −43,384 Ⓑ −864
Ⓒ 56 Ⓓ 43,384

8. Chelsea randomly chooses a marble from a bag containing 7 blue, 4 red, 2 yellow, and 1 black marble. What are the odds of *not* choosing a red marble? C

Ⓐ 2 : 7 Ⓑ 2 : 5 Ⓒ 5 : 2 Ⓓ 7 : 2

9. What is the probability that a dart thrown at the target below lands in the shaded area? B

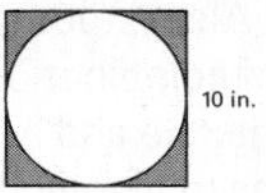

Ⓐ 1.2% Ⓑ 21.5%
Ⓒ 78.5% Ⓓ 99.7%

10. You buy a package of beads that contains red, blue, yellow, and orange beads. Out of 35 beads, there are 10 that are orange. What is the experimental probability that you pick an orange bead when randomly selecting the first one from the package? B

Ⓐ $\frac{1}{4}$ Ⓑ $\frac{2}{7}$ Ⓒ $\frac{1}{3}$ Ⓓ $\frac{1}{2}$

11. The distribution of the number of pets per household is shown in the table below. What is the probability that the number of pets per household is at least 3? A

Pets	0	1	2	3+
Households	50	100	75	75

Ⓐ 0.25 Ⓑ 0.50
Ⓒ 0.75 Ⓓ 1.00

12. What is the probability of $P(A \text{ and } B)$ given $P(A) = 0.20$, $P(B) = 0.45$, and $P(A \text{ or } B) = 0.58$? A

Ⓐ 0.07 Ⓑ 0.93
Ⓒ 0.97 Ⓓ 1.00

13. If $P(A) = 0.1997$, what is $P(\overline{A})$? B

Ⓐ 0.0003 Ⓑ 0.8003
Ⓒ 0.9003 Ⓓ 1.1997

14. You toss a coin and roll a six-sided die simultaneously. What is the probability of tossing a head and rolling a 5? A

Ⓐ $\frac{1}{12}$ Ⓑ $\frac{1}{6}$ Ⓒ $\frac{2}{3}$ Ⓓ $\frac{5}{6}$

15. What is the probability that you consecutively draw four aces from a standard deck without replacement? C

Ⓐ $\frac{1}{7,311,616}$ Ⓑ $\frac{3}{913,952}$
Ⓒ $\frac{1}{270,725}$ Ⓓ $\frac{1}{13}$

16. Out of the 40 students on student council, 35 are either on the honor roll *or* play for the school band. There are 27 student council members who are on the honor roll and 25 that play for the school band. What is the probability that a randomly selected student council member is both on the honor roll *and* plays for the school band? C

Ⓐ $\frac{1}{20}$ Ⓑ $\frac{1}{8}$ Ⓒ $\frac{17}{40}$ Ⓓ $\frac{7}{10}$

17. You perform a binomial experiment which consists of 20 trials with a probability of 27% success on each trial. What is the probability of exactly three successful outcomes? B

Ⓐ 0.00009 Ⓑ 0.10653
Ⓒ 0.45629 Ⓓ 2.10553

Gridded Answer

18. What is the coefficient of x^8 in the expansion of $(x^2 + 2)^6$?

		6	0

Short Response

19. A committee of 5 is to be selected from 10 men and 8 women. In how many ways can at least two women be selected? Explain how you determined this.
6636; Explanations will vary.

Extended Response

20. The baseball team in your community is playing for the championship. They will play seven games against the opposing team.

a. If the probability for your team to win is 74%, what is the probability for the other team to win? 26%

b. Is this a binomial distribution? Why or why not? yes; Answers will vary.

c. What is the probability that your team will win 4 of the 7 games? 18%

Journal **1.** Compare and contrast the following. Include a description of how to find the probability of each type of event. Give an example of each to show how they are different.

a. Independent events vs. dependent events

b. Disjoint events vs. overlapping events

Multi-Step Problem **2.** Your school holds a Spring Carnival each year to raise money for local charities. You are running a carnival game called Lucky Seven. The player must choose whether to throw a dart at the target shown or roll 2 dice to get the number 7. The target is 36 inches square, and the area of each region is a multiple of the area of the region containing the number 7.

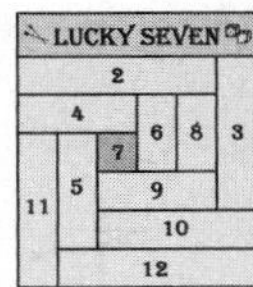

a. Find the probability of hitting each number on the target with a dart. Assume the dart is equally likely to hit any point inside the target.

b. Find the probability of rolling 2 dice that total each number from 2 to 12.

c. Use your answers from parts (a) and (b) to compare the design of the two versions of the game. Are the probabilities of getting each number the same for both versions?

d. **Writing** Considering that the goal is to get a 7, should the player choose to throw a dart or roll 2 dice? Explain.

e. The player can still receive a prize if he gets a 2 or a 12. For which version of the game is it easier to get a 2 or a 12? Use probabilities to support your answer.

f. Design a target so that the probabilities of getting each number from 2 to 12 is the same as rolling 2 dice.

g. **Critical Thinking** Using your target design from part (g), would you still want 7 to be the number that wins? If not, what number would be a better choice? Explain.

1. a. if two events are independent, the occurrence of one has no effect on the occurrence of the other, and if two events are dependent, the occurrence of one affects the occurrence of the other; a description of how to find the probability of two independent events and two dependent events, along with examples of each. **b.** disjoint events cannot both occur, while overlapping events could both occur; a description of how to find the probability of two disjoint event and two overlapping events, along with examples of each. **2. a.** Probabilities from 2 to 12: 0.139, 0.111, 0.083, 0.083, 0.056, 0.028, 0.056, 0.083, 0.111, 0.111, 0.139 **b.** 0.028, 0.056, 0.083, 0.111, 0.139, 0.167, 0.139, 0.111, 0.083, 0.056, 0.028 **c.** No, 2, 3, and 10 through 12 are easier to get by throwing a dart. Five through 9 are easier to get by rolling two dice. The chance of getting a 4 is the same. **d.** Roll two dice. $P(7) \approx 0.167$ with dice. $P(7) \approx 0.028$ with a dart. **e.** Throwing a dart; $P(2 \text{ or } 12) \approx 0.278$ with a dart. $P(2 \text{ or } 12) \approx 0.056$ with dice. **f.** Answers will vary. **g.** No. The number 2 or 12 would be a better choice, because more money goes to charity.

PLAN AND PREPARE

Main Ideas

Students learn the fundamental counting principle and the formulas for permutations and combinations of *n* objects taken *r* at a time. They apply those ideas to problems involving counting. Also, students examine patterns of combinations found in Pascal's triangle and apply these patterns to binomial expansions. Students then expand counting methods to the study of theoretical, experimental, and geometric probability and to odds in favor of an event or against an event. Finally, they learn how to find probabilities of compound, independent, and dependent events and they construct and interpret binomial distributions.

Prerequisite Skills

- Simplifying expressions
- Multiplying binomials
- Finding areas

Additional resources for reviewing prerequisite skills are:

- Skills Review Handbook, pp. 975–1009
- @HomeTutor

10 Counting Methods and Probability

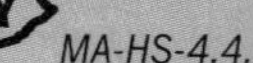

Before

In previous chapters, you learned the following skills, which you'll use in Chapter 10: simplifying expressions, multiplying binomials, and finding areas.

Prerequisite Skills

VOCABULARY CHECK

Copy and complete the statement.

1. The **coefficient** of x^2 in the expression $3x^3 - 15x^2 + 4$ is _?_. −15
2. Written as a fraction in lowest terms, the **ratio** of 18 to 45 is _?_. $\frac{2}{5}$
3. The expressions $x + 3$ and $2x - 1$ are examples of **binomials** because they have _?_ terms. 2

SKILLS CHECK

Simplify the expression. *(Review p. 2 for 10.1.)*

4. $\frac{6 \cdot 5 \cdot 4 \cdot 3}{2 \cdot 1}$ 180
5. $\frac{13 \cdot 12 \cdot 11}{10 \cdot 9 \cdot 8}$ $\frac{143}{60}$
6. $\frac{8 \cdot 7 \cdot 6 \cdot 5 \cdot 4}{5 \cdot 4 \cdot 3 \cdot 2 \cdot 1}$ 56

Find the product. *(Review p. 346 for 10.2.)*

7. $(x + y)^3$ $x^3 + 3x^2y + 3xy^2 + y^3$
8. $(5x + 1)^3$ $125x^3 + 75x^2 + 15x + 1$
9. $(3x - 2y)^3$ $27x^3 - 54x^2y + 36xy^2 - 8y^3$

Find the area of the shaded region. Assume all shapes are circles or squares. *(Review pp. 991–992 for 10.3.)*

10. 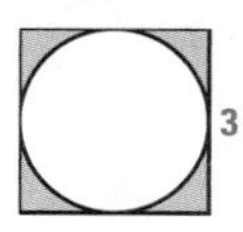

about 1.93 ft²

11. 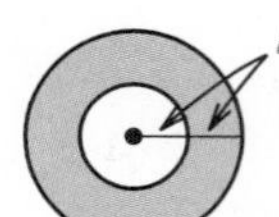

about 151 m²

12. 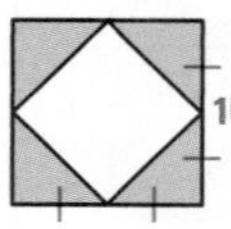

50 in.²

Chapter Planning Guide

Chapter 10 Resource Book
- Teaching Guide/Lesson Plan (pp. 3, 14, 26, 37, 49, 59)
- Project with Rubric (p. 71)

Assessment and Intervention
- Assessment Book (pp. 139–153)
- Benchmark Tests
- Remediation Book

Interactive Technology
- Easy Planner
- Power Presentations CD-ROM
- Activity Generator CD-ROM
- Animated Algebra
- Test Generator CD-ROM
- Online Quizzes
- eWorkbook
- eEdition
- @HomeTutor

Resources for English Learners
- Quick Reference for English Learners
- Spanish Study Guide
- Multi-Language Visual Glossary
- Student Resources in Spanish

Now

In Chapter 10, you will apply the big ideas listed below and reviewed in the Chapter Summary on page 733. You will also use the key vocabulary listed below.

Big Ideas

1. **Using permutations and combinations**
2. **Finding probabilities**
3. **Constructing binomial distributions**

KEY VOCABULARY

- permutation, *p. 684*
- combination, *p. 690*
- binomial theorem, *p. 693*
- probability, *p. 698*
- compound event, *p. 707*
- overlapping events, *p. 707*
- disjoint events, *p. 707*
- independent events, *p. 717*
- dependent events, *p. 718*
- conditional probability, *p. 718*
- random variable, *p. 724*
- binomial distribution, *p. 725*

Why?

You can use the fundamental counting principle and permutations to calculate the number of choices for a situation. For example, you can count the number of possible outcomes of an event or the number of ways to complete a task.

Animated Algebra

The animation illustrated below for Exercise 69 on page 689 helps you answer this question: How does the number of clothing choices affect the number of different ways can you dress mannequins in a display?

Different outfits for a store display can be made using several tops and bottoms.

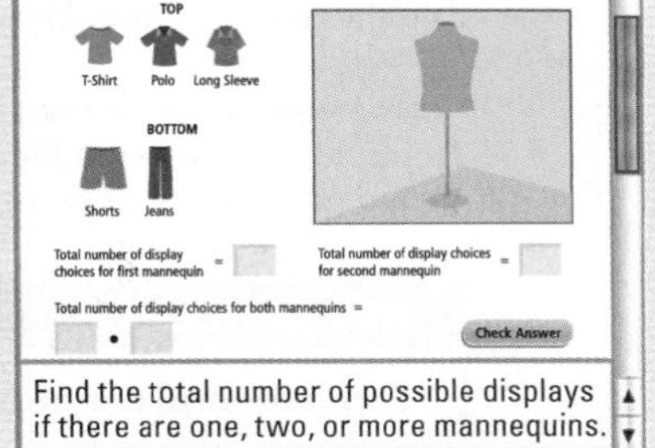

Find the total number of possible displays if there are one, two, or more mannequins.

Animated Algebra at classzone.com

Other animations for Chapter 10: pages 701, 711, 716, 722, and 726

Algebra 2 Toolkit

- Reading Strategies for Chapter 10, pp. 27–28
- Differentiated Instruction Notes, pp. 79–82
- English Learners Notes, pp. 119–120
- Inclusion Notes, pp. 153–154
- Teaching Strategies with Sample Worksheets, pp. 163–186
- Using Technology in the Classroom, pp. 187–192
- Tips for New Teachers, pp. 211–212
- Math Background Notes, pp. 250–253
- Pre-AP Strategies and Copymasters, pp. 329–330, 425–428
- Teacher Survival Activities, pp. 487–488, 515–516
- Bulletin Board Idea, p. 534
- Teacher Tool Transparencies, following p. 538

10.1 Apply the Counting Principle and Permutations

MA-HS-4.4.2 *Students will recognize and identify the differences between combinations and permutations and use them to count discrete quantities.*

Before You counted the number of different ways to perform a task.

Now You will use the fundamental counting principle and permutations.

Why? So you can find numbers of racing outcomes, as in Example 4.

Key Vocabulary
- **permutation**
- **factorial**

In many real-life problems, you want to count the number of ways to perform a task. One way to do this is to use a *tree diagram*.

EXAMPLE 1 Use a tree diagram

SNOWBOARDING A sporting goods store offers 3 types of snowboards (all-mountain, freestyle, and carving) and 2 types of boots (soft and hybrid). How many choices does the store offer for snowboarding equipment?

Solution

Draw a tree diagram and count the number of branches.

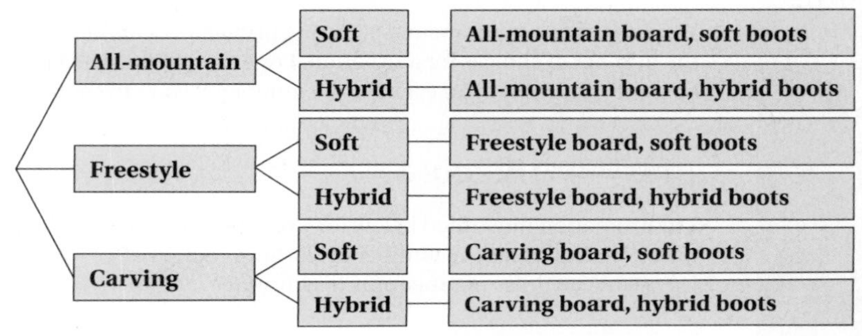

▸ The tree has 6 branches. So, there are 6 possible choices.

FUNDAMENTAL COUNTING PRINCIPLE Another way to count the choices in Example 1 is to use the *fundamental counting principle*. You have 3 choices for the board and 2 choices for the boots, so the total number of choices is $3 \cdot 2 = 6$.

KEY CONCEPT *For Your Notebook*

Fundamental Counting Principle

Two Events If one event can occur in m ways and another event can occur in n ways, then the number of ways that *both* events can occur is $m \cdot n$.

Three or More Events The fundamental counting principle can be extended to three or more events. For example, if three events can occur in m, n, and p ways, then the number of ways that *all* three events can occur is $m \cdot n \cdot p$.

1 PLAN AND PREPARE

Warm-Up Exercises

Transparency Available

Evaluate the expression.

1. $5 \times 4 \times 3 \times 2 \times 1$ 120
2. $\dfrac{7 \times 6 \times 5 \times 4 \times 3 \times 2 \times 1}{6 \times 5 \times 4 \times 3 \times 2 \times 1 \times 2 \times 3}$ $\dfrac{7}{6}$
3. The number of choices Meghan has for displaying her trophies is represented by the expression $a \cdot b$. If $a = 4$ and $b = 3$, how many choices does Meghan have? 12

Notetaking Guide

Transparency Available

Promotes interactive learning and notetaking skills, pp. 259–262.

Pacing

Basic: 1 day

Average: 1 day

Advanced: 1 day

Block: 0.5 block with 10.2

- See *Teaching Guide/Lesson Plan.*

2 FOCUS AND MOTIVATE

Essential Question

Big Idea 1, p. 681

How do you determine the number of distinguishable permutations in the letters of a word? **Tell students they will learn how to answer this question by determining the number of letters in the word that repeat.**

Resource Planning Guide

Chapter Resource Book
- Teaching Guide/Lesson Plan (pp. 3–4)
- Activity Master (p. 5)
- Practice levels A, B, C (pp. 6–8)
- Study Guide (pp. 9–10)
- Catch-up for Absent Students (p. 11)
- Problem Solving Workshop (p. 12)
- Challenge (p. 13)

Workbooks
- Notetaking Guide (pp. 259–262)
- Practice Workbook (pp. 149–150)

Teaching Options
- **Power Presentations CD-ROM** provides dynamic electronic teaching resources for the classroom.
- **Activity Generator CD-ROM** provides editable activities for all ability levels.

Interactive Technology
- Easy Planner
- Power Presentations CD-ROM
- Activity Generator CD-ROM
- Animated Algebra
- Test Generator CD-ROM
- Online Quiz
- eWorkbook
- eEdition
- @HomeTutor

Resources for English Learners
- Quick Reference for English Learners
- Spanish Study Guide
- Multi-Language Visual Glossary
- Student Resources in Spanish

See also the *Algebra 2 Toolkit* for more strategies for meeting individual needs.

EXAMPLE 2 Use the fundamental counting principle

PHOTOGRAPHY You are framing a picture. The frames are available in 12 different styles. Each style is available in 55 different colors. You also want blue mat board, which is available in 11 different shades of blue. How many different ways can you frame the picture?

Solution

You can use the fundamental counting principle to find the total number of ways to frame the picture. Multiply the number of frame styles (12), the number of frame colors (55), and the number of mat boards (11).

Number of ways $= 12 \cdot 55 \cdot 11 = 7260$

▶ The number of different ways you can frame the picture is 7260.

EXAMPLE 3 Use the counting principle with repetition

LICENSE PLATES The standard configuration for a Texas license plate is 1 letter followed by 2 digits followed by 3 letters.

a. How many different license plates are possible if letters and digits can be repeated?

b. How many different license plates are possible if letters and digits cannot be repeated?

Solution

a. There are 26 choices for each letter and 10 choices for each digit. You can use the fundamental counting principle to find the number of different plates.

Number of plates $= 26 \cdot 10 \cdot 10 \cdot 26 \cdot 26 \cdot 26 = 45{,}697{,}600$

▶ With repetition, the number of different license plates is 45,697,600.

b. If you cannot repeat letters there are still 26 choices for the first letter, but then only 25 remaining choices for the second letter, 24 choices for the third letter, and 23 choices for the fourth letter. Similarly, there are 10 choices for the first digit and 9 choices for the second digit. You can use the fundamental counting principle to find the number of different plates.

Number of plates $= 26 \cdot 10 \cdot 9 \cdot 25 \cdot 24 \cdot 23 = 32{,}292{,}000$

▶ Without repetition, the number of different license plates is 32,292,000.

OID ERRORS
a given situation, number of choices hout repetition is ays less than the mber of choices with etition.

✓ **GUIDED PRACTICE** for Examples 1, 2, and 3

1. **SPORTING GOODS** The store in Example 1 also offers 3 different types of bicycles (mountain, racing, and BMX) and 3 different wheel sizes (20 in., 22 in., and 24 in.). How many bicycle choices does the store offer? **9 bicycles**

2. **WHAT IF?** In Example 3, how do the answers change for the standard configuration of a New York license plate, which is 3 letters followed by 4 numbers? **a. The number of plates would increase to 175,760,000.** **b. The number of plates would increase to 78,624,000.**

Motivating the Lesson

A palindrome is any word that reads the same backward or forward, such as *madam* or *radar.* Ask students if 2002 was a palindromic year in the twenty-first century. Then ask them to list other 21st-century palindromic years. In this lesson students will learn counting methods that will allow them to calculate, for example, that there are 30 palindromic years in the 21st through 23rd centuries.

3 TEACH

Extra Example 1

At a blood drive, blood can be labeled one of four types (A, B, AB, or O), one of two Rh factors (+ or −), and one of two genders (F or M). How many different ways can blood be labeled? **16**

Extra Example 2

At a used book sale, you are interested in 5 novels, 3 books of nonfiction, and 7 comic books. If you buy one of each kind, how many different choices do you have? **105**

Key Question to Ask for Example 2

- If you model this problem with a tree diagram, how many branches would the tree have? **7260**

Extra Example 3

The digits 0, 1, 2, 3, and 4 are used to generate four-digit customer codes. How many different codes are possible if digits

a. can be repeated? **625**

b. cannot be repeated? **120**

PERMUTATIONS An ordering of n objects is a **permutation** of the objects. For instance, there are 6 permutations of the letters **A**, **B**, and **C**:

ABC **ACB** **BAC** **BCA** **CAB** **CBA**

You can use the fundamental counting principle to find the number of permutations of **A**, **B**, and **C**. There are 3 choices for the first letter. After the first letter has been chosen, 2 choices remain for the second letter. Finally, after the first two letters have been chosen, there is only 1 choice remaining for the final letter. So, the number of permutations is $3 \cdot 2 \cdot 1 = 6$.

DEFINE FACTORIALS
Zero factorial is defined as $0! = 1$.

The expression $3 \cdot 2 \cdot 1$ can also be written as 3!. The symbol ! is the **factorial** symbol, and 3! is read as "three factorial." In general, $n!$ is defined where n is a positive integer as follows:

$$n! = n \cdot (n - 1) \cdot (n - 2) \cdot \ldots \cdot 3 \cdot 2 \cdot 1$$

The number of permutations of n distinct objects is $n!$.

EXAMPLE 4 Find the number of permutations

OLYMPICS Ten teams are competing in the final round of the Olympic four-person bobsledding competition.

a. In how many different ways can the bobsledding teams finish the competition? (Assume there are no ties.)

b. In how many different ways can 3 of the bobsledding teams finish first, second, and third to win the gold, silver, and bronze medals?

Solution

a. There are 10! different ways that the teams can finish the competition.

$$10! = 10 \cdot 9 \cdot 8 \cdot 7 \cdot 6 \cdot 5 \cdot 4 \cdot 3 \cdot 2 \cdot 1 = 3{,}628{,}800$$

b. Any of the 10 teams can finish first, then any of the remaining 9 teams can finish second, and finally any of the remaining 8 teams can finish third. So, the number of ways that the teams can win the medals is:

$$10 \cdot 9 \cdot 8 = 720$$

✓ **GUIDED PRACTICE** for Example 4

3. **WHAT IF?** In Example 4, how would the answers change if there were 12 bobsledding teams competing in the final round of the competition?
   a. The number of ways to finish would increase to 479,001,600.
   b. The number of ways to finish would increase to 1320.

The answer to part (b) of Example 4 is called the number of permutations of 10 objects taken 3 at a time. It is denoted by ${}_{10}P_3$. Notice that this permutation can be computed using factorials:

$${}_{10}P_3 = 10 \cdot 9 \cdot 8 = \frac{10 \cdot 9 \cdot 8 \cdot 7 \cdot 6 \cdot 5 \cdot 4 \cdot 3 \cdot 2 \cdot 1}{7 \cdot 6 \cdot 5 \cdot 4 \cdot 3 \cdot 2 \cdot 1} = \frac{10!}{7!} = \frac{10!}{(10 - 3)!}$$

This result is generalized at the top of the next page.

Extra Example 4

A television news director has 8 news stories to present on the evening news.

a. How many different ways can the stories be presented? 40,320

b. If only 3 of the stories will be presented, how many possible ways can a lead story, a second story, and a closing story be presented? 336

Key Questions to Ask for Example 4

- Which principle is applied in both solutions? **the fundamental counting principle**
- In part (b) why do you stop multiplying after you calculate $10 \cdot 9 \cdot 8$? **Only three medals will be awarded.**

Differentiated Instruction

Kinesthetic Learners Before proceeding to **Example 4**, students may need more practice with the concept of a permutation. Have student work in pairs. Give each pair a set of four index cards, with the first card labeled A, the second B, and so on. Have students use the cards to make a list of all permutations of the letters A through D.

See also the *Algebra 2 Toolkit* for more strategies.

KEY CONCEPT — *For Your Notebook*

Permutations of *n* Objects Taken *r* at a Time

The number of permutations of *r* objects taken from a group of *n* distinct objects is denoted by ${}_nP_r$ and is given by this formula:

$${}_nP_r = \frac{n!}{(n-r)!}$$

EXAMPLE 5 Find permutations of *n* objects taken *r* at a time

MUSIC You are burning a demo CD for your band. Your band has 12 songs stored on your computer. However, you want to put only 4 songs on the demo CD. In how many orders can you burn 4 of the 12 songs onto the CD?

ALUATE RMUTATIONS
st scientific and phing calculators e a key or menu n for evaluating ${}_nP_r$.

Solution

Find the number of permutations of 12 objects taken 4 at a time.

$${}_{12}P_4 = \frac{12!}{(12-4)!} = \frac{12!}{8!} = \frac{479{,}001{,}600}{40{,}320} = 11{,}880$$

▶ You can burn 4 of the 12 songs in 11,880 different orders.

✓ GUIDED PRACTICE for Example 5

Find the number of permutations.

4. ${}_5P_3$ 60 **5.** ${}_4P_1$ 4 **6.** ${}_8P_5$ 6720 **7.** ${}_{12}P_7$ 3,991,680

PERMUTATIONS WITH REPETITION If you consider the letters E and E to be *distinct*, there are six permutations of the letters E, E, and Y:

EEY EYE YEE
EEY EYE YEE

However, if the two occurrences of E are considered interchangeable, then there are only three distinguishable permutations:

EEY EYE YEE

Each of these permutations corresponds to two of the original six permutations because there are 2!, or 2, permutations of E and E. So, the number of permutations of **E**, **E**, and **Y** can be written as $\frac{3!}{2!} = \frac{6}{2} = 3$.

KEY CONCEPT — *For Your Notebook*

Permutations with Repetition

The number of distinguishable permutations of *n* objects where one object is repeated s_1 times, another is repeated s_2 times, and so on, is:

$$\frac{n!}{s_1! \cdot s_2! \cdot \ldots \cdot s_k!}$$

Extra Example 5

How many different ways can 4 raffle tickets be selected from 50 tickets if each ticket wins a different prize? 5,527,200

Key Questions to Ask for Example 5

- Why can the formula for the permutations of *n* objects taken *r* at a time be applied to this example? There are 12 distinct songs and 4 of them will be burned in a specific order on the CD.
- What are the values of *n* and *r*? $n = 12, r = 4$
- How can you use the fundamental counting principle to solve this problem? $12 \cdot 11 \cdot 10 \cdot 9 = 11{,}880$

Avoiding Common Errors

Make sure students don't evaluate $\frac{n!}{(n-r)!}$ incorrectly as $\left(\frac{n}{n-r}\right)!$. You can have students calculate $\frac{8!}{4!}$ and $\left(\frac{8}{4}\right)!$ to demonstrate that $\frac{8!}{4!} \neq \left(\frac{8}{4}\right)!$.

Graphing Calculator

Some calculators require you to enter the value of *n* before choosing an ${}_nP_r$ menu item; others require that *n* and *r* be entered after choosing the ${}_nP_r$ menu item. Students should be familiar with how to enter ${}_nP_r$ to avoid errors.

Differentiated Instruction

Advanced Challenge students to show that ${}_nP_r$ is a special case of the fundamental counting principle. Ask them to describe two real-world situations that involve the permutation of *n* distinguishable objects taken *r* at a time, one where $r = n$ and another where $r < n$. Then have them demonstrate the solution using both the fundamental counting principle and the formula for ${}_nP_r$. From this they should write a general rule using the fundamental counting principle for finding ${}_nP_r$. This will help them distinguish between permutations and combinations in Lesson 10.2.

See also the *Algebra 2 Toolkit* for more strategies.

Extra Example 6

Find the number of distinguishable permutations of the letters in (a) SOCCER and (b) SWIMMING. 360; 10,080

Key Questions to Ask for Example 6

- Why does it make sense to divide by the permutations of repeated letters? **If a letter repeats t times, then $t!$ of the permutations will be identical.**
- Why do the fractions not include factors of 1! for each nonrepeated letter of the word? **Since $1! = 1$, dividing by 1! does not affect the value.**

Closing the Lesson

Have students summarize the major points of the lesson and answer the Essential Question: How do you determine the number of distinguishable permutations in the letters of a word?

- **If one event can occur in m ways and another event can occur in n ways, then the number of ways that both events can occur is $m \cdot n$.**
- **The number of permutations of n distinct objects is $n!$.**
- **You can use the formula $_nP_r = \frac{n!}{(n-r)!}$ to determine the number of permutations of r objects taken from a group of n distinct objects.**

The number of distinguishable permutations of n objects where one object is repeated s_1 times, another is repeated s_2 times, and so on for k items, is $\frac{n!}{s_1! \cdot s_2! \cdot \ldots \cdot s_k!}$.

3–6. See Additional Answers beginning on p. AA1.

EXAMPLE 6 Find permutations with repetition

Find the number of distinguishable permutations of the letters in (a) MIAMI and (b) TALLAHASSEE.

Solution

a. MIAMI has 5 letters of which M and I are each repeated 2 times. So, the number of distinguishable permutations is $\frac{5!}{2! \cdot 2!} = \frac{120}{2 \cdot 2} = 30$.

b. TALLAHASSEE has 11 letters of which A is repeated 3 times, and L, S, and E are each repeated 2 times. So, the number of distinguishable permutations is $\frac{11!}{3! \cdot 2! \cdot 2! \cdot 2!} = \frac{39{,}916{,}800}{6 \cdot 2 \cdot 2 \cdot 2} = 831{,}600$.

GUIDED PRACTICE for Example 6

Find the number of distinguishable permutations of the letters in the word.

8. MALL 12 **9.** KAYAK 30 **10.** CINCINNATI 50,400

10.1 EXERCISES

HOMEWORK KEY
◯ = **WORKED-OUT SOLUTIONS** on p. WS18 for Exs. 13, 35, and 65
★ = **STANDARDIZED TEST PRACTICE** Exs. 2, 17, 42, 55, 57, and 68

SKILL PRACTICE

1. VOCABULARY What is a permutation of n objects? The number of ways n objects can be ordered.

2. ★ WRITING Simplify the formula for $_nP_r$ when $r = 0$. *Explain* why this result makes sense. *Sample answer:* When $r = 0$, the permutation simplifies to $\frac{n!}{n!}$, which is equal to 1.

EXAMPLE 1 on p. 682 for Exs. 3–6

TREE DIAGRAMS An object has an attribute from each list. Make a tree diagram that shows the number of different objects that can be created. 3–6. See margin.

3.

T-Shirts
Size: M, L, XL
Type: long-sleeved, short-sleeved

4.

Toast
Bread: white, wheat
Spread: jam, margarine

5.

Meal
Entrée: chicken, fish, pasta
Side: corn, green beans, potato

6.

Furniture
Wood: cherry, mahogany, oak, pine
Finish: stained, painted, unfinished

EXAMPLE 2 on p. 683 for Exs. 7–10

FUNDAMENTAL COUNTING PRINCIPLE Each event can occur in the given number of ways. Find the number of ways all of the events can occur.

7. Event A: 2 ways; Event B: 4 ways 8 ways

8. Event A: 5 ways; Event B: 2 ways 10 ways

9. Event A: 4 ways; Event B: 3 ways; Event C: 5 ways 60 ways

10. Event A: 3 ways; Event B: 6 ways; Event C: 5 ways; Event D: 2 ways 180 ways

XAMPLE 3 on p. 683 for Exs. 11–17

LICENSE PLATES For the given configuration, determine how many different license plates are possible if (a) digits and letters can be repeated, and (b) digits and letters cannot be repeated. 11–16. See margin.

11. 4 letters followed by 3 digits
12. 2 letters followed by 5 digits
13. 4 letters followed by 2 digits
14. 5 digits followed by 3 letters
15. 1 digit followed by 5 letters
16. 6 letters

17. ★ **MULTIPLE CHOICE** How many different license plates with 2 letters followed by 4 digits are possible if digits and letters cannot be repeated? A

(A) 3,276,000 (B) 6,760,000 (C) 32,292,000 (D) 45,697,600

EXAMPLES 4 and 5 on pp. 684–685 for Exs. 18–41

FACTORIALS Evaluate the expression.

18. 7! 5040
19. 11! 39,916,800
20. 1! 1
21. 8! 40,320
22. 4! 24
23. 0! 1
24. 12! 479,001,600
25. 6! 720
26. 3! • 4! 144
27. 3(4!) 72
28. $\frac{8!}{(8-5)!}$ 6720
29. $\frac{9!}{4! \cdot 4!}$ 630

PERMUTATIONS Find the number of permutations.

30. ${}_4P_4$ 24
31. ${}_6P_2$ 30
32. ${}_{10}P_1$ 10
33. ${}_8P_7$ 40,320
34. ${}_7P_4$ 840
35. ${}_9P_2$ 72
36. ${}_{13}P_8$ 51,891,840
37. ${}_7P_7$ 5040
38. ${}_5P_0$ 1
39. ${}_9P_4$ 3024
40. ${}_{11}P_4$ 7920
41. ${}_{15}P_0$ 1

42. ★ **SHORT RESPONSE** Let n be a positive integer. Find the number of permutations of n objects taken $n - 1$ at a time. *Compare* your answer with the number of permutations of all n objects. Does this make sense? *Explain.*
$n!$; they are the same; yes; the permutation simplifies to $\frac{n!}{1!}$, which is equal to $n!$.

EXAMPLE 6 on p. 686 for Exs. 43–55

B **PERMUTATIONS WITH REPETITION Find the number of distinguishable permutations of the letters in the word.**

43. OFF 3
44. TREE 12
45. SKILL 60
46. YELLOW 360
47. GRAVEL 720
48. PANAMA 120
49. ARKANSAS 3360
50. FACTORIAL 181,440
51. MAGNETIC 40,320
52. HONOLULU 5040
53. CLEVELAND 90,720
54. MISSISSIPPI 34,650

55. ★ **MULTIPLE CHOICE** What is the number of distinguishable permutations of the letters in the word HAWAII? B

(A) 24 (B) 180 (C) 360 (D) 720

56. **ERROR ANALYSIS** In bingo, balls labeled from 1 to 75 are drawn from a container without being replaced. *Describe* and correct the error in finding the number of ways the first 4 numbers can be chosen for a game of bingo.

75 • 75 • 75 • 75
= 31,640,625 ✗

56. The numbers are not replaced, so the number of balls must decrease by 1 after each drawing; 75 • 74 • 73 • 72 = 29,170,800.

C 57. ★ **SHORT RESPONSE** *Explain* how the fundamental counting principle can be used to justify the formula for the number of permutations of n distinct objects. See margin.

SOLVING EQUATIONS Solve for n.

58. ${}_nP_4 = 8({}_nP_3)$ 11
59. ${}_nP_6 = 5({}_nP_5)$ 10
60. ${}_nP_5 = 9({}_nP_4)$ 13

61. **CHALLENGE** Find the number of distinguishable permutations of 6 letters that are chosen from the letters in the word MANATEE. 1260

4 PRACTICE AND APPLY

Assignment Guide

Answer Transparencies available for all exercises

Basic:
Day 1: pp. 686–689
Exs. 1–4, 7, 8, 11–13, 17–21, 30–33, 42–46, 62–68, 72

Average:
Day 1: pp. 686–689
Exs. 1, 2, 4, 5, 8, 9, 13, 14, 17, 22–25, 34–37, 42, 47–50, 55, 56, 62–70, 73

Advanced:
Day 1: pp. 686–689
Exs. 1, 2, 6, 10, 15–17, 26–29, 38–42, 51–61*, 63, 65–71*

Block:
pp. 686–689
Exs. 1, 2, 4, 5, 8, 9, 13, 14, 17, 22–25, 34–37, 42, 47–50, 55, 56, 62–70, 73 (with 10.2)

Differentiated Instruction

See *Algebra 2 Best Practices Toolkit* for suggestions on addressing the needs of a diverse classroom.

Homework Check

For a quick check of student understanding of key concepts, go over the following exercises:
Basic: 4, 12, 20, 32, 64
Average: 14, 24, 36, 48, 65
Advanced: 16, 28, 40, 52, 66

Extra Practice

- Student Edition, p. 1019
- Chapter 10 Resource Book: Practice levels A, B, C, pp. 6–8

Practice Worksheet

An easily-readable reduced practice page (with answers) for this lesson can be found on p. 680C.

11a. 456,976,000 license plates
11b. 258,336,000 license plates
12a. 67,600,000 license plates
12b. 19,656,000 license plates
13a. 45,697,600 license plates
13b. 32,292,000 license plates
14a. 1,757,600,000 license plates
14b. 471,744,000 license plates
15a. 118,813,760 license plates
15b. 78,936,000 license plates
16a. 308,915,776 license plates
16b. 165,765,600 license plates
57. See Additional Answers beginning on p. AA1.

Study Strategy

Exercises 62–70 Students should follow the same general pattern for these exercises: use the fundamental counting principle to solve problems involving consecutive choices.

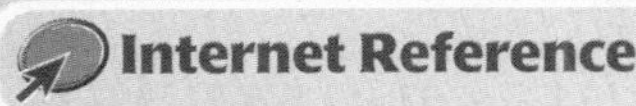

Exercise 63 More information about the Goldman Environmental Prize can be found at www.goldmanprize.org/prize/about.html

An **Animated Algebra** activity is available on-line for **Exercise 69**. This activity is also available on the **Power Presentations CD-ROM**.

PROBLEM SOLVING

EXAMPLE 2 A on p. 683 for Exs. 62–63

62. **CLASS RINGS** You want to purchase a class ring. The ring can be made from 3 different metals. You can choose from 6 different side designs and 12 different stones. How many different class rings are possible? **216 class rings**

Metal	Side Design		Stone
Auralite	Academics	Literature	
Gold	Art	Music	
Silver	Athletics	Technology	

@HomeTutor for problem solving help at classzone.com

63. **ENVIRONMENT** Since 1990, the Goldman Environmental Prize has been awarded annually to 6 grassroots environmentalists, one from each of 6 regions. The regions consist of 52 countries in Africa, 47 in Europe, 45 in Asia, 36 in island nations, 19 in South and Central America, and 3 in North America. How many different sets of 6 countries can be represented by the prize winners in a given year? **225,678,960 sets**

@HomeTutor for problem solving help at classzone.com

EXAMPLES 4, 5, and 6 on pp. 684–686 for Exs. 64–66

64. **PHOTOGRAPHY** A photographer lines up the 15 members of a family in a single line in order to take a photograph. How many different ways can the photographer arrange the family members for the picture? **1,307,674,368,000 ways**

65. **SCHOOL CLUBS** A Spanish club is electing a president, vice president, and secretary. The club has 9 members who are eligible for these offices. How many different ways can the 3 offices be filled? **504 ways**

66. **MUSIC** The window of a music store has 8 stands in fixed positions where instruments can be displayed. In how many ways can 3 identical guitars, 2 identical keyboards, and 3 identical violins be displayed? **560 ways**

67a. 240 selections
67b. 252 selections
67c. 60,480 selections

67. **MULTI-STEP PROBLEM** You are designing an entertainment center. You want to include three audio components and three video components.

a. You want one of each audio component listed at the right. How many selections of audio components are possible?

b. You want one of each video component listed at the right. How many selections of video components are possible?

c. How many selections of all six audio and video components are possible?

Entertainment Center	
Audio Components	**Video Components**
5 receivers	7 TV sets
8 CD players	9 DVD players
6 speakers	4 game systems

68c. Passwords when characters can be repeated; there are more possible choices for these passwords which makes it harder to randomly guess, making them more secure.

B

68. ★ **EXTENDED RESPONSE** To keep computer files secure, many programs require the user to enter a password. The shortest allowable passwords are typically 6 characters long and can contain both letters and digits.

a. **Calculate** How many 6-character passwords are possible if characters can be repeated? **2,176,782,336 passwords**

b. **Calculate** How many 6-character passwords are possible if characters cannot be repeated? **1,402,410,240 passwords**

c. **Draw Conclusions** Which type of password is more secure? *Explain.*

○ = WORKED-OUT SOLUTIONS on p. WS1

★ = STANDARDIZED TEST PRACTICE

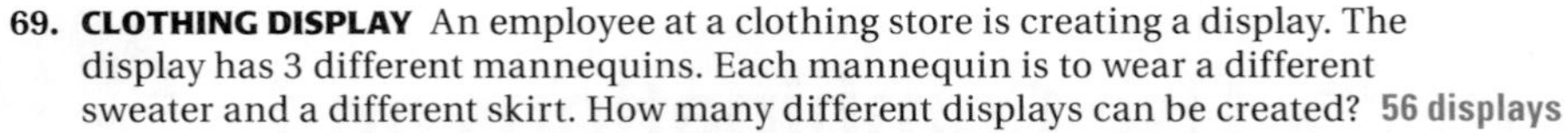

69. CLOTHING DISPLAY An employee at a clothing store is creating a display. The display has 3 different mannequins. Each mannequin is to wear a different sweater and a different skirt. How many different displays can be created? **56 displays**

Just Arrived......
7 NEW SKIRT STYLES
Sweaters On Sale.....
8 DIFFERENT COLORS

Animated Algebra at classzone.com

70. CROSS COUNTRY Three schools are competing in a cross country meet. School A has 6 runners, school B has 5 runners, and school C has 4 runners. For scoring purposes, the finishing order of the meet only considers the school of each runner. How many different finishing orders are there for scoring purposes? **6 finishing orders**

C **71. CHALLENGE** You have learned that $n!$ represents the number of ways that n objects can be placed in a *linear* order, where it matters which object is placed first. Now consider *circular* permutations in which objects are placed in a circle, so that it does *not* matter which object is placed first.

a. Suppose you are seating 5 people at a circular table. How many different ways can you arrange the people around the table? **24 ways**

b. Find a formula for the number of permutations of n objects placed in clockwise order around a circle when only the relative order of the objects matters. *Explain* how you derived your formula.

(n − 1)!; e there ɔ object ed first, ɔnd, third, so on, allow person to esent a ed" position, he remaining ple (n − 1), be arranged 1)! ways.

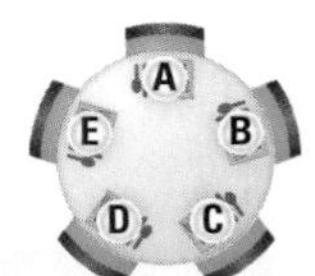

The two arrangements shown represent the same permutation.

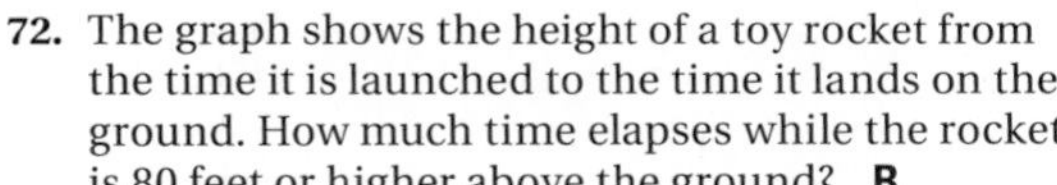

KENTUCKY MIXED REVIEW

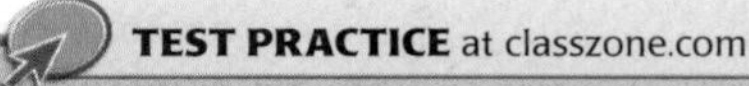

TEST PRACTICE at classzone.com

72. The graph shows the height of a toy rocket from the time it is launched to the time it lands on the ground. How much time elapses while the rocket is 80 feet or higher above the ground? **B**

(A) 3 sec (B) 4 sec
(C) 6 sec (D) 8 sec

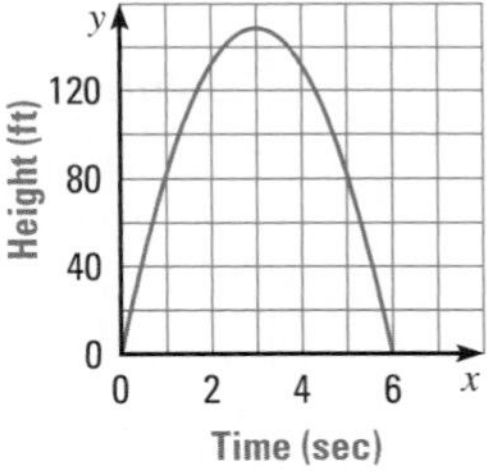

73. Paul makes a scale model of an airplane. The actual airplane is 56 feet long with a wingspan of 37.5 feet. Paul's model is 14 inches long. What is the approximate wingspan of his model? **B**

(A) 9.0 in. (B) 9.4 in. (C) 18.7 in. (D) 22.5 in.

5 ASSESS AND RETEACH

Daily Homework Quiz

Transparency Available

1. Find $_{11}P_5$. **55,440**
2. Find the number of distinguishable permutations of the letters in BASKETBALL. **453,600**
3. How many different 3-digit IDs can be made if the first digit must be a 7 and no digits may be repeated? **72**
4. How many different ways can a chairperson and an assistant be selected for a research project if there are 7 scientists for the two positions? **42**

Available at **classzone.com**

Diagnosis/Remediation

- Practice A, B, C in Chapter 10 Resource Book, pp. 6–8
- Study Guide in Chapter 10 Resource Book, pp. 9–10
- Practice Workbook, pp. 149–150
- @HomeTutor

Challenge

Additional challenge is available in the Chapter 10 Resource Book, p. 13.

1 PLAN AND PREPARE

Warm-Up Exercises

Transparency Available

Evaluate the expression.

1. 5! 120

2. (4 − 2)!3! 12

3. $\frac{8!}{5!}$ 336

4. ${}_7P_5$ 2520

5. In how many ways can 6 people line up to buy tickets for a movie? 720

Notetaking Guide

Transparency Available

Promotes interactive learning and notetaking skills, pp. 263–267.

Pacing

Basic: 1 day

Average: 1 day

Advanced: 1 day

Block: 0.5 block with 10.1

- See *Teaching Guide/Lesson Plan*.

2 FOCUS AND MOTIVATE

Essential Question

Big Idea 1, p. 681

How can you determine the value of ${}_nC_r$ besides applying the formula? **Tell students they will learn how to answer this question by using Pascal's triangle.**

10.2 Use Combinations and the Binomial Theorem

MA-HS-4.4.2 *Students will recognize and identify the differences between combinations and permutations and use them to count discrete quantities.*

Before You used the counting principle and permutations.

Now You will use combinations and the binomial theorem.

Why? So you can find ways to form a set, as in Example 2.

Key Vocabulary
- combination
- Pascal's triangle
- binomial theorem

In Lesson 10.1, you learned that order is important for some counting problems. For other counting problems, order is not important. For instance, if you purchase a package of trading cards, the order of the cards inside the package is not important. A **combination** is a selection of r objects from a group of n objects where the order is not important.

KEY CONCEPT *For Your Notebook*

Combinations of n Objects Taken r at a Time

The number of combinations of r objects taken from a group of n distinct objects is denoted by ${}_nC_r$ and is given by this formula:

$${}_nC_r = \frac{n!}{(n-r)! \cdot r!}$$

EXAMPLE 1 Find combinations

CARDS A standard deck of 52 playing cards has 4 suits with 13 different cards in each suit.

a. If the order in which the cards are dealt is not important, how many different 5-card hands are possible?

b. In how many 5-card hands are all 5 cards of the same color?

Standard 52-Card Deck

K ♠	K ♥	K ♦	K ♣
Q ♠	Q ♥	Q ♦	Q ♣
J ♠	J ♥	J ♦	J ♣
10 ♠	10 ♥	10 ♦	10 ♣
9 ♠	9 ♥	9 ♦	9 ♣
8 ♠	8 ♥	8 ♦	8 ♣
7 ♠	7 ♥	7 ♦	7 ♣
6 ♠	6 ♥	6 ♦	6 ♣
5 ♠	5 ♥	5 ♦	5 ♣
4 ♠	4 ♥	4 ♦	4 ♣
3 ♠	3 ♥	3 ♦	3 ♣
2 ♠	2 ♥	2 ♦	2 ♣
A ♠	A ♥	A ♦	A ♣

Solution

a. The number of ways to choose 5 cards from a deck of 52 cards is:

$${}_{52}C_5 = \frac{52!}{47! \cdot 5!} = \frac{52 \cdot 51 \cdot 50 \cdot 49 \cdot 48 \cdot \cancel{47!}}{\cancel{47!} \cdot 5!} = 2{,}598{,}960$$

b. For all 5 cards to be the same color, you need to choose 1 of the 2 colors and then 5 of the 26 cards in that color. So, the number of possible hands is:

$${}_2C_1 \cdot {}_{26}C_5 = \frac{2!}{1! \cdot 1!} \cdot \frac{26!}{21! \cdot 5!} = \frac{2}{1 \cdot 1} \cdot \frac{26 \cdot 25 \cdot 24 \cdot 23 \cdot 22 \cdot \cancel{21!}}{\cancel{21!} \cdot 5!} = 131{,}560$$

Resource Planning Guide

Chapter Resource Book
- Teaching Guide/Lesson Plan (pp. 14–15)
- Activity Master (p. 16)
- Practice levels A, B, C (pp. 18–20)
- Study Guide (pp. 21–22)
- Catch-up for Absent Students (p. 23)
- Problem Solving Workshop (p. 24)
- Challenge (p. 25)

Workbooks
- Notetaking Guide (pp. 263–267)
- Practice Workbook (pp. 151–152)

Teaching Options
- **Power Presentations CD-ROM** provides dynamic electronic teaching resources for the classroom.
- **Activity Generator CD-ROM** provides editable activities for all ability levels.

Interactive Technology
- Easy Planner
- Power Presentations CD-ROM
- Activity Generator CD-ROM
- Animated Algebra
- Test Generator CD-ROM
- Online Quiz
- eWorkbook
- eEdition
- @HomeTutor

Resources for English Learners
- Quick Reference for English Learners
- Spanish Study Guide
- Multi-Language Visual Glossary
- Student Resources in Spanish

See also the *Algebra 2 Toolkit* for more strategies for meeting individual needs.

MULTIPLE EVENTS When finding the number of ways both an event A *and* an event B can occur, you need to multiply, as in part (b) of Example 1. When finding the number of ways that event A *or* event B can occur, you add instead.

EXAMPLE 2 Decide to multiply or add combinations

THEATER William Shakespeare wrote 38 plays that can be divided into three genres. Of the 38 plays, 18 are comedies, 10 are histories, and 10 are tragedies.

a. How many different sets of *exactly* 2 comedies and 1 tragedy can you read?

b. How many different sets of *at most* 3 plays can you read?

Solution

a. You can choose 2 of the 18 comedies and 1 of the 10 tragedies. So, the number of possible sets of plays is:

$${}_{18}C_2 \cdot {}_{10}C_1 = \frac{18!}{16! \cdot 2!} \cdot \frac{10!}{9! \cdot 1!} = \frac{18 \cdot 17 \cdot \cancel{16!}}{\cancel{16!} \cdot 2 \cdot 1} \cdot \frac{10 \cdot \cancel{9!}}{\cancel{9!} \cdot 1} = 153 \cdot 10 = 1530$$

b. You can read 0, 1, 2, or 3 plays. Because there are 38 plays that can be chosen, the number of possible sets of plays is:

$${}_{38}C_0 + {}_{38}C_1 + {}_{38}C_2 + {}_{38}C_3 = 1 + 38 + 703 + 8436 = 9178$$

AVOID ERRORS
When finding the number of ways to select *at most n* objects, be sure to include the possibility of selecting 0 objects.

SUBTRACTING POSSIBILITIES Counting problems that involve phrases like "at least" or "at most" are sometimes easier to solve by subtracting possibilities you do not want from the total number of possibilities.

EXAMPLE 3 Solve a multi-step problem

BASKETBALL During the school year, the girl's basketball team is scheduled to play 12 home games. You want to attend *at least* 3 of the games. How many different combinations of games can you attend?

Solution

Of the 12 home games, you want to attend 3 games, or 4 games, or 5 games, and so on. So, the number of combinations of games you can attend is:

$${}_{12}C_3 + {}_{12}C_4 + {}_{12}C_5 + \cdots + {}_{12}C_{12}$$

Instead of adding these combinations, use the following reasoning. For each of the 12 games, you can choose to attend or not attend the game, so there are 2^{12} total combinations. If you attend at least 3 games, you do not attend only a total of 0, 1, or 2 games. So, the number of ways you can attend at least 3 games is:

$$2^{12} - ({}_{12}C_0 + {}_{12}C_1 + {}_{12}C_2) = 4096 - (1 + 12 + 66) = 4017$$

✓ GUIDED PRACTICE for Examples 1, 2, and 3

Find the number of combinations.

1. ${}_8C_3$ 56
2. ${}_{10}C_6$ 210
3. ${}_7C_2$ 21
4. ${}_{14}C_5$ 2002
5. **WHAT IF?** In Example 2, how many different sets of *exactly* 3 tragedies and 2 histories can you read? 5400 sets

Motivating the Lesson

Ask students how they can find $(x + y)^5$. Tell them that in this lesson they will learn a formula to expand this binomial and others.

3 TEACH

Extra Example 1

Parents have 10 books that they can read to their children this week. Five of the books are nonfiction and 5 are fiction.

a. If the order in which they read the books is not important, how many different sets of 4 books can they choose? 210

b. In how many groups of 4 books are all the books either nonfiction or fiction? 10

Extra Example 2

The Student Senate consists of 6 seniors, 5 juniors, 4 sophomores, and 3 freshmen.

a. How many different committees of exactly 2 seniors and 2 juniors can be chosen? 150

b. How many different committees of at most 4 students can be chosen? 4047

Key Question to Ask for Example 2

- How is the question in part (b) different from the question in part (a)? The question in part (a) asks how several events can occur together; the question in part (b) asks how one event or another event can occur.

Extra Example 3

You are going to toss 10 different coins. How many different ways will at least 4 of the coins show heads? 848

Differentiated Instruction

Visual Learners Before discussing **Example 2**, encourage students to look for key phrases like "at least," "at most," and "exactly." Suggest that students develop an understanding of these phrases by drawing number lines that represent the quantities described. For example, "at most 3" translates to any whole number between 0 and 3, inclusive. Remind students that, for application problems like these, decimals, fractions, and numbers less than 0 do not make sense.

See also the *Algebra 2 Toolkit* for more strategies.

Extra Example 4

From a collection of 7 baseball caps, you want to trade 3. Use Pascal's triangle to find the number of combinations of 3 caps that can be traded. 35

Key Question to Ask for Example 4

- How many numbers are in the seventh row of Pascal's triangle? the eighth row? the ninth row? the nth row? 8; 9; 10; $n + 1$

Mathematical Reasoning

Multiple Representations Pascal's triangle provides a visual representation of related values of ${}_nC_r$. Be sure to point out the symmetry in the triangle, so that students can see, for example, that ${}_6C_2 = {}_6C_4$.

Study Strategy

Students should see from Pascal's triangle that ${}_nC_0 = {}_nC_n = 1$. This should allow them to more quickly evaluate expressions of this form.

PASCAL'S TRIANGLE If you arrange the values of ${}_nC_r$ in a triangular pattern in which each row corresponds to a value of n, you get what is called **Pascal's triangle**. Pascal's triangle is named after the French mathematician Blaise Pascal (1623–1662).

KEY CONCEPT — *For Your Notebook*

Pascal's Triangle

Pascal's triangle is shown below with its entries represented by combinations and with its entries represented by numbers. The first and last numbers in each row are 1. Every number other than 1 is the sum of the closest two numbers in the row directly above it.

	Pascal's triangle as combinations	Pascal's triangle as numbers
$n = 0$ (0th row)	${}_0C_0$	1
$n = 1$ (1st row)	${}_1C_0 \quad {}_1C_1$	1 1
$n = 2$ (2nd row)	${}_2C_0 \quad {}_2C_1 \quad {}_2C_2$	1 2 1
$n = 3$ (3rd row)	${}_3C_0 \quad {}_3C_1 \quad {}_3C_2 \quad {}_3C_3$	1 3 3 1
$n = 4$ (4th row)	${}_4C_0 \quad {}_4C_1 \quad {}_4C_2 \quad {}_4C_3 \quad {}_4C_4$	1 4 6 4 1
$n = 5$ (5th row)	${}_5C_0 \quad {}_5C_1 \quad {}_5C_2 \quad {}_5C_3 \quad {}_5C_4 \quad {}_5C_5$	1 5 10 10 5 1

EXAMPLE 4 Use Pascal's triangle

SCHOOL CLUBS The 6 members of a Model UN club must choose 2 representatives to attend a state convention. Use Pascal's triangle to find the number of combinations of 2 members that can be chosen as representatives.

Solution

Because you need to find ${}_6C_2$, write the 6th row of Pascal's triangle by adding numbers from the previous row.

$n = 5$ (5th row)   1   5   10   10   5   1

$n = 6$ (6th row)   1   6   15   20   15   6   1

${}_6C_0 \quad {}_6C_1 \quad {}_6C_2 \quad {}_6C_3 \quad {}_6C_4 \quad {}_6C_5 \quad {}_6C_6$

▸ The value of ${}_6C_2$ is the third number in the 6th row of Pascal's triangle, as shown above. Therefore, ${}_6C_2 = 15$. There are 15 combinations of representatives for the convention.

✓ GUIDED PRACTICE for Example 4

6. **WHAT IF?** In Example 4, use Pascal's triangle to find the number of combinations of 2 members that can be chosen if the Model UN club has 7 members. 21 combinations

BINOMIAL EXPANSIONS There is an important relationship between powers of binomials and combinations. The numbers in Pascal's triangle can be used to find coefficients in binomial expansions. For example, the coefficients in the expansion of $(a + b)^4$ are the numbers of combinations in the row of Pascal's triangle for $n = 4$:

$$\begin{array}{ccccc} (a+b)^4 = 1a^4 & + 4a^3b & + 6a^2b^2 & + 4ab^3 & + 1b^4 \\ {}_4C_0 & {}_4C_1 & {}_4C_2 & {}_4C_3 & {}_4C_4 \end{array}$$

This result is generalized in the **binomial theorem**.

KEY CONCEPT *For Your Notebook*

Binomial Theorem

For any positive integer n, the binomial expansion of $(a + b)^n$ is:

$$(a + b)^n = {}_nC_0a^nb^0 + {}_nC_1a^{n-1}b^1 + {}_nC_2a^{n-2}b^2 + \cdots + {}_nC_na^0b^n$$

Notice that each term in the expansion of $(a + b)^n$ has the form ${}_nC_r\,a^{n-r}b^r$ where r is an integer from 0 to n.

EXAMPLE 5 Expand a power of a binomial sum

Use the binomial theorem to write the binomial expansion.

$$\begin{aligned}(x^2 + y)^3 &= {}_3C_0(x^2)^3y^0 + {}_3C_1(x^2)^2y^1 + {}_3C_2(x^2)^1y^2 + {}_3C_3(x^2)^0y^3 \\ &= (1)(x^6)(1) + (3)(x^4)(y) + (3)(x^2)(y^2) + (1)(1)(y^3) \\ &= x^6 + 3x^4y + 3x^2y^2 + y^3\end{aligned}$$

POWERS OF BINOMIAL DIFFERENCES To expand a power of a binomial difference, you can rewrite the binomial as a sum. The resulting expansion will have terms whose signs alternate between + and −.

EXAMPLE 6 Expand a power of a binomial difference

Use the binomial theorem to write the binomial expansion.

$$\begin{aligned}(a - 2b)^4 &= [a + (-2b)]^4 \\ &= {}_4C_0a^4(-2b)^0 + {}_4C_1a^3(-2b)^1 + {}_4C_2a^2(-2b)^2 + {}_4C_3a^1(-2b)^3 + {}_4C_4a^0(-2b)^4 \\ &= (1)(a^4)(1) + (4)(a^3)(-2b) + (6)(a^2)(4b^2) + (4)(a)(-8b^3) + (1)(1)(16b^4) \\ &= a^4 - 8a^3b + 24a^2b^2 - 32ab^3 + 16b^4\end{aligned}$$

GUIDED PRACTICE for Examples 5 and 6

Use the binomial theorem to write the binomial expansion.

7. $(x + 3)^5$
8. $(a + 2b)^4$
9. $(2p - q)^4$
10. $(5 - 2y)^3$

Extra Example 5

Use the binomial theorem to write the binomial expansion of $(x + y)^6$. $x^6 + 6x^5y + 15x^4y^2 + 20x^3y^3 + 15x^2y^4 + 6xy^5 + y^6$

Key Question to Ask for Example 5

- What term represents a in the expansion? What term represents b? a is represented by x^2. b is represented by y.

Extra Example 6

Use the binomial theorem to write the binomial expansion of $(3x - 2)^4$. $81x^4 - 216x^3 + 216x^2 - 96x + 16$

Key Questions to Ask for Example 6

- In the expansion of $(x - y)^m$, if the coefficient of the nth term is negative, is the coefficient of the $(n + 1)$st term negative or positive? positive
- Why are the coefficients of the terms different from the numbers in Pascal's triangle? The coefficient of b is −2 rather than 1.

Reading Strategy

Students are accustomed to seeing terms of a polynomial with numerical coefficients. They should realize that the expression ${}_nC_r$ represents a number.

$^5 + 15x^4 + 90x^3 +$
$x^2 + 405x + 243$

OID ERRORS
en a binomial has
erm or terms with a
efficient other than
he coefficients of
binomial expansion
not the same as the
rresponding row of
scal's triangle.

$+ 8a^3b +$
$^2b^2 + 32ab^3 +$

$p^4 - 32p^3q +$
$^2q^2 - 8pq^3 + q^4$

$-8y^3 + 60y^2 -$
$y + 125$

Extra Example 7

Find the coefficient of x^3y^4 in $(2x - y)^7$. 280

Key Questions to Ask for Example 7

- How do you know that the term containing x^4 occurs when $r = 6$? **Each term is ${}_{10}C_r(3x)^{10-r}(2)^r$. So if the exponent $10 - r$ is 4, then $r = 6$.**
- Why is 210 a factor of the coefficient of x^4? ${}_{10}C_6 = 210$
- What is the sixth value in the tenth row of Pascal's triangle? 210

Closing the Lesson

Have students summarize the major points of the lesson and answer the Essential Question: How can you determine the value of ${}_nC_r$ besides applying the formula?

- **The formula for the number of combinations of r objects taken from a group of n distinct objects is ${}_nC_r = \frac{n!}{(n-r)! \cdot r!}$.**
- **Multiply when counting the number of ways two events can occur together. Add when counting the number of ways that either one event or another event can occur.**
- **The binomial theorem provides a technique for expanding a binomial or finding the coefficient of a particular term in the expansion.**

You can use Pascal's triangle to determine ${}_nC_r$. In Pascal's triangle, the rth value in the nth row is ${}_nC_{r-1}$.

EXAMPLE 7 Find a coefficient in an expansion

Find the coefficient of x^4 in the expansion of $(3x + 2)^{10}$.

Solution

From the binomial theorem, you know the following:

$$(3x + 2)^{10} = {}_{10}C_0(3x)^{10}(2)^0 + {}_{10}C_1(3x)^9(2)^1 + \cdots + {}_{10}C_{10}(3x)^0(2)^{10}$$

Each term in the expansion has the form ${}_{10}C_r(3x)^{10-r}(2)^r$. The term containing x^4 occurs when $r = 6$:

$${}_{10}C_6(3x)^4(2)^6 = (210)(81x^4)(64) = 1{,}088{,}640x^4$$

▶ The coefficient of x^4 is 1,088,640.

✓ GUIDED PRACTICE for Example 7

11. Find the coefficient of x^5 in the expansion of $(x - 3)^7$. 189
12. Find the coefficient of x^3 in the expansion of $(2x + 5)^8$. 1,400,000

10.2 EXERCISES

HOMEWORK KEY
○ = **WORKED-OUT SOLUTIONS** on p. WS18 for Exs. 17, 29, and 49
★ = **STANDARDIZED TEST PRACTICE** Exs. 2, 35, 40, 41, and 52

SKILL PRACTICE

A

EXAMPLES 1, 2, and 3 on pp. 690–691 for Exs. 3–18

1. **VOCABULARY** Copy and complete: The binomial expansion of $(a + b)^n$ is given by the _?_. nth row of Pascal's triangle
2. ★ **WRITING** *Explain* the difference between permutations and combinations. In a permutation the order of the events is important, but in a combination the order is not important.

COMBINATIONS **Find the number of combinations.**

3. ${}_5C_2$ 10
4. ${}_{10}C_3$ 120
5. ${}_9C_6$ 84
6. ${}_8C_2$ 28
7. ${}_{11}C_{11}$ 1
8. ${}_{12}C_4$ 495
9. ${}_7C_5$ 21
10. ${}_{14}C_6$ 3003

ERROR ANALYSIS ***Describe*** **and correct the error in finding the number of combinations.**

11. ${}_6C_2 = \frac{6!}{(6-2)!} = \frac{720}{24} = 30$ ✗

11. The denominator should have been multiplied by 2!; $\frac{6!}{(6-2)! \cdot 2!} = \frac{720}{48} = 15.$

12. ${}_8C_3 = \frac{8!}{3!} = \frac{40{,}320}{6} = 6720$ 

12. The denominator should have been multiplied by $(8 - 3)!$; $\frac{8!}{(8-3)! \cdot 3!} = \frac{40{,}320}{720} = 56.$

CARD HANDS **Find the number of possible 5-card hands that contain the cards specified. The cards are taken from a standard 52-card deck.**

13. 5 face cards (kings, queens, or jacks) 792 hands
14. 4 kings and 1 other card 48 hands
15. 1 ace and 4 cards that are not aces 778,320 hands
16. 5 hearts or 5 diamonds 2574 hands
17. At most 1 queen 2,490,624 hands
18. At least 1 spade 2,023,203 hands

19.

1 6 15 20 15 6 1
1 7 21 35 35 21 7 1
1 8 28 56 70 56 28 8 1
1 9 36 84 126 126 84 36 9 1
1 10 45 120 210 252 210 120 45 10 1

20. $x^6 + 18x^5 + 135x^4 + 540x^3 + 1215x^2 + 1458x + 729$

21. $y^{10} - 30y^9z + 405y^8z^2 - 3240y^7z^3 + 17{,}010y^6z^4 - 61{,}236y^5z^5 + 153{,}090y^4z^6 - 262{,}440y^3z^7 + 295{,}245y^2z^8 - 196{,}830yz^9 + 59{,}049z^{10}$

22. $a^8 + 8a^7b^2 + 28a^6b^4 + 56a^5b^6 + 70a^4b^8 + 56a^3b^{10} + 28a^2b^{12} + 8ab^{14} + b^{16}$

23. $128s^7 - 448s^6t^4 + 672s^5t^8 - 560s^4t^{12} + 280s^3t^{16} - 84s^2t^{20} + 14st^{24} - t^{28}$

EXAMPLE 4
on p. 692
for Exs. 19–23

19. **USING PATTERNS** Copy Pascal's triangle on page 692 and add rows for $n = 6, 7, 8, 9$, and 10. **See margin.**

PASCAL'S TRIANGLE **Use the rows of Pascal's triangle from Exercise 19 to write the binomial expansion.** 20–23. See margin.

20. $(x + 3)^6$
21. $(y - 3z)^{10}$
22. $(a + b^2)^8$
23. $(2s - t^4)^7$

EXAMPLES 5 and 6
on p. 693
for Exs. 24–31

BINOMIAL THEOREM **Use the binomial theorem to write the binomial expansion.** 24–31. See margin.

24. $(x + 2)^3$
25. $(c - 4)^5$
26. $(a + 3b)^4$
27. $(4p - q)^6$
28. $(w^3 - 3)^4$
29. $(2s^4 + 5)^5$
30. $(3u + v^2)^6$
31. $(x^3 - y^2)^4$

EXAMPLE 7
on p. 694
for Exs. 32–35

32. Find the coefficient of x^5 in the expansion of $(x - 2)^{10}$. **−8064**
33. Find the coefficient of x^3 in the expansion of $(3x + 2)^5$. **1080**
34. Find the coefficient of x^6 in the expansion of $(x^2 - 3)^8$. **−13,608**

35. ★ **MULTIPLE CHOICE** Which is the coefficient of x^4 in the expansion of $(x - 3)^7$? **A**

(A) −945 (B) −35 (C) −27 (D) 2835

B

PASCAL'S TRIANGLE **In Exercises 36 and 37, use the diagrams shown.**

36. What is the sum of the numbers in each of rows 0–4 of Pascal's triangle? What is the sum in row n?

row 0: 1, row 1: 2, row 2: 4, row 3: 8, row 4: 16; row n: 2^n

37. *Describe* the pattern formed by the sums of the numbers along the diagonal segments of Pascal's triangle.

The sum along each diagonal segment is equal to the sum of the two previous diagonal segment sums.

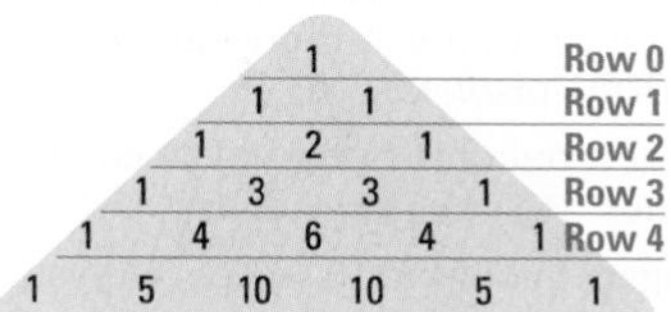

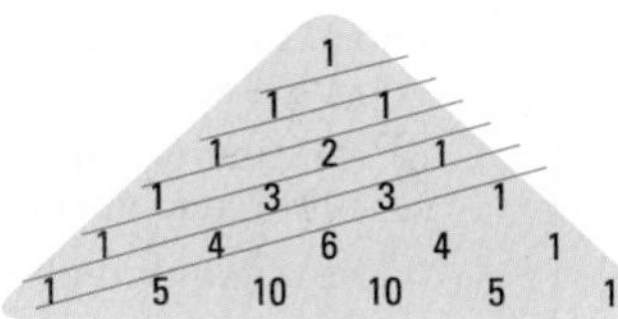

REASONING **In Exercises 38 and 39, decide whether the problem requires *combinations* or *permutations* to find the answer. Then solve the problem.**

38. **NEWSPAPER** Your school newspaper has an editor-in-chief and an assistant editor-in-chief. The staff of the newspaper has 12 students. In how many ways can students be chosen for these two positions? **permutations; 132 ways**

39. **STUDENT COUNCIL** Five representatives from a senior class of 280 students are to be chosen for the student council. In how many ways can students be chosen to represent the senior class on the student council? **combinations; 13,836,130,056 ways**

40. ★ **MULTIPLE CHOICE** A relay race has a team of 4 runners who run different parts of the race. There are 20 students on your track squad. In how many ways can the coach select students to compete on the relay team? **C**

(A) 4845 (B) 40,000 (C) 116,280 (D) 160,000

41. ★ **SHORT RESPONSE** *Explain* how the formula for ${}_nC_n$ suggests the definition $0! = 1$. $1 = {}_nC_n = \frac{n!}{(n-n)!\,n!} = \frac{n!}{0!\,n!} = \frac{1}{0!}$, so 0! must equal 1.

C

CHALLENGE **Verify the identity. *Justify* each of your steps.** 42–47. See margin.

42. ${}_nC_0 = 1$
43. ${}_nC_n = 1$
44. ${}_nC_r \cdot {}_rC_m = {}_nC_m \cdot {}_{n-m}C_{r-m}$
45. ${}_nC_1 = {}_nP_1$
46. ${}_nC_r = {}_nC_{n-r}$
47. ${}_{n+1}C_r = {}_nC_r + {}_nC_{r-1}$

4 PRACTICE AND APPLY

Assignment Guide

Answer Transparencies available for all exercises

Basic:
Day 1: pp. 694–697
Exs. 1–5, 11–14, 19–21, 24–26, 32–37, 48–51, 54

Average:
Day 1: pp. 694–697
Exs. 1, 2, 6–8, 11, 12, 15, 16, 19, 21, 22, 27–29, 32–41, 48–52, 55

Advanced:
Day 1: pp. 694–697
Exs. 1, 2, 9, 10, 17–19, 22, 23, 30–47*, 49–53*

Block:
pp. 694–697
Exs. 1, 2, 6–8, 11, 12, 15, 16, 19, 21, 22, 27–29, 32–41, 48–52, 55 (with 10.1)

Differentiated Instruction

See *Algebra 2 Best Practices Toolkit* for suggestions on addressing the needs of a diverse classroom.

Homework Check

For a quick check of student understanding of key concepts, go over the following exercises:

Basic: 4, 14, 20, 26, 48
Average: 8, 16, 22, 28, 49
Advanced: 10, 18, 30, 34, 50

Extra Practice

- Student Edition, p. 1019
- Chapter 10 Resource Book: Practice levels A, B, C, pp. 18–20

Practice Worksheet

An easily-readable reduced practice page (with answers) for this lesson can be found on p. 680C.

24. $x^3 + 6x^2 + 12x + 8$
25. $c^5 - 20c^4 + 160c^3 - 640c^2 + 1280c - 1024$
26. $a^4 + 12a^3b + 54a^2b^2 + 108ab^3 + 81b^4$
27. $4096p^6 - 6144p^5q + 3840p^4q^2 - 1280p^3q^3 + 240p^2q^4 - 24pq^5 + q^6$
28. $w^{12} - 12w^9 + 54w^6 - 108w^3 + 81$
29. $32s^{20} + 400s^{16} + 2000s^{12} + 5000s^8 + 6250s^4 + 3125$
30. $729u^6 + 1458u^5v^2 + 1215u^4v^4 + 540u^3v^6 + 135u^2v^8 + 18uv^{10} + v^{12}$
31. $x^{12} - 4x^9y^2 + 6x^6y^4 - 4x^3y^6 + y^8$

42–47. See Additional Answers beginning on p. AA1.

Avoiding Common Errors

Exercises 20–35 Students may forget to take into account coefficients, negative signs, and exponents when working these exercises. Refer these students to Examples 5–7 to demonstrate how to solve exercises involving these concepts.

Teaching Strategy

Exercise 46 After students have shown an algebraic representation that ${}_nC_r = {}_nC_{n-r}$, demonstrate how Pascal's triangle also models the equivalency. For example, ${}_7C_3 = {}_7C_4$ and ${}_{10}C_7 = {}_{10}C_3$.

52a. $\frac{15!}{5! \cdot 7! \cdot 3!}$; 360,360 assignments

52b. $\frac{15!}{10! \cdot 5!} \cdot \frac{10!}{3! \cdot 7!} \cdot \frac{3!}{0! \cdot 3!}$; 360,360 assignments

52c. They are the same. *Sample answer:* They are two different ways of counting the same situation. The additional factorials in the numerators and denominators of the expression in part (b) simplify to become the numerator and denominator of the expression in part (a).

PROBLEM SOLVING

EXAMPLES 1, 2, and 3 on pp. 690–691 for Exs. 48–50

A

48. MUSIC You want to purchase 3 CDs from an online collection that contains the types of music shown at the right. You want each CD to contain a different type of music such that 2 CDs are different types of contemporary music and 1 CD is a type of classical music. How many different sets of music types can you choose? **30 sets**

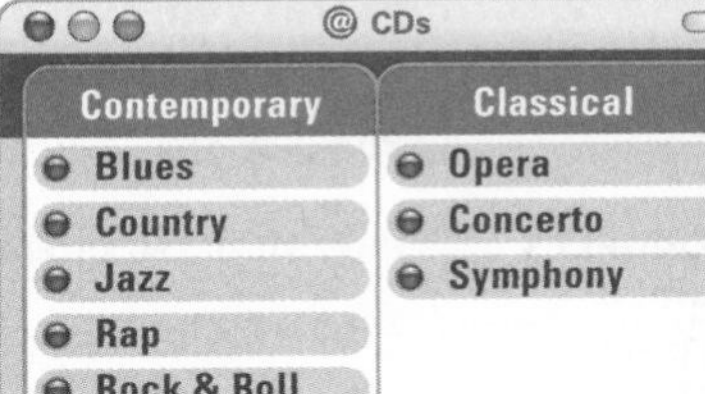

@HomeTutor for problem solving help at classzone.com

49. FLOWERS You are buying a bouquet. The florist has 18 types of flowers that you can use to make the bouquet. You want to use *exactly* 3 types of flowers. How many different combinations of flower types can you use in your bouquet? **816 combinations**

@HomeTutor for problem solving help at classzone.com

50. ARCADE GAMES An arcade has 20 different arcade games. You want to play at least 14 of them. How many different combinations of arcade games can you play? **38,760 combinations**

B

51. MULTI-STEP PROBLEM A televised singing competition picks a winner from 20 original contestants over the course of five episodes. During each of the first, second, and third episodes, 5 singers are eliminated by the end of the episode. The fourth episode eliminates 2 more singers, and the winner is selected at the end of the fifth episode.

a. How many combinations of 5 singers out of the original 20 can be eliminated during the first episode? **15,504 combinations**

b. How many combinations of 5 singers out of the 15 singers who started the second episode can be eliminated during the second episode? **3,003 combinations**

c. How many combinations of singers can be eliminated during the third episode? during the fourth episode? during the fifth episode? **252 combinations; 10 combinations; 3 combinations**

d. Find the total number of ways in which the 20 original contestants can be eliminated to produce a winner. **351,982,350,720 ways**

52. ★ EXTENDED RESPONSE A group of 15 high school students is volunteering at a local fire station. Of these students, 5 will be assigned to wash fire trucks, 7 will be assigned to repaint the station's interior, and 3 will be assigned to do maintenance on the station's exterior. **a–c. See margin.**

a. **Calculate** One way to count the number of possible job assignments is to find the number of permutations of 5 W's (for "wash"), 7 R's (for "repainting"), and 3 M's (for "maintenance"). Use this method to write the number of possible job assignments first as an expression involving factorials and then as a number.

b. **Calculate** Another way to count the number of possible job assignments is to first choose the 5 W's, then choose the 7 R's, and then choose the 3 M's. Use this method to write the number of possible job assignments first as an expression involving factorials and then as a number.

c. **Analyze** *Compare* your results from parts (a) and (b). *Explain* why they make sense.

Volunteers in Aniak, Alaska

◯ = WORKED-OUT SOLUTIONS on p. WS1 ★ = STANDARDIZED TEST PRACTICE

C **53. CHALLENGE** A polygon is *convex* if no line that contains a side of the polygon contains a point in the interior of the polygon. Consider a convex polygon with n sides.

a. Use the combinations formula to write an expression for the number of line segments that join pairs of vertices on an n-sided polygon. ${}_nC_{n-2}$

b. Use your result from part (a) to write a formula for the number of diagonals of an n-sided convex polygon. $\frac{n(n-3)}{2}$

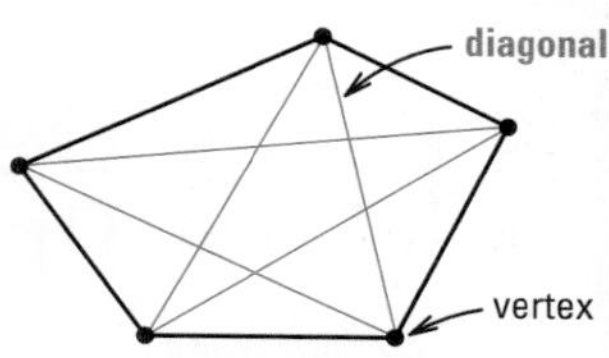

KENTUCKY MIXED REVIEW

TEST PRACTICE at classzone.com

54. Ellen's next math test is worth 150 points and contains 42 questions. Each question is worth either 5 points or 3 points. Which system of equations can be used to determine the number f of 5 point questions and the number t of 3 point questions? **C**

Ⓐ $f - t = 42$, $5f + 3t = 150$ Ⓑ $f + t = 42$, $3f + 5t = 150$

Ⓒ $f + t = 42$, $5f + 3t = 150$ Ⓓ $f + t = 42$, $5f + 5t = 150$

55. An equilateral triangle is inscribed in a circle with a radius of 6 centimeters. What is the approximate area of the shaded region? **B**

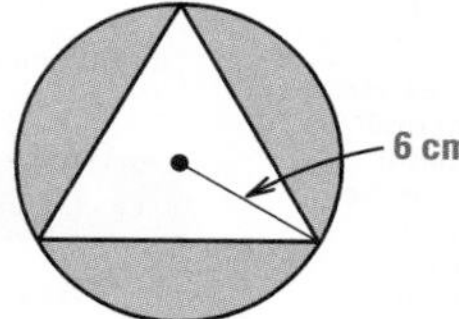

Ⓐ 19.6 cm^2 Ⓑ 66.3 cm^2

Ⓒ 74.9 cm^2 Ⓓ 81.9 cm^2

QUIZ for Lessons 10.1–10.2

For the given license plate configuration, find how many plates are possible if letters and digits (a) can be repeated and (b) cannot be repeated. *(p. 682)*

1. 2 letters followed by 3 digits 676,000 license plates; 468,000 license plates
2. 3 digits followed by 3 letters 17,576,000 license plates; 11,232,000 license plates

Find the number of distinguishable permutations of the letters in the word. *(p. 682)*

3. AWAY **12**
4. IDAHO **120**
5. LETTER **180**
6. TENNESSEE **3780**

Find the number of combinations. *(p. 690)*

7. ${}_8C_6$ **28**
8. ${}_7C_4$ **35**
9. ${}_9C_0$ **1**
10. ${}_{12}C_{11}$ **12**

Use the binomial theorem to write the binomial expansion. *(p. 690)* **11–14. See margin.**

11. $(x + 5)^5$
12. $(2s - 3)^6$
13. $(3u + v)^4$
14. $(2x^3 - 3y)^5$
15. Find the coefficient of x^3 in the expansion of $(x + 2)^9$. *(p. 690)* **5376**

16. **MENU CHOICES** A pizza parlor runs a special where you can buy a large pizza with 1 cheese, 1 vegetable, and 2 meats for $12. You have a choice of 5 cheeses, 10 vegetables, and 6 meats. How many different variations of the pizza special are possible? *(p. 682)* **750 variations**

5 ASSESS AND RETEACH

Daily Homework Quiz

Transparency Available

1. Find ${}_9C_5$. **126**
2. The manager of a chain of restaurants must choose 6 restaurants from 11 for a promotion. How many different selections can be made? **462 selections**
3. A committee consists of 10 Republicans and 8 Democrats. In how many ways can a subcommittee be chosen if it has 5 Republicans and 4 Democrats? **17,640 ways**
4. Use the binomial theorem to expand $(3 - x^2)^3$. $27 - 27x^2 + 9x^4 - x^6$
5. What is the coefficient of x^2y^3 in $(x - 5y)^5$? **−1250**

Online Quiz

Available at **classzone.com**

Diagnosis/Remediation

- Practice A, B, C in Chapter 10 Resource Book, pp. 18–20
- Study Guide in Chapter 10 Resource Book, pp. 21–22
- Practice Workbook, pp. 151–152
- @HomeTutor

Challenge

Additional challenge is available in the Chapter 10 Resource Book, p. 25.

Quiz

An easily-readable reduced copy of the quiz (with answers) on Lessons 10.1–10.2 from the Assessment Book can be found on p. 680E.

11. $x^5 + 25x^4 + 250x^3 + 1250x^2 + 3125x + 3125$
12. $64s^6 - 576s^5 + 2160s^4 - 4320s^3 + 4860s^2 - 2916s + 729$
13. $81u^4 + 108u^3v + 54u^2v^2 + 12uv^3 + v^4$
14. $32x^{15} - 240x^{12}y + 720x^9y^2 - 1080x^6y^3 + 810x^3y^4 - 243y^5$

10.3 Define and Use Probability

MA-HS-4.4.1

Before You determined the number of ways an event could occur.

Now You will find the likelihood that an event will occur.

Why? So you can find real-life geometric probabilities, as in Ex. 39.

1 PLAN AND PREPARE

Warm-Up Exercises

Transparency Available

Write the number as a percent.

1. 0.03 3%

2. $1\frac{2}{5}$ 140%

3. $\frac{5}{8}$ 62.5%

4. 0.0045 0.45%

5. Two-thirds of the senior class work more than 20 hours per week. Write that fraction to the nearest tenth of a percent. 66.7%

Notetaking Guide

Transparency Available

Promotes interactive learning and notetaking skills, pp. 268–271.

Pacing

Basic: 1 day

Average: 1 day

Advanced: 1 day

Block: 0.5 block with 10.4

- See *Teaching Guide/Lesson Plan.*

2 FOCUS AND MOTIVATE

Essential Question

Big Idea 2, p. 681

How can you find the probability that when 5 cards are drawn from a deck, 4 of them will be aces? **Tell students they will learn how to answer this question by using combinations and theoretical probability.**

Key Vocabulary
- probability
- theoretical probability
- odds
- experimental probability
- geometric probability

MA-HS-4.4.1
Students will: determine theoretical and experimental (from given data) probabilities; make predictions and draw inferences from probabilities; compare theoretical and experimental probabilities and determine probabilities involving replacement and non-replacement. DOK 3

When you roll a standard six-sided die, the possible results are called *outcomes*. The outcomes of rolling a die are 1, 2, 3, 4, 5, and 6. An *event* is an outcome or a collection of outcomes. For example, the event "rolling an odd number" consists of the outcomes 1, 3, and 5.

The **probability** of an event is a number from 0 to 1 that indicates the likelihood the event will occur, as shown on the number line below. Probabilities can be written as fractions, decimals, or percents.

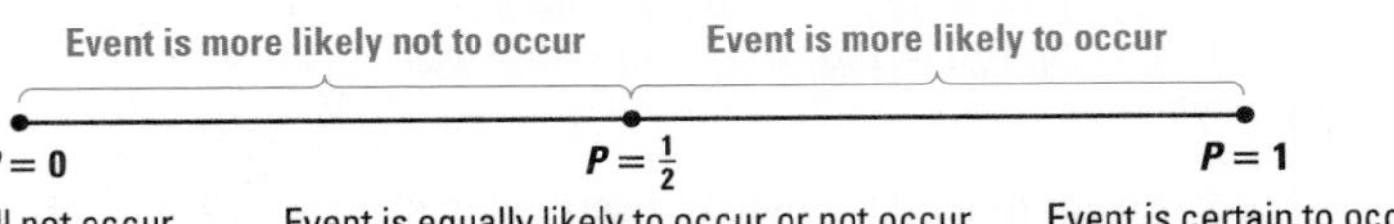

Event will not occur. Event is equally likely to occur or not occur. Event is certain to occur.

KEY CONCEPT *For Your Notebook*

Theoretical Probability of an Event

When all outcomes are equally likely, the **theoretical probability** that an event A will occur is:

$$P(A) = \frac{\text{Number of outcomes in event } A}{\text{Total number of outcomes}}$$

The theoretical probability of an event is often simply called the probability of the event.

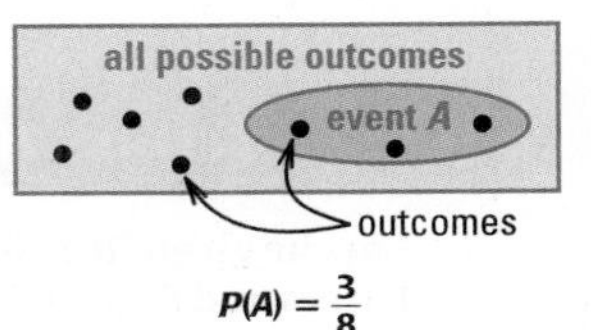

$P(A) = \frac{3}{8}$

EXAMPLE 1 Find probabilities of events

You roll a standard six-sided die. Find the probability of (a) rolling a 5 and (b) rolling an even number.

a. There are 6 possible outcomes. Only 1 outcome corresponds to rolling a 5.

$$P(\text{rolling a 5}) = \frac{\text{Number of ways to roll a 5}}{\text{Number of ways to roll the die}} = \frac{1}{6}$$

b. A total of 3 outcomes correspond to rolling an even number: a 2, 4, or 6.

$$P(\text{rolling even number}) = \frac{\text{Number of ways to roll an even number}}{\text{Number of ways to roll the die}} = \frac{3}{6} = \frac{1}{2}$$

Resource Planning Guide

Chapter Resource Book
- Teaching Guide/Lesson Plan (pp. 26–27)
- Practice levels A, B, C (pp. 28–30)
- Study Guide (pp. 31–32)
- Catch-up for Absent Students (p. 33)
- Problem Solving Workshop (p. 34)
- Challenge (p. 36)

Workbooks
- Notetaking Guide (pp. 268–271)
- Practice Workbook (pp. 153–154)

Teaching Options
- **Power Presentations CD-ROM** provides dynamic electronic teaching resources for the classroom.
- **Activity Generator CD-ROM** provides editable activities for all ability levels.

Interactive Technology
- Easy Planner
- Power Presentations CD-ROM
- Activity Generator CD-ROM
- Animated Algebra
- Test Generator CD-ROM
- Online Quiz
- eWorkbook
- eEdition
- @HomeTutor

Resources for English Learners
- Quick Reference for English Learners
- Spanish Study Guide
- Multi-Language Visual Glossary
- Student Resources in Spanish

See also the *Algebra 2 Toolkit* for more strategies for meeting individual needs.

EXAMPLE 2 Use permutations or combinations

ENTERTAINMENT A community center hosts a talent contest for local musicians. On a given evening, 7 musicians are scheduled to perform. The order in which the musicians perform is randomly selected during the show.

a. What is the probability that the musicians perform in alphabetical order by their last names? (Assume that no two musicians have the same last name.)

b. You are friends with 4 of the musicians. What is the probability that the first 2 performers are your friends?

Solution

a. There are 7! different *permutations* of the 7 musicians. Of these, only 1 is in alphabetical order by last name. So, the probability is:

$$P(\text{alphabetical order}) = \frac{1}{7!} = \frac{1}{5040} \approx 0.000198$$

b. There are ${}_7C_2$ different *combinations* of 2 musicians. Of these, ${}_4C_2$ are 2 of your friends. So, the probability is:

$$P(\text{first 2 performers are your friends}) = \frac{{}_4C_2}{{}_7C_2} = \frac{6}{21} = \frac{2}{7} \approx 0.286$$

GUIDED PRACTICE for Examples 1 and 2

You have an equally likely chance of choosing any integer from 1 through 20. Find the probability of the given event.

1. A perfect square is chosen. $\frac{1}{5}$
2. A factor of 30 is chosen. $\frac{7}{20}$
3. **WHAT IF?** In Example 2, how do your answers to parts (a) and (b) change if there are 9 musicians scheduled to perform?

The probability would [de]crease to $\frac{1}{362,880}$.

[T]he probability [wo]uld decrease to $\frac{1}{6}$.

ODDS You can also use **odds** to measure the likelihood that an event will occur. Odds measure the chances in *favor* of an event occurring or the chances *against* an event occurring.

KEY CONCEPT *For Your Notebook*

Odds in Favor of or Odds Against an Event

When all outcomes are equally likely, the odds in favor of an event A and the odds against an event A are defined as follows:

$$\text{Odds in favor of event } A = \frac{\text{Number of outcomes in } A}{\text{Number of outcomes not in } A}$$

$$\text{Odds against event } A = \frac{\text{Number of outcomes not in } A}{\text{Number of outcomes in } A}$$

You can write the odds in favor of or against an event in the form $\frac{a}{b}$ or in the form $a : b$.

Motivating the Lesson

Mathematicians in the seventeenth century developed probability theory to analyze games of chance. Today, probability theory provides us with tools for answering questions that involve uncertainty, such as "What is the likelihood of rain on graduation night?"

3 TEACH

Extra Example 1

You pick a card from a standard deck of 52 playing cards. Find the probability of (a) picking an 8 and (b) picking a red king. $\frac{1}{13}, \frac{1}{26}$

Extra Example 2

A cereal company plans to put 5 new cereals on the market: a wheat cereal, a rice cereal, a corn cereal, an oat cereal, and a multigrain cereal. The order in which the cereals are introduced will be randomly selected. Each cereal will have a different price.

a. What is the probability that the cereals are introduced in order of their suggested retail price? $\frac{1}{120}$ or about 0.0083

b. What is the probability that the first cereal introduced will be the multigrain cereal? $\frac{1}{5}$ or 0.2

Key Question to Ask for Example 2

- Why is the permutation formula used in part (a) but not in part (b)? Order is important in part (a), but does not matter in part (b).

Extra Example 3

A standard six-sided die is rolled. Find (a) the odds *in favor of* rolling a 6 and (b) the odds *against* rolling an odd number. 1:6; 1:1

Key Question to Ask for Example 3

- If the odds *against* an event are $a:b$, what are the odds *in favor of* the event? $b:a$

Extra Example 4

The blood types for a sample of donors at a blood drive are displayed in the bar graph. Find the experimental probability that a randomly selected blood donor would have blood type O.

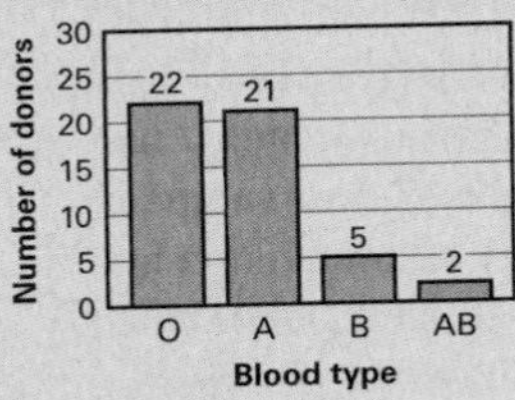

0.44

Mathematical Reasoning

Multiple Representations The odds *for* and *against* an event can also be expressed as ratios of probabilities. Odds *against* an event is $\frac{P(\text{event fails to occur})}{P(\text{event occurs})}$. Odds *for* an event is $\frac{P(\text{event occurs})}{P(\text{event fails to occur})}$.

EXAMPLE 3 Find odds

AVOID ERRORS

Note that the odds in favor of drawing a 10, which are $\frac{1}{12}$, do not equal the probability of drawing a 10, which is $\frac{4}{52} = \frac{1}{13}$.

A card is drawn from a standard deck of 52 cards. Find (a) the odds in *favor* of drawing a 10 and (b) the odds *against* drawing a club.

Solution

a. Odds in favor of drawing a 10 $= \frac{\text{Number of tens}}{\text{Number of non-tens}} = \frac{4}{48} = \frac{1}{12}$, or 1 : 12

b. Odds against drawing a club $= \frac{\text{Number of non-clubs}}{\text{Number of clubs}} = \frac{39}{13} = \frac{3}{1}$, or 3 : 1

EXPERIMENTAL PROBABILITY Sometimes it is not possible or convenient to find the theoretical probability of an event. In such cases, you may be able to calculate an *experimental probability* by performing an experiment, conducting a survey, or looking at the history of the event.

KEY CONCEPT *For Your Notebook*

Experimental Probability of an Event

When an experiment is performed that consists of a certain number of trials, the **experimental probability** of an event A is given by:

$$P(A) = \frac{\text{Number of trials where } A \text{ occurs}}{\text{Total number of trials}}$$

EXAMPLE 4 Find an experimental probability

SURVEY The bar graph shows how old adults in a survey would choose to be if they could choose any age. Find the experimental probability that a randomly selected adult would prefer to be at least 40 years old.

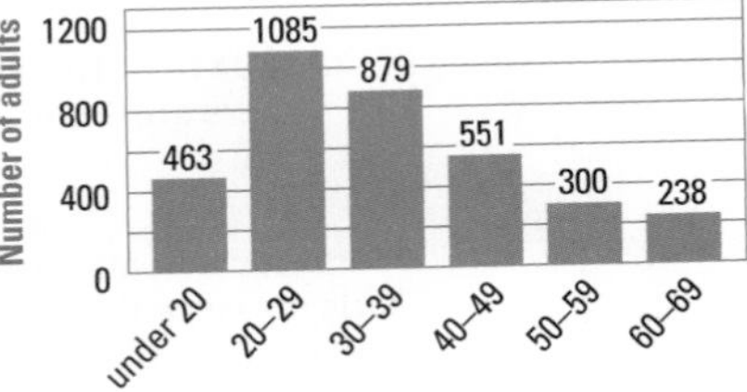

Solution

The total number of people surveyed is:

$$463 + 1085 + 879 + 551 + 300 + 238 = 3516$$

Of those surveyed, $551 + 300 + 238 = 1089$ would prefer to be at least 40.

$$P(\text{at least 40 years old}) = \frac{1089}{3516} \approx 0.310$$

GUIDED PRACTICE for Examples 3 and 4

A card is randomly drawn from a standard deck. Find the indicated odds.

4. In favor of drawing a heart $\frac{1}{3}$

5. Against drawing a queen $\frac{12}{1}$

6. **WHAT IF?** In Example 4, what is the experimental probability that an adult would prefer to be **(a)** at most 39 years old and **(b)** at least 30 years old?

6a. about 0.69

6b. about 0.56

Differentiated Instruction

Advanced The odds in favor of an event can also be expressed as $\frac{P(\text{the event occurs})}{P(\text{the event does not occur})}$. Challenge students to express **Example 3a** in terms of this definition. Then ask them to show how they can use a formula that involves combinations and probabilities to model this situation. Doing so will help them relate combinations, probability, and odds.

See also the *Algebra 2 Toolkit* for more strategies.

heoretical bability is the bability if all comes are equally ely to occur, ile experimental bability is the bability of an eriment of a tain number of ls. *Sample answer:* sume a spinner has ifferent colors. An ample of theoretical bability is what he probability of nning one of the ors. An example experimental bability would be spin the spinner times and then ermine the bability for a color.

GEOMETRIC PROBABILITY Some probabilities are found by calculating a ratio of two lengths, areas, or volumes. Such probabilities are **geometric probabilities**.

EXAMPLE 5 Find a geometric probability

DARTS You throw a dart at the square board shown. Your dart is equally likely to hit any point inside the board. Are you more likely to get 10 points or 0 points?

3 in.
10
5
2
0
18 in.

Solution

$$P(10\text{ points}) = \frac{\text{Area of smallest circle}}{\text{Area of entire board}}$$

$$= \frac{\pi \cdot 3^2}{18^2} = \frac{9\pi}{324} = \frac{\pi}{36} \approx 0.0873$$

$$P(0\text{ points}) = \frac{\text{Area outside largest circle}}{\text{Area of entire board}}$$

$$= \frac{18^2 - (\pi \cdot 9^2)}{18^2} = \frac{324 - 81\pi}{324} = \frac{4 - \pi}{4} \approx 0.215$$

▶ Because $0.215 > 0.0873$, you are more likely to get 0 points.

Animated Algebra at classzone.com

GUIDED PRACTICE for Example 5

7. **WHAT IF?** In Example 5, are you more likely to get 5 points or 0 points? 5 points

10.3 EXERCISES

HOMEWORK KEY
○ = **WORKED-OUT SOLUTIONS** on p. WS18 for Exs. 7, 17, and 39
★ = **STANDARDIZED TEST PRACTICE** Exs. 2, 19, 26, 27, 32, and 42
◆ = **MULTIPLE REPRESENTATIONS** Ex. 40

SKILL PRACTICE

A

1. **VOCABULARY** Copy and complete: A probability that is the ratio of two lengths, areas, or volumes is called a(n) __?__ probability. geometric

2. ★ **WRITING** *Explain* the difference between theoretical probability and experimental probability. Give an example of each. See margin.

XAMPLE 1 n p. 698 r Exs. 3–16

CHOOSING NUMBERS **You have an equally likely chance of choosing any integer from 1 through 50. Find the probability of the given event.**

3. An even number is chosen. $\frac{1}{2}$
4. A number less than 35 is chosen. $\frac{17}{25}$
5. A perfect square is chosen. $\frac{7}{50}$
6. A prime number is chosen. $\frac{3}{10}$
7. A factor of 150 is chosen. $\frac{1}{5}$
8. A multiple of 4 is chosen. $\frac{6}{25}$
9. A two-digit number is chosen. $\frac{41}{50}$
10. A perfect cube is chosen. $\frac{3}{50}$

Extra Example 5

Find the probability that a dart thrown at the rectangular board hits one of the triangles. Assume that the dart is equally likely to hit any point inside the board.

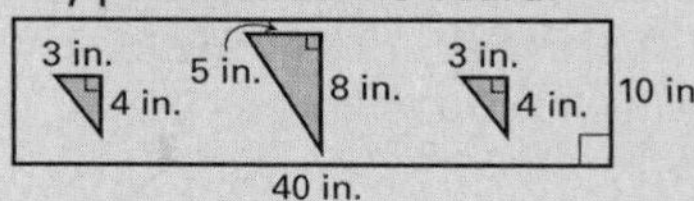

0.08

Key Question to Ask for Example 5

- In part (b), how do you determine the area of the black region? Subtract the area of the largest circle from the area of the square.

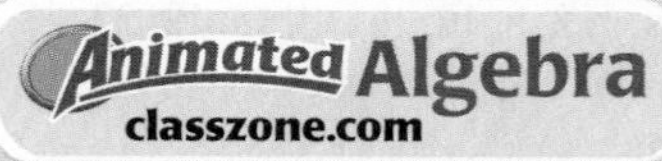

An **Animated Algebra** activity is available on-line for **Example 5**. This activity is also available on the **Power Presentations CD-ROM**.

Closing the Lesson

Have students summarize the major points of the lesson and answer the Essential Question: How do you find the probability that when 5 cards are drawn from a deck, 4 of them will be aces?

- When all outcomes are equally likely, the theoretical probability than an event A will occur is: $P(A) = \frac{\text{Number of outcomes in event } A}{\text{Total number of outcomes}}$.
- The experimental probability of an event A is the ratio of the number of trials where A occurs to the total number of trials.
- When all outcomes are equally likely, the odds *in favor of* an event A is the ratio of the number of outcomes in A to the number of outcomes not in A. The odds *against* A is the ratio of the number of outcomes not in A to the number of outcomes in A.
- Geometric probability is computed as the ratio of two lengths, areas, or volumes.

Use the formula $P(4\text{ aces}) = \frac{{}_4C_4 \cdot 48}{{}_{52}C_5}$.

Differentiated Instruction

Inclusion Some students may need help organizing their thinking. Certain scenarios may be more difficult to interpret than others, making it hard to determine which formula to use. Have students rewrite **Example 5** in their own words. Then have them describe what the goal of the problem is, what formula they should use, and discuss the significance of the solution.

See also the *Algebra 2 Toolkit* for more strategies.

4 PRACTICE AND APPLY

Assignment Guide

Answer Transparencies available for all exercises

Basic:
Day 1: SRH p. 992 Exs. 1–4
pp. 701–704
Exs. 1, 2, 3–9 odd, 11–13, 17–21, 24–28, 35–41, 44

Average:
Day 1: pp. 701–704
Exs. 1, 2, 4–8 even, 13, 14, 17–19, 22–32, 35–42, 45

Advanced:
Day 1: pp. 701–704
Exs. 1, 2, 9, 10, 15, 16, 18, 19, 22, 23, 26–34*, 36–43*

Block:
pp. 701–704
Exs. 1, 2, 4–8 even, 13, 14, 17–19, 22–32, 35–42, 45 (with 10.4)

Differentiated Instruction

See *Algebra 2 Best Practices Toolkit* for suggestions on addressing the needs of a diverse classroom.

Homework Check

For a quick check of student understanding of key concepts, go over the following exercises:

Basic: 5, 17, 20, 28, 35
Average: 6, 18, 21, 30, 36
Advanced: 10, 19, 22, 31, 37

Extra Practice

- Student Edition, p. 1019
- Chapter 10 Resource Book: Practice levels A, B, C, pp. 28–30

Practice Worksheet

An easily-readable reduced practice page (with answers) for this lesson can be found on p. 680C.

CHOOSING CARDS **A card is randomly drawn from a standard deck of 52 cards. Find the probability of drawing the given card.**

11. The king of diamonds $\frac{1}{52}$
12. A king $\frac{1}{13}$
13. A spade $\frac{1}{4}$
14. A black card $\frac{1}{2}$
15. A card other than a 2 $\frac{12}{13}$
16. A face card (a king, queen, or jack) $\frac{3}{13}$

EXAMPLE 2 on p. 699 for Exs. 17–19

LOTTERIES **In Exercises 17 and 18, find the probability of winning the lottery according to the given rules. Assume numbers are selected at random.**

17. You must correctly select 6 out of 48 numbers. The order of the numbers is not important. $\frac{1}{12{,}271{,}512}$

18. You must correctly select 4 numbers, each an integer from 0 to 9. The order of the numbers is important. $\frac{1}{5040}$

19. ★ **MULTIPLE CHOICE** What is the probability (rounded to three decimal places) that 2 randomly selected months both have 31 days? C

Ⓐ 0.159 Ⓑ 0.227 Ⓒ 0.318 Ⓓ 0.340

EXAMPLE 3 on p. 700 for Exs. 20–25

ODDS **You randomly choose a marble from a bag. The bag contains 10 black, 8 red, 4 white, and 6 blue marbles. Find the indicated odds.**

20. In favor of choosing white $\frac{1}{6}$
21. In favor of choosing blue $\frac{3}{11}$
22. Against choosing red $\frac{5}{2}$
23. Against choosing black $\frac{9}{5}$

ERROR ANALYSIS ***Describe* and correct the error in calculating the odds against getting a 5 or 6 when rolling a six-sided die.**

24. Odds against 5 or 6 $= \frac{4}{6} = \frac{2}{3}$ ✗

25. Odds against 5 or 6 $= \frac{2}{4} = \frac{1}{2}$ ✗

24. The denominator should be the number of outcomes in the event, which is 2; $\frac{4}{2} = \frac{2}{1}$.

25. The fraction should be outcomes not in the event, 4, to outcomes in the event, 2; $\frac{4}{2} = \frac{2}{1}$.

B

26. ★ **OPEN-ENDED MATH** Flip a coin 10 times. What is the experimental probability of getting heads? Check students' work.

27. ★ **SHORT RESPONSE** The probability of event A is 0.3. What are the odds in favor of event A? *Explain.* See margin.

EXAMPLE 4 on p. 700 for Exs. 28–32

ROLLING A DIE **The results of rolling a six-sided die 150 times are shown. Use the table to find the experimental probability of the given event. *Compare* your answer to the theoretical probability of the event.** 28–31. See margin.

28. Rolling a 5
29. Rolling an even number
30. Rolling a number less than 5
31. Rolling any number but a 3

Roll	1	2	3	4	5	6
Number of occurrences	27	22	18	26	27	30

32. ★ **MULTIPLE CHOICE** You flip a coin 80 times. You get heads 37 times and tails 43 times. What is the experimental probability of getting heads? A

Ⓐ 0.4625 Ⓑ 0.5 Ⓒ 0.5375 Ⓓ 0.8605

C

33. **REASONING** Find the probability that the vertex of the graph of $y = x^2 - 6x + c$ is above the x-axis if c is a randomly chosen integer from 1 to 20. $\frac{11}{20}$

○ = WORKED-OUT SOLUTIONS on p. WS1 ★ = STANDARDIZED TEST PRACTICE  = MULTIPLE REPRESENTATIONS

27. $\frac{3}{7}$. *Sample answer:* Since the probability is 0.3, there are 3 out of 10 chances of the event occurring. The number of outcomes against event A is $10 - 3 = 7$. So the odds in favor of event A is the ratio of the number of favorable outcomes, 3, to the number of unfavorable outcomes, 7.

28. $\frac{9}{50}$; the experimental probability is slightly greater than the theoretical probability of $\frac{1}{6}$.

34. **CHALLENGE** Suppose you throw a dart at each square target below. Assume that the dart is equally likely to hit any point inside the target.

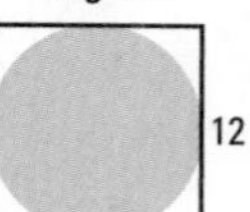

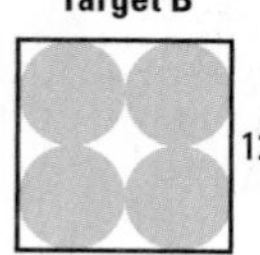

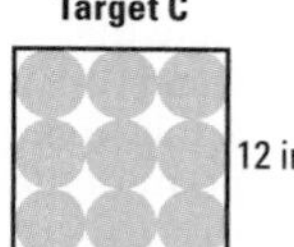

a. **Calculate** What is the probability that the dart lands inside the circle in target A? inside a circle in target B? inside a circle in target C? $\frac{\pi}{4}, \frac{\pi}{4}, \frac{\pi}{4}$

b. **Generalize** Consider the general case where a square target with sides 12 inches long contains n^2 identical circles arranged in n rows and n columns. Make a conjecture about the probability that a dart lands inside one of the circles. Then prove your conjecture. See margin.

PROBLEM SOLVING

EXAMPLE 5 A
on p. 701
for Exs. 35–37

GEOMETRIC PROBABILITY **Find the probability that a dart thrown at the given target will hit the shaded region. Assume the dart is equally likely to hit any point inside the target.**

35. 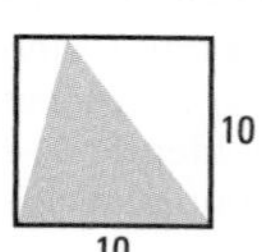

$\frac{1}{2}$

36. 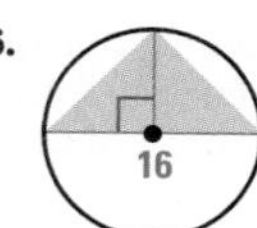

$\frac{1}{\pi}$ or about 0.318

37. 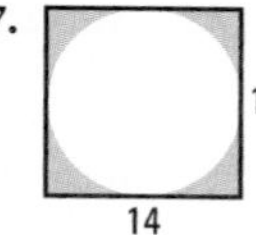

$1 - \frac{\pi}{4}$ or about 0.215

@HomeTutor for problem solving help at classzone.com

38. **JURY SELECTION** A jury of 12 people is selected from a pool of 30 people that includes 12 men and 18 women. What is the probability that the jury will be composed of 12 women? about 0.000215

@HomeTutor for problem solving help at classzone.com

39. **ARCHERY** The standard archery target used in competition has a diameter of 80 centimeters. Find the probability that an arrow shot at the target will hit the center circle, which has a diameter of 16 centimeters. Assume the arrow is equally likely to hit any point inside the target. $\frac{1}{25}$

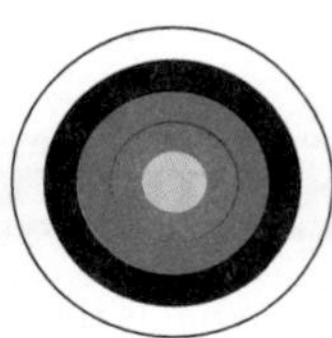

40. **MULTIPLE REPRESENTATIONS** On a typical weekday, there are 1,181,100 one-way trips taken on the public transportation system operated by the Massachusetts Bay Transit Authority. Of these trips, 376,900 are bus rides. Suppose a one-way trip is selected at random.

a. **Using Fractions** What is the probability, expressed as a fraction, that the trip was taken on a bus? $\frac{3769}{11,811}$

b. **Using Decimals** What is the probability, expressed as a decimal, that the trip was taken on a bus? about 0.319

c. **Using Percents** What is the probability, expressed as a percent, that the trip was taken on a bus? about 32%

d. **Using Odds** What are the odds in favor of the trip having been on a bus? $\frac{3769}{8042}$

Avoiding Common Errors

Exercise 19 Students may use incorrect calculations to arrive at the correct answer. Because $\frac{{}_nC_r}{{}_mC_r} = \frac{{}_nP_r}{{}_mP_r}$, make sure students understand why this exercise involves *combinations* of 2 of 12 months, not *permutations* of 2 of 12 months.

Teaching Strategy

Exercise 33 Students may find it easiest to apply a guess and check strategy using their calculators to solve this problem. Use this exercise as an opportunity to review characteristics of the graphs of parabolas. Specifically, help students see that $y = x^2 - 6x + 9$ has its vertex on the x-axis, so for $c > 9$ the vertex is above the x-axis and for $c \leq 9$ the vertex is on or below the x-axis.

Internet Reference

Exercise 41 Additional information about the Gulf of Mexico can be found at gulfsci.usgs.gov

31. $\frac{22}{25}$; the experimental probability is slightly greater than the theoretical probability of $\frac{5}{6}$.

34b. $\frac{\pi}{4}$; the radius of a circle is $\frac{6}{n}$ inches and since there are n^2 circles, the area of all of the circles is $\pi n^2\left(\frac{6}{n}\right)^2 = 36\pi$ square inches. The area of the square is 144 square inches, so the probability is $\frac{36\pi}{144} = \frac{\pi}{4}$.

29. $\frac{13}{25}$; the experimental probability is slightly greater than the theoretical probability of $\frac{1}{2}$.

30. $\frac{31}{50}$; the experimental probability is slightly less than the theoretical probability of $\frac{2}{3}$.

5 ASSESS AND RETEACH

Daily Homework Quiz

Transparency Available

1. Find the probability of drawing all diamonds when you draw 5 cards from a deck of cards. $\frac{33}{66,640} \approx 0.0005$
2. Find the odds in favor of drawing a heart when you draw 1 card from a deck of cards. 1:3
3. The responses to a survey are shown in the table. What is the experimental probability that a randomly chosen subject said "yes"?

Yes	No	Undecided
18	8	2

$\frac{9}{14} \approx 0.643$

4. Find the probability that a dart thrown at the target will hit outside the square. The dart is equally likely to hit any point inside the target. about 0.363

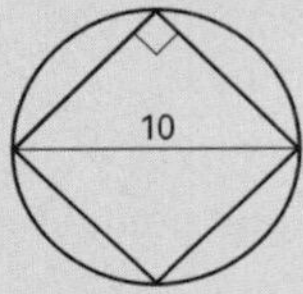

Available at **classzone.com**

Diagnosis/Remediation

- Practice A, B, C in Chapter 10 Resource Book, pp. 28–30
- Study Guide in Chapter 10 Resource Book, pp. 31–32
- Practice Workbook, pp. 153–154
- @HomeTutor

Challenge

Additional challenge is available in the Chapter 10 Resource Book, p. 36.

B

41. **GULF COAST** The map shows the length of shoreline (in miles) along the Gulf of Mexico for each state that borders the body of water. What is the probability that a ship coming ashore at a random point in the Gulf of Mexico lands in the given state?

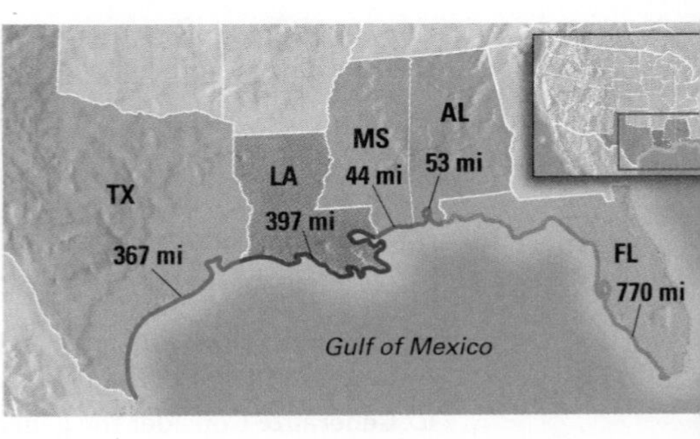

a. Texas $\frac{367}{1631}$

b. Florida $\frac{110}{233}$

c. Alabama $\frac{53}{1631}$

42. ★ **EXTENDED RESPONSE** A magician claims to be able to read minds. To test this claim, five cards numbered 1 through 5 are used. A subject selects two cards from the five cards and concentrates on the numbers.

a. What is the probability that the two numbers chosen are 3 and 4? $\frac{1}{10}$

b. What is the probability that the magician can correctly identify the two numbers by guessing? $\frac{1}{10}$

c. Suppose the magician is able to consistently identify the two numbers about half the time. Does this support the magician's claim to be a mind reader? *Explain.* No. *Sample answer:* If the magician were really a mind reader, the magician would be able to identify the numbers more than half of the time.

C

43. **CHALLENGE** In a guessing game, one player secretly places four different-colored pegs on a board in each of four positions: A, B, C, or D. A second player guesses the configuration of the pegs by placing an identical set of pegs in slots A, B, C, and D on an identical board. The second player is then told how many of the pegs are in the correct slot.

a. What is the probability that the second player has all four pegs correct on the first guess? $\frac{1}{24}$

b. What is the probability that the second player has exactly one peg correct on the first guess? $\frac{1}{3}$

c. The second player is told she has placed two pegs in the correct slot. The player then switches two of the pegs. What is the probability that the player now has all four pegs in the correct slot? $\frac{1}{12}$

KENTUCKY MIXED REVIEW

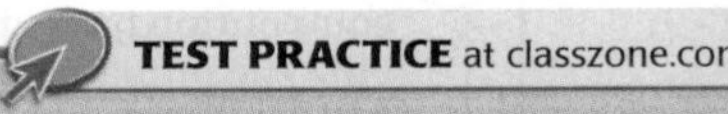

44. What is the area of the figure shown? **B**

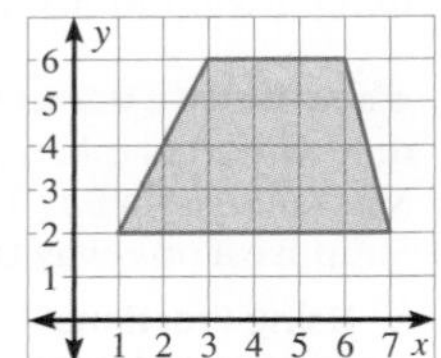

Ⓐ 14 square units

Ⓑ 18 square units

Ⓒ 20 square units

Ⓓ 36 square units

45. What is the midpoint of the line segment connecting points (−4, −1) and (7, 3)? **C**

Ⓐ $\left(-\frac{3}{2}, 1\right)$ Ⓑ $\left(\frac{3}{2}, \frac{1}{2}\right)$ Ⓒ $\left(\frac{3}{2}, 1\right)$ Ⓓ $\left(\frac{3}{2}, 2\right)$

EXTRA PRACTICE for Lesson 10.3, p. 1019 **ONLINE QUIZ** at classzone.com

44–49. See Additional Answers beginning on p. AA1.

Lessons 10.1–10.3

1. **MOVIE THEATER SEATING** Five people walk into a movie theater and look for empty seats in which to sit. What is the number of ways the people can be seated if there are 8 empty seats?

A. 20 B. 56
C. 336 D. 6720

2. **ARRIVAL TIMES** Every day, Ashley and Juan arrive separately at a gym. Let x and y be their arrival times, respectively, in minutes after 9:00 A.M. If they each arrive at a random time between 9:00 A.M. and 9:30 A.M., the point (x, y) will fall in the shaded square in the graph below.

Whoever arrives first waits for the other up to 10 minutes before working out alone. The diagonal shaded region represents pairs of arrival times when they meet. What is the approximate probability that Ashley and Juan will meet under these conditions?

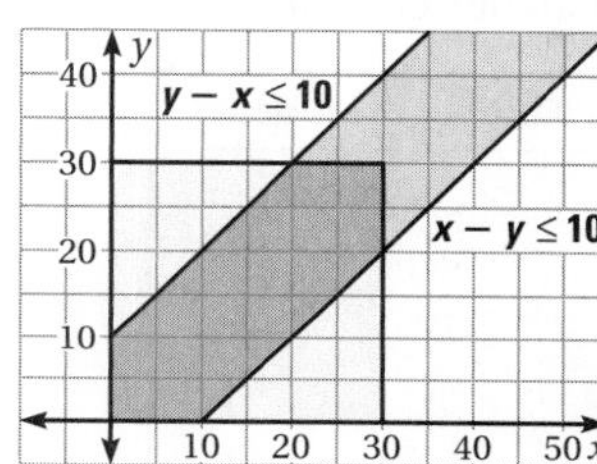

A. 0.333 B 0.444
C. 0.556 D 0.889

3. **GRADUATION REQUIREMENTS** Mark must take 18 elective courses to meet graduation requirements for college. There are 30 courses that he is interested in. How many different course selections are possible?

A. 30,045,015
B. 86,493,225
C. 4.1×10^{16}
D. 5.5×10^{23}

4. **SUMMER OLYMPICS** The graph shows the results of a survey in 2004 that asked U.S. adults which sport they would most like to participate in at the Summer Olympics. What is the approximate probability that a randomly selected U.S. adult would most like to participate in track and field?

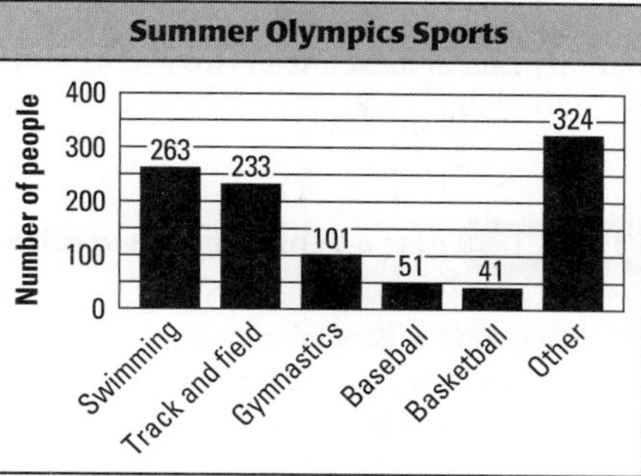

A. 0.23 B. 0.26
C. 0.3 D. 0.338

5. **OMELETS** A restaurant offers 8 different ingredients for an omelet. In a deluxe omelet, you can have up to 6 ingredients. How many different combinations of ingredients can you have?

A. 28 B. 218
C. 219 D. 247

6. **OPEN-RESPONSE** A café that serves fruit smoothies offers 8 different fruits, as shown in the list below.

Available Fruits	
Orange	Strawberry
Banana	Pineapple
Kiwi	Watermelon
Canteloupe	Peach

a. How many different smoothies can you make using 3 different fruits?

b. How many different smoothies can you make using 5 different fruits?

c. *Explain* the relationship between the values of the two answers.

Kentucky Mixed Review

1. D
2. C
3. B
4. A
5. D
6. a. 56
b. 56
c. The answers are the same because the number of ways to choose 3 fruits is the same as the number of ways to *reject* 3 fruits, i.e. choose 5 fruits.

1 PLAN AND PREPARE

Explore the Concept

- Students will use Venn diagrams to find probabilities of overlapping events.
- This activity leads into the study of using intersection to find probability in Lesson 10.4, Example 2.

Materials

Each student or pair of students will need:

- Activity Support Master (*Chapter 10 Resource Book*, p. 40)

Recommended Time

Work activity: 10 min

Discuss results: 5 min

Grouping

Students can work individually or in pairs. If students work in pairs, each can survey half the class about siblings and they can take turns filling in the table in Step 2.

2 TEACH

Tips for Success

Make sure that students write each name in only one section of the Venn diagram. For example, the name of anyone who has both a brother and sister should appear only in the purple section and not also in the blue and orange sections.

Key Discovery

You can use Venn diagrams to model and compute the probabilities of two events that can occur simultaneously.

3 ASSESS AND RETEACH

1. If two overlapping circles in a Venn diagram represent events *A* and *B*, what probability can be calculated from the rectangular region outside the two circles? **the probability that neither *A* nor *B* occurs**

10.4 Find Probabilities Using Venn Diagrams

QUESTION How can you use a Venn diagram to find probabilities involving two events?

In Lesson 10.3, you learned how to compute the probability of one event. In some situations, however, you might be interested in the probability that two events will occur simultaneously. You also might be interested in the probability that at least one of two events will occur. This activity demonstrates how a Venn diagram is useful for computing such probabilities.

EXPLORE Use a Venn diagram to collect data

STEP 1 ***Complete a Venn diagram***

Copy the Venn diagram shown below. Ask the members of your class if they have a sister, have a brother, have both, or have neither. Write their names in the appropriate part of the Venn diagram.

No sister or brother

Have a sister

Have a brother

STEP 2 ***Complete a table***

Copy and complete the frequency table. When determining the frequency for a category, be sure to include all the students who are in the category. Note that a student can belong to more than one category.

Category	Number of students
Have a sister	?
Have a brother	?
Have both a sister and brother	?
Do not have a sister or brother	?

DRAW CONCLUSIONS Use your data to complete these exercises **1–3. Check students' work.**

1. A student from your class is selected at random. Find the probability of each event. *Explain* how you found your answers.
   - **a.** The student has a sister.
   - **b.** The student has a brother.
   - **c.** The student has a sister and a brother.
   - **d.** The student does not have a sister or a brother.
2. Find the probability that a randomly selected student from your class has either a sister or a brother. *Explain* how you found your answer.
3. How could you calculate the answer to Exercise 2 using your answers from Exercise 1?

10.4 Find Probabilities of Disjoint and Overlapping Events

 MA-HS-4.4.1

Before You found probabilities of simple events.

Now You will find probabilities of compound events.

Why? So you can solve problems about meteorology, as in Ex. 44.

ey Vocabulary
- ompound event
- verlapping events
- isjoint or mutually xclusive events

1A-HS-4.4.1
tudents will: etermine theoretical nd experimental rom given data) robabilities; make redictions and raw inferences om probabilities; mpare theoretical nd experimental robabilities and etermine probabilities volving replacement nd non-replacement. OK 3

When you consider all the outcomes for either of two events A and B, you form the *union* of A and B. When you consider only the outcomes shared by both A and B, you form the *intersection* of A and B. The union or intersection of two events is called a **compound event**.

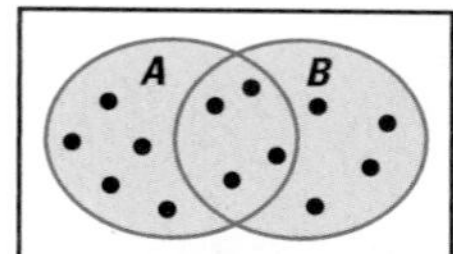

Union of A and B

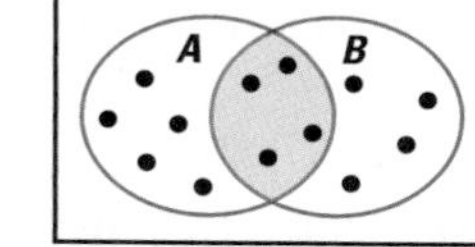

Intersection of A and B

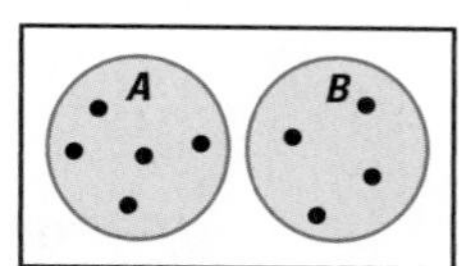

Intersection of A and B is empty.

To find $P(A \text{ or } B)$ you must consider what outcomes, if any, are in the intersection of A and B. Two events are **overlapping** if they have one or more outcomes in common, as shown in the first diagram. Two events are **disjoint**, or **mutually exclusive**, if they have no outcomes in common, as shown in the third diagram.

KEY CONCEPT *For Your Notebook*

Probability of Compound Events

If A and B are any two events, then the probability of A or B is:

$$P(A \text{ or } B) = P(A) + P(B) - P(A \text{ and } B)$$

If A and B are disjoint events, then the probability of A or B is:

$$P(A \text{ or } B) = P(A) + P(B)$$

EXAMPLE 1 Find probability of disjoint events

A card is randomly selected from a standard deck of 52 cards. What is the probability that it is a 10 *or* a face card?

Solution

Let event A be selecting a 10 and event B be selecting a face card. A has 4 outcomes and B has 12 outcomes. Because A and B are disjoint, the probability is:

$$P(A \text{ or } B) = P(A) + P(B) = \frac{4}{52} + \frac{12}{52} = \frac{16}{52} = \frac{4}{13} \approx 0.308$$

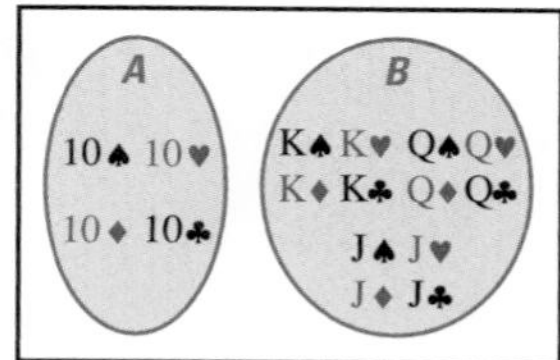

1 PLAN AND PREPARE

Warm-Up Exercises

Transparency Available

A card is drawn from a standard deck of 52 cards. Find each probability.

1. $P(\text{a red card})$ $\frac{1}{2}$
2. $P(\text{a ten})$ $\frac{1}{13}$
3. What is the probability that two flipped coins show heads? $\frac{1}{4}$

Notetaking Guide

Transparency Available

Promotes interactive learning and notetaking skills, pp. 272–274.

Pacing

Basic: 1 day
Average: 1 day
Advanced: 1 day
Block: 0.5 block with 10.3
- See *Teaching Guide/Lesson Plan.*

2 FOCUS AND MOTIVATE

Essential Question

Big Idea 2, p. 681

A problem such as "find the probability of getting 0, 1, 2, 3, or 4 red cards when you draw 5 cards" can require many computations. How can you simplify the solution? **Tell students they will learn how to answer this question by finding the complement of an event.**

Resource Planning Guide

Chapter Resource Book
- Teaching Guide/Lesson Plan (pp. 37–38)
- Practice levels A, B, C (pp. 41–43)
- Study Guide (pp. 44–45)
- Catch-up for Absent Students (p. 46)
- Application (p. 47)
- Challenge (p. 48)

Workbooks
- Notetaking Guide (pp. 272–274)
- Practice Workbook (pp. 155–156)

Teaching Options
- **Power Presentations CD-ROM** provides dynamic electronic teaching resources for the classroom.
- **Activity Generator CD-ROM** provides editable activities for all ability levels.

Interactive Technology
- Easy Planner
- Power Presentations CD-ROM
- Activity Generator CD-ROM
- Animated Algebra
- Test Generator CD-ROM
- Online Quiz
- eWorkbook
- eEdition
- @HomeTutor

Resources for English Learners
- Quick Reference for English Learners
- Spanish Study Guide
- Multi-Language Visual Glossary
- Student Resources in Spanish

See also the *Algebra 2 Toolkit* for more strategies for meeting individual needs.

Motivating the Lesson

Have students divide into two groups, girls and boys. Then ask them to divide into two different groups, those with boy cousins and those with girl cousins. Students should see that the groups in this second division may overlap because some students belong to both groups. In this lesson, students will learn how to determine probabilities for events that overlap.

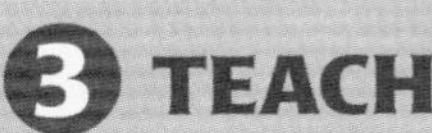

3 TEACH

Extra Example 1

A six-sided die is rolled. What is the probability that the number rolled is less than 3 *or* greater than 5? $\frac{1}{2}$

Key Question to Ask for Example 1

- Why are the two events disjoint? **A card cannot be both a ten and a face card.**

Extra Example 2

A six-sided die is rolled. What is the probability of rolling a number greater than 4 *or* even? **C**

Ⓐ $\frac{1}{6}$ Ⓒ $\frac{2}{3}$

Ⓑ $\frac{1}{3}$ Ⓓ $\frac{5}{6}$

Extra Example 3

Of 100 students surveyed, 92 own either a car or a computer. Also, 65 own cars and 82 own computers. What is the probability that a randomly selected student owns both a car and a computer? **0.55**

EXAMPLE 2 Standardized Test Practice

A card is randomly selected from a standard deck of 52 cards. What is the probability that it is a face card *or* a spade?

Ⓐ $\frac{3}{52}$ Ⓑ $\frac{11}{26}$ Ⓒ $\frac{25}{52}$ Ⓓ $\frac{7}{13}$

Solution

AVOID ERRORS
When two events *A* and *B* overlap, as in Example 2, *P*(*A* or *B*) does not equal *P*(*A*) + *P*(*B*).

Let event *A* be selecting a face card and event *B* be selecting a spade. *A* has 12 outcomes and *B* has 13 outcomes. Of these, 3 outcomes are common to *A* and *B*. So, the probability of selecting a face card *or* a spade is:

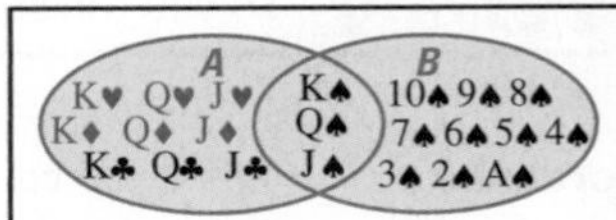

$$P(A \text{ or } B) = P(A) + P(B) - P(A \text{ and } B) = \frac{12}{52} + \frac{13}{52} - \frac{3}{52} = \frac{22}{52} = \frac{11}{26}$$

▸ The correct answer is B. Ⓐ Ⓑ Ⓒ Ⓓ

EXAMPLE 3 Use a formula to find *P*(*A* and *B*)

SENIOR CLASS Out of 200 students in a senior class, 113 students are either varsity athletes *or* on the honor roll. There are 74 seniors who are varsity athletes and 51 seniors who are on the honor roll. What is the probability that a randomly selected senior is both a varsity athlete *and* on the honor roll?

Solution

Let event *A* be selecting a senior who is a varsity athlete and event *B* be selecting a senior on the honor roll. From the given information you know that $P(A) = \frac{74}{200}$, $P(B) = \frac{51}{200}$, and $P(A \text{ or } B) = \frac{113}{200}$. Find *P*(*A* and *B*).

$P(A \text{ or } B) = P(A) + P(B) - P(A \text{ and } B)$ **Write general formula.**

$\frac{113}{200} = \frac{74}{200} + \frac{51}{200} - P(A \text{ and } B)$ **Substitute known probabilities.**

$P(A \text{ and } B) = \frac{74}{200} + \frac{51}{200} - \frac{113}{200}$ **Solve for *P*(*A* and *B*).**

$P(A \text{ and } B) = \frac{12}{200} = \frac{3}{50} = 0.06$ **Simplify.**

GUIDED PRACTICE for Examples 1, 2, and 3

A card is randomly selected from a standard deck of 52 cards. Find the probability of the given event.

1. Selecting an ace *or* an eight $\frac{2}{13}$
2. Selecting a 10 *or* a diamond $\frac{4}{13}$
3. **WHAT IF?** In Example 3, suppose 32 seniors are in the band and 64 seniors are in the band *or* on the honor roll. What is the probability that a randomly selected senior is both in the band *and* on the honor roll? **0.095**

Differentiated Instruction

English Learners For students whose main language is not English, the phrase "overlapping events" may be unclear. Separate the class into groups. Have students work together to create lists of overlapping events other than those in the examples in this lesson.

See also the *Algebra 2 Toolkit* for more strategies.

COMPLEMENTS The event $\overline{A}$, called the *complement* of event A, consists of all outcomes that are not in A. The notation $\overline{A}$ is read as "A bar."

KEY CONCEPT *For Your Notebook*

Probability of the Complement of an Event

The probability of the complement of A is $P(\overline{A}) = 1 - P(A)$.

EXAMPLE 4 Find probabilities of complements

NOTHER WAY
or an alternative
ıethod for solving the
roblem in Example 4,
ırn to page 714 for
ıe **Problem Solving**
Vorkshop.

DICE When two six-sided dice are rolled, there are 36 possible outcomes, as shown. Find the probability of the given event.

a. The sum is not 6.

b. The sum is less than or equal to 9.

Solution

a. $P(\text{sum is not } 6) = 1 - P(\text{sum is } 6) = 1 - \frac{5}{36} = \frac{31}{36} \approx 0.861$

b. $P(\text{sum} \le 9) = 1 - P(\text{sum} > 9) = 1 - \frac{6}{36} = \frac{30}{36} = \frac{5}{6} \approx 0.833$

EXAMPLE 5 Use a complement in real life

FORTUNE COOKIES A restaurant gives a free fortune cookie to every guest. The restaurant claims there are 500 different messages hidden inside the fortune cookies. What is the probability that a group of 5 people receive at least 2 fortune cookies with the same message inside?

Solution

The number of ways to give messages to the 5 people is 500^5. The number of ways to give *different* messages to the 5 people is $500 \cdot 499 \cdot 498 \cdot 497 \cdot 496$. So, the probability that at least 2 of the 5 people have the same message is:

$$P(\text{at least 2 are the same}) = 1 - P(\text{none are the same})$$

$$= 1 - \frac{500 \cdot 499 \cdot 498 \cdot 497 \cdot 496}{500^5}$$

$$\approx 0.0199$$

GUIDED PRACTICE for Examples 4 and 5

Find $P(\overline{A})$.

4. $P(A) = 0.45$ 0.55

5. $P(A) = \frac{1}{4}$ $\frac{3}{4}$

6. $P(A) = 1$ 0

7. $P(A) = 0.03$ 0.97

8. WHAT IF? In Example 5, how does the answer change if there are only 100 different messages hidden inside the fortune cookies? The probability increases to about 0.097.

Extra Example 4

A card is drawn from a standard deck of 52 cards. Find the probability of each event.

a. The card is not a 7. $\frac{12}{13}$ or about 0.923

b. The card is not a red face card. $\frac{46}{52}$ or about 0.885

Key Question to Ask for Example 4

- When is it more convenient to find the probability of the complement of an event rather than the probability of the event itself? Use the complement when the number of outcomes of the event is much greater than the number of outcomes of the complement.

Extra Example 5

There are 10 people at a dinner party. What is the probability that at least 2 people have the same birthday? about 0.117

Closing the Lesson

Have students summarize the major points of the lesson and answer the Essential Question: A problem such as "find the probability of getting 0, 1, 2, 3, or 4 red cards when you draw 5 cards" can require many computations. How can you simplify the solution?

- If A and B are not disjoint events, to find $P(A \text{ or } B)$ you find $P(A) + P(B)$, and subtract $P(A \text{ and } B)$.
- If A and B are disjoint events, to find $P(A \text{ or } B)$ you find $P(A) + P(B)$.
- $P(\overline{A}) = 1 - P(A)$

If you know $P(\overline{A})$, the probability of the complement of the event, then $P(A) = 1 - P(\overline{A})$.

10.4 EXERCISES

HOMEWORK KEY
◯ = WORKED-OUT SOLUTIONS on p. WS18 for Exs. 11, 21, and 45
★ = STANDARDIZED TEST PRACTICE Exs. 2, 15, 34, 39, 40, 44, and 47

4 PRACTICE AND APPLY

Assignment Guide

Answer Transparencies available for all exercises

Basic:
Day 1: SRH p. 1004 Exs. 1–9
pp. 710–713
Exs. 1–5, 9–11, 15–22, 26–30, 42–47, 51

Average:
Day 1: pp. 710–713
Exs. 1, 2, 5–7, 11–13, 15–17, 22–24, 26, 27, 30–39, 42–49, 52

Advanced:
Day 1: pp. 710–713
Exs. 1, 2, 7, 8, 13–15, 18, 19, 24, 25, 31–50*

Block:
pp. 710–713
Exs. 1, 2, 5–7, 11–13, 15–17, 22–24, 26, 27, 30–39, 42–49, 52 (with 10.3)

Differentiated Instruction

See *Algebra 2 Best Practices Toolkit* for suggestions on addressing the needs of a diverse classroom.

Homework Check

For a quick check of student understanding of key concepts, go over the following exercises:

Basic: 4, 10, 16, 42, 43
Average: 6, 12, 17, 42, 44
Advanced: 8, 14, 19, 43, 44

Extra Practice

- Student Edition, p. 1019
- Chapter 10 Resource Book: Practice levels A, B, C, pp. 41–43

Practice Worksheet

An easily-readable reduced practice page (with answers) for this lesson can be found on p. 680D.

SKILL PRACTICE

A

1. **VOCABULARY** Copy and complete: The union or intersection of two events is called a(n) __?__. compound event

2. ★ **WRITING** Are the events A and $\overline{A}$ disjoint? *Explain*. Then give an example of a real-life event and its complement. Yes; the events in $\overline{A}$ are those events that are not in A. *Sample answer:* Event: You go on a rafting trip. Complement: You do not go on a rafting trip.

EXAMPLE 1 on p. 707 for Exs. 3–8

DISJOINT EVENTS **Events A and B are disjoint. Find $P(A \text{ or } B)$.**

3. $P(A) = 0.3, P(B) = 0.1$ 0.4
4. $P(A) = 0.55, P(B) = 0.2$ 0.75
5. $P(A) = 0.41, P(B) = 0.24$ 0.65
6. $P(A) = \frac{2}{5}, P(B) = \frac{3}{5}$ 1
7. $P(A) = \frac{1}{3}, P(B) = \frac{1}{4}$ $\frac{7}{12}$
8. $P(A) = \frac{2}{3}, P(B) = \frac{1}{5}$ $\frac{13}{15}$

EXAMPLES 2 and 3 on p. 708 for Exs. 9–15

OVERLAPPING EVENTS **Find the indicated probability.**

9. $P(A) = 0.5, P(B) = 0.35$
   $P(A \text{ and } B) = 0.2$
   $P(A \text{ or } B) =$ __?__ 0.65
10. $P(A) = 0.6, P(B) = 0.2$
    $P(A \text{ or } B) = 0.7$
    $P(A \text{ and } B) =$ __?__ 0.1
11. $P(A) = 0.28, P(B) = 0.64$
    $P(A \text{ or } B) = 0.71$
    $P(A \text{ and } B) =$ __?__ 0.21
12. $P(A) = 0.46, P(B) = 0.37$
    $P(A \text{ and } B) = 0.31$
    $P(A \text{ or } B) =$ __?__ 0.52
13. $P(A) = \frac{2}{7}, P(B) = \frac{4}{7}$
    $P(A \text{ and } B) = \frac{1}{7}$
    $P(A \text{ or } B) =$ __?__ $\frac{5}{7}$
14. $P(A) = \frac{6}{11}, P(B) = \frac{3}{11}$
    $P(A \text{ or } B) = \frac{7}{11}$
    $P(A \text{ and } B) =$ __?__ $\frac{2}{11}$

15. ★ **MULTIPLE CHOICE** What is $P(A \text{ or } B)$ if $P(A) = 0.41, P(B) = 0.53$, and $P(A \text{ and } B) = 0.27$? B

    (A) 0.12 (B) 0.67 (C) 0.80 (D) 0.94

EXAMPLE 4 on p. 709 for Exs. 16–19

FINDING PROBABILITIES OF COMPLEMENTS **Find $P(\overline{A})$.**

16. $P(A) = 0.5$ 0.5
17. $P(A) = 0$ 1
18. $P(A) = \frac{1}{3}$ $\frac{2}{3}$
19. $P(A) = \frac{5}{8}$ $\frac{3}{8}$

CHOOSING CARDS **A card is randomly selected from a standard deck of 52 cards. Find the probability of drawing the given card.**

20. A king *and* a diamond $\frac{1}{52}$
21. A king *or* a diamond $\frac{4}{13}$
22. A spade *or* a club $\frac{1}{2}$
23. A 4 *or* a 5 $\frac{2}{13}$
24. A 6 *and* a face card 0
25. *Not* a heart $\frac{3}{4}$

ERROR ANALYSIS ***Describe*** **and correct the error in finding the probability of randomly drawing the given card from a standard deck of 52 cards.** 26, 27. See margin.

26.
P(heart or face card)
$= P(\text{heart}) + P(\text{face card})$
$= \frac{13}{52} + \frac{12}{52}$
$= \frac{25}{52}$ ✗

27.
P(club or 9)
$= P(\text{club}) + P(9) + P(\text{club and } 9)$
$= \frac{13}{52} + \frac{4}{52} + \frac{1}{52}$
$= \frac{9}{26}$ ✗

26. The events overlap, so $\frac{3}{52}$ needs to be subtracted from the probability; $P(\text{heart}) + P(\text{face card}) - P(\text{heart and face card}) = \frac{13}{52} + \frac{12}{52} - \frac{3}{52} = \frac{22}{52}$ or $\frac{11}{26}$.

27. The probability of a club and 9 must be subtracted instead of added; $P(\text{club}) + P(9) - P(\text{club and } 9) = \frac{13}{52} + \frac{4}{52} - \frac{1}{52} = \frac{16}{52}$ or $\frac{4}{13}$.

B **FINDING PROBABILITIES** **Find the indicated probability. State whether A and B are disjoint events.**

28. $P(A) = 0.25$
$P(B) = 0.4$
$P(A \text{ or } B) = 0.50$
$P(A \text{ and } B) = \underline{\ ?\ }$
0.15; not disjoint

29. $P(A) = 0.6$
$P(B) = 0.32$
$P(A \text{ or } B) = \underline{\ ?\ }$
$P(A \text{ and } B) = 0.25$
0.67; not disjoint

30. $P(A) = \underline{\ ?\ }$
$P(B) = 0.38$
$P(A \text{ or } B) = 0.65$
$P(A \text{ and } B) = 0$
0.27; disjoint

31. $P(A) = \frac{8}{15}$
$P(B) = \underline{\ ?\ }$
$P(A \text{ or } B) = \frac{3}{5}$
$P(A \text{ and } B) = \frac{2}{15}$
$\frac{1}{5}$; not disjoint

32. $P(A) = \frac{1}{2}$
$P(B) = \frac{1}{6}$
$P(A \text{ or } B) = \frac{2}{3}$
$P(A \text{ and } B) = \underline{\ ?\ }$
0; disjoint

33. $P(A) = 16\%$
$P(B) = \underline{\ ?\ }$
$P(A \text{ or } B) = 32\%$
$P(A \text{ and } B) = 8\%$
24%; not disjoint

Sample *swer:* Jordan ll either biking or imming 4 P.M.; Mr. terson has students rolled in his rtial arts urses, he has enrolled in rate and he s 13 enrolled Muay Thai.

34. ★ **OPEN-ENDED MATH** *Describe* a real-life situation that involves two disjoint events A and B. Then describe a real-life situation that involves two overlapping events C and D.

ROLLING DICE **Two six-sided dice are rolled. Find the probability of the given event. (Refer to Example 4 on page 709 for the possible outcomes.)**

35. The sum is 3 or 4. $\frac{5}{36}$

36. The sum is not 7. $\frac{5}{6}$

37. The sum is greater than or equal to 5. $\frac{5}{6}$

38. The sum is less than 8 or greater than 11. $\frac{11}{18}$

39. ★ **MULTIPLE CHOICE** Two six-sided dice are rolled. What is the probability that the sum is a prime number? **C**

Ⓐ $\frac{13}{36}$ Ⓑ $\frac{7}{18}$ Ⓒ $\frac{5}{12}$ Ⓓ $\frac{5}{11}$

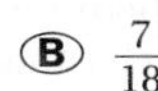

C **40.** ★ **SHORT RESPONSE** Use the first diagram at the right to explain why this equation is true:

$$P(A) + P(B) = P(A \text{ or } B) + P(A \text{ and } B)$$

See margin.

41. **CHALLENGE** Use the second diagram at the right to derive a formula for $P(A \text{ or } B \text{ or } C)$.
$P(A \text{ or } B \text{ or } C) = P(A) + P(B) + P(C) - P(A \text{ and } B) - P(B \text{ and } C) - P(A \text{ and } C) + P(A \text{ and } B \text{ and } C)$

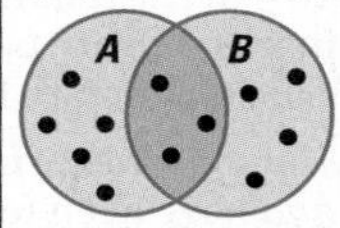

Ex. 40

Ex. 41

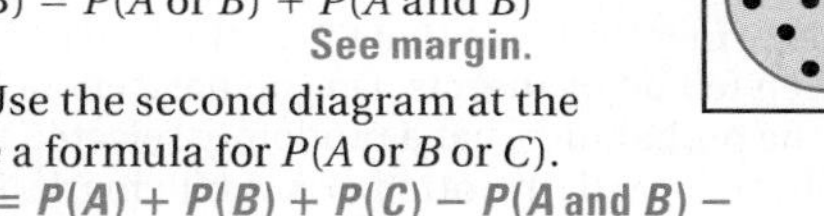

PROBLEM SOLVING

XAMPLES **A** , 2, and 3 n pp. 707–708 or Exs. 42–44

42. **CLASS ELECTIONS** You and your best friend are among several candidates running for class president. You estimate that there is a 45% chance you will win and a 25% chance your best friend will win. What is the probability that either you or your best friend win the election? **70%**

@HomeTutor for problem solving help at classzone.com

43. **BIOLOGY** You are performing an experiment to determine how well plants grow under different light sources. Out of the 30 plants in the experiment, 12 receive visible light, 15 receive ultraviolet light, and 6 receive both visible and ultraviolet light. What is the probability that a plant in the experiment receives either visible light or ultraviolet light? **0.7**

Animated Algebra at classzone.com

Mathematical Reasoning

Multiple Representations

Exercises 9–14, 28–33 Suggest to students that they use both Venn diagrams and the algebraic formula for the probability of compound events to check their answers.

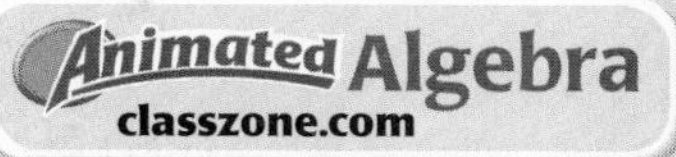

An **Animated Algebra** activity is available on-line for **Exercise 43.** This activity is also available on the **Power Presentations CD-ROM.**

40. $P(A) + P(B) = \frac{8}{12} + \frac{7}{12} = \frac{12}{12} + \frac{3}{12} = P(A \text{ or } B) + P(A \text{ and } B)$; **in $P(A) + P(B)$, the intersection of A and B is counted twice so it has to be added to the probability of $P(A \text{ or } B)$ to make the two sides equal.**

EXAMPLES 4 and 5
on p. 709 for Exs. 44–46

44. ★ **MULTIPLE CHOICE** Refer to the chart below. Which of the following probabilities is greatest? D

Ⓐ P(rains on Sunday) Ⓑ P(does not rain on Saturday)

Ⓒ P(rains on Monday) Ⓓ P(does not rain on Friday)

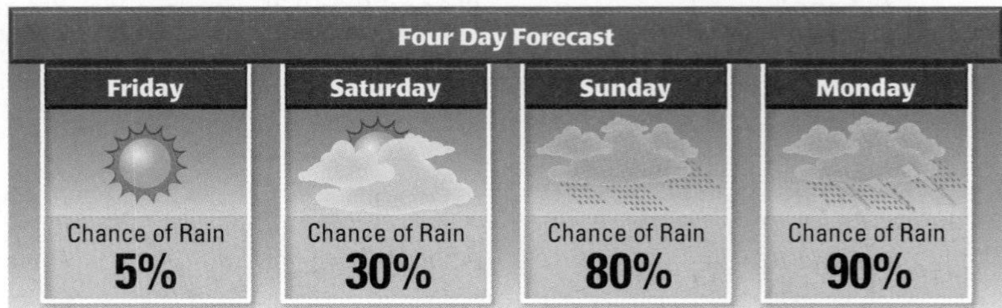

45. **DRAMA CLUB** The organizer of a cast party for a drama club asks each of 6 cast members to bring one food item from a list of 10 items. What is the probability that at least 2 of the 6 cast members bring the same item? 0.8488

46. **HOME ELECTRONICS** A development has 6 houses with the same model of garage door opener. Each opener has 4096 possible transmitter codes. What is the probability that at least 2 of the 6 houses have the same code? about 0.00366

B

47. ★ **EXTENDED RESPONSE** Use the given information about a farmer's tomato crop to complete parts (a)–(c).

   a. 40% of the tomatoes are partially rotten, 30% of the tomatoes have been fed on by insects, and 12% are partially rotten *and* have been fed on by insects. What is the probability that a randomly selected tomato is partially rotten *or* has been fed on by insects? 58%

   b. 20% of the tomatoes have bite marks from a chipmunk and 7% have bite marks *and* are partially rotten. What is the probability that a randomly selected tomato has bite marks *or* is partially rotten? 53%

   c. Suppose the farmer finds out that 6% of the tomatoes have bite marks *and* have been fed on by insects. Do you have enough information to determine the probability that a randomly selected tomato has been fed on by insects *or* is partially rotten *or* has bite marks from a chipmunk? If not, what other information do you require?
   No; what percent of the tomatoes have bite marks.

48. **MULTI-STEP PROBLEM** Follow the steps below to explore a famous probability problem called the *birthday problem.* (Assume that there are 365 possible birthdays.)

   a. **Calculate** Suppose that 6 people are chosen at random. Find the probability that at least 2 of the people share the same birthday. about 0.04

   b. **Calculate** Suppose that 10 people are chosen at random. Find the probability that at least 2 of the people share the same birthday. about 0.12

   c. **Model** Generalize the results from parts (a) and (b) by writing a formula for the probability $P(x)$ that at least 2 people in a group of x people share the same birthday. (*Hint:* Use ${}_nP_r$ notation in your formula.) $P(x) = 1 - \frac{{}_{365}P_x}{365^x}$

   d. **Analyze** Enter the formula from part (c) into a graphing calculator. Use the *table* feature to make a table of values. For what group size does the probability that at least 2 people share the same birthday first exceed 50%? 23 people

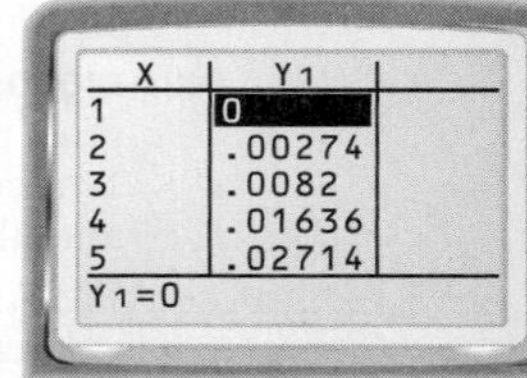

X	Y1
1	0
2	.00274
3	.0082
4	.01636
5	.02714

Y1=0

◯ = WORKED-OUT SOLUTIONS on p. WS1 ★ = STANDARDIZED TEST PRACTICE

712

49. **PET STORE** A pet store has 8 black Labrador retriever puppies (5 females and 3 males) and 12 yellow Labrador retriever puppies (4 females and 8 males). You randomly choose one of the Labrador retriever puppies. What is the probability that it is a female or a yellow Labrador retriever? $\frac{17}{20}$

C 50. **CHALLENGE** You own 50 DVDs consisting of 25 comedies, 15 dramas, and 10 thrillers. You randomly pick 4 movies to watch during a long train ride. What is the probability that you pick at least one DVD of each type of movie? about 0.03

KENTUCKY MIXED REVIEW

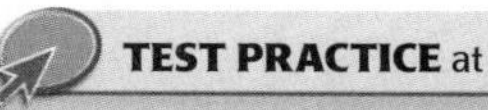

TEST PRACTICE at classzone.com

51. Amy and 7 other students have a bowling party for the math club. The club will pay for bowling, shoe rental, and snacks for all 8 students. The total cost must be at most \$80. Each person bowls the same number of games. What is the maximum number of games that each student can bowl? **B**

Bowling	\$2.70 per person, per game
Shoe rental	\$1.25 per person
Snacks	\$2.80 per person

Ⓐ 1 Ⓑ 2 Ⓒ 3 Ⓓ 4

52. A centrifuge used to train pilots can move 98 ft/sec while making 47 rotations per minute (rpm). If the centrifuge is moving 80 ft/sec, what is a reasonable estimate of its rotational speed? **A**

Ⓐ 38.4 rpm Ⓑ 39.6 rpm Ⓒ 57.6 rpm Ⓓ 166.8 rpm

QUIZ *for Lessons 10.3–10.4*

A card is randomly drawn from a standard deck of 52 cards. Find the probability of drawing the given card. *(p. 698)*

1. The queen of hearts $\frac{1}{52}$
2. An ace $\frac{1}{13}$
3. A diamond $\frac{1}{4}$
4. A red card $\frac{1}{2}$
5. A card other than a 10 $\frac{12}{13}$
6. The 6 of clubs $\frac{1}{52}$

You randomly select a marble from a bag. The bag contains 8 black, 13 red, 7 white, and 12 blue marbles. Find the indicated odds. *(p. 698)*

7. In favor of choosing blue $\frac{3}{7}$
8. In favor of choosing black or white $\frac{3}{5}$
9. Against choosing red $\frac{27}{13}$
10. Against choosing red or white $\frac{1}{1}$

Find the indicated probability. *(p. 707)*

11. $P(A) = 0.6$
$P(B) = 0.35$
$P(A \text{ or } B) = \underline{\ ?\ }$
$P(A \text{ and } B) = 0.2$
0.75

12. $P(A) = \underline{\ ?\ }$
$P(B) = 0.44$
$P(A \text{ or } B) = 0.56$
$P(A \text{ and } B) = 0.12$
0.24

13. $P(A) = 0.75$
$P(B) = \underline{\ ?\ }$
$P(A \text{ or } B) = 0.83$
$P(A \text{ and } B) = 0.25$
0.33

14. $P(A) = 8\%$
$P(B) = 33\%$
$P(A \text{ or } B) = 41\%$
$P(A \text{ and } B) = \underline{\ ?\ }$
0%

15. **COMPUTERS** A manufacturer of computer chips finds that 1% of the chips produced are defective. What is the probability that out of 8 chips, at least 2 are defective? *(p. 707)* about 0.00269

5 ASSESS AND RETEACH

Daily Homework Quiz

Transparency Available

1. A card is randomly selected from a standard deck of 52 cards. What is the probability that it is a queen or an ace? $\frac{2}{13}$
2. Of 200 students at a school, 58 play football, 40 play basketball, and 93 play both. What is the probability that a randomly selected student plays either football or basketball but not both? 0.025
3. When 2 six-sided dice are rolled, what is the probability that the sum is neither 2 nor 12? $\frac{17}{18}$
4. A committee of 3 students is chosen at random from a group of 4 seniors and 6 juniors. What is the probability that the committee will have at least 1 senior? $\frac{5}{6}$

Online Quiz

Available at **classzone.com**

Diagnosis/Remediation

- Practice A, B, C in Chapter 10 Resource Book, pp. 41–43
- Study Guide in Chapter 10 Resource Book, pp. 44–45
- Practice Workbook, pp. 155–156
- @HomeTutor

Challenge

Additional challenge is available in the Chapter 10 Resource Book, p. 48.

Quiz

An easily-readable reduced copy of the quiz (with answers) on Lessons 10.3–10.4 from the Assessment Book can be found on p. 680E.

Alternative Strategy

Example 4 on page 709 can be simulated on a graphing calculator. This simulation can help students visualize the relationship between experimental and theoretical probabilities of a given event.

Graphing Calculator

Students must have the list name selected when entering the formulas for L1, L2, and L3.

Teaching Strategy

Exercise 4 After students answer this exercise, have pairs of students generate random integers and then pool their results to increase the number of data values for this exercise. Have them compare their results with the theoretical probabilities.

PROBLEM SOLVING WORKSHOP LESSON 10.4

Using ALTERNATIVE METHODS

Another Way to Solve Example 4, page 709

MULTIPLE REPRESENTATIONS In Example 4 on page 709, you found theoretical probabilities involving the sum of two dice. You can also perform a *simulation* to estimate these probabilities.

PROBLEM

DICE When two six-sided dice are rolled, there are 36 possible outcomes. Find the probability of the given event.

a. The sum is not 6.

b. The sum is less than or equal to 9.

METHOD

Using a Simulation An alternative approach is to use the random number feature of a graphing calculator to simulate rolling two dice. You can then use the results of the simulation to find the experimental probabilities for the problem.

STEP 1 **Generate** two lists of 120 random integers from 1 to 6 by entering randInt(1,6,120) into lists L_1 and L_2. Define list L_3 to be the sum of lists L_1 and L_2.

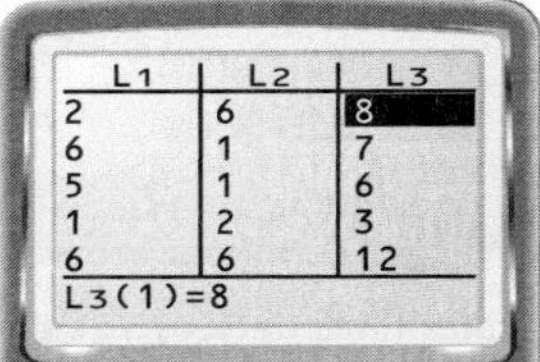

STEP 2 **Sort** the sums in list L_3 in ascending order using the command SortA(L_3). Scroll through the list and count the frequency of each sum.

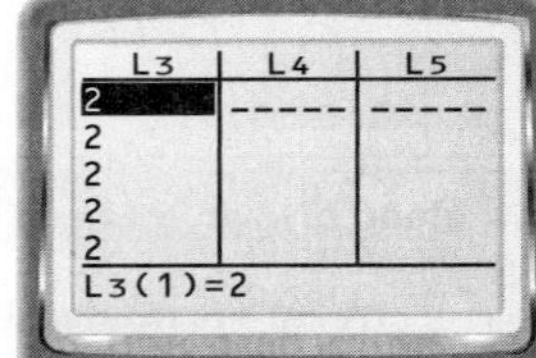

STEP 3 **Find** the probabilities.

a. Divide the number of times the sum was 6 by the total number of simulated rolls, then subtract the result from 1.

b. Divide the number of times the sum was greater than 9 by the total number of simulated rolls, then subtract the result from 1.

PRACTICE

1–4. Check students' work.

1. **WRITING** *Compare* the probabilities found in the simulation above with the theoretical probabilities found in Example 4 on page 709.

2. **SIMULATIONS** Use the results of the simulation above to find the experimental probability that the sum is greater than or equal to 4. *Compare* this to the theoretical probability of the event.

3. **SIMULATIONS** Use the results of the simulation above to find the experimental probability that the sum is not 8 or 9. *Compare* this to the theoretical probability of the event.

4. **REASONING** How could you change the simulation above so that the results would be closer to the theoretical probabilities of the events? *Explain.*

Apply Set Theory

GOAL Define the concepts of sets, operations on sets, and subsets.

y Vocabulary

ion
ersection
mplement
bset

A **set** is a collection of distinct objects. Each object in a set is called an **element** or **member** of the set. A set is denoted by enclosing its elements in braces. For example, if A is the set of positive integers less than 5, then $A = \{1, 2, 3, 4\}$.

There are two special sets that are often used. The set with no elements is called the **empty set** and is denoted by $\emptyset$. The set of all elements under consideration is called the **universal set** and is denoted by U.

KEY CONCEPT *For Your Notebook*

Operations on Sets

The **union** of two sets A and B is written as $A \cup B$ and is the set of all elements in *either* A or B.

$A \cup B$

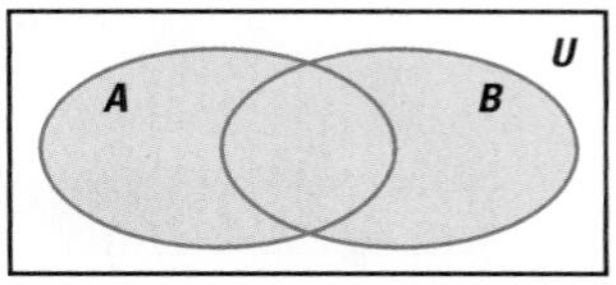

The **intersection** of two sets A and B is written as $A \cap B$ and is the set of all elements in *both* A and B.

$A \cap B$

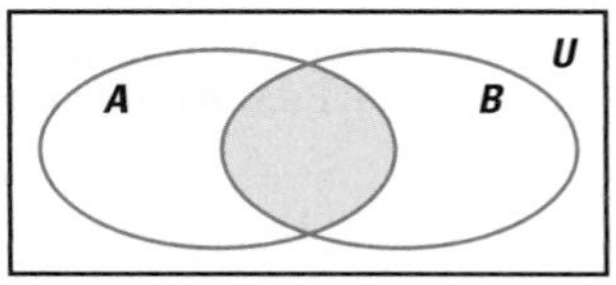

The **complement** of a set A is written as $\overline{A}$ and is the set of all elements in the universal set U that are *not* in A.

$\overline{A}$

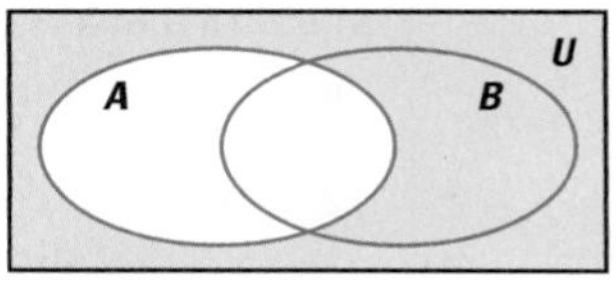

EXAMPLE 1 Perform operations on sets

Let U be the set of all integers from 1 to 10. Let $A = \{1, 2, 4, 8\}$ and let $B = \{2, 4, 6, 8, 10\}$. Find the indicated set.

a. $A \cup B$ **b.** $A \cap B$ **c.** $\overline{A}$ **d.** $\overline{A \cup B}$

Solution

a. $A \cup B = \{1, 2, 4, 8\} \cup \{2, 4, 6, 8, 10\} = \{1, 2, 4, 6, 8, 10\}$

b. $A \cap B = \{1, 2, 4, 8\} \cap \{2, 4, 6, 8, 10\} = \{2, 4, 8\}$

c. $\overline{A} = \overline{\{1, 2, 4, 8\}} = \{3, 5, 6, 7, 9, 10\}$

d. $\overline{A \cup B} = \overline{\{1, 2, 4, 8\} \cup \{2, 4, 6, 8, 10\}} = \overline{\{1, 2, 4, 6, 8, 10\}} = \{3, 5, 7, 9\}$

1 PLAN AND PREPARE

Warm-Up Exercises

1. If $P(A) = 0.25$, $P(B) = 0.40$, and $P(A \text{ and } B) = 0.05$, find $P(A \text{ or } B)$. 0.60
2. If $P(A) = 0.62$, $P(B) = 0.28$, and $P(A \text{ or } B) = 0.80$, find $P(A \text{ and } B)$. 0.10

2 FOCUS AND MOTIVATE

Essential Question

Big Idea 2, p. 681

How do you identify the intersection of two sets? Tell students they will learn how to answer this question by examining the common elements in the two sets.

3 TEACH

Extra Example 1

Let $U = \{0, 5, 10, 15, 20, 25, 30, 35, 40\}$, let $A = \{0, 10, 20, 30, 40\}$ and let $B = \{5, 10, 15, 20, 25\}$. Find the indicated set.

a. $A \cup B$ $\{0, 5, 10, 15, 20, 25, 30, 40\}$
b. $A \cap B$ $\{10, 20\}$
c. $\overline{A}$ $\{5, 15, 25, 35\}$
d. $\overline{A \cap B}$ $\{0, 5, 15, 25, 30, 35, 40\}$

Key Questions to Ask for Example 1

- Which set is $A \cup \overline{A}$? U
- Which operation is performed first in part (d)? $A \cup B$

NCTM STANDARDS

Standard 10: Create representations to communicate mathematical ideas; Use representations to communicate mathematical ideas

Extra Example 2

Let $A = \{-6, -\sqrt{2}, 0, 3, 7, 8\}$, $B = \{-\sqrt{2}, 7, 8\}$, and $C = \{-6, 0, 3\}$.

a. Is $B \subseteq A$? Yes

b. Is $A \subseteq C$? No

c. Is $A \subseteq (B \cap C)$? No

Vocabulary

Call students' attention to the different spellings of *compliment*, which means a polite expression of praise, and *complement*, which derives from the verb *to complete*. Thus, the complement of A *completes* A to produce U.

Closing the Lesson

Have students summarize the major points of the lesson and answer the Essential Question: How do you identify the intersection of two sets?

- The union of two sets contains all the elements that are in at least one of the sets.
- The complement of a set A contains all the elements of the universal set that are not in A.
- If every element of a set A is also an element of a set B, then A is a subset of B.

The elements in the intersection of two sets are those elements common to both sets.

4 PRACTICE AND APPLY

Study Strategy

Exercises 1–11 Students may wish to create Venn diagrams before beginning these exercises.

An **Animated Algebra** activity is available on-line for **Exercise 18**. This activity is also available on the **Power Presentations CD-ROM**.

SUBSETS If every element of a set A is also an element of a set B, then A is a **subset** of B. This relationship is written as $A \subseteq B$. For any set A, $\emptyset \subseteq A$ and $A \subseteq A$. In the diagram at the right, A is a subset of B.

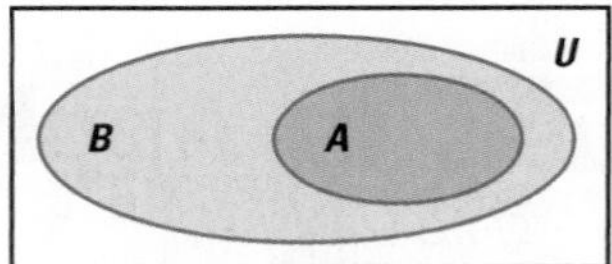

EXAMPLE 2 Identify subsets

Let $A = \{-2, 1, \sqrt{3}, \pi\}$, $B = \{1, \pi, 5\}$, and $C = \{-2, 1, 3, \pi, 5\}$.

a. Is $B \subseteq A$? **b.** Is $B \subseteq C$? **c.** Is $C \subseteq (A \cup B)$?

Solution

a. Not every element of B is an element of A, because 5 is not an element of A. So, B is *not* a subset of A.

b. Every element of B is an element of C. So, B *is* a subset of C.

c. Note that $A \cup B = \{-2, 1, \sqrt{3}, \pi\} \cup \{1, \pi, 5\} = \{-2, 1, \sqrt{3}, \pi, 5\}$. Not every element of C is an element of $A \cup B$, because 3 is not an element of $A \cup B$. So, C is *not* a subset of $A \cup B$.

1. $\{1, 2, 3, 4, 5, 7, 9, 11, 13, 16, 17\}$

3. $\{1, 4, 6, 8, 9, 10, 12, 14, 15, 16, 18, 19, 20\}$

PRACTICE

EXAMPLE 1 on p. 715 for Exs. 1–8

OPERATIONS ON SETS **Let U be the set of all whole numbers from 1 to 20. Let $A = \{2, 3, 5, 7, 11, 13, 17\}$, $B = \{1, 4, 9, 16\}$, and $C = \{2, 5, 8, 11, 14, 17, 20\}$. Find the indicated set.**

1. $A \cup B$ See margin. **2.** $A \cap B$ $\emptyset$ **3.** $\overline{A}$ See margin. **4.** $\overline{B}$

5. $A \cup B \cup C$ See margin. **6.** $\overline{A} \cap C$ $\{8, 14, 20\}$ **7.** $\overline{C \cup B}$ See margin. **8.** $B \cup (A \cap C)$ See margin.

4. $\{2, 3, 5, 6, 7, 8, 10, 11, 12, 13, 14, 15, 17, 18, 19, 20\}$

EXAMPLE 2 on p. 716 for Exs. 9–12

SUBSETS **Let $A = \{-5, \pi, 10\}$, $B = \{-5, 1, \sqrt{5}, 10\}$, and $C = \{-5, 2, \pi, 10\}$.**

9. Is $A \subseteq B$? no **10.** Is $A \subseteq C$? yes **11.** Is $(A \cap B) \subseteq C$? yes

12. REASONING List all the subsets of the set $A = \{-2, 4, 9\}$.
$\{-2\}, \{4\}, \{9\}, \{-2, 4\}, \{-2, 9\}, \{4, 9\}, \{-2, 4, 9\}, \emptyset$

OPERATIONS ON SETS **Consider the sets defined below. Find the indicated set.**

U = the set of all 12 months X = the set of all 30 day months

Y = the set of all 31 day months Z = the set of all months ending with "r"

13. $X \cup Z$ **14.** $X \cap Y$ $\emptyset$ **15.** $\overline{Z}$ **16.** $\overline{X \cup Y}$ February

5. $\{1, 2, 3, 4, 5, 7, 8, 9, 11, 13, 14, 16, 17, 20\}$

7. $\{3, 6, 7, 10, 12, 13, 15, 18, 19\}$

8. $\{1, 2, 4, 5, 9, 11, 16, 17\}$

13. April, June, September, October, November, December

15. January, February, March, April, May, June, July, August

17. REASONING Is the set of all irrational numbers a subset of the real numbers? of the integers? *Explain.* Yes; no; an irrational is a real number but is not an integer.

18. RADIO Two radio towers are set up at points A and B on the map at the right. Each radio tower has a signal that can reach towns up to 50 miles away. Find the set of all towns that can receive a signal from both of the towers.

Animated Algebra at classzone.com

Centerville, Lakeville, Midland, Jackson, Newton

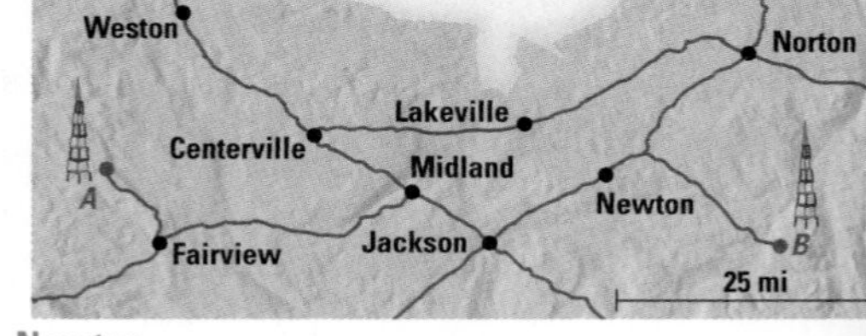

10.5 Find Probabilities of Independent and Dependent Events

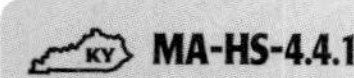

MA-HS-4.4.1

Before You found probabilities of compound events.

Now You will examine independent and dependent events.

Why? So you can formulate coaching strategies, as in Ex. 41.

Key Vocabulary
- independent events
- dependent events
- conditional probability

MA-HS-4.4.1
Students will: determine theoretical and experimental (from given data) probabilities; make predictions and draw inferences from probabilities; compare theoretical and experimental probabilities and determine probabilities involving replacement and non-replacement.
DOK 3

Two events are **independent** if the occurrence of one has no effect on the occurrence of the other. For instance, if a coin is tossed twice, the outcome of the first toss (heads or tails) has no effect on the outcome of the second toss.

KEY CONCEPT *For Your Notebook*

Probability of Independent Events

If A and B are independent events, then the probability that both A and B occur is:

$$P(A \text{ and } B) = P(A) \cdot P(B)$$

More generally, the probability that n independent events occur is the product of the n probabilities of the individual events.

★ **EXAMPLE 1 Standardized Test Practice**

For a fundraiser, a class sells 150 raffle tickets for a mall gift certificate and 200 raffle tickets for a booklet of movie passes. You buy 5 raffle tickets for each prize. What is the probability that you win both prizes?

Ⓐ $\frac{1}{6000}$ Ⓑ $\frac{1}{1200}$ Ⓒ $\frac{1}{350}$ Ⓓ $\frac{1}{70}$

Solution

Let events A and B be getting the winning ticket for the gift certificate and movie passes, respectively. The events are independent. So, the probability is:

$$P(A \text{ and } B) = P(A) \cdot P(B) = \frac{5}{150} \cdot \frac{5}{200} = \frac{1}{30} \cdot \frac{1}{40} = \frac{1}{1200}$$

▸ The correct answer is B. Ⓐ Ⓑ Ⓒ Ⓓ

GUIDED PRACTICE for Example 1

1. **WHAT IF?** In Example 1, what is the probability that you win the mall gift certificate but not the booklet of movie passes? $\frac{13}{400}$

1 PLAN AND PREPARE

Warm-Up Exercises

Transparency Available

Two six-sided die are rolled. Find the probability of each sum.

1. 7 $\frac{1}{6}$ **2.** 5 or 7 $\frac{5}{18}$

3. A coin is going to be tossed 3 times. What is the probability of getting 3 heads? $\frac{1}{8}$

Notetaking Guide

Transparency Available

Promotes interactive learning and notetaking skills, pp. 275–278.

Pacing

Basic: 2 days
Average: 2 days
Advanced: 2 days
Block: 1 block
- See *Teaching Guide/Lesson Plan.*

2 FOCUS AND MOTIVATE

Essential Question

Big Idea 2, p. 681

If you draw two cards from a standard deck of 52 cards, is the probability that the second card is red affected by the color of the first card? **Tell students they will learn how to answer this question by distinguishing between dependent and independent events.**

Resource Planning Guide

Chapter Resource Book
- Teaching Guide/Lesson Plan (pp. 49–50)
- Practice levels A, B, C (pp. 51–53)
- Study Guide (pp. 54–55)
- Catch-up for Absent Students (p. 56)
- Application (p. 57)
- Challenge (p. 58)

Workbooks
- Notetaking Guide (pp. 275–278)
- Practice Workbook (pp. 157–158)

Teaching Options
- **Power Presentations CD-ROM** provides dynamic electronic teaching resources for the classroom.
- **Activity Generator CD-ROM** provides editable activities for all ability levels.

Interactive Technology
- Easy Planner
- Power Presentations CD-ROM
- Activity Generator CD-ROM
- Animated Algebra
- Test Generator CD-ROM
- Online Quiz
- eWorkbook
- eEdition
- @HomeTutor

Resources for English Learners
- Quick Reference for English Learners
- Spanish Study Guide
- Multi-Language Visual Glossary
- Student Resources in Spanish

See also the *Algebra 2 Toolkit* for more strategies for meeting individual needs.

Motivating the Lesson

Jasmine is going to buy one of 5 prom dresses, of which 3 are black and 2 are red. So the probability of choosing a black dress is $\frac{3}{5}$. Then her best friend buys one of the black dresses, so Jasmine won't buy that dress. The probability that Jasmine will randomly choose a black dress from the remaining 4 dresses is $\frac{2}{4}$ or $\frac{1}{2}$. In this chapter you will learn how to compute the probability of two events when the occurrence of one affects the probability of the other.

3 TEACH

Extra Example 1

In a survey at a football game, 50 of 75 male fans and 40 of 50 female fans said that they favor the new team mascot. If 1 male and 1 female fan are randomly selected, what is the probability that both favor the new mascot? **B**

Ⓐ $\frac{1}{5}$ Ⓒ $\frac{18}{25}$

Ⓑ $\frac{8}{15}$ Ⓓ $\frac{11}{15}$

Extra Example 2

A survey found that 46% of parents surveyed say that they read to their children at least once a week. If 3 parents are selected at random, what is the probability that all 3 will say that they read to their children at least once a week? **about 0.097**

Key Question to Ask for Example 2

- If $P(A) = P(B) = P(C)$, does $P(A \text{ and } B \text{ and } C) = P(A)^3$? **yes**

EXAMPLE 2 Find probability of three independent events

RACING In a BMX meet, each heat consists of 8 competitors who are randomly assigned lanes from 1 to 8. What is the probability that a racer will draw lane 8 in the 3 heats in which the racer participates?

Solution

Let events A, B, and C be drawing lane 8 in the first, second, and third heats, respectively. The three events are independent. So, the probability is:

$$P(A \text{ and } B \text{ and } C) = P(A) \cdot P(B) \cdot P(C) = \frac{1}{8} \cdot \frac{1}{8} \cdot \frac{1}{8} = \frac{1}{512} \approx 0.00195$$

EXAMPLE 3 Use a complement to find a probability

MUSIC While you are riding to school, your portable CD player randomly plays 4 different songs from a CD with 16 songs on it. What is the probability that you will hear your favorite song on the CD at least once during the week (5 days)?

Solution

For one day, the probability of *not* hearing your favorite song is:

$$P(\text{not hearing song}) = \frac{{}_{15}C_4}{{}_{16}C_4}$$

Hearing or not hearing your favorite song on Monday, on Tuesday, and so on are independent events. So, the probability of hearing the song at least once is:

$$P(\text{hearing song}) = 1 - [P(\text{not hearing song})]^5 = 1 - \left(\frac{{}_{15}C_4}{{}_{16}C_4}\right)^5 \approx 0.763$$

✓ **GUIDED PRACTICE** for Examples 2 and 3

2. **SPINNER** A spinner is divided into ten equal regions numbered 1 to 10. What is the probability that 3 consecutive spins result in perfect squares? **0.027**
3. **WHAT IF?** In Example 3, how does your answer change if the CD has only 12 songs on it? **It increases to about 0.87.**

CONDITIONAL PROBABILITIES
The conditional probability of B given A can be greater than, less than, or equal to the probability of B.

DEPENDENT EVENTS Two events A and B are **dependent events** if the occurrence of one affects the occurrence of the other. The probability that B will occur given that A has occurred is called the **conditional probability** of B given A and is written as $P(B|A)$.

KEY CONCEPT *For Your Notebook*

Probability of Dependent Events

If A and B are dependent events, then the probability that both A and B occur is:

$$P(A \text{ and } B) = P(A) \cdot P(B|A)$$

Differentiated Instruction

Below Level The language and notation of conditional probability can be difficult for many students. Explain that problems involving conditional probability are concerned with sequential events and ask the question, "After A occurs, what is the probability of B?"

See also the *Algebra 2 Toolkit* for more strategies.

EXAMPLE 4 Find a conditional probability

WEATHER The table shows the numbers of tropical cyclones that formed during the hurricane seasons from 1988 to 2004. Use the table to estimate **(a)** the probability that a future tropical cyclone is a hurricane and **(b)** the probability that a future tropical cyclone in the Northern Hemisphere is a hurricane.

Type of Tropical Cyclone	Northern Hemisphere	Southern Hemisphere
Tropical depression	199	18
Tropical storm	398	200
Hurricane	545	215

Solution

a. $P(\text{hurricane}) = \dfrac{\text{Number of hurricanes}}{\text{Total number of cyclones}} = \dfrac{760}{1575} \approx 0.483$

b. $P(\text{hurricane} \mid \text{Northern Hemisphere})$

$$= \frac{\text{Number of hurricanes in Northern Hemisphere}}{\text{Total number of cyclones in Northern Hemisphere}} = \frac{545}{1142} \approx 0.477$$

EXAMPLE 5 Comparing independent and dependent events

SELECTING CARDS You randomly select two cards from a standard deck of 52 cards. What is the probability that the first card is not a heart and the second is a heart if **(a)** you replace the first card before selecting the second, and **(b)** you do *not* replace the first card?

AVOID ERRORS
It is important to first determine whether A and B are independent or dependent in order to calculate $P(A \text{ and } B)$ correctly.

Solution

Let A be "the first card is not a heart" and B be "the second card is a heart."

a. If you replace the first card before selecting the second card, then A and B are independent events. So, the probability is:

$$P(A \text{ and } B) = P(A) \cdot P(B) = \frac{39}{52} \cdot \frac{13}{52} = \frac{3}{16} \approx 0.188$$

b. If you do not replace the first card before selecting the second card, then A and B are dependent events. So, the probability is:

$$P(A \text{ and } B) = P(A) \cdot P(B \mid A) = \frac{39}{52} \cdot \frac{13}{51} = \frac{13}{68} \approx 0.191$$

✓ GUIDED PRACTICE for Examples 4 and 5

4. **WHAT IF?** Use the information in Example 4 to find **(a)** the probability that a future tropical cyclone is a tropical storm and **(b)** the probability that a future tropical cyclone in the Southern Hemisphere is a tropical storm. a. about 0.38 b. about 0.46

Find the probability of drawing the given cards from a standard deck of 52 cards (a) with replacement and (b) without replacement.

5. A spade, then a club a. $\frac{1}{16}$ b. $\frac{13}{204}$

6. A jack, then another jack a. $\frac{1}{169}$ b. $\frac{1}{221}$

Extra Example 3

During each of the 5 days of a special week, an employee is randomly given 1 of 10 prizes. All prizes are available each day, and one of the prizes is a $500 gift certificate. What is the probability that an employee receives the $500 prize at least once? about 0.41

Key Question to Ask for Example 3

- In the solution, why is P(not hearing the song) raised to the fifth power? The probability of not hearing the song occurs as a factor for each of five days.

Extra Example 4

The table shows the status of 200 registered college students. What is the probability that a randomly selected student (a) is female and (b) if female, is a full time student?

	Part Time	Full Time
Female	80	40
Male	60	20

$\frac{3}{5} = 0.6$; $\frac{2}{5} = 0.4$

Extra Example 5

You randomly select 2 cards from a standard deck of 52 cards. What is the probability that the first card is a heart and the second is a club if (a) you replace the first card before selecting the second, and (b) you do *not* replace the first card?

$\frac{1}{16} = 0.0625$; $\frac{1}{3} = 0.\overline{3}$

Avoiding Common Errors

Make sure that students do not misinterpret the vertical line in $P(B \mid A)$ as a division symbol.

Differentiated Instruction

Below Level It may be helpful to demonstrate the difference between the two situations in **Example 5** using a smaller sample space, the queen and king of hearts and the queen and king of spades. Draw probability trees for the two experiments, both involving a favorable result of drawing a spade first and then a heart, but one should involve replacement of the first card and the other should not. Write the probability for each branch of the probability trees and use them to compute the probability of drawing a spade and then a heart in each experiment.

See also the *Algebra 2 Toolkit* for more strategies.

Extra Example 6

Suppose your area has 8 different Internet Service Providers (ISPs) and you and 3 friends randomly select your own ISP. What is the probability that you all choose different ISPs? **about 0.41**

Extra Example 7

On a manufacturing line, 20% of all the items produced are defective. Although all the items are inspected before they are shipped, 10% of the items are incorrectly classified as either defective or not defective. What percent of the items will be classified as not defective? **74%**

Key Question to Ask for Example 7

- What operation is represented as you move from one branch to a successive branch on the tree? **multiplication**

Closing the Lesson

Have students summarize the major points of the lesson and answer the Essential Question: If you draw 2 cards from a standard deck of 52 cards, is the probability that the second card is red affected by the color of the first card?

- **The probability that n independent events occur is the product of the n probabilities of the individual events. For independent events A and B, $P(A \text{ and } B) = P(A) \cdot P(B)$.**
- **The conditional probability of B given A is written as $P(B|A)$.**
- **The probability that two dependent events A and B will occur is given by the formula $P(A \text{ and } B) = P(A) \cdot P(B|A)$.**

The probability of the color of the second card is affected by the color of the first card if the first card is not replaced before drawing the second card.

THREE OR MORE DEPENDENT EVENTS The formula for finding probabilities of dependent events can be extended to three or more events, as shown below.

EXAMPLE 6 Find probability of three dependent events

COSTUME PARTY You and two friends go to the same store at different times to buy costumes for a costume party. There are 15 different costumes at the store, and the store has at least 3 duplicates of each costume. What is the probability that you each choose different costumes?

ANOTHER WAY

You can also use the fundamental counting principle.

$P(\text{all different})$

$= \frac{\text{different costumes}}{\text{possible costumes}}$

$= \frac{15 \cdot 14 \cdot 13}{15 \cdot 15 \cdot 15} \approx 0.809$

Solution

Let event A be that you choose a costume, let event B be that one friend chooses a different costume, and let event C be that your other friend chooses a third costume. These events are dependent. So, the probability is:

$$P(A \text{ and } B \text{ and } C) = P(A) \cdot P(B|A) \cdot P(C|A \text{ and } B)$$

$$= \frac{15}{15} \cdot \frac{14}{15} \cdot \frac{13}{15} = \frac{182}{225} \approx 0.809$$

EXAMPLE 7 Solve a multi-step problem

SAFETY Using observations made of drivers arriving at a certain high school, a study reports that 69% of adults wear seat belts while driving. A high school student also in the car wears a seat belt 66% of the time when the adult wears a seat belt, and 26% of the time when the adult does not wear a seat belt. What is the probability that a high school student in the study wears a seat belt?

Solution

A probability tree diagram, where the probabilities are given along the branches, can help you solve the problem. Notice that the probabilities for all branches from the same point must sum to 1.

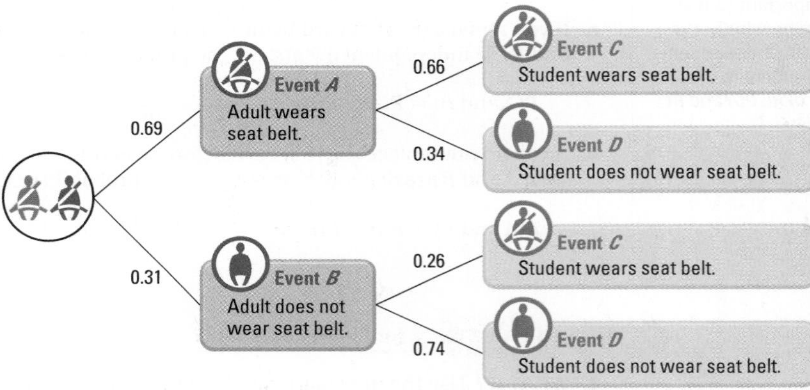

So, the probability that a high school student wears a seat belt is:

$$P(C) = P(A \text{ and } C) + P(B \text{ and } C)$$

$$= P(A) \cdot P(C|A) + P(B) \cdot P(C|B)$$

$$= (0.69)(0.66) + (0.31)(0.26) = 0.536$$

Differentiated Instruction

Auditory Learners When students start finding probabilities of three or more dependent events, such as in **Example 7**, it is easy to confuse the context. Have students read each example aloud and record the key words and phrases. They will be more organized when it comes to solving this problem and others similar to it.

See also the *Algebra 2 Toolkit* for more strategies.

GUIDED PRACTICE for Examples 6 and 7

7. **WHAT IF?** In Example 6, what is the probability that you and your friends choose different costumes if the store sells 20 different costumes? **0.855**

8. **BASKETBALL** A high school basketball team leads at halftime in 60% of the games in a season. The team wins 80% of the time when they have the halftime lead, but only 10% of the time when they do not. What is the probability that the team wins a particular game during the season? **52%**

10.5 EXERCISES

HOMEWORK KEY
○ = **WORKED-OUT SOLUTIONS** on p. WS18 for Exs. 13, 25, and 39
★ = **STANDARDIZED TEST PRACTICE** Exs. 2, 15, 32, 34, and 41

SKILL PRACTICE

A

1. **VOCABULARY** Copy and complete: The probability that B will occur given that A has occurred is called the __?__ of B given A. **conditional probability**

2. ★ **WRITING** *Explain* the difference between dependent events and independent events, and give an example of each. **See margin.**

XAMPLES and 2
n pp. 717–718
r Exs. 3–15

INDEPENDENT EVENTS **Events A and B are independent. Find the indicated probability.**

3. $P(A) = 0.4$
$P(B) = 0.6$
$P(A \text{ and } B) =$ __?__ **0.24**

4. $P(A) = 0.3$
$P(B) = 0.4$
$P(A \text{ and } B) =$ __?__ **0.12**

5. $P(A) = 0.25$
$P(B) =$ __?__
$P(A \text{ and } B) = 0.2$ **0.8**

6. $P(A) = 0.5$
$P(B) =$ __?__
$P(A \text{ and } B) = 0.1$ **0.2**

7. $P(A) =$ __?__
$P(B) = 0.8$
$P(A \text{ and } B) = 0.6$ **0.75**

8. $P(A) =$ __?__
$P(B) = 0.9$
$P(A \text{ and } B) = 0.45$ **0.5**

SPINNING A WHEEL **You are playing a game that involves spinning the wheel shown. Find the probability of spinning the given colors.**

9. green, then blue **about 0.047**
10. red, then yellow **about 0.078**
11. blue, then red **about 0.059**
12. yellow, then green **about 0.063**
13. blue, then green, then red **about 0.015**
14. green, then red, then yellow **about 0.020**

15. ★ **MULTIPLE CHOICE** Events A and B are independent. What is $P(A \text{ and } B)$ if $P(A) = 0.3$ and $P(B) = 0.2$? **A**

Ⓐ 0.06 Ⓑ 0.1 Ⓒ 0.5 Ⓓ 0.6

XAMPLE 4
n p. 719
r Exs. 16–25

DEPENDENT EVENTS **Events A and B are dependent. Find the indicated probability.**

16. $P(A) = 0.3$
$P(B|A) = 0.6$
$P(A \text{ and } B) =$ __?__ **0.18**

17. $P(A) = 0.7$
$P(B|A) = 0.5$
$P(A \text{ and } B) =$ __?__ **0.35**

18. $P(A) = 0.8$
$P(B|A) =$ __?__
$P(A \text{ and } B) = 0.32$ **0.4**

19. $P(A) = 0.6$
$P(B|A) =$ __?__
$P(A \text{ and } B) = 0.45$ **0.75**

20. $P(A) =$ __?__
$P(B|A) = 0.4$
$P(A \text{ and } B) = 0.2$ **0.5**

21. $P(A) = 0.7$
$P(B|A) =$ __?__
$P(A \text{ and } B) = 0.63$ **0.9**

2. Two events are dependent if the occurrence of one affects the occurrence of the other, while events are independent if the occurrence of one does not affect the occurrence of the other. *Sample answer:* Dependent: drawing two cards from a standard deck without replacing the first card drawn, independent: rolling a fair die two times.

4 PRACTICE AND APPLY

Assignment Guide

Answer Transparencies available for all exercises

Basic:
Day 1: pp. 721–723
Exs. 1–7, 9–13, 15, 37
Day 2: pp. 721–723
Exs. 16–19, 22–28, 38–40, 43–44

Average:
Day 1: pp. 721–723
Exs. 1, 2, 4–7, 10–15, 33, 37
Day 2: pp. 721–723
Exs. 17–20, 23–31 odd, 32, 34, 38–41, 43–44

Advanced:
Day 1: pp. 721–723
Exs. 1, 2, 5–15, 33, 37
Day 2: pp. 721–723
Exs. 19–21, 24–32, 34–42*, 44

Block:
pp. 721–723
Exs. 1, 2, 4–7, 10–15, 17–20, 23–31 odd, 32–34, 37–41, 43–44

Differentiated Instruction

See *Algebra 2 Best Practices Toolkit* for suggestions on addressing the needs of a diverse classroom.

Homework Check

For a quick check of student understanding of key concepts, go over the following exercises:

Basic: 4, 16, 26, 37, 39
Average: 6, 18, 28, 37, 40
Advanced: 8, 24, 30, 38, 40

Extra Practice

- Student Edition, p. 1019
- Chapter 10 Resource Book: Practice levels A, B, C, pp. 51–53

Practice Worksheet

An easily-readable reduced practice page (with answers) for this lesson can be found on p. 680D.

Study Strategy

Exercises 3–8 Suggest that students use Venn diagrams to model and check their answers.

Teaching Strategy

Exercises 22–24 Students should understand that $P(A|B)$ is not necessarily equal to $P(B|A)$. To demonstrate that fact, calculate both probabilities for one or more of these exercises with your students.

An **Animated Algebra** activity is available on-line for **Exercise 34**. This activity is also available on the **Power Presentations CD-ROM**.

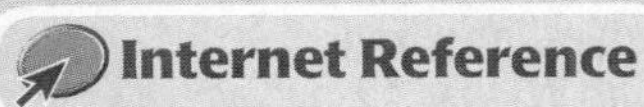

Exercise 38 For more information about endangered and threatened species in the United States, visit www.fws.gov/endangered/wildlife.html

Exercise 42 More information about diabetes can be found at the American Diabetes Association website www.diabetes.org/about-diabetes.jsp

B **CONDITIONAL PROBABILITY Let n be a randomly selected integer from 1 to 20. Find the indicated probability.**

22. n is 2 given that it is even $\frac{1}{10}$

23. n is 5 given that it is less than 8 $\frac{1}{7}$

24. n is prime given that it has 2 digits $\frac{4}{11}$

25. n is odd given that it is prime $\frac{7}{8}$

EXAMPLES 5 and 6 on pp. 719–720 for Exs. 26–32

DRAWING CARDS Find the probability of drawing the given cards from a standard deck of 52 cards (a) with replacement and (b) without replacement.

26. A club, then a spade a. $\frac{1}{16}$ b. $\frac{13}{204}$

27. A queen, then an ace a. $\frac{1}{169}$ b. $\frac{4}{663}$

28. A face card, then a 6 a. $\frac{3}{169}$ b. $\frac{4}{221}$

29. A 10, then a 2 a. $\frac{1}{169}$ b. $\frac{4}{663}$

30. A king, then a queen, then a jack

30a. $\frac{1}{2197}$

30b. $\frac{8}{16,575}$

31. A spade, then a club, then another spade a. $\frac{1}{64}$ b. $\frac{13}{850}$

32. ★ **MULTIPLE CHOICE** What is the approximate probability of drawing 3 consecutive hearts from a standard deck of 52 cards without replacement? B

Ⓐ 0.0122 Ⓑ 0.0129 Ⓒ 0.0156 Ⓓ 0.0166

33. **ERROR ANALYSIS** Events A and B are independent. *Describe* and correct the error in finding $P(A \text{ and } B)$. The probabilities should be multiplied instead of added; $P(A \text{ and } B) = 0.4 \cdot 0.5 = 0.2$.

$P(A) = 0.4, P(B) = 0.5$

$P(A \text{ and } B) = 0.4 + 0.5 = 0.9$

34. ★ **OPEN-ENDED MATH** Flip a set of 3 coins and record the number of coins that come up heads. Repeat until you have a total of 10 trials. a, b. Check students' work.

a. What is the experimental probability that a trial results in 2 heads?

b. *Compare* your answer from part (a) with the theoretical probability that a trial results in 2 heads.

Animated Algebra at classzone.com

C 35. **REASONING** Let A and B be independent events. What is the relationship between $P(B)$ and $P(B|A)$? *Explain.* Since A and B are independent events, $P(A)$ has no affec on $P(B|A)$ so $P(B|A) = P(B)$.

36. **CHALLENGE** How many times must you roll two six-sided dice for there to be at least a 50% chance that you roll two 6's at least once? 18 times

PROBLEM SOLVING

EXAMPLES 3 and 4 on pp. 718–719 for Exs. 37–38

A 37. **SCHOOL BUS** Angela usually rushes to make it to the bus stop in time to catch the school bus, and will often miss the bus if it is early. The bus comes early to Angela's stop 28% of the time. What is the probability that the bus will come early at least once during a 5 day school week? about 81%

@HomeTutor for problem solving help at classzone.com

38. **ENVIRONMENT** The table shows the numbers of species in the United States listed as endangered or threatened as of September, 2004. Find **(a)** the probability that a listed animal is a bird and **(b)** the probability that an endangered animal is a bird. a. about 0.18 b. about 0.20

	Endangered	Threatened
Mammals	69	9
Birds	77	14
Reptiles	14	22
Amphibians	11	10
Other	219	74

@HomeTutor for problem solving help at classzone.com

○ = WORKED-OUT SOLUTIONS on p. WS1 ★ = STANDARDIZED TEST PRACTICE

EXAMPLE 7
on p. 720
for Exs. 39–40

(39.) **TENNIS** A tennis player wins a match 55% of the time when she serves first and 47% of the time when her opponent serves first. The player who serves first is determined by a coin toss before the match. What is the probability that the player wins a given match? 51%

B

40. ACCIDENT REENACTMENT You are a juror for a trial involving a nighttime car accident in a certain city. Use the tree diagram and the facts below to determine the probability that the car involved in the accident was blue.

- The make of the car is known. Of the cars in the city matching this make, 85% are green and 15% are blue.
- A witness of the accident identified the car as blue.
- In reenactments of the accident, the witness correctly reported the color of the car 80% of the time. 0.414

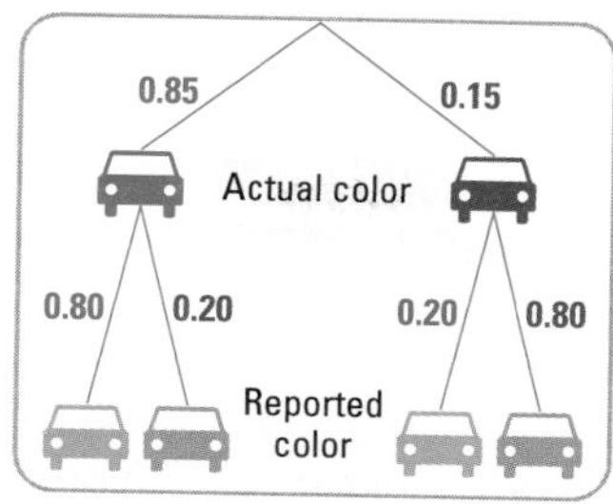

1c. Yes; go for 1 points after the first touchdown. If the 2 points are scored, go for 1 point after the second touchdown. If the two points are not scored, go for 2 points after the second touchdown; win: about 45%, lose: about 30%.

41. ★ **EXTENDED RESPONSE** A football team is losing by 14 points near the end of a game. The team scores two touchdowns (worth 6 points each) before the end of the game. After each touchdown, the coach must decide whether to go for 1 point with a kick (which is successful 99% of the time) or 2 points with a run or pass (which is successful 45% of the time).

a. **Calculate** If the team goes for 1 point after each touchdown, what is the probability that the coach's team wins? loses? ties? 0%; about 2%; about 98%

b. **Calculate** If the team goes for 2 points after each touchdown, what is the probability that the coach's team wins? loses? ties? about 20%, about 30%, about 50%

c. **Reasoning** Can you develop a strategy so that the coach's team has a probability of winning the game that is greater than the probability of losing? If so, explain your strategy and calculate the probabilities of winning and losing using your strategy.

C

42. CHALLENGE It is estimated that 5.9% of Americans have diabetes. Suppose a medical lab uses a test for diabetes that is 98% accurate for people who have the disease and 95% accurate for people who do not have it. Find the conditional probability that a randomly selected person actually has diabetes given that the lab test says they have it. about 0.05

KENTUCKY MIXED REVIEW

KY

TEST PRACTICE at classzone.com

43. What are the slope and y-intercept of the line that contains the point $(4, -2)$ and is parallel to the line $y = -2x + 1$? **C**

Ⓐ $m = -2$, $b = 0$ Ⓑ $m = -\frac{3}{4}$, $b = 1$ Ⓒ $m = -2$, $b = 6$ Ⓓ $m = \frac{1}{2}$, $b = -4$

44. What is the solution set for the equation $7 - 12x^2 = -1$? **B**

Ⓐ $\left\{-\frac{\sqrt{6}}{2}, \frac{\sqrt{6}}{2}\right\}$ Ⓑ $\left\{-\frac{\sqrt{6}}{3}, \frac{\sqrt{6}}{3}\right\}$

Ⓒ $\left\{-\frac{\sqrt{3}}{2}, \frac{\sqrt{3}}{2}\right\}$ Ⓓ $\left\{-\frac{\sqrt{2}}{2}, \frac{\sqrt{2}}{2}\right\}$

5 ASSESS AND RETEACH

Daily Homework Quiz

Transparency Available

1. One red and one green die are rolled. Find the probability that the sum of their numbers is 7 *and* that the number on the green die is larger than the number on the red die. $\frac{1}{12}$

2. A collection of 30 CDs includes 5 CDs by a top female vocalist. Two CDs are selected at random. What is the probability that both are by that female vocalist? $\frac{2}{87}$

3. Find the probability of drawing a 4 and then an 8 from a standard deck of 52 cards (a) with replacement and (b) without replacement. $\frac{1}{169} \approx 0.0059$; $\frac{4}{663} \approx 0.0060$

Online Quiz

Available at **classzone.com**

Diagnosis/Remediation

- Practice A, B, C in Chapter 10 Resource Book, pp. 51–53
- Study Guide in Chapter 10 Resource Book, pp. 54–55
- Practice Workbook, pp. 157–158
- @HomeTutor

Challenge

Additional challenge is available in the Chapter 10 Resource Book, p. 58.

1 PLAN AND PREPARE

Warm-Up Exercises

Transparency Available

1. Use the binomial theorem to expand $(x - 3)^5$. $x^5 - 15x^4 + 90x^3 - 270x^2 + 405x - 243$

Evaluate the expression.

2. ${}_3C_0$ 1
3. ${}_8C_5$ 56

4. A coin is going to be tossed 5 times. What is the probability of getting exactly 4 heads? $\frac{5}{32}$

Notetaking Guide

Transparency Available

Promotes interactive learning and notetaking skills, pp. 279–283.

Pacing

Basic: 2 days

Average: 2 days

Advanced: 2 days

Block: 1 block

• See *Teaching Guide/Lesson Plan.*

2 FOCUS AND MOTIVATE

Essential Question

Big Idea 3, p. 681

What is a binomial distribution? Tell students they will learn how to answer this question by listing all the possible outcomes of an event and calculating the probability of each outcome.

10.6 Construct and Interpret Binomial Distributions

KY MA-HS-4.2.1

Before	You found probabilities of events.
Now	You will study probability distributions.
Why?	So you can describe interest in museums, as in Ex. 46.

Key Vocabulary
- random variable
- probability distribution
- binomial distribution
- binomial experiment
- symmetric
- skewed

MA-HS-4.2.1
Students will describe and compare data distributions and make inferences from the data based on the shapes of graphs, measures of center (mean, median, mode) and measures of spread (range, standard deviation). DOK 2

A **random variable** is a variable whose value is determined by the outcomes of a random event. For example, when you roll a six-sided die, you can define a random variable X that represents the number showing on the die. So, the possible values of X are 1, 2, 3, 4, 5, and 6. For every random variable, a *probability distribution* can be defined.

KEY CONCEPT *For Your Notebook*

Probability Distributions

A **probability distribution** is a function that gives the probability of each possible value of a random variable. The sum of all the probabilities in a probability distribution must equal 1.

Probability Distribution for Rolling a Die						
X	1	2	3	4	5	6
$P(X)$	$\frac{1}{6}$	$\frac{1}{6}$	$\frac{1}{6}$	$\frac{1}{6}$	$\frac{1}{6}$	$\frac{1}{6}$

EXAMPLE 1 Construct a probability distribution

Let X be a random variable that represents the sum when two six-sided dice are rolled. Make a table and a histogram showing the probability distribution for X.

REVIEW COMPOUND EVENTS
Recall that there are 36 possible outcomes when rolling two six-sided dice. These are listed in Example 4 on page 709.

Solution

The possible values of X are the integers from 2 to 12. The table shows how many outcomes of rolling two dice produce each value of X. Divide the number of outcomes for X by 36 to find $P(X)$.

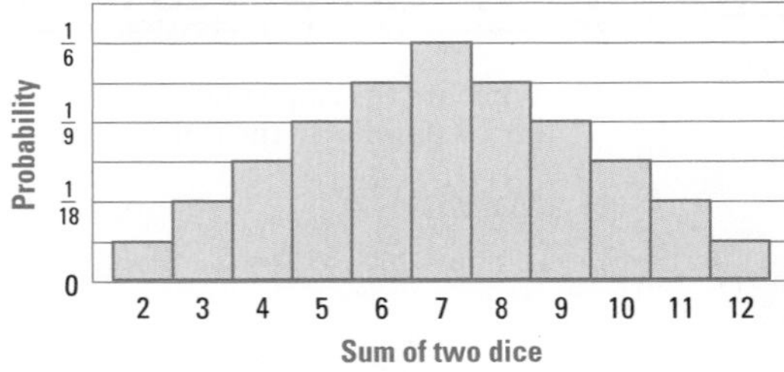

X (sum)	2	3	4	5	6	7	8	9	10	11	12
Outcomes	1	2	3	4	5	6	5	4	3	2	1
$P(X)$	$\frac{1}{36}$	$\frac{1}{18}$	$\frac{1}{12}$	$\frac{1}{9}$	$\frac{5}{36}$	$\frac{1}{6}$	$\frac{5}{36}$	$\frac{1}{9}$	$\frac{1}{12}$	$\frac{1}{18}$	$\frac{1}{36}$

Resource Planning Guide

Chapter Resource Book
- Teaching Guide/Lesson Plan (pp. 59–60)
- Practice levels A, B, C (pp. 62–64)
- Study Guide (pp. 65–66)
- Catch-up for Absent Students (p. 67)
- Problem Solving Workshop (p. 68)
- Challenge (p. 69)

Workbooks
- Notetaking Guide (pp. 279–283)
- Practice Workbook (pp. 159–160)

Teaching Options
- **Power Presentations CD-ROM** provides dynamic electronic teaching resources for the classroom.
- **Activity Generator CD-ROM** provides editable activities for all ability levels.

Interactive Technology
- Easy Planner
- Power Presentations CD-ROM
- Activity Generator CD-ROM
- Animated Algebra
- Test Generator CD-ROM
- Online Quiz
- eWorkbook
- eEdition
- @HomeTutor

Resources for English Learners
- Quick Reference for English Learners
- Spanish Study Guide
- Multi-Language Visual Glossary
- Student Resources in Spanish

See also the *Algebra 2 Toolkit* for more strategies for meeting individual needs.

EXAMPLE 2 Interpret a probability distribution

Use the probability distribution in Example 1 to answer each question.

a. What is the most likely sum when rolling two six-sided dice?

b. What is the probability that the sum of the two dice is at least 10?

Solution

a. The most likely sum when rolling two six-sided dice is the value of X for which $P(X)$ is greatest. This probability is greatest for $X = 7$. So, the most likely sum when rolling the two dice is 7.

b. The probability that the sum of the two dice is at least 10 is:

$$P(X \geq 10) = P(X = 10) + P(X = 11) + P(X = 12)$$

$$= \frac{3}{36} + \frac{2}{36} + \frac{1}{36}$$

$$= \frac{6}{36}$$

$$= \frac{1}{6}$$

$$\approx 0.167$$

GUIDED PRACTICE for Examples 1 and 2

A tetrahedral die has four sides numbered 1 through 4. Let X be a random variable that represents the sum when two such dice are rolled.

1. Make a table and a histogram showing the probability distribution for X. See margin.
2. What is the most likely sum when rolling the two dice? What is the probability that the sum of the two dice is at most 3? sum of 5; $\frac{3}{16}$

BINOMIAL DISTRIBUTIONS One type of probability distribution is a **binomial distribution**. A binomial distribution shows the probabilities of the outcomes of a *binomial experiment*.

KEY CONCEPT *For Your Notebook*

Binomial Experiments

A **binomial experiment** meets the following conditions:

- There are n independent trials.
- Each trial has only two possible outcomes: success and failure.
- The probability of success is the same for each trial. This probability is denoted by p. The probability of failure is given by $1 - p$.

For a binomial experiment, the probability of exactly k successes in n trials is:

$$P(k \text{ successes}) = {}_nC_k p^k (1 - p)^{n-k}$$

Motivating the Lesson

In some carnival games you buy a ticket and then have several chances to win a prize. These situations can be modeled by binomial experiments. This lesson explores the outcomes and probabilities of binomial experiments.

Extra Example 1

Let X be a random variable that represents the number of heads when 4 coins are tossed. Make a table and histogram showing the probability distribution for X.

X (Number of heads)	0	1	2	3	4
Outcomes	1	4	6	4	1
$P(X)$	$\frac{1}{16}$	$\frac{1}{4}$	$\frac{3}{8}$	$\frac{1}{4}$	$\frac{1}{16}$

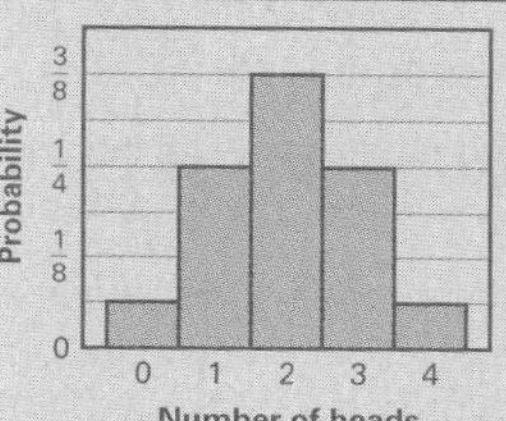

Key Question to Ask for Example 1

- Why is 1 not included as a possible value? **It is not possible to roll a 1 with two dice.**

Extra Example 2

Use the probability distribution in Extra Example 1 to answer each question.

a. What is the most likely outcome of tossing 4 coins? **2 heads**

b. What is the probability that at least 2 heads are tossed? $\frac{11}{16}$

1. See Additional Answers beginning on p. AA1.

Extra Example 3

A health clinic knows that 80% of their patients visited the clinic in the last month. The clinic will call 5 randomly selected patients and ask if they have visited the clinic in the last month. Draw a histogram of the binomial distribution for the survey.

Number of Patients Who Visited Clinic Last Month

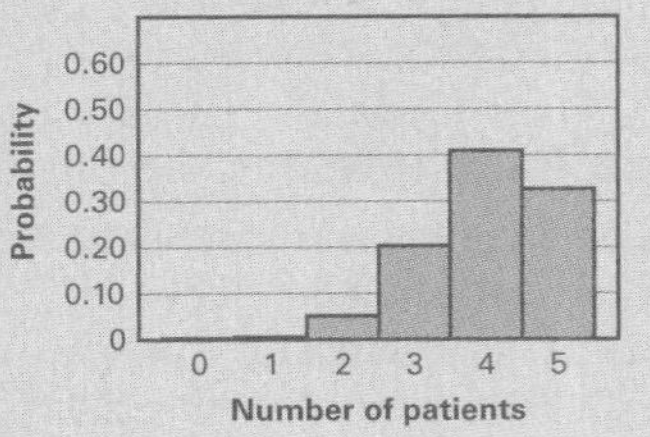

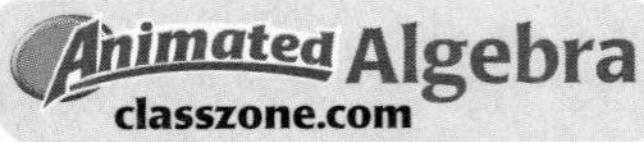

An **Animated Algebra** activity is available on-line for **Example 3**. This activity is also available on the **Power Presentations CD-ROM**.

Key Questions to Ask for Example 3

- What kind of outcome is a *success* for each trial? **A household has a soccer ball.**
- What is the probability of success for this experiment? What is the probability of failure? **success: 0.41; failure: 0.59**

Extra Example 4

Use the probability distribution in Extra Example 3 to answer each question.

a. What is the most likely outcome of the selection? **Of the 5 selected patients, 4 visited the clinic last month.**

b. What is the probability that at most 3 people visited the clinic? **about 26%**

Key Question to Ask for Example 4

- What is the probability that more than 2 households surveyed have a soccer ball? **about 48%**

EXAMPLE 3 Construct a binomial distribution

SPORTS SURVEYS According to a survey, about 41% of U.S. households have a soccer ball. Suppose you ask 6 randomly chosen U.S. households whether they have a soccer ball. Draw a histogram of the binomial distribution for your survey.

Solution

The probability that a randomly selected household has a soccer ball is $p = 0.41$. Because you survey 6 households, $n = 6$.

AVOID ERRORS
You can check your calculations for a binomial distribution by adding all the probabilities. The sum should always be 1.

$P(k = 0) = {}_6C_0(0.41)^0(0.59)^6 \approx 0.042$

$P(k = 1) = {}_6C_1(0.41)^1(0.59)^5 \approx 0.176$

$P(k = 2) = {}_6C_2(0.41)^2(0.59)^4 \approx 0.306$

$P(k = 3) = {}_6C_3(0.41)^3(0.59)^3 \approx 0.283$

$P(k = 4) = {}_6C_4(0.41)^4(0.59)^2 \approx 0.148$

$P(k = 5) = {}_6C_5(0.41)^5(0.59)^1 \approx 0.041$

$P(k = 6) = {}_6C_6(0.41)^6(0.59)^0 \approx 0.005$

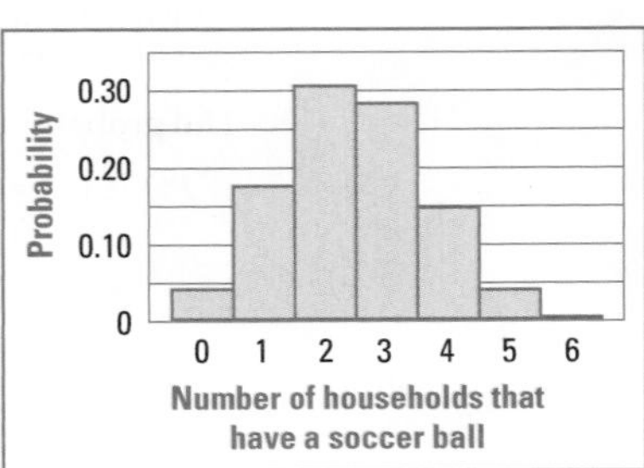

A histogram of the distribution is shown.

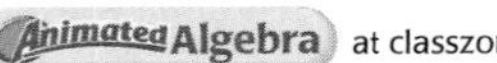

at classzone.com

EXAMPLE 4 Interpret a binomial distribution

Use the binomial distribution in Example 3 to answer each question.

a. What is the most likely outcome of the survey?

b. What is the probability that at most 2 households have a soccer ball?

Solution

a. The most likely outcome of the survey is the value of k for which $P(k)$ is greatest. This probability is greatest for $k = 2$. So, the most likely outcome is that 2 of the 6 households have a soccer ball.

b. The probability that at most 2 households have a soccer ball is:

$$P(k \le 2) = P(k = 2) + P(k = 1) + P(k = 0)$$
$$\approx 0.306 + 0.176 + 0.042$$
$$\approx 0.524$$

▶ So, the probability is about 52%.

✓ GUIDED PRACTICE for Examples 3 and 4

In Sweden, 61% of households have a soccer ball. Suppose you ask 6 randomly chosen Swedish households whether they have a soccer ball.

3. Draw a histogram showing the binomial distribution for your survey. **See margin.**

4. What is the most likely outcome of your survey? What is the probability that at most 2 households you survey have a soccer ball? **4 households; about 0.166**

3.

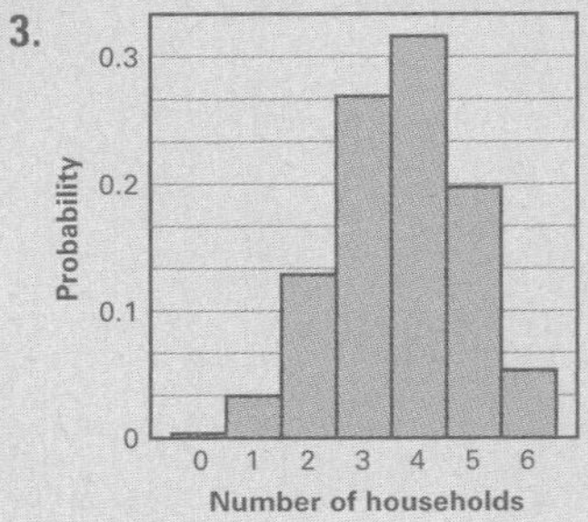

LASSIFY ISTRIBUTIONS

ote that the stribution in xample 1 on p. 724 symmetric, while e distribution in xample 3 on p. 726 skewed.

SYMMETRIC AND SKEWED DISTRIBUTIONS Suppose a probability distribution is represented by a histogram. The distribution is **symmetric** if you can draw a vertical line that divides the histogram into two parts that are mirror images. A distribution that is *not* symmetric is called **skewed**.

EXAMPLE 5 Classify distributions as symmetric or skewed

Describe the shape of the binomial distribution that shows the probability of exactly k successes in 8 trials if (a) $p = 0.5$ and (b) $p = 0.9$.

Solution

a.

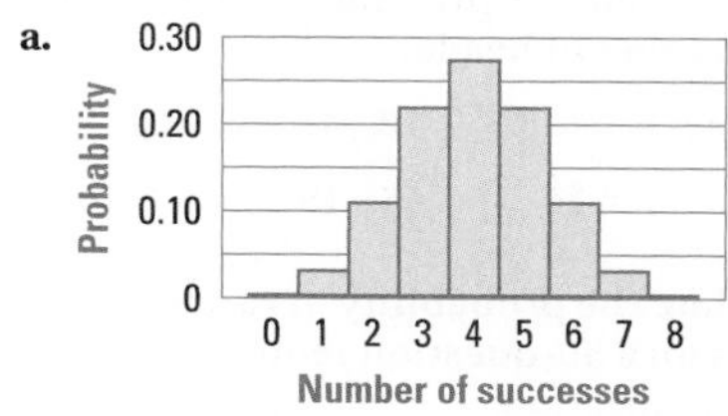

Symmetric; the left half is a mirror image of the right half.

b.

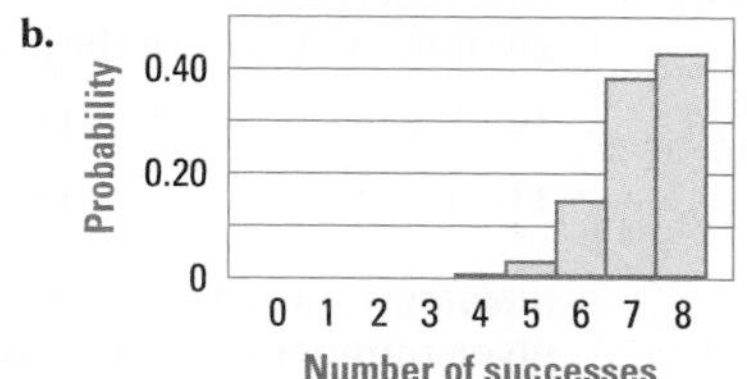

Skewed; the distribution is not symmetric about any vertical line.

✓ **GUIDED PRACTICE** for Example 5

5. A binomial experiment consists of 5 trials with probability p of success on each trial. Describe the shape of the binomial distribution that shows the probability of exactly k successes if (**a**) $p = 0.4$ and (**b**) $p = 0.5$.

a. The distribution is skewed since it is not symmetric about a vertical line.
b. The distribution is symmetric since it is symmetric about a vertical line.

10.6 EXERCISES

HOMEWORK KEY

○ = **WORKED-OUT SOLUTIONS** on p. WS19 for Exs. 5, 21, and 45

★ = **STANDARDIZED TEST PRACTICE** Exs. 2, 9, 32, 39, and 48

◆ = **MULTIPLE REPRESENTATIONS** Ex. 47

SKILL PRACTICE

A

1. **VOCABULARY** Copy and complete: A probability distribution represented by a histogram is _?_ if you can draw a vertical line dividing the histogram into two parts that are mirror images. symmetric

2. ★ **WRITING** *Explain* the difference between a binomial experiment and a binomial distribution. *Sample answer:* A binomial experiment is an experiment that has only two outcomes: success and failure. A binomial distribution shows the outcomes of a binomial experiment.

XAMPLE 1 p. 724 Exs. 3–5

CONSTRUCTING PROBABILITY DISTRIBUTIONS **Make a table and a histogram showing the probability distribution for the random variable.** 3–5. See margin.

3. X = the number on a table tennis ball randomly chosen from a bag that contains 5 balls labeled "1," 3 balls labeled "2," and 2 balls labeled "3."

4. $W = 1$ if a randomly chosen letter is A, E, I, O, or U and 2 otherwise.

(5.) N = the number of digits in a random integer from 0 through 999.

Differentiated Instruction

Inclusion Students with difficulty processing charts and graphs may not recognize from a histogram whether a binomial distribution is symmetric or skewed. Ask students to translate the histograms in **Example 5** into tables that list the number of successes and their respective probabilities. Then have students use their tables to determine the shape of each binomial distribution.

See also the *Algebra 2 Toolkit* for more strategies.

Extra Example 5

Describe the shape of the binomial distribution that shows the probability of exactly k successes in 10 trials if (a) $p = 0.2$ and if (b) $p = 0.5$.
(a) skewed; (b) symmetric

Key Questions to Ask for Example 5

- What happens to the shape of a binomial distribution as p gets farther from 0.5? Its shape becomes more skewed.
- Does the distribution in part (a) have a line of symmetry? If so, describe it. Yes; it is a vertical line through the center of the bar that represents 4 successes.

Study Strategy

When constructing a histogram for a problem that can be modeled by a binomial distribution, first identify what *successful outcome* means and identify its probability. The probability of failure is $1 - P(\text{success})$.

Closing the Lesson

Have students summarize the major points of the lesson and answer the Essential Question: What is a binomial distribution?

- A probability distribution is a function that gives the probability of each possible outcome for a random variable.
- The sum of all probabilities in a probability distribution must equal 1.
- For a binomial experiment, the probability of exactly k successes in n trials can be calculated from ${}_nC_k p^k(1 - p)^{n-k}$, where n is the number of independent trials and p is the probability of success.

A binomial distribution is a probability distribution that shows the probabilities of the outcomes of a binomial experiment. To construct a binomial distribution, list each of the possible outcomes. Then calculate the probability of each of the outcomes.

3–5. See Additional Answers beginning on p. AA1.

4 PRACTICE AND APPLY

Assignment Guide

Answer Transparencies available for all exercises

Basic:
Day 1: SRH p. 799 Exs. 46, 50
pp. 727–730
Exs. 1–9, 47
Day 2: pp. 727–730
Exs. 10–13, 18–21, 26–34, 43–46, 50–51

Average:
Day 1: pp. 727–730
Exs. 1–9, 39, 47
Day 2: pp. 727–730
Exs. 13–15, 21–23, 26, 27, 30–38, 43–46, 48, 50–51

Advanced:
Day 1: pp. 727–730
Exs. 1–9, 39, 47
Day 2: pp. 727–730
Exs. 15–17, 23–25, 30–38, 40–51*

Block:
pp. 727–730
Exs. 1–9, 13–15, 21–23, 26, 27, 30–39, 43–48, 50–51

Differentiated Instruction

See *Algebra 2 Best Practices Toolkit* for suggestions on addressing the needs of a diverse classroom.

Homework Check

For a quick check of student understanding of key concepts, go over the following exercises:

Basic: 3, 6, 12, 33, 43
Average: 4, 7, 22, 34, 44
Advanced: 4, 8, 24, 36, 46

Extra Practice

- Student Edition, p. 1019
- Chapter 10 Resource Book: Practice levels A, B, C, pp. 62–64

Practice Worksheet

An easily-readable reduced practice page (with answers) for this lesson can be found on p. 680D.

EXAMPLE 2 on p. 725 for Exs. 6–9

INTERPRETING PROBABILITY DISTRIBUTIONS In Exercises 6–9, use the given histogram of a probability distribution for a random variable *X*.

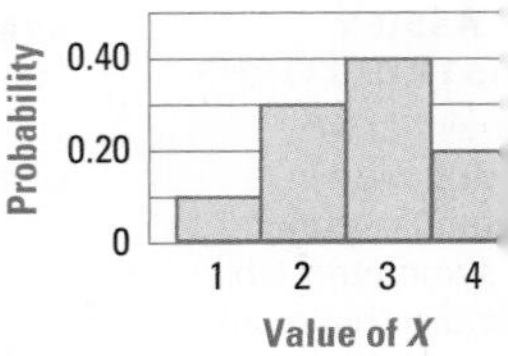

6. What is the probability that X is equal to 1? 0.1
7. What is the most likely value for X? 3
8. What is the probability that X is odd? 0.5
9. ★ **MULTIPLE CHOICE** What is the probability that X is at least 3? C

   (A) 0.2 (B) 0.4 (C) 0.6 (D) 0.8

EXAMPLES 3 and 4 on p. 726 for Exs. 10–32

CALCULATING PROBABILITIES Calculate the probability of tossing a coin 20 times and getting the given number of heads.

10. 1 about 0.000019
11. 2 about 0.00018
12. 4 about 0.0046
13. 6 about 0.037
14. 9 about 0.160
15. 12 about 0.120
16. 15 about 0.015
17. 18 about 0.00018

BINOMIAL PROBABILITIES Calculate the probability of randomly guessing the given number of correct answers on a 30-question multiple choice exam that has choices A, B, C, and D for each question.

18. 0 about 0.00018
19. 2 about 0.0086
20. 6 about 0.145
21. 11 about 0.055
22. 15 about 0.0019
23. 21 about 0.00000024
24. 26
25. 30

24, 25. See margin.

ERROR ANALYSIS *Describe* and correct the error in calculating the probability of rolling a 1 exactly 3 times in 5 rolls of a six-sided die. 26, 27. See margin.

26.
$$P(k = 3) = {}_5C_3\left(\frac{1}{6}\right)^{5-3}\left(\frac{5}{6}\right)^3$$
$$\approx 0.161$$

27.
$$P(k = 3) = \left(\frac{1}{6}\right)^3\left(\frac{5}{6}\right)^{5-3}$$
$$\approx 0.003$$

B

BINOMIAL DISTRIBUTIONS Calculate the probability of k successes for a binomial experiment consisting of n trials with probability p of success on each trial.

28. $k \le 3$, $n = 7$, $p = 0.3$ about 0.874
29. $k \ge 5$, $n = 8$, $p = 0.6$ about 0.594
30. $k \le 2$, $n = 5$, $p = 0.12$ about 0.986
31. $k \ge 10$, $n = 15$, $p = 0.75$ about 0.852
32. ★ **MULTIPLE CHOICE** You perform a binomial experiment consisting of 10 trials with a probability of success of 36% on each trial. What is the most likely number of successes? A

    (A) 3 (B) 4 (C) 6 (D) 7

EXAMPLE 5 on p. 727 for Exs. 33–38

HISTOGRAMS A binomial experiment consists of n trials with probability p of success on each trial. Draw a histogram of the binomial distribution that shows the probability of exactly k successes. *Describe* the distribution as either *symmetric* or *skewed*. Then find the most likely number of successes. 33–38. See margin.

33. $n = 3$, $p = 0.3$
34. $n = 6$, $p = 0.5$
35. $n = 4$, $p = 0.16$
36. $n = 7$, $p = 0.85$
37. $n = 8$, $p = 0.025$
38. $n = 12$, $p = 0.5$
39. ★ **OPEN-ENDED MATH** Construct a symmetric probability distribution for a random variable X and a skewed probability distribution for a random variable Y. Make a table and a histogram for each distribution. Check students' work.

○ = WORKED-OUT SOLUTIONS on p. WS1 ★ = STANDARDIZED TEST PRACTICE ◆ = MULTIPLE REPRESENTATIC

24. about 0.0000000000019
25. about 0.00000000000000000087
26. The exponents on the two probabilities are switched around; ${}_5C_3\left(\frac{1}{6}\right)^3\left(\frac{5}{6}\right)^{5-3} \approx 0.03$.
27. The ${}_5C_3$ was left out of the equation; ${}_5C_3\left(\frac{1}{6}\right)^3\left(\frac{5}{6}\right)^{5-3} \approx 0.03$.

33–38. See Additional Answers beginning on p. AA1.

C In Exercises 40–42, you will derive the binomial probability formula on page 725. Consider a binomial experiment with n trials and probability p of success on each trial.

40. For any particular sequence of k successes and $n - k$ failures, what is the probability that the sequence occurs? *Explain.* See margin.

41. How many sequences of k successes and $n - k$ failures are there? *Explain.* See margin.

42. **CHALLENGE** Use your results from Exercises 40 and 41 to justify the binomial probability formula. The probability of one sequence is $(p)^k(1 - p)^{n-k}$ and there are ${}_nC_k$ sequences, so the probability of having a sequence of n items with k successes that have probability p is ${}_nC_k(p)^k(1 - p)^{n-k}$, which is the binomial probability formula.

PROBLEM SOLVING

EXAMPLES A 3 and 4 on p. 726 for Exs. 43–46

43. **HEALTH** About 1% of people are allergic to bee stings. What is the probability that exactly 1 person in a class of 25 is allergic to bee stings? about 0.196

@HomeTutor for problem solving help at classzone.com

44. **BASKETBALL** Predrag Stojakovic of the Sacramento Kings made 92.7% of his free throw attempts in the 2003–2004 NBA regular season. What is the probability that he will make exactly 10 of his next 15 free throw attempts? about 0.0029

@HomeTutor for problem solving help at classzone.com

45. **BLOOD TYPE** The chart shows the distribution of blood types (O, A, B, AB) and Rh factor ($^+$ or $^-$) for human blood. If, at random, 10 people donate blood to a blood bank during a certain hour, find the probability of each event.

Percent of Population by Blood Type							
O^+	O^-	A^+	A^-	B^+	B^-	AB^+	AB^-
37%	6%	34%	6%	10%	2%	4%	1%

a. Exactly 5 of the people are type A^+. about 0.143

b. Exactly 2 of the people are Rh^-. about 0.276

c. At most 2 of the people are type O. about 0.124

d. At least 5 of the people are Rh^+. about 0.999

46. **FINE ARTS** A survey states that 35% of people in the United States visited an art museum in a certain year. You randomly select 10 U.S. citizens.

a. Draw a histogram showing the binomial distribution of the number of people who visited an art museum. See margin.

b. What is the probability that at most 4 people visited an art museum? about 0.751

B **47.** **MULTIPLE REPRESENTATIONS** An average of 7 gopher holes appear on the farm shown each week. Let X represent how many of the 7 gopher holes appear in the carrot patch. Assume that a gopher hole has an equal chance of appearing at any point on the farm. a–c. See margin.

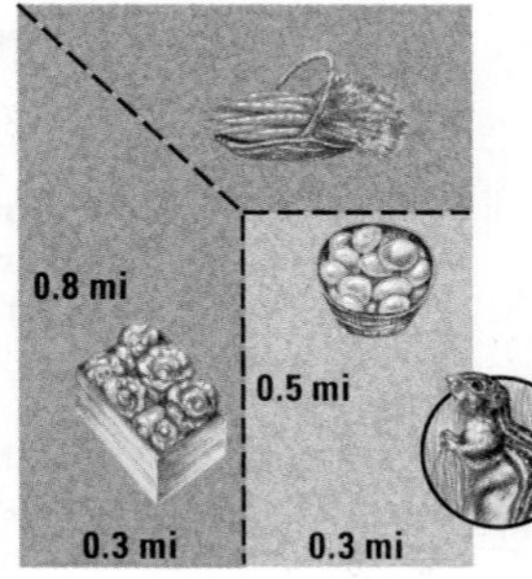

a. Calculating Probabilities Find $P(X)$ for $X = 0, 1, 2, \ldots, 7$.

b. Making a Table Make a table showing the probability distribution for X.

c. Making a Histogram Make a histogram showing the probability distribution for X.

Avoiding Common Errors

Exercises 33–38 Help students learn how to use the results of Example 5 as a rough check of each histogram. When $p < 0.5$, the smaller frequencies should appear on the right of the histogram. When $p > 0.5$, the smaller frequencies should appear on the left of the histogram.

40. $(p)^k(1 - p)^{n-k}$; the probability of k successes is p^k and the probability of $n - k$ failures is $(1 - p)^{n-k}$. To find the probability of a sequence with k successes and $n - k$ failures you must multiply the individual probabilities.

41. ${}_nC_k$; since order does not matter, find the combination of n things taken k at a time.

46a.

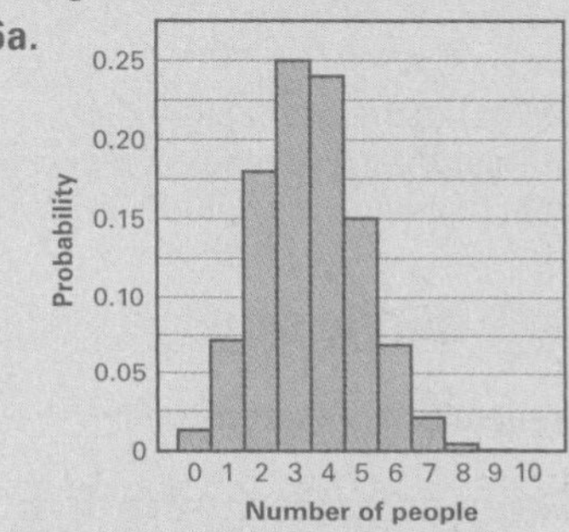

47a. $P(0) \approx 0.099$, $P(1) \approx 0.271$, $P(2) \approx 0.319$, $P(3) = 0.208$, $P(4) \approx 0.081$, $P(5) \approx 0.019$, $P(6) \approx 0.0025$, $P(7) \approx 0.00014$

47b.

x	$P(x)$
0	0.099
1	0.271
2	0.319
3	0.208
4	0.081
5	0.019
6	0.0025
7	0.00014

47c.

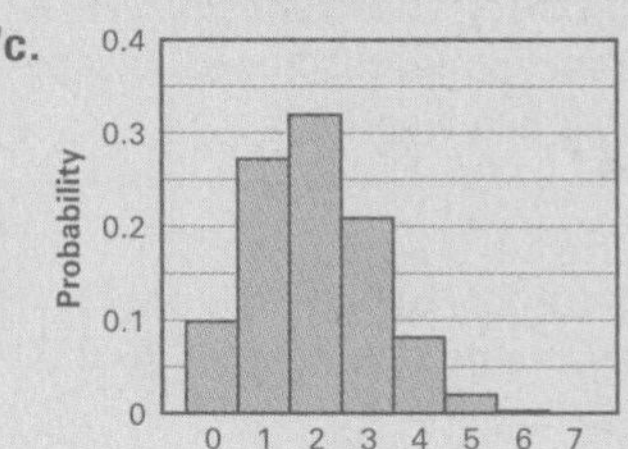

48. ★ **EXTENDED RESPONSE** Assume that having a male child and having a female child are independent events and that the probability of each is 0.5.

a. A couple has 4 male children. Evaluate the validity of this statement: "The first 4 kids were all boys, so the next one will probably be a girl." **Not a valid statement because the events are independent.**

b. What is the probability of having 4 male children and then a female child? **0.03125**

c. Let X be a random variable that represents the number of children a couple already has when they have their first female child. Draw a histogram of the distribution of $P(X)$ for $0 \le X \le 10$ and describe its shape. **See margin for art; skewed.**

C 49. **CHALLENGE** An entertainment system has n speakers. Each speaker will function properly with probability p, independent of whether the other speakers are functioning. The system will operate effectively if at least 50% of its speakers are functioning. For what values of p is a 5-speaker system more likely to operate than a 3-speaker system? **$p > 0.5$**

KY KENTUCKY MIXED REVIEW

TEST PRACTICE at classzone.com

50. For an emergency service call, an electrician charges a base fee of \$65 plus \$36.50 per hour of work. Which equation best represents the relationship between the total cost, c, of the emergency service call and the number of hours worked, n? **B**

Ⓐ $c = 65 + 36.5$ Ⓑ $c = 65 + 36.5n$

Ⓒ $c = 65n + 36.5$ Ⓓ $c = 65n + 36.5n$

51. What is the solution of the equation $3(4x - 5) = -4(-x + 6) - 8x$? **B**

Ⓐ $-\frac{3}{5}$ Ⓑ $-\frac{9}{16}$ Ⓒ $\frac{3}{8}$ Ⓓ $\frac{9}{16}$

QUIZ *for Lessons 10.5–10.6*

Find the probability of randomly drawing the given marbles from a bag of 6 red, 9 green, and 5 blue marbles without replacement. *(p. 717)*

1. red, then green $\frac{27}{190}$ 2. blue, then red $\frac{3}{38}$ 3. green, then green $\frac{18}{95}$

Calculate the probability of getting the given number of 6's when rolling a six-sided die 10 times. *(p. 724)*

4. 0 **about 0.162** 5. 1 **about 0.323** 6. 4 **about 0.054** 7. 8 **about 0.000019**

A binomial experiment consists of n trials with probability p of success on each trial. Draw a histogram of the binomial distribution that shows the probability of exactly k successes. *(p. 724)* **8–10. See margin.**

8. $n = 5, p = 0.2$ 9. $n = 8, p = 0.5$ 10. $n = 6, p = 0.72$

11. **MENU CHOICES** You and 4 friends are in line at lunch and are each selecting a beverage. There are 5 types of beverages available. What is the probability that all of you will select different beverages? *(p. 717)* **0.00032**

EXTRA PRACTICE for Lesson 10.6, p. 1019 **ONLINE QUIZ** at classzone.com

5 ASSESS AND RETEACH

Daily Homework Quiz

Transparency Available

1. A modified die has faces labeled 1, 2, 2, 3, 3, and 3. If two of these dice are rolled, what is the probability that the sum is at most 3? $\frac{5}{36}$

A survey found that 32% of teenagers work part time jobs. You randomly survey 5 teenagers.

2. Draw a histogram of the binomial distribution of the survey.

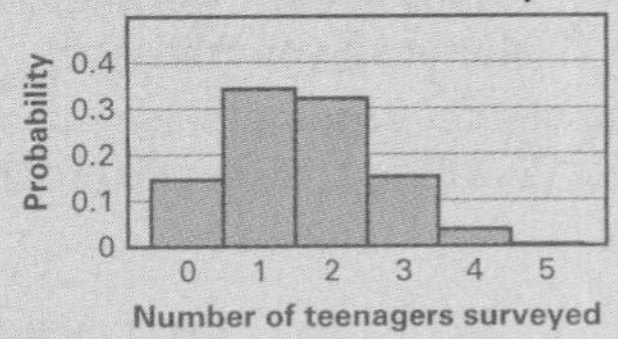

3. What is the probability that fewer than 2 teenagers work part time jobs? **about 0.487**

Online Quiz

Available at **classzone.com**

Diagnosis/Remediation

- Practice A, B, C in Chapter 10 Resource Book, pp. 62–64
- Study Guide in Chapter 10 Resource Book, pp. 65–66
- Practice Workbook, pp. 159–160
- @HomeTutor

Challenge

Additional challenge is available in the Chapter 10 Resource Book, p. 69.

Quiz

An easily-readable reduced copy of the quiz (with answers) on Lessons 10.5–10.6 from the Assessment Book can be found on p. 680E.

48c, Quiz 8–10. See Additional Answers beginning on p. AA1.

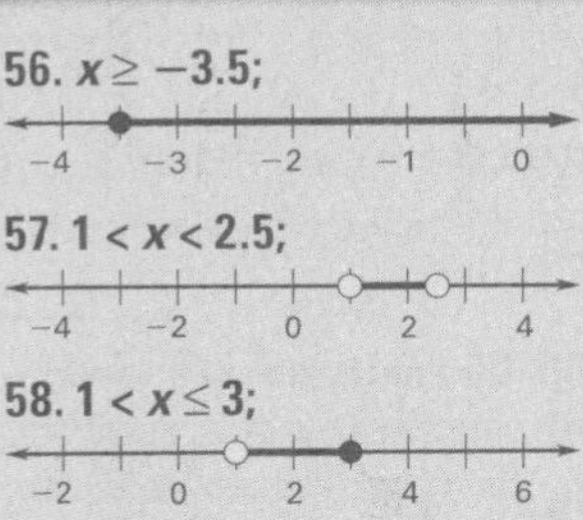

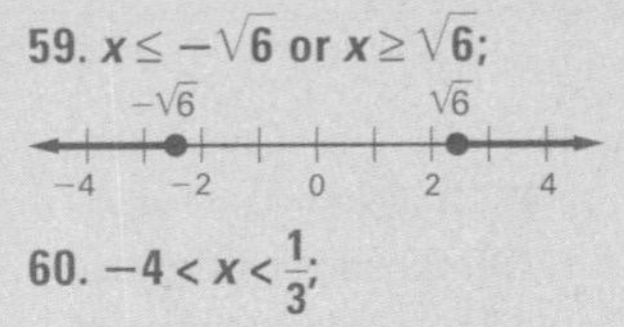

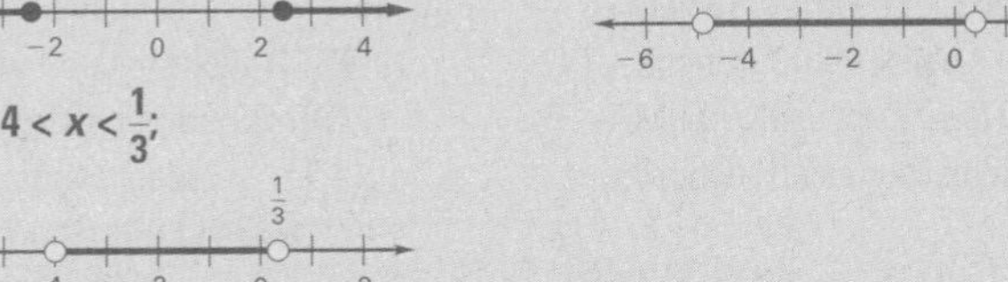

Graphing Calculator **ACTIVITY** *Use after Lesson 10.6*

@HomeTutor
classzone.com
Keystrokes

10.6 Create a Binomial Distribution

QUESTION How can you use a graphing calculator to calculate binomial probabilities?

Some calculators have a binomial probability distribution function that you can use to calculate binomial probabilities. You can then use the calculator to draw a histogram of the distribution.

EXAMPLE Calculate binomial probabilities

TV NEWS According to a survey, 38% of U.S. adults get their news primarily from television. Suppose you survey 6 adults at random. Draw a histogram of the binomial distribution showing the probability that television is the primary news source for exactly k adults. What is the most likely number of adults in your survey who get their news primarily through television?

STEP 1 *Enter values of k*

Let $p = 0.38$ be the probability that television is a person's primary news source. Enter the k-values 0 through 6 into list L_1 on the graphing calculator.

STEP 2 *Find values of P(k)*

Enter the binomial probability command to generate $P(k)$ for all seven k-values. Store the results in list L_2.

STEP 3 *Draw histogram*

Set up the histogram to use the numbers in list L_1 as x-values and the numbers in list L_2 as frequencies. Draw the histogram in a suitable viewing window.

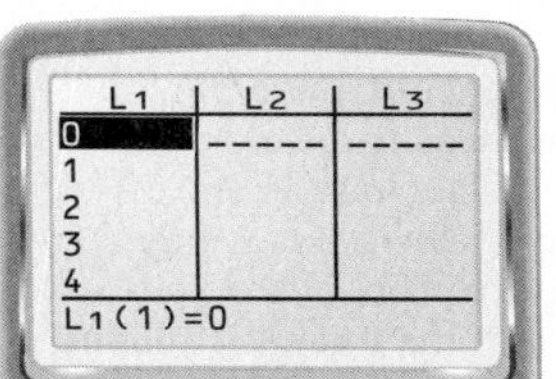

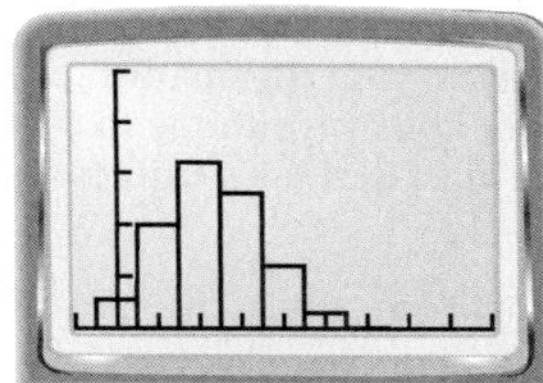

From the histogram in Step 3, you can see that $k = 2$ is the most likely number of the 6 adults surveyed who get their news primarily through television.

PRACTICE

A binomial experiment consists of n trials with probability p of success on each trial. Use a graphing calculator to draw a histogram of the binomial distribution that shows the probability of exactly k successes. Then find the most likely number of successes.

1. $n = 12, p = 0.29$ 3 successes
2. $n = 14, p = 0.58$ 8 successes
3. $n = 15, p = 0.805$ 12 successes
4. **WHAT IF?** In the example, how do your histogram and the most likely number of adults change if you survey 14 adults at random? The most likely number of adults is 5 and the histogram would be spread wider with the probabilities not being as great as the original.

1 PLAN AND PREPARE

Learn the Method

- Students will use a graphing calculator to calculate binomial probabilities and draw histograms.
- Students can use this technique to answers the questions in Lesson 10.6, Examples 1–4.

Keystroke Help

Keystrokes for several models of calculators are available in blackline format in the *Chapter 10 Resource Book.*

2 TEACH

Tips for Success

After students enter List 1, have them quit that screen before beginning Step 2. Some calculators generate an error message if students enter the binomial distribution command while in the List Editor.

Extra Example

In a survey, 13% of businesses reported that they had eliminated jobs. You survey 5 businesses at random. Draw a histogram of a binomial distribution showing the probability that a business eliminated jobs for exactly k businesses. What is the most likely number of businesses that eliminated jobs? zero

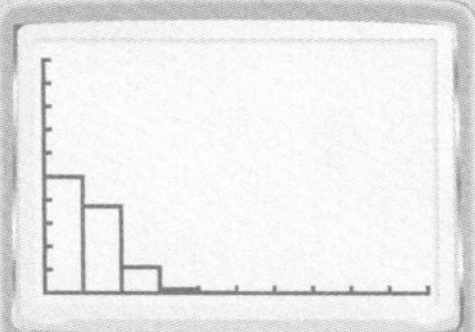

3 ASSESS AND RETEACH

A binomial distribution consists of n trials with probability p of success on each trial. Which situation has a histogram that is closest to being symmetric? A

Ⓐ $n = 10, p = 0.47$
Ⓑ $n = 18, p = 0.79$
Ⓒ $n = 15, p = 0.32$
Ⓓ $n = 16, p = 0.25$

Kentucky Mixed Review

1. C
2. A
3. D
4. B
5. C
6. a. 0.14%
   b. 99.86%
   c. The answers sum to 1 because they are complimentary events.

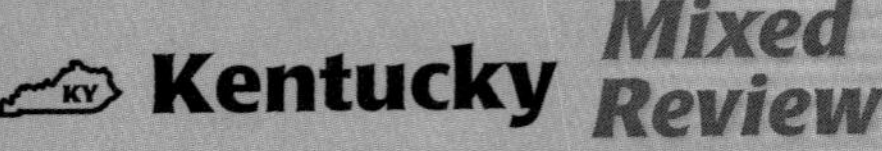

Lessons 10.4–10.6

1. **WORD GAME** You and a friend are playing a word game that involves 100 lettered tiles. The distribution of letters is shown below. You randomly draw 2 tiles without replacement. What is the probability (rounded to 3 decimal places) of getting 2 vowels? (Assume that Y is a consonant.)

Tile	Count	Tile	Count	Tile	Count	Tile	Count
A	9	H	2	O	8	V	2
B	2	I	9	P	2	W	2
C	2	J	1	Q	1	X	1
D	4	K	1	R	6	Y	2
E	12	L	4	S	4	Z	1
F	2	M	2	T	6	Blank	2
G	3	N	6	U	4		

A. 0.112 B. 0.142
C. 0.174 D. 0.178

2. **MANUFACTURING** A manufacturer makes briefcases with numbered locks. The locks can be set so that any one of 1000 different codes will open the briefcase. If 4 friends have briefcases from this manufacturer, what is the probability (rounded to 3 decimal places) that at least 2 of the 4 briefcases have the same code?

A. 0.006 B. 0.059
C. 0.496 D. 0.903

3. **STUDENT SURVEY** A survey finds that 61% of students in the United States like school, that 95% of students who like school plan to attend college, and that 70% of students who do not like school plan to attend college. What is the probability (rounded to 3 decimal places) that a randomly selected high school student in the United States plans to attend college? Use a probabilty tree diagram to find the answer.

A. 0.58 B. 0.822
C. 0.832 D. 0.853

4. **READING SURVEY** According to a survey, 24% of U.S. adults say that reading is their favorite leisure activity. You randomly select 14 adults to survey. What is the probability (rounded to 3 decimal places) that at least 7 adults say reading is their favorite leisure activity?

A. 0.008 B. 0.031
C. 0.971 D. 0.992

5. **MARKET TEST** A computer software company is performing a market test on two versions, A and B, for its new software program. Out of 250 people who view the versions, 85 like version A, 135 like version B, and 45 people like both versions. What is the probability that a person likes one or both of these two versions?

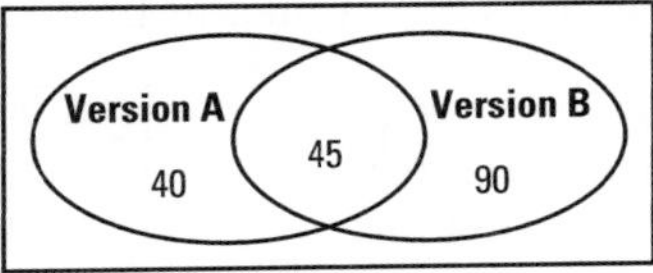

A. 0.66 B. 0.68
C. 0.7 D. 0.88

6. **OPEN-RESPONSE** The owner of a one-person lawn mowing business owns three old and unreliable riding mowers. As long as one of the mowers is working, the owner can stay productive. From past experience, the first mower is unusable 10% of the time, the second is unusable 8% of the time, and the third is unusable 18% of the time.

   a. If the usability of each lawnmower is independent of the usability of the others, what is the probability that all three mowers are unusable on a given day? Round your answer to the nearest hundredth of a percent.

   b. What is the probability that at least one of the mowers is usable on a given day? Round your answer to the nearest hundredth of a percent.

   c. *Explain* the relationship between the two answers.

CHAPTER SUMMARY

BIG IDEAS

For Your Notebook

Idea 1 Using Permutations and Combinations

PERMUTATIONS **Order is important**	Permutations of n distinct objects	$n!$	Number of ways to arrange 10 students at 10 desks: $10! = 3{,}628{,}800$
	Permutations of n distinct objects taken r at a time	${}_nP_r = \frac{n!}{(n-r)!}$	Number of ways to arrange 8 students at 10 desks: $\frac{10!}{2!} = 1{,}814{,}400$
	Permutations of n objects where one object is repeated s_1 times, another is repeated s_2 times, and so on	$\frac{n!}{s_1! \cdot s_2! \cdot \ldots \cdot s_k!}$	Number of distinguishable permutations of the letters in STUDENTS: $\frac{8!}{2! \cdot 2!} = 10{,}080$
COMBINATIONS **Order is not important**	Combinations of r objects taken from a group of n distinct objects	${}_nC_r = \frac{n!}{(n-r)! \cdot r!}$	Number of ways to choose 8 students from a set of 10 students: $\frac{10!}{2! \cdot 8!} = 45$

Idea 2 Finding Probabilities

The following table shows which formula to use when finding probabilities involving two events A and B.

Overlapping Events	Independent Events	Dependent Events
$P(A \text{ or } B) = P(A) + P(B) - P(A \text{ and } B)$	$P(A \text{ and } B) = P(A) \cdot P(B)$	$P(A \text{ and } B) = P(A) \cdot P(B\|A)$

Idea 3 Constructing Binomial Distributions

For a binomial experiment, the probability of exactly k successes in n trials is

$$P(k \text{ successes}) = {}_nC_k p^k (1-p)^{n-k}$$

where the probability of success on each trial is p.

A binomial distribution shows the probabilities of all possible outcomes in a binomial experiment. The distribution is skewed if $p \neq 0.5$.

Binomial Distribution for $n = 6, p = 0.6$

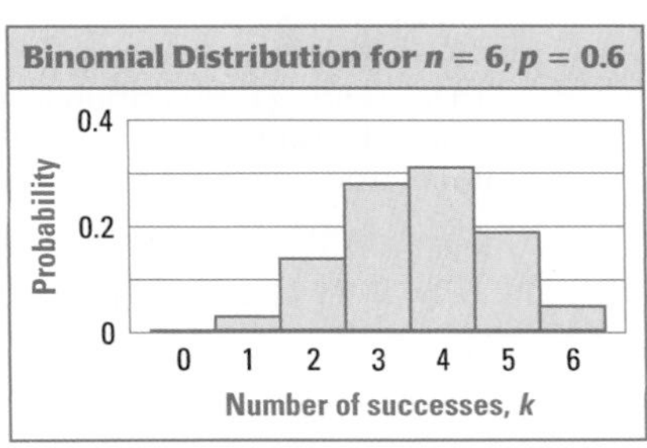

Additional Resources

The following resources are available to help review the materials in this chapter.

Chapter 10 Resource Book
- Chapter Review Games and Activities, p. 70
- Cumulative Practice, Chs. 1–10, pp. 72–73

Student Resources in Spanish

eWorkbook

@HomeTutor

Vocabulary Practice

Vocabulary practice is available at **classzone.com**

Extra Example 10.1

In a photography exhibit, 6 photographs will be displayed in a row along one wall. How many different ways can the photographs be displayed? How many different ways can 3 of the photographs receive first prize, second prize, and honorable mention? 720; 120

10 CHAPTER REVIEW

@HomeTutor
classzone.com
- Multi-Language Glossary
- Vocabulary practice

REVIEW KEY VOCABULARY

- permutation, *p. 684*
- factorial, *p. 684*
- combination, *p. 690*
- Pascal's triangle, *p. 692*
- binomial theorem, *p. 693*
- probability, *p. 698*
- theoretical probability, *p. 698*
- odds, *p. 699*
- experimental probability, *p. 700*
- geometric probability, *p. 701*
- compound event, *p. 707*
- overlapping events, *p. 707*
- disjoint or mutually exclusive events, *p. 707*
- independent events, *p. 717*
- dependent events, *p. 718*
- conditional probability, *p. 718*
- random variable, *p. 724*
- probability distribution, *p. 724*
- binomial distribution, *p. 725*
- binomial experiment, *p. 725*
- symmetric distribution, *p. 727*
- skewed distribution, *p. 727*

VOCABULARY EXERCISES

2. The probability of an event is the ratio of the number of ways the event can occur to the total number of outcomes, while the odds in favor of an event is the ratio of the number of ways the event can occur to the number of ways the event cannot occur.

1. Copy and complete: A(n) _?_ is a selection of r objects from a group of n objects where the order of the objects selected is not important. combination

2. **WRITING** *Explain* the difference between the probability of an event and the odds in favor of the event.

3. **WRITING** You randomly select 10 cards, one by one, from a standard deck of 52 cards without replacement. You record the number of diamonds you get. Is this a binomial experiment? *Explain.* No; there are more than two outcomes for each card selection.

4. **WRITING** Let event A be randomly selecting a green marble from a bag that contains red, green, and blue marbles. Let event B be randomly selecting a marble that is not red from the same bag. Are events A and B disjoint events? *Explain.* No; the events have 1 outcome in common, selecting a green marble.

REVIEW EXAMPLES AND EXERCISES

Use the review examples and exercises below to check your understanding of the concepts you have learned in each lesson of Chapter 10.

10.1 Apply the Counting Principle and Permutations *pp. 682–689*

EXAMPLE

An ice skating competition features 8 skaters. How many different ways can the skaters finish the competition? How many different ways can 3 of the skaters finish first, second, and third?

There are 8! ways the skaters can finish the competition.

$$8! = 8 \cdot 7 \cdot 6 \cdot 5 \cdot 4 \cdot 3 \cdot 2 \cdot 1 = 40{,}320$$

There are ${}_8P_3$ ways that 3 of the skaters can finish first, second, and third.

$${}_8P_3 = \frac{8!}{(8-3)!} = \frac{8!}{5!} = 336$$

@HomeTutor
classzone.com
Chapter Review Practice

AMPLES
nd 5
pp. 684–685
Exs. 5–9

EXERCISES

5. **PHOTOGRAPHY** You are placing 12 pictures on separate pages in an album. How many different ways can you order the 12 pictures in the album? How many different ways can 4 of the 12 pictures be placed on the first 4 pages? **479,001,600 ways; 11,880 ways**

Find the number of permutations.

6. ${}_9P_1$ 9
7. ${}_5P_5$ 120
8. ${}_6P_3$ 120
9. ${}_{10}P_2$ 90

10.2 Use Combinations and the Binomial Theorem

pp. 690–697

EXAMPLE

Use the binomial theorem to expand $(x + 5y)^4$.

$$(x+5y)^4 = {}_4C_0x^4(5y)^0 + {}_4C_1x^3(5y)^1 + {}_4C_2x^2(5y)^2 + {}_4C_3x^1(5y)^3 + {}_4C_4x^0(5y)^4$$
$$= (1)(x^4)(1) + (4)(x^3)(5y) + (6)(x^2)(25y^2) + (4)(x)(125y^3) + (1)(1)(625y^4)$$
$$= x^4 + 20x^3y + 150x^2y^2 + 500xy^3 + 625y^4$$

AMPLES
5, and 6
pp. 691–693
Exs. 10–14

EXERCISES

Use the binomial theorem to write the binomial expansion. 10–13. See margin.

10. $(t + 3)^6$
11. $(2a + b^2)^4$
12. $(w - 8v)^4$
13. $(r^3 - 4s)^5$

14. **ICE CREAM** An ice cream vendor sells 15 flavors of ice cream. You want to sample *at least* 4 of the flavors. How many different combinations of ice cream flavors can you sample? **32,192 combinations**

10.3 Define and Use Probability

pp. 698–704

EXAMPLE

You roll a standard six-sided die. Find the probability of rolling a number less than 3.

Two outcomes correspond to rolling a number less than 3: rolling a 1 or 2.

$$P(\text{rolling less than 3}) = \frac{\text{Number of ways to roll less than 3}}{\text{Number of ways to roll the die}} = \frac{2}{6} = \frac{1}{3}$$

AMPLES
and 4
pp. 698–700
Exs. 15–19

EXERCISES

You have an equally likely chance of choosing any integer from 1 through 30. Find the probability of the given event.

15. An even number is chosen. $\frac{1}{2}$
16. A multiple of 5 is chosen. $\frac{1}{5}$
17. A factor of 60 is chosen. $\frac{11}{30}$
18. A prime number is chosen. $\frac{1}{3}$
19. **COMMUTING** Out of 250 work days, a commuter arrived at work on time 47 times on Mondays, 43 times on Tuesdays, 48 times on Wednesdays, 39 times on Thursdays, and 40 times on Fridays. For a randomly selected work day, what is the probability that the commuter arrived at work on time? **0.868**

Extra Example 10.2

Use the binomial theorem to expand $(x + 3y)^4$. $x^4 + 12x^3y + 54x^2y^2 + 108xy^3 + 81y^4$

Extra Example 10.3

You are going to draw a card from a standard deck of 52 cards. Find the probability of drawing a 4. $\frac{1}{13}$

10. $t^6 + 18t^5 + 135t^4 + 540t^3 + 1215t^2 + 1458t + 729$

11. $16a^4 + 32a^3b^2 + 24a^2b^4 + 8ab^6 + b^8$

12. $4096v^4 - 2048v^3w + 384v^2w^2 - 32vw^3 + w^4$

13. $r^{15} - 20r^{12}s + 160r^9s^2 - 640r^6s^3 + 1280r^3s^4 - 1024s^5$

Extra Example 10.4

Let A and B be events such that $P(A) = \frac{4}{5}$, $P(B) = \frac{3}{10}$, and $P(A \text{ and } B) = \frac{3}{25}$. Find $P(A \text{ or } B)$. $\frac{49}{50}$

Extra Example 10.5

Find the probability of selecting a 9 and then another 9 from a standard deck of 52 cards if (a) you replace the first card before selecting the second, and (b) you do not replace the first card. $\frac{1}{169}$; $\frac{1}{221}$

Extra Example 10.6

An exam has 20 true-false questions. If you randomly fill in an answer page, what is the probability of getting exactly 15 answers correct? about 0.015

10 CHAPTER REVIEW

10.4 Probabilities of Disjoint and Overlapping Events *pp. 707–713*

EXAMPLE

Let A and B be events such that $P(A) = \frac{2}{3}$, $P(B) = \frac{1}{2}$, and $P(A \text{ and } B) = \frac{1}{3}$. Find $P(A \text{ or } B)$.

$$P(A \text{ or } B) = P(A) + P(B) - P(A \text{ and } B) = \frac{2}{3} + \frac{1}{2} - \frac{1}{3} = \frac{5}{6}$$

EXERCISES

EXAMPLES 2 and 4 on pp. 708–709 for Exs. 20–22

Let A and B be events such that $P(A) = 0.32$, $P(B) = 0.48$, and $P(A \text{ and } B) = 0.12$. Find the indicated probability.

20. $P(A \text{ or } B)$ 0.68 **21.** $P(\overline{A})$ 0.68 **22.** $P(\overline{B})$ 0.52

10.5 Probabilities of Independent and Dependent Events *pp. 717–723*

EXAMPLE

Find the probability of selecting a club and then another club from a standard deck of 52 cards if (a) you replace the first card before selecting the second, and (b) you do *not* replace the first card.

Let event A be "the first card is a club" and B be "the second card is a club."

a. $P(A \text{ and } B) = P(A) \cdot P(B) = \frac{13}{52} \cdot \frac{13}{52} = \frac{1}{16} = 0.0625$

b. $P(A \text{ and } B) = P(A) \cdot P(B|A) = \frac{13}{52} \cdot \frac{12}{51} = \frac{1}{17} \approx 0.0588$

EXERCISES

EXAMPLE 5 on p. 719 for Exs. 23–25

Find the probability of randomly selecting the given marbles from a bag of 5 red, 8 green, and 3 blue marbles if (a) you replace the first marble before drawing the second and (b) you do *not* replace the first marble.

23. red, then green a. $\frac{5}{32}$ b. $\frac{1}{6}$ **24.** blue, then red a. $\frac{15}{256}$ b. $\frac{1}{16}$ **25.** green, then green a. $\frac{1}{4}$ b. $\frac{7}{30}$

10.6 Construct and Interpret Binomial Distributions *pp. 724–730*

EXAMPLE

Find the probability of tossing a coin 12 times and getting exactly 4 heads.

$$P(k = 4) = {}_nC_k p^k(1 - p)^{n-k} = {}_{12}C_4(0.5)^4(1 - 0.5)^8 = 495(0.5)^4(0.5)^8 \approx 0.121$$

EXERCISES

EXAMPLE 3 on p. 726 for Exs. 26–29

Find the probability of tossing a coin 8 times and getting the given number of heads.

26. 6 about 0.109 **27.** 4 about 0.273 **28.** 7 about 0.031 **29.** 0 about 0.0039

10 CHAPTER TEST

Find the number of permutations or combinations.

1. ${}_5P_2$ 20
2. ${}_8P_3$ 336
3. ${}_{12}P_7$ 3,991,680
4. ${}_{17}P_{10}$ 70,572,902,400
5. ${}_4C_3$ 4
6. ${}_7C_7$ 1
7. ${}_{18}C_4$ 3060
8. ${}_9C_5$ 126

Use the binomial theorem to write the binomial expansion. 9–12. See margin.

9. $(x + 5)^3$
10. $(3a - 3)^5$
11. $(s + t^2)^4$
12. $(c^3 - 2d^2)^6$

A card is randomly drawn from a standard deck of 52 cards. Find the probability of drawing the given card.

13. A queen $\frac{1}{13}$
14. A red king $\frac{1}{26}$
15. A diamond $\frac{1}{4}$
16. Not a club $\frac{3}{4}$

Find the indicated probability.

17. $P(A) = 0.3$
$P(B) = 0.6$
$P(A \text{ or } B) = \underline{\ ?\ }$
$P(A \text{ and } B) = 0.1$ 0.8
18. $P(A) = 35\%$
$P(B) = \underline{\ ?\ }$
$P(A \text{ or } B) = 80\%$
$P(A \text{ and } B) = 20\%$ 65%
19. $P(A) = \underline{\ ?\ }$
$P(\overline{A}) = \frac{2}{5}$ $\frac{3}{5}$
20. A and B are independent.
$P(A) = 0.15$
$P(B) = 0.6$
$P(A \text{ and } B) = \underline{\ ?\ }$ 0.09
21. A and B are dependent.
$P(A) = 60\%$
$P(B|A) = \underline{\ ?\ }$
$P(A \text{ and } B) = 25\%$ about 41.7%
22. A and B are dependent.
$P(A) = \underline{\ ?\ }$
$P(B|A) = 0.4$
$P(A \text{ and } B) = 0.36$ 0.9

Calculate the probability of k successes for a binomial experiment consisting of n trials with probability p of success on each trial.

23. $k = 4, n = 11, p = 0.4$ about 0.236
24. $k \leq 2, n = 5, p = 0.7$ about 0.163
25. $k \geq 8, n = 9, p = 0.9$ about 0.775
26. **TRUE-OR-FALSE QUIZ** Calculate the probability of randomly guessing at least 8 correct answers on a 10 question true-or-false quiz. about 0.055
27. **GOVERNMENT** There are 15 members on a city council. On a recent agenda item, 8 of the council members voted in favor of a budget increase for city park improvements. How many combinations of council members could have voted in favor of the budget increase? 6435 combinations
28. **PARACHUTING** A parachuter is attempting to land within a square in the middle of a circular landing area. The square has sides 25 feet long, and the diameter of the landing area is 40 feet. If the parachuter is equally likely to first touch the ground at any point within the landing area, what is the probability that the parachuter first touches the ground within the square? about 0.497
29. **EDUCATION** A high school has an enrollment of 1800 students. There are 1050 females enrolled in the school. The high school has 1200 students who are involved in an after-school activity, 725 of whom are female. What is the probability that a randomly selected student at the school is a female who is not involved in an after-school activity? about 0.18
30. **FISHING** A study found that 9% of people cite fishing as their favorite leisure-time activity. Suppose you randomly survey 8 people about their leisure-time activities. What is the probability that at least 2 of the people cite fishing as their favorite? about 0.158

Additional Resources

Assessment Book

- Chapter Test, Levels A, B, C, pp. 142–147
- Standardized Chapter Test, pp. 148–149
- SAT/ACT Chapter Test, pp. 150–151
- Alternative Assessment, pp. 152–153

Test Generator CD-ROM

Chapter Test

Easily-readable reduced copies (with answers) of Chapter Test B, the Standardized Chapter Test, and the Alternative Assessment from the Assessment Book can be found on pp. 680E–680F.

9. $x^3 + 15x^2 + 75x + 125$
10. $243a^5 - 1215a^4 + 2430a^3 - 2430a^2 + 1215a - 243$
11. $s^4 + 4s^3t^2 + 6s^2t^4 + 4st^6 + t^8$
12. $c^{18} - 12c^{15}d^2 + 60c^{12}d^4 - 160c^9d^6 + 240c^6d^8 - 192c^3d^{10} + 64d^{12}$

MULTIPLE-CHOICE QUESTIONS

Some of the information you need to solve a multiple-choice question may appear in a table, a diagram, or a graph.

PROBLEM 1

A dart is thrown at the square target shown. Assume the dart is equally likely to hit any point inside the target. What is the approximate probability that the dart lands in the shaded region outside of the diamond but inside the circle?

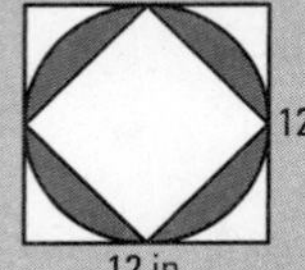

A. 0.285 B. 0.411

C. 0.500 D. 0.785

Plan

INTERPRET THE DIAGRAM The probability of a dart landing in the shaded region is equivalent to the fraction of the area represented by the shaded re

Solution

STEP 1 Find the areas of the different shapes in the diagram.

Area of the square: Each side has a length of 12 inches, so the area is:

$$A_S = 12 \text{ in.} \cdot 12 \text{ in.} = 144 \text{ in.}^2$$

Area of the circle: The diameter of the circle is 12 inches, so the radius half of that, or 6 inches. The area of the circle is:

$$A_C = \pi r^2 = \pi (6 \text{ in.})^2 = 36\pi \text{ in.}^2$$

Area of the diamond: The diamond can be broken horizontally into tw triangles that are each 12 inches wide and 6 inches high. The area is:

$$A_D = 2A_T = 2(0.5)bh = 1 \cdot 12 \text{ in.} \cdot 6 \text{ in.} = 72 \text{ in.}^2$$

STEP 2 Find the ratio.

Compute the probability as a ratio of the shaded area to the total area.

$$\text{Probability} = \frac{A_C - A_D}{A_S} = \frac{36\pi - 72}{144} \approx 0.285$$

Check

Since the shaded area of the diagram is clearly less than one-half of the entire target, 0.285 is a reasonable value. Moreover, answer choices C and D, which ar equal to or greater than 0.5, can clearly be eliminated.

▶ The correct answer is A.

Kentucky Test Preparation

1. The number of arrangements, without considering repetition, is 7! = 5040. The number of *distinct* arrangements must be less.

2. The chance of scoring 60% (12 out 20) or better must be less than one-half.

PROBLEM 2

What is the approximate probability that tossing a fair coin 20 times results in exactly 5 heads?

A. 0 B. 0.015

C. 0.25 D. 0.5

Plan

Each flip of a coin is an event. "Success" is flipping a head. Since the 20 trials are independent and the probability of a success is always the same value (0.5), the number of heads has a binomial distribution.

Solution

For this problem, the probability of success is $p = 0.5$, and the probability of failure is $1 - p = 0.5$. The number of trials is $n = 20$, and the targeted number of successes is $k = 5$.

To find the probability, apply the binomial formula:

$$P(k \text{ successes}) = {}_nC_k p^k (1 - p)^{n-k}$$

$$P(5 \text{ successes}) = {}_{20}C_5 0.5^5 (0.5)^{15}$$

$$= \frac{20 \cdot 19 \cdot 18 \cdot 17 \cdot 16}{5!} 0.5^{20}$$

$$\approx 0.015$$

Check

Since it is unreasonable to expect *exactly* 5 heads with great frequency, answer choices C and D are unreasonably high and can be eliminated. On the other hand, we would expect exactly 5 heads in 20 flips *occasionally*, so the probability of 0.015 is more reasonable than the probability of 0 in answer choice A.

▶ The correct answer is B.

PRACTICE

Explain **why you can eliminate the highlighted answer choice.**

1. What is the number of distinct arrangements of the letters in the word ARRANGE?

   A. 42 B. 128 C. 1260 D.✗ 5040

2. A test includes 20 True/False questions. If you guess randomly, what is the approximate probability that you will get 12 or more of them correct and pass the test?

   A. 0.13 B. 0.25 C.✗ 0.60 D. 0.86

TEST PREPARATION

Kentucky Test Practice

1. B
2. C
3. A
4. D
5. B
6. B
7. A
8. C

MULTIPLE-CHOICE

1. A jar contains 4 yellow marbles, 3 red marbles, and 2 green marbles. To the nearest percent, what is the probability that a randomly selected marble will be green?

A. 11% B. 22%

C. 29% D. 50%

2. How many different four-digit numbers can be made from the digits 1, 3, 4, and 7 if the digits cannot be repeated?

A. 4 B. 16

C. 24 D. 256

3. Find the number of distinguishable permutations of the letters in the word WEEKEND.

A. 840

B. 1680

C. 5040

D. 30,240

4. The table shows the numbers of Democratic and Republican Presidents born in different regions of the United States. The table includes the Presidents in office from 1853 to 2005.

	Democrat	Republican
Midwest	2	9
Northeast	6	5
South	4	3
West	0	1

A President between 1853 and 2005 is chosen at random. Which event is the most probable?

A. The President was born in the South.

B. The President was a Republican, given that he was born in the South.

C. The President was not only a Democrat but also from the West.

D. The President was born in the Midwest.

5. Find $P(A \text{ and } B)$ given that $P(A) = 0.52$, $P(B) = 0.24$, and $P(A \text{ or } B) = 0.61$. Approximate your answer to two decimal places.

A. 0.13

B. 0.15

C. 0.49

D. 0.64

6. Larry is giving two of his friends a ride home from football practice. After leaving practice, he will drop off Teshawn first, then drop off Mark, and finally head home. Between each destination, there are several different routes. The number of routes for each part of the drive is represented by a variable, as shown below.

Part of the Drive Home	Number of Possible Routes
Practice to Teshawn's house	x
Teshawn's house to Mark's house	y
Mark's house to Larry's house	z

Which expression represents the total number of possible routes that Larry can drive?

A. $x + y + z$

B. xyz

C. $2^x2^y2^z$

D. $(x + y + z)^2$

7. Find the value of the expression ${}_5C_2 - {}_5C_3$.

A. 0

B. 5

C. 30

D. 40

8. What is the coefficient of x^3 in the expansion of $(4x - 1)^9$?

A. 64 B. 84

C. 5376 D. 262,144

TEST PREPARATION

MULTIPLE-CHOICE

9. Two dice are rolled in a trivia board game. You roll a 6-sided die to find the number of spaces to advance. You roll a 10-sided die to find which type of question you must answer. How many possible outcomes are there when rolling these two dice?

A. 16 B. 60
C. 210 D. 5040

10. A card is randomly selected from a standard deck of 52 cards. The probability of drawing which type of card is 25%?

A. A spade B. The 3 of hearts
C. A queen D. A red card

11. Which binomial expansion includes the term $40x^2$?

A. $(x + 1)^5$ B. $(x + 5)^5$
C. $(2x + 1)^5$ D. $(2x + 5)^5$

12. A satellite has two independent power systems. The space agency expects that within a 10-year period, the probability that the main source will fail is 0.1, and probability that the backup source will fail is 0.2. What is the probability that the satellite will still have at least one functional power source after 10 years?

A. 0.02 B. 0.7
C. 0.72 D. 0.98

13. In a previous survey of adults who follow more than one sport, 30% listed football as their favorite sport. In a particular group of 15 adults who each follow more than one sport, what is the probability rounded to the nearest thousandth that fewer than 4 of them will say that football is their favorite sport?

A. 0.219 B. 0.297
C. 0.516 D. 0.781

OPEN-RESPONSE

14. For a checking account, you must choose a personal identification number (PIN). The PIN must be between 6 and 8 characters and may contain letters or digits.

a. How many different PINs are possible, assuming the digits and letters can be repeated?

b. *Explain* how your answer would change if no digits can be included.

15. A survey asked adults who use the Internet how frequently they send or receive e-mail. The results of the survey are shown in the bar graph at the right.

a. Find the experimental probability that a randomly selected adult Internet user uses the Internet to send or receive e-mail often or very often.

b. If the survey had polled computer programmers instead of all adults, describe how you think the results of the survey would be different.

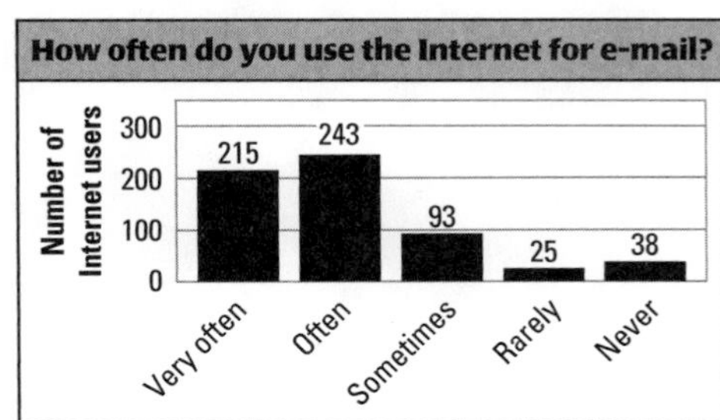

TEST PREPARATION

9. B
10. A
11. C
12. D
13. B
14. a. $36^6 + 36^7 + 36^8 =$ 2,901,650,853,888
b. $26^6 + 26^7 + 26^8 =$ 217,167,790,528
15. a. About 0.75.
b. *Sample answer:* The number of *very often* and *often* responders would be much higher; the number of *rarely* and *never* responders would be much smaller because computer programmers use computers on a regular basis whereas not all adults do.

11 Pacing and Assignment Guide

REGULAR SCHEDULE

Pre-AP For pacing and assignments for a Pre-AP course, see the *Algebra 2 Toolkit*.

Lesson	Les. Day	BASIC	AVERAGE	ADVANCED
11.1 MA-HS-4.2.1	Day 1	SRH p. 1005 Exs. 5–9; pp. 747–749 Exs. 1–19, 26–29, 32–34	pp. 747–749 Exs. 1–14, 19–23, 26–30, 33	pp. 747–749 Exs. 1, 2, 5–8, 14–31*, 33
11.2 MA-HS-4.2.1	Day 1	pp. 753–755 Exs. 1–16, 18–22, 26	pp. 753–755 Exs. 1–16, 18–24, 27	pp. 753–755 Exs. 1–8, 12–25*, 27
11.3 MA-HS-4.2.2	Day 1	pp. 760–762 Exs. 1–5, 9–22, 31–34, 37	pp. 760–762 Exs. 1, 2, 4–6, 9–18, 22–24, 28, 29, 31–35, 38	pp. 760–762 Exs. 1, 2, 7, 8, 11–18, 24–36*, 37
11.4 MA-HS-4.3.1	Day 1	SRH p. 976 Exs. 21–25; pp. 769–771 Exs. 1–5, 28, 29, 33–34	pp. 769–771 Exs. 1–5, 28, 29, 33–34	pp. 769–771 Exs. 1–5, 28, 29, 33–34
	Day 2	pp. 769–771 Exs. 6–24, 27, 30	pp. 769–771 Exs. 8–14, 17–25, 27, 30, 31	pp. 769–771 Exs. 9–14, 17–27*, 30–32*
11.5 MA-HS-4.2.3	Day 1	pp. 778–780 Exs. 1–6, 10–13, 16–17	pp. 778–780 Exs. 1–8, 10–14, 16	pp. 778–780 Exs. 1–15*
Review	Day 1	pp. 784–786 Exs. 1–23	pp. 784–786 Exs. 1–23	pp. 784–786 Exs. 1–23
Assess	Day 1	Chapter 11 Test	Chapter 11 Test	Chapter 11 Test

Yearly Pacing Chapter 11 Total – 8 days Chapters 1–11 Total – 130 days Remaining – 30 days

*Challenge Exercises EP = Extra Practice SRH = Skills Review Handbook

BLOCK SCHEDULE

DAY 1	DAY 2	DAY 3	DAY 4
11.1	**11.3**	**11.4 (CONT.)**	**REVIEW**
pp. 747–749 Exs. 1–14, 19–23, 26–30, 33	pp. 760–762 Exs. 1, 2, 4–6, 9–18, 22–24, 28, 29, 31–35, 38	pp. 769–771 Exs. 8–14, 17–25, 27, 30, 31	pp. 784–786 Exs. 1–23
11.2	**11.4**	**11.5**	**ASSESS**
pp. 753–755 Exs. 1–16, 18–24, 27	pp. 769–771 Exs. 1–5, 28, 29, 33–34	pp. 778–780 Exs. 1–8, 10–14, 16	Chapter 11 Test

Yearly Pacing Chapter 11 Total – 4 days Chapters 1–11 Total – 65 days Remaining – 15 days

Chapter Resource Guide 11

RESOURCE MANAGER

Chapter Resource Book					
CHAPTER SUPPORT					
Parents as Partners (Chapter Overview with home involvement exercises and activity)					p. 1
LESSON SUPPORT	**11.1**	**11.2**	**11.3**	**11.4**	**11.5**
Standards	**MA-HS-4.2.1**	**MA-HS-4.2.1**	MA-HS-4.2.2	**MA-HS-4.3.1**	**MA-HS-4.2.3**
Teaching Guide/Lesson Plan	p. 3	p. 14	p. 26	p. 38	p. 50
Activity Masters		p. 16	p. 28		
Technology Activities & Keystrokes	p. 5		p. 29	p. 40	p. 52
Activity Support Masters					
Practice (3 levels)	p. 6	p. 17	p. 30	p. 42	p. 56
Study Guide	p. 9	p. 20	p. 33	p. 45	p. 59
Catch-Up for Absent Students	p. 11	p. 22	p. 35	p. 47	p. 61
Problem Solving/Application	p. 12	p. 23	p. 36	p. 48	p. 62
Challenge Practice	p. 13	p. 25	p. 37	p. 49	p. 63
REVIEW					
Chapter Review Games and Activities		p. 64	Cumulative Practice		p. 66
Project with Rubric		p. 65	Resource Book Answers		A1

Transparencies	11.1	11.2	11.3	11.4	11.5
Warm-Up/Daily Homework Quiz	✔	✔	✔	✔	✔
Notetaking Guide	✔	✔	✔	✔	✔
Teacher Support					
Answer Transparencies	✔	✔	✔	✔	✔

ASSESSMENT BOOK

Quizzes	p. 154	SAT/ACT Chapter Test	p. 164
Chapter Tests (3 levels)	p. 156	Alternative Assessment with Rubric	p. 166
Standardized Chapter Test	p. 162		

TECHNOLOGY

- Easy Planner
- Test and Practice Generator
- Power Presentations
- @HomeTutor
- Activity Generator
- Animated Algebra
- Classzone.com
- eEdition Plus Online
- eWorkbook Plus Online
- ML Assessment System

ADDITIONAL RESOURCES

KY **Kentucky**

- Additional Lesson C Parameters and Statistics
- Additional Lesson D Evaluating Reports
- Additional Lesson E Misleading Data Displays
- Additional Lesson H Organizing and Displaying Data
- Additional Lesson K Causation vs. Correlation
- Worked-Out Solution Key
- Notetaking Guide
- Practice Workbook
- Benchmark Tests
- Remediation Workbook
- Spanish Study Guide
- Spanish Assessment Book
- Spanish Resources in Spanish
- Multi-Language Visual Glossary

11 Lesson Practice Level B

LESSON 11.1 Practice B
For use with pages 744–749

Find the mean, median, and mode of the data set.

1. 6, 22, 4, 15, 10, 8, 8, 7, 14, 20 11.4; 9; 8
2. 10, 15, 12, 20, 25, 22, 28, 24, 22, 26
3. 53, 52, 48, 44, 60, 48, 44, 57, 44 50; 48; 44
4. 100, 150, 100, 130, 125, 135, 140, 145, 100

2. 20.4; 22; 22 4. 125; 130; 100

Find the range and standard deviation of the data set.

5. 47, 18, 65, 28, 43, 18 47; 18.56
6. 70, 27, 41, 30, 10, 47, 11 60; 19.6
7. 29.4, 22.9, 15.7, 26.9, 24.0, 27.5, 11.4 18; 6.1
8. 35.8, 29.4, 32.1, 24.9, 30.5, 20.3 15.5; 5.49

Identify the outlier in the data set. Then find the mean, median, mode, range, and standard deviation of the data set when the outlier is included and when it is not.

9. 4, 6, 10, 2, 90, 3, 10, 5, 1
   90; 5.1, 4.5, 10, 9, 3.2; 14.6, 5, 10, 89, 26.8
10. 52, 61, 55, 1, 59, 68, 69, 55
   1; 59.9, 59, 55, 17, 6.1; 52.5, 57, 55, 68, 20.3

In Exercises 11–14, find the mean, median, mode, range, and standard deviation of the data set.

11. **Cordless Phones** The data set below gives the prices (in dollars) of cordless phones at an electronics store.

    35, 50, 60, 60, 75, 65, 80 60.7, 60, 60, 45, 14.0

12. **Baseball** The data set below gives the numbers of homeruns for the 10 batters who hit the most homeruns during the 2005 Major League Baseball regular season.

    51, 48, 47, 46, 45, 43, 41, 40, 40, 39 44, 44, 40, 12, 3.8

13. **Department of Motor Vehicles** The data set below gives the waiting times (in minutes) of several people at a department of motor vehicles service center.

    11, 7, 14, 2, 8, 13, 3, 6, 10, 3, 8, 4, 8, 4, 7 7.2, 7, 8, 12, 3.5

14. **Cereal** The data set below gives the calories in a 1-ounce serving of several breakfast cereals.

    135, 115, 120, 110, 110, 100, 105, 110, 125 114.4, 110, 110, 35, 10.1

In Exercises 15–17, use the following information.

High Temperatures The data set below gives a city's high temperatures (in degrees Fahrenheit) during a 15-day period.

36, 37, 36, 34, 49, 33, 30, 30, 32, 31, 31, 32, 32, 33, 35

15. Identify the outlier in the data set. 49
16. Find the mean, median, mode, range, and standard deviation of the data set when the outlier is included and when it is not. 33, 32.5, 32, 7, 2.2; 34.1, 33, 32, 19, 4.5
17. *Describe* the outlier's effect on the measures of central tendency and dispersion.
    The mean is affected the most by the additional temperature. The mode is affected the least. The standard deviation and the range increase with the addition of an outlier.

LESSON 11.1

LESSON 11.2 Practice B
For use with pages 751–755

Find the mean, median, mode, range, and standard deviation of the given data set and of the data set obtained by adding the given constant to each data value. See below.

1. 25, 13, 19, 20, 19, 16, 15; constant: 5
2. 40, 48, 44, 40, 35, 47, 36; constant: 16
3. 89, 87, 76, 66, 93, 66, 85, 67; constant: 19
4. 177, 203, 185, 202, 179, 185; constant: 135
5. 55, 59, 52, 65, 56, 59, 58; constant: −26
6. 318, 306, 306, 314, 310, 319; constant: −52

Find the mean, median, mode, range, and standard deviation of the given data set and of the data set obtained by multiplying each data value by the given constant.

7. 19, 25, 28, 20, 27, 8, 25; constant: 2 21.7, 25, 25, 20, 6.4; 43.4, 50, 50, 40, 12.8
8. 64, 69, 68, 71, 73, 64, 73; constant: 5 68.9, 69, 73, 9, 3.5; 344.3, 345, 365, 45, 17.6
9. 27, 24, 26, 30, 34, 30, 18; constant: 1.1 27, 27, 30, 16, 4.8; 29.7, 29.7, 33, 17.6, 5.2
10. 100, 101, 101, 105, 99, 104, 102; constant: 2.2 101.7, 101, 101, 6, 2.0; 223.8, 222.2, 222.2, 13.2, 4.4
11. 150, 156, 163, 156, 165, 155; constant: 0.4 157.5, 156, 156, 15, 5.1; 63, 62.4, 62.4, 6, 2.0
12. 287, 297, 301, 287, 283, 298; constant: 0.7 292.2, 292, 287, 18, 6.7; 204.5, 204.4, 200.9, 12.6, 4.7

In Exercises 13 and 14, use the following information.

Test Scores The data set below gives the test scores of several students.

92, 97, 95, 93, 84, 85, 92, 87, 100, 94

13. Find the mean, median, mode, range, and standard deviation of the test scores. 91.9, 92.5, 92, 16, 4.9
14. Each student receives 10 points for correctly answering a bonus question. Find the mean, median, mode, range, and standard deviation of the test scores including the bonus points. 101.9, 102.5, 102, 16, 4.9

In Exercises 15 and 16, use the following information.

Auto Batteries The data set below gives the prices (in dollars) of auto batteries at an auto parts store.

80, 60, 65, 90, 45, 55, 70, 55, 65, 90, 65

15. Find the mean, median, mode, range, and standard deviation of the prices. 67.3, 65, 65, 45, 13.7
16. The store has a sale in which all auto batteries are 20% off. Find the mean, median, mode, range, and standard deviation of the sale prices. 53.8, 52, 52, 36, 11.0

1. 18.1, 19, 19, 12, 3.6; 23.1, 24, 24, 12, 3.6
2. 41.4, 40, 40, 13, 4.7; 57.4, 56, 56, 13, 4.7
3. 78.6, 80.5, 66, 27, 10.5; 97.6, 99.5, 85, 27, 10.5
4. 188.5, 185, 185, 26, 10.3; 323.5, 320, 320, 26, 10.3
5. 57.7, 58, 59, 13, 3.8; 31.7, 32, 33, 13, 3.8
6. 312.2, 312, 306, 13, 5.2; 260.2, 260, 254, 13, 5.2

LESSON 11.2

LESSON 11.3 Practice B
For use with pages 757–762

A normal distribution has mean $\bar{x}$ and standard deviation σ. Find the indicated probability for a randomly selected *x*-value from the distribution.

1. $P(x \geq \bar{x} + \sigma)$ 0.16
2. $P(x \leq \bar{x} + 2\sigma)$ 0.975
3. $P(x \geq \bar{x} - 3\sigma)$ 0.9985

Give the percent of the area under the normal curve represented by the shaded region.

4. 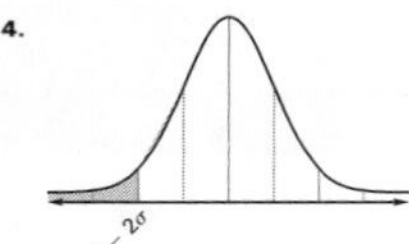

   2.5%

5. $\bar{x} - 3\sigma$ $\bar{x} + 3\sigma$ 0.3%

A normal distribution has a mean of 27 and a standard deviation of 5. Find the probability that a randomly selected *x*-value from the distribution is in the given interval.

6. Between 22 and 32 0.68
7. Between 12 and 27 0.4985
8. Between 17 and 37 0.95
9. At least 22 0.84
10. At least 37 0.025
11. At most 32 0.84

A normal distribution has a mean of 75 and a standard deviation of 10. Use the standard normal table on page 759 of your textbook to find the indicated probability for a randomly selected *x*-value from the distribution.

12. $P(x \leq 70)$ 0.3085
13. $P(x \leq 52)$ 0.0107
14. $P(x \leq 78)$ 0.6179
15. $P(x \leq 96)$ 0.9821
16. $P(x \leq 44)$ 0.0010
17. $P(x \leq 106)$ 0.9990

18. **Biology** The weights of adult male rhesus monkeys are normally distributed with a mean of 17 pounds and a standard deviation of 3 pounds. What is the probability that a randomly selected adult male rhesus monkey has a weight less than 14 pounds? 0.16

In Exercises 19 and 20, use the following information.

Apples The annual per capita consumption of apples in the United States is normally distributed with a mean of 16 pounds and a standard deviation of 4 pounds.

19. Find the *z*-score for an annual per capita consumption of 22 pounds. 1.5
20. What is the probability that a randomly selected person in the United States has an annual per capita consumption of apples less than 22 pounds? 0.9332

LESSON 11.3

LESSON 11.4

Practice B

For use with pages 766–771

1. random sample; unbiased; the sample is representative of the population (car owners)

Identify the type of sample described. Then tell if the sample is biased. *Explain* your reasoning.

1. A consumer advocacy group wants to know if car owners believe their car is reliable. The group randomly selects 1020 car owners and mails out a survey to each one. See above.
2. A grocery store wants to know which day of the week consumers prefer to do their grocery shopping. Everyone who shops at the store on Friday is asked which day of the week they prefer to do their grocery shopping. See below.
3. A survey of students' favorite school subjects is being conducted. Every other student in the math club is asked "Which school subject is your favorite? See below.

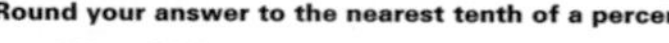

Find the margin of error for a survey that has the given sample size. Round your answer to the nearest tenth of a percent.

4. 200 $\pm 7.1\%$ 5. 350 $\pm 5.3\%$ 6. 1100 $\pm 3.0\%$ 7. 2600 $\pm 2.0\%$

8. 5200 $\pm 1.4\%$ 9. 495 $\pm 4.5\%$ 10. 280 $\pm 6.0\%$ 11. 9000 $\pm 1.1\%$

Find the sample size required to achieve the given margin of error. Round your answer to the nearest whole number.

12. $\pm 2\%$ 2500 13. $\pm 4\%$ 625 14. $\pm 9.5\%$ 111 15. $\pm 2.7\%$ 1372

16. $\pm 4.5\%$ 494 17. $\pm 0.5\%$ 40,000 18. $\pm 3.6\%$ 772 19. $\pm 7.5\%$ 178

In Exercises 20 and 21, use the following information.

Technology Survey In a survey of 504 people in the United States, about 11% said that the influx of new technologies such as computers has left them feeling overwhelmed.

20. What is the margin of error for the survey? Round your answer to the nearest tenth of a percent. 4.5%
21. Give an interval that is likely to contain the exact percent of all people in the United States who feel overwhelmed by the influx of new technologies. between 6.5% and 15.5%

In Exercises 22–25, use the following information.

TV in the Bedroom A survey reported that 510 kids ages 8 to 18, or 68% of those surveyed, have a TV in their bedroom.

22. How many kids ages 8 to 18 were surveyed? 750
23. What is the margin of error for the survey? Round your answer to the nearest tenth of a percent. 3.7%
24. Give an interval that is likely to contain the exact percent of all kids ages 8 to 18 who have a TV in their bedroom. between 64.3% and 71.7%
25. About how many kids ages 8 to 18 should be surveyed to have a margin of error of 2.5%? 1600

2. convenience sample; biased; interviewing consumers while they are shopping on a Friday probably prefer to shop on that day
3. systematic; biased; students in the math club are more likely to prefer math than other students

LESSON 11.5

Practice B

For use with pages 775–780

Determine which type of function best models the data points. Explain.

1. 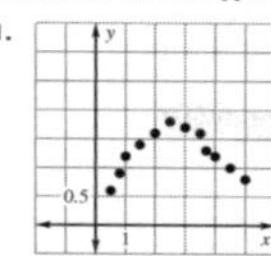

quadratic

2. 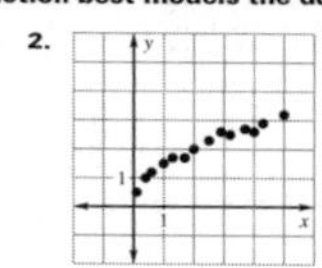

power

3. 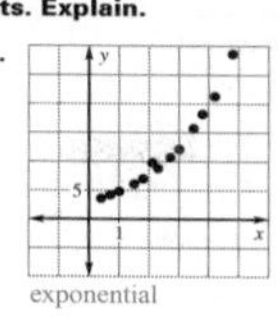

exponential

Determine the equation that best models the data.

4. C

x	2	6	9	15	17	23	27
y	5	2	1	2	4	9	15

A. $y = 1.54x^{0.37}$ B. $y = 0.4x - 0.28$

C. $y = 0.05x^2 - 1.18x + 7.14$ D. $y = 1.44(1.07)^x$

5. A

x	2	5	7	10	13	15	19
y	24	14	10	6	4	3	1

A. $y = 35.3(0.84)^x$ B. $y = -1.24x + 21.48$

C. $y = 86.46x^{-1.27}$ D. $y = 0.095x^2 - 3.22x + 28.91$

6. B

x	3	6	9	12	15	18	21	24
y	26	37	49	56	67	74	83	96

A. $y = 25.86(1.06)^x$ B. $y = 3.2x + 17.82$

C. $y = 12.63x^{0.62}$ D. $y = 0.01x^3 - 0.2x^2 + 5.6x + 10.4$

7. **Black Bears** The table shows the weight w (in kilograms) and the chest-girth circumference c (in centimeters) for 9 male black bears in West Virginia. Use a regression feature of a graphing calculator to find a function that models the data. What is the weight of a male black bear that has a chest-girth circumference of 119 centimeters? $y = 0.4x + 58.4$; 106 kg

w	82	90	101	112	125	136	144	152	160
c	91	94	99	103	108	112	116	119	122

CHAPTER 11

Quiz 1

For use after Lessons 11.1–11.2

Find the mean, median, mode, range, and standard deviation of the data set.

1. 3, 2, 6, 5, 2, 2, 1, 3
2. 6, 3, 5, 7, 4, 8, 4, 6
3. 9, 6, 6, 10, 12, 16, 8, 12, 17
4. 9, 11, 6, 10, 19, 6, 5, 7, 8
5. 17, 18, 22, 16, 18, 14, 13, 23, 20
6. 55, 44, 47, 46, 55, 54, 42, 43
7. **Television Sets** The data set below gives the prices of 6 different televisions at an electronics store. Find the mean, median, mode, range, and standard deviation of the prices.

   \$80, \$100, \$200, \$400, \$400, \$600

Answers

1. $\bar{x} = 3$; median $= 2.5$; mode $= 2$; range $= 5$; $\sigma = 1.58$
2. $\bar{x} = 5.375$; median $= 5.5$; mode $= 4, 6$; range $= 5$; $\sigma = 1.58$
3. $\bar{x} = 10.67$; median $= 10$; mode $= 6, 12$; range $= 11$; $\sigma = 3.74$
4. $\bar{x} = 9$; median $= 8$; mode $= 6$; range $= 14$; $\sigma = 4$
5. $\bar{x} = 17.89$; median $= 18$; mode $= 18$; range $= 10$; $\sigma = 3.18$
6. $\bar{x} = 48.25$; median $= 46.5$; mode $= 55$; range $= 13$; $\sigma = 5.19$
7. $\bar{x} = \$296.67$; median $= \$300$; mode $= \$400$; range $= \$520$; $\sigma = \$186.34$

CHAPTER 11

Quiz 2

For use after Lessons 11.3–11.5

A normal distribution has a mean of 37 and a standard deviation of 4. Find the probability that a randomly selected *x*-value is in the given interval.

1. Between 29 and 49
2. At least 33
3. At most 25

Find the smallest sample size required to achieve the given margin of error. Round your answer to the nearest whole number.

4. 5%
5. 2%
6. 0.9%
7. 1.4%
8. **Baking** You are baking a ham in the oven. The table shows the temperature *y* of the ham (in degrees Fahrenheit) after *x* minutes in the oven. Use a graphing calculator to find an exponential regression model for the data.

x	0	30	60	90	120	150
y	32°	40°	55°	80°	110°	140°

Answers

1. 97.35%
2. 84%
3. 0.15%
4. 400
5. 2500
6. 12,346
7. 5,102
8. $y = 30.79(1.01)^x$

CHAPTER 11

Chapter Test B

For use after Chapter 11

Find the mean, median, and mode of the data set.

1. The number of radio stations per state: 161, 104, 371, 508, 214, 861, 263, 86
2. Home electricity consumption, in kilowatt-hours, over a 12-month period: 843.3, 862.9, 811.1, 753.6, 726.3, 748.8, 882.9, 897.4, 812.3, 791.1, 757.7, 816.3
3. Identify the outlier in the data set. Then find the mean, median, mode, range, and standard deviation of the data set when the outlier is included and when it is not.

   32, 36, 29, 41, 27, 62, 33, 36, 43
4. Find the mean, median, mode, range, and standard deviation of the given data set and of the data set obtained by adding the given constant to each data value.

   56, 51, 48, 62, 57, 64, 51; constant: 12
5. **Restaurant Wages** The data set below gives the wages, in dollars, of eight restaurant workers for one day. On a holiday, each server earns a 20% bonus to their wage. Find the mean, median, mode, range, and standard deviation of their wages and their wages with the bonus.

   36.04, 33.23, 42.14, 63.11, 29.43, 47.66, 55.81, 82.14

A normal distribution has a mean of 81 and a standard deviation of 9. Find the probability that a randomly selected *x*-value from the distribution is in the given interval.

6. Between 90 and 100
7. At least 70
8. **Ceramic Furnace** A study found that the temperature of a ceramic furnace is normally distributed with mean temperature of 1425 degrees Fahrenheit and standard deviation of 40 degrees. What is the probability that a randomly selected furnace will have a temperature less than 1505 degrees Fahrenheit?

Identify the type of sample described. Then tell if the sample is biased.

9. A newspaper is sponsoring a poll, and wants to find out the preferences of farmers across the state regarding the state governor's election. The newspaper surveys farmers in the local area to gather their data.

Answers

1. $\bar{x}$: 321, median: 238.5, mode: none
2. $\bar{x}$: 808.6, median: 811.7, mode: none
3. 62; $\bar{x}$: 37.7, median: 36, mode: 36, range: 35, σ: 10.5; $\bar{x}$: 34.6, median: 34.5, mode: 36, range: 16, σ: 5.53
4. $\bar{x}$: 55.6, median: 56, mode: 51, range: 16, σ: 5.97; $\bar{x}$: 67.6, median: 68, mode: 63, range: 16, σ: 5.97
5. $\bar{x}$: 48.7, median: 44.9, mode: none, range: 52.7, σ: 17.7; $\bar{x}$: 58.4, median: 53.9, mode: none, range: 63.3, σ: 21.2
6. 0.141
7. 0.889
8. 0.977
9. convenience; biased

CHAPTER 11

Chapter Test B *continued*

For use after Chapter 11

Find the margin of error for a survey with the given sample size. Round your answer to the nearest tenth of a percent.

10. 2400
11. 180

Find the sample size required to achieve the given margin of error. Round your answer to the nearest whole number.

12. 10%
13. 1%
14. **Track and Field** In a survey of 212 people at the local track and field championship, 72% favored the home team winning. Find the margin of error for the survey, and give an interval that is likely to contain the exact percent of all people who favor the home team winning.
15. **Ocean Floor** The depth *y*, in miles, of the ocean floor over a horizontal distance *x*, in miles, is shown in the table below. Use a graphing calculator to find a model for the data.

x	2	4	6	8	10	12
y	−1.20	−3.07	−4.19	−4.56	−4.17	−3.04

16. **Warehouse Shipments** The number of packages *y*, in thousands, shipped through a new warehouse *x* days after opening is shown in the table below. Use a graphing calculator to find a model for the data.

x	1	3	6	10	15	21
y	2.26	7.13	15.1	19.8	27.8	39.3

17. **Weed Growth** The number of weeds *y*, in a field after *x* weeks is shown in the table below. Use a graphing calculator to find a model for the data.

x	1	2	3	4	5	6
y	42	99	253	761	2319	7021

Answers

10. 2.0%
11. 7.5%
12. 100
13. 10,000
14. 6.9%; 65.1% to 78.9%
15. $y = 0.09x^2 - 1.5x + 1.42$
16. $y = 1.78x + 1.96$
17. $y = 13.05 \cdot 2.81^x$

CHAPTER 11 Standardized Test
For use after Chapter 11

Multiple Choice

1. What is the median of the data set: 0.3, 0.32, 5.6, −1.2, 3.4, 4.7, 2.1? C
   - Ⓐ −1.2 Ⓑ 1.0
   - Ⓒ 2.1 Ⓓ 2.75

2. What is the mean of the data set: 1, 3, 3, 5, 9, 11, 13, 13, 20, 21? B
   - Ⓐ 8.8 Ⓑ 9.9 Ⓒ 10.0 Ⓓ 13.0

3. What is the range of the data set: −1, 2, 56, −3, 4, 17? D
   - Ⓐ 16 Ⓑ 18 Ⓒ 53 Ⓓ 59

4. What is the standard deviation of a student's test scores of 87, 92, 79, 81, and 93? A
   - Ⓐ 5.64 Ⓑ 12.62
   - Ⓒ 31.84 Ⓓ 159.20

5. Given the data set below, which statement is *false*?
   104, 112, 100, 135, 142, 124, 92, 183 A
   - Ⓐ The mean and median are equal.
   - Ⓑ There is no mode.
   - Ⓒ The range is 91.
   - Ⓓ The outlier of the data set is 183.

6. An algebra teacher calculates the mean of the latest test scores to be 72 and the standard deviation to be 12. Realizing that the test scores are below average for her brilliant class, the teacher decides to raise everyone's score by 5 points. What are the mean and standard deviation of the higher scores? C
   - Ⓐ Mean 72, standard deviation 12
   - Ⓑ Mean 72, standard deviation 17
   - Ⓒ Mean 77, standard deviation 12
   - Ⓓ Mean 77, standard deviation 17

7. An hourly wage is normally distributed with a mean of \$6.75 and a standard deviation of \$.55. What is the probability that an employee's hourly wage is *not* between \$5.65 and \$7.85? B
   - Ⓐ 0.025 Ⓑ 0.05
   - Ⓒ 0.34 Ⓓ 0.68

8. A gardener calculates that each tomato plant he planted last season grew a mean of 9 pounds of tomatoes. If the standard deviation is 3 pounds, then what is the probability that a plant will produce at least 6 pounds of tomatoes? C
   - Ⓐ 16% Ⓑ 32%
   - Ⓒ 84% Ⓓ 95%

9. A normal distribution has a mean of 72 and a standard deviation of 4. What is the z-score corresponding to an x-value of 78? D
   - Ⓐ 0.51 Ⓑ 0.56 Ⓒ 0.92 Ⓓ 1.50

10. A telemarketer decides to contact every third person in the phone book. Which type of sample does this represent? B
    - Ⓐ Self-selected Ⓑ Systematic
    - Ⓒ Convenience Ⓓ Random

11. A recent survey of 1000 shoppers showed that 70% were planning to charge their purchases. What is the margin of error for this survey? B
    - Ⓐ ±0.1% Ⓑ ±3.2%
    - Ⓒ ±7.0% Ⓓ ±10.0%

12. An election poll reveals that 54% of voters favor the incumbent, with a margin of error of ±2.5%. How many voters were polled? C
    - Ⓐ 250 Ⓑ 400
    - Ⓒ 1600 Ⓓ 2500

CHAPTER 11 Standardized Test *continued*
For use after Chapter 11

13. Which type of function best models the data points on the graph? B

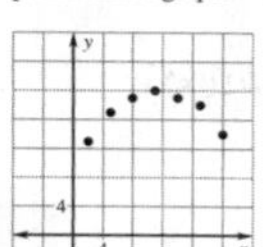

   - Ⓐ Linear Ⓑ Quadratic
   - Ⓒ Cubic Ⓓ Exponential

14. Based on the data set below, which function best models the data? D

x	3	4	7	10	13	16	19
y	27	28	23	20	12	10	9

   - Ⓐ $y = -1.30x + 31.83$
   - Ⓑ $y = 0.02x^2 - 1.81x + 33.80$
   - Ⓒ $y = 0.01x^3 - 0.36x^2 + 1.84x + 24.86$
   - Ⓓ $y = 37.36(0.93)^x$

Gridded Answer

15. What is the z-score corresponding to an x-value of 48 for a normal distribution with a mean of 41 and a standard deviation of 5?

1.4

17. a. See part (b) for graph.; quadratic
b.

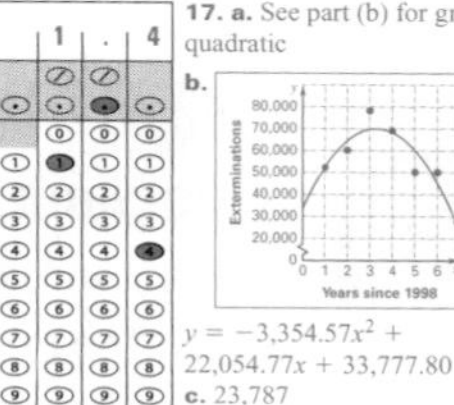

$y = -3{,}354.57x^2 + 22{,}054.77x + 33{,}777.80$
c. 23,787

Short Response

16. Your local grocer would like to conduct a survey about his business.
    a. If he would like to survey customers on their satisfaction, what type of sampling should he obtain? *Explain.*
    b. If he wants to increase his business by determining what services the public would like him to provide, whom should he poll? What type of sampling should he get? *Explain.*

16. a. Answers and explanations will vary.
b. Answers and explanations will vary.

Extended Response

17. Bug-B-Gone Extermination Service has been tracking the numbers of yellow jacket exterminations they have done over the past 6 years. The data is as follows: See left.

Year	Exterminations
1999	52,348
2000	60,259
2001	78,309
2002	69,210
2003	50,231
2004	50,194

   a. Let $x = 1$ represent the year 1999, $x = 2$ represent 2000, and so on. Graph a scatter plot of the data. Which function best models the data?
   b. Find the regression equation which best fits the data and graph the function. What is the equation?
   c. Based on your regression equation, what can Bug-B-Gone predict their numbers of yellow jacket exterminations to be in 2005?

CHAPTER 11 Alternative Assessment and Math Journal
For use after Chapter 11

Journal

1. Explain the difference between a measure of central tendency and a measure of dispersion. Give a real-life example of when it might be preferable to represent a data set using the median or mode, instead of the mean. Explain your reasoning.

Multi-Step Problem

2. The student council at your school is responsible for surveying the students to determine whether they would prefer the school to offer study halls and limited electives or no study halls and a broad range of electives. Because 1740 students attend your school, the council decides to survey a sample of the students.
   a. A student council member suggests that the four representatives from each class (grades 9–12) be surveyed during the next student council meeting. Identify the type of sample described. Then tell if the sample is biased. Explain your reasoning.
   b. How many students would participate in the survey described in part (a)? Calculate the margin of error for a survey with this sample size. Is it acceptable, why or why not?
   c. The student council would like the survey to have a margin of error of no more than ±2% and include no more than one quarter of the student body. Is this possible? If not, explain why and find the least margin of error (to the nearest percent) that can be achieved by surveying one quarter of the student body?
   d. **Writing** Describe how the student council might achieve an unbiased, random sample of one quarter of the student body.
   e. **Critical Thinking** The student council administers the survey as described in part (d). 46% of the students want study halls and limited electives, and 54% of the students want no study halls and a broad range of electives. From this survey, can the school determine which option the student body prefers? Explain.

1. Complete answers should include: an explanation that a measure of central tendency represents the center or middle of a set of data values, while a measure of dispersion indicates how spread out the data values are; a real-life example of a data set with a mean that does not represent a typical data value, usually due to an outlier; an explanation that an outlier often has a greater effect on the mean than on the median or mode. **2. a.** Convenience sample; *Sample answer:* The sample is biased because students on student council may be more motivated, higher-achieving students who would prefer a broader range of electives. **b.** 16 students; ±25%; *Sample answer:* No. A margin of error that large will probably make it impossible to determine a majority opinion. **c.** *Sample answer:* No. A margin of error of ±2% requires a sample size of 2500. One quarter of the student body is 435 students. The least margin of error possible for a survey with that sample size is ±5%. **d.** *Sample answer:* The student council could use a computer to randomly generate 435 student ID numbers. **e.** *Sample answer:* No. Because the margin of error is ±5%, the exact percent of the student body who wants study halls and limited electives is likely between 41% and 51%. Similarly, the exact percent of the student body who wants no study halls and a broad range of electives is likely between 49% and 59%. The overlap in the intervals makes it impossible to determine for sure what the majority of the student body prefers.

CHAPTER 11 Alternative Assessment Rubric *continued*
For use after Chapter 11

Journal Solution

1. Complete answers should include:
   - an explanation that a measure of central tendency represents the center or middle of a set of data values, while a measure of dispersion indicates how spread out the data values are.
   - a real-life example of a data set with a mean that does not represent a typical data value, usually due to an outlier.
   - an explanation that an outlier often has a greater effect on the mean than on the median or mode.

Multi-Step Problem Solution

2. a. Convenience sample; *Sample answer:* The sample is biased because students on student council may be more motivated, higher-achieving students who would prefer a broader range of electives over extra study time.
   b. 16 students; ±25%; *Sample answer:* No. A margin of error that large will probably make it impossible to determine a majority opinion.
   c. *Sample answer:* No. A margin of error of ±2% requires a sample size of 2500, which is more students than attend your school. One quarter of the student body is 435 students. The least margin of error possible for a survey with that sample size is ±5%.
   d. *Sample answer:* The student council could use a computer to randomly generate 435 student ID numbers to determine which students to survey.
   e. *Sample answer:* No. Because the margin of error is ±5%, the exact percent of the student body who wants study halls and limited electives is likely between 41% and 51%. Similarly, the exact percent of the student body who wants no study halls and a broad range of electives is likely between 49% and 59%. The overlap in the intervals makes it impossible to determine for sure what the majority of the student body prefers.

Multi-Step Problem Rubric

4 The student answers all parts of the problem correctly and completely, showing a complete understanding of the relationship between sample size and margin of error. The student shows all work. The student's work is neat.

3 The student answers all parts of the problem, showing nearly complete understanding of the relationship between sample size and margin of error. The student's work may contain one or two errors in the calculations or explanations. The student shows most work. The student's work is neat.

2 The student answers all parts of the problem, showing some understanding of the relationship between sample size and margin of error. The student's work contains more than two errors in the calculations or explanations. The student shows some work. The student's work is sloppy.

1 The student does not complete all parts of the problem and shows little understanding of the relationship between sample size and margin of error. The student's work has several errors in the calculations or explanations. The student's work is sloppy, or no work is shown.

PLAN AND PREPARE

Main Ideas

Students first learn how to calculate the mean, median, mode, and standard deviation and to examine the effect of outliers on a data set. They then learn what the effect is on statistics when they add a constant to the data values or multiply data values by a constant. Students next extend their understanding of probability distributions and measures of central tendency to the study of normal distributions. They learn how the area under the normal curve is related to standard deviations from a mean. They also learn to calculate *z*-scores using the standard normal table. The students then study sampling methods for collecting data, how to identify biased samples, and how to calculate a margin of error. In the final lesson, students apply their understanding of the forms and behavior of linear, quadratic, cubic, exponential, and power functions as they learn to choose the best model to represent a set of data. They will use a graphing calculator to find equations of the models.

Prerequisite Skills

- Arranging a set of real numbers in increasing order
- Finding the probability of an event

Additional resources for reviewing prerequisite skills are:

- Skills Review Handbook, pp. 975–1009
- @HomeTutor

11 Data Analysis and Statistics

MA-HS-4.2.1	11.1 Find Measures of Central Tendency and Dispersion
MA-HS-4.2.1	11.2 Apply Transformations to Data
MA-HS-4.2.2	11.3 Use Normal Distributions
MA-HS-4.3.1	11.4 Select and Draw Conclusions from Samples
MA-HS-4.2.3	11.5 Choose the Best Model for Two-Variable Data

Before

In previous chapters, you learned the following skills, which you'll use in Chapter 11: describing distributions, ordering real numbers, and finding probabilities.

Prerequisite Skills

VOCABULARY CHECK

Copy and complete the statement.

1. The **probability** of an event is a number from _?_ to _?_ that indicates the likelihood the event will occur. 0, 1
2. The **binomial distribution** at the right is not skewed. Instead, it is _?_. normal

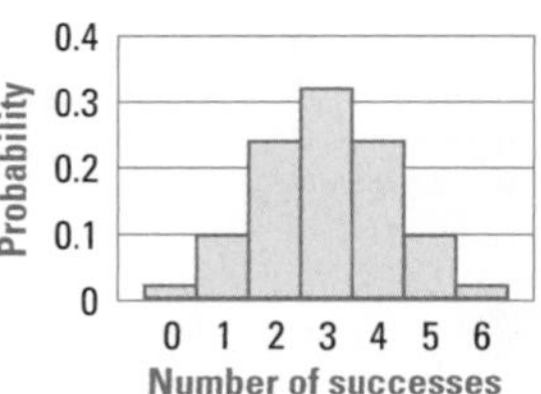

SKILLS CHECK

Graph the numbers on a number line. Then write the numbers in increasing order. *(Review p. 2 for 11.1.)* 3, 4. See margin for art.

3. $-\frac{3}{4}, 0.4, \sqrt{7}, -1.3, \frac{2}{3}, -\sqrt{12}$ $-\sqrt{12}, -1.3, -\frac{3}{4}, 0.4, \frac{2}{3}, \sqrt{7}$
4. $1.5, \frac{4}{3}, -1.24, \sqrt{2}, -\sqrt{3}, \frac{6}{5}$ $-\sqrt{3}, -1.24, \frac{6}{5}, \frac{4}{3}, \sqrt{2}, 1.5$

You have an equally likely chance of choosing any integer from 1 through 20. Find the probability of the event. *(Review p. 698 for 11.3.)*

5. An odd number is chosen. $\frac{1}{2}$
6. A perfect square is chosen. $\frac{1}{5}$
7. A multiple of 3 is chosen. $\frac{3}{10}$
8. A factor of 50 is chosen. $\frac{1}{5}$

Chapter Planning Guide

Chapter 11 Resource Book
- Teaching Guide/Lesson Plan (pp. 3, 14, 26, 38, 50)
- Project with Rubric (p. 65)

Assessment and Intervention
- Assessment Book (pp. 154–167)
- Benchmark Tests
- Remediation Book

Interactive Technology
- Easy Planner
- Power Presentations CD-ROM
- Activity Generator CD-ROM
- Animated Algebra
- Test Generator CD-ROM
- Online Quizzes
- eWorkbook
- eEdition
- @HomeTutor

Resources for English Learners
- Quick Reference for English Learners
- Spanish Study Guide
- Multi-Language Visual Glossary
- Student Resources in Spanish

Now

In Chapter 11, you will apply the big ideas listed below and reviewed in the Chapter Summary on page 783. You will also use the key vocabulary listed below.

Big Ideas

1. Finding measures of central tendency and dispersion
2. Using normal distributions
3. Working with samples

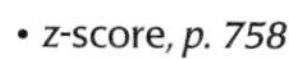

KEY VOCABULARY

- statistics, *p. 744*
- mean, *p. 744*
- median, *p. 744*
- mode, *p. 744*
- range, *p. 745*
- standard deviation, *p. 745*
- normal distribution, *p. 757*
- normal curve, *p. 757*
- standard normal distribution, *p. 758*
- z-score, *p. 758*
- sample, *p. 766*
- unbiased sample, *p. 767*
- biased sample, *p. 767*
- margin of error, *p. 768*

Why?

You can use statistics to compare two or more sets of data. For example, you can compare data for two athletes to see who performs better.

Animated Algebra

The animation illustrated below for Exercise 28 on page 748 helps you answer this question: Which contestant has the best average score after four rounds of an archery competition?

Several contestants shoot arrows at archery targets.

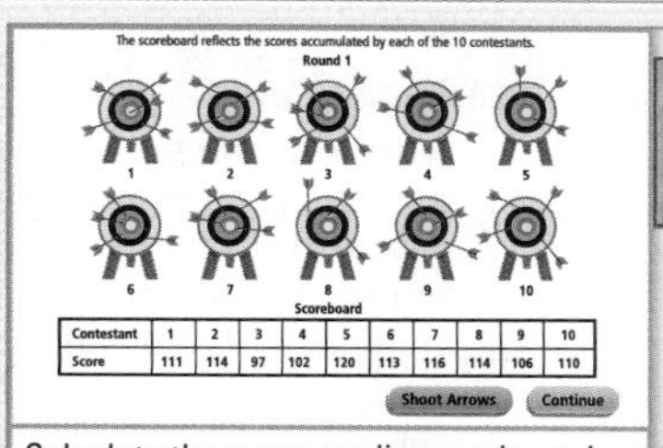

The scoreboard reflects the scores accumulated by each of the 10 contestants.
Round 1
Scoreboard
Contestant 1 2 3 4 5 6 7 8 9 10
Score 111 114 97 102 120 113 116 114 106 110
Shoot Arrows
Continue

Calculate the mean, median, mode, and standard deviation of the scores.

Animated Algebra at classzone.com

Other animations for Chapter 11: pages 744, 754, 757, and 776

Algebra 2 Toolkit

- Reading Strategies for Chapter 11, pp. 29–30
- Differentiated Instruction Notes, pp. 83–86
- English Learners Notes, pp. 121–122
- Inclusion Notes, pp. 155–156
- Teaching Strategies with Sample Worksheets, pp. 163–186
- Using Technology in the Classroom, pp. 187–192
- Tips for New Teachers, pp. 213–214
- Math Background Notes, pp. 254–257
- Pre-AP Strategies and Copymasters, pp. 331–332, 429–430
- Teacher Survival Activities, pp. 489–490, 517–518
- Bulletin Board Idea, p. 535
- Teacher Tool Transparencies, following p. 538

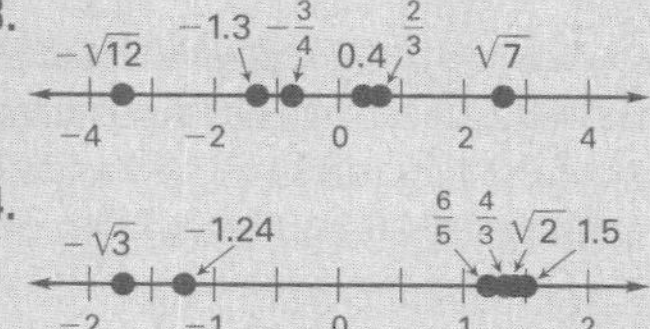

1 PLAN AND PREPARE

Warm-Up Exercises

Transparency Available

Simplify the expression. Round the answer to the nearest tenth.

1. $\sqrt{\frac{145}{10}}$ 3.8 **2.** $\sqrt{\frac{402}{8}}$ 7.1

3. The monthly profit from team jackets can be modeled by $1600 - (p - 60)$, where p is the price in dollars of a jacket. What is the value of the expression when $p = 80$? **$1580**

Notetaking Guide

Transparency Available

Promotes interactive learning and notetaking skills, pp. 286–289.

Pacing

Basic: 1 day

Average: 1 day

Advanced: 1 day

Block: 0.5 block with 11.2

- See *Teaching Guide/Lesson Plan*.

2 FOCUS AND MOTIVATE

Essential Question

Big Idea 1, p. 743

When will the mean of a data set differ significantly from the median of the data set? **Tell students they will learn how to answer this question by examining the outliers of the data set.**

11.1 Find Measures of Central Tendency and Dispersion

 **MA-HS-4.2.1**

Before You displayed data using graphs.

Now You will describe data using statistical measures.

Why? So you can calculate softball statistics, as in Ex. 27.

Key Vocabulary
- statistics
- measure of central tendency
- measure of dispersion
- standard deviation
- outlier

MA-HS-4.2.1
Students will describe and compare data distributions and make inferences from the data based on the shapes of graphs, measures of center (mean, median, mode) and measures of spread (range, standard deviation). DOK 2

Statistics are numerical values used to summarize and compare sets of data. Two important types of statistics are *measures of central tendency* and *measures of dispersion.*

A **measure of central tendency** is a number used to represent the center or middle of a set of data values. The *mean, median,* and *mode* are three commonly used measures of central tendency.

KEY CONCEPT *For Your Notebook*

Measures of Central Tendency

- The **mean**, or *average*, of n numbers is the sum of the numbers divided by n. The mean is denoted by $\overline{x}$, which is read as "x-bar." For the data set $x_1, x_2, \ldots, x_n$, the mean is $\overline{x} = \frac{x_1 + x_2 + \cdots + x_n}{n}$.
- The **median** of n numbers is the middle number when the numbers are written in order. (If n is even, the median is the mean of the two middle numbers.)
- The **mode** of n numbers is the number or numbers that occur most frequently. There may be one mode, no mode, or more than one mode.

EXAMPLE 1 **Find measures of central tendency**

WAITING TIMES The data sets at the right give the waiting times (in minutes) of several people at two veterinary offices. Find the mean, median, and mode of each data set.

Office A	Office B
14, 17, 18, 19, 20, 24, 24, 30, 32	8, 11, 12, 16, 18, 18, 18, 20, 23

AVOID ERRORS
Before identifying the median as the middle number in a list, make sure the numbers are ordered from least to greatest or from greatest to least.

Solution

Office A: Mean: $\overline{x} = \frac{14 + 17 + \cdots + 32}{9} = \frac{198}{9} = 22$ Median: 20 Mode: 24

Office B: Mean: $\overline{x} = \frac{8 + 11 + \cdots + 23}{9} = \frac{144}{9} = 16$ Median: 18 Mode: 18

Animated Algebra at classzone.com

Resource Planning Guide

Chapter Resource Book
- Teaching Guide/Lesson Plan (pp. 3–4)
- Practice levels A, B, C (pp. 6–8)
- Study Guide (pp. 9–10)
- Catch-up for Absent Students (p. 11)
- Problem Solving Workshop (p. 12)
- Challenge (p. 13)

Workbooks
- Notetaking Guide (pp. 286–289)
- Practice Workbook (pp. 161–162)

Teaching Options
- **Power Presentations CD-ROM** provides dynamic electronic teaching resources for the classroom.
- **Activity Generator CD-ROM** provides editable activities for all ability levels.

Interactive Technology
- Easy Planner
- Power Presentations CD-ROM
- Activity Generator CD-ROM
- Animated Algebra
- Test Generator CD-ROM
- Online Quiz
- eWorkbook
- eEdition
- @HomeTutor

Resources for English Learners
- Quick Reference for English Learners
- Spanish Study Guide
- Multi-Language Visual Glossary
- Student Resources in Spanish

See also the *Algebra 2 Toolkit* for more strategies for meeting individual needs.

GUIDED PRACTICE for Example 1

1. **TRANSPORTATION** The data set below gives the waiting times (in minutes) of 10 students waiting for a bus. Find the mean, median, and mode of the data set. 7.4, 7.5, 8

4, 8, 12, 15, 3, 2, 6, 9, 8, 7

MEASURES OF DISPERSION A **measure of dispersion** is a statistic that tells you how *dispersed*, or spread out, data values are. One simple measure of dispersion is the **range**, which is the difference between the greatest and least data values.

EXAMPLE 2 Find ranges of data sets

Find the range of the waiting times in each data set in Example 1.

Solution

Office A: Range = 32 − 14 = 18 **Office B:** Range = 23 − 8 = 15

Because the range for office A is greater, its waiting times are more spread out.

STANDARD DEVIATION Another measure of dispersion is *standard deviation*, which describes the typical difference (or *deviation*) between a data value and the mean.

KEY CONCEPT *For Your Notebook*

Standard Deviation of a Data Set

The **standard deviation** σ (read as "sigma") of $x_1, x_2, \dots, x_n$ is:

$$\sigma = \sqrt{\frac{(x_1 - \bar{x})^2 + (x_2 - \bar{x})^2 + \cdots + (x_n - \bar{x})^2}{n}}$$

EXAMPLE 3 Standardized Test Practice

What is the standard deviation of the waiting times in each data set in Example 1?

Ⓐ 4.7 and 5.2 Ⓑ 5.7 and 5.2 Ⓒ 4.7 and 4.5 Ⓓ 5.7 and 4.5

Solution

Office A: $\sigma = \sqrt{\frac{(14-22)^2 + (17-22)^2 + \cdots + (32-22)^2}{9}} = \sqrt{\frac{290}{9}} \approx 5.7$

Office B: $\sigma = \sqrt{\frac{(8-16)^2 + (11-16)^2 + \cdots + (23-16)^2}{9}} = \sqrt{\frac{182}{9}} \approx 4.5$

▶ The correct answer is D. Ⓐ Ⓑ Ⓒ Ⓓ

Motivating the Lesson

Ask your students to work in groups of 4 and describe the variations in their heights, their favorite school subjects, and their hobbies. In this lesson students will learn how variation can be measured and how it can help describe a data set.

3 TEACH

Extra Example 1

The data sets give the times in minutes for runners in two races. Find the mean, median, and mode(s) of each data set.

Race A	Race B
4, 7, 8, 8, 9, 9, 10, 11, 12	5, 6, 6, 7, 8, 8, 8, 10, 11

Race A: mean ≈ 8.7, median = 9, modes = 8 and 9;
Race B: mean ≈ 7.7, median = 8, mode = 8

An **Animated Algebra** activity is available on-line for **Example 1**. This activity is also available on the **Power Presentations CD-ROM**.

Extra Example 2

Find the range of the times in each data set in Extra Example 1.
Race A: 8; Race B: 6

Extra Example 3

What is the standard deviation of the times in each data set in Extra Example 1? D

Ⓐ 2.3 and 5.2 Ⓑ 1.9 and 2.2
Ⓒ 1.9 and 2.3 Ⓓ 2.2 and 1.8

Key Question to Ask for Example 3

- Which office shows more variability in waiting times? Office A

Differentiated Instruction

Advanced It is important to know how a data set is dispersed as well as its measures of central tendency in order to describe the set accurately. To demonstrate this, ask students to describe two data sets with the same mean and median, but different ranges and standard deviations. Have them discuss the differences in the data sets.

See also the *Algebra 2 Toolkit* for more strategies.

✓ **GUIDED PRACTICE** for Examples 2 and 3

2. Find the range and standard deviation of the data set in Guided Practice Exercise 1 on page 745. **13, 3.8**

OUTLIERS Measures of central tendency and dispersion can give misleading impressions of a data set if the set contains one or more *outliers*. An **outlier** is a value that is much greater than or much less than most of the other values in a data set.

EXAMPLE 4 Examine the effect of an outlier

AIR HOCKEY You are competing in an air hockey tournament. The winning scores for the first 10 games are given below.

14, 15, 15, 17, 11, 15, 13, 12, 15, 13

a. Find the mean, median, mode, range, and standard deviation of the data set.

b. The winning score in the next game is an outlier, 3. Find the new mean, median, mode, range, and standard deviation.

c. Which measure of central tendency does the outlier affect the most? the least?

d. What effect does the outlier have on the range and standard deviation?

Solution

a. **Mean:** $\bar{x} = \frac{14 + 15 + \cdots + 13}{10} = 14$ **Median:** 14.5 **Mode:** 15

Range: $17 - 11 = 6$

Std. Dev.: $\sigma = \sqrt{\frac{(14 - 14)^2 + (15 - 14)^2 + \cdots + (13 - 14)^2}{10}} \approx 1.7$

b. **Mean:** $\bar{x} = \frac{14 + 15 + \cdots + 3}{11} = 13$ **Median:** 14 **Mode:** 15

Range: $17 - 3 = 14$

Std. Dev.: $\sigma = \sqrt{\frac{(14 - 13)^2 + (15 - 13)^2 + \cdots + (3 - 13)^2}{11}} \approx 3.5$

c. The mean is most affected by the outlier. The mode is least affected by the outlier.

d. The outlier causes both the range and standard deviation to increase.

 **GUIDED PRACTICE** for Example 4

3. **WHAT IF?** In part (b) of Example 4, suppose the winning score in the next game is 25 instead of 3. Find the new mean, median, mode, range, and standard deviation of the data set. **15, 15, 15, 14, about 3.5**

Extra Example 4

You are training for a triathlon. The miles that you ride your bicycle for 7 weeks are given below.

17, 20, 16, 18, 22, 19, 20

a. Find the mean, median, mode, range, and standard deviation of the data set. **mean: 18.9, median: 19, mode: 20, range: 6, standard deviation: 1.9**

b. Your mileage the next week is an outlier, 3. Find the new mean, median, mode, range, and standard deviation. **mean: 16.9, median: 18.5, mode: 20, range: 19, standard deviation: 5.2**

c. Which measure of central tendency does the outlier effect the most? the least? **mean; mode**

d. What effect does the outlier have on the range and standard deviation? **The outlier causes both the range and standard deviation to increase.**

Closing the Lesson

Have students summarize the major points of the lesson and answer the Essential Question: When will the mean of a data set differ significantly from the median of the data set?

- **A measure of central tendency represents the middle of a data set. The mean, median, and mode are measures of central tendency.**
- **A data set can also be described by how dispersed its data values are. The range and standard deviation are measures of dispersion.**
- **An outlier is a value that is much larger or smaller than the other members of the data set.**

A data set with an outlier will show a greater difference between the mean and the median than will the data set with the outlier excluded.

Differentiated Instruction

Visual Learners The concept of an outlier can be a difficult one to master. Have students create visual representations of a set of data, such as plotting the data and outlier given in **Example 4** on a number line. Then have students identify any outliers visually.

See also the *Algebra 2 Toolkit* for more strategies.

11.1 EXERCISES

HOMEWORK KEY
○ = WORKED-OUT SOLUTIONS on p. WS19 for Exs. 5, 15, and 29
★ = STANDARDIZED TEST PRACTICE Exs. 2, 7, 8, 23, 24, and 30

SKILL PRACTICE

A

1. **VOCABULARY** Copy and complete: Measures of _?_ represent the center or middle of a data set. Measures of _?_ tell you how spread out the values in a data set are. central tendency; dispersion

2. ★ **WRITING** Define the mean, median, and mode of a set of n numbers. See margin.

XAMPLE 1
on p. 744
or Exs. 3–10

MEASURES OF CENTRAL TENDENCY In Exercises 3–6, find the mean, median, and mode of the data set.

3. The numbers of mice born in nine different litters: 5, 7, 6, 3, 8, 6, 4, 5, 4 about 5.3; 5; 4, 5 and 6

4. A student's quiz scores for the first semester of an algebra class: 18, 20, 14, 15, 20, 17, 16 about 17.1, 17, 20

5. The heights (in inches) of the members of a men's college basketball team: 69, 70, 75, 84, 73, 78, 74, 73, 78, 71 74.5, 73.5, 73 and 78

6. The waiting times (in minutes) of several people at a doctor's office: 24, 19, 30, 39, 22, 19, 26, 35, 42, 15, 25 about 26.9, 25, 19

7. ★ **MULTIPLE CHOICE** What is the median of 0.5, 0.6, 0.7, 1.2, 1.5, and 1.5? B
   (A) 0.7 (B) 0.95 (C) 1 (D) 1.5

8. ★ **MULTIPLE CHOICE** What is the mean of 2, 2, 6, 7, 9, and 10? B
   (A) 2 (B) 6 (C) 6.5 (D) 7.2

ERROR ANALYSIS ***Describe*** **and correct the error in finding the measure of central tendency.**

9. The median of the data set below is 5 because 5 is the middle number.
   12, 8, 9, 5, 10, 10, 3

10. The only mode of the data set below is 12 because 12 occurs most frequently.
    12, 9, 24, 12, 18, 9, 12, 11, 9

The mean is the average of the n numbers; the median is the middle number of n numbers when the numbers are written in increasing order; the mode is the number(s) that occurs most frequently. The numbers need to be written in increasing order prior to choosing the median; 9. There are two modes because the numbers 9 and 12 both occur three times; 9 and 12.

XAMPLES 2 and 3
on p. 745
or Exs. 11–16

MEASURES OF DISPERSION Find the range and standard deviation of the data set.

11. 7, 4, 6, 8, 5, 9, 5, 7 5, about 1.6
12. 10, 12, 7, 11, 20, 7, 6, 8, 9 14, 4
13. 3.1, 2.7, 6.0, 5.6, 2.3, 2.0, 1.3 4.7, about 1.7
14. 44, 47, 45, 48, 45, 47, 50, 44, 48, 42 8, about 2.3
15. 135, 142, 148, 136, 152, 140, 158, 154 23, about 8.1
16. 301, 312, 308, 320, 318, 315, 325, 336 35, about 10.0

XAMPLE 4
on p. 746
or Exs. 17–22

B

IDENTIFYING OUTLIERS Identify the outlier in the data set. Then find the mean, median, mode, range, and standard deviation of the data set when the outlier is included and when it is not. 17–22. See margin.

17. 2, 2, 3, 3, 4, 4, 4, 6, 68
18. 0, 72, 75, 75, 83, 83, 83, 91
19. 10.9, 12.4, 0.7, 11.6, 12.8, 11.6
20. 28, 20, 25, 28, 100, 25, 20
21. 60, 68, 75, 78, 152, 71, 66, 72, 66, 80
22. 184, 192, 173, 181, 199, 65, 190, 188

4 PRACTICE AND APPLY

Assignment Guide

Answer Transparencies available for all exercises

Basic:
Day 1: SRH p. 1005 Exs. 5–9
pp. 747–749
Exs. 1–19, 26–29, 32–34 even

Average:
Day 1: pp. 747–749
Exs. 1–14, 19–23, 26–30, 33

Advanced:
Day 1: pp. 747–749
Exs. 1, 2, 5–8, 14–31*, 33

Block:
pp. 747–749
Exs. 1–14, 19–23, 26–30, 33
(with 11.2)

Differentiated Instruction

See *Algebra 2 Best Practices Toolkit* for suggestions on addressing the needs of a diverse classroom.

Homework Check

For a quick check of student understanding of key concepts, go over the following exercises:
Basic: 3, 12, 18, 26, 27
Average: 4, 14, 20, 26, 28
Advanced: 6, 16, 22, 27, 28

Extra Practice

- Student Edition, p. 1020
- Chapter 11 Resource Book: Practice levels A, B, C, pp. 6–8

Practice Worksheet

An easily-readable reduced practice page (with answers) for this lesson can be found on p. 742C.

17. 68; about 10.7, 4, 4, 66, about 20.3; 3.5, 3.5, 4, 4, about 1.2
18. 0; about 70.3, 79, 83, 91, about 27.2; 80.3, 83, 83, 19, about 6.1
19. 0.7; 10, 11.6, 11.6, 12.1, about 4.2; about 11.9, 11.6, 11.6, 1.9, about 0.67
20. 100; about 35.1; 25; 20, 25, and 28; 80; about 26.7; about 24.3, 25, no mode, 8, about 3.3
21. 152; 78.8, 71.5, 66, 92, about 25.1; about 70.7, 71, 66, 20, about 6.0
22. 65; about 172, 186, no mode, 134, about 40.9; about 186.7, 188, no mode, 26, about 7.7

Vocabulary

Exercises 1–8 Even though a measure of central tendency represents the middle of a data set, except in the case of the median, it does not equal the middle number of the data set. It may be helpful to think of a measure of central tendency as a typical number in a data set.

Avoiding Common Errors

Exercises 11–22, 24, 27–29 Students may forget to square the difference of x_i and the mean when calculating the standard deviation. Explain that since some values are less than the mean, some values of $x_i - \overline{x}$ will be negative. Because the mean is the point at which the positive deviations from the mean equal the negative deviations, the sum of the deviations would be zero. Thus the deviations must first be squared and then summed.

An **Animated Algebra** activity is available on-line for **Exercise 28**. This activity is also available on the **Power Presentations CD-ROM**.

---

23. ★ **OPEN-ENDED MATH** Create a data set with a mean of 10, a median of 11, and a mode of 8. *Sample answer:* **8, 8, 8, 8, 11, 11, 12, 12, 12**

24a. 6; $\frac{|6 - 62.1|}{18.2} > 3$
24b. 88; $\frac{|88 - 27.1|}{17.7} > 3$
24c. 199; $\frac{|199 - 90.9|}{33.2} > 3$

C

24. ★ **SHORT RESPONSE** An outlier can be defined as a value in a data set that lies more than three standard deviations from the mean. So, x is an outlier if $\frac{|x - \overline{x}|}{\sigma} > 3$. In parts (a)–(c), use this definition to identify the outlier(s) in the data set. *Justify* your answers mathematically.

a. 70, 55, 54, 75, 60, 58, 55, 56, 6, 62, 68, 94, 55, 82, 69, 74

b. 18, 20, 22, 25, 16, 40, 24, 19, 38, 3, 21, 27, 88, 24, 23, 26

c. 50, 93, 81, 84, 88, 85, 90, 99, 92, 199, 96, 89, 87, 94, 37

25. CHALLENGE The formula for standard deviation can also be written as:

$$\sigma = \sqrt{\frac{x_1^2 + x_2^2 + \cdots + x_n^2}{n} - \overline{x}^2}$$

For $n = 3$, show that this formula is equivalent to the formula given on page 745. (*Hint:* You will need to show that $x_1 + x_2 + x_3 = 3\overline{x}$.) **See margin.**

PROBLEM SOLVING

EXAMPLES 1, 2, and 3 on pp. 744–745 for Exs. 26–28

A

26. FOOTBALL The data set below gives the numbers of passing touchdowns for the 12 quarterbacks who threw the most touchdowns during the 2004 NFL regular season. Find the mean, median, mode, range, and standard deviation. **about 29.3, 27.5, 27, 28, about 7.6**

49, 39, 31, 30, 29, 28, 27, 27, 27, 22, 21, 21

@HomeTutor for problem solving help at classzone.com

27. OLYMPIC SOFTBALL The data set below gives the total number of at-bats for each player on the 2004 U.S. women's Olympic softball team. Find the mean, median, and mode of the data set. **about 17.8, 20, 6 and 20**

2, 6, 6, 16, 19, 20, 20, 21, 22, 25, 26, 30

@HomeTutor for problem solving help at classzone.com

28. ARCHERY The data set below gives the scores of the contestants in the first round of a junior archery competition. Find the mean, median, mode, range, and standard deviation. **about 110, 112, 114, 23, about 6.5**

111, 114, 97, 102, 120, 113, 116, 114, 106, 110

Animated Algebra at classzone.com

29b. 20.2, 22, 23, 20, about 5.4; about 21.9, 23, 23, 6, about 2.1

29c. *Sample answer:* The mean and the median increase when the outlier is removed and the range and standard deviation decrease.

EXAMPLE 4 on p. 746 for Ex. 29

B

29. MULTI-STEP PROBLEM The data set below gives the numbers of trials required by 10 puppies to learn a trick.

20, 23, 19, 25, 21, 23, 5, 24, 19, 23

a. **Analyze** Identify the outlier of the data set. **5**

b. **Calculate** Find the mean, median, mode, range, and standard deviation of the data set when the outlier is included and when it is not.

c. **Reasoning** *Describe* the outlier's effect on the measures of central tendency and dispersion.

◯ = WORKED-OUT SOLUTIONS on p. WS1

★ = STANDARDIZED TEST PRACTICE

25. *Sample answer:* $\sqrt{\frac{(x_1 - \overline{x})^2 + (x_2 - \overline{x})^2 + (x_3 - \overline{x})^2}{3}} =$

$\sqrt{\frac{x_1^2 - 2\overline{x}x_1 + \overline{x}^2 + x_2^2 - 2\overline{x}x_2 + \overline{x}^2 + x_3^2 - 2\overline{x}x_3 + \overline{x}^2}{3}} =$

$\sqrt{\frac{x_1^2 + x_2^2 + x_3^2}{3} - \frac{2\overline{x}(x_1 + x_2 + x_3)}{3} + \frac{3\overline{x}^2}{3}} =$

$\sqrt{\frac{x_1^2 + x_2^2 + x_3^2}{3} - 2\overline{x}^2 + \overline{x}^2} = \sqrt{\frac{x_1^2 - x_2^2 + x_3^2}{3} - \overline{x}^2}$

748

30. ★ **EXTENDED RESPONSE** The table shows the results (in meters) for the final round of the 2004 and 1964 men's Olympic javelin throw events.

Men's Olympic Javelin Throw	
2004 data	**1964 data**
86.50, 84.95, 84.84, 84.13, 83.31, 83.25, 83.14, 83.01, 80.59, 80.28, 79.43, 74.36	82.66, 82.32, 80.57, 80.17, 78.72, 76.94, 74.72, 74.26

a. **Calculate** Find the mean, median, mode, range, and standard deviation of the 2004 data. about 82.32, about 83.20, no mode, 12.14, about 3.11

b. **Calculate** Find the mean, median, mode, range, and standard deviation of the 1964 data. about 78.80, about 79.45, no mode, 8.40, about 3.02

c. **Analyze** *Compare* the statistics for each set of data. Draw one or more conclusions about the data.

c. *Sample* *swer:* While e distances ere more nsistent 1964; the erage stance was eater in 2004.

C 31. **CHALLENGE** The mean discussed in this lesson is called the *arithmetic mean*. Another type of mean is the *geometric mean*. The geometric mean of two positive numbers a and b is $\sqrt{ab}$. Use the steps below to prove that the arithmetic mean of a and b is always greater than or equal to the geometric mean of a and b.

a. *Explain* why $(a - b)^2 \geq 0$. The result of squaring any real number is always greater than or equal to zero.

b. Use the inequality in part (a) to show that $(a + b)^2 \geq 4ab$. b, c. See margin.

c. Use the inequality in part (b) to show that the arithmetic mean of a and b is greater than or equal to the geometric mean of a and b, or $\frac{a+b}{2} \geq \sqrt{ab}$.

d. Under what condition is the arithmetic mean of a and b equal to the geometric mean of a and b? when a and b are equal

KY KENTUCKY MIXED REVIEW

TEST PRACTICE at classzone.com

32. Which best describes the effect on the graph of $y = -\frac{2}{3}x - 1$ when the slope is doubled? **D**

Ⓐ The y-intercept decreases.

Ⓑ The y-intercept increases.

Ⓒ The x-intercept decreases.

Ⓓ The x-intercept increases.

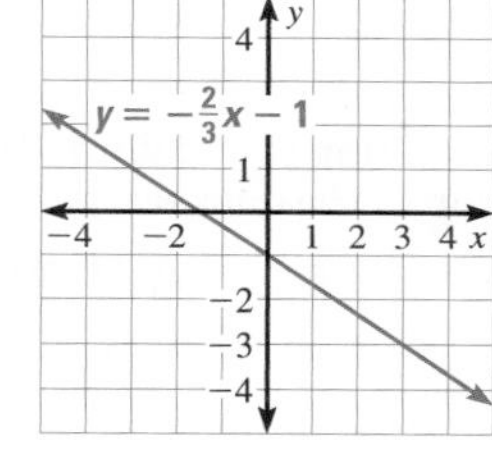

33. What is the length of the line segment joining the points (8, 3) and (2, −1)? **C**

Ⓐ $2\sqrt{5}$ Ⓑ $\sqrt{34}$ Ⓒ $2\sqrt{13}$ Ⓓ $2\sqrt{26}$

34. Which equation describes a relationship in which every real number x corresponds to a negative real number y? **D**

Ⓐ $y = x$ Ⓑ $y = x^2$ Ⓒ $y = |-x|$ Ⓓ $y = -|x|$

5 ASSESS AND RETEACH

Daily Homework Quiz

Transparency Available

A sample of the numbers of hours 10 students worked during a school vacation week are given below.

24, 32, 54, 31, 16, 18, 19, 14, 17, 20

1. Identify the outlier in the data set. 54
2. Find the mean and median of the data set when the outlier is included and when it is not. mean; 24.5, 21.2; median: 19.5, 19
3. Find the mode and range of the data set when the outlier is included and when it is not. mode: no mode, no mode; range: 40, 18
4. Find the standard deviation of the data set when the outlier is included and when it is not. 11.4; 6.1

Online Quiz

Available at **classzone.com**

Diagnosis/Remediation

- Practice A, B, C in Chapter 11 Resource Book, pp. 6–8
- Study Guide in Chapter 11 Resource Book, pp. 9–10
- Practice Workbook, pp. 161–162
- @HomeTutor

Challenge

Additional challenge is available in the Chapter 11 Resource Book, p. 13.

31b.
$$(a - b)^2 \geq 0$$
$$a^2 - 2ab + b^2 \geq 0$$
$$(a^2 - 2ab + b^2) + 4ab \geq 0 + 4ab$$
$$(a^2 + 2ab + b^2) \geq 4ab$$
$$(a + b)^2 \geq 4ab$$

31c.
$$(a + b)^2 \geq 4ab$$
$$\sqrt{(a + b)^2} \geq \sqrt{4ab}$$
$$a + b \geq 2\sqrt{ab}$$
$$\frac{a + b}{2} \geq \sqrt{ab}$$

@HomeTutor
classzone.com
Keystrokes

1 PLAN AND PREPARE

Learn the Method

Students will use a graphing calculator to calculate the mean, median, range, and standard deviation of a data set. Students can use their graphing calculators to calculate the statistics in Exercises 17–22 on page 747.

Keystroke Help

Keystrokes for several models of calculators are available in blackline format in the *Chapter 11 Resource Book*.

2 TEACH

Tips for Success

Make sure students completely clear L1 before entering the age data. Tell students that they do not have to enter the ages in numerical order.

Extra Example 1

The data set below gives the number of children of the first 43 Presidents of the United States. Use a graphing calculator to find the mean, median, range, and standard deviation.

0, 5, 6, 0, 3, 4, 0, 4, 10, 15, 0, 2, 2, 3, 0, 4, 5, 4, 8, 7, 3, 0, 3, 5, 2, 6, 3, 3, 0, 2, 2, 6, 1, 2, 3, 2, 2, 4, 4, 4, 6, 1, 2

mean: 3.44 median: 3, range: 15, standard deviation: 2.9

3 ASSESS AND RETEACH

Suppose you enter a set of data into a list on your graphing calculator then calculate statistics for the data set.

1. Which symbol in the list of statistics represents the standard deviation for your data set? σx
2. How do you find the range of your data set? Calculate maxX − minX.

11.1 Calculate One-Variable Statistics

QUESTION How can you use a graphing calculator to find statistics?

EXAMPLE Calculate statistics for a data set

The data set below gives the ages of the first 43 Presidents of the United States when they first took office. Use a graphing calculator to find the mean, median, range, and standard deviation of the data set.

57, 61, 57, 57, 58, 57, 61, 54, 68, 51, 49, 64, 50, 48, 65, 52, 56, 46, 54, 49, 51, 47, 55, 55, 54, 42, 51, 56, 55, 51, 54, 51, 60, 62, 43, 55, 56, 61, 52, 69, 64, 46, 54

STEP 1 *Calculate statistics*
Enter the data in list L_1. Then press STAT, choose the CALC menu, and select 1-Var Stats.

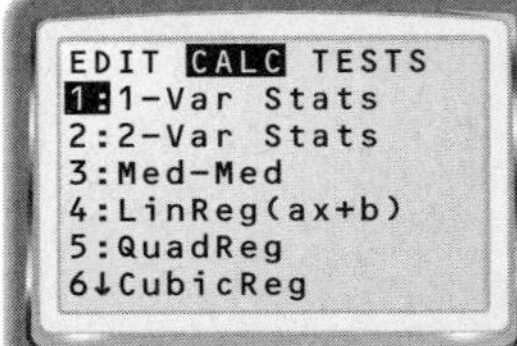

STEP 2 *Read statistics*
The screen shows a list of statistics. The mean is $\bar{x} \approx 54.8$. The standard deviation is $\sigma x \approx 6.15$.

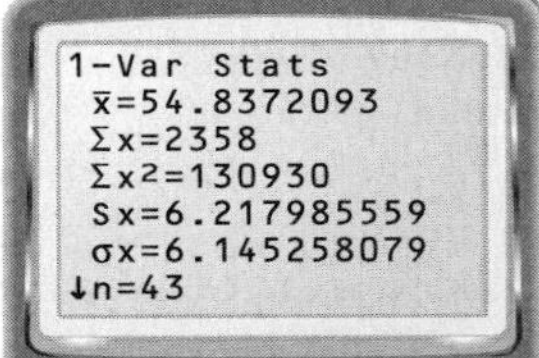

STEP 3 *Scroll down*
Scroll down to find that the median (Med) is 55. The range is maxX − minX, or 27.

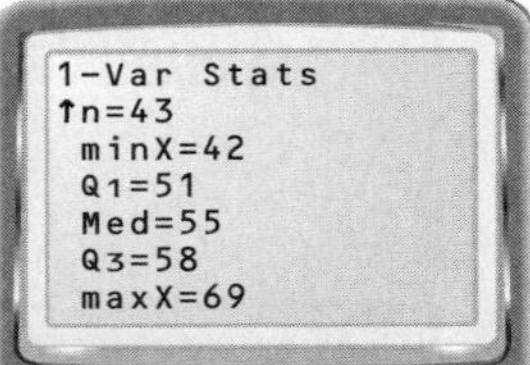

PRACTICE

Use a graphing calculator to find the mean, median, range, and standard deviation of the data set.

1. 43, 46, 47, 48, 51, 54, 58, 40, 52 about 48.8, 48, 18, about 5.3
2. 3.1, 2.7, 6.0, 5.6, 2.3, 2.0, 1.3, 3.4 3.3, 2.9, 4.7, about 1.6
3. 88, 83, 91, 82, 78, 81, 91, 95, 98 about 87.4, 88, 20, about 6.4
4. 19.4, 16.3, 12.7, 24.8, 19.2, 15.4 about 18.0, about 17.8, 12.1, about 3.8
5. 110, 107, 101, 108, 106, 112, 104 about 106.9, 107, 11, about 3.4
6. 265, 252, 257, 298, 275, 281, 276 272, 275, 46, about 14.4
7. **VICE PRESIDENTS' AGES** The data set below gives the ages of the first 46 vice presidents of the United States when they first took office. Use a graphing calculator to find the mean, median, range, and standard deviation of the data set. about 54.0, 53, 35, about 8.4

   53, 53, 45, 65, 68, 42, 42, 50, 56, 50, 52, 49, 66, 36, 51, 56, 45, 61, 57, 51, 65, 64, 57, 52, 42, 52, 53, 58, 48, 59, 69, 64, 52, 60, 71, 40, 52, 53, 51, 60, 66, 49, 56, 41, 44, 59

11.2 Apply Transformations to Data

MA-HS-4.2.1

Before You calculated statistics for data sets.

Now You will learn how transformations of data affect statistics.

Why? So you can solve problems about space travel, as in Example 1.

Key Vocabulary
- mean, *p. 744*
- median, *p. 744*
- mode, *p. 744*
- range, *p. 745*
- standard deviation, *p. 745*

MA-HS-4.2.1
Students will describe and compare data distributions and make inferences from the data based on the shapes of graphs, measures of center (mean, median, mode) and measures of spread (range, standard deviation). **DOK 2**

The following statistics describe the data set 7, 12, 16, 20, and 20.

Mean: 15 **Median:** 16 **Mode:** 20 **Range:** 13 **Std. Dev.:** 5.0

Adding 10 to each data value produces the data set 17, 22, 26, 30, and 30. The statistics for this data set are shown below.

Mean: 25 **Median:** 26 **Mode:** 30 **Range:** 13 **Std. Dev.:** 5.0

Notice that the mean, median, and mode have each increased by 10, but the range and standard deviation are unchanged. These results can be generalized.

KEY CONCEPT *For Your Notebook*

Adding a Constant to Data Values

When a constant is added to every value in a data set, the following are true:

- The mean, median, and mode of the new data set can be obtained by adding the same constant to the mean, median, and mode of the original data set.
- The range and standard deviation are unchanged.

EXAMPLE 1 Add a constant to data values

ASTRONAUTS The data set below gives the weights (in pounds) on Earth of eight astronauts without their space suits. A space suit weighs 250 pounds on Earth. Find the mean, median, mode, range, and standard deviation of the weights of the astronauts without their space suits and with their space suits.

142, 150, 155, 156, 160, 160, 166, 175

Solution

	Weights without suits	Weights with suits
Mean	158	158 + **250** = 408
Median	158	158 + **250** = 408
Mode	160	160 + **250** = 410
Range	33	33 (unchanged)
Standard deviation	9.3	9.3 (unchanged)

1 PLAN AND PREPARE

Warm-Up Exercises

Transparency Available

The water temperatures for one week in July in Key West, Florida, are listed below.

85°, 87°, 87°, 84°, 84°, 86°, 87°

1. Find the mean. 85.7°
2. Find the median. 86°
3. Find the mode. 87°
4. Find the range. 3°
5. Find the standard deviation. 1.3°

Notetaking Guide

Transparency Available

Promotes interactive learning and notetaking skills, pp. 290–291.

Pacing

Basic: 1 day
Average: 1 day
Advanced: 1 day
Block: 0.5 block with 11.1
- See *Teaching Guide/Lesson Plan.*

2 FOCUS AND MOTIVATE

Essential Question

Big Idea 1, p. 743

Are all the statistics of a data set affected when you transform the values in a data set? **Tell students they will learn how to answer this question by applying transformations to data.**

Resource Planning Guide

Chapter Resource Book
- Teaching Guide/Lesson Plan (pp. 14–15)
- Activity Master (p. 16)
- Practice levels A, B, C (pp. 17–19)
- Study Guide (pp. 20–21)
- Catch-up for Absent Students (p. 22)
- Problem Solving Workshop (p. 23)
- Challenge (p. 25)

Workbooks
- Notetaking Guide (pp. 290–291)
- Practice Workbook (pp. 163–164)

Teaching Options
- **Power Presentations CD-ROM** provides dynamic electronic teaching resources for the classroom.
- **Activity Generator CD-ROM** provides editable activities for all ability levels.

Interactive Technology
- Easy Planner
- Power Presentations CD-ROM
- Activity Generator CD-ROM
- Animated Algebra
- Test Generator CD-ROM
- Online Quiz
- eWorkbook
- eEdition
- @HomeTutor

Resources for English Learners
- Quick Reference for English Learners
- Spanish Study Guide
- Multi-Language Visual Glossary
- Student Resources in Spanish

See also the *Algebra 2 Toolkit* for more strategies for meeting individual needs.

Motivating the Lesson

Determine the mean and range of the ages of the students in your class. Then determine what the mean and range would be 5 years from now. In this lesson, students will learn how these statistics are affected by the addition.

3 TEACH

Extra Example 1

The data below give the weights of 5 people. At the end of a month, each person had lost 3 pounds. Give the mean, median, mode, range, and standard deviation of the starting weights and the weights at the end of the month.

138, 142, 155, 140, 155

$\bar{x}$: 146 and 143, median: 142 and 139, mode: 155 and 152, range: 17 and 17, std. dev.: 7.46 and 7.46

Extra Example 2

Give the mean, median, mode, range, and standard deviation for the starting weights of the 5 people in Extra Example 1 in kilograms. (*Note:* 1 kilogram ≈ 0.45 pound.)

$\bar{x}$: 65.7, median: 63.9, mode: 69.75, range: 7.65, std. dev.: 3.36

Closing the Lesson

Have students summarize the major points of the lesson and answer the Essential Question: Are all the statistics of a data set affected when you add or multiply the values in a data set?

- **When a constant is added to every value in a data set, the mean, median, and mode are increased by the same constant. The range and standard deviation remain unchanged.**
- **When each value of a data set is multiplied by a constant, the mean, median, mode, range, and standard deviation are multiplied by the same constant.**

The range and standard deviation are not affected by an addition transformation.

TRANSFORMING DATA BY MULTIPLICATION Another type of transformation you can apply to a data set is to *multiply* each data value by the same constant.

KEY CONCEPT *For Your Notebook*

Multiplying Data Values by a Constant

When each value of a data set is multiplied by a constant, the new mean, median, mode, range, and standard deviation can be found by multiplying each original statistic by the same constant.

EXAMPLE 2 Multiply data values by a constant

OLYMPICS The data set below gives the winning distances (in meters) in the men's Olympic triple jump events from 1964 to 2004. Find the mean, median, mode, range, and standard deviation of the distances in meters and of the distances in feet. (*Note:* 1 meter ≈ 3.28 feet.)

16.85, 17.39, 17.35, 17.29, 17.35, 17.26, 17.61, 18.17, 18.09, 17.71, 17.79

Solution

	Distances in meters	Distances in feet
Mean	17.53	**3.28**(17.53) ≈ 57.50
Median	17.39	**3.28**(17.39) ≈ 57.04
Mode	17.35	**3.28**(17.35) ≈ 56.91
Range	1.32	**3.28**(1.32) ≈ 4.33
Standard deviation	0.37	**3.28**(0.37) ≈ 1.21

✓ **GUIDED PRACTICE** for Examples 1 and 2

1. **ASTRONAUTS** The Manned Maneuvering Unit (MMU) is equipment that latches onto an astronaut's space suit and enables the astronaut to move around outside the spacecraft. The MMU weighs about 300 pounds on Earth. Find the mean, median, mode, range, and standard deviation of the weights of the astronauts in Example 1 with their space suits and MMUs. **708, 708, 710, 33, 9.3**
2. **WHAT IF?** In Example 2, find the mean, median, mode, range, and standard deviation of the distances in yards. (*Note:* 1 meter ≈ 1.09 yards.) **about 19.11, about 18.96, about 18.91, about 1.44, about 0.40**

Differentiated Instruction

Inclusion For application problems like those in **Example 2**, it is important that students set up their conversions correctly before they perform any data analysis. Have students practice setting up various tables to organize different unit conversions properly before having them analyze sets of data.

See also the *Algebra 2 Toolkit* for more strategies.

11.2 EXERCISES

HOMEWORK KEY
- ○ = WORKED-OUT SOLUTIONS on p. WS20 for Exs. 5, 11, and 19
- ★ = STANDARDIZED TEST PRACTICE Exs. 2, 16, 20, 22, and 23
- ◆ = MULTIPLE REPRESENTATIONS Ex. 21

SKILL PRACTICE

A

1. VOCABULARY Copy and complete: Multiplying each value in a data set by a constant is an example of a(n) __?__ of the data. transformation

2. ★ WRITING *Describe* how adding the same constant to every value in a data set affects the mean, median, mode, range, and standard deviation. The mean, median, and mode increase by the value of the constant, but the range and standard deviation remain the same.

XAMPLE 1
n p. 751
r Exs. 3–9

ADDING A CONSTANT **Find the mean, median, mode, range, and standard deviation of the given data set and of the data set obtained by adding the given constant to each data value.**

3. 14, 15, 17, 17, 19, 21, 23; constant: 6
18, 17, 17, 9, about 3.0; 24, 23, 23, 9, about 3.0

4. 31, 35, 38, 39, 42, 42, 48; constant: 18

5. 74, 76, 77, 77, 78, 81, 83; constant: 17
78, 77, 77, 9, about 2.8; 95, 94, 94, 9, about 2.8

6. 178, 193, 204, 211, 211, 216; constant: 155

7. 53, 64, 51, 60, 53, 45, 66; constant: −21
56, 53, 53, 21, about 7.0; 35, 32, 32, 21, about 7.0

8. 295, 279, 278, 282, 279, 301; constant: −45

about 39.3, 39,
17, about 5.1;
out 57.3, 57, 60,
about 5.1

9. ERROR ANALYSIS The standard deviation of a data set is 10. *Describe* and correct the error in finding the standard deviation if 3 is added to each data value.
The standard deviation does not change when adding a constant; 10.

New standard deviation:
10 + 3 = 13

XAMPLE 2
n p. 752
r Exs. 10–16

MULTIPLYING BY A CONSTANT **Find the mean, median, mode, range, and standard deviation of the given data set and of the data set obtained by multiplying each data value by the given constant.** 10–15. See margin.

10. 19, 23, 23, 26, 30, 31, 34; constant: 3

11. 58, 58, 59, 62, 64, 65, 67; constant: 4

12. 28, 31, 32, 35, 35, 39, 40; constant: 1.5

13. 88, 91, 99, 102, 102, 107; constant: 2.5

14. 130, 121, 132, 115, 130, 108; constant: 0.5

15. 222, 231, 222, 212, 250, 235; constant: 0.9

about 202,
out 208, 211,
about 13.0;
out 357, about
, 366, 38,
out 13.0

B

16. ★ MULTIPLE CHOICE The range of a data set is 21. Each value in the data set is multiplied by 3. What is the new range? D

Ⓐ 7 Ⓑ 21 Ⓒ 24 Ⓓ 63

about 286,
out 281, 279,
about 9.0;
out 241, about
, 234, 23,
out 9.0

C

17. CHALLENGE Let $x_1, x_2, \ldots, x_n$ be the values in a data set, and let $\overline{x}$ be the mean of the data set. Show that the mean of $ax_1, ax_2, \ldots, ax_n$ is $a\overline{x}$.

$$\frac{ax_1 + ax_2 + \ldots + ax_n}{n} = \frac{a(x_1 + x_2 + \ldots + x_n)}{n} = a\overline{x}$$

PROBLEM SOLVING

XAMPLES A
and 2
pp. 751–752
Exs. 18–22

18. SALARIES The data set below gives the annual salaries (in thousands of dollars) of nine DJs working at a local radio station.

39, 29, 42.5, 28.5, 48, 45, 38, 36.5, 28.5

a. Find the mean, median, mode, range, and standard deviation of the salaries.
about 37.2, 38, 28.5, 19.5, about 6.9

b. Each DJ receives an annual bonus of $1200. Find the mean, median, mode, range, and standard deviation of the salaries including the bonus.
about 38.4, 39.2, 29.7, 19.5, about 6.9

@HomeTutor for problem solving help at classzone.com

10. about 26.6, 26, 23, 15, about 4.9; about 79.8, 78, 69, 45, about 14.7
11. about 61.9, 62, 58, 9, about 3.36; about 248, 248, 232, 36, about 13.4
12. about 34.3, 35, 35, 12, about 4.0; about 51.5, 52.5, 52.5, 18, about 6.0
13. about 98.2, 100.5, 102, 19, about 6.62; about 245.5, about 251.3, 255, 47.5, about 16.6
14. about 123, 125.5, 130, 24, about 8.86; about 61.5, about 62.8, 65, 12, about 4.43
15. about 229, 226.5, 222, 38, about 12.0; about 206.1, about 203.9, 199.8, 34.2, about 10.8

4 PRACTICE AND APPLY

Assignment Guide

Answer Transparencies available for all exercises

Basic:
Day 1: pp. 753–755
Exs. 1–16, 18–22, 26

Average:
Day 1: pp. 753–755
Exs. 1–16, 18–24, 27

Advanced:
Day 1: pp. 753–755
Exs. 1–8, 12–25*, 27

Block:
pp. 753–755
Exs. 1–16, 18–24, 27 (with 11.1)

Differentiated Instruction

See *Algebra 2 Best Practices Toolkit* for suggestions on addressing the needs of a diverse classroom.

Homework Check

For a quick check of student understanding of key concepts, go over the following exercises:

Basic: 4, 7, 10, 18, 19
Average: 6, 12, 13, 20, 21
Advanced: 8, 14, 16, 21, 22

Extra Practice

- Student Edition, p. 1020
- Chapter 11 Resource Book: Practice levels A, B, C, pp. 17–19

Practice Worksheet

An easily-readable reduced practice page (with answers) for this lesson can be found on p. 742C.

Avoiding Common Errors

Exercises 3–16, 18–24 Many students have difficulty remembering which operations affect which statistics. One way to help them remember is to suggest that they associate the 3 letters in the word *add* with the 3 statistics that begin with the letter *m* – mean, median, and mode. These three statistics increase by the same constant that is added to the values in a data set. All the statistics are multiplied by the constant that multiplies the values in a data set.

Graphing Calculator

Exercises 3–8, 10–15 As students are learning the rules for applying transformations to data, they can apply the techniques they learned in the Graphing Calculator Activity in Lesson 11.1. After they enter an instruction in L2 to add or multiply the values of L1 by the given constants, they can calculate the 1-VAR statistics on L2.

An **Animated Algebra** activity is available on-line for **Exercise 19**. This activity is also available on the **Power Presentations CD-ROM**.

Exercise 22 Addition information about smokejumpers can be found at www.fs.fed.us/fire/people/smokejumpers

19. **CONSTRUCTION** People who plaster ceilings sometimes walk on stilts. This allows them to reach high ceilings without having to move a ladder. The data set below gives the heights (in inches) of nine plasterers.

72, 73, 71, 66, 74, 68, 72, 69, 72

a. Find the mean, median, mode, range, and standard deviation of the given heights. **about 70.8, 72, 72, 8, about 2.4**

b. The plasterers use stilts that are 28 inches high. Find the mean, median, mode, range, and standard deviation of the plasterers' heights with stilts. **about 98.8, 100, 100, 8, about 2.4**

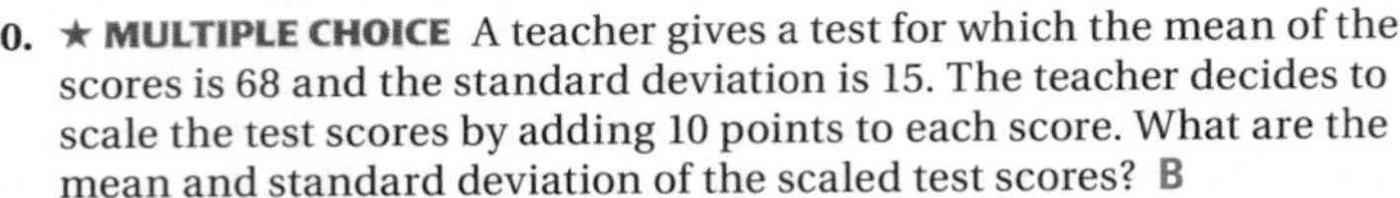

20. ★ **MULTIPLE CHOICE** A teacher gives a test for which the mean of the scores is 68 and the standard deviation is 15. The teacher decides to scale the test scores by adding 10 points to each score. What are the mean and standard deviation of the scaled test scores? **B**

Ⓐ mean: 68, standard deviation: 25 Ⓑ mean: 78, standard deviation: 15

Ⓒ mean: 78, standard deviation: 25 Ⓓ mean: 78, standard deviation: 5

B

21. ◆ **MULTIPLE REPRESENTATIONS** The data set gives the winning distances (in meters) in the women's Olympic long jump event from 1952 to 2004.

6.24, 6.35, 6.37, 6.76, 6.82, 6.78, 6.72, 7.06, 6.96, 7.40, 7.14, 7.12, 6.99, 7.07

a. **Find Statistics in Meters** Find the mean, median, mode, range, and standard deviation of the distances in meters. **about 6.84, 6.89, no mode, 1.16, about 0.324**

b. **Find Statistics in Feet** Find the statistics listed in part (a) for the distances in feet. (*Note:* 1 meter ≈ 3.28 feet.) **about 22.4, about 22.6, no mode, about 3.80, about 1.06**

22. ★ **SHORT RESPONSE** The data set below gives the weights (in pounds) of eight smokejumpers with their equipment.

287, 265, 273, 275, 295, 280, 290, 280

a. Find the mean, median, mode, range, and standard deviation of the given weights. **about 281, 280, 280, 30, about 9.2**

b. The equipment each smokejumper carries weighs about 115 pounds. Find the mean, median, mode, range, and standard deviation of the weights of the smokejumpers without their equipment. *Explain* your reasoning.

22b. about 166, 165, 165, 30, about 9.2; a constant of −115 is added to the original mean, median, and mode to determine the values. The range and standard deviation remain the same.

23. ★ **EXTENDED RESPONSE** The water temperature in an outdoor pool is measured 12 times during a certain week. The temperatures (in degrees Fahrenheit) are listed below.

74.5, 81.9, 72.5, 73.4, 78.4, 72.6, 76.8, 74.5, 77.6, 72.0, 79.2, 76.2

a. Find the mean, median, mode, range, and standard deviation of the Fahrenheit temperatures. **75.8, about 75.4, 74.5, 9.9, about 3.0**

b. Convert all of the Fahrenheit temperatures F to Celsius temperatures C using the formula $C = \frac{5}{9}(F - 32)$. **about 23.6, about 27.7, 22.5, 23.0, about 25.8, about 22.6, about 24.9, about 23.6, about 25.3, about 22.2, about 26.2, about 24.6**

c. Find the mean, median, mode, range, and standard deviation of the Celsius temperatures. **about 24.3, 24.1, 23.6, 5.5, about 1.6**

d. *Describe* the effects of converting from Fahrenheit to Celsius on the measures of central tendency and dispersion. **The effect is a multiplication transformation of $\frac{5}{9}$, along with an addition transformation of about −17.8 for the mean, median, and mode.**

◯ = **WORKED-OUT SOLUTIONS** on p. WS1 ★ = **STANDARDIZED TEST PRACTICE** ◆ = **MULTIPLE REPRESENTATIONS**

. $50,250, 2,000; the tal salary id increases $75,000 thus creasing e average lary by $750. nce all of the pervisor's laries are eater than e median fore and after e increase in y the median ays the same.

24. **WEATHER** The graph shows the average rainfall (in centimeters) for New York's Central Park during each month of the year. Find the mean, median, mode, range, and standard deviation of the rainfall amounts in centimeters and in inches. (*Note:* 1 centimeter ≈ 0.3937 inch.) **10 cm, 10.05 cm, 9.9 cm, 3.1 cm, about 1.0 cm; about 3.9 in., about 4.0 in., about 3.9 in., about 1.2 in., about 0.39 in.**

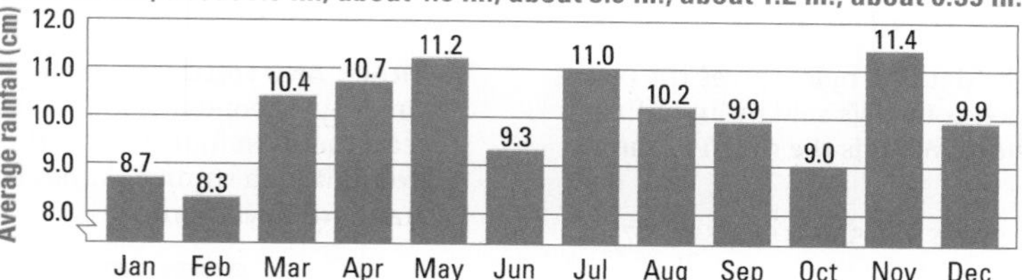

C 25. **CHALLENGE** A company has 5 executives, 15 supervisors, and 80 production workers. The salary ranges are $100,000–$140,000 for the executives, $60,000–$90,000 for the supervisors, and $30,000–$50,000 for the production workers. The mean of all the salaries is $49,500, and the median is $42,000. Each supervisor gets a $5000 raise and no one else gets a raise. What are the new mean and median? *Explain.*

KENTUCKY MIXED REVIEW

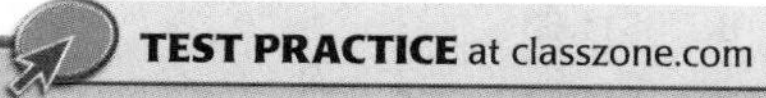
TEST PRACTICE at classzone.com

26. Maria packs 4 different pairs of shorts and 7 different shirts for a vacation with her family. How many different outfits are possible? **C**

Ⓐ 11 Ⓑ 18 Ⓒ 28 Ⓓ 30

27. The quadrilaterals shown at the right are similar. What is the value of x? **D**

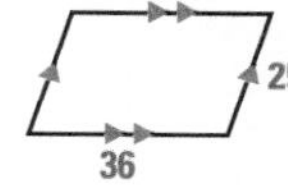

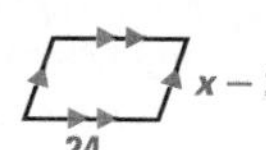

Ⓐ $\frac{50}{3}$ Ⓑ $\frac{56}{3}$

Ⓒ $\frac{83}{4}$ Ⓓ 27

QUIZ *for Lessons 11.1–11.2*

Find the mean, median, mode, range, and standard deviation of the data set. *(p. 744)*

1. 8, 5, 5, 9, 11, 15, 7, 11, 16 **about 9.7, 9, 5 and 11, 11, about 3.7**
2. 18, 19, 23, 17, 19, 15, 14, 24, 21 **about 18.9, 19, 19, 10, about 3.2**
3. 56, 45, 48, 47, 56, 55, 43, 44 **about 49.3, 47.5, 56, 13, about 5.2**
4. 67, 70, 73, 68, 71, 73, 74, 73, 70 **71, 71, 73, 7, about 2.3**
5. 145, 181, 163, 150, 158, 172, 159 **about 161, 159, no mode, 36, about 11.4**
6. 246, 231, 261, 244, 250, 232, 246, 258 **246, 246, 246, 30, about 10.1**
7. **DIGITAL CAMERAS** The data set below gives the original prices of nine different digital cameras at an electronics store. The store is offering a promotion in which all digital cameras ordered online are 20% off. Find the mean, median, mode, range, and standard deviation of the original prices and of the sale prices. *(p. 751)*

$120, $130, $150, $180, $230, $280, $320, $320, $350

about 231, 230, 320, 230, about 84.4; about 185, 184, 256, 184, about 67.5

EXTRA PRACTICE for Lesson 11.2, p. 1020

ONLINE QUIZ at classzone.com

5 ASSESS AND RETEACH

Daily Homework Quiz

Transparency Available

The data set below gives the original price per share of 5 stocks that your parents own.

$33, $18, $18, $22, $35

1. Suppose the stocks double in value by the time you go to college. Find the mean, median, mode, range, and standard deviation of the original values and the doubled values. **mean: $25.20 and $50.40, median: $22 and $44, mode: $18 and $36, range: $17 and $34, standard deviation: $7.36 and $14.72**
2. Find the mean, median, mode, range, and standard deviation if the original values increase by $30. **mean: $55.20, median: $52, mode: $48, range: $17, standard deviation: $7.36**

Online Quiz

Available at **classzone.com**

Diagnosis/Remediation

- Practice A, B, C in Chapter 11 Resource Book, pp. 17–19
- Study Guide in Chapter 11 Resource Book, pp. 20–21
- Practice Workbook, pp. 163–164
- @HomeTutor

Challenge

Additional challenge is available in the Chapter 11 Resource Book, p. 25.

Quiz

An easily-readable reduced copy of the quiz (with answers) on Lessons 11.1–11.2 from the Assessment Book can be found on p. 742E.

Kentucky Mixed Review

1. C
2. B
3. B
4. B
5. B
6. C
7. a. Average score is 84. Standard deviation is 5.40
   b. 84 − x; 5.40. *Sample answer:* The mean will decrease by x because the center of the scores decreases when the scores all decrease by the same amount; however, the standard deviation will not change because the spread of the scores stays the same.

Lessons 11.1–11.2

1. **TV PRICES** The data set below gives the prices of eight 13-inch color TVs sold by an online electronics store. What is the mean of the TV prices?

   \$84, \$75, \$70, \$100, \$80, \$120, \$80, \$75

   A. \$76.13 B. \$80

   C. \$85.50 D. \$87

2. **SALE PRICES** The online electronics store from Exercise 1 is having a three-day sale in which all 13-inch color TVs are 25% off. What is the approximate standard deviation of the sale prices of the eight 13-inch TVs in Exercise 1?

   A. \$3.88

   B. \$11.63

   C. \$15.51

   D. \$60

3. **TEMPERATURES** The table below shows the average temperature (in degrees Fahrenheit) for each month of the year in Buffalo, New York. What is the range of these temperatures?

Average Monthly Temperatures in Buffalo, NY
23.7, 24.6, 33.8, 45.1, 56.5, 65.8, 71.1, 68.9, 61.9, 51.1, 40.5, 29.1

   A. 24 B. 45.2

   C. 46.4 D. 46.6

4. **SALARIES** The data set below gives the salaries (in thousands of dollars) of eight employees of an advertising agency after they receive an annual bonus of \$2500. What is the approximate mean of the salaries *without* the annual bonus?

   49, 52, 46.5, 43, 59.5, 54, 49.5, 61.5

   A. 48.3 B. 49.4

   C. 51.9 D. 54.4

5. **TRACK AND FIELD** The table shows the trial times (in seconds) of four track-and-field teammates in four trials of the 100 meter sprint event. Which runner's times have the lowest standard deviation?

	Trial 1	Trial 2	Trial 3	Trial 4
Runner 1	14.0	13.5	13.1	12.5
Runner 2	13.4	13.3	13.3	13.2
Runner 3	11.9	11.7	11.5	11.2
Runner 4	15.5	14	13.2	16.1

   A. Runner 1

   B. Runner 2

   C. Runner 3

   D. Runner 4

6. **MOUNTAIN BIKES** The data set below gives the prices of 14 mountain bikes. What is the approximate mean of the prices?

   \$155, \$250, \$290, \$200, \$150, \$200, \$270, \$670, \$250, \$230, \$200, \$150, \$270, \$850

   A. \$240

   B. \$253

   C. \$295

   D. \$303

7. **OPEN-RESPONSE** The data set below gives the score of each member of a high school golf team in the first round of the season.

   76, 84, 81, 92, 87

   a. Find the average score and standard deviation for the team.

   b. Suppose that each player decreased his or her score by x strokes. What is the new average score and standard deviation, in terms of x? *Explain.*

11.3 Use Normal Distributions

MA-HS-4.2.2 Students will know the characteristics of the Gaussian normal distribution (bell-shaped curve).

Before You interpreted probability distributions.

Now You will study normal distributions.

Why? So you can model animal populations, as in Example 3.

Key Vocabulary
- **normal distribution**
- **normal curve**
- **standard normal distribution**
- ***z*-score**

In Lesson 10.6, you studied probability distributions. One type of probability distribution is a *normal distribution*. A **normal distribution** is modeled by a bell-shaped curve called a **normal curve** that is symmetric about the mean.

KEY CONCEPT *For Your Notebook*

Areas Under a Normal Curve

A normal distribution with mean $\overline{x}$ and standard deviation σ has the following properties:

- The total area under the related normal curve is 1.
- About 68% of the area lies within 1 standard deviation of the mean.
- About 95% of the area lies within 2 standard deviations of the mean.
- About 99.7% of the area lies within 3 standard deviations of the mean.

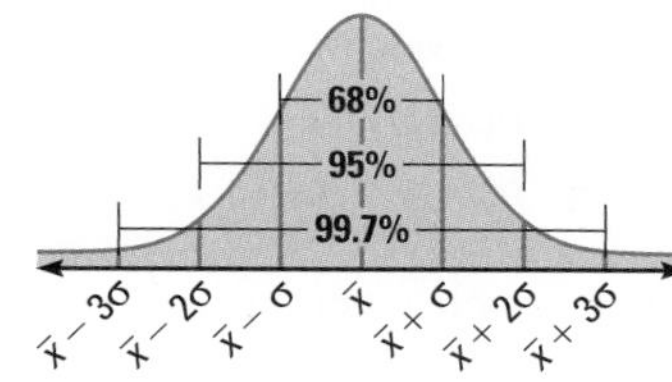

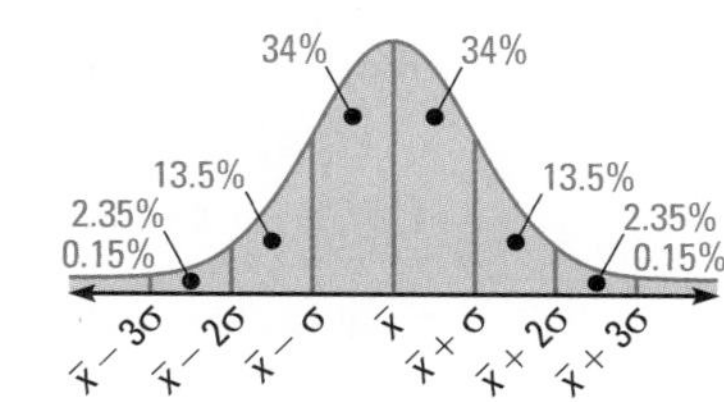

INTERPRET GRAPHS

An area under a normal curve can be interpreted either as a percentage of the data values in the distribution or as a probability.

EXAMPLE 1 Find a normal probability

A normal distribution has mean $\overline{x}$ and standard deviation σ. For a randomly selected x-value from the distribution, find $P(\overline{x} - 2\sigma \le x \le \overline{x})$.

Solution

The probability that a randomly selected x-value lies between between $\overline{x} - 2\sigma$ and $\overline{x}$ is the shaded area under the normal curve shown.

$P(\overline{x} - 2\sigma \le x \le \overline{x}) = 0.135 + 0.34 = 0.475$

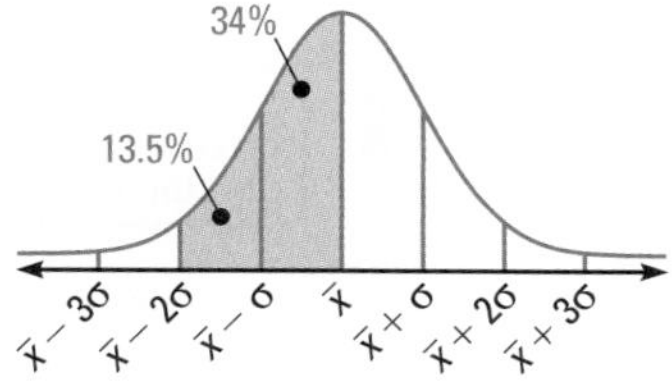

Animated Algebra at classzone.com

1 PLAN AND PREPARE

Warm-Up Exercises

Transparency Available

Simplify the expression.

1. $\frac{93 - 97}{1.5}$ **−2.67** 2. $\frac{20 - 18}{0.8}$ **2.5**
3. 2(0.34) + 2(0.135) **0.95**
4. Sixty-eight percent of a sample of cars tested got between 27 and 32 miles per gallon of gasoline. What percent of the cars tested got less than 27 miles per gallon or more than 32 miles per gallon? **32%**

Notetaking Guide

Transparency Available

Promotes interactive learning and notetaking skills, pp. 292–294.

Pacing

Basic: 1 day
Average: 1 day
Advanced: 1 day
Block: 0.5 block with 11.4
- See *Teaching Guide/Lesson Plan*.

2 FOCUS AND MOTIVATE

Essential Question

Big Idea 2, p. 743

Where are the values in a normal distribution that rarely occur displayed on a normal curve? **Tell students they will learn how to answer this question by examining the areas under the normal curve.**

Resource Planning Guide

Chapter Resource Book
- Teaching Guide/Lesson Plan (pp. 26–27)
- Activity Master (p. 28)
- Practice levels A, B, C (pp. 30–32)
- Study Guide (pp. 33–34)
- Catch-up for Absent Students (p. 35)
- Application (p. 36)
- Challenge (p. 37)

Workbooks
- Notetaking Guide (pp. 292–294)
- Practice Workbook (pp. 165–166)

Teaching Options
- **Power Presentations CD-ROM** provides dynamic electronic teaching resources for the classroom.
- **Activity Generator CD-ROM** provides editable activities for all ability levels.

Interactive Technology
- Easy Planner
- Power Presentations CD-ROM
- Activity Generator CD-ROM
- Animated Algebra
- Test Generator CD-ROM
- Online Quiz
- eWorkbook
- eEdition
- @HomeTutor

Resources for English Learners
- Quick Reference for English Learners
- Spanish Study Guide
- Multi-Language Visual Glossary
- Student Resources in Spanish

See also the *Algebra 2 Toolkit* for more strategies for meeting individual needs.

Motivating the Lesson

Have students calculate the mean and standard deviation of their heights. Then ask them to determine how many of them are within 1, 2, and 3 standard deviations of their mean height. In this lesson, students will study how the values in a special distribution are distributed about the mean.

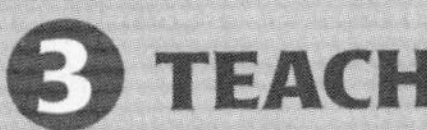

3 TEACH

Extra Example 1

A normal distribution has mean $\overline{x}$ and standard deviation σ. For a randomly selected x-value from the distribution, find $P(\overline{x} - \sigma \leq x \leq \overline{x} + 3\sigma)$ 0.8385

An **Animated Algebra** activity is available on-line for **Example 1**. This activity is also available on the **Power Presentations CD-ROM**.

Extra Example 2

The score on an exam for entrance to a firefighter program are normally distributed with a mean of 200 points and standard deviation of 20 points.

a. About what percent of the candidates score lower than 160 points? 2.5%

b. Candidates with scores above 220 are admitted into the training program. About what percent of the candidates are accepted into the program? 16%

EXAMPLE 2 Interpret normally distributed data

READING The abbreviation "mg/dl" stands for "milligrams per deciliter."

HEALTH The blood cholesterol readings for a group of women are normally distributed with a mean of 172 mg/dl and a standard deviation of 14 mg/dl.

a. About what percent of the women have readings between 158 and 186?

b. Readings higher than 200 are considered undesirable. About what percent of the readings are undesirable?

Solution

a. The readings of 158 and 186 represent one standard deviation on either side of the mean, as shown below. So, 68% of the women have readings between 158 and 186.

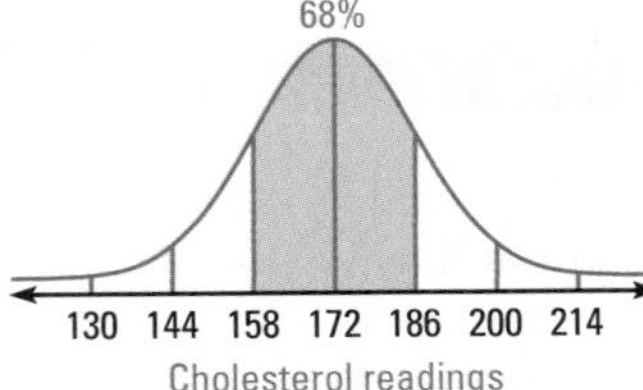

b. A reading of 200 is two standard deviations to the right of the mean, as shown. So, the percent of readings that are undesirable is 2.35% + 0.15%, or 2.5%.

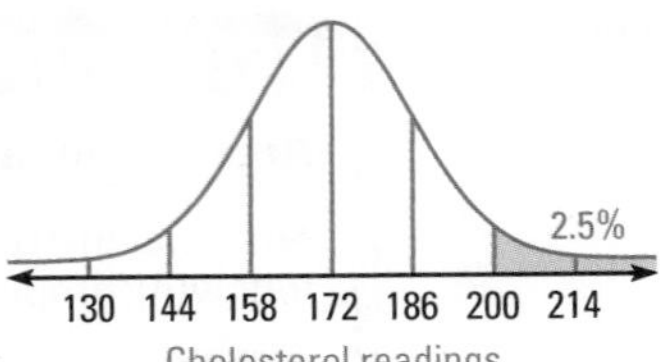

✓ GUIDED PRACTICE for Examples 1 and 2

A normal distribution has mean $\overline{x}$ and standard deviation σ. Find the indicated probability for a randomly selected x-value from the distribution.

1. $P(x \leq \overline{x})$ 0.5
2. $P(x \geq \overline{x})$ 0.5
3. $P(\overline{x} \leq x \leq \overline{x} + 2\sigma)$ 0.475
4. $P(\overline{x} - \sigma \leq x \leq \overline{x})$ 0.34
5. $P(x \leq \overline{x} - 3\sigma)$ 0.0015
6. $P(x \geq \overline{x} + \sigma)$ 0.16
7. **WHAT IF?** In Example 2, what percent of the women have readings between 172 and 200? 47.5%

STANDARD NORMAL DISTRIBUTION The **standard normal distribution** is the normal distribution with mean 0 and standard deviation 1. The formula below can be used to transform x-values from a normal distribution with mean $\overline{x}$ and standard deviation σ into z-values having a standard normal distribution.

Formula: $z = \dfrac{x - \overline{x}}{\sigma}$

Subtract the mean from the given x-value, then divide by the standard deviation.

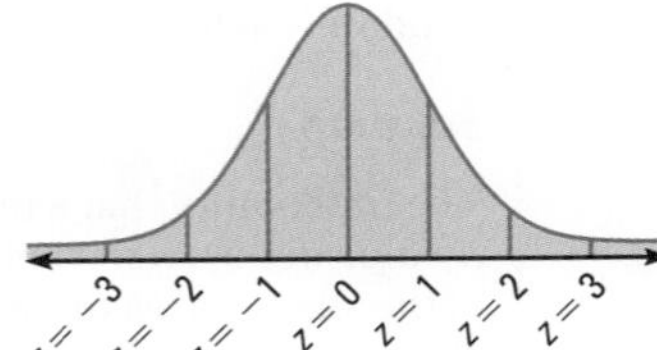

The z-value for a particular x-value is called the **z-score** for the x-value and is the number of standard deviations the x-value lies above or below the mean $\overline{x}$.

Differentiated Instruction

Below Level To help students see the relationship between the area under the normal curve and the distributions of normally distributed data, explain that normal distributions are all bell-shaped, but the bells come in various shapes and sizes. Ask these students to draw several different bell curves, some tall, skinny bells, and some short, fat bells.

See also the *Algebra 2 Toolkit* for more strategies.

STANDARD NORMAL TABLE If z is a randomly selected value from a standard normal distribution, you can use the table below to find the probability that z is less than or equal to some given value. For example, the table shows that $P(z \le -0.4) = 0.3446$. You can find the value of $P(z \le -0.4)$ in the table by finding the value where row -0 and column $.4$ intersect.

Standard Normal Table

z	.0	.1	.2	.3	.4	.5	.6	.7	.8	.9
−3	.0013	.0010	.0007	.0005	.0003	.0002	.0002	.0001	.0001	.0000+
−2	.0228	.0179	.0139	.0107	.0082	.0062	.0047	.0035	.0026	.0019
−1	.1587	.1357	.1151	.0968	.0808	.0668	.0548	.0446	.0359	.0287
−0	.5000	.4602	.4207	.3821	.3446	.3085	.2743	.2420	.2119	.1841
0	.5000	.5398	.5793	.6179	.6554	.6915	.7257	.7580	.7881	.8159
1	.8413	.8643	.8849	.9032	.9192	.9332	.9452	.9554	.9641	.9713
2	.9772	.9821	.9861	.9893	.9918	.9938	.9953	.9965	.9974	.9981
3	.9987	.9990	.9993	.9995	.9997	.9998	.9998	.9999	.9999	1.0000−

ADING

the table, the value 00+ means "slightly re than 0" and the ue 1.0000− means ghtly less than 1."

You can also use the standard normal table to find probabilities for *any* normal distribution by first converting values from the distribution to z-scores.

EXAMPLE 3 Use a *z*-score and the standard normal table

BIOLOGY Scientists conducted aerial surveys of a seal sanctuary and recorded the number x of seals they observed during each survey. The numbers of seals observed were normally distributed with a mean of 73 seals and a standard deviation of 14.1 seals. Find the probability that at most 50 seals were observed during a survey.

Solution

STEP 1 **Find** the z-score corresponding to an x-value of 50.

$$z = \frac{x - \overline{x}}{\sigma} = \frac{50 - 73}{14.1} \approx -1.6$$

STEP 2 **Use** the table to find $P(x \le 50) \approx P(z \le -1.6)$.

The table shows that $P(z \le -1.6) = 0.0548$. So, the probability that at most 50 seals were observed during a survey is about 0.0548.

z	.0	.1	.2	.3	.4	.5	.6	.7	.8	.9
−3	.0013	.0010	.0007	.0005	.0003	.0002	.0002	.0001	.0001	.0000+
−2	.0228	.0179	.0139	.0107	.0082	.0062	.0047	.0035	.0026	.0019
−1	.1587	.1357	.1151	.0968	.0808	.0668	.0548	.0446	.0359	.0287
−0	.5000	.4602	.4207	.3821	.3446	.3085	.2743	.2420	.2119	.1841
0	.5000	.5398	.5793	.6179	.6554	.6915	.7257	.7580	.7881	.8159

✓ **GUIDED PRACTICE** for Example 3

8. **WHAT IF?** In Example 3, find the probability that at most 90 seals were observed during a survey. **0.8849**

9. **REASONING** *Explain* why it makes sense that $P(z \le 0) = 0.5$. **The standard normal distribution is symmetric about its mean of 0, so half the values have z-scores less than or equal to zero.**

Extra Example 3

A survey of 20 colleges found that the average credit card debt for seniors was \$3450. The debt was normally distributed with a standard deviation of \$1175. Find the probability that the credit card debt of the seniors was at most \$3600. **about 0.5398**

Key Questions to Ask for Example 3

- What does the z-score represent? **An observation of 50 seals is 1.6 standard deviations below the mean.**
- How does the probability of 0.0548 correspond to the areas given in the Key Concept box on page 757? **The area under the curve at $\overline{x} - 1.6\sigma$ is between 0.025 and 0.16, but closer to 0.025.**

Closing the Lesson

Have students summarize the major points of the lesson and answer the Essential Question: Where are the values in a normal distribution that rarely occur displayed on a normal curve?

- **The bell-shaped normal curve models a normal distribution.**
- **In a normal distribution with mean $\overline{x}$ and standard deviation σ, the total area under the curve is 1. About 68% of the area lies withing 1 standard deviation of the mean, about 95% of the area lies within 2 standard deviations of the mean, and about 99.7% of the area lies within 3 standard deviations of the mean.**
- **The formula $z = \frac{x - \overline{x}}{\sigma}$ can be used to transform x-values from a normal distribution with mean $\overline{x}$ and standard deviation σ into z-values having a standard normal distribution with mean 0 and standard deviation 1.**

The values occur in the ends of the curve.

Differentiated Instruction

Kinesthetic Learners Some students will struggle with using the standard normal table. Have students work in pairs and create sample problems for one another. Have them trace each row and column with their two index fingers, or use a pair of rulers, to find the intersection of the row and column relevant to their problem.

See also the *Algebra 2 Toolkit* for more strategies.

11.3 EXERCISES

HOMEWORK KEY ○ = WORKED-OUT SOLUTIONS on p. WS20 for Exs. 3, 11, and 33
★ = STANDARDIZED TEST PRACTICE Exs. 2, 17, 18, 28, and 35

4 PRACTICE AND APPLY

Assignment Guide

Answer Transparencies available for all exercises

Basic:
Day 1: pp. 760–762
Exs. 1–5, 9–22, 31–34, 37

Average:
Day 1: pp. 760–762
Exs. 1, 2, 4–6, 9–18, 22–24, 28, 29, 31–35, 38

Advanced:
Day 1: pp. 760–762
Exs. 1, 2, 7, 8, 11–18, 24–36*, 37

Block:
pp. 760–762
Exs. 1, 2, 4–6, 9–18, 22–24, 28, 29, 31–35, 38 (with 11.4)

Differentiated Instruction

See *Algebra 2 Best Practices Toolkit* for suggestions on addressing the needs of a diverse classroom.

Homework Check

For a quick check of student understanding of key concepts, go over the following exercises:

Basic: 4, 12, 20, 31, 32
Average: 6, 14, 22, 32, 33
Advanced: 8, 16, 26, 33, 34

Extra Practice

- Student Edition, p. 1020
- Chapter 11 Resource Book: Practice levels A, B, C, pp. 30–32

Practice Worksheet

An easily-readable reduced practice page (with answers) for this lesson can be found on p. 742C.

SKILL PRACTICE

A

1. **VOCABULARY** Copy and complete: A(n) __?__ is a bell-shaped curve that is symmetric about the mean. normal curve

2. ★ **WRITING** *Describe* how to use the standard normal table to find $P(z \le 1.4)$.
In the table, find the value where row 1 and column .4 intersect.

EXAMPLE 1 on p. 757 for Exs. 3–10

FIND A NORMAL PROBABILITY **A normal distribution has mean $\bar{x}$ and standard deviation σ. Find the indicated probability for a randomly selected x-value from the distribution.**

3. $P(x \le \bar{x} - \sigma)$ 0.16
4. $P(x \ge \bar{x} + 2\sigma)$ 0.025
5. $P(x \le \bar{x} + \sigma)$ 0.84
6. $P(x \ge \bar{x} - \sigma)$ 0.84
7. $P(\bar{x} - \sigma \le x \le \bar{x} + \sigma)$ 0.68
8. $P(\bar{x} - 3\sigma \le x \le \bar{x})$ 0.4985

USING A NORMAL CURVE **Give the percent of the area under the normal curve represented by the shaded region.**

9. 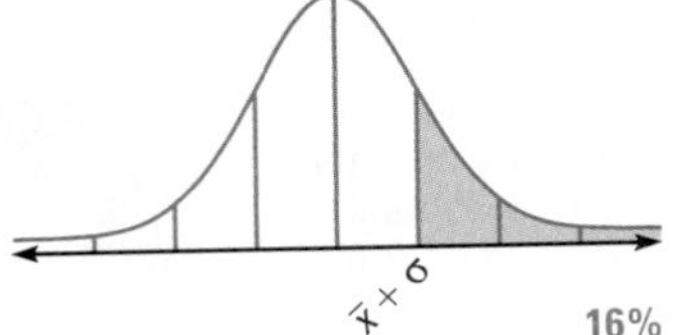

16%

10. 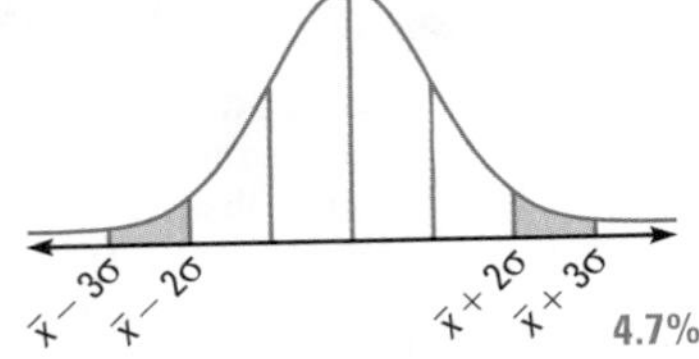

4.7%

EXAMPLE 2 on p. 758 for Exs. 11–18

NORMAL DISTRIBUTIONS **A normal distribution has a mean of 33 and a standard deviation of 4. Find the probability that a randomly selected x-value from the distribution is in the given interval.**

11. Between 29 and 37 0.68
12. Between 33 and 45 0.4985
13. Between 21 and 41 0.9735
14. At least 25 0.975
15. At least 29 0.84
16. At most 37 0.84

17. ★ **MULTIPLE CHOICE** A normal distribution has a mean of 84 and a standard deviation of 5. What is the probability that a randomly selected x-value from the distribution is between 74 and 94? C

Ⓐ 0.475 Ⓑ 0.68 Ⓒ 0.95 Ⓓ 0.997

18. ★ **MULTIPLE CHOICE** A normal distribution has a mean of 51 and a standard deviation of 3. What is the probability that a randomly selected x-value from the distribution is at most 48? B

Ⓐ 0.025 Ⓑ 0.16 Ⓒ 0.84 Ⓓ 0.975

EXAMPLE 3 on p. 759 for Exs. 19–27

B

STANDARD NORMAL TABLE **A normal distribution has a mean of 64 and a standard deviation of 7. Use the standard normal table on page 759 to find the indicated probability for a randomly selected x-value from the distribution.**

19. $P(x \le 68)$ 0.7257
20. $P(x \le 80)$ 0.9893
21. $P(x \le 45)$ 0.0035
22. $P(x \le 54)$ 0.0808
23. $P(x \le 64)$ 0.5
24. $P(x \ge 59)$ 0.758
25. $P(x \ge 75)$ 0.0548
26. $P(60 \le x \le 75)$ 0.6709
27. $P(45 \le x \le 65)$ 0.5363

28. ★ **SHORT RESPONSE** Let x be a randomly selected value from a normal distribution with mean 80 and standard deviation 10. If $P(x \le k) = 0.9192$, what is the value of k? *Explain.* 94; 0.9192 corresponds to a z-score of 1.4, so $1.4 = \frac{x - 80}{10}$.

29. **ERROR ANALYSIS** In a study, the wheat yields (in bushels) for several plots of land were normally distributed with a mean of 4 bushels and a standard deviation of 0.25 bushel. *Describe* and correct the error in finding the probability that a plot yielded at least 3.8 bushels. The table was interpreted incorrectly; $P(z \ge -0.8) = 1 - 0.2119 = 0.7881$.

$$z = \frac{x - \bar{x}}{\sigma} = \frac{3.8 - 4}{0.25} = -0.8$$

From the standard normal table, $P(z \ge -0.8) = 0.2119$. So, the probability that a plot yielded at least 3.8 bushels is 0.2119.

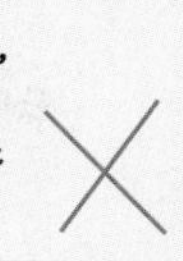

C 30. **CHALLENGE** A normal curve is defined by an equation of this form:

$$y = \frac{1}{\sigma\sqrt{2\pi}} e^{-\frac{1}{2}\left(\frac{x - \bar{x}}{\sigma}\right)^2}$$

a. **Graphing Calculator** Graph three equations of the given form. The equations should use the same mean but different standard deviations. See margin.

b. **Reasoning** *Describe* the effect of the standard deviation on the shape of a normal curve. *Sample answer:* As the standard deviation decreases, the normal curve gets steeper.

PROBLEM SOLVING

EXAMPLES A **2 and 3** on pp. 758–759 for Exs. 31–34

31. **BIOLOGY** The illustration shows a housefly at several times its actual size and indicates the fly's wing length. A study found that the wing lengths of houseflies are normally distributed with a mean of about 4.6 millimeters and a standard deviation of about 0.4 millimeter. What is the probability that a randomly selected housefly has a wing length of at least 5 millimeters? 0.16

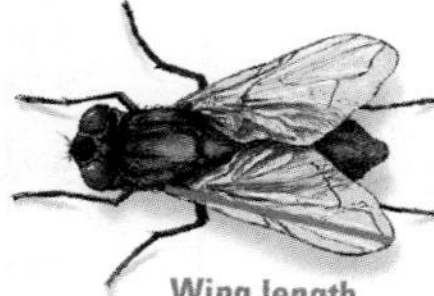

@HomeTutor for problem solving help at classzone.com

32. **FIRE DEPARTMENT** The time a fire department takes to arrive at the scene of an emergency is normally distributed with a mean of 6 minutes and a standard deviation of 1 minute.

a. What is the probability that the fire department takes at most 8 minutes to arrive at the scene of an emergency? 0.975

b. What is the probability that the fire department takes between 4 minutes and 7 minutes to arrive at the scene of an emergency? 0.815

@HomeTutor for problem solving help at classzone.com

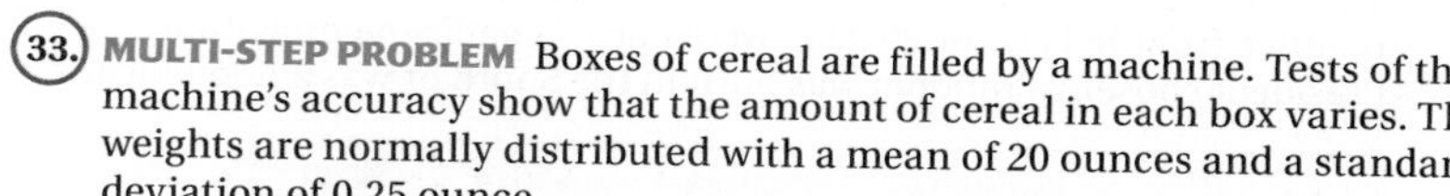

(33.) **MULTI-STEP PROBLEM** Boxes of cereal are filled by a machine. Tests of the machine's accuracy show that the amount of cereal in each box varies. The weights are normally distributed with a mean of 20 ounces and a standard deviation of 0.25 ounce.

a. Find the z-scores for weights of 19.4 ounces and 20.4 ounces. −2.4, 1.6

b. What is the probability that a randomly selected cereal box weighs at most 19.4 ounces? 0.0082

c. What is the probability that a randomly selected cereal box weighs between 19.4 ounces and 20.4 ounces? *Explain* your reasoning. 0.937; $P(z \le 1.6) - P(z \le -2.4)$

Mathematical Reasoning

Exercises 11–18 Students can draw and shade normal curves to model each exercise. Then they can show how their models and probabilities relate to the diagrams given in the Key Concept box on page 757.

Avoiding Common Errors

Exercises 19–33 To help students in subtracting $\bar{x}$ from x when finding a z-score, ask them to first determine whether an x-value lies above or below the mean on the normal curve. A value that lies above the mean should have a positive z-value and a value that lies below the mean should have a negative z-value.

Internet Reference

Exercise 34 More information about guayule plants can be found at www.uswcl.ars.ag.gov/EPD/NewCrops/Guayule.htm

30a. *Sample answer:* $y_1 = \frac{1}{5\sqrt{2\pi}} e^{-\frac{1}{2}\left(\frac{x-50}{5}\right)^2}$, $y_2 = \frac{1}{10\sqrt{2\pi}} e^{-\frac{1}{2}\left(\frac{x-50}{10}\right)^2}$, $y_3 = \frac{1}{15\sqrt{2\pi}} e^{-\frac{1}{2}\left(\frac{x-50}{15}\right)^2}$

Daily Homework Quiz

Transparency Available

1. A normal distribution has mean $\bar{x}$ and standard deviation σ. For a randomly selected x-value from the distribution, find $P(x \le \bar{x} - 2\sigma)$ **0.025**
2. The average donation during a fund drive was $75. The donations were normally distributed with a standard deviation of $15. Use a standard normal table to find the probability that a donation is at most $115. **0.9965**

Online Quiz

Available at **classzone.com**

Diagnosis/Remediation

- Practice A, B, C in Chapter 11 Resource Book, pp. 30–32
- Study Guide in Chapter 11 Resource Book, pp. 33–34
- Practice Workbook, pp. 165–166
- @HomeTutor

Challenge

Additional challenge is available in the Chapter 11 Resource Book, p. 37.

34. **BOTANY** The guayule plant, which grows in the southwestern United States and in Mexico, is one of several plants that can be used as a source of rubber. In a large group of guayule plants, the heights of the plants are normally distributed with a mean of 12 inches and a standard deviation of 2 inches.
    a. What percent of the plants are taller than 16 inches? **2.5%**
    b. What percent of the plants are at most 13 inches? **69.15%**
    c. What percent of the plants are between 7 inches and 14 inches? **83.51%**
    d. What percent of the plants are at least 3 inches taller than or shorter than the mean height? **86.64%**

Guayule plants

B 35. ★ **EXTENDED RESPONSE** Lisa and Ann took different college entrance tests. The scores on the test that Lisa took are normally distributed with a mean of 20 points and a standard deviation of 4.2 points. The scores on the test that Ann took are normally distributed with a mean of 500 points and a standard deviation of 90 points. Lisa scored 30 on her test, and Ann scored 610 on her test.
    a. **Calculate** Find the z-score for Lisa's test score. **2.4**
    b. **Calculate** Find the z-score for Ann's test score. **1.2**
    c. **Interpret** Which student scored better on her college entrance test? *Explain* your reasoning. **Lisa; in a standard normal distribution Lisa's score is higher.**

C 36. **CHALLENGE** According to a survey by the National Center for Health Statistics, the heights of adult men in the United States are normally distributed with a mean of 69 inches and a standard deviation of 2.75 inches.
    a. If you randomly choose 3 adult men, what is the probability that all of them are more than 6 feet tall? **0.0025**
    b. What is the probability that 5 randomly selected men all have heights between 65 inches and 75 inches? **0.657**

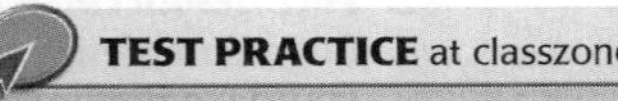

KY KENTUCKY MIXED REVIEW

TEST PRACTICE at classzone.com

37. What is the value of $5x^2 - 2x + 3$ when $x = -3$? **B**

    (A) −48 (B) −36 (C) 41 (D) 54

38. The table shows the regions of the United States in which the Presidents in office from 1853 through 2005 were born. What is the probability that a President chosen at random was born in the South or was a Republican? **B**

	Midwest	Northeast	South	West
Democrat	2	6	4	0
Republican	9	5	3	1

(A) $\frac{1}{10}$ (B) $\frac{11}{15}$ (C) $\frac{4}{5}$ (D) $\frac{5}{6}$

Extension
Use after Lesson 11.3

Approximate Binomial Distributions and Test Hypotheses

GOAL Use normal distributions to approximate binomial distributions.

In Lesson 10.6, you found probabilities related to a binomial distribution using the formula $P(k) = {}_nC_k p^k(1 - p)^{n-k}$. However, it can be tedious to use this formula when the number of probabilities to compute is large. In such cases, you may be able to use a normal distribution to approximate the binomial distribution.

KEY CONCEPT *For Your Notebook*

Normal Approximation of a Binomial Distribution

Consider the binomial distribution consisting of n trials with probability p of success on each trial. If $np \geq 5$ and $n(1 - p) \geq 5$, then the binomial distribution can be approximated by a normal distribution with the following mean and standard deviation.

Mean: $\bar{x} = np$ **Standard Deviation:** $\sigma = \sqrt{np(1 - p)}$

EXAMPLE 1 Find a binomial probability

SURVEYS According to a survey conducted by the Harris Poll, 24% of adults in the United States say that their favorite leisure-time activity is reading. You are conducting a random survey of 250 adults. What is the probability that you will find at most 53 adults who say that reading is their favorite leisure-time activity?

Solution

The number x of adults in your survey who say reading is their favorite leisure-time activity has a binomial distribution with $n = 250$ and $p = 0.24$. To solve the problem using the binomial probability formula, you would have to calculate the following:

$$P(x \leq 53) = P(x = 0) + P(x = 1) + P(x = 2) + \cdots + P(x = 53)$$

This would be tedious. Instead, you can approximate the answer using a normal distribution with the mean and standard deviation given below.

$\bar{x} = np = 250(0.24) = 60$ **Find mean.**

$\sigma = \sqrt{np(1 - p)} = \sqrt{250(0.24)(0.76)} \approx 7$ **Find standard deviation.**

For this normal distribution, 53 is about one standard deviation to the left of the mean. Therefore:

$$P(x \leq 53) \approx 0.0015 + 0.0235 + 0.135 = 0.16$$

▶ The probability that at most 53 of the people surveyed say reading is their favorite leisure-time activity is about 0.16.

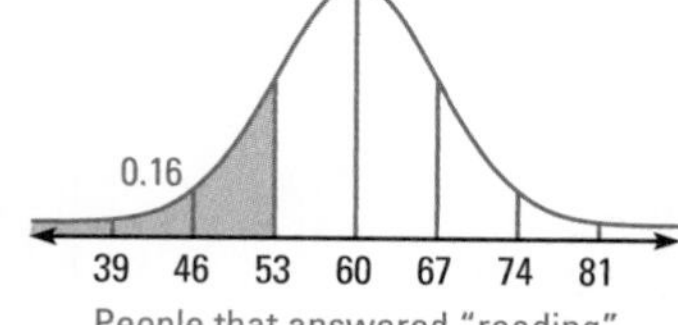

People that answered "reading"

[C]HECK [R]EASONABLENESS
[In] Example 1, note that $np = 60 \geq 5$ [a]nd that $n(1 - p) = 190 \geq 5$. [S]o, it is reasonable [to] use a normal [a]pproximation.

1 PLAN AND PREPARE

Warm-Up Exercises

Solve the equation $\sigma = \sqrt{np(1 - p)}$ for the given values of n and p.

1. $n = 25$ and $p = 0.35$ 2.38
2. $n = 32$ and $p = 0.78$ 2.34
3. $n = 178$ and $p = 0.5$ 6.67
4. $n = 450$ and $p = 0.18$ 8.15
5. Fourteen of 120 seniors surveyed said they had been accepted to the college of their choice. What percent is this? 11.7%

2 FOCUS AND MOTIVATE

Essential Question

Big Idea 2, p. 743

How can you compute a probability related to a binomial distribution or test a statistic from the distribution when the number of probabilities you must compute is very large? **Tell students they will learn how to answer this question by applying the normal distribution to a probability distribution and by using statistical methods of hypothesis testing.**

NCTM STANDARDS

Standard 5: Apply basic concepts of probability

Standard 7: Use types of reasoning/methods of proof

3 TEACH

Extra Example 1

According to a survey conducted by a research company, 55% of female scientists say their first area of interest in science is in the biological sciences. You are conducting a random survey of 300 female scientists. What is the probability that you will find at most 139 female scientists who say that their first area of interest in the sciences is in the biological sciences? **0.0015**

Extra Example 2

In a poll of 905 U.S. adult citizens from one state, 43% reported that they thought their senior U.S. Senator was doing a good job. To test this finding, you survey 50 adults and find that 12 of them think their senior U.S. Senator is doing a good job. Should you reject the survey's findings? **In a random sample of 50 U.S. adult citizens, there is about a 0.35% probability of finding 12 or fewer adult citizens who think their senior senator is doing a good job. With a probability this small, you should reject the hypothesis.**

Closing the Lesson

Have students summarize the major points of the lesson and answer the Essential Question: How can you compute a probability related to a binomial distribution or test a statistic from the distribution when the number of probabilities you must compute is very large?

- **A normal approximation of a binomial distribution has mean $\overline{x} = np$ and standard deviation $\sigma = \sqrt{np(1-p)}$.**
- **Hypothesis testing involves stating the hypothesis you are testing, computing a statistical measure, and calculating a resulting probability to determine if the hypothesis should or should not be rejected.**

You can use a normal approximation of a binomial distribution and hypothesis testing.

HYPOTHESIS TESTING You can use the following procedure to test a hypothesis about a statistical measure for a population.

KEY CONCEPT *For Your Notebook*

Hypothesis Testing

STEP 1 **State** the hypothesis you are testing. The hypothesis should make a statement about some statistical measure of a population (such as the percent of the population that has a certain characteristic).

STEP 2 **Collect** data from a random sample of the population and compute the statistical measure of the sample.

STEP 3 **Assume** that the hypothesis is true and calculate the resulting probability p of obtaining the sample statistical measure *or a more extreme* sample statistical measure. If this probability is small (typically $p < 0.05$), you should reject the hypothesis.

CHOOSE CRITERION
In Step 3, some statisticians use $p < 0.1$ or $p < 0.01$ as a condition for rejecting a hypothesis.

EXAMPLE 2 Test a hypothesis

FIREFIGHTING A recent Harris Poll claimed that 48% of adults consider firefighting to be a prestigious occupation. To test this finding, you survey 40 adults and find that 15 of them do consider firefighting a prestigious occupation. Should you reject the Harris Poll's findings? *Explain.*

Solution

STEP 1 **State** the hypothesis.

48% of adults consider firefighting a prestigious occupation.

STEP 2 **Collect** data and calculate a statistical measure.

In your survey, 15 out of 40 people, or 37.5%, consider firefighting to b a prestigious occupation.

STEP 3 **Assume** that the hypothesis in Step 1 is true. Find the resulting probability that you could randomly select 15 *or fewer* adults out of 4C who consider firefighting a prestigious occupation. This probability is

$$P(x \le 15) = P(x = 0) + P(x = 1) + P(x = 2) + \cdots + P(x = 15)$$

where each term in the sum is a binomial probability with $n = 40$ and $p = 0.48$.

You can approximate the binomial distribution with a normal distribution having the following mean and standard deviation:

$$\overline{x} = np = 40(0.48) = 19.2$$

$$\sigma = \sqrt{np(1-p)} = \sqrt{40(0.48)(0.52)} \approx 3.16$$

Using a z-score and the standard normal table on page 759 gives:

$$P(x \le 15) \approx P\left(z \le \frac{15 - 19.2}{3.16}\right) \approx P(z \le -1.3) = 0.0968$$

▶ So, if it is true that *48% of adults consider firefighting a prestigious occupation,* then there is about a 10% probability of finding 15 or fewer adults who conside firefighting prestigious in a random sample of 40 adults. With a probability th large, you should *not* reject the hypothesis.

PRACTICE

EXAMPLE 1 on p. 763 for Exs. 1–18

APPROXIMATING BINOMIAL DISTRIBUTIONS **Find the mean and standard deviation of a normal distribution that approximates the binomial distribution with n trials and probability p of success on each trial.**

1. $n = 24, p = 0.4$ 9.6, 2.4
2. $n = 40, p = 0.6$ 24, about 3.1
3. $n = 46, p = 0.3$ 13.8, about 3.1
4. $n = 55, p = 0.15$ 8.25, about 2.6
5. $n = 36, p = 0.7$ 25.2, about 2.7
6. $n = 66, p = 0.2$ 13.2, about 3.2
7. $n = 110, p = 0.08$ 8.8, about 2.8
8. $n = 125, p = 0.35$ about 43.8, about 5.3
9. $n = 140, p = 0.75$ 105, about 5.1

COLORBLINDNESS **Use the fact that approximately 4% of people are colorblind. Consider a class of 460 students.**

10. What is the probability that 15 or fewer students are colorblind? about 0.21
11. What is the probability that 12 or more students are colorblind? about 0.93
12. What is the probability that between 6 and 18 students are colorblind? about 0.46

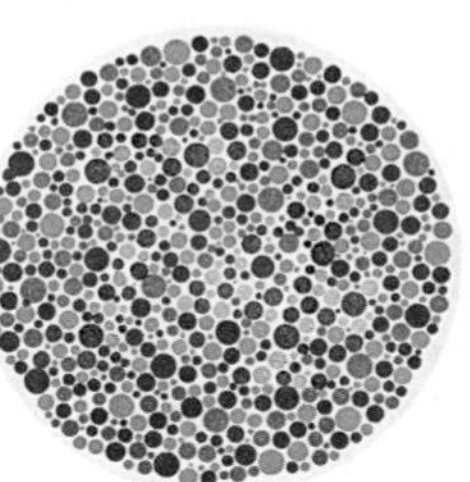

Color vision test

LEFT-HANDEDNESS **Use the fact that approximately 9% of people are left-handed. Consider a high school with 1221 students.**

13. What is the probability that at least 140 students are left-handed? about 0.0013
14. What is the probability that at most 100 students are left-handed? about 0.16
15. What is the probability that between 80 and 130 students are left-handed? about 0.98

MYOPIA **Use the fact that myopia, or nearsightedness, is a condition that affects approximately 25% of the adult population in the United States. Consider a random sample of 192 U.S. adults.**

16. What is the probability that 42 or more people are nearsighted? about 0.84
17. What is the probability that 66 or fewer people are nearsighted? about 0.9987
18. What is the probability that between 36 and 60 people are nearsighted? about 0.95

EXAMPLE 2 on p. 764 for Exs. 19–22

19. **SURVEYS** A survey that asked people in the United States about their feelings of personal well-being found that 85% are generally happy. To test this finding, you question 75 people at random and find that 56 consider themselves generally happy. Would you reject the survey's findings? *Explain.* Yes; $P(x \le 56) \approx 0.01$, which is less than 0.05.
20. **CLASS RINGS** You read an article that claims 30% of graduating seniors will buy a class ring. To test this claim, you survey 45 randomly selected seniors in your school and find that 9 are planning to buy a class ring. Should you reject the article's claim? *Explain.* No; $P(x \le 9) \approx P(z \le -1.5) \approx 0.07$, which is greater than 0.05.
21. **COMPUTERS** A manufacturer of personal computers claims that under normal work use only 1% of its computers will fail to operate at some point during a month. A business uses 600 of the manufacturer's computers under normal work use and has 12 failures in a month. Would you reject the manufacturer's claim? *Explain.* Yes; $P(x \ge 12) \approx 1 - P(z \le 2.5) \approx 1 - 0.9938 = 0.0062$, which is less than 0.05.
22. **JUICE PREFERENCES** A company that makes bottled juices has created a new brand of apple juice. The company claims 80% of people prefer the new apple juice over a competitor's apple juice. A taste test is conducted to test this claim. Of 50 people, 34 prefer the new apple juice. Would you reject the company's claim? *Explain.* Yes; $P(x \le 34) \approx P(z \le -2.1) \approx 0.0179$ which is less than 0.05.

4 PRACTICE AND APPLY

Mathematical Reasoning

Exercises 19–22 Make sure that students understand that hypothesis testing allows the tester to reject or not reject an hypothesis. It does not make claims about the veracity of the hypothesis.

11.4 Select and Draw Conclusions from Samples

MA-HS-4.3.1

Before You used statistics to describe sets of data.

Now You will study different sampling methods for collecting data.

Why? So you can interpret the results of a survey, as in Ex. 27.

1 PLAN AND PREPARE

Warm-Up Exercises

Transparency Available

1. Solve $E = \frac{1}{\sqrt{305}}$. 0.057
2. Solve $0.025 = \frac{1}{\sqrt{n}}$. 1600
3. The mean score on an exam was 78. You scored within 5 points of the mean. If $x = 78 \pm 5$ represents your possible score x on the exam, what is the range of your score? $73 \leq x \leq 83$

Notetaking Guide

Transparency Available

Promotes interactive learning and notetaking skills, pp. 295–297.

Pacing

Basic: 2 days
Average: 2 days
Advanced: 2 days
Block: 0.5 block with 11.3
0.5 block with 11.5

- See *Teaching Guide/Lesson Plan.*

2 FOCUS AND MOTIVATE

Essential Question

Big Idea 3, p. 743

What should be true of the sample when you conduct a survey?

Tell students they will learn how to answer this question by learning about unbiased samples and margin of error.

Key Vocabulary
- population
- sample
- unbiased sample
- biased sample
- margin of error

MA-HS-4.3.1
Students will recognize potential for bias resulting from the misuse of sampling methods (e.g., non-random sampling, polling only a specific group of people, using limited or extremely small sample sizes) and explain why these samples can lead to inaccurate inferences. DOK 2

A **population** is a group of people or objects that you want information about. When it is too difficult, time-consuming, or expensive to survey everyone in a population, information is gathered from a **sample**, or subset, of the population. Some methods for selecting a sample are described below.

In a *self-selected sample*, members of a population can volunteer to be in the sample.

In a *systematic sample*, a rule is used to select members of a population, such as selecting every other person.

In a *convenience sample*, easy-to-reach members of a population are selected, such as those in the first row.

In a *random sample*, each member of a population has an equal chance of being selected.

EXAMPLE 1 Classify samples

BASEBALL A sportswriter wants to survey college baseball coaches about whether they think wooden bats should be mandatory throughout college baseball. Identify the type of sample described.

a. The sportswriter contacts only the coaches that he has cell phone numbers for in order to get quick responses.

b. The sportswriter mails out surveys to all the coaches and uses only the surveys that are returned.

Solution

a. The sportswriter selected coaches that are easily accessible. So, the sample is a convenience sample.

b. The coaches can choose whether or not to respond. So, the sample is a self-selected sample.

Resource Planning Guide

Chapter Resource Book
- Teaching Guide/Lesson Plan (pp. 38–39)
- Activity Master (p. 40)
- Practice levels A, B, C (pp. 42–44)
- Study Guide (pp. 45–46)
- Catch-up for Absent Students (p. 47)
- Problem Solving Workshop (p. 48)
- Challenge (p. 49)

Workbooks
- Notetaking Guide (pp. 295–297)
- Practice Workbook (pp. 167–168)

Teaching Options
- **Power Presentations CD-ROM** provides dynamic electronic teaching resources for the classroom.
- **Activity Generator CD-ROM** provides editable activities for all ability levels.

Interactive Technology
- Easy Planner
- Power Presentations CD-ROM
- Activity Generator CD-ROM
- Animated Algebra
- Test Generator CD-ROM
- Online Quiz
- eWorkbook
- eEdition
- @HomeTutor

Resources for English Learners
- Quick Reference for English Learners
- Spanish Study Guide
- Multi-Language Visual Glossary
- Student Resources in Spanish

See also the *Algebra 2 Toolkit* for more strategies for meeting individual needs.

BIAS IN SAMPLING In order to draw accurate conclusions about a population from a sample, you should select an *unbiased sample*. An **unbiased sample** is representative of the population you want information about. A sample that overrepresents or underrepresents part of the population is a **biased sample**.

EXAMPLE 2 Identify a biased sample

CONCERT ATTENDANCE The manager of a concert hall wants to know how often people in the community attend concerts. The manager asks 50 people standing in line for a rock concert how many concerts per year they attend. Tell whether the sample is *biased* or *unbiased*. Explain your reasoning.

Solution

The sample is biased because people standing in line for a rock concert are more likely to attend concerts than people in general.

CHOOSING UNBIASED SAMPLES Although there are many ways of sampling a population, a random sample is preferred because it is most likely to be representative of the population.

EXAMPLE 3 Choose an unbiased sample

SENIOR CLASS PROM You are a member of the prom committee. You want to poll members of the senior class to find out where they want to hold the prom. There are 324 students in the senior class. Describe a method for selecting a random sample of 40 seniors to poll.

Solution

STEP 1 **Make** a list of all 324 seniors. Assign each senior a different integer from 1 to 324.

STEP 2 **Generate** 40 unique random integers from 1 to 324 using the *randInt* feature of a graphing calculator. The screen at the right shows six such random integers.

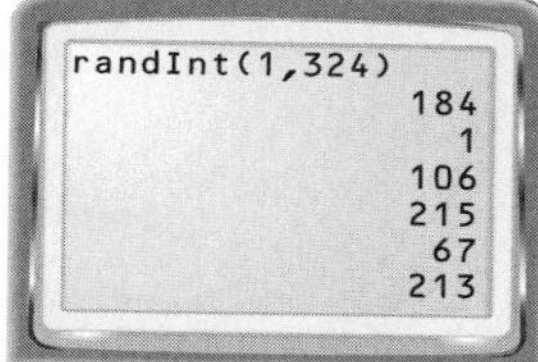

If while generating the integers you obtain a duplicate, discard it and generate a new, unique integer as a replacement.

STEP 3 **Choose** the 40 students that correspond to the 40 integers you generated in Step 2.

GUIDED PRACTICE for Examples 1, 2, and 3

1. **SCHOOL WEBSITE** A computer science teacher wants to know if students would like the morning announcements posted on the school's website. He surveys students in one of his computer science classes. Identify the type of sample described, and tell whether the sample is biased. **convenience sample, biased**

2. **WHAT IF?** In Example 3, what is another method you could use to generate a random sample of 40 students? ***Sample answer:*** **Place each student's name on a small piece of paper in a hat and draw 40 names.**

Motivating the Lesson

Suppose your school district is facing budget cuts. You decide to survey the cheerleaders and football players to find out whether the fine arts program or the sports program should be cut. Have students discuss the value of the possible results of the survey. In this lesson they will learn how to conduct good surveys.

3 TEACH

Extra Example 1

A manufacturer wants to sample the parts from a production line for defects. Identify the type of sample described.

a. The manufacturer has every 5th item on the production line tested for defects. **systematic**

b. The manufacturer has the first 50 items on the production line tested. **convenience**

Extra Example 2

A magazine asked its readers to send in their responses to several questions regarding healthy eating. Tell whether the sample of responses is biased or unbiased. Explain. **The sample is biased because only readers with strong opinions are likely to respond.**

Extra Example 3

The owner of a company with 300 employees wants to survey them about their preference for a regular 5-day, 8-hour workweek or a 4-day, 10-hour workweek. Describe a method for selecting a random sample of 50 employees to poll. ***Sample answer:*** **Place each employee's name in a hat. Then draw 50 names.**

SAMPLE SIZE When conducting a survey, you need to make the size of your sample large enough so that it accurately represents the population. As the sample size increases, the *margin of error* decreases.

The **margin of error** gives a limit on how much the responses of the sample would differ from the responses of the population. For example, if 40% of the people in a poll prefer candidate A, and the margin of error is ±4%, then it is likely that between 36% and 44% of the entire population prefer candidate A.

KEY CONCEPT *For Your Notebook*

Margin of Error Formula

When a random sample of size n is taken from a large population, the margin of error is approximated by this formula:

$$\textbf{Margin of error} = \pm\frac{1}{\sqrt{n}}$$

This means that if the percent of the sample responding a certain way is p (expressed as a decimal), then the percent of the population that would respond the same way is likely to be between $p - \frac{1}{\sqrt{n}}$ and $p + \frac{1}{\sqrt{n}}$.

EXAMPLE 4 Find a margin of error

MEDIA SURVEY In a survey of 1011 people, 52% said that television is their main source of news.

a. What is the margin of error for the survey?

b. Give an interval that is likely to contain the exact percent of all people who use television as their main source of news.

Main Source of News

Television 52%
Newspaper 29%
Radio 10%
Internet 5%
Other 4%

Solution

a. Use the margin of error formula.

$$\text{Margin of error} = \pm\frac{1}{\sqrt{n}} \qquad \textbf{Write margin of error formula.}$$

$$= \pm\frac{1}{\sqrt{1011}} \qquad \textbf{Substitute 1011 for } n.$$

$$\approx \pm 0.031 \qquad \textbf{Use a calculator.}$$

▸ The margin of error for the survey is about ±3.1%.

b. To find the interval, subtract and add 3.1% to the percent of people surveyed who said television is their main source of news (52%).

52% − 3.1% = 48.9%   52% + 3.1% = 55.1%

▸ It is likely that the exact percent of all people who use television as their main source of news is between 48.9% and 55.1%.

Mathematical Reasoning

In many cases, results from convenience samples may be seriously biased. However, point out that convenience sampling can produce good results. For example, if students were to conduct a survey to identify what percent of the population is left-handed, it would be convenient to survey their classmates. Such a survey could produce good results, even though the sample was not randomly chosen.

Extra Example 4

In a survey of 1535 people, 48% preferred Brand A over Brand B and Brand C.

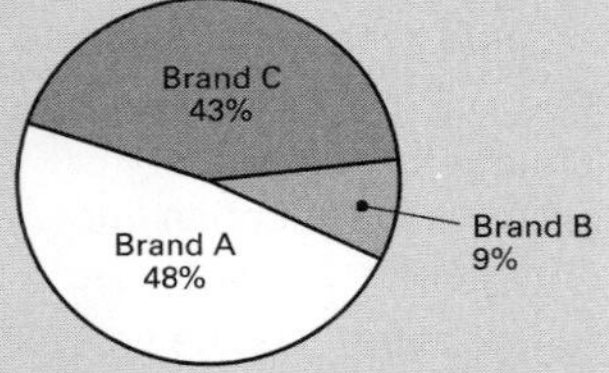

a. What is the margin of error for the survey? ±0.026

b. Give an interval that is likely to obtain the exact percent of all people who prefer Brand A. between 45.4% and 50.6%

Key Questions to Ask for Example 4

- What is the probability that a randomly chosen person from the sample uses television as her or his main source of news? between 0.489 and 0.551
- What is the probability that a randomly chosen person does not use television as her or his main source of news? between 0.449 and 0.551

Differentiated Instruction

Auditory Learners Arrange students in small groups. Have each group work together to poll their fellow classmates on a particular topic. Once they obtain their results, have them explain to one another the margin of error and its possible impact upon their results.

See also the *Algebra 2 Toolkit* for more strategies.

EXAMPLE 5 Standardized Test Practice

A polling company conducts a poll for a U.S. presidential election. How many people did the company survey if the margin of error is ±5%?

Ⓐ 25 people Ⓑ 250 people Ⓒ 400 people Ⓓ 625 people

REVIEW RADICALS
For help with solving equations involving square roots, see p. 452.

Solution

Use the margin of error formula.

$$\text{Margin of error} = \pm\frac{1}{\sqrt{n}}$$ **Write margin of error formula.**

$$\pm 0.05 = \pm\frac{1}{\sqrt{n}}$$ **Substitute ±0.05 for margin of error.**

$$0.0025 = \frac{1}{n}$$ **Square each side.**

$$n = 400$$ **Solve for n.**

There were 400 people surveyed.

▶ The correct answer is C. Ⓐ Ⓑ Ⓒ Ⓓ

GUIDED PRACTICE for Examples 4 and 5

3. **INTERNET** In a survey of 1202 people, 11% said that they use the Internet or e-mail more than 10 hours per week. What is the margin of error for the survey? How many people would need to be surveyed to reduce the margin of error to ±2%? **about ±2.9%; 2500 people**

11.4 EXERCISES

HOMEWORK KEY
○ = **WORKED-OUT SOLUTIONS** on p. WS20 for Exs. 7, 19, and 29
★ = **STANDARDIZED TEST PRACTICE** Exs. 2, 14, 23, 29, and 31

SKILL PRACTICE

A

1. **VOCABULARY** Copy and complete: A sample for which each member of a population has an equal chance of being selected is a(n) __?__ sample. **random**

2. ★ **WRITING** *Describe* the difference between an unbiased sample and a biased sample. **An unbiased sample is representative of the population being sampled, while a biased sample overrepresents/underrepresents part of the population.**

EXAMPLES 1 and 2
on pp. 766–767 for Exs. 3–5

CLASSIFYING SAMPLES Identify the type of sample described. Then tell if the sample is biased. *Explain* your reasoning.

3. A taxicab company wants to know if its customers are satisfied with the service. Each driver surveys every tenth customer during the day. **Systematic; unbiased; the sample is representative of the customers.**

4. A town council wants to know if residents support having an off-leash area for dogs in the town park. Eighty dog owners are surveyed at the park. **Convenience; biased. *Sample answer:* The opinions of the sampled dog owners may not represent the population.**

5. An English teacher needs to pick 5 students to present book reports to the class. The teacher writes the names of all students in the class on pieces of paper, puts the pieces in a hat, and chooses 5 names without looking. **Random; unbiased; each student has an equal chance of being selected.**

Extra Example 5

A state legislator conducts a poll to determine if the voters want to increase their property tax to make highway improvements. How many people were surveyed if the margin of error was ±3%? **B**

Ⓐ 577 people
Ⓑ 1111 people
Ⓒ 1732 people
Ⓓ 90,000 people

Key Question to Ask for Example 5

- How are the formulas in Example 4 and Example 5 related? **The same formula is used in both examples. In Example 4, the formula is solved for the margin of error. In Example 5 the formula is solved for n.**

Closing the Lesson

Have students summarize the major points of the lesson and answer the Essential Question: What should be true of the sample when you conduct a survey?

- **Methods for collecting a sample or subset of a population include a self-selected sample, a systematic sample, a convenience sample, and a random sample.**
- **An unbiased sample is representative of a population of interest. A biased sample overrepresents or underrepresents part of the population.**
- **If the percent of a sample of size n responding a certain way is p, then the percent of the population that would respond the same way is likely to be between $p - \frac{1}{\sqrt{n}}$ and $p + \frac{1}{\sqrt{n}}$, where $\pm\frac{1}{\sqrt{n}}$ is the margin of error for the sample.**

The survey should include a random sample of the population of interest and the sample should be large enough to guarantee a reasonable margin of error.

4 PRACTICE AND APPLY

Assignment Guide

Answer Transparencies available for all exercises

Basic:
Day 1: SRH p. 976 Exs. 21–25
pp. 769–771
Exs. 1–5, 28, 29, 33–34
Day 2: pp. 769–771
Exs. 6–24, 27, 30

Average:
Day 1: pp. 769–771
Exs. 1–5, 28, 29, 33–34
Day 2: pp. 769–771
Exs. 8–14, 17–25, 27, 30, 31

Advanced:
Day 1: pp. 769–771
Exs. 1–5, 28, 29, 33–34
Day 2: pp. 769–771
Exs. 9–14, 17–27*, 30–32*

Block:
pp. 769–771
Exs. 1–5, 28, 29, 33–34 (with 11.3)
pp. 769–771
Exs. 8–14, 17–25, 27, 30, 31
(with 11.5)

Differentiated Instruction

See *Algebra 2 Best Practices Toolkit* for suggestions on addressing the needs of a diverse classroom.

Homework Check

For a quick check of student understanding of key concepts, go over the following exercises:

Basic: 3, 8, 12, 16, 27

Average: 4, 10, 18, 28, 29

Advanced: 5, 12, 22, 30, 31

Extra Practice

- Student Edition, p. 1020
- Chapter 11 Resource Book: Practice levels A, B, C, pp. 42–44

Practice Worksheet

An easily-readable reduced practice page (with answers) for this lesson can be found on p. 742D.

EXAMPLE 4 on p. 768 for Exs. 6–14

FINDING MARGIN OF ERROR **Find the margin of error for a survey that has the given sample size. Round your answer to the nearest tenth of a percent.**

6. 260 $\pm$6.2% **(7.)** 1000 $\pm$3.2% **8.** 750 $\pm$3.7% **9.** 6400 $\pm$1.3%

10. 3275 $\pm$1.7% **11.** 525 $\pm$4.4% **12.** 2024 $\pm$2.2% **13.** 10,000 $\pm$1.0%

14. ★ **MULTIPLE CHOICE** In a survey of 2000 voters, 45% said they planned to vote for candidate A. What is the margin of error for the survey? B

Ⓐ $\pm$1.8% Ⓑ $\pm$2.2% Ⓒ $\pm$3.6% Ⓓ $\pm$4.5%

EXAMPLE 5 on p. 769 for Exs. 15–23

FINDING SAMPLE SIZES **Find the sample size required to achieve the given margin of error. Round your answer to the nearest whole number.**

15. $\pm$3% 1111 people **16.** $\pm$8% 156 people **17.** $\pm$10% 100 people **18.** $\pm$4.2% 567 people

(19.) $\pm$5.6% 319 people **20.** $\pm$1.5% 4444 people **21.** $\pm$6.5% 237 people **22.** $\pm$2.5% 1600 people

23. ★ **MULTIPLE CHOICE** The margin of error for a poll is $\pm$2%. What is the size of the sample? D

Ⓐ 200 Ⓑ 400 Ⓒ 1000 Ⓓ 2500

B **24. ERROR ANALYSIS** In a survey of high school students, 13% said that they play basketball regularly. The margin of error is $\pm$4%. *Describe* and correct the error in calculating the sample size.

$$\pm 0.13 = \pm\frac{1}{\sqrt{n}}$$
$$0.0169 = \frac{1}{n}$$
$$n \approx 59$$

In the calculation 4% should be used instead of 13%; $\pm 0.04 = \pm\frac{1}{\sqrt{n}}$, $0.0016 = \frac{1}{n}$, $n = 625$

25. REASONING A survey claims the percent of a city's residents that favor building a new football stadium is likely between 52.3% and 61.7%. How many people were surveyed? about 453 people

C **26. CHALLENGE** Suppose a random sample of size n is required to produce a margin of error of $\pm E$. Write an expression in terms of n for the sample size needed to reduce the margin of error to $\pm\frac{1}{2}E$. By how many times must the sample size be increased in order to cut the margin of error in half? $4n$; 4

PROBLEM SOLVING

EXAMPLES 3, 4, and 5 on pp. 767–769 for Exs. 27–31

A **27. VACATION SURVEY** In a survey of 439 teenagers in the United States, 14% said that they worked during their summer vacation.

a. What is the margin of error for the survey? about $\pm$4.8%

b. Give an interval that is likely to contain the exact percent of all U.S. teenagers who worked during their summer vacation. between 9.2% and 18.8%

@HomeTutor for problem solving help at classzone.com

28. NEWSLETTER The staff for a student newsletter wants to conduct a survey of students' favorite TV shows. There are 1225 students in the school. The newsletter staff would like to survey 250 students. *Describe* a method for selecting an unbiased, random sample of students. *Sample answer:* Assign each student a number from 1 to 1225 and use a random number generator to generate 250 unique numbers from the given set of numbers.

@HomeTutor for problem solving help at classzone.com

○ = WORKED-OUT SOLUTIONS on p. WS1 ★ = STANDARDIZED TEST PRACTICE

. No. *Sample* *swer:* Since e margin of ror is ±5%, sta could have % of the votes d Murdock uld have 51% the votes.

29. ★ **SHORT RESPONSE** Based on the newspaper report shown below, is it reasonable to assume that Kosta is certain to win the election? *Explain.*

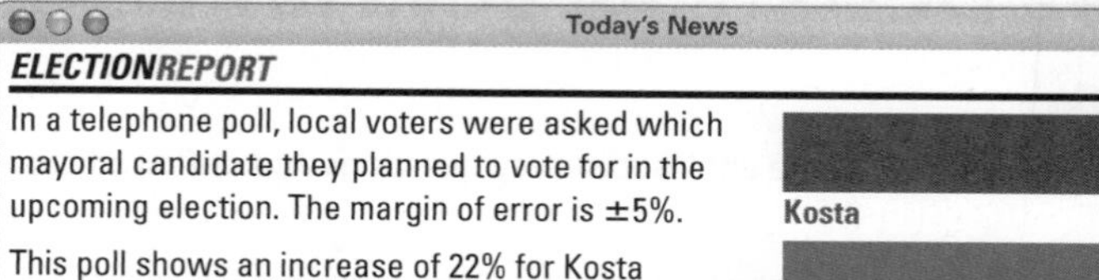
Today's News

ELECTION**REPORT**

In a telephone poll, local voters were asked which mayoral candidate they planned to vote for in the upcoming election. The margin of error is ±5%.

This poll shows an increase of 22% for Kosta since the beginning of the year, while support for Murdock continues to decline.

B

30. **MULTI-STEP PROBLEM** A Gallup Youth Survey reported that 23% of students surveyed, or about 181 students, say that math is their favorite subject in school.
    a. How many students were surveyed? about 787 students
    b. What is the margin of error for the survey? about ±3.6%
    c. Give an interval that is likely to contain the exact percent of all students who would say that math is their favorite subject. between 19.4% and 26.6%

31. ★ **EXTENDED RESPONSE** A survey reported that 235 out of 500 voters in a sample voted for candidate A and the remainder voted for candidate B.
    a. **Find Percents** What percent of the voters in the sample voted for candidate A? for candidate B? 47%, 53%
    b. **Find Margin of Error** What is the margin of error for the survey? about ±4.5%
    c. **Find Intervals** For each candidate, find an interval that is likely to contain the exact percent of all voters who voted for the candidate.
    d. **Reasoning** Based on your intervals, can you be confident that candidate B won? If not, how many people in the sample would need to vote for candidate B for you to be confident of her victory? (*Hint:* Find the least number of voters for candidate B such that the intervals do not overlap.) no; 273 people

c. between .5% and 51.5%, tween 48.5% d 57.5%

C

32. **CHALLENGE** In a survey, 52% of the respondents said they prefer cola X and 48% said they prefer cola Y. How many people would have to be surveyed for you to be confident that cola X is truly preferred by more than half the population? *Explain* your reasoning. 2501 people. *Sample answer:* The margin of error would then be less than 2%.

KENTUCKY MIXED REVIEW

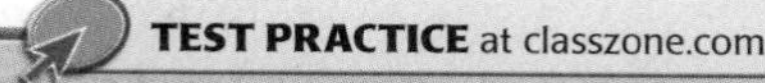

33. What is the solution set for the equation $5x^2 - 7x + 6 = 3x^2 + 4x - 8$? **D**

    Ⓐ $\left\{-4, -\frac{7}{2}\right\}$ Ⓑ $\left\{-4, \frac{7}{2}\right\}$ Ⓒ $\left\{-2, \frac{7}{2}\right\}$ Ⓓ $\left\{2, \frac{7}{2}\right\}$

34. In the figure, $\overline{MN}$ is parallel to $\overline{QP}$, $\overline{MQ}$ is **perpendicular** to $\overline{QP}$, and $m\angle MNR$ is 145°. What is $m\angle RPQ$? **C**

    Ⓐ 90° Ⓑ 105°
    Ⓒ 125° Ⓓ 135°

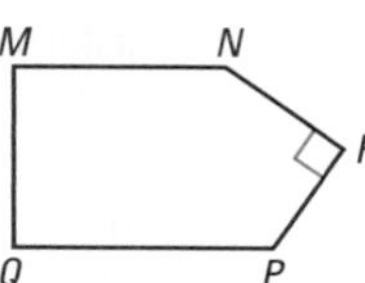

5 ASSESS AND RETEACH

Daily Homework Quiz

Transparency Available

A cafeteria buys grated cheese from a food service. The cheese is packed in boxes labeled 10 pounds. To test that the weight is correct, the cafeteria manager weighs the first 5 boxes in a recent order.

1. Identify the type of sample and explain why it is biased. **Convenience; the sample may be biased if the same production line packed the first 5 boxes and other lines packed other boxes.**
2. In a random sample of 550 boxes, 52% weighed more than 10 pounds. Give the interval that is likely to contain the exact percent that weighed over 10 pounds. How many boxes would need to be weighed if the margin of error was ±3.8%? **between 47.7% and 56.3%; 693 boxes**

Available at **classzone.com**

Diagnosis/Remediation

- Practice A, B, C in Chapter 11 Resource Book, pp. 42–44
- Study Guide in Chapter 11 Resource Book, pp. 45–46
- Practice Workbook, pp. 167–168
- @HomeTutor

Challenge

Additional challenge is available in the Chapter 11 Resource Book, p. 49.

1 PLAN AND PREPARE

Warm-Up Exercises

A survey is conducted by calling randomly selected phone numbers at 1:00 P.M. during the week.

1. Tell whether the sample is biased or unbiased. biased
2. Identify the type of sample used. convenience

2 FOCUS AND MOTIVATE

Essential Question

Big Idea 3, p. 743

How can you identify flaws in survey questions and experiments? Tell students they will learn how to answer this question by studying the features of biased questions and experimental procedures.

3 TEACH

Extra Example 1

Tell if the question is biased. Describe how to correct it.

a. *"What is your height in inches?"* The question requires a calculation, which may be done incorrectly; "What is your height?"

b. *"Should motorcycle helmets be mandatory to save lives?"* This is a leading question because it encourages people to answer "yes"; "Should motorcycle helmets be mandatory?"

NCTM STANDARDS

Standard 5: Collect, organize, and display data

Standard 8: Communicate thinking clearly to others

Extension — Design Surveys and Experiments

Use after Lesson 11.4

GOAL Write unbiased survey questions and unflawed experimental procedures.

Key Vocabulary
- biased question
- experimental group
- control group

When designing a survey, it is important that the survey questions be carefully written. If a question is poorly written, then the responses of the people surveyed may not accurately reflect their opinions or actions. These types of flawed questions are called **biased questions**.

There are several reasons why a question may be biased:

- The question may encourage the respondent to answer in a particular way.
- The question may be perceived as too sensitive to answer truthfully.
- The question may not provide the respondent with enough information to give an accurate opinion.

Bias may also be introduced through the order in which the questions are asked or may result when the person conducting the interview intentionally or unintentionally influences the responses of those interviewed.

EXAMPLE 1 Identify and correct bias in survey questions

Tell why the question may be biased. Describe how to correct the flaw.

a. *"Many national parks are being heavily damaged by acid rain. Do you favor government funding to help prevent acid rain?"*

This is an example of a *leading question*. Respondents may think a "no" response means they are not in favor of supporting national parks. In this way, the question encourages the respondent to answer "yes."

A better way to ask this question is to eliminate the first sentence and just ask, "Do you favor government funding to help prevent acid rain?"

b. *"Do you agree with the amendments to the Clean Air Act?"*

The question assumes that the respondent is familiar with the amendments to the Clean Air Act. Responses by people unfamiliar with the amendments could lead to misleading conclusions.

A better way to ask this question is to first state each amendment and then ask, "Do you agree with this amendment?"

c. Police officers ask mall visitors, *"Do you wear your seat belt regularly?"*

Many motorists may answer untruthfully because a police officer is asking the question, especially if the law requires seat belt use. The data collected might not accurately represent the percent of people who wear seat belts regularly.

In this case, the correction is to have the question be asked by someone not involved in law enforcement.

EXPERIMENTS An experiment is often conducted with two groups. One group, called the **experimental group**, undergoes some procedure or treatment. The other group, called the **control group**, does not undergo the procedure or treatment.

In a well-designed experiment, everything else about the experimental group and the control group is as similar as possible so that the effect of the procedure or treatment can be determined.

EXAMPLE 2 Identify flaws in an experiment

RESEARCH A drug company conducts an experiment to test whether a new pain relief medication is effective at relieving headaches. The experimental group consists of college students who are given the medication. The control group consists of college professors who are not given the medication.

The company finds that the headaches of people in the experimental group are of shorter duration than those of people in the control group. As a result, the company concludes that the medication is effective. Identify any flaws in this experiment, and describe how they can be corrected.

Solution

On average, college students are likely to be younger than college professors. So, it could be age rather than the medication that explains why the experimental group had shorter-lasting headaches than the control group.

To correct this flaw, the drug company could redesign the experiment so that the ages of the people in the experimental group are similar to the ages of the people in the control group.

PRACTICE

EXAMPLE 1
on p. 772
for Exs. 1–6

In Exercises 1–6, tell why the question may be biased. *Describe* how to correct the flaw. 1–3. Sample answers are given.

1. "Do you agree that building a beautiful new baseball stadium would be a good investment for the city to make?" This is a leading question. Respondents may think a "no" response means they are not supporters of city growth.
2. "A survey of the voters in this state shows that 85% favor a tax cut. Do you favor a tax cut?" This is a leading question. A person might want to be part of the majority. Omit the first sentence.
3. A dentist asks her patients, "Do you floss every day?" 3–6. See margin.
4. "Don't you think that renovating the old town hall would be a mistake?"
5. "Do you think the defendant in the Carter case was given a fair trial?"
6. "Which city council candidate's platform do you support?"

EXAMPLE 2
on p. 773
for Ex. 7

7. **EDUCATION** A research company conducts an experiment to test whether a new mathematics software program will increase test scores of students. The experimental group consists of students enrolled in Algebra 2 who are given the software. The control group consists of students enrolled in Algebra 1 who are not given the software.

   The company finds that the students in the experimental group test higher than the students in the control group and concludes that the software is effective at increasing test scores. Identify any flaws in the experiment, and describe how they can be corrected. ***Sample answer:*** The flaw is that Algebra 2 students are the experimental group and Algebra 1 students are the control group; the experimental and control groups should both be Algebra 2 students.

3–6. See Additional Answers beginning on p. AA1.

c. *"Does it seem possible or impossible to you that it has never rained on prom night?"* The double negative may confuse many of the respondents; "Do you think that it has ever rained on prom night?"

Extra Example 2

A researcher conducts an experiment to see if a new medication is effective in preventing strokes. An experimental group of accountants suffers more strokes than a control group of professional baseball players. Identify any flaws in this experiment and describe how they can be corrected. The average age of the accountants is likely to be higher than that of the baseball players, which may account for the increased number of strokes in spite of the medication. To correct the flaw, the company should redesign the experiment so that the ages and activity level in both groups are similar.

Closing the Lesson

Have students summarize the major points of the lesson and answer the Essential Question: How can you identify flaws in survey questions and experiments?

- Biased questions are likely to produce unreliable responses.
- An experimental group undergoes some procedure or treatment that the control group does not undergo.

Check that there are no biased questions and that the experimental and control groups are as similar as possible.

4 PRACTICE AND APPLY

Study Strategy

Exercises 1–6 To further test their understanding of biased questions, students can make up their own leading questions.

1 PLAN AND PREPARE

Explore the Concept

- Students will use a graphing calculator to make a scatter plot and to find a regression model for the data.
- This activity leads into the study of choosing the best model for data in Example 1 in Lesson 11.5.

Materials

Each pair of students will need:

- 20 index cards
- graphing calculator

Recommended Time

Work activity: 10 min

Discuss results: 10 min

Grouping

Students should work in pairs. They can repeat the activity, changing roles.

2 TEACH

Tips for Success

Before students begin the exercises, review the graphs of functions they have studied so far.

Alternative Strategy

Pool the students' data and have all students complete Step 3 and Exercises 1-3 using the pooled data.

Key Discovery

You can use a good model for a set of data to predict values outside the domain of the data set.

3 ASSESS AND RETEACH

Explain why you think the model you chose is a good fit for your data. *Sample answer:* The points fall rapidly and then seem to level off. This suggests an exponential decay model.

@HomeTutor classzone.com Keystrokes

11.5 Fitting a Model to Data

MATERIALS • 20 index cards • graphing calculator

QUESTION How can you choose a mathematical model for a data set?

In this activity, you will measure the time it takes to learn a new task as it becomes more familiar. You will then find a function that models the data you collect. Work with a partner.

EXPLORE Collect data on learning time

STEP 1 Perform task

Write a different word on each index card. Shuffle the cards, then have your partner put them in alphabetical order. Measure the time your partner takes to complete the task.

STEP 2 Record data

Have your partner repeat the task described in Step 1 at least five more times. Record your partner's completion times in a table like the one shown below.

Task number	Time (sec)
1	89
2	70
3	64
4	58
5	58
6	57

STEP 3 Make scatter plot

Let x be the task number and let y be the completion time. Use a graphing calculator to make a scatter plot of the data pairs (x, y) from the table in Step 2.

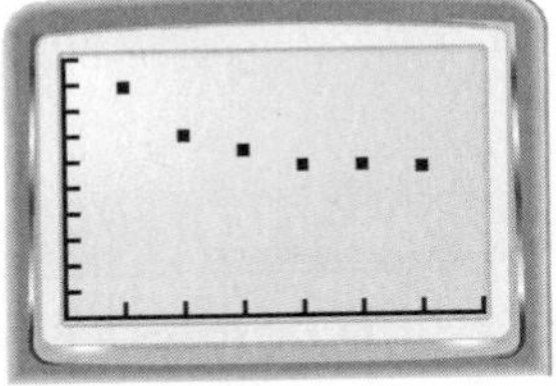

DRAW CONCLUSIONS Use your observations to complete these exercises

1. *Describe* the pattern shown in your scatter plot from Step 3. *Explain* why the pattern makes sense. **The time to complete the activity is decreasing; your partner is familiar with the words on each card and their alphabetical order.**
2. Find a function that is a good model for the data in your scatter plot. You can use one of the graphing calculator's regression features to find a model, or you may experiment with other types of functions that the regression features cannot generate. **Check students' work.**
3. Use the function you chose in Exercise 2 to predict the time your partner would take to alphabetize the index cards on the 10th trial. **Check students' work.**
4. Work with a second partner and repeat the experiment. Find a mathematical model to describe this partner's learning times. Do you get similar or different results? *Explain* why you might expect similar or different results. **Check students' work; similar; while the data is different the pattern should be similar since the new partner would become more familiar with words on the cards.**

11.5 Choose the Best Model for Two-Variable Data

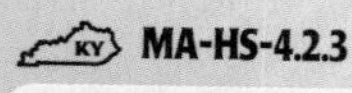
MA-HS-4.2.3

Before You wrote different types of functions to model sets of data.

Now You will choose the best model to represent a set of data.

Why? So you can relate engine speed and horsepower, as in Ex. 14.

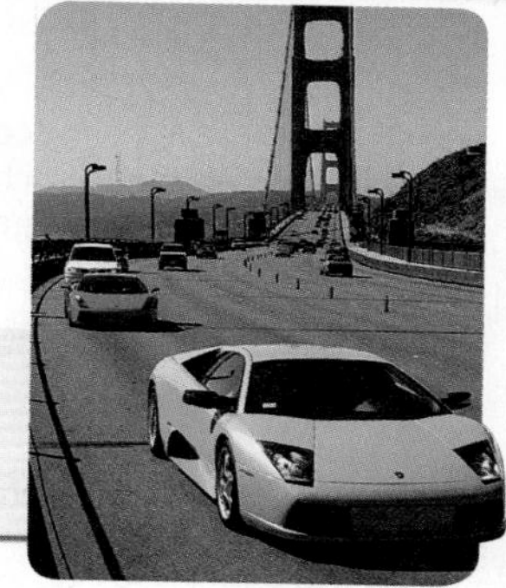

Key Vocabulary
- **linear function,** *p. 75*
- **quadratic function,** *p. 236*
- **cubic function,** *p. 337*
- **exponential function,** *p. 478*
- **power function,** *p. 531*

MA-HS-4.2.3
Students will: identify an appropriate curve of best fit (linear, quadratic, exponential) for a set of two-variable data; determine a line of best fit equation for a set of linear two-variable data and apply a line of best fit to make predictions within and beyond a given set of two-variable data. DOK 3

You have used the functions shown at the right to model sets of data.

To find the best model for a set of data pairs (x, y), make a scatter plot of the data and determine the type of function suggested by the pattern in the data points. Then find a model of this type using one of the regression features of a graphing calculator.

Function	General form
Linear	$y = ax + b$
Quadratic	$y = ax^2 + bx + c$
Cubic	$y = ax^3 + bx^2 + cx + d$
Exponential	$y = ab^x$
Power	$y = ax^b$

EXAMPLE 1 Use a linear model

TUITION The table shows the average tuition y (in dollars) for a private four-year college in the United States from 1995 to 2002, where x is the number of years since 1995. Use a graphing calculator to find a model for the data.

x	0	1	2	3	4	5	6	7
y	14,537	15,605	16,552	17,229	18,340	19,307	20,106	21,183

Solution

STEP 1 **Make** a scatter plot. The points lie approximately on a line. This suggests a linear model.

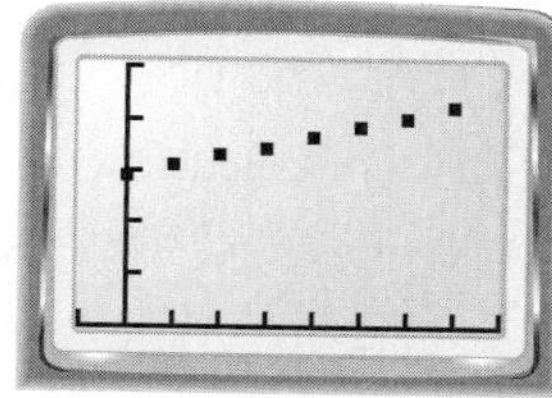

STEP 2 **Use** the linear regression feature to find an equation of the model.

STEP 3 **Graph** the model along with the data to verify that the model fits the data well.

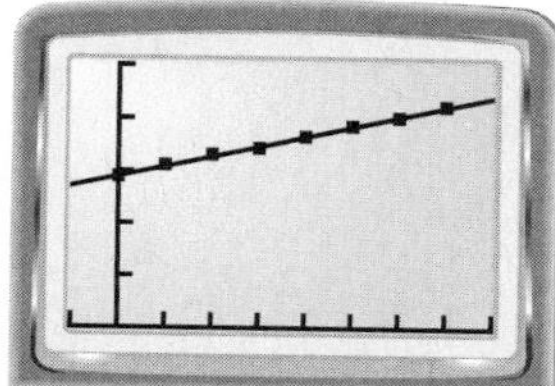

▶ A model for the data is $y = 933x + 14,600$.

1 PLAN AND PREPARE

Warm-Up Exercises
Transparency Available

Find the value of y if $x = 15$.

1. $y = -0.05x^2 + 0.7x + 10.2$ **9.45**
2. $y = 68.3(0.878)^x$ **9.7015**
3. $y = 57.3x^2 - 16.9x$ **12,639**
4. The equation $y = 21.1x^2 + 1364$ models the amount x (in dollars) that your family has spent each year y since 1995 on vacations. How much did your family spend on vacation in 2005? **$3474**

Notetaking Guide
Transparency Available

Promotes interactive learning and notetaking skills, pp. 298–300.

Pacing
Basic: 1 day
Average: 1 day
Advanced: 1 day
Block: 0.5 block with 11.4
- See *Teaching Guide/Lesson Plan.*

2 FOCUS AND MOTIVATE

Essential Question
Big Idea 3, p. 743

How can you choose the best model for two-variable data?
Tell students they will learn how to answer this question by examining scatter plots and using their graphing calculators.

Resource Planning Guide

Chapter Resource Book
- Teaching Guide/Lesson Plan (pp. 50–51)
- Practice levels A, B, C (pp. 56–58)
- Study Guide (pp. 59–60)
- Catch-up for Absent Students (p. 61)
- Problem Solving Workshop (p. 62)
- Challenge (p. 63)

Workbooks
- Notetaking Guide (pp. 298–300)
- Practice Workbook (pp. 169–170)

Teaching Options
- **Power Presentations CD-ROM** provides dynamic electronic teaching resources for the classroom.
- **Activity Generator CD-ROM** provides editable activities for all ability levels.

Interactive Technology
- Easy Planner
- Power Presentations CD-ROM
- Activity Generator CD-ROM
- Animated Algebra
- Test Generator CD-ROM
- Online Quiz
- eWorkbook
- eEdition
- @HomeTutor

Resources for English Learners
- Quick Reference for English Learners
- Spanish Study Guide
- Multi-Language Visual Glossary
- Student Resources in Spanish

See also the *Algebra 2 Toolkit* for more strategies for meeting individual needs.

Motivating the Lesson

It is generally true that an increase in time spent studying results in higher tests scores. But a point might be reached when more time spent studying will not result in significantly higher scores. Ask students what kind of function could model this situation.

3 TEACH

Extra Example 1

The table shows the cost of a meal x (in dollars) and the tip y (in dollars) for parties of 6 at a restaurant. Use a graphing calculator to find a model for the data. $y = 0.17x + 0.44$

x	y	x	y
34.48	5.50	100.76	16
52.54	11	65.60	12
89.64	15	109.34	21

Extra Example 2

The table shows the expenses x (in thousands) and the revenues y (in thousands) for ten years for a small company. Use a graphing calculator to find a model for the data. $y = 2001x^{0.40}$

x	y	x	y
1	2000	31	7900
2	2640	41	8830
5	3810	46	9250
11	5220	48	9400
20	6630	50	9560

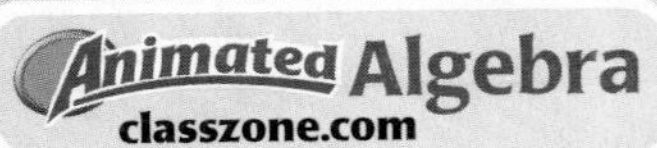

An **Animated Algebra** activity is available on-line for **Example 2**. This activity is also available on the **Power Presentations CD-ROM**.

EXAMPLE 2 Use an exponential model

COOLING RATES You are storing leftover chili in a freezer. The table shows the chili's temperature y (in degrees Fahrenheit) after x minutes in the freezer. Use a graphing calculator to find a model for the data.

x	0	10	20	30	40	50	60
y	100	75	50	35	28	20	15

ANOTHER WAY
For an extension of the problem in Example 2, turn to page 781 for the **Problem Solving Workshop**.

Solution

STEP 1 **Make** a scatter plot. The points fall rapidly at first and then begin to level off. This suggests an exponential decay model.

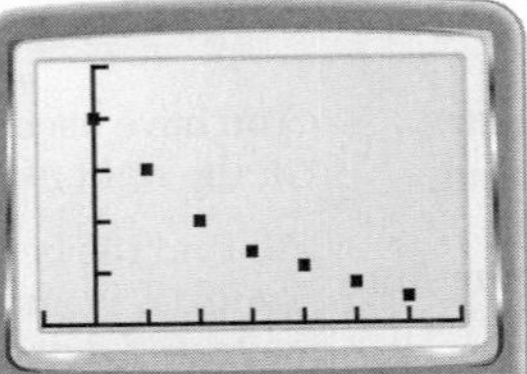

STEP 2 **Use** the exponential regression feature to find an equation of the model.

STEP 3 **Graph** the model along with the data to verify that the model fits the data well.

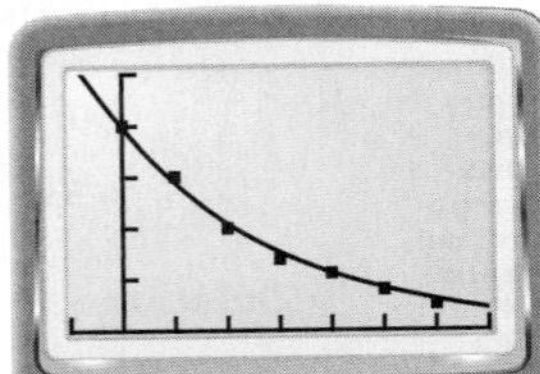

▸ A model for the data is $y = 98.2(0.969)^x$.

Animated Algebra at classzone.com

GUIDED PRACTICE for Examples 1 and 2

Use a graphing calculator to find a model for the data. Then graph the model and the data in the same coordinate plane. 1, 2. See margin for art.

1.

x	10	20	30	40	50	60	70	80
y	23.1	28.9	34.9	43.7	53.2	66.5	80.8	99.3

$f(x) = 0.0106x^2 + 0.116x + 21.6$

2.

x	0	1	2	3	4	5	6	7
y	33	41	52	68	80	89	102	118

$f(x) = 12.2x + 30.3$

Differentiated Instruction

English Learners Students whose first language is not English may struggle with the commands in their graphing calculator. Prior to discussing **Example 1**, have students work in pairs to create a list of calculator menus and commands they will be using for this lesson.

See also the *Algebra 2 Toolkit* for more strategies.

EXAMPLE 3 Use a quadratic model

FUEL EFFICIENCY A study compared the speed x (in miles per hour) and the average fuel efficiency y (in miles per gallon) of cars. The results are shown in the table. Use a graphing calculator to find a model for the data.

x	15	20	25	30	35	40	45	50	55	60	65
y	22.3	25.5	27.5	29.0	28.8	30.0	29.9	30.2	30.4	28.8	27.4

Solution

STEP 1 **Make** a scatter plot. The points form an inverted U-shape. This suggests a quadratic model.

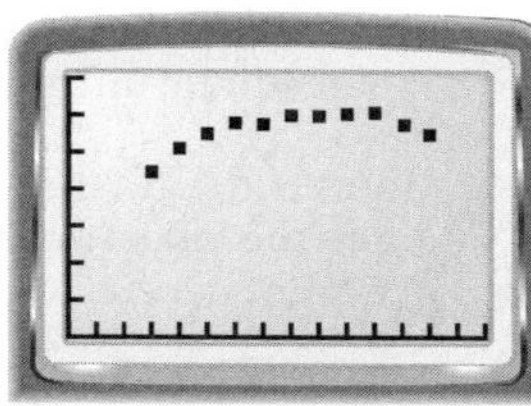

CHOOSE A MODEL

The data in Example 3 can be modeled by both a quadratic function and a cubic function. When this occurs, it is often better to choose the simpler model.

STEP 2 **Use** the quadratic regression feature to find an equation of the model.

STEP 3 **Graph** the model along with the data to verify that the model fits the data well.

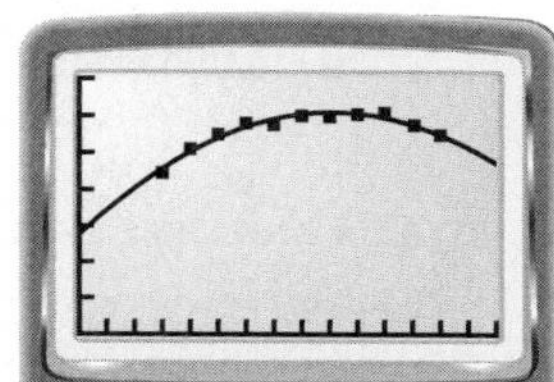

▶ A model for the data is $y = -0.00793x^2 + 0.727x + 13.8$.

GUIDED PRACTICE for Example 3

3. **FUEL EFFICIENCY** Use the model from Example 3 to predict the average fuel efficiency of a car traveling 70 miles per hour. **about 25.8 mi per gal**

Use a graphing calculator to find a model for the data. Then graph the model and the data in the same coordinate plane. **4, 5. See margin for art.**

4.

x	100	200	300	400	500	600	700
y	16	35	55	70	68	56	38

$f(x) = -0.000451x^2 + 0.404x - 23.1$

5.

x	−5	−4	−3	−2	−1	1	2
y	−20	0	3	0	−4	0	18

$f(x) = 0.868x^3 + 4.00x^2 + 0.902x - 6.41$

Extra Example 3

The table shows the amount y (in dollars) of money in your savings account after x weeks. Use a graphing calculator to find a model for the data. **$y = 3.24x^3 - 44.90x^2 + 201.81x + 12.17$**

x	y
0	0
1	200
2	250
3	300
4	300

x	y
5	300
6	315
7	340
8	405

Key Question to Ask for Example 3

- What is the approximate y-coordinate of the vertex of the model? How does it compare to the corresponding value in the table? **30.4; the maximum y-value in the table is also 30.4.**

Closing the Lesson

Have students summarize the major points of the lesson and answer the Essential Question: How can you choose the best model for two-variable data?

- **A linear regression model is the best model for a set of points that lie approximately on a line.**
- **Points that rise or fall rapidly at first and then begin to level off are best modeled by an exponential regression model.**
- **Points that form a U-shape or an inverted U-shape suggest a quadratic regression model.**

To find the best model for a set of data pairs (x, y), determine the type of function suggested by the pattern of data points in a scatter plot of the points. To find a model of this type, use one of the regression features of a graphing calculator.

1.

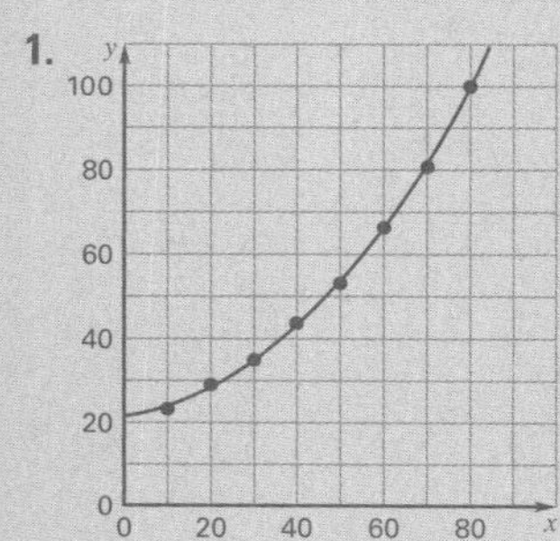

2.

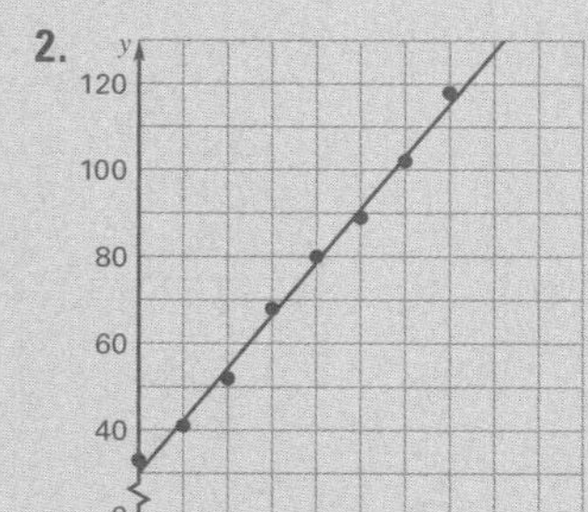

4.

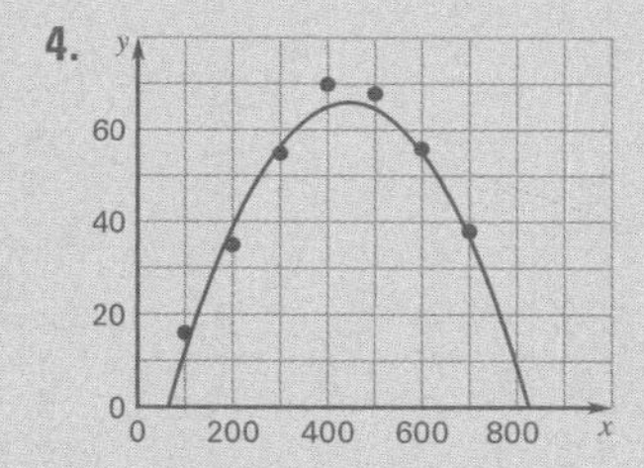

5.

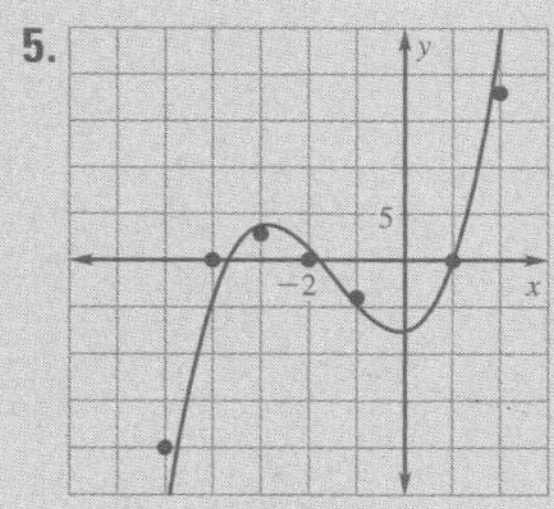

4 PRACTICE AND APPLY

Assignment Guide

Answer Transparencies available for all exercises

Basic:
Day 1: pp. 778–780
Exs. 1–6, 10–13, 16–17

Average:
Day 1: pp. 778–780
Exs. 1–8, 10–14, 16

Advanced:
Day 1: pp. 778–780
Exs. 1–15*

Block:
pp. 778–780
Exs. 1–8, 10–14, 16 (with 11.4)

Differentiated Instruction

See *Algebra 2 Best Practices Toolkit* for suggestions on addressing the needs of a diverse classroom.

Homework Check

For a quick check of student understanding of key concepts, go over the following exercises:

Basic: 3, 4, 6, 10, 11
Average: 4, 5, 6, 11, 12
Advanced: 4, 7, 11, 12, 13

Extra Practice

- Student Edition, p. 1020
- Chapter 11 Resource Book: Practice levels A, B, C, pp. 56–58

Practice Worksheet

An easily-readable reduced practice page (with answers) for this lesson can be found on p. 742D.

11.5 EXERCISES

HOMEWORK KEY
○ = WORKED-OUT SOLUTIONS on p. WS20 for Exs. 3 and 11
★ = STANDARDIZED TEST PRACTICE Exs. 2, 5, 6, 8, and 13
◆ = MULTIPLE REPRESENTATIONS Ex. 12

SKILL PRACTICE

A

1. **VOCABULARY** Copy and complete: A function of the form $y = ab^x$ is a(n) __?__ function. exponential

2. ★ **WRITING** *Explain* how you can determine whether a linear function or a quadratic function is a better model for a set of data.

EXAMPLES 1, 2, and 3 on pp. 775–777 for Exs. 3–7

2. *Sample answer:* Plot the data points in a coordinate plane. If the points appear to lie on a straight line, then a linear model is appropriate. If the points appear to lie on a parabola, then a quadratic model is appropriate.

MODELING DATA Use a graphing calculator to find a model for the data. Then graph the model and the data in the same coordinate plane. 3, 4. See margin for art.

3.

x	1	2	3	4	5	6	7
y	16	17	16	14	11	9	5

$f(x) = -0.381x^2 + 1.12x + 15.7$

4.

x	1	2	3	4	5	6	7
y	26	32	34	37	42	45	49

$f(x) = 3.68x + 23.1$

B

5. ★ **MULTIPLE CHOICE** Which type of function best models the data points? D

(A) Linear (B) Quadratic
(C) Cubic (D) Exponential

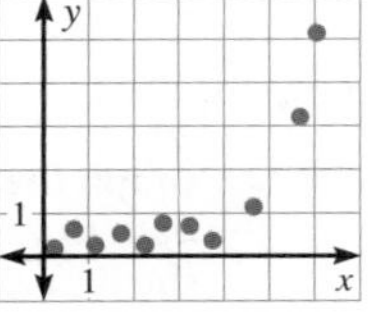

6. ★ **MULTIPLE CHOICE** Which equation best models the data? B

x	0	5	10	15	20	25	30	35
y	125	90	63	43	28	20	16	10

(A) $y = -3.14x + 104$ (B) $y = 126(0.931)^x$
(C) $y = 125x^{-0.6}$ (D) $y = 0.12x^2 + 124$

7. **ERROR ANALYSIS** *Describe* and correct the error made in using the information on a graphing calculator screen to write a model. The x and the value of b have been interchanged; $y = 9.71(1.55)^x$.

The ExpReg screen shows:
y=a*b^x
a=9.714963274
b=1.550355116

A model for the data is:
$y = 9.71x^{1.55}$

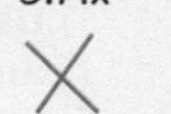

8. ★ **OPEN-ENDED MATH** Write a table of values that can be modeled by a quadratic function. See margin.

C

9. **CHALLENGE** The function $y = 5x^{2.3}$ models a table of data in which x-values are measured in inches and y-values are measured in pounds. If the table is changed to give the x-values in feet, what function models the revised data?

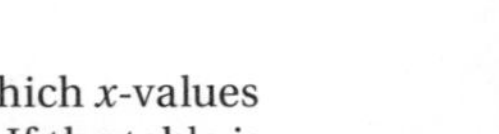
$y = 5\left(\frac{x}{12}\right)^{2.3}$

3.

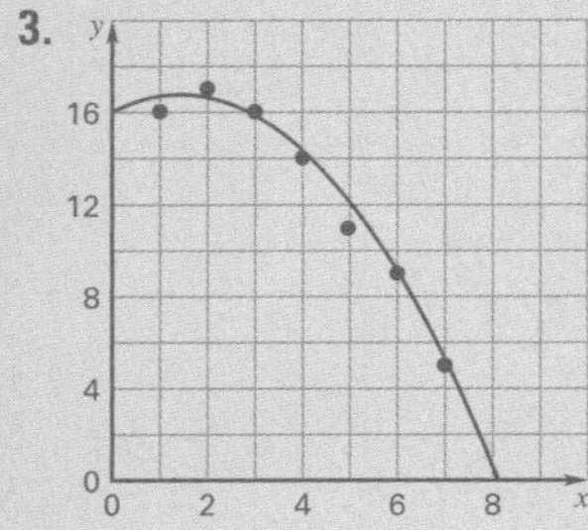

4.

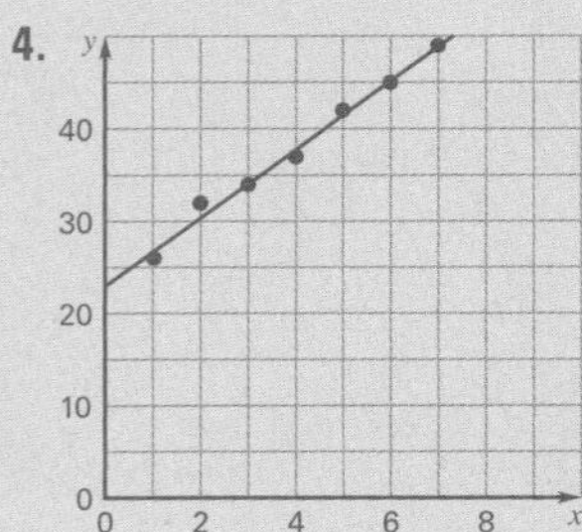

8. *Sample answer:*

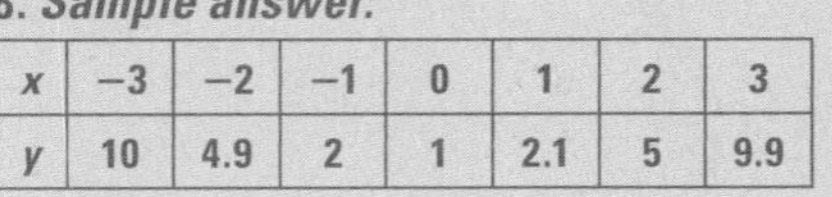

x	−3	−2	−1	0	1	2	3
y	10	4.9	2	1	2.1	5	9.9

PROBLEM SOLVING

EXAMPLES A **1, 2, and 3** on pp. 775–777 for Exs. 10–13

10. **ECONOMICS** The gross domestic product (GDP) is the total value of goods and services produced by a country in any given year. The table shows the GDP y (in billions of dollars) of the United States for selected years from 1930 to 2000. In the table, x represents the number of years since 1930. Use a graphing calculator to find a model for the data. ***Sample answer:*** $y = 67.4(1.07)^x$

x	0	10	20	30	40	50	60	70
y	91.3	101.3	294.3	527.4	1039.7	2795.6	5803.2	9824.6

@HomeTutor for problem solving help at classzone.com

11. **AGRICULTURE** The table shows the ages x (in years) and trunk diameters y (in inches) of several Texas grapefruit trees. Use a graphing calculator to find a model for the data. ***Sample answer:*** $y = 0.00211x^3 - 0.0766x^2 + 1.26x - 0.0664$

x	1	4	8	12	16	20	24
y	1.1	3.9	6.2	7.6	9.1	11.4	15.2

@HomeTutor for problem solving help at classzone.com

12. **MULTIPLE REPRESENTATIONS** The graph below shows the price of a first-class stamp in the United States for selected years from 1975 to 2002. Use a graphing calculator to find a model for the data. Then graph the model and the data in the same coordinate plane. ***Sample answer:*** $f(x) = 0.847x + 13.7$; **see margin for art.**

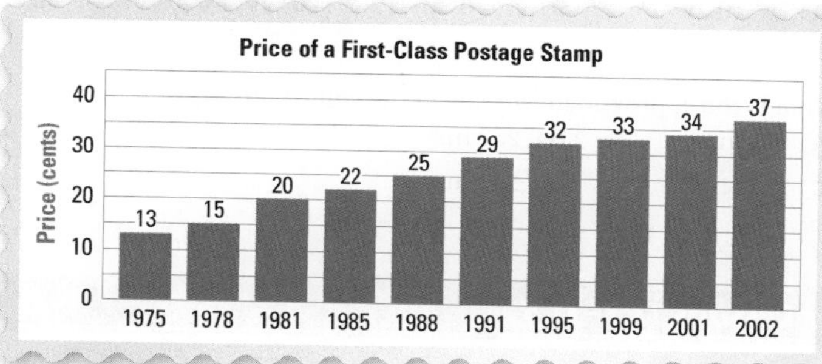

B 13. ★ **EXTENDED RESPONSE** The manager of a restaurant kept a record of the number y of customers each hour, where $x = 3$ represents 3:00 P.M.

x	3	4	5	6	7	8	9	10
y	9	24	44	56	48	42	38	22

a. Make a scatter plot of the data and determine the type of function that best models the data. **quadratic**

b. Use a regression feature of a graphing calculator to find a function that models the data. $y = -2.97x^2 + 40.4x - 85.9$

c. Graph the function and data to verify that the function is a good model. **See margin.**

d. Do you think the function you found would accurately predict the number of customers at 1 P.M.? *Explain.* **No; at 1:00 PM, the function predicts a negative number of customers.**

Avoiding Common Errors

Exercises 3, 4, 6, 10–15 Students who receive a "domain error" message on their calculators when graphing the scatter plots should check to see that they entered all x- and y-coordinates of the data pairs into the lists on their calculators.

Mathematical Reasoning

Exercises 3, 4, 6, 10–15 These exercises ask students to represent data several different ways. This allows them to visualize the correlation between the independent and dependent variables. It will prepare them for using regression models as prediction models in their further study of statistics.

Internet Reference

Exercise 12 For more information about the history of postal rates, visit www.usps.com/history/history/his4.htm#RATES

12.

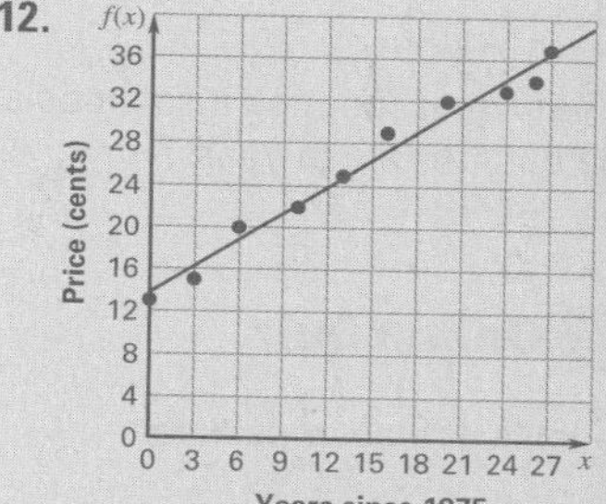

13c.

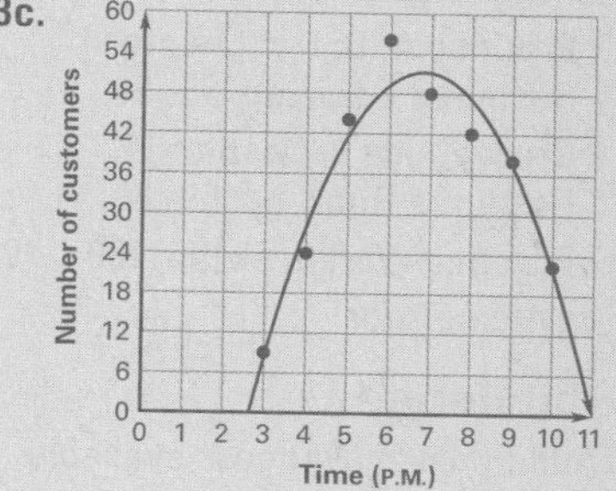

5 ASSESS AND RETEACH

Daily Homework Quiz

Transparency Available

The table shows the number of tuberculosis case rates y per 100,000 people in the United States in the 11 years from 1993 through 2003.

x	0	1	2	3	4	5
y	9.8	9.4	8.7	8	7.4	6.8

x	6	7	8	9	10
y	6.4	5.8	5.6	5.2	5.1

1. Use a graphing calculator to find a model for the data. $y = 9.86(0.932)^x$
2. Then graph the model and the data in the same coordinate plane.

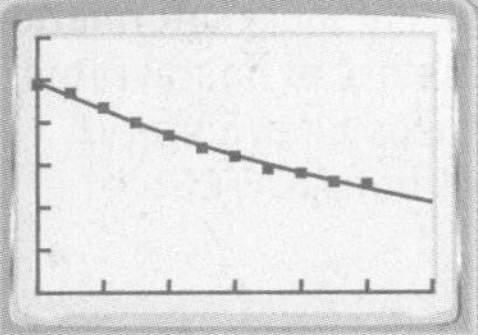

3. What linear function also models the data for these years? $y = -0.5x + 9.61$

Online Quiz

Available at **classzone.com**

Diagnosis/Remediation

- Practice A, B, C in Chapter 11 Resource Book, pp. 56–58
- Study Guide in Chapter 11 Resource Book, pp. 59–60
- Practice Workbook, pp. 169–170
- @HomeTutor

Challenge

Additional challenge is available in the Chapter 11 Resource Book, p. 63.

Quiz

An easily-readable reduced copy of the quiz (with answers) on Lessons 11.3–11.5 from the Assessment Book can be found on p. 742E.

14. **CAR ENGINES** The table shows the relationship between a car's engine speed (in revolutions per minute) and the power (in horsepower) that the engine produces. Use a graphing calculator to find a model for the data. What engine speed maximizes this car's engine power?

Engine speed (rpm)	1000	2000	3000	4000	5000	6000
Engine power (hp)	16	35	55	72	77	68

Sample answer: $f(x) = -0.00000357x^2 + 0.0365x - 19.8$; about 5112 rpm

C 15. **CHALLENGE** As a chair manufacturer produces more chairs, the production cost per chair decreases. The table shows the number x of chairs produced and the production cost y (in dollars) per chair. Model the data with a function whose graph has a horizontal asympote. What does the asymptote represent in this situation?

x	50	300	800	2000	3000	4000
y	260	180	95	45	35	30

Sample answer: $f(x) = 9004x^{-0.609} + 100$; the minimum production cost

TEST PRACTICE at classzone.com

KENTUCKY MIXED REVIEW

16. A sporting goods store has a 20%-off sale on all golf equipment. Which equation describes the relationship between the original price, x, of a piece of golf equipment and the sale price, y? **D**

   (A) $x = 0.2y$ (B) $x = 0.8y$ (C) $y = 0.2x$ (D) $y = 0.8x$

17. What is the approximate volume of the volleyball? **D**

   (A) 77 in.^{3} (B) 232 in.^{3}

   (C) 250 in.^{3} (D) 333 in.^{3}

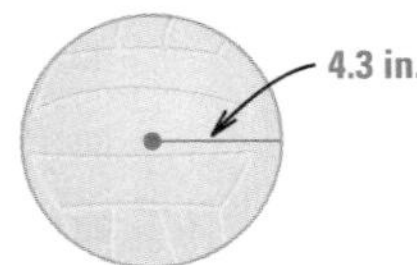

QUIZ *for Lessons 11.3–11.5*

A normal distribution has a mean of 47 and a standard deviation of 6. Find the probability that a randomly selected x-value is in the given interval. *(p. 757)*

1. Between 35 and 65 **0.9735**
2. At least 41 **0.84**
3. At most 29 **0.0015**

Find the sample size required to achieve the given margin of error. Round your answer to the nearest whole number. *(p. 766)*

4. ±3% **1111 people**
5. ±7% **204 people**
6. ±4.5% **494 people**
7. ±0.8% **15,625 people**

8. **SPORTS** The table shows the winning times y (in seconds) for various men's races of length x (in meters) at the 2004 Summer Olympics. Use a graphing calculator to find a model for the data. *(p. 775)* $f(x) = 0.164 - 20.9$

x	100	200	400	800	1500	5000	10,000
y	9.85	19.79	44.00	104.45	214.18	794.39	1625.10

EXTRA PRACTICE for Lesson 11.5, p. 1020

ONLINE QUIZ at classzone.com

Using ALTERNATIVE METHODS

Extending Example 2, page 776

MULTIPLE REPRESENTATIONS In Example 2 on page 776, you used a graphing calculator to find an exponential model of the form $y = ab^x$ for a data set. You can extend this method to find exponential models of the form $y = ab^x + c$.

PROBLEM

COOLING RATES You are storing leftover chili in a refrigerator. The table shows the chili's temperature y (in degrees Fahrenheit) after x minutes in the refrigerator. Use a graphing calculator to find a model for the data.

x	0	10	20	30	40	50	60
y	100	84	72	63	57	52	49

METHOD

Transforming Data One approach to solving the problem is to perform a transformation on the data and then find a model for the transformed data.

STEP 1 **Enter** the data in lists L_1 and L_2. Then make a scatter plot. The temperature appears to decay exponentially to 40°F. So the model has the form $y = ab^x + 40$, or $y - 40 = ab^x$.

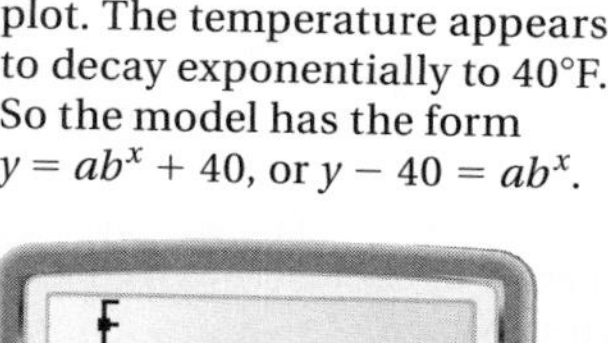

STEP 2 **Define** a new variable $y_1 = y - 40$. Then the data pairs (x, y_1) are modeled by a function of the form $y_1 = ab^x$. Make a list of the values of y_1 by defining L_3 as $L_2 - 40$.

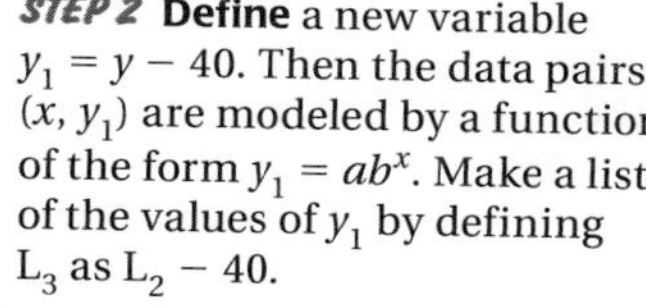

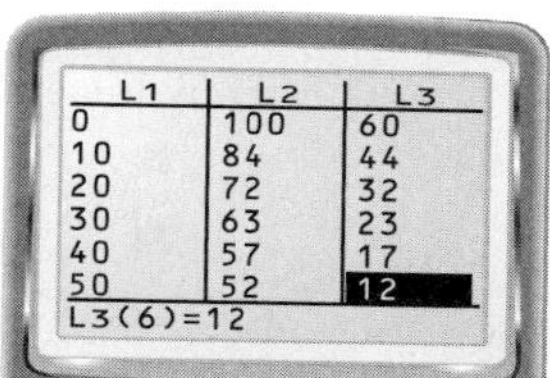

STEP 3 **Use** exponential regression to find a model for the data in lists L_1 and L_3. The model is $y_1 = 60.2(0.969)^x$. So, a model for the original data is $y = 60.2(0.969)^x + 40$.

▶ A model for the original data is $y = 60.2(0.969)^x + 40$. Graph the model along with the original data to verify that the model fits the data well.

PRACTICE

1. The data pairs (x, y) below give the temperature y (in degrees Fahrenheit) of a hot cup of soup after it sits for x minutes at room temperature. Estimate the temperature of the room. Then find a model for the data.

   (0, 132.8), (10, 105.8), (30, 92.3), (50, 84.2), (70, 79.2), (90, 76.1), (110, 75), (120, 74.7), (130, 74.2) **about 74°F; $y = 61.3(0.962)^x + 74$**

2. The data pairs (x, y) below give the temperature y (in degrees Celsius) of a cold glass of water after it sits x minutes at room temperature. Estimate the temperature of the room. Then find a model for the data.

   (0, 3.5), (20, 8.1), (40, 12.2), (60, 15.4), (80, 17), (100, 18.2), (110, 18.6), (120, 18.9) **about 19°C; $y = 24.88(1.004)^x - 19$**

Alternative Strategy

Students learn how to graph an exponential regression model of the form $y = ab^x + c$, where c is an asymptote for the model. This method allows students to visualize the minimum temperature that the chili approaches.

Teaching Strategy

Ask students to compare the graph of the exponential model of the form $y = ab^x$ with the model of the form $y = ab^x + c$ and discuss why the second model is a better model for the data.

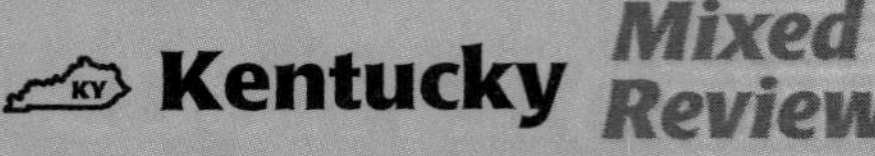

Kentucky Mixed Review

1. D
2. B
3. C
4. C
5. A
6. D
7. a. 16%
   b. 220 cm is 1 standard deviation above the mean, 200 cm. Using the 68-95-99.7 rule, 100% − 68% = 32% of the trees will be taller than 220 cm or shorter than 180 cm. Half of these, or 16%, are taller than 220 cm.

Lessons 11.3–11.5

1. **BIOLOGY** A biologist caught, measured, weighed, and then released eight Maine landlocked salmon. The table shows each fish's length x (in inches) and weight y (in pounds). Which equation is the best model for the data? Use a graphing calculator to find the answer.

x	10.3	15.2	16.2	16.4
y	0.4	1.0	1.3	1.3
x	17.5	18.1	22	23.6
y	1.7	2.0	3.5	4.2

A. $y = 0.0688(1.20)^x$

B. $y = 0.525x^2 - 0.502x + 3.18$

C. $y = 0.332x - 3.84$

D. $y = 0.000321x^{3.01}$

2. **SHOPPING SURVEY** In a survey of 1022 people who shop online, 73% said that they do so because of the convenience. What is the approximate margin of error for the survey?

A. ±2.9%

B. ±3.1%

C. ±3.7%

D. ±7.3%

3. **SHOE SIZE** The table shows the shoe size of a certain boy at different ages (in years). What is the most reasonable prediction for the boy's shoe size at age 17? Use a quadratic model obtained from a graphing calculator to find the answer.

Age	6	7	8	10
Shoe size	5	6	7	9
Age	12	14	15	16
Shoe size	10	11	11	12

A. 10 B. 11

C. 12 D. 13

4. **SPORTS SURVEY** A local sports TV station wants to determine the average number of hours per week people in the viewing area watch sporting events on television. The station surveys people at a nearby sports stadium. Which type of sample is described?

A. Self-selected B. Systematic

C. Convenience D. Random

5. **SUPERMARKET SURVEY** A survey shows that the time spent by shoppers in a certain supermarket is normally distributed with a mean of 45 minutes and a standard deviation of 12 minutes. What is the approximate probability that a randomly chosen shopper spends between 45 and 69 minutes in the supermarket?

A. 0.475

B. 0.4985

C. 0.95

D. 0.997

6. **STUDENT SURVEY** A survey claims that 15% of high school students prefer having gym class during the last period of the day. The survey reports a margin of error of ±5%. About how many students were surveyed?

A. 20

B. 44

C. 133

D. 400

7. **OPEN-RESPONSE** At a tree nursery, the heights of scotch pine trees are normally distributed with a mean of 200 centimeters and a standard deviation of 20 centimeters.

a. Find the percent of scotch pine trees that have a height of at least 220 centimeters. Round your answer to the nearest whole number.

b. *Explain* your answer.

11 CHAPTER SUMMARY

BIG IDEAS — For Your Notebook

Big Idea 1

Finding Measures of Central Tendency and Dispersion

The table shows common measures of central tendency and dispersion for a data set. It also shows how these measures are affected when a constant is added to each data value or when each data value is multiplied by a constant.

	Data: 1, 4, 4, 5, 8, 9, 9, 15	Add 5 to each value in data set	Multiply each value in data set by 3
Mean	6.875	$6.875 + 5 = 11.875$	$3(6.875) = 20.625$
Median	6.5	$6.5 + 5 = 11.5$	$3(6.5) = 19.5$
Mode	4 and 9	$4 + 5 = 9$ and $9 + 5 = 14$	$3(4) = 12$ and $3(9) = 27$
Range	$15 - 1 = 14$	14	$3(14) = 42$
Standard deviation	4.04	4.04	$3(4.04) = 12.12$

Big Idea 2

Using Normal Distributions

A normal distribution is modeled by a symmetric, bell-shaped curve. The area under a normal curve is distributed as shown below. A z-score is the number of standard deviations a data value lies above or below the mean. You can use z-scores and the standard normal table on page 759 to find probabilities related to any normal distribution.

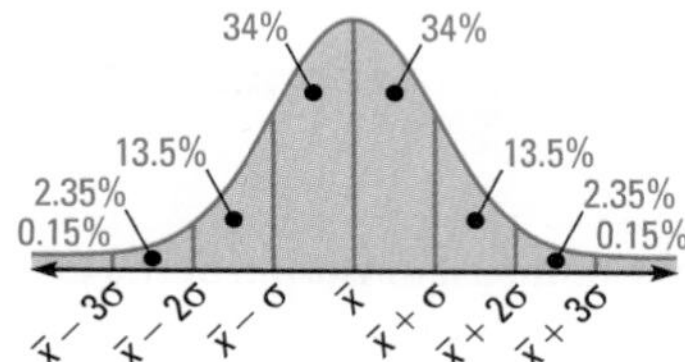

$$z\text{-score} = \frac{x - \bar{x}}{\sigma}$$

Big Idea 3

Working with Samples

You can use several different methods to choose a sample from a population. Random sampling is most likely to produce an unbiased sample.

Self-selected sample	Members volunteer.	Often biased
Systematic sample	A rule is used to select members.	Sometimes biased
Convenience sample	Easy-to-reach members are selected.	Often biased
Random sample	Every member has an equal chance of being selected.	Unbiased

Additional Resources

The following resources are available to help review the materials in this chapter.

Chapter 11 Resource Book

- Chapter Review Games and Activities, p. 64
- Cumulative Practice, Chs. 1–11, pp. 66–67

Student Resources in Spanish

eWorkbook

@HomeTutor

Vocabulary Practice

Vocabulary practice is available at **classzone.com**

Extra Example 11.1

Find the mean, median, mode, range, and standard deviation of the following data set: 26, 29, 29, 31, 34, 34, 42, 43, 45, 48 mean: 36.1, median: 34, modes: 29 and 34, range: 22, standard deviation: 7.4

11 CHAPTER REVIEW

@HomeTutor
classzone.com
- Multi-Language Glossary
- Vocabulary practice

REVIEW KEY VOCABULARY

- statistics, *p. 744*
- measure of central tendency, *p. 744*
- mean, median, mode, *p. 744*
- measure of dispersion, *p. 745*
- range, *p. 745*
- standard deviation, *p. 745*
- outlier, *p. 746*
- normal distribution, *p. 757*
- normal curve, *p. 757*
- standard normal distribution, *p. 758*
- *z*-score, *p. 758*
- population, *p. 766*
- sample, *p. 766*
- unbiased sample, *p. 767*
- biased sample, *p. 767*
- margin of error, *p. 768*

VOCABULARY EXERCISES

1. Copy and complete: _?_ is a measure of dispersion that describes the typical difference between a value in a data set and the mean. Standard deviation
2. **WRITING** *Describe* how multiplying every value in a data set by the same constant affects the mean, median, mode, range, and standard deviation.
3. Copy and complete: The _?_ for an x-value from a normal distribution represents the number of standard deviations the x-value lies above or below the mean. *z*-score

2. The mean, median, mode, range, and standard deviation are all multiplied by the given constant.

REVIEW EXAMPLES AND EXERCISES

Use the review examples and exercises below to check your understanding of the concepts you have learned in each lesson of Chapter 11.

11.1 Find Measures of Central Tendency and Dispersion *pp. 744–749*

EXAMPLE

Find the mean, median, mode, range, and standard deviation of the following data set: 13, 13, 13, 19, 24, 24, 27, 28, 34, 35.

Mean: $\bar{x} = \frac{13 + 13 + 13 + 19 + \cdots + 35}{10} = 23$

Median: 24 **Mode:** 13 **Range** = 35 − 13 = 22

Standard Deviation: $\sigma = \sqrt{\frac{(13-23)^2 + (13-23)^2 + \cdots + (35-23)^2}{10}} \approx 7.9$

EXERCISES

EXAMPLES 1 and 2 on pp. 744–745 for Exs. 4–8

Find the mean, median, mode, range, and standard deviation of the data set.

4. 35, 36, 36, 38, 41, 42, 45, 48 about 40.1, 39.5, 36, 13, about 4.4
5. 75, 76, 79, 85, 88, 88, 90, 92 about 84.1, 86.5, 88, 17, about 6.2
6. 76, 102, 87, 85, 91, 92, 91, 97 about 90.1, 91, 91, 26, about 7.3
7. 103, 155, 140, 125, 130, 140, 115 about 130, 130, 140, 52, about 16.1
8. **GAS PRICES** The list shows the average price of a gallon of gasoline each year from 1994 to 2004. Find the median and standard deviation of the prices.

   \$1.04, \$1.13, \$1.13, \$1.26, \$1.13, \$.97, \$1.30, \$1.47, \$1.14, \$1.47, \$1.59 \$1.14, about \$.19

@HomeTutor
classzone.com
Chapter Review Practice

11.2 Apply Transformations to Data

pp. 751–755

EXAMPLE

Find the mean, median, mode, range, and standard deviation of the data set below and of the data set obtained by multiplying each data value by 0.8.

200, 220, 280, 290, 320, 320, 340, 380

	Original data	Transformed data
Mean	293.75	0.8(293.75) = 235
Median	305	0.8(305) = 244
Mode	320	0.8(320) = 256
Range	180	0.8(180) = 144
Standard deviation	56.33	0.8(56.33) ≈ 45.06

EXERCISES

AMPLES
nd 2
pp. 751–752
Exs. 9–11

Find the mean, median, mode, range, and standard deviation of the given data set and of the data set obtained by performing the given transformation.

9. 34, 35, 37, 37, 38, 41, 42, 46, 48; add −7 to each data value
   about 39.8, 38, 37, 14, about 4.6; about 32.8, 31, 30, 14, about 4.6
10. 62, 66, 66, 68, 74, 76, 78, 80, 82; multiply each data value by 1.2
   about 72.4, 74, 66, 20, about 6.7; about 86.9, 88.8, 79.2, 24, about 8.0
11. **RAINFALL** The list below shows the average rainfall (in millimeters) for Lubbock, Texas, during each month of the year. Find the mean, median, mode, range, and standard deviation of the data in millimeters and of the data in inches. (*Note:* 1 mm ≈ 0.03937 in.)

    14.9, 14.3, 20.1, 30.5, 76.9, 59.8, 57.2, 40.2, 59.8, 46.5, 16.4, 18.8
    about 38.0, about 35.4, 59.8, 62.6, about 20.8; about 1.50, about 1.39, about 2.35, about 2.46, about 0.8

11.3 Use Normal Distributions

pp. 757–762

EXAMPLE

A normal distribution has a mean of 76 and a standard deviation of 9. Use the standard normal table on page 759 to find the probability that a randomly selected x-value from the distribution is at most 64.

$z = \frac{x - \overline{x}}{\sigma} = \frac{64 - 76}{9} \approx -1.3$ **Find z-score for $x = 64$.**

$P(x \le 64) \approx P(z \le -1.3) = 0.0968$ **Use the standard normal table.**

EXERCISES

AMPLE 3
p. 759
Exs. 12–17

A normal distribution has a mean of 95 and a standard deviation of 7. Use the standard normal table on page 759 to find the indicated probability for a randomly selected x-value from the distribution.

12. $P(x \le 89)$ about 0.1841
13. $P(x \le 84)$ about 0.0548
14. $P(91 < x \le 100)$ about 0.4837
15. $P(x \le 50)$ about 0
16. $P(x > 100)$ about 0.242
17. $P(50 < x \le 80)$ about 0.0179

Extra Example 11.2

Find the mean, median, mode, range, and standard deviation of the data set below and of the data set obtained by adding 50 to each data value.

35, 40, 45, 50, 51, 55, 60, 60

Original Data	
Mean	49.5
Median	50.5
Mode	60
Range	25
Standard deviation	8.47

Transformed Data	
Mean	99.5
Median	100.5
Mode	110
Range	25
Standard deviation	8.47

Extra Example 11.3

A normal distribution has a mean of 210 and a standard deviation of 8. Use the standard normal table on page 759 to find the probability that a randomly selected x-value from the distribution is less than 192.
about 0.0107

Extra Example 11.4

In a survey of 512 people, 62% said that they own a DVD player. What is the margin of error for the survey? **about ±4.4%**

Extra Example 11.5

Use a graphing calculator to find a model for the data. Then graph the model and the data in the same coordinate plane.

x	0	2	4	6	8	10
y	15	12	9	7	5	4

$y = 15.38(0.873)^x$

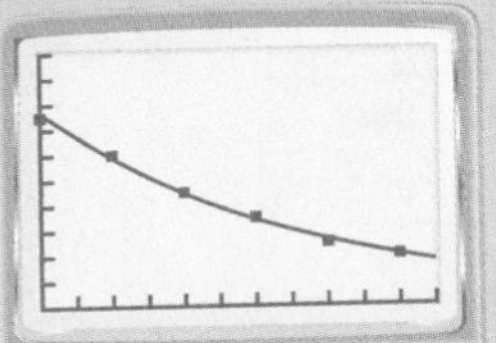

23.

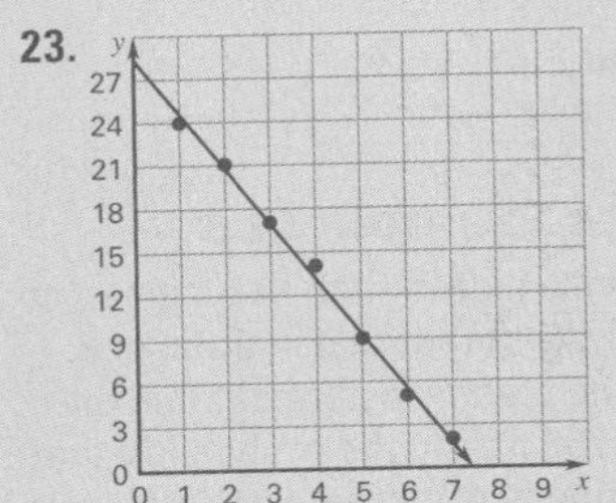

11 CHAPTER REVIEW

11.4 Select and Draw Conclusions from Samples *pp. 766–771*

EXAMPLE

In a survey of 582 people, 57% said that summer is their favorite season. What is the margin of error for the survey?

$$\text{Margin of error} = \pm\frac{1}{\sqrt{n}} = \pm\frac{1}{\sqrt{582}} \approx \pm 0.041 = \pm 4.1\%$$

EXERCISES

EXAMPLE 4 on p. 768 for Exs. 18–22

Find the margin of error for a survey that has the given sample size. Round your answer to the nearest tenth of a percent.

18. 300 **±5.8%** **19.** 2500 **±2%** **20.** 800 **±3.5%** **21.** 4900 **±1.4%**

22. SURVEYS In a Gallup Youth Survey of 517 teenagers, 34% said that their favorite way to spend an evening was to hang out with family or friends. What is the margin of error for the survey? **±4.4%**

11.5 Choose the Best Model for Two-Variable Data *pp. 775–780*

EXAMPLE

Use a graphing calculator to find a model for the data. Then graph the model and the data in the same coordinate plane.

x	20	30	40	50	60	70	80
y	42	48	53	52	49	40	32

Make a scatter plot. The points form an inverted U-shape. This suggests a quadratic model.

Use the quadratic regression feature to find an equation of the model.

Graph the model along with the data to verify that the model fits the data well.

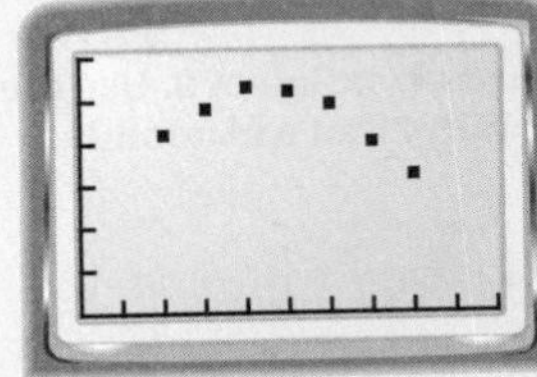

```
QuadReg
 y=ax²+bx+c
 a=-.0171428571
 b=1.535714286
 c=18.07142857
```

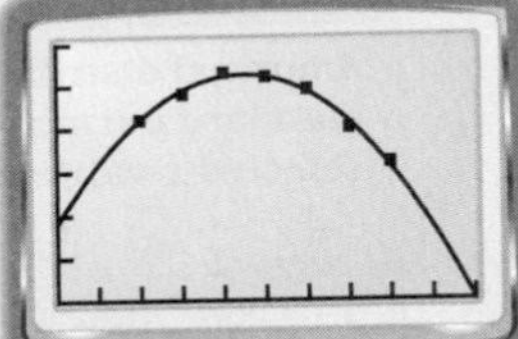

▸ A model for the data is $y = -0.0171x^2 + 1.54x + 18.1$.

EXERCISES

EXAMPLES 1, 2, and 3 on pp. 775–777 for Ex. 23

23. Use a graphing calculator to find a model for the data. Then graph the model and the data in the same coordinate plane.

x	1	2	3	4	5	6	7
y	24	21	17	14	9	5	2

$y = -3.79x + 28.3$; see margin for art.

11 CHAPTER TEST

Find the mean, median, mode, range, and standard deviation of the given data set and of the data set obtained by performing the given transformation.

1. 41, 38, 42, 41, 45, 44, 48, 35; multiply each data value by 3
   41.75, 41.5, 41, 13, about 3.8; about 125.3, 124.5, 123, 39, about 11.4
2. 16, 21, 19, 21, 17, 25, 15, 18; add 14 to each data value
   19, 18.5, 21, 10, about 3.0; 33, 32.5, 35, 10, about 3.0
3. 108, 92, 102, 99, 116, 92; multiply each data value by 4.5
   101.5, 100.5, 92, 24, about 8.6; about 456.8, about 452.3, 414, 108, about 38.7

A normal distribution has a mean of 72 and a standard deviation of 5. Find the probability that a randomly selected x-value from the distribution is in the given interval.

4. Between 67 and 77 **0.68**
5. Between 57 and 72 **0.4985**
6. At least 62 **0.975**

Find the margin of error for a survey that has the given sample size. Round your answer to the nearest tenth of a percent.

7. 340 ±5.4%
8. 8125 ±1.1%
9. 931 ±3.3%
10. 1560 ±2.5%

11. **FOOTBALL** Teams in the National Football League are divided into two conferences, the American Football Conference (AFC) and the National Football Conference (NFC). The table below shows the margin of victory in each conference's championship game for the 1990–2004 seasons.

AFC Championship margins of victory	NFC Championship margins of victory
48, 3, 19, 17, 4, 4, 14, 3, 13, 19, 13, 7, 17, 10, 14	2, 31, 10, 17, 10, 11, 17, 13, 3, 5, 41, 5, 17, 11, 17

   a. Find the mean, median, mode, range, and standard deviation of the AFC margins of victory. **about 13.7; 13; 3, 4, 13, 14, 17, 19; 45; about 10.7**

   b. Find the mean, median, mode, range, and standard deviation of the NFC margins of victory. **14, 11, 17, 39, about 10.1**

   c. *Compare* the statistics for each set of data and make a conclusion about the data. ***Sample answer:*** **The data are very similar except the margins of victory for the NFC are slightly more spread out.**

12. **TEST SCORES** The scores on a standardized test administered to 10,000 students have a mean of 50 and a standard deviation of 10. Find the z-score for each student whose score is given.

   a. Kevin: 55 **0.5**
   b. Manuel: 70 **2**
   c. Colby: 40 **−1**
   d. Neal: 47 **−0.3**

13. **SHOPPING SURVEY** In a survey of 1600 U.S. adults, 61% said that they have purchased a product online. Find the margin of error for the survey. Then give an interval that is likely to contain the exact percent of all U.S. adults who have purchased a product online. **±2.5%; between 58.5% and 63.5%**

14. **TYPING ERRORS** The table shows the average number y of errors made by students in a typing course when they took tests given x days after the start of the course. Use a graphing calculator to find a model for the data. ***Sample answer:*** $y = 48.9(0.967)^x$

x	2	10	14	21	30	45	63	70	91
y	45.2	36.1	30.2	23.1	18.7	11.0	5.6	4.3	2.4

Additional Resources

Assessment Book

- Chapter Test, Levels A, B, C, pp. 156–161
- Standardized Chapter Test, pp. 162–163
- SAT/ACT Chapter Test, pp. 164–165
- Alternative Assessment, pp. 166–167

Test Generator CD-ROM

Chapter Test

Easily-readable reduced copies (with answers) of Chapter Test B, the Standardized Chapter Test, and the Alternative Assessment from the Assessment Book can be found on pp. 742E–742F.

MULTIPLE-CHOICE QUESTIONS

If you have difficulty solving a multiple-choice problem directly, you may be able to use another approach to eliminate incorrect answer choices and obtain the correct answer.

PROBLEM 1

In a survey of 5000 households, 9.2% watched a certain television program. What interval is likely to contain the percent of *all* U.S. households that watched the program?

A. 4.0% to 14.0%
B. 7.8% to 10.6%
C. 8.3% to 10.3%
D. 9.2% to 9.6%

METHOD 1

SOLVE DIRECTLY Calculate the margin of error. Then use the margin of error and the percent given in the problem to find the interval.

STEP 1 **Calculate** the margin of error.

$$\text{Margin of error} = \pm\frac{1}{\sqrt{n}}$$
$$= \pm\frac{1}{\sqrt{5000}}$$
$$\approx \pm 0.014$$
$$= \pm 1.4\%$$

STEP 2 **Find** the lower bound for the interval.

$$\text{Lower bound} = 9.2\% - 1.4\%$$
$$= 7.8\%$$

STEP 3 **Find** the upper bound for the interval.

$$\text{Upper bound} = 9.2\% + 1.4\%$$
$$= 10.6\%$$

STEP 4 **Write** the interval.

The interval is 7.8% to 10.6%.

▸ The correct answer is B.

METHOD 2

ELIMINATE CHOICES Another method is to chec the intervals given in the answer choices.

You know that 9.2% must fall exactly in the mic of the interval.

Choice A: $\frac{4.0 + 14.0}{2} = \frac{18.0}{2} = 9.0$, so 9.2% does fall exactly in the middle of the inter You can eliminate choice A. ✗

Choice B: $\frac{7.8 + 10.6}{2} = \frac{18.4}{2} = 9.2$, so 9.2% falls exactly in the middle of the interval

Choice C: $\frac{8.3 + 10.3}{2} = \frac{18.6}{2} = 9.3$, so 9.2% does fall exactly in the middle of the inte You can eliminate choice C. ✗

Choice D: $\frac{9.2 + 9.6}{2} = \frac{18.8}{2} = 9.4$, so 9.2% does fall exactly in the middle of the inte You can eliminate choice D. ✗

▸ The correct answer is B.

ROBLEM 2

At a local bank, the waiting times for an available teller are normally distributed with a mean of 10 minutes and a standard deviation of 2 minutes. What is the approximate probability that a randomly selected customer at the bank waits no more than 13 minutes for a teller?

A. 60.7% B. 82.0% C. 93.3% D. 98.5%

ETHOD 1

LVE DIRECTLY Use a z-score and the ndard normal table on page 759 to find desired probability.

P 1 **Find** the z-score for a waiting time of 13 minutes.

$$z = \frac{x - \overline{x}}{\sigma}$$

$$= \frac{13 - 10}{2}$$

$$= 1.5$$

P 2 **Use** the standard normal table to find $P(z \leq 1.5)$.

$P(z \leq 1.5) = 0.9332 \approx 93.3\%$

The probability of waiting no more than 13 minutes is about 93.3%.

he correct answer is C.

METHOD 2

ELIMINATE CHOICES Use the facts about normal distributions on page 757 to eliminate incorrect answer choices.

For a randomly selected customer with a waiting time of x minutes, you know the following:

$$P(x \leq 12) = P(x \leq \overline{x} + \sigma)$$

$$= 50\% + 34\%$$

$$= 84\%$$

$$P(x \leq 14) = P(x \leq \overline{x} + 2\sigma)$$

$$= 50\% + 34\% + 13.5\%$$

$$= 97.5\%$$

It follows that $P(x \leq 13)$ is between 84% and 97.5%. Only the probability of 93.3% in answer choice C satisfies this condition.

▶ The correct answer is C.

TEST PREPARATION

RACTICE

plain **why you can eliminate the highlighted answer choice.**

. A normal distribution has a mean of 4.06 and a standard deviation of 0.04. What is the probability that a randomly selected value from the distribution is between 4.06 and 4.14?

A. 0.01 B. 0.475 C. 0.68 D.✕ 0.99

. If you add the same nonzero constant to each value in a data set, which statistic does not change?

A. Mean B. Median C.✕ Mode D. Range

. Which type of function best models the data represented by the scatter plot at the right?

A. Linear B. Quadratic

C. Cubic D.✕ Exponential

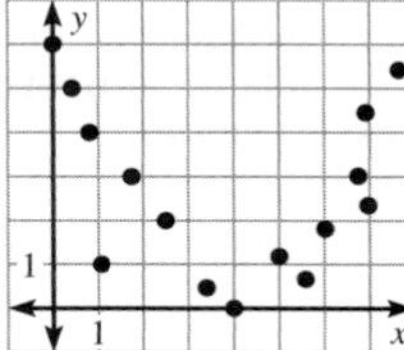

Kentucky Test Preparation

1. ***Sample answer:*** **The interval from 4.06 to 4.14 represents two standard deviations to the right of the mean whose probability is much smaller than 0.99.**
2. ***Sample answer:*** **Adding a nonzero constant only changes the mean, median, and mode.**
3. ***Sample answer:*** **An exponential function is strictly increasing or decreasing.**

Kentucky Test Practice

1. B
2. B
3. D
4. C
5. A
6. B
7. C
8. A
9. D

TEST PREPARATION

Kentucky Test Practice

MULTIPLE-CHOICE

In Exercises 1 and 2, use the data below giving the lengths (in minutes) of the movies showing at a local movie theater.

94, 109, 166, 136, 97, 110, 113, 114, 94, 101

1. What is the median of the data set?

   A. 94 min B. 109.5 min
   C. 110 min D. 111.5 min

2. To the nearest tenth of a minute, what is the standard deviation of the data set?

   A. 7.2 min B. 21.2 min
   C. 25.6 min D. 67.0 min

3. According to a survey from the National Center for Health Statistics, the heights of adult women in the United States are normally distributed with a mean of 64 inches and a standard deviation of 2.7 inches. What is the approximate probability that 4 randomly selected women are all between 58.6 inches and 66.7 inches tall?

   A. 34% B. 44%
   C. 68% D. 81.5%

4. What is the percent of the area under a normal curve that is represented by the shaded region?

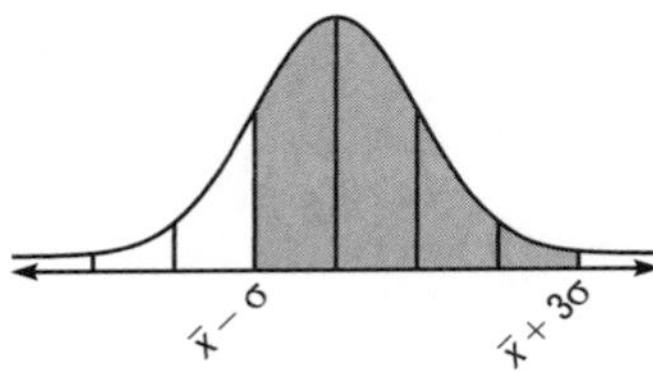

   A. 50% B. 81.5%
   C. 83.85% D. 84%

5. Rachel scored an 88 on her physics test. The class average was 79.3, and the standard deviation was 7.5. What is the *z*-score for Rachel's test score?

   A. 1.16 B. 1.30
   C. 1.45 D. 1.60

6. The data set below gives the numbers of pages in five high school textbooks.

   384, 480, 576, 640, 768

   Which statement is *false*?

   A. There is no mode.
   B. The mean is greater than the median.
   C. The mean is 569.6 pages.
   D. The range is 384 pages.

7. In a nationwide poll of 1015 U.S. adults, Tom Hanks was voted America's favorite movie star. What is the approximate margin of error for the survey?

   A. ±0.031% B. ±0.31%
   C. ±3.1% D. ±31%

8. The table shows the attendance (in millions) at Boston Red Sox games in Fenway Park from 1995 to 2004. Which type of function best models the data?

Year	Attendance	Year	Attendance
1995	2.16	2000	2.59
1996	2.32	2001	2.63
1997	2.23	2002	2.65
1998	2.31	2003	2.72
1999	2.45	2004	2.84

   A. Linear B. Quadratic
   C. Exponential D. Power

9. The delays (in minutes) for a commercial airline flight are listed below for Sunday through Friday of a certain week.

   20, 10, 0, 30, 0, 45

   On Saturday, the flight is delayed 150 minutes. Which statistic is most affected when this outlier is added to the given data set?

   A. Mean B. Median
   C. Mode D. Range

MULTIPLE-CHOICE

0. A normal distribution has a mean of 77 and a standard deviation of 4. What is the z-score corresponding to an x-value of 80?

   A. -0.91 B. -0.75
   C. 0.75 D. 0.91

1. The standard deviation of a data set is 12.2. A new data set is created by adding 5.1 to each data value. To the nearest tenth, what is the standard deviation of the new data set?

   A. 7.1 B. 12.2
   C. 13.2 D. 17.3

12. The mean of the numbers 5, 8, 7, 2, and x is 6. What is the value of x?

    A. 2 B. 5.25
    C. 6.75 D. 8

13. In a normal distribution, about what percent of the area under the related normal curve lies within 2 standard deviations of the mean?

    A. 2.5% B. 5%
    C. 95% D. 97.5%

OPEN-RESPONSE

4. The data set below gives the average rainfall for each month in San Antonio, Texas, and Chicago, Illinois.

   San Antonio, Texas (in inches):
   1.5, 1.8, 1.8, 2.8, 3.4, 3.1, 2.2, 2.5, 3.4, 2.5, 2.2, 1.8

   Chicago, Illinois (in millimeters):
   48.2, 41.8, 72.2, 96.6, 82.5, 103.4, 102.7, 89.3, 78.6, 69.7, 72.7, 64.8

   a. Find the mean, median, mode, range, and standard deviation for each city's rainfall data.
   b. *Compare* the statistics for each city. Make a conclusion about the data. (*Hint:* 1 millimeter ≈ 0.03937 inch.)

5. The table shows the numbers of people (in millions) who voted in U.S. Presidential elections since 1940.

Years since 1940	0	4	8	12	16	20	24	28
Voters (millions)	49.90	47.98	48.79	61.55	62.03	68.84	70.65	73.21
Years since 1940	32	36	40	44	48	52	56	60
Voters (millions)	77.72	81.56	86.52	92.65	91.60	104.43	96.28	105.40

   a. Make a scatter plot of the data.
   b. Find the equation of the linear regression model for this set of data, where time is the independent variable.
   c. Graph the equation along with the data to verify that the equation fits the data well.
   d. Use your equation to predict the number of people who voted in the 2004 U.S. Presidential election. *Compare* your prediction to the actual number of voters in that election, which was 122.30 million voters.

TEST PREPARATION

10. C
11. B
12. D
13. C
14. a. San Antonio: about 2.4, about 2.4, 1.8, 1.9, about 0.6 Chicago: about 76.9, about 75.7, no mode, 61.6, about 18.8
b. *Sample answer:* Chicago gets more rain on average than San Antonio.
15. a. See graph in part C.
b. $y = 0.986x + 46.6$
c.

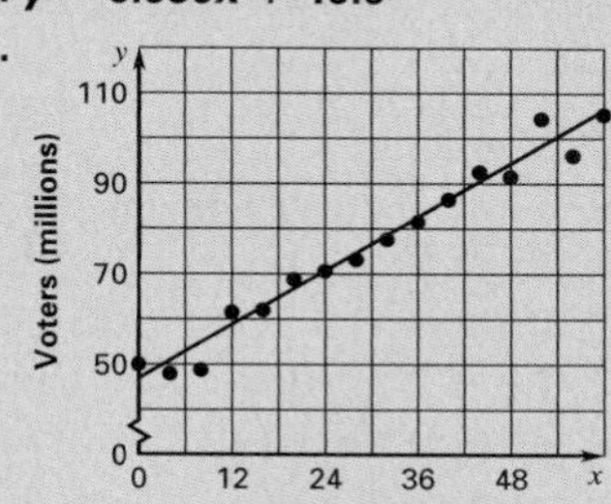

d. about 109.70 million voters; the equation's prediction is an underestimate.

12 Pacing and Assignment Guide

REGULAR SCHEDULE

Pre-AP For pacing and assignments for a Pre-AP course, see the *Algebra 2 Toolkit.*

Lesson	Les. Day	BASIC	AVERAGE	ADVANCED
12.1 MA-HS-1.3.2	Day 1	pp. 798–800 Exs. 1–7, 15–20, 27–31, 37–39, 45–48, 63–66, 69	pp. 798–800 Exs. 1, 2, 8–11, 20–23, 27, 31–33, 40–42, 49–52, 57, 58, 63–67, 70	pp. 798–800 Exs. 1, 2, 12–14, 24–27, 34–36, 43, 44, 53–68*
12.2 MA-HS-1.3.2	Day 1	pp. 806–809 Exs. 1–6, 12–15, 21–25, 29–32, 39–42, 49–51, 63–66, 70	pp. 806–809 Exs. 1, 2, 7–9, 16–18, 21, 22, 25, 26, 29, 33–35, 39, 43–45, 52–54, 63–68, 71	pp. 806–809 Exs. 1, 2, 9–11, 18–20, 26–29, 36–39, 46–48, 51–69*
12.3 MA-HS-1.3.2	Day 1	pp. 814–817 Exs. 1–8, 15–20, 27–32, 37, 38	pp. 814–817 Exs. 1, 2, 6–11, 18–23, 27, 31–35, 37, 38	pp. 814–817 Exs. 1, 2, 9–14, 21–27, 31–36
	Day 2	pp. 814–817 Exs. 39–44, 48–50, 57–60, 63–64	pp. 814–817 Exs. 42–47, 51–54, 57–61, 63–64	pp. 814–817 Exs. 45–47, 51–62*, 63
12.4 MA-HS-1.3.4	Day 1	pp. 823–825 Exs. 1–6, 7–29 odd, 37–40, 43	pp. 823–825 Exs. 1, 2, 4–6, 8–14 even, 19, 20–32 even, 33, 34, 37–41, 44	pp. 823–825 Exs. 1, 2, 5, 6, 15–18, 22–42*, 44
12.5 MA-HS-1.3.2	Day 1	pp. 830–833 Exs. 1–7, 12–16, 22–28, 33–36, 43–46, 49–50	pp. 830–833 Exs. 1, 2, 7–9, 12, 17–19, 22, 23, 28–30, 33–41, 43–47, 49–50	pp. 830–833 Exs. 1, 2, 10–12, 19–21, 30–50*
Review	Day 1	pp. 840–842 Exs. 1–38	pp. 840–842 Exs. 1–38	pp. 840–842 Exs. 1–38
Assess	Day 1	Chapter 12 Test	Chapter 12 Test	Chapter 12 Test

Yearly Pacing Chapter 12 Total – 8 days Chapters 1–12 Total – 138 days Remaining – 22 days

*Challenge Exercises EP = Extra Practice SRH = Skills Review Handbook

BLOCK SCHEDULE

DAY 1	DAY 2	DAY 3	DAY 4
12.1	**12.3**	**12.4**	**REVIEW**
pp. 798–800 Exs. 1, 2, 8–11, 20–23, 27, 31–33, 40–42, 49–52, 57, 58, 63–67, 70	pp. 814–817 Exs. 1, 2, 6–11, 18–23, 27, 31–35, 37, 38, 42–47, 51–54, 57–61, 63–64	pp. 823–825 Exs. 1, 2, 4–6, 8–14 even, 19, 20–32 even, 33, 34, 37–41, 44	pp. 840–842 Exs. 1–38
12.2		**12.5**	**ASSESS**
pp. 806–809 Exs. 1, 2, 7–9, 16–18, 21, 22, 25, 26, 29, 33–35, 39, 43–45, 52–54, 63–68, 71		pp. 830–833 Exs. 1, 2, 7–9, 12, 17–19, 22, 23, 28–30, 33–41, 43–47, 49–50	Chapter 12 Test

Yearly Pacing Chapter 12 Total – 4 days Chapters 1–12 Total – 69 days Remaining – 11 days

Chapter Resource Guide 12

RESOURCE MANAGER

Chapter Resource Book

CHAPTER SUPPORT					
Parents as Partners (Chapter Overview with home involvement exercises and activity)					p. 1
LESSON SUPPORT Standards	12.1 MA-HS-1.3.2	12.2 MA-HS-1.3.2	12.3 MA-HS-1.3.2	12.4 MA-HS-1.3.4	12.5 MA-HS-1.3.2
Teaching Guide/Lesson Plan	p. 3	p. 14	p. 25	p. 38	p. 48
Activity Masters		p. 16			
Technology Activities & Keystrokes	p. 5		p. 27		p. 50
Activity Support Masters					
Practice (3 levels)	p. 6	p. 17	p. 29	p. 40	p. 52
Study Guide	p. 9	p. 20	p. 32	p. 43	p. 55
Catch-Up for Absent Students	p. 11	p. 22	p. 34	p. 45	p. 57
Problem Solving/Application	p. 12	p. 23	p. 35	p. 46	p. 58
Challenge Practice	p. 13	p. 24	p. 37	p. 47	p. 59
REVIEW					
Chapter Review Games and Activities		p. 60	Cumulative Practice		p. 62
Project with Rubric		p. 61	Resource Book Answers		A1

Transparencies	12.1	12.2	12.3	12.4	12.5
Warm-Up/Daily Homework Quiz	✔	✔	✔	✔	✔
Notetaking Guide	✔	✔	✔	✔	✔
Teacher Support	✔	✔	✔		
Answer Transparencies	✔	✔	✔	✔	✔

ASSESSMENT BOOK

Quizzes	p. 168	SAT/ACT Chapter Test	p. 178
Chapter Tests (3 levels)	p. 170	Alternative Assessment with Rubric	p. 180
Standardized Chapter Test	p. 176		

TECHNOLOGY

- Easy Planner
- Test and Practice Generator
- Power Presentations
- @HomeTutor
- Activity Generator
- Animated Algebra
- Classzone.com
- eEdition Plus Online
- eWorkbook Plus Online
- ML Assessment System

ADDITIONAL RESOURCES

Kentucky

- Worked-Out Solution Key
- Notetaking Guide
- Practice Workbook
- Algebra 2 Toolkit
- Benchmark Tests
- Remediation Workbook
- Spanish Study Guide
- Spanish Assessment Book
- Spanish Resources in Spanish
- Multi-Language Visual Glossary

12 Lesson Practice Level B

LESSON 12.1 Practice B
For use with pages 794–800

Write the first six terms of the sequence. See below.

1. $a_n = n^2 + 6$
2. $a_n = n^2 - 3$
3. $a_n = 3^{n+1}$
4. $f(n) = 2^{n-1}$
5. $f(n) = -\frac{4}{3n}$
6. $f(n) = \frac{n}{3n+2}$

For the sequence, describe the pattern, write the next term, and write a rule for the *n*th term. 10. $\frac{1+3}{3}, \frac{2+3}{3}, \frac{3+3}{3}, \frac{4+3}{3}, \frac{8}{3}; a_n = \frac{n+3}{3}$

7. 2, 4, 8, 16 $2^1, 2^2, 2^3, 2^4$; 32; $a_n = 2^n$
8. 1, 8, 27, 64 $1^3, 2^3, 3^3, 4^3$; 125; $a_n = n^3$
9. $\frac{1}{1}, \frac{1}{4}, \frac{1}{9}, \frac{1}{16}$ $\frac{1}{1^2}, \frac{1}{2^2}, \frac{1}{3^2}, \frac{1}{4^2}; \frac{1}{25}; a_n = \frac{1}{n^2}$
10. $\frac{4}{3}, \frac{5}{3}, \frac{6}{3}, \frac{7}{3}$ See above.
11. 3, 5, 7, 9 $2(1) + 1, 2(2) + 1, 2(3) + 1, 2(4) + 1$; 11; $a_n = 2n + 1$
12. $\frac{4}{2}, \frac{8}{3}, \frac{12}{4}, \frac{16}{5}$ $\frac{4(1)}{1+1}, \frac{4(2)}{2+1}, \frac{4(3)}{3+1}, \frac{4(4)}{4+1}; \frac{20}{6}; a_n = \frac{4n}{n+1}$
13. 0.7, 1.3, 1.9, 2.5 $0.6(1) + 0.1, 0.6(2) + 0.1, 0.6(3) + 0.1, 0.6(4) + 0.1$; 3.1; $a_n = 0.6n + 0.1$
14. 1.0, 0.5, 0.0, −0.5 $1.5 - 0.5(1), 1.5 - 0.5(2), 1.5 - 0.5(3), 1.5 - 0.5(4)$; −1.0; $a_n = 1.5 - 0.5n$

Graph the sequence.

15. 1, 2, 3, 4, 5
16. 2, 4, 6, 8, 10
17. $\frac{1}{2}, 1, \frac{3}{2}, 2, \frac{5}{2}$

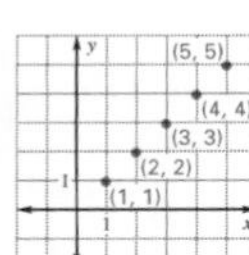

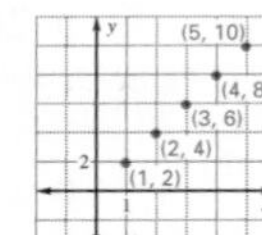

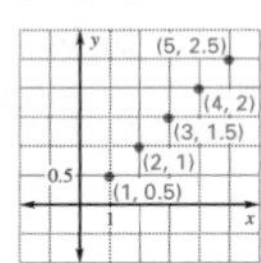

Write the series using summation notation.

18. $-2 + 1 + 6 + 13 + 22 + \cdots$ $\sum_{i=1}^{\infty} i^2 - 3$
19. $\frac{2}{3} + \frac{4}{5} + \frac{6}{6} + \frac{8}{7}$ $\sum_{i=1}^{4} \frac{2i}{i+3}$

Find the sum of the series.

20. $\sum_{k=4}^{8} 3k - 2$ 80
21. $\sum_{i=2}^{4} i^2 + i + 4$ 50
22. $\sum_{i=1}^{22} i$ 253

23. **Jacket** You want to save \$30 to buy a jacket. You begin by saving a dollar in the first week. You plan to save an additional dollar each week after that. For example, you will save \$2 in the second week, \$3 in the third week, and so on. How many weeks must you save to have saved \$30? 8

1. 7, 10, 15, 22, 31, 42
2. −2, 1, 6, 13, 22, 33
3. 9, 27, 81, 243, 729, 2187
4. 1, 2, 4, 8, 16, 32
5. $-\frac{4}{3}, -\frac{2}{3}, -\frac{4}{9}, -\frac{1}{3}, -\frac{4}{15}, -\frac{2}{9}$
6. $\frac{1}{5}, \frac{1}{4}, \frac{3}{11}, \frac{2}{7}, \frac{5}{17}, \frac{3}{10}$

LESSON 12.1

Algebra 2
Chapter 12 Resource Book 7

LESSON 12.2 Practice B
For use with pages 802–809

Tell whether the sequence is arithmetic. *Explain* why or why not. See below.

1. 2, −5, −12, −19, −26
2. 3, 5.5, 8, 10.5, 13
3. 0, −5, −10, −12, −20
4. 2, 4, 8, 16, 32
5. 1, 2, 4, 7, 11
6. $\frac{3}{4}, \frac{7}{8}, 1, \frac{9}{8}, \frac{5}{4}$

Write a rule for the *n*th term of the arithmetic sequence. Then find a_{10}.

7. −4, 2, 8, 14, 20 $a_n = 6n - 10$; 50
8. −25, −29, −33, −37, −41 $a_n = -4n - 21$; −61
9. $\frac{1}{4}, 0, -\frac{1}{4}, -\frac{1}{2}, -\frac{3}{4}$ $a_n = \frac{1}{2} - \frac{1}{4}n$; −2
10. $d = 5, a_5 = 33$ $a_n = 5n + 8$; 58
11. $d = 2, a_6 = 10$ $a_n = 2n - 2$; 18
12. $d = -3, a_{12} = -34.5$ $a_n = -3n + 1.5$; −28.5

Write a rule for the *n*th term of the arithmetic sequence that has the two given terms. 13. $a_n = 14n - 40$ 14. $a_n = \frac{3}{2}n + 4$ 15. $a_n = -5 - n$

13. $a_{20} = 240, a_{15} = 170$
14. $a_6 = 13, a_{14} = 25$
15. $a_9 = -14, a_{15} = -20$
16. $a_8 = -44, a_5 = -32$ $a_n = -12 - 4n$
17. $a_{16} = 6, a_{20} = 7$ $a_n = \frac{n}{4} + 2$
18. $a_7 = \frac{6}{7}, a_9 = \frac{2}{3}$ $\frac{6}{n}$

Find the sum of the arithmetic series.

19. $\sum_{i=1}^{8} 3n - 1$ 100
20. $\sum_{i=1}^{20} -2n + 14$ −140
21. $\sum_{i=1}^{15} -n - 6$ −210
22. $\sum_{i=6}^{12} -5n + 17$ −196
23. $\sum_{i=4}^{9} 6n - 30$ 54
24. $\sum_{i=8}^{16} -11 + 4n$ 333

Write a rule for the sequence whose graph is shown.

25.

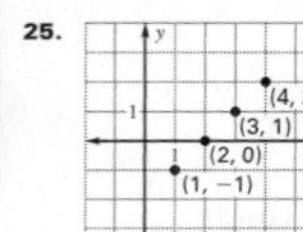

$a_n = n - 2$

26.

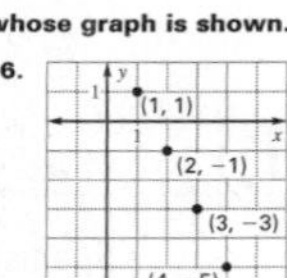

$a_n = -2n + 3$

27.

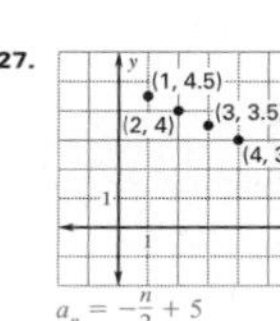

$a_n = -\frac{n}{2} + 5$

28. **Auditorium** An auditorium has 25 rows. The first row has 10 seats, and each row after the first has 1 more seat that the row before it.
    a. Write a rule for the number of seats in the *n*th row. $a_n = n + 9$
    b. Find the total number of seats in the auditorium. 550

1. yes; each difference is −7
2. yes; each difference is 2.5
3. no; differences are not constant
4. no; differences are not constant
5. no; differences are not constant
6. yes; each difference is $\frac{1}{8}$

LESSON 12.2

18 Algebra 2
Chapter 12 Resource Book

LESSON 12.3 Practice B
For use with pages 810–817

Tell whether the sequence is geometric. *Explain* why or why not.

1. 3, 5, 7, 9, 11, . . . no; the ratios are different
2. 5, 10, 20, 40, 80, . . . yes; each ratio is $\frac{2}{1}$
3. 100, 50, 25, $\frac{25}{2}, \frac{25}{4}$, . . . yes; each ratio is $\frac{1}{2}$
4. 1, 3, 7, 15, 31, . . . no; the ratios are different
5. 3, 9, 27, 81, 243, . . . yes; each ratio is $\frac{3}{1}$
6. $-6, -2, -\frac{2}{3}, -\frac{2}{9}, -\frac{2}{27}$, . . . yes; each ratio is $\frac{1}{3}$

Write a rule for the *n*th term of the geometric sequence. Find a_6. Then graph the first five terms of the sequence.

7. $r = 3, a_1 = 2$
8. $r = \frac{1}{10}, a_2 = 4$
9. $r = -\frac{1}{2}, a_3 = 8$

(5, 162) (4, 54) (3, 18) (2, 6) (1, 2)

$a_n = 2(3)^{n-1}$; 486

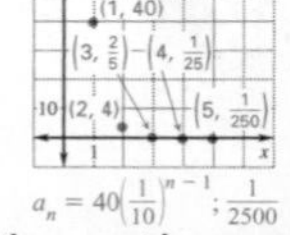

$a_n = 40\left(\frac{1}{10}\right)^{n-1}$; $\frac{1}{2500}$

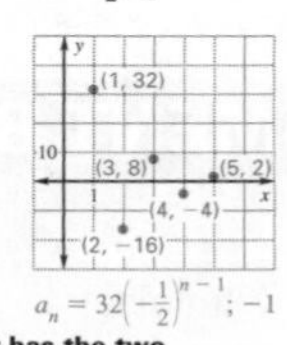

$a_n = 32\left(-\frac{1}{2}\right)^{n-1}$; −1

Write a rule for the *n*th term of the geometric sequence that has the two given terms. 10. $a_n = 1(3)^{n-1}$ 11. $a_n = 6(2)^{n-1}$ 12. $a_n = \frac{1}{2}(4)^{n-1}$

10. $a_1 = 1, a_3 = 9$
11. $a_3 = 24, a_5 = 96$
12. $a_2 = 2, a_6 = 512$
13. $a_2 = 2, a_5 = \frac{1}{4}$ $a_n = 4\left(\frac{1}{2}\right)^{n-1}$
14. $a_3 = 25, a_6 = -\frac{25}{64}$ $a_n = 400\left(-\frac{1}{4}\right)^{n-1}$
15. $a_4 = -\frac{8}{9}, a_7 = -\frac{64}{243}$ $a_n = -3\left(\frac{2}{3}\right)^{n-1}$

Find the sum of the geometric series.

16. $\sum_{i=1}^{5} 3(2)^{i-1}$ 93
17. $\sum_{i=1}^{8} 90\left(\frac{1}{3}\right)^{i-1}$ $\frac{32,800}{243}$
18. $\sum_{i=1}^{10} 32\left(\frac{1}{2}\right)^{i-1}$ $\frac{1023}{16}$
19. $\sum_{i=1}^{10} 8(3)^{i-1}$ 236,192
20. $\sum_{i=0}^{7} 2\left(\frac{3}{2}\right)^{i-1}$ $\frac{6305}{96}$
21. $\sum_{i=0}^{10} 1000\left(\frac{1}{2}\right)^{i-1}$ $\frac{255,875}{64}$

22. **Retirement** You invest \$20,000 in a retirement plan. The plan is expected to have an annual return of 12%. Write a rule for the amount of money a_n available in the plan at the beginning of the *n*th year. What is the balance of the account at the beginning of the 20th year? $a_n = 20,000(1.12)^{n-1}$; \$172,255.23

LESSON 12.3

30 Algebra 2
Chapter 12 Resource Book

LESSON 12.4

Practice B

For use with pages 820–825

For the given series, find and graph the partial sums S_n for $n = 1, 2, 3, 4,$ and 5. *Describe* what happens to S_n as n increases.

1. $1 + \frac{1}{2} + \frac{1}{4} + \frac{1}{8} + \frac{1}{16} + \cdots$

$1; \frac{3}{2}; \frac{7}{4}; \frac{15}{8}; \frac{31}{16}$
As n increases, S_n approaches 2.

2. $3 + \frac{3}{4} + \frac{3}{16} + \frac{3}{64} + \frac{3}{256} + \cdots$

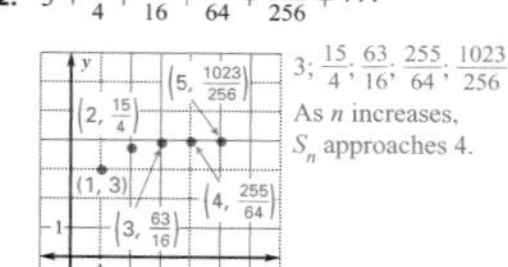

$3; \frac{15}{4}; \frac{63}{16}; \frac{255}{64}; \frac{1023}{256}$
As n increases, S_n approaches 4.

Find the sum of the infinite geometric series, if it exists.

3. $\sum_{i=1}^{\infty} 5\left(\frac{1}{2}\right)^{i-1}$ 10

4. $\sum_{i=1}^{\infty} \left(\frac{1}{5}\right)^{i-1}$ $\frac{5}{4}$

5. $\sum_{i=1}^{\infty} 3\left(-\frac{2}{5}\right)^{i-1}$ $\frac{15}{7}$

6. $\sum_{i=0}^{\infty} 2(6)^{i-1}$ no sum

7. $\sum_{i=1}^{\infty} 6\left(\frac{2}{3}\right)^{i-1}$ 18

8. $\sum_{i=1}^{\infty} 8\left(\frac{1}{3}\right)^{i-1}$ 12

9. $\sum_{i=1}^{\infty} \left(\frac{5}{2}\right)^{i-1}$ no sum

10. $\sum_{i=0}^{\infty} 2\left(-\frac{3}{4}\right)^{i}$ $\frac{8}{7}$

11. $\sum_{i=0}^{\infty} 7\left(\frac{4}{7}\right)^{i}$ $\frac{49}{3}$

Find the sum of the infinite geometric series, if it exists.

12. $2 + \frac{2}{3} + \frac{2}{9} + \frac{2}{27} + \frac{2}{81} + \cdots$ 3

13. $\frac{1}{3} + \frac{1}{4} + \frac{3}{16} + \frac{9}{64} + \frac{27}{256} + \cdots$ $\frac{4}{3}$

14. $\frac{1}{2} + \frac{3}{4} + \frac{9}{8} + \frac{27}{16} + \frac{81}{32} + \cdots$ no sum

15. $\frac{2}{3} + \frac{2}{5} + \frac{6}{25} + \frac{18}{125} + \frac{54}{625} + \cdots$ $\frac{5}{3}$

Write the repeating decimal as a fraction in lowest terms.

16. 0.555 . . . $\frac{5}{9}$

17. 0.262626 . . . $\frac{26}{99}$

18. 0.538538538 . . . $\frac{538}{999}$

19. 17.171717 . . . $\frac{1700}{99}$

20. 311.311311311 . . . $\frac{311{,}00}{999}$

21. 0.040404 . . . $\frac{4}{99}$

22. **Retirement** You invest $15,000 in a retirement plan. The plan is expected to have an annual return of 9%. Write a rule for the amount of money a_n available in the plan at the beginning of the nth year. What is the balance of the account at the beginning of the 25th year? $a_n = 15{,}000(1.09)^{n-1}$; $118,666.25

23. **Ball Bounce** A ball is dropped from a height of 40 feet. Each time it hits the ground, it bounces three-fourths of its previous height. Find the total distance the ball has traveled before coming to rest. 280 ft

LESSON 12.5

Practice B

For use with pages 827–833

Write the first five terms of the sequence. See below.

1. $a_0 = 3$
   $a_n = a_{n-1} + 7$

2. $a_0 = -4$
   $a_n = 2a_{n-1}$

3. $a_0 = 243$
   $a_n = \frac{1}{3}a_{n-1} + 9$

4. $a_0 = 2$
   $a_n = n^2 - 3n + 2a_{n-1}$

5. $a_0 = 2$
   $a_n = (a_{n-1})^2 - 3$

6. $a_1 = 3, a_2 = 1$
   $a_n = a_{n-1} - a_{n-2}$

Write a recursive rule for the sequence. The sequence may be arithmetic, geometric or neither.

7. 2, 4, 6, 8, 10, . . . $a_1 = 2, a_n = a_{n-1} + 2$

8. 6, 10, 14, 18, 22, . . . $a_1 = 6, a_n = a_{n-1} + 4$

9. 2, 6, 18, 54, 162, . . . $a_1 = 2, a_n = 3a_{n-1}$

10. −3, 15, −75, 375, −1875, . . . $a_1 = -3, a_n = -5a_{n-1}$

11. 10, 4, −2, −8, −14, . . . $a_1 = 10, a_n = a_{n-1} - 6$

12. 32, 16, 8, 4, 2, . . . $a_1 = 32, a_n = \frac{1}{2}a_{n-1}$

13. 1, 3, 4, 7, 11, . . . $a_1 = 1, a_2 = 3, a_n = a_{n-1} + a_{n-2}$

14. 2, 4, 16, 256, 65536, . . . $a_1 = 2, a_n = (a_{n-1})^2$

Find the first three iterates of the function for the given initial value.

15. $f(x) = x + 2, x_0 = 0$ 2, 4, 6

16. $f(x) = x - 3, x_0 = 12$ 9, 6, 3

17. $f(x) = 2x - 6, x_0 = 4$ 2, −2, −10

18. $f(x) = 4x + 5, x_0 = 3$ 17, 73, 297

19. $f(x) = -3x + 2, x_0 = -2$ 8, −22, 68

20. $f(x) = x^2 + 3, x_0 = 1$ 4, 19, 364

21. $f(x) = \frac{1}{2}x^2 - 4, x_0 = 6$ 14, 94, 4414

22. $f(x) = x^2 - x - 2, x_0 = 2$ 0, −2, 4

In Exercises 23–25, use the following information.

Tree Farm A tree farm initially has 5000 trees. Each year 10% of the trees are harvested and 450 seedlings are planted.

23. Write a recursive rule for the number of trees on the tree farm at the beginning of the nth year. $a_1 = 5000, a_n = (0.9)a_{n-1} + 450$

24. How many trees remain at the beginning of the fifth year? 4828

25. What happens to the tree population over time? population approaches 4500

In Exercises 26 and 27, use the following information.

Savings Account On January 1, 2006, you have $500 in a savings account which earns 0.25% per month. On the last day of every month you deposit $80.

26. Write a recursive rule for the account balance at the beginning of the nth month. $a_1 = 500, a_n = (1.0025)a_{n-1} + 80$

27. Assuming you do not withdraw any money from the account, what will the balance be on August 1, 2006? $1073.03

1. 3, 10, 17, 24, 31 2. −4, −8, −16, −32, −64 3. 243, 90, 39, 22, $\frac{49}{3}$
4. 2, 2, 2, 4, 12 5. 2, 1, −2, 1, −2 6. 3, 1, −2, −3, −1

12 Assessment

CHAPTER 12 Quiz 1
For use after Lessons 12.1–12.3

Write the next term in the sequence. Then write a rule for the *n*th term.

1. 2, 4, 6, 8, . . . **2.** 6, 7, 8, 9, . . . **3.** $\frac{1}{2}, \frac{2}{3}, \frac{3}{4}, \frac{4}{5}, \ldots$

Find the sum of the series.

4. $\sum_{i=1}^{3} 2i$ **5.** $\sum_{k=1}^{4} k^2 + 1$ **6.** $\sum_{n=3}^{6} \frac{1}{n-2}$

Write a rule for the *n*th term a_n of the arithmetic or geometric sequence. Find a_{10}, then find the sum of the first 10 terms of the sequence.

7. 1, 6, 11, 16, . . . **8.** 3, 9, 27, 81, . . . **9.** −5, −1, 3, 7, . . .

10. Seating The first row of an auditorium has 20 seats. Each row after the first one has 2 more seats than the row before it. There are 30 rows of seats. Write a rule for the number of seats in the *n*th row.

Answers

1. $10, a_n = 2n$
2. $10, a_n = n + 5$
3. $\frac{5}{6}, a_n = \frac{n}{n+1}$
4. 12
5. 34
6. $\frac{25}{12}$
7. $a_n = -4 + 5n$, $a_{10} = 46$, $S_{10} = 235$
8. $a_n = 3(3)^{n-1}$, $a_{10} = 59{,}049$, $S_{10} = 88{,}572$
9. $a_n = 4n - 9$, $a_{10} = 31$, $S_{10} = 130$
10. $a_n = 18 + 2n$

CHAPTER 12 Quiz 2
For use after Lessons 12.4–12.5

Find the sum of the infinite geometric series, if it exists.

1. $\sum_{n=1}^{\infty} 3\left(\frac{2}{5}\right)^{n-1}$

2. $\sum_{n=1}^{\infty} 2\left(-\frac{1}{4}\right)^{n-1}$

3. $\frac{1}{2} + \frac{3}{4} + \frac{9}{8} + \frac{27}{16} + \cdots$

Write the repeating decimal as a fraction in lowest terms.

4. 0.4444 . . . **5.** 13.1313 . . .

Write the first five terms of the sequence.

6. $a_1 = 3$, $a_n = a_{n-1} + 5$ **7.** $a_1 = 2, a_2 = 5$, $a_n = a_{n-1} + a_{n-2}$

Write the recursive rule for the sequence. The sequence may be arithmetic, geometric, or neither.

8. 4, 10, 16, 22, 28, . . .

9. 3, 4, 12, 48, 576, . . .

10. 5, 15, 45, 135, 405, . . .

Find the first three iterates of the function for the given initial value.

11. $f(x) = -2x - 1, x_0 = 2$ **12.** $g(x) = 5x + 2, x_0 = -1$

13. Pendulums A pendulum that is released to swing freely travels 30 inches on the first swing. On each successive swing, the pendulum travels 75% as far as the previous swing. What is the total distance the pendulum swings?

Answers

1. 5
2. $\frac{8}{5}$
3. sum doesn't exist, $|r| > 1$
4. $\frac{4}{9}$
5. $\frac{1300}{99}$
6. 3, 8, 13, 18, 23
7. 2, 5, 7, 12, 19
8. $a_1 = 4$, $a_n = a_{n-1} + 6$
9. $a_1 = 3, a_2 = 4$, $a_n = a_{n-1} \cdot a_{n-2}$
10. $a_1 = 5, a_n = 3(a_{n-1})$
11. −5, 9, −19
12. −3, −13, −63
13. 120 in.

CHAPTER 12 Chapter Test B
For use after Chapter 12

For Exercises 1 and 2, write the first six terms of the sequence.

1. $a_n = n - 4$

2. $a_n = n(n - 1)$

3. Write the series −5 + 5 + 15 + 25 + 35 using summation notation.

4. Find the sum of the series $\sum_{i=1}^{6} 4i$.

5. Tell whether the sequence −7, −1, 5, 11, 17, 23, . . . is arithmetic.

6. Write a rule for the *n*th term of the arithmetic sequence 2, 9, 16, 23, 30, ... What is a_{16}?

7. Write a rule for the *n*th term of the arithmetic sequence that has the terms $a_3 = 17$ and $a_{14} = 50$.

8. Find the sum of the arithmetic series $\sum_{i=3}^{7} (4 + i)$.

9. Tell whether the sequence $\frac{2}{3}$, 4, 24, 144, 864, . . . is geometric.

10. Write a rule for the *n*th term of the geometric sequence with $a_1 = 2$ and $a_4 = -16$. What is a_7?

11. Find the sum of the geometric series $\sum_{i=1}^{5} 3\left(\frac{2}{3}\right)^i$.

12. Stock Price Stock from a troubled company loses $\frac{1}{8}$ of its market price each day. The value of the stock after day 1 is \$144. Find a rule for the value of the stock after *n* days. What is the value of the stock after the 7th day?

For Exercises 13 and 14, find the sum of the infinite geometric series, if it exists.

13. $\sum_{k=1}^{\infty} 2\left(\frac{3}{4}\right)^{k-1}$

14. $\frac{3}{2} - \frac{3}{4} + \frac{3}{8} - \frac{3}{16} + \cdots$

Answers

1. −3, −2, −1, 0, 1, 2
2. 0, 2, 6, 12, 20, 30
3. $\sum_{n=0}^{4} 10n - 5$
4. 84
5. yes
6. $a_n = 7n - 5$; 107
7. $a_n = 3n + 8$
8. 45
9. yes
10. $a_n = \frac{1}{2}(-2)^{n+1}$; 128
11. $\frac{422}{81}$
12. $a_n = 144\left(\frac{7}{8}\right)^{(n-1)}$; \$64.63
13. 8
14. 1

CHAPTER 12 Chapter Test B *continued*
For use after Chapter 12

15. Write the repeating decimal 0.232323. . . as a fraction.

16. Write the first five terms of the sequence where $a_1 = -2$ and $a_n = 3a_{n-1}$.

17. Strikeouts A baseball pitcher records 153 strikeouts in his first year pitching. Since then, the number of yearly strikeouts for this pitcher has decreased by 31%. If this trend continues, what is an upper limit on the total number of strikeouts over the pitcher's lifetime?

For Exercises 18 and 19, write a recursive rule for the sequence. The sequence may be arithmetic, geometric, or neither.

18. 7, 20, 33, 46, 59, . . .

19. 27, 36, 48, 64, $\frac{256}{3}$, . . .

20. Find the first three iterates of the function $f(x) = x^2 - 2x + 1$ with initial value $x_0 = 3$.

Answers

15. $\frac{23}{99}$
16. −2, −6, −18, −54, −162
17. 494
18. $a_1 = 7$, $a_n = 13 + a_{n-1}$
19. $a_1 = 27$, $a_n = \frac{4}{3}a_{n-1}$
20. 4, 9, 64

CHAPTER 12

Standardized Test

For use after Chapter 12

Multiple Choice

1. What is the fifth term of the sequence $a_n = 2n(n^2 - 1)$? C

Ⓐ 120 Ⓑ 180
Ⓒ 240 Ⓓ 420

2. For the sequence $\frac{3}{4}, \frac{3}{8}, \frac{3}{16}, \frac{3}{32}, \ldots$ which rule determines the nth term? B

Ⓐ $a_n = \frac{3}{2n+2}$ Ⓑ $a_n = \frac{3}{2^{n+1}}$
Ⓒ $a_n = \frac{3}{2^n}$ Ⓓ $a_n = \frac{3}{2^{n-1}}$

3. Which sequence is shown in the graph? D

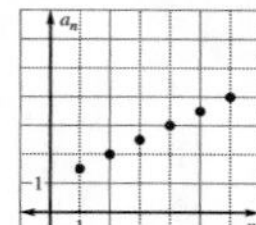

Ⓐ $a_n = 2n + 1$ Ⓑ $a_n = 2n - 1$
Ⓒ $a_n = \frac{1}{2}n - 1$ Ⓓ $a_n = \frac{1}{2}n + 1$

4. Which summation notation represents the series $5 + 8 + 13 + 20 + 29 + \cdots$? C

Ⓐ $\sum_{i=1}^{\infty} 3i + 2$
Ⓑ $\sum_{i=1}^{\infty} i^2 + 3i + 2$
Ⓒ $\sum_{i=1}^{\infty} i^2 + 4$
Ⓓ $\sum_{i=1}^{\infty} (2i - 1)^2 + 4$

5. What is the sum of the series $\sum_{k=1}^{15} k$? B

Ⓐ 15 Ⓑ 120
Ⓒ 225 Ⓓ 1240

6. Which of the following sequences is *not* arithmetic? D

Ⓐ $\frac{1}{2}, 2, \frac{7}{2}, 5, \frac{13}{2}, \ldots$
Ⓑ 7, 10, 13, 16, 19, . . .
Ⓒ 12, 3, −6, −15, −24, . . .
Ⓓ $7, \frac{7}{2}, \frac{7}{4}, \frac{7}{8}, \frac{7}{16}, \ldots$

7. If $a_{16} = 25$ and $d = 3$, what is the rule for the nth term of the sequence? B

Ⓐ $a_n = 3n - 26$ Ⓑ $a_n = 3n - 23$
Ⓒ $a_n = 3n - 20$ Ⓓ $a_n = 3n - 15$

8. What is the rule for the nth term of the sequence shown in the graph? C

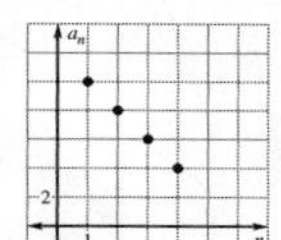

Ⓐ $a_n = 10 - 2n$ Ⓑ $a_n = 10 + 2n$
Ⓒ $a_n = 12 - 2n$ Ⓓ $a_n = 12 + 2n$

9. What is the common ratio for the geometric sequence shown in the graph? B

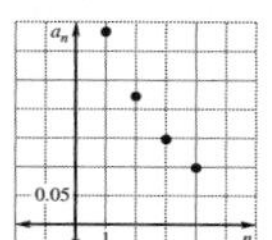

Ⓐ $\frac{2}{9}$ Ⓑ $\frac{2}{3}$ Ⓒ $\frac{3}{2}$ Ⓓ 2

CHAPTER 12

Standardized Test *continued*

For use after Chapter 12

10. What is the sum of the arithmetic series $\sum_{i=1}^{13} 1 + 5i$? D

Ⓐ 36 Ⓑ 39 Ⓒ 429 Ⓓ 468

11. The probability that a 21-year old male driver causes an auto accident decreases by 2% every year starting at age 21. If the initial probability is 25%, which equation models this probability? A

Ⓐ $a_n = 0.25(0.98)^{n-1}$
Ⓑ $a_n = 0.25(1.02)^{n-1}$
Ⓒ $a_n = 0.75(0.98)^{n-1}$
Ⓓ $a_n = 0.75(1.02)^{n-1}$

12. For the series $\frac{2}{3} + \frac{2}{9} + \frac{2}{27} + \frac{2}{81} + \cdots$ what is S_6? C

Ⓐ $\frac{80}{81}$ Ⓑ $\frac{242}{243}$
Ⓒ $\frac{728}{729}$ Ⓓ 1

13. If the series in Exercise 12 has an infinite sum, what is it? C

Ⓐ No infinite sum Ⓑ $\frac{2}{3}$
Ⓒ 1 Ⓓ 2

14. Which fraction is equal to the repeating decimal 2.343434? D

Ⓐ $\frac{234}{999}$ Ⓑ $\frac{34}{99}$
Ⓒ $\frac{68}{99}$ Ⓓ $\frac{232}{99}$

17. a. Answers will vary.; 5%
b. $a_0 = \$1100$; It is the initial amount invested.
c. $a_n = 1100(1.05)^n$

Gridded Answer

15. What is the value of the third iterate for $f(x) = -x + 7$, where $x_0 = -2$? 9

Short Response

16. A firefighter calculates that for a 1.75-inch hose, 40 pounds per square inch of pressure (psi) is lost due to friction for every 100 feet of hose.

a. Determine the explicit and recursive rules for the sequences which calculate friction loss for n feet of hose. $a_n = 0.4n$; $a_n = a_{n-1} + 0.4$

b. If the water pressure is to be 55 psi at the nozzle and you have 250 feet of 1.75-inch hose, the firefighter should adjust the valve on the truck for what pressure? 155 psi

Extended Response

17. You deposit a sum of money into a college fund. Interest on the fund is compounded annually. After one year, there is \$1,155.00 in the account. After 2 years, there is \$1,212.75.

a. How might you determine the interest rate, assuming it remains constant? What is the interest rate? See left.

b. What is the initial value? What is its significance? See left.

c. Determine the general rule for a_n. See left.

d. If you leave the funds untouched, how much will you have in the account after 6 years? \$1474.11

CHAPTER 12

Alternative Assessment and Math Journal

For use after Chapter 12

Journal

1. What is the difference between an arithmetic sequence and a geometric sequence? Is it possible for a sequence to be both arithmetic and geometric? If yes, give an example and identify the common difference and the common ratio. If no, explain why.

Multi-Step Problem

2. You tee up on a 200-yard hole at a local golf course. You make an initial drive (first shot) directly toward the hole. Your second shot travels 50 yards, your third travels 25 yards, your fourth 12.5 yards, and so on. Assume that the first shot fits the pattern and that the ball continues directly toward the hole on each shot.

a. Classify the sequence of shots as *arithmetic, geometric,* or *neither.*
b. How long is your drive (first shot)?
c. Write a recursive rule to model the distance of each shot.
d. Use the rule from part (c) to find the distance of the sixth shot.
e. Write an explicit rule to model the distance of each shot.
f. Use the rule from part (e) to find the distance of the tenth shot.
g. **Writing** Is it more convenient to determine the distance of a particular shot with a recursive rule or an explicit rule? Explain.
h. Find the first shot less than 10 yards from the hole and the first shot less than 5 yards from the hole.
i. **Critical Thinking** Explain why a geometric series can be used to represent the total distance traveled by the ball. Theoretically, will the ball travel 200 yards if you represent the total distance with a finite geometric series? an infinite geometric series? Explain your reasoning.

1. Complete answers should include: an explanation that in an arithmetic sequence, the difference between consecutive terms is constant and in a geometric sequence, the ratio of any term to the previous term is constant; an example of a sequence that is both arithmetic and geometric (ie. a sequence with a common difference of 0 and a common ratio of 1). **2. a.** geometric **b.** 100 yd **c.** $a_1 = 100$, $a_n = 0.5a_{n-1}$ **d.** 3.125 yd **e.** $a_n = 100(0.5)^{n-1}$ **f.** about 0.195 yd **g.** *Sample answer:* It is more convenient to determine the distance of a particular shot using an explicit rule, especially for larger values of n, because you do not need to know the previous term(s) of the sequence. **h.** fifth shot; sixth shot **i.** *Sample answer:* Because a geometric series is the expression formed by adding the terms of a geometric sequence, it represents the sum of the distances of each shot, or the total distance traveled by the ball. No. Yes. Using a finite geometric series, the total distance will always be less than 200 yards. Using an infinite geometric series, the total distance will be the sum of the series, or 200 yards.

CHAPTER 12

Alternative Assessment Rubric *continued*

For use after Chapter 12

Journal Solution

1. Complete answers should include:

- an explanation that in an arithmetic sequence, the difference between consecutive terms is constant and in a geometric sequence, the ratio of any term to the previous term is constant.
- an example of a sequence that is both arithmetic and geometric (ie. a sequence with a common difference of 0 and a common ratio of 1).

Multi-Step Problem Solution

2. a. geometric
b. 100 yd
c. $a_1 = 100$, $a_n = 0.5a_{n-1}$
d. 3.125 yd
e. $a_n = 100(0.5)^{n-1}$
f. about 0.195 yd
g. *Sample answer:* It is more convenient to determine the distance of a particular shot using an explicit rule, especially for larger values of n, because you do not need to know the previous term(s) of the sequence.
h. fifth shot; sixth shot
i. *Sample answer:* Because a geometric series is the expression formed by adding the terms of a geometric sequence, it represents the sum of the distances of each shot, or the total distance traveled by the ball. No. Yes. Using a finite geometric series, the total distance will always be less than 200 yards. Using an infinite geometric series, the total distance will be the sum of the series, or 200 yards.

Multi-Step Problem Rubric

4 The student answers all parts of the problem correctly and completely, showing a complete understanding of the relationship between sequences and series. The student shows all work. The student's work is neat.

3 The student answers all parts of the problem, showing nearly complete understanding of the relationship between sequences and series. The student's work may contain one or two errors in the calculations, rules, or explanations. The student shows most work. The student's work is neat.

2 The student answers all parts of the problem, showing some understanding of the relationship between sequences and series. The student's work contains more than two errors in the calculations, rules, or explanations. The student shows some work. The student's work is sloppy.

1 The student does not complete all parts of the problem and shows little understanding of the relationship between sequences and series. The student's work has several errors in the calculations, rules, or explanations. The student's work is sloppy, or no work is shown.

PLAN AND PREPARE

Main Ideas

In this chapter students explore sequences and series. They define explicit rules that generate number sequences whose terms have a common difference or a common ratio, and they use summation notation to represent and find the sum of the terms of a series. They use rules for the sum of arithmetic series, finite geometric series, and infinite geometric series. Also, students define recursive rules for generating arithmetic and geometric sequences and they investigate how to use iteration to generate a sequence recursively given a function rule.

Prerequisite Skills

- Solving linear equations
- Solving systems of linear equations
- Identifying a composite function and its domain

Additional resources for reviewing prerequisite skills are:

- Skills Review Handbook, pp. 975–1009
- @HomeTutor

12 Sequences and Series

KY

Before

In previous chapters, you learned the following skills, which you'll use in Chapter 12: solving equations, solving systems of equations, and performing function composition.

Prerequisite Skills

VOCABULARY CHECK

Copy and complete the statement using $f(x) = \frac{1}{x}$ and $g(x) = 4x + 2$.

1. The **domain** of $f(x)$ is _?_. $x \neq 0$
2. The **range** of $g(x)$ is _?_. all real numbers
3. The **composition** $f(g(x))$ is equal to _?_. $\frac{1}{4x+2}$

SKILLS CHECK

Solve the equation. Check your solution. *(Review p. 18 for 12.2.)*

4. $7x + 3 = 31$ 4
5. $9 = 2x - 7$ 8
6. $14 = -3x + 8$ -2
7. $10 - 3x = 28$ -6
8. $11x + 9 = 3x + 17$ 1
9. $2x + 3 = -6 - x$ -3

Solve the system using any algebraic method. *(Review p. 160 for 12.3.)*

10. $3x + y = 0$; $-2x - 4y = -30$ $(-3, 9)$
11. $2x - 2y = 10$; $x + y = -10$ $\left(-\frac{5}{2}, -\frac{15}{2}\right)$
12. $4x - 5y = 25$; $0.5x + 1.5y = 18.5$ $\left(\frac{260}{17}, \frac{123}{17}\right)$

Let $f(x) = 2x - 1$ and $g(x) = -2x^{-1}$. Perform the indicated operation and state the domain. *(Review p. 428 for 12.5.)*

13. $f(g(x))$ $-4x^{-1} - 1$, all real numbers except $x = 0$
14. $f(f(x))$ $4x - 3$, all real numbers
15. $g(g(x))$ x, all real numbers except $x = 0$

792

Chapter Planning Guide

Chapter 12 Resource Book
- Teaching Guide/Lesson Plan (pp. 3, 14, 25, 38, 48)
- Project with Rubric (p. 61)

Assessment and Intervention
- Assessment Book (pp. 168–181)
- Benchmark Tests
- Remediation Book

Interactive Technology
- Easy Planner
- Power Presentations CD-ROM
- Activity Generator CD-ROM
- Animated Algebra
- Test Generator CD-ROM
- Online Quizzes
- eWorkbook
- eEdition
- @HomeTutor

Resources for English Learners
- Quick Reference for English Learners
- Spanish Study Guide
- Multi-Language Visual Glossary
- Student Resources in Spanish

Now

In Chapter 12, you will apply the big ideas listed below and reviewed in the Chapter Summary on page 839. You will also use the key vocabulary listed below.

Big Ideas

1. Analyze sequences
2. Find sums of series
3. Use recursive rules

KEY VOCABULARY

- sequence, *p. 794*
- terms of a sequence, *p. 794*
- series, *p. 796*
- summation notation, *p. 796*
- sigma notation, *p. 796*
- arithmetic sequence, *p. 802*
- common difference, *p. 802*
- arithmetic series, *p. 804*
- geometric sequence, *p. 810*
- common ratio, *p. 810*
- geometric series, *p. 812*
- partial sum, *p. 820*
- explicit rule, *p. 827*
- recursive rule, *p. 827*
- iteration, *p. 830*

Why?

You can use sequences to describe patterns in the real world. For example, you can use the Fibonacci sequence to describe patterns in nature.

Animated Algebra

The animation illustrated below for Example 3 on page 828 helps you answer this question: How can you generate Fibonacci numbers?

Start
Fibonacci numbers are seen in objects such as shells, pinecones, and broccoli.

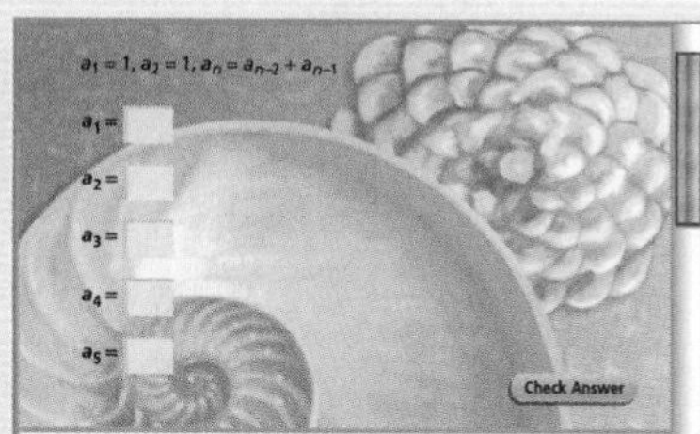

Animated Algebra at classzone.com

Other animations for Chapter 12: pages 805, 811, 820, and 832

Algebra 2 Toolkit

- Reading Strategies for Chapter 12, pp. 31–32
- Differentiated Instruction Notes, pp. 87–90
- English Learners Notes, pp. 123–124
- Inclusion Notes, pp. 157–158
- Teaching Strategies with Sample Worksheets, pp. 163–186
- Using Technology in the Classroom, pp. 187–192
- Tips for New Teachers, pp. 215–216
- Math Background Notes, pp. 258–261
- Pre-AP Strategies and Copymasters, pp. 333–334, 431–438
- Teacher Survival Activities, pp. 491–492, 519–520
- Bulletin Board Idea, p. 536
- Teacher Tool Transparencies, following p. 538

1 PLAN AND PREPARE

Warm-Up Exercises

Transparency Available

1. Evaluate $x^2 + 3$ for $x = 1, 2, 3,$ and 4. 4, 7, 12, 19
2. Find $f(1)$, $f(2)$, and $f(3)$ for $f(n) = n^3 + 2$. 3, 10, 29
3. The volume V of a cube with side length e is modeled by the function $V = e^3$. What is the range of the function for the domain 1, 2, 3, 4? 1, 8, 27, 64

Notetaking Guide

Transparency Available

Promotes interactive learning and notetaking skills, pp. 303–306.

Pacing

Basic: 1 day
Average: 1 day
Advanced: 1 day
Block: 0.5 block with 12.2
• See *Teaching Guide/Lesson Plan.*

2 FOCUS AND MOTIVATE

Essential Question

Big Idea 2, p. 793

How can you write an expression for sums such as $5 + 10 + 15 + \ldots + 50$ or $\frac{1}{2} + \frac{1}{4} + \frac{1}{8} + \ldots$? Tell students they will learn how to answer this question by using summation notation.

12.1 Define and Use Sequences and Series

MA-HS-1.3.2

Before You identified and wrote functions.
Now You will recognize and write rules for number patterns.
Why? So you can find angle measures, as in Ex. 63.

Key Vocabulary
- sequence
- terms of a sequence
- series
- summation notation
- sigma notation

MA-HS-1.3.2
Students will: describe and extend arithmetic and geometric sequences; determine a specific term of a sequence given an explicit formula; determine an explicit rule for the nth term of an arithmetic sequence and apply sequences to solve real-world problems. DOK 3

KEY CONCEPT — *For Your Notebook*

Sequences

A **sequence** is a function whose domain is a set of consecutive integers. If a domain is not specified, it is understood that the domain starts with 1. The values in the range are called the **terms** of the sequence.

Domain:	$1 \quad 2 \quad 3 \quad 4 \ldots n$	The relative position of each term
	$\downarrow \quad \downarrow \quad \downarrow \quad \downarrow \quad\quad \downarrow$	
Range:	$a_1 \quad a_2 \quad a_3 \quad a_4 \ldots a_n$	Terms of the sequence

A *finite sequence* has a limited number of terms. An *infinite sequence* continues without stopping.

Finite sequence: 2, 4, 6, 8 **Infinite sequence:** 2, 4, 6, 8, . . .

A sequence can be specified by an equation, or *rule*. For example, both sequences above can be described by the rule $a_n = 2n$ or $f(n) = 2n$.

EXAMPLE 1 Write terms of sequences

Write the first six terms of (a) $a_n = 2n + 5$ and (b) $f(n) = (-3)^{n-1}$.

Solution

a.		b.	
$a_1 = 2(1) + 5 = 7$	1st term	$f(1) = (-3)^{1-1} = 1$	1st term
$a_2 = 2(2) + 5 = 9$	2nd term	$f(2) = (-3)^{2-1} = -3$	2nd term
$a_3 = 2(3) + 5 = 11$	3rd term	$f(3) = (-3)^{3-1} = 9$	3rd term
$a_4 = 2(4) + 5 = 13$	4th term	$f(4) = (-3)^{4-1} = -27$	4th term
$a_5 = 2(5) + 5 = 15$	5th term	$f(5) = (-3)^{5-1} = 81$	5th term
$a_6 = 2(6) + 5 = 17$	6th term	$f(6) = (-3)^{6-1} = -243$	6th term

GUIDED PRACTICE for Example 1

Write the first six terms of the sequence.

1. $a_n = n + 4$ 5, 6, 7, 8, 9, 10
2. $f(n) = (-2)^{n-1}$ 1, −2, 4, −8, 16, −32
3. $a_n = \frac{n}{n+1}$ $\frac{1}{2}, \frac{2}{3}, \frac{3}{4}, \frac{4}{5}, \frac{5}{6}, \frac{6}{7}$

Resource Planning Guide

Chapter Resource Book
- Teaching Guide/Lesson Plan (pp. 3–4)
- Practice levels A, B, C (pp. 6–8)
- Study Guide (pp. 9–10)
- Catch-up for Absent Students (p. 11)
- Problem Solving Workshop (p. 12)
- Challenge (p. 13)

Workbooks
- Notetaking Guide (pp. 303–306)
- Practice Workbook (pp. 171–172)

Teaching Options
- **Power Presentations CD-ROM** provides dynamic electronic teaching resources for the classroom.
- **Activity Generator CD-ROM** provides editable activities for all ability levels.

Interactive Technology
- Easy Planner
- Power Presentations CD-ROM
- Activity Generator CD-ROM
- Animated Algebra
- Test Generator CD-ROM
- Online Quiz
- eWorkbook
- eEdition
- @HomeTutor

Resources for English Learners
- Quick Reference for English Learners
- Spanish Study Guide
- Multi-Language Visual Glossary
- Student Resources in Spanish

See also the *Algebra 2 Toolkit* for more strategies for meeting individual needs.

WRITING RULES If the terms of a sequence have a recognizable pattern, then you may be able to write a rule for the *n*th term of the sequence.

EXAMPLE 2 Write rules for sequences

Describe the pattern, write the next term, and write a rule for the *n*th term of the sequence (a) −1, −8, −27, −64, . . . and (b) 0, 2, 6, 12, ...

Solution

a. You can write the terms as $(-1)^3$, $(-2)^3$, $(-3)^3$, $(-4)^3$, ... The next term is $a_5 = (-5)^3 = -125$. A rule for the *n*th term is $a_n = (-n)^3$.

b. You can write the terms as 0(1), 1(2), 2(3), 3(4), ... The next term is $f(5) = 4(5) = 20$. A rule for the *n*th term is $f(n) = (n - 1)n$.

WRITE RULES
you are given only
ne first several terms
f a sequence, there is
o *single* rule for the *n*th
erm. For instance, the
equence 2, 4, 8, . . . can
e given by $a_n = 2^n$ or
$_n = n^2 - n + 2$.

GRAPHING SEQUENCES To graph a sequence, let the horizontal axis represent the position numbers (the domain) and the vertical axis represent the terms (the range).

EXAMPLE 3 Solve a multi-step problem

RETAIL DISPLAYS You work in a grocery store and are stacking apples in the shape of a square pyramid with 7 layers. Write a rule for the number of apples in each layer. Then graph the sequence.

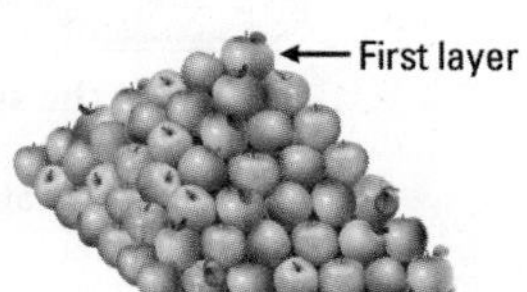

Solution

STEP 1 **Make** a table showing the number of fruit in the first three layers. Let a_n represent the number of apples in layer *n*.

Layer, *n*	1	2	3
Number of apples, a_n	$1 = 1^2$	$4 = 2^2$	$9 = 3^2$

STEP 2 **Write** a rule for the number of apples in each layer. From the table, you can see that $a_n = n^2$.

STEP 3 **Plot** the points (1, 1), (2, 4), (3, 9), . . . , (7, 49). The graph is shown at the right.

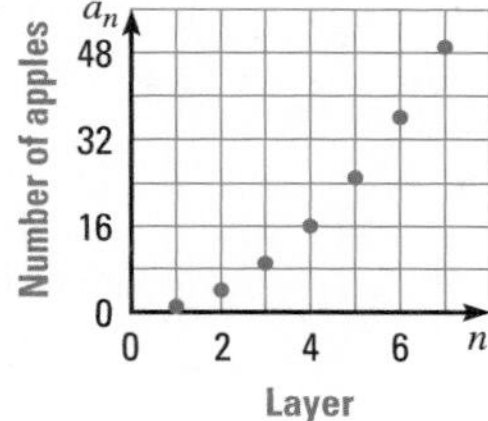

AVOID ERRORS
lthough the plotted
oints in Example 3
ollow a curve, do *not*
raw the curve because
ne sequence is defined
nly for integer values
f *n*.

✓ **GUIDED PRACTICE** for Examples 2 and 3

4. For the sequence 3, 8, 15, 24, . . . , describe the pattern, write the next term, graph the first five terms, and write a rule for the *n*th term. **You can write the terms as 1 • 3, 2 • 4, 3 • 5, 4 • 6, . . .; $a_5 = 5 \cdot 7 = 35$, see margin for art, $a_n = n(n + 2)$.**
5. **WHAT IF?** In Example 3, suppose there are 9 layers of apples. How many apples are in the 9th layer? **81 apples**

Motivating the Lesson

Ask students to think about an exercise program such as running 5 miles the first week, and increasing the distance by 3 miles per week. In this lesson they will learn to use sequences and series to represent the number of miles run each week and the total number of miles run.

3 TEACH

Extra Example 1

Write the first five terms of (a) $a_n = 5n - 1$ and (b) $f(n) = 2^n - 3$. **(a) 4, 9, 14, 19, 24; (b) −1, 1, 5, 13, 29**

Extra Example 2

Describe the pattern, write the next term, and write a rule for the *n*th term of the sequence (a) 2, 5, 10, 17, . . . and (b) −4, −8, −12, −16, −20, ... **(a) Pattern: Square the number and add 1; $a^5 = 5^2 + 1 = 26$; $a_n = n^2 + 1$; (b) Pattern: −4 times 1, 2, 3, . . . ; $a^5 = -4(5) = -20$; $a_n = -4n$**

Extra Example 3

At the beginning of the summer, you walk a mile in 9 minutes. At the end of the first week you walk a mile in 5 fewer seconds. At the end of the second week, you decrease your time by another 10 seconds. At the end of third week, you decrease your time by 20 more seconds, and at the end of the fourth week, you decrease your time by another 40 seconds. Write a rule for the number of seconds you decrease your time by each week. Then graph the sequence for the first five weeks. $a_n = 5(2)^{n-1}$

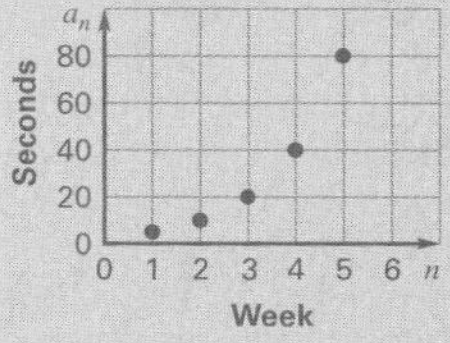

4.

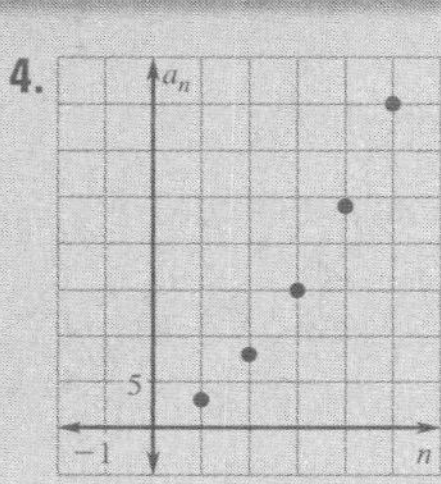

Extra Example 4

Write the series using summation notation.

a. $1 + 8 + 27 + 64 + \ldots + 729$ $\sum_{i=1}^{9} i^3$

b. $1 + \frac{1}{2} + \frac{1}{4} + \frac{1}{8} + \ldots$ $\sum_{i=1}^{\infty} \frac{1}{2^{i-1}}$

Key Questions to Ask for Example 4

- Which series is finite? Which series is infinite? **the series in part (a) is finite; the series in part (b) is infinite.**
- What is the nth term in each series? **(a) $25n$; (b) $\frac{n}{n+1}$**

Reading Strategy

The notation $\sum_{i=1}^{n} a_i$ is an instruction that tells us to calculate the values of $a_i, a_2, \ldots, a_n$, and add them. The notation can be read "the sum of a-sub-i from $i = 1$ to $i = n$."

KEY CONCEPT *For Your Notebook*

Series and Summation Notation

When the terms of a sequence are added together, the resulting expression is a **series**. A series can be finite or infinite.

Finite series: $2 + 4 + 6 + 8$ **Infinite series:** $2 + 4 + 6 + 8 + \cdots$

You can use **summation notation** to write a series. For example, the two series above can be written in summation notation as follows:

$$2 + 4 + 6 + 8 = \sum_{i=1}^{4} 2i \qquad 2 + 4 + 6 + 8 + \cdots = \sum_{i=1}^{\infty} 2i$$

For both series, the *index of summation* is i and the *lower limit of summation* is 1. The *upper limit of summation* is 4 for the finite series and ∞ (infinity) for the infinite series. Summation notation is also called **sigma notation** because it uses the uppercase Greek letter *sigma*, written Σ.

READING
When written in summation notation, this series is read as "the sum of $2i$ for values of i from 1 to 4."

EXAMPLE 4 Write series using summation notation

Write the series using summation notation.

a. $25 + 50 + 75 + \cdots + 250$ **b.** $\frac{1}{2} + \frac{2}{3} + \frac{3}{4} + \frac{4}{5} + \cdots$

Solution

a. Notice that the first term is 25(1), the second is 25(2), the third is 25(3), and the last is 25(10). So, the terms of the series can be written as:

$$a_i = 25i \text{ where } i = 1, 2, 3, \ldots, 10$$

The lower limit of summation is 1 and the upper limit of summation is 10.

▶ The summation notation for the series is $\sum_{i=1}^{10} 25i$.

b. Notice that for each term the denominator of the fraction is 1 more than the numerator. So, the terms of the series can be written as:

$$a_i = \frac{i}{i+1} \text{ where } i = 1, 2, 3, 4, \ldots$$

The lower limit of summation is 1 and the upper limit of summation is infinity.

▶ The summation notation for the series is $\sum_{i=1}^{\infty} \frac{i}{i+1}$.

GUIDED PRACTICE for Example 4

Write the series using summation notation.

6. $5 + 10 + 15 + \cdots + 100$ $\sum_{i=1}^{20} 5i$

7. $\frac{1}{2} + \frac{4}{5} + \frac{9}{10} + \frac{16}{17} + \cdots$ $\sum_{i=1}^{\infty} \frac{i^2}{i^2+1}$

8. $6 + 36 + 216 + 1296 + \cdots$ $\sum_{i=1}^{\infty} 6^i$

9. $5 + 6 + 7 + \cdots + 12$ $\sum_{i=1}^{8} 4 + i$

Differentiated Instruction

Advanced Learners Have students show that $\sum_{i=1}^{n} c = c + c + \ldots + c = nc$. Then ask them to find the value of $\sum_{i=1}^{n+1} c$. Help them see that $\sum_{i=1}^{n+1} c = \sum_{i=1}^{n} c + (n+1)c = nc + (n+1)c = c(2n+1)$. Tell them that they will see similar uses of summation notation when they explore mathematical induction in the Lesson 12.5 Extension.

See also the *Algebra 2 Toolkit* for more strategies.

INDEX OF SUMMATION The index of summation for a series does not have to be i—any letter can be used. Also, the index does not have to begin at 1. For instance, the index begins at 4 in the next example.

EXAMPLE 5 Find the sum of a series

AVOID ERRORS
Be sure to use the correct lower and upper limits of summation when finding the sum of a series.

Find the sum of the series.

$$\sum_{k=4}^{8}(3 + k^2) = (3 + 4^2) + (3 + 5^2) + (3 + 6^2) + (3 + 7^2) + (3 + 8^2)$$
$$= 19 + 28 + 39 + 52 + 67$$
$$= 205$$

SPECIAL FORMULAS For series with many terms, finding the sum by adding the terms can be tedious. Below are formulas you can use to find the sums of three special types of series.

KEY CONCEPT *For Your Notebook*

Formulas for Special Series

Sum of n terms of 1	Sum of first n positive integers	Sum of squares of first n positive integers
$\sum_{i=1}^{n} 1 = n$	$\sum_{i=1}^{n} i = \frac{n(n+1)}{2}$	$\sum_{i=1}^{n} i^2 = \frac{n(n+1)(2n+1)}{6}$

EXAMPLE 6 Use a formula for a sum

RETAIL DISPLAYS How many apples are in the stack in Example 3 on page 795?

Solution

From Example 3 you know that the ith term of the series is given by $a_i = i^2$ where $i = 1, 2, 3, \ldots, 7$. Using summation notation and the third formula listed above, you can find the total number of apples as follows:

$$1^2 + 2^2 + \cdots + 7^2 = \sum_{i=1}^{7} i^2 = \frac{7(7+1)(2 \cdot 7 + 1)}{6} = \frac{7(8)(15)}{6} = 140$$

▸ There are 140 apples in the stack. Check this by actually adding the number of apples in each of the seven layers.

GUIDED PRACTICE for Examples 5 and 6

Find the sum of the series.

10. $\sum_{i=1}^{5} 8i$ 120
11. $\sum_{k=3}^{7} (k^2 - 1)$ 130
12. $\sum_{i=1}^{34} 1$ 34
13. $\sum_{n=1}^{6} n$ 21

14. **WHAT IF?** Suppose there are 9 layers in the apple stack in Example 3. How many apples are in the stack? 285 apples

Extra Example 5

Find the sum of the series.

$\sum_{k=3}^{5}(3k^2 - 7)$ 129

Key Questions to Ask for Example 5

- What are the lower and upper limits of the summation? 4 and 8
- What are the values of k? 4, 5, 6, 7, and 8

Extra Example 6

You have a stack of apples similar to the stack in Example 3, but there are 8 layers. Use a formula to find how many apples are in the stack. 204

Key Question to Ask for Example 6

- Write an expression for the number of apples if the stack has 10 layers. $\sum_{i=1}^{10} i^2 = \frac{10(11)(21)}{6}$

Closing the Lesson

Have students summarize the major points of the lesson and answer the Essential Question: How can you write an expression for sums such as $5 + 10 + 15 + \ldots + 50$ or $\frac{1}{2} + \frac{1}{4} + \frac{1}{8} + \ldots$?

- **A sequence is a function whose domain is a set of consecutive integers. A sequence can be described by rule that generates its nth term.**
- **A series is the sum of the terms of a sequence. You can use summation notation to write a series.**
- $\sum_{i=1}^{n} 1 = n$, $\sum_{i=1}^{n} i = \frac{n(n+1)}{2}$, and $\sum_{i=1}^{n} i^2 = \frac{n(n+1)(2n+1)}{6}$.

$5 + 10 + 15 + \ldots + 50 = \sum_{i=1}^{10} 5n$;

$\frac{1}{2} + \frac{1}{4} + \frac{1}{8} + \ldots = \sum_{i=1}^{\infty} \frac{1}{2^n}$

Differentiated Instruction

Inclusion To reaffirm the methods they have learned, have students repeat the steps in **Examples 3 and 6** for 8 layers of apples. Then have the students compare the work side by side with that for 7 layers, and make observations about any similarities and differences. Ask students to create a table listing the advantages and disadvantages of the two methods.

See also the *Algebra 2 Toolkit* for more strategies.

12.1 EXERCISES

HOMEWORK KEY
○ = **WORKED-OUT SOLUTIONS** on p. WS20 for Exs. 19, 47, and 65
★ = **STANDARDIZED TEST PRACTICE** Exs. 2, 27, 58, 64, and 67

SKILL PRACTICE

A

1. **VOCABULARY** Copy and complete: Another name for summation notation is ___?___. sigma notation

2. ★ **WRITING** *Explain* the difference between a sequence and a series.
A sequence is a list of numbers, and a series is the sum of the terms of a sequence.

EXAMPLE 1 on p. 794 for Exs. 3–14

WRITING TERMS **Write the first six terms of the sequence.** 3–10. See margin.

3. $a_n = n + 2$
4. $a_n = 6 - n$
5. $a_n = n^2$
6. $f(n) = n^3 + 2$
7. $a_n = 4^{n-1}$
8. $a_n = -n^2$
9. $f(n) = n^2 - 5$
10. $a_n = (n + 3)^2$
11. $f(n) = -\frac{4}{n}$ $-4, -2, -\frac{4}{3}, -1, -\frac{4}{5}, -\frac{2}{3}$
12. $a_n = \frac{3}{n}$ $3, \frac{3}{2}, 1, \frac{3}{4}, \frac{3}{5}, \frac{1}{2}$
13. $a_n = \frac{2n}{n+2}$ $\frac{2}{3}, 1, \frac{6}{5}, \frac{4}{3}, \frac{10}{7}, \frac{3}{2}$
14. $f(n) = \frac{n}{2n-1}$ $1, \frac{2}{3}, \frac{3}{5}, \frac{4}{7}, \frac{5}{9}, \frac{6}{11}$

EXAMPLE 2 on p. 795 for Exs. 15–27

WRITING RULES **For the sequence, describe the pattern, write the next term, and write a rule for the *n*th term.** 15–26. See margin.

15. 1, 6, 11, 16, . . .
16. 1, 2, 4, 8, . . .
17. −4, 8, −12, 16, . . .
18. 2, 9, 28, 65, . . .
19. $\frac{2}{3}, \frac{2}{6}, \frac{2}{9}, \frac{2}{12}, \ldots$
20. $\frac{2}{3}, \frac{4}{4}, \frac{6}{5}, \frac{8}{6}, \ldots$
21. $\frac{1}{4}, \frac{2}{4}, \frac{3}{4}, \frac{4}{4}, \frac{5}{4}, \ldots$
22. $\frac{1}{10}, \frac{3}{20}, \frac{5}{30}, \frac{7}{40}, \ldots$
23. 3.1, 3.8, 4.5, 5.2, . . .
24. 4.2, 2.6, 1, −0.6, −2.2, . . .
25. 1.2, 4.2, 9.2, 16.2, . . .
26. 9, 16.8, 24.6, 32.4, . . .

27. ★ **MULTIPLE CHOICE** Which rule gives the total number of squares in the *n*th figure of the pattern shown? D

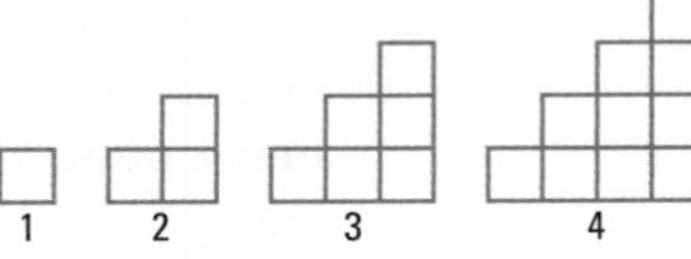

Ⓐ $a_n = 3n - 3$ Ⓑ $a_n = 4n - 5$ Ⓒ $a_n = n$ Ⓓ $a_n = \frac{n(n+1)}{2}$

EXAMPLE 3 on p. 795 for Exs. 28–36

GRAPHING SEQUENCES **Graph the sequence.** 28–36. See margin.

28. −2, −5, −8, −11, −14
29. 2, 4, 8, 16, 32, 64
30. 1, 5, 9, 13, . . . , 29
31. −2, 4, −6, 8, . . . , −22
32. 0, 3, 8, 15, 24, 35
33. −1, 0, 1, 8, 27
34. 4, −9, 14, −19, 24
35. $\frac{1}{2}, \frac{3}{2}, \frac{5}{2}, \ldots, \frac{13}{2}$
36. $\frac{1}{9}, \frac{2}{8}, \frac{3}{7}, \frac{4}{6}, \ldots, \frac{9}{1}$

EXAMPLE 4 on p. 796 for Exs. 37–44

WRITING SUMMATION NOTATION **Write the series using summation notation.**

37. $7 + 10 + 13 + 16 + 19$ $\sum_{i=1}^{5} 3i + 4$
38. $5 + 11 + 17 + 23 + 29$ $\sum_{i=1}^{5} 6i - 1$
39. $-1 + 1 + 3 + 5 + 7 + \cdots$
40. $-2 + 4 - 8 + 16 - 32 + \cdots$
41. $3 + 10 + 17 + 24 + 31 + \cdots$ $\sum_{i=1}^{\infty} 7i - 4$
42. $\frac{1}{3} + \frac{1}{9} + \frac{1}{27} + \frac{1}{81}$ $\sum_{i=1}^{4} \frac{1}{3^i}$
43. $\frac{1}{4} + \frac{2}{5} + \frac{3}{6} + \frac{4}{7} + \frac{5}{8} + \frac{6}{9} + \frac{7}{10}$ $\sum_{i=1}^{7} \frac{i}{3+i}$
44. $-1 + 2 + 7 + 14 + 23 + \cdots$ $\sum_{i=1}^{\infty} i^2 - 2$

3. 3, 4, 5, 6, 7, 8
4. 5, 4, 3, 2, 1, 0
5. 1, 4, 9, 16, 25, 36
6. 3, 10, 29, 66, 127, 218
7. 1, 4, 16, 64, 256, 1024
8. −1, −4, −9, −16, −25, −36
9. −4, −1, 4, 11, 20, 31
10. 16, 25, 36, 49, 64, 81
39. $\sum_{i=1}^{\infty} 2i - 3$
40. $\sum_{i=1}^{\infty} (-2)^i$

4 PRACTICE AND APPLY

Assignment Guide

Answer Transparencies available for all exercises

Basic:
Day 1: pp. 798–800
Exs. 1–7, 15–20, 27–31, 37–39, 45–48, 63–66, 69

Average:
Day 1: pp. 798–800
Exs. 1, 2, 8–11, 20–23, 27, 31–33, 40–42, 49–52, 57, 58, 63–67, 70

Advanced:
Day 1: pp. 798–800
Exs. 1, 2, 12–14, 24–27, 34–36, 43, 44, 53–68*

Block:
pp. 798–800
Exs. 1, 2, 8–11, 20–23, 27, 31–33, 40–42, 49–52, 57, 58, 63–67, 70 (with 12.2)

Differentiated Instruction

See *Algebra 2 Best Practices Toolkit* for suggestions on addressing the needs of a diverse classroom.

Homework Check

For a quick check of student understanding of key concepts, go over the following exercises:
Basic: 4, 16, 30, 38, 63
Average: 8, 20, 32, 50, 63
Advanced: 12, 26, 36, 54, 64

Extra Practice

- Student Edition, p. 1021
- Chapter 12 Resource Book: Practice levels A, B, C, pp. 6–8

Practice Worksheet

An easily-readable reduced practice page (with answers) for this lesson can be found on p. 792C.

15. You can write the terms as $5(1) - 4, 5(2) - 4, 5(3) - 4, 5(4) - 4$, $a_5 = 21$, $a_n = 5n - 4$.

16. You can write the terms as $2^{1-1}, 2^{2-1}, 2^{3-1}, 2^{4-1}$, $a_5 = 16$, $a_n = 2^{n-1}$.

17. You can write the terms as $(-1)^1(4 \cdot 1), (-1)^2(4 \cdot 2), (-1)^3(4 \cdot 3), (-1)^4(4 \cdot 4)$, $a_5 = -20$, $a_n = (-1)^n(4 \cdot n)$.

18. You can write the terms as $1^3 + 1, 2^3 + 1, 3^3 + 1, 4^3 + 1$, $a_5 = 126$, $a_n = n^3 + 1$.

19. You can write the terms as $\frac{2}{3(1)}, \frac{2}{3(2)}, \frac{2}{3(3)}, \frac{2}{3(4)}$, $a_5 = \frac{2}{15}$, $a_n = \frac{2}{3n}$.

20. You can write the terms as $\frac{2(1)}{1+2}, \frac{2(2)}{2+2}, \frac{2(3)}{3+2}, \frac{2(4)}{4+2}$, $a_5 = \frac{10}{7}$, $a_n = \frac{2n}{n+2}$.

XAMPLES B and 6
n p. 797 r Exs. 45–58

USING SUMMATION NOTATION Find the sum of the series.

45. $\sum_{i=1}^{6} 2i$ 42
46. $\sum_{i=1}^{5} 7i$ 105
47. $\sum_{n=0}^{4} n^3$ 100
48. $\sum_{k=1}^{4} 3k^2$ 90
49. $\sum_{k=3}^{6} (5k - 2)$ 82
50. $\sum_{n=1}^{5} (n^2 - 1)$ 50
51. $\sum_{i=1}^{8} \frac{2}{i}$ $\frac{761}{140}$
52. $\sum_{k=1}^{6} \frac{k}{k+1}$ $\frac{617}{140}$
53. $\sum_{i=1}^{35} 1$ 35
54. $\sum_{n=1}^{16} n$ 136
55. $\sum_{i=1}^{25} i$ 325
56. $\sum_{n=1}^{18} n^2$ 2109

57. **ERROR ANALYSIS** *Describe* and correct the error in finding the sum of the series.

$\sum_{i=0}^{5} (2i + 3) = 5 + 7 + 9 + 11 + 13 = 45$

The lower limit is zero, so the first term should be 3; 3 + 5 + 7 + 9 + 11 + 13 = 48.

58. ★ **MULTIPLE CHOICE** What is the sum of the series $\sum_{i=1}^{20} i$? B

Ⓐ 20 Ⓑ 210 Ⓒ 420 Ⓓ 2870

EVIEW OGIC C
or help with counter-examples see 1002.

CHALLENGE Tell whether the statement about summation notation is *true* or *false*. If the statement is true, prove it. If the statement is false, give a counterexample.

59. $\sum_{i=1}^{n} ka_i = k\sum_{i=1}^{n} a_i$ true; $\sum_{i=1}^{n} ka_i = (ka_1 + ka_2 + ka_3 + \ldots + ka_n) = k(a_1 + a_2 + a_3 + \ldots + a_n) = k\sum_{i=1}^{n} a_i$

60. $\sum_{i=1}^{n} (a_i + b_i) = \sum_{i=1}^{n} a_i + \sum_{i=1}^{n} b_i$ See margin.

61. $\sum_{i=1}^{n} a_i b_i = \left(\sum_{i=1}^{n} a_i\right)\left(\sum_{i=1}^{n} b_i\right)$ False. *Sample answer:* $\sum_{i=1}^{4} (2i)(-4i) \neq \left(\sum_{i=1}^{4} 2i\right)\left(\sum_{i=1}^{4} -4i\right)$

62. $\sum_{i=1}^{n} (a_i)^k = \left(\sum_{i=1}^{n} a_i\right)^k$ False. *Sample answer:* $\sum_{i=1}^{4} (2x)^2 \neq \left(\sum_{i=1}^{4} 2x\right)^2$

Margin: true; $\sum_{i=1}^{n} (a_i + b_i) = (a_1 + b_1) + (a_2 + b_2) + (a_3 + b_3) + \ldots (a_n + b_n) = (a_1 + a_2 + a_3 + \ldots + a_n) + (b_1 + b_2 + b_3 + \ldots + b_n) = \sum_{i=1}^{n} a_i + \sum_{i=1}^{n} b_i$

PROBLEM SOLVING

XAMPLES A and 6
n pp. 795–797 r Exs. 63–64

63. **GEOMETRY** For a regular n-sided polygon ($n \geq 3$), the measure a_n of an interior angle is given by this formula:

$$a_n = \frac{180(n - 2)}{n}$$

Write the first five terms of the sequence. Write a rule for the sequence giving the total measure T_n of the interior angles in each regular n-sided polygon. Use the rule to find the total measure of the angles in the Guggenheim Museum skylight, which is a regular dodecagon.

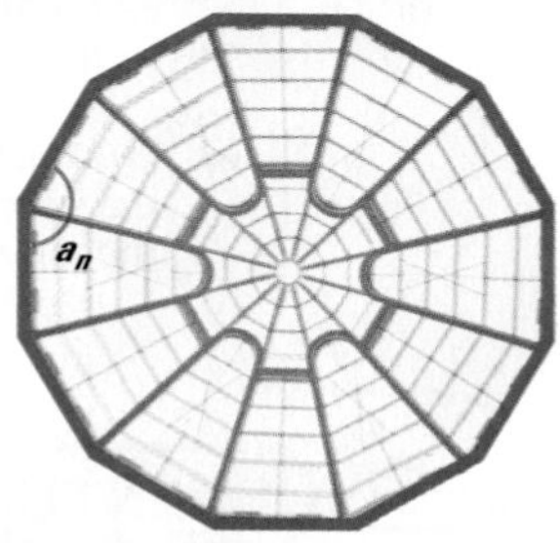

Guggenheim Museum Skylight

@HomeTutor for problem solving help at classzone.com

60°, 90°, 108°, °, about .57°; = 180(n − 2); 0°

64. ★ **SHORT RESPONSE** You want to save $500 for a school trip. You begin by saving a penny on the first day. You plan to save an additional penny each day after that. For example, you will save 2 pennies on the second day, 3 pennies on the third day, and so on. How much money will you have saved after 100 days? How many days must you save to have saved $500? *Explain* how you used a series to find your answer.

@HomeTutor for problem solving help at classzone.com

$50.50; 316 ys. *Sample swer:* I used special ies formula the sum he first n sitive integers d set it equal 0,000 (since re are 50,000 nnies in $500) d solved.

Avoiding Common Errors

Exercises 45–56 Watch for students who calculate only the last term in the sequence rather than the sum of all the terms. Remind them that they must find the sum of *all* the terms in each sequence.

Mathematical Reasoning

Exercise 64 Tell students that some good strategies are to draw a chart, use a guess and check strategy, or find the intersection of $y = \frac{x(x+1)}{2}$ and $f(n) = 50{,}000$ to help them determine their answer. Ask students who use those strategies to share their representations with the rest of the class.

Internet Reference

Exercise 65 More information about the Tower of Hanoi can be found at www.lhs.berkeley.edu/Java/Tower/towerhistory.html

24. You can write the terms as 5.8 − 1.6(1), 5.8 − 1.6(2), 5.8 − 1.6(3), 5.8 − 1.6(4), 5.8 − 1.6(5), $a_6 = -3.8$, $a_n = 5.8 - 1.6n$.
25. You can write the terms as $1^2 + 0.2, 2^2 + 0.2, 3^2 + 0.2, 4^2 + 0.2$, $a_5 = 25.2$, $a_n = n^2 + 0.2$.
26. You can write the terms as 7.8(1) + 1.2, 7.8(2) + 1.2, 7.8(3) + 1.2, 7.8(4) + 1.2, $a_5 = 40.2$, $a_n = 7.8n + 1.2$.
28–36. See Additional Answers beginning on p. AA1.

21. You can write the terms as $\frac{1}{4}, \frac{2}{4}, \frac{3}{4}, \frac{4}{4}, \frac{5}{4}$, $a_6 = \frac{6}{4}$, $a_n = \frac{n}{4}$.
22. You can write the terms as $\frac{2(1) - 1}{1(10)}, \frac{2(2) - 1}{2(10)}, \frac{2(3) - 1}{3(10)}, \frac{2(4) - 1}{4(10)}$, $a_5 = \frac{9}{50}$, $a_n = \frac{2n - 1}{10n}$.
23. You can write the terms as 0.7(1) + 2.4, 0.7(2) + 2.4, 0.7(3) + 2.4, 0.7(4) + 2.4, $a_5 = 5.9$, $a_n = 0.7n + 2.4$.

5 ASSESS AND RETEACH

Daily Homework Quiz

Transparency Available

The rule $a_n = 1.4n + 9.6$ models the expected sales in millions of in-vehicle navigation systems for 6 years from 2004 to 2009.

1. Write the first 6 terms of the sequence. **11, 12.4, 13.8, 15.2, 16.6, 18**
2. Use summation notation to write the sum of the first 6 terms of the sequence. Then find the sum. $\sum_{i=1}^{6}(1.4i + 9.6)$; **87**
3. Describe the pattern for the sequence 1, 2, 4, 8, 16, ... Then write the next term and the general term. **You can write the terms as $2^0, 2^1, 2^2, 2^3$; $a_6 = 2^{6-1} = 2^5 = 32$; $a_n = 2^{n-1}$**

Online Quiz

Available at **classzone.com**

Diagnosis/Remediation

- Practice A, B, C in Chapter 12 Resource Book, pp. 6–8
- Study Guide in Chapter 12 Resource Book, pp. 9–10
- Practice Workbook, pp. 171–172
- @HomeTutor

Challenge

Additional challenge is available in the Chapter 12 Resource Book, p. 13.

66c.

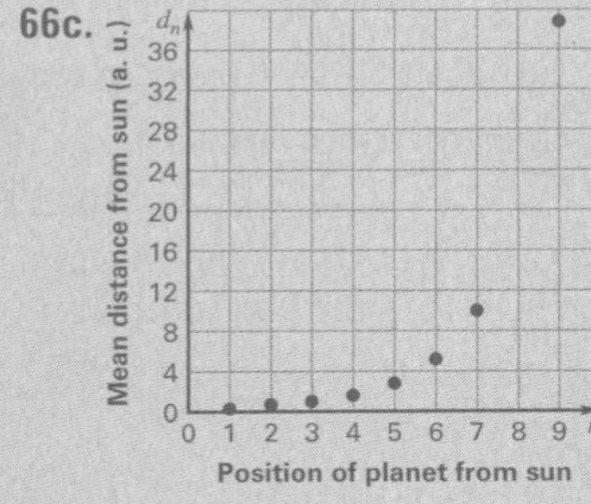

65. **TOWER OF HANOI** In the puzzle called the Tower of Hanoi, the object is to use a series of moves to take the rings from one peg and stack them in order on another peg. A move consists of moving exactly one ring, and no ring may be placed on top of a smaller ring. The minimum number a_n of moves required to move n rings is 1 for 1 ring, 3 for 2 rings, 7 for 3 rings, 15 for 4 rings, and 31 for 5 rings. Find a formula for the sequence. What is the minimum number of moves required to move 6 rings? 7 rings? 8 rings? **$a_n = 2^n - 1$; 63 moves, 127 moves, 255 moves**

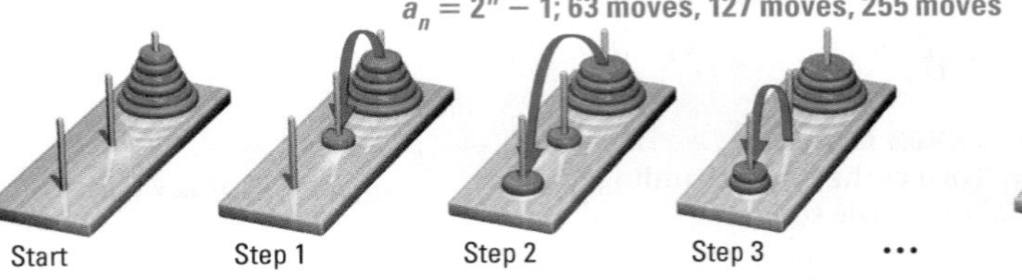

B

66. **MULTI-STEP PROBLEM** The mean distance d_n (in astronomical units) of each planet (except Neptune) from the sun is approximated by the Titius-Bode rule, $d_n = 0.3(2)^{n-2} + 0.4$, where n is a positive integer representing the position of the planet from the sun.
   a. **Evaluate** The value of n is 4 for Mars. Use the Titius-Bode rule to approximate the distance of Mars from the sun. **about 1.6 astronomical units**
   b. **Convert** One astronomical unit is equal to about 149,600,000 kilometers. How far is Mars from the sun in kilometers? **about 239,356,592 km**
   c. **Graph** Graph the sequence given by the Titius-Bode rule. **See margin.**

67c. Except for layer 1, there are always more balls in the same layer of the square pyramid. The difference in the number of balls is $\frac{n(n-1)}{2}$.

67. ★ **EXTENDED RESPONSE** For a display at a sports store, you are stacking soccer balls in a pyramid whose base is an equilateral triangle. The number a_n of balls per layer is given by $a_n = \frac{n(n+1)}{2}$ where $n = 1$ represents the top layer.
   a. How many balls are in the fifth layer? **15 balls**
   b. How many balls are in a stack with five layers? **35 balls**
   c. *Compare* the number of balls in a layer of a triangular pyramid with the number of balls in the same layer of a square pyramid.

C

68. **CHALLENGE** Using the true statements from Exercises 59–62 on page 799 and the special formulas on page 797, find a formula for the number of balls in the top n layers of the pyramid from Exercise 67. **$S_n = \frac{1}{2}\left(\frac{n(n+1)(2n+1)}{6} + \frac{n(n+1)}{2}\right)$**

KY KENTUCKY MIXED REVIEW

TEST PRACTICE at classzone.com

69. The sale price, y, for a pair of tennis shoes is $\frac{2}{3}$ of the original price, x. **Which** equation represents this relationship? **A**

   Ⓐ $y = \frac{2}{3}x$ Ⓑ $y = \frac{3}{2}x$ Ⓒ $y = x + \frac{2}{3}$ Ⓓ $y = x - \frac{2}{3}$

70. Which equation represents a line with a slope of -5 and a y-intercept of 2? **A**

   Ⓐ $y = -5x + 2$ Ⓑ $y = -5x + 10$ Ⓒ $y = 2x - 5$ Ⓓ $y = 2x + 10$

Graphing Calculator ACTIVITY *Use after Lesson 12.1*

@HomeTutor
classzone.com
Keystrokes

12.1 Work with Sequences

QUESTION How can you use a graphing calculator to perform operations with sequences?

EXAMPLE Find, graph, and sum terms of a sequence

Use a graphing calculator to find the first eight terms of $a_n = 5n - 3$. Graph the sequence. Then find the sum of the first eight terms of the sequence.

STEP 1 *Enter sequence*

Put the graphing calculator in *sequence* mode and *dot* mode. Enter the sequence. Note that the calculator uses $u(n)$ rather than a_n.

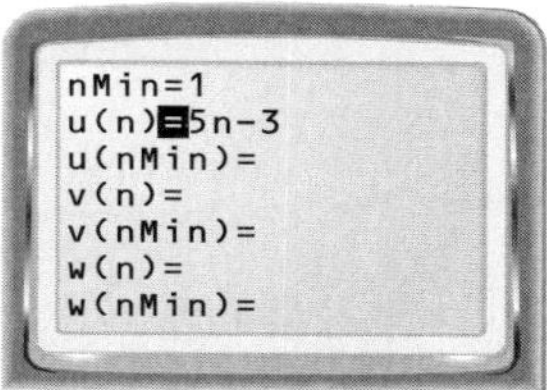

STEP 2 *Calculate terms*

Use the *table* feature to view the terms of the sequence. The first eight terms are 2, 7, 12, 17, 22, 27, 32, and 37.

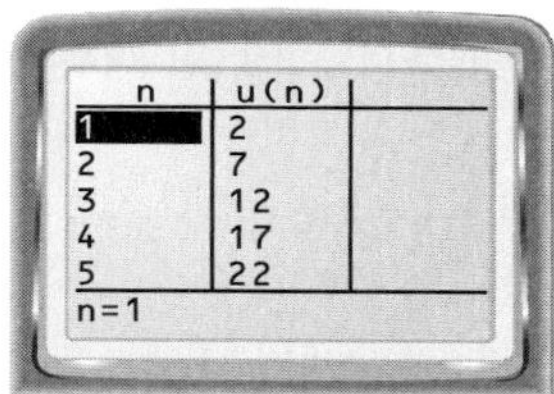

STEP 3 *Graph sequence*

Set the viewing window so that $1 \le n \le 8$, $0 \le x \le 9$, and $0 \le y \le 40$. Graph the sequence. Use the *trace* feature to view the terms of the sequence.

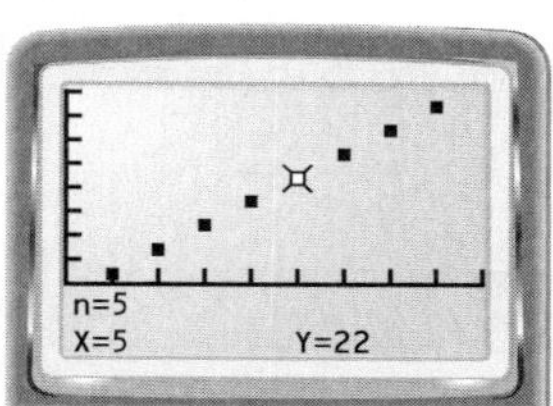

STEP 4 *Find sum of terms*

Use the *summation* feature to find the sum of the first eight terms of the sequence. The screen shows that the sum is 156.

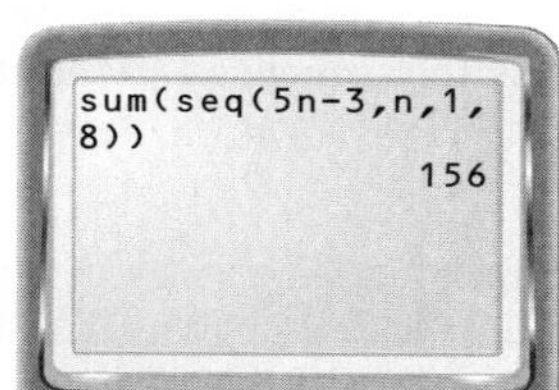

PRACTICE

Use a graphing calculator to (a) find the first ten terms of the sequence, (b) graph the sequence, and (c) find the sum of the first ten terms of the sequence. 1–6. See margin.

1. $a_n = 4n + 1$ **2.** $a_n = 3(n + 2)$ **3.** $a_n = 35 - 3n$

4. $a_n = 15 + 2n$ **5.** $a_n = 3 + n^2$ **6.** $a_n = 2^{n-1}$

1–6. For part (b), see Additional answers beginning on p. AA1.
1a. 5, 9, 13, 17, 21, 25, 29, 33, 37, 41
1c. 230
2a. 9, 12, 15, 18, 21, 24, 27, 30, 33, 36
2c. 225
3a. 32, 29, 26, 23, 20, 17, 14, 11, 8, 5
3c. 185
4a. 17, 19, 21, 23, 25, 27, 29, 31, 33, 35
4c. 260
5a. 4, 7, 12, 19, 28, 39, 52, 67, 84, 103
5c. 415
6a. 1, 2, 4, 8, 16, 32, 64, 128, 256, 512
6c. 1023

1 PLAN AND PREPARE

Learn the Method

- Students use the sequence mode of a graphing calculator to find the first n terms in a sequence, graph the sequence, and find the sum of the n terms.
- Students can use the techniques they learn in this activity to check their answers in Exercises 3–14, 28–36, and 45–56 in Lesson 12.1.

Keystroke Help

Keystrokes for several models of calculators are available in blackline format in the *Chapter 12 Resource Book*.

2 TEACH

Tips for Success

Make sure students clear functions from the Y= editor and the Stat Plot editor before graphing the sequences.

Extra Example 1

Use a graphing calculator to find the first eight terms of $a_n = 3n + 2$. Graph the sequence. Then find the sum of the first eight terms of the sequence. 5, 8, 11, 14, 17, 20, 23, 26;

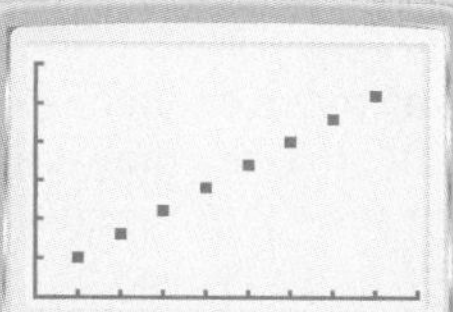

Sum: 124

3 ASSESS AND RETEACH

1. In Step 2 of the Example, what are the numbers in the left column? What do they represent? 1 through 8; the values of n

2. In Step 4 of the Example, what do the 1 and the 8 represent? the lower and upper limits of the summation

1 PLAN AND PREPARE

Warm-Up Exercises

Transparency Available

How is each term in the sequence related to the previous term?

1. 0, 3, 6, 9, 12, . . . Each is 3 more than the previous term.
2. 13, 8, 3, −2, −7, . . . Each is 5 less than the previous term.

Write a rule for the *n*th term of the sequence. Then find a_5.

3. 3, 6, 9, 12, . . . $a_n = 3n$; $a_5 = 15$
4. −8, −16, −24, −32, . . . $a_n = -8n$; $a_5 = -40$

Notetaking Guide

Transparency Available

Promotes interactive learning and notetaking skills, pp. 307–310.

Pacing

Basic: 1 day
Average: 1 day
Advanced: 1 day
Block: 0.5 block with 12.1
• See *Teaching Guide/Lesson Plan.*

2 FOCUS AND MOTIVATE

Essential Question

Big Idea 1, p. 793

How can you tell that a sequence is arithmetic? Tell students they will learn how to answer this question by examining the differences of consecutive terms of a sequence.

12.2 Analyze Arithmetic Sequences and Series

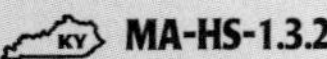

MA-HS-1.3.2

Before You worked with general sequences and series.

Now You will study arithmetic sequences and series.

Why? So you can arrange a marching band, as in Ex. 64.

Key Vocabulary
- arithmetic sequence
- common difference
- arithmetic series

MA-HS-1.3.2
Students will: describe and extend arithmetic and geometric sequences; determine a specific term of a sequence given an explicit formula; determine an explicit rule for the nth term of an arithmetic sequence and apply sequences to solve real-world problems. DOK 3

In an **arithmetic sequence**, the difference of consecutive terms is constant. This constant difference is called the **common difference** and is denoted by d.

EXAMPLE 1 Identify arithmetic sequences

Tell whether the sequence is arithmetic.

a. −4, 1, 6, 11, 16, . . .

b. 3, 5, 9, 15, 23, . . .

Solution

Find the differences of consecutive terms.

a. $a_2 - a_1 = 1 - (-4) = 5$

$a_3 - a_2 = 6 - 1 = 5$

$a_4 - a_3 = 11 - 6 = 5$

$a_5 - a_4 = 16 - 11 = 5$

▶ Each difference is 5, so the sequence is arithmetic.

b. $a_2 - a_1 = 5 - 3 = 2$

$a_3 - a_2 = 9 - 5 = 4$

$a_4 - a_3 = 15 - 9 = 6$

$a_5 - a_4 = 23 - 15 = 8$

▶ The differences are not constant, so the sequence is not arithmetic.

GUIDED PRACTICE for Example 1

1. Tell whether the sequence 17, 14, 11, 8, 5, . . . is arithmetic. *Explain* why or why not. Arithmetic; there is a common difference of −3.

KEY CONCEPT *For Your Notebook*

Rule for an Arithmetic Sequence

Algebra The nth term of an arithmetic sequence with first term a_1 and common difference d is given by:

$$a_n = a_1 + (n - 1)d$$

Example The nth term of an arithmetic sequence with a first term of 2 and common difference 3 is given by:

$$a_n = 2 + (n - 1)3, \text{ or } a_n = -1 + 3n$$

Resource Planning Guide

Chapter Resource Book
- Teaching Guide/Lesson Plan (pp. 14–15)
- Activity Master (p. 16)
- Practice levels A, B, C (pp. 17–19)
- Study Guide (pp. 20–21)
- Catch-up for Absent Students (p. 22)
- Problem Solving Workshop (p. 23)
- Challenge (p. 24)

Workbooks
- Notetaking Guide (pp. 307–310)
- Practice Workbook (pp. 173–174)

Teaching Options
- **Power Presentations CD-ROM** provides dynamic electronic teaching resources for the classroom.
- **Activity Generator CD-ROM** provides editable activities for all ability levels.

Interactive Technology
- Easy Planner
- Power Presentations CD-ROM
- Activity Generator CD-ROM
- Animated Algebra
- Test Generator CD-ROM
- Online Quiz
- eWorkbook
- eEdition
- @HomeTutor

Resources for English Learners
- Quick Reference for English Learners
- Spanish Study Guide
- Multi-Language Visual Glossary
- Student Resources in Spanish

See also the *Algebra 2 Toolkit* for more strategies for meeting individual needs.

EXAMPLE 2 Write a rule for the *n*th term

Write a rule for the *n*th term of the sequence. Then find a_{15}.

a. 4, 9, 14, 19, . . .

b. 60, 52, 44, 36, . . .

Solution

a. The sequence is arithmetic with first term $a_1 = 4$ and common difference $d = 9 - 4 = 5$. So, a rule for the *n*th term is:

$a_n = a_1 + (n - 1)d$ — Write general rule.

$= 4 + (n - 1)5$ — Substitute 4 for a_1 and 5 for d.

$= -1 + 5n$ — Simplify.

The 15th term is $a_{15} = -1 + 5(15) = 74$.

b. The sequence is arithmetic with first term $a_1 = 60$ and common difference $d = 52 - 60 = -8$. So, a rule for the *n*th term is:

$a_n = a_1 + (n - 1)d$ — Write general rule.

$= 60 + (n - 1)(-8)$ — Substitute 60 for a_1 and -8 for d.

$= 68 - 8n$ — Simplify.

The 15th term is $a_{15} = 68 - 8(15) = -52$.

AVOID ERRORS

In the general rule for an arithmetic sequence, note that the common difference d is multiplied by $n - 1$, not n.

EXAMPLE 3 Write a rule given a term and common difference

One term of an arithmetic sequence is $a_{19} = 48$. The common difference is $d = 3$.

a. Write a rule for the *n*th term.

b. Graph the sequence.

Solution

a. Use the general rule to find the first term.

$a_n = a_1 + (n - 1)d$ — Write general rule.

$a_{19} = a_1 + (19 - 1)d$ — Substitute 19 for n.

$48 = a_1 + 18(3)$ — Substitute 48 for a_{19} and 3 for d.

$-6 = a_1$ — Solve for a_1.

So, a rule for the *n*th term is:

$a_n = a_1 + (n - 1)d$ — Write general rule.

$= -6 + (n - 1)3$ — Substitute -6 for a_1 and 3 for d.

$= -9 + 3n$ — Simplify.

b. Create a table of values for the sequence. The graph of the first 6 terms of the sequence is shown. Notice that the points lie on a line. This is true for *any* arithmetic sequence.

n	1	2	3	4	5	6
a_n	−6	−3	0	3	6	9

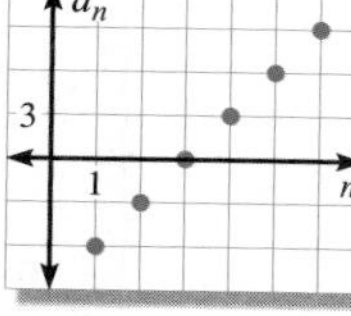

Motivating the Lesson

Suppose your annual salary at a job is $40,000. You hope to increase your salary by $2000 each year. You can calculate what your salary will be after 10 years using properties of arithmetic sequences, which are introduced in this lesson.

3 TEACH

Extra Example 1

Tell whether the sequence is arithmetic.

a. 7, 13, 19, 25, . . . yes

b. −8, −4, 0, 6, 12, . . . no

Key Question to Ask for Example 1

- In part (a) what is $a_{33} - a_{32}$? What is $a_{50} - a_{49}$? 5; 5

Extra Example 2

Write a rule for the *n*th term of the sequence. Then find a_{20}.

a. −7, −10, −13, −16, . . . $a_n = -4 - 3n$; $a_{20} = -64$

b. 59, 68, 77, 86, . . . $a_n = 50 + 9n$; $a_{20} = 230$

Key Questions to Ask for Example 2

- In part (a), what is the relationship between the coefficient of n in $-1 + 5n$ and the common difference? They are the same.
- In part (b), what is the relationship between the coefficient of n in $68 - 8n$ and the common difference? They are the same.

Extra Example 3

One term of an arithmetic sequence is $a_{27} = 263$. The common difference is $d = 11$.

a. Write a rule for the nth term.
$a_n = -34 + 11n$

b. Graph the first 6 terms of the sequence.

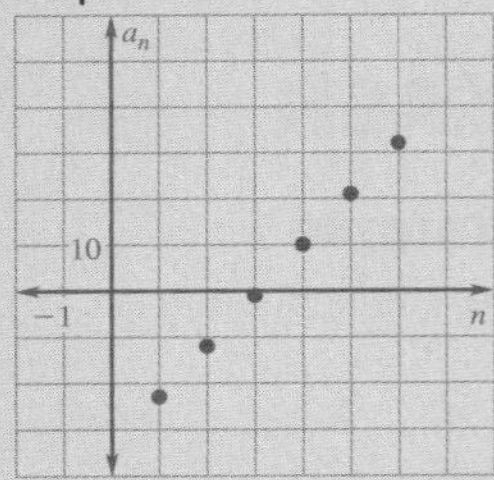

Teaching Strategy

Ask students to look at the graph in Example 3, part (b). Help them see that the slope of the line through the points is d.

Extra Example 4

Two terms of an arithmetic sequence are $a_{10} = 148$ and $a_{44} = 556$. Find a rule for the nth term.
$a_n = 28 + 12n$

Key Question to Ask for Example 4

- How can you use the values of a_8 and a_{27} to find the values of a_9 and a_{28}? What are the values? **Add the common difference 4; 25, 101.**

Vocabulary

The Key Concept box uses the term *mean*. Remind students that the mean of two numbers is one half of their sum.

EXAMPLE 4 Write a rule given two terms

Two terms of an arithmetic sequence are $a_8 = 21$ and $a_{27} = 97$. Find a rule for the nth term.

Solution

STEP 1 **Write** a system of equations using $a_n = a_1 + (n - 1)d$ and substituting 27 for n (Equation 1) and then 8 for n (Equation 2).

$a_{27} = a_1 + (27 - 1)d \Rightarrow 97 = a_1 + 26d$ **Equation 1**

$a_8 = a_1 + (8 - 1)d \Rightarrow 21 = a_1 + 7d$ **Equation 2**

STEP 2 **Solve** the system.

$76 = 19d$ **Subtract.**

$4 = d$ **Solve for *d*.**

$97 = a_1 + 26(4)$ **Substitute for *d* in Equation 1.**

$-7 = a_1$ **Solve for a_1.**

STEP 3 **Find** a rule for a_n.

$a_n = a_1 + (n - 1)d$ **Write general rule.**

$= -7 + (n - 1)4$ **Substitute for a_1 and *d*.**

$= -11 + 4n$ **Simplify.**

GUIDED PRACTICE for Examples 2, 3, and 4

Write a rule for the nth term of the arithmetic sequence. Then find a_{20}.

2. 17, 14, 11, 8, . . .
$a_n = 20 - 3n$; −40

3. $a_{11} = -57$, $d = -7$
$a_n = 20 - 7n$; −120

4. $a_7 = 26$, $a_{16} = 71$
$a_n = -9 + 5n$; 91

ARITHMETIC SERIES The expression formed by adding the terms of an arithmetic sequence is called an **arithmetic series**. The sum of the first n terms of an arithmetic series is denoted by S_n. To find a rule for S_n, you can write S_n in two different ways and add the results.

$$S_n = a_1 + (a_1 + d) + (a_1 + 2d) + \cdots + a_n$$
$$S_n = a_n + (a_n - d) + (a_n - 2d) + \cdots + a_1$$
$$2S_n = (a_1 + a_n) + (a_1 + a_n) + (a_1 + a_n) + \cdots + (a_1 + a_n)$$

You can conclude that $2S_n = n(a_1 + a_n)$, which leads to the following result.

KEY CONCEPT *For Your Notebook*

The Sum of a Finite Arithmetic Series

The sum of the first n terms of an arithmetic series is:

$$S_n = n\left(\frac{a_1 + a_n}{2}\right)$$

In words, S_n is the mean of the first and nth terms, multiplied by the number of terms.

Differentiated Instruction

Below Level To help students get familiar with the formula $S_n = n\left(\frac{a_1 + a_2}{2}\right)$, have them check the formula values for S_4, S_5, and S_6 by finding the sums of the first 4, 5, and 6 numbers. This may help them see that the formula for S_n is a shortcut for finding the sum of a series.

See also the *Algebra 2 Toolkit* for more strategies.

EXAMPLE 5 Standardized Test Practice

What is the sum of the arithmetic series $\sum_{i=1}^{20} (3 + 5i)$?

Ⓐ 103 Ⓑ 111 Ⓒ 1110 Ⓓ 2220

LASSIFY SERIES
ou can verify that the eries in Example 5 is rithmetic by evaluating + $5i$ for the first few alues of the index i. he resulting terms re 8, 13, 18, 23, . . . , hich have a common ifference of 5.

Solution

$a_1 = 3 + 5(1) = 8$ **Identify first term.**

$a_{20} = 3 + 5(20) = 103$ **Identify last term.**

$S_{20} = 20\left(\frac{8 + 103}{2}\right)$ **Write rule for S_{20}, substituting 8 for a_1 and 103 for a_{20}.**

$= 1110$ **Simplify.**

▶ The correct answer is C. Ⓐ Ⓑ Ⓒ Ⓓ

EXAMPLE 6 Use an arithmetic sequence and series in real life

HOUSE OF CARDS You are making a house of cards similar to the one shown.

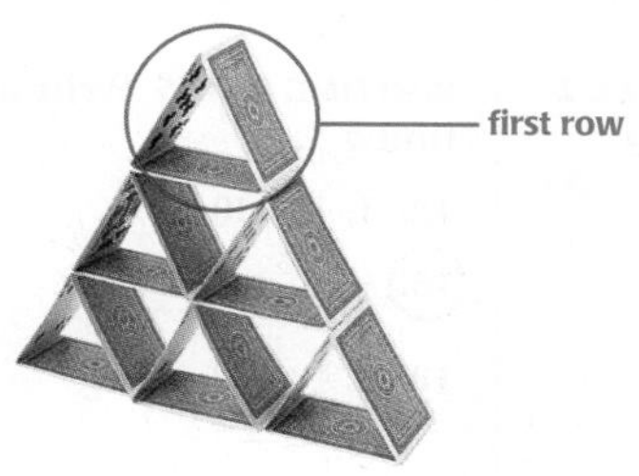

a. Write a rule for the number of cards in the nth row if the top row is row 1.

b. What is the total number of cards if the house of cards has 14 rows?

Solution

a. Starting with the top row, the numbers of cards in the rows are 3, 6, 9, 12, ... These numbers form an arithmetic sequence with a first term of 3 and a common difference of 3. So, a rule for the sequence is:

$a_n = a_1 + (n - 1)d$ **Write general rule.**

$= 3 + (n - 1)3$ **Substitute 3 for a_1 and 3 for d.**

$= 3n$ **Simplify.**

b. Find the sum of an arithmetic series with first term $a_1 = 3$ and last term $a_{14} = 3(14) = 42$.

$$\text{Total number of cards} = S_{14} = 14\left(\frac{a_1 + a_{14}}{2}\right) = 14\left(\frac{3 + 42}{2}\right) = 315$$

GUIDED PRACTICE for Examples 5 and 6

5. Find the sum of the arithmetic series $\sum_{i=1}^{12} (2 + 7i)$. **570**

6. **WHAT IF?** In Example 6, what is the total number of cards if the house of cards has 8 rows? **108 cards**

Extra Example 5

What is the sum of the arithmetic series $\sum_{i=1}^{28} (-2 + 4i)$? **D**

Ⓐ 14 Ⓑ 420
Ⓒ 870 Ⓓ 1568

Key Question to Ask for Example 5

- Why do you calculate a_1 and a_{20}? **a_1 is the first term, and for $n = 20$, a_{20} is the last term.**

Extra Example 6

A tall brick building has a decoration as shown.

a. Write a rule for the number of bricks in the nth row if the top row is row 1. **$a_n = n$**

b. What is the total number of bricks if the bottom row has 44 bricks? **990**

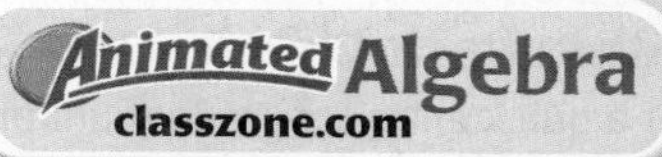

An **Animated Algebra** activity is available on-line for **Example 6.** This activity is also available on the **Power Presentations CD-ROM**.

Closing the Lesson

Have students summarize the major points of the lesson and answer the Essential Question: How can you tell that a sequence is arithmetic?

- **The nth term of an arithmetic sequence is given by $a_n = a_1 + (n - 1)d$, where a_1 is the first term and the common difference is d.**
- **The sum of the first n terms of an arithmetic series is $S_n = n\left(\frac{a_1 + a_2}{2}\right)$.**

A sequence is an arithmetic sequence if the difference of consecutive terms is constant.

Differentiated Instruction

Kinesthetic Learners For students who have trouble determining the initial pattern of numbers of cards in **Example 6**, it might be helpful for groups of students to draw or build a house of cards, adding rows until they can ascertain the properties of the sequence. By actually adding the cards themselves each time, students will experience how a sequence is formed.

See also the *Algebra 2 Toolkit* for more strategies.

4 PRACTICE AND APPLY

Assignment Guide

Answer Transparencies available for all exercises

Basic:
Day 1: pp. 806–809
Exs. 1–6, 12–15, 21–25, 29–32, 39–42, 49–51, 63–66, 70

Average:
Day 1: pp. 806–809
Exs. 1, 2, 7–9, 16–18, 21, 22, 25, 26, 29, 33–35, 39, 43–45, 52–54, 63–68, 71

Advanced:
Day 1: pp. 806–809
Exs. 1, 2, 9–11, 18–20, 26–29, 36–39, 46–48, 51–69*

Block:
pp. 806–809
Exs. 1, 2, 7–9, 16–18, 21, 22, 25, 26, 29, 33–35, 39, 43–45, 52–54, 63–68, 71 (with 12.1)

Differentiated Instruction

See *Algebra 2 Best Practices Toolkit* for suggestions on addressing the needs of a diverse classroom.

Homework Check

For a quick check of student understanding of key concepts, go over the following exercises:

Basic: 4, 14, 24, 32, 42
Average: 8, 16, 34, 44, 63
Advanced: 10, 20, 36, 46, 64

Extra Practice

- Student Edition, p. 1021
- Chapter 12 Resource Book: Practice levels A, B, C, pp. 17–19

Practice Worksheet

An easily-readable reduced practice page (with answers) for this lesson can be found on p. 792C.

12.2 EXERCISES

HOMEWORK KEY
○ = WORKED-OUT SOLUTIONS on p. WS21 for Exs. 15, 41, and 65
★ = STANDARDIZED TEST PRACTICE Exs. 2, 29, 39, 52, and 68
◆ = MULTIPLE REPRESENTATIONS Ex. 66

SKILL PRACTICE

A

1. **VOCABULARY** Copy and complete: The constant difference between consecutive terms of an arithmetic sequence is called the _?_. common difference

2. ★ **WRITING** *Explain* the difference between an arithmetic sequence and an arithmetic series. An arithmetic sequence is a list of numbers that have the same common difference between consecutive terms. An arithmetic series is the sum of the terms of an arithmetic sequence.

EXAMPLE 1 on p. 802 for Exs. 3–11

IDENTIFYING ARITHMETIC SEQUENCES Tell whether the sequence is arithmetic. *Explain* why or why not. 3–11. See margin.

3. $1, -2, -5, -8, -11, \ldots$
4. $16, 14, 11, 6, 3, \ldots$
5. $5, 14, 23, 32, 41, \ldots$
6. $-10, -7, -5, -2, 0, \ldots$
7. $0.5, 1, 1.5, 2, 2.5, \ldots$
8. $20, 10, 5, 2.5, 1.25, \ldots$
9. $\frac{7}{4}, \frac{5}{4}, \frac{3}{4}, -\frac{3}{4}, -\frac{5}{4}, \ldots$
10. $\frac{1}{7}, \frac{2}{7}, \frac{4}{7}, \frac{8}{7}, \frac{16}{7}, \ldots$
11. $-\frac{5}{2}, -1, \frac{1}{2}, 2, \frac{7}{2}, \ldots$

EXAMPLE 2 on p. 803 for Exs. 12–22

WRITING RULES Write a rule for the nth term of the arithmetic sequence. Then find a_{20}.

12. $1, 4, 7, 10, 13, \ldots$ $a_n = 3n - 2$; 58
13. $5, 11, 17, 23, 29, \ldots$ $a_n = -1 + 6n$; 119
14. $8, 21, 34, 47, 60, \ldots$ $a_n = -5 + 13n$; 255
15. $-3, -1, 1, 3, 5, \ldots$ $a_n = -5 + 2n$; 35
16. $6, 2, -2, -6, -10, \ldots$ $a_n = 10 - 4n$; -70
17. $25, 14, 3, -8, -19, \ldots$ $a_n = 36 - 11n$; -184
18. $0, \frac{2}{3}, \frac{4}{3}, 2, \frac{8}{3}, \ldots$ $a_n = -\frac{2}{3} + \frac{2}{3}n$; $\frac{38}{3}$
19. $2, \frac{5}{3}, \frac{4}{3}, 1, \frac{2}{3}, \ldots$ $a_n = \frac{7}{3} - \frac{1}{3}n$; $-\frac{13}{3}$
20. $1.5, 3.6, 5.7, 7.8, 9.9, \ldots$ $a_n = -0.6 + 2.1n$; 41.4

ERROR ANALYSIS *Describe* and correct the error in writing the rule for the nth term of the arithmetic sequence $37, 24, 11, -2, -15, \ldots$.

21.
Use $a_1 = 37$ and $d = -13$.
$a_n = a_1 + nd$
$a_n = 37 + n(-13)$
$a_n = 37 - 13n$

22.
The first term is 37 and the common difference is -13.
$a_n = -13 + (n - 1)(37)$
$a_n = -50 + 37n$

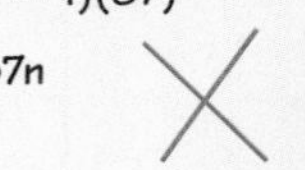

21. The equation for and arithmetic sequence is not correct; $a_n = a_1 + (n - 1)d$, $a_n = 37 + (n - 1)(-13)$, $a_n = 50 - 13n$.

22. The terms were substituted into the wrong places; $37 = (n - 1)(-13)$, $a_n = 50 - 13n$.

EXAMPLE 3 on p. 803 for Exs. 23–29

WRITING RULES Write a rule for the nth term of the arithmetic sequence. Then graph the first six terms of the sequence. 23–28. See margin for art.

23. $a_{16} = 52, d = 5$ $a_n = -28 + 5n$
24. $a_6 = -16, d = 9$ $a_n = -70 + 9n$
25. $a_4 = 96, d = -14$ $a_n = 152 - 14n$
26. $a_{12} = -3, d = -7$ $a_n = 81 - 7n$
27. $a_{10} = 30, d = \frac{7}{2}$ $a_n = -5 + \frac{7}{2}n$
28. $a_{11} = \frac{1}{2}, d = -\frac{1}{2}$ $a_n = 6 - \frac{1}{2}n$

29. ★ **MULTIPLE CHOICE** For a certain arithmetic sequence, $a_{30} = 57$ and $d = 4$. What is a rule for the nth term of the sequence? C

Ⓐ $a_n = -63 - 4n$
Ⓑ $a_n = -59 - 4n$
Ⓒ $a_n = -63 + 4n$
Ⓓ $a_n = -59 + 4n$

3. Arithmetic; there is a common difference of 3 between consecutive terms.
4. Not arithmetic; there is not a common difference between consecutive terms.
5. Arithmetic; there is a common difference of 9 between consecutive terms.
6. Not arithmetic; there is not a common difference between consecutive terms.
7. Arithmetic; there is a common difference of 0.5 between consecutive terms.
8. Not arithmetic; there is not a common difference between consecutive terms.
9. Not arithmetic; there is not a common difference between consecutive terms.
10. Not arithmetic; there is not a common difference between consecutive terms.
11. Arithmetic; there is a common difference of 1.5 between consecutive terms.

EXAMPLE 4 on p. 804 for Exs. 30–39

WRITING RULES Write a rule for the *n*th term of the arithmetic sequence that has the two given terms.

30. $a_4 = 31, a_{10} = 85$ $a_n = -5 + 9n$
31. $a_6 = 39, a_{14} = 79$ $a_n = 9 + 5n$
32. $a_3 = -2, a_{17} = 40$ $a_n = -11 + 3n$
33. $a_8 = -10, a_{20} = -58$ $a_n = 22 - 4n$
34. $a_9 = 89, a_{15} = 137$ $a_n = 17 + 8n$
35. $a_2 = 17, a_{11} = 35$ $a_n = 13 + 2n$
36. $a_7 = 4, a_{12} = -9$ $a_n = \frac{111}{5} - \frac{13}{5}n$
37. $a_5 = 15, a_9 = 24$ $a_n = \frac{15}{4} + \frac{9}{4}n$
38. $a_6 = 0, a_{11} = -2$ $a_n = \frac{12}{5} - \frac{2}{5}n$

39. ★ **MULTIPLE CHOICE** For a certain arithmetic sequence, $a_6 = -6$ and $a_{13} = -48$. What is a rule for the *n*th term of the sequence? B

Ⓐ $a_n = 18 + 6n$ Ⓑ $a_n = 30 - 6n$

Ⓒ $a_n = -6 + 24n$ Ⓓ $a_n = -36 - 6n$

EXAMPLE 5 on p. 805 for Exs. 40–48

FINDING SUMS Find the sum of the arithmetic series.

40. $\sum_{i=1}^{10}(1 + 3i)$ 175
41. $\sum_{i=1}^{8}(-3 - 2i)$ −96
42. $\sum_{i=1}^{18}(14 - 6i)$ −774
43. $\sum_{i=1}^{22}(-9 + 11i)$ 2585
44. $\sum_{i=3}^{9}(72 - 6i)$ 252
45. $\sum_{i=5}^{14}(-54 + 9i)$ 315
46. $2 + 6 + 10 + \cdots + 58$ 450
47. $-1 + 4 + 9 + \cdots + 34$ 132
48. $44 + 37 + 30 + \cdots + 2$ 161

B **USING GRAPHS Write a rule for the sequence whose graph is shown.**

49. 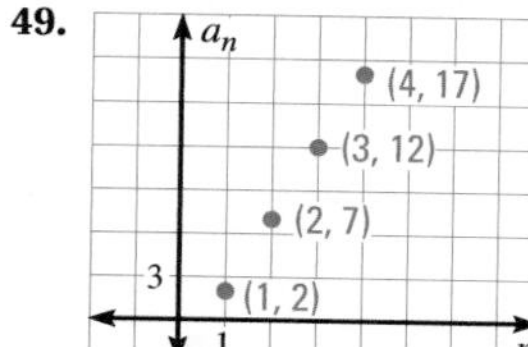

$a_n = -3 + 5n$

50. 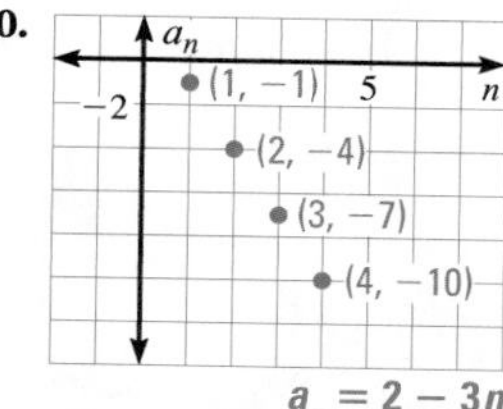

$a_n = 2 - 3n$

51. 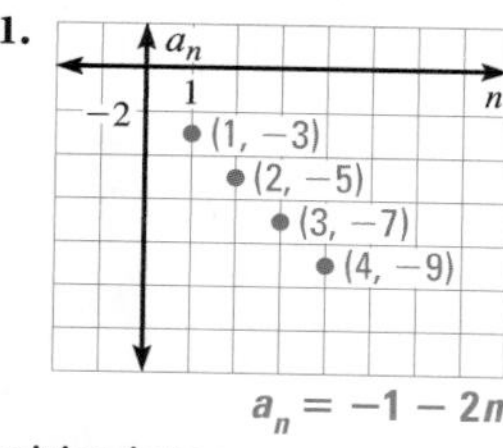

$a_n = -1 - 2n$

52. ★ **WRITING** *Compare* the graph of $a_n = 3n + 2$, where *n* is a positive integer, with the graph of $f(x) = 3x + 2$, where *x* is a real number. Discuss how the graph of an arithmetic sequence is similar to and different from the graph of a linear function. *Sample answer:* The graph of a_n is just points at every integer *n* and the graph of $f(x)$ is a line. Both graphs have the same rate of change between points.

REASONING Tell whether the statement is *true* or *false*. *Explain* your answer.

53. If the common difference of an arithmetic series is doubled while the first term and number of terms in the series remain unchanged, then the sum of the series is doubled. False. *Sample answer:* Doubling the common difference alone does not double the sum.

54. If the numbers *a*, *b*, and *c* are the first three terms of an arithmetic sequence, then *b* is half the sum of *a* and *c*. true; $a + c = 2b$

C **SOLVING EQUATIONS Find the value of *n*.**

55. $\sum_{i=1}^{n}(-5 + 7i) = 486$ 12
56. $\sum_{i=1}^{n}(10 - 3i) = -28$ 8
57. $\sum_{i=1}^{n}(58 - 8i) = -1150$ 25
58. $\sum_{i=1}^{n}(5 - 5i) = -50$ 5
59. $\sum_{i=3}^{n}(-3 - 4i) = -507$ 15
60. $\sum_{i=5}^{n}(7 + 12i) = 455$ 9

61. **REASONING** Find the sum of all positive odd integers less than 300. 22,500

62. **CHALLENGE** The numbers $3 - x$, x, and $1 - 3x$ are the first three terms in an arithmetic sequence. Find the value of *x* and the next term in the sequence. $\frac{2}{3}, -\frac{8}{3}$

Study Strategy

Exercise 39 Ask students how they can check the rule they chose. One strategy is to use that rule to evaluate a_6 and a_{13}.

Avoiding Common Errors

Exercises 40–45 Make sure that students use the entire expression in parentheses and not just the term that includes *i* to evaluate a_1 and a_n. For instance, point out that in Exercise 40, $S_n = 10\left(\frac{4 + 31}{2}\right)$ and in Exercise 41, $S_n = 8\left(\frac{-5 + (-19)}{2}\right)$.

Mathematical Reasoning

Exercise 52 Students can graph several points (n, a_n) for $a_n = 3n + 2$ and draw a line through them to see the relationship between (n, a_n) and $f(x) = 3x + 2$.

26. 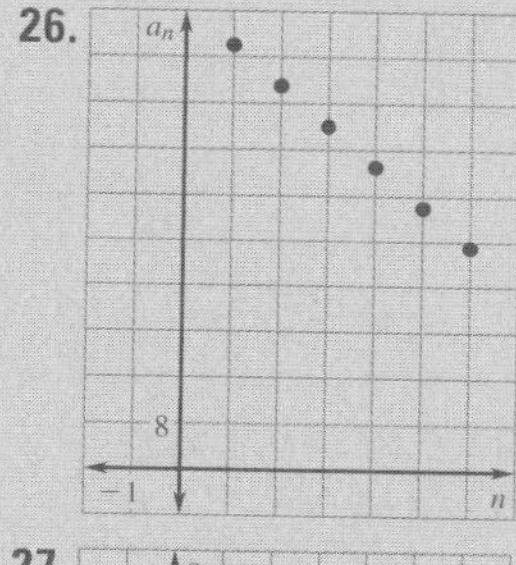

27. 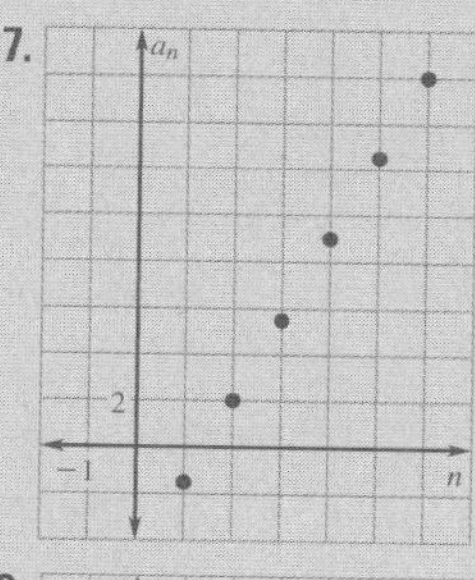

28. 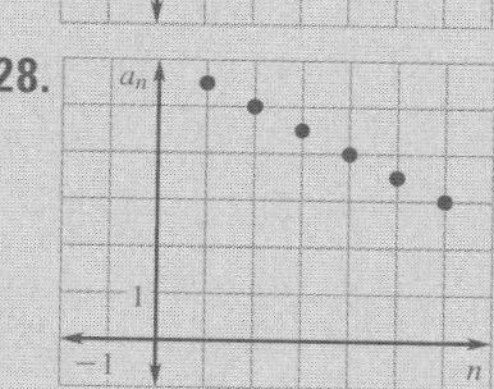

23. 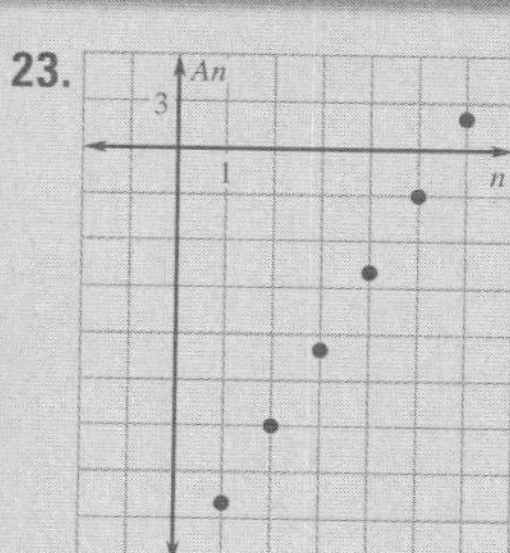

24. 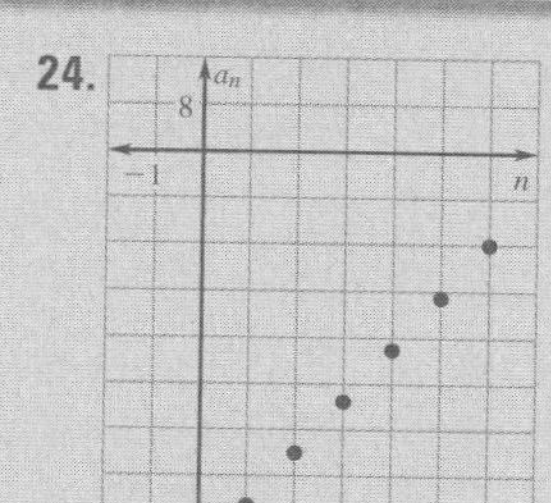

25. 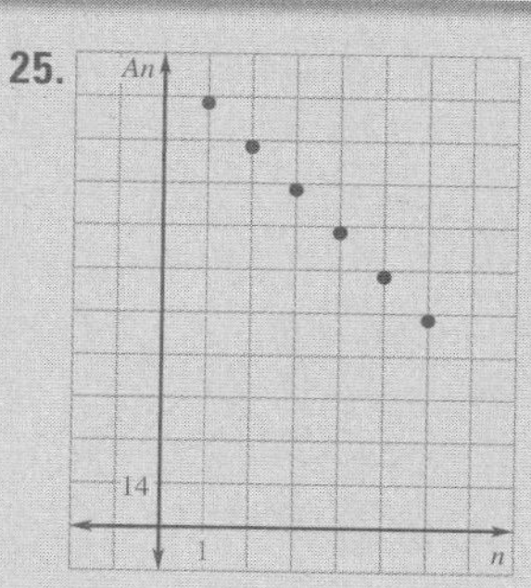

Teaching Strategy

Exercise 63 Ask students to recall that the honeycomb represents a tessellation of a regular hexagon in a plane. Students may find it helpful to cut out a hexagon and tessellate it to confirm that each number $a_2, a_3, a_4, \ldots$ is 6 more than the previous number.

Exercise 65 Additional information about the *Four-Sided Pyramid* can be found at the National Gallery of Art's website www.nga.gov/feature/sculpturegarden/sculpture/sculpture10.shtm

66a.

n	$d(n)$
1	16
2	48
3	80
4	112

66c.

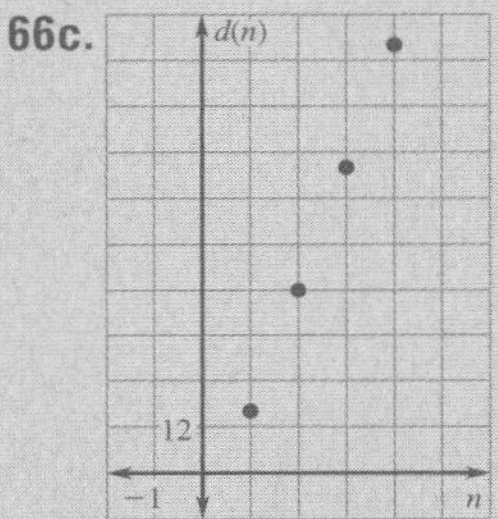

PROBLEM SOLVING

EXAMPLE 6 on p. 805 for Exs. 63–65

A

63. HONEYCOMBS Domestic bees make their honeycomb by starting with a single hexagonal cell, then forming ring after ring of hexagonal cells around the initial cell, as shown. The numbers of cells in successive rings form an arithmetic sequence.

Initial cell | 1 ring | 2 rings

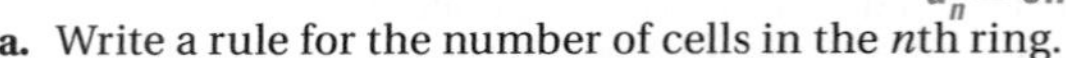

a. Write a rule for the number of cells in the nth ring. $a_n = 6n$

b. What is the total number of cells in the honeycomb after the 9th ring is formed? (*Hint:* Do not forget to count the initial cell.) 271 cells

@HomeTutor for problem solving help at classzone.com

64. MARCHING BAND A marching band is arranged in 7 rows. The first row has 3 band members, and each row after the first has 2 more band members than the row before it. Write a rule for the number of band members in the nth row. Then find the total number of band members. $a_n = 1 + 2n$; 63 band members

@HomeTutor for problem solving help at classzone.com

65. SCULPTURE Sol LeWitt's sculpture *Four-Sided Pyramid* in the National Gallery of Art Sculpture Garden is made of concrete blocks. As shown in the diagram, each layer has 8 more visible blocks than the layer in front of it.

a. Write a rule for the number of visible blocks in the nth layer where $n = 1$ represents the front layer. $a_n = -4 + 8n$

b. When you view the pyramid from one corner, a total of 12 layers are visible. How many of the pyramid's blocks are visible? 576 blocks

B

66. **MULTIPLE REPRESENTATIONS** The distance D (in feet) that an object falls in t seconds can be modeled by $D(t) = 16t^2$.

a. Making a Table Let $d(n)$ represent the distance the object falls in the nth second. Make a table of values showing $d(1)$, $d(2)$, $d(3)$, and $d(4)$. (*Hint:* The distance $d(1)$ that the object falls in the first second is $D(1) - D(0)$.) See margin.

b. Writing a Rule Write a rule for the sequence of distances given by $d(n)$. $d(n) = -16 + 3$

c. Drawing a Graph Graph the sequence from part (b). See margin.

67. ENTERTAINMENT During a high school spirit week, students dress up in costumes. A cash prize is given each day to the student with the best costume. The organizing committee has \$1000 to give away over five days. The committee wants to increase the amount of the prize by \$50 each day. How much should the committee give away on the first day? \$100

○ = WORKED-OUT SOLUTIONS on p. WS1 ★ = STANDARDIZED TEST PRACTICE

= MULTIPLE REPRESENTATIO

68. ★ **EXTENDED RESPONSE** A paper towel manufacturer sells paper towels rolled onto cardboard dowels. The thickness of the paper is 0.0004 inch. The diameter of a dowel is 2 inches, and the total diameter of a roll is 5 inches.

n	d_n (in.)	ℓ_n (in.)
1	2	2π
2	?	?
3	?	?
4	?	?

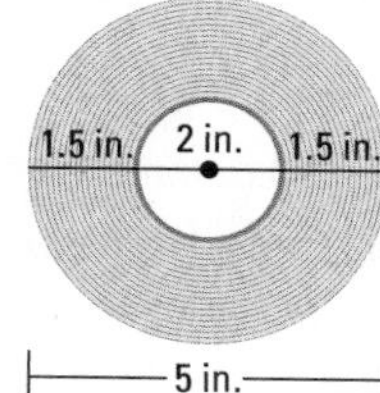

a. **Calculate** Let n be the number of times the paper towel is wrapped around the dowel, let d_n be the diameter of the roll just before the nth wrap, and let ℓ_n be the length of paper added in the nth wrap. Copy and complete the table. See margin.

b. **Model** What kind of sequence is $\ell_1, \ell_2, \ell_3, \ell_4, \ldots$? Write a rule for the nth term of the sequence. arithmetic; $a_n = [2 + 0.0008(n - 1)]\pi$

c. **Apply** Find the number of times the paper must be wrapped around the dowel to create a roll with a 5 inch diameter. Use your answer and the rule from part (b) to find the length of paper in a roll with a 5 inch diameter. 3750 times; 41,228.7 in.

d. **Interpret** Suppose a roll with a 5 inch diameter costs \$1.50. How much would you expect to pay for a roll with a 7 inch diameter whose dowel also has a diameter of 2 inches? *Explain* your reasoning and any assumptions you make. *Sample answer:* \$2.10; a 5 inch roll costs \$1.50 which breaks down to \$0.30 per inch, so a 7 inch roll should costs $7 \cdot 0.3$.

C 69. **CHALLENGE** A theater has n rows of seats, and each row has d more seats than the row in front of it. There are x seats in the last (nth) row and a total of y seats in the entire theater. How many seats are in the front row of the theater? Write your answer in terms of n, x, and y. $a_1 = \frac{2y}{n} - x$

KY KENTUCKY MIXED REVIEW

TEST PRACTICE at classzone.com

70. What is the approximate perimeter of the trapezoid? **B**

Ⓐ 17.0 units

Ⓑ 17.8 units

Ⓒ 24.6 units

Ⓓ 29.0 units

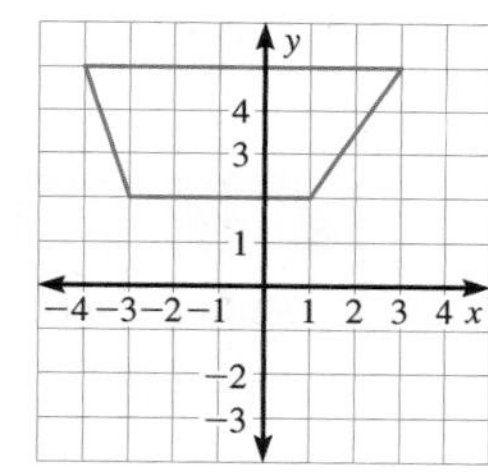

71. Sam randomly selects one card from a standard deck of 52 cards. Which of the following events has a probability of occurring that is about 8%? **C**

Ⓐ The card is a spade.

Ⓑ The card is the 3 of hearts.

Ⓒ The card is a queen.

Ⓓ The card is a red card.

5 ASSESS AND RETEACH

Daily Homework Quiz

Transparency Available

1. Is the sequence 2, 103, 204, 305, 406, . . . arithmetic? Explain your answer. Yes; the common difference is 101.

2. Write a rule for the nth term of the sequence 5, 2, −1, −4, ... Then find a_5. $a_n = 8 - 3n$; $a_5 = -7$

3. Two terms of an arithmetic sequence are $a_5 = 14$ and $a_{30} = 89$. Find a rule for the nth term. $a_n = -1 + 3n$

A movie theater has 24 seats in the first row and each successive row contains one additional seat. There are 30 rows in all.

4. Write a rule for the number of seats in the nth row. $a_n = 23 + n$

5. How many seats are in the theater? 1155 seats

Online Quiz

Available at **classzone.com**

Diagnosis/Remediation

- Practice A, B, C in Chapter 12 Resource Book, pp. 17–19
- Study Guide in Chapter 12 Resource Book, pp. 20–21
- Practice Workbook, pp. 173–174
- @HomeTutor

Challenge

Additional challenge is available in the Chapter 12 Resource Book, p. 24.

68a.

n	d_n (in.)	ℓ_n (in.)
1	2	2π
2	2.0008	2.0008π
3	2.0016	2.0016π
4	2.0024	2.0024π

12.3 Analyze Geometric Sequences and Series

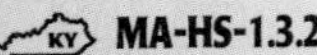 MA-HS-1.3.2

Before You studied arithmetic sequences and series.

Now You will study geometric sequences and series.

Why? So you can solve problems about sports tournaments, as in Ex. 58.

Key Vocabulary
- geometric sequence
- common ratio
- geometric series

MA-HS-1.3.2
Students will: describe and extend arithmetic and geometric sequences; determine a specific term of a sequence given an explicit formula; determine an explicit rule for the nth term of an arithmetic sequence and apply sequences to solve real-world problems. DOK 3

In a **geometric sequence**, the ratio of any term to the previous term is constant. This constant ratio is called the **common ratio** and is denoted by r.

EXAMPLE 1 Identify geometric sequences

Tell whether the sequence is geometric.

a. 4, 10, 18, 28, 40, . . .

b. 625, 125, 25, 5, 1, . . .

Solution

To decide whether a sequence is geometric, find the ratios of consecutive terms.

a. $\frac{a_2}{a_1} = \frac{10}{4} = \frac{5}{2}$ $\quad \frac{a_3}{a_2} = \frac{18}{10} = \frac{9}{5}$ $\quad \frac{a_4}{a_3} = \frac{28}{18} = \frac{14}{9}$ $\quad \frac{a_5}{a_4} = \frac{40}{28} = \frac{10}{7}$

▸ The ratios are different, so the sequence is not geometric.

b. $\frac{a_2}{a_1} = \frac{125}{625} = \frac{1}{5}$ $\quad \frac{a_3}{a_2} = \frac{25}{125} = \frac{1}{5}$ $\quad \frac{a_4}{a_3} = \frac{5}{25} = \frac{1}{5}$ $\quad \frac{a_5}{a_4} = \frac{1}{5}$

▸ Each ratio is $\frac{1}{5}$, so the sequence is geometric.

GUIDED PRACTICE for Example 1

Tell whether the sequence is geometric. *Explain* why or why not.

1. 81, 27, 9, 3, 1, . . . Geometric; there is a common ratio of $\frac{1}{3}$.

2. 1, 2, 6, 24, 120, . . . Not geometric; there is no common ratio.

3. −4, 8, −16, 32, −64, . . . Geometric; there is a common ratio of −2.

KEY CONCEPT *For Your Notebook*

Rule for a Geometric Sequence

Algebra The nth term of a geometric sequence with first term a_1 and common ratio r is given by:

$$a_n = a_1 r^{n-1}$$

Example The nth term of a geometric sequence with a first term of 3 and common ratio 2 is given by:

$$a_n = 3(2)^{n-1}$$

1 PLAN AND PREPARE

Warm-Up Exercises

Transparency Available

Find the next term in each sequence

1. 3, 6, 9, 12, . . . 15
2. 0.25, 0.50, 1, 2, . . . 4
3. A high school graduated 250 seniors in 2004. In 2005 the number of graduating seniors increased by 4%. How many seniors graduated in 2005? 260 seniors

Notetaking Guide

Transparency Available

Promotes interactive learning and notetaking skills, pp. 311–314.

Pacing

Basic: 2 days
Average: 2 days
Advanced: 2 days
Block: 1 block
- See *Teaching Guide/Lesson Plan.*

2 FOCUS AND MOTIVATE

Essential Question

Big Idea 2, p. 793

How can you find the sum of the terms of a geometric series? Tell students they will learn how to answer this question by using the formula $S_n = a_1\left(\frac{1 - r^n}{1 - r}\right)$.

Resource Planning Guide

Chapter Resource Book
- Teaching Guide/Lesson Plan (pp. 25–26)
- Activity Master (p. 27)
- Practice levels A, B, C (pp. 29–31)
- Study Guide (pp. 32–33)
- Catch-up for Absent Students (p. 34)
- Problem Solving Workshop (p. 35)
- Challenge (p. 37)

Workbooks
- Notetaking Guide (pp. 311–314)
- Practice Workbook (pp. 175–176)

Teaching Options
- **Power Presentations CD-ROM** provides dynamic electronic teaching resources for the classroom.
- **Activity Generator CD-ROM** provides editable activities for all ability levels.

Interactive Technology
- Easy Planner
- Power Presentations CD-ROM
- Activity Generator CD-ROM
- Animated Algebra
- Test Generator CD-ROM
- Online Quiz
- eWorkbook
- eEdition
- @HomeTutor

Resources for English Learners
- Quick Reference for English Learners
- Spanish Study Guide
- Multi-Language Visual Glossary
- Student Resources in Spanish

See also the *Algebra 2 Toolkit* for more strategies for meeting individual needs.

EXAMPLE 2 Write a rule for the *n*th term

Write a rule for the *n*th term of the sequence. Then find a_7.

a. 4, 20, 100, 500, . . .

b. 152, −76, 38, −19, . . .

Solution

a. The sequence is geometric with first term $a_1 = 4$ and common ratio $r = \frac{20}{4} = 5$. So, a rule for the *n*th term is:

$a_n = a_1 r^{n-1}$ — **Write general rule.**

$= 4(5)^{n-1}$ — **Substitute 4 for a_1 and 5 for r.**

The 7th term is $a_7 = 4(5)^{7-1} = 62{,}500$.

b. The sequence is geometric with first term $a_1 = 152$ and common ratio $r = \frac{-76}{152} = -\frac{1}{2}$. So, a rule for the *n*th term is:

$a_n = a_1 r^{n-1}$ — **Write general rule.**

$= 152\left(-\frac{1}{2}\right)^{n-1}$ — **Substitute 152 for a_1 and $-\frac{1}{2}$ for r.**

The 7th term is $a_7 = 152\left(-\frac{1}{2}\right)^{7-1} = \frac{19}{8}$.

OID ERRORS
he general rule for
eometric sequence,
e that the exponent
− 1, not *n*.

EXAMPLE 3 Write a rule given a term and common ratio

One term of a geometric sequence is $a_4 = 12$. The common ratio is $r = 2$.

a. Write a rule for the *n*th term.

b. Graph the sequence.

Solution

a. Use the general rule to find the first term.

$a_n = a_1 r^{n-1}$ — **Write general rule.**

$a_4 = a_1 r^{4-1}$ — **Substitute 4 for n.**

$12 = a_1(2)^3$ — **Substitute 12 for a_4 and 2 for r.**

$1.5 = a_1$ — **Solve for a_1.**

So, a rule for the *n*th term is:

$a_n = a_1 r^{n-1}$ — **Write general rule.**

$= 1.5(2)^{n-1}$ — **Substitute 1.5 for a_1 and 2 for r.**

b. Create a table of values for the sequence. The graph of the first 6 terms of the sequence is shown. Notice that the points lie on an exponential curve. This is true for *any* geometric sequence with $r > 0$.

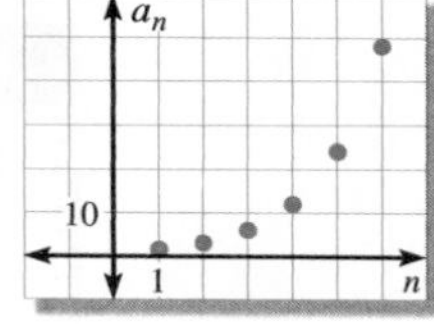

n	1	2	3	4	5	6
a_n	1.5	3	6	12	24	48

Animated Algebra at classzone.com

Motivating the Lesson

Have students list in order the numbers of parents they have, the number of grandparents, and the number of great-grandparents. In this lesson students will learn a formula which can be used to show they have 2046 ancestors in the 10 previous generations.

3 TEACH

Extra Example 1

Tell whether the sequence is geometric.

a. 2, 6, 18, 54, 162, . . . yes

b. 2, 7, 12, 17, 22, . . . no

Extra Example 2

Write a rule for the *n*th term of the sequence. Then find a_6.

a. 3, 12, 48, 192, . . .

$a_n = 3(4)^{n-1}$; $a_6 = 3072$

b. 36, −12, 4, $-\frac{4}{3}$, . . .

$a_n = 36\left(-\frac{1}{3}\right)^{n-1}$; $a_6 = -\frac{4}{27}$

Extra Example 3

One term of a geometric sequence is $a_5 = 54$. The common ratio is $r = 3$.

a. Write a rule for the *n*th term.

$a_n = \frac{2}{3}(3)^{n-1}$

b. Graph the sequence.

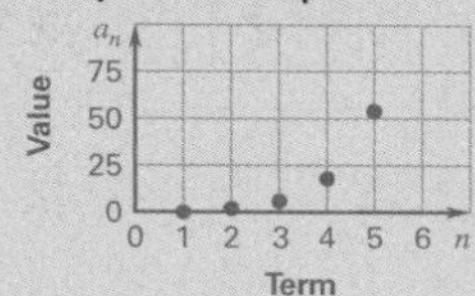

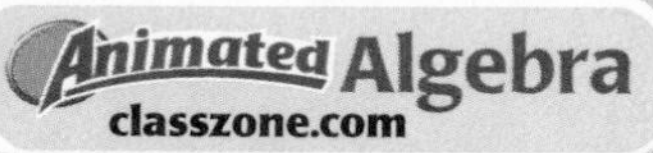

An **Animated Algebra** activity is available on-line for **Example 3.** This activity is also available on the **Power Presentations CD-ROM.**

Differentiated Instruction

Below Level To help students understand the difference between arithmetic sequences and geometric sequences, ask them to compare the graph in Example 3 to the graph in Lesson 12.2, Example 3. The visualization of the graphs of the two sequences should help them see that the arithmetic sequence is modeled by points on a line, while the geometric sequence is modeled by points on an exponential function. Point out that the common difference and the common ratio define the rate at which the terms of the sequences increase.

See also the *Algebra 2 Toolkit* for more strategies.

Extra Example 4

Two terms of a geometric sequence are $a_3 = 45$ and $a_5 = 405$. Find a rule for the nth term. $a_n = 5(3)^{n-1}$ or $a_n = 5(-3)^{n-1}$

Key Questions to Ask for Example 4

- What is the common ratio of the sequence? -4
- What is the first term of the sequence? What is the second term? -3, 12
- Will a^7 be positive or negative? Explain. a_n is the product of -3 and $(-4)^{n-1}$. When $n - 1$ is odd, both factors are negative so a_n is positive. When $n - 1$ is even (so n is odd), a_n will be negative. For a_7, n is odd so a_n is negative.

EXAMPLE 4 Write a rule given two terms

Two terms of a geometric sequence are $a_3 = -48$ and $a_6 = 3072$. Find a rule for the nth term.

Solution

STEP 1 **Write** a system of equations using $a_n = a_1r^{n-1}$ and substituting 3 for n (Equation 1) and then 6 for n (Equation 2).

$a_3 = a_1r^{3-1} \longrightarrow -48 = a_1r^2$ Equation 1

$a_6 = a_1r^{6-1} \longrightarrow 3072 = a_1r^5$ Equation 2

STEP 2 **Solve** the system.

$\frac{-48}{r^2} = a_1$ Solve Equation 1 for a_1.

$3072 = \frac{-48}{r^2}(r^5)$ Substitute for a_1 in Equation 2.

$3072 = -48r^3$ Simplify.

$-4 = r$ Solve for r.

$-48 = a_1(-4)^2$ Substitute for r in Equation 1.

$-3 = a_1$ Solve for a_1.

STEP 3 **Find** a rule for a_n.

$a_n = a_1r^{n-1}$ Write general rule.

$a_n = -3(-4)^{n-1}$ Substitute for a_1 and r.

✓ GUIDED PRACTICE for Examples 2, 3, and 4

Write a rule for the nth term of the geometric sequence. Then find a_8.

4. 3, 15, 75, 375, . . . $a_n = 3(5)^{n-1}$; 234,375

5. $a_6 = -96$, $r = 2$ $a_n = -3(2)^{n-1}$; -384

6. $a_2 = -12$, $a_4 = -3$ $a_n = -24\left(\frac{1}{2}\right)^{n-1}$; -0.1875

GEOMETRIC SERIES The expression formed by adding the terms of a geometric sequence is called a **geometric series**. The sum of the first n terms of a geometric series is denoted by S_n. You can develop a rule for S_n as follows.

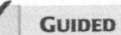

$$\begin{aligned} S_n &= a_1 + a_1r + a_1r^2 + a_1r^3 + \cdots + a_1r^{n-1} \\ -rS_n &= \quad - a_1r - a_1r^2 - a_1r^3 - \cdots - a_1r^{n-1} - a_1r^n \\ \hline S_n(1 - r) &= a_1 + 0 + 0 + 0 + \cdots + 0 - a_1r^n \end{aligned}$$

So, $S_n(1 - r) = a_1(1 - r^n)$. If $r \neq 1$, you can divide each side of this equation by $1 - r$ to obtain the following rule for S_n.

KEY CONCEPT *For Your Notebook*

The Sum of a Finite Geometric Series

The sum of the first n terms of a geometric series with common ratio $r \neq 1$ is:

$$S_n = a_1\left(\frac{1 - r^n}{1 - r}\right)$$

EXAMPLE 5 Find the sum of a geometric series

Find the sum of the geometric series $\sum_{i=1}^{16} 4(3)^{i-1}$.

$a_1 = 4(3)^{1-1} = 4$ **Identify first term.**

$r = 3$ **Identify common ratio.**

$S_{16} = a_1\left(\frac{1 - r^{16}}{1 - r}\right)$ **Write rule for S_{16}.**

$= 4\left(\frac{1 - 3^{16}}{1 - 3}\right)$ **Substitute 4 for a_1 and 3 for r.**

$= 86{,}093{,}440$ **Simplify.**

▶ The sum of the series is 86,093,440.

EXAMPLE 6 Use a geometric sequence and series in real life

MOVIE REVENUE In 1990, the total box office revenue at U.S. movie theaters was about \$5.02 billion. From 1990 through 2003, the total box office revenue increased by about 5.9% per year.

a. Write a rule for the total box office revenue a_n (in billions of dollars) in terms of the year. Let $n = 1$ represent 1990.

b. What was the total box office revenue at U.S. movie theaters for the entire period 1990–2003?

Solution

a. Because the total box office revenue increased by the same percent each year, the total revenues from year to year form a geometric sequence. Use $a_1 = 5.02$ and $r = 1 + 0.059 = 1.059$ to write a rule for the sequence.

$a_n = 5.02(1.059)^{n-1}$ **Write a rule for a_n.**

b. There are 14 years in the period 1990–2003, so find S_{14}.

$$S_{14} = a_1\left(\frac{1 - r^{14}}{1 - r}\right) = 5.02\left(\frac{1 - (1.059)^{14}}{1 - 1.059}\right) \approx 105$$

▶ The total movie box office revenue for the period 1990–2003 was about \$105 billion.

 **GUIDED PRACTICE** for Examples 5 and 6

7. Find the sum of the geometric series $\sum_{i=1}^{8} 6(-2)^{i-1}$. **−510**

8. **MOVIE REVENUE** Use the rule in part (a) of Example 6 to estimate the total box office revenue at U.S. movie theaters in 2000. **about \$8.91 billion**

Extra Example 5

Find the sum of the geometric series $\sum_{i=1}^{6} 4\left(\frac{3}{2}\right)^{i-1}$. **$\frac{665}{8}$**

Key Question to Ask for Example 5

- How many terms are in the series? **16**

Extra Example 6

In 1999 about 586 thousand used cars were sold in Maryland. From 1999 through 2004, the number of used cars sold increased by about 3.8% per year.

a. Write a rule for the total number of used cars sold a_n (in thousands) in terms of the year. Let $n = 1$ represent 1999. **$a_n = 586(1.038)^{n-1}$**

b. What was the total number of used cars sold in Maryland from 1999 to 2004? **about 3,867,000 cars**

Key Question to Ask for Example 6

- Why is $r = 1.059$ and not 0.059? **Each year's revenue is 105.9% of the previous year's revenue.**

Closing the Lesson

Have students summarize the major points of the lesson and answer the Essential Question: How can you find the sum of the terms of a geometric series?

- **In a geometric sequence, the ratio of any term to the previous term is constant. That ratio is called the common ratio.**
- **The nth term of a geometric sequence is given by $a_n = a_1r^{n-1}$, where a_1 is the first term and r is the common ratio.**

The sum S_n of the first n terms of a geometric series with common ratio r ($r \neq 1$) is $S_n = a_1\left(\frac{1 - r^n}{1 - r}\right)$.

Differentiated Instruction

Auditory Learners Have students read **Example 6** aloud. They should write a list of key words, phrases, and/or numbers—for instance, "1990 *through* 2003"—that will help them determine how to solve the problem. Have them keep the list in their notebooks to expand and use throughout the chapter. See also the *Algebra 2 Toolkit* for more strategies.

12.3 EXERCISES

HOMEWORK KEY

○ = **WORKED-OUT SOLUTIONS** on p. WS21 for Exs. 19, 49, and 59

★ = **STANDARDIZED TEST PRACTICE** Exs. 2, 27, 54, 55, and 59

◆ = **MULTIPLE REPRESENTATIONS** Ex. 61

4 PRACTICE AND APPLY

Assignment Guide

Answer Transparencies available for all exercises

Basic:
Day 1: pp. 814–817
Exs. 1–8, 15–20, 27–32, 37, 38
Day 2: pp. 814–817
Exs. 39–44, 48–50, 57–60, 63–64

Average:
Day 1: pp. 814–817
Exs. 1, 2, 6–11, 18–23, 27, 31–35, 37, 38
Day 2: pp. 814–817
Exs. 42–47, 51–54, 57–61, 63–64

Advanced:
Day 1: pp. 814–817
Exs. 1, 2, 9–14, 21–27, 31–36
Day 2: pp. 814–817
Exs. 45–47, 51–62*, 63

Block:
pp. 814–817
Exs. 1, 2, 6–11, 18–23, 27, 31–35, 37, 38, 42–47, 51–54, 57–61, 63–64

Differentiated Instruction

See *Algebra 2 Best Practices Toolkit* for suggestions on addressing the needs of a diverse classroom.

Homework Check

For a quick check of student understanding of key concepts, go over the following exercises:

Basic: 4, 16, 30, 40, 57
Average: 8, 20, 32, 44, 58
Advanced: 24, 34, 46, 52, 59

Extra Practice

- Student Edition, p. 1021
- Chapter 12 Resource Book: Practice levels A, B, C, pp. 29–31

Practice Worksheet

An easily-readable reduced practice page (with answers) for this lesson can be found on p. 792C.

3–14. See Additional Answers beginning on p. AA1.

SKILL PRACTICE

A

1. **VOCABULARY** Copy and complete: The constant ratio of consecutive terms in a geometric sequence is called the ___?___. common ratio

2. ★ **WRITING** How can you determine whether a sequence is geometric? When you divide consecutive terms you have the same ratio.

EXAMPLE 1 on p. 810 for Exs. 3–14

IDENTIFYING GEOMETRIC SEQUENCES **Tell whether the sequence is geometric. *Explain* why or why not.** 3–14. See margin.

3. $1, 4, 8, 16, 32, \ldots$
4. $4, 16, 64, 256, 1024, \ldots$
5. $216, 36, 6, 1, \frac{1}{6}, \ldots$
6. $\frac{1}{3}, \frac{2}{3}, \frac{4}{3}, \frac{8}{3}, \frac{16}{3}, \ldots$
7. $\frac{1}{2}, 1, \frac{3}{2}, 2, \frac{5}{2}, \ldots$
8. $-\frac{1}{4}, \frac{3}{8}, -\frac{3}{16}, \frac{1}{32}, -\frac{3}{64}, \ldots$
9. $10, 5, 2.5, 1.25, 0.625, \ldots$
10. $-3, -6, 12, 24, -48, \ldots$
11. $-4, 12, -36, 108, -324, ..$
12. $0.2, 0.6, 1.8, 5.4, 16.2, \ldots$
13. $-5, 10, 20, 40, 80, \ldots$
14. $0.75, 1.5, 2.25, 3, 3.75, \ldots$

EXAMPLE 2 on p. 811 for Exs. 15–27

WRITING RULES **Write a rule for the *n*th term of the geometric sequence. Then find a_7.**

15. $1, -4, 16, -64, \ldots$ $a_n = (-4)^{n-1}$; 4096
16. $6, 18, 54, 162, \ldots$ $a_n = 6(3)^{n-1}$; 4374
17. $4, 24, 144, 864, \ldots$ $a_n = 4(6)^{n-1}$; 186,624
18. $7, -35, 175, -875, \ldots$ $a_n = 7(-5)^{n-1}$; 109,375
19. $2, \frac{3}{2}, \frac{9}{8}, \frac{27}{32}, \ldots$ $a_n = 2\left(\frac{3}{4}\right)^{n-1}$; $\frac{729}{2048}$
20. $3, -\frac{6}{5}, \frac{12}{25}, -\frac{24}{125}, \ldots$
21. $4, 2, 1, 0.5, \ldots$
22. $-0.3, 0.6, -1.2, 2.4, \ldots$ $a_n = -0.3(-2)^{n-1}$; -19.2
23. $-2, -0.8, -0.32, -0.128, \ldots$ $a_n = -2(0.4)^{n-1}$; -0.008192
24. $7, -4.2, 2.52, -1.512, \ldots$ $a_n = 7(-0.6)^{n-1}$; 0.326592
25. $5, -14, 39.2, -109.76, \ldots$ $a_n = 5(-2.8)^{n-1}$; 2409.45152
26. $120, 180, 270, 405, \ldots$ $a_n = 120(1.5)^{n-1}$; 1366.875

20. $3\left(-\frac{2}{5}\right)^{n-1}$; $\frac{192}{15{,}625}$

21. $4\left(\frac{1}{2}\right)^{n-1}$; $\frac{1}{16}$

27. ★ **MULTIPLE CHOICE** What is a rule for the *n*th term of the geometric sequence $5, 20, 80, 320, \ldots$? B

Ⓐ $a_n = 5(2)^{n-1}$ Ⓑ $a_n = 5(4)^{n-1}$

Ⓒ $a_n = 5(-4)^{n-1}$ Ⓓ $a_n = 5(-2)^{n-1}$

EXAMPLE 3 on p. 811 for Exs. 28–38

WRITING RULES **Write a rule for the *n*th term of the geometric sequence. Then graph the first six terms of the sequence.** 28–36. See margin for art.

28. $a_1 = 5, r = 3$ $a_n = 5(3)^{n-1}$
29. $a_1 = -2, r = 6$ $a_n = -2(6)^{n-1}$
30. $a_2 = 6, r = 2$ $a_n = 3(2)^{n-}$
31. $a_2 = 15, r = \frac{1}{2}$ $a_n = 30\left(\frac{1}{2}\right)^{n-1}$
32. $a_5 = 1, r = \frac{1}{8}$ $a_n = 4096\left(\frac{1}{8}\right)^{n-1}$
33. $a_4 = -12, r = -\frac{1}{4}$ $a_n = 768\left(-\frac{1}{4}\right)^{n-1}$
34. $a_3 = 75, r = 5$ $a_n = 3(5)^{n-1}$
35. $a_2 = 8, r = 4$ $a_n = 2(4)^{n-1}$
36. $a_4 = 500, r = 5$ $a_n = 4(5)^{n-1}$

ERROR ANALYSIS ***Describe*** **and correct the error in writing the rule for the *n*th term of the geometric sequence for which $a_1 = 3$ and $r = 2$.**

37. $a_n = a_1 r^n$
$a_n = 3(2)^n$
The exponent should be $n - 1$ instead of n; $a_n = 3(2)^{n-1}$.

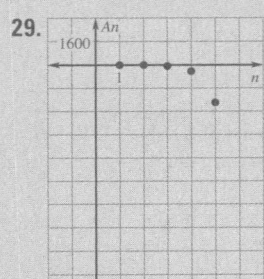

38. $a_n = r a_1^{\,n-1}$
$a_n = 2(3)^{n-1}$
r and a_1 are switched arou in the formula; $a_n = a_1 r^{n-1}$, $a_n = 3(2)^{n-1}$.

28.
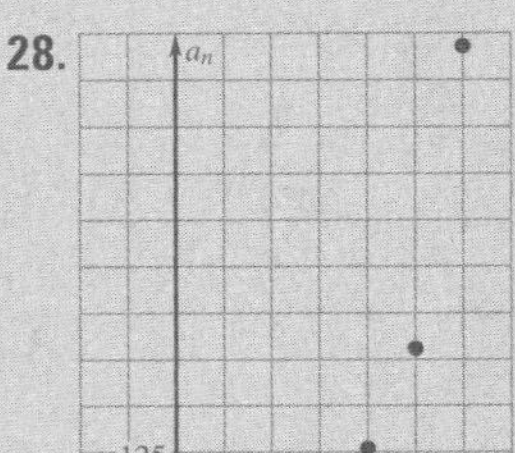

29.
A_n
1600
1
n

30.
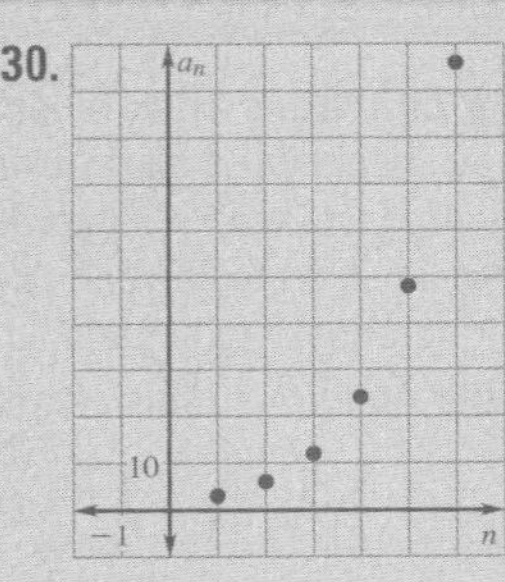

EXAMPLE 4 B
p. 812
Exs. 39–47

WRITING RULES **Write a rule for the nth term of the geometric sequence that has the two given terms.**

39. $a_1 = 3, a_3 = 12$

40. $a_1 = 1, a_5 = 625$

41. $a_1 = -\frac{1}{4}, a_4 = -16$ $a_n = \left(-\frac{1}{4}\right)(4)^{n-1}$

42. $a_3 = 10, a_6 = 270$ $a_n = \left(\frac{10}{9}\right)(3)^{n-1}$

43. $a_2 = -40, a_4 = -10$

44. $a_2 = -24, a_5 = 1536$ $a_n = 6(-4)^{n-1}$

45. $a_4 = 162, a_7 = 4374$

46. $a_3 = \frac{7}{4}, a_5 = \frac{7}{16}$

47. $a_4 = 6, a_7 = \frac{243}{8}$ $a_n = \frac{32}{27}\left(\frac{3\sqrt[3]{12}}{4}\right)^{n-1}$

$= 3(2)^{n-1}$ or $= 3(-2)^{n-1}$

$= 1(5)^{n-1}$ or $= 1(-5)^{n-1}$

$= -80\left(\frac{1}{2}\right)^{n-1}$ C

$a_n = \ldots\left(-\frac{1}{2}\right)^{n-1}$

$= 7\left(\frac{1}{2}\right)^{n-1}$

$a_n = 7\left(-\frac{1}{2}\right)^{n-1}$

EXAMPLE 5
p. 813
Exs. 48–54

FINDING SUMS **Find the sum of the geometric series.**

48. $\sum_{i=1}^{10} 5(2)^{i-1}$ 5115

49. $\sum_{i=1}^{8} 6(4)^{i-1}$ 131,070

50. $\sum_{i=0}^{7} 12\left(-\frac{1}{2}\right)^{i}$ $\frac{255}{32}$

51. $\sum_{i=1}^{6} 4\left(\frac{1}{4}\right)^{i-1}$ $\frac{1365}{256}$

52. $\sum_{i=1}^{12} 8\left(\frac{3}{2}\right)^{i-1}$ $\frac{527{,}345}{256}$

53. $\sum_{i=0}^{10} (-4)^{i}$ 838,861

54. ★ **MULTIPLE CHOICE** What is the sum of the geometric series $\sum_{i=1}^{9} 2(3)^{i-1}$? C

Ⓐ 19,680 Ⓑ 19,681 Ⓒ 19,682 Ⓓ 19,683

55. ★ **OPEN-ENDED MATH** Write a geometric series with 5 terms such that the sum of the series is 100. (*Hint:* Choose a value of r and then find a_1.) *Sample answer:* $\frac{100}{31}, \frac{200}{31}, \frac{400}{31}, \frac{800}{31}, \frac{1600}{31}$

56. **CHALLENGE** Using the rule for the sum of a finite geometric series, write each polynomial as a rational expression.

a. $1 + x + x^2 + x^3 + x^4$ $S_5 = \left(\frac{1 - x^5}{1 - x}\right)$

b. $3x + 6x^3 + 12x^5 + 24x^7$ $S_4 = 3x\left(\frac{1 - 16x^8}{1 - 2x^2}\right)$

PROBLEM SOLVING

EXAMPLE 6 A
p. 813
Exs. 57–59

57. **SKYDIVING** In a skydiving formation with R rings, each ring after the first has twice as many skydivers as the preceding ring. The formation for $R = 2$ is shown.

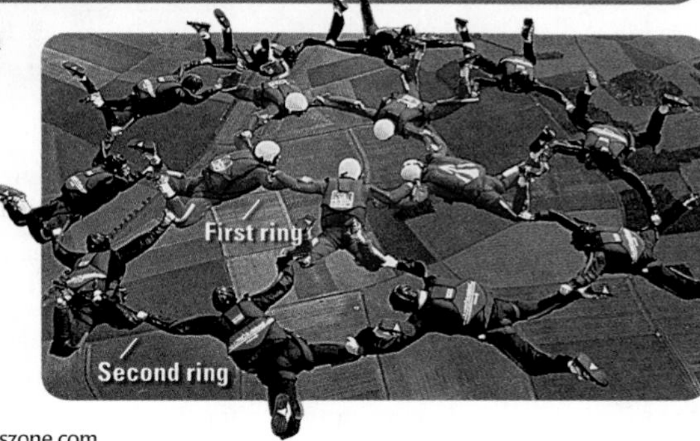

a. Let a_n be the number of skydivers in the nth ring. Find a rule for a_n. $a_n = 5(2)^{n-1}$

b. Find the total number of skydivers if there are $R = 4$ rings. 75 skydivers

@HomeTutor for problem solving help at classzone.com

58. **SOCCER** A regional soccer tournament has 64 participating teams. In the first round of the tournament, 32 games are played. In each successive round, the number of games played decreases by one half.

a. Find a rule for the number of games played in the nth round. For what values of n does your rule make sense? $a_n = 32\left(\frac{1}{2}\right)^{n-1}$; $1 \le n \le 6$

b. Find the total number of games played in the regional soccer tournament. 63 games

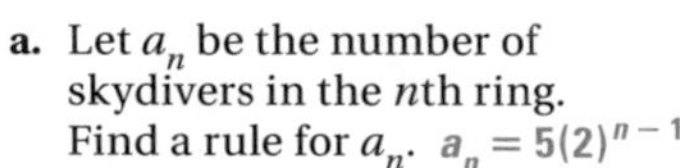

@HomeTutor for problem solving help at classzone.com

Study Strategy

Exercise 39 Another way to find r is to use the proportion $\frac{a_3}{a_2} = \frac{a_2}{a_1}$. Then $a_1a_3 = (a_2)^2$, so $(a_2)^2 = 36$ and $a_2 = \pm 6$. That means $r = 2$ or $r = -2$. This method of finding r can be used any time you are given a_n and a_{n+2}. The general formula is $\frac{a_{n+2}}{a_{n+1}} = \frac{a_{n+1}}{a_n}$.

Avoiding Common Errors

Exercises 48–53 Some students mistakenly write the right hand side of the sum formula as $a_1\frac{(1-r)^n}{(1-r)}$.

Suggest that students write the formula and check it before substituting values for a_1 and r.

34.

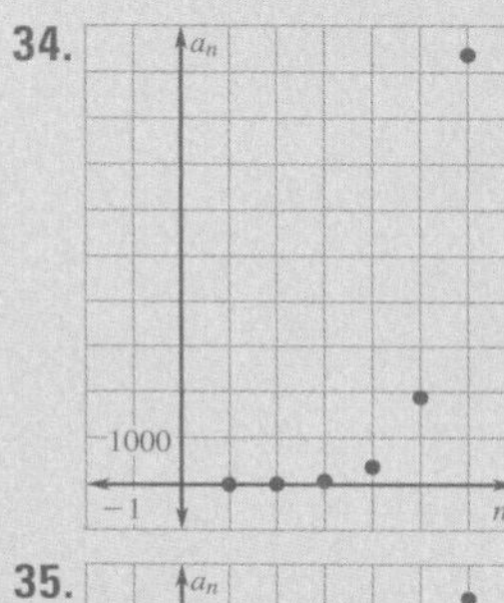

35.

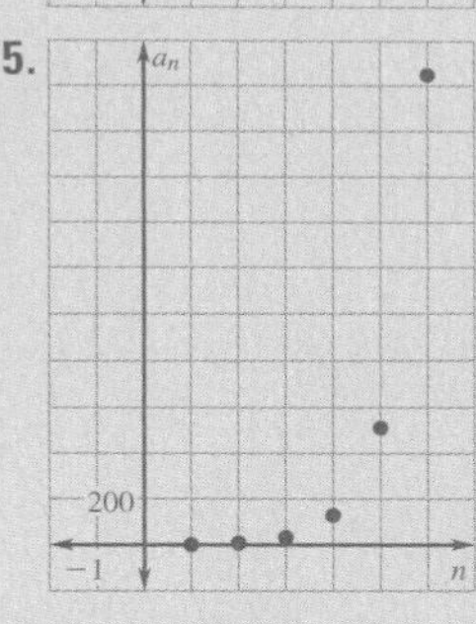

36.

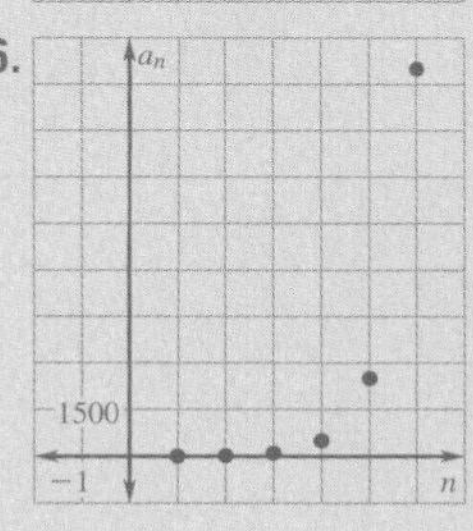

31.

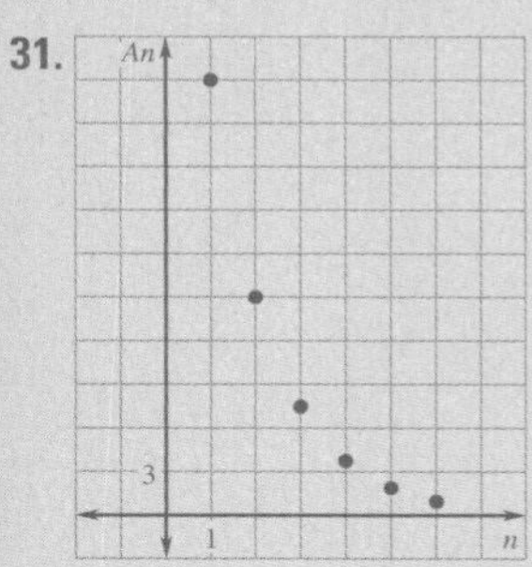

32.

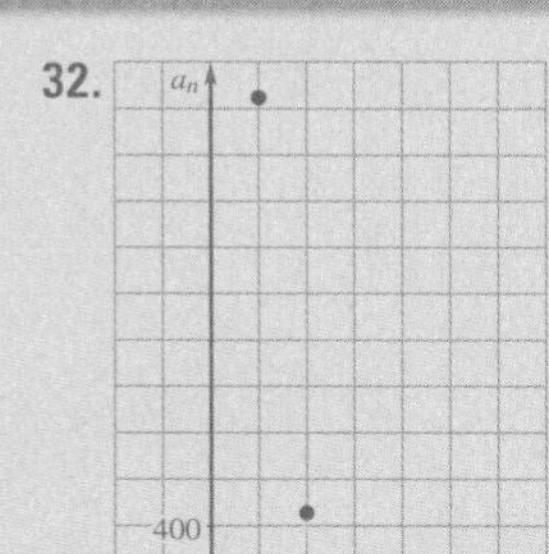

33.

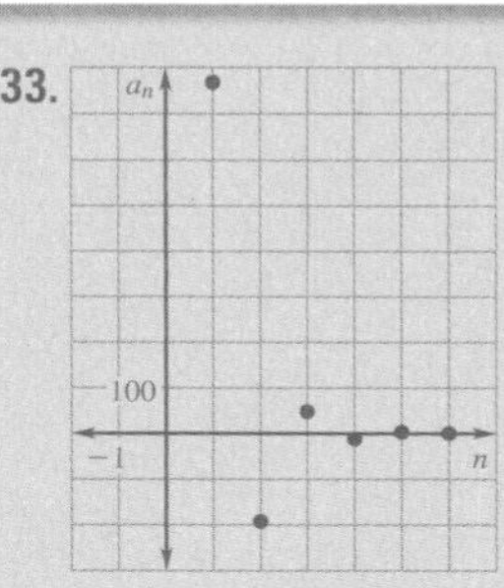

Vocabulary

Exercise 59 The search is called a *binary* search because at each stage, the set of data is divided into two parts.

61b.

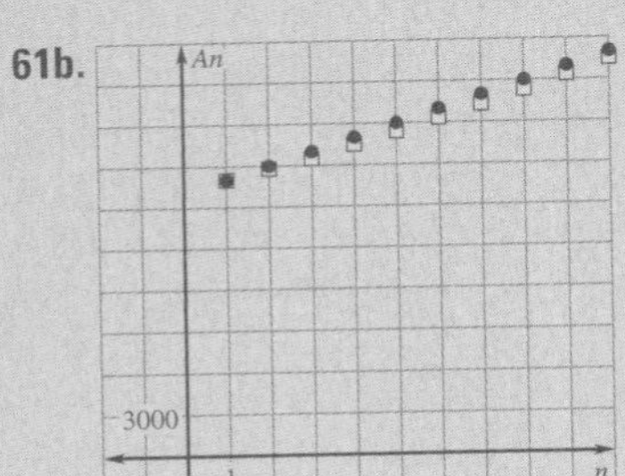

59. ★ **SHORT RESPONSE** A *binary search* technique used on a computer involves jumping to the middle of an ordered list of data (such as an alphabetical list of names) and deciding whether the item being searched for is there. If not, the computer decides whether the item comes before or after the middle. Half of the list is ignored on the next pass, and the computer jumps to the middle of the remaining list. This is repeated until the item is found.

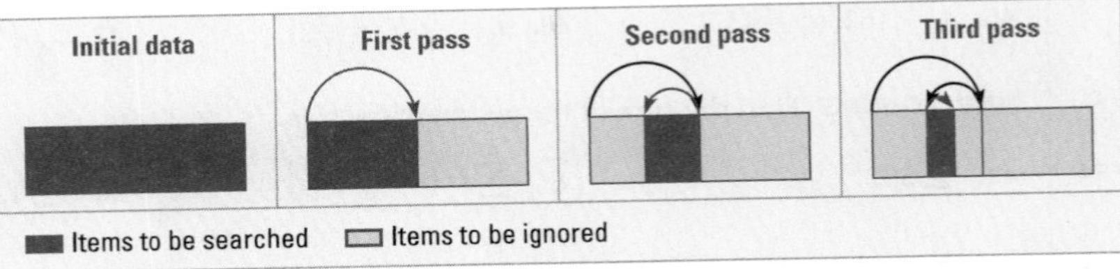

a. Find a rule for the number of items remaining after the nth pass through an ordered list of 1024 items. $a_n = 1024\left(\frac{1}{2}\right)^{n-1}$

b. In the worst case, the item to be found is the only one left in the list after n passes through the list. What is the worst-case value of n for a binary search of a list with 1024 items? *Explain.* 11. *Sample answer:* On the 11th pass, there is only 1 term to choose from so it must be the answer.

B

60. **FRACTALS** The *Sierpinski carpet* is a fractal created using squares. The process involves removing smaller squares from larger squares. First, divide a large square into nine congruent squares. Remove the center square. Repeat these steps for each smaller square, as shown below. Assume that each side of the initial square is one unit long.

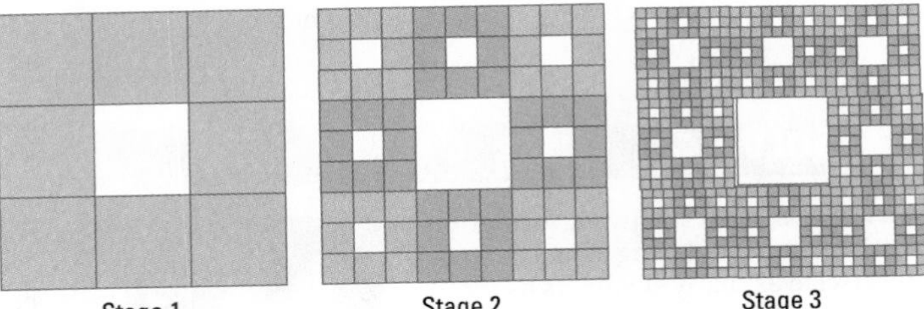

Stage 1 Stage 2 Stage 3

a. Let a_n be the number of squares removed at the nth stage. Find a rule for a_n. Then find the total number of squares removed through stage 8. $a_n = (8)^{n-1}$; 2,396,745 squares

b. Let b_n be the remaining area of the original square after the nth stage. Find a rule for b_n. Then find the remaining area of the original square after stage 12. $a_n = \frac{8}{9}\left(\frac{8}{9}\right)^{n-1}$; about 0.2433

61a. $a_n = 19{,}000 + 1000n$, arithmetic; $b_n = 20{,}000(1.04)^{n-1}$, geometric

61.  **MULTIPLE REPRESENTATIONS** Two companies, company A and company B, offer the same starting salary of $20,000 per year. Company A gives a raise of $1000 each year. Company B gives a raise of 4% each year.

a. **Writing Rules** Write rules giving the salaries a_n and b_n in the nth year at companies A and B, respectively. Tell whether the sequence represented by each rule is *arithmetic, geometric,* or *neither.*

b. **Drawing Graphs** Graph each sequence in the same coordinate plane. See margin.

c. **Finding Sums** For each company, find the sum of wages earned during the first 20 years of employment. Company A: $590,000; Company B: about $595,562

d. **Using Technology** Use a graphing calculator or spreadsheet to find after how many years the total amount earned at company B is greater than the total amount earned at company A. 19 yr

○ = WORKED-OUT SOLUTIONS on p. WS1 ★ = STANDARDIZED TEST PRACTICE ◆ = MULTIPLE REPRESENTATIONS

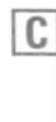

C **62. CHALLENGE** On January 1 of each year, you deposit \$2000 in an individual retirement account (IRA) that pays 5% annual interest. You make a total of 30 deposits. How much money do you have in your IRA immediately after you make your last deposit? **\$139,521.58**

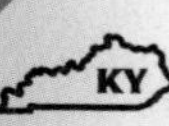

KY KENTUCKY MIXED REVIEW

TEST PRACTICE at classzone.com

63. The total cost of carnival tickets for 3 adults and 5 children is \$49. The total cost of carnival tickets for 5 adults and 3 children is \$55. What is the price, a, of one adult ticket and the price, c, of one child ticket? **C**

Ⓐ $a = \$5; c = \$8$ Ⓑ $a = \$7.25; c = \$6.25$

Ⓒ $a = \$8; c = \$5$ Ⓓ $a = \$10; c = \$3.80$

64. What is the relationship between the graphs of $y = 3x^2$ and $y = 1.5x^2$? **D**

Ⓐ The graph of $y = 1.5x^2$ is a reflection of the graph of $y = 3x^2$ in the x-axis.

Ⓑ The graph of $y = 1.5x^2$ is a 90° rotation of the graph of $y = 3x^2$ about the origin.

Ⓒ The graph of $y = 1.5x^2$ is narrower than the graph of $y = 3x^2$.

Ⓓ The graph of $y = 1.5x^2$ is wider than the graph of $y = 3x^2$.

QUIZ for Lessons 12.1–12.3

Write the next term in the sequence. Then write a rule for the nth term. *(p. 794)*

1. 1, 3, 5, 7, . . . **9; $a_n = -1 + 2n$**
2. −5, 10, −15, 20, . . . **−25; $a_n = (-1)^n(5n)$**
3. $\frac{1}{20}, \frac{2}{30}, \frac{3}{40}, \frac{4}{50}, \ldots$ **$\frac{5}{60}$; $a_n = \frac{n}{10(n+1)}$**
4. 4, 16, 64, 256, . . . **1024; $a_n = 4^n$**
5. 2, 6, 12, 20, . . . **30; $a_n = n(n + 1)$**
6. 9, 36, 81, 144, . . . **36; $a_n = n^2 + 4n - 9$**

Find the sum of the series. *(p. 794)*

7. $\sum_{i=1}^{4} 2i^3$ **200**
8. $\sum_{k=1}^{5} (k^2 + 3)$ **70**
9. $\sum_{n=2}^{6} \frac{1}{n-1}$ **$\frac{137}{60}$**

Write a rule for the nth term a_n of the arithmetic or geometric sequence. Find a_{15}, then find the sum of the first 15 terms of the sequence.

10. 1, 7, 13, 19, . . . *(p. 802)* **$a_n = -5 + 6n$; 85, 645**
11. $\frac{1}{2}, 2, \frac{7}{2}, 5, \ldots$ *(p. 802)* **$a_n = -1 + \frac{3}{2}n$; $\frac{43}{2}$, 165**
12. 5, 2, −1, −4, −7, . . . *(p. 802)* **$a_n = 8 - 3n$; −37, −240**
13. 2, 8, 32, 128, . . . *(p. 810)* **$a_n = 2(4)^{n-1}$; ...,870,912; ...,827,882**
14. $2, \frac{4}{3}, \frac{8}{9}, \frac{16}{27}, \ldots$ *(p. 810)* **$a_n = \ldots)^{n-1}$; ...,768 / ...2,969, about 5.99**
15. −3, 15, −75, 375, . . . *(p. 810)* **$a_n = \ldots(-5)^{n-1}$; ...8,310,546,875, ...5,258,789,063**

16. **COLLEGE TUITION** In 1995, the average tuition at a public college in the United States was \$2057. From 1995 through 2002, the average tuition at public colleges increased by about 6% per year. Write a rule for the average tuition a_n in terms of the year. Let $n = 1$ represent 1995. What was the average tuition at a public college in 2002? *(p. 810)* **$a_n = 2057(1.06)^{n-1}$**

5 ASSESS AND RETEACH

Daily Homework Quiz

Transparency Available

1. Tell whether the sequence 5, 10, 20, 40, . . . is geometric. If so, write a rule for the nth term of the sequence and find a_6. **Yes; $a_n = 5(2)^{n-1}$; $a_6 = 160$**
2. One term of a geometric sequence is $a_5 = 48$. The common ratio is $r = 2$. Write a rule for the nth term. **$a_n = 3(2)^{n-1}$**
3. Two terms of a geometric sequence are $a_2 = -2000$ and $a_5 = 16{,}000{,}000$. Find a rule for the nth term. **$a_n = 100(-20)^{n-1}$**
4. Find the sum of the geometric series $\sum_{i=1}^{5} 5(3)^{i-1}$. **605**

Online Quiz

Available at **classzone.com**

Diagnosis/Remediation

- Practice A, B, C in Chapter 12 Resource Book, pp. 29–31
- Study Guide in Chapter 12 Resource Book, pp. 32–33
- Practice Workbook, pp. 175–176
- @HomeTutor

Challenge

Additional challenge is available in the Chapter 12 Resource Book, p. 37.

Quiz

An easily-readable reduced copy of the quiz (with answers) on Lessons 12.1–12.3 from the Assessment Book can be found on p. 792E.

Kentucky Mixed Review

1. C
2. C
3. B
4. C
5. a. 105 pieces of chalk
   b. the total is the sum $15 + 14 + \ldots + 6$. There are 10 terms, so the sum is $\frac{1}{2}n(n+1) = \frac{1}{2}(10)(15+6) = 105$.
6. a. geometric; there is a constant ratio of $\frac{1}{2}$ between terms
   b. $a_n = 66(0.5)^{n-1}$
   c. 14 hours

Kentucky *Mixed Review*

Lessons 12.1–12.3

1. **TARGETS** The rings of a target alternate between dark and light. The three innermost rings of the target are shown below. Which expression is a series that gives the total area of the innermost *light* rings of target n?

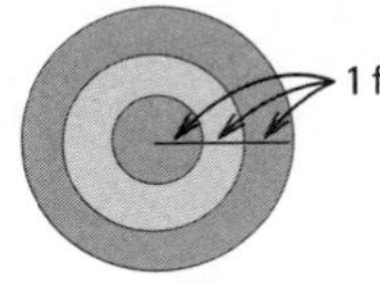

The 3 innermost rings of the target

A. $\sum_{i=1}^{n}(2i-1)\pi$

B. $\sum_{i=1}^{n}(4i-3)\pi$

C. $\sum_{i=1}^{n}(4i-1)\pi$

D. $\sum_{i=1}^{n}i^2\pi$

2. **SALARY** Maria has an annual salary of $45,000 during her first year of employment. Her salary increases 3.5% per year. What will Maria's salary be during her 5th year of employment?

A. $49,672
B. $51,241
C. $51,639
D. $53,446

3. **CONSTRUCTION** A staircase is being built that leads from the ground to an elevated deck. The base of the staircase is a concrete slab that is 2 inches tall. Each stair is 7 inches tall. What is the height of the bottom of the 10th stair?

A. 60 inches
B. 65 inches
C. 70 inches
D. 72 inches

4. **SEATING ARRANGEMENT** At a restaurant, rectangular tables are placed together along their shared edges, as shown in the diagram below. How many people can be seated around 8 tables arranged in this way?

A. 30 people B. 32 people
C. 34 people D. 36 people

5. **OPEN-RESPONSE** Pieces of chalk are stacked in a pile. Part of the pile is shown below.

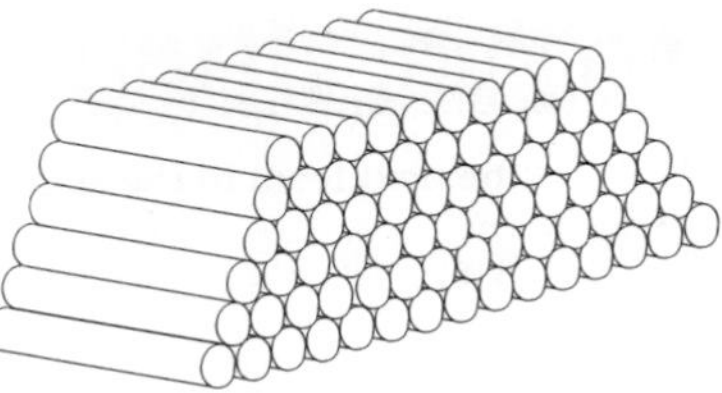

a. The bottom row has 15 pieces of chalk and the top row has 6 pieces of chalk. Each row has one less piece of chalk than the row below it. How many pieces of chalk are in the pile?

b. Justify your answer.

6. **OPEN-RESPONSE** A scientist is studying the radioactive decay of Platinum-197. The scientist starts with a 66 gram sample of Platinum-197 and measures the amount remaining every two hours. The recorded amounts (in grams) are 66, 33, 16.5, 8.25, . . .

a. Is this sequence *arithmetic*, *geometric*, or *neither*? *Explain* how you know.

b. Write a rule for the nth term of the sequence.

c. After how many hours will the sample have a mass of less than 1 gram?

12.4 Investigating an Infinite Geometric Series

MATERIALS • scissors • paper

QUESTION What is the sum of an infinite geometric series?

You can illustrate an infinite geometric series by cutting a piece of paper into smaller and smaller pieces.

EXPLORE Model an infinite geometric series

Start with a rectangular piece of paper. Define its area to be 1 square unit.

STEP 1 *Cut paper in half*

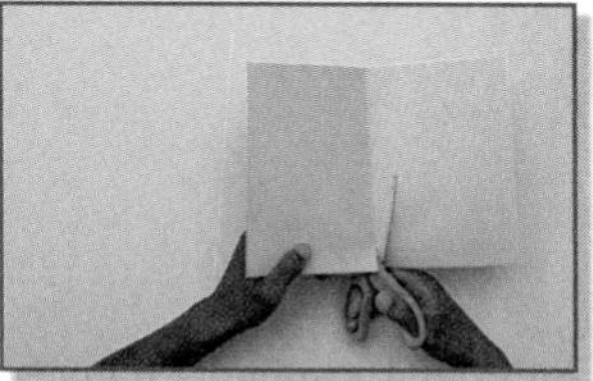

Fold the paper in half and cut along the fold. Place one half on a desktop and hold the remaining half.

STEP 2 *Cut paper again*

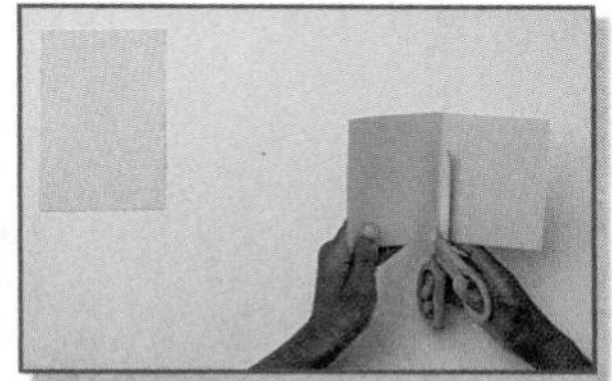

Fold the piece of paper you are holding in half and cut along the fold. Place one half on the desktop and hold the remaining half.

STEP 3 *Repeat steps*

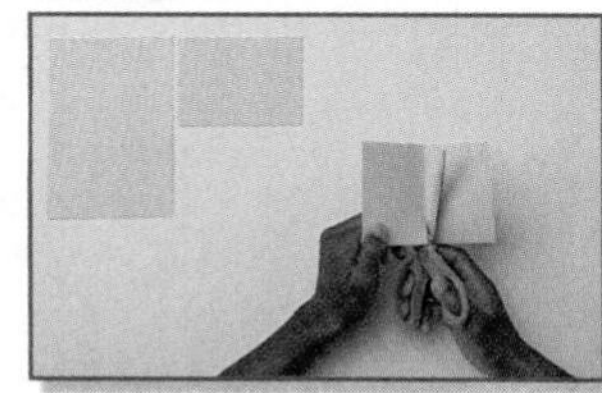

Repeat Steps 1 and 2 until you find it too difficult to fold and cut the piece of paper you are holding.

STEP 4 *Find areas* The first piece of paper on the desktop has an area of $\frac{1}{2}$ square unit. The second piece has an area of $\frac{1}{4}$ square unit. Write the areas of the next three pieces of paper. Explain why these areas form a geometric sequence. $\frac{1}{8}, \frac{1}{16}, \frac{1}{32}$; there is a common ratio of $\frac{1}{2}$

STEP 5 *Make a table* Copy and complete the table by recording the number of pieces of paper on the desktop and the combined area of the pieces at each step. See margin.

Number of pieces	1	2	3	4	. . .
Combined area	$\frac{1}{2}$	$\frac{1}{2}+\frac{1}{4}=?$	?	?	. . .

DRAW CONCLUSIONS Use your observations to complete these exercises

1. Based on your table, what number does the combined area of the pieces of paper appear to be approaching? 1

2. Using the formula for the sum of a finite geometric series, write and simplify a rule for the combined area A_n of the pieces of paper after n cuts. What happens to A_n as $n \to \infty$? *Justify* your answer mathematically.

   $A_n = 1 - \left(\frac{1}{2}\right)^n$; A_n gets closer to 1; $n = 7 \to 0.9921875$, $n = 10 \to 0.9990234375$, $n = 100 \to 1$.

Step 5.

Number of pieces	1	2	3	4	5	6	7
Combined area	$\frac{1}{2}$	$\frac{3}{4}$	$\frac{7}{8}$	$\frac{15}{16}$	$\frac{31}{32}$	$\frac{63}{64}$	$\frac{127}{128}$

1 PLAN AND PREPARE

Explore the Concept

- Students will use paper cutting to investigate the sum of an infinite geometric series.
- This activity leads into the study of using partial sums to find the limiting value of an infinite geometric series in Lesson 12.4, Example 1.

Materials

Each student will need:
- paper
- scissors

Recommended Time

Work activity: 10 min
Discuss results: 5 min

Grouping

Students should work individually.

2 TEACH

Tips for Success

Below Level students may need a review of adding fractions with unlike denominators prior to completing Step 5.

Key Questions

- What is the common ratio of the series? $\frac{1}{2}$
- Why does this activity model an infinite series? Theoretically, the paper can be folded and cut an unlimited number of times.

Key Discovery

If the terms of a geometric series have a common ratio that is less than 1, then the partial sum of the series appears to approach a limit.

3 ASSESS AND RETEACH

If the terms of a geometric series have a common ratio greater than 1, do you think the partial sums will approach a limit? Explain. No; the terms become greater and greater, so the partial sums cannot be approaching a limit.

12.4 Find Sums of Infinite Geometric Series

MA-HS-1.3.4

Before You found the sums of finite geometric series.

Now You will find the sums of infinite geometric series.

Why? So you can analyze a fractal, as in Ex. 42.

1 PLAN AND PREPARE

Warm-Up Exercises

Transparency Available

Find each sum.

1. $100 + 50 + 25$ 175
2. $100 + 50 + 25 + \frac{25}{2}$ 187.5
3. $100 + 50 + 25 + \frac{25}{2} + \frac{25}{4}$ 193.75
4. $100 + 50 + 25 + \frac{25}{2} + \frac{25}{4} + \frac{25}{8}$ 196.875

Notetaking Guide

Transparency Available

Promotes interactive learning and notetaking skills, pp. 315–317.

Pacing

Basic: 1 day
Average: 1 day
Advanced: 1 day
Block: 0.5 block with 12.5
- See *Teaching Guide/Lesson Plan.*

2 FOCUS AND MOTIVATE

Essential Question

Big Idea 2, p. 793

When does an infinite geometric series have a sum, and when does it not have a sum? **Tell students they will learn how to answer this question by determining the absolute value of the common ratio of the series.**

Key Vocabulary
- **partial sum**

MA-HS-1.3.4
Students will recognize and solve problems that can be modeled using a finite geometric series, such as home mortgage problems and other compound interest problems.

The sum S_n of the first n terms of an infinite series is called a **partial sum**. The partial sums of an infinite geometric series may approach a limiting value.

EXAMPLE 1 Find partial sums

Consider the infinite geometric series $\frac{1}{2} + \frac{1}{4} + \frac{1}{8} + \frac{1}{16} + \frac{1}{32} + \cdots$. Find and graph the partial sums S_n for $n = 1, 2, 3, 4,$ and 5. Then describe what happens to S_n as n increases.

Solution

$S_1 = \frac{1}{2} = 0.5$

$S_2 = \frac{1}{2} + \frac{1}{4} = 0.75$

$S_3 = \frac{1}{2} + \frac{1}{4} + \frac{1}{8} \approx 0.88$

$S_4 = \frac{1}{2} + \frac{1}{4} + \frac{1}{8} + \frac{1}{16} \approx 0.94$

$S_5 = \frac{1}{2} + \frac{1}{4} + \frac{1}{8} + \frac{1}{16} + \frac{1}{32} \approx 0.97$

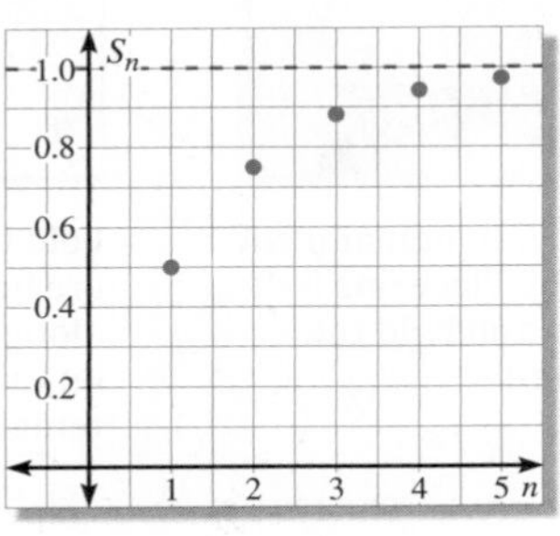

From the graph, S_n appears to approach 1 as n increases.

Animated Algebra at classzone.com

SUMS OF INFINITE SERIES In Example 1, you can understand why S_n approaches 1 as n increases by considering the rule for S_n:

$$S_n = a_1\left(\frac{1 - r^n}{1 - r}\right) = \frac{1}{2}\left(\frac{1 - \left(\frac{1}{2}\right)^n}{1 - \frac{1}{2}}\right) = 1 - \left(\frac{1}{2}\right)^n$$

As n increases, $\left(\frac{1}{2}\right)^n$ approaches 0, so S_n approaches 1. Therefore, 1 is defined to be the sum of the infinite geometric series in Example 1. More generally, as n increases for *any* infinite geometric series with common ratio r between -1 and 1, the value of $S_n = a_1\left(\frac{1 - r^n}{1 - r}\right) \approx a_1\left(\frac{1 - 0}{1 - r}\right) = \frac{a_1}{1 - r}$.

Resource Planning Guide

Chapter Resource Book
- Teaching Guide/Lesson Plan (pp. 38–39)
- Practice levels A, B, C (pp. 40–42)
- Study Guide (pp. 43–44)
- Catch-up for Absent Students (p. 45)
- Application (p. 46)
- Challenge (p. 47)

Workbooks
- Notetaking Guide (pp. 315–317)
- Practice Workbook (pp. 177–178)

Teaching Options
- **Power Presentations CD-ROM** provides dynamic electronic teaching resources for the classroom.
- **Activity Generator CD-ROM** provides editable activities for all ability levels.

Interactive Technology
- Easy Planner
- Power Presentations CD-ROM
- Activity Generator CD-ROM
- Animated Algebra
- Test Generator CD-ROM
- Online Quiz
- eWorkbook
- eEdition
- @HomeTutor

Resources for English Learners
- Quick Reference for English Learners
- Spanish Study Guide
- Multi-Language Visual Glossary
- Student Resources in Spanish

See also the *Algebra 2 Toolkit* for more strategies for meeting individual needs.

KEY CONCEPT *For Your Notebook*

The Sum of an Infinite Geometric Series

The sum of an infinite geometric series with first term a_1 and common ratio r is given by

$$S = \frac{a_1}{1 - r}$$

provided $|r| < 1$. If $|r| \geq 1$, the series has no sum.

EXAMPLE 2 Find sums of infinite geometric series

Find the sum of the infinite geometric series.

a. $\sum_{i=1}^{\infty} 5(0.8)^{i-1}$

b. $1 - \frac{3}{4} + \frac{9}{16} - \frac{27}{64} + \cdots$

Solution

a. For this series, $a_1 = 5$ and $r = 0.8$.

$$S = \frac{a_1}{1 - r} = \frac{5}{1 - 0.8} = 25$$

b. For this series, $a_1 = 1$ and $r = -\frac{3}{4}$.

$$S = \frac{a_1}{1 - r} = \frac{1}{1 - \left(-\frac{3}{4}\right)} = \frac{4}{7}$$

EXAMPLE 3 Standardized Test Practice

What is the sum of the infinite geometric series $1 - 3 + 9 - 27 + \cdots$?

Ⓐ $\frac{1}{4}$ Ⓑ $\frac{4}{3}$ Ⓒ 3   Ⓓ Does not exist

Solution

You know that $a_1 = 1$ and $a_2 = -3$. So, $r = \frac{-3}{1} = -3$.

Because $|-3| \geq 1$, the sum does not exist.

▶ The correct answer is D. Ⓐ Ⓑ Ⓒ Ⓓ

AVOID ERRORS

If you substitute 1 for a_1 and -3 for r in the formula $S = \frac{a_1}{1 - r}$, you get an answer of $S = \frac{1}{4}$ for the sum. However, this answer is not correct because the sum formula does not apply when $|r| \geq 1$.

GUIDED PRACTICE for Examples 1, 2, and 3

1. Consider the series $\frac{2}{5} + \frac{4}{25} + \frac{8}{125} + \frac{16}{625} + \frac{32}{3125} + \cdots$. Find and graph the partial sums S_n for $n = 1, 2, 3, 4,$ and 5. Then describe what happens to S_n as n increases. **$S_1 = \frac{2}{5}$, $S_2 \approx 0.56$, $S_3 \approx 0.62$, $S_4 \approx 0.65$, $S_5 \approx 0.66$, S_n appears to be approaching $\frac{2}{3}$. See margin for art.**

Find the sum of the infinite geometric series, if it exists.

2. $\sum_{n=1}^{\infty} \left(-\frac{1}{2}\right)^{n-1}$ **$\frac{2}{3}$**

3. $\sum_{n=1}^{\infty} 3\left(\frac{5}{4}\right)^{n-1}$ **no sum**

4. $3 + \frac{3}{4} + \frac{3}{16} + \frac{3}{64} + \cdots$ **4**

Motivating the Lesson

Discuss this famous "paradox" with students: "You shoot an arrow toward a target. It travels half the distance to the target, then half the remaining distance, then half the rest, and so on. Since this process can continue indefinitely, the arrow will never reach the target." Tell students that this lesson explores the sum of an infinite geometric series, which will let the students conclude that yes, the arrow *will* reach the target.

3 TEACH

Extra Example 1

Consider the infinite geometric series $2 + \frac{2}{3} + \frac{2}{9} + \frac{2}{27} + \frac{2}{81} + \cdots$. Find and graph the partial sums S_n for $n = 1, 2, 3, 4,$ and 5. Then describe what happens to S_n as n increases.

$S_1 = 2$, $S_2 \approx 2.67$, $S_3 \approx 2.89$, $S_4 \approx 2.96$, $S_5 \approx 2.99$

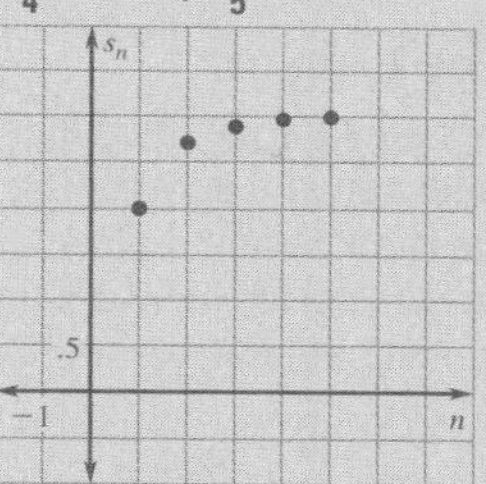

As n increases, S_n appears to approach 3.

An **Animated Algebra** activity is available on-line for **Example 1**. This activity is also available on the **Power Presentations CD-ROM**.

1. See Additional Answers beginning on p. AA1.

Extra Example 2

Find the sum of the infinite geometric series.

a. $\sum_{i=1}^{\infty} 3\left(\frac{1}{4}\right)^{i-1}$ 4

b. $-\frac{1}{2} + \frac{1}{4} - \frac{1}{8} + \frac{1}{16} + \ldots$ $-\frac{1}{3}$

Extra Example 3

What is the sum of the infinite series $1 + \frac{3}{2} + \frac{9}{4} + \frac{27}{8} + \ldots$? D

(A) −2 (B) $-\frac{1}{2}$

(C) 2 (D) Does not exist

Extra Example 4

A rubber ball is dropped from a height of 60 feet. Each bounce takes it to $\frac{2}{3}$ of its previous height. What is the total vertical distance the ball travels? 300 ft

Extra Example 5

Write 5.146146146. . . as a fraction in lowest terms. $\frac{5141}{999}$

Closing the Lesson

Have students summarize the major points of the lesson and answer the Essential Question: When does an infinite geometric series have a sum and when does it not have a sum?

- The sum S_n of the first n terms of an infinite series is called a partial sum. The partial sums of an infinite geometric series may approach a limiting value.
- If the common ratio r of a geometric series is between −1 and 1, then S_n approaches $\frac{a_1}{1-r}$ as n increases.
- You can express a repeating decimal as an infinite geometric series, and you can use the sum of the series to write the decimal as a fraction in lowest terms.

If $|r| < 1$ for an infinite geometric series, the series has the sum $S = \frac{a_1}{1-r}$. If $|r| \geq 1$ for an infinite geometric series, the series has no sum.

EXAMPLE 4 Use an infinite series as a model

PENDULUMS A pendulum that is released to swing freely travels 18 inches on the first swing. On each successive swing, the pendulum travels 80% of the distance of the previous swing. What is the total distance the pendulum swings?

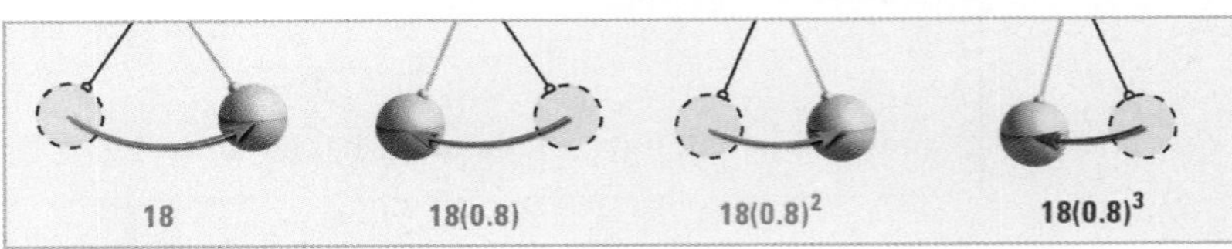

Solution

The total distance traveled by the pendulum is:

$d = 18 + 18(0.8) + 18(0.8)^2 + 18(0.8)^3 + \cdots$

$= \frac{a_1}{1-r}$ Write formula for sum.

$= \frac{18}{1-0.8}$ Substitute 18 for a_1 and 0.8 for r.

$= 90$ Simplify.

▶ The pendulum travels a total distance of 90 inches, or 7.5 feet.

EXAMPLE 5 Write a repeating decimal as a fraction

Write 0.242424. . . as a fraction in lowest terms.

$0.242424\ldots = 24(0.01) + 24(0.01)^2 + 24(0.01)^3 + \cdots$

$= \frac{a_1}{1-r}$ Write formula for sum.

$= \frac{24(0.01)}{1-0.01}$ Substitute 24(0.01) for a_1 and 0.01 for r.

$= \frac{0.24}{0.99}$ Simplify.

$= \frac{24}{99}$ Write as a quotient of integers.

$= \frac{8}{33}$ Reduce fraction to lowest terms.

▶ The repeating decimal 0.242424. . . is $\frac{8}{33}$ as a fraction.

✓ GUIDED PRACTICE for Examples 4 and 5

5. **WHAT IF?** In Example 4, suppose the pendulum travels 10 inches on its first swing. What is the total distance the pendulum swings? 50 in.

Write the repeating decimal as a fraction in lowest terms.

6. 0.555. . . $\frac{5}{9}$

7. 0.727272. . . $\frac{8}{11}$

8. 0.131313. . . $\frac{13}{99}$

Differentiated Instruction

Kinesthetic Learners It is tempting for students to enter a repeating decimal, up to a few decimal places, into their calculator and use the calculator functions to express the decimal as a fraction. Have students use their calculators to write 0.24 and 0.24242424 as fractions. Discuss their observations as a class, particularly with respect to the results of **Example 5**.

See also the *Algebra 2 Toolkit* for more strategies.

12.4 EXERCISES

HOMEWORK KEY
○ = **WORKED-OUT SOLUTIONS** on p. WS21 for Exs. 13, 27, and 39
★ = **STANDARDIZED TEST PRACTICE** Exs. 2, 32, 34, 39, 40, and 41

SKILL PRACTICE

A

1. **VOCABULARY** Copy and complete: The sum S_n of the first n terms of an infinite series is called a(n) _?_. partial sum

2. ★ **WRITING** *Explain* how to tell whether the series $\sum_{i=1}^{\infty} a_1 r^{i-1}$ has a sum. If $|r| < 1$, then the series has a sum.

AMPLE 1
p. 820
Exs. 3–6

PARTIAL SUMS For the given series, find and graph the partial sums S_n for $n = 1, 2, 3, 4,$ and 5. *Describe* what happens to S_n as n increases. 3–6. See margin.

3. $\frac{1}{2} + \frac{1}{6} + \frac{1}{18} + \frac{1}{54} + \frac{1}{162} + \cdots$

4. $\frac{2}{3} + \frac{1}{3} + \frac{1}{6} + \frac{1}{12} + \frac{1}{24} + \cdots$

5. $4 + \frac{12}{5} + \frac{36}{25} + \frac{108}{125} + \frac{324}{625} + \cdots$

6. $\frac{1}{4} + \frac{5}{4} + \frac{25}{4} + \frac{125}{4} + \frac{625}{4} + \cdots$

AMPLES
and 3
p. 821
Exs. 7–23

FINDING SUMS Find the sum of the infinite geometric series, if it exists.

7. $\sum_{n=1}^{\infty} 8\left(\frac{1}{5}\right)^{n-1}$ 10

8. $\sum_{k=1}^{\infty} -6\left(\frac{3}{2}\right)^{k-1}$ no sum

9. $\sum_{i=1}^{\infty} \frac{2}{5}\left(\frac{5}{3}\right)^{i-1}$ no sum

10. $\sum_{k=1}^{\infty} \frac{11}{3}\left(\frac{3}{8}\right)^{k-1}$ $\frac{88}{15}$

11. $\sum_{i=1}^{\infty} 2\left(\frac{1}{6}\right)^{i-1}$ $\frac{12}{5}$

12. $\sum_{n=1}^{\infty} -5\left(\frac{2}{5}\right)^{n-1}$ $-\frac{25}{3}$

(13.) $\sum_{k=1}^{\infty} 7\left(-\frac{8}{9}\right)^{k-1}$ $\frac{63}{17}$

14. $\sum_{n=1}^{\infty} \frac{1}{2}\left(-\frac{10}{3}\right)^{n-1}$ no sum

15. $\sum_{k=1}^{\infty} 9(4)^{k-1}$ no sum

16. $\sum_{i=1}^{\infty} -2\left(-\frac{1}{4}\right)^{i-1}$ $-\frac{8}{5}$

17. $\sum_{i=0}^{\infty} \left(-\frac{3}{7}\right)^{i}$ $\frac{7}{10}$

18. $\sum_{n=0}^{\infty} \frac{5}{6}(3)^{n}$ no sum

19. **ERROR ANALYSIS** *Describe* and correct the error in finding the sum of the infinite geometric series $\sum_{n=1}^{\infty} \left(\frac{7}{2}\right)^{n-1}$.
Since $r > 1$, the infinite geometric series has no sum.

For this series, $a_1 = 1$ and $r = \frac{7}{2}$.

$$S = \frac{a_1}{1 - r} = \frac{1}{1 - \frac{7}{2}} = \frac{1}{-\frac{5}{2}} = -\frac{2}{5}$$

FINDING SUMS Find the sum of the infinite geometric series, if it exists.

20. $-\frac{1}{8} - \frac{1}{12} - \frac{1}{18} - \frac{1}{27} + \cdots$ $-\frac{3}{8}$

21. $\frac{2}{3} - \frac{2}{9} + \frac{2}{27} - \frac{2}{81} + \cdots$ $\frac{1}{2}$

22. $\frac{4}{15} + \frac{4}{9} + \frac{20}{27} + \frac{100}{81} + \cdots$ no sum

23. $3 + \frac{5}{2} + \frac{25}{12} + \frac{125}{72} + \cdots$ 18

AMPLE 5 B
p. 822
Exs. 24–32

REWRITING DECIMALS Write the repeating decimal as a fraction in lowest terms.

24. 0.222. . . $\frac{2}{9}$

25. 0.444. . . $\frac{4}{9}$

26. 0.161616. . . $\frac{16}{99}$

(27.) 0.625625625. . . $\frac{625}{999}$

28. 32.3232. . . $\frac{3200}{99}$

29. 130.130130. . . $\frac{130,000}{999}$

30. 0.090909. . . $\frac{1}{11}$

31. 0.2777. . . $\frac{5}{18}$

32. ★ **MULTIPLE CHOICE** Which fraction is equal to the repeating decimal 18.1818. . . ? C

Ⓐ $\frac{2}{11}$ Ⓑ $\frac{1836}{101}$ Ⓒ $\frac{200}{11}$ Ⓓ $\frac{181}{9}$

33. **REASONING** Show that 0.999. . . is equal to 1. $\frac{0.9}{1 - 0.1} = \frac{0.9}{0.9} = 1$

4 PRACTICE AND APPLY

Assignment Guide

Answer Transparencies available for all exercises

Basic:
Day 1: pp. 823–825
Exs. 1–6, 7–29 odd, 37–40, 43

Average:
Day 1: pp. 823–825
Exs. 1, 2, 4–6, 8–14 even, 19, 20–32 even, 33, 34, 37–41, 44

Advanced:
Day 1: pp. 823–825
Exs. 1, 2, 5, 6, 15–18, 22–42*, 44

Block:
pp. 823–825
Exs. 1, 2, 4–6, 8–14 even, 19, 20–32 even, 33, 34, 37–41, 44 (with 12.5)

Differentiated Instruction

See *Algebra 2 Best Practices Toolkit* for suggestions on addressing the needs of a diverse classroom.

Homework Check

For a quick check of student understanding of key concepts, go over the following exercises:

Basic: 4, 9, 15, 25, 37
Average: 5, 10, 12, 28, 38
Advanced: 6, 16, 18, 30, 39

Extra Practice

- Student Edition, p. 1021
- Chapter 12 Resource Book: Practice levels A, B, C, pp. 40–42

Practice Worksheet

An easily-readable reduced practice page (with answers) for this lesson can be found on p. 792D.

3–6. See Additional Answers beginning on p. AA1.

Reading Strategy

Exercises 7–18 Remind students that the ∞ symbol above the summation symbol indicates that the series has no upper limit.

Avoiding Common Errors

Exercises 7–18, 20–23 Some students may describe the sum of a series as $-\infty$ or ∞ when partial sums have no limit. Encourage students to describe the sum as "does not exist" because the symbols $-\infty$ and ∞ do not refer to specific real numbers.

Mathematical Reasoning

Exercise 33 This exercise demonstrates that a repeating decimal and an infinite geometric series can be two representations of the same number.

34. Sample answer: $\sum_{i=1}^{\infty} 2.5\left(\frac{1}{2}\right)^{i-1}$, $\sum_{i=1}^{\infty} \frac{10}{3}\left(\frac{1}{3}\right)^{i-1}$

34. ★ **OPEN-ENDED MATH** Find two infinite geometric series whose sums are each 5.

C **CHALLENGE Specify the values of x for which the given infinite geometric series has a sum. Then find the sum in terms of x.**

35. $1 + 4x + 16x^2 + 64x^3 + \cdots$ $-\frac{1}{4} < x < \frac{1}{4}$; $S = \frac{1}{1-4x}$

36. $6 + \frac{3}{2}x + \frac{3}{8}x^2 + \frac{3}{32}x^3 + \cdots$ $-4 < x < 4$; $S = \frac{6}{1-\frac{1}{4}x}$

PROBLEM SOLVING

EXAMPLE 4 on p. 822 for Exs. 37–39

A **37. TIRE SWING** A person is given one push on a tire swing and then allowed to swing freely. On the first swing, the person travels a distance of 14 feet. On each successive swing, the person travels 80% of the distance of the previous swing. What is the total distance the person swings? 70 ft

@HomeTutor for problem solving help at classzone.com

38. BUSINESS A company had a profit of \$350,000 in its first year. Since then, the company's profit has decreased by 12% per year. If this trend continues, what is an upper limit on the total profit the company can make over the course of its lifetime? *Justify* your answer using an infinite geometric series. \$2,916,666.67; $s = \frac{350{,}0}{1-0}$

@HomeTutor for problem solving help at classzone.com

39. ★ **MULTIPLE CHOICE** In 1994, the number of cassette tapes shipped in the United States was 345 million. In each successive year, the number decreased by about 21.7%. What is the total number of cassettes that will ship in 1994 and after if this trend continues? D

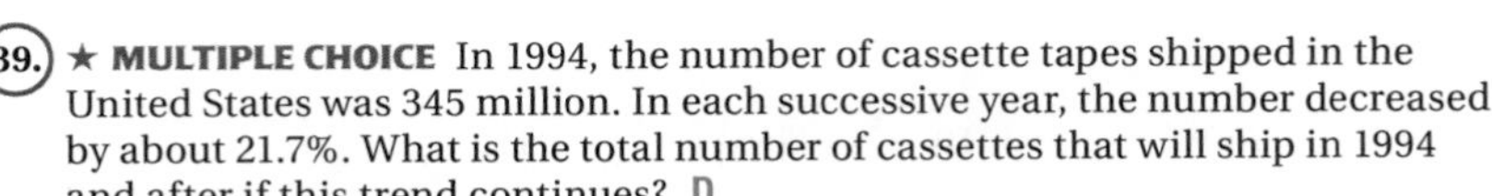

Ⓐ 420 million Ⓑ 440 million Ⓒ 615 million Ⓓ 1.59 billion

B **40.** ★ **SHORT RESPONSE** Can the Greek hero Achilles, running at 20 feet per second, ever catch up to a tortoise that runs 10 feet per second if the tortoise has a 20 foot head start? The Greek mathematician Zeno said no. He reasoned as follows:

When Achilles runs 20 feet, the tortoise will be in a new spot, 10 feet away.

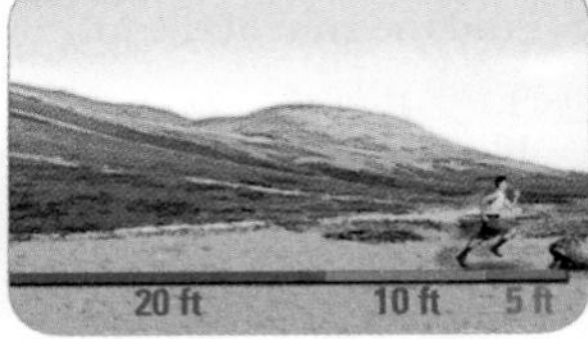

Then, when Achilles gets to that spot, the tortoise will be 5 feet away.

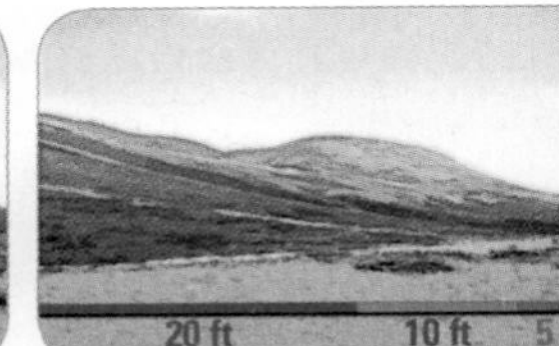

Achilles will keep halving the distance but will never catch up to the tortoise.

In actuality, looking at the race as Zeno did, you can see that both the distances and the times Achilles required to traverse them form infinite geometric series. Using the table, show that both series have finite sums. Does Achilles catch up to the tortoise? *Explain.*

Distance (ft)	20	10	5	2.5	1.25	0.625	...
Time (sec)	1	0.5	0.25	0.125	0.0625	0.03125	...

$S_d = 40$ ft, $S_t = 2$ sec; Yes; the total distance traveled is 40 feet and it occurs after 2 seconds.

◯ = WORKED-OUT SOLUTIONS on p. WS1 ★ = STANDARDIZED TEST PRACTICE

41\. b. $\sum_{i=1}^{\infty} 12(0.75)^{i-1}$

41. ★ **EXTENDED RESPONSE** A student drops a rubber ball from a height of 8 feet. Each time the ball hits the ground, it bounces to 75% of its previous height.

8 ft; 6 ft + 6 ft; 4.5 ft + 4.5 ft; 3.375 ft + 3.375 ft; 2.531 ft + 2.531 ft
1 2 3 4 5
Bounce number

a. How far does the ball travel between the first and second bounces? between the second and third bounces? **12 ft; 9 ft**

b. Write an infinite series to model the total distance traveled by the ball, excluding the distance traveled before the first bounce.

c. Find the total distance traveled by the ball, including the distance traveled before the first bounce. **56 ft**

d. Show that if the ball is dropped from a height of h feet, then the total distance traveled by the ball (including the distance traveled before the first bounce) is $7h$ feet. $\frac{2(0.75h)}{1-0.75} + h = 7h$

C **42.** **CHALLENGE** The *Sierpinski triangle* is a fractal created using equilateral triangles. The process involves removing smaller triangles from larger triangles by joining the midpoints of the sides of the larger triangles as shown below. Assume that the initial triangle has an area of 1 square unit.

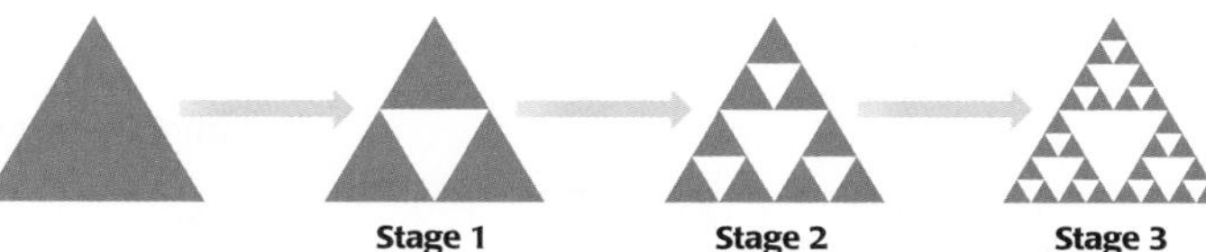

a. Let a_n be the total area of all the triangles that are removed at stage n. Write a rule for a_n. $a_n = \frac{3^{n-1}}{4^n}$

b. Find $\sum_{n=1}^{\infty} a_n$. What does your answer mean in the context of this problem? **1; eventually no area remains.**

KENTUCKY MIXED REVIEW

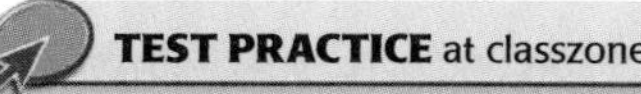

43. Rectangle P represents 150 people who were surveyed about pet ownership. Circle D represents the 75 people who said they owned a dog. Circle C represents the 40 people who said they owned a cat. How many people do not own a dog or a cat? **C**

P D C 15

Ⓐ 20 Ⓑ 35

Ⓒ 50 Ⓓ 85

44. $\triangle PQR$ is a right triangle. What is the length of $\overline{PR}$? **B**

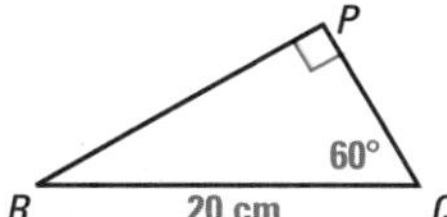

Ⓐ 10 cm Ⓑ $10\sqrt{3}$ cm

Ⓒ $20\sqrt{3}$ cm Ⓓ 40 cm

5 ASSESS AND RETEACH

Daily Homework Quiz

Transparency Available

Find the sum of the infinite geometric series if it exists.

1. $\sum_{i=1}^{\infty} 5\left(\frac{1}{2}\right)^{n-1}$ **10**

2. $1 - \frac{1}{2} + \frac{1}{4} - \frac{1}{8} + \dots$ $\frac{2}{3}$

3. $\frac{1}{4} + \frac{1}{2} + 1 + 2 + \dots$ **does not exist**

4. Write 0.378378378... as a fraction in lowest terms. $\frac{126}{333}$

5. A pendulum travels a distance of 24 centimeters on its first swing. On each successive swing, the pendulum travels $\frac{5}{6}$ of the previous swing. What is the total distance the pendulum swings? **144 cm**

Online Quiz

Available at **classzone.com**

Diagnosis/Remediation

- Practice A, B, C in Chapter 12 Resource Book, pp. 40–42
- Study Guide in Chapter 12 Resource Book, pp. 43–44
- Practice Workbook, pp. 177–178
- @HomeTutor

Challenge

Additional challenge is available in the Chapter 12 Resource Book, p. 47.

1 PLAN AND PREPARE

Explore the Concept

- Students will use a spreadsheet to generate the terms of a sequence defined by a recursive rule.
- This activity leads into the study of using recursive rules to generate sequences in Lesson 12.5, Example 1.

Recommended Time

Work activity: 10 min

Discuss results: 5 min

Grouping

Students can work individually or in pairs. If students work in pairs, they can take turns filling in the spreadsheet. They should discuss their conclusions.

2 TEACH

Tips for Success

The direction line for Step 2 tells students to enter "=A1 + 7". Be sure students enter the equal sign, but not the quotation marks.

Key Question

How is each term related to the previous term? **Each term is 7 more than the previous term.**

Key Discovery

A recursive rule for a sequence provides a value for a_1 and describes the value of a_n in terms of the value of the previous term a_{n-1}.

3 ASSESS AND RETEACH

How is the term a_{n-1} related to the term a_n? **The term a_{n-1} is the term just before a_n.**

@HomeTutor classzone.com Keystrokes

12.5 Exploring Recursive Rules

MATERIALS • computer with spreadsheet program

QUESTION How can you evaluate a recursive rule for a sequence?

A *recursive rule* for a sequence gives the beginning term or terms of the sequence and then an equation relating the nth term a_n to one or more preceding terms. For example, the rule $a_1 = 4$, $a_n = a_{n-1} + 7$ defines a sequence recursively.

EXPLORE Find terms of a sequence given by a recursive rule

Find the first eight terms of the sequence defined by $a_1 = 4$, $a_n = a_{n-1} + 7$. What type of sequence does this rule represent?

STEP 1 *Enter first term*
Enter the value of a_1 into cell A1.

A1	4		
	A	B	C
1	4		
2			
3			
4			
5			
6			
7			
8			

STEP 2 *Enter recursive equation*
Enter the formula "=A1+7" into cell A2.

A2	=A1+7		
	A	B	C
1	4		
2	11		
3			
4			
5			
6			
7			
8			

STEP 3 *Fill cells*
Use the *fill down* command to copy the recursive equation into the rest of column A.

A8	=A7+7		
	A	B	C
1	4		
2	11		
3	18		
4	25		
5	32		
6	39		
7	46		
8	53		

STEP 4 *Identify terms and type of sequence*
The first eight terms of the sequence are 4, 11, 18, 25, 32, 39, 46, and 53. This sequence is an arithmetic sequence because the difference of consecutive terms is always 7.

DRAW CONCLUSIONS Use your observations to complete these exercises

1. Find the first eight terms of the sequence defined by $a_1 = 4$, $a_n = 7a_{n-1}$. What type of sequence does this rule represent? **4; 28; 196; 1372; 9604; 67,228; 470,596; 3,294,172; geometric**
2. Write a recursive rule for the sequence 15, 11, 7, 3, −1, −5, ... **$a_1 = 15$, $a_n = a_{n-1} - 4$**
3. Write a recursive rule for the sequence 81, 27, 9, 3, 1, $\frac{1}{3}$, ... **$a_1 = 81$, $a_n = \frac{1}{3}a_{n-1}$**
4. What equation relates the nth term a_n to the preceding term a_{n-1} for an arithmetic sequence with common difference d? for a geometric sequence with common ratio r? **$a_n = a_{n-1} + d$; $a_n = ra_{n-1}$**

12.5 Use Recursive Rules with Sequences and Functions

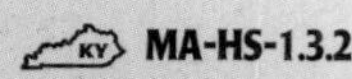

MA-HS-1.3.2

Before	You used explicit rules for sequences.
Now	You will use recursive rules for sequences.
Why?	So you can model evaporation from a pool, as in Ex. 44.

Key Vocabulary
- explicit rule
- recursive rule
- iteration

MA-HS-1.3.2
Students will: describe and extend arithmetic and geometric sequences; determine a specific term of a sequence given an explicit formula; determine an explicit rule for the nth term of an arithmetic sequence and apply sequences to solve real-world problems. DOK 3

So far in this chapter you have worked with *explicit rules* for the *n*th term of a sequence, such as $a_n = 3n - 2$ and $a_n = 3(2)^n$. An **explicit rule** gives a_n as a function of the term's position number *n* in the sequence.

In this lesson you will learn another way to define a sequence—by a *recursive rule*. A **recursive rule** gives the beginning term or terms of a sequence and then a *recursive equation* that tells how a_n is related to one or more preceding terms.

EXAMPLE 1 Evaluate recursive rules

Write the first six terms of the sequence.

a. $a_0 = 1, a_n = a_{n-1} + 4$

b. $a_1 = 1, a_n = 3a_{n-1}$

Solution

a. $a_0 = 1$

$a_1 = a_0 + 4 = 1 + 4 = 5$

$a_2 = a_1 + 4 = 5 + 4 = 9$

$a_3 = a_2 + 4 = 9 + 4 = 13$

$a_4 = a_3 + 4 = 13 + 4 = 17$

$a_5 = a_4 + 4 = 17 + 4 = 21$

b. $a_1 = 1$

$a_2 = 3a_1 = 3(1) = 3$

$a_3 = 3a_2 = 3(3) = 9$

$a_4 = 3a_3 = 3(9) = 27$

$a_5 = 3a_4 = 3(27) = 81$

$a_6 = 3a_5 = 3(81) = 243$

ARITHMETIC AND GEOMETRIC SEQUENCES In part (a) of Example 1, observe that the *differences* of consecutive terms of the sequence are constant, so the sequence is arithmetic. In part (b), the *ratios* of consecutive terms are constant, so the sequence is geometric. In general, rules for arithmetic and geometric sequences can be written recursively as follows.

KEY CONCEPT *For Your Notebook*

Recursive Equations for Arithmetic and Geometric Sequences

Arithmetic Sequence

$a_n = a_{n-1} + d$ where *d* is the common difference

Geometric Sequence

$a_n = r \cdot a_{n-1}$ where *r* is the common ratio

1 PLAN AND PREPARE

Warm-Up Exercises

Transparency Available

Find the common difference or common ratio for each sequence.

1. 5, 10, 15, 20, . . . $d = 5$

2. 8, 4, 0, −4, . . . $d = -4$

3. 216, −36, 6, −1, . . . $r = -\frac{1}{6}$

4. 99, 200, 301, 402, . . . $d = 101$

Notetaking Guide

Transparency Available

Promotes interactive learning and notetaking skills, pp. 318–320.

Pacing

Basic: 1 day
Average: 1 day
Advanced: 1 day
Block: 0.5 block with 12.4
- See *Teaching Guide/Lesson Plan.*

2 FOCUS AND MOTIVATE

Essential Question

Big Idea 3, p. 793

How do you write a recursive rule for an arithmetic sequence and for a geometric sequence? **Tell students they will learn how to answer this question by writing a specific value for the first term and relating each other term to the term that precedes it.**

Resource Planning Guide

Chapter Resource Book
- Teaching Guide/Lesson Plan (pp. 48–49)
- Practice levels A, B, C (pp. 52–54)
- Study Guide (pp. 55–56)
- Catch-up for Absent Students (p. 57)
- Problem Solving Workshop (p. 58)
- Challenge (p. 59)

Workbooks
- Notetaking Guide (pp. 318–320)
- Practice Workbook (pp. 179–180)

Teaching Options
- **Power Presentations CD-ROM** provides dynamic electronic teaching resources for the classroom.
- **Activity Generator CD-ROM** provides editable activities for all ability levels.

Interactive Technology
- Easy Planner
- Power Presentations CD-ROM
- Activity Generator CD-ROM
- Animated Algebra
- Test Generator CD-ROM
- Online Quiz
- eWorkbook
- eEdition
- @HomeTutor

Resources for English Learners
- Quick Reference for English Learners
- Spanish Study Guide
- Multi-Language Visual Glossary
- Student Resources in Spanish

See also the *Algebra 2 Toolkit* for more strategies for meeting individual needs.

Motivating the Lesson

In many situations, such as growth, decay, compound interest, and so on, each value is a function of the previous value. In this lesson students will learn about recursive formulas, which describe such situations.

3 TEACH

Extra Example 1

Write the first six terms of the sequence.

a. $a_1 = -2$, $a_n = a_{n-1} + 3$
−2, 1, 4, 7, 10, 13

b. $a_1 = 32$, $a_n = \frac{1}{2}a_{n-1}$
32, 16, 8, 4, 2, 1

Key Question to Ask for Example 1

- What does a_{n-1} represent? **a_{n-1} is the term that precedes a_n.**

Extra Example 2

Write a recursive rule for the sequence.

a. 100, 40, 16, $\frac{32}{5}$, $\frac{64}{25}$, . . . **$a_1 = 100$, $a_n = \frac{2}{5}a_{n-1}$**

b. 8, 28, 48, 68, 88, . . . **$a_1 = 8$, $a_n = a_{n-1} + 20$**

Extra Example 3

Write a recursive rule for the sequence.

a. −10, 8, 18, 10, −8, −18, . . . **$a_1 = -10$, $a_2 = 8$, $a_n = a_{n-1} - a_{n-2}$**

b. 1, $\frac{1}{2}$, $\frac{1}{6}$, $\frac{1}{24}$, $\frac{1}{120}$, . . . **$a_1 = 1$, $a_n = \frac{a_{n-1}}{n}$**

EXAMPLE 2 Write recursive rules

Write a recursive rule for the sequence.

a. 3, 13, 23, 33, 43, . . . **b.** 16, 40, 100, 250, 625, . . .

Solution

a. The sequence is arithmetic with first term $a_1 = 3$ and common difference $d = 13 - 3 = 10$.

$a_n = a_{n-1} + d$ **General recursive equation for a_n**

$= a_{n-1} + 10$ **Substitute 10 for *d*.**

▶ So, a recursive rule for the sequence is $a_1 = 3$, $a_n = a_{n-1} + 10$.

AVOID ERRORS
A recursive *equation* for a sequence does not include the initial term. To write a recursive *rule* for a sequence, the initial term must be included.

b. The sequence is geometric with first term $a_1 = 16$ and common ratio $r = \frac{40}{16} = 2.5$.

$a_n = r \cdot a_{n-1}$ **General recursive equation for a_n**

$= 2.5a_{n-1}$ **Substitute 2.5 for *r*.**

▶ So, a recursive rule for the sequence is $a_1 = 16$, $a_n = 2.5a_{n-1}$.

✓ GUIDED PRACTICE for Examples 1 and 2

Write the first five terms of the sequence.

1. $a_1 = 3$, $a_n = a_{n-1} - 7$ **3, −4, −11, −18, −25**
2. $a_0 = 162$, $a_n = 0.5a_{n-1}$ **162, 81, 40.5, 20.25, 10.125**
3. $a_0 = 1$, $a_n = a_{n-1} + n$ **1, 2, 4, 7, 11**
4. $a_1 = 4$, $a_n = 2a_{n-1} - 1$ **4, 7, 13, 25, 49**

Write a recursive rule for the sequence.

5. 2, 14, 98, 686, 4802, . . . **$a_1 = 2$, $a_n = 7a_{n-1}$**
6. 19, 13, 7, 1, −5, . . . **$a_1 = 19$, $a_n = a_{n-1} - 6$**
7. 11, 22, 33, 44, 55, . . . **$a_1 = 11$, $a_n = a_{n-1} + 11$**
8. 324, 108, 36, 12, 4, . . . **$a_1 = 324$, $a_n = \frac{1}{3}a_{n-1}$**

RECURSIVE RULES FOR SPECIAL SEQUENCES For some sequences, it is difficult to write an explicit rule but relatively easy to write a recursive rule.

EXAMPLE 3 Write recursive rules for special sequences

Write a recursive rule for the sequence.

a. 1, 1, 2, 3, 5, . . . **b.** 1, 1, 2, 6, 24, . . .

Solution

a. Beginning with the third term in the sequence, each term is the sum of the two previous terms.

▶ So, a recursive rule is $a_1 = 1$, $a_2 = 1$, $a_n = a_{n-2} + a_{n-1}$.

NAME SEQUENCES
The sequence in part (a) of Example 3 is called the *Fibonacci sequence*. The sequence in part (b) of Example 3 lists the factorial numbers you studied in Chapter 10.

b. Denote the first term by $a_0 = 1$. Then note that $a_1 = 1 = 1 \cdot a_0$, $a_2 = 2 = 2 \cdot a_1$, $a_3 = 6 = 3 \cdot a_2$, and so on.

▶ So, a recursive rule is $a_0 = 1$, $a_n = n \cdot a_{n-1}$.

EXAMPLE 4 Solve a multi-step problem

MUSIC SERVICE An online music service initially has 50,000 annual members. Each year it loses 20% of its current members and adds 5000 new members.

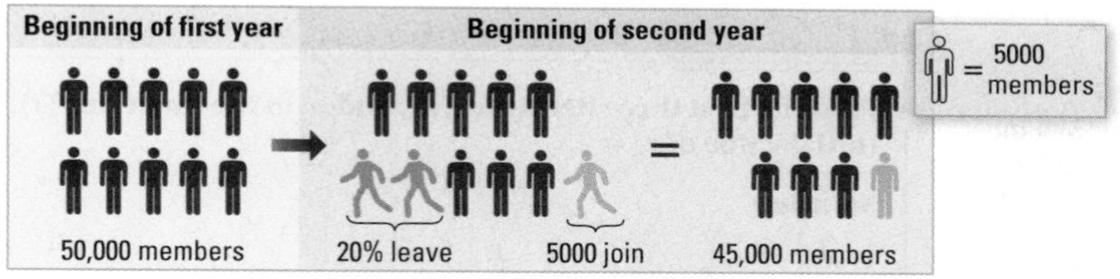

- Write a recursive rule for the number a_n of members at the start of the nth year.
- Find the number of members at the start of the 5th year.
- Describe what happens to the number of members over time.

OTHER WAY
alternative methods solving the problem xample 4, turn age 834 for the blem Solving rkshop.

Solution

STEP 1 **Write** a recursive rule. Because the number of members declines 20% each year, 80% of the members are retained from one year to the next. Also, 5000 new members are added each year.

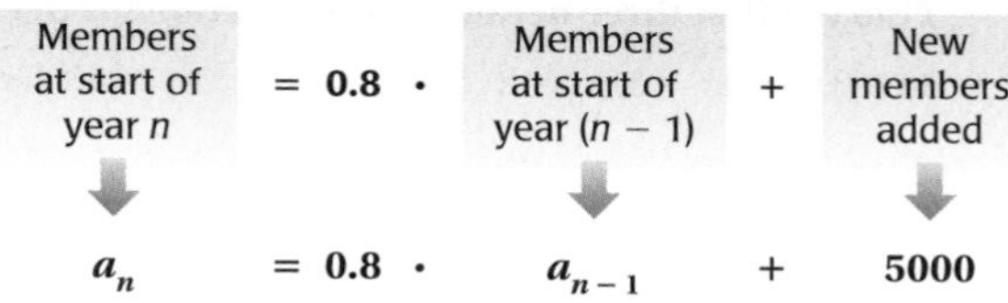

Members at start of year n
= 0.8 ·
Members at start of year (n − 1)
+
New members added

$$a_n = 0.8 \cdot a_{n-1} + 5000$$

▶ A recursive rule is $a_1 = 50{,}000$, $a_n = 0.8a_{n-1} + 5000$.

STEP 2 **Find** the number of members at the start of the 5th year. Enter 50,000 (the value of a_1) into a graphing calculator. Then enter the rule $0.8 \times \text{Ans} + 5000$ to find a_2. Press ENTER three more times to find a_5.

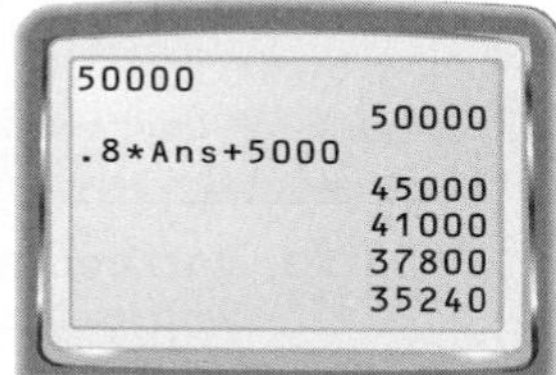

▶ There are about 35,240 members at the start of the 5th year.

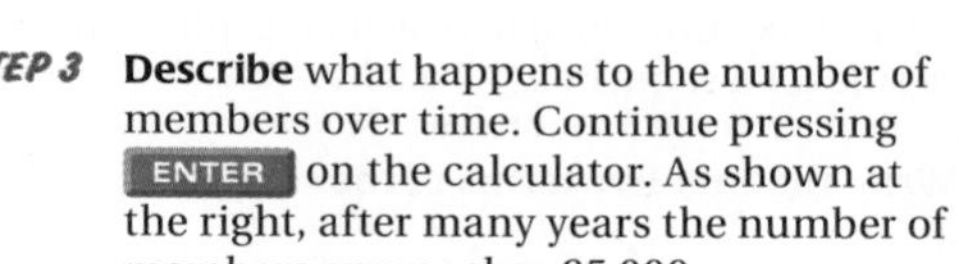

STEP 3 **Describe** what happens to the number of members over time. Continue pressing ENTER on the calculator. As shown at the right, after many years the number of members approaches 25,000.

▶ The number of members stabilizes at about 25,000 members.

✓ GUIDED PRACTICE for Examples 3 and 4

9. Write a recursive rule for the sequence 1, 2, 2, 4, 8, 32, ...
   $a_1 = 1$, $a_2 = 2$ $a_n = (a_{n-2})(a_{n-1})$
10. **WHAT IF?** In Example 4, suppose 70% of the members are retained each year. What happens to the number of members over time?
    The number of members stabilizes at about 16,667 members.

Extra Example 4

A mosquito population in a controlled laboratory condition is estimated to be about 500. Each day an additional 100 mosquitoes are hatched. The population also declines by 85% every day from a pesticide and other natural causes. Write a recursive rule for the number a_n of mosquitoes at the start of the nth day. Find the number of mosquitoes after the 5th day. Describe what happens to the number of mosquitoes over time. $a_1 = 500$, $a_n = 0.15a_{n-1} + 100$; There are about 118 mosquitoes after 5 days. Over time, the number of mosquitoes stabilizes at about 118 mosquitoes.

Key Questions to Ask for Example 4

- What percent of its members does the service retain each year? 80%
- If you graph the data points for the first thirty years, what horizontal line is an asymptote for the points? $y = 25{,}000$

Mathematical Reasoning

Multiple Representations When discussing Example 4, the iterations from $n = 2$ to $n = 20$ can be entered in the list editor of a graphing calculator. Then a scatter plot of the data over time can be graphed. Students can use the graph to visualize the limit of the number of members over time.

Differentiated Instruction

English Learners Students should work cooperatively to overcome language barriers that might inhibit their progress in solving problems such as the one in **Example 4**. Have students make and retain a list of key phrases and concepts that they can use to translate similar word problems into mathematical statements. For instance, losing 20% of the members means that 80% of the members stay (are retained). Encourage students to share their results with the class.

See also the *Algebra 2 Toolkit* for more strategies.

Extra Example 5

Find the first three iterates x_1, x_2, and x_3 of the function $f(x) = 5x - 3$ for an initial value of $x_0 = 1$. 2, 7, 32

Key Question to Ask for Example 5

- What is a recursive rule for the sequence? $a_0 = 2$, $a_n = -3a_{n-1} + 1$

Avoiding Common Errors

Be sure students are evaluating $f(x_1)$, $f(x_2)$, and $f(x_3)$ and NOT evaluating $f(1)$, $f(2)$, and $f(3)$. Remind them that an iteration is a repeated composition of a function so it acts like a recursive rule for generating a sequence.

Closing the Lesson

Have students summarize the major points of the lesson and answer the Essential Question: How do you write a recursive rule for an arithmetic sequence and a geometric sequence?

- A recursive equation for an arithmetic sequence is $a_n = a_{n-1} + d$, where d is the common difference.
- A recursive equation for a geometric sequence is $a_n = r \cdot a_{n-1}$, where r is the common ratio.
- You can use iteration to generate a sequence recursively. Begin with an initial value x_0 and let $x_1 = f(x_0)$, $x_2 = f(x_1)$, $x_3 = f(x_2)$, and so on.

Write the value of the first term of the sequence. Then write a recursive equation that explains how each term a_n is related to one or more previous terms.

ITERATING FUNCTIONS **Iteration** involves the repeated composition of a function f with itself. The result of one iteration is $f(f(x))$. The result of two iterations is $f(f(f(x)))$. You can use iteration to generate a sequence recursively. Begin with an initial value x_0, and let $x_1 = f(x_0)$, $x_2 = f(x_1) = f(f(x_0))$, and so on.

EXAMPLE 5 Iterate a function

READING
An *iterate* is a number that is the result of iterating a function.

Find the first three iterates x_1, x_2, and x_3 of the function $f(x) = -3x + 1$ for an initial value of $x_0 = 2$.

Solution

$x_1 = f(x_0)$	$x_2 = f(x_1)$	$x_3 = f(x_2)$
$= f(2)$	$= f(-5)$	$= f(16)$
$= -3(2) + 1$	$= -3(-5) + 1$	$= -3(16) + 1$
$= -5$	$= 16$	$= -47$

▶ The first three iterates are −5, 16, and −47.

GUIDED PRACTICE for Example 5

Find the first three iterates of the function for the given initial value.

11. $f(x) = 4x - 3$, $x_0 = 2$ 5, 17, 65

12. $f(x) = x^2 - 5$, $x_0 = -1$ −4, 11, 116

12.5 EXERCISES

HOMEWORK KEY
○ = **WORKED-OUT SOLUTIONS** p. WS21 for Exs. 15, 27, and 45
★ = **STANDARDIZED TEST PRACTICE** Exs. 2, 12, 33, 40, 45, and 47

SKILL PRACTICE

1. VOCABULARY Copy and complete: The repeated composition of a function with itself is called __?__. iteration

2. ★ WRITING *Explain* the difference between an explicit rule for a sequence and a recursive rule for a sequence. An explicit rule gives the value based on the position of the term in the sequence while a recursive rule gives the value based on previous term(s) in the sequence

EXAMPLE 1
on p. 827 for Exs. 3–12

WRITING TERMS **Write the first five terms of the sequence.**

3. $a_1 = 1$, $a_n = a_{n-1} + 3$ 1, 4, 7, 10, 13

4. $a_0 = 4$, $a_n = 2a_{n-1}$ 4, 8, 16, 32, 64

5. $a_1 = -1$, $a_n = a_{n-1} - 5$ −1, −6, −11, −16, −21

6. $a_0 = 3$, $a_n = a_{n-1} - n^2$ 3, 2, −2, −11, −27

7. $a_1 = 2$, $a_n = (a_{n-1})^2 + 1$ 2; 5; 26; 677; 458,330

8. $a_0 = 4$, $a_n = (a_{n-1})^2 - 10$ 4; 6; 26; 666; 443,546

9. $a_1 = 2$, $a_n = n^2 + 3n - a_{n-1}$ 2, 8, 10, 18, 22

10. $a_0 = 2$, $a_1 = 4$, $a_n = a_{n-1} - a_{n-2}$ 2, 4, 2, −2, −4

11. $a_1 = 2$, $a_2 = 3$, $a_n = a_{n-1} \cdot a_{n-2}$ 2, 3, 6, 18, 108

12. ★ MULTIPLE CHOICE What are the first four terms of the sequence for which $a_1 = 1$, $a_2 = 4$, and $a_n = a_{n-1} \cdot a_{n-2}$? A

Ⓐ 1, 4, 4, 16 Ⓑ 1, 4, 16, 64 Ⓒ 1, 4, 8, 16 Ⓓ 1, 4, 4, 8

XAMPLES and 3
n p. 828
or Exs. 13–23

. When
iting a
cursive rule,
u must define
e previous
formation
eded; $a_1 = 5$,
$= 2$, $a_n =$
$_{-2} - a_{n-1}$.

WRITING RULES **Write a recursive rule for the sequence. The sequence may be arithmetic, geometric, or neither.**

13. 21, 14, 7, 0, −7, . . . $a_1 = 21, a_n = a_{n-1} - 7$

14. 3, 12, 48, 192, 768, . . . $a_1 = 3, a_n = 4a_{n-1}$

15. 4, −12, 36, −108, 324, . . . $a_1 = 4, a_n = -3a_{n-1}$

16. 1, 8, 15, 22, 29, . . . $a_1 = 1, a_n = a_{n-1} + 7$

17. 44, 11, $\frac{11}{4}$, $\frac{11}{16}$, $\frac{11}{64}$, . . . $a_1 = 44, a_n = \frac{1}{4}a_{n-1}$

18. 1, 4, 5, 9, 14, . . . $a_1 = 1, a_2 = 4, a_n = a_{n-2} + a_{n-1}$

19. 54, 43, 32, 21, 10, . . . $a_1 = 54, a_n = a_{n-1} - 11$

20. 3, 5, 15, 75, 1125, . . . $a_1 = 3, a_2 = 5, a_n = a_{n-2} \cdot a_{n-1}$

21. 16, 9, 7, 2, 5, . . . $a_1 = 16, a_2 = 9, a_n = a_{n-2} - a_{n-1}$

ERROR ANALYSIS ***Describe*** **and correct the error in writing a recursive rule for the sequence 5, 2, 3, −1, 4, ...**

22.

> Beginning with the third term in the sequence, each term a_n equals $a_{n-2} - a_{n-1}$. So a recursive rule is given by:
>
> $a_n = a_{n-2} - a_{n-1}$ ✗

. The rule does
t work for all
the terms of
e sequence;
$= 5$, $a_2 = 2$,
$= a_{n-2} -$
$_{-1}$.

23.

> Beginning with the second term in the sequence, each term a_n is $a_{n-1} - 3$. So a recursive rule is given by:
>
> $a_1 = 5, a_n = a_{n-1} - 3$ ✗

XAMPLE 5
n p. 830
or Exs. 24–33

ITERATING FUNCTIONS **Find the first three iterates of the function for the given initial value.**

24. $f(x) = 3x - 2, x_0 = 2$ 4, 10, 28

25. $f(x) = 5x + 6, x_0 = -2$ −4, −14, −64

26. $g(x) = -4x + 7, x_0 = 1$ 3, −5, 27

27. $f(x) = \frac{1}{2}x - 3, x_0 = 2$ −2, −4, −5

28. $f(x) = \frac{2}{3}x + 5, x_0 = 6$ 9, 11, $12\frac{1}{3}$

29. $h(x) = x^2 - 4, x_0 = -3$ 5, 21, 437

30. $f(x) = 2x^2 + 1, x_0 = -1$ 3, 19, 723

31. $f(x) = x^2 - x + 2, x_0 = 1$ 2, 4, 14

32. $g(x) = -3x^2 + 2x, x_0 = 2$ −8, −208, −130,208

33. ★ **MULTIPLE CHOICE** What are the first three iterates x_1, x_2, and x_3 of the function $f(x) = -2x + 3$ for an initial value of $x_0 = 2$? C

Ⓐ −1, 1, 3 Ⓑ 1, −5, 7 Ⓒ −1, 5, −7 Ⓓ 1, −1, −3

B **WRITING RULES** **Write a recursive rule for the sequence.** 34–39. See margin.

34. 3, 8, 17, 81, 370, . . .

35. 1, 2, 12, 56, 272, . . .

36. 5, $5\sqrt{3}$, 15, $15\sqrt{3}$, 45, . . .

37. 2, 5, 11, 26, 59, . . .

38. 8, 4, 2, 2, 1, . . .

39. −3, −2, 5, −3, −2, . . .

40. ★ **OPEN-ENDED MATH** Give an example of a sequence in which each term after the third term is a function of the three terms preceding it. Write a recursive rule for the sequence and find its first eight terms.
Sample answer: $a_1 = 2, a_2 = 4, a_3 = 7, a_n = a_{n-3} + a_{n-2} + a_{n-1}$; 2, 4, 7, 13, 24, 44, 81, 149

C **41.** **REASONING** *Explain* why there are not a function f and an initial value x_0 such that the function's first three iterates are $x_1 = 2$, $x_2 = 2$, and $x_3 = 8$.
Sample answer: If the first two iterates are 2, the given rule must not be a function.

42. **CHALLENGE** You can define a sequence using a piecewise rule. The following is an example of a piecewise-defined sequence.

$$a_1 = 5, a_n = \begin{cases} \frac{a_{n-1}}{2}, \text{ if } a_{n-1} \text{ is even} \\ 3a_{n-1} + 3, \text{ if } a_{n-1} \text{ is odd} \end{cases}$$

a. Write the first ten terms of the sequence. 5, 18, 9, 30, 15, 48, 24, 12, 6, 3

b. Choose three different positive integer values for a_1 (other than $a_1 = 5$). For each value of a_1, find the first ten terms of the sequence. What conclusions can you make about the behavior of this sequence of integers?

b. *Sample swer:* $a_1 = 2$: 1, 6, 3, 12, 6, 3, 6, 3; $a_1 = 3$: 12, 6, 3, 12, 6, 3, 6, 3; $a_1 = 6$: 3, 12, 6, 3, 12, 6, 12, 6; the terms the sequence ll eventually peat the mbers 3, 12, 6.

4 PRACTICE AND APPLY

Assignment Guide

Answer Transparencies available for all exercises

Basic:
Day 1: pp. 830–833
Exs. 1–7, 12–16, 22–28, 33–36, 43–46, 49–50

Average:
Day 1: pp. 830–833
Exs. 1, 2, 7–9, 12, 17–19, 22, 23, 28–30, 33–41, 43–47, 49–50

Advanced:
Day 1: pp. 830–833
Exs. 1, 2, 10–12, 19–21, 30–50*

Block:
pp. 830–833
Exs. 1, 2, 7–9, 12, 17–19, 22, 23, 28–30, 33–41, 43–47, 49–50 (with 12.4)

Differentiated Instruction

See *Algebra 2 Best Practices Toolkit* for suggestions on addressing the needs of a diverse classroom.

Homework Check

For a quick check of student understanding of key concepts, go over the following exercises:

Basic: 4, 14, 16, 26, 43
Average: 8, 18, 28, 43, 44
Advanced: 10, 20, 32, 44, 45

Extra Practice

- Student Edition, p. 1021
- Chapter 12 Resource Book: Practice levels A, B, C, pp. 52–54

Practice Worksheet

An easily-readable reduced practice page (with answers) for this lesson can be found on p. 792D.

34. $a_1 = 3, a_2 = 8, a_n = (a_{n-2})^2 + a_{n-1}$
35. $a_1 = 1, a_2 = 2, a_n = 4(a_{n-2} + a_{n-1})$
36. $a_1 = 5, a_n = \sqrt{3}\,a_{n-1}$
37. $a_1 = 2, a_2 = 5, a_n = 3a_{n-2} + a_{n-1}$
38. $a_1 = 8, a_2 = 4, a_n = \frac{a_{n-2}}{a_{n-1}}$
39. $a_1 = -3, a_2 = -2, a_n = -1(a_{n-2} + a_{n-1})$

Avoiding Common Errors

Exercises 43–44 Students may use the percents given in each problem to write the recursive equations. Remind them that the equation should model how much of the population or concentration *remains* at each stage.

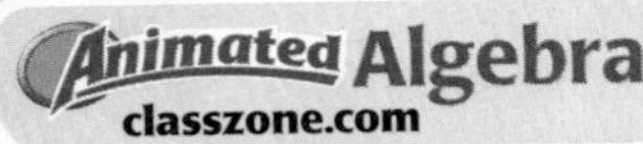

An **Animated Algebra** activity is available on-line for **Exercise 46**. This activity is also available on the **Power Presentations CD-ROM**.

PROBLEM SOLVING

EXAMPLE 4 A on p. 829 for Exs. 43–45

43a. $a_1 = 5000$, $a_n = 0.8a_{n-1} + 500$; 3524 fish

43. FISH POPULATION A lake initially contains 5000 fish. Each year the population declines 20% due to fishing and other causes, and the lake is restocked with 500 fish.

a. Write a recursive rule for the number a_n of fish at the beginning of the nth year. How many fish are there at the beginning of the 5th year?

b. What happens to the population of fish in the lake over time? The population of the lake approaches 2500 fish.

@HomeTutor for problem solving help at classzone.com

44. $a_1 = 34$, $a_n = 0.6a_{n-1} + 16$; the amount of chlorine in the pool approaches 40 ounces.

44. POOL CARE You are adding chlorine to a swimming pool. You add 34 ounces of chlorine the first week and 16 ounces every week thereafter. Each week 40% of the chlorine in the pool evaporates. Write a recursive rule for the amount of chlorine in the pool each week. What happens to the amount of chlorine in the pool over time?

First week

34 oz of chlorine are added

Each successive week

16 oz of chlorine are added
40% of chlorine has evaporated

@HomeTutor for problem solving help at classzone.com

45. $a_1 = 2000$, $a_n = 1.014a_{n-1} - 100$; 24 mo. *Sample answer:* As long Gladys does not add anything to her credit card and continues her payments, her 24th payment will only be \$62.14.

(45.) ★ SHORT RESPONSE Gladys owes \$2000 to a credit card company that charges interest at a rate of 1.4% per month. At the end of each month she makes a payment of \$100. Write a recursive rule for the balance a_n of the account at the beginning of the nth month. How long will it take to pay off the account? *Explain* your reasoning.

B

46. FIBONACCI SEQUENCE The Fibonacci sequence, which is defined recursively in Example 3 on page 828, occurs many places in nature. This sequence can also be defined explicitly as follows:

$$f_n = \frac{1}{\sqrt{5}}\left(\frac{1+\sqrt{5}}{2}\right)^n - \frac{1}{\sqrt{5}}\left(\frac{1-\sqrt{5}}{2}\right)^n,\ n \ge 1$$

Use the explicit rule to find the first five terms of the Fibonacci sequence. 1, 1, 2, 3, 5

Animated Algebra at classzone.com

47. ★ EXTENDED RESPONSE A person repeatedly takes 20 milligrams of a prescribed drug every 4 hours. Thirty percent of the drug is removed from the bloodstream every 4 hours.

a. Write a recursive rule for the amount of the drug in the bloodstream after n doses. $a_1 = 20$, $a_n = 0.7a_{n-1} + 20$

b. The value that a drug level in a person's body approaches after an extended period of time is called the *maintenance level.* What is the maintenance level of this drug, given a dosage of 20 milligrams? $66\frac{2}{3}$ mg

c. How does doubling the dosage affect the maintenance level of the drug? *Justify* your answer mathematically. The maintenance level of the drug doubles as well; $a_1 = 20$, $a_n = 0.7(2a_{n-1}) + 2(20)$.

○ = WORKED-OUT SOLUTIONS on p. WS1

★ = STANDARDIZED TEST PRACTICE

C **48. CHALLENGE** You are saving money for retirement. You plan to withdraw $30,000 at the beginning of each year for 20 years after you retire. Based on the type of investment you are making, you can expect to earn an annual return of 8% on your savings after you retire.

a. Let a_n be your balance n years after retiring. Write a recursive equation that shows how a_n is related to a_{n-1}. $a_n = 1.08a_{n-1} - 30{,}000$

b. Solve the equation from part (a) for a_{n-1}. Find a_0, the minimum amount of money you should have in your account when you retire. (*Hint:* Let $a_{20} = 0$.) $a_{n-1} = \frac{a_n + 30{,}000}{1.08}$; $a_0 =$ about 294,544.42

KENTUCKY MIXED REVIEW

TEST PRACTICE at classzone.com

49. What is the solution of $\frac{1}{3}(8x - 5) = 4x + 7$? **A**

Ⓐ $-\frac{13}{2}$ Ⓑ 4 Ⓒ 9 Ⓓ 29

50. To the nearest tenth of a square foot, what is the area of a rectangular garden with a 25-foot-long side and a 50-foot diagonal? **B**

Ⓐ 892.5 ft^2 Ⓑ 1082.5 ft^2 Ⓒ 1107.5 ft^2 Ⓓ 2165.0 ft^2

QUIZ for Lessons 12.4–12.5

Find the sum of the infinite geometric series, if it exists. *(p. 820)*

1. $\sum_{n=1}^{\infty} 2\left(\frac{3}{7}\right)^{n-1}$ 3.5

2. $\sum_{n=0}^{\infty} 4\left(-\frac{5}{6}\right)^{n}$ $\frac{24}{11}$

3. $\frac{3}{4} + \frac{15}{8} + \frac{75}{16} + \frac{375}{32} + \cdots$ no sum

Write the repeating decimal as a fraction in lowest terms. *(p. 820)*

4. 0.777. . . $\frac{7}{9}$

5. 0.393939. . . $\frac{13}{33}$

6. 123.123123. . . $\frac{41{,}000}{333}$

Write the first five terms of the sequence. *(p. 827)*

7. $a_1 = 2$, $a_n = a_{n-1} + 4$ 2, 6, 10, 14, 18

8. $a_0 = 3$, $a_n = (a_{n-1})^2 - 5$ 3, 4, 11, 116, 13,451

9. $a_1 = 1, a_2 = 4$, $a_n = a_{n-1} - a_{n-2}$ 1, 4, 3, −1, −4

Write a recursive rule for the sequence. The sequence may be arithmetic, geometric, or neither. *(p. 827)*

10. $5, \frac{17}{4}, \frac{7}{2}, \frac{11}{4}, 2, \ldots$ $a_1 = 5, a_n = a_{n-1} - \frac{3}{4}$

11. 2, 6, 12, 72, 864, . . . $a_1 = 2, a_2 = 6, a_n = a_{n-2} \cdot a_{n-1}$

12. 8, 24, 72, 216, 648, . . . $a_1 = 8, a_n = 3a_{n-1}$

Find the first three iterates of the function for the given initial value. *(p. 827)*

13. $f(x) = -3x - 2, x_0 = 1$ −5, 13, −41

14. $g(x) = 4x + 1, x_0 = 2$ 9, 37, 149

15. $f(x) = -2x + 3, x_0 = -2$ 7, −11, 25

16. $f(x) = 5x - 7, x_0 = -3$ −22, −117, −592

17. $h(x) = x^2 - 6, x_0 = -1$ −5, 19, 355

18. $f(x) = 3x^2 + 2, x_0 = 0$ 2, 14, 590

19. PENDULUMS A pendulum that is released to swing freely travels 25 inches on the first swing. On each successive swing, the pendulum travels 85% as far as the previous swing. What is the total distance the pendulum swings? *(p. 820)* $166\frac{2}{3}$ in.

5 ASSESS AND RETEACH

Daily Homework Quiz

Transparency Available

Write the first six terms of the sequence.

1. $a_0 = -1, a_n = a_{n-1} + 3$ −1, 2, 5, 8, 11, 14

2. $a_1 = 4, a_n = 2a_{n-1}$ 4, 8, 16, 32, 64, 128

3. Write a recursive rule for the sequence 128, 32, 8, 2, $\frac{1}{2}$, ... $a_1 = 128, a_n = \frac{1}{4}a_{n-1}$

4. A mortgage is $140,000. On the first of each month the bank charges 0.5% interest, and on the 15th of the month the family makes a payment of $840. Write a recursive rule for the balance owed at the end of each month. Find the balance after 3 months. $a_1 = 140{,}000, a_n = 1.005a_{n-1} - 840$; $139,577.90

5. Find the first three iterates of $f(x) = 3x + 2$ for an initial value of $x_0 = 5$. $x_1 = 17, x_2 = 53, x_3 = 161$

Available at **classzone.com**

Diagnosis/Remediation

- Practice A, B, C in Chapter 12 Resource Book, pp. 52–54
- Study Guide in Chapter 12 Resource Book, pp. 55–56
- Practice Workbook, pp. 179–180
- @HomeTutor

Challenge

Additional challenge is available in the Chapter 12 Resource Book, p. 59.

Quiz

An easily-readable reduced copy of the quiz (with answers) on Lessons 12.4–12.5 from the Assessment Book can be found on p. 792E.

Using ALTERNATIVE METHODS

Alternative Strategy

Students can also solve Example 4 on page 829 by graphing the sequence or by solving a linear equation for the limit of the sequence. Graphing will allow students to visualize what happens to the number of members over time. Solving an equation will help students relate a recursion formula to an algebraic equation. Both methods will prepare students for the idea of a limit of a function that they will study in a calculus course.

Graphing Calculator

Make sure that students understand that the settings for the window are based on the parameters of the recursion formula.

Another Way to Solve Example 4, page 829

MULTIPLE REPRESENTATIONS In Example 4 on page 829, you found the number that a real-life sequence approaches over time by using a calculator to evaluate the rule for the sequence. You can also solve this problem using a graph or an algebraic method.

PROBLEM

MUSIC SERVICE An online music service initially has 50,000 annual members. Each year the music service loses 20% of its current members and adds 5000 new members. What happens to the number of members over time?

METHOD 1

Using a Graph A recursive rule for the number a_n of members at the beginning of the nth year is $a_1 = 50{,}000$, $a_n = 0.8a_{n-1} + 5000$. One alternative method for finding the number this sequence approaches is to graph the sequence on a graphing calculator.

STEP 1 **Set** the calculator to *sequence* mode and *dot* mode.

STEP 2 **Press** Y= and enter the equations $n\text{Min} = 1$, $u(n) = 0.8u(n - 1) + 5000$, and $u(n\text{Min}) = 50{,}000$. Press WINDOW and enter the following parameters:

nMin = 1	Xmin = 0	Ymin = 15,000
nMax = 100	Xmax = 100	Ymax = 35,000
PlotStart = 1	Xscl = 10	Yscl = 5000
PlotStep = 1		

STEP 3 **Graph** the sequence. Use the *trace* feature to find the value that the sequence approaches as n becomes large. From the graph, you can see that the sequence approaches 25,000.

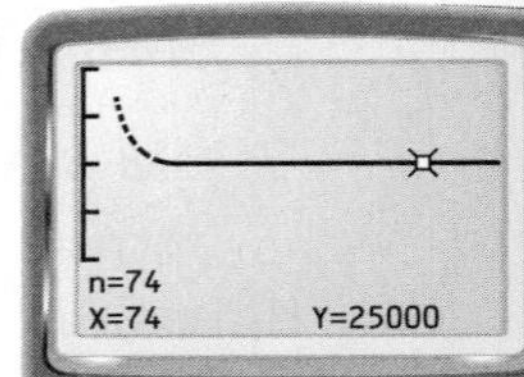

▶ Over time, the number of members of the music service approaches 25,000.

METHOD 2 **Using Algebra** Another approach is to use an algebraic method to determine what happens to the number of members over time.

STEP 1 **Write** the recursive rule.

$a_1 = 50{,}000,\ a_n = 0.8a_{n-1} + 5000.$

STEP 2 **Assume** that the sequence has a limit L, which is the value that the sequence approaches as n becomes large.

STEP 3 **Consider** what happens to the equation $a_n = 0.8a_{n-1} + 5000$ as n becomes large. The value of a_n (the left-hand side) approaches L while the value of $0.8a_{n-1} + 5000$ (the right-hand side) approaches $0.8L + 5000$. So, you can conclude that $L = 0.8L + 5000$.

STEP 4 **Solve** the equation $L = 0.8L + 5000$ for L.

$L = 0.8L + 5000$	**Write equation.**
$0.2L = 5000$	**Subtract $0.8L$ from each side.**
$L = 25{,}000$	**Divide each side by 0.2.**

▶ The sequence approaches the limit $L = 25{,}000$ as n becomes large. So, over time the number of members of the music service approaches 25,000.

PRACTICE

Describe **what happens to the terms of the sequence as n becomes large.**

1. $a_1 = 3000,\ a_n = 0.25a_{n-1} + 300$ The sequence approaches 400.
2. $a_1 = 1700,\ a_n = 0.38a_{n-1} + 512$
The sequence approaches 825.8.
3. **WHAT IF?** Suppose the online music service in the problem on page 834 loses 8% of its current members and adds 1200 new members each year. Use the graphing method and the algebraic method to determine what happens to the number of members over time.
The number of members approaches 15,000.
4. **TOWN LIBRARY** A town library initially has 54,000 books in its collection. Each year 2% of the books are lost or discarded. The library can afford to purchase 1150 new books each year. Write a recursive rule for the number a_n of books in the library at the beginning of the nth year. Use the graphing method and the algebraic method to determine what happens to the number of books in the library over time.
$a_1 = 54{,}000,\ a_n = 0.98a_{n-1} + 1150$; the number of books in the library approaches 57,500
5. **ERROR ANALYSIS** A student attempted to solve the problem in Exercise 4 as shown below. *Describe* and correct the error in the student's work.

$a_1 = 54{,}000,\ a_n = 0.02a_{n-1} + 1150$
Let L be the limit of the sequence. Then:

$L = 0.02L + 1150$

$0.98L = 1150$

$L \approx 1173$

So, over time the number of books in the library approaches about 1173.

See margin.

6. **REASONING** Give an example of a real-life situation which you can represent with a recursive rule that does not approach a limit. Write a recursive rule that represents the situation. *Sample answer:* Save a penny on day one and increase each day by a penny; $a_1 = 0.01,\ a_n = a_{n-1} + 0.01$.

5. *Sample answer:* 2% of the books are lost or discarded, so 98% are retained; $a_n = 0.98a_{n-1} + 1150$.

1 PLAN AND PREPARE

Warm-Up Exercises

Simplify.

1. $\frac{x(x+1)}{3} + (x+1)$ $\frac{(x+1)(x+3)}{3}$

2. $3\left(\frac{3^x - 1}{5}\right) + 5$ $\frac{3^{x+1} + 22}{5}$

3. Factor $3n(n+2) + 4(n+2)$. $(n+2)(3n+4)$

4. Let $a_1 = 4$ and $a_n = a_{n-1} + n + 2$. Find the value of a_8. 53

2 FOCUS AND MOTIVATE

Essential Question

Big Idea 2, p. 793

What is the sum of the first 100 natural numbers? Tell students they will learn how to answer this question by proving an explicit rule for the sum of the first n natural numbers.

3 TEACH

Extra Example 1

Use mathematical induction to prove that $4 + 8 + 12 + \ldots + 4n = 2n(n+1)$. Basis Step: For $n = 1$, $2n(n+1) = 2(1)(1+1) = 4 = 4(1) = 4n$; Inductive Step: Assume that $4 + 8 + 12 + \ldots + 4k = 2k(k+1)$. Then $4 + 8 + 12 + 4k + 4(k+1) = 2k(k+1) + 4(k+1) = (k+1)(2k+4) = 2(k+1)(k+2) = 2(k+1)[(k+1)+1]$. Therefore $4 + 8 + 12 + \ldots + 4n = 2n(n+1)$.

NCTM STANDARDS

Standard 7: Develop mathematical arguments and proofs; Use types of reasoning/methods of proof

Extension

Use after Lesson 12.5

Prove Statements Using Mathematical Induction

GOAL Use mathematical induction to prove statements about all positive integers.

In Lesson 12.1, you saw the rule for the sum of the first n positive integers:

$$\sum_{i=1}^{n} i = 1 + 2 + \cdots + n = \frac{n(n+1)}{2}$$

You can use *mathematical induction* to prove statements about positive integers.

KEY CONCEPT *For Your Notebook*

Mathematical Induction

To show that a statement is true for all positive integers n, perform these steps.

Basis Step: Show that the statement is true for $n = 1$.

Inductive Step: Assume that the statement is true for $n = k$ where k is any positive integer. Show that this implies the statement is true for $n = k + 1$.

EXAMPLE 1 Use mathematical induction

Use mathematical induction to prove that $1 + 2 + \cdots + n = \frac{n(n+1)}{2}$.

UNDERSTAND INDUCTION

If you know from the basis step that a statement is true for $n = 1$, then the inductive step implies that it is true for $n = 2$, and therefore for $n = 3$, and so on for all positive integers n.

Solution

Basis Step: Check that the formula works for $n = 1$.

$1 \stackrel{?}{=} \frac{1(1+1)}{2} \rightarrow 1 = 1$ ✓

Inductive Step: Assume that $1 + 2 + \cdots + k = \frac{k(k+1)}{2}$.

Show that $1 + 2 + \cdots + k + (k+1) = \frac{(k+1)[(k+1)+1]}{2}$.

$1 + 2 + \cdots + k = \frac{k(k+1)}{2}$ **Assume true for k.**

$1 + 2 + \cdots + k + (k+1) = \frac{k(k+1)}{2} + (k+1)$ **Add $k + 1$ to each side.**

$= \frac{k(k+1) + 2(k+1)}{2}$ **Add.**

$= \frac{(k+1)(k+2)}{2}$ **Factor out $k + 1$.**

$= \frac{(k+1)[(k+1)+1]}{2}$ **Rewrite $k + 2$ as $(k + 1) + 1$.**

Therefore, $1 + 2 + \cdots + n = \frac{n(n+1)}{2}$ for all positive integers n.

EXAMPLE 2 Use mathematical induction

Let $a_n = 5a_{n-1} + 2$ with $a_1 = 2$. Use mathematical induction to prove that an explicit rule for the nth term is $a_n = \frac{5^n - 1}{2}$.

Solution

Basis Step: Check that the formula works for $n = 1$.

$$a_1 \stackrel{?}{=} \frac{5^1 - 1}{2} \longrightarrow 2 = 2 \checkmark$$

Inductive Step: Assume that $a_k = \frac{5^k - 1}{2}$. Show that $a_{k+1} = \frac{5^{k+1} - 1}{2}$.

$a_{k+1} = 5a_k + 2$ — **Definition of a_n for $n = k + 1$**

$= 5\left(\frac{5^k - 1}{2}\right) + 2$ — **Substitute for a_k.**

$= \frac{5^{k+1} - 5}{2} + 2$ — **Multiply.**

$= \frac{5^{k+1} - 5 + 4}{2}$ — **Add.**

$= \frac{5^{k+1} - 1}{2}$ — **Simplify.**

Therefore, an explicit rule for the nth term is $a_n = \frac{5^n - 1}{2}$ for all positive integers n.

PRACTICE

EXAMPLES 1 and 2 on pp. 836–837 for Exs. 1–8

Use mathematical induction to prove the statement. **1–6. See margin.**

1. $\sum_{i=1}^{n} (2i - 1) = n^2$

2. $\sum_{i=1}^{n} i^2 = \frac{n(n+1)(2n+1)}{6}$

3. $\sum_{i=1}^{n} 2^{i-1} = 2^n - 1$

4. $\sum_{i=1}^{n} a_1 r^{i-1} = a_1\left(\frac{1 - r^n}{1 - r}\right)$

5. $\sum_{i=1}^{n} \frac{1}{i(i+1)} = \frac{n}{n+1}$

6. $\sum_{i=1}^{n} (2i)^2 = \frac{2n(n+1)(2n+1)}{3}$

7. **GEOMETRY** The numbers 1, 6, 15, 28, . . . are called *hexagonal numbers* because they represent the numbers of dots used to make hexagons, as shown below. Prove that the nth hexagonal number H_n is given by $H_n = n(2n - 1)$. **See margin.**

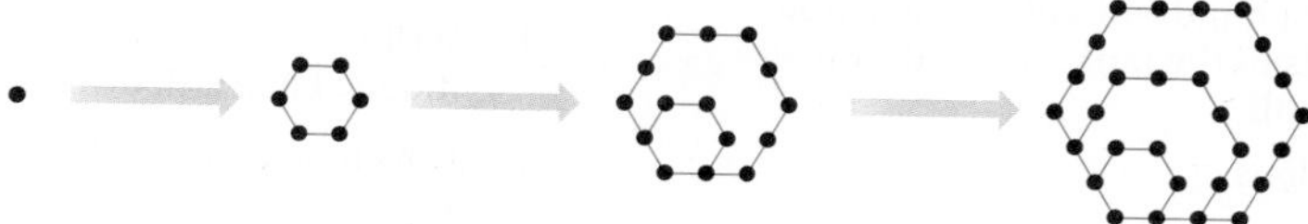

8. **REASONING** Let $f_1, f_2, \ldots, f_n, \ldots$ be the Fibonacci sequence. Prove that $f_1 + f_2 + \cdots + f_n = f_{n+2} - 1$ for all positive integers n. **See margin.**

Key Question to Ask for Example 1

- Which step in the proof shows that $n = \frac{n(n+1)}{2}$ for $n = 1$? **the basis step**

Extra Example 2

Let $a_n = 3a_{n-1}$ with $a_1 = 3$. Use mathematical induction to prove that an explicit rule for the nth term is $a_n = 3^n$. **Basis Step: For $n = 1, 3^n = 3^1 = 3 = a_1$; Inductive Step: Assume that $a_k = 3^k$. Then $a_{k+1} = 3a_k = 3(3^k) = 3^{k+1}$.**

Mathematical Reasoning

You can use a set of dominoes to demonstrate mathematical induction. The dominoes can be arranged to create a chain reaction if (1) The first domino is knocked down, and (2) You know that if any domino falls, then the one after it will fall. Help students relate the chain of dominos to the natural numbers.

Closing the Lesson

Have students summarize the major points of the lesson and answer the Essential Question: What is the sum of the first 100 natural numbers?

- **The principle of mathematical induction states that a statement is true for all positive integers n if (1) the statement is true for $n = 1$ and (2) if the statement is true for $n = k$, then the statement must be true for $n = k + 1$.**

$1 + 2 + 3 + \ldots + 100 = \frac{100(101)}{2} = 5050$

4 PRACTICE AND APPLY

Teaching Strategy

Exercises 1–6 Because mathematical induction is a difficult topic for students, have students work in pairs as they prove the statements. Suggest that they begin by writing the first several terms of each series.

1–7. See Additional Answers beginning on p. AA1.

8. Basis Step: Check that the formula works for $n = 1$.
$f_1 = f_{1+2} - 1 \rightarrow 1 = f_3 - 1 \rightarrow 1 = 2 - 1 \rightarrow 1 = 1 \checkmark$
Inductive Step: Assume that $f_1 + f_2 + \ldots + f_k = f_{k+2} - 1$.
Show that $f_1 + f_2 + \ldots + f_k + f_{k+1} = f_{k+3} - 1$.
$f_1 + f_2 + \ldots + f_k + f_{k+1} = (f_{k+2} - 1) + f_{k+1}$
$= (f_{k+2} + f_{k+1}) - 1$
$= f_{k+3} - 1 \checkmark$

Kentucky Mixed Review

1. D
2. A
3. D
4. B
5. D
6. C
7. a. 0.54%
   b. $a_n = 1.0054a_{n-1} - 196$
   c. \$8244.47

Kentucky Mixed Review

Lessons 12.4–12.5

1. **TOTAL DISTANCE** A ball is dropped from a height of 12 feet. Each time the ball hits the ground, it bounces to 70% of its previous height. What is the total distance traveled by the ball, including the distance traveled before the first bounce?

   A. 28 feet B. 40 feet
   C. 56 feet D. 68 feet

2. **FRACTAL TREE** A fractal tree starts with a single branch (the trunk) and "grows" as shown. What is a recursive rule for the number of new branches in each stage?

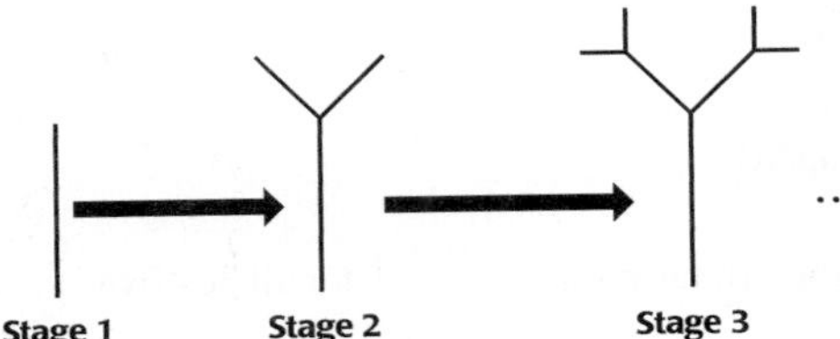

   A. $a_1 = 1, a_n = 2a_n - 1$
   B. $a_1 = 1, a_n = a_n - 1 + (n - 1)$
   C. $a_n = 2^{n-1}$
   D. $a_n = \frac{1}{2}n(n - 1) + 1$

3. **TREE FARM** A tree farm currently has 8000 trees. Each year 10% of the trees are harvested and 500 seedlings are planted. After an extended period of time, how many trees exist on the farm?

   A. 500 trees B. 1250 trees
   C. 2500 trees D. 5000 trees

4. **FISH TANK** Paul owns a 40 gallon fish tank that leaks 5% of its water every day. Paul replaces 1 gallon each day to make up for the loss. To the nearest hundredth of a gallon, how much water is in the tank 4 days after it was completely full?

   A. 1.05 gallons
   B. 36.29 gallons
   C. 37.15 gallons
   D. 38.75 gallons

5. **SPRINGS** The length ℓ_1 of the first loop of a spring is 16 inches. The length ℓ_2 of the second loop is 0.9 times the length of the first loop. The length ℓ_3 of the third loop is 0.9 times the length of the second loop, and so on. If the spring could have infinitely many loops, what would be its total length?

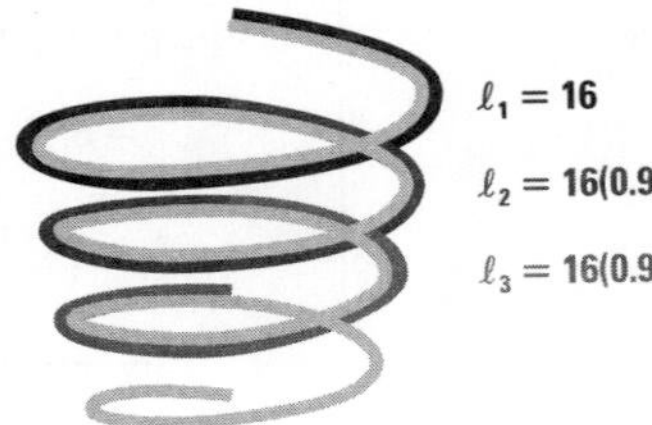

   A. 17.8 inches B. 80 inches
   C. 150 inches D. 160 inches

6. **GEOMETRIC SERIES** Which statement below is a FALSE statement about an infinite geometric series $\{a_n\}$ with a common ratio r?

   A. The sum of series exists only if $|r| < 1$.
   B. For all n, $\frac{a_n}{a_{n+1}} = \frac{1}{r}$.
   C. The sum of the series does not exist if r has a negative value.
   D. If the sum exists, the sum of the series is $\frac{a_1}{1 - r}$.

7. **OPEN-RESPONSE** Leah takes a five year loan of \$10,000 to buy a car. The loan has an annual interest rate of 6.5%, compounded monthly. Each month, Leah makes a payment of \$196 (except for the last month, when she makes a payment of \$165).

   a. Find the monthly interest rate.
   b. Write a recursive rule for the amount of money Leah still owes after n months.
   c. How much money does Leah owe after 12 months?

CHAPTER SUMMARY

BIG IDEAS

For Your Notebook

ig Idea 1

Analyze Sequences

The information below highlights the similarities and differences between arithmetic and geometric sequences.

Arithmetic Sequence

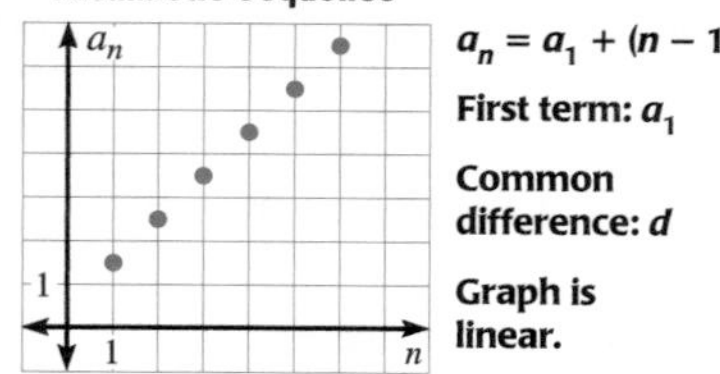

$a_n = a_1 + (n - 1)d$

First term: a_1

Common difference: d

Graph is linear.

Geometric Sequence

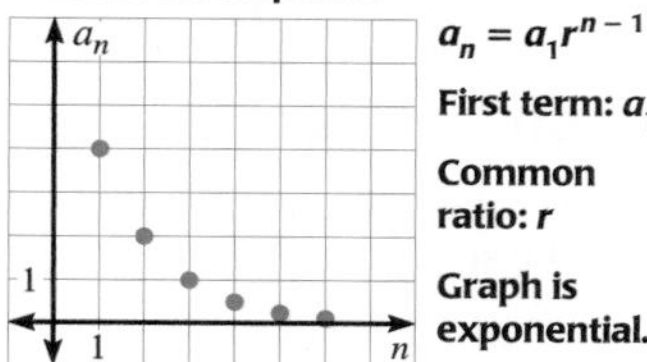

$a_n = a_1 r^{n-1}$

First term: a_1

Common ratio: r

Graph is exponential.

ig Idea 2

Find Sums of Series

The most common formulas for sums of series are shown below.

Arithmetic Series	Geometric Series	Infinite Geometric Series
Sum of the first n terms: $S_n = n\left(\frac{a_1 + a_n}{2}\right)$	Sum of the first n terms: $S_n = a_1\left(\frac{1 - r^n}{1 - r}\right), r \neq 1$	Sum of the series: $S = \frac{a_1}{1 - r}, \lvert r \rvert < 1$
Example: $4 + 9 + 14 + 19 + 24$	Example: $3 + 6 + 12 + 24$	Example: $5 + 1 + 0.2 + 0.04 + \cdots$
$S_5 = 5\left(\frac{4 + 24}{2}\right) = 70$	$S_4 = 3\left(\frac{1 - 2^4}{1 - 2}\right) = 45$	$S = \frac{5}{1 - 0.2} = 6.25$

Other common sum formulas:

$$\sum_{i=1}^{n} 1 = n \qquad \sum_{i=1}^{n} i = \frac{n(n+1)}{2} \qquad \sum_{i=1}^{n} i^2 = \frac{n(n+1)(2n+1)}{6}$$

g Idea 3

Use Recursive Rules

The table shows explicit and recursive rules for arithmetic and geometric sequences.

	Explicit Rule	Recursive Rule
Arithmetic Sequence	$a_n = a_1 + (n - 1)d$	$a_n = a_{n-1} + d$
Example: 3, 5, 7, 9, 11, . . .	$a_n = 1 + 2n$	$a_1 = 3, a_n = a_{n-1} + 2$
Geometric Sequence	$a_n = a_1 r^{n-1}$	$a_n = r \cdot a_{n-1}$
Example: 8, 4, 2, 1, 0.5, . . .	$a_n = 8(0.5)^{n-1}$	$a_1 = 8, a_n = 0.5a_{n-1}$

Additional Resources

The following resources are available to help review the materials in this chapter.

Chapter 12 Resource Book

- Chapter Review Games and Activities, p. 60
- Cumulative Practice, Chs. 1–12, pp. 62–63

Student Resources in Spanish

eWorkbook

@HomeTutor

Vocabulary Practice

Vocabulary practice is available at **classzone.com**

839

Extra Example 12.1

Find the sum of the series $\sum_{i=1}^{5}(5i - 4)$. 55

12 CHAPTER REVIEW

@HomeTutor
classzone.com
- Multi-Language Glossary
- Vocabulary practice

REVIEW KEY VOCABULARY

- sequence, *p. 794*
- terms of a sequence, *p. 794*
- series, *p. 796*
- summation notation, *p. 796*
- sigma notation, *p. 796*
- arithmetic sequence, *p. 802*
- common difference, *p. 802*
- arithmetic series, *p. 804*
- geometric sequence, *p. 810*
- common ratio, *p. 810*
- geometric series, *p. 812*
- partial sum, *p. 820*
- explicit rule, *p. 827*
- recursive rule, *p. 827*
- iteration, *p. 830*

VOCABULARY EXERCISES

1. Copy and complete: The values in the range of a sequence are called the _?_ of the sequence. terms
2. **WRITING** How can you determine whether a sequence is arithmetic? A sequence is arithmetic if the difference between consecutive terms is constant.
3. Copy and complete: A(n) _?_ rule gives a_n as a function of the term's position number n in the sequence. explicit
4. Copy and complete: In a(n) _?_ sequence, the ratio of any term to the previous term is constant. geometric

REVIEW EXAMPLES AND EXERCISES

Use the review examples and exercises below to check your understanding of the concepts you have learned in each lesson of Chapter 12.

12.1 Define and Use Sequences and Series *pp. 794–800*

EXAMPLE

Find the sum of the series $\sum_{i=1}^{4}(i^2 - 4)$.

$a_1 = 1^2 - 4 = -3$ **First term**

$a_2 = 2^2 - 4 = 0$ **Second term**

$a_3 = 3^2 - 4 = 5$ **Third term**

$a_4 = 4^2 - 4 = 12$ **Fourth term**

The sum of the series is $\sum_{i=1}^{4}(i^2 - 4) = -3 + 0 + 5 + 12 = 14$.

EXERCISES

EXAMPLES 5 and 6 on p. 797 for Exs. 5–8

Find the sum of the series.

5. $\sum_{n=1}^{6}(n^2 + 7)$ 133
6. $\sum_{i=2}^{6}(10 - 4i)$ −30
7. $\sum_{i=1}^{17} i$ 153
8. $\sum_{k=1}^{25} k^2$ 5525

@HomeTutor
classzone.com
Chapter Review Practice

12.2 Analyze Arithmetic Sequences and Series
pp. 802–809

EXAMPLE

Write a rule for the nth term of the sequence 9, 13, 17, 21, 25, ...

The sequence is arithmetic with first term $a_1 = 9$ and common difference $d = 4$. So, a rule for the nth term is:

$a_n = a_1 + (n - 1)d$ **Write general rule.**

$= 9 + (n - 1)(4)$ **Substitute 9 for a_1 and 4 for d.**

$= 5 + 4n$ **Simplify.**

EXERCISES

XAMPLES
, 3, 4, and 5
n pp. 803–805
or Exs. 9–16

Write a rule for the nth term of the arithmetic sequence.

9. 8, 5, 2, −1, −4, . . . $a_n = 11 - 3n$

10. $d = 7, a_8 = 54$ $a_n = -2 + 7n$

11. $a_4 = 27, a_{11} = 69$ $a_n = 3 + 6n$

Find the sum of the series.

12. $\sum_{i=1}^{15}(3 + 2i)$ 285

13. $\sum_{i=1}^{26}(25 - 3i)$ −403

14. $\sum_{i=1}^{22}(6i - 5)$ 1408

15. $\sum_{i=1}^{30}(-84 + 8i)$ 1200

16. COMPUTER Joe buys a $600 computer on layaway by making a $200 down payment and then paying $25 per month. Write a rule for the total amount of money paid on the computer after n months. $a_n = 200 + 25n$

12.3 Analyze Geometric Sequences and Series
pp. 810–817

EXAMPLE

Find the sum of the series $\sum_{i=1}^{7} 5(3)^{i-1}$.

The series is geometric with first term $a_1 = 5$ and common ratio $r = 3$.

$S_7 = a_1\left(\frac{1 - r^7}{1 - r}\right)$ **Write rule for S_7.**

$= 5\left(\frac{1 - 3^7}{1 - 3}\right)$ **Substitute 5 for a_1 and 3 for r.**

$= 5465$ **Simplify.**

EXERCISES

XAMPLES
, 3, 4, and 5
n pp. 811–813
r Exs. 17–23

Write a rule for the nth term of the geometric sequence.

17. 256, 64, 16, 4, 1, . . . $a_n = 256\left(\frac{1}{4}\right)^{n-1}$

18. $r = 5, a_2 = 200$ $a_n = 40(5)^{n-1}$

19. $a_1 = 144, a_3 = 16$ $a_n = 144\left(\frac{1}{3}\right)^{n-1}$ or $a_n = 144\left(-\frac{1}{3}\right)^{n-1}$

Find the sum of the series.

20. $\sum_{i=1}^{6} 3(5)^{i-1}$ 11,718

21. $\sum_{i=1}^{9} 8(2)^{i-1}$ 4088

22. $\sum_{i=1}^{5} 15\left(\frac{2}{3}\right)^{i-1}$ $\frac{1055}{27}$

23. $\sum_{i=1}^{7} 40\left(\frac{1}{2}\right)^{i-1}$ $\frac{635}{8}$

Extra Example 12.2

Write a rule for the nth term of the sequence −4, −7, −10, −13, −16, ... $a_n = -1 - 3n$

Extra Example 12.3

Find the sum of the series $\sum_{i=1}^{10} 6(2)^i$. 12,276

12 CHAPTER REVIEW

Extra Example 12.4

Find the sum of the series $\sum_{i=1}^{\infty} (1.6)^i$.

does not exist

Extra Example 12.5

Write a recursive rule for the sequence 125, 25, 5, 1, $\frac{1}{5}$, ...

$a_1 = 125$, $a_n = \frac{1}{5}a_{n-1}$

12.4 Find Sums of Infinite Geometric Series

pp. 820–825

EXAMPLE

Find the sum of the series $\sum_{i=1}^{\infty} \left(\frac{4}{5}\right)^{i-1}$, if it exists.

For this series, $a_1 = 1$ and $r = \frac{4}{5}$. Because $|r| < 1$, the sum of this series exists.

The sum is $S = \frac{a_1}{1-r} = \frac{1}{1-\frac{4}{5}} = 5$.

EXERCISES

EXAMPLES 2 and 5 on pp. 821–822 for Exs. 24–31

Find the sum of the infinite geometric series, if it exists.

24. $\sum_{i=1}^{\infty} 3\left(\frac{5}{8}\right)^{i-1}$ 8
25. $\sum_{i=1}^{\infty} 7\left(-\frac{3}{4}\right)^{i-1}$ 4
26. $\sum_{i=1}^{\infty} 4(1.3)^{i-1}$ no sum
27. $\sum_{i=1}^{\infty} -0.2(0.5)^{i-1}$ −0.4

Write the repeating decimal as a fraction in lowest terms.

28. 0.888. . . $\frac{8}{9}$
29. 0.546546546. . . $\frac{182}{333}$
30. 0.3787878. . . $\frac{25}{66}$
31. 0.7838383. . . $\frac{388}{495}$

12.5 Use Recursive Rules with Sequences and Functions

pp. 827–833

EXAMPLE

Write a recursive rule for the sequence 6, 10, 14, 18, 22, ...

The sequence is arithmetic with first term $a_1 = 6$ and common difference $d = 10 - 6 = 4$.

$a_n = a_{n-1} + d$ **General recursive rule for a_n**

$= a_{n-1} + 4$ **Substitute 4 for *d*.**

So, a recursive rule for the sequence is $a_1 = 6$, $a_n = a_{n-1} + 4$.

EXERCISES

EXAMPLES 1, 2, and 3 on pp. 827–828 for Exs. 32–38

Write the first five terms of the sequence.

32. $a_1 = 4$, $a_n = a_{n-1} + 9$ 4, 13, 22, 31, 40
33. $a_1 = 8$, $a_n = 5a_{n-1}$ 8, 40, 200, 1000, 5000
34. $a_1 = 2$, $a_n = n \cdot a_{n-1}$ 2, 4, 12, 48, 240

Write a recursive rule for the sequence.

35. 6, 18, 54, 162, 486, . . . $a_1 = 6$, $a_n = 3a_{n-1}$
36. 4, 6, 9, 13, 18, . . . $a_1 = 4$, $a_n = a_{n-1} + n$
37. 7, 13, 19, 25, 31, . . . $a_1 = 7$, $a_n = a_{n-1} + 6$
38. **POPULATION** A town's population increases at a rate of about 1% per year. In 2000, the town had a population of 26,000. Write a recursive rule for the town's population P_n in year n. Let $n = 1$ represent 2000. $a_1 = 26{,}000$, $a_n = 1.01a_{n-1}$

CHAPTER TEST

Tell whether the sequence is *arithmetic, geometric,* or *neither. Explain.*

1. 5, 9, 13, 17, . . .   2. 3, 6, 12, 24, . . .   3. $40, 10, \frac{5}{2}, \frac{5}{8}, \ldots$ 4. 4, 7, 12, 19, . . .

1. Arithmetic; there is a common difference of 4.
2. Geometric; there is a common ratio of 2.
3. Geometric; there is a common ratio of $\frac{1}{4}$.
4. Neither; there is no common ratio or common difference.

Write the first six terms of the sequence.

5. $a_n = 6 - n^2$ 5, 2, −3, −10, −19, −30
6. $a_n = 7n^3$ 7, 56, 189, 448, 875, 1512
7. $a_1 = 4$, $a_n = 5a_{n-1}$ 4, 20, 100, 500, 2500, 12,500
8. $a_1 = -1$, $a_n = a_{n-1} + 6$ −1, 5, 11, 17, 23, 29

Write the next term of the sequence, and then write a rule for the *n*th term.

9. 5, 11, 17, 23, . . . 29, $a_n = -1 + 6n$
10. 3, 15, 75, 375, . . . 1875, $a_n = 3 \cdot 5^{n-1}$
11. $\frac{6}{5}, \frac{7}{10}, \frac{8}{15}, \frac{9}{20}, \ldots$ $\frac{10}{25}$, $a_n = \frac{n+5}{5n}$
12. 1.6, 3.2, 4.8, 6.4, . . . 8, $a_n = 1.6n$

Find the sum of the series.

13. $\sum_{i=1}^{48} i$ 1176
14. $\sum_{n=1}^{28} n^2$ 7714
15. $\sum_{i=1}^{10} (4i - 9)$ 130
16. $\sum_{i=1}^{19} (2i + 5)$ 475
17. $\sum_{i=1}^{5} 9(2)^{i-1}$ 279
18. $\sum_{i=1}^{6} 12\left(\frac{1}{3}\right)^{i-1}$ $\frac{1456}{81}$
19. $\sum_{i=1}^{\infty} 8\left(\frac{3}{4}\right)^{i-1}$ 32
20. $\sum_{i=1}^{\infty} 20\left(\frac{3}{10}\right)^{i-1}$ $\frac{200}{7}$

Write the repeating decimal as a fraction in lowest terms.

21. 0.111. . . $\frac{1}{9}$
22. 0.464646. . . $\frac{46}{99}$
23. 0.187187187. . . $\frac{187}{999}$
24. 0.3252525. . . $\frac{161}{495}$

Write a recursive rule for the sequence.

25. 2, 12, 72, 432, . . . $a_1 = 2, a_n = 6a_{n-1}$
26. 3, 10, 17, 24, . . . $a_1 = 3, a_n = a_{n-1} + 7$
27. 135, 45, 15, 5, . . . $a_1 = 135, a_n = \frac{1}{3}a_{n-1}$
28. 1, −3, 9, −27, . . . $a_1 = 1, a_n = -3a_{n-1}$

Find the first three iterates of the function for the given initial value.

29. $f(x) = 3x - 7, x_0 = 4$ 5, 8, 17
30. $f(x) = 8 - 5x, x_0 = 1$ 3, −7, 43
31. $f(x) = x^2 + 2, x_0 = -1$ 3, 11, 123

32. **QUILTS** Use the pattern of checkerboard quilts shown.

$n = 1, a_n = 1$

$n = 2, a_n = 2$

$n = 3, a_n = 5$

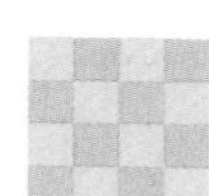
$n = 4, a_n = 8$

a. What does n represent for each quilt? What does a_n represent?

b. Make a table that shows n and a_n for $n = 1, 2, 3, 4, 5, 6, 7,$ and 8. See margin.

c. Use the rule $a_n = \frac{n^2}{2} + \frac{1}{4}[1 - (-1)^n]$ to find a_n for $n = 1, 2, 3, 4, 5, 6, 7,$ and 8. *Compare* these values with the results in your table. What can you conclude about the sequence defined by this rule?

a. the number of …s and columns; number of blue …ares

c. 1, 2, 5, 8, 13, 18, … 32; the values … the same; … rule defines … sequence … resented by … checkerboard … lts.

33. **AUDITIONS** Several rounds of auditions are being held to cast the three main parts in a play. There are 3072 actors at the first round of auditions. In each successive round of auditions, one fourth of the actors from the previous round remain. Find a rule for the number a_n of actors in the nth round of auditions. For what values of n does your rule make sense? $a_n = 3072\left(\frac{1}{4}\right)^{n-1}$; $1 \le n \le 5$

32b.

n	1	2	3	4	5	6	7	8
a_n	1	2	5	8	13	18	25	32

Additional Resources

Assessment Book

- Chapter Test, Levels A, B, C, pp. 170–175
- Standardized Chapter Test, pp. 176–177
- SAT/ACT Chapter Test, pp. 178–179
- Alternative Assessment, pp. 180–181

Test Generator CD-ROM

Chapter Test

Easily-readable reduced copies (with answers) of Chapter Test B, the Standardized Chapter Test, and the Alternative Assessment from the Assessment Book can be found on pp. 792E–792F.

TEST PREPARATION

MULTIPLE-CHOICE QUESTIONS

Some of the information you need to solve a multiple-choice question may appear in a table, a diagram, or a graph.

PROBLEM 1

The frequencies (in hertz) of the notes on a piano form a geometric sequence. The frequencies of G (labeled "8") and A (labeled "10") are shown in the diagram. What is the approximate frequency of E flat (labeled "4")?

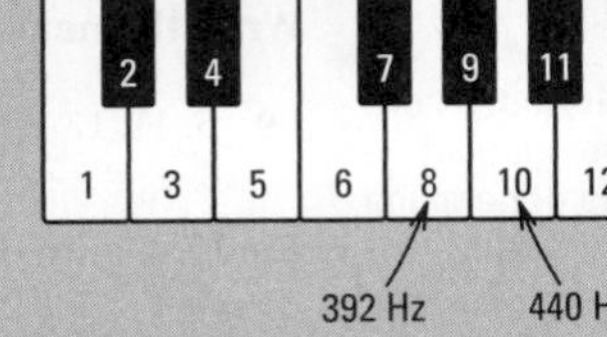

A. 247 Hz B. 311 Hz

C. 330 Hz D. 554 Hz

Plan

INTERPRET THE DIAGRAM The diagram gives you the frequencies of the 8th 10th notes. Use these frequencies to find the frequency of the 4th note.

Solution

STEP 1 Write a system of equations.

Let a_n be the frequency (in hertz) of the nth note. Because the frequencies f a geometric sequence, a rule for a_n has the form $a_n = a_1r^{n-1}$. From the diag $a_8 = 392$ and $a_{10} = 440$. Use these values to write a system of equations.

$a_8 = a_1r^{8-1} \longrightarrow 392 = a_1r^7$ **Equation 1**

$a_{10} = a_1r^{10-1} \longrightarrow 440 = a_1r^9$ **Equation 2**

STEP 2 Solve the system of equations to find the values of r and a_1.

$a_1 = \frac{392}{r^7}$ **Solve Equation 1 for a_1.**

$440 = \frac{392}{r^7} \cdot r^9$ **Substitute $\frac{392}{r^7}$ for a_1 in Equatio**

$440 = 392r^2$ **Simplify.**

$1.12 \approx r^2$ **Divide each side by 392.**

$1.06 \approx r$ **Take positive square root of each side.**

Find a_1 by substituting the value of r into revised Equation 1.

$$a_1 = \frac{392}{r^7} = \frac{392}{(1.06)^7} \approx 261$$

STEP 3 Write a rule for the nth term and find a_4.

A rule for the sequence is $a_n = a_1r^{n-1} = 261(1.06)^{n-1}$.

So, $a_4 = 261(1.06)^3 \approx 311$.

▸ The correct answer is B.

TEST PRACTICE
classzone.com

Kentucky Test Preparation

1. B
2. A

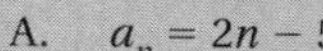

PROBLEM 2

The first 4 terms of an infinite arithmetic sequence are shown in the graph. Which rule describes the nth term in the sequence?

A. $a_n = 2n - 5$ B. $a_n = 2n + 5$

C. $a_n = 5n - 2$ D. $a_n = n + 5$

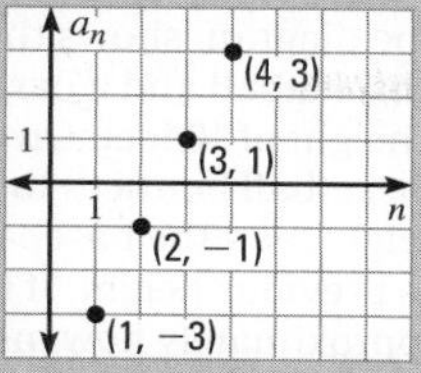

Plan

INTERPRET THE GRAPH In order to find a rule for the sequence, you must first use the graph to write the terms of the sequence.

Solution

1 ... e the terms of the ...ence.

The points shown in the graph are:

(1, −3), (2, −1), (3, 1), (4, 3)

Therefore, the sequence is −3, −1, 1, 3, ...

2 ... the first term and ...ommon difference.

The first term a_1 of the sequence is −3.

Because each term after the first is 2 more than the previous term, the common difference d is 2.

3 ... e a rule for the nth

$a_n = \mathbf{a_1} + (n - 1)\mathbf{d}$	**Write general rule for an arithmetic sequence.**
$= \mathbf{-3} + (n - 1)\mathbf{2}$	**Substitute −3 for a_1 and 2 for d.**
$= -3 + 2n - 2$	**Distributive property**
$= 2n - 5$	**Simplify.**

▶ The correct answer is A.

PRACTICE

In Exercises 1 and 2, use the graph in Problem 2.

1. What is the value of a_{15}?

A. −35 B. 25

C. 30 D. 165

2. Which statement is true about the sequence that is graphed?

A. The sum of the first 14 terms is 140.

B. The value of a_{20} is 40.

C. A recursive rule for the sequence is $a_1 = 2, a_n = a_{n-1} - 5$.

D. The ratio of any term to the previous term is constant.

TEST PREPARATION

Kentucky Test Practice

1. C
2. C
3. D
4. B
5. D
6. B
7. D

Kentucky Test Practice

TEST PREPARATION

MULTIPLE-CHOICE

1. The diagram shows the bounce heights of a basketball and a baseball dropped from a height of 10 feet. On each bounce, the basketball bounces to 36% of its previous height, and the baseball bounces to 30% of its previous height. If both patterns continue, approximately how much greater is the total distance traveled by the basketball than the total distance traveled by the baseball?

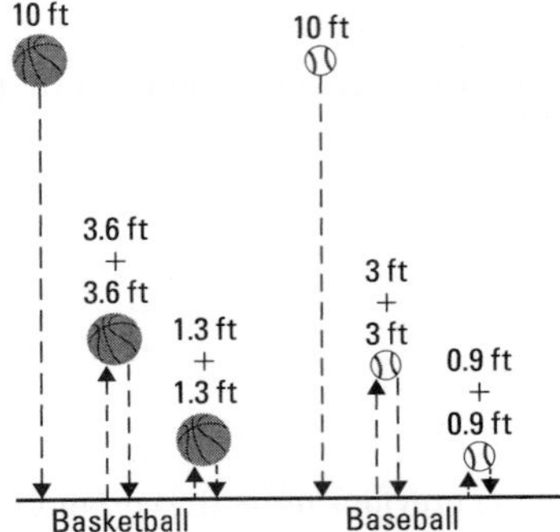

A. 1.34 feet B. 2.00 feet
C. 2.62 feet D. 5.63 feet

2. The table shows the domain and range of a sequence. Which recursive rule describes the sequence?

Domain	1	2	3	4	5
Range	20	10	5	2.5	1.25

A $a_1 = 20, a_n = a_{n-1} + 10$
B. $a_1 = 20, a_n = a_{n-1} - 10$
C. $a_1 = 20, a_n = 0.5a_{n-1}$
D. $a_1 = 20, a_n = 2a_{n-1}$

3. What type of sequence is graphed at the right?

a_n, 3, 1, n

A. Arithmetic
B. Geometric with $0 < r < 1$
C. Geometric with $r > 1$
D. Neither arithmetic nor geometric

In Exercises 4 and 5, use the information below. Cheryl is researching her lineage for a history project. So far, she has created a family tree for three generations, as shown below. Cheryl is only including relatives from whom she is directly descended. Siblings are not included.

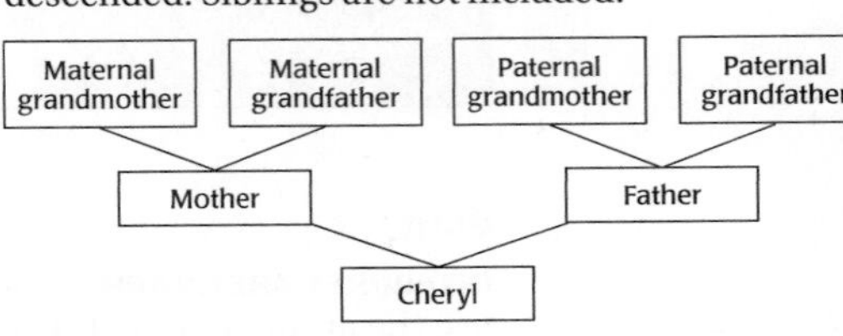

4. Assume that Cheryl is in generation 1, her parents are in generation 2, and so on. Let a_n be the number of relatives in generation n. What is a rule for a_n?

A. $a_n = n + 2$ B. $a_n = 2^{n-1}$
C. $a_n = 2^n$ D. $a_n = 2^{n+1}$

5. Cheryl creates a family tree with 8 generations of her family. How many people are in her family tree?

A. 8 B. 64
C. 128 D. 255

In Exercises 6 and 7, use the diagram of a stack of blocks.

6. Which rule describes the number of blocks in the nth layer, where $n = 1$ represents the top layer?

A. $a_n = n + 1$ B. $a_n = n(n + 1)$
C. $a_n = 2n^2$ D. $a_n = n^2 + 1$

7. Which sum gives the number of blocks shown?

A. $\sum_{i=2}^{20} (i + 1)$ B. $\sum_{i=1}^{4} (i + 1)$
C. $\sum_{i=2}^{20} i(i + 1)$ D. $\sum_{i=1}^{4} i(i + 1)$

TEST PRACTICE
classzone.com

MULTIPLE-CHOICE

8. Two terms of a geometric sequence are $a_3 = 12$ and $a_5 = 48$. What is the value of a_1?

A. −24 B. 1
C. 3 D. 4

9. Write the repeating decimal 0.1515... as a fraction in lowest terms.

A. $\frac{3}{20}$ B. $\frac{5}{33}$
C. $\frac{303}{2000}$ D. $\frac{50}{33}$

10. What is the sum of the following series?

$$\sum_{i=1}^{5} 0.5(2)^{i-1}$$

A. 0.5 B. 7.5
C. 8 D. 15.5

11. What is the eighth term of the sequence below?

−4, 12, −36, 108, ...

A. −8748 B. −684
C. 684 D. 8748

12. What is the sum of the first 15 terms of the sequence $a_n = 6n + 3$?

A. 93 B. 667
C. 723 D. 765

13. Person *A* sends an e-mail to 10 friends. Each of those 10 friends forwards the e-mail to 10 more friends. Through how many stages has the e-mail been forwarded if you are among a group of 100 million people receiving it?

A. 7 B. 8
C. 9 D. 10

OPEN-RESPONSE

14. A running track is shaped like a rectangle with two semicircular ends, as shown. The track has 8 lanes that are each 1.22 meters wide. The lanes are numbered from 1 to 8 starting from the inside lane. The length of each line segment that extends from the center of the left semicircle to the inside of a lane is called the lane's curve radius.

Not drawn to scale

a. Is the sequence formed by the curve radii *arithmetic*, *geometric*, or *neither*? *Explain.*

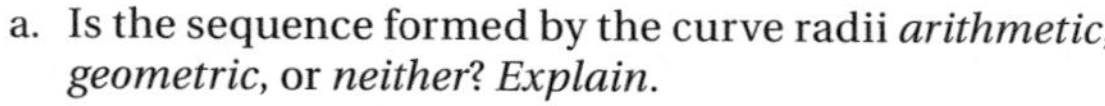

b. Write a formula for the sequence from part (a).

c. World records must be set on tracks that have a curve radius of at most 50 meters in the outside lane. Does the track shown meet the requirement? *Explain.*

15. Mark takes out a loan for $16,000 with an interest rate of 0.75% per month. At the end of each month he makes a payment of $300.

a. Write a recursive rule for the balance a_n of the loan at the beginning of the *n*th month.

b. How much will Mark owe at the beginning of the 18th month?

c. How long will it take Mark to pay off the loan?

TEST PREPARATION

8. C
9. B
10. D
11. D
12. D
13. B
14. a. Arithmetic; each lane adds 1.22 meters to the radius. This represents the common difference of an arithmetic sequence.
b. $a_n = 35.28 + 1.22n$
c. Yes; the curve radius of lane 8 is about 45 meters, which is less than 50 meters.
15. a. $a_1 = 16{,}000$; $a_n = 1.0075a_{n-1} - 300$
b. $12,749.33
c. 69 months

Additional Resources

The following resources are available to help review the materials in Chapters 10–12.

Chapter Resource Books

- Chapter 10 CRB, Cumulative Review, pp. 72–73
- Chapter 11 CRB, Cumulative Review, pp. 66–67
- Chapter 12 CRB, Cumulative Review, pp. 62–63

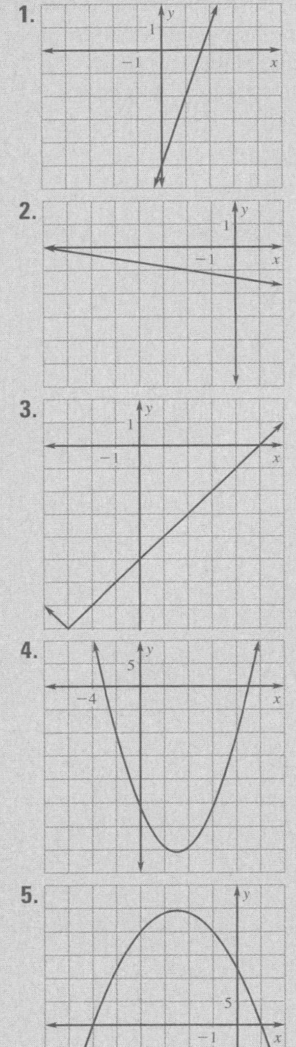

Graph the function. 1–12. See margin.

1. $3x - y = 5$ *(p. 89)*
2. $\frac{1}{2}x + 3y = -4$ *(p. 89)*
3. $y = |x + 3| - 8$ *(p. 123)*
4. $y = x^2 - 6x - 27$ *(p. 236)*
5. $y = -2(x + 6)(x - 1)$ *(p. 245)*
6. $y = (x - 3)^2 + 4$ *(p. 245)*
7. $y = \sqrt{x + 6}$ *(p. 446)*
8. $y = \sqrt[3]{x} - 2$ *(p. 446)*
9. $y = 3 \cdot 4^{x-2}$ *(p. 478)*
10. $y = 12\left(\frac{1}{8}\right)^x$ *(p. 486)*
11. $y = \frac{2}{x - 3} + 5$ *(p. 558)*
12. $y = \frac{6}{x^2 - 4}$ *(p. 565)*

Evaluate the determinant of the matrix. *(p. 203)*

13. $\begin{bmatrix} 2 & 3 \\ 1 & 8 \end{bmatrix}$ 13
14. $\begin{bmatrix} 12 & 3 \\ -7 & 8 \end{bmatrix}$ 117
15. $\begin{bmatrix} 0 & 5 & 2 \\ 10 & 13 & -4 \\ -5 & 4 & -1 \end{bmatrix}$ 360
16. $\begin{bmatrix} 5 & -9 & 4 \\ 4 & 2 & 1 \\ 0 & 1 & 1 \end{bmatrix}$ 57

The variables *x* and *y* vary inversely. Use the given values to write an equation relating *x* and *y*. Then find the value of *y* when $x = -8$. *(p. 551)*

17. $x = 3, y = 6$ $y = \frac{18}{x}$; $-\frac{9}{4}$
18. $x = -4, y = 9$ $y = -\frac{36}{x}$; $\frac{9}{2}$
19. $x = 4, y = \frac{1}{8}$ $y = \frac{\frac{1}{2}}{x}$; $-\frac{1}{16}$
20. $x = 9, y = \frac{2}{5}$ $y = \frac{\frac{18}{5}}{x}$; $-\frac{9}{20}$

Graph the equation. 21–23. See margin.

21. $\frac{x^2}{36} + \frac{y^2}{4} = 1$ *(p. 634)*
22. $\frac{y^2}{100} - \frac{x^2}{49} = 1$ *(p. 642)*
23. $(x - 3)^2 = 16y$ *(p. 650)*

Find the number of permutations or combinations.

24. ${}_9P_3$ *(p. 682)* 504
25. ${}_{16}P_5$ *(p. 682)* 524,160
26. ${}_7C_2$ *(p. 690)* 21
27. ${}_6C_6$ *(p. 690)* 1

Find the indicated probability.

28. $P(A) = 0.32$
$P(B) = 0.6$
$P(A \text{ or } B) = 0.85$
$P(A \text{ and } B) = \underline{\ ?\ }$ *(p. 707)* 0.07
29. *A* and *B* are dependent events.
$P(A) = 0.5$
$P(B|A) = 0.3$
$P(A \text{ and } B) = \underline{\ ?\ }$ *(p. 717)* 0.15
30. *A* and *B* are independent events.
$P(A) = 0.25$
$P(B) = \underline{\ ?\ }$
$P(A \text{ and } B) = 0.2$ *(p. 717)* 0.8

Find the mean, median, mode, range, and standard deviation of the data set. *(p. 744)*

31. 19, 11, 8, 10, 11, 15, 16 about 12.857, 11, 11, 11, about 3.603
32. 54, 58, 49, 60, 63, 58, 42 about 54.857, 58, 58, 21, about 6.685
33. 216, 203, 225, 216, 212, 228, 209 about 215.571, 216, 216, 25, about 8.086
34. −3, 5, −11, 6, −3, 2
35. 99, 92, 93, 82, 88, 71, 97 about 88.857, 92, no mode, 28, about 8.967
36. 78, 4, 28, 57, 88, 24, 57, 37, 65 $48\frac{2}{3}$, 57, 57, 84, about 25.777

34. $-\frac{2}{3}, -\frac{1}{2}, -3, 17,$ about 5.793

Find the sum of the series.

37. $\sum_{i=1}^{6} 3i^2$ *(p. 794)* 273
38. $\sum_{i=1}^{16} (-2 + i)$ *(p. 802)* 104
39. $\sum_{i=1}^{12} \left(\frac{2}{3}\right)^{i-1}$ *(p. 810)* about 2.977
40. $\sum_{i=1}^{\infty} 5\left(\frac{1}{3}\right)^{i-1}$ *(p. 820)* 7.5

Write an explicit rule and a recursive rule for the sequence. *(p. 827)*

41. −7, −3, 1, 5, . . .
42. 1, −14, −29, −44, . . .
43. 3, 12, 48, 192, . . .

41. $a_n = -11 + 4n$, $a_1 = -7$, $a_n = a_{n-1} + 4$

42. $a_n = 16 - 15n$, $a_1 = 1$, $a_n = a_{n-1} - 15$

43. $a_n = 3(4)^{n-1}$, $a_1 = 3$, $a_n = 4a_{n-1}$

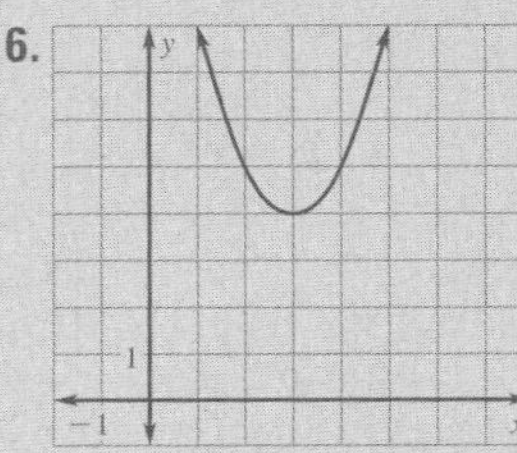

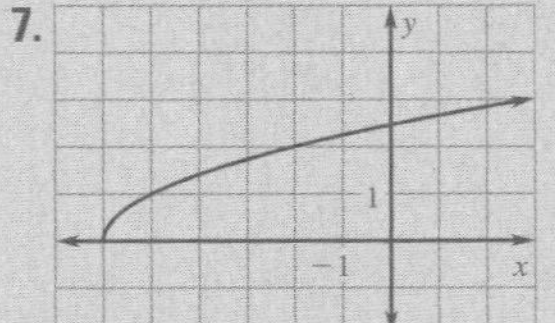

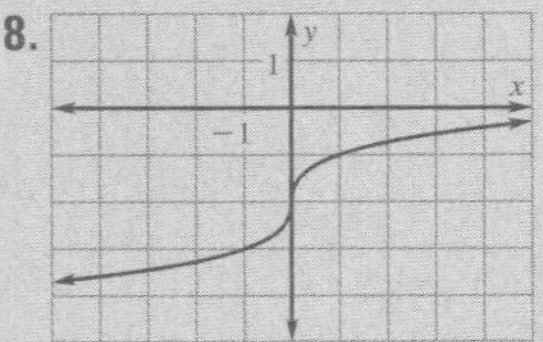

44. **FUNDRAISER** You are organizing a school fundraiser that involves selling holiday cookies and decorative calendars. You want to raise $2400. You charge $2 for a bag of cookies and $7 for a calendar. Write and graph an equation to represent the situation. If you sell 200 calendars, how many bags of cookies do you need to sell in order to meet your goal? *(p. 98)* **$2x + 7y = 2400$, see margin for art; 500 bags of cookies.**

45. **GEOMETRY** A designer is creating a kit for making sand castles. The designer wants one of the molds to be a cone that will hold 75π cubic inches of sand. What should the dimensions of the cone be if the height should be 4 inches more than the radius of the base? *(p. 370)* **5 in.**

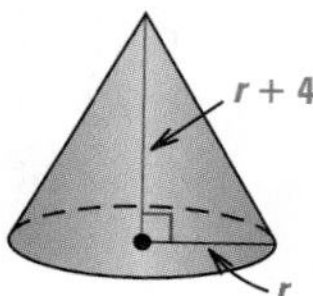

46. **ELECTRICITY** The current I (in amperes) required for an electrical appliance is given by $I = \sqrt{\frac{P}{R}}$ where P is the power (in watts) and R is the resistance (in ohms). Find the power consumed by a portable hair dryer for which $I = 17$ amperes and $R = 6.5$ ohms. *(p. 452)* **1878.5 watts**

47. **DEPRECIATION** Rachel buys a new car for $18,600. The value of the car decreases by 15.5% each year. Estimate when the car will have a value of $8000. *(p. 486)* **in 5 yr**

48. **GEOMETRY** Steve is a lifeguard at a pond. The pond is approximately circular in shape with a diameter of 330 feet. He ropes off a section of the pond for swimming. The rope forms a chord of the circle and is a maximum distance of 50 feet from the edge of the pond. What is the length of the rope? *(p. 626)* **about 237 ft**

49. **DINING OUT** You and three friends go to a restaurant for dinner. There are 20 different items on the menu. Each of you is equally likely to order any item. What is the probability that each of you orders a different item from the menu? *(p. 717)* **about 0.727**

50. **REAL ESTATE COMMISSIONS** The data set below gives the selling prices of seven homes that are being sold by one real estate agent. The agent will receive 5% of the selling price of each home as a commission. *(pp. 744, 751)*

Selling Prices of Homes
$201,900; $205,200; $195,800; $210,300; $199,900; $215,500; $192,100

a. Find the mean, median, mode, range, and standard deviation of the data.

b. Find the agent's commission for each home. Then find the mean, median, mode, range, and standard deviation of the commissions.

c. *Compare* the statistics from parts (a) and (b).

a. $202,957.14, 01,900, none, 3,400, $7519.85

b. $10,095, 0,260, $9790, 0,515, $9995, 0,775, $9605; 0,147.86, 0,095, none, 170, $375.99

c. *Sample swer:* Each atistical measure part (b) is 5% of e corresponding atistical measure part (a).

51. **SALARY** An accountant takes a job that pays an annual salary of $31,000 for the first year. The employer offers a $1600 raise for each of the next 8 years. Write a rule for the accountant's salary in the nth year. What will the accountant's salary be in the 9th year? *(p. 802)* **$a_n = 29,400 + 1600n$; $43,800**

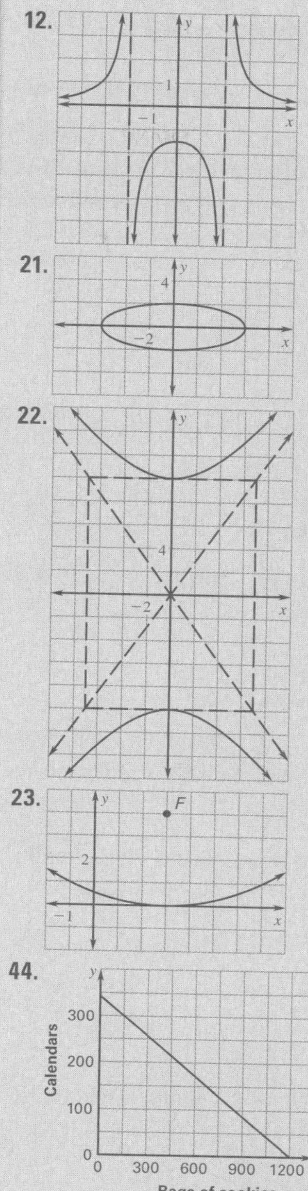

9.
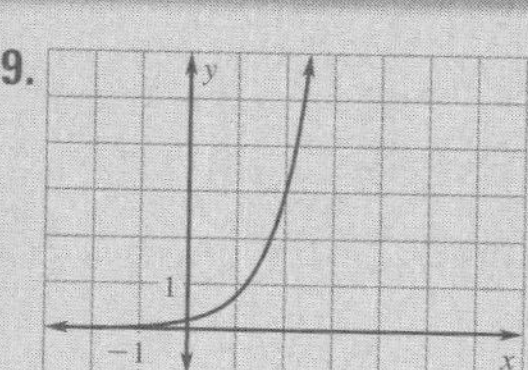

10.
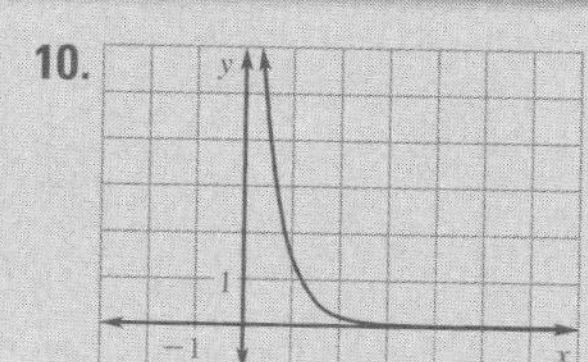

11.
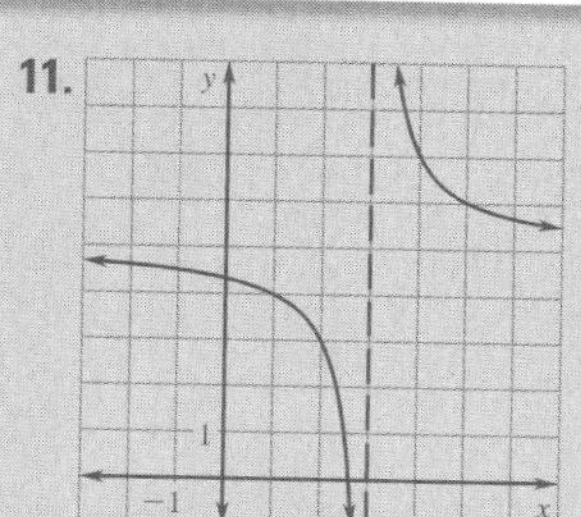

13 Pacing and Assignment Guide

REGULAR SCHEDULE

Pre-AP For pacing and assignments for a Pre-AP course, see the *Algebra 2 Toolkit*.

Lesson	Les. Day	BASIC	AVERAGE	ADVANCED
13.1 MA-HS-2.1.3	Day 1	SRH p. 995 Exs. 5–8; pp. 856–858 Exs. 1–11, 15–23, 30–34, 38	pp. 856–858 Exs. 1, 2, 4–6, 10–12, 15–20, 23–28, 30–36, 39	pp. 856–858 Exs. 1, 2, 7, 8, 15–20, 24–29*, 32–37*, 39
13.2 *MA-HS-2.2.1*	Day 1	pp. 862–865 Exs. 1–11, 14–18, 23–37 odd, 38, 48–51, 55	pp. 862–865 Exs. 1–5, 9–11, 14, 18–20, 25–28, 31–45 odd, 48–53, 56	pp. 862–865 Exs. 1, 2, 11–14, 20–22, 28–31, 35–54*
13.3 MA-HS-2.1.3	Day 1	pp. 870–872 Exs. 1–15	pp. 870–872 Exs. 1, 2, 4–15, 32	pp. 870–872 Exs. 1, 2, 5–15, 32, 33
	Day 2	pp. 870–872 Exs. 16–27, 35–38, 41–43	pp. 870–872 Exs. 17–21, 25–29, 35–39, 41–43	pp. 870–872 Exs. 20–23, 28–31, 34–43*
13.4 MA-HS-2.1.3	Day 1	pp. 878–880 Exs. 1–7, 11–15, 20–23, 26, 35–38, 42	pp. 878–880 Exs. 1, 2, 5–8, 11, 14–16, 22–31, 35–39, 42	pp. 878–880 Exs. 1, 2, 8–11, 17–19, 23–40*
13.5 MA-HS-3.1.7	Day 1	SRH p. 980 Exs. 21, 23, 26, 28; pp. 886–888 Exs. 1–6, 12–14, 18–20, 27–32, 43–47, 50	pp. 886–888 Exs. 1, 2, 7–9, 14–16, 21–23, 27, 28, 32–34, 38–41, 43–48, 51	pp. 886–888 Exs. 1, 2, 10, 11, 16, 17, 24–28, 32–49*
13.6 MA-HS-3.1.7	Day 1	pp. 892–894 Exs. 1–20	pp. 892–894 Exs. 1–10, 14–17, 20, 36–41	pp. 892–894 Exs. 1–7, 15–20, 36–42*
	Day 2	pp. 892–894 Exs. 21–29, 33, 43–46, 49–50	pp. 892–894 Exs. 24–35, 43–47, 49–50	pp. 892–894 Exs. 26–35, 43–50
Review	Day 1	pp. 898–900 Exs. 1–24	pp. 898–900 Exs. 1–24	pp. 898–900 Exs. 1–24
Assess	Day 1	Chapter 13 Test	Chapter 13 Test	Chapter 13 Test
Yearly Pacing		Chapter 13 Total – 10 days	Chapters 1–13 Total – 148 days	Remaining – 12 days

*Challenge Exercises EP = Extra Practice SRH = Skills Review Handbook

BLOCK SCHEDULE

DAY 1	DAY 2	DAY 3	DAY 4	DAY 5
13.1	**13.3**	**13.4**	**13.6**	**REVIEW**
pp. 856–858 Exs. 1, 2, 4–6, 10–12, 15–20, 23–28, 30–36, 39	pp. 870–872 Exs. 1, 2, 4–15, 17–21, 25–29, 32, 35–39, 41–43	pp. 878–880 Exs. 1, 2, 5–8, 11, 14–16, 22–31, 35–39, 42	pp. 892–894 Exs. 1–10, 14–17, 20, 24–41, 43–47, 49–50	pp. 898–900 Exs. 1–24
13.2		**13.5**		**ASSESS**
pp. 862–865 Exs. 1–5, 9–11, 14, 18–20, 25–28, 31–45 odd, 48–53, 56		pp. 886–888 Exs. 1, 2, 7–9, 14–16, 21–23, 27, 28, 32–34, 38–41, 43–48, 51		Chapter 13 Test
Yearly Pacing	Chapter 13 Total – 5 days	Chapters 1–13 Total – 74 days	Remaining – 6 days	

Chapter Resource Guide 13

RESOURCE MANAGER

Chapter Resource Book

CHAPTER SUPPORT						
Parents as Partners (Chapter Overview with home involvement exercises and activity)					p. 1	
LESSON SUPPORT **Standards**	**13.1** **MA-HS-2.1.3**	**13.2** *MA-HS-2.2.1*	**13.3** **MA-HS-2.1.3**	**13.4** **MA-HS-2.1.3**	**13.5** **MA-HS-3.1.7**	**13.6** **MA-HS-3.1.7**
Teaching Guide/Lesson Plan	p. 3	p. 14	p. 24	p. 36	p. 47	p. 59
Activity Masters	p. 5		p. 26			
Technology Activities & Keystrokes					p. 49	p. 61
Activity Support Masters				p. 38		
Practice (3 levels)	p. 6	p. 16	p. 27	p. 39	p. 51	p. 63
Study Guide	p. 9	p. 19	p. 30	p. 42	p. 54	p. 66
Catch-Up for Absent Students	p. 11	p. 21	p. 32	p. 44	p. 56	p. 68
Problem Solving/Application	p. 12	p. 22	p. 33	p. 45	p. 57	p. 69
Challenge Practice	p. 13	p. 23	p. 35	p. 46	p. 58	p. 70

REVIEW			
Chapter Review Games and Activities	p. 71	Cumulative Practice	p. 73
Project with Rubric	p. 72	Resource Book Answers	A1

Transparencies	*13.1*	*13.2*	*13.3*	*13.4*	*13.5*	*13.6*
Warm-Up/Daily Homework Quiz	✔	✔	✔	✔	✔	✔
Notetaking Guide	✔	✔	✔	✔	✔	✔
Teacher Support						
Answer Transparencies	✔	✔	✔	✔	✔	✔

ASSESSMENT BOOK

Quizzes	p. 182	SAT/ACT Chapter Test	p. 193
Chapter Tests (3 levels)	p. 185	Alternative Assessment with Rubric	p. 195
Standardized Chapter Test	p. 191		

TECHNOLOGY

- Easy Planner
- Test and Practice Generator
- Power Presentations
- @HomeTutor
- Activity Generator
- Animated Algebra
- Classzone.com
- eEdition Plus Online
- eWorkbook Plus Online
- ML Assessment System

ADDITIONAL RESOURCES

Kentucky

- Worked-Out Solution Key
- Notetaking Guide
- Practice Workbook
- Algebra 2 Toolkit
- Benchmark Tests
- Remediation Workbook

- Spanish Study Guide
- Spanish Assessment Book
- Spanish Resources in Spanish
- Multi-Language Visual Glossary

13 Lesson Practice Level B

LESSON 13.1 **Practice B**
For use with pages 852–858

Evaluate the six trigonometric functions of the angle θ.

1. 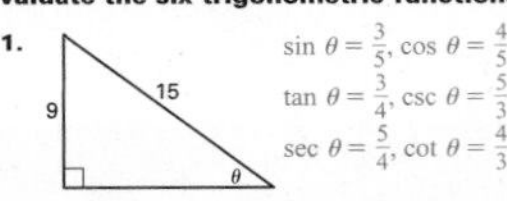

$\sin\theta = \frac{3}{5}, \cos\theta = \frac{4}{5}, \tan\theta = \frac{3}{4}, \csc\theta = \frac{5}{3}, \sec\theta = \frac{5}{4}, \cot\theta = \frac{4}{3}$

2. 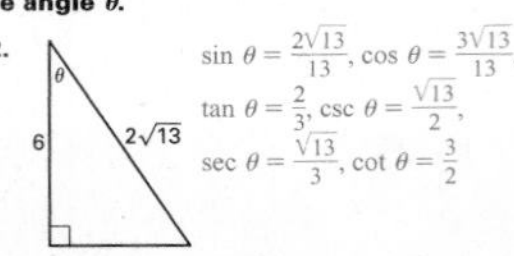

$\sin\theta = \frac{2\sqrt{13}}{13}, \cos\theta = \frac{3\sqrt{13}}{13}, \tan\theta = \frac{2}{3}, \csc\theta = \frac{\sqrt{13}}{2}, \sec\theta = \frac{\sqrt{13}}{3}, \cot\theta = \frac{3}{2}$

Let θ be an acute angle of a right triangle. Find the values of the other five trigonometric functions of θ.

3. $\sin\theta = \frac{4}{5}$ $\cos\theta = \frac{3}{5}, \tan\theta = \frac{4}{3}, \csc\theta = \frac{5}{4}, \sec\theta = \frac{5}{3}, \cot\theta = \frac{3}{4}$

4. $\cos\theta = \frac{5}{6}$ $\sin\theta = \frac{\sqrt{11}}{6}, \tan\theta = \frac{\sqrt{11}}{5}, \csc\theta = \frac{6\sqrt{11}}{11}, \sec\theta = \frac{6}{5}, \cot\theta = \frac{5\sqrt{11}}{11}$

5. $\sec\theta = \frac{\sqrt{73}}{8}$ $\sin\theta = \frac{3\sqrt{73}}{73}, \cos\theta = \frac{8\sqrt{73}}{73}, \tan\theta = \frac{3}{8}, \csc\theta = \frac{\sqrt{73}}{3}, \cot\theta = \frac{8}{3}$

6. $\cot\theta = \sqrt{3}$ $\sin\theta = \frac{1}{2}, \cos\theta = \frac{\sqrt{3}}{2}, \tan\theta = \frac{\sqrt{3}}{3}, \csc\theta = 2, \sec\theta = \frac{2\sqrt{3}}{3}$

Find the exact values of x and y.

7. 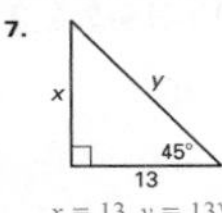

$x = 13, y = 13\sqrt{2}$

8. $x = \frac{4\sqrt{3}}{3}, y = \frac{8\sqrt{3}}{3}$

9. 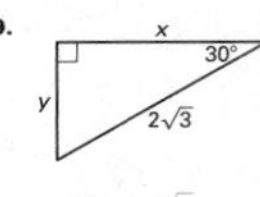

$x = 3, y = \sqrt{3}$

Solve $\triangle DEF$ using the diagram and the given measurements.

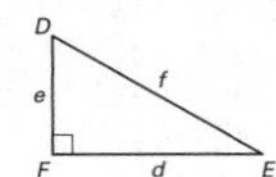

10. $D = 40°, f = 8$ $E = 50°, d \approx 5.14, e \approx 6.13$

11. $E = 53°, d = 13$ $D = 37°, e \approx 17.25, f \approx 21.60$

12. $D = 67°, e = 10.5$ $E = 23°, d \approx 24.74, f \approx 26.87$

13. **Shadow** A person casts the shadow shown. What is the approximate height of the person? about 6 ft

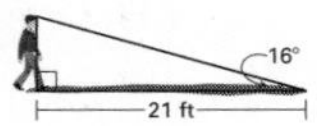

14. **Mountains** A hiker at the top of a mountain sees a farm and an airport in the distance.
    a. What is the distance d from the hiker to the farm? about 10,313 ft
    b. What is the distance y from the farm to the airport? about 9640 ft

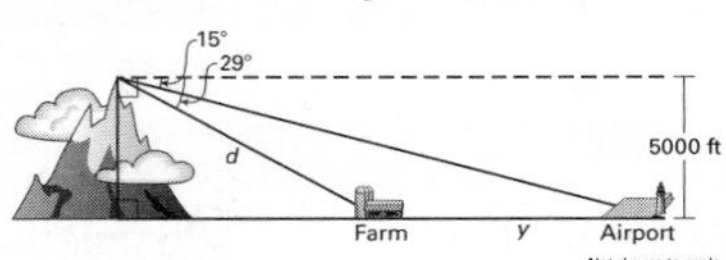

LESSON 13.1

LESSON 13.2 **Practice B**
For use with pages 859–865

Draw an angle with the given measure in standard position.

1. $130°$ 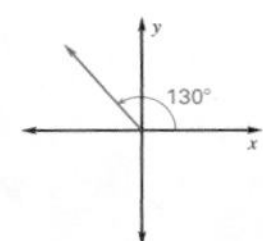
2. $\frac{5\pi}{4}$ 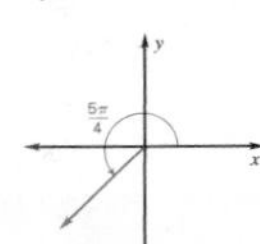
3. $-\frac{2\pi}{3}$ 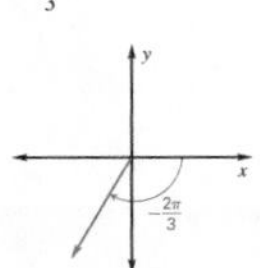

Find one positive angle and one negative angle that are coterminal with the given angle.

4. $-35°$ $325°, -395°$
5. $280°$ $640°, -80°$
6. $-\frac{\pi}{6}$ $\frac{11\pi}{6}, -\frac{13\pi}{6}$
7. $\frac{7\pi}{5}$ $\frac{17\pi}{5}, -\frac{3\pi}{5}$

Convert the degree measure to radians or the radian measure to degrees.

8. $270°$ $\frac{3\pi}{2}$
9. $-135°$ $-\frac{3\pi}{4}$
10. $\frac{11\pi}{6}$ $330°$
11. $-\frac{\pi}{18}$ $-10°$

Find the arc length and area of a sector with the given radius r and central angle θ.

12. $r = 5$ m, $\theta = \frac{\pi}{2}$ $\frac{5\pi}{2}$ m, $\frac{25\pi}{4}$ m²
13. $r = 7$ in., $\theta = \frac{3\pi}{4}$ $\frac{21\pi}{4}$ in., $\frac{147\pi}{8}$ in.²
14. $r = 11$ ft, $\theta = 200°$ $\frac{110\pi}{9}$ ft, $\frac{605\pi}{9}$ ft²

Evaluate the trigonometric function using a calculator if necessary. If possible, give an exact answer.

15. $\cos\frac{\pi}{4}$  $\frac{\sqrt{2}}{2}$
16. $\sin\frac{\pi}{6}$ $\frac{1}{2}$
17. $\cot\frac{\pi}{9}$ about 2.7475
18. $\csc\frac{4\pi}{5}$ about 1.7013

19. **Swing** At an amusement park, you ride a swing that takes you several revolutions counter clockwise as shown in the diagram. Find the measure of the angle generated as you are on the ride. Give the answer in both degrees and radians. $2030°, \frac{203\pi}{18}$

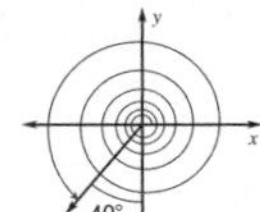

20. **Cheese** A circular piece of cheese has a portion cut out as shown.
    a. What is the approximate arc length of the portion that is missing?
    b. What is the approximate area of the portion that is missing?

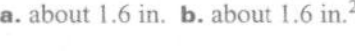
a. about 1.6 in. b. about 1.6 in.²

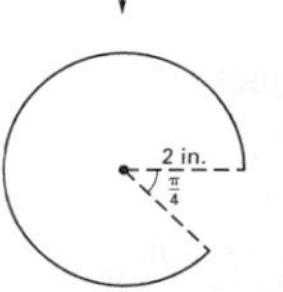

LESSON 13.2

LESSON 13.3 **Practice B**
For use with pages 866–872

Use the given point on the terminal side of an angle θ in standard position to evaluate the six trigonometric functions of θ.

1. $(8, -15)$ See above.
2. $(-7, -2)$ See below.

1. $\sin\theta = -\frac{15}{17}, \cos\theta = \frac{8}{17}, \tan\theta = -\frac{15}{8}, \csc\theta = -\frac{17}{15}, \sec\theta = \frac{17}{8}, \cot\theta = -\frac{8}{15}$

Evaluate the six trigonometric functions of θ.

3. $\theta = 90°$ $\sin\theta = 1, \cos\theta = 0, \tan\theta$ is undefined, $\csc\theta = 1, \sec\theta$ is undefined, $\cot\theta = 0$
4. $\theta = -\pi$ $\sin\theta = 0, \cos\theta = -1, \tan\theta = 0, \csc\theta$ is undefined, $\sec\theta = -1, \cot\theta$ is undefined

Sketch the angle. Then find its reference angle.

5. $-115°$ $65°$
6. $125°$ $55°$ 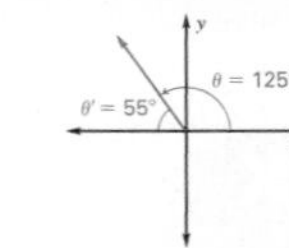

7. $325°$ $35°$ 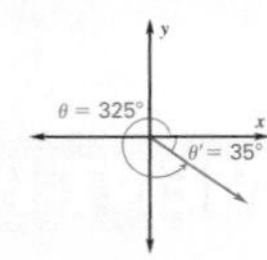

8. $-\frac{17\pi}{6}$ $\frac{\pi}{6}$
9. $-\frac{7\pi}{4}$ $\frac{\pi}{4}$ 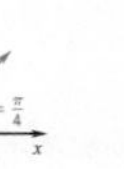 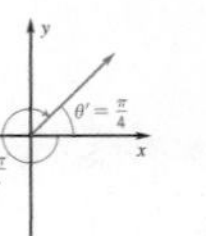
10. $\frac{11\pi}{3}$ 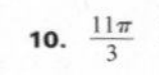 $\frac{\pi}{3}$ 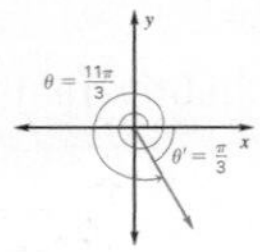

Evaluate the function without using a calculator.

11. $\sin 240°$ $-\frac{\sqrt{3}}{2}$
12. $\tan 150°$ $-\frac{\sqrt{3}}{3}$
13. $\sec(-315°)$ $\sqrt{2}$
14. $\cot(-150°)$ $\sqrt{3}$
15. $\cos\left(-\frac{3\pi}{4}\right)$ $-\frac{\sqrt{2}}{2}$
16. $\csc\frac{7\pi}{6}$ -2
17. $\tan\frac{8\pi}{3}$ $-\sqrt{3}$
18. $\sin\left(-\frac{5\pi}{6}\right)$ $-\frac{1}{2}$

19. **Distance** A projectile is launched with an initial speed of 42 feet per second. It is projected at an angle of 50°. How far does the projectile travel? How much farther does it travel if it is launched with an initial speed of 84 feet per second? about 54.3 ft, about 163 ft

20. **Baseball** A baseball player hits a ball projected at an angle of 40°. The height at which the ball is hit is the same as the height of the fence. At what speed must the baseball player hit the ball in order for it to clear a fence that is 385 feet away? about 112 ft/sec

2. $\sin\theta = -\frac{2\sqrt{53}}{53}, \cos\theta = -\frac{7\sqrt{53}}{53}, \tan\theta = \frac{2}{7}, \csc\theta = -\frac{\sqrt{53}}{2}, \sec\theta = -\frac{\sqrt{53}}{7}, \cot\theta = \frac{7}{2}$

LESSON 13.3

LESSON 13.4 Practice B
For use with pages 875–880

Evaluate the expression without using a calculator. Give your answer in both radians and degrees.

1. $\cos^{-1}(-1)$ $\pi, 180°$ **2.** $\tan^{-1}\frac{\sqrt{3}}{3}$ $\frac{\pi}{6}, 30°$ **3.** $\sin^{-1} 0$ $0\pi, 0°$

4. $\sin^{-1}\left(-\frac{\sqrt{2}}{2}\right)$ $-\frac{\pi}{4}, -45°$ **5.** $\tan^{-1}(1)$ $\frac{\pi}{4}, 45°$ **6.** $\cos^{-1}(2)$ undefined

Use a calculator to evaluate the expression in both radians and degrees.

7. $\tan^{-1}(-1.7)$ $-1.04, -59.5°$ **8.** $\cos^{-1} 0.24$ $1.33, 76.1°$ **9.** $\sin^{-1} 0.85$ $1.02, 58.2°$

10. $\tan^{-1}(4.1)$ $1.33, 76.3°$ **11.** $\sin^{-1}(-0.99)$ $-1.43, -81.9°$ **12.** $\cos^{-1}(-0.1)$ $1.67, 95.7°$

Solve the equation for θ.

13. $\sin\theta = -0.71;\ 270° < \theta < 360°$ $314.8°$ **14.** $\tan\theta = 1.6;\ 180° < \theta < 270°$ $238.0°$

15. $\cos\theta = 0.22;\ 270° < \theta < 360°$ $282.7°$ **16.** $\cos\theta = -0.22;\ 180° < \theta < 270°$ $257.3°$

Find the measure of the angle θ.

17. 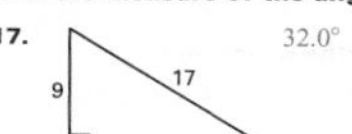

32.0°

18. 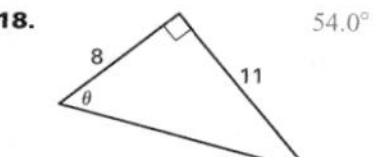

54.0°

19. 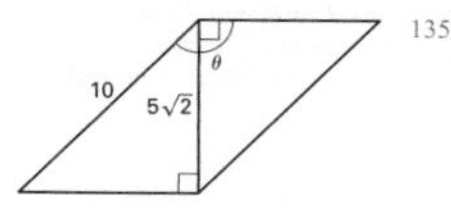

135°

20. Carpentry You are making a door stopper from a block of wood. When the door rests against the stopper, you want the corner of the stopper to extend through the width of the door. If the bottom of the 1.7-inch wide door is 0.7 inch off the ground, what is the angle θ of the door stopper? about 22.4°

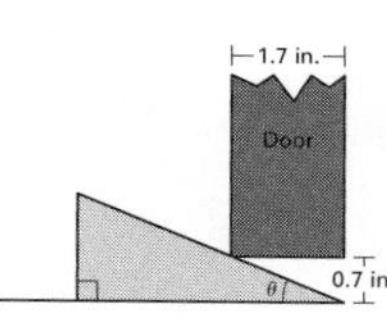

21. Flight A falcon perched at a height of 100 feet descends straight toward a prey that is 125 feet away. At what angle does it descend? If the falcon ascends along the same path as it descended, at what angle does it ascend? about 36.9°, about 53.1°

LESSON 13.5 Practice B
For use with pages 882–888

Solve $\triangle ABC$. (*Hint:* Some of the "triangles" have no solution and some have two solutions.)

1. A, B, C; 28°, 71°, 15
$A = 81°, b \approx 7.1, c \approx 14.4$

2. 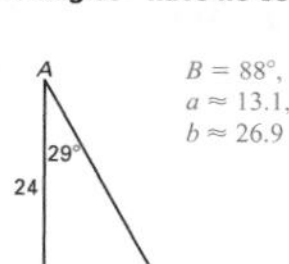

$C = 73°, a \approx 20.9, b \approx 12.6$

$B = 88°, a \approx 13.1, b \approx 26.9$

3. 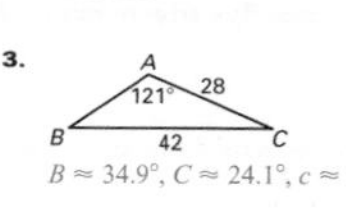

$B \approx 34.9°, C \approx 24.1°, c \approx 20.0$

4. $A = 72°, B = 35°, c = 21$ $B = 50°, a \approx 31.3, b \approx 24.0$ **5.** $A = 95°, C = 35°, c = 18$

6. $A = 105°, a = 11, b = 13$ no triangle **7.** $B = 10°, C = 23°, a = 15$ $A = 147°, b \approx 4.8, c \approx 10.8$

8. $A = 60°, B = 32°, b = 26$ $C = 88°, a \approx 42.5, c \approx 49.0$ **9.** $C = 49°, a = 24, c = 19$ $A \approx 72.4°, B \approx 58.6°, b \approx 21.5$; $A \approx 107.6°, B \approx 23.4°, b \approx 10.0$

Find the area of $\triangle ABC$.

10. $B = 141°, a = 7, c = 8$ 17.6 units^2 **11.** $C = 70°, a = 30, b = 24$ 338.3 units^2

12. $A = 99°, b = 20, c = 27$ 266.7 units^2 **13.** $B = 32°, a = 18, c = 13$ 62.0 units^2

14. 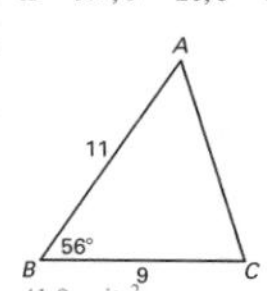

41.0 units^2

15. 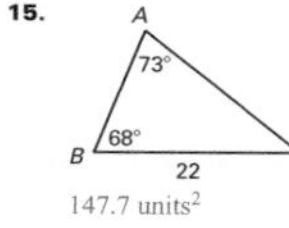

147.7 units^2

16. 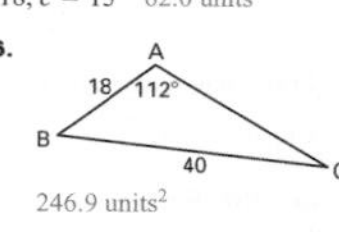

246.9 units^2

17. Utility Poles After a storm, two street lights with the same length are leaning against each other. The bases of the poles are 45 feet apart. The angles that the poles make with the ground are 50° and 60°. Using the diagram shown at the right, find c. about 4.8 ft

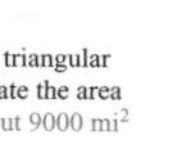

18. Maps The state of New Hampshire is approximately triangular in shape. Use the diagram shown at the right to estimate the area of the state to the nearest thousand square miles. about 9000 mi²

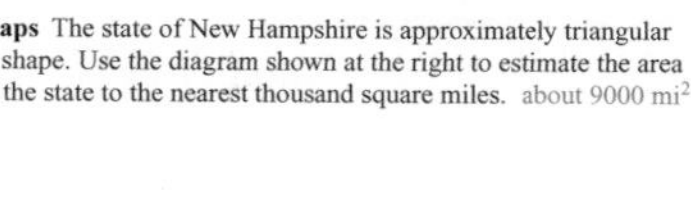

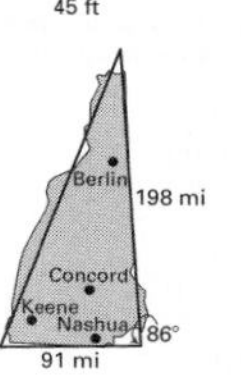

LESSON 13.6 Practice B
For use with pages 889–894

Solve $\triangle ABC$.

1. 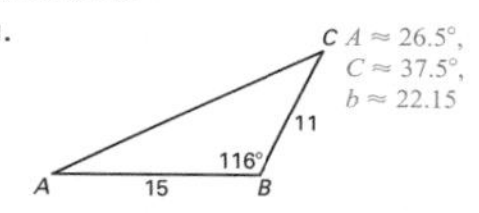

$A \approx 26.5°, C \approx 37.5°, b \approx 22.15$

2. 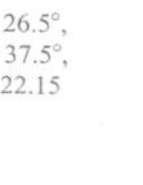

$A \approx 35.5°, B \approx 69.2°, C \approx 75.3°$

3. $a = 12, b = 13, c = 20$ $A \approx 35.2°, B \approx 38.6°, C \approx 106.2$ **4.** $B = 135°, a = 19, c = 7$ $A \approx 33.3°, C \approx 11.7°, b \approx 24.5$

5. $A = 46°, b = 24, c = 10$ $B \approx 111.1°, C \approx 22.9°, a \approx 18.5$ **6.** $C = 3°, a = 16, b = 33$ $A \approx 2.8°, B \approx 174.2°, c \approx 17.0$

7. $a = 17, b = 37, c = 23$ $A = 19.0°, B \approx 134.8°, C \approx 26.2°$ **8.** $a = 42, b = 43, c = 38$ $A = 62.1°, B \approx 64.8°, C \approx 53.1°$

Find the area of $\triangle ABC$.

9. 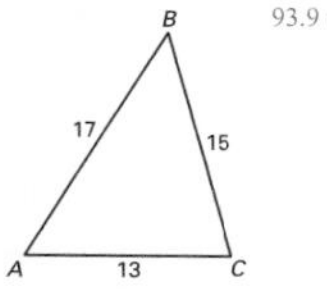

93.9 units^2

10. 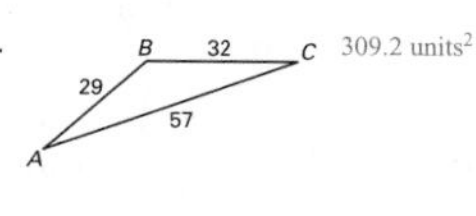

309.2 units^2

11. $a = 6, b = 8, c = 12$ 21.3 units^2 **12.** $a = 15, b = 10, c = 9$ 43.6 units^2

13. $a = 20, b = 25, c = 14$ 139.8 units^2 **14.** $a = 32, b = 37, c = 7$ 84.1 units^2

15. $a = 55, b = 50, c = 42$ 1003.3 units^2 **16.** $a = 38, b = 50, c = 72$ 898.0 units^2

17. Flagpole A 5-foot long flagpole that is angled on the side of a building is casting a 3 foot long shadow. The distance from the end of the flagpole to the end of the shadow is 4.1 feet. Use the diagram to find θ. about 55.0°

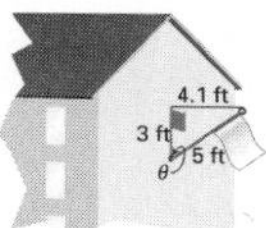

18. Distance The distance between Miami, Florida and Bermuda is about 1042 miles. The distance from Bermuda to San Juan, Puerto Rico is about 965 miles, and the distance from San Juan to Miami is about 1038 miles. Find the area of the triangle formed by the three locations. about 445,000 mi²

CHAPTER 13 Quiz 1
For use after Lessons 13.1–13.2

Solve $\triangle ABC$ using the diagram at the right and the given measurements.

1. $A = 40°, a = 13$
2. $B = 55°, b = 15$
3. $B = 66°, a = 9$
4. $B = 37°, c = 18$

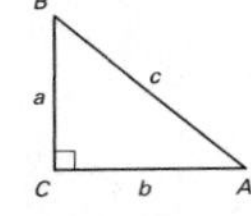

Find one positive angle and one negative angle that is coterminal with the given angle.

5. $125°$
6. $280°$
7. $\frac{2\pi}{3}$
8. $\frac{5\pi}{4}$
9. Find the arc length and the area of the sector with a radius of 10 inches and a central angle of $\theta = 100°$.
10. **Stepladder** A stepladder has an angle of elevation 60° with the front of the house. The length of the stepladder is 24 feet. At what height does the stepladder meet the house?

Answers

1. $B = 50°, b = 15.49,$ $c = 20.22$
2. $A = 35°, a = 10.50,$ $c = 18.31$
3. $A = 24°, b = 20.21,$ $c = 22.13$
4. $A = 53°, a = 14.38,$ $b = 10.83$
5. *Sample answer:* $485°, -235°$
6. *Sample answer:* $640°, -80°$
7. *Sample answer:* $\frac{8\pi}{3}, -\frac{4\pi}{3}$
8. *Sample answer:* $\frac{13\pi}{4}, -\frac{3\pi}{4}$
9. $\frac{50\pi}{9}$ in., $\frac{250\pi}{9}$ in.^{2}
10. 20.78 ft

CHAPTER 13 Quiz 2
For use after Lessons 13.3–13.4

Use the given point on the terminal side of an angle θ in standard position to evaluate the six trigonometric functions of θ.

1. $(9, -3)$
2. $(3, 6)$

Evaluate the expression without using a calculator.

3. $\cos 120°$
4. $\tan \frac{4\pi}{3}$
5. $\sin(-750°)$
6. $\sec\left(-\frac{5\pi}{4}\right)$

Evaluate the expression without using a calculator. Give your answer in both radians and degrees.

7. $\sin^{-1}\left(\frac{\sqrt{2}}{2}\right)$
8. $\cos^{-1}(-1)$
9. $\tan^{-1}\sqrt{3}$
10. $\sin^{-1}\left(\frac{1}{2}\right)$

Solve the equation for θ.

11. $\sin\theta = 0.4, 90° < \theta < 180°$
12. $\cos\theta = -0.52, 90° < \theta < 180°$
13. **Car Ramp** A car drives on a ramp in order to enter the parking garage. The ramp has a height of 4 feet and a horizontal length of 20 feet. What is the angle θ of the ramp?

Answers

1. $\sin\theta = -\frac{\sqrt{10}}{10}, \cos\theta = \frac{3\sqrt{10}}{10}, \tan\theta = -\frac{1}{3},$ $\csc\theta = -\sqrt{10}, \sec\theta = \frac{\sqrt{10}}{3}, \cot\theta = -3$
2. $\sin\theta = \frac{2\sqrt{5}}{5}, \cos\theta = \frac{\sqrt{5}}{5}, \tan\theta = 2,$ $\csc\theta = \frac{\sqrt{5}}{2}, \sec\theta = \sqrt{5}, \cot\theta = \frac{1}{2}$
3. $-\frac{1}{2}$
4. $\sqrt{3}$
5. $-\frac{1}{2}$
6. $-\sqrt{2}$
7. $45°, \frac{\pi}{4}$
8. $180°, \pi$
9. $60°, \frac{\pi}{3}$
10. $30°, \frac{\pi}{6}$
11. $156.42°$
12. $121.33°$
13. $11.31°$

CHAPTER 13 Quiz 3
For use after Lessons 13.5–13.6

Solve $\triangle ABC$.

1. $A = 60°, B = 84°, c = 12$
2. $a = 13, b = 18, c = 27$
3. $C = 40°, a = 30, b = 30$
4. $A = 50°, B = 43°, c = 12$

Find the area of $\triangle ABC$.

5. $a = 5, b = 7, C = 36°$
6. $a = 16, b = 20, C = 83°$
7. $b = 21, c = 18, A = 110°$
8. $a = 25, b = 23, c = 14$
9. **Geometry** The base of a right triangular prism has edges of length 9 centimeters, 11 centimeters, and 14 centimeters. The height of the prism is 6 centimeters. What is the volume of the prism?

Answers

1. $C = 36°,$ $a = 17.68,$ $b = 20.3$
2. $A = 24.57°,$ $B = 35.15°,$ $C = 120.28°$
3. $A = 70°,$ $B = 70°,$ $c = 20.52$
4. $C = 87°,$ $a = 9.21,$ $b = 8.2$
5. 10.29
6. 158.81
7. 177.6
8. 159.05
9. 296.86 cm^3

CHAPTER 13 Chapter Test B
For use after Chapter 13

Let θ be an acute angle of a right triangle. Find the value of the other five trigonometric functions of θ.

1. $\sin\theta = \frac{5}{13}$
2. $\tan\theta = \frac{2}{5}$

Find the exact values of x and y.

3.

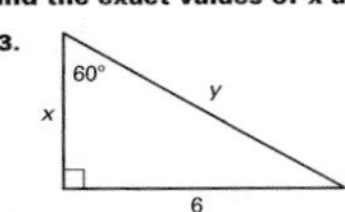

4.

5. Find one positive angle and one negative angle that are coterminal with the angle $\frac{5\pi}{3}$.

Convert the degree measure to radians or the radian measure to degrees.

6. $390°$
7. $-\frac{3\pi}{4}$
8. Find the arc length and area of a sector with a radius of 8 feet and central angle of $\theta = 135°$.

Use the given point on the terminal side at angle θ in standard position to evaluate the six trigonometric functions of θ.

9. $(-4, 2)$
10. $(-1, -2)$

Answers

1. $\cos\theta = \frac{12}{13}, \tan\theta = \frac{5}{12}, \csc\theta = \frac{13}{5},$ $\sec\theta = \frac{13}{12},$ $\cot\theta = \frac{12}{5}$
2. $\sin\theta = \frac{2\sqrt{29}}{29},$ $\cos\theta = \frac{5\sqrt{29}}{29}, \csc\theta = \frac{\sqrt{29}}{2}, \sec\theta = \frac{\sqrt{29}}{5},$ $\cot\theta = \frac{5}{2}$
3. $x = 2\sqrt{3}, y = 4\sqrt{3}$
4. $x = 6, y = 6$
5. *Sample answer:* $\frac{11\pi}{3}, -\frac{\pi}{3}$
6. $\frac{13\pi}{6}$
7. $-135°$
8. 6π ft; 24π ft^2
9. $\sin\theta = \frac{\sqrt{5}}{5}, \cos\theta = -\frac{2\sqrt{5}}{5}, \tan\theta = -\frac{1}{2},$ $\csc\theta = \sqrt{5}, \sec\theta = -\frac{\sqrt{5}}{2}, \cot\theta = -2$
10. $\sin\theta = -\frac{2\sqrt{5}}{5}, \cos\theta = -\frac{\sqrt{5}}{5}, \tan\theta = 2,$ $\csc\theta = -\frac{\sqrt{5}}{2}, \sec\theta = -\sqrt{5}, \cot\theta = \frac{1}{2}$

CHAPTER 13 Chapter Test B *continued*

For use after Chapter 13

Evaluate the function without using a calculator.

11. $\sin(-120°)$

12. $\tan 225°$

Evaluate the expression without using a calculator. Give your answer in both radians and degrees.

13. $\cos^{-1}\left(\frac{1}{2}\right)$

14. $\tan^{-1} 1$

15. Solve the equation for θ.

$\sin \theta = -0.72;\ 270° \le \theta \le 360°$

16. **Escalator** An escalator ascends 45 feet over a horizontal distance of 30 feet. What is the angle of elevation?

Solve $\triangle ABC$.

17. $B = 105°, C = 36°, b = 8$

18. $A = 46°, b = 4, a = 6$

Find the area of $\triangle ABC$ with the given side lengths and included angle.

19. $C = 112°, b = 5, a = 10$

20. $B = 8°, a = 42, c = 44$

Solve $\triangle ABC$.

21. $C = 64°, a = 3, b = 9$

22. $a = 8, b = 5, c = 8$

23. Find the area of $\triangle ABC$ with side lengths $a = 20$, $b = 12$, and $c = 16$.

24. A sign in the shape of a triangle has sides of 4 feet, 5 feet, and 6 feet. What is the area of this sign?

Answers

11. $-\frac{\sqrt{3}}{2}$
12. 1
13. $60°, \frac{\pi}{3}$
14. $45°, \frac{\pi}{4}$
15. 314°
16. 56.3°
17. $A \approx 39°, a \approx 5.2,$ $c \approx 4.9$
18. $B \approx 28.7°,$ $C \approx 105.3°, c \approx 8.0$
19. 23.18
20. 128.6
21. $c \approx 8.1, A \approx 19.4°,$ $B \approx 96.6°$
22. $A \approx 71.8°,$ $B \approx 36.4°, C \approx 71.8°$
23. 96
24. 9.9 ft^2

CHAPTER 13 Standardized Test

For use after Chapter 13

Multiple Choice

1. If θ is an acute angle of a right triangle and $\tan \theta = \frac{3}{5}$, what is the value of $\cos \theta$? C

Ⓐ $\frac{\sqrt{34}}{5}$ Ⓑ $\frac{3\sqrt{34}}{34}$

Ⓒ $\frac{5\sqrt{34}}{34}$ Ⓓ $\frac{5}{3}$

2. What is the value of x in the triangle shown? B

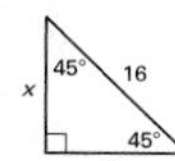

Ⓐ 8 Ⓑ $8\sqrt{2}$

Ⓒ $8\sqrt{3}$ Ⓓ $16\sqrt{2}$

3. You've let out 125 feet of string from the reel while flying a kite. If the angle of elevation is 60°, how much higher is the kite than the reel? C

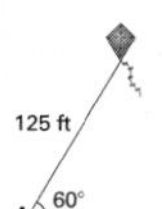

Ⓐ 62.5 feet Ⓑ $\frac{125\sqrt{2}}{2}$ feet

Ⓒ $\frac{125\sqrt{3}}{2}$ feet Ⓓ 250 feet

4. How many degrees is $\frac{12\pi}{5}$ radians? C

Ⓐ 72° Ⓑ 216°

Ⓒ 432° Ⓓ 864°

5. Which angle is illustrated in the diagram? A

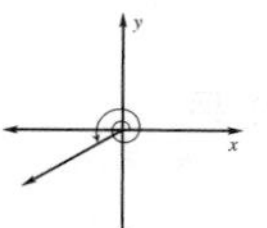

Ⓐ $-\frac{19\pi}{6}$ Ⓑ $-\frac{7\pi}{6}$

Ⓒ $\frac{7\pi}{6}$ Ⓓ $\frac{19\pi}{6}$

6. If $(3, -4)$ is a point on the terminal side of an angle θ, what is $\cos \theta$? B

Ⓐ $-\frac{4}{3}$ Ⓑ $\frac{3}{5}$ Ⓒ $\frac{3}{4}$ Ⓓ $\frac{4}{5}$

7. What is the reference angle for $-\frac{7\pi}{4}$? B

Ⓐ $\frac{\pi}{6}$ Ⓑ $\frac{\pi}{4}$ Ⓒ $\frac{\pi}{3}$ Ⓓ $\frac{\pi}{2}$

8. What is the value of the expression $\cos^{-1}\left(\frac{\sqrt{3}}{2}\right)$? A

Ⓐ 30° Ⓑ 45° Ⓒ 60° Ⓓ 90°

9. What is the value of $\tan(-135°)$? D

Ⓐ -1 Ⓑ $-\frac{\sqrt{2}}{2}$

Ⓒ $\frac{\sqrt{2}}{2}$ Ⓓ 1

10. What is the measure of $\angle A$ rounded to two decimal places? B

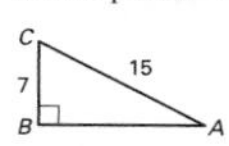

Ⓐ 25.02° Ⓑ 27.82°

Ⓒ 62.18° Ⓓ 64.98°

CHAPTER 13 Standardized Test *continued*

For use after Chapter 13

11. Which dimensions approximate the lengths of the remaining sides of $\triangle ABC$? A

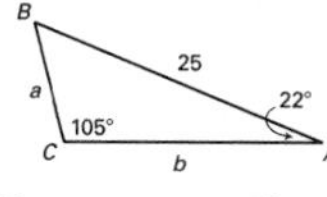

Ⓐ $a = 10, b = 21$ Ⓑ $a = 21, b = 10$

Ⓒ $a = 29, b = 64$ Ⓓ $a = 64, b = 29$

12. What are the remaining angle measures of the triangle with $A = 120°$, $a = 35$, and $b = 10$? A

Ⓐ $B = 14°, C = 46°$

Ⓑ $B = 46°, C = 14°$

Ⓒ $B = 3°, C = 57°$

Ⓓ $B = 57°, C = 3°$

13. If the area of $\triangle ABC$ is 42 square inches, with $a = 12$ inches and $b = 8$ inches, what is the measure of $\angle C$, rounded to the nearest thousandths of a degree? D

Ⓐ 0.875° Ⓑ 11.143°

Ⓒ 12.636° Ⓓ 61.045°

14. Which dimensions could not be the dimensions of any triangle? A

Ⓐ $A = 123°, a = 29, b = 54$

Ⓑ $A = 123°, a = 29, b = 17$

Ⓒ $A = 57°, a = 29, b = 17$

Ⓓ $A = 57°, a = 54, b = 29$

Gridded Answer

15. What is the area in square feet of a triangle with sides of 8 feet, 13 feet, and 17 feet?

		5	0

Short Response

16. Write a problem to solve a triangle that has two solutions. What are the angles and side lengths of the two triangles? Describe your process. Answers will vary.

Extended Response

17. Fred decides to take a drive in the country. He travels due east along one route for 35 miles and then turns southwest along onto another route for 23 miles.

a. Given that the angle between the two routes is 49°, draw a diagram of Fred's trip. See below.

b. Upon completing the 23 miles along the second route, Fred decides to take a direct route home. He estimates that he has enough fuel to travel another 45 miles. Will Fred make it home without stopping at a gas station? Why or why not? Yes; by using the Law of Cosines, you can determine that he will travel approximately 26 miles back home.

17. a. 35 mi, 49°, 23 mi

CHAPTER 13 Alternative Assessment and Math Journal

For use after Chapter 13

Journal **1.** Make a table containing the defined domain restrictions for sine, cosine, and tangent so that their inverse functions exist. Explain why the domain restrictions are necessary. Are the defined domains the only domains for which the inverse trigonometric functions exist? Explain why or why not using examples to support your answer when possible

Multi-Step Problem **2.** Cubbenah (of Jamaican descent) and his history class have been discussing the recent resurgence of interest in geneaology. With the availability of information on the Internet, it is now easier to trace families back over many generations. The teacher asks each student to complete a physical project that represents his/her heritage. Cubbenah wants to make a Jamaican flag that is 3 feet by 1.5 feet. The Jamaican flag consists of two green triangles (one is $\triangle ABC$), two black triangles (one is $\triangle DEF$), and yellow diagonals.

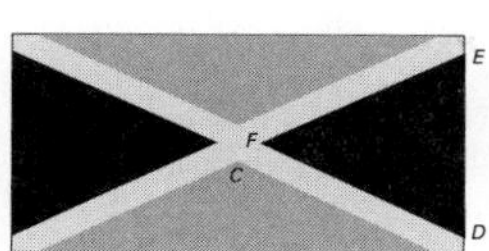

a. Solve isosceles $\triangle ABC$ where $a = 17.7$ inches and $C = 130°$.

b. Solve isosceles $\triangle DEF$ where $f = 15$ inches and $E = 65°$.

c. **Writing** Did you use the law of sines or the law of cosines to solve $\triangle ABC$? $\triangle DEF$? Explain your choice of method for each triangle.

d. Describe another way to solve $\triangle ABC$.

e. How much green fabric and black fabric is needed to make the flag? Use two different methods for finding area.

f. **Critical Thinking** How much yellow fabric is needed to make the flag?

1. Complete answers should include: a table containing the defined restricted domains for which sine, cosine, and tangent have inverses; an explanation that the domains of the original trigonometric functions (sine, cosine, and tangent) must be restricted so that the function produces all of its possible values without these values repeating. If there was repetition, the inverse would not be a function (horizontal line test); an explanation that because the range values of the sine, cosine, and tangent functions repeat periodically, there is an infinite number of domains for which the inverse trigonometric functions exist; examples of other possible restricted domains for which the inverses of the sine, cosine, and tangent exist, such as $\frac{\pi}{2} \le \theta \le \frac{3\pi}{2}$ for sine, $\pi \le \theta \le 2\pi$ for cosine, and $\frac{\pi}{2} < \theta < \frac{3\pi}{2}$ for tangent. **2. a.** $A \approx 25°$; $B \approx 25°$; $b = 17.7$ in.; $c \approx 32.1$ in. **b.** $D = 65°$; $F = 50°$; $d \approx 17.7$ in.; $e \approx 17.7$ in. **c.** *Sample answer:* I used the law of cosines for $\triangle ABC$ and the law of sines for $\triangle DEF$. Because $\triangle ABC$ is isosceles, $b = 17.7$ in. This information creates the SAS case, so the triangle can be solved using law of cosines. Because $\triangle DEF$ is isosceles, $D = 65°$. This information creates the ASA case, so the triangle can be solved using the law of sines. **d.** *Sample answer:* Another way to solve $\triangle ABC$ is to use the law of sines. Because $\triangle ABC$ is isosceles, A and B must have the same measure, 25°. This information creates the ASA case or the AAS case, so the triangle can be solved using the law of sines. **e.** about 240 in.^{2}; about 240 in.^{2} **f.** about 168 in.^{2}

PLAN AND PREPARE

Main Ideas

First, students will learn the right triangle definitions of the six trigonometric functions and how to use right triangle trigonometry. Next, they will learn to use radian measure and to evaluate trigonometric functions of any angle. Then, they will learn to evaluate and use inverse trigonometric functions. Finally, students will learn to apply the law of sines and the law of cosines to solve triangles and applied problems.

Prerequisite Skills

- Using the Pythagorean theorem
- Solving equations using inverse functions
- Finding angle measures in triangles

Additional resources for reviewing prerequisite skills are:

- Skills Review Handbook, pp. 975–1009
- @HomeTutor

13 Trigonometric Ratios and Functions

KY

Before

In previous courses and in previous chapters, you learned the following skills, which you'll use in Chapter 13: using the Pythagorean theorem, solving equations using inverse functions, and finding angle measures in triangles.

Prerequisite Skills

VOCABULARY CHECK

Copy and complete the statement.

1. The **reciprocal** of $\frac{4}{5}$ is _?_. $\frac{5}{4}$
2. Functions f and g are **inverses** of each other if _?_ and _?_. $f(g(x)) = x, g(f(x)) = x$
3. An equation of the **circle** with center (0, 0) and a radius of 1 unit is _?_. $x^2 + y^2 = 1$

SKILLS CHECK

A right triangle has legs with lengths a and b and a hypotenuse with length c. Find the unknown side length. *(Review p. 995 for 13.1.)*

4. $a = 8, b = 10$ $c = 2\sqrt{41}$
5. $a = 2.5, c = 6.5$ $b = 6$
6. $b = 9, c = 11$ $a = 2\sqrt{10}$

Solve the equation. *(Review p. 515 for 13.4.)*

7. $4^x - 5 = 3$ $\frac{3}{2}$
8. $\log_2 x = -1$ $\frac{1}{2}$
9. $-5 + 2 \ln 3x = 20$ about 89,446

The measures of the angles of a triangle are given. Find the value of x. *(Review p. 995 for 13.5, 13.6.)*

10. $x°, 65°, 55°$ 60
11. $90°, x°, x°$ 45
12. $41°, 107°, x°$ 32

850

Chapter Planning Guide

Chapter 13 Resource Book
- Teaching Guide/Lesson Plan (pp. 3, 14, 24, 36, 47, 59)
- Project with Rubric (p. 72)

Assessment and Intervention
- Assessment Book (pp. 182–196)
- Benchmark Tests
- Remediation Book

Interactive Technology
- Easy Planner
- Power Presentations CD-ROM
- Activity Generator CD-ROM
- Animated Algebra
- Test Generator CD-ROM
- Online Quizzes
- eWorkbook
- eEdition
- @HomeTutor

Resources for English Learners
- Quick Reference for English Learners
- Spanish Study Guide
- Multi-Language Visual Glossary
- Student Resources in Spanish

Now

In Chapter 13, you will apply the big ideas listed below and reviewed in the Chapter Summary on page 897. You will also use the key vocabulary listed below.

Big Ideas

1. **Using trigonometric functions**
2. **Using inverse trigonometric functions**
3. **Applying the law of sines and law of cosines**

KEY VOCABULARY

- sine, *p. 852*
- cosine, *p. 852*
- tangent, *p. 852*
- cosecant, *p. 852*
- secant, *p. 852*
- cotangent, *p. 852*
- radian, *p. 860*
- central angle, *p. 861*
- unit circle, *p. 867*
- reference angle, *p. 868*
- inverse sine, *p. 875*
- inverse cosine, *p. 875*
- inverse tangent, *p. 875*
- law of sines, *p. 882*
- law of cosines, *p. 889*

Why?

You can use angle measures and trigonometry to find lengths and areas in real life. For example, you can use an angle measure to find the area of each step in a spiral staircase.

Animated Algebra

The animation illustrated below for Exercise 53 on page 864 helps you answer this question: How does the central angle of a step in a spiral staircase affect the step's area?

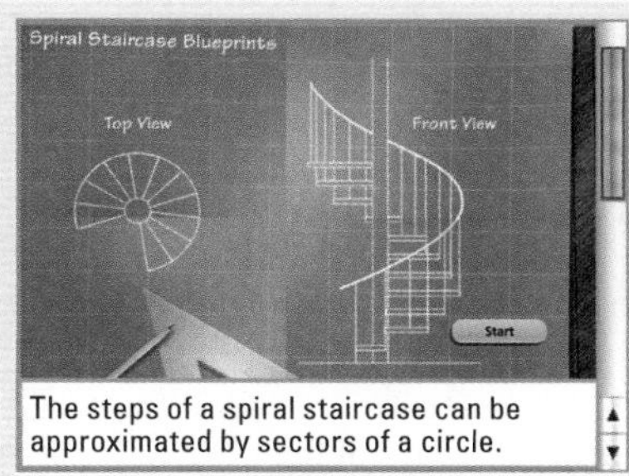

The steps of a spiral staircase can be approximated by sectors of a circle.

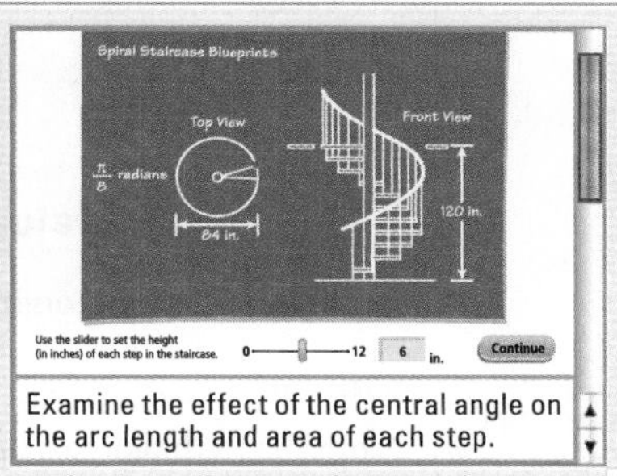

Examine the effect of the central angle on the arc length and area of each step.

Animated Algebra at classzone.com

Other animations for Chapter 13: pages 854, 867, 884, and 897

Algebra 2 Toolkit

- Reading Strategies for Chapter 13, pp. 33–34
- Differentiated Instruction Notes, pp. 91–94
- English Learners Notes, pp. 125–126
- Inclusion Notes, pp. 159–160
- Teaching Strategies with Sample Worksheets, pp. 163–186
- Using Technology in the Classroom, pp. 187–192
- Tips for New Teachers, pp. 217–218
- Math Background Notes, pp. 262–265
- Pre-AP Strategies and Copymasters, pp. 335–336, 439–442
- Teacher Survival Activities, pp. 493–494, 521–522
- Bulletin Board Idea, p. 537
- Teacher Tool Transparencies, following p. 538

1 PLAN AND PREPARE

Warm-Up Exercises

Transparency Available

In right triangle *ABC*, *a* and *b* are the lengths of the legs and *c* is the length of the hypotenuse. Find the missing length. Give exact values.

1. $a = 6$, $b = 8$ $c = 10$

2. $c = 10$, $b = 7$ $a = \sqrt{51}$

3. If you walk 2.0 kilometers due east and then 1.5 kilometers due north, how far will you be from your starting point? 2.5 km

Notetaking Guide

Transparency Available

Promotes interactive learning and notetaking skills, pp. 323–326.

Pacing

Basic: 1 day

Average: 1 day

Advanced: 1 day

Block: 0.5 block with 13.2

- See *Teaching Guide/Lesson Plan.*

2 FOCUS AND MOTIVATE

Essential Question

Big Idea 1, p. 851

How are trigonometric functions used in right triangles? Tell students they will learn how to answer this question by learning to solve right triangles.

13.1 Use Trigonometry with Right Triangles

MA-HS-2.1.3

Before	You used the Pythagorean theorem to find lengths.
Now	You will use trigonometric functions to find lengths.
Why?	So you can measure distances indirectly, as in Example 5.

Key Vocabulary
- **sine**
- **cosine**
- **tangent**
- **cosecant**
- **secant**
- **cotangent**

MA-HS-2.1.3
Students will apply definitions and properties of right triangle relationships (right triangle trigonometry and the Pythagorean theorem) to determine length and angle measures to solve real-world and mathematical problems. DOK 3

Consider a right triangle that has an acute angle θ (the Greek letter *theta*). The three sides of the triangle are the *hypotenuse*, the side *opposite* θ, and the side *adjacent* to θ.

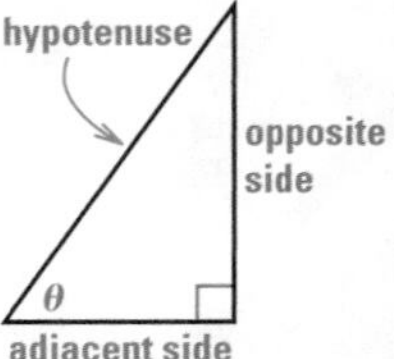

Ratios of a right triangle's side lengths are used to define the six trigonometric functions: **sine**, **cosine**, **tangent**, **cosecant**, **secant**, and **cotangent**. These six functions are abbreviated sin, cos, tan, csc, sec, and cot, respectively.

KEY CONCEPT *For Your Notebook*

Right Triangle Definitions of Trigonometric Functions

Let θ be an acute angle of a right triangle. The six trigonometric functions of θ are defined as follows:

$$\sin\theta = \frac{\text{opposite}}{\text{hypotenuse}} \qquad \cos\theta = \frac{\text{adjacent}}{\text{hypotenuse}} \qquad \tan\theta = \frac{\text{opposite}}{\text{adjacent}}$$

$$\csc\theta = \frac{\text{hypotenuse}}{\text{opposite}} \qquad \sec\theta = \frac{\text{hypotenuse}}{\text{adjacent}} \qquad \cot\theta = \frac{\text{adjacent}}{\text{opposite}}$$

The abbreviations *opp*, *adj*, and *hyp* are often used to represent the side lengths of the right triangle. Note that the ratios in the second row are reciprocals of the ratios in the first row:

$$\csc\theta = \frac{1}{\sin\theta} \qquad \sec\theta = \frac{1}{\cos\theta} \qquad \cot\theta = \frac{1}{\tan\theta}$$

EXAMPLE 1 Evaluate trigonometric functions

Evaluate the six trigonometric functions of the angle θ.

θ, 5, hypotenuse, 12

Solution

REVIEW GEOMETRY
For help with the Pythagorean theorem, see p. 995.

From the Pythagorean theorem, the length of the hypotenuse is $\sqrt{5^2 + 12^2} = \sqrt{169} = 13$.

$$\sin\theta = \frac{\text{opp}}{\text{hyp}} = \frac{12}{13} \qquad \cos\theta = \frac{\text{adj}}{\text{hyp}} = \frac{5}{13} \qquad \tan\theta = \frac{\text{opp}}{\text{adj}} = \frac{12}{5}$$

$$\csc\theta = \frac{\text{hyp}}{\text{opp}} = \frac{13}{12} \qquad \sec\theta = \frac{\text{hyp}}{\text{adj}} = \frac{13}{5} \qquad \cot\theta = \frac{\text{adj}}{\text{opp}} = \frac{5}{12}$$

Resource Planning Guide

Chapter Resource Book
- Teaching Guide/Lesson Plan (pp. 3–4)
- Activity Master (p. 5)
- Practice levels A, B, C (pp. 6–8)
- Study Guide (pp. 9–10)
- Catch-up for Absent Students (p. 11)
- Application (p. 12)
- Challenge (p. 13)

Workbooks
- Notetaking Guide (pp. 323–326)
- Practice Workbook (pp. 181–182)

Teaching Options
- **Power Presentations CD-ROM** provides dynamic electronic teaching resources for the classroom.
- **Activity Generator CD-ROM** provides editable activities for all ability levels.

Interactive Technology
- Easy Planner
- Power Presentations CD-ROM
- Activity Generator CD-ROM
- Animated Algebra
- Test Generator CD-ROM
- Online Quiz
- eWorkbook
- eEdition
- @HomeTutor

Resources for English Learners
- Quick Reference for English Learners
- Spanish Study Guide
- Multi-Language Visual Glossary
- Student Resources in Spanish

See also the *Algebra 2 Toolkit* for more strategies for meeting individual needs.

EXAMPLE 2 Standardized Test Practice

If θ is an acute angle of a right triangle and $\sin\theta = \frac{4}{7}$, what is $\tan\theta$?

Ⓐ $\frac{3}{7}$ Ⓑ $\frac{4\sqrt{33}}{33}$ Ⓒ $\frac{\sqrt{33}}{7}$ Ⓓ $\frac{4}{3}$

Solution

STEP 1 **Draw** a right triangle with acute angle θ such that the leg opposite θ has length 4 and the hypotenuse has length 7. By the Pythagorean theorem, the length x of the other leg is $x = \sqrt{7^2 - 4^2} = \sqrt{33}$.

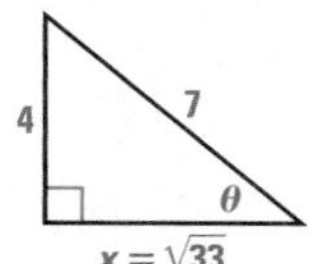
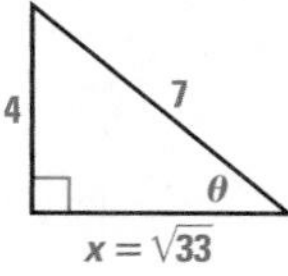

STEP 2 **Find** the value of $\tan\theta$.

$$\tan\theta = \frac{\text{opp}}{\text{adj}} = \frac{4}{\sqrt{33}} = \frac{4\sqrt{33}}{33}$$

▶ The correct answer is B. Ⓐ Ⓑ Ⓒ Ⓓ

✓ GUIDED PRACTICE for Examples 1 and 2

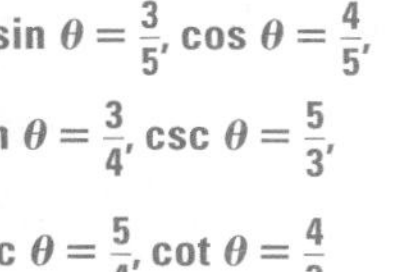

Evaluate the six trigonometric functions of the angle θ.

1. (triangle with legs 4 and 3)

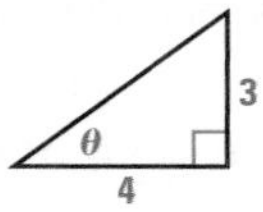

2. 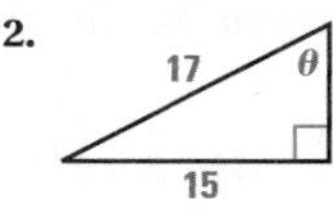

3. 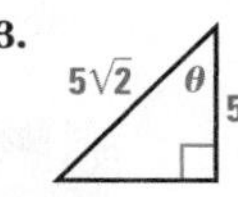

4. In a right triangle, θ is an acute angle and $\cos\theta = \frac{7}{10}$. What is $\sin\theta$? $\frac{\sqrt{51}}{10}$

Margin answers (partially visible): $\sin\theta = \frac{3}{5}, \cos\theta = \frac{4}{5}$, …$n\,\theta = \frac{3}{4}, \csc\theta = \frac{5}{3}$, …$c\,\theta = \frac{5}{4}, \cot\theta = \frac{4}{3}$; $\sin\theta = \frac{15}{17}, \cos\theta =$ …, $\tan\theta = \frac{15}{8}, \csc\theta =$ …, $\sec\theta = \frac{17}{8}, \cot\theta =$ …; $\sin\theta = \frac{\sqrt{2}}{2}, \cos\theta =$ …, $\tan\theta = 1, \csc\theta =$ …, $\sec\theta = \sqrt{2}$, …$t\,\theta = 1$

SPECIAL ANGLES The angles 30°, 45°, and 60° occur frequently in trigonometry. You can use the trigonometric values for these angles to find unknown side lengths in special right triangles.

KEY CONCEPT *For Your Notebook*

Trigonometric Values for Special Angles

The table below gives the values of the six trigonometric functions for the angles 30°, 45°, and 60°. You can obtain these values from the triangles shown.

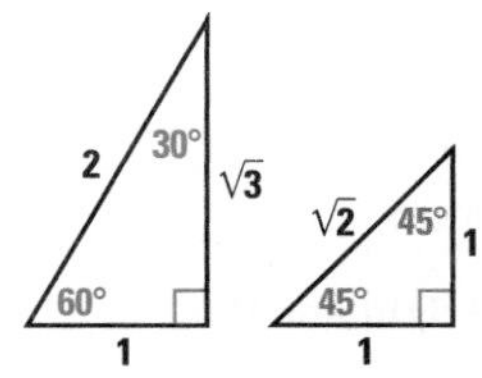

θ	$\sin\theta$	$\cos\theta$	$\tan\theta$	$\csc\theta$	$\sec\theta$	$\cot\theta$
30°	$\frac{1}{2}$	$\frac{\sqrt{3}}{2}$	$\frac{\sqrt{3}}{3}$	2	$\frac{2\sqrt{3}}{3}$	$\sqrt{3}$
45°	$\frac{\sqrt{2}}{2}$	$\frac{\sqrt{2}}{2}$	1	$\sqrt{2}$	$\sqrt{2}$	1
60°	$\frac{\sqrt{3}}{2}$	$\frac{1}{2}$	$\sqrt{3}$	$\frac{2\sqrt{3}}{3}$	2	$\frac{\sqrt{3}}{3}$

Motivating the Lesson

You are on a camping trip and have set up camp on the banks of a river. You think it would be fun to canoe across the river, but want to know how wide the river is before you try it. By measuring a distance and an angle on the ground, you can use trigonometry with a right triangle to calculate the width of the river.

3 TEACH

Extra Example 1

Evaluate the six trigonometric functions of the angle θ.

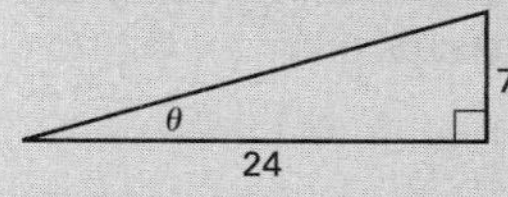

$\sin\theta = \frac{7}{25}, \cos\theta = \frac{24}{25}, \tan\theta = \frac{7}{24}$, $\csc\theta = \frac{25}{7}, \sec\theta = \frac{25}{24}, \cot\theta = \frac{24}{7}$

Extra Example 2

If θ is an acute angle of a right triangle and $\cos\theta = \frac{3}{8}$, what is the value of $\csc\theta$? C

Ⓐ $\frac{3\sqrt{55}}{55}$

Ⓑ $\frac{\sqrt{55}}{8}$

Ⓒ $\frac{8\sqrt{55}}{55}$

Ⓓ $\frac{8}{3}$

Key Question to Ask for Example 2

- In Example 2, why do you need to use the Pythagorean theorem before you can find the value of $\tan\theta$? **The tangent function involves a ratio of the two legs of a right triangle. Because the length of one of the legs is not given, you need to use the Pythagorean theorem to find it.**

Extra Example 3

Find the value for x in the right triangle shown.

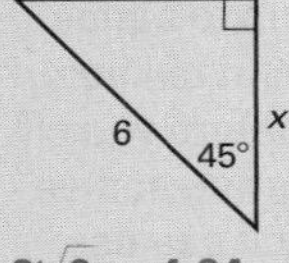

$3\sqrt{2} \approx 4.24$

An **Animated Algebra** activity is available on-line for **Example 3**. This activity is also available on the **Power Presentations CD-ROM**.

Extra Example 4

Solve $\triangle ABC$.

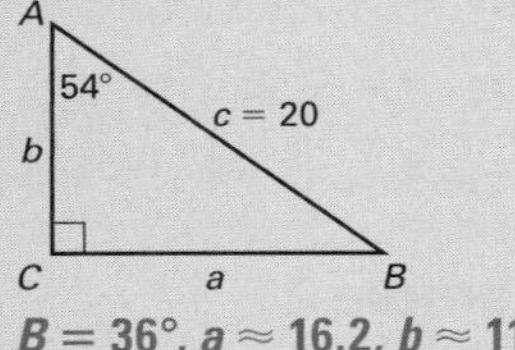

$B = 36°, a \approx 16.2, b \approx 11.8$

Key Question to Ask for Example 4

- In Example 4, once you have found a, how could you find c without using a trigonometric function? **Use the Pythagorean theorem: $c = \sqrt{15^2 + 7.98^2}$**

Avoiding Common Errors

When using the keys for trigonometric functions on a calculator, students may need to be reminded to enter a closing parenthesis before multiplying a value by another number.

EXAMPLE 3 Find an unknown side length of a right triangle

Find the value of x for the right triangle shown.

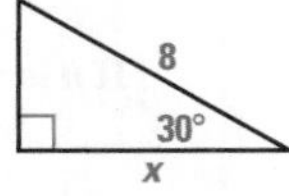

Solution

Write an equation using a trigonometric function that involves the ratio of x and 8. Solve the equation for x.

$\cos 30° = \frac{\text{adj}}{\text{hyp}}$ **Write trigonometric equation.**

$\frac{\sqrt{3}}{2} = \frac{x}{8}$ **Substitute.**

$4\sqrt{3} = x$ **Multiply each side by 8.**

▶ The length of the side is $x = 4\sqrt{3} \approx 6.93$.

SOLVING A TRIANGLE Finding *all* unknown side lengths and angle measures of a triangle is called *solving* the triangle. Solving right triangles that have acute angles other than 30°, 45°, and 60° may require the use of a calculator.

To find values of the sine, cosine, and tangent functions on a calculator, use the keys SIN, COS, and TAN. Use these keys and the reciprocal key for cosecant, secant, and cotangent. Be sure the calculator is set in degree mode.

EXAMPLE 4 Use a calculator to solve a right triangle

Solve $\triangle ABC$.

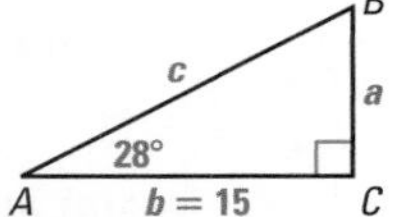

Solution

READING Throughout this chapter, a capital letter is used to denote both an angle of a triangle and its measure. The same letter in lowercase is used to denote the length of the side opposite that angle.

A and B are complementary angles, so $B = 90° - 28° = 62°$.

$\tan 28° = \frac{\text{opp}}{\text{adj}}$	$\sec 28° = \frac{\text{hyp}}{\text{adj}}$	**Write trigonometric equation.**
$\tan 28° = \frac{a}{15}$	$\sec 28° = \frac{c}{15}$	**Substitute.**
$15(\tan 28°) = a$	$15\left(\frac{1}{\cos 28°}\right) = c$	**Solve for the variable.**
$7.98 \approx a$	$17.0 \approx c$	**Use a calculator.**

▶ So, $B = 62°$, $a \approx 7.98$, and $c \approx 17.0$.

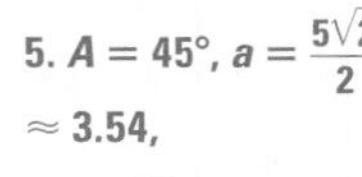

GUIDED PRACTICE for Examples 3 and 4

Solve $\triangle ABC$ using the diagram at the right and the given measurements.

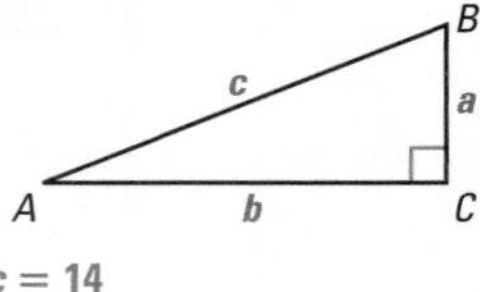

5. $B = 45°, c = 5$

5. $A = 45°, a = \frac{5\sqrt{2}}{2} \approx 3.54, b = \frac{5\sqrt{2}}{2} \approx 3.54$

6. $A = 32°, b = 10$ **$B = 58°, a \approx 6.25, c \approx 11.8$**

7. $A = 71°, c = 20$ **$B = 19°, a \approx 18.9, b \approx 6.51$**

8. $B = 60°, a = 7$ **$A = 30°, b = \frac{14\sqrt{3}}{2} \approx 12.1, c = 14$**

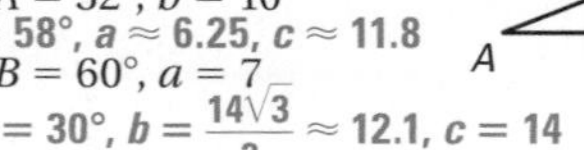

EXAMPLE 5 Use indirect measurement

GRAND CANYON While standing at Yavapai Point near the Grand Canyon, you measure an angle of 90° between Powell Point and Widforss Point, as shown. You then walk to Powell Point and measure an angle of 76° between Yavapai Point and Widforss Point. The distance between Yavapai Point and Powell Point is about 2 miles. How wide is the Grand Canyon between Yavapai Point and Widforss Point?

Solution

CHOOSE FUNCTIONS
The tangent function is used to find the unknown distance because it involves the ratio of x and 2.

$\tan 76° = \frac{x}{2}$ **Write trigonometric equation.**

$2(\tan 76°) = x$ **Multiply each side by 2.**

$8.0 \approx x$ **Use a calculator.**

▶ The width is about 8.0 miles.

ANGLES OF SIGHT If you look at a point above you, such as the top of a building, the angle that your line of sight makes with a line parallel to the ground is called the **angle of elevation**. At the top of the building, the angle between a line parallel to the ground and your line of sight is called the **angle of depression**. These two angles have the same measure.

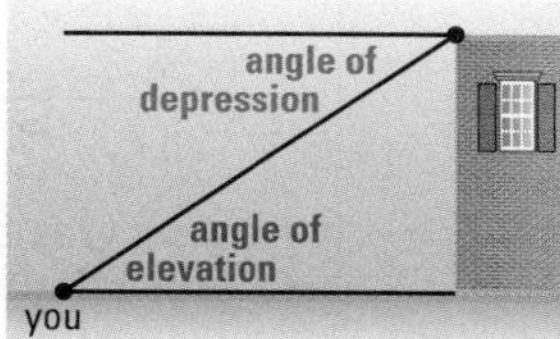

EXAMPLE 6 Use an angle of elevation

PARASAILING A parasailer is attached to a boat with a rope 300 feet long. The angle of elevation from the boat to the parasailer is 48°. Estimate the parasailer's height above the boat.

Solution

STEP 1 **Draw** a diagram that represents the situation.

STEP 2 **Write** and solve an equation to find the height h.

$\sin 48° = \frac{h}{300}$ **Write trigonometric equation.**

$300(\sin 48°) = h$ **Multiply each side by 300.**

$223 \approx h$ **Use a calculator.**

▶ The height of the parasailer above the boat is about 223 feet.

GUIDED PRACTICE for Examples 5 and 6

9. **GRAND CANYON** In Example 5, find the distance between Powell Point and Widforss Point. about 8.27 mi

10. **WHAT IF?** In Example 6, estimate the height of the parasailer above the boat if the angle of elevation is 38°. about 185 ft

Extra Example 5

You are hiking toward a main road, but reach a point where the road is flooded. To avoid the flooded area, you turn onto a diagonal road that meets your original road at a 48° angle and follow that road for 3.6 miles until you hit the main road. How far were you from the main road when you turned onto the diagonal road?

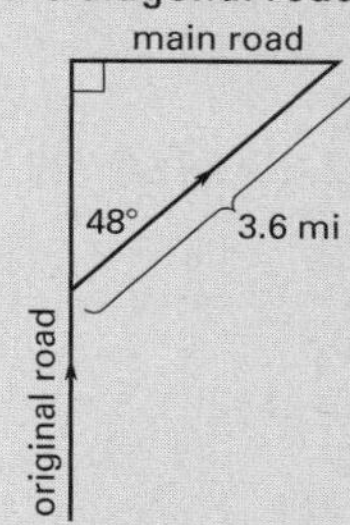

about 2.4 mi

Extra Example 6

From a point on the ground 28 feet from the base of a flagpole, the angle of elevation to the top of the flagpole is 63°. Estimate the height of the flagpole. about 55 ft

Closing the Lesson

Have students summarize the major points of the lesson and answer the Essential Question: How are trigonometric functions used in right triangles?

- **The six trigonometric ratios, sine, cosine, tangent, cosecant, secant, and cotangent, are the six possible ratios of pairs of sides of a right triangle.**
- **If you know the length of any side and the measure of either of the acute angles, you can find all remaining parts of a right triangle.**

The trigonometric functions are used in right triangles to find missing side lengths.

13.1 EXERCISES

HOMEWORK KEY

○ = WORKED-OUT SOLUTIONS on p. WS21 for Exs. 5, 11, and 33

★ = STANDARDIZED TEST PRACTICE Exs. 2, 15, 20, 33, and 36

◆ = MULTIPLE REPRESENTATIONS Ex. 34

4 PRACTICE AND APPLY

Assignment Guide

Answer Transparencies available for all exercises

Basic:
Day 1: SRH p. 995 Exs. 5–8
pp. 856–858
Exs. 1–11, 15–23, 30–34, 38

Average:
Day 1: pp. 856–858
Exs. 1, 2, 4–6, 10–12, 15–20, 23–28, 30–36, 39

Advanced:
Day 1: pp. 856–858
Exs. 1, 2, 7, 8, 15–20, 24–29*, 32–37*, 39

Block:
pp. 856–858
Exs. 1, 2, 4–6, 10–12, 15–20, 23–28, 30–36, 39 (with 13.2)

Differentiated Instruction

See *Algebra 2 Best Practices Toolkit* for suggestions on addressing the needs of a diverse classroom.

Homework Check

For a quick check of student understanding of key concepts, go over the following exercises:

Basic: 4, 10, 17, 22, 32
Average: 6, 12, 18, 24, 34
Advanced: 8, 15, 19, 26, 35

Extra Practice

- Student Edition, p. 1022
- Chapter 13 Resource Book: Practice levels A, B, C, pp. 6–8

Practice Worksheet

An easily-readable reduced practice page (with answers) for this lesson can be found on p. 850C.

SKILL PRACTICE

A

1. **VOCABULARY** What is an angle of elevation? The angle formed by the line of sight to an object and a line parallel to the ground.
2. ★ **WRITING** *Explain* what it means to solve a right triangle. Find any missing information so the measures of all 3 angles and sides are known.

EXAMPLE 1 on p. 852 for Exs. 3–8

EVALUATING FUNCTIONS Evaluate the six trigonometric functions of the angle θ. 3–8. See margin.

3. 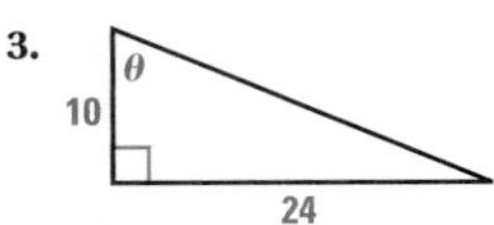

4. 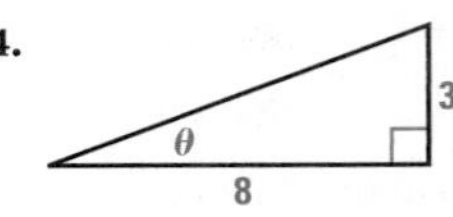

5. 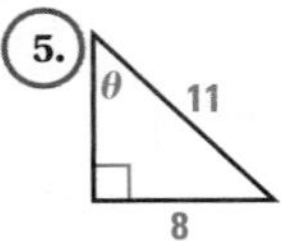

6. 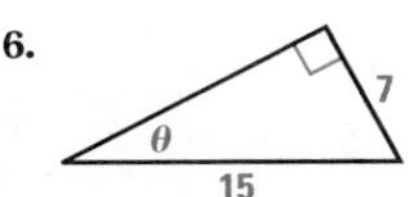

7. 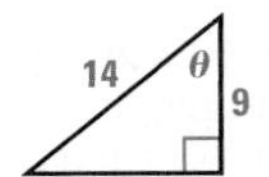

8. 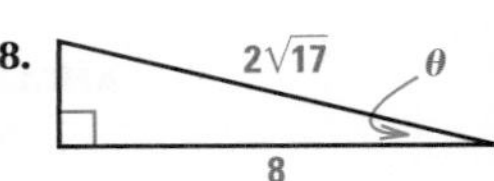

EXAMPLE 2 on p. 853 for Exs. 9–16

FINDING VALUES Let θ be an acute angle of a right triangle. Find the values of the other five trigonometric functions of θ. 9–14. See margin.

9. $\sin\theta = \frac{5}{6}$
10. $\cos\theta = \frac{5}{8}$
11. $\tan\theta = \frac{7}{3}$
12. $\csc\theta = \frac{10}{7}$
13. $\sec\theta = \frac{12}{5}$
14. $\cot\theta = \frac{6}{11}$

15. ★ **MULTIPLE CHOICE** In a right triangle, θ is an acute angle and $\cos\theta = \frac{4}{9}$. What is the value of $\tan\theta$? C

Ⓐ $\frac{4\sqrt{65}}{65}$ Ⓑ $\frac{\sqrt{65}}{9}$ Ⓒ $\frac{\sqrt{65}}{4}$ Ⓓ $\frac{9}{4}$

16. **ERROR ANALYSIS** *Describe* and correct the error in finding $\csc\theta$, given that θ is an acute angle of a right triangle and $\cos\theta = \frac{7}{11}$.

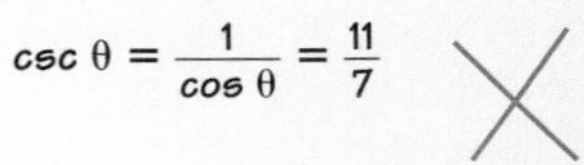

16. Cosecant is not the reciprocal of cosine, it is the reciprocal of sine; $\sin\theta = \frac{6\sqrt{2}}{11}$, $\csc\theta = \frac{1}{\sin\theta} = \frac{11}{6\sqrt{2}} = \frac{11\sqrt{2}}{12}$.

EXAMPLE 3 on p. 854 for Exs. 17–20

B

FINDING SIDE LENGTHS Find the exact values of x and y.

17. 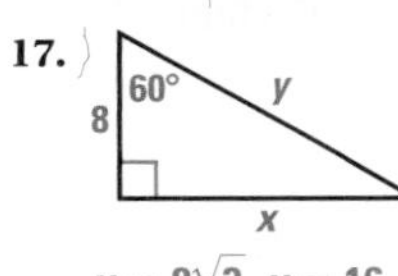

$x = 8\sqrt{3}, y = 16$

18. 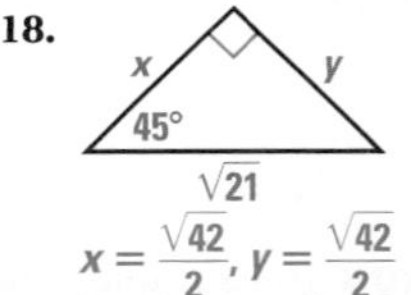

$x = \frac{\sqrt{42}}{2}, y = \frac{\sqrt{42}}{2}$

19. 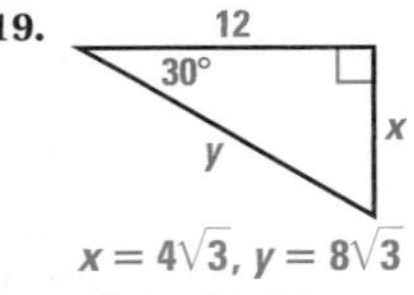

$x = 4\sqrt{3}, y = 8\sqrt{3}$

20. ★ **MULTIPLE CHOICE** In a 30°-60°-90° triangle, the longer leg has a length of 5. What is the length of the shorter leg? A

Ⓐ $\frac{5\sqrt{3}}{3}$ Ⓑ $\frac{5\sqrt{3}}{2}$ Ⓒ $\frac{10\sqrt{3}}{3}$ Ⓓ $5\sqrt{3}$

3–8. See Additional Answers beginning on p. AA1.

9. $\cos\theta = \frac{\sqrt{11}}{6}$, $\tan\theta = \frac{5\sqrt{11}}{11}$, $\csc\theta = \frac{6}{5}$, $\sec\theta = \frac{6\sqrt{11}}{11}$, $\cot\theta = \frac{\sqrt{11}}{5}$

10. $\sin\theta = \frac{\sqrt{39}}{8}$, $\tan\theta = \frac{\sqrt{39}}{5}$, $\csc\theta = \frac{8\sqrt{39}}{39}$, $\sec\theta = \frac{8}{5}$, $\cot\theta = \frac{5\sqrt{39}}{39}$

11. $\sin\theta = \frac{7\sqrt{58}}{58}$, $\cos\theta = \frac{3\sqrt{58}}{58}$, $\csc\theta = \frac{\sqrt{58}}{7}$, $\sec\theta = \frac{\sqrt{58}}{3}$, $\cot\theta = \frac{3}{7}$

EXAMPLE 4
on p. 854
for Exs. 21–28

SOLVING TRIANGLES **Solve $\triangle ABC$ using the diagram and the given measurements.**

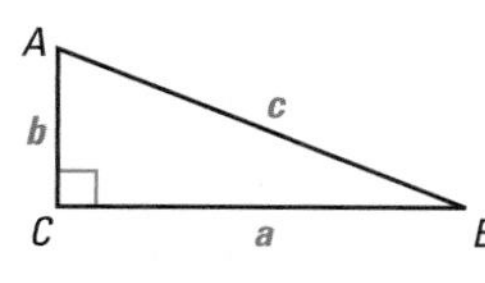

21. $A = 35°, c = 16$ $B = 55°, a \approx 9.18, b \approx 13.11$
22. $B = 53°, a = 12$ $A = 37°, b \approx 15.92, c \approx 19.94$
23. $B = 18°, c = 24$ $A = 72°, a \approx 22.83, b \approx 7.42$
24. $A = 67°, b = 7$ $B = 23°, a \approx 16.49, c \approx 17.92$
25. $B = 75°, a = 15$ $A = 15°, b \approx 55.98, c \approx 57.96$
26. $A = 49°, c = 27$ $B = 41°, a \approx 20.38, b \approx 17.71$
27. $A = 64°, b = 32$ $B = 26°, a \approx 65.61, c \approx 73.0$
28. $B = 24°, c = 10.8$ $A = 66°, a \approx 9.87, b \approx 4.39$

C

29. **CHALLENGE** A procedure for approximating π based on the work of Archimedes is to inscribe a regular hexagon in a circle.

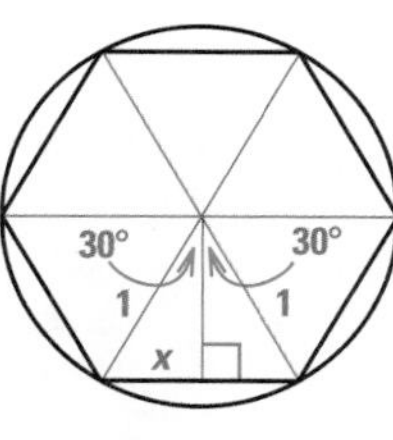

   a. Use the diagram at the right to solve for x. What is the perimeter of the hexagon? $\frac{1}{2}$, 6 units

   b. Show that a regular n-sided polygon inscribed in a circle of radius 1 has a perimeter of $2n \cdot \sin\left(\frac{180}{n}\right)^\circ$. See margin.

   c. Use the result from part (b) to find an expression in terms of n that approximates π. Then evaluate the expression when $n = 50$. $n \sin\left(\frac{180}{n}\right)^\circ$; about 3.14

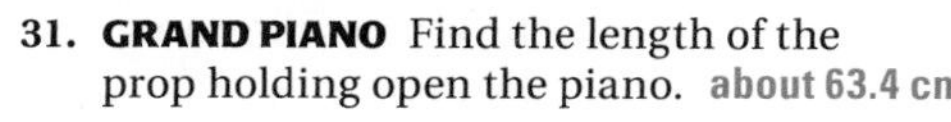

PROBLEM SOLVING

EXAMPLES 5 and 6 A
on p. 855
for Exs. 30–35

In Exercises 30 and 31, use the information in the diagram to solve the problem.

30. **TREE HEIGHT** A tree casts the shadow shown. What is the height of the tree? about 15 ft

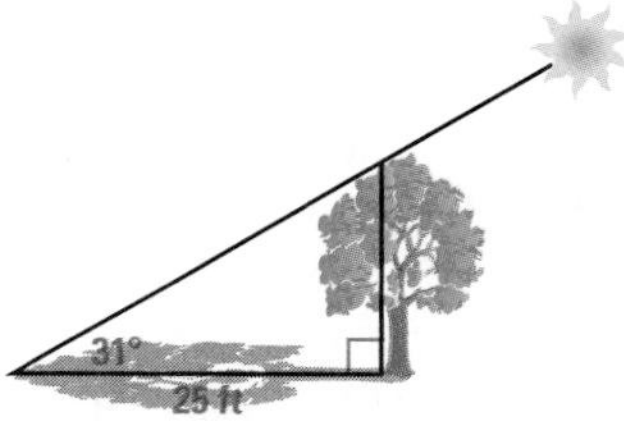

31. **GRAND PIANO** Find the length of the prop holding open the piano. about 63.4 cm

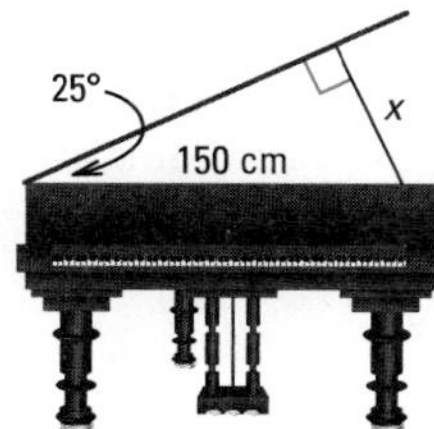

@HomeTutor for problem solving help at classzone.com

32. **RAILWAY** The Falls Incline Railway at Niagara Falls has an angle of elevation of 36°. The railway extends a horizontal distance of about 138 feet. Find the height and length of the railway. height: about 100 ft, length: about 171 ft

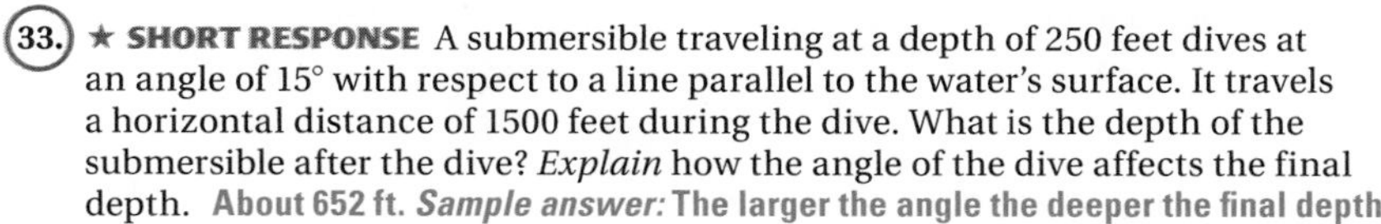

33. ★ **SHORT RESPONSE** A submersible traveling at a depth of 250 feet dives at an angle of 15° with respect to a line parallel to the water's surface. It travels a horizontal distance of 1500 feet during the dive. What is the depth of the submersible after the dive? *Explain* how the angle of the dive affects the final depth. About 652 ft. *Sample answer:* The larger the angle the deeper the final depth.

B

34. **MULTIPLE REPRESENTATIONS** You are climbing Mount Massive in Colorado. You are at an altitude of 11,200 feet. You measure the angle of elevation to a ridge above you to be 29.4°. The distance (along the face of the mountain) between you and the ridge is 6315 feet.

   a. **Drawing a Diagram** Draw a diagram that represents this situation. See margin.

   b. **Writing an Equation** Write and solve an equation to find the altitude of the ridge. $\sin 29.4° = \frac{h - 11{,}200}{6315}$, $h \approx 14{,}300$ ft

12. $\sin\theta = \frac{7}{10}, \cos\theta = \frac{\sqrt{51}}{10}, \tan\theta = \frac{7\sqrt{51}}{51}, \sec\theta = \frac{10\sqrt{51}}{51}, \cot\theta = \frac{\sqrt{51}}{7}$

13. $\sin\theta = \frac{\sqrt{119}}{12}, \cos\theta = \frac{5}{12}, \tan\theta = \frac{\sqrt{119}}{5}, \csc\theta = \frac{12\sqrt{119}}{119}, \cot\theta = \frac{5\sqrt{119}}{119}$

14. $\sin\theta = \frac{11\sqrt{157}}{157}, \cos\theta = \frac{6\sqrt{157}}{157}, \tan\theta = \frac{11}{6}, \csc\theta = \frac{\sqrt{157}}{11}, \sec\theta = \frac{\sqrt{157}}{6}$

29b. See Additional Answers beginning on p. AA1.

Study Strategy

Exercises 17 and 19 Students often have trouble remembering the exact values of the trigonometric functions of 30° and 60° angles, so it is helpful to show them a way to figure these out for themselves. Tell them to write in their notebooks and remember, "The side opposite the 30° angle is half the hypotenuse." From that, the length of the side opposite the 60° angle can be calculated by the Pythagorean theorem, and then the values of all six functions of both of these angles follow.

Teaching Strategy

Exercises 17–19 Show students how an equilateral triangle can be cut in half to form two 30°-60°-90° triangles, which will illustrate *why* the side opposite the 30° angle is half as long as the hypotenuse. Also show how it is easy to find the values of the six trigonometric functions of a 45° angle by applying the definition of an isosceles triangle and the Pythagorean theorem. This approach will give students tools for figuring out the values of the trigonometric functions of the special angles on their own rather than depending on memorization.

Avoiding Common Errors

Exercises 21–28 Some students make errors in solving right triangles because they incorrectly identify the sides that are adjacent and opposite a certain angle, especially if the triangle is oriented differently from the figure on the top of page 852. Guide these students to first locate the acute angle whose measure is given and then go across from its vertex to find the opposite side for *that* angle.

Internet Reference

Exercise 32 More information about the Falls Incline Railway can be found at www.niagaraparks.com/nfgg/firailway.php

34a.

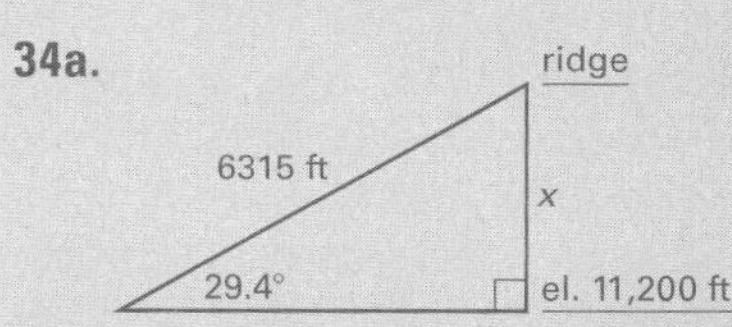

5 ASSESS AND RETEACH

Daily Homework Quiz

Transparency Available

1. Evaluate the six trigonometric functions of the angle θ.

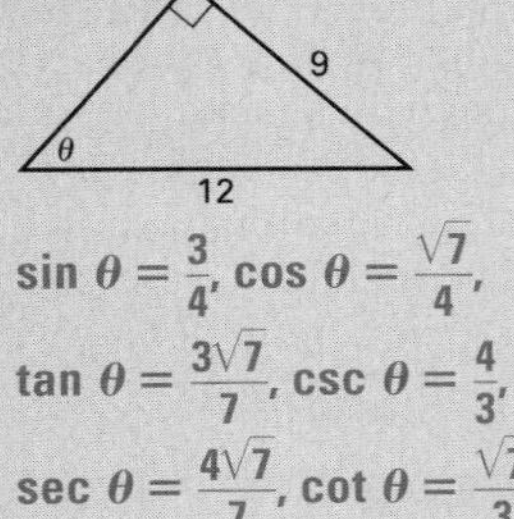

$\sin\theta = \frac{3}{4}$, $\cos\theta = \frac{\sqrt{7}}{4}$,

$\tan\theta = \frac{3\sqrt{7}}{7}$, $\csc\theta = \frac{4}{3}$,

$\sec\theta = \frac{4\sqrt{7}}{7}$, $\cot\theta = \frac{\sqrt{7}}{3}$

2. Solve $\triangle ABC$.

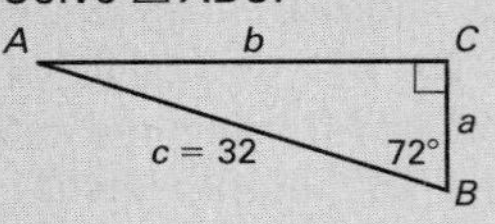

$A = 18°$, $a \approx 9.89$, $b \approx 30.4$

3. From a point on the ground 64 feet from the base of a tree, the angle of elevation to the top of the tree is 28°. Estimate the height of the tree. about 34 ft

Available at **classzone.com**

Diagnosis/Remediation

- Practice A, B, C in Chapter 13 Resource Book, pp. 6–8
- Study Guide in Chapter 13 Resource Book, pp. 9–10
- Practice Workbook, pp. 181–182
- @HomeTutor

Challenge

Additional challenge is available in the Chapter 13 Resource Book, p. 13.

---

35. **TROPIC OF CANCER** The Tropic of Cancer is the circle of latitude farthest north of the equator where the sun can appear directly overhead. It lies 23.5° north of the equator, as shown.

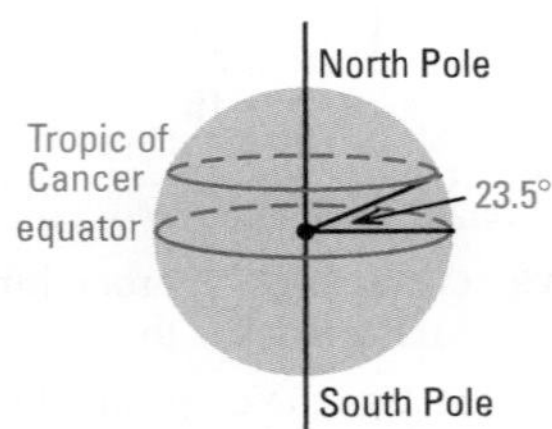

   a. Find the circumference of the Tropic of Cancer using 3960 miles as Earth's approximate radius. **about 22,818 mi**

   b. What is the distance between two points on the Tropic of Cancer that lie directly across from each other? **about 7263 mi**

36c. About 39,688 ft; first find the horizontal distance, $x + y$, between the airplane and the second town to be about 93,301 feet. Then subtract 53,613 feet to find the distance between the two towns.

36. ★ **EXTENDED RESPONSE** A passenger in an airplane sees two towns directly to the left of the plane.

   a. What is the distance d from the airplane to the first town? **about 59,155 ft**

   b. What is the horizontal distance x from the airplane to the first town? **about 53,613 ft**

   c. What is the distance y between the two towns? *Explain* the process you used to find your answer. **See margin.**

C 37. **CHALLENGE** You measure the angle of elevation from the ground to the top of a building as 32°. When you move 50 meters closer to the building, the angle of elevation is 53°. How high is the building? **about 59 m**

KENTUCKY MIXED REVIEW

38. The height h (in feet) of a horseshoe tossed during a game of horseshoes is $h = -16t^2 + 30t + 2$ where t is the time (in seconds). About how long is the horseshoe in the air? **B**

   Ⓐ 1.4 sec Ⓑ 1.9 sec
   Ⓒ 2.9 sec Ⓓ 3.6 sec

39. Rectangle $KLMN$ has diagonals that intersect at point P. What are the coordinates of point L? **D**

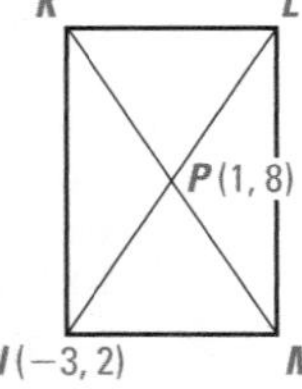

   Ⓐ (−1, 5)
   Ⓑ (−1, 14)
   Ⓒ (5, 5)
   Ⓓ (5, 14)

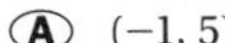

13.2 Define General Angles and Use Radian Measure

MA-HS-2.2.1 Students will continue to apply to both real-world and mathematical problems U.S. customary and metric systems of measurement.

Before You used acute angles measured in degrees.

Now You will use general angles that may be measured in radians.

Why? So you can find the area of a curved playing field, as in Example 4.

Key Vocabulary
- initial side
- terminal side
- standard position
- coterminal
- radian
- sector
- central angle

In Lesson 13.1, you worked only with acute angles. In this lesson, you will study angles with measures that can be any real numbers.

KEY CONCEPT *For Your Notebook*

Angles in Standard Position

In a coordinate plane, an angle can be formed by fixing one ray, called the **initial side**, and rotating the other ray, called the **terminal side**, about the vertex.

An angle is in **standard position** if its vertex is at the origin and its initial side lies on the positive x-axis.

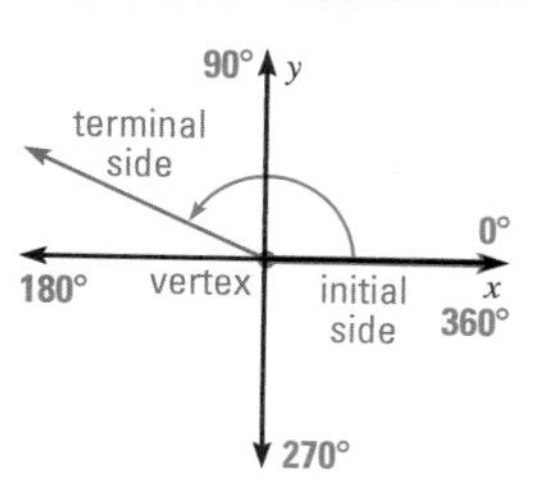

The measure of an angle is positive if the rotation of its terminal side is counterclockwise, and negative if the rotation is clockwise. The terminal side of an angle can make more than one complete rotation.

EXAMPLE 1 **Draw angles in standard position**

Draw an angle with the given measure in standard position.

a. 240° **b.** 500° **c.** −50°

Solution

a. Because 240° is 60° more than 180°, the terminal side is 60° counterclockwise past the negative x-axis.

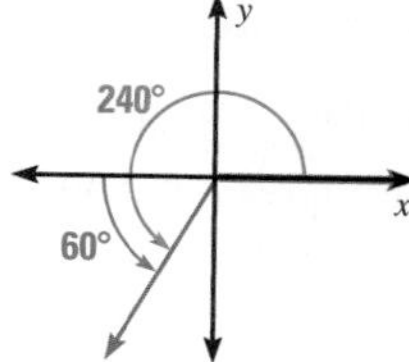

b. Because 500° is 140° more than 360°, the terminal side makes one whole revolution counterclockwise plus 140° more.

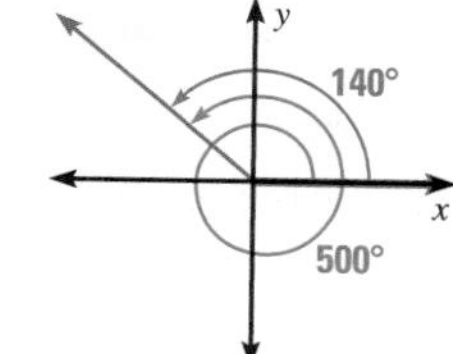

c. Because −50° is negative, the terminal side is 50° clockwise from the positive x-axis.

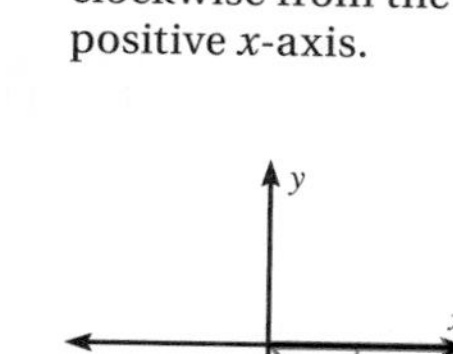

1 PLAN AND PREPARE

Warm-Up Exercises

Transparency Available

Write the expression in simplest form.

1. $\frac{5}{6}(180°)$ 150°
2. $\frac{115°}{180°}$ $\frac{23}{36}$
3. $\frac{11}{12}(180°)$ 165°
4. $\frac{135°}{180°}$ $\frac{3}{4}$
5. A compact disk has radius 6 centimeters. Find its circumference and area to the nearest tenth. $C \approx 37.7$ cm; $A \approx 113.1$ cm^2

Notetaking Guide

Transparency Available

Promotes interactive learning and notetaking skills, pp. 327–330.

Pacing

Basic: 1 day
Average: 1 day
Advanced: 1 day
Block: 0.5 block with 13.1
- See *Teaching Guide/Lesson Plan.*

2 FOCUS AND MOTIVATE

Essential Question

Big Idea 1, p. 851

What is radian measure? Tell students they will learn how to answer this question by working with angles related to central angles of circles.

Resource Planning Guide

Chapter Resource Book
- Teaching Guide/Lesson Plan (pp. 14–15)
- Practice levels A, B, C (pp. 16–18)
- Study Guide (pp. 19–20)
- Catch-up for Absent Students (p. 21)
- Problem Solving Workshop (p. 22)
- Challenge (p. 23)

Workbooks
- Notetaking Guide (pp. 327–330)
- Practice Workbook (pp. 183–184)

Teaching Options
- **Power Presentations CD-ROM** provides dynamic electronic teaching resources for the classroom.
- **Activity Generator CD-ROM** provides editable activities for all ability levels.

Interactive Technology
- Easy Planner
- Power Presentations CD-ROM
- Activity Generator CD-ROM
- Animated Algebra
- Test Generator CD-ROM
- Online Quiz
- eWorkbook
- eEdition
- @HomeTutor

Resources for English Learners
- Quick Reference for English Learners
- Spanish Study Guide
- Multi-Language Visual Glossary
- Student Resources in Spanish

See also the *Algebra 2 Toolkit* for more strategies for meeting individual needs.

COTERMINAL ANGLES In Example 1, the angles 500° and 140° are **coterminal** because their terminal sides coincide. An angle coterminal with a given angle can be found by adding or subtracting multiples of 360°.

EXAMPLE 2 Find coterminal angles

Find one positive angle and one negative angle that are coterminal with (a) −45° and (b) 395°.

Solution

There are many such angles, depending on what multiple of 360° is added or subtracted.

a. $-45° + 360° = 315°$
$-45° - 360° = -405°$

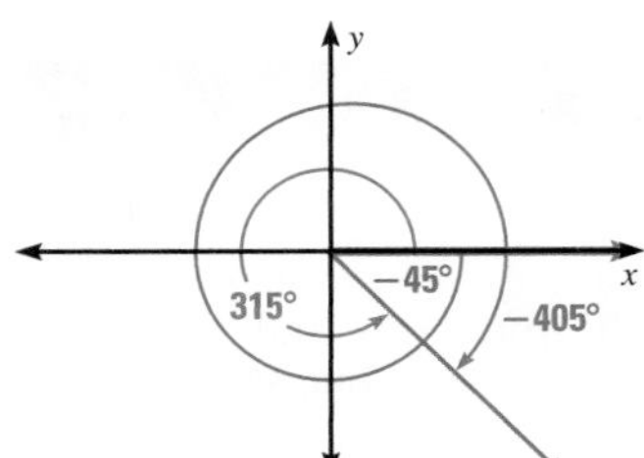

b. $395° - 360° = 35°$
$395° - 2(360°) = -325°$

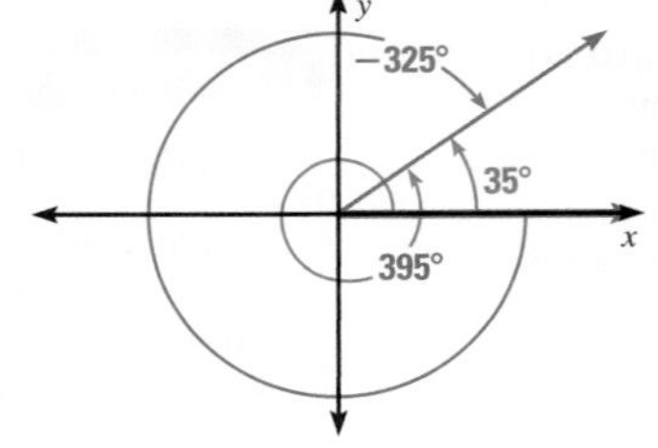

✓ GUIDED PRACTICE for Examples 1 and 2

Draw an angle with the given measure in standard position. Then find one positive coterminal angle and one negative coterminal angle.

1–4. See margin for art. Sample answers are given.

1. 65° 425°, −295° **2.** 230° 590°, −130° **3.** 300° 660°, −60° **4.** 740° 20°, −340°

RADIAN MEASURE Angles can also be measured in *radians.* To define a radian, consider a circle with radius r centered at the origin as shown. One **radian** is the measure of an angle in standard position whose terminal side intercepts an arc of length r.

Because the circumference of a circle is $2\pi r$, there are 2π radians in a full circle. Degree measure and radian measure are therefore related by the equation $360° = 2\pi$ radians, or $180° = \pi$ radians.

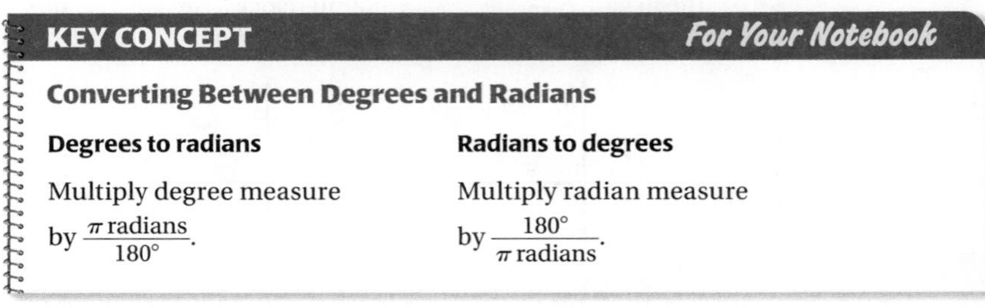

KEY CONCEPT *For Your Notebook*

Converting Between Degrees and Radians

Degrees to radians	**Radians to degrees**
Multiply degree measure by $\frac{\pi \text{ radians}}{180°}$.	Multiply radian measure by $\frac{180°}{\pi \text{ radians}}$.

Motivating the Lesson

Ask students for examples that involve the location of a point on a circle. They may think of examples from everyday objects, such as the motion of a point on the edge of a compact disk, or from sports, geography, or astronomy. Tell them that some of the formulas used to describe circular motion involve angles measured in radians.

3 TEACH

Extra Example 1

Draw an angle with the given measure in standard position.

a. 135°

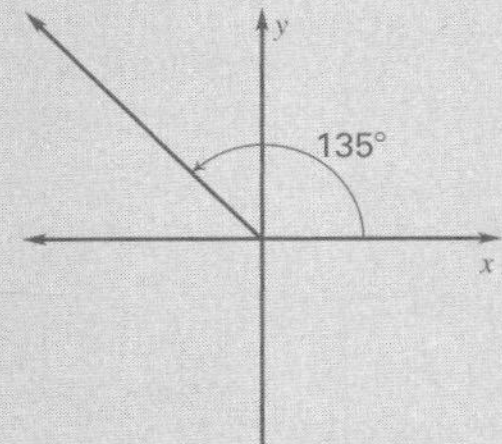

b. 640°

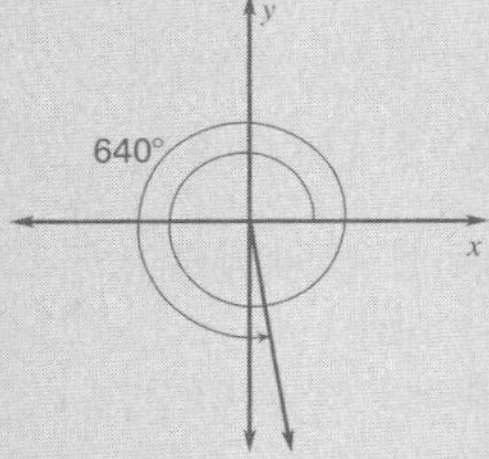

c. −105°

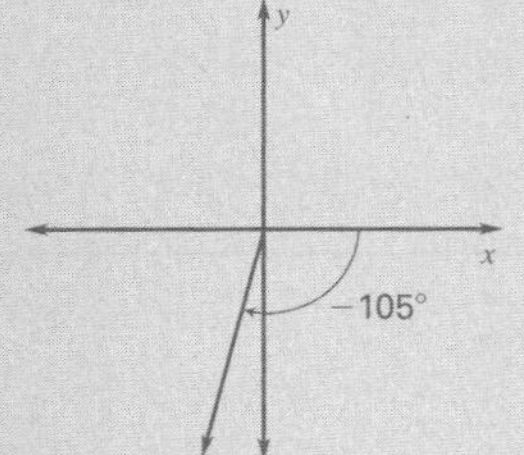

Differentiated Instruction

Below Level Draw a large circle with a compass. Measure the radius with string, and cut a piece of string that has the length of the radius. Place the string on the circle so that it becomes an arc, and mark the endpoints of the arc. Draw segments to connect the center to the endpoints of the arc to form a central angle of 1 radian. Then, by marking off adjacent arcs on the circle, students will see that it takes about $6\frac{1}{4}$, or 2π, of these arcs to get around the circle.

See also the *Algebra 2 Toolkit* for more strategies.

EXAMPLE 3 Convert between degrees and radians

READING
The unit "radians" is often omitted. For instance, the measure $-\frac{\pi}{12}$ radians may be written simply as $-\frac{\pi}{12}$.

Convert (a) 125° to radians and (b) $-\frac{\pi}{12}$ radians to degrees.

a. $125° = 125°\left(\frac{\pi \text{ radians}}{180°}\right)$

$= \frac{25\pi}{36}$ radians

b. $-\frac{\pi}{12} = \left(-\frac{\pi}{12} \text{ radians}\right)\left(\frac{180°}{\pi \text{ radians}}\right)$

$= -15°$

CONCEPT SUMMARY *For Your Notebook*

Degree and Radian Measures of Special Angles

The diagram shows equivalent degree and radian measures for special angles from 0° to 360° (0 radians to 2π radians).

You may find it helpful to memorize the equivalent degree and radian measures of special angles in the first quadrant and for $90° = \frac{\pi}{2}$ radians. All other special angles are just multiples of these angles.

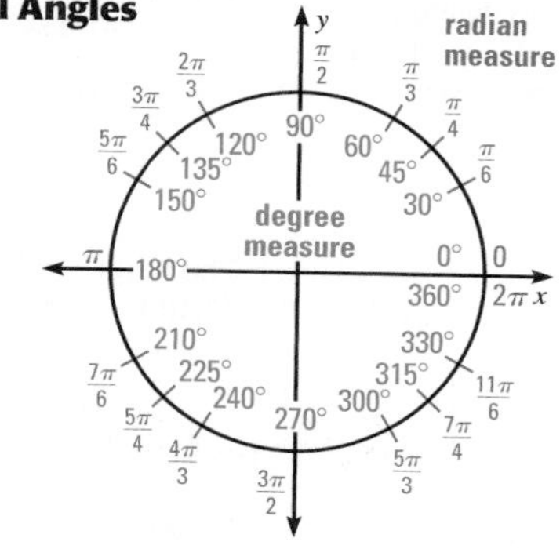

✓ GUIDED PRACTICE for Example 3

Convert the degree measure to radians or the radian measure to degrees.

5. 135° $\frac{3\pi}{4}$ **6.** −50° $-\frac{5\pi}{18}$ **7.** $\frac{5\pi}{4}$ 225° **8.** $\frac{\pi}{10}$ 18°

SECTORS OF CIRCLES A **sector** is a region of a circle that is bounded by two radii and an arc of the circle. The **central angle** θ of a sector is the angle formed by the two radii. There are simple formulas for the arc length and area of a sector when the central angle is measured in radians.

KEY CONCEPT *For Your Notebook*

Arc Length and Area of a Sector

The arc length s and area A of a sector with radius r and central angle θ (measured in radians) are as follows.

Arc length: $s = r\theta$

Area: $A = \frac{1}{2}r^2\theta$

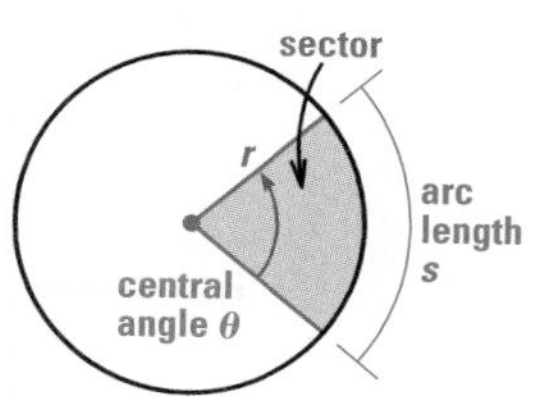

Extra Example 2

Find one positive angle and one negative angle that are coterminal with the angle.

a. −215° 145°; −575°

b. 570° 210°; −150°

Extra Example 3

Convert the given angle measure.

a. 75° to radians $\frac{5\pi}{12}$ radians

b. $-\frac{5\pi}{4}$ radians to degrees −225°

Key Questions to Ask for Example 3

- How could you use a proportion to convert 125° to radians? Solve the proportion $\frac{x \text{ radians}}{\pi \text{ radians}} = \frac{125°}{180°}$.
- How could you use a proportion to convert $-\frac{\pi}{12}$ radians to degrees? Solve the proportion $\frac{-\frac{\pi}{12} \text{ radians}}{\pi \text{ radians}} = \frac{x°}{180°}$.

Study Strategy

Show students how to use the unit circle to remember the relationship between radians and degrees: The radius of the unit circle is 1, so its circumference is 2π. Since a complete circle is 360°, this tells you that 2π radians = 360°, or π radians = 180°.

2.

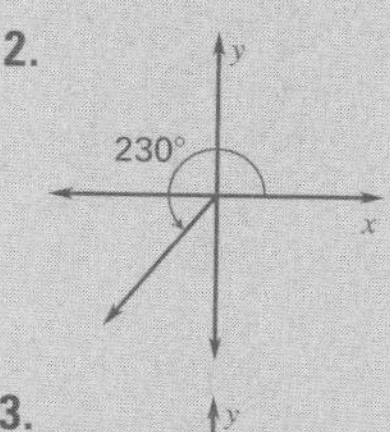

3.

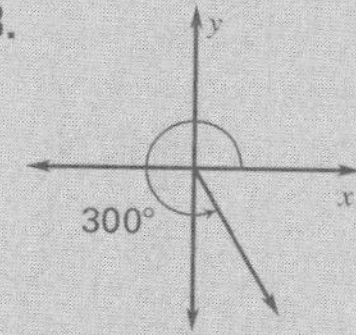

4.

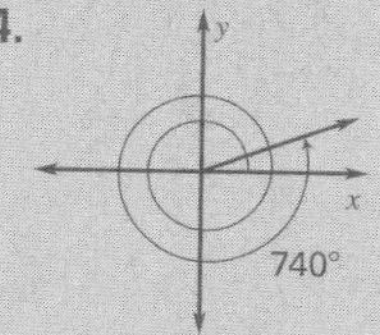

Differentiated Instruction

Advanced Challenge students to derive the formulas for arc length and area of a sector shown in the Key Concept box. Ask for volunteers to show and explain their derivations to the class. If students see where these formulas come from, they will most likely understand and remember them better.

See also the *Algebra 2 Toolkit* for more strategies.

1.

y
65°
x

Extra Example 4

Children at a day camp are playing a game on a circular field. The shaded sector in the figure is called the "safe zone," and is marked off by rope along its outer edge. Find the length of the rope and the area of the safe zone.

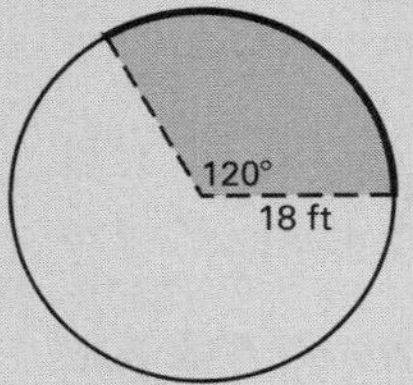

about 37.7 ft; about 339 ft^2

Key Question to Ask for Example 4

- How does arc length relate to the circumference of the entire circle? The circumference of the complete circle is 4 times the arc length.

Closing the Lesson

Have students summarize the major points of the lesson and answer the Essential Question: What is radian measure?

- Angles with positive measure result from counterclockwise rotation; negative measures result from clockwise rotation.
- The formulas for arc length and area of a sector of a circle use radian measure for the central angle.

Radian measure and degree measure are two different systems for measuring angles. One radian is the measure of an angle in standard position whose terminal sides intercept an arc whose length is equal to the radius of the circle.

6.

7.

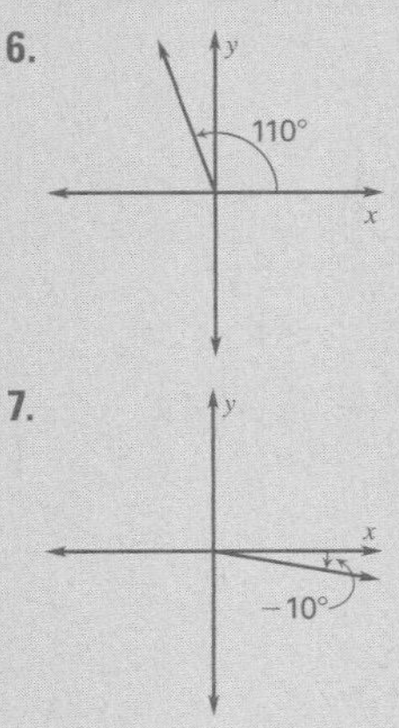

8.

450°

EXAMPLE 4 Solve a multi-step problem

SOFTBALL A softball field forms a sector with the dimensions shown. Find the length of the outfield fence and the area of the field.

Outfield fence

90°

180 ft

Solution

AVOID ERRORS
You must write the measure of an angle in radians when using the formulas for the arc length and area of a sector.

STEP 1 **Convert** the measure of the central angle to radians.

$$90° = 90°\left(\frac{\pi \text{ radians}}{180°}\right) = \frac{\pi}{2} \text{ radians}$$

STEP 2 **Find** the arc length and the area of the sector.

Arc length: $s = r\theta = 180\left(\frac{\pi}{2}\right) = 90\pi \approx 283$ feet

Area: $A = \frac{1}{2}r^2\theta = \frac{1}{2}(180)^2\left(\frac{\pi}{2}\right) = 8100\pi \approx 25{,}400 \text{ ft}^2$

▶ The length of the outfield fence is about 283 feet. The area of the field is about 25,400 square feet.

GUIDED PRACTICE for Example 4

9. **WHAT IF?** In Example 4, estimate the length of the outfield fence and the area of the field if the outfield fence is 220 feet from home plate. about 346 ft, about 38,013 ft^2

13.2 EXERCISES

HOMEWORK KEY
○ = WORKED-OUT SOLUTIONS on p. WS22 for Exs. 11, 23, and 51
★ = STANDARDIZED TEST PRACTICE Exs. 2, 14, 31, 50, and 53

SKILL PRACTICE

1. **VOCABULARY** Copy and complete: An angle is in standard position if its vertex is at the __?__ and its __?__ lies on the positive x-axis. origin, initial side

2. ★ **WRITING** How does the sign of an angle's measure determine its direction of rotation? If the angle is positive you travel counter-clockwise from the initial position on the x-axis. If the angle is negative you travel clockwise from the initial position.

EXAMPLES 1 and 3
on pp. 859–861 for Exs. 3–14

VISUAL THINKING **Match the angle measure with the angle.**

3. −240° B

4. 600° C

5. $-\frac{9\pi}{4}$ A

A.

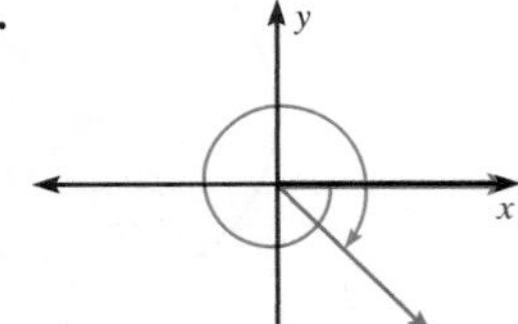

B.

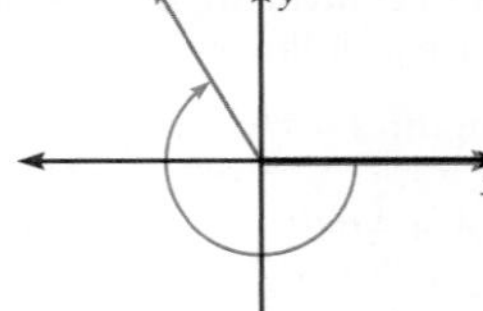

C.

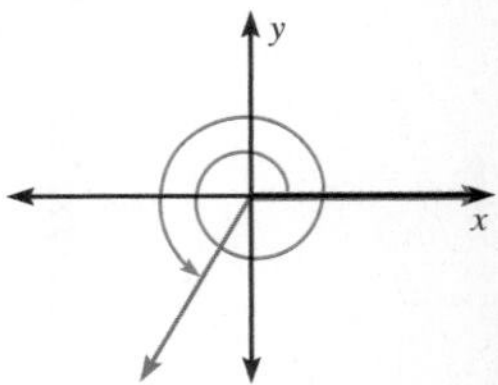

Differentiated Instruction

Visual Learners Suggest that students create a visual representation of the softball field described in **Example 4**. Have students superimpose a coordinate plane over their drawing, and then have them label the initial side, vertex, terminal side, and label the angle measure. Such a visual representation will help students set up their calculations correctly and calculate the proper solution.

See also the *Algebra 2 Toolkit* for more strategies.

DRAWING ANGLES **Draw an angle with the given measure in standard position.** 6–13. See margin.

6. 110°
7. −10°
8. 450°
9. −900°
10. 6π
11. $\frac{5\pi}{18}$
12. $-\frac{5\pi}{3}$
13. $\frac{26\pi}{9}$

14. ★ **MULTIPLE CHOICE** Which angle measure is shown in the diagram? C

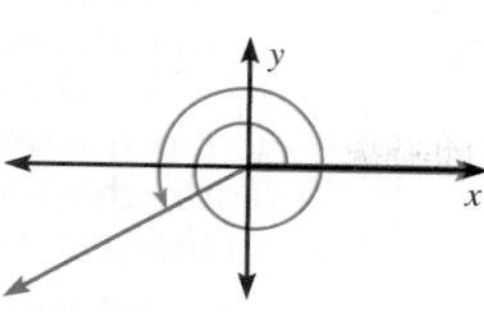

Ⓐ −150° Ⓑ 210°
Ⓒ 570° Ⓓ 930°

EXAMPLES 2 and 3 on pp. 860–861 for Exs. 15–22

FINDING COTERMINAL ANGLES **Find one positive angle and one negative angle that are coterminal with the given angle.** 15–22. Sample answers are given.

15. 70° 430°, −290°
16. 255° 615°, −105°
17. −125° 235°, −485°
18. 820° 100°, −260°
19. $\frac{9\pi}{2}$ $\frac{\pi}{2}, -\frac{3\pi}{2}$
20. $-\frac{7\pi}{6}$ $\frac{5\pi}{6}, -\frac{19\pi}{6}$
21. $\frac{28\pi}{9}$ $\frac{10\pi}{9}, -\frac{8\pi}{9}$
22. $\frac{20\pi}{3}$ $\frac{2\pi}{3}, -\frac{4\pi}{3}$

EXAMPLE 3 on p. 861 for Exs. 23–31

CONVERTING MEASURES **Convert the degree measure to radians or the radian measure to degrees.**

23. 40° $\frac{2\pi}{9}$
24. 315° $\frac{7\pi}{4}$
25. −260° $-\frac{13\pi}{9}$
26. 500° $\frac{25\pi}{9}$
27. $\frac{\pi}{9}$ 20°
28. $-\frac{\pi}{4}$ −45°
29. 5π 900°
30. $\frac{14\pi}{15}$ 168°

31. ★ **MULTIPLE CHOICE** Which angle measure is equivalent to $\frac{13\pi}{6}$ radians? B

Ⓐ 30° Ⓑ 390° Ⓒ 750° Ⓓ 1110°

EXAMPLE 4 B on p. 862 for Exs. 32–38

FINDING ARC LENGTH AND AREA **Find the arc length and area of a sector with the given radius r and central angle θ.**

32. $r = 4$ in., $\theta = \frac{\pi}{6}$ about 2.09 in., about 4.19 in.^{2}
33. $r = 3$ m, $\theta = \frac{5\pi}{12}$ about 3.93 m, about 5.89 m^2
34. $r = 15$ cm, $\theta = 45°$ about 11.8 cm, about 88.4 cm^2
35. $r = 12$ ft, $\theta = 150°$ about 31.4 ft, about 188 ft^2
36. $r = 18$ m, $\theta = 25°$ about 7.85 m, about 70.7 m^2
37. $r = 25$ in., $\theta = 270°$ about 118 in., about 1470 in.^{2}

38. **ERROR ANALYSIS** *Describe* and correct the error in finding the area of a sector with a radius of 6 centimeters and a central angle of 40°.

$A = \frac{1}{2}(6)^2(40) = 720$ cm^2

The angle measure must be in radians before using the formula; $A = \frac{1}{2}(6)^2\left(\frac{2\pi}{9}\right) \approx 12.6$ cm^2.

HINT For Exs. 39–46, set your calculator in radian mode.

EVALUATING FUNCTIONS **Evaluate the trigonometric function using a calculator if necessary. If possible, give an exact answer.**

39. $\cos\frac{\pi}{3}$ $\frac{1}{2}$
40. $\sin\frac{\pi}{4}$ $\frac{\sqrt{2}}{2}$
41. $\tan\frac{\pi}{6}$ $\frac{\sqrt{3}}{3}$
42. $\sec\frac{\pi}{9}$ about 1.06
43. $\cot\frac{\pi}{8}$ about 2.41
44. $\cos\frac{\pi}{6}$ $\frac{\sqrt{3}}{2}$
45. $\sin\frac{3\pi}{7}$ about 0.975
46. $\csc\frac{4\pi}{15}$ about 1.35

C 47. **CHALLENGE** A rotating object that passes through an angle θ during time t has an angular velocity v given by the formula $v = \frac{\theta}{t}$. Find the angular velocity of the hour hand, the minute hand, and the second hand on a 12 hour clock. Give all answers in degrees per hour. 30° per h, 360° per h, 21,600° per h

4 PRACTICE AND APPLY

Assignment Guide

Answer Transparencies available for all exercises

Basic:
Day 1: pp. 862–865
Exs. 1–11, 14–18, 23–37 odd, 38, 48–51, 55

Average:
Day 1: pp. 862–865
Exs. 1–5, 9–11, 14, 18–20, 25–28, 31–45 odd, 48–53, 56

Advanced:
Day 1: pp. 862–865
Exs. 1, 2, 11–14, 20–22, 28–31, 35–54*

Block:
pp. 862–865
Exs. 1–5, 9–11, 14, 18–20, 25–28, 31–45 odd, 48–53, 56 (with 13.1)

Differentiated Instruction

See *Algebra 2 Best Practices Toolkit* for suggestions on addressing the needs of a diverse classroom.

Homework Check

For a quick check of student understanding of key concepts, go over the following exercises:

Basic: 8, 16, 23, 33, 48
Average: 10, 18, 26, 35, 50
Advanced: 12, 22, 28, 36, 52

Extra Practice

- Student Edition, p. 1022
- Chapter 13 Resource Book: Practice levels A, B, C, pp. 16–18

Practice Worksheet

An easily-readable reduced practice page (with answers) for this lesson can be found on p. 850C.

9.
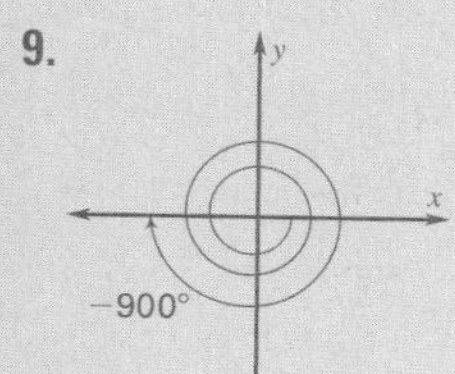

10.
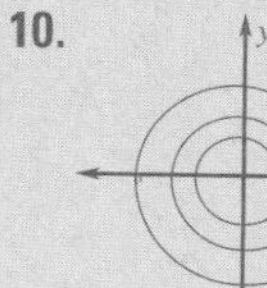

11.
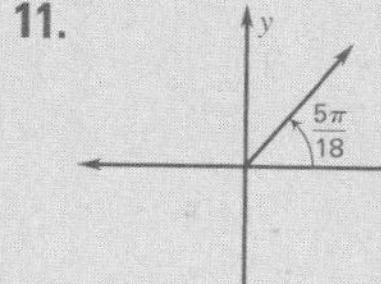

12.
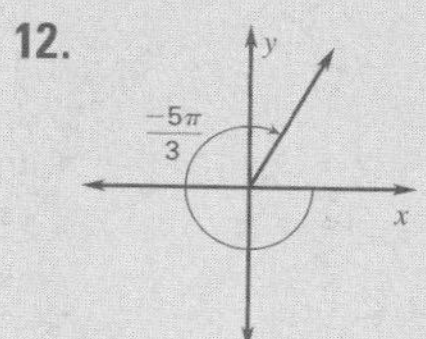

13.
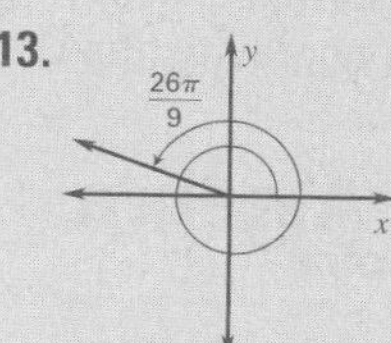

Avoiding Common Errors

Exercises 39–46 A common error in exercises like these is not having the calculator set in radian mode. Since students have probably not used radian mode before, show them how to make this selection from the mode settings. Tell them that they will sometimes be working in degree mode and sometimes in radian mode in this chapter, so they should get in the habit of checking the mode setting whenever they start working with their calculators.

Graphing Calculator

Exercises 42, 43, 46 Since there are no keys for the cosecant, secant, and cotangent functions, students should not be expected to know how to evaluate these functions without some help. Ask them how they think this might be done. It is likely that some students will suggest using the second function keys for $\sin^{-1}$, $\cos^{-1}$, and $\tan^{-1}$, based on the reciprocal relationships $\csc\theta = \frac{1}{\sin\theta}$, $\sec\theta = \frac{1}{\cos\theta}$, and $\cot\theta = \frac{1}{\tan\theta}$, which they learned in Lesson 13.1. Tell students that this is a good guess, but then have them test it with one of the special angles to discover that it is incorrect. Then tell them those keys are used to find inverse functions, which they will learn about in Lesson 13.4. Show them, for example, that $\sec\frac{\pi}{9}$ can be keystroked as $\frac{1}{\cos\frac{\pi}{9}}$ *or* by first evaluating $\cos\frac{\pi}{9}$ and then using the x^{-1} key.

Internet Reference

Exercise 51 For additional information about the use of a centrifuge, visit NASA's website at science.nasa.gov/headlines/y2003/07feb_stronggravity.htm

An **Animated Algebra** activity is available on-line for **Exercise 53**. This activity is also available on the **Power Presentations CD-ROM**.

PROBLEM SOLVING

EXAMPLES 1 and 3 on pp. 859–861 for Exs. 48–50

48. ASTRONOMY In astronomy, the *terminator* is the day-night line on a planet that divides the planet into daytime and nighttime regions. The terminator moves across the planet's surface as the planet rotates. It takes about 4 hours for Earth's terminator to move across the continental United States. Through what angle has Earth rotated during this time? Give the answer in both degrees and radians. $60°, \frac{\pi}{3}$

@HomeTutor for problem solving help at classzone.com

49. CD PLAYER When a CD player reads information from the outer edge of a CD, the CD spins about 200 revolutions per minute. At that speed, through what angle does a point on the CD spin in one minute? Give the answer in both degrees and radians. $72{,}000°, 400\pi$

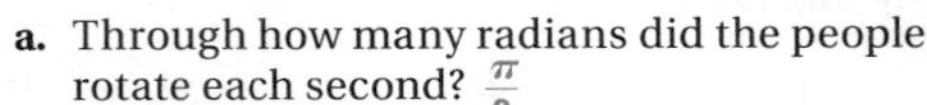

@HomeTutor for problem solving help at classzone.com

50. See margin for art; $-240°$, $-\frac{4\pi}{3}$. *Sample answer:* The minute hand travels 12 times farther than the hour hand in the 8 hours of work.

50. ★ SHORT RESPONSE You work every Saturday from 9:00 A.M. to 5:00 P.M. Draw a diagram that shows the rotation completed by the hour hand of a clock during this time. Find the measure of the angle generated by the hour hand in both degrees and radians. *Compare* this angle with the angle generated by the minute hand from 9:00 A.M. to 5:00 P.M.

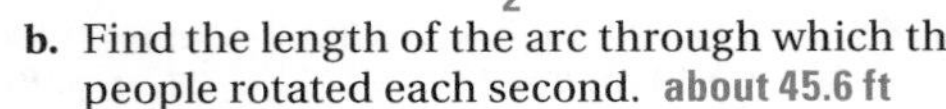

EXAMPLE 4 on p. 862 for Exs. 51–53

51. MULTI-STEP PROBLEM A scientist performed an experiment to study the effects of gravitational force on humans. In order for humans to experience twice Earth's gravity, they were placed in a centrifuge 58 feet long and spun at a rate of about 15 revolutions per minute.

a. Through how many radians did the people rotate each second? $\frac{\pi}{2}$

b. Find the length of the arc through which the people rotated each second. about 45.6 ft

52. MULTI-STEP PROBLEM In the shot put event at the 2004 Summer Olympic Games, the winning shot was 21.16 meters. For a shot put to be fair, it must land within a sector having a central angle of 34.92°.

a. If the officials drew an arc across the fair landing area marking the farthest throw, how long would the arc be? about 12.9 m

b. All fair shot puts in the 2004 Olympics landed within a sector bounded by the arc from part (a). What is the area of this sector? about 136 m^2

53b. 360°. *Sample answer:* Since each step has a central angle of $\frac{\pi}{8}$ and there are 16 steps, the staircase will cover $16\left(\frac{\pi}{8}\right)$ or 2π, which is equivalent to 360°.

53. ★ EXTENDED RESPONSE A spiral staircase has 15 steps. Each step is a sector with a radius of 42 inches and a central angle of $\frac{\pi}{8}$.

a. What is the length of the arc formed by the outer edge of a step? about 16.5 in.

b. Through what angle would you rotate by climbing the stairs? Include a sixteenth turn for stepping up on the landing. *Explain* your reasoning.

c. How many square inches of carpeting would you need to cover the 15 steps? about 5195.4 in.^2

Animated Algebra at classzone.com

○ = WORKED-OUT SOLUTIONS on p. WS1 ★ = STANDARDIZED TEST PRACTICE

50.

12 1 2 3 4 5 6 7 8 9 10 11 −240°

C **54. CHALLENGE** A dartboard is divided into 20 sectors. Each sector is worth a point value from 1 to 20 and has shaded regions that double or triple this value. A sector is shown below.

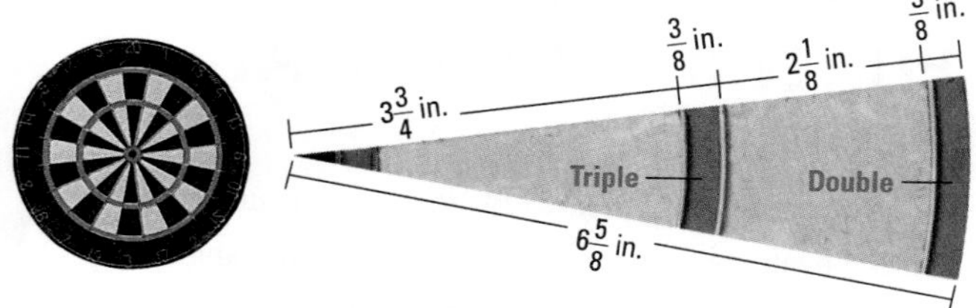

a. Find the areas of the entire sector, the double region, and the triple region. about 6.9 in.^{2}, 0.76 in.^{2}, 0.46 in.^{2}

b. A dart you throw randomly lands somewhere inside the sector. What is the probability that it lands in the double region? in the triple region? about 0.11; about 0.07

KENTUCKY MIXED REVIEW

TEST PRACTICE at classzone.com

55. Lou saves \$12 per week to buy an acoustic guitar that costs \$280. Which equation best represents the relationship between the amount of money Lou still needs to save, m, and the number of weeks, n, that he has been saving? **B**

Ⓐ $m = 280 + 12n$ Ⓑ $m = 280 - 12n$

Ⓒ $m = (280 + 12)n$ Ⓓ $m = (280 - 12)n$

56. Stewart randomly selects two cards from a standard deck of 52 cards. What is the probability that the first card is a heart and the second card is red if he replaces the first card before selecting the second? **C**

Ⓐ 0.063 Ⓑ 0.123 Ⓒ 0.125 Ⓓ 0.75

QUIZ *for Lessons 13.1–13.2*

Solve $\triangle ABC$ using the diagram and the given measurements. *(p. 852)*

1. $A = 50°, a = 14$ $B = 40°, b \approx 11.7, c \approx 18.3$
2. $A = 25°, b = 10$ $B = 65°, a \approx 4.66, c \approx 11.0$
3. $B = 70°, a = 5$ $A = 20°, b \approx 13.7, c \approx 14.6$
4. $B = 42°, c = 18$ $A = 48°, a \approx 13.4, b \approx 12.0$
5. $A = 15°, a = 9$ $B = 75°, b \approx 33.6, c \approx 34.8$
6. $B = 37°, c = 12$ $A = 53°, a \approx 9.58, b \approx 7.22$

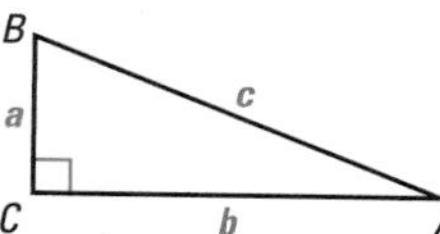

Find one positive angle and one negative angle that are coterminal with the given angle. *(p. 859)* 7–10. Sample answers are given.

7. 115° 475°, −245°
8. 290° 650°, −70°
9. $\frac{4\pi}{9}$ $\frac{22\pi}{9}, -\frac{14\pi}{9}$
10. $\frac{7\pi}{5}$ $\frac{17\pi}{5}, -\frac{3\pi}{5}$

11. Find the arc length and area of a sector with a radius of 8 inches and a central angle of $\theta = 115°$. *(p. 859)* about 16.1 in., about 64.2 in.^{2}

12. **ESCALATOR** The escalator at the Wilshire/Vermont Metro Rail Station in Los Angeles has an angle of elevation of 30°. The length of the escalator is 152 feet. What is the height of the escalator? *(p. 852)* 76 ft

5 ASSESS AND RETEACH

Daily Homework Quiz

Transparency Available

1. Find one positive angle and one negative angle that are coterminal with 475°. 115°; −245°
2. Convert 315° to radians and $\frac{17\pi}{6}$ radians to degrees. $\frac{7\pi}{4}$ radians; 510°
3. You are planting a vegetable garden on a plot of land that is a sector of a circle. You want fencing along only the curved edge of the garden. Use the figure to find the length of fencing you will need and the area that will be available for planting. about 19.6 ft; about 147 ft^2

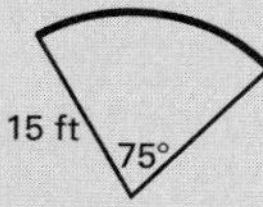

Available at **classzone.com**

Diagnosis/Remediation

- Practice A, B, C in Chapter 13 Resource Book, pp. 16–18
- Study Guide in Chapter 13 Resource Book, pp. 19–20
- Practice Workbook, pp. 183–184
- @HomeTutor

Challenge

Additional challenge is available in the Chapter 13 Resource Book, p. 23.

Quiz

An easily-readable reduced copy of the quiz (with answers) on Lessons 13.1–13.2 from the Assessment Book can be found on p. 850E.

1 PLAN AND PREPARE

Warm-Up Exercises

Transparency Available

1. In right triangle ABC, $a = 3$, $b = 5$, and c is the length of the hypotenuse. Evaluate sin A, cos A, and tan A. $\sin A = \frac{3\sqrt{34}}{34}$, $\cos A = \frac{5\sqrt{34}}{34}$, $\tan A = \frac{3}{5}$
2. Evaluate cos 60°. $\frac{1}{2}$
3. Evaluate sec 45°. $\sqrt{2}$
4. Evaluate cot 30°. $\sqrt{3}$

Notetaking Guide

Transparency Available

Promotes interactive learning and notetaking skills, pp. 331–335.

Pacing

Basic: 2 days
Average: 2 days
Advanced: 2 days
Block: 1 block
- See *Teaching Guide/Lesson Plan.*

2 FOCUS AND MOTIVATE

Essential Question

Big Idea 1, p. 851

How can you evaluate trigonometric functions of any angle? Tell students they will learn how to answer this question by learning several methods for evaluating trigonometric functions.

13.3 Evaluate Trigonometric Functions of Any Angle

MA-HS-2.1.3

Before You evaluated trigonometric functions of an acute angle.
Now You will evaluate trigonometric functions of any angle.
Why? So you can calculate distances involving rotating objects, as in Ex. 37.

Key Vocabulary
- unit circle
- quadrantal angle
- reference angle

MA-HS-2.1.3
Students will apply definitions and properties of right triangle relationships (right triangle trigonometry and the Pythagorean theorem) to determine length and angle measures to solve real-world and mathematical problems. DOK 3

You can generalize the right-triangle definitions of trigonometric functions from Lesson 13.1 so that they apply to *any* angle in standard position.

KEY CONCEPT — *For Your Notebook*

General Definitions of Trigonometric Functions

Let θ be an angle in standard position, and let (x, y) be the point where the terminal side of θ intersects the circle $x^2 + y^2 = r^2$. The six trigonometric functions of θ are defined as follows:

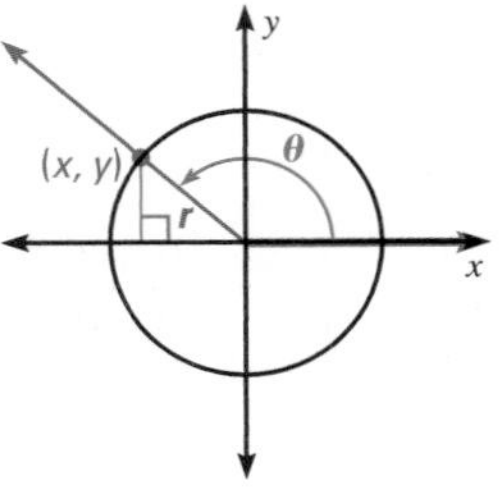

$\sin\theta = \frac{y}{r}$ $\qquad \csc\theta = \frac{r}{y}, y \neq 0$

$\cos\theta = \frac{x}{r}$ $\qquad \sec\theta = \frac{r}{x}, x \neq 0$

$\tan\theta = \frac{y}{x}, x \neq 0$ $\qquad \cot\theta = \frac{x}{y}, y \neq 0$

These functions are sometimes called *circular functions.*

EXAMPLE 1 Evaluate trigonometric functions given a point

Let $(-4, 3)$ be a point on the terminal side of an angle θ in standard position. Evaluate the six trigonometric functions of θ.

Solution

Use the Pythagorean theorem to find the value of r.

$$r = \sqrt{x^2 + y^2} = \sqrt{(-4)^2 + 3^2} = \sqrt{25} = 5$$

Using $x = -4$, $y = 3$, and $r = 5$, you can write the following:

$\sin\theta = \frac{y}{r} = \frac{3}{5}$ $\qquad \cos\theta = \frac{x}{r} = -\frac{4}{5}$ $\qquad \tan\theta = \frac{y}{x} = -\frac{3}{4}$

$\csc\theta = \frac{r}{y} = \frac{5}{3}$ $\qquad \sec\theta = \frac{r}{x} = -\frac{5}{4}$ $\qquad \cot\theta = \frac{x}{y} = -\frac{4}{3}$

Resource Planning Guide

Chapter Resource Book
- Teaching Guide/Lesson Plan (pp. 24–25)
- Activity Master (p. 26)
- Practice levels A, B, C (pp. 27–29)
- Study Guide (pp. 30–31)
- Catch-up for Absent Students (p. 32)
- Problem Solving Workshop (p. 33)
- Challenge (p. 35)

Workbooks
- Notetaking Guide (pp. 331–335)
- Practice Workbook (pp. 185–186)

Teaching Options
- **Power Presentations CD-ROM** provides dynamic electronic teaching resources for the classroom.
- **Activity Generator CD-ROM** provides editable activities for all ability levels.

Interactive Technology
- Easy Planner
- Power Presentations CD-ROM
- Activity Generator CD-ROM
- Animated Algebra
- Test Generator CD-ROM
- Online Quiz
- eWorkbook
- eEdition
- @HomeTutor

Resources for English Learners
- Quick Reference for English Learners
- Spanish Study Guide
- Multi-Language Visual Glossary
- Student Resources in Spanish

See also the *Algebra 2 Toolkit* for more strategies for meeting individual needs.

KEY CONCEPT — *For Your Notebook*

The Unit Circle

The circle $x^2 + y^2 = 1$, which has center (0, 0) and radius 1, is called the **unit circle**. The values of $\sin\theta$ and $\cos\theta$ are simply the y-coordinate and x-coordinate, respectively, of the point where the terminal side of θ intersects the unit circle.

$$\sin\theta = \frac{y}{r} = \frac{y}{1} = y \qquad \cos\theta = \frac{x}{r} = \frac{x}{1} = x$$

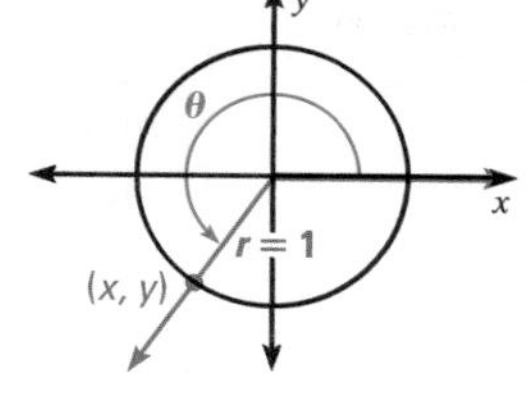

It is convenient to use the unit circle to find trigonometric functions of *quadrantal angles*. A **quadrantal angle** is an angle in standard position whose terminal side lies on an axis. The measure of a quadrantal angle is always a multiple of 90°, or $\frac{\pi}{2}$ radians.

EXAMPLE 2 Use the unit circle

Use the unit circle to evaluate the six trigonometric functions of $\theta = 270°$.

ANOTHER WAY

The general circle $x^2 + y^2 = r^2$ can also be used to find the trigonometric functions of $\theta = 270°$. The terminal side of θ intersects the circle at $(0, -r)$. Therefore:

$\sin\theta = \frac{y}{r} = \frac{-r}{r} = -1$

The other functions can be evaluated similarly.

Solution

Draw the unit circle, then draw the angle $\theta = 270°$ in standard position. The terminal side of θ intersects the unit circle at $(0, -1)$, so use $x = 0$ and $y = -1$ to evaluate the trigonometric functions.

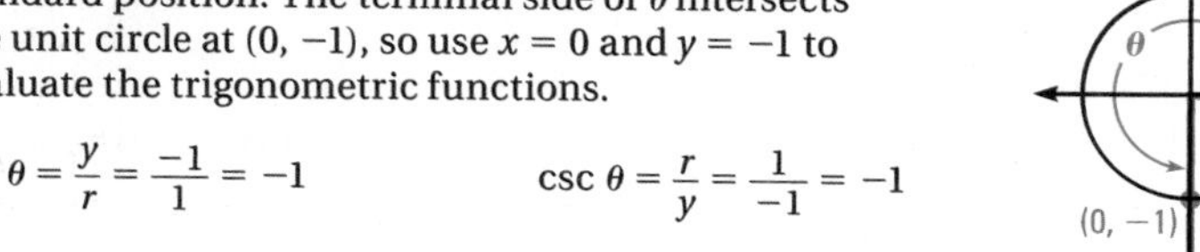

$\sin\theta = \frac{y}{r} = \frac{-1}{1} = -1$ $\qquad$ $\csc\theta = \frac{r}{y} = \frac{1}{-1} = -1$

$\cos\theta = \frac{x}{r} = \frac{0}{1} = 0$ $\qquad$ $\sec\theta = \frac{r}{x} = \frac{1}{0}$ undefined

$\tan\theta = \frac{y}{x} = \frac{-1}{0}$ undefined $\qquad$ $\cot\theta = \frac{x}{y} = \frac{0}{-1} = 0$

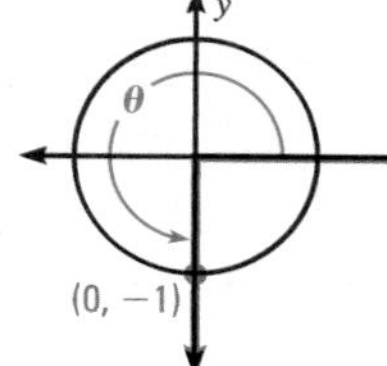

Animated Algebra at classzone.com

✓ GUIDED PRACTICE for Examples 1 and 2

Evaluate the six trigonometric functions of θ.

1. 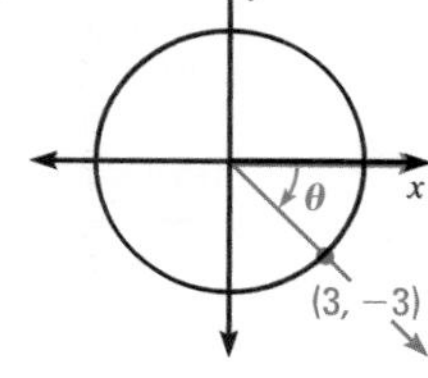

2. (−8, 15), θ

3. 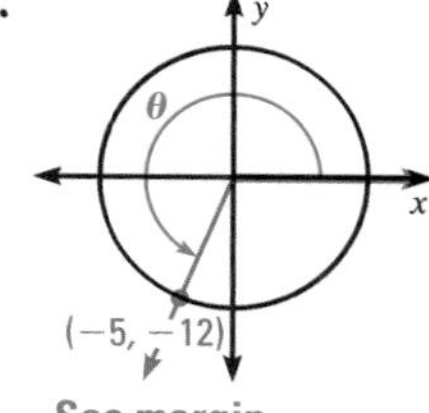

See margin.

4. Use the unit circle to evaluate the six trigonometric functions of $\theta = 180°$.
$\sin\theta = 0$, $\cos\theta = -1$, $\tan\theta = 0$, $\csc\theta$ = undefined, $\sec\theta = -1$, $\cot\theta$ = undefined

Margin answers:

1. $\sin\theta = -\frac{\sqrt{2}}{2}$, $\cos\theta =$ …, $\tan\theta = -1$, $\csc\theta =$ …$\sqrt{2}$, $\sec\theta = \sqrt{2}$, $\cot\theta = -1$

2. $\sin\theta = \frac{15}{17}$, $\cos\theta =$ …$\frac{8}{17}$, $\tan\theta = -\frac{15}{8}$, $\csc\theta = \frac{17}{15}$, $\sec\theta = -\frac{17}{8}$, $\cot\theta = -\frac{8}{15}$

3. $\sin\theta = -\frac{12}{13}$, $\cos\theta = -\frac{5}{13}$, $\tan\theta = \frac{12}{5}$, $\csc\theta = -\frac{13}{12}$, $\sec\theta = -\frac{13}{5}$, $\cot\theta = \frac{5}{12}$

Motivating the Lesson

You are on your school's soccer team and are working on improving how far you can kick the ball. If you can measure the initial speed of your kick and the angle of the kick, you can use a formula that involves the sine function to calculate how far the ball will travel before it hits the ground.

3 TEACH

Extra Example 1

Let $(-9, -40)$ be a point on the terminal side of an angle θ in standard position. Evaluate the six trigonometric functions of θ.
$\sin\theta = -\frac{40}{41}$, $\cos\theta = -\frac{9}{41}$, $\tan\theta = \frac{40}{9}$, $\csc\theta = -\frac{41}{40}$, $\sec\theta = -\frac{41}{9}$, $\cot\theta = \frac{9}{40}$

Key Question to Ask for Example 1

- What must always be true about the value of r? Explain. The value of r must always be positive because r is the radius of a circle.

Extra Example 2

Use the unit circle to evaluate the six trigonometric functions of $\theta = 2\pi$. $\sin\theta = 0$, $\cos\theta = 1$, $\tan\theta = 0$, $\csc\theta$ is undefined, $\sec\theta = 1$, $\cot\theta$ is undefined.

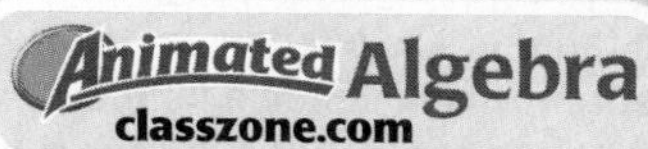

An **Animated Algebra** activity is available on-line for **Example 2**. This activity is also available on the **Power Presentations CD-ROM**.

Extra Example 3

Find the reference angle θ' for the given angle.

a. $\theta = \frac{7\pi}{12}$ $\theta' = \frac{5\pi}{12}$

b. $\theta = -295°$ $\theta' = 65°$

Key Questions to Ask for Example 3

- If θ is its own reference angle, what do you know about θ? θ is an acute (or first quadrant) angle.
- Can a reference angle ever have a negative measure? Explain. No; a reference angle is always an acute angle, which means its measure is between 0° and 90° $\left(\text{or } 0 \text{ and } \frac{\pi}{2}\right)$.

Study Strategy

The Key Concept box at the bottom of this page shows the signs of the values of the six trigonometric functions in the four quadrants. Students may find this information easier to remember if they use this simpler diagram:

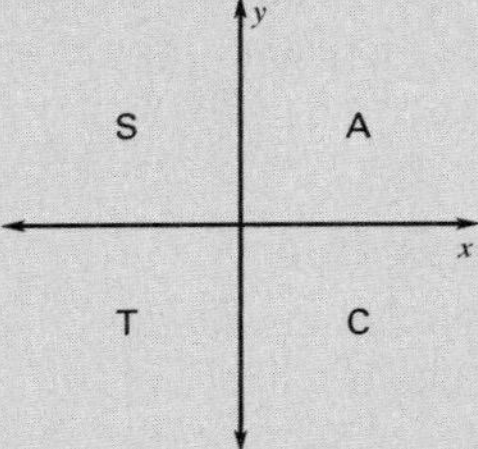

Here, A = all, S = sine, T = tangent, and C = cosine. This diagram shows which functions among sine, cosine, and tangent are positive in each quadrant. Then, since a number and its reciprocal always have the same sign, the signs of the values of the cosecant, cotangent, and secant follow. Some students like to just remember "ASTC," remembering that they must start in Quadrant I and move through the quadrants in the order in which they are numbered.

READING The symbol θ' is read as "theta prime."

KEY CONCEPT *For Your Notebook*

Reference Angle Relationships

Let θ be an angle in standard position. The **reference angle** for θ is the acute angle θ' formed by the terminal side of θ and the x-axis. The relationship between θ and θ' is shown below for nonquadrantal angles θ such that $90° < \theta < 360°$ $\left(\frac{\pi}{2} < \theta < 2\pi\right)$.

Quadrant II

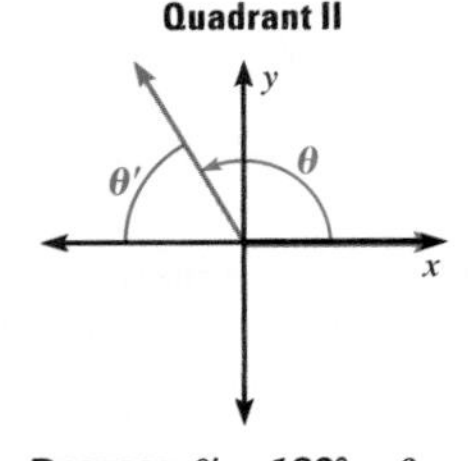

Degrees: $\theta' = 180° - \theta$
Radians: $\theta' = \pi - \theta$

Quadrant III

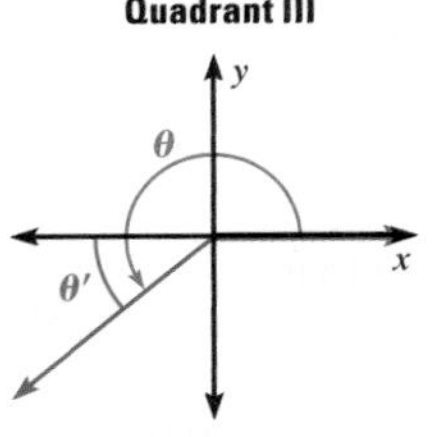

Degrees: $\theta' = \theta - 180°$
Radians: $\theta' = \theta - \pi$

Quadrant IV

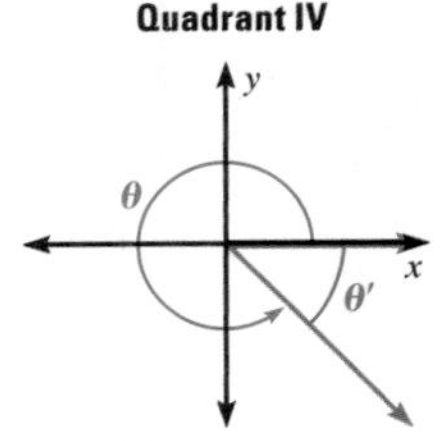

Degrees: $\theta' = 360° - \theta$
Radians: $\theta' = 2\pi - \theta$

EXAMPLE 3 Find reference angles

Find the reference angle θ' for (a) $\theta = \frac{5\pi}{3}$ and (b) $\theta = -130°$.

Solution

a. The terminal side of θ lies in Quadrant IV. So, $\theta' = 2\pi - \frac{5\pi}{3} = \frac{\pi}{3}$.

b. Note that θ is coterminal with 230°, whose terminal side lies in Quadrant III. So, $\theta' = 230° - 180° = 50°$.

EVALUATING TRIGONOMETRIC FUNCTIONS Reference angles allow you to evaluate a trigonometric function for any angle θ. The sign of the trigonometric function value depends on the quadrant in which θ lies.

KEY CONCEPT *For Your Notebook*

Evaluating Trigonometric Functions

Use these steps to evaluate a trigonometric function for any angle θ:

STEP 1 **Find** the reference angle θ'.

STEP 2 **Evaluate** the trigonometric function for θ'.

STEP 3 **Determine** the sign of the trigonometric function value from the quadrant in which θ lies.

Signs of Function Values

Quadrant II	Quadrant I
$\sin\theta, \csc\theta$: +	$\sin\theta, \csc\theta$: +
$\cos\theta, \sec\theta$: −	$\cos\theta, \sec\theta$: +
$\tan\theta, \cot\theta$: −	$\tan\theta, \cot\theta$: +
Quadrant III	**Quadrant IV**
$\sin\theta, \csc\theta$: −	$\sin\theta, \csc\theta$: −
$\cos\theta, \sec\theta$: −	$\cos\theta, \sec\theta$: +
$\tan\theta, \cot\theta$: +	$\tan\theta, \cot\theta$: −

5. 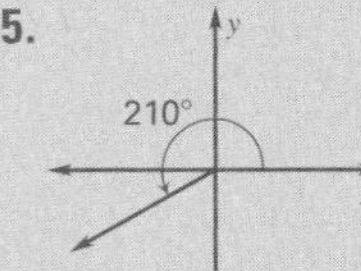

6. 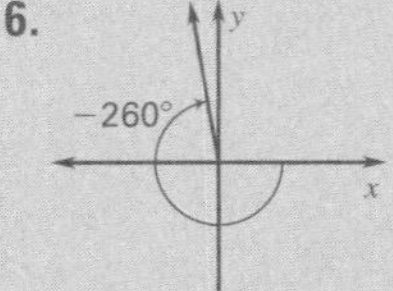

7. 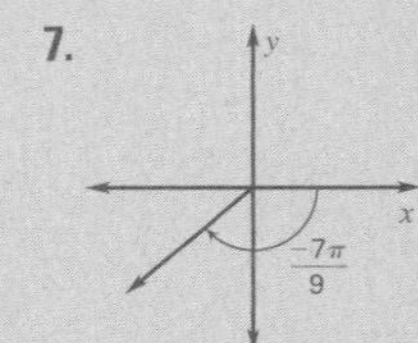

8. 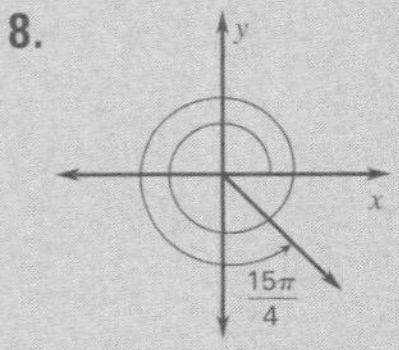

EXAMPLE 4 Use reference angles to evaluate functions

Evaluate (a) tan (−240°) and (b) csc $\frac{17\pi}{6}$.

Solution

a. The angle −240° is coterminal with 120°. The reference angle is $\theta' = 180° - 120° = 60°$. The tangent function is negative in Quadrant II, so you can write:

$$\tan(-240°) = -\tan 60° = -\sqrt{3}$$

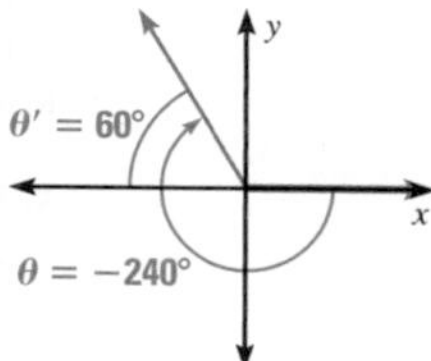

b. The angle $\frac{17\pi}{6}$ is coterminal with $\frac{5\pi}{6}$. The reference angle is $\theta' = \pi - \frac{5\pi}{6} = \frac{\pi}{6}$. The cosecant function is positive in Quadrant II, so you can write:

$$\csc\frac{17\pi}{6} = \csc\frac{\pi}{6} = 2$$

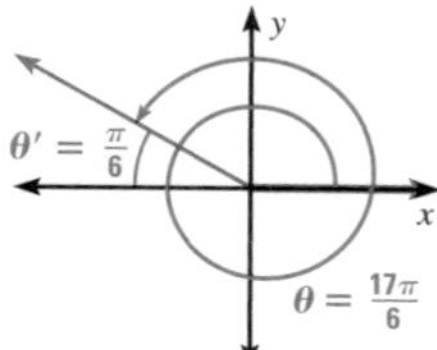

✓ GUIDED PRACTICE for Examples 3 and 4

Sketch the angle. Then find its reference angle. 5–8. See margin for art.

5. 210° 30°
6. −260° 80°
7. $-\frac{7\pi}{9}$ $\frac{2\pi}{9}$
8. $\frac{15\pi}{4}$ $\frac{\pi}{4}$
9. Evaluate cos (−210°) without using a calculator. $-\frac{\sqrt{3}}{2}$

EXAMPLE 5 Calculate horizontal distance traveled

ROBOTICS The "frogbot" is a robot designed for exploring rough terrain on other planets. It can jump at a 45° angle and with an initial speed of 16 feet per second. On Earth, the horizontal distance d (in feet) traveled by a projectile launched at an angle θ and with an initial speed v (in feet per second) is given by:

Frogbot

ITERPRET MODELS ɪis model neglects air sistance and assumes at the projectile's arting and ending ɪights are the same.

$$d = \frac{v^2}{32}\sin 2\theta$$

How far can the frogbot jump on Earth?

Solution

$d = \frac{v^2}{32}\sin 2\theta$ **Write model for horizontal distance.**

$= \frac{16^2}{32}\sin(2 \cdot 45°)$ **Substitute 16 for v and 45° for θ.**

$= 8$ **Simplify.**

▶ The frogbot can jump a horizontal distance of 8 feet on Earth.

Extra Example 4

Evaluate.

a. sin (−225°) $\frac{\sqrt{2}}{2}$

b. cot $\frac{5\pi}{3}$ $-\frac{\sqrt{3}}{3}$

Key Question to Ask for Example 4

- What should you do differently when finding the reference angle for an angle measured in radians, rather than degrees? Use π instead of 180° and 2π instead of 360°.

Avoiding Common Errors

A common error when using reference angles to evaluate trigonometric functions is to use the angle formed by the terminal side of the angle and the y-axis, rather than the x-axis, or to go to whichever axis forms a smaller angle with the terminal side. When you discuss Example 4, use the diagrams to emphasize that you must always use the terminal side of the angle and the x-axis to form the reference angle. Require that students draw diagrams for each of the Guided Practice exercises for Examples 3 and 4.

Extra Example 5

You kick a soccer ball at an initial speed of 46 feet per second, projected at an angle of 30°. How far will the ball travel horizontally before hitting the ground? about 57.3 ft

Differentiated Instruction

Kinesthetic Learners Encourage students to use a pencil, ruler, or straightedge to trace the motion of the terminal side of the angles in **Example 4**. Remind students to start their tracing at the x-axis and move counterclockwise about the origin, calculating the measure of the angle where the terminal side is located. Remind students that a full revolution corresponds to an angle of 360° or 2π radians.

See also the *Algebra 2 Toolkit* for more strategies.

Extra Example 6

The Navy Pier Ferris wheel in Chicago has a diameter of 140 feet and its base is 10 feet off the ground. You board a gondola on the Ferris wheel and rotate 158° counterclockwise before the wheel temporarily stops. How high above the ground are you when the wheel stops? **about 145 ft**

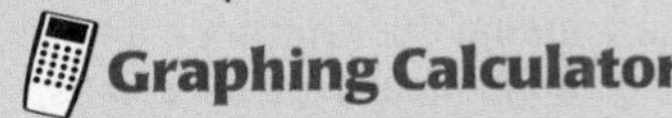

Graphing Calculator

Make sure that students understand when they use their calculators in Example 6, they can enter sin 110° directly. It is not necessary to use reference angles when you are using a calculator.

Closing the Lesson

Have students summarize the major points of the lesson and answer the Essential Question: How can you evaluate trigonometric functions of any angle?

- **The six trigonometric functions can be defined for any angle, positive or negative, and measured in degrees or radians.**
- **The reference angle for an angle θ is the acute angle θ' formed by the terminal side of θ and the x-axis.**

If you know the coordinates of a point on the terminal side of the angle, use the general definitions of the six functions. For a quadrantal angle, use the unit circle. If the reference angle is 30°, 45°, or 60°, find the function value for the reference angle and adjust the sign as needed for the quadrant of the angle. If you cannot use any of these methods to find exact values, use a calculator to find approximate function values.

EXAMPLE 6 Model with a trigonometric function

ROCK CLIMBING A rock climber is using a rock climbing treadmill that is 10.5 feet long. The climber begins by lying horizontally on the treadmill, which is then rotated about its midpoint by 110° so that the rock climber is climbing towards the top. If the midpoint of the treadmill is 6 feet above the ground, how high above the ground is the top of the treadmill?

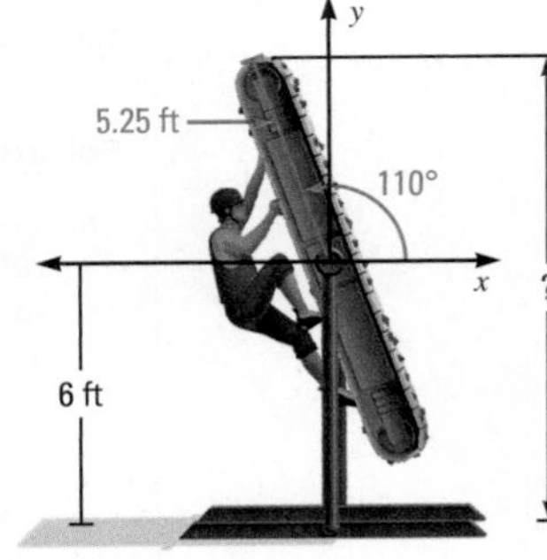

Solution

$\sin\theta = \frac{y}{r}$ — **Use definition of sine.**

$\sin 110° = \frac{y}{5.25}$ — **Substitute 110° for θ and $\frac{10.5}{2} = 5.25$ for r.**

$4.9 \approx y$ — **Solve for y.**

▶ The top of the treadmill is about $6 + 4.9 = 10.9$ feet above the ground.

GUIDED PRACTICE for Examples 5 and 6

10. **TRACK AND FIELD** Estimate the horizontal distance traveled by a track and field long jumper who jumps at an angle of 20° and with an initial speed of 27 feet per second. **about 14.64 ft**

11. **WHAT IF?** In Example 6, how high is the top of the rock climbing treadmill if it is rotated 100° about its midpoint? **about 11.2 ft**

13.3 EXERCISES

HOMEWORK KEY
○ = **WORKED-OUT SOLUTIONS** on p. WS22 for Exs. 5, 17, and 37
★ = **STANDARDIZED TEST PRACTICE** Exs. 2, 11, 33, 37, and 39

SKILL PRACTICE

A

1. **VOCABULARY** Copy and complete: A(n) _?_ is an angle in standard position whose terminal side lies on an axis. **quadrantal angle**

2. ★ **WRITING** Given an angle θ in Quadrant III, explain how you can use a reference angle to find $\cos\theta$. ***Sample answer:*** **Subtract 180° from the angle measure to determine the reference angle. Then, compute the cosine of this angle and make it negative.**

EXAMPLE 1 on p. 866 for Exs. 3–11

USING A POINT **Use the given point on the terminal side of an angle θ in standard position to evaluate the six trigonometric functions of θ.** **3–10. See margin.**

3. (8, 15)
4. (−9, 12)
5. (−7, −24)
6. (5, −12)
7. (2, −2)
8. (−6, 9)
9. (−3, −5)
10. $(5, -\sqrt{11})$

11. ★ **MULTIPLE CHOICE** Let (−7, −4) be a point on the terminal side of an angle θ in standard position. What is the value of $\tan\theta$? **C**

Ⓐ $-\frac{7}{4}$ Ⓑ $-\frac{4}{7}$ Ⓒ $\frac{4}{7}$ Ⓓ $\frac{7}{4}$

3–10. See Additional Answers beginning on p. AA1.

:XAMPLE 2
on p. 867
or Exs. 12–15

QUADRANTAL ANGLES **Evaluate the six trigonometric functions of θ.** 12–15. See margin.

12. $\theta = 0°$ **13.** $\theta = \frac{\pi}{2}$ **14.** $\theta = 540°$ **15.** $\theta = \frac{7\pi}{2}$

:XAMPLE 3
on p. 868
or Exs. 16–23

FINDING REFERENCE ANGLES **Sketch the angle. Then find its reference angle.** 16–23. See margin for art.

16. $-100°$ 80° **17.** $150°$ 30° **18.** $320°$ 40° **19.** $-370°$ 10°

20. $-\frac{5\pi}{6}$ $\frac{\pi}{6}$ **21.** $\frac{8\pi}{3}$ $\frac{\pi}{3}$ **22.** $\frac{15\pi}{4}$ $\frac{\pi}{4}$ **23.** $-\frac{13\pi}{6}$ $\frac{\pi}{6}$

:XAMPLE 4 B
on p. 869
or Exs. 24–31

EVALUATING FUNCTIONS **Evaluate the function without using a calculator.**

24. $\sec 135°$ $-\sqrt{2}$ **25.** $\tan 240°$ $\sqrt{3}$ **26.** $\sin(-150°)$ $-\frac{1}{2}$ **27.** $\csc(-420°)$ $-\frac{2\sqrt{3}}{3}$

28. $\cos \frac{7\pi}{4}$ $\frac{\sqrt{2}}{2}$ **29.** $\cot\left(-\frac{8\pi}{3}\right)$ $\frac{\sqrt{3}}{3}$ **30.** $\tan\left(-\frac{3\pi}{4}\right)$ 1 **31.** $\sec \frac{11\pi}{6}$ $\frac{2\sqrt{3}}{3}$

32. **ERROR ANALYSIS** Let (4, 3) be a point on the terminal side of an angle θ in standard position. *Describe* and correct the error in finding $\tan \theta$.

$\tan \theta = \frac{x}{y} = \frac{4}{3}$ ✗

The equation for tangent is $\tan \theta = \frac{y}{x}$; $\tan \theta = \frac{3}{4}$.

C **33.** ★ **SHORT RESPONSE** Write $\tan \theta$ as the ratio of two other trigonometric functions. Use this ratio to explain why $\tan 90°$ is undefined but $\cot 90° = 0$. See margin.

34. **CHALLENGE** Five of the most famous numbers in mathematics — 0, 1, π, e, and i — are related by the simple equation $e^{\pi i} + 1 = 0$. Derive this equation using Euler's formula: $e^{a+bi} = e^a(\cos b + i \sin b)$. See margin.

PROBLEM SOLVING

XAMPLE 5 A
on p. 869
or Exs. 35–36

In Exercises 35 and 36, use the formula in Example 5 on page 869.

35. **FOOTBALL** You and a friend each kick a football with an initial speed of 49 feet per second. Your kick is projected at an angle of 45° and your friend's kick is projected at an angle of 60°. About how much farther will your football travel than your friend's football? about 10 ft

@HomeTutor for problem solving help at classzone.com

36. **IN-LINE SKATING** At what speed must the in-line skater launch himself off the ramp in order to land on the other side of the ramp? about 16.5 ft/sec

@HomeTutor for problem solving help at classzone.com

XAMPLE 6
on p. 870
or Exs. 37–38

37. ★ **SHORT RESPONSE** A Ferris wheel has a radius of 75 feet. You board a car at the bottom of the Ferris wheel, which is 10 feet above the ground, and rotate 255° counterclockwise before the ride temporarily stops. How high above the ground are you when the ride stops? If the radius of the Ferris wheel is doubled, is your height above the ground doubled? *Explain.*

About 104 ft; no. *Sample answer:* The initial height of the Ferris wheel is above the ground is not doubled so the entire height is not doubled.

4 PRACTICE AND APPLY

Assignment Guide

Answer Transparencies available for all exercises

Basic:
Day 1: pp. 870–872
Exs. 1–15
Day 2: pp. 870–872
Exs. 16–27, 35–38, 41–43

Average:
Day 1: pp. 870–872
Exs. 1, 2, 4–15, 32
Day 2: pp. 870–872
Exs. 17–21, 25–29, 35–39, 41–43

Advanced:
Day 1: pp. 870–872
Exs. 1, 2, 5–15, 32, 33
Day 2: pp. 870–872
Exs. 20–23, 28–31, 34–43*

Block:
pp. 870–872
Exs. 1, 2, 4–15, 17–21, 25–29, 32, 35–39, 41–43

Differentiated Instruction

See *Algebra 2 Best Practices Toolkit* for suggestions on addressing the needs of a diverse classroom.

Homework Check

For a quick check of student understanding of key concepts, go over the following exercises:

Basic: 4, 12, 18, 24, 35
Average: 6, 14, 20, 28, 36
Advanced: 8, 15, 22, 30, 38

Extra Practice

- Student Edition, p. 1022
- Chapter 13 Resource Book: Practice levels A, B, C, pp. 27–29

Practice Worksheet

An easily-readable reduced practice page (with answers) for this lesson can be found on p. 850C.

12. $\sin \theta = 0$, $\cos \theta = 1$, $\tan \theta = 0$, $\csc \theta =$ undefined, $\sec \theta = 1$, $\cot \theta =$ undefined
13. $\sin \theta = 1$, $\cos \theta = 0$, $\tan \theta =$ undefined, $\csc \theta = 1$, $\sec \theta =$ undefined, $\cot \theta = 0$
14. $\sin \theta = 0$, $\cos \theta = -1$, $\tan \theta = 0$, $\csc \theta =$ undefined, $\sec \theta = -1$, $\cot \theta =$ undefined
15. $\sin \theta = -1$, $\cos \theta = 0$, $\tan \theta =$ undefined, $\csc \theta = -1$, $\sec \theta =$ undefined, $\cot \theta = 0$
16–23. See Additional Answers beginning on p. AA1.

33. $\tan \theta = \frac{\sin \theta}{\cos \theta}$; $\sin 90° = 1$ and $\cos 90° = 0$ so $\tan 90°$ is undefined because you cannot divide by zero but $\cot 90° = \frac{0}{1} = 0$.

34. See Additional Answers beginning on p. AA1.

5 ASSESS AND RETEACH

Daily Homework Quiz

Transparency Available

1. Let (8, −10) be a point on the terminal side of an angle θ in standard position. Evaluate $\cos\theta$. $\frac{4\sqrt{41}}{41}$
2. Use the unit circle to evaluate $\csc 540°$. undefined
3. Find the reference angle θ' for $\theta = \frac{11\pi}{8}$. $\theta' = \frac{3\pi}{8}$
4. Evaluate $\cot(-225°)$. −1
5. You kick a football at an initial speed of 50 feet per second, projected at an angle of 36°. About how far will the ball travel horizontally before hitting the ground? about 74.3 ft

Available at **classzone.com**

Diagnosis/Remediation

- Practice A, B, C in Chapter 13 Resource Book, pp. 27–29
- Study Guide in Chapter 13 Resource Book, pp. 30–31
- Practice Workbook, pp. 185–186
- @HomeTutor

Challenge

Additional challenge is available in the Chapter 13 Resource Book, p. 35.

B

38. MULTI-STEP PROBLEM When two atoms in a molecule are bonded to a common atom, chemists are interested in both the bond angle and the lengths of the bonds. An ozone molecule (O_3) is made up of two oxygen atoms bonded to a third oxygen atom, as shown.

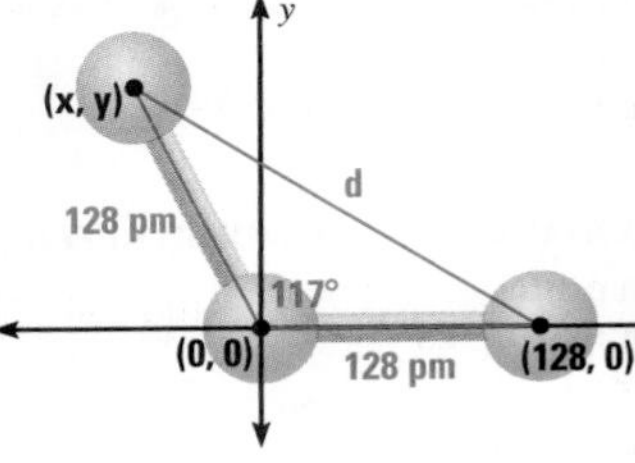

a. In the diagram, coordinates are given in picometers (pm). (*Note:* 1 pm = 10^{-12} m.) Find the coordinates (x, y) of the center of the oxygen atom in Quadrant II. (58.1, 114)

b. Find the distance d (in picometers) between the centers of the two unbonded oxygen atoms. about 134 pm

39. ★ EXTENDED RESPONSE A sprinkler at ground level is used to water a garden. The water leaving the sprinkler has an initial speed of 25 feet per second.

a. **Calculate** Copy the table below. Use the formula in Example 5 on page 869 to complete the table.

Angle of sprinkler, θ	25°	30°	35°	40°	45°	50°	55°	60°	65°
Horizontal distance water travels, d	? 15.0	? 16.9	? 18.4	? 19.2	? 19.5	? 19.2	? 18.4	? 16.9	? 15.0

b. **Interpret** What value of θ appears to maximize the horizontal distance traveled by the water? Use the formula for horizontal distance traveled and the unit circle to explain why your answer makes sense.

39b. 45°; since $\frac{v^2}{32}$ is constant in this situation, the maximum distance traveled will occur when $\sin 2\theta$ is as large as possible. The maximum value of sine occurs when $\theta = 90°$, so $2\theta = 90°$, $\theta = 45°$.

c. **Compare** *Compare* the horizontal distance traveled by the water when $\theta = (45 - k)°$ with the distance when $\theta = (45 + k)°$. The distances are the same.

C

40. CHALLENGE The latitude of a point on Earth is the degree measure of the shortest arc from that point to the equator. For example, the latitude of point P in the diagram equals the degree measure of arc PE. At what latitude θ is the circumference of the circle of latitude at P half the distance around the equator? 60°

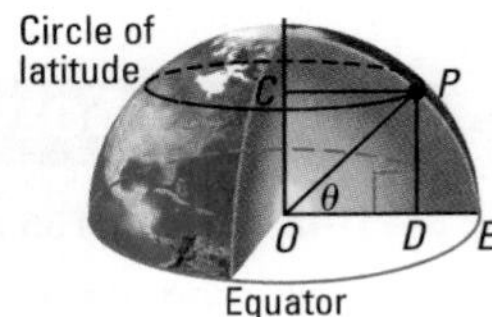

KENTUCKY MIXED REVIEW

TEST PRACTICE at classzone.com

41. Jamal drives 100 miles in 1.75 hours. He averages 70 miles per hour on the highway and 30 miles per hour for the remainder of the trip. About how many hours did he spend driving on the highway? **C**

Ⓐ 0.25 h Ⓑ 0.55 h Ⓒ 1.2 h Ⓓ 1.6 h

42. Jaime builds a bicycle ramp that is 6 feet long and rises at an angle of 30°. What is the value of x, the height of the ramp? **A**

6 ft, x, 30°

Ⓐ 3 ft Ⓑ $3\sqrt{2}$ ft

Ⓒ $3\sqrt{3}$ ft Ⓓ 12 ft

43. What are the coordinates of the y-intercept of the graph of the equation $3y = 12 - 2x$? **B**

Ⓐ $\left(0, -\frac{2}{3}\right)$ Ⓑ (0, 4) Ⓒ (6, 0) Ⓓ (12, 0)

Lessons 13.1–13.3

1. **MARCHING BAND** Your school's marching band is performing at halftime during a football game. In the final formation, the band members form a circle 100 feet wide in the center of the field. You start at a point on the circle 100 feet from the goal line, march 300° around the circle, and then walk toward the goal line to exit the field. How far from the goal line are you at the point where you leave the circle?

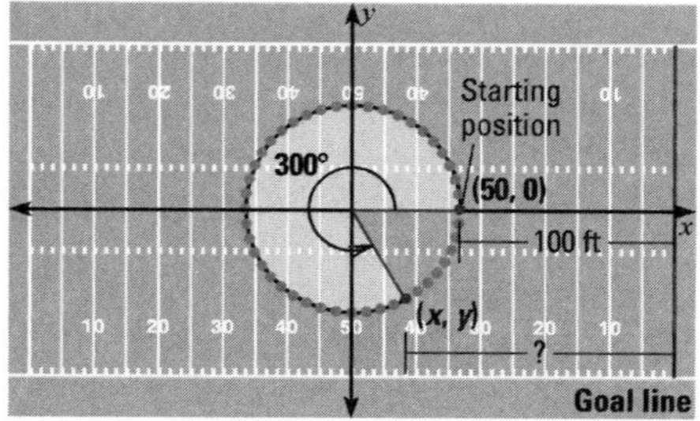

A. 30 feet
B. 120 feet
C. 125 feet
D. 314 feet

2. **KITE FLYING** You are flying a kite at an angle of 70°. You have let out a total of 400 feet of string and are holding the reel steady 4 feet above the ground. A friend watching the kite estimates that the angle of elevation to the kite is 85°. About how far from your friend are you standing?

A. 33 feet B. 104 feet
C. 170 feet D. 171.2 feet

3. **SEARS TOWER** You are standing 100 meters from the main entrance of the Sears Tower in Chicago, Illinois. You estimate that the angle of elevation to the top of the building is 77°. A friend is at the top of the building. What is the approximate straight-line distance between you and your friend?

A. 386 meters B. 433 meters
C. 445 meters D. 622 meters

4. **PIZZERIA** A pizzeria has two sizes of pizza. A large pizza has a radius of 8 inches and a small pizza has a radius of 6 inches. What is the angle measure of a slice of a small pizza that has approximately the same area as a 30° slice of a large pizza?

A. 35.9° B. 40.0°
C. 53.3° D. 96.0°

5. **ANGLE MEASURES** For which of the following angles is the secant positive and the cotangent negative?

A. 50° B. 130°
C. 230° D. 310°

6. **OPEN-RESPONSE** The top of the Space Needle in Seattle, Washington, is a revolving, circular restaurant. The restaurant has a radius of 47.25 feet and makes one complete revolution in about an hour. You have dinner at a window table from 7:00 P.M. to 8:55 P.M.

a. How many feet do you revolve? Round your answer to the nearest tenth of a foot.

b. Do diners seated 5 feet away from the window revolve the same distance? *Explain.*

Kentucky Mixed Review

1. C
2. C
3. C
4. C
5. D
6. a. About 569 feet
b. No; the radius of their circle is only 42.25, so the arc length that corresponds to their revolution is less.

1 PLAN AND PREPARE

Explore the Concept

- Students will use tables of values for the sine and cosine functions to determine whether these functions have inverses.
- This activity leads into the study of inverse trigonometric functions in Example 1 in Lesson 13.4.

Materials

Each student will need:

- Activity Support Master (*Chapter 13 Resource Book*, p. 38)

Recommended Time

Work activity: 10 min

Discuss results: 10 min

Grouping

Students should work individually.

2 TEACH

Tips for Success

In Steps 2 and 3, have students list and analyze the pairs (sin θ, θ) and (cos θ, θ) to explain why the functions do not have inverses over the given domains.

Key Discovery

If the domains of the sine and cosine functions are restricted in ways such that no *y*-values are repeated, then the functions will have inverses.

3 ASSESS AND RETEACH

Would you also have to use restricted domains for the other four trigonometric functions to have inverse functions? Explain. Yes. If the domains are not restricted, *y*-values will be repeated, so the inverses would not be functions.

Steps 1–3. See Additional Answers beginning on p. AA1.

13.4 Investigating Inverse Trigonometric Functions

MATERIALS • paper and pencil

QUESTION Do the sine and cosine functions have inverse functions?

EXPLORE Determine if a trigonometric function has an inverse function

STEP 1 ***Make a table*** Copy and complete the table to find the values of $f(\theta) = \sin \theta$ and $g(\theta) = \cos \theta$ for each of the given values of θ. Steps 1–3. See margin.

θ	$-\pi$	$-\frac{3\pi}{4}$	$-\frac{\pi}{2}$	$-\frac{\pi}{4}$	0	$\frac{\pi}{4}$	$\frac{\pi}{2}$	$\frac{3\pi}{4}$	π
$f(\theta) = \sin \theta$	?	?	?	?	?	?	?	?	?
$g(\theta) = \cos \theta$	?	?	?	?	?	?	?	?	?

STEP 2 ***Analyze sine*** Use the table to explain why $f(\theta) = \sin \theta$ does not have an inverse function on the domain $-\pi \le \theta \le \pi$.

STEP 3 ***Analyze cosine*** Does $g(\theta) = \cos \theta$ have an inverse function on the domain $-\pi \le \theta \le \pi$? Explain why or why not.

STEP 4 ***Use graphs*** The graphs of $f(\theta) = \sin \theta$ and $g(\theta) = \cos \theta$ are shown for the domain $-\pi \le \theta \le \pi$. Explain how the graphs justify your answers in Steps 2 and 3. The graphs fail the horizontal line test.

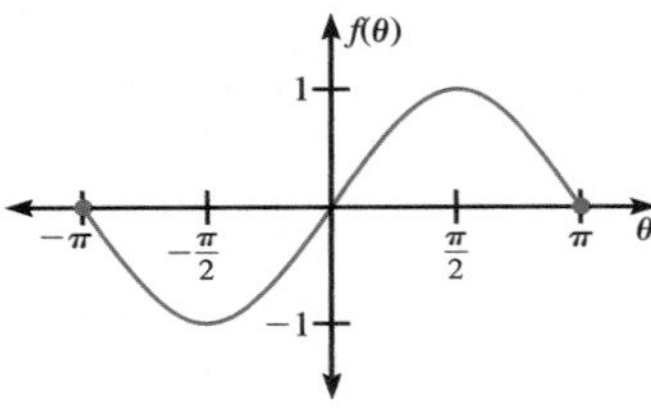

$f(\theta) = \sin \theta$

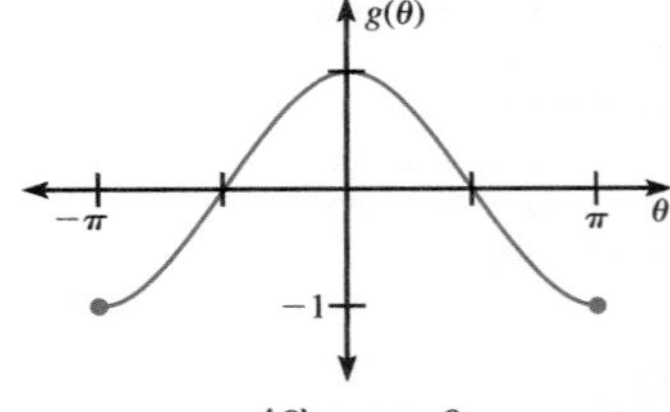

$g(\theta) = \cos \theta$

DRAW CONCLUSIONS Use your observations to complete these exercises 1–3. See margin.

1. Use the graph of $f(\theta) = \sin \theta$ in Step 4 to choose a restricted domain for which the sine function does have an inverse function. *Explain* how you made your choice.
2. Give a restricted domain for which $g(\theta) = \cos \theta$ has an inverse function. *Explain* how you chose the domain.
3. Are the domains that you wrote in Exercises 1 and 2 the *only* domains for which the trigonometric functions have inverse functions? *Explain.*

1. *Sample answer:* $-\frac{\pi}{2} < \theta < \frac{\pi}{2}$; this represents the largest continuous section with no duplicate values for $f(\theta)$.
2. *Sample answer:* $0 < \theta < \pi$; this represents the largest continuous section with no duplicate values for $f(\theta)$.
3. No. *Sample answer:* The domain can be shifted as long as there are no duplicate values for the function.

13.4 Evaluate Inverse Trigonometric Functions

MA-HS-2.1.3

Before You found values of trigonometric functions given angles.

Now You will find angles given values of trigonometric functions.

Why? So you can find launch angles, as in Example 4.

Key Vocabulary
- inverse sine
- inverse cosine
- inverse tangent

MA-HS-2.1.3
Students will apply definitions and properties of right triangle relationships (right triangle trigonometry and the Pythagorean theorem) to determine length and angle measures to solve real-world and mathematical problems. DOK 3

So far in this chapter, you have learned to evaluate trigonometric functions of a given angle. In this lesson, you will study the reverse problem—finding an angle that corresponds to a given value of a trigonometric function.

Suppose you were asked to find an angle θ whose sine is 0.5. After considering the problem, you would realize *many* such angles exist. For instance, the angles

$$\frac{\pi}{6}, \frac{5\pi}{6}, \frac{13\pi}{6}, \frac{17\pi}{6}, \text{ and } -\frac{7\pi}{6}$$

all have a sine value of 0.5. To obtain a unique angle θ such that $\sin \theta = 0.5$, you must restrict the domain of the sine function. Domain restrictions allow the *inverse sine*, *inverse cosine*, and *inverse tangent* functions to be defined.

KEY CONCEPT *For Your Notebook*

Inverse Trigonometric Functions

If $-1 \le a \le 1$, then the **inverse sine** of a is an angle θ, written $\theta = \sin^{-1} a$, where:

(1) $\sin \theta = a$

(2) $-\frac{\pi}{2} \le \theta \le \frac{\pi}{2}$ (or $-90° \le \theta \le 90°$)

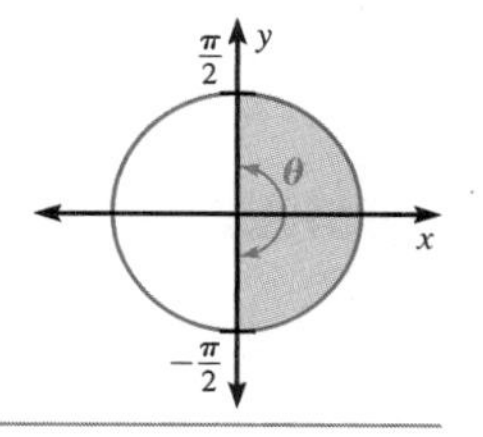

If $-1 \le a \le 1$, then the **inverse cosine** of a is an angle θ, written $\theta = \cos^{-1} a$, where:

(1) $\cos \theta = a$

(2) $0 \le \theta \le \pi$ (or $0° \le \theta \le 180°$)

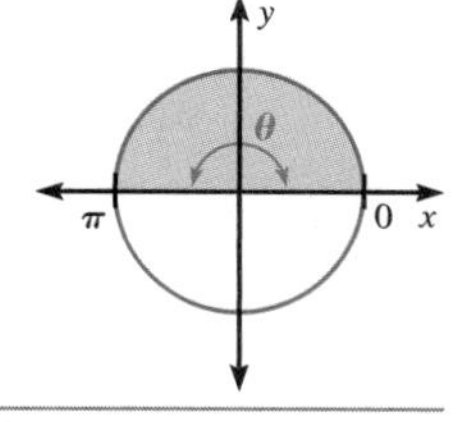

If a is any real number, then the **inverse tangent** of a is an angle θ, written $\theta = \tan^{-1} a$, where:

(1) $\tan \theta = a$

(2) $-\frac{\pi}{2} < \theta < \frac{\pi}{2}$ (or $-90° < \theta < 90°$)

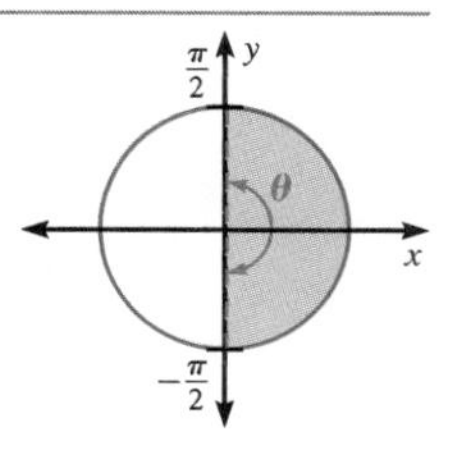

1 PLAN AND PREPARE

Warm-Up Exercises

Transparency Available

Evaluate the expression.

1. $\cos 45°$ $\frac{\sqrt{2}}{2}$
2. $\sin \frac{5\pi}{6}$ $\frac{1}{2}$
3. $\tan(-60°)$ $-\sqrt{3}$
4. $\cos \pi$ -1
5. $\tan\left(-\frac{\pi}{6}\right)$ $-\frac{\sqrt{3}}{3}$

Notetaking Guide

Transparency Available

Promotes interactive learning and notetaking skills, pp. 336–338.

Pacing

Basic: 1 day
Average: 1 day
Advanced: 1 day
Block: 0.5 block with 13.5
- See *Teaching Guide/Lesson Plan.*

2 FOCUS AND MOTIVATE

Essential Question

Big Idea 2, p. 851

How are inverse trigonometric functions used? Tell students they will learn how to answer this question by using inverse trigonometric functions to solve trigonometric equations and find angles of triangles.

Resource Planning Guide

Chapter Resource Book
- Teaching Guide/Lesson Plan (pp. 36–37)
- Practice levels A, B, C (pp. 39–41)
- Study Guide (pp. 42–43)
- Catch-up for Absent Students (p. 44)
- Problem Solving Workshop (p. 45)
- Challenge (p. 46)

Workbooks
- Notetaking Guide (pp. 336–338)
- Practice Workbook (pp. 187–188)

Teaching Options
- **Power Presentations CD-ROM** provides dynamic electronic teaching resources for the classroom.
- **Activity Generator CD-ROM** provides editable activities for all ability levels.

Interactive Technology
- Easy Planner
- Power Presentations CD-ROM
- Activity Generator CD-ROM
- Animated Algebra
- Test Generator CD-ROM
- Online Quiz
- eWorkbook
- eEdition
- @HomeTutor

Resources for English Learners
- Quick Reference for English Learners
- Spanish Study Guide
- Multi-Language Visual Glossary
- Student Resources in Spanish

See also the *Algebra 2 Toolkit* for more strategies for meeting individual needs.

Motivating the Lesson

Suppose you want a ladder to reach 6 feet up a wall. When you are leaning the ladder against the wall, you can use an inverse trigonometric function to estimate at what angle with the ground you should set the ladder.

3 TEACH

Extra Example 1

Evaluate the expression in both radians and degrees.

a. $\sin^{-1}(-1)$ $-\frac{\pi}{2}$ **or** $-90°$

b. $\cos^{-1}\left(-\frac{\sqrt{2}}{2}\right)$ $\frac{3\pi}{4}$ **or** $135°$

c. $\tan^{-1}\frac{\sqrt{3}}{3}$ $\frac{\pi}{6}$ **or** $30°$

Key Question to Ask for Example 1

- If you used a calculator to try to find $\cos^{-1}(-1.5)$, what do you think would happen? *Explain.* **You would get an ERROR message because there is no angle whose cosine is −1.5.**

Extra Example 2

Solve the equation $\cos\theta = \frac{3}{4}$ where $270° < \theta < 360°$. **318.6°**

Key Question to Ask for Example 2

- Does the equation in Example 2 have another solution in addition to $\theta \approx 218.7°$, where $0° < \theta < 360°$? If so, state the quadrant in which it is located and show how to find it. **Yes; Quadrant IV; $-38.7° + 360° = 321.3°$**

EXAMPLE 1 Evaluate inverse trigonometric functions

Evaluate the expression in both radians and degrees.

a. $\cos^{-1}\frac{\sqrt{3}}{2}$ **b.** $\sin^{-1} 2$ **c.** $\tan^{-1}(-\sqrt{3})$

Solution

a. When $0 \le \theta \le \pi$, or $0° \le \theta \le 180°$, the angle whose cosine is $\frac{\sqrt{3}}{2}$ is:

$$\theta = \cos^{-1}\frac{\sqrt{3}}{2} = \frac{\pi}{6} \quad \text{or} \quad \theta = \cos^{-1}\frac{\sqrt{3}}{2} = 30°$$

b. There is no angle whose sine is 2. So, $\sin^{-1} 2$ is undefined.

c. When $-\frac{\pi}{2} < \theta < \frac{\pi}{2}$, or $-90° < \theta < 90°$, the angle whose tangent is $-\sqrt{3}$ is:

$$\theta = \tan^{-1}(-\sqrt{3}) = -\frac{\pi}{3} \quad \text{or} \quad \theta = \tan^{-1}(-\sqrt{3}) = -60°$$

EXAMPLE 2 Solve a trigonometric equation

Solve the equation $\sin\theta = -\frac{5}{8}$ where $180° < \theta < 270°$.

Solution

USE A CALCULATOR
On most calculators, you can evaluate inverse trigonometric functions using the keys 2nd SIN for inverse sine, 2nd COS for inverse cosine, and 2nd TAN for inverse tangent.

STEP 1 **Use** a calculator to determine that in the interval $-90° \le \theta \le 90°$, the angle whose sine is $-\frac{5}{8}$ is $\sin^{-1}\left(-\frac{5}{8}\right) \approx -38.7°$. This angle is in Quadrant IV, as shown.

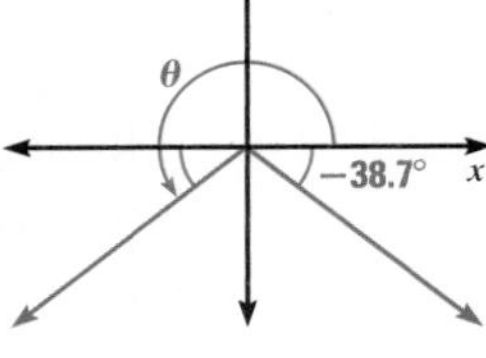

STEP 2 **Find** the angle in Quadrant III (where $180° < \theta < 270°$) that has the same sine value as the angle in Step 1. The angle is:

$$\theta \approx 180° + 38.7° = 218.7°$$

CHECK Use a calculator to check the answer.

$$\sin 218.7° \approx -0.625 = -\frac{5}{8} \checkmark$$

✓ GUIDED PRACTICE for Examples 1 and 2

Evaluate the expression in both radians and degrees.

1. $\sin^{-1}\frac{\sqrt{2}}{2}$ **$\frac{\pi}{4}$, 45°**
2. $\cos^{-1}\frac{1}{2}$ **$\frac{\pi}{3}$, 60°**
3. $\tan^{-1}(-1)$ **$-\frac{\pi}{4}$, −45°**
4. $\sin^{-1}\left(-\frac{1}{2}\right)$ **$-\frac{\pi}{6}$, −30°**

Solve the equation for θ.

5. $\cos\theta = 0.4$; $270° < \theta < 360°$ **about 293.6°**
6. $\tan\theta = 2.1$; $180° < \theta < 270°$ **about 244.5°**
7. $\sin\theta = -0.23$; $270° < \theta < 360°$ **about 346.7°**
8. $\tan\theta = 4.7$; $180° < \theta < 270°$ **about 258.0°**
9. $\sin\theta = 0.62$; $90° < \theta < 180°$ **about 141.7°**
10. $\cos\theta = -0.39$; $180° < \theta < 270°$ **about 247.0°**

EXAMPLE 3 Standardized Test Practice

What is the measure of the angle θ in the triangle shown?

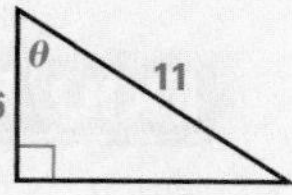

Ⓐ 28.6° Ⓑ 33.1°

Ⓒ 56.9° Ⓓ 61.4°

AVOID ERRORS

All the answer choices are in degrees. Therefore, check that your calculator is set in degree mode, not radian mode.

Solution

In the right triangle, you are given the lengths of the side adjacent to θ and the hypotenuse, so use the inverse cosine function to solve for θ.

$$\cos\theta = \frac{\text{adj}}{\text{hyp}} = \frac{6}{11} \longrightarrow \theta = \cos^{-1}\frac{6}{11} \approx 56.9°$$

▶ The correct answer is C. Ⓐ Ⓑ Ⓒ Ⓓ

EXAMPLE 4 Write and solve a trigonometric equation

MONSTER TRUCKS A monster truck drives off a ramp in order to jump onto a row of cars. The ramp has a height of 8 feet and a horizontal length of 20 feet. What is the angle θ of the ramp?

Solution

STEP 1 **Draw** a triangle that represents the ramp.

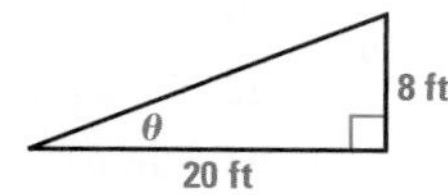

STEP 2 **Write** a trigonometric equation that involves the ratio of the ramp's height and horizontal length.

$$\tan\theta = \frac{\text{opp}}{\text{adj}} = \frac{8}{20}$$

STEP 3 **Use** a calculator to find the measure of θ.

$$\theta = \tan^{-1}\frac{8}{20} \approx 21.8°$$

▶ The angle of the ramp is about 22°.

✓ GUIDED PRACTICE for Examples 3 and 4

Find the measure of the angle θ.

11. about 63.6°

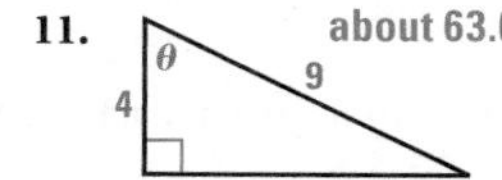

12. about 51.3°

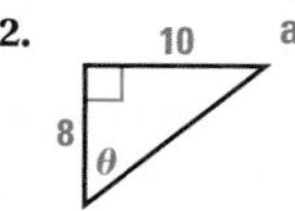
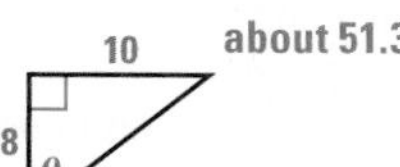

13. about 24.6°

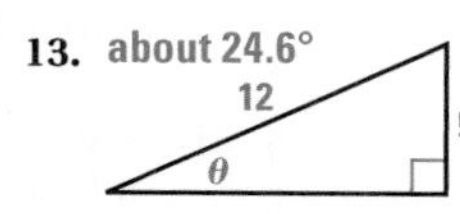

14. **WHAT IF?** In Example 4, suppose a monster truck drives 26 feet on a ramp before jumping onto a row of cars. If the ramp is 10 feet high, what is the angle θ of the ramp? about 22.6°

Extra Example 3

What is the measure of the angle in the triangle shown? D

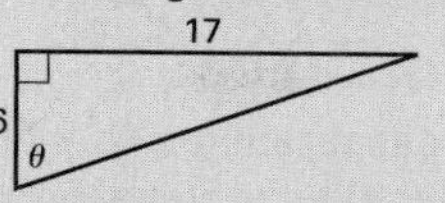

Ⓐ 19.4°
Ⓑ 20.7°
Ⓒ 69.3°
Ⓓ 70.6°

Key Question to Ask for Example 3

- How much information must be given about side lengths in a right triangle in order for you to be able to find the measures of its acute angles? **the lengths of any two sides**

Extra Example 4

If a building that is 52 feet tall casts a 23-foot shadow, what is the angle of elevation of the Sun? **about 66°**

Closing the Lesson

Have students summarize the major points of the lesson and answer the Essential Question: How are inverse trigonometric functions used?

- **In order to define the inverse sine, inverse cosine, and inverse tangent functions, the domains of the sine, cosine, and tangent functions must be restricted.**

Inverse trigonometric functions are used to solve trigonometric equations and to find the measure of an angle in a right triangle if you know the lengths of two of its sides.

Differentiated Instruction

Kinesthetic Learners Organize students in groups and pass out large sheets of paper. Have students draw the triangle from **Example 4** on their paper, changing feet to inches and drawing it full size. Remind students to be careful in their measurements and in creating the right angle. Then have students use a protractor to measure the unknown angle measure. Have them compare their results to the answer to the problem.

See also the *Algebra 2 Toolkit* for more strategies.

4 PRACTICE AND APPLY

Assignment Guide

Answer Transparencies available for all exercises

Basic:
Day 1: pp. 878–880
Exs. 1–7, 11–15, 20–23, 26, 35–38, 42

Average:
Day 1: pp. 878–880
Exs. 1, 2, 5–8, 11, 14–16, 22–31, 35–39, 42

Advanced:
Day 1: pp. 878–880
Exs. 1, 2, 8–11, 17–19, 23–40*

Block:
pp. 878–880
Exs. 1, 2, 5–8, 11, 14–16, 22–31, 35–39, 42 (with 13.5)

Differentiated Instruction

See *Algebra 2 Best Practices Toolkit* for suggestions on addressing the needs of a diverse classroom.

Homework Check

For a quick check of student understanding of key concepts, go over the following exercises:

Basic: 4, 14, 25, 35, 36
Average: 6, 16, 28, 35, 37
Advanced: 10, 18, 29, 36, 37

Extra Practice

- Student Edition, p. 1022
- Chapter 13 Resource Book: Practice levels A, B, C, pp. 39–41

Practice Worksheet

An easily-readable reduced practice page (with answers) for this lesson can be found on p. 850D.

13.4 EXERCISES

HOMEWORK KEY
○ = **WORKED-OUT SOLUTIONS on p. WS22 for Exs. 7, 23, and 37**
★ = **STANDARDIZED TEST PRACTICE Exs. 2, 11, 30, 31, 37, and 38**

SKILL PRACTICE

A

1. VOCABULARY Copy and complete: The __?__ sine of $\frac{1}{2}$ is $\frac{\pi}{6}$, or 30°. **inverse**

2. ★ WRITING *Explain* why $\tan^{-1} 3$ is defined, but $\cos^{-1} 3$ is undefined. ***Sample answer:* The range of tan θ is all real numbers but the range for cos θ is $-1 \le \cos\theta \le 1$ and 3 is not in the range.**

EXAMPLE 1 on p. 876 for Exs. 3–11

EVALUATING EXPRESSIONS **Evaluate the expression without using a calculator. Give your answer in both radians and degrees.**

3. $\sin^{-1} 1$ **$\frac{\pi}{2}$, 90°**
4. $\tan^{-1}(-1)$ **$-\frac{\pi}{4}$, −45°**
5. $\cos^{-1} 0$ **$\frac{\pi}{2}$, 90°**
6. $\cos^{-1}(-2)$ **undefined**
7. $\sin^{-1}\frac{\sqrt{3}}{2}$ **$\frac{\pi}{3}$, 60°**
8. $\sin^{-1}\frac{1}{2}$ **$\frac{\pi}{6}$, 30°**
9. $\tan^{-1}\left(-\frac{\sqrt{3}}{3}\right)$ **$-\frac{\pi}{6}$, −30°**
10. $\cos^{-1}\left(-\frac{1}{2}\right)$ **$\frac{2\pi}{3}$, 120°**

11. ★ MULTIPLE CHOICE What is the value of the expression $\cos^{-1}\frac{\sqrt{2}}{2}$? **C**

Ⓐ 0° Ⓑ 30° Ⓒ 45° Ⓓ 60°

USING A CALCULATOR **Use a calculator to evaluate the expression in both radians and degrees.**

12. $\sin^{-1} 0.18$ **about 0.18, about 10.4°**
13. $\tan^{-1} 2.6$ **about 1.20, about 69.0°**
14. $\cos^{-1} 0.36$ **about 1.20, about 68.9°**
15. $\cos^{-1}(-0.4)$ **about 1.98, about 113.6°**
16. $\tan^{-1}(-0.75)$ 16. about −0.64, about −36.9°
17. $\sin^{-1}(-0.2)$ 17. about −0.20, about −11.5°
18. $\sin^{-1} 0.8$ **about 0.93, about 53.1°**
19. $\cos^{-1} 0.99$ **about 0.14, about 8.1°**

EXAMPLE 2 on p. 876 for Exs. 20–26

B

SOLVING EQUATIONS **Solve the equation for θ.**

20. $\cos\theta = -0.82$; $180° < \theta < 270°$ **about 214.9°**
21. $\sin\theta = -0.45$; $180° < \theta < 270°$ **about 206.7°**
22. $\sin\theta = 0.15$; $90° < \theta < 180°$ **about 171.4°**
23. $\tan\theta = 3.2$; $180° < \theta < 270°$ **about 252.6°**
24. $\tan\theta = -5.3$; $90° < \theta < 180°$ **about 100.7°**
25. $\cos\theta = 0.25$; $270° < \theta < 360°$ **about 284.5°**

26. ERROR ANALYSIS *Describe* and correct the error in solving the equation $\sin\theta = 0.7$ where $90° < \theta < 180°$. **The domain restriction is $90° < \theta < 180°$ and 44.4° is not in the domain; 135.6°.**

The angle whose sine is 0.7 is $\sin^{-1} 0.7 \approx 44.4°$, so $\theta \approx 44.4°$.

EXAMPLE 3 on p. 877 for Exs. 27–29

FINDING ANGLES **Find the measure of the angle θ.**

27. **about 38.7°**

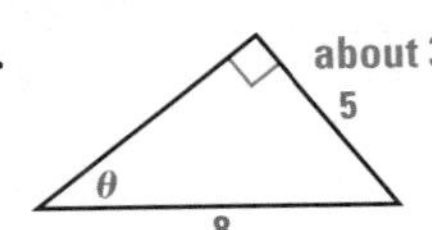

28. **about 80.5°**

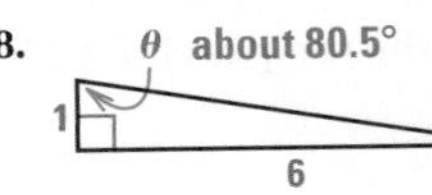

29. **120°**

θ, 4, $2\sqrt{3}$

30. ★ OPEN-ENDED MATH Suppose $\cos\theta > 0$ and $\sin\theta < 0$. Give a possible value of θ such that $-360° \le \theta \le 0°$. ***Sample answer:* −45°**

31. ★ OPEN-ENDED MATH Suppose $\sin\theta < 0$ and $\tan\theta > 0$. Give a possible value of θ such that $360° \le \theta \le 720°$. ***Sample answer:* 600°**

C

CHALLENGE **Rewrite the expression so that it does not involve trigonometric functions or inverse trigonometric functions.**

32. $\csc(\sin^{-1} x)$ **x^{-1}**
33. $\cot(\tan^{-1} x)$ **x^{-1}**
34. $\sec(\cos^{-1} x)$ **x^{-1}**

PROBLEM SOLVING

EXAMPLE 4 A
on p. 877
for Exs. 35–37

35. **LADDER ANGLE** A fire truck has a 100 foot ladder whose base is 10 feet above the ground. A firefighter extends a ladder toward a burning building to reach a window 90 feet above the ground. Draw a diagram to represent this situation. At what angle should the firefighter set the ladder? **See margin for art; about 53°**

@HomeTutor for problem solving help at classzone.com

37. About 32.9°; about 46.4 ft. *Sample answer:* The pile is 15 feet high and the angle of repose is about 32.9°, the base of the right triangle formed is about 23.2 feet. Since this represents the radius of the pile, you need to multiply by 2 to get the diameter.

36. **ANGLE OF DESCENT** An airplane is flying at an altitude of 31,000 feet when it begins its descent for landing. If the runway is 104 miles away, at what angle does the airplane descend? **about 3.23°**

@HomeTutor for problem solving help at classzone.com

37. ★ **SHORT RESPONSE** Different types of granular substances naturally settle at different angles when stored in cone-shaped piles. The angle θ is called the *angle of repose.* When rock salt is stored in a cone-shaped pile 11 feet high, the diameter of the pile's base is about 34 feet. Find the angle of repose for rock salt. If another pile of rock salt is 15 feet high, what is the diameter of its base? *Explain.*

B

38. ★ **EXTENDED RESPONSE** If you are in shallow water and look at an object below the surface of the water, the object will look farther away from you than it really is. This is because when light rays pass between air and water, the water *refracts,* or bends, the light rays. The *index of refraction* for water is 1.333. This is the ratio of the sine of θ_1 to the sine of θ_2 for the angles θ_1 and θ_2 shown below.

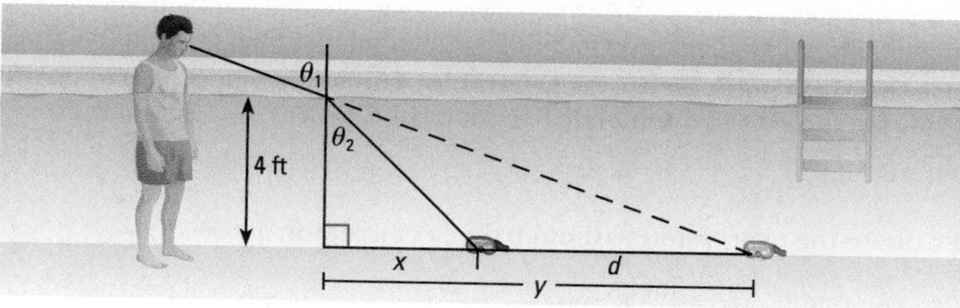

a. You are in 4 feet of water in the shallow end of a pool. You look down at some goggles at angle $\theta_1 = 70°$ (measured from a line perpendicular to the surface of the water). Find θ_2. **about 44.8°**

b. Find the distances x and y. **about 3.97 ft, about 11.0 ft**

c. Find the distance d between where the goggles are and where they appear to be. **about 7.03 ft**

d. *Explain* what happens to d as you move closer to the goggles. **The distance decreases.**

39. **CYCLING** As a spectator at a cycling road race, you are sitting 100 feet from the center of a straightaway. A cyclist traveling 30 miles per hour passes in front of you. At what angle do you have to turn your head to see the cyclist t seconds later? Assume the cyclist is still on the straightaway and is traveling at a constant speed. (*Hint:* First convert 30 miles per hour to a speed v in feet per second. The expression vt represents the distance, in feet, traveled by the cyclist.) $\theta = \tan^{-1}\left(\frac{44t}{100}\right)$

Graphing Calculator

Exercises 12–19 Show students how to evaluate these expressions directly in radian mode, which is more efficient than having to convert each angle from degree mode to radian mode.

Avoiding Common Errors

Exercises 20–25 When solving trigonometric equations with a calculator, a common error is to have the calculator set in the wrong mode. Make sure that all students know how to switch between degree and radian mode and tell them to get in the habit of checking which mode their calculator is in each time they start to use it in this chapter. As a quick check, if they are in the home screen, they can just enter sin (90). If the calculator returns 1, it is in degree mode; if not, it is in radian mode.

35.

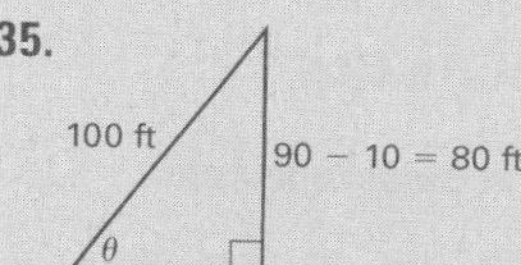

5 ASSESS AND RETEACH

Daily Homework Quiz

Transparency Available

1. Evaluate $\sin^{-1}\left(-\frac{\sqrt{3}}{2}\right)$ in both radians and degrees. $-\frac{\pi}{3}$ or $-60°$
2. Solve the equation $\tan \theta = -2.5$ where $90° < \theta < 180°$. **111.8°**
3. What is the measure of the angle θ in the triangle shown?

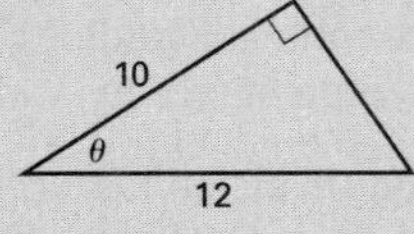

33.6°

4. A ramp goes from the ground to the entrance to a building. If the height of the ramp is 27 inches and the horizontal distance is 58 inches, what is the angle of the ramp? **about 25°**

Available at **classzone.com**

Diagnosis/Remediation

- Practice A, B, C in Chapter 13 Resource Book, pp. 39–41
- Study Guide in Chapter 13 Resource Book, pp. 42–43
- Practice Workbook, pp. 187–188
- @HomeTutor

Challenge

Additional challenge is available in the Chapter 13 Resource Book, p. 46.

Quiz

An easily-readable reduced copy of the quiz (with answers) on Lessons 13.3–13.4 from the Assessment Book can be found on p. 850E.

Quiz 1–4. See Additional Answers beginning on p. AA1.

C **40. CHALLENGE** You want to photograph a painting with a camera mounted on a tripod. The painting is 3 feet tall, and the bottom of the painting is 1 foot above the camera lens, as shown. How far should the camera be positioned from the wall in order to have the largest possible viewing angle θ when you take the photograph? (*Hint:* Write an equation for θ in terms of x only, and then use a graphing calculator to find the value of x that maximizes θ.) **about 37°**

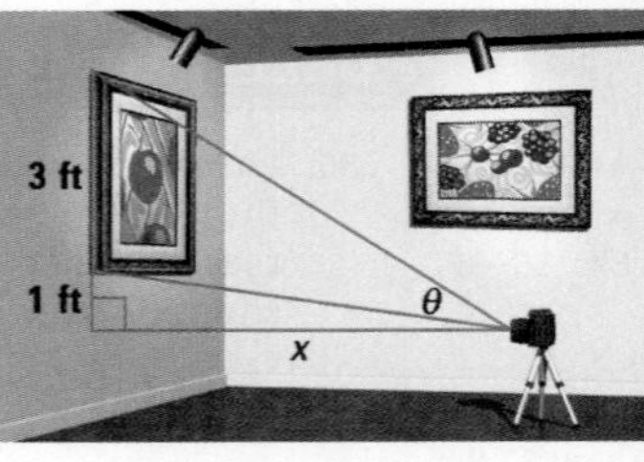

KY KENTUCKY MIXED REVIEW

TEST PRACTICE at classzone.com

41. The graph of which linear equation has a slope of $-\frac{2}{5}$? **C**

Ⓐ $-5x - 2y = -15$ Ⓑ $2x - 5y = -15$

Ⓒ $2x + 5y = -15$ Ⓓ $5x + 2y = -15$

42. Steve plants a flower bed next to a corner of a building. The flower bed forms part of a circle with a radius of 10 feet. What is the flower bed's approximate area? **D**

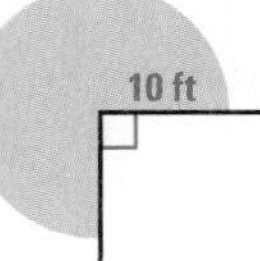

Ⓐ 47.1 ft^2 Ⓑ 78.5 ft^2

Ⓒ 226.9 ft^2 Ⓓ 235.6 ft^2

QUIZ *for Lessons 13.3–13.4*

Use the given point on the terminal side of an angle θ in standard position to evaluate the six trigonometric functions of θ. *(p. 866)* **1–4. See margin.**

1. $(6, -2)$ **2.** $(-7, 5)$ **3.** $(4, 8)$ **4.** $(-12, -3)$

Evaluate the expression without using a calculator. *(p. 866)*

5. $\cos 150°$ $-\frac{\sqrt{3}}{2}$ **6.** $\tan \frac{8\pi}{3}$ $-\sqrt{3}$ **7.** $\sin(-840°)$ $-\frac{\sqrt{3}}{2}$ **8.** $\sec\left(-\frac{15\pi}{4}\right)$ $\sqrt{2}$

Evaluate the expression without using a calculator. Give your answer in both radians and degrees. *(p. 875)*

9. $\cos^{-1}\left(-\frac{\sqrt{2}}{2}\right)$ $\frac{3\pi}{4}$, 135° **10.** $\sin^{-1}(-1)$ $-\frac{\pi}{2}$, $-90°$ **11.** $\tan^{-1}\frac{\sqrt{3}}{3}$ $\frac{\pi}{6}$, 30° **12.** $\cos^{-1}\frac{1}{2}$ $\frac{\pi}{3}$, 60°

Solve the equation for θ. *(p. 875)*

13. $\sin \theta = 0.3$; $90° < \theta < 180°$ **about 162.5°** **14.** $\tan \theta = 6$; $180° < \theta < 270°$ **about 260.5°**

15. $\cos \theta = -0.72$; $90° < \theta < 180°$ **about 136.1°** **16.** $\sin \theta = -0.55$; $270° < \theta < 360°$ **about 326.6°**

17. ACROBATICS A stuntman uses a 30 foot rope to swing 136° between two platforms of equal height, grazing the ground in the middle of the swing. If the rope stays taut throughout the swing, how far above the ground was the stuntman at the beginning and the end of the swing? How far apart are the two platforms? *(p. 875)* **about 18.8 ft; about 55.6 ft**

@HomeTutor
classzone.com
Keystrokes

13.5 Explore the Law of Sines

QUESTION How can you use geometry software to explore the law of sines?

EXPLORE Investigate a relationship between the angles and sides of a triangle

STEP 1 *Draw a triangle*

Draw $\triangle ABC$. Label the vertices and sides as shown.

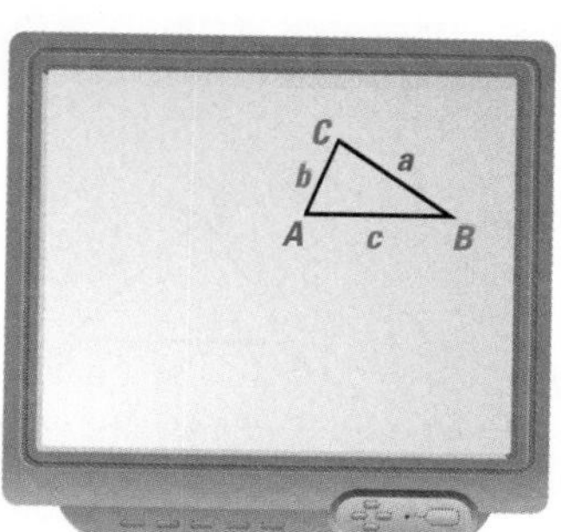

STEP 2 *Measure parts of triangle*

Find the side lengths a, b, and c. Also find the measures of angles A, B, and C.

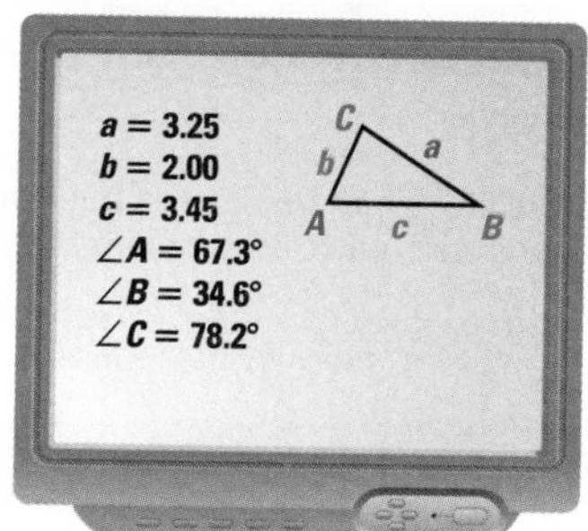

STEP 3 *Calculate ratios*

Find the ratios $\frac{\sin A}{a}$, $\frac{\sin B}{b}$, and $\frac{\sin C}{c}$.

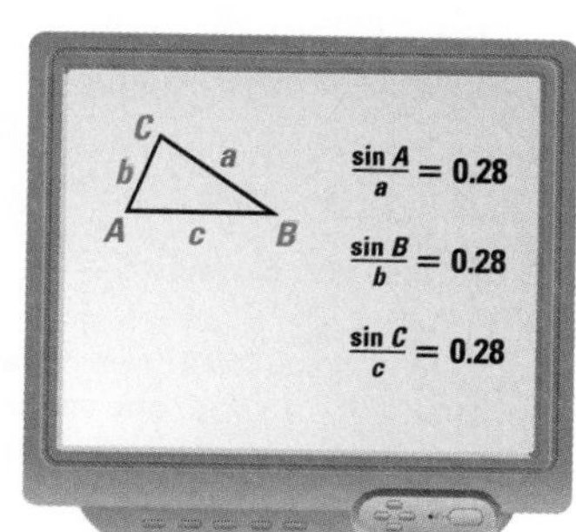

DRAW CONCLUSIONS Use your observations to complete these exercises

1. What are the values of the ratios $\frac{\sin A}{a}$, $\frac{\sin B}{b}$, and $\frac{\sin C}{c}$ for your triangle? What do you notice about these values? **Check student's work; all of the ratios are the same.**
2. Change the shape of your triangle by dragging its vertices, and observe how the ratios you found in Step 3 change. Make a conjecture about how these ratios are related for *any* triangle. **The ratios are always equal.**

1 PLAN AND PREPARE

Explore the Concept

- Students will use geometry software to explore the law of sines.
- This activity leads into the study of using the law of sines to solve triangles in Examples 1–4 of Lesson 13.5.

Materials

Each student will need a computer with geometry software.

Recommended Time

Work activity: 10 min
Discuss results: 10 min

Grouping

Students should work individually.

2 TEACH

Tips for Success

Make sure that students try acute, right, and obtuse triangles.

Key Discovery

In any triangle ABC, $\frac{\sin A}{a} = \frac{\sin B}{b} = \frac{\sin C}{c}$.

3 ASSESS AND RETEACH

Is there any kind of triangle in which the relationship you discovered in this activity will not work? If so, what kind of triangle? **No; it is true for any triangle.**

13.5 Apply the Law of Sines

1 PLAN AND PREPARE

Warm-Up Exercises

Transparency Available

1. Solve $\triangle ABC$.

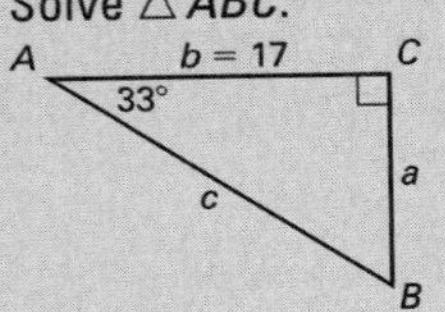

$B = 57°$, $a \approx 11.0$, $c \approx 20.3$

2. Solve $\triangle ABC$ with $B = 41°$, $C = 90°$, and $c = 22$. $A = 49°$, $a \approx 16.6$, $b \approx 14.4$

Notetaking Guide

Transparency Available

Promotes interactive learning and notetaking skills, pp. 339–343.

Pacing

Basic: 1 day

Average: 1 day

Advanced: 1 day

Block: 0.5 block with 13.4

- See *Teaching Guide/Lesson Plan.*

2 FOCUS AND MOTIVATE

Essential Question

Big Idea 3, p. 851

When can the law of sines be used to solve a triangle? Tell students they will learn how to answer this question by using the law of sines to solve triangles.

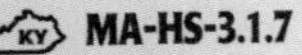

MA-HS-3.1.7

Before	You solved right triangles.
Now	You will solve triangles that have no right angle.
Why?	So you can find the distance between faraway objects, as in Ex. 44.

Key Vocabulary
- law of sines

MA-HS-3.1.7
Students will solve real-world and mathematical problems by applying properties of triangles (e.g., Triangle Sum theorem and Isosceles Triangle theorems). DOK 2

In Lesson 13.1, you solved right triangles. To solve a triangle with no right angle, you need to know the length of at least one side and any two other parts of the triangle. The **law of sines** can be used to solve triangles when two angles and the length of any side are known (AAS or ASA cases), or when the lengths of two sides and an angle opposite one of the two sides are known (SSA case).

KEY CONCEPT — For Your Notebook

Law of Sines

The law of sines can be written in either of the following forms for $\triangle ABC$ with sides of length a, b, and c.

$$\frac{\sin A}{a} = \frac{\sin B}{b} = \frac{\sin C}{c} \qquad \frac{a}{\sin A} = \frac{b}{\sin B} = \frac{c}{\sin C}$$

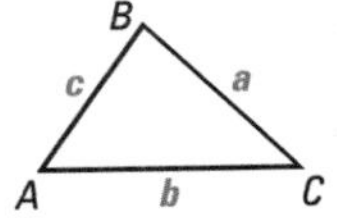

EXAMPLE 1 Solve a triangle for the AAS or ASA case

Solve $\triangle ABC$ with $C = 107°$, $B = 25°$, and $b = 15$.

Solution

First find the angle: $A = 180° - 107° - 25° = 48°$.

By the law of sines, you can write $\frac{a}{\sin 48°} = \frac{15}{\sin 25°} = \frac{c}{\sin 107°}$.

$\frac{a}{\sin 48°} = \frac{15}{\sin 25°}$	Write two equations, each with one variable.	$\frac{c}{\sin 107°} = \frac{15}{\sin 25°}$
$a = \frac{15 \sin 48°}{\sin 25°}$	Solve for each variable.	$c = \frac{15 \sin 107°}{\sin 25°}$
$a \approx 26.4$	Use a calculator.	$c \approx 33.9$

▶ In $\triangle ABC$, $A = 48°$, $a \approx 26.4$, and $c \approx 33.9$.

GUIDED PRACTICE for Example 1

Solve $\triangle ABC$.

1. $B = 34°$, $C = 100°$, $b = 8$
$A = 46°$, $a \approx 10.3$, $c \approx 14.1$

2. $A = 51°$, $B = 44°$, $c = 11$
$C = 85°$, $a \approx 8.6$, $b \approx 7.7$

Resource Planning Guide

Chapter Resource Book
- Teaching Guide/Lesson Plan (pp. 47–48)
- Practice levels A, B, C (pp. 51–53)
- Study Guide (pp. 54–55)
- Catch-up for Absent Students (p. 56)
- Application (p. 57)
- Challenge (p. 58)

Workbooks
- Notetaking Guide (pp. 339–343)
- Practice Workbook (pp. 189–190)

Teaching Options
- **Power Presentations CD-ROM** provides dynamic electronic teaching resources for the classroom.
- **Activity Generator CD-ROM** provides editable activities for all ability levels.

Interactive Technology
- Easy Planner
- Power Presentations CD-ROM
- Activity Generator CD-ROM
- Animated Algebra
- Test Generator CD-ROM
- Online Quiz
- eWorkbook
- eEdition
- @HomeTutor

Resources for English Learners
- Quick Reference for English Learners
- Spanish Study Guide
- Multi-Language Visual Glossary
- Student Resources in Spanish

See also the *Algebra 2 Toolkit* for more strategies for meeting individual needs.

DESCRIBE CASES Because the SSA case can result in 0, 1, or 2 triangles, it is called the *ambiguous case.*

SSA CASE Two angles and one side (AAS or ASA) determine exactly one triangle. Two sides and an angle opposite one of the sides (SSA) may determine no triangle, one triangle, or two triangles.

KEY CONCEPT *For Your Notebook*

Possible Triangles in the SSA Case

Consider a triangle in which you are given a, b, and A. By fixing side b and angle A, you can sketch the possible positions of side a to figure out how many triangles can be formed. In the diagrams below, note that $h = b \sin A$.

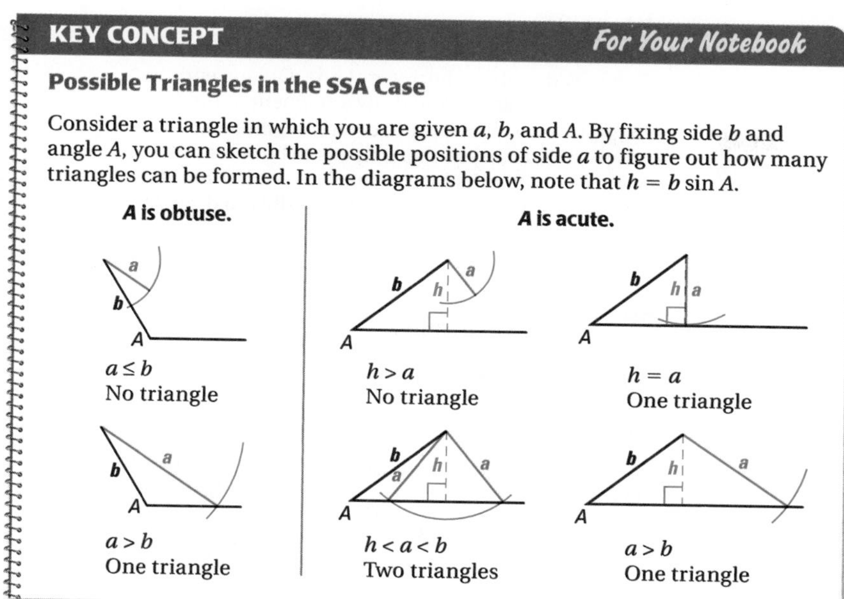

EXAMPLE 2 Solve the SSA case with one solution

Solve $\triangle ABC$ with $A = 115°$, $a = 20$, and $b = 11$.

Solution

First make a sketch. Because A is obtuse and the side opposite A is longer than the given adjacent side, you know that only one triangle can be formed. Use the law of sines to find B.

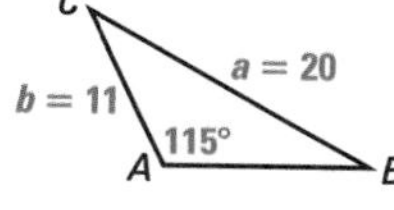

$\frac{\sin B}{11} = \frac{\sin 115°}{20}$ **Law of sines**

$\sin B = \frac{11 \sin 115°}{20} \approx 0.4985$ **Multiply each side by 11.**

$B \approx 29.9°$ **Use inverse sine function.**

You then know that $C \approx 180° - 115° - 29.9° = 35.1°$. Use the law of sines again to find the remaining side length c of the triangle.

$\frac{c}{\sin 35.1°} = \frac{20}{\sin 115°}$ **Law of sines**

$c = \frac{20 \sin 35.1°}{\sin 115°}$ **Multiply each side by sin 35.1°.**

$c \approx 12.7$ **Use a calculator.**

▸ In $\triangle ABC$, $B \approx 29.9°$, $C \approx 35.1°$, and $c \approx 12.7$.

Motivating the Lesson

If you know the lengths of any two sides of a triangular region and the measure of the angle between the two sides, you can use these three measures to find the area of the region.

3 TEACH

Extra Example 1

Solve $\triangle ABC$ with $A = 94°$, $C = 67°$, and $b = 25$. $B = 19°$, $a \approx 76.6$, $c \approx 70.7$

Key Question to Ask for Example 1

- When you are given the measures of two angles and one side of a triangle, why does it not matter whether the given side is the one included between the two angles? Since you are given the measures of any two angles, you can always find the third angle measure.

Extra Example 2

Solve $\triangle ABC$ with $A = 127°$, $a = 63$, and $b = 42$. $B \approx 32.2°$, $C \approx 20.8°$, $c \approx 28.0$

Key Question to Ask for Example 2

- How is the SSA case different from the AAS and ASA cases? The SSA combination, which means two sides and a non-included angle are given, does not always determine exactly one triangle.

Differentiated Instruction

Below Level In order to understand the work they will be doing in Lessons 13.5 and 13.6, it is essential that students know that ASA, AAS, SAS, and SSS are all congruence conditions, which means that exactly one triangle is determined, while SSA is not. Do not assume that students remember this from their geometry classes. Provide them with a construction activity to do with compass and straightedge to gain hands-on knowledge of what combinations of given parts will determine exactly one triangle. See also the *Algebra 2 Toolkit* for more strategies.

Extra Example 3

Solve $\triangle ABC$ with $B = 52°$, $a = 6.5$, and $b = 4.7$. No solution (The triangle is not possible.)

Key Question to Ask for Example 3

- What will happen if you try to solve the triangle described in Example 3 by applying the law of sines and using your calculator? First try to find B: $\sin B = \frac{5 \sin 51°}{3.5} \approx 1.1102$. Trying to find $\sin^{-1} 1.1102$ will give an ERROR message, since the value of the sine function is never greater than 1.

Extra Example 4

Solve $\triangle ABC$ with $A = 62°$, $a = 32$, and $b = 34$. Triangle 1: $B \approx 69.7°$, $C \approx 48.3°$, $c \approx 27.1$; Triangle 2: $B \approx 110.3°$, $C \approx 7.7°$, $c \approx 4.86$

Key Question to Ask for Example 4

- In Example 4, how do you know that there are two different angles B for which $\sin B = 0.7911$? The values of the sine function are positive in quadrants I and II. These two quadrants (in addition to the quadrantal angle 90°, whose sine is 1) include all of the angles that can be angles in a triangle. There is one angle in Quadrant I and one in Quadrant II that have as their sine any given number between 0 and 1.

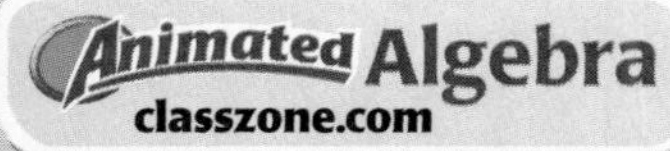

An **Animated Algebra** activity is available on-line for **Example 4**. This activity is also available on the **Power Presentations CD-ROM**.

EXAMPLE 3 Examine the SSA case with no solution

Solve $\triangle ABC$ with $A = 51°$, $a = 3.5$, and $b = 5$.

Solution

Begin by drawing a horizontal line. On one end form a 51° angle (A) and draw a segment 5 units long ($\overline{AC}$, or b). At vertex C, draw a segment 3.5 units long (a). You can see that a needs to be at least $5 \sin 51° \approx 3.9$ units long to reach the horizontal side and form a triangle. So, it is not possible to draw the indicated triangle.

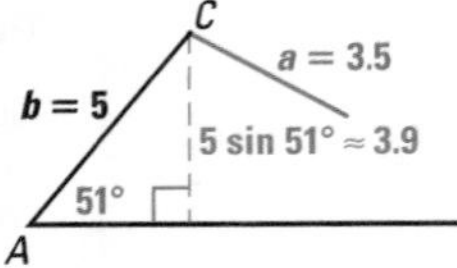

EXAMPLE 4 Solve the SSA case with two solutions

Solve $\triangle ABC$ with $A = 40°$, $a = 13$, and $b = 16$.

Solution

First make a sketch. Because $b \sin A = 16 \sin 40° \approx 10.3$, and $10.3 < 13 < 16$ ($h < a < b$), two triangles can be formed.

Triangle 1

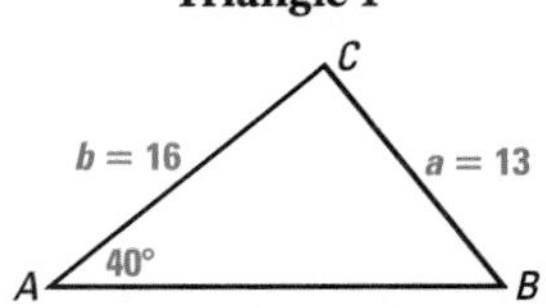

Triangle 2

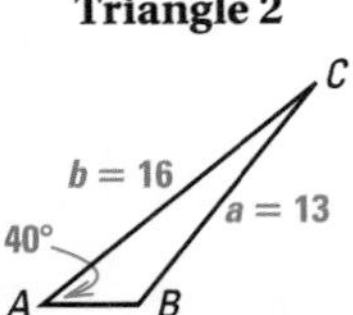

Use the law of sines to find the possible measures of B.

$$\frac{\sin B}{16} = \frac{\sin 40°}{13}$$ Law of sines

$$\sin B = \frac{16 \sin 40°}{13} \approx 0.7911$$ Use a calculator.

There are two angles B between 0° and 180° for which $\sin B \approx 0.7911$. One is acute and the other is obtuse. Use your calculator to find the acute angle: $\sin^{-1} 0.7911 \approx 52.3°$.

The obtuse angle has 52.3° as a reference angle, so its measure is $180° - 52.3° = 127.7°$. Therefore, $B \approx 52.3°$ or $B \approx 127.7°$.

Now find the remaining angle C and side length c for each triangle.

Triangle 1

$C \approx 180° - 40° - 52.3° = 87.7°$

$$\frac{c}{\sin 87.7°} = \frac{13}{\sin 40°}$$

$$c = \frac{13 \sin 87.7°}{\sin 40°} \approx 20.2$$

▶ In Triangle 1, $B \approx 52.3°$, $C \approx 87.7°$, and $c \approx 20.2$.

Triangle 2

$C \approx 180° - 40° - 127.7° = 12.3°$

$$\frac{c}{\sin 12.3°} = \frac{13}{\sin 40°}$$

$$c = \frac{13 \sin 12.3°}{\sin 40°} \approx 4.3$$

▶ In Triangle 2, $B \approx 127.7°$, $C \approx 12.3°$, and $c \approx 4.3$.

Animated Algebra at classzone.com

✓ **GUIDED PRACTICE** for Examples 2, 3, and 4

Solve $\triangle ABC$.

3. $A = 122°, a = 18, b = 12$
$B \approx 34.4°, C \approx 23.6°, c \approx 8.5$

4. $A = 36°, a = 9, b = 12$
$B \approx 51.6°, C \approx 92.4°, c \approx 15.3$ or $B \approx 128.4°, C \approx 15.6°, c \approx 4.$

5. $A = 50°, a = 2.8, b = 4$
no triangle

6. $B = 105°, b = 13, a = 6$
$A \approx 26.5°, C \approx 48.5°, c \approx 10.1$

AREA OF A TRIANGLE You can use the following result to find the area of a triangle when you know the lengths of two sides and the measure of the included angle. This result can also be used to derive the law of sines (see Exercise 42).

KEY CONCEPT *For Your Notebook*

Area of a Triangle

The area of any triangle is given by one half the product of the lengths of two sides times the sine of their included angle. For $\triangle ABC$ shown, there are three ways to calculate the area:

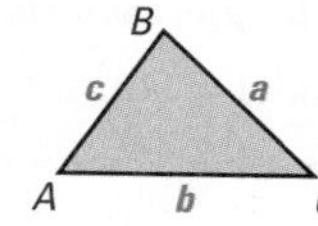

$$\text{Area} = \frac{1}{2}bc \sin A \qquad \text{Area} = \frac{1}{2}ac \sin B \qquad \text{Area} = \frac{1}{2}ab \sin C$$

EXAMPLE 5 Find the area of a triangle

BIOLOGY Black-necked stilts are birds that live throughout Florida and surrounding areas but breed mostly in the triangular region shown on the map. Find the area of this region.

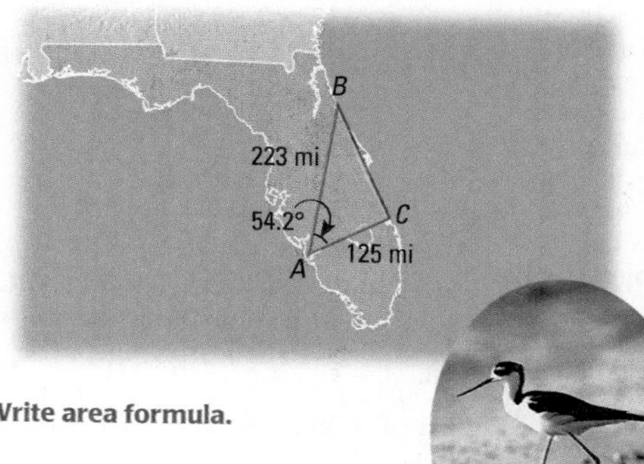

Solution

The area of the region is:

$\text{Area} = \frac{1}{2}bc \sin A$ **Write area formula.**

$= \frac{1}{2}(125)(223) \sin 54.2°$ **Substitute.**

$\approx 11{,}300$ **Use a calculator.**

▶ The area of the region is about 11,300 square miles.

 **GUIDED PRACTICE** for Example 5

Find the area of $\triangle ABC$ with the given side lengths and included angle.

7. $a = 10, b = 14, C = 46°$ **about 50.4**

8. $a = 19, c = 8, B = 75°$ **about 73.4**

9. $b = 11, c = 7, A = 120°$ **about 33.3**

10. $a = 20, b = 24, C = 87°$ **about 239.7**

Extra Example 5

- You are setting up a triangular flower garden in your back yard. If you lay off lengths of 15 feet and 11 feet for two sides of the garden with a 62° angle between these two sides, what will be the area of the garden? **about 72.8 ft^2**

Key Question to Ask for Example 5

- How do you know that the area formula used in Example 5 will never give a negative value for the area of a triangle? **The value of the sine function is positive for all angles that can possibly be angles in triangles.**

Closing the Lesson

Have students summarize the major points of the lesson and answer the Essential Question: When can the law of sines be used to solve a triangle?

- **The law of sines says that in any triangle ABC, $\frac{\sin A}{a} = \frac{\sin B}{b} = \frac{\sin C}{c}$.**
- **In the SSA case, there may be one triangle, two triangles, or no triangles with the given measurements.**

The law of sines is used to solve triangles with no right angle in the AAS, ASA, and SSA cases.

Differentiated Instruction

Auditory Learners Have students read aloud the three formulas for the area of a triangle given in the Key Concept box. Ask them what they notice about the variables in each formula. Students should compare the formulas to the sketch in the Key Concept box and conclude that when using the given angle to find the area of the triangle, the two side lengths used in the formula are those that make up the sides of the angle in the formula. Also, they should notice that each variable appears only once in each formula.

See also the *Algebra 2 Toolkit* for more strategies.

4 PRACTICE AND APPLY

Assignment Guide

Answer Transparencies available for all exercises

Basic:
Day 1: SRH p. 980 Exs. 21, 23, 26, 28
pp. 886–888
Exs. 1–6, 12–14, 18–20, 27–32, 43–47, 50

Average:
Day 1: pp. 886–888
Exs. 1, 2, 7–9, 14–16, 21–23, 27, 28, 32–34, 38–41, 43–48, 51

Advanced:
Day 1: pp. 886–888
Exs. 1, 2, 10, 11, 16, 17, 24–28, 32–49*

Block:
pp. 886–888
Exs. 1, 2, 7–9, 14–16, 21–23, 27, 28, 32–34, 38–41, 43–48, 51 (with 13.4)

Differentiated Instruction

See *Algebra 2 Best Practices Toolkit* for suggestions on addressing the needs of a diverse classroom.

Homework Check

For a quick check of student understanding of key concepts, go over the following exercises:

Basic: 4, 6, 20, 30, 43, 45
Average: 8, 22, 32, 44, 45
Advanced: 10, 26, 36, 44, 46

Extra Practice

- Student Edition, p. 1022
- Chapter 13 Resource Book: Practice levels A, B, C, pp. 51–53

Practice Worksheet

An easily-readable reduced practice page (with answers) for this lesson can be found on p. 850D.

13.5 EXERCISES

HOMEWORK KEY
○ = **WORKED-OUT SOLUTIONS** on p. WS23 for Exs. 13, 31, and 45
★ = **STANDARDIZED TEST PRACTICE** Exs. 2, 28, 41, 47, and 48
◆ = **MULTIPLE REPRESENTATIONS** Ex. 45

SKILL PRACTICE

A

1. **VOCABULARY** What information do you need to use the law of sines? **two angle measures and the length of a side, or the lengths of two sides and the measure of an angle opposite one of the two sides**

2. ★ **WRITING** Suppose a, b, and A are given for $\triangle ABC$ where $A < 90°$. Under what conditions would you have no triangle? one triangle? two triangles? **See margin.**

EXAMPLES 1, 2, 3, and 4 on pp. 882–884 for Exs. 3–28

IDENTIFYING CASES **State the case (AAS, ASA, or SSA) applicable to the given measurements. Then decide whether the measurements determine *one triangle, two triangles,* or *no triangle.***

3. $A = 112°, a = 9, b = 4$ **SSA; one triangle**
4. $A = 40°, C = 75°, c = 20$ **AAS; one triangle**
5. $A = 52°, a = 32, b = 42$ **SSA; no triangle**
6. $A = 37°, a = 8, b = 14$ **SSA; no triangle**
7. $A = 28°, B = 64°, c = 55$ **ASA; one triangle**
8. $A = 149°, a = 7, b = 10$ **SSA; no triangle**
9. $B = 34°, b = 5, a = 16$ **SSA; no triangle**
10. $B = 70°, b = 85, c = 88$ **SSA; two triangles**
11. $C = 48°, c = 28, b = 20$ **SSA; one triangle**

SOLVING TRIANGLES **Solve $\triangle ABC$.**

12.
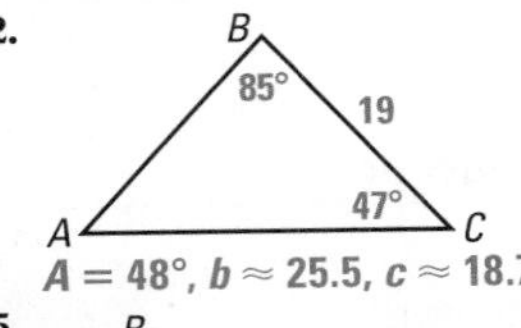

$A = 48°, b \approx 25.5, c \approx 18.7$

13.
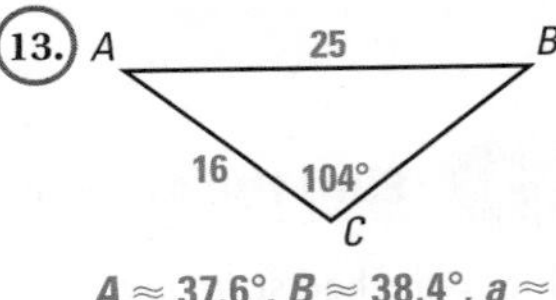

$A \approx 37.6°, B \approx 38.4°, a \approx 15.7$

14.
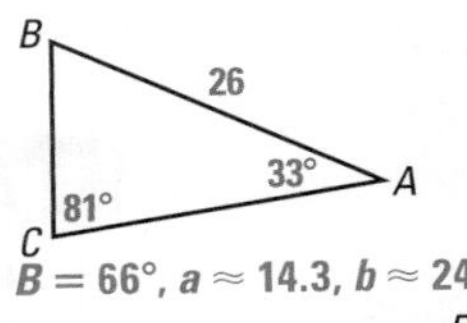

$B = 66°, a \approx 14.3, b \approx 24.0$

15.
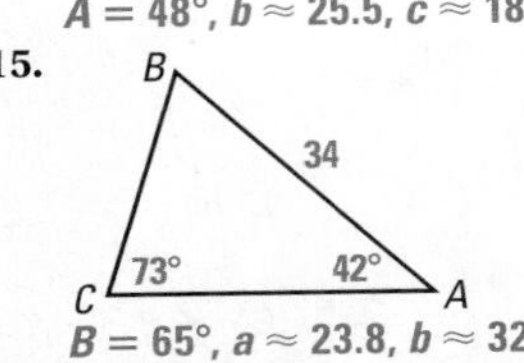

$B = 65°, a \approx 23.8, b \approx 32.2$

16.
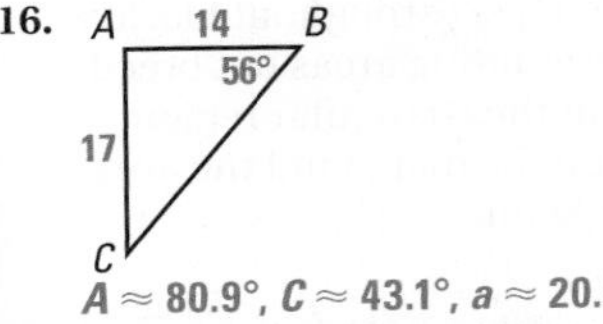

$A \approx 80.9°, C \approx 43.1°, a \approx 20.2$

17.
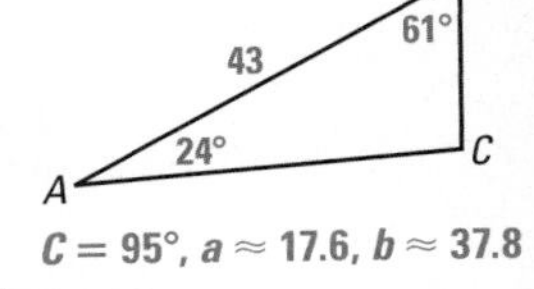

$C = 95°, a \approx 17.6, b \approx 37.8$

SOLVING TRIANGLES **Solve $\triangle ABC$. (*Hint:* Some of the "triangles" have no solution and some have two solutions.)**

18. $A = 73°, a = 18, b = 11$ $B \approx 35.8°, C \approx 71.2°, c \approx 17.8$
19. $A = 26°, C = 35°, b = 13$ $B = 119°, a \approx 6.5, c \approx 8.5$
20. $B = 102°, C = 43°, b = 21$ $A = 35°, a \approx 12.3, c \approx 14.6$
21. $A = 38°, a = 19, b = 25$
22. $A = 55°, B = 64°, c = 34$ $C = 61°, a \approx 31.8, b \approx 34.9$
23. $A = 114°, a = 15, b = 10$ $B \approx 37.5°, C \approx 28.5°, c \approx 7.8$
24. $C = 98°, c = 29, a = 33$ **no triangle**
25. $A = 49°, B = 32°, b = 44$ $C = 99°, a \approx 62.7, c \approx 82.0$
26. $B = 21°, b = 17, c = 32$

27. **ERROR ANALYSIS** *Describe* and correct the error in finding the measure of angle C in the triangle below.

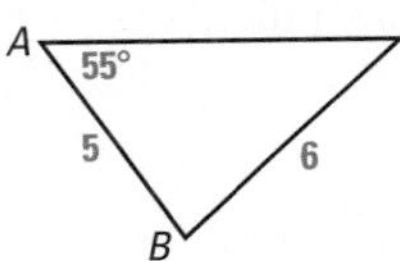

The sides were not paired with their opposite angles; $\frac{\sin C}{5} = \frac{\sin 55°}{6}$, $\sin C = \frac{5 \sin 55°}{6} \approx 0.6826$, $C \approx 43.0°$.

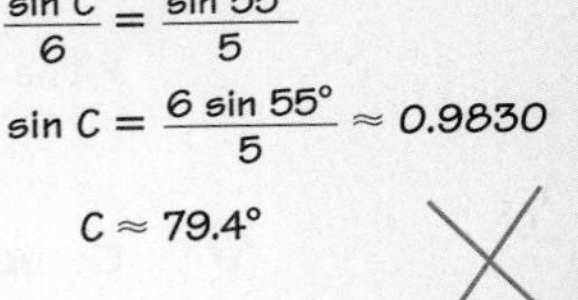

28. ★ **MULTIPLE CHOICE** What is the side length c in $\triangle ABC$ if $A = 32°$, $C = 67°$, and $b = 31$ ft? **B**

Ⓐ 16.6 ft Ⓑ 28.9 ft Ⓒ 33.3 ft Ⓓ 57.8 ft

2. when the height of the triangle is greater than the side opposite the given angle; when the height is equal to the side opposite the given angle or when the side opposite the given angle is greater than the other given side; when the height of the triangle is less than the side opposite the given angle and this is less than the other given side

21. $B \approx 54.1°$, $C \approx 87.9°$, $c \approx 30.8$, or $B \approx 125.9°$, $C \approx 16.1°$, $c \approx 8.6$

26. $A \approx 116.6°$, $C \approx 42.4°$, $a \approx 42.4$, or $A \approx 21.4°$, $C \approx 137.6°$, $a \approx 17.3$

EXAMPLE 5 B
on p. 885
for Exs. 29–41

FINDING AREA **Find the area of $\triangle ABC$ with the given side lengths and included angle.**

29. $B = 124°, a = 9, c = 11$ about 41.0
30. $A = 68°, b = 13, c = 7$ about 42.2
31. $A = 34°, b = 29, c = 36$ about 291.9
32. $C = 79°, a = 25, b = 17$ about 208.6
33. $B = 57°, a = 9, c = 5$ about 18.9
34. $C = 96°, a = 7, b = 15$ about 52.2
35. $A = 130°, b = 23, c = 20$ about 176.2
36. $B = 60°, a = 19, c = 14$ about 115.2
37. $C = 29°, a = 38, b = 31$ about 285.6

FINDING AREA **Find the area of $\triangle ABC$.**

38. about 81.8

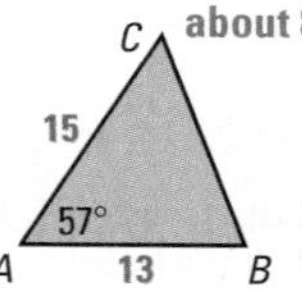

39. about 205.3

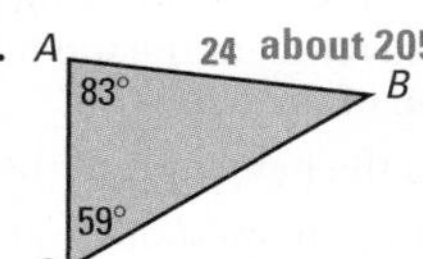

40. about 147.3

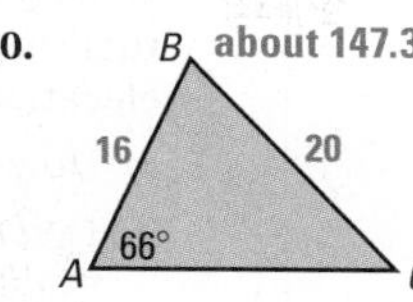

41. ★ **MULTIPLE CHOICE** What is the area of $\triangle ABC$ if $B = 52°$, $a = 29$, and $c = 24$? A

Ⓐ 274 units^2 Ⓑ 348 units^2 Ⓒ 548 units^2 Ⓓ 696 units^2

C

42. **CHALLENGE** Using the triangle shown at the right as a reference, derive the formulas for the area of a triangle given on page 885. Then use the area formulas to derive the law of sines. See margin.

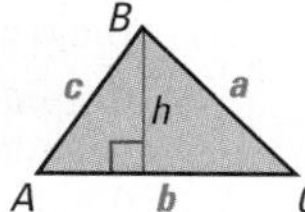

PROBLEM SOLVING

EXAMPLE 1 A
on p. 882
for Ex. 43

43. about 193.6 ft, about 212.9 ft

43. **LIFEGUARDS** Two lifeguards are watching a windsurfer. Use the information in the diagram to find the distance from each lifeguard to the windsurfer.

@HomeTutor for problem solving help at classzone.com

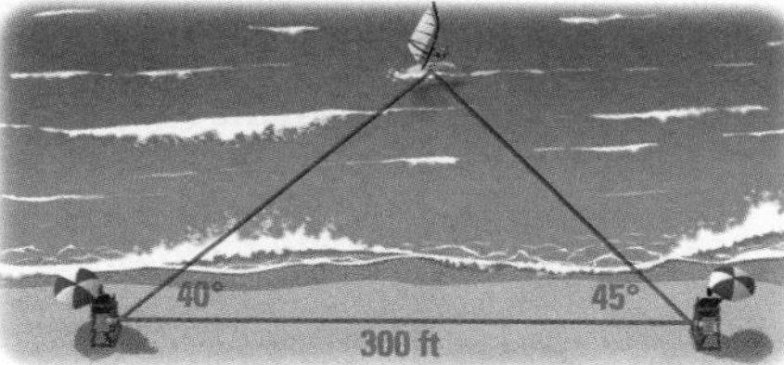

EXAMPLE 2
on p. 883
for Ex. 44

44. **NEW YORK CITY** You are on the observation deck of the Empire State Building looking at the Chrysler Building. When you turn 145° clockwise, you see the Statue of Liberty. You know that the Chrysler Building and the Empire State Building are about 0.6 mile apart and that the Chrysler Building and the Statue of Liberty are about 5.7 miles apart. Estimate the distance between the Empire State Building and the Statue of Liberty. about 5.2 mi

@HomeTutor for problem solving help at classzone.com

EXAMPLE 5
on p. 885
for Exs. 45–46

45. ◆ **MULTIPLE REPRESENTATIONS** You are fertilizing a triangular garden. One side of the garden is 62 feet long and another side is 54 feet long. The angle opposite the 62 foot side is 58°.

a. **Drawing a Diagram** Draw a diagram to represent this situation. See margin.

b. **Solving a Triangle** Use the law of sines to solve the triangle you drew in part (a). third side: about 70.4 ft; other angles: about 47.6°, about 74.4°

c. **Applying a Formula** One bag of fertilizer covers an area of 200 square feet. How many bags of fertilizer will you need to cover the entire garden? 9 bags

Avoiding Common Errors

Exercises 3–11 Some students may try to find two different triangles for the AAS and ASA cases. Remind them that only the SSA case does not determine exactly one triangle, which means it is the only case in which there may be 0, 1, or 2 triangles. Use the term "ambiguous case" to emphasize this point.

Mathematical Reasoning

Exercises 18–26 Sometimes students have trouble solving triangles because they do not know in what order they should try to find the missing parts. Have them work individually or with partners to develop an organized strategy for solving a triangle for each of the cases discussed in this lesson. Encourage them to find effective ways to present this information. A flow chart is one way that will work well. After you discuss the SAS and SSS cases in Lesson 13.6, students should go back and add that information to what they have put together for the AAS, ASA, and SSA cases here.

Study Strategy

Exercises 29–41 Some students may benefit from a hint for remembering the new formula for the area of a triangle. If they forget whether the formula includes sin *A* or cos *A*, suggest that they try this test: What if the included angle is 90°? Since $\sin 90° = 1$, if $C = 90°$, this would give Area $= \frac{1}{2}ab$. This says that the area of a right triangle is half the product of the lengths of its legs, which is correct. But since $\cos 90° = 0$, using cos *C* in the formula would give an area of 0, which cannot be correct.

45a.

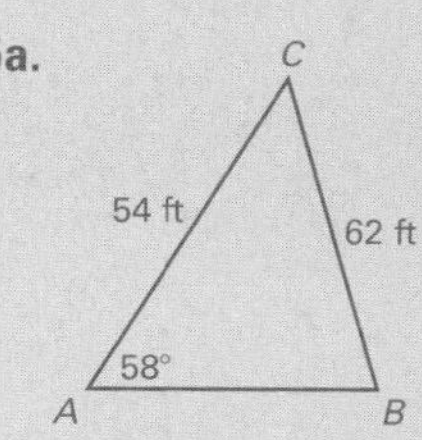

42. *Sample answer:* $\sin A = \frac{h}{c}$, $h = c \sin A$. To compute the area of a triangle use the equation $A = \frac{1}{2}bh$ and by substituting for h you would get $A = \frac{1}{2}bc \sin A$. You get similar results by using angles B and C ($\sin C = \frac{h}{a}$, $h = a \sin C \rightarrow A = \frac{1}{2}ab \sin C$). Since all of these equations represent the area of the same triangle, you can set them equal to each other. This results in $\frac{1}{2}bc \sin A = \frac{1}{2}ac \sin B = \frac{1}{2}ab \sin C$. If you simplify this, you end up with $\frac{\sin A}{a} = \frac{\sin B}{b} = \frac{\sin C}{c}$, which is the law of sines.

5 ASSESS AND RETEACH

Daily Homework Quiz

Transparency Available

Solve $\triangle ABC$ with the given parts.

1. $A = 112°$, $a = 24$, $B = 29°$
   $C = 39°$, $b \approx 12.5$, $c \approx 16.3$
2. $A = 96°$, $a = 16$, $b = 7$
   $B \approx 25.8°$, $C \approx 58.2°$, $c \approx 13.7$

Decide if the given measurements determine *one triangle*, *two triangles*, or *no triangle*.

3. $A = 71°$, $a = 45$, $c = 47$
   two triangles
4. $C = 85°$, $b = 33$, $c = 28$
   no triangle
5. Two sides of a sports pennant are each 18 inches long, and the angle between these two sides is 50°. What is the area of the pennant? about 124 in.^{2}

Online Quiz

Available at classzone.com

Diagnosis/Remediation

- Practice A, B, C in Chapter 13 Resource Book, pp. 51–53
- Study Guide in Chapter 13 Resource Book, pp. 54–55
- Practice Workbook, pp. 189–190
- @HomeTutor

Challenge

Additional challenge is available in the Chapter 13 Resource Book, p. 58.

47b. See Additional Answers beginning on p. AA1.

---

46. **MULTI-STEP PROBLEM** Quadrilateral *ABCD* shown at the right is a kite.

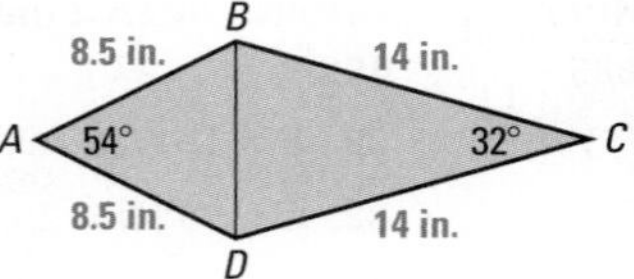

   a. Find the area of $\triangle ABD$. about 29.2 in.^{2}
   b. Find the area of $\triangle BCD$. about 51.9 in.^{2}
   c. What is the area of the kite? about 81.1 in.^{2}

B 47. ★ **SHORT RESPONSE** A building is constructed on top of a cliff that is 300 meters high. A person standing on level ground below the cliff observes that the angle of elevation to the top of the building is 72°, and the angle of elevation to the top of the cliff is 63°.
   a. How far away is the person from the base of the cliff? about 152.9 m
   b. *Describe* two different methods you can use to find the height of the building. Use one of these methods to find the building's height. See margin.

48a. *Sample answer:* $A = 24 \sin x$, where the length of the sides of the triangle are 6 and 8.

48b. No; x increases to 90° where the equation reaches a maximum and then begins to decrease.

48. ★ **EXTENDED RESPONSE** Use a graphing calculator to explore how the included angle in the formulas on page 885 affects a triangle's area.
   a. **Model** Choose lengths for two sides of the triangle. Let x represent the measure (in degrees) of the included angle. Write an equation that gives the triangle's area y as a function of x.
   b. **Graphing Calculator** Enter the equation from part (a) into a graphing calculator. Use the *table* feature to examine values of the area for $0° < x° < 180°$. Does the area always increase as x increases? *Explain.*
   c. **Interpret** What value of x maximizes the triangle's area? What is the maximum area, and how is it related to the side lengths you chose in part (a)? 90°. *Sample answer:* 24, it is equal to one-half of the product of the side lengths.

C 49. **CHALLENGE** The distance between Mercury and the sun is approximately 36 million miles. The distance between Earth and the sun is approximately 93 million miles. If on a certain day the angle (measured from Earth) between the sun and Mercury is 22°, what are the possible distances between Mercury and Earth? about 95 million mi or about 77 million mi

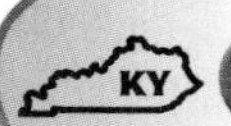

KENTUCKY MIXED REVIEW

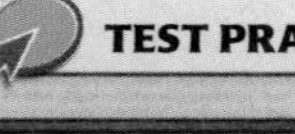

TEST PRACTICE at classzone.com

50. Amy uses 100 of the tiles shown to tile a square room. What is the perimeter of the room? **B**

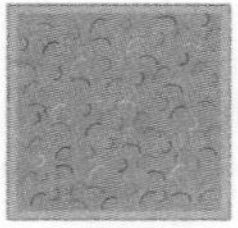

   Ⓐ 24 ft　　Ⓑ 32 ft
   Ⓒ 36 ft　　Ⓓ 80 ft

51. The ages of the first 20 people entering an amusement park are 12, 16, 35, 24, 40, 48, 15, 18, 20, 50, 38, 14, 11, 28, 18, 19, 26, 15, 16, and 21. What is an acceptable set of intervals to use when making a histogram of the ages? **C**
   Ⓐ 10–20, 21–40, and 41–50
   Ⓑ 10–15, 16–20, 21–30, and 31–50
   Ⓒ 11–20, 21–30, 31–40, and 41–50
   Ⓓ 15–25, 26–35, 36–45, and 46–55

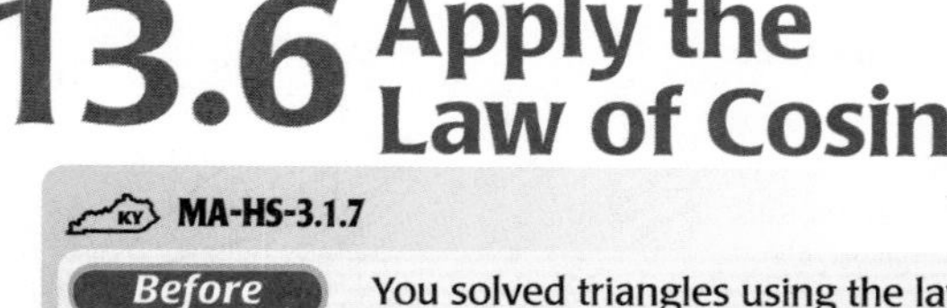

13.6 Apply the Law of Cosines

MA-HS-3.1.7

Before You solved triangles using the law of sines.

Now You will solve triangles using the law of cosines.

Why? So you can find angles formed by trapeze artists, as in Ex. 43.

Key Vocabulary
- law of cosines

MA-HS-3.1.7
Students will solve real-world and mathematical problems by applying properties of triangles (e.g., Triangle Sum theorem and Isosceles Triangle theorems). DOK 2

In Lesson 13.5, you solved triangles for the AAS, ASA, and SSA cases. In this lesson, you will use the **law of cosines** to solve triangles when two sides and the included angle are known (SAS), or when all three sides are known (SSS).

KEY CONCEPT *For Your Notebook*

Law of Cosines

If $\triangle ABC$ has sides of length a, b, and c as shown, then:

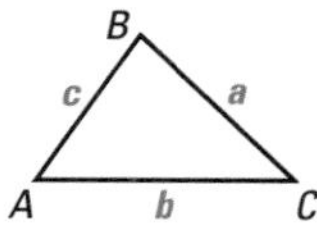

$$a^2 = b^2 + c^2 - 2bc\cos A$$

$$b^2 = a^2 + c^2 - 2ac\cos B$$

$$c^2 = a^2 + b^2 - 2ab\cos C$$

EXAMPLE 1 Solve a triangle for the SAS case

Solve $\triangle ABC$ with $a = 11$, $c = 14$, and $B = 34°$.

B, $c = 14$, A, 34°, $a = 11$, b, C

Solution

Use the law of cosines to find side length b.

$b^2 = a^2 + c^2 - 2ac\cos B$	Law of cosines
$b^2 = 11^2 + 14^2 - 2(11)(14)\cos 34°$	Substitute for a, c, and B.
$b^2 \approx 61.7$	Simplify.
$b \approx \sqrt{61.7} \approx 7.85$	Take positive square root.

ANOTHER WAY
When you know all three sides and one angle, you can use the law of cosines *or* the law of sines to find the measure of a second angle.

Use the law of sines to find the measure of angle A.

$\frac{\sin A}{a} = \frac{\sin B}{b}$	Law of sines
$\frac{\sin A}{11} = \frac{\sin 34°}{7.85}$	Substitute for a, b, and B.
$\sin A = \frac{11\sin 34°}{7.85} \approx 0.7836$	Multiply each side by 11 and simplify.
$A \approx \sin^{-1} 0.7836 \approx 51.6°$	Use inverse sine.

The third angle C of the triangle is $C \approx 180° - 34° - 51.6° = 94.4°$.

▸ In $\triangle ABC$, $b \approx 7.85$, $A \approx 51.6°$, and $C \approx 94.4°$.

1 PLAN AND PREPARE

Warm-Up Exercises

Transparency Available

Solve $\triangle ABC$ with the given parts.

1. $A = 75°$, $B = 82°$, $c = 16$
   $C = 23°$, $a \approx 39.6$, $b \approx 40.6$
2. $B = 131°$, $b = 52$, $c = 38$
   $C \approx 33.5°$, $A \approx 15.5°$, $a \approx 18.4$
3. Two sides of a triangular lot are each 80 feet long, and the angle between these two sides is 110°. Find the area of the lot. about 3007 ft^2

Notetaking Guide

Transparency Available

Promotes interactive learning and notetaking skills, pp. 344–347.

Pacing

Basic: 2 days
Average: 2 days
Advanced: 2 days
Block: 1 block
- See *Teaching Guide/Lesson Plan.*

2 FOCUS AND MOTIVATE

Essential Question

Big Idea 3, p. 851

In which cases can the law of cosines be used to solve a triangle? **Tell students they will learn how to answer this question by using the law of cosines to solve triangles.**

Resource Planning Guide

Chapter Resource Book
- Teaching Guide/Lesson Plan (pp. 59–60)
- Activity Master (p. 61)
- Practice levels A, B, C (pp. 63–65)
- Study Guide (pp. 66–67)
- Catch-up for Absent Students (p. 68)
- Problem Solving Workshop (p. 69)
- Challenge (p. 70)

Workbooks
- Notetaking Guide (pp. 344–347)
- Practice Workbook (pp. 191–192)

Teaching Options
- **Power Presentations CD-ROM** provides dynamic electronic teaching resources for the classroom.
- **Activity Generator CD-ROM** provides editable activities for all ability levels.

Interactive Technology
- Easy Planner
- Power Presentations CD-ROM
- Activity Generator CD-ROM
- Animated Algebra
- Test Generator CD-ROM
- Online Quiz
- eWorkbook
- eEdition
- @HomeTutor

Resources for English Learners
- Quick Reference for English Learners
- Spanish Study Guide
- Multi-Language Visual Glossary
- Student Resources in Spanish

See also the *Algebra 2 Toolkit* for more strategies for meeting individual needs.

Motivating the Lesson

You and a friend are hiking together, but then decide to follow different paths. You measure the obtuse angle between the two paths before starting. After an hour of walking, you check your pedometer and call your friend on your cell phone to find out how far she has walked. Putting together the information you now have, you can use the law of cosines to figure out how far apart you are.

TEACH

Extra Example 1

Solve $\triangle ABC$ with $a = 22$, $b = 15$, and $C = 108°$. $c \approx 30.2$, $A \approx 43.8°$, $B \approx 28.2°$

Extra Example 2

Solve $\triangle ABC$ with $a = 19$, $b = 26$, and $c = 31$. $A \approx 37.7°$, $B \approx 56.7°$, $C \approx 85.6°$

Key Question to Ask for Example 2

- What is a different way that you could find A? Use the law of cosines again, this time in the form $a^2 = b^2 + c^2 - 2bc \cos A$.

Extra Example 3

The lengths of the sides of a triangular plot of land are 120 feet, 150 feet, and 175 feet. Find the largest angle of the triangle. about 80.0°

AVOID ERRORS

In Example 2, the largest angle is found first to make sure that the other two angles are acute. This way, when you use the law of sines to find another angle measure, you will know that it is between 0° and 90°.

EXAMPLE 2 Solve a triangle for the SSS case

Solve $\triangle ABC$ with $a = 12$, $b = 27$, and $c = 20$.

Solution

First find the angle opposite the longest side, $\overline{AC}$. Use the law of cosines to solve for B.

$b^2 = a^2 + c^2 - 2ac \cos B$ **Law of cosines**

$27^2 = 12^2 + 20^2 - 2(12)(20) \cos B$ **Substitute.**

$\frac{27^2 - 12^2 - 20^2}{-2(12)(20)} = \cos B$ **Solve for cos B.**

$-0.3854 \approx \cos B$ **Simplify.**

$B \approx \cos^{-1}(-0.3854) \approx 112.7°$ **Use inverse cosine.**

Now use the law of sines to find A.

$\frac{\sin A}{a} = \frac{\sin B}{b}$ **Law of sines**

$\frac{\sin A}{12} = \frac{\sin 112.7°}{27}$ **Substitute for a, b, and B.**

$\sin A = \frac{12 \sin 112.7°}{27} \approx 0.4100$ **Multiply each side by 12 and simplify.**

$A \approx \sin^{-1} 0.4100 \approx 24.2°$ **Use inverse sine.**

The third angle C of the triangle is $C \approx 180° - 24.2° - 112.7° = 43.1°$.

▶ In $\triangle ABC$, $A \approx 24.2°$, $B \approx 112.7°$, and $C \approx 43.1°$.

EXAMPLE 3 Use the law of cosines in real life

SCIENCE Scientists can use a set of footprints to calculate an organism's *step angle*, which is a measure of walking efficiency. The closer the step angle is to 180°, the more efficiently the organism walked.

The diagram at the right shows a set of footprints for a dinosaur. Find the step angle B.

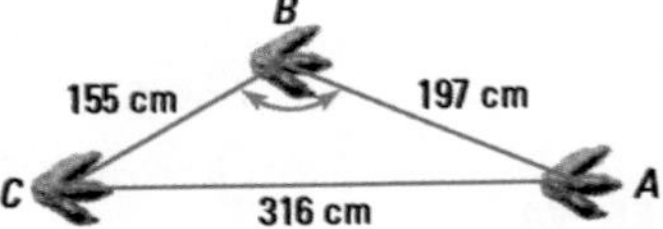

Solution

$b^2 = a^2 + c^2 - 2ac \cos B$ **Law of cosines**

$316^2 = 155^2 + 197^2 - 2(155)(197) \cos B$ **Substitute.**

$\frac{316^2 - 155^2 - 197^2}{-2(155)(197)} = \cos B$ **Solve for cos B.**

$-0.6062 \approx \cos B$ **Simplify.**

$B \approx \cos^{-1}(-0.6062) \approx 127.3°$ **Use inverse cosine.**

▶ The step angle B is about 127.3°.

Differentiated Instruction

Below Level Guide students to organize the information from Lessons 13.5 and 13.6 in a chart. Provide the outline of the chart on a handout, and work with them to complete it accurately. The chart should list each of the cases discussed (AAS, ASA, SSA, SAS, SSS), indicate how many solutions there might be, and show whether the law of sines or law of cosines should be used first in solving the triangle. Also, have students draw a sketch for each case, marking the given parts, to help them form a mental picture of the different cases.

See also the *Algebra 2 Toolkit* for more strategies.

✓ GUIDED PRACTICE for Examples 1, 2, and 3

Solve $\triangle ABC$.

1. $a = 8, c = 10, B = 48°$
   $A \approx 52.2°, C \approx 79.8°, b \approx 7.55$

2. $a = 14, b = 16, c = 9$
   $A \approx 60.7°, B \approx 85.2°, C \approx 34.1°$

3. **WHAT IF?** In Example 3, suppose that $a = 193$ cm, $b = 335$ cm, and $c = 186$ cm. Find the step angle θ. about 124°

HERON'S AREA FORMULA The law of cosines can be used to establish the following formula for the area of a triangle. The formula is credited to the Greek mathematician Heron (circa A.D. 100).

KEY CONCEPT *For Your Notebook*

Heron's Area Formula

The area of the triangle with sides of length a, b, and c is

$$\text{Area} = \sqrt{s(s-a)(s-b)(s-c)}$$

where $s = \frac{1}{2}(a + b + c)$. The variable s is called the *semiperimeter*, or half-perimeter, of the triangle.

EXAMPLE 4 Solve a multi-step problem

URBAN PLANNING The intersection of three streets forms a piece of land called a traffic triangle. Find the area of the traffic triangle shown.

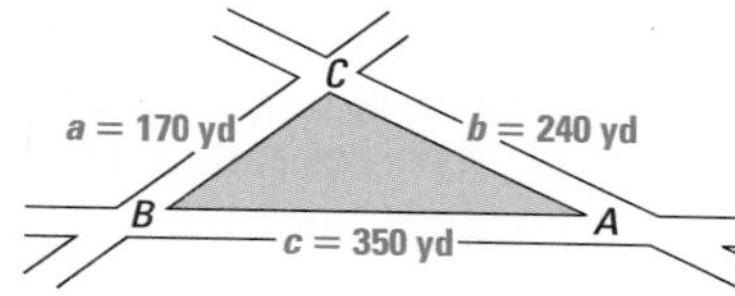

ANOTHER WAY
For an alternative method for solving the problem in Example 4, turn to page 895 for the **Problem Solving Workshop**.

Solution

STEP 1 **Find** the semiperimeter s.

$$s = \frac{1}{2}(a + b + c) = \frac{1}{2}(170 + 240 + 350) = 380$$

STEP 2 **Use** Heron's formula to find the area of $\triangle ABC$.

$$\text{Area} = \sqrt{s(s-a)(s-b)(s-c)}$$

$$= \sqrt{380(380-170)(380-240)(380-350)} \approx 18{,}300$$

▶ The area of the traffic triangle is about 18,300 square yards.

✓ GUIDED PRACTICE for Example 4

Find the area of $\triangle ABC$.

4.
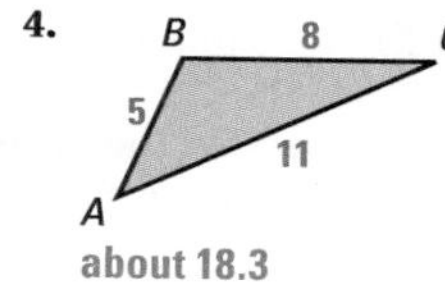

about 18.3

5.
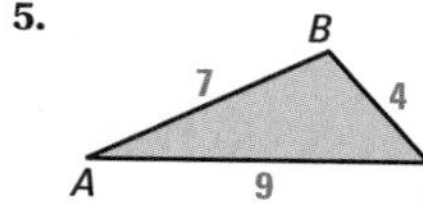

about 13.4

6.
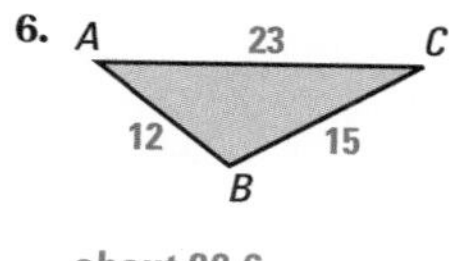

about 80.6

Extra Example 4

Find the area of the traffic triangle shown in the figure.

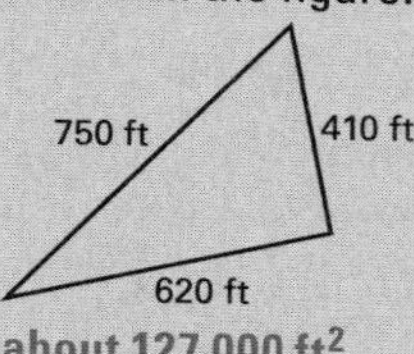

about 127,000 ft^2

Key Question to Ask for Example 4

- What is the first step in using Heron's formula? calculating the semiperimeter

Mathematical Reasoning

Students have now learned three formulas for finding the area of a triangle: the "regular" formula, $A = \frac{1}{2}bh$, the formula from Lesson 13.5, $A = \frac{1}{2}ab \sin C$, and Heron's formula. Lead a class discussion comparing these three formulas. You might ask these questions: (1) What measurements must be known in order to use each formula? (2) What are the advantages and disadvantages of each formula? (3) Which formula is easiest to use?

Closing the Lesson

Have students summarize the major points of the lesson and answer the Essential Question: In which cases can the law of cosines be used to solve a triangle?

- For $\triangle ABC$, the law of cosines says that $a^2 = b^2 + c^2 - 2bc \cos A$. Different forms of this equation can be written by switching the variables.
- Heron's formula can be used to find the area of any triangle if you know the lengths of all three sides.

The law of cosines is used to solve triangles with no right angle in the SAS and SSS cases.

Differentiated Instruction

Inclusion When first learning Heron's formula, students will benefit from having an organized method of applying the formula. For each problem a student attempts, have the student create a table with columns for "$s =$," "$a =$," "$b =$," and "$c =$." After students have identified the values of the variables, have them create columns for the differences "$s - a =$," "$s - b =$," and "$s - c =$." Finally, have them use their table entries in the formula to find the area of the triangle.

See also the *Algebra 2 Toolkit* for more strategies.

4 PRACTICE AND APPLY

Assignment Guide

Answer Transparencies available for all exercises

Basic:
Day 1: pp. 892–894
Exs. 1–20
Day 2: pp. 892–894
Exs. 21–29, 33, 43–46, 49–50

Average:
Day 1: pp. 892–894
Exs. 1–10, 14–17, 20, 36–41
Day 2: pp. 892–894
Exs. 24–35, 43–47, 49–50

Advanced:
Day 1: pp. 892–894
Exs. 1–7, 15–20, 36–42*
Day 2: pp. 892–894
Exs. 26–35, 43–50*

Block:
pp. 892–894
Exs. 1–10, 14–17, 20, 24–41, 43–47, 49–50

Differentiated Instruction

See *Algebra 2 Best Practices Toolkit* for suggestions on addressing the needs of a diverse classroom.

Homework Check

For a quick check of student understanding of key concepts, go over the following exercises:

Basic: 8, 14, 24, 43, 44
Average: 10, 16, 28, 43, 45
Advanced: 16, 18, 30, 44, 45

Extra Practice

- Student Edition, p. 1022
- Chapter 13 Resource Book: Practice levels A, B, C, pp. 63–65

Practice Worksheet

An easily-readable reduced practice page (with answers) for this lesson can be found on p. 850D.

13.6 EXERCISES

HOMEWORK KEY
○ = WORKED-OUT SOLUTIONS on p. WS23 for Exs. 17, 25, and 45
★ = STANDARDIZED TEST PRACTICE Exs. 2, 20, 33, 34, 45, and 47

SKILL PRACTICE

A

1. **VOCABULARY** Copy and complete: In a triangle with sides of length a, b, and c, $\frac{1}{2}(a+b+c)$ is called the _?_. semiperimeter

2. ★ **WRITING** Express Heron's formula in words. See margin.

2. The area of a triangle is equal to the square root of the product of the semiperimeter of the triangle and the difference between the semiperimeter and each of the sides of the triangle.

EXAMPLES 1 and 2 on pp. 889–890 for Exs. 3–20

CHOOSING A METHOD **For the given case, tell whether you would use the *law of sines* or the *law of cosines* to solve the triangle.**

3. SSS law of cosines
4. ASA law of sines
5. SSA law of sines
6. SAS law of cosines
7. AAS law of sines

SOLVING TRIANGLES **Solve $\triangle ABC$.**

8. 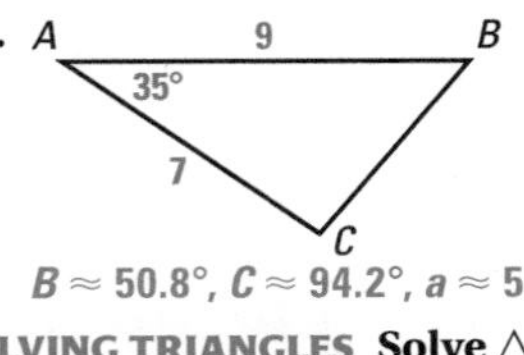

$B \approx 50.8°, C \approx 94.2°, a \approx 5.18$

9. 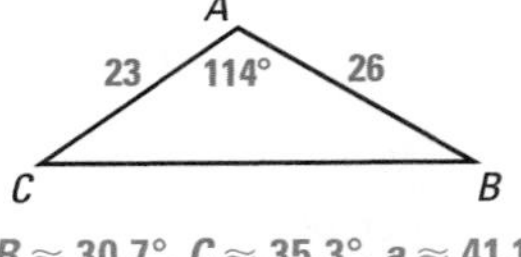

$B \approx 30.7°, C \approx 35.3°, a \approx 41.1$

10. 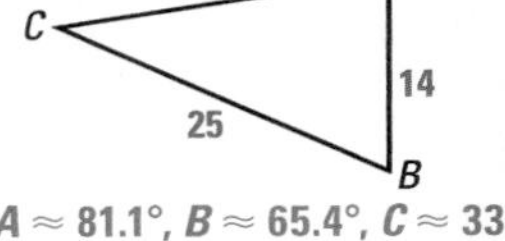

$A \approx 81.1°, B \approx 65.4°, C \approx 33.5$

SOLVING TRIANGLES **Solve $\triangle ABC$.**

11. $B = 25°, a = 8, c = 6$ $A \approx 110.4°, C \approx 44.6°, b \approx 3.60$
12. $A = 103°, b = 15, c = 24$ $B \approx 28.0°, C \approx 49.0°, a \approx 31.0$
13. $a = 18, b = 28, c = 13$ $A \approx 30.3°, B \approx 128.4°, C \approx 21.$
14. $a = 38, b = 31, c = 35$ $A \approx 70.0°, B \approx 50.1°, C \approx 59.9°$
15. $C = 48°, a = 17, b = 20$ $A \approx 55.7°, B \approx 76.3°, c \approx 15.3$
16. $B = 63°, a = 29, c = 38$ $A \approx 46.0°, C \approx 71.0°, b \approx 35.$
17. $a = 10, b = 3, c = 12$ $A \approx 42.6°, B \approx 11.7°, C \approx 125.7°$
18. $a = 23, b = 24, c = 20$ $A \approx 62.2°, B \approx 67.4°, C \approx 50.4°$
19. $C = 96°, a = 35, b = 43$ $A \approx 36.7°, B \approx 47.3°, c \approx 58.$

20. ★ **MULTIPLE CHOICE** What is the measure of angle B in $\triangle ABC$ if $a = 17$, $b = 29$, and $c = 14$? D

Ⓐ 18.7° Ⓑ 22.9° Ⓒ 111.2° Ⓓ 138.4°

B

EXAMPLE 4 on p. 891 for Exs. 21–33

FINDING AREA **Find the area of $\triangle ABC$.**

21. 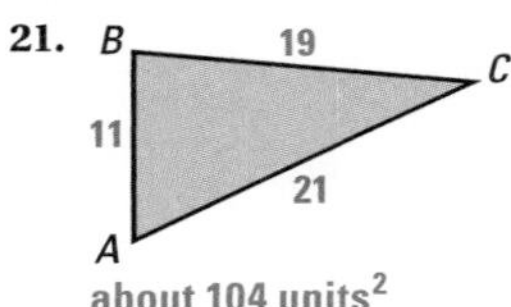

about 104 units^2

22. 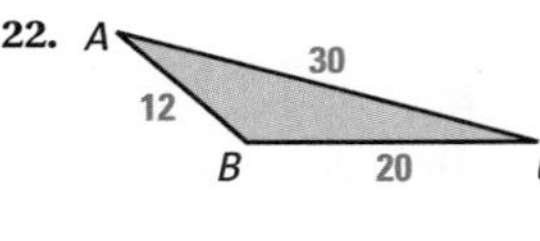

about 80.5 units^2

23. 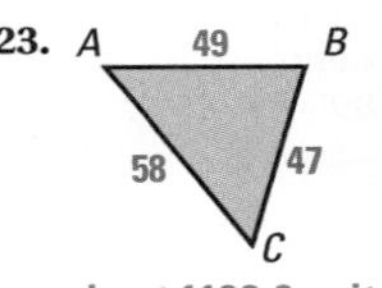

about 1108.6 units^2

FINDING AREA **Find the area of $\triangle ABC$ with the given side lengths.**

24. $a = 12, b = 7, c = 8$ about 26.9
25. $a = 5, b = 11, c = 10$ about 25.0
26. $a = 25, b = 24, c = 19$ about 214.2
27. $a = 14, b = 20, c = 28$ about 131.9
28. $a = 31, b = 23, c = 17$ about 192.2
29. $a = 81, b = 67, c = 71$ about 2259.7
30. $a = 43, b = 59, c = 48$ about 1018.2
31. $a = 51, b = 51, c = 43$ about 994.3
32. $a = 38, b = 25, c = 61$ about 234.6

33. ★ **MULTIPLE CHOICE** What is the area of $\triangle ABC$ if $a = 21$, $b = 16$, and $c = 13$? B

Ⓐ 66 units^2 Ⓑ 104 units^2 Ⓒ 1350 units^2 Ⓓ 4368 units^2

34. ★ **SHORT RESPONSE** Use the law of cosines to show that the measure of each angle of an equilateral triangle is 60°. *Explain* your reasoning. See margin.

34. $x^2 = x^2 + x^2 - 2(x)(x)\cos A \rightarrow \frac{-x^2}{-2x^2} = \cos A \rightarrow \frac{1}{2} = \cos A \rightarrow A = 60°$.
Sample answer: Since all of the sides are the same, the angles opposite those sides will also be the same.

35. **ERROR ANALYSIS** *Describe* and correct the error in finding the measure of angle A in $\triangle ABC$ if $a = 18$, $b = 15$, and $c = 10$.

$$\cos A = \frac{15^2 + 10^2 - 18^2}{2(18)(15)} \approx 0.0019$$

$$A \approx \cos^{-1} 0.0019 \approx 89.9°$$

Since you are looking for A the equation should be $a^2 = b^2 + c^2 - 2bc \cos A$; $18^2 = 15^2 + 10^2 - 2(15)(10) \cos A$, $A \approx \cos^{-1} 0.0033 \approx 89.8°$.

CHOOSING A METHOD **Use the law of sines, the law of cosines, or the Pythagorean theorem to solve $\triangle ABC$.**

40. $A \approx 81.0°$, $B \approx 59.0°$, $a \approx 41.5$ or $A \approx 19.0°$, $B \approx 121.0°$, $a \approx 13.7$

36. $A = 72°$, $B = 44°$, $b = 14$ $C = 64°$, $a \approx 19.2$, $c \approx 18.1$

37. $B = 98°$, $C = 37°$, $a = 18$ $A = 45°$, $b \approx 25.2$, $c \approx 15.3$

38. $C = 65°$, $a = 12$, $b = 21$ $A \approx 34.3°$, $B \approx 80.7°$, $c \approx 19.3$

39. $B = 90°$, $a = 15$, $c = 6$ $A \approx 68.2°$, $C \approx 21.8°$, $b \approx 16.2$

40. $C = 40°$, $b = 36$, $c = 27$

41. $a = 34$, $b = 19$, $c = 27$ $A \approx 93.7°$, $B \approx 33.9°$, $C \approx 52.4°$

C 42. **CHALLENGE** Given $\triangle ABC$ with height h, derive the law of cosines. *Explain* how the Pythagorean theorem is related to the law of cosines. See margin.

PROBLEM SOLVING

EXAMPLE 3 A on p. 890 for Ex. 43

43. **TRAPEZE ARTISTS** The diagram shows the paths of two trapeze artists who are both 5 feet long when hanging by their knees. The "flyer" on the left bar is preparing to make hand-to-hand contact with the "catcher" on the right bar. At what angle θ will the two meet? about 119.6°

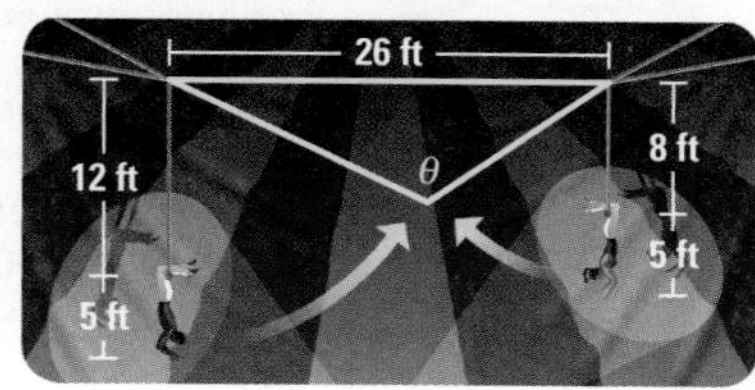

@HomeTutor for problem solving help at classzone.com

EXAMPLE 4 on p. 891 for Exs. 44–45

44. **RESEARCH TRIANGLE** Raleigh, Durham, and Chapel Hill are three cities in North Carolina that form what is known as the Research Triangle. It is about 18 miles from Raleigh to Durham, 23 miles from Raleigh to Chapel Hill, and 8 miles from Chapel Hill to Durham. Find the area of the Research Triangle. about 63 mi^2

@HomeTutor for problem solving help at classzone.com

45. ★ **SHORT RESPONSE** The diagram shows the dimensions of a plot of land. What is the area of the land in acres? (Use the fact that 1 acre = 43,560 square feet.) *Explain* how you could also determine the area by first finding the length of $\overline{AC}$. About 19.8 acres. *Sample answer:* Find AC then find the area of $\triangle ACD$ and $\triangle ABC$ using Heron's formula.

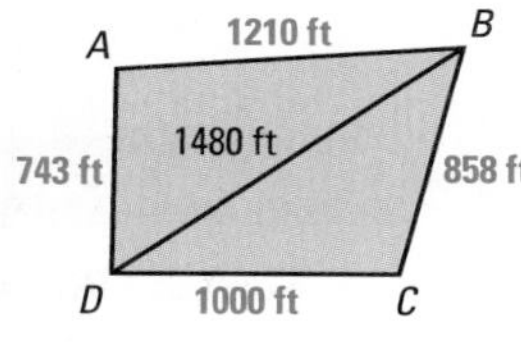

B 46. **MULTI-STEP PROBLEM** A golfer hits a drive 260 yards on a hole that is 400 yards long. The shot is 15° off target.

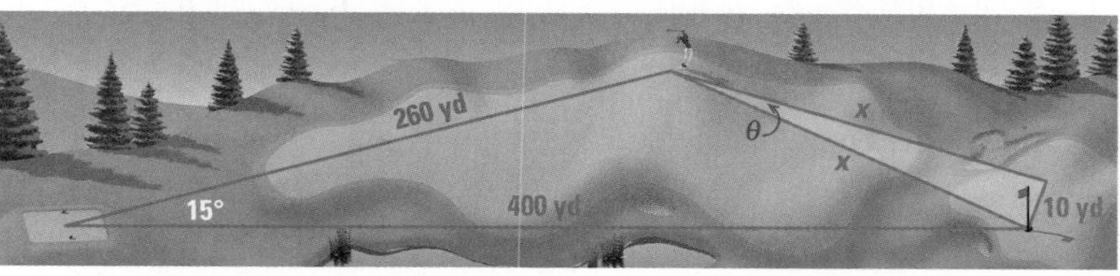

a. What is the distance x from the golfer's ball to the hole? about 163 yd

b. Assume the golfer is able to hit the ball precisely the distance found in part (a). What is the maximum angle θ by which the ball can be off target in order to land no more than 10 yards from the hole? about 3.52°

Avoiding Common Errors

Exercises 8–33 When students use calculators, emphasize that they must take care in entering numbers and symbols. They should pay special attention to the need for parentheses. Once they have an answer, they should check to see that it makes sense. If not, they may have made errors in keying in numbers or symbols.

Exercises 24–32 Some students may use the perimeter, rather than the semiperimeter, in one or more places where s appears in Heron's formula. Have these students write the formula in their notebooks, along with the equation $s = \frac{1}{2}(a + b + c)$. Teach them to always compute the semiperimeter first, and to write down the value of s, but *not* the perimeter of the triangle before they start substituting into Heron's formula.

Teaching Strategy

Exercises 13, 14, 17, 18, 20 Although it is true that three sides determine exactly one triangle (or, equivalently, that SSS is a congruence condition), students should understand that this does not mean that a triangle exists with *any* three side lengths. After they have solved $\triangle ABC$ with the side lengths given in Exercise 13, ask them to repeat the process with $a = 18$, $b = 28$, and $c = 9$. The first time they try to find an angle measure with the law of cosines, using their calculators, they will get an ERROR message. Ask them why this happens. This provides a good opportunity to review the triangle inequality from their geometry course.

42. See Additional Answers beginning on p. AA1.

5 ASSESS AND RETEACH

Daily Homework Quiz

Transparency Available

Solve $\triangle ABC$ with the given parts.

1. $B = 77°$, $a = 25$, $c = 35$
   $b \approx 38.2$, $A \approx 39.7°$, $C \approx 63.3°$
2. $a = 45$, $b = 56$, $c = 78$
   $A \approx 34.5°$, $B \approx 44.9°$, $C \approx 100.6°$
3. Two people start walking on straight paths that make an angle of 112°. After one person has walked 1.2 miles and the other has walked 1.8 miles, how far apart are they? **about 2.5 mi**
4. What is the area of a triangular banner with sides of length 28 cm, 35 cm, and 47 cm? **about 487 cm^2**

Online Quiz

Available at **classzone.com**

Diagnosis/Remediation

- Practice A, B, C in Chapter 13 Resource Book, pp. 63–65
- Study Guide in Chapter 13 Resource Book, pp. 66–67
- Practice Workbook, pp. 191–192
- @HomeTutor

Challenge

Additional challenge is available in the Chapter 13 Resource Book, p. 70.

Quiz

An easily-readable reduced copy of the quiz (with answers) on Lessons 13.5–13.6 from the Assessment Book can be found on p. 850E.

47c. About 1 h 46 min; 79.2° W of N. ***Sample answer:*** **The angle at hiker 1 is 79.2° and you have parallel lines at each hiker pointing in the North direction. The angle at hiker 2 is then an alternate interior angle, and is congruent.**

47. ★ **EXTENDED RESPONSE** Starting at the same point in a forest, two hikers take different paths. The first hiker walks due north at a speed of 2 miles per hour. The second hiker walks 60° east of north at a speed of 3 miles per hour.

a. How far apart are the hikers after 1 hour? **about 2.6 mi**

b. The two hikers carry walkie-talkies with a range of 10 miles. After how much time are the hikers out of range of each other? **about 3 h 45 min**

c. Suppose after two hours the first hiker stops and tells the second hiker to meet her. How long will it take the second hiker to meet the first hiker? In what direction should the second hiker walk? *Explain* your reasoning.

C **48. CHALLENGE** An airplane flies 55° east of north from city A to city B, a distance of 470 miles. Another airplane flies 7° north of east from city A to city C, a distance of 890 miles. What is the distance between cities B and C? **about 524 mi**

KENTUCKY MIXED REVIEW

TEST PRACTICE at classzone.com

49. The scatter plot shows the atmospheric temperature at various altitudes. What is the approximate temperature at an altitude of 5 kilometers? **C**

Ⓐ −32°C Ⓑ −25°C
Ⓒ −20°C Ⓓ −12°C

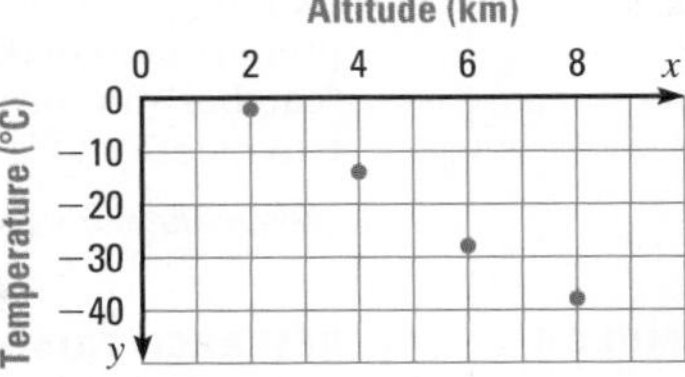

50. Which equation best represents the line that contains the point (4, 4) and is perpendicular to the line $y = -3x + 5$? **C**

Ⓐ $y = 3x - 8$ Ⓑ $y = -3x + 16$

Ⓒ $y = \frac{1}{3}x + \frac{8}{3}$ Ⓓ $y = -\frac{1}{3}x + \frac{8}{3}$

QUIZ *for Lessons 13.5–13.6*

Solve $\triangle ABC$. *(pp. 882 and 889)*

1. $A = 50°$, $B = 74°$, $c = 12$
   $C = 56°$, $a \approx 11.1$, $b \approx 13.9$
2. $C = 66°$, $a = 18$, $c = 17$ $A \approx 75.3°$, $B \approx 38.7°$, $b \approx 11.6$ or $A \approx 104.7°$, $B \approx 9.3°$, $b \approx 3.0$
3. $a = 20$, $b = 14$, $c = 23$
   $A \approx 59.7°$, $B \approx 37.2°$, $C \approx 83.1°$
4. $C = 118°$, $a = 26$, $b = 34$
   $A \approx 26.4°$, $B \approx 35.6°$, $c \approx 51.6$
5. $A = 102°$, $C = 25°$, $a = 31$
   $B = 53°$, $b \approx 25.3$, $c \approx 13.4$
6. $a = 49$, $b = 52$, $c = 38$
   $A \approx 63.8°$, $B \approx 72.2°$, $C \approx 44.0°$
7. $B = 53°$, $a = 41$, $c = 29$
   $A \approx 82.4°$, $C \approx 44.6°$, $b \approx 33.0$
8. $A = 112°$, $B = 48°$, $c = 5$
   $C = 20°$, $a \approx 13.6$, $b \approx 10.9$

Find the area of $\triangle ABC$. *(pp. 882 and 889)*

9. $B = 94°$, $a = 13$, $c = 15$ **about 97.3**
10. $C = 18°$, $a = 16$, $b = 11$ **about 27.2**
11. $a = 18$, $b = 25$, $c = 19$ **about 170.3**
12. $a = 27$, $b = 21$, $c = 37$ **about 279.1**
13. $a = 62$, $b = 47$, $c = 53$ **about 1210.4**
14. $A = 70°$, $b = 44$, $c = 36$ **about 744.2**
15.  **GEOMETRY** The base of a right triangular prism has sides of length 8 centimeters, 10 centimeters, and 13 centimeters. The height of the prism is 5 centimeters. What is the volume of the prism? *(p. 889)* **about 200 cm^3**

EXTRA PRACTICE for Lesson 13.6, p. 1022 **ONLINE QUIZ** at classzone.com

PROBLEM SOLVING WORKSHOP
LESSON 13.6

Using ALTERNATIVE METHODS

Another Way to Solve Example 4, page 891

MULTIPLE REPRESENTATIONS In Example 4 on page 891, you found the area of a triangle given the lengths of its sides by using Heron's formula. You can also find the area of the triangle by writing and solving a system of equations.

PROBLEM

URBAN PLANNING The intersection of three streets forms a piece of land called a traffic triangle. Find the area of the traffic triangle shown.

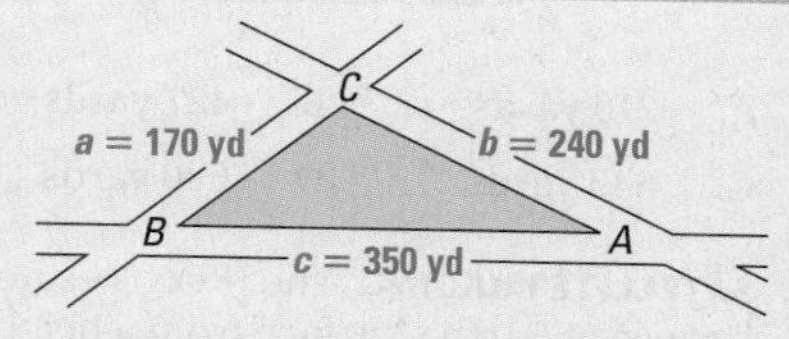

METHOD

Using a System of Equations Use a system of quadratic equations to find the triangle's height h. Then find the area of the triangle using the formula $A = \frac{1}{2}bh$.

STEP 1 **Draw** a new diagram of the triangle as shown. Let h be the height of the triangle. The altitude labeled by h divides $\overline{AB}$ into two segments of length x and $350 - x$.

STEP 2 **Use** the Pythagorean theorem to write a system of quadratic equations.

$$h^2 + x^2 = 170^2$$
$$h^2 + (350 - x)^2 = 240^2$$

STEP 3 **Solve** the first equation for h^2 to get $h^2 = 170^2 - x^2$. Substitute this expression for h^2 in the second equation, and solve for x.

$$170^2 - x^2 + (350 - x)^2 = 240^2$$
$$28{,}900 - x^2 + 122{,}500 - 700x + x^2 = 57{,}600$$
$$-700x = -93{,}800$$
$$x = 134$$

STEP 4 **Use** the Pythagorean theorem to find that $h = \sqrt{170^2 - 134^2} \approx 104.6$. So the area of the triangle is $A = \frac{1}{2}bh \approx \frac{1}{2}(350)(104.6) \approx 18{,}300$.

▶ The area of the triangle is about 18,300 square yards.

PRACTICE

FINDING AREAS **Use the method above to find the area of $\triangle ABC$ with the given side lengths.**

1. $a = 12$, $b = 17$, $c = 26$ **about 81.9**
2. $a = 63$, $b = 92$, $c = 87$ **about 2630.5**
3. $a = 101$, $b = 94$, $c = 153$ **about 4619.5**
4. **WHAT IF?** Suppose $a = 200$ yd in the problem above. Find the area of the triangle. **about 23,200 yd^2**
5. **GARDEN AREA** A triangular garden has sides with lengths 50 feet, 38 feet, and 43 feet. Use the method above to find the area of the garden. **about 792.6 ft^2**

Alternative Strategy

Example 4 on page 891 can be solved by using a system of equations. This method allows students to see how they can use the usual area formula $A = \frac{1}{2}bh$ to find the area of any triangle given the lengths of the three sides.

Avoiding Common Errors

In Step 3 of the method shown, some students may make errors in squaring the binomial. If this happens, have them write out the equation $(a - b)^2 = a^2 - 2ab + b^2$ and then substitute 350 for a and x for b.

Teaching Strategy

Your may need to explain that the substitution method for solving a linear system can also be used for a quadratic system. Show students how solving for h^2 works well in this situation and makes the algebra easier.

1. D
2. C
3. A
4. D
5. C
6. a. 8.5°
   b. 20.22 feet

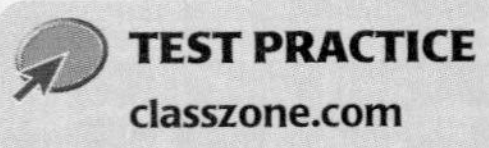

Kentucky Mixed Review

Lessons 13.4–13.6

1. **AREA OF A PROPERTY** You are buying the triangular piece of property shown. What is the approximate length of the third side?

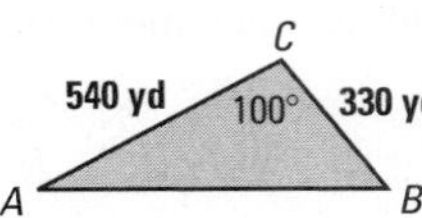

A. 210 yards B 427 yards
C. 633 yards D 680 yards

2. **SATELLITE IMAGING** The IKONOS satellite takes images of Earth's surface from a height of about 423 miles. The largest region IKONOS can view is about 1045 miles across. IKONOS can take photographs that show objects 1 meter across provided the objects lie within a region 413 miles across. What is the approximate angle IKONOS rotates as it pans across a region this size?

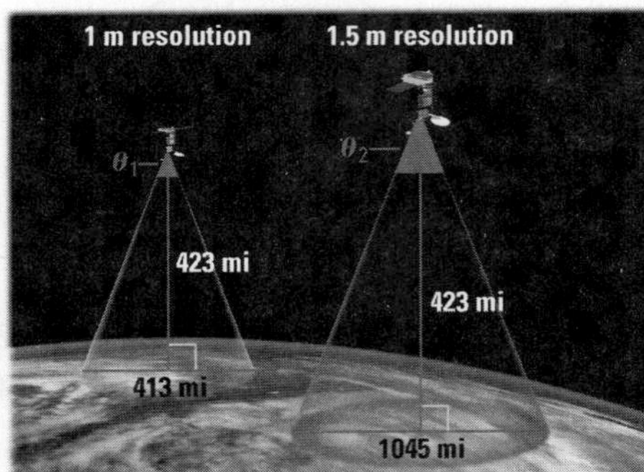

A. 26.0° B. 44.3°
C. 52.0° D. 64.0°

3. **CONSTRUCTION** You want to build a triangular concrete patio that has sides of length 8 feet, 11 feet, and 15 feet, and a thickness of 0.5 foot. One bag of cement makes 0.33 cubic foot of concrete. How many bags of cement do you need to make the patio?

A. 65 bags B. 79 bags
C. 109 bags D. 130 bags

4. **THROWING DISTANCE** On a baseball field, the pitcher's mound at P is 60.5 feet from home plate at H and 95 feet from an arc where the outfield grass begins. A ball is hit 25° to the right of the pitcher's mound and travels to the edge of the grass. What approximate distance d must an outfielder throw the ball to make an out at home plate?

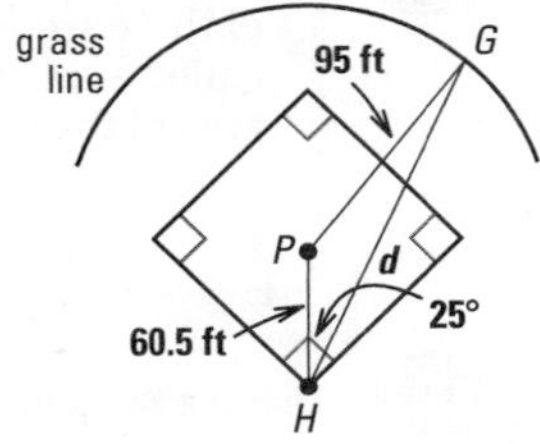

A. 47.6 feet B. 112.6 feet
C. 131.4 feet D. 146.3 feet

5. **MAXIMUM VOLUME** A trough can be made by folding a rectangular piece of metal in half and then enclosing the ends. The volume of water the trough can hold depends on how far you bend the metal. Use a graphing calculator to estimate the maximum volume of the trough. (*Hint:* First find the volume of the trough as a function of θ.)

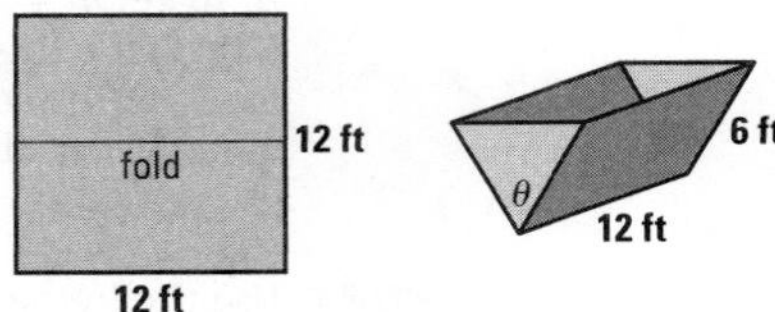

A. 54 ft^3 B. 72 ft^3
C. 216 ft^3 D. 218 ft^3

6. **OPEN-RESPONSE** After walking 20 feet into the water at a beach, you notice that the depth of the water is 3 feet.

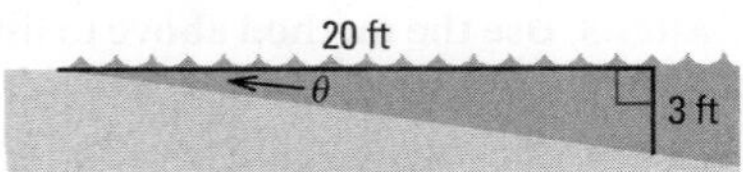

a. Find the angle θ at which the beach slopes.

b. How far would you walk diagonally to reach a depth of 3 feet?

Animated Algebra classzone.com Electronic Function Library

BIG IDEAS *For Your Notebook*

Big Idea 1

Using Trigonometric Functions

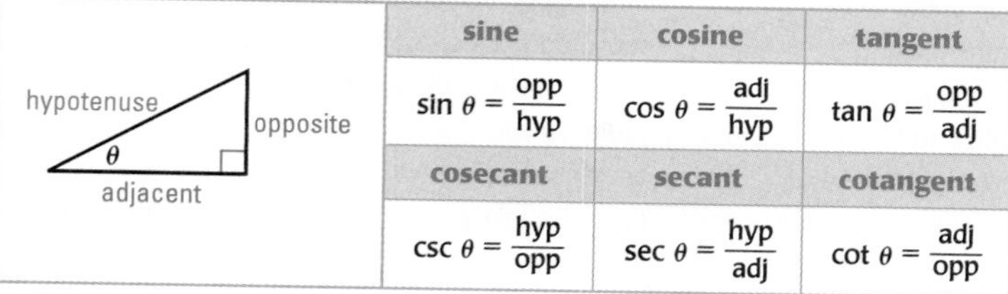

sine	cosine	tangent
$\sin\theta = \frac{\text{opp}}{\text{hyp}}$	$\cos\theta = \frac{\text{adj}}{\text{hyp}}$	$\tan\theta = \frac{\text{opp}}{\text{adj}}$
cosecant	**secant**	**cotangent**
$\csc\theta = \frac{\text{hyp}}{\text{opp}}$	$\sec\theta = \frac{\text{hyp}}{\text{adj}}$	$\cot\theta = \frac{\text{adj}}{\text{opp}}$

Using Inverse Trigonometric Functions

Inverse trigonometric functions can be used to solve trigonometric equations.

If $-1 \le a \le 1$, then the inverse sine of a is an angle θ, written $\sin^{-1} a = \theta$, where $\sin\theta = a$ and $-\frac{\pi}{2} \le \theta \le \frac{\pi}{2}$.

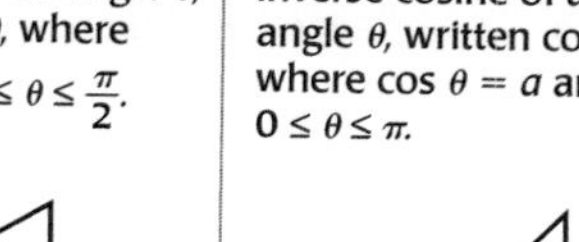

$\sin^{-1}\frac{1}{2} = 30°$

If $-1 \le a \le 1$, then the inverse cosine of a is an angle θ, written $\cos^{-1} a = \theta$, where $\cos\theta = a$ and $0 \le \theta \le \pi$.

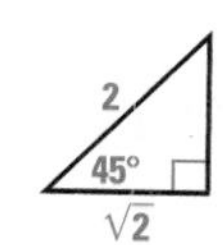

$\cos^{-1}\frac{\sqrt{2}}{2} = 45°$

If a is any real number, then the inverse tangent of a is an angle θ, written $\tan^{-1} a = \theta$, where $\tan\theta = a$ and $-\frac{\pi}{2} < \theta < \frac{\pi}{2}$.

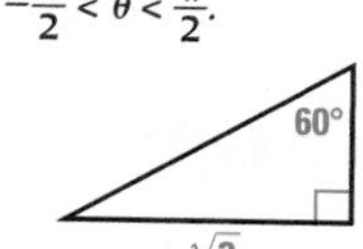

$\tan^{-1}\sqrt{3} = 60°$

Applying the Law of Sines and Law of Cosines

Use the table below to help you remember when to apply each law.

If you know this information . . .	use this law . . .	to find this information.
angle-angle-side	Law of sines	remaining sides*
angle-side-angle	Law of sines	remaining sides*
side-side-angle	Law of sines	remaining side and one angle*
side-angle-side	Law of cosines	remaining side and one angle*
side-side-side	Law of cosines	two angles*

* Find the remaining angle by using the triangle sum theorem.

Additional Resources

The following resources are available to help review the materials in this chapter.

Chapter 13 Resource Book

- Chapter Review Games and Activities, p. 71
- Cumulative Practice, Chs. 1–13, pp. 73–74

Student Resources in Spanish

eWorkbook

@HomeTutor

Vocabulary Practice

Vocabulary practice is available at **classzone.com**

Extra Example 13.1

Evaluate the six trigonometric functions of angle θ.

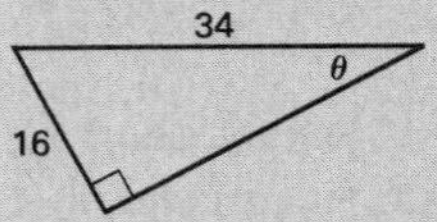

$\sin\theta = \frac{8}{17}$, $\cos\theta = \frac{15}{17}$, $\tan\theta = \frac{8}{15}$,
$\csc\theta = \frac{17}{8}$, $\sec\theta = \frac{17}{15}$, $\cot\theta = \frac{15}{8}$

13 CHAPTER REVIEW

@HomeTutor
classzone.com
• Multi-Language Glossary
• Vocabulary practice

REVIEW KEY VOCABULARY

- sine, *p. 852*
- cosine, *p. 852*
- tangent, *p. 852*
- cosecant, *p. 852*
- secant, *p. 852*
- cotangent, *p. 852*
- angle of elevation, *p. 855*
- angle of depression, *p. 855*
- initial side of an angle, *p. 859*
- terminal side of an angle, *p. 859*
- standard position of an angle, *p. 859*
- coterminal angles, *p. 860*
- radian, *p. 860*
- sector, *p. 861*
- central angle, *p. 861*
- unit circle, *p. 867*
- quadrantal angle, *p. 867*
- reference angle, *p. 868*
- inverse sine, *p. 875*
- inverse cosine, *p. 875*
- inverse tangent, *p. 875*
- law of sines, *p. 882*
- law of cosines, *p. 889*

VOCABULARY EXERCISES

1. An angle in standard position has its vertex at the origin, and its initial side lies on the positive *x*-axis.

1. **WRITING** *Describe* an angle in standard position.
2. Identify the relationship between the angles −225° and 135°. *Sample answer:* The angles are coterminal with a 45° reference angle.
3. What is the name of a circle with center at the origin and radius 1 unit? unit circle
4. Copy and complete: If $\cos\theta = a$ and $0 \le \theta \le \pi$, then the _?_ of a equals θ. inverse cosine
5. **WRITING** State the law of sines in words. *Sample answer:* The law of sines is a ratio relating the sine of an angle and its corresponding side to the other angles and corresponding sides.

REVIEW EXAMPLES AND EXERCISES

Use the review examples and exercises below to check your understanding of the concepts you have learned in each lesson of Chapter 13.

13.1 Use Trigonometry with Right Triangles *pp. 852–858*

EXAMPLE

Evaluate the six trigonometric functions of the angle θ.

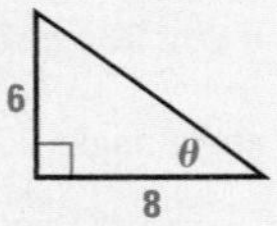

From the Pythagorean theorem, the length of the hypotenuse is $\sqrt{6^2 + 8^2} = \sqrt{100} = 10$.

$$\sin\theta = \frac{\text{opp}}{\text{hyp}} = \frac{6}{10} = \frac{3}{5} \quad \cos\theta = \frac{\text{adj}}{\text{hyp}} = \frac{8}{10} = \frac{4}{5} \quad \tan\theta = \frac{\text{opp}}{\text{adj}} = \frac{6}{8} = \frac{3}{4}$$

$$\csc\theta = \frac{\text{hyp}}{\text{opp}} = \frac{10}{6} = \frac{5}{3} \quad \sec\theta = \frac{\text{hyp}}{\text{adj}} = \frac{10}{8} = \frac{5}{4} \quad \cot\theta = \frac{\text{adj}}{\text{opp}} = \frac{8}{6} = \frac{4}{3}$$

EXERCISES

EXAMPLES 1 and 3 on pp. 852–854 for Exs. 6–7

6. In $\triangle ABC$, $a = 4$, $b = 5$, and $C = 90°$. Evaluate the six trigonometric functions of angle B. $\sin B = \frac{5\sqrt{41}}{41}$, $\cos B = \frac{4\sqrt{41}}{41}$, $\tan B = \frac{5}{4}$, $\csc B = \frac{\sqrt{41}}{5}$, $\sec B = \frac{\sqrt{41}}{4}$, $\cot B = \frac{4}{5}$
7. **HOT AIR BALLOON** You are standing 50 meters from a hot air balloon that is preparing to take off. The angle of elevation to the top of the balloon is 28°. Find the height of the balloon. about 26.6 m

@HomeTutor
classzone.com
Chapter Review Practice

13.2 Define General Angles and Use Radian Measure *pp. 859–865*

EXAMPLE

Convert 110° to radians and $\frac{7\pi}{12}$ radians to degrees.

$$110° = 110°\left(\frac{\pi \text{ radians}}{180°}\right) = \frac{11\pi}{18} \text{ radians}$$

$$\frac{7\pi}{12} \text{ radians} = \left(\frac{7\pi}{12} \text{ radians}\right)\left(\frac{180°}{\pi \text{ radians}}\right) = 105°$$

EXERCISES

XAMPLE 3
n p. 861
r Exs. 8–11

Convert the degree measure to radians or the radian measure to degrees.

8. 145° $\frac{29\pi}{36}$
9. −80° $-\frac{4\pi}{9}$
10. $\frac{4\pi}{3}$ 240°
11. $\frac{11\pi}{6}$ 330°

13.3 Evaluate Trigonometric Functions of Any Angle *pp. 866–872*

EXAMPLE

Evaluate sec 120°.

The reference angle is $\theta' = 180° - 120° = 60°$. The secant function is negative in Quadrant II, so you can write:

$$\sec 120° = -\sec 60° = -2$$

EXERCISES

XAMPLE 4
n p. 869
r Exs. 12–15

Evaluate the function without using a calculator.

12. tan 330° $-\frac{\sqrt{3}}{3}$
13. csc (−405°) $-\sqrt{2}$
14. $\sin \frac{13\pi}{6}$ $\frac{1}{2}$
15. $\sec \frac{11\pi}{3}$ 2

13.4 Evaluate Inverse Trigonometric Functions *pp. 875–880*

EXAMPLE

Evaluate $\tan^{-1} 1$ in both radians and degrees.

When $-\frac{\pi}{2} < \theta < \frac{\pi}{2}$, or $-90° < \theta < 90°$, the angle θ whose tangent is 1 is:

$$\theta = \tan^{-1} 1 = \frac{\pi}{4} \quad \text{or} \quad \theta = \tan^{-1} 1 = 45°$$

EXERCISES

KAMPLES
and 4
pp. 876–877
Exs. 16–17

16. Evaluate $\sin^{-1}(-0.5)$ in both radians and degrees. $-\frac{\pi}{6}$, −30°
17. **RAMP** You use a 12 foot ramp to load items into a van. If the floor of the van is 4 feet off the ground, what is the angle of elevation of the ramp? about 19.5°

Extra Example 13.2
Convert 260° to radians and $\frac{9\pi}{5}$ radians to degrees. $\frac{13\pi}{9}$ radians; 324°

Extra Example 13.3
Evaluate cot 330°. $-\sqrt{3}$

Extra Example 13.4
Evaluate $\cos^{-1}(-1)$ in both radians and degrees. π radians or 180°

13 CHAPTER REVIEW

Extra Example 13.5

Solve $\triangle ABC$ with $B = 27°$, $C = 54°$, and $c = 36$. $A = 99°$, $a \approx 44.0$, $b \approx 20.2$

Extra Example 13.6

Solve $\triangle ABC$ with $a = 13$, $b = 8$, and $c = 11$. $A \approx 84.8°$, $B \approx 37.8°$, $C \approx 57.4°$

13.5 Apply the Law of Sines

pp. 882–888

EXAMPLE

Solve $\triangle ABC$ with $A = 28°$, $C = 74°$, and $b = 22$.

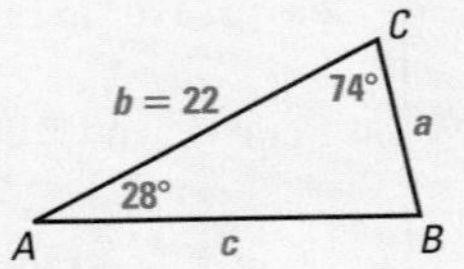

Find angle B: $B = 180° - 28° - 74° = 78°$.

Use the law of sines to solve for a and c.

$$\frac{a}{\sin 28°} = \frac{22}{\sin 78°} \qquad \frac{c}{\sin 74°} = \frac{22}{\sin 78°}$$

$$a = \frac{22 \sin 28°}{\sin 78°} \approx 10.6 \qquad c = \frac{22 \sin 74°}{\sin 78°} \approx 21.6$$

▶ For $\triangle ABC$, $B = 78°$, $a \approx 10.6$, and $c \approx 21.6$.

EXERCISES

EXAMPLES 1, 2, 3 and 4 on pp. 882–884 for Exs. 18–21

Solve $\triangle ABC$. (*Hint:* Some of the "triangles" may have no solution and some may have two solutions.)

18. $A = 43°$, $C = 83°$, $b = 12$
$B = 54°$, $a \approx 10.1$, $c \approx 14.7$

19. $B = 104°$, $b = 25$, $c = 18$
$A \approx 31.7°$, $C \approx 44.3°$, $a \approx 13.5$

20. $C = 55°$, $a = 17$, $c = 15$
$A \approx 68.2°$, $B \approx 56.8°$, $b \approx 15.3$, or $A \approx 111.8°$, $B \approx 13.2°$, $b \approx 4.2$

21. $B = 60°$, $C = 73°$, $b = 20$
$A = 47°$, $a \approx 16.9$, $c \approx 22.1$

13.6 Apply the Law of Cosines

pp. 889–894

EXAMPLE

Solve $\triangle ABC$ with $A = 66°$, $b = 16$, and $c = 21$.

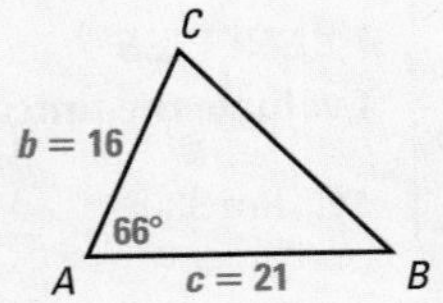

Use the law of cosines to find the length a.

$$a^2 = b^2 + c^2 - 2bc \cos A$$

$$a^2 = 16^2 + 21^2 - 2(16)(21) \cos 66°$$

$$a^2 \approx 423.7$$

$$a \approx 20.6$$

Now find angle B and angle C.

$$\frac{\sin B}{16} = \frac{\sin 66°}{20.6}$$

$$\sin B = \frac{16 \sin 66°}{20.6} \approx 0.7095$$

$$B = \sin^{-1} 0.7095 \approx 45.2°$$

$$C \approx 180° - 66° - 45.2° \approx 68.8°$$

▶ For $\triangle ABC$, $B \approx 45.2°$, $C \approx 68.8°$, and $a \approx 20.6$.

EXERCISES

EXAMPLES 1 and 2 on pp. 889–890 for Exs. 22–24

Solve $\triangle ABC$.

22. $a = 19$, $b = 11$, $c = 14$
$A \approx 98.2°$, $B \approx 35.0°$, $C \approx 46.8°$

23. $B = 75°$, $a = 20$, $c = 17$
$A \approx 58.7°$, $C \approx 46.3°$, $b \approx 22.6$

24. $a = 30$, $b = 35$, $c = 39$
$A \approx 47.4°$, $B \approx 59.3°$, $C \approx 73$

13 CHAPTER TEST

1. $\sin\theta = \frac{4\sqrt{97}}{97}$, $\cos\theta = \frac{9\sqrt{97}}{97}$, $\tan\theta = \frac{4}{9}$, csc $\theta = \frac{\sqrt{97}}{4}$, sec $\theta = \frac{\sqrt{97}}{9}$, $\cot\theta = \frac{9}{4}$

2. $\sin\theta = \frac{\sqrt{57}}{11}$, $\cos\theta = \frac{8}{11}$, $\tan\theta = \frac{\sqrt{57}}{8}$, $\csc\theta = \frac{11\sqrt{57}}{57}$, $\sec\theta = \frac{11}{8}$, $\cot\theta = \frac{8\sqrt{57}}{57}$

3. $\sin\theta = \frac{\sqrt{13}}{7}$, $\cos\theta = \frac{6}{7}$, $\tan\theta = \frac{\sqrt{13}}{6}$, $\csc\theta = \frac{7\sqrt{13}}{13}$, $\sec\theta = \frac{7}{6}$, $\cot\theta = \frac{6\sqrt{13}}{13}$

Evaluate the six trigonometric functions of the angle θ.

1.

4
9
θ

2.

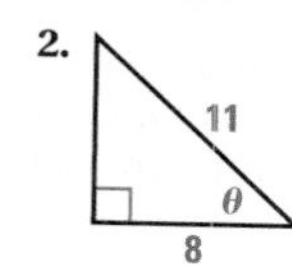

3.

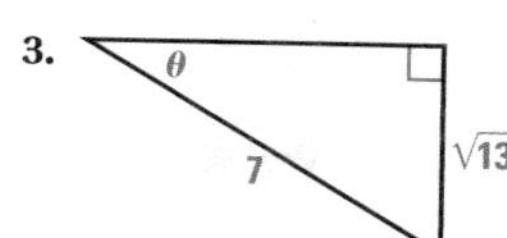

Convert the degree measure to radians or the radian measure to degrees.

4. $260°$ $\frac{13\pi}{9}$ **5.** $-50°$ $-\frac{5\pi}{18}$ **6.** $\frac{4\pi}{5}$ $144°$ **7.** $\frac{8\pi}{3}$ $480°$

Evaluate the function without using a calculator.

8. $\tan 150°$ $-\frac{\sqrt{3}}{3}$ **9.** $\sec(-480°)$ -2 **10.** $\sin\left(-\frac{5\pi}{3}\right)$ $\frac{\sqrt{3}}{2}$ **11.** $\cos\frac{11\pi}{6}$ $\frac{\sqrt{3}}{2}$

Evaluate the expression in both radians and degrees without using a calculator.

12. $\cos^{-1} 1$ $0, 0°$ **13.** $\tan^{-1}\sqrt{3}$ $\frac{\pi}{3}, 60°$ **14.** $\sin^{-1}\left(-\frac{\sqrt{2}}{2}\right)$ $-\frac{\pi}{4}, -45°$ **15.** $\cos^{-1}\left(-\frac{\sqrt{3}}{2}\right)$ $\frac{5\pi}{6}, 150°$

Solve $\triangle ABC$. (*Hint:* Some of the "triangles" may have no solution and some may have two solutions.)

16. $A = 47°, C = 32°, c = 12$ $B = 101°, a \approx 16.6, b \approx 22.2$

17. $a = 24, b = 12, c = 17$ $A \approx 110.5°, B \approx 27.9°, C \approx 41.6°$

18. $B = 63°, a = 11, b = 8$ no triangle

19. $C = 101°, a = 23, b = 19$ $A \approx 44.0°, B \approx 35.0°, c \approx 32.5$

20. $a = 24, b = 30, c = 21$ $A \approx 52.6°, B \approx 83.3°, C \approx 44.1°$

21. $A = 26°, B = 77°, c = 50$ $C = 77°, a \approx 22.5, b = 50$

Find the area of $\triangle ABC$.

22. $A = 81°, b = 16, c = 18$ about 142.2

23. $a = 8, b = 6, c = 7$ about 20.3

24. $a = 25, b = 24, c = 38$ about 293.8

25. $C = 111°, a = 7, b = 13$ about 42.5

26. $a = 16, b = 33, c = 24$ about 180.9

27. $B = 61°, a = 12, c = 18$ about 94.5

28. SURVEYING To measure the width of a river, you plant a stake at point A on one side of the riverbank, directly across from a tree stump at point B on the other side of the riverbank. From point A, you walk 80 meters along the riverbank to point C. You find the measure of angle C to be 39°. What is the width w of the river? about 64.8 m

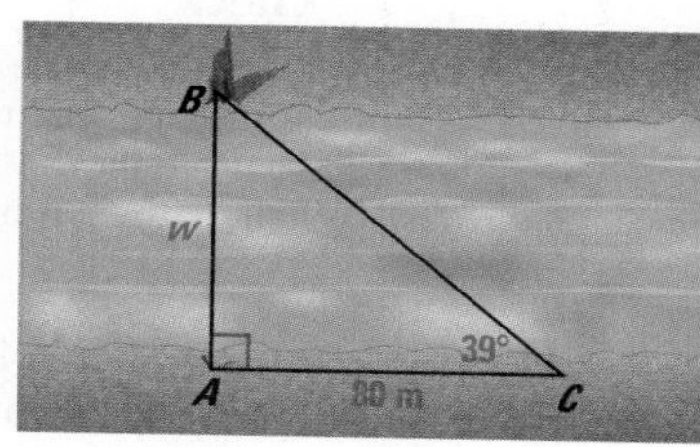

29. CONSTRUCTION A crane has a 200 foot arm with a lower end that is 5 feet off the ground. The arm has to reach to the top of a building that is 160 feet high. At what angle θ should the arm be set? about 50.8°

30. NAVIGATION A boat travels 40 miles due west before turning 20° and traveling an additional 25 miles. How far is the boat from its point of departure? about 64.1 mi

Additional Resources

Assessment Book

- Chapter Test, Levels A, B, C, pp. 185–190
- Standardized Chapter Test, pp. 191–192
- SAT/ACT Chapter Test, pp. 193–194
- Alternative Assessment, pp. 195–196

Test Generator CD-ROM

Chapter Test

Easily-readable reduced copies (with answers) of Chapter Test B, the Standardized Chapter Test, and the Alternative Assessment from the Assessment Book can be found on pp. 850E–850F.

MULTIPLE-CHOICE QUESTIONS

After solving a multiple-choice problem, use estimation to check your answer. Eliminate unreasonably small or unreasonably large values to increase confidence in your answer.

PROBLEM 1

What is the volume of the right triangular prism shown?

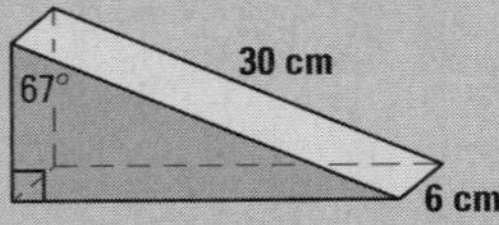

A. 969 cm^3 B. 1,938 cm^3

C. 2,485 cm^3 D. 12,060 cm^3

Plan

The volume of the prism shown is the area of its triangular cross section times the depth, 6 cm. To find the area of the triangle, the base and height are needed. These can be found using trigonometry.

Solution

Base of the triangle: $\sin 67° \times 30 \text{ cm} \approx 27.6 \text{ cm}$
Height of the triangle: $\cos 67° \times 30 \text{ cm} \approx 11.7 \text{ cm}$

We can use these values to find the area of the triangular cross-section:

$$A = \frac{1}{2}bh = \frac{1}{2} \cdot 27.6 \cdot 11.7 = 161.46 \text{ cm}^2$$

Finally, the volume of the prism is the area of cross section times the depth:

$$V = A \times \text{depth} \approx 161.46 \times 6 \approx 969 \text{ cm}^3$$

Check

The hypotenuse of the triangular cross section is 30 cm. That means that the base of the triangle must be *less* than 30 cm. The triangle is approximately a 30°-60°-90° triangle, the "legs" of which are always in a 1 : 2 ratio. A rough estimate of the height, then, is half of 30 cm, or 15 cm. Finally, a rough estimate of the volume is

$$\frac{1}{2} \times 30 \text{ cm} \times 15 \text{ cm} \times 6 \text{ cm} = 1{,}350 \text{ cm}^3$$

Answer choices C and D are substantially larger than 1350 cm^3. Since this value above is based on an overestimate of the length of the base, answer choice A is more reasonable than answer choice B.

▸ The correct answer is A.

TEST PREPARATION

PROBLEM 2

Marta kicks a soccer ball with an initial velocity of 40.0 feet per second at an angle of 45°. Luisa kicks another soccer ball at an angle of 25°. The balls traveled the same horizontal distance. With what initial velocity did Luisa kick the ball?

A. 20.9 ft/sec B. 40.0 ft/sec

C. 45.7 ft/sec D. 49.89 ft/sec

Plan

First, use the formula $d = \frac{v^2}{32}\sin 2\theta$ to find the distance of Marta's ball. Then use this result to solve for the velocity of Luisa's ball.

Solution

Using the initial velocity of 40 feet per second and the angle 45°, the horizontal distance traveled by Marta's ball is:

$$d = \frac{v^2}{32}\sin 2\theta = \frac{(40.0)^2}{32}\sin\left(2(45^\circ)\right) = 50 \sin 90^\circ = 50 \text{ feet}$$

Luisa's ball also traveled 50 feet. Find the initial velocity of Luisa's ball by solving the equation $d = \frac{v^2}{32}\sin 2\theta$ with the value $d = 50$ and $\theta = 25°$.

$$50 = \frac{v^2}{32}\text{si}\,(2(25^\circ)) \qquad v = +\sqrt{\frac{50 \cdot 32}{\sin(50^\circ)}} \approx 45.7 \text{ feet/second}$$

Check

Because Marta's angle of elevation was optimal (45°), she needs to kick the ball with less velocity than anyone else kicking it the same distance. So Luisa's velocity must be greater. This confirms that the answer 45.7 feet/second is reasonable.

▶ The correct answer is C.

PRACTICE

Explain why you can eliminate the highlighted answer choice.

1. What is the angle of the ramp shown below, to the nearest hundredth of a degree?

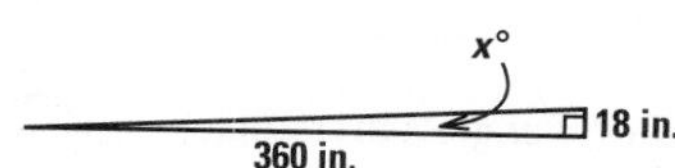

A. 0.05° B. 2.86° C. 30.96° D.✗ 87.14°

2. According to the ADA Accessibility Guidelines, the maximum slope of a wheelchair ramp is 1:12. What is the maximum angle of elevation of such a ramp?

A.✗ 0.08° B. 4.76° C. 4.76° D. 85.24°

TEST PREPARATION

Kentucky Test Preparation

KY

1. **The angle is unreasonable because it is too large. In fact, the correct answer is the complement of this angle.**
2. **This angle is unreasonable because it is only a fraction of 1 degree and is therefore too small.**

1. C
2. D
3. D
4. B
5. A
6. A
7. B
8. A

Kentucky Test Practice

TEST PREPARATION

MULTIPLE-CHOICE

1. Kepler's second law states that an imaginary line connecting the center of a planet and the center of the sun sweeps out equal areas in equal time intervals. The diagram below shows the orbit of Mars over a ten day period.

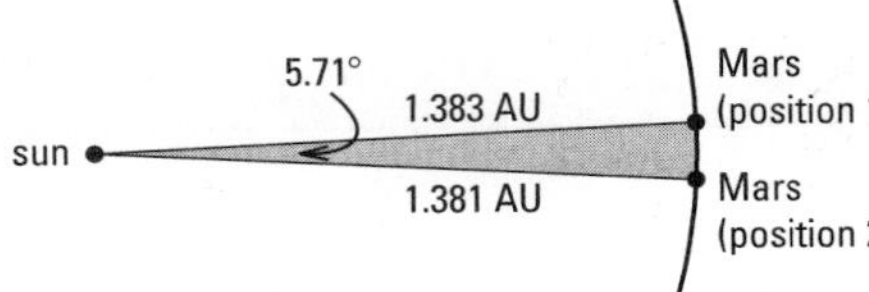

What is the approximate area Mars swept out during this time? (*Note:* 1 AU is 1 astronomical unit, which equals about 93 million miles.)

A. 8.8×10^6 mi^2 B. 8.8×10^7 mi^2

C. 8.2×10^{14} mi^2 D. 8.2×10^{15} mi^2

2. A unicyclist is traveling forward in a straight line. The diameter of the wheel of her unicycle is 24 inches. How far does the unicycle travel if the wheel rotates 2160°?

A. 6 ft, 3 in. B. 12 ft

C. 18 ft, 10 in. D. 37 ft, 8 in.

3. You are standing 30 feet from the base of a tree. The angle of elevation from your eyes to the top of the tree is 70°. If the height at eye level is 5 feet, what is the height of the tree to the nearest foot?

A. 15 ft B. 16 ft

C. 33 ft D. 87 ft

4. What is the radius of a sector whose arc length is $\frac{10\pi}{3}$ inches and whose area is $\frac{25\pi}{3}$ in.^{2}?

A. $\sqrt{5}$ inches B. 5 inches

C. 5π inches D. 25 inches

5. What is the degree measure of angle A in triangle ABC if $a = 13$, $b = 9$, and $c = 77$?

A. 108° B. 128°

C. 142° D. 162°

6. A tennis player is practicing her serve. She aims for a mark 57 feet along the ground from her. She hits the ball when it is 9 feet in the air. The ball travels in a straight line and hits the mark. Which equation below can be used to find the angle θ that the path of the ball makes with the ground?

A. $\tan \theta = \frac{9}{57}$ B. $\sin \theta = \frac{9}{57}$

C. $\tan \theta = \frac{57}{9}$ D. $\sin \theta = \frac{57}{9}$

7. The diagrams below show the distances between atoms in a water molecule in liquid and ice forms. The measurements are given in picometers (pm), where 1 pm = 10^{-12} m.

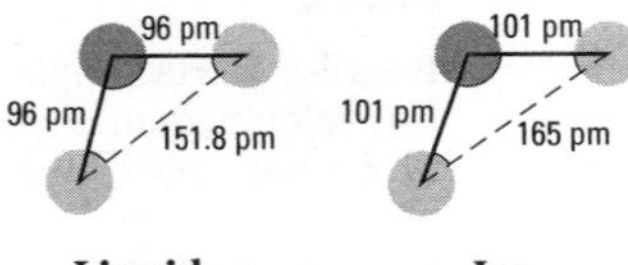

Which statement describes the obtuse angles?

A. The obtuse angle for liquid is larger.

B. The obtuse angle for ice is larger.

C. The obtuse angles are equal in size.

D. The angles cannot be determined.

8. To the nearest whole number, what is the approximate area of the triangle below?

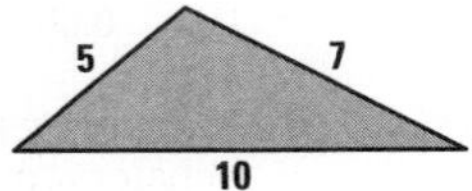

A. 16 B. 18 C. 25 D. 35

MULTIPLE-CHOICE

9. Which angle measure is shown in the diagram?

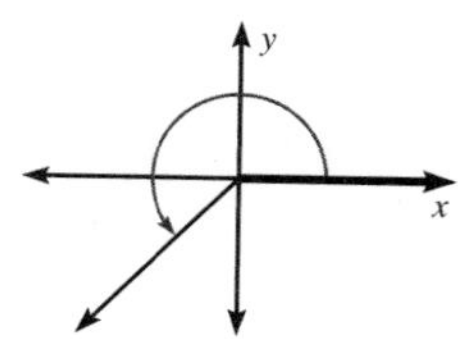

A. $\frac{\pi}{4}$ radians B. $\frac{3\pi}{4}$ radians

C. $\frac{5\pi}{4}$ radians D. $\frac{3\pi}{2}$ radians

10. What is the approximate value of a in $\triangle ABC$ if $A = 85°$, $B = 27°$, and $c = 5.0$ cm?

A. 1.0 cm B. 5.4 cm

C. 5.9 cm D. 11.0 cm

11. What is the reference angle for 300°?

A. 30° B. 60°

C. 120° D. 240°

12. If θ is an acute angle of a right triangle and $\sin\theta = \frac{3}{5}$, what is the value of $\cos\theta$?

A. $\frac{2}{5}$ B $\frac{3}{5}$ C. $\frac{3}{4}$ D. $\frac{4}{5}$

13. What angle, in degrees, is equivalent to $\frac{5\pi}{6}$ radians?

A. 30° B. 150°

C. 300° D. 330°

14. What is the value of $\sin^{-1} 0.5$ in degrees?

A. 0.008° B. 0.47°

C. 0.52° D. 30°

15. Let (10, 24) be a point on the terminal side of an angle θ in standard position. What is the value of $\sec\theta$?

A. $\frac{10}{24}$ B. $\frac{26}{24}$ C. $\frac{24}{10}$ D. $\frac{26}{10}$

OPEN-RESPONSE

16. A boat uses 50 feet of rope to drop anchor in a lake. The angle θ that the rope makes with the bottom of the lake is 20°.

a. Find the depth of the water.

b. The boat moves to deeper water but still lets out the same amount of rope when dropping anchor. If the horizontal distance from the boat to the anchor is 37 feet, what is the new measure of θ?

c. *Describe* how θ changes as the boat travels to deeper water with 50 feet of anchor rope. Assume the rope is always taut.

17. You are making a lampshade out of fabric for the lamp shown. The pattern for the lampshade is shown in the diagram.

a. Use the smaller sector to write an equation that relates θ and x.

b. Use the larger sector to write an equation that relates θ and $x + 10$.

c. Solve the system of equations from parts (a) and (b) to find x and θ.

d. Find the amount of fabric (in square inches) that you will use.

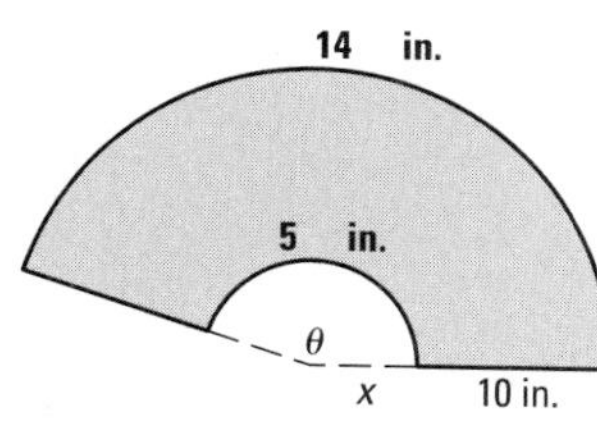

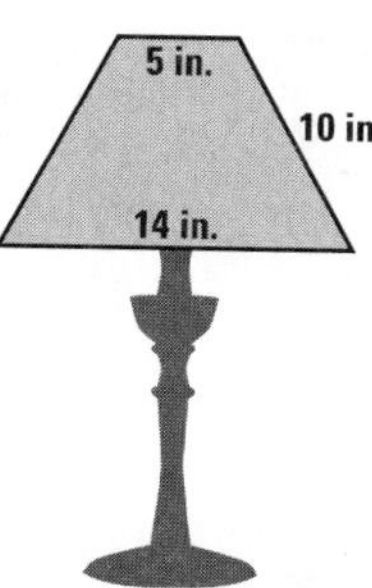

TEST PREPARATION

9. C
10. B
11. B
12. D
13. B
14. D
15. D
16. a. 17.1 feet
b. about 42.3°
c. *Sample answer:* The angle gets larger.
17. a. $5\pi = x\theta$
b. $14\pi = (x + 10)\theta$
c. $5\frac{5}{9}, \frac{9\pi}{10}$
d. about 298.5 in.^{2}

14 Pacing and Assignment Guide

REGULAR SCHEDULE

Pre-AP For pacing and assignments for a Pre-AP course, see the *Algebra 2 Toolkit.*

Lesson	Les. Day	BASIC	AVERAGE	ADVANCED
14.1 *MA-HS-5.1.3*	Day 1	pp. 912–914 Exs. 1–15	pp. 912–914 Exs. 1–15	pp. 912–914 Exs. 1–15
	Day 2	pp. 912–914 Exs. 16–19, 29–31, 34–35	pp. 912–914 Exs. 16–25, 29–32, 34–35	pp. 912–914 Exs. 19–35*
14.2 *MA-HS-5.1.3*	Day 1	pp. 919–922 Exs. 1–14, 21, 50, 51	pp. 919–922 Exs. 1–8, 12–17, 21, 50, 51	pp. 919–922 Exs. 1–8, 15–21, 50, 51
	Day 2	pp. 919–922 Exs. 22–30, 34–38, 53, 56–57	pp. 919–922 Exs. 25–30, 34, 35, 38–40, 42–47, 52–54, 56–57	pp. 919–922 Exs. 30–35, 39–49*, 52–57*
14.3	Day 1	pp. 927–930 Exs. 1–5, 9–15, 22–28, 40–42, 47	pp. 927–930 Exs. 1, 2, 4–6, 9, 14–18, 22–24, 28–32, 35, 39–44, 46	pp. 927–930 Exs. 1, 2, 7–9, 18–21, 24, 29–45*
14.4 **MA-HS-5.3.6**	Day 1	EP p. 1014 Exs. 15–18, 20; pp. 935–937 Exs. 1–6, 9–15 odd, 16–18, 22–26, 30, 31, 41–43, 47	pp. 935–937 Exs. 1, 2, 5–7, 10–12, 15, 18–23, 26–28, 30–33, 36–39, 41–44, 47	pp. 935–937 Exs. 1, 2, 7, 8, 13–15, 19–21, 27–29, 32–40*, 42–45
14.5 *MA-HS-5.1.3*	Day 1	pp. 944–947 Exs. 1–14, 23–27, 31	pp. 944–947 Exs. 1–8, 12–21, 23–28, 30	pp. 944–947 Exs. 1, 5, 6, 13–29*
14.6	Day 1	pp. 952–954 Exs. 1–14, 18–24, 31–34, 40–42, 46	pp. 952–954 Exs. 1, 2, 6–8, 11, 14–18, 24–27, 31–38, 40–44, 47	pp. 952–954 Exs. 1, 2, 9–11, 16–18, 27–30, 32–45*, 47
14.7	Day 1	EP p. 1017 Exs. 30–32; pp. 959–962 Exs. 1–7, 11–14, 16–19, 21–23, 27–29, 50, 51	pp. 959–962 Exs. 1, 2, 5–9, 11, 13–20, 23–25, 28, 29, 50, 51	pp. 959–962 Exs. 1, 2, 6–15, 18–20, 23–29, 50, 51
	Day 2	pp. 959–962 Exs. 30–33, 36–38, 42–44, 52–54, 57–58	pp. 959–962 Exs. 30–47, 52–55, 57	pp. 959–962 Exs. 30–49*, 52–56*
Review	Day 1	pp. 965–968 Exs. 1–35	pp. 965–968 Exs. 1–35	pp. 965–968 Exs. 1–35
Assess	Day 1	Chapter 14 Test	Chapter 14 Test	Chapter 14 Test
Yearly Pacing		Chapter 14 Total – 12 days	Chapters 1–14 Total – 160 days	Remaining – 0 days

*Challenge Exercises EP = Extra Practice SRH = Skills Review Handbook

BLOCK SCHEDULE

DAY 1	DAY 2	DAY 3	DAY 4	DAY 5	DAY 6
14.1	**14.2**	**14.3**	**14.5**	**14.7**	**REVIEW**
pp. 912–914 Exs. 1–25, 29–32, 34–35	pp. 919–922 Exs. 1–8, 12–17, 21, 25–30, 34, 35, 38–40, 42–47, 50–54, 56–57	pp. 927–930 Exs. 1, 2, 4–6, 9, 14–18, 22–24, 28–32, 35, 39–44, 46	pp. 944–947 Exs. 1–8, 12–21, 23–28, 30	pp. 959–962 Exs. 1, 2, 5–9, 11, 13–20, 23–25, 28–47, 50–55, 57	pp. 965–968 Exs. 1–35
		14.4	**14.6**		**ASSESS**
		pp. 935–937 Exs. 1, 2, 5–7, 10–12, 15, 18–23, 26–28, 30–33, 36–39, 41–44, 47	pp. 952–954 Exs. 1, 2, 6–8, 11, 14–18, 24–27, 31–38, 40–44, 47		Chapter 14 Test

Yearly Pacing Chapter 14 Total – 6 days Chapters 1–14 Total – 80 days Remaining – 0 days

Chapter Resource Guide 14

RESOURCE MANAGER

Chapter Resource Book

CHAPTER SUPPORT							
Parents as Partners (Chapter Overview with home involvement exercises and activity)						p. 1	
LESSON SUPPORT **Standards**	14.1 *MA-HS-5.1.3*	14.2 *MA-HS-5.1.3*	14.3	14.4 **MA-HS-5.3.6**	14.5 *MA-HS-5.1.3*	14.6	14.7
Teaching Guide/Lesson Plan	p. 3	p. 15	p. 26	p. 38	p. 50	p. 62	p. 72
Activity Masters	p. 5	p. 17					
Technology Activities & Keystrokes			p. 28	p. 40	p. 52		p. 74
Activity Support Masters							
Practice (3 levels)	p. 7	p. 18	p. 30	p. 41	p. 54	p. 64	p. 77
Study Guide	p. 10	p. 21	p. 33	p. 44	p. 57	p. 67	p. 80
Catch-Up for Absent Students	p. 12	p. 23	p. 35	p. 46	p. 59	p. 69	p. 82
Problem Solving/Application	p. 13	p. 24	p. 36	p. 47	p. 60	p. 70	p. 83
Challenge Practice	p. 14	p. 25	p. 37	p. 49	p. 61	p. 71	p. 84

REVIEW			
Chapter Review Games and Activities	p. 85	Cumulative Practice	p. 87
Project with Rubric	p. 86	Resource Book Answers	A1

Transparencies	*14.1*	*14.2*	*14.3*	*14.4*	*14.5*	*14.6*	*14.7*
Warm-Up/Daily Homework Quiz	✔	✔	✔	✔	✔	✔	✔
Notetaking Guide	✔	✔	✔	✔	✔	✔	✔
Teacher Support	✔	✔					
Answer Transparencies	✔	✔	✔	✔	✔	✔	✔

ASSESSMENT BOOK

Quizzes	p. 197	SAT/ACT Chapter Test	p. 208
Chapter Tests (3 levels)	p. 200	Alternative Assessment with Rubric	p. 210
Standardized Chapter Test	p. 206	Cumulative Test	p. 212

TECHNOLOGY

- Easy Planner
- Test and Practice Generator
- Power Presentations
- @HomeTutor
- Activity Generator
- Animated Algebra
- Classzone.com
- eEdition Plus Online
- eWorkbook Plus Online
- ML Assessment System

ADDITIONAL RESOURCES

Kentucky

- Worked-Out Solution Key
- Notetaking Guide
- Practice Workbook
- Algebra 2 Toolkit
- Benchmark Tests
- Remediation Workbook
- Spanish Study Guide
- Spanish Assessment Book
- Spanish Resources in Spanish
- Multi-Language Visual Glossary

14 Lesson Practice Level B

LESSON 14.1 Practice B
For use with pages 908–914

Match the function with its graph.

1. $y = 3 \sin 2x$ B **2.** $y = 3 \sin \frac{1}{2}x$ C **3.** $y = 3 \cos 2x$ A

A. 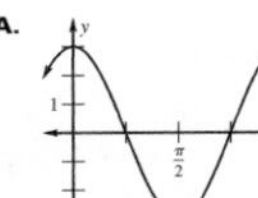

B. 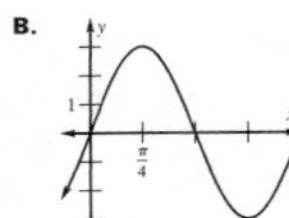

C. 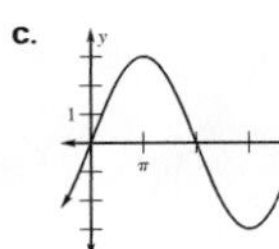

Graph one cycle of the function. Identify the amplitude and period.

4. $y = 5 \tan 3x$ amplitude: 5, period: $\frac{\pi}{3}$ **5.** $y = 3 \cos \frac{2}{3}x$ amplitude: 3, period: 3π **6.** $y = \pi \sin 2x$ amplitude: π, period: π

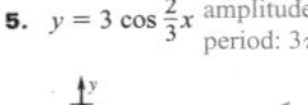

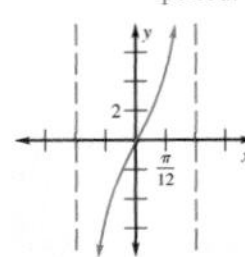

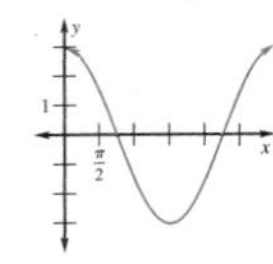

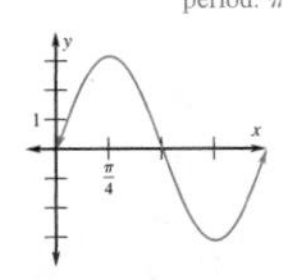

7. $y = \frac{1}{2} \cos 3\pi x$ **8.** $y = 2 \sin \pi x$ **9.** $y = 3 \tan \frac{1}{3}\pi x$

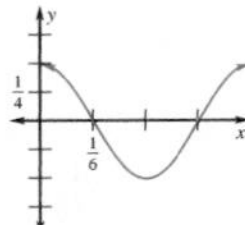

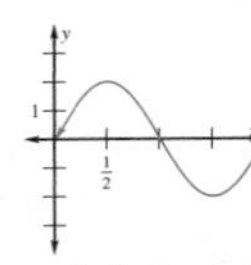

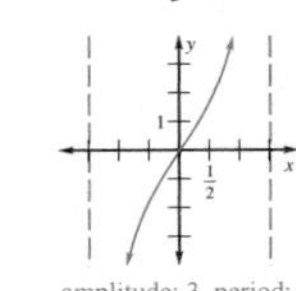

amplitude: $\frac{1}{2}$, period: $\frac{2}{3}$ amplitude: 2, period: 2 amplitude: 3, period: 3

10. Tuning Forks A tuning fork vibrates with a frequency of 220 hertz (cycles per second). You strike the tuning fork with a force that produces a maximum pressure of 3 pascals. Write and graph a sine model that gives the pressure P as a function of the time t (in seconds). What is the period of the sound wave?
$P = 3 \sin 440\pi t$; $\frac{1}{220}$

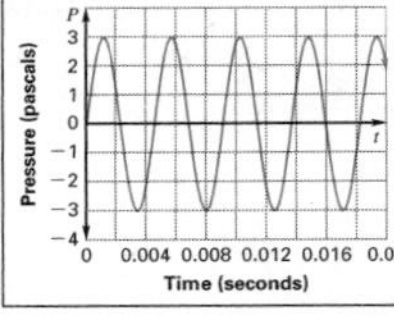

LESSON 14.2 Practice B
For use with pages 915–922

Graph the function.

1. $y = -\sin\left(x - \frac{\pi}{3}\right) - 3$ **2.** $y = -\tan\left(x + \frac{\pi}{2}\right) - 2$ **3.** $y = 2 - \cos(2x + \pi)$

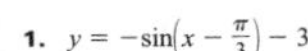

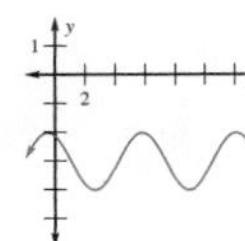

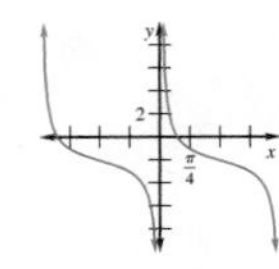

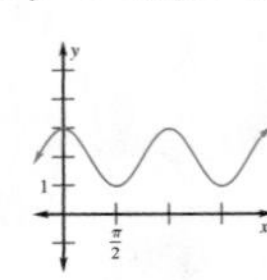

4. $y = 1 - \tan\left(x - \frac{\pi}{4}\right)$ **5.** $y = 3 - \cos\left(x + \frac{3\pi}{2}\right)$ **6.** $y = -\frac{1}{2} \sin(2x + 3\pi)$

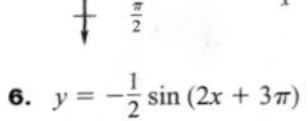

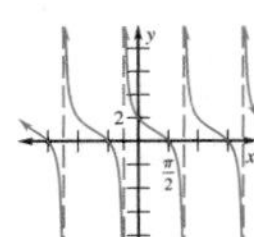

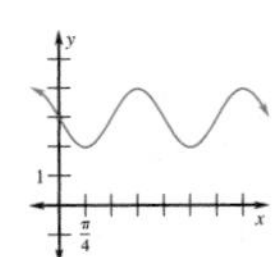

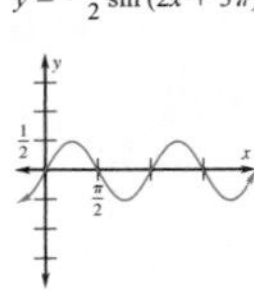

Write an equation of the graph described.

7. The graph of $y = -2 \tan 5x$ translated down 4 units and left π units $y = -2 \tan 5(x + \pi) - 4$

8. The graph of $y = \frac{1}{4} \cos 2x$ translated up 4 units and then reflected in the x-axis $y = -\frac{1}{4} \cos 2x - 4$

9. The graph of $y = \frac{1}{2} \sin 4x$ translated right 3 units and then reflected in the line $y = -2$ $y = -\frac{1}{2} \sin 4(x - 3) - 4$

10. Window Washers You are standing 70 feet from a 200 foot building, watching as a window washer lowers himself to the ground. Write an equation that gives the window washer's distance d (in feet) from the top of the building as a function of the angle of elevation θ. State the domain of the function. Then graph the function. What is the angle of elevation if the window washer has lowered himself halfway down the building?
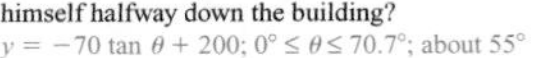
$y = -70 \tan \theta + 200$; $0° \le \theta \le 70.7°$; about 55°

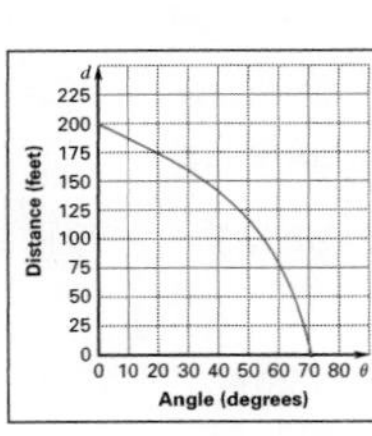

LESSON 14.3 Practice B
For use with pages 924–930

Find the values of the other five trigonometric functions of θ. See below.

1. $\sin \theta = -\frac{15}{17}, \pi < \theta < \frac{3\pi}{2}$ **2.** $\tan \theta = \frac{3}{4}, 0 < \theta < \frac{\pi}{2}$

3. $\cos \theta = -\frac{1}{2}, \frac{\pi}{2} < \theta < \pi$ **4.** $\sec \theta = \sqrt{5}, \frac{3\pi}{2} < \theta < 2\pi$

Simplify the expression.

5. $\sec(-x)\cot(-x)\sin(-x)$ 1 **6.** $\frac{\cos^2 x}{\sin x} + \sin x$ $\csc x$

7. $\frac{1 - \cos^2 x}{\cos^2 x}$ $\tan^2 x$ **8.** $\sin^3 x + \cos\left(\frac{\pi}{2} - x\right)\cos^2 x$ $\sin x$

9. $\csc(-x) - \csc(-x)\cos^2 x$ $-\sin x$ **10.** $\frac{1 + \sec(-x)}{\sin(-x) + \tan(-x)}$ $-\csc x$

Verify the identity. See below.

11. $\cos x \sec x = 1$ **12.** $1 - \tan^2 x = 2 - \sec^2 x$

13. $\frac{\tan^2 x}{\sec x} = \sec x - \cos x$ **14.** $\tan\left(\frac{\pi}{2} - x\right)\sin x = \cos x$

15. $\frac{\cos^2 x}{1 + \tan^2 x} + \frac{\sin^2 x}{\sec^2 x} = \cos^2 x$ **16.** $\frac{\sin\left(\frac{\pi}{2} - x\right) - 1}{1 - \cos(-x)} = -1$

17. Rate of Change In calculus, it can be shown that the rate of change of the function $f(x) = \sec x \cot x$ is given by the expression: $-\csc^2 x \sec x + \cot x \sec x \tan x$. Show that this expression for the rate of change can be written as $-\csc x \cot x$.
$-\csc^2 x \sec x + \cot x \sec x \tan x = -\csc^2 x \sec x + \sec x = \sec x(1 - \csc^2 x) = \sec x(-\cot^2 x) = \frac{1}{\cos x}\left(-\frac{\cos^2 x}{\sin^2 x}\right) = -\frac{\cos x}{\sin^2 x} = -\cot x \csc x$

18. Using Identities Use the cotangent identity to describe what happens to the value of $\cot \theta$ as the value of $\cos \theta$ decreases and the value of $\sin \theta$ increases. On what intervals does this happen? The cotangent is decreasing. This occurs on the intervals from $n\pi$
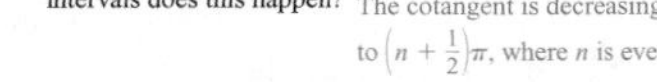
to $\left(n + \frac{1}{2}\right)\pi$, where n is even.

1. $\cos \theta = -\frac{8}{17}$, $\tan \theta = \frac{15}{8}$, $\sec \theta = -\frac{17}{8}$, $\csc \theta = -\frac{17}{15}$, $\cot \theta = \frac{8}{15}$

2. $\sin \theta = \frac{3}{5}$, $\cos \theta = \frac{4}{5}$, $\sec \theta = \frac{5}{4}$, $\csc \theta = \frac{5}{3}$, $\cot \theta = \frac{4}{3}$

3. $\sin \theta = \frac{\sqrt{3}}{2}$, $\tan \theta = -\sqrt{3}$, $\sec \theta = -2$, $\csc \theta = \frac{2}{\sqrt{3}}$, $\cot \theta = -\frac{1}{\sqrt{3}}$

4. $\sin \theta = -\frac{2}{\sqrt{5}}$, $\cos \theta = \frac{1}{\sqrt{5}}$, $\tan \theta = -2$, $\csc \theta = -\frac{\sqrt{5}}{2}$, $\cot \theta = -\frac{1}{2}$

11. $\cos x \sec x = \cos x\left(\frac{1}{\cos x}\right) = 1$

12. $1 - \tan^2 x = 1 - (\sec^2 x - 1) = 2 - \sec^2 x$

13. $\frac{\tan^2 x}{\sec x} = \frac{\sec^2 x - 1}{\sec x} = \frac{\sec^2 x}{\sec x} - \frac{1}{\sec x} = \sec x - \cos x$

14. $\tan\left(\frac{\pi}{2} - x\right)\sin x = \cot x \sin x = \frac{\cos x}{\sin x} \cdot \sin x = \cos x$

15. $\frac{\cos^2 x}{1 + \tan^2 x} + \frac{\sin^2 x}{\sec^2 x} = \frac{\cos^2 x}{\sec^2 x} + \frac{\sin^2 x}{\sec^2 x} = \frac{\cos^2 x + \sin^2 x}{\sec^2 x} = \frac{1}{\sec^2 x} = \cos^2 x$

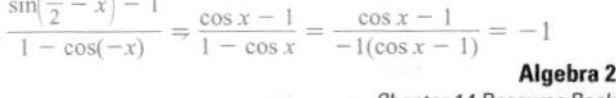

16. $\frac{\sin\left(\frac{\pi}{2} - x\right) - 1}{1 - \cos(-x)} = \frac{\cos x - 1}{1 - \cos x} = \frac{\cos x - 1}{-1(\cos x - 1)} = -1$

LESSON 14.4 Practice B
For use with pages 931–937

Find the general solution of the equation.

1. $\sqrt{2}\cos x - 1 = 0$ $\frac{\pi}{4} + 2n\pi, \frac{7\pi}{4} + 2n\pi$ **2.** $7 \sec x - 7 = 0$ $2n\pi$

3. $5 \cos x - \sqrt{3} = 3 \cos x$ $\frac{\pi}{6} + 2n\pi, \frac{11\pi}{6} + 2n\pi$ **4.** $\csc x - 2 = 0$ $\frac{\pi}{6} + 2n\pi, \frac{5\pi}{6} + 2n\pi$

Solve the equation in the interval $0 \le x < 2\pi$. 10. $\frac{\pi}{2}, \frac{3\pi}{2}, \frac{\pi}{6}, \frac{5\pi}{6}, \frac{7\pi}{6}, \frac{11\pi}{6}$

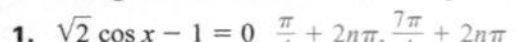

5. $2 \cot^4 x - \cot^2 x - 15 = 0$ $\frac{\pi}{6}, \frac{5\pi}{6}, \frac{7\pi}{6}, \frac{11\pi}{6}$ **6.** $2 \sin^4 x - \sin^2 x = 0$ $0, \pi, \frac{\pi}{4}, \frac{3\pi}{4}, \frac{5\pi}{4}, \frac{7\pi}{4}$

7. $2 \csc x + 17 = 15 + \csc x$ $\frac{7\pi}{6}, \frac{11\pi}{6}$ **8.** $\sec x \csc x - 2 \csc x = 0$ $\frac{\pi}{3}, \frac{5\pi}{3}$

9. $3 \tan^3 x - \tan x = 0$ $0, \pi, \frac{\pi}{6}, \frac{5\pi}{6}, \frac{7\pi}{6}, \frac{11\pi}{6}$ **10.** $\cos x \csc^2 x + 3 \cos x = 7 \cos x$ See above.

11. $\sqrt{2}\cos x \sin x - \cos x = 0$ $\frac{\pi}{2}, \frac{3\pi}{2}, \frac{\pi}{4}, \frac{3\pi}{4}$ **12.** $3 \sec^2 x - 4 = 0$ $\frac{\pi}{6}, \frac{5\pi}{6}, \frac{7\pi}{6}, \frac{11\pi}{6}$

13. Approximate Solutions Use a graphing calculator to approximate the solutions of $3 \tan^2 2x = 1$ in the interval $0 \le x < \pi$. Round your answer to two decimal places. 0.26, 1.31, 1.83, 2.88

14. Find Points of Intersection Find the points of intersection of the graphs of the given functions in the interval $0 \le x < 2\pi$.

$y = \sin x \tan x$ $\left(\frac{\pi}{3}, \frac{3}{2}\right), \left(\frac{5\pi}{3}, \frac{3}{2}\right)$

$y = 2 - \cos x$

15. Calculus In calculus, it can be shown that the function $y = 2 \sin x - \cos 2x$ has minimum and maximum values when $2 \cos x + 4 \cos x \sin x = 0$. Find all solutions of $2 \cos x + 4 \cos x \sin x = 0$ in the interval $0 \le x < 2\pi$. Verify your solutions with a graphing calculator. $\frac{\pi}{2}, \frac{3\pi}{2}, \frac{7\pi}{6}, \frac{11\pi}{6}$

In Exercises 16 and 17, use the following information.

Area The area A of a rectangle inscribed in one arch of the graph of $y = \cos x$ is given by $A = 2x \cos x$ for $0 \le x \le \frac{\pi}{2}$.

16. Use a graphing utility to graph the area function, and approximate the area of the largest inscribed rectangle. $A \approx 1.12$

17. Determine the values of x for which $A \ge 1$. $0.61 < x < 1.1$

LESSON 14.5 Practice B
For use with pages 941–946

Write a function for the sinusoid. See below.

1. 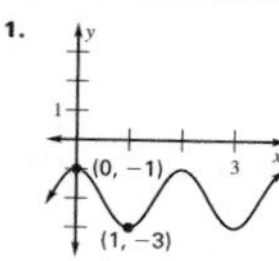

2. 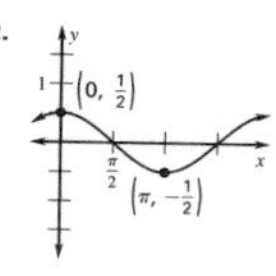

3. 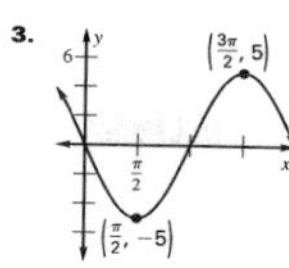

4. 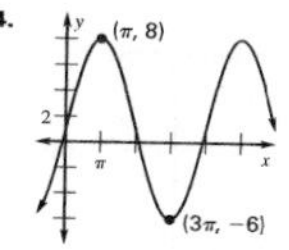

5. 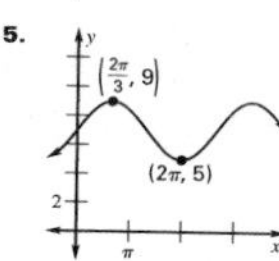

6. 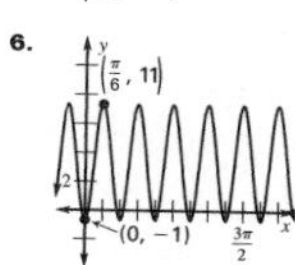

Write a trigonometric function for the sinusoid with maximum at point *A* and minimum at point *B*.

7. $A(3, 7), B(1, -3)$ $y = -5 \sin \frac{\pi x}{2} + 2$
8. $A(0, 3), B(2\pi, -3)$ $y = 3 \cos \frac{x}{2}$
9. $A(0.5, 5), B(1.5, -15)$ $y = 10 \sin \pi x - 5$
10. $A\left(\frac{1}{4}, 2\right), B\left(\frac{3}{4}, 0\right)$ $y = \sin 2\pi x + 1$
11. $A\left(\frac{\pi}{3}, 4\right), B(0, 2)$ $y = -\cos 3x + 3$
12. $A(9\pi, 1), B(3\pi, -5)$ $y = -3 \sin \frac{x}{6} - 2$

13. **Temperature** The average daily temperature T (in degrees Fahrenheit) in Detroit, Michigan is given in the table. Time t is measured in months, with $t = 0$ representing January 1. Use a graphing calculator to write a sinusoidal model that gives T as a function of t. $T = 24.6 \sin(0.5x - 1.8) + 48.9$

t	0.5	1.5	2.5	3.5	4.5	5.5
T	24.5	27.2	36.9	48.1	59.8	69.0

t	6.5	7.5	8.5	9.5	10.5	11.5
T	73.5	71.8	63.9	51.9	40.7	29.6

1. $y = \cos \pi x - 2$ **2.** $y = \frac{1}{2} \cos x$
3. $y = -5 \sin x$ **4.** $y = 7 \sin \frac{x}{2} + 1$
5. $y = 2 \sin \frac{3x}{4} + 7$ **6.** $y = -6 \cos 6x + 5$

LESSON 14.5

LESSON 14.6 Practice B
For use with pages 949–954

Find the exact value of the expression.

1. $\cos 105°$ $\frac{\sqrt{2} - \sqrt{6}}{4}$
2. $\sin 195°$ $\frac{\sqrt{2} - \sqrt{6}}{4}$
3. $\tan 165°$ $\sqrt{3} - 2$
4. $\tan \frac{\pi}{12}$ $2 - \sqrt{3}$
5. $\sec \frac{19\pi}{12}$ $\sqrt{2} + \sqrt{6}$
6. $\sin \frac{13\pi}{12}$ $\frac{\sqrt{2} - \sqrt{6}}{4}$

Evaluate the expression given $\cos u = \frac{4}{5}$ with $0 < u < \frac{\pi}{2}$ and $\tan v = \frac{8}{15}$ with $\pi < v < \frac{3\pi}{2}$.

7. $\sin(u + v)$ $-\frac{77}{85}$
8. $\cos(u + v)$ $-\frac{36}{85}$
9. $\tan(u + v)$ $\frac{77}{36}$
10. $\sin(u - v)$ $-\frac{13}{85}$
11. $\cos(u - v)$ $-\frac{84}{85}$
12. $\tan(u - v)$ $\frac{13}{84}$

Simplify, but do *not* evaluate, the expression.

13. $\sin 20° \cos 50° + \cos 20° \sin 50°$ $\sin 70°$
14. $\cos \frac{\pi}{4} \cos \frac{\pi}{3} - \sin \frac{\pi}{4} \sin \frac{\pi}{3}$ $\cos \frac{7\pi}{12}$
15. $\frac{\tan 68° - \tan 54°}{1 + \tan 68° \tan 54°}$ $\tan 14°$
16. $\frac{1 - \tan \frac{5\pi}{3} \tan \frac{\pi}{4}}{\tan \frac{5\pi}{3} + \tan \frac{\pi}{4}}$ $\cot \frac{23\pi}{12}$

Solve the equation for $0 \le x < 2\pi$.

17. $\cos\left(x + \frac{\pi}{4}\right) - \cos\left(x - \frac{\pi}{4}\right) = 1$ $\frac{5\pi}{4}, \frac{7\pi}{4}$
18. $\sin\left(x + \frac{\pi}{6}\right) - \sin\left(x - \frac{\pi}{6}\right) = \frac{1}{2}$ $\frac{\pi}{3}, \frac{5\pi}{3}$
19. $\tan(x + \pi) + \cos\left(x - \frac{\pi}{2}\right) = 0$ $0, \pi$
20. $\sin(x + \pi) + \sin(x - \pi) = 2$ $\frac{3\pi}{2}$

In Exercises 21 and 22, use the following information.

Geometry In the figure shown, the acute angle of intersection, $\theta_2 - \theta_1$, of two lines with slopes m_1 and m_2 is given by $\tan(\theta_2 - \theta_1) = \frac{m_2 - m_1}{1 + m_1 m_2}$.

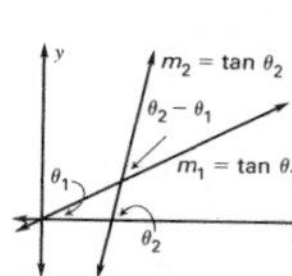

21. Find the acute angle of intersection of the lines $y = \frac{1}{4}x - 2$ and $y = 4x + 5$. 61.9°

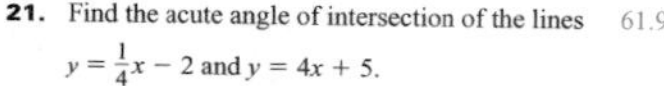

22. Find the acute angle of intersection of the lines $y = x + 2$ and $y = 3x + 2$. 26.6°

LESSON 14.6

LESSON 14.7 Practice B
For use with pages 955–962

Find the exact value of the expression.

1. $\tan 67.5°$ $\sqrt{2} + 1$
2. $\sin \frac{5\pi}{8}$ $\frac{\sqrt{2 + \sqrt{2}}}{2}$
3. $\cos \frac{3\pi}{8}$ $\frac{\sqrt{2 - \sqrt{2}}}{2}$

Find the exact values of $\sin \frac{u}{2}$, $\cos \frac{u}{2}$, and $\tan \frac{u}{2}$. See below.

4. $\tan u = \frac{3}{4}, \pi < u < \frac{3\pi}{2}$
5. $\sin u = -\frac{5}{13}, \frac{3\pi}{2} < u < 2\pi$

Find the exact values of $\sin 2x$, $\cos 2x$, and $\tan 2x$. See below.

6. $\cos x = \frac{12}{13}, 0 < x < \frac{\pi}{2}$
7. $\sin x = -\frac{4}{5}, \frac{3\pi}{2} < x < 2\pi$

Rewrite the expression without double angles or half angles, given that $0 < x < \frac{\pi}{2}$. Then simplify the expression.

8. $2 \csc 2x$ $\csc x \sec x$
9. $\frac{\sin \frac{x}{2} \tan \frac{x}{2}}{1 - \cos x}$ $\frac{\sqrt{2 - 2\cos x}}{2 \sin x}$
10. $\frac{1 + \cos 2x}{\cot x}$ $2 \sin x \cos x$

Verify the identity.

11. $\cos 4x = 8 \cos^4 x - 8 \cos^2 x + 1$ $\cos 4x = \cos 2(2x) = 2\cos^2 2x - 1 = 2(\cos 2x)(\cos 2x) - 1 = 2(2\cos^2 x - 1)(2\cos^2 x - 1) - 1 = 8\cos^4 x - 8\cos^2 x + 1$
12. $4 \sin \frac{x}{2} \cos \frac{x}{2} = 2 \sin x$ $4 \sin \frac{x}{2} \cos \frac{x}{2} = 2\left(2 \sin \frac{x}{2} \cos \frac{x}{2}\right) = 2\left(\sin 2\left(\frac{x}{2}\right)\right) = 2 \sin x$
13. $(\sin x + \cos x)^2 = 1 + \sin 2x$ $(\sin x + \cos x)^2 = \sin^2 x + 2 \sin x \cos x + \cos^2 x = 1 + 2 \sin x \cos x = 1 + \sin 2x$
14. $\cos 3x = 4 \cos^3 x - 3 \cos x$ See below.

Solve the equation for $0 \le x < 2\pi$.

15. $\sec 2x = 2$ $\frac{\pi}{6}, \frac{5\pi}{6}, \frac{7\pi}{6}, \frac{11\pi}{6}$
16. $\cos 2x = \cos x$ $0, \frac{2\pi}{3}, \frac{4\pi}{3}$
17. $\sin 2x \sin x = \cos x$ $\frac{\pi}{4}, \frac{\pi}{2}, \frac{3\pi}{4}, \frac{5\pi}{4}, \frac{3\pi}{2}, \frac{7\pi}{4}$

18. **Calculus** A graph of $y = \cos 2x + 2 \cos x$ in the interval $0 \le x < 2\pi$ is shown in the figure. In calculus, it can be shown that the function $y = \cos 2x + 2 \cos x$ has turning points when $\sin 2x + \sin x = 0$. Find the coordinates of these turning points.
$(0, 3), \left(\frac{2\pi}{3}, -\frac{3}{2}\right), (\pi, -1), \left(\frac{4\pi}{3}, -\frac{3}{2}\right)$

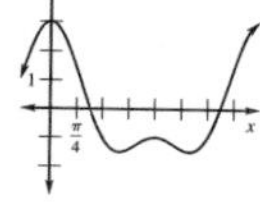

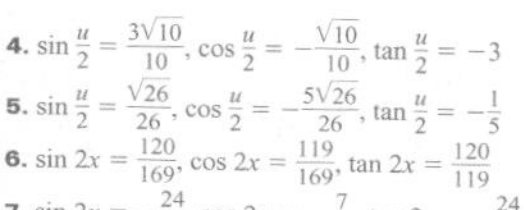

4. $\sin \frac{u}{2} = \frac{3\sqrt{10}}{10}, \cos \frac{u}{2} = -\frac{\sqrt{10}}{10}, \tan \frac{u}{2} = -3$
5. $\sin \frac{u}{2} = \frac{\sqrt{26}}{26}, \cos \frac{u}{2} = -\frac{5\sqrt{26}}{26}, \tan \frac{u}{2} = -\frac{1}{5}$
6. $\sin 2x = \frac{120}{169}, \cos 2x = \frac{119}{169}, \tan 2x = \frac{120}{119}$
7. $\sin 2x = -\frac{24}{25}, \cos 2x = -\frac{7}{25}, \tan 2x = -\frac{24}{7}$

14. $\cos 3x = \cos(x + 2x) = \cos x \cos 2x - \sin x \sin 2x = \cos x(2\cos^2 x - 1) - 2\sin^2 x \cos x = 2\cos^3 x - \cos x - 2\cos x(1 - \cos^2 x) = 2\cos^3 x - \cos x - 2\cos x + 2\cos^3 x = 4\cos^3 x - 3\cos x$

LESSON 14.7

CHAPTER 14 Quiz 1

For use after Lessons 14.1–14.2

Find the amplitude and the period of the graph of the function.

1. $y = \sin 3x$
2. $y = \frac{1}{2}\cos 4x$
3. $y = 3\sin 2\pi x$
4. $f(x) = 4\cos\frac{\pi}{3}x$

Graph the function.

5. $y = 4\cos \pi x$
6. $y = \frac{1}{2}\sin\frac{5}{4}\pi x$

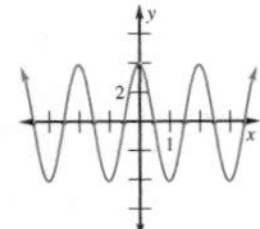

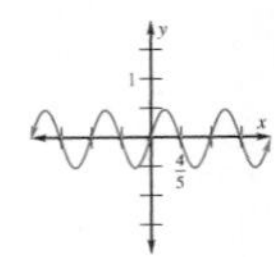

7. $y = 1 + 2\cos 2x$
8. $y = \tan 2\left(x - \frac{\pi}{2}\right)$

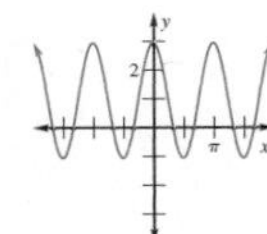

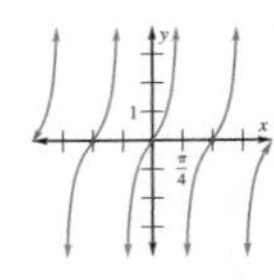

9. Write an equation of the graph of $y = 2\sin x$ translated up 3 units and right π units.

Answers

1. amplitude: 1, period: $\frac{2\pi}{3}$
2. amplitude: $\frac{1}{2}$, period: $\frac{\pi}{2}$
3. amplitude: 3, period: 1
4. amplitude: 4, period: 6
5. See left.
6. See left.
7. See left.
8. See left.
9. $y = 3 + 2\sin(x - \pi)$

CHAPTER 14 Quiz 2

For use after Lessons 14.3–14.5

Simplify the expression.

1. $\cos\theta\csc\theta$
2. $\sin^2\theta + \cos^2\theta + \cot^2\theta$
3. $\cos\left(\frac{\pi}{2} - \theta\right)\sin\theta + \cos^2\theta$
4. $\frac{\sin(-\theta)}{\cos(-\theta)}$

Find the general solution of the equation.

5. $\sin(-x) - \sin x = 1$
6. $\sqrt{2}\sin x\cos x - \sin x = 0$

Write a function for the sinusoid.

7.

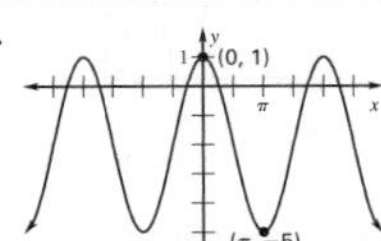

8.

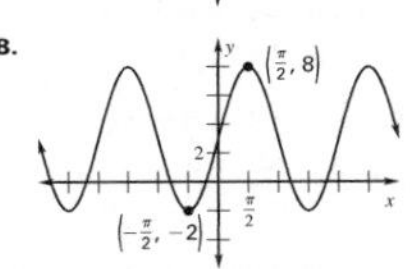

9. During one cycle, a sinusoid has a minimum at $(13, -3)$ and a maximum at $(5, 13)$. What is the amplitude of this sinusoid?

Answers

1. $\cot\theta$
2. $\csc^2\theta$
3. 1
4. $-\tan\theta$
5. $\frac{7\pi}{6} + 2n\pi$, $\frac{11\pi}{6} + 2n\pi$
6. $2n\pi$, $\pi + 2n\pi$, $\frac{\pi}{4} + 2n\pi$, $\frac{7\pi}{4} + 2n\pi$
7. $y = -2 + 3\cos x$
8. $y = 3 + 5\sin x$
9. 8

CHAPTER 14 Quiz 3

For use after Lessons 14.6–14.7

Find the exact value of the expression.

1. $\cos 75°$
2. $\sin\left(-\frac{\pi}{12}\right)$
3. $\cos 15°$
4. $\tan\left(\frac{5\pi}{12}\right)$

Solve the equation for $0 \le x \le 2\pi$.

5. $\sin\left(x + \frac{\pi}{4}\right) - \sin\left(x - \frac{\pi}{4}\right) = 1$
6. $\cos 2x - \cos x = 0$

Find the exact values of $\sin\frac{a}{2}$, $\cos\frac{a}{2}$ *and* $\tan\frac{a}{2}$.

7. $\cos a = -\frac{2}{7}$, $\frac{\pi}{2} < a < \pi$
8. $\sin a = -\frac{4}{5}$, $\frac{3\pi}{2} < a < 2\pi$

9. **Golf Ball** Use the equation $x = \frac{1}{32}v^2\sin 2\theta$ to find the horizontal distance a golf ball will travel if it is hit at an initial speed of 60 feet per second and at an initial angle of 50°.

Answers

1. $\frac{\sqrt{6} - \sqrt{2}}{4}$
2. $\frac{\sqrt{2} - \sqrt{6}}{4}$
3. $\frac{\sqrt{6} + \sqrt{2}}{4}$
4. $2 + \sqrt{3}$
5. $\frac{\pi}{4}$, $\frac{7\pi}{4}$
6. $0, \frac{2\pi}{3}, \frac{4\pi}{3}, 2\pi$
7. $\sin\frac{a}{2} = \frac{3\sqrt{14}}{14}$, $\cos\frac{a}{2} = \frac{\sqrt{70}}{14}$, $\tan\frac{a}{2} = \frac{3\sqrt{5}}{5}$
8. $\sin\frac{a}{2} = \frac{\sqrt{5}}{5}$, $\cos\frac{a}{2} = -\frac{2\sqrt{5}}{5}$, $\tan\frac{a}{2} = -\frac{1}{2}$
9. 110.79 ft

CHAPTER 14 Chapter Test B

For use after Chapter 14

Graph the function.

1. $y = 3\cos\left(\frac{\pi}{2}x\right)$
2. $f(x) = 2\tan(2x)$

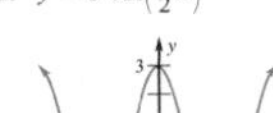

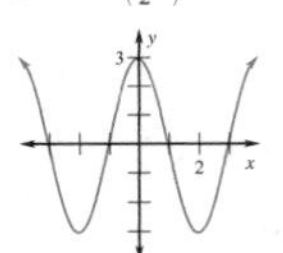

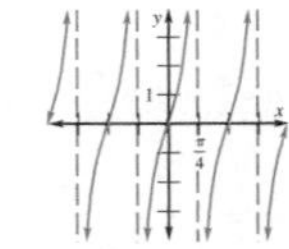

3. $y = 1 + \sin(2x)$
4. $f(x) = \tan\left(x - \frac{\pi}{2}\right) - 2$

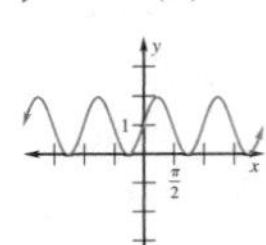

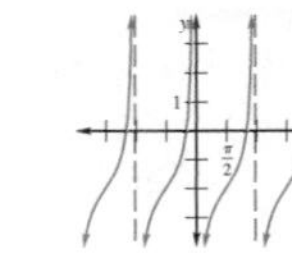

5. Write an equation of the graph $y = \cos(2x) + 3$ translated down 1 unit and then reflected in the y-axis.
6. Find the values of the other five trigonometric functions of θ, given that $\sec\theta = \frac{5}{3}$, $\frac{3\pi}{2} < \theta < 2\pi$.

Simplify the expression.

7. $\sin^2\left(\frac{\pi}{2} - \theta\right) + \cos^2\left(\frac{\pi}{2} - \theta\right)$
8. $\tan^2\left(\frac{\pi}{2} - \theta\right) + 1$
9. Verify the identity $1 - \sin^2(-\theta) = \cos^2(-\theta)$.
10. Solve the equation $\cot^2 x - 2 = 1$ in the interval $0 < x < \pi$.
11. Find the general solution of the equation $\cos^2 x + \sin^2 x = 2\sin x$.

Answers

1. See left.
2. See left.
3. See left.
4. See left.
5. $y = \cos(2x) + 2$
6. $\cos\theta = \frac{3}{5}$, $\sin\theta = -\frac{4}{5}$, $\csc\theta = -\frac{5}{4}$, $\tan\theta = -\frac{4}{3}$, $\cot\theta = -\frac{3}{4}$
7. 1
8. $\csc^2\theta$
9. $1 - \sin^2(-\theta) = 1 - (-\sin\theta)^2 = 1 - \sin^2\theta = 1 - (1 - \cos^2\theta) = \cos^2\theta = \cos^2(-\theta)$
10. $\frac{\pi}{6}$, $\frac{5\pi}{6}$
11. $\frac{\pi}{6} + 2n\pi$, $\frac{5\pi}{6} + 2n\pi$

CHAPTER 14

Chapter Test B *continued*

For use after Chapter 14

12. Write a function for the sinusoid with a maximum at point $(\pi, 2.5)$ and a minimum at point $(3\pi, 1.5)$.

13. Storm Surge Storm surge from a hurricane causes a large sinusoidal wave pattern to develop near the shore. The highest wave reached the top of a wall 20 feet above sea level. The low point immediately behind this wave was 6 feet below sea level, and was 20 feet behind the peak. What is the amplitude of the sinusoid? What is the vertical shift of the sinusoid from a wave at ground level?

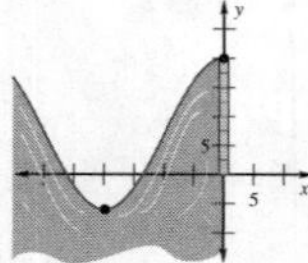

14. Find the exact value of $\cos\left(\frac{7\pi}{12}\right)$.

15. Find $\cos(a + b)$ given that $\cos a = -\frac{4}{5}$ with $\pi < a < \frac{3\pi}{2}$ and $\sin b = \frac{7}{25}$ with $\frac{\pi}{2} < b < \pi$.

16. Simplify $\tan(x - \pi)$.

17. Find the exact value of $\sin 15°$.

18. Given $\sin a = \frac{12}{13}$, $0 < a < \frac{\pi}{2}$, find $\cos 2a$.

19. Given $\tan a = \frac{3}{4}$, $\pi < a < \frac{3\pi}{2}$, find $\cos \frac{a}{2}$.

20. Solve the equation $\cos x - \sin 2x = 0$ in the interval $0 \le x < 2\pi$.

Answers

12. $y = \frac{1}{2}\sin\left(\frac{1}{2}x\right) + 2$

13. amplitude: 13 ft; vertical shift: 7 ft

14. $\frac{\sqrt{2} - \sqrt{6}}{4}$

15. $\frac{117}{125}$

16. $\tan x$

17. $\frac{\sqrt{2 - \sqrt{3}}}{2}$

18. $-\frac{119}{169}$

19. $-\frac{\sqrt{10}}{10}$

20. $\frac{\pi}{6}, \frac{\pi}{2}, \frac{5\pi}{6}, \frac{3\pi}{2}$

CHAPTER 14

Standardized Test

For use after Chapter 14

Multiple Choice

1. Which function has an amplitude of 3 and a period of $\frac{1}{2}$? A

Ⓐ $y = -3 \sin 4\pi x$
Ⓑ $y = -3 \cos 4x$
Ⓒ $y = 3 \sin\left(\frac{\pi}{2}\right)x$
Ⓓ $y = \frac{1}{2} \cos 3\pi x$

2. Which function is represented by the graph shown? D

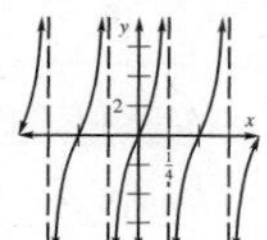

Ⓐ $y = 3 \tan 2x$ Ⓑ $y = 3 \tan\left(\frac{1}{2}\right)x$
Ⓒ $y = 3 \tan \pi x$ Ⓓ $y = 3 \tan 2\pi x$

3. Which function represents a horizontal shift of 2π units and a vertical shift of 3 units? B

Ⓐ $y = 2\pi + \cos 3x$
Ⓑ $y = 3 + \cos(x + 2\pi)$
Ⓒ $y = \cos(x + 3 + 2\pi)$
Ⓓ $y = 3 \cos(x + 2\pi)$

4. Which is a minimum point of the graph of $y = -2 \cos(x + \pi)$? A

Ⓐ $(-\pi, -2)$ Ⓑ $\left(-\frac{\pi}{2}, -2\right)$
Ⓒ $\left(\frac{\pi}{4}, -2\right)$ Ⓓ $\left(\frac{\pi}{2}, -2\right)$

5. Which expression is equivalent to the expression $\sin\left(\frac{\pi}{2} - \theta\right) \tan \theta$? B

Ⓐ $\cos \theta$ Ⓑ $\sin \theta$
Ⓒ $\frac{\cos^2 \theta}{\sin \theta}$ Ⓓ $\frac{\sin^2 \theta}{\cos \theta}$

6. Given that $\sin A = \frac{5}{13}$ and $\pi < A < \frac{3\pi}{2}$, what is $\tan A$? C

Ⓐ $-\frac{5}{12}$ Ⓑ $-\frac{12}{13}$
Ⓒ $\frac{5}{12}$ Ⓓ $\frac{12}{13}$

7. Which expression is equivalent to $\sin x$? D

Ⓐ $\tan^2 x \cos^2\left(\frac{\pi}{2} - x\right)$
Ⓑ $\tan^2 x \sin^2\left(\frac{\pi}{2} - x\right)$
Ⓒ $\tan^2 x \cos^2\left(\frac{\pi}{2} - x\right)\csc x$
Ⓓ $\tan^2 x \sin^2\left(\frac{\pi}{2} - x\right)\csc x$

8. What are the general solutions to the equation $\sin^2 x + \frac{5}{2} \sin x - \frac{3}{2} = 0$? C

Ⓐ $x = \frac{\pi}{6} + 2n\pi$
Ⓑ $x = \frac{\pi}{3} + 2n\pi$
Ⓒ $x = \frac{\pi}{6} + 2n\pi, x = \frac{5\pi}{6} + 2n\pi$
Ⓓ $x = \frac{\pi}{3} + 2n\pi, x = \frac{2\pi}{3} + 2n\pi$

CHAPTER 14

Standardized Test *continued*

For use after Chapter 14

9. Which is an intersection point of the graphs of $y = 7 \cos x + 1$ and $y = 5 \cos x$ on the interval $\frac{\pi}{2} \le x \le \pi$? B

Ⓐ $\left(\frac{11\pi}{6}, -\frac{1}{2}\right)$ Ⓑ $\left(\frac{2\pi}{3}, -\frac{5}{2}\right)$
Ⓒ $\left(\frac{5\pi}{6}, -\frac{1}{2}\right)$ Ⓓ $\left(\frac{5\pi}{6}, \frac{1}{2}\right)$

10. A sinusoid reaches a maximum value of $\left(\frac{\pi}{2}, 28\right)$ and a minimum value of $(\pi, 12)$ during a single cycle. What is its amplitude? B

Ⓐ $\frac{\pi}{2}$ Ⓑ 8
Ⓒ 2π Ⓓ 20

11. If $\tan A = \frac{2}{3}$ and $\tan B = \frac{1}{5}$, what is $\tan(A + B)$? C

Ⓐ $\frac{12}{15}$ Ⓑ $\frac{12}{13}$
Ⓒ 1 Ⓓ 2

12. What is the simplified expression for $\sin\left(x + \frac{\pi}{6}\right)$? C

Ⓐ $\cos x$
Ⓑ $\sin x$
Ⓒ $\frac{1}{2} \cos x + \frac{\sqrt{3}}{2} \sin x$
Ⓓ $\frac{1}{2} \sin x + \frac{\sqrt{3}}{2} \cos x$

13. What is the solution to $\cos(x + 300) + \sin\left(\frac{1}{4}x\right) = 1$? B

Ⓐ 45° Ⓑ 120°
Ⓒ 135° Ⓓ 180°

14. What is the solution to $\sin 2x + \cos x = 0$ on the interval $\pi \le x < \frac{3\pi}{2}$? A

Ⓐ $x = \frac{7\pi}{6}$ Ⓑ $x = \frac{5\pi}{4}$
Ⓒ $x = \frac{4\pi}{3}$ Ⓓ $x = \frac{3\pi}{2}$

Gridded Answer

15. What is the vertical shift of a graph which reaches it maximum at (45°, 37) and its minimum at (135°, −5)?

		1	6

17. a. shift: 6, amplitude: 6, period: 2π **b.** $y = 6 + 6 \sin x$

c.

Short Response

16. Find an equivalent expression for $\sin 4x$ in terms of $\sin x$ and $\cos x$. Show the full detail of your simplification. Is there only one possible answer? *Explain.* See below.

Extended Response

17. A sound wave models a sinusoidal function. See above.

a. If the wave reaches its maximum at $\left(\frac{\pi}{2}, 12\right)$ and its minimum at $\left(\frac{3\pi}{2}, 0\right)$, what are the shift, amplitude, and period of the function?

b. Write the function which models this sound wave.

c. Graph the function.

16. *Sample answer:* $\sin 4x = \sin 2(2x) = 2 \sin(2x) \cos(2x) = 2(2 \sin x \cos x)(1 - 2 \sin^2 x)$; Explanations will vary.

CHAPTER 14

Alternative Assessment and Math Journal

For use after Chapter 14

Journal

1. Is the function $y = -2 \sin\left(2x - \frac{\pi}{2}\right) + 3$ in the form $y = a \sin b(x - h) + k$? Why or why not? How does the amplitude and period of the function compare to the amplitude and period of $y = \sin x$? How does the graph of the function compare to the graph of $y = 2 \sin 2x$?

Multi-Step Problem

2. The table shows the number C of cars in an office parking lot over the course of a work day. The time t is measured in hours, with $t = 0$ representing 7:00 A.M.

t	0	1	2	3	4	5	6	7	8	9	10	11	12
C	13	67	92	108	82	52	15	75	100	110	86	34	12

a. Writing You want to write a sinusoidal model for the data in the table without using a graphing calculator. Is it more convenient to model the data with a sine or cosine function? Explain.

b. Write a sinusoidal model for the number C of cars as a function of the time t (in hours) without using a graphing calculator. Identify and explain how you calculated your values for the amplitude, period, horizontal shift, and vertical shift.

c. Use a graphing calculator to write a sinusoidal model that gives C as a function of t.

d. Using your model from part (c), at about what time(s) will there be 45 cars in the parking lot?

e. Critcal Thinking Consider the reflection of the function from part (c) in the midline. What type of business' parking lot might be represented by this sinusoid? Explain.

1. Complete answers should include: an explanation that the function is not in the form $y = a \sin b(x - h) + k$ because the coefficient of x must be factored outside of the parentheses in order for h to represent the correct horizontal shift; an explanation that $y = -2 \sin\left(2x - \frac{\pi}{2}\right) + 3$ has a larger amplitude (double) and shorter period (half) than $y = \sin x$; an explanation that the graph of $y = -2 \sin\left(2x - \frac{\pi}{2}\right) + 3$ is the graph of $y = 2 \sin 2x$ translated right $\frac{\pi}{4}$ units and up 3 units, then reflected in the line $y = 3$. **2. a.** *Sample answer:* Because the number of cars is at its minimum at $t = 0$, it is more convenient to model the data with a cosine function reflected in the t-axis. That way, the function does not require a horizontal shift. **b.** $C = -49 \cos \frac{\pi}{3}t + 61$; *Sample answer:* The amplitude is half the difference of the maximum (110) and the minimum (12), or 49. The number of cars in the parking lot completed two cycles in 12 hours, so the period is 6 hours. No horizontal shift is necessary, and the vertical shift is the average of the maximum and minimum, or 61. **c.** $C = 46.1 \sin(1.045t - 1.3) + 68.4$ **d.** 7:45 A.M., 11:45 A.M., 1:45 P.M., 5:45 P.M. **e.** *Sample answer:* restaurant; A restaurant might have the maximum number of cars in its parking lot at 7:00 A.M., 1 P.M., and 7 P.M. because those times coincide with mealtimes.

PLAN AND PREPARE

Main Ideas

Students are introduced to the graphs of sine, cosine, and tangent functions. They learn how to use amplitudes, periods, and asymptotes to graph these functions as well as translations and reflections of the functions. Then students learn how trigonometric identities can be generated from the unit circle. They apply identities to solve trigonometric equations. Next students apply their understanding of the graphs of sine and cosine functions to write sinusoidal functions and models, including sinusoidal regression equations. Finally, students extend their understanding of trigonometric identities to problems involving trigonometric sum and difference formulas and double-angle and half-angle formulas.

Prerequisite Skills

- Evaluating functions
- Sketching angles and finding the reference angles
- Evaluating expressions

Additional resources for reviewing prerequisite skills are:

- Skills Review Handbook, pp. 975–1009
- @HomeTutor

14 Trigonometric Graphs, Identities, and Equations

KY

Before

In Chapter 13, you learned the following skills, which you'll use in Chapter 14: evaluating trigonometric functions, finding reference angles, and evaluating inverse trigonometric functions.

Prerequisite Skills

VOCABULARY CHECK

Copy and complete the statement.

1. The **sine** of θ is _?_. $\frac{5}{13}$
2. The **cosine** of θ is _?_. $\frac{12}{13}$
3. The **tangent** of θ is _?_. $\frac{5}{12}$

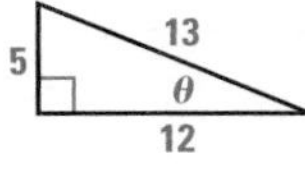

SKILLS CHECK

Evaluate the expression. *(Review p. 866 for 14.1.)*

4. $\sin 45°$ $\frac{\sqrt{2}}{2}$
5. $\cos \frac{\pi}{2}$ 0
6. $\tan \frac{\pi}{3}$ $\sqrt{3}$

Sketch the angle. Then find its reference angle. *(Review p. 866 for 14.1.)*
7–9. See margin for art.

7. $-165°$ 15°
8. $285°$ 75°
9. $-\frac{5\pi}{8}$ $\frac{3\pi}{8}$

Evaluate the expression. *(Review p. 875 for 14.4.)*

10. $\sin^{-1} \frac{\sqrt{3}}{2}$ 60° or $\frac{\pi}{3}$
11. $\cos^{-1} 1$ 0
12. $\tan^{-1} \sqrt{3}$ 60° or $\frac{\pi}{3}$

Chapter Planning Guide

Chapter 14 Resource Book
- Teaching Guide/Lesson Plan (pp. 3, 15, 26, 38, 50, 62, 72)
- Project with Rubric (p. 86)

Assessment and Intervention
- Assessment Book (pp. 197–211)
- Benchmark Tests
- Remediation Book

Interactive Technology
- Easy Planner
- Power Presentations CD-ROM
- Activity Generator CD-ROM
- Animated Algebra
- Test Generator CD-ROM
- Online Quizzes
- eWorkbook
- eEdition
- @HomeTutor

Resources for English Learners
- Quick Reference for English Learners
- Spanish Study Guide
- Multi-Language Visual Glossary
- Student Resources in Spanish

Now

In Chapter 14, you will apply the big ideas listed below and reviewed in the Chapter Summary on page 964. You will also use the key vocabulary listed below.

Big Ideas

1. **Graphing trigonometric functions**
2. **Solving trigonometric equations**
3. **Applying trigonometric formulas**

KEY VOCABULARY

- amplitude, *p. 908*
- periodic function, *p. 908*
- cycle, *p. 908*
- period, *p. 908*
- frequency, *p. 910*
- trigonometric identity, *p. 924*
- sinusoid, *p. 941*

Why?

You can use trigonometric functions to model characteristics of a projectile's path. For example, you can find the horizontal distance traveled by a soccer ball using trigonometric functions.

Animated Algebra

The animation illustrated below for Exercise 51 on page 961 helps you answer this question: How does changing the initial speed and angle of a soccer ball kicked from ground level affect the horizontal distance the ball travels?

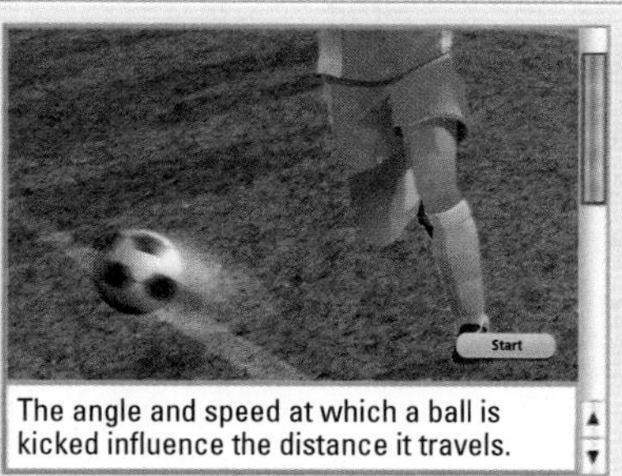

The angle and speed at which a ball is kicked influence the distance it travels.

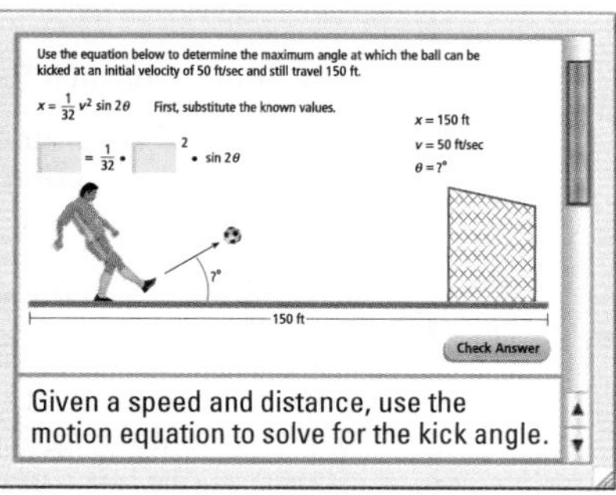

Given a speed and distance, use the motion equation to solve for the kick angle.

Animated Algebra at classzone.com

Other animations for Chapter 14: pages 912, 917, and 964

Algebra 2 Toolkit

- Reading Strategies for Chapter 14, pp. 35–36
- Differentiated Instruction Notes, pp. 95–96
- English Learners Notes, pp. 127–128
- Inclusion Notes, pp. 161–162
- Teaching Strategies with Sample Worksheets, pp. 163–186
- Using Technology in the Classroom, pp. 187–192
- Tips for New Teachers, pp. 219–220
- Math Background Notes, pp. 266–267
- Pre-AP Strategies and Copymasters, pp. 337–338, 443–448
- Teacher Survival Activities, pp. 495–496, 523–524
- Bulletin Board Idea, p. 538
- Teacher Tool Transparencies, following p. 538

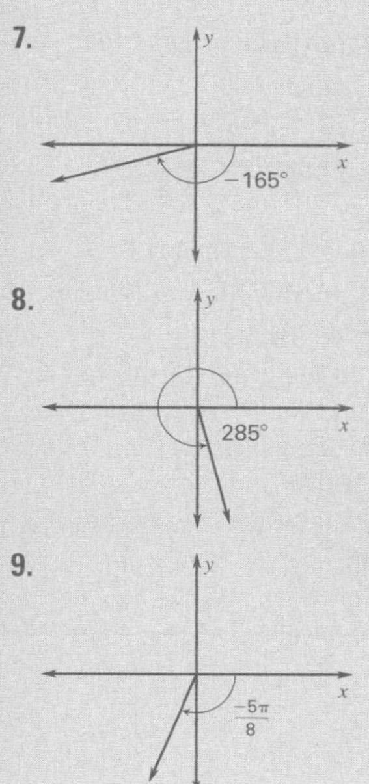

1 PLAN AND PREPARE

Warm-Up Exercises

Transparency Available

Find the sine, cosine, and tangent.

1. $\frac{\pi}{2}$ **sin: 1, cos: 0, tan: undefined**
2. 2π **sin: 0, cos: 1, tan: 0**
3. The diameter of a wheel is 27 inches. Through how many radians does a point on the wheel move when the wheel moves 15 feet? **about 13.3 radians**

Notetaking Guide

Transparency Available

Promotes interactive learning and notetaking skills, pp. 350–353.

Pacing

Basic: 2 days
Average: 2 days
Advanced: 2 days
Block: 1 block
- See *Teaching Guide/Lesson Plan.*

2 FOCUS AND MOTIVATE

Essential Question

Big Idea 1, p. 907

Compare the graphs of $y = \sin x$ and $y = \cos x$ to the graph of $y = \tan x$. **Tell students they will learn how to answer this question by examining specific values of the graphs as well as the repeating behavior of the graphs.**

14.1 Graph Sine, Cosine, and Tangent Functions

MA-HS-5.1.3

Before	You evaluated sine, cosine, and tangent functions.
Now	You will graph sine, cosine, and tangent functions.
Why?	So you can model oscillating motion, as in Ex. 31.

Key Vocabulary
- **amplitude**
- **periodic function**
- **cycle**
- **period**
- **frequency**

MA-HS-5.1.3
Students will demonstrate how equations and graphs are models of the relationship between two real-world quantities (e.g., the relationship between degrees Celsius and degrees Fahrenheit).

In this lesson, you will learn to graph functions of the form $y = a \sin bx$ and $y = a \cos bx$ where a and b are positive constants and x is in radian measure. The graphs of all sine and cosine functions are related to the graphs of the parent functions $y = \sin x$ and $y = \cos x$, which are shown below.

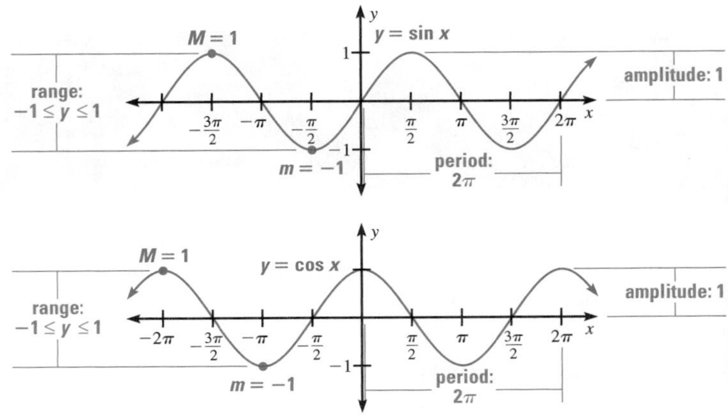

KEY CONCEPT — *For Your Notebook*

Characteristics of $y = \sin x$ and $y = \cos x$

- The domain of each function is all real numbers.
- The range of each function is $-1 \le y \le 1$. Therefore, the minimum value of each function is $m = -1$ and the maximum value is $M = 1$.
- The **amplitude** of each function's graph is half the difference of the maximum M and the minimum m, or $\frac{1}{2}(M - m) = \frac{1}{2}[1 - (-1)] = 1$.
- Each function is **periodic**, which means that its graph has a repeating pattern. The shortest repeating portion of the graph is called a **cycle**. The horizontal length of each cycle is called the **period**. Each graph shown above has a period of 2π.
- The x-intercepts for $y = \sin x$ occur when $x = 0, \pm\pi, \pm 2\pi, \pm 3\pi, \ldots$.
- The x-intercepts for $y = \cos x$ occur when $x = \pm\frac{\pi}{2}, \pm\frac{3\pi}{2}, \pm\frac{5\pi}{2}, \pm\frac{7\pi}{2}, \ldots$.

Resource Planning Guide

Chapter Resource Book
- Teaching Guide/Lesson Plan (pp. 3–4)
- Activity Master (p. 5)
- Practice levels A, B, C (pp. 7–9)
- Study Guide (pp. 10–11)
- Catch-up for Absent Students (p. 12)
- Application (p. 13)
- Challenge (p. 14)

Workbooks
- Notetaking Guide (pp. 350–353)
- Practice Workbook (pp. 193–194)

Teaching Options
- **Power Presentations CD-ROM** provides dynamic electronic teaching resources for the classroom.
- **Activity Generator CD-ROM** provides editable activities for all ability levels.

Interactive Technology
- Easy Planner
- Power Presentations CD-ROM
- Activity Generator CD-ROM
- Animated Algebra
- Test Generator CD-ROM
- Online Quiz
- eWorkbook
- eEdition
- @HomeTutor

Resources for English Learners
- Quick Reference for English Learners
- Spanish Study Guide
- Multi-Language Visual Glossary
- Student Resources in Spanish

See also the *Algebra 2 Toolkit* for more strategies for meeting individual needs.

KEY CONCEPT — *For Your Notebook*

Amplitude and Period

The amplitude and period of the graphs of $y = a \sin bx$ and $y = a \cos bx$, where a and b are nonzero real numbers, are as follows:

$$\text{Amplitude} = |a| \qquad \text{Period} = \frac{2\pi}{|b|}$$

GRAPHING KEY POINTS Each graph below shows five key x-values on the interval $0 \le x \le \frac{2\pi}{b}$ that you can use to sketch the graphs of $y = a \sin bx$ and $y = a \cos bx$ for $a > 0$ and $b > 0$. These are the x-values where the **maximum** and **minimum** values occur and the **x-intercepts**.

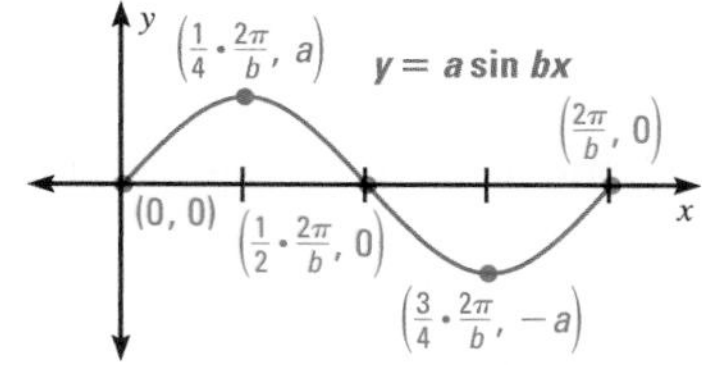

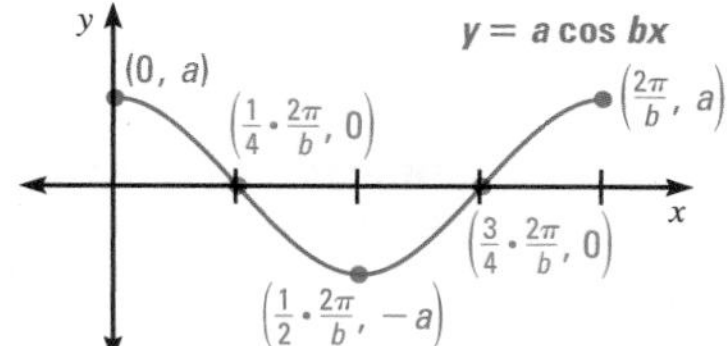

EXAMPLE 1 Graph sine and cosine functions

Graph (a) $y = 4 \sin x$ and (b) $y = \cos 4x$.

VARY CONSTANTS
Notice how changes in a and b affect the graphs of $y = a \sin bx$ and $y = a \cos bx$. When the value of a increases, the amplitude increases. When the value of b increases, the period decreases.

Solution

a. The amplitude is $a = 4$ and the period is $\frac{2\pi}{b} = \frac{2\pi}{1} = 2\pi$.

Intercepts: $(0, 0)$; $\left(\frac{1}{2} \cdot 2\pi, 0\right) = (\pi, 0)$; $(2\pi, 0)$

Maximum: $\left(\frac{1}{4} \cdot 2\pi, 4\right) = \left(\frac{\pi}{2}, 4\right)$

Minimum: $\left(\frac{3}{4} \cdot 2\pi, -4\right) = \left(\frac{3\pi}{2}, -4\right)$

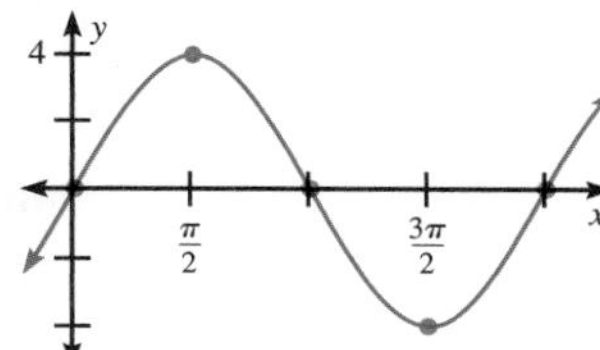

b. The amplitude is $a = 1$ and the period is $\frac{2\pi}{b} = \frac{2\pi}{4} = \frac{\pi}{2}$.

Intercepts: $\left(\frac{1}{4} \cdot \frac{\pi}{2}, 0\right) = \left(\frac{\pi}{8}, 0\right)$; $\left(\frac{3}{4} \cdot \frac{\pi}{2}, 0\right) = \left(\frac{3\pi}{8}, 0\right)$

Maximums: $(0, 1)$; $\left(\frac{\pi}{2}, 1\right)$

Minimum: $\left(\frac{1}{2} \cdot \frac{\pi}{2}, -1\right) = \left(\frac{\pi}{4}, -1\right)$

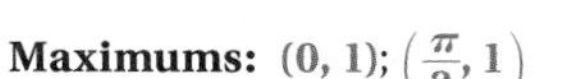

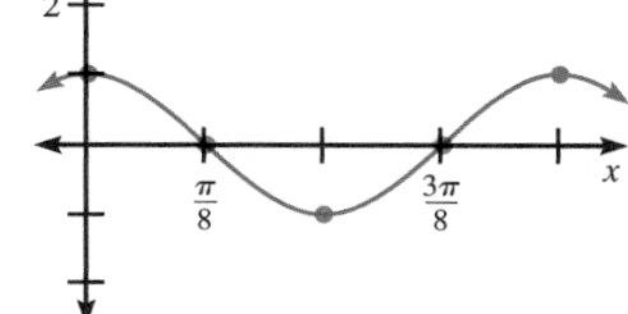

GUIDED PRACTICE for Example 1

Graph the function. 1–4. See margin.

1. $y = 2 \cos x$
2. $y = 5 \sin x$
3. $f(x) = \sin \pi x$
4. $g(x) = \cos 4\pi x$

Motivating the Lesson

Have students make a table that shows the time in 15-minute increments from noon until 6 P.M. Corresponding to each time in the table, ask them to indicate how many minutes it is from the nearest hour. Then ask students to use a timeline to graph the number of minutes against the time. Their graphs will show an example of a periodic function. In this lesson students will learn about the characteristics of graphs that are periodic.

3 TEACH

Extra Example 1

Graph (a) $y = \sin 3x$ and (b) $y = 3 \cos x$.

a.

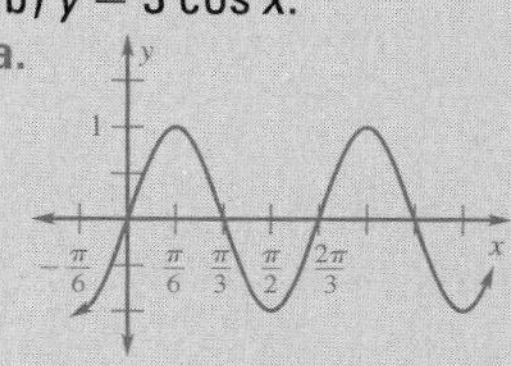

b.

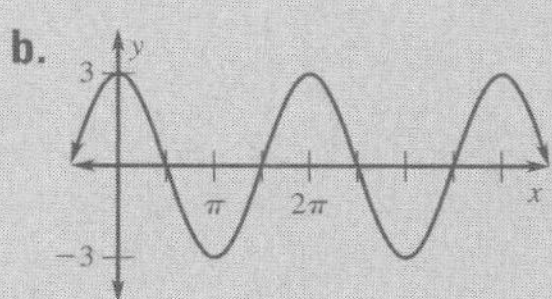

1–4. See Additional Answers beginning on p. AA1.

Differentiated Instruction

Inclusion Before discussing **Example 1**, give students the opportunity to obtain some practice with the material discussed in the two Key Concept boxes. Give students a worksheet displaying a few graphs of sine and cosine functions. Have students give the coordinates of several points on each curve and identify the amplitude and period of each graph.

See also the *Algebra 2 Toolkit* for more strategies.

Extra Example 2

Graph $y = 3\cos\frac{\pi}{2}x$.

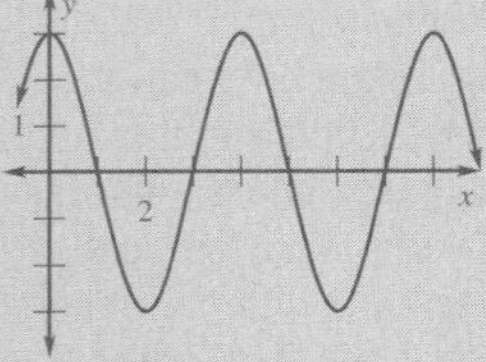

Extra Example 3

Hydraulic engineers use cosine models to predict high and low tides. At one point along a coastline the maximum mean tide level over the course of a year is 2 feet. If high tides occur every 12.5 hours, write and graph a cosine model that predicts the tide level T as a function of time t (in hours).

$T = 2\cos\left(\frac{2\pi t}{12.5}\right)$

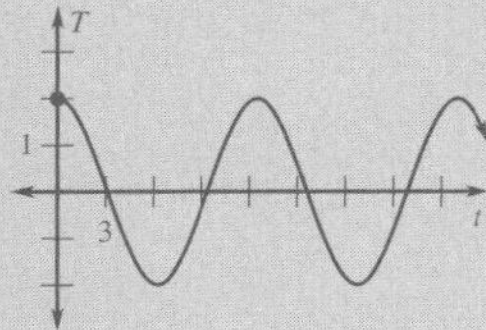

EXAMPLE 2 Graph a cosine function

Graph $y = \frac{1}{2}\cos 2\pi x$.

SKETCH A GRAPH

After you have drawn one complete cycle of the graph in Example 2 on the interval $0 \le x \le 1$, you can extend the graph by copying the cycle as many times as desired to the left and right of $0 \le x \le 1$.

Solution

The amplitude is $a = \frac{1}{2}$ and the period is $\frac{2\pi}{b} = \frac{2\pi}{2\pi} = 1$.

Intercepts: $\left(\frac{1}{4} \cdot 1, 0\right) = \left(\frac{1}{4}, 0\right)$;

$\left(\frac{3}{4} \cdot 1, 0\right) = \left(\frac{3}{4}, 0\right)$

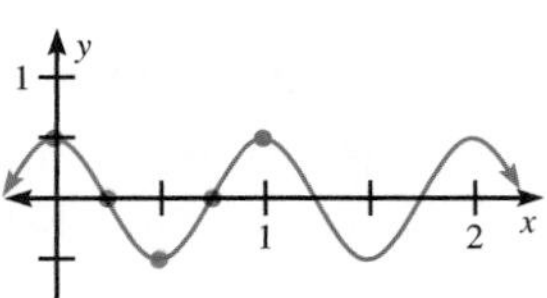

Maximums: $\left(0, \frac{1}{2}\right)$; $\left(1, \frac{1}{2}\right)$

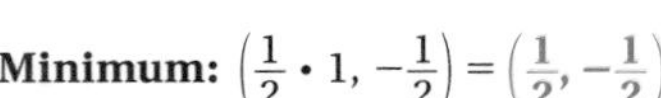

Minimum: $\left(\frac{1}{2} \cdot 1, -\frac{1}{2}\right) = \left(\frac{1}{2}, -\frac{1}{2}\right)$

MODELING WITH TRIGONOMETRIC FUNCTIONS The periodic nature of trigonometric functions is useful for modeling *oscillating* motions or repeating patterns that occur in real life. Some examples are sound waves, the motion of a pendulum, and seasons of the year. In such applications, the reciprocal of the period is called the **frequency**, which gives the number of cycles per unit of time.

EXAMPLE 3 Model with a sine function

AUDIO TEST A sound consisting of a single frequency is called a pure tone. An *audiometer* produces pure tones to test a person's auditory functions. Suppose an audiometer produces a pure tone with a frequency f of 2000 hertz (cycles per second). The maximum pressure P produced from the pure tone is 2 millipascals. Write and graph a sine model that gives the pressure P as a function of the time t (in seconds).

Solution

STEP 1 **Find** the values of a and b in the model $P = a\sin bt$. The maximum pressure is 2, so $a = 2$. You can use the frequency f to find b.

$$\text{frequency} = \frac{1}{\text{period}} \longrightarrow 2000 = \frac{b}{2\pi} \longrightarrow 4000\pi = b$$

The pressure P as a function of time t is given by $P = 2\sin 4000\pi t$.

STEP 2 **Graph** the model. The amplitude is $a = 2$ and the period is $\frac{1}{f} = \frac{1}{2000}$.

Intercepts: $(0, 0)$;

$\left(\frac{1}{2} \cdot \frac{1}{2000}, 0\right) = \left(\frac{1}{4000}, 0\right)$; $\left(\frac{1}{2000}, 0\right)$

Maximum: $\left(\frac{1}{4} \cdot \frac{1}{2000}, 2\right) = \left(\frac{1}{8000}, 2\right)$

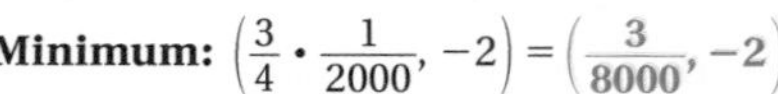

Minimum: $\left(\frac{3}{4} \cdot \frac{1}{2000}, -2\right) = \left(\frac{3}{8000}, -2\right)$

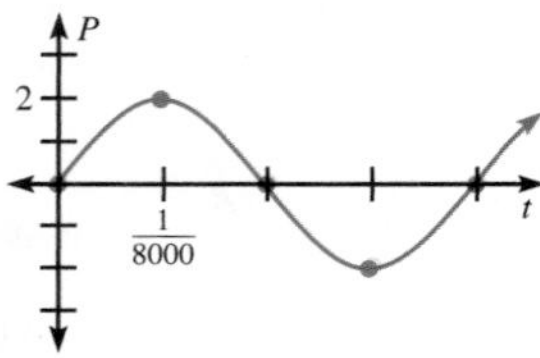

Differentiated Instruction

Below Level Have students begin by making a table of values for $y = \sin x$, $-2\pi \le x \le 2\pi$ and graphing the curve. Have them repeat the process for $y = \cos x$, $-2\pi \le x \le 2\pi$ on a piece of tracing paper. Tell them to place the graph of $y = \cos x$ over the graph of $y = \sin x$ and have them compare the maximum, minimum, and intercepts of the two graphs.

See also the *Algebra 2 Toolkit* for more strategies.

GUIDED PRACTICE for Examples 2 and 3

Graph the function. 5–8. See margin.

5. $y = \frac{1}{4} \sin \pi x$
6. $y = \frac{1}{3} \cos \pi x$
7. $f(x) = 2 \sin 3x$
8. $g(x) = 3 \cos 4x$

9. **WHAT IF?** In Example 3, how would the function change if the audiometer produced a pure tone with a frequency of 1000 hertz?
The period would increase because the frequency is decreased, $P = 2 \sin 2000\pi t$.

GRAPH OF $Y = \tan X$ The graphs of all tangent functions are related to the graph of the parent function $y = \tan x$, which is shown below.

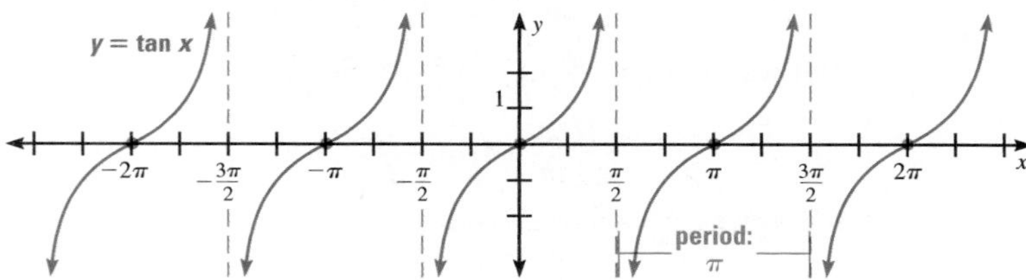

FIND ODD MULTIPLES
Odd multiples of $\frac{\pi}{2}$ are values such as these:
$\pm 1 \cdot \frac{\pi}{2} = \pm\frac{\pi}{2}$
$\pm 3 \cdot \frac{\pi}{2} = \pm\frac{3\pi}{2}$
$\pm 5 \cdot \frac{\pi}{2} = \pm\frac{5\pi}{2}$

The function $y = \tan x$ has the following characteristics:

1. The domain is all real numbers except odd multiples of $\frac{\pi}{2}$. At these x-values, the graph has vertical asymptotes.
2. The range is all real numbers. So, the function $y = \tan x$ does not have a maximum or minimum value, and therefore the graph of $y = \tan x$ does not have an amplitude.
3. The graph has a period of π.
4. The x-intercepts of the graph occur when $x = 0, \pm\pi, \pm 2\pi, \pm 3\pi, \ldots$.

KEY CONCEPT *For Your Notebook*

Characteristics of $y = a \tan bx$

The period and vertical asymptotes of the graph of $y = a \tan bx$, where a and b are nonzero real numbers, are as follows:

- The period is $\frac{\pi}{|b|}$.
- The vertical asymptotes are at odd multiples of $\frac{\pi}{2|b|}$.

GRAPHING KEY POINTS The graph at the right shows five key x-values that can help you sketch the graph of $y = a \tan bx$ for $a > 0$ and $b > 0$. These are the **x-intercept**, the x-values where the **asymptotes** occur, and the x-values **halfway between** the x-intercept and the asymptotes. At each halfway point, the function's value is either a or $-a$.

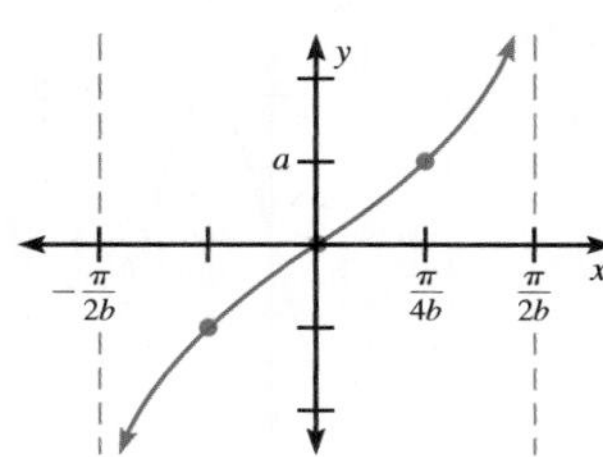

Extra Example 4

Graph one period of the function $y = 2 \tan \frac{1}{2}x$.

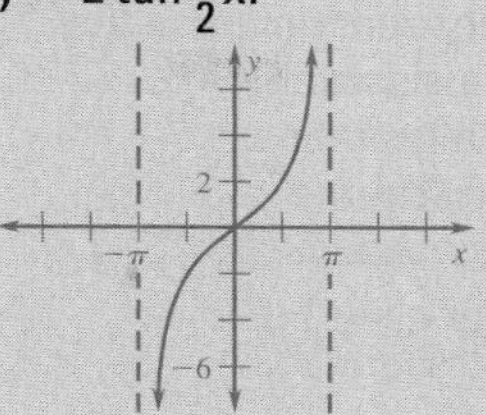

Avoiding Common Errors

Some students may have trouble calculating the halfway points for the tangent function in Example 4. An alternative method is to see that since 6 is half of 12, the graph has halfway points at $\frac{\pi}{12}$ and $-\frac{\pi}{12}$.

An **Animated Algebra** activity is available on-line for **Example 4**. This activity is also available on the **Power Presentations CD-ROM**.

8.
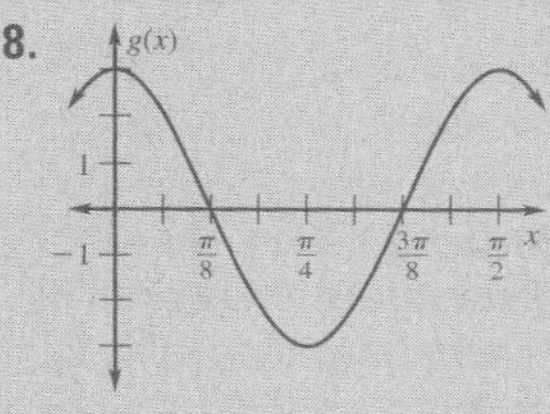

5.
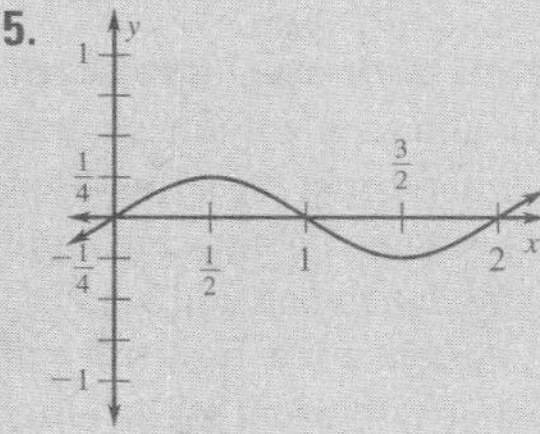

6.
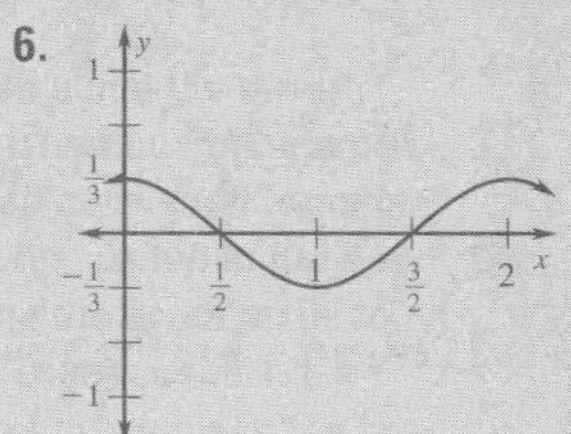

7.
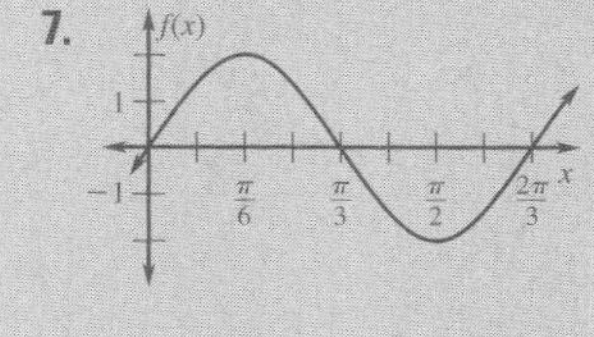

Closing the Lesson

Have students summarize the major points of the lesson and answer the Essential Question: Compare the graphs of $y = \sin x$ and $y = \cos x$ to the graph of $y = \tan x$.

- The graphs of $y = a \sin bx$ and $y = a \cos bx$, where a and b are nonzero numbers and x is in radian measure, have amplitude $|a|$ and period $\frac{2\pi}{|b|}$.
- You can use the maximum and minimum values and the x-intercepts to graph $y = \sin x$ and $y = \cos x$.
- The graph of $y = a \tan bx$, where a and b are nonzero real numbers, has period $\frac{\pi}{|b|}$ and vertical asymptotes at odd multiples of $\frac{\pi}{2|b|}$.
- You can use the asymptotes, the x-intercepts, and the x-values halfway between the x-intercepts and the asymptotes to graph $y = \tan x$.

The graphs of $y = \sin x$, $y = \cos x$, and $y = \tan x$ are all periodic. Whereas the graphs of $y = \sin x$ and $y = \cos x$ have maximum and minimum values, the graph of $y = \tan x$ has asymptotes at every odd multiple of $x = \pm\frac{\pi}{2}$.

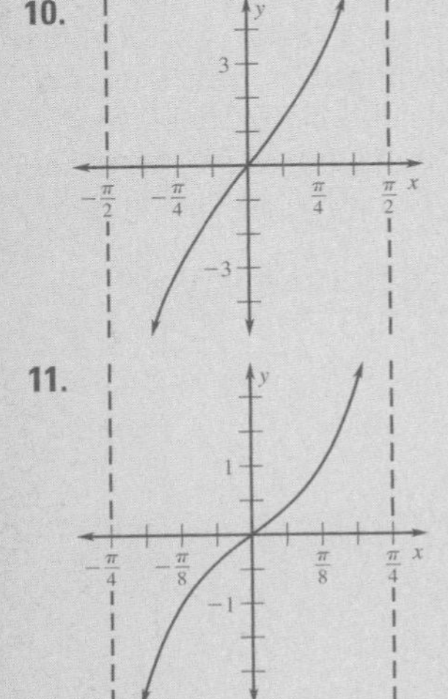

EXAMPLE 4 Graph a tangent function

Graph one period of the function $y = 2 \tan 3x$.

Solution

The period is $\frac{\pi}{b} = \frac{\pi}{3}$.

Intercept: $(0, 0)$

Asymptotes: $x = \frac{\pi}{2b} = \frac{\pi}{2 \cdot 3}$, or $x = \frac{\pi}{6}$;

$x = -\frac{\pi}{2b} = -\frac{\pi}{2 \cdot 3}$, or $x = -\frac{\pi}{6}$

Halfway points: $\left(\frac{\pi}{4b}, a\right) = \left(\frac{\pi}{4 \cdot 3}, 2\right) = \left(\frac{\pi}{12}, 2\right)$;

$\left(-\frac{\pi}{4b}, -a\right) = \left(-\frac{\pi}{4 \cdot 3}, -2\right) = \left(-\frac{\pi}{12}, -2\right)$

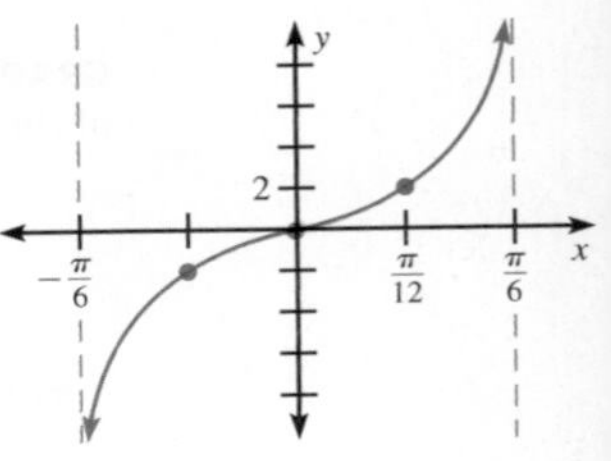

Animated Algebra at classzone.com

✓ GUIDED PRACTICE for Example 4

Graph one period of the function. 10–13. See margin.

10. $y = 3 \tan x$ **11.** $y = \tan 2x$ **12.** $f(x) = 2 \tan 4x$ **13.** $g(x) = 5 \tan \pi x$

14.1 EXERCISES

HOMEWORK KEY
- ○ = WORKED-OUT SOLUTIONS on p. WS23 for Exs. 5, 17, and 31
- ★ = STANDARDIZED TEST PRACTICE Exs. 2, 15, 24, 25, and 31
- ◆ = MULTIPLE REPRESENTATIONS Ex. 32

SKILL PRACTICE

A

1. VOCABULARY Copy and complete: The graphs of the functions $y = \sin x$ and $y = \cos x$ both have a(n) _?_ of 2π. period

2. ★ WRITING *Compare* the domains and ranges of the functions $y = a \sin bx$, $y = a \cos bx$, and $y = a \tan bx$ where a and b are positive constants. See margin.

EXAMPLE 1 on p. 909 for Exs. 3–14

ANALYZING FUNCTIONS **Identify the amplitude and the period of the graph of the function.**

3.

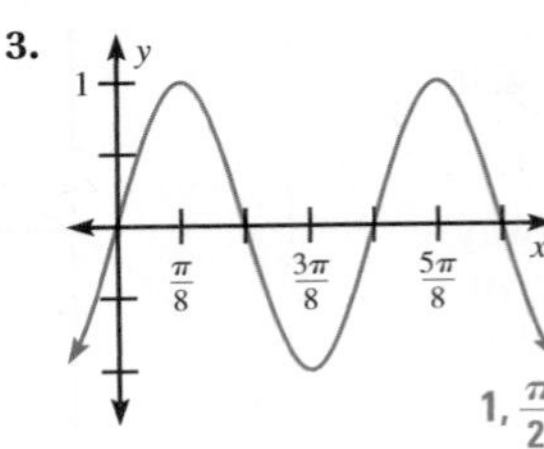

$1, \frac{\pi}{2}$

4.

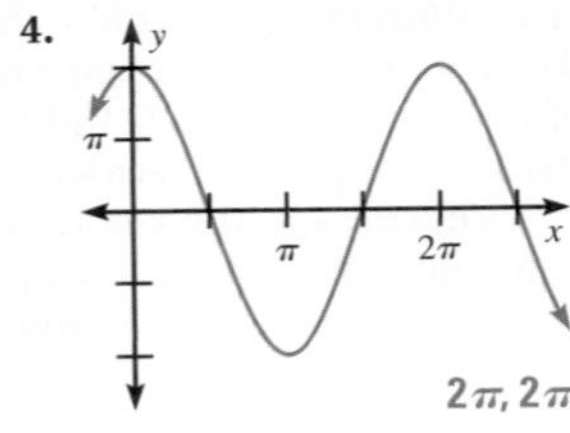

$2\pi, 2\pi$

5.

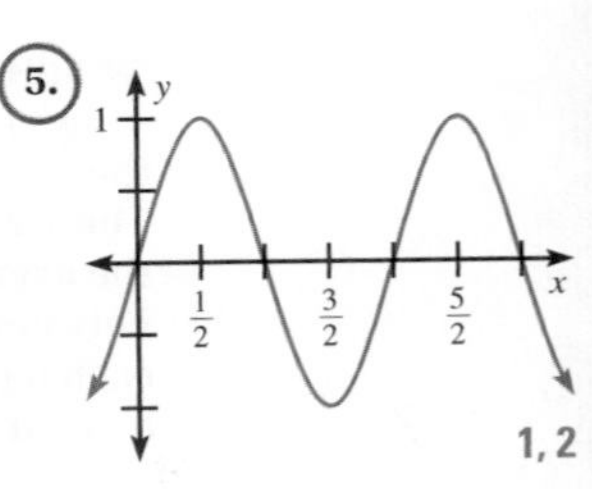

1, 2

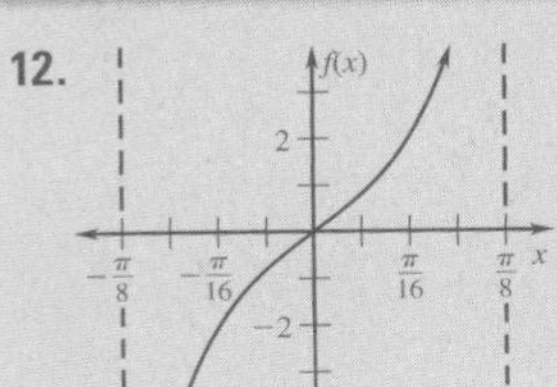

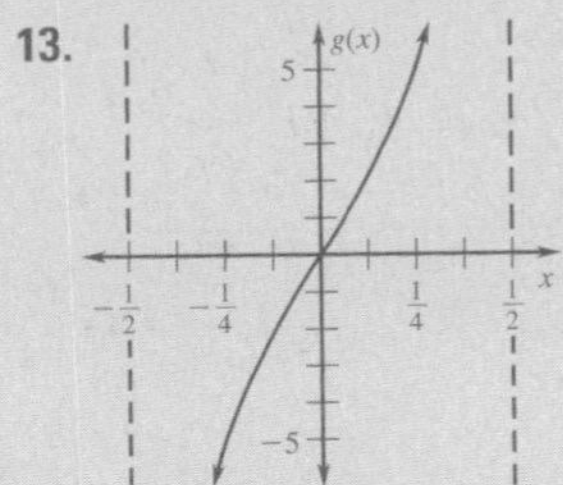

Skill Practice

2. The domains and ranges are the same for sine and cosine (all real numbers and $-1 \le y \le 1$). For tangent, the domain is all real numbers except multiples of $\frac{\pi}{2}$ and the range is all real numbers.

GRAPHING **Graph the function.** **6–13. See margin.**

6. $y = \sin \frac{1}{5}x$
7. $y = 4 \cos x$
8. $f(x) = \cos \frac{2}{5}x$
9. $y = \sin \pi x$
10. $f(x) = \frac{2}{3} \sin x$
11. $f(x) = \sin \frac{\pi}{2}x$
12. $y = \frac{\pi}{4} \cos x$
13. $f(x) = \cos 24x$

14. **ERROR ANALYSIS** *Describe* and correct the error in finding the period of the function $y = \sin \frac{2}{3}x$. **See margin.**

$$\text{Period} = \frac{|b|}{2\pi} = \frac{\left|\frac{2}{3}\right|}{2\pi} = \frac{1}{3\pi}$$

15. ★ **MULTIPLE CHOICE** The graph of which function has an amplitude of 4 and a period of 2? **C**

Ⓐ $y = 4 \cos 2x$ Ⓑ $y = 2 \sin 4x$ Ⓒ $y = 4 \sin \pi x$ Ⓓ $y = 2 \cos \frac{1}{2}\pi x$

EXAMPLES 2, 3, and 4 on pp. 910–912 for Exs. 16–24

B **GRAPHING** **Graph the function.** **16–23. See margin.**

16. $y = 2 \sin 8x$
17. $f(x) = 4 \tan x$
18. $y = 3 \cos \pi x$
19. $y = 5 \sin 2x$
20. $f(x) = 2 \tan 4x$
21. $y = 2 \cos \frac{1}{4}\pi x$
22. $f(x) = 4 \tan \pi x$
23. $y = \pi \cos 4\pi x$

24. ★ **MULTIPLE CHOICE** Which of the following is an asymptote of the graph of $y = 2 \tan 3x$? **A**

Ⓐ $x = \frac{\pi}{6}$ Ⓑ $x = -\pi$ Ⓒ $x = \frac{1}{6}$ Ⓓ $x = -\frac{\pi}{12}$

C 25. ★ **OPEN-ENDED MATH** *Describe* a real-life situation that can be modeled by a periodic function. ***Sample answer:*** **The rise and fall of the tides versus time.**

CHALLENGE **Sketch the graph of the function by plotting points. Then state the function's domain, range, and period.** **26–28. See margin.**

26. $y = \csc x$
27. $y = \sec x$
28. $y = \cot x$

PROBLEM SOLVING

EXAMPLE 3 on p. 910 for Exs. 29–30

A 29. **PENDULUMS** The motion of a certain pendulum can be modeled by the function $d = 4 \cos \pi t$ where d is the pendulum's horizontal displacement (in inches) relative to its position at rest and t is the time (in seconds). Graph the function. What is the greatest horizontal distance the pendulum will travel from its position at rest? **See margin for art; 8 in.**

@HomeTutor for problem solving help at classzone.com

30. **TUNING FORKS** A tuning fork produces a sound pressure wave that can be modeled by

$$P = 0.001 \sin 880t$$

where P is the pressure (in pascals) and t is the time (in seconds). Find the period and frequency of this function. Then graph the function. $\frac{\pi}{440}, \frac{440}{\pi}$; **see margin for art.**

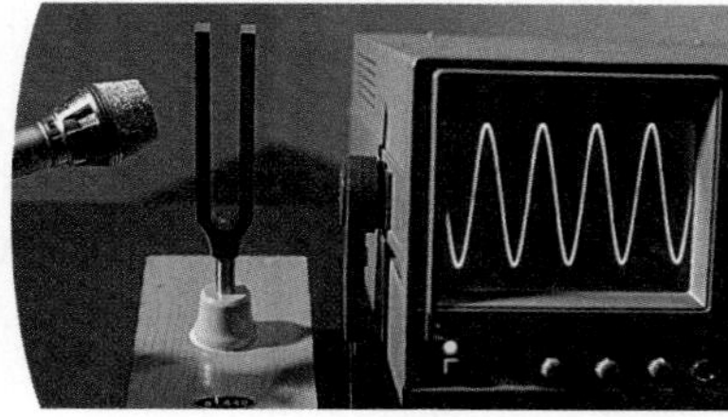

 for problem solving help at classzone.com

4 PRACTICE AND APPLY

Assignment Guide

Answer Transparencies available for all exercises

Basic:
Day 1: pp. 912–914
Exs. 1–15
Day 2: pp. 912–914
Exs. 16–19, 29–31, 34–35 odd

Average:
Day 1: pp. 912–914
Exs. 1–15
Day 2: pp. 912–914
Exs. 16–25, 29–32, 34–35

Advanced:
Day 1: pp. 912–914
Exs. 1–15, 40–51 odd
Day 2: pp. 912–914
Exs. 19–35*

Block:
pp. 912–914
Exs. 1–25, 29–32, 34–35

Differentiated Instruction

See *Algebra 2 Best Practices Toolkit* for suggestions on addressing the needs of a diverse classroom.

Homework Check

For a quick check of student understanding of key concepts, go over the following exercises:

Basic: 3, 8, 16, 18, 29
Average: 4, 10, 18, 20, 30
Advanced: 10, 12, 20, 22, 30

Extra Practice

- Student Edition, p. 1023
- Chapter 14 Resource Book: Practice levels A, B, C, pp. 7–9

Practice Worksheet

An easily-readable reduced practice page (with answers) for this lesson can be found on p. 906C.

6–13. See Additional Answers beginning on p. AA1.

14. To find the period, use the expression $\frac{2\pi}{|b|}$; period $= \frac{2\pi}{\left|\frac{2}{3}\right|} = 3\pi$.

16–23, 26–28. See Additional Answers beginning on p. AA1.

29.

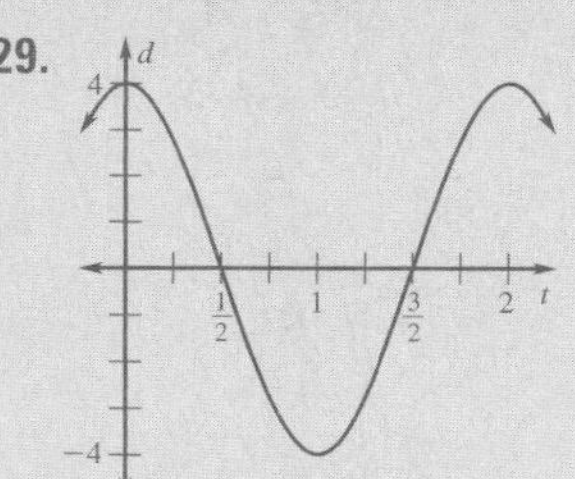

30.

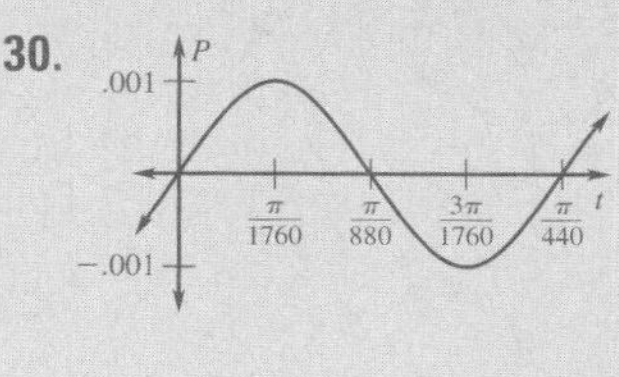

5 ASSESS AND RETEACH

Daily Homework Quiz

Transparency Available

Graph each function.

1. $y = \sin 2\pi x$

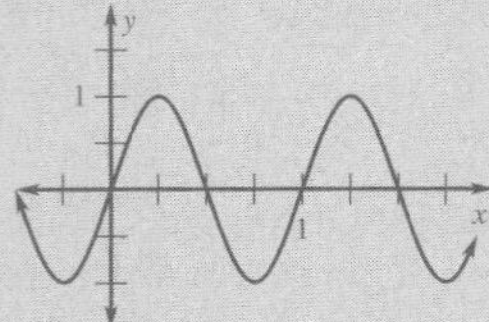

2. $y = 4 \tan x$

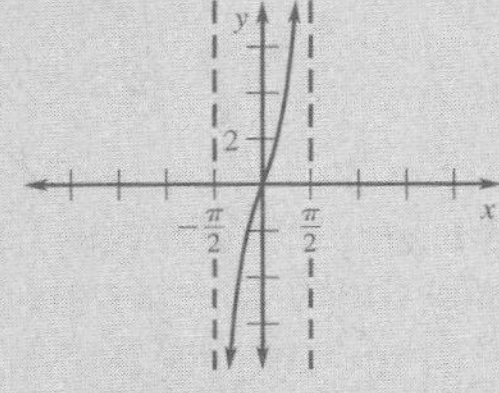

The typical voltage V supplied by an electrical outlet in the U.S. oscillates between about -170 volts and $+170$ volts with a frequency of 60 cycles per second.

3. Write a sine model that gives the number of volts V as a function of time t (in seconds). $V = 170 \sin 120\pi t$

4. Graph the function.

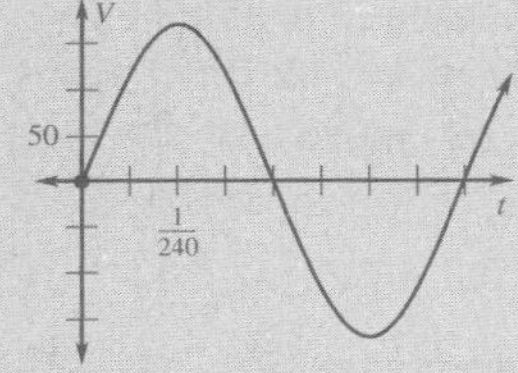

Available at **classzone.com**

Diagnosis/Remediation

- Practice A, B, C in Chapter 14 Resource Book, pp. 7–9
- Study Guide in Chapter 14 Resource Book, pp. 10–11
- Practice Workbook, pp. 193–194
- @HomeTutor

Challenge

Additional challenge is available in the Chapter 14 Resource Book, p. 14.

32b–c, 33a–b. See Additional Answers beginning on p. AA1.

B

31. ★ **SHORT RESPONSE** A buoy oscillates up and down as waves go past. The buoy moves a total of 3.5 feet from its low point to its high point, and then returns to its high point every 6 seconds.

a. Write an equation that gives the buoy's vertical position y at time t if the buoy is at its highest point when $t = 0$. $y = 1.75 \cos \frac{\pi}{3}t$

b. *Explain* why you chose $y = a \sin bt$ or $y = a \cos bt$ for part (a). Since the high point occurs at $t = 0$, the cosine function best represents situation.

32. ◆ **MULTIPLE REPRESENTATIONS** You are standing on a bridge, 140 feet above the ground. You look down at a car traveling away from the underpass.

a. Writing an Equation Write an equation that gives the car's distance d from the base of the bridge as a function of the angle θ. $\tan \theta = \frac{d}{140}$

b. Drawing a Graph Graph the function found in part (a). *Explain* how the graph relates to the given situation. See margin.

c. Making a Table Make a table of values for the function. Use the table to find the car's distance from the bridge when $\theta = 20°$, $40°$, and $60°$. See margin.

C

33. **CHALLENGE** The motion of a spring can be modeled by $y = A \cos kt$ where y is the spring's vertical displacement (in feet) relative to its position at rest, A is the initial displacement (in feet), k is a constant that measures the elasticity of the spring, and t is the time (in seconds).

a. Suppose you have a spring whose motion can be modeled by the function $y = 0.2 \cos 6t$. Find the initial displacement and the period of the spring. Then graph the given function. $0.2, \frac{\pi}{3}$; see margin for art.

b. Graphing Calculator If a damping force is applied to the spring, the motion of the spring can be modeled by the function $y = 0.2e^{-4.5t} \cos 4t$. Graph this function. What effect does damping have on the motion? See margin for art; the function is no longer periodic, it appears to be a decay function.

KENTUCKY MIXED REVIEW

TEST PRACTICE at classzone.com

34. What is the area of $\triangle MNP$? **B**

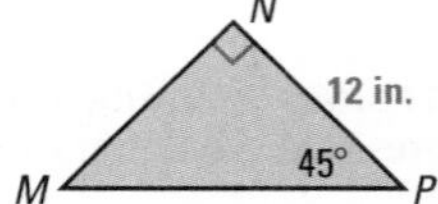

Ⓐ 36 in.^{2} Ⓑ 72 in.^{2}
Ⓒ 109 in.^{2} Ⓓ 144 in.^{2}

35. The length of $\overline{ST}$ is $7\sqrt{5}$ and the coordinates of its endpoints are $(x, -10)$ and $(-8, 4)$. What are the possible values of x? **D**

Ⓐ −15 Ⓑ 1
Ⓒ −15, −1 Ⓓ 15, −1

14.2 Translate and Reflect Trigonometric Graphs

MA-HS-5.1.3

Before You graphed sine, cosine, and tangent functions.

Now You will translate and reflect trigonometric graphs.

Why? So you can model predator-prey populations, as in Ex. 54.

Key Vocabulary
- translation, p. 123
- reflection, p. 124
- amplitude, p. 908
- period, p. 908

MA-HS-5.1.3
Students will demonstrate how equations and graphs are models of the relationship between two real-world quantities (e.g., the relationship between degrees Celsius and degrees Fahrenheit).

KEY CONCEPT *For Your Notebook*

Translations of Sine and Cosine Graphs

To graph $y = a \sin b(x - h) + k$ or $y = a \cos b(x - h) + k$ where $a > 0$ and $b > 0$, follow these steps:

STEP 1 **Identify** the amplitude a, the period $\frac{2\pi}{b}$, the horizontal shift h, and the vertical shift k of the graph.

STEP 2 **Draw** the horizontal line $y = k$, called the *midline* of the graph.

STEP 3 **Find** the five key points by translating the key points of $y = a \sin bx$ or $y = a \cos bx$ horizontally h units and vertically k units.

STEP 4 **Draw** the graph through the five translated key points.

EXAMPLE 1 Graph a vertical translation

Graph $y = 2 \sin 4x + 3$.

Solution

STEP 1 **Identify** the amplitude, period, horizontal shift, and vertical shift.

Amplitude: $a = 2$ Horizontal shift: $h = 0$

Period: $\frac{2\pi}{b} = \frac{2\pi}{4} = \frac{\pi}{2}$ Vertical shift: $k = 3$

STEP 2 **Draw** the midline of the graph, $y = 3$.

STEP 3 **Find** the five key points.

FIND KEY POINTS Because the graph is shifted up 3 units, the y-coordinates of the five key points will be increased by 3.

On $y = k$: $(0, 0 + 3) = (0, 3)$;

$\left(\frac{\pi}{4}, 0 + 3\right) = \left(\frac{\pi}{4}, 3\right)$; $\left(\frac{\pi}{2}, 0 + 3\right) = \left(\frac{\pi}{2}, 3\right)$

Maximum: $\left(\frac{\pi}{8}, 2 + 3\right) = \left(\frac{\pi}{8}, 5\right)$

Minimum: $\left(\frac{3\pi}{8}, -2 + 3\right) = \left(\frac{3\pi}{8}, 1\right)$

STEP 4 **Draw** the graph through the key points.

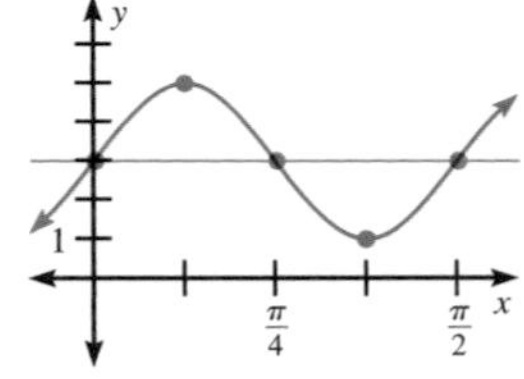

1 PLAN AND PREPARE

Warm-Up Exercises

Transparency Available

Describe the translation of the graph of $y = x^2$ that produces the graph of the given function.

1. $y = x^2 + 2$ 2 units up
2. $y = x^2 - 5$ 5 units down
3. $y = (x - 1)^2$ 1 unit right
4. $y = (x + 3) + 4$ 3 units left and 4 units up

Notetaking Guide

Transparency Available

Promotes interactive learning and notetaking skills, pp. 354–357.

Pacing

Basic: 2 days
Average: 2 days
Advanced: 2 days
Block: 1 block
- See *Teaching Guide/Lesson Plan.*

2 FOCUS AND MOTIVATE

Essential Question

Big Idea 1, p. 907

Describe the values of a, h, and k if the graph of $y = a \tan b(x - h) + k$ is a reflection and a translation up and left of the graph of $y = |a| \tan bx$.

Tell students they will learn how to answer this question by studying the properties of translations and reflections of trigonometric graphs.

Resource Planning Guide

Chapter Resource Book
- Teaching Guide/Lesson Plan (pp. 15–16)
- Activity Master (p. 17)
- Practice levels A, B, C (pp. 18–20)
- Study Guide (pp. 21–22)
- Catch-up for Absent Students (p. 23)
- Application (p. 24)
- Challenge (p. 25)

Workbooks
- Notetaking Guide (pp. 354–357)
- Practice Workbook (pp. 195–196)

Teaching Options
- **Power Presentations CD-ROM** provides dynamic electronic teaching resources for the classroom.
- **Activity Generator CD-ROM** provides editable activities for all ability levels.

Interactive Technology
- Easy Planner
- Power Presentations CD-ROM
- Activity Generator CD-ROM
- Animated Algebra
- Test Generator CD-ROM
- Online Quiz
- eWorkbook
- eEdition
- @HomeTutor

Resources for English Learners
- Quick Reference for English Learners
- Spanish Study Guide
- Multi-Language Visual Glossary
- Student Resources in Spanish

See also the *Algebra 2 Toolkit* for more strategies for meeting individual needs.

Motivating the Lesson

Show students a picture of a person flying a kite. Discuss how the height of the kite is dependent on the length of the string attached to the kite, the angle the string makes with the ground, and the height of the person holding the string. Tell students that sine functions representing translations of the function $y = \sin x$ can represent different heights of the kite.

3 TEACH

Extra Example 1

Graph $y = \frac{1}{2} \cos 2x - 2$.

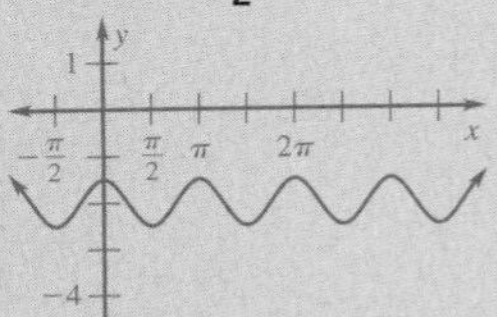

Extra Example 2

Graph $y = 2 \sin \frac{1}{2}(x - 4\pi)$.

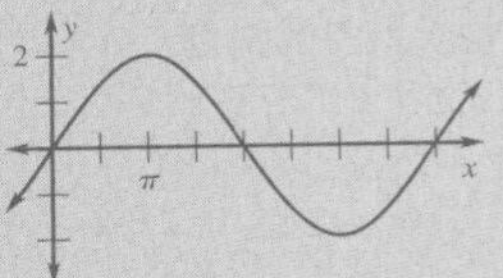

Guided Practice, p. 917

1.

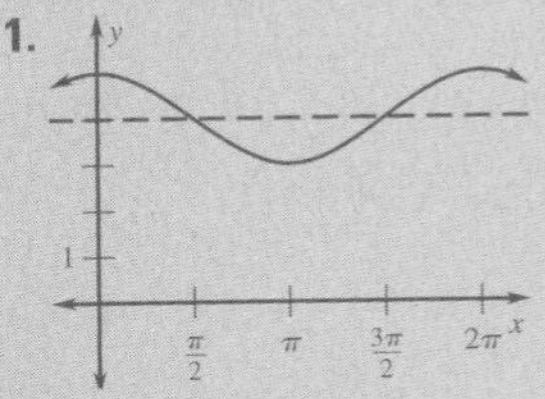

2.

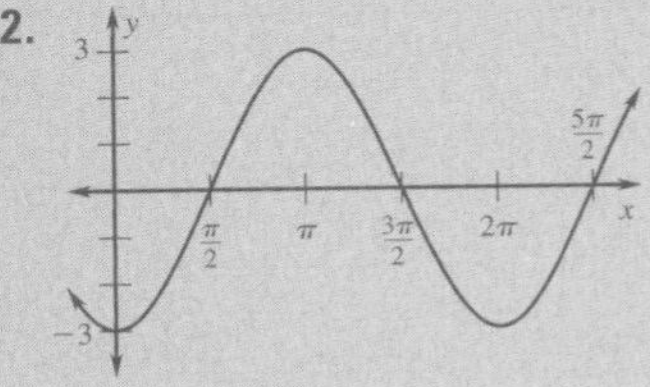

EXAMPLE 2 Graph a horizontal translation

Graph $y = 5 \cos 2(x - 3\pi)$.

Solution

STEP 1 **Identify** the amplitude, period, horizontal shift, and vertical shift.

Amplitude: $a = 5$ Horizontal shift: $h = 3\pi$

Period: $\frac{2\pi}{b} = \frac{2\pi}{2} = \pi$ Vertical shift: $k = 0$

STEP 2 **Draw** the midline of the graph. Because $k = 0$, the midline is the x-axis.

FIND KEY POINTS Because the graph is shifted to the right 3π units, the x-coordinates of the five key points will be increased by 3π.

STEP 3 **Find** the five key points.

On $y = k$: $\left(\frac{\pi}{4} + 3\pi, 0\right) = \left(\frac{13\pi}{4}, 0\right)$;

$\left(\frac{3\pi}{4} + 3\pi, 0\right) = \left(\frac{15\pi}{4}, 0\right)$

Maximums: $(0 + 3\pi, 5) = (3\pi, 5)$;
$(\pi + 3\pi, 5) = (4\pi, 5)$

Minimum: $\left(\frac{\pi}{2} + 3\pi, -5\right) = \left(\frac{7\pi}{2}, -5\right)$

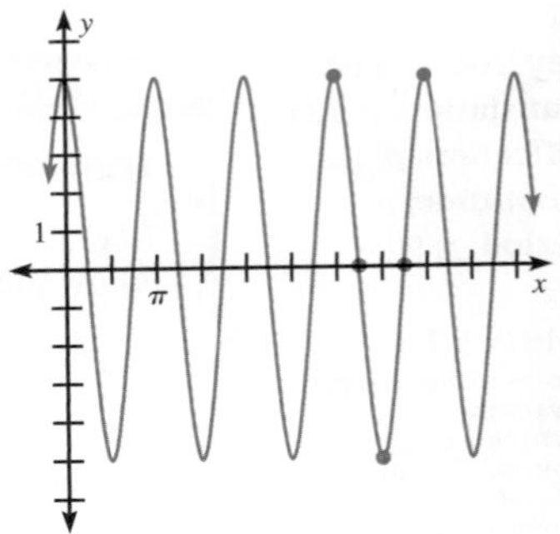

STEP 4 **Draw** the graph through the key points.

EXAMPLE 3 Graph a model for circular motion

FERRIS WHEEL Suppose you are riding a Ferris wheel that turns for 180 seconds. Your height h (in feet) above the ground at any time t (in seconds) can be modeled by the equation $h = 85 \sin \frac{\pi}{20}(t - 10) + 90$.

a. Graph your height above the ground as a function of time.

b. What are your maximum and minimum heights?

Solution

a. The amplitude is 85 and the period is $\frac{2\pi}{\frac{\pi}{20}} = 40$. The wheel turns $\frac{180}{40} = 4.5$ times in 180 seconds, so the graph below shows 4.5 cycles.

The five key points are (10, 90), (20, 175), (30, 90), (40, 5), and (50, 90).

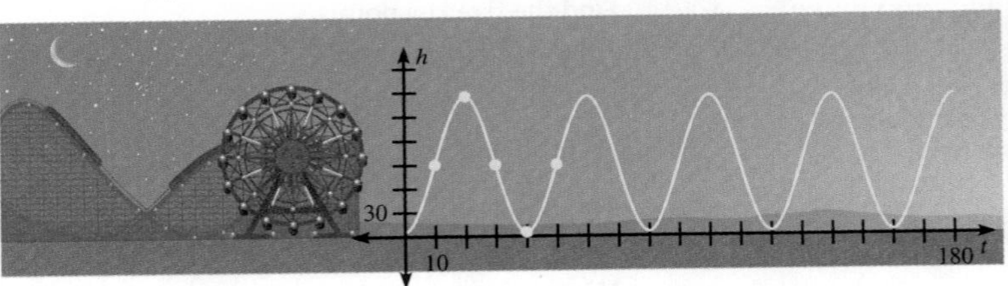

b. Your maximum height is $90 + 85 = 175$ feet and your minimum height is $90 - 85 = 5$ feet.

✓ GUIDED PRACTICE for Examples 1, 2, and 3

Graph the function. 1–3. See margin.

1. $y = \cos x + 4$
2. $y = 3\sin\left(x - \frac{\pi}{2}\right)$
3. $f(x) = \sin(x + \pi) - 1$

REFLECTIONS You have graphed functions of the form $y = a\sin b(x - h) + k$ and $y = a\cos b(x - h) + k$ where $a > 0$. To see what happens when $a < 0$, consider the graphs of $y = -\sin x$ and $y = -\cos x$.

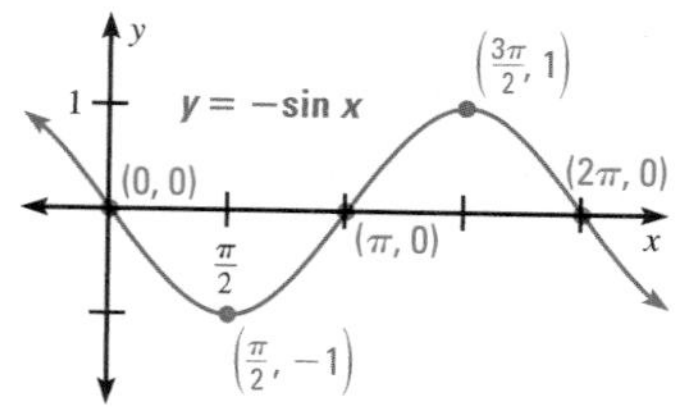

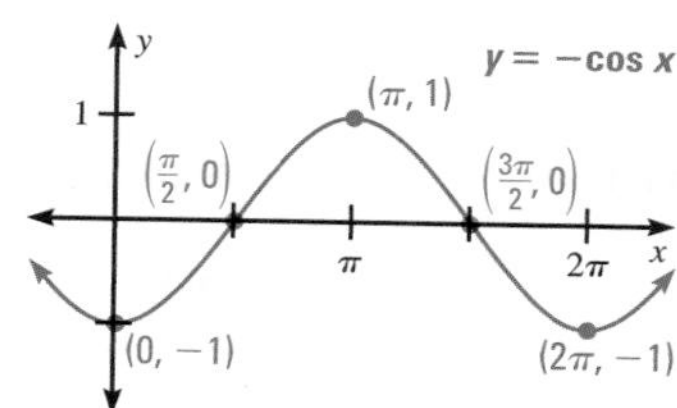

Notice that the graphs are reflections of the graphs of $y = \sin x$ and $y = \cos x$ in the x-axis. In general, when $a < 0$ the graphs of $y = a\sin b(x - h) + k$ and $y = a\cos b(x - h) + k$ are reflections of the graphs of $y = |a|\sin b(x - h) + k$ and $y = |a|\cos b(x - h) + k$, respectively, in the midline $y = k$.

EXAMPLE 4 Combine a translation and a reflection

Graph $y = -2\sin\frac{2}{3}\left(x - \frac{\pi}{2}\right)$.

Solution

STEP 1 **Identify** the amplitude, period, horizontal shift, and vertical shift.

Amplitude: $|a| = |-2| = 2$ Horizontal shift: $h = \frac{\pi}{2}$

Period: $\frac{2\pi}{b} = \frac{2\pi}{\frac{2}{3}} = 3\pi$ Vertical shift: $k = 0$

STEP 2 **Draw** the midline of the graph. Because $k = 0$, the midline is the x-axis.

STEP 3 **Find** the five key points of $y = |-2|\sin\frac{2}{3}\left(x - \frac{\pi}{2}\right)$.

On $y = k$: $\left(0 + \frac{\pi}{2}, 0\right) = \left(\frac{\pi}{2}, 0\right)$; $\left(\frac{3\pi}{2} + \frac{\pi}{2}, 0\right) = (2\pi, 0)$; $\left(3\pi + \frac{\pi}{2}, 0\right) = \left(\frac{7\pi}{2}, 0\right)$

Maximum: $\left(\frac{3\pi}{4} + \frac{\pi}{2}, 2\right) = \left(\frac{5\pi}{4}, 2\right)$ **Minimum:** $\left(\frac{9\pi}{4} + \frac{\pi}{2}, -2\right) = \left(\frac{11\pi}{4}, -2\right)$

GRAPH REFLECTIONS The maximum and minimum of the original graph become the minimum and maximum, respectively, of the reflected graph.

STEP 4 **Reflect** the graph. Because $a < 0$, the graph is reflected in the midline $y = 0$. So, $\left(\frac{5\pi}{4}, 2\right)$ becomes $\left(\frac{5\pi}{4}, -2\right)$ and $\left(\frac{11\pi}{4}, -2\right)$ becomes $\left(\frac{11\pi}{4}, 2\right)$.

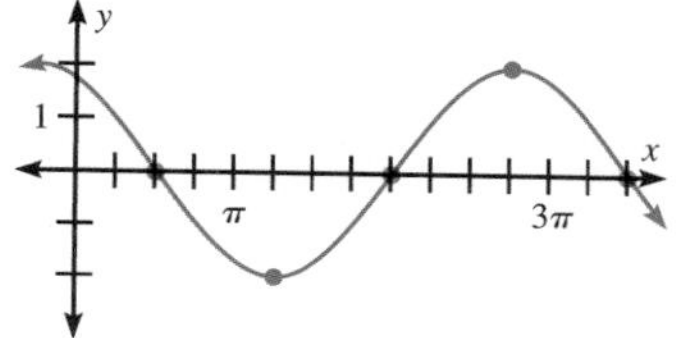

STEP 5 **Draw** the graph through the key points.

Animated Algebra at classzone.com

Differentiated Instruction

Visual Learners Have students graph functions similar to those in **Guided Practice Exercises 1–3**. Change the values of the constants and have students graph the new functions alongside the first ones that were given. Then, have students work in small groups to identify the effects on the graph of changing the constants of these trigonometric functions.

See also the *Algebra 2 Toolkit* for more strategies.

3.

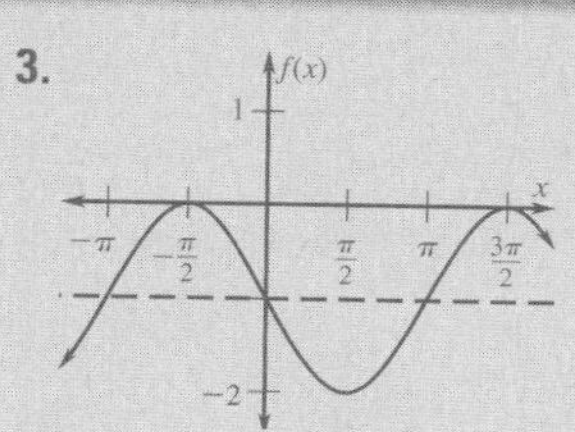

Extra Example 3

An outboard motor rotates its propeller at 5000 revolutions per minute. The center of the propeller is 18 inches below the surface of the water. The depth $D(t)$ (in feet) of a point on the propeller at time t (in seconds) can be modeled by the equation $D(t) = 5\cos\left(\frac{500\pi}{3}t\right) + 18$.

a. Graph the depth of the point below water as function of time.

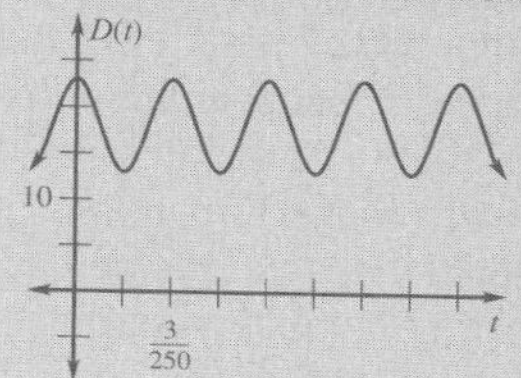

b. Where are the maximum and minimum depths? max. depth: 23 in., min. depth: 13 in.

Extra Example 4

Graph $y = -\cos 4x + 1$.

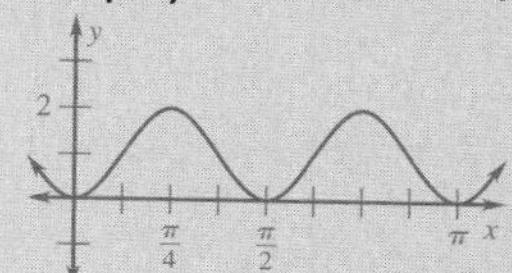

Key Question to Ask for Example 4

- How can you translate the graph of $y = \sin x$ to obtain the graph of $y = -2\sin\frac{2}{3}\left(x - \frac{\pi}{2}\right)$? Double the amplitude, increase the period to 3π, shift the graph $\frac{\pi}{2}$ units right, then reflect the graph over the x-axis.

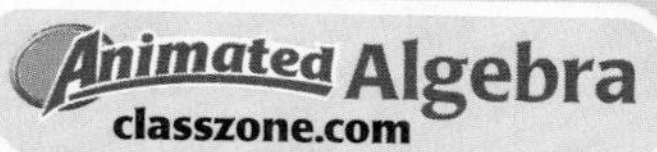

An **Animated Algebra** activity is available on-line for **Example 4**. This activity is also available on the **Power Presentations CD-ROM**.

Avoiding Common Errors

If students have trouble graphing the function on a graphing calculator, it may be that their graphing calculators are in degree mode. Remind them that the values of θ are angle measures, measured in radians.

Extra Example 5

Graph $y = -2\tan\left(x - \frac{\pi}{2}\right)$.

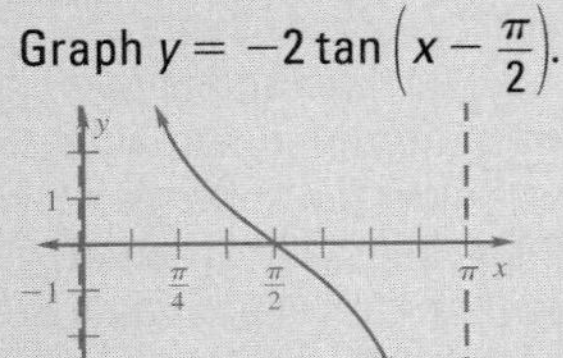

Extra Example 6

The Mars Exploration Rover, Spirit, has a robotic arm with a maximum height of about 85 centimeters when fully extended. Suppose that Spirit's shoulder is about 30 centimeters from a Martian rock. Write and graph a model that gives the height h of the arm as a function of its vertical angle θ. $h = -30\tan\theta + 85$

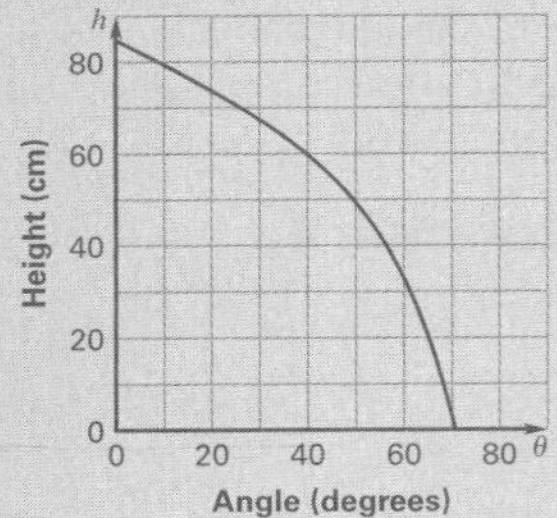

Closing the Lesson

Have students summarize the major points of the lesson and answer the Essential Question: Describe the values of a, h, and k if the graph of $y = a\tan b(x - h) + k$ is a reflection and a translation left and up of the graph of $y = |a| \tan bx$.

- The graphs of $y = a\sin b(x - h) + k$ and $y = a\cos b(x - h) + k$, where $a > 0$ and $b > 0$, are horizontal translations h units and vertical translations k units of the graphs of $y = a\sin bx$ and $y = a\cos bx$ respectively, and have amplitude a, period $\frac{2\pi}{b}$, and midline $y = k$.
- In general, when $a < 0$, the graphs of $y = a\sin bx$ and $y = a\cos bx$ are the reflections of the graphs of $y = |a| \sin bx$ and $y = |a| \cos bx$, respectively, in the midline $y = k$.
- Graphing tangent functions using translations and reflections is similar to graphing sine and cosine functions. When a tangent funtion has a horizontal shift, the asymptotes also have a horizontal shift.

$a < 0$, $h < 0$, and $k > 0$

TANGENT FUNCTIONS Graphing tangent functions using translations and reflections is similar to graphing sine and cosine functions.

EXAMPLE 5 Combine a translation and a reflection

Graph $y = -3\tan x + 5$.

Solution

STEP 1 **Identify** the period, horizontal shift, and vertical shift.

Period: π Horizontal shift: $h = 0$ Vertical shift: $k = 5$

STEP 2 **Draw** the midline of the graph, $y = 5$.

STEP 3 **Find** the asymptotes and key points of $y = |-3| \tan x + 5$.

FIND ASYMPTOTES
Notice that the asymptotes are not shifted. This is because there is no horizontal shift.

Asymptotes: $x = -\frac{\pi}{2 \cdot 1} = -\frac{\pi}{2}$; $x = \frac{\pi}{2 \cdot 1} = \frac{\pi}{2}$

On $y = k$: $(0, 0 + 5) = (0, 5)$

Halfway points: $\left(-\frac{\pi}{4}, -3 + 5\right) = \left(-\frac{\pi}{4}, 2\right)$; $\left(\frac{\pi}{4}, 3 + 5\right) = \left(\frac{\pi}{4}, 8\right)$

STEP 4 **Reflect** the graph. Because $a < 0$, the graph is reflected in the midline $y = 5$. So, $\left(-\frac{\pi}{4}, 2\right)$ becomes $\left(-\frac{\pi}{4}, 8\right)$ and $\left(\frac{\pi}{4}, 8\right)$ becomes $\left(\frac{\pi}{4}, 2\right)$.

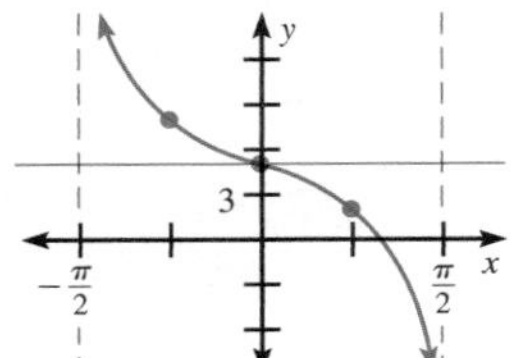

STEP 5 **Draw** the graph through the key points.

EXAMPLE 6 Model with a tangent function

GLASS ELEVATOR You are standing 120 feet from the base of a 260 foot building. You watch your friend go down the side of the building in a glass elevator. Write and graph a model that gives your friend's distance d (in feet) from the top of the building as a function of the angle of elevation θ.

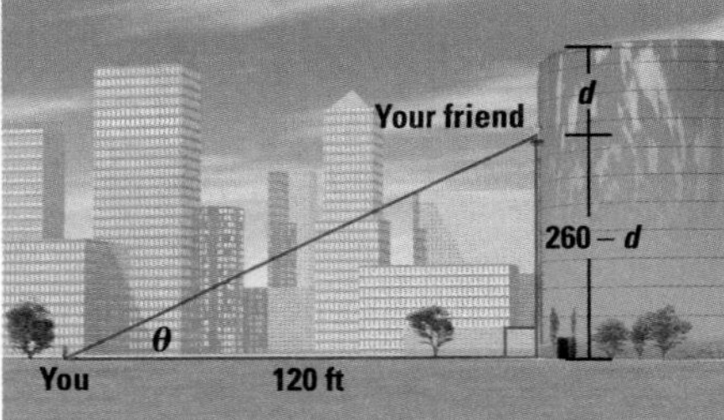

Solution

Use a tangent function to write an equation relating d and θ.

$\tan\theta = \frac{\text{opp}}{\text{adj}} = \frac{260 - d}{120}$	**Definition of tangent**
$120\tan\theta = 260 - d$	**Multiply each side by 120.**
$120\tan\theta - 260 = -d$	**Subtract 260 from each side.**
$-120\tan\theta + 260 = d$	**Solve for *d*.**

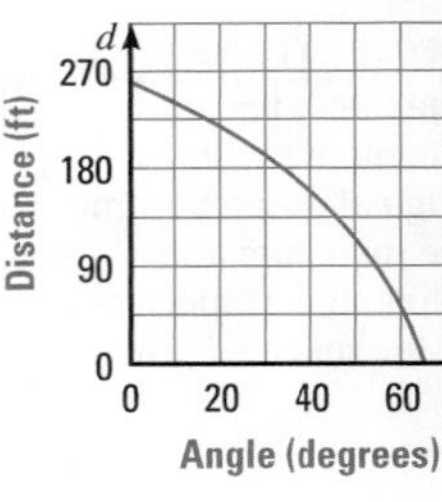

The graph of $d = -120\tan\theta + 260$ is shown at the right.

GUIDED PRACTICE for Examples 4, 5, and 6

Graph the function. 4–6. See margin.

4. $y = -\cos\left(x + \frac{\pi}{2}\right)$
5. $y = -3\sin\frac{1}{2}x + 2$
6. $f(x) = -\tan 2x - 1$
7. **WHAT IF?** In Example 6, how does the model change if you are standing 150 feet from a building that is 400 feet tall? The graph is shifted 400 units up instead of 260. The new equation would be $d = -150\tan\theta + 400$.

14.2 EXERCISES

HOMEWORK KEY
○ = **WORKED-OUT SOLUTIONS** on p. WS23 for Exs. 11, 23, and 53
★ = **STANDARDIZED TEST PRACTICE** Exs. 2, 21, 35, 48, and 54

SKILL PRACTICE

A

1. **VOCABULARY** Copy and complete: The graph of $y = \cos 2(x - 3)$ is the graph of $y = \cos 2x$ translated _?_ units to the right. 3
2. ★ **WRITING** *Describe* the difference between the graphs of $y = \tan x$ and $y = -\tan x$. How are the graphs related? $y = -\tan x$ is a reflection of $y = \tan x$ over the y-axis.

EXAMPLES and 2 on pp. 915–916 for Exs. 3–21

MATCHING **Match the function with its graph.**

3. $y = \sin 2\left(x + \frac{\pi}{2}\right)$ E
4. $f(x) = \cos(x + \pi)$ C
5. $y = \cos x - 2$ D
6. $y = \sin\left(x + \frac{\pi}{4}\right)$ B
7. $y = \cos\frac{1}{2}x + 1$ A
8. $f(x) = \sin\frac{1}{2}(x - \pi)$ F

A. 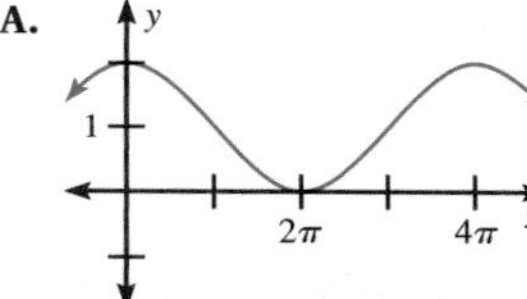

B. 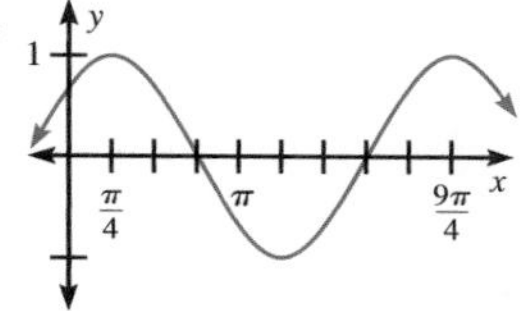

C. 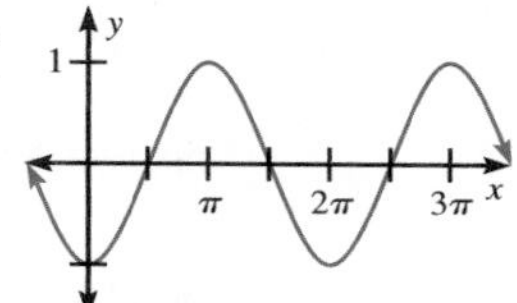

D. 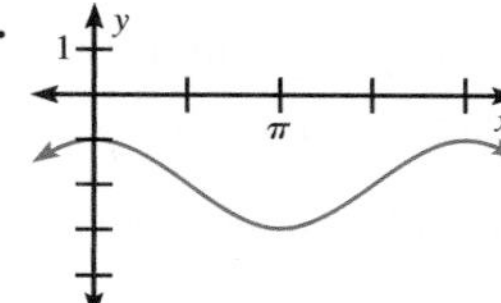

E. 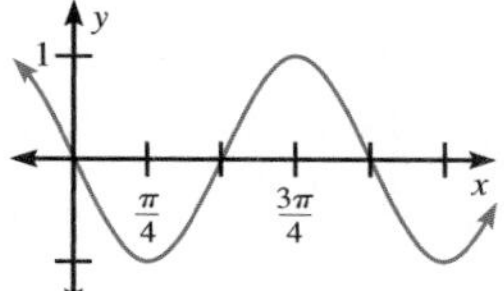

F. 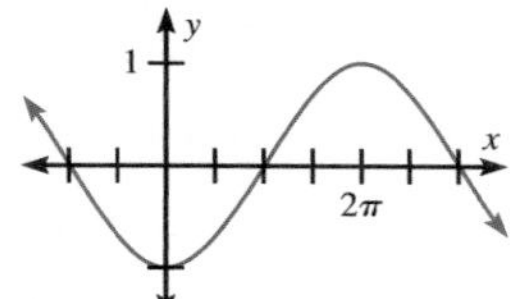

GRAPHING **Graph the sine or cosine function.** 9–20. See margin.

9. $y = \sin x + 3$
10. $y = \cos x - 5$
11. $y = 2\cos x + 1$
12. $y = \sin 3x - 4$
13. $f(x) = \sin\left(x + \frac{\pi}{4}\right)$
14. $y = \cos\left(x - \frac{\pi}{2}\right)$
15. $y = \cos 2(x + \pi)$
16. $f(x) = \frac{1}{2}\sin\left(x - \frac{3\pi}{2}\right)$
17. $y = 4\sin\frac{1}{3}\left(x + \frac{\pi}{2}\right)$
18. $f(x) = \cos\left(x - \frac{\pi}{8}\right) + 2$
19. $y = 3\cos\left(x + \frac{3\pi}{4}\right) - 1$
20. $y = \sin 2(x + 2\pi) - 3$

Guided Practice

4. 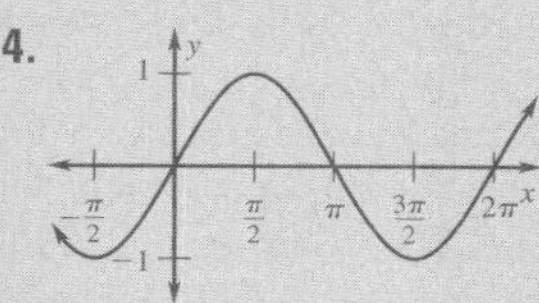

5. 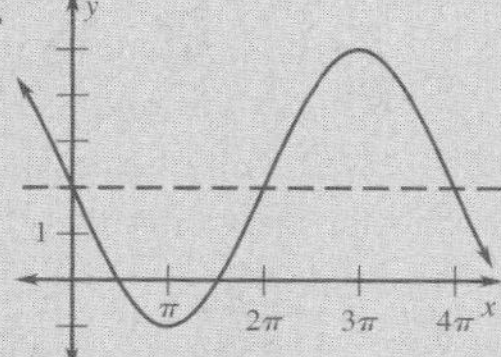

6. 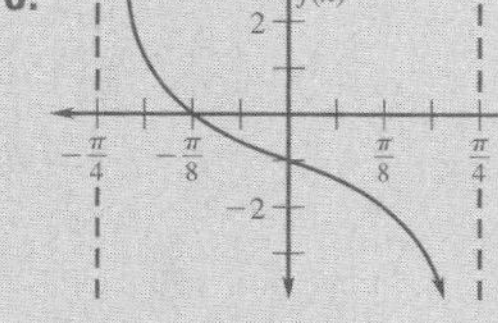

4 PRACTICE AND APPLY

Assignment Guide

Answer Transparencies available for all exercises

Basic:
Day 1: pp. 919–922
Exs. 1–14, 21, 50, 51
Day 2: pp. 919–922
Exs. 22–30, 34–38, 53, 56–57

Average:
Day 1: pp. 919–922
Exs. 1–8, 12–17, 21, 50, 51
Day 2: pp. 919–922
Exs. 25–30, 34, 35, 38–40, 42–47, 52–54, 56–57

Advanced:
Day 1: pp. 919–922
Exs. 1–8, 15–21, 50, 51
Day 2: pp. 919–922
Exs. 30–35, 39–49*, 51–57*

Block:
pp. 919–922
Exs. 1–8, 12–17, 21, 25–30, 34, 35, 38–40, 42–47, 50–54, 56–57

Differentiated Instruction

See *Algebra 2 Best Practices Toolkit* for suggestions on addressing the needs of a diverse classroom.

Homework Check

For a quick check of student understanding of key concepts, go over the following exercises:
Basic: 12, 24, 36, 50, 53
Average: 16, 28, 38, 50, 53
Advanced: 18, 32, 40, 51, 53

Extra Practice

- Student Edition, p. 1023
- Chapter 14 Resource Book: Practice levels A, B, C, pp. 18–20

Practice Worksheet

An easily-readable reduced practice page (with answers) for this lesson can be found on p. 906C.

Skill Practice

9–20. See Additional Answers beginning on p. AA1.

Mathematical Reasoning

Exercise 48 To visually confirm their responses, ask students to graph two or more tangent functions that pass through the origin and have asymptotes $x = \pm\pi$ on tracing paper. Then have them overlay one graph on another to confirm the similar asymptotes and x-intercept at the origin.

Vocabulary

Exercise 53 Explain to students unfamiliar with the word "rappelling" that this technique is used to lower oneself down a cliff at a controlled rate by means of friction on the rope. In the picture, the climber is using his left hand to control the speed of his descent. Thus the rope behind the climber falls at a different angle than does the rope above the climber. For purposes of this exercise, students should draw a sketch in which the angle of depression for the rope above the climber is equal to the angle of elevation for the rope below the climber.

22.

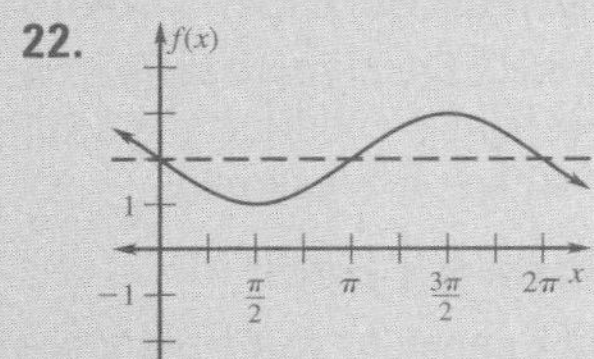

23.

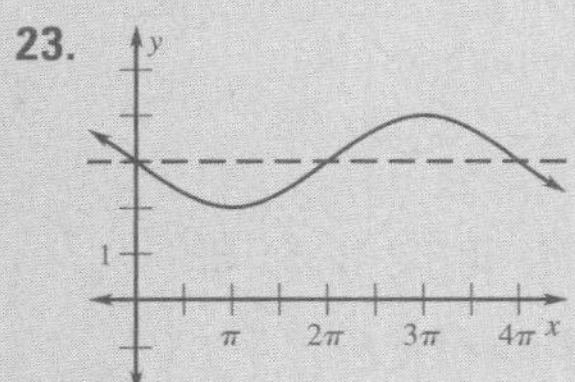

24.

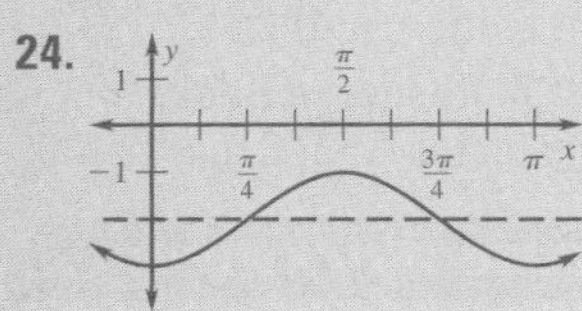

25.

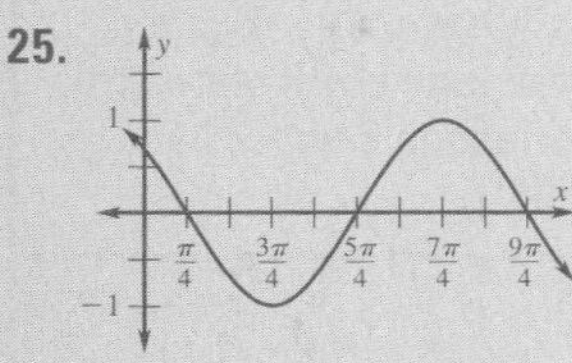

26.

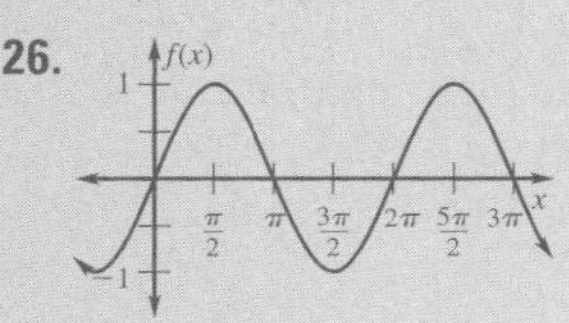

21. ★ **MULTIPLE CHOICE** The graph of which function is shown? **C**

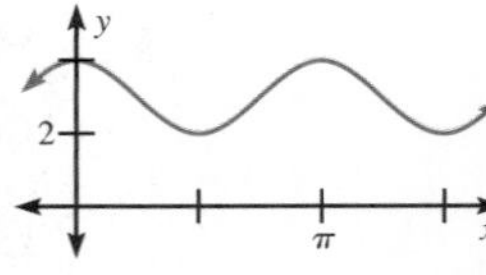

Ⓐ $y = \cos \frac{1}{2}x + 3$ Ⓑ $y = \cos x + 3$

Ⓒ $y = \cos 2x + 3$ Ⓓ $y = \cos (x + \pi) + 3$

EXAMPLE 4 [B] on p. 917 for Exs. 22–33

GRAPHING **Graph the sine or cosine function.** 22–33. See margin.

22. $f(x) = -\sin x + 2$
23. $y = -\sin \frac{1}{2}x + 3$
24. $y = -\cos 2x - 2$
25. $y = -\sin \left(x - \frac{\pi}{4}\right)$
26. $f(x) = -\sin (x - \pi)$
27. $y = -2 \cos \frac{1}{4}x$
28. $y = -3 \cos (x - \pi) + 4$
29. $y = -\cos (x + \pi) + 1$
30. $f(x) = 1 - 3 \sin (x + \pi)$
31. $y = -\sin \left(x - \frac{3\pi}{2}\right) + 2$
32. $f(x) = -\cos \left(x + \frac{\pi}{2}\right) - 2$
33. $y = -4 \cos 2\left(x - \frac{\pi}{4}\right)$

34. **ERROR ANALYSIS** *Describe* and correct the error in determining the maximum point of the function $y = 2 \sin \left(x - \frac{\pi}{2}\right)$.

Maximum: $\left(\left(\frac{1}{4} \cdot 2\pi\right) - \frac{\pi}{2}, 2\right) = \left(\frac{\pi}{2} - \frac{\pi}{2}, 2\right) = (0, 2)$ ✗

34. To determine the maximum, take the coordinate of the maximum of $y = \sin x$, which is $\left(\frac{\pi}{2}, 1\right)$, and add this to the horizontal shift of the x-value; maximum: $\left(\frac{\pi}{2} + \frac{\pi}{2}, 2\right) = (\pi, 2)$.

35. ★ **MULTIPLE CHOICE** Which of the following is a maximum point of the graph of $y = -4 \cos \left(x - \frac{\pi}{2}\right)$? **A**

Ⓐ $\left(-\frac{\pi}{2}, 4\right)$ Ⓑ $(0, 4)$ Ⓒ $\left(\frac{\pi}{2}, 4\right)$ Ⓓ $(\pi, 4)$

EXAMPLE 5 on p. 918 for Exs. 36–41

GRAPHING **Graph the tangent function.** 36–41. See margin.

36. $y = -\frac{1}{2} \tan x$
37. $y = \tan 2x - 3$
38. $y = -\tan 4x + 2$
39. $y = 2 \tan \left(x + \frac{\pi}{2}\right)$
40. $y = -\tan 2\left(x - \frac{\pi}{2}\right)$
41. $y = -\frac{1}{2} \tan \left(x - \frac{\pi}{4}\right)$

WRITING EQUATIONS **In Exercises 42–46, write an equation of the graph described.**

42. The graph of $y = \cos 2\pi x$ translated down 4 units and left 3 units **$y = \cos (2\pi x + 3) - 4$**
43. The graph of $y = 3 \sin x$ translated up 2 units and right π units **$y = 3 \sin (x - \pi) + 2$**
44. The graph of $y = 5 \tan x$ translated right $\frac{\pi}{4}$ unit and then reflected in the x-axis **$y = -5 \tan \left(x - \frac{\pi}{4}\right)$**
45. The graph of $y = \frac{1}{3} \cos \pi x$ translated down 1 unit and then reflected in the line $y = -1$ **$y = -\frac{1}{3} \cos \pi x - 1$**
46. The graph of $y = \frac{1}{2} \sin 6x$ translated down $\frac{3}{2}$ units and right 1 unit, and then reflected in the line $y = -\frac{3}{2}$ **$y = -\frac{1}{2} \sin (6x - 1) - \frac{3}{2}$**

47. **REASONING** *Explain* how you can obtain the graph of $y = \cos x$ by translating the graph of $y = \sin x$. **The graph of $y = \cos x$ can be obtained by translating the graph of $y = \sin x$ either to the left by $\frac{\pi}{2}$ or to the right $\frac{3\pi}{2}$.**

◯ = **WORKED-OUT SOLUTIONS** on p. WS1 ★ = **STANDARDIZED TEST PRACTICE**

27.

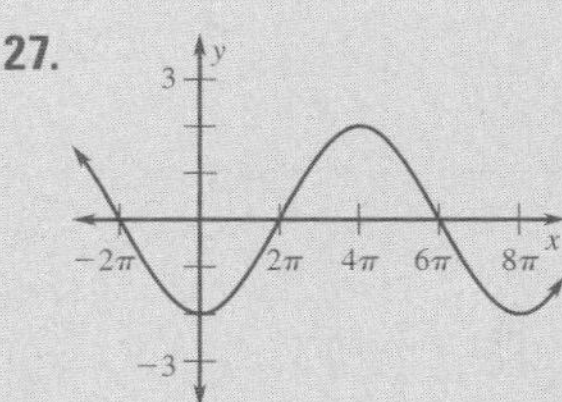

28.

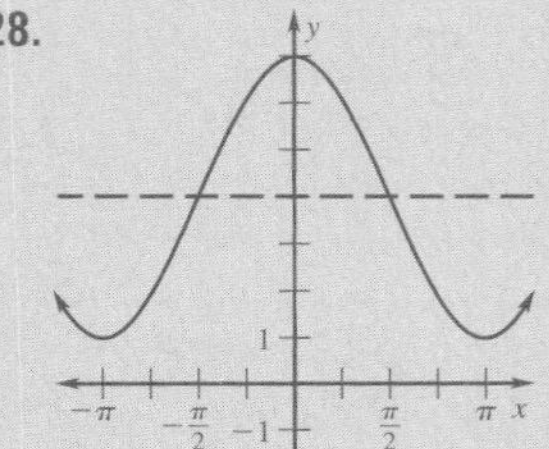

29.

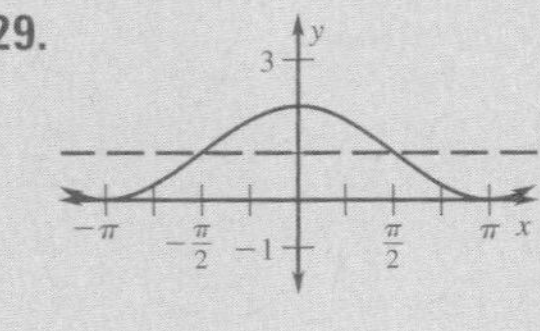

C 48. ★ **SHORT RESPONSE** *Explain* why there is more than one tangent function whose graph passes through the origin and has asymptotes at $x = -\pi$ and $x = \pi$. **Any change of amplitude will create a different curve that still passes through the origin and has the same asymptotes.**

49. **CHALLENGE** Find a tangent function whose graph intersects the graph of $y = 2 + 2 \sin x$ only at minimum points of the sine graph. ***Sample answer:*** $y = 5 \tan\left(\frac{1}{2}x - \frac{3\pi}{4}\right)$

PROBLEM SOLVING

EXAMPLE 3 A on p. 916 for Exs. 50–51

50. **WATER WHEEL** The Great Laxey wheel, located on the Isle of Man, is one of the largest working water wheels in the world. The wheel was built in 1854 to pump water from the mines underneath it. The height h (in feet) above the viewing platform of a bucket on the wheel can be approximated by the function

$$h = 36.25 \sin \frac{\pi}{12}t + 34.25$$

where t is time (in seconds). Graph the function. Find the diameter of the wheel if the lowest point on the wheel is 2 feet below the viewing platform. **See margin for art; 72.5 ft.**

@HomeTutor for problem solving help at classzone.com

51. **AUTOMOTIVE MECHANICS** The pistons in an engine force the crank pins to rotate in a circle around the center of the crankshaft. The graph shows the height h (in inches) of a crank pin relative to the axle as a function of time t (in seconds). Write a cosine function for the height of the crank pin. $h = 3.75 \cos (200\pi t)$

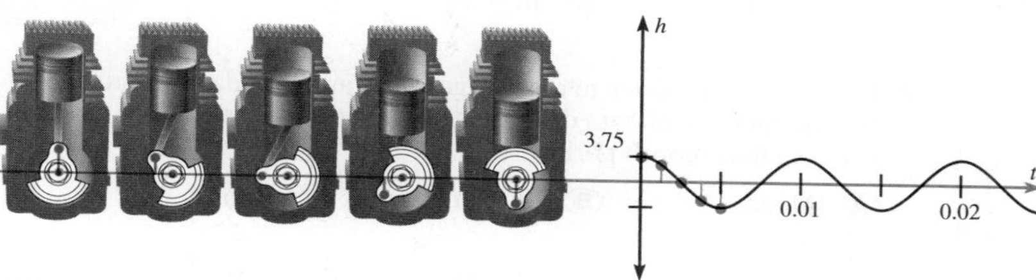

@HomeTutor for problem solving help at classzone.com

52. **BLOOD PRESSURE** For a certain person at rest, the blood pressure P (in millimeters of mercury) at time t (in seconds) is given by this function:

$$P = 100 - 20 \cos \frac{8\pi}{3}t$$

Graph the function. If one cycle is equivalent to one heartbeat, what is the person's pulse rate in heartbeats per minute? **See margin for art; 80 heartbeats per minute.**

EXAMPLE 6 B on p. 918 for Ex. 53

53. **MULTI-STEP PROBLEM** You are standing 300 feet from the base of a 200 foot cliff. Your friend is rappelling down the cliff.

a. Write a model that gives your friend's distance d (in feet) from the top of the cliff as a function of the angle of elevation θ. $d = -300 \tan \theta + 200$

b. Graph the function from part (a). **See margin.**

c. Determine the angle of elevation if your friend has rappelled halfway down the cliff. **about 18.4°**

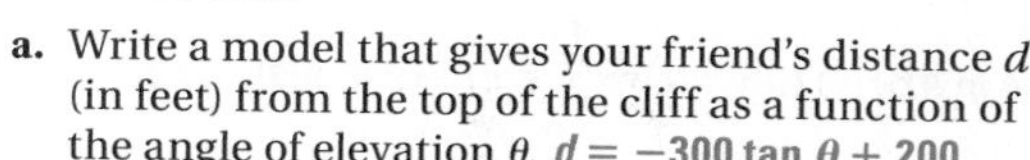

Internet Reference

Exercise 50 Additional information about the Great Laxey wheel can be found at www.gov.im/mnh/heritage/museums/laxeywheel.xml

33.

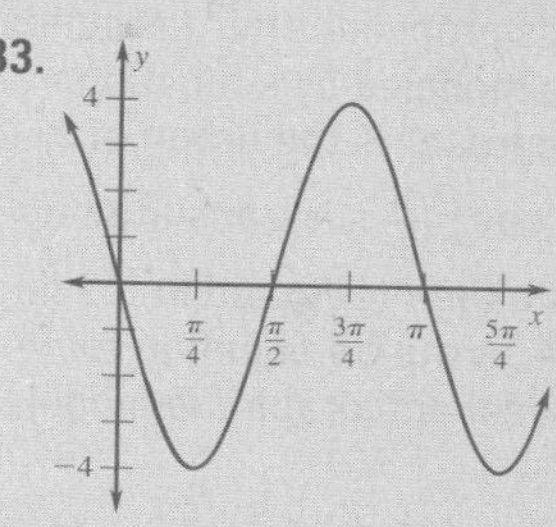

36–41. See Additional Answers beginning on p. AA1.

50.

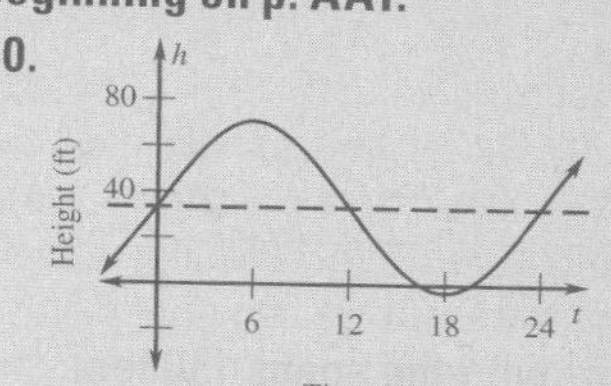

52.

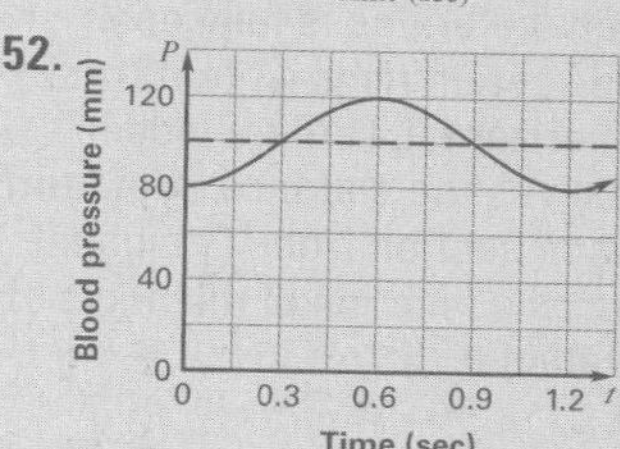

53b.

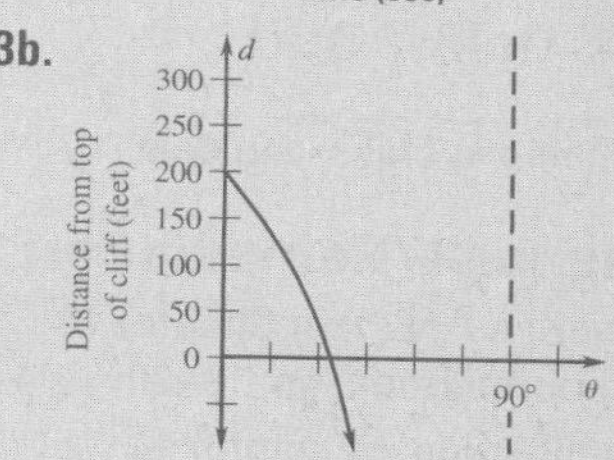

30.

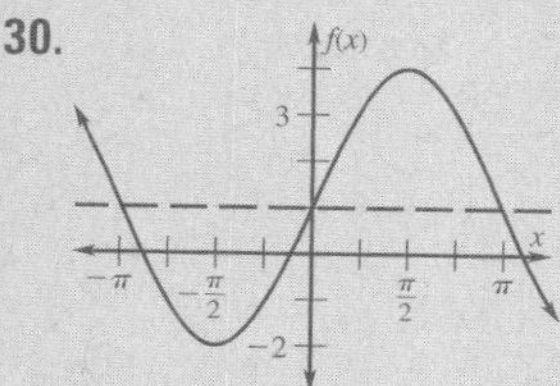

31.

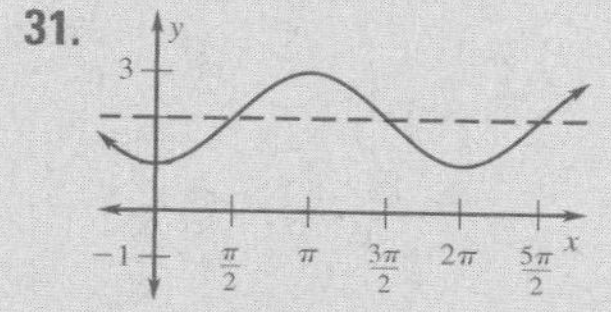

32.

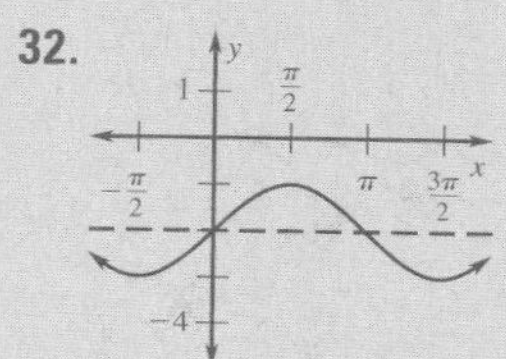

54. ★ **EXTENDED RESPONSE** In a particular region, the population C of coyotes (the predator) and the population R of rabbits (the prey) can be modeled by

$$C = 9000 + 3000 \sin \frac{\pi}{12}t \quad \text{and} \quad R = 20{,}000 + 8000 \cos \frac{\pi}{12}t$$

where t is the time in months.

a. Determine the ratio of rabbits to coyotes when $t = 0, 6, 12$, and 18 months. $\frac{28}{9}, \frac{5}{3}, \frac{4}{3}, \frac{10}{3}$

b. Graph both functions in the same coordinate plane. **See margin.**

c. Use the graphs to explain how the changes in the two populations appear to be related. **See margin.**

C 55. **CHALLENGE** Suppose a Ferris wheel has a radius of 25 feet and operates at a speed of 2 revolutions per minute. The bottom car is 5 feet above the ground. Write a model for a person's height h (in feet) above the ground if the value of h is 44 feet when $t = 0$. $h = 25 \cos (2\pi t + 0.976) + 30$

KENTUCKY MIXED REVIEW

56. The cylindrical tube shown is metal. It has an inner radius of 10 inches, an outer radius of 12 inches, and a height of 23 inches. What is the approximate amount of metal needed to make this tube? **C**

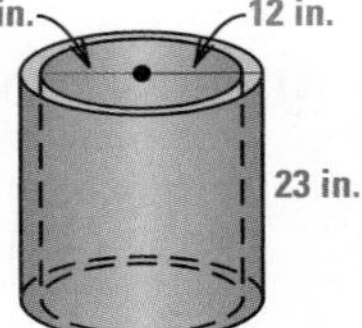

Ⓐ 289 in.^{3} Ⓑ 1012 in.^{3}

Ⓒ 3179 in.^{3} Ⓓ 4625 in.^{3}

57. Lisa records the price of regular gasoline every Friday for four months. Which measure of data describes the most frequent price of gasoline over the four month period? **C**

Ⓐ Mean Ⓑ Median Ⓒ Mode Ⓓ Range

QUIZ for Lessons 14.1–14.2

Find the amplitude and the period of the graph of the function. *(p. 908)*

1. $y = \cos 4x$ $1, \frac{\pi}{2}$
2. $y = \frac{3}{2} \sin 5x$ $\frac{3}{2}, \frac{2\pi}{5}$
3. $f(x) = \frac{1}{4} \sin x$ $\frac{1}{4}, 2\pi$
4. $y = \frac{1}{2} \cos 2\pi x$ $\frac{1}{2}, 1$
5. $y = \sin \pi x$ $1, 2$
6. $g(x) = 3 \cos \frac{\pi}{2}x$ $3, 4$

Graph the function. 7–12. See margin.

7. $y = 4 \sin \pi x$ *(p. 908)*
8. $y = \frac{1}{2} \cos \frac{3}{2}\pi x$ *(p. 908)*
9. $g(x) = 2 \tan \frac{1}{4}x$ *(p. 908)*
10. $f(x) = -2 \sin 3x + 4$ *(p. 915)*
11. $y = \cos (x + \pi) + 2$ *(p. 915)*
12. $y = -\tan 2\left(x + \frac{\pi}{2}\right)$ *(p. 915)*
13. **WINDOW WASHERS** You are standing 70 feet from the base of a 250 foot building watching a window washer lower himself to the ground. Write and graph a model that gives the window washer's distance d (in feet) from the top of the building as a function of the angle of elevation θ. *(p. 915)* $d = 250 - 70 \tan \theta$; see margin for art.

EXTRA PRACTICE for Lesson 14.2, p. 1023

5 ASSESS AND RETEACH

Daily Homework Quiz

Transparency Available

1. The depth d (in feet) of a point on a boat's propeller after t seconds can be modeled by a function that represents the graph of $d = 7 \cos\left(\frac{550}{3}\pi t\right)$ translated up 24 units then reflected in the line $y = 24$. Write an equation for the model and graph the model. $D = -7 \cos\left(\frac{550}{3}\pi t\right) + 24$

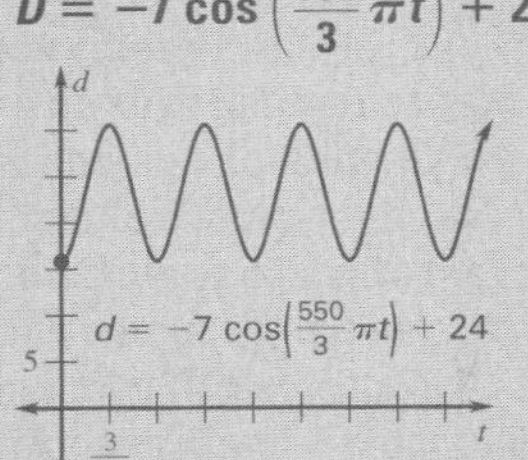

2. A drawbridge spans 150 feet. When the bridge is fully open, each section rises 43 feet from the horizontal. Write a model that gives the distance d (in feet) of each section from its highest point as a function of the angle of elevation θ. $d = -75 \tan \theta + 43$

Available at **classzone.com**

Diagnosis/Remediation

- Practice A, B, C in Chapter 14 Resource Book, pp. 18–20
- Study Guide in Chapter 14 Resource Book, pp. 21–22
- Practice Workbook, pp. 195–196
- @HomeTutor

Challenge

Additional challenge is available in the Chapter 14 Resource Book, p. 25.

Quiz

An easily-readable reduced copy of the quiz (with answers) on Lessons 14.1–14.2 from the Assessment Book can be found on p. 906E.

54b–c, Quiz 7–13. See Additional Answers beginning on p. AA1.

@HomeTutor classzone.com Keystrokes

14.3 Investigating Trigonometric Identities

MATERIALS • graphing calculator

QUESTION How can you use a graphing calculator to verify trigonometric identities?

EXPLORE Investigate a trigonometric identity

Determine whether the equation $\sin^2 x + \cos^2 x = 1$ is true for *no x-values, some x-values,* or *all x-values.*

STEP 1 Enter equations
Enter the left side of the equation as y_1 and the right side as y_2. Use the "thick" graph style for y_2 to distinguish the graphs.

STEP 2 Set viewing window
Set your calculator in radian mode. Adjust the viewing window so that the x-axis shows $-2\pi \le x \le 2\pi$ and the y-axis shows $-2 \le y \le 2$.

STEP 3 Graph equations
Graph the equations. The calculator first graphs $y_1 = \sin^2 x + \cos^2 x$ and then $y_2 = 1$ as a thicker line over the graph of y_1.

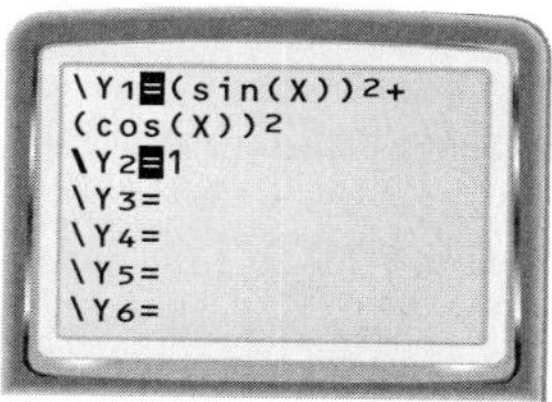

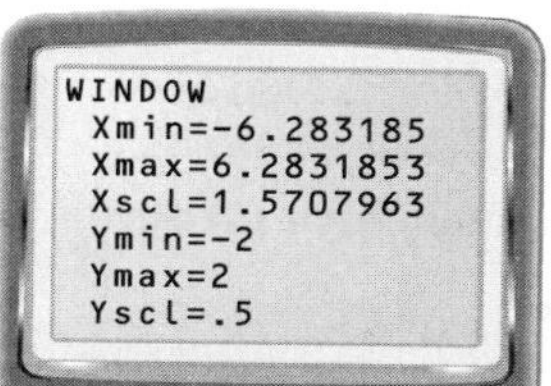

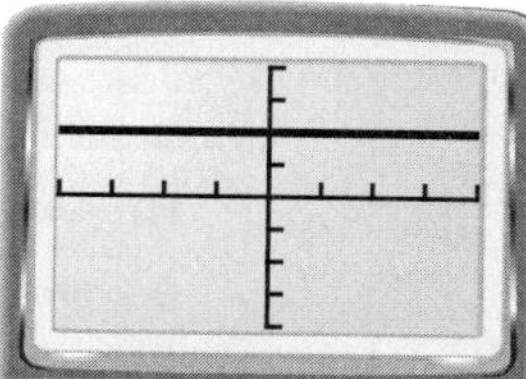

▶ The graphs of each side of the equation $\sin^2 x + \cos^2 x = 1$ are the same. So, the equation is true for all x-values.

DRAW CONCLUSIONS Use your observations to complete these exercises

Use a graphing calculator to determine whether the equation is true for *no x-values, some x-values,* or *all x-values.* (Set your calculator in radian mode and use $-2\pi \le x \le 2\pi$ and $-2 \le y \le 2$ for the viewing window.)

1. $\tan x = \frac{\sin x}{\cos x}$ all x-values
2. $\sin x = -\cos x$ some x-values
3. $\tan x = \frac{1}{x}$ some x-values
4. $\cos(-3x) = \cos 3x$ all x-values
5. $\cos x = 1.5$ no x-values
6. $\sin(x - \pi) = \cos x$ some x-values
7. $\sin(-x) = -\sin x$ all x-values
8. $\cos \frac{x}{2} = \frac{1}{2}\cos x$ some x-values
9. $\cos\left(x - \frac{\pi}{2}\right) = \sin x$ all x-values
10. **REASONING** Trigonometric equations that are true for *all* values of x (in their domain) are called trigonometric identities. Which trigonometric equations in Exercises 1–9 are trigonometric identities? $\tan x = \frac{\sin x}{\cos x}$, $\cos(-3x) = \cos 3x$, $\sin(-x) = -\sin x$, $\cos\left(x - \frac{\pi}{2}\right) = \sin x$

1 PLAN AND PREPARE

Explore the Concept

- Students will use graphing calculators to verify trigonometric identities.
- This activity leads into the study of verifying a trigonometric identity in Example 4 in Lesson 14.3.

Materials

Each student or pair of students will need a graphing calculator.

Recommended Time

Work activity: 10 min
Discuss results: 5 min

Grouping

Students can work individually or in pairs. If students work in pairs, they can take turns entering and graphing the equations. They should discuss the significance of each graph.

2 TEACH

Alternative Strategy

Demonstrate the activity on an overhead or chalkboard. Choose other equations that are true for only some values of x or for no values of x.

Key Discovery

When the graphs of both sides of a trigonometric equation are the same, then the equation is called a trigonometric identity and is true for all values of x.

3 ASSESS AND RETEACH

Use the Pythagorean theorem to verify that $\sin^2 + \cos^2 = 1$.

$\sin = \frac{\text{opp}}{\text{hyp}}$; $\cos = \frac{\text{adj}}{\text{hyp}}$; $\left(\frac{\text{opp}}{\text{hyp}}\right)^2 + \left(\frac{\text{adj}}{\text{hyp}}\right)^2 = \frac{\text{opp}^2 + \text{adj}^2}{\text{hyp}^2} = \frac{\text{hyp}^2}{\text{hyp}^2} = 1$

1 PLAN AND PREPARE

Warm-Up Exercises

Transparency Available

Identify the trigonometric function equivalent to the given function.

1. $\frac{1}{\tan \theta}$ **cot θ**
2. $\frac{\sin \theta}{\cos \theta}$ **tan θ**
3. $\frac{1}{\sec \theta}$ **cos θ**
4. $\frac{1}{\csc \theta}$ **sin θ**
5. You are in an airplane that takes off at a 10° angle and travels at a rate of 250 feet per second. About how long does it take the plane to reach an altitude of 15,000 feet? **5.76 min**

Notetaking Guide

Transparency Available

Promotes interactive learning and notetaking skills, pp. 358–361.

Pacing

Basic: 1 day
Average: 1 day
Advanced: 1 day
Block: 0.5 block with 14.4
• See *Teaching Guide/Lesson Plan.*

2 FOCUS AND MOTIVATE

Essential Question

Big Idea 2, p. 907

How can you verify that a trigonometric equation is an identity? **Tell students they will learn how to answer this question by transforming one side of the equation.**

14.3 Verify Trigonometric Identities

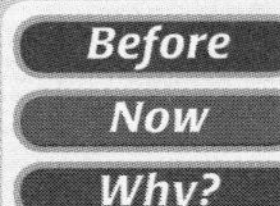

Before You graphed trigonometric functions.
Now You will verify trigonometric identities.
Why? So you can model the path of Halley's comet, as in Ex. 41.

Key Vocabulary
• **trigonometric identity**

Recall from Lesson 13.3 that if an angle θ is in standard position with its terminal side intersecting the unit circle at (x, y), then $x = \cos \theta$ and $y = \sin \theta$. Because (x, y) is on a circle centered at the origin with radius 1, it follows that:

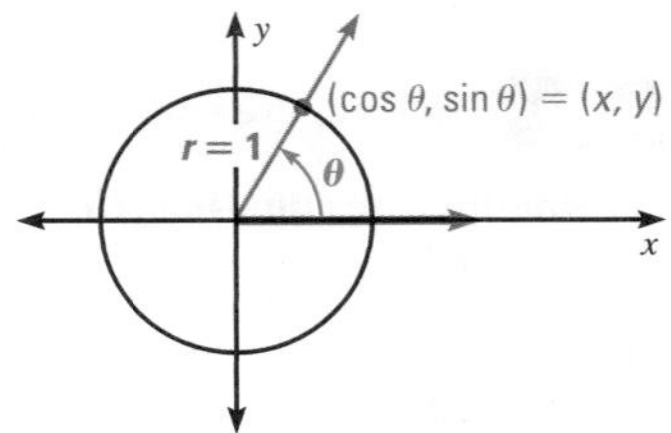

$$x^2 + y^2 = 1$$
$$\cos^2 \theta + \sin^2 \theta = 1$$

The equation $\cos^2 \theta + \sin^2 \theta = 1$ is true for any value of θ. A trigonometric equation that is true for all values of θ (in its domain) is called a **trigonometric identity**. Several fundamental trigonometric identities are listed below, some of which you have already learned.

KEY CONCEPT — *For Your Notebook*

Fundamental Trigonometric Identities

Reciprocal Identities

$\csc \theta = \frac{1}{\sin \theta}$ $\qquad \sec \theta = \frac{1}{\cos \theta}$ $\qquad \cot \theta = \frac{1}{\tan \theta}$

Tangent and Cotangent Identities

$\tan \theta = \frac{\sin \theta}{\cos \theta}$ $\qquad \cot \theta = \frac{\cos \theta}{\sin \theta}$

Pythagorean Identities

$\sin^2 \theta + \cos^2 \theta = 1$ $\qquad 1 + \tan^2 \theta = \sec^2 \theta$ $\qquad 1 + \cot^2 \theta = \csc^2 \theta$

Cofunction Identities

$\sin\left(\frac{\pi}{2} - \theta\right) = \cos \theta$ $\qquad \cos\left(\frac{\pi}{2} - \theta\right) = \sin \theta$ $\qquad \tan\left(\frac{\pi}{2} - \theta\right) = \cot \theta$

Negative Angle Identities

$\sin(-\theta) = -\sin \theta$ $\qquad \cos(-\theta) = \cos \theta$ $\qquad \tan(-\theta) = -\tan \theta$

You can use trigonometric identities to evaluate trigonometric functions, simplify trigonometric expressions, and verify other identities.

Resource Planning Guide

Chapter Resource Book
• Teaching Guide/Lesson Plan (pp. 26–27)
• Practice levels A, B, C (pp. 30–32)
• Study Guide (pp. 33–34)
• Catch-up for Absent Students (p. 35)
• Problem Solving Workshop (p. 36)
• Challenge (p. 37)

Workbooks
• Notetaking Guide (pp. 358–361)
• Practice Workbook (pp. 197–198)

Teaching Options
• **Power Presentations CD-ROM** provides dynamic electronic teaching resources for the classroom.
• **Activity Generator CD-ROM** provides editable activities for all ability levels.

Interactive Technology
• Easy Planner
• Power Presentations CD-ROM
• Activity Generator CD-ROM
• Animated Algebra
• Test Generator CD-ROM
• Online Quiz
• eWorkbook
• eEdition
• @HomeTutor

Resources for English Learners
• Quick Reference for English Learners
• Spanish Study Guide
• Multi-Language Visual Glossary
• Student Resources in Spanish

See also the *Algebra 2 Toolkit* for more strategies for meeting individual needs.

EXAMPLE 1 Find trigonometric values

Given that $\sin\theta = \frac{4}{5}$ and $\frac{\pi}{2} < \theta < \pi$, find the values of the other five trigonometric functions of θ.

Solution

STEP 1 **Find** $\cos\theta$.

$\sin^2\theta + \cos^2\theta = 1$ — Write Pythagorean identity.

$\left(\frac{4}{5}\right)^2 + \cos^2\theta = 1$ — Substitute $\frac{4}{5}$ for $\sin\theta$.

$\cos^2\theta = 1 - \left(\frac{4}{5}\right)^2$ — Subtract $\left(\frac{4}{5}\right)^2$ from each side.

$\cos^2\theta = \frac{9}{25}$ — Simplify.

$\cos\theta = \pm\frac{3}{5}$ — Take square roots of each side.

$\cos\theta = -\frac{3}{5}$ — Because θ is in Quadrant II, $\cos\theta$ is negative.

REVIEW TRIGONOMETRY
For help with finding the sign of a trigonometric function value, see p. 866.

STEP 2 **Find** the values of the other four trigonometric functions of θ using the known values of $\sin\theta$ and $\cos\theta$.

$$\tan\theta = \frac{\sin\theta}{\cos\theta} = \frac{\frac{4}{5}}{-\frac{3}{5}} = -\frac{4}{3} \qquad \cot\theta = \frac{\cos\theta}{\sin\theta} = \frac{-\frac{3}{5}}{\frac{4}{5}} = -\frac{3}{4}$$

$$\csc\theta = \frac{1}{\sin\theta} = \frac{1}{\frac{4}{5}} = \frac{5}{4} \qquad \sec\theta = \frac{1}{\cos\theta} = \frac{1}{-\frac{3}{5}} = -\frac{5}{3}$$

EXAMPLE 2 Simplify a trigonometric expression

Simplify the expression $\tan\left(\frac{\pi}{2} - \theta\right)\sin\theta$.

$\tan\left(\frac{\pi}{2} - \theta\right)\sin\theta = \cot\theta\sin\theta$ — Cofunction identity

$= \left(\frac{\cos\theta}{\sin\theta}\right)(\sin\theta)$ — Cotangent identity

$= \cos\theta$ — Simplify.

EXAMPLE 3 Simplify a trigonometric expression

Simplify the expression $\csc\theta\cot^2\theta + \frac{1}{\sin\theta}$.

$\csc\theta\cot^2\theta + \frac{1}{\sin\theta} = \csc\theta\cot^2\theta + \csc\theta$ — Reciprocal identity

$= \csc\theta(\csc^2\theta - 1) + \csc\theta$ — Pythagorean identity

$= \csc^3\theta - \csc\theta + \csc\theta$ — Distributive property

$= \csc^3\theta$ — Simplify.

Motivating the Lesson

Introduce the expressions *student identity card, student identity number, identity theft,* and *physical marks of identity.* Ask students to discuss the meaning of *identity* in each expression. They can give examples of student identity numbers and identity theft. They may be able to describe physical marks of identity such as a tattoo of a rose on a shoulder. In this lesson students will explore trigonometric identities.

3 TEACH

Extra Example 1

Given that $\tan\theta = \frac{5}{12}$ and $\pi < \theta < \frac{3\pi}{2}$, find the values of the other five trigonometric functions of θ.
$\sin\theta = -\frac{5}{13}$, $\cos\theta = -\frac{12}{13}$, $\sec\theta = -\frac{13}{12}$, $\csc\theta = -\frac{13}{5}$, $\cot\theta = \frac{12}{5}$

Extra Example 2

Simplify the expression $\tan(-\theta)\cos\theta$. $-\sin\theta$

Key Question to Ask for Example 2

- Compare the graphs of $\tan\left(\frac{\pi}{2} - \theta\right)\sin\theta$ and $\cos\theta$.
The graphs coincide.

Extra Example 3

Simplify the expression $\sin\theta + \cos\theta\cot\theta$. $\csc\theta$

GUIDED PRACTICE for Examples 1, 2, and 3

Find the values of the other five trigonometric functions of θ. 1, 2. See margin.

1. $\cos\theta = \frac{1}{6}, 0 < \theta < \frac{\pi}{2}$

2. $\sin\theta = -\frac{3}{7}, \pi < \theta < \frac{3\pi}{2}$

Simplify the expression.

3. $\sin x \cot x \sec x$ 1

4. $\frac{\tan x \csc x}{\sec x}$ 1

5. $\frac{\cos\left(\frac{\pi}{2} - \theta\right) - 1}{1 + \sin(-\theta)}$ −1

VERIFYING IDENTITIES You can use the fundamental identities on page 924 to verify new trigonometric identities. When verifying an identity, begin with the expression on one side. Use algebra and trigonometric properties to manipulate the expression until it is identical to the other side.

EXAMPLE 4 Verify a trigonometric identity

Verify the identity $\frac{\sec^2\theta - 1}{\sec^2\theta} = \sin^2\theta$.

$\frac{\sec^2\theta - 1}{\sec^2\theta} = \frac{\sec^2\theta}{\sec^2\theta} - \frac{1}{\sec^2\theta}$ Write as separate fractions.

$= 1 - \left(\frac{1}{\sec\theta}\right)^2$ Simplify.

$= 1 - \cos^2\theta$ Reciprocal identity

$= \sin^2\theta$ Pythagorean identity

EXAMPLE 5 Verify a trigonometric identity

Verify the identity $\sec x + \tan x = \frac{\cos x}{1 - \sin x}$.

$\sec x + \tan x = \frac{1}{\cos x} + \tan x$ Reciprocal identity

$= \frac{1}{\cos x} + \frac{\sin x}{\cos x}$ Tangent identity

$= \frac{1 + \sin x}{\cos x}$ Add fractions.

$= \frac{1 + \sin x}{\cos x} \cdot \frac{1 - \sin x}{1 - \sin x}$ Multiply by $\frac{1 - \sin x}{1 - \sin x}$.

$= \frac{1 - \sin^2 x}{\cos x(1 - \sin x)}$ Simplify numerator.

$= \frac{\cos^2 x}{\cos x(1 - \sin x)}$ Pythagorean identity

$= \frac{\cos x}{1 - \sin x}$ Simplify.

VERIFY IDENTITIES
To verify the identity, you must introduce $1 - \sin x$ into the denominator. Multiply the numerator and the denominator by $1 - \sin x$ so you get an equivalent expression.

Extra Example 4

Verify that $\sec\theta - \cos\theta = \sin\theta\tan\theta$.

$\sec\theta - \cos\theta$

$= \frac{1}{\cos\theta} - \cos\theta$ (reciprocal identity)

$= \frac{1 - \cos^2\theta}{\cos\theta}$ (Write as single fraction.)

$= \frac{\sin^2\theta}{\cos\theta}$ (Pythagorean identity)

$= \sin\theta \cdot \frac{\sin\theta}{\cos\theta}$ (Write equivalent expression.)

$= \sin\theta\tan\theta$ (tangent identity)

Key Question to Ask for Example 4

- Why do you think it is easier to transform the expression on the left to the expression on the right rather than the other way around? It is easier to "break down" $\frac{\sec^2\theta - 1}{\sec^2\theta}$ than to try to "build up" $\sin^2\theta$.

Extra Example 5

Verify the identity $\sin\theta(\tan\theta + \cot\theta) = \sec\theta$.

$\sin\theta(\tan\theta + \cot\theta)$

$= \sin\theta\left(\frac{\sin\theta}{\cos\theta} + \frac{\cos\theta}{\sin\theta}\right)$ (tangent and cotangent identities)

$= \sin\theta\left(\frac{\sin^2\theta + \cos^2\theta}{\cos\theta\sin\theta}\right)$ (Add fractions.)

$= \sin\theta\left(\frac{1}{\cos\theta\sin\theta}\right)$ (Pythagorean identity)

$= \frac{1}{\cos\theta}$ (Simplify.)

$= \sec\theta$ (reciprocal identity)

Key Question to Ask for Example 5

- For what values of x is the equation not defined? multiples of $\frac{\pi}{2}$

Avoiding Common Errors

Students can easily confuse the two Pythagorean identities that involve $\tan\theta$ and $\cot\theta$. To help them remember the identities, point out one identity relates two functions that begin with "c," cotangent and cosecant. The other identity relates the other two functions, tangent and secant.

1. $\sin\theta = \frac{\sqrt{35}}{6}$, $\tan\theta = \sqrt{35}$, $\csc\theta = \frac{6\sqrt{35}}{35}$, $\sec\theta = 6$, $\cot\theta = \frac{\sqrt{35}}{35}$

2. $\cos\theta = \frac{-2\sqrt{10}}{7}$, $\tan\theta = \frac{3\sqrt{10}}{20}$, $\csc\theta = -\frac{7}{3}$, $\sec\theta = \frac{-7\sqrt{10}}{20}$, $\cot\theta = \frac{2\sqrt{10}}{3}$

Differentiated Instruction

Advanced You might wish to consider pairing advanced students with students who have trouble verifying trigonometric identities. Both students will benefit from the interaction. Advanced students will be forced to supply reasons for the steps in their verification which they might avoid when working alone. The students who are being helped will receive necessary guidance.

See also the *Algebra 2 Toolkit* for more strategies.

EXAMPLE 6 Verify a real-life trigonometric identity

SHADOW LENGTH A vertical *gnomon* (the part of a sundial that projects a shadow) has height h. The length s of the shadow cast by the gnomon when the angle of the sun above the horizon is θ can be modeled by the equation below. Show that the equation is equivalent to $s = h \cot \theta$.

$$s = \frac{h \sin (90° - \theta)}{\sin \theta}$$

Solution

Simplify the equation.

$s = \frac{h \sin (90° - \theta)}{\sin \theta}$ **Write original equation.**

$= \frac{h \sin \left(\frac{\pi}{2} - \theta\right)}{\sin \theta}$ **Convert 90° to radians.**

$= \frac{h \cos \theta}{\sin \theta}$ **Cofunction identity**

$= h \cot \theta$ **Cotangent identity**

GUIDED PRACTICE for Examples 4, 5, and 6

Verify the identity. 6–9. See margin.

6. $\cot (-\theta) = -\cot \theta$
7. $\csc^2 x (1 - \sin^2 x) = \cot^2 x$
8. $\cos x \csc x \tan x = 1$
9. $(\tan^2 x + 1)(\cos^2 x - 1) = -\tan^2 x$

14.3 EXERCISES

HOMEWORK KEY

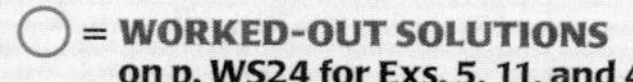
= WORKED-OUT SOLUTIONS on p. WS24 for Exs. 5, 11, and 41

★ = STANDARDIZED TEST PRACTICE Exs. 2, 9, 24, 42, 43, and 44

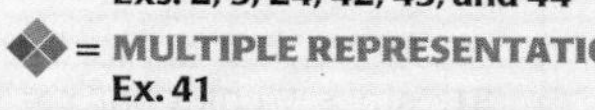
= MULTIPLE REPRESENTATIONS Ex. 41

SKILL PRACTICE

A

1. **VOCABULARY** What is a trigonometric identity? A trigonometric equation that is true for all values of θ in its domain

2. ★ **WRITING** What does the cofunction identity $\sin\left(\frac{\pi}{2} - \theta\right) = \cos \theta$ tell you about the graphs of $y = \sin x$ and $y = \cos x$? You obtain the graph of $y = \cos x$ if you translate the graph of $y = \sin x$ to the right $\frac{\pi}{2}$ units and reflect it in the x-axis.

EXAMPLE 1 on p. 925 for Exs. 3–9

FINDING VALUES **Find the values of the other five trigonometric functions of θ.** 3–8. See margin.

3. $\sin \theta = \frac{1}{3}, 0 < \theta < \frac{\pi}{2}$
4. $\tan \theta = \frac{3}{7}, 0 < \theta < \frac{\pi}{2}$

5. $\cos \theta = \frac{5}{6}, \frac{3\pi}{2} < \theta < 2\pi$
6. $\sin \theta = -\frac{7}{10}, \pi < \theta < \frac{3\pi}{2}$
7. $\cot \theta = -\frac{2}{5}, \frac{\pi}{2} < \theta < \pi$
8. $\sec \theta = -\frac{9}{4}, \frac{\pi}{2} < \theta < \pi$

Extra Example 6

The population p_1 of insects in a colony is dependent on the population p_2 of another insect in the colony and can be modeled by the function $p_1 = \frac{45 \sin (-\theta)}{\tan (-\theta)} \cdot \cos \theta + p_2$. Show that the equation is equivalent to $p_1 = 45 \cos^2 \theta + p_2$.

$\frac{45 \sin (-\theta)}{\tan (-\theta)} \cdot \cos \theta + p_2$

$= \frac{45 \sin \theta}{\tan \theta} \cdot \cos \theta + p_2$ (negative angle identities)

$= \frac{45 \sin \theta}{\frac{\sin \theta}{\cos \theta}} \cdot \cos \theta + p_2$ (tangent identity)

$= 45 \cos^2 \theta + p_2$ (Simplify.)

Key Question to Ask for Example 6

- How can you relate the cofunction identity for cosine to the graphs of $y = \cos x$ and $y = \sin x$? If you shift the graph of $y = \cos x$ to the right 90°, it coincides with the graph of $y = \sin x$.

Closing the Lesson

Have students summarize the major points of the lesson and answer the Essential Question: How can you verify that a trigonometric equation is an identity?

- A trigonometric equation that is true for all values of θ in the domain is called a trigonometric identity.
- The reciprocal functions and the relationship of $\sin \theta$ and $\cos \theta$ to $\tan \theta$ and $\cot \theta$ define trigonometric identities.
- Other trigonometric identities are the Pythagorean identities, the cofunction identities, and the negative angle identitites.

Using the fundamental trigonometric identities and properties of algebra, you can transform the expression on one side of the equation so that it is identical to the expression on the other side.

Guided Practice

6. $\cot (-\theta) = \frac{1}{\tan (-\theta)} = \frac{1}{-\tan \theta} = -\cot \theta$

7. $\csc^2 x (1 - \sin^2 x) = \left(\frac{1}{\sin^2 x}\right) \cos^2 x = \frac{\cos^2 x}{\sin^2 x} = \cot^2 x$

8. $\cos x \csc x \tan x = \cos x \cdot \frac{1}{\sin x} \cdot \frac{\sin x}{\cos x} = 1$

9. $(\tan^2 x + 1)(\cos^2 x - 1) = (\sec^2 x)(-\sin^2 x) = \left(\frac{1}{\cos^2 x}\right)(-\sin^2 x) = -\frac{\sin^2 x}{\cos^2 x} = -\tan^2 x$

Skill Practice

3–8. See Additional Answers beginning on p. AA1.

4 PRACTICE AND APPLY

Assignment Guide

Answer Transparencies available for all exercises

Basic:
Day 1: pp. 927–930
Exs. 1–5, 9–15, 22–28, 40–42, 47

Average:
Day 1: pp. 927–930
Exs. 1, 2, 4–6, 9, 14–18, 22–24, 28–32, 35, 39–44, 46

Advanced:
Day 1: pp. 927–930
Exs. 1, 2, 7–9, 18–21, 24, 29–45*

Block:
pp. 927–930
Exs. 1, 2, 4–6, 9, 14–18, 22–24, 28–32, 35, 39–44, 46 (with 14.4)

Differentiated Instruction

See *Algebra 2 Best Practices Toolkit* for suggestions on addressing the needs of a diverse classroom.

Homework Check

For a quick check of student understanding of key concepts, go over the following exercises:

Basic: 4, 12, 14, 26, 39
Average: 6, 16, 28, 30, 40
Advanced: 8, 20, 32, 34, 41

Extra Practice

- Student Edition, p. 1023
- Chapter 14 Resource Book: Practice levels A, B, C, pp. 30–32

Practice Worksheet

An easily-readable reduced practice page (with answers) for this lesson can be found on p. 906C.

9. ★ **MULTIPLE CHOICE** If $\csc\theta = \frac{3}{2}$ and $\frac{\pi}{2} < \theta < \pi$, what is the value of $\tan\theta$? **A**

   (A) $-\frac{2\sqrt{5}}{5}$ (B) $-\frac{2\sqrt{13}}{13}$ (C) $\frac{2\sqrt{13}}{13}$ (D) $\frac{2\sqrt{5}}{5}$

EXAMPLES 2 and 3 on p. 925 for Exs. 10–24

SIMPLIFYING EXPRESSIONS Simplify the expression.

10. $\sin x \cot x$ **$\cos x$**
11. $\frac{\sin(-\theta)}{\cos(-\theta)}$ **$-\tan\theta$**
12. $\csc\theta\sin\theta + \cot^2\theta$ **$\csc^2\theta$**
13. $\cos\theta(1+\tan^2\theta)$ **$\sec\theta$**
14. $1+\tan^2\left(\frac{\pi}{2}-x\right)$ **$\csc^2 x$**
15. $\frac{\cos\left(\frac{\pi}{2}-x\right)}{\csc x}$ **$\sin^2 x$**
16. $\frac{\cos\left(\frac{\pi}{2}-\theta\right)}{\csc\theta} + \cos^2\theta$ **1**
17. $\sin\left(\frac{\pi}{2}-\theta\right)\sec\theta$ **1**
18. $\frac{\cos^2 x}{\cot^2 x}$ **$\sin^2 x$**
19. $\frac{\sec x\sin x + \cos\left(\frac{\pi}{2}-x\right)}{1+\sec x}$ **$\sin x$**
20. $\frac{\csc^2 x - \cot^2 x}{\sin(-x)\cot x}$ **$-\sec x$**
21. $\frac{\cos^2 x\tan^2(-x) - 1}{\cos^2 x}$ **-1**

ERROR ANALYSIS *Describe* and correct the error in simplifying the expression.

22. $1-\sin^2\theta = 1-(1-\cos^2\theta)$
    $= 1-1-\cos^2\theta$
    $= -\cos^2\theta$ ✗

23. $\tan(-x)\csc x = \frac{\sin x}{\cos x}\cdot\frac{1}{\sin x}$
    $= \frac{1}{\cos x}$
    $= \sec x$ ✗

22. The negative sign was not distributed through the parentheses; $1-1+\cos^2\theta = \cos^2\theta$.

23. $\tan(-x) = -\tan(x)$ so step 1 used an incorrect substitution; $-\frac{\sin x}{\cos x}\cdot\frac{1}{\sin x} = -\frac{1}{\cos x} = -\sec x$.

24. ★ **MULTIPLE CHOICE** Which of the following is the simplified form of the expression $\cos\theta\sec\theta$? **B**

   (A) $\tan\theta$ (B) 1 (C) 2 (D) $1-\sin^2\theta$

EXAMPLES 4 and 5 on p. 926 for Exs. 25–34

B **VERIFYING IDENTITIES** Verify the identity. **25–34. See margin.**

25. $\sin x\csc x = 1$
26. $\tan\theta\csc\theta\cos\theta = 1$
27. $\frac{\cos\left(\frac{\pi}{2}-\theta\right)+1}{1-\sin(-\theta)} = 1$
28. $\sin\left(\frac{\pi}{2}-x\right)\tan x = \sin x$
29. $\frac{\csc^2\theta - \cot^2\theta}{1-\sin^2\theta} = \sec^2\theta$
30. $2-\cos^2\theta = 1+\sin^2\theta$
31. $\sin x + \cos x\cot x = \csc x$
32. $\frac{\sin^2(-x)}{\tan^2 x} = \cos^2 x$
33. $\frac{1+\cos x}{\sin x} + \frac{\sin x}{1+\cos x} = 2\csc x$
34. $\frac{\sin x}{1-\cos(-x)} = \csc x + \cot x$
35. **ODD AND EVEN FUNCTIONS** A function f is *odd* if $f(-x) = -f(x)$. A function f is *even* if $f(-x) = f(x)$. Which of the six trigonometric functions are odd? Which are even? **$\sin x$, $\csc x$, $\tan x$, $\cot x$; $\cos x$, $\sec x$**

C **VERIFYING IDENTITIES** Verify the identity. **36, 37. See margin.**

36. $\ln|\sec\theta| = -\ln|\cos\theta|$
37. $\ln|\tan\theta| = \ln|\sin\theta| - \ln|\cos\theta|$
38. **CHALLENGE** Use the Pythagorean identity $\sin^2\theta+\cos^2\theta = 1$ to derive the other Pythagorean identities, $1+\tan^2\theta = \sec^2\theta$ and $1+\cot^2\theta = \csc^2\theta$. **See margin.**

○ = WORKED-OUT SOLUTIONS on p. WS1 ★ = STANDARDIZED TEST PRACTICE  = MULTIPLE REPRESENTATIO

25. $\sin x\csc x = \sin x\left(\frac{1}{\sin x}\right) = 1$

26. $\tan\theta\csc\theta\cos\theta = \left(\frac{\sin\theta}{\cos\theta}\right)\left(\frac{1}{\sin\theta}\right)\cos\theta = 1$

27. $\frac{\cos\left(\frac{\pi}{2}-\theta\right)+1}{1-(-\sin\theta)} = \frac{\sin\theta+1}{1+\sin\theta} = 1$

28. $\sin\left(\frac{\pi}{2}-x\right)\tan x = \cos x\left(\frac{\sin x}{\cos x}\right) = \sin x$

29. $\frac{\csc^2\theta-\cot^2\theta}{1-\sin^2\theta} = \frac{\frac{1-\cos^2\theta}{\sin^2\theta}}{\cos^2\theta} = \frac{\frac{\sin^2\theta}{\sin^2\theta}}{\cos^2\theta} = \frac{1}{\cos^2\theta} = \sec^2\theta$

PROBLEM SOLVING

EXAMPLE 6 A on p. 927 for Exs. 39–41

39. **RATE OF CHANGE** In calculus, it can be shown that the rate of change of the function $f(x) = \sec x + \cos x$ is given by this expression:

$$\sec x \tan x - \sin x$$

Show that the expression for the rate of change can be written as $\sin x \tan^2 x$. **See margin.**

@HomeTutor for problem solving help at classzone.com

40. **PHYSICAL SCIENCE** Static friction is the amount of force necessary to keep a stationary object on a flat surface from moving. Suppose a book weighing W pounds is lying on a ramp inclined at an angle θ. The coefficient of static friction u for the book can be found using this equation:

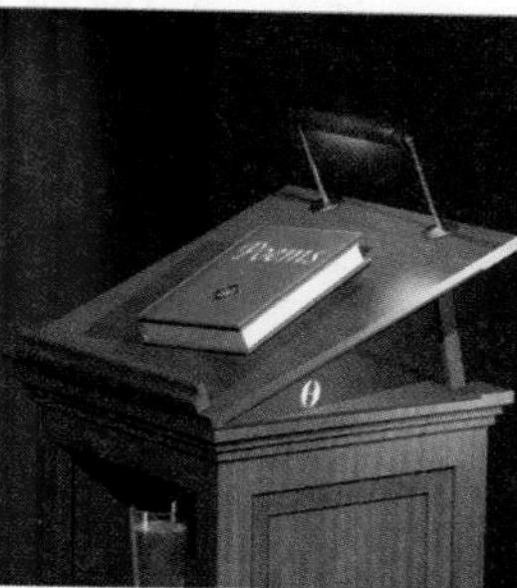

$$uW \cos \theta = W \sin \theta$$

a. Solve the equation for u and simplify the result. $u = \tan \theta$

b. Use the equation from part (a) to determine what happens to the value of u as the angle θ increases from 0° to 90°. **u increase from 0 to ∞.**

@HomeTutor for problem solving help at classzone.com

B 41. ◆ **MULTIPLE REPRESENTATIONS** The path of Halley's comet is an ellipse with the sun as a focus. The equation below gives the comet's distance r from the sun (in astronomical units) as a fuction of the angle θ (in radians) between the major axis and the comet.

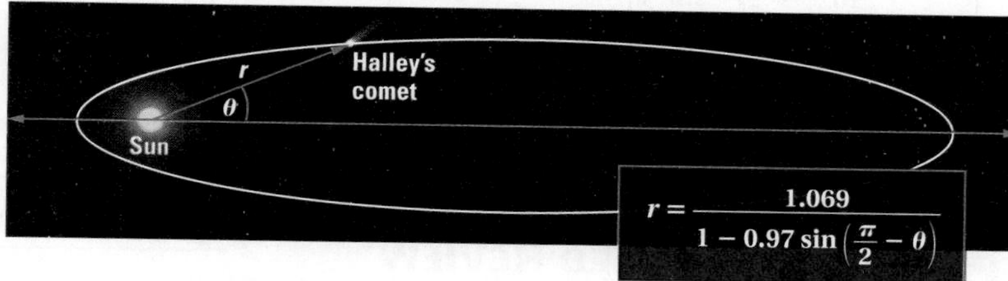

$$r = \frac{1.069}{1 - 0.97 \sin\left(\frac{\pi}{2} - \theta\right)}$$

a. **Writing an Equation** Simplify the equation given above. $r = \frac{1.069}{1 - 0.97 \cos \theta}$

b. **Drawing a Graph** Use a graphing calculator to graph the equation from part (a). **See margin.**

c. **Making a Table** Make a table of values for the equation from part (a) in which θ starts at 0 and increases in increments of $\frac{\pi}{4}$. Use the table to approximate the closest and farthest distance, in miles, that Halley's comet is from the sun. (*Note:* 1 astronomical unit ≈ 93 million miles.) **See margin.**

42. ★ **SHORT RESPONSE** Use a reciprocal identity to describe what happens to the value of $\sec \theta$ as the value of $\cos \theta$ increases. On what intervals does this happen? **The value of $\sec \theta$ decreases as the value of $\cos \theta$ increases; $\pi \le \theta \le 2\pi$, $3\pi \le \theta \le 4\pi$, $5\pi \le \theta \le 6\pi$, and so on.**

43. ★ **SHORT RESPONSE** Use the tangent identity to describe what happens to the value of $\tan \theta$ as the value of $\sin \theta$ increases and the value of $\cos \theta$ decreases. On what intervals does this happen? **The value of $\tan \theta$ increases as the value of $\sin \theta$ increases and the value of $\cos \theta$ decreases; $0 \le \theta \le \frac{\pi}{2}$, $2\pi \le \theta \le \frac{5\pi}{2}$, $4\pi \le \theta \le \frac{9\pi}{2}$, and so on.**

30. $2 - \cos^2 \theta = 2 - (1 - \sin^2 \theta) = 2 - 1 + \sin^2 \theta = 1 + \sin^2 \theta$

31. $\sin x + \cos x \cot x = \sin x + \cos x\left(\frac{\cos x}{\sin x}\right) = \sin x + \frac{\cos^2 x}{\sin x} = \frac{\sin^2 x + \cos^2 x}{\sin x} = \frac{1}{\sin x} = \csc x$

32. $\frac{\sin^2(-x)}{\tan^2 x} = \frac{(-\sin x)^2}{\tan^2 x} = \frac{\sin^2 x}{\tan^2 x} = \frac{\sin^2 x}{\left(\frac{\sin^2 x}{\cos^2 x}\right)} = \sin^2 x\left(\frac{\cos^2 x}{\sin^2 x}\right) = \cos^2 x$

Study Strategy

Exercises 25–34 After students complete an exercise, they can work backwards from the verification to check for errors in reasoning.

Teaching Strategy

Exercises 25–34, 39–41 Point out that there is not necessarily only one way to verify an identity. After students have completed these exercises, have them compare their answers with a partner to see if there was more than one way to complete any of the exercises.

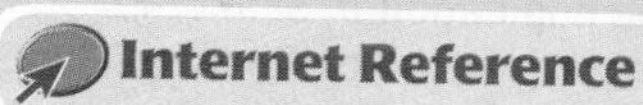

Internet Reference

Exercise 41 Additional information about Halley's comet can be found at csep10.phys.utk.edu/astr161/lect/comets/halley.html

33. $\frac{1 + \cos x}{\sin x} + \frac{\sin x}{1 + \cos x} = \frac{1 + 2\cos x + \cos^2 x + \sin^2 x}{(1 + \cos x)(\sin x)} = \frac{1 + 2\cos x + 1}{(1 + \cos x)(\sin x)} = \frac{2 + 2\cos x}{(1 + \cos x)(\sin x)} = \frac{2(1 + \cos x)}{(1 + \cos x)(\sin x)} = \frac{2}{\sin x} = 2 \csc x$

34. $\frac{\sin x}{1 - \cos(-x)} = \frac{\sin x}{1 - \cos x} = \frac{(\sin x)(1 + \cos x)}{(1 - \cos x)(1 + \cos x)} = \frac{(\sin x)(1 + \cos x)}{1 - \cos^2 x} = \frac{(\sin x)(1 + \cos x)}{\sin^2 x} = \frac{1 + \cos x}{\sin x} = \frac{1}{\sin x} + \frac{\cos x}{\sin x} = \csc x + \cot x$

36. $\ln |\sec \theta| = \ln \frac{1}{|\cos \theta|} = \ln |(\cos \theta)^{-1}| = -1 \ln |\cos \theta| = -\ln |\cos \theta|$

37. $\ln |\tan \theta| = \ln \left|\frac{\sin \theta}{\cos \theta}\right| = \ln |\sin \theta| - \ln |\cos \theta|$

38, 39, 41b–c. See Additional Answers beginning on p. AA1.

5 ASSESS AND RETEACH

Daily Homework Quiz

Transparency Available

1. Given that $\cos\theta = \frac{8}{17}$ and $\frac{3\pi}{2} < \theta < 2\pi$, find the values of $\csc\theta$ and $\cot\theta$. **$\csc\theta = -\frac{17}{15}$, $\cot\theta = -\frac{8}{15}$**

2. The population b_1 of bacteria in a culture is dependent on the population b_2 of another bacteria in the culture and can be modeled by the function $b_1 = \frac{b_2 \tan\left(\frac{\pi}{2} - \theta\right)}{\csc\theta}$. Simplify $\frac{b_2 \tan\left(\frac{\pi}{2} - \theta\right)}{\csc\theta}$ to show that the equation is equivalent to $b_1 = b_2\cos\theta$.

$\frac{b_2 \tan\left(\frac{\pi}{2} - \theta\right)}{\csc\theta}$

$= \frac{b_2\cot\theta}{\csc\theta}$ (cofunction identity)

$= \frac{\frac{b_2\cos\theta}{\sin\theta}}{\frac{1}{\sin\theta}}$ (cotangent and reciprocal identities)

$= b_2\cos\theta$ (Simplify.)

Available at **classzone.com**

Diagnosis/Remediation

- Practice A, B, C in Chapter 14 Resource Book, pp. 30–32
- Study Guide in Chapter 14 Resource Book, pp. 33–34
- Practice Workbook, pp. 197–198
- @HomeTutor

Challenge

Additional challenge is available in the Chapter 14 Resource Book, p. 37.

44a, 45a–c. See Additional Answers beginning on p. AA1.

44. ★ **EXTENDED RESPONSE** When light traveling in a medium (such as air) strikes the surface of a second medium (such as water) at an angle θ_1, the light begins to travel at a different angle θ_2. This change of direction is defined by Snell's law, $n_1 \sin\theta_1 = n_2 \sin\theta_2$, where n_1 and n_2 are the *indices of refraction* for the two mediums. Snell's law can be derived from the equation:

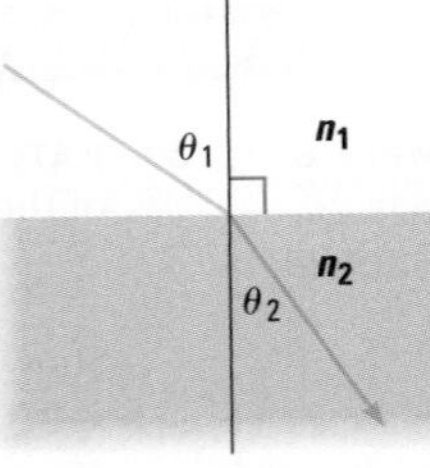

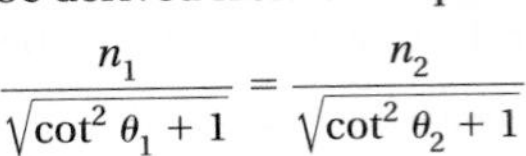

$$\frac{n_1}{\sqrt{\cot^2\theta_1 + 1}} = \frac{n_2}{\sqrt{\cot^2\theta_2 + 1}}$$

a. Derive Simplify the equation to derive Snell's law: $n_1 \sin\theta_1 = n_2 \sin\theta_2$. **See margin.**

b. Solve If $\theta_1 = 55°$, $\theta_2 = 35°$, and $n_2 = 2$, what is the value of n_1? **about 1.4**

c. Interpret If $\theta_1 = \theta_2$, what must be true about the values of n_1 and n_2? *Explain* when this situation would occur.
$n_1 = n_2$; this situation could occur when the mediums have the same composition.

C **45. CHALLENGE** Brewster's angle is the angle θ_1, at which light reflected off water is completely polarized, so that glare is minimized when you look at the water with polarized sunglasses. Brewster's angle can be found using Snell's law (see Exercise 44). **a–c. See margin.**

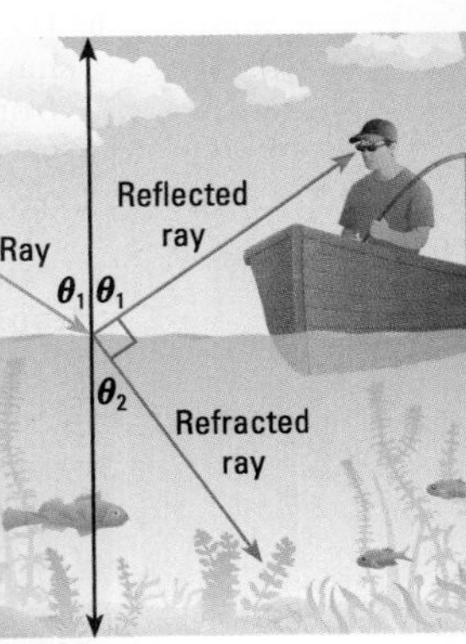

a. Let $\sin^2\theta_2 = \left(\frac{n_1}{n_2}\sin\theta_1\right)^2$ and $\cos^2\theta_2 = \left(\frac{n_2}{n_1}\cos\theta_1\right)^2$.

Add the two equations to show that

$$\frac{n_1^2}{n_2^2}\sin^2\theta_1 + \frac{n_2^2}{n_1^2}\cos^2\theta_1 = 1.$$

b. Show that the equation from part (a) can be simplified to $\frac{n_2^2 - n_1^2}{n_2^2}\sin^2\theta_1 = \frac{n_2^2 - n_1^2}{n_1^2}\cos^2\theta_1$.

c. Solve the equation from part (b) to find Brewster's angle:

$$\theta_1 = \tan^{-1}\left(\frac{n_2}{n_1}\right)$$

KY KENTUCKY MIXED REVIEW

46. Which equation will produce the widest parabola when graphed? **B**

Ⓐ $y = -3x^2$ Ⓑ $y = -\frac{2}{5}x^2$ Ⓒ $y = 1.5x^2$ Ⓓ $y = \frac{5}{2}x^2$

47. Reflect $\triangle RST$ in the line $x = -1$. In which quadrant will the image of point R appear? **A**

Ⓐ Quadrant I Ⓑ Quadrant II
Ⓒ Quadrant III Ⓓ Quadrant IV

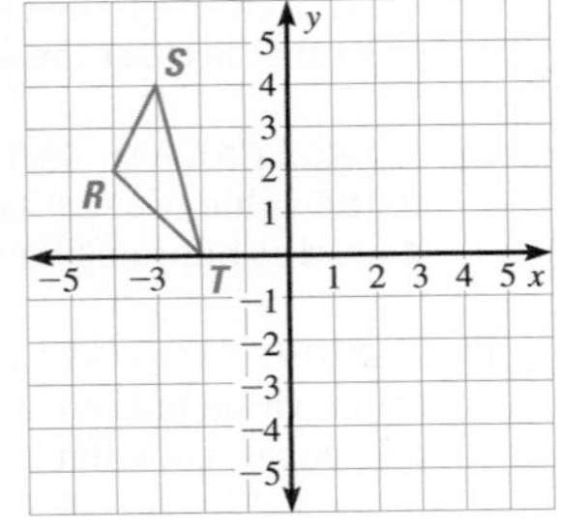

14.4 Solve Trigonometric Equations

MA-HS-5.3.6 Students will model, solve and graph quadratic equations in real-world and mathematical problems. DOK 2

Before You verified trigonometric identities.

Now You will solve trigonometric equations.

Why? So you can solve surface area problems, as in Ex. 43.

Key Vocabulary
- **extraneous solution,** p. 52

In Lesson 14.3, you verified trigonometric identities. In this lesson, you will solve trigonometric equations. To see the difference, consider the following:

$$\sin^2 x + \cos^2 x = 1 \qquad \textbf{Equation 1}$$

$$\sin x = 1 \qquad \textbf{Equation 2}$$

Equation 1 is an identity because it is true for all real values of x. Equation 2, however, is true only for some values of x. When you find these values, you are solving the equation.

EXAMPLE 1 Solve a trigonometric equation

Solve $2 \sin x - \sqrt{3} = 0$.

Solution

First isolate $\sin x$ on one side of the equation.

$2 \sin x - \sqrt{3} = 0$ **Write original equation.**

$2 \sin x = \sqrt{3}$ **Add $\sqrt{3}$ to each side.**

$\sin x = \frac{\sqrt{3}}{2}$ **Divide each side by 2.**

One solution of $\sin x = \frac{\sqrt{3}}{2}$ in the interval $0 \le x < 2\pi$ is $x = \sin^{-1} \frac{\sqrt{3}}{2} = \frac{\pi}{3}$. The other solution in the interval is $x = \pi - \frac{\pi}{3} = \frac{2\pi}{3}$. Moreover, because $y = \sin x$ is periodic, there will be infinitely many solutions.

WRITE GENERAL SOLUTION
To write the general solution of a trigonometric equation, you can add multiples of the period to all the solutions from one cycle.

You can use the two solutions found above to write the general solution:

$$x = \frac{\pi}{3} + 2n\pi \quad \text{or} \quad x = \frac{2\pi}{3} + 2n\pi \quad \text{(where } n \text{ is any integer)}$$

CHECK You can check the answer by graphing $y = \sin x$ and $y = \frac{\sqrt{3}}{2}$ in the same coordinate plane. Then find the points where the graphs intersect. You can see that there are infinitely many such points.

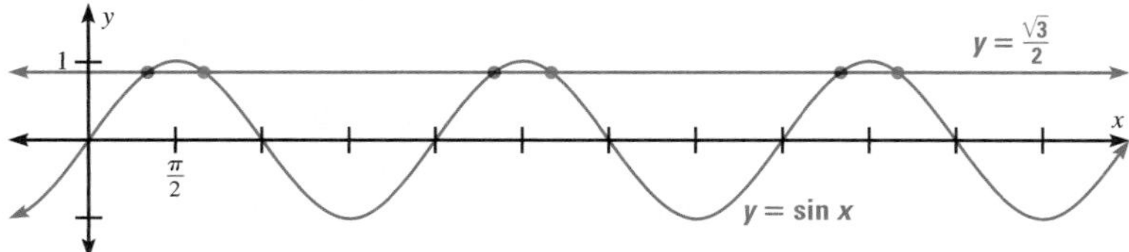

1 PLAN AND PREPARE

Warm-Up Exercises

Transparency Available

Solve each equation.

1. $(x + 3)^2 = 5$ $x = -3 \pm \sqrt{5}$
2. $x^2 + 16 = 8x$ $x = 4$
3. The height h of a toy rocket t seconds after it is launched is given by $h = -16t^2 + 120t$. When will the rocket be 180 feet above the ground? **after about 2.07 sec and about 5.43 sec**

Notetaking Guide

Transparency Available

Promotes interactive learning and notetaking skills, pp. 362–365.

Pacing

Basic: 1 day
Average: 1 day
Advanced: 1 day
Block: 0.5 block with 14.3
- See *Teaching Guide/Lesson Plan.*

2 FOCUS AND MOTIVATE

Essential Question

Big Idea 2, p. 907

How can you write the general solution of a trigonometric equation?

Tell students they will learn how to answer this question by solving trigonometric equations and observing the periodic behavior of the function over its domain.

Resource Planning Guide

Chapter Resource Book
- Teaching Guide/Lesson Plan (pp. 38–39)
- Practice levels A, B, C (pp. 41–43)
- Study Guide (pp. 44–45)
- Catch-up for Absent Students (p. 46)
- Problem Solving Workshop (p. 47)
- Challenge (p. 49)

Workbooks
- Notetaking Guide (pp. 362–365)
- Practice Workbook (pp. 199–200)

Teaching Options
- **Power Presentations CD-ROM** provides dynamic electronic teaching resources for the classroom.
- **Activity Generator CD-ROM** provides editable activities for all ability levels.

Interactive Technology
- Easy Planner
- Power Presentations CD-ROM
- Activity Generator CD-ROM
- Animated Algebra
- Test Generator CD-ROM
- Online Quiz
- eWorkbook
- eEdition
- @HomeTutor

Resources for English Learners
- Quick Reference for English Learners
- Spanish Study Guide
- Multi-Language Visual Glossary
- Student Resources in Spanish

See also the *Algebra 2 Toolkit* for more strategies for meeting individual needs.

Motivating the Lesson

Discuss with students cyclical change, such as high and low tide or the phases of the moon, whose regularity we can count on. Tell them that trigonometric equations model cyclical change and can help us control our environment.

3 TEACH

Extra Example 1

Solve $2\cos x + 1 = 0$.
$x = \frac{2\pi}{3} + 2n\pi$ or $x = \frac{4\pi}{3} + 2n\pi$

Key Question to Ask for Example 1

- Explain, in terms of degrees, why one solution of the equation is $\frac{\pi}{3} + 2n\pi$ and another solution is $\frac{2\pi}{3} + 2n\pi$. $\sin 60° = \frac{\sqrt{3}}{2} = \sin(60° + 60°) = \sin 120°$. Thus, for each additional 360° rotation around the unit circle from either $\frac{\pi}{3}$ or $\frac{2\pi}{3}$, $\sin\theta = \frac{\sqrt{3}}{2}$.

Extra Example 2

Solve $3 - \tan^2 x = 0$ in the interval $0 \le x < 2\pi$. $\frac{\pi}{3}, \frac{2\pi}{3}, \frac{4\pi}{3}, \frac{5\pi}{3}$

Extra Example 3

Suppose the average monthly high temperature (°F) T in a Midwestern U. S. city can be modeled by $T = 27\sin\left(\frac{\pi}{6}t - \frac{2\pi}{3}\right) + 57$ when t is in months and $t = 1$ corresponds to January. In which month is the average high temperature 84°? July

EXAMPLE 2 Solve a trigonometric equation in an interval

Solve $9\tan^2 x + 2 = 3$ in the interval $0 \le x < 2\pi$.

$9\tan^2 x + 2 = 3$	Write original equation.
$9\tan^2 x = 1$	Subtract 2 from each side.
$\tan^2 x = \frac{1}{9}$	Divide each side by 9.
$\tan x = \pm\frac{1}{3}$	Take square roots of each side.

REVIEW INVERSE FUNCTIONS
For help with inverse trigonometric functions, see p. 875.

Using a calculator, you find that $\tan^{-1}\frac{1}{3} \approx 0.322$ and $\tan^{-1}\left(-\frac{1}{3}\right) \approx -0.322$. Therefore, the general solution of the equation is:

$x \approx 0.322 + n\pi$ or $x \approx -0.322 + n\pi$ (where n is any integer)

▶ The specific solutions in the interval $0 \le x < 2\pi$ are:

$x \approx 0.322$	$x \approx -0.322 + \pi \approx 2.820$
$x \approx 0.322 + \pi \approx 3.464$	$x \approx -0.322 + 2\pi \approx 5.961$

EXAMPLE 3 Solve a real-life trigonometric equation

OCEANOGRAPHY The water depth d for the Bay of Fundy can be modeled by

$$d = 35 - 28\cos\frac{\pi}{6.2}t$$

where d is measured in feet and t is the time in hours. If $t = 0$ represents midnight, at what time(s) is the water depth 7 feet?

High tide

Low tide

ANOTHER WAY
For alternative methods for solving the problem in Example 3, turn to page 938 for the **Problem Solving Workshop**.

Solution

Substitute 7 for d in the model and solve for t.

$35 - 28\cos\frac{\pi}{6.2}t = 7$	Substitute 7 for d.
$-28\cos\frac{\pi}{6.2}t = -28$	Subtract 35 from each side.
$\cos\frac{\pi}{6.2}t = 1$	Divide each side by −28.
$\frac{\pi}{6.2}t = 2n\pi$	$\cos\theta = 1$ when $\theta = 2n\pi$.
$t = 12.4n$	Solve for t.

▶ On the interval $0 \le t \le 24$ (representing one full day), the water depth is 7 feet when $t = 12.4(0) = 0$ (that is, at midnight) and when $t = 12.4(1) = 12.4$ (that is, at 12:24 P.M.).

Differentiated Instruction

Auditory Learners Before working through the solution to **Example 3**, have students read the question aloud. Ask students to write down the goal of the problem (i.e., the value for which they are solving). When they have reached the end of the solution, ask students what they have found; students should explain the meaning of the value they found. Have students make sure they have answered the question asked by writing a sentence in their own words describing the answer they found.

See also the *Algebra 2 Toolkit* for more strategies.

GUIDED PRACTICE for Examples 1, 2, and 3

1. Find the general solution of the equation $2 \sin x + 4 = 5$. $\frac{\pi}{6} + 2n\pi$ or $\frac{5\pi}{6} + 2n\pi$
2. Solve the equation $3 \csc^2 x = 4$ in the interval $0 \le x < 2\pi$. $\frac{\pi}{3}, \frac{2\pi}{3}, \frac{4\pi}{3}, \frac{5\pi}{3}$
3. **OCEANOGRAPHY** In Example 3, at what time(s) is the water depth 63 feet? 6:12 A.M. and 6:36 P.M.

EXAMPLE 4 Standardized Test Practice

What is the general solution of $\sin^3 x - 4 \sin x = 0$?

Ⓐ $x = \frac{\pi}{2} + 2n\pi$ or $x = \frac{3\pi}{2} + 2n\pi$ Ⓑ $x = \frac{\pi}{2} + 2n\pi$ or $x = \pi + 2n\pi$

Ⓒ $x = \pi + 2n\pi$ Ⓓ $x = 2n\pi$ or $x = \pi + 2n\pi$

Solution

$\sin^3 x - 4 \sin x = 0$ **Write original equation.**

$\sin x (\sin^2 x - 4) = 0$ **Factor out sin x.**

$\sin x (\sin x + 2)(\sin x - 2) = 0$ **Factor difference of squares.**

Set each factor equal to 0 and solve for x, if possible.

$\sin x = 0$	$\sin x + 2 = 0$	$\sin x - 2 = 0$
$x = 0$ or $x = \pi$	$\sin x = -2$	$\sin x = 2$

ELIMINATE SOLUTIONS
Because $\sin x$ is never less than -1 or greater than 1, there are no solutions of $\sin x = -2$ and $\sin x = 2$.

The only solutions in the interval $0 \le x < 2\pi$ are $x = 0$ and $x = \pi$.

The general solution is $x = 2n\pi$ or $x = \pi + 2n\pi$ where n is any integer.

▶ The correct answer is D. Ⓐ Ⓑ Ⓒ Ⓓ

EXAMPLE 5 Use the quadratic formula

Solve $\cos^2 x - 5 \cos x + 2 = 0$ in the interval $0 \le x \le \pi$.

Solution

Because the equation is in the form $au^2 + bu + c = 0$ where $u = \cos x$, you can use the quadratic formula to solve for $\cos x$.

$\cos^2 x - 5 \cos x + 2 = 0$ **Write original equation.**

$\cos x = \frac{-(-5) \pm \sqrt{(-5)^2 - 4(1)(2)}}{2(1)}$ **Quadratic formula**

$= \frac{5 \pm \sqrt{17}}{2}$ **Simplify.**

≈ 4.56 or 0.44 **Use a calculator.**

$x = \cos^{-1} 4.56$ | $x = \cos^{-1} 0.44$ **Use inverse cosine.**

No solution | ≈ 1.12 **Use a calculator, if possible.**

▶ In the interval $0 \le x \le \pi$, the only solution is $x \approx 1.12$.

Extra Example 4

What is the general solution of $2 \cos^3 x - \cos x = 0$? A

Ⓐ $x = \frac{\pi}{2} + 2n\pi$ or $x = \pi + n\pi$

Ⓑ $x = \frac{\pi}{2} + 2n\pi$ or $x = \pi + 2n\pi$

Ⓒ $x = \frac{\pi}{2} + 2n\pi$

Ⓓ $x = n\pi$ or $x = \pi + n\pi$

Key Question to Ask for Example 4

- Which solutions does answer C omit? ... $-2\pi, 0, 2\pi, 4\pi, 6\pi, 8\pi, \ldots$

Extra Example 5

Solve $\sin^2 x - 4 \sin x + 1 = 0$ in the interval $0 \le x \le \pi$. $x \approx 0.27$ or $x \approx 2.87$

Key Question to Ask for Example 5

- Why is there no solution for $x = \cos^{-1} 4.56$? $\cos x$ is never greater than 1.

Avoiding Common Errors

Example 5 Watch for students who mistakenly evaluate $\cos^{-1} 0.44$ as $\frac{1}{\cos 0.44}$. Remind these students that $\cos^{-1} 0.44$ represents an angle whose cosine is 0.44, and that $\frac{1}{\cos 0.44}$ represents the reciprocal of $\cos 0.44$.

Extra Example 6

Solve $\sin x - \cos x = 1$ in the interval $0 \le x < 2\pi$. $x = \frac{\pi}{2}$ and $x = \pi$

Key Question to Ask for Example 6

- Why is it necessary to square both sides of the equation in the first step of the solution? **You must express both trigonometric functions in terms of a single function. Squaring will allow you to express $(\sin x)^2$ in terms of $\cos x$.**

Closing the Lesson

Have students summarize the major points of the lesson and answer the Essential Question: How can you write the general solution of a trigonometric equation?

- **You can use factoring, the quadratic equation, or trigonometric identities to solve a trigonometric equation.**
- **When solving a trigonometric equation, you must identify all solutions for the given domain.**
- **When solving a trigonometric equation, you should always check your solutions in the original equation to verify that none of the solutions is an extraneous solution.**

For the given domain, you can add multiples of the period to all solutions from one cycle.

EXTRANEOUS SOLUTIONS When solving a trigonometric equation, it is possible to obtain extraneous solutions. So, you should always check your solutions in the original equation.

EXAMPLE 6 Solve an equation with an extraneous solution

Solve $1 + \cos x = \sin x$ in the interval $0 \le x < 2\pi$.

REVIEW FOIL METHOD
For help multiplying binomials, see p. 245.

$1 + \cos x = \sin x$	Write original equation.
$(1 + \cos x)^2 = (\sin x)^2$	Square both sides.
$1 + 2\cos x + \cos^2 x = \sin^2 x$	Multiply.
$1 + 2\cos x + \cos^2 x = 1 - \cos^2 x$	Pythagorean identity
$2\cos^2 x + 2\cos x = 0$	Quadratic form
$2\cos x(\cos x + 1) = 0$	Factor out $2\cos x$.
$2\cos x = 0$ or $\cos x + 1 = 0$	Zero product property
$\cos x = 0$ or $\cos x = -1$	Solve for $\cos x$.

On the interval $0 \le x < 2\pi$, $\cos x = 0$ has two solutions: $x = \frac{\pi}{2}$ or $x = \frac{3\pi}{2}$.

On the interval $0 \le x < 2\pi$, $\cos x = -1$ has one solution: $x = \pi$.

Therefore, $1 + \cos x = \sin x$ has three possible solutions: $x = \frac{\pi}{2}$, π, and $\frac{3\pi}{2}$.

CHECK To check the solutions, substitute them into the original equation and simplify.

$1 + \cos x = \sin x$	$1 + \cos x = \sin x$	$1 + \cos x = \sin x$
$1 + \cos\frac{\pi}{2} \stackrel{?}{=} \sin\frac{\pi}{2}$	$1 + \cos\pi \stackrel{?}{=} \sin\pi$	$1 + \cos\frac{3\pi}{2} \stackrel{?}{=} \sin\frac{3\pi}{2}$
$1 + 0 \stackrel{?}{=} 1$	$1 + (-1) \stackrel{?}{=} 0$	$1 + 0 \stackrel{?}{=} -1$
$1 = 1$ ✓	$0 = 0$ ✓	$1 \ne -1$

▶ The apparent solution $x = \frac{3\pi}{2}$ is extraneous because it does not check in the original equation. The only solutions in the interval $0 \le x < 2\pi$ are $x = \frac{\pi}{2}$ and $x = \pi$. Graphs of each side of the original equation confirm the solutions.

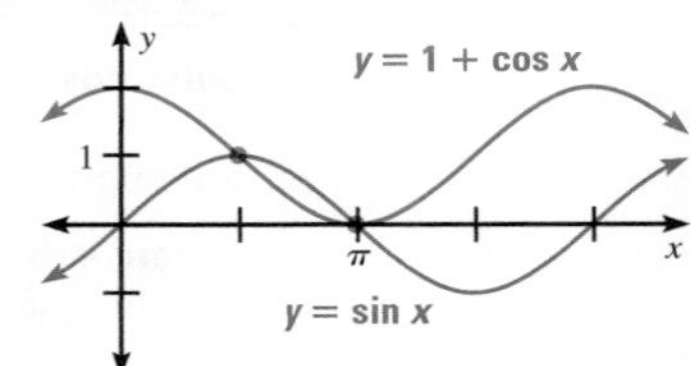

✓ GUIDED PRACTICE for Examples 4, 5, and 6

Find the general solution of the equation.

4. $\sin^3 x - \sin x = 0$ $0 + n\pi$ or $\frac{\pi}{2} + n\pi$

5. $1 - \cos x = \sqrt{3}\sin x$ $0 + 2n\pi$ or $\frac{2\pi}{3} + 2n\pi$

Solve the equation in the interval $0 \le x \le \pi$.

6. $2\sin x = \csc x$ $\frac{\pi}{4}, \frac{3\pi}{4}$

7. $\tan^2 x - \sin x\tan^2 x = 0$ $0, \pi$ or $\frac{\pi}{2}$

14.4 EXERCISES

HOMEWORK KEY

- ◯ = **WORKED-OUT SOLUTIONS** on p. WS24 for Exs. 5, 13, and 43
- ★ = **STANDARDIZED TEST PRACTICE** Exs. 2, 15, 36, 42, and 44
- ◆ = **MULTIPLE REPRESENTATIONS** Ex. 43

SKILL PRACTICE

A

1. VOCABULARY What is the difference between a trigonometric equation and a trigonometric identity? A trigonometric identity is true for all real values of x where a trigonometric equation is only true for some specific value(s) of x.

2. ★ WRITING *Describe* several techniques for solving trigonometric equations. See margin.

EXAMPLE 1 on p. 931 for Exs. 3–15

CHECKING SOLUTIONS **Verify that the given x-value is a solution of the equation.**

3. $2 + 3\cos x - 5 = 0, x = 4\pi$
$2 + 3\cos(4\pi) - 5 = 2 + 3(1) - 5 = 0$

4. $\pi \sec x + \pi = 0, x = \pi$
$\pi \sec(\pi) + \pi = -\pi + \pi = 0$

5. $12\sin^2 x - 3 = 0, x = \frac{\pi}{6}$
See margin.

6. $5\tan^3 x - 5 = 0, x = \frac{\pi}{4}$
$5\tan^3\left(\frac{\pi}{4}\right) - 5 = 5(1)^3 - 5 = 0$

7. $2\cos^4 x - \cos^2 x = 0, x = \frac{\pi}{2}$
$2\cos^4\left(\frac{\pi}{2}\right) - \cos^2\left(\frac{\pi}{2}\right) = 2(0)^4 - (0)^2 = 0$

8. $3\cot^4 x - \cot^2 x - 24 = 0, x = \frac{7\pi}{6}$
$3\cot^4\left(\frac{7\pi}{6}\right) - \cot^2\left(\frac{7\pi}{6}\right) - 24 = 3(9) - 3 - 24 = 0$

GENERAL SOLUTIONS **Find the general solution of the equation.**

9. $2\sin x - 1 = 0$

10. $\sqrt{3}\csc x + 2 = 0$

11. $3\tan x - \sqrt{3} = 0$

12. $\sin x + \sqrt{2} = -\sin x$

13. $4\cos^2 x - 3 = 0$

14. $3\tan^2 x - 9 = 0$

15. ★ MULTIPLE CHOICE What is the general solution of the equation $4\sin x = 2\sin x + 1$? C

(A) $x = \frac{\pi}{6} + 2n\pi$ or $x = \frac{7\pi}{6} + 2n\pi$

(B) $x = \frac{\pi}{6} + n\pi$ or $x = \frac{5\pi}{6} + n\pi$

(C) $x = \frac{\pi}{6} + 2n\pi$ or $x = \frac{5\pi}{6} + 2n\pi$

(D) $x = \frac{\pi}{6} + n\pi$ or $x = \frac{7\pi}{6} + n\pi$

EXAMPLE 2 on p. 932 for Exs. 16–23

SOLVING EQUATIONS **Solve the equation in the interval $0 \le x < 2\pi$.**

16. $5 + 2\sin x - 7 = 0$ $\frac{\pi}{2}$

17. $3\tan x - \sqrt{3} = 0$ $\frac{\pi}{6}, \frac{7\pi}{6}$

18. $3\cos x = \cos x - 1$ $\frac{2\pi}{3}, \frac{4\pi}{3}$

19. $2\sin^2 x - 1 = 0$

20. $5\tan^2 x - 15 = 0$

21. $4\cos^2 x - 1 = 0$

19–21. See margin.

ERROR ANALYSIS ***Describe*** **and correct the error in solving the equation in the interval $0 \le x \le \frac{\pi}{2}$.** 22, 23. See margin.

22.
$\sin^2 x = \frac{1}{2}\sin x$
$\sin x = \frac{1}{2}$
$x = \frac{\pi}{6}$ ✗

23.
$-2\cos x = -1$
$\cos x = -\frac{1}{2}$
$x = \frac{2\pi}{3}$ ✗

B

EXAMPLE 4 on p. 933 for Exs. 24–29

GENERAL SOLUTIONS **Find the general solution of the equation.**

24. $\sin x\cos x - 3\cos x = 0$ $\frac{\pi}{2} + n\pi$

25. $\sqrt{3}\cos x\tan x - \cos x = 0$ $\frac{\pi}{6} + n\pi$

26. $2\sin^3 x = \sin x$ $0 + n\pi$ or $\frac{\pi}{4} + n\pi$ or $\frac{7\pi}{4} + n\pi$

27. $2\tan^4 x - \tan^2 x - 15 = 0$ $\frac{\pi}{3} + n\pi$ or $\frac{2\pi}{3} + n\pi$

28. $\sqrt{\cos x} = 2\cos x - 1$ $0 + 2n\pi$

29. $1 + \cos x = \sqrt{3}\sin x$ $\frac{\pi}{3} + 2n\pi$ or $\pi + 2n\pi$

2. *Sample answer:* Factoring, using the quadratic formula, substitution of other trigonometric identities

9. $\frac{\pi}{6} + 2n\pi$ or $\frac{5\pi}{6} + 2n\pi$

10. $\frac{4\pi}{3} + 2n\pi$ or $\frac{5\pi}{3} + 2n\pi$

11. $\frac{\pi}{6} + n\pi$

12. $\frac{5\pi}{4} + 2n\pi$ or $\frac{7\pi}{4} + 2n\pi$

13. $\frac{\pi}{6} + n\pi$ or $\frac{5\pi}{6} + n\pi$

14. $\frac{\pi}{3} + n\pi$ or $\frac{2\pi}{3} + n\pi$

19. $\frac{\pi}{4}, \frac{3\pi}{4}, \frac{5\pi}{4}, \frac{7\pi}{4}$

20. $\frac{\pi}{3}, \frac{2\pi}{3}, \frac{4\pi}{3}, \frac{5\pi}{3}$

21. $\frac{\pi}{3}, \frac{2\pi}{3}, \frac{4\pi}{3}, \frac{5\pi}{3}$

4 PRACTICE AND APPLY

Assignment Guide

Answer Transparencies available for all exercises

Basic:
Day 1: EP p. 1014 Exs. 15–18, 20
pp. 935–937
Exs. 1–6, 9–15 odd, 16–18, 22–26, 30, 31, 41–43, 47

Average:
Day 1: pp. 935–937
Exs. 1, 2, 5–7, 10–12, 15, 18–23, 26–28, 30–33, 36–39, 41–44, 47

Advanced:
Day 1: pp. 935–937
Exs. 1, 2, 7, 8, 13–15, 19–21, 27–29, 32–40*, 42–45

Block:
pp. 935–937
Exs. 1, 2, 5–7, 10–12, 15, 18–23, 26–28, 30–33, 36–39, 41–44, 47 (with 14.3)

Differentiated Instruction

See *Algebra 2 Best Practices Toolkit* for suggestions on addressing the needs of a diverse classroom.

Homework Check

For a quick check of student understanding of key concepts, go over the following exercises:

Basic: 15, 16, 24, 30, 41

Average: 12, 18, 26, 32, 41

Advanced: 14, 20, 28, 34, 42

Extra Practice

- Student Edition, p. 1023
- Chapter 14 Resource Book: Practice levels A, B, C, pp. 41–43

Practice Worksheet

An easily-readable reduced practice page (with answers) for this lesson can be found on p. 906C.

5. $12\sin^2\left(\frac{\pi}{6}\right) - 3 = 12\left(\frac{1}{2}\right)^2 - 3 = 0$

22. When you divide by a trigonometric function, you are possibly dividing by 0 and that is not allowed. You must add or subtract to eliminate values.
$\sin^2 x - \frac{1}{2}\sin x = 0$
$\sin x\left(\sin x - \frac{1}{2}\right) = 0$
$\sin x = 0$ or $\sin x = \frac{1}{2}$
$x = 0, \pi$ or $x = \frac{\pi}{6}, \frac{5\pi}{6}$

23. When two negative values are divided, the quotient is positive.
$\cos x = \frac{1}{2}$
$x = \frac{\pi}{3}, \frac{5\pi}{3}$

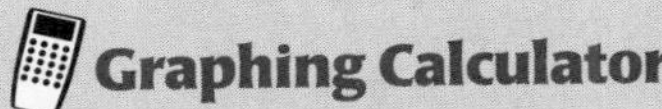

Graphing Calculator

Exercises 9–14 If students solve these equations on their graphing calculators, their graphing window may identify only the basic solutions. Remind them to use the period of the function to determine all solutions.

Avoiding Common Errors

Exercise 26 Students may begin the proof by dividing both sides by $\sin x$. Remind them that the division is undefined for $\sin x = 0$.

43a. $S = \frac{27}{4} + \frac{27}{32}\left(\frac{\sqrt{3} - \cos\theta}{\sin\theta}\right)$

43b. *Sample answer:*

θ	16	17	18	19
S	9.1095	8.9887	8.8825	8.7884

θ	120	121	122	123
S	8.9246	8.9619	9.0005	9.0405

about 17° and about 122°

43c.

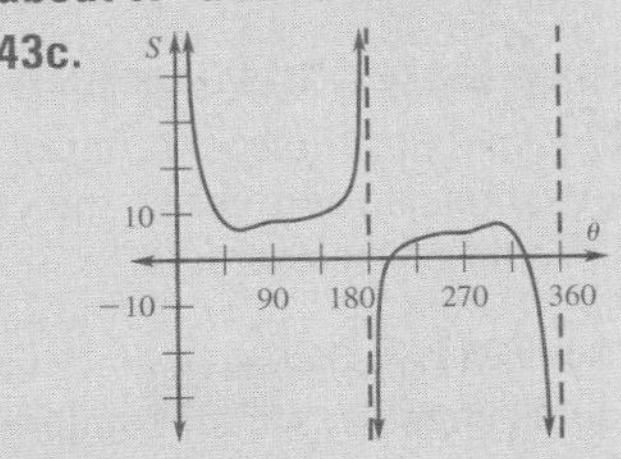

about 54.7°

EXAMPLES 5 and 6 on pp. 933–934 for Exs. 30–35

30. $\frac{\pi}{4}, \frac{3\pi}{4}, \frac{5\pi}{4}, \frac{7\pi}{4}$

32. $\frac{\pi}{3}, \pi, \frac{5\pi}{3}$

39. $\left(\frac{\pi}{6}, \frac{\sqrt{3}}{3}\right), \left(\frac{2\pi}{3}, 3\sqrt{3}\right), \left(\frac{7\pi}{6}, \frac{\sqrt{3}}{3}\right), \left(\frac{5\pi}{3}, 3\sqrt{3}\right)$

40a. The x and y coordinates are the same sign in the first and third quadrants which give the same point of reference.

SOLVING **Solve the equation in the given interval. Check your solutions.**

30. $\sec x \csc^2 x = 2 \sec x;\ 0 \le x < 2\pi$

31. $\sqrt{3}\cos^2 x = \cos^2 x \tan x;\ 0 \le x \le \pi$ $\frac{\pi}{3}, \frac{\pi}{2}$

32. $2\sin^2 x - \cos x - 1 = 0;\ 0 \le x < 2\pi$

33. $\sin^2 x + 5\sin x - 3 = 0;\ -\frac{\pi}{2} \le x < \frac{\pi}{2}$ about 0.572

34. $\tan^2 x - 3\tan x + 2 = 0;\ 0 \le x \le \pi$ $\frac{\pi}{4}$, about 1.11

35. $\cos x + \sin x \tan x = 2;\ \pi \le x < 2\pi$ $\frac{5\pi}{3}$

36. ★ **MULTIPLE CHOICE** What are the points of intersection of the graphs of $y = 4\sin x + 1$ and $y = 2\sin x + 2$ on the interval $0 \le x < 2\pi$? **B**

Ⓐ $\left(\frac{\pi}{6}, -3\right), \left(\frac{\pi}{2}, -3\right)$

Ⓑ $\left(\frac{\pi}{6}, 3\right), \left(\frac{5\pi}{6}, 3\right)$

Ⓒ $\left(\frac{\pi}{2}, 3\right), \left(\frac{7\pi}{6}, 3\right)$

Ⓓ $\left(\frac{\pi}{6}, 3\right), \left(\frac{11\pi}{6}, 3\right)$

C **INTERSECTION POINTS** **Find the points of intersection of the graphs of the given functions in the interval $0 \le x < 2\pi$.**

37. $y = \cos^2 x$
$y = 2\cos x - 1$ (0, 1)

38. $y = 9\sin^2 x$
$y = \sin^2 x + 8\sin x - 2$ $\left(\frac{\pi}{6}, 2.25\right), \left(\frac{5\pi}{6}, 2.25\right)$

39. $y = \sqrt{3}\tan^2 x$
$y = \sqrt{3} - 2\tan x$

40. **CHALLENGE** A number c is a *fixed point* of a function f if $f(c) = c$. For example, 0 is a fixed point of $f(x) = \sin x$ because $f(0) = \sin 0 = 0$.

a. **Reasoning** Use graphs to explain why the function $g(x) = \cos x$ has only one fixed point.

b. **Graphing Calculator** Find the fixed point of $g(x) = \cos x$. about 0.739

PROBLEM SOLVING

EXAMPLE 3 A on p. 932 for Exs. 41–42

42. May 2 and August 11. *Sample answer:* Graph the function $D(t)$ and $y = 20$ and use the calculator to locate the points of intersection, rounding up for the next day.

41. **WIND SPEED** The average wind speed s (in miles per hour) in the Boston Harbor can be approximated by $s = 3.38 \sin \frac{\pi}{180}(t + 3) + 11.6$ where t is the time in days, with $t = 0$ representing January 1. On which days of the year is the average wind speed 10 miles per hour? **July 26 and November 26**

@HomeTutor for problem solving help at classzone.com

42. ★ **SHORT RESPONSE** The number of degrees θ north of due east ($\theta > 0$) or south of due east ($\theta < 0$) that the sun rises in Cheyenne, Wyoming, can be modeled by

$$\theta(t) = 31 \sin\left(\frac{2\pi}{365}t - 1.4\right)$$

where t is the time in days, with $t = 1$ representing January 1. Use an algebraic method to find at what day(s) the sun is 20° north of due east at sunrise. *Explain* how you can use the graph of $\theta(t)$ to check your answer.

@HomeTutor for problem solving help at classzone.com

○ = WORKED-OUT SOLUTIONS on p. WS1

★ = STANDARDIZED TEST PRACTICE

 = MULTIPLE REPRESENTATIONS

43. **MULTIPLE REPRESENTATIONS** The surface area S of a honeycomb cell can be estimated by the equation shown at the right. In the equation, h is the height (in inches), s is the width of a side (in inches), and θ is the angle (in degrees) indicated in the diagram. **a–c. See margin.**

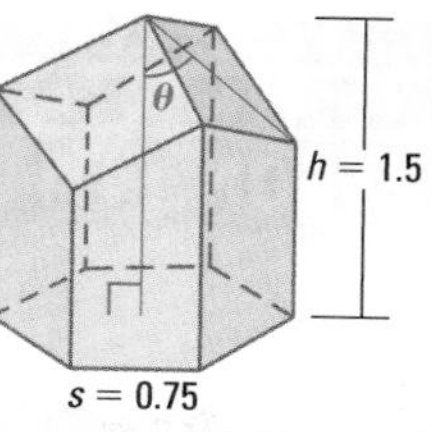

$S = 6hs + \frac{3}{2}s^2\left(\frac{\sqrt{3} - \cos\theta}{\sin\theta}\right)$

a. **Using a Diagram** Use the values of h and s in the diagram to simplify the equation.

b. **Making a Table** Use a graphing calculator to make a table for the function from part (a). For what value(s) of θ does $S = 9$ square inches?

c. **Drawing a Graph** Use a graphing calculator to graph the function from part (a). What value of θ minimizes the surface area?

44. ★ **EXTENDED RESPONSE** The power P (in watts) used by a microwave oven is the product of the voltage V (in volts) and the current I (in amperes). Suppose the voltage and current can be modeled by

$$V = 170\cos 120\pi t \quad \text{and} \quad I = 11.3\cos 120\pi t$$

where t is the time (in seconds).

a. **Model** Write the function $P(t)$ for the power used by the microwave. **$P(t) = 1921\cos^2 120\pi t$**

b. **Solve** At what times does the microwave use 375 watts of power?

c. **Graphing Calculator** Graph the function $P(t)$. *Describe* how the graph differs from that of a cosine function of the form $y = a\cos bt$. **The graph of $P(t)$ never goes below the x-axis.**

44b. about $0.00295 + 0.00833n$ sec and about $0.00538 + 0.00833n$ sec

C **45.** **CHALLENGE** Matrix multiplication can be used to rotate a point (x, y) counterclockwise about the origin through an angle θ. The coordinates of the resulting point (x', y') are determined by the matrix equation shown at the right.

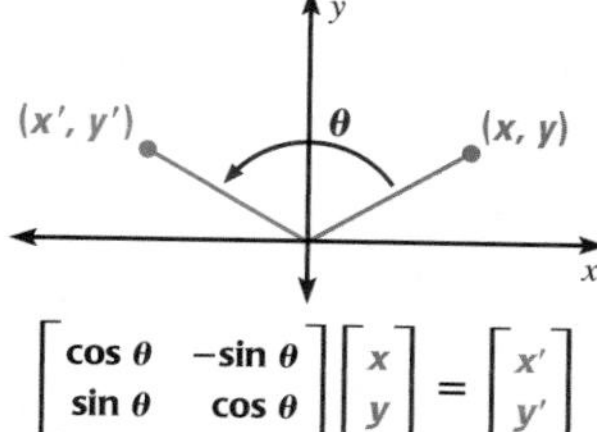

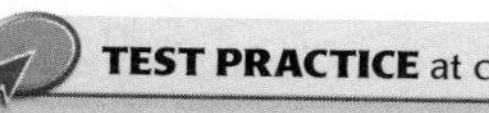

$$\begin{bmatrix}\cos\theta & -\sin\theta\\ \sin\theta & \cos\theta\end{bmatrix}\begin{bmatrix}x\\ y\end{bmatrix} = \begin{bmatrix}x'\\ y'\end{bmatrix}$$

a. The point (2, 3) is rotated counterclockwise about the origin through an angle of $\frac{\pi}{3}$. What are the coordinates of the resulting point? $\left(1 - \frac{3\sqrt{3}}{2}, \sqrt{3} + \frac{3}{2}\right)$

b. Through what angle θ must the point (6, 2) be rotated to produce $(x', y') = (3\sqrt{3} - 1, \sqrt{3} + 3)$? $\frac{\pi}{6}$

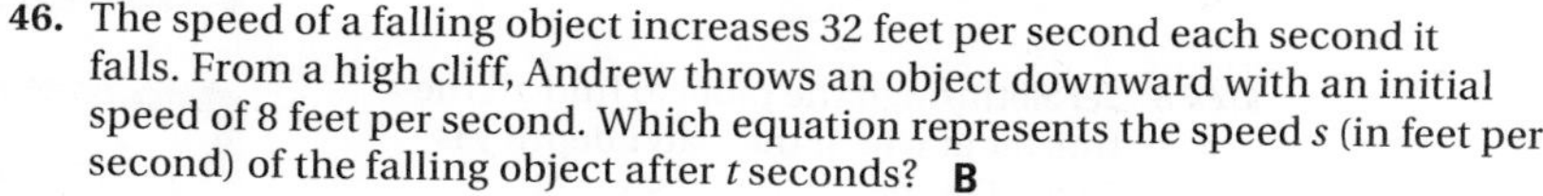

KENTUCKY MIXED REVIEW

TEST PRACTICE at classzone.com

46. The speed of a falling object increases 32 feet per second each second it falls. From a high cliff, Andrew throws an object downward with an initial speed of 8 feet per second. Which equation represents the speed s (in feet per second) of the falling object after t seconds? **B**

Ⓐ $s = -32t + 8$ Ⓑ $s = 32t + 8$

Ⓒ $s = 8t + 32$ Ⓓ $s = 32t$

47. What are the coordinates of the y-intercept of the graph of $-3x + 4y = 24$? **C**

Ⓐ $(-8, 0)$ Ⓑ $\left(0, \frac{4}{3}\right)$

Ⓒ $(0, 6)$ Ⓓ $(0, 8)$

EXTRA PRACTICE for Lesson 14.4, p. 1023

ONLINE QUIZ at classzone.com

5 ASSESS AND RETEACH

Daily Homework Quiz

Transparency Available

1. Find the general solution of $\tan x + \tan^2 x = 0$. $x = n\pi$ or $x = \frac{3\pi}{4} + n\pi$

Solve the equation in the given interval.

2. $2 - 8\cos^2 x = 0$; $0 \le x \le \pi$ $\frac{\pi}{3}, \frac{2\pi}{3}$

3. $\tan x \sin^2 x = 3\tan x$; $0 \le x \le \pi$ $0, \pi$

4. $\cos^2 x - 4\cos x = -2$; $0 \le x \le \pi$ 0.95

5. Suppose the average monthly high temperature T(°F) in a U. S. city can be modeled by $T = 12\cos\left(\frac{\pi}{6}t - \pi\right) + 75$ where t is in months and $t = 1$ corresponds to January. In which month is the average high temperature 63°? **December**

Online Quiz

Available at **classzone.com**

Diagnosis/Remediation

- Practice A, B, C in Chapter 14 Resource Book, pp. 41–43
- Study Guide in Chapter 14 Resource Book, pp. 44–45
- Practice Workbook, pp. 199–200
- @HomeTutor

Challenge

Additional challenge is available in the Chapter 14 Resource Book, p. 49.

Using ALTERNATIVE METHODS

Alternative Strategy

Example 3 on page 932 can be solved by using a table or a graph. These methods emphasize an important point about problem solving strategies, namely that there is likely to be more than one approach to solving a mathematical problem. Both methods allow student to see the periodic rhythm of the tides. Graphing the function relates an algebraic solution to a geometric solution.

Another Way to Solve Example 3, page 932

MULTIPLE REPRESENTATIONS In Example 3 on page 932, you solved a trigonometric equation algebraically. You can also solve a trigonometric equation using a table or using a graph.

PROBLEM

OCEANOGRAPHY The water depth d for the Bay of Fundy can be modeled by

$$d = 35 - 28 \cos \frac{\pi}{6.2}t$$

where d is measured in feet and t is the time in hours. If $t = 0$ represents midnight, at what time(s) is the water depth 7 feet?

METHOD 1

Using a Table The problem requires solving the equation $35 - 28 \cos \frac{\pi}{6.2}t = 7$. One way to solve this equation is to make a table of values. You can use a graphing calculator to make the table.

STEP 1 **Enter** the function $y = 35 - 28 \cos \frac{\pi}{6.2}x$ into a graphing calculator. Note that time is now represented by x and water depth is now represented by y.

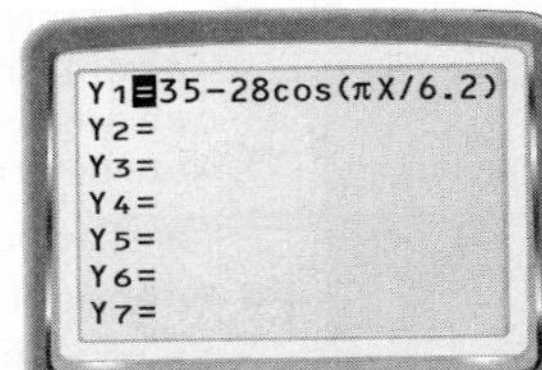

STEP 2 **Make** a table of values for the function. Set the table so that the x-values start at 0 and increase in increments of 0.1. (Be sure that the calculator is set in radian mode.)

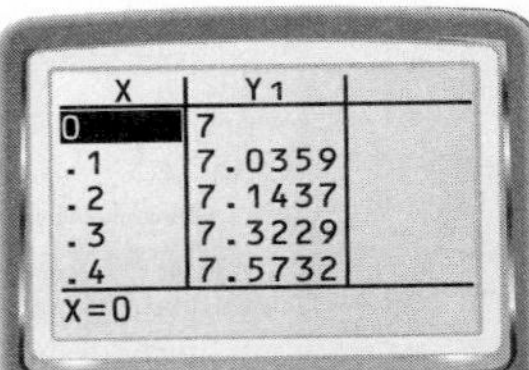

STEP 3 **Scroll** through the table to find all the times x at which the water depth y is 7 feet. On the interval $0 \le x \le 24$ (which represents one full day), you can see that the function equals 7 when x is 0 and 12.4.

X	Y1
12.1	7.3229
12.2	7.1437
12.3	7.0359
12.4	7
12.5	7.0359

X=12.4

▶ The water depth is 7 feet when $x = 0$ (that is, at midnight) and when $x = 12.4$ (that is, at 12:24 P.M.).

METHOD 2 **Using a Graph** Another approach is to use a graph to solve the equation $35 - 28 \cos \frac{\pi}{6.2} t = 7$. You can use a graphing calculator to make the graph.

STEP 1 **Enter** the functions $y = 35 - 28 \cos \frac{\pi}{6.2} x$ and $y = 7$ into a graphing calculator. Again, note that time is now represented by x and water depth is now represented by y.

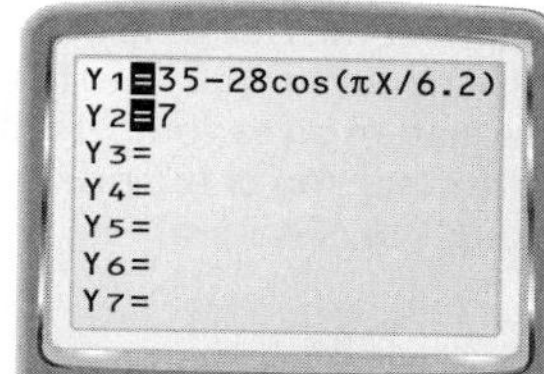

STEP 2 **Graph** the functions. Set your calculator in radian mode. Adjust the viewing window so that you can see where the graphs intersect on the interval $0 \le x \le 24$.

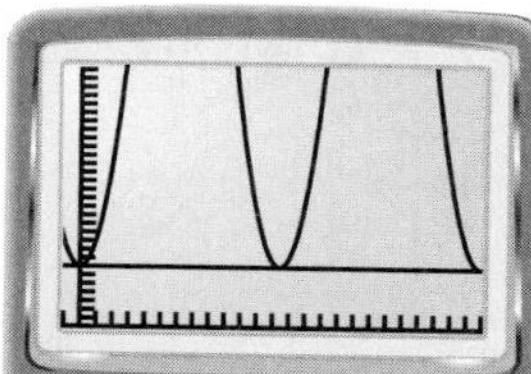

STEP 3 **Find** the intersection points of the two graphs using the *intersect* feature of the graphing calculator. On the interval $0 \le x \le 24$, the graphs intersect at (0, 7) and (12.4, 7). Because x represents the number of hours since midnight, you know that the water depth is 7 feet at midnight and 12:24 P.M.

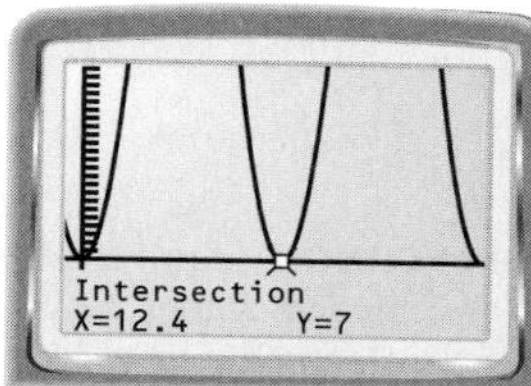

PRACTICE

SOLVING EQUATIONS Solve the equation using a table and using a graph.

1. $20 \sin \frac{\pi}{4} x - 6 = 8$ **about 0.987, about 3.01**
2. $5 \cos \frac{\pi}{6} x + 6 = 2$ **about 4.77, about 7.23**
3. $-10 \cos 2\pi x = 3$ **about 0.298, about 0.702**
4. $3 + 4 \sin \frac{\pi}{2} x = 2$ **about 2.16, about 3.84**
5. $-15 - 10 \sin \frac{\pi}{20} x = -11$ **about 22.6, about 37.4**
6. $-34 \cos \frac{\pi}{5}\left(x - \frac{\pi}{10}\right) + 22 = 17$ **about 2.58, about 8.05**
7. **WHAT IF?** In the problem on page 938, suppose you want to find the time(s) when the depth of the water in the Bay of Fundy is 15 feet. Find the time(s) using a table and using a graph. **1:32 A.M., 10:52 A.M., 1:56 P.M., 11:16 P.M.**
8. **WRITING** *Explain* why the equation $2 \sin x + 3 = 0$ has no solution. How does a graph show this? **See margin.**
9. **BUOY** An ocean buoy bobs up and down as waves travel past it. The buoy's displacement d (in feet) with respect to sea level can be modeled by $d = 3 \sin \pi t$ where t is the time (in seconds). During the one second interval $0 \le t \le 1$, when is the buoy 1.5 feet above sea level? Solve the problem using a table and using a graph. **about 0.17 sec and about 0.83 sec**

8. The range for sine is $-1 \le y \le 1$ and when you solve for sine, you get -1.5. Since this is not in the range, there is no solution; the graph of $2 \sin x + 3$ does not cross the x-axis, which means that there are no x-values where the expression is equal to 0.

Kentucky Mixed Review

1. B
2. D
3. D
4. C
5. B
6. a. 365 days
   b. the amount of ice cream produced should have a period of roughly 1 year; 137.5 million gallons
   c. Highest production: Day 196 (July 15); Lowest Production: Day 13 (January 13)

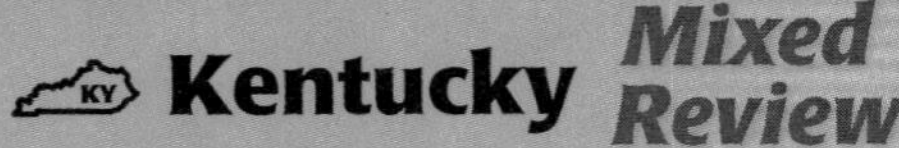

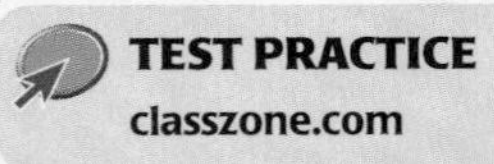

Lessons 14.1–14.4

1. **AMUSEMENT PARK** At an amusement park, you watch your friend go on a ride that simulates free-fall. You are standing 200 feet from the base of the ride as it slowly begins to pull your friend to the top. The ride is 120 feet tall. Which equation gives your friend's distance d (in feet) from the top of the ride as a function of the angle of elevation?

A. $d = \frac{200}{\tan \theta}$ B. $d = 120 - 200 \tan \theta$

C. $d = 200 \tan \theta$ D. $d = 120 - \frac{200}{\tan \theta}$

2. **BICYCLING** You put a reflector on a spoke of your bicycle wheel. As you ride your bicycle, the reflector's height h (in inches) above the ground is modeled by

$$h = 13.5 + 11.5 \cos 2\pi t$$

where t is the time (in seconds). What is the frequency of the function?

A. 1 B. $\frac{\pi}{2}$

C. π D. 2π

3. **HOT AIR BALLOON** You stand 80 feet from the launch site of a hot air balloon traveling directly upward. What is the angle of elevation from you to the balloon when the balloon's height is 150 feet?

A. 28.1°

B. 32.2°

C. 57.8°

D. 61.9°

4. **RATE OF CHANGE** In calculus, it can be shown that the rate of change of the function $f(x) = -\csc x - \sin x$ is given by this expression:

$$\csc x \cot x - \cos x$$

Which expression is equivalent to $\csc x \cot x - \cos x$?

A. $\cos x$

B. $\cot^2 x$

C. $\cos x \cot^2 x$

D. $\cos x \csc^2 x$

5. **AMPLITUDE** What is the amplitude of the graph shown?

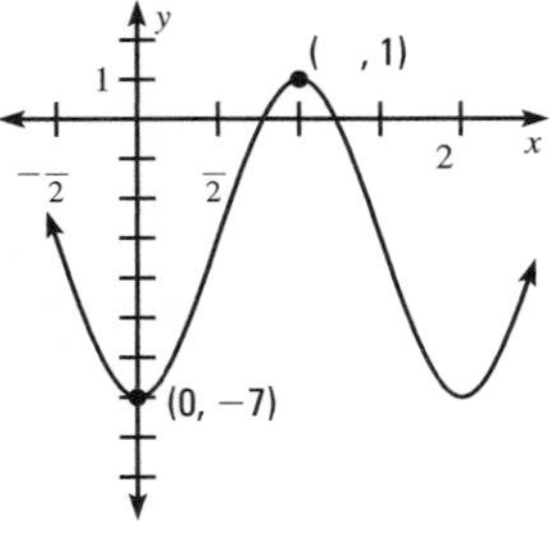

A. 1 B. 4

C. 6 D. 8

6. **OPEN-RESPONSE** The number n of millions of gallons of ice cream produced in the U.S. can be approximated by the function

$$n(t) = 113 + 24.5 \sin (0.0172(t - 105))$$

where t is the time in days with $t = 1$ representing January 1.

a. What is the period of this function, to the nearest number of days? *Explain* why this answer is reasonable.

b. According to the model, what is the maximum number of gallons of ice cream produced any one day of the year?

c. According to the model, what days of the year correspond to the highest and lowest production of ice cream?

14.5 Write Trigonometric Functions and Models

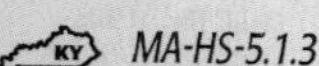
MA-HS-5.1.3

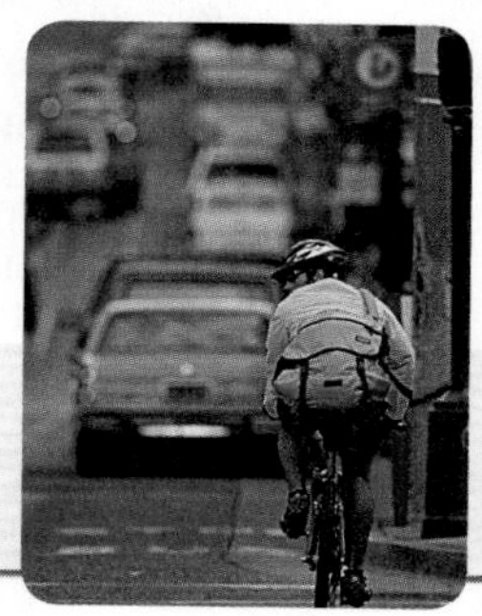

Before You graphed sine and cosine functions.

Now You will model data using sine and cosine functions.

Why? So you can model the number of bicyclists, as in Ex. 26.

Key Vocabulary
- **sinusoid**

Graphs of sine and cosine functions are called **sinusoids**. One method to write a sine or cosine function that models a sinusoid is to find the values of a, b, h, and k for

$$y = a \sin b(x - h) + k \qquad \text{or} \qquad y = a \cos b(x - h) + k$$

where $|a|$ is the amplitude, $\frac{2\pi}{b}$ is the period ($b > 0$), h is the horizontal shift, and k is the vertical shift.

MA-HS-5.1.3
Students will demonstrate how equations and graphs are models of the relationship between two real-world quantities (e.g., the relationship between degrees Celsius and degrees Fahrenheit).

EXAMPLE 1 Solve a multi-step problem

Write a function for the sinusoid shown below.

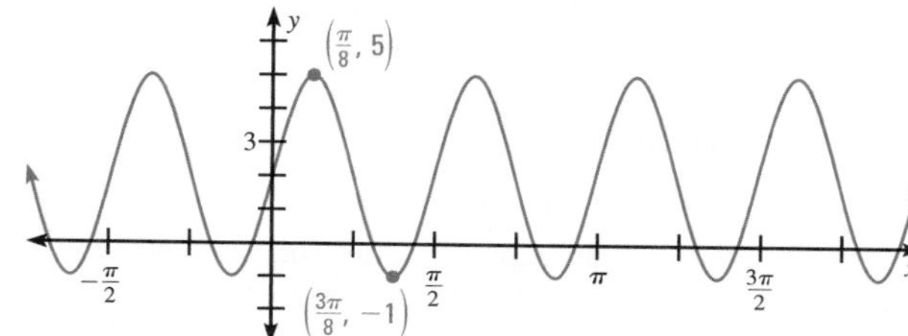

Solution

STEP 1 **Find** the maximum value M and minimum value m. From the graph, $M = 5$ and $m = -1$.

STEP 2 **Identify** the vertical shift, k. The value of k is the mean of the maximum and minimum values. The vertical shift is $k = \frac{M + m}{2} = \frac{5 + (-1)}{2} = \frac{4}{2} = 2$. So, $k = 2$.

STEP 3 **Decide** whether the graph should be modeled by a sine or cosine function. Because the graph crosses the midline $y = 2$ on the y-axis, the graph is a sine curve with no horizontal shift. So, $h = 0$.

FIND PERIOD
Because the graph repeats every $\frac{\pi}{2}$ units, the period is $\frac{\pi}{2}$.

STEP 4 **Find** the amplitude and period. The period is $\frac{\pi}{2} = \frac{2\pi}{b}$. So, $b = 4$.

The amplitude is $|a| = \frac{M - m}{2} = \frac{5 - (-1)}{2} = \frac{6}{2} = 3$. The graph is not a reflection, so $a > 0$. Therefore, $a = 3$.

▶ The function is $y = 3 \sin 4x + 2$.

1 PLAN AND PREPARE

Warm-Up Exercises
Transparency Available
The average monthly precipitation in inches at a lake in California can be approximated by the function $y = a \sin\left(\frac{\pi}{6}x + \frac{\pi}{3}\right) + 3$.

1. If the minimum precipitation is 0 and the maximum is 6, what is the value of a? 3
2. What is the period of the function? 12

Notetaking Guide
Transparency Available
Promotes interactive learning and notetaking skills, pp. 366–367.

Pacing
Basic: 1 day
Average: 1 day
Advanced: 1 day
Block: 0.5 block with 14.6
- See *Teaching Guide/Lesson Plan.*

2 FOCUS AND MOTIVATE

Essential Question
Big Idea 3, p. 907
Describe three ways to determine a trigonometric equation for modeling sinusoidal data. **Tell students they will learn how to answer this question by analyzing the data or the graph of the data.**

Resource Planning Guide

Chapter Resource Book
- Teaching Guide/Lesson Plan (pp. 50–51)
- Practice levels A, B, C (pp. 54–56)
- Study Guide (pp. 57–58)
- Catch-up for Absent Students (p. 59)
- Application (p. 60)
- Challenge (p. 61)

Workbooks
- Notetaking Guide (pp. 366–367)
- Practice Workbook (pp. 201–202)

Teaching Options
- **Power Presentations CD-ROM** provides dynamic electronic teaching resources for the classroom.
- **Activity Generator CD-ROM** provides editable activities for all ability levels.

Interactive Technology
- Easy Planner
- Power Presentations CD-ROM
- Activity Generator CD-ROM
- Animated Algebra
- Test Generator CD-ROM
- Online Quiz
- eWorkbook
- eEdition
- @HomeTutor

Resources for English Learners
- Quick Reference for English Learners
- Spanish Study Guide
- Multi-Language Visual Glossary
- Student Resources in Spanish

See also the *Algebra 2 Toolkit* for more strategies for meeting individual needs.

Motivating the Lesson

Ask students to describe situations that can be modeled by linear regressions and quadratic regressions. Then ask them how they think they could model the average number of daylight hours in your city per month over the course of a year. Explain that sinusoidal regression models can be used for situations with cyclical behavior, such as the average number of daylight hours per month in a year.

3 TEACH

Extra Example 1

Write a function for the sinusoid shown below. $y = 2\cos(3x - \pi)$

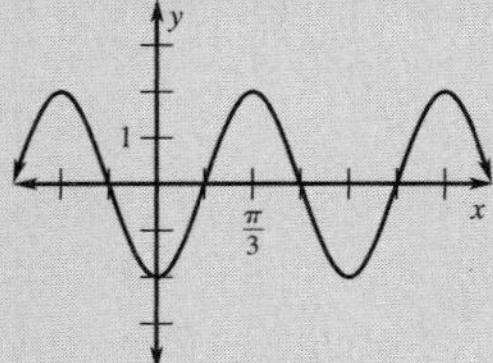

Extra Example 2

A physical therapist recommends an exercise for a patient recovering from shoulder surgery. The patient extends his arm and rotates it in a circular motion. At the highest point in the circle, the patient's arm is 65 inches above the floor. His arm is 40 inches above the floor at the circle's lowest point. His arm makes 4 revolutions per second. Write a model for the height (in inches) of the arm as a function of the time t (in seconds) if the arm is at its highest point when $t = 0$.

$y = 12.5\cos 8\pi t + 52.5$

EXAMPLE 2 Model circular motion

JUMP ROPE At a Double Dutch competition, two people swing jump ropes as shown in the diagram below. The highest point of the middle of each rope is 75 inches above the ground, and the lowest point is 3 inches. The rope makes 2 revolutions per second. Write a model for the height h (in feet) of a rope as a function of the time t (in seconds) if the rope is at its lowest point when $t = 0$.

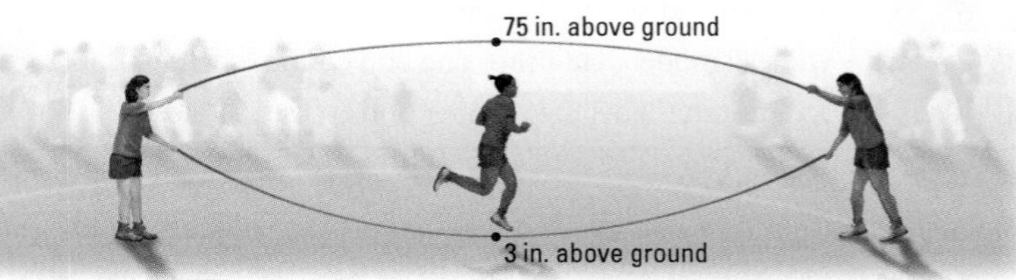

Solution

STEP 1 **Find** the maximum and minimum values of the function. A rope's maximum height is 75 inches, so $M = 75$. A rope's minimum height is 3 inches, so $m = 3$.

STEP 2 **Identify** the vertical shift. The vertical shift for the model is:

$$k = \frac{M + m}{2} = \frac{75 + 3}{2} = \frac{78}{2} = 39$$

STEP 3 **Decide** whether the height should be modeled by a sine or cosine function. When $t = 0$, the height is at its minimum. So, use a cosine function whose graph is a reflection in the x-axis with no horizontal shift ($h = 0$).

STEP 4 **Find** the amplitude and period.

The amplitude is $|a| = \frac{M - m}{2} = \frac{75 - 3}{2} = 36$.

Because the graph is a reflection, $a < 0$. So, $a = -36$. Because a rope is rotating at a rate of 2 revolutions per second, one revolution is completed in 0.5 second. So, the period is $\frac{2\pi}{b} = 0.5$, and $b = 4\pi$.

▶ A model for the height of a rope is $h = -36\cos 4\pi t + 39$.

✓ GUIDED PRACTICE for Examples 1 and 2

Write a function for the sinusoid.

1. (graph: y-axis 3; points $(0, 2)$, $\left(\frac{\pi}{3}, -2\right)$; x-axis mark $\frac{2\pi}{3}$)

Sample answer: $y = 2\cos 3x$

2. (graph: y-axis 1; points $\left(\frac{1}{2}, 1\right)$, $\left(\frac{3}{2}, -3\right)$; x-axis mark 2)

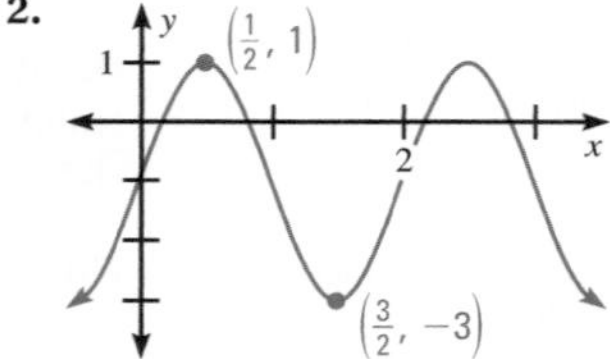

Sample answer: $y = 2\sin \pi x - 1$

3. **WHAT IF?** *Describe* how the model in Example 2 would change if the lowest point of a rope is 5 inches above the ground and the highest point is 70 inches above the ground. **The amplitude changes to 32.5 and the vertical shift becomes 37.5, but the period is not affected**

Differentiated Instruction

Visual Learners Have students draw a diagram of the situation described in **Example 2**. Students should label all parts of their diagram with an appropriate value and a vocabulary term. Then, have students work through the solution, translating their diagram into an equation to be solved.

See also the *Algebra 2 Toolkit* for more strategies.

SINUSOIDAL REGRESSION Another way to model sinusoids is to use a graphing calculator that has a sinusoidal regression feature. The advantage of this method is that it uses all of the data points to find the model.

EXAMPLE 3 Use sinusoidal regression

ENERGY The table below shows the number of kilowatt hours K (in thousands) used each month for a given year by a hangar at the Cape Canaveral Air Station in Florida. The time t is measured in months, with $t = 1$ representing January. Write a trigonometric model that gives K as a function of t.

t	1	2	3	4	5	6	7	8	9	10	11	12
K	61.9	59	62	70.1	81.4	93.1	102.3	106.8	105.4	92.9	81.2	69.9

Solution

STEP 1 **Enter** the data in a graphing calculator.

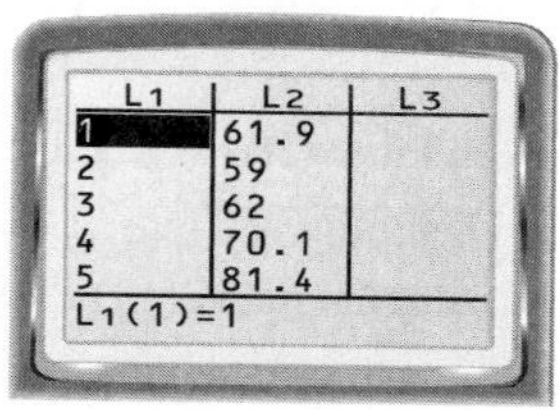

STEP 2 **Make** a scatter plot.

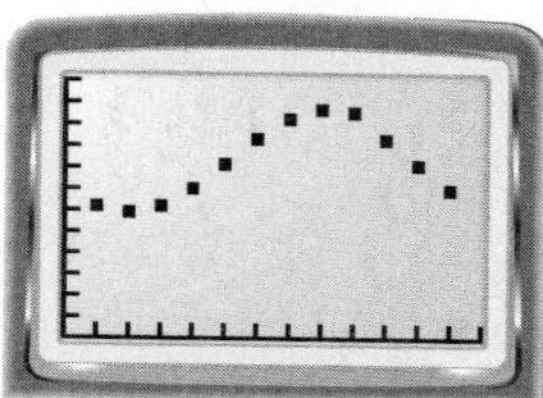

STEP 3 **Perform** a sinusoidal regression, because the scatter plot appears sinusoidal.

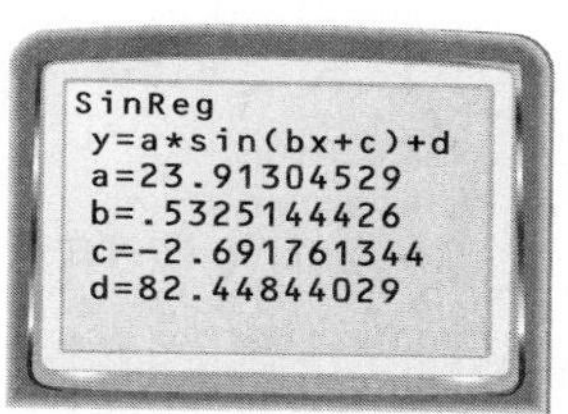

STEP 4 **Graph** the model and the data in the same viewing window.

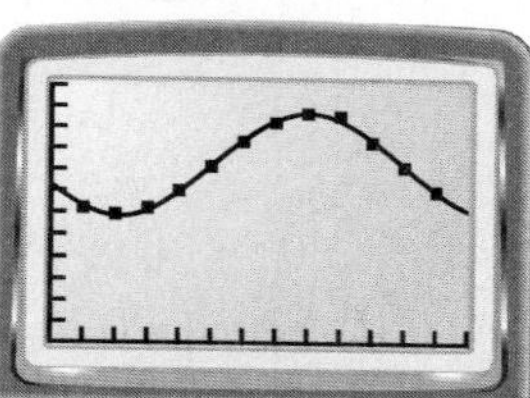

▶ The model appears to be a good fit. So, a model for the data is $K = 23.9 \sin(0.533t - 2.69) + 82.4$.

✓ GUIDED PRACTICE for Example 3

4. **METEOROLOGY** Use a graphing calculator to write a sine model that gives the average daily temperature T (in degrees Fahrenheit) for Boston, Massachusetts, as a function of the time t (in months), where $t = 1$ represents January. **$T = 21.8 \sin(0.514t - 2.18) + 51.3$**

t	1	2	3	4	5	6	7	8	9	10	11	12
T	29	32	39	48	59	68	74	72	65	54	45	35

Extra Example 3

The table below shows the number of sunlight hours h for each month during one year in Anchorage, Alaska. The time t is measured in months with $t = 1$ representing January. Write a trigonometric model that gives h as a function of t.

t	1	2	3	4
h	5.7	7.8	10.4	13.4

t	5	6	7	8
h	16.9	18.7	19.2	17.1

t	9	10	11	12
h	14.3	11.4	8.5	6.1

$h = 6.64 \sin(0.512t - 1.82) + 12.31$

Closing the Lesson

Have students summarize the major points of the lesson and answer the Essential Question: Describe three ways to determine a trigonometric equation for modeling sinusoidal data.

- To write a function for a sinusoid, find the values of a, b, h, and k for $y = a \sin b(x - h) + k$ or $y = a \cos b(x - h) + k$. Use the values to write a function.
- To model a situation with a circular function interpret the characteristics of the data to find the values of a, b, h, and k and to determine whether the graph should be modeled by a sine function or a cosine function.
- If you have all data points for a discrete data set, you can use a graphing calculator that has a sinusoidal regression feature to model the data.

You can find the values of a, b, h, and k for $y = a \sin b(x - h) + k$ or $y = a \cos b(x - h) + k$ from a graph of the function, from a description of the function's behavior, or you can use a calculator to find a sinusoidal regression model for the data.

14.5 EXERCISES

HOMEWORK KEY
○ = **WORKED-OUT SOLUTIONS** on p. WS24 for Exs. 5, 9, and 25
★ = **STANDARDIZED TEST PRACTICE** Exs. 2, 18, 19, 20, and 28

4 PRACTICE AND APPLY

Assignment Guide

Answer Transparencies available for all exercises

Basic:
Day 1: pp. 944–947
Exs. 1–14, 23–27, 31

Average:
Day 1: pp. 944–947
Exs. 1–8, 12–21, 23–28, 30

Advanced:
Day 1: pp. 944–947
Exs. 1, 5, 6, 13–29*

Block:
pp. 944–947
Exs. 1–8, 12–21, 23–28, 30
(with 14.6)

Differentiated Instruction

See *Algebra 2 Best Practices Toolkit* for suggestions on addressing the needs of a diverse classroom.

Homework Check

For a quick check of student understanding of key concepts, go over the following exercises:

Basic: 4, 10, 23, 25, 26
Average: 6, 12, 24, 25, 26
Advanced: 14, 16, 24, 25, 27

Extra Practice

- Student Edition, p. 1023
- Chapter 14 Resource Book: Practice levels A, B, C, pp. 54–56

Practice Worksheet

An easily-readable reduced practice page (with answers) for this lesson can be found on p. 906D.

SKILL PRACTICE

A

1. **VOCABULARY** What is a sinusoid? The graph of a sine or cosine function

2. ★ **WRITING** *Describe* two methods you can use to model a sinusoid. See margin.

EXAMPLE 1 on p. 941 for Exs. 3–19

WRITING FUNCTIONS **Write a function for the sinusoid.** 3–6. Sample answers are given.

3.

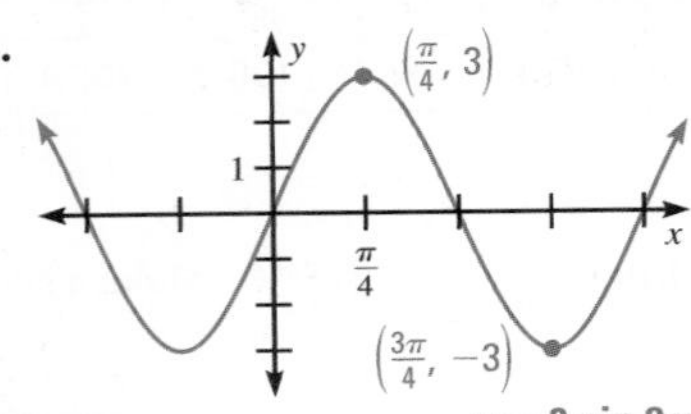

$y = 3 \sin 2x$

4.

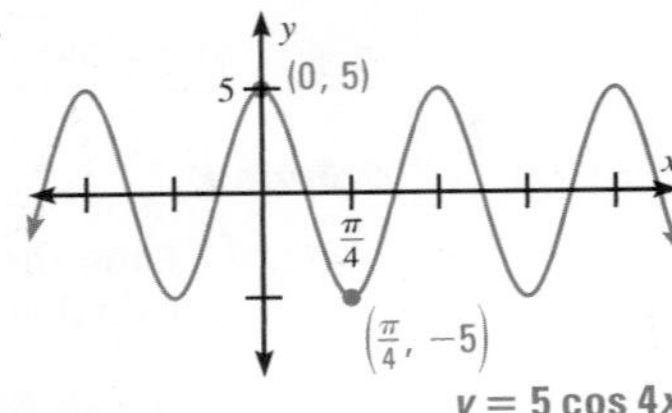

$y = 5 \cos 4x$

5.

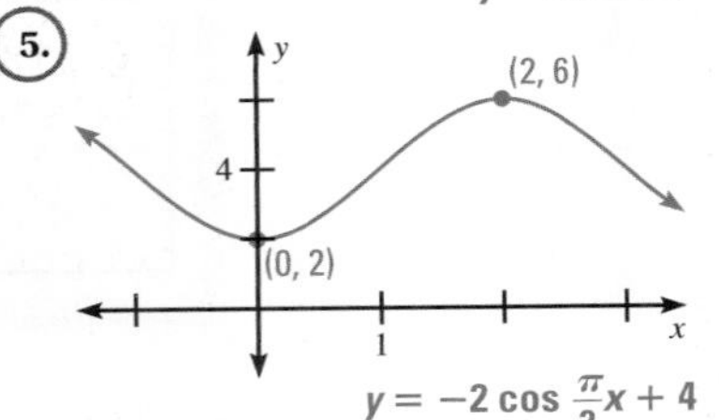

$y = -2 \cos \frac{\pi}{2}x + 4$

6.

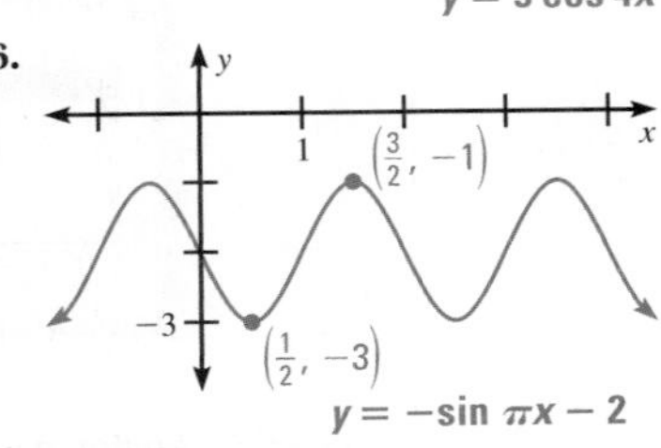

$y = -\sin \pi x - 2$

ERROR ANALYSIS ***Describe*** **and correct the error in finding the amplitude and vertical shift for a sinusoid with a maximum point at (2, 10) and a minimum point at (4, −6).**

7.

$|a| = \frac{M - m}{2}$

$= \frac{10 - 6}{2}$

$= 2$ ✗

8.

$k = \frac{M + m}{2}$

$= \frac{2 + 4}{2}$

$= 3$ ✗

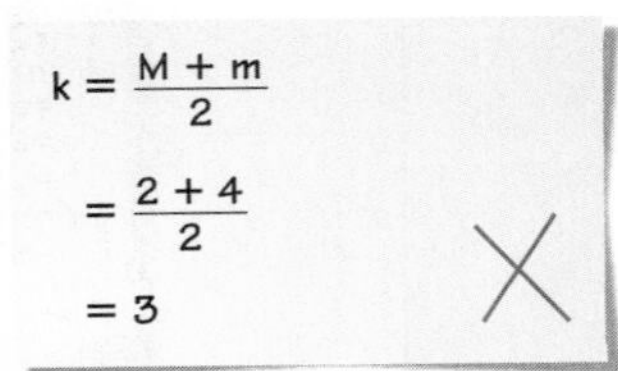

7. To determine the amplitude, you must take half of the difference between the maximum and the minimum; $\frac{10 - (-6)}{2} = 8$.

8. To determine the vertical shift, you use the y-coordinates of the points; $\frac{10 + (-6)}{2} = 2$.

B

WRITING FUNCTIONS **Write a function for the sinusoid with maximum at point A and minimum at point B.** 9–17. Sample answers are given.

9. $A(\pi, 6), B(3\pi, -6)$ $y = 6 \sin \frac{1}{2}x$

10. $A(0, 4), B(\pi, -4)$ $y = 4 \cos x$

11. $A\left(\frac{\pi}{3}, 5\right), B(0, 3)$ $y = -\cos 3x + 4$

12. $A\left(\frac{\pi}{6}, 8\right), B(0, -6)$ $y = -7 \cos 6x + 1$

13. $A\left(\frac{3\pi}{4}, 9\right), B(2\pi, 5)$ $y = 2 \cos \frac{4}{5}\left(x - \frac{3\pi}{4}\right) + 7$

14. $A(0, 5), B(6, -11)$ $y = 8 \sin \frac{\pi}{6}(x + 3) - 3$

15. $A(0, 0), B(4\pi, -4)$ $y = 2 \sin \frac{1}{4}(x + 2\pi) - 2$

16. $A\left(\frac{\pi}{3}, -3\right), B\left(\frac{\pi}{12}, -7\right)$ $y = -2 \cos 4\left(x - \frac{\pi}{12}\right) - 5$

17. $A\left(\frac{2\pi}{3}, 0\right), B(0, -12)$ $y = -6 \cos \frac{3}{2}x - 6$

18. ★ **MULTIPLE CHOICE** During one cycle, a sinusoid has a minimum at (16, 38) and a maximum at (24, 60). What is the amplitude of this sinusoid? B

Ⓐ 8 Ⓑ 11 Ⓒ 22 Ⓓ 49

2. *Sample answer:* Method 1: graphing calculator — enter the data points into the calculator and have the calculator create a sinusoid regression of the data. Method 2: construct the model yourself by finding the vertical shift, the horizontal shift, and the period. Then substitute all of these values into the general form for the appropriate sinusoid curve.

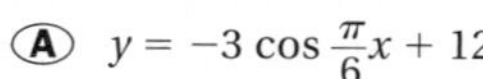

19. ★ **MULTIPLE CHOICE** What is an equation of the graph shown at the right? B

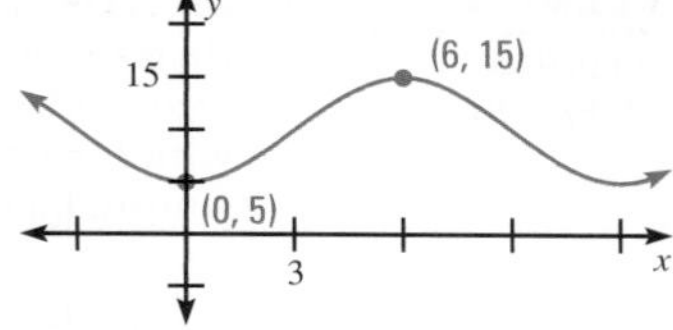

Ⓐ $y = -3\cos\frac{\pi}{6}x + 12$ Ⓑ $y = -5\cos\frac{\pi}{6}x + 10$

Ⓒ $y = 3\sin\frac{\pi}{6}x + 12$ Ⓓ $y = -5\sin\frac{\pi}{6}x + 10$

20. A cosine function, because it does not require determining a horizontal shift.

20. ★ **WRITING** Any sinusoid can be modeled by both a sine function and a cosine function. Therefore, you can choose the type of function that is more convenient. *Explain* which type of function you would choose to model a sinusoid whose y-intercept occurs at the minimum value of the function.

C

21. **REASONING** Model the sinusoid in Example 1 on page 941 with a cosine function of the form $y = a\cos b(x - h) + k$. Use identities to show that the model you found is equivalent to the sine model in Example 1. **See margin.**

22. **CHALLENGE** Write a sine function for the sinusoid with a minimum at $\left(\frac{\pi}{2}, 3\right)$ and a maximum at $\left(\frac{\pi}{4}, 8\right)$. ***Sample answer:*** $y = 2.5\sin 4\left(x - \frac{\pi}{8}\right) + 5.5$

PROBLEM SOLVING

EXAMPLE 1 A
on p. 941
for Exs. 23–24

23. **CIRCUITS** A circuit has an alternating voltage of 100 volts that peaks every 0.5 second. Use the graph shown at the right to write a sinusoidal model for the voltage V as a function of the time t (in seconds). $V = 100\sin 4\pi t$

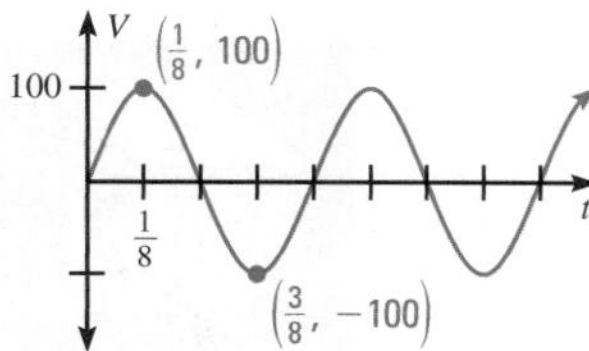

@HomeTutor for problem solving help at classzone.com

24. **CLIMATOLOGY** The graph below shows the average daily temperature of Houston, Texas. Write a sinusoidal model for the average daily temperature T (in degrees Fahrenheit) as a function of time t (in months). $y = -16\cos\frac{\pi}{6}x + 68$

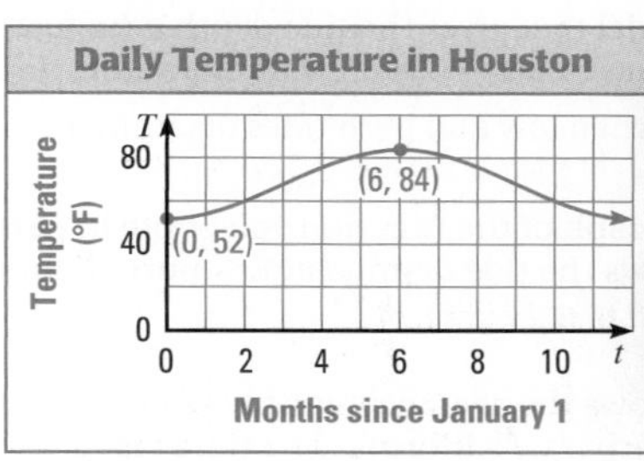

@HomeTutor for problem solving help at classzone.com

EXAMPLE 2
on p. 942
for Ex. 25

25. **CIRCULAR MOTION** One of the largest sewing machines in the world has a *flywheel* (which turns as the machine sews) that is 5 feet in diameter. Write a model for the height h (in feet) of the handle at the edge of the flywheel as a function of the time t (in seconds). Assume that the wheel makes a complete turn every 2 seconds and the handle is at its minimum height of 4 feet above the ground when $t = 0$. $h = -2.5\cos\pi t + 6.5$

Vocabulary

Exercise 1 Students may be confused about why the graphs of cosine functions are also called sinusoids. Discuss the relationship between the graphs of $y = \sin x$ and $y = \cos x$. Explain that a sinusoid is any curve similar to the sine curve, meaning that it can be a sine curve that is stretched, reflected, and/or translated.

Teaching Strategy

Exercises 9–17 Pair students so that a more advanced student can work with a student who is having difficulty with the lesson. Ask them to write both a sine and a cosine function for each equation. This will make Exercises 21 and 29 accessible to more students and will provide a review of sine and cosine cofunction identities.

Study Strategy

Exercise 25 Encourage students to draw a sketch of the flywheel first. Then they should label the maximum and minimum points.

21. $y = 3\cos 4\left(x - \frac{\pi}{8}\right) + 2$; $y = 3\cos\left(4x - \frac{\pi}{2}\right) + 2$. **Using the cofunction identity, this simplifies to** $y = 3\sin 4x + 2$.

Avoiding Common Errors

Exercise 29 Students may incorrectly enter the cosine function in their calculators and produce a different graph from that of the sine regression model. Remind them that since $\cos \theta = \sin\left(\frac{\pi}{2} - \theta\right)$, they must use parentheses to subtract the value of $b(x - h)$ from $\frac{\pi}{2}$.

EXAMPLE 3 on p. 943 for Exs. 26–27

B

26. **BICYCLISTS** The table below shows the number of adult residents R (in millions) in the United States who rode a bicycle during the months of October 2001 through September 2002. The time t is measured in months, with $t = 1$ representing October 2001. Use a graphing calculator to write a sinusoidal model that gives R as a function of t. **$R = 8.94 \sin(0.520t + 2.54) + 33.3$**

t	1	2	3	4	5	6	7	8	9	10	11	12
R	35	30	24	24	26	29	35	34	39	43	44	37

27. **MULTI-STEP PROBLEM** The table below shows the number of employees N (in thousands) at a sporting goods company each year for eleven years. The time t is measured in years, with $t = 1$ representing the first year.

t	1	2	3	4	5	6	7	8	9	10	11
N	20.8	22.7	24.6	23.2	20	17.5	16.7	17.8	21	22	24.1

a. **Model** Use a graphing calculator to write a sinusoidal model that gives N as a function of t. **$N = 3.68 \sin(0.776t - 0.703) + 20.4$**

b. **Calculate** Predict the number of employees in the twelfth year. **about 23,100 employees**

28. ★ **EXTENDED RESPONSE** The low tide at Eastport, Maine, is 3.5 feet and occurs at midnight. After 6 hours, Eastport is at high tide, which is 16.5 feet.

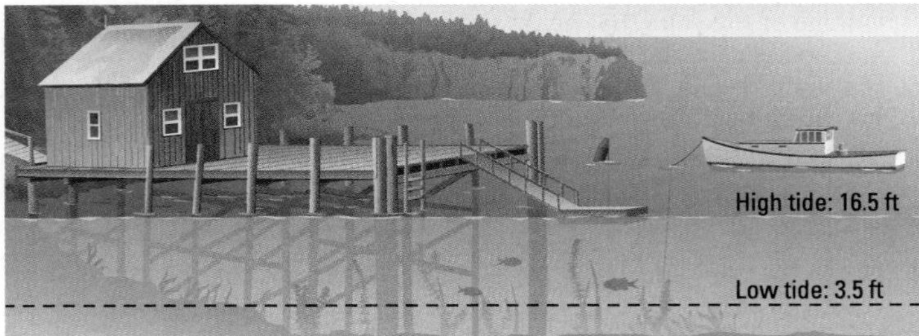

a. **Model** Write a sinusoidal model that gives the tide depth d (in feet) as a function of the time t (in hours). Let $t = 0$ represent midnight. **$d = -6.5 \cos \frac{\pi}{6}t + 10$**

b. **Calculate** Find all the times when low and high tides occur in a 24 hour period. **low tide: 12:00 A.M., 12:00 P.M., high tide: 6:00 A.M., 6:00 P.M.**

c. **Reasoning** *Explain* how the graph of the function you wrote in part (a) is related to a graph that shows the tide depth d at Eastport t hours after 3:00 A.M. **It is a horizontal shift to the right by $\frac{1}{4}$.**

C

29. **CHALLENGE** The table below shows the average monthly sea temperatures T (in degrees Celsius) for Santa Barbara, California. The time t is measured in months, with $t = 1$ representing January.

t	1	2	3	4	5	6	7	8	9	10	11	12
T	14	13.6	13.4	12.5	13.9	15.6	16.8	17.2	17.7	17.1	15.5	14.1

a. Use a graphing calculator to write a sine model that gives T as a function of t. **$T = 2.43 \sin(0.578t + 2.89) + 15.2$**

b. Find a cosine model for the data. **$T = 2.43 \cos(0.578(t + 2.28)) + 15.2$**

30. The top, front, and side views of a solid built with cubes are shown below. How many cubes are needed to construct this solid? **B**

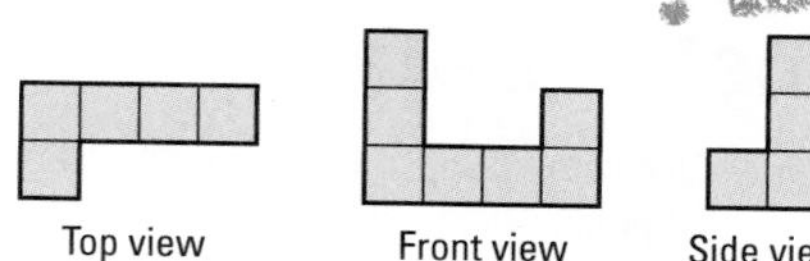

Top view Front view Side view

Ⓐ 7 Ⓑ 8 Ⓒ 9 Ⓓ 10

31. What is the area of the blue figure shown at the right? **C**

Ⓐ 48.5 cm^2 Ⓑ 113.0 cm^2

Ⓒ 141.5 cm^2 Ⓓ 283.0 cm^2

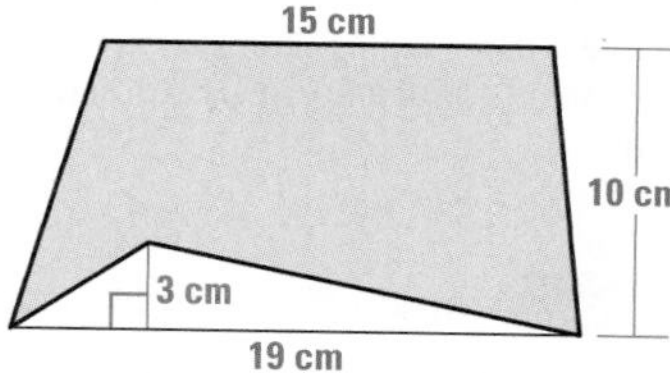

QUIZ for Lessons 14.3–14.5

Simplify the expression. *(p. 924)*

1. $\sin x \sec x$ $\tan x$
2. $\sin\theta(1+\cot^2\theta)$ $\csc\theta$
3. $\tan\left(\frac{\pi}{2}-\theta\right)\cot\theta - \csc^2\theta$ -1
4. $\cos^2\theta+\sin^2\theta+\tan^2\theta$ $\sec^2\theta$
5. $\dfrac{\tan\left(\frac{\pi}{2}-x\right)\sec x}{1-\csc^2 x}$ $-\tan x \sec x$
6. $\dfrac{\sin(-x)}{\csc x}+\dfrac{\cos(-x)}{\sec x}$ $2\cos^2 x - 1$

Find the general solution of the equation. *(p. 931)*

7. $\cos x + \cos(-x) = 1$ $\frac{\pi}{3}+2n\pi$ or $\frac{5\pi}{3}+2n\pi$
8. $\sqrt{2}\cos x\sin x - \cos x = 0$ $\frac{\pi}{2}+n\pi$ or $\frac{\pi}{4}+2n\pi$ or $\frac{3\pi}{4}+2n\pi$
9. $2\sin^2 x - \sin x = 1$ $\frac{\pi}{2}+2n\pi$ or $\frac{7\pi}{6}+2n\pi$ or $\frac{11\pi}{6}+2n\pi$

Write a function for the sinusoid. *(p. 941)*

10. 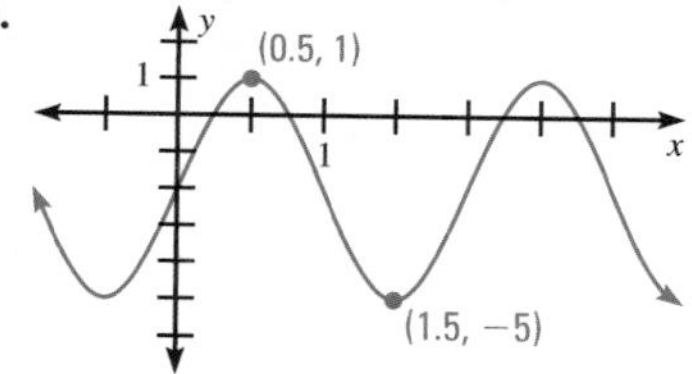

Sample answer: $y = 3\sin\pi x - 2$

11. 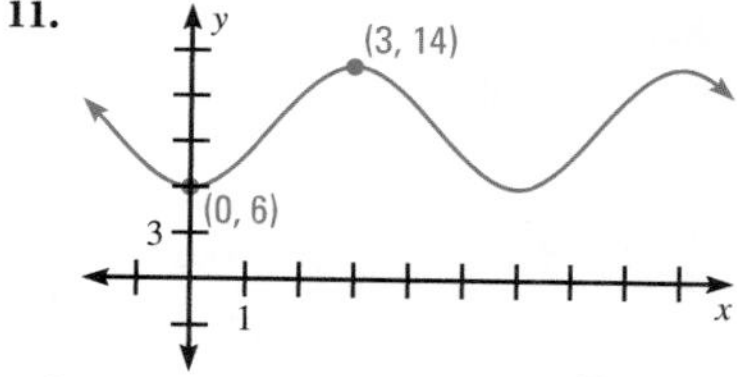

Sample answer: $y = -4\cos\frac{\pi}{3}x + 10$

12. **DAILY TEMPERATURES** The table below shows the average daily temperature D (in degrees Fahrenheit) in Detroit, Michigan. The time t is measured in months, with $t = 1$ representing January. Use a graphing calculator to write a sinusoidal model that gives D as a function of t. *(p. 941)*

t	1	2	3	4	5	6	7	8	9	10	11	12
D	24.5	27.2	36.9	48.1	59.8	69	73.5	71.8	63.9	51.9	40.7	29.6

$D = 24.6\sin(0.506t - 2.06) + 48.9$

5 ASSESS AND RETEACH

Daily Homework Quiz

Transparency Available

1. The highest point in the rotation of a robotic arm is 30 inches above the ground and the lowest point is 12 inches above the ground. The arm makes $\frac{1}{2}$ revolution per second. Write a model for the height h (in inches) of the arm as a function of time t (in seconds) if the arm is at its lowest point when $t = 0$. $h = -9\cos\pi t + 21$
2. The table below shows the maximum monthly temperature t (°F) for Death Valley, California. Write a trigonometric model that gives t as a function of m.

m	1	2	3	4	5	6	7	8	9	10	11	12
t	66.3	73.7	81.5	89.9	99.2	109.0	115.1	113.2	105.5	92.5	73.7	65.7

$t = 24.2\sin(0.52m - 2.1) + 90.5$

Online Quiz

Available at **classzone.com**

Diagnosis/Remediation

- Practice A, B, C in Chapter 14 Resource Book, pp. 54–56
- Study Guide in Chapter 14 Resource Book, pp. 57–58
- Practice Workbook, pp. 201–202
- @HomeTutor

Challenge

Additional challenge is available in the Chapter 14 Resource Book, p. 61.

Quiz

An easily-readable reduced copy of the quiz (with answers) on Lessons 14.3–14.5 from the Assessment Book can be found on p. 906E.

1 PLAN AND PREPARE

Explore the Concept

Students will use a Calculator Based Laboratory to model the sound waves produced by a musical instrument with sine functions. This activity leads into the study of the sum formula for sin $(a + b)$ in Lesson 14.6.

Materials

Each group of students will need:

- a musical instrument
- Calculator Based Laboratory
- graphing calculator

Recommended Time

Work activity: 10 min
Discuss results: 5 min

Grouping

Students should work in pairs. The students can take turns playing the instrument and graphing the sine function.

2 TEACH

Tips for Success

Make sure students know how to use a CBL.

Key Discovery

The sound of a pure note can be represented using a sine wave.

3 ASSESS AND RETEACH

Why do you think that a note is modeled by different sine functions when played on different instruments? *Sample answer:* **Different instruments are designed to create different pressure when sound is transmitted through breathing or touch.**

CBL ACTIVITY *Use after Lesson 14.5*

@HomeTutor
classzone.com
Keystrokes

14.5 Collect and Model Trigonometric Data

MATERIALS • musical instrument • CBL microphone • Calculator Based Laboratory (CBL) • graphing calculator

QUESTION How is music related to trigonometry?

Sound is a variation in pressure transmitted through air, water, or other matter. Sound travels as a wave. The sound of a pure note can be represented using a sine (or cosine) wave. More complicated sounds can be modeled by the sum of several sine waves.

EXPLORE Analyze the sound of a musical instrument

Play a note on a musical instrument. Write a sine function to describe the note.
Steps 1–4. Check students' work.

STEP 1 *Play note*

Play a pure note on a musical instrument. Use the CBL and the CBL microphone to collect the sound data and store it in a graphing calculator.

STEP 2 *Graph function*

Use the graphing calculator to graph the pressure of the sound as a function of time.

STEP 3 *Find characteristics of graph*

Use the graph of the sound data to calculate the note's amplitude and frequency (the number of cycles in one second).

STEP 4 *Write function*

Write a sine function for the note.

DRAW CONCLUSIONS Use your observations to complete these exercises

1. Choose a note to play and have a classmate also choose a note. Find two sine functions $y = f(x)$ and $y = g(x)$ that model the two notes. Then play the notes simultaneously and use the CBL and a graphing calculator to graph the resulting sound wave. *Compare* this graph with the graph of $y = f(x) + g(x)$. What do you notice? **Check students' work; the graph is the same as the graph of $y = f(x) + g(x)$**
2. The pitch of a sound wave is determined by the wave's frequency. The greater the frequency, the higher the pitch. Which of the notes in Exercise 1 had a higher pitch? **Check students' work.**
3. When you change the volume of a note, what happens to the graph of the sound wave? **Increasing the volume does not change the graph of the note.**
4. *Compare* the sine waves for different instruments playing the same note. **Check students' work.**

14.6 Apply Sum and Difference Formulas

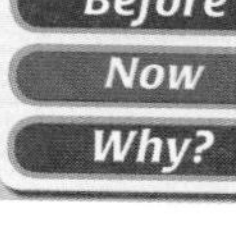

Before You found trigonometric functions of a given angle.

Now You will use trigonometric sum and difference formulas.

Why? So you can simplify a ratio used for aerial photography, as in Ex. 43.

Key Vocabulary
- **trigonometric identity,** *p. 924*

In this lesson, you will study formulas that allow you to evaluate trigonometric functions of the sum or difference of two angles.

KEY CONCEPT *For Your Notebook*

Sum and Difference Formulas

Sum Formulas	Difference Formulas
$\sin(a+b) = \sin a \cos b + \cos a \sin b$	$\sin(a-b) = \sin a \cos b - \cos a \sin b$
$\cos(a+b) = \cos a \cos b - \sin a \sin b$	$\cos(a-b) = \cos a \cos b + \sin a \sin b$
$\tan(a+b) = \dfrac{\tan a + \tan b}{1 - \tan a \tan b}$	$\tan(a-b) = \dfrac{\tan a - \tan b}{1 + \tan a \tan b}$

In general, $\sin(a+b) \neq \sin a + \sin b$. Similar statements can be made for the other trigonometric functions of sums and differences.

EXAMPLE 1 **Evaluate a trigonometric expression**

Find the exact value of (a) sin 15° and (b) $\tan \frac{7\pi}{12}$.

a. $\sin 15° = \sin(60° - 45°)$ — **Substitute 60° − 45° for 15°.**

$= \sin 60° \cos 45° - \cos 60° \sin 45°$ — **Difference formula for sine**

$= \frac{\sqrt{3}}{2}\left(\frac{\sqrt{2}}{2}\right) - \frac{1}{2}\left(\frac{\sqrt{2}}{2}\right)$ — **Evaluate.**

$= \frac{\sqrt{6} - \sqrt{2}}{4}$ — **Simplify.**

b. $\tan \frac{7\pi}{12} = \tan\left(\frac{\pi}{3} + \frac{\pi}{4}\right)$ — **Substitute $\frac{\pi}{3} + \frac{\pi}{4}$ for $\frac{7\pi}{12}$.**

$= \dfrac{\tan \frac{\pi}{3} + \tan \frac{\pi}{4}}{1 - \tan \frac{\pi}{3} \tan \frac{\pi}{4}}$ — **Sum formula for tangent**

$= \dfrac{\sqrt{3} + 1}{1 - \sqrt{3} \cdot 1}$ — **Evaluate.**

$= -2 - \sqrt{3}$ — **Simplify.**

REVIEW CONJUGATES
For help with using conjugates to rationalize denominators, see p. 266.

1 PLAN AND PREPARE

Warm-Up Exercises

Transparency Available

Find the exact value.

1. sin 30° $\frac{1}{2}$ **2.** $\cos \frac{\pi}{4}$ $\frac{\sqrt{2}}{2}$

3. tan 60° $\sqrt{3}$ **4.** tan 45° 1

5. A ladder leaning against a building makes a 75° angle with the ground The bottom of the ladder is 3 feet from the base of a building. How high up the building is the top of the ladder? **about 11 ft**

Notetaking Guide

Transparency Available

Promotes interactive learning and notetaking skills, pp. 368–371.

Pacing

Basic: 1 day
Average: 1 day
Advanced: 1 day
Block: 0.5 block with 14.5
- See *Teaching Guide/Lesson Plan.*

2 FOCUS AND MOTIVATE

Essential Question

Big Idea 3, p. 907

How do the sum and difference formulas for tangent differ from the sum and difference formulas for sine and cosine? **Tell students they will learn how to answer this question by applying sum and difference formulas.**

Resource Planning Guide

Chapter Resource Book
- Teaching Guide/Lesson Plan (pp. 62–63)
- Practice levels A, B, C (pp. 64–66)
- Study Guide (pp. 67–68)
- Catch-up for Absent Students (p. 69)
- Problem Solving Workshop (p. 70)
- Challenge (p. 71)

Workbooks
- Notetaking Guide (pp. 368–371)
- Practice Workbook (pp. 203–204)

Teaching Options
- **Power Presentations CD-ROM** provides dynamic electronic teaching resources for the classroom.
- **Activity Generator CD-ROM** provides editable activities for all ability levels.

Interactive Technology
- Easy Planner
- Power Presentations CD-ROM
- Activity Generator CD-ROM
- Animated Algebra
- Test Generator CD-ROM
- Online Quiz
- eWorkbook
- eEdition
- @HomeTutor

Resources for English Learners
- Quick Reference for English Learners
- Spanish Study Guide
- Multi-Language Visual Glossary
- Student Resources in Spanish

See also the *Algebra 2 Toolkit* for more strategies for meeting individual needs.

Motivating the Lesson

Students will not have an intuitive basis for identifying the sum and difference formulas for trigonometric functions. Ask them to make a conjecture about $\sin(a + b)$. They are likely to state incorrectly that $\sin(a + b) = \sin a + \sin b$. Ask them to give several examples to show that $\sin(a + b) \neq \sin a + \sin b$.

3 TEACH

Extra Example 1

Find the exact value of (a) $\sin \frac{7\pi}{12}$ and (b) $\cos 15°$. $\sin \frac{7\pi}{12} = \frac{\sqrt{6} + \sqrt{2}}{4}$; $\cos 15° = \frac{\sqrt{6} + \sqrt{2}}{4}$

Extra Example 2

Find $\tan (a - b)$ given that $\tan a = -\frac{7}{24}$ with $\frac{\pi}{2} < a < \pi$ and $\tan b = \frac{4}{5}$ for $\pi < b < \frac{3\pi}{2}$. $-\frac{131}{92}$

Extra Example 3

Simplify the expression $\sin\left(x - \frac{5\pi}{2}\right)$. $-\cos x$

Extra Example 4

Solve $\cos (x + \pi) + \cos (x - \pi) = 0$ for $0 \leq x \leq 2\pi$. $\frac{\pi}{2}, \frac{3\pi}{2}$

Key Question to Ask for Example 4

- Why is $\sin\left(x + \frac{\pi}{3}\right) + \sin\left(x - \frac{\pi}{3}\right) = 1$ not an identity? The equation is true only for $x = \frac{\pi}{2} + 2n\pi$.

EXAMPLE 2 Use a difference formula

Find $\cos (a - b)$ given that $\cos a = -\frac{4}{5}$ with $\pi < a < \frac{3\pi}{2}$ and $\sin b = \frac{5}{13}$ with $0 < b < \frac{\pi}{2}$.

Solution

Using a Pythagorean identity and quadrant signs gives $\sin a = -\frac{3}{5}$ and $\cos b = \frac{12}{13}$.

$\cos (a - b) = \cos a \cos b + \sin a \sin b$ **Difference formula for cosine**

$= -\frac{4}{5}\left(\frac{12}{13}\right) + \left(-\frac{3}{5}\right)\left(\frac{5}{13}\right)$ **Substitute.**

$= -\frac{63}{65}$ **Simplify.**

✓ **GUIDED PRACTICE** for Examples 1 and 2

Find the exact value of the expression.

1. $\sin 105°$ $\frac{\sqrt{2} + \sqrt{6}}{4}$
2. $\cos 75°$ $\frac{\sqrt{6} - \sqrt{2}}{4}$
3. $\tan \frac{5\pi}{12}$ $2 + \sqrt{3}$
4. $\cos \frac{\pi}{12}$ $\frac{\sqrt{6} + \sqrt{2}}{4}$
5. Find $\sin (a - b)$ given that $\sin a = \frac{8}{17}$ with $0 < a < \frac{\pi}{2}$ and $\cos b = -\frac{24}{25}$ with $\pi < b < \frac{3\pi}{2}$. $-\frac{87}{425}$

EXAMPLE 3 Simplify an expression

Simplify the expression $\cos (x + \pi)$.

$\cos (x + \pi) = \cos x \cos \pi - \sin x \sin \pi$ **Sum formula for cosine**

$= (\cos x)(-1) - (\sin x)(0)$ **Evaluate.**

$= -\cos x$ **Simplify.**

EXAMPLE 4 Solve a trigonometric equation

Solve $\sin\left(x + \frac{\pi}{3}\right) + \sin\left(x - \frac{\pi}{3}\right) = 1$ for $0 \leq x < 2\pi$.

ANOTHER WAY

You can also solve by using a graphing calculator. First graph each side of the original equation and then use the *intersect* feature to find the x-value(s) where the expressions are equal.

$\sin\left(x + \frac{\pi}{3}\right) + \sin\left(x - \frac{\pi}{3}\right) = 1$ **Write equation.**

$\sin x \cos \frac{\pi}{3} + \cos x \sin \frac{\pi}{3} + \sin x \cos \frac{\pi}{3} - \cos x \sin \frac{\pi}{3} = 1$ **Use formulas.**

$\frac{1}{2} \sin x + \frac{\sqrt{3}}{2} \cos x + \frac{1}{2} \sin x - \frac{\sqrt{3}}{2} \cos x = 1$ **Evaluate.**

$\sin x = 1$ **Simplify.**

▶ In the interval $0 \leq x < 2\pi$, the only solution is $x = \frac{\pi}{2}$.

Differentiated Instruction

Advanced The tangent identity tells us that $\tan (a + b) = \frac{\sin (a + b)}{\cos (a + b)}$. Applying the formulas for sums of sines and cosines to the numerator and denominator of this fraction, dividing both numerator and denominator by $\cos a \cos b$, then simplifying and applying the tangent identity will allow the students to derive the identify for $\tan (a + b)$.

See also the *Algebra 2 Toolkit* for more strategies.

EXAMPLE 5 Solve a multi-step problem

DAYLIGHT HOURS The number h of hours of daylight for Dallas, Texas, and Anchorage, Alaska, can be approximated by the equations below, where t is the time in days and $t = 0$ represents January 1. On which days of the year will the two cities have the same amount of daylight?

Dallas: $h_1 = 2\sin\left(\frac{\pi t}{182} - 1.35\right) + 12.1$ **Anchorage:** $h_2 = -6\cos\left(\frac{\pi t}{182}\right) + 12.1$

Solution

STEP 1 **Solve** the equation $h_1 = h_2$ for t.

$$2\sin\left(\frac{\pi t}{182} - 1.35\right) + 12.1 = -6\cos\left(\frac{\pi t}{182}\right) + 12.1$$

$$\sin\left(\frac{\pi t}{182} - 1.35\right) = -3\cos\left(\frac{\pi t}{182}\right)$$

$$\sin\left(\frac{\pi t}{182}\right)\cos 1.35 - \cos\left(\frac{\pi t}{182}\right)\sin 1.35 = -3\cos\left(\frac{\pi t}{182}\right)$$

$$\sin\left(\frac{\pi t}{182}\right)(0.219) - \cos\left(\frac{\pi t}{182}\right)(0.976) = -3\cos\left(\frac{\pi t}{182}\right)$$

$$0.219\sin\left(\frac{\pi t}{182}\right) = -2.024\cos\left(\frac{\pi t}{182}\right)$$

$$\tan\left(\frac{\pi t}{182}\right) = -9.242$$

$$\frac{\pi t}{182} = \tan^{-1}(-9.242) + n\pi$$

$$\frac{\pi t}{182} \approx -1.463 + n\pi$$

$$t \approx -84.76 + 182n$$

STEP 2 **Find** the days within one year (365 days) for which Dallas and Anchorage will have the same amount of daylight.

$t \approx -84.76 + 182(1) \approx 97$, or on April 8

$t \approx -84.76 + 182(2) \approx 279$, or on October 7

GUIDED PRACTICE for Examples 3, 4, and 5

Simplify the expression.

6. $\sin(x + 2\pi)$ $\sin x$
7. $\cos(x - 2\pi)$ $\cos x$
8. $\tan(x - \pi)$ $\tan x$
9. Solve $6\cos\left(\frac{\pi t}{75}\right) + 5 = -24\sin\left(\frac{\pi t}{75} + 22\right) + 5$ for $0 \le t < 2\pi$. about 5.65

Extra Example 5

The equations $d = \sin\left(\frac{\pi}{2} - \frac{\pi t}{6}\right) + 9$ and $d = 3\cos\frac{\pi t}{6} + 9$ model the water depth d (in feet) of two different boat docks t hours after midnight. At what time in the next 24 hours will the water depth at both docks be the same? **3 A.M., 9 A.M., 3 P.M., and 9 P.M.**

Key Question to Ask for Example 5

- Why is it necessary to add $n\pi$ to $\tan^{-1}(-9.242)$? **The solution of $\tan\frac{\pi t}{182} = -9.242$ will give the reference angle for which $\frac{\pi t}{182} = \tan^{-1}(-9.242)$. Since the graph of $y = \tan x$ has a period of π, $\frac{\pi t}{182} = \tan^{-1}(-9.242) + n\pi$.**

Closing the Lesson

Have students summarize the major points of the lesson and answer the Essential Question: How do the sum and difference formulas for tangent differ from the sum and difference formulas for sine and cosine?

- **The sum formulas are $\sin(a + b) = \sin a\cos b + \cos a\sin b$, $\cos(a + b) = \cos a\cos b - \sin a\sin b$, and $\tan(a + b) = \frac{\tan a + \tan b}{1 - \tan a\tan b}$.**
- **The difference formulas are $\sin(a + b) = \sin a\cos b - \cos a\sin b$, $\cos(a - b) = \cos a\cos b + \sin a\sin b$, and $\tan(a - b) = \frac{\tan a - \tan b}{1 + \tan a\tan b}$**

The sum and difference formulas for the tangent function involve fractions and only the tangent function; the same formulas for the sine and cosine functions do not involve fractions and the formulas for both functions involve both the sine and cosine functions.

Differentiated Instruction

English Learners When some students need to use the sum and difference formulas, they may become confused and attempt to add or subtract the two given equations. Remind students that they will apply the sum and difference *formulas* to solve the given equations.

See also the *Algebra 2 Toolkit* for more strategies.

14.6 EXERCISES

HOMEWORK KEY

○ = **WORKED-OUT SOLUTIONS** on p. WS25 for Exs. 9, 23, and 43

★ = **STANDARDIZED TEST PRACTICE** Exs. 2, 11, 18, 32, and 44

4 PRACTICE AND APPLY

Assignment Guide

Answer Transparencies available for all exercises

Basic:
Day 1: pp. 952–954
Exs. 1–14, 18–24, 31–34, 40–42, 46

Average:
Day 1: pp. 952–954
Exs. 1, 2, 6–8, 11, 14–18, 24–27, 31–38, 40–44, 47

Advanced:
Day 1: pp. 952–954
Exs. 1, 2, 9–11, 16–18, 27–30, 32–45*, 47

Block:
pp. 952–954
Exs. 1, 2, 6–8, 11, 14–18, 24–27, 31–38, 40–44, 47 (with 14.5)

Differentiated Instruction

See *Algebra 2 Best Practices Toolkit* for suggestions on addressing the needs of a diverse classroom.

Homework Check

For a quick check of student understanding of key concepts, go over the following exercises:

Basic: 6, 12, 22, 34, 40
Average: 8, 14, 26, 36, 40
Advanced: 10, 16, 30, 38, 41

Extra Practice

- Student Edition, p. 1023
- Chapter 14 Resource Book: Practice levels A, B, C, pp. 64–66

Practice Worksheet

An easily-readable reduced practice page (with answers) for this lesson can be found on p. 906D.

SKILL PRACTICE

A

1. **VOCABULARY** Give the sum and difference formulas for sine, cosine, and tangent. **See margin.**

2. ★ **WRITING** *Explain* how you can evaluate tan 75° using either the sum or difference formula for tangent. **Use the sum formula for tangent and the fact that 45° + 30° = 75° or use the difference formula and the fact that 135° − 60° = 75°.**

EXAMPLE 1 on p. 949 for Exs. 3–10

FINDING VALUES **Find the exact value of the expression.**

3. $\tan(-15°)$ $\sqrt{3}-2$
4. $\sin(-165°)$ $\frac{-\sqrt{6}+\sqrt{2}}{4}$
5. $\tan 195°$ $2-\sqrt{3}$
6. $\cos 15°$ $\frac{\sqrt{2}+\sqrt{6}}{4}$
7. $\sin\frac{23\pi}{12}$ $\frac{\sqrt{2}-\sqrt{6}}{4}$
8. $\tan\frac{17\pi}{12}$ $2+\sqrt{3}$
9. $\cos\left(-\frac{5\pi}{12}\right)$ $\frac{\sqrt{6}-\sqrt{2}}{4}$
10. $\sin\left(-\frac{7\pi}{12}\right)$ $\frac{-\sqrt{6}-\sqrt{}}{4}$

11. ★ **SHORT RESPONSE** Derive the cofunction identity $\sin\left(\frac{\pi}{2}-\theta\right)=\cos\theta$ using the difference formula for sine. **See margin.**

EXAMPLE 2 on p. 950 for Exs. 12–18

EVALUATING EXPRESSIONS **Evaluate the expression given that $\cos a=\frac{4}{5}$ with $0<a<\frac{\pi}{2}$ and $\sin b=-\frac{15}{17}$ with $\frac{3\pi}{2}<b<2\pi$.**

12. $\sin(a+b)$ $-\frac{36}{85}$
13. $\cos(a+b)$ $\frac{77}{85}$
14. $\tan(a+b)$ $-\frac{36}{77}$
15. $\sin(a-b)$ $\frac{84}{85}$
16. $\cos(a-b)$ $-\frac{13}{85}$
17. $\tan(a-b)$ $-\frac{84}{13}$

18. ★ **MULTIPLE CHOICE** What is the value of $\sin(a-b)$ given that $\sin a=-\frac{3}{5}$ with $\pi<a<\frac{3\pi}{2}$ and $\cos b=\frac{12}{13}$ with $0<b<\frac{\pi}{2}$? **B**

Ⓐ $-\frac{18}{55}$ Ⓑ $-\frac{16}{65}$ Ⓒ $\frac{14}{45}$ Ⓓ $\frac{20}{43}$

EXAMPLE 3 on p. 950 for Exs. 19–31

SIMPLIFYING EXPRESSIONS **Simplify the expression.**

19. $\tan(x+\pi)$ $\tan x$
20. $\sin(x+\pi)$ $-\sin x$
21. $\cos(x+2\pi)$ $\cos x$
22. $\tan(x-2\pi)$ $\tan x$
23. $\sin\left(x-\frac{3\pi}{2}\right)$ $\cos x$
24. $\tan\left(x+\frac{\pi}{2}\right)$ $-\cot x$
25. $\sin\left(x+\frac{3\pi}{2}\right)$ $-\cos x$
26. $\cos\left(x-\frac{3\pi}{2}\right)$ $-\sin$
27. $\tan\left(x+\frac{3\pi}{2}\right)$ $-\cot x$
28. $\cos\left(x-\frac{\pi}{2}\right)$ $\sin x$
29. $\tan\left(x+\frac{5\pi}{2}\right)$ $-\cot x$
30. $\cos\left(x+\frac{5\pi}{2}\right)$ $-\sin$

31. **ERROR ANALYSIS** *Describe* and correct the error in simplifying the expression. **The sign in the denominator should be negative when using the sum formula; $\frac{\tan x+\tan\frac{\pi}{4}}{1-\tan x\tan\frac{\pi}{4}}=\frac{\tan x+1}{1-\tan x}$.**

$$\tan\left(x+\frac{\pi}{4}\right)=\frac{\tan x+\tan\frac{\pi}{4}}{1+\tan x\tan\frac{\pi}{4}}=\frac{\tan x+1}{1+\tan x}=1$$ ✗

EXAMPLE 4 on p. 950 for Exs. 32–38

B

32. ★ **MULTIPLE CHOICE** What is a solution of the equation $\sin(x-2\pi)+\tan(x-2\pi)=0$ on the interval $\pi<x<3\pi$? **C**

Ⓐ $\frac{\pi}{2}$ Ⓑ $\frac{3\pi}{2}$ Ⓒ 2π Ⓓ 3π

1. $\sin(a+b)=\sin a\cos b+\cos a\sin b$, $\sin(a-b)=\sin a\cos b-\cos a\sin b$, $\cos(a+b)=\cos a\cos b-\sin a\sin b$, $\cos(a-b)=\cos a\cos b+\sin a\sin b$, $\tan(a+b)=\frac{\tan a+\tan b}{1-\tan a\tan b}$, $\tan(a-b)=\frac{\tan a-\tan b}{1+\tan a\tan b}$

11. $\sin\left(\frac{\pi}{2}-\theta\right)=\sin\frac{\pi}{2}\cos\theta-\cos\frac{\pi}{2}\sin\theta=1(\cos\theta)-0(\sin\theta)=\cos\theta$

SOLVING TRIGONOMETRIC EQUATIONS **Solve the equation for $0 \le x < 2\pi$.**

33. $\cos\left(x + \frac{\pi}{6}\right) - 1 = \cos\left(x - \frac{\pi}{6}\right)$ $\frac{3\pi}{2}$

34. $\sin\left(x + \frac{\pi}{4}\right) + \sin\left(x - \frac{\pi}{4}\right) = 0$ $0, \pi$

35. $\sin\left(x + \frac{5\pi}{6}\right) + \sin\left(x - \frac{5\pi}{6}\right) = 1$ **about 3.757, about 5.668**

36. $\tan(x + \pi) + \cos\left(x + \frac{\pi}{2}\right) = 0$ $0, \pi$

37. $\tan(x + \pi) + 2\sin(x + \pi) = 0$ $0, \frac{\pi}{3}, \pi, \frac{5\pi}{3}$

38. $\sin(x + \pi) + \cos(x + \pi) = 0$ $\frac{3\pi}{4}, \frac{7\pi}{4}$

C 39. **CHALLENGE** Consider a complex number $z = a + bi$ in the complex plane shown. Let r be the length of the line segment joining z and the origin, and let θ be the angle that this segment makes with the positive real axis, as shown. **a–c. See margin.**

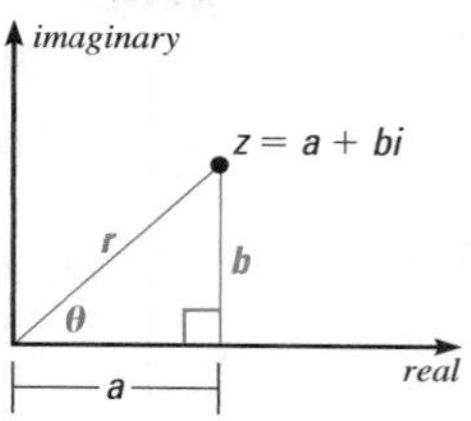

a. *Explain* why $a = r\cos\theta$ and $b = r\sin\theta$, so that $z = (r\cos\theta) + i(r\sin\theta)$.

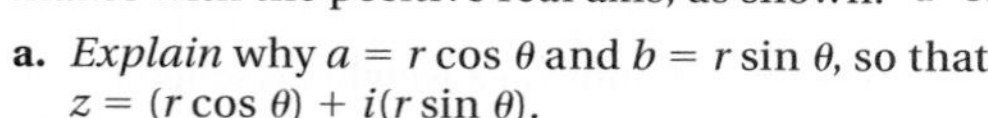

b. Use the result from part (a) to show the following:

$$z^2 = r^2[(\cos\theta\cos\theta - \sin\theta\sin\theta) + i(\sin\theta\cos\theta + \cos\theta\sin\theta)]$$

c. Use the sum and difference formulas to show that the equation in part (b) can be written as $z^2 = r^2(\cos 2\theta + i\sin 2\theta)$.

PROBLEM SOLVING

EXAMPLE 5 A on p. 951 for Exs. 40–41

40. **METEOROLOGY** The number h of hours of daylight for Rome, Italy, and Miami, Florida, can be approximated by the equations below, where t is the time in days and $t = 0$ represents January 1.

Rome: $h_1 = 2.7\sin\left(\frac{\pi t}{182} - 4.94\right) + 12.1$ **Miami:** $h_2 = -1.6\cos\frac{\pi t}{182} + 12.1$

On which days of the year will the cities have the same amount of daylight? **April 9 and Oct 9**

@HomeTutor for problem solving help at classzone.com

1. about 15 min
8 sec

41. **CLOCK TOWER** The heights m and h (in feet) of a clock tower's minute hand and hour hand, respectively, can be approximated by

$$m = 182.5 - 11.5\sin\left(\frac{\pi t}{30} - \frac{\pi}{2}\right) \quad \text{and} \quad h = 182.5 - 7\sin\left(\frac{\pi t}{360}\right)$$

where t is the time in minutes and $t = 0$ represents 3:00 P.M. Use a graphing calculator to find how long it takes for the height of the minute hand to equal the height of the hour hand.

@HomeTutor for problem solving help at classzone.com

B 42. **PHYSICAL SCIENCE** When a wave travels through a taut string, the displacement y of each point on the string depends on the time t and the point's position x. The equation of a *standing wave* can be obtained by adding the displacements of two waves traveling in opposite directions. Suppose two waves can be modeled by these equations:

$$y_1 = A\cos\left(\frac{2\pi t}{3} - \frac{2\pi x}{5}\right) \qquad y_2 = A\cos\left(\frac{2\pi t}{3} + \frac{2\pi x}{5}\right)$$

Show that $y_1 + y_2 = 2A\cos\left(\frac{2\pi t}{3}\right)\cos\left(\frac{2\pi x}{5}\right)$. **See margin.**

Teaching Strategy

Exercises 3–10, 12–30 All of the sum and difference formulas can be difficult for students to memorize and they are likely to confuse the operation signs involved with each formula. It may help them to remember the signs for the formulas, by associating the signs with the initial letters of *sine* and *cosine* and remembering that *sine* = same sign and *cosine* = change sign. Thus the formula for $\sin(a + b)$ keeps the *same* addition sign, and the formula for $\sin(a - b)$ keeps the *same* subtraction sign. By contrast, the formulas for $\cos(a + b)$ and $\cos(a - b)$ *change* the addition sign to subtraction and the subtraction to addition. Finally, since $\tan x = \frac{\sin x}{\cos x}$, $\tan(a + b)$ and $\tan(a - b)$ can be associated with $\frac{\textit{same}\text{ sign}}{\textit{change}\text{ sign}}$.

Study Strategy

Exercises 3–32, 33–38 Suggest that students copy the sum and difference formulas into their notebooks and refer to the formulas as they complete Exercises 3–32. Then suggest that they try to complete Exercises 33–38 without referring to their notes for the formulas.

Mathematical Reasoning

Exercise 12 Since a is in Quadrant I, $\cos a = \frac{4}{5}$ implies that $a = \cos^{-1}\frac{4}{5}$. Since b is in Quadrant IV, $\sin b = -\frac{15}{17}$ implies that $b = \sin^{-1}\left(-\frac{15}{17}\right)$. Use these relations to find $\sin(a + b)$ on a graphing calculator by storing $\cos^{-1}\frac{4}{5}$ in A and by storing $\sin^{-1}\left(-\frac{15}{17}\right)$ in B. Then you can calculate $\sin(A + B)$→Frac to find the value of $\sin(a + b)$.

39a. Using the triangle, $\cos\theta = \frac{a}{r} \rightarrow a = r\cos\theta$. Similarly, $\sin\theta = \frac{b}{r} \rightarrow b = r\sin\theta$. Since $z = a + bi$, substitution yields $z = (r\cos\theta) + i(r\sin\theta)$.

39b. $z = a + bi$, so $z^2 = (a + bi)^2$ which expands to $a^2 + 2abi - b^2$; substituting the facts found in part (a) gives

$$z^2 = (r\cos\theta)^2 + 2i(r\cos\theta)(r\sin\theta) - (r\sin\theta)^2$$
$$= r^2\cos^2\theta + 2ir^2\cos\theta\sin\theta - r^2\sin^2\theta$$
$$= r^2[(\cos\theta\cos\theta - \sin\theta\sin\theta) + i(\sin\theta\cos\theta + \cos\theta\sin\theta)]$$

39c. $z^2 = r^2(\cos\theta\cos\theta - \sin\theta\sin\theta) + i(\sin\theta\cos\theta + \cos\theta\sin\theta)$

$z^2 = r^2[\cos(\theta + \theta) + i\sin(\theta + \theta)]$

$z^2 = r^2(\cos 2\theta + i\sin 2\theta)$

42. See Additional Answers beginning on p. AA1.

5 ASSESS AND RETEACH

Daily Homework Quiz

Transparency Available

1. Find the exact value of sin 75°. $\frac{\sqrt{6}+\sqrt{2}}{4}$
2. Find tan $(a - b)$ given that $\cos a = -\frac{5}{13}$ with $\frac{\pi}{2} < a < \pi$ and $\sin b = \frac{3}{5}$ with $0 < b < \frac{\pi}{2}$. $\frac{63}{16}$
3. Simplify the expression $\sin\left(x + \frac{5\pi}{2}\right)$. $\cos x$
4. Two objects are attached to coiled springs. The objects are pulled down and then released at the same time. The equations $d = 16 \sin\left(\frac{\pi t}{2} - \frac{\pi}{2}\right) + 20$ and $d = -8 \cos\frac{\pi t}{2} + 20$ represent the distance d (in inches) of each object from its resting position t seconds after the objects are released. After how many seconds are the two objects first at the same height? **1 sec**

Available at **classzone.com**

Diagnosis/Remediation

- Practice A, B, C in Chapter 14 Resource Book, pp. 64–66
- Study Guide in Chapter 14 Resource Book, pp. 67–68
- Practice Workbook, pp. 203–204
- @HomeTutor

Challenge

Additional challenge is available in the Chapter 14 Resource Book, p. 71.

44b–c, 45. See Additional Answers beginning on p. AA1.

43. **MULTI-STEP PROBLEM** A photographer is at a height h taking aerial photographs. The ratio of the image length WQ to the length NA of the actual object is

$$\frac{WQ}{NA} = \frac{f \tan(\theta - t) + f \tan t}{h \tan \theta}$$

where f is the focal length of the camera, θ is the angle between the vertical line perpendicular to the ground and the line from the camera to point A, and t is the tilt angle of the film.

a. Use the difference formula for tangent to simplify the ratio.

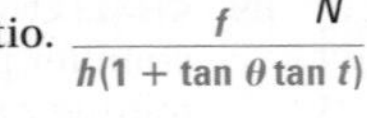

b. Show that $\frac{WQ}{NA} = \frac{f}{h}$ when $t = 0$. $\frac{f}{h(1 + \tan\theta \tan 0)} = \frac{f}{h}$

44. ★ **EXTENDED RESPONSE** Your friend pulls on a weight attached to a spring and then releases it. A split second later, you begin filming the spring to analyze its motion. You find that the spring's distance y (in inches) from its equilibrium point can be modeled by $y = 5 \sin(2t + C)$ where $C = \tan^{-1}\frac{3}{4}$ and t is the elapsed time (in seconds) since you began filming.

44a. $\frac{3}{5}, \frac{4}{5}$

a. Find the values of sin C and cos C.

b. Use a sum formula to show that $y = 5 \sin(2t + C)$ can be written as $y = 4 \sin 2t + 3 \cos 2t$. **See margin.**

c. Graph the function found in part (b) and find its maximum value. *Explain* what this value represents. **See margin.**

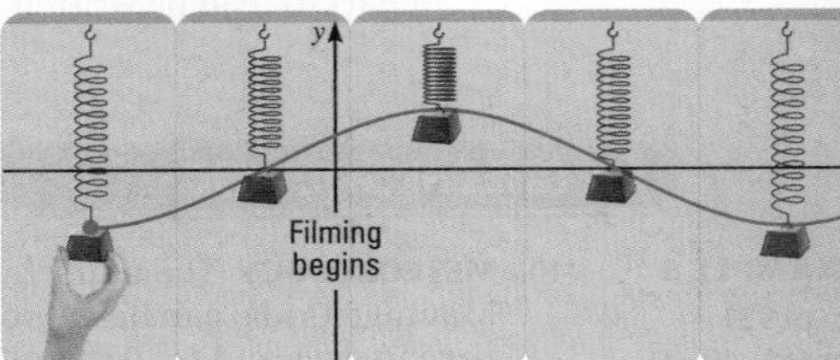

C 45. **CHALLENGE** The busy signal on a touch-tone phone is a combination of two tones with frequencies of 480 hertz and 620 hertz. The individual tones can be modeled by the following equations:

480 hertz: $y_1 = \cos 960\pi t$ **620 hertz:** $y_2 = \cos 1240\pi t$

The sound of the busy signal can be modeled by $y_1 + y_2$. Show that:

$$y_1 + y_2 = 2 \cos 1100\pi t \cos 140\pi t$$ **See margin.**

KENTUCKY MIXED REVIEW

TEST PRACTICE at classzone.com

46. A stack of boxes forms a square pyramid. The diagram shows the top three layers of the pyramid. Which rule gives the number a_n of boxes in the nth layer of the pyramid? **D**

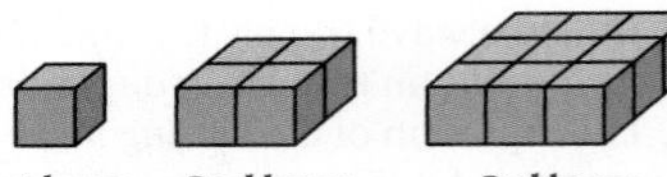

Ⓐ $a_n = 2n$ Ⓑ $a_n = 2(n + 1)$ Ⓒ $a_n = n(n + 1)$ Ⓓ $a_n = n^2$

47. What is the solution of $2(x - 2) - 1.45 = 3(x - 3)$? **B**

Ⓐ −12.14   Ⓑ 3.55   Ⓒ 6.08   Ⓓ 11.25

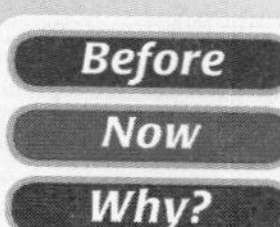

14.7 Apply Double-Angle and Half-Angle Formulas

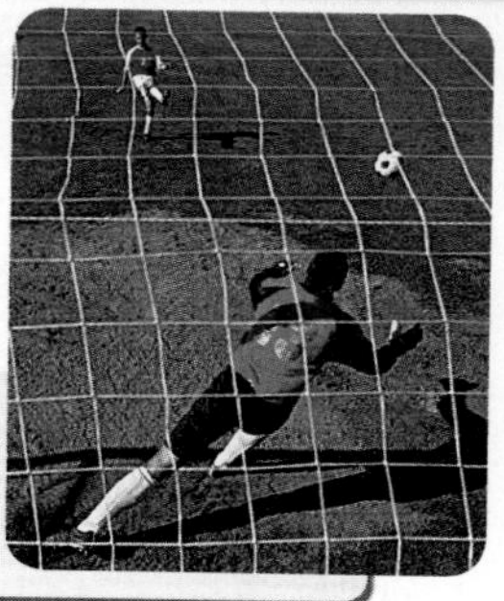

Before You evaluated expressions using sum and difference formulas.

Now You will use double-angle and half-angle formulas.

Why? So you can find the distance an object travels, as in Example 4.

Key Vocabulary
- **sine,** *p. 852*
- **cosine,** *p. 852*
- **tangent,** *p. 852*

In this lesson, you will use formulas for double angles (angles of measure $2a$) and half angles $\left(\text{angles of measure } \frac{a}{2}\right)$.

KEY CONCEPT *For Your Notebook*

Double-Angle and Half-Angle Formulas

Double-Angle Formulas

$\sin 2a = 2\sin a \cos a$

$\cos 2a = 1 - 2\sin^2 a$

$\cos 2a = 2\cos^2 a - 1$

$\cos 2a = \cos^2 a - \sin^2 a$

$\tan 2a = \dfrac{2\tan a}{1 - \tan^2 a}$

Half-Angle Formulas

$\sin\dfrac{a}{2} = \pm\sqrt{\dfrac{1-\cos a}{2}}$

$\cos\dfrac{a}{2} = \pm\sqrt{\dfrac{1+\cos a}{2}}$

$\tan\dfrac{a}{2} = \dfrac{1-\cos a}{\sin a}$

$\tan\dfrac{a}{2} = \dfrac{\sin a}{1+\cos a}$

The signs of $\sin\frac{a}{2}$ and $\cos\frac{a}{2}$ depend on the quadrant in which $\frac{a}{2}$ lies.

EXAMPLE 1 Evaluate trigonometric expressions

Find the exact value of (a) cos 165° and (b) $\tan\frac{\pi}{12}$.

a. $\cos 165° = \cos\frac{1}{2}(330°)$

$= -\sqrt{\dfrac{1+\cos 330°}{2}}$

$= -\sqrt{\dfrac{1+\frac{\sqrt{3}}{2}}{2}}$

$= -\dfrac{\sqrt{2+\sqrt{3}}}{2}$

b. $\tan\frac{\pi}{12} = \tan\frac{1}{2}\left(\frac{\pi}{6}\right)$

$= \dfrac{1-\cos\frac{\pi}{6}}{\sin\frac{\pi}{6}}$

$= \dfrac{1-\frac{\sqrt{3}}{2}}{\frac{1}{2}}$

$= 2-\sqrt{3}$

CHOOSE SIGNS
Because 165° is in Quadrant II and the value of cosine is negative in Quadrant II, the following formula is used:
$\cos\frac{a}{2} = -\sqrt{\frac{1+\cos a}{2}}$

1 PLAN AND PREPARE

Warm-Up Exercises
Transparency Available
Simplify the expression.

1. $-\sqrt{\frac{3}{4}}$ $-\frac{\sqrt{3}}{2}$ **2.** $\sqrt{\frac{1+\frac{7}{25}}{2}}$ $\frac{4}{5}$

3. You are designing a logo on a coordinate plane. The tangent of an angle in the logo is positive. In which quadrant(s) can the angle lie? I or III

Notetaking Guide
Transparency Available
Promotes interactive learning and notetaking skills, pp. 372–374.

Pacing
Basic: 2 days
Average: 2 days
Advanced: 2 days
Block: 1 block
- See *Teaching Guide/Lesson Plan.*

2 FOCUS AND MOTIVATE

Essential Question
Big Idea 3, p. 907
If you are given the values of sin *a*, cos *a*, and tan *a*, what identity formulas can you use to determine a trigonometric function's value for either $2a$ or $\frac{a}{2}$? **Tell students they will learn how to answer this question by applying the double-angle and half-angle formulas.**

Resource Planning Guide

Chapter Resource Book
- Teaching Guide/Lesson Plan (pp. 72–73)
- Activity Master (p. 74)
- Practice levels A, B, C (pp. 77–79)
- Study Guide (pp. 80–81)
- Catch-up for Absent Students (p. 82)
- Problem Solving Workshop (p. 83)
- Challenge (p. 84)

Workbooks
- Notetaking Guide (pp. 372–374)
- Practice Workbook (pp. 205–206)

Teaching Options
- **Power Presentations CD-ROM** provides dynamic electronic teaching resources for the classroom.
- **Activity Generator CD-ROM** provides editable activities for all ability levels.

Interactive Technology
- Easy Planner
- Power Presentations CD-ROM
- Activity Generator CD-ROM
- Animated Algebra
- Test Generator CD-ROM
- Online Quiz
- eWorkbook
- eEdition
- @HomeTutor

Resources for English Learners
- Quick Reference for English Learners
- Spanish Study Guide
- Multi-Language Visual Glossary
- Student Resources in Spanish

See also the *Algebra 2 Toolkit* for more strategies for meeting individual needs.

Motivating the Lesson

Discuss with students the fact that the distance any object can be thrown is determined by the initial speed of the object and the angle above the horizontal at which the object is thrown. In this lesson students will learn about trigonometric identities that can be used to determine the distance an object has been thrown.

3 TEACH

Extra Example 1

Find the exact value of (a) $\tan \frac{3\pi}{8}$ and (b) sin 15°. **$\tan \frac{3\pi}{8} = \sqrt{2} + 1$; $\sin 15° = \frac{\sqrt{2 - \sqrt{3}}}{2}$**

Key Question to Ask for Example 1

- In part b, why is it easier to use $\tan \frac{a}{2} = \frac{1 - \cos a}{\sin a}$ than $\tan \frac{a}{2} = \frac{\sin a}{1 + \cos a}$? **You do not need to rationalize the denominator.**

Extra Example 2

Given $\tan a = \frac{3}{4}$ with $\pi < a < \frac{3\pi}{2}$, find (a) $\cos 2a$ and (b) $\cos \frac{a}{2}$.

$\cos 2a = \frac{7}{25}$; $\cos \frac{a}{2} = -\frac{\sqrt{10}}{10}$

Extra Example 3

Which expression is equivalent to $4\left(\frac{\sin \theta}{2}\right)\left(\frac{\cos \theta}{2}\right)$? **A**

Ⓐ $\frac{1}{2} \sin 2\theta$ Ⓑ $2 \cos \theta$

Ⓒ $\tan 2\theta$ Ⓓ $\cos 2\theta$

Key Question to Ask for Example 3

- Describe the error in this reasoning: $\frac{\sin 2\theta}{1 - \cos 2\theta} = \frac{2 \sin \theta}{2 \sin^2 \theta} = \frac{1}{\sin \theta} = \csc \theta$ **$\sin 2\theta \neq 2 \sin \theta$**

EXAMPLE 2 Evaluate trigonometric expressions

Given $\cos a = \frac{5}{13}$ with $\frac{3\pi}{2} < a < 2\pi$, find (a) $\sin 2a$ and (b) $\sin \frac{a}{2}$.

MULTIPLY AN INEQUALITY

In part (b), you can multiply through the inequality $\frac{3\pi}{2} < a < 2\pi$ by $\frac{1}{2}$ to get $\frac{3\pi}{4} < \frac{a}{2} < \pi$. So, $\frac{a}{2}$ is in Quadrant II.

Solution

a. Using a Pythagorean identity gives $\sin a = -\frac{12}{13}$.

$$\sin 2a = 2 \sin a \cos a = 2\left(-\frac{12}{13}\right)\left(\frac{5}{13}\right) = -\frac{120}{169}$$

b. Because $\frac{a}{2}$ is in Quadrant II, $\sin \frac{a}{2}$ is positive.

$$\sin \frac{a}{2} = \sqrt{\frac{1 - \cos a}{2}} = \sqrt{\frac{1 - \frac{5}{13}}{2}} = \sqrt{\frac{4}{13}} = \frac{2\sqrt{13}}{13}$$

EXAMPLE 3 Standardized Test Practice

Which expression is equivalent to $\frac{\sin 2\theta}{1 - \cos 2\theta}$?

Ⓐ $\sin \theta$ Ⓑ $\cot \theta$ Ⓒ $\csc \theta$ Ⓓ $\cos \theta$

Solution

$\frac{\sin 2\theta}{1 - \cos 2\theta} = \frac{2 \sin \theta \cos \theta}{1 - (1 - 2 \sin^2 \theta)}$	**Use double-angle formulas.**
$= \frac{2 \sin \theta \cos \theta}{2 \sin^2 \theta}$	**Simplify denominator.**
$= \frac{\cos \theta}{\sin \theta}$	**Divide out common factor 2 sin θ.**
$= \cot \theta$	**Use cotangent identity.**

▶ The correct answer is B. Ⓐ Ⓑ Ⓒ Ⓓ

GUIDED PRACTICE for Examples 1, 2, and 3

Find the exact value of the expression.

1. $\tan \frac{\pi}{8}$ **$\sqrt{2} - 1$**

2. $\sin \frac{5\pi}{8}$ **$\frac{\sqrt{2 + \sqrt{2}}}{2}$**

3. $\cos 15°$ **$\frac{\sqrt{2 + \sqrt{3}}}{2}$**

4. Given $\sin a = \frac{\sqrt{2}}{2}$ with $0 < a < \frac{\pi}{2}$, find $\cos 2a$ and $\tan \frac{a}{2}$. **0, $\sqrt{2} - 1$**

5. Given $\cos a = -\frac{3}{5}$ with $\pi < a < \frac{3\pi}{2}$, find $\sin 2a$ and $\sin \frac{a}{2}$. **$\frac{24}{25}$, $\frac{2\sqrt{5}}{5}$**

Simplify the expression.

6. $\frac{\cos 2\theta}{\sin \theta + \cos \theta}$ **$\cos \theta - \sin \theta$**

7. $\frac{\tan 2x}{\tan x}$ **$\frac{2}{1 - \tan^2 x}$**

8. $\sin 2x \tan \frac{x}{2}$ **$2 \cos x(1 - \cos x)$**

PATH OF A PROJECTILE The path traveled by an object that is projected at an initial height of h_0 feet, an initial speed of v feet per second, and an initial angle θ is given by

$$y = -\frac{16}{v^2 \cos^2 \theta}x^2 + (\tan \theta)x + h_0$$

where x is the horizontal distance (in feet) and y is the vertical distance (in feet). (This model neglects air resistance.)

EXAMPLE 4 Derive a trigonometric model

SOCCER Write an equation for the horizontal distance traveled by a soccer ball kicked from ground level ($h_0 = 0$) at speed v and angle θ.

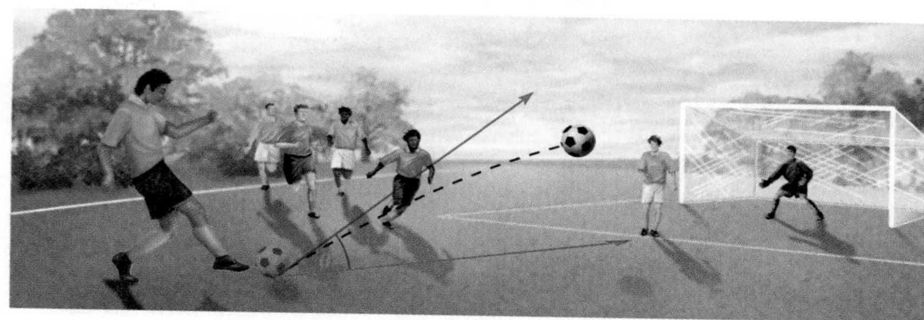

Solution

$-\frac{16}{v^2 \cos^2 \theta}x^2 + (\tan \theta)x + 0 = 0$	Let $h_0 = 0$.
$-x\left(\frac{16}{v^2 \cos^2 \theta}x - \tan \theta\right) = 0$	Factor.
$\frac{16}{v^2 \cos^2 \theta}x - \tan \theta = 0$	Zero product property
$\frac{16}{v^2 \cos^2 \theta}x = \tan \theta$	Add $\tan \theta$ to each side.
$x = \frac{1}{16}v^2 \cos^2 \theta \tan \theta$	Multiply each side by $\frac{1}{16}v^2 \cos^2 \theta$.
$x = \frac{1}{16}v^2 \cos \theta \sin \theta$	Use $\cos \theta \tan \theta = \sin \theta$.
$x = \frac{1}{32}v^2 (2 \cos \theta \sin \theta)$	Rewrite $\frac{1}{16}$ as $\frac{1}{32} \cdot 2$.
$x = \frac{1}{32}v^2 \sin 2\theta$	Use a double-angle formula.

USE ZERO PRODUCT PROPERTY
One solution of this equation is $x = 0$, which corresponds to the point where the ball leaves the ground. This solution is ignored in later steps, because the problem requires finding where the ball *lands*.

✓ GUIDED PRACTICE for Example 4

9. **WHAT IF?** Suppose you kick a soccer ball from ground level with an initial speed of 70 feet per second. Can you make the ball travel 200 feet? no

10. **REASONING** Use the equation $x = \frac{1}{32}v^2 \sin 2\theta$ to explain why the projection angle that maximizes the distance a soccer ball travels is $\theta = 45°$.
Sample answer: $\sin 2(45°) = \sin 90° = 1$, this is the only value that will not decrease the velocity of the ball since it is the only non-fractional value.

Extra Example 4

The entryway to a house is in the shape of an isosceles triangle with legs a units long, height h, and base $2k$. Write a formula for the area A of the triangle in terms of a and the angle θ between the two legs.
$A = \frac{1}{2}a^2 \sin \theta$

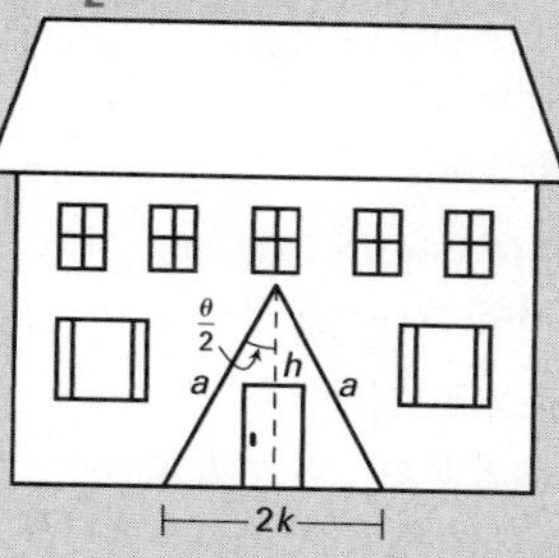

Key Question to Ask for Example 4

- If you graph the function for a given value of v, what would the maximum height of the sine curve represent? The maximum height the soccer ball could reach for the given value of v.

Mathematical Reasoning

Multiple Representations Solving $\cos 2\theta = 1 - 2\sin^2 \theta$ for $\sin^2 \theta$ gives the formula $\sin^2 \theta = \frac{1 - \cos 2\theta}{2}$. Similarly, solving $\cos 2\theta = 2\cos^2 \theta - 1$ for $\cos^2 \theta$ gives the formula $\cos^2 \theta = \frac{1 + \cos 2\theta}{2}$. These formulas are useful in calculus where they can be used to explore how a function changes at every unit of time.

Extra Example 5

Verify the identity $\tan \theta = \frac{1 - \cos 2\theta}{\sin 2\theta}$.

$\frac{1 - \cos 2\theta}{\sin 2\theta}$

$= \frac{1 - (1 - 2\sin^2 \theta)}{2 \sin \theta \cos \theta}$ (double angle identities)

$= \frac{2\sin^2 \theta}{2 \sin \theta \cos \theta}$ (Simplify numerator.)

$= \frac{\sin \theta}{\cos \theta}$ (Divide numerator and denominator by $2 \sin \theta$.)

$= \tan \theta$ (tangent identity)

Extra Example 6

Solve $\cos x + \cos 2x = 0$ for $0 \le x \le 2\pi$. $\frac{\pi}{3}, \pi, \frac{5\pi}{3}$

Extra Example 7

Find the general solution of $\sin x = -\sin 2x$. $x = n\pi$ or $\frac{2\pi}{3} + 2n\pi$ or $\frac{4\pi}{3} + 2n\pi$

Key Question to Ask for Example 7

- What expression could you evaluate to find the reference angle for $\sin \frac{x}{2} = \frac{1}{2}$? $2 \sin^{-1} \frac{1}{2}$

Closing the Lesson

Have students summarize the major points of the lesson and answer the Essential Question: If you are given the values of sin *a*, cos *a*, and tan *a*, what identity formulas can you use to determine a trigonometric function's value for either $2a$ or $\frac{a}{2}$?

- The double-angle formulas are: $\cos 2a = \cos^2 a - \sin^2 a = 2\cos^2 a - 1 = 1 - 2\sin^2 a$, $\sin 2a = 2 \sin a \cos a$, and $\tan 2a = \frac{2 \tan a}{1 - \tan^2 a}$.
- The half-angle formulas are: $\sin \frac{a}{2} = \pm\sqrt{\frac{1 - \cos a}{2}}$, $\cos \frac{a}{2} = \pm\sqrt{\frac{1 + \cos a}{2}}$, and $\tan \frac{a}{2} = \frac{1 - \cos a}{\sin a} = \frac{\sin a}{1 + \cos a}$.
- The signs of $\sin \frac{a}{2}$ and $\cos \frac{a}{2}$ depend on the quadrant in which $\frac{a}{2}$ lies.

You can use either a double-angle formula or a half-angle formula to find either value.

EXAMPLE 5 Verify a trigonometric identity

Verify the identity $\cos 3x = 4\cos^3 x - 3\cos x$.

$\cos 3x = \cos (2x + x)$	Rewrite $\cos 3x$ as $\cos (2x + x)$.
$= \cos 2x \cos x - \sin 2x \sin x$	Use a sum formula.
$= (2\cos^2 x - 1)\cos x - (2 \sin x \cos x) \sin x$	Use double-angle formulas.
$= 2\cos^3 x - \cos x - 2\sin^2 x \cos x$	Multiply.
$= 2\cos^3 x - \cos x - 2(1 - \cos^2 x)\cos x$	Use a Pythagorean identity.
$= 2\cos^3 x - \cos x - 2\cos x + 2\cos^3 x$	Distributive property
$= 4\cos^3 x - 3\cos x$	Combine like terms.

EXAMPLE 6 Solve a trigonometric equation

Solve $\sin 2x + 2\cos x = 0$ for $0 \le x < 2\pi$.

Solution

$\sin 2x + 2\cos x = 0$	Write original equation.
$2 \sin x \cos x + 2\cos x = 0$	Use a double-angle formula.
$2\cos x (\sin x + 1) = 0$	Factor.

Set each factor equal to 0 and solve for x.

$2\cos x = 0$	$\sin x + 1 = 0$
$\cos x = 0$	$\sin x = -1$
$x = \frac{\pi}{2}, \frac{3\pi}{2}$	$x = \frac{3\pi}{2}$

CHECK Graph the function $y = \sin 2x + 2\cos x$ on a graphing calculator. Then use the *zero* feature to find the x-values on the interval $0 \le x < 2\pi$ for which $y = 0$. The two x-values are:

$$x = \frac{\pi}{2} \approx 1.57 \quad \text{and} \quad x = \frac{3\pi}{2} \approx 4.71$$

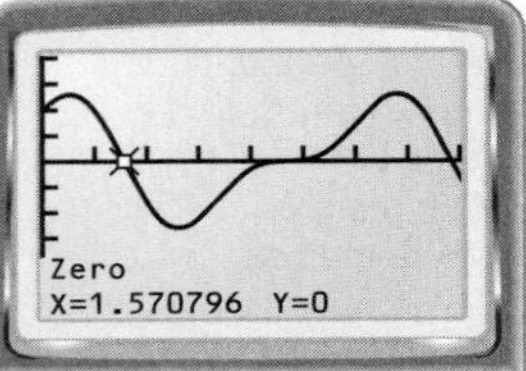

EXAMPLE 7 Find a general solution

Find the general solution of $2 \sin \frac{x}{2} = 1$.

$2 \sin \frac{x}{2} = 1$	Write original equation.
$\sin \frac{x}{2} = \frac{1}{2}$	Divide each side by 2.
$\frac{x}{2} = \frac{\pi}{6} + 2n\pi$ or $\frac{5\pi}{6} + 2n\pi$	General solution for $\frac{x}{2}$
$x = \frac{\pi}{3} + 4n\pi$ or $\frac{5\pi}{3} + 4n\pi$	General solution for x

SOLVE EQUATIONS
As seen in Example 7, some equations that involve double or half angles can be solved without resorting to double- or half-angle formulas.

Guided Practice, p. 959

11. $\sin 3x = \sin (2x + x)$
$= \sin 2x \sin x + \cos 2x \cos x$
$= 2 \sin x \cos x \cos x + (1 - 2\sin^2 x)\sin x$
$= 2 \sin x \cos^2 x + \sin x - 2\sin^3 x$
$= 2 \sin x(1 - \sin^2 x) + \sin x - 2\sin^3 x$
$= 2 \sin x - 2\sin^3 x + \sin x - 2\sin^3 x$
$= 3 \sin x - 4\sin^3 x$

12. $1 + \cos 10x = 2\cos^2 5x$
$= 1 + \cos 2(5x)$
$= 1 + 2\cos^2 (5x) - 1$
$= 2\cos^2 5x$

 **GUIDED PRACTICE** for Examples 5, 6, and 7

Verify the identity. 11, 12. See margin.

11. $\sin 3x = 3 \sin x - 4 \sin^3 x$

12. $1 + \cos 10x = 2 \cos^2 5x$

Solve the equation.

13. $\tan 2x + \tan x = 0$ for $0 \le x < 2\pi$ $0, \frac{\pi}{3}, \frac{2\pi}{3}, \pi, \frac{4\pi}{3}, \frac{5\pi}{3}$

14. $2 \cos \frac{x}{2} + 1 = 0$ $\frac{4\pi}{3} + 4n\pi$ or $\frac{8\pi}{3} + 4n\pi$

14.7 EXERCISES

HOMEWORK KEY

○ = WORKED-OUT SOLUTIONS on p. WS25 for Exs. 7, 13, and 53

★ = STANDARDIZED TEST PRACTICE Exs. 2, 11, 27, 54, and 55

SKILL PRACTICE

1. VOCABULARY Copy and complete: $\sin 2a = 2 \sin a \cos a$ is called the __?__ formula for sine. double angle

2. ★ WRITING *Explain* how to determine the sign of the answer when evaluating a half-angle formula for sine or cosine. See margin.

EXAMPLE 1 on p. 955 for Exs. 3–11

EVALUATING EXPRESSIONS **Find the exact value of the expression.**

3. $\sin 105°$ $\frac{\sqrt{2+\sqrt{3}}}{2}$

4. $\tan 112.5°$ $-\sqrt{2} - 1$

5. $\tan (-165°)$ $2 - \sqrt{3}$

6. $\cos (-75°)$ $\frac{\sqrt{2-\sqrt{3}}}{2}$

7. $\cos \frac{\pi}{8}$ $\frac{\sqrt{\sqrt{2}+2}}{2}$

8. $\sin \frac{5\pi}{12}$ $\frac{\sqrt{2+\sqrt{3}}}{2}$

9. $\tan\left(-\frac{5\pi}{8}\right)$ $\sqrt{2} + 1$

10. $\sin\left(-\frac{11\pi}{12}\right)$ $-\frac{\sqrt{2-\sqrt{3}}}{2}$

11. ★ MULTIPLE CHOICE What is the exact value of tan 15°? B

Ⓐ $-\sqrt{3}$ Ⓑ $2 - \sqrt{3}$ Ⓒ $\sqrt{3}$ Ⓓ $2 + \sqrt{3}$

EXAMPLE 2 on p. 956 for Exs. 12–20

HALF-ANGLE FORMULAS **Find the exact values of $\sin \frac{a}{2}$, $\cos \frac{a}{2}$, and $\tan \frac{a}{2}$.**

12. $\cos a = \frac{4}{5}, 0 < a < \frac{\pi}{2}$ $\frac{\sqrt{10}}{10}, \frac{3\sqrt{10}}{10}, \frac{1}{3}$

13. $\cos a = \frac{1}{3}, \frac{3\pi}{2} < a < 2\pi$ $\frac{\sqrt{3}}{3}, -\frac{\sqrt{6}}{3}, -\frac{\sqrt{2}}{2}$

14. $\sin a = \frac{12}{13}, \frac{\pi}{2} < a < \pi$ $\frac{2\sqrt{13}}{13}, \frac{2\sqrt{13}}{13}, -\frac{2}{3}$

15. $\sin a = -\frac{3}{5}, \pi < a < \frac{3\pi}{2}$ $\frac{3\sqrt{10}}{10}, -\frac{\sqrt{10}}{10}, -3$

16. ERROR ANALYSIS *Describe* and correct the error in finding the exact value of $\sin \frac{a}{2}$ given that $\cos a = -\frac{3}{5}$ with $\frac{\pi}{2} < a < \pi$. $\frac{a}{2}$ is in quadrant I, so the value for sine should be positive; $\frac{2\sqrt{5}}{5}$.

$$\sin \frac{a}{2} = -\sqrt{\frac{1 - \cos a}{2}} = -\sqrt{\frac{1 + \frac{3}{5}}{2}} = -\sqrt{\frac{4}{5}} = -\frac{2\sqrt{5}}{5} \quad ✗$$

DOUBLE-ANGLE FORMULAS **Find the exact values of sin 2*a*, cos 2*a*, and tan 2*a*.**

17. $\tan a = 2, \pi < a < \frac{3\pi}{2}$ $\frac{4}{5}, -\frac{3}{5}, -\frac{4}{3}$

18. $\tan a = -\sqrt{3}, \frac{\pi}{2} < a < \pi$ $-\frac{\sqrt{3}}{2}, -\frac{1}{2}, \sqrt{3}$

19. $\sin a = -\frac{2}{3}, \pi < a < \frac{3\pi}{2}$ $\frac{4\sqrt{5}}{9}, \frac{1}{9}, 4\sqrt{5}$

20. $\cos a = \frac{2}{5}, -\frac{\pi}{2} < a < 0$ $-\frac{4\sqrt{21}}{25}, -\frac{17}{25}, \frac{4\sqrt{21}}{17}$

2. Determine what quadrant the angle, $\frac{a}{2}$, is in and the sign that corresponds to the trigonometric value you are seeking is the sign that applies.

4 PRACTICE AND APPLY

Assignment Guide

Answer Transparencies available for all exercises

Basic:
Day 1: EP p. 1017 Exs. 30–32
pp. 959–962
Exs. 1–7, 11–14, 16–19, 21–23, 27–29, 50, 51
Day 2: pp. 959–962
Exs. 30–33, 36–38, 42–44, 52–54, 57–58

Average:
Day 1: pp. 959–962
Exs. 1, 2, 5–9, 11, 13–20, 23–25, 28, 29, 50, 51
Day 2: pp. 959–962
Exs. 30–47, 52–55, 57

Advanced:
Day 1: pp. 959–962
Exs. 1, 2, 6–15, 18–20, 23–29, 50, 51
Day 2: pp. 959–962
Exs. 30–49*, 52–56*

Block:
pp. 959–962
Exs. 1, 2, 5–9, 11, 13–20, 23–25, 28–47, 50–55, 57

Differentiated Instruction

See *Algebra 2 Best Practices Toolkit* for suggestions on addressing the needs of a diverse classroom.

Homework Check

For a quick check of student understanding of key concepts, go over the following exercises:

Basic: 6, 12, 22, 32, 50
Average: 14, 24, 38, 42, 50
Advanced: 18, 34, 40, 44, 51

Extra Practice

- Student Edition, p. 1023
- Chapter 14 Resource Book: Practice levels A, B, C, pp. 77–79

Practice Worksheet

An easily-readable reduced practice page (with answers) for this lesson can be found on p. 906D.

Study Strategy

Exercises 12–15, 17–20 To help students determine the sign of a trigonometric value, they can make a table or a sketch in their notebooks that shows in which quadrants the sine, cosine, and tangent functions are positive. They can refer to the table or sketch as they complete these exercises.

Avoiding Common Errors

Exercises 21–26, 30–41 Watch for students who incorrectly assume that $\sin 2\theta = 2\sin\theta$, $\cos 2\theta = 2\cos\theta$, and $\tan 2\theta = 2\tan\theta$. Ask these students to graph $y = \sin 2\theta$ and $y = 2\sin\theta$ to confirm that the graphs do not coincide. They can also confirm that the graphs of the two cosine equations do not coincide, nor do the graphs of the two tangent equations. These graphs should also suggest to students that $\sin\frac{\theta}{2} = \frac{1}{2}\sin\theta$, $\cos\frac{\theta}{2} = \frac{1}{2}\cos\theta$, and $\tan\frac{\theta}{2} = \frac{1}{2}\tan\theta$ are not identities.

28. You cannot cancel out $\cos^2 x$ because it is not a part of a product in the numerator; $\frac{\cos 2x}{\cos^2 x} = \frac{2\cos^2 x - 1}{\cos^2 x} = 2 - \sec^2 x$.

29. The correct half angle formula is $\pm\sqrt{\frac{1-\cos a}{2}}$; $\sqrt{\frac{1-\frac{\sqrt{2}}{2}}{2}} = \sqrt{\frac{\frac{2-\sqrt{2}}{2}}{2}} = \sqrt{\frac{2-\sqrt{2}}{4}} = \frac{\sqrt{2-\sqrt{2}}}{2}$.

30. $2\cos^2\theta = 1 + 2\cos^2\theta - 1 = 1 + \cos 2\theta$

31. $\sin 3\theta = \sin(2\theta + \theta) = \sin 2\theta\cos\theta + \cos 2\theta\sin\theta = 2\sin\theta\cos\theta\cos\theta + (2\cos^2\theta - 1)\sin\theta = 2\sin\theta\cos^2\theta + (2\cos^2\theta - 1)\sin\theta = \sin\theta(2\cos^2\theta + 2\cos^2\theta - 1) = \sin\theta(4\cos^2\theta - 1)$

32. $\frac{1}{2}\sin\frac{2x}{3} = \frac{1}{2}\sin 2\left(\frac{x}{3}\right) = \frac{1}{2}\left(2\sin\frac{x}{3}\cos\frac{x}{3}\right) = \sin\frac{x}{3}\cos\frac{x}{3}$

EXAMPLE 3 on p. 956 for Exs. 21–29

SIMPLIFYING EXPRESSIONS **Rewrite the expression without double angles or half angles, given that $0 < \theta < \frac{\pi}{2}$. Then simplify the expression.**

21. $\frac{\cos 2\theta}{1 - 2\sin^2\theta}$ **1**

22. $\frac{\sin 2\theta}{2\cos\theta}$ **$\sin\theta$**

23. $(1 - \tan\theta)\tan 2\theta$ **$\frac{2\tan\theta}{1+\tan\theta}$**

24. $\frac{\cos 2\theta}{\sin\theta - \cos\theta}$ **$-\cos\theta - \sin\theta$**

25. $\frac{-\tan\frac{\theta}{2}}{\csc\theta}$ **$\cos\theta - 1$**

26. $2\sin\frac{\theta}{2}\cos\frac{\theta}{2}$ **$\sin\theta$**

27. ★ **MULTIPLE CHOICE** Which expression is equivalent to $\cot\theta + \tan\theta$? **B**

Ⓐ $\csc 2\theta$ Ⓑ $2\csc 2\theta$ Ⓒ $\sec 2\theta$ Ⓓ $2\sec 2\theta$

ERROR ANALYSIS ***Describe*** **and correct the error in simplifying the expression.** **28, 29. See margin.**

28. $\frac{\cos 2x}{\cos^2 x} = \frac{\cos^2 x - \sin^2 x}{\cos^2 x} = \frac{1}{\cos^2 x} = \sec^2 x$ ✗

29. $\sin 22.5° = \sin\frac{1}{2}(45°) = 2\sin 45°\cos 45° = 2\left(\frac{\sqrt{2}}{2}\right)\left(\frac{\sqrt{2}}{2}\right) = 1$ ✗

EXAMPLE 5 B on p. 958 for Exs. 30–35

VERIFYING IDENTITIES **Verify the identity.** **30–35. See margin.**

30. $2\cos^2\theta = 1 + \cos 2\theta$

31. $\sin 3\theta = \sin\theta(4\cos^2\theta - 1)$

32. $\frac{1}{2}\sin\frac{2x}{3} = \sin\frac{x}{3}\cos\frac{x}{3}$

33. $2\sin^2 x\tan\frac{x}{2} = 2\sin x - \sin 2x$

34. $-\frac{\cos 2\theta}{\sin\theta} = 2\sin\theta - \csc\theta$

35. $\cos 4\theta = \cos^4\theta - 6\sin^2\theta\cos^2\theta + \sin^4\theta$

EXAMPLE 6 on p. 958 for Exs. 36–41

SOLVING EQUATIONS **Solve the equation for $0 \le x < 2\pi$.**

36. $\sin\frac{x}{2} = 1$ **π**

37. $2\cos\frac{x}{2} + 1 = 0$ **$\frac{4\pi}{3}$**

38. $\tan x - \tan 2x = 0$ **$0, \pi$**

39. $\tan\frac{x}{2} = \frac{2-\sqrt{2}}{2\sin x}$ **$\frac{\pi}{4}, \frac{7\pi}{4}$**

40. $\cos 2x = -2\cos^2 x$ **$\frac{\pi}{3}, \frac{2\pi}{3}, \frac{4\pi}{3}, \frac{5\pi}{3}$**

41. $2\sin 2x\sin x = 3\cos x$ **$\frac{\pi}{3}, \frac{\pi}{2}, \frac{2\pi}{3}, \frac{4\pi}{3}, \frac{3\pi}{2}, \frac{5\pi}{3}$**

EXAMPLE 7 on p. 958 for Exs. 42–47

FINDING GENERAL SOLUTIONS **Find the general solution of the equation.**

42. $\cos\frac{x}{2} = 1$ **$0 + 4n\pi$**

43. $\tan\frac{x}{2} = \sin x$ **$0 + 2n\pi$ or $\frac{\pi}{2} + n\pi$**

44. $\sin 2x = \sin x$ **$0 + n\pi$ or $\frac{\pi}{3} + 2n\pi$ or $\frac{5\pi}{3} + 2n\pi$**

45. $\cos 2x + \cos x = 0$ **$\frac{\pi}{3} + 2n\pi$ or $\frac{5\pi}{3} + 2n\pi$ or $\pi + 2n\pi$**

46. $\cos\frac{x}{2} + \sin x = 0$ **$\pi + 2n\pi$**

47. $\sin\frac{x}{2} + \cos x = 0$ **$\pi + 2n\pi$**

C

48. **REASONING** Show that the three double-angle formulas for cosine are equivalent. **See margin.**

49. **CHALLENGE** Use the diagram shown at the right to derive the formulas for $\sin\frac{\theta}{2}$, $\cos\frac{\theta}{2}$, and $\tan\frac{\theta}{2}$ when θ is an acute angle. **See margin.**

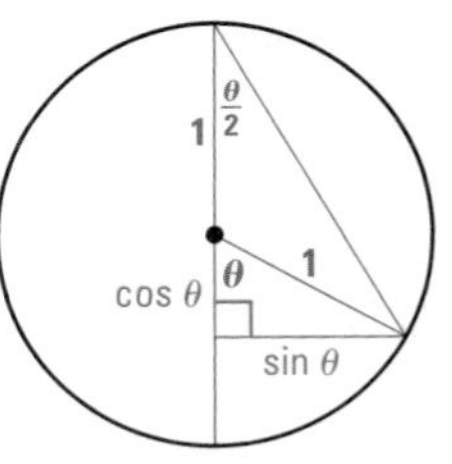

◯ = WORKED-OUT SOLUTIONS on p. WS1

★ = STANDARDIZED TEST PRACTICE

33. $2\sin^2 x\tan\frac{x}{2} = 2\sin^2 x\left(\frac{1-\cos x}{\sin x}\right) = 2\sin x(1-\cos x) = 2\sin x - 2\sin x\cos x = 2\sin x - \sin 2x$

34. $-\frac{\cos 2\theta}{\sin\theta} = -\frac{1 - 2\sin^2\theta}{\sin\theta} = \frac{2\sin^2\theta}{\sin\theta} - \frac{1}{\sin\theta} = 2\sin\theta - \csc\theta$

35. $\cos 4\theta = \cos(2\theta + 2\theta) = \cos 2\theta\cos 2\theta - \sin 2\theta\sin 2\theta = (\cos^2\theta - \sin^2\theta)^2 - (2\sin\theta\cos\theta)^2 = \cos^4\theta - 2\cos^2\theta\sin^2\theta + \sin^4\theta - 4\sin^2\theta\cos^2\theta = \cos^4\theta - 6\sin^2\theta\cos^2\theta + \sin^4\theta$

PROBLEM SOLVING

EXAMPLE 4 A on p. 957 for Exs. 50–51

50. GOLF Use the equation $x = \frac{1}{32}v^2 \sin 2\theta$ from Example 4 on page 957 to find the horizontal distance a golf ball will travel if it is hit at an initial speed of 50 feet per second and at an initial angle of 40°. **about 76.9 ft**

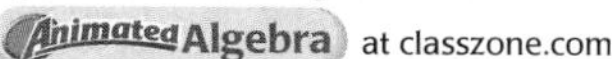

51. SOCCER Suppose you are attempting to kick a soccer ball from ground level. Through what range of angles can you kick the soccer ball with an initial speed of 80 feet per second to make it travel at least 150 feet? **$24.3° \le \theta \le 65.7°$**

Animated Algebra at classzone.com

52. MULTI-STEP PROBLEM At latitude L, the acceleration due to gravity g (in centimeters per second squared) at sea level can be approximated by:

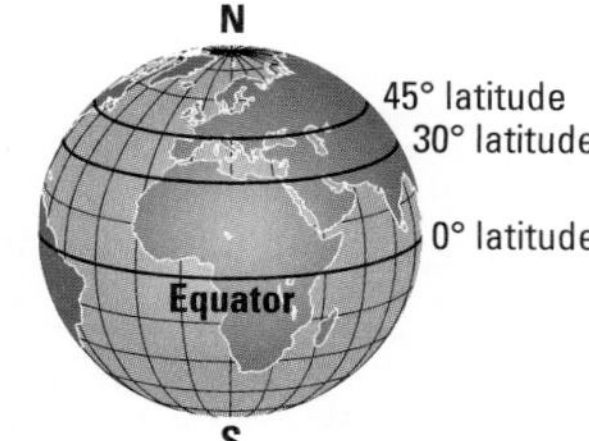

$$g = 978 + 5.17 \sin^2 L - 0.014 \sin L \cos L$$

a. Simplify the equation above to show that $g = 978 + 5.17 \sin^2 L - 0.007 \sin 2L$.

b. Graph the function from part (a). **See margin.**

c. Use the graph to approximate the acceleration due to gravity when the latitude is 45°, 30°, and 0°. **about 981 cm/sec², about 979 cm/sec², about 978 cm/sec²**

52a. Since $0.014 \sin L \cos L$ can be written as $0.007 \sin 2L$, you get $g = 978 + 5.17 \sin^2 L - 0.007 \sin 2L$.

53. MACH NUMBER An airplane's Mach number M is the ratio of its speed to the speed of sound. When an airplane travels faster than the speed of sound, the sound waves form a cone behind the airplane. The Mach number is related to the apex angle θ of the cone by the equation $\sin \frac{\theta}{2} = \frac{1}{M}$. Find the angle θ that corresponds to a Mach number of 2.5. **about 47.2°**

B

54. ★ SHORT RESPONSE A *Mercator projection* is a map projection of the globe onto a plane that preserves angles. On a globe with radius r, consider a point P that has latitude L and longitude T. The coordinates (x, y) of the corresponding point P' on the plane can be found using these equations:

$$x = rT \qquad y = r \ln\left[\tan\left(\frac{\frac{\pi}{2} + L}{2}\right)\right]$$

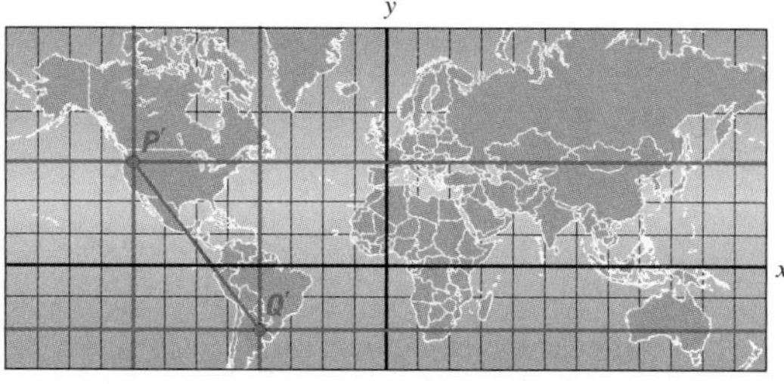

a. Use half-angle and sum formulas to show that the equation for the y-coordinate can be written as $y = r \ln\left(\frac{1 + \sin L}{\cos L}\right)$. **See margin.**

b. What is a reasonable domain for the equation in part (a)? *Explain.* **All latitudes except $90° < L < 270°$; $\cos 90° = 0$ and division by zero is undefined and the natural log of negative values is also undefined.**

An **Animated Algebra** activity is available on-line for **Exercise 51**. This activity is also available on the **Power Presentations CD-ROM**.

Exercise 53 More information about Mach numbers can be found at www.grc.nasa.gov/WWW/K-12/airplane/mach.html

49. $\sin \frac{\theta}{2} = \frac{\sin\theta}{\sqrt{2\cos\theta + 2}}$
$= \frac{\sqrt{1 - \cos^2\theta}}{\sqrt{2(\cos\theta + 1)}}$
$= \sqrt{\frac{(1 - \cos\theta)(1 + \cos\theta)}{2(\cos\theta + 1)}}$
$= \sqrt{\frac{1 - \cos\theta}{2}}$;
$\cos \frac{\theta}{2} = \frac{\cos\theta + 1}{\sqrt{2\cos\theta + 2}}$
$= \sqrt{\frac{(1 + \cos\theta)(1 + \cos\theta)}{2(\cos\theta + 1)}}$
$= \sqrt{\frac{1 + \cos\theta}{2}}$;
$\tan \frac{\theta}{2} = \frac{\sin\theta}{1 + \cos\theta}$
$= \frac{\sin\theta}{1 + \cos\theta} \cdot \frac{1 - \cos\theta}{1 - \cos\theta}$
$= \frac{\sin\theta(1 - \cos\theta)}{1 - \cos^2\theta}$
$= \frac{\sin\theta(1 - \cos\theta)}{\sin^2\theta}$
$= \frac{1 - \cos\theta}{\sin\theta}$

52b.

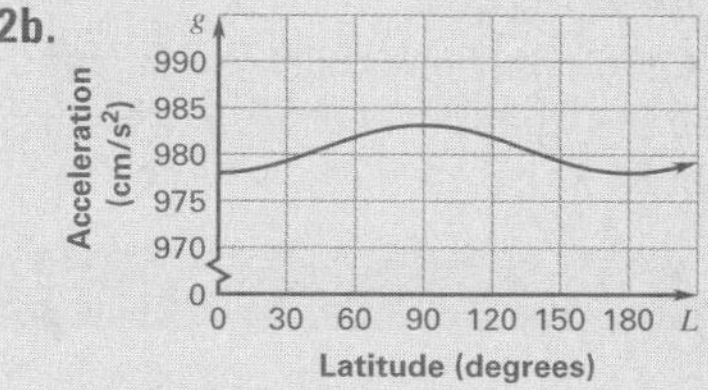

54a. See Additional Answers beginning on p. AA1.

48. $\cos 2a = \cos(a + a) = \cos a \cos a - \sin a \sin a = \cos^2 a - \sin^2 a$; and $\cos 2a = \cos^2 a - \sin^2 a = (1 - \sin^2 a) - \sin^2 a = 1 - 2\sin^2 a$; and $\cos 2a = \cos^2 a - \sin^2 a = \cos^2 a - (1 - \cos^2 a) = 2\cos^2 a - 1$

5 ASSESS AND RETEACH

Daily Homework Quiz

Transparency Available

1. Find the exact value of tan 75°. $2 + \sqrt{3}$

2. Given $\tan a = -\frac{7}{24}$, with $\frac{3\pi}{2} < a < 2\pi$, find $\tan \frac{a}{2}$. $-\frac{1}{7}$

3. Verify the identity $\csc x - \cot x = \tan \frac{x}{2}$.

$\csc x - \cot x$

$= \frac{1}{\sin x} - \frac{\cos x}{\sin x}$ (cosecant and cotangent identities)

$= \frac{1 - \cos x}{\sin x}$ (Write as single fraction.)

$= \tan \frac{x}{2}$ (half-angle formula)

4. Find the general solution of $\cos x = \sin 2x$. $x = \frac{\pi}{2} + n\pi$ or $\frac{\pi}{6} + 2n\pi$ or $\frac{5\pi}{6} + 2n\pi$

Online Quiz

Available at **classzone.com**

Diagnosis/Remediation

- Practice A, B, C in Chapter 14 Resource Book, pp. 77–79
- Study Guide in Chapter 14 Resource Book, pp. 80–81
- Practice Workbook, pp. 205–206
- @HomeTutor

Challenge

Additional challenge is available in the Chapter 14 Resource Book, p. 84.

Quiz

An easily-readable reduced copy of the quiz (with answers) on Lessons 14.6–14.7 from the Assessment Book can be found on p. 906E.

55a. $y = -\frac{16}{(40)^2 \cos^2 \theta}(41.75)^2 + \tan \theta\,(41.75) + 6$

Quiz 7. See Additional Answers beginning on p. AA1.

55b. $y = -\frac{1743.0625}{100 \cos^2 \theta} + 41.75 \tan \theta + 6$; about 36.7° or about 58.8°

55. ★ **EXTENDED RESPONSE** At a basketball game, a person has a chance to win 1 million dollars by making a half court shot. The distance from half court to the point below the 10-foot-high basketball rim is 41.75 feet.

a. Write an equation that models the path of the basketball if the person releases the ball 6 feet high with an initial speed of 40 feet per second. **See margin.**

b. Simplify the equation. Use a calculator to find the angles at which the person can make the half court shot.

c. Assume the person releases the ball at one of the angles found in part (b). What other assumption(s) must you make to say that the shot is made? **The person is aiming at the rim and the ball follows the prescribed path.**

C 56. **CHALLENGE** A rectangle is inscribed in a semicircle with radius 1, as shown. What value of θ creates the rectangle with the largest area? **45°**

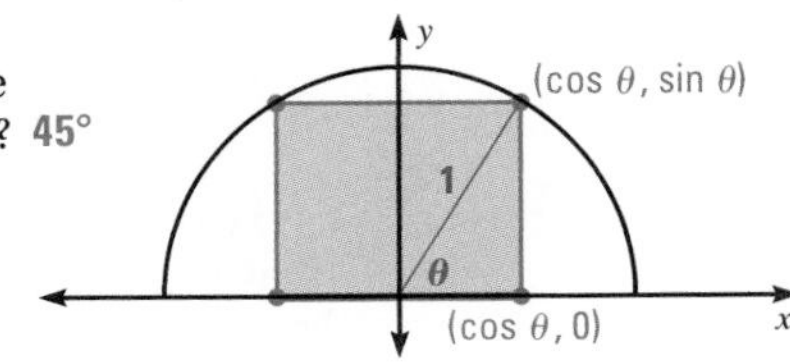

KENTUCKY MIXED REVIEW

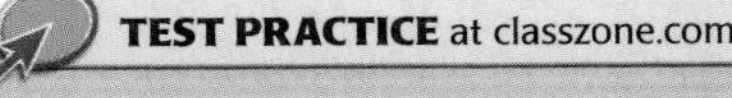

57. $\angle MNO$ and $\angle PQR$ are supplementary angles. Which of the following statements is true? **D**

Ⓐ $\angle MNO = \angle PQR$ Ⓑ $\angle MNO \perp \angle PQR$

Ⓒ $m\angle MNO + m\angle PQR = 90°$ Ⓓ $m\angle MNO + m\angle PQR = 180°$

58. What is the approximate length of arc MN? **B**

Ⓐ 30.5 ft Ⓑ 33.0 ft

Ⓒ 39.6 ft Ⓓ 55.0 ft

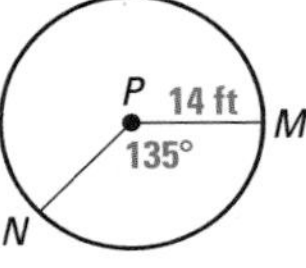

QUIZ for Lessons 14.6–14.7

Find the exact value of the expression. *(pp. 949, 955)*

1. $\sin \frac{\pi}{12}$ $\frac{\sqrt{2 - \sqrt{3}}}{2}$
2. $\sin(-22.5°)$ $-\frac{\sqrt{2 - \sqrt{2}}}{2}$
3. $\tan(-345°)$ $-\sqrt{3} + 2$
4. $\cos \frac{\pi}{8}$ $\frac{\sqrt{2 + \sqrt{2}}}{2}$

Solve the equation for $0 \le x < 2\pi$.

5. $\sin\left(x + \frac{\pi}{2}\right) - \sin\left(x - \frac{\pi}{2}\right) = 0$ *(p. 949)* $\frac{\pi}{2}, \frac{3\pi}{2}$
6. $\cos 2x = 3 \sin x + 2$ *(p. 955)* $\frac{7\pi}{6}, \frac{3\pi}{2}, \frac{11\pi}{6}$

Find the exact values of $\sin \frac{a}{2}$, $\cos \frac{a}{2}$, and $\tan 2a$. *(p. 955)*

7. $\tan a = \frac{3}{5}, 0 < a < \frac{\pi}{2}$ **See margin.**
8. $\cos a = -\frac{4}{7}, \pi < a < \frac{3\pi}{2}$ $\frac{\sqrt{154}}{14}, -\frac{\sqrt{42}}{14}, -\frac{8\sqrt{33}}{17}$

9. **FOOTBALL** Use the formula $x = \frac{1}{32}v^2 \sin 2\theta$ to find the horizontal distance x (in feet) that a football travels if it is kicked from ground level with an initial speed of 25 feet per second at an angle of 30°. *(p. 955)* **about 16.9 ft**

Lessons 14.5–14.7

1. **PHYSICAL SCIENCE** The force F (in pounds) on a person's back when he or she bends over at an angle of θ is given by

$$F = \frac{0.6W \sin(\theta + 90°)}{\sin 12°}$$

where W is the person's weight (in pounds). Which of the following is equivalent to the given formula?

A. $24.8W \sin \theta$ B. $20.6 \cos \theta$
C. $2.89 \sin \theta$ D. $2.89W \cos \theta$

2. **INDEX OF REFRACTION** The index of refraction n of a transparent material is the ratio of the speed of light in a vacuum to the speed of light in the material. The index of glass is 1.5. Triangular prisms are often used to measure the index of refraction based on the formula shown below. If the given prism is made of glass and $\alpha = 60°$, what is the approximate value of θ? (*Hint:* Write the formula for the index of refraction in terms of $\cot \frac{\theta}{2}$.)

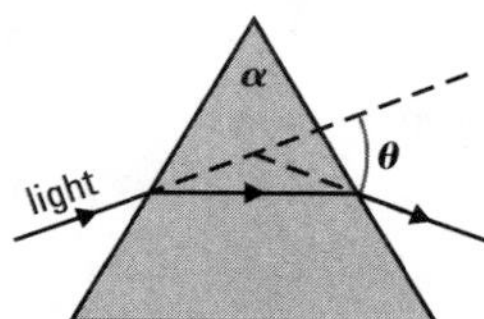

A. 38.3° B. 76.5°
C. 82.0° D. 126.7°

3. **EVALUATING EXPRESSIONS** What is the value of $\tan(a + b)$ given that $\sin a = \frac{3}{5}$ with $0 < a < \frac{\pi}{2}$ and $\cos b = \frac{\sqrt{2}}{2}$ with $0 < b < \frac{\pi}{2}$?

A. -1 B. $2\frac{1}{7}$
C. 3 D. 7

4. **AVERAGE TEMPERATURE** The graph below shows the average daily temperature T (in degrees Fahrenheit) in Denver, Colorado. The time t is measured in months, with $t = 0$ representing January 1. Use a trigonometric model to estimate the days of the year when the average daily temperature in Denver, Colorado, is 65°F.

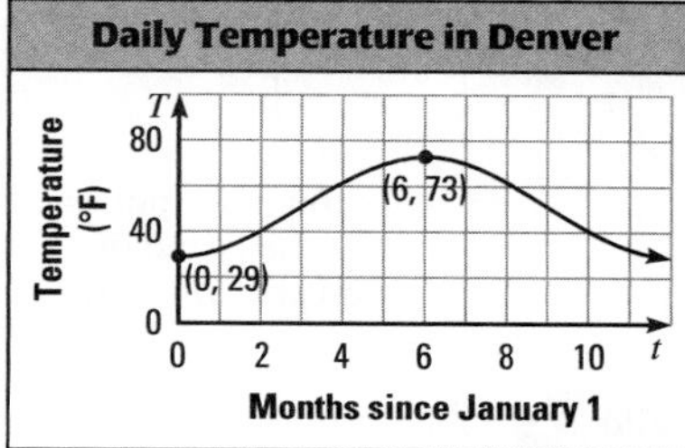

A. March 16 and August 15
B. March 25 and August 6
C. April 10 and July 21
D. April 27 and July 3

5. **OPEN-RESPONSE** In the figure shown below, the acute angle of intersection, $\theta_2 - \theta_1$, of two lines with slopes m_1 and m_2 is given by this equation:

$$\tan(\theta_2 - \theta_1) = \frac{m_2 - m_1}{1 + m_1 m_2}$$

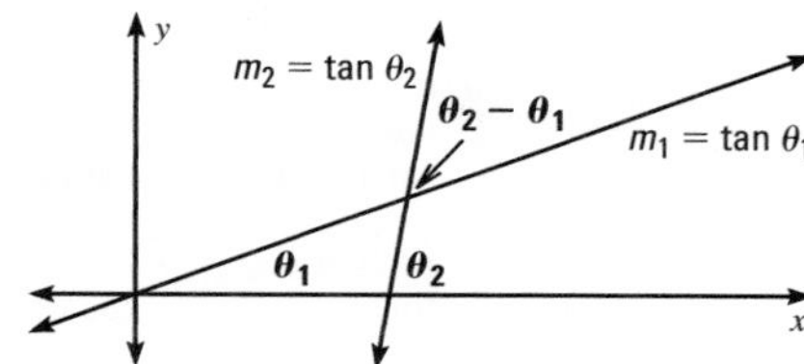

a. Find the acute angle of intersection of the lines $y = \frac{1}{2}x$ and $y = 2x - 4$. Round your answer to the nearest tenth of a degree.

b. *Explain* your reasoning.

Kentucky Mixed Review

1. D
2. B
3. D
4. C
5. a. 36.9°
b. *Sample answer*: The slopes of the lines are $\frac{1}{2}$ and 2. So the angle a between them is the solution to the equation below:

$$\tan(a) = \frac{2 - \frac{1}{2}}{1 + 2 \cdot \frac{1}{2}} = 0.75$$

Therefore, the angle a is arc tan (0.75) = 36.9°.

14 CHAPTER SUMMARY

Animated Algebra
classzone.com
Electronic Function Library

Additional Resources

The following resources are available to help review the materials in this chapter.

Chapter 14 Resource Book
- Chapter Review Games and Activities, p. 85
- Cumulative Practice, Chs. 1–14, pp. 87–88

Student Resources in Spanish

eWorkbook

@HomeTutor

Vocabulary Practice
Vocabulary practice is available at **classzone.com**

BIG IDEAS — For Your Notebook

Big Idea 1: Graphing Trigonometric Functions

The graphs of $y = a \sin bx$ and $y = a \cos bx$ are shown below for $a > 0$ and $b > 0$.

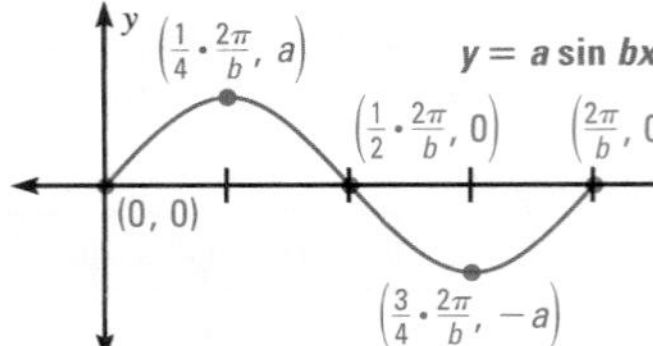

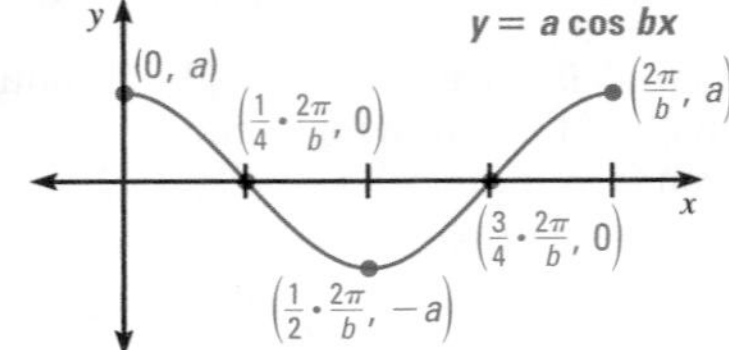

To graph a function of the form $y = a \sin b(x - h) + k$ or $y = a \cos b(x - h) + k$, shift the graph of $y = a \sin bx$ or $y = a \cos bx$, respectively, horizontally h units and vertically k units. Then, if $a < 0$, reflect the graph in the midline $y = k$.

Big Idea 2: Solving Trigonometric Equations

The table below shows strategies that may help you solve trigonometric equations. Only the first few steps are shown.

Factor	Use the quadratic formula	Use an identity
$x \sin^2 x - x = 0$	$\cos^2 x - 6 \cos x + 1 = 0$	$\cos^2 x - 1 = 9 \sin^2 x$
$x(\sin^2 x - 1) = 0$	$\cos x = \frac{6 \pm \sqrt{36 - 4(1)(1)}}{2(1)}$	$\cos^2 x - 1 = 9(1 - \cos^2 x)$
$x(\sin x + 1)(\sin x - 1) = 0$	$\cos x = 3 \pm 2\sqrt{2}$	$10 \cos^2 x = 10$
		$\cos^2 x = 1$

Big Idea 3: Applying Trigonometric Formulas

Use the formulas below to evaluate trigonometric functions of certain angles.

Sum formulas	$\sin(a + b) = \sin a \cos b + \cos a \sin b$ $\cos(a + b) = \cos a \cos b - \sin a \sin b$	$\tan(a + b) = \frac{\tan a + \tan b}{1 - \tan a \tan b}$
Difference formulas	$\sin(a - b) = \sin a \cos b - \cos a \sin b$ $\cos(a - b) = \cos a \cos b + \sin a \sin b$	$\tan(a - b) = \frac{\tan a - \tan b}{1 + \tan a \tan b}$
Double-angle formulas	$\cos 2a = \cos^2 a - \sin^2 a$ $\cos 2a = 2\cos^2 a - 1$ $\cos 2a = 1 - 2\sin^2 a$ $\sin 2a = 2 \sin a \cos a$	$\tan 2a = \frac{2 \tan a}{1 - \tan^2 a}$
Half-angle formulas	$\sin \frac{a}{2} = \pm\sqrt{\frac{1 - \cos a}{2}}$ $\cos \frac{a}{2} = \pm\sqrt{\frac{1 + \cos a}{2}}$	$\tan \frac{a}{2} = \frac{1 - \cos a}{\sin a}$ $\tan \frac{a}{2} = \frac{\sin a}{1 + \cos a}$

CHAPTER REVIEW

@HomeTutor
classzone.com
• Multi-Language Glossary
• Vocabulary practice

REVIEW KEY VOCABULARY

- amplitude, *p. 908*
- periodic function, *p. 908*
- cycle, *p. 908*
- period, *p. 908*
- frequency, *p. 910*
- trigonometric identity, *p. 924*
- sinusoid, *p. 941*

VOCABULARY EXERCISES

1. Copy and complete: Frequency gives the number of _?_ per unit of time. cycles

2. **WRITING** *Explain* how to find the period of $y = a \sin b(x - h) + k$. The period of sine is determined by the expression $\frac{2\pi}{b}$.

Determine whether the given number is the *amplitude, period,* or *frequency* of the graph of $y = \pi \cos \frac{\pi x}{2}$.

3. 4 period
4. π amplitude
5. 0.25 frequency

REVIEW EXAMPLES AND EXERCISES

Use the review examples and exercises below to check your understanding of the concepts you have learned in each lesson of Chapter 14.

14.1 Graph Sine, Cosine, and Tangent Functions

pp. 908–914

EXAMPLE

Graph (a) $y = \frac{1}{2} \cos 2x$ and (b) $y = 3 \tan \frac{x}{2}$.

a. Amplitude: $a = \frac{1}{2}$ **Period:** $\frac{2\pi}{2} = \pi$

Intercepts: $(0, 0); \left(\frac{\pi}{2}, 0\right); (\pi, 0)$

Maximum: $\left(\frac{\pi}{4}, \frac{1}{2}\right)$ **Minimum:** $\left(\frac{3\pi}{4}, -\frac{1}{2}\right)$

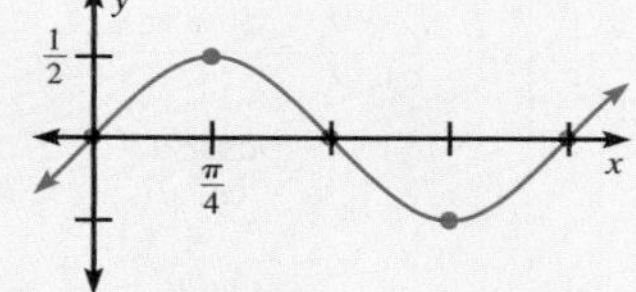

b. Period: $\frac{\pi}{\frac{1}{2}} = 2\pi$ **Intercept:** $(0, 0)$

Asymptotes: $x = -\pi; x = \pi$

Halfway points: $\left(-\frac{\pi}{2}, -3\right); \left(\frac{\pi}{2}, 3\right)$

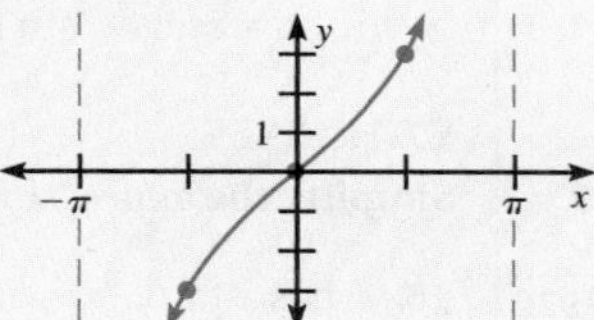

EXAMPLES 1, 2, and 4 on pp. 909–912 for Exs. 6–9

EXERCISES

Graph the function. 6–9. See margin.

6. $y = \sin 2x$
7. $f(x) = \frac{1}{2} \cos \frac{x}{2}$
8. $g(x) = 5 \sin \pi x$
9. $y = 2 \tan \frac{1}{3}x$

Extra Example 14.1

Graph (a) $y = \sin \pi x$ and (b) $y = 2 \tan \frac{3}{2}x$.

a.

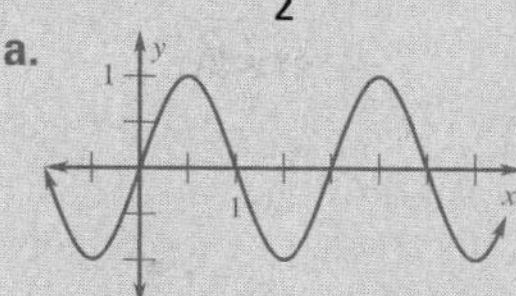

b.

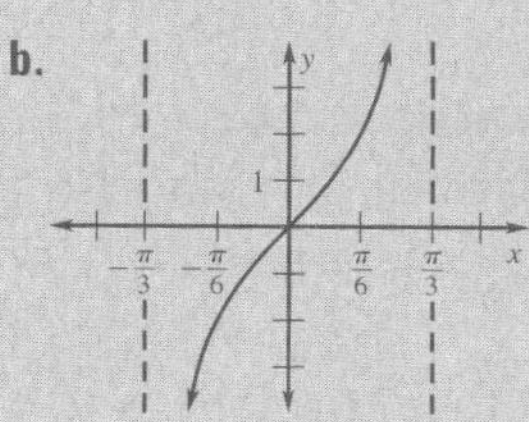

6.

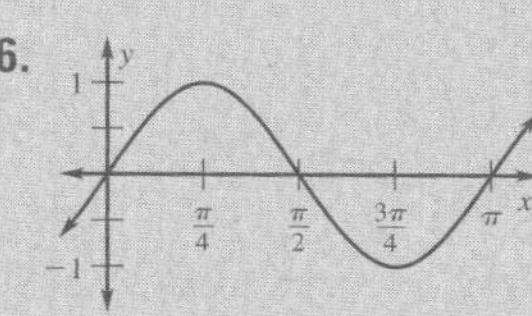

7.

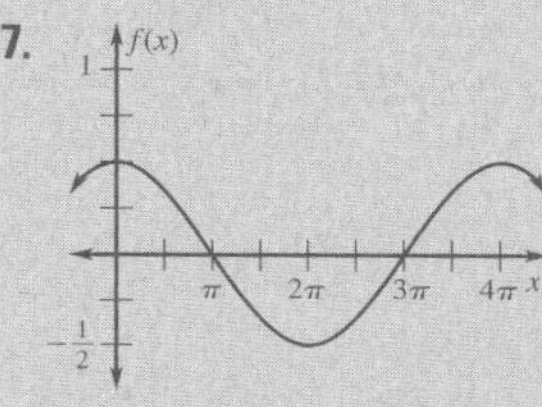

8.

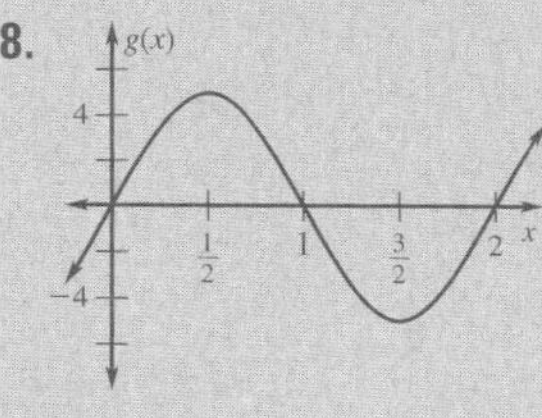

9.

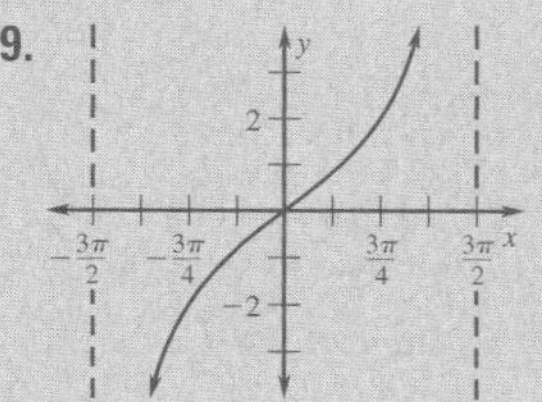

14 CHAPTER REVIEW

14.2 Translate and Reflect Trigonometric Graphs

pp. 915–922

EXAMPLE

Graph $y = 3\cos(x - \pi) - 1$.

To graph $y = 3\cos(x - \pi) - 1$, start with the graph of $y = 3\cos x$. Then, translate the graph right π units and down 1 unit.

Amplitude: $|3| = 3$ **Period:** 2π

Horizontal shift: π **Vertical shift:** -1

On $y = k$: $\left(\frac{3\pi}{2}, -1\right)$; $\left(\frac{5\pi}{2}, -1\right)$

Minimum: $(2\pi, -4)$

Maximums: $(\pi, 2)$; $(3\pi, 2)$

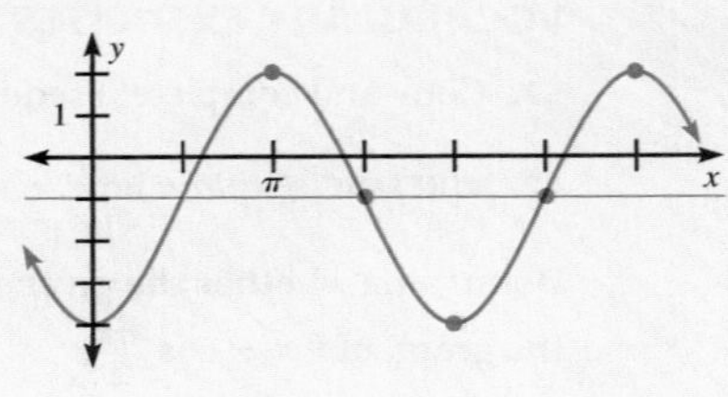

EXERCISES

EXAMPLES 1, 2, and 4 on pp. 915–917 for Exs. 10–15

Graph the function. 10–15. See margin.

10. $f(x) = \cos 2x + 4$ **11.** $y = \frac{1}{2}\sin 5(x - \pi)$ **12.** $y = 2\sin\left(x - \frac{\pi}{2}\right) + 3$

13. $y = 2\cos\frac{1}{3}x + 3$ **14.** $g(x) = -1 - 3\cos 4x$ **15.** $y = 4 - \sin 3\left(x - \frac{\pi}{3}\right)$

14.3 Verify Trigonometric Identities

pp. 924–930

EXAMPLE

Verify the identity $\frac{\cot^2\theta}{\csc\theta} = \csc\theta - \sin\theta$.

$\frac{\cot^2\theta}{\csc\theta} = \frac{\csc^2\theta - 1}{\csc\theta}$ **Pythagorean identity**

$= \frac{\csc^2\theta}{\csc\theta} - \frac{1}{\csc\theta}$ **Write as separate fractions.**

$= \csc\theta - \frac{1}{\csc\theta}$ **Simplify.**

$= \csc\theta - \sin\theta$ **Reciprocal identity**

EXERCISES

EXAMPLES 2, 3, 4, and 5 on pp. 925–926 for Exs. 16–20

Simplify the expression.

16. $-\cos x \tan(-x)$ $\sin x$ **17.** $\sec x \tan^2 x + \sec x$ $\sec^3 x$ **18.** $\sin\left(\frac{\pi}{2} - x\right)\tan x$ $\sin x$

Verify the identity. 19, 20. See margin.

19. $\frac{\sin^2(-x) - 1}{\cot^2 x} = -\sin^2 x$ **20.** $\tan\left(\frac{\pi}{2} - x\right)\cot x = \csc^2 x - 1$

Extra Example 14.2

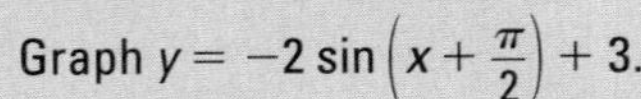
Graph $y = -2\sin\left(x + \frac{\pi}{2}\right) + 3$.

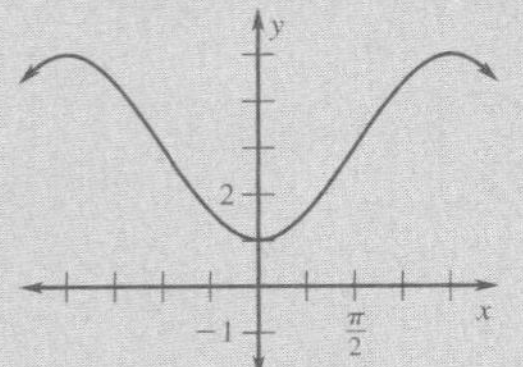

Extra Example 14.3

Verify the identity $\frac{1}{\sin\theta} - \sin\theta = \cos\theta\cot\theta$.

$\frac{1}{\sin\theta} - \sin\theta$

$= \frac{1 - \sin^2\theta}{\sin\theta}$ (Write as a single fraction.)

$= \frac{\cos^2\theta}{\sin\theta}$ (Pythagorean identity)

$= \frac{\cos\theta \cdot \cos\theta}{\sin\theta}$ (Write as multiplication.)

$= \cos\theta\cot\theta$ (cotangent identity)

10.

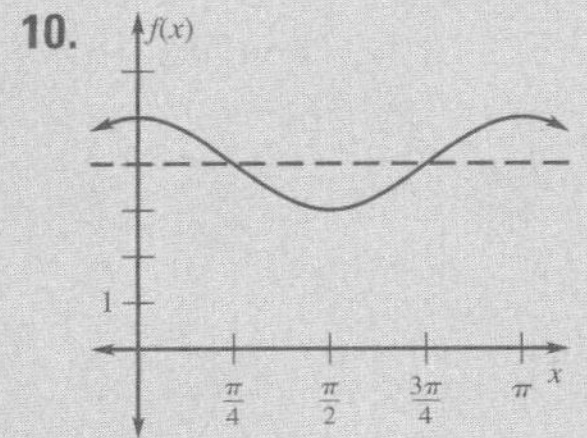

11.

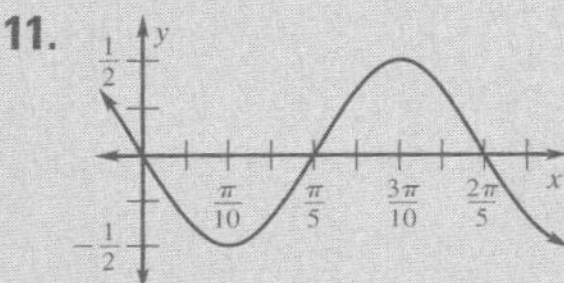

12.

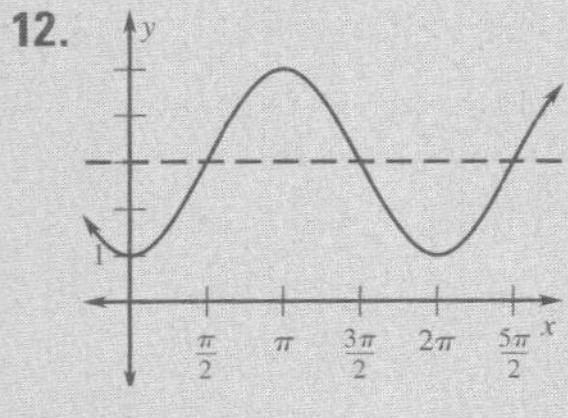

13.

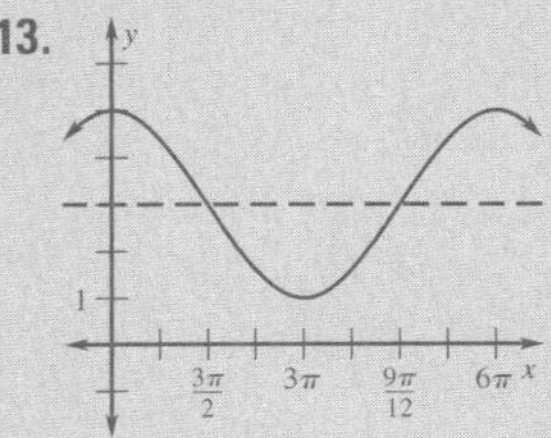

14.

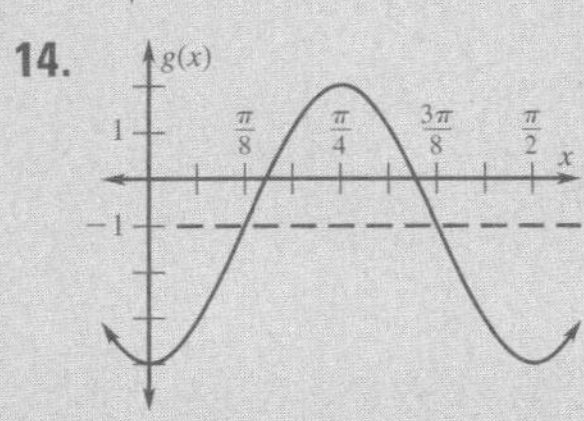

15.

19. $\frac{\sin^2(-x) - 1}{\cot^2 x} = \frac{-(1 - \sin^2 x)}{\frac{\cos^2 x}{\sin^2 x}} = \frac{-\cos^2 x}{\frac{\cos^2 x}{\sin^2 x}} = -\sin^2 x$

20. $\tan\left(\frac{\pi}{2} - x\right)\cot x = \cot x \cot x = \cot^2 x = \csc^2 x - 1$

@HomeTutor
classzone.com
Chapter Review Practice

14.4 Solve Trigonometric Equations

pp. 931–937

EXAMPLE

Solve $2\cos^2 x = 1$ in the interval $0 \le x < 2\pi$.

$2\cos^2 x = 1$ **Write original equation.**

$\cos^2 x = \frac{1}{2}$ **Divide each side by 2.**

$\cos x = \pm\frac{\sqrt{2}}{2}$ **Take square roots of each side.**

▸ In the interval $0 \le x < 2\pi$, the solutions are $x = \frac{\pi}{4}, \frac{3\pi}{4}, \frac{5\pi}{4}$, and $\frac{7\pi}{4}$.

EXAMPLES 1 and 4 on pp. 931–933 for Exs. 21–23

EXERCISES

Solve the equation in the interval $0 \le x < 2\pi$.

21. $-4\sin^2 x = -3$ $\frac{\pi}{3}, \frac{2\pi}{3}, \frac{4\pi}{3}, \frac{5\pi}{3}$ **22.** $\cos^2 x = \cos x$ $0, \frac{\pi}{2}, \frac{3\pi}{2}$ **23.** $\tan^2 4x = 3$ See margin.

14.5 Write Trigonometric Functions and Models

pp. 941–947

EXAMPLE

Write a function for the sinusoid.

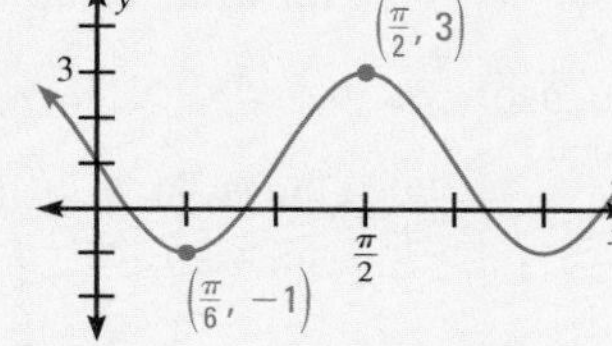

STEP 1 **Find** the maximum value M and minimum value m. From the graph, $M = 3$ and $m = -1$.

STEP 2 **Identify** the vertical shift, k.

$k = \frac{M + m}{2} = \frac{3 + (-1)}{2} = \frac{2}{2} = 1$

STEP 3 **Decide** whether the graph should be modeled by a sine or cosine function. Because the graph crosses the midline, $y = 1$, on the y-axis and then decreases to its minimum value, the graph is a sine curve with a reflection but no horizontal shift. So, $a < 0$ and $h = 0$.

STEP 4 **Find** the amplitude and period. The period is $\frac{2\pi}{3} = \frac{2\pi}{b}$. So, $b = 3$.

The amplitude is $|a| = \frac{M - m}{2} = \frac{3 - (-1)}{2} = \frac{4}{2} = 2$. So, $a = -2$.

A function for the sinusoid is $y = -2\sin 3x + 1$.

EXAMPLE 1 on p. 941 for Exs. 24–25

EXERCISES

Write a function for the sinusoid.

24.

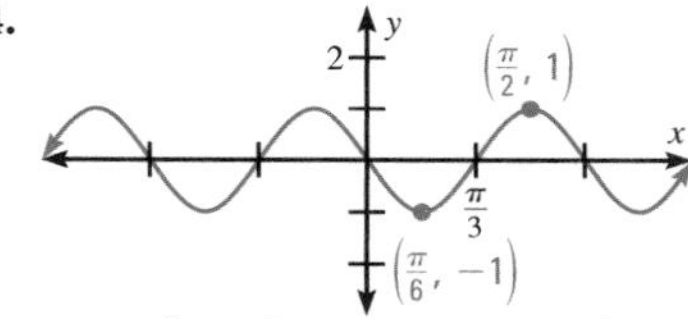

Sample answer: $y = -\sin 3x$

25.

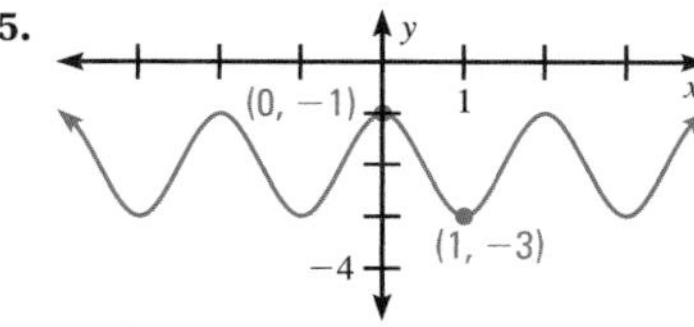

Sample answer: $y = \cos \pi x - 2$

Extra Example 14.4

Solve $\sin\theta\cos\theta = \cos\theta$ in the interval $0 \le x \le 2\pi$. $x = \frac{\pi}{2}$ and $\frac{3\pi}{2}$

Extra Example 14.5

Write a function for the sinusoid shown. $y = 3\cos\frac{x}{2} - 2$

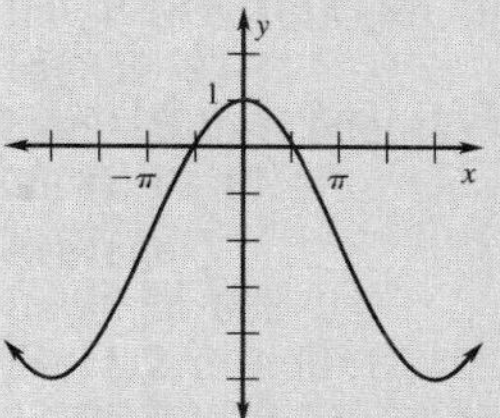

23. $\frac{\pi}{12}, \frac{\pi}{6}, \frac{\pi}{3}, \frac{5\pi}{12}, \frac{7\pi}{12}, \frac{2\pi}{3}, \frac{5\pi}{6}, \frac{11\pi}{12}, \frac{13\pi}{12}, \frac{7\pi}{6}, \frac{4\pi}{3}, \frac{17\pi}{12}, \frac{19\pi}{12}, \frac{5\pi}{3}, \frac{11\pi}{6}, \frac{23\pi}{12}$

Extra Example 14.6

Find the exact value of the expression.

a. $\cos \frac{\pi}{12}$ $\frac{\sqrt{2}+\sqrt{6}}{4}$

b. $\tan 225°$ 1

Extra Example 14.7

Find the exact value of the expression.

a. $\sin 165°$ $\frac{\sqrt{2-\sqrt{3}}}{2}$

b. $\tan \frac{4}{3}\pi$ $\sqrt{3}$

14 CHAPTER REVIEW

14.6 Apply Sum and Difference Formulas

pp. 949–954

EXAMPLE

Find the exact value of the expression.

a. $\cos 225° = \cos(270° - 45°)$ — **Substitute 270° − 45° for 225°.**

$= \cos 270° \cos 45° + \sin 270° \sin 45°$ — **Difference formula for cosine**

$= 0\left(\frac{\sqrt{2}}{2}\right) - 1\left(\frac{\sqrt{2}}{2}\right)$ — **Evaluate.**

$= -\frac{\sqrt{2}}{2}$ — **Simplify.**

b. $\sin \frac{7\pi}{12} = \sin\left(\frac{\pi}{3} + \frac{\pi}{4}\right)$ — **Substitute $\frac{\pi}{3} + \frac{\pi}{4}$ for $\frac{7\pi}{12}$.**

$= \sin \frac{\pi}{3} \cos \frac{\pi}{4} + \cos \frac{\pi}{3} \sin \frac{\pi}{4}$ — **Sum formula for sine**

$= \frac{\sqrt{3}}{2}\left(\frac{\sqrt{2}}{2}\right) + \frac{1}{2}\left(\frac{\sqrt{2}}{2}\right)$ — **Evaluate.**

$= \frac{\sqrt{6}+\sqrt{2}}{4}$ — **Simplify.**

EXERCISES

EXAMPLES 1 and 2 on pp. 949–950 for Exs. 26–30

Find the exact value of the expression.

26. $\cos 195°$ $\frac{-\sqrt{2}-\sqrt{6}}{4}$ **27.** $\tan 75°$ $2+\sqrt{3}$ **28.** $\sin \frac{13\pi}{12}$ $\frac{\sqrt{2}-\sqrt{6}}{4}$ **29.** $\cos \frac{5\pi}{6}$ $-\frac{\sqrt{3}}{2}$

30. Find $\cos(a - b)$, given that $\sin a = \frac{8}{17}$ with $\frac{\pi}{2} < a < \pi$ and $\cos b = \frac{1}{2}$ with $0 < b < \frac{\pi}{2}$. $\frac{-15+8\sqrt{3}}{34}$

14.7 Apply Double-Angle and Half-Angle Formulas

pp. 955–962

EXAMPLE

Find the exact value of the expression.

a. $\tan 135° = \tan \frac{1}{2}(270°) = \frac{1-\cos 270°}{\sin 270°} = \frac{1-0}{-1} = -1$

b. $\sin \frac{\pi}{12} = \sin \frac{1}{2}\left(\frac{\pi}{6}\right) = \sqrt{\frac{1-\cos\frac{\pi}{6}}{2}} = \sqrt{\frac{1-\frac{\sqrt{3}}{2}}{2}} = \frac{1}{2}\sqrt{2-\sqrt{3}}$

EXERCISES

EXAMPLES 1 and 2 on pp. 955–956 for Exs. 31–35

Find the exact value of the expression.

31. $\sin 75°$ $\frac{\sqrt{2+\sqrt{3}}}{2}$ **32.** $\tan(-15°)$ $-2+\sqrt{3}$ **33.** $\cos \frac{\pi}{12}$ $\frac{\sqrt{2+\sqrt{3}}}{2}$ **34.** $\cos \frac{3\pi}{4}$ $-\frac{\sqrt{2}}{2}$

35. Given $\cos a = \frac{1}{2}$ with $0 < a < \frac{\pi}{2}$, find $\sin 2a$ and $\tan \frac{a}{2}$. $\frac{\sqrt{3}}{2}, \frac{\sqrt{3}}{3}$

14 CHAPTER TEST

Graph the function. 1–6. See margin.

1. $f(x) = 4 \cos 2x$
2. $y = \frac{3}{2} \sin \pi x$
3. $f(x) = -4 \tan \frac{\pi}{2}x$
4. $y = \sin (x - \pi) - 2$
5. $f(x) = 3 \tan \left(x - \frac{\pi}{2}\right)$
6. $y = -2 \cos \frac{1}{3}x + 3$

Simplify the expression.

7. $\frac{\sin (-\theta)}{\tan (-\theta)}$ **$\cos \theta$**
8. $\cos^2 x + \sin^2 x - \csc^2 x$ **$-\cot^2 x$**
9. $\frac{\sin \left(\frac{\pi}{2} - x\right)}{\sec x}$ **$\cos^2 x$**

Write a function for the sinusoid.

10.

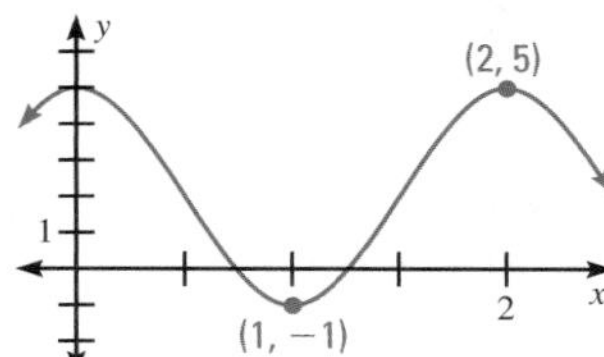

Sample answer: $y = 3 \cos \pi x + 2$

11.

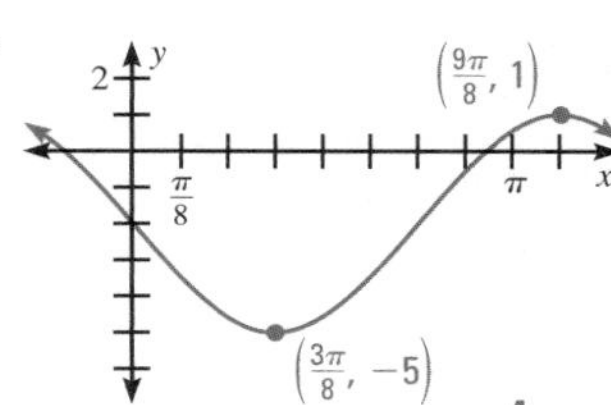

Sample answer: $y = -3 \sin \frac{4}{3}x - 2$

12. Verify the identity $\cos 3x = 4 \cos^3 x - 3 \cos x$. See margin.

Solve the equation in the interval $0 \le x < 2\pi$.

13. $9 \sin^2 x \tan x = 16 \tan x$ **$0, \pi$**
14. $(1 - \tan^2 x) \tan 2x = 2\sqrt{3}$ **$\frac{\pi}{3}, \frac{4\pi}{3}$**
15. $\sin \frac{x}{2} = \frac{\sqrt{2}}{2}$ **$\frac{\pi}{2}, \frac{3\pi}{2}$**

Find the general solution of the equation.

16. $6 \tan^2 x - 2 = 0$ **$\frac{\pi}{6} + n\pi, \frac{5\pi}{6} + n\pi$**
17. $\cos x = \sin 2x \sin x$ **$\frac{\pi}{4} + n\pi$ or $\frac{\pi}{2} + n\pi$ or $\frac{3\pi}{4} + n\pi$**
18. $\sin \frac{x}{2} = 1 - \cos x$ **$\frac{\pi}{3} + 2n\pi$ or $\frac{5\pi}{3} + 2n\pi$**

Find the exact value of the expression.

19. $\sin 255°$ **$-\frac{\sqrt{2 + \sqrt{3}}}{2}$**
20. $\cos \left(-\frac{\pi}{8}\right)$ **$\frac{\sqrt{2 + \sqrt{2}}}{2}$**
21. $\tan \frac{5\pi}{12}$ **$2 + \sqrt{3}$**
22. $\sin \frac{10\pi}{3}$ **$-\frac{\sqrt{3}}{2}$**

23. **BOATING** The paddle wheel of a ship is 11 feet in diameter, revolves 15 times per minute when moving at top speed, and is 2 feet below the water's surface at its lowest point. Using this speed and starting from a point at the very top of the wheel, write a model for the height h (in feet) of the end of the paddle relative to the water's surface as a function of time t (in minutes). *Sample answer:* $y = 5.5 \cos (30\pi t) + 3.5$

24. **PRECIPITATION** The table below shows the monthly precipitation P (in inches) in Bismarck, North Dakota. The time t is measured in months, with $t = 1$ representing January. Use a graphing calculator to write a sinusoidal model that gives P as a function of t. $P = 1.08 \sin (0.585t - 2.33) + 1.53$

t	1	2	3	4	5	6	7	8	9	10	11	12
P	0.5	0.5	0.9	1.5	2.2	2.6	2.6	2.2	1.6	1.3	0.7	0.4

1. [graph]

2.

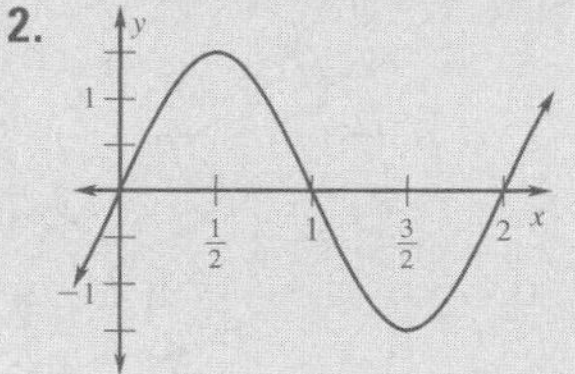

3.

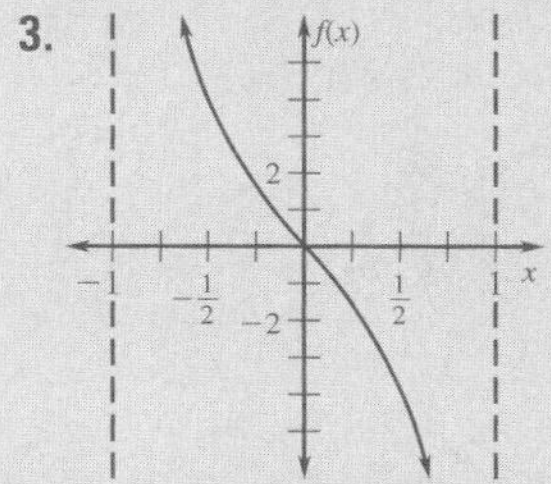

Additional Resources

Assessment Book

- Chapter Test, Levels A, B, C, pp. 200–205
- Standardized Chapter Test, pp. 206–207
- SAT/ACT Chapter Test, pp. 208–209
- Alternative Assessment, pp. 210–211

Test Generator CD-ROM

Chapter Test

Easily-readable reduced copies (with answers) of Chapter Test B, the Standardized Chapter Test, and the Alternative Assessment from the Assessment Book can be found on pp. 906E–906F.

4.

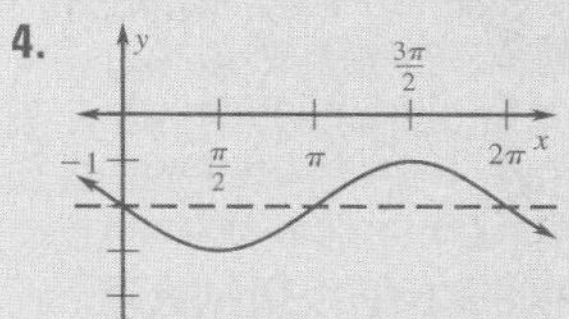

5.

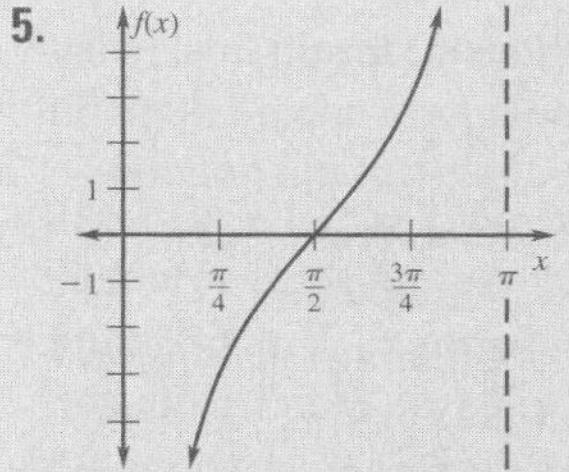

6.

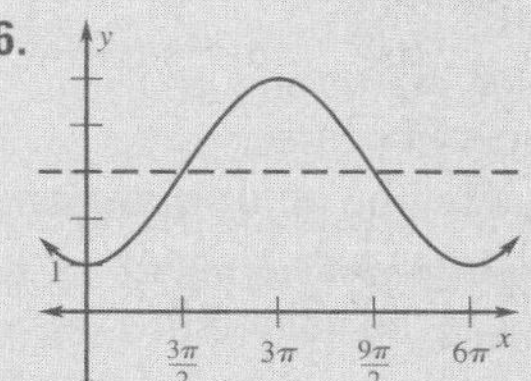

12. $\cos 3x = \cos (2x + x)$
$= \cos 2x \cos x - \sin 2x \sin x$
$= (2 \cos^2 x - 1)(\cos x) - (2 \sin x \cos x) \sin x$
$= 2 \cos^3 x - \cos x - 2 \sin^2 x \cos x$
$= 2 \cos^3 x - \cos x - 2(1 - \cos^2 x)\cos x$
$= 2 \cos^3 x - \cos x - 2 \cos x + 2 \cos^3 x$
$= 4 \cos^3 x - 3 \cos x$

Kentucky General Scoring Rubric

4 Points (Full credit)
- You complete all important components of the question and communicate ideas clearly.
- You demonstrate in-depth understanding of the relevant concepts and/or processes.
- Where appropriate, you choose more efficient and/or sophisticated processes.
- Where appropriate, you offer insightful interpretations or extensions (generalizations, applications, analogies).

3 Points (Full or Partial Credit)
- You complete most important components of the question and communicate clearly.
- You demonstrate an understanding of major concepts even though you overlook or misunderstand some less-important ideas or details.

2 Points (Partial Credit)
- You complete some important components of the question and communicate those components clearly.
- You demonstrate that there are gaps in your conceptual understanding.

1 Point (Partial Credit)
- You show minimal understanding of the question.
- You address only a small portion of the question.

0 Points (No Credit)
- Your answer is totally incorrect or irrelevant.

BLANK (No Credit)
- You did not give any answer at all.

TEST PREPARATION

Scoring Rubric

Full Credit
- solution is complete and correct

Partial Credit
- solution is complete but has errors,

or
- solution is without error but incomplete

No Credit
- no solution is given,

or
- solution makes no sense

OPEN-RESPONSE QUESTIONS

PROBLEM

The horizontal distance x (in feet) traveled by a football kicked from ground level at speed v and angle θ can be modeled by $x = \frac{1}{32}v^2 \sin 2\theta$.

a. Write an expression for half of the horizontal distance. How is this expression related to the football's maximum height?

b. Write a simplified expression for the football's maximum height.

c. What is the maximum height of a football kicked from ground level with a speed of 80 feet per second and an angle of 35°?

Below are sample solutions to the problem. Read each solution and the comments on the left to see why the sample represents *full credit, partial credit,* or *no credit.*

SAMPLE 1: Full credit solution

The expression is correct, and its significance is fully explained.

a. Half of the horizontal distance $= \frac{1}{2} \cdot \frac{1}{32}v^2 \sin 2\theta = \frac{1}{64}v^2 \sin 2\theta$

Because the ball travels in a parabolic path, the maximum height occurs at half the horizontal distance.

The correct formula is used for the path of a projectile.

b. Substitute the expression from part (a) for x in the equation for the path of a projectile. Note that the initial height h_0 is 0.

$$y = -\frac{16}{v^2 \cos^2 \theta}x^2 + (\tan \theta)x + h_0$$

$$y = -\frac{16}{v^2 \cos^2 \theta}\left(\frac{1}{64}v^2 \sin 2\theta\right)^2 + (\tan \theta)\left(\frac{1}{64}v^2 \sin 2\theta\right) + 0$$

$$= -\frac{v^2 (\sin 2\theta)(\sin 2\theta)}{256 \cos^2 \theta} + \frac{(v^2 \sin 2\theta)\tan \theta}{64}$$

A double-angle formula is used correctly, and the resulting expression is correctly simplified.

$$= -\frac{v^2(2 \sin \theta \cos \theta)(2 \sin \theta \cos \theta)}{256 \cos \theta \cos \theta} + \frac{v^2(2 \sin \theta)(\cos \theta \tan \theta)}{64}$$

$$= -\frac{\overset{1}{v^2} (2 \sin \theta \cos \theta)(2 \sin \theta \cos \theta)}{\underset{64}{256} \cos \theta \cos \theta} + \frac{v^2 (2 \sin \theta)(\sin \theta)}{64}$$

$$= -\frac{v^2 \sin^2 \theta}{64} + \frac{2v^2 \sin^2 \theta}{64}$$

$$= \frac{1}{64}v^2 \sin^2 \theta$$

c. To find the maximum height of the ball, substitute 80 for v and 35° for θ.

The answer is correct.

Maximum height $= \frac{1}{64}v^2 \sin^2 \boldsymbol{\theta} = \frac{1}{64} \cdot \mathbf{80}^2 \sin^2 \mathbf{35°} \approx 33$ feet answer is correct, but k is not shown and explanation is given.

expression is not simplified.

answer is correct.

SAMPLE 2: Partial credit solution

a. $\frac{1}{64}v^2 \sin 2\theta$

b. $y = -\frac{16}{v^2 \cos^2 \theta}x^2 + (\tan \theta)x + h_0$

$= -\frac{16}{v^2 \cos^2 \theta}\left(\frac{1}{64}v^2 \sin 2\theta\right)^2 + (\tan \theta)\left(\frac{1}{64}v^2 \sin 2\theta\right) + 0$

$= -\frac{16}{v^2 \cos^2 \theta}\left(\frac{1}{4096}v^4 \sin^2 2\theta\right) + (\tan \theta)\left(\frac{1}{64}v^2 \sin 2\theta\right)$

$= -\frac{v^2 \sin^2 2\theta}{256 \cos^2 \theta} + \frac{v^2 \tan \theta \sin 2\theta}{64}$

c. The maximum height of the football is:

$-\frac{v^2 \sin^2 2\theta}{256 \cos^2 \theta} + \frac{v^2 \tan \theta \sin 2\theta}{64} = -\frac{80^2 \sin^2 70°}{256 \cos^2 35°} + \frac{80^2 \tan 35° \sin 70°}{64} \approx 33$ feet

expressions in parts d b are incorrect, no work is shown.

values are stituted incorrectly. answer is wrong.

SAMPLE 3: No credit solution

a. $x = \frac{1}{64}v^2 \sin \theta$

b. The maximum height is given by $\frac{1}{64}v^2 \sin \theta$.

c. $x = \frac{1}{64}v^2 \sin \theta = \frac{1}{64} \cdot 35^2 \sin 80° \approx 19$ feet

The maximum height is about 19 feet.

PRACTICE Apply the Scoring Rubric

Score the following solution to the problem on the previous page as *full credit, partial credit,* or *no credit. Explain* your reasoning. If you choose *partial credit* or *no credit,* explain how you would change the solution so that it earns a score of full credit.

a. Half of the total horizontal distance is $\frac{1}{64}v^2 \sin 2\theta$. This is the horizontal distance when the ball is at its maximum height.

b. A simplified expression for the maximum height of the ball is $\frac{1}{64}v^2 \sin^2 \theta$.

c. Substitute 80 for v and 35° for θ in the expression from part (b) to find the maximum height of the football.

$\frac{1}{64}v^2 \sin^2 \theta = \frac{1}{64} \cdot 80^2 \sin^2 35° \approx \frac{1}{64} \cdot 6400(0.574)^2 \approx 33$ feet

TEST PREPARATION

Kentucky Test Preparation

Partial credit; the answer is correct, no work is shown for part (b), but part (c) is explained correctly and the answer is correct; the steps need to be shown as to how the student came up with the simplified equation in part (b).

OPEN-RESPONSE

1. Sound travels in waves that can be represented using sine functions. When two notes are played at the same time on a musical instrument, the resulting sound wave can be modeled by the sum of two sound waves.

a. Playing C and G together creates harmony and produces a pleasant sound. Use a graphing calculator to graph the sound wave that results from playing C and G at the same time.

b. Playing C and B together creates dissonance and produces an unpleasant sound. Use a graphing calculator to graph the sound wave that results from playing B and C at the same time.

Note	Sound wave
C	$y = \sin 523.26t$
G	$y = \sin 784t$
B	$y = \sin 987.76t$

c. Make a conjecture about the relationship between how the notes sound when played together and the resulting sound wave. *Explain* your reasoning.

2. The blades of a fan rotate counterclockwise at a speed of 800 rotations per minute. The length of each blade is 9 inches. The maximum height of the tip of a fan blade above the ground is 48 inches.

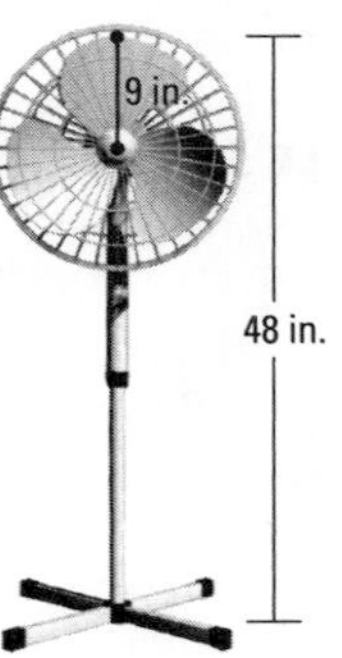

a. What is the minimum height of the tip of a fan blade above the ground?

b. Write a function that models the height of the tip of the highest fan blade as a function of time. Assume that the blade starts in the position shown in the diagram.

c. Do your answers to parts (a) and (b) change if the fan rotates clockwise? *Explain* why or why not.

3. The chart shows the average monthly temperature (in degrees Fahrenheit) and a household's gas usage (in cubic feet) for 12 months.

a. Use the chart to make a table of values giving the month t (with January corresponding to $t = 0$), the average monthly temperature y_1, and the gas usage y_2 (in thousands of cubic feet).

b. Use the table from part (a) and a graphing calculator to find trigonometric models for the average monthly temperature y_1 as a function of time and the gas usage y_2 as a function of time.

c. Graph the two regression equations on your graphing calculator. *Describe* the relationship between the temperature and gas usage trend.

January	February	March	April
32°F 20,000 ft^3	21°F 27,000 ft^3	15°F 23,000 ft^3	22°F 22,000 ft^3
May	**June**	**July**	**August**
35°F 21,000 ft^3	49°F 14,000 ft^3	62°F 8,000 ft^3	78°F 9,000 ft^3
September	**October**	**November**	**December**
71°F 13,000 ft^3	63°F 15,000 ft^3	55°F 19,000 ft^3	40°F 23,000 ft^3

TEST PREPARATION

Kentucky Test Practice

1. a.

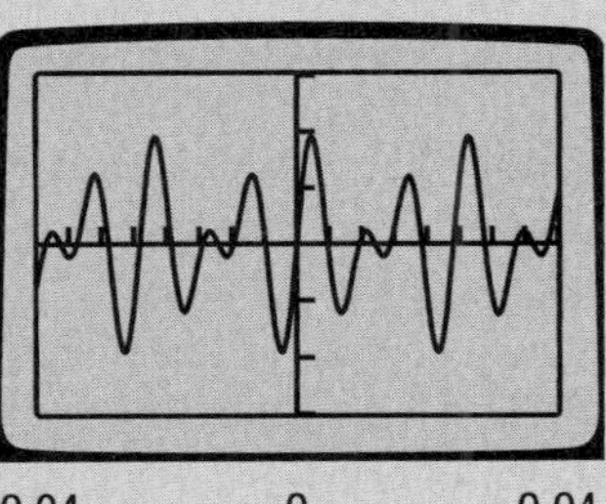

b.

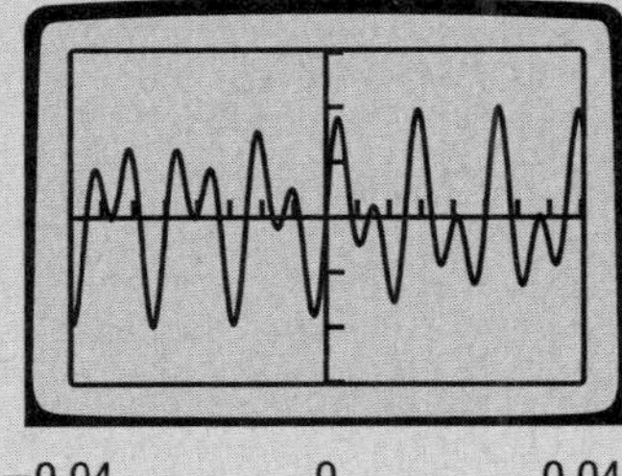

c. When two notes that produce a pleasant sound are played together, the resulting graph has a shorter repeating pattern than the resulting graph of two notes that produce a dissonant sound.

2. a. 30 inches

b. $y = 9 \cos 1600\pi t + 39$

c. No; the height of the tip of the fan blade does not change based on the direction of the rotation of the fan.

3. a.

T	0	1	2	3	4	5	6	7	8	9	10	11
y_1	32	21	15	22	35	49	62	78	71	63	55	40
y_2	20	27	23	22	21	14	8	9	13	15	19	23

b. Temperature:

$y_1 = 28.5 \sin(0.547x - 2.61) + 45.7$

Gas:

$y_2 = 7.89 \sin(0.610x + 0.519) + 17.1$

c. The trend is that when the temperature rises, the gas usage falls.

OPEN-RESPONSE

4. A basketball is dropped from a height of 15 feet.
   a. Can the height of the basketball over time be modeled by a trigonometric function?
   b. If so, write the function. If not, explain why not.

5. Consider the following function:

$$f(x) = \sin x \cos x$$

   a. Without graphing the function, what would you expect the graph to look like? *Explain* your reasoning.
   b. Copy and complete the table below and determine whether your prediction was correct.

x	$-\pi$	$-\frac{3\pi}{4}$	$-\frac{\pi}{2}$	$-\frac{\pi}{4}$	0	$\frac{\pi}{4}$	$\frac{\pi}{2}$	$\frac{3\pi}{4}$	π
$f(x)$	?	?	?	?	?	?	?	?	?

MULTIPLE-CHOICE

6. The graph of which function is shown?

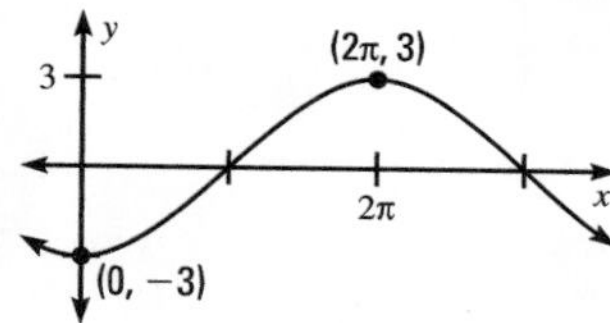

   A. $y = -3 \cos 2x$ B. $y = -2 \cos 3x$
   C. $y = -\frac{1}{2} \cos 3x$ D. $y = -3 \cos \frac{1}{2}x$

7. Which expression is *not* equivalent to 1?

   A. $\tan x \sec x \cos x$ B. $\sin^2 x + \cos^2 x$
   C. $\frac{\cos^2(-x) \tan^2 x}{\sin^2(-x)}$ D. $\cos\left(\frac{\pi}{2} - x\right) \csc x$

8. What is the general solution of the equation $\cos^3 x = 25 \cos x$?

   A. $\frac{\pi}{2} + 2n\pi$ B. $\frac{3\pi}{2} + 2n\pi$
   C. $\frac{\pi}{2} + n\pi$ D. $\frac{\pi}{4} + 2n\pi$

9. What is the x-intercept of the graph of $y = \sin \frac{1}{2}\pi x$ on the interval $0 < x < 3$?

   A. $\frac{1}{2}$ B. 1
   C. 2 D. 0

10. Find the y-coordinate of the point of intersection of the graphs of $y = 2 + \sin x$ and $y = 3 - \sin x$ in the interval $0 < x < \frac{\pi}{2}$.

   A. $\frac{\pi}{6}$ B. $\frac{1}{2}$
   C. $2\frac{1}{2}$ D. $\frac{\pi}{3}$

11. Find the amplitude of the sinusoid shown below.

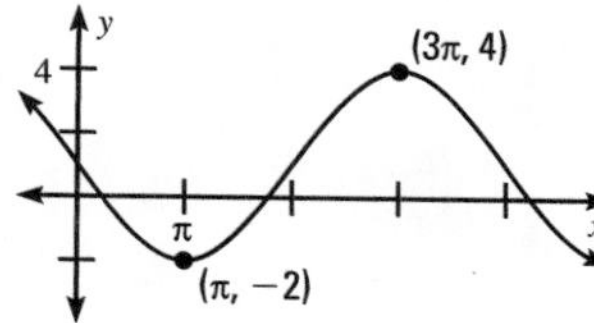

   A. −2 B. 2 C. 3 D. 4

TEST PREPARATION

4. a. No
b. As the ball bounces it does not return to its original height. The amplitude changes as does the timing of each bounce. Therefore the ball's height cannot be modeled by the cosine function.
5. a. *Sample answer*: The graph should look like $y = 0.5 \sin 2x$ because of the identity $\sin 2x = 2 \sin x \cos x$.
b. 0, 0.5, 0, −0.5, 0, 0.5, 0, −0.5, 0.
6. D
7. A
8. C
9. C
10. C
11. C

ADDITIONAL LESSONS

ALGEBRA 2

The additional lessons have been written to ensure complete state standard coverage. These lessons provide content addressing material to encompass individual state needs. They are offered to help teach all of the standards or to provide enrichment and challenge opportunities.

ADDITIONAL LESSONS

Essential Question:
Why is it important for you to know both the U.S. Customary system and the metric measuring system? *Sample answer:* Traveling to a different country; buying a product made in another country.

Key Question for Ex. 1:
Does it matter which measuring system you use? Explain your reasoning. No; it depends on what you are measuring and what measuring tools you have access to.

Extra Example 1:
Choose an appropriate customary unit and metric unit for the measurement. Explain your reasoning.

a. **Height of a building in New York City** feet, yards, or meters; The height of a building in New York City is much greater than either one inch or one centimeter and is also much less than either one mile or one kilometer.

b. **Weight or mass of a textbook** pounds or kilograms; The weight or mass of a textbook is much greater than either one ounce or one gram and is also much less than either one ton or one metric ton.

c. **Capacity of a swimming pool** gallons or kiloliters; The capacity of a swimming pool is much greater than either one cup or one liter.

Common Problem:
Students might incorrectly multiply or divide when converting units of measure. The use of ratios for the conversion might make this clearer.

Ratios used to solve Example 2:

a. $3400\ \text{mg} \times \frac{1\ \text{g}}{1000\ \text{mg}} = 3.4\ \text{g}$

Divide because 1000 is in the denominator.

b. $3.5\ \text{lb} \times \frac{16\ \text{oz}}{1\ \text{lb}} = 56\ \text{oz}$

Multiply because 16 is in the numerator.

Closing Question:
Which measuring system do you prefer? Explain your reasoning. Answers will vary.

Additional Lesson A Measurement

Use after Chapter 1

Key Vocabulary
- **metric system**
- **U.S. Customary system**

MA-HS-M-S-SM3 **Students will make decisions about units and scales that are appropriate for problem solving situations involving measurement.**

MA-HS-M-S-SM5 **Students will compare and contrast the use of U.S. Customary and metric systems of measurement.**

MEASUREMENT SYSTEMS Recall from previous courses that the **metric system** is a decimal system of measurement. It contains units of measurement for length, mass, and capacity. The **U.S. Customary system** is the system used in the United States. It contains units of measurement for length, weight, and capacity. Review metric units and U.S. Customary units on page 1025.

EXAMPLE 1 Choose appropriate units of measurement

Choose an appropriate customary unit and metric unit for the measurement. Explain your reasoning.

a. Distance from Boston to Cleveland

b. Weight or mass of a dog

c. Capacity of an eyedropper

Solution

a. The distance from Boston to Cleveland is much greater than either one yard or one meter. So, use miles or kilometers.

b. The weight or mass of a dog is much greater than either one ounce or one gram. The weight or mass is also much less than either one ton or one metric ton. So, use pounds or kilograms.

c. The capacity of an eyedropper is much less than either one cup or one liter. So, use fluid ounces or milliliters.

EXAMPLE 2 Convert units

Copy and complete the statement.

a. 3400 mg = __?__ g **b.** 3.5 lb = __?__ oz

Solution

a. To convert from milligrams to grams, divide by 1000.

$3400 \div 1000 = 3.4$, so $3400\ \text{mg} = 3.4\ \text{g}$.

b. To convert from pounds to ounces, multiply by 16.

$3.5 \times 16 = 56$, so $3.5\ \text{lb} = 56\ \text{oz}$.

CONVERSIONS Conversions in the metric system are based on powers of 10, as shown in Example 2. Conversions in the U.S. Customary system are based on relationships between units that typically do not involve powers of 10. This difference creates a wider use of fractions in the U.S. Customary system than in the metric system.

EXAMPLE 3 Units in real life

COOKING A recipe calls for $2\frac{3}{4}$ cups (or about 650 milliliters) of water. You want to divide the recipe in half. Is one unit of measurement easier to use than the other? Explain.

Solution

Find the number of cups and milliliters of water needed.

Cups	Milliliters
$2\frac{3}{4} \div 2 = \frac{11}{4} \times \frac{1}{2} = \frac{11}{8} = 1\frac{3}{8}$	$650 \div 2 = 325$

The arithmetic with milliliters is simple, and it may be more convenient to measure 325 milliliters rather than $1\frac{3}{8}$ cups. So, it may be easier to use milliliters. However, note that $1\frac{3}{8}$ cups $\approx$ 325 milliliters, so either unit of measurement can be used.

PRACTICE

Choose an appropriate customary unit and metric unit for the measurement. Explain your reasoning.

EXAMPLE 1 for Exs. 1–4

1. Distance from a bird nest to the ground
2. Weight or mass of Mars
3. Length of a pencil
4. Capacity of a bathtub

Copy and complete the statement.

EXAMPLE 2 for Exs. 5–10

5. 6.2 kg = _?_ g
6. 13 yd = _?_ ft
7. 5250 lb = _?_ ton
8. 10 kL = _?_ L
9. 1.4 mm = _?_ m
10. 52 c = _?_ gal

EXAMPLE 3 for Ex. 11

11. **CONSTRUCTION** The instructions for building a bird house call for sawing a 2-meter (or about 6.5-foot) board into four pieces. Is either unit of measurement easier to use than the other? Explain.

Answers to Additional Lessons

1. **feet, yards, meters; The distance from a bird nest to the ground is much greater than either one inch or one centimeter and is much less than either one mile or one kilometer.**
2. **tons, metric tons; The weight or mass of Mars is much greater than either one pound or one kilogram.**
3. **inches, centimeters; The length of a pencil is less than either one foot or one meter.**
4. **gallons, liters; The capacity of a bathtub is much greater than either one cup or one milliliter and is less than one kiloliter.**
5. **6200 g**
6. **39 ft**
7. **2.625 ton**
8. **10,000 L**
9. **0.0014 m**
10. **3.25 gal**
11. **2-meter; The arithmetic with meters is simple, and it may be more convenient to measure $\frac{1}{2}$ meter rather than 3.25 feet.**

Essential Question:

Why is it important to know more than one coordinate system? Sometimes you do not know the horizontal and vertical distances, but you know a distance and an angle. For example, a kite is flying on 100 feet of string and at an angle of 65° to the ground.

Key Question for Ex. 3:

Why is there a need for latitude and longitude? Latitude and longitude are needed to locate points in the world in a consistent manner.

Extra Example 3:

Other examples for the use of a navigational system are using a compass and giving directions. For navigation, the coordinate plane is called a left-handed system. North is 0° at the top and you move in a clockwise direction as shown in the figure. Give directions for walking from *A* to *B*.

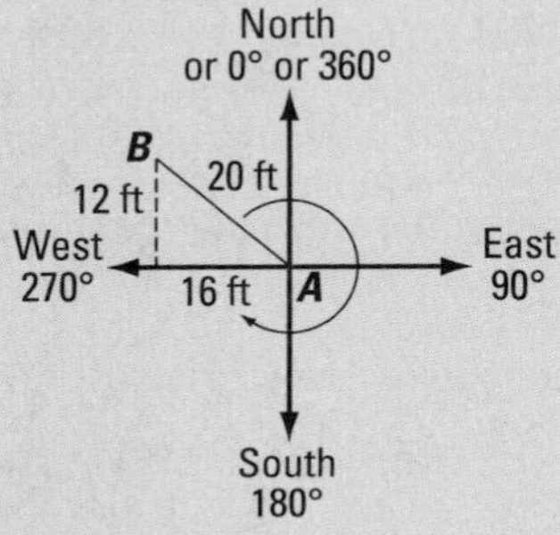

Sample answers:
1. Walk west 16 feet, then north 12 feet.
2. Walk 20 feet northwest of *A*.
3. Walk 20 feet at 307°.

Common Problem:

Once students see that they can move clockwise as in the navigational system in Extra Example 3, they may mistakenly move clockwise in the polar coordinate system.

Closing Question:

What would be the spherical coordinates for Guatemala City? Guatemala City is 90° west (of the prime meridian) and 15° north of the equator (75° down from the North Pole). Assume the radius of the Earth is 4000 miles. So, its spherical coordinates would be (4000, –90°, 75°).

Additional Lesson B Other Coordinate Systems

Use after Chapter 1

MA-HS-G-S-CG6 Students will use Cartesian coordinates and **other coordinate systems (e.g., navigational, polar, spherical systems) to analyze geometric situations.**

Key Vocabulary
- **polar coordinate system**
- **polar axis**
- **polar coordinates**
- **spherical coordinate system**

POLAR COORDINATE SYSTEM You are familiar with representing graphs of equations as collections of points (x, y) on the two-dimensional rectangular coordinate system.

Now you will study a coordinate system called the **polar coordinate system**. To form the polar coordinate system in the coordinate plane, fix a point O, called the pole (or origin), and construct from O an initial ray called the **polar axis** as shown to the right. Then each point P in the plane can be assigned **polar coordinates** (r, θ).

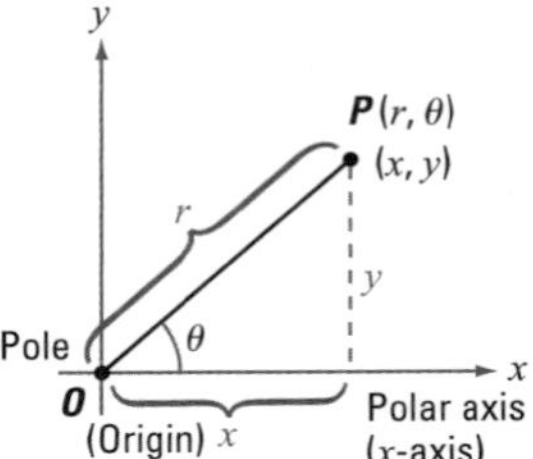

KEY CONCEPT *For Your Notebook*

Polar Coordinate System

In a polar coordinate system, a point P in the plane has two coordinates (r, θ).

1. r is the distance from O to P.
2. θ is the angle, counterclockwise from the polar axis to segment $\overline{OP}$.

EXAMPLE 1 Plot a point in the polar coordinate system

The highest point of a pine tree is given by the polar coordinate (4, 30°).

a. Graph the polar coordinate.

b. Find the height of the pine tree.

Solution

a. The point (4, 30°) lies four units from the pole (or origin) and 30° counterclockwise from the polar axis as shown.

90°
(4, 30°)
180°
30°
1 2 3 4
0°
270°

b. From the diagram, you can see that the ray, the polar axis, and the pine tree form a 30°-60°-90° triangle. Using the 30°-60°-90° Triangle Theorem, you know the hypotenuse is twice as long as the shorter leg. Because the pine tree is the shorter leg of the triangle, the height of the pine tree is $4 \div 2 = 2$ units.

GEOMETRY
In a 30°-60°-90° triangle, the hypotenuse is twice as long as the shorter leg, and the longer leg is $\sqrt{3}$ times as long as the shorter leg.

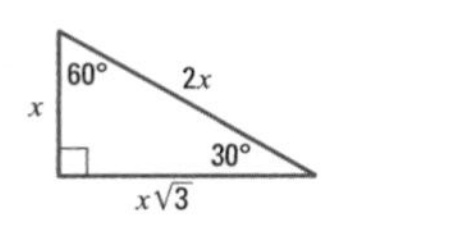

SPHERICAL COORDINATE SYSTEM Recall that a point in space has three coordinates (x, y, z), as shown in Figure B.1. From the origin, a point can be forward or back on the x-axis, left or right on the y-axis, and up or down on the z-axis. In the **spherical coordinate system**, as shown in Figure B.2, each point is represented by three coordinates: the first coordinate is a distance, and the second and third coordinates are angles. A point P is represented by (p, θ, ϕ).

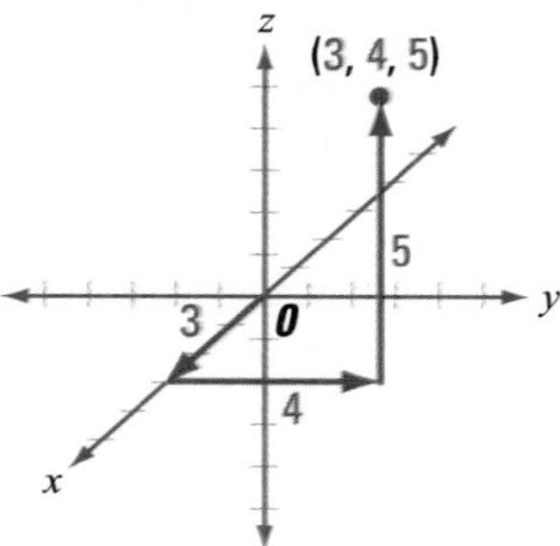

Figure B.1

Figure B.2

KEY CONCEPT *For Your Notebook*

Spherical Coordinate System

In a sperical coordinate system, a point P in space has three coordinates (p, θ, ϕ). See Figure B.2.

1. p is the distance between P and the origin.
2. (r, θ) is the projection of point P in the xy-plane.
3. ϕ is the angle between the positive z-axis and the line segment $\overline{OP}$.

EXAMPLE 2 Use coordinates in the spherical coordinate system

Use the spherical coordinate in the diagram to find (a) the angle between the positive z-axis and the line segment $\overline{OP}$ and (b) the distance between P and the origin.

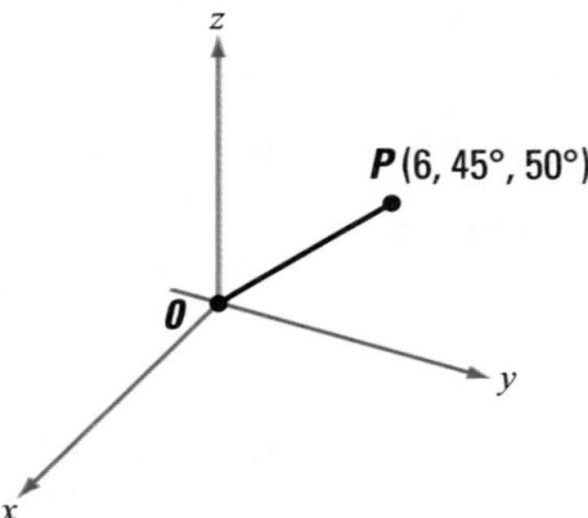

Solution

a. You know the angle between the positive z-axis and segment $\overline{OP}$ is ϕ. From the diagram, ϕ is 50°.

b. You know the distance between P and the origin is p. From the diagram, p is 6 units.

Answers to Additional Lessons

1.

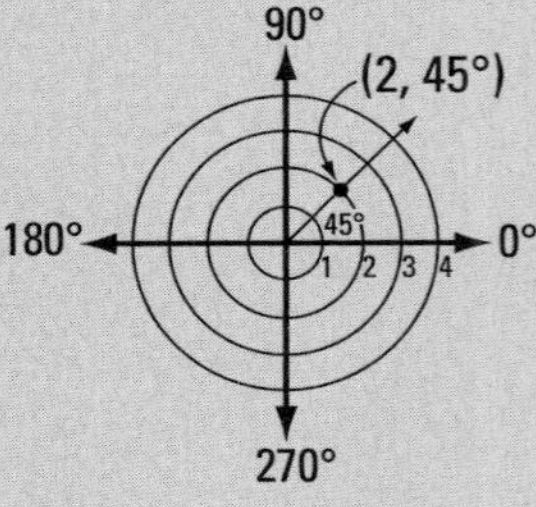

2.

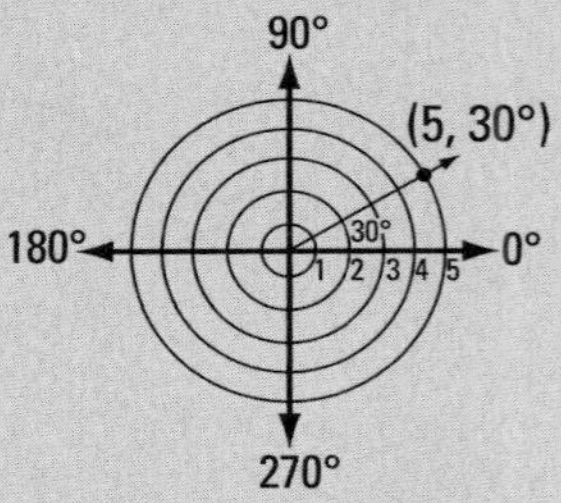

3.

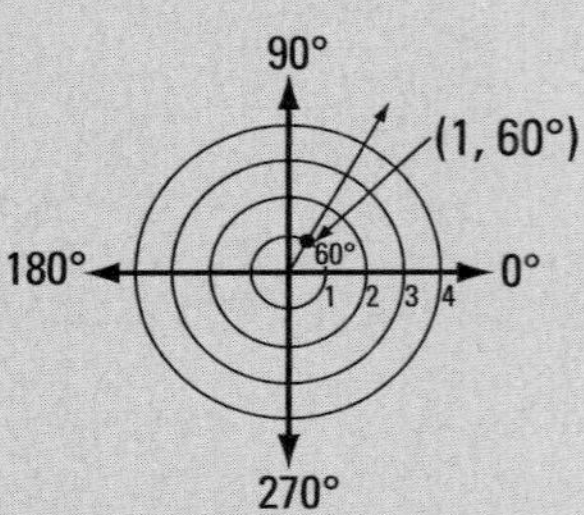

4.

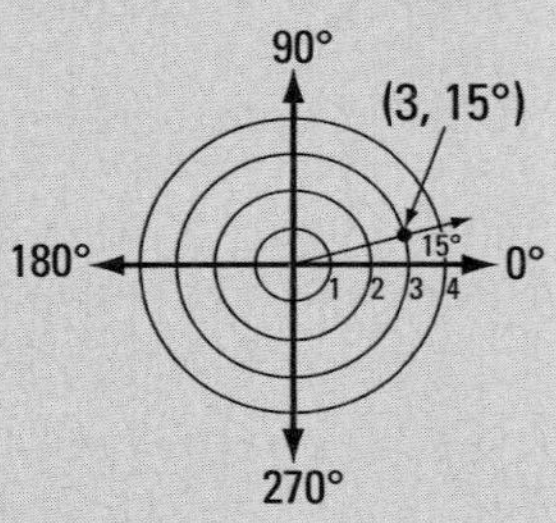

5. 60°
6. 3 units
7. South America
8. North America

NAVIGATIONAL SYSTEM As shown in the map below, latitude lines run horizontally. Zero degrees latitude is the equator and the degrees continue 90° north and 90° south. Longitude lines run vertically. Zero degrees longitude passes through Greenwich, England and the degrees continue 180° east and 180° west.

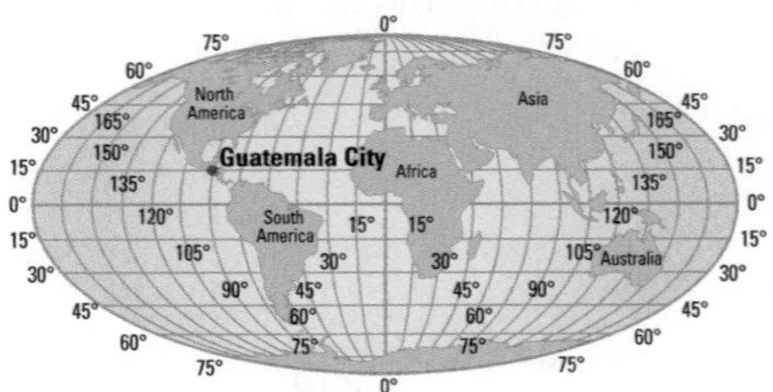

EXAMPLE 3 Find latitude and longitude

Use the map shown above to answer the following.

a. Find the approximate latitude and longitude of Guatemala City, Guatemala.

b. A city is located at approximately 32° south latitude and 116° east longitude. In which continent is the city located?

Solution

a. From the map, you can see that Guatemala City is located at approximately 15° north latitude and 90° west longitude.

b. From the map, you can see that 32° south latitude and 116° east longitude is located in Australia.

PRACTICE

EXAMPLE 1 for Exs. 1–4

Graph the polar coordinate.

1. (2, 45°)
2. (5, 30°)
3. (1, 60°)
4. (3, 15°)

EXAMPLE 2 for Exs. 5–6

In Exercises 5 and 6, use the spherical coordinate in the diagram.

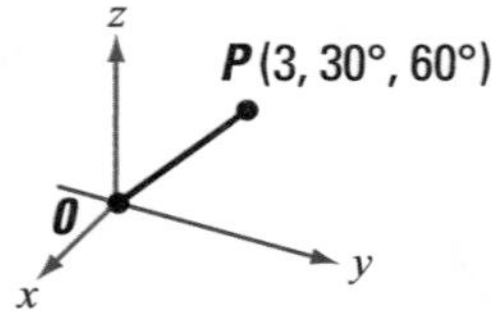

5. Find the angle between the positive z-axis and the line segment $\overline{OP}$.

6. Find the distance between P and the origin.

EXAMPLE 3 for Exs. 7–8

In Exercises 7 and 8, use the map from Example 3. Determine which continent contains the location with the given latitude and longitude.

7. 15° south latitude, 60° west longitude

8. 45° north latitude, 90° west longitude

Additional Lesson C

Parameters and Statistics

Use after Chapter 11

Key Vocabulary

- **parameter**
- **statistic**

MA-HS-DAP-S-CDS1 **Students will understand the distinction between a statistic and a parameter.**

MA-HS-DAP-S-CDS9 **Students will explore how basic statistical techniques monitor process characteristics in the workplace.**

Recall that a *population* is a group of people or objects that you want information about and a *sample* is a subset of the population. Examples of populations and samples are shown below.

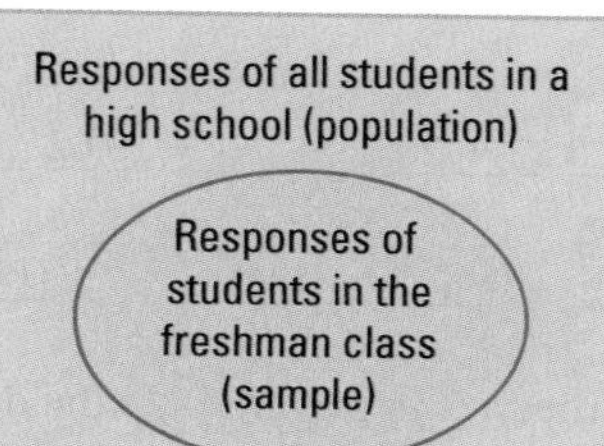

Registered voters in Jefferson County (population)

Registered voters in Jefferson county who responded to a survey (sample)

In statistics it is important to distinguish whether a numerical value describes a population characteristic or a sample characteristic. A **parameter** is a numerical value that describes a population characteristic. A **statistic** is a numerical value that describes a sample characteristic.

EXAMPLE 1 Distinguish between a parameter and a statistic

Decide whether the numerical value describes a *population parameter* or a *sample statistic*. Explain your reasoning.

a. A survey of a sample of students who took the most recent American history exam reported that the average score was 88%.

b. The average score of the 120 students who took the most recent American history exam increased by 7% from the previous exam.

c. In a random check of a sample of students' most recent American history exams, the teacher found that 68% of the students answered Question 4 incorrectly.

Solution

a. Because the 88% average score was based on a subset of the population, it is a sample statistic.

b. Because the 7% increase is based on the scores of all 120 students who took the exam, it is a population parameter.

c. Because 68% is based on a subset of the population, it is a sample statistic.

Essential Question:

When you need to calculate an average, is it always possible to survey the *entire* population? no

Key Question for Ex. 1:

Ask yourself, "Do I have the entire population or a sample from the population?" a 7sample7from7the7 population77 7entire7popul ation7 c 7sample7from7the7population

Extra Example 1:

Decide whether the numerical value describes a *population parameter* or a *sample statistic*. Explain your reasoning.

The average height of the freshman class was 5 feet 4 inches.

population7parameter 7 ecause7the7 average7height7of757feet747inches7is7 ased7on7the7heights7of7all7of7the7 students7in7the7freshman7 class 7it7is7a7 population7parameter

Common Problem:

Students may not understand that a population can sometimes be a portion of a larger population. For Example 1(b), there are many students in the school but only 120 of them took the American history exam, so this group represents the entire population and the calculated values are *population parameters*. If the average score on the exam was calculated using only one class of 20 students, then the average score would be a *sample statistic*.

Closing Question:

Why would it be important for you to know if published numbers are parameters or statistics? *Sample answer:*7 o7distinguish7w hether7 the7pu lished7num er7descri es7a7 population7characteristic7or7 a7sample7 characteristic

Answers to Additional Lessons

1. **sample statistic; 83% is based on a subset of the population.**
2. **population parameter; The average critical reading score of 502 on the SAT is based on the scores of all college-bound seniors.**
3. **population parameter; 46% is based on all first-year students at the University of Kentucky.**
4. **sample statistic; 850 adults is based on a subset of the population.**
5. **mean: 180.2; standard deviation: about 27.203; While the mean is approximately the desired talking time, the standard deviation is too large. So, the process should be adjusted to make the talking times for the batteries more consistent.**

STATISTICS IN THE WORKPLACE Sample statistics can be used in the manufacturing industry to monitor product quality.

EXAMPLE 2 Use sample statistics in the workplace

WATER CONTENT During a quality assurance check, the actual water contents (in fluid ounces) of 15 bottles of purified water were recorded as

20.23, 20.05, 20.52, 19.71, 20.35, 19.92, 20.38, 19.82,
19.45, 19.96, 20.28, 19.78, 20.61, 19.92, 19.62.

The desired volume of water is 20 fluid ounces with a standard deviation of 0.1 fluid ounce. Find the mean and standard deviation of the sample. Using this information, what conclusion can you make about the manufacturing process?

Solution

$$\text{Mean: } \bar{x} = \frac{20.23 + 20.05 + \cdots + 19.62}{15} = \frac{300.6}{15} = 20.04$$

$$\text{Std. Dev.: } \sigma = \sqrt{\frac{(20.23 - 20.04)^2 + \cdots + (19.62 - 20.04)^2}{15}} \approx 0.331$$

While the the mean is approximately the desired volume of water, the standard deviation is too large. So, the process should be adjusted to fill eac bottle more consistently.

PRACTICE

Decide whether the numerical value describes a *population parameter* or a *sample statistic*. Explain your reasoning.

EXAMPLE 1 for Exs. 1–4

1. In a survey of a sample of high school students, 83% said that they have a profile on social networking website.
2. In a recent year, the average critical reading score for all college-bound seniors on th SAT was 502.
3. In a survey of all first-year students at the University of Kentucky, 46% had a high school GPA of 3.75 or higher.
4. In a survey of a sample of 2500 adults in the United States, 850 said that they know someone whose child is currently homeschooled.

EXAMPLE 2 for Ex. 5

5. **CELL PHONE BATTERIES** During a quality assurance check, the talking times (in minutes) of 20 cell phone batteries were recorded as

   170, 198, 181, 155, 208, 148, 165, 200, 215, 145,
   150, 170, 215, 225, 200, 152, 190, 145, 218, 154.

   The desired talking time for a battery is 180 minutes with a standard deviation of 10 minutes. Find the mean and standard deviation of the sample talking times. Using this information, what conclusions can you make about the manufacturing process

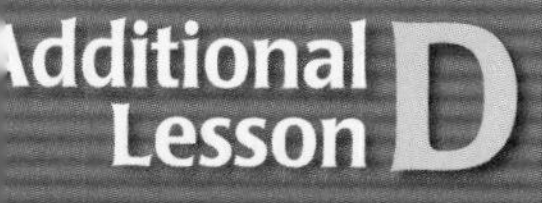

Evaluating Reports

Use after Chapter 11

MA-HS-DAP-S-CDS12	**Students will evaluate reports based on data published in the media by considering the source of the data, the design of the study and the way the data are displayed and analyzed.**
MA-HS-DAP-S-ES4	**Students will evaluate published reports that are based on interpretations of data by examining the design of the study, the appropriateness of the data analysis and the validity of the conclusions.**

PUBLISHED DATA It is important to evaluate reports that are prepared using data published in the media. A few important aspects to examine are the source of the data, the design of the study, and the way the data are analyzed and displayed.

EXAMPLE 1 Evaluate a report

Consider the following report about gas prices.

The majority of adults believe that high gasoline prices reflect a permanent change

Do you think the higher gas prices this year compared with last year represent a temporary fluctuation or a more permanent change?

Source: Experian-Gallup Personal Credit index survey of 3017 adults 18 and older conducted April through June 2006.

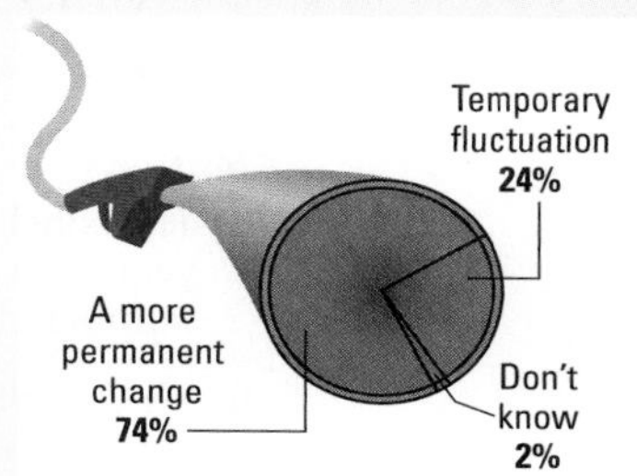

a. Identify the source of the data used to create the data display.

b. Explain the design of the study.

c. How are the data displayed? How are the data analyzed?

Solution

a. The source of the data is located at the bottom of the report. The data is from an Experian-Gallup survey.

b. The study was conducted through a survey. The report displays the question and results of the survey, preceded by a conclusion drawn from the results.

c. The data are displayed in a circle graph. The conclusion is based on the 74% of people surveyed who replied that higher gas prices reflect a more permanent change.

Essential Question:

Should all data sources be trusted? No; some data sources could present biased results.

Key Question for Ex. 1:

Do you think surveying 3017 people is a large enough sample to make this a strong conclusion? No; not if making a national conclusion from the survey.

Extra Example 1:

Consider the following report about teens.

News flash: America's teens read newspapers!

Where do you get most of your news?

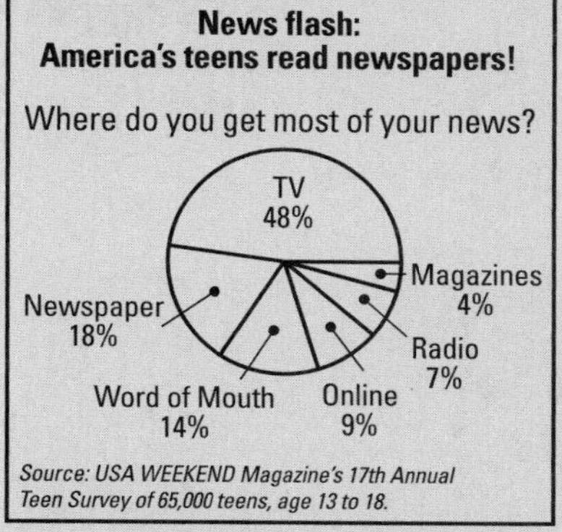

Source: USA WEEKEND Magazine's 17th Annual Teen Survey of 65,000 teens, age 13 to 18.

a. **Identify the source of the data used to create the data display.** USA WEEKEND Magazine's 17th Annual Teen Survey

b. **Explain the design of the study.** The study was conducted through a survey. The report displays the question and results of the survey, preceded by a conclusion drawn from the results.

c. **How are the data displayed? How are the data analyzed?** The data are displayed in a circle graph. The conclusion is based on the 18% of teens surveyed who replied that they get most of their news from a newspaper.

Common Problem:

Students may overlook the fine print in a graph which might provide information about how the data were collected.

Closing Question:

Why should you analyze a graph and its data before you make any conclusions? *Sample answer:* To make sure the source of the data is reliable and the way the data are analyzed and displayed is done correctly.

EXAMPLE 2 Determine the validity of conclusions

BIRD FLU The double bar graph shown consists of data published by the World Health Organization about the total number of laboratory confirmed cases of the bird flu and the number of laboratory confirmed cases of the bird flu in Vietnam for the years 2003 to 2006. Determine whether each conclusion below the graph is valid. Explain.

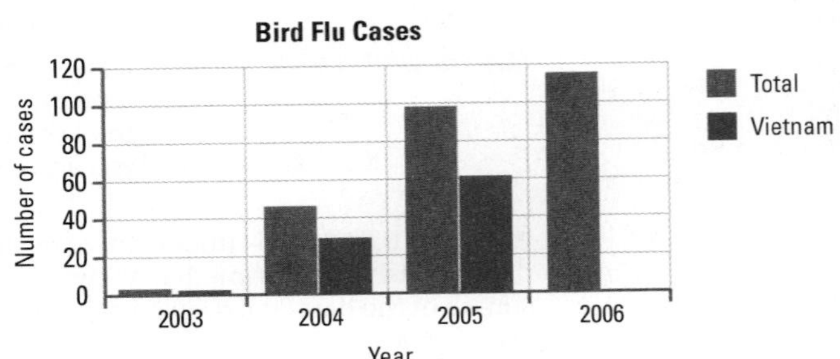

a. Because the total number of cases increased each year from 2003 to 2006 the total number of cases in 2007 will be greater than 115.

b. The majority of the cases each year from 2003 to 2005 occurred in Vietnam.

c. There were no cases of bird flu in Vietnam in 2006, so there will be no cases in 2007.

d. The country with the majority of the cases changed from 2005 to 2006.

Solution

a. The conclusion is not valid. The total number of cases did increase each year from 2003 to 2006, but other factors will determine whether the number of cases increases in 2007.

b. The conclusion is valid. Vietnam accounted for $\frac{3}{4} = 75\%$ of all cases in 2003, $\frac{29}{46} \approx 63\%$ in 2004, and $\frac{61}{98} \approx 62\%$ in 2005.

c. The conclusion is not valid. There were no bird flu cases in Vietnam in 2006, but other factors will determine whether there are any cases in 2007.

d. The conclusion is valid. Vietnam accounted for about 62% of all cases in 2005 and 0% of all cases in 2006. So, Vietnam had the majority in 2005 and another country had the majority in 2006.

PRACTICE

EXAMPLE 1 for Ex. 1

1. For the report below, (a) identify the source of the data used to create the data display, (b) explain the design of the study, and (c) explain how the data are displayed and analyzed.

Job Satisfaction Decreasing

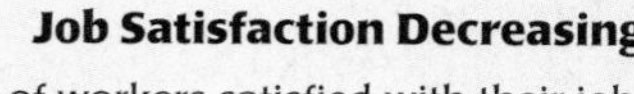

Percentage of workers satisfied with their jobs:

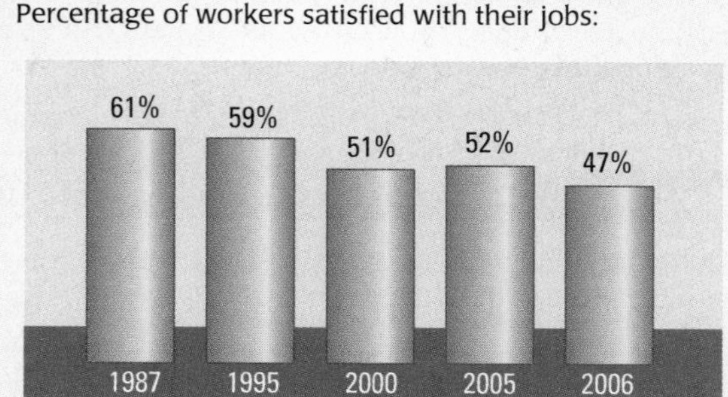

Source: The Conference Board, TNS survey of 5000 U.S. households.

EXAMPLE 2 for Ex. 2

2. Determine whether each conclusion listed below the report are valid. Explain.

Doctor-Diagnosed Arthritis

The percentage of the U.S. population with arthritis is shown for 2005 and the projection is shown for 2030.

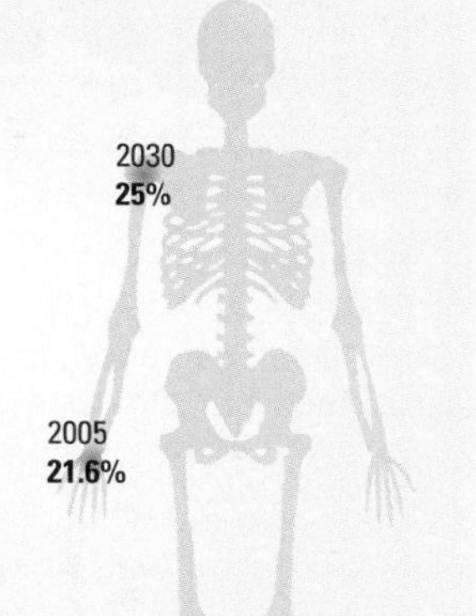

Source: Centers for Disease Control and Prevention

a. By 2030, a quarter of the adult U.S. population is projected to have doctor-diagnosed arthritis.

b. In 2005, 21.6% of the adult U.S. population had arthritis of the wrist and by 2030, 25% of the population will have arthritis of the shoulder.

Answers to Additional Lessons

1. (a) The Conference Board
   (b) The study was conducted through a survey. The report displays the results of the survey, preceded by a conclusion drawn from the results.
   (c) bar graph; The conclusion is based on the fact that for each year represented in the bar graph, the percentage of workers satisfied with their jobs decreases, with the exception of 2005.
2. (a) valid; The circle graph shows that 25% of the adult U.S. population is projected to have doctor-diagnosed arthritis in 2030.
   (b) not valid; In 2005, 21.6% of the adult U.S. population had doctor-diagnosed arthritis and by 2030, 25% of the adult U.S. population is projected to have doctor-diagnosed arthritis.

Essential Question:

What elements of a graph make it misleading? *Sample answer:* Broken vertical axis, large increments, small intervals

Key Question for Ex. 1:

What are the similarities and differences between the two graphs shown in the example? Similarities: They both are bar graphs, have the same years on the horizontal axis, and the price is in dollars per troy ounce.
Differences: The second graph has a break in the vertical axis.

Extra Example 1:

Which of the line graphs that show the number of cellular subscribers from 2000 to 2005 could be misleading? Explain.

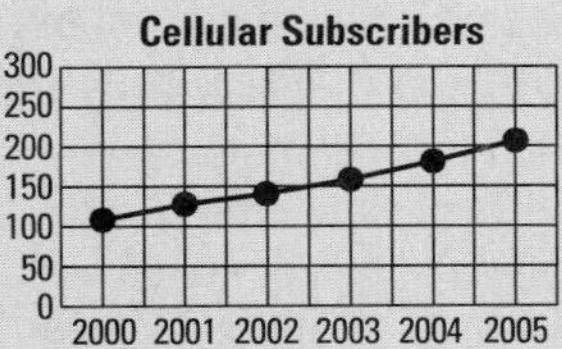

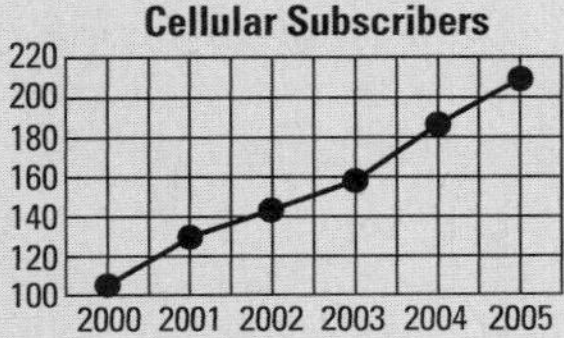

Source: Cellular Telecommunications & Internet Association

The second graph has a break in the vertical axis, so comparing the points on the graph may lead to incorrect conclusions. It looks as if the number of cellular subscribers multiplied by 6 from 2000 to 2005, but you can determine that the number of cellular subscribers just about doubled in this amount of time. The first graph is less likely to be misleading.

Common Problem:

Students may forget to look at the range and scale for the numbers on the vertical axis, especially if the physical spacing between the numbers on both graphs is about the same.

Closing Question:

Why would someone intentionally use a misleading graph? *Sample answer:* to be more dramatic with the data

Additional Lesson E — Misleading Data Displays

Use after Chapter 11

MA-HS-DAP-S-CDS13 Students will identify and explain misleading uses of data.

DATA DISPLAYS It is important to realize that data displays can be deceiving. The next two examples show how data displays can be manipulated to distort the relationship between data.

EXAMPLE 1 Recognize a misleading data display

PLATINUM Which of the bar graphs that show the average dealer price of platinum from 2001 to 2005 could be misleading? Explain.

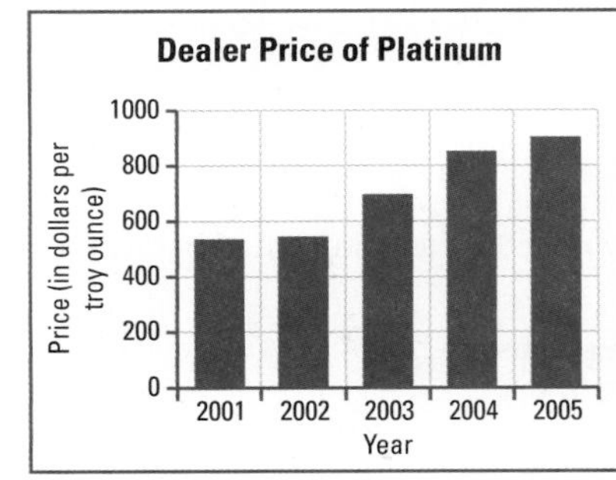

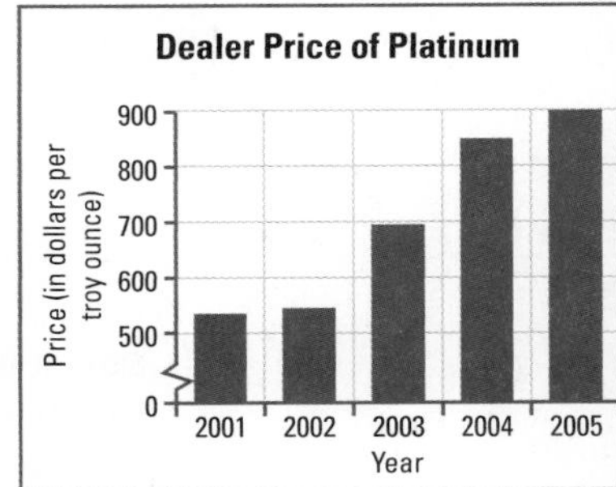

Solution

The second graph has a break in the vertical axis, so comparing the heights of the bars may lead to incorrect conclusions. It looks as if the average price tripled from 2001 to 2005, but you can determine that the average price did not even double in this amount of time. The first graph is less likely to be misleading.

EXAMPLE 2 Analyze a misleading data display

BUSINESS The line graph displays a company's profits for the years 2006 to 2010. What is misleading about the graph?

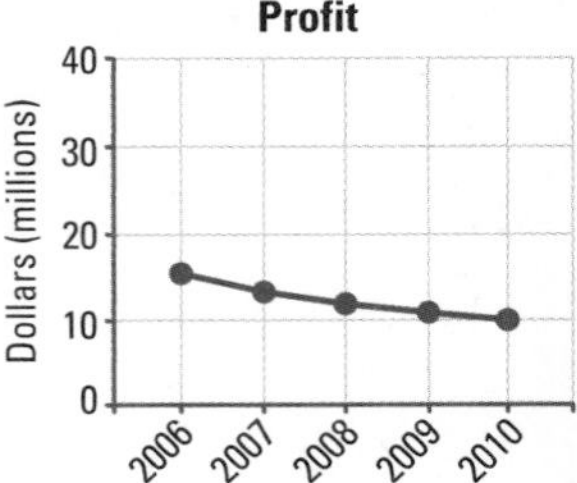

Solution

The range on the vertical scale is greater than needed. The graph suggests that profits have decreased only slightly, when they have decreased by a third.

EXAMPLE 3 Analyze a misleading data display

COMPOSTING The graph shows the amounts of waste recovered for composting in the United States. What is misleading about the graph?

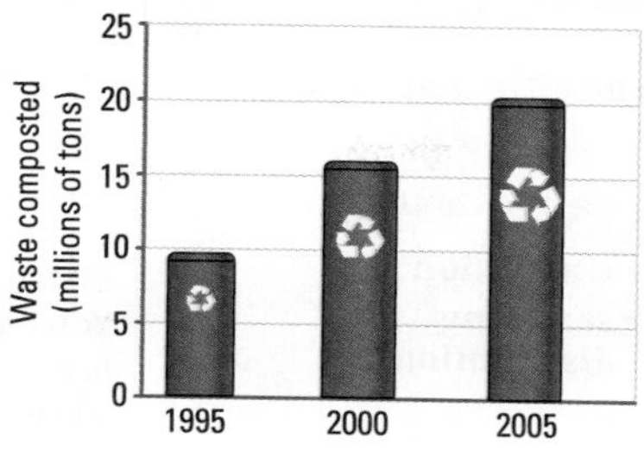

Solution

The widths of the trash cans increase, which makes data values look larger in comparison to earlier years. The 1995 value is about one half the 2005 value, but a comparison of the sizes of the trash cans makes it appear to be about one fourth of the 2005 value.

PRACTICE

EXAMPLE 1 for Ex. 1

1. **ATTENDANCE** Which of the bar graphs that show attendance at an annual rock festival from 2006 to 2010 could be misleading? Explain.

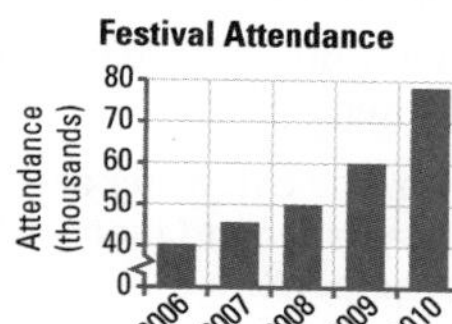

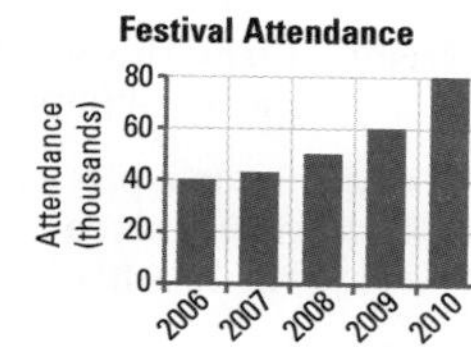

EXAMPLE 2 for Ex. 2

2. **TRAVELING** Explain what is misleading about each line graph below. Which graph might a travel agent use to convince people that train travel is becoming too expensive? Explain your reasoning.

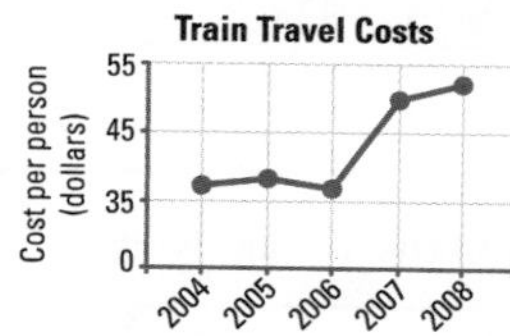

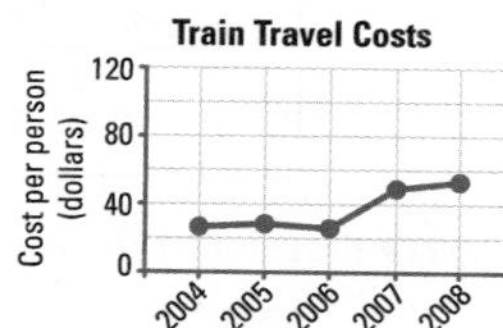

EXAMPLE 3 for Ex. 3

3. **BASKETBALL** The graph shows the numbers of games lost by the Kentucky Wildcats in three consecutive seasons. What is misleading about the graph?

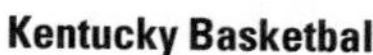

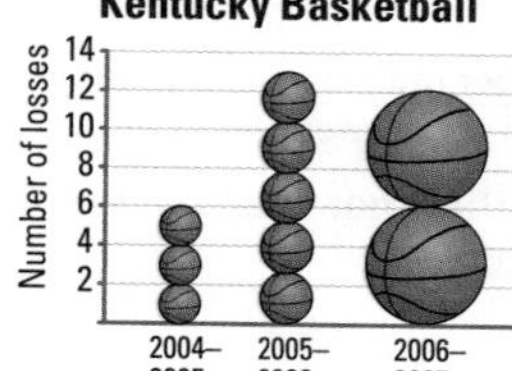

Answers to Additional Lessons

1. **The first graph has a break in the vertical axis, so comparing the bars may lead to incorrect conclusions. It looks as if attendance in 2010 was three or four times as great as in 2006, but attendance only doubled during this time. The second graph is less likely to be misleading.**
2. **The first line graph has a break in the vertical axis, so comparing years on the line graph may lead to incorrect conclusions. The second line graph has a range on the vertical scale that is greater than needed. A travel agent might use the graph with the break in the vertical axis to show that train travel is becoming too expensive, because it makes the increase from 2006 to 2007 seem much larger and more significant than the other graph.**
3. ***Sample answer:* The sizes and numbers of basketballs used for each season are different. From the graph it looks like there were 3 losses in the 2004-2005 season, 5 losses in the 2005-2006 season, and 2 losses in the 2006-2007 season.**

Essential Question:

When would you use a simulation? You would use a simulation when you could feasibly perform an experiment to determine the likelihood of an event.

Key Question for Ex. 1:

If you were to perform this experiment again, would you get the same result? No, because simulations rely on chance.

Extra Example 1:

The movie times for three movies at a local theater are $1\frac{1}{2}$, 2, and $2\frac{1}{2}$ hours. You randomly choose two movies. Estimate the probability that the average movie length is 1 hour 45 minutes. *Sample answer:* 0.3

Common Problem:

Students may not perform an experiment enough times to be able to make valid conclusions.

Closing Question:

Come up with another example where you can use a simulation. Answers will vary.

Additional Lesson F

Simulations and Sampling Distributions

Use after Chapter 10

MA-HS-DAP-S-ES3 **Students will use simulations to explore the variability of sample statistics from a known population and to construct sampling distributions.**

Key Vocabulary
- **simulation**
- **sampling distribution**

SIMULATIONS Recall that you have found the theoretical probability of events. You can also perform a *simulation* to estimate these probabilities. A **simulation** is an experiment that you can perform to make predictions about real-world situations.

EXAMPLE 1 Perform a simulation

WAIT TIMES The wait times of three rides at an amusement park are 1, 2, and 3 hours. You randomly choose two rides and you are able to choose the same ride twice. Estimate the probability that your average wait time is 2.5 hours.

Solution

You can perform a simulation to answer the question.

STEP 1 **Write** the wait time of each ride on a separate piece of paper. Put the pieces of paper in a container.

STEP 2 **Draw** a piece of paper from the container at random. Record the result and replace the paper. Draw a second piece of paper at random. Record the result and replace the paper.

STEP 3 **Repeat** this process 49 more times.

STEP 4 **Calculate** the average wait time for each simulation to complete the table.

Wait for ride 1	Wait for ride 2	Average wait time
3	2	2.5
1	1	1.0

STEP 5 **Record** the frequency of the average wait times in a table.

Average wait time	1.0	1.5	2.0	2.5	3.0
Frequency	2	9	20	13	6

STEP 6 **Find** the probability that your average wait time is 2.5 hours.

$$P(2.5 \text{ hours}) = \frac{\text{Number of favorable outcomes}}{\text{Total number of outcomes}} = \frac{13}{50} = 0.26$$

In this simulation, the probability that your the average wait time is 2.5 hours is 0.26.

SAMPLING DISTRIBUTIONS Recall that a *probability distribution* is a function that gives the probability of each possible value of a random variable. A **sampling distribution** is the probability distribution of a sample statistic that is formed when samples of size n are repeatedly taken from a population.

EXAMPLE 2 Create a sampling distribution

WAIT TIMES List all possible samples of size $n = 2$ from Example 1 and calculate the average of each. Make a table showing the sampling distribution of the sample averages. Compare the theoretical probability of an average wait time of 2.5 hours to the estimated probability.

STEP 1 **List** all nine samples of size 2 from the population {1, 2, 3} and the average of each sample.

Sample	1, 1	1, 2	1, 3	2, 1	2, 2	2, 3	3, 1	3, 2	3, 3
Sample average, $\bar{x}$	1	1.5	2	1.5	2	2.5	2	2.5	3

STEP 2 **Make** a table of the sampling distribution of the sample averages.

$\bar{x}$	1	1.5	2	2.5	3
Frequency	1	2	3	2	1
Probability	0.111	0.222	0.333	0.222	0.111

STEP 3 **Compare** the estimated probability to the theoretical probability.

The estimated probability 0.26 is very close to the theoretical probability 0.222.

PRACTICE

EXAMPLES 1 AND 2 for Exs. 1–3

In Exercises 1 and 2, use the information in Examples 1 and 2.

1. Estimate the probability that your average wait time is 1 hour.
2. Compare the theoretical probability of an average wait time of 1 hour to the estimated probability in Exercise 1.
3. **PROJECT TIMES** You have a list of four projects to complete. The times to complete the projects are 10, 30, 50, and 70 minutes. You randomly select two of the projects.
   a. Repeat a simulation 50 times to estimate the probability that your average project time is 40 minutes.
   b. List all possible samples of size $n = 2$ and calculate the average of each. Make a table showing the sampling distribution of the sample averages. Round your results to four decimal places.
   c. Compare the theoretical probability of an average project time of 40 minutes to the estimated probability.

Answers to Additional Lessons

1. **0.04**
2. **The estimated probability 0.04 is less than the theoretical probability 0.111.**
3. **(a) *Sample answer:***

Average project time	20	30	40	50	60
Frequency	5	9	18	10	8

The probability that your average project time is 40 minutes is 0.36.

(b) *Sample answer:* See below

(c) *Sample answer:* The estimated probability 0.36 is very close to the theoretical probability 0.3333.

Sample	10, 30	10, 50	10, 70	30, 10	30, 50	30, 70	50, 10	50, 30	50, 70	70, 10	70, 30	70, 50
Sample average, $\bar{x}$	20	30	40	20	40	50	30	40	60	40	50	60

$\bar{x}$	20	30	40	50	60
Frequency	2	2	4	2	2
Probability	0.1667	0.1667	0.3333	0.1667	0.1667

Essential Question:

Do you think the number of times you perform an experiment has an impact on the sample statistics you calculate? Yes; as the number of trials in an experiment increases, the experimental probability of an event approaches the theoretical probability of the event.

Key Question for Ex. 2:

Why do you think the experimental probability is not equal to the theoretical probability? There were not enough trials done in the experiment.

Extra Example 3:

A bag contains 3 red, 2 yellow, and 5 green marbles. You randomly choose one marble, record its color, and replace the marble. Repeat this process 50 times. Use your results to find the experimental probability of randomly choosing a red marble? How close are your results to the theoretical probability of choosing a red marble? *Sample answer:* 0.24; The experimental probability of randomly choosing a red marble is close to the theoretical probability of choosing a red marble.

Common Problem:

Students may have a difficult time deciding the number of trials needed to produce accurate results.

Closing Question:

What might cause the experimental probability to differ from the theoretical probability? The number of trials

Additional Lesson G Law of Large Numbers

Use after Chapter 10

MA-HS-DAP-S-P9 **Students will explain how the law of large numbers can be applied in simple examples.**

Key Vocabulary

- **law of large numbers**

THEORETICAL PROBABILITY You learned that the *theoretical probability* of an event can be found using the following:

$$\text{Theoretical probability} = \frac{\text{Number of favorable outcomes}}{\text{Total number of outcomes}}$$

EXAMPLE 1 Find a theoretical probability

You flip a coin. Find the probability of getting tails.

Solution

There are 2 possible outcomes. Only 1 outcome corresponds to getting tails.

$$P(\text{tails}) = \frac{\text{Number of ways to get tails}}{\text{Number of ways to flip the coin}} = \frac{1}{2} = 0.5$$

EXPERIMENTAL PROBABILITY You also learned that an *experimental probability* is based on repeated trials of an experiment.

$$\text{Experimental probability} = \frac{\text{Number of successes}}{\text{Number of trials}}$$

EXAMPLE 2 Find an experimental probability

The results of flipping a coin 50 times are shown. Use the table to find the experimental probability of getting tails.

Result	(heads)	(tails)
Number of occurrences	28	22

Solution

$$P(\text{tails}) = \frac{\text{Number of tails}}{\text{Number of trials}} = \frac{22}{50} = 0.44$$

EXAMPLE 3 Increase the number of trials

The results of flipping a coin 500 times are shown. Use the table to find the experimental probability of getting tails.

Result	Heads	Tails
Number of occurrences	240	260

Solution

$P(\text{tails}) = \frac{\text{Number of tails}}{\text{Number of trials}} = \frac{260}{500} = 0.52$

In Examples 2 and 3, notice that as the number of trials increased, the experimental probability became closer to the theoretical probability. This relationship between theoretical and experimental probabilities is described in the **law of large numbers.**

KEY CONCEPT *For Your Notebook*

Law of Large Numbers

As the number of trials in an experiment increases, the experimental probability of an event approaches the theoretical probability of the event.

PRACTICE

EXAMPLE 1 for Exs. 1–4

You roll a six-sided die. Find the probability of the given event.

1. Rolling a 1
2. Rolling a number greater than 2
3. Rolling an odd number
4. Rolling a number divisible by 3

EXAMPLES 2 AND 3 for Exs. 5–6

You roll a six-sided die n times. Use the results in the table to find the experimental probability of each event in Exercises 1–4.

5. $n = 100$

Roll	1	2	3	4	5	6
Number of occurrences	11	20	16	17	14	22

6. $n = 1000$

Roll	1	2	3	4	5	6
Number of occurrences	160	172	163	181	152	172

7. Explain why the law of large numbers can be applied to the experiment in Exercises 5 and 6. Use the experiment results to justify your answer.

Answers to Additional Lessons

1. $\frac{1}{6}$

2. $\frac{2}{3}$

3. $\frac{1}{2}$

4. $\frac{1}{3}$

5. $\frac{11}{100}, \frac{69}{100}, \frac{41}{100}, \frac{19}{50}$

6. $\frac{4}{25}, \frac{167}{250}, \frac{19}{40}, \frac{67}{200}$

7. As the number of trials in the experiment increased from 100 trials in Exercise 5 to 1000 trials in Exercise 6, the experimental probability of the event became closer to the theoretical probability of the event.

Essential Question:

What are the different ways you can display data? Circle graph, line graph, stem-and-leaf plot, box-and-whisker plot, bar graph, Venn diagram, and histogram

Key Question for Ex. 2:

Is there another way you could display the data? line graph

Extra Example 2:

The table shows the average wait time (in minutes) for the number of park visitors waiting for a ride. Choose an appropriate display for the data. Use a spreadsheet or a graphing calculator to organize and display the data.

Riders	10	20	30	40
Wait Time	1	1.5	2.5	3

Bar graph or line graph;

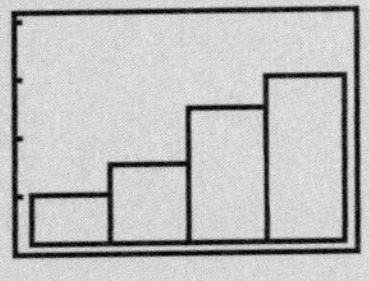

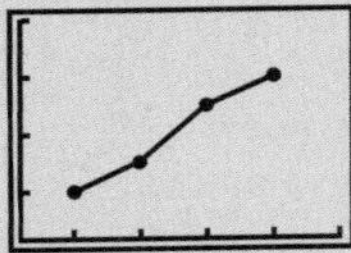

Common Problem:

Remind students to enter data carefully and to check that the data are correct before displaying and analyzing their graphs.

Closing Question:

Why is it important to choose an appropriate display for data? By choosing an appropriate display for data, you can make meaningful conclusions about the data.

Additional Lesson H Organizing and Displaying Data

Use after Chapter 11

Key Vocabulary

- estimation

MA-HS-DAP-S-DR6 **Students will organize and display data using appropriate methods (e.g., spreadsheets and graphing calculators) to detect patterns and departures from patterns.**

DATA AND TECHNOLOGY You can use spreadsheet programs and graphing calculators to organize and display data. These displays can be used to recognize patterns and departures from patterns.

EXAMPLE 1 Use a spreasheet to organize and display data

BIRDS The table shows the weight (in ounces) and wingspan (in inches) of several small birds known to host the West Nile Virus. Use a spreadsheet to organize and display the data in a scatter plot. Describe any pattern in the data.

Wingspan (in inches)	18	25	13	12	16	14	15.5	15
Weight (in ounces)	2.5	6	1.8	1.5	2.9	2.1	2.2	2.3

Solution

STEP 1 **Enter** the wingspans and weights in a spreadsheet.

	A	B
1	Wingspan	Weight
2	18	2.5
3	25	6
4	13	1.8
5	12	1.5
6	16	2.9
7	14	2.1
8	15.5	2.2
9	15	2.3

STEP 2 **Organize** the data by sorting th wingspans in ascending order.

	A	B
1	Wingspan	Weight
2	12	1.5
3	13	1.8
4	14	2.1
5	15	2.3
6	15.5	2.2
7	16	2.9
8	18	2.5
9	25	6

STEP 3 **Create** the graph by selecting the scatter plot chart type.

STEP 4 **Describe** the pattern.

By viewing either the ordered data in Step 2 or the scatter plot at the right, you can see that the general pattern is that weight increases as wingspan increases. However, two values, (15.5, 2.2) and (18, 2.5), depart from this pattern slightly.

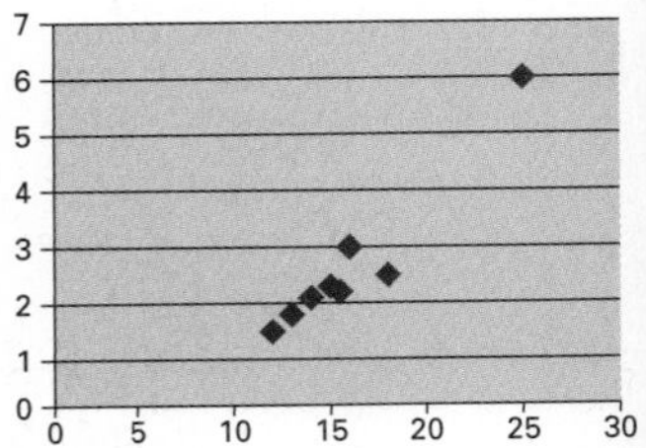

EXAMPLE 2 Use a graphing calculator to organize and display data

PROFIT The table shows the profits (in millions of dollars) of a company when different numbers of salespeople were employed. Use a graphing calculator to organize and display the data in a bar graph. Describe any pattern in the data.

Salespeople	3	6	5	8	7	10	9
Profit (in millions of dollars)	1.6	3.2	2.3	3.8	3.6	3.4	3.7

Solution

STEP 1 **Enter** the salespeople data in a list and the profits in a list.

L1	L2	L3 3
3	1.6	
6	3.2	
5	2.3	
8	3.8	
7	3.6	
10	3.4	
9	3.7	

L3(1)=

STEP 2 **Order** the data using the *sort* feature.

L1	L2	L3 3
3	1.6	
5	2.3	
6	3.2	
7	3.6	
8	3.8	
9	3.7	
10	3.4	

L3(1)=

STEP 3 **Change** the type of plot to a bar graph.

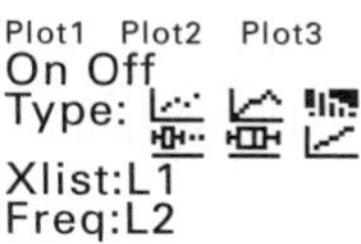

STEP 4 **Create** the graph. Use domain $3 \le x \le 11$ and range $0 \le y \le 4$.

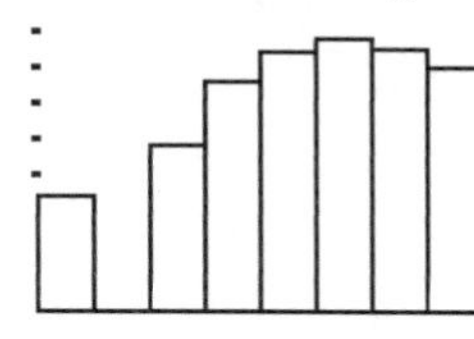

By viewing either the ordered data in Step 2 or the bar graph in Step 4, you can see that the general pattern is that profit increases as the number of salespeople increases. However, the profit begins to decrease as the number of salespeople increases beyond 8.

PRACTICE

XAMPLES AND 2 ›r Exs. 1–2

1. **BOWLING** The table shows a bowler's six best games and the number of spares converted in each game. Use a graphing calculator and a spreadsheet program to organize and display the data in a bar graph. Describe any pattern in the data.

Number of spares	3	2	5	1	0	4
Score	197	205	193	217	246	208

2. **ADVERTISING** The table shows a company's annual advertising expenditures and sales. Use a graphing calculator and a spreadsheet program to organize and display the data in a scatter plot. Describe any pattern in the data.

Advertising	$7000	$9000	$8000	$12,000	$10,500
Sales	$90,000	$95,000	$98,000	$130,000	$118,000

Answers to Additional Lessons

1.

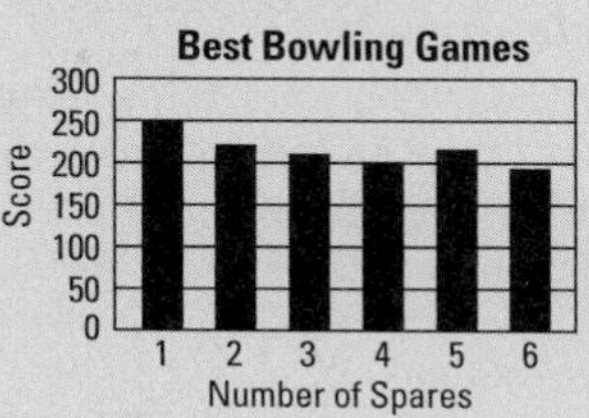

The general pattern is that the score decreases as the number of spares converted increases. However, one value, (5, 193), departs from this pattern slightly.

2.

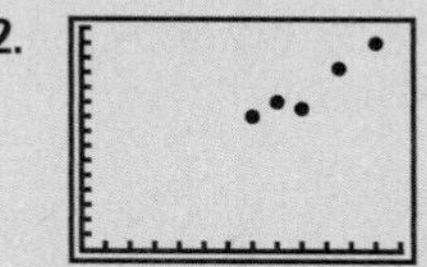

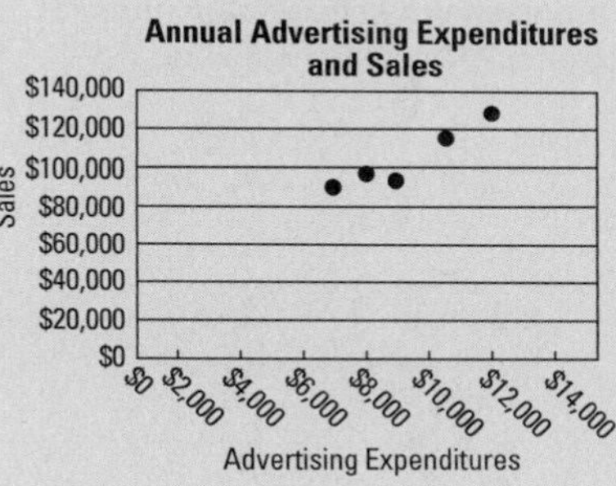

The general pattern is that sales increase as the advertising expenditures increase. However, one value, ($9000, $95,000), departs from this pattern slightly.

Essential Question:

If you repeatedly toss three coins, on average how many heads can you expect on each toss? Answers will vary. Class discussion; the teacher should record responses on the board. The actual answer is in Example 2.

Key Question for Ex. 1:

How many items are in the sample space? How do you calculate this total? 8; 2·2·2 by the counting principle

Extra Example 2:

Two six-sided dice are tossed. Find the expected value for the sum of the points. 7; You can expect, on average, for the sum to be 7.

Common Problem:

Students may omit items in the sample space of the experiment and therefore incorrectly calculate the frequencies and probabilities.

Closing Question:

How do you think expected values are used when designing carnival games? Answers will vary.

Additional Lesson I

Expected Value

Use after Chapter 10

MA-HS-DAP-S-P4 **Students will compute and interpret the expected val of random variables in simple cases.**

Key Vocabulary

- **sample space**
- **random variable**
- **discrete random variable**
- **frequency**
- **expected value**

RANDOM VARIABLE The collection of all possible outcomes of a probability experiment is the **sample space** *S*. A **random variable** *x* represents a numeric value associated with each outcome of a probability experiment. If the set of values taken on by the random variable is finite, then the random variable is **discrete**. The number of times a specific value of *x* occurs is the **frequency** of

EXAMPLE 1 Find frequencies and probabilities

COIN TOSS Three coins are tossed. Let a random variable represent the number of heads in each outcome, which are 0, 1, 2, and 3.

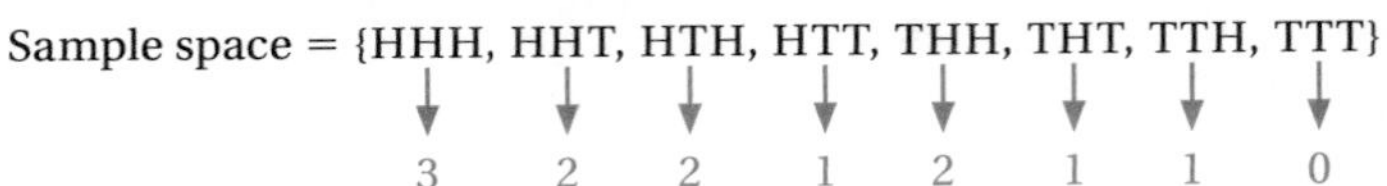

a. Find the frequency of each value of the random variable.

b. Find the probability of each value of the random variable.

Solution

a. To find the frequencies, simply count the number of occurrences of eac value of the random variable.

Random variable, *x*	0	1	2	3
Frequency of *x*	1	3	3	1

b. Use the number of outcomes in the sample space, 8, and the frequencie to find the probability of each value of the random variable.

Random variable, *x*	0	1	2	3
Probability of *x*, *P*(*x*)	$\frac{1}{8}$	$\frac{3}{8}$	$\frac{3}{8}$	$\frac{1}{8}$

EXPECTED VALUE Suppose you repeat the coin toss in Example 1 several time and want to find the average number of heads in the outcome. This average o *mean* is the **expected value** of the random variable.

KEY CONCEPT — *For Your Notebook*

Expected Value

If the range of a discrete random variable consists of m different values $\{x_1, x_2, x_3, \ldots, x_m\}$, then the expected value E of the random variable is

$$E(x) = x_1P(x_1) + x_2P(x_2) + x_3P(x_3) + \cdots + x_mP(x_m).$$

The expected value is also called the *mean* of the random variable.

EXAMPLE 2 Find an expected value

Three coins are tossed. Find the expected value for the number of heads in the outcome.

Solution

Using the results of Example 1, you obtain the expected value as shown.

$$E(x) = \underbrace{(0)\left(\frac{1}{8}\right)}_{\text{0 Heads}} + \underbrace{(1)\left(\frac{3}{8}\right)}_{\text{1 Head}} + \underbrace{(2)\left(\frac{3}{8}\right)}_{\text{2 Heads}} + \underbrace{(3)\left(\frac{1}{8}\right)}_{\text{3 Heads}}$$

$$= 0 + \frac{3}{8} + \frac{6}{8} + \frac{3}{8}$$

$$= 1.5$$

So, the average number of heads in the outcome is 1.5.

PRACTICE

XAMPLES AND 2 ......> or Exs. 1–2

1. **EXAM** Two students answer a true-false question on an exam. Let a random variable represent the number of answers of *true* among the two students, which are 0, 1, and 2.
   a. Find the frequency of each value of the random variable.
   b. Find the probability of each value of the random variable.
   c. Find the expected value for the number of answers of true among the two students.
2. **COIN TOSS** Four coins are tossed. Let a random variable represent the number of heads in each outcome, which are 0, 1, 2, 3, and 4.
   a. Find the frequency of each value of the random variable.
   b. Find the probability of each value of the random variable.
   c. Find the expected value for the number of heads in the outcome.

Answers to Additional Lessons

1.

(a)

Random variable, x	0	1	2
Frequency of x	1	2	1

(b)

Random variable, x	0	1	2
Probability of x, $P(x)$	$\frac{1}{4}$	$\frac{1}{2}$	$\frac{1}{4}$

(c) $E(x) = 1$

2. **(a)** See below
(b) See below
(c) $E(x) = 2$

2. a.

Random variable, x	0	1	2	3	4
Frequency of x	1	4	4	4	1

b.

Random variable, x	0	1	2	3	4
Probability of x, $P(x)$	$\frac{1}{14}$	$\frac{2}{7}$	$\frac{2}{7}$	$\frac{2}{7}$	$\frac{1}{14}$

Essential Question:

Why are parametric equations studied? Parametric equations are useful for modeling the path of an object.

Key Question for Ex. 1:

Which values in the table do you calculate? You calculate the x- and y-values.

Extra Example 1:

Sketch the curve given by each pair of parametric equations.

a. $x = t^2 - 4$ **and** $y = \frac{t}{2}$, $-2 \le t \le 2$

a.

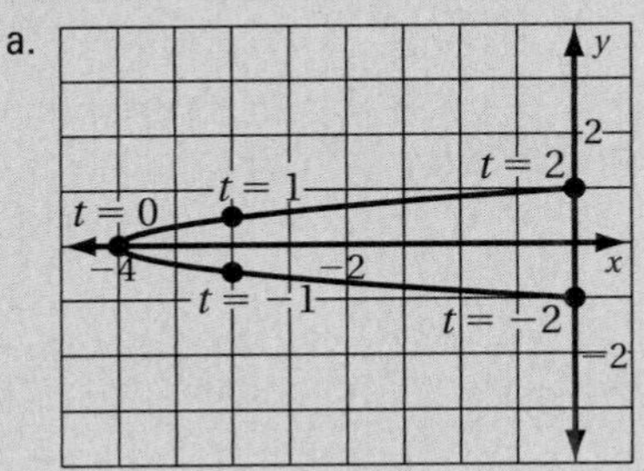

b. $x = 4t^2 - 4$ **and** $y = t$, $-1 \le t \le 1$

b.

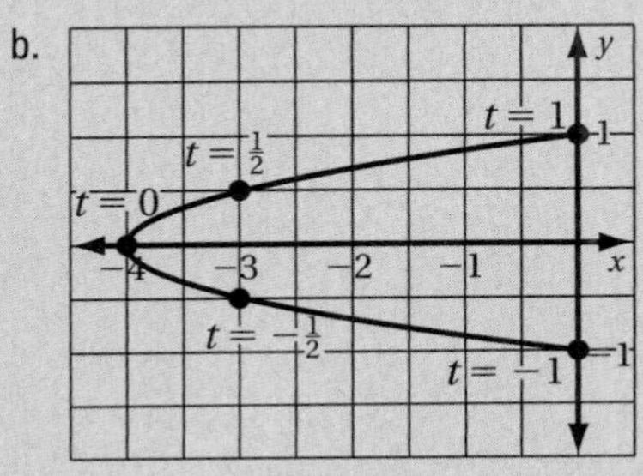

Common Problem:

Students may incorrectly plot the (x, y) ordered pairs. They may confuse parametric equations with $f(t)$ functions where the t-values are plotted on the horizontal axis. Also, you may want to require the students to label all points.

Closing Question:

Can different parametric equations produce the same curve? How are they different? Yes; *Sample answer:* If t is time, then the speed that one graph is traced is either faster or slower than the speed that the other graph is traced.

Additional Lesson J — Parametric Equations

Use after Chapter 4

Key Vocabulary
- **parametric equation**
- **parameter**

MA-HS-AT-S-PRF7 **Students will use a variety of symbolic representations including recursive and parametric equations, for functions and relations.**

You have been representing a graph by a single equation in *two* variables. Now you will use *three* variables to represent a curve in a plane.

KEY CONCEPT *For Your Notebook*

Parametric Equation

If f and g are continuous functions of t on an interval I, then the equations

$$x = f(t) \qquad \text{and} \qquad y = g(t)$$

are called **parametric equations**, and t is called the **parameter**.

SKETCHING CURVES When sketching a curve represented by a pair of parametric equations, the points are plotted in the xy-plane. Each set of coordinates (x, y) is found from a value chosen for the parameter t.

EXAMPLE 1 Sketch a curve

Sketch the curve given by the parametric equations $x = t - 1$ and $y = t^2 + 1$ on the interval $-2 \le t \le 2$.

Solution

STEP 1 **Make** a table of values.

t	−2	−1	0	1	2
x	−3	−2	−1	0	1
y	5	2	1	2	5

STEP 2 **Plot** the points (x, y). Notice that the points lie on a curve.

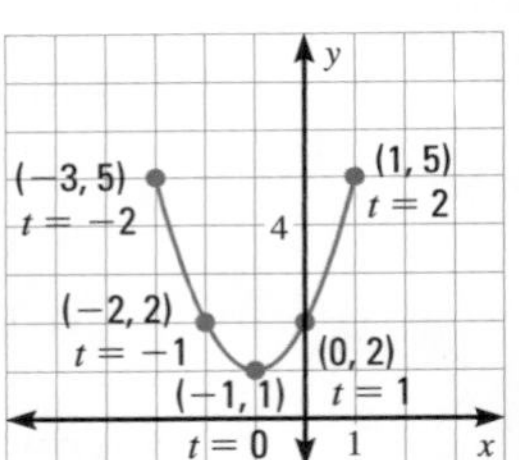

PARAMETRIC EQUATIONS In Example 2, you will use parametric equations to model the path of an object. The variables x and y represent the horizontal and vertical position of the object, and the parameter t represents the time.

EXAMPLE 2 Model the path of an object

VOLLEYBALL The path of a volleyball can be modeled by the parametric equations $x = 22t$ and $y = -16t^2 + 22t + 3$ on the interval $0 \le t \le 1.5$, where x and y are in feet and t is the time (in seconds) since the volleyball was hit.

a. Sketch the curve.

b. Interpret the meaning of x and y when $t = 0.5$.

c. How long was the ball in the air?

Solution

a. Make a table and plot the points.

t	0	0.5	1	1.5
x	0	11	22	33
y	3	10	9	0

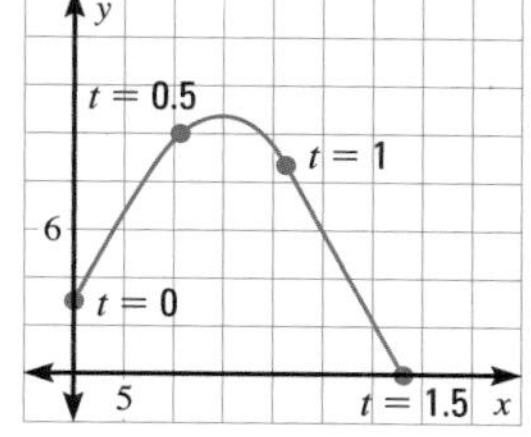

b. When $t = 0.5$, $x = 11$ and $y = 10$. This indicates that 0.5 second after the volleyball was hit, it had traveled $x = 11$ feet horizontally and was at a height of $y = 10$ feet.

c. When $t = 1.5$, $x = 33$ and $y = 0$. This indicates that 1.5 seconds after the volleyball was hit, it struck the ground because the height was $y = 0$ feet. So, the ball was in the air 1.5 seconds.

PRACTICE

Sketch the curve given by the parametric equations on the interval $-2 \le t \le 2$.

EXAMPLE 1 for Exs. 1–6

1. $x = t + 1$, $y = 3t - 2$
2. $x = 5 + 2t$, $y = 3 - t$
3. $x = 0.2t$, $y = t^2$
4. $x = 2t$, $y = -t^2$
5. $x = t + 3$, $y = t^2 - 1$
6. $x = 1 - t$, $y = t^2 + 2$

EXAMPLE 2 for Exs. 7–8

7. **BASEBALL** The path of a baseball can be modeled by the parametric equations $x = 54t$ and $y = -16t^2 + 54t + 7$ on the interval $0 \le t \le 3.5$, where x and y are in feet and t is the time (in seconds) since the baseball was thrown.
   a. Sketch the curve.
   b. Interpret the meaning of x and y when $t = 2$.
   c. How long was the ball in the air?

8. **SOCCER** The path of a ball can be modeled by the parametric equations $x = 16\sqrt{3}t$ and $y = -16t^2 + 16t$ on the interval $0 \le t \le 1$, where x and y are in feet and t is the time (in seconds) since the ball was kicked.
   a. Sketch the curve.
   b. Interpret the meaning of x and y when $t = 0.5$.
   c. Approximate the maximum height of the ball.

Answers to Additional Lessons

1. 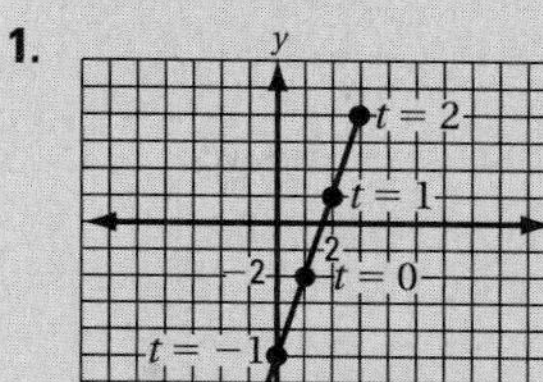

2. 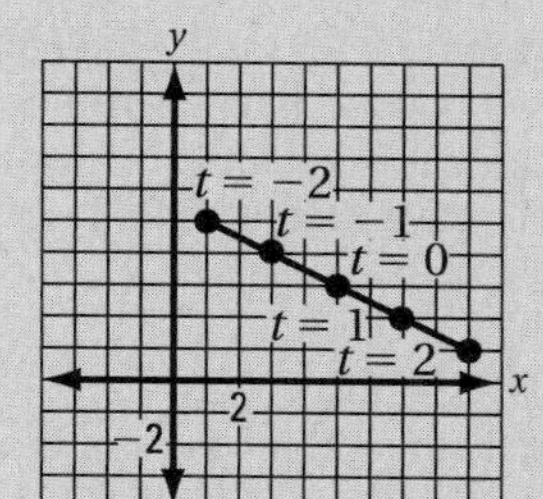

3. 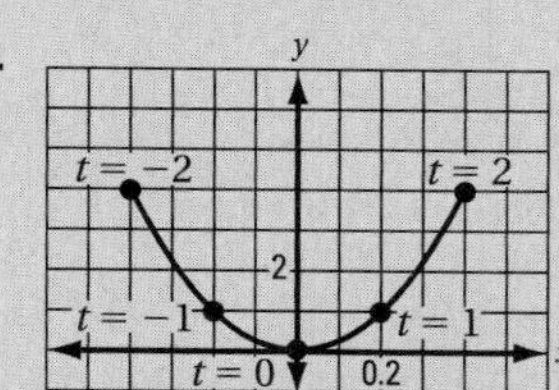

4. 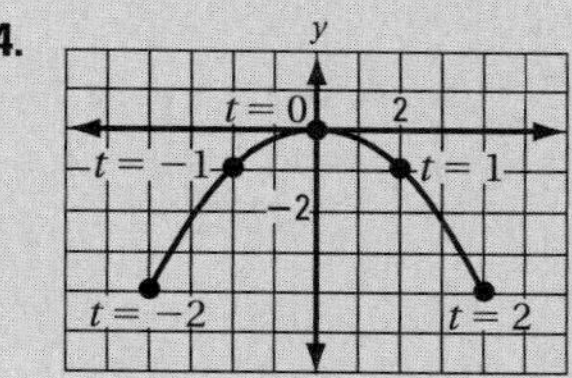

5. 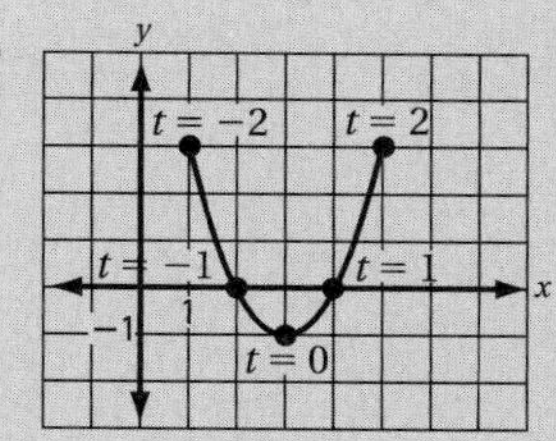

6. 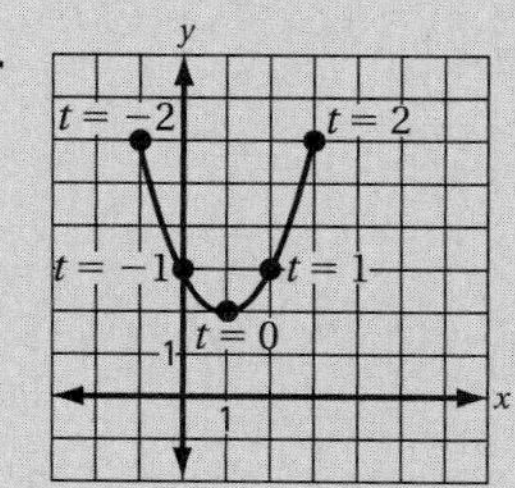

7. (a) 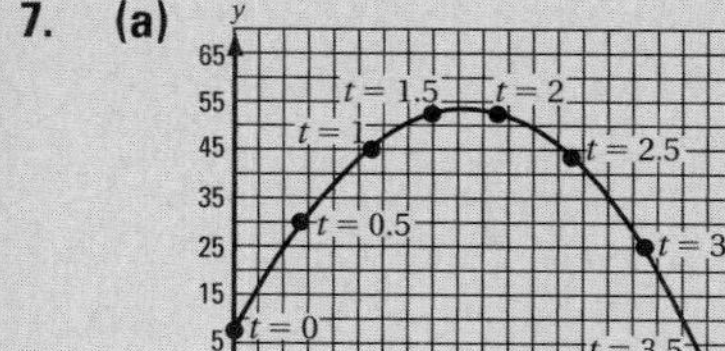

(b) **When $t = 2$, $x = 108$ and $y = 51$. This indicates that 2 seconds after the baseball was thrown, it had traveled 108 feet horizontally and was at a height of 51 feet.**

(c) **When $t = 3.5$, $x = 189$ and $y = 0$. This indicates that 3.5 seconds after the baseball was thrown, it struck the ground because the height was $y = 0$ feet. So, the ball was in the air 3.5 seconds.**

8. (a) 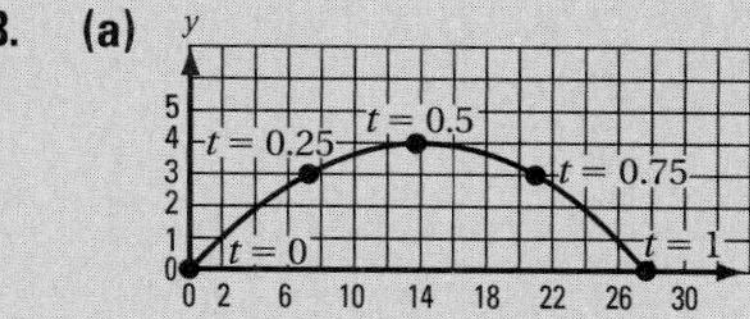

(b) **When $t = 0.5$, $x = 8\sqrt{3}$ and $y = 4$. This indicates that 0.5 second after the ball was kicked, it had traveled $8\sqrt{3}$ feet horizontally and was at a height of 4 feet.**

(c) **4 ft**

Essential Question:

What would you look for to show that data has a strong correlation? The closer the data appears to be linear, the stronger the correlation.

Key Question for Ex. 1:

Could this also be an example of causation? Yes, of course; as you practice more your speed will increase.

Extra Example:

Would "people who smoke have lung cancer" be causation or correlation? Correlation, the medical data is not enough to prove that everybody who smokes has lung cancer.

Common Problem:

Deciding if something is a true cause and effect.

Closing Question:

Would you consider the following statement to illustrate correlation and/or causation: "people who don't go to the gym will be fat?" Correlation, there is nothing that says being fat is associated with not going to the gym.

Additional Lesson K Causation vs. Correlation

Use after Chapter 11

Key Vocabulary

- **correlation**
- **causation**

MA-HS-4.2.4 **Students will recognize when arguments based on data confuse correlation and causation.**

There is often a relationship between two variables in a set of data. It is easiest to see if the data is graphed in the form of a scatter plot. For data that appears linear, a line of best fit can be drawn.

Correlation describes the relationship or lack thereof, between two variables in a data set, and measures the strength of these linear relationships. With some data, there is also a **causation,** where a change in one variable results in a change in the other. But be careful: a strong correlation between variables in a set of data does not necessarily mean there is a causation between the variables.

EXAMPLE 1 Analyze a set of data to determine a correlation

The following set of data shows the number of hours a student has practiced typing and his typing speed, measured in words per minute. Describe the correlation, if any, between practice time and typing speed.

Hours of Practice	5	6	9	10	12	15	16	17
Typing Speed (WPM)	4	5	12	14	18	20	22	25

Graph the data as a scatter plot on a coordinate grid.

Draw a line of best fit.

As can be seen from the graph, there appears to be a very strong correlation between hours of practice and typing speed.

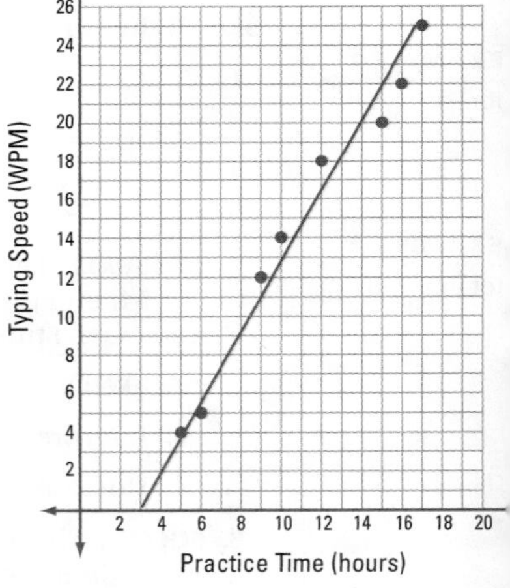

EXAMPLE 2 Analyze a set of data to determine a causation

The following data lists the shoe size and vocabulary size (number of known words) of several children that were studied. Determine if there is a causal relationship between shoe size and vocabulary size.

Graph the data.

Shoe Size	Vocabulary Size (known words)
1	15,000
2	20,000
4	38,000
7	62,000
9	79,000
10	103,000
11	121,000

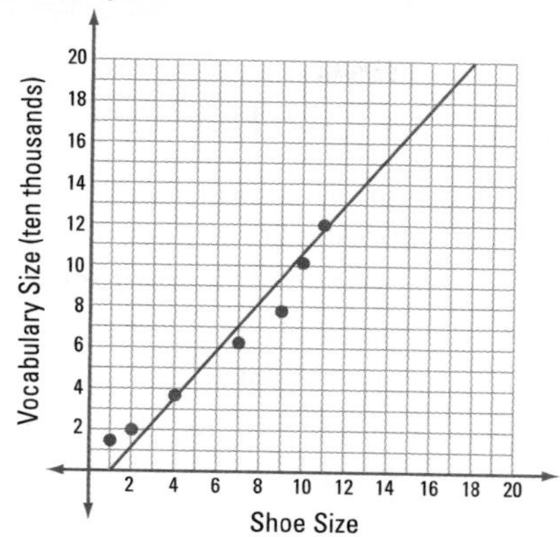

Draw a line of best fit.

There appears to be a strong relationship between shoe size and vocabulary size.

However, this is not a causal relationship.

Larger shoe size does not cause a larger vocabulary. There is a hidden variable at play here, which is age. As children get older, there shoe size and vocabulary size both happen to get larger.

PRACTICE

Complete the following exercises.

For each set of data, describe the correlation, if any, which exists between the variables. Then determine whether or not there is a causal relationship between the variables in the data.

EXAMPLE 1 for Exs. 1–3

1. The data shows the age of a car (number of years old) and its resale value, in dollars.

Age of Car (years)	Resale Value (US $)
1	21,200
2	18,600
5	13,100
8	8,800
10	3,400

2. The data represents the height and IQ (Intelligence Quotient) of six people selected at random.

Height (inches)	53	58	60	62	63	68
IQ	147	128	152	136	131	149

3. The data in the table below represents several approximate house sizes in square feet, and the average amount of money that people who lived in a home of that size spent per week at a coffee shop.

House Size (thousands of sq. ft.)	1	2	3	4	5	6	7
Weekly $ Spent at Coffee Shop	5	128	18	19	27	32	38

Answers to Additional Lessons

1. **strong positive correlation; causation**

2. **no correlation; no causation**

3. **positive correlation; no causation**

Contents of Student Resources

Operations with Positive and Negative Numbers

To add positive and negative numbers, you can use a number line.

To subtract any number, add its opposite.

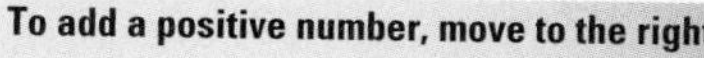

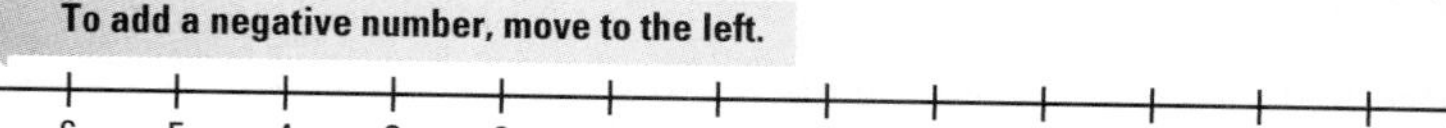

EXAMPLE **Add or subtract.**

a. $1 + (-5)$

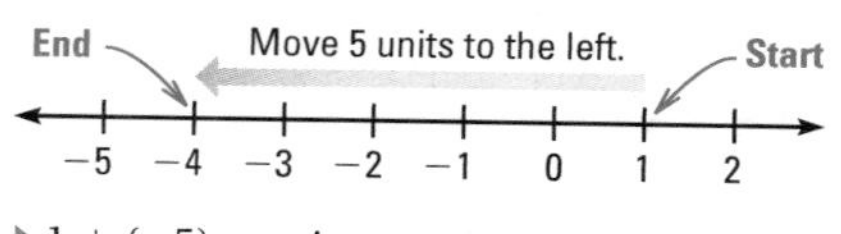

▶ $1 + (-5) = -4$

b. $-2 - (-5) = -2 + 5$ **The opposite of −5 is 5.**

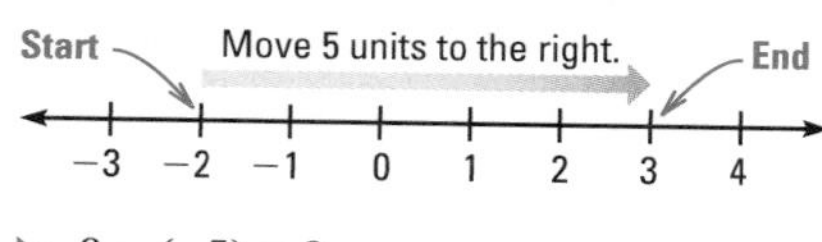

▶ $-2 - (-5) = 3$

To multiply or divide positive and negative numbers, use the following rules.

- The product or quotient of two numbers with the *same* sign is *positive*.
- The product or quotient of two numbers with *different* signs is *negative*.

EXAMPLE **Multiply or divide.**

a. $3 \cdot 7 = 21$ **b.** $-3(-7) = 21$

c. $18 \div 2 = 9$ **d.** $-18 \div (-2) = 9$

e. $-3(7) = -21$ **f.** $3(-7) = -21$

g. $-18 \div 2 = -9$ **h.** $18 \div (-2) = -9$

PRACTICE

Perform the indicated operation.

1. $2 + (-8)$ **−6** **2.** $5 - 12$ **−7** **3.** $-6(10)$ **−60** **4.** $-30 \div (-2)$ **15** **5.** $-4 + 6$ **2**

6. $7(-5)$ **−35** **7.** $18 - 10$ **8** **8.** $-7 + (-12)$ **−19** **9.** $11(4)$ **44** **10.** $81 \div (-9)$ **−9**

11. $-12 \div 3$ **−4** **12.** $-9(-8)$ **72** **13.** $-1 + 13$ **12** **14.** $45 \div (-9)$ **−5** **15.** $-6(12)$ **−72**

16. $14 - (-9)$ **23** **17.** $-32 \div 16$ **−2** **18.** $-23 + (-5)$ **−28** **19.** $-8 - (-5)$ **−3** **20.** $17 - (-18)$ **35**

21. $-9(-1)$ **9** **22.** $-3 - (-11)$ **8** **23.** $-18 \div (-3)$ **6** **24.** $14 + (-7)$ **7** **25.** $5(-3)$ **−15**

26. $21 + (-8)$ **13** **27.** $-2 - 10$ **−12** **28.** $-9 + 26$ **17** **29.** $-20 \div (-4)$ **5** **30.** $22 \div (-2)$ **−11**

31. $-7(-6)$ **42** **32.** $1 - 24$ **−23** **33.** $-15 - 2$ **−17** **34.** $0 + (-4)$ **−4** **35.** $16 \div 8$ **2**

SKILLS REVIEW HANDBOOK

Fractions, Decimals, and Percents

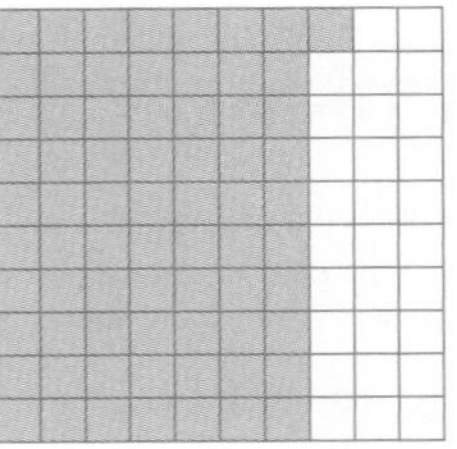

A **percent** is a ratio with a denominator of 100. The word *percent* means "per hundred," or "out of one hundred." The symbol for percent is %.

In the model at the right, 71 of the 100 squares are shaded. You can write the shaded part of the model as a fraction, a decimal, or a percent.

Fraction: seventy-one divided by one hundred, or $\frac{71}{100}$

Decimal: seventy-one hundredths, or 0.71

Percent: seventy-one percent, or 71%

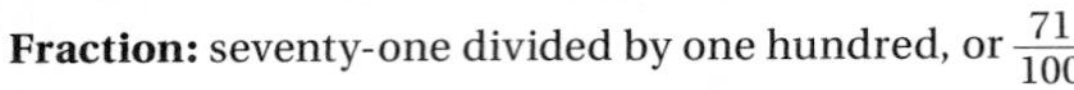

EXAMPLE Write as a fraction.

a. $94\% = \frac{94}{100} = \frac{47}{50}$ **b.** $20\% = \frac{20}{100} = \frac{1}{5}$ **c.** $0.3 = \text{three tenths} = \frac{3}{10}$

EXAMPLE Write as a decimal.

a. $15\% = \frac{15}{100} = 0.15$ **b.** $106\% = \frac{106}{100} = 1.06$ **c.** $\frac{5}{8} = 5 \div 8 = 0.625$

EXAMPLE Write as a percent.

a. $0.41 = \frac{41}{100} = 41\%$ **b.** $0.8 = \frac{8}{10} = \frac{80}{100} = 80\%$ **c.** $\frac{5}{4} = \frac{5 \cdot 25}{4 \cdot 25} = \frac{125}{100} = 125\%$

PRACTICE

Write as a fraction.

1. 0.65 $\frac{13}{20}$ **2.** 0.08 $\frac{2}{25}$ **3.** 1.5 $\frac{3}{2}$ **4.** 0.13 $\frac{13}{100}$ **5.** 0.7 $\frac{7}{10}$

6. 50% $\frac{1}{2}$ **7.** 26% $\frac{13}{50}$ **8.** 3% $\frac{3}{100}$ **9.** 95% $\frac{19}{20}$ **10.** 110% $\frac{11}{10}$

Write as a decimal.

11. $\frac{1}{4}$ 0.25 **12.** $\frac{9}{10}$ 0.9 **13.** $\frac{30}{25}$ 1.2 **14.** $\frac{2}{5}$ 0.4 **15.** $\frac{3}{8}$ 0.375

16. 16% 0.16 **17.** 142% 1.42 **18.** 1% 0.01 **19.** 30% 0.3 **20.** 6.5% 0.065

Write as a percent.

21. 0.6 60% **22.** 0.24 24% **23.** 1.3 130% **24.** 0.07 7% **25.** 0.45 45%

26. $\frac{1}{10}$ 10% **27.** $\frac{4}{5}$ 80% **28.** $\frac{17}{20}$ 85% **29.** $\frac{5}{2}$ 250% **30.** $\frac{3}{16}$ 18.75%

Calculating with Percents

You can use equations to calculate with percents. Replace words with symbols as shown in the table at the right. Below are three types of questions you can answer with percents.

Word	what	of	is
Symbol	n	$\times$	$=$

SKILLS REVIEW HANDBOOK

EXAMPLE **Answer the question.**

a. What is 15% of 20?

$n = 0.15 \times 20$

$n = 3$

3 is 15% of 20.

b. What percent of 8 is 6?

$n \times 8 = 6$

$n = 6 \div 8 = 0.75 = 75\%$

75% of 8 is 6.

c. 80% of what number is 4?

$0.8 \times n = 4$

$n = 4 \div 0.8 = 5$

80% of 5 is 4.

To find a percent of change, calculate $\frac{\text{Amount of increase or decrease}}{\text{Original amount}}$.

EXAMPLE **Find the percent of change.**

a. A class increases from 21 students to 25 students.

$\frac{25 - 21}{21} = \frac{4}{21} \approx 0.19 = 19\%$ increase

b. A price decreases from \$12 to \$9.

$\frac{12 - 9}{12} = \frac{3}{12} = 0.25 = 25\%$ decrease

PRACTICE

Answer the question.

1. What is 98% of 200? 196
2. What is 25% of 8? 2
3. What is 30% of 128? 38.4
4. What is 5% of 700? 35
5. What is 100% of 17? 17
6. What is 150% of 14? 21
7. What is 0.2% of 500? 1
8. What is 6.5% of 3000? 195
9. What percent of 100 is 54? 54%
10. What percent of 18 is 9? 50%
11. What percent of 80 is 8? 10%
12. What percent of 15 is 20? $133\frac{1}{3}\%$
13. What percent of 30 is 6? 20%
14. What percent of 5 is 8? 160%
15. What percent of 50 is 1? 2%
16. 50% of what number is 6? 12
17. 55% of what number is 44? 80
18. 10% of what number is 6? 60
19. 75% of what number is 45? 60
20. 1% of what number is 2? 200
21. 90% of what number is 63? 70
22. 12% of what number is 60? 500
23. 200% of what number is 16? 8

Find the percent of change. Round to the nearest percent if necessary.

24. A class increases from 20 to 28 students. 40% increase
25. Time decreases from 60 to 45 minutes. 25% decrease
26. A price is reduced from \$200 to \$180. 10% decrease
27. Votes increase from 200 to 300. 50% increase
28. A test is shortened from 40 to 32 items. 20% decrease
29. Membership increases from 820 to 1605. 96% increase
30. A wage rises from \$8.75 to \$10.00. 14% increase
31. The temperature drops from 24°F to 5°F. 79% decrease

SKILLS REVIEW HANDBOOK

Factors and Multiples

Factors are numbers or expressions that are multiplied together. A **prime number** is a whole number greater than 1 that has exactly two whole number factors, 1 and itself. The table shows all the prime numbers less than 100. A **composite number** is a whole number greater than 1 that has more than two whole number factors.

Prime Numbers Less Than 100
2, 3, 5, 7, 11, 13, 17, 19, 23, 29, 31, 37, 41, 43, 47, 53, 59, 61, 67, 71, 73, 79, 83, 89, 97

When you write a composite number as a product of prime numbers, you are writing its **prime factorization**.

EXAMPLE **Write the prime factorization of 60.**

Use a *factor tree*. Write 60 at the top. Then draw two branches and write 60 as the product of two factors. Continue to draw branches until all the factors are prime numbers. Two factor trees for 60 are given at the right. Both show $60 = 2 \cdot 2 \cdot 3 \cdot 5$.

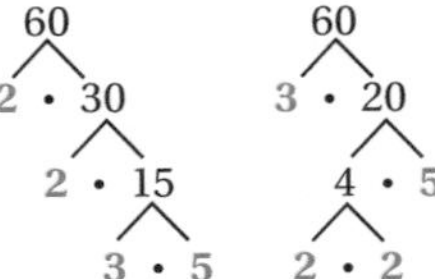

▶ The prime factorization of 60 is $2^2 \cdot 3 \cdot 5$.

A whole number that is a factor of two or more nonzero whole numbers is a **common factor** of the numbers. The largest of the common factors is the **greatest common factor (GCF)**.

EXAMPLE **Find the greatest common factor (GCF) of 18 and 45.**

Method 1 **List factors.**

Factors of 18: 1, 2, 3, 6, 9, 18

Factors of 45: 1, 3, 5, 9, 15, 45

The GCF is 9, the greatest of the common factors.

Method 2 **Use prime factorization.**

Prime factorization of 18: $2 \cdot 3 \cdot 3$

Prime factorization of 45: $3 \cdot 3 \cdot 5$

The GCF is the product of the common prime factors: $3 \cdot 3 = 9$.

A **multiple** of a whole number is the product of the number and any nonzero whole number. A **common multiple** of two or more numbers is a multiple of all of the numbers. The **least common multiple (LCM)** is the smallest of the common multiples.

EXAMPLE **Find the least common multiple (LCM) of 12 and 15.**

Method 1 **List multiples.**

Multiples of 12: 12, 24, 36, 48, 60, . . .

Multiples of 15: 15, 30, 45, 60, . . .

The LCM is 60, the least of the common multiples.

Method 2 **Use prime factorization.**

Prime factorization of 12: $2^2 \cdot 3$

Prime factorization of 15: $3 \cdot 5$

Form the LCM of the numbers by writing each prime factor to the highest power it occurs in either number: $2^2 \cdot 3 \cdot 5 = 60$.

The **least common denominator (LCD)** of two fractions is the least common multiple of the denominators. Use the LCD to add or subtract fractions with different denominators.

EXAMPLE **Add:** $\frac{3}{10} + \frac{5}{8}$

The least common multiple of the denominators, 10 and 8, is 40.
So, the least common denominator (LCD) of the fractions is 40.

Rewrite the fractions using the LCD of 40: $\frac{3}{10} = \frac{3 \cdot 4}{10 \cdot 4} = \frac{12}{40}$ and $\frac{5}{8} = \frac{5 \cdot 5}{8 \cdot 5} = \frac{25}{40}$

Add the numerators and keep the same denominator: $\frac{3}{10} + \frac{5}{8} = \frac{12}{40} + \frac{25}{40} = \frac{37}{40}$

PRACTICE

Write the prime factorization of the number. If the number is prime, write *prime*.

1. 42 $2 \cdot 3 \cdot 7$ **2.** 104 $2^3 \cdot 13$ **3.** 75 $3 \cdot 5^2$ **4.** 23 prime **5.** 70 $2 \cdot 5 \cdot 7$

6. 27 3^3 **7.** 72 $2^3 \cdot 3^2$ **8.** 180 $2^2 \cdot 3^2 \cdot 5$ **9.** 47 prime **10.** 100 $2^2 \cdot 5^2$

11. 88 $2^3 \cdot 11$ **12.** 49 7^2 **13.** 83 prime **14.** 142 $2 \cdot 71$ **15.** 32 2^5

Find the greatest common factor (GCF) of the numbers.

16. 4, 6 2 **17.** 24, 40 8 **18.** 10, 25 5 **19.** 55, 44 11 **20.** 28, 35 7

21. 8, 20 4 **22.** 5, 8 1 **23.** 15, 12 3 **24.** 16, 32 16 **25.** 70, 90 10

26. 2, 18 2 **27.** 9, 21 3 **28.** 36, 42, 54 6 **29.** 7, 12, 17 1 **30.** 45, 63, 81 9

Find the least common multiple (LCM) of the numbers.

31. 4, 16 16 **32.** 2, 14 14 **33.** 5, 6 30 **34.** 16, 24 48 **35.** 6, 8 24

36. 12, 20 60 **37.** 3, 6 6 **38.** 18, 8 72 **39.** 9, 12 36 **40.** 9, 5 45

41. 10, 15 30 **42.** 7, 9 63 **43.** 40, 4, 5 40 **44.** 25, 30, 3 150 **45.** 27, 81, 33 891

Perform the indicated operation(s). Simplify the result.

46. $\frac{1}{2} + \frac{3}{8}$ $\frac{7}{8}$ **47.** $\frac{3}{4} - \frac{5}{16}$ $\frac{7}{16}$ **48.** $\frac{7}{10} - \frac{3}{5}$ $\frac{1}{10}$ **49.** $\frac{1}{2} + \frac{1}{3}$ $\frac{5}{6}$

50. $\frac{5}{12} + \frac{1}{3}$ $\frac{3}{4}$ **51.** $\frac{4}{5} + \frac{1}{8}$ $\frac{37}{40}$ **52.** $\frac{1}{10} + \frac{3}{4}$ $\frac{17}{20}$ **53.** $\frac{5}{6} - \frac{1}{2}$ $\frac{1}{3}$

54. $\frac{7}{8} - \frac{11}{16}$ $\frac{3}{16}$ **55.** $\frac{9}{10} - \frac{1}{3}$ $\frac{17}{30}$ **56.** $\frac{2}{3} - \frac{1}{6}$ $\frac{1}{2}$ **57.** $\frac{1}{4} + \frac{2}{5}$ $\frac{13}{20}$

58. $\frac{4}{5} + \frac{1}{12} - \frac{5}{6}$ $\frac{1}{20}$ **59.** $\frac{3}{2} - \frac{3}{10} - \frac{3}{4}$ $\frac{9}{20}$ **60.** $\frac{9}{10} - \frac{1}{5} - \frac{1}{2}$ $\frac{1}{5}$ **61.** $\frac{7}{8} + \frac{3}{16} - \frac{1}{4}$ $\frac{13}{16}$

62. $\frac{8}{9} + \frac{2}{3} - \frac{7}{12}$ $\frac{35}{36}$ **63.** $\frac{1}{6} + \frac{4}{15} + \frac{1}{3}$ $\frac{23}{30}$ **64.** $\frac{1}{2} + \frac{2}{3} + \frac{1}{4}$ $\frac{17}{12} = 1\frac{5}{12}$ **65.** $\frac{15}{16} - \frac{7}{10} + \frac{1}{2}$ $\frac{59}{80}$

66. $\frac{5}{24} - \frac{1}{6} + \frac{7}{12}$ $\frac{5}{8}$ **67.** $\frac{1}{2} + \frac{3}{5} - \frac{1}{4}$ $\frac{17}{20}$ **68.** $\frac{5}{6} - \frac{3}{5} - \frac{2}{15}$ $\frac{1}{10}$ **69.** $\frac{4}{9} + \frac{3}{4} - \frac{7}{12}$ $\frac{11}{18}$

SKILLS REVIEW HANDBOOK

Ratios and Proportions

A **ratio** uses division to compare two quantities.

You can write a ratio of two quantities a and b, where b is not equal to 0, in three ways.

You should write ratios in simplest form.

Three Ways to Write the Ratio of a to b		
a to b	$a:b$	$\frac{a}{b}$

EXAMPLE **Write the ratio of 12 boys to 16 girls in three ways.**

First write the ratio as a fraction in simplest form: $\frac{\text{Boys}}{\text{Girls}} = \frac{12}{16} = \frac{12 \div 4}{16 \div 4} = \frac{3}{4}$

▶ Three ways to write the ratio of boys to girls are 3 to 4, 3:4, and $\frac{3}{4}$.

A **proportion** is an equation stating that two ratios are equal.

You can use cross multiplication to solve a proportion.

Using Cross Multiplication to Solve Proportions
If $\frac{a}{b} = \frac{c}{d}$, where $b \neq 0$ and $d \neq 0$, then $ad = bc$.

EXAMPLE **Solve the proportion.**

a. $\frac{5}{9} = \frac{n}{54}$

$5 \cdot 54 = 9 \cdot n$ Cross multiply.

$270 = 9n$ Simplify.

$30 = n$ Solve for n.

b. $\frac{x}{40} = \frac{3}{8}$

$x \cdot 8 = 40 \cdot 3$ Cross multiply.

$8x = 120$ Simplify.

$x = 15$ Solve for x.

PRACTICE

Write the ratio in simplest form. Express the answer in three ways.

1. 3 to 9 1 to 3, 1:3, $\frac{1}{3}$
2. 16 to 24 2 to 3, 2:3, $\frac{2}{3}$
3. 10 to 8 5 to 4, 5:4, $\frac{5}{4}$
4. 6 to 2 3 to 1, 3:1, $\frac{3}{1}$
5. 25 to 30 5 to 6, 5:6, $\frac{5}{6}$
6. 60 to 10 6 to 1, 6:1, $\frac{6}{1}$
7. 4 to 4 1 to 1, 1:1, $\frac{1}{1}$
8. 8 to 20 2 to 5, 2:5, $\frac{2}{5}$
9. 32 to 72 4 to 9, 4:9, $\frac{4}{9}$
10. 42 to 15 14 to 5, 14:5, $\frac{14}{5}$
11. 14 to 2 7 to 1, 7:1, $\frac{7}{1}$
12. 12 to 15 4 to 5, 4:5, $\frac{4}{5}$

Solve the proportion.

13. $\frac{x}{14} = \frac{12}{24}$ 7
14. $\frac{8}{24} = \frac{d}{36}$ 12
15. $\frac{15}{n} = \frac{3}{4}$ 20
16. $\frac{9}{45} = \frac{5}{h}$ 25
17. $\frac{a}{6} = \frac{4}{12}$ 2
18. $\frac{13}{t} = \frac{91}{7}$ 1
19. $\frac{75}{120} = \frac{r}{8}$ 5
20. $\frac{b}{90} = \frac{2}{3}$ 60
21. $\frac{4}{11} = \frac{n}{110}$ 40
22. $\frac{5}{z} = \frac{150}{90}$ 3
23. $\frac{9}{8} = \frac{x}{6}$ 6.75
24. $\frac{72}{105} = \frac{24}{m}$ 35
25. $\frac{17}{33} = \frac{51}{a}$ 99
26. $\frac{20}{125} = \frac{24}{n}$ 150
27. $\frac{16}{144} = \frac{8}{x}$ 72
28. $\frac{96}{6} = \frac{t}{3}$ 48

Converting Units of Measurement

The table of measures on page 1025 gives many statements of equivalent measures. Using each statement, you can write two different conversion factors.

Statement of Equivalent Measures	Conversion Factors
100 cm = 1 m	$\frac{100\text{ cm}}{1\text{ m}} = 1$ and $\frac{1\text{ m}}{100\text{ cm}} = 1$

To convert from one unit of measurement to another, multiply by a conversion factor. Use the one that will eliminate the starting unit and keep the desired unit.

EXAMPLE **Copy and complete.**

a. 3.5 m = _?_ cm

$3.5\text{ m} \times \frac{100\text{ cm}}{1\text{ m}} = (3.5 \times 100)\text{ cm} = 350\text{ cm}$

▶ So, 3.5 m = 350 cm.

b. 620 cm = _?_ m

$620\text{ cm} \times \frac{1\text{ m}}{100\text{ cm}} = \frac{620}{100}\text{ m} = 6.2\text{ m}$

▶ So, 620 cm = 6.2 m.

Sometimes you need to use more than one conversion factor.

EXAMPLE **Copy and complete: 7 days = _?_ sec**

Find the appropriate statements of equivalent measures.

24 h = 1 day, 60 min = 1 h, and 60 sec = 1 min

Write conversion factors: $\frac{24\text{ h}}{1\text{ day}}$, $\frac{60\text{ min}}{1\text{ h}}$, and $\frac{60\text{ sec}}{1\text{ min}}$

Multiply by conversion factors to eliminate days and keep seconds.

$7\text{ days} \times \frac{24\text{ h}}{1\text{ day}} \times \frac{60\text{ min}}{1\text{ h}} \times \frac{60\text{ sec}}{1\text{ min}} = (7 \times 24 \times 60 \times 60)\text{ sec} = 604{,}800\text{ sec}$

▶ So, 7 days = 604,800 sec.

PRACTICE

Copy and complete.

1. 6 L = _?_ mL 6000
2. 2 mi = _?_ ft 10,560
3. 80 oz = _?_ lb 5
4. 4 days = _?_ h 96
5. 77 mm = _?_ cm 7.7
6. 5 gal = _?_ qt 20
7. 48 ft = _?_ yd 16
8. 1500 mL = _?_ L 1.5
9. 40 m = _?_ cm 4000
10. 125 lb = _?_ oz 2000
11. 800 g = _?_ kg 0.8
12. 900 sec = _?_ min 15
13. 72 in. = _?_ ft 6
14. 2.5 ton = _?_ lb 5000
15. 90 min = _?_ h 1.5
16. 65,000 mg = _?_ g 65
17. 100 yd = _?_ in. 3600
18. 3.5 kg = _?_ g 3500
19. 6 pt = _?_ qt 3
20. 1 week = _?_ min 10,080
21. 2 oz = _?_ lb $\frac{1}{8}$
22. 1 km = _?_ mm 1,000,000
23. 1 mi = _?_ in. 63,360
24. 5 gal = _?_ c 80
25. 288 in.^{2} = _?_ ft^2 2
26. 24 pt = _?_ gal 3
27. 4 kg = _?_ g 4000
28. 7 hr = _?_ sec 25,200

981

SKILLS REVIEW HANDBOOK

Scientific Notation

Scientific notation is a way to write numbers using powers of 10. A number is written in **scientific notation** if it has the form $c \times 10^n$ where $1 \le c < 10$ and n is an integer. The table shows some powers of ten in order from least to greatest.

Power of Ten	10^{-3}	10^{-2}	10^{-1}	10^0	10^1	10^2	10^3
Value	0.001	0.01	0.1	1	10	100	1000

EXAMPLE Write the number in scientific notation.

a. 12,800,000 — Standard form

12,800,000 — Move the decimal point 7 places to the left.

1.28×10^7 — Use 7 as an exponent of 10.

b. 0.0000039 — Standard form

0.0000039 — Move the decimal point 6 places to the right.

3.9×10^{-6} — Use −6 as an exponent of 10.

EXAMPLE Write the number in standard form.

a. 6.1×10^4 — Scientific notation

6.1×10^4 — The exponent of 10 is 4.

61,000 — Move the decimal point 4 places to the right.

61,000 — Standard form

b. 5.74×10^{-5} — Scientific notation

5.74×10^{-5} — The exponent of 10 is −5.

0.0000574 — Move the decimal point 5 places to the left.

0.0000574 — Standard form

PRACTICE

Write the number in scientific notation.

1. 0.6 6×10^{-1}
2. 25,000,000 2.5×10^7
3. 0.08 8×10^{-2}
4. 0.00542 5.42×10^{-3}
5. 40.8 4.08×10^1
6. 7 7×10^0
7. 0.000385 3.85×10^{-4}
8. 8,145,000 8.145×10^6
9. 41,236 4.1236×10^4
10. 0.0000016 1.6×10^{-6}
11. 486,000 4.86×10^5
12. 0.000000009 9×10^{-9}
13. 0.01002 1.002×10^{-2}
14. 1,000,000,000 1×10^9
15. 7050.5 7.0505×10^3
16. 0.37 3.7×10^{-1}
17. 9850 9.85×10^3
18. 0.0000206 2.06×10^{-5}
19. 805 8.05×10^2
20. 0.0005 5×10^{-4}

Write the number in standard form.

21. 5×10^3 5000
22. 4×10^{-2} 0.04
23. 8.2×10^{-1} 0.82
24. 6.93×10^2 693
25. 3.2×10^{-3} 0.0032
26. 9.01×10^{-5} 0.0000901
27. 7.345×10^5 734,500
28. 2.38×10^{-2} 0.0238
29. 1.814×10^0 1.814
30. 2.7×10^8 270,000,000
31. 1×10^6 1,000,000
32. 4.9×10^{-4} 0.00049
33. 8×10^{-6} 0.000008
34. 5.6×10^4 56,000
35. 1.87×10^9 1,870,000,000
36. 7×10^{-4} 0.0007
37. 6.08×10^6 6,080,000
38. 9.009×10^{-3} 0.009009
39. 3.401×10^7 34,010,000
40. 5.32×10^1 53.2

Significant Digits

Significant digits indicate how precisely a number is known. Use the following guidelines to determine the number of significant digits.

- All nonzero digits are significant.
- All zeros that appear between two nonzero digits are significant.
- For a decimal, all zeros that appear after the last nonzero digit are significant. For a whole number, you cannot tell whether any zeros after the last nonzero digit are significant, so you should assume that they are not significant.

Sometimes calculations involve measurements that have various numbers of significant digits. In this case, a general rule is to carry all digits through the calculation and then round the result to the same number of significant digits as the measurement with the *fewest* significant digits. When you calculate with units that cannot be divided into fractional parts, such as number of people, consider only the significant digits of the other number(s).

SKILLS REVIEW HANDBOOK

EXAMPLE **Perform the calculation. Write your answer with the appropriate number of significant digits.**

a.

12.6	**3 significant digits**
× 0.05	**1 significant digit**
0.63	**The product has 2 significant digits.**
0.6	**Round to 1 significant digit.**

b.

840	**2 significant digits**
+ 702	**3 significant digits**
1542	**The sum has 4 significant digits.**
1500	**Round to 2 significant digits.**

c. \$61.20 restaurant bill ÷ 6 people

The number of people is exact, so consider only the 4 significant digits of the bill, \$61.20. The answer should have 4 significant digits.

\$61.20 ÷ 6 = \$10.20

▶ Each person pays \$10.20.

PRACTICE

Perform the calculation. Write your answer with the appropriate number of significant digits.

1. 600 + 30 **600**

2. 5 − 2.6 **2**

3. 12 • 6.75 **81**

4. 0.098 + 0.14 + 0.369 **0.61**

5. 3.6053 − 1.720 **1.885**

6. 40 ÷ 3.5 **10**

7. 8.0 − 3.1 **4.9**

8. 31.7 • 6.8 • 0.435 **94**

9. 30.5 • 6.40 **195**

10. 3.18 + 2.0005 **5.18**

11. 0.088 ÷ 2.44 **0.036**

12. 8650 + 380 − 49 **9000**

13. 4016 − 3007 **1009**

14. 1.35 + 14.8 **16.2**

15. 320 ÷ 18 **18**

16. 38.1 • 3.04 ÷ 0.024 **4800**

17. \$1.45 per notebook • 12 notebooks **\$17.40**

18. 10.0 liters of water − 4.5 liters of water **5.5 L**

19. 260 pints of milk ÷ 106 students **2.5 pints per student**

20. 0.5 yard of fabric + 0.87 yard of fabric **1 yd**

21. 27,973 books ÷ 11 libraries **2543 books per library**

22. 12.76 gallons of gas + 6.08 gallons of gas **18.8 gallons of gas**

23. \$6.95 per ticket • 180 tickets **\$1250**

24. 1540 pounds − 160 pounds − 85 pounds **1300 lb**

SKILLS REVIEW HANDBOOK

Writing Algebraic Expressions

To solve a problem using algebra, you often need to write a phrase as an algebraic expression.

EXAMPLE **Write the phrase as an algebraic expression.**

a. 6 less than a number

"Less than" indicates subtraction.

▸ $n - 6$

b. The cube of a number

"Cube" indicates raising to the third power.

▸ n^3

c. Double a number

"Double" indicates multiplication by 2.

▸ $2n$

EXAMPLE **Write an algebraic expression to answer the question.**

a. Rebecca walks three times as far to school as Meghan does. If Meghan walks m blocks to school, how many blocks to school does Rebecca walk?

▸ $3m$

b. Kate is 8 inches taller than Noah. If Noah is n inches tall, how tall is Kate?

▸ $n + 8$

PRACTICE

Write the phrase as an algebraic expression.

1. 8 more than a number $n + 8$

2. 10 times a number $10n$

3. Twice a number $2n$

4. 6 less than a number $n - 6$

5. One fifth of a number $\frac{1}{5}n$

6. 4 greater than a number $n + 4$

7. 5 times a number $5n$

8. A number squared n^2

9. 25% of a number $0.25n$

10. Half a number $\frac{1}{2}n$

11. 2 less than a number $n - 2$

12. The square root of a number $\sqrt{n}$

Write an algebraic expression to answer the question.

13. Allison is 4 years younger than her sister Camille. If Camille is c years old, how old is Allison? $c - 4$ yr

14. Ryan bought a movie ticket for x dollars. He paid with a $20 bill. How much change should Ryan get? $20 - x$ dollars

15. Bridget spent $5 more than Tom spent at the mall. If Tom spent x dollars, how much did Bridget spend? $x + 5$ dollars

16. Marc has twice as many baseball cards as hockey cards. If Marc has h hockey cards, how many baseball cards does he have? $2h$ baseball cards

17. Elizabeth's ballet class is 45 minutes long. If Elizabeth is m minutes late for ballet class, how many minutes will she spend in class? $45 - m$ min

18. Steve drove x miles per hour for 5 hours. How many miles did Steve drive? $5x$ mi

19. Wendy bought 10 pens priced at x dollars each. How much did she spend? $10x$ dollars

984

3inomial Products

monomial is a number, a variable, or the product of a number and one or more ariables. A **binomial** is the sum of two monomials. In other words, a binomial is polynomial with two terms. You can use a geometric model to find the product f two binomials.

EXAMPLE **Simplify $(2x + 1)(x + 3)$.**

Draw a rectangle with dimensions $2x + 1$ and $x + 3$. Use the dimensions to divide the rectangle into parts. Then find the area of each part. The binomial product $(2x + 1)(x + 3)$ is the sum of the areas of all the parts.

There are 2 blue parts with area x^2, 7 green parts with area x, and 3 yellow parts with area 1.

$$(2x + 1)(x + 3) = 2x^2 + 7x + 3$$

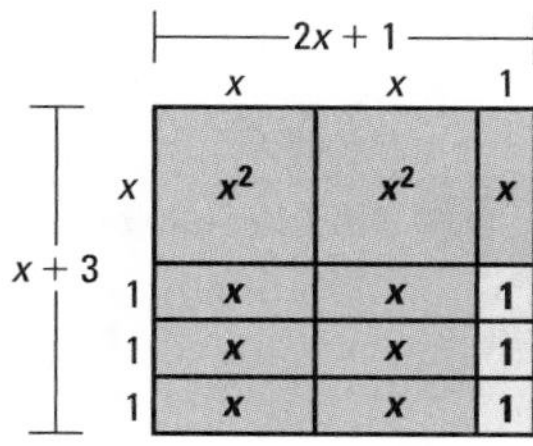

nother way to find the product of two binomials is to use the distributive roperty systematically. Multiply the *first* terms, the *outer* terms, the *inner* terms, nd the *last* terms of the binomials. This is called **FOIL** for the words **F**irst, **O**uter, nner, and **L**ast.

EXAMPLE **Simplify $(x + 2)(4x - 5)$.**

	First / Outer / Inner / Last	
$(x + 2)(4x - 5)$	$= x(4x) + x(-5) + 2(4x) + 2(-5)$	**Use FOIL.**
	$= 4x^2 - 5x + 8x - 10$	**Multiply.**
	$= 4x^2 + 3x - 10$	**Combine like terms.**

PRACTICE

Simplify.

1. $(a + 5)(a + 3)$ $a^2 + 8a + 15$
2. $(m + 4)(m + 11)$ $m^2 + 15m + 44$
3. $(t + 8)(t + 7)$ $t^2 + 15t + 56$
4. $(z + 1)(z + 6)$ $z^2 + 7z + 6$
5. $(y + 4)(y + 2)$ $y^2 + 6y + 8$
6. $(x + 9)(x + 9)$ $x^2 + 18x + 81$
7. $(y - 2)^2$ $y^2 - 4y + 4$
8. $(n + 6)^2$ $n^2 + 12n + 36$
9. $(4 - z)^2$ $z^2 - 8z + 16$
10. $(a + 10)(a - 10)$ $a^2 - 100$
11. $(y + 3)(y - 7)$ $y^2 - 4y - 21$
12. $(k + 1)^2$ $k^2 + 2k + 1$
13. $(5x - 4)(5x + 4)$ $25x^2 - 16$
14. $(3 + n)^2$ $n^2 + 6n + 9$
15. $(c + 5)(2c - 7)$ $2c^2 + 3c - 35$
16. $(a + 5)(a + 5)$ $a^2 + 10a + 25$
17. $(7 - z)(7 + z)$ $-z^2 + 49$
18. $(3x - 8)(x - 6)$ $3x^2 - 26x + 48$
19. $(4a + 3)^2$ $16a^2 + 24a + 9$
20. $(3 - g)(2g + 3)$ $-2g^2 + 3g + 9$
21. $(4 - x)(8 + x)$ $-x^2 - 4x + 32$
22. $(3n - 1)(n - 4)$ $3n^2 - 13n + 4$
23. $(-a + 9)(a - 9)$ $-a^2 + 18a - 81$
24. $(8x + 1)(x + 1)$ $8x^2 + 9x + 1$
25. $(5x + 2)(2x - 5)$ $10x^2 - 21x - 10$
26. $(2d - 5)(3d - 1)$ $6d^2 - 17d + 5$
27. $(-4z + 3)(6z - 1)$ $-24z^2 + 22z - 3$

985

SKILLS REVIEW HANDBOOK

LCDs of Rational Expressions

A **rational expression** is a fraction whose numerator and denominator are nonzero polynomials. The **least common denominator (LCD)** of two rational expressions is the least common multiple of the denominators. To find the LCD, follow these three steps:

STEP 1 **Write** each denominator as the product of its factors.

STEP 2 **Write** the product consisting of the highest power of each factor that appears in either denominator.

STEP 3 **Simplify** the product from Step 2 to write the LCD.

EXAMPLE **Find the least common denominator of the rational expressions.**

a. $\frac{2}{5xy}$ and $\frac{2}{y^3}$

STEP 1 **Factors:** $5xy = 5 \cdot x \cdot y$; $y^3 = y^3$

STEP 2 **Product:** $5 \cdot x \cdot y^3$

STEP 3 **LCD:** $5xy^3$

b. $\frac{3}{8x^2}$ and $\frac{1}{12x}$

Factors: $8x^2 = 2^3 \cdot x^2$; $12x = 2^2 \cdot 3 \cdot x$

Product: $2^3 \cdot 3 \cdot x^2$

LCD: $24x^2$

c. $\frac{-1}{3x+6}$ and $\frac{x}{x^2-3x-10}$

Factors: $3x + 6 = 3 \cdot (x + 2)$; $x^2 - 3x - 10 = (x + 2) \cdot (x - 5)$

Product: $3 \cdot (x + 2) \cdot (x - 5)$

LCD: $3(x + 2)(x - 5)$

PRACTICE

Find the least common denominator of the rational expressions.

1. $\frac{1}{2ab}$ and $\frac{4}{a^2}$ $2a^2b$
2. $\frac{5}{6k^2}$ and $\frac{6}{7k^2}$ $42k^2$
3. $\frac{2}{z^3}$ and $\frac{2}{z^2}$ z^3
4. $\frac{4}{5x}$ and $\frac{-3}{10x}$ $10x$
5. $\frac{m}{14}$ and $\frac{1}{18m}$ $126m$
6. $\frac{19}{20xy}$ and $\frac{3}{16xy}$ $80xy$
7. $\frac{1}{3y^2}$ and $\frac{1}{3y}$ $3y^2$
8. $\frac{-4}{9ab^2}$ and $\frac{2}{21a^2b}$ $63a^2b^2$
9. $\frac{n}{n+2}$ and $\frac{n^2}{n-2}$ $(n + 2)(n - 2)$
10. $\frac{-1}{x-1}$ and $\frac{3}{x+3}$ $(x - 1)(x + 3)$
11. $\frac{-8}{5n+5}$ and $\frac{4}{n+1}$ $5(n + 1)$
12. $\frac{y}{8}$ and $\frac{1}{2y+8}$ $8(y + 4)$
13. $\frac{1}{2m-6}$ and $\frac{2}{3m-9}$ $6(m - 3)$
14. $\frac{a}{n^2}$ and $\frac{-a}{n^2-6n}$ $n^2(n - 6)$
15. $\frac{1}{x-4}$ and $\frac{1}{(x-4)^2}$ $(x - 4)^2$
16. $\frac{3}{4x+12}$ and $\frac{4}{6x+18}$ $12(x + 3)$
17. $\frac{1}{2n^3}$ and $\frac{-9}{10n^2+8n}$ $2n^3(5n + 4)$
18. $\frac{10}{15b-30}$ and $\frac{17b}{9b-18}$ $45(b - 2)$
19. $\frac{-5}{(k+3)^4}$ and $\frac{3}{(k+3)^2}$ $(k + 3)^4$
20. $\frac{1}{y-5}$ and $\frac{8}{3y-15}$ $3(y - 5)$
21. $\frac{n^2}{10n+20}$ and $\frac{n}{7n+14}$ $70(n + 2)$
22. $\frac{20}{5z-40}$ and $\frac{1}{9z-56}$ $5(z - 8)(9z - 56)$
23. $\frac{2a}{a^2+4a+4}$ and $\frac{2}{a+2}$ $(a + 2)^2$
24. $\frac{1}{2z-6}$ and $\frac{-1}{z^2-z-6}$ $2(z + 2)(z - 3)$
25. $\frac{3k}{k-3}$ and $\frac{-k}{k^2-5k+6}$ $(k - 3)(k - 2)$
26. $\frac{x}{x^2-9}$ and $\frac{-x}{x^2+3x-18}$ $(x + 6)(x - 3)(x + 3)$
27. $\frac{m^2}{m^2-11m+28}$ and $\frac{-5}{m^2+5m-4}$ $(m - 7)(m - 4)(m^2 + 5m - 45$

The Coordinate Plane

A **coordinate plane** is formed by the intersection of a horizontal number line called the ***x*-axis** and a vertical number line called the ***y*-axis**. The axes meet at a point called the **origin** and divide the coordinate plane into four **quadrants**, numbered I, II, III, and IV.

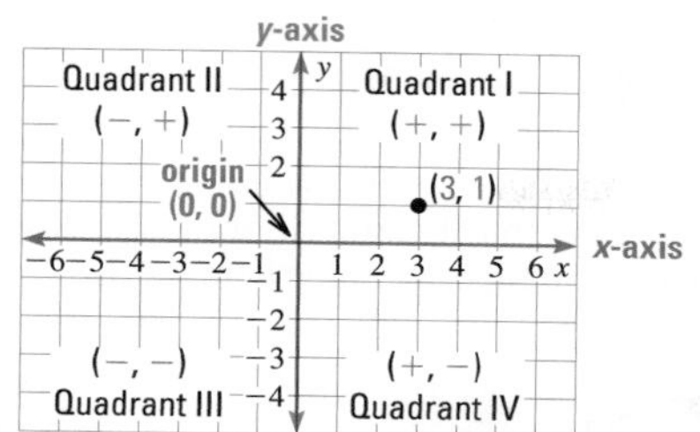

Each point in a coordinate plane is represented by an **ordered pair**. The first number is the ***x*-coordinate**, and the second number is the ***y*-coordinate**.

The ordered pair (3, 1) is graphed at the right. The x-coordinate is 3, and the y-coordinate is 1. So, the point is right 3 units and up 1 unit from the origin.

SKILLS REVIEW HANDBOOK

1–20.

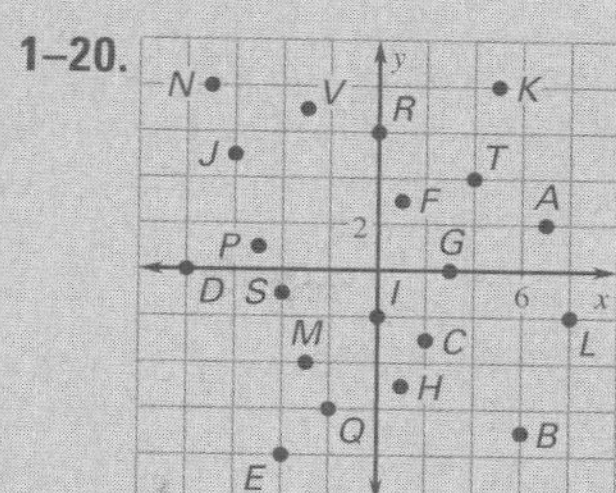

EXAMPLE **Graph the points $A(2, -1)$ and $B(-4, 0)$ in a coordinate plane.**

$A(2, -1)$ Start at the origin.
The x-coordinate is 2, so move right 2 units.
The y-coordinate is −1, so move down 1 unit.
Draw a point at (2, −1) and label it A.

$B(-4, 0)$ Start at the origin.
The x-coordinate is −4, so move left 4 units.
The y-coordinate is 0, so move up 0 units.
Draw a point at (−4, 0) and label it B.

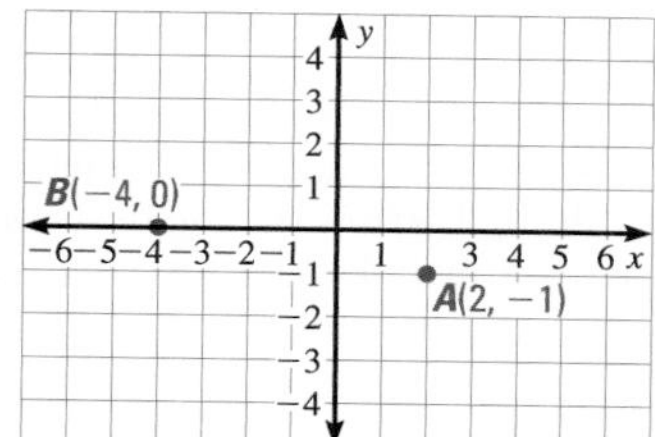

PRACTICE

Graph the points in a coordinate plane. 1–20. See margin.

1. $A(7, 2)$	**2.** $B(6, -7)$	**3.** $C(2, -3)$	**4.** $D(-8, 0)$	**5.** $E(-4, -8)$
6. $F(1, 3)$	**7.** $G(3, 0)$	**8.** $H(1, -5)$	**9.** $I(0, -2)$	**10.** $J(-6, 5)$
11. $K(5, 8)$	**12.** $L(8, -2)$	**13.** $M(-3, -4)$	**14.** $N(-7, 8)$	**15.** $P(-5, 1)$
16. $Q(-2, -6)$	**17.** $R(0, 6)$	**18.** $S(-4, -1)$	**19.** $T(4, 4)$	**20.** $V(-3, 7)$

Give the coordinates and the quadrant or axis of the point.

21. A (2, 5)	**22.** B (−1, −2)	**23.** C (5, −5)
24. D (−4, 1)	**25.** E (4, 0)	**26.** F (−5, 4)
27. G (5, 4)	**28.** H (−5, −4)	**29.** J (4, −2)
30. K (−5, −1)	**31.** L (−2, 0)	**32.** M (0, 3)
33. N (−2, 2)	**34.** O (0, 0)	**35.** P (2, −4)
36. Q (−3, −5)	**37.** R (2, −1)	**38.** S (3, 3)
39. T (−1, 5)	**40.** U (5, 2)	**41.** V (−4, −3)
42. W (1, 1)	**43.** X (1, −3)	**44.** Y (0, −5)

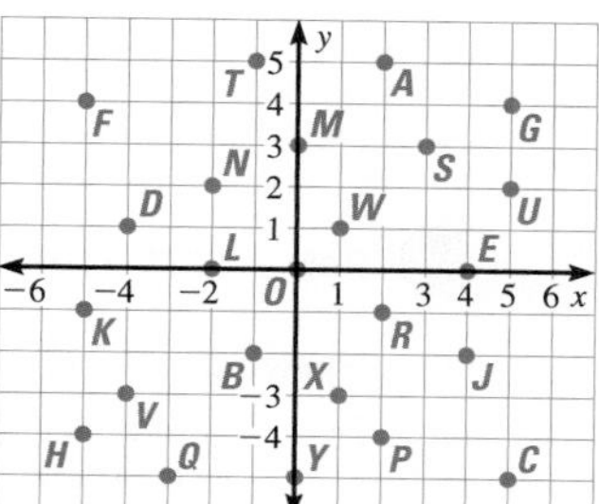

p. 989

9. 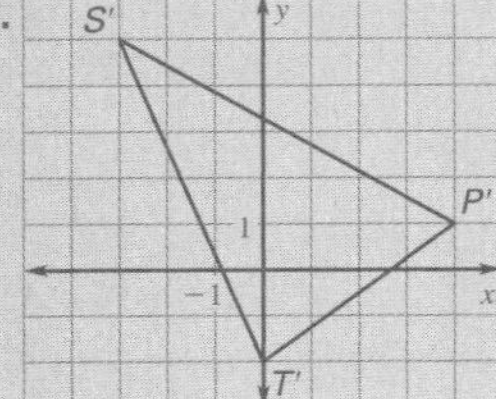

10.

11. 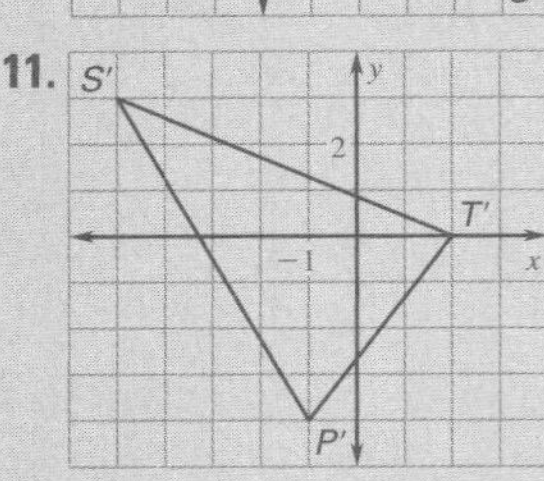

12. 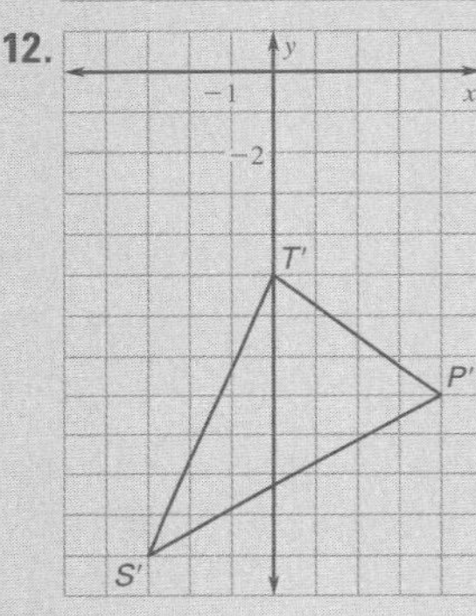

13. 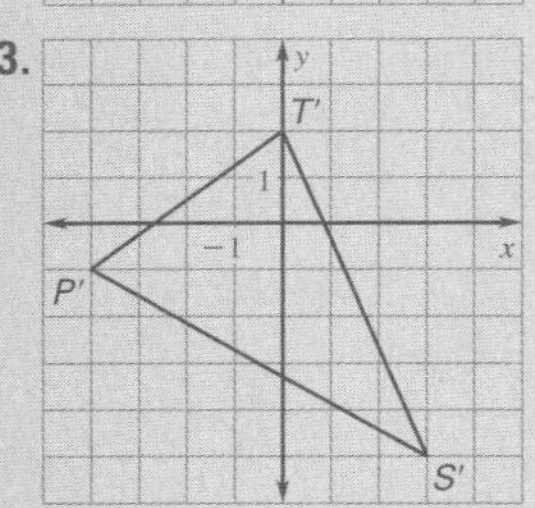

SKILLS REVIEW HANDBOOK

Transformations

A **transformation** is a change made to the position or to the size of a figure. Each point (x, y) of the figure is mapped to a new point, and the new figure is called an **image**.

A **translation** is a transformation in which each point of a figure moves the same distance in the same direction. A figure and its translated image are congruent.

Translation *a* Units Horizontally and *b* Units Vertically
$(x, y) \rightarrow (x + a, y + b)$

EXAMPLE **Translate $\overline{FG}$ right 3 units and down 1 unit.**

To move right 3 units, use $a = 3$. To move down 1 unit, use $b = -1$. So, use $(x, y) \rightarrow (x + 3, y + (-1))$ with each endpoint.

$F(2, 4) \rightarrow F'(2 + 3, 4 + (-1)) = F'(5, 3)$
$G(1, 1) \rightarrow G'(1 + 3, 1 + (-1)) = G'(4, 0)$

Graph the endpoints (5, 3) and (4, 0). Then draw the image.

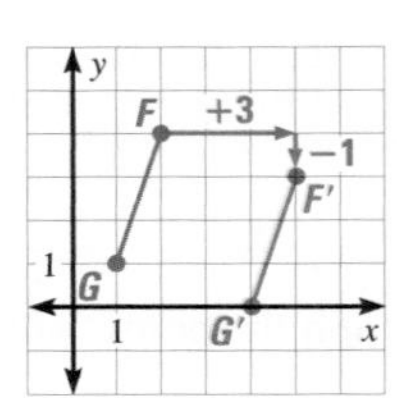

A **reflection** is a transformation in which a figure is reflected, or flipped, in a line, called the **line of reflection**. A figure and its reflected image are congruent.

Reflection in *x*-axis	Reflection in *y*-axis
$(x, y) \rightarrow (x, -y)$	$(x, y) \rightarrow (-x, y)$

EXAMPLE **Reflect $\triangle ABC$ in the *y*-axis.**

Use $(x, y) \rightarrow (-x, y)$ with each vertex.

$A(4, 3) \rightarrow A'(-4, 3)$ **Change each**
$B(1, 2) \rightarrow B'(-1, 2)$ ***x*-coordinate**
$C(3, 1) \rightarrow C'(-3, 1)$ **to its opposite.**

Graph the new vertices. Then draw the image.

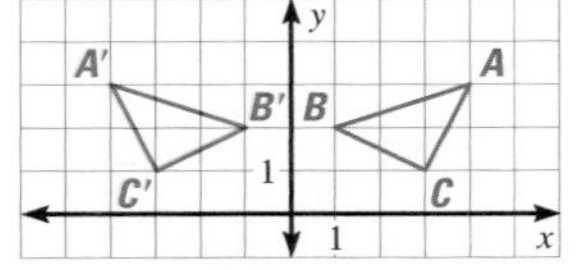

A **rotation** is a transformation in which a figure is turned about a fixed point, called the **center of rotation**. The direction can be clockwise or counterclockwise. A figure and its rotated image are congruent.

Rotation About the Origin	
180° either direction	$(x, y) \rightarrow (-x, -y)$
90° clockwise	$(x, y) \rightarrow (y, -x)$
90° counterclockwise	$(x, y) \rightarrow (-y, x)$

EXAMPLE **Rotate *RSTV* 180° about the origin.**

Use $(x, y) \rightarrow (-x, -y)$ with each vertex.

$R(2, 2) \rightarrow R'(-2, -2)$ **Change every**
$S(4, 2) \rightarrow S'(-4, -2)$ **coordinate**
$T(4, 1) \rightarrow T'(-4, -1)$ **to its opposite.**
$V(1, 0) \rightarrow V'(-1, 0)$

Graph the new vertices. Then draw the image.

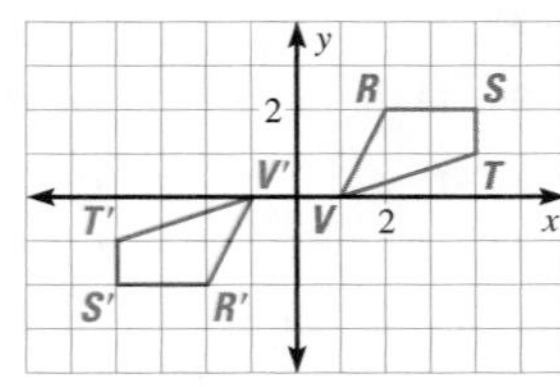

A **dilation** is a transformation in which a figure stretches or shrinks depending on the dilation's **scale factor**. A figure *stretches* if $k > 1$ and *shrinks* if $0 < k < 1$. A figure and its dilated image are similar.

Dilation with Scale Factor k with Respect to the Origin
$(x, y) \rightarrow (kx, ky)$

EXAMPLE **Dilate *JKLM* using a scale factor of 0.5.**

The scale factor is $k = 0.5$, so multiply every coordinate by 0.5. Use $(x, y) \rightarrow (0.5x, 0.5y)$ with each vertex.

$J(4, 4) \rightarrow J'(0.5 \cdot 4, 0.5 \cdot 4) = J'(2, 2)$
$K(6, 4) \rightarrow K'(0.5 \cdot 6, 0.5 \cdot 4) = K'(3, 2)$
$L(6, -1) \rightarrow L'(0.5 \cdot 6, 0.5 \cdot (-1)) = L'(3, -0.5)$
$M(4, -1) \rightarrow M'(0.5 \cdot 4, 0.5 \cdot (-1)) = M'(2, -0.5)$

Graph the new vertices. Then draw the image.

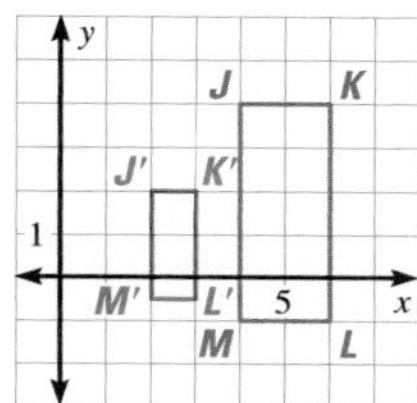

PRACTICE

Find the coordinates of $N(-3, 8)$ after the given transformation. For rotations, rotate about the origin.

1. Rotate 180°. (3, −8)
2. Reflect in x-axis. (−3, −8)
3. Translate up 3 units. (−3, 11)
4. Reflect in y-axis. (3, 8)
5. Rotate 90° clockwise. (8, 3)
6. Translate left 5 units. (−8, 8)
7. Rotate 90° counterclockwise. (−8, −3)
8. Translate right 2 units and down 9 units. (−1, −1)

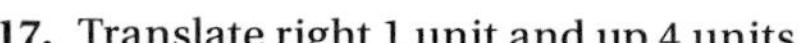

Transform $\triangle PST$. Graph the result. For rotations, rotate about the origin. 9–18. See margin.

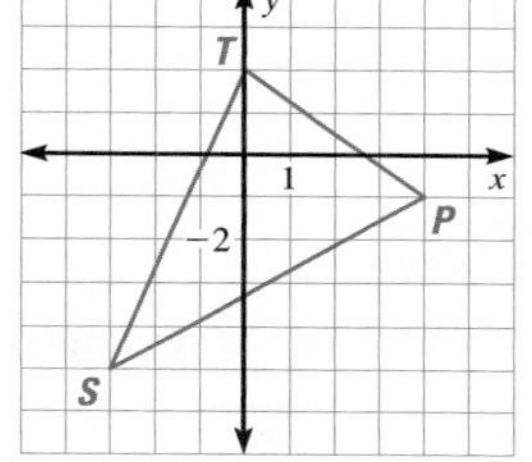
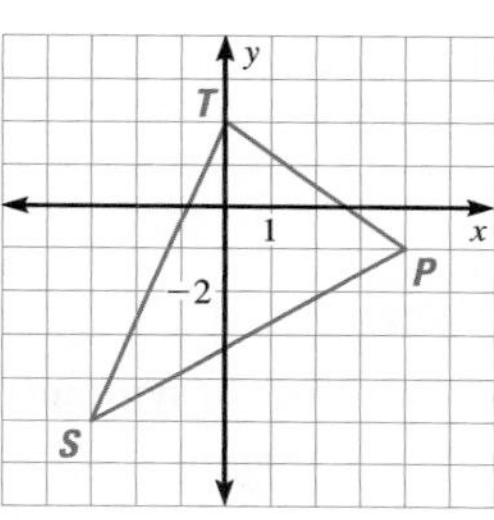

9. Reflect in x-axis.
10. Rotate 90° counterclockwise.
11. Rotate 90° clockwise.
12. Translate down 7 units.
13. Reflect in y-axis.
14. Translate left 4 units.
15. Rotate 180°.
16. Translate right 2 units.
17. Translate right 1 unit and up 4 units.
18. Translate left 6 units and up 2 units.

The coordinates of the vertices of a polygon are given. Draw the polygon. Then find the coordinates of the vertices of the image after the specified dilation, and draw the image. 19–23. See margin.

19. (1, 3), (3, 2), (2, 5); dilate using a scale factor of 3
20. (2, 8), (2, 4), (6, 8), (6, 4); dilate using a scale factor of $\frac{3}{2}$
21. (3, 3), (6, 3), (3, −3), (6, −3); dilate using a scale factor of $\frac{1}{3}$
22. (2, 2), (2, 7), (5, 7); dilate using a scale factor of 2
23. (2, −2), (6, −2), (4, −6), (0, −6); dilate using a scale factor of $\frac{1}{2}$

14.

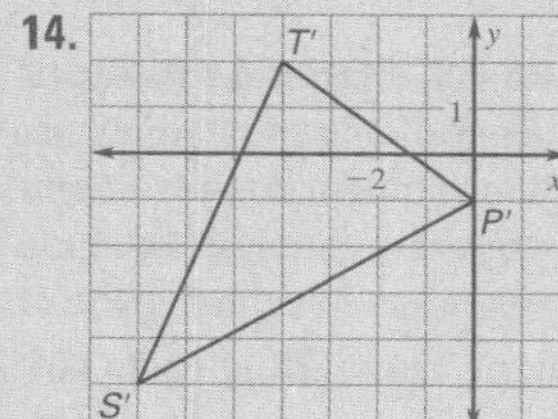

15.

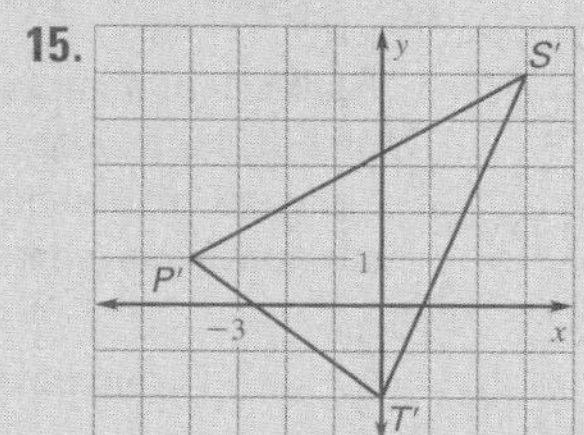

16.

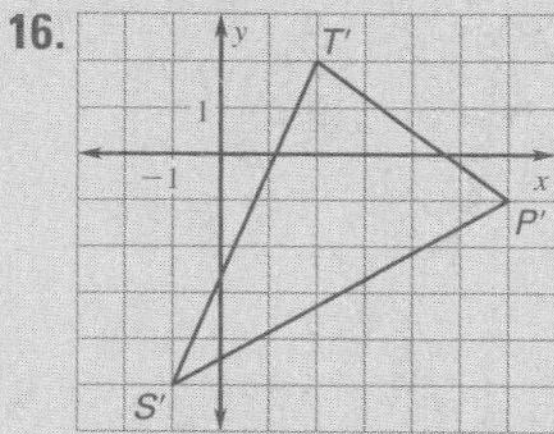

17.–22.

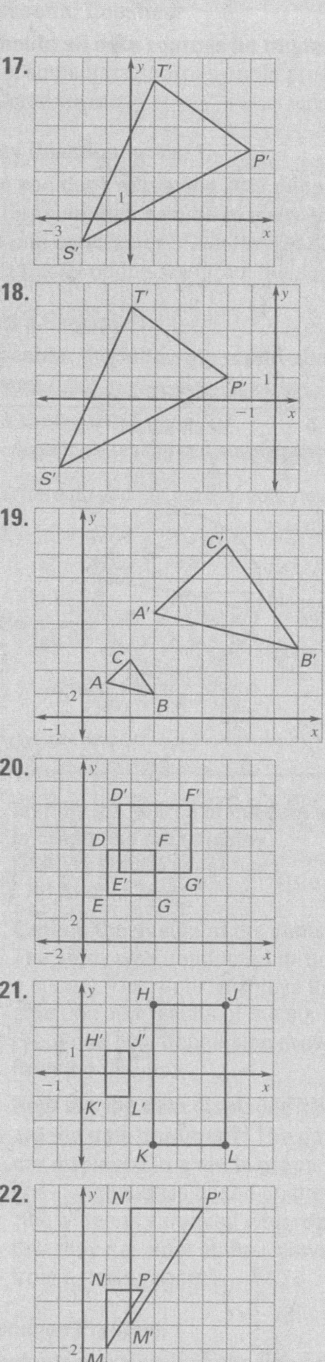

23.

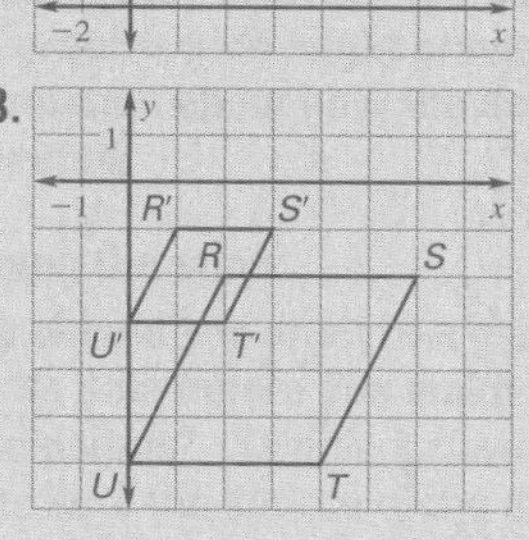

Line Symmetry

A figure has **line symmetry** if a line, called a **line of symmetry**, divides the figure into two parts that are mirror images of each other. Below are four figures with their lines of symmetry shown in red.

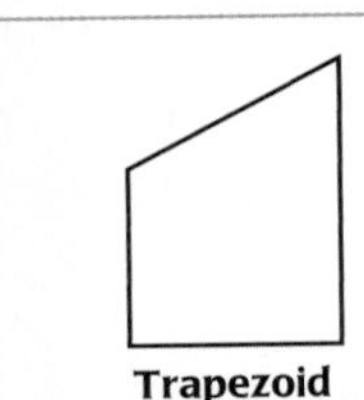	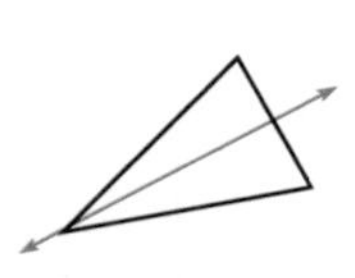	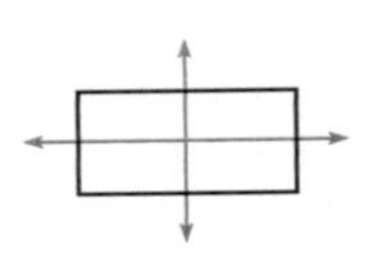	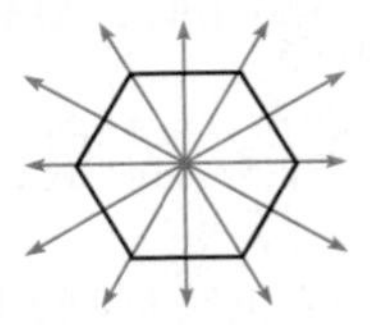
Trapezoid No lines of symmetry	**Isosceles Triangle** 1 line of symmetry	**Rectangle** 2 lines of symmetry	**Regular Hexagon** 6 lines of symmetry

EXAMPLE **A line of symmetry for the figure is shown in red. Find the coordinates of point *A*.**

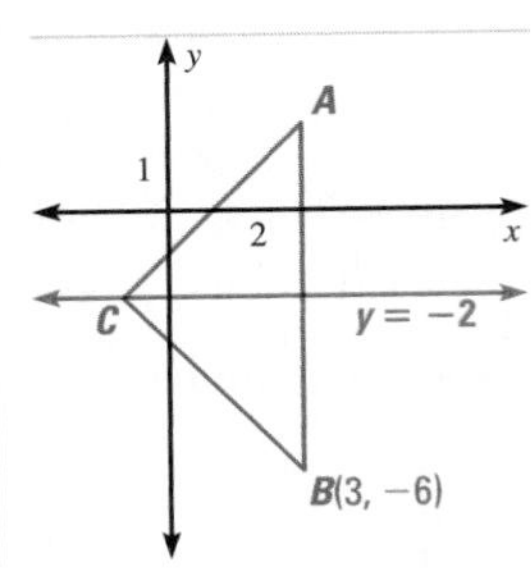

Point A is the mirror image of the point $(3, -6)$ with respect to the line of symmetry $y = -2$. The x-coordinate of A is 3, the same as the x-coordinate of $(3, -6)$. Because -6 is the y-coordinate of $(3, -6)$, and $-2 - (-6) = 4$, the point $(3, -6)$ is *down* 4 units from the line of symmetry. Therefore, point A must be *up* 4 units from the line of symmetry. So, the y-coordinate of A is $-2 + 4 = 2$. The coordinates of point A are $(3, 2)$.

PRACTICE

Tell how many lines of symmetry the figure has.

1. 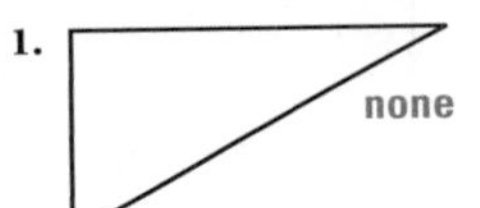 none
2. 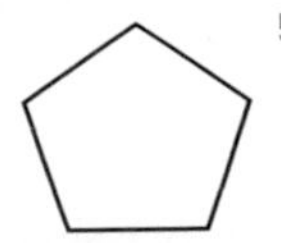 5
3. 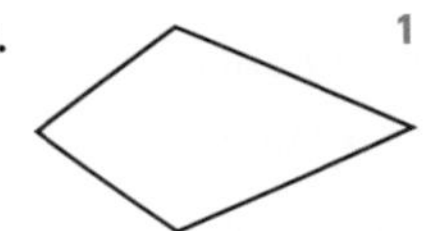 1
4. 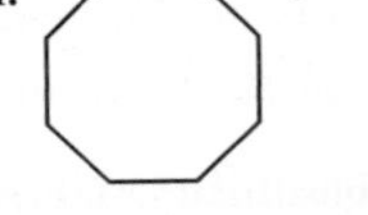 8

5. A parallelogram none
6. A square 4
7. A rhombus 2
8. An equilateral triangle 3

A line of symmetry for the figure is shown in red. Find the coordinates of point *A*.

9. 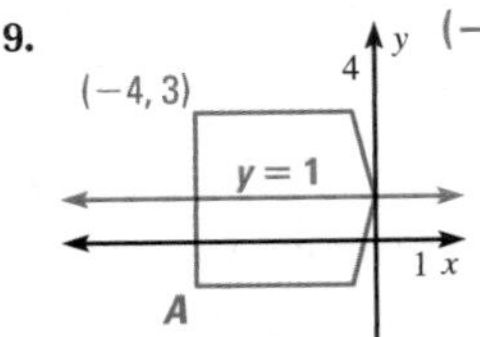

(−4, −1)

10. 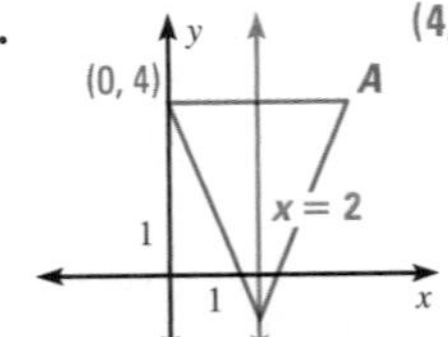

(4, 4)

11. 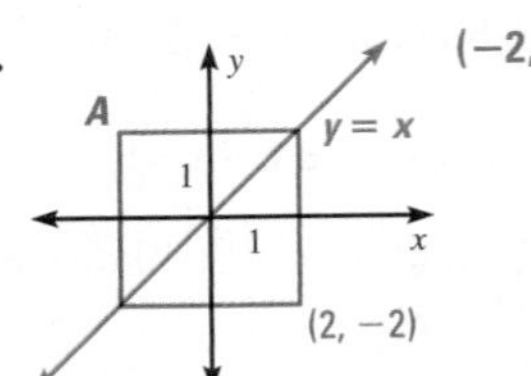

(−2, 2)

Perimeter and Area

The **perimeter** P of a figure is the distance around it. To find the perimeter of a figure, add the side lengths.

EXAMPLE **Find the perimeter of the figure.**

a.

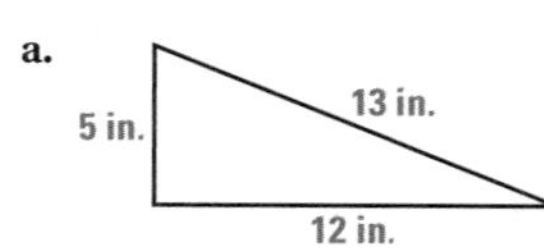

$P = 5 + 12 + 13 = 30$ in.

b.

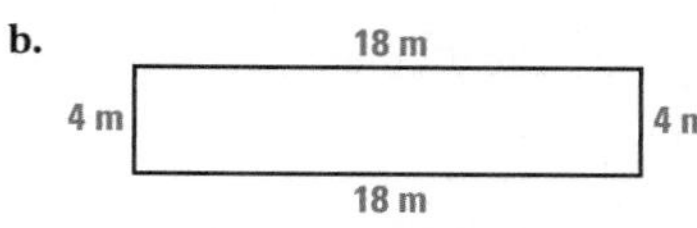

$P = 2(4) + 2(18) = 8 + 36 = 44$ m

The **area** A of a figure is the number of square units enclosed by the figure.

Area of a Triangle	Area of a Rectangle	Area of a Parallelogram	Area of a Trapezoid
h, b	w, ℓ	h, b	b_1, h, b_2
$A = \frac{1}{2}bh$	$A = \ell w$	$A = bh$	$A = \frac{1}{2}(b_1 + b_2)h$

EXAMPLE **Find the area of the figure.**

a.

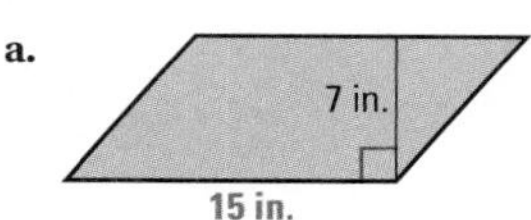

$A = (15)(7) = 105 \text{ in.}^2$

b.

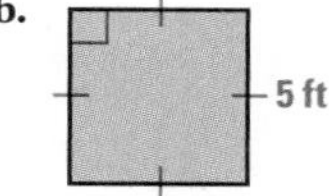

$A = (5)(5) = 25 \text{ ft}^2$

c.

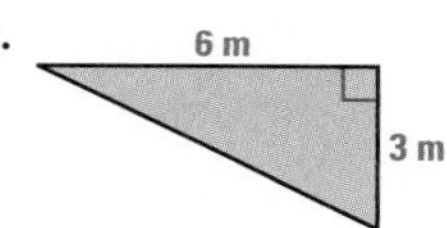

$A = \frac{1}{2}(6)(3) = 9 \text{ m}^2$

PRACTICE

Find the perimeter and area of the figure.

1.

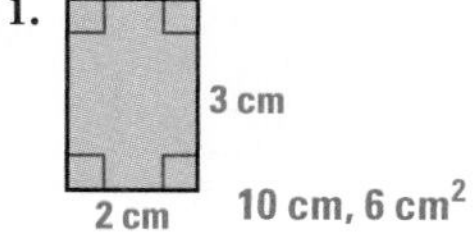

10 cm, 6 cm^2

2.

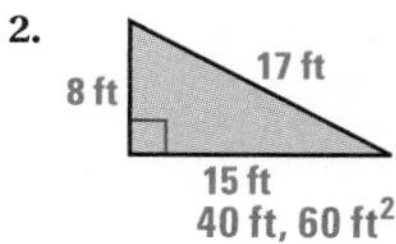

40 ft, 60 ft^2

3.

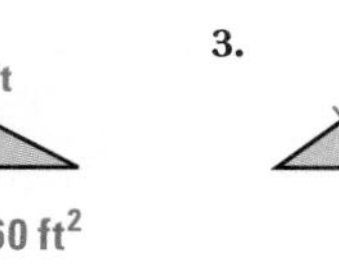

26 in., 24 in.^2

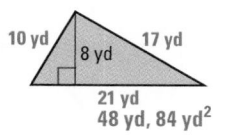

4.

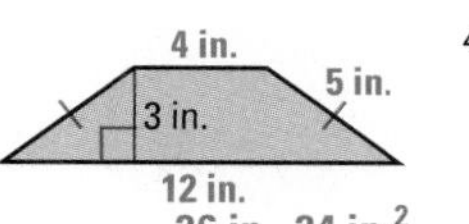

24 m, 30 m^2

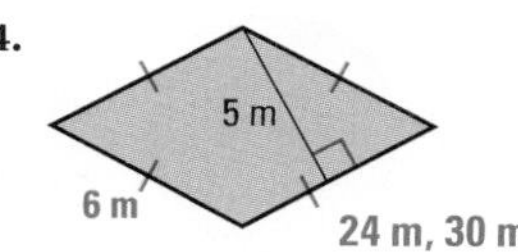

5.

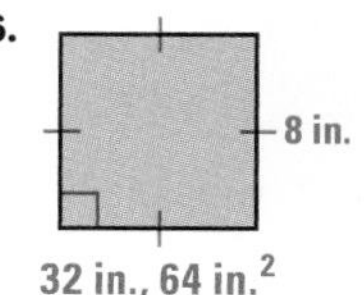

48 yd, 84 yd^2

6.

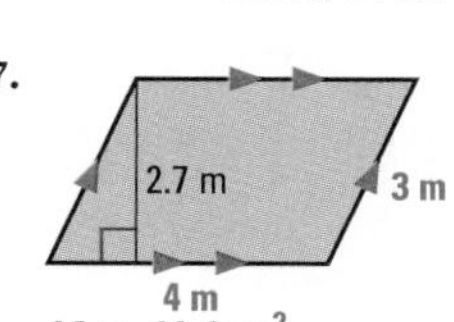

32 in., 64 in.^2

7.

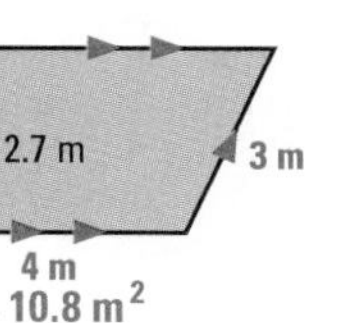

14 m, 10.8 m^2

8.

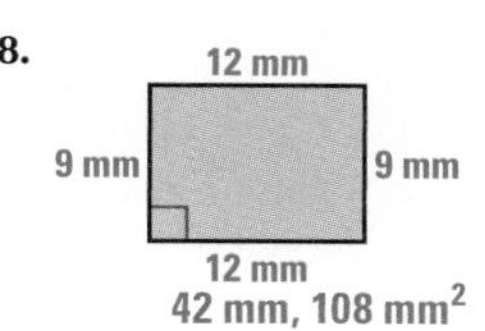

42 mm, 108 mm^2

991

Circumference and Area of a Circle

A **circle** consists of all points in a plane that are the same distance from a fixed point called the **center**.

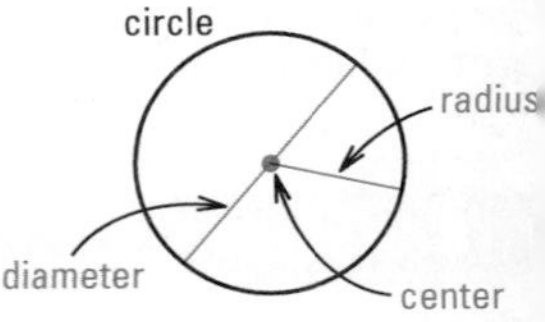

The distance between the center and any point on the circle is the **radius**. The distance across the circle through the center is the **diameter**. The diameter is twice the radius.

The **circumference** of a circle is the distance around the circle. For any circle, the ratio of the circumference to the diameter is π (pi), an irrational number that is approximately 3.14 or $\frac{22}{7}$.

To find the circumference C of a circle with radius r, use the formula $C = 2\pi r$.

To find the area A of a circle with radius r, use the formula $A = \pi r^2$.

EXAMPLE **Find the circumference and area of a circle with radius 6 cm. Give an exact answer and an approximate answer for each.**

Circumference

$C = 2\pi r$

$= 2\pi(6)$

$= 12\pi$

$\approx 12(3.14)$

≈ 37.7

▶ The circumference is 12π centimeters, or about 37.7 centimeters.

Area

$A = \pi r^2$

$= \pi(6)^2$

$= 36\pi$

$\approx 36(3.14)$

≈ 113

▶ The area is 36π square centimeters, or about 113 square centimeters.

6 cm

PRACTICE

Find the circumference and area of the circle. Give an exact answer and an approximate answer for each. 1–12. See margin.

1.

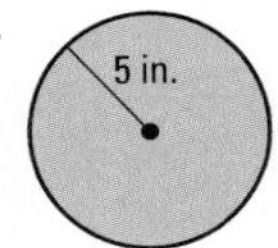

2.

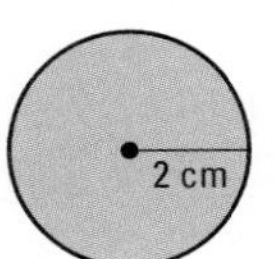

3.

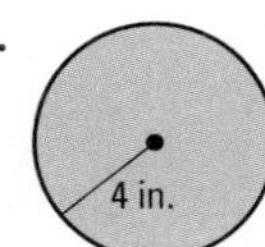

4.

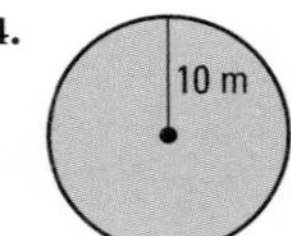

5.

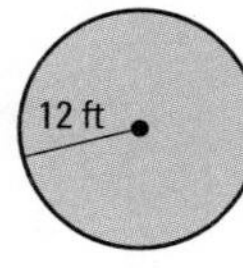

6.

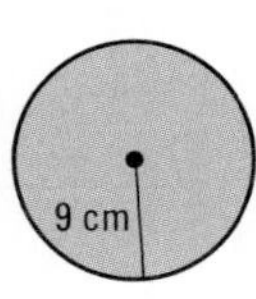

7.

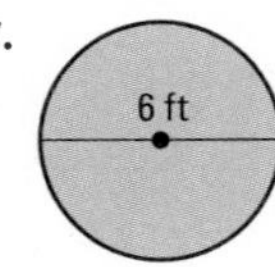

8.

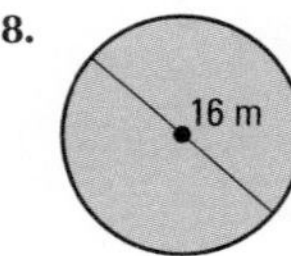

9. 2 cm

10. 14 ft

11. 22 in.

12.

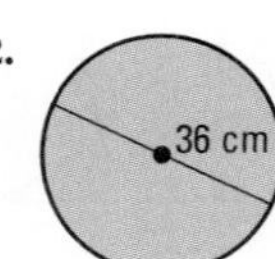

1. $C = 10\pi$ in. or about 31 in., $A = 25\pi$ in.^{2} or about 79 in.^{2}
2. $C = 4\pi$ cm or about 13 cm, $A = 4\pi$ cm^2 or about 13 cm^2
3. $C = 8\pi$ in. or about 25 in., $A = 16\pi$ in.^{2} or about 50 in.^{2}
4. $C = 20\pi$ m or about 63 m, $A = 100\pi$ m^2 or about 314 m^2
5. $C = 24\pi$ ft or about 75 ft, $A = 144\pi$ ft^2 or about 452 ft^2
6. $C = 18\pi$ cm or about 57 cm, $A = 81\pi$ cm^2 or about 254 cm^2
7. $C = 6\pi$ ft or about 19 ft, $A = 9\pi$ ft^2 or about 28 ft^2
8. $C = 16\pi$ m or about 50 m, $A = 64\pi$ m^2 or about 201 m^2
9. $C = 2\pi$ cm or about 6 cm, $A = \pi$ cm^2 or about 3 cm^2
10. $C = 14\pi$ ft or about 44 ft, $A = 49\pi$ ft^2 or about 154 ft^2
11. $C = 22\pi$ in. or about 69 in., $A = 121\pi$ in.^{2} or about 380 in.^{2}
12. $C = 36\pi$ cm or about 113 cm, $A = 324\pi$ cm^2 or about 1017 cm^2

Surface Area and Volume

A **solid** is a three-dimensional figure that encloses part of space.

The **surface area** S of a solid is the area of the solid's outer surface(s).

The **volume** V of a solid is the amount of space that the solid occupies.

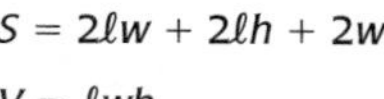

Rectangular Prism

$S = 2\ell w + 2\ell h + 2wh$

$V = \ell wh$

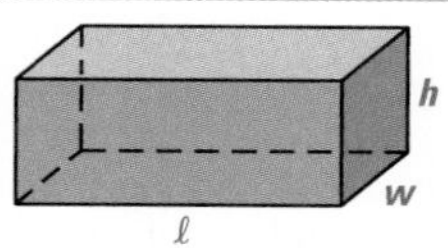

Cylinder

$S = 2\pi r^2 + 2\pi rh$

$V = \pi r^2 h$

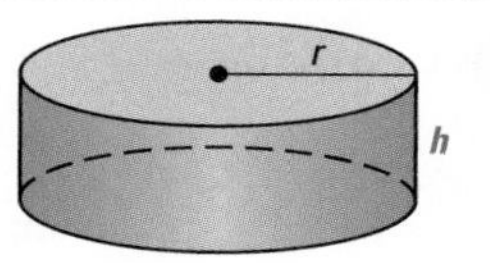

EXAMPLE Find the surface area and volume of the rectangular prism.

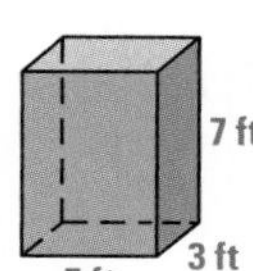

Surface area

$S = 2\ell w + 2\ell h + 2wh$

$= 2(5)(3) + 2(5)(7) + 2(3)(7)$

$= 30 + 70 + 42$

$= 142 \text{ ft}^2$

Volume

$V = \ell wh$

$= (5)(3)(7)$

$= 105 \text{ ft}^3$

EXAMPLE Find the surface area and volume of the cylinder.

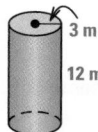

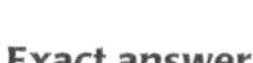

Surface area

$S = 2\pi r^2 + 2\pi rh$

$= 2\pi(3)^2 + 2\pi(3)(12)$

$= 90\pi \text{ m}^2$ **Exact answer**

$\approx 283 \text{ m}^2$ **Approximate answer**

Volume

$V = \pi r^2 h$

$= \pi(3)^2(12)$

$= 108\pi \text{ m}^3$ **Exact answer**

$\approx 339 \text{ m}^3$ **Approximate answer**

PRACTICE

Find the surface area and volume of the solid.

1. 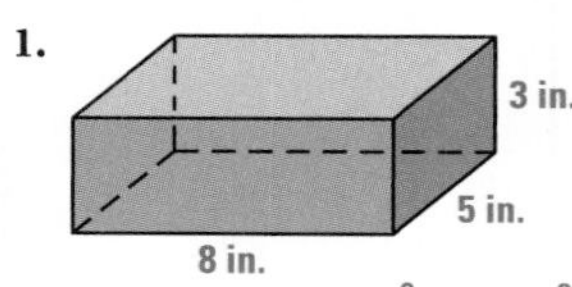

158 in.^{2}, 120 in.^{3}

2. 
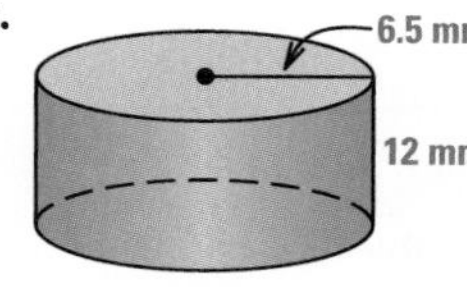
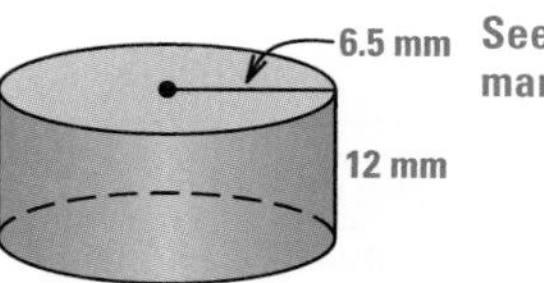

See margin.

3. 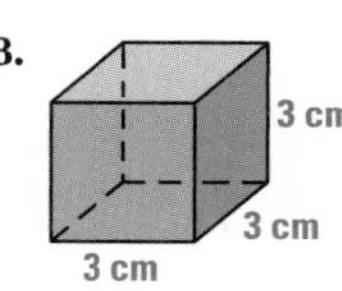

54 cm^2, 27 cm^3

4. 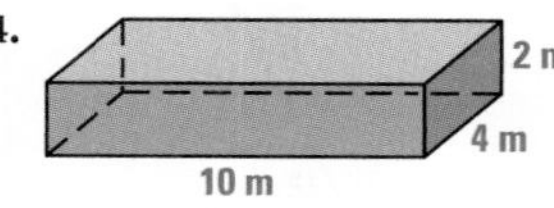

136 m^2, 80 m^3

5. 14 yd, 4 yd

See margin.

6. 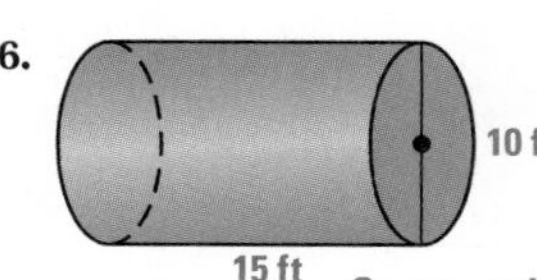

See margin.

2. 240.5π mm^2 or about 756 mm^2, 507π mm^3 or about 1592 mm^3

5. 154π yd^2 or about 484 yd^2, 196π yd^3 or about 615 yd^3

6. 200π ft^2 or about 628 ft^2, 375π ft^3 or about 1178 ft^2

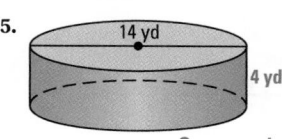

Angle Relationships

An **angle bisector** is a ray that divides an angle into two congruent angles.
Two angles are **complementary angles** if the sum of their measures is 90°.
Two angles are **supplementary angles** if the sum of their measures is 180°.

EXAMPLE Find the value of *x*.

a. $\overrightarrow{BD}$ bisects $\angle ABC$ and $m\angle ABC = 64°$.

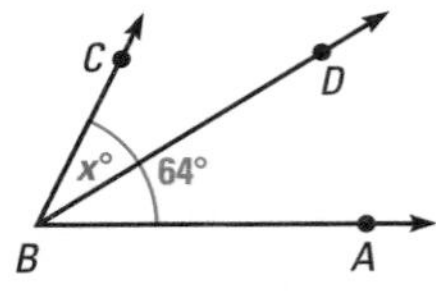

Because $\overrightarrow{BD}$ bisects $\angle ABC$, the value of x is half $m\angle ABC$.

$$x = \frac{64}{2} = 32$$

b. $\angle GFJ$ and $\angle HFJ$ are complementary.

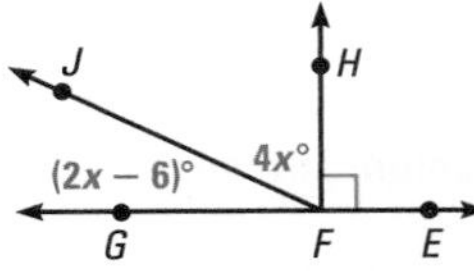

Because $\angle GFJ$ and $\angle HFJ$ are complementary angles, their sum is 90°.

$$(2x - 6) + 4x = 90$$
$$6x - 6 = 90$$
$$x = 16$$

c. $\angle CBD$ and $\angle ABD$ are supplementary.

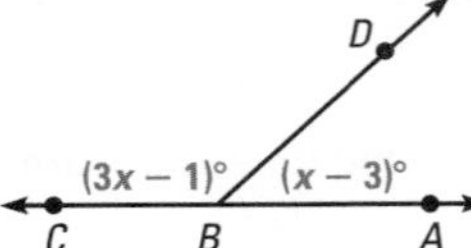

Because $\angle CBD$ and $\angle ABD$ are supplementary angles, their sum is 180°.

$$(3x - 1) + (x - 3) = 180$$
$$4x - 4 = 180$$
$$x = 46$$

PRACTICE

$\overrightarrow{BD}$ is the angle bisector of $\angle ABC$. Find the value of x.

1. 39

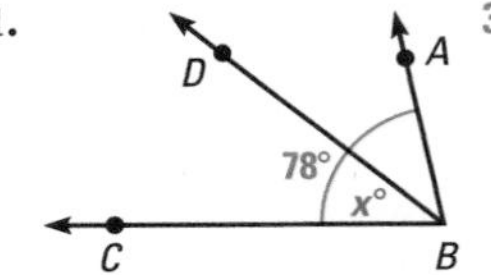

2. 26

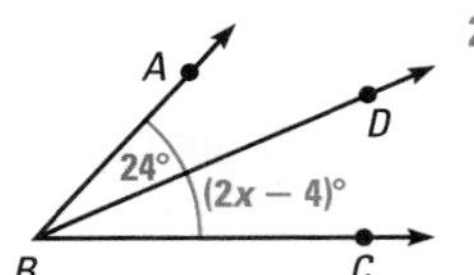

3. 8

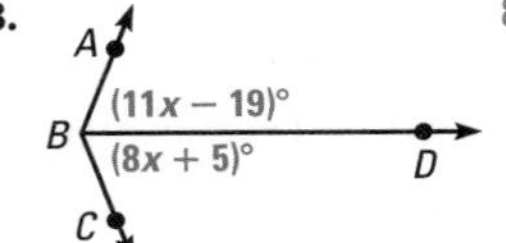

$\angle ABD$ and $\angle DBC$ are complementary. Find the value of x.

4. 12

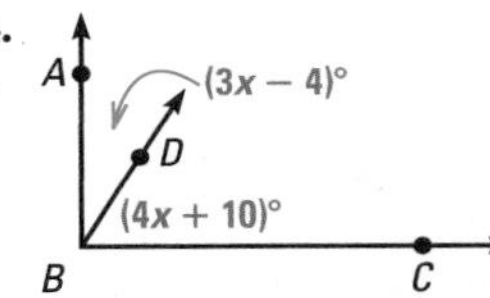

5. 16

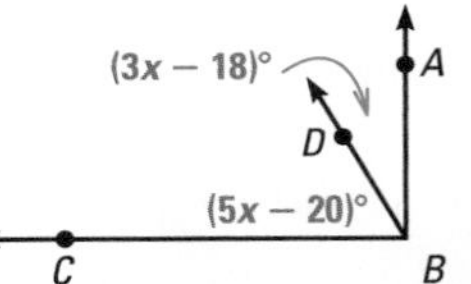

6. 7

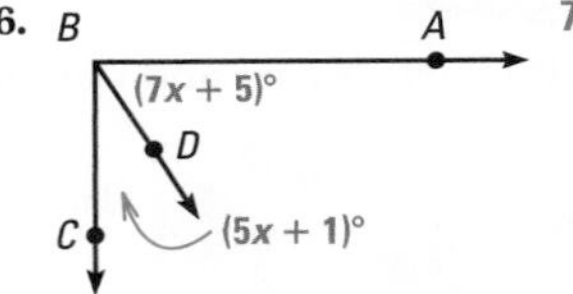

$\angle ABD$ and $\angle DBC$ are supplementary. Find the value of x.

7. 23

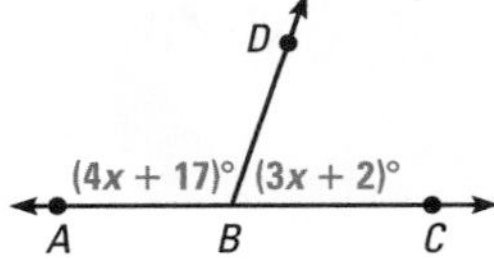

8. 52

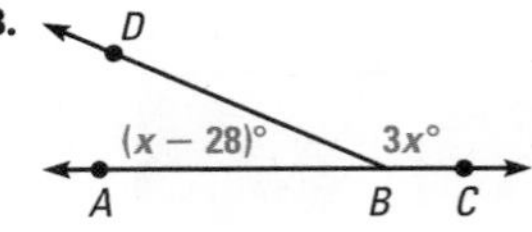

9. 29

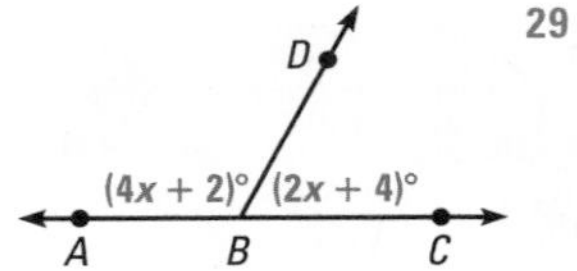

994

Triangle Relationships

he sum of the angle measures of any triangle is 180°.

EXAMPLE **Find the value of *x*.**

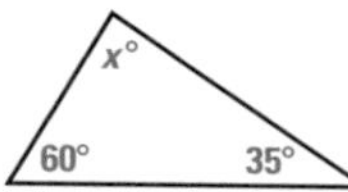

$60 + 35 + x = 180$	**The sum of the angle measures is 180°.**
$95 + x = 180$	**Simplify.**
$x = 85$	**Solve for *x*.**

n a right triangle, the **hypotenuse** is the side opposite the ight angle. The **legs** are the sides that form the right angle. he **Pythagorean theorem** states that the sum of the squares f the lengths of the legs equals the square of the length of he hypotenuse.

Pythagorean Theorem

$a^2 + b^2 = c^2$

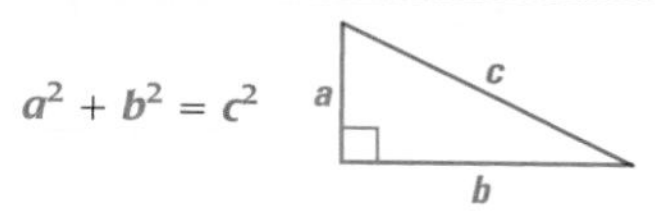

EXAMPLE **Find the value of *x*.**

a.

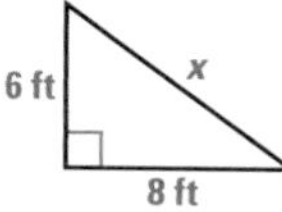

$6^2 + 8^2 = x^2$	**Pythagorean theorem**
$36 + 64 = x^2$	**Simplify.**
$100 = x^2$	**Simplify.**
$x = 10$ ft	**Solve for *x*.**

b.

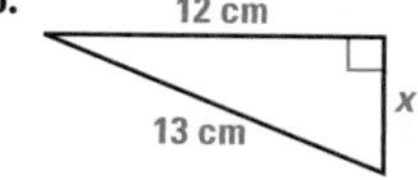

$x^2 + 12^2 = 13^2$	**Pythagorean theorem**
$x^2 + 144 = 169$	**Simplify.**
$x^2 = 25$	**Solve for x^2.**
$x = 5$ cm	**Solve for *x*.**

PRACTICE

Find the value of *x*.

1. 40

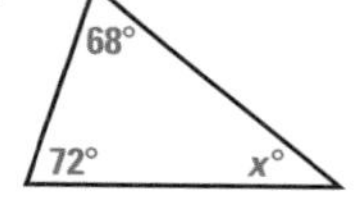

2. 109

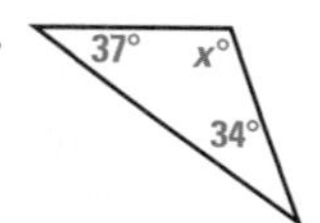
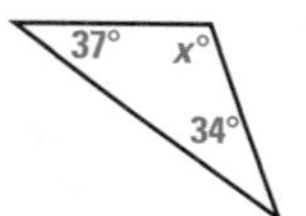

3. 60

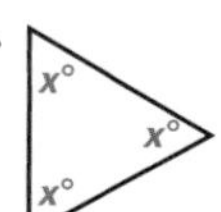
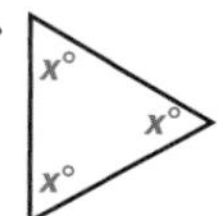

4. 34

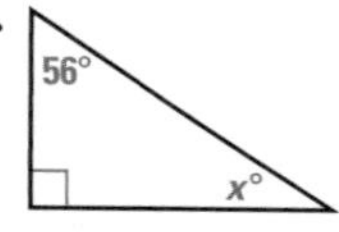

5. 50 cm

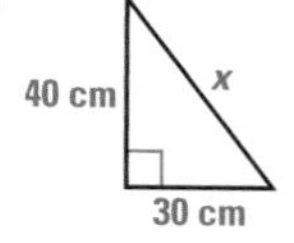

6. $8\sqrt{2}$ in.

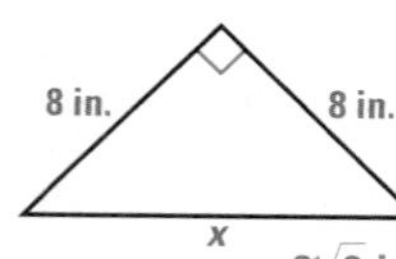

7. 12 ft

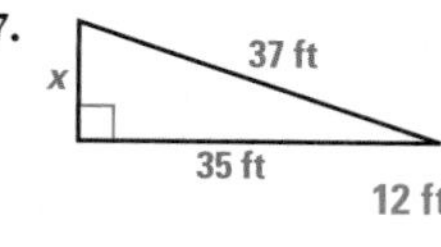

8. $\sqrt{11}$ m

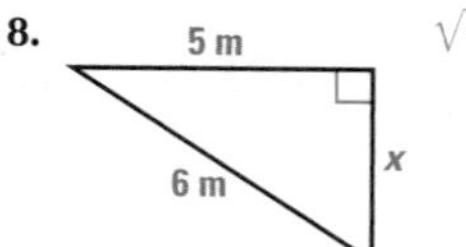

9. A triangle with angles that measure $x°$, $x°$, and 70° 55°

995

SKILLS REVIEW HANDBOOK

Congruent and Similar Figures

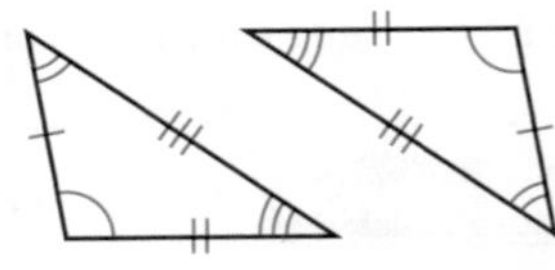

Two figures are **congruent** if they have the same shape and the same size. If two figures are congruent, then corresponding angles are congruent and corresponding sides are congruent. The triangles at the right are congruent. Matching arcs show congruent angles, and matching tick marks show congruent sides.

Two figures are **similar** if they have the same shape but not necessarily the same size. If two figures are similar, then corresponding angles are congruent and the ratios of the lengths of corresponding sides are equal.

EXAMPLE Tell whether the figures are *congruent, similar,* or *neither.*

a.

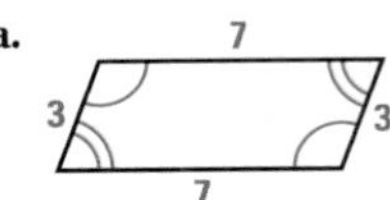

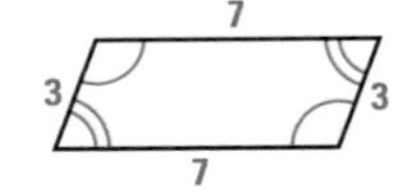

As shown, corresponding angles are congruent and corresponding sides are congruent. So, the figures are congruent.

b.

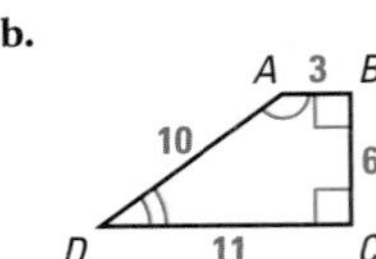

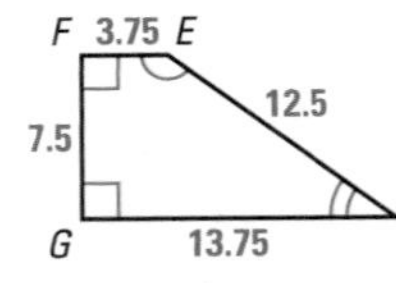

As shown, corresponding angles are congruent, but corresponding sides have different lengths. So, the figures are not congruent, but they may be similar.

The figures are similar if the ratios of the lengths of corresponding sides are equal.

$\frac{AB}{EF} = \frac{3}{3.75} = 0.8 \quad \frac{BC}{FG} = \frac{6}{7.5} = 0.8 \quad \frac{CD}{GH} = \frac{11}{13.75} = 0.8 \quad \frac{AD}{EH} = \frac{10}{12.5} = 0.8$

▶ Because corresponding angles are congruent and the ratios of the lengths of corresponding sides are equal, *ABCD* is similar to *EFGH*.

EXAMPLE The two polygons are similar. Find the value of *x*.

a.

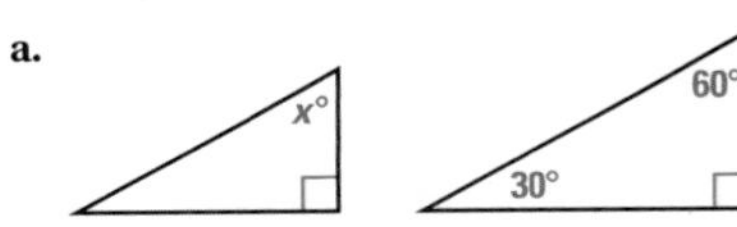

The angle with measure $x°$ corresponds to the angle with measure 60°, so $x = 60$.

b.

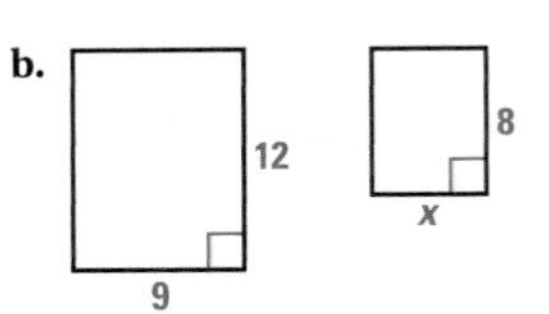

The side with length 12 corresponds to the side with length 8, and the side with length 9 corresponds to the side with length x.

$\frac{12}{8} = \frac{9}{x}$ **Write a proportion.**

$12x = 72$ **Cross multiply.**

$x = 6$ **Solve for *x*.**

PRACTICE

Tell whether the figures are *congruent, similar,* or *neither. Explain.*

1.

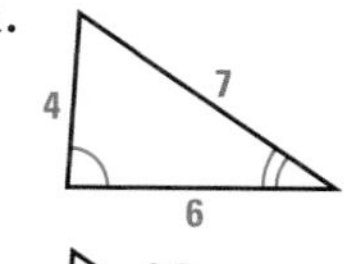

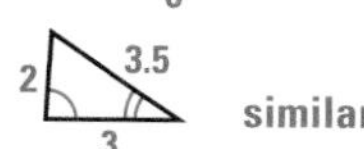

similar

2.

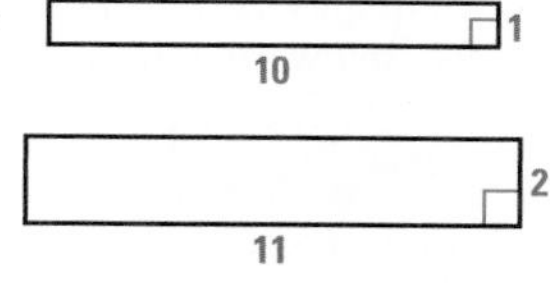

neither

3.

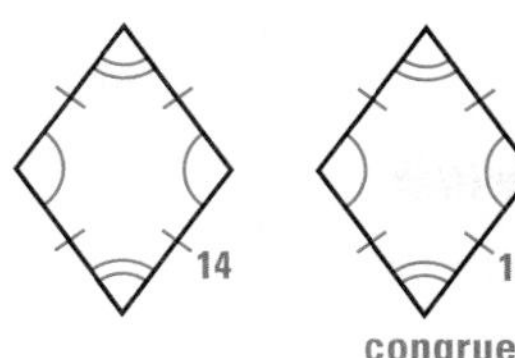

congruent

4.

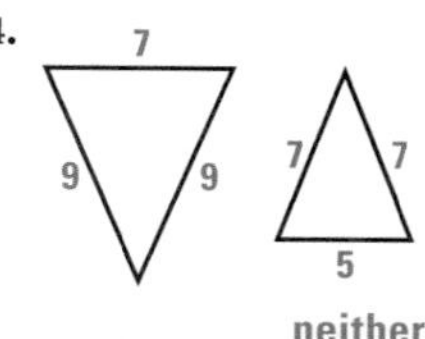

neither

5.

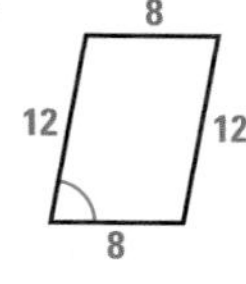

congruent

6.

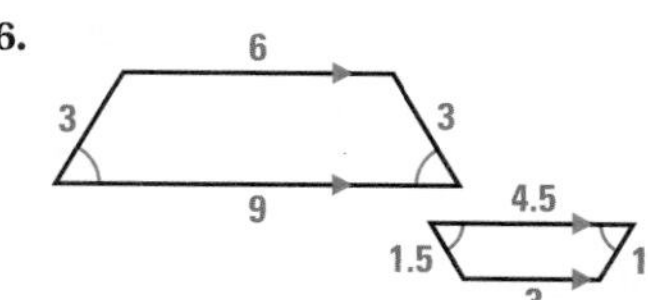

similar

7.

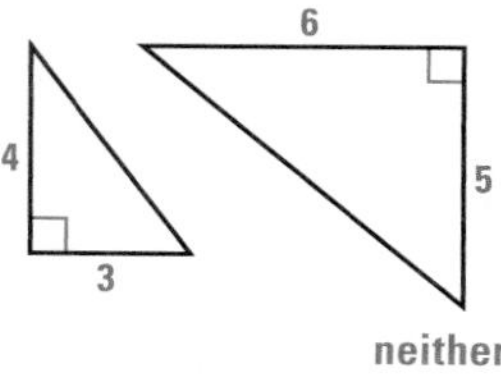

neither

8.

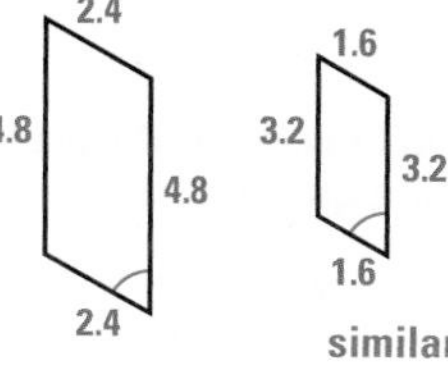

similar

9.

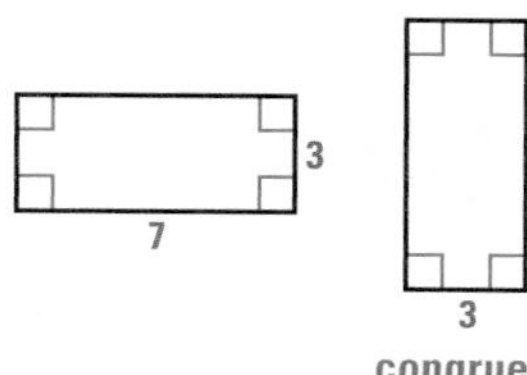

congruent

The two polygons are similar. Find the value of *x*.

10. 43°

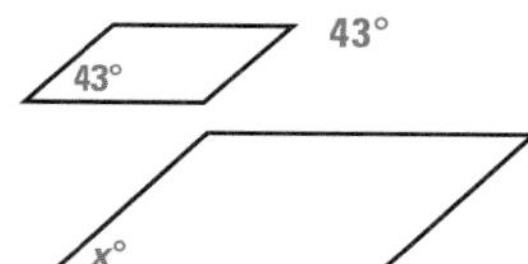

11. 11.5

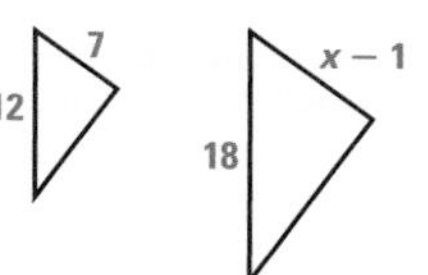

12. 8

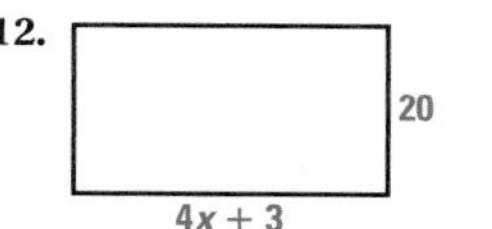

13. 14

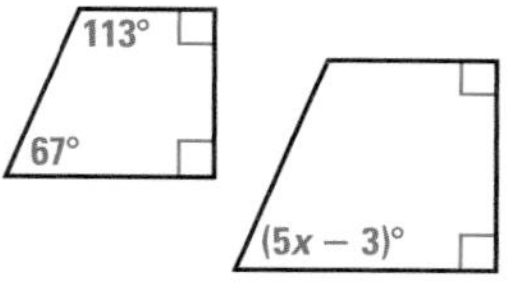

14. 6

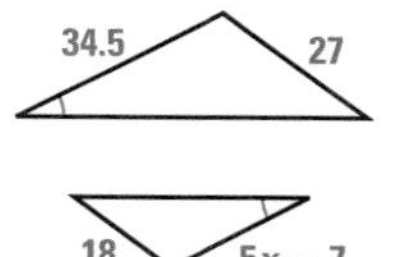

15. 40

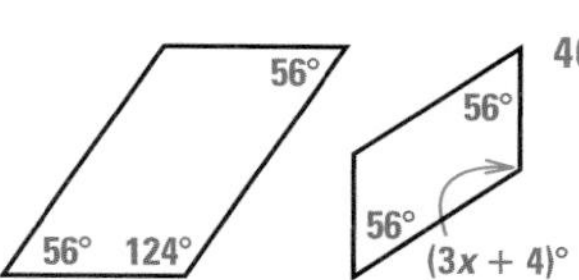

16. 7.5

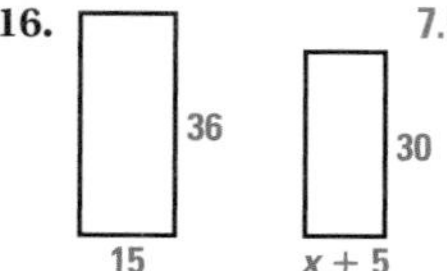

17. 7

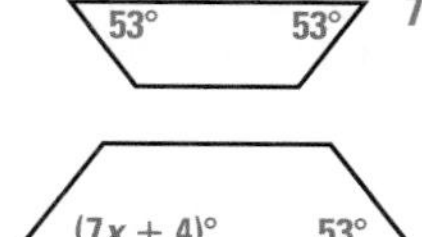

18. 6

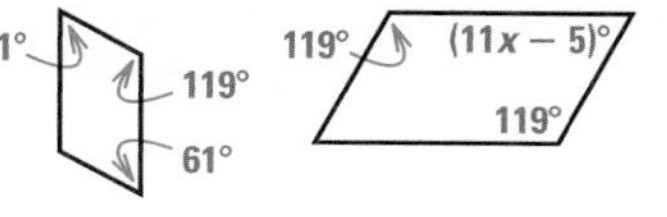

SKILLS REVIEW HANDBOOK

SKILLS REVIEW HANDBOOK

More Problem Solving Strategies

Problem solving strategies can help you solve mathematical and real-life problems. Lesson 1.5 shows how to apply the strategies *use a formula, look for a pattern, draw a diagram,* and *use a verbal model.* Below are four more strategies.

Strategy	When to Use	How to Use
Make a list or table	Make a list or table when a problem requires you to record, generate, or organize information.	Make a table with columns, rows, and any given information. Generate a systematic list that can help you solve the problem.
Work backward	Work backward when a problem gives you an end result and you need to find beginning conditions.	Work backward from the given information until you solve the problem. Work forward through the problem to check your answer.
Guess, check, and revise	Guess, check, and revise when you need a place to start or you want to see how the problem works.	Make a reasonable guess. Check to see if your guess solves the problem. If it does not, revise your guess and check again.
Solve a simpler problem	Solve a simpler problem when a problem can be made easier by using simpler numbers.	Think of a way to make the problem simpler. Solve the simpler problem, then use what you learned to solve the original problem.

EXAMPLE **Lee works as a cashier. In how many different ways can Lee make $.50 in change using quarters, dimes, and nickels?**

Use the strategy *make a list or table.* Then count the number of different ways.

Quarters	Dimes	Nickels
2	0	0
1	2	1
1	1	3
1	0	5
0	5	0
0	4	2
0	3	4
0	2	6
0	1	8
0	0	10

Start with the greatest number of quarters.

Then list all the possibilities with 1 quarter, starting with the greatest number of dimes.

Then list all the possibilities with 0 quarters, starting with the greatest number of dimes.

▶ Lee can make $.50 in quarters, dimes, and nickels in 10 different ways.

EXAMPLE **In a cafeteria, 3 cookies cost $.50 less than a sandwich. If a sandwich costs $4.25, how much does one cookie cost?**

Use the strategy *work backward.*

$4.25 - 0.50 = 3.75$ **Cost of 3 cookies**

$3.75 \div 3 = 1.25$ **Cost of 1 cookie**

CHECK $1.25 \times 3 = 3.75$ **Cost of 3 cookies**

$3.75 + 0.50 = 4.25$ **Cost of sandwich**

▶ One cookie costs $1.25.

EXAMPLE **Nolan's class has 6 more boys than girls. There are 28 students altogether. How many girls are in Nolan's class?**

Use the strategy *guess, check, and revise.* Guess a number of girls that is less than half of 28.

First guess:	12 girls, $12 + 6 = 18$ boys, $12 + 18 = 30$ students	**Too high** ✗
Second guess:	10 girls, $10 + 6 = 16$ boys, $10 + 16 = 26$ students	**Too low** ✗
Third guess:	11 girls, $11 + 6 = 17$ boys, $11 + 17 = 28$ students	**Correct** ✓

▶ There are 11 girls in Nolan's class.

EXAMPLE **How many diagonals does a regular decagon have?**

Use the strategy *solve a simpler problem.* A decagon has 10 sides, so find the number of diagonals of polygons with fewer sides and look for a pattern.

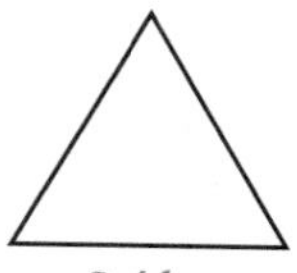

3 sides
0 diagonals

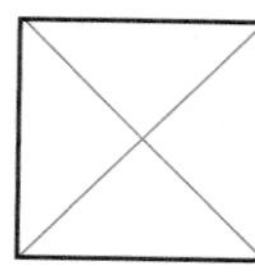

4 sides
2 diagonals

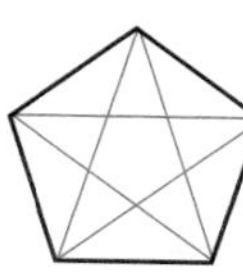

5 sides
5 diagonals

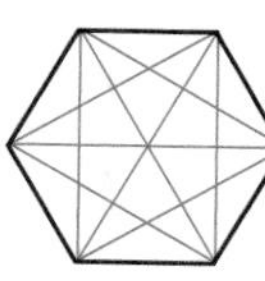

6 sides
9 diagonals

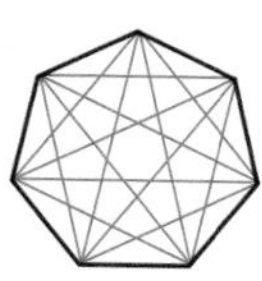

7 sides
14 diagonals

Notice that the difference of the numbers of diagonals for consecutive figures keeps increasing by 1:

$2 - 0 = 2$ $\quad 5 - 2 = 3$ $\quad 9 - 5 = 4$ $\quad 14 - 9 = 5$

So, an 8-sided polygon has $14 + 6 = 20$ diagonals, a 9-sided polygon has $20 + 7 = 27$ diagonals, and a 10-sided polygon has $27 + 8 = 35$ diagonals.

▶ A regular decagon (a 10-sided polygon) has 35 diagonals.

PRACTICE

1. Ben has a concert at 7:30 P.M. First he must do 2 hours of homework. Then, dinner and a shower will take about 45 minutes. Ben wants to allow a half hour to get to the concert. What time should Ben start his homework? **4:15 P.M.**
2. Quinn and Kyle collected 87 aluminum cans to recycle. Quinn collected twice as many cans as Kyle. How many cans did each person collect? **Kyle: 29 cans, Quinn: 58 cans**
3. In how many different ways can three sisters form a line at a ticket booth? **6 ways**
4. The 8×8 grid at the right has some 1×1 squares, some 2×2 squares, some 3×3 squares, and so on. How many total squares does the grid have? **204 squares**

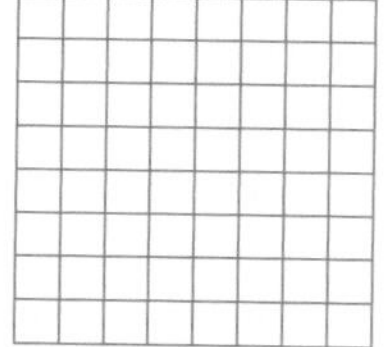

5. If Kaleigh draws 20 different diameters in a circle, into how many parts will the circle be divided? **40 parts**
6. Six friends form a tennis league. Each friend will play a match with every other friend. How many matches will be played? **15 matches**
7. Susan has 13 coins in her pocket with a total value of \$1.05. She has only dimes and nickels. How many of each type of coin does Susan have? **8 dimes, 5 nickels**

999

Logical Argument

A logical argument has two given statements, called **premises**, and a statement, called a **conclusion**, that follows from the premises. Below is an example.

Premise 1	If a triangle has a right angle, then it is a right triangle.
Premise 2	In $\triangle ABC$, $\angle B$ is a right angle.
Conclusion	$\triangle ABC$ is a right triangle.

Letters are often used to represent the statements of a logical argument and to write a pattern for the argument. The table below gives five types of logical arguments. In the examples, *p*, *q*, and *r* represent the following statements.

p: a figure is a square   *q*: a figure is a rectangle   *r*: a figure is a parallelogram

Type of Argument	Pattern	Example
Direct Argument	If *p* is true, then *q* is true. *p* is true. Therefore, *q* is true.	If *ABCD* is a square, then it is a rectangle. *ABCD* is a square. Therefore, *ABCD* is a rectangle.
Indirect Argument	If *p* is true, then *q* is true. *q* is not true. Therefore, *p* is not true.	If *ABCD* is a square, then it is a rectangle. *ABCD* is not a rectangle. Therefore, *ABCD* is not a square.
Chain Rule	If *p* is true, then *q* is true. If *q* is true, then *r* is true. Therefore, if *p*, then *r*.	If *ABCD* is a square, then it is a rectangle. If *ABCD* is a rectangle, then it is a parallelogram. Therefore, if *ABCD* is a square, then it is a parallelogram.
Or Rule	*p* is true or *q* is true. *p* is not true. Therefore, *q* is true.	*ABCD* is a square or a rectangle. *ABCD* is not a square. Therefore, *ABCD* is a rectangle.
And Rule	*p* and *q* are not both true. *q* is true. Therefore, *p* is not true.	*ABCD* is not both a square and a rectangle. *ABCD* is a rectangle. Therefore, *ABCD* is not a square.

An argument that follows one of these patterns correctly has a **valid conclusion**.

EXAMPLE **State whether the conclusion is *valid* or *invalid*. If the conclusion is valid, name the type of logical argument used.**

a. If it is raining at noon, Peter's family will not have a picnic lunch. Peter's family had a picnic lunch. Therefore, it was not raining at noon.

▸ The conclusion is valid. This is an example of indirect argument.

b. If a triangle is equilateral, then it is an acute triangle. Triangle *XYZ* is an acute triangle. Therefore, triangle *XYZ* is equilateral.

▸ The conclusion is invalid.

c. If $x = 4$, then $2x - 7 = 1$. If $2x - 7 = 1$, then $2x = 8$. $x = 4$. Therefore, if $x = 4$, then $2x = 8$.

▸ The conclusion is valid. This is an example of the chain rule.

d. If it is at least 80°F outside today, you will go swimming. It is 85°F outside today. Therefore, you will go swimming.

▸ The conclusion is valid. This is an example of direct argument.

A **compound statement** has two or more parts joined by *or* or *and*.

- For an *and* compound statement to be true, each part must be true.
- For an *or* compound statement to be true, at least one part must be true.

EXAMPLE **State whether the compound statement is *true* or *false*.**

a. $\underline{12 < 20}$ and $\underline{-12 > -20}$
True True
▸ True, because each part is true.

b. $\underline{2 < 4}$ and $\underline{4 < 3}$
True False
▸ False, because one part is false.

c. $\underline{10 > 0}$ or $\underline{-10 > 0}$
True False
▸ True, because at least one part is true.

d. $\underline{-8 > -7}$ or $\underline{-7 > -6}$ or $\underline{-6 > -5}$
False False False
▸ False, because every part is false.

PRACTICE

State whether the conclusion is *valid* or *invalid*. If the conclusion is valid, name the type of logical argument used.

1. If Scott goes to the store, then he will buy sugar. If he buys sugar, then he will bake cookies. Scott goes to the store. Therefore, he will bake cookies. **valid; Chain Rule**
2. If a triangle has at least two congruent sides, then it is isosceles. Triangle *MNP* has sides 5 in., 6 in., and 5 in. long. Therefore, triangle *MNP* is isosceles. **valid; Direct Argument**
3. If a horse is an Arabian, then it is less than 16 hands tall. Andrea's horse is 13 hands tall. Therefore, Andrea's horse is an Arabian. **invalid**
4. If a figure is a rhombus, then it has four sides. Figure *WXYZ* has four sides. Therefore, *WXYZ* is a rhombus. **invalid**
5. Jeff cannot buy both a new coat and new boots. Jeff decides to buy new boots. Therefore, Jeff cannot buy a new coat. **valid; *And* Rule**
6. If $x = 0$, then $y = 4$. If $y = 4$, then $z = 7$. Therefore, if $z = 7$, then $x = 0$. **invalid**
7. Kate will order either tacos or burritos for lunch. Kate does not order tacos for lunch. Therefore, Kate orders burritos for lunch. **valid; *Or* Rule**
8. If a triangle is equilateral, then it is equiangular. Triangle *ABC* is not equiangular. Therefore, triangle *ABC* is not equilateral. **valid; Indirect Argument**
9. An animal cannot be both a fish and a bird. Courtney's pet is not a fish. Therefore, Courtney's pet must be a bird. **invalid**

State whether the compound statement is *true* or *false*.

10. $-7 < -5$ and $-5 < -6$ **false**
11. $6 > 2$ or $8 < 4$ **true**
12. $0 \le -1$ or $5 \ge 5$ **true**
13. $4 \le 3$ or $12 \ge 13$ **false**
14. $3 < 5$ and $-3 < -5$ **false**
15. $1 = -1$ or $1 = 1$ or $1 = 0$ **true**
16. $7 < 8$ and $8 < 12$ **true**
17. $-2 < 2$ and $3 \ge 2$ **true**
18. $3(-4) = 12$ or $-3(4) = 12$ **false**
19. $-8 > 8$ or $-8 = 8$ or $-8 \ge 0$ **false**
20. $140 \ne 145$ or $140 > -145$ or $-140 < -145$ **true**
21. $-8(9) = -72$ and $8(-9) = -72$ **true**
22. $22 \le 23$ and $-22 < -23$ and $23 > 22$ **false**

Conditional Statements and Counterexamples

A **conditional statement** has two parts, a hypothesis and a conclusion. When a conditional statement is written in **if-then form**, the "if" part contains the **hypothesis** and the "then" part contains the **conclusion**. An example of a conditional statement is shown below.

If a triangle is equiangular, then each angle of the triangle measures 60°.

Hypothesis: a triangle is equiangular
Conclusion: each angle of the triangle measures 60°

The **converse** of a conditional statement is formed by switching the hypothesis and the conclusion. The converse of the statement above is as follows:

If each angle of a triangle measures 60°, then the triangle is equiangular.

EXAMPLE **Rewrite the conditional statement in if-then form. Then write its converse and tell whether the converse is *true* or *false*.**

a. Bob will earn $20 by mowing the lawn.

If-then form: If Bob mows the lawn, then he will earn $20.

Converse: If Bob earns $20, then he mowed the lawn. False

b. $x = 8$ when $5x + 1 = 41$.

If-then form: If $5x + 1 = 41$, then $x = 8$.

Converse: If $x = 8$, then $5x + 1 = 41$. True

A **biconditional statement** is a statement that has the words "if and only if." You can write a conditional statement and its converse together as a biconditional statement.

A triangle is equiangular if and only if each angle of the triangle measures 60°.

A biconditional statement is true only when the conditional statement and its converse are both true.

EXAMPLE **Tell whether the biconditional statement is *true* or *false*. Explain.**

a. An angle measures 90° if and only if it is a right angle.

Conditional: If an angle is a right angle, then it measures 90°. True
Converse: If an angle measures 90°, then it is a right angle. True

▶ The biconditional statement is true because the conditional and its converse are both true.

b. Bonnie has $.50 if and only if she has two quarters.

Conditional: If Bonnie has two quarters, then she has $.50. True
Converse: If Bonnie has $.50, then she has two quarters. False

▶ The biconditional statement is false because the converse is not true.

A **counterexample** is an example that shows that a statement is false.

EXAMPLE **Tell whether the statement is *true* or *false*. If false, give a counterexample.**

a. If a polygon has four sides and opposite sides are parallel, then it is a rectangle.

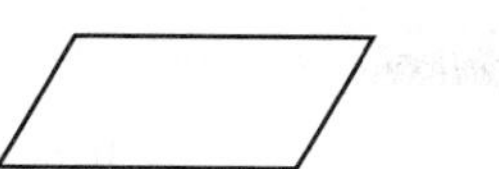

▸ False. A counterexample is the parallelogram shown.

b. If $x^2 = 49$, then $x = 7$.

▸ False. A counterexample is $x = -7$, because $(-7)^2 = 49$.

PRACTICE

Rewrite the conditional statement in if-then form. Then write its converse and tell whether the converse is *true* or *false*.

1. The graph of the equation $y = mx + b$ is a line. If you have the equation $y = mx + b$, then you have the graph of a line; if you have the graph of a line, then you have the equation $y = mx + b$, false.
2. You will earn \$35 for working 5 hours. If you work 5 hours, then you will earn \$35; if you earn \$35, then you worked 5 hours, false.
3. Abby can go swimming if she finishes her homework. If Abby finishes her homework, then she can go swimming; if Abby goes swimming, then she finished her homework, false.
4. In a right triangle, the sum of the squares of the lengths of the legs equals the square of the length of the hypotenuse. See margin.
5. $x = 5$ when $4x + 8 = 28$. If $4x + 8 = 28$, then $x = 5$; if $x = 5$, then $4x + 8 = 28$, true.
6. The sum of two even numbers is an even number. If you add two even numbers, then the sum is an even number; if the sum is an even number, then you added two even numbers, false.

Tell whether the biconditional statement is *true* or *false*. *Explain*.

7. Two lines are perpendicular if and only if they intersect to form a right angle. See margin.
8. $x^3 = 27$ if and only if $x = 3$. True; if $x^3 = 27$, then $x = 3$ and if $x = 3$ then $x^3 = 27$.
9. A vegetable is a carrot if and only if it is orange. False; not all orange vegetables are carrots.
10. A rhombus is a square if and only if it has four right angles. True; if a rhombus is a square then it has four right angles and if a rhombus has four right angles then it is a square.
11. The graph of a function is a parabola if and only if the function is $y = x^2$. False; the converse is not true.
12. An integer is odd if and only if it is not even. True; if an integer is odd then it is not even and if an integer is not even, then it is odd.

Tell whether the statement is *true* or *false*. If false, give a counterexample.

13. If an integer is not negative, then it is positive. False; zero is neither positive nor negative.
14. If you were born in the summer, then you were born in July. False. *Sample answer:* You are born in August and you are still born in the summer.
15. If a polygon has exactly 5 congruent sides, then the polygon is a pentagon. False. *Sample answer:* An octagon could have exactly 5 congruent sides.
16. If $x = -6$, then $x^2 = 36$. true
17. If B is 6 inches from A and 8 inches from C, then A is 14 inches from C. False; A could be in between B and C and therefore would only be 2 inches from C.
18. If a triangle is isosceles, then it is obtuse. False. *Sample answer:* The triangle is an acute isosceles triangle.
19. If Charlie has \$1.00 in coins, then he has four quarters. False. *Sample answer:* Charlie could have 10 dimes.
20. If you are in Montana, then you are in the United States. true

4. If you have a right triangle, then the sum of the squares of the lengths of the legs equals the square of the length of the hypotenuse; if the sum of the squares of the lengths of the legs of a triangle equals the square of the length of the hypotenuse, then you have a right triangle, true.

7. True; if two lines are perpendicular, then they intersect to form a right angle and if two lines intersect to form a right angle, then they are perpendicular.

1. 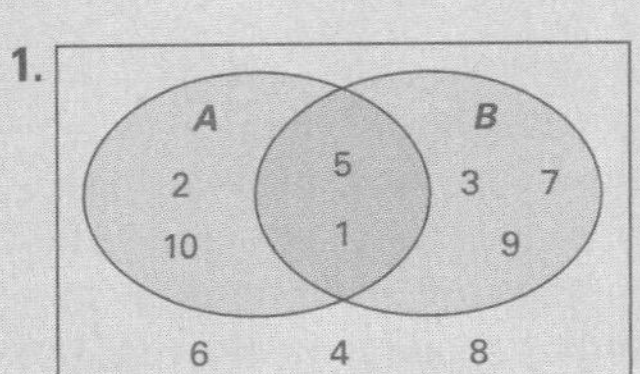

2. 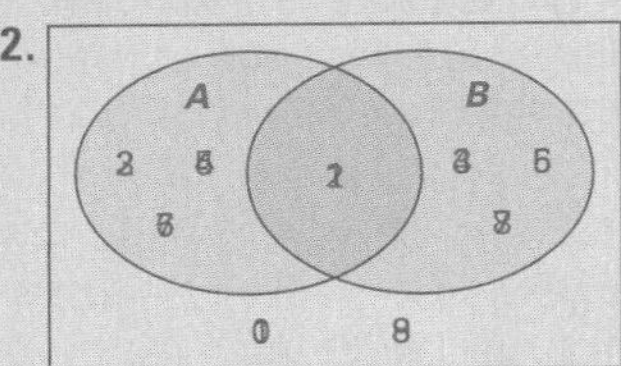

3. 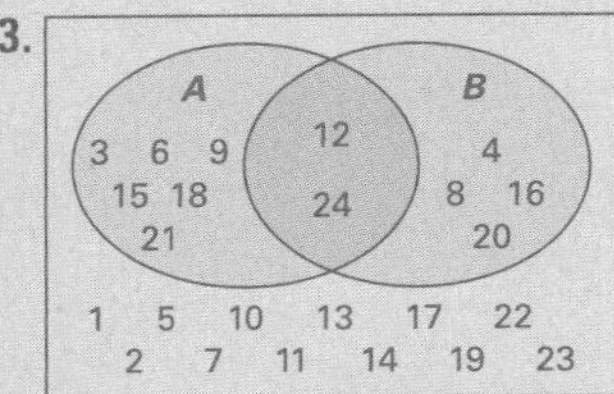

SKILLS REVIEW HANDBOOK

Venn Diagrams

A **Venn diagram** uses shapes to show how sets are related.

EXAMPLE **Draw a Venn diagram of the positive integers less than 13 where set *A* consists of factors of 12 and set *B* consists of even numbers.**

Positive integers less than 13:
1, 2, 3, 4, 5, 6, 7, 8, 9, 10, 11, 12

Set *A* (factors of 12): 1, 2, 3, 4, 6, 12

Set *B* (even numbers): 2, 4, 6, 8, 10, 12

Both set *A* and set *B*: 2, 4, 6, 12

Neither set *A* nor set *B*: 5, 7, 9, 11

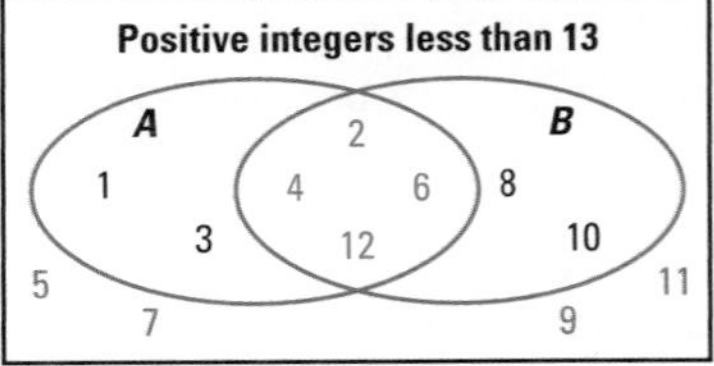

EXAMPLE **Use the Venn diagram above to decide if the statement is *true* or *false*. Explain your reasoning.**

a. If a positive integer less than 13 is not even, then it is not a factor of 12.

▸ False. 1 and 3 are not even, but they are factors of 12.

b. All positive integers less than 13 that are even are factors of 12.

▸ False. 8 and 10 are even, but they are not factors of 12.

PRACTICE

Draw a Venn diagram of the sets described. 1–3. See margin.

1. Of the positive integers less than 11, set *A* consists of factors of 10 and set *B* consists of odd numbers.
2. Of the positive integers less than 10, set *A* consists of prime numbers and set *B* consists of even numbers.
3. Of the positive integers less than 25, set *A* consists of multiples of 3 and set *B* consists of multiples of 4.

Use the Venn diagrams you drew in Exercises 1–3 to decide if the statement is *true* or *false*. Explain your reasoning.

4. The only factors of 10 less than 11 that are not odd are 2 and 10. True; the factors of 10 are 1, 2, 5, and 10.
5. If a number is neither a multiple of 3 nor a multiple of 4, then it is odd. False. *Sample answer:* 10 is even, but not a multiple of 3 or 4.
6. All prime numbers less than 10 are not even. False; 2 is even and prime.
7. If a positive odd integer less than 11 is a factor of 10, then it is 5. False; 1 is a positive odd integer and a factor of 10.
8. There are 2 positive integers less than 25 that are both a multiple of 3 and a multiple of 4. True; 12 and 24 are the only positive integers less than 25 that are multiples of 3 and 4.
9. If a positive even integer less than 10 is prime, then it is 2. True; 2 is the only even prime number.

Mean, Median, Mode, and Range

Mean, median, and mode are measures of central tendency; they measure the center of data. Range is a measure of dispersion; it measures the spread of data.

The **mean** of a data set is the sum of the values divided by the number of values. The mean is also called the *average*.	The **median** of a data set is the middle value when the values are written in numerical order. If a data set has an even number of values, the median is the mean of the two middle values.	The **mode** of a data set is the value that occurs most often. A data set can have no mode, one mode, or more than one mode.	The **range** of a data set is the difference between the greatest value and the least value.

EXAMPLE **Find the mean, median, mode(s), and range of the data.**

Daily High Temperatures, Week of June 21–27							
Day	Sunday	Monday	Tuesday	Wednesday	Thursday	Friday	Saturday
Temperature (°F)	76	74	70	69	70	75	78

Mean Add the values. Then divide by the number of values.

$76 + 74 + 70 + 69 + 70 + 75 + 78 = 512$

mean $= 512 \div 7 \approx 73$ The **mean** of the data is about 73°F.

Median Write the values in order from least to greatest. Find the middle value(s).

69, 70, 70, <u>74</u>, 75, 76, 78

median $= 74$ The **median** of the data is 74°F.

Mode Find the value that occurs most often.

mode $= 70$ The **mode** of the data is 70°F.

Range Subtract the least value from the greatest value.

range $= 78 - 69 = 9$ The **range** of the data is 9°F.

PRACTICE

Find the mean, median, mode(s), and range of the data.

1. Apartment rents: $650, $800, $700, $525, $675, $750, $500, $650, $725 about $664, $675, $650, $300
2. Ages of new drivers: 15, 15, 15, 15, 16, 16, 16, 16, 16, 17, 17, 17, 18, 18 about 16.2 yr, 16 yr, 16 yr, 3 yr
3. Monthly cell-phone minutes: 581, 713, 423, 852, 948, 337, 810, 604, 897 685 min, 713 min, none, 611 min
4. Prices of a CD: $12.98, $14.99, $13.49, $12.98, $13.89, $16.98, $11.98 $13.90, $13.49, $12.98, $5
5. Cookies in a batch: 36, 60, 52, 44, 48, 45, 48, 41, 60, 45, 38, 55, 60, 48, 40 48 cookies, 48 cookies, 48 cookies, 24 cookies
6. Ages of family members: 41, 45, 8, 10, 40, 44, 3, 5, 42, 42, 13, 14, 67, 70 about 31.7 yr, 40.5 yr, 42 yr, 67 yr
7. Hourly rates of pay: $8.80, $6.50, $10.85, $7.90, $9.50, $9, $8.70, $12.35 $9.20, $8.90, none, $5.85
8. Weekly quiz scores: 8, 9, 8, 10, 10, 7, 9, 8, 9, 9, 10, 7, 8, 6, 10, 9, 9, 8, 8, 10 8.6, 9, 8 and 9, 4
9. People on a bus: 9, 14, 5, 22, 18, 30, 6, 25, 18, 12, 15, 10, 8, 22, 10, 11, 20 15 people, 14 people, 10 people and 18 people and 22 people, 25 people

Graphing Statistical Data

There are many ways to display data. An appropriate graph can help you analyze data. The table at the right summarizes how data are shown in some statistical graphs.

Bar Graph	Compares data in categories.
Circle Graph	Compares data as parts of a whole.
Line Graph	Shows data change over time.

EXAMPLE Use the bar graph to answer the questions.

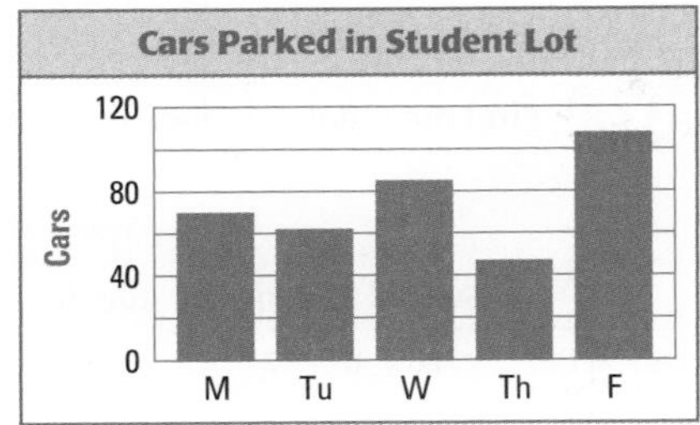

a. On which day of the week were the greatest number of cars parked in the student lot?

▶ The tallest bar on the graph is for Friday. So, the answer is Friday.

b. How many cars were parked in the student lot on Monday?

▶ The bar for Monday shows that about 70 cars were parked in the student lot.

EXAMPLE Use the circle graph to answer the questions.

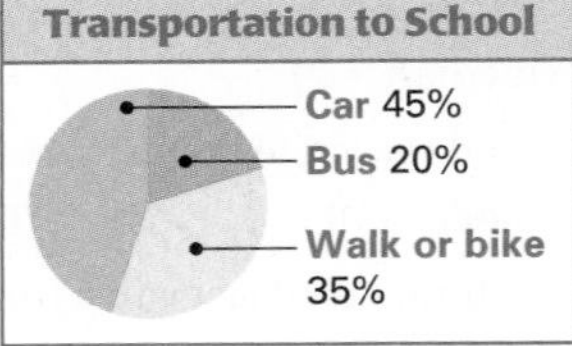

a. Which type of transportation is used almost half the time?

▶ Almost half of the total area of the circle is labeled "Car 45%." So, a car is used almost half the time.

b. Which type of transportation is used the least often?

▶ The smallest part of the circle is labeled "Bus 20%." So, a bus is used the least often.

EXAMPLE Use the line graph to answer the questions.

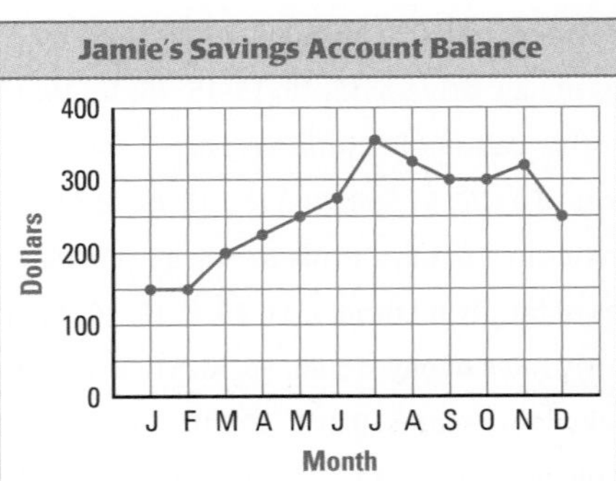

a. In which month(s) was Jamie's balance $250?

▶ The points on the graph to the right of $250 show that Jamie's balance was $250 in May and December.

b. Between which two consecutive months did Jamie's balance increase the most?

▶ Of the graph's line segments that have positive slope, the graph is steepest from June to July. So, Jamie's balance increased the most between June and July.

PRACTICE

Use the line graph to answer Exercises 1–5.

1. At which hour did Ferraro's have 22 diners? **6 P.M.**
2. At which hour did Ferraro's have the most diners? **7 P.M.**
3. How many diners were at Ferraro's at 11 P.M.? Were they gone by midnight? **5 diners; yes**
4. Between which two consecutive hours did the number of diners at Ferraro's change the most? **9 P.M. and 10 P.M.**
5. How many fewer diners were at Ferraro's at 10 P.M. than at 6 P.M.? **14 diners**

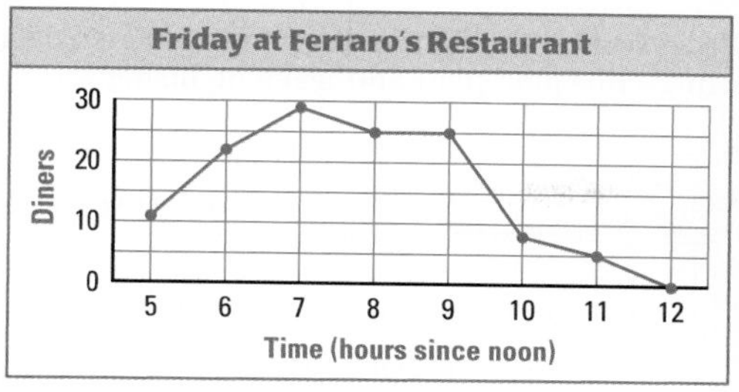

Use the bar graph to answer Exercises 6–8.

6. In which season were the fewest students born? **fall**
7. In which season(s) were 7 students born? **winter and summer**
8. How many more students were born in spring than in summer? **3 students**

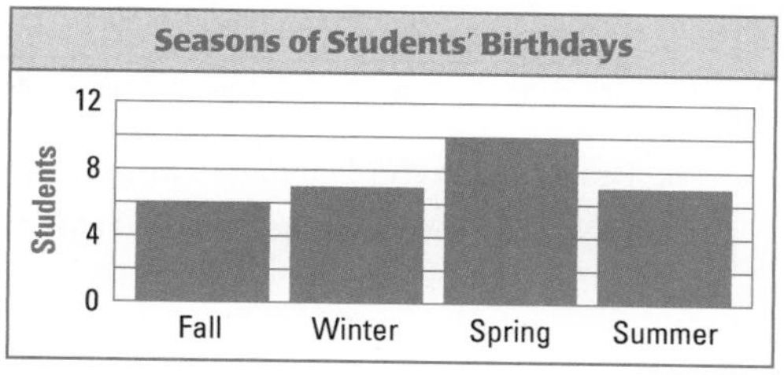

Use the circle graph to answer Exercises 9–11.

9. What is the heat source of more than half the homes in the United States? **natural gas**
10. What percent of homes in the United States are heated with electricity? **22%**
11. If you randomly selected 500 U.S. homes, about how many would be heated with fuel oil? **50 homes**

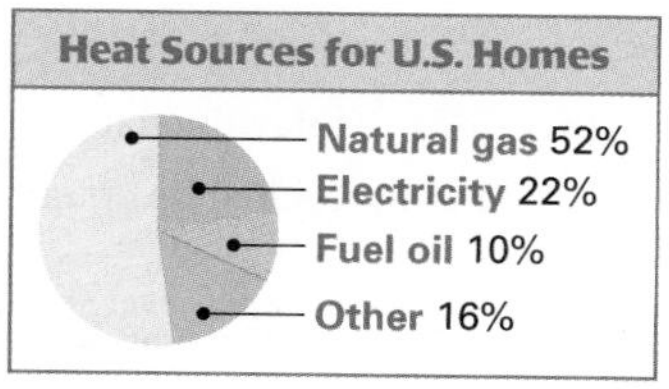

12. The table below shows the high temperatures in degrees Fahrenheit for one week. Display the data in a line graph. **See margin.**

Mon.	Tues.	Wed.	Thurs.	Fri.	Sat.	Sun.
83	89	79	73	69	67	71

13. A high school conducted a survey to determine the numbers of students involved in various school activities. Display the survey results in a bar graph. **See margin.**

Computer club	Music club	Yearbook club	Drama club	Student council	Chess club
34	75	16	57	28	12

14. The table below shows the items sold at a café in one day. Display the data in a circle graph. **See margin.**

Juice	Soda	Water	Muffin	Cookie
95	180	100	55	40

12.

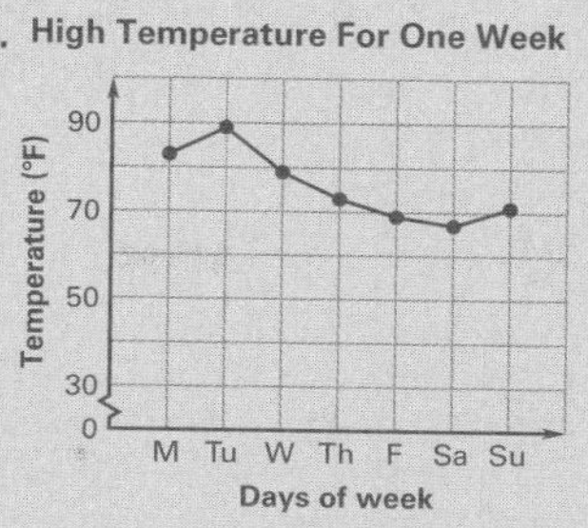

13.

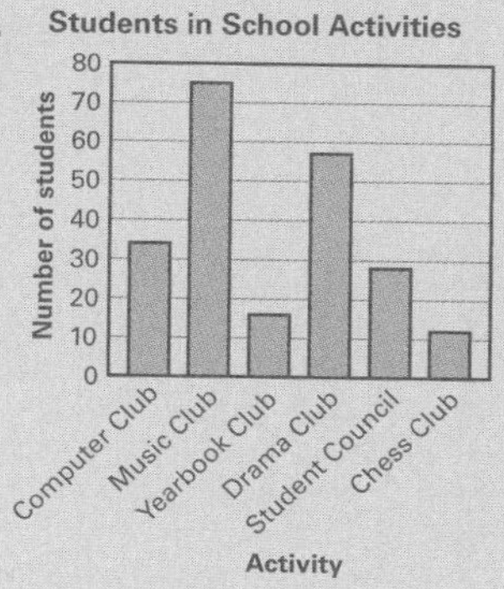

14.

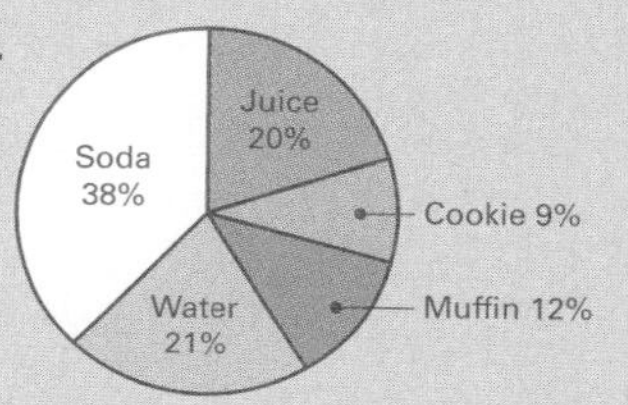

Organizing Statistical Data

Because it is difficult to analyze unorganized data, it is helpful to organize data using a line plot, stem-and-leaf plot, histogram, or box-and-whisker plot.

EXAMPLE **Sydney's math test scores are 90, 85, 88, 95, 100, 77, 85, 100, 80, 77, and 90.**

a. Draw a line plot to display the data.

Make a number line from 75 to 100. Each time a value is listed in the data set, draw an X above the value on the number line.

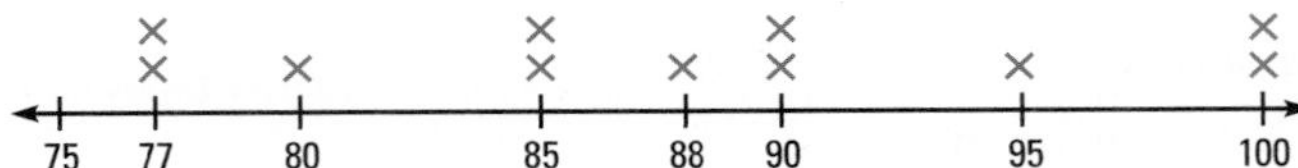

b. Draw a stem-and-leaf plot to display the data.

First write the leaves next to their stems.

Stem	Leaves
7	7 7
8	5 8 5 0
9	0 5 0
10	0 0

Key: 7 | 7 = 77

Then order the leaves from least to greatest.

Stem	Leaves
7	7 7
8	0 5 5 8
9	0 0 5
10	0 0

Key: 7 | 7 = 77

c. Draw a histogram to display the data.

First make a frequency table. Use equal intervals.

Score	Tally	Frequency
71–80	III	3
81–90	~~IIII~~	5
91–100	III	3

Then make a histogram.

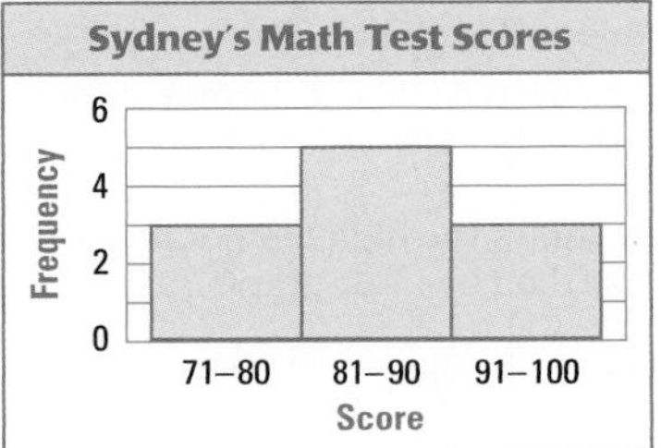

d. Draw a box-and-whisker plot to display the data.

Write the data in order from least to greatest. Ordered data are divided into a lower half and an upper half by the median. The median of the lower half is the **lower quartile**, and the median of the upper half is the **upper quartile**.

77	77	80	85	85	88	90	90	95	100	100
Low value		Lower quartile			Median			Upper quartile		High value

Plot the median, quartiles, and low and high values below a number line. Draw a box between quartiles with a vertical line through the median as shown. Draw whiskers to the low and high values.

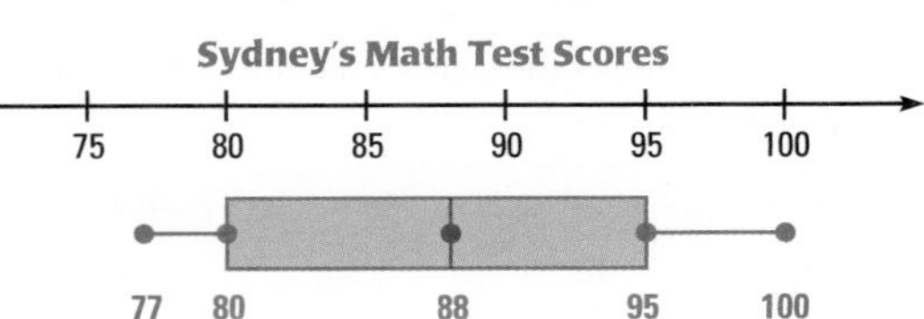

PRACTICE

Use the following list of ticket prices to answer Exercises 1–4: $50, $42, $65, $54, $70, $65, $59, $30, $67, $49, $54, $30, $73, $47, and $54.

1. Draw a line plot to display the data. See margin.
2. How many ticket prices are $50 or less? 6 ticket prices
3. Draw a stem-and-leaf plot to display the data. See margin.
4. What is the range of ticket prices costs? $43

Use the following list of hourly wages of employees to answer Exercises 5–8: $8.50, $6, $10, $14.25, $5.75, $7, $6.50, $14, $10, $9, $6.50, $8.25, $8.50, $11.25, $7, $16, $12, $6, $6.75.

5. Draw a histogram to display the data. Begin with the interval $5.00 to $6.99. See margin.
6. Copy and complete: The greatest number of employees earn from _?_ to _?_ per hour. $5.00, $6.99
7. Draw a box-and-whisker plot to display the data. See margin.
8. Copy and complete: About half of the employees have an hourly wage of _?_ or less. $8.50

Use the line plot, which shows the results of a survey asking people the average number of e-mails they receive daily, to answer Exercises 9 and 10.

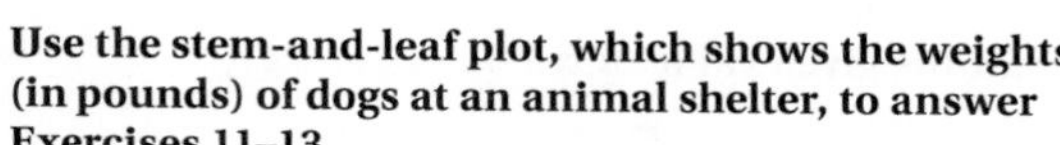

9. Copy and complete: Most people surveyed receive an average of _?_ e-mails per day. 5
10. How many people receive an average of more than 10 e-mails per day? 4 people

Use the stem-and-leaf plot, which shows the weights (in pounds) of dogs at an animal shelter, to answer Exercises 11–13.

Stem	Leaves
2	2 5 5 9
3	1 3 5 8
4	0 0 1 2 2 5 6 7
5	0 3 5 8 9
6	4 5

Key: 2 | 2 = 22

11. How many dogs were at the shelter? 23 dogs
12. Find the median of the data. 42 lb
13. Find the range of the data. 43 lb

Use the histogram to answer Exercises 14–16.

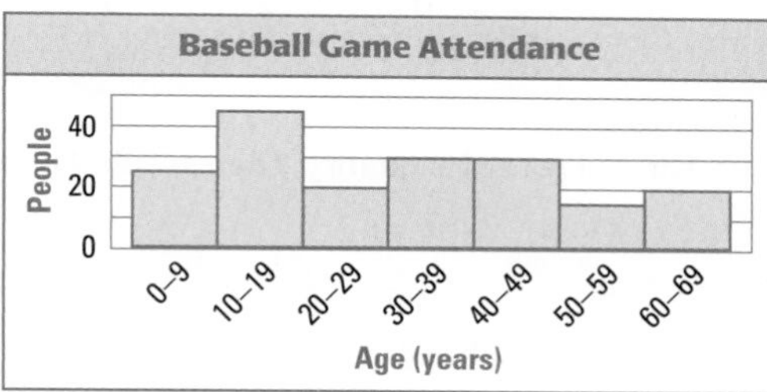

14. Which age group had the greatest attendance at the baseball game? Which had the least? 10–19 yr; 50–59 yr
15. How many children up to the age of 9 years attended the baseball game? 25 children
16. Which age group had the same attendance as the oldest group? 20–29 yr

Use the box-and-whisker plot to answer Exercises 17–19.

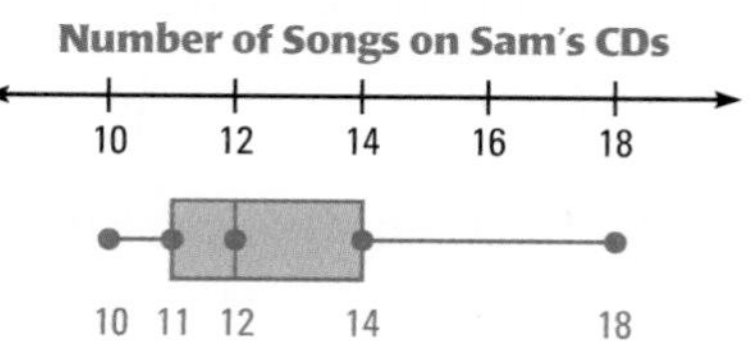

17. What is the median number of songs on Sam's CDs? 12 songs
18. What is the upper quartile of songs on Sam's CDs? 14 songs
19. What is the least number of songs on one of Sam's CDs? What is the greatest number? 10 songs; 18 songs

SKILLS REVIEW HANDBOOK

1. See below.

3.

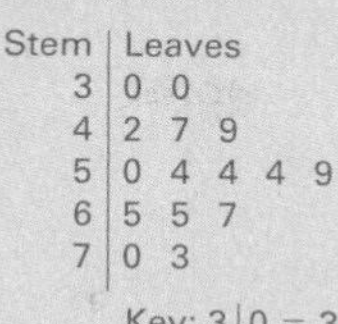

Stem	Leaves
3	0 0
4	2 7 9
5	0 4 4 4 9
6	5 5 7
7	0 3

Key: 3 | 0 = 30

5.

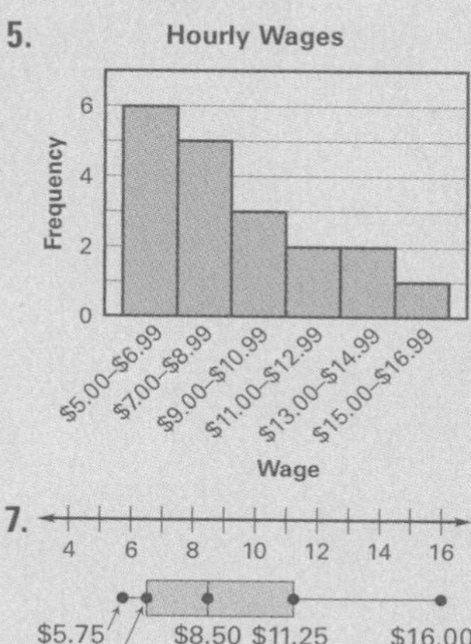

7. 4 6 8 10 12 14 16

$5.75 $6.50 $8.50 $11.25 $16.00

1.

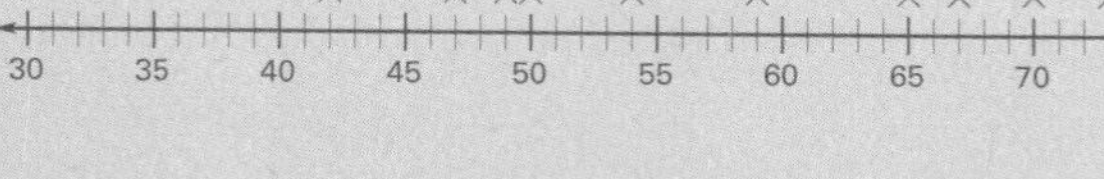

Extra Practice

Chapter 1

1.1 Graph the numbers on a number line. 1–3. See margin.

1. $-2, \frac{5}{3}, 0.2, -\sqrt{2}, -\frac{5}{4}$
2. $-\frac{4}{3}, 1, -1.2, \sqrt{3}, 1.9$
3. $3.7, -\sqrt{7}, -\frac{1}{2}, 4, \sqrt{15}$

1.1 Perform the indicated conversion.

4. 18 feet to inches 216 in.
5. 20 ounces to pounds 1.25 lb
6. 3 years to hours 26,280 h

1.2 Evaluate the expression for the given value of the variable.

7. $-2p + 5$ when $p = -5$ 15
8. $3x^2 - x + 7$ when $x = -1$ 11
9. $8z^3 - 6z$ when $z = 2$ 52

1.2 Simplify the expression.

10. $2y^2 - 3y + 5y^2$ $7y^2 - 3y$
11. $4r^2 - 5r + 2r^2 + 12$ $6r^2 - 5r + 12$
12. $-w^3 + w^2 - 7w^2 - 8w^3$ $-9w^3 - 6w^2$
13. $2(b + 5) + 3(2b - 10)$ $8b - 20$
14. $-7(t^2 + 2) + 9(t - 2)$ $-7t^2 + 9t - 32$
15. $4(m - 3) - 5(m^2 - m)$ $-5m^2 + 9m - 12$

1.3 Solve the equation. Check your solution.

16. $3a + 2 = 11$ 3
17. $-9 = b - 14$ 5
18. $8 - 0.5c = 1$ 14
19. $-3n - 7 = -n + 17$ -12
20. $12m = 15m - 7.5$ 2.5
21. $6p + 1 = 21 - 4p$ 2
22. $6(x + 1) = 2x - 10$ -4
23. $4(y - 3) = 2(y + 8)$ 14
24. $11(z - 5) = 2(z + 6) - 13$ 6

1.4 Solve the equation for y. Then find the value of y for the given value of x. 25–30. See margin.

25. $6y - x = 18; x = 2$
26. $2x + 3y = 12; x = -6$
27. $4y - 9x = -30; x = 6$
28. $3x - xy = 20; x = 8$
29. $4y + 6xy = 10; x = -2$
30. $5x + 8y + 4xy = 0; x = -1$

1.5 Look for a pattern in the table. Then write an equation that represents the table.

31.

x	0	1	2	3
y	25	22	19	16

$y = -3x + 25$

32.

x	0	1	2	3
y	1.5	4	6.5	9

$y = 2.5x + 1.5$

1.6 Solve the inequality. Then graph the solution. 33–41. See margin for art.

33. $x + 2 > 9$ $x > 7$
34. $-13 - 3x < 11$ $x > -8$
35. $4x - 9 \le 2x + 1$ $x \le 5$
36. $-3x - 8 \ge -9x + 10$ $x \ge 3$
37. $-7 < x + 3 \le 1$ $-10 < x \le -2$
38. $-4 \le 3x - 7 \le 4$ $1 \le x \le \frac{11}{3}$
39. $-9 \le 5 - 2x < 7$ $-1 < x \le 7$
40. $x + 3 < -2$ or $x - 7 > 0$ $x < -5$ or $x > 7$
41. $2x + 9 \ge 3$ or $-5x + 1 \le 0$ $x \ge -3$

1.7 Solve the equation. Check for extraneous solutions.

42. $|g + 5| = 4$ $-9, -1$
43. $\left|\frac{1}{3}q - \frac{2}{3}\right| = 1$ $-1, 5$
44. $|10 - 3t| = t + 4$ 1.5, 7
45. $|3z + 1| = -6z$ $-\frac{1}{9}$

1.7 Solve the inequality. Then graph the solution. 46–53. See margin for art.

46. $|a| < 2$ $-2 < a < 2$
47. $|2c| > 14$ $c < -7$ or $c > 7$
48. $|g + 11| \ge 2$ $g \le -13$ or $g \ge -9$
49. $|4j - 7| \le 9$ $-\frac{1}{2} \le j \le 4$
50. $|0.25m + 3| \ge 1$ $m \le -16$ or $m \ge -8$
51. $|10 - 2p| > 9$ $p < \frac{1}{2}$ or $p > 9.5$
52. $|0.6r + 8| \le 17$ $-\frac{125}{3} \le r \le 15$
53. $|5t - 9| + 9 < 10$ $\frac{8}{5} < t < 2$

EXTRA PRACTICE

1.
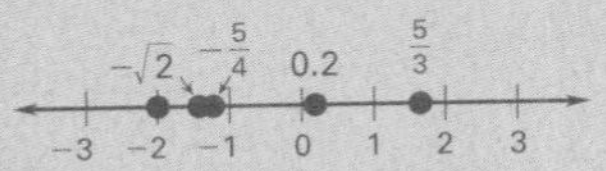

2.
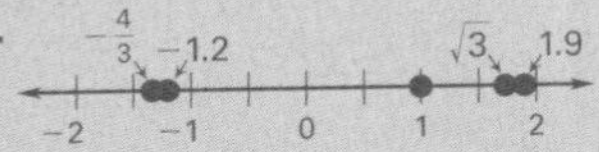

3.
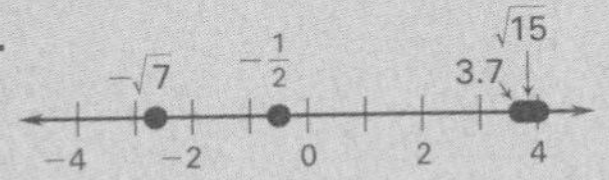

25. $y = \frac{1}{6}x + 3; \frac{10}{3}$

26. $y = -\frac{2}{3}x + 4; 8$

27. $y = \frac{9}{4}x - \frac{15}{2}; 6$

28. $y = -\frac{20}{x} + 3; \frac{1}{2}$

29. $y = \frac{5}{2 + 3x}; -\frac{5}{4}$

30. $y = \frac{-5x}{8 + 4x}; \frac{5}{4}$

33.
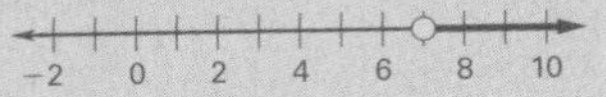

34.

35.
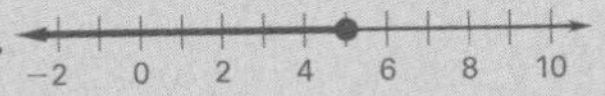

36.
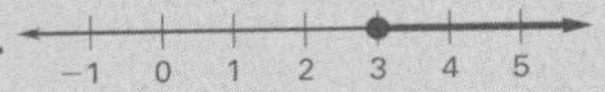

37.
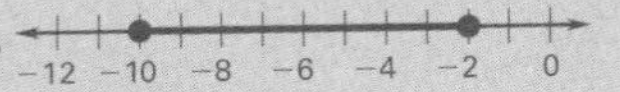

38.
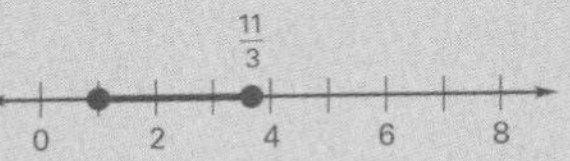

39.
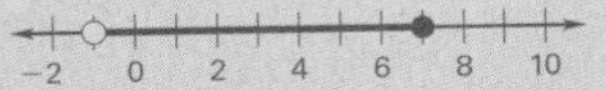

40.
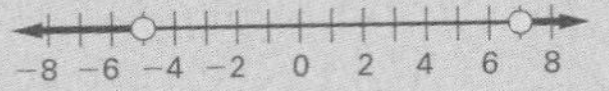

41.
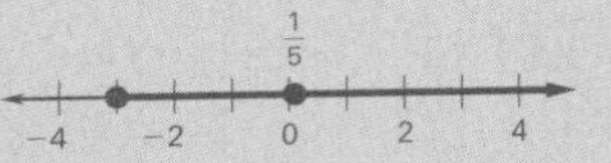

46.
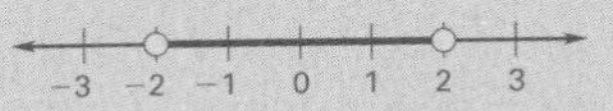

47.
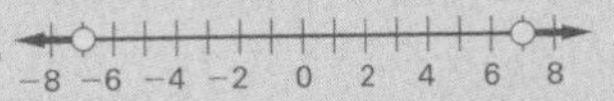

48.
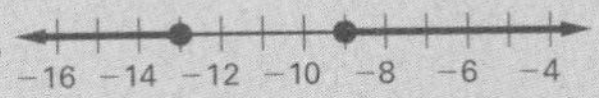

49.
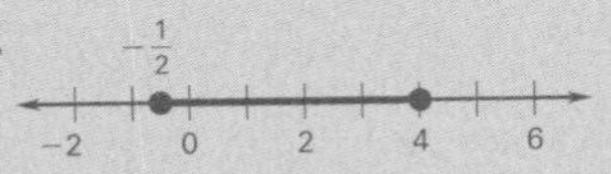

50.
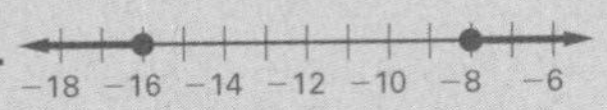

51.
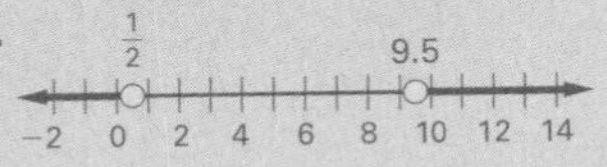

52.
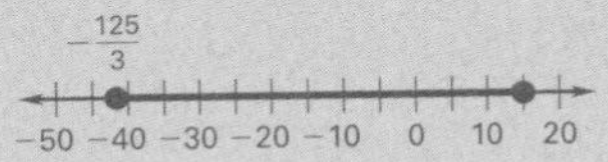

53.
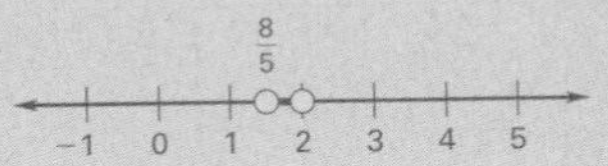

Chapter 2

2.1 Tell whether the relation is a function. *Explain.* 1–4. See margin.

1. 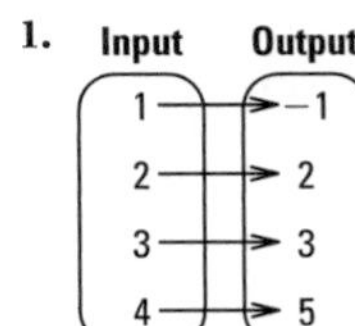

2. 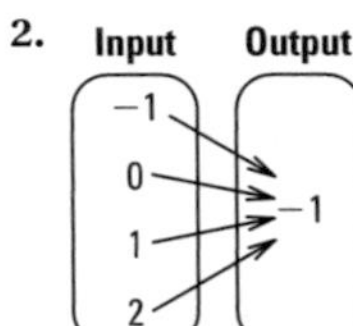

3. 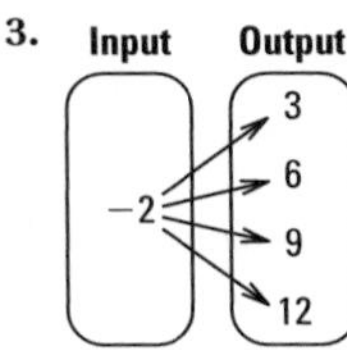

4. 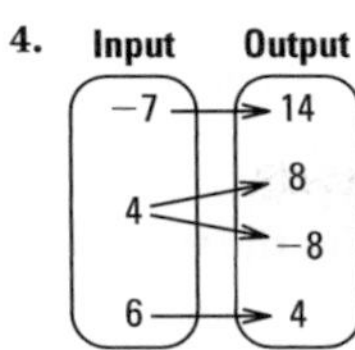

2.2 Find the slope of the line passing through the given points. Then tell whether the line *rises, falls, is horizontal,* or *is vertical.*

5. $(-3, 0), (5, -4)$ $-\frac{1}{2}$; falls
6. $(2, -1), (8, -1)$ 0; is horizontal
7. $(3, 5), (3, -12)$ undefined; is vertical
8. $(1, 8), (-1, -4)$ 6; rises

2.2 Tell whether the lines are *parallel, perpendicular,* or *neither.*

9. Line 1: through $(5, -4)$ and $(-4, 2)$
Line 2: through $(-5, -4)$ and $(-2, -2)$ neither
10. Line 1: through $(0, -4)$ and $(-2, 2)$
Line 2: through $(4, -3)$ and $(5, -6)$ parallel

2.3 Graph the equation using any method. 11–18. See margin.

11. $y = 2x - 2$
12. $y = -x + 2$
13. $f(x) = \frac{2}{3}x - 1$
14. $x + 2y = -6$
15. $-4x + 5y = 10$
16. $y - 2 = 0$
17. $-2x = 6y + 5$
18. $2y + 10 = -2.5x$

2.4 Write an equation of the line that satisfies the given conditions.

19. $m = 7, b = -3$ $y = 7x - 3$
20. $m = \frac{1}{3}, b = 4$ $y = \frac{1}{3}x + 4$
21. $m = 0$, passes through $(7, -2)$ $y = -2$
22. $m = -\frac{1}{4}$, passes through $(3, 6)$ $y = -\frac{1}{4}x + 6\frac{3}{4}$
23. passes through $(-1, -3)$ and $(2, 7)$ $y = \frac{10}{3}x + \frac{1}{3}$
24. passes through $(4, -2)$ and $(0, 4)$ $y = -\frac{3}{2}x + 4$

2.5 The variables x and y vary directly. Write an equation that relates x and y. Then find y when $x = -2$.

25. $x = 2, y = 4$ $y = 2x$; -4
26. $x = -1, y = 3$ $y = -3x$; 6
27. $x = -28, y = -7$ $y = \frac{1}{4}x$; $-\frac{1}{2}$
28. $x = 6, y = -4$ $y = -\frac{2}{3}x$; $\frac{4}{3}$

2.6 In Exercises 29 and 30, (a) draw a scatter plot of the data, (b) approximate the best-fitting line, and (c) estimate y when $x = 12$. 29, 30. See margin for art.

29.

x	1	2	3	4	5
y	8	11	13	16	18

c. about 36

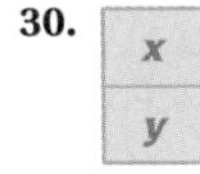

30.

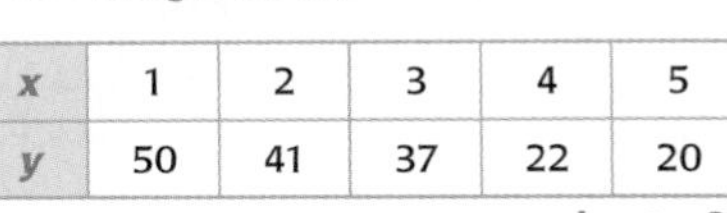

x	1	2	3	4	5
y	50	41	37	22	20

c. about −37

2.7 Graph the function. *Compare* the graph with the graph of $y = |x|$. 31–34. See margin.

31. $y = |x + 3|$
32. $y = -2|x - 5|$
33. $y = 3|x + 1| - 2$
34. $y = -\frac{1}{2}|x + 2| + 3$

2.8 Graph the inequality in a coordinate plane. 35–42. See margin.

35. $x < 4$
36. $y \geq -2$
37. $y \leq -x - 1$
38. $x + 2y > 8$
39. $-x - 4y \leq 6$
40. $3x + 4y > 12$
41. $y < |x + 1|$
42. $y \geq 3|x - 2| - 1$

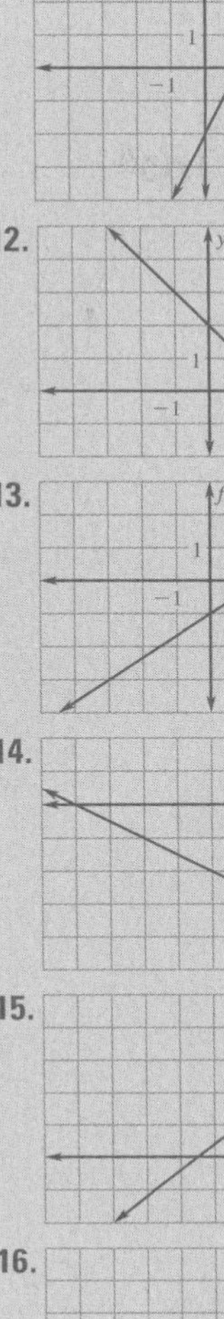

11. 12. 13. 14.

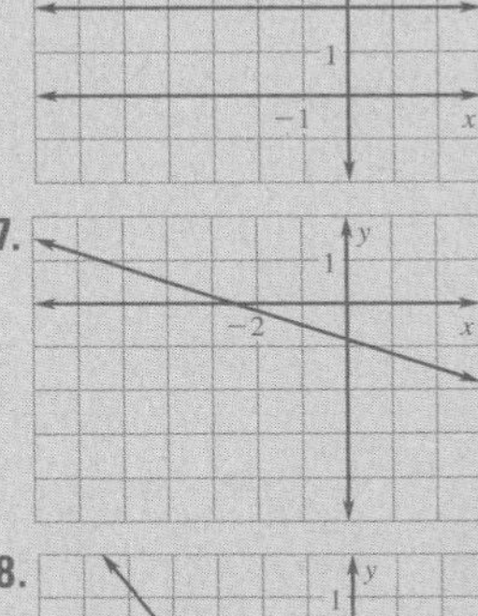

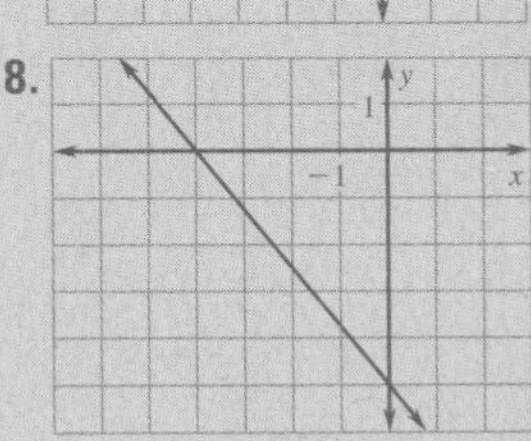

29a–b, 30a–b, 31–42. See Additional Answers beginning on p. AA1.

1. Function; for each input there is exactly one output.
2. Function; for each input there is exactly one output.
3. Not a function; there is more than one output for the input −2.
4. Not a function; there is more than one output for the input 4.

1.

2.

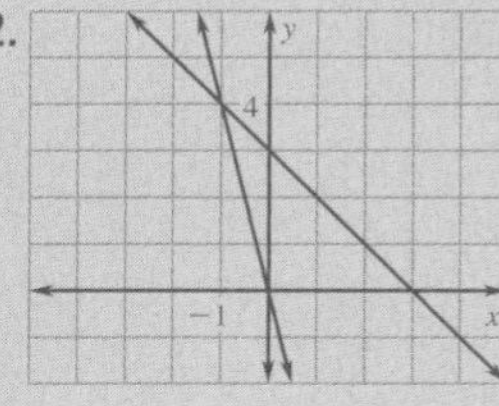

3.

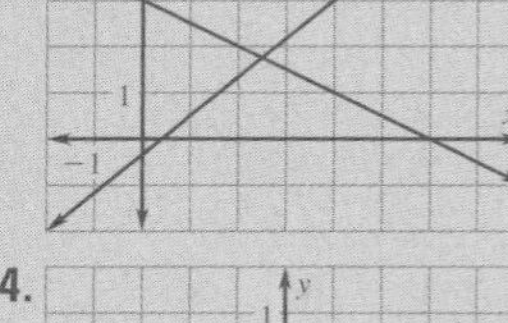

4.

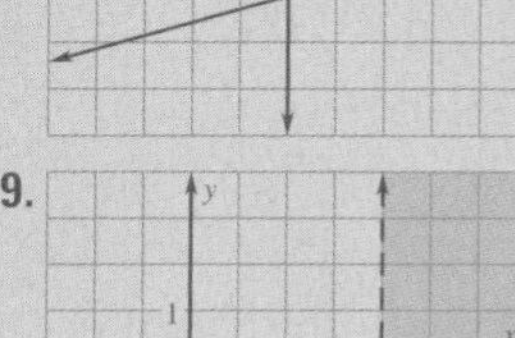

9.

10.

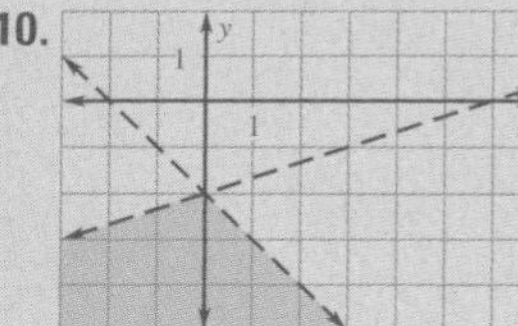

11.

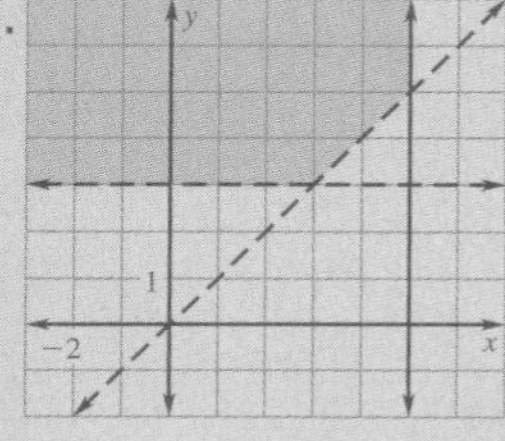

12.

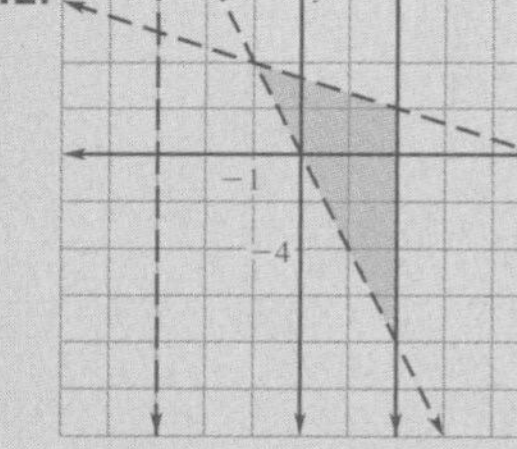

Chapter 3

EXTRA PRACTICE

3.1 Graph the linear system and estimate the solution. Then check the solution algebraically. 1–4. See margin for art.

1. $y = 2x - 1$
   $y = x - 4$ (−3, −7)
2. $y = -x + 3$
   $y = -4x$ (−1, 4)
3. $x + 2y = 6$
   $-5x + 6y = -2$
   (2.5, 1.75)
4. $-2x + 7y = -7$
   $4x - 14y = 14$
   infinitely many solutions

3.2 Solve the system using any algebraic method.

5. $-5x - y = -3$
   $x - 4y = 9$ (1, −2)
6. $4x - 2y = -6$
   $-3x + y = -3$ (6, 15)
7. $4x + 3y = -5$
   $12x + 4y = 10$ $\left(\frac{5}{2}, -5\right)$
8. $3x + 2y = 4$
   $-7x - 5y = -7$ (6, −7)

3.3 Graph the system of inequalities. 9–12. See margin.

9. $x > 4$
   $y \geq -1$
10. $x + y < -2$
    $x - 3y > 6$
11. $x \leq 5$
    $y > 3$
    $y > x$
12. $x > -3$
    $x \leq 2$
    $2x + 3y < 10$
    $y > -4x$

3.4 Solve the system using any algebraic method.

13. $3x + y - z = -6$
    $-x + 2y + 3z = -1$
    $5x - 2y + 6z = 54$
    (2, −7, 5)
14. $x + y - z = 7$
    $2x - 3y + z = 2$
    $4x + 2y - 2z = 20$
    (3, 0, −4)
15. $-x + y - 2z = 1.5$
    $4x - y + 5z = -6$
    $2x + y - 2z = 6$
    $\left(\frac{3}{2}, -3, -3\right)$
16. $-6x + y + 9z = 4$
    $2x - 3y - z = -6$
    $8x + 5y - 4z = 10$
    $\left(\frac{1}{6}, 2, \frac{1}{3}\right)$

3.5 Perform the indicated operation. 17–19. See margin.

17. $\begin{bmatrix} -6 & 7 \\ 0 & 3 \end{bmatrix} + \begin{bmatrix} -6 & 2 \\ -8 & 1 \end{bmatrix}$
18. $-\frac{2}{3}\begin{bmatrix} -9 & 3 \\ 4 & -1 \end{bmatrix}$
19. $\begin{bmatrix} 10 & 17 & -9 \\ -6 & 4 & 11 \end{bmatrix} - \begin{bmatrix} -6 & 8 & -2 \\ -4 & -9 & 4 \end{bmatrix}$

3.6 Find the product. If the product is not defined, state the reason. 20–22. See margin.

20. $\begin{bmatrix} 4 & 1 \\ -3 & 0 \end{bmatrix}\begin{bmatrix} -7 & 5 \\ 7 & -3 \end{bmatrix}$
21. $\begin{bmatrix} -16 \\ 2 \end{bmatrix}\begin{bmatrix} 4 \\ 15 \end{bmatrix}$
22. $\begin{bmatrix} 5 & -1 & 0 \\ 4 & -2 & 9 \end{bmatrix}\begin{bmatrix} 12 \\ -7 \\ 3 \end{bmatrix}$

3.7 Evaluate the determinant of the matrix.

23. $\begin{bmatrix} 5 & 8 \\ -2 & 10 \end{bmatrix}$ 66
24. $\begin{bmatrix} 13 & 7 \\ -11 & -4 \end{bmatrix}$ 25
25. $\begin{bmatrix} 1 & -3 & -2 \\ 7 & 4 & 0 \\ -7 & 2 & 3 \end{bmatrix}$ −9
26. $\begin{bmatrix} 6 & 0 & 5 \\ -4 & 2 & 1 \\ 1 & 0 & 0.5 \end{bmatrix}$ −4

3.7 Use Cramer's rule to solve the linear system.

27. $2x + y = -8$
    $-5x - 2y = 13$
    (3, −14)
28. $8x + 3y = 1$
    $7x + 3y = -1$
    (2, −5)
29. $2x - 2y - 3z = 9$
    $3x + z = 10$
    $x + y = 0$
    (3, −3, 1)
30. $2x + y + 3z = 4$
    $-8x + 4y + z = -7$
    $x + 2y + 3z = -1$
    (−2, −7, 5)

3.8 Find the inverse of the matrix. 31–34. See margin.

31. $\begin{bmatrix} 3 & 7 \\ 3 & 8 \end{bmatrix}$
32. $\begin{bmatrix} 1 & 4 \\ 0 & 5 \end{bmatrix}$
33. $\begin{bmatrix} -2 & -5 \\ 3 & 8 \end{bmatrix}$
34. $\begin{bmatrix} 9 & 2 \\ 18 & 5 \end{bmatrix}$

3.8 Use an inverse matrix to solve the linear system.

35. $x + 3y = -4$
    $-2x + y = -34$
    (14, −6)
36. $2x + 3y = 6$
    $-x - 6y = -9$ $\left(1, \frac{4}{3}\right)$
37. $3x - 8y = 0$
    $2x + y = -19$
    (−8, −3)
38. $x + y = 7$
    $-5x + 3y = -3$
    (3, 4)

17. $\begin{bmatrix} -12 & 9 \\ -8 & 4 \end{bmatrix}$ 18. $\begin{bmatrix} 6 & -2 \\ -\frac{8}{3} & \frac{2}{3} \end{bmatrix}$ 19. $\begin{bmatrix} 16 & 9 & -7 \\ -2 & 13 & 7 \end{bmatrix}$ 20. $\begin{bmatrix} -21 & 17 \\ 21 & -15 \end{bmatrix}$

21. Not defined; the number of columns in the left matrix does not equal the number of rows in the right matrix.

22. $\begin{bmatrix} 67 \\ 89 \end{bmatrix}$ 31. $\begin{bmatrix} \frac{8}{3} & -\frac{7}{3} \\ -1 & 1 \end{bmatrix}$ 32. $\begin{bmatrix} 1 & -\frac{4}{5} \\ 0 & \frac{1}{5} \end{bmatrix}$ 33. $\begin{bmatrix} -8 & -5 \\ 3 & 2 \end{bmatrix}$ 34. $\begin{bmatrix} \frac{5}{9} & -\frac{2}{9} \\ -2 & 1 \end{bmatrix}$

Chapter 4

4.1 Graph the function. Label the vertex and axis of symmetry. 1–4. See margin.

1. $y = 3x^2 + 5$
2. $y = -x^2 - 4x - 4$
3. $y = -2x^2 + 4x + 1$
4. $y = 2x^2 + 5x + 6$

4.2 Graph the function. Label the vertex and axis of symmetry. 5–8. See margin.

5. $y = 4(x - 2)^2 + 1$
6. $y = -(x + 3)^2 - 2$
7. $y = 3(x - 1)(x - 5)$
8. $y = \frac{1}{2}(x + 3)(x + 2)$

4.2 Write the quadratic function in standard form.

9. $y = 7(x + 2)(x + 4)$ $y = 7x^2 + 42x + 56$
10. $y = 2(x + 5)(x - 3)$ $y = 2x^2 + 4x - 30$
11. $y = (x - 7)^2 + 7$ $y = x^2 - 14x + 56$
12. $y = -(x + 1)^2 - 4$ $y = -x^2 - 2x - 5$

4.3 Factor the expression. If the expression cannot be factored, say so.

13. $x^2 - 4x + 4$ $(x - 2)^2$
14. $t^2 - 11t - 26$ $(t - 13)(t + 2)$
15. $x^2 + 21x + 108$ $(x + 9)(x + 12)$
16. $b^2 - 400$ $(b - 20)(b + 20)$

4.3 Solve the equation.

17. $x^2 + 5x - 14 = 0$ $-7, 2$
18. $x^2 - 11x + 24 = 0$ $3, 8$
19. $c^2 + 6c = 55$ $-11, 5$
20. $n^2 = 5n$ $0, 5$

4.4 Factor the expression. If the expression cannot be factored, say so.

21. $2x^2 + x - 15$ $(2x - 5)(x + 3)$
22. $10a^2 - 19a + 7$ $(5a - 7)(2a - 1)$
23. $3r^2 + 9r - 4$ not factorable
24. $4t^2 + 8t + 3$ $(2t + 1)(2t + 3)$

4.4 Find the zeros of the function by rewriting the function in intercept form.

25. $y = 81x^2 - 16$ $-\frac{4}{9}, \frac{4}{9}$
26. $y = 2x^2 - 9x - 5$ $-\frac{1}{2}, 5$
27. $y = 4x^2 + 18x + 18$ $-3, -\frac{3}{2}$
28. $y = -3x^2 - 30x - 27$ $-9, -1$

4.5 Simplify the expression.

29. $\sqrt{56}$ $2\sqrt{14}$
30. $3\sqrt{2} \cdot \sqrt{50}$ 30
31. $\sqrt{\frac{4}{7}}$ $\frac{2\sqrt{7}}{7}$
32. $\frac{6}{1 + \sqrt{2}}$ $-6 + 6\sqrt{2}$

4.5 Solve the equation.

33. $b^2 = 8$ $\pm 2\sqrt{2}$
34. $p^2 + 6 = 127$ ± 11
35. $(x - 5)^2 = 10$ $5 \pm \sqrt{10}$
36. $3(x + 2)^2 - 4 = 11$ $-2 \pm \sqrt{5}$

4.6 Write the expression as a complex number in standard form.

37. $(5 + 2i) + (6 - 5i)$ $11 - 3i$
38. $-3i(7 + i)$ $3 - 21i$
39. $\frac{1 + 2i}{3 - 8i}$ $-\frac{13}{73} + \frac{14}{73}i$
40. $\frac{(3 - 2i) + 2i}{(-1 + 7i) - (2 + 3i)}$ $-\frac{9}{25} - \frac{12}{25}i$

4.7 Solve the equation by completing the square.

41. $x^2 + 6x = 10$ $-3 \pm \sqrt{19}$
42. $x^2 - 9x - 2 = 0$ $\frac{9}{2} \pm \frac{\sqrt{89}}{2}$
43. $2c^2 - 12c + 6 = 0$ $3 \pm \sqrt{6}$
44. $3z^2 - 3z + 9 = 0$ $\frac{1}{2} \pm \frac{\sqrt{11}}{2}i$

4.8 Use the quadratic formula to solve the equation.

45. $x^2 + 10x - 10 = 0$ $-5 \pm \sqrt{35}$
46. $x^2 - x - 1 = 0$ $\frac{1}{2} \pm \frac{\sqrt{5}}{2}$
47. $4s^2 + 3s = 12$ $-\frac{3}{8} \pm \frac{\sqrt{201}}{8}$
48. $-2r^2 = r + 17$ $-\frac{1}{4} \pm \frac{3\sqrt{15}}{4}i$

4.9 Solve the inequality using any method.

49. $x^2 - 10x \geq 0$ $x \leq 0$ or $x \geq 10$
50. $x^2 - 8x + 12 < 0$ $2 < x < 6$
51. $-x^2 + 7x + 6 > 1$ $-0.653 < x < 7.65$
52. $3x^2 + 16x + 2 \leq 3x$ $-4.17 \leq x \leq -0.160$

4.10 Write a quadratic function in standard form for the parabola that passes through the given points.

53. $(-1, -6), (0, -7), (2, 9)$ $y = 3x^2 + 2x - 7$
54. $(-2, -1), (1, 2), (3, -6)$ $y = -x^2 + 3$
55. $(-3, 36), (0, 36), (2, 16)$ $y = -2x^2 - 6x + 36$

EXTRA PRACTICE

4.
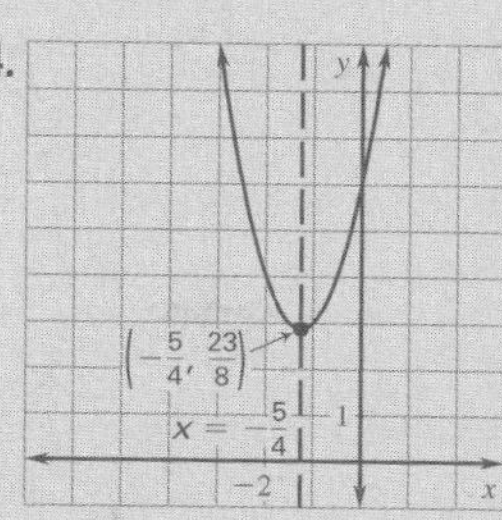

5.
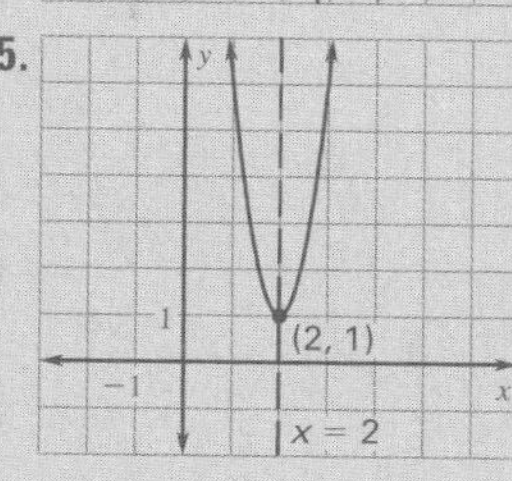

6.
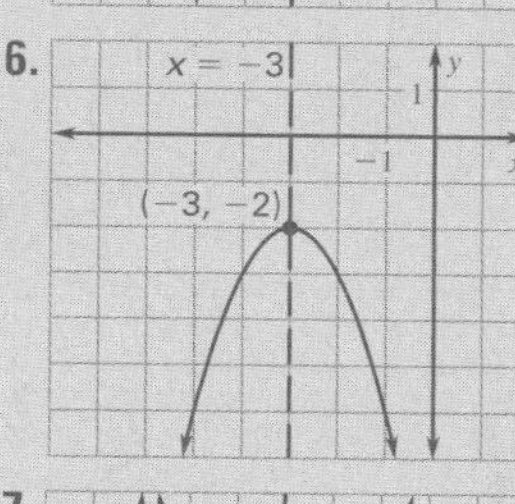

7.
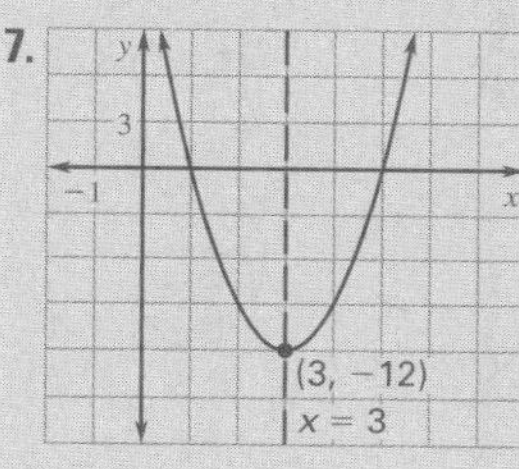

8.
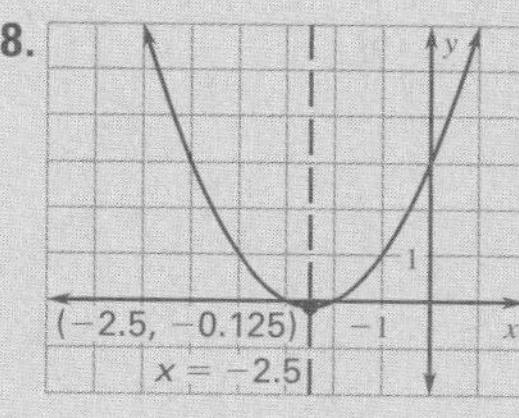

1.
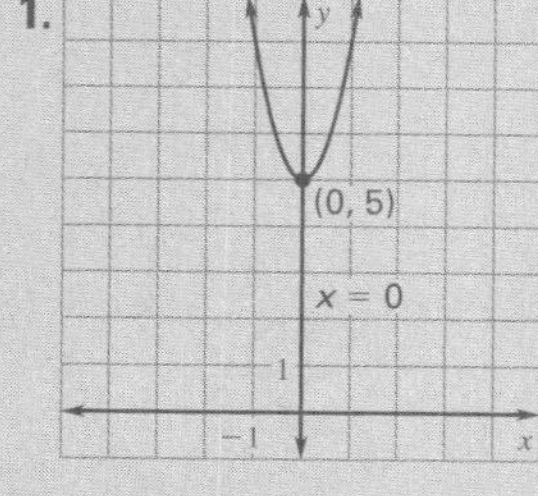

2.
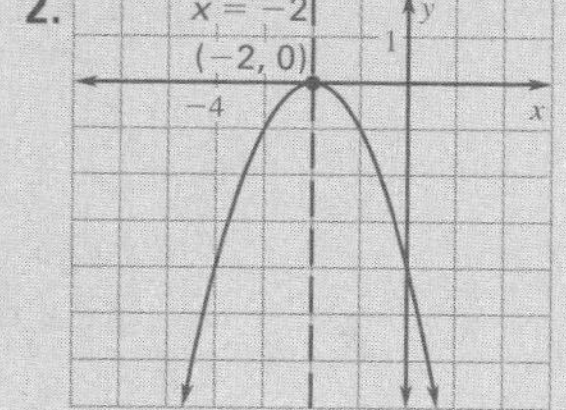

3.
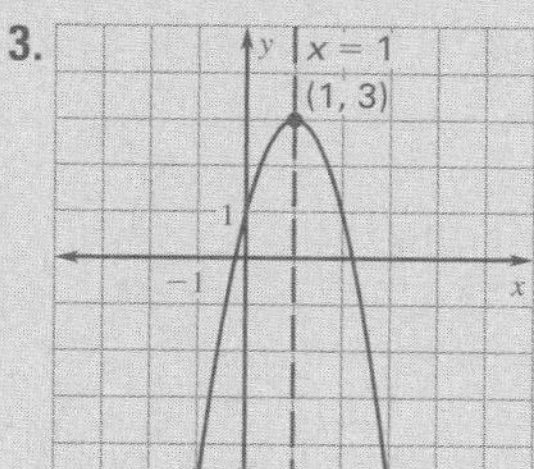

4. $\frac{-2y^2}{5x^4}$; quotient of powers property, negative exponent property, product of powers property

5. $\frac{b^6}{64a^{15}}$; power of a product property, negative exponent property

6. $\frac{2s^8}{r^4}$; product of powers property, negative exponent property

7. $7x^2y^2$; product of powers property, quotient of powers property, negative exponent property

8.

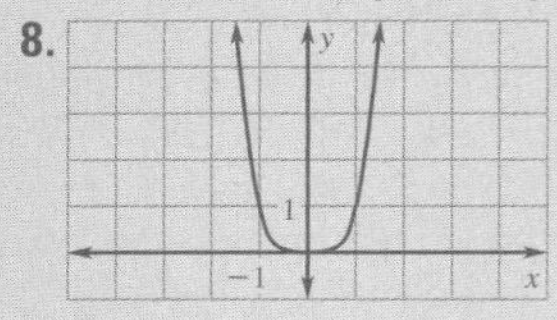

9.

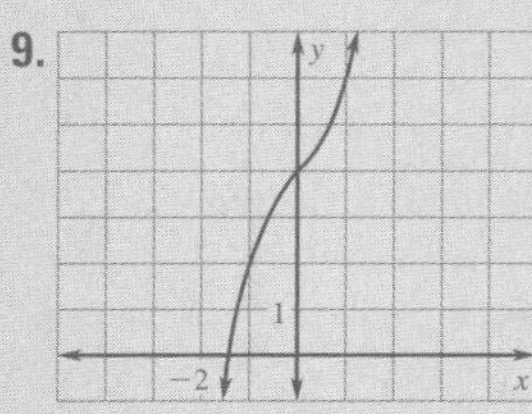

10.

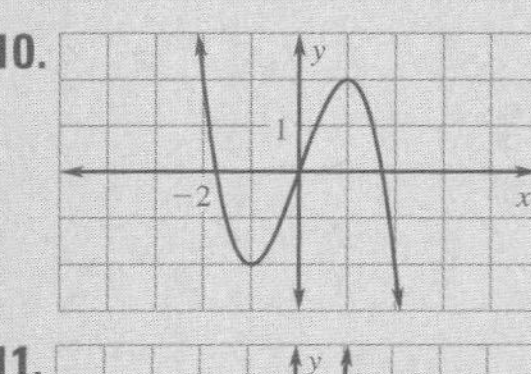

11.

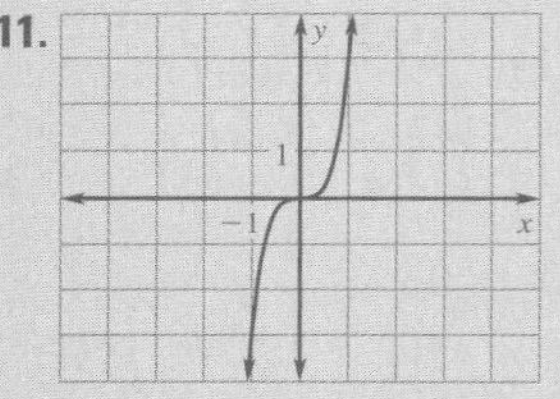

25. positive: 2 or 0, negative: 1, imaginary: 2 or 0

26. positive: 1, negative: 2 or 0, imaginary: 4 or 2

27. positive: 1, negative: 1, imaginary: 2

Chapter 5

EXTRA PRACTICE

5.1 Write the answer in scientific notation.

1. $(3.4 \times 10^3)(2.8 \times 10^8)$ 9.52×10^{11}
2. $(5.8 \times 10^{-6})^4$ $1.1316496 \times 10^{-21}$
3. $\frac{4.6 \times 10^{-7}}{9.2 \times 10^{-9}}$ 5×10^1

5.1 Simplify the expression. Tell which properties of exponents you used. 4–7. See margin.

4. $\frac{-14x^{-3}y^5}{35xy^3}$
5. $(4a^5b^{-2})^{-3}$
6. $(2r^3s^3)(r^{-7}s^5)$
7. $\frac{xy^{-1}}{x^2y} \cdot \frac{7x^3}{y^{-4}}$

5.2 Graph the polynomial function. 8–11. See margin.

8. $f(x) = x^4$
9. $f(x) = x^3 + x + 4$
10. $f(x) = -x^3 + 3x$
11. $f(x) = x^5 + 2x^3$

5.3 Perform the indicated operation.

12. $(4z^3 + 9) + (3z^2 - 4z - 2)$ $4z^3 + 3z^2 - 4z + 7$
13. $(x^2 + 3x - 1) - (4x^2 + 7)$ $-3x^2 + 3x - 8$
14. $(3x - 4)^3$ $27x^3 - 108x^2 + 144x - 64$

5.4 Factor the polynomial completely using any method.

15. $3x^4 + 18x^3 + 27x^2$ $3x^2(x + 3)^2$
16. $343x^3 + 1000$ $(7x + 10)(49x^2 - 70x + 100)$
17. $2x^3 + x^2 - 8x - 4$ $(x - 2)(x + 2)(2x + 1)$

5.4 Find the real-number solutions of the equation.

18. $3x^3 + 18x^2 = 48x$ $-8, 0, 2$
19. $x^4 + 32 = 14x^2$ $\pm\sqrt{7 \pm \sqrt{17}}$
20. $2x^3 + 48 = 3x^2 + 32x$ $-4, \frac{3}{2}, 4$

5.5 Divide using polynomial long division or synthetic division.

21. $(2x^3 + 4x^2 - 5x + 16) \div (x - 3)$ $2x^2 + 10x + 25 + \frac{91}{x - 3}$
22. $(x^4 + 2x^3 - 7x^2 - 14) \div (x + 2)$ $x^3 - 7x + 14 + \frac{-42}{x + 2}$

5.6 Find all real zeros of the function.

23. $f(x) = 2x^3 + 3x^2 - 8x + 3$ $-3, \frac{1}{2}, 1$
24. $f(x) = 2x^4 + x^3 - 53x^2 - 14x + 20$ $-3 \pm \sqrt{5}, \frac{1}{2}, 5$

5.7 Determine the possible numbers of positive real zeros, negative real zeros, and imaginary zeros of the function. 25–27. See margin.

25. $f(x) = -x^3 + 2x^2 - 11x - 1$
26. $f(x) = 4x^5 + 3x^2 - 8x - 10$
27. $f(x) = x^4 - 3x^3 - 7x - 13$

5.8 Estimate the coordinates of each turning point and state whether each corresponds to a local maximum or a local minimum. Then estimate all real zeros and determine the least degree the function can have. 28–30. See margin.

28.

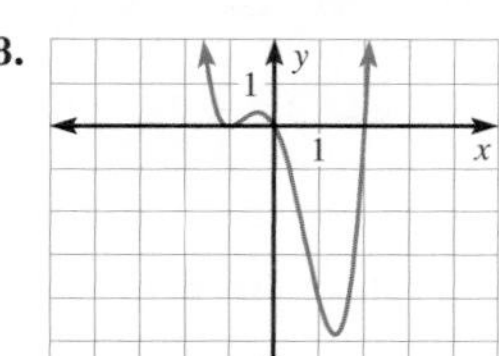

29.

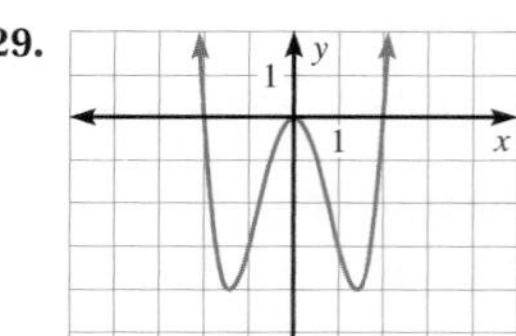

30.

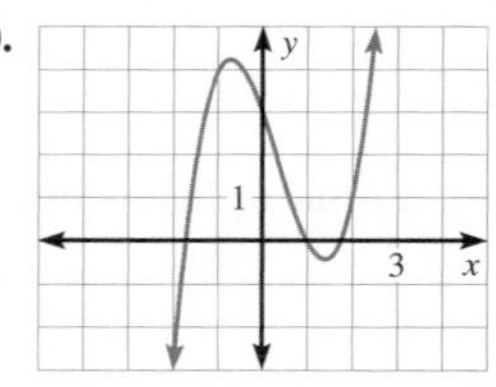

5.9 Use finite differences and a system of equations to find a polynomial function that fits the data in the table.

31.

x	1	2	3	4	5	6
y	2.5	11	27.5	55	96.5	155

$y = 0.5x^3 + x^2 + 2x - 1$

32.

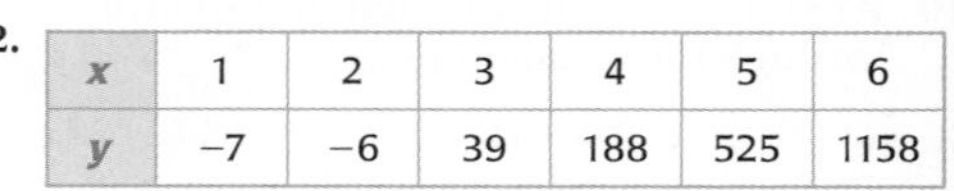

x	1	2	3	4	5	6
y	−7	−6	39	188	525	1158

$y = x^4 - 3x^2 - 5x$

28. (−1, 0) local minimum, (−0.5, 0.25) local maximum, (1.5, −4.9) local minimum; (−1, 0), (−1, 0), (0, 0), (2, 0), degree 4

29. (−1.5, −4) local minimum, (0, 0) local maximum, (1.5, −4) local minimum; (−2, 0), (0, 0), (0, 0), (2, 0), degree 4

30. (−0.75, 4.25) local maximum, (1.25, −0.25) local minimum; (−1.75, 0), (1, 0), (1.75, 0), degree 3

Chapter 6

6.1 Find the indicated real nth root(s) of a.

1. $n = 4, a = 81$ ± 3
2. $n = 3, a = 512$ 8
3. $n = 5, a = -243$ -3

6.1 Evaluate the expression without using a calculator.

4. $36^{-1/2}$ $\frac{1}{6}$
5. $64^{5/6}$ 32
6. $(\sqrt[3]{216})^{-2}$ $\frac{1}{36}$
7. $(\sqrt[5]{-32})^4$ 16

6.1 Solve the equation. Round the result to two decimal places when appropriate.

8. $x^3 = -8$ -2
9. $x^4 + 9 = 90$ ± 3
10. $(x - 3)^5 = 60$ 5.27
11. $-4x^6 = -400$ ± 2.15

6.2 Simplify the expression.

12. $4^{5/2} \cdot 4^{-1/2}$ 16
13. $\frac{17^{3/7}}{17^{4/7}}$ $\frac{1}{17^{1/7}}$
14. $(\sqrt[4]{5} \cdot \sqrt{5})^4$ 125
15. $\frac{\sqrt[3]{135}}{\sqrt[3]{5}}$ 3
16. $5\sqrt[5]{7} - 7\sqrt[5]{7}$ $-2\sqrt[5]{7}$
17. $\sqrt[3]{2} + 2\sqrt[3]{128}$ $9\sqrt[3]{2}$
18. $\frac{324^{1/4}}{4^{-1/4}}$ 6
19. $4\sqrt[3]{108} \cdot 2\sqrt[3]{4}$ $48\sqrt[3]{2}$

6.2 Write the expression in simplest form. Assume all variables are positive.

20. $\sqrt{20x^6y^7}$ $2x^3y^3\sqrt{5y}$
21. $\sqrt[5]{18x^3y^{14}z^{20}}$ $y^2z^4\sqrt[5]{18x^3y^4}$
22. $\sqrt[4]{\frac{x^5}{y^{16}}}$ $\frac{x}{y^4}\sqrt[4]{x}$
23. $\sqrt[3]{16x^7y^2} \cdot \sqrt[3]{6xy^5}$ $2x^2y^2\sqrt[3]{12x^2y}$

6.3 Let $f(x) = -x + 4$, $g(x) = x^3$, and $h(x) = \frac{x}{4}$. Perform the indicated operation and state the domain. 24–31. See margin.

24. $f(x) + g(x)$
25. $g(x) - f(x)$
26. $g(x) \cdot h(x)$
27. $\frac{f(x)}{g(x)}$
28. $f(g(x))$
29. $g(h(x))$
30. $h(f(x))$
31. $f(f(x))$

6.4 Verify that f and g are inverse functions. 32–33. See margin.

32. $f(x) = 2x - 4$, $g(x) = \frac{1}{2}x + 2$
33. $f(x) = 3x^2 + 1, x \geq 0$; $g(x) = \left(\frac{x-1}{3}\right)^{1/2}$

6.4 Find the inverse of the function.

34. $f(x) = 5x - 3$ $f^{-1}(x) = \frac{x+3}{5}$
35. $f(x) = \frac{4}{3}x + 2$ $f^{-1}(x) = \frac{3}{4}x - \frac{3}{2}$
36. $f(x) = \frac{1}{2}x^2, x \geq 0$ $f^{-1}(x) = \sqrt{2x}$
37. $f(x) = -x^6 + 2, x \leq 0$ $f^{-1}(x) = -\sqrt[6]{-x+2}$
38. $f(x) = \frac{4x^4 - 1}{18}, x \geq 0$ $f^{-1}(x) = \sqrt[4]{\frac{18x+1}{4}}$
39. $f(x) = 32x^5 + 4$ $f^{-1}(x) = \frac{\sqrt[5]{x-4}}{2}$

6.5 Graph the function. Then state the domain and range. 40–47. See margin for art.

40. $y = -\frac{1}{3}\sqrt{x}$ domain: $x \geq 0$, range: $y \leq 0$
41. $y = \frac{2}{5}\sqrt[3]{x}$ See margin.
42. $y = \frac{5}{6}\sqrt{x}$ domain: $x \geq 0$, range: $y \geq 0$
43. $y = \sqrt{x+2} - 3$ domain: $x \geq -2$, range: $y \geq -3$
44. $y = -2\sqrt[3]{x-1} + 2$ See margin.
45. $f(x) = 3\sqrt[3]{x}$ See margin.
46. $g(x) = -\frac{1}{2}\sqrt{x-2}$ domain: $x \geq 2$, range: $y \leq 0$
47. $h(x) = -\sqrt{x+3} + 4$ domain: $x \geq -3$, range: $y \leq 4$

6.6 Solve the equation. Check your solution.

48. $\sqrt{2x+3} = 7$ 23
49. $-5\sqrt{x+1} + 12 = 2$ 3
50. $\sqrt[3]{5x-1} + 6 = 10$ 13
51. $2\sqrt[3]{8x} + 9 = 5$ -1
52. $7x^{4/3} = 175$ $\pm 5\sqrt{5}$
53. $(x-2)^{3/4} = 1$ 3
54. $x - 8 = \sqrt{18x}$ 32
55. $x = \sqrt{4x-3}$ $1, 3$
56. $\sqrt{2x+1} + 5 = \sqrt{x+12} - 8$ no solution

EXTRA PRACTICE

40. 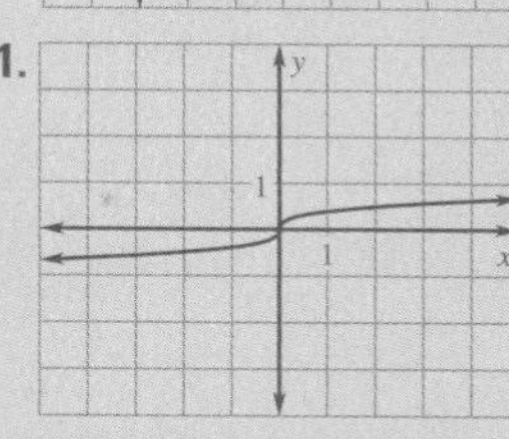

41. 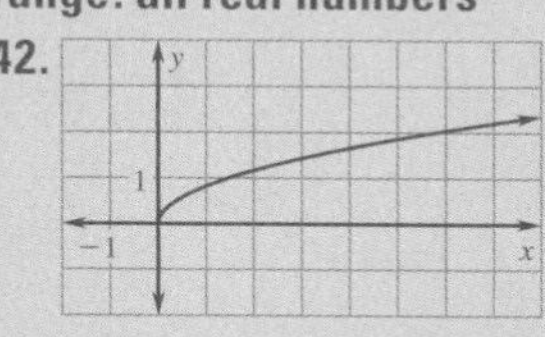

domain: all real numbers, range: all real numbers

42. 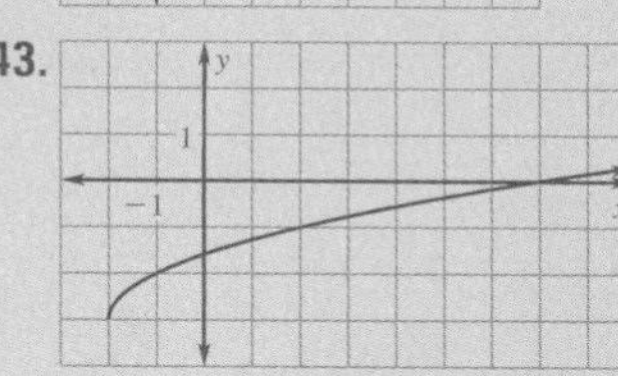

43. 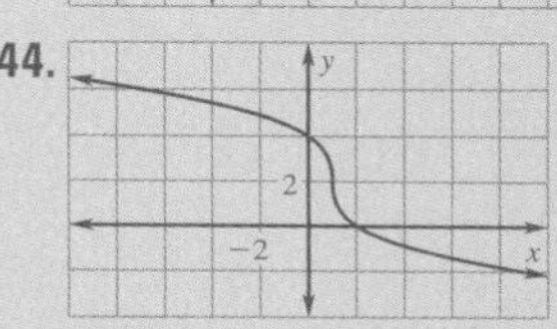

44. 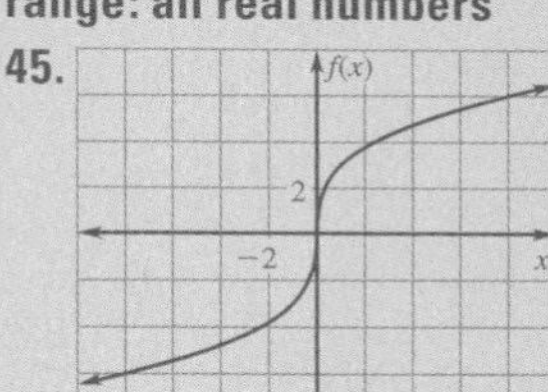

domain: all real numbers, range: all real numbers

45. 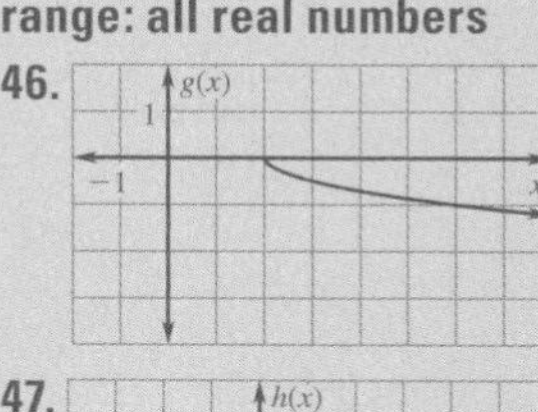

domain: all real numbers, range: all real numbers

46. 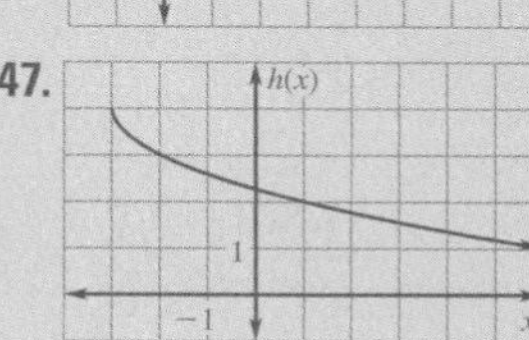

47.

24. $x^3 - x + 4$, all real numbers
25. $x^3 + x - 4$, all real numbers
26. $\frac{x^4}{4}$, all real numbers
27. $\frac{-x+4}{x^3}$, all real numbers except $x = 0$
28. $-x^3 + 4$, all real numbers
29. $\frac{x^3}{64}$, all real numbers
30. $-\frac{x}{4} + 1$, all real numbers
31. x, all real numbers
32, 33. See Additional Answers beginning on p. AA1.

1.

2.

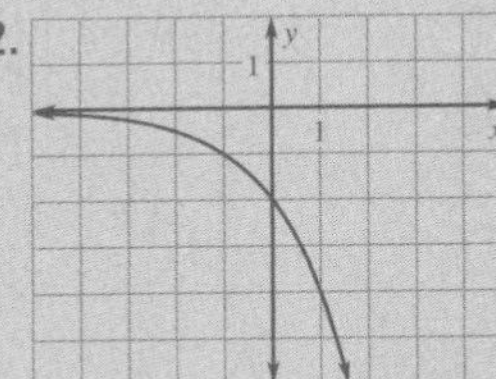

3.

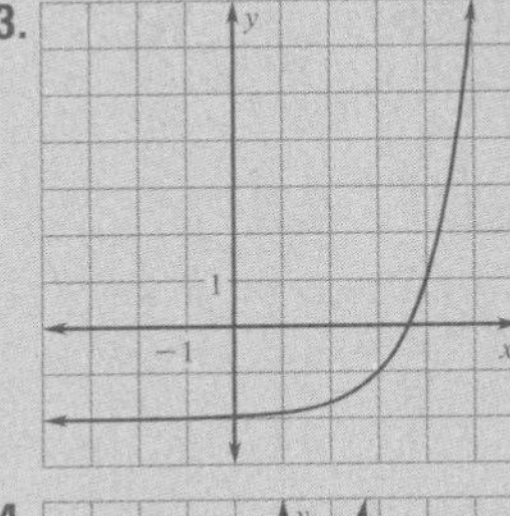

4.

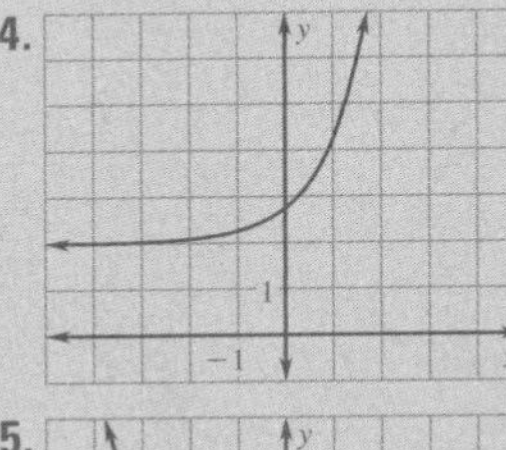

5.

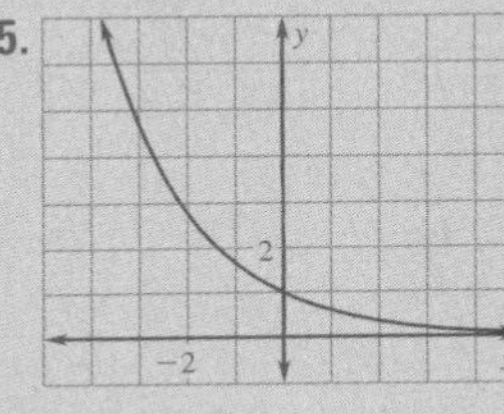

6.

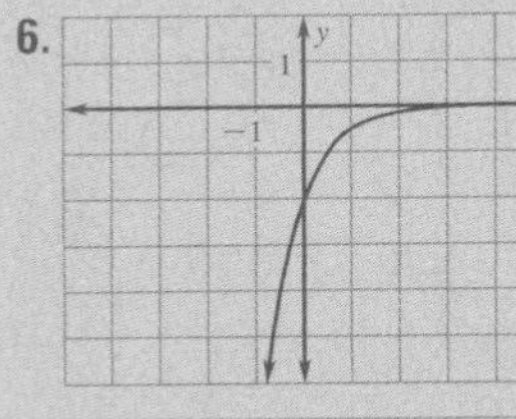

7.

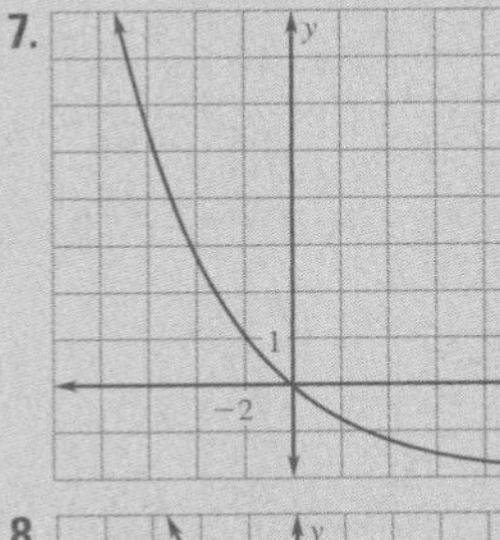

8.

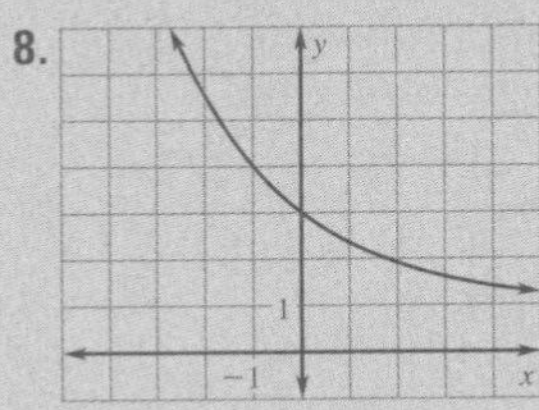

EXTRA PRACTICE

Chapter 7

7.1 Graph the function. State the domain and range. 1–4. See margin for art.

1. $y = \left(\frac{4}{3}\right)^x$ domain: all real numbers, range: $y > 0$

2. $y = -2 \cdot 2^x$ domain: all real numbers, range: $y < 0$

3. $y = 3^{x-3} - 2$ domain: all real numbers, range: $y > -2$

4. $y = \frac{1}{4} \cdot 3^{x+1} + 2$ domain: all real numbers, range: $y > 2$

7.2 Graph the function. State the domain and range. 5–8. See margin for art.

5. $y = \left(\frac{3}{5}\right)^x$ domain: all real numbers, range: $y > 0$

6. $y = -2\left(\frac{1}{4}\right)^x$ domain: all real numbers, range: $y < 0$

7. $y = (0.8)^{x-3} - 2$ domain: all real numbers, range: $y > -2$

8. $y = 2\left(\frac{2}{3}\right)^x + 1$ domain: all real numbers, range: $y > 1$

7.3 Simplify the expression.

9. $e^{-3} \cdot e^{-8}$ $\frac{1}{e^{11}}$

10. $(2e^{2x})^{-5}$ $\frac{1}{32e^{10x}}$

11. $\sqrt{81e^{8x}}$ $9e^{4x}$

12. $\frac{28e^{3x}}{21e^{-x}}$ $\frac{4}{3}e^{4x}$

7.3 Graph the function. State the domain and range. 13–16. See margin for art.

13. $y = 0.5e^{3x}$ domain: all real numbers, range: $y > 0$

14. $y = 2e^{-x} - 2$ See margin.

15. $y = 1.5e^{x+1} + 3$ domain: all real numbers, range: $y > 3$

16. $y = e^{3(x-2)} + 1$ domain: all real numbers, range: $y > 1$

7.4 Evaluate the logarithm without using a calculator.

17. $\log_4 \frac{1}{16}$ -2

18. $\log_6 6$ 1

19. $\log_5 125$ 3

20. $\log_{3/4} \frac{64}{27}$ -3

7.4 Simplify the expression.

21. $5^{\log_5 x}$ x

22. $10^{\log 9}$ 9

23. $\log_4 16^x$ $2x$

24. $e^{\ln 5}$ 5

7.4 Graph the function. State the domain and range. 25–28. See margin for art.

25. $y = \log_7 x$ domain: $x > 0$, range: all real numbers

26. $y = \log_{1/2}(x - 4)$ domain: $x > 4$, range: all real numbers

27. $y = \log_5 x + 3$ domain: $x > 0$, range: all real numbers

28. $y = \log_3(x - 2) + 1$ domain: $x > 2$, range: all real numbers

7.5 Expand the expression.

29. $\log_5 \frac{2x}{5}$ $\log_5 2 + \log_5 x - 1$

30. $\log \frac{100x^2}{y}$ $2 + 2\log x - \log y$

31. $\ln 20x^3y^2$ $\ln 20 + 3\ln x + 2\ln y$

32. $\log_2 \sqrt[3]{8x^4}$ $1 + \frac{4}{3}\log_2 x$

7.5 Condense the expression.

33. $\log_4 20 + 4\log_4 x$ $\log_4 20x^4$

34. $\log 7 + 2\log x - 5\log y$ $\log \frac{7x^2}{y^5}$

35. $0.5\ln 100 - 2\ln x + 8\ln y$ $\ln \frac{10y^8}{x^2}$

7.5 Use the change-of-base formula to evaluate the logarithm.

36. $\log_2 5$ about 2.322

37. $\log_4 80$ about 3.161

38. $\log_5 100$ about 2.861

39. $\log_7 27$ about 1.694

7.6 Solve the equation. Check for extraneous solutions.

40. $2^{4x+2} = 8^{x+2}$ 4

41. $\left(\frac{1}{9}\right)^{x-3} = 3^{3x+1}$ 1

42. $7^{9x} = 18$ about 0.165

43. $\ln(3x + 7) = \ln(x - 1)$ no solution

44. $\log_5(3x + 2) = 3$ 41

45. $\log_6(x + 9) + \log_6 x = 2$ 3

7.7 Write an exponential function $y = ab^x$ whose graph passes through the given points.

46. (1, 8), (2, 32) $y = 2 \cdot 4^x$

47. (1, 3), (3, 12) $y = \frac{3}{2} \cdot 2^x$ or $y = -\frac{3}{2} \cdot (-2)^x$

48. (2, −9), (5, −243) $y = -1 \cdot 3^x$

49. (1, 4), (2, 4) $y = 4 \cdot 1^x$

7.7 Write a power function $y = ax^b$ whose graph passes through the given points.

50. (2, 2), (5, 16) $y = 0.415\,x^{2.27}$

51. (3, 27), (6, 432) $y = \frac{1}{3} \cdot x^4$

52. (1, 4), (8, 17) $y = 4 \cdot x^{0.696}$

53. (5, 36), (10, 220) $y = 0.538 \cdot x^{2.611}$

13–16, 25–28. See Additional Answers beginning on p. AA1.

Chapter 8

8.1 **The variables x and y vary inversely. Use the given values to write an equation relating x and y. Then find y when $x = -5$.**

1. $x = 2, y = -10$ $\quad y = \frac{-20}{x}$; 4
2. $x = \frac{1}{3}, y = 24$ $\quad y = \frac{8}{x}$; $-\frac{8}{5}$
3. $x = -3, y = -5$ $\quad y = \frac{15}{x}$; -3
4. $x = 25, y = -\frac{2}{5}$ $\quad y = \frac{-10}{x}$; 2

8.1 **Determine whether x and y show *direct variation*, *inverse variation*, or *neither*.**

5.

x	y
2.5	32
4	20
5	16
6.4	12.5
8	10

inverse variation

6.

x	y
1	2.5
3.5	8.75
5	12.5
8	20
9	22.5

direct variation

7.

x	y
11	30
14	61
16	85
24	92
27	105

neither

8.

x	y
1	12
3	4
8	1.5
12	1
15	0.8

inverse variation

8.2 **Graph the function. State the domain and range.** 9–12. See margin.

9. $y = \frac{6}{x}$
10. $y = \frac{-2}{x} + 3$
11. $y = \frac{5}{x-1} - 2$
12. $y = \frac{4x+19}{x+3}$

8.3 **Graph the function.** 13–16. See margin.

13. $y = \frac{x}{x^2 - 4}$
14. $y = \frac{x^2+1}{x^2+4x+3}$
15. $y = \frac{x^2+2x-3}{x+2}$
16. $f(x) = \frac{2x^2-8}{x^2-2x}$

8.4 **Simplify the rational expression, if possible.**

17. $\frac{x^2+x-6}{x^2+9x+18}$ $\quad \frac{x-2}{x+6}$
18. $\frac{x^3-100x}{x^4+20x^3+100x^2}$ $\quad \frac{x-10}{x(x+10)}$
19. $\frac{x^2-5x-84}{2x^2-98}$ $\quad \frac{x-12}{2(x-7)}$
20. $\frac{x^2+7x+10}{x^2-7x+10}$ $\quad$ simplified

8.4 **Multiply or divide the expressions. Simplify the result.**

21. $\frac{6x^2y}{xy^2} \cdot \frac{2y}{9x^3}$ $\quad \frac{4}{3x^2}$
22. $\frac{2x^2-x-6}{2x^2+5x+3} \cdot \frac{x^2+x}{x^2-4}$ $\quad \frac{x}{x+2}$
23. $\frac{3x^2+15x}{x^2-12x+36} \cdot (x^2-x-30)$ $\quad \frac{3x(x+5)^2}{x-6}$
24. $\frac{12x^8y}{5y^5} \div \frac{3y^2}{x^2}$ $\quad \frac{4x^{10}}{5y^6}$
25. $\frac{6x^2+x-1}{4x^3+4x^2} \div \frac{6x^2-2x}{x^2-4x-5}$ $\quad \frac{(2x+1)(x-5)}{8x^3}$
26. $\frac{x^2-4x-32}{2x^2-13x-24} \div \frac{x}{4x^2-9}$ $\quad \frac{(x+4)(2x-3)}{x}$

8.5 **Add or subtract the expressions. Simplify the result.**

27. $\frac{x^2}{x+1} - \frac{1}{x+1}$ $\quad x-1$
28. $\frac{x+5}{x+6} + \frac{1}{x-2}$ $\quad \frac{x^2+4x-4}{(x+6)(x-2)}$
29. $\frac{5}{x+2} + \frac{35}{x^2-3x-10}$ $\quad \frac{5}{(x-5)}$

8.5 **Simplify the complex fraction.**

30. $\frac{\frac{x}{2x+1}}{5+\frac{3}{x}}$ $\quad \frac{x^2}{(5x+3)(2x+1)}$
31. $\frac{\frac{x}{3}+2}{\frac{1}{x}+3}$ $\quad \frac{x(x+6)}{3(1+3x)}$
32. $\frac{\frac{3}{x^2-4}}{\frac{2}{x+2} - \frac{x+1}{x^2-x-6}}$ $\quad \frac{3(x-3)}{(x-2)(x-7)}$

8.6 **Solve the equation. Check for extraneous solutions.**

33. $\frac{7}{3x-7} = \frac{14}{x+1}$ $\quad 3$
34. $\frac{1}{3} + \frac{2}{x} = -\frac{3}{x^2}$ $\quad -3$
35. $2 - \frac{4}{x+2} = \frac{2}{x}$ $\quad -1, 2$
36. $\frac{4}{x-2} + \frac{6x^2}{x^2-4} = \frac{3x}{x+2}$ $\quad -\frac{4}{3}$

EXTRA PRACTICE

10.
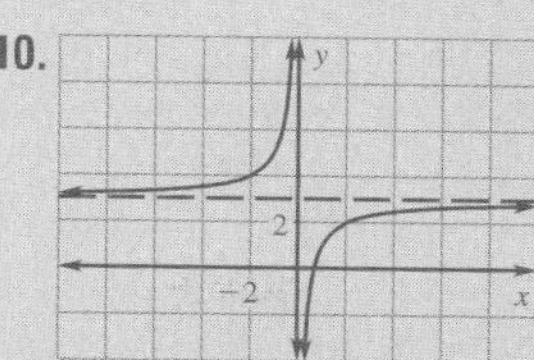

domain: all real numbers except 0, range: all real numbers except 3

11.
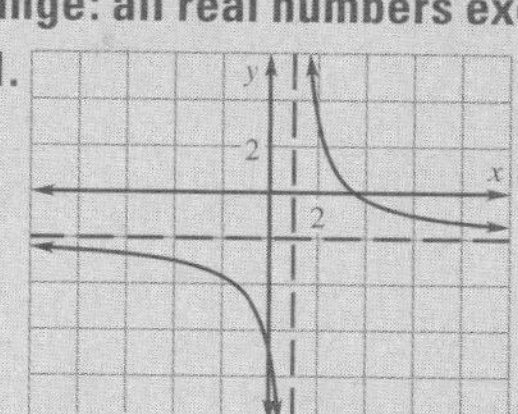

domain: all real numbers except 1, range: all real numbers except −2

12.
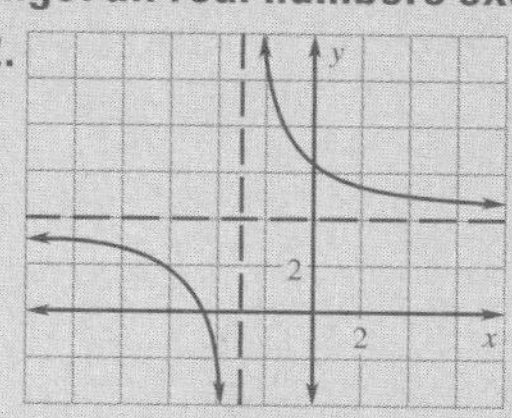

domain: all real numbers except −3, range: all real numbers except 4

13.
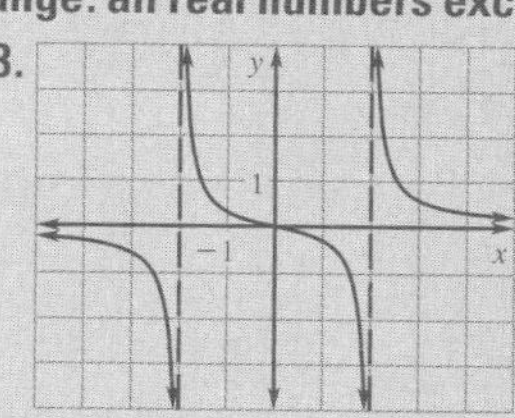

14.
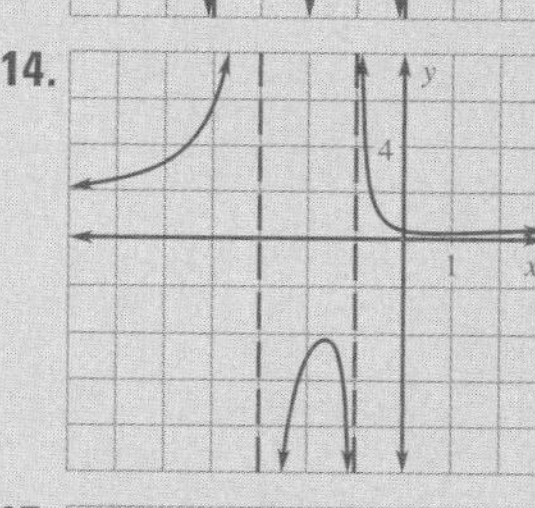

15.
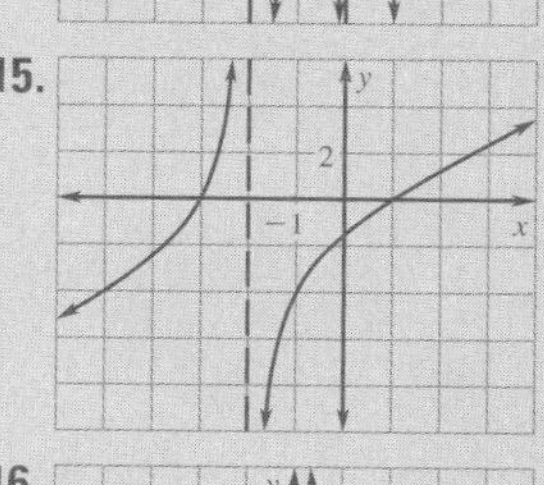

16.
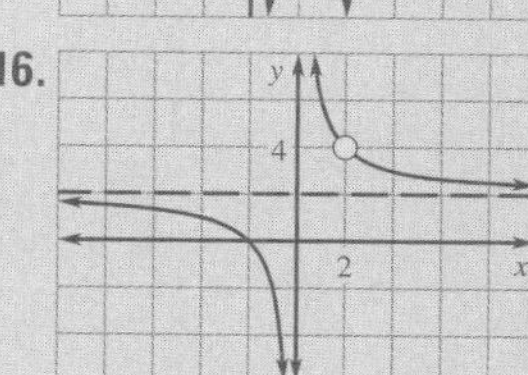

9.
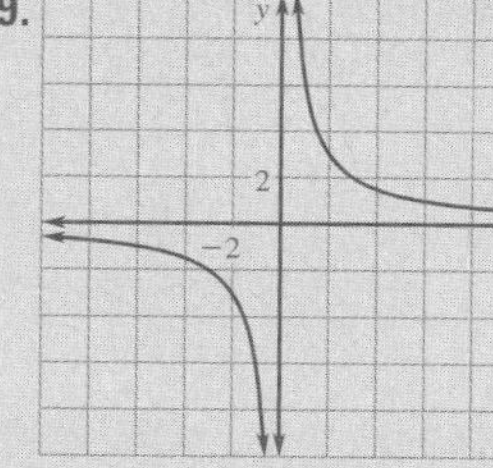

domain: all real numbers except 0, range: all real numbers except 0

5.

6.

7.

8.

9.

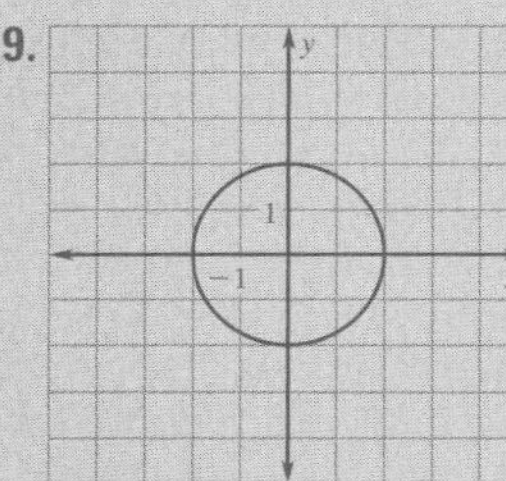

10.

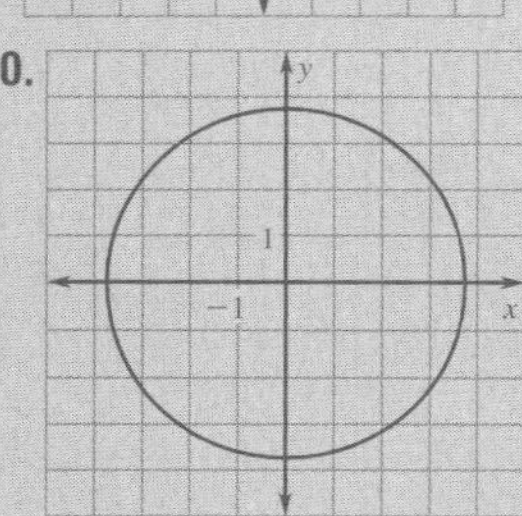

11.

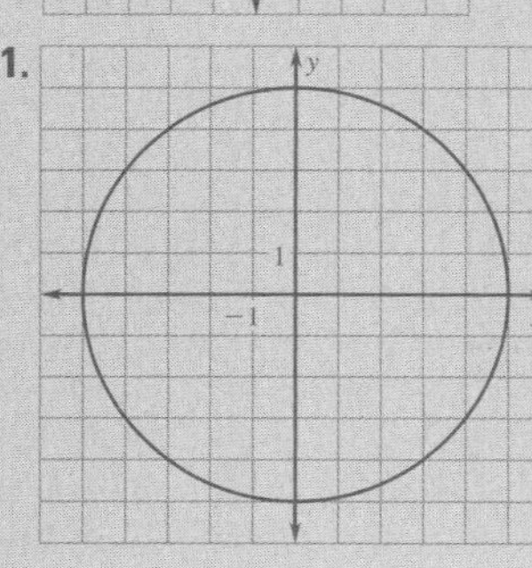

12.

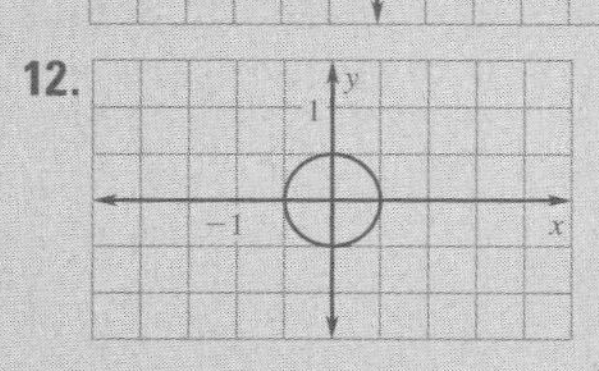

EXTRA PRACTICE

Chapter 9

9.1 Find the distance between the two points. Then find the midpoint of the line segment joining the two points.

1. $(-5, 0), (5, 4)$ $2\sqrt{29}; (0, 2)$
2. $(2, 1), (3, 7)$ $\sqrt{37}; \left(\frac{5}{2}, 4\right)$
3. $(-12, 12), (14, -4)$ $2\sqrt{233}; (1, 4)$
4. $(12, -1), (18, -9)$ $10; (15, -5)$

9.2 Graph the equation. Identify the focus, directrix, and axis of symmetry of the parabola. 5–8. See margin for art.

5. $y^2 = 2x$ $\left(\frac{1}{2}, 0\right), x = -\frac{1}{2}, y = 0$
6. $x^2 = -4y$ $(0, -1), y = 1, x = 0$
7. $14x^2 = -21y$ $\left(0, -\frac{3}{8}\right), y = \frac{3}{8}, x = 0$
8. $12y^2 + 3x = 0$ $\left(-\frac{1}{16}, 0\right), x = \frac{1}{16}, y = 0$

9.3 Graph the equation. Identify the radius of the circle. 9–12. See margin for art.

9. $x^2 + y^2 = 4$ 2
10. $x^2 + y^2 = 14$ $\sqrt{14}$
11. $3x^2 + 3y^2 = 75$ 5
12. $16x^2 + 16y^2 = 4$ $\frac{1}{2}$

9.3 Write the standard form of the equation of the circle that passes through the given point and whose center is at the origin.

13. $(8, 0)$ $x^2 + y^2 = 64$
14. $(0, -9)$ $x^2 + y^2 = 81$
15. $(7, -1)$ $x^2 + y^2 = 50$
16. $(-5, -11)$ $x^2 + y^2 = 146$

9.4 Graph the equation. Identify the vertices, co-vertices, and foci of the ellipse. 17–20. See margin for art.

17. $\frac{x^2}{81} + \frac{y^2}{16} = 1$ $(\pm 9, 0), (0, \pm 4), (\pm\sqrt{65}, 0)$
18. $x^2 + \frac{y^2}{9} = 1$ $(0, \pm 3), (\pm 1, 0), (0, \pm 2\sqrt{2})$
19. $9x^2 + 4y^2 = 576$ $(0, \pm 12), (\pm 8, 0), (0, \pm 4\sqrt{5})$
20. $49x^2 + 64y^2 = 12{,}544$ $(\pm 16, 0), (0, \pm 14), (\pm 2\sqrt{15}, 0)$

9.4 Write an equation of the ellipse with the given characteristics and center at (0, 0).

21. Vertex: $(4, 0)$ Co-vertex: $(0, 2)$ $\frac{x^2}{16} + \frac{y^2}{4} = 1$
22. Vertex: $(0, -5)$ Co-vertex: $(4, 0)$ $\frac{x^2}{16} + \frac{y^2}{25} = 1$
23. Vertex: $(9, 0)$ Focus: $(-3, 0)$ $\frac{x^2}{81} + \frac{y^2}{72} = 1$
24. Co-vertex: $(0, 10)$ Focus: $(8, 0)$ $\frac{x^2}{164} + \frac{y^2}{100} = 1$

9.5 Graph the equation. Identify the vertices, foci, and asymptotes of the hyperbola. 25–27. See margin for art.

25. $\frac{x^2}{36} - \frac{y^2}{16} = 1$ $(\pm 6, 0), (\pm 2\sqrt{13}, 0), y = \pm\frac{2}{3}x$
26. $x^2 - y^2 = 4$ $(\pm 2, 0), (\pm 2\sqrt{2}, 0), y = \pm x$
27. $49y^2 - 81x^2 = 3969$ $(0, \pm 9), (0, \pm\sqrt{130}), y = \pm\frac{9}{7}x$

9.5 Write an equation of the hyperbola with the given foci and vertices.

28. Foci: $(0, -8), (0, 8)$ Vertices: $(0, -6), (0, 6)$ $\frac{y^2}{36} - \frac{x^2}{28} = 1$
29. Foci: $(-2, 0), (2, 0)$ Vertices: $(-1, 0), (1, 0)$ $\frac{x^2}{1} - \frac{y^2}{3} = 1$
30. Foci: $(0, -5), (0, 5)$ Vertices: $(0, -3\sqrt{2}), (0, 3\sqrt{2})$ $\frac{y^2}{18} - \frac{x^2}{7} = 1$

9.6 Graph the equation. Identify the important characteristics of the graph. 31–33. See margin.

31. $\frac{(x-3)^2}{25} + \frac{y^2}{9} = 1$
32. $(x + 2)^2 + (y - 1)^2 = 4$
33. $(y - 4)^2 - \frac{(x+1)^2}{16} = 1$

9.6 Classify the conic section and write its equation in standard form. Then graph the equation. 34–37. See margin for art.

34. $x^2 + y^2 + 2x + 2y - 7 = 0$ circle, $(x + 1)^2 + (y + 1)^2 = 9$
35. $9x^2 + 4y^2 - 72x + 16y + 16 = 0$ ellipse, $\frac{(x-4)^2}{16} + \frac{(y+2)^2}{36} = 1$
36. $9x^2 - 4y^2 + 16y - 52 = 0$ hyperbola, $\frac{x^2}{4} - \frac{(y-2)^2}{9} = 1$
37. $x^2 - 6x - 4y + 17 = 0$ parabola, $(x - 3)^2 = 4(y - 2)$

9.7 Solve the system.

38. $x^2 + y^2 = 4$; $9x^2 - 4y^2 = 36$ $(-2, 0)\ (2, 0)$
39. $y = x - 2$; $x^2 + y^2 - 6x - 4y - 12 = 0$ $(0, -2)\ (7, 5)$
40. $y^2 = x - 5$; $9x^2 - 25y^2 = 225$ $(5, 0)$

17.

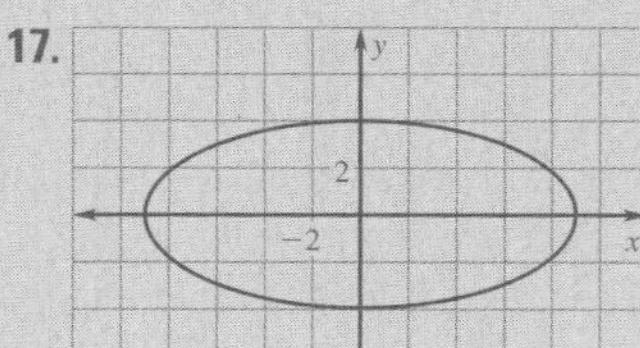

18.

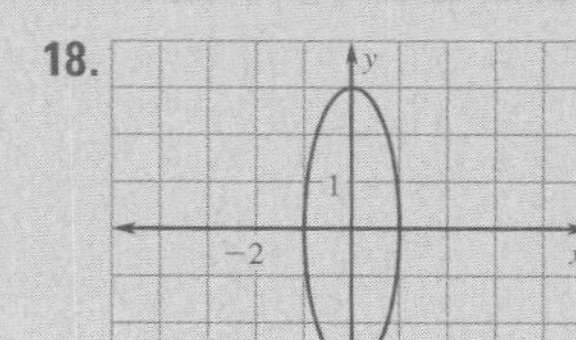

19.

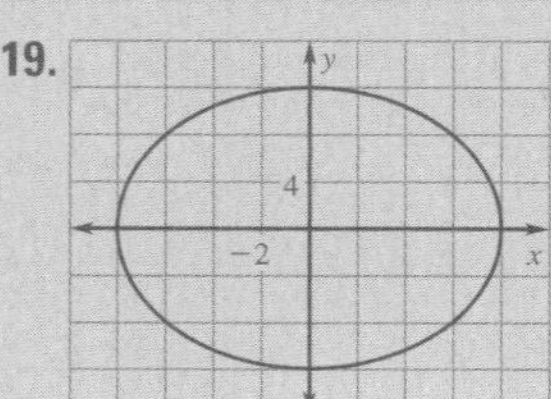

Chapter 10

10.1 For the given password configuration, determine how many passwords are possible if (a) digits and letters can be repeated, and (b) digits and letters cannot be repeated.

1. 8 digits a. 100,000,000 passwords b. 1,814,400 passwords
2. 8 letters a. 208,827,064,576 passwords b. 62,990,928,000 passwords
3. 5 letters followed by 1 digit a. 118,813,760 passwords, b. 78,936,000 passwords
4. 2 digits followed by 2 letters a. 67,600 passwords b. 58,500 passwords

10.1 Find the number of permutations.

5. ${}_5P_2$ 20
6. ${}_6P_1$ 6
7. ${}_9P_9$ 362,880
8. ${}_{12}P_4$ 11,880

10.1 Find the number of distinguishable permutations of the letters in the word.

9. VANILLA 1260
10. CHOCOLATE 90,720
11. STRAWBERRY 604,800
12. COFFEE 180

10.2 Find the number of combinations.

13. ${}_7C_3$ 35
14. ${}_4C_1$ 4
15. ${}_{10}C_9$ 10
16. ${}_{15}C_6$ 5005

10.2 Use the binomial theorem to write the binomial expansion.

17. $(x - 3)^3$ $x^3 - 9x^2 + 27x - 27$
18. $(2x + 3y)^4$
19. $(p^2 + 4)^5$
20. $(x^3 + y^2)^6$

18–20. See margin.

10.3 You have an equally likely chance of choosing any integer from 1 through 25. Find the probability of the given event.

21. An odd number is chosen. $\frac{13}{25}$
22. A multiple of 3 is chosen. $\frac{8}{25}$

10.3 Find the probability that a dart thrown at the given target will hit the shaded region. Assume the dart is equally likely to hit any point inside the target.

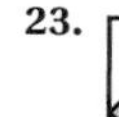

23. $\frac{1}{2}$

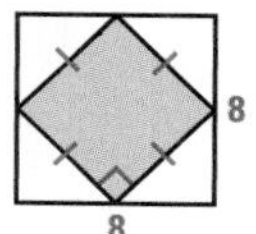

24. $1 - \frac{2}{\pi}$

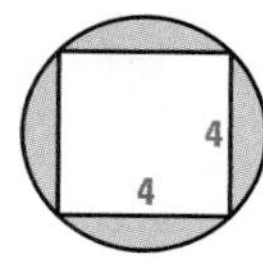

25. $1 - \frac{\pi}{4}$

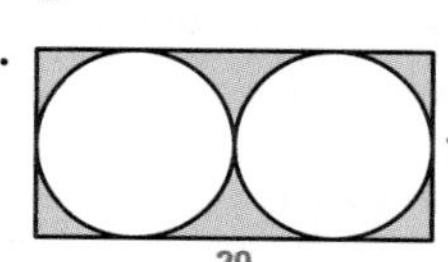

10.4 Events *A* and *B* are disjoint. Find *P*(*A* or *B*).

26. $P(A) = 0.4$, $P(B) = 0.15$ 0.55
27. $P(A) = 0.3$, $P(B) = 0.5$ 0.8
28. $P(A) = 0.7$, $P(B) = 0.21$ 0.91

10.4 Find the indicated probability. State whether *A* and *B* are disjoint events.

29. $P(A) = 0.25$
$P(B) = 0.55$
$P(A \text{ or } B) = $?
$P(A \text{ and } B) = 0.2$
0.6; not disjoint

30. $P(A) = 0.52$
$P(B) = 0.15$
$P(A \text{ or } B) = 0.67$
$P(A \text{ and } B) = $?
0; disjoint

31. $P(A) = 0.54$
$P(B) = 0.28$
$P(A \text{ or } B) = 0.65$
$P(A \text{ and } B) = $?
0.17; not disjoint

32. $P(A) = 0.5$
$P(B) = 0.4$
$P(A \text{ or } B) = $?
$P(A \text{ and } B) = 0.3$
0.6; not disjoint

10.5 Find the probability of drawing the given cards from a standard deck of 52 cards (a) with replacement and (b) without replacement.

33. A jack, then a 3 a. $\frac{1}{169}$, b. $\frac{4}{663}$
34. A club, then another club a. $\frac{1}{16}$, b. $\frac{1}{17}$
35. A black ace, then a red card a. $\frac{1}{52}$, b. $\frac{1}{51}$

10.6 Calculate the probability of tossing a coin 15 times and getting the given number of heads.

36. 1 about 0.000458
37. 4 about 0.0417
38. 7 about 0.196
39. 15 about 0.0000305

EXTRA PRACTICE

18. $16x^4 + 96x^3y + 216x^2y^2 + 216xy^3 + 81y^4$
19. $p^{10} + 20p^8 + 160p^6 + 640p^4 + 1280p^2 + 1024$
20. $x^{18} + 6x^{15}y^2 + 15x^{12}y^4 + 20x^9y^6 + 15x^6y^8 + 6x^3y^{10} + y^{12}$

p. 1018

20.

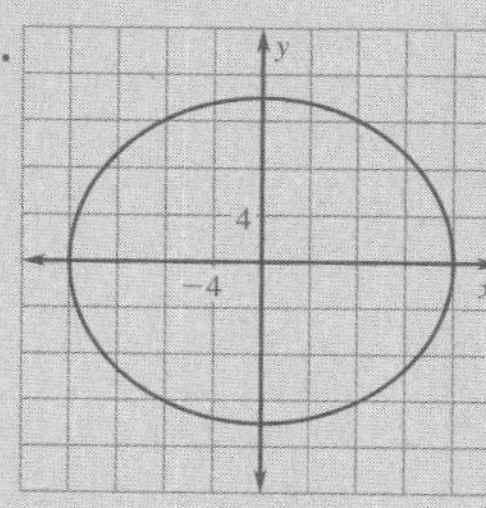

25–27, 31–37. See Additional Answers beginning on p. AA1.

24.

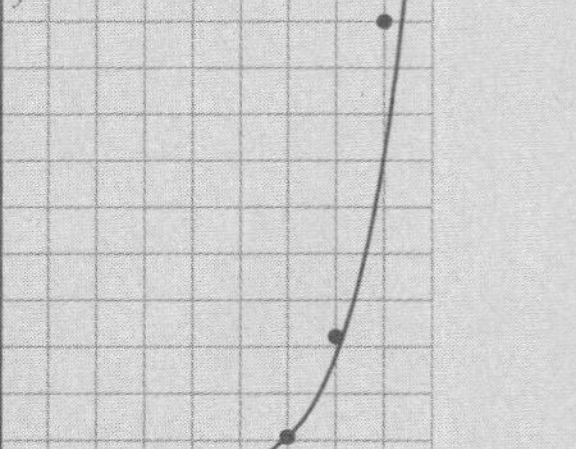

25.

EXTRA PRACTICE

Chapter 11

11.1 Find the mean, median, mode, range, and standard deviation of the data set.

1. 5, 5, 6, 9, 11, 12, 14, 16, 16, 16
11, 11.5, 16, 11, 4.313

2. 16, 18, 29, 30, 34, 35, 35, 38, 46
about 31.2, 34, 35, 30, 8.90

3. −4, −3, −3, 4, 1, 0, 0, −3, −2, 10, 11
1, 0, −3, 15, 4.991

4. 1.7, 2.2, 1.8, 3.0, 0.4, 1.2, 2.8, 2.9
2, 2, no mode, 2.6, 0.853

5. 4.5, 5.7, 4.3, 6.9, −2.1, 5.7, −1.2, 3.8
3.45, 4.4, 5.7, 9, 3.09

6. −7.2, 3.9, 2.6, −9.1, 2.5, −7.2, 3.9, −7.2
−2.225, −2.35, −7.2, 13, 5.502

11.2 Find the mean, median, mode, range, and standard deviation of the given data set and of the data set obtained by adding the given constant to each data value.

7. 33, 36, 36, 39, 49, 56; constant: 2
41.5, 37.5, 36, 23, 8.221; 43.5, 39.5, 38, 23, 8.221

8. 10, 12, 14, 16, 16, 18, 19; constant: −1
15, 16, 16, 9, 2.976; 14, 15, 15, 9, 2.976

11.2 Find the mean, median, mode, range, and standard deviation of the given data set and of the data set obtained by multiplying each data value by the given constant.

9. −2, −2, 5, 4, 2, −2, 8, 3; constant: 1.5
2, 2.5, −2, 10, 3.5; 3, 3.75, −3, 15, 5.25

10. 52, 52, 76, 56, 67, 89, 70; constant: 3
66, 67, 52, 37, 12.75; 198, 201, 156, 111, 38.25

11.3 A normal distribution has a mean of 2.7 and a standard deviation of 0.3. Find the probability that a randomly selected x-value from the distribution is in the given interval.

11. Between 2.4 and 2.7 0.34

12. At least 3.0 0.16

13. At most 2.1 0.025

11.4 Identify the type of sample described. Then tell if the sample is biased. *Explain* your reasoning.

14. The owner of a movie rental store wants to know how often her customers rent movies. She asks every tenth customer how many movies the customer rents each month. Systematic; not biased; the owner took a random selection of customers.

15. A school wants to consult parents about updating its attendance policy. Each student is sent home with a survey for a parent to complete. The school uses only surveys that are returned within one week. Self-selected; biased; only those parents who received the survey and feel strongly about the attendance policy are likely to respond.

11.4 Find the margin of error for a survey that has the given sample size. Round your answer to the nearest tenth of a percent.

16. 100 ± 10%

17. 600 ± 4.1%

18. 2900 ± 1.9%

19. 5000 ± 1.4%

11.4 Find the sample size required to achieve the given margin of error. Round your answer to the nearest whole number.

20. ±1% 10,000

21. ±2% 2500

22. ±5.5% 331

23. ±6.2% 260

11.5 Use a graphing calculator to find a model for the data. Then graph the model and the data in the same coordinate plane. 24–25. See margin for art.

24.

x	0	2	4	6	8	10	12	14
y	−10	−3	4	10	14	20	21	36

$y = 2.94x - 9.08$

25.

x	1	2	3	4	5	6	7	8
y	0.5	0.8	1.1	3	9	30	90	280

$y = 0.108(2.56)^x$

Chapter 12

12.1 For the sequence, describe the pattern, write the next term, and write a rule for the nth term. 1–3. See margin.

1. 9, 16, 25, 36, . . . 2. $\frac{1}{3}, \frac{2}{3}, 1, \frac{4}{3}, \ldots$ 3. 12.5, 7, 1.5, −4, . . .

12.1 Write the series using summation notation.

4. 16 + 32 + 48 + 64 + · · · + 144 $\sum_{n=1}^{9} 16n$ 5. $\frac{1}{6} + \frac{2}{7} + \frac{3}{8} + \frac{4}{9} + \frac{1}{2} + \cdots$ $\sum_{n=1}^{\infty} \frac{n}{5+n}$

12.1 Find the sum of the series.

6. $\sum_{i=1}^{5} (3i + 2)$ 55 7. $\sum_{i=0}^{5} 4i^2$ 220 8. $\sum_{n=4}^{6} \frac{n}{n+3}$ $\frac{313}{168}$ 9. $\sum_{k=6}^{8} k^3$ 1071

12.2 Write a rule for the nth term of the arithmetic sequence. Then graph the first six terms of the sequence. 10–12. See margin for art.

10. $a_5 = 15, d = 6$ $a_n = 6n - 15$ 11. $a_{10} = -78, d = -10$ $a_n = -10n + 22$ 12. $a_6 = -\frac{11}{5}, d = -\frac{2}{5}$ $a_n = -\frac{2}{5}n + \frac{1}{5}$

12.2 Write a rule for the nth term of the arithmetic sequence. Then find a_{15}.

13. 11, 20, 29, 38, . . . $a_n = 9n + 2$; 137 14. −8, −15, −22, −29, . . . $a_n = -7n - 1$; −106 15. $3, \frac{7}{3}, \frac{5}{3}, 1, \ldots$ $a_n = -\frac{2}{3}n + \frac{11}{3}$; $-\frac{19}{3}$

12.2 Write a rule for the nth term of the arithmetic sequence that has the two given terms.

16. $a_2 = 9, a_7 = 37$ $a_n = 5.6n - 2.2$ 17. $a_8 = 10.5, a_{16} = 18.5$ $a_n = 2.5 + n$ 18. $a_3 = -\frac{14}{5}, a_{10} = -\frac{42}{5}$ $a_n = -\frac{4}{5}n - \frac{2}{5}$

12.3 Write a rule for the nth term of the geometric sequence. Then find a_{10}.

19. $\frac{1}{27}, \frac{1}{9}, \frac{1}{3}, 1, \ldots$ $a_n = \frac{1}{27} \cdot 3^{n-1}$; 729 20. 5, 4, 3.2, 2.56, . . . $a_n = 5 \cdot \left(\frac{4}{5}\right)^{n-1}$; about 0.671 21. $4, \frac{16}{3}, \frac{64}{9}, \frac{256}{27}, \ldots$ $a_n = 4 \cdot \left(\frac{4}{3}\right)^{n-1}$; $\frac{1,048,576}{19,683}$

12.3 Find the sum of the geometric series.

22. $\sum_{i=1}^{4} 3(4)^{i-1}$ 255 23. $\sum_{i=1}^{7} 0.5(-3)^{i-1}$ 273.5 24. $\sum_{i=1}^{5} 10\left(\frac{3}{5}\right)^{i-1}$ 23.056 25. $\sum_{i=1}^{7} 2(1.2)^{i-1}$ about 25.8

12.4 Find the sum of the infinite geometric series, if it exists.

26. 8 + 4 + 2 + 1 + · · · 16 27. 2 − 4 + 8 − 16 + · · · no sum 28. −6.75 + 4.5 − 3 + 2 − · · · −4.05

12.4 Write the repeating decimal as a fraction in lowest terms.

29. 0.333. . . $\frac{1}{3}$ 30. 0.898989. . . $\frac{89}{99}$ 31. 0.212121. . . $\frac{7}{33}$ 32. 1.50150150. . . $\frac{500}{333}$

12.5 Write a recursive rule for the sequence. The sequence may be arithmetic, geometric, or neither.

33. 2.5, 5, 10, 20, . . . $a_1 = 2.5, a_n = 2a_{n-1}$ 34. 2, −2, −6, −10, . . . $a_1 = 2, a_n = a_{n-1} - 4$ 35. 1, 2, 2, 4, 8, 32, . . . $a_1 = 1$ and $a_2 = 2$, $a_n = (a_{n-2})(a_{n-1})$

12.5 Find the first three iterates of the function for the given initial value.

36. $f(x) = 2x - 5, x_0 = 3$ 1, −3, −11 37. $f(x) = \frac{4}{5}x - 2, x_0 = -10$ −10, −10, −10 38. $f(x) = 3x^2 + x, x_0 = -1$ 2, 14, 602

EXTRA PRACTICE

1. perfect squares beginning with $3^2 = 9$; 49; $a_n = (n + 2)^2$

2. multiples of $\frac{1}{3}$; $\frac{5}{3}$; $a_n = \frac{n}{3}$

3. each term is decreased by 5.5; −9.5; $a_n = 18 - 5.5n$

10.

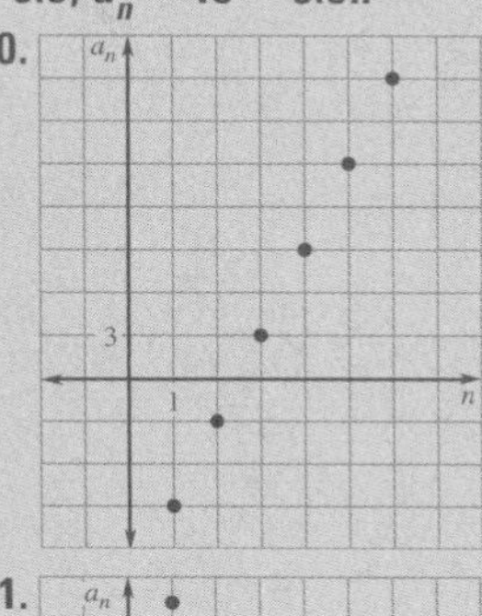

11.

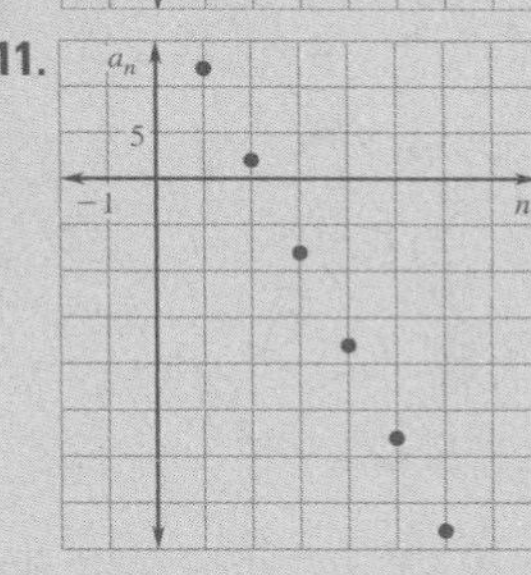

12.

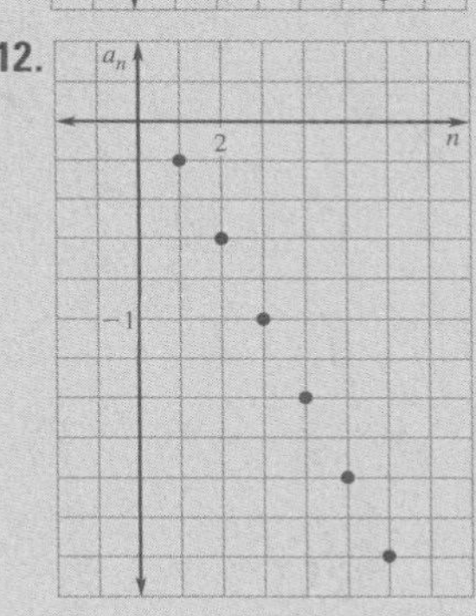

1. $\cos\theta = \frac{4}{5}$, $\tan\theta = \frac{3}{4}$, $\csc\theta = \frac{5}{3}$, $\sec\theta = \frac{5}{4}$, $\cot\theta = \frac{4}{3}$

2. $\sin\theta = \frac{8}{17}$, $\cos\theta = \frac{15}{17}$, $\csc\theta = \frac{17}{8}$, $\sec\theta = \frac{17}{15}$, $\cot\theta = \frac{15}{8}$

3. $\sin\theta = \frac{\sqrt{3}}{2}$, $\cos\theta = \frac{1}{2}$, $\tan\theta = \sqrt{3}$, $\csc\theta = \frac{2\sqrt{3}}{3}$, $\cot\theta = \frac{\sqrt{3}}{3}$

4. $\sin\theta = \frac{3}{4}$, $\tan\theta = \frac{3\sqrt{7}}{7}$, $\csc\theta = \frac{4}{3}$, $\sec\theta = \frac{4\sqrt{7}}{7}$, $\cot\theta = \frac{\sqrt{7}}{3}$

18.

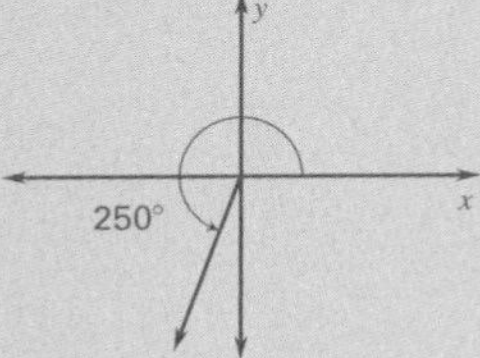

19.

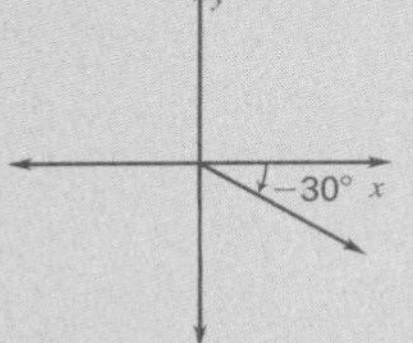

20.

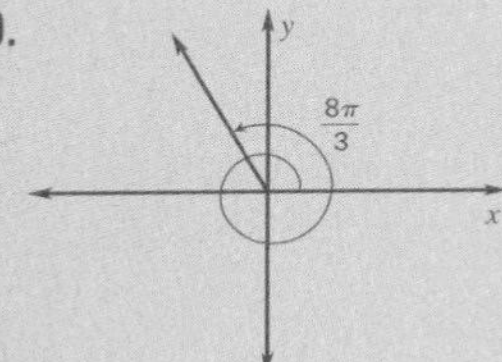

21.

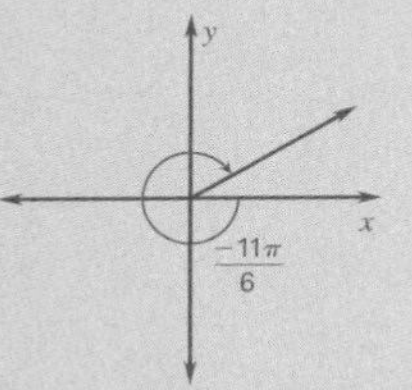

33. $B \approx 40.7°$, $C \approx 105.3°$, $c \approx 10.35$ or $B \approx 139.3°$, $C \approx 6.7°$, $c \approx 1.25°$

EXTRA PRACTICE

Chapter 13

13.1 Let θ be an acute angle of a right triangle. Find the values of the other five trigonometric functions of θ. 1–4. See margin.

1. $\sin\theta = \frac{3}{5}$
2. $\tan\theta = \frac{8}{15}$
3. $\sec\theta = 2$
4. $\cos\theta = \frac{\sqrt{7}}{4}$

13.1 Solve $\triangle ABC$ using the diagram and the given measurements.

5. $A = 21°, c = 8$ — $B = 69°, a \approx 2.867, b \approx 7.469$
6. $B = 66°, a = 14$ — $A = 24°, b \approx 31.445, c \approx 34.420$
7. $B = 60°, c = 20$ — $A = 30°, a = 10, b = 10\sqrt{3}$
8. $A = 29°, b = 6$ — $B = 61°, a \approx 3.326, c \approx 6.860$
9. $A = 18°, c = 18$ — $B = 72°, a \approx 5.562, b \approx 17.119$
10. $B = 56°, c = 7$ — $A = 34°, a \approx 3.914, b \approx 5.803$

13.2 Convert the degree measure to radians or the radian measure to degrees.

11. $100°$ $\frac{5\pi}{9}$
12. $-6°$ $-\frac{\pi}{30}$
13. $\frac{3\pi}{4}$ $135°$
14. $-\frac{\pi}{6}$ $-30°$

13.2 Find the arc length and area of a sector with the given radius r and central angle θ.

15. $r = 5$ ft, $\theta = 90°$ $\frac{5\pi}{2}$ ft, $\frac{25\pi}{4}$ ft^2
16. $r = 2$ in., $\theta = 300°$ $\frac{10\pi}{3}$ in., $\frac{10\pi}{3}$ in.^{2}
17. $r = 12$ cm, $\theta = \pi$ 12π cm, 72π cm^2

13.3 Sketch the angle. Then find its reference angle. 18–21. See margin for art.

18. $250°$ $70°$
19. $-30°$ $30°$
20. $\frac{8\pi}{3}$ $\frac{\pi}{3}$
21. $-\frac{11\pi}{6}$ $\frac{\pi}{6}$

13.3 Evaluate the function without using a calculator.

22. $\sin(-60°)$ $-\frac{\sqrt{3}}{2}$
23. $\csc 240°$ $-\frac{2\sqrt{3}}{3}$
24. $\tan\frac{7\pi}{4}$ -1
25. $\cos\left(-\frac{5\pi}{4}\right)$ $-\frac{\sqrt{2}}{2}$

13.4 Evaluate the expression without using a calculator. Give your answer in both radians and degrees.

26. $\sin^{-1} 0$ $0, 0°$
27. $\cos^{-1}\left(-\frac{\sqrt{3}}{2}\right)$ $\frac{5\pi}{6}, 150°$
28. $\cos^{-1} 3$ undefined
29. $\tan^{-1} 1$ $\frac{\pi}{4}, 45°$

13.4 Solve the equation for θ.

30. $\sin\theta = 0.25$; $90° < \theta < 180°$ about $165.52°$
31. $\cos\theta = 0.9$; $270° < \theta < 360°$ about $334.16°$
32. $\tan\theta = 2$; $180° < \theta < 270°$ about $243.43°$

13.5 Solve $\triangle ABC$. (*Hint:* Some of the "triangles" may have no solution and some may have two solutions.)

33. $A = 34°, a = 6, b = 7$ See margin.
34. $A = 50°, C = 65°, b = 60$ — $B = 65°, a \approx 50.71, c = 60$
35. $B = 86°, b = 13, c = 11$ — $A \approx 36.4°, C \approx 57.6°, a \approx 7.73$

13.5 Find the area of $\triangle ABC$ with the given side lengths and included angle.

36. $A = 35°, b = 50, c = 120$ about 1720
37. $B = 35°, a = 7, c = 12$ about 24.1
38. $C = 20°, a = 10, b = 16$ about 27.4

13.6 Solve $\triangle ABC$.

39. $a = 16, b = 23, c = 17$ — $A \approx 44.1°, B \approx 88.3°, C \approx 47.6°$
40. $C = 50°, a = 12, b = 14$ — $A \approx 55.7°, B \approx 74.3°, c \approx 11.14$
41. $A = 80°, b = 7, c = 5$ — $B \approx 61.3°, C \approx 38.7°, a \approx 7.86$

13.6 Find the area of $\triangle ABC$ with the given side lengths.

42. $a = 6, b = 3, c = 4$ about 5.33
43. $a = 14, b = 30, c = 27$ about 189
44. $a = 16, b = 16, c = 20$ about 125

p. 1023

1.

Chapter 14

14.1 Graph the function. 1–4. See margin.

1. $y = \cos \frac{1}{4}x$ 2. $y = 3 \sin x$ 3. $y = \sin 2\pi x$ 4. $y = 2 \tan 2x$

14.2 Graph the sine or cosine function. 5–7. See margin.

5. $y = \sin 2\left(x - \frac{\pi}{4}\right) + 1$ 6. $y = -\sin\left(x + \frac{\pi}{4}\right)$ 7. $y = 2 \cos x + 3$

14.2 Graph the tangent function. 8–10. See margin.

8. $y = 2 \tan x + 2$ 9. $y = -\frac{1}{4} \tan 2x$ 10. $y = \tan\left(x - \frac{\pi}{2}\right) - 1$

14.3 Simplify the expression.

11. $\cos^2\left(\frac{\pi}{2} - x\right) + \cos^2(-x)$ **1** 12. $\frac{(\sec x - 1)(\sec x + 1)}{\tan x}$ **$\tan x$** 13. $\tan\left(\frac{\pi}{2} - x\right) \cot x - \csc^2 x$ **-1**

14.3 Verify the identity. 14–16. See margin.

14. $\frac{\cos(-x)}{1 + \sin(-x)} = \sec x + \tan x$ 15. $\frac{\cos^2 x + \sin^2 x}{\tan^2 x + 1} = \cos^2 x$ 16. $2 - \sec^2 x = 1 - \tan^2 x$

14.4 Find the general solution of the equation.

17. $12 \tan^2 x - 4 = 0$ **$\frac{\pi}{6} + n\pi, \frac{5\pi}{6} + n\pi$** 18. $3 \sin x = -2 \sin x + 3$ **$0.6435 + 2n\pi, 2.498 + 2n\pi$** 19. $\tan^2 x - 2 \tan x = -1$ **$\frac{\pi}{4} + n\pi$**

14.4 Solve the equation in the given interval. Check your solutions.

20. $\cos^2 x \sin x = 5 \sin x;\ 0 \le x < 2\pi$ **$0, \pi$** 21. $2 - 2\cos^2 x = 3 + 5 \sin x;\ 0 \le x < 2\pi$ **$\frac{7\pi}{6}, \frac{11\pi}{6}$**

22. $8 \cos x = 4 \sec x;\ 0 \le x < \pi$ **$\frac{\pi}{4}, \frac{3\pi}{4}$** 23. $\cos^2 x - 4 \cos x + 1 = 0;\ 0 \le x < \pi$ **about 1.2995**

14.5 Write a function for the sinusoid.

24. 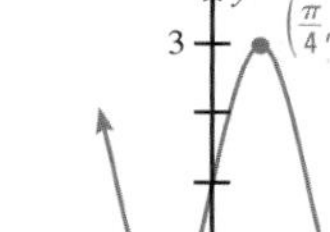  **$y = 1 + 2 \sin 2x$**

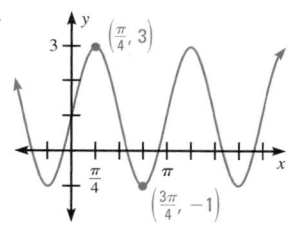

25. 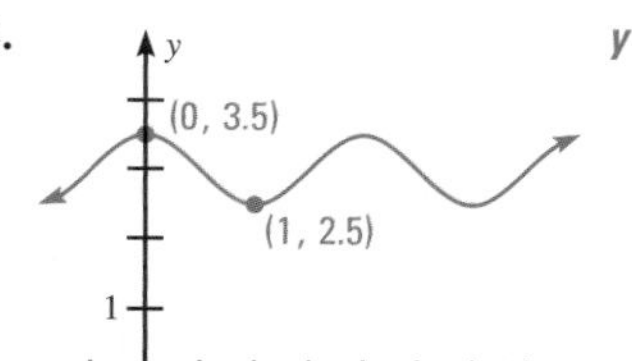 **$y = 3 + \frac{1}{2} \cos \pi x$**

14.6 Find the exact value of the expression.

26. $\sin(-15°)$ **$\frac{\sqrt{2} - \sqrt{6}}{4}$** 27. $\cos 165°$ **$\frac{-\sqrt{2} - \sqrt{6}}{4}$** 28. $\tan \frac{11\pi}{12}$ **$-2 + \sqrt{3}$** 29. $\cos \frac{\pi}{12}$ **$\frac{\sqrt{2} + \sqrt{6}}{4}$**

14.7 Find the exact values of sin 2*a*, cos 2*a*, and tan 2*a*.

30. $\tan a = \frac{2}{3}, \pi < a < \frac{3\pi}{2}$ **$\frac{12}{13}, \frac{5}{13}, \frac{12}{5}$** 31. $\cos a = \frac{9}{10}, 0 < a < \frac{\pi}{2}$ **$\frac{9\sqrt{19}}{50}, \frac{31}{50}, \frac{9\sqrt{19}}{31}$** 32. $\sin a = -\frac{3}{5}, \frac{3\pi}{2} < a < 2\pi$ **$-\frac{24}{25}, \frac{7}{25}, -\frac{24}{7}$**

14.7 Find the general solution of the equation.

33. $\cos 2x - \cos x = 0$ **$\frac{2\pi}{3} + 2n\pi, \frac{4\pi}{3} + 2n\pi, 0 + 2n\pi$** 34. $\cos \frac{x}{2} = \sin x$ **$\frac{\pi}{3} + 2n\pi, \pi + 2n\pi, \frac{5\pi}{3} + 2n\pi$** 35. $\sin 2x = -1$ **$\frac{3\pi}{4} + 2n\pi$**

EXTRA PRACTICE

2. 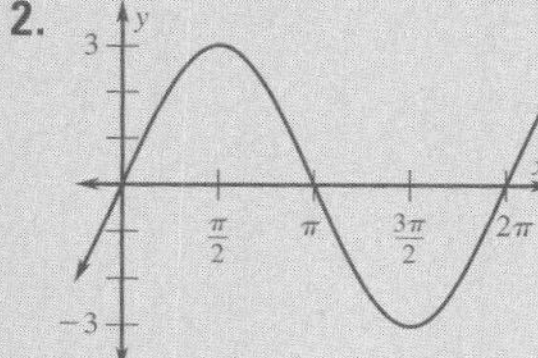

3. 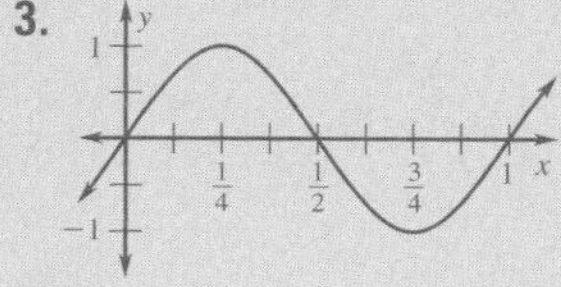

4. 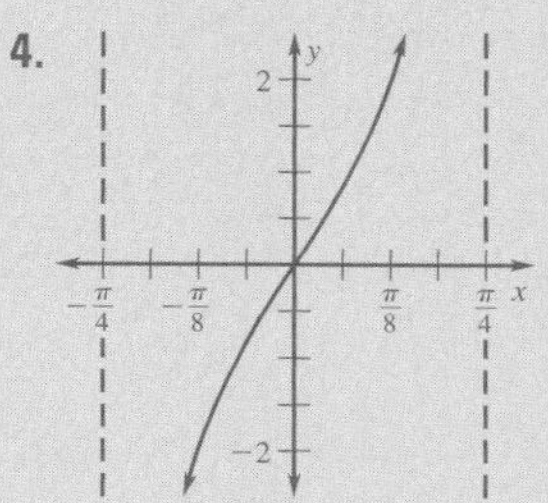

5.

6. 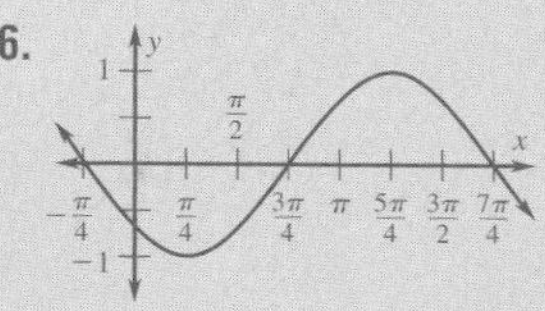

7. 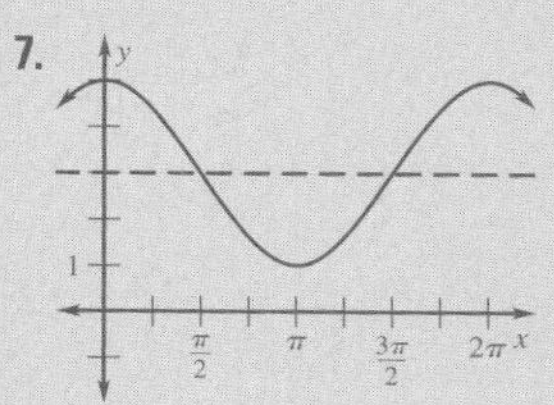

8. 9. 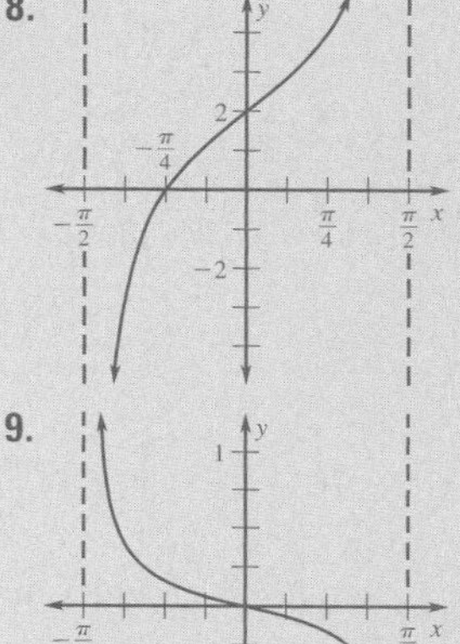

10. 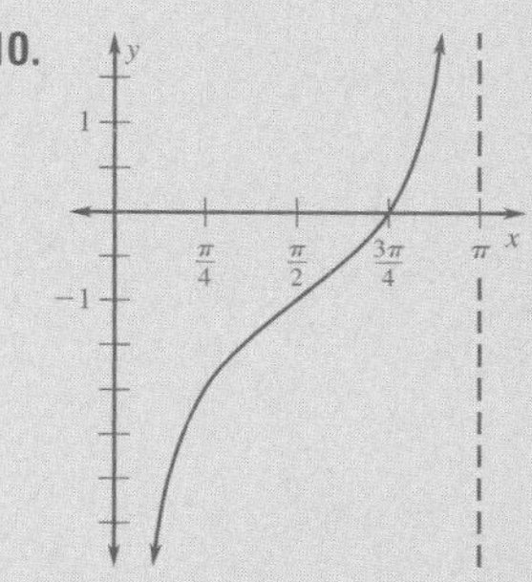

14. $\frac{\cos(-x)}{1 + \sin(-x)} = \frac{\cos x}{1 - \sin x}$
$= \frac{\cos x + \cos x \sin x}{1 - \sin^2 x}$
$= \frac{\cos x + \cos x \sin x}{\cos^2 x}$
$= \frac{1}{\cos x} + \frac{\sin x}{\cos x}$
$= \sec x + \tan x$

15. $\frac{\cos^2 x + \sin^2 x}{\tan^2 x + 1} = \frac{1}{\sec^2 x}$
$= \cos^2 x$

16. $2 - \sec^2 x = 2 - (1 - \tan^2 x)$
$= 1 + \tan^2 x$

Symbols

Symbol	Meaning	Page
$\ldots$	and so on	2
$\approx$	is approximately equal to	2
$\cdot$	multiplication, times	3
$-a$	opposite of a	4
$\frac{1}{a}$	reciprocal of a, $a \neq 0$	4
b_1	b sub 1	26
π	pi; irrational number ≈ 3.14	26
$<$	is less than	41
$>$	is greater than	41
$\leq$	is less than or equal to	41
$\geq$	is greater than or equal to	41
$\lvert x \rvert$	absolute value of x	51
$\neq$	is not equal to	52
(x, y)	ordered pair	72
$f(x)$	f of x, or the value of f at x	75
m	slope	82
$\parallel$	is parallel to	84
$\perp$	is perpendicular to	84
(x, y, z)	ordered triple	178
$\begin{bmatrix} 1 & 0 \\ 0 & 1 \end{bmatrix}$	matrix	187
$\lvert A \rvert$	determinant of matrix A	203
A^{-1}	inverse of matrix A	210
$\sqrt{a}$	the nonnegative square root of a	266
i	imaginary unit equal to $\sqrt{-1}$	275
$\lvert z \rvert$	absolute value of complex number z	279
$x \to +\infty$	x approaches positive infinity	339
$\sqrt[n]{a}$	nth root of a	414
f^{-1}	inverse of function f	438
e	irrational number ≈ 2.718	492
$\log_b y$	log base b of y	499
$\log x$	log base 10 of x	500
$\ln x$	log base e of x	500
$n!$	n factorial; number of permutations of n objects	684
${}_nP_r$	number of permutations of r objects from n distinct objects	685
${}_nC_r$	number of combinations of r objects from n distinct objects	690
$P(A)$	probability of event A	698
$P(\overline{A})$	probability of the complement of event A	709
$\cup$	union of two sets	715
$\cap$	intersection of two sets	715
$\emptyset$	empty set	715
$\subseteq$	is a subset of	716
$P(B \mid A)$	probability of event B given that event A has occurred	718
$\overline{x}$	x-bar; the mean of a data set	744
σ	sigma; the standard deviation of a data set	745
Σ	summation	796
θ	theta	852
sin	sine	852
cos	cosine	852
tan	tangent	852
csc	cosecant	852
sec	secant	852
cot	cotangent	852
$\sin^{-1}$	inverse sine	875
$\cos^{-1}$	inverse cosine	875
$\tan^{-1}$	inverse tangent	875

TABLES

1024

Measures

Time	
60 seconds (sec) = 1 minute (min) 60 minutes = 1 hour (h) 24 hours = 1 day 7 days = 1 week 4 weeks (approx.) = 1 month	365 days, 52 weeks (approx.), 12 months = 1 year 10 years = 1 decade 100 years = 1 century

Metric	United States Customary
Length 10 millimeters (mm) = 1 centimeter (cm) 100 cm, 1000 mm = 1 meter (m) 1000 m = 1 kilometer (km)	**Length** 12 inches (in.) = 1 foot (ft) 36 in., 3 ft = 1 yard (yd) 5280 ft, 1760 yd = 1 mile (mi)
Area 100 square millimeters (mm^2) = 1 square centimeter (cm^2) 10,000 cm^2 = 1 square meter (m^2) 10,000 m^2 = 1 hectare (ha)	**Area** 144 square inches ($in.^2$) = 1 square foot (ft^2) 9 ft^2 = 1 square yard (yd^2) 43,560 ft^2, 4840 yd^2 = 1 acre (A)
Volume 1000 cubic millimeters (mm^3) = 1 cubic centimeter (cm^3) 1,000,000 cm^3 = 1 cubic meter (m^3)	**Volume** 1728 cubic inches ($in.^3$) = 1 cubic foot (ft^3) 27 ft^3 = 1 cubic yard (yd^3)
Liquid Capacity 1000 milliliters (mL), 1000 cubic centimeters (cm^3) = 1 liter (L) 1000 L = 1 kiloliter (kL)	**Liquid Capacity** 8 fluid ounces (fl oz) = 1 cup (c) 2 c = 1 pint (pt) 2 pt = 1 quart (qt) 4 qt = 1 gallon (gal)
Mass 1000 milligrams (mg) = 1 gram (g) 1000 g = 1 kilogram (kg) 1000 kg = 1 metric ton (t)	**Weight** 16 ounces (oz) = 1 pound (lb) 2000 lb = 1 ton
Temperature Degrees Celsius (°C) 0°C = freezing point of water 37°C = normal body temperature 100°C = boiling point of water	**Temperature Degrees Fahrenheit (°F)** 32°F = freezing point of water 98.6°F = normal body temperature 212°F = boiling point of water

TABLES

1025

Formulas

Formulas from Coordinate Geometry

Slope of a line (p. 82)	$m = \frac{y_2 - y_1}{x_2 - x_1}$ where m is the slope of the nonvertical line through points (x_1, y_1) and (x_2, y_2)
Parallel and perpendicular lines (p. 84)	If line l_1 has slope m_1 and line l_2 has slope m_2, then: $l_1 \parallel l_2$ if and only if $m_1 = m_2$; $l_1 \perp l_2$ if and only if $m_1 = -\frac{1}{m_2}$, or $m_1 m_2 = -1$
Distance formula (p. 615)	$d = \sqrt{(x_2 - x_1)^2 + (y_2 - y_1)^2}$ where d is the distance between points (x_1, y_1) and (x_2, y_2)
Midpoint formula (p. 615)	$M\left(\frac{x_1 + x_2}{2}, \frac{y_1 + y_2}{2}\right)$ is the midpoint of the line segment joining points (x_1, y_1) and (x_2, y_2).

TABLES

Formulas from Matrix Algebra

Determinant of a 2 × 2 matrix (p. 203)	$\det\begin{bmatrix} a & b \\ c & d \end{bmatrix} = \begin{vmatrix} a & b \\ c & d \end{vmatrix} = ad - cb$
Determinant of a 3 × 3 matrix (p. 203)	$\det\begin{bmatrix} a & b & c \\ d & e & f \\ g & h & i \end{bmatrix} = \begin{vmatrix} a & b & c \\ d & e & f \\ g & h & i \end{vmatrix} = (aei + bfg + cdh) - (gec + hfa + idb)$
Area of a triangle (p. 204)	The area of a triangle with vertices (x_1, y_1), (x_2, y_2), and (x_3, y_3) is given by $\text{Area} = \pm\frac{1}{2}\begin{vmatrix} x_1 & y_1 & 1 \\ x_2 & y_2 & 1 \\ x_3 & y_3 & 1 \end{vmatrix}$ where the appropriate sign (±) should be chosen to yield a positive value.
Cramer's rule (p. 205)	Let $A = \begin{bmatrix} a & b \\ c & d \end{bmatrix}$ be the coefficient matrix of this linear system: $ax + by = e$, $cx + dy = f$. If $\det A \neq 0$, then the system has exactly one solution. The solution is $x = \frac{\begin{vmatrix} e & b \\ f & d \end{vmatrix}}{\det A}$ and $y = \frac{\begin{vmatrix} a & e \\ c & f \end{vmatrix}}{\det A}$.
Inverse of a 2 × 2 matrix (p. 210)	The inverse of the matrix $A = \begin{bmatrix} a & b \\ c & d \end{bmatrix}$ is $A^{-1} = \frac{1}{\lvert A \rvert}\begin{bmatrix} d & -b \\ -c & a \end{bmatrix} = \frac{1}{ad - cb}\begin{bmatrix} d & -b \\ -c & a \end{bmatrix}$ provided $ad - cb \neq 0$.

Formulas and Theorems from Algebra

Quadratic formula (p. 292)	The solutions of $ax^2 + bx + c = 0$ are $$x = \frac{-b \pm \sqrt{b^2 - 4ac}}{2a}$$ where a, b, and c are real numbers such that $a \neq 0$.
Discriminant of a quadratic equation (p. 294)	The expression $b^2 - 4ac$ is called the discriminant of the associated equation $ax^2 + bx + c = 0$. The value of the discriminant can be positive, zero, or negative, which corresponds to an equation having two real solutions, one real solution, or two imaginary solutions, respectively.
Special product patterns (p. 347)	**Sum and difference:** $(a + b)(a - b) = a^2 - b^2$ **Square of a binomial:** $(a + b)^2 = a^2 + 2ab + b^2$ $(a - b)^2 = a^2 - 2ab + b^2$ **Cube of a binomial:** $(a + b)^3 = a^3 + 3a^2b + 3ab^2 + b^3$ $(a - b)^3 = a^3 - 3a^2b + 3ab^2 - b^3$
Special factoring patterns (p. 354)	**Sum of two cubes:** $a^3 + b^3 = (a + b)(a^2 - ab + b^2)$ **Difference of two cubes:** $a^3 - b^3 = (a - b)(a^2 + ab + b^2)$
Remainder theorem (p. 363)	If a polynomial $f(x)$ is divided by $x - k$, then the remainder is $r = f(k)$.
Factor theorem (p. 364)	A polynomial $f(x)$ has a factor $x - k$ if and only if $f(k) = 0$.
Rational zero theorem (p. 370)	If $f(x) = a_nx^n + \cdots + a_1x + a_0$ has *integer* coefficients, then every rational zero of f has this form: $$\frac{p}{q} = \frac{\text{factor of constant term } a_0}{\text{factor of leading coefficient } a_n}$$
Fundamental theorem of algebra (p. 379)	If $f(x)$ is a polynomial of degree n where $n > 0$, then the equation $f(x) = 0$ has at least one solution in the set of complex numbers.
Corollary to the fundamental theorem of algebra (p. 379)	If $f(x)$ is a polynomial of degree n where $n > 0$, then the equation $f(x) = 0$ has exactly n solutions provided each solution repeated twice is counted as 2 solutions, each solution repeated three times is counted as 3 solutions, and so on.
Complex conjugates theorem (p. 380)	If f is a polynomial function with real coefficients, and $a + bi$ is an imaginary zero of f, then $a - bi$ is also a zero of f.
Irrational conjugates theorem (p. 380)	Suppose f is a polynomial function with rational coefficients, and a and b are rational numbers such that $\sqrt{b}$ is irrational. If $a + \sqrt{b}$ is a zero of f, then $a - \sqrt{b}$ is also a zero of f.
Descartes' rule of signs (p. 381)	Let $f(x) = a_nx^n + a_{n-1}x^{n-1} + \cdots + a_2x^2 + a_1x + a_0$ be a polynomial function with real coefficients. • The number of *positive real zeros* of f is equal to the number of changes in sign of the coefficients of $f(x)$ or is less than this by an even number. • The number of *negative real zeros* of f is equal to the number of changes in sign of the coefficients of $f(-x)$ or is less than this by an even number.

TABLES

Formulas and Theorems from Algebra *(continued)*

Discriminant of a general second-degree equation (p. 653)	Any conic can be described by a general second-degree equation in x and y: $Ax^2 + Bxy + Cy^2 + Dx + Ey + F = 0$. The expression $B^2 - 4AC$ is the discriminant of the conic equation and can be used to identify it. **Discriminant** — **Type of Conic** $B^2 - 4AC < 0$, $B = 0$, and $A = C$ — Circle $B^2 - 4AC < 0$, and either $B \neq 0$ or $A \neq C$ — Ellipse $B^2 - 4AC = 0$ — Parabola $B^2 - 4AC > 0$ — Hyperbola If $B = 0$, each axis of the conic is horizontal or vertical.

Formulas from Combinatorics

Fundamental counting principle (p. 682)	If one event can occur in m ways and another event can occur in n ways, then the number of ways that both events can occur is $m \cdot n$.
Permutations of n objects taken r at a time (p. 685)	The number of permutations of r objects taken from a group of n distinct objects is denoted by ${}_nP_r$ and is given by: $${}_nP_r = \frac{n!}{(n-r)!}$$
Permutations with repetition (p. 685)	The number of distinguishable permutations of n objects where one object is repeated s_1 times, another is repeated s_2 times, and so on is: $$\frac{n!}{s_1! \cdot s_2! \cdot \ldots \cdot s_k!}$$
Combinations of n objects taken r at a time (p. 690)	The number of combinations of r objects taken from a group of n distinct objects is denoted by ${}_nC_r$ and is given by: $${}_nC_r = \frac{n!}{(n-r)! \cdot r!}$$
Pascal's triangle (p. 692)	If you arrange the values of ${}_nC_r$ in a triangular pattern in which each row corresponds to a value of n, you get what is called Pascal's triangle. ${}_0C_0$ — 1 ${}_1C_0 \quad {}_1C_1$ — 1 1 ${}_2C_0 \quad {}_2C_1 \quad {}_2C_2$ — 1 2 1 ${}_3C_0 \quad {}_3C_1 \quad {}_3C_2 \quad {}_3C_3$ — 1 3 3 1 ${}_4C_0 \quad {}_4C_1 \quad {}_4C_2 \quad {}_4C_3 \quad {}_4C_4$ — 1 4 6 4 1 The first and last numbers in each row are 1. Every number other than 1 is the sum of the closest two numbers in the row directly above it.
Binomial theorem (p. 693)	The binomial expansion of $(a + b)^n$ for any positive integer n is: $$(a+b)^n = {}_nC_0a^nb^0 + {}_nC_1a^{n-1}b^1 + {}_nC_2a^{n-2}b^2 + \cdots + {}_nC_na^0b^n$$ $$= \sum_{r=0}^{n} {}_nC_ra^{n-r}b^r$$

TABLES

1028

Formulas from Probability

Theoretical probability of an event (p. 698)	When all outcomes are equally likely, the theoretical probability that an event A will occur is: $P(A) = \frac{\text{Number of outcomes in } A}{\text{Total number of outcomes}}$
Odds in favor of an event (p. 699)	When all outcomes are equally likely, the odds in favor of an event A are: $\frac{\text{Number of outcomes in } A}{\text{Number of outcomes not in } A}$
Odds against an event (p. 699)	When all outcomes are equally likely, the odds against an event A are: $\frac{\text{Number of outcomes not in } A}{\text{Number of outcomes in } A}$
Experimental probability of an event (p. 700)	When an experiment is performed that consists of a certain number of trials, the experimental probability of an event A is given by: $P(A) = \frac{\text{Number of trials where } A \text{ occurs}}{\text{Total number of trials}}$
Probability of compound events (p. 707)	If A and B are any two events, then the probability of A or B is: $P(A \text{ or } B) = P(A) + P(B) - P(A \text{ and } B)$ If A and B are disjoint events, then the probability of A or B is: $P(A \text{ or } B) = P(A) + P(B)$
Probability of the complement of an event (p. 709)	The probability of the complement of event A, denoted $\overline{A}$, is: $P(\overline{A}) = 1 - P(A)$
Probability of independent events (p. 717)	If A and B are independent, the probability that both A and B occur is: $P(A \text{ and } B) = P(A) \cdot P(B)$
Probability of dependent events (p. 718)	If A and B are dependent, the probability that both A and B occur is: $P(A \text{ and } B) = P(A) \cdot P(B \mid A)$
Binomial probabilities (p. 725)	For a binomial experiment consisting of n trials where the probability of success on each trial is p, the probability of exactly k successes is: $P(k \text{ successes}) = {}_nC_k p^k (1-p)^{n-k}$

Formulas from Statistics

Mean of a data set (p. 744)	$\overline{x} = \frac{x_1 + x_2 + \cdots + x_n}{n}$ where $\overline{x}$ (read "x-bar") is the mean of the data $x_1, x_2, \ldots, x_n$
Standard deviation of a data set (p. 745)	$\sigma = \sqrt{\frac{(x_1 - \overline{x})^2 + (x_2 - \overline{x})^2 + \ldots + (x_n - \overline{x})^2}{n}}$ where σ (read "sigma") is the standard deviation of the data $x_1, x_2, \ldots, x_n$
Areas under a normal curve (p. 757)	A normal distribution with mean $\overline{x}$ and standard deviation σ has these properties: • The total area under the related normal curve is 1. • About 68% of the area lies within 1 standard deviation of the mean. • About 95% of the area lies within 2 standard deviations of the mean. • About 99.7% of the area lies within 3 standard deviations of the mean.
***z*-score** (p. 758)	$z = \frac{x - \overline{x}}{\sigma}$ where x is a data value, $\overline{x}$ is the mean, and σ is the standard deviation

TABLES

Formulas for Sequences and Series

Formulas for sums of special series (p. 797)	$\sum_{i=1}^{n} 1 = n$ $\sum_{i=1}^{n} i = \frac{n(n+1)}{2}$ $\sum_{i=1}^{n} i^2 = \frac{n(n+1)(2n+1)}{6}$
Explicit rule for an arithmetic sequence (p. 802)	The nth term of an arithmetic sequence with first term a_1 and common difference d is: $a_n = a_1 + (n-1)d$
Sum of a finite arithmetic series (p. 804)	The sum of the first n terms of an arithmetic series is: $S_n = n\left(\frac{a_1 + a_n}{2}\right)$
Explicit rule for a geometric sequence (p. 810)	The nth term of a geometric sequence with first term a_1 and common ratio r is: $a_n = a_1 r^{n-1}$
Sum of a finite geometric series (p. 812)	The sum of the first n terms of a geometric series with common ratio $r \neq 1$ is: $S_n = a_1\left(\frac{1 - r^n}{1 - r}\right)$
Sum of an infinite geometric series (p. 821)	The sum of an infinite geometric series with first term a_1 and common ratio r is $S = \frac{a_1}{1 - r}$ provided $\lvert r \rvert < 1$. If $\lvert r \rvert \geq 1$, the series has no sum.
Recursive equation for an arithmetic sequence (p. 827)	$a_n = a_{n-1} + d$ where d is the common difference
Recursive equation for a geometric sequence (p. 827)	$a_n = r \cdot a_{n-1}$ where r is the common ratio

TABLES

Formulas and Identities from Trigonometry

Conversion between degrees and radians (p. 860)	To rewrite a degree measure in radians, multiply by $\frac{\pi \text{ radians}}{180°}$. To rewrite a radian measure in degrees, multiply by $\frac{180°}{\pi \text{ radians}}$.
Definition of trigonometric functions (p. 866)	Let θ be an angle in standard position and (x, y) be any point (except the origin) on the terminal side of θ. Let $r = \sqrt{x^2 + y^2}$. $\sin \theta = \frac{y}{r}$ $\cos \theta = \frac{x}{r}$ $\tan \theta = \frac{y}{x}, x \neq 0$ $\csc \theta = \frac{r}{y}, y \neq 0$ $\sec \theta = \frac{r}{x}, x \neq 0$ $\cot \theta = \frac{x}{y}, y \neq 0$
Law of sines (p. 882)	If $\triangle ABC$ has sides of length a, b, and c, then: $\frac{\sin A}{a} = \frac{\sin B}{b} = \frac{\sin C}{c}$
Area of a triangle (given two sides and the included angle) (p. 885)	If $\triangle ABC$ has sides of length a, b, and c, then its area is: Area $= \frac{1}{2}bc \sin A$ Area $= \frac{1}{2}ac \sin B$ Area $= \frac{1}{2}ab \sin C$

1030

Formulas and Identities from Trigonometry *(continued)*

Law of cosines (p. 889)	If $\triangle ABC$ has sides of length a, b, and c, then: $a^2 = b^2 + c^2 - 2bc\cos A$ $b^2 = a^2 + c^2 - 2ac\cos B$ $c^2 = a^2 + b^2 - 2ab\cos C$
Heron's area formula (p. 891)	The area of the triangle with sides of length a, b, and c is $\text{Area} = \sqrt{s(s-a)(s-b)(s-c)}$ where $s = \frac{1}{2}(a + b + c)$.
Reciprocal identities (p. 924)	$\csc\theta = \frac{1}{\sin\theta}$ $\sec\theta = \frac{1}{\cos\theta}$ $\cot\theta = \frac{1}{\tan\theta}$
Tangent and cotangent identities (p. 924)	$\tan\theta = \frac{\sin\theta}{\cos\theta}$ $\cot\theta = \frac{\cos\theta}{\sin\theta}$
Pythagorean identities (p. 924)	$\sin^2\theta + \cos^2\theta = 1$ $1 + \tan^2\theta = \sec^2\theta$ $1 + \cot^2\theta = \csc^2\theta$
Cofunction identities (p. 924)	$\sin\left(\frac{\pi}{2} - \theta\right) = \cos\theta$ $\cos\left(\frac{\pi}{2} - \theta\right) = \sin\theta$ $\tan\left(\frac{\pi}{2} - \theta\right) = \cot\theta$
Negative angle identities (p. 924)	$\sin(-\theta) = -\sin\theta$ $\cos(-\theta) = \cos\theta$ $\tan(-\theta) = -\tan\theta$
Sum formulas (p. 949)	$\sin(a + b) = \sin a\cos b + \cos a\sin b$ $\cos(a + b) = \cos a\cos b - \sin a\sin b$ $\tan(a + b) = \frac{\tan a + \tan b}{1 - \tan a\tan b}$
Difference formulas (p. 949)	$\sin(a - b) = \sin a\cos b - \cos a\sin b$ $\cos(a - b) = \cos a\cos b + \sin a\sin b$ $\tan(a - b) = \frac{\tan a - \tan b}{1 + \tan a\tan b}$
Double-angle formulas (p. 955)	$\cos 2a = \cos^2 a - \sin^2 a$ $\sin 2a = 2\sin a\cos a$ $\cos 2a = 2\cos^2 a - 1$ $\tan 2a = \frac{2\tan a}{1 - \tan^2 a}$ $\cos 2a = 1 - 2\sin^2 a$
Half-angle formulas (p. 955)	$\sin\frac{a}{2} = \pm\sqrt{\frac{1 - \cos a}{2}}$ $\tan\frac{a}{2} = \frac{1 - \cos a}{\sin a}$ $\cos\frac{a}{2} = \pm\sqrt{\frac{1 + \cos a}{2}}$ $\tan\frac{a}{2} = \frac{\sin a}{1 + \cos a}$ The signs of $\sin\frac{a}{2}$ and $\cos\frac{a}{2}$ depend on the quadrant in which $\frac{a}{2}$ lies.

TABLES

TABLES

Formulas from Geometry

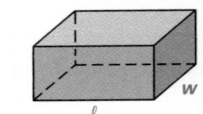

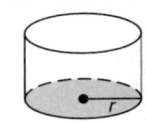

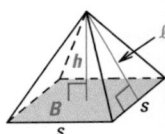

Basic geometric figures	See pages 991–993 for area formulas for basic two-dimensional geometric figures.
Area of an equilateral triangle	Area $= \frac{\sqrt{3}}{4}s^2$ where s is the length of a side
Arc length and area of a sector	Arc length $= r\theta$ where r is the radius and θ is the radian measure of the central angle that intercepts the arc Area $= \frac{1}{2}r^2\theta$
Area of an ellipse	Area $= \pi ab$ where a and b are half the lengths of the major and minor axes of the ellipse
Volume and surface area of a right rectangular prism	Volume $= \ell wh$ where ℓ is the length, w is the width, and h is the height Surface area $= 2(\ell w + wh + \ell h)$
Volume and surface area of a right cylinder	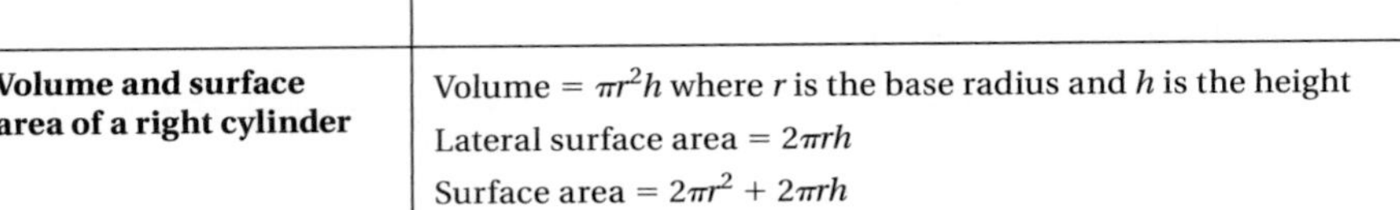 Volume $= \pi r^2 h$ where r is the base radius and h is the height Lateral surface area $= 2\pi rh$ Surface area $= 2\pi r^2 + 2\pi rh$
Volume and surface area of a right regular pyramid	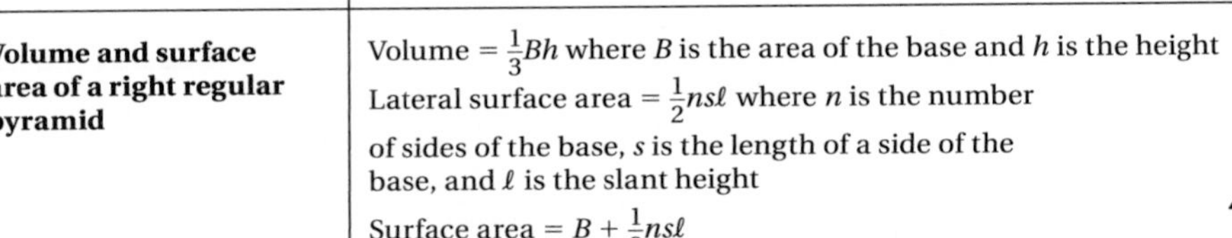 Volume $= \frac{1}{3}Bh$ where B is the area of the base and h is the height Lateral surface area $= \frac{1}{2}ns\ell$ where n is the number of sides of the base, s is the length of a side of the base, and ℓ is the slant height Surface area $= B + \frac{1}{2}ns\ell$
Volume and surface area of a right circular cone	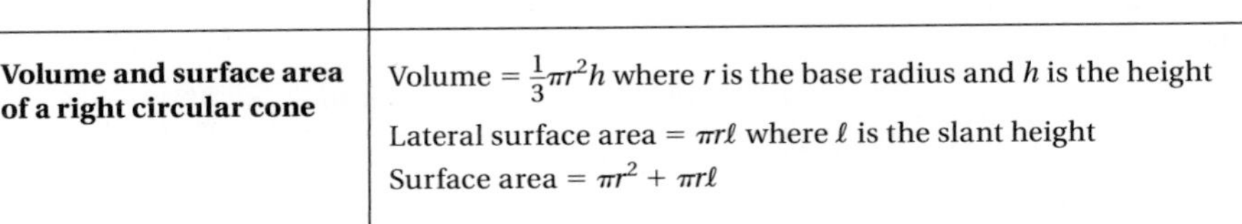 Volume $= \frac{1}{3}\pi r^2 h$ where r is the base radius and h is the height Lateral surface area $= \pi r\ell$ where ℓ is the slant height Surface area $= \pi r^2 + \pi r\ell$ 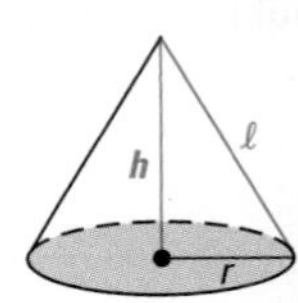
Volume and surface area of a sphere	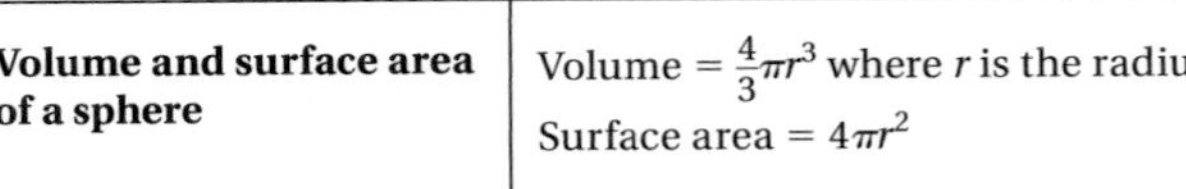 Volume $= \frac{4}{3}\pi r^3$ where r is the radius Surface area $= 4\pi r^2$ 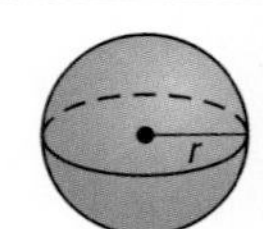

1032

Properties

Properties of Real Numbers

	Let a, b, and c be real numbers.	
	Addition	**Multiplication**
Closure Property (p. 3)	$a + b$ is a real number.	ab is a real number.
Commutative Property (p. 3)	$a + b = b + a$	$ab = ba$
Associative Property (p. 3)	$(a + b) + c = a + (b + c)$	$(ab)c = a(bc)$
Identity Property (p. 3)	$a + 0 = a, 0 + a = a$	$a \cdot 1 = a, 1 \cdot a = a$
Inverse Property (p. 3)	$a + (-a) = 0$	$a \cdot \frac{1}{a} = 1, a \neq 0$
Distributive Property (p. 3)	The distributive property involves both addition and multiplication: $a(b + c) = ab + ac$	
Zero Product Property (p. 253)	Let A and B be real numbers or algebraic expressions. If $AB = 0$, then $A = 0$ or $B = 0$.	

Properties of Matrices

	Let A, B, and C be matrices, and let k be a scalar.
Associative Property of Addition (p. 188)	$(A + B) + C = A + (B + C)$
Commutative Property of Addition (p. 188)	$A + B = B + A$
Distributive Property of Addition (p. 188)	$k(A + B) = kA + kB$
Distributive Property of Subtraction (p. 188)	$k(A - B) = kA - kB$
Associative Property of Matrix Multiplication (p. 197)	$(AB)C = A(BC)$
Left Distributive Property of Matrix Multiplication (p. 197)	$A(B + C) = AB + AC$
Right Distributive Property of Matrix Multiplication (p. 197)	$(A + B)C = AC + BC$
Associative Property of Scalar Multiplication (p. 197)	$k(AB) = (kA)B = A(kB)$
Multiplicative Identity (p. 210)	An $n \times n$ matrix with 1's on the main diagonal and 0's elsewhere is an identity matrix, denoted I. For any $n \times n$ matrix A, $AI = IA = A$.
Inverse Matrices (p. 210)	If the determinant of an $n \times n$ matrix A is nonzero, then A has an inverse, denoted A^{-1}, such that $AA^{-1} = A^{-1}A = I$.

Properties of Exponents

	Let a and b be real numbers, and let m and n be integers.
Product of Powers Property (p. 330)	$a^m \cdot a^n = a^{m+n}$
Power of a Power Property (p. 330)	$(a^m)^n = a^{mn}$
Power of a Product Property (p. 330)	$(ab)^m = a^m b^m$
Negative Exponent Property (p. 330)	$a^{-m} = \frac{1}{a^m}, a \neq 0$
Zero Exponent Property (p. 330)	$a^0 = 1, a \neq 0$
Quotient of Powers Property (p. 330)	$\frac{a^m}{a^n} = a^{m-n}, a \neq 0$
Power of a Quotient Property (p. 330)	$\left(\frac{a}{b}\right)^m = \frac{a^m}{b^m}, b \neq 0$

TABLES

Properties of Radicals and Rational Exponents

Number of Real nth Roots (p. 414)	Let n be an integer greater than 1, and let a be a real number. • If n is odd, then a has one real nth root: $\sqrt[n]{a} = a^{1/n}$ • If n is even and $a > 0$, then a has two real nth roots: $\pm\sqrt[n]{a} = \pm a^{1/n}$ • If n is even and $a = 0$, then a has one nth root: $\sqrt[n]{0} = 0^{1/n} = 0$ • If n is even and $a < 0$, then a has no real nth roots.
Radicals and Rational Exponents (p. 415)	Let $a^{1/n}$ be an nth root of a, and let m be a positive integer. • $a^{m/n} = (a^{1/n})^m = (\sqrt[n]{a})^m$ • $a^{-m/n} = \frac{1}{a^{m/n}} = \frac{1}{(a^{1/n})^m} = \frac{1}{(\sqrt[n]{a})^m}, a \neq 0$
Properties of Rational Exponents (p. 420)	All of the properties of exponents listed on the previous page apply to rational exponents as well as integer exponents.
Product and Quotient Properties of Radicals (p. 421)	Let n be an integer greater than 1, and let a and b be positive real numbers. Then $\sqrt[n]{a \cdot b} = \sqrt[n]{a} \cdot \sqrt[n]{b}$ and $\sqrt[n]{\frac{a}{b}} = \frac{\sqrt[n]{a}}{\sqrt[n]{b}}$.

Properties of Logarithms

	Let a, b, c, m, n, x, and y be positive real numbers such that $b \neq 1$ and $c \neq 1$.
Logarithms and Exponents (p. 499)	$\log_b y = x$ if and only if $b^x = y$
Special Logarithm Values (p. 499)	$\log_b 1 = 0$ because $b^0 = 1$ and $\log_b b = 1$ because $b^1 = b$
Common and Natural Logarithms (p. 500)	$\log_{10} x = \log x$ and $\log_e x = \ln x$
Product Property of Logarithms (p. 507)	$\log_b mn = \log_b m + \log_b n$
Quotient Property of Logarithms (p. 507)	$\log_b \frac{m}{n} = \log_b m - \log_b n$
Power Property of Logarithms (p. 507)	$\log_b m^n = n \log_b m$
Change of Base (p. 508)	$\log_c a = \frac{\log_b a}{\log_b c}$

Properties of Functions

Operations on Functions (pp. 428, 430)	Let f and g be any two functions. A new function h can be defined using any of the following operations. **Addition:** $h(x) = f(x) + g(x)$ **Subtraction:** $h(x) = f(x) - g(x)$ **Multiplication:** $h(x) = f(x) \cdot g(x)$ **Division:** $h(x) = \frac{f(x)}{g(x)}$ **Composition:** $h(x) = g(f(x))$ For addition, subtraction, multiplication, and division, the domain of h consists of the x-values that are in the domains of both f and g. Additionally, the domain of the quotient does not include x-values for which $g(x) = 0$. For composition, the domain of h is the set of all x-values such that x is in the domain of f and $f(x)$ is in the domain of g.
Inverse Functions (p. 438)	Functions f and g are inverses of each other provided: $f(g(x)) = x$ and $g(f(x)) = x$

TABLES

English–Spanish Glossary

A

absolute value (p. 51) The absolute value of a number x, represented by the symbol $\|x\|$, is the distance the number is from 0 on a number line. **valor absoluto** (pág. 51) El valor absoluto de un número x, representado por el símbolo $\|x\|$, es la distancia a la que está el número de 0 en una recta numérica.	$\left\|\frac{2}{3}\right\| = \frac{2}{3}$, $\|-4.3\| = 4.3$, and $\|0\| = 0$. $\left\|\frac{2}{3}\right\| = \frac{2}{3}$, $\|-4.3\| = 4.3$ y $\|0\| = 0$.
absolute value function (p. 123) A function that contains an absolute value expression. **función de valor absoluto** (pág. 123) Función que contiene una expresión de valor absoluto.	$y = \|x\|$, $y = \|x - 3\|$, and $y = 4\|x + 8\| - 9$ are absolute value functions. $y = \|x\|$, $y = \|x - 3\|$ e $y = 4\|x + 8\| - 9$ son funciones de valor absoluto.
absolute value of a complex number (p. 279) If $z = a + bi$, then the absolute value of z, denoted $\|z\|$, is a nonnegative real number defined as $\|z\| = \sqrt{a^2 + b^2}$. **valor absoluto de un número complejo** (pág. 279) Si $z = a + bi$, entonces el valor absoluto de z, denotado por $\|z\|$, es un número real no negativo definido como $\|z\| = \sqrt{a^2 + b^2}$.	$\|-4 + 3i\| = \sqrt{(-4)^2 + 3^2} = \sqrt{25} = 5$
algebraic expression (p. 11) An expression that consists of numbers, variables, operations, and grouping symbols. Also called variable expression. **expresión algebraica** (pág. 11) Expresión formada por números, variables, operaciones y signos de agrupación.	$\frac{2}{3}p$, $\frac{8}{7 - r}$, $k - 5$, and $n^2 + 2n$ are algebraic expressions. $\frac{2}{3}p$, $\frac{8}{7 - r}$, $k - 5$ y $n^2 + 2n$ son expresiones algebraicas.
amplitude (p. 908) The amplitude of the graph of a sine or cosine function is $\frac{1}{2}(M - m)$, where M is the maximum value of the function and m is the minimum value of the function. **amplitud** (pág. 908) La amplitud de la grafica de una función seno o coseno es $\frac{1}{2}(M - m)$, donde M es el valor máximo de la función y m es el valor mínimo de la función.	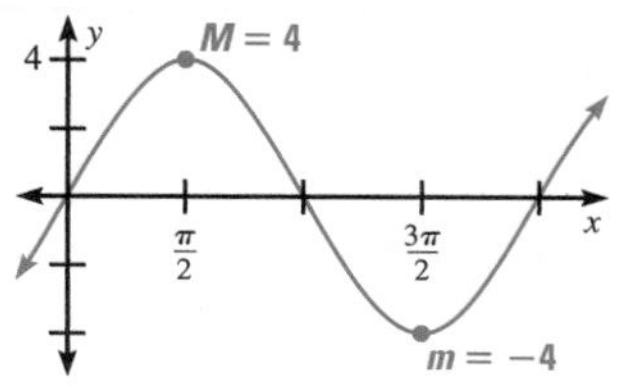 The graph of $y = 4 \sin x$ has an amplitude of $\frac{1}{2}(4 - (-4)) = 4$. La gráfica de $y = 4$ sen x tiene una amplitud de $\frac{1}{2}(4 - (-4)) = 4$.
angle of depression (p. 855) The angle by which an observer's line of sight must be depressed from the horizontal to the point observed. **ángulo de depresión** (pág. 855) El ángulo con el que se debe bajar la línea de visión de un observador desde la horizontal hasta el punto observado.	*See* angle of elevation. *Ver* ángulo de elevación.

ENGLISH-SPANISH GLOSSARY

angle of elevation (p. 855) The angle by which an observer's line of sight must be elevated from the horizontal to the point observed. **ángulo de elevación** (pág. 855) El ángulo con el que se debe elevar la línea de visión de un observador desde la horizontal hasta el punto observado.	
arithmetic sequence (p. 802) A sequence in which the difference of consecutive terms is constant. **progresión aritmética** (pág. 802) Progresión en la que la diferencia entre los términos consecutivos es constante.	$-4, 1, 6, 11, 16, \ldots$ is an arithmetic sequence with common difference 5. $-4, 1, 6, 11, 16, \ldots$ es una progresión aritmética con una diferencia común de 5.
arithmetic series (p. 804) The expression formed by adding the terms of an arithmetic sequence. **serie aritmética** (pág. 804) La expresión formada al sumar los términos de una progresión aritmética.	$\sum_{i=1}^{5} 2i = 2 + 4 + 6 + 8 + 10$
asymptote (p. 478) A line that a graph approaches more and more closely. **asíntota** (pág. 478) Recta a la que se aproxima una gráfica cada vez más.	 The asymptote for the graph shown is the line $y = 3$. La asíntota para la gráfica que se muestra es la recta $y = 3$.
axis of symmetry of a parabola (pp. 236, 620) The line perpendicular to the parabola's directrix and passing through its focus and vertex. **eje de simetría de una parábola** (págs. 236, 620) La recta perpendicular a la directriz de la parábola y que pasa por su foco y su vértice.	*See* parabola. *Ver* parábola.

B

base of a power (p. 10) The number or expression that is used as a factor in a repeated multiplication. **base de una potencia** (pág. 10) El número o la expresión que se usa como factor en la multiplicación repetida.	In the power 2^5, the base is 2. En la potencia 2^5, la base es 2.

best-fitting line (p. 114) The line that lies as close as possible to all the data points in a scatter plot.

mejor recta de regresión (pág. 114) La recta que se ajusta lo más posible a todos los puntos de datos de un diagrama de dispersión.

best-fitting quadratic model (p. 311) The model given by using quadratic regression on a set of paired data.

modelo cuadrático con mejor ajuste (pág. 311) El modelo dado al realizar una regresión cuadrática sobre un conjunto de pares de datos.

biased question (p. 772) A question that elicits responses that do not accurately reflect the opinions or actions of the people surveyed.

pregunta capciosa (pág. 772) Pregunta que induce a respuestas que no reflejan con exactitud las opiniones o acciones de los encuestados.

"Would you rather see an exciting laser show or a boring movie?" is a biased question.

"¿Preferirías ver un emocionante espectáculo de láser o una película aburrida?" es una pregunta capciosa.

biased sample (p. 767) A sample that overrepresents or underrepresents part of a population.

muestra sesgada (pág. 767) Muestra que representa de forma excesiva o insuficiente a parte de una población.

The members of a school's basketball team would form a biased sample for a survey about whether to build a new gym.

Los miembros del equipo de baloncesto de una escuela formarían una muestra sesgada si participaran en una encuesta sobre si quieren que se construya un nuevo gimnasio.

binomial (p. 252) The sum of two monomials.

binomio (pág. 252) La suma de dos monomios.

$3x - 1$ and $t^3 - 4t$ are binomials.

$3x - 1$ y $t^3 - 4t$ son binomios.

binomial distribution (p. 725) The probability distribution associated with a binomial experiment.

distribución binomial (pág. 725) La distribución de probabilidades asociada a un experimento binomial.

Probability
Probabilidad
0.30
0.20
0.10
0
0 1 2 3 4 5 6 7 8
Number of successes
Número de éxitos

Binomial distribution for 8 trials with $p = 0.5$.

Distribución binomial de 8 pruebas con $p = 0.5$.

1037

binomial experiment (p. 725) An experiment that meets the following conditions. (1) There are n independent trials. (2) Each trial has only two possible outcomes: success and failure. (3) The probability of success is the same for each trial. **experimento binomial** (pág. 725) Experimento que satisface las siguientes condiciones. (1) Hay n pruebas independientes. (2) Cada prueba tiene sólo dos resultados posibles: éxito y fracaso. (3) La probabilidad de éxito es igual para cada prueba.	A fair coin is tossed 12 times. The probability of getting exactly 4 heads is as follows: **Una moneda normal se lanza 12 veces. La probabilidad de sacar exactamente 4 caras es la siguiente:** $P(k=4) = {}_nC_k p^k(1-p)^{n-k}$ $= {}_{12}C_4(0.5)^4(1-0.5)^8$ $= 495(0.5)^4(0.5)^8$ ≈ 0.121
binomial theorem (p. 693) The binomial expansion of $(a+b)^n$ for any positive integer n: $(a+b)^n = {}_nC_0a^nb^0 + {}_nC_1a^{n-1}b^1 + {}_nC_2a^{n-2}b^2 + \cdots + {}_nC_na^0b^n$. **teorema binomial** (pág. 693) La expansión binomial de $(a+b)^n$ para cualquier número entero positivo n: $(a+b)^n = {}_nC_0a^nb^0 + {}_nC_1a^{n-1}b^1 + {}_nC_2a^{n-2}b^2 + \cdots + {}_nC_na^0b^n$.	$(x^2+y)^3$ $= {}_3C_0(x^2)^3y^0 + {}_3C_1(x^2)^2y^1 + {}_3C_2(x^2)^1y^2 + {}_3C_3(x^2)^0y^3$ $= (1)(x^6)(1) + (3)(x^4)(y) + (3)(x^2)(y^2) + (1)(1)(y^3)$ $= x^6 + 3x^4y + 3x^2y^2 + y^3$

C

center of a circle (p. 626) *See* circle. **centro de un círculo** (pág. 626) *Ver* círculo.	The circle with equation $(x-3)^2 + (y+5)^2 = 36$ has its center at $(3, -5)$. *See also* circle. **El círculo con la ecuación $(x-3)^2 + (y+5)^2 = 36$ tiene el centro en $(3, -5)$. *Ver también* círculo.**
center of a hyperbola (p. 642) The midpoint of the transverse axis of a hyperbola. **centro de una hipérbola** (pág. 642) El punto medio del eje transverso de una hipérbola.	*See* hyperbola. ***Ver* hipérbola.**
center of an ellipse (p. 634) The midpoint of the major axis of an ellipse. **centro de una elipse** (pág. 634) El punto medio del eje mayor de una elipse.	*See* ellipse. ***Ver* elipse.**
central angle (p. 861) An angle formed by two radii of a circle. **ángulo central** (pág. 861) Ángulo formado por dos radios de un círculo.	*See* sector. ***Ver* sector.**

1038

circle (p. 626) The set of all points (x, y) in a plane that are of distance r from a fixed point, called the center of the circle. **círculo** (pág. 626) El conjunto de todos los puntos (x, y) de un plano que están a una distancia r de un punto fijo, llamado centro del círculo.	
coefficient (p. 12) When a term is the product of a number and a power of a variable, the number is the coefficient of the power. **coeficiente** (pág. 12) Cuando un término es el producto de un número y una potencia de una variable, el número es el coeficiente de la potencia.	In the algebraic expression $2x^2 + (-4x) + (-1)$, the coefficient of $2x^2$ is 2 and the coefficient of $-4x$ is -4. **En la expresión algebraica $2x^2 + (-4x) + (-1)$, el coeficiente de $2x^2$ es 2 y el coeficiente de $-4x$ es -4.**
coefficient matrix (p. 205) The coefficient matrix of the linear system $ax + by = e, cx + dy = f$ is $\begin{bmatrix} a & b \\ c & d \end{bmatrix}$. **matriz coeficiente** (pág. 205) La matriz coeficiente del sistema lineal $ax + by = e, cx + dy = f$ es $\begin{bmatrix} a & b \\ c & d \end{bmatrix}$.	$9x + 4y = -6$ $3x - 5y = -21$ coefficient matrix: **matriz coeficiente:** $\begin{bmatrix} 9 & 4 \\ 3 & -5 \end{bmatrix}$ matrix of constants: **matriz de constantes:** $\begin{bmatrix} -6 \\ -21 \end{bmatrix}$ matrix of variables: **matriz de variables:** $\begin{bmatrix} x \\ y \end{bmatrix}$
combination (p. 690) A selection of r objects from a group of n objects where the order is not important, denoted $_nC_r$ where $_nC_r = \frac{n!}{(n-r)! \cdot r!}$. **combinación** (pág. 690) Selección de r objetos de un grupo de n objetos en el que el orden no importa, denotado $_nC_r$, donde $_nC_r = \frac{n!}{(n-r)! \cdot r!}$.	There are 6 combinations of the $n = 4$ letters A, B, C, and D selected $r = 2$ at a time: AB, AC, AD, BC, BD, and CD. **Hay 6 combinaciones de las letras $n = 4$ A, B, C y D seleccionadas $r = 2$ cada vez: AB, AC, AD, BC, BD y CD.**
common difference (p. 802) The constant difference of consecutive terms of an arithmetic sequence. **diferencia común** (pág. 802) La diferencia constante entre los términos consecutivos de una progresión aritmética.	*See* arithmetic sequence. ***Ver* progresión aritmética.**
common logarithm (p. 500) A logarithm with base 10. It is denoted by $\log_{10}$ or simply by log. **logaritmo común** (pág. 500) Logaritmo con base 10. Se denota por $\log_{10}$ ó simplemente por log.	$\log_{10} 100 = \log 100 = 2$ because $10^2 = 100$. **$\log_{10} 100 = \log 100 = 2$ ya que $10^2 = 100$.**

ENGLISH-SPANISH GLOSSARY

common ratio (p. 810) The constant ratio of consecutive terms of a geometric sequence. **razón común** (pág. 810) La razón constante entre los términos consecutivos de una progresión geométrica.	*See* geometric sequence. *Ver* progresión geométrica.
complement of a set (p. 715) The complement of a set A, written $\overline{A}$, is the set of all elements in the universal set U that are *not* in A. **complemento de un conjunto** (pág. 715) El complemento de un conjunto A, escrito $\overline{A}$, es el conjunto de todos los elementos del conjunto universal U que *no* están en A.	Let U be the set of all integers from 1 to 10 and let $A = \{1, 2, 4, 8\}$. Then $\overline{A} = \{3, 5, 6, 7, 9, 10\}$. Sea U el conjunto de todos los números enteros entre 1 y 10 y sea $A = \{1, 2, 4, 8\}$. Por lo tanto, $\overline{A} = \{3, 5, 6, 7, 9, 10\}$.
completing the square (p. 284) The process of adding a term to a quadratic expression of the form $x^2 + bx$ to make it a perfect square trinomial. **completar el cuadrado** (pág. 284) El proceso de sumar un término a una expresión cuadrática de la forma $x^2 + bx$, de modo que sea un trinomio cuadrado perfecto.	To complete the square for $x^2 + 16x$, add $\left(\frac{16}{2}\right)^2 = 64: x^2 + 16x + 64 = (x + 8)^2$. Para completar el cuadrado para $x^2 + 16x$, suma $\left(\frac{16}{2}\right)^2 = 64: x^2 + 16x + 64 = (x + 8)^2$.
complex conjugates (p. 276) Two complex numbers of the form $a + bi$ and $a - bi$. **números complejos conjugados** (pág. 276) Dos números complejos de la forma $a + bi$ y $a - bi$.	$2 + 4i, 2 - 4i$
complex fraction (p. 584) A fraction that contains a fraction in its numerator or denominator. **fracción compleja** (pág. 584) Fracción que tiene una fracción en su numerador o en su denominador.	$\dfrac{\frac{5}{x+4}}{\frac{6x}{3x^2}}, \dfrac{1}{\frac{1}{p} + \frac{1}{q}}$
complex number (p. 276) A number $a + bi$ where a and b are real numbers and i is the imaginary unit. **número complejo** (pág. 276) Un número $a + bi$, donde a y b son números reales e i es la unidad imaginaria.	$0, 2.5, \sqrt{3}, \pi, 5i, 2 - i$
complex plane (p. 278) A coordinate plane in which each point (a, b) represents a complex number $a + bi$. The horizontal axis is the real axis and the vertical axis is the imaginary axis. **plano complejo** (pág. 278) Plano de coordenadas en el que cada punto (a, b) representa un número complejo $a + bi$. El eje horizontal es el eje real, y el eje vertical es el eje imaginario.	imaginary imaginario $-2 + 4i$ $3i$ i 1 real real $3 - 2i$ $-4 - 3i$
composition of functions (p. 430) The composition of a function g with a function f is $h(x) = g(f(x))$. **composición de funciones** (pág. 430) La composición de una función g con una función f es $h(x) = g(f(x))$.	$f(x) = 5x - 2,\ g(x) = 4x^{-1}$ $g(f(x)) = g(5x - 2) = 4(5x - 2)^{-1} = \frac{4}{5x - 2}, x \neq \frac{2}{5}$

compound event (p. 707) The union or intersection of two events. **suceso compuesto** (pág. 707) La unión o la intersección de dos sucesos.	When you roll a six-sided die, the event "roll a 2 or an odd number" is a compound event. **Cuando lanzas un cubo numerado de seis lados, el suceso "salir el 2 ó un número impar" es un suceso compuesto.**
compound inequality (p. 41) Two simple inequalities joined by "and" or "or." **desigualdad compuesta** (pág. 41) Dos desigualdades simples unidas por "y" u "o".	$2x > 0$ or $x + 4 < -1$ is a compound inequality. **$2x > 0$ ó $x + 4 < -1$ es una desigualdad compuesta.**
conditional probability (p. 718) The conditional probability of B given A, written $P(B \mid A)$, is the probability that event B will occur given that event A has occurred. **probabilidad condicional** (pág. 718) La probabilidad condicional de B dado A, escrito $P(B \mid A)$, es la probabilidad de que ocurra el suceso B dado que ha ocurrido el suceso A.	Two cards are randomly selected from a standard deck of 52 cards. Let event A be "the first card is a club" and let event B be "the second card is a club." Then $P(B \mid A) = \frac{12}{51} = \frac{4}{17}$ because there are 12 (out of 13) clubs left among the remaining 51 cards. **Dos cartas se seleccionan al azar de una baraja normal de 52 cartas. Sea el suceso A "la primera carta es de tréboles" y sea el suceso B "la segunda carta es de tréboles". Entonces $P(B \mid A) = \frac{12}{51} = \frac{4}{17}$ ya que quedan 12 (del total de 13) cartas de tréboles entre las 51 cartas restantes.**
conic (p. 650) *See* conic section. **cónica** (pág. 650) *Ver* sección cónica.	*See* conic section. ***Ver* sección cónica.**
conic section (p. 650) A curve formed by the intersection of a plane and a double-napped cone. Conic sections are also called conics. **sección cónica** (pág. 650) Una curva formada por la intersección de un plano y un cono doble. Las secciones cónicas también se llaman cónicas.	*See* circle, ellipse, hyperbola, *and* parabola. ***Ver* círculo, elipse, hipérbola *y* parábola.**
conjugates (p. 267) The expressions $a + \sqrt{b}$ and $a - \sqrt{b}$ where a and b are rational numbers. **conjugados** (pág. 267) Las expresiones $a + \sqrt{b}$ y $a - \sqrt{b}$ cuando a y b son números racionales.	The conjugate of $7 + \sqrt{2}$ is $7 - \sqrt{2}$. **El conjugado de $7 + \sqrt{2}$ es $7 - \sqrt{2}$.**
consistent system (p. 154) A system of equations that has at least one solution. **sistema compatible** (pág. 154) Sistema de ecuaciones que tiene al menos una solución.	$y = 2 + 3x$ $6x + 2y = 4$ The system above is consistent, with solution (0, 2). **El sistema de arriba es compatible, con la solución (0, 2).**

constant of variation (pp. 107, 551, 553) The nonzero constant a in a direct variation equation $y = ax$, an inverse variation equation $y = \frac{a}{x}$, or a joint variation equation $z = axy$. **constante de variación** (págs. 107, 551, 553) La constante distinta de cero a de una ecuación de variación directa $y = ax$, de una ecuación de variación inversa $y = \frac{a}{x}$ o de una ecuación de variación conjunta $z = axy$.	In the direct variation equation $y = -\frac{5}{2}x$, the constant of variation is $-\frac{5}{2}$. **En la ecuación de variación directa $y = -\frac{5}{2}x$, la constante de variación es $-\frac{5}{2}$.**
constant term (pp. 12, 337) A term that has a number part but no variable part. **término constante** (págs. 12, 337) Término que tiene una parte numérica pero sin variable.	The constant term of the algebraic expression $3x^2 + 5x + (-7)$ is -7. **El término constante de la expresión algebraica $3x^2 + 5x + (-7)$ es -7.**
constraints (p. 174) In linear programming, the linear inequalities that form a system. **restricciones** (pág. 174) En la programación lineal, las desigualdades lineales que forman un sistema.	*See* linear programming. ***Ver* programación lineal.**
continuous function (p. 80) A function whose graph is unbroken. **función continua** (pág. 80) Función que tiene una gráfica no interrumpida.	Any linear function, such as $y = 2x + 4$, is a continuous function. **Cualquier función lineal, como $y = 2x + 4$, es una función continua.**
control group (p. 773) A group that does not undergo a procedure or treatment when an experiment is conducted. *See also* experimental group. **grupo de control** (pág. 773) Grupo que no se somete a ningún procedimiento o tratamiento durante la realización de un experimento. *Ver también* grupo experimental.	*See* experimental group. ***Ver* grupo experimental.**
correlation coefficient (p. 114) A measure, denoted by r where $-1 \le r \le 1$, of how well a line fits a set of data pairs (x, y). **coeficiente de correlación** (pág. 114) Medida denotada por r, donde $-1 \le r \le 1$, y que describe el ajuste de una recta a un conjunto de pares de datos (x, y).	A data set that shows a strong positive correlation has a correlation coefficient of $r \approx 1$. *See also* positive correlation *and* negative correlation. **Un conjunto de datos que muestra una correlación positiva fuerte tiene un coeficiente de correlación de $r \approx 1$. *Ver también* correlación positiva *y* correlación negativa.**
cosecant function (p. 852) If θ is an acute angle of a right triangle, the cosecant of θ is the length of the hypotenuse divided by the length of the side opposite θ. **función cosecante** (pág. 852) Si θ es un ángulo agudo de un triángulo rectángulo, la cosecante de θ es la longitud de la hipotenusa dividida por la longitud del lado opuesto a θ.	*See* sine function. ***Ver* función seno.**

cosine function (p. 852) If θ is an acute angle of a right triangle, the cosine of θ is the length of the side adjacent to θ divided by the length of the hypotenuse. **función coseno** (pág. 852) Si θ es un ángulo agudo de un triángulo rectángulo, el coseno de θ es la longitud del lado adyacente a θ dividida por la longitud de la hipotenusa.	*See* sine function. *Ver* función seno.
cotangent function (p. 852) If θ is an acute angle of a right triangle, the cotangent of θ is the length of the side adjacent to θ divided by the length of the side opposite θ. **función cotangente** (pág. 852) Si θ es un ángulo agudo de un triángulo rectángulo, la cotangente de θ es la longitud del lado adyacente a θ dividida por la longitud del lado opuesto a θ.	*See* sine function. *Ver* función seno.
coterminal angles (p. 860) Angles in standard position with terminal sides that coincide. **ángulos coterminales** (pág. 860) Ángulos en posición normal cuyos lados terminales coinciden.	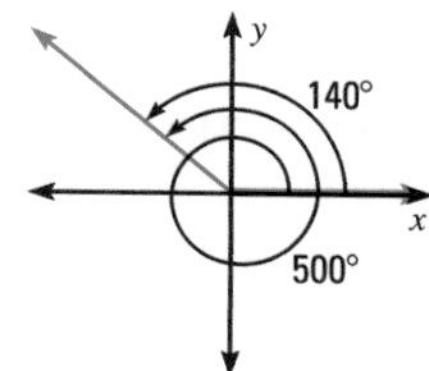 The angles with measures 500° and 140° are coterminal. **Los ángulos que miden 500° y 140° son coterminales.**
co-vertices of an ellipse (p. 634) The points of intersection of an ellipse and the line perpendicular to the major axis at the center. **puntos extremos del eje menor de una elipse** (pág. 634) Los puntos de intersección de una elipse y la recta perpendicular al eje mayor en el centro.	*See* ellipse. *Ver* elipse.
Cramer's rule (p. 205) A method for solving a system of linear equations using determinants: For the linear system $ax + by = e, cx + dy = f$, let A be the coefficient matrix. If $\det A \neq 0$, the solution of the system is as follows: $$x = \frac{\begin{vmatrix} e & b \\ f & d \end{vmatrix}}{\det A}, y = \frac{\begin{vmatrix} a & e \\ c & f \end{vmatrix}}{\det A}$$ **regla de Cramer** (pág. 205) Método para resolver un sistema de ecuaciones lineales usando determinantes: Para el sistema lineal $ax + by = e, cx + dy = f$, sea A la matriz coeficiente. Si $\det A \neq 0$, la solución del sistema es la siguiente: $$x = \frac{\begin{vmatrix} e & b \\ f & d \end{vmatrix}}{\det A}, y = \frac{\begin{vmatrix} a & e \\ c & f \end{vmatrix}}{\det A}$$	$$\begin{matrix} 9x + 4y = -6 \\ 3x - 5y = -21; \end{matrix} \begin{vmatrix} 9 & 4 \\ 3 & -5 \end{vmatrix} = -57$$ Applying Cramer's rule gives the following: **Al aplicar la regla de Cramer se obtiene lo siguiente:** $$x = \frac{\begin{vmatrix} -6 & 4 \\ -21 & -5 \end{vmatrix}}{-57} = \frac{114}{-57} = -2$$ $$y = \frac{\begin{vmatrix} 9 & -6 \\ 3 & -21 \end{vmatrix}}{-57} = \frac{-171}{-57} = 3$$

ENGLISH-SPANISH GLOSSARY

cross multiplying (p. 589) A method for solving a simple rational equation for which each side of the equation is a single rational expression. **multiplicar en cruz** (pág. 589) Método para resolver una ecuación racional simple en la que cada lado es una sola expresión racional.	To solve $\frac{3}{x+1} = \frac{9}{4x+5}$, cross multiply. **Para resolver $\frac{3}{x+1} = \frac{9}{4x+5}$, multiplica en cruz.** $3(4x + 5) = 9(x + 1)$ $12x + 15 = 9x + 9$ $3x = -6$ $x = -2$
cycle (p. 908) The shortest repeating portion of the graph of a periodic function. **ciclo** (pág. 908) En una función periódica, la parte más corta de la gráfica que se repite.	*See* periodic function. ***Ver* función periódica.**

D

decay factor (p. 486) The quantity b in the exponential decay function $y = ab^x$ with $a > 0$ and $0 < b < 1$. **factor de decrecimiento** (pág. 486) La cantidad b de la función de decrecimiento exponencial $y = ab^x$, con $a > 0$ y $0 < b < 1$.	The decay factor for the function $y = 3(0.5)^x$ is 0.5. **El factor de decrecimiento de la función $y = 3(0.5)^x$ es 0.5.**
degree of a polynomial function (p. 337) The exponent in the term of a polynomial function where the variable is raised to the greatest power. **grado de una función polinómica** (pág. 337) En una función polinómica, el exponente del término donde la variable se eleva a la mayor potencia.	*See* polynomial function. ***Ver* función polinómica.**
dependent events (p. 718) Two events such that the occurrence of one event affects the occurrence of the other event. **sucesos dependientes** (pág. 718) Dos sucesos tales que la ocurrencia de uno de ellos afecta a la ocurrencia del otro.	Two cards are drawn from a deck without replacement. The events "the first is a 3" and "the second is a 3" are dependent. **Se sacan dos cartas de una baraja y no se reemplazan. Los sucesos "la primera es un 3" y "la segunda es un 3" son dependientes.**
dependent system (p. 154) A consistent system of equations that has infinitely many solutions. **sistema dependiente** (pág. 154) Sistema compatible de ecuaciones que tiene infinitas soluciones.	$2x - y = 3$ $4x - 2y = 6$ Any ordered pair $(x, 2x - 3)$ is a solution of the system above, so there are infinitely many solutions. **Cualquier par ordenado $(x, 2x - 3)$ es una solución del sistema que figura arriba, por lo que hay infinitas soluciones.**

dependent variable (p. 74) The output variable in an equation in two variables. **variable dependiente** (pág. 74) La variable de salida de una ecuación con dos variables.	*See* independent variable. *Ver* variable independiente.
determinant (p. 203) A real number associated with any square matrix A, denoted by $\det A$ or $\lvert A \rvert$. **determinante** (pág. 203) Número real asociado a toda matriz cuadrada A, denotada por $\det A$ o $\lvert A \rvert$.	$\det \begin{bmatrix} 5 & 4 \\ 3 & 1 \end{bmatrix} = 5(1) - 3(4) = -7$ $\det \begin{bmatrix} a & b \\ c & d \end{bmatrix} = ad - cb$
dimensions of a matrix (p. 187) The dimensions of a matrix with m rows and n columns are $m \times n$. **dimensiones de una matriz** (pág. 187) Las dimensiones de una matriz con m filas y n columnas son $m \times n$.	A matrix with 2 rows and 3 columns has the dimensions 2×3 (read "2 by 3"). Una matriz con 2 filas y 3 columnas tiene por dimensiones 2×3 (leído "2 por 3").
direct variation (p. 107) Two variables x and y show direct variation provided that $y = ax$ where a is a nonzero constant. **variación directa** (pág. 107) Dos variables x e y indican una variación directa siempre que $y = ax$, donde a es una constante distinta de cero.	The equation $5x + 2y = 0$ represents direct variation because it is equivalent to the equation $y = -\frac{5}{2}x$. La ecuación $5x + 2y = 0$ representa una variación directa ya que es equivalente a la ecuación $y = -\frac{5}{2}x$.
directrix of a parabola (p. 620) *See* parabola. **directriz de una parábola** (pág. 620) *Ver* parábola.	*See* parabola. *Ver* parábola.
discrete function (p. 80) A function whose graph consists of separate points. **función discreta** (pág. 80) Función cuya gráfica consiste en puntos aislados.	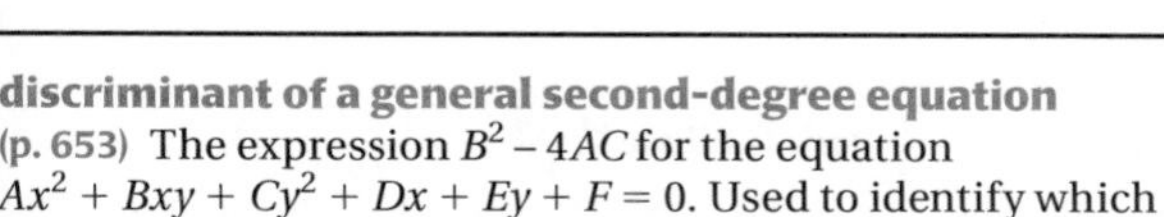
discriminant of a general second-degree equation (p. 653) The expression $B^2 - 4AC$ for the equation $Ax^2 + Bxy + Cy^2 + Dx + Ey + F = 0$. Used to identify which type of conic the equation represents. **discriminante de una ecuación general de segundo grado** (pág. 653) La expresión $B^2 - 4AC$ para la ecuación $Ax^2 + Bxy + Cy^2 + Dx + Ey + F = 0$. Se usa para identificar qué tipo de cónica representa la ecuación.	For the equation $4x^2 + y^2 - 8x - 8 = 0$, $A = 4$, $B = 0$, and $C = 1$. $B^2 - 4AC = 0^2 - 4(4)(1) = -16$ Because $B^2 - 4AC < 0$, $B = 0$, and $A \neq C$, the conic is an ellipse. Para la ecuación $4x^2 + y^2 - 8x - 8 = 0$, $A = 4$, $B = 0$ y $C = 1$. $B^2 - 4AC = 0^2 - 4(4)(1) = -16$ Debido a que $B^2 - 4AC < 0$, $B = 0$ y $A \neq C$, la cónica es un elipse.

ENGLISH-SPANISH GLOSSARY

discriminant of a quadratic equation (p. 294) The expression $b^2 - 4ac$ for the quadratic equation $ax^2 + bx + c = 0$; also the expression under the radical sign in the quadratic formula. **discriminante de una ecuación cuadrática** (pág. 294) La expresión $b^2 - 4ac$ para la ecuación cuadrática $ax^2 + bx + c = 0$; es también la expresión situada bajo el signo radical de la fórmula cuadrática.	The value of the discriminant of $2x^2 - 3x - 7 = 0$ is $b^2 - 4ac = (-3)^2 - 4(2)(-7) = 65$. **El valor del discriminante de $2x^2 - 3x - 7 = 0$ es $b^2 - 4ac = (-3)^2 - 4(2)(-7) = 65$.**
disjoint events (p. 707) Events A and B are disjoint if they have no outcomes in common; also called mutually exclusive events. **sucesos disjuntos** (pág. 707) Los sucesos A y B son disjuntos si no tienen casos en común; también se llaman sucesos mutuamente excluyentes.	When you randomly select a card from a standard deck of 52 cards, selecting a club and selecting a heart are disjoint events. **Al seleccionar al azar una carta de una baraja normal de 52 cartas, sacar una de tréboles y sacar una de corazones son sucesos disjuntos.**
distance formula (p. 614) The distance d between any two points (x_1, y_1) and (x_2, y_2) is $d = \sqrt{(x_2 - x_1)^2 + (y_2 - y_1)^2}$. **fórmula de la distancia** (pág. 614) La distancia d entre dos puntos cualesquiera (x_1, y_1) y (x_2, y_2) es $d = \sqrt{(x_2 - x_1)^2 + (y_2 - y_1)^2}$.	The distance between $(-3, 5)$ and $(4, -1)$ is $\sqrt{(4 - (-3))^2 + (-1 - 5)^2} = \sqrt{49 + 36} = \sqrt{85}$. **La distancia entre $(-3, 5)$ y $(4, -1)$ es $\sqrt{(4 - (-3))^2 + (-1 - 5)^2} = \sqrt{49 + 36} = \sqrt{85}$.**
domain (p. 72) The set of input values of a relation. **dominio** (pág. 72) El conjunto de los valores de entrada de una relación.	*See* relation. ***Ver* relación.**

E

eccentricity of a conic section (p. 665) The eccentricity e of a hyperbola or an ellipse is $\frac{c}{a}$ where c is the distance from each focus to the center and a is the distance from each vertex to the center. The eccentricity of a circle is $e = 0$. The eccentricity of a parabola is $e = 1$. **excentricidad de una sección cónica** (pág. 665) La excentricidad e de una hipérbola o de una elipse es $\frac{c}{a}$, donde c es la distancia entre cada foco y el centro y a es la distancia entre cada vértice y el centro. La excentricidad de un círculo es $e = 0$. La excentricidad de una parábola es $e = 1$.	For the ellipse $\frac{(x+4)^2}{36} + \frac{(y-2)^2}{16} = 1$, $c = \sqrt{36 - 16} = 2\sqrt{5}$, so the eccentricity is $e = \frac{c}{a} = \frac{2\sqrt{5}}{\sqrt{36}} = \frac{\sqrt{5}}{3} \approx 0.745$. **Para la elipse $\frac{(x+4)^2}{36} + \frac{(y-2)^2}{16} = 1$, $c = \sqrt{36 - 16} = 2\sqrt{5}$, por lo tanto la excentricidad es $e = \frac{c}{a} = \frac{2\sqrt{5}}{\sqrt{36}} = \frac{\sqrt{5}}{3} \approx 0.745$.**
element of a matrix (p. 187) Each number in a matrix. **elemento de una matriz** (pág. 187) Cada número de una matriz.	*See* matrix. ***Ver* matriz.**

ENGLISH-SPANISH GLOSSARY

element of a set (p. 715) Each object in a set; also called a member of the set.

elemento de un conjunto (pág. 715) Cada objeto de un conjunto; también se llama miembro del conjunto.

The elements of the set $A = \{1, 2, 3, 4\}$ are 1, 2, 3, and 4.

Los elementos del conjunto $A = \{1, 2, 3, 4\}$ son 1, 2, 3 y 4.

elimination method (p. 161) A method of solving a system of equations by multiplying equations by constants, then adding the revised equations to eliminate a variable.

método de eliminación (pág. 161) Método para resolver un sistema de ecuaciones en el que se multiplican ecuaciones por constantes y se agregan luego las ecuaciones revisadas para eliminar una variable.

To use the elimination method to solve the system with equations $3x - 7y = 10$ and $6x - 8y = 8$, multiply the first equation by -2 and add the equations to eliminate x.

Para usar el método de eliminación a fin de resolver el sistema con las ecuaciones $3x - 7y = 10$ y $6x - 8y = 8$, multiplica la primera ecuación por -2 y suma las ecuaciones para eliminar x.

ellipse (p. 634) The set of all points P in a plane such that the sum of the distances between P and two fixed points, called the foci, is a constant.

elipse (pág. 634) El conjunto de todos los puntos P de un plano tales que la suma de las distancias entre P y dos puntos fijos, llamados focos, es una constante.

y
co-vertex
puntos extremos
(0, b)
center
centro
vertex
vértice
(−a, 0)
d_1
P
d_2
vertex
vértice
(a, 0)
x
(−c, 0)
focus
foco
(c, 0)
focus
foco
major axis
eje mayor
minor axis
eje menor
(0, −b)
co-vertex
puntos extremos
$d_1 + d_2 =$ constant
constante

empty set (p. 715) The set with no elements, denoted Ø.

conjunto vacío (pág. 715) El conjunto que no tiene elementos, indicado Ø.

The set of positive integers less than 0 is the empty set, Ø.

El conjunto de los números enteros positivos menores que 0 es el conjunto vacío, Ø.

end behavior (p. 339) The behavior of the graph of a function as x approaches positive infinity $(+\infty)$ or negative infinity $(-\infty)$.

comportamiento (pág. 339) El comportamiento de la gráfica de una función al aproximarse x a infinito positivo $(+\infty)$ o a infinito negativo $(-\infty)$.

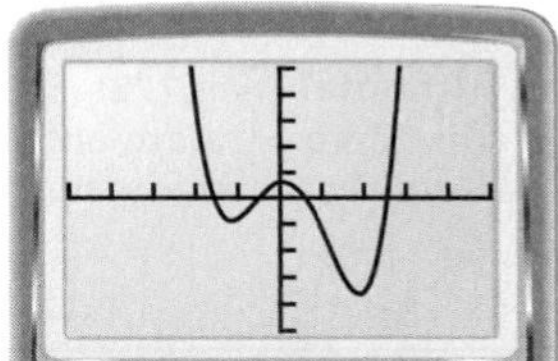

$f(x) \rightarrow +\infty$ as $x \rightarrow -\infty$ or as $x \rightarrow +\infty$.

$f(x) \rightarrow +\infty$ según $x \rightarrow -\infty$ o según $x \rightarrow +\infty$.

equal matrices (p. 187) Matrices that have the same dimensions and equal elements in corresponding positions.

matrices iguales (pág. 187) Matrices que tienen las mismas dimensiones y elementos iguales en posiciones correspondientes.

$$\begin{bmatrix} 6 & 0 \\ -\frac{4}{4} & \frac{3}{4} \end{bmatrix} = \begin{bmatrix} 3 \cdot 2 & -1 + 1 \\ -1 & 0.75 \end{bmatrix}$$

equation (p. 18) A statement that two expressions are equal. **ecuación** (pág. 18) Enunciado que establece la igualdad de dos expresiones.	$2x - 3 = 7$, $2x^2 = 4x$
equation in two variables (p. 74) An equation that contains two variables. **ecuación con dos variables** (pág. 74) Ecuación que tiene dos variables.	$y = 3x - 5$, $d = -16t^2 + 64$
equivalent equations (p. 18) Equations that have the same solution(s). **ecuaciones equivalentes** (pág. 18) Ecuaciones que tienen la misma solución o soluciones.	$x + 8 = 3$ and $4x = -20$ are equivalent because both have the solution -5. $x + 8 = 3$ y $4x = -20$ son equivalentes porque tienen ambas la solución -5.
equivalent expressions (p. 12) Two algebraic expressions that have the same value for all values of their variable(s). **expresiones equivalentes** (pág. 12) Dos expresiones algebraicas que tienen el mismo valor para todos los valores de la variable o variables.	$8x + 3x$ and $11x$ are equivalent expressions, as are $2(x - 3)$ and $2x - 6$. $8x + 3x$ y $11x$ son expresiones equivalentes, como también lo son $2(x - 3)$ y $2x - 6$.
equivalent inequalities (p. 42) Inequalities that have the same solution. **desigualdades equivalentes** (pág. 42) Desigualdades que tienen la misma solución.	$3n - 1 \leq 8$ and $n + 1.5 \leq 4.5$ are equivalent inequalities because the solution of both inequalities is all numbers less than or equal to 3. $3n - 1 \leq 8$ y $n + 1.5 \leq 4.5$ son desigualdades equivalentes ya que la solución de ambas son todos los números menores o iguales a 3.
experimental group (p. 773) A group that undergoes some procedure or treatment when an experiment is conducted. *See also* control group. **grupo experimental** (pág. 773) Grupo que se somete a algún procedimiento o tratamiento durante la realización de un experimento. *Ver también* grupo de control.	One group of headache sufferers, the experimental group, is given pills containing medication. Another group, the control group, is given pills containing no medication. Un grupo de personas que sufren de dolores de cabeza, el grupo experimental, recibe píldoras que contienen el medicamento. Otro grupo, el grupo de control, recibe píldoras sin el medicamento.
experimental probability (p. 700) A probability based on performing an experiment, conducting a survey, or looking at the history of an event. **probabilidad experimental** (pág. 700) Probabilidad basada en la realización de un experimento o una encuesta o en el estudio de la historia de un suceso.	You roll a six-sided die 100 times and get a 4 nineteen times. The experimental probability of rolling a 4 with the die is $\frac{19}{100} = 0.19$. Lanzas 100 veces un dado de seis caras y sale diecinueve veces el 4. La probabilidad experimental de que salga el 4 al lanzar el dado es $\frac{19}{100} = 0.19$.

explicit rule (p. 827) A rule for a sequence that gives the nth term a_n as a function of the term's position number n in the sequence.

The rules $a_n = -11 + 4n$ and $a_n = 3(2)^{n-1}$ are explicit rules for sequences.

regla explícita (pág. 827) Regla de una progresión que expresa el término enésimo a_n en función del número de posición n del término en la progresión.

Las reglas $a_n = -11 + 4n$ y $a_n = 3(2)^{n-1}$ son reglas explícitas de progresiones.

exponent (p. 10) The number or variable that represents the number of times the base of a power is used as a factor.

In the power 2^5, the exponent is 5.

exponente (pág. 10) El número o la variable que representa la cantidad de veces que la base de una potencia se usa como factor.

En la potencia 2^5, el exponente es 5.

exponential decay function (p. 486) If $a > 0$ and $0 < b < 1$, then the function $y = ab^x$ is an exponential decay function with decay factor b.

función de decrecimiento exponencial (pág. 486) Si $a > 0$ y $0 < b < 1$, entonces la función $y = ab^x$ es una función de decrecimiento exponencial con factor de decrecimiento b.

$y = 2\left(\frac{1}{4}\right)^x$

exponential equation (p. 515) An equation in which a variable expression occurs as an exponent.

$4^x = \left(\frac{1}{2}\right)^{x-3}$ is an exponential equation.

ecuación exponencial (pág. 515) Ecuación que tiene como exponente una expresión algebraica.

$4^x = \left(\frac{1}{2}\right)^{x-3}$ es una ecuación exponencial.

exponential function (p. 478) A function of the form $y = ab^x$, where $a \neq 0$, $b > 0$, and $b \neq 1$.

See exponential growth function *and* exponential decay function.

función exponencial (pág. 478) Función de la forma $y = ab^x$, donde $a \neq 0$, $b > 0$ y $b \neq 1$.

Ver función de crecimiento exponencial *y* función de decrecimiento exponencial.

exponential growth function (p. 478) If $a > 0$ and $b > 1$, then the function $y = ab^x$ is an exponential growth function with growth factor b.

función de crecimiento exponencial (pág. 478) Si $a > 0$ y $b > 1$, entonces la función $y = ab^x$ es una función de crecimiento exponencial con factor de crecimiento b.

$y = \frac{1}{2} \cdot 4^x$

extraneous solution (p. 52) An apparent solution that must be rejected because it does not satisfy the original equation.

Solving $|2x + 12| = 4x$ gives the apparent solutions $x = 6$ and $x = -2$. The apparent solution -2 is extraneous because it does not satisfy the original equation.

solución extraña (pág. 52) Solución aparente que debe rechazarse ya que no satisface la ecuación original.

Al resolver $|2x + 12| = 4x$ se obtienen las soluciones aparentes $x = 6$ y $x = -2$. La solución aparente -2 es extraña ya no satisface la ecuación original.

1049

F

factor by grouping (p. 354) To factor a polynomial with four terms by grouping, factor common monomials from pairs of terms, and then look for a common binomial factor. **factorizar por grupos** (pág. 354) Para factorizar por grupos un polinomio con cuatro términos, factoriza unos monomios comunes a partir de los pares de términos y luego busca un factor binómico común.	$x^3 - 3x^2 - 16x + 48$ $= x^2(x-3) - 16(x-3)$ $= (x^2 - 16)(x-3)$ $= (x+4)(x-4)(x-3)$
factored completely (p. 353) A factorable polynomial with integer coefficients is factored completely if it is written as a product of unfactorable polynomials with integer coefficients. **completamente factorizado** (pág. 353) Un polinomio que puede factorizarse y que tiene coeficientes enteros está completamente factorizado si está escrito como producto de polinomios que no pueden factorizarse y que tienen coeficientes enteros.	$3x(x-5)$ is factored completely. $(x+2)(x^2-6x+8)$ is *not* factored completely because x^2-6x+8 can be factored as $(x-2)(x-4)$. $3x(x-5)$ está completamente factorizado. $(x+2)(x^2-6x+8)$ *no* está completamente factorizado ya que x^2-6x+8 puede factorizarse como $(x-2)(x-4)$.
factorial (p. 684) For any positive integer n, the expression $n!$, read "n factorial," is the product of all the integers from 1 to n. Also, 0! is defined to be 1. **factorial** (pág. 684) Para cualquier número entero positivo n, la expresión $n!$, leída "factorial de n", es el producto de todos los números enteros entre 1 y n. También, 0! se define como 1.	$6! = 6 \cdot 5 \cdot 4 \cdot 3 \cdot 2 \cdot 1 = 720$
feasible region (p. 174) In linear programming, the graph of the system of constraints. **región factible** (pág. 174) En la programación lineal, la gráfica del sistema de restricciones.	*See* linear programming. *Ver* programación lineal.
finite differences (p. 393) When the x-values in a data set are equally spaced, the differences of consecutive y-values are called finite differences. **diferencias finitas** (pág. 393) Cuando los valores de x de un conjunto de datos están a igual distancia entre sí, las diferencias entre los valores de y consecutivos se llaman diferencias finitas.	$f(x) = x^2$ $f(1)$ $f(2)$ $f(3)$ $f(4)$ 1 4 9 16 $4 - 1 = 3$ $9 - 4 = 5$ $16 - 9 = 7$ The first-order finite differences are 3, 5, and 7. Las diferencias finitas de primer orden son 3, 5 y 7.
foci of a hyperbola (p. 642) *See* hyperbola. **focos de una hipérbola** (pág. 642) *Ver* hipérbola.	*See* hyperbola. *Ver* hipérbola.
foci of an ellipse (p. 634) *See* ellipse. **focos de una elipse** (pág. 634) *Ver* elipse.	*See* ellipse. *Ver* elipse.

ENGLISH-SPANISH GLOSSARY

focus of a parabola (p. 620) *See* parabola. **foco de una parábola** (pág. 620) *Ver* parábola.	*See* parabola. *Ver* parábola.
formula (p. 26) An equation that relates two or more quantities, usually represented by variables. **fórmula** (pág. 26) Ecuación que relaciona dos o más cantidades que generalmente se representan por variables.	The formula $P = 2\ell + 2w$ relates the length and width of a rectangle to its perimeter. La fórmula $P = 2\ell + 2w$ relaciona el largo y el ancho de un rectángulo con su perímetro.
frequency of a periodic function (p. 910) The reciprocal of the period. Frequency is the number of cycles per unit of time. **frecuencia de una función periódica** (pág. 910) El recíproco del período. La frecuencia es el número de ciclos por unidad de tiempo.	$P = 2 \sin 4000\pi t$ has period $\frac{2\pi}{4000\pi} = \frac{1}{2000}$, so its frequency is 2000 cycles per second (hertz) when t represents time in seconds. $P = 2 \text{ sen } 4000\pi t$ tiene período $\frac{2\pi}{4000\pi} = \frac{1}{2000}$, por lo que su frecuencia es de 2000 ciclos por segundo (hertzios) cuando t representa el tiempo en segundos.
function (p. 73) A relation for which each input has exactly one output. **función** (pág. 73) Relación para la que cada entrada tiene exactamente una salida.	The relation $(-4, 6)$, $(3, -9)$, and $(7, -9)$ is a function. The relation $(0, 3)$, $(0, 6)$, and $(10, 8)$ is not a function because the input 0 is mapped onto both 3 and 6. La relación $(-4, 6)$, $(3, -9)$ y $(7, -9)$ es una función. La relación $(0, 3)$, $(0, 6)$ y $(10, 8)$ no es una función ya que la entrada 0 se hace corresponder tanto con 3 como con 6.
function notation (p. 75) Using $f(x)$ (or a similar symbol such as $g(x)$ or $h(x)$) to represent the dependent variable of a function. **notación de función** (pág. 75) Usar $f(x)$ (o un símbolo semejante como $g(x)$ o $h(x)$) para representar la variable dependiente de una función.	The linear function $y = mx + b$ can be written using function notation as $f(x) = mx + b$. La función lineal $y = mx + b$ escrita en notación de función es $f(x) = mx + b$.

G

general second-degree equation in *x* and *y* (p. 653) The form $Ax^2 + Bxy + Cy^2 + Dx + Ey + F = 0$. **ecuación general de segundo grado en *x* e *y*** (pág. 653) La forma $Ax^2 + Bxy + Cy^2 + Dx + Ey + F = 0$.	$16x^2 - 9y^2 - 96x + 36y - 36 = 0$ and $4x^2 + y^2 - 8x - 8 = 0$ are second-degree equations in x and y. $16x^2 - 9y^2 - 96x + 36y - 36 = 0$ y $4x^2 + y^2 - 8x - 8 = 0$ son ecuaciones de segundo grado en x e y.

ENGLISH-SPANISH GLOSSARY

geometric probability (p. 701) A probability found by calculating a ratio of two lengths, areas, or volumes. **probabilidad geométrica** (pág. 701) Probabilidad hallada al calcular una razón entre dos longitudes, áreas o volúmenes.	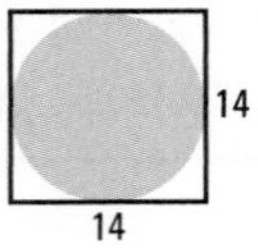 14 14 The probability that a dart that hits the square at random lands inside the circle is $\frac{\pi \cdot 7^2}{14^2} \approx 0.785$. La probabilidad de que un dardo que da con el blanco cuadrado, dé al azar en el interior del círculo es $\frac{\pi \cdot 7^2}{14^2} \approx 0.785$.
geometric sequence (p. 810) A sequence in which the ratio of any term to the previous term is constant. **progresión geométrica** (pág. 810) Progresión en la que la razón entre cualquier término y el término precedente es constante.	−19, 38, −76, 152 is a geometric sequence with common ratio −2. −19, 38, −76, 152 es una progresión geométrica con una razón común de −2.
geometric series (p. 812) The expression formed by adding the terms of a geometric sequence. **serie geométrica** (pág. 812) La expresión formada al sumar los términos de una progresión geométrica.	$\sum_{i=1}^{5} 4(3)^{i-1} = 4 + 12 + 36 + 108 + 324$
graph of a linear inequality in two variables (p. 132) The set of all points in a coordinate plane that represent solutions of the inequality. **gráfica de una desigualdad lineal con dos variables** (pág. 132) El conjunto de todos los puntos de un plano de coordenadas que representan las soluciones de la desigualdad.	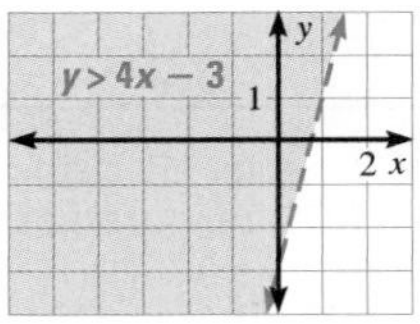 $y > 4x - 3$ y, 1, 2, x
graph of a system of linear inequalities (p. 168) The graph of all solutions of the system. **gráfica de un sistema de desigualdades lineales** (pág. 168) La gráfica de todas las soluciones del sistema.	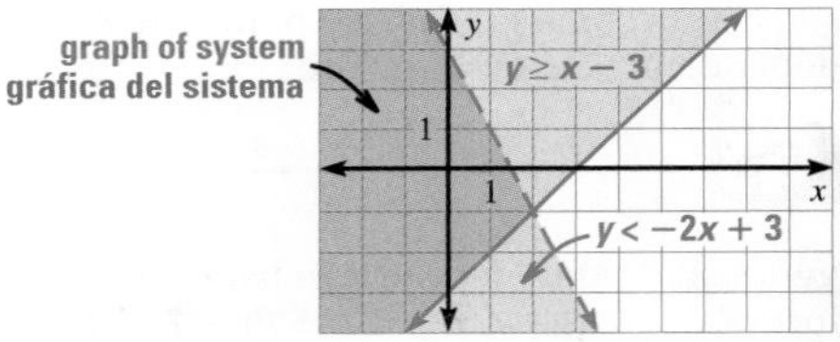 graph of system gráfica del sistema $y \geq x - 3$ $y < -2x + 3$ y, 1, 1, x
graph of an equation in two variables (p. 74) The set of all points (x, y) that represent solutions of the equation. **gráfica de una ecuación con dos variables** (pág. 74) El conjunto de todos los puntos (x, y) que representan soluciones de la ecuación.	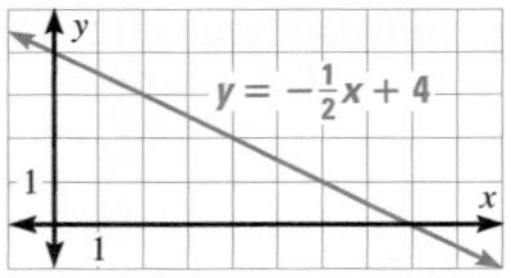 $y = -\frac{1}{2}x + 4$ y, 1, 1, x

ENGLISH-SPANISH GLOSSARY

graph of an inequality in one variable (p. 41) All points on a number line that represent solutions of the inequality.

gráfica de una desigualdad con una variable (pág. 41) Todos los puntos de una recta numérica que representan soluciones de la desigualdad.

growth factor (p. 478) The quantity b in the exponential growth function $y = ab^x$ with $a > 0$ and $b > 1$.

factor de crecimiento (pág. 478) La cantidad b de la función de crecimiento exponencial $y = ab^x$, con $a > 0$ y $b > 1$.

The growth factor for the function $y = 8(3.4)^x$ is 3.4.

El factor de crecimiento de la función $y = 8(3.4)^x$ es 3.4.

H

half-planes (p. 132) The two regions into which the boundary line of a linear inequality divides the coordinate plane.

semiplanos (pág. 132) Las dos regiones en que la recta límite de una desigualdad lineal divide al plano de coordenadas.

The solution of $y < 3$ is the half-plane consisting of all the points below the line $y = 3$.

La solución de $y < 3$ es el semi-plano que consta de todos los puntos que se encuentran debajo de la recta $y = 3$.

hyperbola (pp. 558, 642) The set of all points P in a plane such that the difference of the distances from P to two fixed points, called the foci, is constant.

hipérbola (págs. 558, 642) El conjunto de todos los puntos P de un plano tales que la diferencia de distancias entre P y dos puntos fijos, llamados focos, es constante.

I

identity (p. 12) A statement that equates two equivalent expressions.

identidad (pág. 12) Enunciado que hace iguales a dos expresiones equivalentes.

$8x + 3x = 11x$ and $2(x - 3) = 2x - 6$ are identities.

$8x + 3x = 11x$ y $2(x - 3) = 2x - 6$ son identidades.

identity matrix (p. 210) The $n \times n$ matrix that has 1's on the main diagonal and 0's elsewhere.

matriz identidad (pág. 210) La matriz $n \times n$ que tiene los 1 en la diagonal principal y los 0 en las otras posiciones.

The 2×2 identity matrix is $\begin{bmatrix} 1 & 0 \\ 0 & 1 \end{bmatrix}$.

La matriz identidad 2×2 es $\begin{bmatrix} 1 & 0 \\ 0 & 1 \end{bmatrix}$.

1053

imaginary number (p. 276) A complex number $a + bi$ where $b \neq 0$. **número imaginario** (pág. 276) Un número complejo $a + bi$, donde $b \neq 0$.	$5i$ and $2 - i$ are imaginary numbers. **$5i$ y $2 - i$ son números imaginarios.**
imaginary unit *i* (p. 275) $i = \sqrt{-1}$, so $i^2 = -1$. **unidad imaginaria *i*** (pág. 275) $i = \sqrt{-1}$, por lo que $i^2 = -1$.	$\sqrt{-3} = i\sqrt{3}$
inconsistent system (p. 154) A system of equations that has no solution. **sistema incompatible** (pág. 154) Sistema de ecuaciones que no tiene solución.	$x + y = 4$ $x + y = 1$ The system above has no solution because the sum of two numbers cannot be both 4 and 1. **El sistema de arriba no tiene ninguna solución porque la suma de dos números no puede ser 4 y 1.**
independent events (p. 717) Two events such that the occurrence of one event has no effect on the occurrence of the other event. **sucesos independientes** (pág. 717) Dos sucesos tales que la ocurrencia de uno de ellos no afecta a la ocurrencia del otro.	If a coin is tossed twice, the outcome of the first toss (heads or tails) and the outcome of the second toss are independent events. **Al lanzar una moneda dos veces, el resultado del primer lanzamiento (cara o cruz) y el resultado del segundo lanzamiento son sucesos independientes.**
independent system (p. 154) A consistent system that has exactly one solution. **sistema independiente** (pág. 154) Sistema compatible que tiene exactamente una solución.	The system consisting of $4x + y = 8$ and $2x - 3y = 18$ has exactly one solution, $(3, -4)$. **El sistema que consiste de $4x + y = 8$ y $2x - 3y = 18$ tiene exactamente una solución, $(3, -4)$.**
independent variable (p. 74) The input variable in an equation in two variables. **variable independiente** (pág. 74) La variable de entrada de una ecuación con dos variables.	In $y = 3x - 5$, the independent variable is x. The dependent variable is y because the value of y depends on the value of x. **En $y = 3x - 5$, la variable independiente es x. La variable dependiente es y ya que el valor de y depende del valor de x.**
index of a radical (p. 414) The integer n, greater than 1, in the expression $\sqrt[n]{a}$. **índice de un radical** (pág. 414) El número entero n, que es mayor que 1 y aparece en la expresión $\sqrt[n]{a}$.	The index of $\sqrt[3]{-216}$ is 3. **El índice de $\sqrt[3]{-216}$ es 3.**
initial side of an angle (p. 859) *See* terminal side of an angle. **lado inicial de un ángulo** (pág. 859) *Ver* lado terminal de un ángulo.	*See* standard position of an angle. ***Ver* posición normal de un ángulo.**

ENGLISH-SPANISH GLOSSARY

1054

intercept form of a quadratic function (p. 246) The form $y = a(x - p)(x - q)$, where the x-intercepts of the graph are p and q. **forma de intercepto de una función cuadrática** (pág. 246) La forma $y = a(x - p)(x - q)$, donde los interceptos en x de la gráfica son p y q.	The function $y = 2(x + 3)(x - 1)$ is in intercept form. La función $y = 2(x + 3)(x - 1)$ está en la forma de intercepto.
intersection of sets (p. 715) The intersection of two sets A and B, written $A \cap B$, is the set of all elements in *both* A and B. **intersección de conjuntos** (pág. 715) La intersección de dos conjuntos A y B, escrita $A \cap B$, es el conjunto de todos los elementos que están *tanto* en A *como* en B.	If $A = \{1, 2, 4, 8\}$ and $B = \{2, 4, 6, 8, 10\}$, then $A \cap B = \{2, 4, 8\}$. Si $A = \{1, 2, 4, 8\}$ y $B = \{2, 4, 6, 8, 10\}$, entonces $A \cap B = \{2, 4, 8\}$.
inverse cosine function (p. 875) If $-1 \le a \le 1$, then the inverse cosine of a is an angle θ, written $\theta = \cos^{-1} a$, where $\cos \theta = a$ and $0 \le \theta \le \pi$ (or $0° \le \theta \le 180°$). **función inversa del coseno** (pág. 875) Si $-1 \le a \le 1$, entonces el coseno inverso de a es un ángulo θ, escrito $\theta = \cos^{-1} a$, donde $\cos \theta = a$ y $0 \le \theta \le \pi$ (ó $0° \le \theta \le 180°$).	When $0° \le \theta \le 180°$, the angle θ whose cosine is $\frac{1}{2}$ is 60°, so $\theta = \cos^{-1} \frac{1}{2} = 60°$ (or $\theta = \cos^{-1} \frac{1}{2} = \frac{\pi}{3}$). Cuando $0° \le \theta \le 180°$, el ángulo θ cuyo coseno es $\frac{1}{2}$ es de 60°, por lo que $\theta = \cos^{-1} \frac{1}{2} = 60°$ (ó $\theta = \cos^{-1} \frac{1}{2} = \frac{\pi}{3}$).
inverse function (p. 438) An inverse relation that is a function. Functions f and g are inverses provided that $f(g(x)) = x$ and $g(f(x)) = x$. **función inversa** (pág. 438) Relación inversa que es una función. Las funciones f y g son inversas siempre que $f(g(x)) = x$ y $g(f(x)) = x$.	$f(x) = x + 5;\ g(x) = x - 5$ $f(g(x)) = (x - 5) + 5 = x$ $g(f(x)) = (x + 5) - 5 = x$ So, f and g are inverse functions. Entonces, f y g son funciones inversas.
inverse matrices (p. 210) Two $n \times n$ matrices are inverses of each other if their product (in both orders) is the $n \times n$ identity matrix. *See also* identity matrix. **matrices inversas** (pág. 210) Dos matrices $n \times n$ son inversas entre sí si su producto (de ambos órdenes) es la matriz identidad $n \times n$. *Ver también* matriz identidad.	$\begin{bmatrix} -5 & 8 \\ 2 & -3 \end{bmatrix}^{-1} = \begin{bmatrix} 3 & 8 \\ 2 & 5 \end{bmatrix}$ because / ya que $\begin{bmatrix} 3 & 8 \\ 2 & 5 \end{bmatrix}\begin{bmatrix} -5 & 8 \\ 2 & -3 \end{bmatrix} = \begin{bmatrix} 1 & 0 \\ 0 & 1 \end{bmatrix}$ and / y $\begin{bmatrix} -5 & 8 \\ 2 & -3 \end{bmatrix}\begin{bmatrix} 3 & 8 \\ 2 & 5 \end{bmatrix} = \begin{bmatrix} 1 & 0 \\ 0 & 1 \end{bmatrix}$.
inverse relation (p. 438) A relation that interchanges the input and output values of the original relation. The graph of an inverse relation is a reflection of the graph of the original relation, with $y = x$ as the line of reflection. **relación inversa** (pág. 438) Relación en la que se intercambian los valores de entrada y de salida de la relación original. La gráfica de una relación inversa es una reflexión de la gráfica de la relación original, con $y = x$ como eje de reflexión.	To find the inverse of $y = 3x - 5$, switch x and y to obtain $x = 3y - 5$. Then solve for y to obtain the inverse relation $y = \frac{1}{3}x + \frac{5}{3}$. Para hallar la inversa de $y = 3x - 5$, intercambia x e y para obtener $x = 3y - 5$. Luego resuelve para y para obtener la relación inversa $y = \frac{1}{3}x + \frac{5}{3}$.

ENGLISH-SPANISH GLOSSARY

inverse sine function (p. 875) If $-1 \le a \le 1$, then the inverse sine of a is an angle θ, written $\theta = \sin^{-1} a$, where $\sin \theta = a$ and $-\frac{\pi}{2} \le \theta \le \frac{\pi}{2}$ (or $-90° \le \theta \le 90°$).

función inversa del seno (pág. 875) Si $-1 \le a \le 1$, entonces el seno inverso de a es un ángulo θ, escrito $\theta = \text{sen}^{-1} a$, donde $\text{sen}\, \theta = a$ y $-\frac{\pi}{2} \le \theta \le \frac{\pi}{2}$ (ó $-90° \le \theta \le 90°$).

When $-90° \le \theta \le 90°$, the angle θ whose sine is $\frac{1}{2}$ is 30°, so $\theta = \sin^{-1} \frac{1}{2} = 30°$ (or $\theta = \sin^{-1} \frac{1}{2} = \frac{\pi}{6}$).

Cuando $-90° \le \theta \le 90°$, el ángulo θ cuyo seno es $\frac{1}{2}$ es de 30°, por lo que $\theta = \text{sen}^{-1} \frac{1}{2} = 30°$ (ó $\theta = \text{sen}^{-1} \frac{1}{2} = \frac{\pi}{6}$).

inverse tangent function (p. 875) If a is any real number, then the inverse tangent of a is an angle θ, written $\theta = \tan^{-1} a$, where $\tan \theta = a$ and $-\frac{\pi}{2} < \theta < \frac{\pi}{2}$ (or $-90° < \theta < 90°$).

función inversa de la tangente (pág. 875) Si a es un número real cualquiera, entonces la tangente inversa de a es un ángulo θ, escrito $\theta = \tan^{-1} a$, donde $\tan \theta = a$ y $-\frac{\pi}{2} < \theta < \frac{\pi}{2}$ (ó $-90° < \theta < 90°$).

When $-90° < \theta < 90°$, the angle θ whose tangent is $-\sqrt{3}$ is $-60°$, so $\theta = \tan^{-1}(-\sqrt{3}) = -60°$ (or $\theta = \tan^{-1}(-\sqrt{3}) = -\frac{\pi}{3}$).

Cuando $-90° < \theta < 90°$, el ángulo θ cuya tangente es $-\sqrt{3}$ es de $-60°$, por lo que $\theta = \tan^{-1}(-\sqrt{3}) = -60°$ (ó $\theta = \tan^{-1}(-\sqrt{3}) = -\frac{\pi}{3}$).

inverse variation (p. 551) The relationship of two variables x and y if there is a nonzero number a such that $y = \frac{a}{x}$.

variación inversa (pág. 551) La relación entre dos variables x e y si hay un número a distinto de cero tal que $y = \frac{a}{x}$.

The equations $xy = 7$ and $y = -\frac{3}{x}$ represent inverse variation.

Las ecuaciones $xy = 7$ e $y = -\frac{3}{x}$ representan la variación inversa.

iteration (p. 830) The repeated composition of a function with itself. The result of one iteration is $f(f(x))$, and of two iterations is $f(f(f(x)))$.

iteración (pág. 830) La composición repetida de una función usando la función misma. El resultado de una iteración es $f(f(x))$, y el de dos iteraciones es $f(f(f(x)))$.

$f(x) = -3x + 1;\ x_0 = 2$

$x_1 = f(x_0) = f(2) = -3(2) + 1 = -5$

$x_2 = f(x_1) = f(-5) = -3(-5) + 1 = 16$

$x_3 = f(x_2) = f(16) = -3(16) + 1 = -47$

joint variation (p. 553) A relationship that occurs when a quantity varies directly with the product of two or more other quantities.

variación conjunta (pág. 553) Relación producida cuando una cantidad varía directamente con el producto de dos o más otras cantidades.

The equation $z = 5xy$ represents joint variation.

La ecuación $z = 5xy$ representa la variación conjunta.

L

law of cosines (p. 889) If $\triangle ABC$ has sides of length a, b, and c as shown, then $a^2 = b^2 + c^2 - 2bc \cos A$, $b^2 = a^2 + c^2 - 2ac \cos B$, and $c^2 = a^2 + b^2 - 2ab \cos C$.

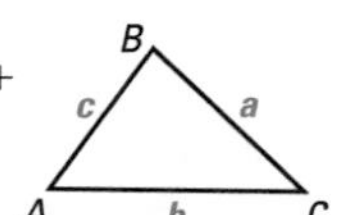

ley de los cosenos (pág. 889) Si $\triangle ABC$ tiene lados de longitud a, b y c como se indica, entonces $a^2 = b^2 + c^2 - 2bc \cos A$, $b^2 = a^2 + c^2 - 2ac \cos B$ y $c^2 = a^2 + b^2 - 2ab \cos C$.

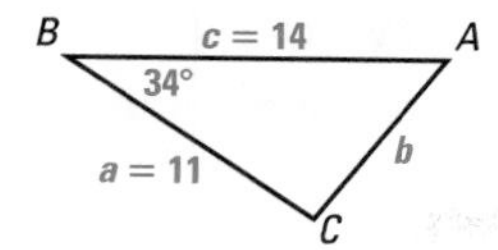

$$b^2 = a^2 + c^2 - 2ac \cos B$$
$$b^2 = 11^2 + 14^2 - 2(11)(14) \cos 34°$$
$$b^2 \approx 61.7$$
$$b \approx 7.85$$

law of sines (p. 882) If $\triangle ABC$ has sides of length a, b, and c as shown, then

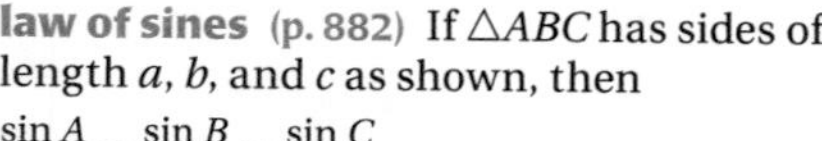

$$\frac{\sin A}{a} = \frac{\sin B}{b} = \frac{\sin C}{c}.$$

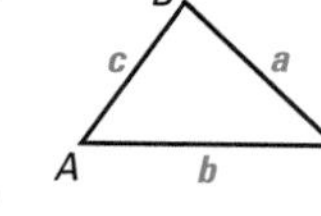

ley de los senos (pág. 882) Si $\triangle ABC$ tiene lados de longitud a, b y c como se indica, entonces $\frac{\text{sen } A}{a} = \frac{\text{sen } B}{b} = \frac{\text{sen } C}{c}$.

$\frac{\sin 25°}{15} = \frac{\sin 107°}{c} \rightarrow c \approx 33.9$

$\frac{\text{sen } 25°}{15} = \frac{\text{sen } 107°}{c} \rightarrow c \approx 33.9$

leading coefficient (p. 337) The coefficient in the term of a polynomial function that has the greatest exponent.

coeficiente inicial (pág. 337) En una función polinómica, el coeficiente del término con el mayor exponente.

See polynomial function.

Ver función polinómica.

like radicals (p. 422) Radical expressions with the same index and radicand.

radicales semejantes (pág. 422) Expresiones radicales con el mismo índice y el mismo radicando.

$\sqrt[4]{10}$ and $7\sqrt[4]{10}$ are like radicals.

$\sqrt[4]{10}$ y $7\sqrt[4]{10}$ son radicales semejantes.

like terms (p. 12) Terms that have the same variable parts. Constant terms are also like terms.

términos semejantes (pág. 12) Términos que tienen las mismas variables. Los términos constantes también son términos semejantes.

In the algebraic expression
$5x^2 + (-3x) + 7 + 4x + (-2)$,
$-3x$ and $4x$ are like terms, and 7 and -2 are like terms.

En la expresión algebraica
$5x^2 + (-3x) + 7 + 4x + (-2)$,
$-3x$ y $4x$ son términos semejantes, y 7 y -2 también lo son.

linear equation in one variable (p. 18) An equation that can be written in the form $ax + b = 0$ where a and b are constants and $a \neq 0$.

ecuación lineal con una variable (pág. 18) Ecuación que puede escribirse en la forma $ax + b = 0$, donde a y b son constantes y $a \neq 0$.

The equation $\frac{4}{5}x + 8 = 0$ is a linear equation in one variable.

La ecuación $\frac{4}{5}x + 8 = 0$ es una ecuación lineal con una variable.

ENGLISH-SPANISH GLOSSARY

linear equation in three variables (p. 178) An equation of the form $ax + by + cz = d$ where a, b, and c are not all zero. **ecuación lineal con tres variables** (pág. 178) Ecuación de la forma $ax + by + cz = d$, donde a, b y c no son todos cero.	$2x + y - z = 5$ is a linear equation in three variables. $2x + y - z = 5$ es una ecuación lineal con tres variables.
linear function (p. 75) A function that can be written in the form $y = mx + b$ where m and b are constants. **función lineal** (pág. 75) Función que puede escribirse en la forma $y = mx + b$, donde m y b son constantes.	The function $y = -2x - 1$ is a linear function with $m = -2$ and $b = -1$. La función $y = -2x - 1$ es una función lineal con $m = -2$ y $b = -1$.
linear inequality in one variable (p. 41) An inequality that can be written in one of the following forms, where a and b are real numbers and $a \neq 0$: $ax + b < 0$, $ax + b \leq 0$, $ax + b > 0$, or $ax + b \geq 0$. **desigualdad lineal con una variable** (pág. 41) Desigualdad que puede escribirse de una de las siguientes formas, donde a y b son números reales y $a \neq 0$: $ax + b < 0$, $ax + b \leq 0$, $ax + b > 0$ ó $ax + b \geq 0$.	$5x + 2 > 0$ is a linear inequality in one variable. $5x + 2 > 0$ es una desigualdad lineal con una variable.
linear inequality in two variables (p. 132) An inequality that can be written in one of the following forms: $Ax + By < C$, $Ax + By \leq C$, $Ax + By > C$, or $Ax + By \geq C$. **desigualdad lineal con dos variables** (pág. 132) Desigualdad que puede escribirse de una de las siguientes formas: $Ax + By < C$, $Ax + By \leq C$, $Ax + By > C$ o $Ax + By \geq C$.	$5x - 2y \geq -4$ is a linear inequality in two variables. $5x - 2y \geq -4$ es una desigualdad lineal con dos variables.
linear programming (p. 174) The process of maximizing or minimizing a linear objective function subject to a system of linear inequalities called constraints. The graph of the system of constraints is called the feasible region. **programación lineal** (pág. 174) El proceso de maximizar o minimizar una función objetivo lineal sujeta a un sistema de desigualdades lineales llamadas restricciones. La gráfica del sistema de restricciones se llama región factible.	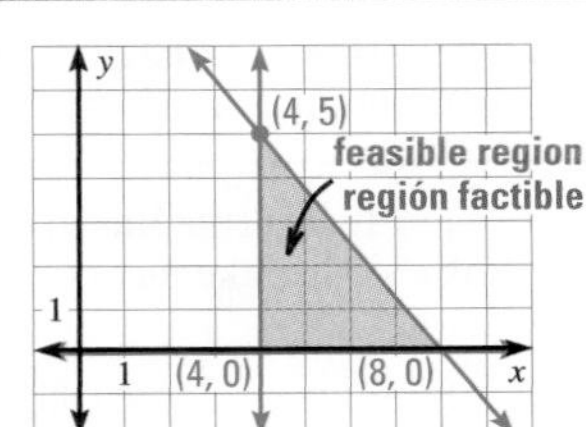 To maximize the objective function $P = 35x + 30y$ subject to the constraints $x \geq 4$, $y \geq 0$, and $5x + 4y \leq 40$, evaluate P at each vertex. The maximum value of 290 occurs at (4, 5). Para maximizar la función objetivo $P = 35x + 30y$ sujeta a las restricciones $x \geq 4$, $y \geq 0$ y $5x + 4y \leq 40$, evalúa P en cada vértice. El valor máximo de 290 ocurre en (4, 5).

ENGLISH-SPANISH GLOSSARY

local maximum (p. 388) The y-coordinate of a turning point of a function if the point is higher than all nearby points. **máximo local** (pág. 388) La coordenada y de un punto crítico de una función si el punto está situado más alto que todos los puntos cercanos.	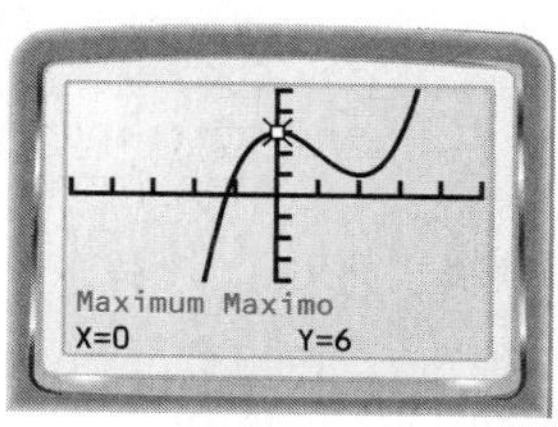 The function $f(x) = x^3 - 3x^2 + 6$ has a local maximum of $y = 6$ when $x = 0$. **La función $f(x) = x^3 - 3x^2 + 6$ tiene un máximo local de $y = 6$ cuando $x = 0$.**
local minimum (p. 388) The y-coordinate of a turning point of a function if the point is lower than all nearby points. **mínimo local** (pág. 388) La coordenada y de un punto crítico de una función si el punto está situado más bajo que todos los puntos cercanos.	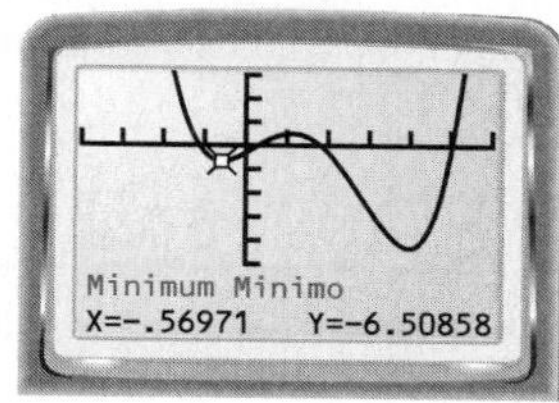 The function $f(x) = x^4 - 6x^3 + 3x^2 + 10x - 3$ has a local minimum of $y \approx -6.51$ when $x \approx -0.57$. **La función $f(x) = x^4 - 6x^3 + 3x^2 + 10x - 3$ tiene un mínimo local de $y \approx -6.51$ cuando $x \approx -0.57$.**
logarithm of y with base b (p. 499) Let b and y be positive numbers with $b \neq 1$. The logarithm of y with base b, denoted $\log_b y$ and read "log base b of y," is defined as follows: $\log_b y = x$ if and only if $b^x = y$. **logaritmo de y con base b** (pág. 499) Sean b e y números positivos, con $b \neq 1$. El logaritmo de y con base b, denotado por $\log_b y$ y leído "log base b de y", se define de esta manera: $\log_b y = x$ si y sólo si $b^x = y$.	$\log_2 8 = 3$ because $2^3 = 8$. $\log_{1/4} 4 = -1$ because $\left(\frac{1}{4}\right)^{-1} = 4$. **$\log_2 8 = 3$ ya que $2^3 = 8$.** **$\log_{1/4} 4 = -1$ ya que $\left(\frac{1}{4}\right)^{-1} = 4$.**
logarithmic equation (p. 517) An equation that involves a logarithm of a variable expression. **ecuación logarítmica** (pág. 517) Ecuación en la que aparece el logaritmo de una expresión algebraica.	$\log_5 (4x - 7) = \log_5 (x + 5)$ is a logarithmic equation. **$\log_5 (4x - 7) = \log_5 (x + 5)$ es una ecuación logarítmica.**

M

major axis of an ellipse (p. 634) The line segment joining the vertices of an ellipse. **eje mayor de una elipse** (pág. 634) El segmento de recta que une los vértices de una elipse.	*See* ellipse. ***Ver* elipse.**

ENGLISH-SPANISH GLOSSARY

margin of error (p. 768) The margin of error gives a limit on how much the response of a sample would be expected to differ from the response of the population. **margen de error** (pág. 768) El margen de error indica un límite acerca de cuánto se prevé que diferirían las respuestas obtenidas en una muestra de las obtenidas en la población.	If 40% of the people in a poll prefer candidate A, and the margin of error is ±4%, then it is expected that between 36% and 44% of the entire population prefer candidate A. **Si el 40% de los encuestados prefiere al candidato A y el margen de error es ±4%, entonces se prevé que entre el 36% y el 44% de la población total prefiere al candidato A.**
matrix, matrices (p. 187) A rectangular arrangement of numbers in rows and columns. Each number in a matrix is an element. **matriz, matrices** (pág. 187) Disposición rectangular de números colocados en filas y columnas. Cada numero de la matriz es un elemento.	$A = \begin{bmatrix} 4 & -1 & 5 \\ 0 & 6 & 3 \end{bmatrix}$ Matrix A has 2 rows and 3 columns. The element in the second row and first column is 0. **La matriz A tiene 2 filas y 3 columnas. El elemento en la segunda fila y en la primera columna es 0.**
matrix of constants (p. 212) The matrix of constants of the linear system $ax + by = e, cx + dy = f$ is $\begin{bmatrix} e \\ f \end{bmatrix}$. **matriz de constantes** (pág. 212) La matriz de constantes del sistema lineal $ax + by = e, cx + dy = f$ es $\begin{bmatrix} e \\ f \end{bmatrix}$.	*See* coefficient matrix. ***Ver* matriz coeficiente.**
matrix of variables (p. 212) The matrix of variables of the linear system $ax + by = e, cx + dy = f$ is $\begin{bmatrix} x \\ y \end{bmatrix}$. **matriz de variables** (pág. 212) La matriz de variables del sistema lineal $ax + by = e, cx + dy = f$ es $\begin{bmatrix} x \\ y \end{bmatrix}$.	*See* coefficient matrix. ***Ver* matriz coeficiente.**
maximum value of a quadratic function (p. 238) The y-coordinate of the vertex for $y = ax^2 + bx + c$ when $a < 0$. **valor máximo de una función cuadrática** (pág. 238) La coordenada y del vértice para $y = ax^2 + bx + c$ cuando $a < 0$.	 The maximum value of $y = -x^2 + 2x - 1$ is 0. **El valor máximo de $y = -x^2 + 2x - 1$ es 0.**
mean (p. 744) For the data set $x_1, x_2, \ldots, x_n$, the mean is $\bar{x} = \frac{x_1 + x_2 + \ldots + x_n}{n}$. Also called average. **media** (pág. 744) Para el conjunto de datos $x_1, x_2, \ldots, x_n$, la media es $\bar{x} = \frac{x_1 + x_2 + \ldots + x_n}{n}$. También se llama promedio.	*See* measure of central tendency. ***Ver* medida de tendencia central.**

ENGLISH-SPANISH GLOSSARY

measure of central tendency (p. 744) A number used to represent the center or middle of a set of data values. Mean, median, and mode are three measures of central tendency.	**14, 17, 18, 19, 20, 24, 24, 30, 32** The mean is $\frac{14 + 17 + 18 + \ldots + 32}{9} = \frac{198}{9} = 22$. The median is the middle number, 20. The mode is 24 because 24 occurs the most frequently.
medida de tendencia central (pág. 744) Número usado para representar el centro o la posición central de un conjunto de valores de datos. La media, la mediana y la moda son tres medidas de tendencia central.	La media es $\frac{14 + 17 + 18 + \ldots + 32}{9} = \frac{198}{9} = 22$. La mediana es el número central, 20. La moda es 24 ya que 24 ocurre más veces.
measure of dispersion (p. 745) A statistic that tells you how dispersed, or spread out, data values are. Range and standard deviation are measures of dispersion.	*See* range *and* standard deviation.
medida de dispersión (pág. 745) Estadística que te indica cómo se dispersan, o distribuyen, los valores de datos. El rango y la desviación típica son medidas de dispersión.	*Ver* rango *y* desviación típica.
median (p. 744) The median of n numbers is the middle number when the numbers are written in numerical order. If n is even, the median is the mean of the two middle numbers.	*See* measure of central tendency.
mediana (pág. 744) La mediana de n números es el número central cuando los números se escriben en orden numérico. Si n es par, la mediana es la media de los dos números centrales.	*Ver* medida de tendencia central.
midpoint formula (p. 615) The midpoint M of the line segment joining $A(x_1, y_1)$ and $B(x_2, y_2)$ is $M\left(\frac{x_1 + x_2}{2}, \frac{y_1 + y_2}{2}\right)$.	The midpoint of the line segment joining $(-2, 3)$ and $(8, 6)$ is $\left(\frac{-2 + 8}{2}, \frac{3 + 6}{2}\right) = \left(3, \frac{9}{2}\right)$.
fórmula del punto medio (pág. 615) El punto medio M del segmento de recta que une $A(x_1, y_1)$ y $B(x_2, y_2)$ es $M\left(\frac{x_1 + x_2}{2}, \frac{y_1 + y_2}{2}\right)$.	El punto medio del segmento de recta que une $(-2, 3)$ y $(8, 6)$ es $\left(\frac{-2 + 8}{2}, \frac{3 + 6}{2}\right) = \left(3, \frac{9}{2}\right)$.
minimum value of a quadratic function (p. 238) The y-coordinate of the vertex for $y = ax^2 + bx + c$ when $a > 0$. **valor mínimo de una función cuadrática** (pág. 238) La coordenada y del vértice para $y = ax^2 + bx + c$ cuando $a > 0$.	y 2 x $y = x^2 - 6x + 5$ (3, −4) The minimum value of $y = x^2 - 6x + 5$ is -4. El valor mínimo de $y = x^2 - 6x + 5$ es -4.
minor axis of an ellipse (p. 634) The line segment joining the co-vertices of an ellipse.	*See* ellipse.
eje menor de una elipse (pág. 634) El segmento de recta que une los puntos extremos de una elipse.	*Ver* elipse.

ENGLISH-SPANISH GLOSSARY

mode (p. 744) The mode of n numbers is the number or numbers that occur most frequently. **moda** (pág. 744) La moda de n números es el número o números que ocurren más veces.	*See* measure of central tendency. ***Ver* medida de tendencia central.**
monomial (p. 252) An expression that is either a number, a variable, or the product of a number and one or more variables with whole number exponents. **monomio** (pág. 252) Expresión que es un número, una variable o el producto de un número y una o más variables con exponentes naturales.	6, $0.2x$, $\frac{1}{2}ab$, and $-5.7n^4$ are monomials. **6, $0.2x$, $\frac{1}{2}ab$ y $-5.7n^4$ son monomios.**
mutually exclusive events (p. 707) *See* disjoint events. **sucesos mutuamente excluyentes** (pág. 707) *Ver* sucesos disjuntos.	*See* disjoint events. ***Ver* sucesos disjuntos.**

N

natural base *e* (p. 492) An irrational number defined as follows: As n approaches $+\infty$, $\left(1 + \frac{1}{n}\right)^n$ approaches $e \approx 2.718281828$. **base natural *e*** (pág. 492) Número irracional definido de esta manera: Al aproximarse n a $+\infty$, $\left(1 + \frac{1}{n}\right)^n$ se aproxima a $e \approx 2.718281828$.	*See* natural logarithm. ***Ver* logaritmo natural.**
natural logarithm (p. 500) A logarithm with base e. It can be denoted $\log_e$, but is more often denoted by ln. **logaritmo natural** (pág. 500) Logaritmo con base e. Puede denotarse $\log_e$, pero es más frecuente que se denote ln.	$\ln 0.3 \approx -1.204$ because $e^{-1.204} \approx (2.7183)^{-1.204} \approx 0.3$. **$\ln 0.3 \approx -1.204$ ya que $e^{-1.204} \approx (2.7183)^{-1.204} \approx 0.3$.**
negative correlation (p. 113) The paired data (x, y) have a negative correlation if y tends to decrease as x increases. **correlación negativa** (pág. 113) Los pares de datos (x, y) presentan una correlación negativa si y tiende a disminuir al aumentar x.	y x
normal curve (p. 757) A smooth, symmetrical, bell-shaped curve that can model normal distributions and approximate some binomial distributions. **curva normal** (pág. 757) Curva lisa, simétrica y con forma de campana que puede representar distribuciones normales y aproximar a algunas distribuciones binomiales.	*See* normal distribution. ***Ver* distribución normal.**

ENGLISH-SPANISH GLOSSARY

normal distribution (p. 757) A probability distribution with mean $\bar{x}$ and standard deviation σ modeled by a bell-shaped curve with the area properties shown at the right.

distribución normal (pág. 757) Una distribución de probabilidad con media $\bar{x}$ y desviación normal σ representada por una curva en forma de campana y que tiene las propiedades vistas a la derecha.

68%
95%
99.7%
$\bar{x}-3\sigma$ $\bar{x}-2\sigma$ $\bar{x}-\sigma$ $\bar{x}$ $\bar{x}+\sigma$ $\bar{x}+2\sigma$ $\bar{x}+3\sigma$

nth root of a (p. 414) For an integer n greater than 1, if $b^n = a$, then b is an nth root of a. Written as $\sqrt[n]{a}$.

raíz enésima de a (pág. 414) Para un número entero n mayor que 1, si $b^n = a$, entonces b es una raíz enésima de a. Se escribe $\sqrt[n]{a}$.

$\sqrt[3]{-216} = -6$ because $(-6)^3 = -216$.

$\sqrt[3]{-216} = -6$ ya que $(-6)^3 = -216$.

numerical expression (p. 10) An expression that consists of numbers, operations, and grouping symbols.

expresión numérica (pág. 10) Expresión formada por números, operaciones y signos de agrupación.

$-4(-3)^2 - 6(-3) + 11$ is a numerical expression.

$-4(-3)^2 - 6(-3) + 11$ es una expresión numérica.

O

objective function (p. 174) In linear programming, the linear function that is maximized or minimized.

función objetivo (pág. 174) En la programación lineal, la función lineal que se maximiza o minimiza.

See linear programming.

Ver programación lineal.

odds against (p. 699) When all outcomes are equally likely,

$$\text{Odds against event } A = \frac{\text{Number of outcomes not in } A}{\text{Number of outcomes in } A}.$$

probabilidad en contra (pág. 699) Cuando todos los casos son igualmente posibles,

$$\text{Probabilidad en contra del suceso } A = \frac{\text{Número de casos no del } A}{\text{Número de casos del } A}.$$

The odds against rolling a 4 using a standard six-sided die are $\frac{5}{1}$, or 5 : 1, because 5 outcomes correspond to not rolling a 4 and only 1 outcome corresponds to rolling a 4.

La probabilidad en contra de sacar el 4 al lanzar un dado normal de seis caras es $\frac{5}{1}$, ó 5 : 1, ya que 5 casos corresponden a un número que no sea el 4 y sólo 1 caso corresponde al 4.

odds in favor (p. 699) When all outcomes are equally likely,

$$\text{Odds in favor of event } A = \frac{\text{Number of outcomes in } A}{\text{Number of outcomes not in } A}.$$

probabilidad a favor (pág. 699) Cuando todos los casos son igualmente posibles,

$$\text{Probabilidad a favor del suceso } A = \frac{\text{Número de casos del } A}{\text{Número de casos no del } A}.$$

The odds in favor of rolling a 4 using a standard six-sided die are $\frac{1}{5}$, or 1 : 5, because only 1 outcome corresponds to rolling a 4 and 5 outcomes correspond to not rolling a 4.

La probabilidad a favor de sacar el 4 al lanzar un dado normal de seis caras es $\frac{1}{5}$, ó 1 : 5, ya que sólo 1 caso corresponde al 4 y 5 casos corresponden a un número que no sea el 4.

opposite (p. 4) The opposite, or additive inverse, of any number b is $-b$. **opuesto** (pág. 4) El opuesto, o inverso aditivo, de cualquier número b es $-b$.	6.2 and -6.2 are opposites. **6.2 y -6.2 son opuestos.**
ordered triple (p. 178) A set of three numbers of the form (x, y, z) that represents a point in space. **terna ordenada** (pág. 178) Un conjunto de tres números de la forma (x, y, z) que representa un punto en el espacio.	The ordered triple $(2, 1, -3)$ is a solution of the equation $4x + 2y + 3z = 1$. **La terna ordenada $(2, 1, -3)$ es una solución de la ecuación $4x + 2y + 3z = 1$.**
outlier (p. 746) A value that is much greater than or much less than most of the other values in a data set. **valor extremo** (pág. 746) Valor que es mucho mayor o mucho menor que la mayoría de los otros valores de un conjunto de datos.	3 is an outlier in the data set 3, 11, 12, 13, 13, 14, 15, 15, 15, 15, 17. **3 es un valor extremo del conjunto de datos 3, 11, 12, 13, 13, 14, 15, 15, 15, 15, 17.**

P

parabola (pp. 236, 620) The set of all points equidistant from a point called the focus and a line called the directrix. The graph of a quadratic function $y = ax^2 + bx + c$ is a parabola. **parábola** (págs. 236, 620) El conjunto de todos los puntos equidistantes de un punto, llamado foco, y de una recta, llamada directriz. La gráfica de una función cuadrática $y = ax^2 + bx + c$ es una parábola.	axis of symmetry eje de simetría focus foco vertex vértice directrix directriz
parallel lines (p. 84) Two lines in the same plane that do not intersect. **rectas paralelas** (pág. 84) Dos rectas del mismo plano que no se cortan.	y x
parent function (p. 89) The most basic function in a family of functions. **función básica** (pág. 89) La función más fundamental de una familia de funciones.	The parent function for the family of all linear functions is $y = x$. **La función básica de la familia de todas las funciones lineales es $y = x$.**
partial sum (p. 820) The sum S_n of the first n terms of an infinite series. **suma parcial** (pág. 820) La suma S_n de los n primeros términos de una serie infinita.	$\frac{1}{2} + \frac{1}{4} + \frac{1}{8} + \frac{1}{16} + \frac{1}{32} + \ldots$ The series above has the partial sums $S_1 = 0.5, S_2 = 0.75, S_3 \approx 0.88, S_4 \approx 0.94, \ldots$. **La serie de arriba tiene las sumas parciales $S_1 = 0.5, S_2 = 0.75, S_3 \approx 0.88, S_4 \approx 0.94, \ldots$.**

ENGLISH-SPANISH GLOSSARY

Pascal's triangle (p. 692) An arrangement of the values of ${}_nC_r$ in a triangular pattern in which each row corresponds to a value of n.

triángulo de Pascal (pág. 692) Disposición de los valores de ${}_nC_r$ en un patrón triangular en el que cada fila corresponde a un valor de n.

$${}_0C_0$$
$${}_1C_0 \quad {}_1C_1$$
$${}_2C_0 \quad {}_2C_1 \quad {}_2C_2$$
$${}_3C_0 \quad {}_3C_1 \quad {}_3C_2 \quad {}_3C_3$$
$${}_4C_0 \quad {}_4C_1 \quad {}_4C_2 \quad {}_4C_3 \quad {}_4C_4$$
$${}_5C_0 \quad {}_5C_1 \quad {}_5C_2 \quad {}_5C_3 \quad {}_5C_4 \quad {}_5C_5$$

period (p. 908) The horizontal length of each cycle of a periodic function.

período (pág. 908) La longitud horizontal de cada ciclo de una función periódica.

See periodic function.

Ver función periódica.

periodic function (p. 908) A function whose graph has a repeating pattern.

función periódica (pág. 908) Función cuya gráfica tiene un patrón que se repite.

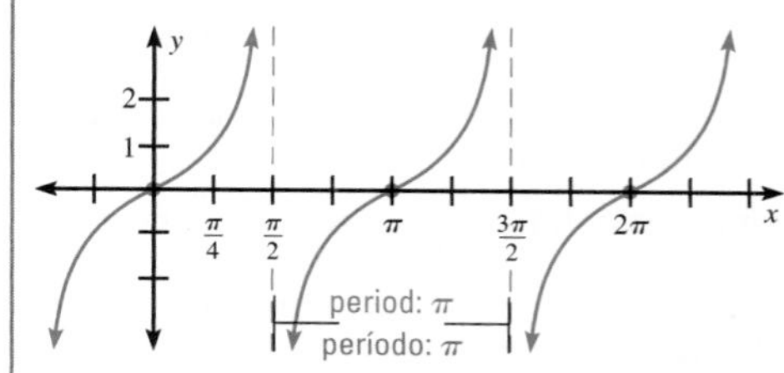

The graph shows 3 cycles of $y = \tan x$, a periodic function with a period of π.

La gráfica muestra 3 ciclos de $y = \tan x$, función periódica con período π.

permutation (p. 684) An ordering of objects. The number of permutations of r objects taken from a group of n distinct objects is denoted ${}_nP_r$ where ${}_nP_r = \frac{n!}{(n-r)!}$.

permutación (pág. 684) Ordenación de objetos. El número de permutaciones de r objetos tomados de un grupo de n objetos diferenciados se indica ${}_nP_r$, donde ${}_nP_r = \frac{n!}{(n-r)!}$.

There are 6 permutations of the $n = 3$ letters A, B, and C taken $r = 3$ at a time: ABC, ACB, BAC, BCA, CAB, and CBA.

Hay 6 permutaciones de las letras $n = 3$ A, B y C tomadas $r = 3$ cada vez: ABC, ACB, BAC, BCA, CAB y CBA.

perpendicular lines (p. 84) Two lines in the same plane that intersect to form a right angle.

rectas perpendiculares (pág. 84) Dos rectas del mismo plano que al cortarse forman un ángulo recto.

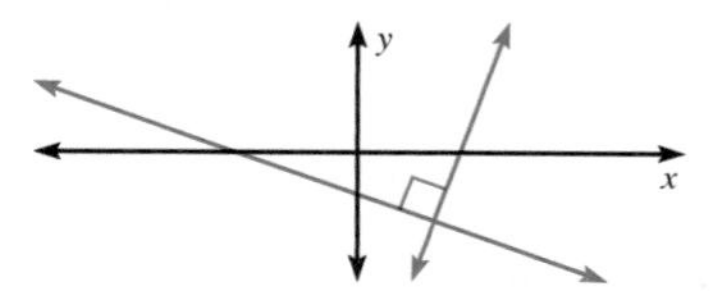

piecewise function (p. 130) A function defined by at least two equations, each of which applies to a different part of the function's domain.

función definida a trozos (pág. 130) Función definida por al menos dos ecuaciones, cada una de las cuales se aplica a una parte diferente del dominio de la función.

$$g(x) = \begin{cases} 3x - 1, & \text{if } x < 1 \\ 0, & \text{if } x = 1 \\ -x + 4, & \text{if } x > 1 \end{cases} \qquad g(x) = \begin{cases} 3x - 1, & \text{si } x < 1 \\ 0, & \text{si } x = 1 \\ -x + 4, & \text{si } x > 1 \end{cases}$$

1065

point-slope form (p. 98) An equation of a line written in the form $y - y_1 = m(x - x_1)$ where the line passes through the point (x_1, y_1) and has a slope of m.

The equation $y + 2 = -4(x - 5)$ is in point-slope form.

forma punto-pendiente (pág. 98) Ecuación de una recta escrita en la forma $y - y_1 = m(x - x_1)$, donde la recta pasa por el punto (x_1, y_1) y tiene pendiente m.

La ecuación $y + 2 = -4(x - 5)$ está en la forma punto-pendiente.

polynomial (p. 337) A monomial or a sum of monomials, each of which is called a term of the polynomial. *See also* monomial.

-14, $x^4 - \frac{1}{4}x^2 + 3$, and $7b - \sqrt{3} + \pi b^2$ are polynomials.

polinomio (pág. 337) Monomio o suma de monomios, cada uno de los cuales se llama término del polinomio. *Ver también* monomio.

-14, $x^4 - \frac{1}{4}x^2 + 3$ y $7b - \sqrt{3} + \pi b^2$ son polinomios.

polynomial function (p. 337) A function of the form $f(x) = a_n x^n + a_{n-1}x^{n-1} + \cdots + a_1 x + a_0$ where $a_n \neq 0$, the exponents are all whole numbers, and the coefficients are all real numbers.

$f(x) = 11x^5 - 0.4x^2 + 16x - 7$ is a polynomial function. The degree of $f(x)$ is 5, the leading coefficient is 11, and the constant term is -7.

función polinómica (pág. 337) Función de la forma $f(x) = a_n x^n + a_{n-1}x^{n-1} + \cdots + a_1 x + a_0$ donde $a_n \neq 0$, los exponentes son todos números enteros y los coeficientes son todos números reales.

$f(x) = 11x^5 - 0.4x^2 + 16x - 7$ es una función polinómica. El grado de $f(x)$ es 5, el coeficiente inicial es 11 y el término constante es -7.

polynomial long division (p. 362) A method used to divide polynomials similar to the way you divide numbers.

división desarrollada polinómica (pág. 362) Método utilizado para dividir polinomios semejante a la manera en que divides números.

$$
\begin{array}{r}
x^2 + 7x + 7 \\
x - 2 \overline{)\, x^3 + 5x^2 - 7x + 2} \\
\underline{x^3 - 2x^2} \qquad\qquad \\
7x^2 - 7x \qquad \\
\underline{7x^2 - 14x} \qquad \\
7x + 2 \\
\underline{7x - 14} \\
16
\end{array}
$$

$$\frac{x^3 + 5x^2 - 7x + 2}{x - 2} = x^2 + 7x + 7 + \frac{16}{x - 2}$$

population (p. 766) A group of people or objects that you want information about.

A sportswriter randomly selects 5% of college baseball coaches for a survey. The population is all college baseball coaches. The 5% of coaches selected is the sample.

población (pág. 766) Grupo de personas u objetos acerca del cual deseas informarte.

Un periodista deportiva selecciona al azar al 5% de los entrenadores universitarios de béisbol para que participe en una encuesta. La población son todos los entrenadores universitarios de béisbol. El 5% de los entrenadores que resultó seleccionado es la muestra.

positive correlation (p. 113) The paired data (x, y) have a positive correlation if y tends to increase as x increases.

correlacion positiva (pág. 113) Los pares de datos (x, y) presentan una correlación positiva si y tiende a aumentar al aumentar x.

power (p. 10) An expression that represents repeated multiplication of the same factor.

potencia (pág. 10) Expresión que representa la multiplicación repetida del mismo factor.

32 is the fifth power of 2 because $32 = 2 \cdot 2 \cdot 2 \cdot 2 \cdot 2 = 2^5$.

32 es la quinta potencia de 2 ya que $32 = 2 \cdot 2 \cdot 2 \cdot 2 \cdot 2 = 2^5$.

power function (p. 428) A function of the form $y = ax^b$, where a is a real number and b is a rational number.

función potencial (pág. 428) Función de la forma $y = ax^b$, donde a es un número real y b es un número racional.

$f(x) = 4x^{3/2}$ is a power function.

$f(x) = 4x^{3/2}$ es una función potencial.

probability distribution (p. 724) A function that gives the probability of each possible value of a random variable. The sum of all the probabilities in a probability distribution must equal 1.

distribución de probabilidades (pág. 724) Función que indica la probabilidad de cada valor posible de una variable aleatoria. La suma de todas las probabilidades de una distribución de probabilidades debe ser igual a 1.

Let the random variable X represent the number showing after rolling a standard six-sided die.

Sea la variable aleatoria X el número que salga al lanzar un dado normal de seis caras.

Probability Distribution for Rolling a Die **Distribución de probabilidad al lanzar un dado**						
X	1	2	3	4	5	6
$P(X)$	$\frac{1}{6}$	$\frac{1}{6}$	$\frac{1}{6}$	$\frac{1}{6}$	$\frac{1}{6}$	$\frac{1}{6}$

probability of an event (p. 698) A number from 0 to 1 that indicates the likelihood that the event will occur.

probabilidad de un suceso (pág. 698) Número entre 0 y 1 que indica la probabilidad de que ocurra el suceso.

See experimental probability, geometric probability, *and* theoretical probability.

***Ver* probabilidad experimental, probabilidad geométrica *y* probabilidad teórica.**

pure imaginary number (p. 276) A complex number $a + bi$ where $a = 0$ and $b \neq 0$.

número imaginario puro (pág. 276) Número complejo $a + bi$, donde $a = 0$ y $b \neq 0$.

$-4i$ and $1.2i$ are pure imaginary numbers.

$-4i$ y $1.2i$ son números imaginarios puros.

Q

quadrantal angle (p. 867) An angle in standard position whose terminal side lies on an axis.

ángulo cuadrantal (pág. 867) Ángulo en posición normal cuyo lado terminal se encuentra en un eje.

quadratic equation in one variable (p. 253) An equation that can be written in the form $ax^2 + bx + c = 0$ where $a \neq 0$.	The equation $x^2 - 5x = 36$ is a quadratic equation in one variable because it can be written in the form $x^2 - 5x - 36 = 0$.
ecuación cuadrática con una variable (pág. 253) Ecuación que puede escribirse en la forma $ax^2 + bx + c = 0$, donde $a \neq 0$.	**La ecuación $x^2 - 5x = 36$ es una ecuación cuadrática con una variable ya que puede escribirse en la forma $x^2 - 5x - 36 = 0$.**
quadratic form (p. 355) The form $au^2 + bu + c$, where u is any expression in x.	The expression $16x^4 - 8x^2 - 8$ is in quadratic form because it can be written as $u^2 - 2u - 8$ where $u = 4x^2$.
forma cuadrática (pág. 355) La forma $au^2 + bu + c$, donde u es cualquier expresión en x.	**La expresión $16x^4 - 8x^2 - 8$ está en la forma cuadrática ya que puede escribirse $u^2 - 2u - 8$, donde $u = 4x^2$.**
quadratic formula (p. 292) The formula $x = \frac{-b \pm \sqrt{b^2 - 4ac}}{2a}$ used to find the solutions of the quadratic equation $ax^2 + bx + c = 0$ when a, b, and c are real numbers and $a \neq 0$.	To solve $3x^2 + 6x + 2 = 0$, substitute 3 for a, 6 for b, and 2 for c in the quadratic formula.
fórmula cuadrática (pág. 292) La fórmula $x = \frac{-b \pm \sqrt{b^2 - 4ac}}{2a}$ que se usa para hallar las soluciones de la ecuación cuadrática $ax^2 + bx + c = 0$ cuando a, b y c son números reales y $a \neq 0$.	**Para resolver $3x^2 + 6x + 2 = 0$, sustituye a por 3, b por 6 y c por 2 en la fórmula cuadrática.** $x = \frac{-6 \pm \sqrt{6^2 - 4(3)(2)}}{2(3)} = \frac{-3 \pm \sqrt{3}}{3}$
quadratic function (p. 236) A function that can be written in the form $y = ax^2 + bx + c$ where $a \neq 0$.	The functions $y = 3x^2 - 5$ and $y = x^2 - 4x + 6$ are quadratic functions.
función cuadrática (pág. 236) Función que puede escribirse en la forma $y = ax^2 + bx + c$, donde $a \neq 0$.	**Las funciones $y = 3x^2 - 5$ e $y = x^2 - 4x + 6$ son funciones cuadráticas.**
quadratic inequality in one variable (p. 302) An inequality that can be written in the form $ax^2 + bx + c < 0$, $ax^2 + bx + c \leq 0$, $ax^2 + bx + c > 0$, or $ax^2 + bx + c \geq 0$.	$x^2 + x \leq 0$ and $2x^2 + x - 4 > 0$ are quadratic inequalities in one variable.
desigualdad cuadrática con una variable (pág. 302) Desigualdad que se puede escribir en la forma $ax^2 + bx + c < 0$, $ax^2 + bx + c \leq 0$, $ax^2 + bx + c > 0$ ó $ax^2 + bx + c \geq 0$.	**$x^2 + x \leq 0$ y $2x^2 + x - 4 > 0$ son desigualdades cuadráticas con una variable.**
quadratic inequality in two variables (p. 300) An inequality that can be written in the form $y < ax^2 + bx + c$, $y \leq ax^2 + bx + c$, $y > ax^2 + bx + c$, or $y \geq ax^2 + bx + c$.	$y > x^2 + 3x - 4$ is a quadratic inequality in two variables.
desigualdad cuadrática con dos variables (pág. 300) Desigualdad que se puede escribir en la forma $y < ax^2 + bx + c$, $y \leq ax^2 + bx + c$, $y > ax^2 + bx + c$ ó $y \geq ax^2 + bx + c$.	**$y > x^2 + 3x - 4$ es una desigualdad cuadrática con dos variables.**

quadratic system (p. 658) A system of equations that includes one or more equations of conics. **sistema cuadrático** (pág. 658) Sistema de ecuaciones que incluye una o más ecuaciones de cónicas.	$y^2 - 7x + 3 = 0$, $2x - y = 3$ $x^2 + 4y^2 + 8y = 16$, $2x^2 - y^2 - 6x - 4 = 0$ The systems above are quadratic systems. **Los sistemas de arriba son sistemas cuadráticos.**

R

radian (p. 860) In a circle with radius r and center at the origin, one radian is the measure of an angle in standard position whose terminal side intercepts an arc of length r. **radián** (pág. 860) En un círculo con radio r y cuyo centro está en el origen, un radián es la medida de un ángulo en posición normal cuyo lado terminal intercepta un arco de longitud r.	y, x, r, r 1 radian 1 radián
radical (pp. 266, 414) An expression of the form $\sqrt{s}$ or $\sqrt[n]{s}$ where s is a number or an expression. **radical** (págs. 266, 414) Expresión de la forma $\sqrt{s}$ o $\sqrt[n]{s}$, donde s es un número o una expresión.	$\sqrt{5}, \sqrt[3]{2x+1}$
radical equation (p. 452) An equation with one or more radicals that have variables in their radicands. **ecuación radical** (pág. 452) Ecuación con uno o más radicales en cuyo radicando aparecen variables.	$\sqrt[3]{2x+7} = 3$
radical function (p. 446) A function that contains a radical with a variable in its radicand. **función radical** (pág. 446) Función que tiene un radical con una variable en su radicando.	$f(x) = \frac{1}{2}\sqrt{x}, g(x) = -3\sqrt[3]{x+5}$
radicand (p. 266) The number or expression beneath a radical sign. **radicando** (pág. 266) El número o la expresión que aparece bajo el signo radical.	The radicand of $\sqrt{5}$ is 5, and the radicand of $\sqrt{8y^2}$ is $8y^2$. **El radicando de $\sqrt{5}$ es 5, y el radicando de $\sqrt{8y^2}$ es $8y^2$.**
radius of a circle (p. 626) The distance from the center of a circle to a point on the circle. Also, a line segment that connects the center of a circle to a point on the circle. *See also* circle. **radio de un círculo** (pág. 626) La distancia desde el centro de un círculo hasta un punto del círculo. También, es un segmento de recta que une el centro de un círculo con un punto del círculo. *Ver también* círculo.	The circle with equation $(x-3)^2 + (y+5)^2 = 36$ has radius $\sqrt{36} = 6$. *See also* circle. **El círculo con la ecuación $(x-3)^2 + (y+5)^2 = 36$ tiene el radio $\sqrt{36} = 6$. *Ver también* círculo.**

ENGLISH-SPANISH GLOSSARY

1069

random variable (p. 724) A variable whose value is determined by the outcomes of a random event. **variable aleatoria** (pág. 724) Variable cuyo valor viene determinado por los resultados de un suceso aleatorio.	The random variable X representing the number showing after rolling a six-sided die has possible values of 1, 2, 3, 4, 5, and 6. **La variable aleatoria X que representa el número que sale al lanzar un dado de seis caras tiene como valores posibles 1, 2, 3, 4, 5 y 6.**
range of a relation (p. 72) The set of output values of a relation. **rango de una relación** (pág. 72) El conjunto de los valores de salida de una relación.	*See* relation. ***Ver* relación.**
range of data values (p. 745) A measure of dispersion equal to the difference between the greatest and least data values. **rango de valores de datos** (pág. 745) Medida de dispersión igual a la diferencia entre el valor máximo y el valor mínimo de los datos.	**14, 17, 18, 19, 20, 24, 24, 30, 32** The range of the data set above is $32 - 14 = 18$. **El rango del conjunto de datos de arriba es $32 - 14 = 18$.**
rate of change (p. 85) A comparison of how much one quantity changes, on average, relative to the change in another quantity. **relación de cambio** (pág. 85) Comparación entre el cambio producido, por término medio, en una cantidad y el cambio producido en otra cantidad.	The temperature rises from 75°F at 8 A.M. to 91°F at 12 P.M. The average rate of change in temperature is $\frac{91°\text{F} - 75°\text{F}}{12 \text{ P.M.} - 8 \text{ A.M.}} = \frac{16°\text{F}}{4 \text{ h}} = 4°/\text{h}$. **La temperatura sube de 75°F a las 8 de la mañana a 91°F a las 12 del mediodía. La relación de cambio media en la temperatura es $\frac{91°\text{F} - 75°\text{F}}{12 \text{ P.M.} - 8 \text{ A.M.}} = \frac{16°\text{F}}{4 \text{ h}} = 4°/\text{h}$.**
rational function (p. 558) A function of the form $f(x) = \frac{p(x)}{q(x)}$, where $p(x)$ and $q(x)$ are polynomials and $q(x) \neq 0$. **función racional** (pág. 558) Función de la forma $f(x) = \frac{p(x)}{q(x)}$, donde $p(x)$ y $q(x)$ son polinomios y $q(x) \neq 0$.	The functions $y = \frac{6}{x}$ and $y = \frac{2x+1}{x-3}$ are rational functions. **Las funciones $y = \frac{6}{x}$ e $y = \frac{2x+1}{x-3}$ son funciones racionales.**
rationalizing the denominator (p. 267) The process of eliminating a radical expression in the denominator of a fraction by multiplying both the numerator and denominator by an appropriate radical expression. **racionalizar el denominador** (pág. 267) El proceso de eliminar una expresión radical del denominador de una fracción al multiplicar tanto el numerador como el denominador por una expresión radical adecuada.	To rationalize the denominator of $\frac{\sqrt{5}}{\sqrt{2}}$, multiply the numerator and denominator by $\sqrt{2}$. **Para racionalizar el denominador de $\frac{\sqrt{5}}{\sqrt{2}}$, multiplica el numerador y el denominador por $\sqrt{2}$.**
reciprocal (p. 4) The reciprocal, or multiplicative inverse, of any nonzero number b is $\frac{1}{b}$. **recíproco** (pág. 4) El recíproco, o inverso multiplicativo, de cualquier número b distinto de cero es $\frac{1}{b}$.	-2 and $\frac{1}{-2} = -\frac{1}{2}$ are reciprocals. **-2 y $\frac{1}{-2} = -\frac{1}{2}$ son recíprocos.**

ENGLISH-SPANISH GLOSSARY

recursive rule (p. 827) A rule for a sequence that gives the beginning term or terms of the sequence and then a recursive equation that tells how the nth term a_n is related to one or more preceding terms.	The recursive rule $a_0 = 1$, $a_n = a_{n-1} + 4$ gives the arithmetic sequence 1, 5, 9, 13, … .
regla recursiva (pág. 827) Regla de una progresión que da el primer término o términos de la progresión y luego una ecuación recursiva que indica qué relación hay entre el término enésimo a_n y uno o más de los términos precedentes.	**La regla recursiva $a_0 = 1$, $a_n = a_{n-1} + 4$ da la progresión aritmética 1, 5, 9, 13, … .**
reference angle (p. 868) If θ is an angle in standard position, its reference angle is the acute angle θ' formed by the terminal side of θ and the x-axis. **ángulo de referencia** (pág. 868) Si θ es un ángulo en posición normal, su ángulo de referencia es el ángulo agudo θ' formado por el lado terminal de θ y el eje de x.	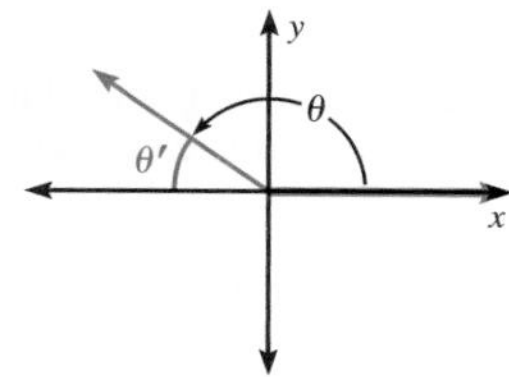 The acute angle θ' is the reference angle for angle θ. **El ángulo agudo θ' es el ángulo de referencia para el ángulo θ.**
reflection (p. 124) A transformation that flips a graph or figure in a line. **reflexión** (pág. 124) Transformación que vuelca una gráfica o una figura en una recta.	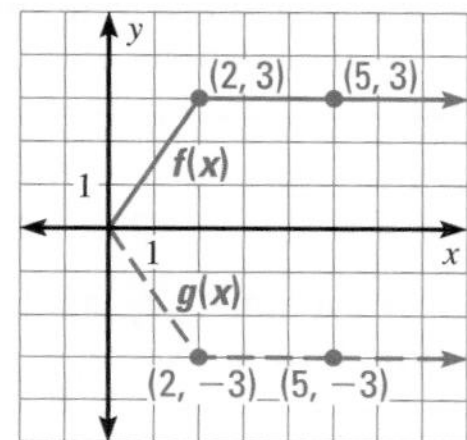 The graph of $g(x)$ is the reflection of the graph of $f(x)$ in the x-axis. **La gráfica de $g(x)$ es la reflexión de la gráfica de $f(x)$ en el eje de x.**
relation (p. 72) A mapping, or pairing, of input values with output values.	The ordered pairs (−2, −2), (−2, 2), (0, 1), and (3, 1) represent the relation with inputs (domain) of −2, 0, and 3 and outputs (range) of −2, 1, and 2.
relación (pág. 72) Correspondencia entre los valores de entrada y los valores de salida.	**Los pares ordenados (−2, −2), (−2, 2), (0, 1) y (3, 1) representan la relación con entradas (dominio) de −2, 0 y 3 y salidas (rango) de −2, 1 y 2.**

repeated solution (p. 379) For the polynomial equation $f(x) = 0$, k is a repeated solution if and only if the factor $x - k$ has an exponent greater than 1 when $f(x)$ is factored completely. **solución repetida** (pág. 379) Para la ecuación polinómica $f(x) = 0$, k es una solución repetida si y sólo si el factor $x - k$ tiene un exponente mayor que 1 cuando $f(x)$ está completamente factorizado.	−1 is a repeated solution of the equation $(x + 1)^2 (x - 2) = 0$. −1 es una solución repetida de la ecuación $(x + 1)^2 (x - 2) = 0$.
root of an equation (p. 253) The solutions of a quadratic equation are its roots. **raíz de una ecuación** (pág. 253) Las soluciones de una ecuación cuadrática son sus raíces.	The roots of the quadratic equation $x^2 - 5x - 36 = 0$ are 9 and −4. Las raíces de la ecuación cuadrática $x^2 - 5x - 36 = 0$ son 9 y −4.

S

sample (p. 766) A subset of a population. **muestra** (pág. 766) Subconjunto de una población.	*See* population. *Ver* población.
scalar (p. 188) A real number by which you multiply a matrix. **escalar** (pág. 188) Número real por el que se multiplica una matriz.	*See* scalar multiplication. *Ver* multiplicación escalar.
scalar multiplication (p. 188) Multiplication of each element of a matrix by a real number, called a scalar. **multiplicación escalar** (pág. 188) Multiplicación de cada elemento de una matriz por un número real llamado escalar.	$-2\begin{bmatrix} 4 & -1 \\ 1 & 0 \\ 2 & 7 \end{bmatrix} = \begin{bmatrix} -8 & 2 \\ -2 & 0 \\ -4 & -14 \end{bmatrix}$
scatter plot (p. 113) A graph of a set of data pairs (x, y) used to determine whether there is a relationship between the variables x and y. **diagrama de dispersión** (pág. 113) Gráfica de un conjunto de pares de datos (x, y) que sirve para determinar si hay una relación entre las variables x e y.	
scientific notation (p. 331) The representation of a number in the form $c \times 10^n$ where $1 \le c < 10$ and n is an integer. **notación científica** (pág. 331) La representación de un número de la forma $c \times 10^n$, donde $1 \le c < 10$ y n es un número entero.	0.693 is written in scientific notation as 6.93×10^{-1}. 0.693 escrito en notación científica es 6.93×10^{-1}.

ENGLISH-SPANISH GLOSSARY

secant function (p. 852) If θ is an acute angle of a right triangle, the secant of θ is the length of the hypotenuse divided by the length of the side adjacent to θ. **función secante** (pág. 852) Si θ es un ángulo agudo de un triángulo rectángulo, la secante de θ es la longitud de la hipotenusa dividida por la longitud del lado adyacente a θ.	*See* sine function. ***Ver* función seno.**
sector (p. 861) A region of a circle that is bounded by two radii and an arc of the circle. The central angle θ of a sector is the angle formed by the two radii. **sector** (pág. 861) Región de un círculo delimitada por dos radios y un arco del círculo. El ángulo central θ de un sector es el ángulo formado por dos radios.	sector sector r arc length s longitud de un arco s central angle θ ángulo central θ
sequence (p. 794) A function whose domain is a set of consecutive integers. The domain gives the relative position of each term of the sequence. The range gives the terms of the sequence. **progresión** (pág. 794) Función cuyo dominio es un conjunto de números enteros consecutivos. El dominio da la posición relativa de cada término de la secuencia. El rango da los términos de la secuencia.	For the domain $n = 1, 2, 3$, and 4, the sequence defined by $a_n = 2n$ has the terms 2, 4, 6, and 8. **Para el dominio $n = 1, 2, 3$ y 4, la secuencia definida por $a_n = 2n$ tiene los términos 2, 4, 6 y 8.**
series (p. 796) The expression formed by adding the terms of a sequence. A series can be finite or infinite. **serie** (pág. 796) La expresión formada al sumar los términos de una progresión. La serie puede ser finita o infinita.	Finite series: $2 + 4 + 6 + 8$ Infinite series: $2 + 4 + 6 + 8 + \cdots$ **Serie finita: $2 + 4 + 6 + 8$** **Serie infinita: $2 + 4 + 6 + 8 + \cdots$**
set (p. 715) A collection of distinct objects. **conjunto** (pág. 715) Colección de objetos diferenciados.	If A is the set of positive integers less than 5, then $A = \{1, 2, 3, 4\}$. **Si A es el conjunto de números enteros positivos menores que 5, entonces $A = \{1, 2, 3, 4\}$.**
sigma notation (p. 796) *See* summation notation. **notación sigma** (pág. 796) *Ver* notación de sumatoria.	*See* summation notation. ***Ver* notación de sumatoria.**
simplest form of a radical (p. 422) A radical with index n is in simplest form if the radicand has no perfect nth powers as factors and any denominator has been rationalized. **forma más simple de un radical** (pág. 422) Un radical con índice n está escrito en la forma más simple si el radicando no tiene como factor ninguna potencia enésima perfecta y el denominador ha sido racionalizado.	$\sqrt[3]{135}$ in simplest form is $3\sqrt[3]{5}$. $\frac{\sqrt[5]{7}}{\sqrt[5]{8}}$ in simplest form is $\frac{\sqrt[5]{28}}{2}$. **$\sqrt[3]{135}$ en la forma más simple es $3\sqrt[3]{5}$.** **$\frac{\sqrt[5]{7}}{\sqrt[5]{8}}$ en la forma más simple es $\frac{\sqrt[5]{28}}{2}$.**

ENGLISH-SPANISH GLOSSARY

simplified form of a rational expression (p. 573) A rational expression in which the numerator and denominator have no common factors other than ± 1.

forma simplificada de una expresión racional (pág. 573) Expresión racional en la que el numerador y el denominador no tienen factores comunes además de ± 1.

$$\frac{x^2 - 2x - 15}{x^2 - 9} = \frac{(x + 3)(x - 5)}{(x + 3)(x - 3)} = \frac{x - 5}{x - 3}$$

↑

Simplified form
Forma simplificada

sine function (p. 852) If θ is an acute angle of a right triangle, the sine of θ is the length of the side opposite θ divided by the length of the hypotenuse.

función seno (pág. 852) Si θ es un ángulo agudo de un triángulo rectángulo, el seno de θ es la longitud del lado opuesto a θ dividida por la longitud de la hipotenusa.

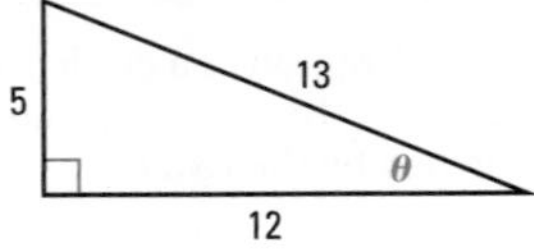

$$\sin\theta = \frac{\text{opp}}{\text{hyp}} = \frac{5}{13} \qquad \csc\theta = \frac{\text{hyp}}{\text{opp}} = \frac{13}{5}$$

$$\cos\theta = \frac{\text{adj}}{\text{hyp}} = \frac{12}{13} \qquad \sec\theta = \frac{\text{hyp}}{\text{adj}} = \frac{13}{12}$$

$$\tan\theta = \frac{\text{opp}}{\text{adj}} = \frac{5}{12} \qquad \cot\theta = \frac{\text{adj}}{\text{opp}} = \frac{12}{5}$$

$$\text{sen}\,\theta = \frac{\text{op}}{\text{hip}} = \frac{5}{13} \qquad \text{cosec}\,\theta = \frac{\text{hip}}{\text{op}} = \frac{13}{5}$$

$$\cos\theta = \frac{\text{ady}}{\text{hip}} = \frac{12}{13} \qquad \sec\theta = \frac{\text{hip}}{\text{ady}} = \frac{13}{12}$$

$$\tan\theta = \frac{\text{op}}{\text{ady}} = \frac{5}{12} \qquad \cot\theta = \frac{\text{ady}}{\text{op}} = \frac{12}{5}$$

sinusoids (p. 941) Graphs of sine and cosine functions.

sinusoides (pág. 941) Gráficas de funciones seno y coseno.

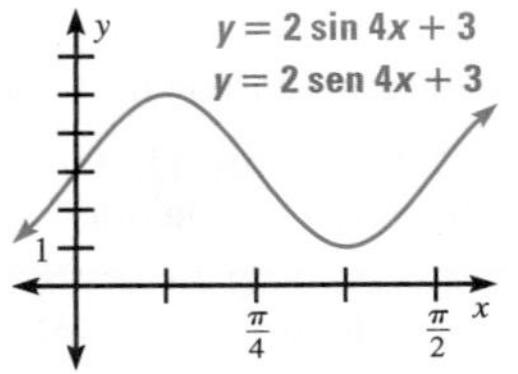

skewed distribution (p. 727) A probability distribution that is not symmetric. *See also* symmetric distribution.

distribución asimétrica (pág. 727) Distribución de probabilidades que no es simétrica. *Ver también* distribución simétrica.

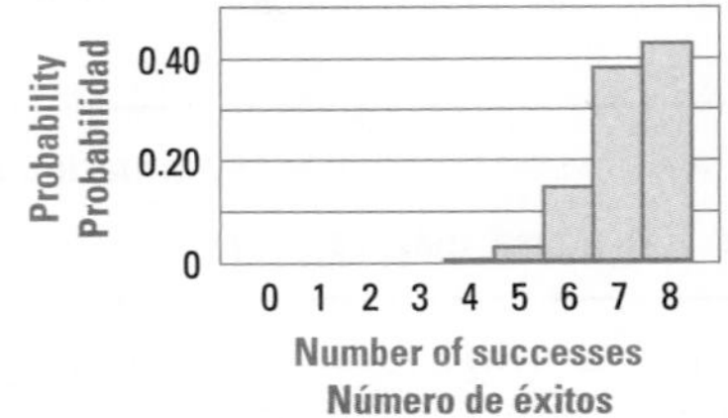

1074

slope (p. 82) The ratio of vertical change (the rise) to horizontal change (the run) for a nonvertical line. For a nonvertical line passing through the points (x_1, y_1) and (x_2, y_2), the slope is $m = \frac{y_2 - y_1}{x_2 - x_1}$. **pendiente** (pág. 82) Para una recta no vertical, la razón entre el cambio vertical (distancia vertical) y el cambio horizontal (distancia horizontal). Para una recta no vertical que pasa por los puntos (x_1, y_1) y (x_2, y_2), la pendiente es $m = \frac{y_2 - y_1}{x_2 - x_1}$.	The slope of the line that passes through the points (−3, 0) and (3, 4) is: **La pendiente de la recta que pasa por los puntos (−3, 0) y (3, 4) es:** $m = \frac{y_2 - y_1}{x_2 - x_1} = \frac{4 - 0}{3 - (-3)} = \frac{4}{6} = \frac{2}{3}$
slope-intercept form (p. 90) A linear equation written in the form $y = mx + b$ where m is the slope and b is the y-intercept of the equation's graph. **forma pendiente-intercepto** (pág. 90) Ecuación lineal escrita en la forma $y = mx + b$, donde m es la pendiente y b es el intercepto en y de la gráfica de la ecuación.	The equation $y = -\frac{2}{3}x - 1$ is in slope-intercept form. **La ecuación $y = -\frac{2}{3}x - 1$ está en la forma pendiente-intercepto.**
solution of a linear inequality in two variables (p. 132) An ordered pair (x, y) that produces a true statement when the values of x and y are substituted into the inequality. **solución de una desigualdad lineal con dos variables** (pág. 132) Par ordenado (x, y) que produce un enunciado verdadero cuando x e y se sustituyen por sus valores en la desigualdad.	The ordered pair (1, 2) is a solution of $3x + 4y > 8$ because $3(1) + 4(2) = 11$, and $11 > 8$. **El par ordenado (1, 2) es una solución de $3x + 4y > 8$ ya que $3(1) + 4(2) = 11$, y $11 > 8$.**
solution of a system of linear equations in three variables (p. 178) An ordered triple (x, y, z) whose coordinates make each equation in the system true. **solución de un sistema de ecuaciones lineales en tres variables** (pág. 178) Terna ordenada (x, y, z) cuyas coordenadas hacen que cada ecuación del sistema sea verdadera.	$4x + 2y + 3z = 1$ $2x - 3y + 5z = -14$ $6x - y + 4z = -1$ (2, 1, −3) is the solution of the system above. **(2, 1, −3) es la solución del sistema de arriba.**
solution of a system of linear equations in two variables (p. 153) An ordered pair (x, y) that satisfies each equation of the system. **solución de un sistema de ecuaciones lineales en dos variables** (pág. 153) Par ordenado (x, y) que satisface cada ecuación del sistema.	$4x + y = 8$ $2x - 3y = 18$ (3, −4) is the solution of the system above. **(3, −4) es la solución del sistema de arriba.**
solution of a system of linear inequalities in two variables (p. 168) An ordered pair (x, y) that is a solution of each inequality in the system. **solución de un sistema de desigualdades lineales en dos variables** (pág. 168) Par ordenado (x, y) que es una solución de cada desigualdad del sistema.	$y > -2x - 5$ $y \leq x + 3$ (−1, 1) is a solution of the system above. **(−1, 1) es una solución del sistema de arriba.**

ENGLISH-SPANISH GLOSSARY

1075

solution of an equation in one variable (p. 18) A number that produces a true statement when substituted for the variable in the equation. **solución de una ecuación con una variable** (pág. 18) Número que produce un enunciado verdadero al sustituir la variable por él en la ecuación.	The solution of the equation $\frac{4}{5}x + 8 = 20$ is 15. **La solución de la ecuación $\frac{4}{5}x + 8 = 20$ es 15.**
solution of an equation in two variables (p. 74) An ordered pair (x, y) that produces a true statement when the values of x and y are substituted in the equation. **solución de una ecuación con dos variables** (pág. 74) Par ordenado (x, y) que produce un enunciado verdadero al sustituir x e y por sus valores en la ecuación.	$(-2, 3)$ is a solution of $y = -2x - 1$. **$(-2, 3)$ es una solución de $y = -2x - 1$.**
solution of an inequality in one variable (p. 41) A number that produces a true statement when substituted for the variable in the inequality. **solución de una desigualdad con una variable** (pág. 41) Número que produce un enunciado verdadero al sustituir la variable por él en la desigualdad.	-1 is a solution of the inequality $5x + 2 > 7x - 4$. **-1 es una solución de la desigualdad $5x + 2 > 7x - 4$.**
solve for a variable (p. 26) Rewrite an equation as an equivalent equation in which the variable is on one side and does not appear on the other side. **resolver para una variable** (pág. 26) Escribir una ecuación como ecuación equivalente que tenga la variable en uno de sus lados pero no en el otro.	When you solve the circumference formula $C = 2\pi r$ for r, the result is $r = \frac{C}{2\pi}$. **Al resolver para r la fórmula de circunferencia $C = 2\pi r$, el resultado es $r = \frac{C}{2\pi}$.**
square root (p. 266) If $b^2 = a$, then b is a square root of a. The radical symbol $\sqrt{\ }$ represents a nonnegative square root. **raíz cuadrada** (pág. 266) Si $b^2 = a$, entonces b es una raíz cuadrada de a. El signo radical $\sqrt{\ }$ representa una raíz cuadrada no negativa.	The square roots of 9 are 3 and -3 because $3^2 = 9$ and $(-3)^2 = 9$. So, $\sqrt{9} = 3$ and $-\sqrt{9} = -3$. **Las raíces cuadradas de 9 son 3 y -3 ya que $3^2 = 9$ y $(-3)^2 = 9$. Así pues, $\sqrt{9} = 3$ y $-\sqrt{9} = -3$.**
standard deviation (p. 745) The typical difference (or deviation) between a data value and the mean. The standard deviation σ of a numerical data set $x_1, x_2, \dots, x_n$ is given by the following formula: $\sigma = \sqrt{\frac{(x_1 - \bar{x})^2 + (x_2 - \bar{x})^2 + \cdots + (x_n - \bar{x})^2}{n}}$ **desviación típica** (pág. 745) La diferencia (o desviación) más común entre un valor de los datos y la media. La desviación típica σ de un conjunto de datos numéricos $x_1, x_2, \dots, x_n$ viene dada por la siguiente fórmula: $\sigma = \sqrt{\frac{(x_1 - \bar{x})^2 + (x_2 - \bar{x})^2 + \cdots + (x_n - \bar{x})^2}{n}}$	**14, 17, 18, 19, 20, 24, 24, 30, 32** Because the mean of the data set is 22, the standard deviation is: **Como la media del conjunto de datos es 22, la desviación típica es:** $\sigma = \sqrt{\frac{(14 - 22)^2 + (17 - 22)^2 + \cdots + (32 - 22)^2}{9}}$ $= \sqrt{\frac{290}{9}} \approx 5.7$

ENGLISH-SPANISH GLOSSARY

standard form of a complex number (p. 276) The form $a + bi$ where a and b are real numbers and i is the imaginary unit. **forma general de un número complejo** (pág. 276) La forma $a + bi$, donde a y b son números reales e i es la unidad imaginaria.	The standard form of the complex number $i(1 + i)$ is $-1 + i$. **La forma general del número complejo $i(1 + i)$ es $-1 + i$.**
standard form of a linear equation (p. 91) A linear equation written in the form $Ax + By = C$ where A and B are not both zero. **forma general de una ecuación lineal** (pág. 91) Ecuación lineal escrita en la forma $Ax + By = C$, donde A y B no son ambos cero.	The linear equation $y = -3x + 4$ can be written in standard form as $3x + y = 4$. **La ecuación lineal $y = -3x + 4$ escrita en la forma general es $3x + y = 4$.**
standard form of a polynomial function (p. 337) The form of a polynomial function that has terms written in descending order of exponents from left to right. **forma general de una función polinómica** (pág. 337) La forma de una función polinómica en la que los términos se ordenan de tal modo que los exponentes disminuyen de izquierda a derecha.	The function $g(x) = 7x - \sqrt{3} + \pi x^2$ can be written in standard form as $g(x) = \pi x^2 + 7x - \sqrt{3}$. **La función $g(x) = 7x - \sqrt{3} + \pi x^2$ escrita en la forma general es $g(x) = \pi x^2 + 7x - \sqrt{3}$.**
standard form of a quadratic equation in one variable (p. 253) The form $ax^2 + bx + c = 0$ where $a \neq 0$. **forma general de una ecuación cuadrática con una variable** (pág. 253) La forma $ax^2 + bx + c = 0$, donde $a \neq 0$.	The quadratic equation $x^2 - 5x = 36$ can be written in standard form as $x^2 - 5x - 36 = 0$. **La ecuación cuadrática $x^2 - 5x = 36$ escrita en la forma general es $x^2 - 5x - 36 = 0$.**
standard form of a quadratic function (p. 236) The form $y = ax^2 + bx + c$ where $a \neq 0$. **forma general de una función cuadrática** (pág. 236) La forma $y = ax^2 + bx + c$, donde $a \neq 0$.	The quadratic function $y = 2(x + 3)(x - 1)$ can be written in standard form as $y = 2x^2 + 4x - 6$. **La función cuadrática $y = 2(x + 3)(x - 1)$ escrita en la forma general es $y = 2x^2 + 4x - 6$.**
standard normal distribution (p. 758) The normal distribution with mean 0 and standard deviation 1. *See also* z-score. **distribución normal típica** (pág. 758) La distribución normal con media 0 y desviación típica 1. *Ver también* puntuación z.	$z = -3$ $z = -2$ $z = -1$ $z = 0$ $z = 1$ $z = 2$ $z = 3$

standard position of an angle (p. 859) In a coordinate plane, the position of an angle whose vertex is at the origin and whose initial side lies on the positive x-axis. **posición normal de un ángulo** (pág. 859) En un plano de coordenadas, la posición de un ángulo cuyo vértice está en el origen y cuyo lado inicial se sitúa en el eje de x positivo.	90° y terminal side lado terminal 0° 180° initial side x lado inicial 360° vertex vértice 270°
statistics (p. 744) Numerical values used to summarize and compare sets of data. **estadística** (pág. 744) Valores numéricos utilizados para resumir y comparar conjuntos de datos.	*See* mean, median, mode, range, *and* standard deviation. *Ver* **media, mediana, moda, rango** *y* **desviación típica.**
step function (p. 131) A piecewise function defined by a constant value over each part of its domain. Its graph resembles a series of stair steps. **función escalonada** (pág. 131) Función definida a trozos y por un valor constante en cada parte de su dominio. Su gráfica parece un grupo de escalones.	$f(x) = \begin{cases} 1, \text{ if } 0 \le x < 1 \\ 2, \text{ if } 1 \le x < 2 \\ 3, \text{ if } 2 \le x < 3 \end{cases}$ $f(x) = \begin{cases} 1, \text{ si } 0 \le x < 1 \\ 2, \text{ si } 1 \le x < 2 \\ 3, \text{ si } 2 \le x < 3 \end{cases}$
subset (p. 716) If every element of a set A is also an element of a set B, then A is a subset of B. This is written as $A \subseteq B$. For any set A, $\emptyset \subseteq A$ and $A \subseteq A$. **subconjunto** (pág. 716) Si cada elemento de un conjunto A es también un elemento de un conjunto B, entonces A es un subconjunto de B. Esto se escribe $A \subseteq B$. Para cualquier conjunto A, $\emptyset \subseteq A$ y $A \subseteq A$.	If $A = \{1, 2, 4, 8\}$ and B is the set of all positive integers, then A is a subset of B, or $A \subseteq B$. **Si $A = \{1, 2, 4, 8\}$ y B es el conjunto de todos los números enteros positivos, entonces A es un subconjunto de B, o $A \subseteq B$.**
substitution method (p. 160) A method of solving a system of equations by solving one of the equations for one of the variables and then substituting the resulting expression in the other equation(s). **método de sustitución** (pág. 160) Método para resolver un sistema de ecuaciones mediante la resolución de una de las ecuaciones para una de las variables seguida de la sustitución de la expresión resultante en la(s) otra(s) ecuación (ecuaciones).	$2x + 5y = -5$ $x + 3y = 3$ Solve equation 2 for x: $x = -3y + 3$. Substitute the expression for x in equation 1 and solve for y: $y = 11$. Use the value of y to find the value of x: $x = -30$. **Resuelve la ecuación 2 para x: $x = -3y + 3$. Sustituye la expresión para x en la ecuación 1 y resuelve para y: $y = 11$. Usa el valor de y para hallar el valor de x: $x = -30$.**
summation notation (p. 796) Notation for a series that uses the uppercase Greek letter sigma, Σ. Also called sigma notation. **notación de sumatoria** (pág. 796) Notación de una serie que usa la letra griega mayúscula sigma, Σ. También se llama notación sigma.	$\sum_{i=1}^{5} 7i = 7(1) + 7(2) + 7(3) + 7(4) + 7(5)$ $= 7 + 14 + 21 + 28 + 35$

ENGLISH-SPANISH GLOSSARY

symmetric distribution (p. 727) A probability distribution, represented by a histogram, in which you can draw a vertical line that divides the histogram into two parts that are mirror images.

distribución simétrica (pág. 727) Distribución de probabilidad representada por un histograma en la que se puede trazar una recta vertical que divida al histograma en dos partes; éstas son imágenes especulares entre sí.

Probability / Probabilidad: 0, 0.10, 0.20, 0.30
Number of successes / Número de éxitos: 0 1 2 3 4 5 6 7 8

synthetic division (p. 363) A method used to divide a polynomial by a divisor of the form $x - k$.

división sintética (pág. 363) Método utilizado para dividir un polinomio por un divisor en la forma $x - k$.

−3	2	1	−8	5
		−6	15	−21
	2	−5	7	−16

$$\frac{2x^3 + x^2 - 8x + 5}{x + 3} = 2x^2 - 5x + 7 - \frac{16}{x + 3}$$

synthetic substitution (p. 338) A method used to evaluate a polynomial function.

sustitución sintética (pág. 338) Método utilizado para evaluar una función polinómica.

3	2	−5	0	−4	8
		6	3	9	15
	2	1	3	5	**23**

The synthetic substitution above indicates that for $f(x) = 2x^4 - 5x^3 - 4x + 8$, $f(3) = 23$.

La sustitución sintética de arriba indica que para $f(x) = 2x^4 - 5x^3 - 4x + 8$, $f(3) = 23$.

system of linear inequalities in two variables (p. 168) A system consisting of two or more linear inequalities in two variables. *See also* linear inequality in two variables.

sistema de desigualdades lineales con dos variables (pág. 168) Sistema que consiste de dos o más desigualdades lineales con dos variables. *Ver también* desigualdad lineal con dos variables.

$$x + y \le 8$$
$$4x - y > 6$$

system of three linear equations in three variables (p. 178) A system consisting of three linear equations in three variables. *See also* linear equation in three variables.

sistema de tres ecuaciones lineales en tres variables (pág. 178) Sistema formado por tres ecuaciones lineales con tres variables. *Ver también* ecuación lineal con tres variables.

$$2x + y - z = 5$$
$$3x - 2y + z = 16$$
$$4x + 3y - 5z = 3$$

system of two linear equations in two variables (p. 153) A system consisting of two equations that can be written in the form $Ax + By = C$ and $Dx + Ey = F$ where x and y are variables, A and B are not both zero, and D and E are not both zero. **sistema de dos ecuaciones lineales con dos variables** (pág. 153) Un sistema que consiste en dos ecuaciones que se pueden escribir de la forma $Ax + By = C$ y $Dx + Ey = F$, donde x e y son variables, A y B no son ambos cero, y D y E tampoco son ambos cero.	$4x + y = 8$ $2x - 3y = 18$

T

tangent function (p. 852) If θ is an acute angle of a right triangle, the tangent of θ is the length of the side opposite θ divided by the length of the side adjacent to θ. **función tangente** (pág. 852) Si θ es un ángulo agudo de un triángulo rectángulo, la tangente de θ es la longitud del lado opuesto a θ dividida por la longitud del lado adyacente a θ.	*See* sine function. *Ver* función seno.
terminal side of an angle (p. 859) In a coordinate plane, an angle can be formed by fixing one ray, called the initial side, and rotating the other ray, called the terminal side, about the vertex. **lado terminal de un ángulo** (pág. 859) En un plano de coordenadas, un ángulo puede formarse al fijar un rayo, llamado lado inicial, y al girar el otro rayo, llamado lado terminal, en torno al vértice.	*See* standard position of an angle. *Ver* posición normal de un ángulo.
terms of a sequence (p. 794) The values in the range of a sequence. **términos de una progresión** (pág. 794) Los valores del rango de una progresión.	The first 4 terms of the sequence 1, −3, 9, −27, 81, −243, . . . are 1, −3, 9, and −27. Los 4 primeros términos de la progresión 1, −3, 9, −27, 81, −243, . . . son 1, −3, 9 y −27.
terms of an expression (p. 12) The parts of an expression that are added together. **términos de una expresión** (pág. 12) Las partes de una expresión que se suman.	The terms of the algebraic expression $3x^2 + 5x + (-7)$ are $3x^2$, $5x$, and -7. Los términos de la expresión algebraica $3x^2 + 5x + (-7)$ son $3x^2$, $5x$ y -7.

ENGLISH-SPANISH GLOSSARY

theoretical probability (p. 698) When all outcomes are equally likely, the theoretical probability that an event A will occur is $P(A) = \frac{\text{Number of outcomes in event } A}{\text{Total number of outcomes}}$. **probabilidad teórica** (pág. 698) Cuando todos los casos son igualmente posibles, la probabilidad teórica de que ocurra un suceso A es $P(A) = \frac{\text{Número de casos del suceso } A}{\text{Número total de casos}}$.	The theoretical probability of rolling an even number using a standard six-sided die is $\frac{3}{6} = \frac{1}{2}$ because 3 outcomes correspond to rolling an even number out of 6 total outcomes . **La probabilidad teórica de sacar un número par al lanzar un dado normal de seis caras es $\frac{3}{6} = \frac{1}{2}$ ya que 3 casos corresponden a un número par del total de 6 casos.**
transformation (p. 123) A transformation changes a graph's size, shape, position, or orientation. **transformación** (pág. 123) Una transformación cambia el tamaño, la forma, la posición o la orientación de una gráfica.	Translations, vertical stretches and shrinks, reflections, and rotations are transformations. **Las traslaciones, las expansiones y contracciones verticales, las reflexiones y las rotaciones son transformaciones.**
translation (p. 123) A transformation that shifts a graph horizontally and/or vertically, but does not change its size, shape, or orientation. **traslación** (pág. 123) Transformación que desplaza una gráfica horizontal o verticalmente, o de ambas maneras, pero que no cambia su tamaño, forma u orientación.	The graph of $y = \lvert x + 4 \rvert - 2$ is the graph of $y = \lvert x \rvert$ translated down 2 units and left 4 units. **La gráfica de $y = \lvert x + 4 \rvert - 2$ es la gráfica de $y = \lvert x \rvert$ al trasladar ésta 2 unidades hacia abajo y 4 unidades hacia la izquierda.**
transverse axis of a hyperbola (p. 642) The line segment joining the vertices of a hyperbola. **eje transverso de una hipérbola** (pág. 642) El segmento de recta que une los vértices de una hipérbola.	*See* hyperbola. ***Ver* hipérbola.**
trigonometric identity (p. 924) A trigonometric equation that is true for all domain values. **identidad trigonométrica** (pág. 924) Ecuación trigonométrica que es verdadera para todos los valores del dominio.	$\sin(-\theta) = -\sin\theta$ $\quad \sin^2\theta + \cos^2\theta = 1$ **sen $(-\theta) = -$sen θ $\quad$ sen$^2\theta + \cos^2\theta = 1$**
trinomial (p. 252) The sum of three monomials. **trinomio** (pág. 252) La suma de tres monomios.	$4x^2 + 3x - 1$ is a trinomial. **$4x^2 + 3x - 1$ es un trinomio.**

U

unbiased sample (p. 767) A sample that is representative of the population you want information about.	You want to poll members of the senior class about where to hold the prom. If every senior has an equal chance of being polled, then the sample is unbiased.
muestra no sesgada (pág. 767) Muestra que es representativa de la población acerca de la cual deseas informarte.	**Quieres encuestar a algunos estudiantes de último curso sobre el lugar donde organizar el baile de fin de año. Si cada estudiante de último curso tiene iguales posibilidades de ser encuestado, entonces es una muestra no sesgada.**
union of sets (p. 715) The union of two sets A and B, written $A \cup B$, is the set of all elements in *either* A or B.	If $A = \{1, 2, 4, 8\}$ and $B = \{2, 4, 6, 8, 10\}$, then $A \cup B = \{1, 2, 4, 6, 8, 10\}$.
unión de conjuntos (pág. 715) La unión de dos conjuntos A y B, escrita $A \cup B$, es el conjunto de todos los elementos que están en A *o* B.	**Si $A = \{1, 2, 4, 8\}$ y $B = \{2, 4, 6, 8, 10\}$, entonces $A \cup B = \{1, 2, 4, 6, 8, 10\}$.**
unit circle (p. 867) The circle $x^2 + y^2 = 1$, which has center (0, 0) and radius 1. For an angle θ in standard position, the terminal side of θ intersects the unit circle at the point $(\cos \theta, \sin \theta)$. **círculo unidad** (pág. 867) El círculo $x^2 + y^2 = 1$, que tiene centro (0, 0) y radio 1. Para un ángulo θ en posición normal, el lado terminal de θ corta al círculo unidad en el punto $(\cos \theta, \text{sen } \theta)$.	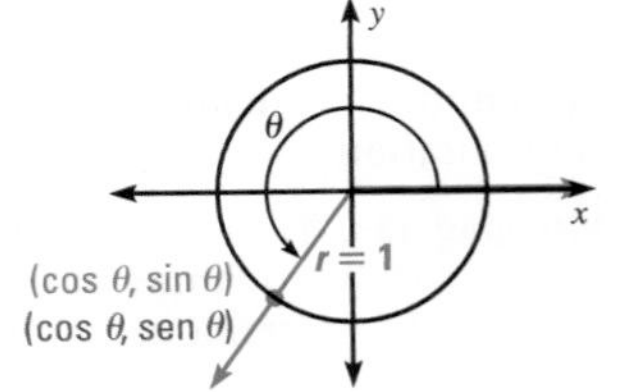
universal set (p. 715) The set of all elements under consideration; denoted U.	*See* complement of a set.
conjunto universal (pág. 715) El conjunto de todos los elementos tenidos en cuenta; se indica U.	***Ver* complemento de un conjunto.**

V

variable (p. 11) A letter that is used to represent one or more numbers.	In the expressions $6x$, $3x^2 + 1$, and $12 - 5x$, the letter x is the variable.
variable (pág. 11) Letra utilizada para representar uno o más números.	**En las expresiones $6x$, $3x^2 + 1$ y $12 - 5x$, la letra x es la variable.**
variable term (p. 12) A term that has a variable part.	The variable terms of the algebraic expression $3x^2 + 5x + (-7)$ are $3x^2$ and $5x$.
término algebraico (pág. 12) Término que tiene variable.	**Los términos algebraicos de la expresión algebraica $3x^2 + 5x + (-7)$ son $3x^2$ y $5x$.**
verbal model (p. 34) A word equation that represents a real-life problem.	Distance (miles) = Rate (miles/hour) • Time (hours)
modelo verbal (pág. 34) Ecuación expresada mediante palabras que representa un problema de la vida real.	**Distancia (millas) = Velocidad (millas/hora) • Tiempo (horas)**

vertex form of a quadratic function (p. 245) The form $y = a(x - h)^2 + k$, where the vertex of the graph is (h, k) and the axis of symmetry is $x = h$.

forma de vértice de una función cuadrática (pág. 245) La forma $y = a(x - h)^2 + k$, donde el vértice de la gráfica es (h, k) y el eje de simetría es $x = h$.

The quadratic function $y = -\frac{1}{4}(x + 2)^2 + 5$ is in vertex form.

La función cuadrática $y = -\frac{1}{4}(x + 2)^2 + 5$ está en la forma de vértice.

vertex of a parabola (pp. 236, 620) The point on a parabola that lies on the axis of symmetry.

vértice de una parábola (págs. 236, 620) El punto de una parábola que se encuentra en el eje de simetría.

See parabola.

Ver parábola.

vertex of an absolute value graph (p. 123) The highest or lowest point on the graph of an absolute value function.

vértice de una gráfica de valor absoluto (pág. 123) El punto más alto o más bajo de la gráfica de una función de valor absoluto.

The vertex of the graph of $y = |x - 4| + 3$ is the point $(4, 3)$.

El vértice de la gráfica de $y = |x - 4| + 3$ es el punto $(4, 3)$.

vertices of a hyperbola (p. 642) The points of intersection of a hyperbola and the line through the foci of the hyperbola.

vértices de una hipérbola (pág. 642) Los puntos de intersección de una hipérbola y la recta que pasa por los focos de la hipérbola.

See hyperbola.

Ver hipérbola.

vertices of an ellipse (p. 634) The points of intersection of an ellipse and the line through the foci of the ellipse.

vértices de una elipse (pág. 634) Los puntos de intersección de una elipse y la recta que pasa por los focos de la elipse.

See ellipse.

Ver elipse.

X

x-intercept (p. 91) The x-coordinate of a point where a graph intersects the x-axis.

intercepto en x (pág. 91) La coordenada x de un punto donde una gráfica corta al eje de x.

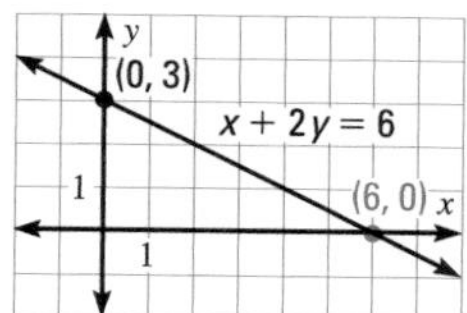

The x-intercept is 6.

El intercepto en x es 6.

1083

Y

y-intercept (p. 89) The y-coordinate of a point where a graph intersects the y-axis.

intercepto en y (pág. 89) La coordenada y de un punto donde una gráfica corta al eje de y.

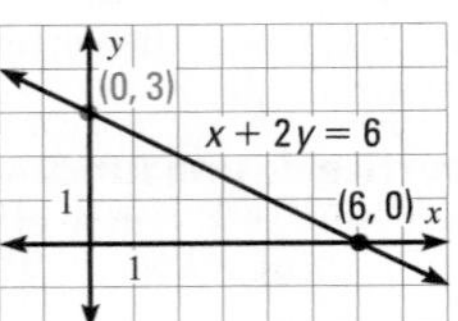

The y-intercept is 3.

El intercepto en y es 3.

Z

zero of a function (p. 254) A number k is a zero of a function f if $f(k) = 0$.

cero de una función (pág. 254) Un número k es un cero de una función f si $f(k) = 0$.

The zeros of the function $f(x) = 2(x + 3)(x - 1)$ are -3 and 1.

Los ceros de la función $f(x) = 2(x + 3)(x - 1)$ son -3 y 1.

z-score (p. 758) The number z of standard deviations that a data value lies above or below the mean of the data set: $z = \frac{x - \bar{x}}{\sigma}$.

puntuación z (pág. 758) El número z de desviaciones típicas que un valor se encuentra por encima o por debajo de la media del conjunto de datos: $z = \frac{x - \bar{x}}{\sigma}$.

A normal distribution has a mean of 76 and a standard deviation of 9. The z-score for $x = 64$ is $z = \frac{x - \bar{x}}{\sigma} = \frac{64 - 76}{9} \approx -1.3$.

Una distribución normal tiene una media de 76 y una desviación típica de 9. La puntuación z para $x = 64$ es $z = \frac{x - \bar{x}}{\sigma} = \frac{64 - 76}{9} \approx -1.3$.

ENGLISH-SPANISH GLOSSARY

Credits

Photographs

Cover Michael Wong/Corbis; **Authors:** *top* Meridian Creative Group, *top center* Robert C. Jenks, Jenks Studio, *bottom center* McDougal Littell, *bottom* Jerry Head Jr.; **Table of Contents: Chapter 1** PhotoDisc/Getty Images; **Chapter 2** Alex Rosenfeld/Science Photo Library; **Chapter 3** Jonathan Nourok/PhotoEdit; **Chapter 4** Mandy Collins/Alamy; **Chapter 5** Dave Bjorn/Photo Resource Hawaii; **Chapter 6** Joe McBride/Getty Images; **Chapter 7** Ron Sanford/Corbis; **Chapter 8** Ralph Wetmore/Getty Images; **Chapter 9** NASA; **Chapter 10** Jerry Wachter/Sportschrome, Inc.; **Chapter 11** AP/Wide World Photos; **Chapter 12** Ted Kinsman/Photo Researchers, Inc.; **Chapter 13** David Madison/Getty Images; **Chapter 14** Thorney Lieberman/Getty Images; **Interior: 1** Jennifer Graylock/AP/Wide World Photos; **2** Sylvain Grandadam/Getty Images; **6** Jason Hawkes/Getty Images; **8** *all* Courtesy NASA/JPL-Caltech; **9** Joel Sartore/Getty Images; **10** Rubberball Productions/Getty Images; **13** Brand X Pictures/Getty Images; **18** PhotoDisc/Getty Images; **20** Creatas/PunchStock; **23** Walter Hodges/Getty Images; **24** *both* Digital Stock/Corbis; **26** Peter Adams/Index Stock Imagery; **29** Rubberball Productions; **33** Gary I. Rothstein/AP/Wide World Photos; **34** PhotoDisc/Getty Images; **35** Jason Reed/Reuters; **38** Eugene Hoshiko/AP/Wide World Photos; **41** Royalty-Free/Corbis; **42** Barbara Leslie/Getty Images; **44** David A. Northcott/Corbis; **50** *all* Jay Penni Photography/McDougal Littell; **51** Digital Vision Ltd./SuperStock; **54** Jim Cummins/Getty Images; **59** Dean Hoffmeyer/AP/Wide World Photos; **70–71** George D. Lepp/Corbis; **72** Tom Stock/Getty Images; **74** Paul Battaglia/AP/Wide World Photos; **76** Stephen Frink/Corbis; **79** D.C. Lowe/SuperStock; **82** Ernest Manewal/Index Stock Imagery; **85** *both* Susan Ragan/AP/Wide World Photos; **89** Angela Wyant/Getty Images; **91** Paul Nicklen/National Geographic/Getty Images; **98** Nancy Richmond/The Image Works; **100** Steve Skjold/PhotoEdit; **103** David Young-Wolff/PhotoEdit; **107** Dave G. Houser/Corbis; **108** Amos Nachoum/Corbis; **112** *all* McDougal Littell; **113** Douglas C. Pizac/AP/Wide World Photos; **115** Sandy Huffaker/Getty Images; **123** *top right* John Coletti/Index Stock Imagery; **132** Digital Vision/Getty Images; **134** *all* Stockbyte/Getty Images; **150–151** Myrleen Ferguson Cate/PhotoEdit; **153** Duomo/Corbis; **155** David Frazier/The Image Works; **160** Rubberball/PictureQuest; **166** Petros Giannakouris/AP/Wide World Photos; **168** Duncan Smith/Getty Images; **170** Viviane Moos/Corbis; **173** Jim Cummins/Getty Images; **174** Brand X/SuperStock; **176** Kelly-Mooney Photography/Corbis; **178** Chris Donahue/AP/Wide World Photos; **185** Manchan/Getty Images; **186** Comstock Images/Alamy; **187** Stephen J. Carrera/AP/Wide World Photos; **192** Brand X Pictures/Alamy; **195** Mike Powell/Getty Images; **203** Tim Wakefield/SuperStock; **210** Lee Strickland/Getty Images; **215** Walter Meayers Edwards/Getty Images; **216** Gianni Cigolini/Getty Images; **220** Tom Bean/Corbis; **234–235** Getty Images; **236** C. B. Knight/Getty Images; **239** Rick Friedman/Corbis; **245** Medford Taylor/Getty Images; **251** David Hall/Nature Picture Library; **252** Kayte M. Deioma/PhotoEdit; **257** Image Source Limited/Index Stock Imagery; **259** Greg Huglin/SuperStock; **261** John Warden/SuperStock; **262** PhotoDisc/Getty Images; **264** *bottom right* Seth Thompson/Getty Images; **266** Hubble Heritage Team/NASA/AP/Wide World Photos; **269** Mike Mergen/AP/Wide World Photos; **270** Steve Allen/Brand X Pictures/PictureQuest; **271** Duomo/Corbis; **274** Cheryl Hatch/AP/Wide World Photos; **275** Dr. Fred Espenak/SPL/Photo Researchers, Inc.; **281** Imagebroker/Alamy; **282** Alfred Pasieka/SPL/Photo Researchers, Inc.; **283** *all* McDougal Littell; **284** Jim Cummins/Getty Images; **287** David Madison/Getty Images; **289** Ron Watts/Corbis; **291** Tom Stewart/Corbis; **292** Mike Yamashita/Corbis; **295** *left* David Madison/Getty Images; **295** *center* Roy Morsch/Corbis; **295** *right* Amwell/Getty Images; **299** Ben Mangor/SuperStock; **300** PhotoDisc/Getty Images; **303** Marcio Jose Sanchez/AP/Wide World Photos; **306** Stephen Frisch/Stock Boston; **309** Photolibrary.com/Index Stock Imagery; **311** Kevin Fleming/Corbis; **314** Michael Wong/Corbis; **316** Stockbyte; **328–329** Reuters/Corbis; **330** NASA/Corbis; **331** *right* Reuters/Corbis; **331** *left* Dex Image/Getty Images; **332** Comstock Images; **337** David Young-Wolff/PhotoEdit; **343** *bottom* ThinkStock LLC/Index Stock Imagery; **344** M. Philip Kahl/Bruce Coleman, Inc.; **346** Tim Larsen/AP/Wide World Photos; **348** David Frazier/Getty Images; **353** Richard T. Nowitz/Corbis; **362** Orlin Wagner/AP/Wide World Photos; **365** Royalty-Free/Corbis; **367** Joe Cavarotta/AP/Wide World Photos; **368** Neil Rabinowitz/Corbis; **370** *top right* Volker Steger/Siemens/SPL/Photo Researchers, Inc.; **376** age fotostock/SuperStock; **379** Peter Correz/Getty Images; **383** PhotoDisc/Getty Images; **385** Peter Yates/SPL/Photo Researchers, Inc.; **387** *top right* Turner & de Vries/Getty Images; **393** Terry Renna/AP/Wide World Photos; **398** Tom Stewart/Corbis; **400** Joe McDonald/Corbis; **412–413** David Bergman/Corbis; **414** Javier Soriano/AFP/Getty Images; **416** Azure Computer & Photo Services/Animals Animals; **419** McDougal Littell/Houghton Mifflin Co.; **420** Cameron Heryet/Getty Images; **426** Lester Lefkowitz/Corbis; **428** Darrell Gulin/Corbis; **431** StreetStock Images/Brand X Pictures/PictureArts; **434** Courtesy of Professor Tim Pennings, Hope College; **436** Royalty-Free/Corbis; **437** *both* RMIP/Richard Haynes/McDougal Littell; **438** Paul A. Souders/Corbis; **441** Gail Burton/AP/Wide World Photos; **444** Rod Taylor/AP/Wide World Photos; **446** Duomo/Corbis; **447** Navaswan/Getty Images; **451** Brian Erler/Getty Images; **452–453** Cathrine Wessel/Corbis; **453** Philippe Giraud/Corbis Sygma; **457** Casey Riffe/Marshfield News-Herald/AP/Wide World Photos; **458** OSF/Colbeck, M./Animals Animals; **476** *background* B.A.E. Inc./Alamy; **478** Greer & Associates, Inc./SuperStock; **484** Bob Daemmrich/Corbis Sygma; **485** Lynda Richardson/Corbis; **486** age fotostock/SuperStock; **488** PhotoDisc/Getty Images; **491** Richard A. Cooke/Corbis; **492** Cousteau Society/Getty Images; **498** Tim Hursley/SuperStock; **499** Chuck Carlton/Index Stock Imagery; **506** Jim McNee/Index Stock Imagery; **507** age fotostock/SuperStock; **509** Royalty-Free/Corbis; **511** *center left* image100/Alamy; **511** *center* Pat LaCroix/Getty Images; **511** *center right* Tony Arruza/Corbis; **512** *center right* Rubberball Productions; **512** *center left* Cathy Melloan/PhotoEdit; **512** *bottom* Rubberball Productions; **515** Roger Ressmeyer/Corbis; **516** Jeff Sherman/Getty Images; **522** *both* AM Corporation/Alamy; **528** *both* Jay Penni Photography/McDougal Littell; **529** Mark Chappell/Animals Animals; **530** Nick Dolding/Getty Images; **532** Gerard Lacz/Animals Animals; **534** Bryn Colton/Assignments Photographers/Corbis; **536** Bettmann/Corbis; **548–549** Jeff Hunter/Getty Images; **550** *both* RMIP/Richard Haynes/McDougal Littell; **551** Lawrence Manning/Corbis; **552** age fotostock/SuperStock; **553** Rick Bowmer/AP/Wide World Photos; **558** Ken Reid/Getty Images; **560** *both* Courtesy of Z Corporation; **565** Bobby Model/National Geographic/Getty Images; **567** Donald C. Johnson/Corbis; **569** The Photolibrary Wales/Alamy; **570** Scaled Composites/SPL/Photo Researchers, Inc.; **572** Michael Newman/PhotoEdit; **573** Mary Ann Chastain/AP/Wide World Photos; **579** Tony McConnell/SPL/Photo Researchers, Inc.; **582** Luca DiCecco/Alamy; **589** Denis Boissavy/Getty Images; **592** don jon red/Alamy; **594** Fédération Internationale de Volleyball/AP/Wide World Photos; **601** PhotoDisc/Getty Images; **612–613** Phototake/Getty Images; **614** Nick Vedros & Assoc./Getty Images; **618** Reuters/Corbis; **620** Stephen Frink/Getty

Images; **624** Hank Morgan/Time Life Pictures/Getty Images; **625** Roger Ressmeyer/Corbis; **626** Royalty-Free/Corbis; **634** Ralph Wetmore/Getty Images; **638** *bottom left* NASA/ARC; **638** *bottom right* Detlev Van Ravenswaay/SPL/Photo Researchers, Inc.; **641** Tom Uhlman/Visuals Unlimited; **642** Paul A. Souders/Corbis; **648** Mike Cartwright/AP/Wide World Photos; **649** RMIP/Richard Haynes/McDougal Littell; **650** Courtesy of Superdairyboy; **656** Erik S. Lesser/AP/Wide World Photos; **658** Yellow Dog Productions/Getty Images; **676** Fermilab Photo; **680–681** Alexander Walter/Getty Images; **682** Douglas C. Pizac/AP/Wide World Photos; **684** Oliver Morin/AFP/Getty Images; **690** Robbie Jack/Corbis; **696** Marc Lester/AP/Wide World Photos; **698** PhotoDisc/Getty Images; **699** Ellen Senisi/The Image Works; **705** *bottom left* Big Cheese Photo/FotoSearch; **707** Jeff Greenberg/The Image Works; **717** Dennis MacDonald/PhotoEdit; **719** NOAA/AP/Wide World Photos; **724** John Russell/AP/Wide World Photos; **742–743** Mark E. Gibson/Getty Images; **744** Omar Torres/AFP/Getty Images; **746** Banana Stock/Alamy; **748** Alan Diaz/AP/Wide World Photos; **749** Andy Lyons/Getty Images; **751** NASA-HQ-GRIN; **754** *bottom* Ric Francis/AP/Wide World Photos; **754** *top* Phil Cantor/Index Stock Imagery; **756** *top* age fotostock/SuperStock; **756** *bottom* Don Heupel/AP/Wide World Photos; **756** *bottom center* ThinkStock/SuperStock; **757** PhotoDisc/Getty Images; **759** Kennan Ward/Corbis; **762** Barbara Novovitch/Reuters; **765** Royalty-Free/Corbis; **766** David Young-Wolff/PhotoEdit; **772** Spencer Grant/PhotoEdit; **774** Jay Penni Photography/McDougal Littell; **775** Ben Margot/AP/Wide World Photos; **780** Jay Penni Photography/McDougal Littell; **782** Dynamic Graphics/PictureQuest; **792–793** Steve Gschmeissner/SPL/Photo Researchers, Inc.; **794** Roger Wood/Corbis; **799** Frank Chmura/PictureQuest; **802** Richard Cummins/Corbis; **805** Stockbyte/PictureQuest; **808** © 2007 Sol LeWitt/Artist Rights Society (ARS), New York. Photo Credit: Mary Ann Sullivan, Bluffton University; **810** PhotoStockFile/Alamy; **813** GDT/Getty Images; **815** Agence Vandystadt/Photo Researchers, Inc.; **819** *all* Jay Penni Photography/McDougal Littell; **820** Courtesy of Gayla Chandler; **827** Popperfoto/Alamy; **838** Gary S. Settles/Photo Researchers, Inc.; **850–851** João Paulo/Getty Images; **852** Hugh Sitton/Getty Images; **859** M. Spencer Green/AP/Wide World Photos; **864** *top* Royalty-Free/Corbis; **864** *center* Courtesy NASA, Life Sciences Division; **865** *both* Royalty-Free/Corbis; **866** age fotostock/SuperStock; **869** Courtesy NASA/JPL-Caltech; **873** *bottom right* Brand X Pictures/Getty Images; **873** *right* Richard Cummins/SuperStock; **873** *bottom right* Yoshio Tomii/SuperStock; **875** Greg Ebersole/AP/Wide World Photos; **879** Paolo Curto/The Image Bank; **882** Richard Berenholtz/Corbis; **885** Steve Bein/Corbis; **889** David Madison/Getty Images; **906–907** Royalty-Free/Corbis; **908** Richard Olseius/National Geographic/Getty Images; **910** Annabella Bluesky/SPL/Photo Researchers, Inc.; **913** Peter Arnold, Inc./Alamy; **915** *both* Craig T. Lorenz/Photo Researchers, Inc.; **921** Image Source/PunchStock; **924** Lowell Observatory/NOAO/AURA/NSF; **931** Scott Camazine/Photo Researchers, Inc.; **932** *both* Christopher Mackay/Tantramar Interactive; **940** PhotoDisc/Getty Images; **941** Lee Cohen/Corbis; **945** Steve Chenn/Corbis; **948** RMIP/Richard Haynes/McDougal Littell; **949** Howard Kingsnorth/Getty Images; **951** *left* Larry Dunmire/SuperStock; **951** *right* Ken Graham/Getty Images; **955** Pascal Rondeau/Getty Images; **963** Bill Ross/Corbis.

Illustrations and Maps

Argosy **1, 51, 70, 151, 235, 329, 413, 477, 549, 557** *top*, **613, 622** *top*, **646, 654, 662, 667** *top left*, **681, 743, 793, 818** *bottom left*; **851, 907, 921, 942, 954, 957**; Kenneth Batelman **504, 636, 752, 766 , 871, 879, 930, 946**; Steve Cowden **15, 32, 39, 95, 241, 243** *top center*, **247, 268, 298** *center*, **434, 439, 457, 464, 535**; Stephen Durke **290** *bottom*, **552, 570, 622** *center*, **660, 689** *top*, **800, 808** *top*, **832, 858, 872** *center right*, **896, 918, 929** *center*, **929** *top right*, **940**; John Francis **580, 761**; Patrick Gnan/Deborah Wolfe, Ltd. **5, 129, 254, 343** *top*, **351, 356, 360, 377, 392, 585, 641, 644, 657, 676, 818** *top right*; **822, 838, 880, 890, 902, 905, 927, 953, 972**; Chris Lyons **139, 158, 647** *center*; Steve McEntee **480, 563, 870, 873** *bottom left*, **877, 887, 893** *bottom*, **893** *center*, **904, 914, 916**; Paul Mirocha **497, 574**; Laurie O'Keefe **88, 494, 729**; Steve Stankiewicz **258, 505**; Doug Stevens **125**; Dan Stuckenschneider **16, 46, 87, 108, 119, 137, 185, 189, 250, 257, 265** *top right*, **369, 373, 426, 450, 519, 524, 556, 557** *center*, **688, 795, 824, 936**; Matt Zang/American Artists **500**; Carol Zuber-Mallison **111, 204, 208, 209, 358, 521, 587, 616, 618, 619, 663, 704, 855, 885, 961** *top right*, **961** *bottom*. All other illustrations © McDougal Littell/Houghton Mifflin Company.

Worked-Out Solutions

This section of the book provides step-by-step solutions to exercises with circled exercise numbers. These solutions provide models that can help guide your work with the homework exercises.

The separate **Selected Answers** section follows this section. It provides numerous answers that you can use to check your own answers.

WORKED-OUT SOLUTIONS

Chapter 1

Lesson 1.1 (pp. 6–9)

21. $7a + (4 + 5a)$

$= 7a + (5a + 4)$ Commutative property of addition

$= (7a + 5a) + 4$ Associative property of addition

$= (7 + 5)a + 4$ Distributive property

$= 12a + 4$ Simplify

31. $350 \text{ feet} \cdot \frac{1 \text{ yard}}{3 \text{ feet}} \approx 116.7 \text{ yards}$

59. a. Pluto, Neptune, Uranus, Saturn, Jupiter, Mars, Earth, Mercury, Venus

b. Mercury, Venus, Earth, Mars, Jupiter, Saturn, Uranus, Neptune, Pluto

c. The greater the distance from the sun, the colder the surface temperature.

d. Venus

Lesson 1.2 (pp. 13–16)

21. When $m = 6$:

$8m + (2m - 9)^3 = 8(6) + (2(6) - 9)^3$

$= 8(6) + (3)^3$

$= 48 + 27 = 75$

29. $7(m - 3) + 4(m + 5) = 7m - 21 + 4m + 20$

$= (7m + 4m) + (-21 + 20) = 11m - 1$

59. $270 - 4.5(x)$. The expression makes sense for all positive integer values of x less than or equal to 60. When $x > 60$, the balance is negative.

Lesson 1.3 (pp. 21–24)

23. $5b - 4 = 2b + 8$

$3b - 4 = 8$

$3b = 12$

$b = 4$

Check:

$5b - 4 = 2b + 8$

$5(4) - 4 \stackrel{?}{=} 2(4) + 8$

$20 - 4 \stackrel{?}{=} 8 + 8$

$16 = 16$ ✓

43. $\frac{1}{2}t + \frac{1}{3}t = 10$

$6\left(\frac{1}{2}t + \frac{1}{3}\right)t = 6(10)$

$3t + 2t = 60$

$5t = 60$

$t = 12$

Check:

$\frac{1}{2}t + \frac{1}{3}t = 10$

$\frac{1}{2}(12) + \frac{1}{3}(12) \stackrel{?}{=} 10$

$6 + 4 \stackrel{?}{=} 10$

$10 = 10$ ✓

71. $7.75(25) + 6.25x = 250$

$193.75 + 6.25x = 250$

$x = 9$

You must work 9 hours/week at the second job.

Lesson 1.4 (pp. 30–32)

3. $A = \ell w \rightarrow \frac{A}{w} = \ell$

When $w = 50$ and $A = 250$: $\ell = \frac{A}{w} = \frac{250}{50} = 5$

The length of the rectangle is 5 millimeters.

9. $6x + 5y = 31 \rightarrow 5y = 31 - 6x \rightarrow y = \frac{31}{5} - \frac{6x}{5}$

When $x = -4$: $y = \frac{31}{5} - \frac{6(-4)}{5} = \frac{55}{5} = 11$

WS1

35. $F = \frac{9}{5}C + 32 \rightarrow F - 32 = \frac{9}{5}C \rightarrow \frac{5}{9}(F - 32) = C$

When $F = 50$: $\frac{5}{9}(50 - 32) = C$

$$\frac{5}{9}(18) = C$$

$$10 = C$$

The temperature of 10°C corresponds to 50°F.

WORKED-OUT SOLUTIONS

Lesson 1.5 (pp. 37–40)

3. $d = rt \rightarrow 20 = 40t \rightarrow \frac{1}{2} = t$; $t = \frac{1}{2}$ hour

11. 11 15 19 23 An equation is $y = 11 + 4x$.

+4 +4 +4

27. 15 16.5 18 19.5 21

+1.5 +1.5 +1.5 +1.5

An equation is $y = 15 + 1.5x$. It is not reasonable to assume the pattern in the table continues indefinitely. If it did, the plant would become indefinitely tall.

Lesson 1.6 (pp. 44–47)

13. $x < -2$ or $x > 4$

25. $15 - 3x > 3$

$x < 4$

0 1 2 3 4 5 6

55. a. Lowland: $0 \le e < 500$

b. Alpine: $2000 \le e < 2429$

Subalpine: $1400 \le e < 2000$

Alpine and subalpine: $1400 \le e < 2429$

c. Not in montane zone: $e < 500$ or $e \ge 1400$

Lesson 1.7 (pp. 55–58)

21. $|2d - 5| = 13$

$2d - 5 = -13$ or $2d - 5 = 13$

$2d = -8$ or $2d = 18$

$d = -4$ or $d = 9$

47. $|d + 4| \ge 3$

−9 −7 −5 −3 −1 1

$d + 4 \le -3$ or $d + 4 \ge 3$

$d \le -7$ or $d \ge -1$

77. Accept: $|b - 21| \le 1$; Reject: $|b - 21| > 1$

Chapter 2

Lesson 2.1 (pp. 76–79)

7. (5, 20), (10, 20), (15, 30), (20, 30)

Domain: 5, 10, 15, and 20; Range: 20 and 30

Graph

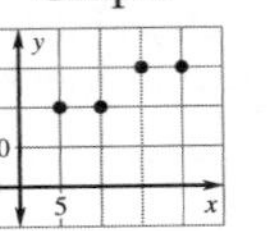

Mapping Diagram

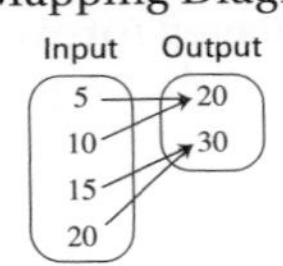

17. The relation is not a function because the input −2 is mapped to both 0 and 5.

45. $V(r) = \frac{4}{3}\pi r^3$

$V(6) = \frac{4}{3}\pi(6)^3 = 288\pi \approx 905$ units^3

$V(6)$ represents the volume of a sphere with a radius of 6 units.

Lesson 2.2 (pp. 86–88)

9. $m = \frac{3 - (-4)}{-1 - (-5)} = \frac{7}{4} > 0$; the line rises.

19. Line 1: through (1, 5) and (3, −2)

Line 2: through (−3, 2) and (4, 0)

$m_1 = \frac{-2 - 5}{3 - 1} = -\frac{7}{2}$

$m_2 = \frac{0 - 2}{4 - (-3)} = -\frac{2}{7}$

Because $m_1 \cdot m_2 = -\frac{7}{2} \cdot -\frac{2}{7} = 1 \neq -1$ and $m_1 \neq m_2$, the lines are neither perpendicular nor parallel.

45. A;

Average rate of change $= \frac{\text{change in gallons}}{\text{change in days}}$

$= \frac{214 \text{ gallons} - 400 \text{ gallons}}{30 \text{ days} - 0 \text{ days}}$

$= \frac{-186 \text{ gallons}}{30 \text{ days}} = -6.2$ gallons per day

WS2

Lesson 2.3 (pp. 93–96)

15.

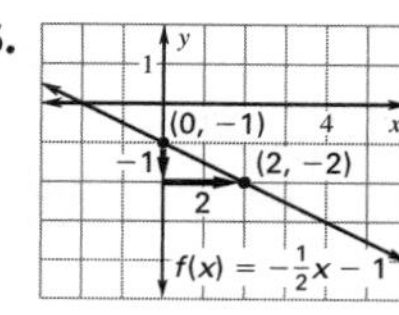

37. $-5x + 10y = 20$

x-intercept:

$-5x + 10(0) = 20$

$x = -4$

y-intercept:

$-5(0) + 10y = 20$

$y = 2$

31.

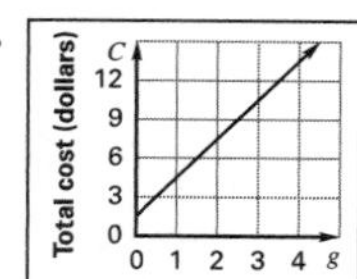

The y-intercept, 1.5, represents the cost to rent shoes, \$1.50. The slope, 3, represents the cost per game, \$3.

Lesson 2.4 (pp. 101–104)

5. Let $(x_1, y_1) = (7, -3)$ and $m = -\frac{4}{7}$.

$y - y_1 = m(x - x_1)$

$y - (-3) = -\frac{4}{7}(x - 7)$

$y = -\frac{4}{7}x + 1$

5. Let $(x_1, y_1) = (-5, -2)$ and $(x_2, y_2) = (-3, 8)$.

$m = \frac{y_2 - y_1}{x_2 - x_1} = \frac{8 - (-2)}{-3 - (-5)} = \frac{10}{2} = 5$

$y - y_1 = m(x - x_1)$

$y - (-2) = 5(x - (-5))$

$y = 5x + 23$

3. An equation is $15x + 9y = 4500$.

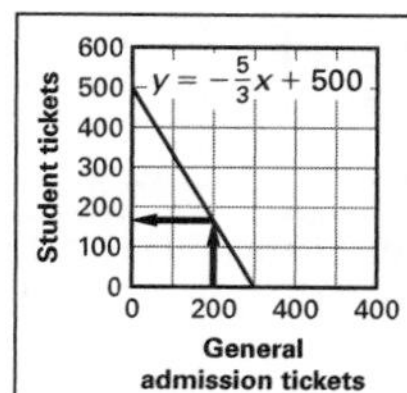

From the graph, you can see that if 200 general admissions tickets were sold, about 167 student tickets were sold.

Lesson 2.5 (pp. 109–111)

5. $y = ax$

$-21 = a(6)$

$-\frac{7}{2} = a$

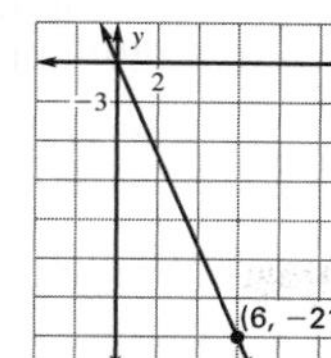

Substitute $-\frac{7}{2}$ for a in $y = ax$. $y = -\frac{7}{2}x$

15. $y = ax$

$-1.6 = a(-4.8)$

$\frac{1}{3} = a$

So, $y = \frac{1}{3}x$.

When $x = 12$:

$y = \frac{1}{3}(12) = 4$

41. $\frac{23}{4.5} \approx 5.1$ $\frac{40}{7.8} \approx 5.1$ $\frac{82}{16} \approx 5.1$

Because the ratios are approximately equal, the data show direct variation. An equation relating s and t is $t = 5.1s$.

Lesson 2.6 (pp. 117–120)

9. The correlation coefficient is closest to −1 because the scatter plot shows a strong negative correlation.

11. a.

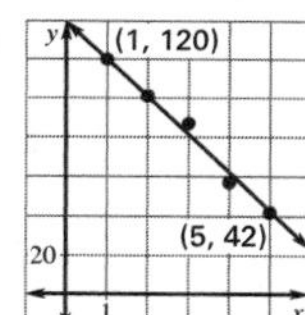

b. The line shown appears to pass through $(x_1, y_1) = (1, 120)$ and $(x_2, y_2) = (5, 42)$.

$m = \frac{y_2 - y_1}{x_2 - x_1} = \frac{42 - 120}{5 - 1} = -\frac{78}{4} = -19.5$

$y - y_1 = m(x - x_1)$

$y - 120 = -19.5(x - 1)$

$y = -19.5x + 139.5$

c. When $x = 20$:

$y = -19.5(20) + 139.5 = -250.5$

WORKED-OUT SOLUTIONS

WS3

25. A scatter plot and possible line of best fit are shown. The line appears to pass through $(x_1, y_1) = (0, 2240)$ and $(x_2, y_2) = (6, 2850)$.

$$m = \frac{y_2 - y_1}{x_2 - x_1} = \frac{2850 - 2240}{6 - 0} = \frac{610}{6} \approx 101.7$$

$$y - y_1 = m(x - x_1)$$

$$y - 2240 = 101.7(x - 0)$$

$$y = 101.7x + 2240$$

An approximation of the best-fitting line is $y = 101.7x + 2240$.

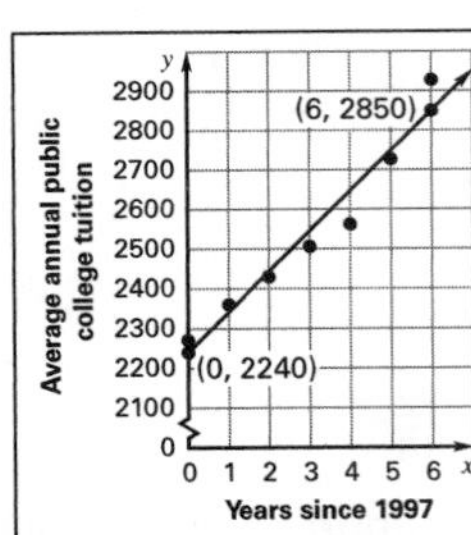

Lesson 2.7 (pp. 127–129)

13. The graph of $f(x) = -\frac{1}{2}|x - 1| + 5$ is the graph of $f(x) = |x|$ reflected in the x-axis, vertically shrunk by a factor of $\frac{1}{2}$, and translated right 1 unit and up 5 units.

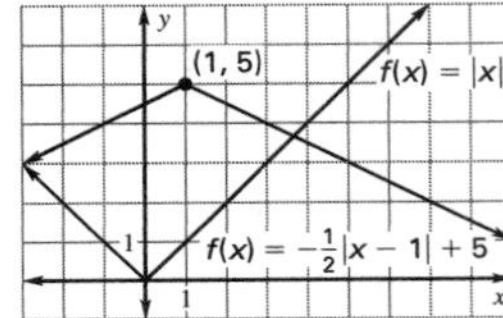

19. Vertex is $(-2, -1)$; $y = a|x + 2| - 1$

Using point $(0, 0)$: $0 = a|0 + 2| - 1$

$$\frac{1}{2} = a$$

An equation is $y = \frac{1}{2}|x + 2| - 1$.

39. Vertex is $(69, 140)$; $y = a|x - 69| + 140$

Using point $(0, 0)$: $0 = a|0 - 69| + 140$

$$-\frac{140}{69} = a$$

An equation is $y = -\frac{140}{69}|x - 69| + 140$.

Lesson 2.8 (pp. 135–138)

15.

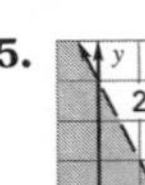
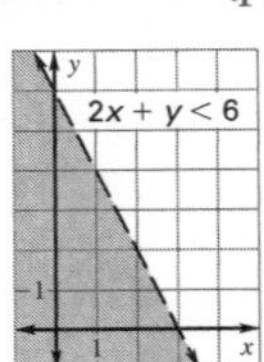

25.

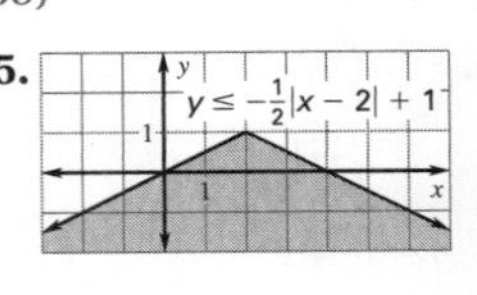

45. x = yards of cotton lace; y = yards of linen lace
$1.5x + 2.5y \le 75$

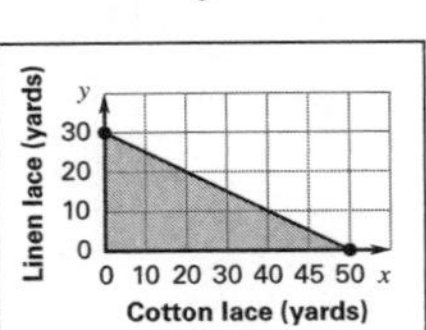

Let $x = 24$:

$$1.5(24) + 2.5y \le 75$$

$$y \le 15.6$$

You can buy 15.6 or less yards of linen lace.

Chapter 3

Lesson 3.1 (pp. 156–158)

9. $y = -3x - 2$

$4 \stackrel{?}{=} -3(-2) - 2$

$4 \stackrel{?}{=} 6 - 2$

$4 = 4$ ✓

$5x + 2y = -2$

$5(-2) + 2(4) \stackrel{?}{=} -2$

$-10 + 8 \stackrel{?}{=} -2$

$-2 = -2$ ✓

The solution is $(-2, 4)$.

21.

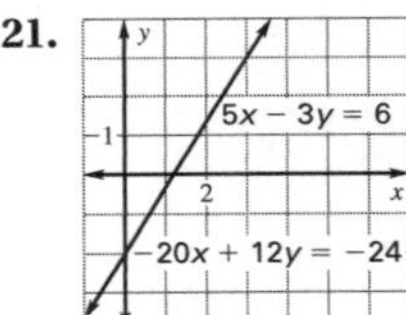

The graphs of the equations are the same line. The system has infinitely many solutions. The system is consistent and dependent.

37. Let y = total cost.

Let x = number of days.

Option A: $y = 121 + x$

Option B: $y = 12x$

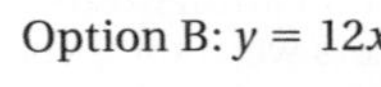

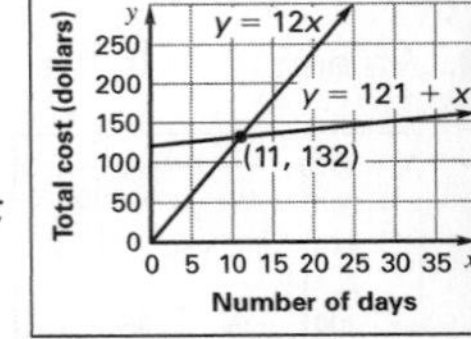

The plans are equal after 11 days. If the daily cost of option B increases, the plans will be equal in fewer days.

WORKED-OUT SOLUTIONS

Lesson 3.2 (pp. 164–167)

5. $6x - 2y = 5$

$-3x + y = 7 \rightarrow y = 3x + 7$

When $y = 3x + 7$:

$6x - 2(3x + 7) = 5$

$6x - 6x - 14 = 5$

$-14 \neq 5$ There is no solution.

29. $2x - 3y = 8$ $\xrightarrow{\times 2}$ $4x - 6y = 16$

$-4x + 5y = -10$ $\longrightarrow$ $-4x + 5y = -10$

$-y = 6$

When $y = -6$:

$2x - 3(-6) = 8$

$x = -5$ The solution is $(-5, -6)$.

59. x = double $\quad x + y = 26 \rightarrow y = 26 - x$

y = singles $\quad 4x + 2y = 76$

$4x + 2(26 - x) = 76 \quad y = 26 - x$

$4x + 52 - 2x = 76 \quad y = 26 - 12$

$x = 12 \quad y = 14$

There were 12 doubles games and 14 singles games in progress.

Lesson 3.3 (pp. 171–173)

9. $4x - 4y \geq -16$

$-x + 2y \geq -4$

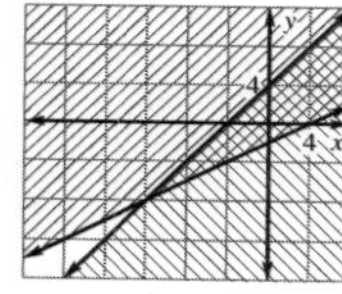

19. $3x + 2y > -6$

$-5 + 2y > -2$

$y < 5$

37. a. $x \geq 2$

$y \geq 2$

$x + y \leq 8$

$x + y \geq 5$

b.

c. *Sample answer:* 3 juniors, 4 seniors; 4 juniors, 4 seniors.

Lesson 3.4 (pp. 182–185)

11. $3x - y + 2z = 4$

$6x - 2y + 4z = -8$

$2x - y + 3z = 10$

$6x - 2y + 4z = -8$ Add -2 times Equation 1

$-6x + 2y - 4z = -8$ to Equation 2.

$0 = -8$

No solution

25. $x + 5y - 2z = -1$

$-x - 2y + z = 6$

$-2x - 7y + 3z = 7$

$x + 5y - 2z = -1$ Add Equation 2 to

$-y - 2y + z = 6$ Equation 1.

$3y - z = 5$ New Equation 1

$-2x - 7y + 3z = 7$ Add 2 times Equation

$2x + 10y - 4z = -2$ 1 to Equation 3.

$3y - z = 5$ New Equation 2

$3y - z = 5$ Add -1 times new Equation

$-3y + z = -5$ 1 to new Equation 2

$0 = 0$

Infinitely many solutions

45. a. f = 1st place; s = 2nd place; t = 3rd place

$f + s + t = 20$ Equation 1

$5f + 3s + t = 68$ Equation 2

$s = f + t$ Equation 3

$f + (f + t) + t = 20 \rightarrow 2f + 2t = 20$ New Eq. 1

$5f + 3(f + t) + t = 68 \rightarrow 8f + 4t = 68$ New Eq. 2

$-8f - 8t = -80$ Add -4 times new

$8f + 4t = 68$ Eq. 1 to new Eq. 2.

$-4t = -12$

$t = 3$

Substitute $t = 3$ into new Equation 1.

$2f + 2(3) = 20 \rightarrow f = 7$

Substitute $f = 7$ and $t = 3$ into Equation 3.

$s = f + t \rightarrow s = 7 + 3 = 10$

7 athletes placed first, 10 athletes placed second, and 3 athletes placed third.

WORKED-OUT SOLUTIONS

WS5

b. $f + s + t = 20$ Equation 1

$5f + 3s + t = 70$ Equation 2

$s = f + t$ Equation 3

$f + (f + t) + t = 20 \rightarrow 2f + 2t = 20$ New Eq. 1

$5f + 3(f + t) + t = 70 \rightarrow 8f + 4t = 70$ New Eq. 2

$-8f - 8t = -80$ Add -4 times new

$\underline{8f + 4t = 70}$ Eq. 1 to new Eq. 2.

$-4t = -10$

$t = \frac{5}{2}$

t cannot be a fraction; you cannot have part of a person. This claim must be false.

Lesson 3.5 (pp. 191–193)

5. $\begin{bmatrix} 10 & -8 \\ 5 & -3 \end{bmatrix} - \begin{bmatrix} 12 & -3 \\ 3 & -4 \end{bmatrix}$

$= \begin{bmatrix} 10 - 12 & -8 - (-3) \\ 5 - 3 & -3 - (-4) \end{bmatrix} = \begin{bmatrix} -2 & -5 \\ 2 & 1 \end{bmatrix}$

21. $\begin{bmatrix} 1.8 & -1.5 & 10.6 \\ -8.8 & 3.4 & 0 \end{bmatrix} + 3\begin{bmatrix} 7.2 & 0 & -5.4 \\ 2.1 & -1.9 & 3.3 \end{bmatrix}$

$= \begin{bmatrix} 1.8 + 21.6 & -1.5 + 0 & 10.6 + (-16.2) \\ -8.8 + 6.3 & 3.4 + (-5.7) & 0 + 9.9 \end{bmatrix}$

$= \begin{bmatrix} 23.4 & -1.5 & -5.6 \\ -2.5 & -2.3 & 9.9 \end{bmatrix}$

33. a.

	May(M) A	B	C	June (J) A	B	C
Downtown	31	42	18	25	36	12
Mall	22	25	11	38	32	15

b. $M + J = \begin{bmatrix} 31 & 42 & 18 \\ 22 & 25 & 11 \end{bmatrix} + \begin{bmatrix} 25 & 36 & 12 \\ 38 & 32 & 15 \end{bmatrix}$

$= \begin{bmatrix} 31 + 25 & 42 + 36 & 18 + 12 \\ 22 + 38 & 25 + 32 & 11 + 15 \end{bmatrix} = \begin{bmatrix} 56 & 78 & 30 \\ 60 & 57 & 26 \end{bmatrix}$

The downtown store sold 56 of Model A, 78 of Model B, and 30 of Model C. The mall store sold 60 of Model A, 57 of Model B, and 26 of Model C.

c. $\frac{1}{2}(M + J) = \frac{1}{2}\begin{bmatrix} 56 & 78 & 30 \\ 60 & 57 & 26 \end{bmatrix}$

$= \begin{bmatrix} 28 & 39 & 15 \\ 30 & 28.5 & 13 \end{bmatrix}$

Lesson 3.6 (pp. 199–202)

13. $\begin{bmatrix} 9 & -3 \\ 0 & 2 \end{bmatrix}\begin{bmatrix} 0 & 1 \\ 4 & -2 \end{bmatrix}$

$= \begin{bmatrix} 9(0) + (-3)(4) & 9(1) + (-3)(-2) \\ 0(0) + 2(4) & 0(1) + 2(-2) \end{bmatrix}$

$= \begin{bmatrix} -12 & 15 \\ 8 & -4 \end{bmatrix}$

23. $-\frac{1}{2}AC = -\frac{1}{2}\begin{bmatrix} 5 & -3 \\ -2 & 4 \end{bmatrix}\begin{bmatrix} -6 & 3 \\ 4 & 1 \end{bmatrix}$

$= -\frac{1}{2}\begin{bmatrix} 5(-6) + (-3)(4) & 5(3) + (-3)(1) \\ (-2)(-6) + (4)(4) & (-2)(3) + (4)(1) \end{bmatrix}$

$= -\frac{1}{2}\begin{bmatrix} -42 & 12 \\ 28 & -2 \end{bmatrix} = \begin{bmatrix} 21 & -6 \\ -14 & 1 \end{bmatrix}$

41. SP: $(3 \times 2)(1 \times 3)$ PS: $(1 \times 3)(3 \times 2)$

not equal equal

So, matrix PS is defined.

$PS = [650 \quad 825 \quad 1050]\begin{bmatrix} 21 & 16 \\ 40 & 33 \\ 15 & 19 \end{bmatrix}$

$= [650(21) + 825(40) + 1050(15) \quad 650(16) + 825(33) + 1050(19)]$

$= [62{,}400 \quad 57{,}575]$

The profit for dealer A is \$62,400 and the profit for dealer B is \$57,575.

Lesson 3.7 (pp. 207–209)

11. $\begin{vmatrix} -1 & 12 & 4 \\ 0 & 2 & -5 \\ 3 & 0 & 1 \end{vmatrix}\begin{matrix} -1 & 12 \\ 0 & 2 \\ 3 & 0 \end{matrix}$

$= (-2 - 180 + 0) - (24 + 0 + 0) = -206$

23. Area $= \pm\frac{1}{2}\begin{vmatrix} 4 & 2 & 1 \\ 4 & 8 & 1 \\ 8 & 5 & 1 \end{vmatrix} = \pm\frac{1}{2}\begin{vmatrix} 4 & 2 & 1 \\ 4 & 8 & 1 \\ 8 & 5 & 1 \end{vmatrix}\begin{matrix} 4 & 2 \\ 4 & 8 \\ 8 & 5 \end{matrix}$

$= \pm\frac{1}{2}[(32 + 16 + 20) - (64 + 20 + 8)] = 12$

The area of the triangle is 12 square units.

43. a. x = single; y = double; z = triple

$x + y + z = 120$

$0.90x + 1.2y + 1.6z = 134$

$x = y + z \rightarrow x - y - z = 0$

$$\left|\begin{array}{ccc|cc} 1 & 1 & 1 & 1 & 1 \\ 0.9 & 1.2 & 1.6 & 0.9 & 1.2 \\ 1 & -1 & -1 & 1 & -1 \end{array}\right|$$

$= (-1.2 + 1.6 - 0.9) - (1.2 - 1.6 - 0.9) = 0.8$

$$x = \frac{\begin{vmatrix} 120 & 1 & 1 \\ 134 & 1.2 & 1.6 \\ 0 & -1 & -1 \end{vmatrix}}{0.8} = \frac{48}{0.8} = 60$$

$$y = \frac{\begin{vmatrix} 1 & 120 & 1 \\ 0.9 & 134 & 1.6 \\ 1 & 0 & -1 \end{vmatrix}}{0.8} = \frac{32}{0.8} = 40$$

$$z = \frac{\begin{vmatrix} 1 & 1 & 120 \\ 0.9 & 1.2 & 134 \\ 1 & -1 & 0 \end{vmatrix}}{0.8} = \frac{16}{0.8} = 20$$

There are 60 single-scoop, 40 double-scoop, and 20 triple-scoop cones sold.

b. New price = $1.1 \times$ old price

1.1($.90) = $.99; 1.1($1.20) = $1.32; 1.1($1.60) = $1.76

New sales = $0.95 \times$ old sales

0.95(60) = 57; 0.95(40) = 38; 0.95(20) = 19

New revenue = $.99(57) + $1.32(38) + $1.76(19) = $140.03

Lesson 3.8 (pp. 214–217)

3. $A = \begin{bmatrix} 1 & -5 \\ -1 & 4 \end{bmatrix}$

$$A^{-1} = \frac{1}{4-5}\begin{bmatrix} 4 & 5 \\ 1 & 1 \end{bmatrix} = -1\begin{bmatrix} 4 & 5 \\ 1 & 1 \end{bmatrix} = \begin{bmatrix} -4 & -5 \\ -1 & -1 \end{bmatrix}$$

25. $\begin{bmatrix} 4 & -1 \\ -7 & -2 \end{bmatrix} \cdot \begin{bmatrix} x \\ y \end{bmatrix} = \begin{bmatrix} 10 \\ -25 \end{bmatrix}$

$$A^{-1} = \frac{1}{-8-7}\begin{bmatrix} -2 & 1 \\ 7 & 4 \end{bmatrix} = \begin{bmatrix} \frac{2}{15} & -\frac{1}{15} \\ -\frac{7}{15} & -\frac{4}{15} \end{bmatrix}$$

$$X = A^{-1}B = \begin{bmatrix} \frac{2}{15} & -\frac{1}{15} \\ -\frac{7}{15} & -\frac{4}{15} \end{bmatrix}\begin{bmatrix} 10 \\ -25 \end{bmatrix} = \begin{bmatrix} 3 \\ 2 \end{bmatrix} = \begin{bmatrix} x \\ y \end{bmatrix}$$

The solution of the system is (3, 2).

47. $\begin{bmatrix} 78 & 104 & 198 \\ 1 & 0 & 0.6 \\ 22 & 255 & 23.8 \end{bmatrix}\begin{bmatrix} b \\ t \\ w \end{bmatrix} = \begin{bmatrix} 500 \\ 3 \\ 100 \end{bmatrix}$

$$X = A^{-1}B = \begin{bmatrix} 2.3 \\ 0.8 \\ 1.2 \end{bmatrix}$$

2.3 oz Bran Crunchies; 0.8 oz Toasted Oats; and 1.2 oz Whole Wheat Flakes

Chapter 4

Lesson 4.1 (pp. 240–243)

15.

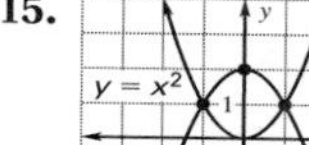

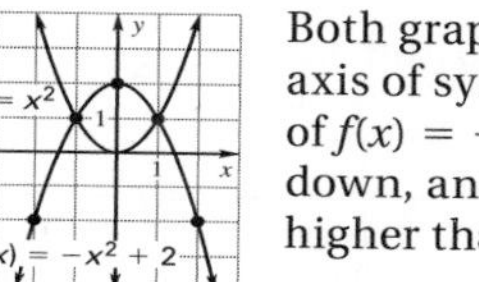

Both graphs have the same axis of symmetry. The graph of $f(x) = -x^2 + 2$ opens down, and its vertex is 2 units higher than that of $y = x^2$.

37. $f(x) = \frac{3}{2}x^2 + 6x + 4$

$a > 0$; the function has a minimum value.

$$x = \frac{-b}{2a} = \frac{-(6)}{2\left(\frac{3}{2}\right)} = -2$$

Minimum: $f(-2) = \frac{3}{2}(-2)^2 + 6(-2) + 4 = -2$

57. $y = \frac{1}{9000}x^2 - \frac{7}{15}x + 500$

$$x = \frac{-b}{2a} = \frac{-\left(\frac{-7}{15}\right)}{2\left(\frac{1}{9000}\right)} = 2100$$

$$y = \frac{1}{9000}(2100)^2 - \frac{7}{15}(2100) + 500 = 10$$

The cable is 10 feet above the road.

WORKED-OUT SOLUTIONS

Lesson 4.2 (pp. 249–251)

19. 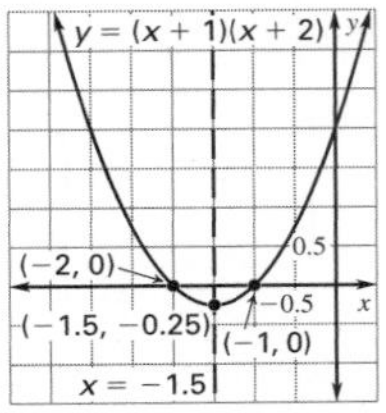 $a = 1, p = -1, \text{ and } q = -2$

x-int.: $x = -2$ and $x = -1$

Axis of sym.:

$$x = \frac{-2 + (-1)}{2} = -1.5$$

Vertex: $(-1.5, -0.25)$

29. $y = (x - 3)^2 + 6 = (x - 3)(x - 3) + 6$

$= (x^2 - 3x - 3x + 9) + 6 = x^2 - 6x + 15$

53. a. $y = -0.000234x(x - 160)$

$= -0.000234(x - 0)(x - 160)$

$p = 0, q = 160$; the field is 160 feet wide.

b. $x = \frac{p + q}{2} = \frac{0 + 160}{2} = 80$

$y = -0.000234(80)(80 - 160) \approx 1.5$

The maximum height is about 1.5 feet.

Lesson 4.3 (pp. 255–258)

33. $z^2 - 3z - 54 = 0 \rightarrow (z - 9)(z + 6) = 0$

$z - 9 = 0 \rightarrow z = 9$ or $z + 6 = 0 \rightarrow z = -6$

47. $y = x^2 + 7x - 30 = (x + 10)(x - 3)$

The zeros are -10 and 3.

67. a. $A = (30)(20) = 600 \text{ ft}^2$

b. New area (feet) = New length (feet) • New width (feet)

$1064 = (x + 30)(x + 20)$

c. $x^2 + 50x + 600 = 1064$

$(x - 58)(x - 8) = 0 \rightarrow x = -58$ or $x = 8$

Expand the length and width by 8 feet.

Lesson 4.4 (pp. 263–265)

27. $20x^2 + 124x + 24 = 4(5x^2 + 31x + 6)$

$= 4(5x + 1)(x + 6)$

39. $6r^2 - 7r - 5 = 0 \rightarrow (3r - 5)(2r + 1) = 0$

$r = \frac{5}{3} = 1\frac{2}{3}$ or $r = -\frac{1}{2}$

63. $96 = (2x + 8)(2x + 12) - 96$

$0 = 4x^2 + 40x - 96$

$0 = (4x - 8)(x + 12)$

$x = 2$ or $x = -12$

The border's width should be 2 feet.

Lesson 4.5 (pp. 269–271)

17. $\frac{\sqrt{2}}{4 + \sqrt{5}} = \frac{\sqrt{2}}{4 + \sqrt{5}} \cdot \frac{4 - \sqrt{5}}{4 - \sqrt{5}} = \frac{4\sqrt{2} - \sqrt{10}}{11}$

27. $-3w^2 = -213 \rightarrow w^2 = 71 \rightarrow w = \pm\sqrt{71}$

41. a. $\pi r^2 = 10^2 = 100$

b. $\pi r^2 = 100 \rightarrow r^2 = \frac{100}{\pi} \rightarrow r \approx 5.6$ feet

c. $\pi r^2 = s^2 \rightarrow r^2 = \frac{s^2}{\pi}$

$r = \sqrt{\frac{s^2}{\pi}} = \frac{s}{\sqrt{\pi}} \cdot \frac{\sqrt{\pi}}{\sqrt{\pi}} = \frac{s\sqrt{\pi}}{\pi}$

Lesson 4.6 (pp. 279–282)

11. $-5(n - 3)^2 = 10 \rightarrow (n - 3)^2 = -2$

$n - 3 = \pm\sqrt{-2} \rightarrow n = 3 \pm i\sqrt{2}$

29. $\frac{6i}{3 - i} = \frac{6i}{3 - i} \cdot \frac{3 + i}{3 + i} = \frac{18i + 6i^2}{9 + 3i - 3i - i^2}$

$= \frac{-6 + 18i}{10} = -\frac{6}{10} + \frac{18}{10}i = -\frac{3}{5} + \frac{9}{5}i$

67. Impedance: $12 + 8i - 6i - 10i = 12 - 8i$ ohms

Lesson 4.7 (pp. 288–291)

27. $x^2 - 2x = -25$

$x^2 - 2x + 1 = -25 + 1$

$(x - 1)^2 = -24$

$x - 1 = \pm\sqrt{-24} \rightarrow x = 1 \pm 2i\sqrt{6}$

45. $y = x^2 - 3x + 4$

$y + \frac{9}{4} = \left(x^2 - 3x + \frac{9}{4}\right) + 4$

$y = \left(x - \frac{3}{2}\right)^2 + \frac{7}{4}$

The vertex is $\left(\frac{3}{2}, \frac{7}{4}\right)$.

65.

$$y = (200 + 10x)(40 - x)$$
$$y = 8000 + 200x - 10x^2$$
$$y - 8000 = -10(x^2 - 20x)$$
$$y - 8000 + (-10)(100) = -10(x^2 - 20x + 100)$$
$$y - 9000 = -10(x - 10)^2$$
$$y = -10(x - 10)^2 + 9000$$

The revenue is maximized when the price is increased 10 times; 10($10) = $100.

Lesson 4.8 (pp. 296–299)

19. $4x^2 + 3 = x^2 - 7x \rightarrow 3x^2 + 7x + 3 = 0$

$$x = \frac{-7 \pm \sqrt{7^2 - 4(3)(3)}}{2(3)} = \frac{-7 \pm \sqrt{13}}{6}$$

39. $7r^2 - s = 2r + 9r^2 \rightarrow -2r^2 - 2r - 5 = 0$

$b^2 - 4ac = (-2)^2 - 4(-2)(-5) = -36 < 0$

Two imaginary: $\dfrac{-(-2) \pm \sqrt{-36}}{2(-2)} = -\dfrac{1}{2} \pm \dfrac{3}{2}i$

71. $S = -0.000013E^2 + 0.042E - 21$

$10 = -0.000013E^2 + 0.042E - 21$

$0 = -0.000013E^2 + 0.042E - 31$

$$E = \frac{-0.042 \pm \sqrt{(0.042)^2 - 4(-0.000013)(-31)}}{2(-0.000013)}$$

$$E = \frac{-0.042 \pm \sqrt{0.000152}}{-0.000026}$$

$E \approx 1141$ meters or $E \approx 2090$ meters

Lesson 4.9 (pp. 304–307)

17. $y \le -\frac{2}{3}x^2 + 3x + 1$

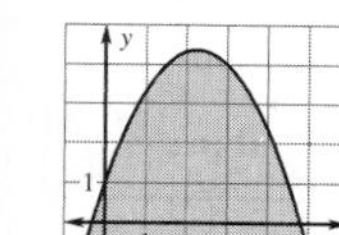

39. $3x^2 + 2x - 8 \le 0$

$(3x - 4)(x + 2) = 0$

$x = \frac{4}{3}$ or $x = -2$

The solution is $-2 \le x \le \frac{4}{3}$.

73. $0.0017x^2 + 0.145x + 2.35 > 10$

$0.0017x^2 + 0.145x - 7.65 > 0$

$$x = \frac{-0.145 \pm \sqrt{0.073045}}{0.0034} \approx 36.84, -122.13$$

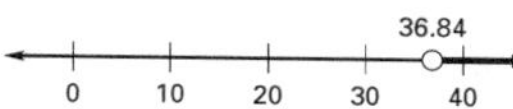

Test values $x = 0$ and $x = 37$ to determine that $x \ge 36.84$. The domain is $0 \le x \le 40$. So, the larvae's length tends to be greater than 10 mm between around 37 to 40 days.

Lesson 4.10 (pp. 312–315)

19. $y = a(x - p)(x - q) \rightarrow y = a(x + 3)(x - 3)$

$-4 = a(1 + 3)(1 - 3) \rightarrow \frac{1}{2} = a$

A quadratic function is $y = \frac{1}{2}(x + 3)(x - 3)$.

35. $y = ax^2 + bx + c$

$9 = a(-1)^2 + b(-1) + c \rightarrow a - b + c = 9$

$1 = a(1)^2 + b(1) + c \rightarrow a + b + c = 1$

$17 = a(3)^2 + b(3) + c \rightarrow 9a + 3b + c = 17$

Using substitution and $c = 9 - a + b$:

$a + b + (9 - a + b) = 1 \rightarrow b = -4$

$9a + 3(-4) + (9 - a - 4) = 17 \rightarrow a = 3$

$3 - (-4) + c = 9 \rightarrow c = 2$

A quadratic function is $y = 3x^2 - 4x + 2$.

49. a.

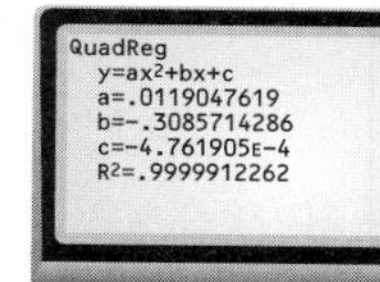

$y = 0.01190x^2 - 0.309x - 0.00048$

b. When $x = 10$, $y \approx -1.90$ seconds

Chapter 5

Lesson 5.1 (pp. 333–335)

17. $(6.3 \times 10^5)(8.9 \times 10^{-12}) = 56.07 \times 10^{-7}$

$= 5.607 \times 10^1 \times 10^{-7} = 5.607 \times 10^{-6}$

31. $\frac{3c^3d}{9cd^{-1}} = \frac{3}{9}c^{3-1}d^{1-(-1)} = \frac{1}{3}c^2d^2$

Quotient of powers property

51. Bead: $d = 6$ mm, $r = 3$ mm

$v = \frac{4}{3}\pi r^3 = \frac{4}{3}\pi(3)^3 = 36\pi$

Pearl: $d = 9$ mm, $r = \frac{9}{2}$ mm

$v = \frac{4}{3}\pi r^3 = \frac{4}{3}\pi\left(\frac{9}{2}\right)^3 = \frac{243\pi}{2}$

$\frac{\text{Volume of pearl}}{\text{Volume of bead}} = \frac{\frac{243\pi}{2}}{36\pi} = \frac{243}{72} = 3.375$

About 3.4 times greater

Lesson 5.2 (pp. 341–344)

21. 3 | −7 11 4 0

3	−7	11	4	0
		−21	−30	−78
	−7	−10	−26	−78

$f(3) = -78$

27. The degree is even and the leading coefficient is negative.

57.

t	0	2	4	6	8	10	12
s	1.2	1.46	1.68	1.59	1.44	1.97	4.41

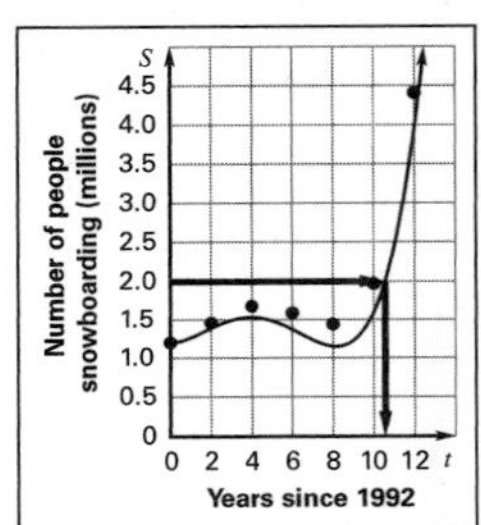

The number of snowboarders was greater than 2 million in 2002 (when $t \approx 10$).

Lesson 5.3 (pp. 349–352)

11. $(5b - 6b^3 + 2b^4) - (9b^3 + 4b^4 - 7)$

$= 2b^4 - 4b^4 - 6b^3 - 9b^3 + 5b + 7$

$= -2b^4 - 15b^3 + 5b + 7$

21. $(2a - 3)(a^2 - 10a - 2)$

$= (2a - 3)(a^2) - (2a - 3)(10a) - (2a - 3)(2)$

$= 2a^3 - 23a^2 + 26a + 6$

61. $P = 0.00267sF = 0.00267s(0.0116s^2 + 0.789)$

$= 0.000030972s^3 + 0.00210663s$

When $s = 10$, $P(10) = 0.0520383$.

About 0.052 horsepower is needed.

Lesson 5.4 (pp. 356–359)

7. $3y^5 - 48y^3 = 3y^3(y^2 - 16) = 3y^3(y + 4)(y - 4)$

23. $4c^3 + 8c^2 - 9c - 18 = 4c^2(c + 2) - 9(c + 2)$

$= (c + 2)(2c + 3)(2c - 3)$

61. $\ell = x$; $h = x - 5$; $w = x - 5$

$v = \ell wh \rightarrow 250 = (x)(x - 5)(x - 5)$

$250 = x(x^2 - 10x + 25)$

$0 = x^3 - 10x^2 + 25x - 250$

$0 = x^2(x - 10) + 25(x - 10)$

$0 = (x^2 + 25)(x - 10) \rightarrow x = 10$

$\ell = 10$ in., $h = 5$ in., $w = 5$ in.

Lesson 5.5 (pp. 366–368)

17.

6	1	−5	−8	13	−12
		6	6	−12	6
	1	1	−2	1	−6

$x^3 + x^2 - 2x + 1 - \frac{6}{x - 6}$

25.

−9	1	2	−51	108
		−9	63	−108
	1	−7	12	0

$f(x) = (x + 9)(x^2 - 7x + 12)$

$= (x + 9)(x - 4)(x - 3)$

43.

$$\begin{array}{r} -0.13x^2 + 11.2x - 560.9 \\ 14.8x + 725 \overline{)\,-1.95x^3 + 70.1x^2 - 188x + 2150} \\ \underline{-1.95x^3 - 95.5x^2} \qquad\qquad\qquad \\ 165.6x^2 - 188x \qquad\quad \\ \underline{165.6x^2 + 8113.3x} \qquad\quad \\ -8301.3x + 2150 \\ \underline{-8301.3x - 406{,}652.5} \\ 408{,}802.5 \end{array}$$

$f(x) = -0.13x^2 + 11.2x - 560.9 + \frac{408{,}802.5}{14.8x + 725}$

WORKED-OUT SOLUTIONS

Lesson 5.6 (pp. 374–377)

7. $g(x) = 4x^5 + 3x^3 - 2x - 14$

Factors of the constant term: $\pm1, \pm2, \pm7, \pm14$

Factors of the leading coefficient: $\pm1, \pm2, \pm4$

Possible rational zeros: $\pm\frac{1}{1}, \pm\frac{2}{1}, \pm\frac{7}{1}, \pm\frac{14}{1}, \pm\frac{1}{2},$

$\pm\frac{2}{2}, \pm\frac{7}{2}, \pm\frac{14}{2}, \pm\frac{1}{4}, \pm\frac{2}{4}, \pm\frac{7}{4}, \pm\frac{14}{4}$

$= \pm1, \pm2, \pm7, \pm14, \pm\frac{1}{2}, \pm\frac{7}{2}, \pm\frac{1}{4}, \pm\frac{7}{4}$

21. Possible rational zeros: $\pm1, \pm3, \pm5, \pm15, \pm\frac{1}{2},$

$\pm\frac{3}{2}, \pm\frac{5}{2}, \pm\frac{15}{2}, \pm\frac{1}{3}, \pm\frac{5}{3}, \pm\frac{1}{6}, \pm\frac{5}{6}$

Reasonable zeros: $x = -3, x = -\frac{5}{3}, x = \frac{1}{2}$

Test $x = -3$:

$$\begin{array}{r|rrrr} -3 & 6 & 25 & 16 & -15 \\ & & -18 & -21 & 15 \\ \hline & 6 & 7 & -5 & 0 \end{array}$$

$f(x) = (x + 3)(6x^2 + 7x - 5)$

$= (x + 3)(2x - 1)(3x + 5)$

Real zeros are $-3, \frac{1}{2}, -\frac{5}{3}$.

47. $V = x(x - 1)(x - 2) \rightarrow 24 = x(x^2 - 3x + 2)$

$0 = x^3 - 3x^2 + 2x - 24$

Possible rational zeros: $\pm1, \pm2, \pm3, \pm4, \pm6, \pm8, \pm12, \pm24$

Lesson 5.7 (pp. 383–386)

15. Possible rational zeros: $\pm1, \pm2, \pm4, \pm8$

$f(x) = x^4 + x^3 + 2x^2 + 4x - 8$

$= (x + 2)(x^3 - x^2 + 4x - 4)$

$= (x + 2)(x - 1)(x^2 + 4)$

$= (x + 2)(x - 1)(x - 2i)(x + 2i)$

The zeros are -2, 1, $2i$, and $-2i$.

37. $h(x) = x^5 - 2x^3 - x^2 + 6x + 5$

2 sign changes; 2 or 0 positive real zeros

$h(-x) = (-x)^5 - 2(-x)^3 - (-x)^2 + 6(-x) + 5$

$= -x^5 + 2x^3 - x^2 - 6x + 5$

3 sign changes; 3 or 1 positive real zeros.

Possible numbers of zeros:

Positive	Negative	Imaginary	Total
2	3	0	5
0	3	2	5
2	1	2	5
0	1	4	5

61. $S = -0.015x^3 + 0.6x^2 - 2.4x + 19$

$0 = -0.015x^3 + 0.6x^2 - 2.4x - 56$

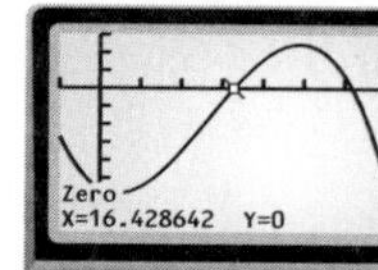

There are two positive zeros of this function, $x \approx 16.4$ and $x \approx 30.9$, but $x \approx 16.4$ is the most likely amount.

Lesson 5.8 (pp. 390–392)

3.

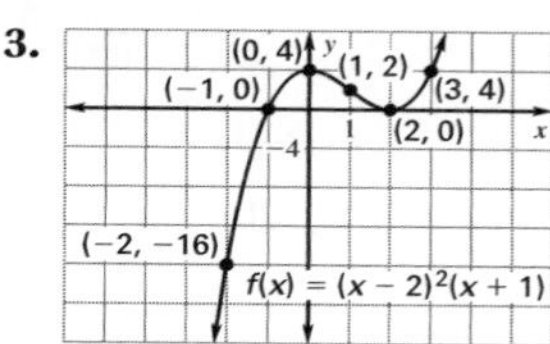

19. Turning pts: $(-2.2, -38)$, local minimum; $(-1.1, 0.8)$, local maximum; $(0.3, -40)$, local minimum; $(1.9, 8)$, local maximum; $(2.75, -10.5)$, local minimum

Zeros: $x \approx -2.6, x \approx -1.4, x \approx -1, x \approx 1.5,$ $x \approx 2.2, x \approx 3$

It must be at least a degree 6 function.

41.

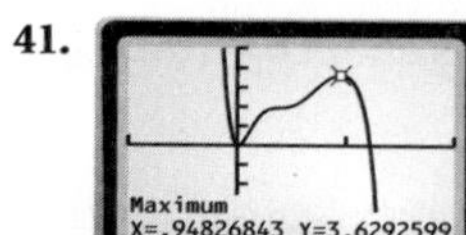

At about 0.95 seconds into the stroke the swimmer is going the fastest.

Lesson 5.9 (pp. 397–399)

9. $f(x) = a(x + 5)(x)(x - 6)$

$-12 = a(1 + 5)(1)(1 - 6) \rightarrow \frac{2}{5} = a$

$f(x) = \frac{2}{5}x(x + 5)(x - 6)$

15. $f(1)$ $f(2)$ $f(3)$ $f(4)$ $f(5)$ $f(6)$

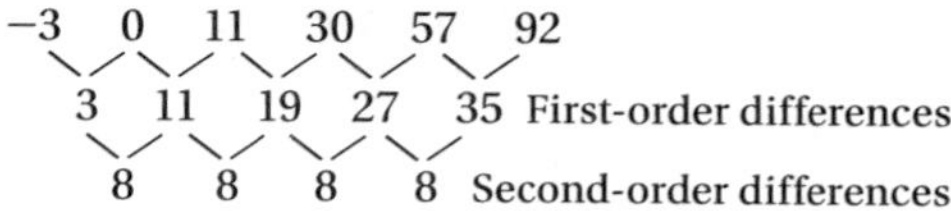

27. a. $m = 0.00081742t^3 - 0.02154t^2 + 0.249t + 3.17$

b. X=27 Y=10.279618

About \$10.30

c. Intersection X=12.354934 Y= 4.5

In 1995 ($t \approx 12.4$)

Chapter 6

Lesson 6.1 (pp. 417–419)

9. $(\sqrt[n]{a})^m = a^{m/n} \to (\sqrt[3]{10})^7 = 10^{7/3}$

25. $27^{2/3} = (27^{1/3})^2 = (3)^2 = 9$

63. $p = ks^3 \to 1.2 = k(1700)^3 \to k = \dfrac{3}{12{,}282{,}500{,}000}$

$p = \dfrac{3}{12{,}282{,}500{,}000}s^3 \to 1.5 = \dfrac{3}{12{,}282{,}500{,}000}s^3$

$\to 6{,}141{,}250{,}000 = s^3 \to s \approx 1831$

About 1800 revolutions per minute

Lesson 6.2 (pp. 424–427)

5. $3^{1/4} \cdot 27^{1/4} = 3^{1/4} \cdot 3^{1/4} \cdot 3^{1/4} \cdot 3^{1/4}$

$= 3^{(1/4 + 1/4 + 1/4 + 1/4)} = 3^1 = 3$

27. $5\sqrt[4]{64} \cdot 2\sqrt[4]{8} = 10\sqrt[4]{512} = 40\sqrt[4]{2}$

85. $d = 1.9[(5.5 \times 10^{-4})\ell]^{1/2}$

$\ell = 10 \text{ cm} = 100 \text{ mm}$

$d = 1.9[(5.5 \times 10^{-4})(100)]^{1/2} \approx 0.4456$

The optimum diameter is about 0.45 mm.

Lesson 6.3 (pp. 432–434)

3. $f(x) + g(x) = -3x^{1/3} + 4x^{1/2} + 5x^{1/3} + 4x^{1/2}$

$= 2x^{1/3} + 8x^{1/2}$

Domain of f: all nonnegative reals

Domain of g: all nonnegative reals

Domain of $f + g$: all nonnegative reals

13. $g(x) \cdot f(x) = (5x^{1/2})(4x^{2/3}) = 20x^{7/6}$

Domain of f: all reals

Domain of g: all nonnegative reals

Domain of $g \cdot f$: all nonnegative reals

45. For \$15 discount: $f(x) = x - 15$

For 10% discount: $g(x) = x - 0.1x = 0.9x$

a. $g(f(x)) = g(x - 15) = 0.9(x - 15)$

$x = 85$: $0.9(85 - 15) = 0.9(70) = \$63.00$

b. $f(g(x)) = f(0.9x) = 0.9x - 15$

$x = 85$: $0.9(85) - 15 = 76.5 - 15 = \$61.50$

c. The 10% discount before the \$15 discount.

Lesson 6.4 (pp. 442–445)

7. $y = 12x + 7 \to x = 12y + 7 \to \dfrac{x}{12} - \dfrac{7}{12} = y$

15. $f(g(x)) = f(x - 4) = (x - 4) + 4 = x$ ✓

$g(f(x)) = g(x + 4) = (x + 4) - 4 = x$ ✓

49. $v = 1.34\sqrt{\ell}$

$\left(\dfrac{v}{1.34}\right)^2 = \ell$

The waterlength should be $\ell = \left(\dfrac{7.5}{1.34}\right)^2 \approx 31.3$ feet.

Lesson 6.5 (pp. 449–451)

11. The domain and range are all real numbers.

17. 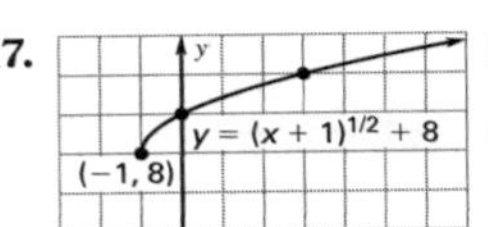

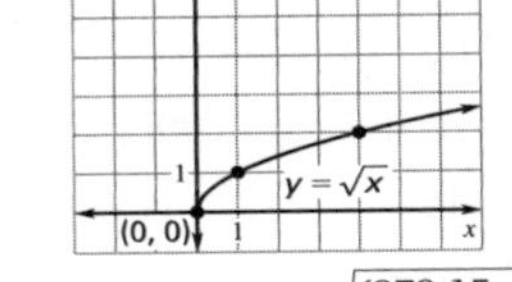

Domain: $x \geq -1$

Range: $y \geq 8$

37. a. $v = 331.5\sqrt{\dfrac{(273.15 + C)}{273.15}} = 331.5\sqrt{1 + \dfrac{C}{273.15}}$

b. Domain: $C \geq -273.15$; range: $v \geq 0$

Lesson 6.6 (pp. 456–459)

5. $\sqrt{9x} + 11 = 14$

$\sqrt{9x} = 3$

$9x = 9 \to x = 1$

Check: $\sqrt{9(1)} + 11 \stackrel{?}{=} 14$

$\sqrt{9} + 11 \stackrel{?}{=} 14$

$14 = 14$ ✓

13. $\sqrt[3]{x} - 10 = -3$

$\sqrt[3]{x} = 7$

$(\sqrt[3]{x})^3 = (7)^3 \to x = 343$

Check: $\sqrt[3]{343} - 10 \stackrel{?}{=} -3$

$7 - 10 \stackrel{?}{=} -3$

$-3 = -3$ ✓

59. $h = 150$: $\quad 150 = 62.5\sqrt[3]{t} + 75.8$

$1.7 \approx t$

$h = 250$: $\quad 250 = 625\sqrt[3]{t} + 75.8$

$21.7 \approx t$

The elephant with a shoulder height of 250 cm is about 20 years older than the elephant with the shoulder height of 150 cm.

Chapter 7

Lesson 7.1 (pp. 482–485)

17. 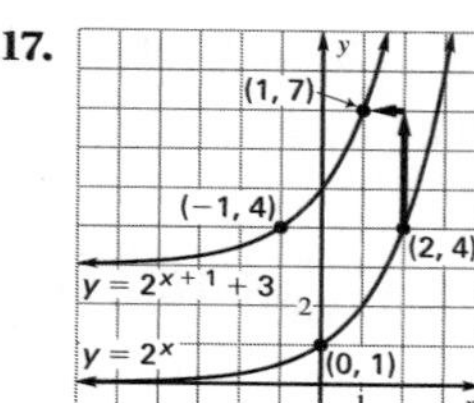

The domain is all real numbers and the range is $y > 3$.

29. $A = P\left(1 + \frac{r}{n}\right)^{nt} = 800\left(1 + \frac{0.02}{365}\right)^{365t}$

37. a. $P = 2200$; $r = 0.03$; $n = 4$; $t = 4$

$A = 2200\left(1 + \frac{0.03}{4}\right)^{4 \cdot 4} \approx 2479.38$

The balance is \$2479.38.

b. $P = 2200$; $r = 0.0225$; $n = 12$; $t = 4$

$A = 2200\left(1 + \frac{0.0225}{12}\right)^{12 \cdot 4} \approx 2406.98$

The balance is \$2406.98.

c. $P = 2200$; $r = 0.02$; $n = 365$; $t = 4$

$A = 2200\left(1 + \frac{0.02}{365}\right)^{365 \cdot 4} \approx 2383.23$

The balance is \$2383.23.

Lesson 7.2 (pp. 489–491)

9. 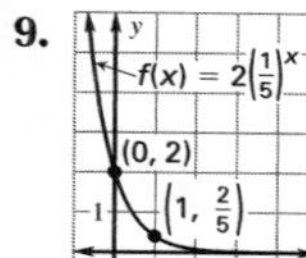

19. 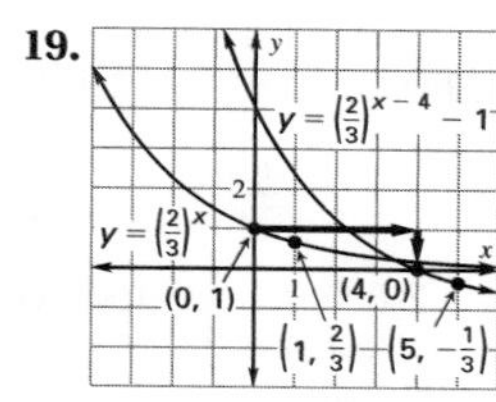

Domain: all real numbers
Range: $y > -1$

33. a. 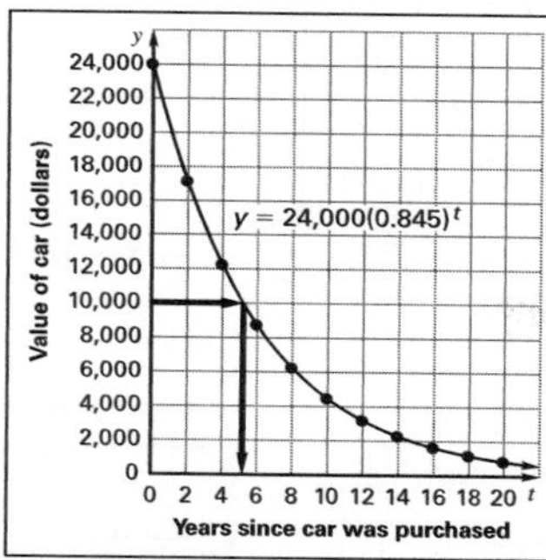

About 5 years after it was purchased

b. $y = 24{,}000(0.845)^{50} \approx \$5.29$; too low

Lesson 7.3 (pp. 495–498)

5. $(2e^{3x})^3 = 2^3(e^{3x})^3 = 8e^{9x}$

35. $f(x) = \frac{1}{4}e^{-5x}$; exponential decay

57. $P = 2000$; $r = 0.04$; $t = 5$

$A = Pe^{rt} = 2000e^{(0.04)(5)} \approx \$2442.81$

Lesson 7.4 (pp. 503–505)

13. $\left(\frac{1}{2}\right)^{-3} = 8$, so $\log_{1/2} 8 = -3$.

33. $\log_3 81^x = \log_3 (3^4)^x = \log_3 3^{4x} = 4x$

61. a. $E = 2.5 \times 10^{24}$

$M = 0.29(\ln(2.5 \times 10^{24})) - 9.9 \approx 6.39$

b. $M = 0.29(\ln E) - 9.9$

$\frac{M + 9.9}{0.29} = \ln E \rightarrow e^{(M + 9.9)/0.29} = E$

This represents the amount of energy released as a function of the energy magnitude.

Lesson 7.5 (pp. 510–513)

11. $\log 144 = \log 12^2 = 2 \log 12 = 2.158$

17. $\log 3x^4 = \log 3 + \log x^4 = \log 3 + 4 \log x$

71. $L(10I) - L(I) = 10 \log \frac{10I}{I_0} - 10 \log \frac{I}{I_0}$

$= 10\left(\log \frac{10I}{I_0} - \log \frac{I}{I_0}\right)$

$= 10\left(\log 10 + \log \frac{I}{I_0} - \log \frac{I}{I_0}\right)$

$= 10 \log 10 = 10$ decibels

Lesson 7.6 (pp. 519–522)

15. $11^{5x} = 33$

$\log_{11} 11^{5x} = \log_{11} 33$

$5x = \log_{11} 33 = \frac{\log 33}{\log 11} \to x \approx 0.2916$

35. $5.2 \log_4 2x = 16$ Check:

$\log_4 2x \approx 3.0769$

$4^{(\log_4 2x)} \approx 4^{3.0769}$

$2x \approx 71.2020$

$x \approx 35.6010$

Intersection X=35.601007 Y=16

57. $R = 100e^{-0.00043t} \to 5 = 100e^{-0.00043t}$

$0.05 = e^{-0.00043t}$

$\ln 0.05 = \ln e^{-0.00043t}$

$-2.9957 \approx -0.00043t$

$t \approx 6967$ years

Lesson 7.7 (pp. 533–536)

11. $m = \frac{5.66 - 2.89}{5 - 1} \approx 0.69$

$\ln y - 2.89 = 0.69(x - 1)$

$\ln y = 0.69x + 2.2$

$y = e^{0.69x + 2.2}$

$y = e^{2.2}(e^{0.69})^x \approx 9(2)^x$

23.

ln x	0	0.693	1.099	1.386	1.609
ln y	−0.511	1.411	2.518	3.296	3.902

$m = \frac{3.902 - (-0.511)}{1.609 - 0} \approx 2.743$

$\ln y - (-0.511) = 2.743(\ln x - 0)$

$\ln y = \ln x^{2.743} - 0.511$

$y = e^{\ln x^{2.743} - 0.511}$

$y = e^{-0.511} \cdot e^{\ln x^{2.743}} \approx 0.6x^{2.743}$

33. a. A model is $y = 0.48(2.08)^x$.

b. Linear if a graph of (x, y) appears linear; exponential if a graph of $(x, \ln y)$ appears linear; power if a graph of $(\ln x, \ln y)$ appears linear. The graph of (x, y) appears linear, so a model is $y = 33.8x + 28$.

Chapter 8

Lesson 8.1 (pp. 554–557)

15. $y = \frac{a}{x} \to 2 = \frac{a}{7} \to 14 = a$

$y = \frac{14}{x} \to y = \frac{14}{3}$

21. $x \cdot y$: $12(132) = 1584$ y/x: $132/12 = 11$

$18(198) = 3564$ $198/18 = 11$

$23(253) = 5819$ $253/23 = 11$

$29(319) = 9251$ $319/29 = 11$

$34(374) = 12{,}716$ $374/34 = 11$

x and y show direct variation because the ratios y/x are equal.

39. Snow shoes: $P = \frac{a}{A} \to 0.43 = \frac{a}{400} \to 172 = a$

An equation is $P = \frac{172}{A}$.

Boots: $P = \frac{172}{60} \to P \approx 2.87$ lb/in.^{2}

Lesson 8.2 (pp. 561–563)

5.

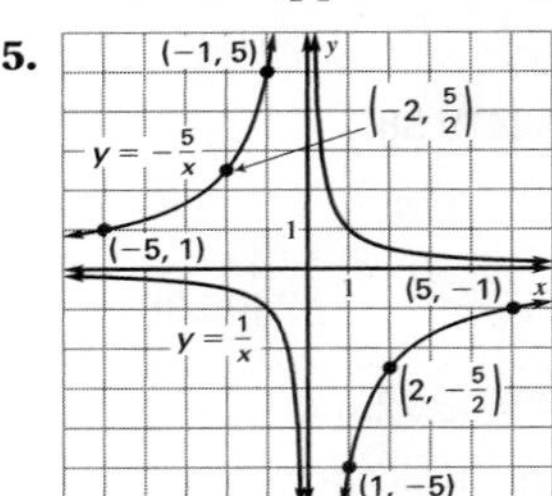

The graph of $y = \frac{-5}{x}$ lies farther from the axes than the graph of $y = \frac{1}{x}$, and it lies in Quadrants II and IV instead of Quadrants I and III.

21.

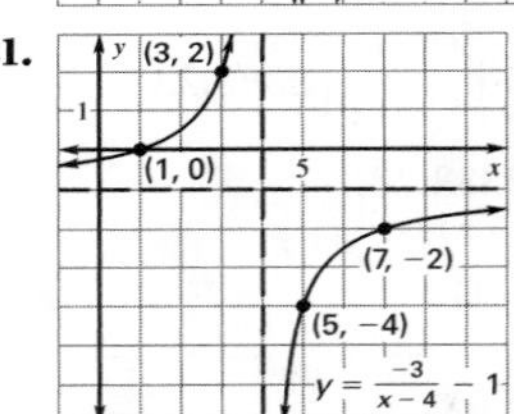

The domain is all real numbers except 4, and the range is all real numbers except −1.

39. a. $t = \frac{1000}{0.6T + 331} = \frac{1000}{0.6(25) + 331} \approx 2.89$

2.89 seconds to travel 1 kilometer; $2.89(5) = 14.45$ seconds to travel 5 kilometers

39. b. From the graph, you can estimate the temperature to be 3.9°C.

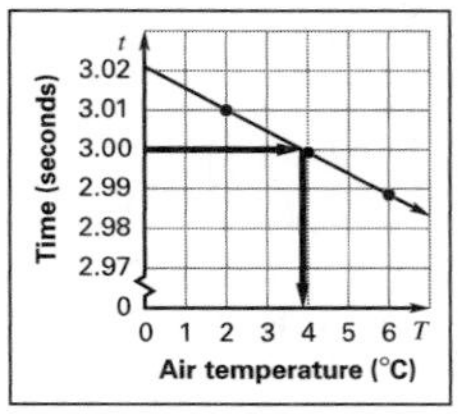

Lesson 8.3 (pp. 568–571)

7. $y = \frac{5}{x^2 - 1} \rightarrow y = \frac{5}{(x + 1)(x - 1)}$

No x-intercept; $x = -1$ and $x = 1$ are vertical asymptotes.

15.

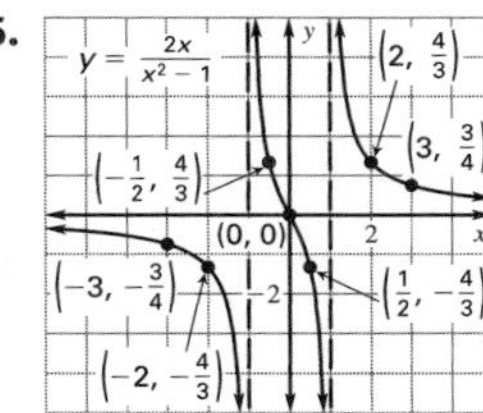

33. a.

Depth	Temp.
1000	4.7634
1050	4.5796
1100	4.4094
1150	4.2515
1200	4.1044
1250	3.9672
1300	3.8389

b. The mean temperature is 4°C at about 1238 meters.

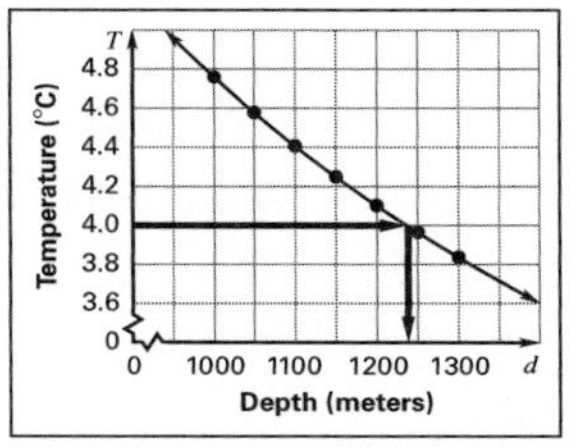

Lesson 8.4 (pp. 577–580)

7. $\frac{(x - 5)(x + 4)}{(x + 5)(x - 3)}$ Cannot be simplified

25. $\frac{48x^7y^4}{6x^3y^6} = \frac{\not{6} \cdot 8 \cdot \not{x^3} \cdot x^4 \cdot \not{y^4}}{\not{6} \cdot \not{x^3} \cdot \not{y^4} \cdot y^2} = \frac{8x^4}{y^2}$

49.

$$S \div A = \frac{-6420t + 292{,}000}{6.02t^2 - 125t + 1000} \div \frac{-407t + 7220}{5.92t^2 - 131t + 1000}$$

$$= \frac{-6420t + 292{,}000}{6.02t^2 - 125t + 1000} \cdot \frac{5.92t^2 - 131t + 1000}{-407t + 7220}$$

For 1999, $t = 7$: $S \div A = \frac{247{,}060}{419.98} \cdot \frac{373.08}{4371} \approx \$50.21$

Lesson 8.5 (pp. 586–588)

5. $\frac{9}{x + 1} - \frac{2x}{x + 1} = \frac{9 - 2x}{x + 1}$

17. $\frac{8}{3x^2} - \frac{5}{4x} = \frac{32}{12x^2} - \frac{15x}{12x^2} = \frac{32 - 15x}{12x^2}$

43. a. $M = \frac{Pi}{1 - \left(\frac{1}{1 + i}\right)^{12t}} = \frac{Pi}{1 - \frac{1}{(1 + i)^{12t}}}$

$$= \frac{Pi}{\frac{(1 + i)^{12t} - 1}{(1 + i)^{12t}}} = \frac{Pi(1 + i)^{12t}}{(1 + i)^{12t} - 1}$$

b. $P = 15{,}500$; $i = 0.06$; $t = 4$

$$m = \frac{15{,}500(0.005)(1 + 0.005)^{48}}{(1 + 0.005)^{48} - 1} \approx \$364.02$$

Lesson 8.6 (pp. 593–595)

5. $\frac{9}{3x} = \frac{4}{x + 2}$ Check: $\frac{9}{3(6)} \stackrel{?}{=} \frac{4}{(6) + 2}$

$4(3x) = 9(x + 2)$ $\frac{9}{18} \stackrel{?}{=} \frac{4}{8}$

$x = 6$ $\frac{1}{2} = \frac{1}{2}$ ✓

15. $\frac{2}{3x} + \frac{1}{6} = \frac{4}{3x}$ Check: $\frac{2}{3(4)} + \frac{1}{6} \stackrel{?}{=} \frac{4}{3(4)}$

$6x\left(\frac{2}{3x} + \frac{1}{6}\right) = 6x\left(\frac{4}{3x}\right)$ $\frac{2}{12} + \frac{1}{6} \stackrel{?}{=} \frac{4}{12}$

$2(2) + 1(x) = 4(2) \rightarrow x = 4$ $\frac{4}{12} = \frac{4}{12}$ ✓

35.

$$n = \frac{635t^2 - 7350t + 27{,}200}{t^2 - 11.5t + 39.4}$$

$$720 = \frac{635t^2 - 7350t + 27{,}200}{t^2 - 11.5t + 39.4}$$

$$720t^2 - 8280t + 28{,}368 = 635t^2 - 7350t + 27{,}200$$

$$85t^2 - 930 + 1168 = 0$$

$$t = \frac{930 \pm \sqrt{(930)^2 - 4(1168)(85)}}{2(85)} \approx 1.45, 9.45$$

Because 9.45 is not in the domain $(0 \le t \le 9)$, $t \approx 1.45 \rightarrow 1995$.

Chapter 9

Lesson 9.1 (pp. 617–619)

7. $d = \sqrt{(6 - 2)^2 + (-5 - (-1))^2} = 4\sqrt{2}$

Midpoint $= \left(\frac{2 + 6}{2}, \frac{-1 + (-5)}{2}\right) = (4, -3)$

WORKED-OUT SOLUTIONS

27. $A(-4, 1), B(-2, 6), C(0, -1)$

$AB = \sqrt{(-2-(-4))^2 + (6-1)^2} = \sqrt{29}$

$BC = \sqrt{(0-(-2))^2 + (-1-6)^2} = \sqrt{53}$

$AC = \sqrt{(0-(-4))^2 + (-1-1)^2} = \sqrt{20} = 2\sqrt{5}$

$AB \neq BC \neq AC$, so $\triangle ABC$ is scalene.

53. a. $M = \left(\frac{-6+3}{2}, \frac{5+11}{2}\right) = \left(-\frac{3}{2}, 8\right)$

b. $VS = \sqrt{(-6-0)^2 + (5-0)^2} = \sqrt{61}$

$SM = \sqrt{\left(-\frac{3}{2} - (-6)\right)^2 + (8-5)^2} = \frac{\sqrt{117}}{2}$

$VS + SM = \sqrt{61} + \frac{\sqrt{117}}{2}$

$\approx 13.2 \text{ units} \cdot \frac{0.1 \text{ mi}}{1 \text{ unit}} = 1.32 \text{ mi}$

c. $MP = \frac{\sqrt{117}}{2}$

$PV = \sqrt{(0-3)^2 + (0-11)^2} = \sqrt{130}$

$MP + PV = \frac{\sqrt{117}}{2} + \sqrt{130}$

$\approx 16.8 \text{ units} \cdot \frac{0.1 \text{ mi}}{1 \text{ unit}} = 1.68 \text{ mi}$

Lesson 9.2 (pp. 623–625)

15. $5x^2 = -15y \rightarrow x^2 = -3y$

$4p = -3 \rightarrow p = -\frac{3}{4}$

Focus: $\left(0, -\frac{3}{4}\right)$

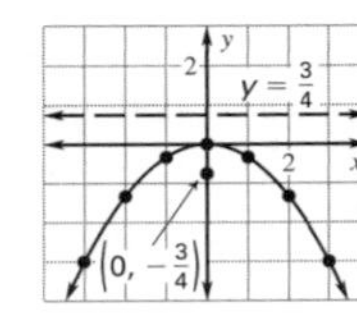

Directrix: $y = \frac{3}{4}$ Axis of symmetry: $x = 0$

27. Focus: $(-5, 0) \rightarrow p = -5 \rightarrow y^2 = -20x$

57. a.

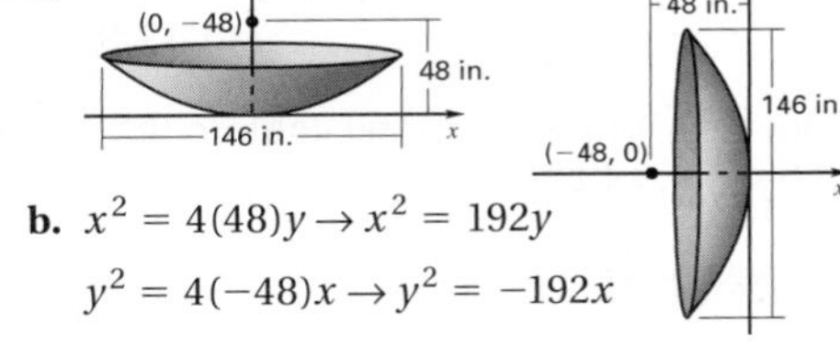

b. $x^2 = 4(48)y \rightarrow x^2 = 192y$

$y^2 = 4(-48)x \rightarrow y^2 = -192x$

c. Using $x^2 = 192y$ and $x = 73$, $y \approx 27.8$

Using $y^2 = -192x$ and $y = 73$, $x \approx -27.8$.

The dish is about 27.8 inches deep.

Lesson 9.3 (pp. 629–632)

17. $15x^2 + 15y^2 = 60$

$x^2 + y^2 = 4$

$r = \sqrt{4} = 2$

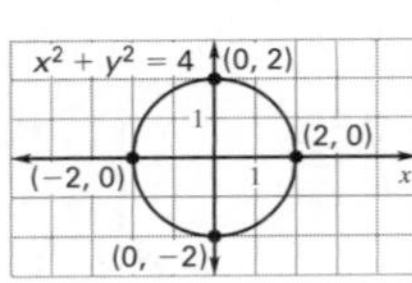

39. $r = \sqrt{(-8-0)^2 + (14-0)^2} = \sqrt{260}$

$x^2 + y^2 = (\sqrt{260})^2 \rightarrow x^2 + y^2 = 260$

65.

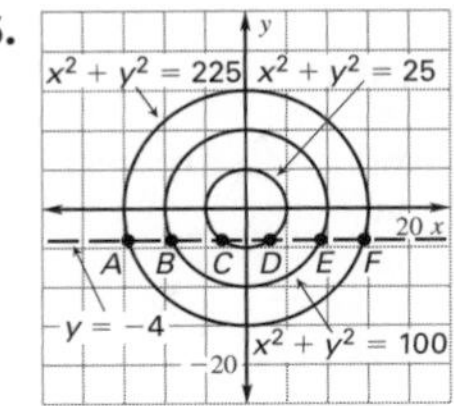

A: $x^2 + (-4)^2 = 225 \rightarrow x \approx \pm 14.5 \rightarrow (-14.5, -4)$

B: $x^2 + (-4)^2 = 100 \rightarrow x \approx \pm 9.2 \rightarrow (-9.2, -4)$

C: $x^2 + (-4)^2 = 25 \rightarrow x = \pm 3 \rightarrow (-3, -4)$

D: $x^2 + (-4)^2 = 25 \rightarrow x = \pm 3 \rightarrow (3, -4)$

E: $x^2 + (-4)^2 = 100 \rightarrow x \approx \pm 9.2 \rightarrow (9.2, -4)$

F: $x^2 + (-4)^2 = 225 \rightarrow x \approx \pm 14.5 \rightarrow (14.5, -4)$

a. $AF \approx |14.5 - (-14.5)| = 29$ mi

b. $BE \approx |9.2 - (-9.2)| = 18.4$ mi

c. $CD \approx |3 - (-3)| = 6$ mi

Lesson 9.4 (pp. 637–639)

11. $16x^2 + 9y^2 = 144$

$\frac{x^2}{9} + \frac{y^2}{16} = 1$; $a = 4$, $b = 3$

Vertices: $(0, \pm 4)$;

Co-vertices: $(\pm 3, 0)$;

Foci: $(0, \pm\sqrt{7})$

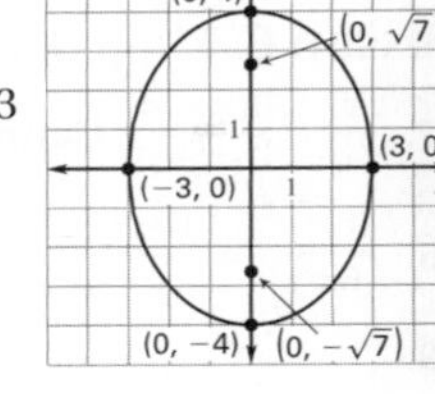

29. $b = \sqrt{7}$; $c = 3$; $a^2 = b^2 + c^2 \rightarrow a = 4$

$\frac{x^2}{4^2} + \frac{y^2}{(\sqrt{7})^2} = 1$, or $\frac{x^2}{16} + \frac{y^2}{7} = 1$

49. Largest field:

$2a = 185 \rightarrow a = 92.5$; $2b = 155 \rightarrow b = 77.5$

$\frac{x^2}{77.5^2} + \frac{y^2}{92.5^2} = 1$, or $\frac{x^2}{6006.25} + \frac{y^2}{8556.25} = 1$

$A = \pi(92.5)(77.5) \approx 22{,}521$ square meters

WS16

Smallest field:

$2a = 135 \rightarrow a = 67.5;\ 2b = 110 \rightarrow b = 55$

$\frac{x^2}{55^2} + \frac{y^2}{67.5^2} = 1$, or $\frac{x^2}{3025} + \frac{y^2}{4556.25} = 1$

$A = \pi(67.5)(55) \approx 11{,}663$ square meters

$11{,}663 \le A \le 22{,}521$

Lesson 9.5 (pp. 645–648)

13. $81x^2 - 16y^2 = 1296$

$\frac{x^2}{16} - \frac{y^2}{81} = 1$

$a = 4;\ b = 9;\ c = \sqrt{97}$

Vertices: $(\pm 4, 0)$

Foci: $(\pm\sqrt{97}, 0)$

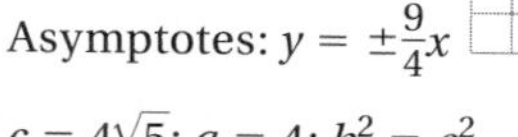

Asymptotes: $y = \pm\frac{9}{4}x$

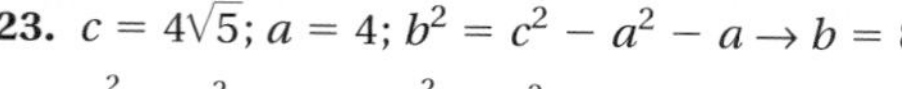

23. $c = 4\sqrt{5};\ a = 4;\ b^2 = c^2 - a^2 - a \rightarrow b = 8$

$\frac{y^2}{4^2} - \frac{x^2}{8^2} = 1$, or $\frac{y^2}{16} - \frac{x^2}{64} = 1$

41. a. $A(30.5, 0);\ B(85, -40)$

b. Vertices: $(\pm 30.5, 0)$; horizontal trans. axis

$\frac{x^2}{a^2} - \frac{y^2}{b^2} = 1 \rightarrow \frac{x^2}{30.5^2} - \frac{y^2}{b^2} = 1$

$\frac{85^2}{30.5^2} - \frac{(-40)^2}{b^2} = 1 \rightarrow b^2 \approx 236.5$

So, an equation is $\frac{x^2}{930.25} - \frac{y^2}{236.5} = 1.$

c. $x = 42$: $\frac{42^2}{930.25} - \frac{y^2}{236.5} = 1 \rightarrow y \approx 14.6$

$h = 40 + 14.6 = 54.6$ feet

Lesson 9.6 (pp. 655–657)

3. $(x + 4)^2 = -8(y - 2)$

Parabola; vertical axis; vertex at $(h, k) = (-4, 2)$.

$4p = -8 \rightarrow p = -2$

Focus: $(h, k + p) = (-4, 0)$

Directrix: $y = k - p \rightarrow y = 4$

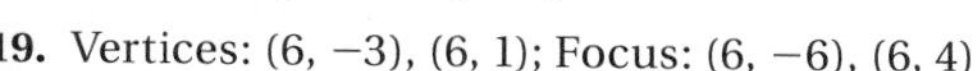

19. Vertices: $(6, -3), (6, 1)$; Focus: $(6, -6), (6, 4)$

Vertical transverse axis; $\frac{(y - k)^2}{a^2} - \frac{(x - h)^2}{b^2} = 1$

Center: $(h, k) = \left(\frac{6 + 6}{2}, \frac{-3 + 1}{2}\right)$

Distance between vertex $(6, -3)$ and (h, k):

$a = |-3 - k| = |-3 - (-1)| = 2$

Distance between focus $(6, -6)$ and (h, k):

$c = |-6 - k| = |-6 - (-1)| = 5$

$b^2 = c^2 - a^2 = 25 - 4 = 21 \rightarrow b = \sqrt{21}$

An equation is $\frac{(y + 1)^2}{4} - \frac{(x - 6)^2}{21} = 1.$

49. $x^2 - 10x + 4y = 0;\ A = 1, B = 0, C = 0$

$B^2 - 4AC = 0 - 4(1)(0) = 0 \rightarrow$ Parabola

$x^2 - 10x + 4y = 0$

$(x^2 - 10x + 25) = -4y + 25$

$(x - 5)^2 = -4\left(y - \frac{25}{4}\right)$

$(h, k) = \left(5, \frac{25}{4}\right)$; height $= \frac{25}{4} = 6.25$ feet

When $y = 0$, the x-intercepts are 0 and 10, so the distance of the jump is 10 feet.

Lesson 9.7 (pp. 661–664)

5.

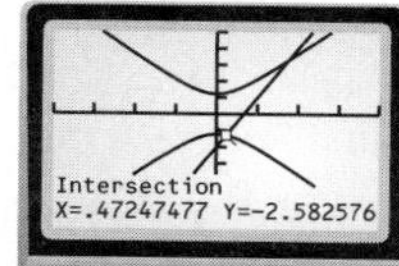

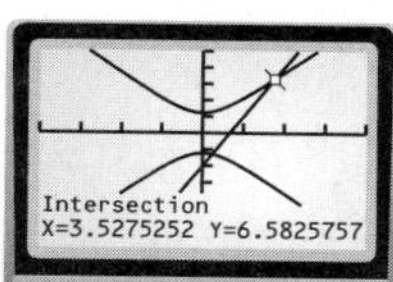

The solutions are approximately $(0.5, -2.6)$ and $(3.5, 6.6)$.

15. $4x^2 - 5y^2 = -76$

$2x + y = -6 \rightarrow y = -2x - 6$

Substitute $-2x - 6$ for y in Equation 1.

$4x^2 - 5(-2x - 6)^2 = -76$

$4x^2 - 20x^2 - 120x - 180 = -76$

$-16x^2 - 120x - 104 = 0$

$2x^2 + 15x + 13 = 0$

$(2x + 2)\left(x + \frac{13}{2}\right) = 0 \rightarrow x = -1, x = -\frac{13}{2}$

When $x = -1$: $y = -2(-1) - 6 = -4$

When $x = -\frac{13}{2}$: $y = -2\left(-\frac{13}{2}\right) - 6 = 7$

The solutions are $(-1, -4)$ and $\left(-\frac{13}{2}, 7\right)$.

WORKED-OUT SOLUTIONS

WS17

41. **a.** Oak Lane: $m = -\frac{1}{7}$, $(x_1, y_1) = (-2, 1)$

$$y - 1 = -\frac{1}{7}(x + 2) \rightarrow y = -\frac{1}{7}x + \frac{5}{7}$$

Circle: $x^2 + y^2 = 1$

b. $$x^2 + \left(-\frac{1}{7}x + \frac{5}{7}\right)^2 = 1$$

$$x^2 + \frac{1}{49}x^2 - \frac{10}{49}x + \frac{25}{49} = 1$$

$$49x^2 + x^2 - 10x + 25 = 49$$

$$50x^2 - 10x - 24 = 0$$

$$(5x - 4)(10x + 6) = 0 \rightarrow x = \frac{4}{5}, x = -\frac{3}{5}$$

$$y = -\frac{1}{7}\left(\frac{4}{5}\right) + \frac{5}{7} = \frac{3}{5}; y = -\frac{1}{7}\left(-\frac{3}{5}\right) + \frac{5}{7} = \frac{4}{5}$$

The solutions are $\left(\frac{4}{5}, \frac{3}{5}\right)$ and $\left(-\frac{3}{5}, \frac{4}{5}\right)$.

c. $d = \sqrt{\left(-\frac{3}{5} - \frac{4}{5}\right)^2 + \left(\frac{4}{5} - \frac{3}{5}\right)^2} = \sqrt{2} \approx 1.4$ mi

WORKED-OUT SOLUTIONS

Chapter 10

Lesson 10.1 (pp. 686–689)

13. **a.** $26 \cdot 26 \cdot 26 \cdot 26 \cdot 10 \cdot 10 = 45{,}697{,}600$

b. $26 \cdot 25 \cdot 24 \cdot 23 \cdot 10 \cdot 9 = 32{,}292{,}000$

35. $${}_9P_2 = \frac{9!}{(9-2)!} = \frac{9!}{7!} = \frac{362{,}880}{5040} = 72$$

65. Permutations of 9 objects taken 3 at a time:

$${}_9P_3 = \frac{9!}{(9-3)!} = \frac{9!}{6!} = \frac{362{,}880}{720} = 504 \text{ ways}$$

Lesson 10.2 (pp. 694–697)

17. *Exactly one queen*: Choose 1 of the 4 queens and 4 of the 48 that are not queens.

$${}_4C_1 \cdot {}_{48}C_4 = \frac{4!}{3!1!} \cdot \frac{48!}{44!4!} = 778{,}320$$

No queen: Choose 5 cards from the 48 in a deck that are not queens.

$${}_{48}C_5 = \frac{48!}{43!5!} = 1{,}712{,}304$$

The total number of possible hands is $778{,}320 + 1{,}712{,}304 = 2{,}490{,}624$.

29. $(2s^4 + 5)^5 = {}_5C_0(2s^4)^5 5^0 + {}_5C_1(2s^4)^4 5^1$
$+ {}_5C_2(2s^4)^3 5^2 + {}_5C_3(2s^4)^2 5^3 + {}_5C_4(2s^4)^1 5^4$
$+ {}_5C_5(2s^4)^0 5^5 = 1(32s^{20}) + 5(16s^{16})(5)$
$+ 10(8s^{12})(25) + 10(4s^8)(125) + 5(2s^4)(625)$
$+ 1(1)(3125) = 32s^{20} + 400s^{16} + 2000s^{12}$
$+ 5000s^8 + 6250s^4 + 3125$

49. You can choose 3 of the 18 types of flowers.

$${}_{18}C_3 = \frac{18!}{15!3!} = \frac{18 \cdot 17 \cdot 16 \cdot \cancel{15!}}{\cancel{15!} \cdot 3!} = 816$$

Lesson 10.3 (pp. 702–704)

7. Factors of 150 from 1 to 50: 1, 2, 3, 5, 6, 10, 15, 25, 30, 50

$$P = \frac{\text{Factors of 150}}{\text{Integers from 1 to 50}} = \frac{10}{50} = \frac{1}{5}$$

17. There are ${}_{48}C_6$ different combinations of 6 numbers. Only 1 is the correct combination.

$$P(\text{correct numbers}) = \frac{1}{{}_{48}C_6} = \frac{1}{12{,}271{,}512}$$

39. $$P = \frac{\text{Area of smallest circle}}{\text{Area of entire target}} = \frac{\pi \cdot 8^2}{\pi \cdot 40^2} = \frac{1}{25} = 0.04$$

Lesson 10.4 (pp. 710–713)

11. $P(A \text{ or } B) = P(A) + P(B) - P(A \text{ and } B)$
$0.71 = 0.28 + 0.64 - P(A \text{ and } B)$
$-0.21 = -P(A \text{ and } B) \rightarrow P(A \text{ and } B) = 0.21$

21. $P(\text{K or } \blacklozenge) = P(\text{K}) + P(\blacklozenge) - P(\text{K and } \blacklozenge)$
$= \left(\frac{4}{52}\right) + \left(\frac{13}{52}\right) - \left(\frac{1}{52}\right) = \frac{4}{13}$

45. The number of combinations of 6 food items is 10^6. The number of combinations of 6 different food items is $10 \cdot 9 \cdot 8 \cdot 7 \cdot 6 \cdot 5$. So, the probability that at least 2 bring the same item is $P = 1 - P(\text{none are the same}) =$
$1 - \frac{10 \cdot 9 \cdot 8 \cdot 7 \cdot 6 \cdot 5}{10^6} = 0.8488$.

Lesson 10.5 (pp. 721–723)

13. $P = P(\text{blue}) \cdot P(\text{green}) \cdot P(\text{red})$
$= \left(\frac{3}{16}\right) \cdot \left(\frac{4}{16}\right) \cdot \left(\frac{5}{16}\right) = \frac{60}{4096} \approx 0.015$

25. Primes from 1 to 20: 2, 3, 5, 7, 11, 13, 17, 19.

$P(\text{odd}|\text{prime}) = \dfrac{P(\text{number of odd primes})}{P(\text{number of primes})} = \dfrac{7}{8}$

39.

Total # of matches —0.5→ Event *A*: player wins toss —0.55→ Event *C*: player wins

Event *A*: player wins toss —0.45→ Event *D*: player loses

Total # of matches —0.5→ Event *B*: player loses toss —0.47→ Event *C*: player wins

Event *B*: player loses toss —0.53→ Event *D*: player loses

$P(C) = P(A \text{ and } C) + P(B \text{ and } C)$

$= P(A) \cdot P(C|A) + P(B) \cdot P(C|B)$

$= (0.50) \cdot (0, 55) + (0, 50)(0.47) = 0.51$

Lesson 10.6 (pp. 727–730)

5.

N	Outcomes	*P*(*N*)
1	10	$\frac{10}{100} = \frac{1}{100}$
2	90	$\frac{90}{1000} = \frac{9}{100}$
3	900	$\frac{900}{1000} = \frac{9}{10}$

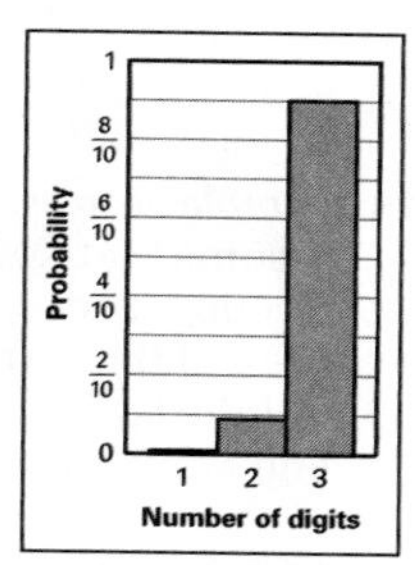

21. Each question has 4 possible answers, so the probability of guessing a correct answer is $p = 0.25$. There are 30 questions, so $n = 30$. The probability of randomly guessing 11 correct answers is $P(k = 11) = {}_{30}C_{11}(0.25)^{11}(1 - 0.25)^{30-11} \approx 0.055$.

45. a. $p = 0.34$;

$P(k = 5) = {}_{10}C_5(0.34)^5(1 - 0.34)^{10-5} \approx 0.14$

b. $p = P(\text{Rh}^-) = P(\text{O}^-) + P(\text{A}^-) + P(\text{B}^-) + P(\text{AB}^-)$

$= 0.15$

$P(k = 2) = {}_{10}C_2(0.15)^2(1 - 0.15)^{10-2} \approx 0.28$

c. $p = P(\text{O}) = P(\text{O}^+) + P(\text{O}^-) = 0.43$

$P(k = 0) = {}_{10}C_0(0.43)^0(1 - 0.43)^{10-0} \approx 0.004$

$P(k = 1) = {}_{10}C_1(0.43)^1(1 - 0.43)^{10-1} \approx 0.027$

$P(k = 2) = {}_{10}C_2(0.43)^2(1 - 0.43)^{10-2} \approx 0.093$

$P(k \le 2) = P(k = 0) + P(k = 1) + P(k = 2)$

≈ 0.124

d. $p = P(\text{Rh}^+) = P(\text{O}^+) + P(\text{A}^+) + P(\text{B}^+)$

$+ P(\text{AB}^+) = 0.85$

$P(k = 5) = {}_{10}C_5(0.85)^5(1 - 0.85)^{10-5} \approx 0.008$

$P(k = 6) = {}_{10}C_6(0.85)^6(1 - 0.85)^{10-6} \approx 0.040$

$P(k = 7) = {}_{10}C_7(0.85)^7(1 - 0.85)^{10-7} \approx 0.130$

$P(k = 8) = {}_{10}C_8(0.85)^8(1 - 0.85)^{10-8} \approx 0.276$

$P(k = 9) = {}_{10}C_9(0.85)^9(1 - 0.85)^{10-9} \approx 0.347$

$P(k = 10) = {}_{10}C_{10}(0.85)^{10}(1 - 0.85)^{10-10} \approx 0.197$

$P(k \ge 5) = P(k = 5) + P(k = 6) + P(k = 7)$

$+ P(k = 8) + P(k = 9) + P(k = 10) \approx 0.998$

Chapter 11

Lesson 11.1 (pp. 747–749)

5. Mean:

$\dfrac{69 + 70 + 75 + 84 + 73 + 78 + 74 + 73 + 78 + 71}{10}$

$= 74.5$

Median: ~~69~~, ~~70~~, ~~71~~, ~~73~~, 73, 74, ~~75~~, ~~78~~, ~~78~~, ~~84~~

$\dfrac{73 + 74}{2} = 73.5$

Mode: 73 and 78

15. Range: $158 - 135 = 23$

$\overline{x} = \dfrac{135 + 142 + 148 + 136 + 152 + 140 + 158 + 154}{8}$

$= 145.625$

$\sigma =$

$\sqrt{\dfrac{(135 - 145.625)^2 + (142 - 145.625)^2 + \cdots + (154 - 145.625)^2}{8}}$

$= \sqrt{\dfrac{519.875}{8}} \approx 8.1$

29. a. The outlier is 5.

b. *With outlier*:

Mean: $\overline{x} = \dfrac{20 + 23 + \cdots + 23}{10} = 20.2$

Median: 22 Mode: 23 Range: $25 - 5 = 20$

Std. Dev.:

$\sigma = \dfrac{(20 - 20.2)^2 + (23 - 20.2)^2 + \cdots + (23 - 20.2)^2}{10}$

≈ 5.4

WS19

WORKED-OUT SOLUTIONS

Without outlier:

Mean: $\overline{x} = \frac{20 + 23 + \cdots + 23}{9} \approx 21.9$

Median: 23 Mode: 23 Range: $25 - 19 = 6$

Std. Dev.:

$$\sigma = \sqrt{\frac{(20 - 20.2)^2 + (23 - 20.2)^2 + \cdots + (23 - 20.2)^2}{9}}$$

≈ 2.1

c. The outlier causes the mean and median to decrease, and the range and standard deviation to increase. The mode stays the same.

Lesson 11.2 (pp. 753–755)

5.

	Original data set	Adding 17 to data values
Mean	78	78 + 17 = 95
Median	77	77 + 17 = 94
Mode	77	77 + 17 = 94
Range	9	9
Standard deviation	2.8	2.8

11.

	Original data set	Multiplying data values by 4
Mean	61.9	61.9(4) = 247.6
Median	62	62(4) = 248
Mode	58	58(4) = 232
Range	9	9(4) = 36
Standard deviation	3.4	3.4(4) = 13.6

19.

	Heights without stilts	Heights with stilts
Mean	70.8	70.8 + 28 = 98.8
Median	72	72 + 28 = 100
Mode	72	72 + 28 = 100
Range	8	8
Standard deviation	2.4	2.4

Lesson 11.3 (pp. 760–762)

3. $P(x \le \overline{x} - \sigma) = 0.0015 + 0.0235 + 0.135 = 0.16$

11. 29 and 37 are one standard deviation on either side of the mean, which accounts for 68% of the data. So, the probability is 0.68.

33. a. 19.4 ounces: $z = \frac{19.4 - 20}{0.25} = -2.4$

20.4 ounces: $z = \frac{20.4 - 20}{0.25} = 1.6$

b. The table shows that $P(x \le -2.4) = 0.0082$. So, the probability is 0.0082.

c. $P(x \le 20.4) = 0.9452$; $P(x \le 19.4) = 0.0082$

$P(x \le 20.4) - P(x \le 19.4) = 0.937$

Lesson 11.4 (pp. 769–771)

7. Margin of error $= \pm\frac{1}{\sqrt{n}} = \pm\frac{1}{\sqrt{1000}} \approx \pm 0.032$

The margin of error is about ±3.2%.

19. Margin of error $= \pm\frac{1}{\sqrt{n}}$

$\pm 0.056 = \pm\frac{1}{\sqrt{n}}$

$0.003136 = \frac{1}{n} \rightarrow n \approx 319$

29. *Sample answer*: It is not reasonable to assume that Kosta is going to win the election, because the margin of error is ±5%. If the margin of error works in favor of Murdock, Kosta will have 49% (54% − 5%) and Murdock will have 51% (46% + 5%).

Lesson 11.5 (pp. 778–780)

3. Model: $y = -0.38x^2 + 1.1x + 16$

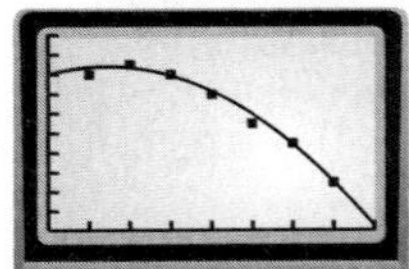

11. A model for the data is $y = 0.00211x^3 - 0.0766x^2 + 1.26x - 0.0664$.

Chapter 12

Lesson 12.1 (pp. 798–800)

19. $\frac{2}{3 \cdot 1}, \frac{2}{3 \cdot 2}, \frac{2}{3 \cdot 3}, \frac{2}{3 \cdot 4}, \ldots$

Next term: $\frac{2}{3 \cdot 5} = \frac{2}{15}$; A rule is $a_n = \frac{2}{3n}$.

47. $\sum_{n=0}^{4} n^3 = 0^3 + 1^3 + 2^3 + 3^3 + 4^3$

$= 0 + 1 + 8 + 27 + 64 = 100$

65.

n	1	2	3	4	5
a_n	1	3	7	15	31

A formula for the sequence is $a_n = 2^n - 1$.

$a_6 = 2^6 - 1 = 63$ moves for 6 rings

$a_7 = 2^7 - 1 = 127$ moves for 7 rings

$a_8 = 2^8 - 1 = 255$ moves for 8 rings

Lesson 12.2 (pp. 806–809)

15. Arithmetic sequence

$a_1 = -3; d = -1 - (-3) = 2$

A rule for the nth term is

$a_n = a_1 + (n - 1)d = -3 + (n - 1)2 = 2n - 5$

$a_{20} = 2(20) - 5 = 35$

41. $\sum_{i=1}^{8} (-3 - 2i)$

$a_1 = -3 - 2(1) = -5; a_8 = -3 - 2(8) = -19$

$S_8 = 8\left(\frac{-5 + (-19)}{2}\right) = -96$

65. a. $a_1 = 4; d = 8$

$a_n = a_1 + (n - 1)d = 4 + (n - 1)8 = -4 + 8n$

b. $a_{12} + a_{11} + \cdots + a_2 + a_1 = 576$ blocks

Lesson 12.3 (pp. 814–817)

19. Geometric sequence; $a_1 = 2; r = \frac{\frac{3}{2}}{2} = \frac{3}{4}$

$a_n = a_1 r^{n-1} = 2\left(\frac{3}{4}\right)^{n-1}$

$a_7 = 2\left(\frac{3}{4}\right)^{7-1} = \frac{1458}{4096} = \frac{729}{2048}$

49. $\sum_{i=1}^{8} 6(4)^{i-1}$

$a_1 = 6(4)^{1-1} = 6; r = 4$

$S_8 = a_1\left(\frac{1 - r^8}{1 - r}\right) = 6\left(\frac{1 - 4^8}{1 - 4}\right) = 131{,}070$

59. a. $a_1 = 1024 \div 2 = 512; r = \frac{1}{2}$

$a_n = a_1(r)^{n-1} = 512\left(\frac{1}{2}\right)^{n-1}$

b. $n = 10$; after 10 passes, the number of items remaining is $a_{10} = 512\left(\frac{1}{2}\right)^{10-1} = 1$.

Lesson 12.4 (pp. 823–825)

13. $\sum_{k=1}^{\infty} 7\left(-\frac{8}{9}\right)^{k-1}$

$a_1 = 7; r = -\frac{8}{9}; S = \frac{a_1}{1 - r} = \frac{7}{1 - \left(-\frac{8}{9}\right)} = \frac{63}{17}$

27. $625(0.001) + 625(0.001)^2 + 625(0.001)^3 + \cdots$

$= \frac{a_1}{1 - r} = \frac{625(0.001)}{1 - 0.001} = \frac{0.625}{0.999} = \frac{625}{999}$

39. D;

$n = 345 + 345(0.783) + 345(0.783)^2 + 345(0.783)^3 + \cdots$

$= \frac{a_1}{1 - r} = \frac{345}{1 - 0.783} \approx 1.59$ billion

Lesson 12.5 (pp. 830–833)

15. Geometric sequence; $a_1 = 4; r = -3$

$a_n = r \cdot a_{n-1} = -3a_{n-1}$

A recursive rule is $a_1 = 4, a_n = -3a_{n-1}$.

27. $f(x) = \frac{1}{2}x - 3, x_0 = 2$

$x_1 = f(x_0)$	$x_2 = f(x_1)$	$x_3 = f(x_2)$
$= f(2)$	$= f(-2)$	$= f(-4)$
$= \frac{1}{2}(2) - 3$	$= \frac{1}{2}(-2) - 3$	$= \frac{1}{2}(-4) - 3$
$= -2$	$= -4$	$= -5$

45. Recursive rule:

$a_1 = 2000, a_n = 1.014a_{n-1} - 100$.

Because $a_{24} = 62.14$, the balance at the beginning of the 24th month is \$62.14. So, she will be able to pay off the balance at the end of the 24th month.

Chapter 13

Lesson 13.1 (pp. 856–858)

5.

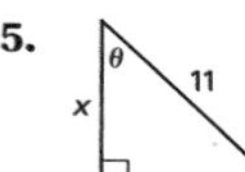

Using the Pythagorean theorem:

$x = \sqrt{11^2 - 8^2} = \sqrt{57}$

$\sin\theta = \frac{8}{11}$ $\cos\theta = \frac{\sqrt{57}}{11}$ $\tan\theta = \frac{8\sqrt{57}}{57}$

$\csc\theta = \frac{11}{8}$ $\sec\theta = \frac{11\sqrt{57}}{57}$ $\cot\theta = \frac{\sqrt{57}}{8}$

WORKED-OUT SOLUTIONS

WORKED-OUT SOLUTIONS

11. $\tan\theta = \frac{\text{opp}}{\text{adj}} = \frac{7}{3}$

$x = \sqrt{7^2 + 3^2} = \sqrt{58}$

$\sin\theta = \frac{7\sqrt{58}}{58}$ $\quad\cos\theta = \frac{3\sqrt{58}}{58}$ $\quad\tan\theta = \frac{7}{3}$

$\csc\theta = \frac{\sqrt{58}}{7}$ $\quad\sec\theta = \frac{\sqrt{58}}{3}$ $\quad\cot\theta = \frac{3}{7}$

33.

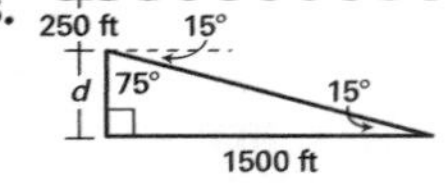

$\tan 15° = \frac{d}{1500}$

$d \approx 402$

The total depth is 402 + 250 = 652 feet.

As the angle of the dive increases, the depth increases.

Lesson 13.2 (pp. 862–865)

11. $\frac{5\pi}{18} = \frac{5\,\cancel{\pi\text{ radians}}}{18}\left(\frac{180°}{\cancel{\pi\text{ radians}}}\right) = 50°$

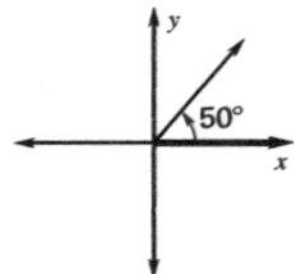

23. $40° = 40°\left(\frac{\pi\text{ radians}}{180°}\right) = \frac{2\pi}{9}\text{ radians}$

51. a. $\frac{15\text{ rev}}{1\text{ min}}\left(\frac{1\text{ min}}{60\text{ sec}}\right)\left(\frac{2\pi\text{ rad}}{1\text{ rev}}\right) = \frac{\pi}{2}\text{ rad/sec}$

b. Arc length: $s = r\theta = 29\left(\frac{\pi}{2}\right) \approx 45.6$ feet

Lesson 13.3 (pp. 870–872)

5. $r = \sqrt{x^2 + y^2} = \sqrt{(-7)^2 + (-24)^2} = \sqrt{625} = 25$

$\sin\theta = \frac{y}{r} = \frac{-24}{25}$ $\quad\cos\theta = \frac{x}{f} = \frac{-7}{25}$

$\tan\theta = \frac{y}{x} = \frac{-24}{-7} = \frac{24}{7}$ $\quad\csc\theta = \frac{r}{y} = \frac{-25}{24}$

$\sec\theta = \frac{r}{x} = \frac{-25}{7}$ $\quad\cot\theta = \frac{x}{y} = \frac{7}{24}$

17. $\theta' = 180° - 150° = 30°$

37.

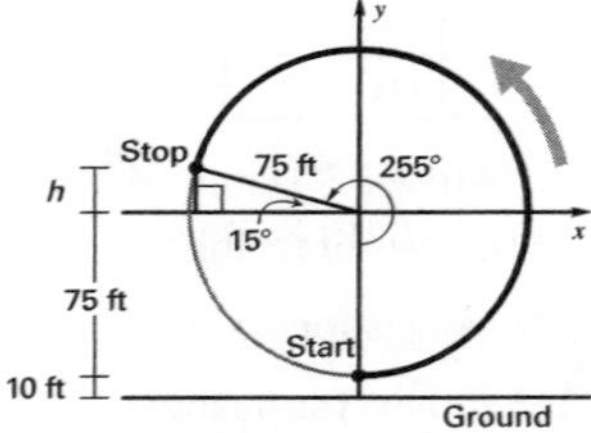

$\theta' = 270° - 255° = 15°$

$\sin 15° = \frac{h}{75}$

$19.4 \approx h$

When the ride stops, you are about 10 + 75 + 19.4 = 104.4 feet above the ground. If the radius is doubled, your height above the ground is doubled only if your starting height above the ground is also doubled.

Lesson 13.4 (pp. 878–880)

7. When $-\frac{\pi}{2} \le \theta \le \frac{\pi}{2}$, or $-90° \le \theta \le 90°$, the angle whose sine is $\frac{\sqrt{3}}{2}$ is $\theta = \sin^{-1}\frac{\sqrt{3}}{2} = \frac{\pi}{3}$, or $\theta = \sin^{-1}\frac{\sqrt{3}}{2} = 60°$.

23. $\tan\theta = 3.2$; $180° < \theta < 270°$

$\tan^{-1}(3.2) \approx 72.6°$, which is in Quadrant I. To find the angle in Quadrant III ($180° < \theta < 270°$): $\theta \approx 180 + 72.6 = 252.6°$

37.

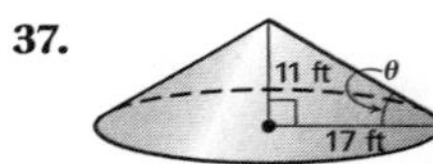

$\tan\theta = \frac{11}{17}$

$\theta = \tan^{-1}\left(\frac{11}{17}\right) \approx 33°$

Because the angle of repose remains the same, you can use $\theta = 33°$ to find the radius of the 15 foot high pile:

$\tan 33° = \frac{15}{r} \rightarrow r = \frac{15}{\tan 33°}$

≈ 23

The diameter is about $d = 2r = 2(23) = 46$ ft.

Lesson 13.5 (pp. 886–888)

13. $\frac{\sin B}{16} = \frac{\sin 104°}{25}$

$\sin B = \frac{16 \sin 104°}{25} \approx 0.6210 \rightarrow B \approx 38.4°$

$A \approx 180° - 104° - 38.4° = 37.6°$

$\frac{a}{\sin 37.6°} = \frac{25}{\sin 104°} \rightarrow a = \frac{25 \sin 37.6°}{\sin 104°} \approx 15.7$

45. a.

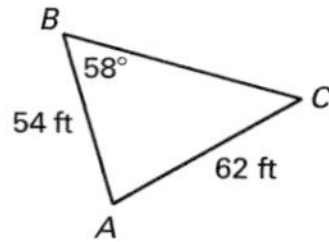

b. $\frac{\sin C}{54} = \frac{\sin 58°}{62}$

$\sin C = \frac{54 \sin 58°}{62} \approx 0.7386 \rightarrow C \approx 47.6°$

$A \approx 180° - 58° - 47.6° = 74.4°$

$\frac{a}{\sin 74.4°} = \frac{62}{\sin 58°} \rightarrow a = \frac{62 \sin 74.4°}{\sin 58°} \approx 70.4$

c. Area $= \frac{1}{2} bc \sin A = \frac{1}{2}(62)(54)(\sin 74.4°)$

≈ 1612

$1612 \text{ ft}^2 \div 200 \text{ ft}^2/\text{bag} \approx 8.1$ bags

You will need 9 bags of fertilizer.

Lesson 13.6 (pp. 892–894)

17. $a^2 = b^2 + c^2 - 2bc \cos A$

$10^2 = 3^2 + 12^2 - 2(3)(12)\cos A$

$\frac{53}{72} = \cos A \rightarrow A \approx 43°$

$\frac{10}{\sin 43°} = \frac{3}{\sin B} \rightarrow \frac{3(\sin 43°)}{10} = \sin B$

$B \approx 12°; C \approx 180 - 43° - 12° = 125°$

In $\triangle ABC$, $A \approx 43°$, $B \approx 12°$, and $C \approx 125°$.

25. $s = \frac{1}{2}(a + b + c) = \frac{1}{2}(5 + 11 + 10) = 13$

Area $= \sqrt{s(s - a)(sb)(s - c)}$

$= \sqrt{13(13 - 5)(13 - 11)(13 - 10)} = \sqrt{624}$

≈ 25 square units

45. $\triangle ADB$: $s = \frac{1}{2}(743 + 1210 + 1480) = 1716.5$

Area =

$\sqrt{1716.5(1716.5 - 743)(1716.5 - 1210)(1716.5 - 1480)}$

$\approx 447{,}399$

$\triangle CDB$: $s = \frac{1}{2}(1000 + 858 + 1480) = 1669$

Area =

$\sqrt{1669(1669 - 1000)(1669 - 858)(1669 - 1480)}$

$\approx 413{,}697$

Area $= (447{,}399 + 413{,}697)\cancel{\text{ft}^2}\left(\frac{1 \text{ acre}}{43{,}560\cancel{\text{ft}^2}}\right)$

≈ 20 acres

If you first found the length of $\overline{AC}$, you could repeat the same process using $\triangle ABC$ and $\triangle ADC$.

Chapter 14

Lesson 14.1 (pp. 912–914)

5. Amplitude: 1; period: 2

17. $f(x) = 4 \tan x$

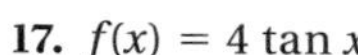

Period: π; intercept: (0, 0)

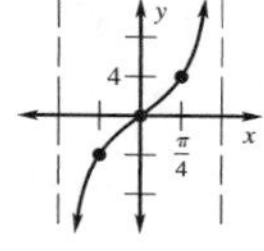

Asymptotes: $x = \pm\frac{\pi}{2}$

Halfway points: $\left(\frac{\pi}{4}, 4\right)\left(-\frac{\pi}{4}, -4\right)$

31. a. Equation has the form $y = a \cos bt$.

$a = \frac{1}{2}(3.5) = 1.75$

Period is 6, so $6 = \frac{2\pi}{b} \rightarrow b = \frac{\pi}{3}$.

Equation is $y = 1.75 \cos \frac{\pi}{3}t$.

b. Choose $y = a \cos bt$ because at $t = 0$, the buoy is at its highest point.

Lesson 14.2 (pp. 919–922)

11. $y = 2 \cos x + 1$

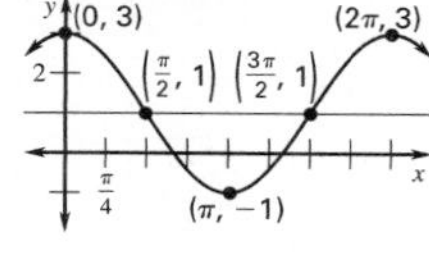

Amplitude: $a = 2$

Period: $\frac{2\pi}{b} = 2\pi$

Horizontal shift: $h = 0$; Vertical shift: $k = 1$

WS23

23. $y = -\sin \frac{1}{2}x + 3$

Amplitude: $|a| = 1$

Period: $\frac{2\pi}{b} = \frac{2\pi}{\frac{1}{2}} = 4\pi$

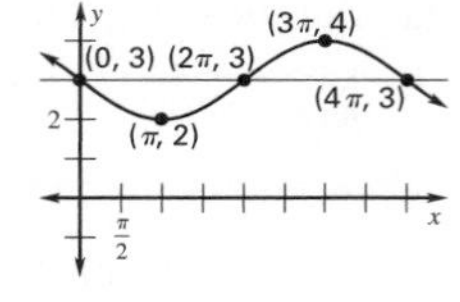

$h = 0$; $k = 3$; $a < 0$, so graph is reflected.

53. a. $\frac{200 - d}{300} = \tan \theta$

$d = -300 \tan \theta + 200$

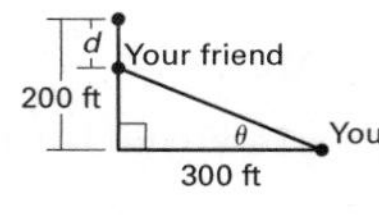

b.

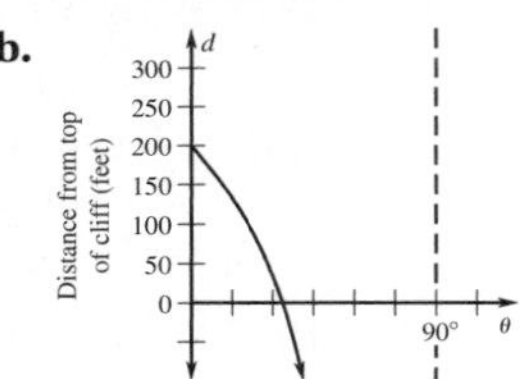

c. $100 = -300 \tan \theta + 200 \rightarrow \theta \approx 18.4°$

Lesson 14.3 (pp. 927–930)

5. $\cos \theta = \frac{5}{6}$, $3\pi < \theta < 2\pi$

$\sin^2 \theta + \cos^2 \theta = 1$

$\sin^2 \theta + \left(\frac{5}{6}\right)^2 = 1$

$\sin \theta = -\frac{\sqrt{11}}{6}$ ← Negative because θ is in Quadrant III

$\tan \theta = \frac{\sin \theta}{\cos \theta} = -\frac{\sqrt{11}}{5}$ $\quad \cot \theta = \frac{\cos \theta}{\sin \theta} = -\frac{5}{\sqrt{11}}$

$\csc \theta = \frac{1}{\sin \theta} = \frac{-6}{\sqrt{11}}$ $\quad \sec \theta = \frac{1}{\cos \theta} = \frac{6}{5}$

11. $\frac{\sin(-\theta)}{\cos(-\theta)} = \frac{-\sin \theta}{\cos \theta} = -\tan \theta$

41. a. $r = \frac{1.069}{1 - 0.97 \sin\left(\frac{\pi}{2} - \theta\right)} = \frac{1.069}{1 - 0.97 \cos \theta}$

b.

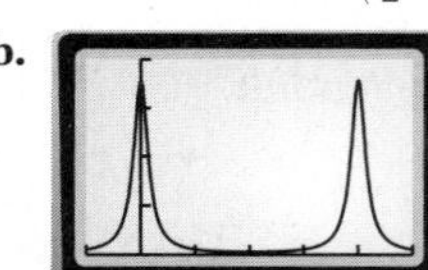

c.

θ	0	$\frac{\pi}{4}$	$\frac{\pi}{2}$	$\frac{3\pi}{4}$	π
r	35.6	3.4	1.1	0.6	0.5

θ	$\frac{5\pi}{4}$	$\frac{3\pi}{2}$	$\frac{7\pi}{4}$	2π
r	0.6	1.1	3.4	35.6

Closest distance:

$0.543 \text{ a.u.} \cdot \frac{93{,}000{,}000 \text{ mi}}{1 \text{ a.u.}} \approx 50.5$ million mi

Farthest distance:

$35.6 \text{ a.u.} \cdot \frac{93{,}000{,}000 \text{ mi}}{1 \text{ a.u.}} \approx 3.31$ billion mi

Lesson 14.4 (pp. 935–937)

5. $12 \sin^2\left(\frac{\pi}{6}\right) - 3 \stackrel{?}{=} 0$

$12\left(\frac{1}{2}\right)^2 - 3 \stackrel{?}{=} 0 \rightarrow 3 - 3 = 0$ ✓

13. $4 \cos^2 x - 3 = 0 \rightarrow \cos^2 x = \frac{3}{4} \rightarrow \cos x = \pm\frac{\sqrt{3}}{2}$

In $0 \le x < \pi$, $x = \frac{\pi}{6}$ and $x = \frac{5\pi}{6}$.

$x = \frac{\pi}{6} + n\pi$ or $x = \frac{5\pi}{6} + n\pi$

43. a. $S = 6(1.5)(0.75) + \frac{3}{2}(0.75)^2\left(\frac{\sqrt{3} - \cos \theta}{\sin \theta}\right)$

$= 6.75 + 0.84375\left(\frac{\sqrt{3} - \cos \theta}{\sin \theta}\right)$

b.

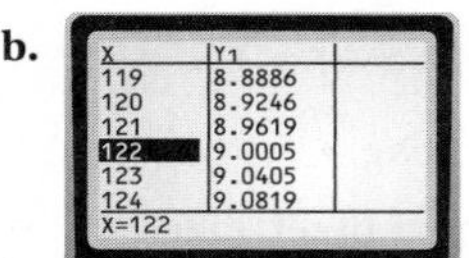

X Y1
119 8.8886
120 8.9246
121 8.9619
122 9.0005
123 9.0405
124 9.0819
X=122

When $\theta \approx 122°$, $S = 9 \text{ in.}^2$

c.

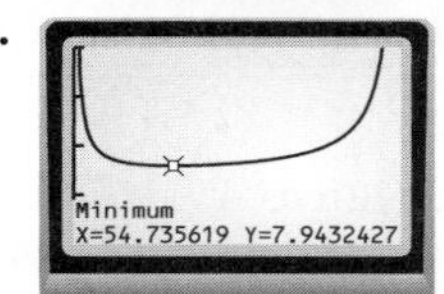

A value of $\theta \approx 54.7°$ minimizes the surface area.

Lesson 14.5 (pp. 944–947)

5. $M = 6$, $m = 2$

Vertical shift: $k = \frac{M + m}{2} = \frac{6 + 2}{2} = 4$

The graph is a cosine curve with $h = 0$.

Period $= 4 = \frac{2\pi}{b} \rightarrow b = \frac{\pi}{2}$

$|a| = \frac{M - m}{2} = \frac{6 - 2}{2} = 2$

The graph is a reflection, so $a = -2$.

The function is $y = -2 \cos \frac{\pi}{2}x + 4$.

9. $M = 6, m = -6$

Vertical shift: $k = \frac{M + m}{2} = \frac{6 + (-6)}{2} = 0$

The graph is a sine curve with $h = 0$.

Period $= 2(3\pi - \pi) = 4\pi = \frac{2\pi}{b} \rightarrow b = \frac{1}{2}$

$|a| = \frac{M - m}{2} = \frac{6 - (-6)}{2} = 6$

The graph is not a reflection, so $a = 6$.

The function is $y = 6 \sin \frac{1}{2}x$.

25. When $t = 0$, $m = 4$; when $t = 1$, $M = 9$.

$k = \frac{M + m}{2} = \frac{9 + 4}{2} = \frac{13}{2}$

The graph is a cosine curve with $h = 0$.

Period $= 2 = \frac{2\pi}{b} \rightarrow b = \pi$

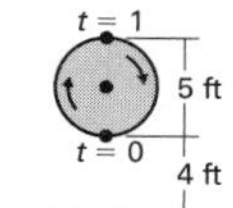

$|a| = \frac{M - m}{2} = \frac{9 - 4}{2} = \frac{5}{2}$

The graph is a reflection, so $a = -\frac{5}{2}$.

A model is $y = -\frac{5}{2} \cos \pi x + \frac{13}{2}$.

Lesson 14.6 (pp. 952–954)

9. $\cos\left(-\frac{5\pi}{12}\right) = \cos\left(\frac{\pi}{3} - \frac{3\pi}{4}\right)$

$= \cos \frac{\pi}{3} \cos \frac{3\pi}{4} + \sin \frac{\pi}{3} \sin \frac{3\pi}{4}$

$= \frac{1}{2}\left(-\frac{\sqrt{2}}{2}\right) + \frac{\sqrt{3}}{2}\left(\frac{\sqrt{2}}{2}\right)$

$= \frac{\sqrt{6} - \sqrt{2}}{4}$

23. $\sin\left(x - \frac{3\pi}{2}\right) = \sin x \cos \frac{3\pi}{2} - \cos x \sin \frac{3\pi}{2}$

$= (\sin x)(0) - (\cos x)(-1) = \cos x$

43. a.

$\frac{WQ}{NA} = \frac{f \tan(\theta - t) + f \tan t}{h \tan \theta}$

$= \frac{f}{h} (\tan(\theta - t) + \tan t)\left(\frac{1}{\tan \theta}\right)$

$= \frac{f}{h}\left(\frac{\tan \theta - \tan t}{1 + \tan \theta \tan t} + \frac{\tan t(1 + \tan \theta \tan t)}{1 + \tan \theta \tan t)}\right)\left(\frac{1}{\tan \theta}\right)$

$= \frac{f}{h}\left(\frac{\tan \theta + \tan \theta \tan^2 t}{1 + \tan \theta \tan t}\right)\left(\frac{1}{\tan \theta}\right)$

$= \frac{f}{h}\left(\frac{\tan \theta(1 + \tan^2 t)}{1 + \tan \theta \tan t}\right)\left(\frac{1}{\tan \theta}\right)$

$= \frac{f}{h}\left(\frac{\sec^2 t}{1 + \tan \theta \tan t}\right)$

b. When $t = 0$:

$\frac{WQ}{NA} = \frac{f}{h}\left(\frac{\sec^2(0)}{1 + \tan \theta \tan(0)}\right) = \frac{f}{h}\left(\frac{1}{1 + 0}\right) = \frac{f}{h}$

Lesson 14.7 (pp. 959–962)

7. $\cos \frac{\pi}{8} = \cos \frac{1}{2}\left(\frac{\pi}{4}\right) = \sqrt{\frac{1 + \cos \frac{\pi}{4}}{2}}$

$= \sqrt{\frac{1 + \frac{\sqrt{2}}{2}}{2}} = \sqrt{\frac{2 + \sqrt{2}}{4}} = \frac{\sqrt{2 + \sqrt{2}}}{2}$

13. $\cos a = \frac{1}{3}, \frac{3\pi}{2} < a < 2\pi$

$\frac{3\pi}{4} < \frac{a}{2} < \pi \rightarrow \frac{a}{2}$ is in Quadrant II.

$\sin \frac{a}{2} = \sqrt{\frac{1 - \cos a}{2}} = \sqrt{\frac{1 - \frac{1}{3}}{2}} = \sqrt{\frac{1}{3}} = \frac{\sqrt{3}}{3}$

$\cos \frac{a}{2} = -\sqrt{\frac{1 + \cos a}{2}} = -\sqrt{\frac{1 + \frac{1}{3}}{2}} = -\sqrt{\frac{2}{3}} = -\frac{\sqrt{6}}{3}$

$\tan \frac{a}{2} = \frac{\sin \frac{a}{2}}{\cos \frac{a}{2}} = \frac{\frac{\sqrt{3}}{3}}{-\frac{\sqrt{6}}{3}} = \frac{\sqrt{3}}{3} \cdot \frac{-3}{\sqrt{6}} = \frac{-\sqrt{3}}{\sqrt{6}} = \frac{-\sqrt{2}}{2}$

53. When $M = 2.5$: $\sin \frac{\theta}{2} = \frac{1}{M} = \frac{1}{2.5}$

Using the Pythagorean Theorem:

$\cos \frac{\theta}{2} = \frac{\sqrt{5.25}}{2.5}$

$\sin \theta = 2 \sin \frac{\theta}{2} \cos \frac{\theta}{2} = 2\left(\frac{1}{2.5}\right)\left(\frac{\sqrt{5.25}}{2.5}\right) \approx 0.7332$

$\theta \approx 47°$

WORKED-OUT SOLUTIONS

Selected Answers

Chapter 1

1.1 Skill Practice (pp. 6–7) **1.** reciprocal

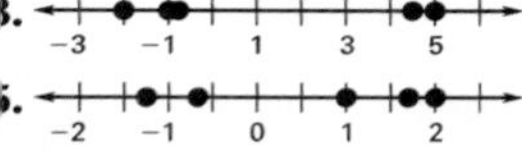

11. Associative property of addition **13.** Commutative property of multiplication **15.** Distributive property

17.

$6 \cdot (a \div 3) = 6 \cdot \left(a \cdot \frac{1}{3}\right)$	Definition of division
$= 6 \cdot \left(\frac{1}{3} \cdot a\right)$	Commutative property of multiplication
$= \left(6 \cdot \frac{1}{3}\right) \cdot a$	Associative property of multiplication
$= 2a$	Multiplication

19.

$(c - 3) + 3 = (c + (-3)) + 3$	Definition of subtraction
$= c + ((-3) + 3)$	Associative property of addition
$= c + 0$	Inverse property of addition
$= c$	Identity property of addition

21.

$7a + (4 + 5a) = 7a + (5a + 4)$	Commutative property of addition
$= (7a + 5a) + 4$	Associative property of addition
$= 12a + 4$	Combine like terms.

23. *Sample answer:* $a = -2, b = \frac{1}{4}$ **25.** \$8.50 per h **27.** \$36.25 **29.** 195 mi **31.** $116\frac{2}{3}$ yd **33.** 2200 g **35.** 1.75 gal **37.** 0.00175 ton **39.** The unit multiplier should be $\frac{0.82 \text{ euro}}{1 \text{ dollar}}$; 25 dollars $\cdot \frac{0.82 \text{ euro}}{1 \text{ dollar}} = 20.5$ euros. **41.** 29.3 ft/sec **43.** 31.1 mi/h **45.** 0.04 oz/sec **47.** 1800 mi/h **49.** Always; this represents the associative property of addition, which is true for all real numbers. **51.** Sometimes; it is true when $c = 0$. **53.** Always; this represents the distributive property, which is true for all real numbers.

55.

$\frac{a}{b} \div \frac{c}{d} = \frac{a}{b} \cdot \frac{d}{c}$	Definition of division
$= \frac{ad}{bc}$	Definition of multiplication of fractions
$= \frac{ad}{cb}$	Commutative property of multiplication
$= \frac{a}{c} \cdot \frac{d}{b}$	Definition of multiplication of fractions
$= \frac{a}{c} \div \frac{b}{d}$	Definition of division

1.1 Problem Solving (pp. 8–9) **57. a.** Lance: 6, Darcy: 2, Javier: 3, Sandra: −2 **b.** Sandra, Darcy, Javier, Lance **59. a.** Pluto, Neptune, Uranus, Saturn, Jupiter, Mars, Earth, Mercury, Venus **b.** Mercury, Venus, Earth, Mars, Jupiter, Saturn, Uranus, Neptune, Pluto **c.** *Sample answer:* The planets are in opposite orders in parts (a) and (b) with the exception of Mercury and Venus. **d.** Mercury or Venus **61. a.** cheetah: 102.67; three-toed sloth: 0.15; squirrel: 17.6; grizzly bear: 30 **b.** *Sample answer:* The cheetah is about 467 times faster than the three-toed sloth.

1.2 Skill Practice (pp. 13–15) **1.** base: 12, exponent: 7 **3.** The negative sign should be applied after evaluating the power, $-3^4 = -81$. **5.** 81 **7.** 49 **9.** −32 **11.** −10,000 **13.** −64 **15.** 64 **17.** −5 **19.** −100 **21.** 75 **23.** 6 **25.** $5x + 5$ **27.** $13z^2 - 2z + 10$ **29.** $11m - 1$ **31.** $-5p^2 + 21$ **35.** $10n + 24$; 44 **37.** 26 **39.** 49 **41.** $\frac{1}{9}$ **43.** $-7d + 11c$ **45.** $2m^2 + n^2 - 8m$ **47.** $13m^2 - 5$ **49.** $-8s + 8t$ **51.** *Sample answer:* $3k + 4k + (-8) - 2j$; $7k - 8 - 2j$ **53.** $(4 + 3) \cdot (5 - 2) = 21$ **55.** $(3 \cdot 4)^2 - (2^3 + 3)^2 = 23$

1.2 Problem Solving (pp. 15–16) **57.** 0, 10, 20, 30; \$1.89, \$3.20, \$4.51, \$5.82 **59.** $270 - 4.5x$; no; when $x > 60$ there will be a negative balance on the card, which means you will have spent more than what you had on the card. **63.** $-6.5x - 6y + 200$; \$88

1.3 Skill Practice (pp. 21–23) **1.** solution **3.** 3 **5.** 12 **7.** 6 **9.** $-\frac{2}{9}$ **11.** 4 **13.** −1 **15.** 18 **17.** −9 **21.** 1 **23.** 4 **25.** −7 **27.** $-1\frac{1}{3}$ **29.** 4 **31.** $-2\frac{2}{3}$ **33.** 4 **35.** −7 **37.** −2 **39.** 28 **41.** Both sides of the equations should be divided by $\frac{3}{7}$ instead of subtracting $\frac{3}{7}$ from each side; $\frac{3}{7}x = 15, x = 15 \div \frac{3}{7}, x = 35$. **43.** 12 **45.** 60 **47.** −23

SELECTED ANSWERS

49. $1\frac{2}{3}$ **51.** 6; 15, 8, 15, 8 **53.** 2; 6, 6, 3 **55.** 4 **57.** 2 **59.** 4 **61.** 2.9 **63.** no solution **65.** all real numbers **67.** $x = \frac{d-b}{a-c}$; $a = c$ and $b \neq d$; $a = c$ and $b = d$

1.3 Problem Solving (pp. 23–24) **69.** 3 h **71.** 9 h **73. a.** $3c + 2g = 8$ **b.** $2\frac{1}{4}, \frac{1}{2}; 2\frac{5}{12}, \frac{1}{4}$ **75.** 18 min

1.4 Skill Practice (pp. 30–31) **1.** formula **3.** $\ell = \frac{A}{w}$; 5 mm **5.** $h = \frac{2A}{b_1 + b_2}$; 6 cm **7.** $y = 26 - 3x$; 5 **9.** $y = -\frac{6}{5}x + \frac{31}{5}$; 11 **11.** $y = \frac{3}{2}x - \frac{21}{2}$; -3 **13.** $y = \frac{7}{4}x - \frac{11}{4}$; 6 **17.** The variable y should only appear on one side of the equation, not both; $4y - xy = 9$, $y(4 - x) = 9$, $y = \frac{9}{4-x}$. **19.** $h = \frac{S}{\pi r} - k$; about 4.96 cm **21.** $y = \frac{40 + 3x}{x}$; 11 **23.** $y = \frac{16x + 28}{3x}$; $7\frac{2}{3}$ **25.** $y = \frac{15}{1 - 2x}$; 5 **27.** Method 1: $y = \frac{5}{3}x - 3$, $y = \frac{5}{3} \cdot 2 - 3$, $y = \frac{1}{3}$; Method 2: $15 \cdot 2 - 9y = 27$, $30 - 9y = 27$, $-9y = -3$, $y = \frac{1}{3}$; *Sample answer:* Method 1 is more efficient because it is already solved for y. **29.** $z = \frac{x + y}{xy - 1}$ **31.** $z = \frac{xy}{xy - y - x}$

1.4 Problem Solving (pp. 31–32) **33.** $d = \frac{C}{\pi}$; about 36 in. **35.** $C = \frac{5}{9}(F - 32)$; 10°C **37.** $R = 80c + 150d$; $d = \frac{R - 80c}{150}$; 80 designer tuxedos; 160 designer tuxedos; 240 designer tuxedos **39.** $V = \frac{\ell^2 w}{4\pi}$; $V = \frac{w^2 \ell}{4\pi}$

1.5 Skill Practice (pp. 37–38) **1.** verbal model **3.** 0.5 h **5.** 90 mi **7.** 54 ft **9.** 20 m **11.** $y = 4x + 11$ **13.** $y = 46 - 10x$ **17.** $4x + 9 = 12$, 0.75 ft **19.** The pattern shows the output is decreased by 10 each time; an equation that represents the table is $y = 75 - 10x$. **23.** $y = 7x - 16$

1.5 Problem Solving (pp. 38–39) **25.** 3.75 km/min **27.** $y = 1.5x + 15$; no; the bamboo shoot will eventually slow its growth rate and stop growing.

29.

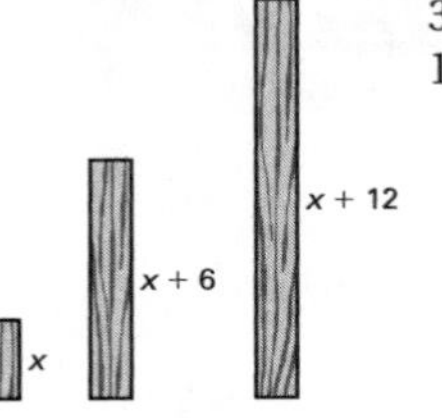

$3x + 18 = 72$, 18 in., 24 in., 30 in.

31. $40x + 7(20 - x) = 404$; 8 boxes of books, 12 boxes of clothes **33.** about 4.07 in.

1.6 Skill Practice (pp. 44–45) **1.** graph

3.

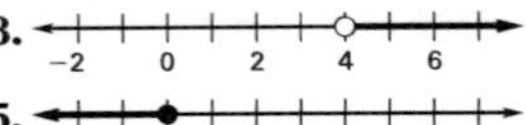

5.

11. $-3 \leq x \leq 1$ **13.** $x < -2$ or $x > 4$

17.

19.

23. $x \leq -2$

25. $x < 4$

35. The inequality symbol should not be reversed when subtracting; $10 > 2x$, $5 > x$.

37. $-6 < x < 3$

39. $1 \leq x < 7$

43. $x < -4$ or $x > 2$

45. $x \leq -\frac{1}{2}$ or $x \geq 1$

49. no solution **51.** no solution

1.6 Problem Solving (pp. 46–47) **53.** $45x + 35 \leq 250$, $x \leq 4\frac{7}{9}$ days; 4 or fewer days **55. a.** $0 \leq e < 500$ **b.** $1400 \leq e < 2429$ **c.** $0 \leq e < 500$ or $1400 \leq e < 2429$ **57.** $50 \leq F \leq 95$; $10 \leq C \leq 35$ **59. a.** Amy: $0.65(84) + 0.15(80) + 0.2w \geq 85$, Brian: $0.65(80) + 0.15(100) + 0.2x \geq 85$, Clara: $0.65(75) + 0.15(95) + 0.2y \geq 85$, Dan: $0.65(80) + 0.15(90) + 0.2z \geq 85$ **b.** $w \geq 92$; $x \geq 90$; $y \geq 110$; $z \geq 97.5$ **c.** Amy, Brian, and Dan. *Sample answer:* It is impossible to score over 100 points on a test, so Clara will not be able to achieve a grade of 85 or better.

1.6 Problem Solving Workshop (p. 49) **1.** $y = -35x + 200$; $x > 20$ **3.** $x \geq \$7000$

1.7 Skill Practice (pp. 55–56) **1.** An apparent solution that must be rejected because it does not satisfy the original equation. **3.** solution **5.** not a solution **7.** solution

9. $-9, 9$

11. 0

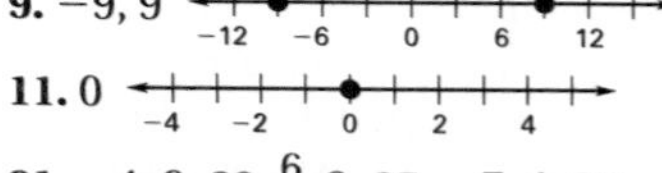

21. $-4, 9$ **23.** $\frac{6}{7}, 2$ **25.** $-7, 4$ **27.** $-7, 2$ **29.** $1\frac{4}{9}; 3$ **31.** $-20, 4$ **33.** No; the equation has no solutions because an absolute value will never be negative. **35.** -3 **37.** $-1\frac{1}{2}, -\frac{1}{2}$, **39.** $-\frac{1}{6}, -3\frac{3}{4}$ **41.** When writing the second equation, the right side of the equation should be $-x - 3$; $5x - 9 = -x - 3$, $6x - 9 = -3$, $6x = 6$, $x = 1$, the solutions are 3 and 1.

43. $-5 \le j \le 5$

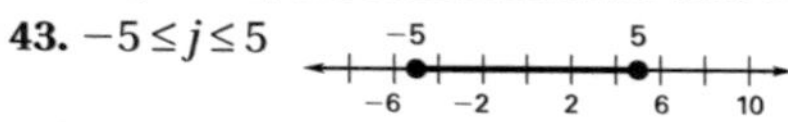

45. $-5 < m < 9$

65. $c > 0$, $c = 0$, $c < 0$ **67.** no solution

69. $x < 9$ or $x > 9$

71. $x \le \frac{-c - b}{a}$ or $x \ge \frac{c - b}{a}$ **73.** $x < \frac{c - b}{a}$ or $x > \frac{-c - b}{a}$

75. $|p - 6.5| \le 1$ **77.** $|b - 21| > 1$ **79.** $|x - 45| \le 15$

81. $|e - 6008| \le 5992$, $|m - 46{,}000| \le 45{,}000$

Chapter Review (pp. 61–64) **1.** exponent, base **3.** extraneous solution **5.** *Sample answer:* $3(x - 4)$ and $3x - 12$ **7.** Inverse property of multiplication **9.** Distributive property **11.** $3x - 6y$ **13.** $18b - 33$ **15.** $-2t^4 + 5t^2$ **17.** $-\frac{1}{6}$ **19.** 9 **21.** -1 **23.** \$74.99 **25.** $y = -10x + 7$; -23 **27.** $y = \frac{-15}{x - 6}$; 15 **29.** $y = \frac{5}{2}x - 5$; -20 **31.** $h = \frac{S - 2\pi r^2}{2\pi r}$; about 7.73 cm **33.** 602 mi

35. $x \le 6$

37. $x \le -\frac{1}{2}$

39. $-3 \le x \le 3$

41. $-3, 1\frac{2}{3}$ **43.** no solution

45. $y < -1$ or $y > 6$

47. $|v - 26| \le 0.5$, 25.5 in. $\le v \le$ 26.5 in.

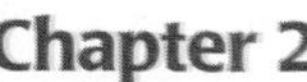

Chapter 2

2.1 Skill Practice (pp. 76–78) **1.** independent, dependent **3.** domain: $-4, -2, 1, 3$, range: $-3, -1, 2, 3$

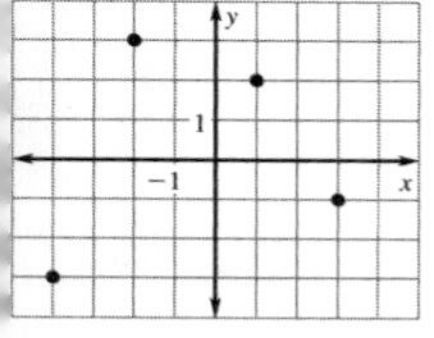

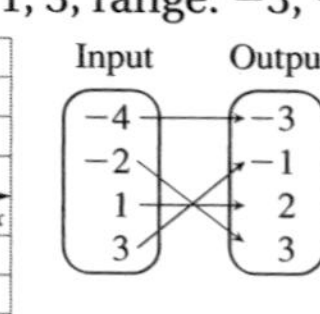

5. domain: $-2, 1, 6$, range: $-3, -1, 5, 8$

11. Yes; each input has exactly one output. **13.** Yes; each input has exactly one output. **15.** x is the input and y is the output, so there should be one value of y for each value of x; the relation given by the table is not a function because the inputs 1 and 0 each have more than one output. **17.** No; the input -2 has more than one output. **19.** No; the input -1 has more than one output. **21.** function **23.** not a function

25. **27.**

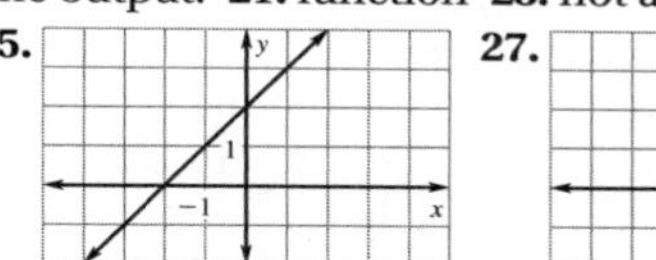

35. not linear; 10 **37.** linear; 6 **39.** linear; -3

2.1 Problem Solving (pp. 78–79) **43.** Yes; each input has exactly one output. **45.** About 905; $V(6)$ represents the volume of a sphere with radius 6.

47. a.

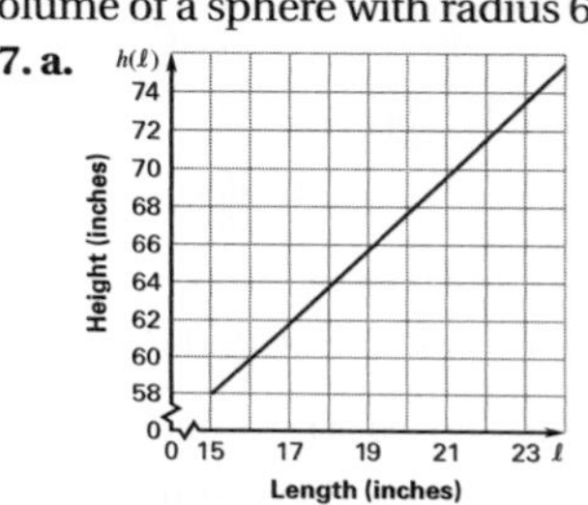

domain: $15 \le \ell \le 24$, range: $57.95 \le h(\ell) \le 75.5$

b. 59 in. or 4 ft 11 in. **c.** 21.7 in. **49. a.** domain: 11,350,000, 12,280,000, 12,420,000, 15,980,000, 18,980,000, 20,850,000, 33,870,000, range: 20, 21, 27, 31, 34, 55 **b.** Yes; each input p has exactly one output. **c.** No; the input 21 has more than one output.

Extension (p. 81)

1.

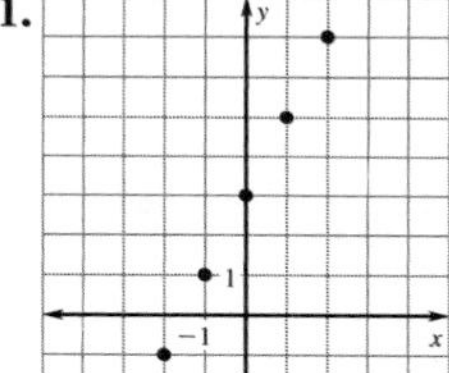

discrete; $-1, 1, 3, 5, 7$

SA3

3. continuous; $y > -6$

5. $d(x) = 3.5x$

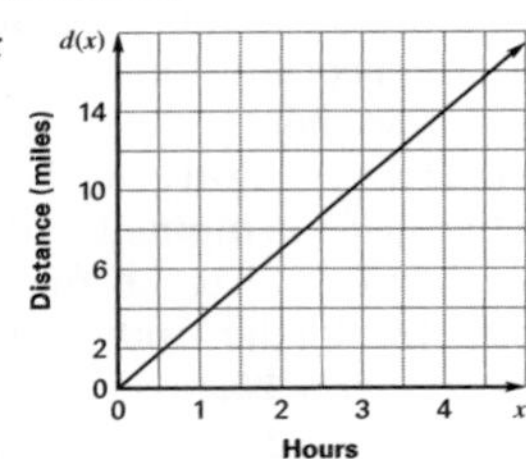

domain: $x \geq 0$, range: $d(x) \geq 0$; continuous

7. $m(x) = 3x$

domain: whole numbers, range: multiples of 3; discrete

2.2 Skill Practice (pp. 86–87) **1.** slope **3.** $\frac{3}{2}$; rises **5.** $-\frac{5}{3}$; falls **7.** -4; falls **9.** $\frac{7}{4}$; rises **11.** undefined; is vertical **13.** 0; is horizontal **15.** The x and y coordinates were not subtracted in the correct order; $\frac{-1-(-3)}{2-(-4)} = \frac{1}{3}$. **19.** neither **21.** perpendicular **23.** parallel **25.** 13 mi/gal **27.** 2 m/sec **29.** 2 **31.** $\frac{1}{6}$ **33.** $-\frac{3}{2}$ **35.** No; no. *Sample answer:* The slope of $\overleftrightarrow{PQ} = \frac{2-1}{-3-(-1)} = -\frac{1}{2}$. The slope of $\overleftrightarrow{QR} = \frac{1-0}{-1-1} = -\frac{1}{2}$. The slope of $\overleftrightarrow{ST} = \frac{-1-(-2)}{3-5} = -\frac{1}{2}$.

2.2 Problem Solving (pp. 87–88) **41.** $\frac{7}{12}$ **43.** 6.5% **47. a.** $\frac{3}{8}$ **b.** yes **c.** $\frac{1}{8}$

2.3 Skill Practice (pp. 93–94) **1.** slope-intercept

3. Both graphs have a y-intercept of 0, but the graph of $y = 3x$ has a slope of 3 instead of 1.

5. Both graphs have a slope of 1, but the graph of $y = x + 5$ has a y-intercept of 5 instead of 0.

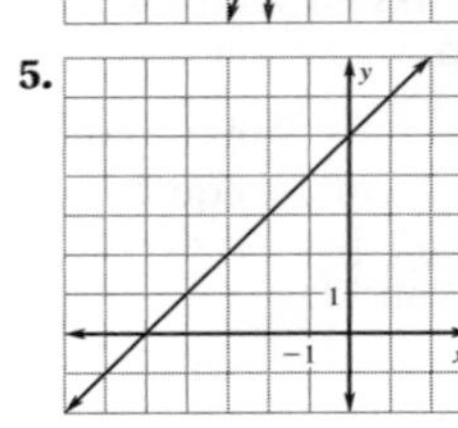

9.

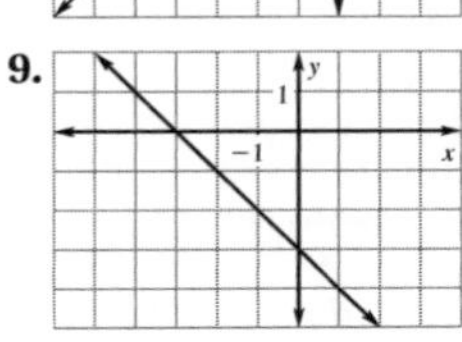

11.

21. The slope and y-intercept were switched around.

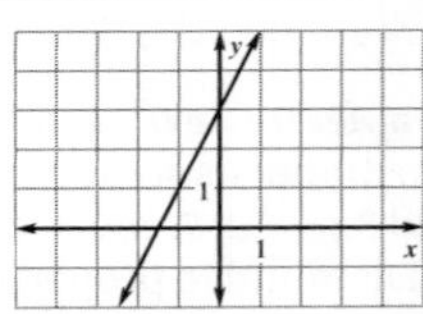

25. x-intercept: -15, y-intercept: -3 **27.** x-intercept: 5, y-intercept: -10 **29.** x-intercept: 6, y-intercept: -4.5

31.

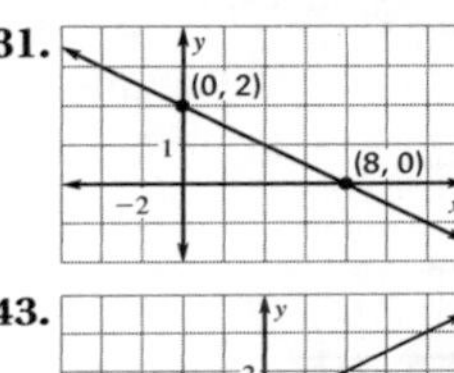

33.

43.

45.

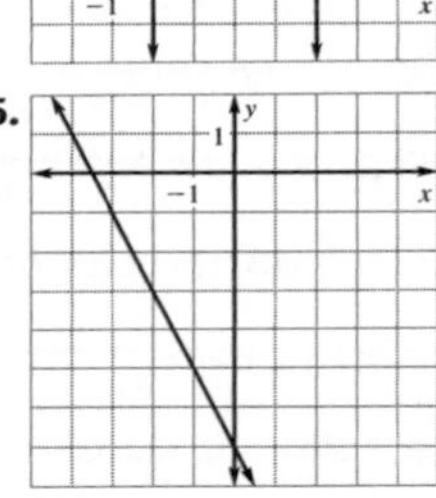

55. *Sample answer:* $x = 3$, $y = -2$ **57.** slope: $-\frac{A}{B}$, y-intercept: $\frac{C}{B}$

SELECTED ANSWERS

2.3 Problem Solving (pp. 94–96)

59. 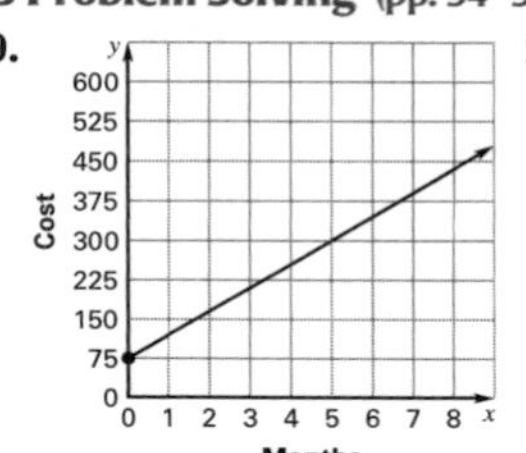 \$480

61. 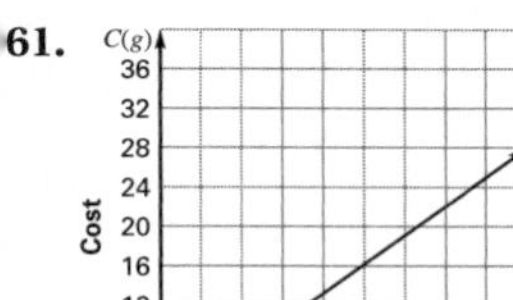 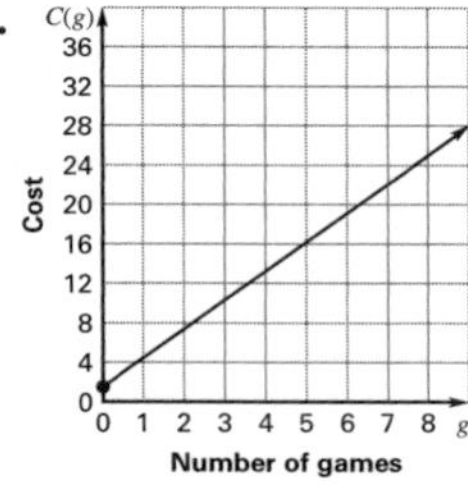 \$1.50; \$3

63. 30; fall; the value of the card will decrease after you buy each smoothie, so the line will fall from left to right.

65. 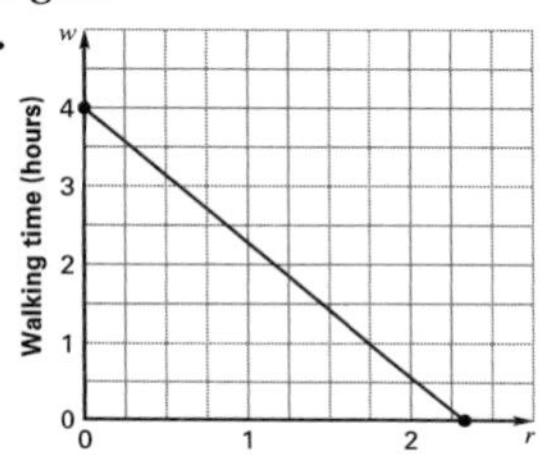 *Sample answer:* $r = 0$ and $w = 4$, $r = 1.75$ and $w = 1$, $r = 0.875$ and $w = 2.5$

67. a.

t (minutes)	h (feet)
0	200
1	350
2	500
3	650
4	800
5	950

b.

c. $h(t) = 150t + 200$

2.4 Skill Practice (pp. 101–103) **1.** standard **3.** $y = 2$ **5.** $y = 6x$ **7.** $y = -\frac{5}{4}x + 7$ **9.** $y = 4x - 2$ **11.** $y = 2x + 11$ **13.** $y = -9x + 85$ **15.** $y = -\frac{4}{7}x + 1$ **17.** $y = -\frac{1}{3}x - 2$ **19.** The x- and y-coordinates were transposed; $y - 1 = -2(x - 5)$, $y - 1 = -2x + 10$, $y = -2x + 11$. **21.** $y = -x + 8$ **23.** $y = -3x + 13$ **25.** $y = -\frac{1}{4}x - \frac{1}{4}$ **27.** $y = -2x + 6$ **29.** $y = -\frac{1}{4}x + \frac{19}{4}$ **31.** $y = -3x + 11$ **33.** $y = -\frac{2}{3}x + 7$ **35.** $y = 5x + 23$ **37.** $y = -3x + 17.5$ **41.** $-4x + y = -3$ **43.** $4x - 5y = -7$ **45.** $4x + 3y = 32$ **47.** *Sample answer:* $y = -\frac{1}{2}x + 8$

2.4 Problem Solving (pp. 103–104) **51.** $n = 15t + 50$ **53.** $15x + 9y = 4500$

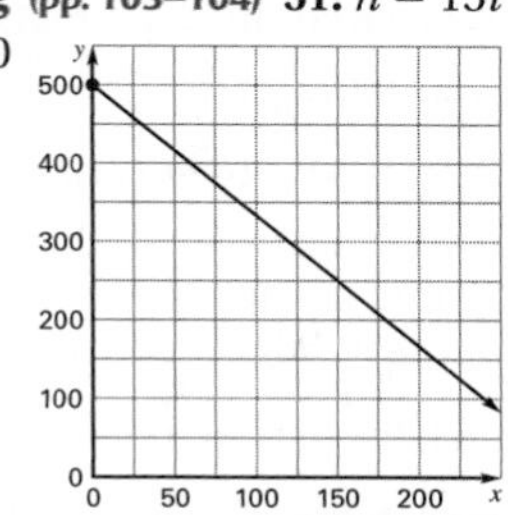

Find the point on the line where x is 200 then the corresponding y-coordinate is how many student tickets were sold. **55.** $y = 1.66x + 21.62$; \$48.18 **57. a.** $2\ell + 2w = 24$

b. 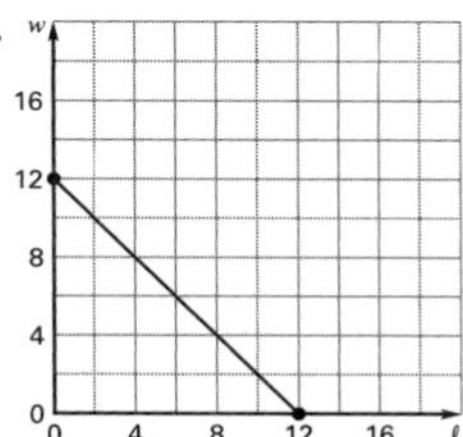

c. *Sample answer:*

ℓ	w
6	6
7	5
8	4
9	3
10	2

2.4 Problem Solving Workshop (p. 105) **1.** $y = 4x + 7$ **3.** $y = -\frac{1}{2}x + 16$ **5.** $y = 32.14x + 1764.36$

2.5 Skill Practice (pp. 109–110) **1.** *Sample answer:* If $y = ax$, then a is the constant of variation. a is a constant ratio of y to x for all ordered pairs (x, y). **3.** $y = 3x$

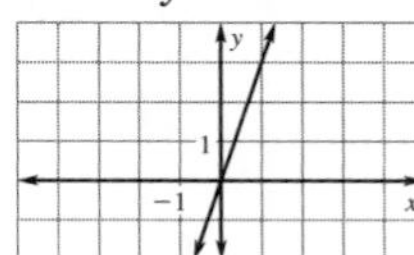

SELECTED ANSWERS

5. $y = -3.5x$

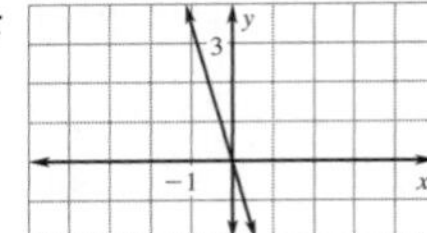

11. $y = 2x$; 24 **13.** $y = -0.2x$; -2.4 **15.** $y = \frac{1}{3}x$; 4 **19.** not direct variation **21.** direct variation; 2.5 **23.** direct variation; $\frac{1}{6}$ **25.** $y = -\frac{4}{3}x$; 3 **27.** $y = -7x$; $\frac{4}{7}$ **29.** $y = -7.2x$; $\frac{5}{9}$ **31.** direct variation; $y = -\frac{1}{3}x$ **33.** direct variation; $y = -4x$ **35.** The quotients need to be compared to each other, not the products; $\frac{24}{1} = 24$, $\frac{12}{2} = 6$, $\frac{8}{3} \approx 2.7$, $\frac{6}{4} = 1.5$, because the ratios are not equal, the data do not show direct variation.

2.5 Problem Solving (pp. 110–111) **39.** $w = 3600d$; 6300 lb **41.** direct variation; $t = 5.1s$ **43. a.** direct variation; $P = 4s$ **b.** Not a direct variation; the ratios of A to s are not equal. **c.** Not a direct variation; the ratios of A to P are not equal.

2.6 Skill Practice (pp. 117–118) **1.** best-fitting line **3.** negative correlation **5.** approximately no correlation **7.** 0 **9.** -1

11. a.

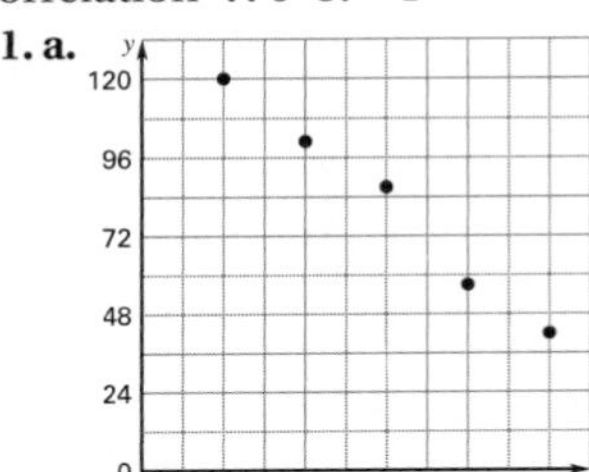

b. *Sample answer:* $y = -20x + 141$ **c.** about -259

13. a.

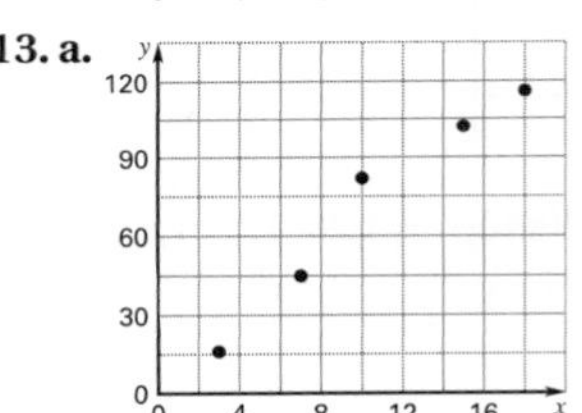

b. *Sample answer:* $y = 6.7x + 1$ **c.** about 135

17. The line should go through the middle of the data points. *Sample answer:*

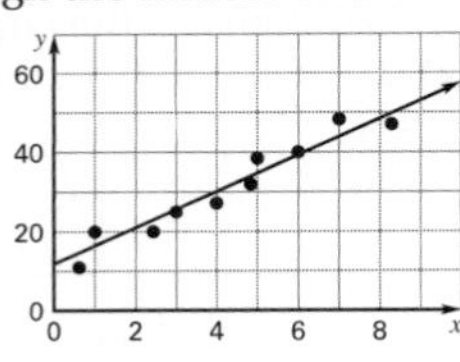

19. $y = 0.05x + 1.14$

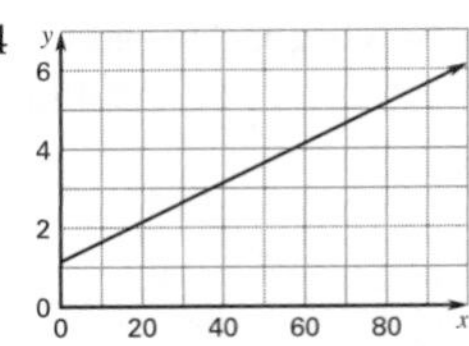

21. a. *Sample answer:* Measuring the depth of water at different times while filling a swimming pool. The number of gallons of milk you buy and the total cost. **b.** *Sample answer:* The age of a car and its current value. The number of miles you have driven since you last put gas in the tank and the amount of gas left in the tank. **c.** *Sample answer:* The height of a person and the month they were born. The age of a person and the number of vehicles they own.

2.6 Problem Solving (pp. 119–120) **25.** *Sample answer:* $y = 101.3x + 2236.6$ **27. a.** (0, 37), (4, 49), (8, 57), (12, 64), (14, 67), (18, 72), (22, 77)

b.

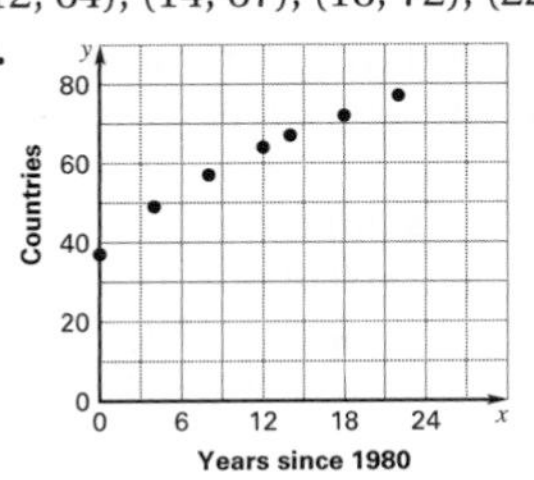

c. *Sample answer:* $y = 1.8x + 40.7$; 102 countries

2.7 Skill Practice (pp. 127–128) **1.** vertex

3.

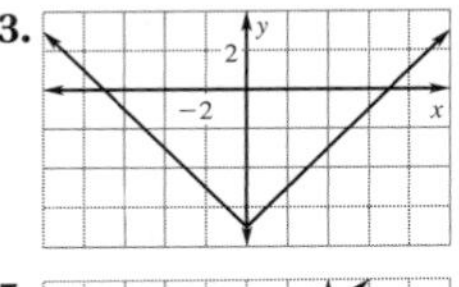

translated down 7 units

5.

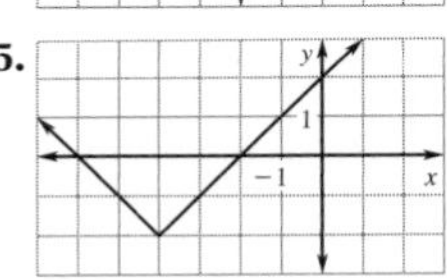

translated left 4 units and down 2 units

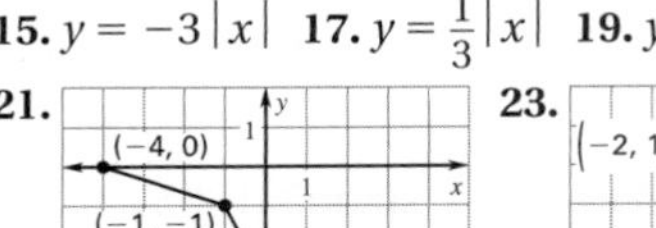

15. $y = -3|x|$ **17.** $y = \frac{1}{3}|x|$ **19.** $y = \frac{1}{2}|x + 2| - 1$

21.

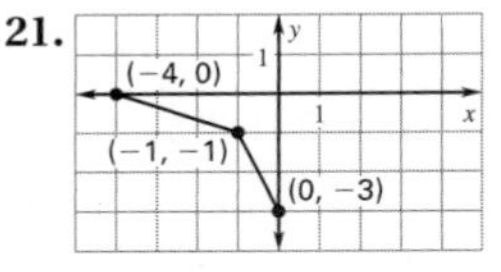

23. (−2, $1\frac{1}{2}$) (1, 1) (2, 0)

29. The graph should be translated left 3 units.

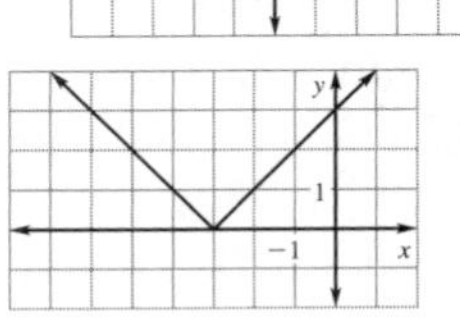

33. No. *Sample answer:* It does not pass the vertical line test.

SELECTED ANSWERS

2.7 Problem Solving (pp. 128–129)

37.

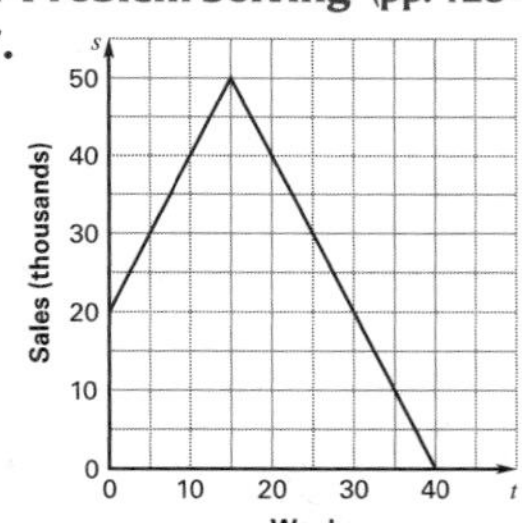

50,000 pairs of shoes

39. $y = -\frac{140}{69}|x - 69| + 140$

41. a.

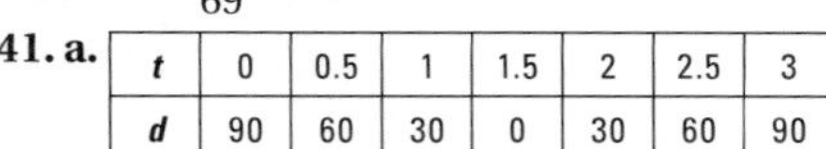

t	0	0.5	1	1.5	2	2.5	3
d	90	60	30	0	30	60	90

b.

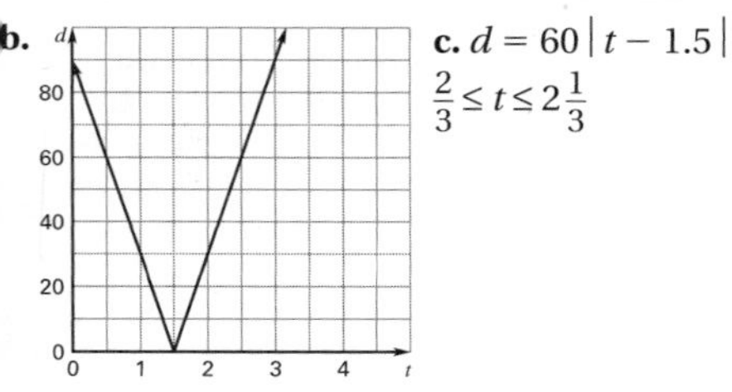

c. $d = 60|t - 1.5|$; $\frac{2}{3} \le t \le 2\frac{1}{3}$

Extension (p. 131) **1.** -1 **3.** $\frac{5}{2}$

5. **7.**

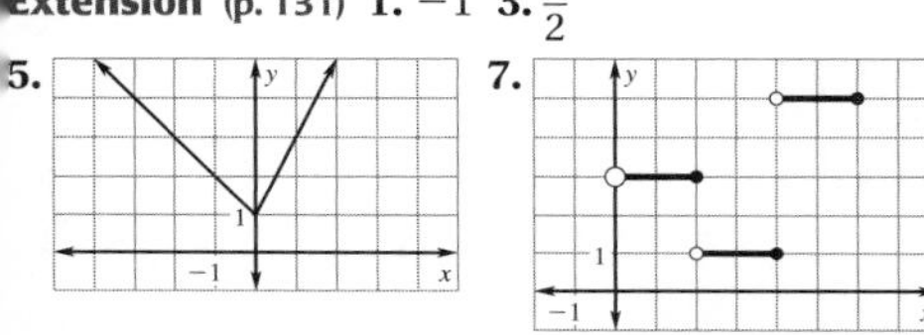

9.

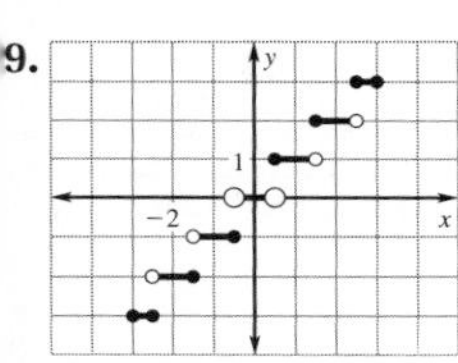

2.8 Skill Practice (pp. 135–136) **1.** half-plane **3.** solution, not a solution **5.** solution, solution

7.

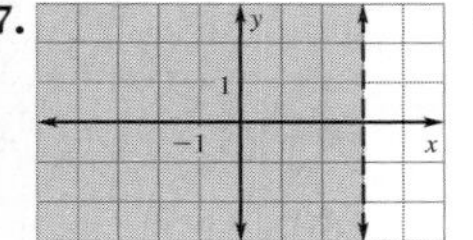

9.

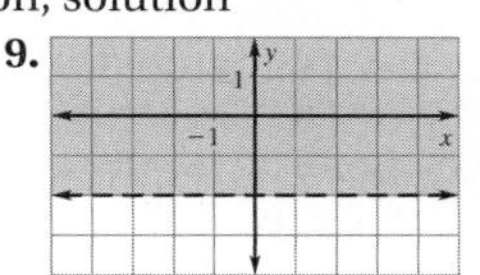

19. The boundary line should be a dashed line.

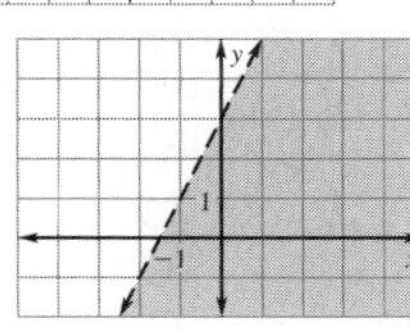

23.

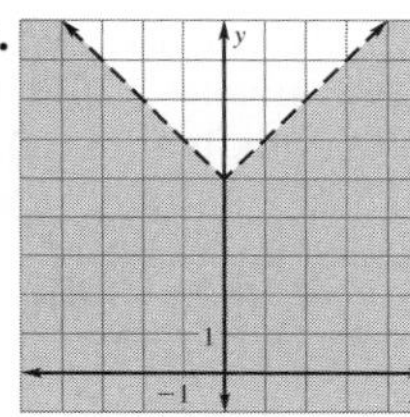

25.

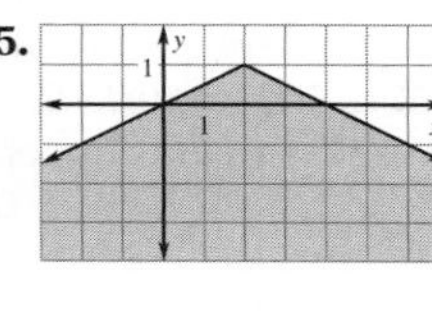

29. solution, not a solution **31.** solution, not a solution

33.

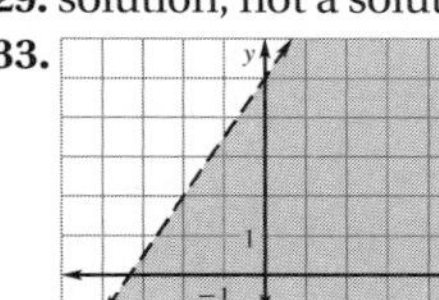

35.

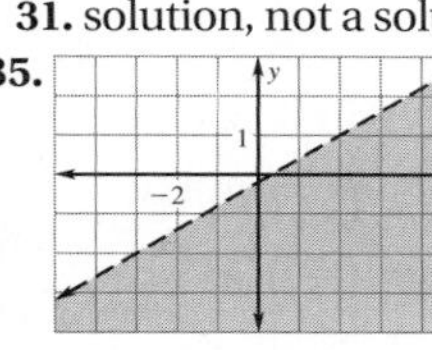

39. *Sample answer:* $y > x + 3$ **41.** $y > -\frac{3}{5}x + 3$; pick two points on the boundary line to find the slope and then use the point-slope form of an equation to find the equation. The boundary line is dotted, so the inequality dos not include points on the boundary. Then choose a point to determine which inequality sign to use. *Sample answer:* You and your sister want to spend at least $15 on your little brother's birthday. You want to buy him some racecars that cost $3 each and some building block sets that cost $5 each.

2.8 Problem Solving (pp. 137–138) **43.** $0.03x + 0.06y \le 20$

45. $1.5x + 2.5y \le 75$

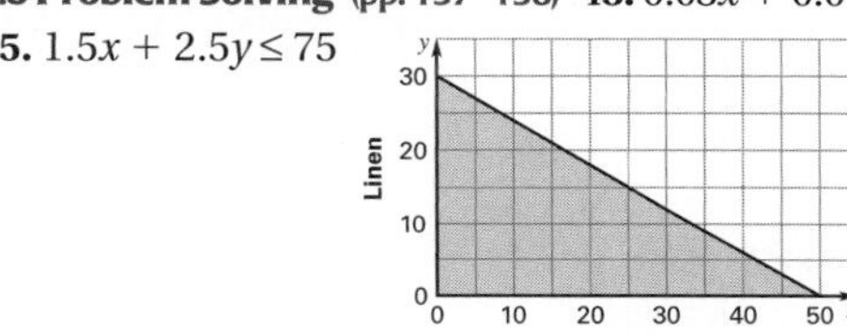

$y \le 15.6$ yd

47. a. $11x + 26y \le 120$

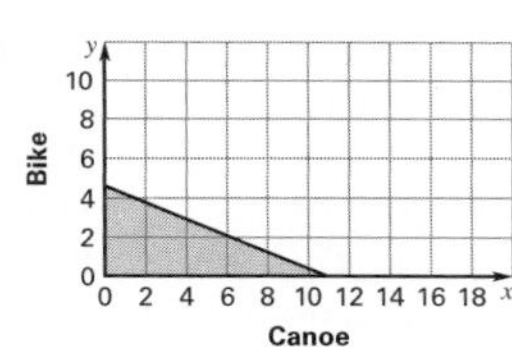

b. *Sample answer:* 2 days canoeing and 5 days biking, 3 days canoeing and 2 days biking, 2 days canoeing and 2 days biking

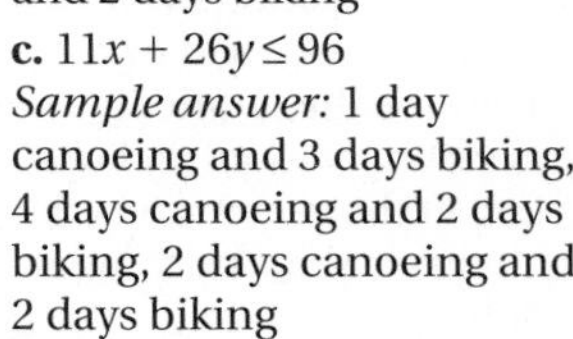

c. $11x + 26y \le 96$ *Sample answer:* 1 day canoeing and 3 days biking, 4 days canoeing and 2 days biking, 2 days canoeing and 2 days biking

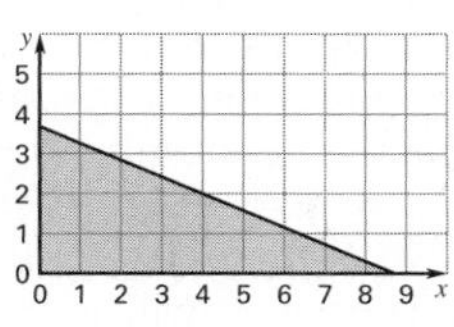

SELECTED ANSWERS

SA7

Chapter Review (pp. 141–144) **1.** standard **3.** direct variation **5.** domain: −2, −1, 2, 3, range: −2, 0, 6, 8; function **7.** linear function; 51 **9.** undefined **11.** 0

13.

15.

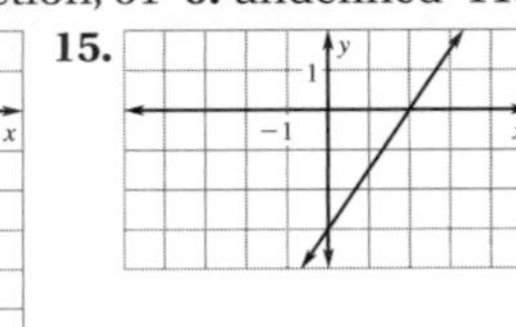

17. $y = -\frac{3}{4}x + 2$ **19.** $y = -8x$; −24 **21.** $y = -0.8x$; −2.4

23. *Sample answer:* $y = -x + 2.3$

25.

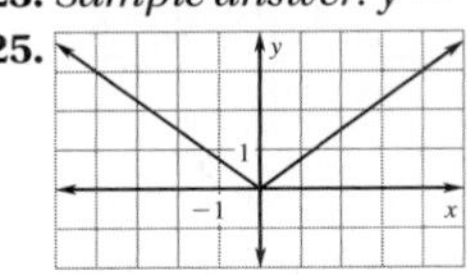

shrunk vertically by a factor of $\frac{3}{4}$

27.

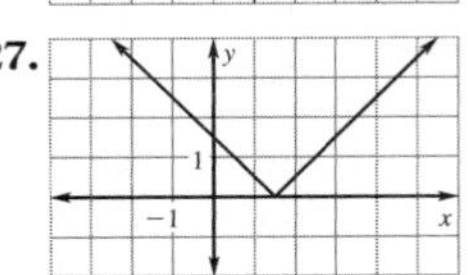

$1.75, $1.25

29. solution

31.

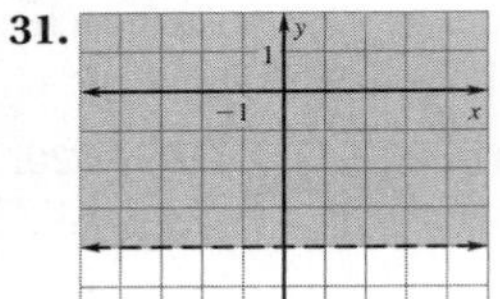

33.

Chapter 3

3.1 Skill Practice (pp. 156–157) **1.** independent **3.** (1, −1) **5.** (4, −1) **7.** (5, 0) **9.** (−2, 4) **11.** infinitely many solutions **13.** (3, 3) **17.** (2, −1); consistent and independent **19.** no solution; inconsistent **21.** infinitely many solutions; consistent and dependent **23.** (2, 0); consistent and independent **25.** (3, −1); consistent and independent **27.** infinitely many solutions; consistent and dependent **31.** no solution **33.** (−4, 2) and (−4, 2)

3.1 Problem Solving (pp. 157–158) **35.** lifeguard: 6 h, cashier: 8 h **37.** 11 days; the number of days will decrease; the number of days will be divided by a larger number, which will decrease the quotient, which is the number of days. **39. a.** $m = -0.0958x + 50.8$ **b.** $w = -0.124x + 57.1$ **c.** in the year 2195 **d.** No. *Sample answer:* It is not likely that the same linear models will apply indefinitely.

3.2 Skill Practice (pp. 164–165) **1.** substitution **3.** (6, −1) **5.** no solution **7.** $\left(\frac{4}{3}, 2\right)$ **9.** (0, 3) **11.** (−3, 8) **13.** (44, −17) **15.** $\left(7, \frac{1}{2}\right)$ **17.** (−6, −2) **19.** $\left(-\frac{1}{2}, \frac{1}{6}\right)$ **21.** (−8, 6) **23.** no solution **25.** (7, 3) **27.** Failed to multiply the constant by −2.

$$\begin{aligned} -6x - 4y &= -14 \\ 5x + 4y &= 15 \\ \hline -x &= 1 \\ x &= -1 \end{aligned}$$

29. (−5, −6) **31.** infinitely many solutions **33.** (−8, 0) **35.** (7, −6) **37.** $\left(-\frac{3}{2}, 4\right)$ **39.** $\left(-\frac{3}{4}, \frac{1}{2}\right)$ **41.** (2, 3) **43.** (3, 2) **45.** about (2.90, −2.16) **47.** (−1, 2) **49.** (7, 1) **51.** $\left(-\frac{1}{9}, 6\right)$ **53.** (5, 4)

3.2 Problem Solving (pp. 165–166) **55.** 5 acoustic, 4 electric **57.** The company can fill its orders by operating Factory A for 5 weeks and Factory B for 3 weeks. **59.** 12 doubles games, 14 singles games **61.** 80 pounds of peanuts, 20 pounds of cashews

3.3 Skill Practice (pp. 171–172) **1.** The ordered pair must satisfy each inequality of the system.

5.

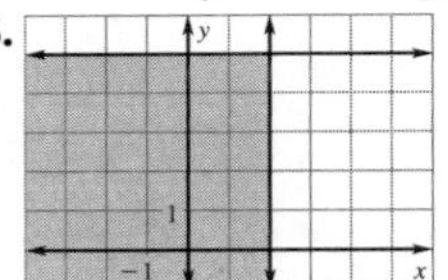

7. no solution

9.

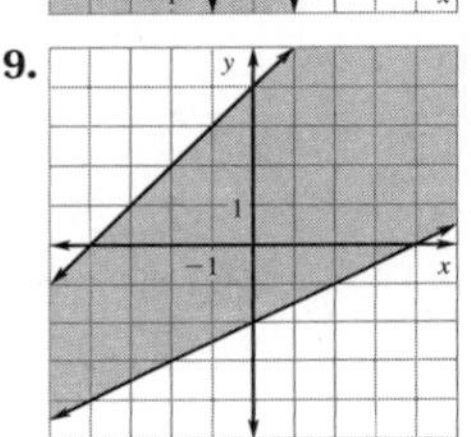

17.

19.

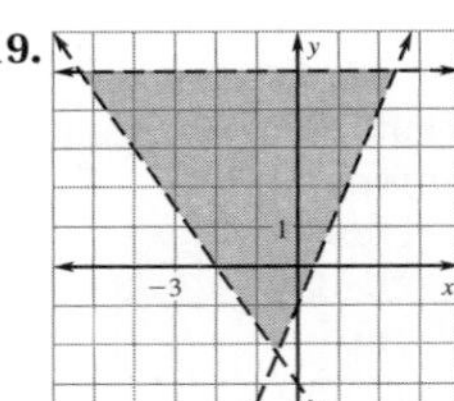

27. *Sample answer:* $y < x - 1$, $y < -\frac{3}{4}x + 4$

29.

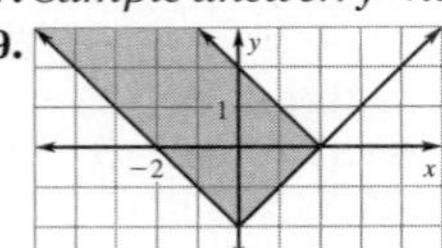

SELECTED ANSWERS

3.3 Problem Solving (pp. 172–173) **35.** $x \ge 20$, $x \le 50$, $y \ge 0.3x$, $y \le 0.7x$, where x represents the regular price and y represents the sale price; $6 \le y \le 14$ **37. a.** $x \ge 2$, $y \ge 2$, $x + y \le 8$, $x + y \ge 5$

b.

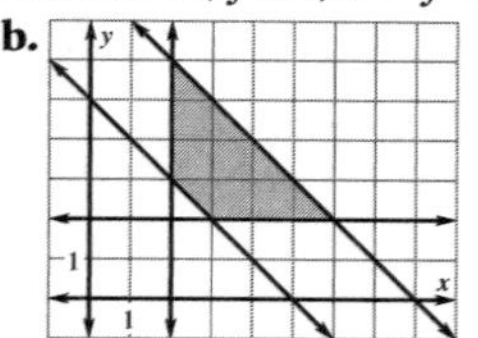

c. *Sample answer:* 3 juniors, 4 seniors; 4 juniors, 4 seniors

39. a. $x \ge 20$, $x \le 65$, $y \ge 0.5(220 - x)$, $y \le 0.75(220 - x)$

b.

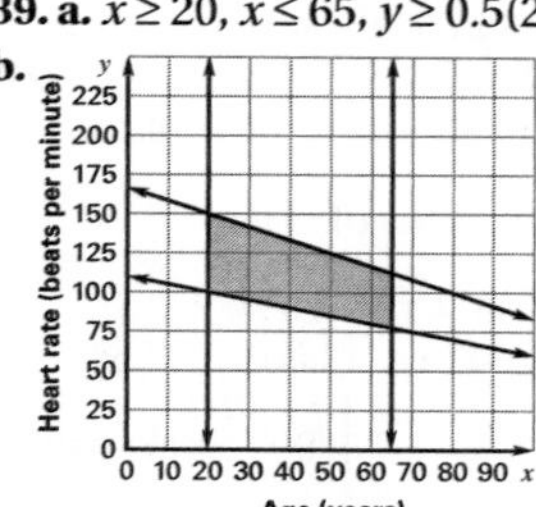

c. No; the person's heart rate is above the target zone. A 40-year old person's heart rate should be between 90 and 135 heartbeats per minute.

Extension (p. 176) **1.** 1; 14 **3.** 170; 580 **5.** 5; 55 **7.** 6 mini piñatas, 6 regular-sized piñatas **9.** 12 jars of tomato sauce, 4 jars of salsa

3.4 Skill Practice (pp. 182–183) **1.** *Sample answer:* $2x - 3y + z = 6$; a plane **3.** no **5.** yes **7.** no **9.** (1, 5, 6) **11.** no solution **13.** (0, 4, −2) **15.** (3, 2, 1) **17.** (−6, 4, −4) **19.** (0, 0, −2) **21.** In the 2nd equation, the coefficient of y was not multiplied by 2;

$$\begin{aligned} 2x + y - 2z &= 23 \\ 6x + 4y + 2z &= 22 \\ \hline 8x + 5y \quad\quad &= 45 \end{aligned}$$

25. infinitely many solutions **27.** (−1, 4, 0) **29.** (−4, 5, −4) **31.** (0, −2, 6) **33.** (2, 6, −5) **35.** (2, 1, 0) **37.** $a = 12$, $b = -4$, $c = 10$; when you substitute −1 for x, 2 for y, and −3 for z into each of the equations, you get the results for a, b, and c.

3.4 Problem Solving (pp. 184–185) **43.** 1st delivery: 300 gal; 2nd delivery: 750 gal; 3rd delivery: 2050 gal **45. a.** $f + s + t = 20$, $5f + 3s + t = 68$, $s = f + t$, where f represents the number of first-place finishes, s represents the number of second-place finishes, and t represents the number of third-place finishes; 7 first-place finishes, 10 second-place finishes, 3 third-place finishes **b.** When you solve for f and t, you get a fractional answer and you cannot have fractions of a person. **47. a.** $2.5r + 4\ell + 2i = 32$, $r + \ell + i = 12$, $r = 2(\ell + i)$ where r represents the number of roses, ℓ represents the number of lilies, and i represents the number of irises **b.** 8 roses, 2 lilies, 2 irises **c.** yes; 8 roses, 2 lilies, 2 irises

3.5 Skill Practice (pp. 190–193) **1.** dimensions **3.** The corresponding entries were not added together to create a 2 × 1 matrix; $\begin{bmatrix} 13.1 \\ -1.2 \end{bmatrix}$ **5.** $\begin{bmatrix} -2 & -5 \\ 2 & 1 \end{bmatrix}$

7. $\begin{bmatrix} 3.6 & 4.7 \\ 6.2 & 7.5 \\ 14.3 & -1.2 \end{bmatrix}$ **9.** $\begin{bmatrix} -2 & -5 \\ 14 & -1 \\ -10 & 6 \end{bmatrix}$ **11.** $\begin{bmatrix} -6 & 0 & 15 \\ -12 & -21 & 9 \end{bmatrix}$

13. $\begin{bmatrix} -3 & 5.1 & 2.4 \\ 8.1 & 0 & -4.5 \end{bmatrix}$ **15.** $\begin{bmatrix} -13.2 & -6.82 & -9.9 \\ 2.2 & 0 & -5.5 \\ -12.1 & 3.96 & -14.08 \end{bmatrix}$

17. $\begin{bmatrix} 13 & -8 \\ -9 & 1 \end{bmatrix}$ **19.** $\begin{bmatrix} 12 & -8 \\ -4 & 0 \end{bmatrix}$ **21.** $\begin{bmatrix} 23.4 & -1.5 & -5.6 \\ -2.5 & -2.3 & 9.9 \end{bmatrix}$

23. $\begin{bmatrix} -6.3 & -0.75 & 10.7 \\ -6.5 & 3.6 & -3.3 \end{bmatrix}$ **25.** $x = \frac{19}{2}$, $y = 4$ **27.** $x = -2$, $y = -16$ **29.** *Sample answer:* $A = \begin{bmatrix} 5.5 & -3 \\ -8 & 7 \end{bmatrix}$, $B = \begin{bmatrix} 2 & -2 \\ -5 & 4 \end{bmatrix}$

3.5 Problem Solving (pp. 192–193)

31. $\begin{bmatrix} 0 & 5 & 1 & -1 \\ -7 & -1 & -5 & -2 \\ 1 & -1 & 4 & 10 \end{bmatrix}$ **33. a.** $M = \begin{matrix} \text{Model A} \\ \text{Model B} \\ \text{Model C} \end{matrix} \begin{bmatrix} 31 & 22 \\ 42 & 25 \\ 18 & 11 \end{bmatrix}$, $J = \begin{matrix} \text{Model A} \\ \text{Model B} \\ \text{Model C} \end{matrix} \begin{bmatrix} 25 & 38 \\ 36 & 32 \\ 12 & 15 \end{bmatrix}$ **b.** $\begin{bmatrix} 56 & 60 \\ 78 & 57 \\ 30 & 26 \end{bmatrix}$; the sum represents the total sales for May and June. **c.** $\begin{bmatrix} 28 & 30 \\ 39 & 28.5 \\ 15 & 13 \end{bmatrix}$

3.6 Skill Practice (pp. 199–200) **1.** columns; rows **3.** defined; 2 × 2 **5.** not defined **7.** not defined

11. $\begin{bmatrix} -2 & 1 \\ -8 & 4 \end{bmatrix}$ **13.** $\begin{bmatrix} -12 & 15 \\ 8 & -4 \end{bmatrix}$ **15.** $\begin{bmatrix} 11 & 35 \\ 8 & 0 \\ -9 & 7 \end{bmatrix}$

17. $\begin{bmatrix} 21 & -8 \\ 74 & -50 \end{bmatrix}$ **19.** The multiplication should be row 1 of left matrix by column 1 of the right matrix; $3(7) + (-1)(1) = 20$. **23.** $\begin{bmatrix} 21 & -6 \\ -14 & 1 \end{bmatrix}$ **25.** $\begin{bmatrix} -10 & 7 \\ -8 & 10 \end{bmatrix}$

27. $\begin{bmatrix} -2 & 4 & 0 \\ 5 & 15 & 8 \\ -16 & 17 & 36 \end{bmatrix}$ **29.** $\begin{bmatrix} -204 & 81 \\ 160 & -38 \end{bmatrix}$ **31.** $x = 3$, $y = 35$

33. $\begin{bmatrix} 18 & -5 \\ -10 & 3 \end{bmatrix}$, $\begin{bmatrix} -82 & 23 \\ 46 & -13 \end{bmatrix}$

35. *Sample answer:* $\begin{bmatrix} 3 & 7 \\ -2 & 5 \end{bmatrix} \begin{bmatrix} 1 & 0 \\ 0 & 1 \end{bmatrix}$

SA9

3.6 Problem Solving (pp. 200–202)

37. $\begin{matrix} \text{Bats} \\ \text{Balls} \\ \text{Uniforms} \end{matrix}\begin{bmatrix} 12 \\ 45 \\ 15 \end{bmatrix}$, $\text{Cost}\overset{\begin{matrix}\text{Bat} & \text{Ball} & \text{Uniform}\end{matrix}}{\begin{bmatrix} 21 & 4 & 30 \end{bmatrix}}$; $\text{Item}\overset{\text{Cost}}{\begin{bmatrix} 882 \end{bmatrix}}$

39. Friday: $1150, Saturday: $1675
41. *PS*; $\begin{bmatrix} 62{,}400 & 57{,}575 \end{bmatrix}$, it shows the profit for all of the cars sold by each dealer. **43. a.** $\begin{bmatrix} 0.8 & 0.05 \\ 0.2 & 0.95 \end{bmatrix}$

b. $M_1 = \begin{bmatrix} 4400 \\ 8600 \end{bmatrix}$; the number of commuters after 1 year

c. $M_2 = \begin{bmatrix} 3950 \\ 9050 \end{bmatrix}$, $M_3 = \begin{bmatrix} 3612.5 \\ 9387.5 \end{bmatrix}$, $M_4 = \begin{bmatrix} 3359.375 \\ 9640.625 \end{bmatrix}$; the number of commuters after 2, 3, and 4 years

3.7 Skill Practice (pp. 207–208) **1.** determinant **3.** −6 **5.** 25 **7.** 8 **9.** 39 **11.** −206 **13.** −34 **15.** 1160 **17.** −480 **19.** The sum of the products for the diagonals that go up should be subtracted from the sum of the products for the diagonals that go down; 10 + 0 + (−8) − (3 + 24 + 0) = −25 **23.** 12 **25.** 21 **27.** 25 **29.** (−4, 3) **31.** (−7, −5) **33.** (6, −3, −7) **35.** (0, 4, 1) **37.** (8, 6, 7)

3.7 Problem Solving (pp. 208–209) **41.** 12 ft^2 **43. a.** 60 single scoop, 40 double scoop, 20 triple scoop **b.** $140.03 **45. a.** 4786 mi^2 **b.** 3201 mi^2 **c.** 7987 mi^2 **d.** Connect Vernal, UT, to Moab, UT.

3.8 Skill Practice (pp. 214–215)

1. matrix of variables $\begin{bmatrix} x \\ y \end{bmatrix}$, matrix of constants $\begin{bmatrix} 4 \\ -2 \end{bmatrix}$

3. $\begin{bmatrix} -4 & -5 \\ -1 & -1 \end{bmatrix}$ **5.** $\begin{bmatrix} 1 & -1 \\ -\frac{5}{2} & 3 \end{bmatrix}$ **7.** $\begin{bmatrix} -\frac{7}{4} & -\frac{3}{2} \\ 1 & 1 \end{bmatrix}$

9. $\begin{bmatrix} -\frac{1}{12} & \frac{1}{6} \\ -\frac{1}{60} & \frac{1}{15} \end{bmatrix}$ **11.** The scalar should be $\frac{1}{\det}$;

$\frac{1}{6}\begin{bmatrix} 5 & -4 \\ -1 & 2 \end{bmatrix} = \begin{bmatrix} \frac{5}{6} & -\frac{2}{3} \\ -\frac{1}{6} & \frac{1}{3} \end{bmatrix}$. **13.** $\begin{bmatrix} 11 & 9 \\ -9 & -6 \end{bmatrix}$

15. $\begin{bmatrix} -3 & 1 \\ \frac{11}{2} & -\frac{1}{4} \end{bmatrix}$ **17.** $\begin{bmatrix} 18 & 19 & 10 \\ -3 & -4 & -2 \end{bmatrix}$

19. $\begin{bmatrix} -\frac{3}{10} & -\frac{1}{5} & \frac{3}{10} \\ \frac{9}{10} & \frac{3}{5} & \frac{1}{10} \\ -\frac{1}{5} & \frac{1}{5} & \frac{1}{5} \end{bmatrix}$ **21.** $\begin{bmatrix} -\frac{1}{2} & 0 & \frac{1}{2} \\ -\frac{17}{16} & \frac{1}{8} & \frac{7}{16} \\ \frac{7}{32} & \frac{1}{16} & -\frac{1}{32} \end{bmatrix}$

23. $\begin{bmatrix} \frac{3}{20} & \frac{3}{10} & \frac{1}{20} \\ -\frac{11}{160} & \frac{9}{80} & \frac{3}{160} \\ -\frac{1}{40} & -\frac{1}{20} & -\frac{7}{40} \end{bmatrix}$ **25.** (3, 2) **27.** (−1, −4)

29. (10, −2) **31.** (1, −8) **33.** (−3, 5) **35.** (−9, 19, −10) **37.** (−1, −2, 3) **39.** (−2, 10, 0)

41. *Sample answer:* $\begin{bmatrix} 2 & 3 \\ 4 & 6 \end{bmatrix}$

3.8 Problem Solving (pp. 215–217) **43.** single-engine: 150 h, twin-engine: 50 h **45. a.** $2x + y = 8$, $3x + y = 11$ where x represents rolls and y represents muffins

b. $\begin{bmatrix} 2 & 1 \\ 3 & 1 \end{bmatrix}\begin{bmatrix} x \\ y \end{bmatrix} = \begin{bmatrix} 8 \\ 11 \end{bmatrix}$ **c.** 3 batches of rolls, 2 batches of muffins **47.** Bran Crunchies: 2.3 oz, Toasted Oats: 0.8 oz, Whole Wheat Flakes: 1.2 oz

49. a. $\begin{bmatrix} 1 & 4 & 2 \\ -1 & -3 & -5 \end{bmatrix}$, $\begin{bmatrix} -1 & -3 & -5 \\ -1 & -4 & -2 \end{bmatrix}$; 90° clockwise rotation **b.** multiply *AAT* by *A* and then again by *A*

3.8 Problem Solving Workshop (p. 219) **1.** DVD: $15, popcorn: $1.75, movie pass: $8 **3.** 11 lbs of sunflower seed, 9 lbs of thistle seed

Chapter Review (pp. 222–226) **1.** consistent, inconsistent **3.** The number of columns in the left hand matrix is the same as the number of rows in the right hand matrix.

5. 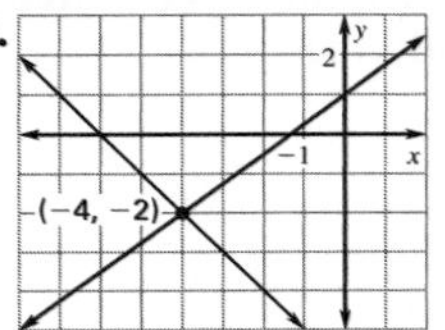

(−4, −2)

7. (−3, 7) **9.** (−6, 7)

11. 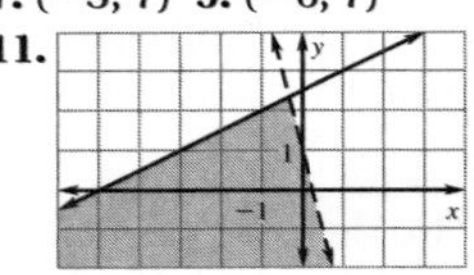

13.

15. (−3, −8, 4) **17.** 10 wind instruments, 3 string instruments, 2 percussion instruments

19. $\begin{bmatrix} 6 & 4 \\ 8 & -4 \end{bmatrix}$ **21.** $\begin{bmatrix} 2 & -4 & 0 \\ 7 & 6 & 7 \end{bmatrix}$ **23.** $\begin{bmatrix} 64 & 32 & 40 \\ -8 & 48 & -16 \end{bmatrix}$

25. $\begin{bmatrix} 28 & -76 \\ -20 & 10 \end{bmatrix}$ **27.** $\begin{bmatrix} -2 & 6 & -15 \\ 6 & 0 & -3 \end{bmatrix}$ **29.** −42 **31.** 18

33. (7, 1) **35.** (−1, −4)

Cumulative Review (pp. 232–233) **1.** $-2x^2 + 7x$ **3.** $-4x^2 + 6x + 15$ **5.** $-\frac{5}{2}$ **7.** −8, 2 **9.** −16, 25

SA10

11. $5 \le x \le 10$

13. $-1 < x < 9$

15. $-4 < x < \frac{11}{3}$

17. $-\frac{7}{12}$; falls **19.** 0; is horizontal

21.

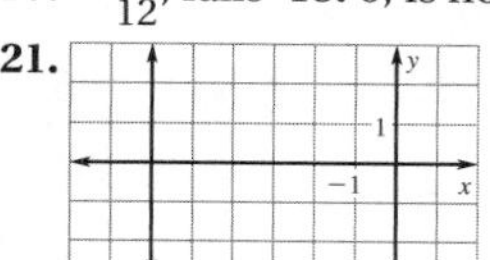

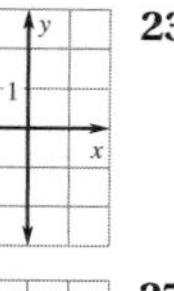

23.

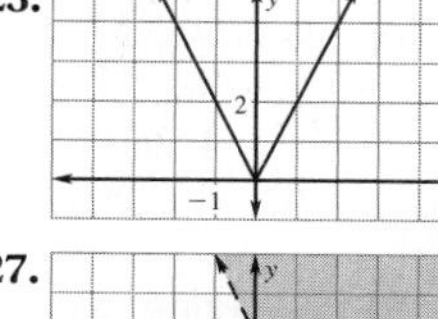

25.

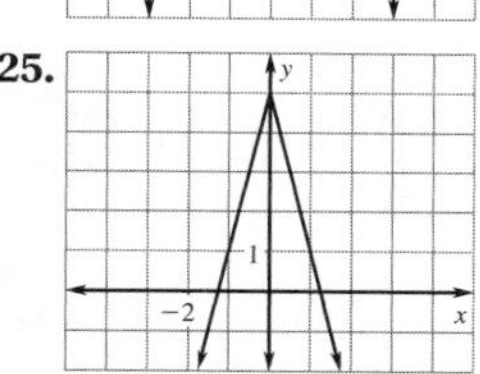

27.

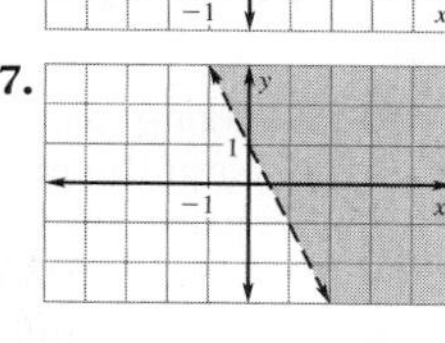

29.

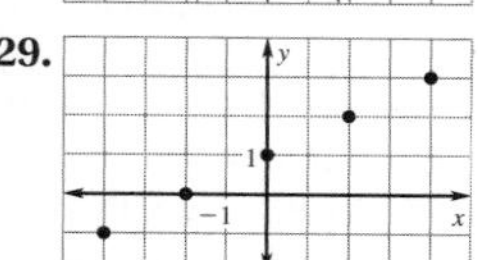

function

31. (5, −4) **33.** (−2, 4, 1) **35.** $\begin{bmatrix} 6 & 2 \\ 19 & 0 \end{bmatrix}$

37. $\begin{bmatrix} -15 & 21 & -3 \\ -30 & 42 & -6 \end{bmatrix}$ **39.** $\begin{bmatrix} -\frac{4}{3} & -3 \\ 1 & 2 \end{bmatrix}$ **41.** $\begin{bmatrix} -\frac{1}{3} & -\frac{1}{3} \\ -\frac{1}{12} & -\frac{5}{24} \end{bmatrix}$

43. a. $W = \frac{TR^2}{R^2 + A^2}$ **b.** About 98 games; it's the same.

45. $c = \frac{1}{20}p$; \$6250 **47.** $s > 213, j < 263, s + j > 472.5$

Chapter 4

4.1 Skill Practice (pp. 240–241) **1.** parabola **3.** 16, 4, 0, 4, 16 **5.** 8, 2, 0, 2, 8

7.

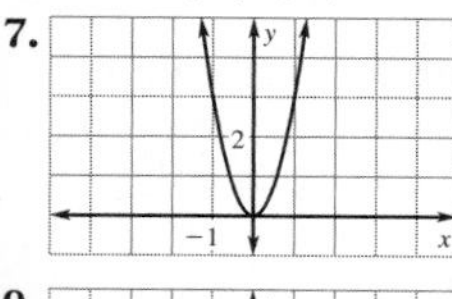

same axis of symmetry and vertex, opens up, and is narrower

9.

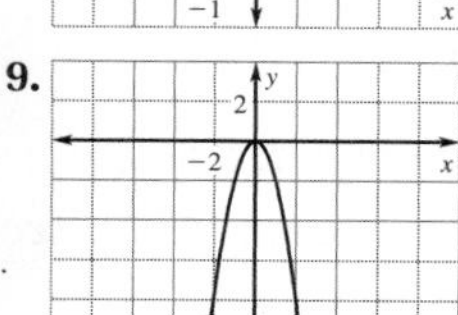

same axis of symmetry and vertex, opens down, and is narrower

19. The formula for the x-coordinate of the vertex is $-\frac{b}{2a}$; $-\frac{24}{2(4)} = -3$.

21.

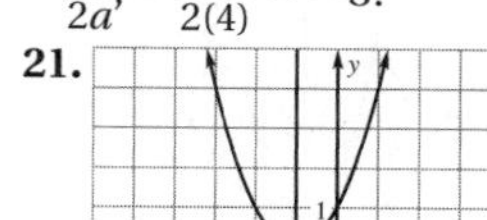

23.

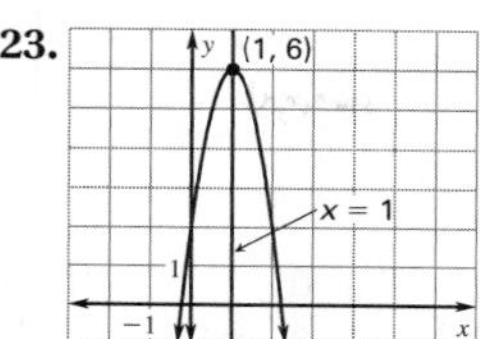

33. maximum value; −1 **35.** minimum value; −1 **37.** minimum value; −2 **41.** $a = -0.02, b = 1, c = 6$ **43.** *Sample answer:* $y = -x^2 + 8x + 3$, $y = 2x^2 - 16x - 1$, $y = x^2 - 8x - 6$

47.

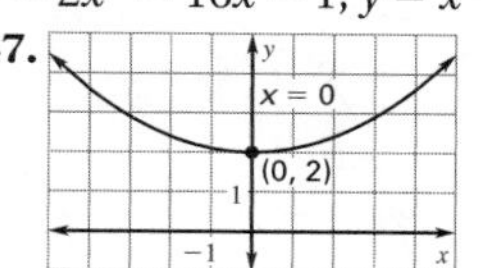

49.

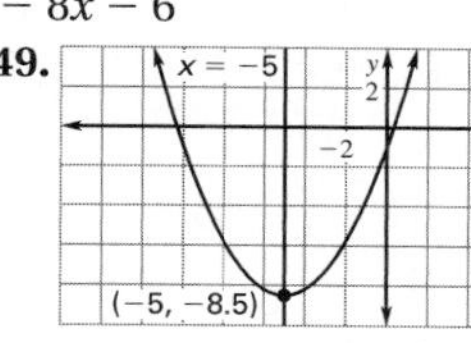

53. The axis of symmetry has to lie half way between the two x-coordinates; $x = -1$.

4.1 Problem Solving (pp. 242–243) **55.** Raise the price by \$0.75 to increase revenue to \$4900 per day. **57.** about 10 ft **59. a.** profit = price • sales − expenses; $P(x) = (20 - x)(150 + 10x) - 1500$

b.

x	$P(x)$
0	1500
1	1540
2	1560
3	1560
4	1540
5	1500

c.

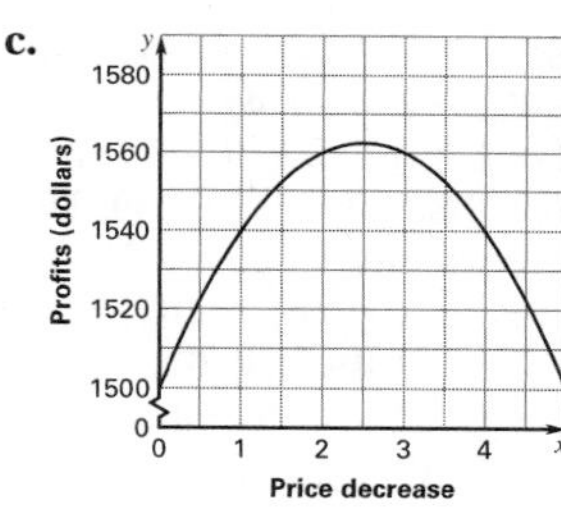

Reduce the price by \$2.50 to increase profits to \$1562.50 per week.

4.2 Skill Practice (pp. 249–250) **1.** vertex

3.

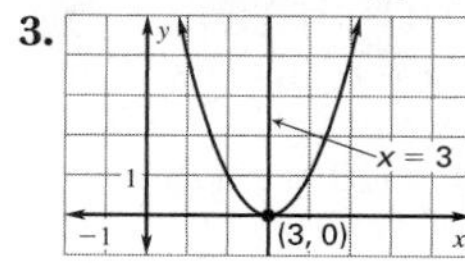

5.

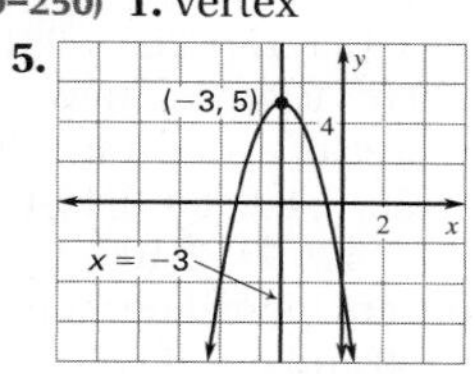

SELECTED ANSWERS

13.

(−3, 0) (3, 0) x = 0 (0, −9)

15. 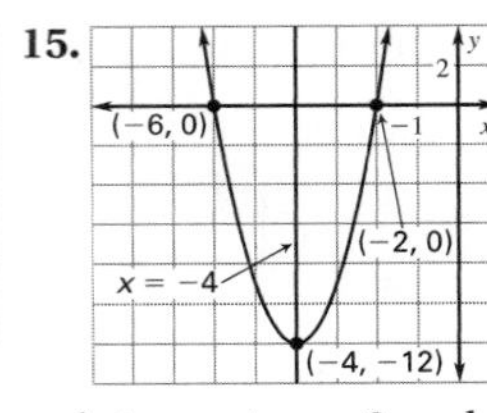

23. $p = 2$ and $q = -3$; the x-intercepts are 2 and -3. **25.** $y = x^2 - 2x - 15$ **27.** $y = -3x^2 + 18x - 24$ **29.** $y = x^2 - 6x + 15$ **31.** $y = 5x^2 + 30x + 41$ **33.** minimum: -4 **35.** minimum: 130 **37.** maximum: 729 **39.** minimum: -450 **41.** maximum: 211.25

43. 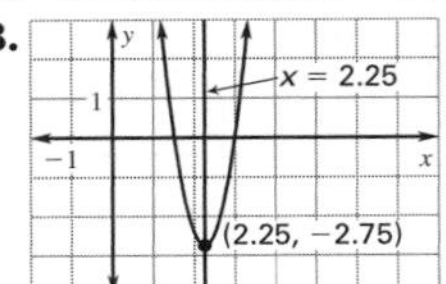

45. 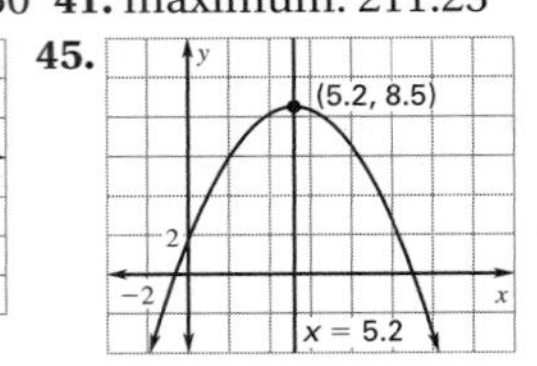

49. *Sample answer:* $y = (x - 8)(x + 2)$, $y = (x - 4)(x - 2)$, $y = (x + 3)(x - 9)$

4.2 Problem Solving (pp. 250–251) **51.** 6 ft; about 28 ft **53. a.** 160 ft **b.** about 1.5 ft **55. a.** about 14%; about 55.5 cm^3 **b.** about 13.6%; about 44.1 cm^3 **c.** hot-air: domain: $5.52 < x < 22.6$, range: $0 < y < 55.5$; hot oil: domain: $5.35 < x < 21.8$, range: $0 < y < 44.1$; since moisture content and popping volume cannot be negative, the domain and range must each be positive numbers. A positive domain occurs between the x-intercepts and the greatest number in the range occurs at the maximum point, which is the vertex.

4.3 Skill Practice (pp. 255–257) **1.** an x value that makes the function equal to zero **3.** $(x + 1)(x + 5)$ **5.** $(a - 11)(a - 2)$ **7.** cannot be factored **9.** $(b + 8)(b - 5)$ **11.** $(x - 9)(x + 2)$ **13.** $(x + 12)(x - 3)$ **15.** $(x + 6)(x - 6)$ **17.** $(x - 12)^2$ **19.** $(x + 4)^2$ **21.** $(n + 7)^2$ **23.** $(z - 11)(z + 11)$ **25.** 5, 6 **27.** -7, 7 **29.** -4, -1 **31.** -5 **33.** -6, 9 **35.** 0, -9 **37.** 7 **39.** The equation was not factored correctly; $x^2 - x - 6 = 0$, $(x - 3)(x + 2) = 0$, $x = 3$ or $x = -2$. **43.** $3(10)(12) = (10 + x)(12 + x)$ **45.** 4 **47.** -10, 3 **49.** 0, 8 **51.** -5, 5 **53.** -12, -7 **55.** -1 **57.** $x^2 - 19x + 88 = 0$ **59.** 4 **61.** 3 **63.** *Sample answer:* $x^2 - 20x + 91 = 0$

4.3 Problem Solving (pp. 257–258) **65.** $3(50)(100) = (50 + x)(100 + x)$, -200, 50; 100 ft by 150 ft **67. a.** 600 ft^2 **b.** area of new patio = area of existing patio + area of expansion, $(30 + x)(20 + x) = 600 + 464$ **c.** -58, 8; 8 ft **69.** $3(18)(15) = (18 + x)(15 + x)$, -45, 12; 114 ft **71.** $2(100) = (10 + x)(10 + x)$; no; there are no real numbers a and b such that $ab = -100$ and $a + b = 20$.

4.4 Skill Practice (pp. 263–264) **1.** 4 **3.** $(2x + 3)(x + 1)$ **5.** $(4r + 1)(r + 1)$ **7.** $(11z - 9)(z + 1)$ **9.** cannot be factored **11.** $(9d + 5)(d - 2)$ **13.** $(3x + 1)(3x - 1)$ **15.** $(7n - 4)(7n + 4)$ **17.** $(7x + 5)^2$ **19.** $(3p - 2)^2$ **21.** $(6x - 7)^2$ **23.** $2(3z + 4)(3z + 2)$ **25.** $6u(u - 4)$ **27.** $4(5x + 1)(x + 6)$ **29.** $-3(6n - 5)(2n - 1)$ **31.** 4 should be factored out of each term in the binomial; $4x^2 - 36 = 4(x^2 - 9) = 4(x + 3)(x - 3)$. **33.** -2, 2 **35.** 0, $-\frac{2}{9}$ **37.** $-1\frac{1}{2}$ **39.** $-\frac{1}{2}$, $1\frac{2}{3}$ **41.** $-\frac{1}{4}$, 5 **43.** $-\frac{3}{5}$, 6 **45.** $-\frac{3}{11}$, 2 **47.** -1, $1\frac{1}{3}$ **49.** -1, $\frac{7}{12}$ **51.** 3 **53.** -1, $2\frac{2}{3}$ **55.** $-\frac{7}{9}$, 2 **57.** 0, 4

4.4 Problem Solving (pp. 264–265) **63.** 2 ft **65.** \$5.75; letting x represent the number of \$.25 decreases in the sandwich price, the revenue R is given by the function $R = (330 + 15x)(6 - 0.25x)$. The zeros of this function are -22 and 24, and their average is 1. So, to maximize the daily revenue, each sandwich should be sold for $6 - 0.25(1)$, or \$5.75. The maximum daily revenue is then $(330 + 15(1))(5.75) = (345)(5.75) = \$1983.75$. **67. a.** 72 in. **b.** $w = 32 - h$; $V = 36(36 - h)(h)$ **c.** 18 in., 18 in., 11,664 in.^{3}; find the roots of the equation in part (b) to be 0 and 36, so the line of symmetry is at $x = \frac{36 + 0}{2} = 18$. To find the maximum volume, substitute 18 for h into the equation from part (b).

4.5 Skill Practice (pp. 269–270) **1.** radicand **3.** $2\sqrt{7}$ **5.** $5\sqrt{6}$ **7.** 24 **9.** $\frac{\sqrt{5}}{4}$ **11.** $\frac{8\sqrt{3}}{3}$ **13.** $\frac{3\sqrt{22}}{11}$ **15.** $-\sqrt{3} - 1$ **17.** $\frac{4\sqrt{2} - \sqrt{10}}{11}$ **21.** The equation has two solutions; $x^2 = 81$, $x = \pm 9$. **23.** $\pm 5\sqrt{2}$ **25.** ± 5 **27.** $\pm\sqrt{71}$ **29.** ± 10 **31.** $1 \pm \sqrt{2}$ **33.** $-2 \pm \frac{\sqrt{26}}{2}$ **35.** Factor: $x^2 - 4 = 0$, $(x + 2)(x - 2) = 0$, $x = -2$ or $x = 2$; Solve the equation $x^2 - 4 = 0$, $x^2 = 4$, $x = \pm 2$.

4.5 Problem Solving (pp. 270–271) **39.** Earth: about 3.1 sec, Mars: 5 sec, Jupiter: about 2.0 sec, Saturn: about 3.2 sec, Pluto: about 12.2 sec **41. a.** $\pi r^2 = 100$ **b.** about 5.6 ft **c.** $\sqrt{\frac{s^2}{\pi}}$; $s^2 = \pi r^2$, $\frac{s^2}{\pi} = r^2$, $\sqrt{\frac{s^2}{\pi}} = r$

4.5 Problem Solving Workshop (p. 273) **1.** 1, 5 **3.** $1\frac{2}{3}$ **5.** about -4.4, about 1.4 **7.** about 108 mph **9.** 1.25 sec

4.6 Skill Practice (pp. 279–280) **1.** $a + bi$ **3.** $\pm 2i\sqrt{7}$ **5.** $\pm 2i$ **7.** $\pm i\sqrt{11}$ **9.** $\pm i$ **11.** $3 \pm i\sqrt{2}$ **13.** $17 - i$ **15.** $-8 + 6i$ **17.** $19 - 9i$ **19.** $21 + 9i$ **23.** $-8 - 4i$ **25.** $-18 - 13i$ **27.** 73 **29.** $-\frac{3}{5} + \frac{9}{5}i$ **31.** $\frac{3}{4} - \frac{1}{3}i$

SELECTED ANSWERS

33. $-\frac{59}{106} - \frac{21}{106}i$ **43.** $\sqrt{109}$ **45.** $\sqrt{37}$ **47.** 4 **49.** $7\sqrt{2}$
51. $-20 + 2i$ **53.** $-125 + 90i$ **55.** $-\frac{5}{26} - \frac{51}{26}i$
57. $i^2 = -1$, so $-2i^2 = 2$; $4 - i + 8i - 2i^2 = 6 + 7i$.
59. **a.** additive: $-2 - i$, multiplicative: $\frac{2}{5} - \frac{1}{5}i$
b. additive: $-5 + i$, multiplicative: $\frac{5}{26} + \frac{1}{26}i$
c. additive: $1 - 3i$, multiplicative: $-\frac{1}{10} - \frac{3}{10}i$

4.6 Problem Solving (pp. 281–282) **65.** $4 - 3i$ ohms
67. $12 - 8i$ ohms
69.

Powers of i	i	i^2	i^3	i^4	i^5	i^6	i^7	i^8
Simplified	i	-1	$-i$	1	i	-1	$-i$	1

The pattern repeats every four powers of i; $i^9 = i$, $i^{10} = -1$, $i^{11} = -i$, $i^{12} = 1$.
71. does not belong to the Mandelbrot set
73. belongs to the Mandelbrot set
75. **a.** $\frac{519}{125} + \frac{167}{125}i$ **b.** $\frac{2326}{265} + \frac{668}{265}i$ **c.** $\frac{98}{37} - \frac{4}{37}i$

4.7 Skill Practice (pp. 288–289) **1.** A binomial is the sum of two monomials and a trinomial is the sum of three monomials. **3.** $-5, 1$ **5.** $-14, -2$ **7.** $11 \pm \sqrt{13}$
9. $-4 \pm 3\sqrt{5}$ **11.** $\frac{2 \pm i\sqrt{3}}{3}$ **13.** 9; $(x + 3)^2$ **15.** 144; $(x - 12)^2$ **17.** 1; $(x - 1)^2$ **19.** $\frac{49}{4}$; $\left(x + \frac{7}{2}\right)^2$ **21.** $\frac{1}{4}$; $\left(x - \frac{1}{2}\right)^2$
23. $-4 \pm \sqrt{15}$ **25.** $-6 \pm 3\sqrt{2}$ **27.** $1 \pm 2i\sqrt{6}$
29. $-7 \pm \sqrt{41}$ **31.** $-1 \pm i\sqrt{2}$ **33.** $-\frac{1}{2} \pm \frac{i\sqrt{7}}{2}$
35. $-5 + 5\sqrt{3}$ **37.** $-2 + 2\sqrt{21}$ **39.** (2.8, 125.44); at 2.8 seconds the water will reach a maximum height of 125.44 feet. **41.** $y = (x - 4)^2 + 3$; (4, 3)
43. $y = (x + 6)^2 + 1$; $(-6, 1)$ **45.** $y = \left(x - \frac{3}{2}\right)^2 + \frac{7}{4}$; $\left(\frac{3}{2}, \frac{7}{4}\right)$ **47.** $y = 2(x + 6)^2 - 47$; $(-6, -47)$
49. $y = 2(x - 7)^2 + 1$; (7, 1) **51.** 36 should be added to each side instead of 9; $4(x^2 + 6x + 9) = 11 + 36$; $4(x + 3)^2 = 47$; $(x + 3)^2 = \frac{47}{4}$; $x + 3 = \pm\frac{\sqrt{47}}{2}$; $x = -3 \pm \frac{\sqrt{47}}{2}$. **53.** $-\frac{3}{2} \pm i\frac{\sqrt{47}}{2}$ **55.** $\frac{1}{6} \pm i\frac{\sqrt{71}}{6}$
57. $-0.5 \pm 0.5i\sqrt{19}$

4.7 Problem Solving (pp. 290–291) **63.** 40 ft **65.** Selling systems for \$300 would maximize monthly revenue at \$9000. **67. a.** $1500 = (120 - 2x)(x)$ **b.** about 17.75, about 42.25; 17.25 must be rejected because it gives a length for the garden that is greater than the length of the side of the school. **c.** about 42.25 ft by 35.5 ft

4.8 Skill Practice (pp. 296–297) **1.** discriminant **3.** $-1, 5$
5. $-4 \pm i\sqrt{3}$ **7.** $\frac{1}{2}$ **9.** $\frac{2 \pm \sqrt{3}}{2}$ **11.** $\frac{4 \pm \sqrt{43}}{3}$ **13.** 2
15. $\frac{-3 \pm i\sqrt{47}}{2}$ **17.** $-\frac{5 \pm 2\sqrt{10}}{5}$ **19.** $\frac{-7 \pm \sqrt{13}}{6}$
21. $\frac{5 \pm \sqrt{31}}{3}$ **23.** 2, 3 **25.** $-1, 3$ **27.** $-2, 4$ **29.** $-5, -3$
31. 0; one real solution **33.** -32; two imaginary solutions **35.** -20; two imaginary solutions
37. -335; two imaginary solutions **39.** -36; two imaginary solutions **41.** $\frac{1 \pm i\sqrt{67}}{2}$ **43.** $-2\frac{1}{2}, \frac{5}{14}$
45. $\frac{1 \pm \sqrt{229}}{12}$ **47.** $0.875 \pm 0.752i$ **49.** $\sqrt{-144} = 12i$; $x = \frac{-6 \pm \sqrt{-144}}{6}$; $x = \frac{-6 \pm 12i}{6}$; $x = -1 \pm 2i$
51. $\dfrac{\frac{-b + \sqrt{b^2 - 4ac}}{2a} + \frac{-b - \sqrt{b^2 - 4ac}}{2a}}{2} = \dfrac{\frac{-2b}{2a}}{2} = \frac{-b}{2a}$, which is the formula for the axis of symmetry.
53. negative **57. a.** $c < 16$ **b.** $c = 16$ **c.** $c > 16$
59. **a.** $c < 48$ **b.** $c = 48$ **c.** $c > 48$ **61. a.** $c < 0.25$
b. $c = 0.25$ **c.** $c > 0.25$ **63.** $-\frac{1}{3}x^2 - \frac{1}{3}x + 4 = 0$
65. $2x^2 + 4x + 4 = 0$

4.8 Problem Solving (pp. 298–299) **71.** 1141 m, 2090 m
73. **a.**

t	0	0.25	.05	0.75	1
(x, y)	(0, 6)	(5, 10.25)	(10, 12.5)	(15, 12.75)	(20, 11)

b.

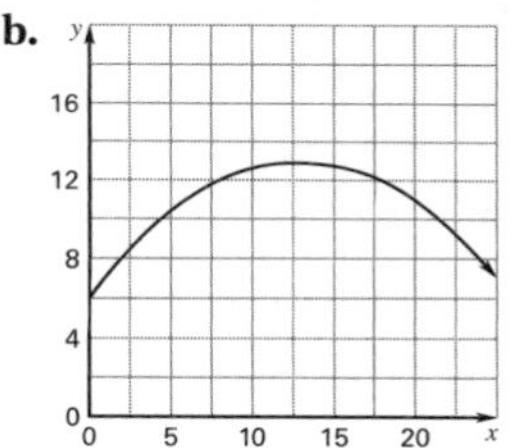

c. No; the height of the ball when $x = 15$ is 12.75 feet, which is above the backboard, so the free throw would not be made.

4.9 Skill Practice (pp. 304–305)
1. *Sample answer:* $3x^2 - 2x + 5 > 0$, $y \geq x^2 + 4x - 8$
7.

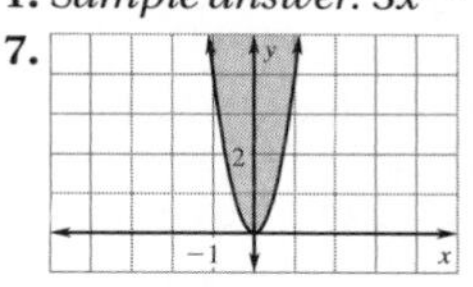

9.

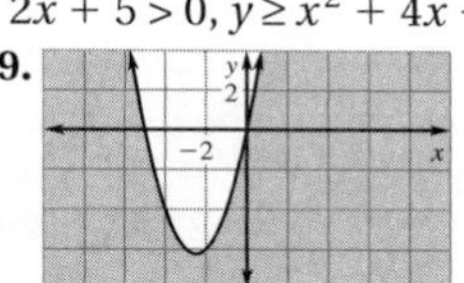

19.

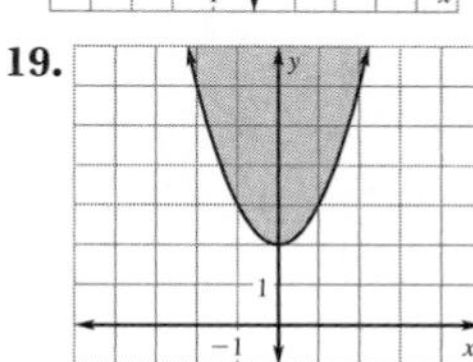

The inside of the parabola should be shaded.

SELECTED ANSWERS

21.

23. 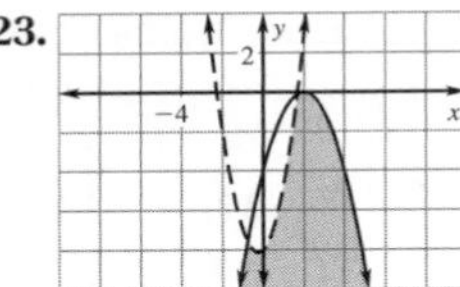

27. $x < -3$ or $x > 1$ **29.** $x \le -2$ or $x \ge 4$ **31.** $2 < x < 8$ **33.** $-1 \le x \le 3$ **35.** $0 < x < 6$ **37.** $x < 0.59$ or $x > 3.4$ **39.** $-2 \le x \le 1.3$ **41.** $0.67 \le x \le 2.5$ **43.** $-1.2 < x < 3.7$ **47.** $-9 < x < -1$ **49.** $x < -\frac{2}{3}$ or $x > 5$ **51.** $x \le -3.5$ or $x \ge 1.5$ **53.** $-0.27 \le x \le 1.5$ **55.** $-2.8 \le x \le -0.72$ **57.** $x < -0.46$ or $x > 1.8$ **59.** $-0.89 < x < 1.3$ **61.** no solution **63.** $x < 0.52$ or $x > 11.5$ **65.** $0 \le x \le 0.5$ **67.** no solution

4.9 Problem Solving (pp. 306–307)

71. 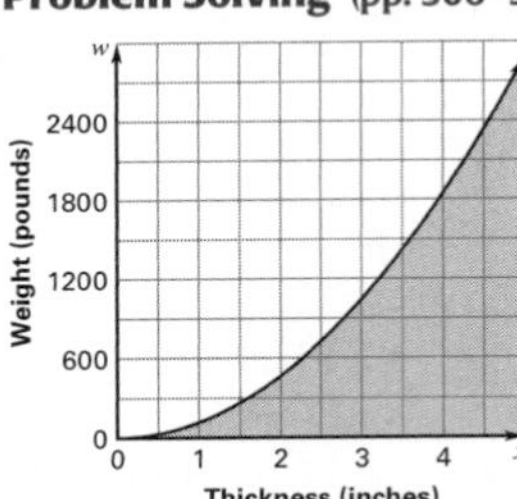

73. $37 \le x \le 40$; the domain restricts the number of days to less than or equal to 40. **75. a.** $-0.054x^2 + 1.43x - 8 < 0$; $x \le 8.0$ or $x \ge 18.5$ **b.** No; the ball will go over the goal by 1.3 feet.

4.10 Skill Practice (pp. 312–313) **1.** best-fitting quadratic model **3.** $y = (x - 3)^2 + 2$ **5.** $y = \frac{1}{2}(x + 1)^2 - 3$ **7.** $y = -(x - 1)^2 + 6$ **9.** $y = -\frac{1}{4}(x + 3)^2 + 3$ **11.** $y = 2(x + 4)^2 - 2$ **13.** $y = \frac{1}{3}(x + 1)^2 - 4$ **17.** $y = -(x - 3)(x + 2)$ **19.** $y = \frac{1}{2}(x + 3)(x - 3)$ **21.** $y = x(x + 3)$ **23.** $y = 3(x - 3)(x - 7)$ **25.** $y = \frac{1}{2}(x + 6)(x - 3)$ **27.** The vertex form of the equation should be used instead of the intercept form; $y = a(x - 2)^2 + 3$; $5 = a(1 - 2)^2 + 3$; $5 = a + 3$; $a = 2$, so $y = 2(x - 2)^2 + 3$. **29.** $y = 2x^2 + 20x + 46$ **31.** $y = \frac{7}{4}x^2 + \frac{29}{4}x - 2$ **33.** $y = -\frac{11}{2}x^2 - \frac{21}{2}x + 5$ **35.** $y = 3x^2 - 4x + 2$ **37.** $y = -\frac{1}{2}x^2 + 4x - 3$ **39.** $y = -\frac{2}{3}x^2 + 2x + 10$ **41.** $y = 8x^2 + 64x - 264$ **43.** *Sample answer:* $y = \frac{3}{4}x^2$

4.10 Problem Solving (pp. 314–315)

47. $y = -\frac{3}{80}(x - 20)^2 + 15$ **49. a.** $y = 0.012x^2 - 0.309x - 0.00048$ **b.** about -1.90 sec

Chapter Review (pp. 318–322) **1.** If $a < 0$, the function has a maximum value and if $a > 0$, then the function has a minimum value. **3.** vertex form

5. 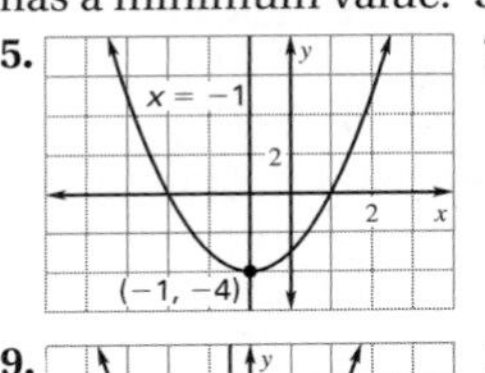

7. 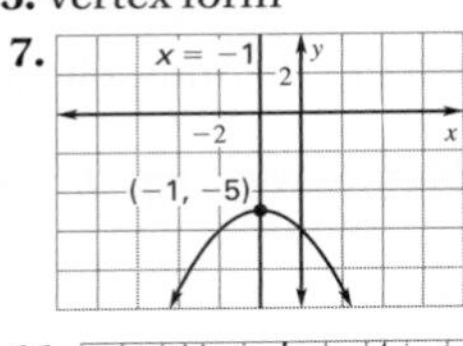

9. 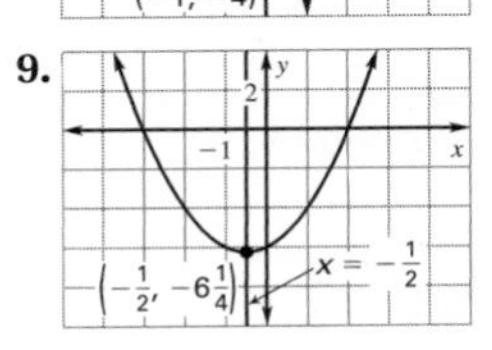

11. 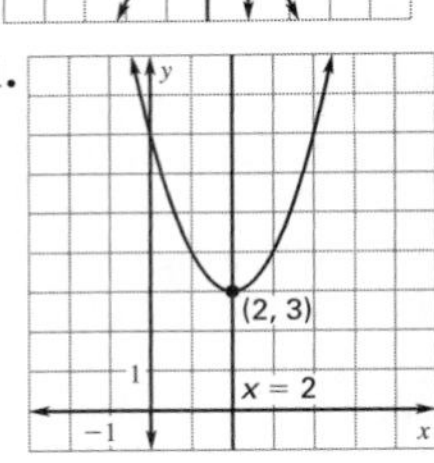

13. 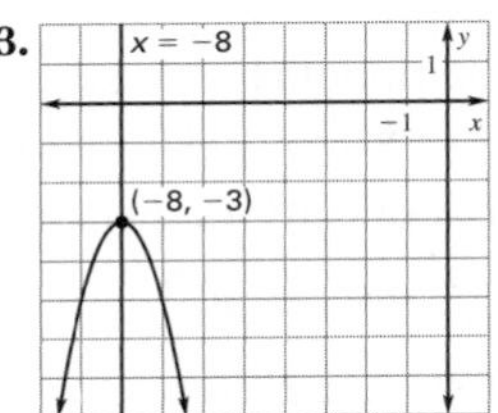

15. $-5, 0$ **17.** $-3, 9$ **19.** -9 **21.** $(72 + x)(48 + x) = 2(72)(48)$; 24 ft **23.** $4 \pm 4\sqrt{2}$ **25.** ± 6 **27.** $-1 \pm 3\sqrt{3}$ **29.** $-9 - 18i$ **31.** 29 **33.** $-4 + 2i$ **35.** $3 \pm 2\sqrt{6}$ **37.** $\frac{-3 \pm \sqrt{13}}{2}$ **39.** $-\frac{1}{3}$ **41.** about 0.2 sec **43.** $-0.65 \le x \le 4.6$ **45.** $y = 2(x + 3)(x - 2)$ **47.** $y = -\frac{5}{4}(x - 2)^2 + 7$

Chapter 5

5.1 Skill Practice (pp. 333–334) **1. a.** Product of powers property **b.** Negative exponent property **c.** Power of a product property **3.** 243; product of powers property **5.** -3125; product of powers property **7.** $\frac{1}{125}$; quotient of powers property **9.** $\frac{343}{8}$; power of a quotient property, negative exponent property **11.** 729; quotient of powers property **13.** $\frac{1}{36}$; product of powers property, negative exponent property **15.** 6.3×10^9 **17.** 5.607×10^{-6} **19.** 9.261×10^{-12} **21.** 1.5×10^3 **23.** 2.25×10^{-2}

SA14

25. $1024y^{15}$; power of a product property, power of a power property **27.** $\frac{w^9}{x^3}$; product of powers property, negative exponent property **29.** $\frac{1}{27a^9b^{15}}$; power of a product property, power of a power property, negative exponent property **31.** $\frac{c^2d^2}{3}$; quotient of powers property **33.** $\frac{2}{3a^2b^2}$; quotient of powers property, negative exponent property **35.** $\frac{x^6}{3y^3}$; product of powers property, quotient of powers property, negative exponent property **37.** The exponents should be subtracted, not divided; x^8. **39.** The base should not change; $(-3)^6$. **41.** $\frac{\pi x^3}{2}$ **43.** $x^{11}y^5z^{-3}$ **45.** $a^{-4}b^9$

5.1 Problem Solving (pp. 334–335) **49.** Pacific: 6.2868×10^{17} m^3, Atlantic: 3.01824×10^{17} m^3, Indian: 2.71656×10^{17} m^3, Arctic: 1.7061×10^{16} m^3 **51.** *Sample answer:* The volume of the pearl is $\frac{27}{8}$ times as large as the volume of the bead. **53. a.** about 4.4225×10^{-7} m^3

5.2 Skill Practice (pp. 341–343) **1.** degree: 4, type: quartic, leading coefficient: -5, constant term: 6 **3.** polynomial function; $f(x) = -x^2 + 8$, degree: 2, type: quadratic, leading coefficient: -1 **5.** polynomial function; $g(x) = \pi x^4 + \sqrt{6}$, degree: 4, type: quartic, leading coefficient: π **7.** polynomial function; $h(x) = -\frac{5}{2}x^3 + 3x - 10$, degree: 3, type: cubic, leading coefficient: $-\frac{5}{2}$ **9.** -32 **11.** 378 **13.** 182 **15.** 109 **17.** 149 **19.** -11 **21.** -78

23. The coefficient of x^3 was left out.

−2	−4	0	9	−21	7
		8	−16	14	14
	−4	8	−7	−7	21

25. degree: even, leading coefficient: positive **27.** degree: even, leading coefficient: negative **29.** $-\infty$, $-\infty$ **31.** $-\infty$, $+\infty$ **33.** $+\infty$, $-\infty$ **35.** $+\infty$, $+\infty$ **37.** *Sample answer:* $f(x) = -x^5 - 2x^4 + 1$

39.

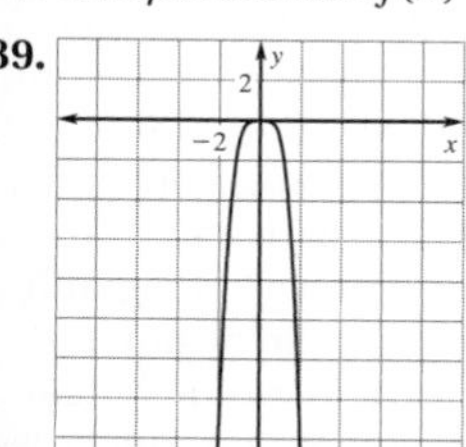

41.

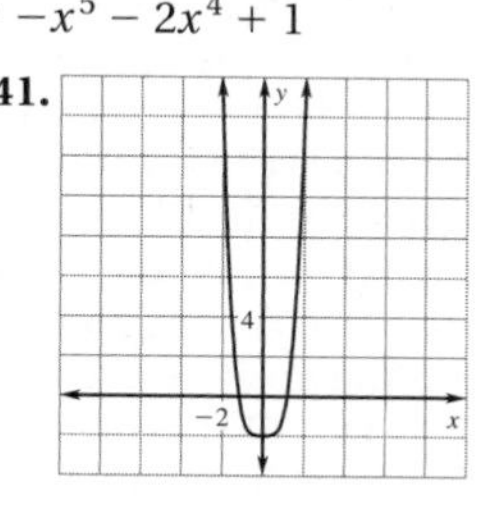

51. $g(x) \to -\infty$ as $x \to -\infty$ and $g(x) \to +\infty$ as $x \to +\infty$

5.2 Problem Solving (pp. 343–344)

55.

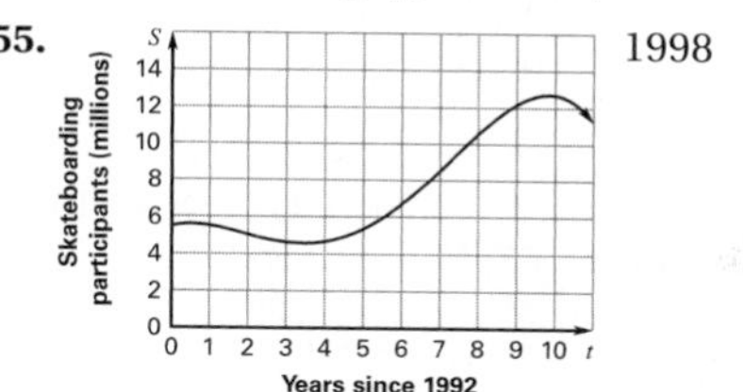

1998

57.

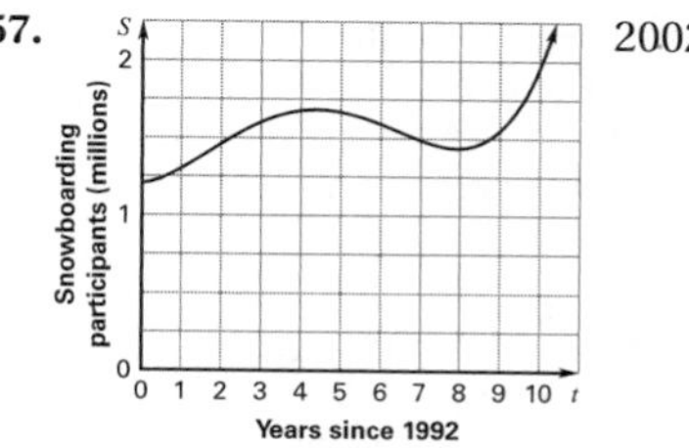

2002

59. a. 35.625 g

b.

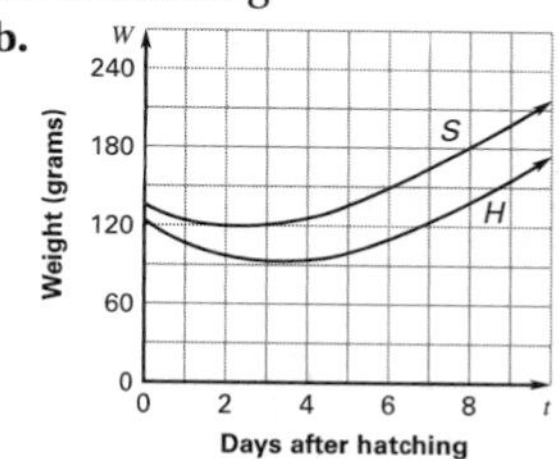

c. Sarus. *Sample answer:* Substituting 3 into each equation gives the Sarus chick weighing about 120 grams and the hooded chick weighing about 92 grams. The weight of the Sarus chick is closer to 130 grams than the weight of the hooded chick is.

5.3 Skill Practice (pp. 349–350) **1.** like terms **3.** $10x^2 - 8$ **5.** $14y - 8$ **7.** $7s^3 - 2s^2 + 8s + 10$ **9.** $2c^3 + 5c^2 + c + 9$ **11.** $-2b^4 - 15b^3 + 5b + 7$ **13.** $2x^4 - x^3$ **17.** $30x^3 + 10x^2$ **19.** $3z^2 - 8z - 3$ **21.** $2a^3 - 23a^2 + 26a + 6$ **23.** $-x^4 + 12x^3 - 34x^2 + 4x + 3$ **25.** $12y^4 - 9y^3 - 85y^2 - 19y + 5$ **27.** The cube of a binomial $(a - b)^3$ is found by $a^3 - 3a^2b + 3ab^2 - b^3$; $(2x - 7)^3 = (2x)^3 - 3(2x)^2(7) + 3(2x)(7)^2 - (7)^3 = 8x^3 - 84x^2 + 294x - 343$. **29.** $x^3 - 3x^2 - 25x - 21$ **31.** $2a^3 - 5a^2 - 37a - 30$ **33.** $-2b^3 + 7b^2 - 7b + 2$ **35.** $-12w^3 + 95w^2 - 143w + 30$ **37.** $-27q^3 + 132q^2 - 172q + 32$ **39.** $w^2 - 18w + 81$ **41.** $4c^2 + 20c + 25$ **43.** $25p^2 - 9$ **45.** $4a^2 - 81b^2$ **49.** $2\pi x^3 - 13\pi x^2 + 8\pi x + 48\pi$ **51.** $4x^3 - \frac{20}{3}x^2 - 7x + 12$ **53.** $(a + b)^2 = (a + b)(a + b) = a^2 + ab + ab + b^2 = a^2 + 2ab + b^2$ **55.** $(a - b)^3 = (a - b)(a - b)(a - b) = (a - b)(a^2 - 2ab + b^2) = a^3 - 2a^2b + ab^2 - a^2b + 2ab^2 - b^3 = a^3 - 3a^2b + 3ab^2 - b^3$

SELECTED ANSWERS

57. a. $(x-1)(x^4+x^3+x^2+x+1)$; $(x-1)(x^5+x^4+x^3+x^2+x+1)$ **b.** $(x-1)(x^{n-1}+x^{n-2}+x^{n-3}+\ldots+1)$

5.3 Problem Solving (pp. 351–352) **59.** $0.281t^3 - 16.8t^2 + 460t + 8600$ **61.** $F = 0.000031s^3 + 0.002107s$; about 0.05 horsepower **63.** $N = -1.51503t^4 - 25.45106t^3 + 215.9226t^2 + 127.75t + 9858.5$; calculate $L_m \cdot S_m + L_w \cdot S_w$.

5.4 Skill Practice (pp. 356–357) **1.** quadratic **3.** $7x(2x-3)$ **5.** $c(c+3)(c+6)$ **7.** $3y^3(y-4)(y+4)$ **11.** $(y-4)(y^2+4y+16)$ **13.** $(5n+6)(25n^2-30n+36)$ **15.** $(2c+7)(4c^2+14c+49)$ **17.** $-5(z-4)(z^2+4z+16)$ **19.** $(y-7)(y^2+4)$ **21.** $(3m-1)(m^2+3)$ **23.** $(c+2)(2c-3)(2c+3)$ **25.** $(a^2+1)(a^2+6)$ **27.** $2z(2z-1)(2z+1)(4z^2+1)$ **29.** $3x(x^2-6)(5x^2+6)$ **31.** The factor $3x$ should also be set equal to 0; $x=0$ or $x=-4$ or $x=4$. **33.** $0, -1\frac{2}{3}, 1\frac{2}{3}$ **35.** 2, −2, −6 **37.** $0, -\sqrt{21}, \sqrt{21}$ **39.** $-\sqrt{3}, \sqrt{3}, 2, -2$ **43.** $(n^2-10)(n^2+6)$ **45.** $(12a-5)(3a^2+7)$ **47.** $(d+3)(d-3)(2d^2+5)$ **49.** $2y^2(y^2-5)(4y^2+1)$ **51.** 2 **53.** 5 **55.** $(c+d)(c-d)(7a+b)$

5.4 Problem Solving (pp. 358–359) **59.** 3 cm by 9 cm by 18 cm **61.** length: 10 in., width: 5 in., height: 5 in. **63.** The volume cannot be $\frac{7}{3}$ because the only x value that corresponds to that volume is about −1.37, which would yield a negative side length.

5.4 Problem Solving Workshop (p. 361) **1.** 4 **3.** 6 **5.** about 1.4, 4 **7.** 2.5 **9.** height: 12 in., width: 8 in., length: 18 in.

5.5 Skill Practice (pp. 366–367) **1.** If a polynomial $f(x)$ is divided by $x-k$, then the remainder is $r=f(k)$. **3.** $x+5+\frac{3}{x-4}$ **5.** $x^2+4x+7+\frac{9}{x-1}$ **7.** $3x+8+\frac{-4x+1}{x^2+x}$ **9.** $5x^2-12x+37+\frac{-122x+109}{x^2+2x-4}$ **11.** $2x+3+\frac{25}{x-5}$ **13.** $x+4+\frac{-15}{x+4}$ **15.** $x^2-x-4+\frac{-18}{x-4}$ **17.** $x^3+x^2-2x+1+\frac{-6}{x-6}$ **19.** The degree of the answer should be reduced by 1; $x^2+2x-1+\frac{1}{x-2}$. **21.** $(x-6)(x-5)(x+1)$ **23.** $(x-8)(x+2)(x+4)$ **25.** $(x-4)(x-3)(x+9)$ **27.** $(2x-7)(x-3)(x-1)$ **29.** −1, 6 **31.** −0.4, 1.5 **33.** $\frac{-4\pm\sqrt{14}}{2}$ **37.** $x+8$

5.5 Problem Solving (pp. 367–368) **41.** 1 million T-shirts **43.** $f(x) = -0.132x^2 + 11.2x - 560.9 + \frac{408{,}803}{14.8x+725}$ **45.** $-0.00233x^3 + 0.249x^2 - 21.0x + 1740 + \frac{-445{,}000}{3.10x+256}$; divided the overnight stays function by the total visits function

5.6 Skill Practice (pp. 374–375) **1.** constant, leading coefficient **3.** ±1, ±2, ±4, ±7, ±14, ±28 **5.** $\pm1, \pm3, \pm9, \pm\frac{1}{2}, \pm\frac{3}{2}, \pm\frac{9}{2}$ **7.** $\pm1, \pm2, \pm7, \pm14, \pm\frac{1}{2}, \pm\frac{7}{2}, \pm\frac{1}{4}, \pm\frac{7}{4}$ **9.** $\pm1, \pm3, \pm5, \pm15, \pm\frac{1}{2}, \pm\frac{3}{2}, \pm\frac{5}{2}, \pm\frac{15}{2}, \pm\frac{1}{4}, \pm\frac{3}{4}, \pm\frac{5}{4}, \pm\frac{15}{4}, \pm\frac{1}{8}, \pm\frac{3}{8}, \pm\frac{5}{8}, \pm\frac{15}{8}$ **11.** 1, 3, 8 **13.** −5, −1, 6 **15.** −2, −1 **17.** −4, −1, 1, 2 **19.** $1, \frac{-1\pm\sqrt{17}}{2}$ **21.** $-3, -\frac{5}{3}, \frac{1}{2}$ **25.** $-1, \frac{3}{2}, 3$ **27.** $-4, -\frac{1}{3}, 3$ **29.** −3.5, −1, 2 **31.** −2, 2 **33.** $-2, 1, \frac{5}{2}, 3$ **35.** $-3, \frac{1}{2}, 1$ **37.** p should be factors of 5 and q should be factors of 6; possible zeros: $\pm1, \pm5, \pm\frac{1}{2}, \pm\frac{5}{2}, \pm\frac{1}{3}, \pm\frac{5}{3}, \pm\frac{1}{6}, \pm\frac{5}{6}$. **41.** −1, 1, 2; B **43.** −2; A

5.6 Problem Solving (pp. 376–377) **45.** length: 3 in., width: 3 in., height: 7 in. **47.** $x^3 - 3x^2 + 2x - 24 = 0$; ±1, ±2, ±3, ±4, ±6, ±8, ±12, ±24 **49. a.** $-10t^3 + 140t^2 - 20t - 2150 = 0$ **b.** 1, 2, 5, **c.** 5; 1999

5.7 Skill Practice (pp. 383–385) **1.** repeated **3.** 4 **5.** 6 **7.** 7 **11.** −5, −3, 1, 2 **13.** −5, −2, 2 **15.** $-2, 1, 2i, -2i$ **17.** $1, -1, 1+\sqrt{3}, 1-\sqrt{3}$ **19.** $-4, -2, -\frac{3}{2}, 1$ **21.** $f(x) = x^3 - 2x^2 - 5x + 6$ **23.** $f(x) = x^3 - 4x^2 - 15x + 18$ **25.** $f(x) = x^4 - 4x^3 + 14x^2 - 36x + 45$ **27.** $f(x) = x^4 - 18x^3 + 122x^2 - 370x + 425$ **29.** $f(x) = x^4 - x^3 - 18x^2 + 10x + 8$ **31.** $f(x) = x^5 - 13x^4 + 60x^3 - 82x^2 - 144x + 360$ **33.** *Sample answer:* $f(x) = x^5 - 4x^4 + 6x^3 - 6x^2 + 5x - 2$ **35.** positive: 1, negative: 0, imaginary: 2 **37.** positive: 2 or 0, negative: 3 or 1, imaginary: 4, 2, or 0 **39.** positive: 3 or 1, negative: 2 or 0, imaginary: 4, 2, or 0 **41.** positive: 2 or 0, negative: 1, imaginary: 6 or 4 **43.** $x \approx -1.1, x \approx 1.3$ **45.** $x \approx -0.58, x \approx 1.9$ **47.** $x \approx -0.42, x \approx 2.0$ **49.** $x \approx -3.5, x \approx -1.1, x = -1, x \approx 2.1, x \approx 3.6$ **51.** There could be 3, 2, 1, or 0 positive zeros, 3, 2, 1, or 0 negative zeros, and 2 or 0 imaginary zeros. **53.** Positive real zeros: 1, negative real zeros: 2, imaginary zeros: 0; the graph crosses the positive x-axis once and the negative x-axis twice. **55.** Positive real zeros: 0, negative real zeros: 1, imaginary zeros: 4; the graph does not cross the positive x-axis and it crosses the negative x-axis once. Since the function has degree 5, the remaining 4 zeros must be imaginary.

5.7 Problem Solving (pp. 385–386) **59.** year 3 and year 9 **61.** about 16.4 g per mL **63.** 0 in., about 59 in.; the bookshelf would have nearly 0 inches of deflection near each end because of the supports holding the bookshelf, so the answers make sense because they represent each end of a 60 inch bookshelf.

5.8 Skill Practice (pp. 390–391) **1.** turning

3.

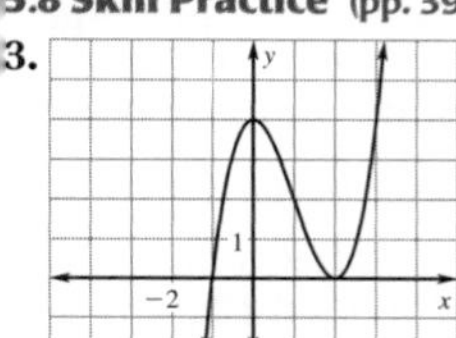

5.

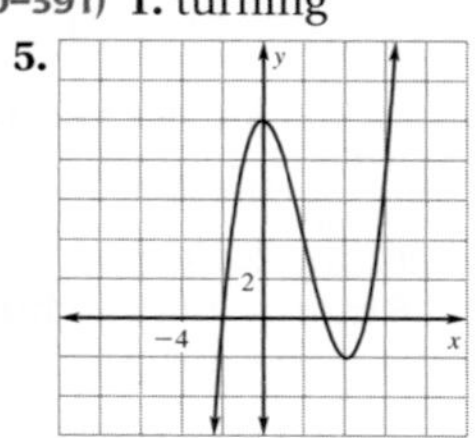

13. The x-intercepts should be at -2 and 1.

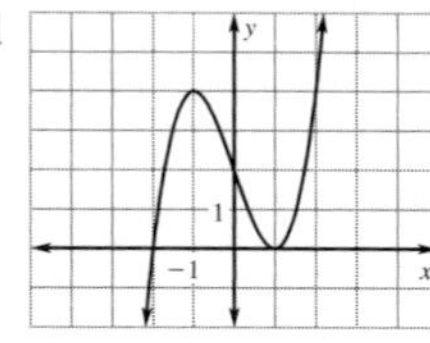

15–19. Sample answers are given. **15.** local maximum: $(-0.3, 0.3)$, local minimum: $(0.9, -1.3)$; zeros: -0.75, 0, 1.4, least degree: 3 **17.** local maximums: $(1, 0)$, $(3, 0)$, local minimum: $(2, -2)$; zeros: 1, 3, least degree: 4 **19.** local maximums: $(-1.1, 0.8)$, $(1.9, 8)$, local minimums: $(-2.2, -38)$, $(0.3, -41)$, $(2.8, -13)$; zeros: -2.6, -1.2, -1, 1.5, 2.2, 3, least degree: 6 **23.** x-intercept: -2.5; local maximum: $(-1.2, 4.0)$; local minimum: $(1.2, 0.96)$ **25.** x-intercepts: -2.2, 1, 1.7; local maximums: $(-1.6, 10.5)$, $(0.17, 2.0)$; local minimums: $(0, 2)$, $(1.5, -1.7)$ **27.** x-intercepts: -0.77, 4.5; local maximum: $(0.47, -2.6)$; local minimums: $(-0.16, -3.1)$, $(3.4, -39.4)$ **29.** x-intercepts: -0.77, 0, 0.82; local maximum: $(0.47, 1.6)$; local minimum: $(-0.46, -1.5)$ **31.** *Sample answer:* Quadratic functions only have one turning point, therefore one maximum or minimum value. Cubic functions can have two turning points, therefore one maximum and one minimum, and the end behavior is to infinity, so there is no real maximum or minimum value. **33.** *Sample answer:* $y = x(x + 2)(x - 4)$, $y = x(x + 2)(x - 4)^2$, $y = x^3(x + 2)(x - 4)$

35.

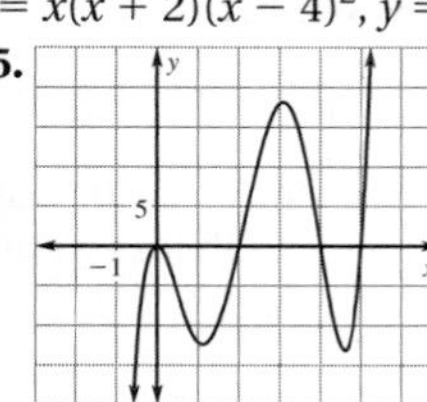

domain: all real numbers, range: all real numbers

37.

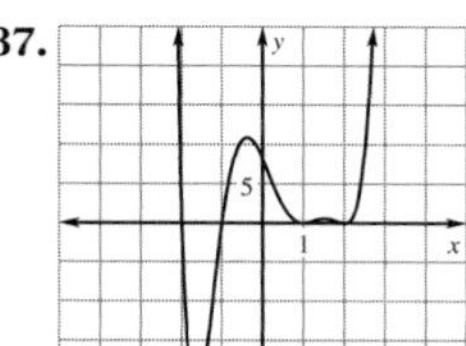

domain: all real numbers, range: $y \geq -21.3$

5.8 Problem Solving (pp. 391–392) **39.** maximum: about 5.8 in. by 13.8 in. by 2.1 in.; about 168 in.^{3}

41.

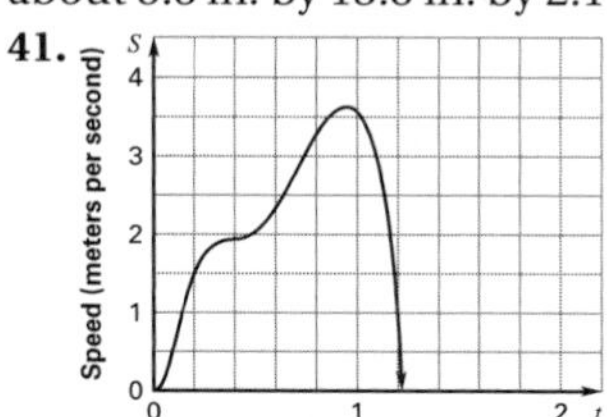

after about 0.95 sec

43. a.

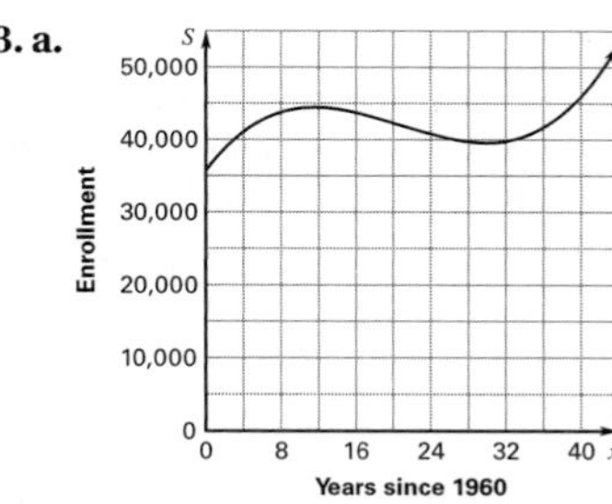

b. Maximum: (11.7, 44,971), minimum: (29.8, 40,078). *Sample answer:* The maximum indicates that in 1972 the number of students enrolled was about 44,971,000. The minimum indicates that in 1990 there were about 40,078,000 students enrolled. **c.** $36{,}300 \leq y \leq 47{,}978$

5.9 Skill Practice (pp. 397–398) **1.** finite differences **3.** $y = 0.5x^3 - 2x^2 + 0.5x + 3$ **5.** $y = \frac{1}{6}x^3 - \frac{1}{3}x^2 - \frac{11}{6}x + 2$ **7.** $y = 2x^3 + 2x^2 - 8x - 8$ **9.** $y = \frac{2}{5}x^3 - \frac{2}{5}x^2 - 12x$ **11.** 1 should have been substituted for x and 3 for y; $3 = a(1 + 1)(1 - 2)(1 - 5)$, $3 = 8a$, $a = \frac{3}{8}$.

13.

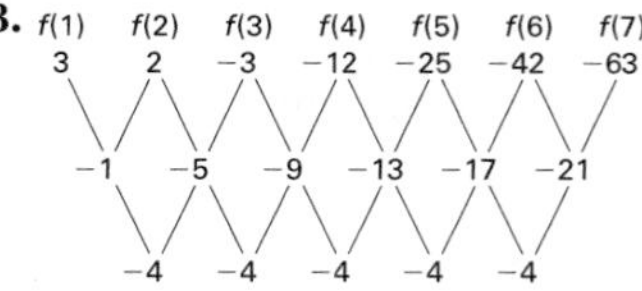

SELECTED ANSWERS

15. f(1) f(2) f(3) f(4) f(5) f(6) f(7)
−3 0 11 30 57 92 135
3 11 19 27 35 43
8 8 8 8 8

19. $f(x) = -4x^2 + 15x$ **21.** $f(x) = -0.5x^3 + 5x^2 - 2.5x + 3$ **23.** 5; 6; there must be one more data point than the degree of the equation.

5.9 Problem Solving (pp. 398–399) **25.** $d = 0.5n^2 - 1.5n$ **27. a.** $m = 0.000817t^3 - 0.0215t^2 + 0.249t + 3.17$ **b.** about \$10.30 **c.** 1995

29.

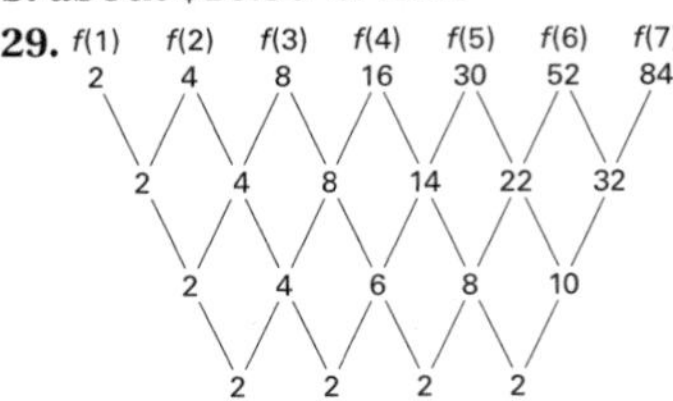

Chapter Review (pp. 402–406) **1.** local maximum, local minimum **3.** If it is in the form $c \times 10^n$ where $1 \le c < 10$ and n is an integer. **5.** 128; product of powers property **7.** $\frac{y^{10}}{x^4}$; power of a power property, negative exponent property **9.** $\frac{16}{9}$; quotient of powers property, negative exponent property **11.** $\frac{1}{x^8y^8}$; power of a quotient property, negative exponent property

13.

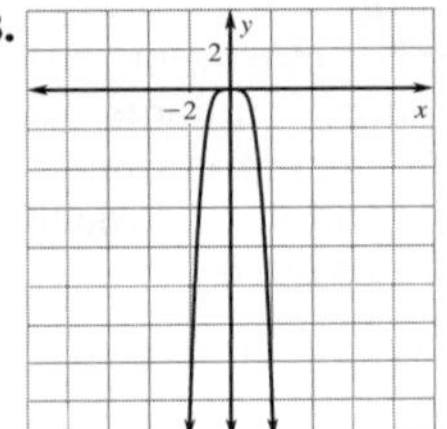

15.

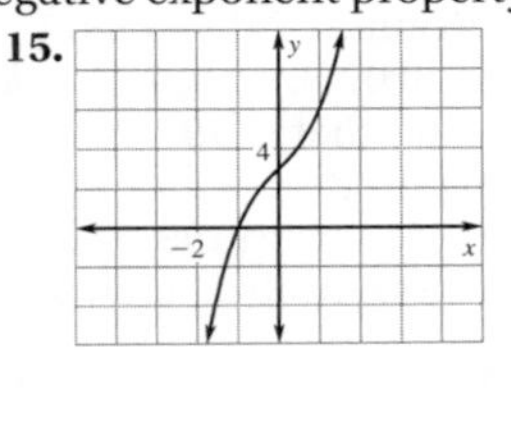

17. $6x^3 - 9x^2 + 3x + 3$ **19.** $5x^3 - 29x^2 - 14x + 48$ **21.** $8(2x - 1)(4x^2 + 2x + 1)$ **23.** $(x - 2)(x + 2)(2x - 7)$ **25.** $x - 6 + \frac{18x - 16}{x^2 + 3x - 1}$ **27.** $2x^2 - x + 8 + \frac{-4}{x - 5}$ **29.** $(x + 2)(x - 3)(x - 4)$ **31.** $(x - 1)(3x - 2)(3x + 2)$ **33.** −3, 2, 5 **35.** $x^3 - 2x^2 - 19x + 20$ **37.** $x^4 - 15x^3 + 72x^2 - 120x + 56$ **39.** x-intercept: −1.7; local maximum: (0, −1); local minimum: (−1, −2) **41.** $y = x^3 - 8x^2 + 2x - 1$

Chapter 6

6.1 Skill Practice (pp. 417–418) **1.** index **7.** $12^{1/3}$ **9.** $10^{7/3}$ **11.** $\sqrt[4]{5}$ **13.** $(\sqrt[5]{14})^2$ **15.** ±8 **17.** 0 **19.** no real roots **21.** 2 **23.** 64 **25.** 9 **27.** $\frac{1}{4}$ **29.** $\frac{1}{128}$ **31.** $\frac{1}{16}$ **35.** 2.89 **37.** 2.10 **39.** 12 **41.** 0.01 **43.** 0.02 **45.** −0.18 **47.** *Sample answer:* $27^{1/3}$, $81^{1/4}$ **49.** There are two real solutions; $x = \pm 3$. **51.** 6 **53.** 1, 9 **55.** ±1.68 **57.** −7.66

6.1 Problem Solving (pp. 418–419) **61.** about 4.30 in. **63.** $\frac{3}{12{,}282{,}500{,}000}$; about 1800 RPM **65. a.** 4096 mm^3 **b.** tetrahedron: about 32.6 mm, octahedron: about 20.6 mm, dodecahedron: about 8.12 mm, icosahedron: about 12.3 mm **c.** No. *Sample answer:* The icosahedron has the greatest number of faces, 20, and an edge length of 12.3 millimeters which is greater than the edge length of the dodecahedron, which has 12 faces.

6.2 Skill Practice (pp. 424–425) **1.** No; they do not have the same index. **3.** 25 **5.** 3 **7.** $2 \cdot 5^{1/2}$ **9.** $\frac{\sqrt[5]{1331}}{11}$ **11.** $7^{3/4}$ **13.** $\frac{\sqrt[3]{50}}{16{,}000}$ **15.** 10 **17.** $2\sqrt{2}$ **19.** 2 **21.** 3 **25.** $2\sqrt[3]{2}$ **27.** $40\sqrt[4]{2}$ **29.** $\frac{\sqrt{3}}{2}$ **31.** $\sqrt[15]{3}$ **33.** $\frac{2}{5}\sqrt[3]{5}$ **35.** $\frac{1}{2}\sqrt[4]{7}$ **37.** $-2\sqrt[7]{2}$ **39.** $-6\sqrt[4]{2}$ **41.** The radicands are not the same, so they cannot be combined; $2\sqrt[3]{10} + 6\sqrt[3]{5}$. **43.** $x^{7/12}$ **45.** $3x$ **47.** $\frac{y^{4/3}}{x^{3/5}}$ **49.** $\frac{1}{x^4}$ **51.** *Sample answer:* $x^{5/4}$ and $x^{1/2}$ **53.** $yz^3\sqrt[4]{12x^2y^2}$ **55.** $x^2z^4\sqrt{xy}$ **57.** $\frac{x\sqrt[3]{y^2}}{y^2}$ **59.** $\sqrt[14]{x^{11}}$ **61.** $\frac{1}{2}y^{3/2}$ **63.** $2x^2y^{1/2}$ **65.** $(2xy + 3y)\sqrt[4]{2x^2}$ **67.** perimeter: $24x^{1/4}$, area: $35x^{1/2}$ **71.** $\frac{1}{y^{6.6}}$ **73.** $\frac{1}{x^{1.2}}$ **75.** $\frac{1}{y^{1.3}}$ **77.** $7z^{0.3}$ **79.** $x^{\sqrt{6}}$ **81.** $4x^2y^{\sqrt{2}}$

6.2 Problem Solving (pp. 426–427) **83. a.** about 580 cm^2 **b.** about 16,671 cm^2 **85.** about 0.45 mm **87. a.** about 2 times fainter **b.** about 1.6 times fainter **c.** about 3 times fainter **89. a.** $r = \sqrt[3]{\frac{3V}{4\pi}}$ **b.** $S = 4\pi\left(\sqrt[3]{\frac{3V}{4\pi}}\right)^2 = 4\pi\left(\frac{3V}{4\pi}\right)^{2/3} = \frac{4\pi(3V)^{2/3}}{(4\pi)^{2/3}} = (4\pi)^{1/3}(3V)^{2/3}$ **c.** The balloon with twice as much water will have $\sqrt[3]{4}$, or about 1.59, times the surface area of the balloon with less water.

6.3 Skill Practice (pp. 432–433) **1.** composition **3.** $2x^{1/3} + 8x^{1/2}$, all nonnegative real numbers **5.** $-6x^{1/3} + 8x^{1/2}$, all nonnegative real numbers

SELECTED ANSWERS

7. $-8x^{1/3}$, all nonnegative real numbers **9.** 0, all nonnegative real numbers **13.** $20x^{7/6}$, nonnegative real numbers **15.** $25x$, all nonnegative real numbers **17.** $\frac{5}{4x^{1/6}}$, positive real numbers **19.** 1, positive real numbers **21.** -64 **23.** $-\frac{36}{25}$ **25.** 71 **27.** -625 **29.** $\frac{6}{x} - 7$, all real numbers except $x = 0$ **31.** $\frac{2x - 13}{3}$, all real numbers **33.** x, all real numbers except $x = 0$ **35.** $4x - 21$, all real numbers **37.** 4 should be distributed to each term, not just the first term; $4x^2 - 12$. **39.** *Sample answer:* $f(x) = 3x$, $g(x) = 2x$

6.3 Problem Solving (pp. 433–434) **43.** $r(w) = 220w^{-0.266}$; about 134 breaths per minute, about 48.3 breaths per minute, about 11.3 breaths per minute **45. a.** \$63 **b.** \$61.50 **c.** Apply the 10% discount before the \$15 discount; you pay \$61.50 using this method and \$63 using the other method.

6.4 Skill Practice (pp. 442–443) **1.** An inverse relation interchanges the input and output values of the original relation. **3.** $y = \frac{x + 1}{4}$ **5.** $y = \frac{x + 6}{7}$ **7.** $y = \frac{x - 7}{12}$ **9.** $y = \frac{1}{5}x - \frac{1}{15}$ **11.** $y = \frac{7 - 5x}{3}$ **13.** Switching the roles of x and y does not include switching the sign of the variables; $x = -y + 3, x - 3 = -y, 3 - x = y$. **15.** $f(g(x)) = x - 4 + 4 = x$, $g(f(x)) = x + 4 - 4 = x$ **17.** $f(g(x)) = \frac{1}{4}((4x)^{1/3})^3 = \frac{1}{4}(4x) = x$, $g(f(x)) = \left(4\left(\frac{1}{4}x^3\right)\right)^{1/3} = (x^3)^{1/3} = x$ **19.** $f(g(x)) = 4\left(\frac{1}{4}x - \frac{9}{4}\right) + 9 = x - 9 + 9 = x$, $g(f(x)) = \frac{1}{4}(4x + 9) - \frac{9}{4} = x + \frac{9}{4} - \frac{9}{4} = x$ **23.** $f^{-1}(x) = \sqrt[4]{\frac{x}{4}}$ **25.** $f^{-1}(x) = \frac{\sqrt[5]{x}}{2}$ **27.** $f^{-1}(x) = -\frac{5}{4}\sqrt{x}$ **29.** function **31.** not a function **33.** function **35.** not a function **37.** not a function **39.** $f^{-1}(x) = \sqrt[3]{x + 2}$ **41.** $f^{-1}(x) = -\sqrt[6]{\frac{40 - 5x}{2}}$ **43.** $f^{-1}(x) = \sqrt[4]{x + 9}$

6.4 Problem Solving (pp. 444–445) **47. a.** $w = 2\ell - 6$ **b.** 7 lb **49.** $\ell = \left(\frac{v}{1.34}\right)^2$; about 31.3 ft

6.5 Skill Practice (pp. 449–450) **1.** radical

3.

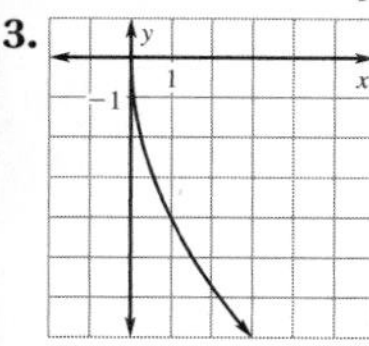

domain: $x \geq 0$, range: $y \leq 0$

5. domain: $x \geq 0$, range: $y \leq 0$

11.

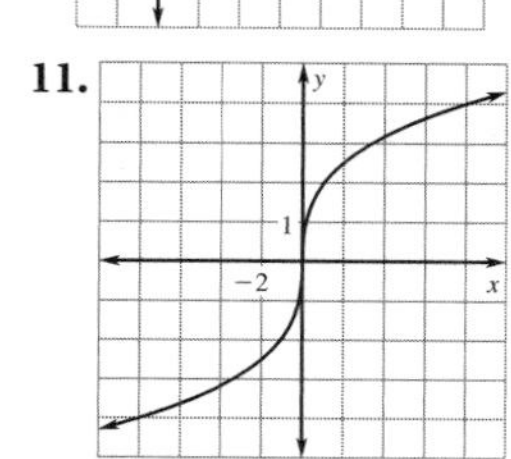

domain: all real numbers, range: all real numbers

13.

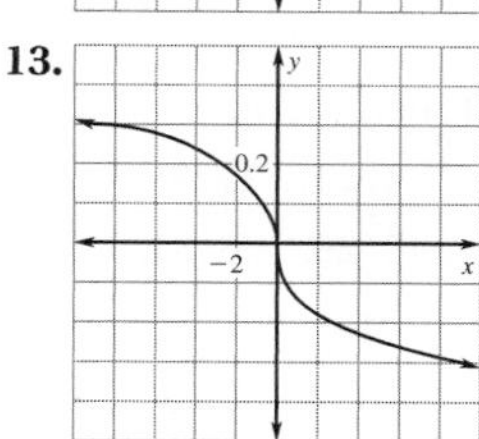

domain: all real numbers, range: all real numbers

17. domain: $x \geq -1$, range: $y \geq 8$

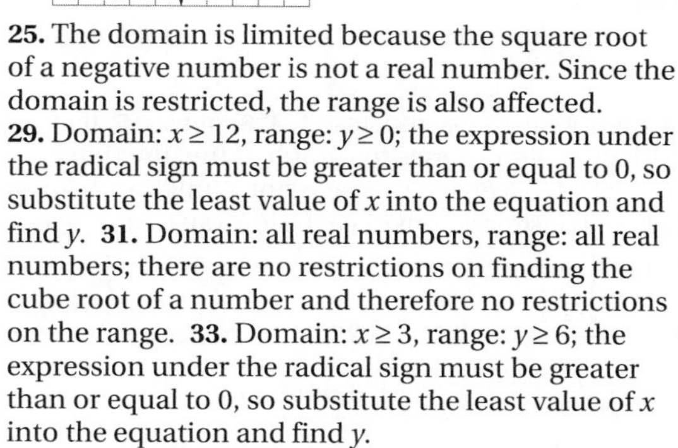

19. domain: all real numbers, range: all real numbers

25. The domain is limited because the square root of a negative number is not a real number. Since the domain is restricted, the range is also affected. **29.** Domain: $x \geq 12$, range: $y \geq 0$; the expression under the radical sign must be greater than or equal to 0, so substitute the least value of x into the equation and find y. **31.** Domain: all real numbers, range: all real numbers; there are no restrictions on finding the cube root of a number and therefore no restrictions on the range. **33.** Domain: $x \geq 3$, range: $y \geq 6$; the expression under the radical sign must be greater than or equal to 0, so substitute the least value of x into the equation and find y.

6.5 Problem Solving (pp. 450–451) **35.** about 43 ft above sea level **37. a.** $v = 331.5\sqrt{1 + \frac{C}{273.15}}$ **b.** domain: $C \geq -273.15$, range: $v \geq 0$ **39. a.** $v_t = 33.7\sqrt{\frac{165}{A}}$

SELECTED ANSWERS

b. *Sample answer:*

A	2	4	6	8	10
v_t	306.1	216.44	176.72	153.05	136.89

c.

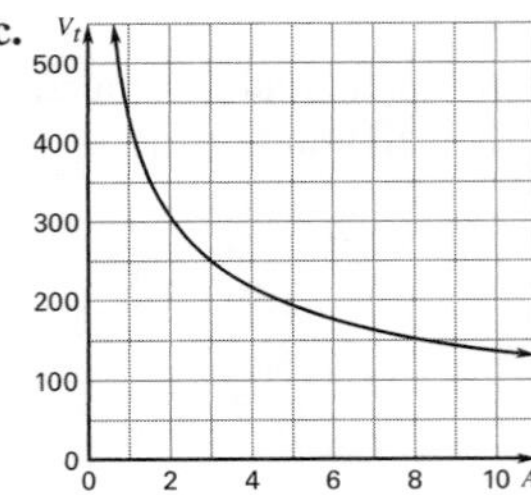

6.6 Skill Practice (pp. 456–457) **1.** extraneous **3.** 7 **5.** 1 **7.** 6 **9.** 29 **11.** $-70\frac{1}{2}$ **13.** 343 **15.** 18 **17.** 8 **19.** 11 **21.** −37 **23.** 4 **25.** 32 **27.** 40 **29.** 108 **31.** 1 **33.** Both sides must be raised to the power; $((x+7)^{1/2})^2 = 5^2$, $x + 7 = 25$, $x = 18$. **35.** 25 **37.** 3, 8 **39.** $-2\frac{1}{10}$ **41.** $\frac{1}{2}$ **45.** 3 **47.** 4 **49.** $\frac{1}{4}$ **51.** −2, 2 **53.** (4, 25)

6.6 Problem Solving (pp. 457–459) **57.** about 391 min **59.** *Sample answer:* The elephant with a shoulder height of 250 centimeters is about 20 years older than the elephant with a shoulder height of 150 centimeters. **61. a.** about 0.162 mi/h **b.** about 80.4 mi/h **c.** $0.162 \le s \le 80.4$

6.6 Problem Solving Workshop (p. 461) **1.** −39 **3.** about 55.7 **5.** about 97 ft **7.** about 37.5 cm

6.6 Extension (p. 463) **1.** $x \ge 16$ **3.** $0 \le x \le 4$ **5.** $x \ge 1$ **7.** $0 \le x \le 6.25$ **9.** $0 \le x < 1.3$ **11.** $0 \le x < 4$ **13.** about 413 m^2

Chapter Review (pp. 466–468) **1.** 4 **3.** power **5.** If a horizontal line crosses the graph of the function more than once, the inverse is not a function. **7.** Take the square root of each side; raise each side to the $\frac{3}{2}$ power. **9.** 0 **11.** 5 **13.** $\frac{1}{9}$ **15.** −8 **17.** $\frac{1}{15}$ **19.** $\frac{3x^2y^2\sqrt{2z}}{7z^2}$ **21.** $3x - 14$ **23.** $4x + 26$ **25.** $y = \frac{\sqrt{x-9}}{2}$

27.

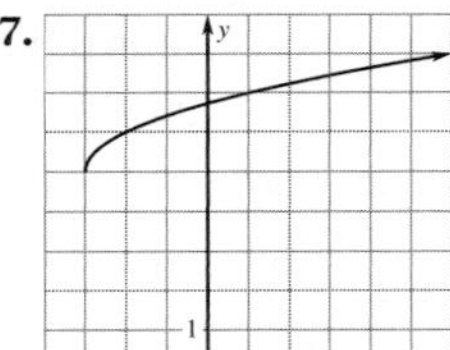

domain: $x \ge -3$, range: $y \ge 5$

29.

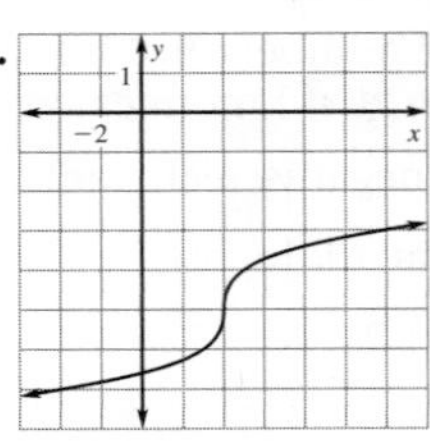

domain: all real numbers, range: all real numbers

31. 16

Cumulative Review (pp. 474–475) **1.** $y = 4x - 11$ **3.** $y = -8x - 22$ **5.** $y = \frac{4}{5}x + 12$ **7.** −4 **9.** 2, 7 **11.** 2, 0, −5

13.

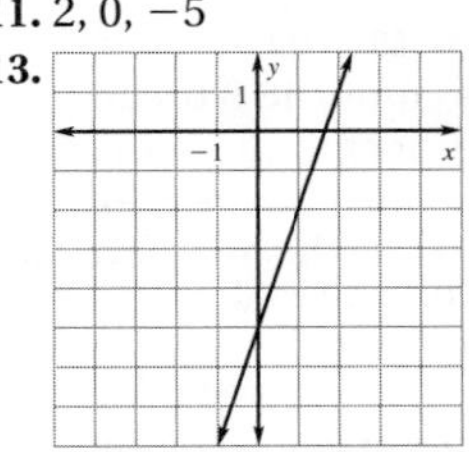

15.

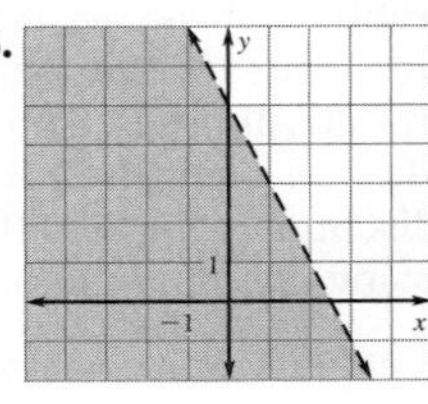

17.

19.

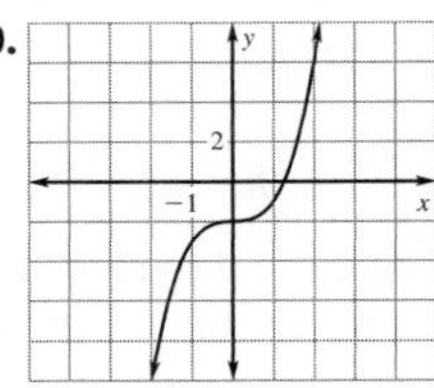

21.

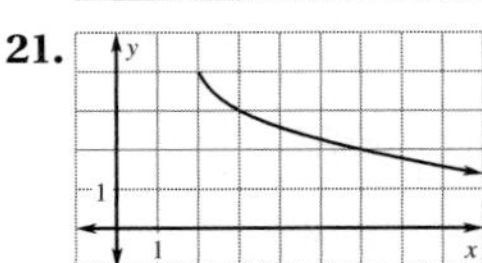

23. (−1, 6) **25.** $9 - i$ **27.** $34 + 8i$ **29.** $y = -(x-6)^2 - 10$ **31.** $8x^9y^6$ **33.** x^7y **35.** $5x^2 + 6x - 16$ **37.** $2x^3 + 3x^2 - 34x + 35$ **39.** $(x^2 - 8)(x^2 + 5)$ **41.** $(x-6)(x-3)(x+3)$ **43.** $10x^2 - 28x - 6$, all real numbers **45.** $10x - 29$, all real numbers **47.** $f^{-1}(x) = \frac{7x - 49}{3}$ **49.** $f^{-1}(x) = \sqrt[3]{6x+5}$ **51.** $f^{-1}(x) = \sqrt[5]{\frac{-9x+18}{8}}$ **53.** $y = 0.499x + 1.25$; about \$5,240,000 **55.** \$4642 **57.** $y = -\frac{1}{8}x^2 + 5x + 6$ **59.** $y = x^3 - 5x + 6$; \$690

Chapter 7

7.1 Skill Practice (pp. 482–483) **1.** 2.4, 1.5, 50%

7.

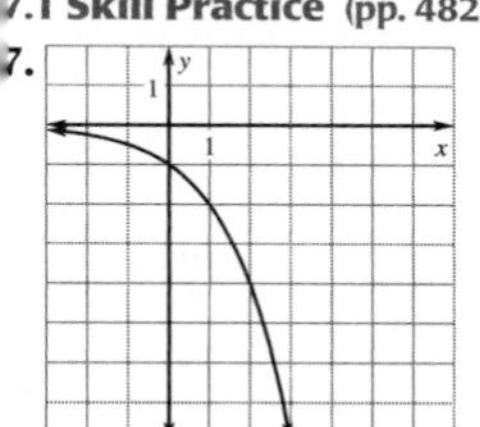

9.

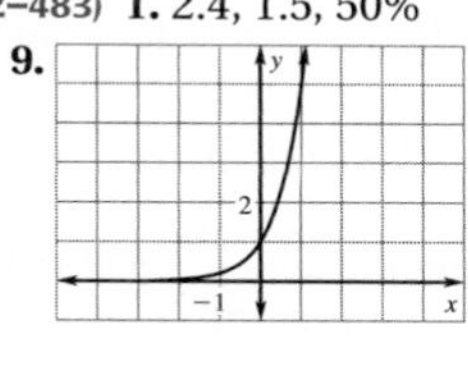

15.

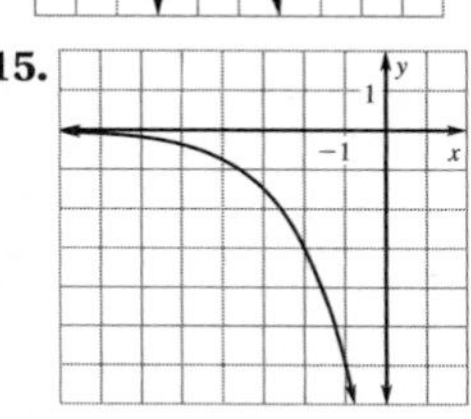

domain: all real numbers, range: $y < 0$

17.

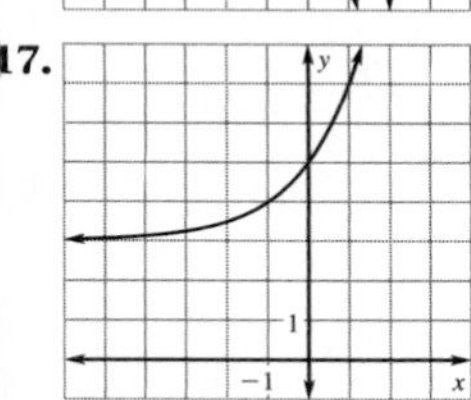

domain: all real numbers, range: $y > 3$

27. The power of $(x - 3)$ translates the parent graph 3 units to the right, not to the left.

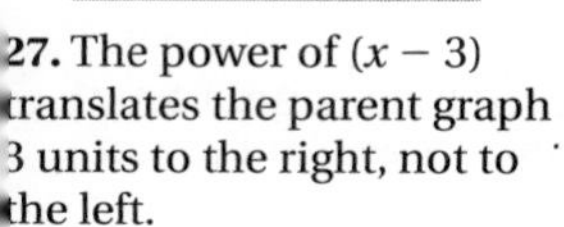

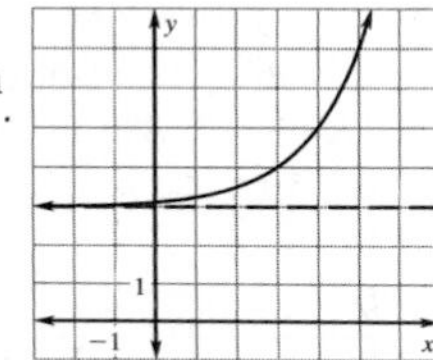

29. $A = 800\left(1 + \frac{0.02}{365}\right)^{365t}$, where A represents the amount in the account after t years. **31. a.** \$1844.81 **b.** 18 yr **33. a.** The graph no longer has a vertical stretch of 2. **b.** The graph will increase slower. **c.** The graph will be translated 3 units to the right instead of 4 units to the left. **d.** The graph will be translated 1 unit down instead of 3 units up.

7.1 Problem Solving (pp. 484–485)

35. a. 0.42 million, 2.47, 147%

b.

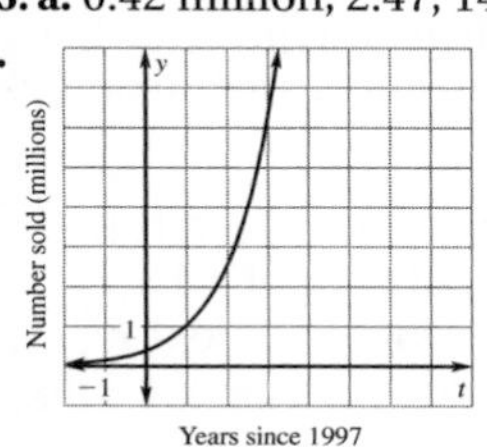

about 16 million DVD players

37. a. \$2479.38 **b.** \$2406.98 **c.** \$2383.23

39. a. $P = 494.29(1.03)^t$; 664,284 people

b.

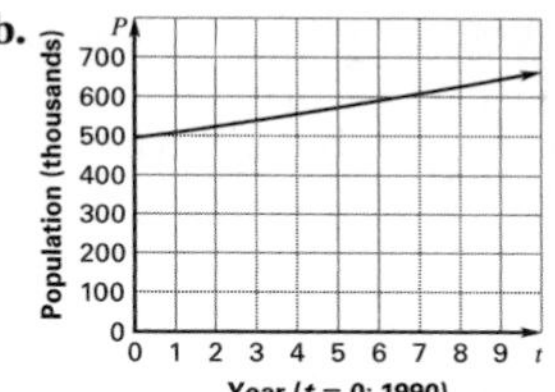

domain: $t \geq 0$, range: $P \geq 494.29$

c. 1996 **41. a.** $p = 48.28(1.06)^t$

b.

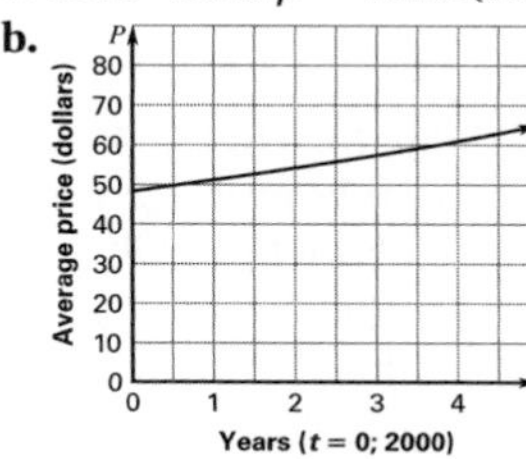

2003

c. *Sample answer:* Since the function is only defined when t is between 0 and 4, you can look at the graph between these values to determine the minimum or maximum that gives meaningful results. **43.** No. *Sample answer:* The amounts are not equal except initially and one year after the investments are made.

7.2 Skill Practice (pp. 489–490) **1.** 1250, 0.85, 15% **3.** exponential decay **5.** exponential growth

7.

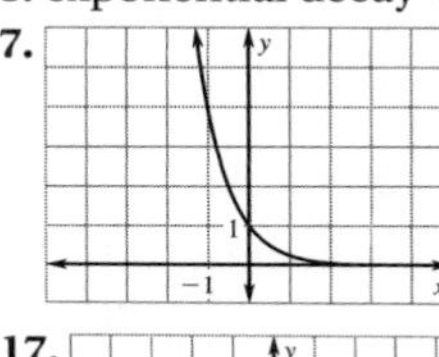

9.

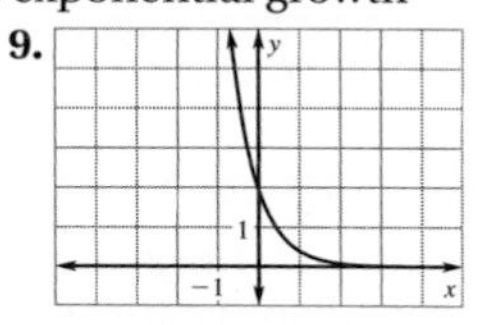

17.

domain: all real numbers, range: $y < 0$

19.

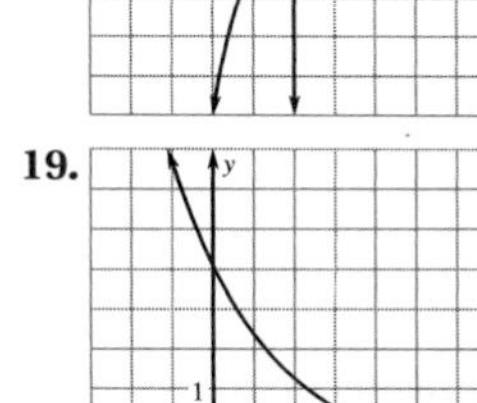

domain: all real numbers, range: $y > -1$

25. a. The graph is a vertical stretch by a factor of $\frac{4}{3}$. **b.** The graph will be steeper because the decay factor is smaller. **c.** The graph moves 5 units to the right instead of 2 units to the right. **d.** The horizontal asymptote moves to $x = 3$.

SELECTED ANSWERS

SELECTED ANSWERS

7.2 Problem Solving (pp. 490–491) **31. a.** $y = 200(0.75)^t$; about \$84.38

b.

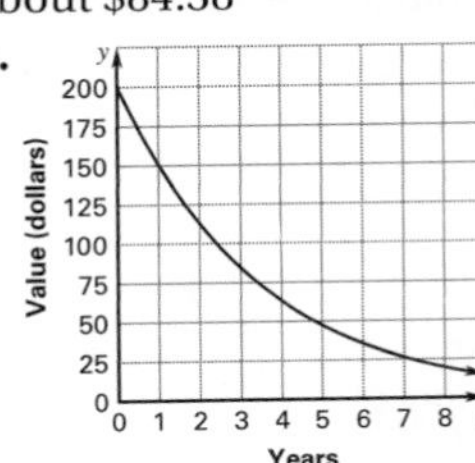
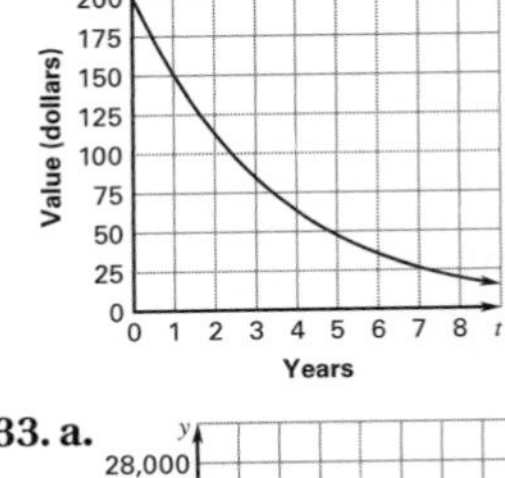

c. after about 2.5 yr

33. a.

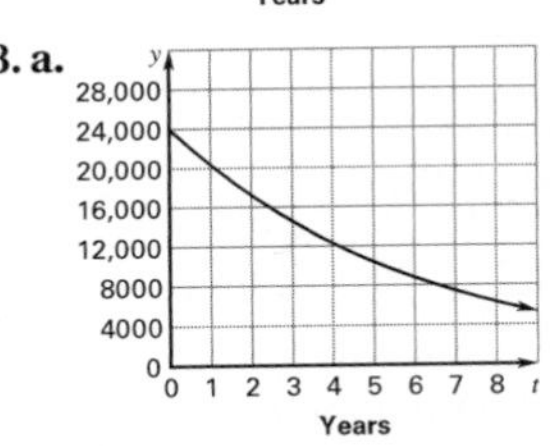

after 5 yr **b.** \$5.29; no. *Sample answer:* A car does not normally last 50 years.

35. a. 0.89, 11%

b.

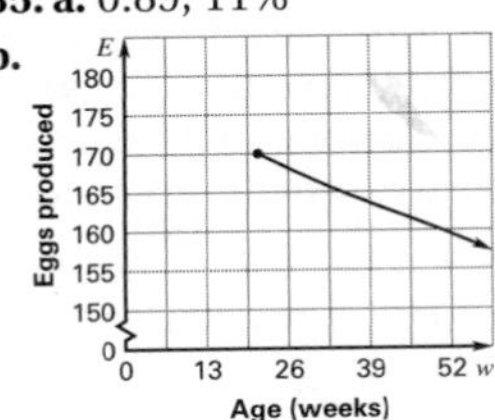

c. about 134 eggs per yr **d.** Change the exponent to just w.

7.3 Skill Practice (pp. 495–496) **1.** e **3.** e^7 **5.** $8e^{9x}$ **7.** $\frac{1}{3e^{5x}}$ **9.** $3e^3$ **11.** $3e^{1-x}$ **13.** $2e^{3x}$ **17.** The 3 should be raised to the second power also; $(3e^{5x})^2 = 3^2e^{(5x)(2)} = 9e^{10x}$. **19.** about 20.086 **21.** about 9.025 **23.** about 0.670 **25.** about 1096.633 **27.** about 1.482 **29.** about -66.139 **31.** exponential decay **33.** exponential decay **35.** exponential decay **37.** exponential growth

43.

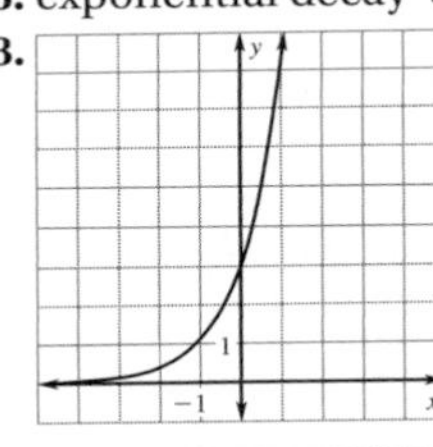

domain: all real numbers, range: $y > 0$

45.

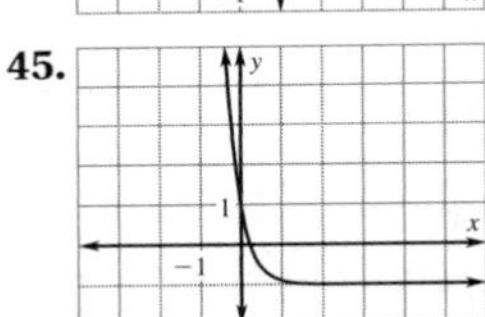

domain: all real numbers, range: $y > -1$

51. 10,000,000,000. *Sample answer:* Since small values of n were increasing the function very slowly, I checked larger intervals. I noticed that every power of 10 gave an answer one digit closer to the actual value of e. **53.** *Sample answer:* $f(x) = \frac{1}{2}e^{-3x}$, $g(x) = \frac{2}{3}e^{-5x}$

7.3 Problem Solving (pp. 497–498) **55.** about 895 million camera phones **57.** \$2442.81 **59. a.** $L(x) = 100e^{-0.02x}$

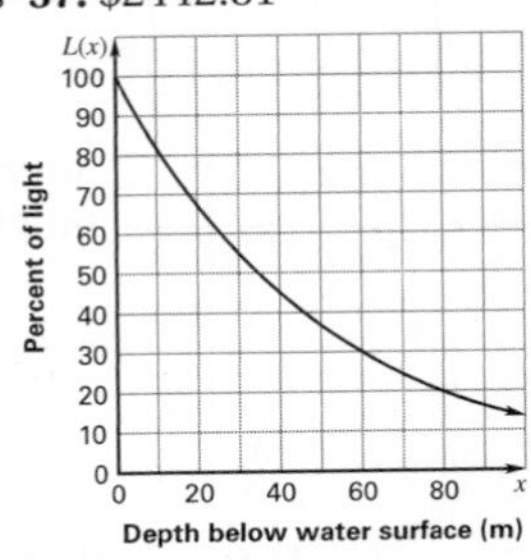

b. about 45% **c.** about 35 m **61.** about 1.986 cm^2

7.4 Skill Practice (pp. 503–504) **1.** common **3.** $4^2 = 16$ **5.** $6^{-2} = \frac{1}{36}$ **7.** *Sample answer:* The -3 and $\frac{1}{8}$ are switched around; $\log_2 \frac{1}{8} = -3$. **9.** 2 **11.** 6 **13.** -3 **15.** $-\frac{1}{2}$ **17.** 3 **19.** 2 **21.** about 1.792 **23.** about 0.793 **25.** about 1.683 **27.** about 4.700 **29.** x **31.** 8 **33.** $4x$ **35.** $5x$ **37.** $y = 8^x$ **39.** $y = \log_{0.4} x$ **41.** $y = \ln x - 2$ **43.** $y = e^x - 1$

45.

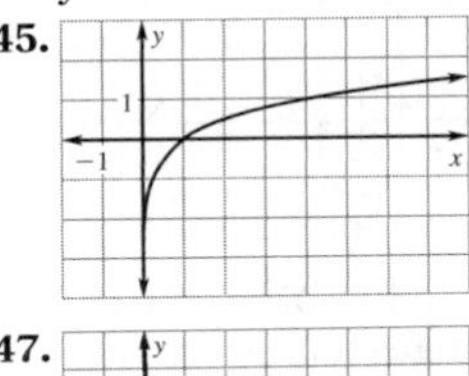

domain: $x > 0$, range: all real numbers

47.

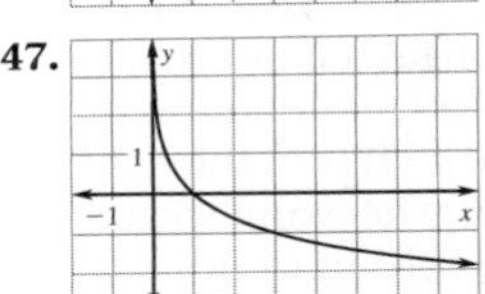

domain: $x > 0$, range: all real numbers

7.4 Problem Solving (pp. 504–505) **59.** 2.3 **61. a.** about 6.4 **b.** $E = e^{(M + 9.9)/0.29}$; the inverse represents the amount of energy released, in ergs, as a function of the energy magnitude.

7.5 Skill Practice (pp. 510–511) **1.** product **7.** 0.477 **9.** 1.204 **11.** 2.158 **13.** -0.602 **15.** $\log_3 4 + \log_3 x$ **17.** $\log 3 + 4\log x$ **19.** $\log_2 2 - \log_2 5$ **21.** $\log_4 x - \log_4 3 - \log_4 y$ **23.** $\log_7 5 + 3\log_7 x + \log_7 y + 2\log_7 z$ **25.** $2\ln x + \frac{1}{3}\ln y$ **27.** $\frac{1}{2}\log_2 x$ **29.** $\frac{3}{4}\ln x$ **31.** The two parts should be added, not multiplied; $\log_2 5 + \log_2 x$.

SA22

33. $\log_4 \frac{7}{10}$ **35.** $\log 11x^2$ **37.** $\log \frac{x^5}{y^4}$ **39.** $\ln 10x$ **41.** $\ln \frac{64}{y^4}$ **45.** about 1.404 **47.** about 2.465 **49.** about 1.631 **51.** about 1.581 **53.** about 1.513 **55.** 1.5 **57.** about 0.875 **59.** about -1.358 **61.** When using the change of base formula, the base goes in the denominator; $\frac{\log 7}{\log 3}$. **63.** 150 decibels

7.5 Problem Solving (pp. 512–513) **69.** about 76 decibels **71.** 10; $L(10I) - L(I) = 10 \log \frac{10I}{I_0} - 10 \log \frac{I}{I_0} = 10\left(\log \frac{10I}{I_0} - \log \frac{I}{I_0}\right) = 10\left(\log 10 + \log \frac{I}{I_0} - \log \frac{I}{I_0}\right) = 10 \log 10 = 10(1) = 10$ **73. a.** $s = 2 \log_2 f$

b.

f	1.414	2.000	2.828	4.000
s	about 1	2	about 3	4

f	5.657	8.000	11.314	16.000
s	about 5	6	about 7	8

Sample answer: The amount of light increases by about 1 each time. **c.** About 22.627; if you set up the equation $9 = 2 \log_2 f$ and solve for f, the result is $2^{9/2}$.

7.6 Skill Practice (pp. 519–520) **1.** exponential **3.** 8 **5.** $\frac{7}{12}$ **7.** $-\frac{5}{7}$ **9.** $-\frac{5}{3}$ **11.** -2 **13.** about -1.609 **15.** about 0.292 **17.** about -0.723 **19.** about 0.650 **21.** about -0.378 **23.** about -0.203 **25.** 6 **27.** no solution **29.** $\frac{31}{15}$ **31.** $\frac{1}{3}$ **33.** e^7 or about 1096.633 **35.** about 35.601 **37.** 4 **39.** about 0.729 **41.** about 2.720 **43.** about 10.243 **45.** The logarithm was not simplified correctly, $x \log_3 6 \neq 2x$; $\log_3 6 \approx 1.631$, $x = 1.585$. **47.** *Sample answer:* $3^x = 81$, $\log_5 (x + 4) = 0$

7.6 Problem Solving (pp. 521–522)
55. about 24°F **57.** about 6967 yr

59. a.

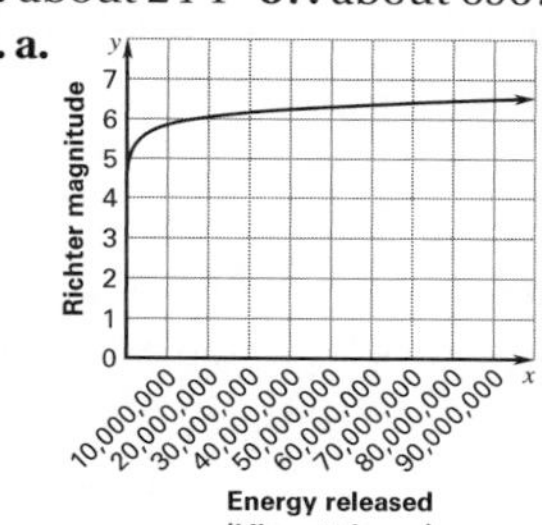

Japan: about 127,000,000 kilowatt-hours, Greece: about 11,500,000 kilowatt-hours, USA: about 23,500 kilowatt-hours

b. Japan: $6.6 = 0.67 \log (0.37E) + 1.46$, 126,893,702 kilowatt-hours; Greece: $5.9 = 0.67 \log (0.37E) + 1.46$, 11,446,269 kilowatt-hours; USA; $4.1 = 0.67 \log (0.37E) + 1.46$, 23,556 kilowatt-hours

7.6 Problem Solving Workshop (p. 525) **1.** about 0.799 **3.** about 2.10 **5.** 0.8 **7.** about 4.48 **9.** 2001 **11.** about 251.19 mm **13.** about 0.03225°C

Extension (p. 527) **1.** $x \le 2.727$ **3.** $x \le 1.51$ **5.** $x \le 6.03$ **7.** $x \ge 27$ **9.** $0 < x \le 36$ **11.** $0 < x < 32$ **13.** after 5.25 yr

7.7 Skill Practice (pp. 533–534) **1.** exponential **3.** $y = \frac{3}{4} \cdot 4^x$ **5.** $y = \frac{1}{8} \cdot 2^x$ **7.** $y = \frac{2}{5} \cdot 5^x$ **9.** $y = 4.99 \cdot 0.499^x$

11.

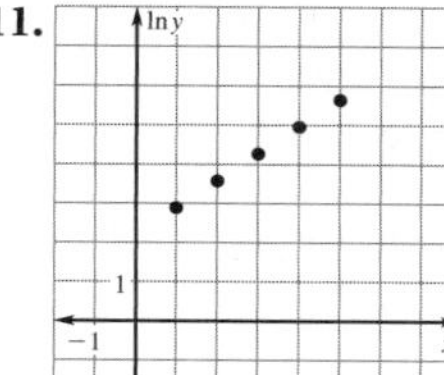

$y = 9(2)^x$

13. $y = 7.83(1.25)^x$

15. $y = 0.12x^{2.32}$ **17.** $y = 1.25x^{1.26}$ **19.** $y = 0.569x^{1.91}$ **21.** $y = 0.241x^{2.34}$

23.

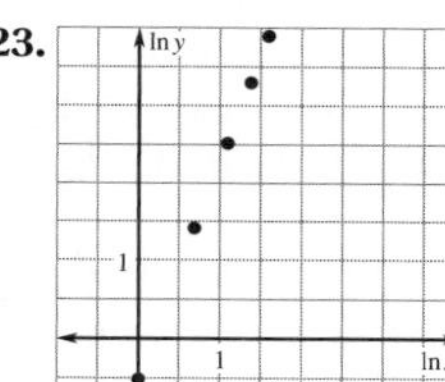

$y = 0.606x^{2.74}$

25.

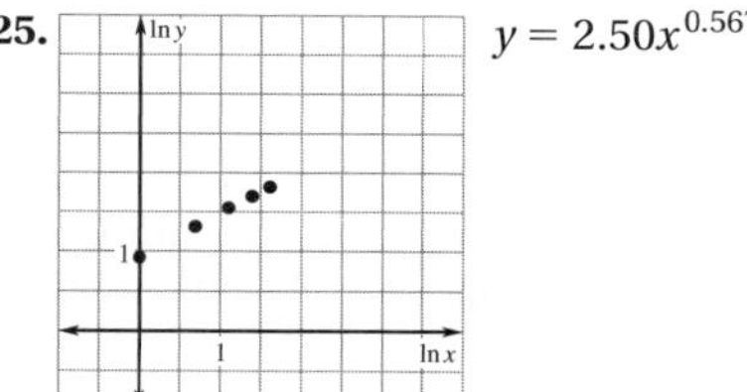

$y = 2.50x^{0.567}$

29. The x should be raised to the 3, not multiplied by it; $\ln y = \ln x^3 - 2$, $y = e^{\ln x^3 - 2}$, $y = e^{\ln x^3} \cdot e^{-2}$, $y = e^{\ln x^3} \cdot e^{-2}$, $y = 0.135x^3$

SELECTED ANSWERS

7.7 Problem Solving (pp. 534–536)

31. a. **b.** $y = 0.000466x^{2.80}$ **c.** about 64.8 kg

33. a. $y = 0.475(2.08)^x$ **b.** Graph the points (x, y); if they appear linear, then a line is the best fit. If not, graph the points $(x, \ln y)$; if these points appear linear, then an exponential model is the best fit for the data. If not, graph the points $(\ln x, \ln y)$; if these points appear linear, then a power model is the best fit for the data; $y = 33.8x + 2.8$.

35. a.

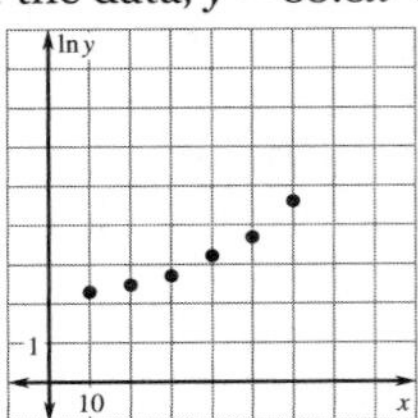

b.

c. Exponential function; the points for $(x, \ln y)$ appear more linear than the points $(\ln x, \ln y)$, so an exponential model appears to be the best fit for the data. **d.** $y = 4.98(1.05)^x$; about 247 cm

Chapter Review (pp. 538–542) **1.** $y = 5$ **3.** *Sample answer:* $\log_b y = x$ if and only if $b^x = y$. **5.** Exponential function. *Sample answer:* The variable is in the exponent.

7.

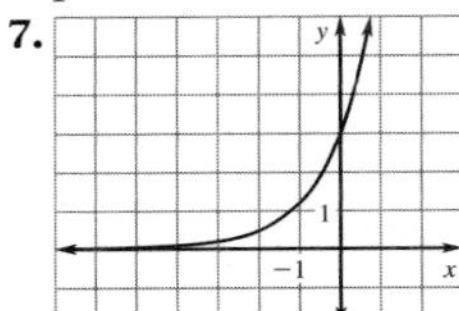

domain: all real numbers, range: $y > 0$

9. \$1725.39

11.

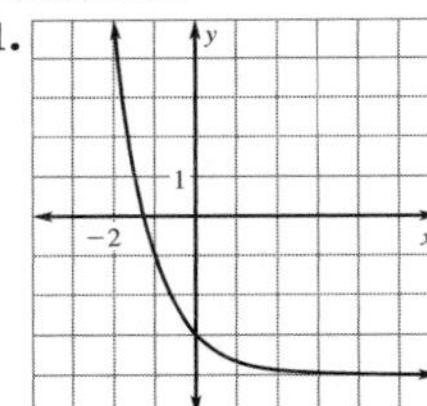

domain: all real numbers, range: $y > -4$

13.

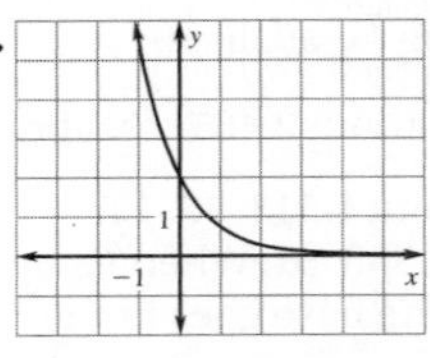

domain: all real numbers, range: $y > 0$

15. domain: all real numbers, range: $y > 6$

17. 5 **19.** −3

21.

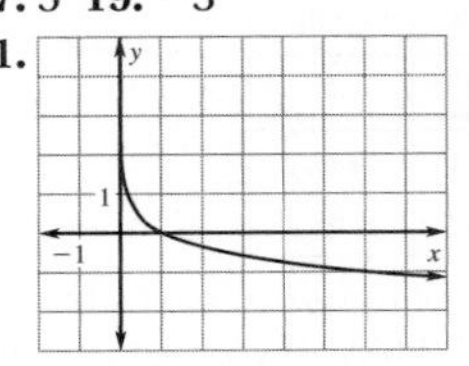

domain: $x > 0$, range: all real numbers

23.

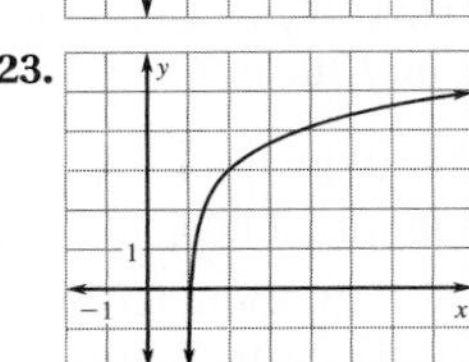

domain: $x > 0$, range: all real numbers

25. $\log_8 3 + \log_8 x + \log_8 y$ **27.** $\log 8 - 4 \log y$ **29.** $\log_7 384$ **31.** $\ln 36$ **33.** 7 **35.** $y = 64\left(\frac{1}{2}\right)^x$ **37.** $y = \frac{1}{4} \cdot 6x$

Chapter 8

8.1 Skill Practice (pp. 555–556) **1.** jointly **3.** inverse variation **5.** direct variation **7.** inverse variation **9.** direct variation **13.** $y = \frac{9}{x}$; 3 **15.** $y = \frac{14}{x}$; $\frac{14}{3}$ **17.** $y = \frac{5}{x}$; $\frac{5}{3}$ **19.** $y = \frac{-35}{3x}$; $-\frac{35}{9}$ **21.** direct variation **23.** inverse variation **25.** $z = \frac{1}{4}xy$; −5 **27.** $z = \frac{1}{14}xy$; $\frac{-10}{7}$ **29.** $z = -5xy$; 100 **31.** $x = \frac{ay}{z}$ **33.** $w = \frac{axz}{y}$ **35.** *Sample answer:* $f(x) = 2x$, $g(x) = \frac{2}{x}$

8.1 Problem Solving (pp. 556–557) **37.** $n = \frac{103.68}{s}$; 26 photos **39.** $P = \frac{172}{A}$; about 2.87 lb/in.^{2} **41. a.** $F = \frac{Gm_1m_2}{d^2}$ **b.** 6.7×10^{-11} **c.** It decreases; it increases.

8.2 Skill Practice (pp. 561–562) **1.** range; domain

3. The graph lies farther from the axes than the graph of $y = \frac{1}{x}$. Both graphs lie in the 1st and 3rd quadrants and have the same asymptotes, domain, and range.

5. 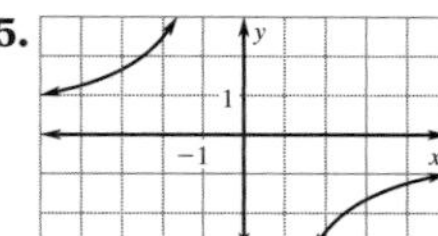
The graph lies farther from the axes than the graph of $y = \frac{1}{x}$ and is located in quadrants 2 and 4. Both graphs have the same asymptotes, domain, and range.

11. 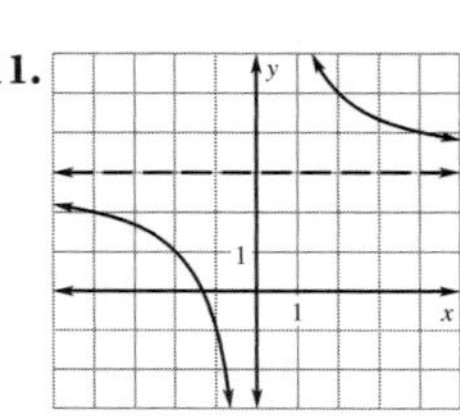
domain: all real numbers except 0, range: all real numbers except 3

13. 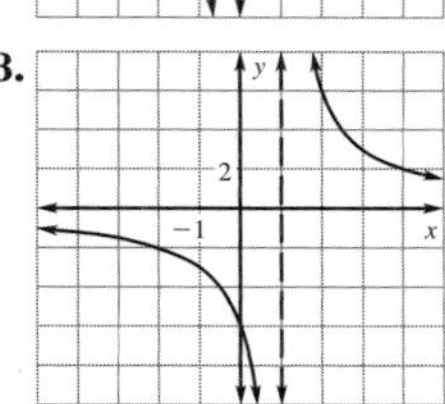
domain: all real numbers except 1, range: all real numbers except 0

25. The graph should be $y = \frac{-8}{x}$ not $y = \frac{8}{x}$.

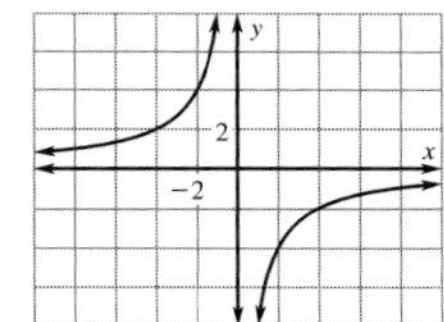

27. domain: all real numbers except 3, range: all real numbers except 1

29. 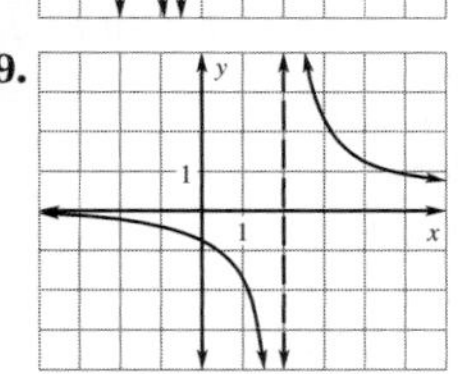
domain: all real numbers except 2, range: all real numbers except $\frac{1}{4}$

35. *Sample answer:* $y = \frac{3x + 1}{x + 8}$

8.2 Problem Solving (pp. 562–563)

37. $c = \frac{43m + 50}{m}$;

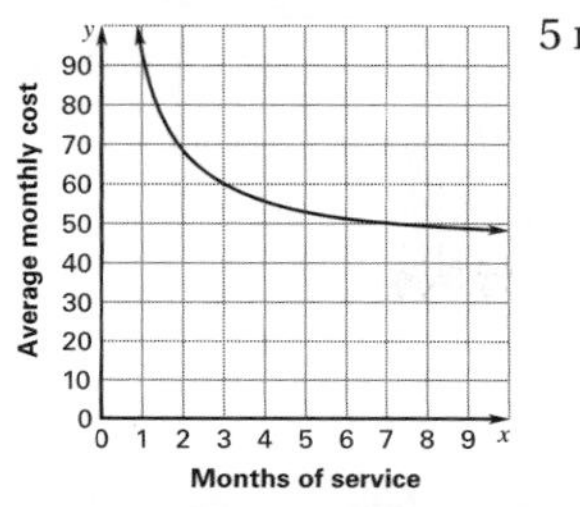

5 mo

39. a. About 14.5 sec. *Sample answer:* Substitute 25 for T to find $t \approx 2.89$. Since you are 5 kilometers away, multiply t by 5 to get $5(2.89) \approx 14.5$ seconds.

b. 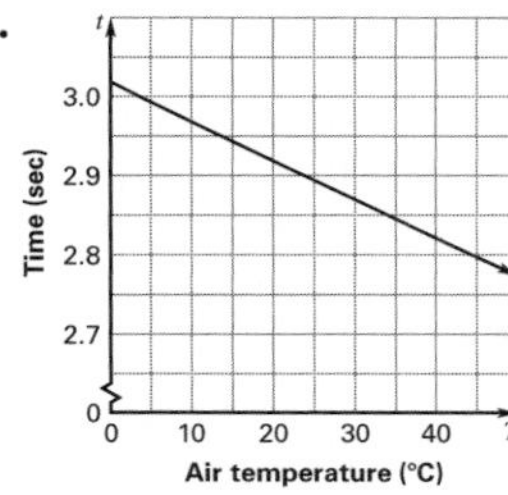

about 3.9°C

41. a. approaching: $f_1 = \frac{1{,}480{,}000}{740 - r}$, moving away: $f_1 = \frac{1{,}480{,}000}{740 + r}$

b. 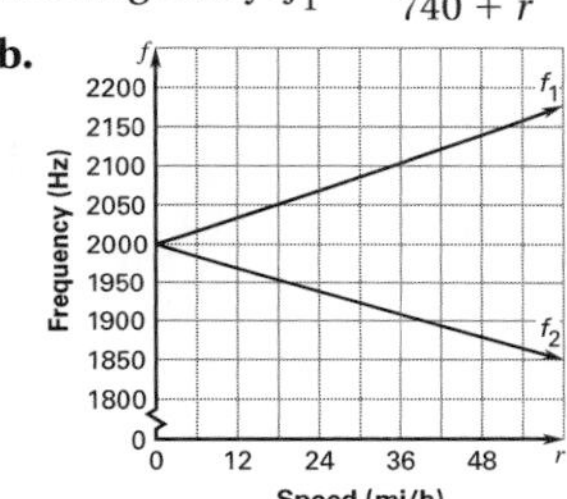

c. The frequency of a sound that is approaching is greater than that of a sound moving away.

8.3 Skill Practice (pp. 568–569) **1.** horizontal asymptote **3.** C **5.** B **7.** none; $x = 1$ and $x = -1$ **9.** none; $x = 5$ and $x = -3$ **11.** -3; $x = 0$ and $x = -\frac{1}{3}$ **13.** The vertical asymptote occurs at the zeros of the denominator not the numerator; the vertical asymptotes occur at the zeros of the denominator $x^2 - 8x + 7$. So, the vertical asymptotes are at $x = 7$ and $x = 1$.

15. 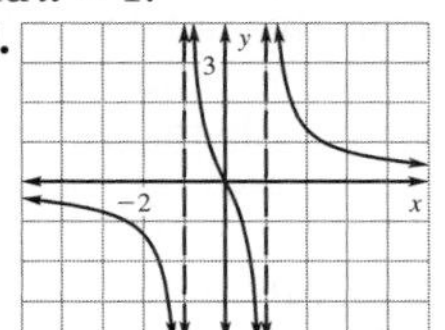

SELECTED ANSWERS

17.

25. $0 < y \le 7.5$ **27.** all real numbers except $-0.209 < y < -4.791$

8.3 Problem Solving (pp. 569–571) **31. a.** $\ell = \frac{100}{\pi r^2}$
b. $S = 2\pi r^2 + \frac{200}{r}$ **c.** $r \approx 2.515$ ft, $\ell \approx 5.032$ ft

33. a.

Depth (m)	Mean Temperature (°C)
1000	4.763
1050	4.580
1100	4.409
1150	4.251
1200	4.104
1250	3.967
1300	3.839

b. about 1238 m

35. a.

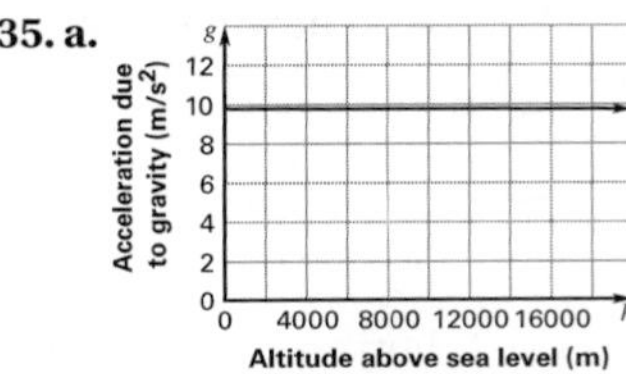

b. about 9.78 m/sec^2 **c.** about 9.47 m/sec^2
d. *Sample answer:* g decreases, but at a very small rate.

8.4 Skill Practice (pp. 577–579) **1.** reciprocal **3.** B **5.** C **7.** simplified form **9.** $\frac{x-3}{x+5}$ **11.** $\frac{2(x-1)}{x-7}$ **13.** $\frac{x-6}{x+6}$ **15.** $\frac{4x-1}{3x+2}$ **17.** $\frac{x^2-3}{x-3}$ **19.** You can only divide out common factors. Since the factors that are divided out are not common factors of the entire numerator and denominator, you cannot divide them out; $\frac{x^2+16x+48}{x^2+8x+16} = \frac{(x+4)(x+12)}{(x+4)(x+4)} = \frac{x+12}{x+4}$ **21.** $\frac{2}{x}$
23. Exercise 21. *Sample answer:* The perimeter of Exercise 21 is smaller and the areas are the same.

25. $\frac{8x^4}{y^2}$ **27.** $\frac{2(x+1)}{x}$ **29.** $\frac{x+4}{2(x-5)}$ **31.** $(x+2)(x+7)$
33. $\frac{4(x+5)(x+4)}{x}$ **35.** $\frac{4x^4y}{5z}$ **37.** $\frac{16x(x-4)}{(x+4)}$
39. $\frac{x-5}{(x+5)^2}$ **41.** $\frac{5(x+1)}{x-1}$ **43.** $\frac{(x+8)(x-7)}{6x}$

45.

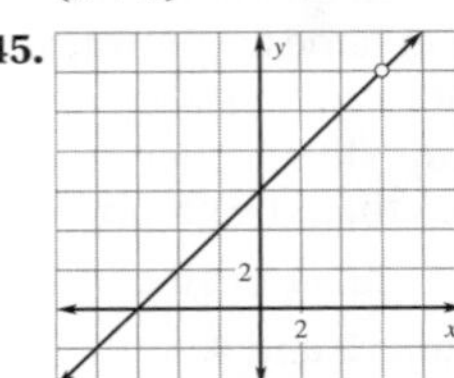

8.4 Problem Solving (pp. 579–580)
49. $\frac{S}{A} = \frac{(-6420t + 292{,}000)(5.92t^2 - 131t + 1000)}{(6.02t^2 - 125t + 1000)(-407t + 7220)}$; \$50.21 **51. a.** $V_{\text{sphere}} = \frac{4}{3}\pi r^3$, $V_{\text{cylinder}} = \pi r^2 h$, since the volumes are the same, set the equations equal to each other resulting in $h = \frac{4}{3}r$. **b.** $S_{\text{sphere}} = 4\pi r^2$, $S_{\text{cylinder}} = \frac{14}{3}\pi r^2$ **c.** $\frac{6}{7}$. *Sample answer:* The spherical tank uses less material.

8.5 Skill Practice (pp. 586–587) **1.** complex fraction **3.** $\frac{5}{x}$ **5.** $\frac{9-2x}{x+1}$ **7.** 5 **9.** $3x(x-2)$ **11.** $2x(x-5)$ **13.** $x(x-5)(x+5)$ **17.** $\frac{32-15x}{12x^2}$ **19.** $\frac{3(x+12)}{(x+8)(x-3)}$ **21.** $\frac{2x^2+3x+9}{(x+1)(x-3)}$ **23.** $\frac{-3(x+16)}{(x-4)^2}$ **25.** You must have a common denominator before you can add values in the numerator; $\frac{x(x-5)+4(x+2)}{(x+2)(x-5)} = \frac{x^2-x+8}{(x-5)(x+2)}$.
27. $\frac{(2x+3)(x-1)}{(x-3)(x+3)^2}$ **29.** $\frac{8x^3-9x^2-28x+8}{x(x-4)(3x-1)}$
31. $\frac{x(x-18)}{6(5x+2)}$ **33.** $\frac{8x(x+1)}{(x-2)(5x+3)}$ **35.** $\frac{3x}{4(x-1)}$
37. *Sample answer:* $\frac{\frac{x^2-x-6}{x^2+4x}}{\frac{x+2}{x}}$, $\frac{\frac{x^2+3x-18}{4}}{\frac{x^2+10x+24}{4}}$

8.5 Problem Solving (pp. 587–588) **41.** $T = \frac{2da}{(a-j)(a+j)}$; about 10.2 h **43. a.** $M = \frac{Pi}{1-\left(\frac{1}{1+i}\right)^{12t}} = \frac{Pi}{1-\frac{1}{(1+i)^{12t}}} = \frac{Pi}{\frac{(1+i)^{12t}-1}{(1+i)^{12t}}} = \frac{Pi(1+i)^{12t}}{(1+i)^{12t}-1}$ **b.** \$364.02

8.6 Skill Practice (pp. 592–593) **1.** cross multiplying **3.** Graph both sides of the equation. If the graphs intersect at a possible solution, then it is a solution. If the graphs do not intersect at a possible solution, then it is an extraneous solution. **5.** 6 **7.** 2 **9.** -1 **11.** no solution **15.** 4 **17.** $-\frac{7}{3}$ **19.** $\frac{-1 \pm \sqrt{79}}{3}$ **21.** 1 **23.** $-\frac{5}{2}$, 8 **25.** 0, 7 **27.** The student simply added numerators and denominators on the left side of the equation. Both sides of the equation should have been multiplied by the LCD, $6x$; $6x\left(\frac{5}{x} + \frac{23}{6}\right) = 6x\left(\frac{45}{x}\right)$, $30 + 23x = 270$. **29.** *Sample answer:* $\frac{6}{x+5} = \frac{2x}{x-1}$; $\frac{4}{x} + \frac{5}{3} = \frac{12}{x}$

8.6 Problem Solving (pp. 594–595) **33.** 26 serves **35.** 1995 **37.** $\frac{1 + \sqrt{5}}{2}$

8.6 Problem Solving Workshop (p. 597) **1.** about ± 5.6 **3.** 9 **5.** about ± 3.2 **7. a.** 99 ft **b.** 33 ft

Extension (p. 600) **1.** $x < 2$ **3.** $x < 3$ **5.** $-1.5 < x < 4$ **7.** $x > -5$ **9.** $-1 \le x \le 1$ **11.** $0 < x < 1$ **13.** $x > -2$ **15.** $-4 < x < -3$ or $x > -2$ **17.** $-3 < x < -2$ or $x \ge 2$ **19.** 1999 to 2002 **21.** at least 13 mo

Chapter Review (pp. 603–606) **1.** inverse variation **3.** rational function **5.** cross multiplying **7.** $y = \frac{24}{x}$; -8 **9.** $y = \frac{-8}{x}$; $\frac{8}{3}$

11.

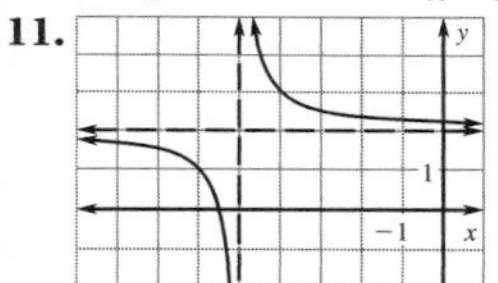

domain: all real numbers except $x = -5$, range: all real numbers except $y = 2$

13.

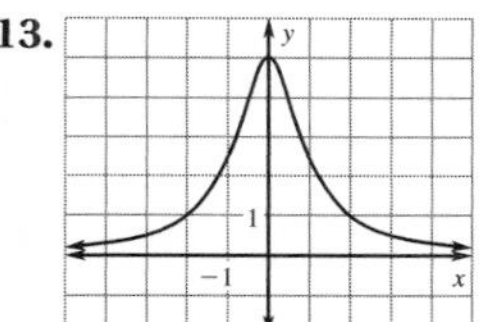

15.

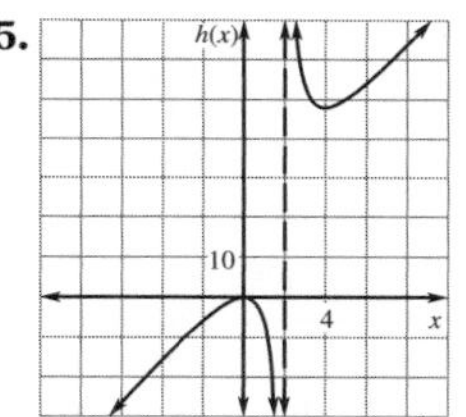

17.

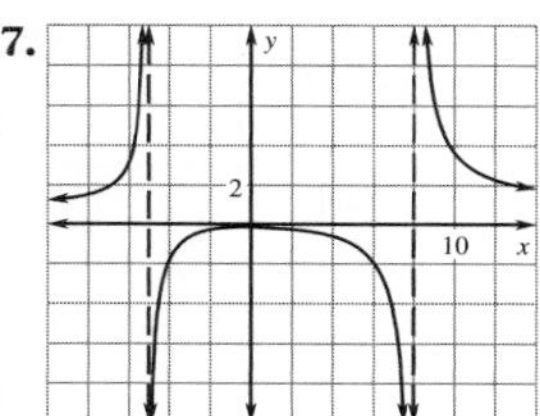

19. $\frac{16x^3}{y^2}$ **21.** $\frac{3x(4x-1)}{(x-4)(x-3)}$ **23.** $\frac{3x^2 + 26x + 36}{6x(x+3)}$ **25.** $\frac{-2(2x^2 + 3x + 3)}{(x-3)(x+3)(x+1)}$ **27.** 5 **29.** -1 **31.** $-\frac{6}{11}$, 0 **33.** 0 **35.** no solution

Chapter 9

9.1 Skill Practice (pp. 617–618)
1. The distance d between (x_1, y_1) and (x_2, y_2) is $d = \sqrt{(x_2 - x_1)^2 + (y_2 - y_1)^2}$; the midpoint of the line segment joining $A(x_1, y_1)$ and $B(x_2, y_2)$ is $M\left(\frac{x_1 + x_2}{2}, \frac{y_1 + y_2}{2}\right)$. **3.** 17; $\left(4, \frac{15}{2}\right)$ **5.** $5\sqrt{5}$; $\left(\frac{5}{2}, 1\right)$ **7.** $4\sqrt{2}$; $(4, -3)$ **9.** $12\sqrt{2}$; $(2, 2)$ **11.** $\sqrt{145}$; $\left(\frac{1}{2}, 0\right)$ **13.** $\sqrt{449}$; $\left(5, \frac{9}{2}\right)$ **15.** $2\sqrt{194}$; $(1.2, 2)$ **17.** $\frac{\sqrt{3221}}{10}$ or about 5.68; $(0.35, -6)$ **21.** The difference of the squares should be added not subtracted; $d = \sqrt{(2 - (-4))^2 + (8 - 3)^2} = \sqrt{36 + 25} = \sqrt{61}$. **23.** isosceles **25.** scalene **27.** scalene **29.** scalene **31.** $y = -\frac{2}{3}x + \frac{43}{3}$ **33.** $y = -\frac{1}{4}x - \frac{5}{2}$ **35.** $y = -4x + \frac{17}{2}$ **37.** *Sample answer:* (6, 4), (2, 0) **39.** $y = -\frac{5}{4}x + \frac{55}{4}$ **41.** ± 6 **43.** -10, 2 **45.** $d(x) = \sqrt{5x^2 - 16x + 13}$; $\left(\frac{1}{5}, \frac{2}{5}\right)$, (3, 6)

9.1 Problem Solving (pp. 618–619) **47.** 17 m **49.** about 6.02 mi **51.** about 4.55 mi **53. a.** $(-1.5, 8)$ **b.** about 1.32 mi **c.** about 1.68 mi **55.** about 550 ft

9.2 Skill Practice (pp. 623–624) **1.** focus, directrix

3.

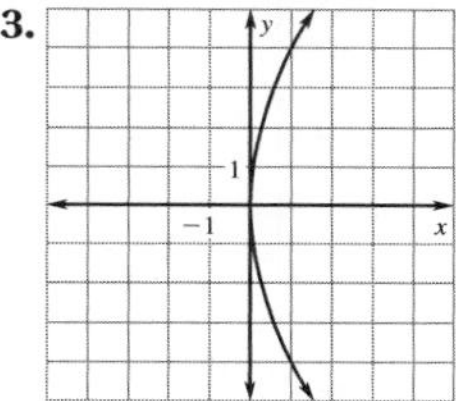

$(4, 0)$, $x = -4$, $y = 0$

5.

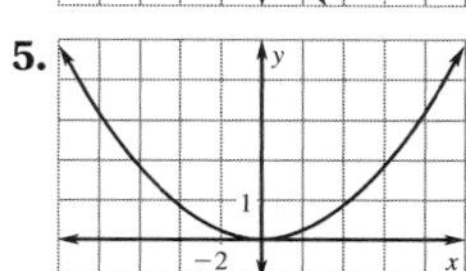

$(0, 5)$, $y = -5$, $x = 0$

23. The parabola should open to the right rather than up;

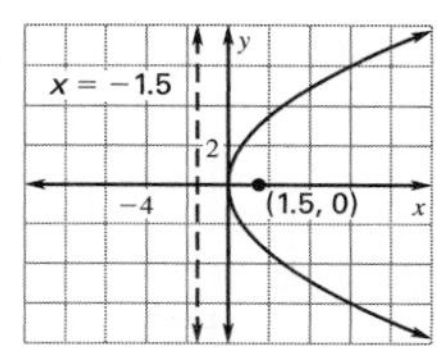

SELECTED ANSWERS

27. $y^2 = -20x$ **29.** $x^2 = -16y$ **31.** $x^2 = -40y$
33. $y^2 = -36x$ **35.** $x^2 = -\frac{3}{2}y$ **37.** $y^2 = -\frac{9}{4}x$
39. $y^2 = -12x$ **41.** $y^2 = 20x$ **43.** $x^2 = 16y$
45. $x^2 = -24y$ **47.** $y^2 = 6x$ **49.** $x^2 = \frac{22}{3}y$

51. a. The new focus will be located at (0, 1) rather than $\left(0, \frac{1}{4}\right)$. The new directrix will be $y = -1$ rather than $y = -\frac{1}{4}$. The parabola will be wider.

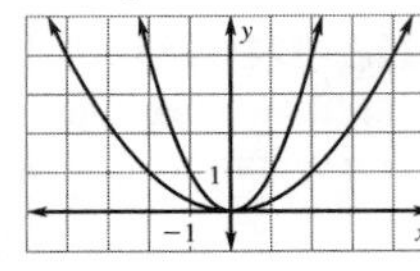

b. The new focus will be located at $\left(-\frac{1}{8}, 0\right)$ rather than $\left(\frac{3}{2}, 0\right)$. The new directrix will be at $x = \frac{1}{8}$ rather than $x = -\frac{3}{2}$. The parabola will open left rather than right and be narrower.

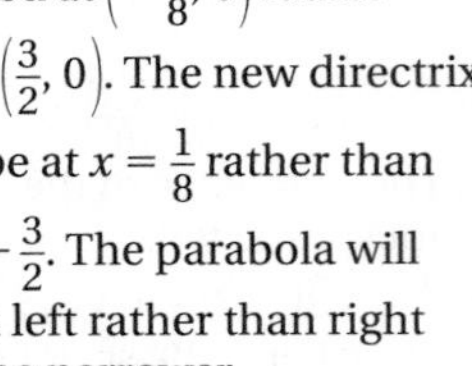

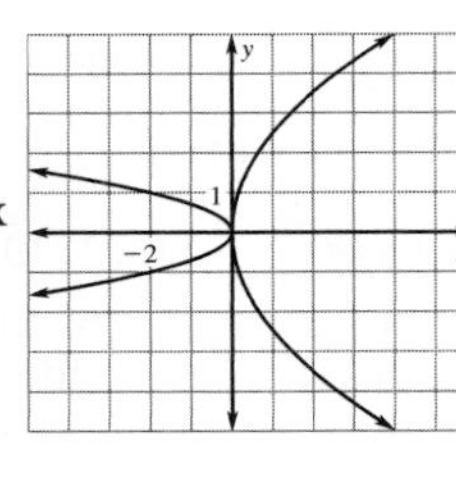

53. The graph gets wider. *Sample answer:* As the value of $|p|$ increases, then the focus and directrix (each of which lie $|p|$ units from the vertex) get further and further away from the vertex and from each other. Since each point on a parabola is equidistant from the focus and the directrix, this has the effect of making the parabola wider and wider as $|p|$ increases.

9.2 Problem Solving (pp. 624–625)

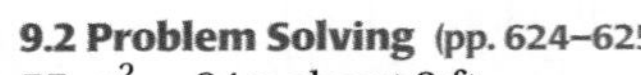

55. $x^2 = 24y$; about 3 ft

57. a.

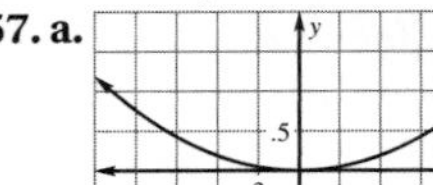

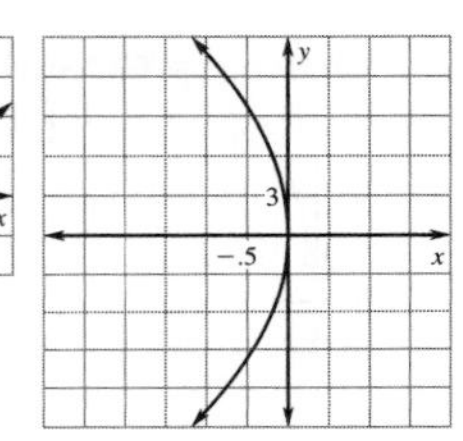

b. $x^2 = 192y$, $y^2 = -192x$ **c.** About 27.8 in.; no. *Sample answer:* Except for the direction they open, they are identical. **59. a.** about 20 in. **b.** *Sample answer:* $x^2 = 50y$; choose a value for p such that $4p > 10.5$; about 43.6 in. **c.** *Sample answer:* $x^2 = 8y$; choose a value for p such that $4p < 10.5$; about 17.4 in.

9.3 Skill Practice (pp. 629–630) **1.** center **3.** C **5.** A **7.** F

9.

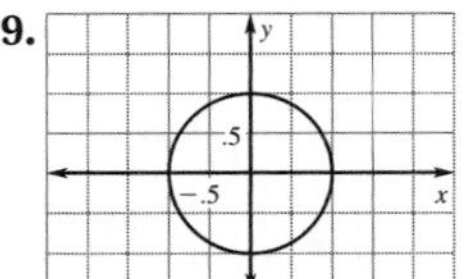

1

11.

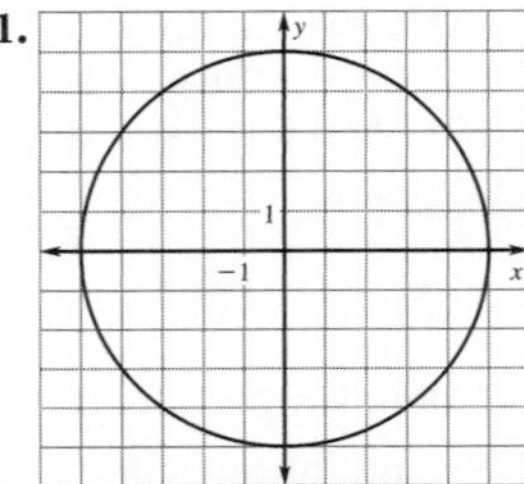

5

23. $x^2 + y^2 = 64$ **25.** $x^2 + y^2 = 256$ **27.** $x^2 + y^2 = 15$
29. $x^2 + y^2 = 96$ **31.** $x^2 + y^2 = 36$ **33.** $x^2 + y^2 = 25$
35. $x^2 + y^2 = 100$ **37.** $x^2 + y^2 = 116$ **39.** $x^2 + y^2 = 260$
41. $x^2 + y^2 = 242$

45.

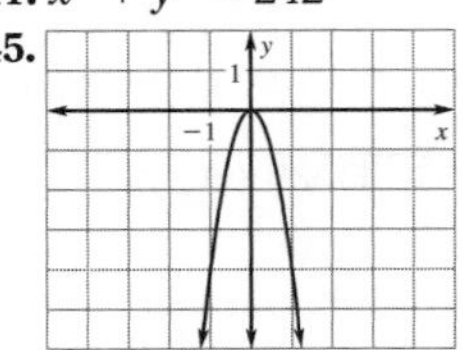

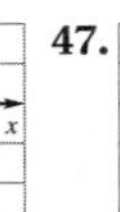

47.

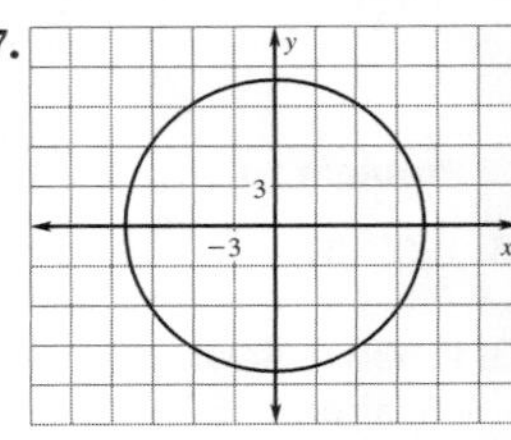

53. $y = -\frac{1}{4}x + \frac{17}{4}$ **55.** $y = \frac{5}{3}x + \frac{34}{3}$ **57.** $y = \frac{5}{9}x + \frac{106}{9}$
59. *Sample answer:* $x^2 + y^2 = 35$, $x^2 + y^2 = 36$, $x^2 + y^2 = 38$

9.3 Problem Solving (pp. 630–632) **63.** yes **65. a.** about 28.9 mi **b.** about 18.3 mi **c.** 6 mi **67.** about 7.94 ft

9.4 Skill Practice (pp. 637–638) **1.** foci

3.

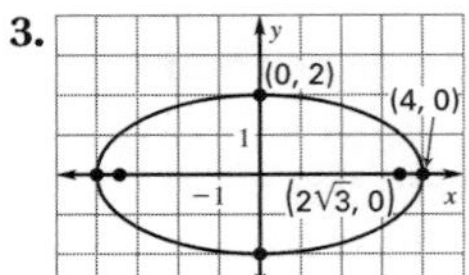

$(\pm 4, 0)$, $(0, \pm 2)$, $(\pm 2\sqrt{3}, 0)$

5.

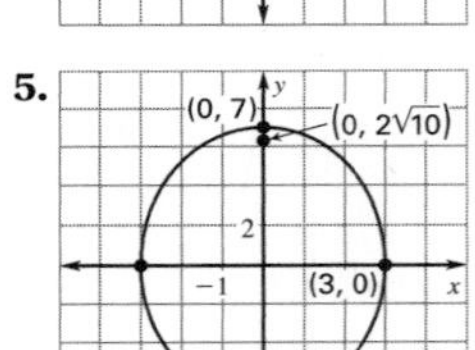

$(0, \pm 7)$, $(\pm 3, 0)$, $(0, \pm 2\sqrt{10})$

15. The major axis should be the y-axis, not the x-axis.

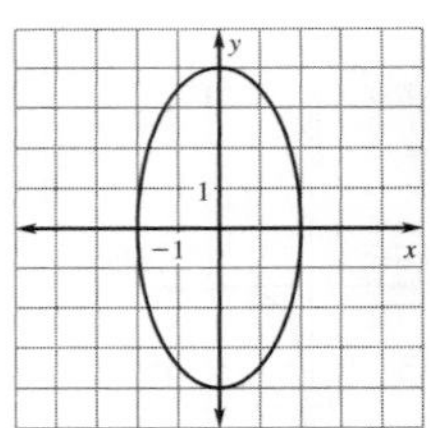

SELECTED ANSWERS

17. $\frac{x^2}{25}+\frac{y^2}{9}=1$ 19. $\frac{x^2}{196}+\frac{y^2}{81}=1$ 21. $\frac{x^2}{121}+\frac{y^2}{144}=1$
23. $\frac{x^2}{28}+\frac{y^2}{64}=1$ 25. $\frac{x^2}{49}+\frac{y^2}{81}=1$ 27. $\frac{x^2}{4}+\frac{y^2}{16}=1$
29. $\frac{x^2}{16}+\frac{y^2}{7}=1$ 31. $\frac{x^2}{400}+\frac{y^2}{175}=1$ 33. $\frac{x^2}{60}+\frac{y^2}{256}=1$

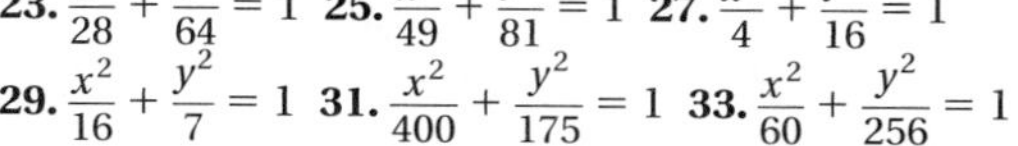

37.

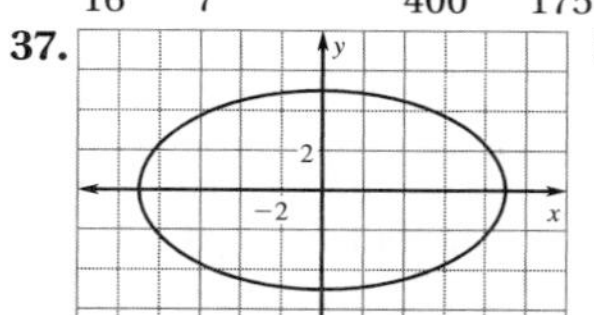

39.

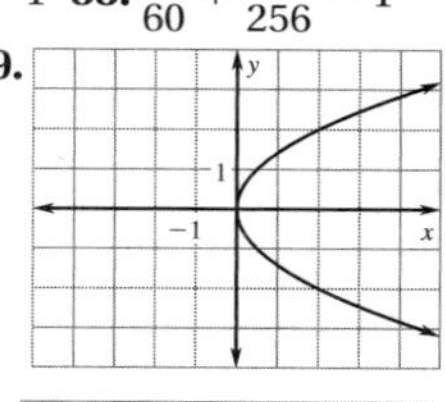

45. The conic changes from an ellipse elongated along the y-axis to a circle to an ellipse elongated along the x-axis.

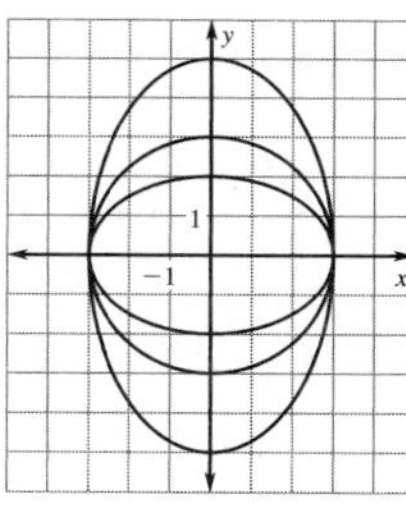

9.4 Problem Solving (pp. 638–639)

49. $\frac{x^2}{(77.5)^2}+\frac{y^2}{(92.5)^2}=1$, $\frac{x^2}{(55)^2}+\frac{y^2}{(67.5)^2}=1$; about $11{,}700 \le A \le 22{,}500$

51.

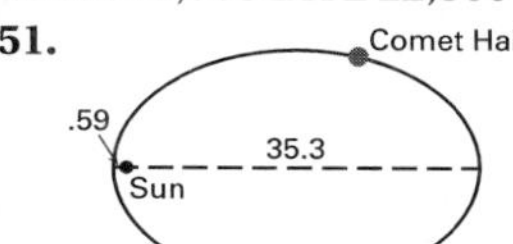

Sample answer: $\frac{x^2}{21.1}+\frac{y^2}{320.4}$

9.4 Problem Solving Workshop (p. 640) 1. About 66,100 m^2; better. *Sample answer:* More rectangles means there is less area of the ellipse not included. 3. a. $\frac{x^2}{125^2}+\frac{y^2}{100^2}=1$ b. about 39,000 m^2

9.5 Skill Practice (pp. 645–646)

1. vertices, transverse axis

3.

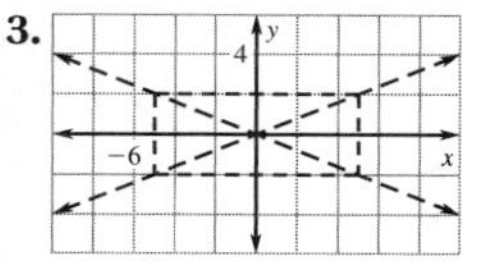

$(\pm 5, 0)$, $(\pm\sqrt{29}, 0)$, $y=\pm\frac{2}{5}x$

5.

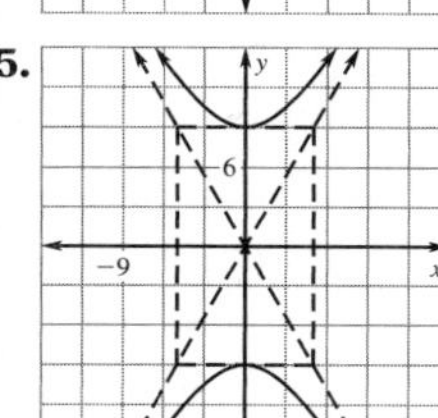

$(0, \pm 9)$, $(0, \pm\sqrt{106})$, $y=\pm\frac{9}{5}x$

17. The equation of a hyperbola must equal one, so the hyperbola's vertices should be located at $(\pm 4, 0)$.

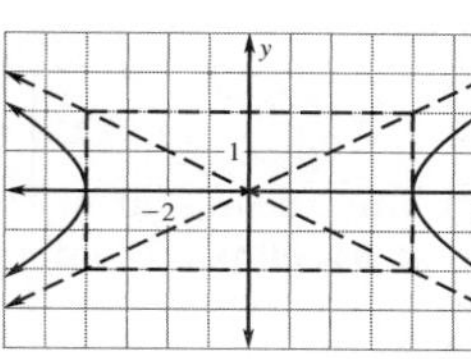

19. $\frac{x^2}{4}-\frac{y^2}{32}=1$ 21. $\frac{y^2}{49}-\frac{x^2}{95}=1$ 23. $\frac{y^2}{16}-\frac{x^2}{64}=1$
25. $\frac{x^2}{4}-\frac{y^2}{50}=1$

27.

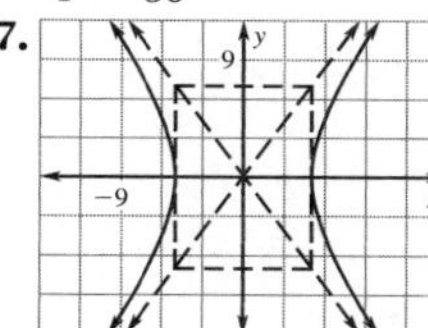

29.

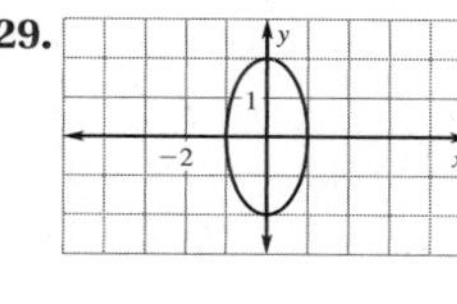

33. a. The hyperbola will be narrower, the vertices are the same, but the foci move to $(\pm\sqrt{13}, 0)$. b. The hyperbola will be wider, the vertices are the same, but the foci move to $(0, \pm\sqrt{41})$. 35. *Sample answer:* $x^2-\frac{y^2}{4}=1$, $\frac{x^2}{4}-\frac{y^2}{16}=1$, $\frac{x^2}{9}-\frac{y^2}{36}=1$; as the value of a gets larger the hyperbola is stretched vertically.

9.5 Problem Solving (pp. 646–647) 39. $\frac{y^2}{\frac{1}{2}}-\frac{x^2}{\frac{1}{4}}=1$

41. a. (30.5, 0), (85, −40) b. $\frac{x^2}{930.25}-\frac{y^2}{236.45}=1$
c. about 54.6 ft 43. a. $\frac{x^2}{16}-\frac{y^2}{20}=1$ b. *Sample answer:* Choose any point on the graph and observe that the difference of the distances from that point and the foci remain constant.

9.6 Skill Practice (pp. 655–656) 1. The intersection of a plane and a double-napped cone form them.

3.

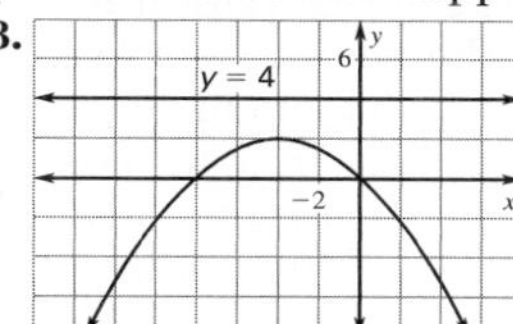

parabola with vertex $(-4, 2)$, focus $(-4, 0)$, and directrix $y = 4$

5.

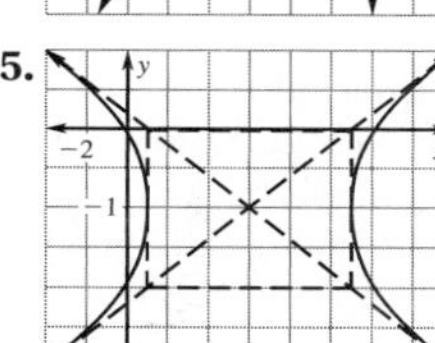

hyperbola with center $(6, -1)$, vertices $(11, -1)$ and $(1, -1)$, asymptotes $y=\frac{1}{5}x-\frac{11}{5}$ and $y=-\frac{1}{5}x+\frac{1}{5}$

13. $(x+5)^2+(y-1)^2=36$ 15. $(y+3)^2=20(x+4)$
17. $\frac{(x-1)^2}{16}+\frac{(y-4)^2}{12}=1$ 19. $\frac{(y+1)^2}{4}-\frac{(x-6)^2}{21}=1$

21. The center is at $(-2, 3)$, not $(2, -3)$; $\frac{(x+2)^2}{25} + \frac{(y-3)^2}{9} = 1$. **23.** $y = 4$ **25.** $x = 3, y = 5$ **27.** any line passing through the point $(-2, -1)$ **29.** circle **31.** ellipse **33.** parabola **35.** hyperbola

37. circle, $(x-7)^2 + (y+2)^2 = 64$

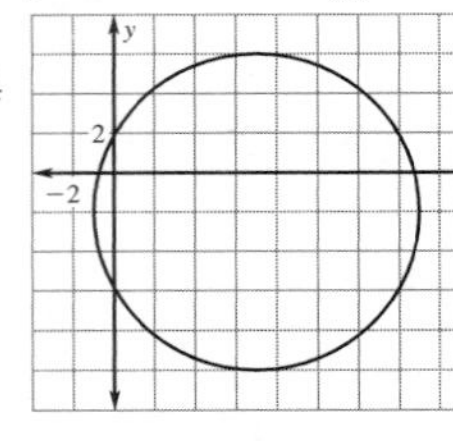

39. parabola, $(x-8)^2 = 8(y-2)$

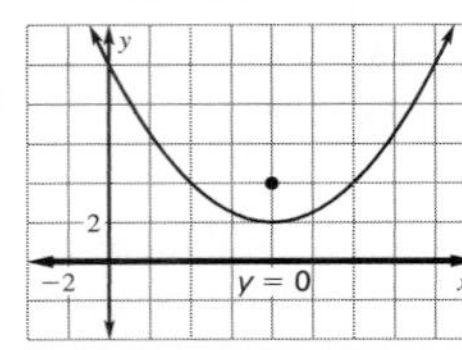

45. If the non-zero coefficients of x^2 and y^2 are the same it's a circle. If the non-zero coefficients of x^2 and y^2 are both positive and different it's an ellipse. If one of the non-zero coefficients of x^2 or y^2 is negative and the other one is positive it's a hyperbola. If one of the coefficients of x^2 or y^2 is zero it's a parabola.

9.6 Problem Solving (pp. 656–657)

49. $(x-5)^2 = -4\left(y - \frac{25}{4}\right)$; $6\frac{1}{4}$ ft, 10 ft

51. a. $(x-100)^2 + (y+60)^2 \le 150^2$, $(x+80)^2 + (y+70)^2 \le 100^2$

b.

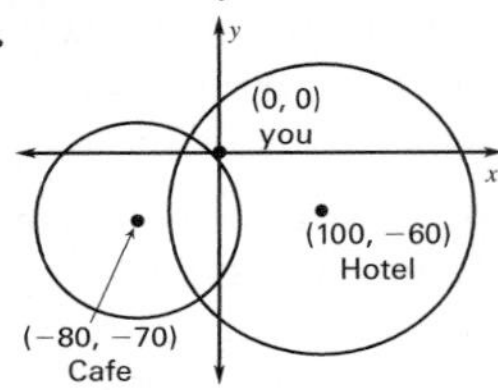

One; the distance from your position to the hotel is less than the radius of the hotel's transmitter, but you are about 106 yards from the café's transmitter which is out of range.

c. *Sample answer:* Find the distance from the hotel to the cafe. If it's greater than 250 yards they do not overlap. It it's less than or equal to 250 yards they overlap.

9.7 Skill Practice (pp. 661–662) **1.** quadratic **3.** $(-4, -4), (4, 4)$ **5.** $(0.472, -2.58), (3.53, 6.58)$ **7.** $(-2.18, -3.36), (1.38, 3.76)$ **9.** $(3, -3), (-2, 2)$

11. $\left(\frac{-64 - 2\sqrt{106}}{17}, \frac{8 - 4\sqrt{106}}{17}\right), \left(\frac{-64 + 2\sqrt{106}}{17}, \frac{4 + 2\sqrt{106}}{17}\right)$

13. $(0, 2), \left(\frac{4}{3}, \frac{2}{3}\right)$ **15.** $(-1, -4), \left(-\frac{13}{2}, 7\right)$ **17.** no solution

19. $\left(\frac{7 + 3\sqrt{3}}{11}, \frac{-1 + 9\sqrt{3}}{11}\right), \left(\frac{7 - 3\sqrt{3}}{11}, \frac{-1 - 9\sqrt{3}}{11}\right)$

23. $(0, \pm\sqrt{5}), (-5, 0)$ **25.** $\left(\frac{1}{2}, \frac{1}{2}\right)$ **27.** no solution **29.** no solution **31.** $(4, 0)$ **33.** $(-1, -2), (2, 1)$ **35.** When $(1 - y^2)^2$ was expanded, the last term should have been y^4; $1 - 2y^2 + y^4 + y^2 - 2 + 2y^2 - 2y = -1$, $y^4 + y^2 - 2y = 0$; (0.1), (1,0). **37.** about $(-2.32, -2.02)$, $(-0.296, -2.82)$

9.7 Problem Solving (pp. 662–664) **39.** $d = 0.8t$, $d = 2.5t^2$, 0.32 min **41. a.** $x^2 + y^2 = 1$, $y = -\frac{1}{7}x + \frac{5}{7}$ **b.** $\left(-\frac{3}{5}, \frac{4}{5}\right), \left(\frac{4}{5}, \frac{3}{5}\right)$ **c.** about 1.41 mi **43. a.** $(1, 1)$ **b.** about $(-8.94, -2.68)$

9.7 Extension (p. 666) **1.** 0 **3.** $\frac{\sqrt{15}}{8} \approx 0.484$ **5.** 1 **7.** $\frac{x^2}{36} + \frac{25(y-4)^2}{756} = 1$ **9.** $\frac{x^2}{49} + \frac{25(y-5)^2}{1176} = 1$ **11.** $\frac{(x-4)^2}{9} - \frac{25(y+4)^2}{504} = 1$ **13.** *Sample answer:* $\frac{x^2}{30.25} + \frac{y^2}{13.19} = 1$ **15.** In the ellipse $0 < c < a$, therefore $0 < \frac{c}{a} < 1$. In the hyperbola $0 < a < c$, therefore $\frac{c}{a} > 1$.

Chapter Review (pp. 669–672) **1.** parabola **3.** transverse axis **5.** $2\sqrt{17}$; $(-2, -4)$ **7.** $\sqrt{106}$; $\left(-\frac{1}{2}, \frac{1}{2}\right)$

9.

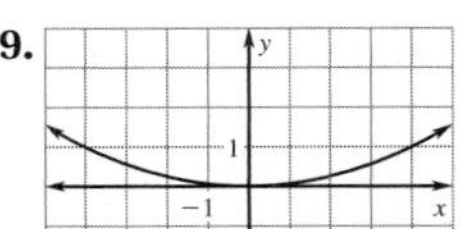

$(0, 4), y = -4, x = 0$

11.

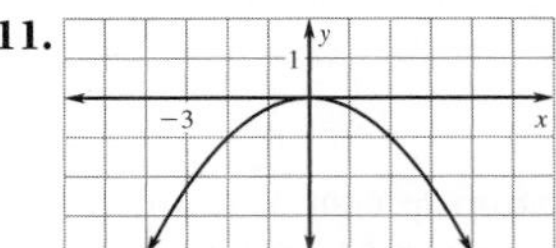

$(0, -1), y = 1, x = 0$

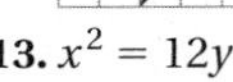

13. $x^2 = 12y$

15.

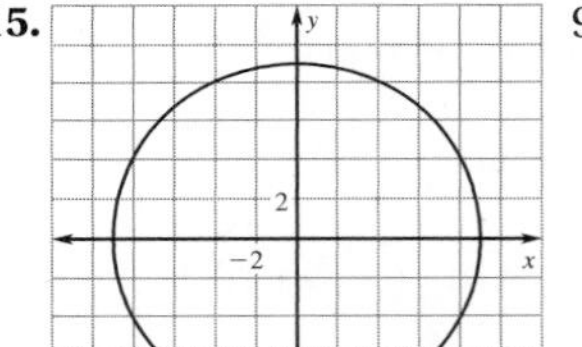

9

17.

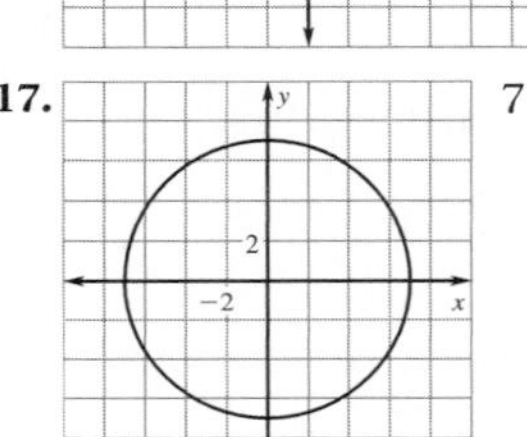

7

19. $x^2 + y^2 = 68$

21. $(\pm5, 0), (0, \pm4), (\pm3, 0)$

23. 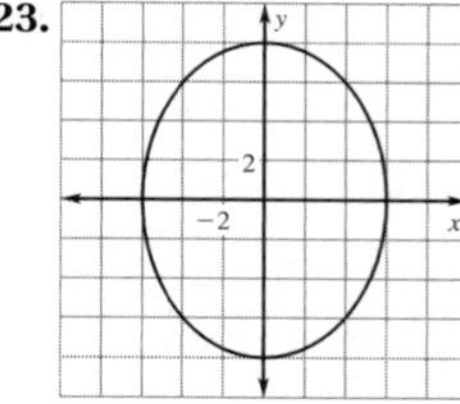 $(0, \pm8), (\pm6, 0), (0, \pm2\sqrt{7})$

25. $\dfrac{y^2}{64} + \dfrac{x^2}{39} = 1$

27. 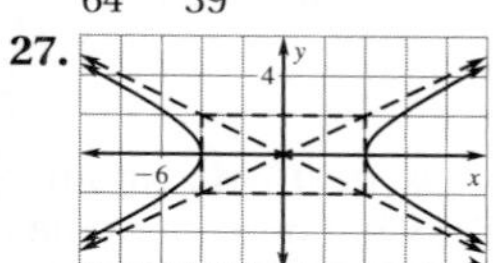 $(\pm4, 0), (\pm2\sqrt{5}, 0)$, $y = \pm\frac{1}{2}x$

29. $\dfrac{y^2}{4} - \dfrac{x^2}{21} = 1$

31. ellipse, $\dfrac{(x+5)^2}{9} + \dfrac{(y+4)^2}{4} = 1$

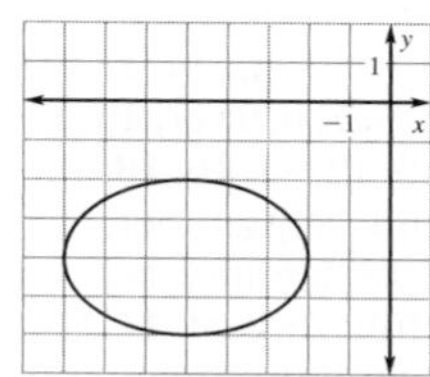

33. hyperbola, $\dfrac{(x-1)^2}{\frac{10}{9}} - \dfrac{(y+2)^2}{10} = 1$

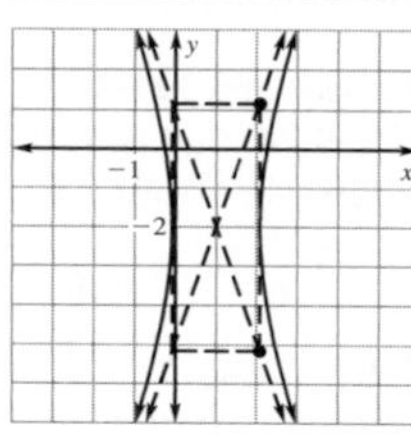

35. (16, 8), (1, 2) **37.** (2, 0)

Cumulative Review (pp. 678–679) **1.** $-\frac{13}{7}$ **3.** 5, 7 **5.** −2, −5, 4 **7.** $\frac{3}{2}$ **9.** 7

11. 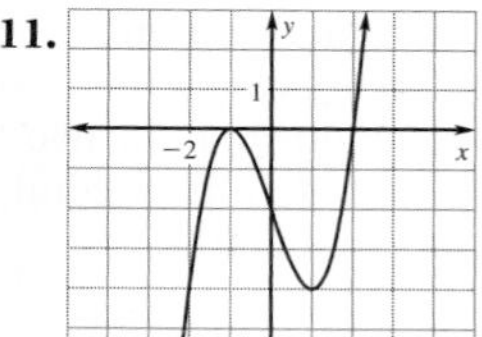

 **13.** 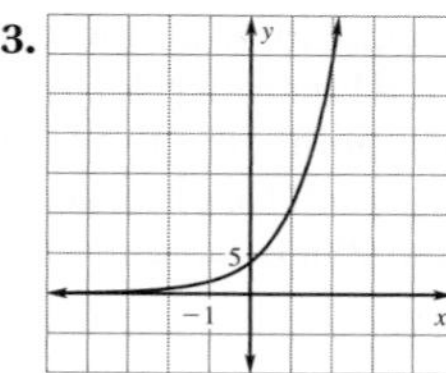

15. 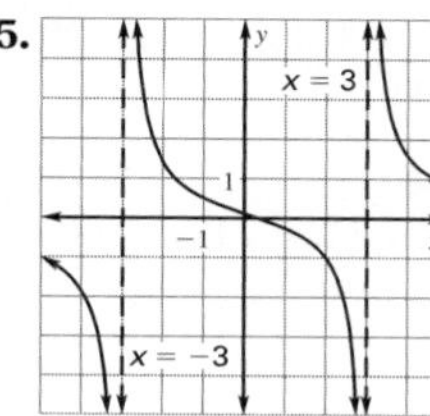

17. $(3x - 4)(2x + 5)$ **19.** $f^{-1}(x) = \dfrac{x+1}{6}$ **21.** $f^{-1}(x) = x^{1/5}$ **23.** decay **25.** $\ln\dfrac{x^3}{5}$ **27.** $\log\dfrac{x^5y}{z^3}$ **29.** $y = \dfrac{-75}{x}$ **31.** $\dfrac{3}{x+5}$ **33.** $\dfrac{x^2+2x+41}{x^2+3x-10}$ **35.** $\sqrt{29}$; $\left(\frac{11}{2}, 6\right)$

37. circle, $(x+6)^2 + (y-2)^2 = 25$;

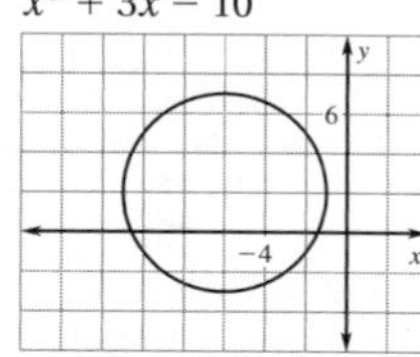

39. parabola, $(y+2)^2 = -6(x+2)$;

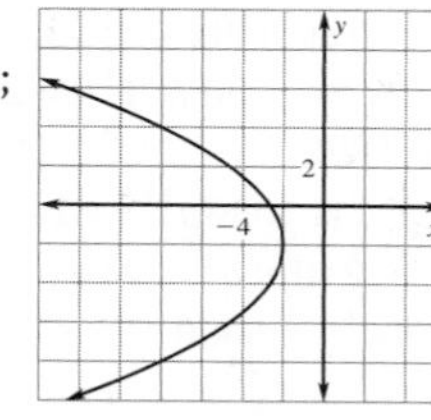

41. 115 ft, 75 ft **43.** 400 adults, 250 students **45.** about 7 mi^2 **47.** $0.85(t - 50)$, \$365.50 **49.** $s = 348(1.02)^t$

Chapter 10

10.1 Skill Practice (pp. 686–687) **1.** The number of ways n objects can be ordered.

3. 

5. 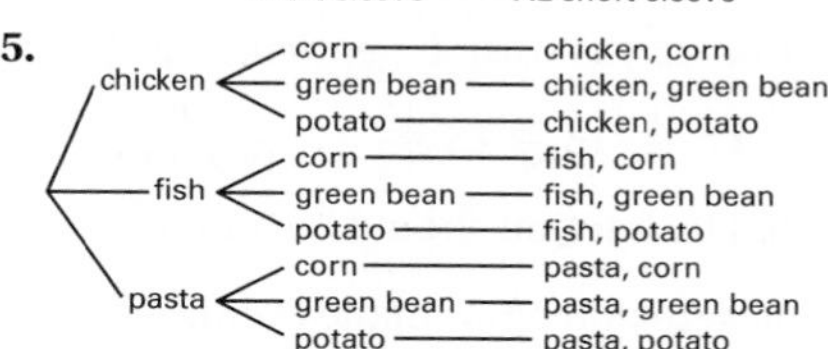

7. 8 ways **9.** 60 ways **11. a.** 456,976,000 license plates **b.** 258,336,000 license plates **13. a.** 45,697,600 license plates **b.** 32,292,000 license plates **15. a.** 118,813,760 license plates **b.** 78,936,000 license plates **19.** 39,916,800 **21.** 40,320 **23.** 1 **25.** 720 **27.** 72 **29.** 630 **31.** 30 **33.** 40,320

SELECTED ANSWERS

35. 72 **37.** 5040 **39.** 3024 **41.** 1 **43.** 3 **45.** 60 **47.** 720 **49.** 3360 **51.** 40,320 **53.** 90,720 **59.** 10

10.1 Problem Solving (pp. 688–689)
63. 225,678,960 sets **65.** 504 ways **67. a.** 240 selections **b.** 252 selections **c.** 60,480 selections **69.** 70,560 displays

10.2 Skill Practice (pp. 694–695) **1.** nth row of Pascal's triangle **3.** 10 **5.** 84 **7.** 1 **9.** 21 **11.** The denominator should have been multiplied by 2!; $\frac{6!}{(6-2)! \cdot 2!} = \frac{720}{48} = 15.$ **13.** 792 hands **15.** 778,320 hands **17.** 2,490,624 hands

19.
1 6 15 20 15 6 1
1 7 21 35 35 21 7 1
1 8 28 56 70 56 28 8 1
1 9 36 84 126 126 84 36 9 1
1 10 45 120 210 252 210 120 45 10 1

21. $y^{10} - 30y^9z + 405y^8z^2 - 3240y^7z^3 + 17{,}010y^6z^4 - 61{,}236y^5z^5 + 153{,}090y^4z^6 - 262{,}440y^3z^7 + 295{,}245y^2z^8 - 196{,}830yz^9 + 59{,}049z^{10}$ **23.** $128s^7 - 448s^6t^4 + 672s^5t^8 - 560s^4t^{12} + 280s^3t^{16} - 84s^2t^{20} + 14st^{24} - t^{28}$ **25.** $c^5 - 20c^4 + 160c^3 - 640c^2 + 1280c - 1024$ **27.** $4096p^6 - 6144p^5q + 3840p^4q^2 - 1280p^3q^3 + 240p^2q^4 - 24pq^5 + q^6$ **29.** $32s^{20} + 400s^{16} + 2000s^{12} + 5000s^8 + 6250s^4 + 3125$ **31.** $x^{12} - 4x^9y^2 + 6x^6y^4 - 4x^3y^6 + y^8$ **33.** 1080 **37.** The sum along each diagonal segment is equal to the sum of the two previous diagonal segment sums. **39.** combinations; 13,836,130,056 ways **41.** $1 = {}_nC_n = \frac{n!}{(n-n)! \cdot n!} = \frac{n!}{0! \cdot n!} = \frac{1}{0!}$, so 0! must equal 1.

10.2 Problem Solving (pp. 696–697)
49. 816 combinations **51. a.** 15,504 combinations **b.** 3,003 combinations **c.** 252 combinations; 10 combinations; 3 combinations **d.** 351,982,350,720 ways

10.3 Skill Practice (pp. 701–703) **1.** geometric **3.** $\frac{1}{2}$ **5.** $\frac{7}{50}$ **7.** $\frac{1}{5}$ **9.** $\frac{41}{50}$ **11.** $\frac{1}{52}$ **13.** $\frac{1}{4}$ **15.** $\frac{12}{13}$ **17.** $\frac{1}{12{,}271{,}512}$ **21.** $\frac{3}{11}$ **23.** $\frac{9}{5}$ **25.** The fraction should be outcomes not in the event, 4, to outcomes in the event, 2; $\frac{4}{2} = \frac{2}{1}$. **27.** $\frac{3}{7}$. *Sample answer:* Since the probability is 0.3, there are 3 out of 10 chances of the event occurring. The number of outcomes against event A is $10 - 3 = 7$. So the odds in favor of event A is the ratio of the number of favorable outcomes, 3, to the number of unfavorable outcomes, 7.

29. $\frac{13}{25}$; the experimental probability is slightly greater than the theoretical probability of $\frac{1}{2}$. **31.** $\frac{22}{25}$; the experimental probability is slightly greater than the theoretical probability of $\frac{5}{6}$. **33.** $\frac{11}{20}$

10.3 Problem Solving (pp. 703–704) **35.** $\frac{1}{2}$ **37.** $1 - \frac{\pi}{4}$ or about 0.215 **39.** $\frac{1}{25}$ **41. a.** $\frac{367}{1631}$ **b.** $\frac{110}{233}$ **c.** $\frac{53}{1631}$

10.4 Skill Practice (pp. 710–711) **1.** compound event **3.** 0.4 **5.** 0.65 **7.** $\frac{7}{12}$ **9.** 0.65 **11.** 0.21 **13.** $\frac{5}{7}$ **17.** 1 **19.** $\frac{3}{8}$ **21.** $\frac{4}{13}$ **23.** $\frac{2}{13}$ **25.** $\frac{3}{4}$ **27.** The probability of a club and 9 must be subtracted instead of added; $P(\text{club}) + P(9) - P(\text{club and } 9) = \frac{13}{52} + \frac{4}{52} - \frac{1}{52} = \frac{4}{13}$. **29.** 0.67; not disjoint **31.** $\frac{1}{5}$; not disjoint **33.** 24%; not disjoint **35.** $\frac{5}{36}$ **37.** $\frac{5}{6}$

10.4 Problem Solving (pp. 711–713) **43.** 0.7 **45.** about 0.8488 **47. a.** 58% **b.** 53% **c.** No; what percent of the tomatoes have bite marks. **49.** $\frac{17}{20}$

Extension (p. 716) **1.** {1, 2, 3, 4, 5, 7, 9, 11, 13, 16, 17} **3.** {1, 4, 6, 8, 9, 10, 12, 14, 15, 16, 18, 19, 20} **5.** {1, 2, 3, 4, 5, 7, 8, 9, 11, 13, 14, 16, 17, 20} **7.** {3, 6, 7, 10, 12, 13, 15, 18, 19} **9.** no **11.** yes **13.** April, June, September, October, November, December **15.** January, February, March, April, May, June, July, August **17.** Yes; no; an irrational is a real number but is not an integer.

10.5 Skill Practice (pp. 721–722) **1.** conditional probability **3.** 0.24 **5.** 0.8 **7.** 0.75 **9.** about 0.047 **11.** about 0.059 **13.** about 0.015 **17.** 0.35 **19.** 0.75 **21.** 0.9 **23.** $\frac{1}{7}$ **25.** $\frac{7}{8}$ **27. a.** $\frac{1}{169}$ **b.** $\frac{4}{663}$ **29. a.** $\frac{1}{169}$ **b.** $\frac{4}{663}$ **31. a.** $\frac{1}{64}$ **b.** $\frac{13}{850}$ **33.** The probabilities should be multiplied instead of added; $P(A \text{ and } B) = 0.4 \cdot 0.5 = 0.2$. **35.** Since A and B are independent events, $P(A)$ has no affect on $P(B \mid A)$ so $P(B \mid A) = P(B)$.

10.5 Problem Solving (pp. 722–723) **37.** about 81% **39.** 51% **41. a.** 0%; about 2%; about 98% **b.** about 20%, about 30%, about 50% **c.** Yes; go for 2 points after the first touchdown. If the 2 points are scored, go for 1 point after the second touchdown. If the two points are not scored, go for 2 points after the second touchdown; win: about 45%, lose: about 30%.

SA32

10.6 Skill Practice (pp. 727–729) **1.** symmetric

3.

x (value)	1	2	3
P(x)	$\frac{1}{2}$	$\frac{3}{10}$	$\frac{1}{5}$

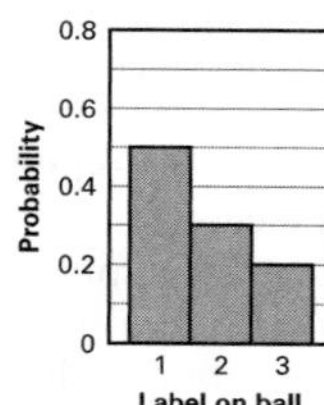

5.

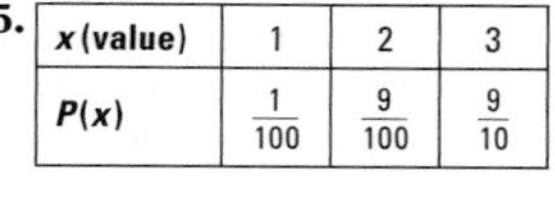

x (value)	1	2	3
P(x)	$\frac{1}{100}$	$\frac{9}{100}$	$\frac{9}{10}$

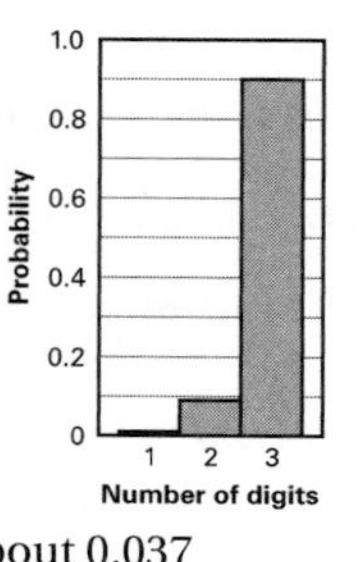

7. 3 **11.** about 0.00018 **13.** about 0.037 **15.** about 0.120 **17.** about 0.00018 **19.** about 0.0086 **21.** about 0.055 **23.** about 0.00000024 **25.** about 0.0000000000000000000087 **27.** The ${}_5C_3$ was left out of the equation; ${}_5C_3\left(\frac{1}{6}\right)^3\left(\frac{5}{6}\right)^{5-3} \approx 0.03$. **29.** about 0.594 **31.** about 0.852

33. skewed; 1 success

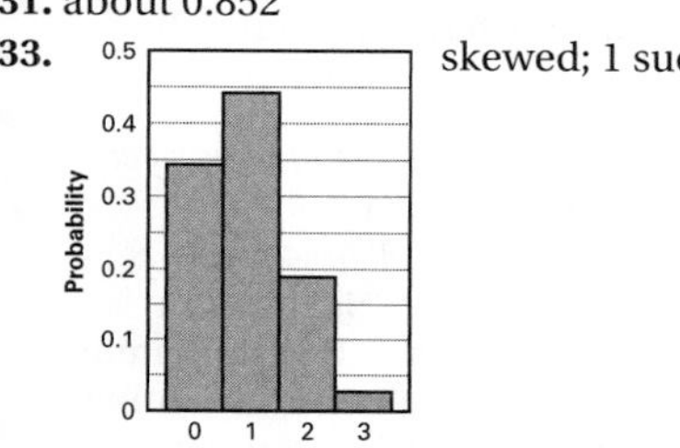

35. skewed; 0 successes

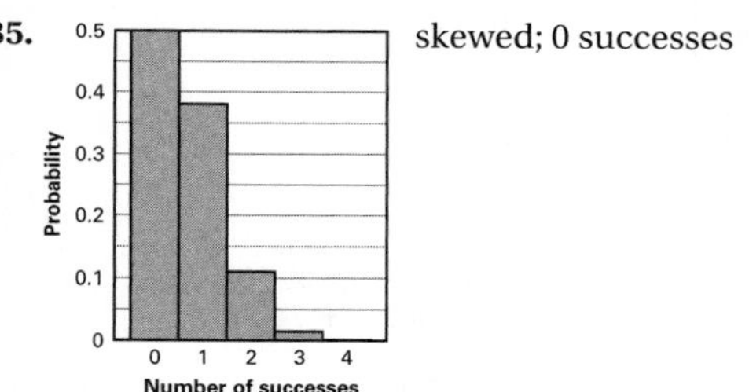

41. ${}_nC_k$; since order does not matter, find the combination of n things taken k at a time.

10.6 Problem Solving (pp. 729–730) **43.** about 0.196 **45. a.** about 0.143 **b.** about 0.276 **c.** about 0.124 **d.** about 0.999

47. a. $P(0)$ = about 0.099, $P(1)$ = about 0.271, $P(2)$ = about 0.319, $P(3) = 0.208$, $P(4)$ = about 0.081, $P(5)$ = about 0.019, $P(6)$ = about 0.0025, $P(7)$ = about 0.00014

b.

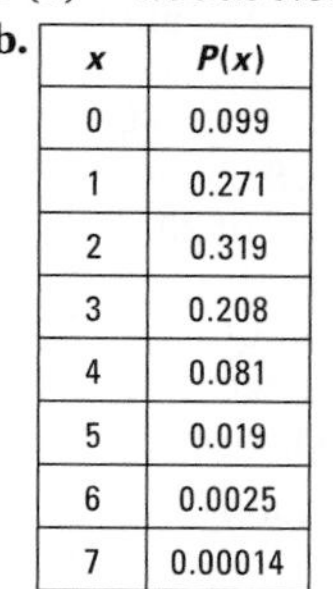

x	P(x)
0	0.099
1	0.271
2	0.319
3	0.208
4	0.081
5	0.019
6	0.0025
7	0.00014

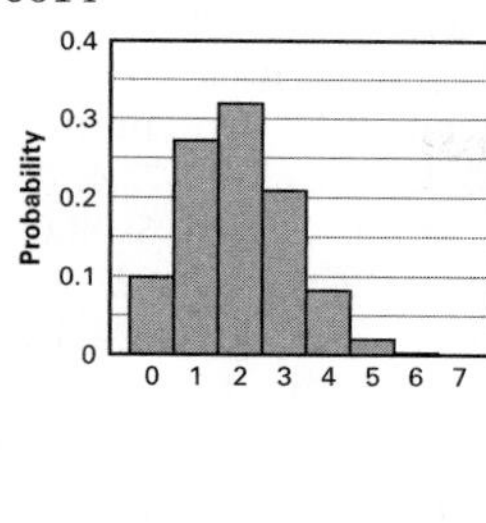

Chapter Review (pp. 734–736) **1.** combination **3.** No; there are more than two outcomes for each card selection. **5.** 479,001,600 ways; 11,880 ways **7.** 120 **9.** 90 **11.** $16a^4 + 32a^3b^2 + 24a^2b^4 + 8ab^6 + b^8$ **13.** $r^{15} - 20r^{12}s + 160r^9s^2 - 640r^6s^3 + 1280r^3s^4 - 1024s^5$ **15.** $\frac{1}{2}$ **17.** $\frac{11}{30}$ **19.** 0.868 **21.** 0.68 **23. a.** $\frac{5}{32}$ **b.** $\frac{1}{6}$ **25. a.** $\frac{1}{4}$ **b.** $\frac{7}{30}$ **27.** about 0.273 **29.** about 0.0039

Chapter 11

11.1 Skill Practice (pp. 747–748) **1.** central tendency; dispersion **3.** about 5.3; 5; 4, 5 and 6 **5.** 74.5, 73.5, 73 and 78 **9.** The numbers need to be written in increasing order prior to choosing the median; 9. **11.** 5, about 1.6 **13.** 4.7, about 1.7 **15.** 23, about 8.1 **17.** 68; about 10.7, 4, 4, 66, about 20.3; 3.5, 3.5, 4, 4, about 1.2 **19.** 0.7; 10, 11.6, 11.6, 12.1, about 4.2; about 11.9, 11.6, 11.6, 1.9, about 0.67 **21.** 152; 78.8, 71.5, 66, 92, about 25.1; about 70.7, 71, 66, 20, about 6.0 **23.** *Sample answer:* 8, 8, 8, 8, 11, 11, 12, 12, 12

11.1 Problem Solving (pp. 748–749) **27.** about 17.8, 20, 6 and 20 **29. a.** 5 **b.** 20.2, 22, 23, 20, about 5.4; about 21.9, 23, 23, 6, about 2.1 **c.** *Sample answer:* The mean and the median increase when the outlier is removed and the range and standard deviation decrease.

11.2 Skill Practice (p. 753) **1.** transformation **3.** 18, 17, 17, 9, about 3.0; 24, 23, 23, 9, about 3.0 **5.** 78, 77, 77, 9, about 2.8; 95, 94, 94, 9, about 2.8 **7.** 56, 53, 53, 21, about 7.0; 35, 32, 32, 21, about 7.0 **9.** The standard deviation does not change when adding a constant; 10. **11.** about 61.9, 62, 58, 9, about 3.36; about 248, 248, 232, 36, about 13.4 **13.** about 98.2, 100.5, 102, 19, about 6.62; about 245.5, about 251.3, 255, 47.5, about 16.6

15. about 229, 226.5, 222, 38, about 12.0; about 206.1, about 203.9, 199.8, 34.2, about 10.8

11.2 Problem Solving (pp. 753–755) **19. a.** about 70.8, 72, 72, 8, about 2.4 **b.** about 98.8, 100, 100, 8, about 2.4 **21. a.** about 6.84, 6.89, no mode, 1.16, about 0.324 **b.** about 22.4, about 22.6, no mode, about 3.80, about 1.06 **23. a.** 75.8, about 75.4, 74.5, 9.9, about 3.0 **b.** about 23.6, about 27.7, 22.5, 23.0, about 25.8, about 22.6, about 24.9, about 23.6, about 25.3, about 22.2, about 26.2, about 24.6 **c.** about 24.3, 24.1, 23.6, 5.5, about 1.6 **d.** The effect is a multiplication transformation with a factor of $\frac{5}{9}$, along with an addition transformation of about −17.8 for the mean, median, and mode.

11.3 Skill Practice (pp. 760–761) **1.** normal curve **3.** 0.16 **5.** 0.84 **7.** 0.68 **9.** 16% **11.** 0.68 **13.** 0.9735 **15.** 0.84 **19.** 0.7257 **21.** 0.0035 **23.** 0.5 **25.** 0.0548 **27.** 0.5363 **29.** The table was interpreted incorrectly; $P(z \geq -0.8) = 1 - 0.2119 = 0.7881$.

11.3 Problem Solving (pp. 761–762) **31.** 0.16 **33. a.** −2.4, 1.6 **b.** 0.0082 **c.** 0.937; $P(z \leq 1.6) - P(z \leq -2.4)$ **35. a.** 2.4 **b.** 1.2 **c.** Lisa; in a standard normal distribution Lisa's score is higher.

Extension (p. 765) **1.** 9.6, 2.4 **3.** 13.8, about 3.1 **5.** 25.2, about 2.7 **7.** 8.8, about 2.8 **9.** 105, about 5.1 **11.** about 0.93 **13.** about 0.0013 **15.** about 0.98 **17.** about 0.9987 **19.** Yes; $P(x \leq 56) \approx 0.01$, which is less than 0.05. **21.** Yes; $P(x \geq 12) \approx 1 - P(z \leq 2.5) \approx 1 - 0.9938 = 0.0062$, which is less than 0.05.

11.4 Skill Practice (pp. 769–770) **1.** random **3.** Systematic; unbiased; the sample is representative of the customers. **5.** Random; unbiased; each student has an equal change of being selected. **7.** ±3.2% **9.** ±1.3% **11.** ±4.4% **13.** ±1.0% **15.** 1111 people **17.** 100 people **19.** 319 people **21.** 237 people **25.** about 453 people

11.4 Problem Solving (pp. 770–771) **27. a.** about ±4.8% **b.** between 9.2% and 18.8% **29.** No. *Sample answer:* Since the margin of error is ±5%, Kosta could have 49% of the votes and Murdock could have 51% of the votes. **31. a.** 47%, 53% **b.** about ±4.5% **c.** between 42.5% and 51.5%, between 48.5% and 57.5% **d.** no; 273 people

Extension (p. 773) **1.** *Sample answer:* This is a leading question. Respondents may think a "no" response means they are not supporters of city growth. **3.** *Sample answer:* Many patients may answer untruthfully because their dentist is asking the question. The information should be collected anonymously. **5.** *Sample answer:* The question assumes that the respondent is familiar with the facts of the case. Any presentation of the facts (as interpreted by the pollster) may be biased as well. It might be best then to ask the question as given only to those who reply affirmatively to the question, "Are you familiar with the facts of the Carter case?" **7.** *Sample answer:* The flaw is that Algebra 2 students are the experimental group and Algebra 1 students are the control group; the experimental and control groups should both be Algebra 2 students.

11.5 Skill Practice (p. 778) **1.** exponential **3.** $f(x) = -0.381x^2 + 1.12x + 15.7$;

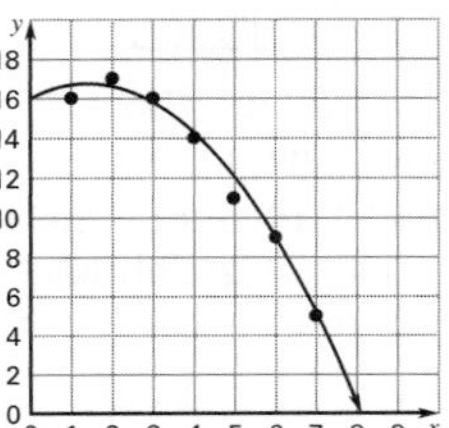

7. The x and the value of b have been interchanged; $y = 9.71(1.55)^x$.

11.5 Problem Solving (p. 779) **11.** *Sample answer:* $y = 0.00211x^3 - 0.0766x^2 + 1.26x - 0.0664$ **13. a.** quadratic **b.** $y = -2.97x^2 + 40.4x - 85.9$

c.

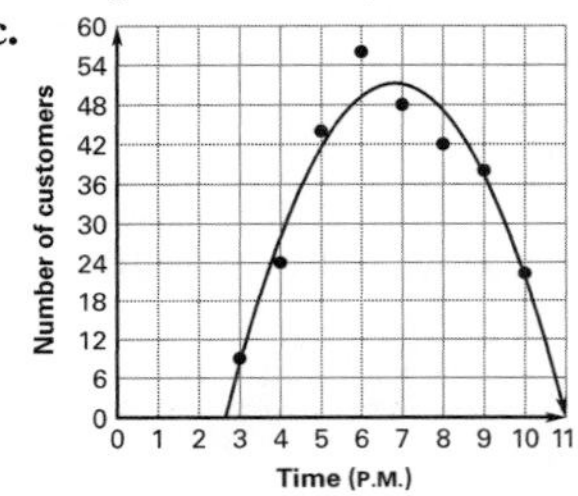

d. No; at 1:00 P.M., the function predicts a negative number of customers.

11.5 Problem Solving Workshop (p. 781) **1.** about 74°F; $y = 61.3(0.962)^x + 74$

Chapter Review (pp. 784–786) **1.** Standard deviation **3.** z-score **5.** about 84.1, 86.5, 88, 17, about 6.2 **7.** about 130, 130, 140, 52, about 16.1 **9.** about 39.8, 38, 37, 14, about 4.6; about 32.8, 31, 30, 14, about 4.6 **11.** about 38.0, about 35.4, 59.8, 62.6, about 20.8; about 1.50, about 1.39, about 2.35, about 2.46, about 0.8 **13.** about 0.0548 **15.** about 0 **17.** about 0.0179 **19.** ±2% **21.** ±1.4%

SA34

23. $y = -3.79x + 28.3$;

Chapter 12

12.1 Skill Practice (pp. 798–799) **1.** sigma notation **3.** 3, 4, 5, 6, 7, 8 **5.** 1, 4, 9, 16, 25, 36 **7.** 1, 4, 16, 64, 256, 1024 **9.** −4, −1, 4, 11, 20, 31 **11.** $-4, -2, -\frac{4}{3}, -1, -\frac{4}{5}, -\frac{2}{3}$ **13.** $\frac{2}{3}, 1, \frac{6}{5}, \frac{4}{3}, \frac{10}{7}, \frac{3}{2}$ **15.** You can write the terms as $(5 \cdot 1 - 4), (5 \cdot 2 - 4), (5 \cdot 3 - 4), (5 \cdot 4 - 4)$, $a_5 = 21$, $a_n = 5n - 4$. **17.** You can write the terms as $(-1)^1(4 \cdot 1), (-1)^2(4 \cdot 2), (-1)^3(4 \cdot 3), (-1)^4(4 \cdot 4)$, $a_5 = -20$, $a_n = (-1)^n(4 \cdot n)$. **19.** You can write the terms as $\frac{2}{3(1)}, \frac{2}{3(2)}, \frac{2}{3(3)}, \frac{2}{3(4)}$, $a_5 = \frac{2}{15}$, $a_n = \frac{2}{3n}$. **21.** You can write the terms as $\frac{1}{4}, \frac{2}{4}, \frac{3}{4}, \frac{4}{4}, \frac{5}{4}$, $a_6 = \frac{6}{4}$, $a_n = \frac{n}{4}$. **23.** You can write the terms as 0.7(1) + 2.4, 0.7(2) + 2.4, 0.7(3) + 2.4, 0.7(4) + 2.4, $a_5 = 5.9$, $a_n = 0.7n + 2.4$. **25.** You can write the terms as $1^2 + 0.2$, $2^2 + 0.2$, $3^2 + 0.2$, $4^2 + 0.2$, $a_5 = 25.2$, $a_n = n^2 + 0.2$.

29.

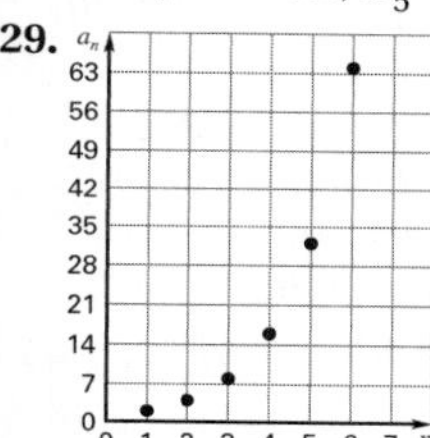

31.

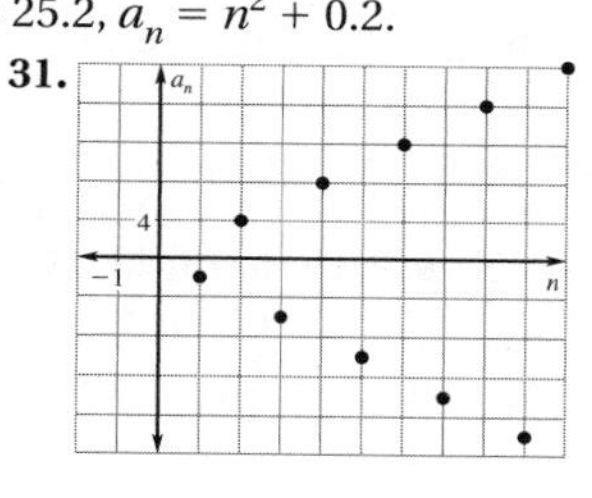

37. $\sum_{i=1}^{5} 3i + 4$ **39.** $\sum_{i=1}^{\infty} 2i - 3$ **41.** $\sum_{i=1}^{\infty} 7i - 4$ **43.** $\sum_{i=1}^{7} \frac{i}{3+i}$ **45.** 42 **47.** 100 **49.** 82 **51.** $\frac{761}{140}$ **53.** 35 **55.** 325 **57.** The lower limit is zero, so the first term should be 3; 3 + 5 + 7 + 9 + 11 + 13 = 48.

12.1 Problem Solving (pp. 799–800) **63.** 60°, 90°, 108°, 120°, about 128.57°; $T_n = 180(n - 2)$; 1800° **65.** $a_n = 2^n - 1$; 63 moves, 127 moves, 255 moves **67. a.** 15 balls **b.** 35 balls **c.** Except for layer 1, there are always more balls in the same layer of the square pyramid. The difference in the number of balls is $\frac{n(n-1)}{2}$.

12.2 Skill Practice (pp. 806–807) **1.** common difference **3.** Arithmetic; there is a common difference of 3 between consecutive terms. **5.** Arithmetic; there is a common difference of 9 between consecutive terms. **7.** Arithmetic; there is a common difference of 0.5 between consecutive terms. **9.** Not arithmetic; there is not a common difference between consecutive terms. **11.** Arithmetic; there is a common difference of 1.5 between consecutive terms. **13.** $a_n = -1 + 6n$; 119 **15.** $a_n = -5 + 2n$; 35 **17.** $a_n = 36 - 11n$; −184 **19.** $a_n = \frac{7}{3} - \frac{1}{3}n$; $-\frac{13}{3}$ **21.** The equation for an arithmetic sequence is not correct; $a_n = a_1 + (n - 1)d$, $a_n = 37 + (n - 1)(-13)$, $a_n = 50 - 13n$.

23. $a_n = -28 + 5n$;

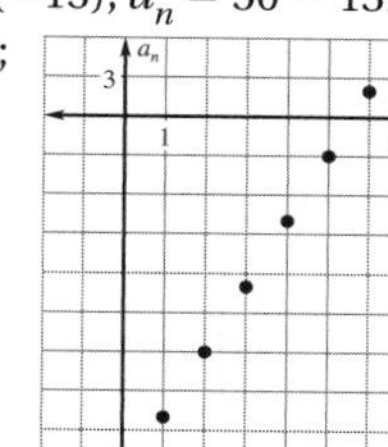

25. $a_n = 152 - 14n$;

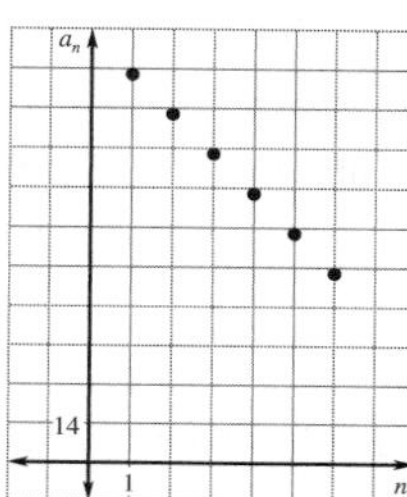

31. $a_n = 9 + 5n$ **33.** $a_n = 22 - 4n$ **35.** $a_n = 13 + 2n$ **37.** $a_n = \frac{15}{4} + \frac{9}{4}n$ **41.** −96 **43.** 2585 **45.** 315 **47.** 132 **49.** $a_n = -3 + 5n$ **51.** $a_n = -1 - 2n$ **53.** False. *Sample answer:* Doubling the common difference alone does not double the sum. **55.** 12 **57.** 25 **59.** 15 **61.** 22,500

12.2 Problem Solving (pp. 808–809) **63. a.** $a_n = 6n$ **b.** 271 cells **65. a.** $a_n = -4 + 8n$ **b.** 576 blocks **67.** $100

12.3 Skill Practice (pp. 814–815) **1.** common ratio **3.** Not geometric; there is no common ratio. **5.** Geometric; there is a common ratio of $\frac{1}{6}$. **7.** Not geometric; there is no common ratio. **9.** Geometric; there is a common ratio of $\frac{1}{2}$. **11.** Geometric; there is a common ratio of −3. **13.** Not geometric; there is no common ratio. **15.** $a_n = (-4)^{n-1}$; 4096

SELECTED ANSWERS

SELECTED ANSWERS

17. $a_n = 4(6)^{n-1}$; 186,624 **19.** $a_n = 2\left(\frac{3}{4}\right)^{n-1}$; $\frac{729}{2048}$ **21.** $a_n = 4\left(\frac{1}{2}\right)^{n-1}$; $\frac{1}{16}$ **23.** $a_n = -2(0.4)^{n-1}$; -0.008192 **25.** $a_n = 5(-2.8)^{n-1}$; 2409.45152 **29.** $a_n = -2(6)^{n-1}$;

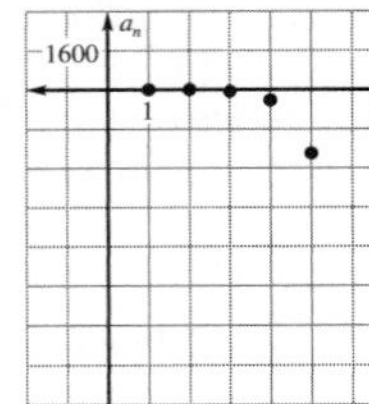

31. $a_n = 30\left(\frac{1}{2}\right)^{n-1}$;

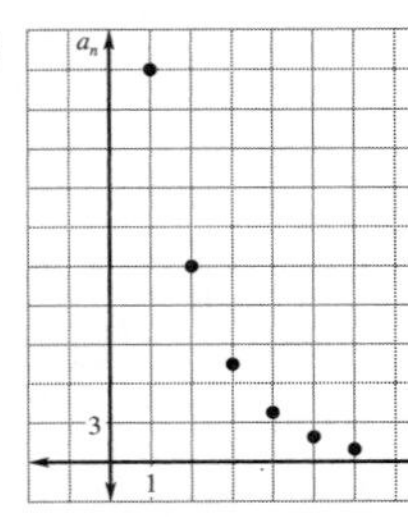

37. The exponent should be $n - 1$ instead of n; $a_n = 3(2)^{n-1}$. **39.** $a_n = 3(2)^{n-1}$ or $a_n = 3(-2)^{n-1}$ **41.** $a_n = \left(-\frac{1}{4}\right)(4)^{n-1}$ **43.** $a_n = -80\left(\frac{1}{2}\right)^{n-1}$ or $a_n = -80\left(-\frac{1}{2}\right)^{n-1}$ **45.** $a_n = 6(3)^{n-1}$ **47.** $a_n = \frac{32}{27}\left(\frac{3\sqrt[3]{12}}{4}\right)^{n-1}$ **49.** 131,070 **51.** $\frac{1365}{256}$ **53.** 838,861 **55.** *Sample answer:* $\frac{100}{31}, \frac{200}{31}, \frac{400}{31}, \frac{800}{31}, \frac{1600}{31}$

12.3 Problem Solving (pp. 815–817) **57. a.** $a_n = 5(2)^{n-1}$ **b.** 75 skydivers **59. a.** $a_n = 1024\left(\frac{1}{2}\right)^{n-1}$ **b.** 11. *Sample answer:* On the 11th pass, there is only 1 term to choose from so it must be the answer **61. a.** $a_n = 19{,}000 + 1000n$, arithmetic; $b_n = 20{,}000(1.04)^{n-1}$, geometric

b.

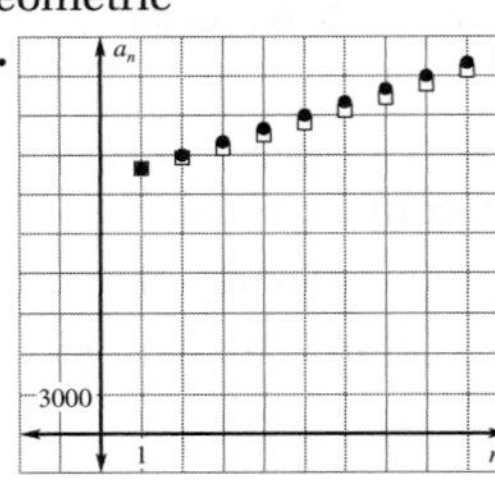

c. Company A: \$590,000; Company B: about \$595,562 **d.** 19 yr

12.4 Skill Practice (pp. 823–824) **1.** partial sum **3.** $S_1 = 0.5$, $S_2 \approx 0.67$, $S_3 \approx 0.72$, $S_4 \approx 0.74$, $S_5 \approx 0.75$; S_n appears to be approaching 0.75.

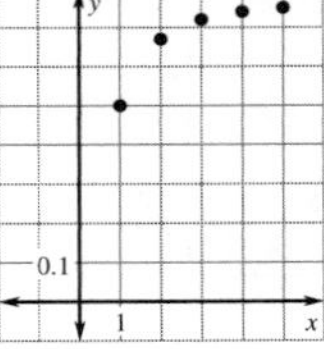

5. $S_1 = 4$, $S_2 = 6.4$, $S_3 = 7.84$, $S_4 \approx 8.71$, $S_5 \approx 9.22$; S_n appears to be approaching 10.

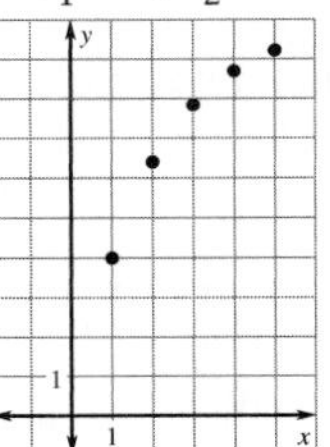

7. 10 **9.** no sum **11.** $\frac{12}{5}$ **13.** $\frac{63}{17}$ **15.** no sum **17.** $\frac{7}{10}$ **19.** Since $r > 1$, the infinite geometric series has no sum. **21.** $\frac{1}{2}$ **23.** 18 **25.** $\frac{4}{9}$ **27.** $\frac{625}{999}$ **29.** $\frac{130{,}000}{999}$ **31.** $\frac{5}{18}$ **33.** $\frac{0.9}{1 - 0.1} = \frac{0.9}{0.9} = 1$

12.4 Problem Solving (pp. 824–825) **37.** 70 ft **41. a.** 12 ft; 9 ft **b.** $\sum_{i=1}^{\infty} 12(0.75)^{i-1}$ **c.** 56 ft **d.** $\frac{2(0.75h)}{1 - 0.75} + h = 7h$

12.5 Skill Practice (pp. 830–831) **1.** iteration **3.** 1, 4, 7, 10, 13 **5.** −1, −6, −11, −16, −21 **7.** 2; 5; 26; 677; 458,330 **9.** 2, 8, 10, 18, 22 **11.** 2, 3, 6, 18, 108 **13.** $a_1 = 21$, $a_n = a_{n-1} - 7$ **15.** $a_1 = 4$, $a_n = -3a_{n-1}$ **17.** $a_1 = 44$, $a_n = \frac{1}{4}a_{n-1}$ **19.** $a_1 = 54$, $a_n = a_{n-1} - 11$ **21.** $a_1 = 16$, $a_2 = 9$, $a_n = a_{n-2} - a_{n-1}$ **23.** The rule does not work for all of the terms of the sequence; $a_1 = 5$, $a_2 = 2$, $a_n = a_{n-2} - a_{n-1}$. **25.** −4, −14, −64 **27.** −2, −4, −5 **29.** 5, 21, 437 **31.** 2, 4, 14 **35.** $a_1 = 1$, $a_2 = 2$, $a_n = 4(a_{n-2} + a_{n-1})$ **37.** $a_1 = 2$, $a_2 = 5$, $a_n = 3a_{n-2} + a_{n-1}$ **39.** $a_1 = -3$, $a_2 = -2$, $a_n = -1(a_{n-2} + a_{n-1})$ **41.** *Sample answer:* If the first two iterates are 2, the given rule must not be a function.

12.5 Problem Solving (pp. 832–833) **43. a.** $a_1 = 5000$, $a_n = 0.8a_{n-1} + 500$; 3524 fish **b.** The population of the lake approaches 2500 fish.

SA36

45. $a_1 = 2000$, $a_n = 1.014a_{n-1} - 100$; 24 mo. *Sample answer:* As long Gladys does not add anything to her credit card and continues her payments, her 24th payment will only be \$62.14.

47. a. $a_1 = 20$, $a_n = 0.7\,a_{n-1} + 20$ **b.** $66\frac{2}{3}$ mg
c. The maintenance level of the drug doubles as well; $a_1 = 20$, $a_n = 0.7\,(2a_{n-1}) + 2(20)$.

12.5 Problem Solving Workshop (p. 835)
1. The sequence approaches 400. **3.** The number of members approaches 15,000. **5.** *Sample answer:* 2% of the books are lost of discarded so 98% are retained; $a_n = 0.98a_{n-1} + 1150$.

Extension (p. 837)
1. Basis Step:
Check that the formula works for $n = 1$.
$2(1) - 1 = 1^2 \rightarrow 1 = 1$ ✓
Inductive Step:
Assume that $1 + 3 + 5 + \ldots + (2k - 1) = k^2$.
Show that $1 + 3 + 5 + \ldots + (2k - 1) + (2(k + 1) - 1)$ $= (k + 1)^2$.
$1 + 3 + 5 + \ldots + (2k - 1) + (2(k + 1) - 1)$
$= k^2 + (2(k + 1) - 1)$
$= k^2 + 2k + 2 - 1$
$= k^2 + 2k + 1$
$= (k + 1)^2$ ✓
3. Basis Step:
Check that the formula works for $n = 1$.
$2^{1-1} = 2^1 - 1 \rightarrow 2^0 = 2 - 1 \rightarrow 1 = 1$ ✓
Inductive Step:
Assume that $1 + 2 + 2^2 + 2^3 + \ldots + 2^{k-1} = 2^k - 1$.
Show that $1 + 2 + 2^2 + 2^3 + \ldots + 2^{k-1} + 2^{(k-1)-1}$ $= 2^{k+1} - 1$.
$1 + 2 + 2^2 + 2^3 + \ldots + 2^{k-1} + 2^{(k-1)-1}$
$= (2^k - 1) + 2^{(k+1)-1}$
$= 2^k - 1 + 2^k$
$= 2(2^k) - 1$
$= 2^{k+1} - 1$ ✓

Chapter Review (pp. 840–842) **1.** terms **3.** explicit **5.** 133 **7.** 153 **9.** $a_n = 11 - 3n$ **11.** $a_n = 3 + 6n$ **13.** −403 **15.** 1200 **17.** $a_n = 256\left(\frac{1}{4}\right)^{n-1}$ **19.** $a_n = 144\left(\frac{1}{3}\right)^{n-1}$ or $a_n = 144\left(-\frac{1}{3}\right)^{n-1}$ **21.** 4088 **23.** $\frac{635}{8}$ **25.** 4 **27.** −0.4 **29.** $\frac{182}{333}$ **31.** $\frac{388}{495}$ **33.** 8, 40, 200, 1000, 5000 **35.** $a_1 = 6$, $a_n = 3a_{n-1}$ **37.** $a_1 = 7$, $a_n = a_{n-1} + 6$

Cumulative Review (pp. 848–849)

1.
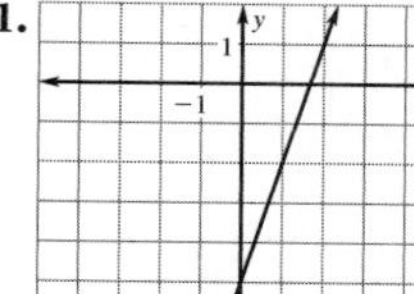

3.
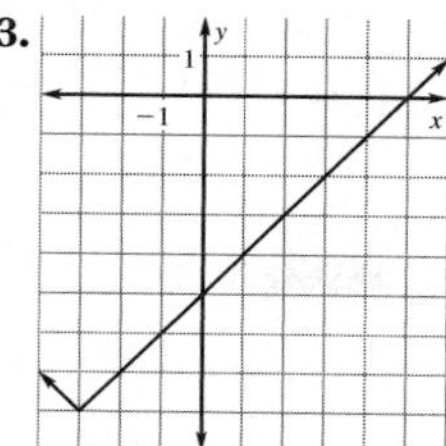

5.
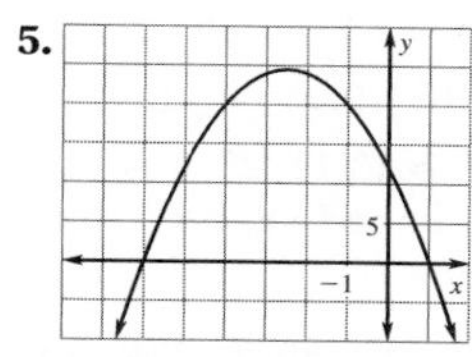

7.
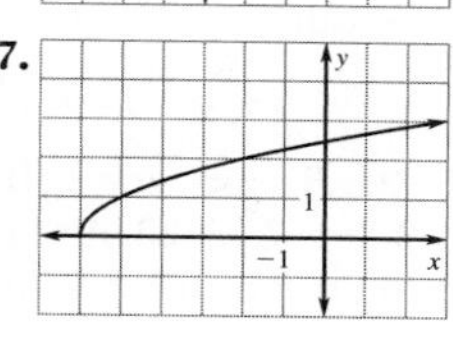

9.
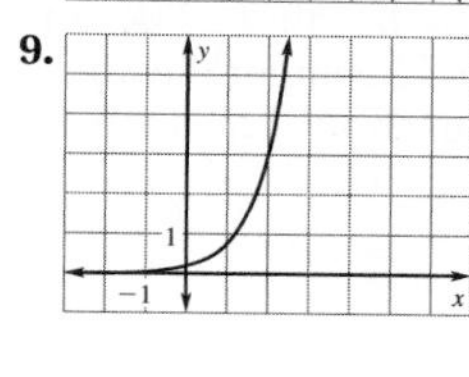

11.
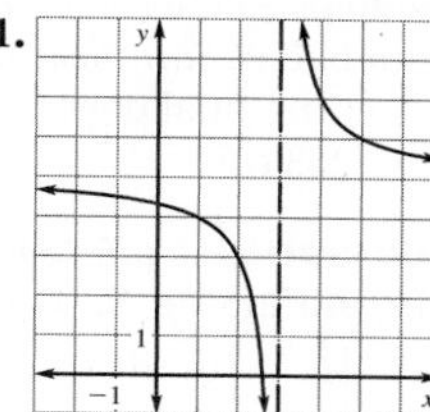

13. 13 **15.** 360 **17.** $y = \frac{18}{x}$; $-\frac{9}{4}$ **19.** $y = \frac{\frac{1}{2}}{x}$; $-\frac{1}{16}$

21.
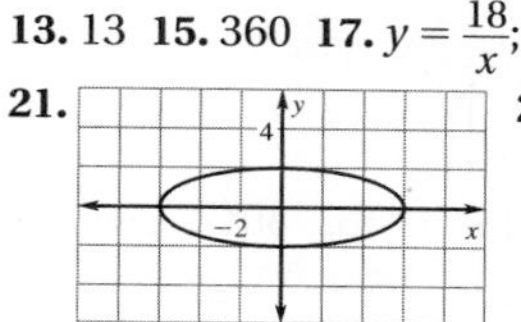

23.
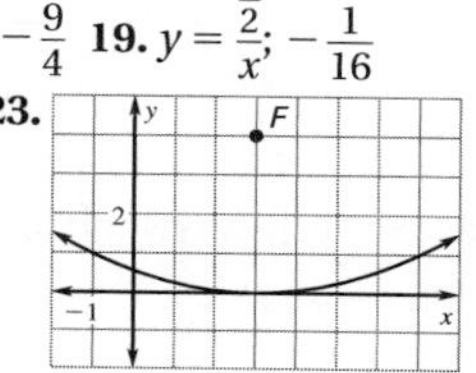

25. 524,160 **27.** 1 **29.** 0.15 **31.** about 12.857, 11, 11, 11, about 3.603 **33.** about 215.571, 216, 216, 25, about 8.086 **35.** about 88.857, 92, no mode, 28, about 8.967 **37.** 273 **39.** about 2.977 **41.** $a_n = -11 + 4n$, $a_1 = -7$, $a_n = a_{n-1} + 4$ **43.** $a_n = 3(4)^{n-1}$, $a_1 = 3$, $a_n = 4a_{n-1}$ **45.** 5 in. **47.** in 5 yr **49.** about 0.727 **51.** $a_n = 29{,}400 + 1600n$; \$43,800

Chapter 13

13.1 Skill Practice (pp. 856–857) **1.** The angle formed by the line of sight to an object and a line parallel to the ground. **3.** $\sin\theta = \frac{12}{13}$, $\cos\theta = \frac{5}{13}$, $\tan\theta = \frac{12}{5}$, $\csc\theta = \frac{13}{12}$, $\sec\theta = \frac{13}{5}$, $\cot\theta = \frac{5}{12}$
5. $\sin\theta = \frac{8}{11}$, $\cos\theta = \frac{\sqrt{57}}{11}$, $\tan\theta = \frac{8\sqrt{57}}{57}$, $\csc\theta = \frac{11}{8}$, $\sec\theta = \frac{11\sqrt{57}}{57}$, $\cot\theta = \frac{\sqrt{57}}{8}$

7. $\sin\theta = \frac{\sqrt{115}}{14}$, $\cos\theta = \frac{9}{14}$, $\tan\theta = \frac{\sqrt{115}}{9}$, $\csc\theta = \frac{14\sqrt{115}}{115}$, $\sec\theta = \frac{14}{9}$, $\cot\theta = \frac{9\sqrt{115}}{115}$ **9.** $\cos\theta = \frac{\sqrt{11}}{6}$, $\tan\theta = \frac{5\sqrt{11}}{11}$, $\csc\theta = \frac{6}{5}$, $\sec\theta = \frac{6\sqrt{11}}{11}$, $\cot\theta = \frac{\sqrt{11}}{5}$ **11.** $\sin\theta = \frac{7\sqrt{58}}{58}$, $\cos\theta = \frac{3\sqrt{58}}{58}$, $\csc\theta = \frac{\sqrt{58}}{7}$, $\sec\theta = \frac{\sqrt{58}}{3}$, $\cot\theta = \frac{3}{7}$ **13.** $\sin\theta = \frac{\sqrt{119}}{12}$, $\cos\theta = \frac{5}{12}$, $\tan\theta = \frac{\sqrt{119}}{5}$, $\csc\theta = \frac{12\sqrt{119}}{119}$, $\cot\theta = \frac{5\sqrt{119}}{119}$ **17.** $x = 8\sqrt{3}$, $y = 16$ **19.** $x = 4\sqrt{3}$, $y = 8\sqrt{3}$ **21.** $B = 55°$, $a \approx 9.18$, $b \approx 13.11$ **23.** $A = 72°$, $a \approx 22.83$, $b \approx 7.42$ **25.** $A = 15°$, $b \approx 55.98$, $c \approx 57.96$ **27.** $B = 26°$, $a \approx 65.61$, $c \approx 73.0$

13.1 Problem Solving (pp. 857–858) **31.** about 63.4 cm **33.** About 652 ft. *Sample answer:* The larger the angle the deeper the final depth. **35. a.** about 22,818 mi **b.** about 7263 mi

13.2 Skill Practice (pp. 862–863)
1. origin, initial side **3.** B **5.** A
7. **9.**

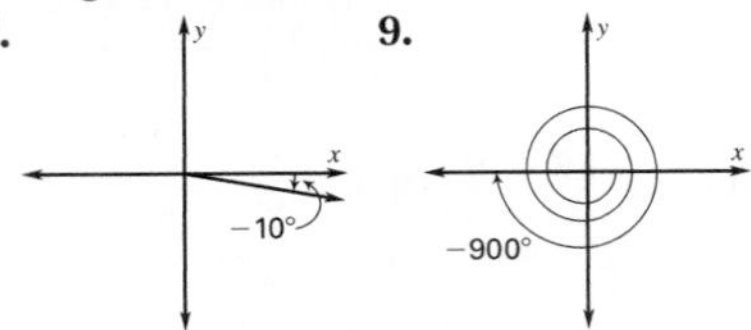

15–21. Sample answers are given. **15.** 430°, −290° **17.** 235°, −485° **19.** $\frac{\pi}{2}$, $-\frac{3\pi}{2}$ **21.** $\frac{10\pi}{9}$, $-\frac{8\pi}{9}$ **23.** $\frac{2\pi}{9}$ **25.** $-\frac{13\pi}{9}$ **27.** 20° **29.** 900° **33.** about 3.93 m, about 5.89 m^2 **35.** about 31.4 ft, about 188 ft^2 **37.** about 118 in., about 1470 in.^{2} **39.** $\frac{1}{2}$ **41.** $\frac{\sqrt{3}}{3}$ **43.** about 2.41 **45.** about 0.975

13.2 Problem Solving (pp. 864–865) **49.** 72,000°, 400π **51. a.** $\frac{\pi}{2}$ **b.** about 45.6 ft **53. a.** about 16.5 in. **b.** 360°. *Sample answer:* Since each step has a central angle of $\frac{\pi}{8}$ and there are 16 steps, the staircase will cover $16\left(\frac{\pi}{8}\right)$ or 2π, which is equivalent to 360°. **c.** about 5195.4 in.^{2}

13.3 Skill Practice (pp. 870–871) **1.** quadrantal angle **3.** $\sin\theta = \frac{15}{17}$, $\cos\theta = \frac{8}{17}$, $\tan\theta = \frac{15}{8}$, $\csc\theta = \frac{17}{15}$, $\sec\theta = \frac{17}{8}$, $\cot\theta = \frac{8}{15}$ **5.** $\sin\theta = -\frac{24}{25}$, $\cos\theta = -\frac{7}{25}$, $\tan\theta = \frac{24}{7}$, $\csc\theta = -\frac{25}{24}$, $\sec\theta = -\frac{25}{7}$, $\cot\theta = \frac{7}{24}$

7. $\sin\theta = -\frac{\sqrt{2}}{2}$, $\cos\theta = \frac{\sqrt{2}}{2}$, $\tan\theta = -1$, $\csc\theta = -\sqrt{2}$, $\sec\theta = \sqrt{2}$, $\cot\theta = -1$ **9.** $\sin\theta = -\frac{5\sqrt{34}}{34}$, $\cos\theta = -\frac{3\sqrt{34}}{34}$, $\tan\theta = \frac{5}{3}$, $\csc\theta = -\frac{\sqrt{34}}{5}$, $\sec\theta = -\frac{\sqrt{34}}{3}$, $\cot\theta = \frac{3}{5}$ **13.** $\sin\theta = 1$, $\cos\theta = 0$, $\tan\theta =$ undefined, $\csc\theta = 1$, $\sec\theta =$ undefined, $\cot\theta = 0$ **15.** $\sin\theta = -1$, $\cos\theta = 0$, $\tan\theta =$ undefined, $\csc\theta = -1$, $\sec\theta =$ undefined, $\cot\theta = 0$
17. 30° **19.** 10°

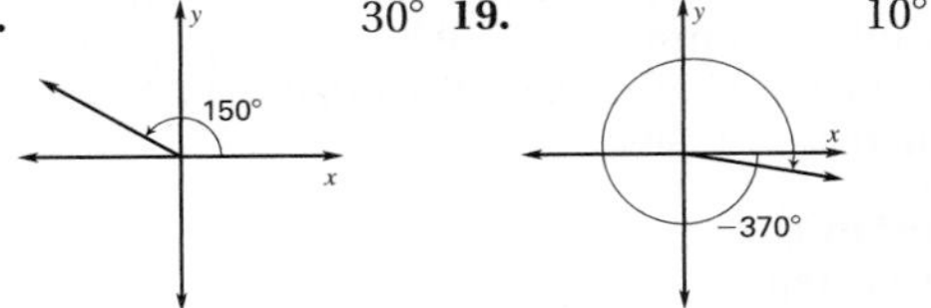

25. $\sqrt{3}$ **27.** $-\frac{2\sqrt{3}}{3}$ **29.** $\frac{\sqrt{3}}{3}$ **31.** $\frac{2\sqrt{3}}{3}$ **33.** $\tan\theta = \frac{\sin\theta}{\cos\theta}$; $\sin 90° = 1$ and $\cos 90° = 0$ so $\tan 90°$ is undefined because you cannot divide by zero but $\cot\theta = \frac{0}{1} = 0$.

13.3 Problem Solving (pp. 871–872) **35.** about 10 ft **37.** About 104 ft; no. *Sample answer:* If your starting height above the ground is not doubled, the entire height is not doubled.

39. a.

Angle of sprinkler, θ	25°	30°	35°	40°	45°
Horizontal distance water travels, d	15.0	16.9	18.4	19.2	19.5

Angle of sprinkler, θ	50°	55°	60°	65°
Horizontal distance water travels, d	19.2	18.4	16.9	15.0

b. 45°; since $\frac{v^2}{32}$ is constant, the maximum distance traveled will occur when $\sin 2\theta$ is as large as possible. The maximum value of sine 2θ occurs when $2\theta = 90°$, that is, when $\theta = 45°$.
c. The distances are the same.

13.4 Skill Practice (p. 878) **1.** inverse **3.** $\frac{\pi}{2}$, 90° **5.** $\frac{\pi}{2}$, 90° **7.** $\frac{\pi}{3}$, 60° **9.** $-\frac{\pi}{6}$, −30° **13.** about 1.20, about 69.0° **15.** about 1.98, about 113.6° **17.** about −0.20, about −11.5° **19.** about 0.14, about 8.1° **21.** about 206.7° **23.** about 252.6° **25.** about 284.5° **27.** about 38.7° **29.** 120° **31.** *Sample answer:* 600°

13.4 Problem Solving (pp. 879–880)
35. about 53°

100 ft
90 − 10 = 80 ft
θ

37. About 32.9°; about 46.4 ft. *Sample answer:* The pile is 15 feet high and the angle of repose is about 32.9°, the base of the right triangle formed is about 23.2 feet. Since this represents the radius of the pile, you need to multiply by 2 to get the diameter.
39. $\theta = \tan^{-1}\left(\frac{44t}{100}\right)$

13.5 Skill Practice (pp. 886–887) **1.** two angle measures and the length of a side, or the lengths of two sides and the measure of an angle opposite one of the two sides **3.** SSA; one triangle **5.** SSA; no triangle **7.** ASA; one triangle **9.** SSA; no triangle **11.** SSA; one triangle **13.** $A \approx 37.6°$, $B \approx 38.4°$, $a \approx 15.7$ **15.** $B = 65°$, $a \approx 23.8$, $b \approx 32.2$ **17.** $C = 95°$, $a \approx 17.6$, $b \approx 37.8$ **19.** $B = 119°$, $a \approx 6.5$, $c \approx 8.5$ **21.** $B \approx 54.1°$, $C \approx 87.9°$, $c \approx 30.8$, or $B \approx 125.9°$, $C \approx 16.1°$, $c \approx 8.6$ **23.** $B \approx 37.5°$, $C \approx 28.5°$, $c \approx 7.8$ **25.** $C = 99°$, $a \approx 62.7$, $c \approx 82.0$ **27.** The sides were not paired with their opposite angles; $\frac{\sin C}{5} = \frac{\sin 55°}{6}$, $\sin C = \frac{\sin 55°}{6} \approx 0.6826$, $C \approx 43.0°$. **29.** about 41.0 **31.** about 291.9 **33.** about 18.9 **35.** about 176.2 **37.** about 285.6 **39.** about 205.3

13.5 Problem Solving (pp. 887–888)
43. about 193.6 ft, about 212.9 ft
45. a. **b.** third side: about 70.4 ft; other angles: about 47.6°, about 74.4° **c.** 9 bags **47. a.** about 152.9 m

13.6 Skill Practice (pp. 892–893) **1.** semiperimeter **3.** law of cosines **5.** law of sines **7.** law of sines **9.** $B \approx 30.7°$, $C \approx 35.3°$, $a \approx 41.1$ **11.** $A \approx 110.4°$, $C \approx 44.6°$, $b \approx 3.60$ **13.** $A \approx 30.3°$, $B \approx 128.4°$, $C \approx 21.3°$ **15.** $A \approx 55.7°$, $B \approx 76.3°$, $c \approx 15.3$ **17.** $A \approx 42.6°$, $B \approx 11.7°$, $C \approx 125.7°$ **19.** $A \approx 36.7°$, $B \approx 47.3°$, $c \approx 58.2$ **21.** about 104 **23.** about 1108.6 **25.** about 25 **27.** about 131.9 **29.** about 2259.7 **31.** about 994.3 **35.** Since you are looking for A the equation should be $a^2 = b^2 + c^2 - 2bc \cos A$; $18^2 = 15^2 + 10^2 - 2(15)(10) \cos A$, $A \approx \cos^{-1} 0.0033 \approx 89.8°$. **37.** $A = 45°$, $b \approx 25.2$, $c \approx 15.3$ **39.** $A \approx 68.2°$, $C \approx 21.8°$, $b \approx 16.2$ **41.** $A \approx 93.7°$, $B \approx 33.9°$, $C \approx 52.4°$

13.6 Problem Solving (pp. 893–894) **43.** about 119.6° **45.** About 19.8 acres. *Sample answer:* Find $\overline{AC}$ then find the area of $\triangle ACD$ and $\triangle ABC$ using Heron's formula. **47. a.** about 2.6 mi **b.** about 3 h 45 min **c.** About 1 h 46 min; 79.2° W of N. *Sample answer:* The angle at hiker 1 is 79.2° and you have parallel lines at each hiker pointing in the North direction. The angle at hiker 2 is then an alternate interior angle, and is congruent.

13.6 Problem Solving Workshop (p. 895)
1. about 81.9 **3.** about 4619.5 **5.** about 792.6 ft^2

Chapter Review (pp. 898–900) **1.** An angle in standard position has its vertex at the origin, and its initial side lies on the positive x-axis. **3.** unit circle **5.** *Sample answer:* The law of sines is a ratio relating the sine of an angle and its corresponding side to the other angles and corresponding sides. **7.** about 26.6 m **9.** $-\frac{4\pi}{9}$ **11.** 330° **13.** $-\sqrt{2}$ **15.** 2 **17.** about 19.5° **19.** $A \approx 31.7°$, $C \approx 44.3°$, $a \approx 13.5$ **21.** $A = 47°$, $a \approx 16.9$, $c \approx 22.1$ **23.** $A \approx 58.7°$, $C \approx 46.3°$, $b \approx 22.6$

Chapter 14

14.1 Skill Practice (pp. 912–913)
1. period **3.** $1, \frac{\pi}{2}$ **5.** 1, 2

7.
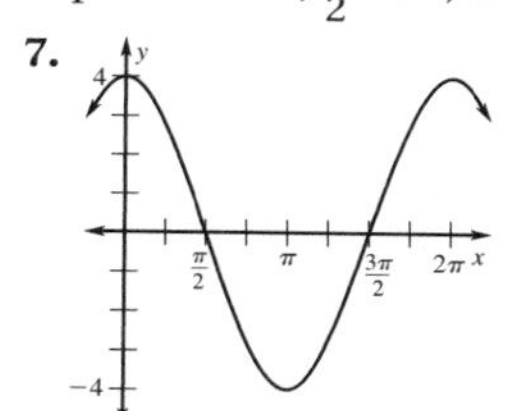

9.
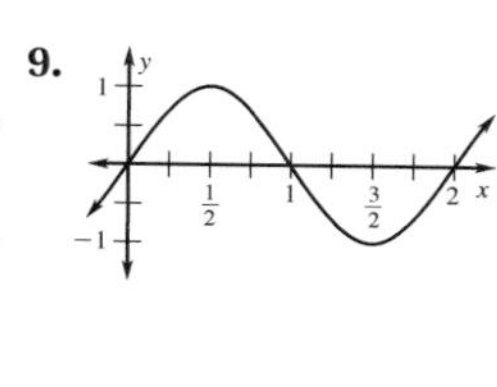

17.
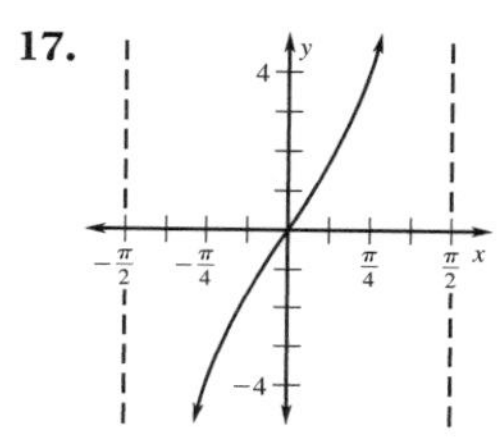

19.
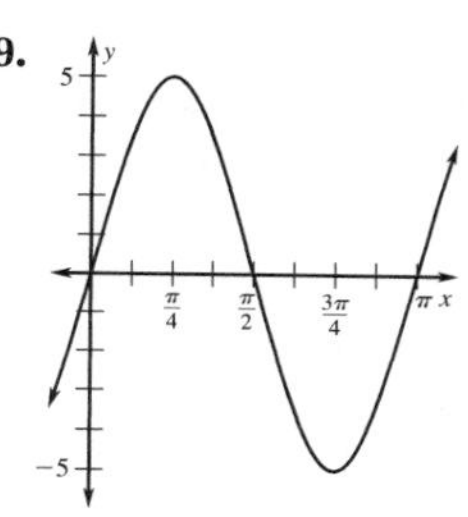

25. *Sample answer:* The rise and fall of the tides versus time.

14.1 Problem Solving (pp. 913–914)
29.
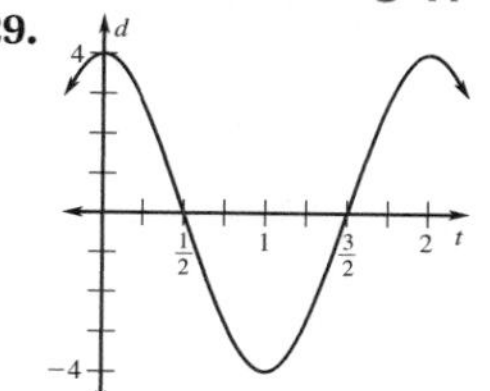
8 in.

31. a. $y = 1.75 \cos \frac{\pi}{3} t$ **b.** Since the high point occurs at $t = 0$, the cosine function best represents situation.

14.2 Skill Practice (pp. 919–921) **1.** 3 **3.** E **5.** D **7.** A

9.

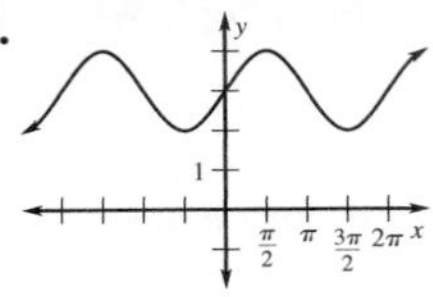

11.

23.

25.

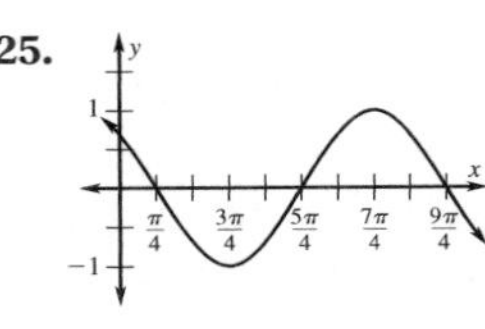

37.

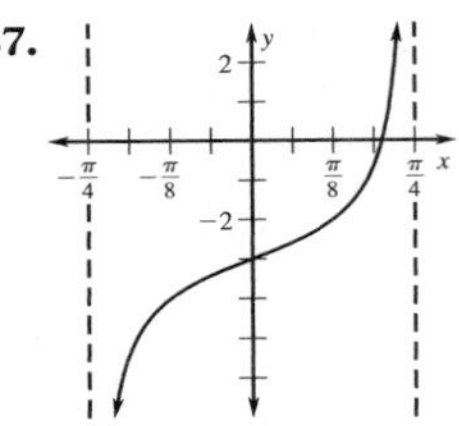

39.

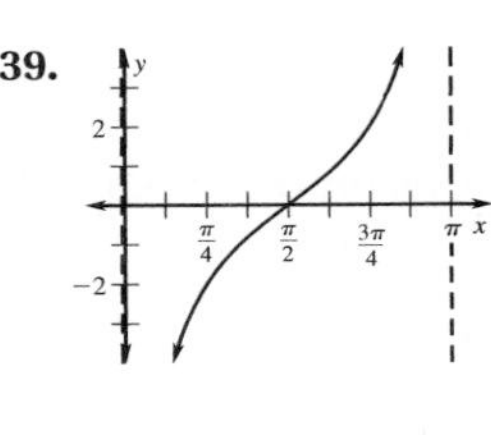

43. $y = 3 \sin (x - \pi) + 2$ **45.** $y = -\frac{1}{3} \cos \pi x - 1$

47. The graph of $y = \cos x$ can be obtained by translating the graph of $y = \sin x$ either to the left by $\frac{\pi}{2}$ or to the right $\frac{3\pi}{2}$.

14.2 Problem Solving (pp. 921–922)

51. $h = 3.75 \cos (200\pi t)$ **53. a.** $d = -300 \tan \theta + 200$

b.

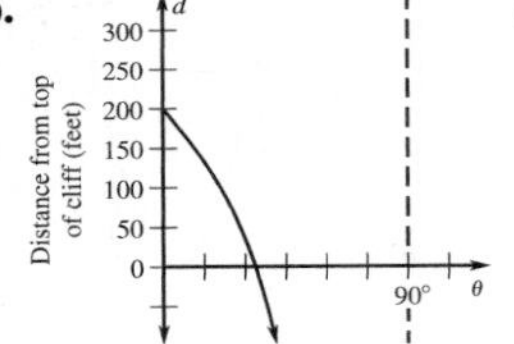

c. about 18.4°

14.3 Skill Practice (pp. 927–928) **1.** A trigonometric equation that is true for all values of θ in its domain

3. $\cos \theta = \frac{2\sqrt{2}}{3}$, $\tan \theta = \frac{\sqrt{2}}{4}$, $\csc \theta = 3$, $\sec \theta = \frac{3\sqrt{2}}{4}$, $\cot \theta = 2\sqrt{2}$ **5.** $\sin \theta = -\frac{\sqrt{11}}{6}$, $\tan \theta = -\frac{\sqrt{11}}{5}$, $\csc \theta = -\frac{6\sqrt{11}}{11}$ $\sec \theta = \frac{6}{5}$, $\cot \theta = -\frac{5\sqrt{11}}{11}$

7. $\sin \theta = \frac{5\sqrt{29}}{29}$, $\cos \theta = -\frac{2\sqrt{29}}{29}$, $\tan \theta = -\frac{5}{2}$, $\csc \theta = \frac{\sqrt{29}}{5}$, $\sec \theta = -\frac{\sqrt{29}}{2}$ **11.** $-\tan \theta$

13. $\sec \theta$ **15.** $\sin^2 x$ **17.** 1 **19.** $\sin x$ **21.** -1

23. $\tan (-x) = -\tan (x)$, so Step 1 used an incorrect substitution; $-\frac{\sin x}{\cos x} \cdot \frac{1}{\sin x} = -\frac{1}{\cos x} = -\sec x$.

25. $\sin x \csc x = \sin x \left(\frac{1}{\sin x}\right) = 1$

27. $\frac{\cos\left(\frac{\pi}{2} - \theta\right) + 1}{1 - \sin(-\theta)} = \frac{\sin \theta + 1}{1 - \sin \theta} = 1$

29. $\frac{\csc^2 \theta - \cot^2 \theta}{1 - \sin^2 \theta} = \frac{1}{\cos^2 \theta} = \sec^2 \theta$

31. $\sin x + \cos x \cot x = \sin x + \cos x \left(\frac{\cos x}{\sin x}\right) = \sin x + \frac{\cos^2 x}{\sin x} = \frac{\sin^2 x + \cos^2 x}{\sin x} = \frac{1}{\sin x} = \csc x$

33. $\frac{1 + \cos x}{\sin x} + \frac{\sin x}{1 + \cos x} = \frac{1 + 2\cos x + \cos^2 x + \sin^2 x}{(1 + \cos x)(\sin x)} = \frac{1 + 2\cos x + 1}{(1 + \cos x)(\sin x)} = \frac{2 + 2\cos x}{(1 + \cos x)(\sin x)} = \frac{2(1 + \cos x)}{(1 + \cos x)(\sin x)} = \frac{2}{\sin x} = 2 \csc x$

35. $\sin x$, $\csc x$, $\tan x$, $\cot x$; $\cos x$, $\sec x$

37. $\ln |\tan \theta| = \ln \left|\frac{\sin \theta}{\cos \theta}\right| = \ln |\sin \theta| - \ln |\cos \theta|$

14.3 Problem Solving (pp. 929–930)

39. $\sec x \tan x - \sin x = \frac{1}{\cos x} \cdot \frac{\sin x}{\cos x} - \sin x = \frac{\sin x}{\cos^2 x} - \frac{\sin x \cos^2 x}{\cos^2 x} = \frac{\sin x - \sin x \cos^2 x}{\cos^2 x} = \frac{\sin x (1 - \cos^2 x)}{\cos^2 x} = \frac{\sin x (\sin^2 x)}{\cos^2 x} = \sin x \tan^2 x$

41. a. $r = \frac{1.069}{1 - 0.97 \cos \theta}$

b.

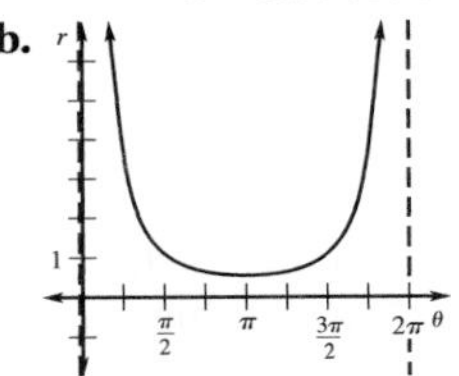

c.

θ	0	$\frac{\pi}{4}$	$\frac{\pi}{2}$	$\frac{3\pi}{4}$	π	$\frac{5\pi}{4}$	$\frac{3\pi}{2}$
r	35.6	3.40	1.07	0.634	0.543	0.634	1.07

about 50,500,000 mi, about 3,310,800,000 mi

43. The value of $\tan \theta$ increases as the value of $\sin \theta$ increases and the value of $\cos \theta$ decreases; $0 \le \theta \le \frac{\pi}{2}$, $2\pi \le \theta \le \frac{5\pi}{2}$, $4\pi \le \theta \le \frac{9\pi}{2}$, and so on.

14.4 Skill Practice (pp. 935–936) **1.** A trigonometric identity is true for all real values of x where a trigonometric equation is only true for some specific value(s) of x. **3.** $2 + 3 \cos (4\pi) - 5 = 2 + 3(1) - 5 = 0$

5. $12 \sin^2\left(\frac{\pi}{6}\right) - 3 = 12\left(\frac{1}{2}\right)^2 - 3 = 0$

7. $2 \cos^4\left(\frac{\pi}{2}\right) - \cos^2\left(\frac{\pi}{2}\right) = 2(0)^4 - (0)^2 = 0$

9. $\frac{\pi}{6} + 2n\pi$ or $\frac{5\pi}{6} + 2n\pi$ **11.** $\frac{\pi}{6} + n\pi$

SA40

13. $\frac{\pi}{6} + n\pi$ or $\frac{5\pi}{6} + n\pi$ **17.** $\frac{\pi}{6}, \frac{7\pi}{6}$ **19.** $\frac{\pi}{4}, \frac{3\pi}{4}, \frac{5\pi}{4}, \frac{7\pi}{4}$ **21.** $\frac{\pi}{3}, \frac{2\pi}{3}, \frac{4\pi}{3}, \frac{5\pi}{3}$ **23.** When two negative values are divided, the quotient is positive; $\cos x = \frac{1}{2}, x = \frac{\pi}{3}, \frac{5\pi}{3}$. **25.** $\frac{\pi}{6} + n\pi$ **27.** $\frac{\pi}{3} + n\pi$ or $\frac{2\pi}{3} + n\pi$ **29.** $\frac{\pi}{3} + 2n\pi$ or $\pi + 2n\pi$ **31.** $\frac{\pi}{3}, \frac{\pi}{2}$ **33.** about 0.572 **35.** $\frac{5\pi}{3}$ **37.** (0, 1) **39.** $\left(\frac{\pi}{6}, \frac{\sqrt{3}}{3}\right), \left(\frac{2\pi}{3}, 3\sqrt{3}\right), \left(\frac{7\pi}{6}, \frac{\sqrt{3}}{3}\right), \left(\frac{5\pi}{3}, 3\sqrt{3}\right)$

14.4 Problem Solving (pp. 936–937) **41.** July 26 and November 26 **43. a.** $S = \frac{27}{4} + \frac{27}{32}\left(\frac{\sqrt{3} - \cos\theta}{\sin\theta}\right)$

b. *Sample:*

θ	16	17	18	19
S	9.1095	8.9887	8.8825	8.7884

θ	120	121	122	123
S	8.9246	8.9619	9.0005	9.0405

about 17° and about 122°

c.

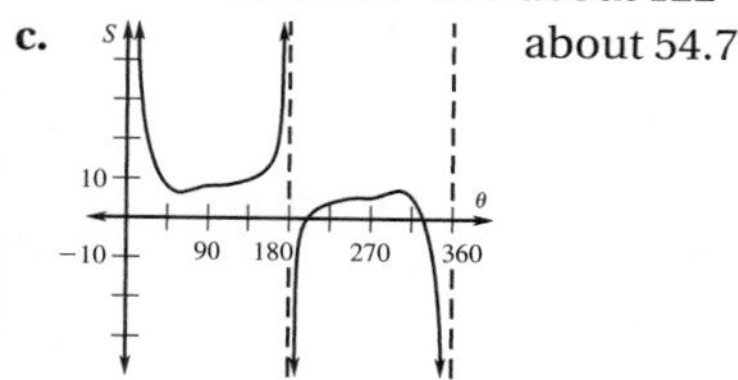

about 54.7°

14.4 Problem Solving Workshop (p. 939) **1.** about 0.987, about 3.01 **3.** about 0.298, about 0.702 **5.** about 22.6, about 37.4 **7.** 1:32 AM, 10:52 AM, 1:56 PM, 11:16 PM **9.** about 0.17 sec and about 0.83 sec

14.5 Skill Practice (pp. 944–945) **1.** The graph of a sine or cosine function **3.** *Sample answer:* $y = 3\sin 2x$ **5.** *Sample answer:* $y = -2\cos\frac{\pi}{2}x + 4$ **7.** To determine the amplitude, you must take half of the difference between the maximum and the minimum; $\frac{10 - (-6)}{2} = 8$.

9–17. Sample answers are given. **9.** $y = 6\sin\frac{1}{2}x$ **11.** $y = -\cos 3x + 4$ **13.** $y = 2\cos\frac{4}{5}\left(x - \frac{3\pi}{4}\right) + 7$ **15.** $y = 2\sin\frac{1}{4}(x + 2\pi) - 2$ **17.** $y = -6\cos\frac{3}{2}x - 6$ **21.** $y = 3\cos 4\left(x - \frac{\pi}{8}\right) + 2$;

$y = 3\cos\left(4x - \frac{\pi}{2}\right) + 2$ (Dist. property);

$y = 3\cos\left(\frac{\pi}{2} - 4x\right) + 2$ (Neg. angle identity);

$y = 3\sin 4x + 2$ (Cofunction identity)

14.5 Problem Solving (pp. 945–946) **23.** $V = 100\sin 4\pi t$ **25.** $h = -2.5 \text{ cas } \pi t + 6.5$ **27. a.** $N = 3.68\sin(0.776t - 0.703) + 20.4$ **b.** about 23,100 employees

14.6 Skill Practice (pp. 952–953) **1.** $\sin(a + b) = \sin a\cos b + \cos a\sin b$, $\sin(a - b) = \sin a\cos b - \cos a\sin b$, $\cos(a + b) = \cos a\cos b - \sin a\sin b$, $\cos(a - b) = \cos a\cos b + \sin a\sin b$, $\tan(a + b) = \frac{\tan a + \tan b}{1 - \tan a\tan b}$, $\tan(a - b) = \frac{\tan a - \tan b}{1 + \tan a\tan b}$ **3.** $\sqrt{3} - 2$ **5.** $2 - \sqrt{3}$ **7.** $\frac{\sqrt{2} - \sqrt{6}}{4}$ **9.** $\frac{\sqrt{6} - \sqrt{2}}{4}$ **11.** $\sin\left(\frac{\pi}{2} - 0\right) = \sin\frac{\pi}{2}\cos\theta - \cos\frac{\pi}{2}\sin\theta = 1(\cos\theta) - 0(\sin\theta) = \cos\theta$ **13.** $\frac{77}{85}$ **15.** $\frac{84}{85}$ **17.** $-\frac{84}{13}$ **19.** $\tan x$ **21.** $\cos x$ **23.** $\cos x$ **25.** $-\cos x$ **27.** $-\cot x$ **29.** $-\cot x$ **31.** The sign in the denominator should be negative when using the sum formula; $\frac{\tan x + \tan\frac{\pi}{4}}{1 - \tan x\tan\frac{\pi}{4}} = \frac{\tan x + 1}{1 - \tan x}$. **33.** $\frac{3\pi}{2}$ **35.** about 3.757, about 5.668 **37.** $0, \frac{\pi}{3}, \pi, \frac{5\pi}{3}$

14.6 Problem Solving (pp. 953–954) **41.** about 15 min 48 sec **43. a.** $\frac{f(1 + \tan^2 t)}{h(1 + \tan\theta\tan t)}$ **b.** $\frac{f(1 + \tan^2 0)}{h(1 + \tan\theta\tan 0)} = \frac{f}{h}$

14.7 Skill Practice (pp. 959–960) **1.** double angle **3.** $\frac{\sqrt{2 + \sqrt{3}}}{2}$ **5.** $2 - \sqrt{3}$ **7.** $\frac{\sqrt{\sqrt{2} + 2}}{2}$ **9.** $\sqrt{2} + 1$ **13.** $\frac{\sqrt{3}}{3}, -\frac{\sqrt{6}}{3}, -\frac{\sqrt{2}}{2}$ **15.** $\frac{3\sqrt{10}}{10}, -\frac{\sqrt{10}}{10}, -3$ **17.** $\frac{4}{5}, -\frac{3}{5}, -\frac{4}{3}$ **19.** $\frac{4\sqrt{5}}{9}, \frac{1}{9}, 4\sqrt{5}$ **21.** 1 **23.** $\frac{2\tan\theta}{1 + \tan\theta}$ **25.** $\cos\theta - 1$ **29.** The correct half angle formula is $\pm\sqrt{\frac{1 - \cos a}{2}}$; $\sqrt{\frac{1 - \frac{\sqrt{2}}{2}}{2}} = \sqrt{\frac{\frac{2 - \sqrt{2}}{2}}{2}} = \sqrt{\frac{2 - \sqrt{2}}{4}} = \frac{\sqrt{2 - \sqrt{2}}}{2}$ **31.** $\sin 3\theta = \sin(2\theta + \theta) = \sin 2\theta\cos\theta + \cos 2\theta\sin\theta = 2\sin\theta\cos\theta\cos\theta + (2\cos^2\theta - 1)\sin\theta = 2\sin\theta\cos^2\theta + (2\cos^2\theta - 1)\sin\theta = \sin\theta(2\cos^2\theta + 2\cos^2\theta - 1) = \sin\theta(4\cos^2\theta - 1)$ **33.** $2\sin^2 x\tan\frac{x}{2} = 2\sin^2 x\left(\frac{1 - \cos x}{\sin x}\right) = 2\sin x(1 - \cos x) = 2\sin x - 2\sin x\cos x = 2\sin x - \sin 2x$ **35.** $\cos 4\theta = \cos(2\theta + 2\theta) = \cos 2\theta\cos 2\theta - \sin 2\theta\sin 2\theta = (\cos^2\theta - \sin^2\theta)^2 - (2\sin\theta\cos\theta)^2 = \cos^4\theta - 2\cos^2\theta\sin^2\theta + \sin^4\theta - 4\sin^2\theta\cos^2\theta = \cos^4\theta - 6\sin^2\theta\cos^2\theta + \sin^4\theta$ **37.** $\frac{4\pi}{3}$ **39.** $\frac{\pi}{4}, \frac{7\pi}{4}$ **41.** $\frac{\pi}{3}, \frac{\pi}{2}, \frac{2\pi}{3}, \frac{4\pi}{3}, \frac{3\pi}{2}, \frac{5\pi}{3}$

43. The value of $\tan\theta$ increases as the value of $\sin\theta$ increases and the value of $\cos\theta$ decreases; $0 \le \theta \le \frac{\pi}{2}$, $2\pi\ \theta \le \frac{5\pi}{2}$, $4\pi\ \theta \le \frac{9\pi}{2}$, and so on.

14.7 Problem Solving (pp. 961–962)
51. $24.3° \le \theta \le 65.7°$ **53.** about 47.2°
55. a. $y = -\frac{16}{(40)^2 \cos^2 \theta}(41.75)^2 + \tan \theta\,(41.75) + 6$
b. $y = -\frac{1743.0625}{100 \cos^2 \theta} + \tan \theta\,(41.75) + 6$; about 36.7° or about 58.8° **c.** *Sample answer:* The person aims toward the basket and the ball does not bounce off the rim.

Chapter Review (pp. 965–968) **1.** cycles **3.** period **5.** frequency

7.
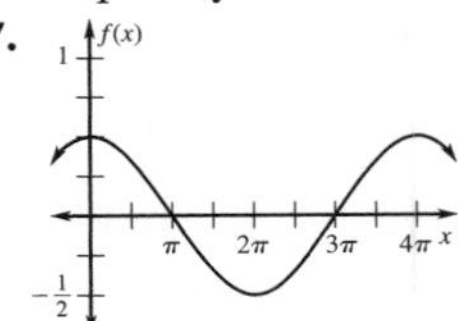

9.
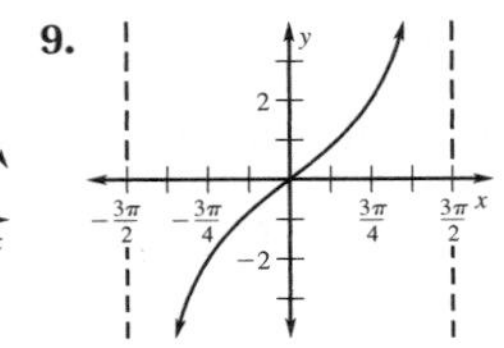

11.
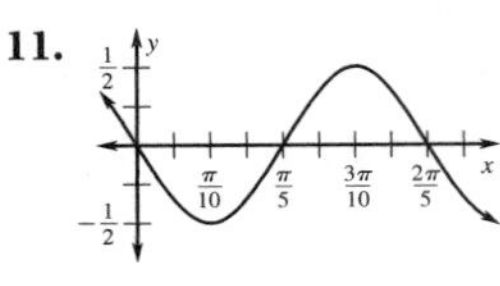

13.
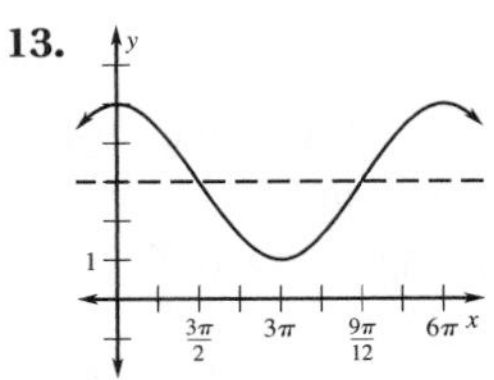

15.
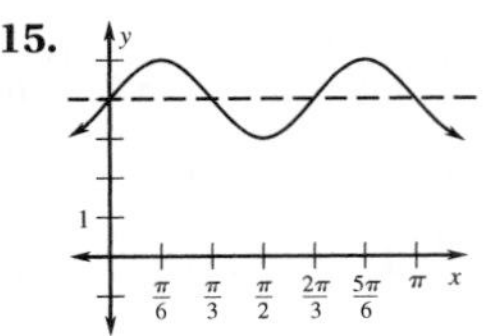

17. $\sec^3 x$ **19.** $\frac{\sin^2(-x) - 1}{\cot^2 x} = \frac{-(1 - \sin^2 x)}{\frac{\cos^2 x}{\sin^2 x}} = \frac{-\cos^2 x}{\frac{\cos^2 x}{\sin^2 x}} = -\sin^2 x$ **21.** $\frac{\pi}{3}, \frac{2\pi}{3}, \frac{4\pi}{3}, \frac{5\pi}{3}$ **23.** $\frac{\pi}{12}, \frac{\pi}{6}, \frac{\pi}{3}, \frac{5\pi}{12}, \frac{7\pi}{12}, \frac{2\pi}{3}, \frac{5\pi}{6}, \frac{11\pi}{12}, \frac{13\pi}{12}, \frac{7\pi}{6}, \frac{4\pi}{3}, \frac{17\pi}{12}, \frac{19\pi}{12}, \frac{5\pi}{3}, \frac{11\pi}{6}, \frac{23\pi}{12}$ **25.** *Sample answer:* $y = \cos \pi x - 2$ **27.** $2 + \sqrt{3}$ **29.** $-\frac{\sqrt{3}}{2}$
31. $\frac{\sqrt{2+\sqrt{3}}}{2}$ **33.** $\frac{\sqrt{2+\sqrt{3}}}{2}$ **35.** $\frac{\sqrt{3}}{2}, \frac{\sqrt{3}}{2}$

Skills Review Handbook

Operations with Positive and Negative Numbers (p. 975)
1. −6 **3.** −60 **5.** 2 **7.** 8 **9.** 44 **11.** −4 **13.** 12 **15.** −72 **17.** −2 **19.** −3 **21.** 9 **23.** 6 **25.** −15 **27.** −12 **29.** 5 **31.** 42 **33.** −17 **35.** 2

Fractions, Decimals, and Percents (p. 976) **1.** $\frac{13}{20}$ **3.** $\frac{3}{2}$ **5.** $\frac{7}{10}$ **7.** $\frac{13}{50}$ **9.** $\frac{19}{20}$ **11.** 0.25 **13.** 1.2 **15.** 0.375 **17.** 1.42 **19.** 0.3 **21.** 60% **23.** 130% **25.** 45% **27.** 80% **29.** 250%

Calculating with Percents (p. 977) **1.** 196 **3.** 38.4 **5.** 17 **7.** 1 **9.** 54% **11.** 10% **13.** 20% **15.** 2% **17.** 80 **19.** 60 **21.** 70 **23.** 8 **25.** 25% decrease **27.** 50% increase **29.** 96% increase **31.** 79% decrease

Factors and Multiples (p. 979) **1.** $2 \cdot 3 \cdot 7$ **3.** $3 \cdot 5^2$ **5.** $2 \cdot 5 \cdot 7$ **7.** $2^3 \cdot 3^2$ **9.** prime **11.** $2^3 \cdot 11$ **13.** prime **15.** 2^5 **17.** 8 **19.** 11 **21.** 4 **23.** 3 **25.** 10 **27.** 3 **29.** 1 **31.** 16 **33.** 30 **35.** 24 **37.** 6 **39.** 36 **41.** 30 **43.** 40 **45.** 891 **47.** $\frac{7}{16}$ **49.** $\frac{5}{6}$ **51.** $\frac{37}{40}$ **53.** $\frac{1}{3}$ **55.** $\frac{17}{30}$ **57.** $\frac{13}{20}$ **59.** $\frac{9}{20}$ **61.** $\frac{13}{16}$ **63.** $\frac{23}{30}$ **65.** $\frac{59}{80}$ **67.** $\frac{17}{20}$ **69.** $\frac{11}{18}$

Ratios and Proportions (p. 980) **1.** 1 to 3, 1 : 3, $\frac{1}{3}$ **3.** 5 to 4, 5 : 4, $\frac{5}{4}$ **5.** 5 to 6, 5 : 6, $\frac{5}{6}$ **7.** 1 to 1, 1 : 1, $\frac{1}{1}$ **9.** 4 to 9, 4 : 9, $\frac{4}{9}$ **11.** 7 to 1, 7 : 1, $\frac{7}{1}$ **13.** 7 **15.** 20 **17.** 2 **19.** 5 **21.** 40 **23.** 6.75 **25.** 99 **27.** 72

Converting Units of Measurement (p. 981) **1.** 6000 **3.** 5 **5.** 7.7 **7.** 16 **9.** 4000 **11.** 0.8 **13.** 6 **15.** 1.5 **17.** 3600 **19.** 3 **21.** $\frac{1}{8}$ **23.** 63,360 **25.** 2 **27.** 4000

Scientific Notation (p. 982) **1.** 6×10^{-1} **3.** 8×10^{-2} **5.** 4.08×10^1 **7.** 3.85×10^{-4} **9.** 4.1236×10^4 **11.** 4.86×10^5 **13.** 1.002×10^{-2} **15.** 7.0505×10^3 **17.** 9.85×10^3 **19.** 8.05×10^2 **21.** 5000 **23.** 0.82 **25.** 0.0032 **27.** 734,500 **29.** 1.814 **31.** 1,000,000 **33.** 0.000008 **35.** 1,870,000,000 **37.** 6,080,000 **39.** 34,010,000

Significant Digits (p. 983) **1.** 600 **3.** 81 **5.** 1.885 **7.** 4.9 **9.** 195 **11.** 0.036 **13.** 1009 **15.** 18 **17.** $17.40 **19.** 2.5 pints per student **21.** 2543 books per library **23.** $1250

Writing Algebraic Expressions (p. 984) **1.** $n + 8$ **3.** $2n$ **5.** $\frac{1}{5}n$ **7.** $5n$ **9.** $0.25n$ **11.** $n - 2$ **13.** $c - 4$ yr **15.** $x + 5$ dollars **17.** $45 - m$ min **19.** $10x$ dollars

Binomial Products (p. 985) **1.** $a^2 + 8a + 15$ **3.** $t^2 + 15t + 56$ **5.** $y^2 + 6y + 8$ **7.** $y^2 - 4y + 4$ **9.** $z^2 - 8z + 16$ **11.** $y^2 - 4y - 21$ **13.** $25x^2 - 16$ **15.** $2c^2 + 3c - 35$ **17.** $-z^2 + 49$ **19.** $16a^2 + 24a + 9$ **21.** $-x^2 - 4x + 32$ **23.** $-a^2 + 18a - 81$ **25.** $10x^2 - 21x - 10$ **27.** $-24z^2 + 22z - 3$

LCDs of Rational Expressions (p. 986) **1.** $2a^2b$ **3.** z^3 **5.** $126m$ **7.** $3y^2$ **9.** $(n + 2)(n - 2)$ **11.** $5(n + 1)$ **13.** $6(m - 3)$ **15.** $(x - 4)^2$ **17.** $2n^3(5n + 4)$ **19.** $(k + 3)^4$ **21.** $70(n + 2)$ **23.** $(a + 2)^2$ **25.** $(k - 3)(k - 2)$ **27.** $(m - 7)(m - 4)(m^2 + 5m - 45)$

SELECTED ANSWERS

The Coordinate Plane (p. 987)

1–20.

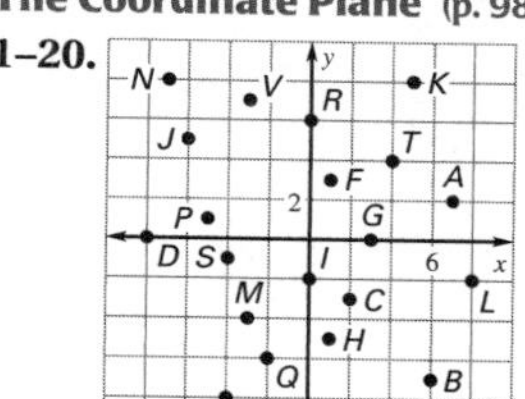

21. (2, 5) **23.** (5, −5) **25.** (4, 0) **27.** (5, 4) **29.** (4, −2) **31.** (−2, 0) **33.** (−2, 2) **35.** (2, −4) **37.** (2, −1) **39.** (−1, 5) **41.** (−4, −3) **43.** (1, −3)

Transformations (p. 989)

1. (3, −8) **3.** (−3, 11) **5.** (8, 3) **7.** (−8, −3)

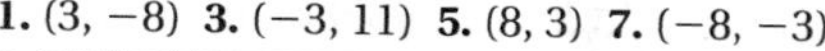

9.

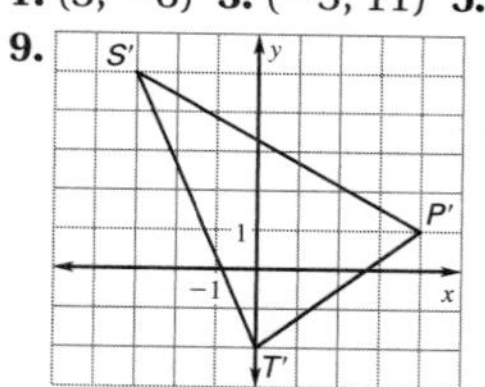

11.

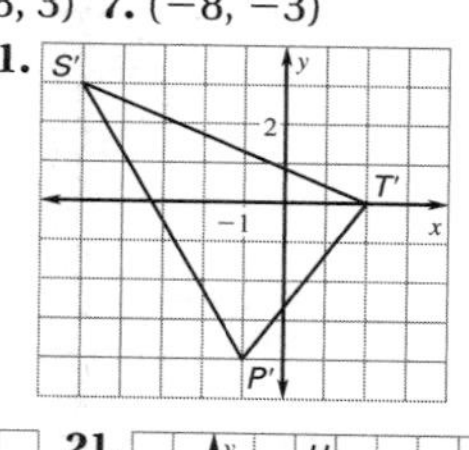

19.

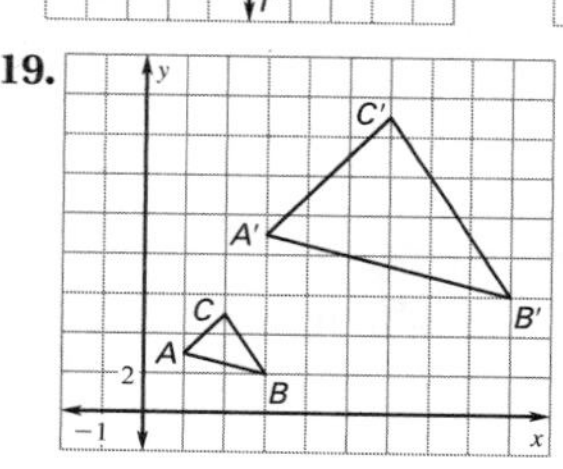

21.

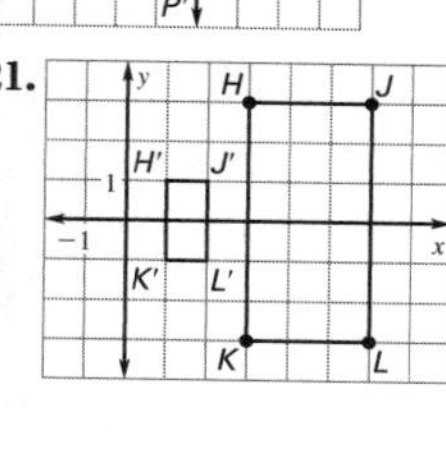

Line Symmetry (p. 990) **1.** none **3.** 1 **5.** none **7.** 2 **9.** (−4, −1) **11.** (−2, 2)

Perimeter and Area (p. 991) **1.** 10 cm, 6 cm^2 **3.** 26 in., 24 in.^{2} **5.** 48 yd, 84 yd^2 **7.** 14 m, 10.8 m^2

Circumference and Area of a Circle (p. 992)
1. $C = 10\pi$ in. or about 31 in., $A = 25\pi$ in.^{2} or about 79 in.^{2} **3.** $C = 8\pi$ in. or about 25 in., $A = 16\pi$ in.^{2} or about 50 in.^{2} **5.** $C = 24\pi$ ft or about 75 ft, $A = 144\pi$ ft^2 or about 452 ft^2 **7.** $C = 6\pi$ ft or about 19 ft, $A = 9\pi$ ft^2 or about 28 ft^2 **9.** $C = 2\pi$ cm or about 6 cm, $A = \pi$ cm^2 or about 3 cm^2 **11.** $C = 22\pi$ in. or about 69 in., $A = 121\pi$ in.^{2} or about 380 in.^{2}

Surface Area and Volume (p. 993) **1.** 158 in.^{2}, 120 in.^{3} **3.** 54 cm^2, 27 cm^3 **5.** 154π yd^2 or about 484 yd^2, 196π yd^3 or about 616 yd^3

Angle Relationships (p. 994) **1.** 39 **3.** 8 **5.** 16 **7.** 23 **9.** 29

Triangle Relationships (p. 995) **1.** 40 **3.** 60 **5.** 50 cm **7.** 12 ft **9.** 55°

Congruent and Similar Figures (p. 997) **1.** similar **3.** congruent **5.** congruent **7.** neither **9.** congruent **11.** 11.5 **13.** 14 **15.** 40 **17.** 7

More Problem Solving Strategies (p. 999) **1.** 4:15 P.M. **3.** 6 ways **5.** 40 parts **7.** 8 dimes, 5 nickels

Logical Argument (p. 1001) **1.** valid; Chain Rule **3.** invalid **5.** valid; *And* Rule **7.** valid; *Or* Rule **9.** invalid **11.** true **13.** false **15.** true **17.** true **19.** false **21.** true

Conditional Statements and Counterexamples (p. 1003)
1. If you have the equation $y = mx + b$, then you have the graph of a line; if you have the graph of a line, then you have the equation $y = mx + b$, false. **3.** If Abby finishes her homework, then she can go swimming; if Abby goes swimming, then she finished her homework, false. **5.** If $4x + 8 = 28$, then $x = 5$; if $x = 5$, then $4x + 8 = 28$, true. **7.** True; if two lines are perpendicular, then they intersect to form a right angle and if two lines intersect to form a right angle, then they are perpendicular. **9.** False; not all orange vegetables are carrots. **11.** False; the converse is not true. **13.** False; zero is neither positive nor negative. **15.** False. *Sample answer:* An octagon could have exactly 5 congruent sides. **17.** False; *A* could be in between *B* and *C* and therefore would only be 2 inches from *C*. **19.** False. *Sample answer:* Charlie could have 10 dimes.

Venn Diagrams (p. 1004)

1.

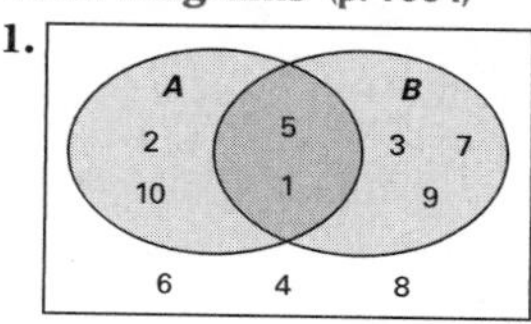

3.

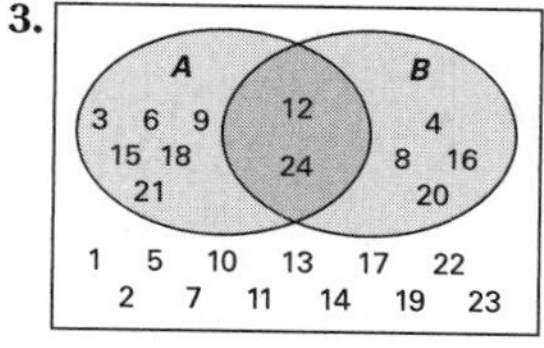

5. False. *Sample answer:* 10 is even, but it is not a multiple of 3 or 4. **7.** False; 1 is a positive odd integer and a factor of 10. **9.** True; 2 is the only even prime number.

Mean, Median, Mode, and Range (p. 1005)
1. about \$664, \$675, \$650, \$300 **3.** 685 min, 713 min, none, 611 min **5.** 48 cookies, 48 cookies, 48 cookies, 24 cookies **7.** \$9.20, \$8.90, none, \$5.85 **9.** 15 people, 14 people, 10 people and 18 people and 22 people, 25 people

Graphing Statistical Data (p. 1006) **1.** 6 P.M. **3.** 5 diners; yes **5.** 14 diners **7.** winter and summer **9.** natural gas **11.** 50 homes

13.

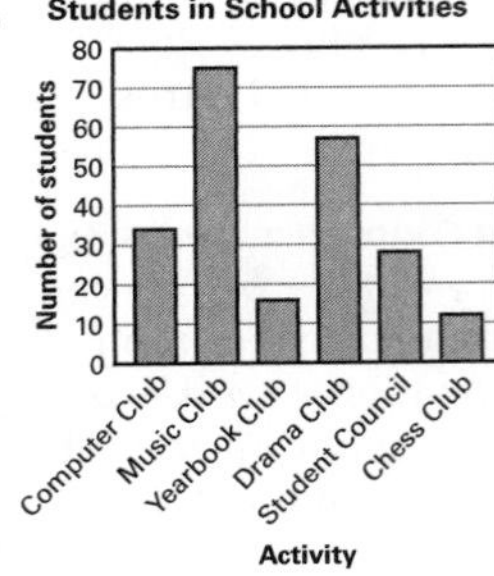

Organizing Statistical Data (p. 1009)

1.

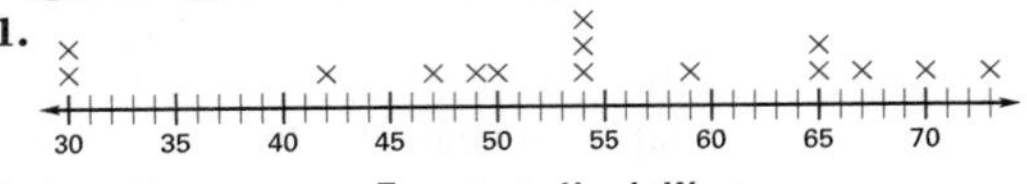

3.

Stem	Leaves
3	0 0
4	2 7 9
5	0 4 4 4 9
6	5 5 7
7	0 3

Key: 3 | 0 = 30

5.

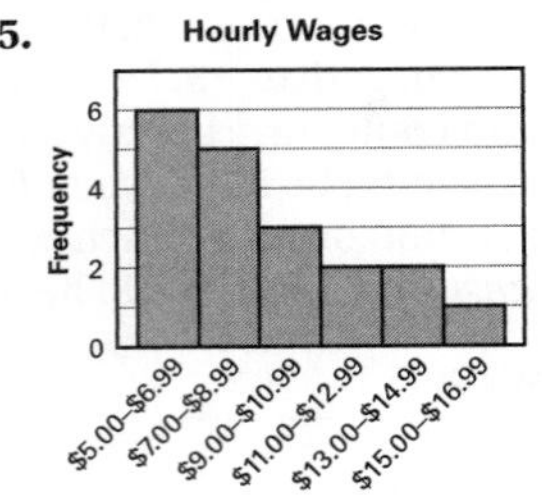

7.

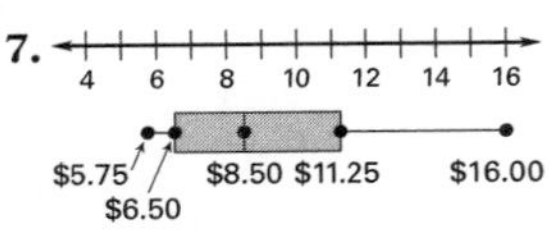

9. 5 **11.** 23 dogs **13.** 43 lb **15.** 25 children **17.** 12 songs **19.** 10 songs; 18 songs

Extra Practice

Chapter 1 (p. 1010)

1.

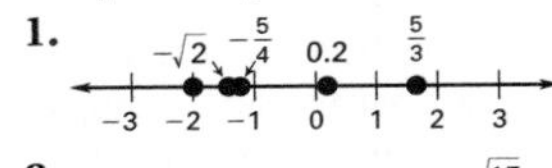

3.

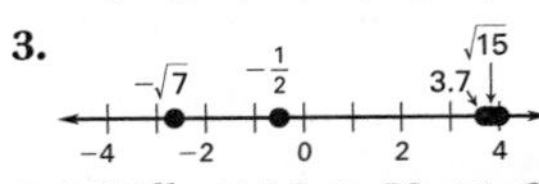

5. 1.25 lb **7.** 15 **9.** 52 **11.** $6r^2 - 5r + 12$ **13.** $8b - 20$ **15.** $-5m^2 + 9m - 12$ **17.** 5 **19.** −12 **21.** 2 **23.** 14 **25.** $y = \frac{1}{6}x + 3$; $\frac{10}{3}$ **27.** $y = \frac{9}{4}x - \frac{15}{2}$; 6 **29.** $y = \frac{5}{2 + 3x}$; $-\frac{5}{4}$ **31.** $y = -3x + 25$

33. $x > 7$

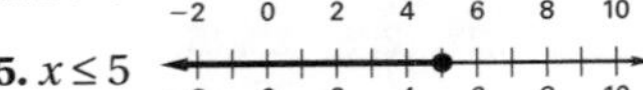

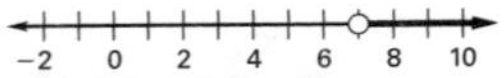

35. $x \le 5$ (number line: −2 0 2 4 6 8 10)

43. −1, 5 **45.** $-\frac{1}{9}$

47. $c < -7$ or $c > 7$ (number line: −8 −6 −4 −2 0 2 4 6 8)

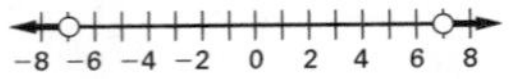

49. $-\frac{1}{2} \le j \le 4$ (number line: $-\frac{1}{2}$; −2 0 2 4 6)

Chapter 2 (p. 1011)

1. Function; for each input there is exactly one output. **3.** Not a function; there is more than one output for the input −2. **5.** $-\frac{1}{2}$; falls **7.** undefined; is vertical **9.** neither

11.

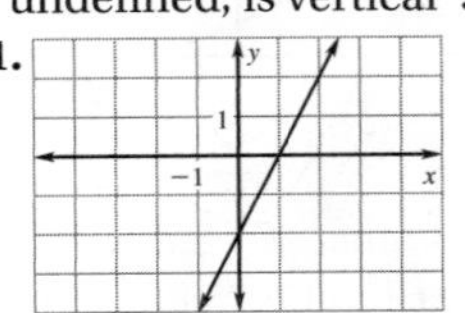

13.

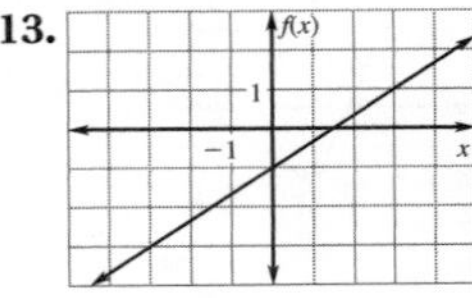

19. $y = 7x - 3$ **21.** $y = -2$ **23.** $y = \frac{10}{3}x + \frac{1}{3}$ **25.** $y = 2x$; −4 **27.** $y = \frac{1}{4}x$; $-\frac{1}{2}$

29. a, b.

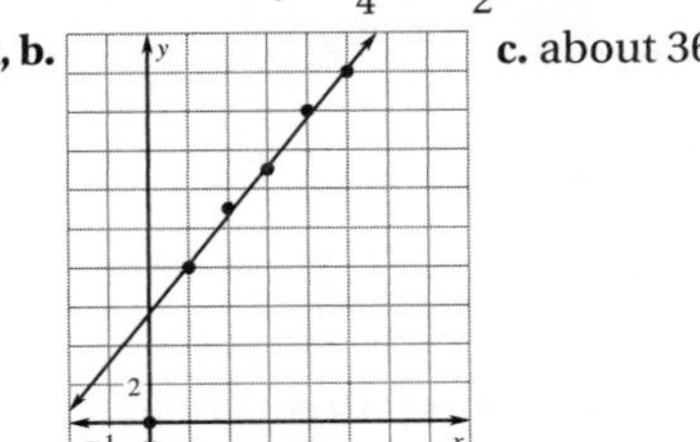

c. about 36

31.

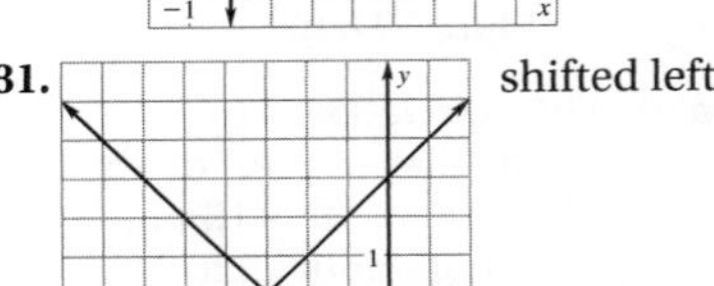

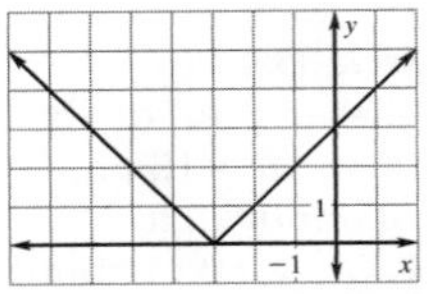

shifted left 3

33.

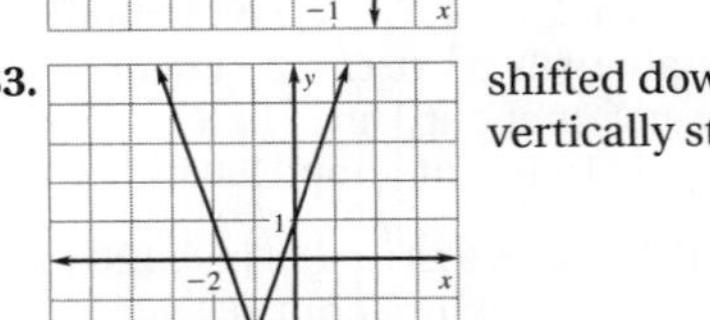

shifted down 2, left 1, and vertically stretched

35. **37.**

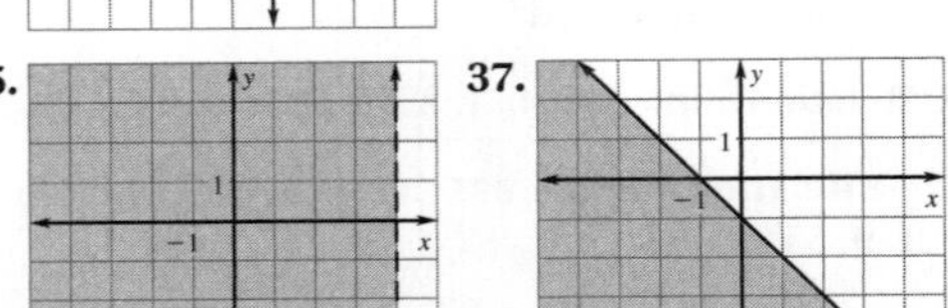

Chapter 3 (p. 1012)

1. $(-3, -7)$

3. $(2.5, 1.75)$

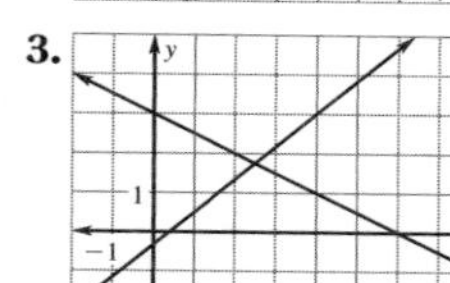

5. $(1, -2)$ **7.** $\left(\frac{5}{2}, -5\right)$

9.

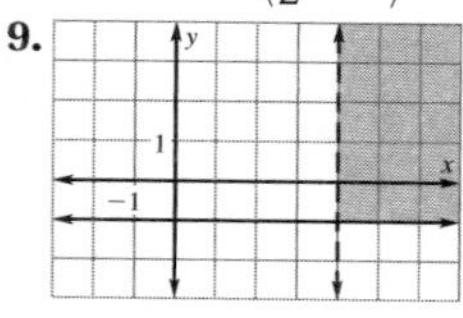

11.

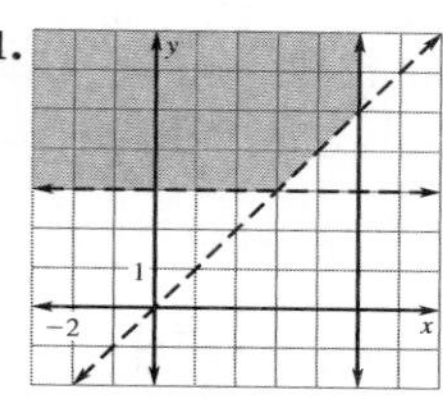

13. $(2, -7, 5)$ **15.** $\left(\frac{3}{2}, -3, -3\right)$ **17.** $\begin{bmatrix} -12 & 9 \\ -8 & 4 \end{bmatrix}$

19. $\begin{bmatrix} 16 & 9 & -7 \\ -2 & 13 & 7 \end{bmatrix}$ **21.** not defined; the number of columns in the left matrix does not equal the number of rows in the right matrix. **23.** 66 **25.** -9 **27.** $(3, -14)$

29. $(3, -3, 1)$ **31.** $\begin{bmatrix} \frac{8}{3} & -\frac{7}{3} \\ -1 & 1 \end{bmatrix}$ **33.** $\begin{bmatrix} -8 & -5 \\ 3 & 2 \end{bmatrix}$

35. $(14, -6)$ **37.** $(-8, -3)$

Chapter 4 (p. 1013)

1.

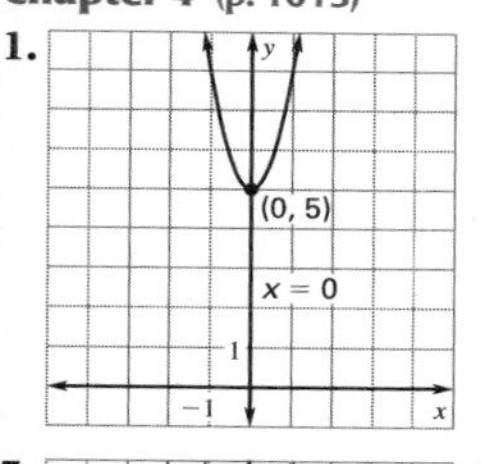

3.

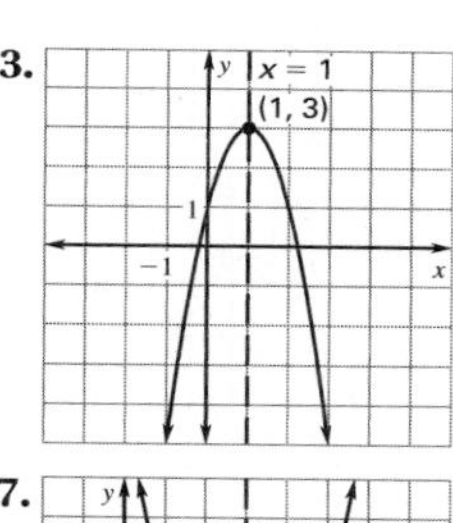

5. **7.**

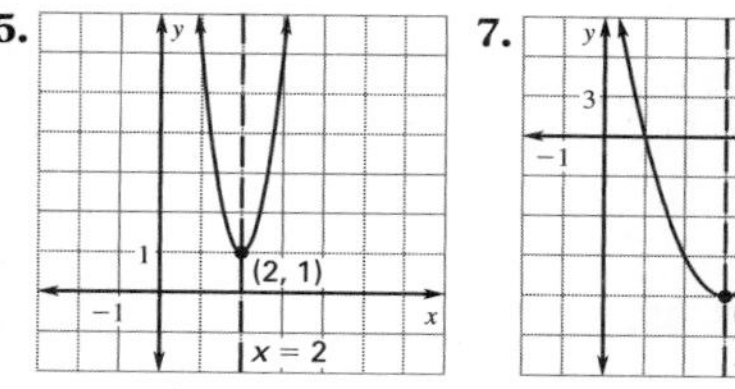

9. $y = 7x^2 + 42x + 56$ **11.** $y = x^2 - 14x + 56$
13. $(x - 2)^2$ **15.** $(x + 9)(x + 12)$ **17.** $-7, 2$ **19.** $-11, 5$
21. $(2x - 5)(x + 3)$ **23.** not factorable **25.** $-\frac{4}{9}, \frac{4}{9}$
27. $-3, -\frac{3}{2}$ **29.** $2\sqrt{14}$ **31.** $\frac{2\sqrt{7}}{7}$ **33.** $\pm 2\sqrt{2}$ **35.** $5 \pm \sqrt{10}$
37. $11 - 3i$ **39.** $-\frac{13}{73} + \frac{14}{73}i$ **41.** $-3 \pm \sqrt{19}$ **43.** $3 \pm \sqrt{6}$
45. $-5 \pm \sqrt{35}$ **47.** $-\frac{3}{8} \pm \frac{\sqrt{201}}{8}$ **49.** $x \le 0$ or $x \ge 10$
51. $-0.653 < x < 7.65$ **53.** $y = 3x^2 + 2x - 7$
55. $y = -2x^2 - 6x + 36$

Chapter 5 (p. 1014) **1.** 9.52×10^{11} **3.** 5×10^1 **5.** $\frac{b^6}{64a^{15}}$; power of a product property, negative exponent property **7.** $7x^2y^2$; product of powers property, quotient of powers property, negative exponent property

9.

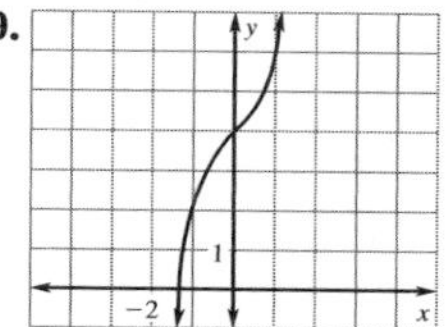

11.

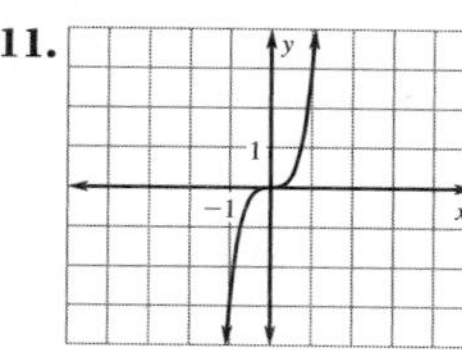

13. $-3x^2 + 3x - 8$ **15.** $3x^2(x + 3)^2$
17. $(x - 2)(x + 2)(2x + 1)$ **19.** $\pm\sqrt{7 \pm \sqrt{17}}$
21. $2x^2 + 10x + 25 + \frac{91}{x - 3}$ **23.** $-3, \frac{1}{2}, 1$
25. positive: 2 or 0, negative: 1, imaginary: 2 or 0
27. positive: 1, negative: 1, imaginary: 2 **29.** $(-1.5, -4)$ local minimum, $(0, 0)$ local maximum, $(1.5, -4)$ local minimum; $(-2, 0)$, $(0, 0)$, $(0, 0)$, $(2, 0)$, degree 4
31. $y = 0.5x^3 + x^2 + 2x - 1$

Chapter 6 (p. 1015) **1.** ± 3 **3.** -3 **5.** 32 **7.** 16 **9.** ± 3
11. ± 2.15 **13.** $\frac{1}{17^{1/7}}$ **15.** 3 **17.** $9\sqrt[3]{2}$ **19.** $48\sqrt[3]{2}$
21. $y^2z^4\sqrt[5]{18x^3y^4}$ **23.** $2x^2y^2\sqrt[3]{12x^2y}$ **25.** $x^3 + x - 4$, all real numbers **27.** $\frac{-x + 4}{x^3}$, all real numbers except $x = 0$ **29.** $\frac{x^3}{64}$, all real numbers **31.** x, all real numbers
33. $f(g(x)) = 3\left(\left(\frac{x - 1}{3}\right)^{1/2}\right)^2 + 1 = x - 1 + 1 = x$,
$g(f(x)) = \left(\frac{(3x^2 + 1) - 1}{3}\right)^{1/2} = \left(\frac{3x^2}{3}\right)^{1/2} = x$
35. $f^{-1}(x) = \frac{3}{4}x - \frac{3}{2}$ **37.** $f^{-1}(x) = -\sqrt[6]{-x + 2}$
39. $f^{-1}(x) = \frac{\sqrt[5]{x - 4}}{2}$

41.

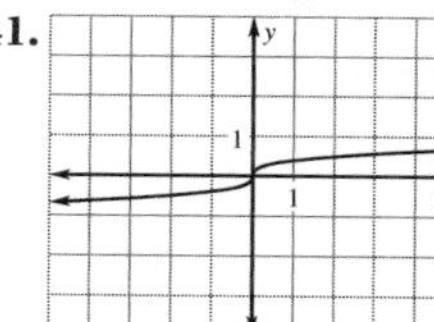

domain: all real numbers, range: all real numbers

SELECTED ANSWERS

43. domain: $x \geq -2$, range: $y \geq -3$

49. 3 **51.** -1 **53.** 3 **55.** 1, 3

Chapter 7 (p. 1016)

1. 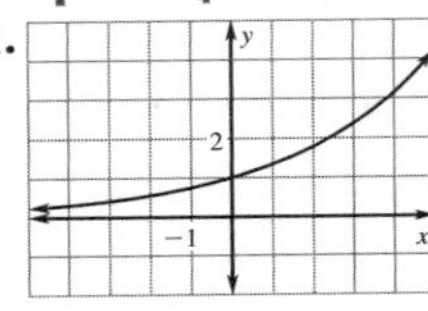 domain: all real numbers, range: $y > 0$

3. 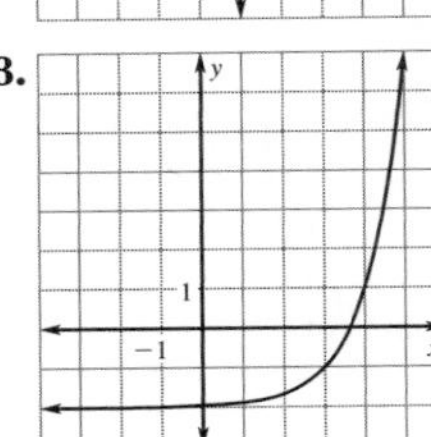 domain: all real numbers, range: $y > -2$

5. 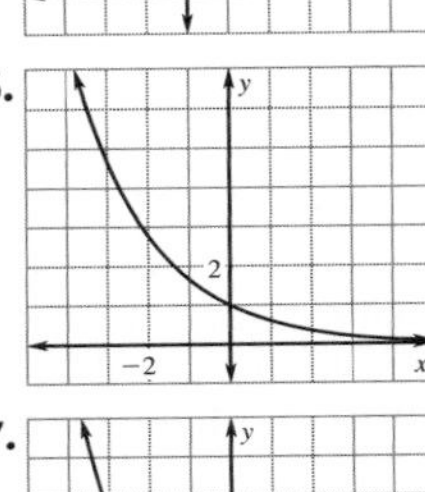 domain: all real numbers, range: $y > 0$

7. 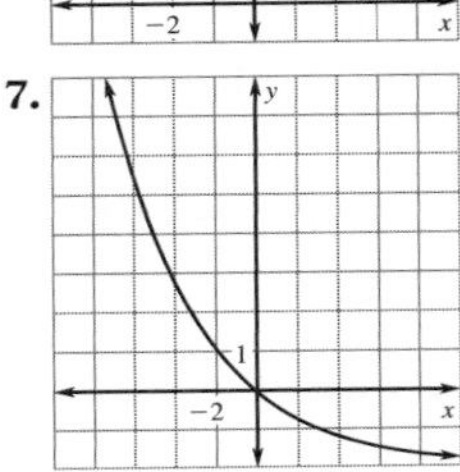 domain: all real numbers, range: $y > -2$

9. $\frac{1}{e^{11}}$ **11.** $9e^{4x}$

13. 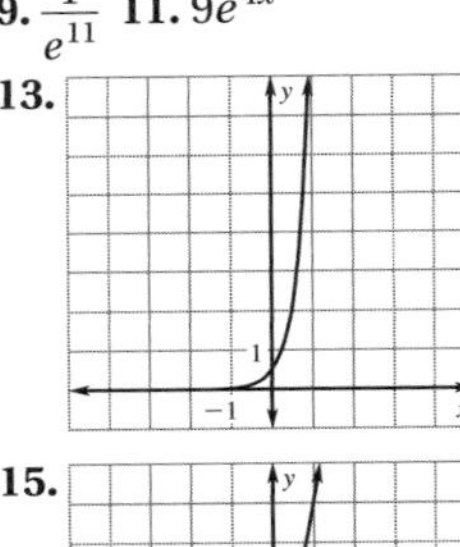 domain: all real numbers, range: $y > 0$

15. 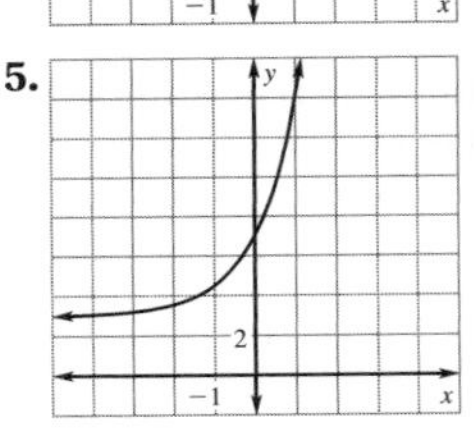 domain: all real numbers, range: $y > 3$

17. -2 **19.** 3 **21.** x **23.** $2x$

25. 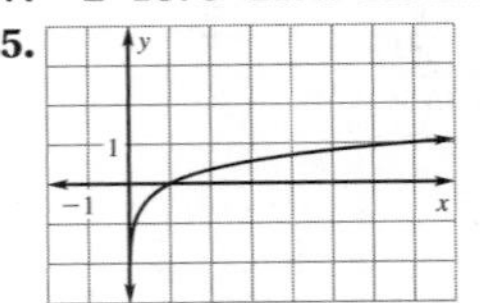 domain: $x > 0$, range: all real numbers

27. 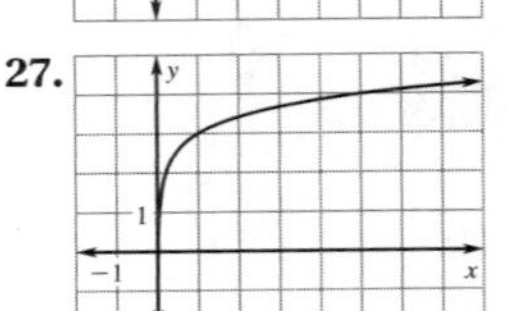 domain: $x > 0$, range: all real numbers

29. $\log_5 2 + \log_5 x - 1$ **31.** $\ln 20 + 3 \ln x + 2 \ln y$ **33.** $\log_4 20x^4$ **35.** $\ln \frac{10y^8}{x^2}$ **37.** about 3.161 **39.** about 1.694 **41.** 1 **43.** no solution **45.** 3 **47.** $y = \frac{3}{2} \cdot 2^x$ or $y = -\frac{3}{2} \cdot (-2)^x$ **49.** $y = 4 \cdot 1^x$ **51.** $y = \frac{1}{3} \cdot x^4$ **53.** $y = 0.538 \cdot x^{2.611}$

Chapter 8 (p. 1017)

1. $y = \frac{-20}{x}$; 4 **3.** $y = \frac{15}{x}$; -3 **5.** inverse variation **7.** neither variation

9. 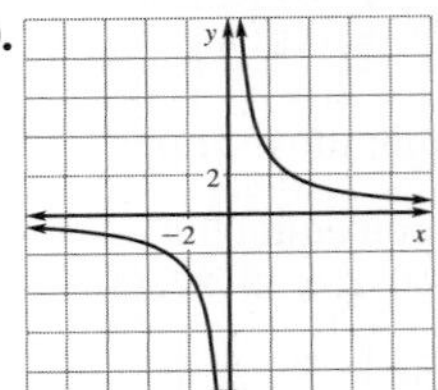 domain: all real numbers except $x = 0$, range: all real numbers except $y = 0$

11. 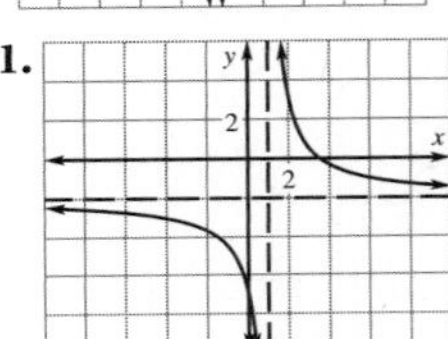 domain: all real numbers except $x = 1$, range: all real numbers except $y = -2$

13. 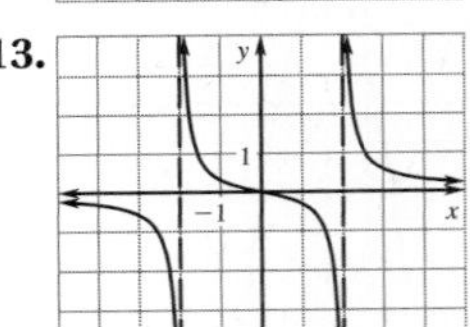 **15.**

17. $\frac{x-2}{x+6}$ **19.** $\frac{x-12}{2(x-7)}$ **21.** $\frac{4}{3x^2}$ **23.** $\frac{3x(x+5)^2}{x-6}$ **25.** $\frac{(2x+1)(x-5)}{8x^3}$ **27.** $x - 1$ **29.** $\frac{5}{x-5}$ **31.** $\frac{x(x+6)}{3(1+3x)}$ **33.** 3 **35.** $-1, 2$

SELECTED ANSWERS

Chapter 9 (p. 1018) **1.** $2\sqrt{29}$; (0, 2) **3.** $2\sqrt{233}$; (1, 4)

5. 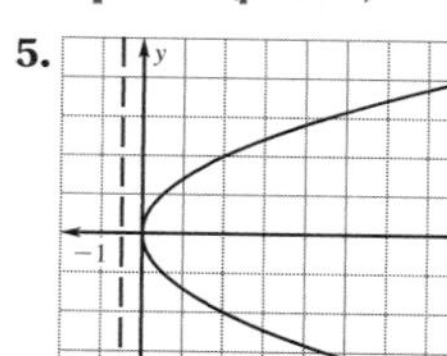 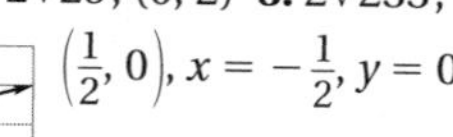 $\left(\frac{1}{2}, 0\right)$, $x = -\frac{1}{2}$, $y = 0$

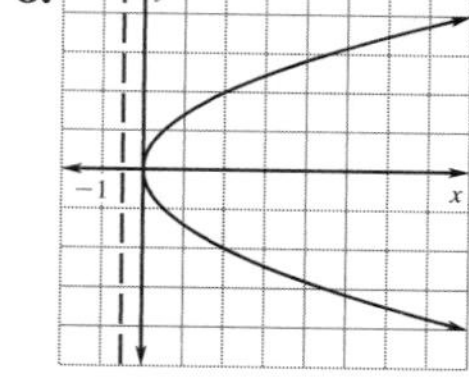

7. 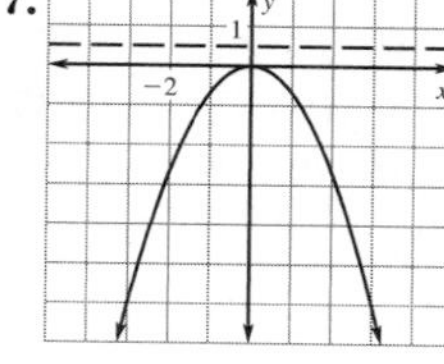 $\left(0, -\frac{3}{8}\right)$, $y = \frac{3}{8}$, $x = 0$

9. 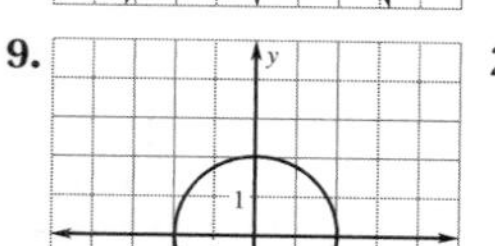 2

11. 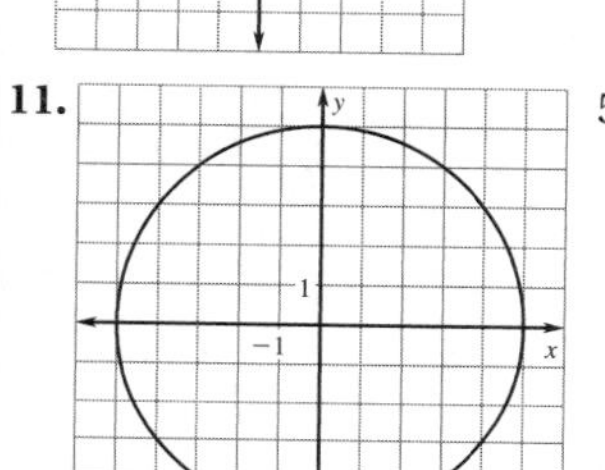 5

13. $x^2 + y^2 = 64$ **15.** $x^2 + y^2 = 50$

17. 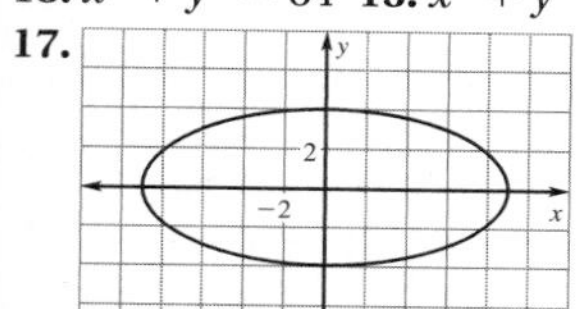 $(\pm 9, 0)$, $(0, \pm 4)$, $\left(\pm\sqrt{65}, 0\right)$

19. 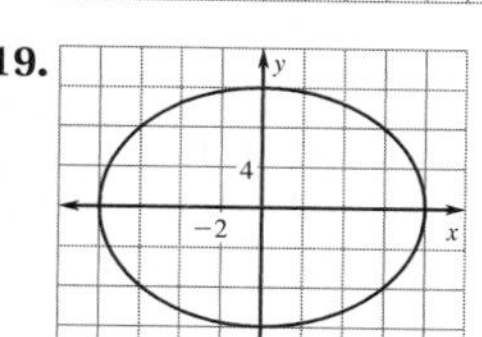 $(0, \pm 12)$, $(\pm 8, 0)$, $\left(0, \pm 4\sqrt{5}\right)$

21. $\frac{x^2}{16} + \frac{y^2}{4} = 1$ **23.** $\frac{x^2}{81} + \frac{y^2}{72} = 1$

25. 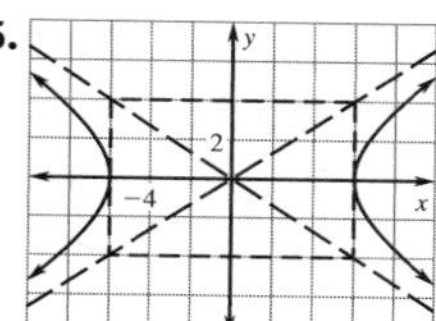 $(\pm 6, 0)$, $\left(\pm 2\sqrt{13}, 0\right)$, $y = \pm\frac{2}{3}x$

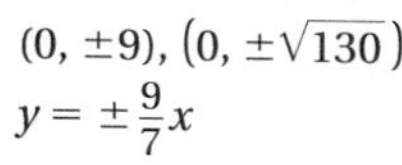

27. 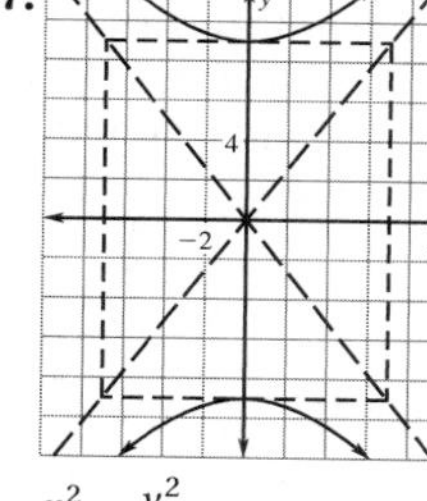 $(0, \pm 9)$, $\left(0, \pm\sqrt{130}\right)$, $y = \pm\frac{9}{7}x$

29. $\frac{x^2}{1} - \frac{y^2}{3} = 1$

31. 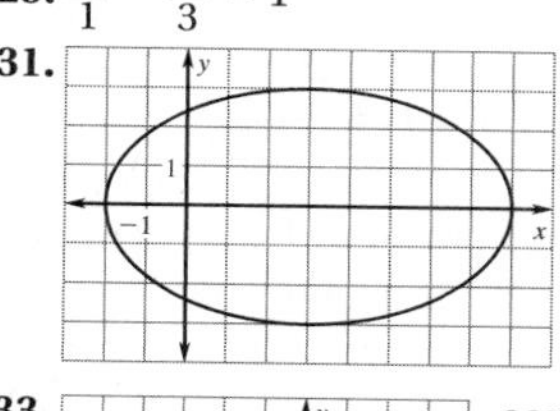 center: (3, 0), vertices: (−2, 0) (8, 0), co-vertices: (3, 3) (3, −3), foci: (−1, 0) (7, 0)

33. 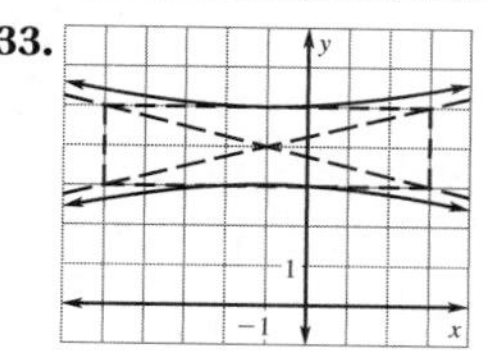 center: (−1, 4), vertices: (−1, 5) (−1, 3), foci: $\left(-1, 4 + \sqrt{17}\right)$ $\left(-1, 4 - \sqrt{17}\right)$, asymptotes: $y = \pm\frac{1}{4}x$

35. ellipse, 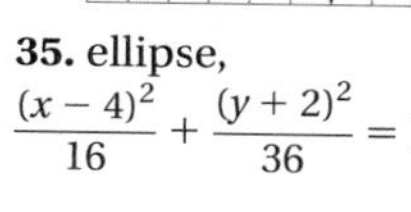 $\frac{(x-4)^2}{16} + \frac{(y+2)^2}{36} = 1$

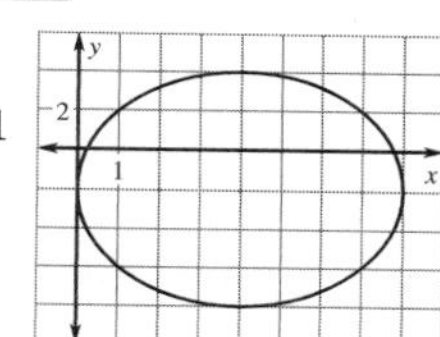

37. parabola, $(x-3)^2 = 4(y-2)$

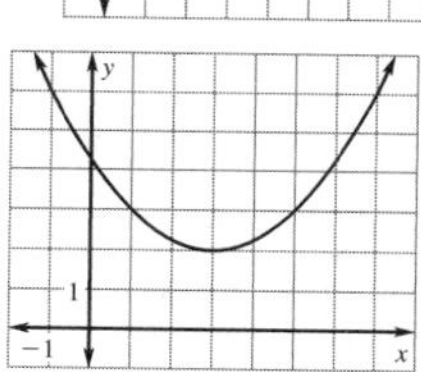

39. (0, −2) (7, 5)

Chapter 10 (p. 1019) **1. a.** 100,000,000 passwords **b.** 1,814,400 passwords **3. a.** 118,813,760 passwords **b.** 78,936,000 passwords **5.** 20 **7.** 362,880 **9.** 1260 **11.** 604,800 **13.** 35 **15.** 10 **17.** $x^3 - 9x^2 + 27x - 27$ **19.** $p^{10} + 20p^8 + 160p^6 + 640p^4 + 1280p^2 + 1024$ **21.** $\frac{13}{25}$ **23.** $\frac{1}{2}$ **25.** $1 - \frac{\pi}{4}$ **27.** 0.8 **29.** 0.6; not disjoint

SELECTED ANSWERS

31. 0.17; not disjoint **33. a.** $\frac{1}{169}$ **b.** $\frac{4}{663}$ **35. a.** $\frac{1}{52}$ **b.** $\frac{1}{51}$ **37.** about 0.0417 **39.** about 0.0000305

Chapter 11 (p. 1020) **1.** 11, 11.5, 16, 11, 4.313 **3.** 1, 0, −3, 15, 4.991 **5.** 3.45, 4.4, 5.7, 9, 3.09 **7.** 41.5, 37.5, 36, 23, 8.221; 43.5, 39.5, 38, 23, 8.221 **9.** 2, 2.5, −2, 10, 3.5; 3, 3.75, −3, 15, 5.25 **11.** 0.34 **13.** 0.025 **15.** Self-selected; biased; only those parents who received the survey and feel strongly about the attendance policy are likely to respond. **17.** $\pm$ 4.1% **19.** $\pm$ 1.4% **21.** 2500 **23.** 260 **25.** $y = 0.108(2.56)^x$

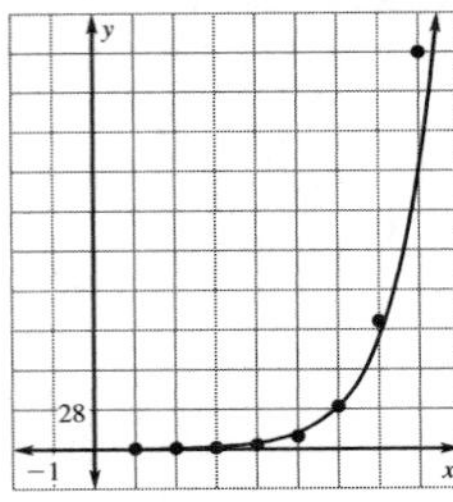

Chapter 12 (p. 1021) **1.** perfect squares listed in order starting at 3, 49, $a_n = (n + 2)^2$ **3.** each term is decreased by 5.5, −9.5, $a_n = 18 - 5.5n$ **5.** $\sum_{n=1}^{\infty} \frac{n}{5+n}$ **7.** 220 **9.** 1071 **11.** $a_n = -10n + 22$

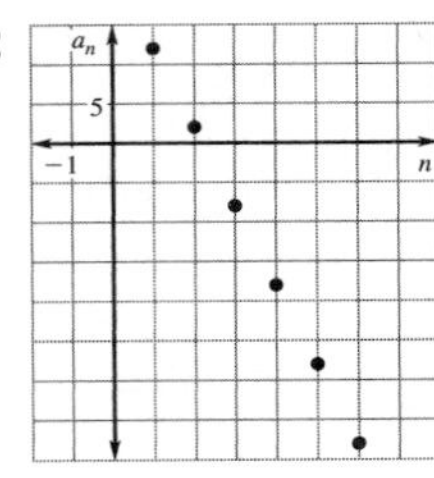

13. $a_n = 9n + 2$; 137 **15.** $a_n = -\frac{2}{3}n + \frac{11}{3}$; $-\frac{19}{3}$ **17.** $a_n = 2.5 + n$ **19.** $a_n = \frac{1}{27} \cdot 3^{n-1}$; 729 **21.** $a_n = 4 \cdot \left(\frac{4}{3}\right)^{n-1}$; about 53.3 **23.** 273.5 **25.** about 25.8 **27.** no sum **29.** $\frac{1}{3}$ **31.** $\frac{7}{33}$ **33.** $a_1 = 2.5$, $a_n = 2(a_{n-1})$ **35.** $a_1 = 1$ and $a_2 = 2$, $a_n = (a_{n-2})(a_{n-1})$ **37.** −10, −10, −10

Chapter 13 (p. 1022) **1.** $\cos \theta = \frac{4}{5}$, $\tan \theta = \frac{3}{4}$, $\csc \theta = \frac{5}{3}$, $\sec \theta = \frac{5}{4}$, $\cot \theta = \frac{4}{3}$ **3.** $\sin \theta = \frac{\sqrt{3}}{2}$, $\cos \theta = \frac{1}{2}$, $\tan \theta = \sqrt{3}$, $\csc \theta = \frac{2\sqrt{3}}{3}$, $\cot \theta = \frac{\sqrt{3}}{3}$ **5.** $B = 69°$, $a \approx 2.867$, $b \approx 7.469$ **7.** $A = 30°$, $a = 10$, $b = 10\sqrt{3}$ **9.** $B = 72°$, $a \approx 5.562$, $b \approx 17.119$ **11.** $\frac{5\pi}{9}$ **13.** 135° **15.** $\frac{5\pi}{2}$ ft, $\frac{25\pi}{4}$ ft^2 **17.** 12π cm, 72π cm^2

19. 30° **21.** $\frac{\pi}{6}$

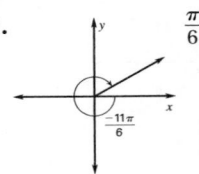

23. $-\frac{2\sqrt{3}}{3}$ **25.** $-\frac{\sqrt{2}}{2}$ **27.** $\frac{5\pi}{6}$, 150° **29.** $\frac{\pi}{4}$, 45° **31.** about 334.16° **33.** $B \approx 40.7°$, $C \approx 105.3°$, $c \approx 10.35$ or $B \approx 139.3°$, $C \approx 6.72°$, $c \approx 1.26$ **35.** $A \approx 36.4°$, $C \approx 57.6°$, $a \approx 7.73$ **37.** about 24.1 **39.** $A \approx 44.1°$, $B \approx 88.3°$, $C \approx 47.6°$ **41.** $B \approx 61.3°$, $C \approx 38.7°$, $a \approx 7.86$ **43.** about 189

Chapter 14 (p. 1023)

1.

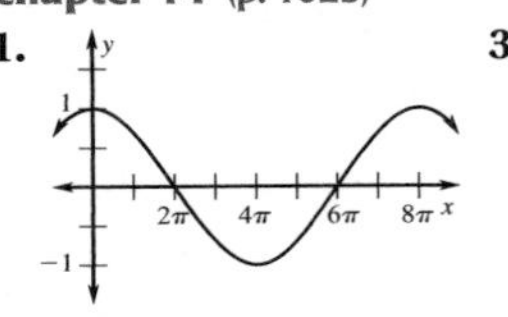

3.

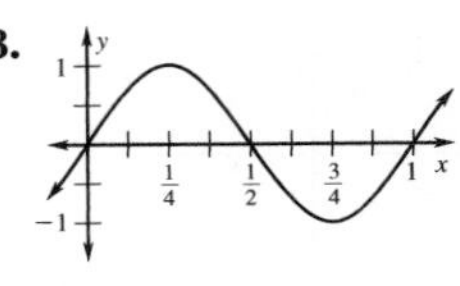

5.

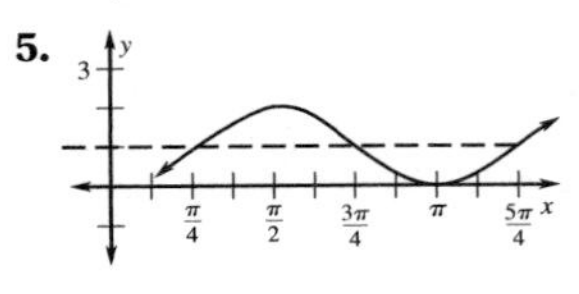

7.

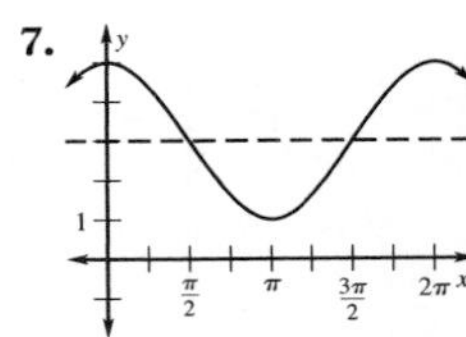

9.

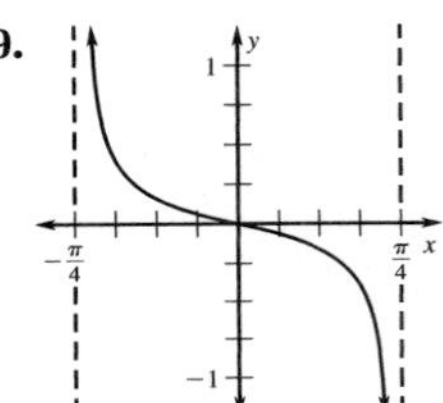

11. 1 **13.** −1 **15.** $\frac{\cos^2 x + \sin^2 x}{\tan^2 x + 1} = \frac{1}{\sec^2 x} = \cos^2 x$ **17.** $\frac{\pi}{6} + n\pi$, $\frac{5\pi}{6} + n\pi$ **19.** $\frac{\pi}{4} + n\pi$ **21.** $\frac{7\pi}{6}$, $\frac{11\pi}{6}$ **23.** about 1.2995 **25.** $y = 3 + \frac{1}{2}\cos \pi x$ **27.** $\frac{-\sqrt{2} - \sqrt{6}}{4}$ **29.** $\frac{\sqrt{2} + \sqrt{6}}{4}$ **31.** $\frac{9\sqrt{19}}{50}$, $\frac{31}{50}$, $\frac{9\sqrt{19}}{31}$ **33.** $\frac{2\pi}{3} + 2n\pi$, $\frac{4\pi}{3} + 2n\pi$, $0 + 2n\pi$ **35.** $\frac{3\pi}{4} + 2n\pi$

Teacher's Edition Index

Pupil's Edition in black
Teacher's Edition in blue

A

INDEX

E

INDEX

F

INDEX

H

I

INDEX

M

INDEX

INDEX

S

INDEX

T

INDEX

INDEX

Additional Answers

Chapter 1

1.1 Skill Practice (pp. 6–7)

17. $6 \cdot (a \div 3) = 6 \cdot \left(a \cdot \frac{1}{3}\right)$ Definition of division
$= 6 \cdot \left(\frac{1}{3} \cdot a\right)$ Commutative property of multiplication
$= \left(6 \cdot \frac{1}{3}\right) \cdot a$ Associative property of multiplication
$= 2a$ Multiplication

18. $15 \cdot (3 \div b) = 15 \cdot \left(3 \cdot \frac{1}{b}\right)$ Definition of division
$= (15 \cdot 3) \cdot \frac{1}{b}$ Associative property of multiplication
$= 45 \cdot \frac{1}{b}$ Multiplication
$= 45 \div b$ Definition of division

19. $(c - 3) + 3 = (c + (-3)) + 3$ Definition of subtraction
$= c + ((-3) + 3)$ Associative property of addition
$= c + 0$ Inverse property of addition
$= c$ Identity property of addition

20. $(a + b) - c = (a + b) + (-c)$ Definition of subtraction
$= a + (b + (-c))$ Associative property of addition
$= a + (b - c)$ Definition of subtraction

21. $7a + (4 + 5a) = 7a + (5a + 4)$ Commutative property of addition
$= (7a + 5a) + 4$ Associative property of addition
$= 12a + 4$ Combine like terms.

22. $(12b + 15) - 3b = (12b + 15) + (-3b)$ Definition of subtraction
$= (15 + 12b) + (-3b)$ Commutative property of addition
$= 15 + (12b + (-3b))$ Associative property of addition
$= 15 + 9b$ Combine like terms.

55. $\frac{a}{b} \div \frac{c}{d} = \frac{a}{b} \cdot \frac{d}{c}$ Definition of division
$= \frac{ad}{bc}$ Definition of multiplication of fractions
$= \frac{ad}{cb}$ Commutative property of multiplication
$= \frac{a}{c} \cdot \frac{d}{b}$ Definition of multiplication of fractions
$= \frac{a}{c} \div \frac{b}{d}$ Definition of division

1.2 Problem Solving (pp. 15–16)

61. a.

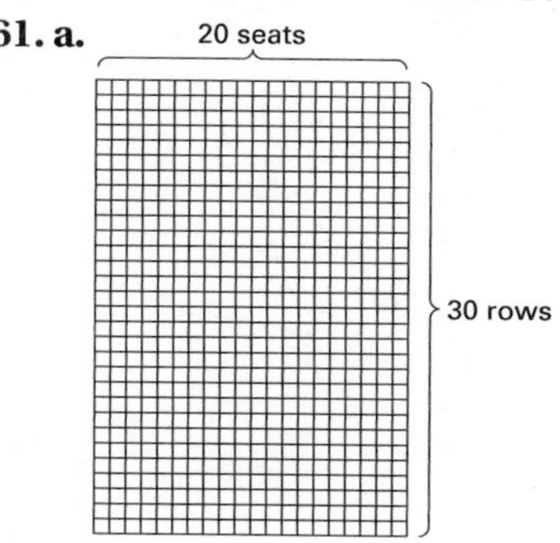

1.6 Skill Practice (pp. 44–45)

22. **23.**

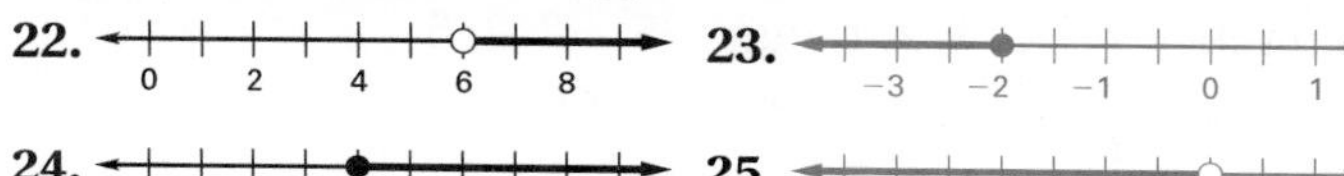

24. **25.**

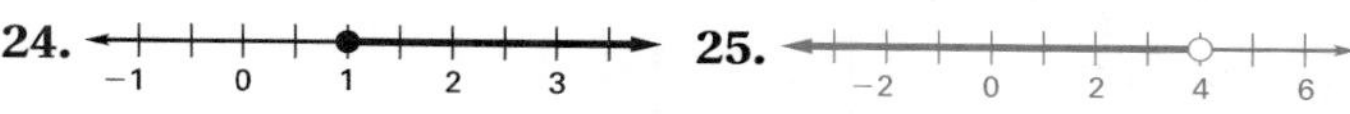

26. **27.**

28. **29.**

30. **31.**

32. **33.**

37. **38.**

39. **40.**

41. **42.**

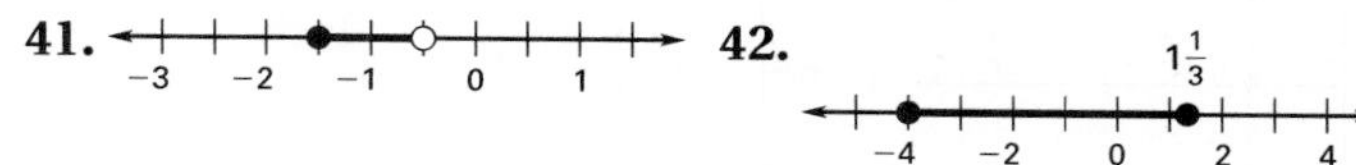

43. **44.**

45. **46.**

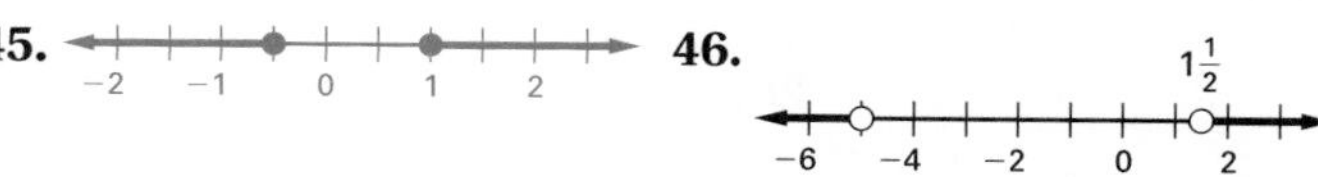

47. **48.**

ADDITIONAL ANSWERS

Chapter 2

2.1 Skill Practice (pp. 76–78)

3. domain: −4, −2, 1, 3, range: −3, −1, 2, 3

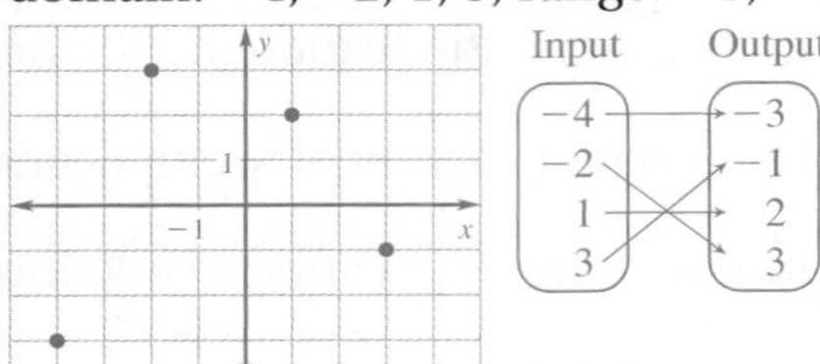

4. domain: −3, −1, 3, 5, range: −2, −1, 3

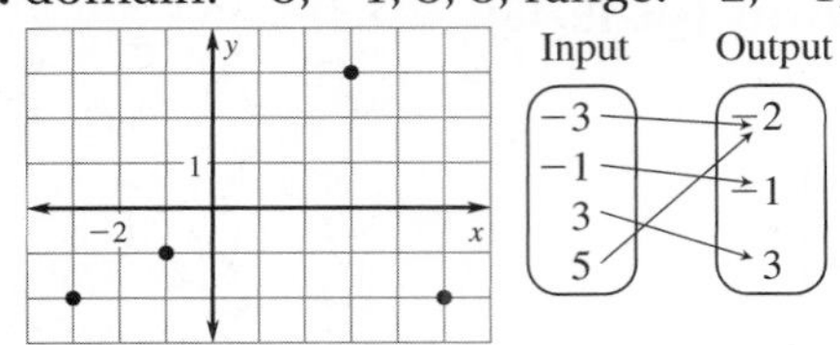

5. domain: −2, 1, 6, range: −3, −1, 5, 8

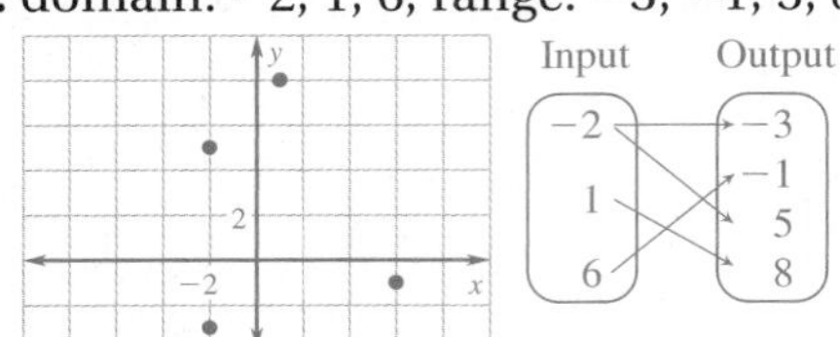

6. domain: −7, −3, 1, 2, range: −5, −2, 4, 6

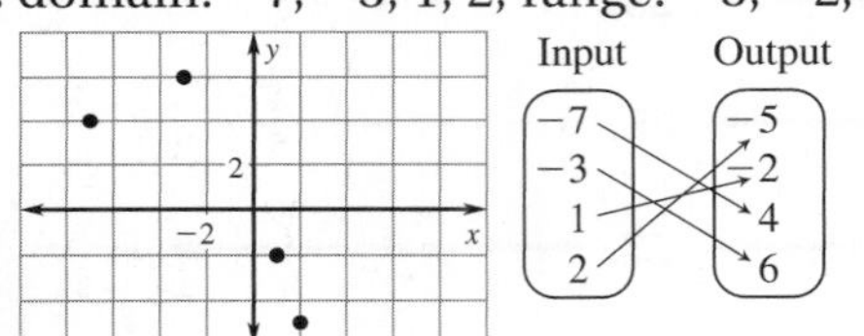

7. domain: 5, 10, 15, 20, range: 20, 30

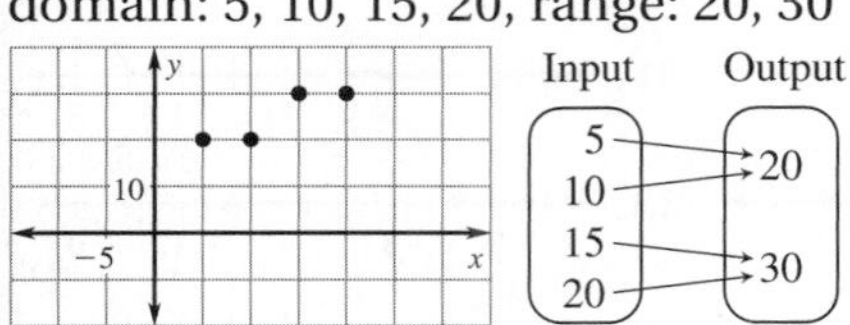

8. domain: 4, 16, range: −4, −2, 2, 4

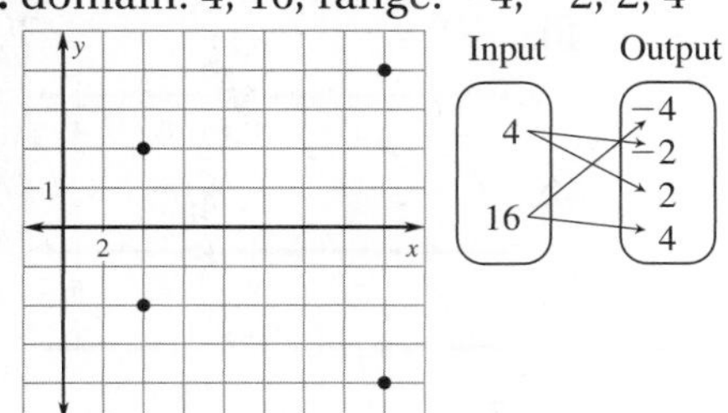

25.

26.

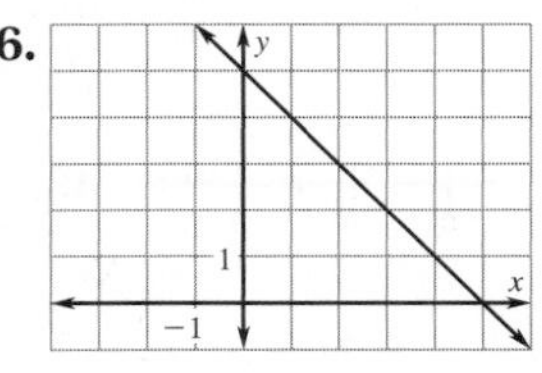

27.

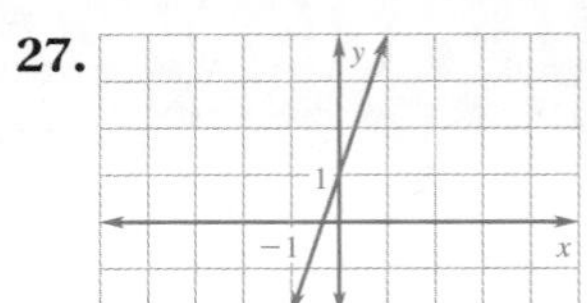

28.

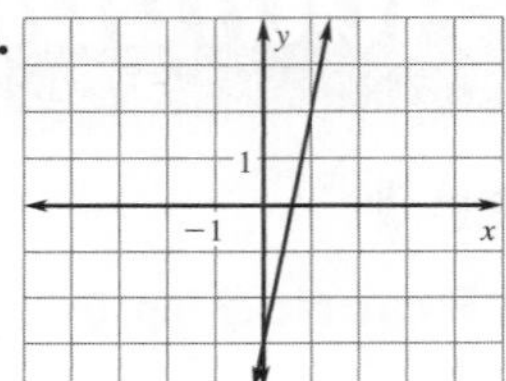

29.

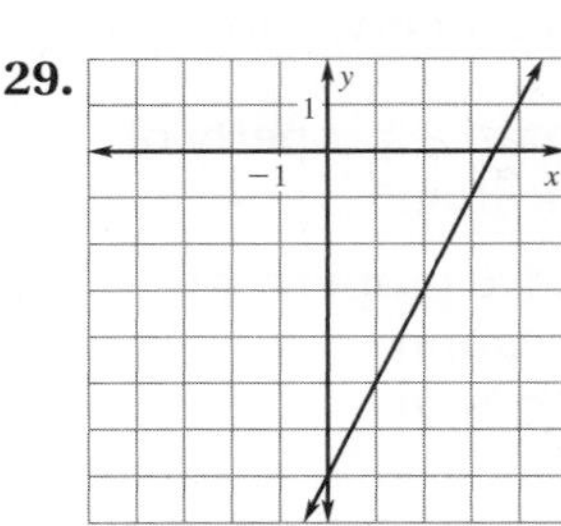

30.

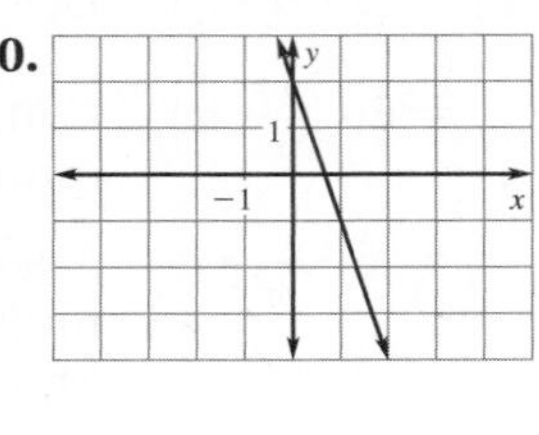

31.

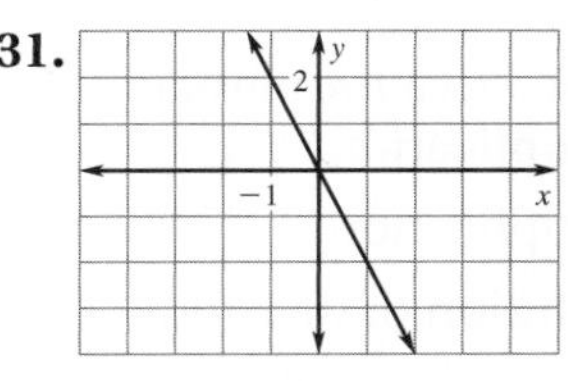

32.

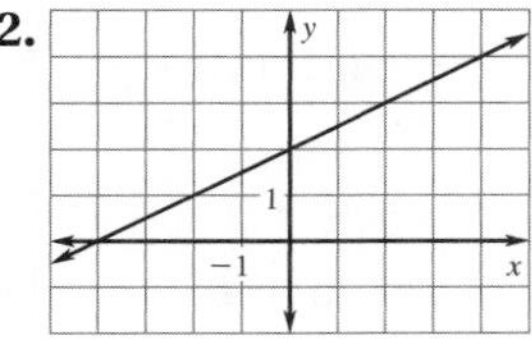

33.

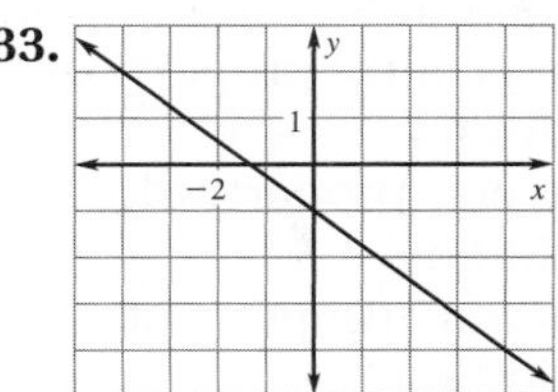

Extension (p. 81)

5.

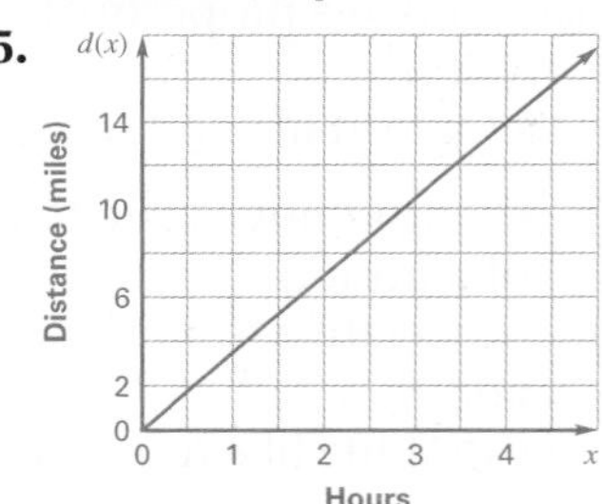

6.

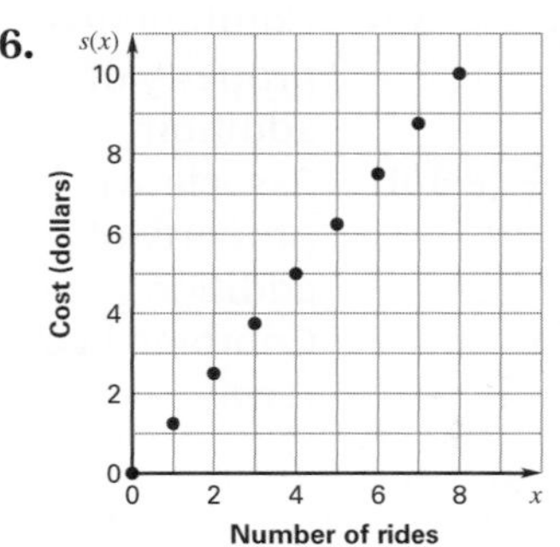

7. 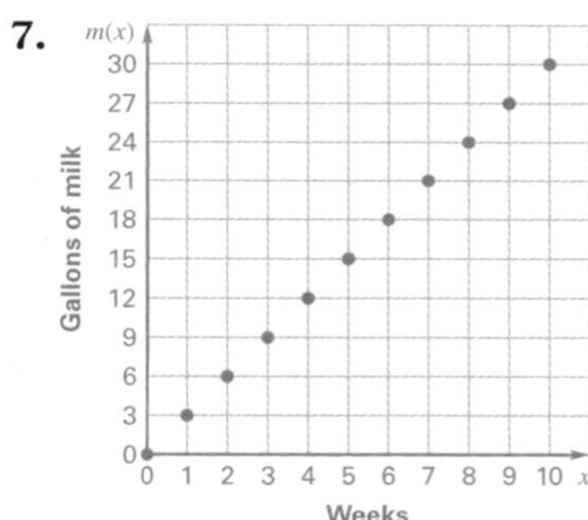

8. 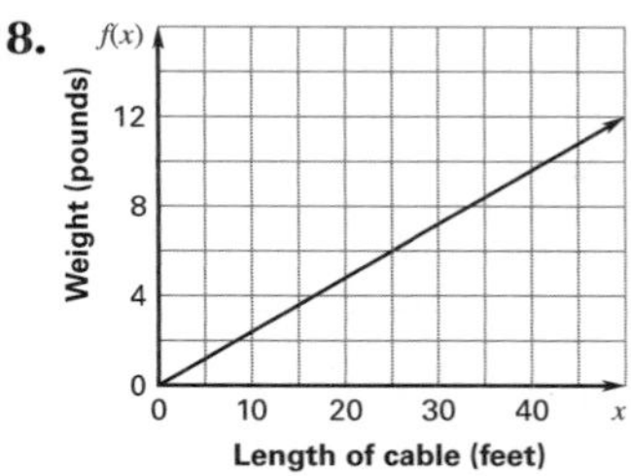

9. 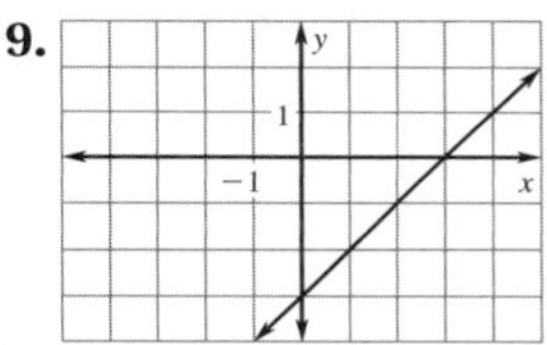

2.3 Guided Practice (pp. 90–92)

1. 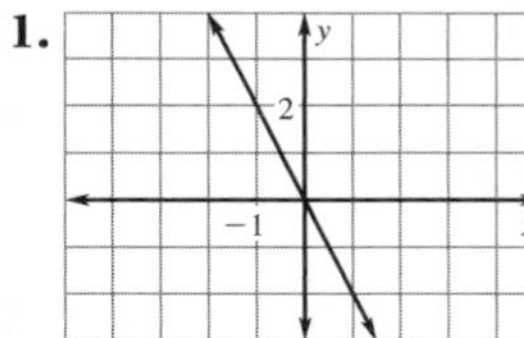
Both graphs have a y-intercept of 0, but the graph of $y = -2x$ has a slope of -2 instead of 1.

2. 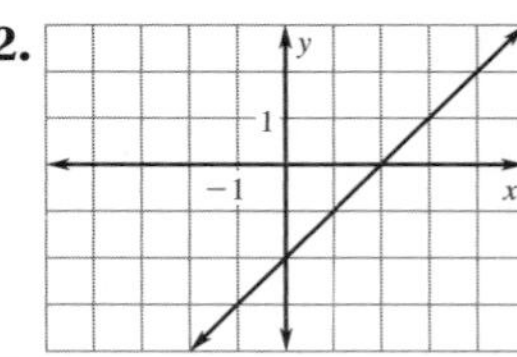
Both graphs have a slope of 1, but the graph of $y = x - 2$ has a y-intercept of -2 instead of 0.

3. 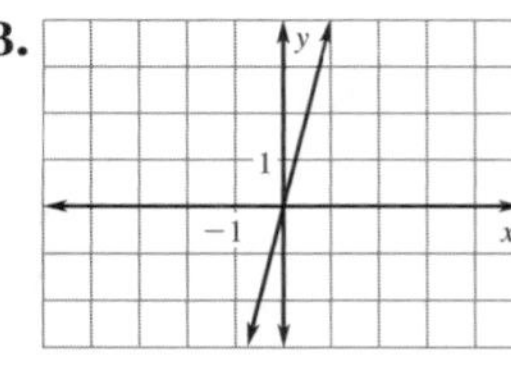
Both graphs have a y-intercept of 0, but the graph of $y = 4x$ has a slope of 4 instead of 1.

4. 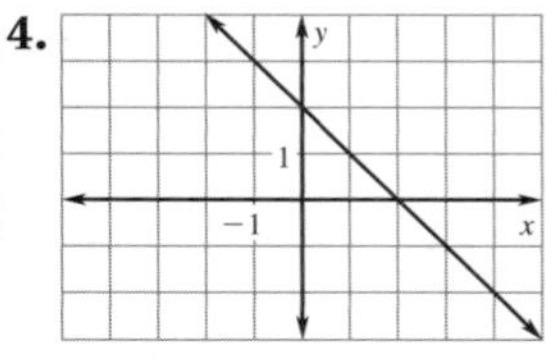

5. 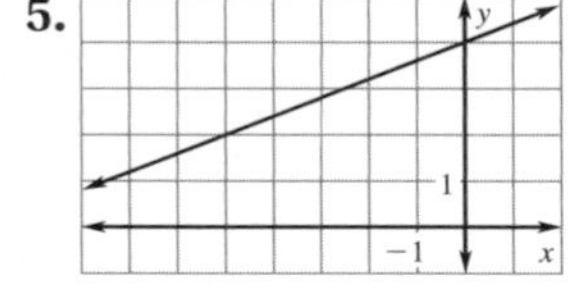

6. 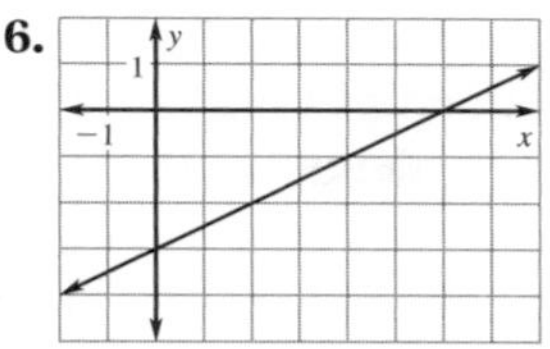

7. 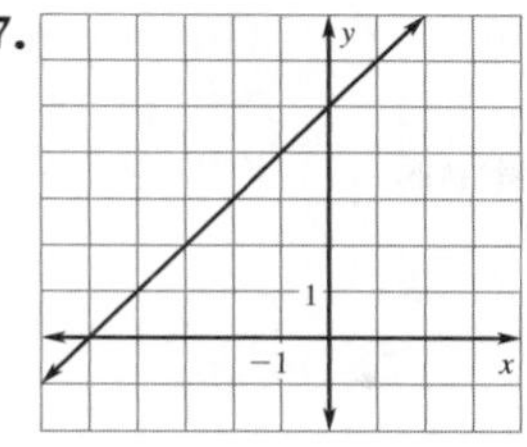

8. 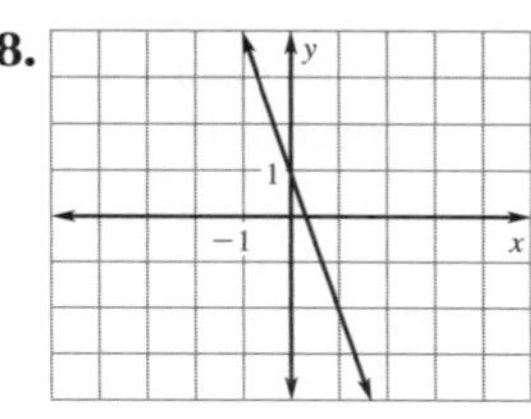

9. 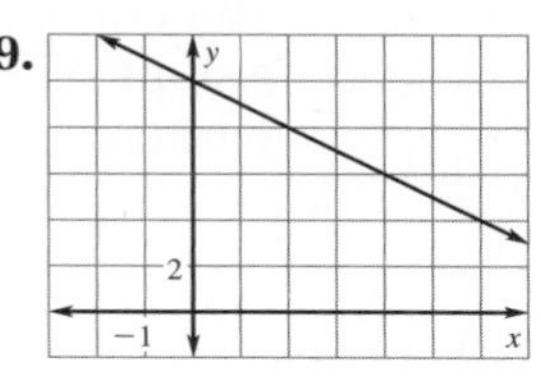

11. 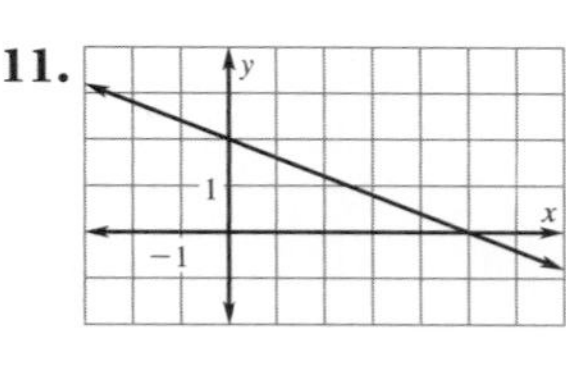

12. 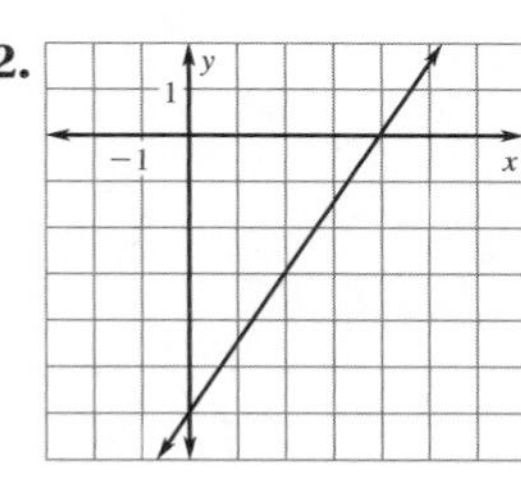

13. 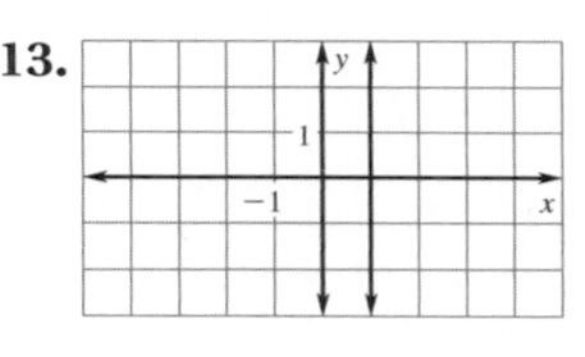

14. 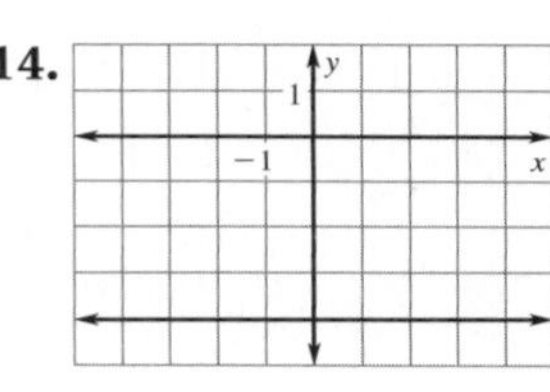

2.3 Skill Practice (pp. 93–94)

3. 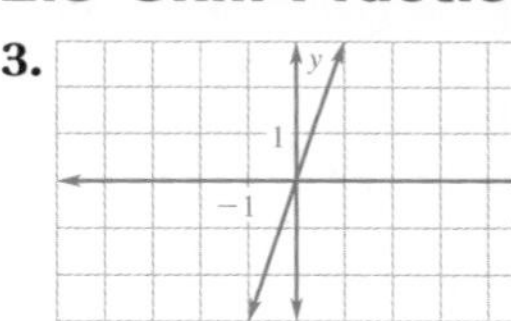
Both graphs have a y-intercept of 0, but the graph of $y = 3x$ has a slope of 3 instead of 1.

4. 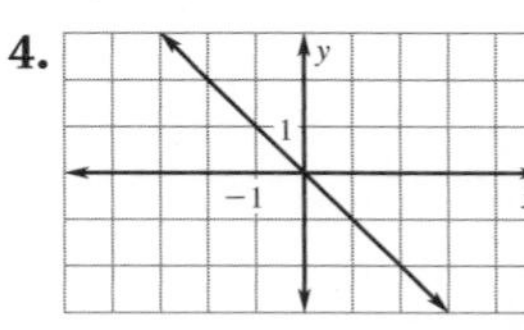
Both graphs have a y-intercept of 0, but the graph of $y = -x$ has a slope of -1 instead of 1.

5. 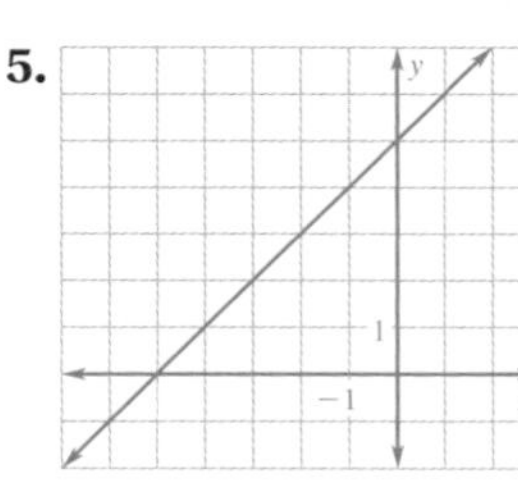
Both graphs have a slope of 1, but the graph of $y = x + 5$ has a y-intercept of 5 instead of 0.

6. 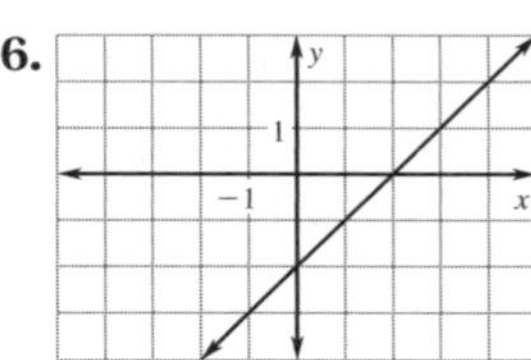
Both graphs have a slope of 1, but the graph of $y = x - 2$ has a y-intercept of -2 instead of 0.

7. 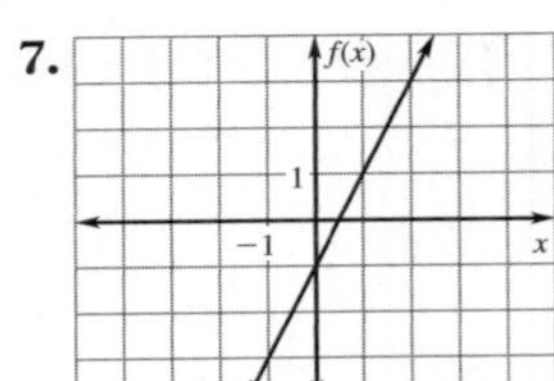

The graph of $f(x) = 2x - 1$ has a slope of 2 instead of 1 and a y-intercept of -1 instead of 0.

8. 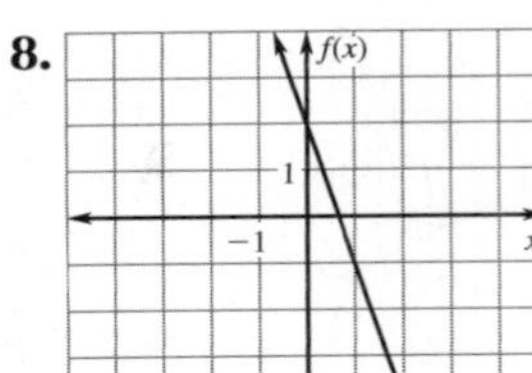

The graph of $f(x) = -3x + 2$ has a slope of -3 instead of 1 and a y-intercept of 2 instead of 0.

9. 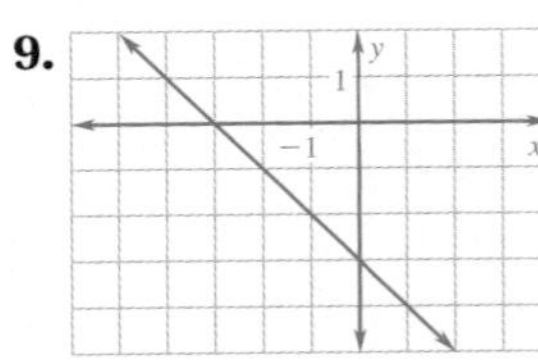

10.

11. 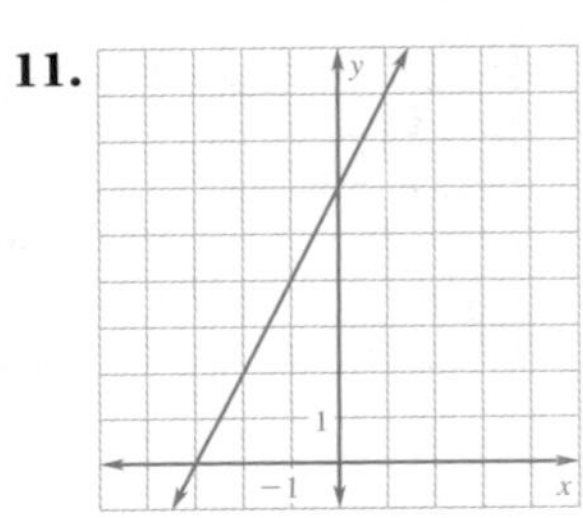

12.

13. 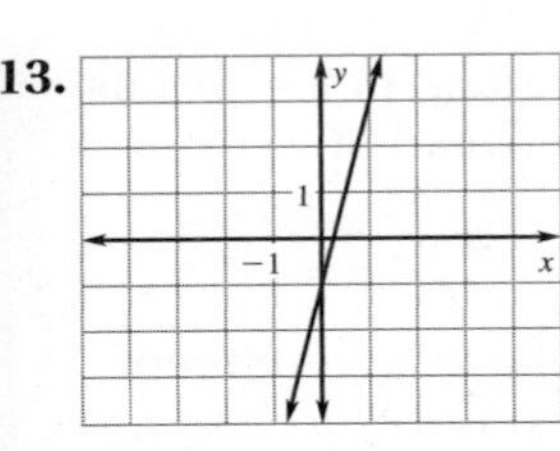

14. 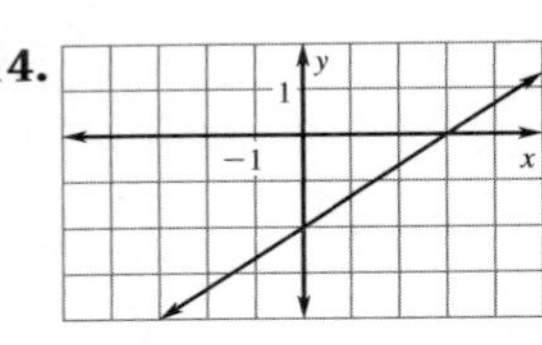

15. 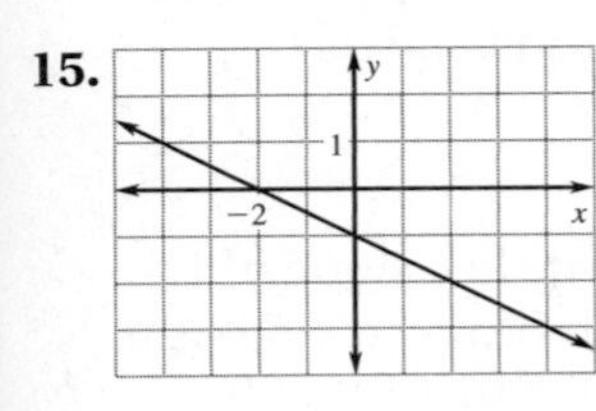

16. 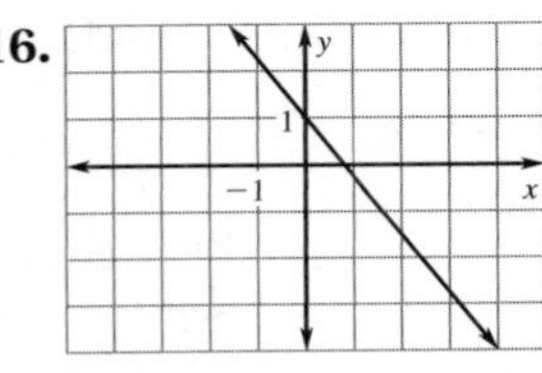

17. 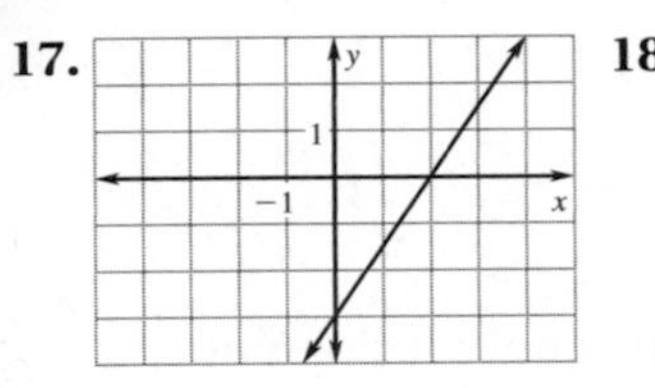

18. 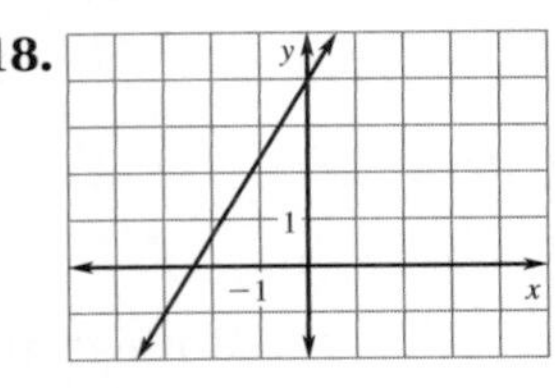

19. 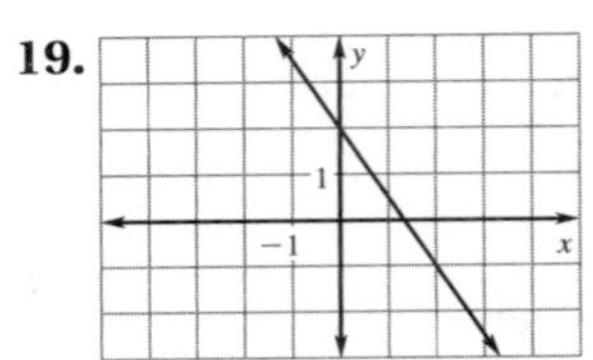

20. 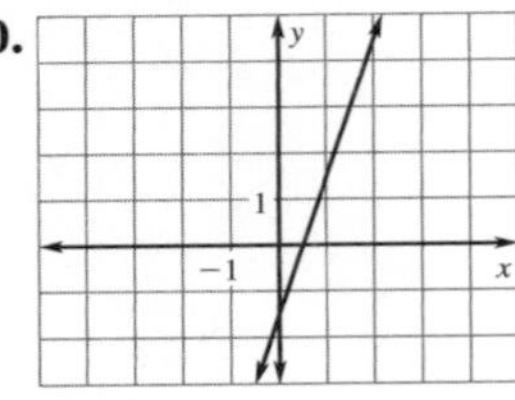

21. The slope and y-intercept were switched around.

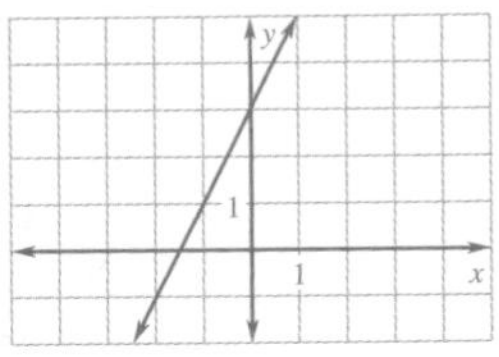

22. The slope is rise over run instead of run over rise.

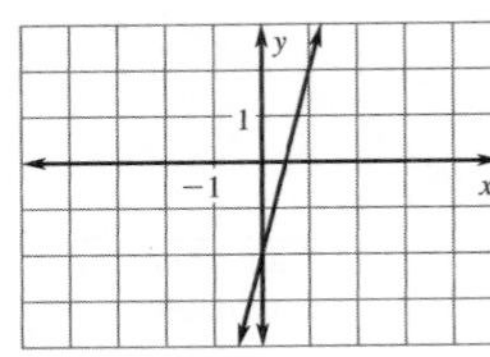

31. 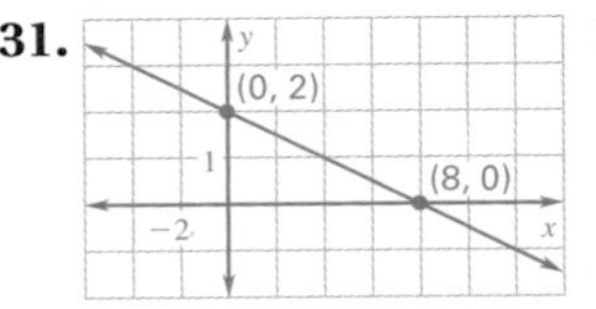

32. 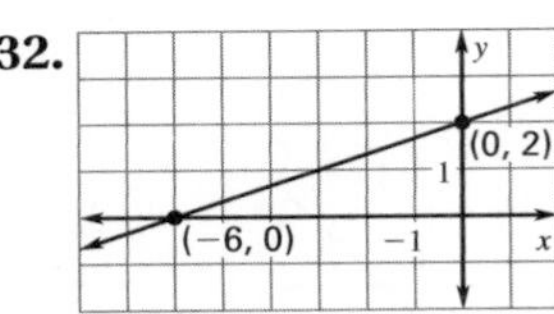

33. 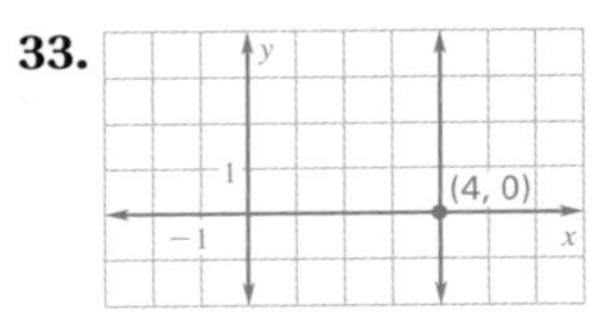

34. 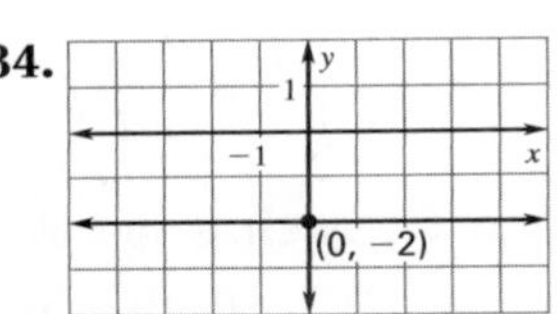

35. 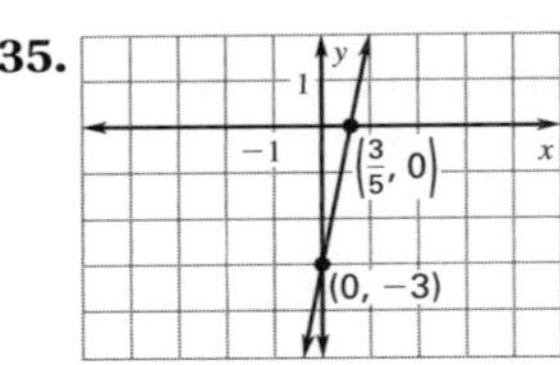

36. 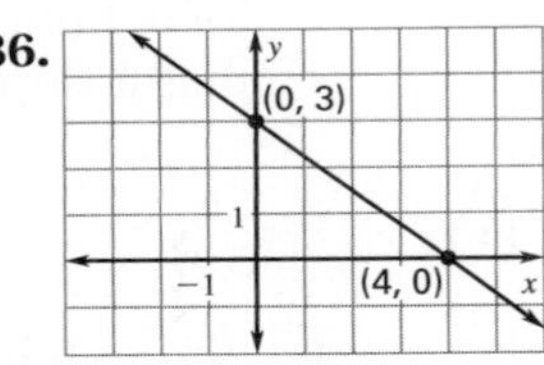

37. 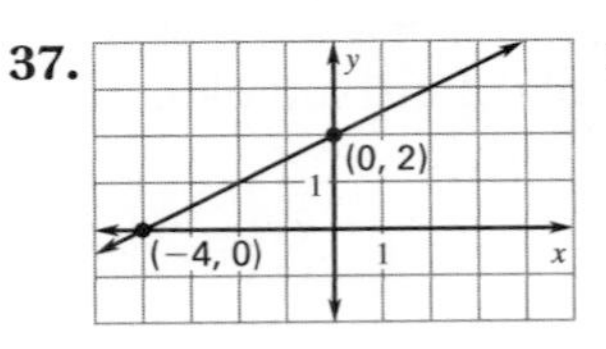

38. 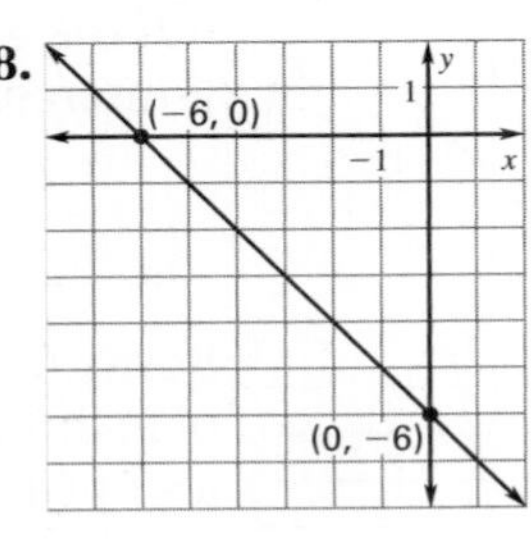

39. 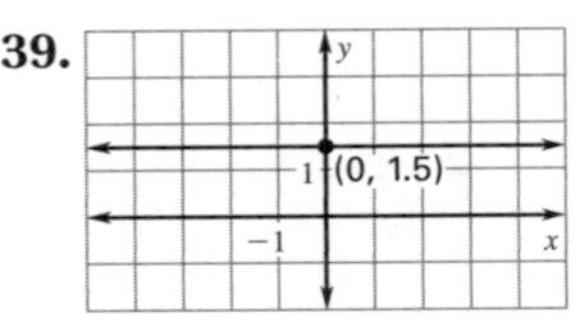

40. 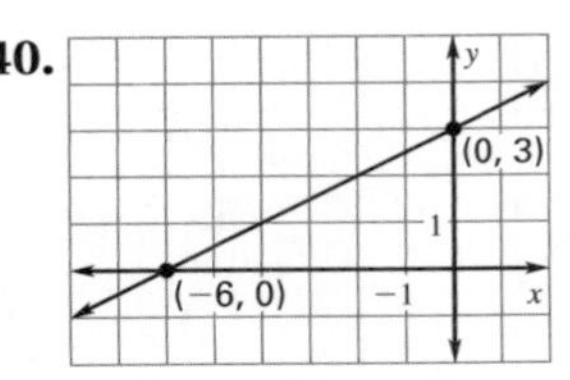

41. 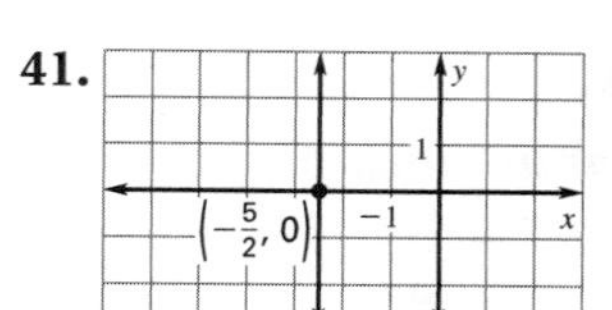

42. 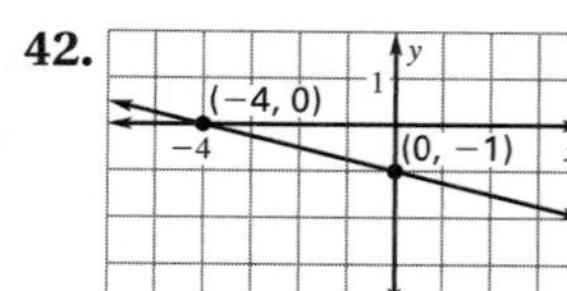

43. 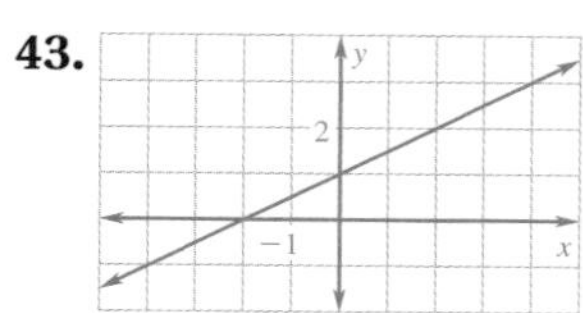

44. 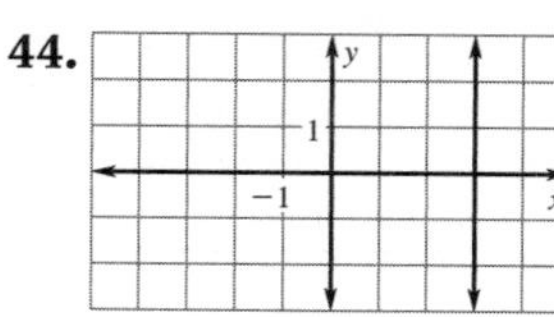

45. 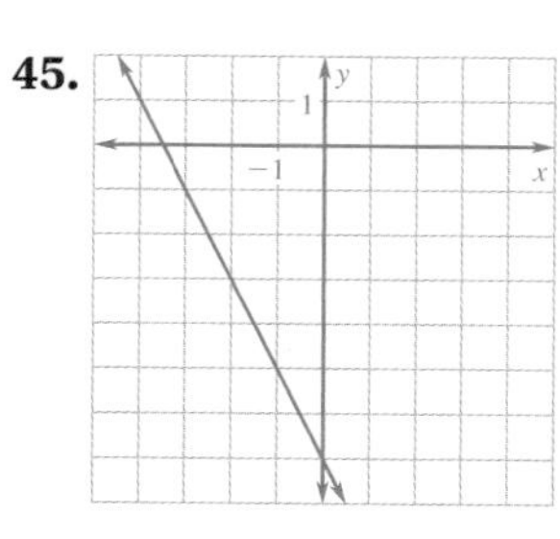

46. 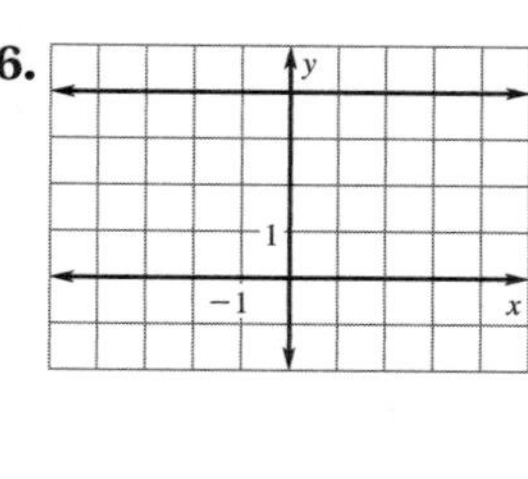

47. 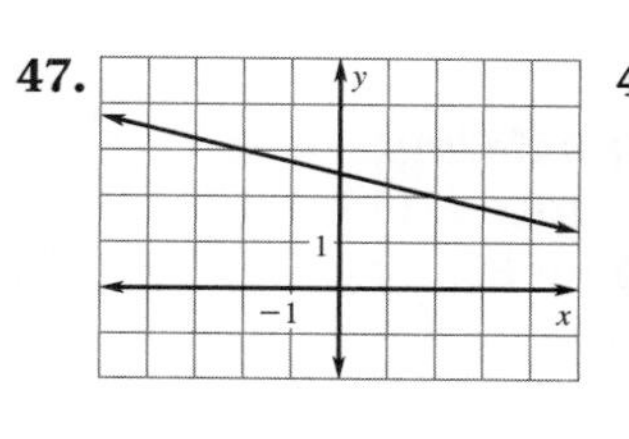

48. 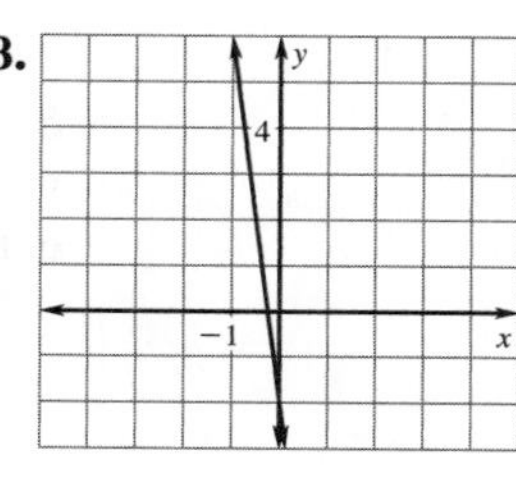

49. 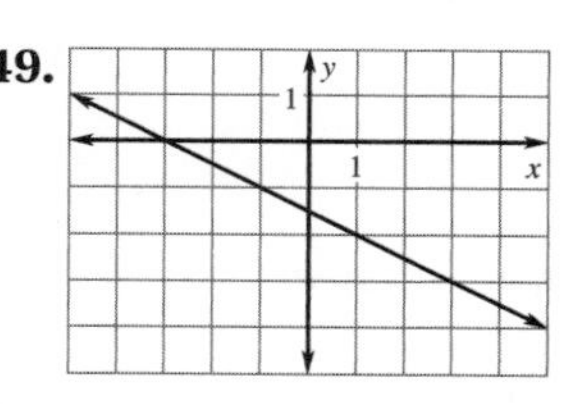

50. 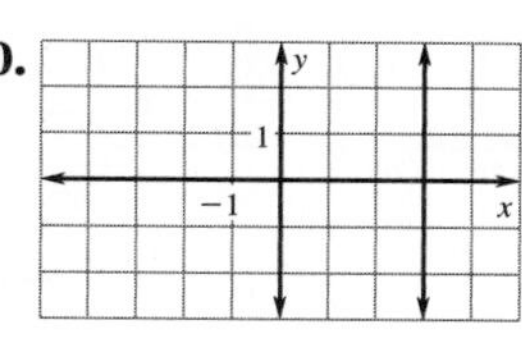

51. 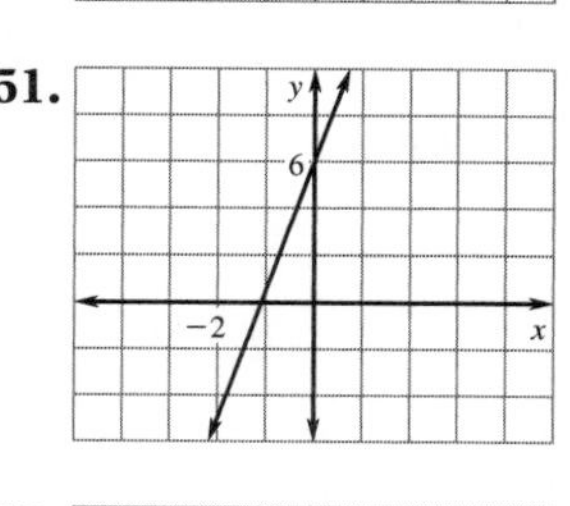

52. 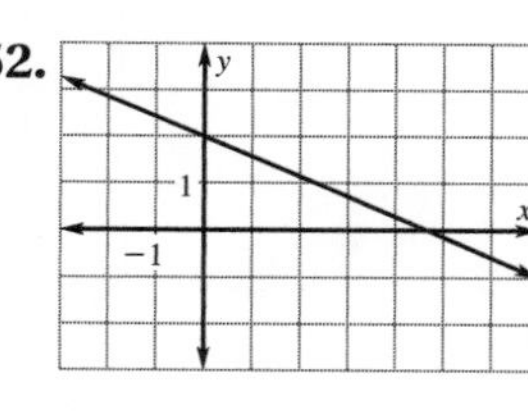

53. 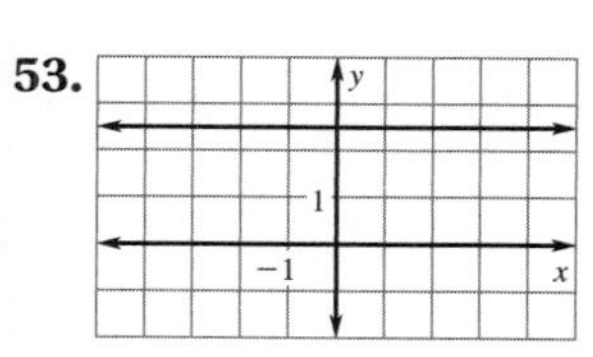

54. 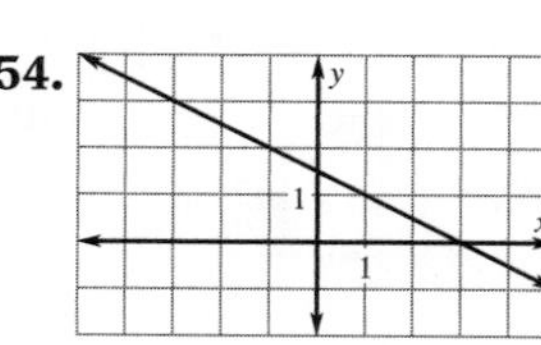

Quiz for Lessons 2.1–2.3 (p. 96)

6. 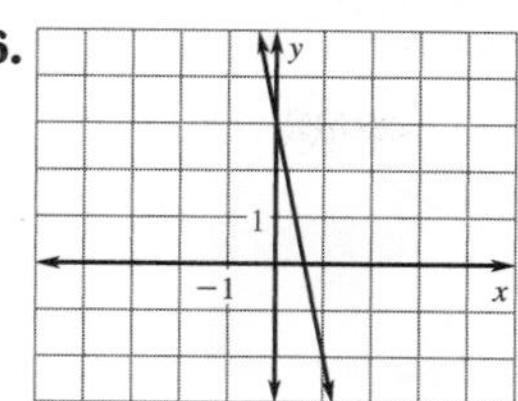

7. 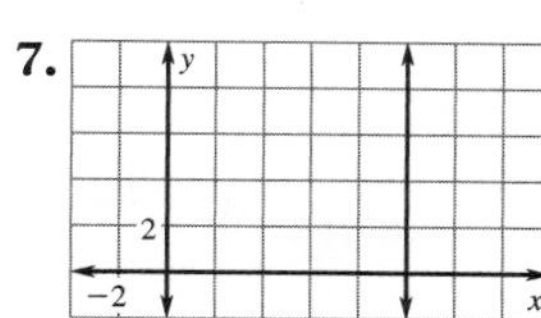

8. 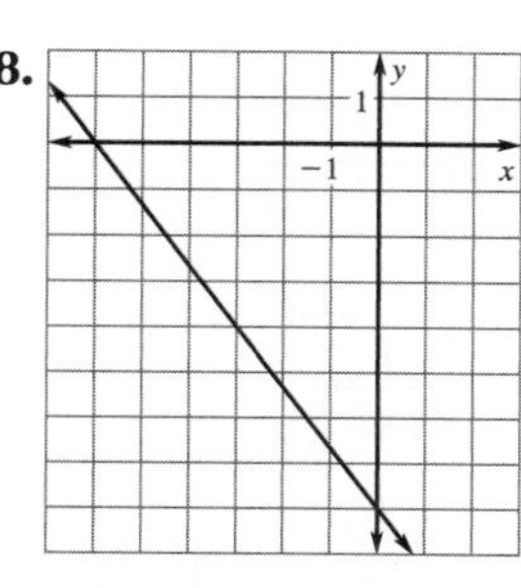

9. 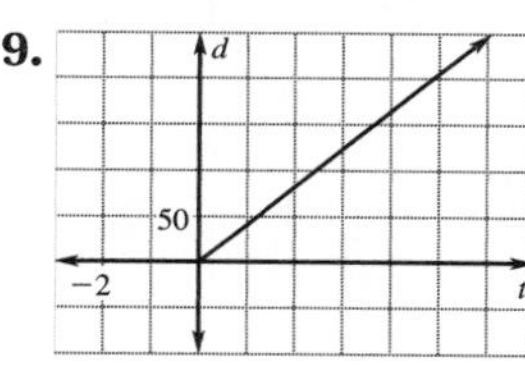

ADDITIONAL ANSWERS

2.3 Graphing Calculator Activity (p. 97)

4. 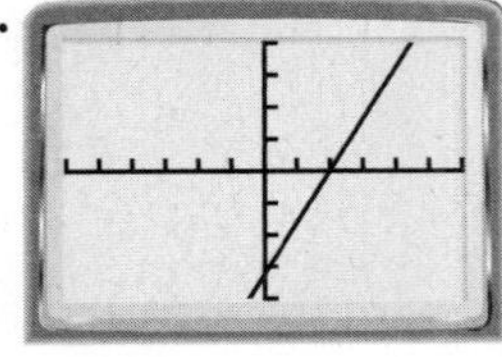

5. 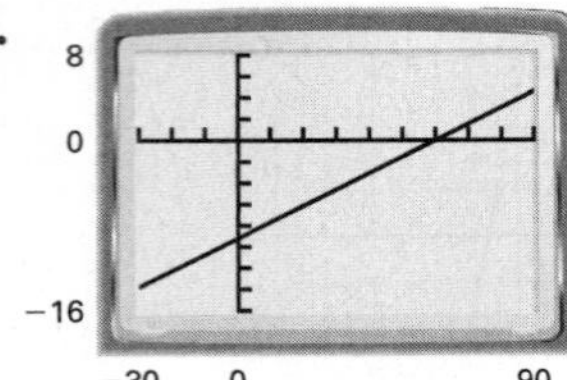

6. 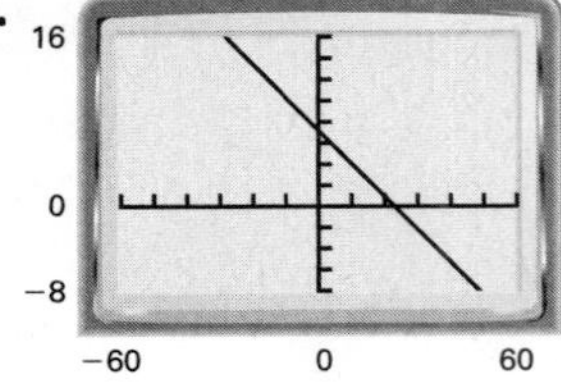

2.4 Problem Solving (pp. 103–104)

57. b. 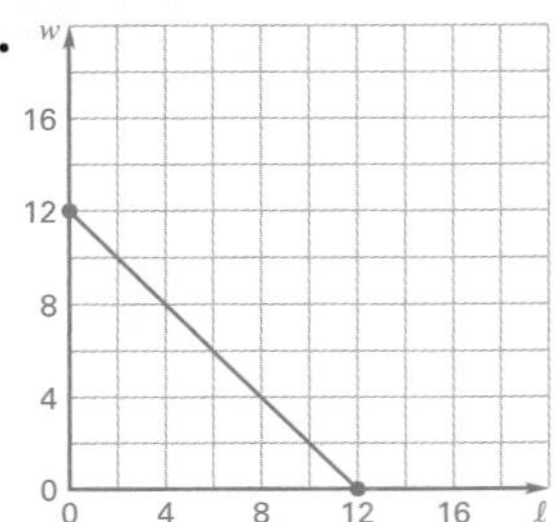

c. *Sample:*

ℓ	w
6	6
7	5
8	4
9	3
10	2

2.5 Guided Practice (pp. 107–109)

1. 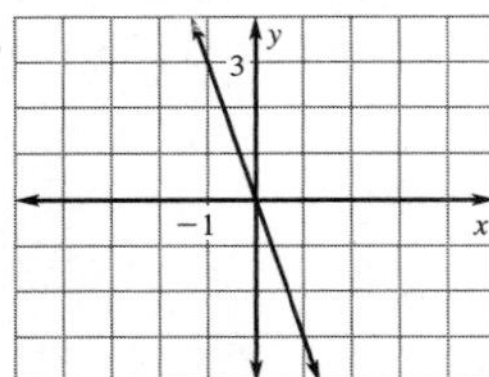

2. 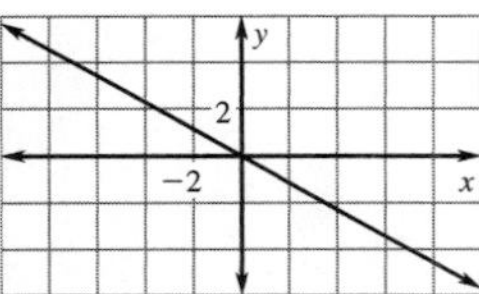

3. 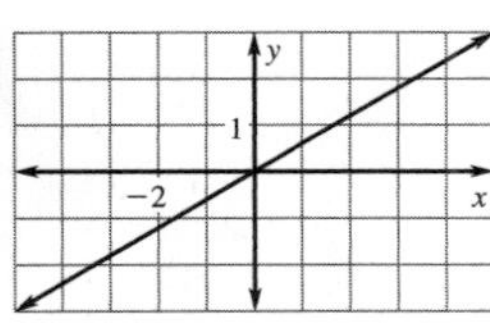

4. 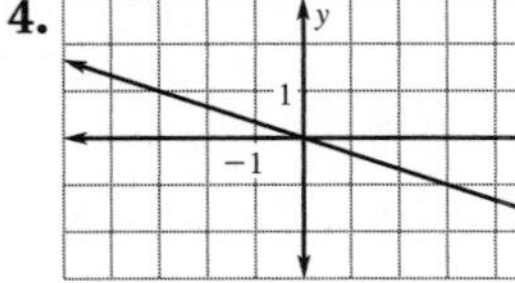

2.6 Skill Practice (pp. 117–118)

10. a. 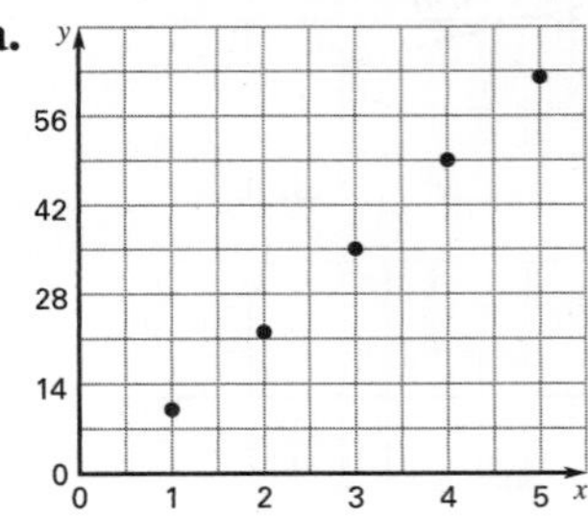

b. *Sample answer:* $y = 13x - 4$
c. about 256

11. a. 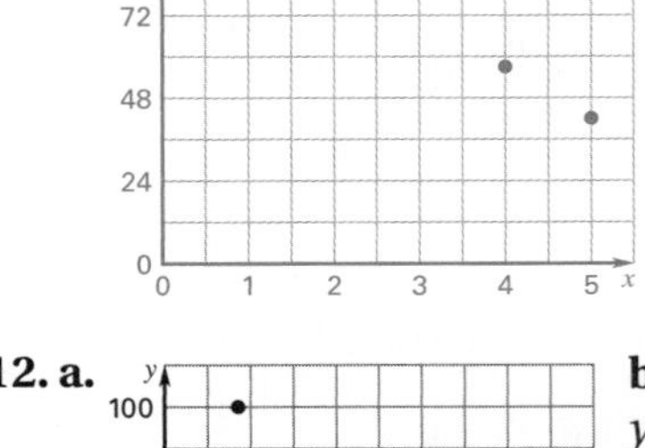

b. *Sample answer:* $y = -20x + 141$
c. about −259

12. a. 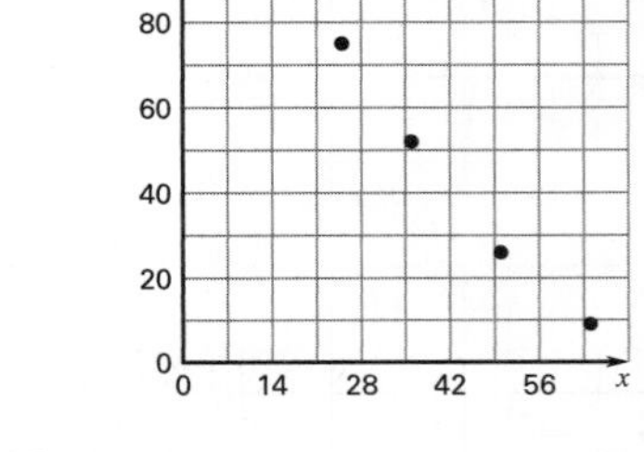

b. *Sample answer:* $y = -1.8x + 119$
c. about 83

13. a. 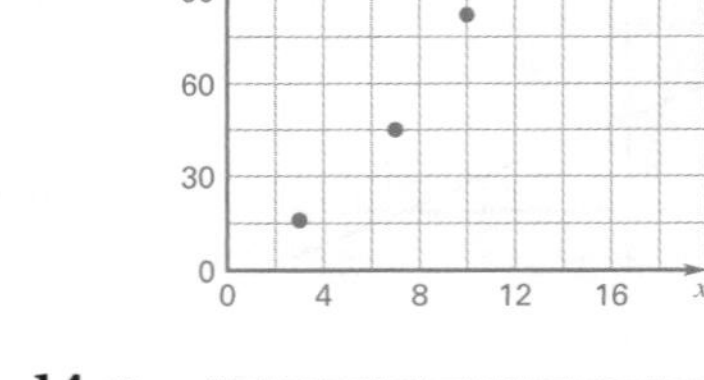

b. *Sample answer:* $y = 6.7x + 1$
c. about 135

14. a. 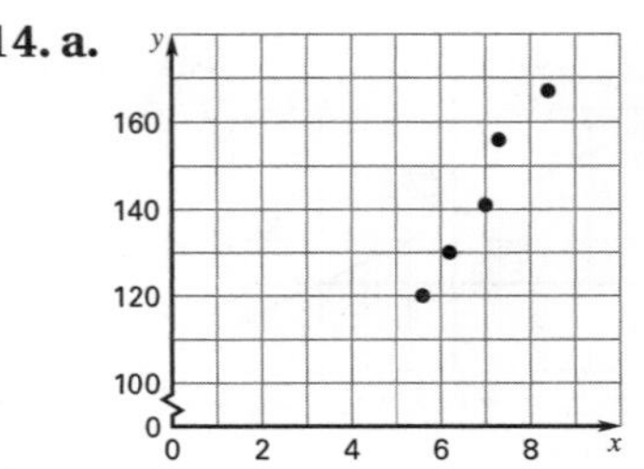

b. *Sample answer:* $y = 17.4x + 22.8$
c. about 371

15. a. 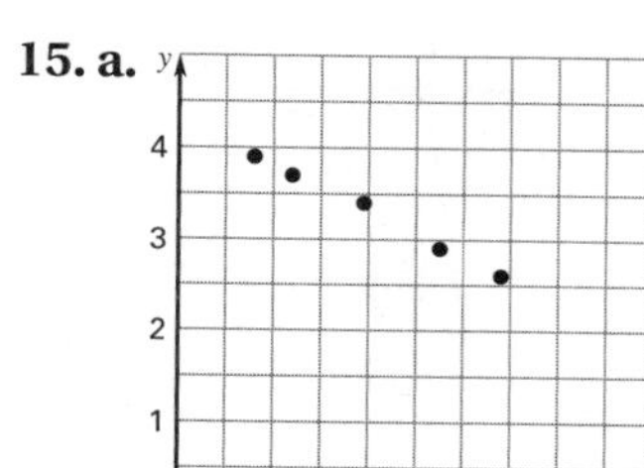

b. *Sample answer:* $y = -0.025x + 4.35$
c. about 3.82

Quiz for Lessons 2.4–2.6 (p. 120)

7. 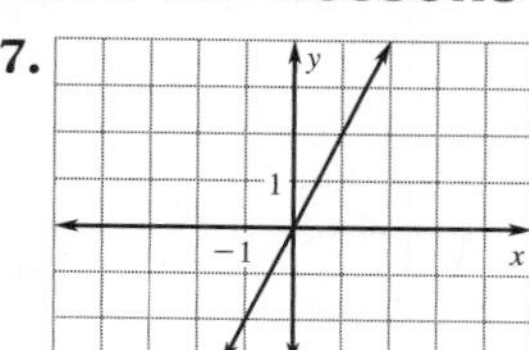
8. 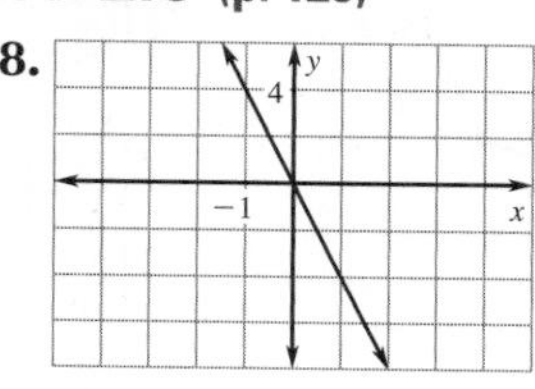
9. 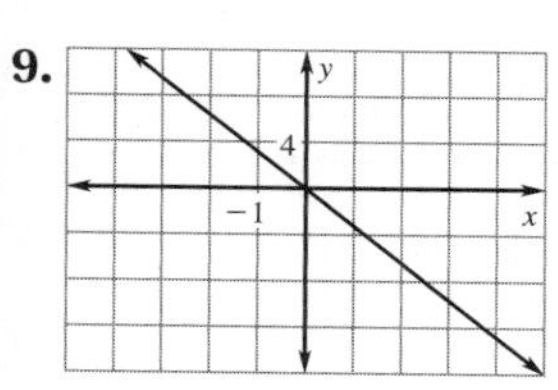
10. 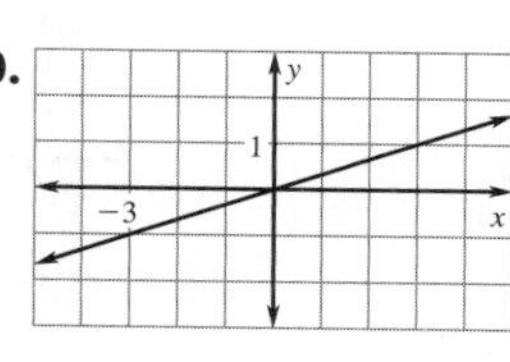

2.7 Investigating Algebra Activity (p. 122)

2. 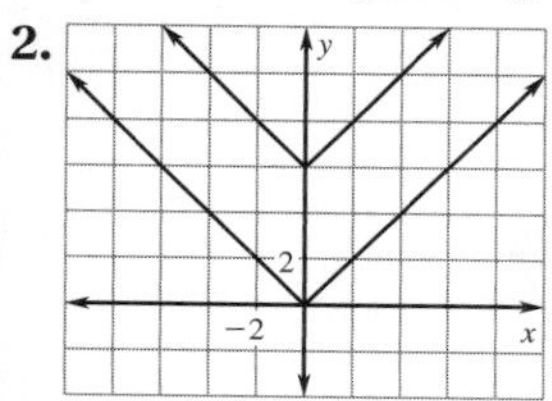
3. 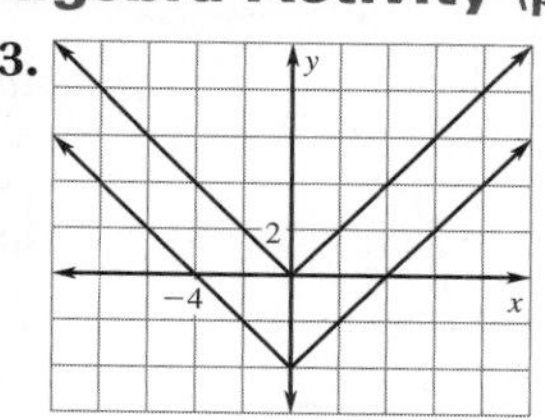
4. 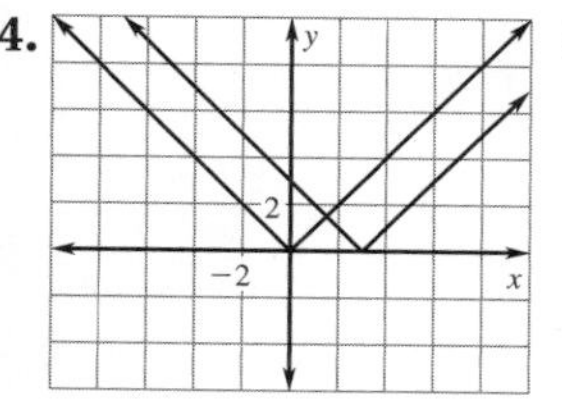
5. 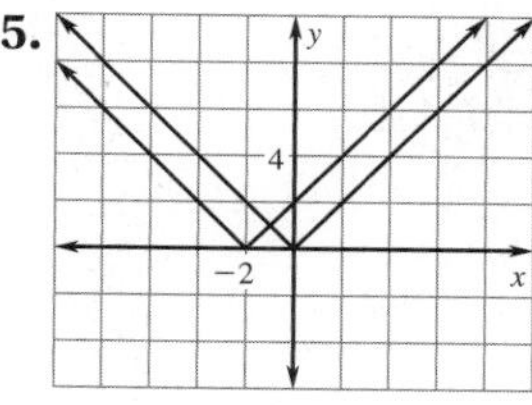
6. 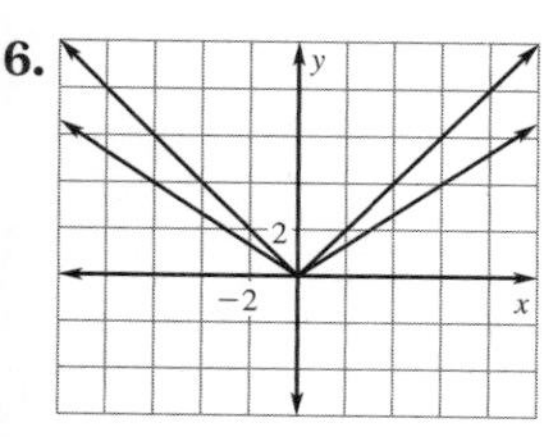
7. 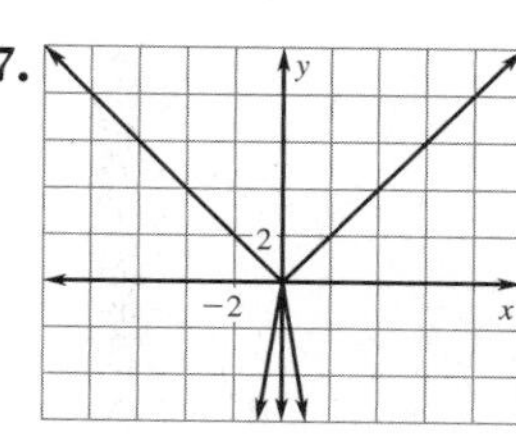
8. 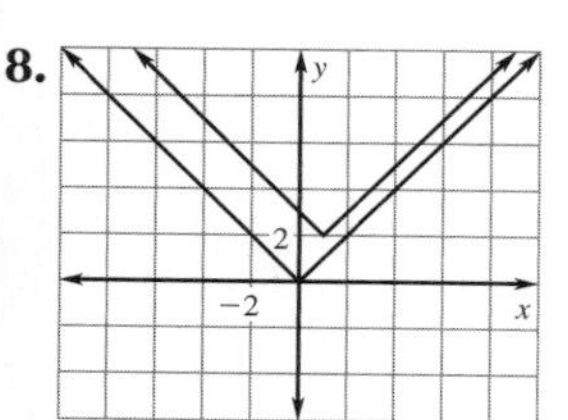
9. 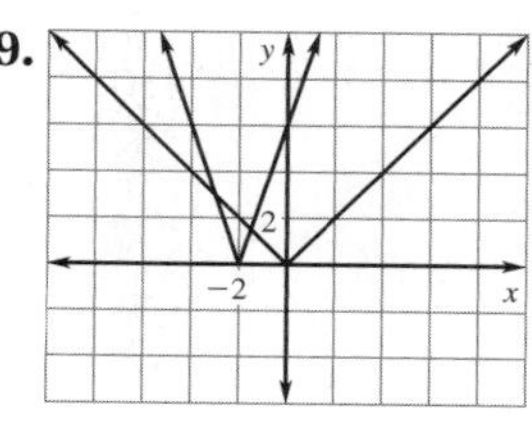

10. 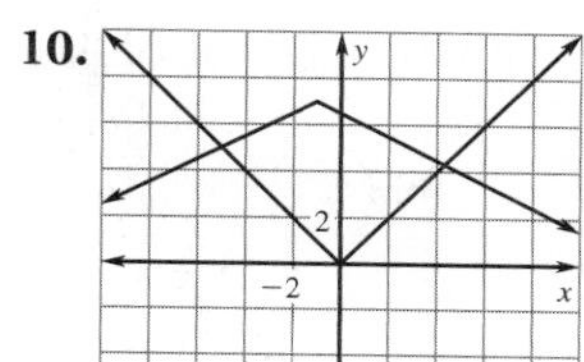

2.7 Skill Practice (pp. 127–128)

3. 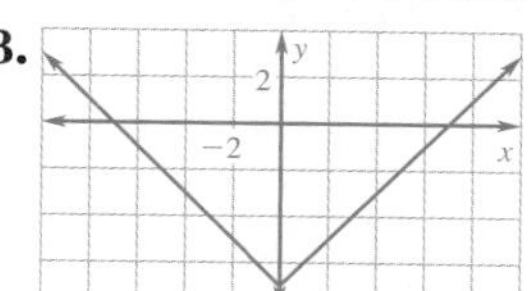 translated down 7 units

4. 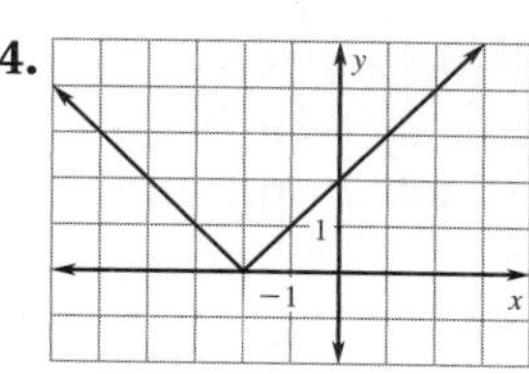 translated left 2 units

5. 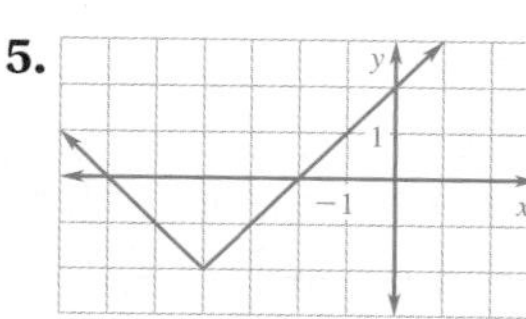 translated left 4 units and down 2 units

6. 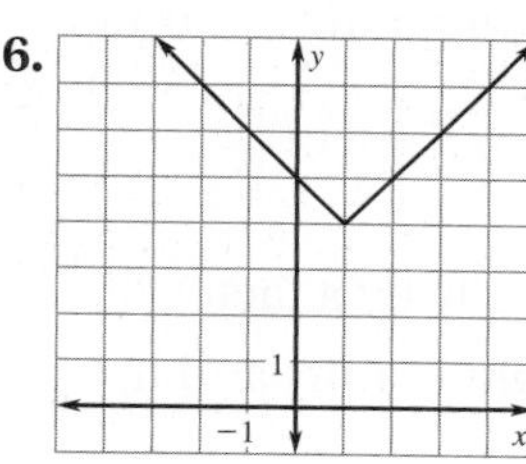 translated right 1 unit and up 4 units

7. 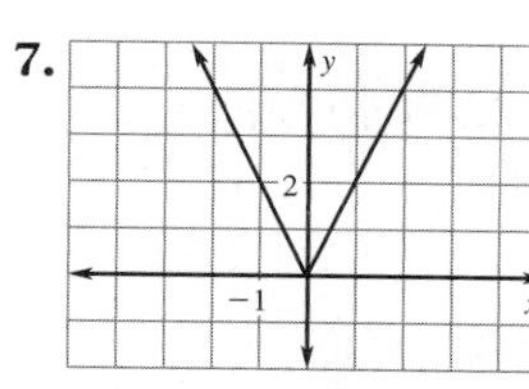 stretched vertically by a factor of 2

8. 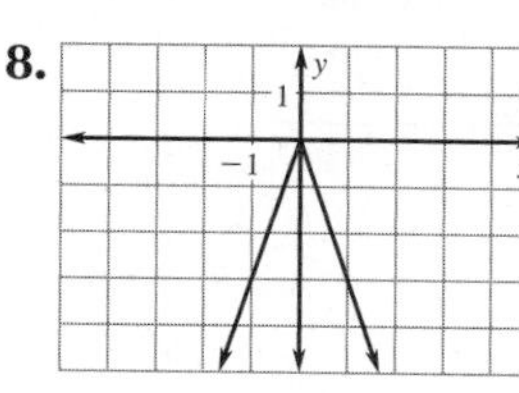 reflected over the *x*-axis and stretched vertically by a factor of 3

9. 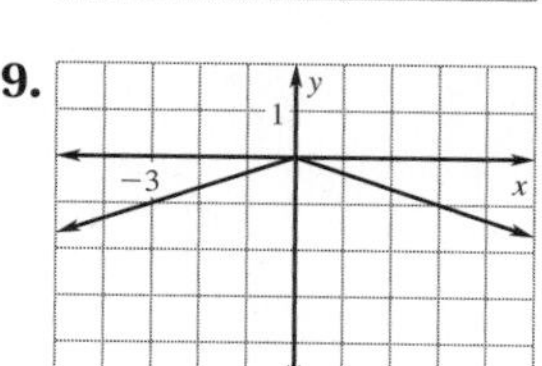 reflected over the *x*-axis and shrunk vertically by a factor of $\frac{1}{3}$

ADDITIONAL ANSWERS

10. 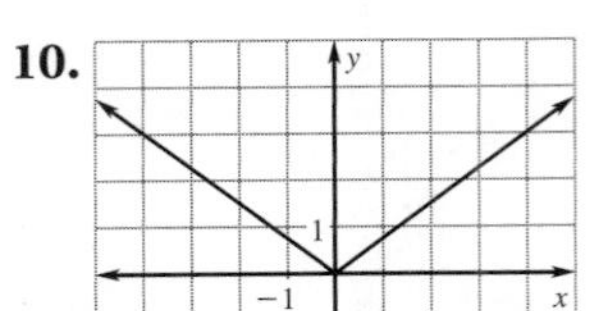

shrunk vertically by a factor of $\frac{3}{4}$

11. 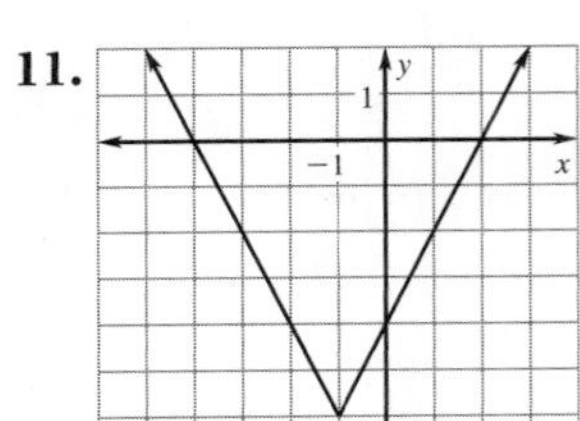

stretched vertically by a factor of 2, translated left 1 unit and down 6 units

12. 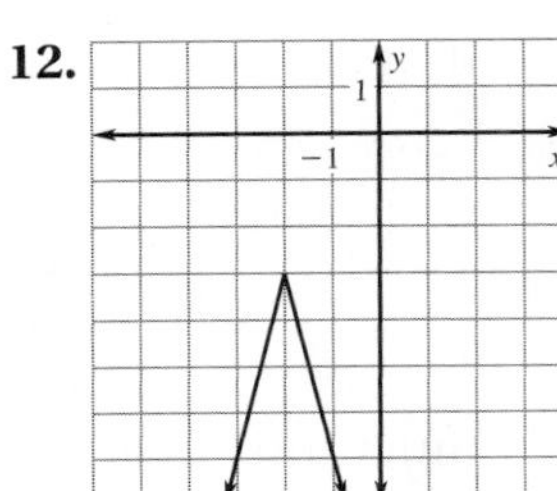

reflected over the x-axis, stretched vertically by a factor of 4, translated left 2 units and down 3 units

13. 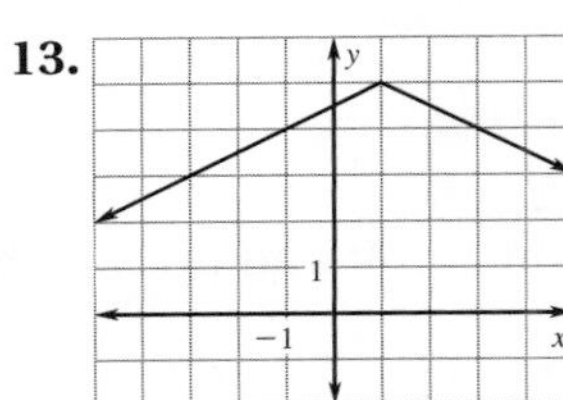

reflected over the x-axis, shrunk vertically by a factor of $\frac{1}{2}$, translated right 1 unit and up 5 units

14. 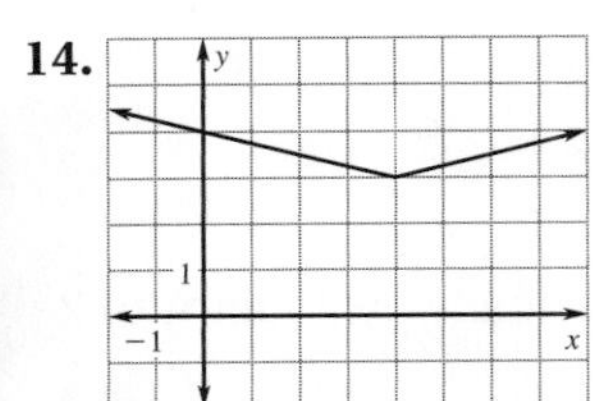

shrunk vertically by a factor of $\frac{1}{4}$, translated right 4 units and up 3 units

21. 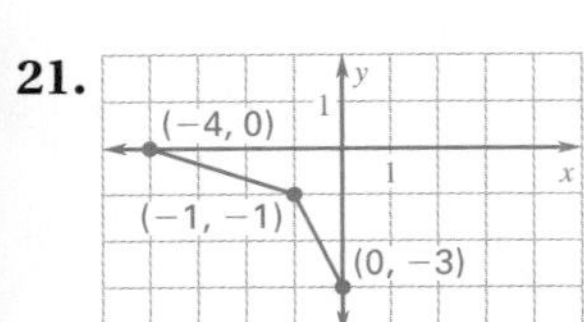

22. 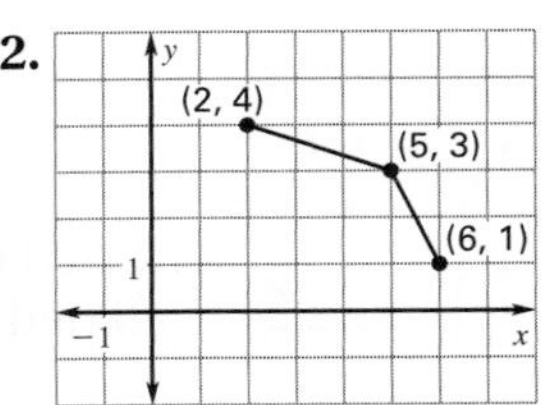

23. 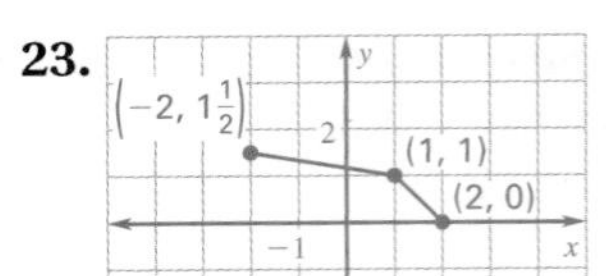

24. 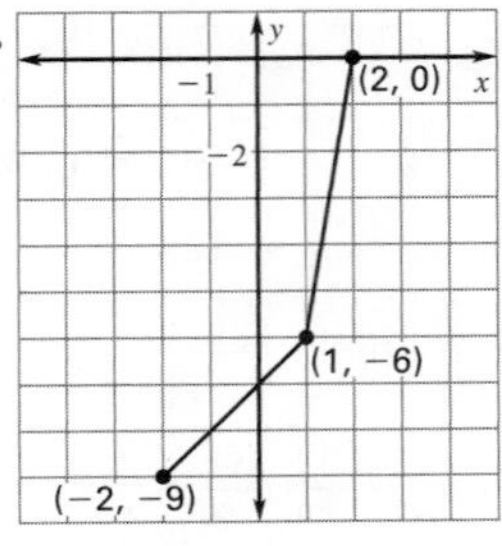

25. 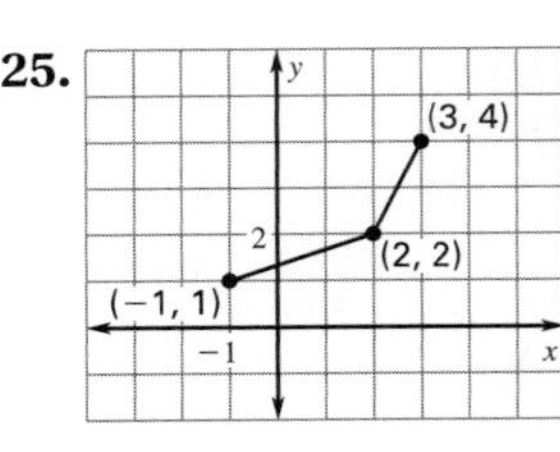

26. 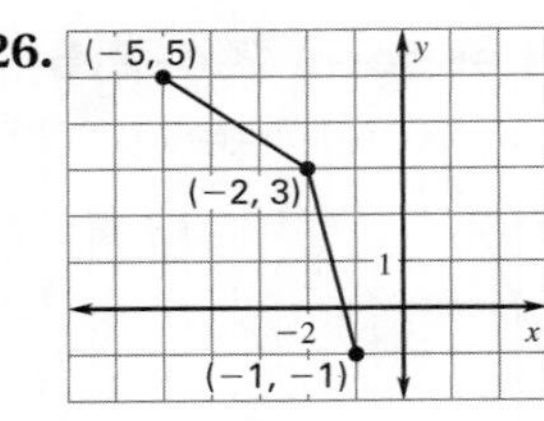

27. *Sample:*

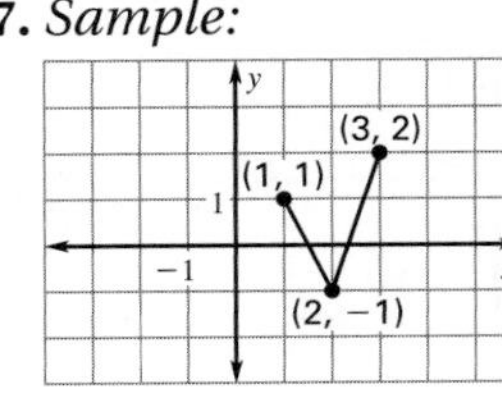

a. *Sample:*

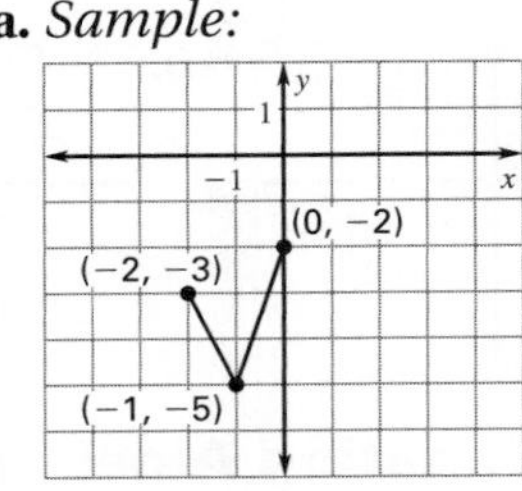

b. *Sample:*

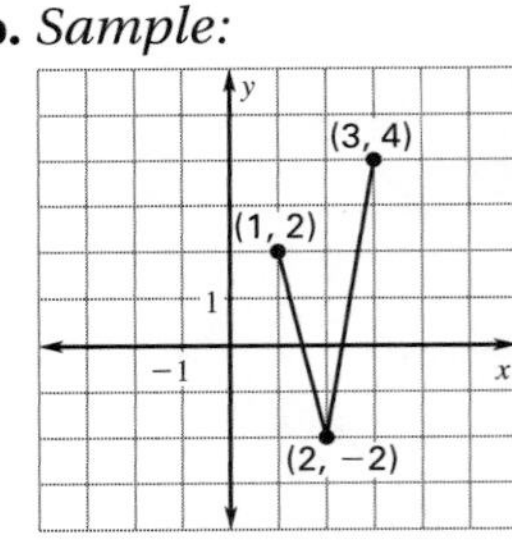

c. *Sample:*

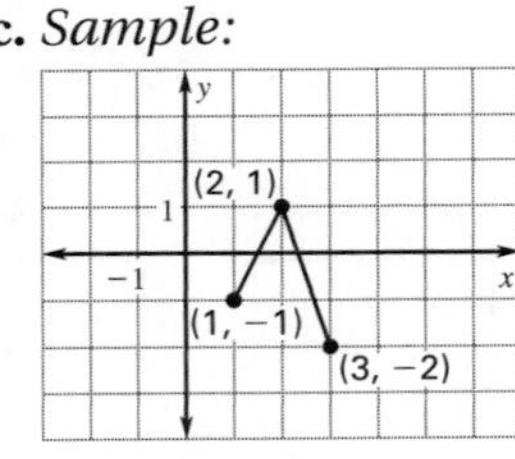

ADDITIONAL ANSWERS

2.8 Guided Practice (pp. 132–135)

11. Step 1: $0.4x + 1.2y \leq 420$

Step 2:

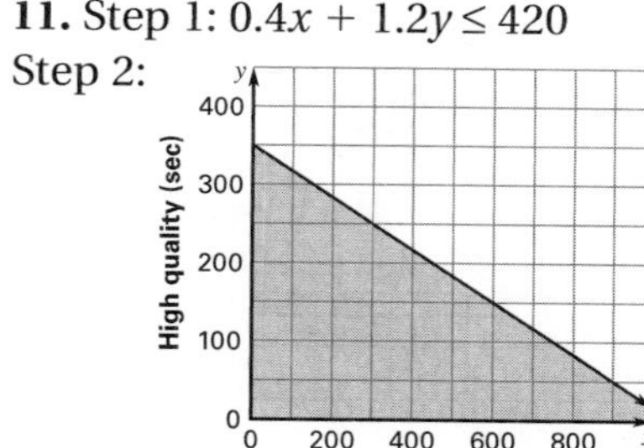

Step 3: *Sample answer:* 300 standard and 200 high quality, 600 standard and 150 high quality, or 100 standard and 300 high quality

12.

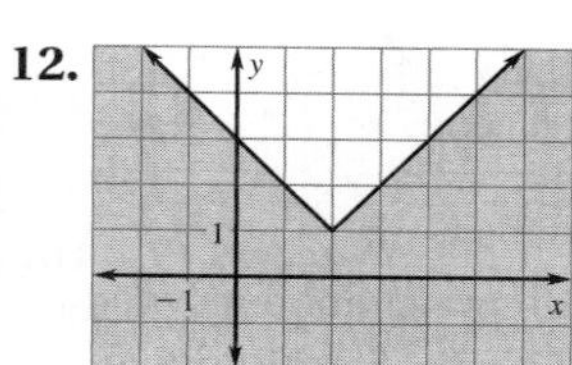

13.

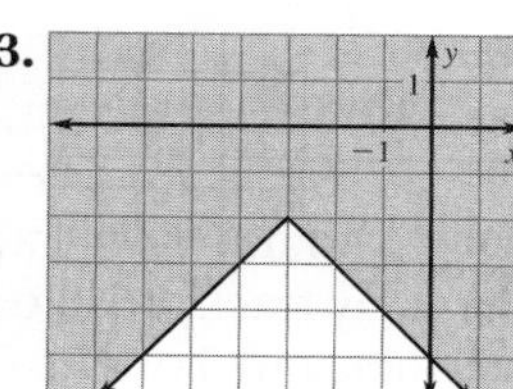

14.

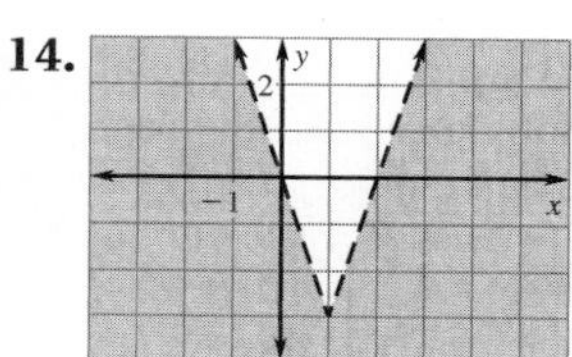

2.8 Skill Practice (pp. 135–136)

7.

8.

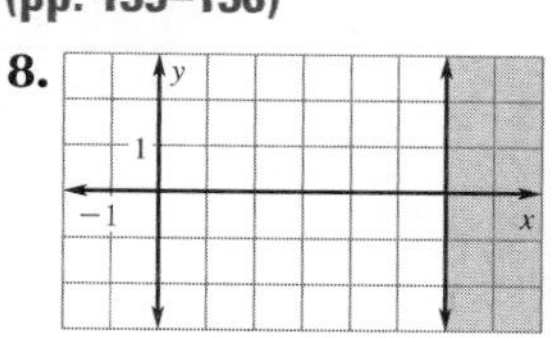

9.

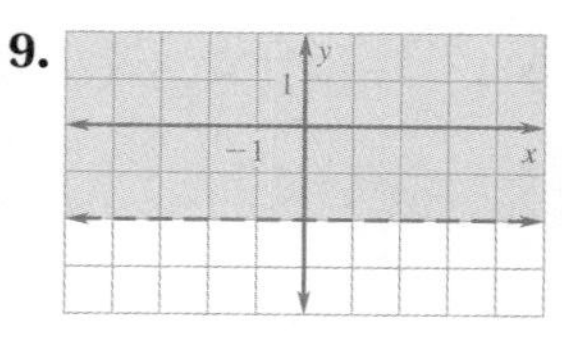

10.

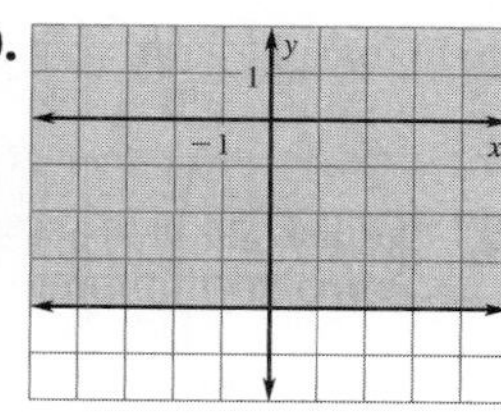

11.

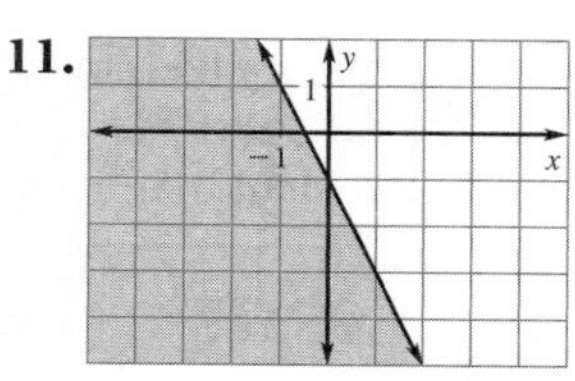

12.

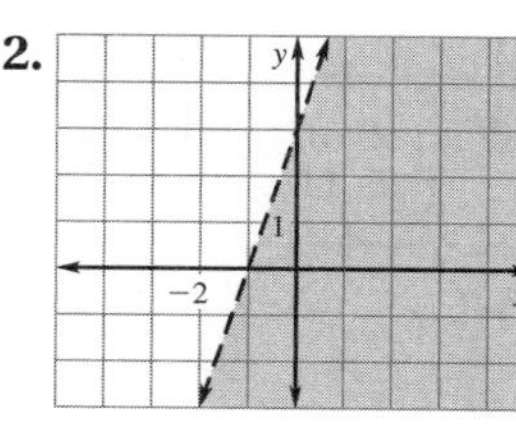

13.

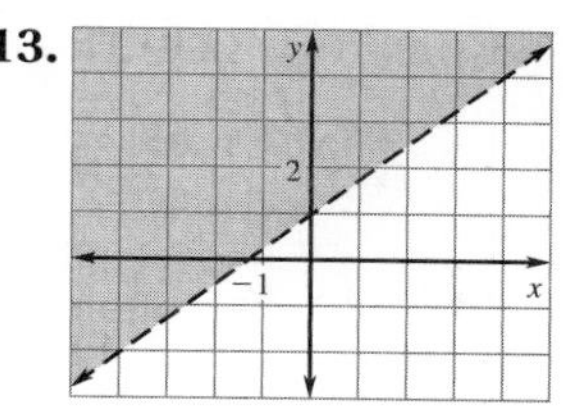

14.

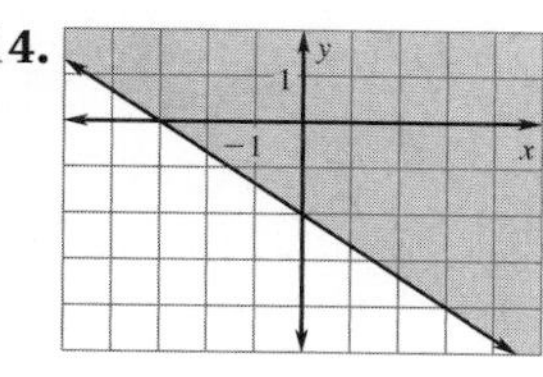

15.

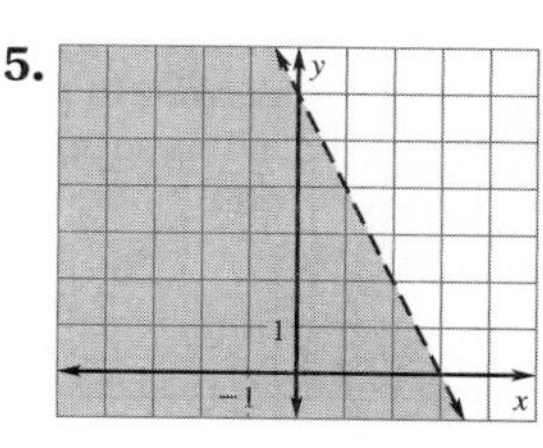

16.

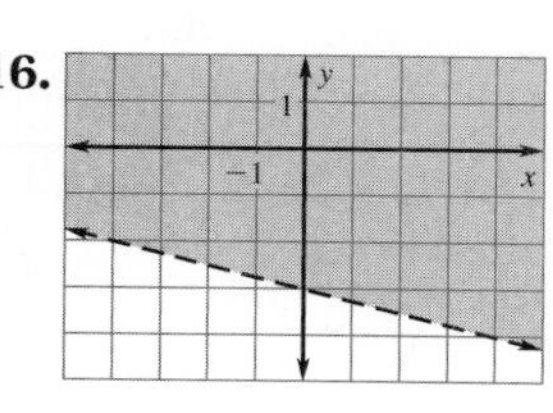

17.

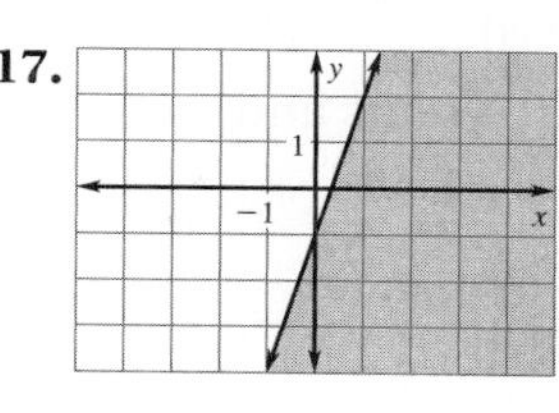

18.

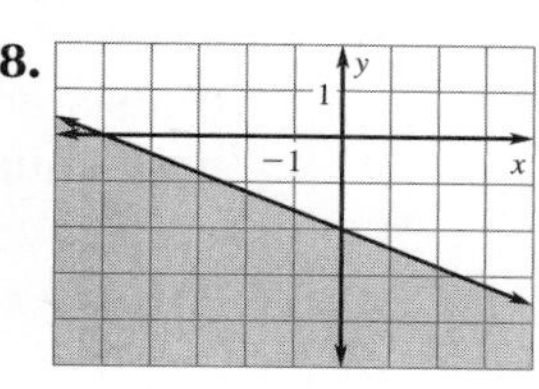

22.

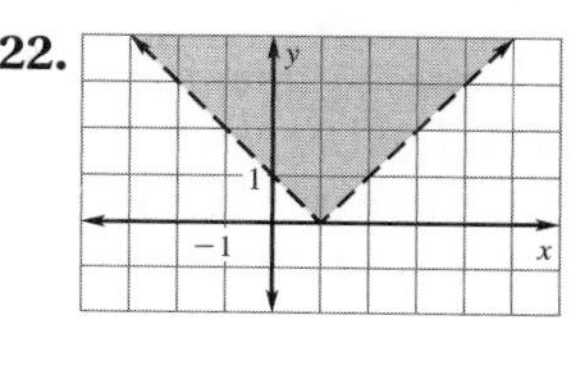

23.

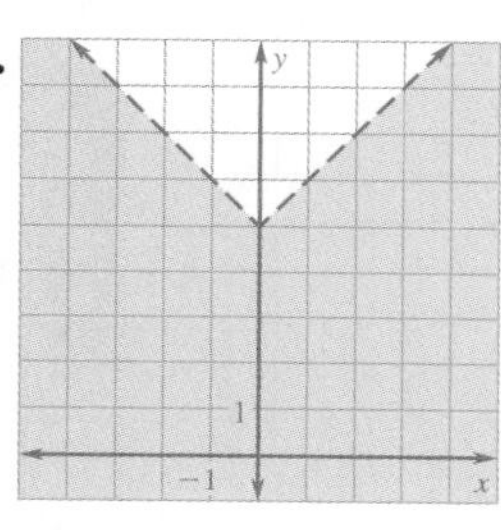

24.

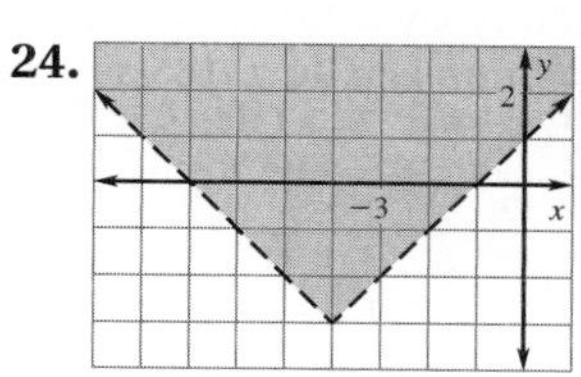

25.

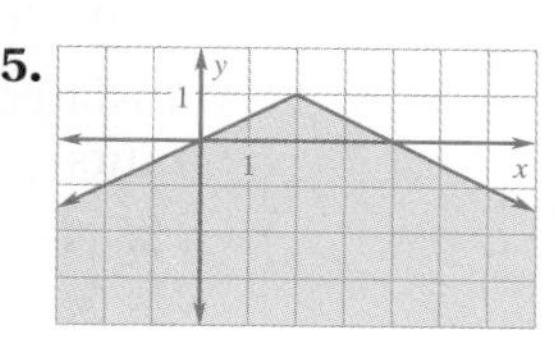

26.

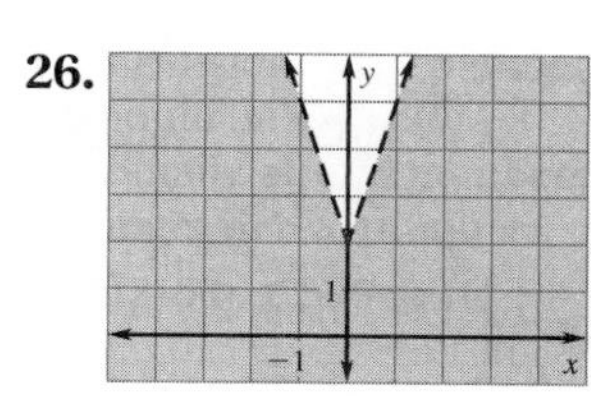

27.

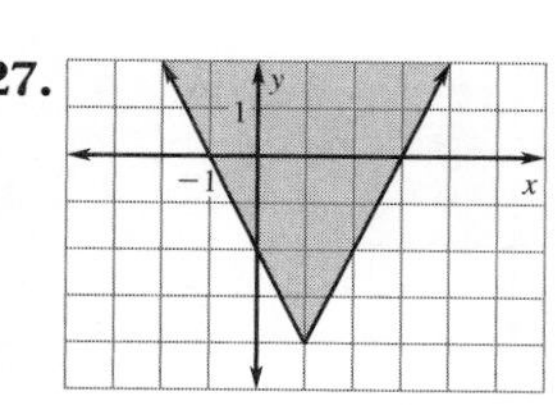

33.

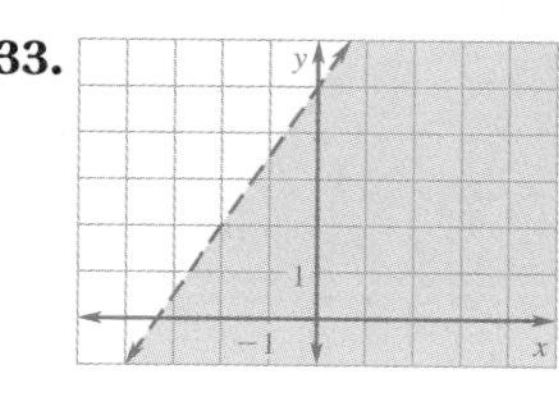

34.

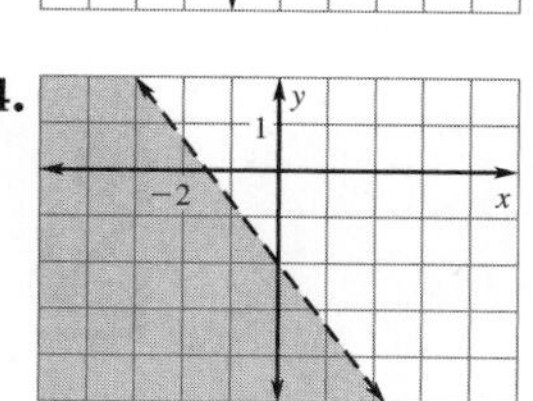

ADDITIONAL ANSWERS

35. 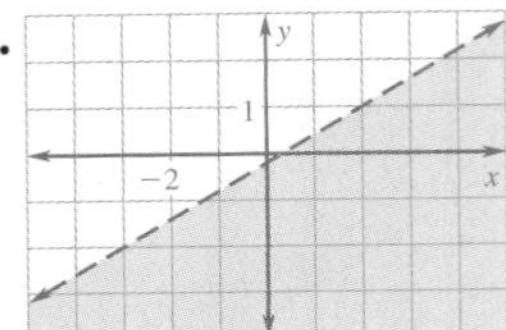

36. 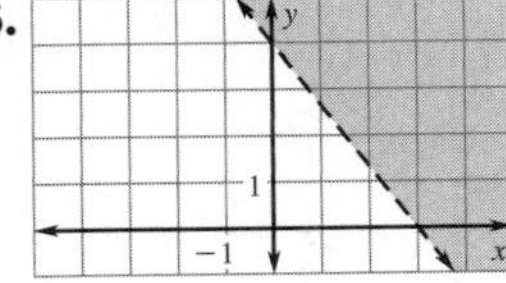

37. 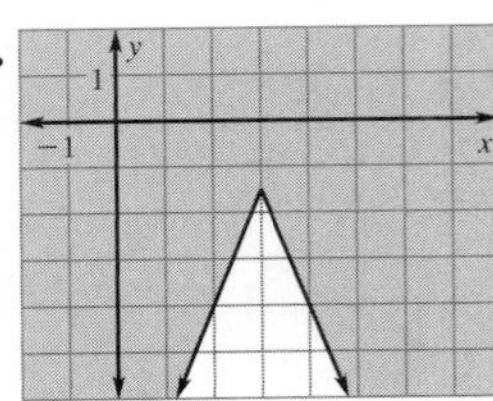

38. 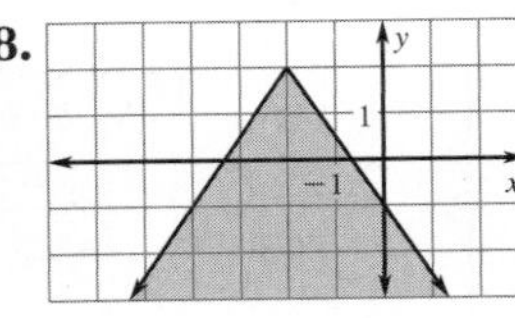

Quiz for Lessons 2.7–2.8 (p. 138)

1. 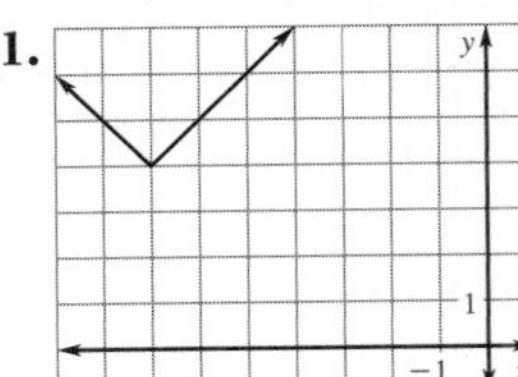 translated left 7 units and up 4 units

2. 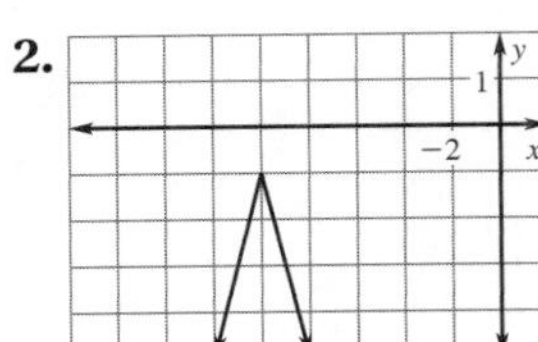 reflected over the x-axis and stretched vertically by a factor of 2, translated left 10 units and down 1 unit

3. 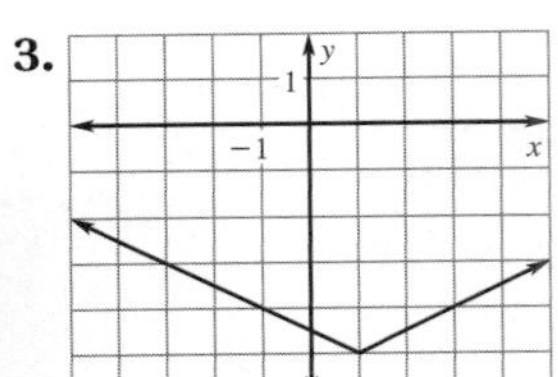 shrunk vertically by a factor of $\frac{1}{2}$, translated right 1 unit and down 5 units

7. 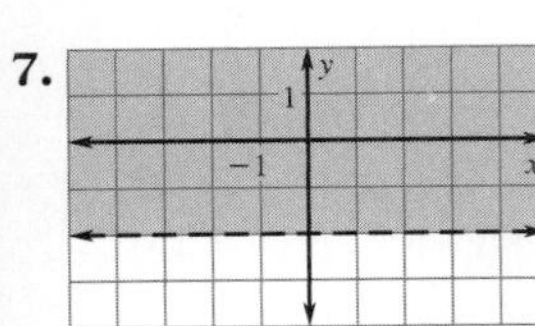

8. 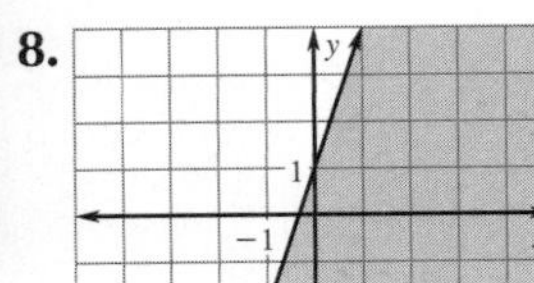

9. 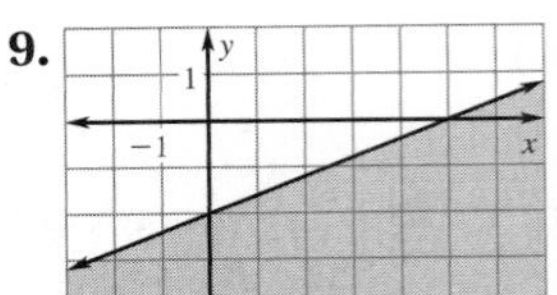

10. $2x + 3y \leq 20$;

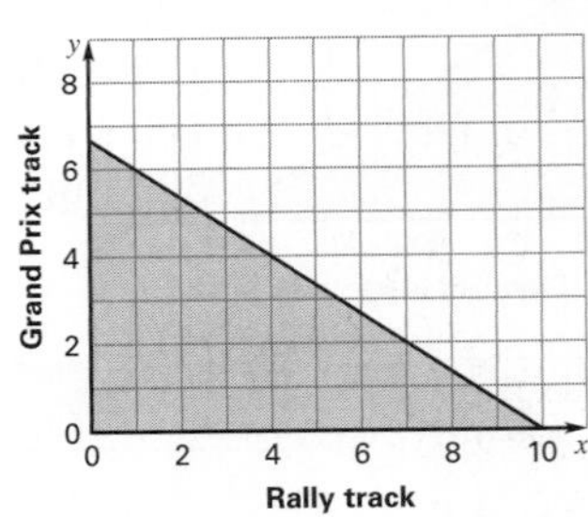

Sample answer: 4 on the Rally track and 4 on the Grand Prix track, 5 on the Rally track and 3 on the Grand Prix track, or 2 on the Rally track and 5 on the Grand Prix

Chapter Review (pp. 141–144)

31. 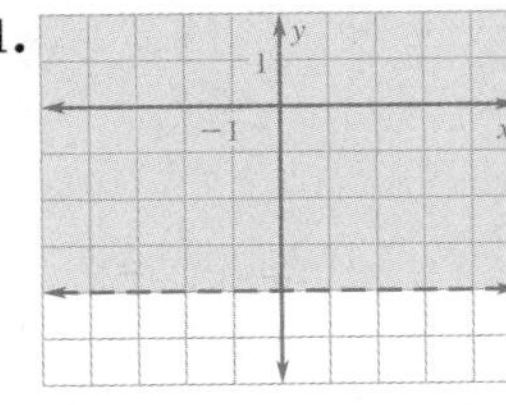

32. 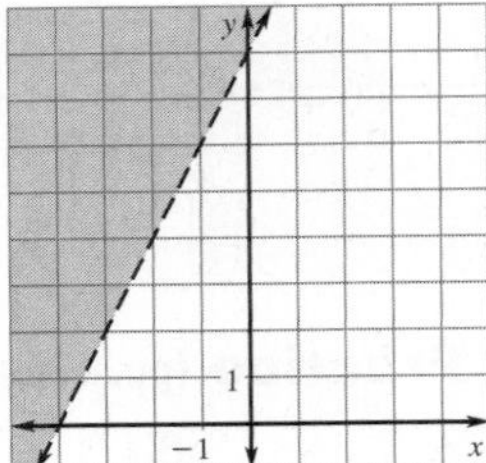

33. 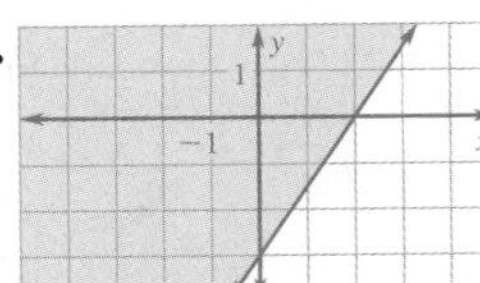

34. $1.5x + 2.5y \geq 180$;

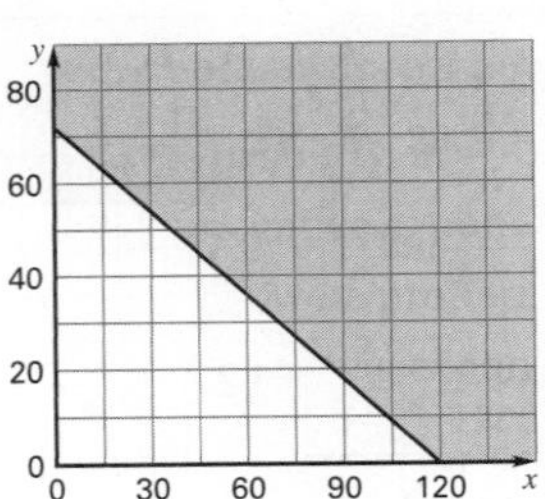

Chapter Test (p. 145)

20. 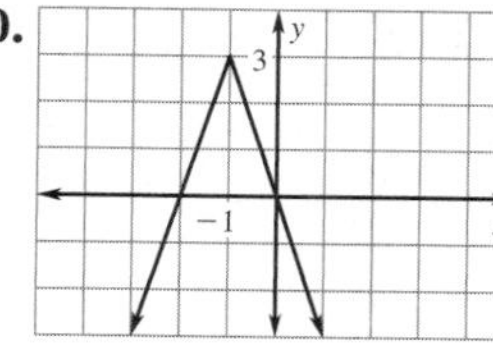

reflected over the x-axis, stretched by a factor of 3, translated left 1 unit and up 3 units

21. 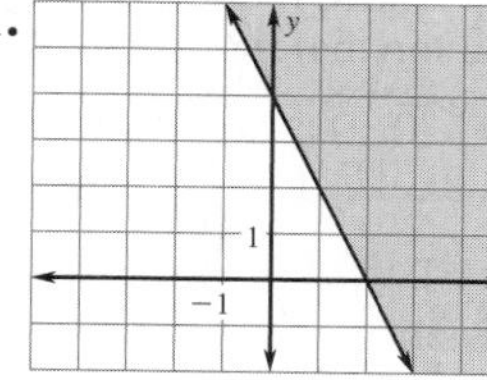

22. 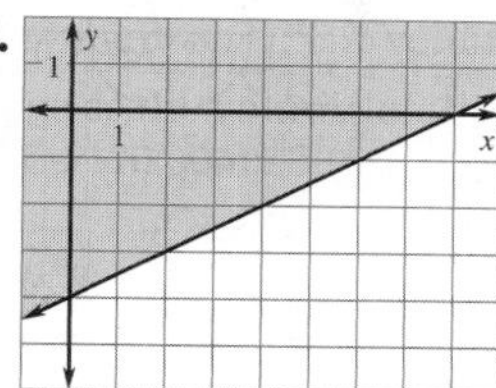

23. 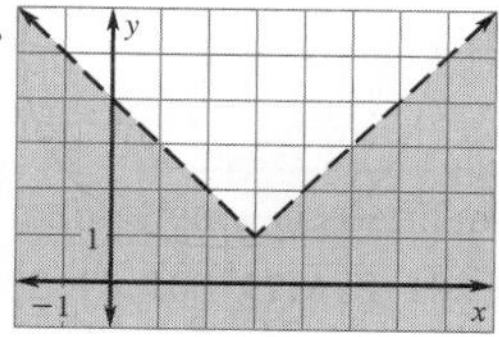

24. 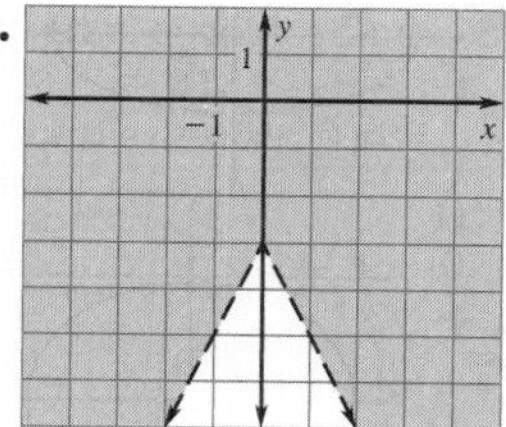

Chapter 3

3.1 Skill Practice (pp. 156–157)

3. 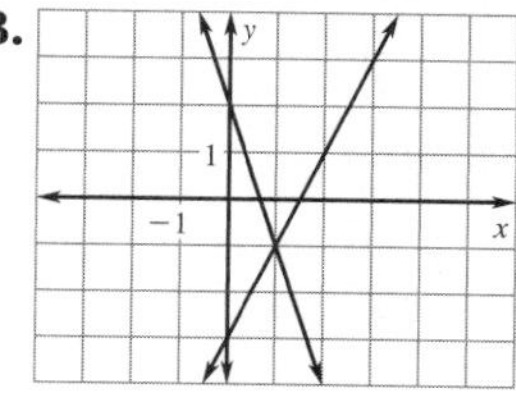

4. 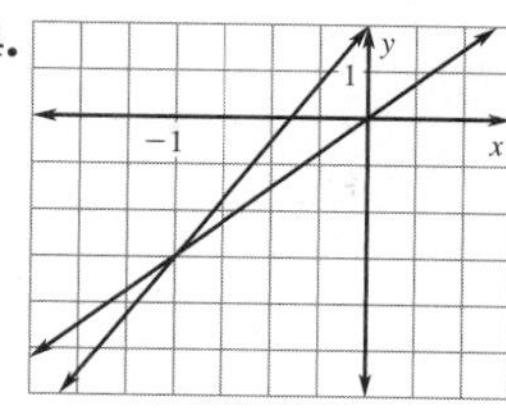

5. 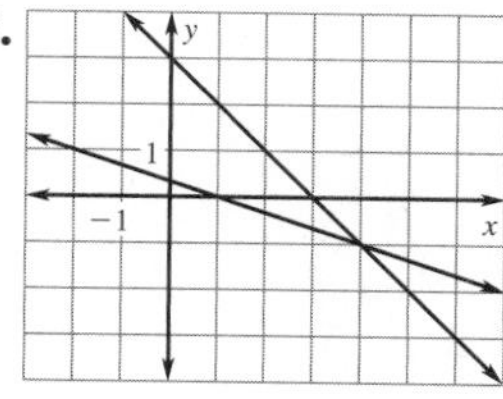

6. 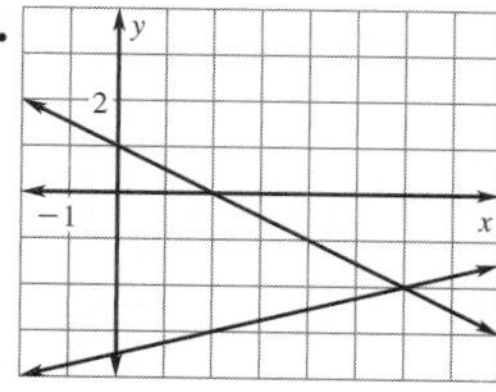

7. 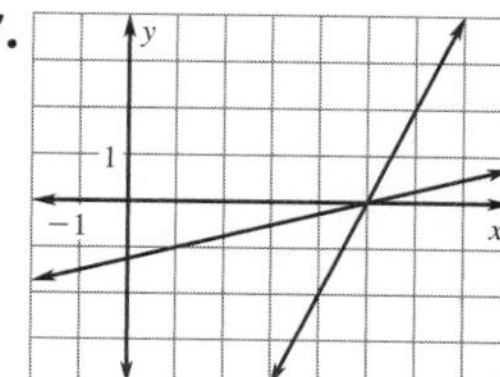

8. 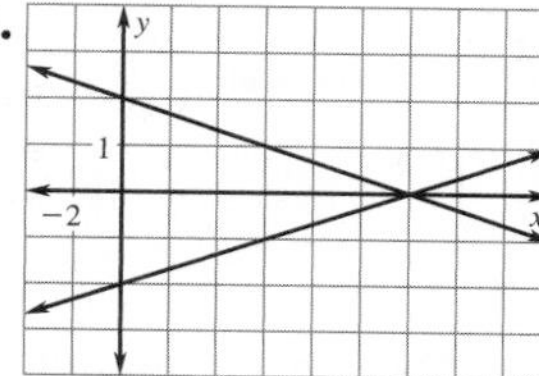

9. 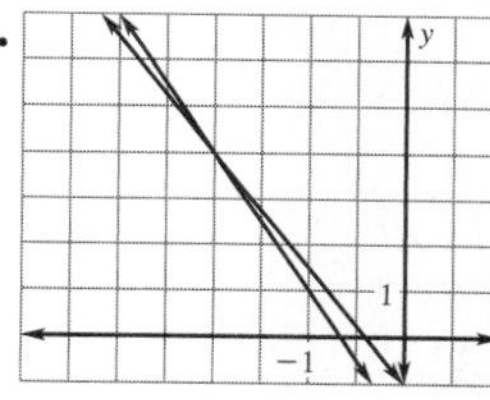

10. 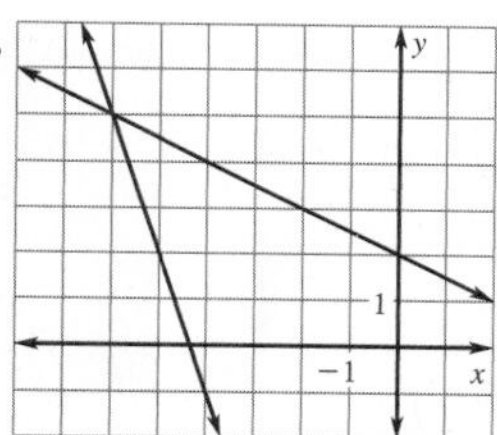

11. 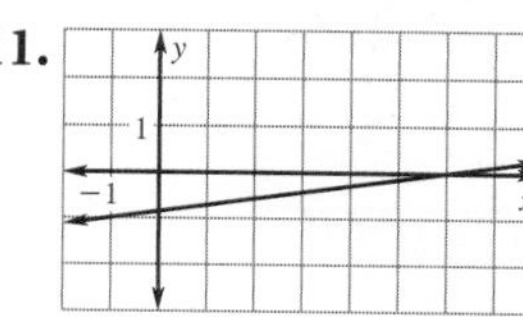

12. 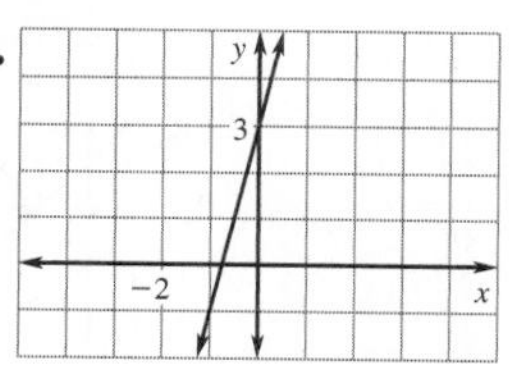

13. 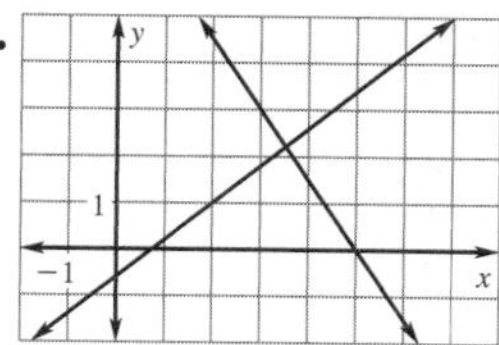

14. 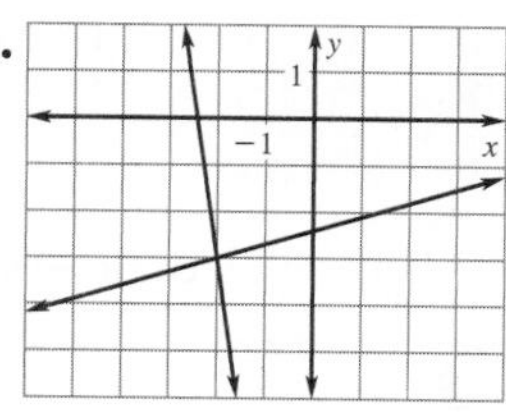

3.1 Problem Solving (pp. 157–158)

40. a.

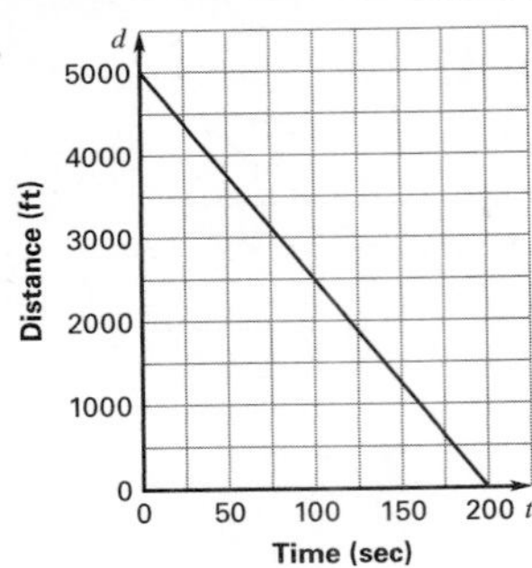

b.

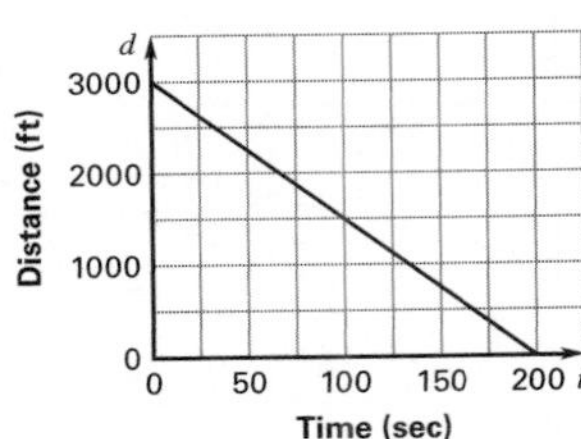

3.3 Guided Practice (pp. 169–170)

1.

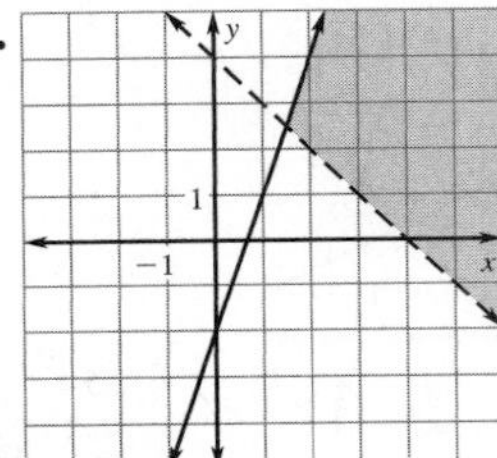

2.

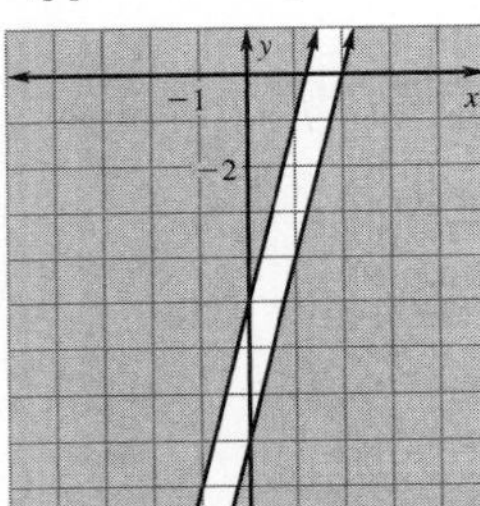

3.

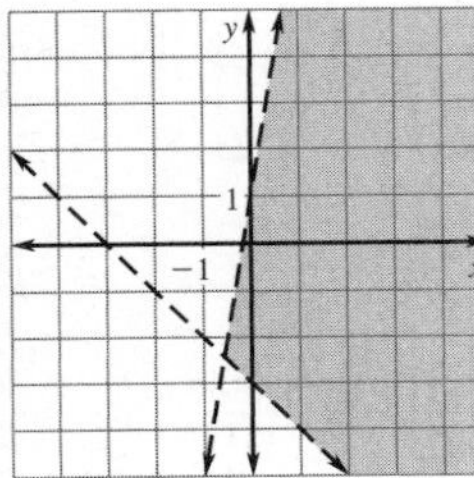

4.

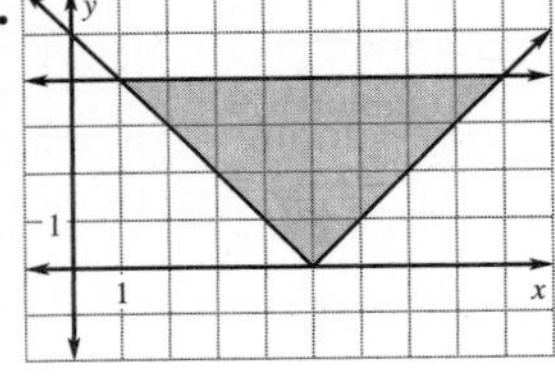

5.

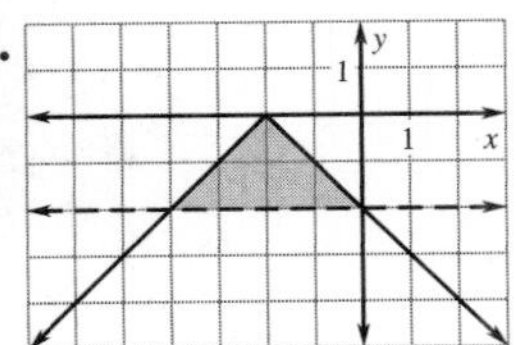

6. no solution

3.3 Skill Practice (pp. 171–173)

4.

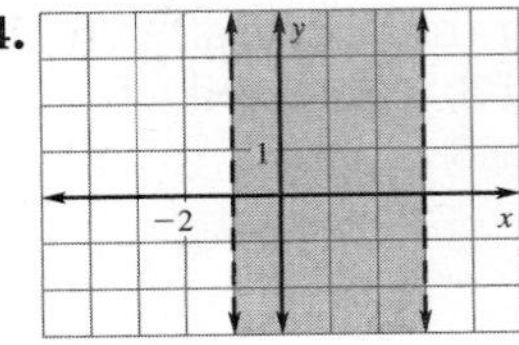

5.

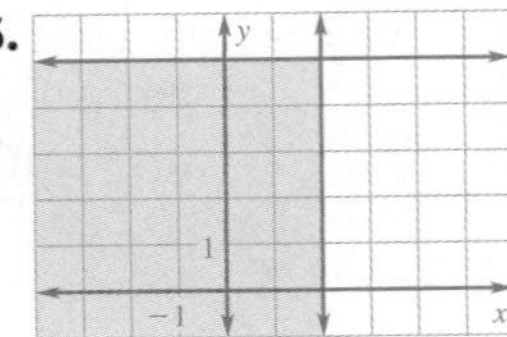

6. no solution

7. no solution

8.

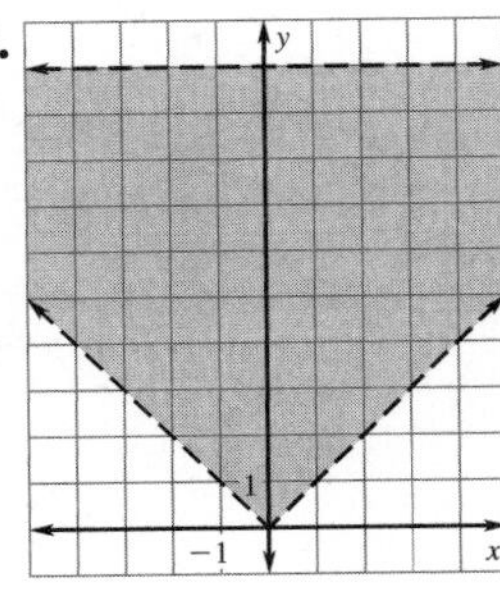

9.

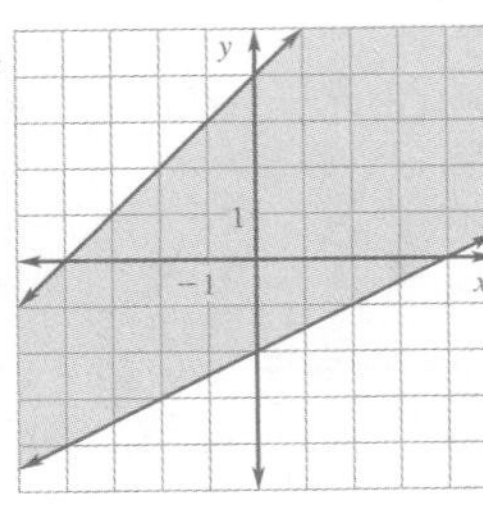

10.

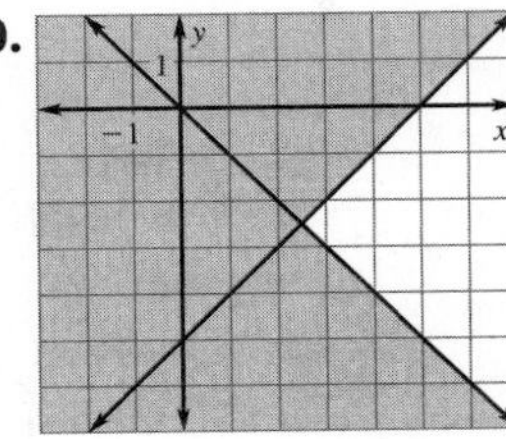

11.

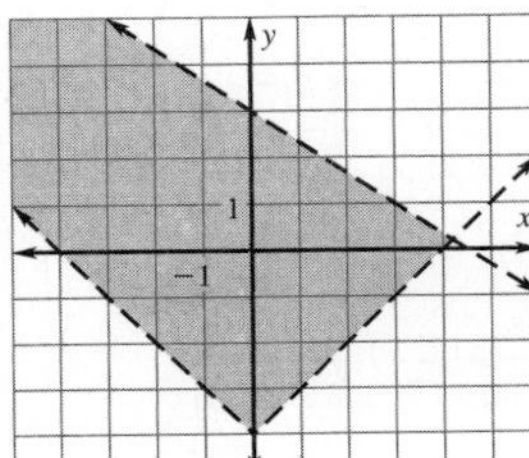

12.

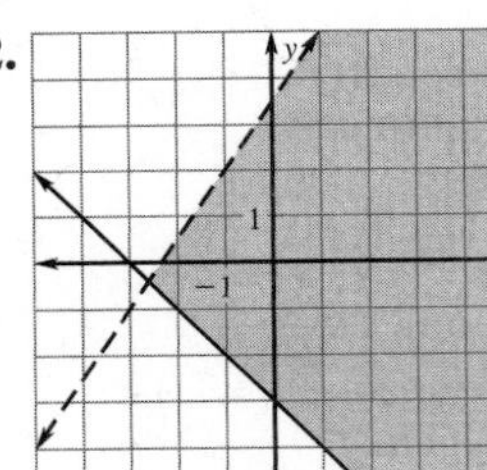

13. no solution

14.

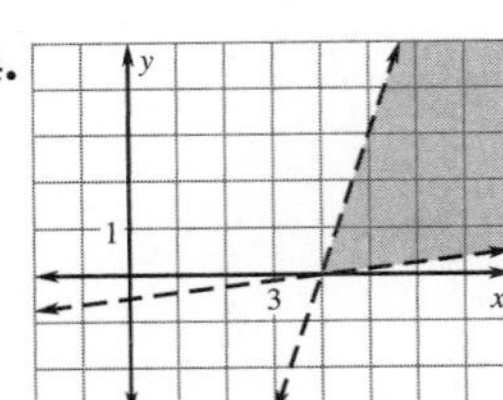

15.

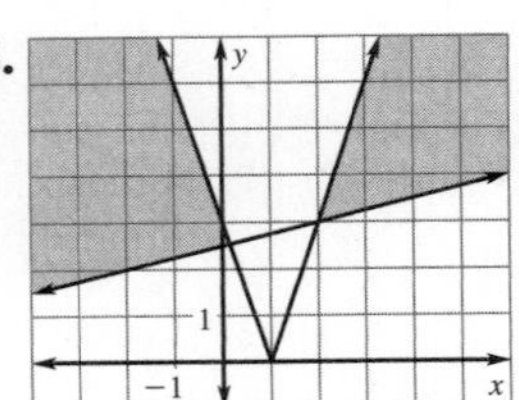

ADDITIONAL ANSWERS

17.
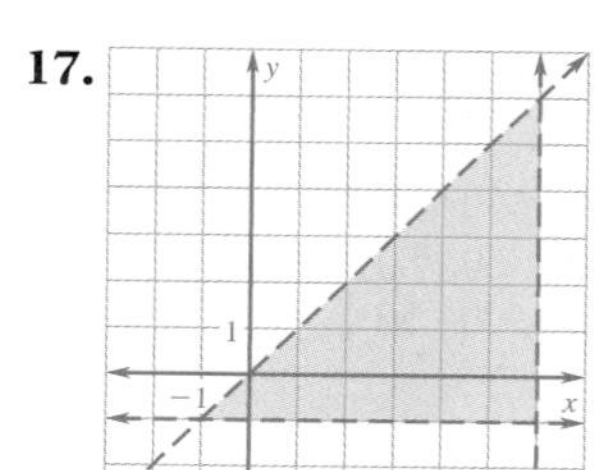

18.
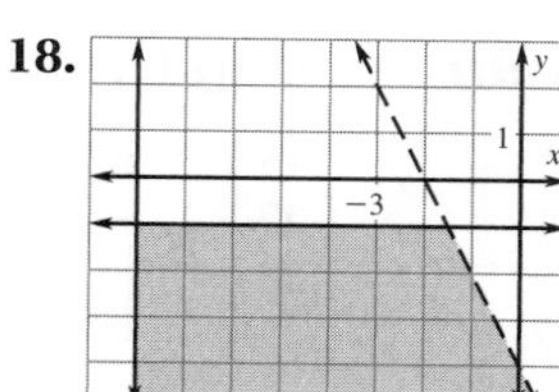

19.
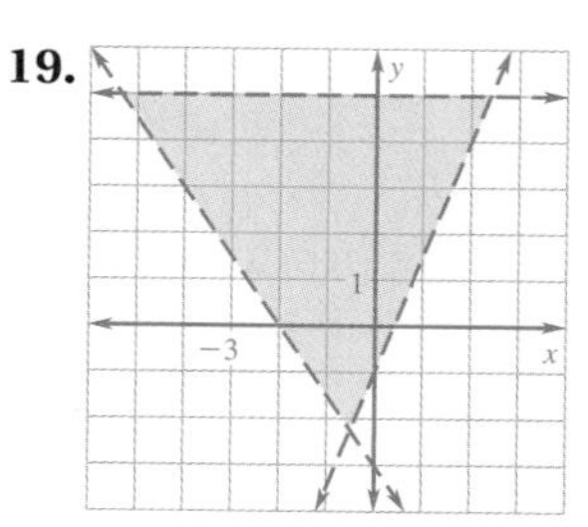

20.
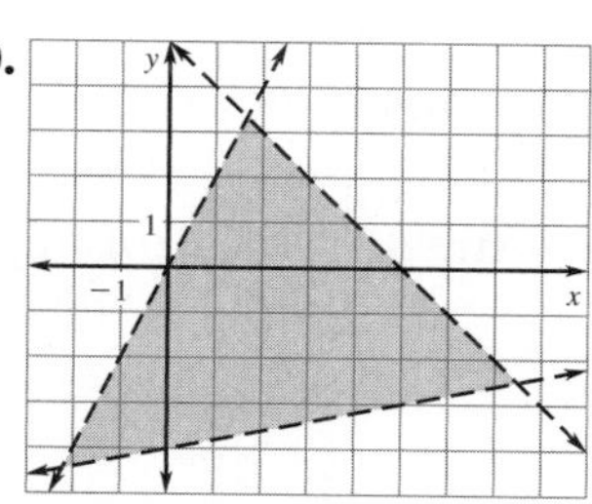

21.
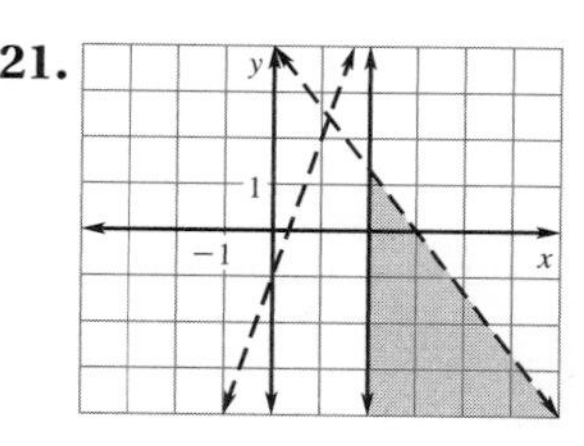

22.
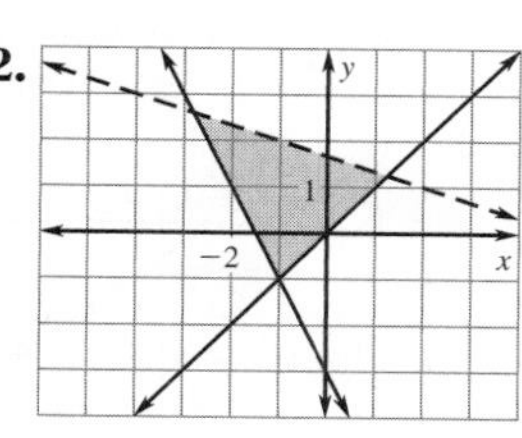

23.
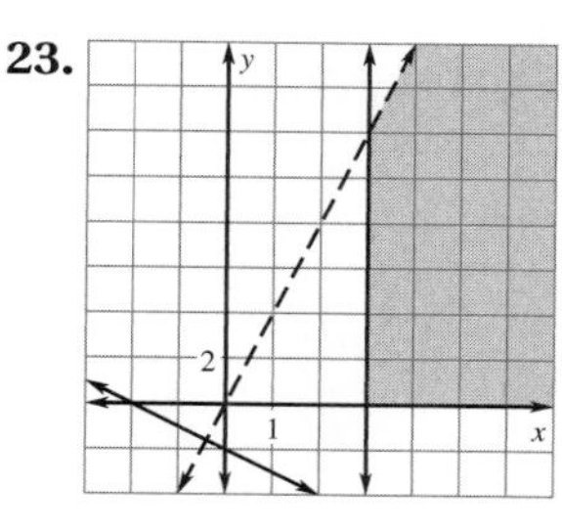

24.
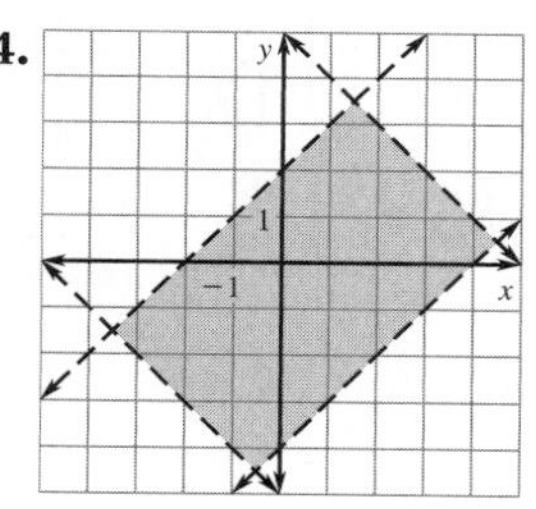

25.
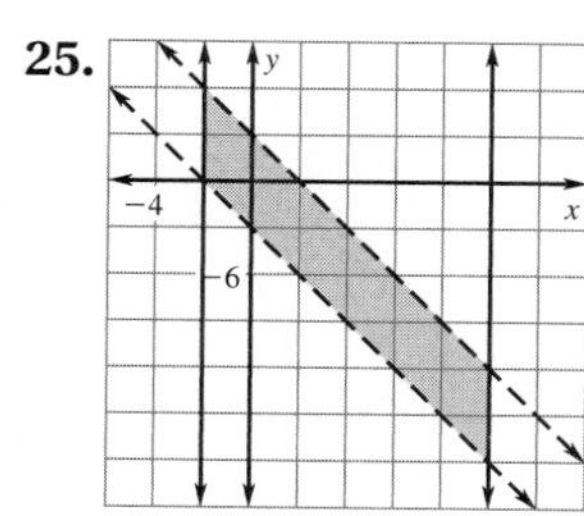

39. b.
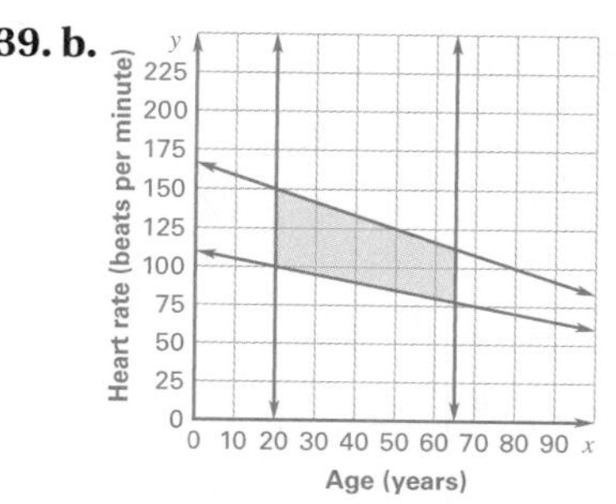

c. No; the person's heart rate is above the target zone. A 40-year old person's heart rate should be between 90 and 135 heartbeats per minute.

40.
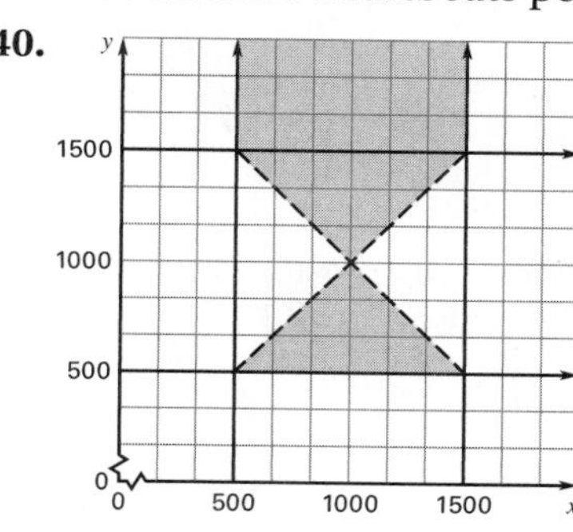

ADDITIONAL ANSWERS

3.5 Skill Practice (pp. 190–193)

10. $\begin{bmatrix} -2 & 8 \\ 6 & -12 \end{bmatrix}$ 11. $\begin{bmatrix} -6 & 0 & 15 \\ -12 & -21 & 9 \end{bmatrix}$ 12. $\begin{bmatrix} -8 & 12 & 8 \\ \frac{5}{2} & -22 & -7 \end{bmatrix}$

13. $\begin{bmatrix} -3 & 5.1 & 2.4 \\ 8.1 & 0 & -4.5 \end{bmatrix}$ 14. $\begin{bmatrix} -1 & 4 & 6 \\ 10 & -\frac{1}{2} & 0 \\ -4 & 5 & 1 \end{bmatrix}$

15. $\begin{bmatrix} -13.2 & -6.82 & -9.9 \\ 2.2 & 0 & -5.5 \\ -12.1 & 3.96 & -14.08 \end{bmatrix}$ 16. $\begin{bmatrix} 23 & -16 \\ -3 & -1 \end{bmatrix}$ 17. $\begin{bmatrix} 13 & -8 \\ -9 & 1 \end{bmatrix}$

18. $\begin{bmatrix} 2 & -4 \\ 18 & -4 \end{bmatrix}$ 19. $\begin{bmatrix} 12 & -8 \\ -4 & 0 \end{bmatrix}$ 20. $\begin{bmatrix} 9 & -1.5 & 5.2 \\ -6.7 & 1.5 & 3.3 \end{bmatrix}$

21. $\begin{bmatrix} 23.4 & -1.5 & -5.6 \\ -2.5 & -2.3 & 9.9 \end{bmatrix}$ 22. $\begin{bmatrix} 3.6 & 3 & -26.6 \\ 19.7 & -8.7 & 3.3 \end{bmatrix}$

23. $\begin{bmatrix} -6.3 & -0.75 & 10.7 \\ -6.5 & 3.6 & -3.3 \end{bmatrix}$

Quiz for Lessons 3.3–3.5 (p. 193)

1. 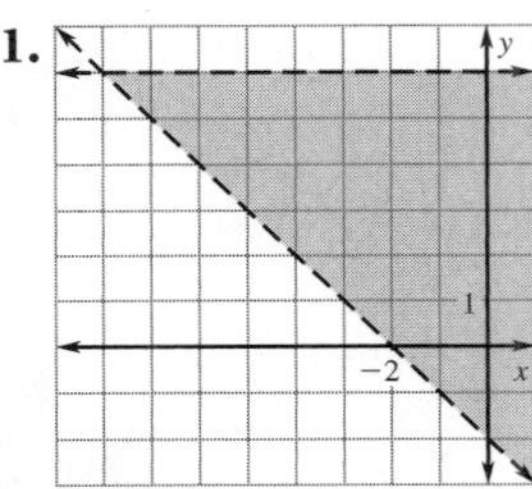

2. 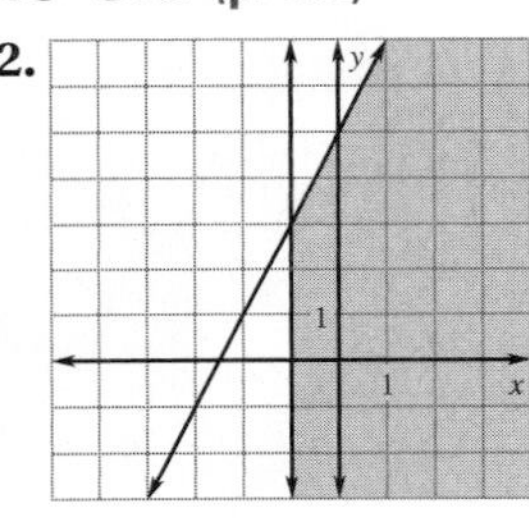

3. no solution

4. 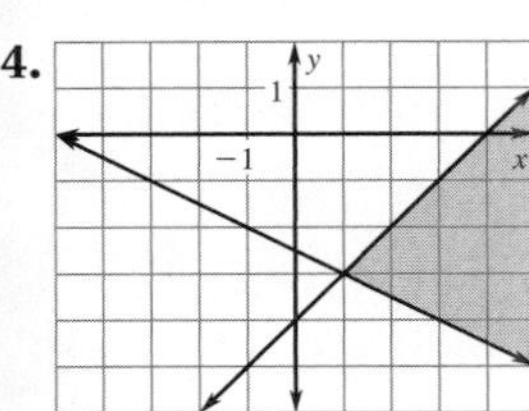

5. 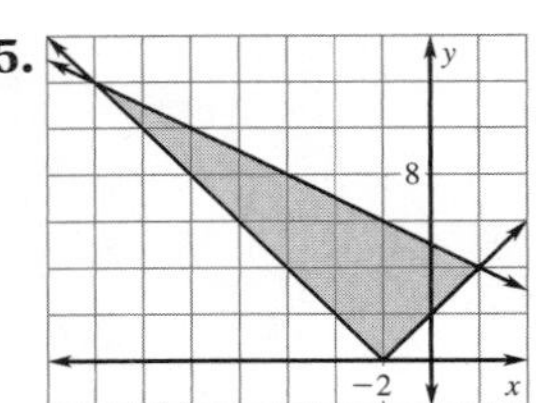

6. 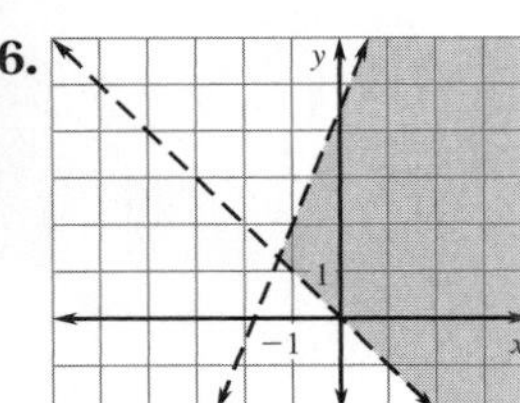

3.6 Problem Solving (pp. 200–202)

44. a. $C = \begin{bmatrix} 10 \\ 15 \\ 20 \\ 20 \end{bmatrix}$, $P = \begin{bmatrix} 15 \\ 20 \\ 25 \\ 30 \end{bmatrix}$ b. $\begin{bmatrix} 0 & 20 & 100 & 0 \\ 10 & 100 & 50 & 30 \\ 20 & 300 & 100 & 50 \end{bmatrix}$

c. $\begin{bmatrix} 2300 \\ 3200 \\ 7700 \end{bmatrix}$, $\begin{bmatrix} 2900 \\ 4300 \\ 10,300 \end{bmatrix}$; *SC* represents the total cost for making the scarves after each year, *SP* represents the total prices for each year. d. $\begin{bmatrix} 600 \\ 1100 \\ 2600 \end{bmatrix}$; this represents the profit made each year.

45. a. $\begin{bmatrix} -4 & -8 & -2 \\ -7 & -4 & -4 \end{bmatrix}$

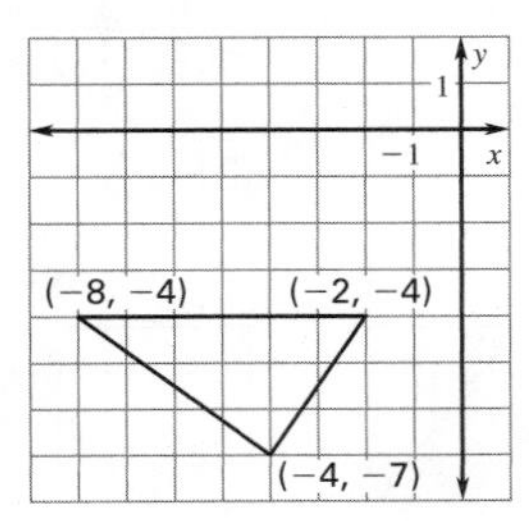

b. $\begin{bmatrix} 7 & 4 & 4 \\ -4 & -8 & -2 \end{bmatrix}$, $\begin{bmatrix} 4 & 8 & 2 \\ 7 & 4 & 4 \end{bmatrix}$; (7, −4), (4, −8), (4, −2); (4, 7), (8, 4), (2, 4)

3.8 Guided Practice (pp. 210–213)

1. $\begin{bmatrix} \frac{2}{11} & -\frac{1}{22} \\ -\frac{1}{11} & \frac{3}{11} \end{bmatrix}$ **2.** $\begin{bmatrix} \frac{2}{3} & -\frac{5}{12} \\ \frac{1}{3} & -\frac{1}{12} \end{bmatrix}$

3. $\begin{bmatrix} -1 & 2 \\ \frac{1}{2} & -\frac{3}{2} \end{bmatrix}$ **4.** $\begin{bmatrix} -1 & -2 \\ 4 & 1 \end{bmatrix}$

3.8 Skill Practice (pp. 214–215)

19. $\begin{bmatrix} -\frac{3}{10} & -\frac{1}{5} & \frac{3}{10} \\ \frac{9}{10} & \frac{3}{5} & \frac{1}{10} \\ -\frac{1}{5} & \frac{1}{5} & \frac{1}{5} \end{bmatrix}$

20. $\begin{bmatrix} -\frac{4}{3} & \frac{4}{3} & -\frac{1}{3} \\ -\frac{5}{6} & \frac{1}{3} & \frac{1}{6} \\ \frac{7}{6} & -\frac{2}{3} & \frac{1}{6} \end{bmatrix}$

21. $\begin{bmatrix} -\frac{1}{2} & 0 & \frac{1}{2} \\ -\frac{17}{16} & \frac{1}{8} & \frac{7}{16} \\ \frac{7}{32} & \frac{1}{16} & -\frac{1}{32} \end{bmatrix}$

22. $\begin{bmatrix} \frac{5}{146} & \frac{5}{146} & \frac{13}{146} \\ \frac{6}{73} & \frac{6}{73} & \frac{1}{73} \\ -\frac{48}{73} & \frac{25}{73} & -\frac{8}{73} \end{bmatrix}$

23. $\begin{bmatrix} \frac{3}{20} & \frac{3}{10} & \frac{1}{20} \\ -\frac{11}{160} & \frac{9}{80} & \frac{3}{160} \\ -\frac{1}{40} & -\frac{1}{20} & -\frac{7}{40} \end{bmatrix}$

24. $\begin{bmatrix} \frac{13}{47} & -\frac{11}{47} & -\frac{9}{47} \\ \frac{15}{47} & \frac{9}{47} & -\frac{14}{47} \\ -\frac{4}{47} & \frac{7}{47} & \frac{10}{47} \end{bmatrix}$

3.8 Problem Solving (pp. 215–217)

50. $AB = \begin{bmatrix} a & b \\ c & d \end{bmatrix} \begin{bmatrix} \frac{d}{ad-cb} & \frac{-b}{ad-cb} \\ \frac{-c}{ad-cb} & \frac{a}{ad-cb} \end{bmatrix} =$

$$\begin{bmatrix} a\left(\frac{d}{ad-cb}\right) + b\left(\frac{-c}{ad-cb}\right) & a\left(\frac{-b}{ad-cb}\right) + b\left(\frac{a}{ad-cb}\right) \\ c\left(\frac{d}{ad-cb}\right) + d\left(\frac{-c}{ad-cb}\right) & c\left(\frac{-b}{ad-cb}\right) + d\left(\frac{a}{ad-cb}\right) \end{bmatrix} = \begin{bmatrix} 1 & 0 \\ 0 & 1 \end{bmatrix},$$

$BA = \begin{bmatrix} \frac{d}{ad-cb} & \frac{-b}{ad-cb} \\ \frac{-c}{ad-cb} & \frac{a}{ad-cb} \end{bmatrix} \begin{bmatrix} a & b \\ c & d \end{bmatrix} =$

$$\begin{bmatrix} \left(\frac{d}{ad-cb}\right)a + \left(\frac{-b}{ad-cb}\right)c & \left(\frac{d}{ad-cb}\right)b + \left(\frac{-b}{ad-cb}\right)d \\ \left(\frac{-c}{ad-cb}\right)a + \left(\frac{a}{ad-cb}\right)c & \left(\frac{-c}{ad-cb}\right)b + \left(\frac{a}{ad-cb}\right)d \end{bmatrix} = \begin{bmatrix} 1 & 0 \\ 0 & 1 \end{bmatrix}$$

Chapter 4

4.1 Guided Practice (pp. 237–239)

1. 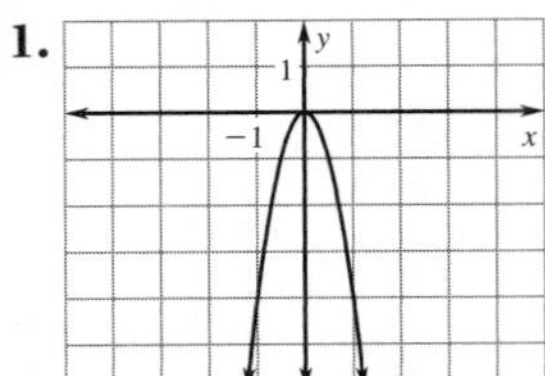

2. 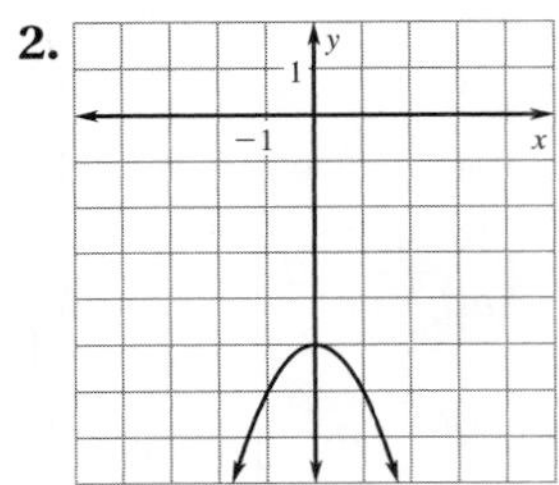

3. 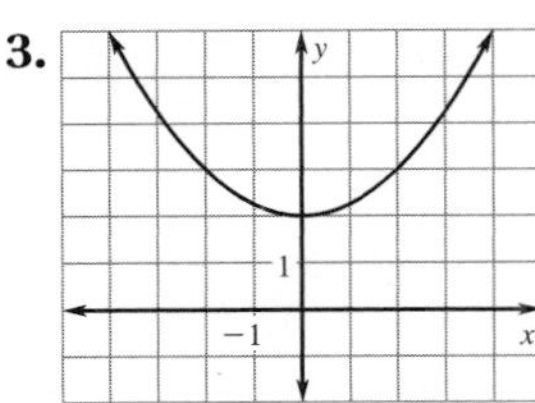

4.1 Skill Practice (pp. 240–241)

7. 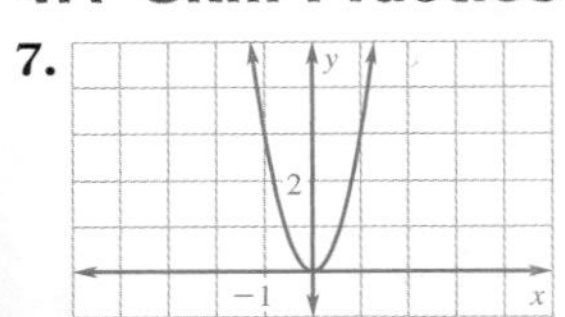

same axis of symmetry and vertex, opens up, and is narrower

8. 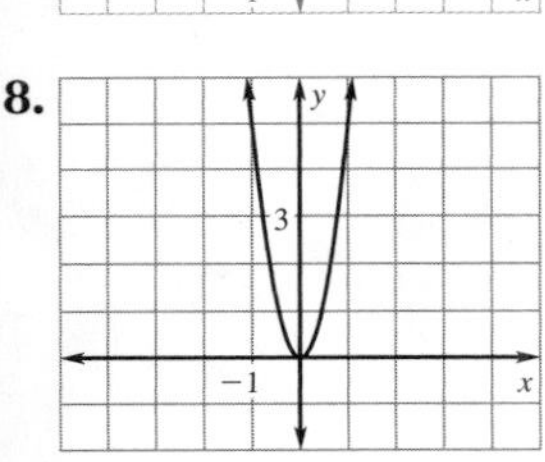

same axis of symmetry and vertex, opens up, and is narrower

9. 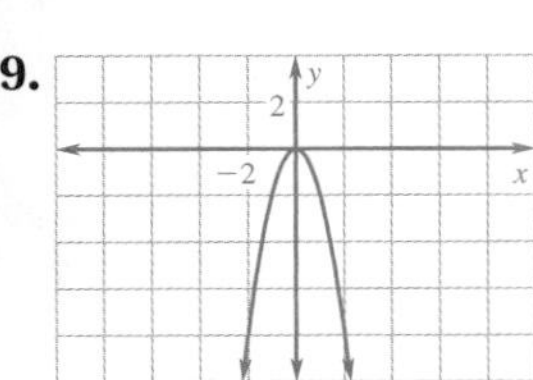

same axis of symmetry and vertex, opens down, and is narrower

10. 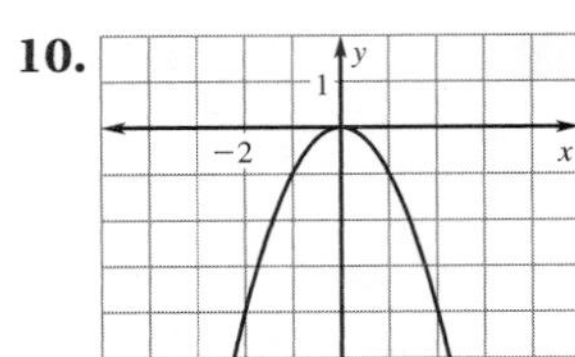

same axis of symmetry and vertex, opens down

11. 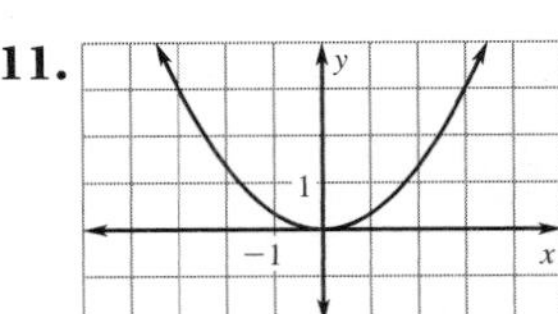

same axis of symmetry and vertex, opens up, and is wider

12. 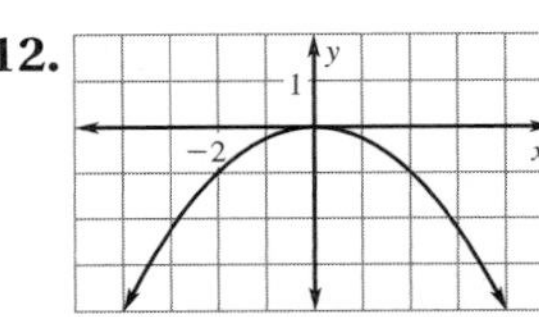

same axis of symmetry and vertex, opens down, and is wider

13. 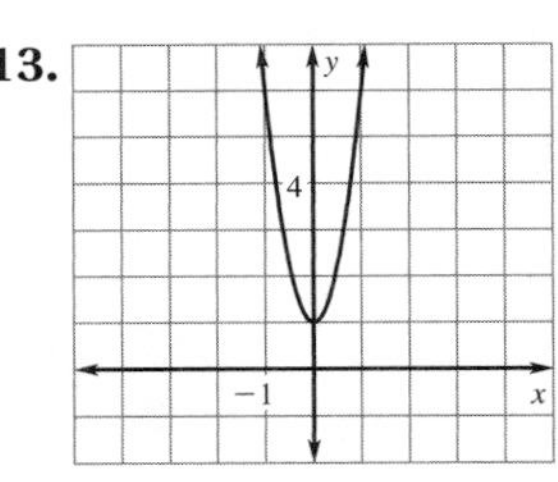

same axis of symmetry, vertex is shifted up 1 unit, opens up, and is narrower

14. 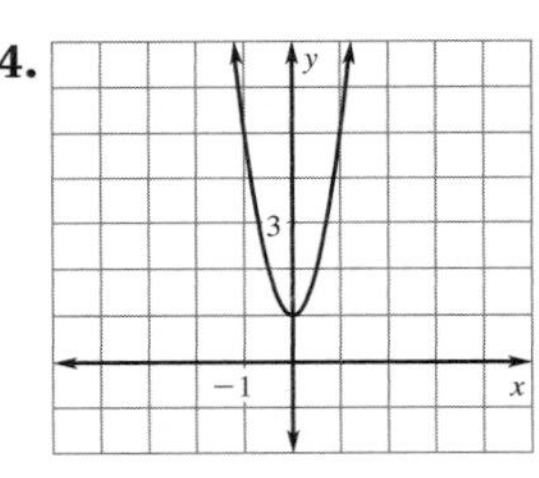

same axis of symmetry, vertex is shifted up 1 unit, opens up, and is narrower

15. 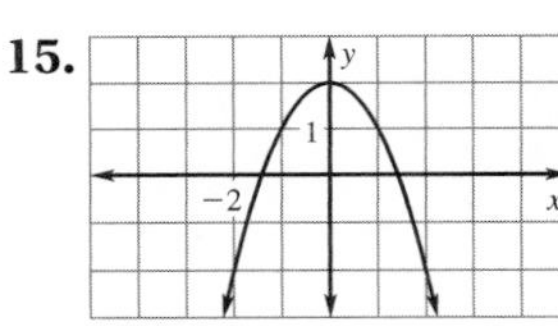

same axis of symmetry, vertex is shifted up 2 units, opens down

16. 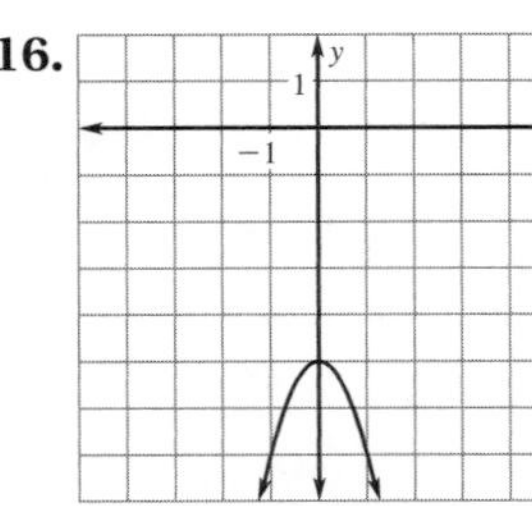

same axis of symmetry, vertex is shifted down 5 units, opens down, and is narrower

17. 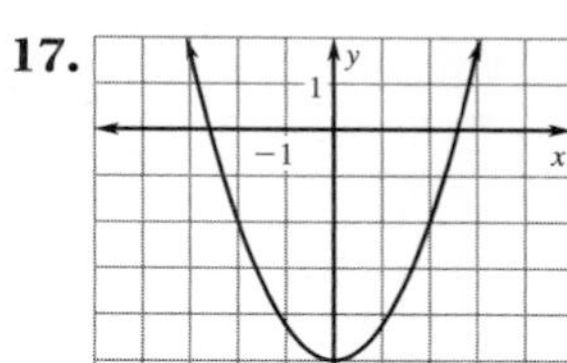
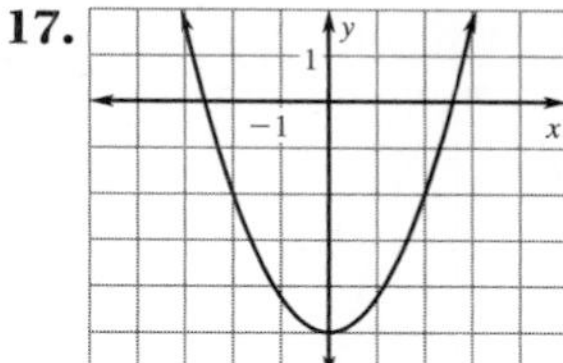

same axis of symmetry, vertex is shifted down 5 units, opens up, and is wider

18. 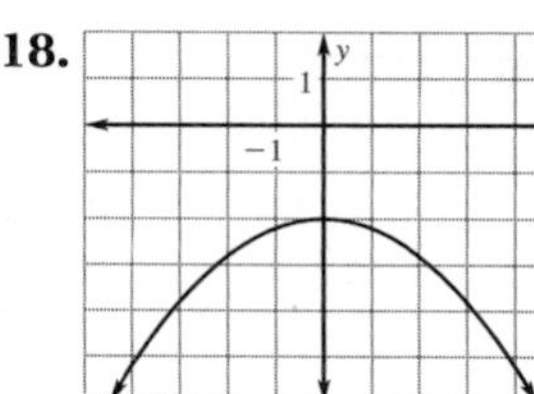

same axis of symmetry, vertex is shifted down 2 units, opens down, and is wide

21.

22. 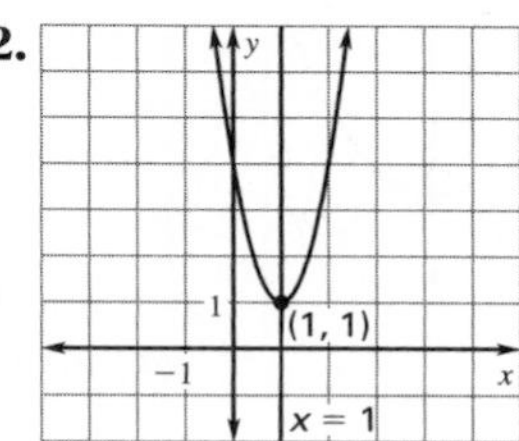

23.

24. 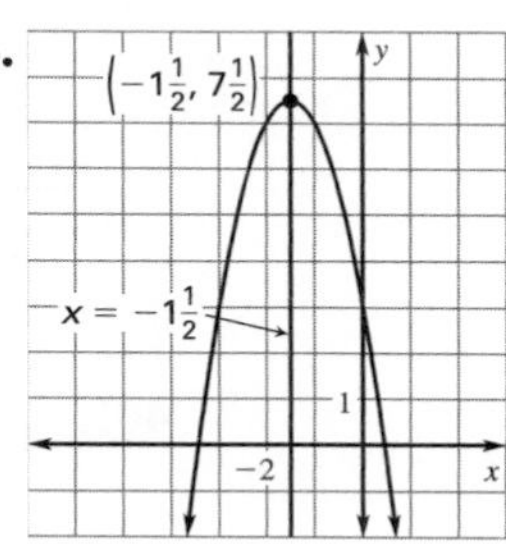

25.

26. 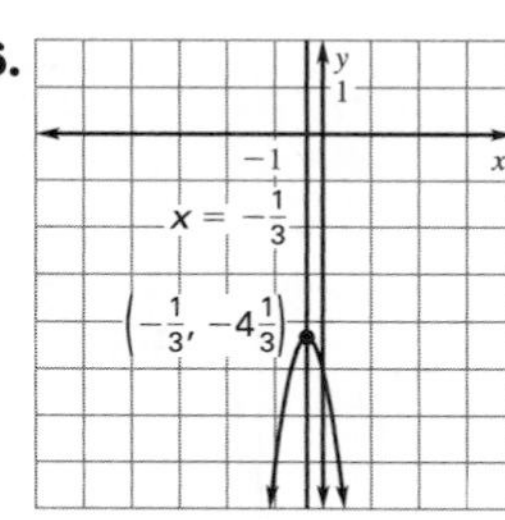

27.

28. 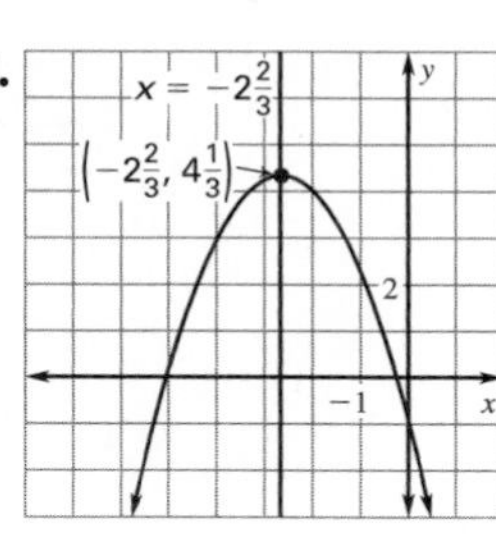

29. 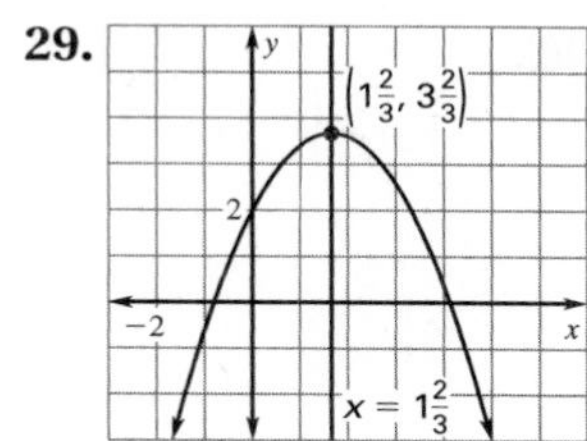

30. 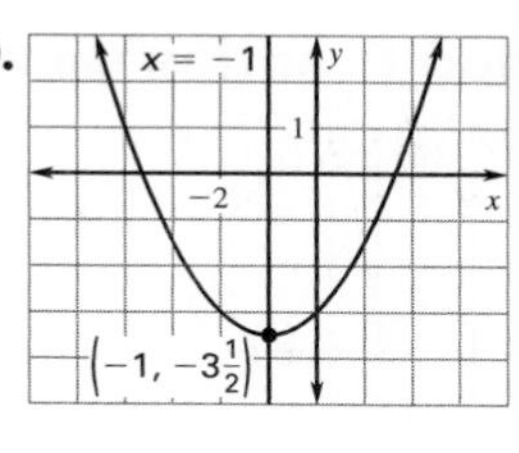

31. 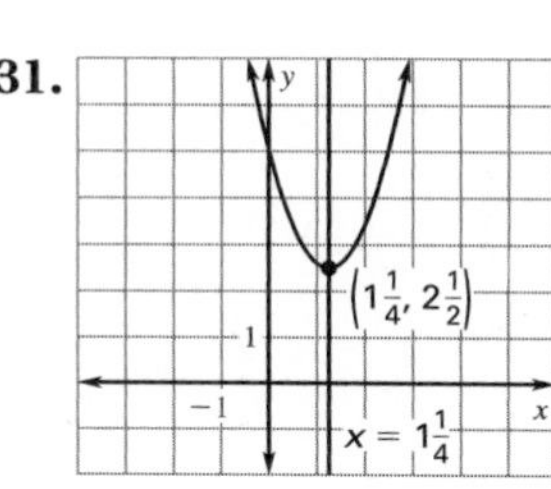

32. 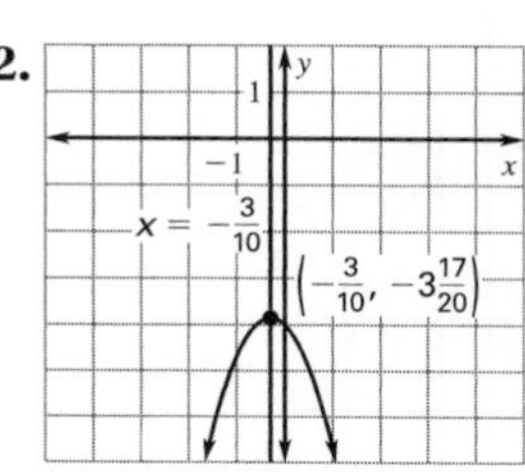

ADDITIONAL ANSWERS

4.2 Guided Practice (pp. 246–248)

1.

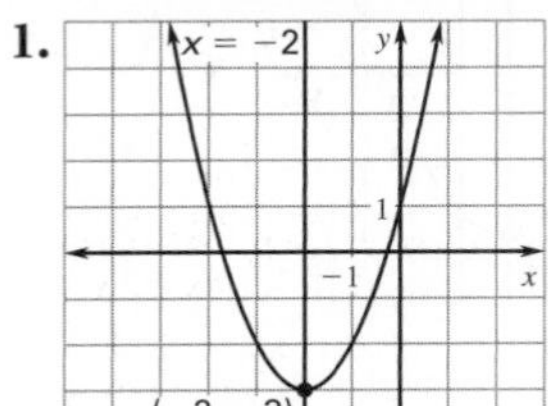

2.

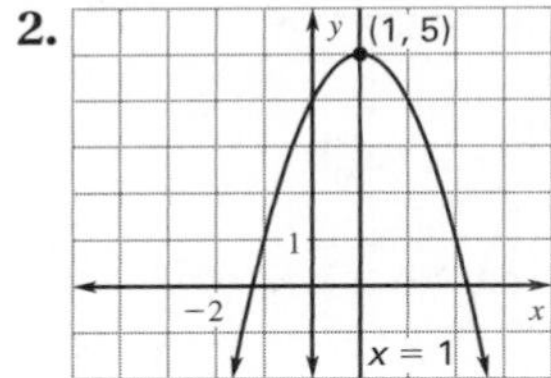

3.

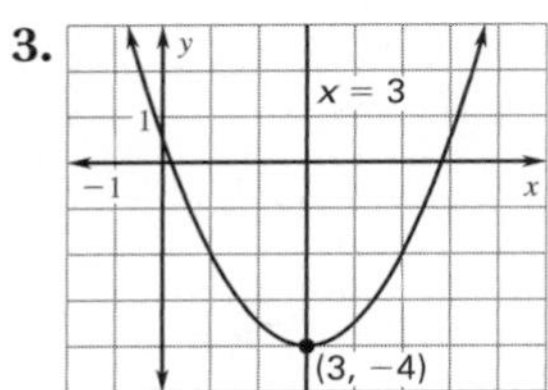

4.2 Skill Practice (pp. 249–250)

13.

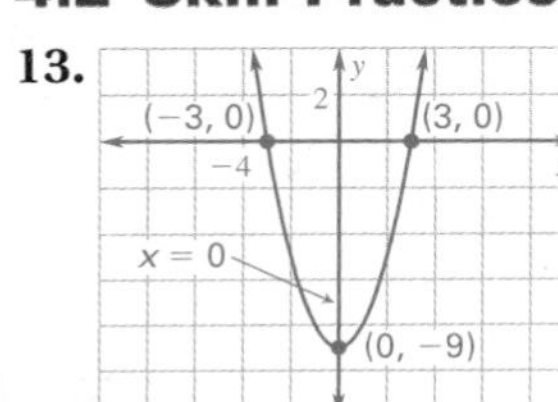

14.

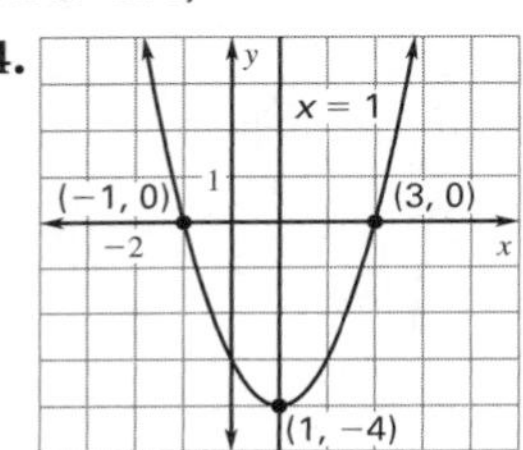

15.

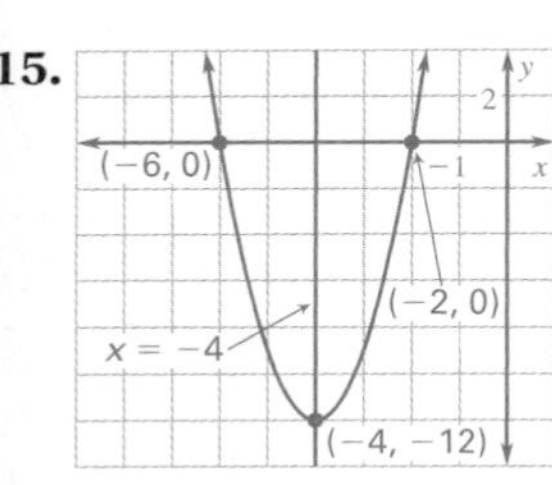

16.

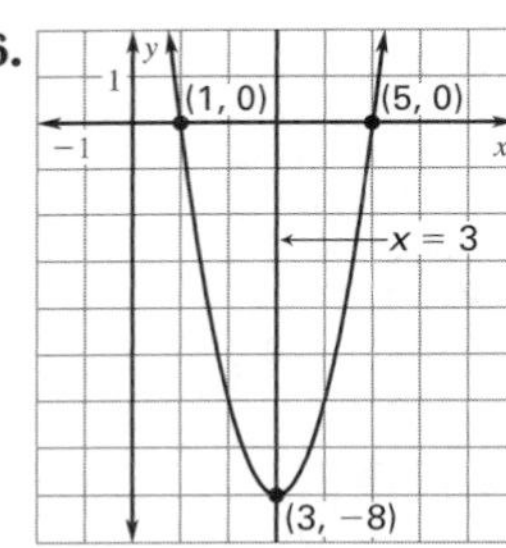

17.

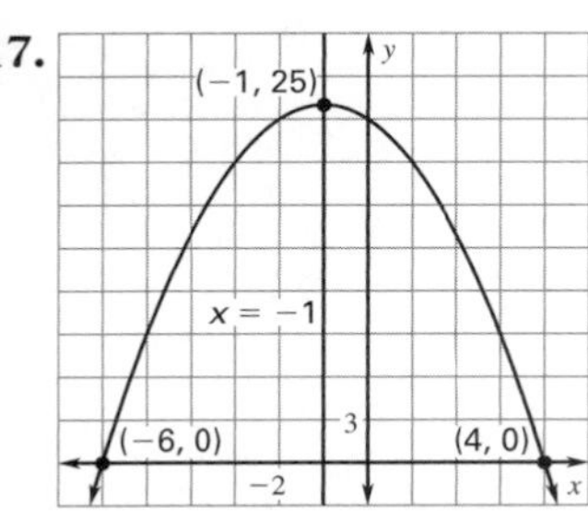

18.

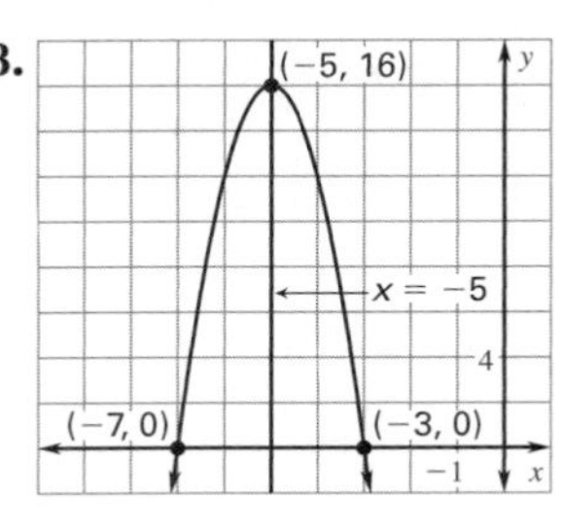

19.

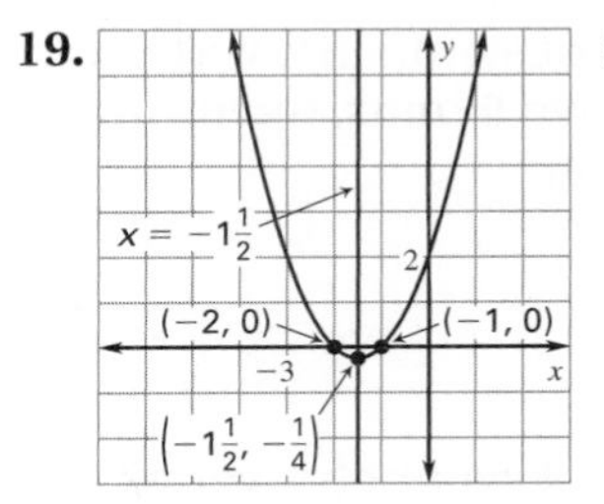

20.

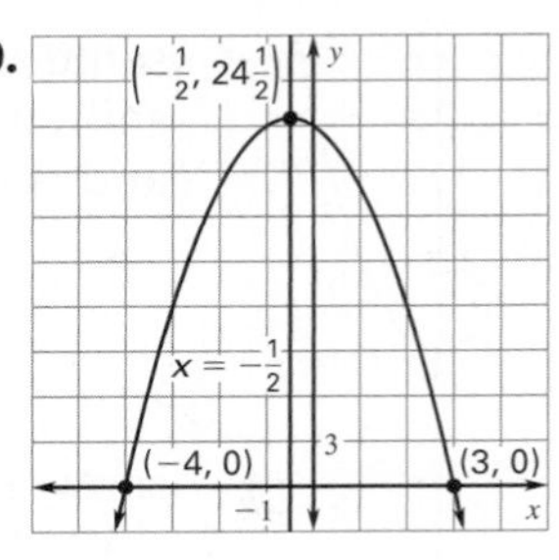

21.

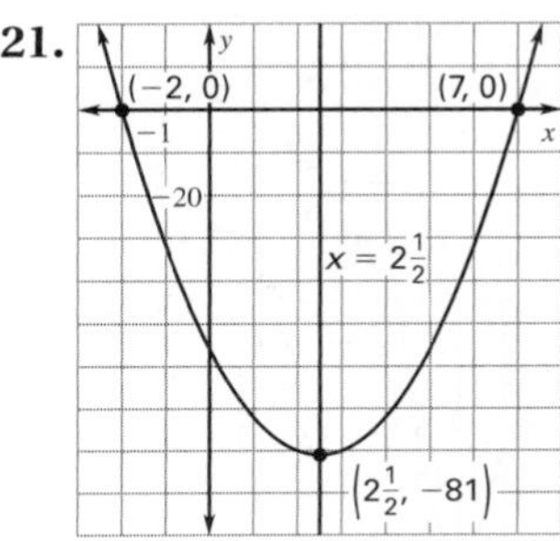

43.

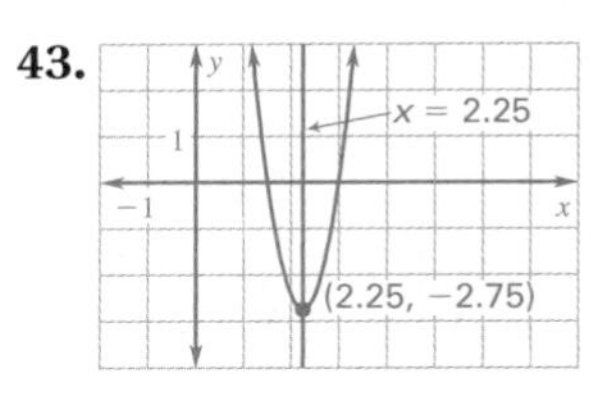

44.

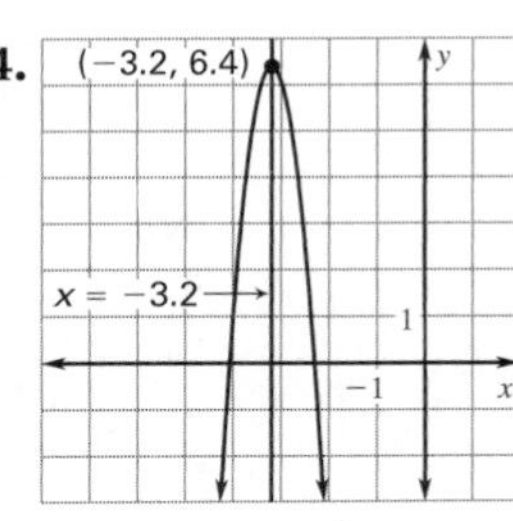

45.

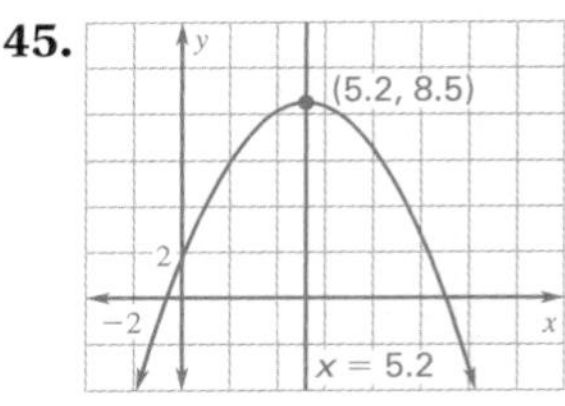

46.

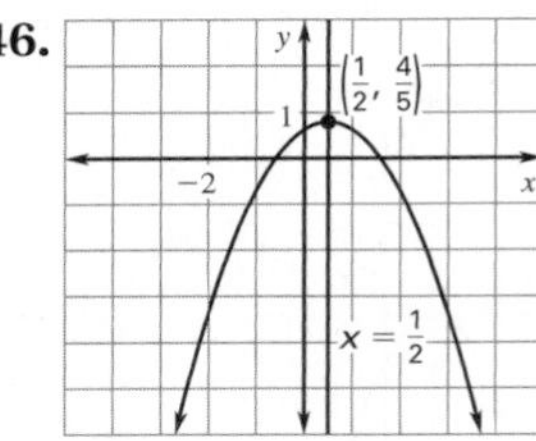

47.

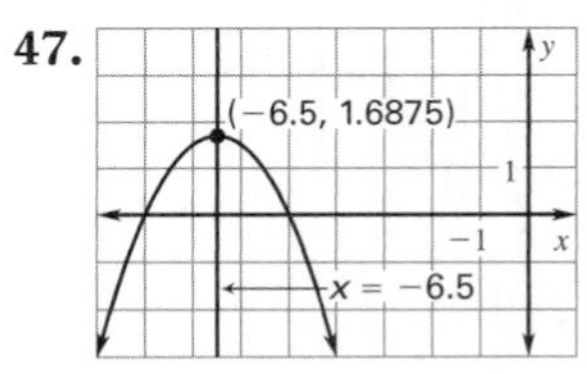

48.

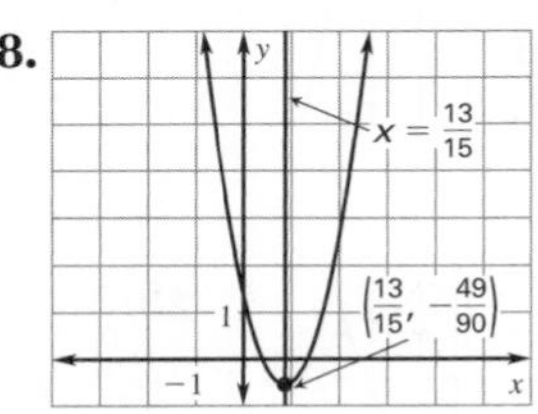

ADDITIONAL ANSWERS

4.8 Skill Practice (pp. 296–297)

67.
$$a\left(x^2 + \frac{b}{a}x\right) = -c$$
$$a\left(x^2 + \frac{b}{a}x + \frac{b^2}{4a^2}\right) = -c + \frac{b^2}{4a}$$
$$a\left(x + \frac{b}{2a}\right)^2 = \frac{b^2 - 4ac}{4a}$$
$$\left(x + \frac{b}{2a}\right)^2 = \frac{b^2 - 4ac}{4a^2}$$
$$x + \frac{b}{2a} = \frac{\pm\sqrt{b^2 - 4ac}}{2a}$$
$$x = \frac{-b \pm\sqrt{b^2 - 4ac}}{2a}$$

4.9 Guided Practice (pp. 301–303)

1. 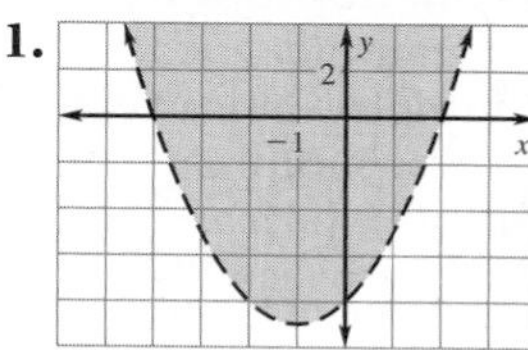

2. 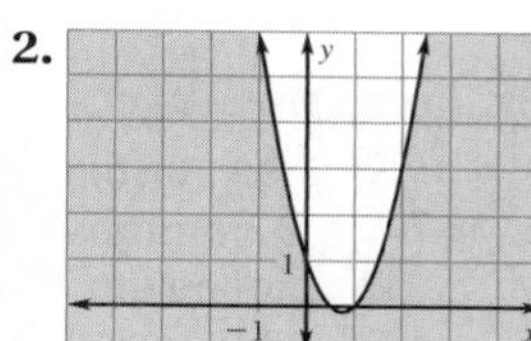

3. 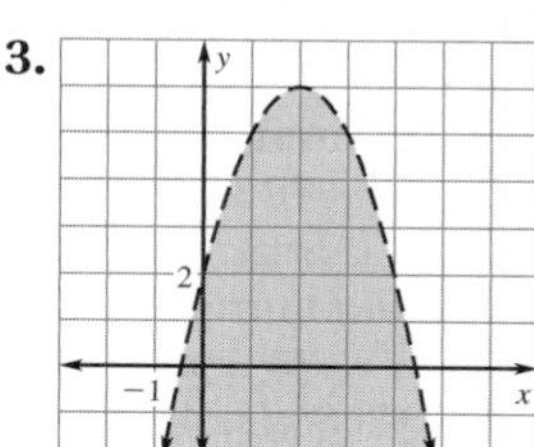

4. 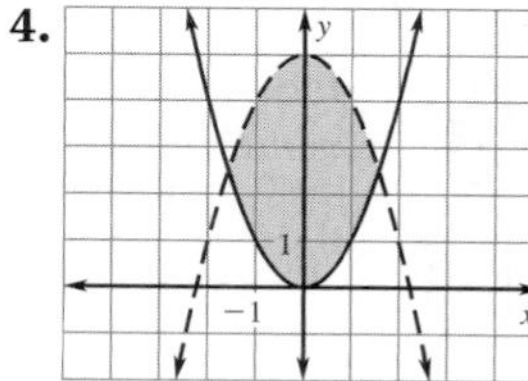

4.9 Skill Practice (pp. 304–305)

6. 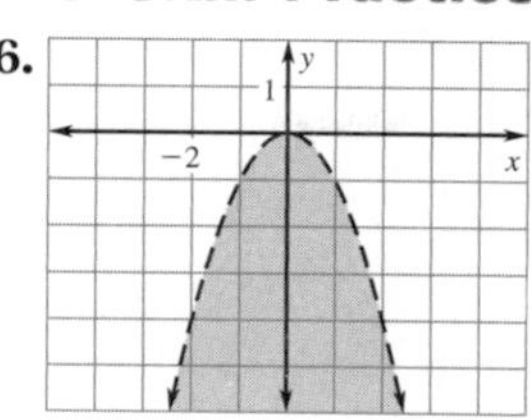

7. 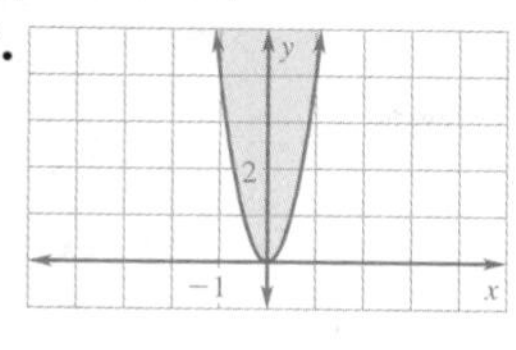

8. 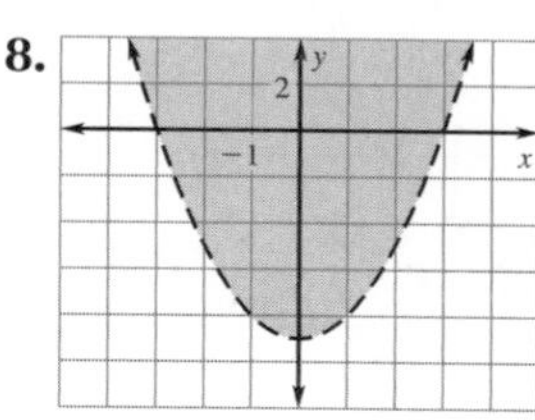

9. 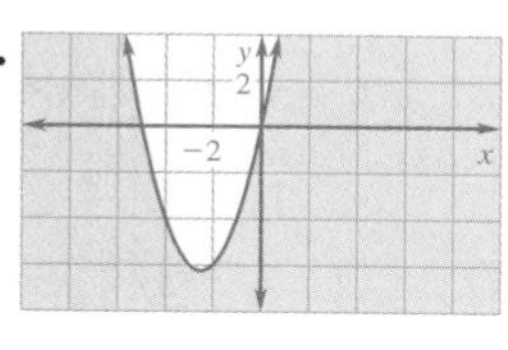

10. 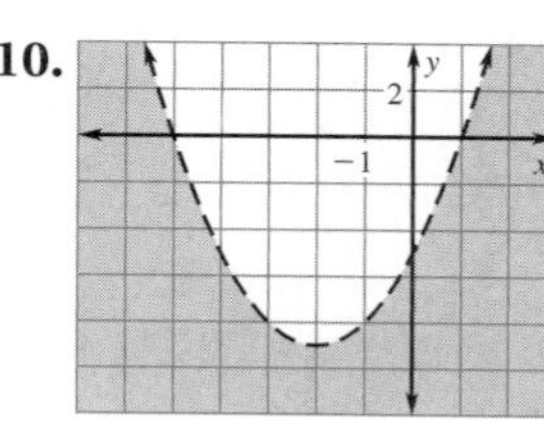

11. 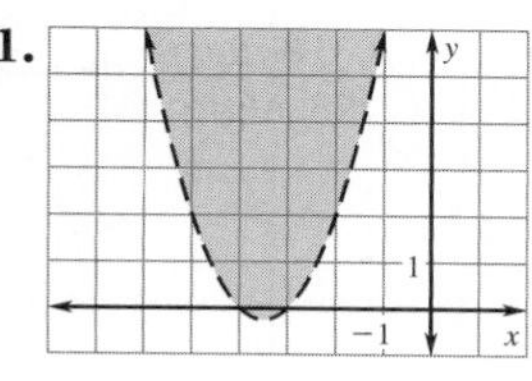

12. 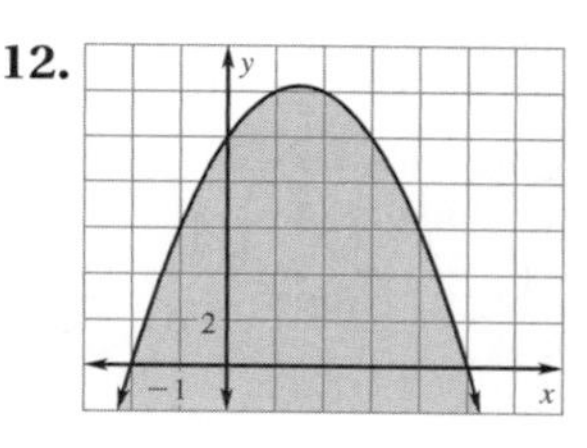

13. 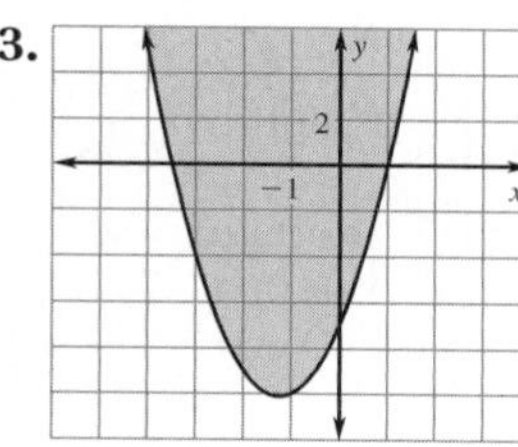

14. 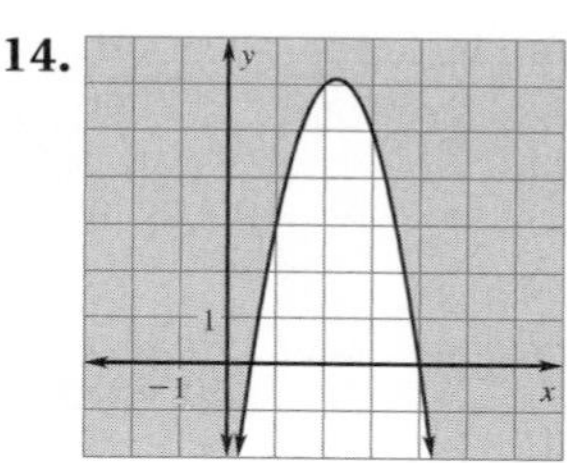

15. 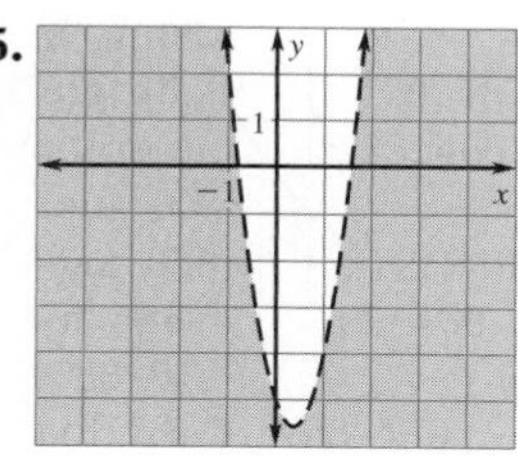

16. 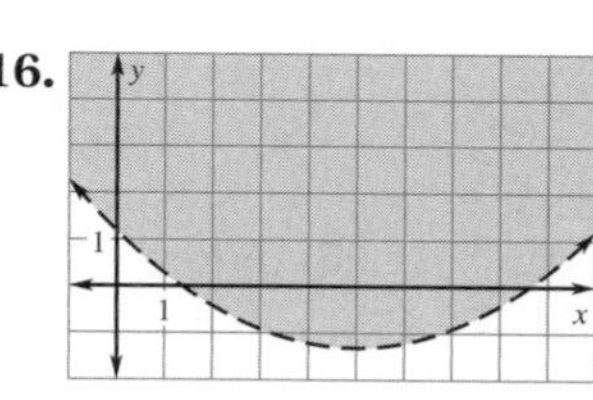

17. 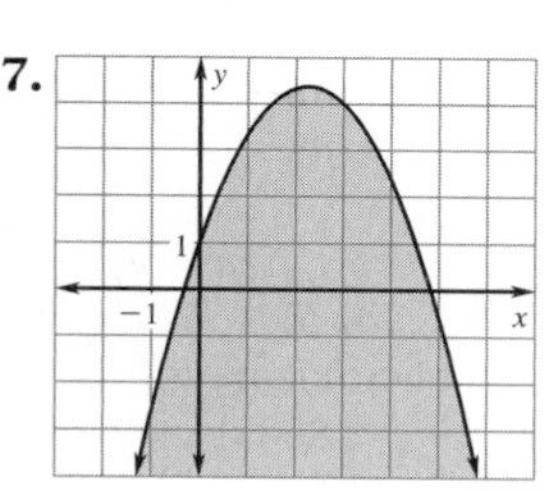

4.9 Problem Solving (pp. 306–307)

78.
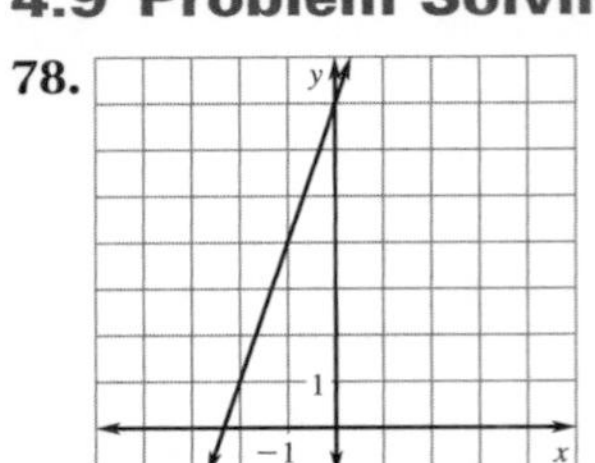

79.
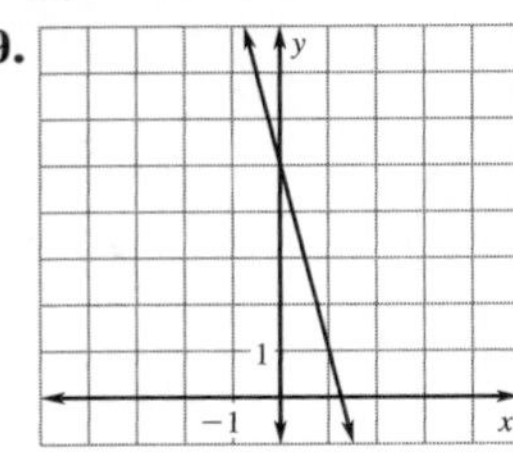

80.
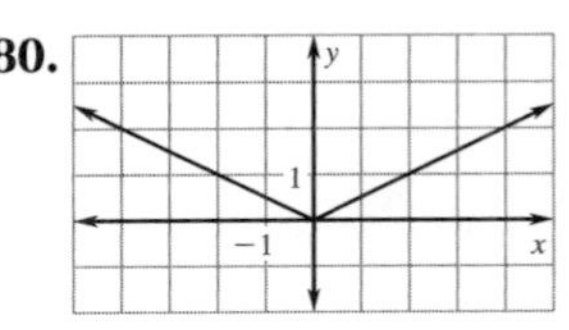

81.
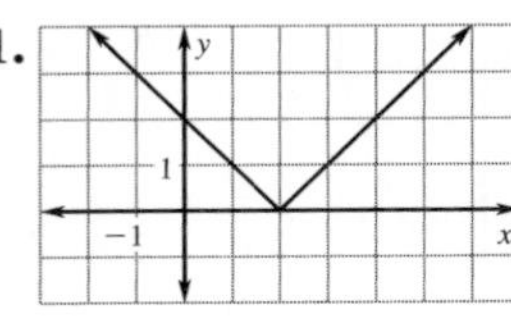

82.
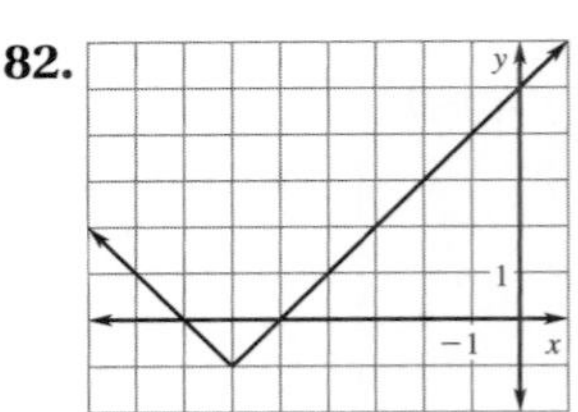

83.
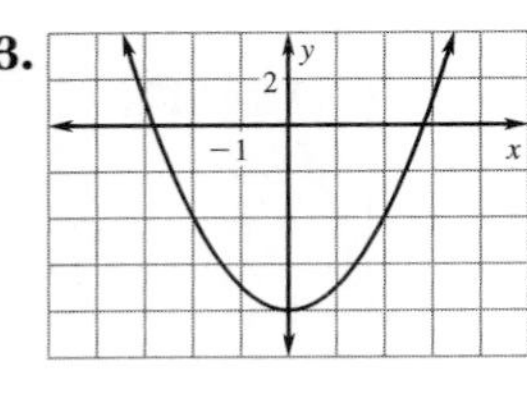

84.
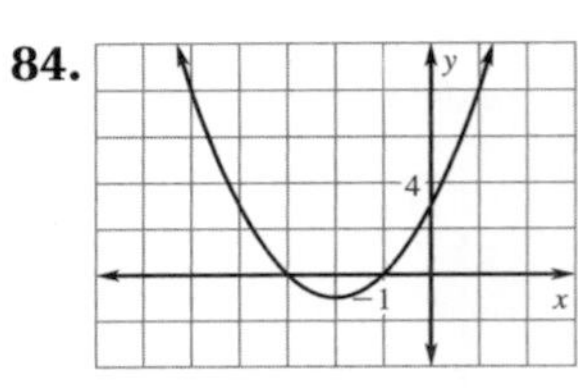

85.
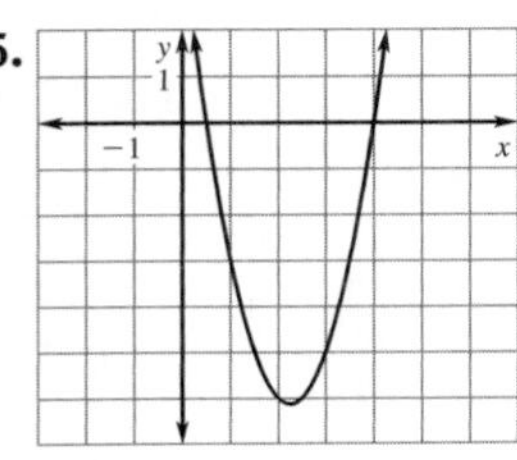

86.
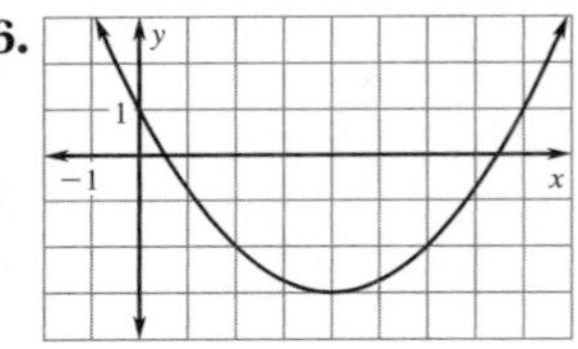

Chapter 5

5.1 Skill Practice (pp. 333–334) **24.** $\frac{1}{w^8}$; quotient of powers property, negative exponent property **25.** $1024y^{15}$; power of a product property, power of a power property **26.** $\frac{1}{p^3q^2}$; power of a product property, negative exponent property, power of a power property **27.** $\frac{w^9}{x^3}$; product of powers property, negative exponent property **28.** $\frac{s^6}{125t^{12}}$; power of a product property, power of a power property, negative exponent property **29.** $\frac{1}{27a^9b^{15}}$; power of a product property, power of a power property, negative exponent property **30.** $\frac{y^3}{x^3}$; negative exponent property, product of powers property **31.** $\frac{c^2d^2}{3}$; quotient of powers property **32.** $\frac{s^{10}}{6}$; quotient of powers property **33.** $\frac{2}{3a^2b^2}$; quotient of powers property, negative exponent property **34.** $2y^4z^4$; quotient of powers property **35.** $\frac{x^6}{3y^3}$; product of powers property, quotient of powers property, negative exponent property

55.
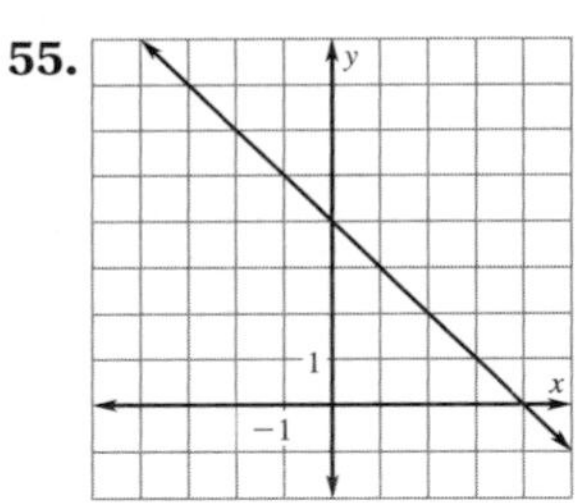

56.
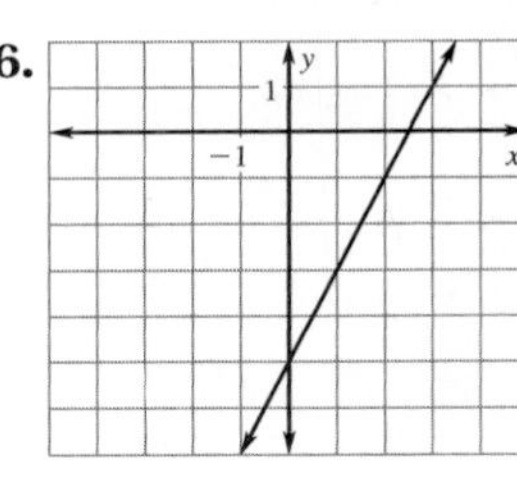

57.
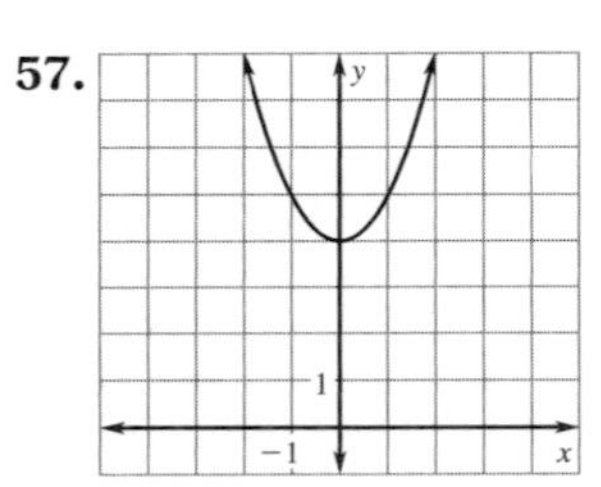

58.
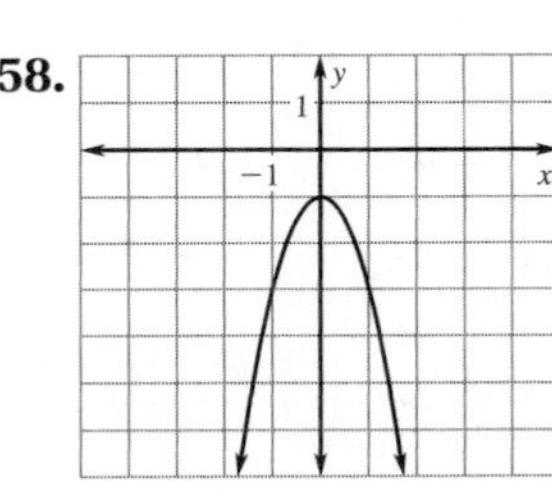

59.
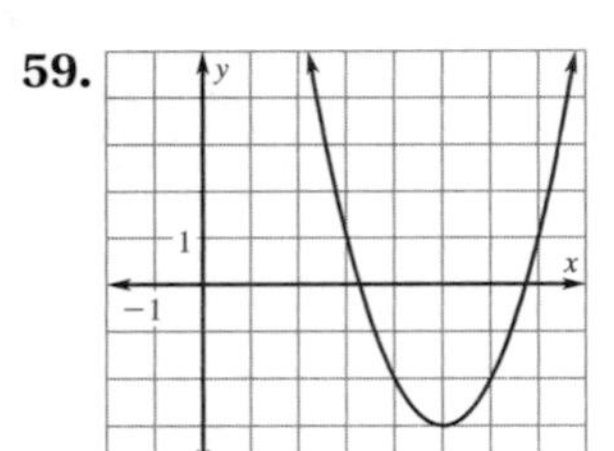

60.
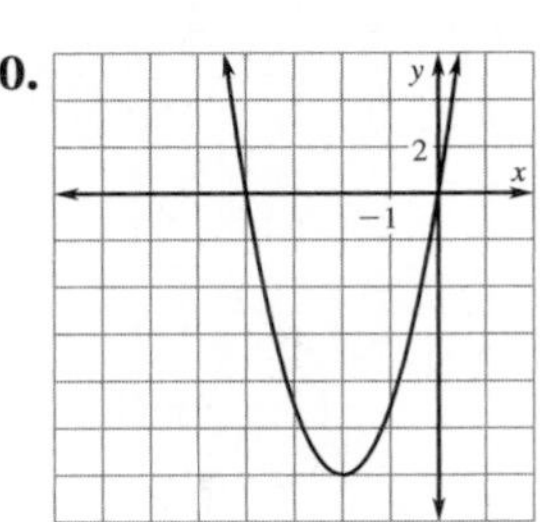

ADDITIONAL ANSWERS

5.2 Investigating Algebra Activity (p. 336)

5. a. $f(x)$ approaches $-\infty$ as x approaches $-\infty$ and $f(x)$ approaches $+\infty$ as x approaches $+\infty$. **b.** $f(x)$ approaches $+\infty$ as x approaches $-\infty$ and $f(x)$ approaches $-\infty$ as x approaches $+\infty$. **c.** $f(x)$ approaches $+\infty$ as x approaches $-\infty$ and $f(x)$ approaches $+\infty$ as x approaches $+\infty$. **d.** $f(x)$ approaches $-\infty$ as x approaches $-\infty$ and $f(x)$ approaches $-\infty$ as x approaches $+\infty$.

5.2 Skill Practice (pp. 341–343)

3. polynomial function; $f(x) = -x^2 + 8$, degree: 2, type: quadratic, leading coefficient: -1 **4.** polynomial function; $f(x) = 8x^4 + 6x - 3$, degree: 4, type: quartic, leading coefficient: 8 **5.** polynomial function; $g(x) = \pi x^4 + \sqrt{6}$, degree: 4, type: quartic, leading coefficient: π **6.** not a polynomial function **7.** polynomial function; $h(x) = -\frac{5}{2}x^3 + 3x - 10$, degree: 3, type: cubic, leading coefficient: $-\frac{5}{2}$ **8.** not a polynomial function

53. a.

x	$f(x)$	$g(x)$	$\frac{f(x)}{g(x)}$
10	1000	840	$\frac{25}{21}$
20	8000	7280	$\frac{100}{91}$
50	125,000	120,000	$\frac{25}{24}$
100	1,000,000	980,400	$\frac{2500}{2451}$
200	8,000,000	7,920,800	$\frac{10,000}{9901}$

5.2 Problem Solving (pp. 343–344)

56. b.

t	0	1	2	3	4	5
M	21,600	21,264	21,396	21,930	22,800	23,940

t	6	7	8	9	10	11
M	25,284	26,766	28,320	29,880	31,380	32,754

t	12	13	14	15	16
M	33,936	34,860	35,460	35,670	35,424

c.

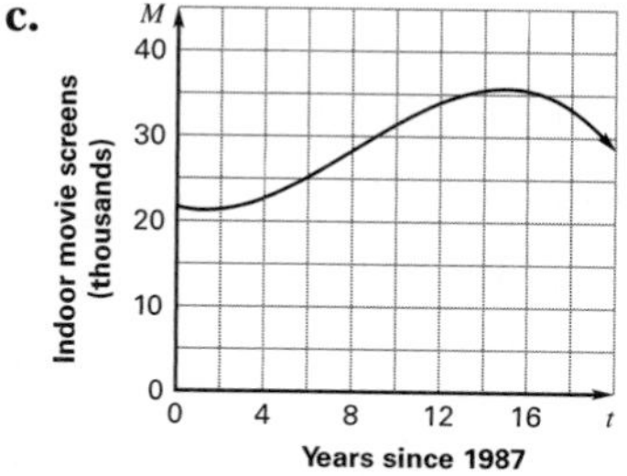

58. b.

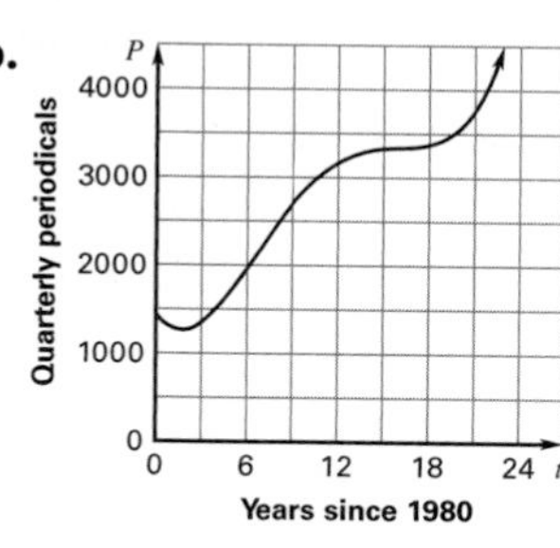

59. b.

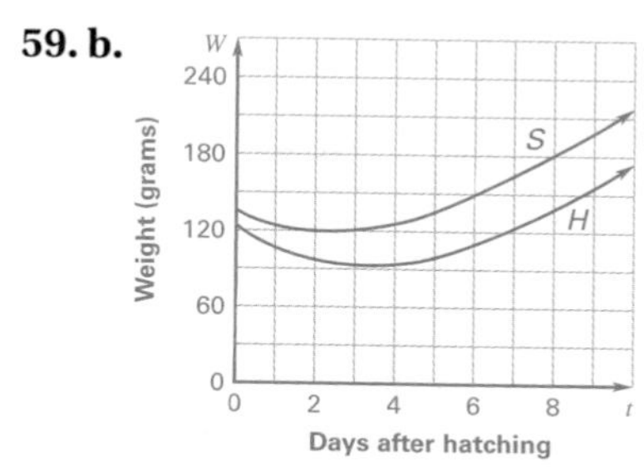

Quiz for Lessons 5.1–5.3 (p. 352)

9.

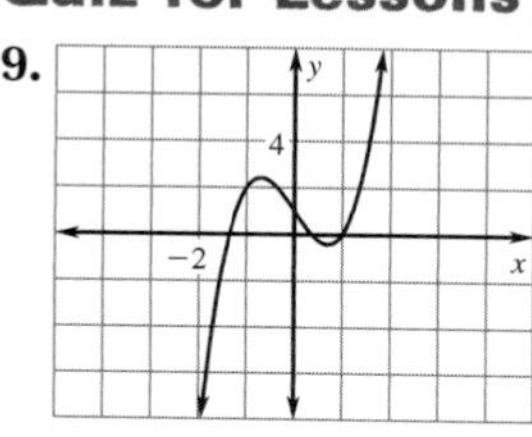

10.

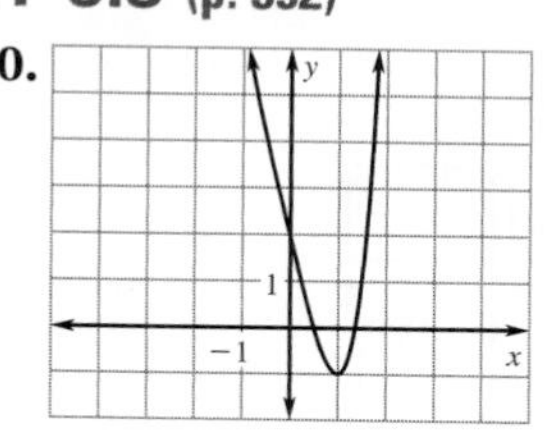

11.

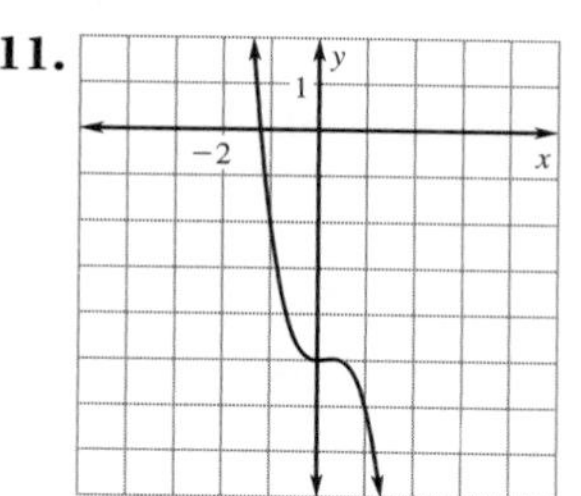

5.8 Skill Practice (pp. 390–391)

3.

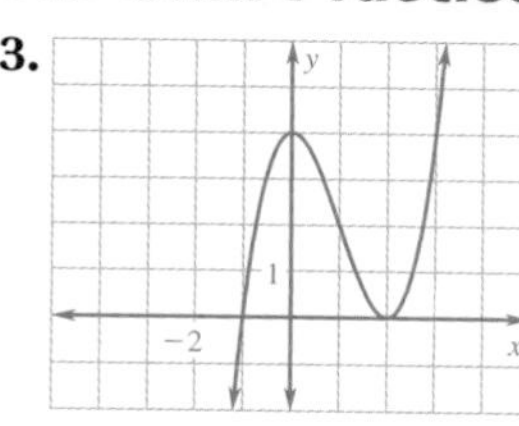

4.

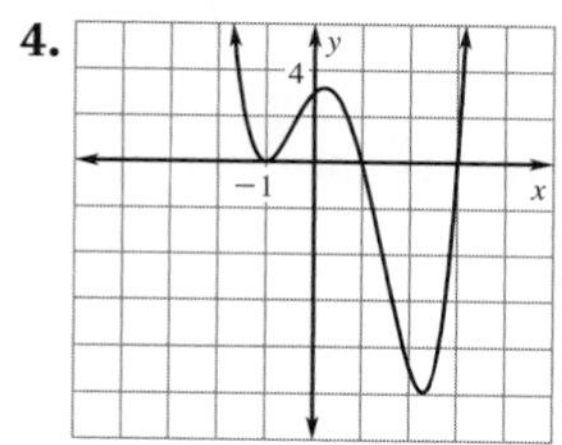

5.

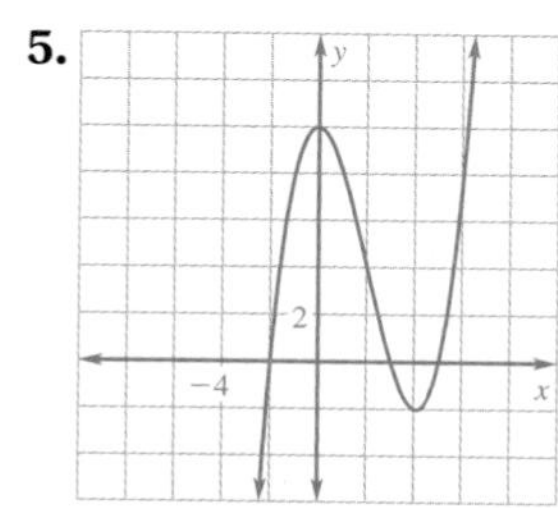

6.

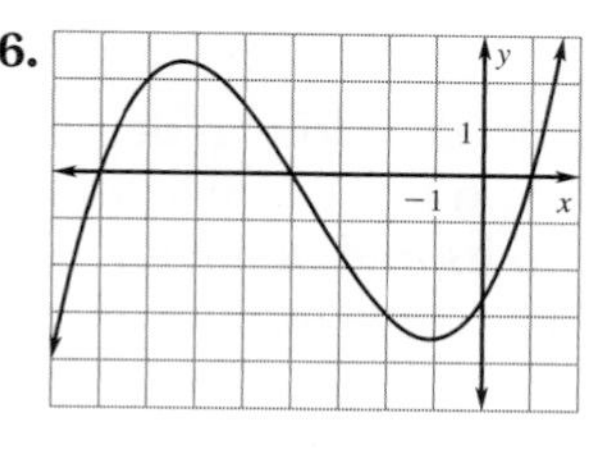

7.

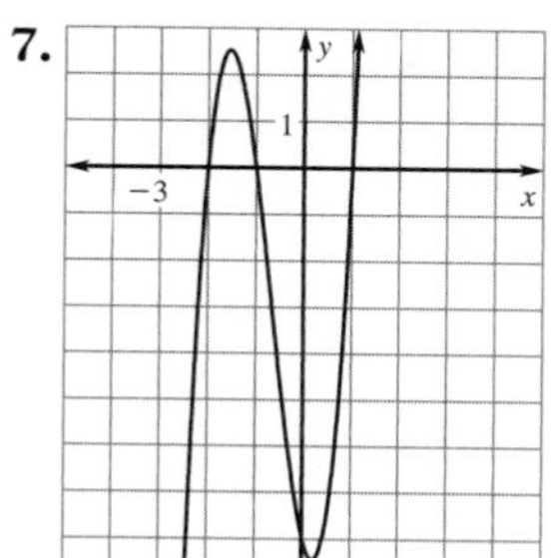

8.

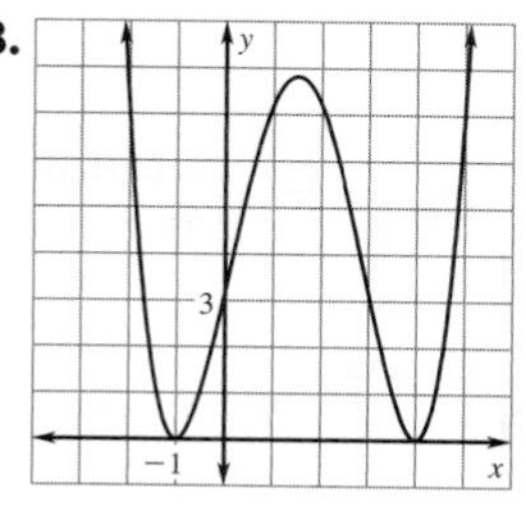

9. 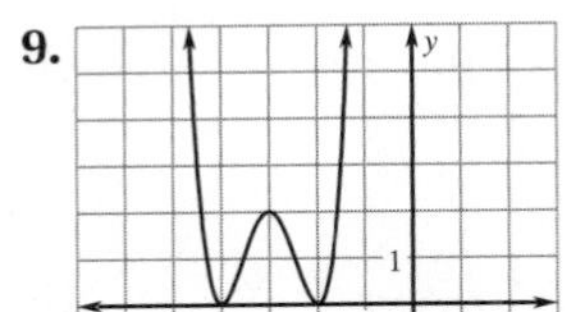

10. 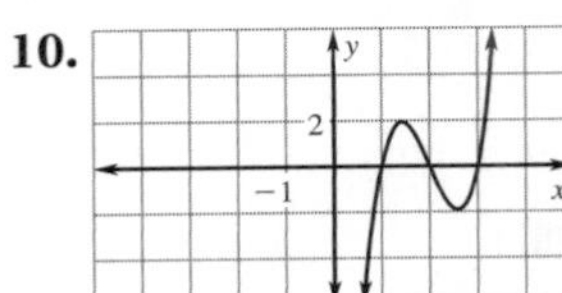

11. 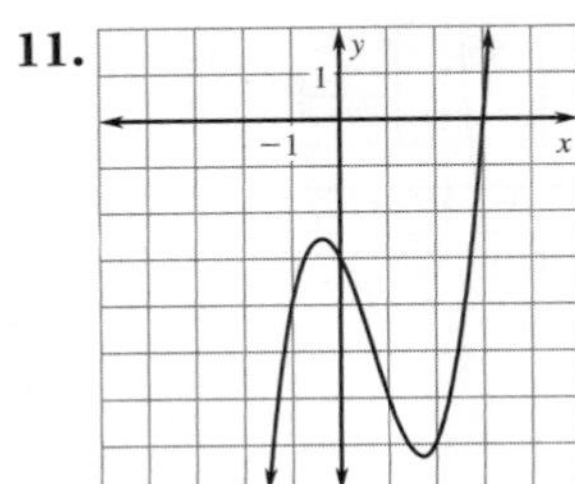

12. 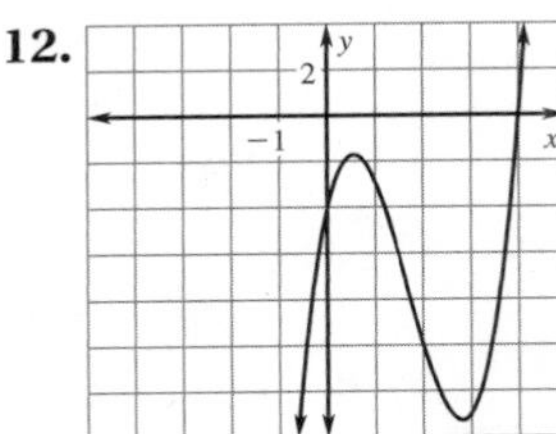

13. The x-intercepts should be at −2 and 1.

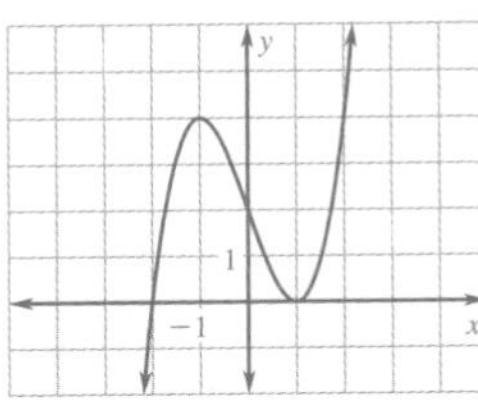

14. The function is a fourth degree polynomial with a positive leading coefficient, so its end behavior should be to positive infinity at both ends.

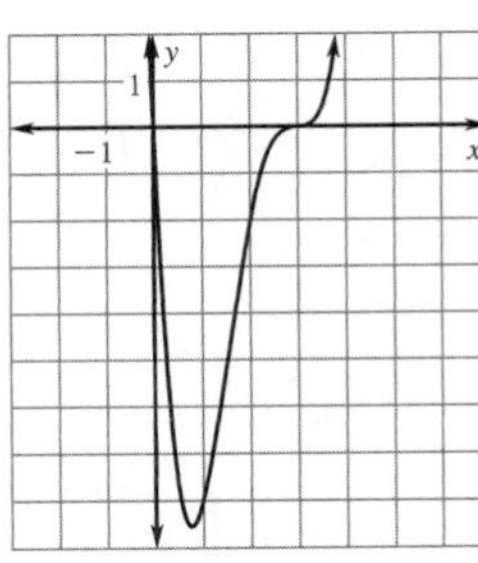

34. 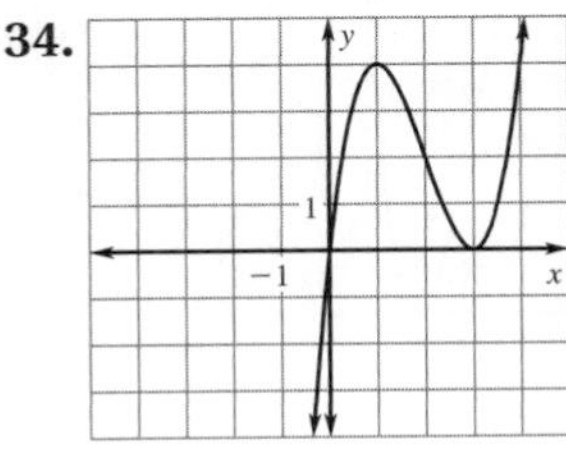

domain: all real numbers, range: all real numbers

35. 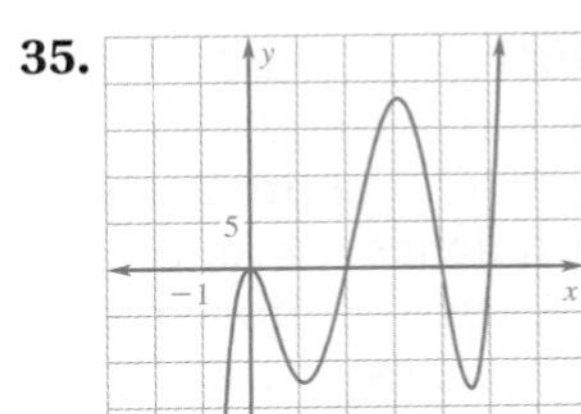

domain: all real numbers, range: all real numbers

36. 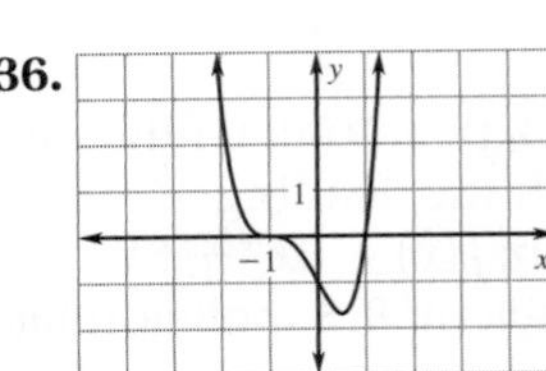

domain: all real numbers, range: $y \geq -1.7$

37. 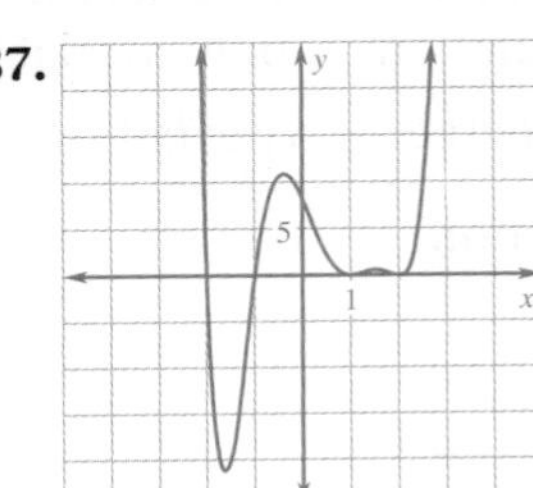

domain: all real numbers, range: $y \geq -21.3$

5.8 Problem Solving (pp. 391–392)

41. 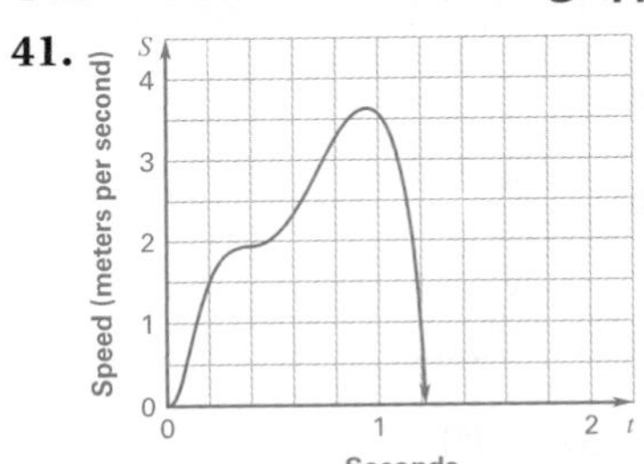

42. c. 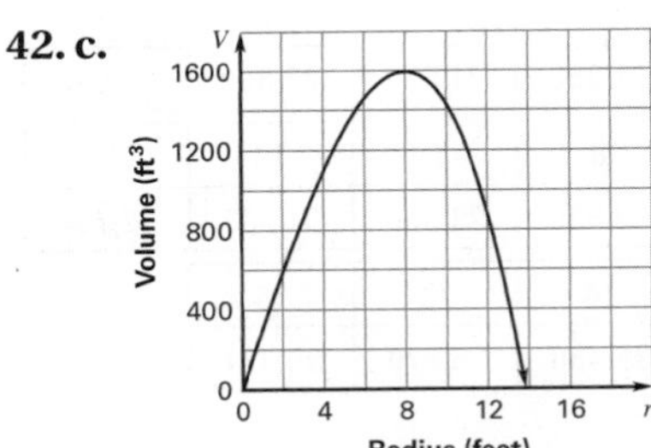

43. a. 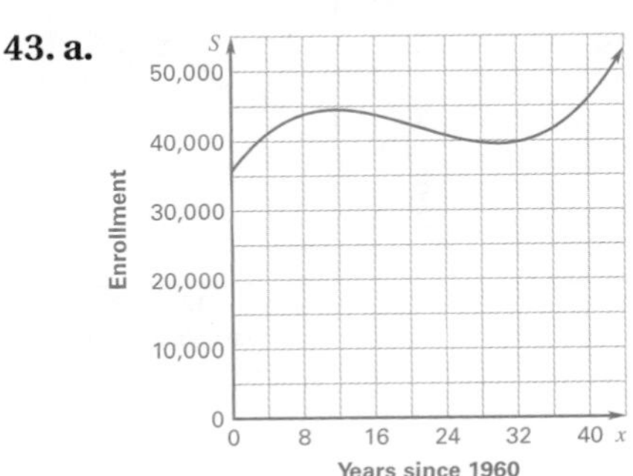

ADDITIONAL ANSWERS

5.9 Skill Practice (pp. 397–398)

12.
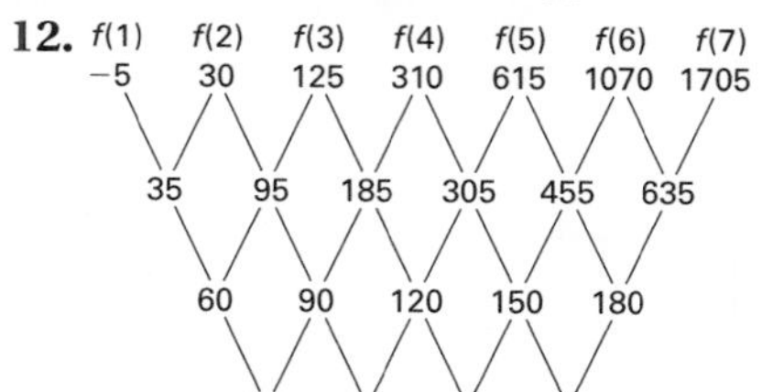

13.
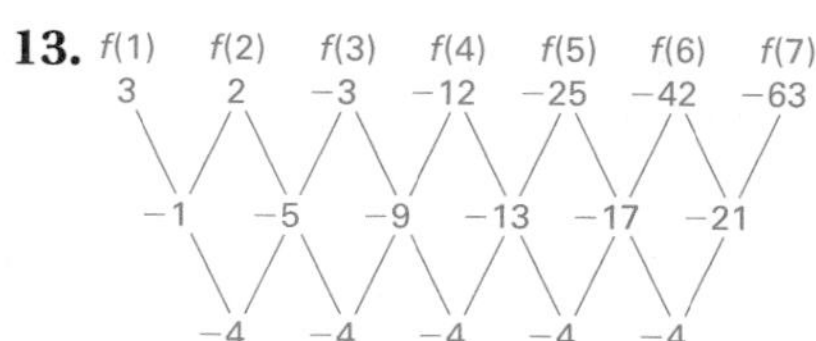

14.
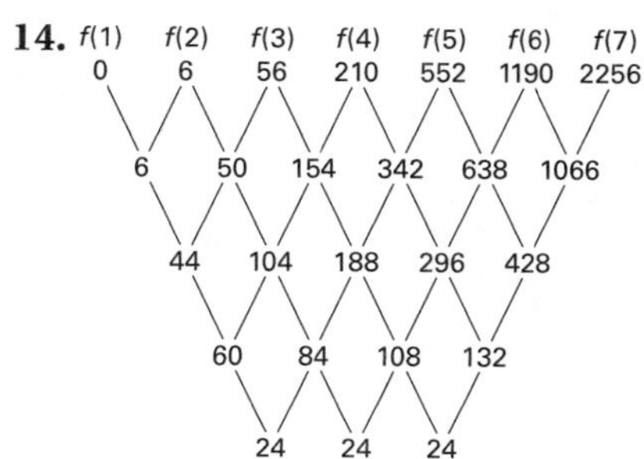

15.
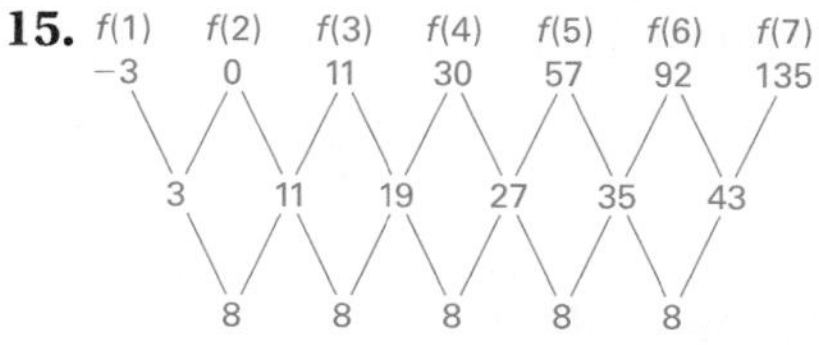

16.
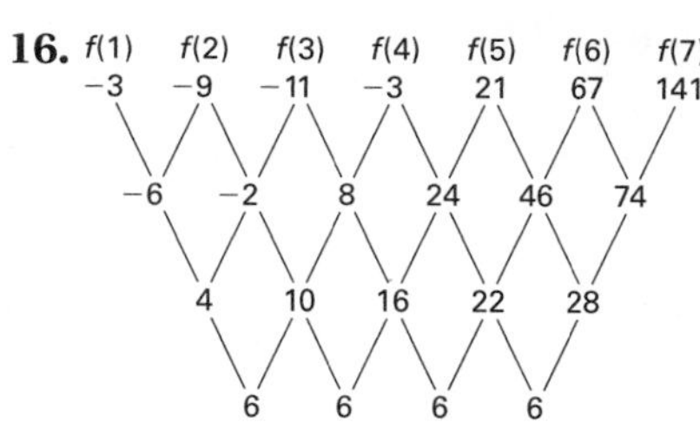

17.
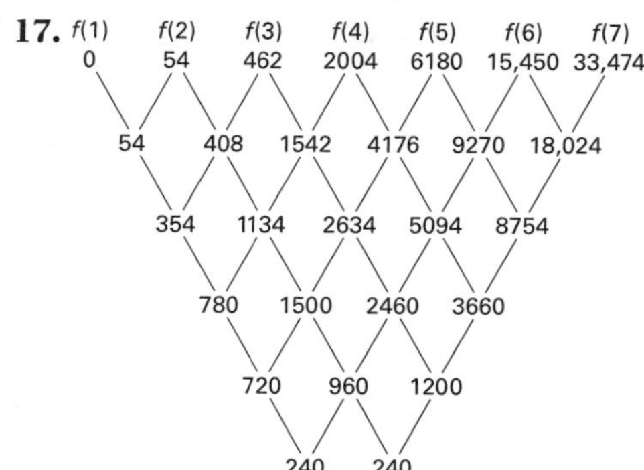

Quiz for Lessons 5.7–5.9 (p. 399)

7.
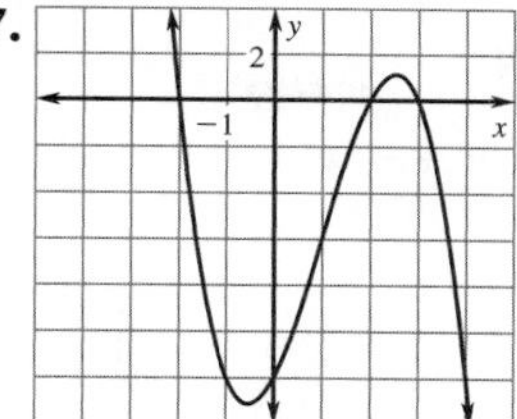

8.
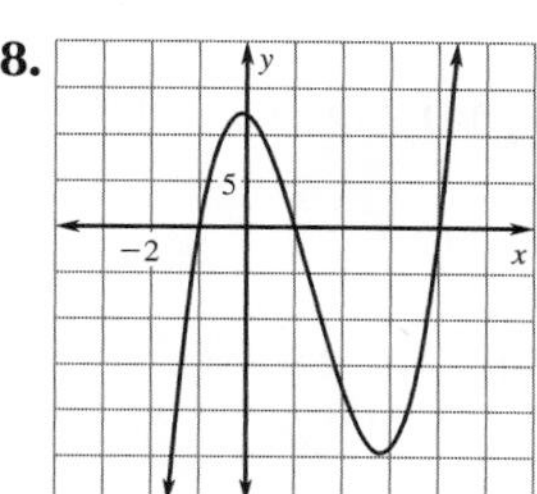

9.
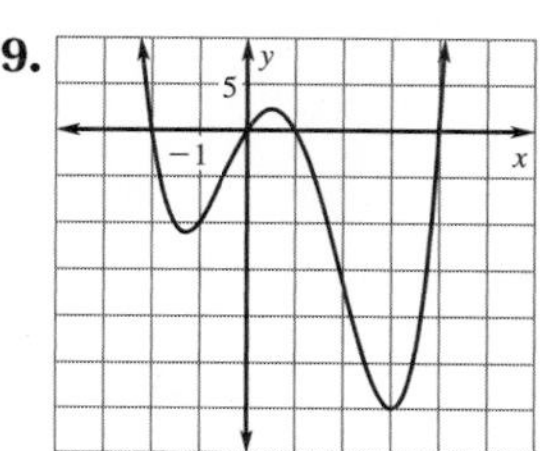

10.
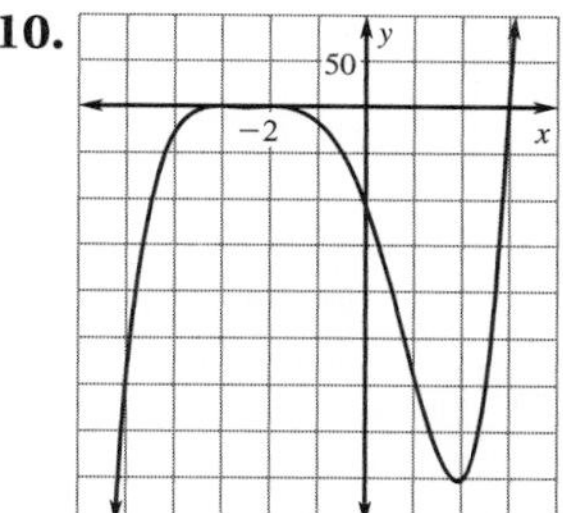

ADDITIONAL ANSWERS

Chapter 6

6.4 Guided Practice (pp. 439–442)

1. $f^{-1}(x) = x - 4$; $f(f^{-1}(x)) = (x - 4) + 4 = x$,
$f^{-1}(f(x)) = (x + 4) - 4 = x$

2. $f^{-1}(x) = \frac{x+1}{2}$; $f(f^{-1}(x)) = 2\left(\frac{x+1}{2}\right) - 1 = x + 1 - 1 = x$,
$f^{-1}(f(x)) = \frac{(2x-1)+1}{2} = \frac{2x}{2} = x$

3. $f^{-1}(x) = \frac{x-1}{-3}$; $f(f^{-1}(x)) = -3\left(\frac{x-1}{-3}\right) + 1 = x - 1 + 1 = x$,
$f^{-1}(f(x)) = \frac{(-3x+1)-1}{-3} = \frac{-3x}{-3} = x$

6.5 Guided Practice (pp. 447–449)

1.
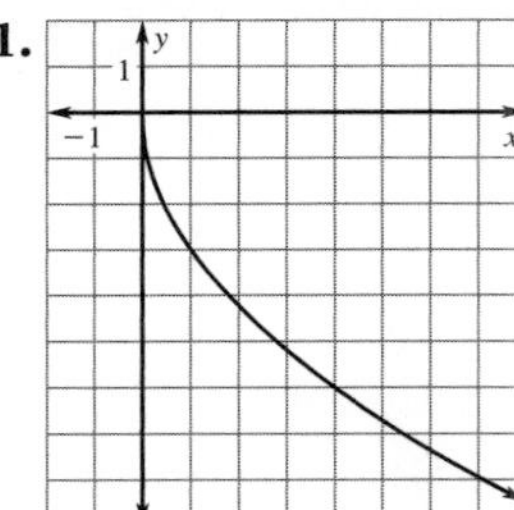

2.
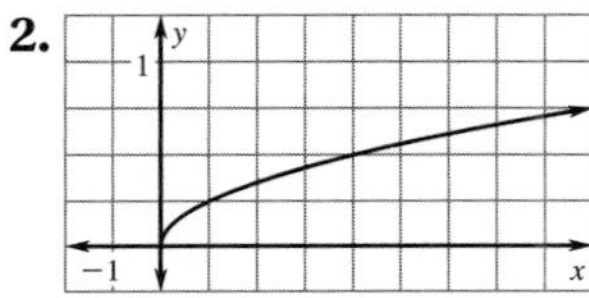

3.
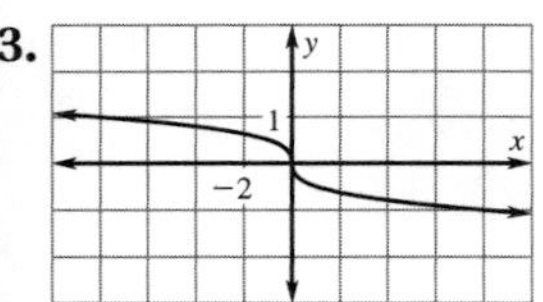

4.
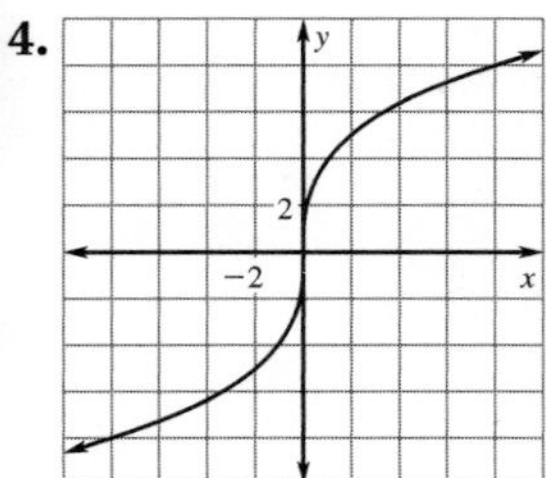

6.5 Skill Practice (pp. 449–450)

3.
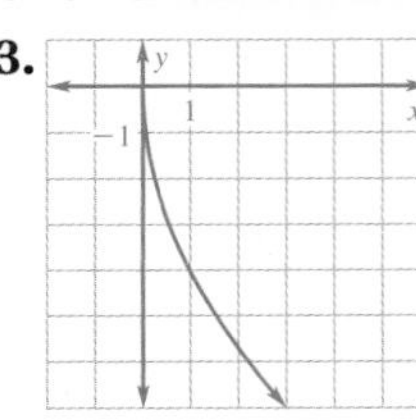

4.
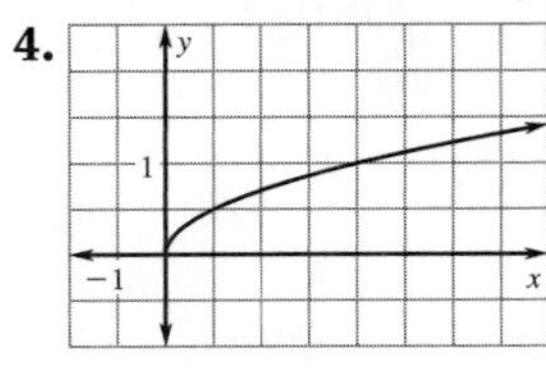

5.
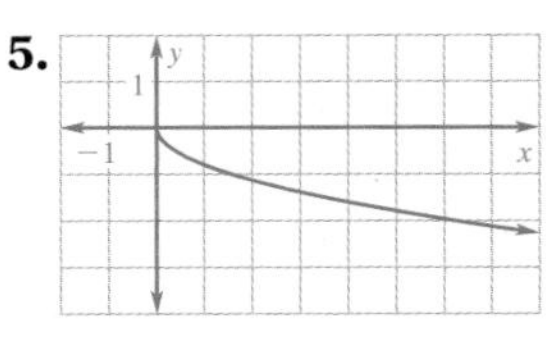

6.
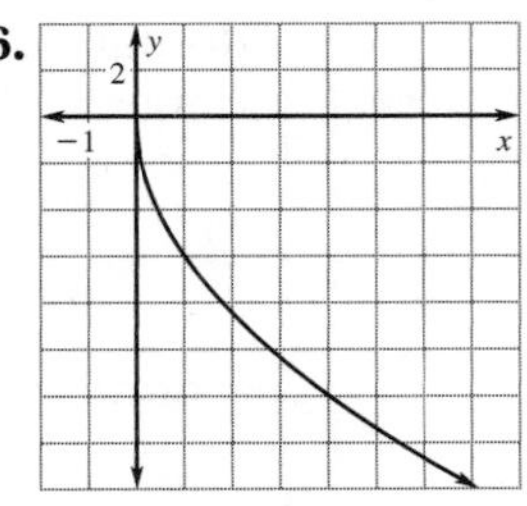

7.
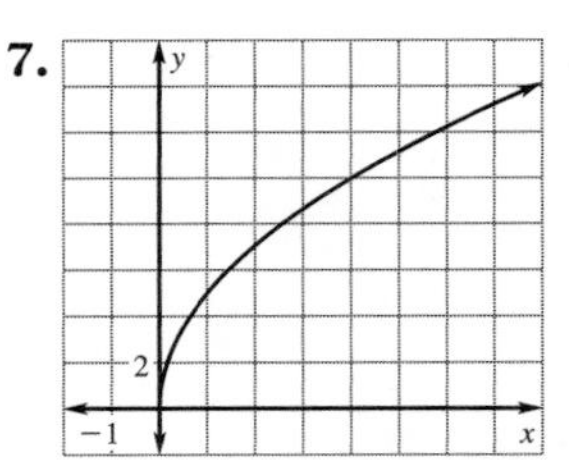

8.
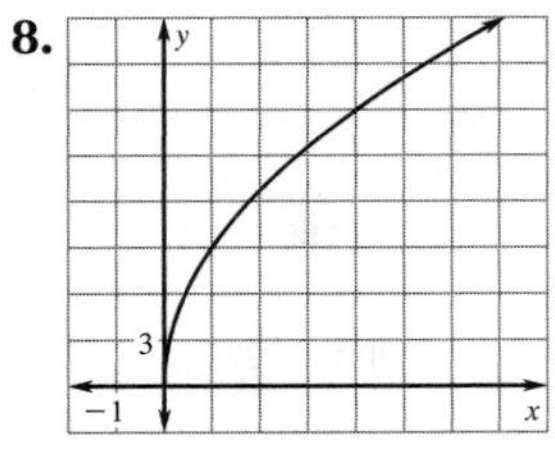

10.
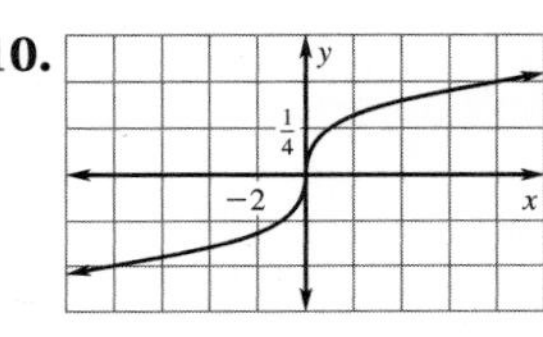
domain: all real numbers, range: all real numbers

11.
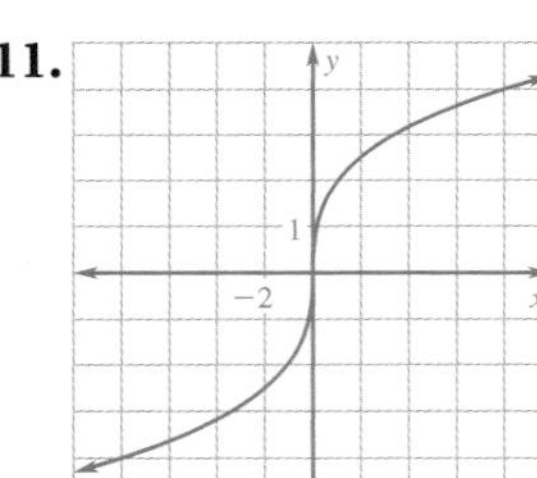
domain: all real numbers, range: all real numbers

12.
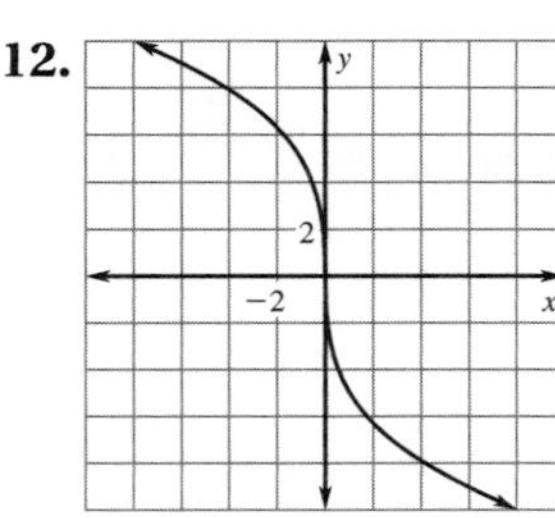
domain: all real numbers, range: all real numbers

13.
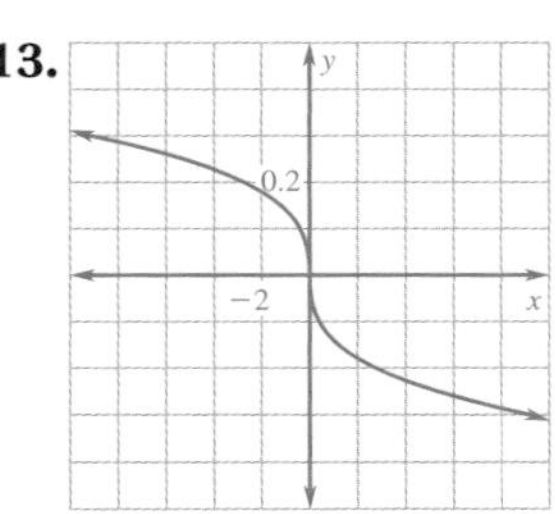
domain: all real numbers, range: all real numbers

ADDITIONAL ANSWERS

14. 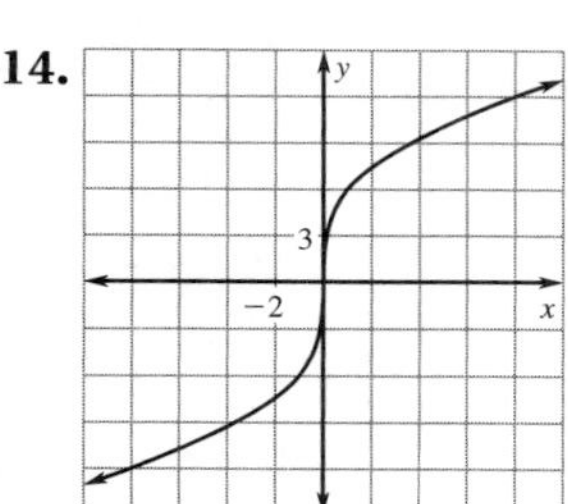

domain: all real numbers, range: all real numbers

15. 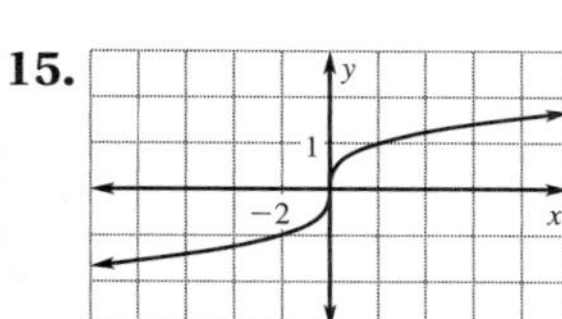

domain: all real numbers, range: all real numbers

16. 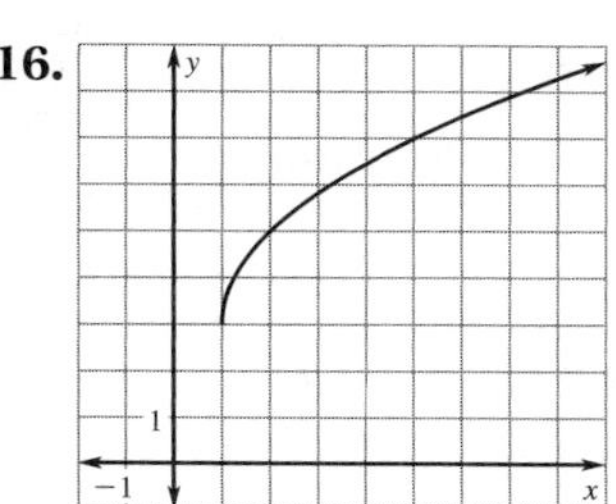

domain: $x \geq 1$, range: $y \geq 3$

17. 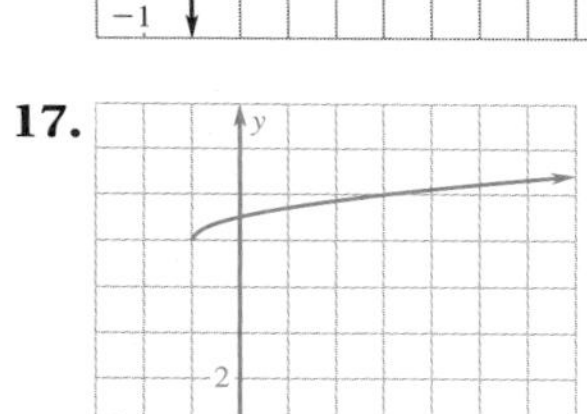

domain: $x \geq -1$, range: $y \geq 8$

18. 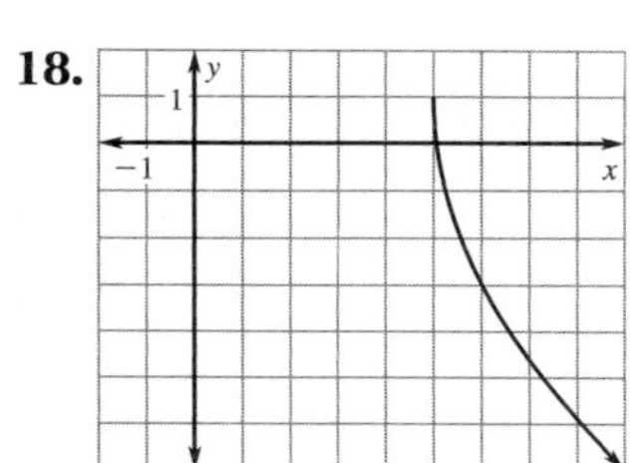

domain: $x \geq 5$, range: $y \leq 1$

19. 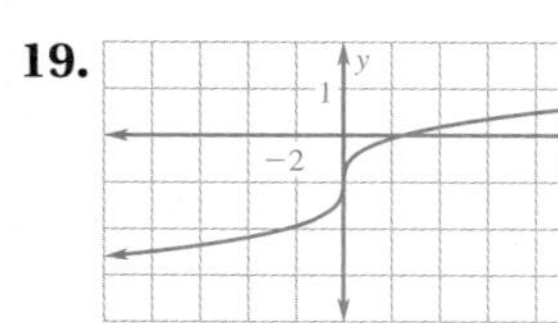

domain: all real numbers, range: all real numbers

20. 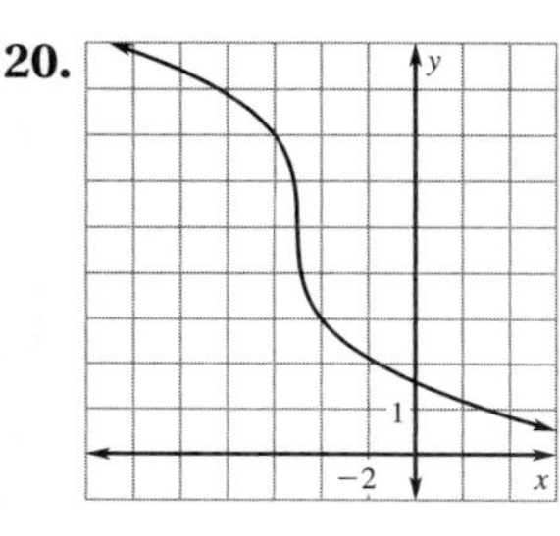

domain: all real numbers, range: all real numbers

21. 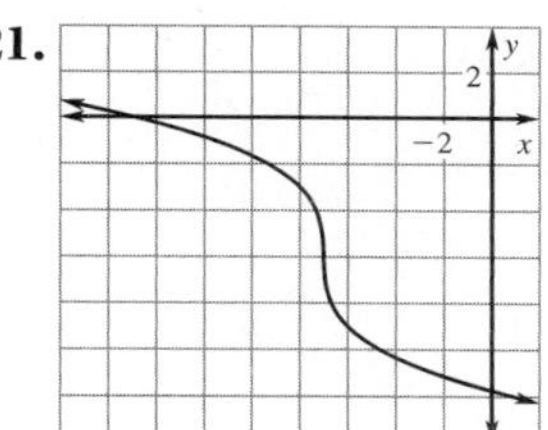

domain: all real numbers, range: all real numbers

22. 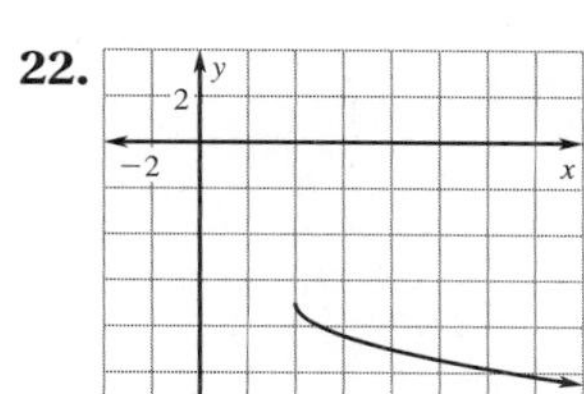

domain: $x \geq 4$, range: $y \leq -7$

23. 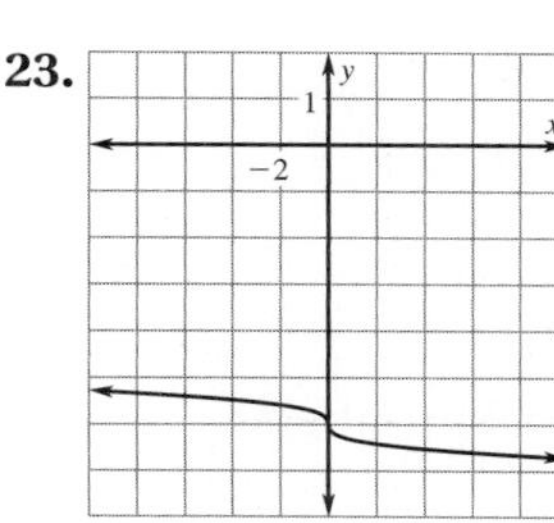

domain: all real numbers, range: all real numbers

24. 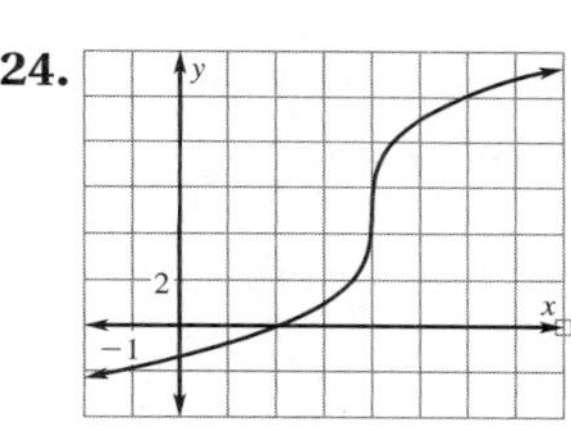

domain: all real numbers, range: all real numbers

28. Domain: $x \geq -5$, range: $y \geq 0$; the expression under the radical sign must be greater than or equal to 0, so substitute the least value of x into the equation and find y.
29. Domain: $x \geq 12$, range: $y \geq 0$; the expression under the radical sign must be greater than or equal to 0, so substitute the least value of x into the equation and find y.
30. Domain: $x \geq 0$, range: $y \geq -4$; the expression under the radical sign must be greater than or equal to 0, so substitute the least value of x into the equation and find y.
31. Domain: all real numbers, range: all real numbers; there are no restrictions on finding the cube root of a number and therefore no restrictions on the range.
32. Domain: all real numbers, range: all real numbers; there are no restrictions on finding the cube root of a number and therefore no restrictions on the range.
33. Domain: $x \geq 3$, range: $y \geq 6$; the expression under the radical sign must be greater than or equal to 0, so substitute the least value of x into the equation and find y.

6.5 Problem Solving (pp. 450–451)

40. a. $S = \pi r^2 + \pi r$, $\frac{S}{\pi} = r^2 + r$, $\frac{S}{\pi} + \frac{1}{4} = r^2 + r + \frac{1}{4}$, $\frac{S}{\pi} + \frac{1}{4} = \left(r + \frac{1}{2}\right)^2$, $\sqrt{\frac{S}{\pi} + \frac{1}{4}} = r + \frac{1}{2}$, $\sqrt{\frac{4S + \pi}{4\pi}} = r + \frac{1}{2}$, $\frac{1}{\sqrt{\pi}}\sqrt{S + \frac{\pi}{4}} = r + \frac{1}{2}$, $\frac{1}{\sqrt{\pi}}\sqrt{S + \frac{\pi}{4}} - \frac{1}{2} = r$

b. 

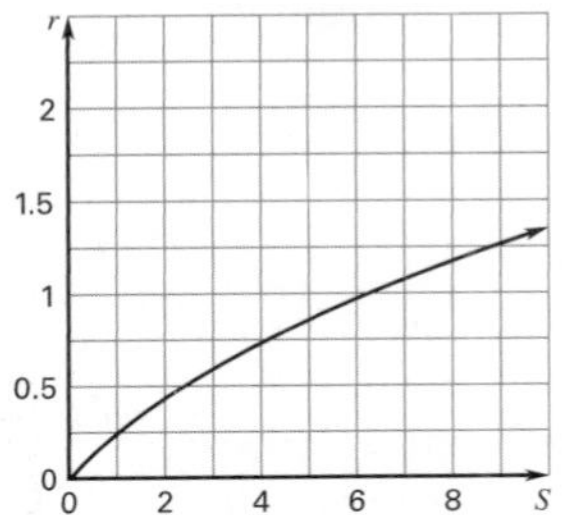

Chapter 7

7.1 Guided Practice (pp. 479–481)

1. 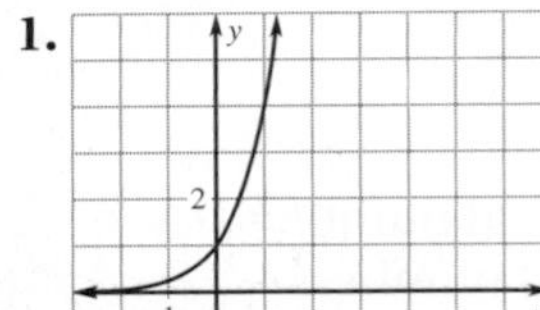
domain: all real numbers, range: $y \geq 0$

2. 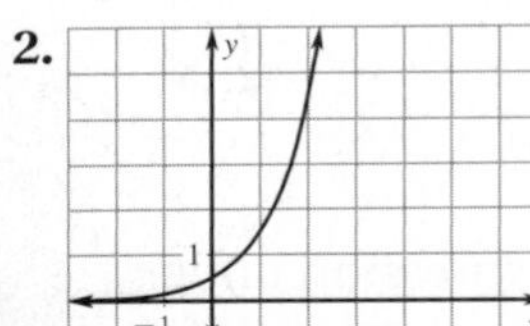
domain: all real numbers, range: $y \geq 0$

3. 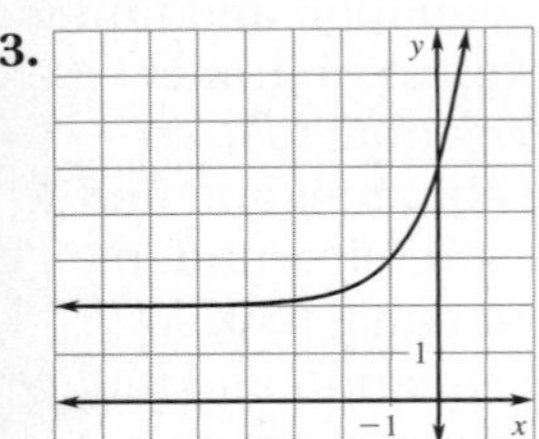
domain: all real numbers, range: $y \geq 2$

7.1 Skill Practice (pp. 482–483)

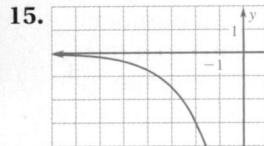

15. 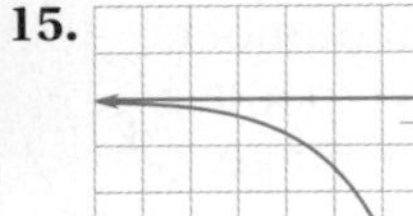
domain: all real numbers, range: $y < 0$

16. 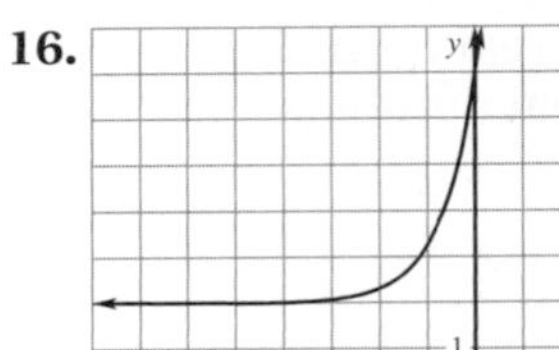
domain: all real numbers, range: $y > 2$

17. 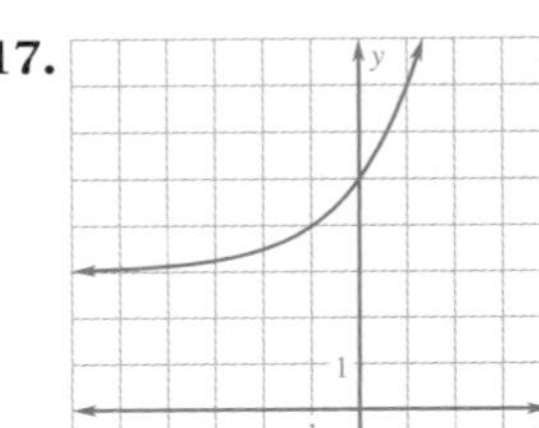
domain: all real numbers, range: $y > 3$

18. 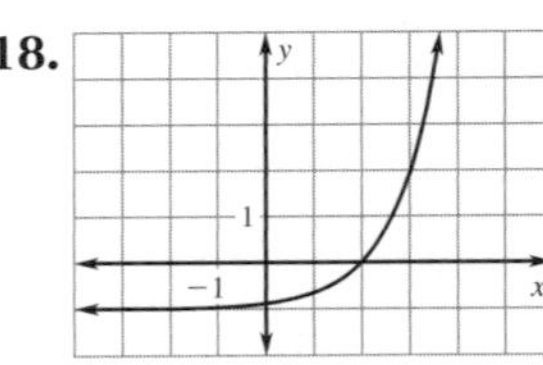
domain: all real numbers, range: $y > -1$

19. 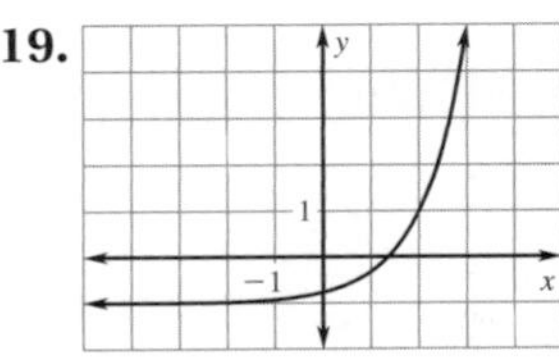
domain: all real numbers, range: $y > -1$

20. 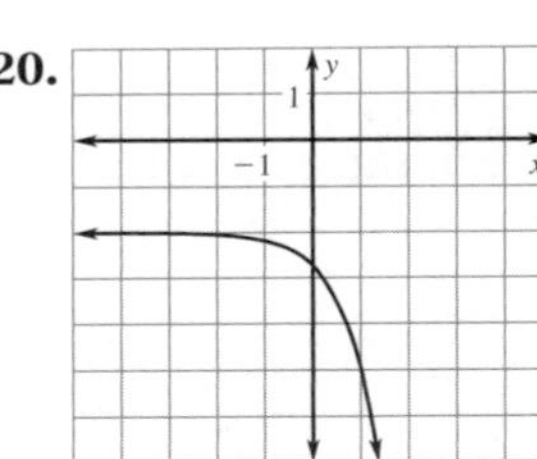
domain: all real numbers, range: $y < -2$

21. 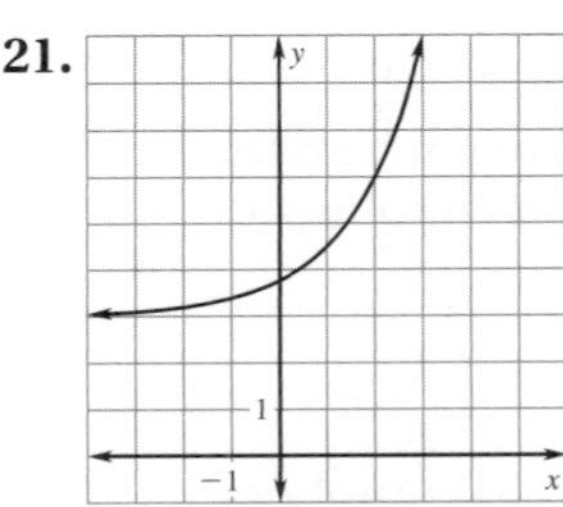
domain: all real numbers, range: $y > 3$

22. 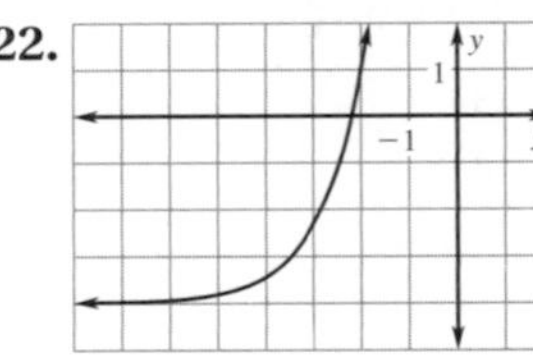
domain: all real numbers, range: $y > -4$

23. 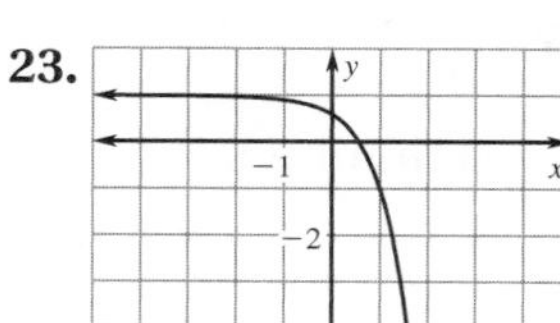

domain: all real numbers, range: $y < 1$

7.2 Guided Practice (pp. 487–488)

1. 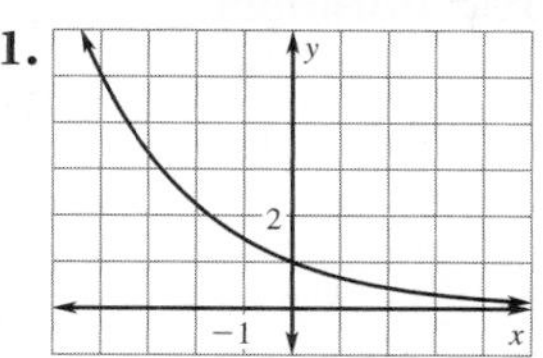

2. 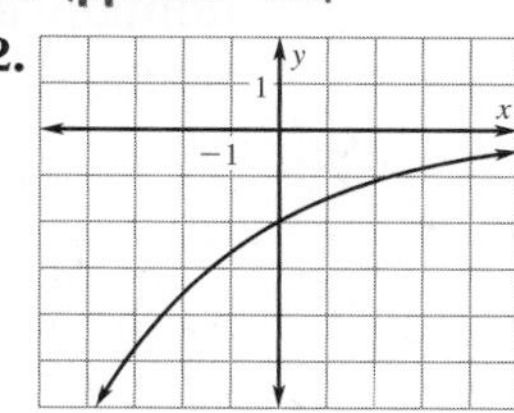

3. 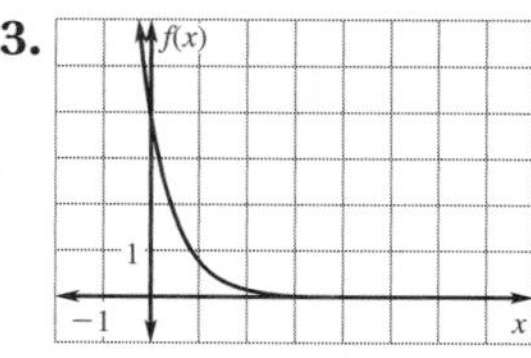

4. 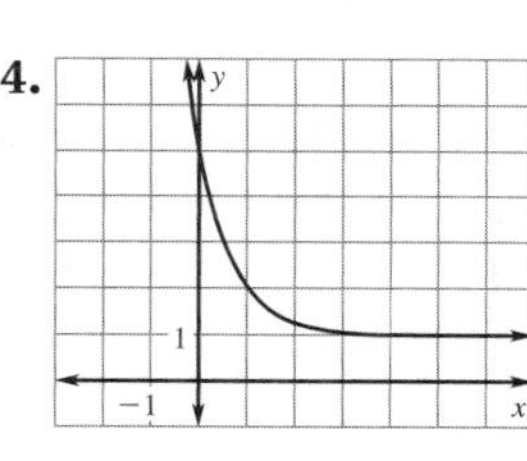

domain: all real numbers, range: $y > 1$

5. 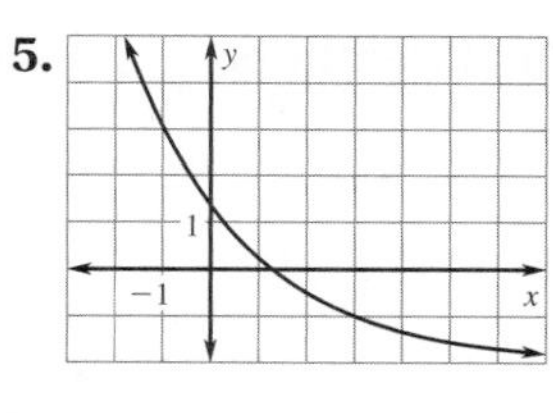

domain: all real numbers, range: $y > -2$

6. 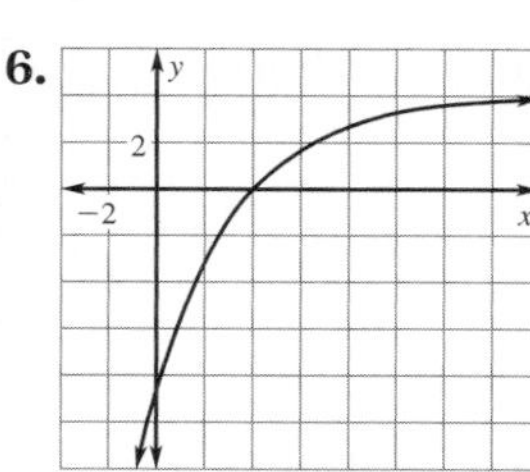

domain: all real numbers, range: $y < 4$

7.2 Skill Practice (pp. 489–490)

7. 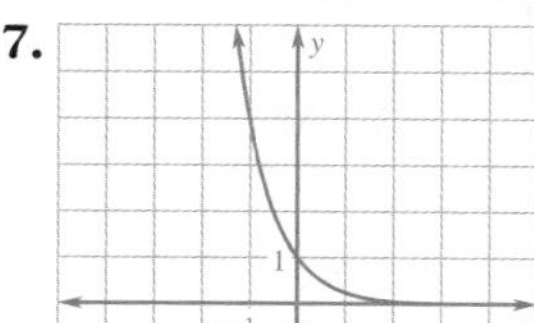

8. 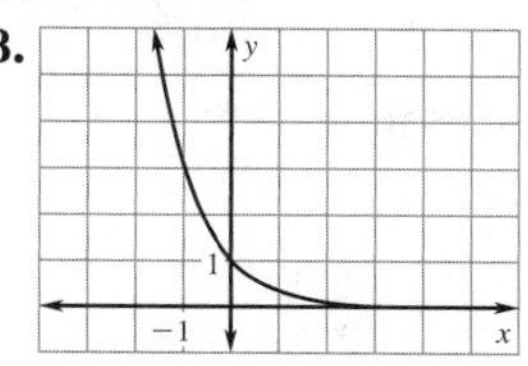

9. 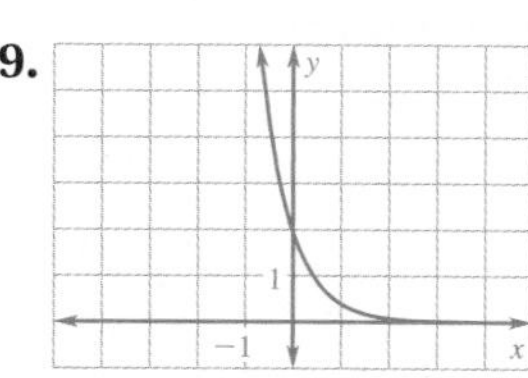

10. 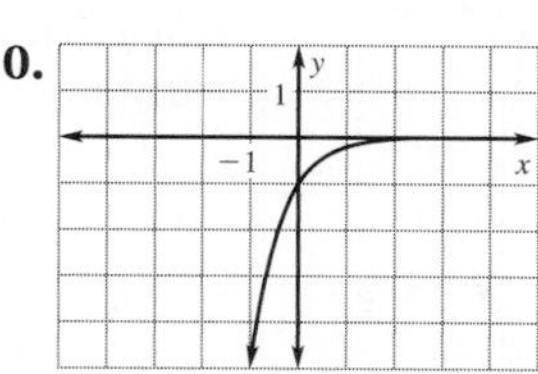

11. 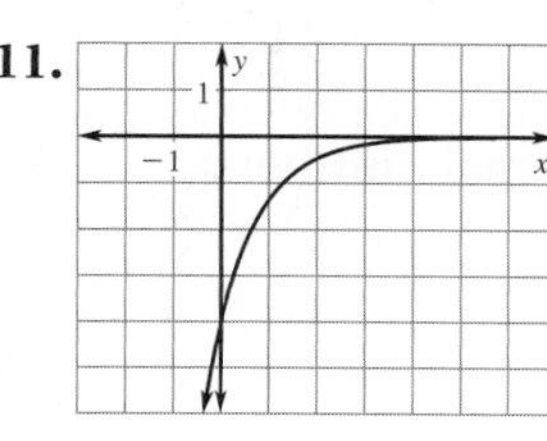

12. 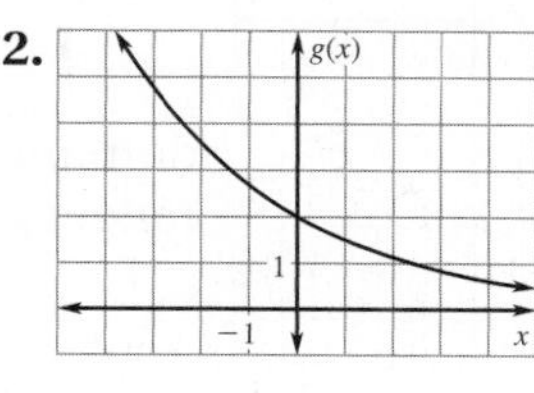

13. 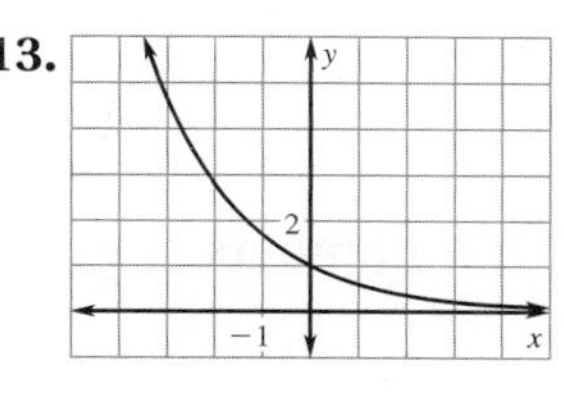

14. 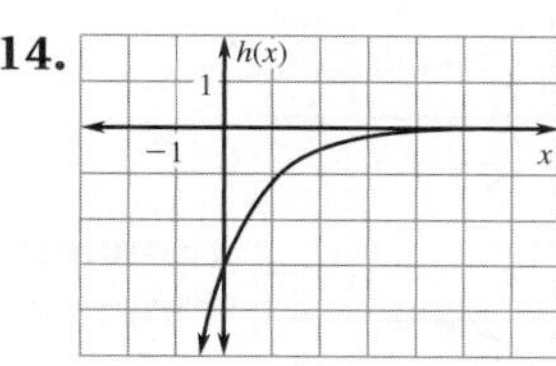

16. 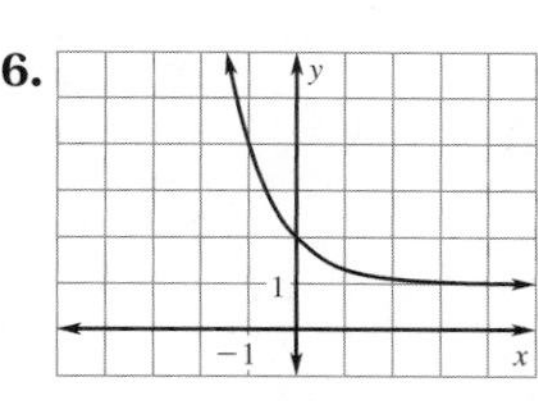

domain: all real numbers, range: $y > 1$

17. 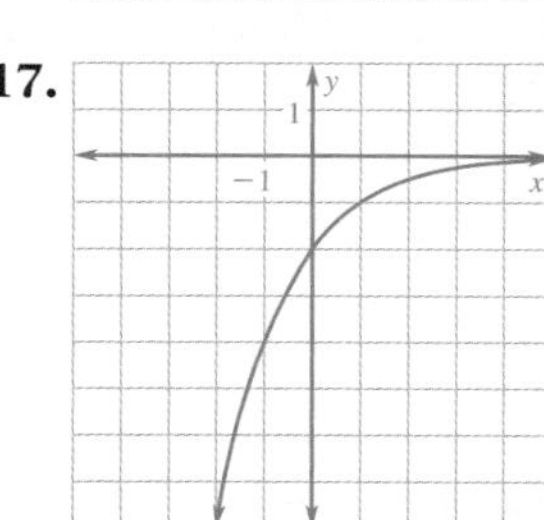

domain: all real numbers, range: $y < 0$

18. 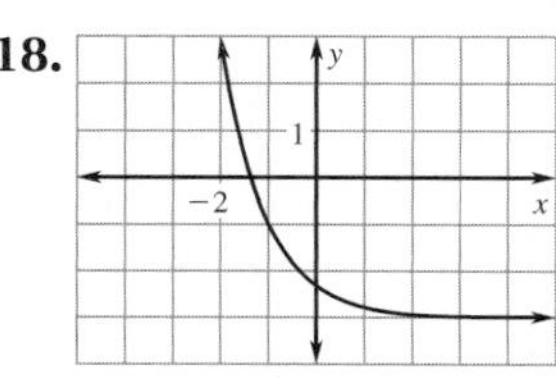

domain: all real numbers, range: $y > -3$

ADDITIONAL ANSWERS

19. 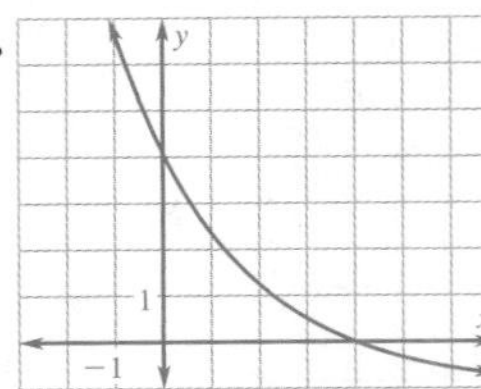
domain: all real numbers, range: $y > -1$

20. 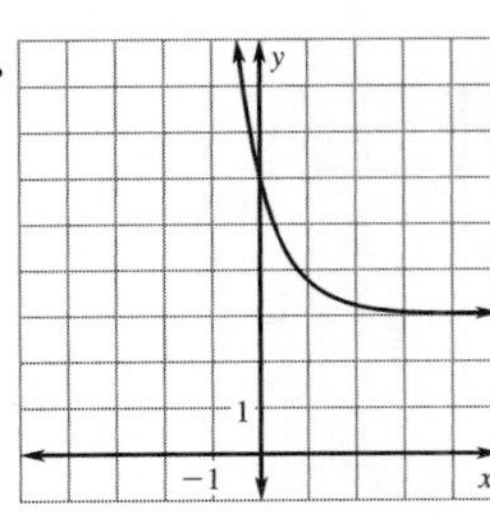
domain: all real numbers, range: $y > 3$

21. 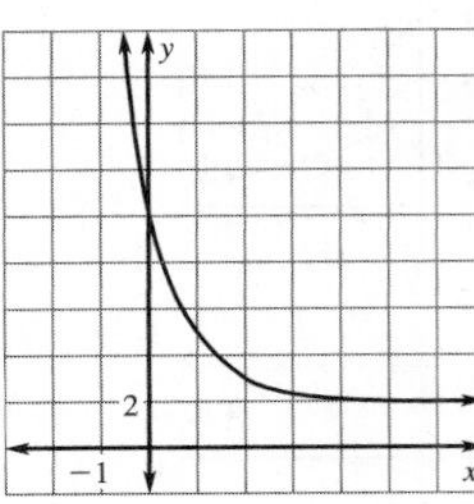
domain: all real numbers, range: $y > 2$

22. 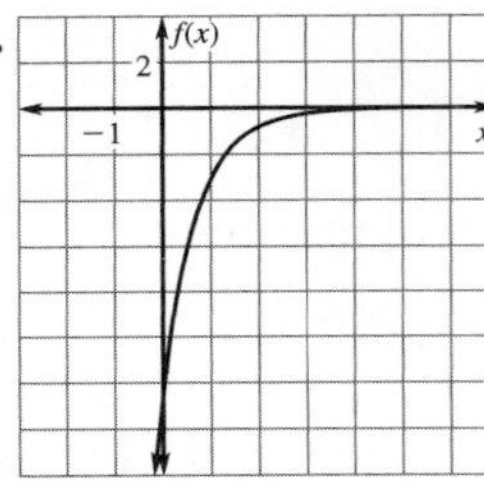
domain: all real numbers, range: $y < 0$

23. 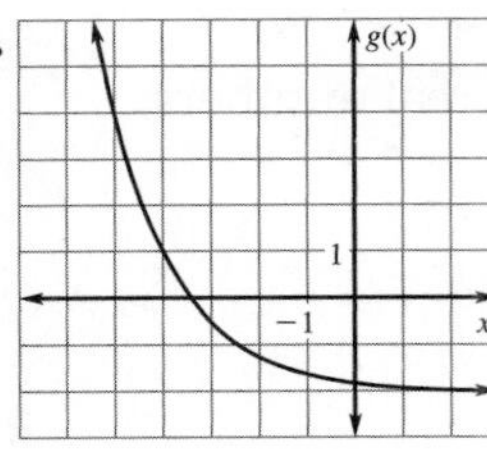
domain: all real numbers, range: $y > -2$

24. 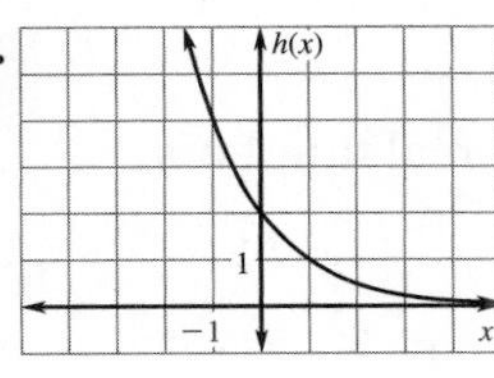
domain: all real numbers, range: $y > 0$

7.3 Skill Practice (pp. 495–496)

42. 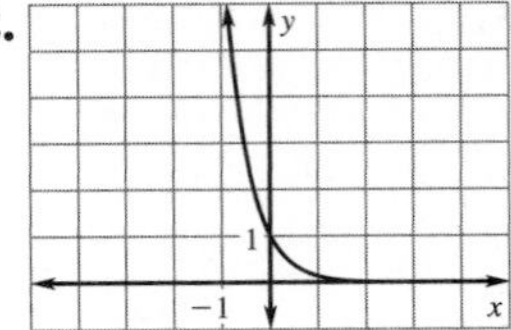
domain: all real numbers, range: $y > 0$

43. 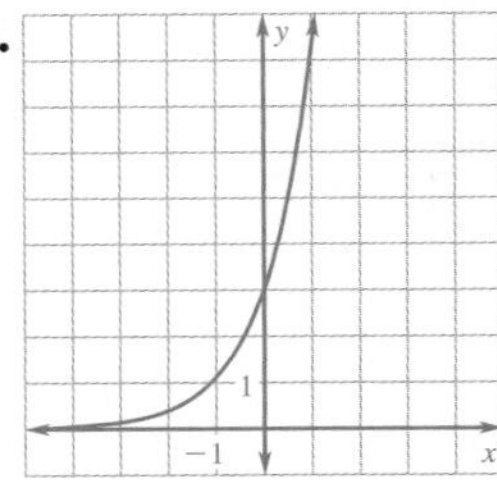
domain: all real numbers, range: $y > 0$

44. 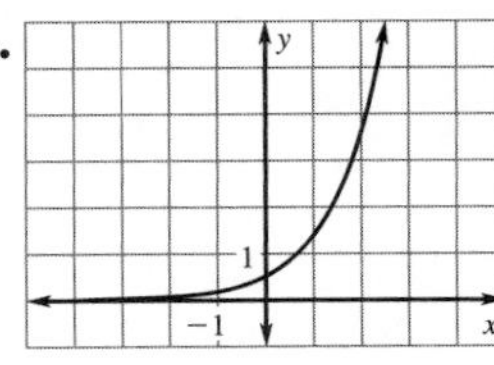
domain: all real numbers, range: $y > 0$

45. 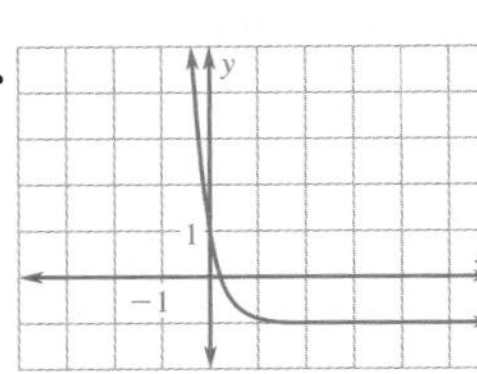
domain: all real numbers, range: $y > -1$

46. 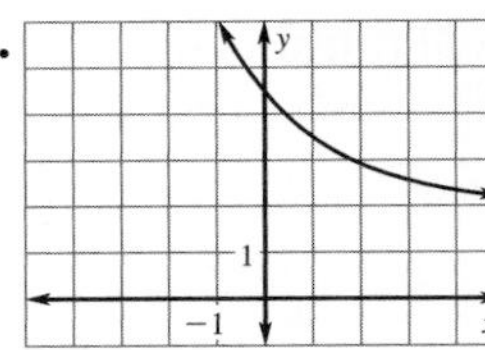
domain: all real numbers, range: $y > 2$

47. 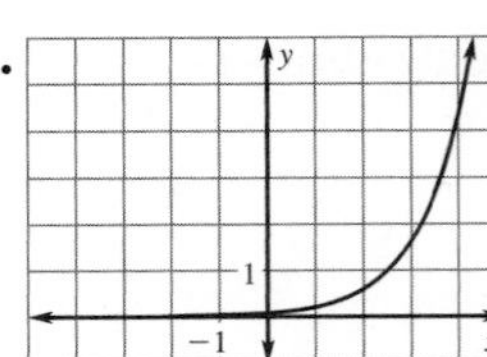
domain: all real numbers, range: $y > 0$

48. 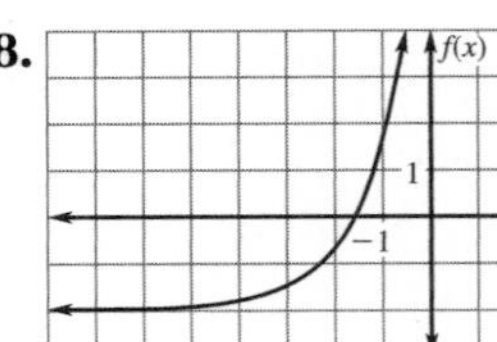
domain: all real numbers, range: $y > -2$

ADDITIONAL ANSWERS

49. 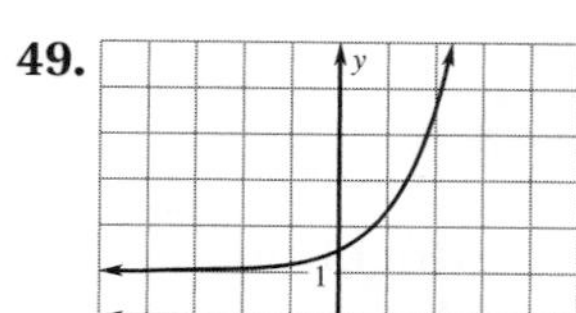
domain: all real numbers,
range: $y > 1$

50. 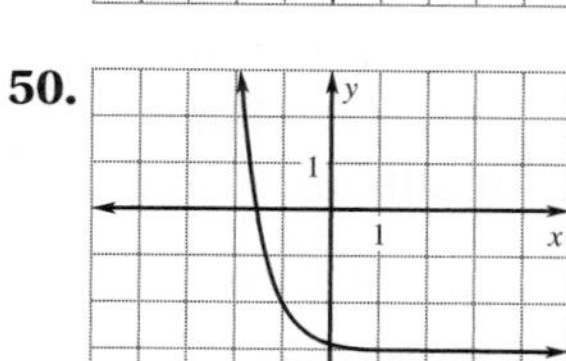
domain: all real numbers,
range: $y > -3$

Quiz for Lessons 7.1–7.3 (p. 498)

1. 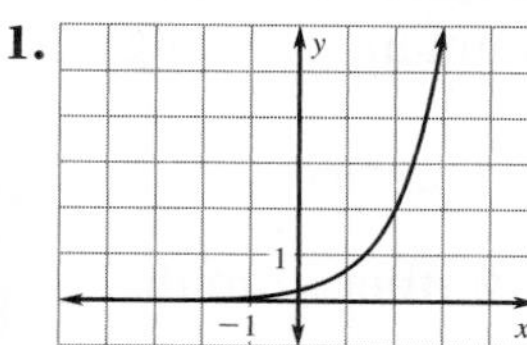

2.

3. 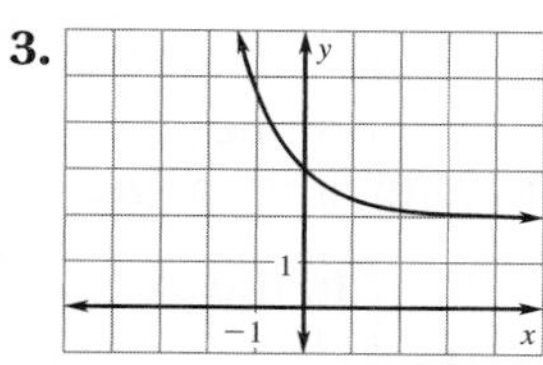

8. domain: all real numbers,
range: $y > 0$

9. 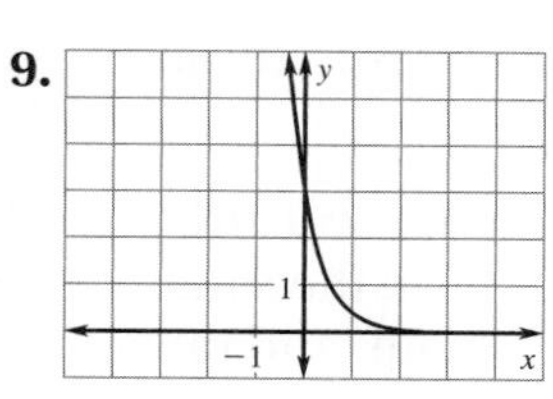
domain: all real numbers,
range: $y > 0$

10. 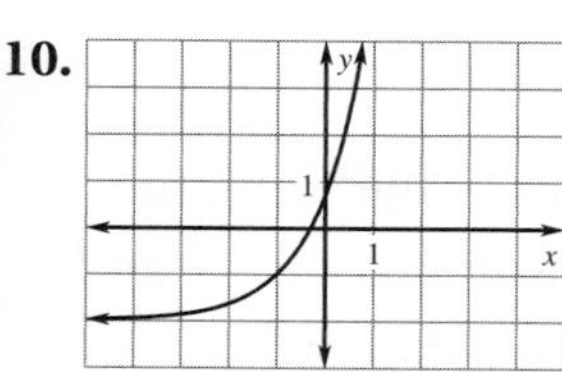
domain: all real numbers,
range: $y > -2$

11. 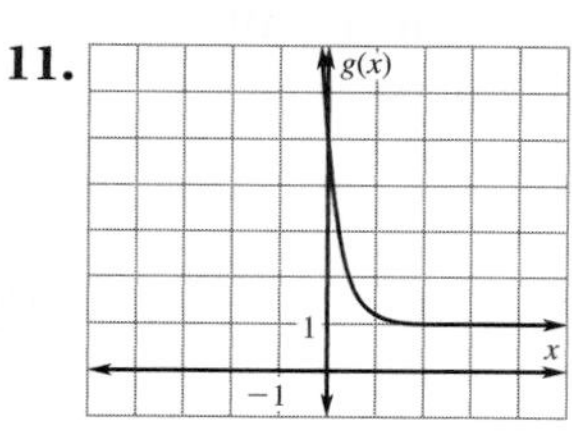
domain: all real numbers,
range: $y > 1$

7.4 Skill Practice (pp. 503–504)

45. 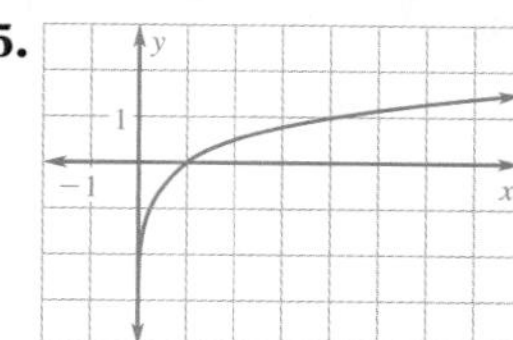
domain: $x > 0$,
range: all real numbers

46. 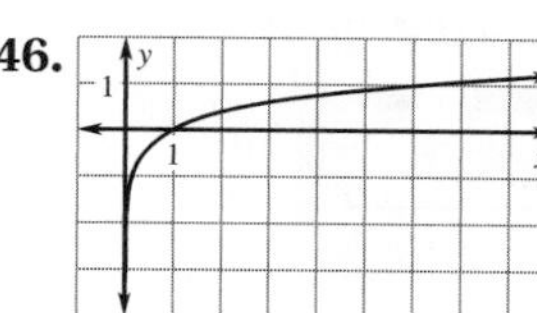
domain: $x > 0$,
range: all real numbers

47. 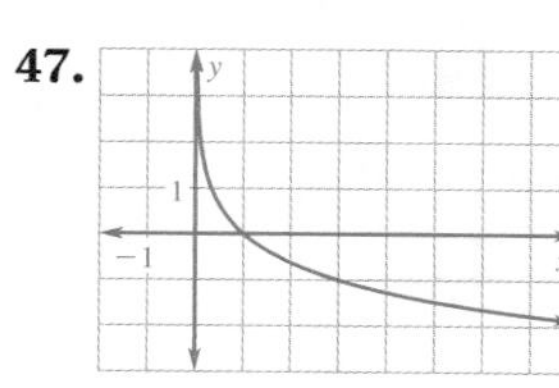
domain: $x > 0$,
range: all real numbers

48. 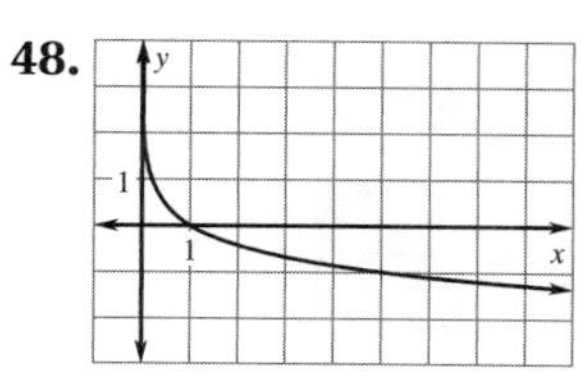
domain: $x > 0$,
range: all real numbers

49. 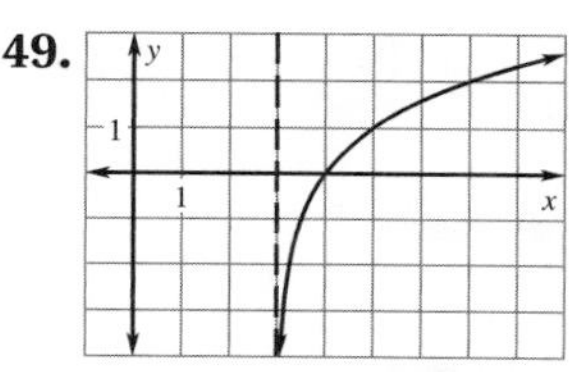
domain: $x > 3$,
range: all real numbers

50. 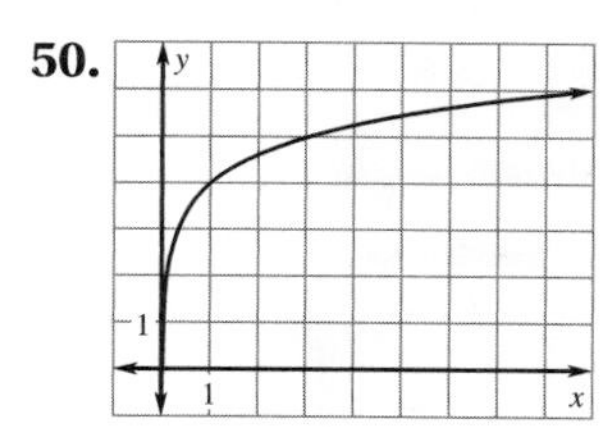
domain: $x > 0$,
range: all real numbers

51. 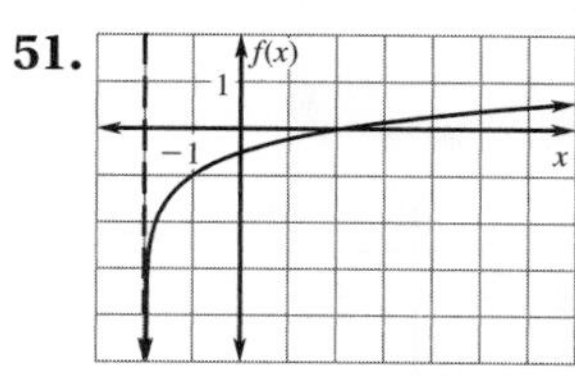
domain: $x > -2$,
range: all real numbers

52. 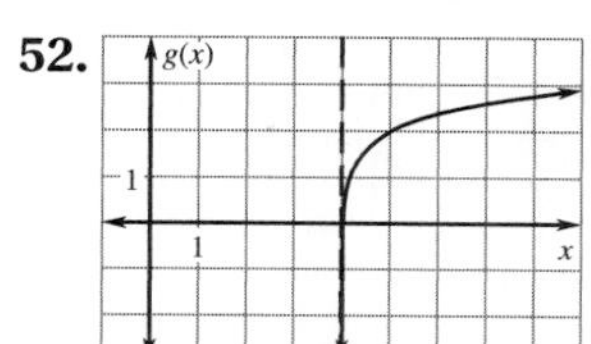
domain: $x > 4$,
range: all real numbers

53. 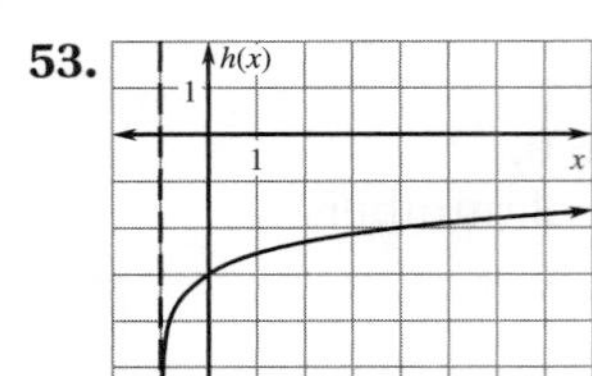

domain: $x > -1$, range: all real numbers

7.5 Graphing Calculator Activity (p. 514)

1. 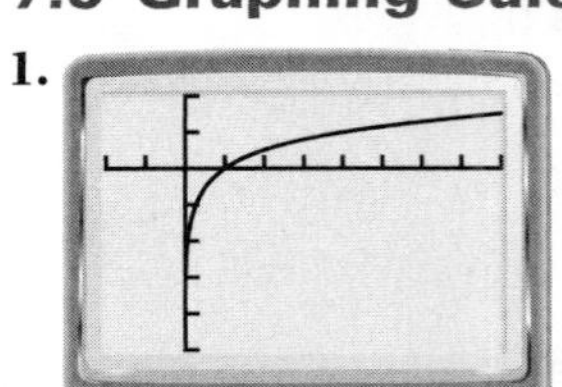

2. 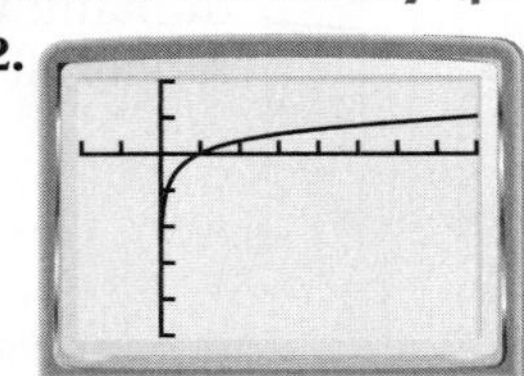

3. 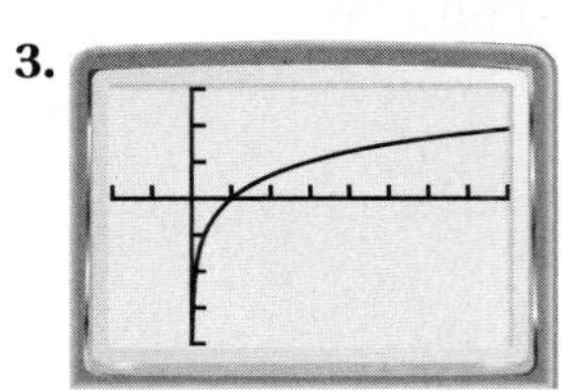

4. 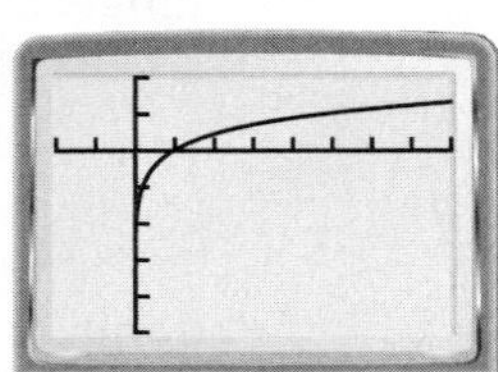

5. 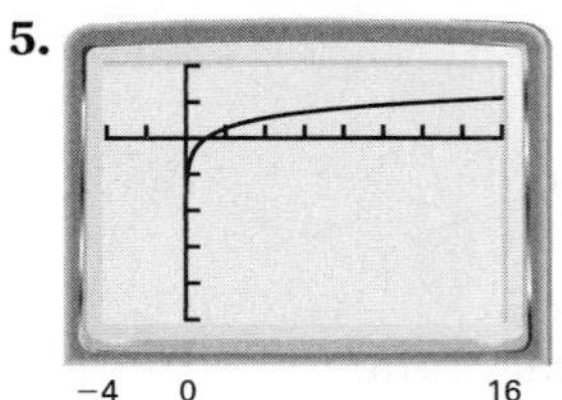

6. 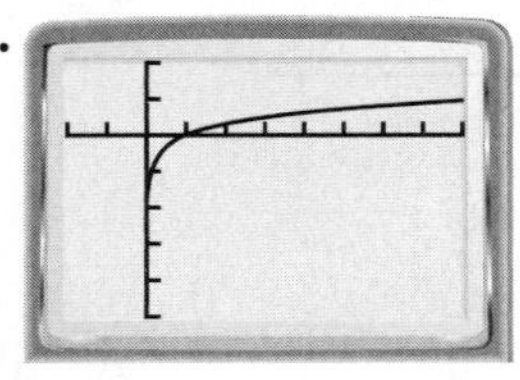

7. 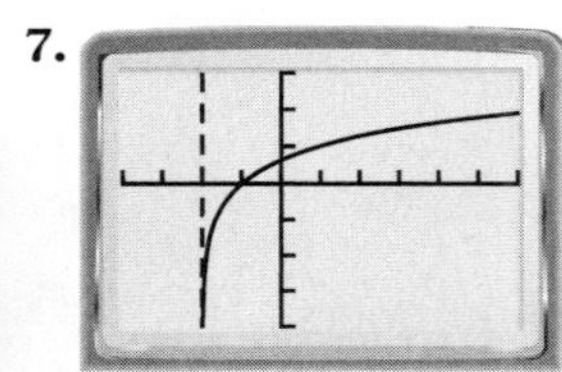

8. 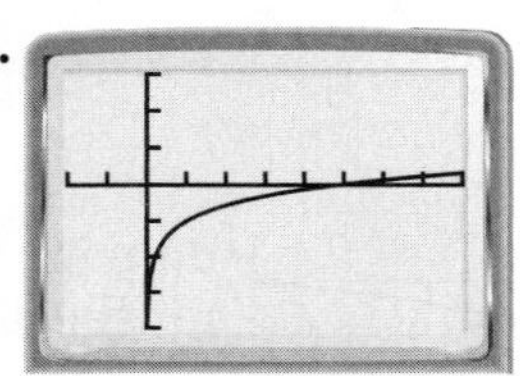

9. 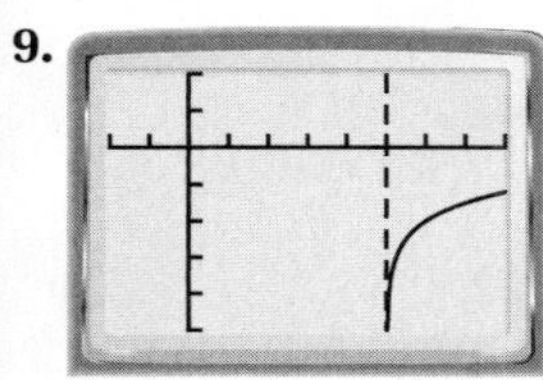

10. 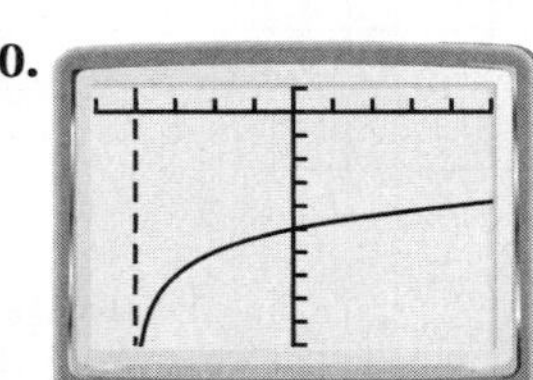

11. 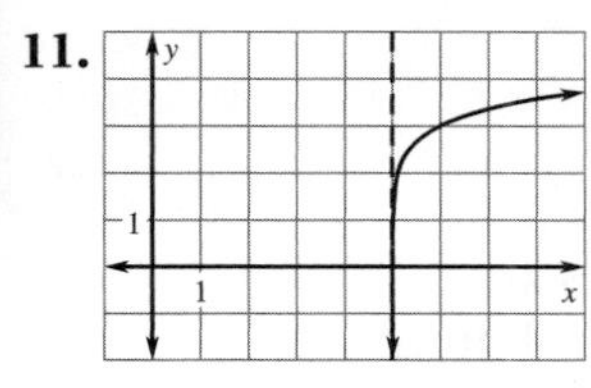

12. 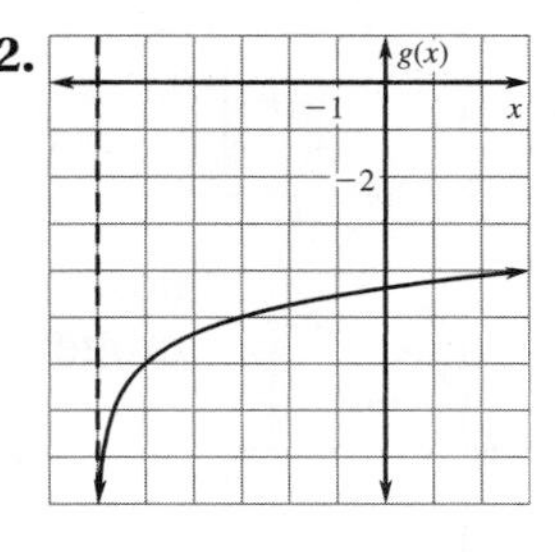

Chapter 8

8.2 Skill Practice (pp. 561–562)

3. 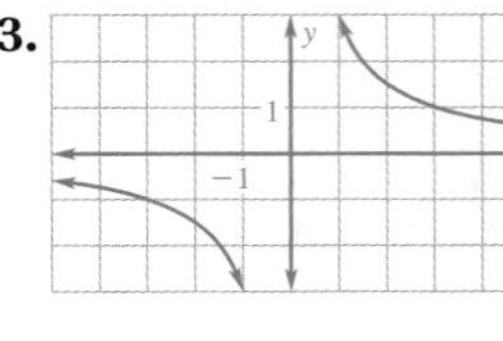

The graph lies farther from the axes than the graph of $y = \frac{1}{x}$. Both graphs lie in the 1st and 3rd quadrants and have the same asymptotes, domain, and range.

4. 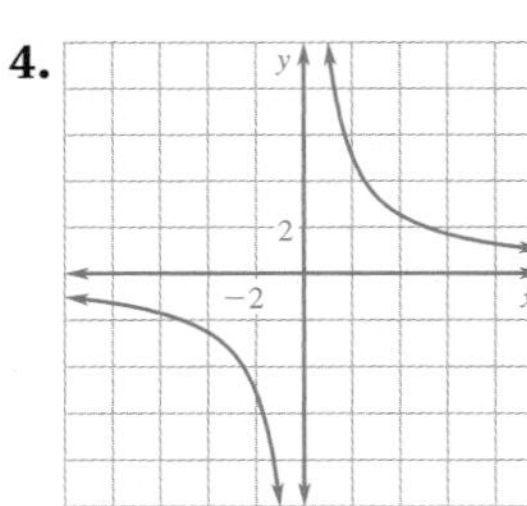

The graph lies farther from the axes than the graph of $y = \frac{1}{x}$. Both graphs lie in the 1st and 3rd quadrants and have the same asymptotes, domain, and range.

5. 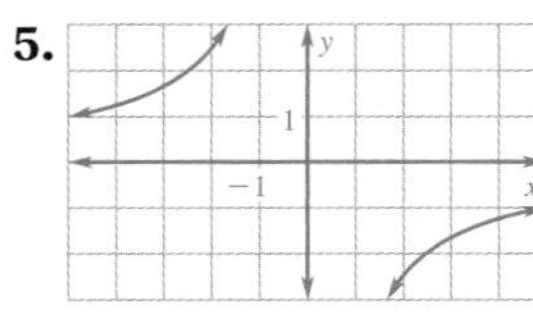

The graph lies farther from the axes than the graph of $y = \frac{1}{x}$ and is located in quadrants 2 and 4. Both graphs have the same asymptotes, domain, and range.

6. 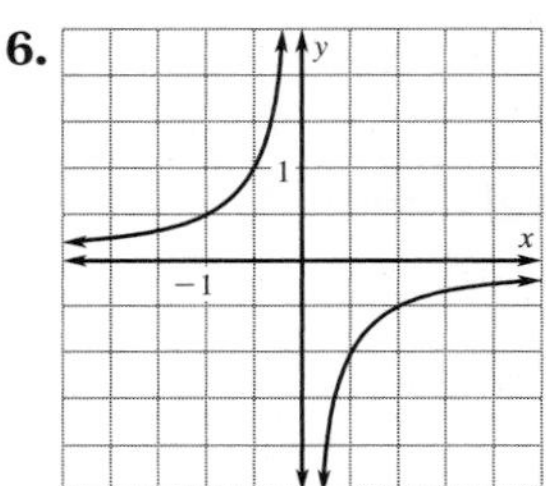

The graph lies closer to the axes than the graph of $y = \frac{1}{x}$. Both graphs lie in the 1st and 3rd quadrants and have the same asymptotes, domain, and range.

7. 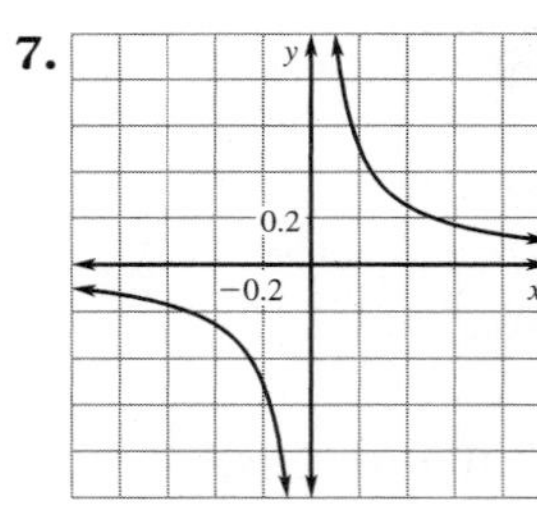

The graph lies closer to the axes than the graph of $y = \frac{1}{x}$. Both graphs lie in the 1st and 3rd quadrants and have the same asymptotes, domain, and range.

8. 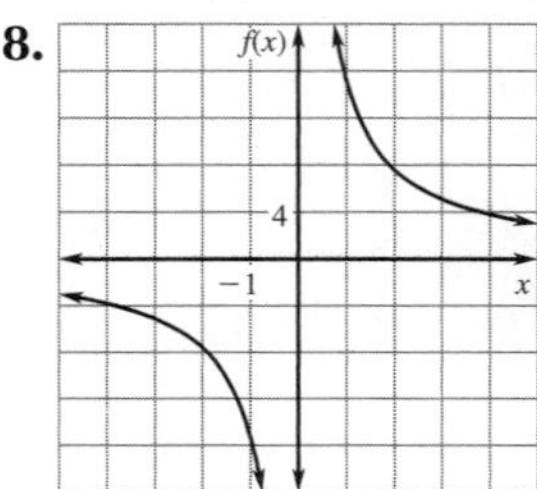

The graph lies farther from the axes than the graph of $y = \frac{1}{x}$ and is located in quadrants 2 and 4. Both have the same asymptotes, domain, and range.

ADDITIONAL ANSWERS

9. 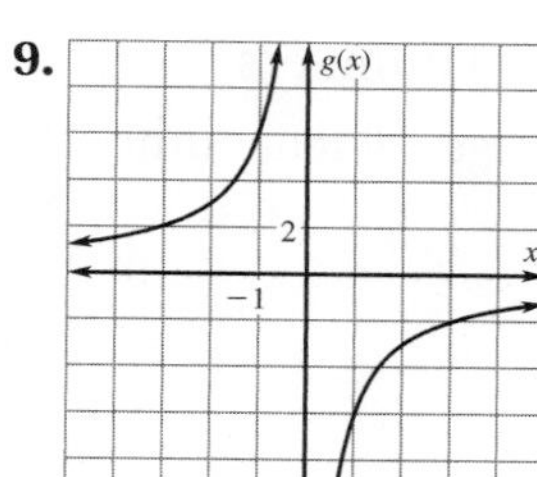

The graph lies farther from the axes than the graph of $y = \frac{1}{x}$ and is located in quadrants 2 and 4. Both graphs have the same asymptotes, domain, and range.

10. 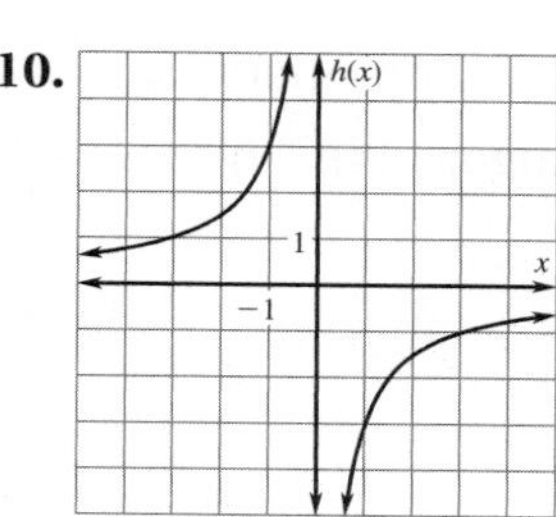

The graph lies farther from the axes than the graph of $y = \frac{1}{x}$ and is located in quadrants 2 and 4. Both graphs have the same asymptotes, domain, and range.

11. 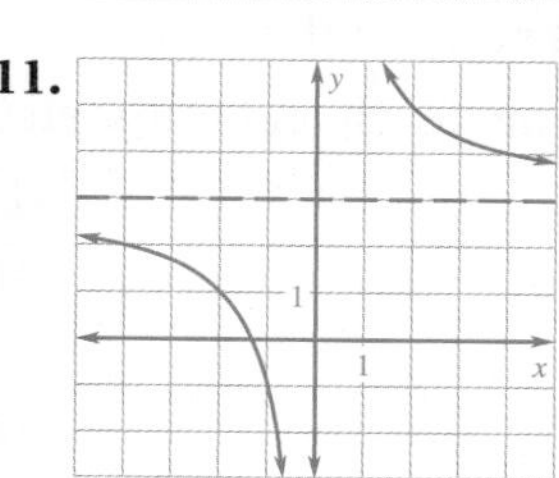

domain: all real numbers except 0, range: all real numbers except 3

12. 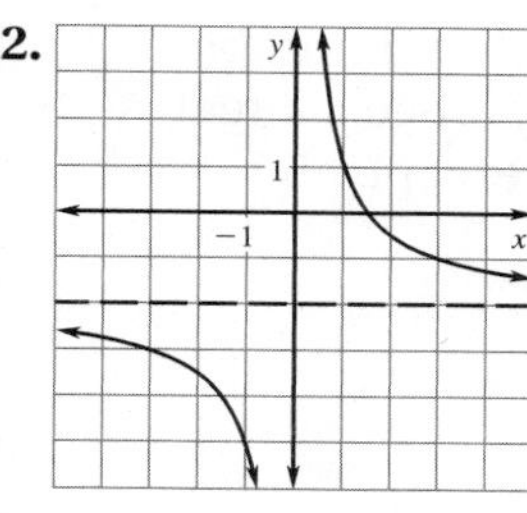

domain: all real numbers except 0, range: all real numbers except −2

13. 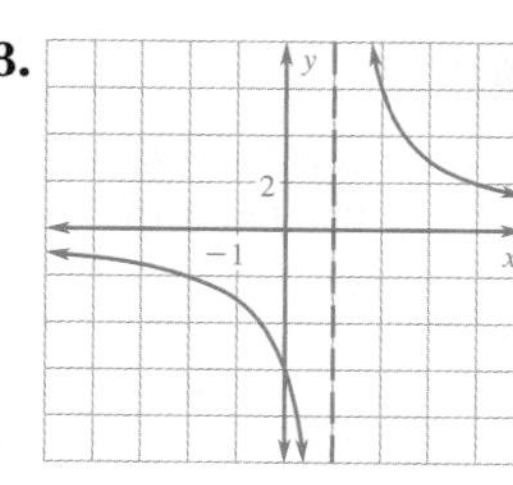

domain: all real numbers except 1, range: all real numbers except 0

14. 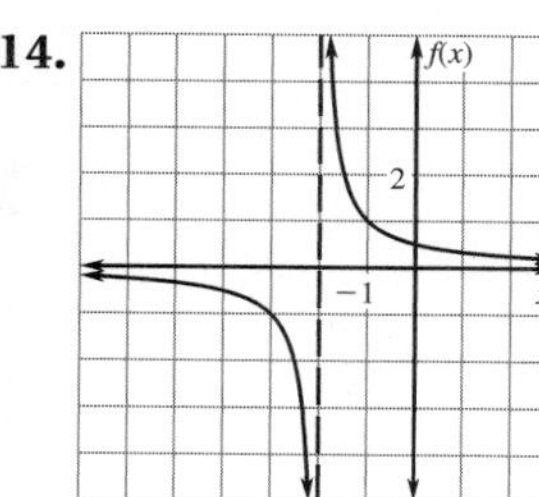

domain: all real numbers except −2, range: all real numbers except 0

15. 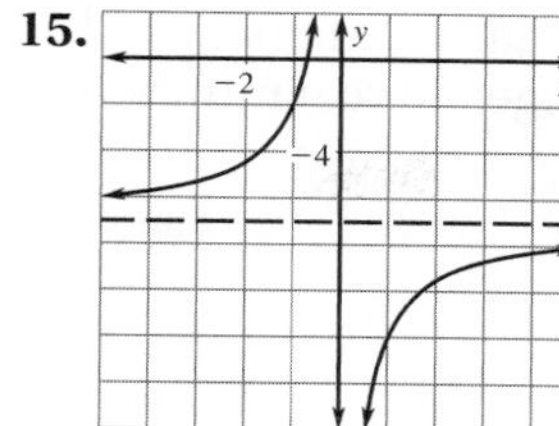

domain: all real numbers except 0, range: all real numbers except −7

16. 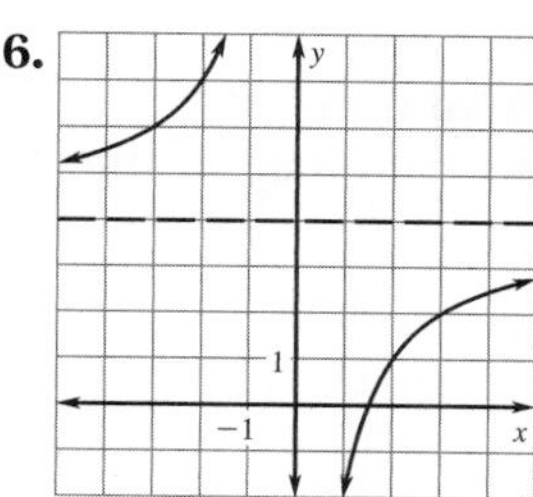

domain: all real numbers except 0, range: all real numbers except 4

17. 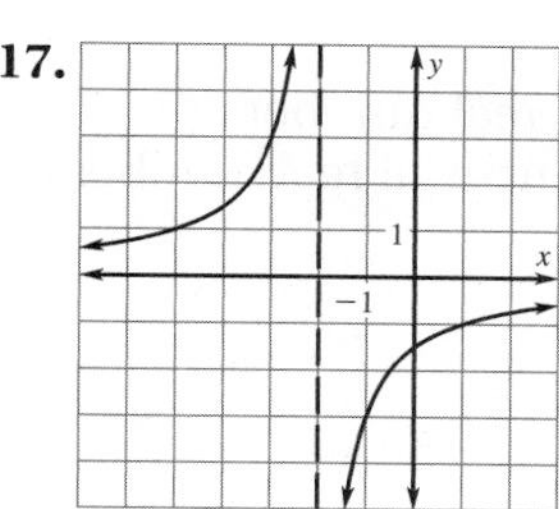

domain: all real numbers except −2, range: all real numbers except 0

18. 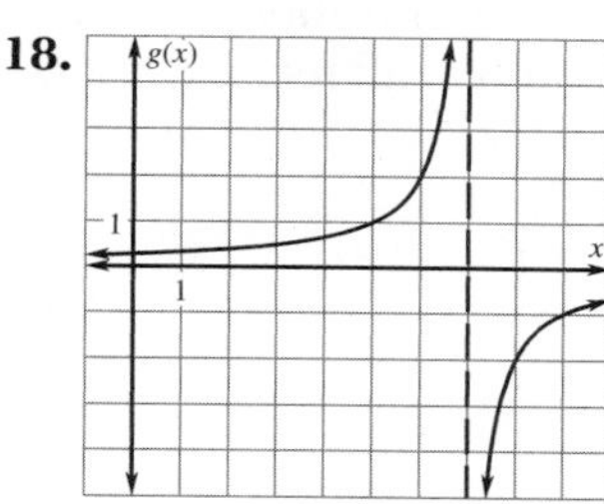

domain: all real numbers except 7, range: all real numbers except 0

19. 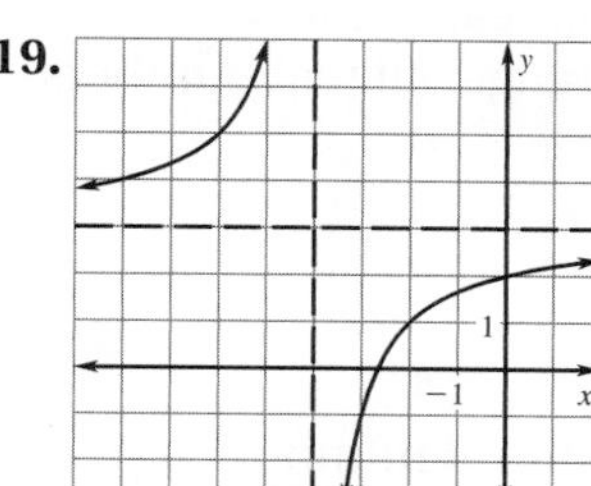

domain: all real numbers except −4, range: all real numbers except 3

20. 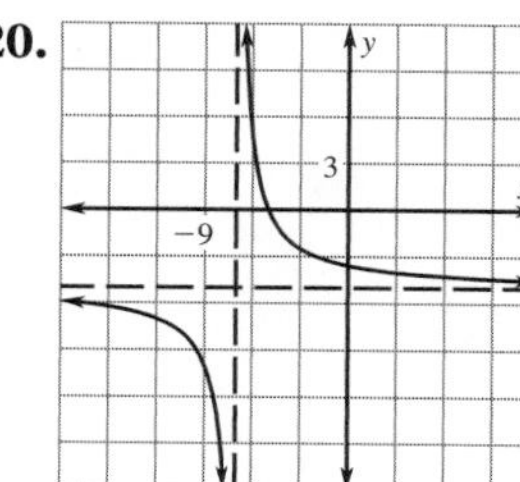

domain: all real numbers except −7, range: all real numbers except −5

ADDITIONAL ANSWERS

21. 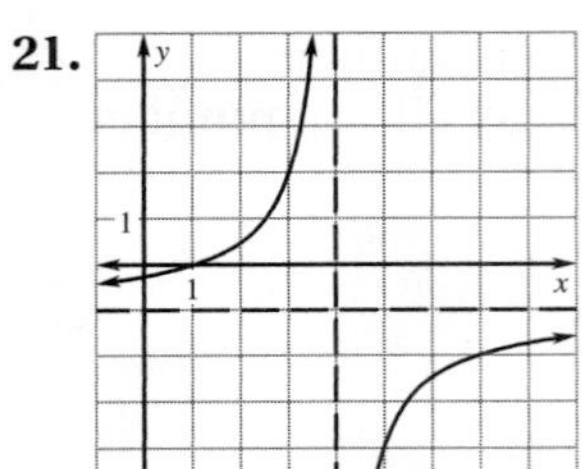 domain: all real numbers except 4, range: all real numbers except −1

22. 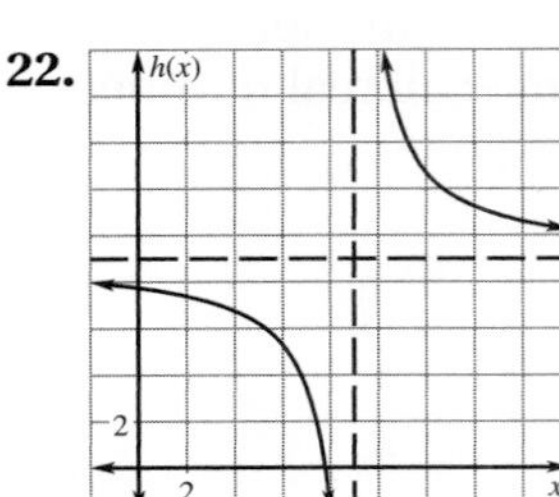 domain: all real numbers except 9, range: all real numbers except 9

27. 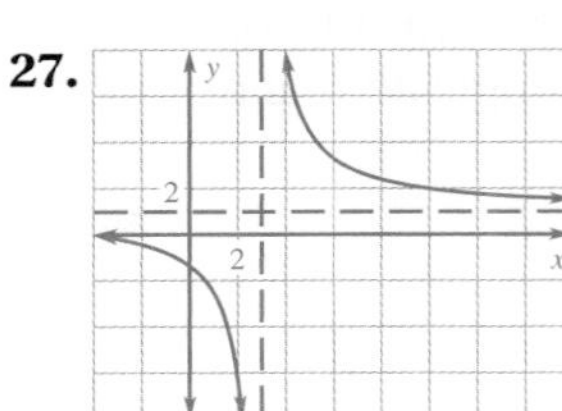 domain: all real numbers except 3, range: all real numbers except 1

28. 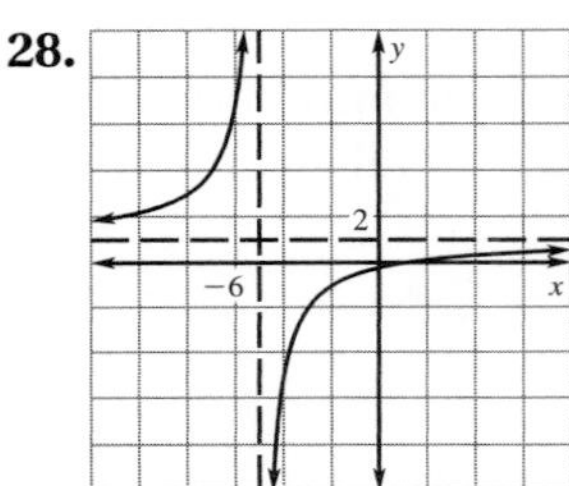 domain: all real numbers except −5, range: all real numbers except 1

29. 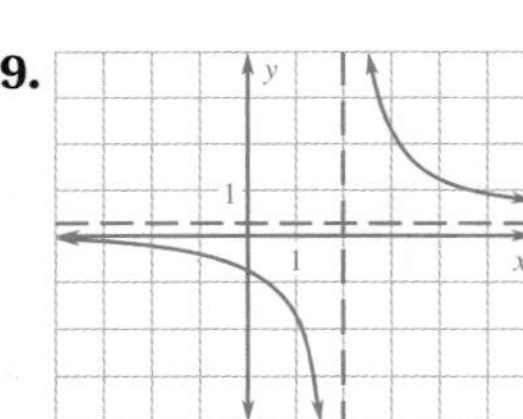 domain: all real numbers except 2, range: all real numbers except $\frac{1}{4}$

30. 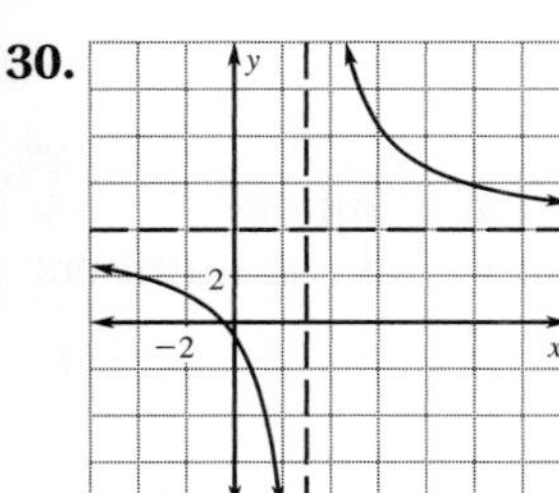 domain: all real numbers except 3, range: all real numbers except 4

31. 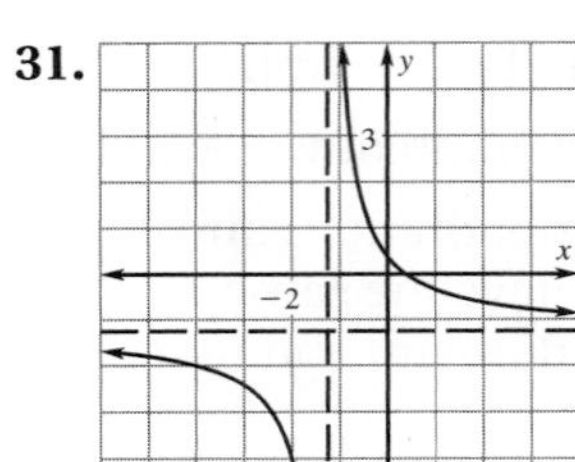 domain: all real numbers except $-\frac{5}{4}$, range: all real numbers except $-\frac{5}{4}$

32. 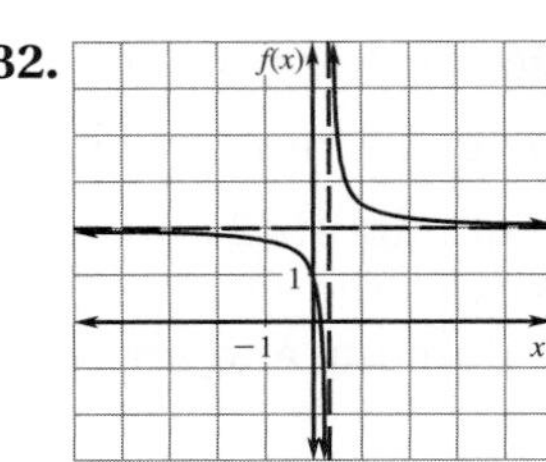 domain: all real numbers except $\frac{1}{3}$, range: all real numbers except 2

33. 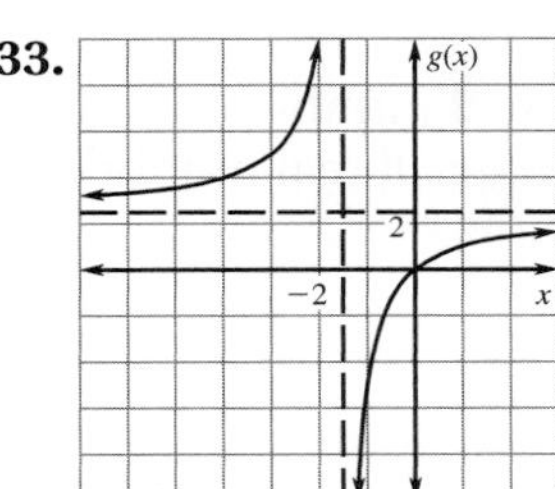 domain: all real numbers except $-\frac{3}{2}$, range: all real numbers except $\frac{5}{2}$

34. 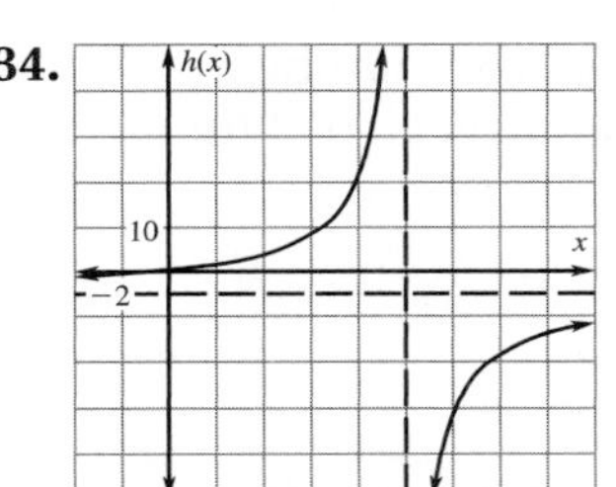 domain: all real numbers except 10, range: all real numbers except −5

8.2 Problem Solving (pp. 562–563)

40. a. 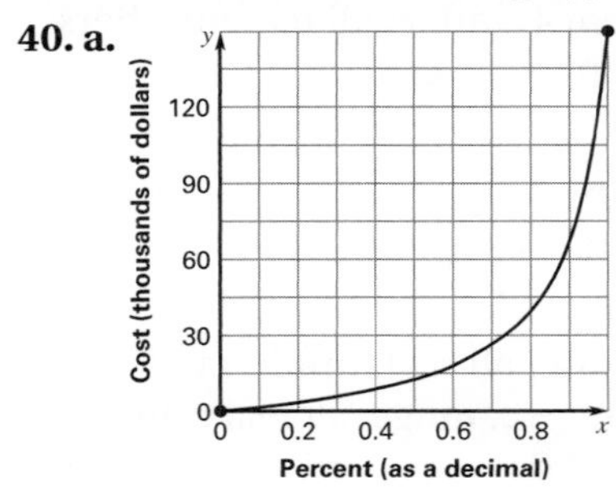

domain: $0 \le x \le 100$, range: $0 \le y \le 150{,}000$

41. b. 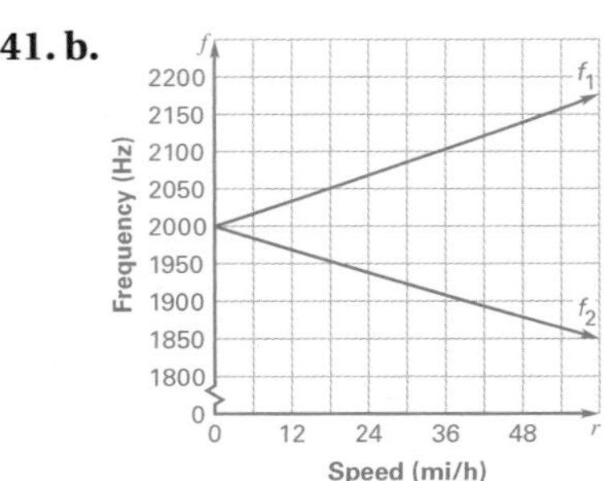

42.

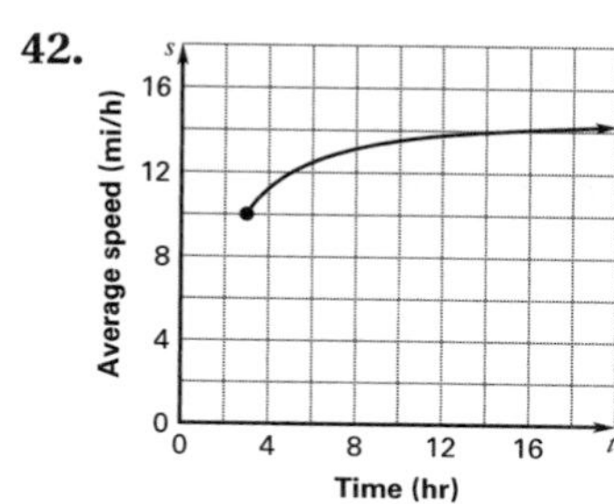

8.2 Graphing Calculator Activity (p. 564)

1–8. Sample viewing windows are given.

1. 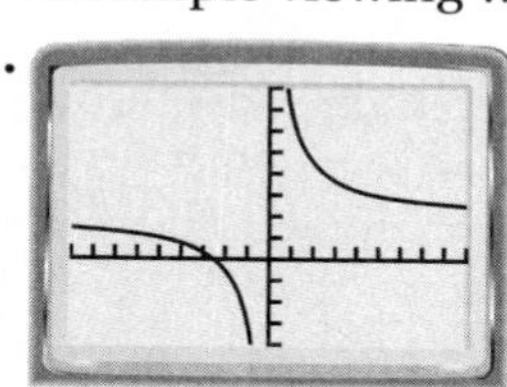 Xmin: −9, Xmax: 9, Xscl: 1, Ymin: −4, Ymax: 8, Yscl: 1

2. 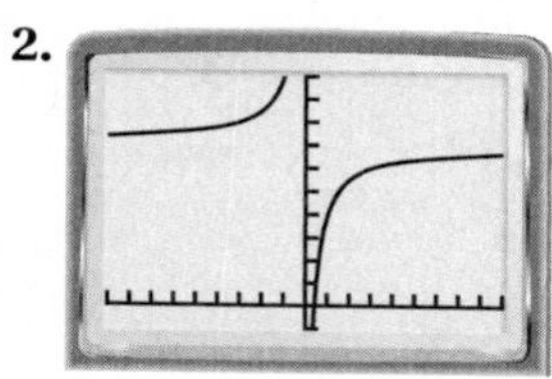 Xmin: −9, Xmax: 9, Xscl: 1, Ymin: −1, Ymax: 11, Yscl: 1

3. 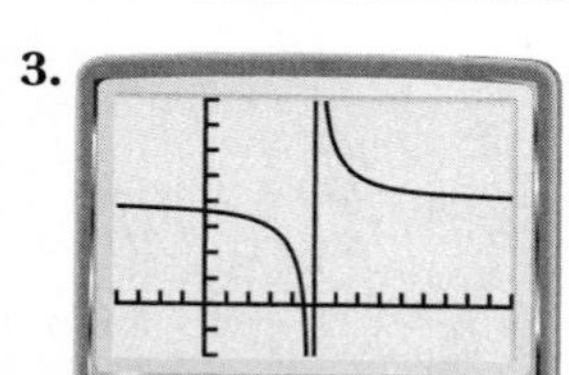 Xmin: −4, Xmax: 14, Xscl: 1, Ymin: −2, Ymax: 10, Yscl: 1

4. 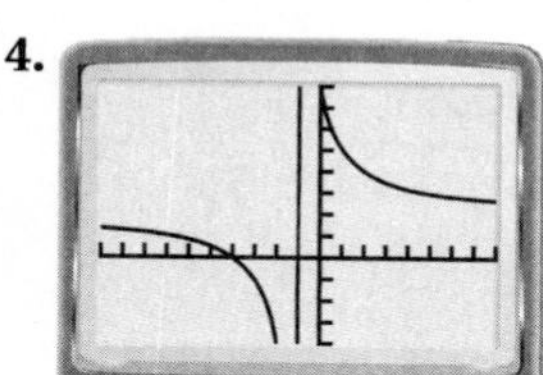 Xmin: −10, Xmax: 8, Xscl: 1, Ymin: −4, Ymax: 8, Yscl: 1

5. 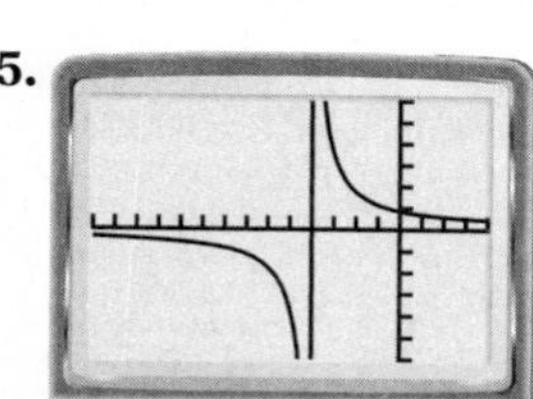 Xmin: −13, Xmax: 5, Xscl: 1, Ymin: −6, Ymax: 6, Yscl: 1

6. 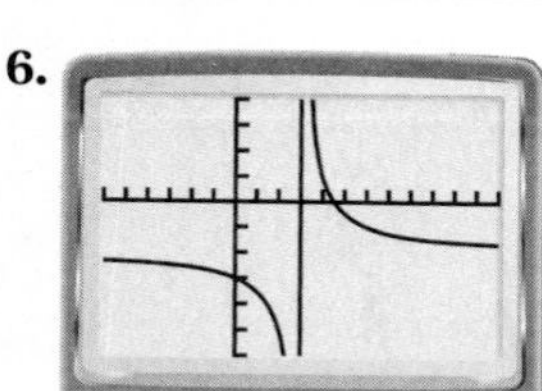 Xmin: −6, Xmax: 12, Xscl: 1, Ymin: −8, Ymax: 4, Yscl: 1

7. 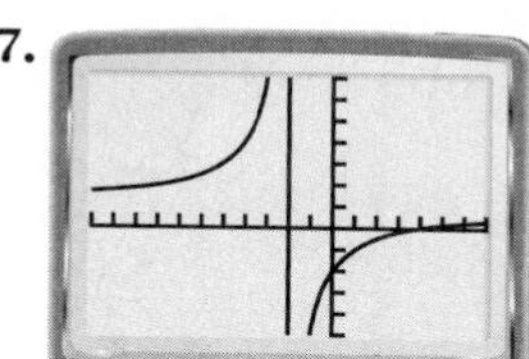 Xmin: −11, Xmax: 7, Xscl: 1, Ymin: −5, Ymax: 7, Yscl: 1

8. 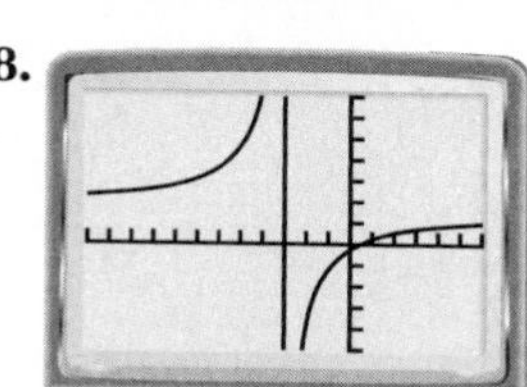 Xmin: −12, Xmax: 6, Xscl: 1, Ymin: −5, Ymax: 7, Yscl: 1

8.3 Guided Practice (p. 567)

1.

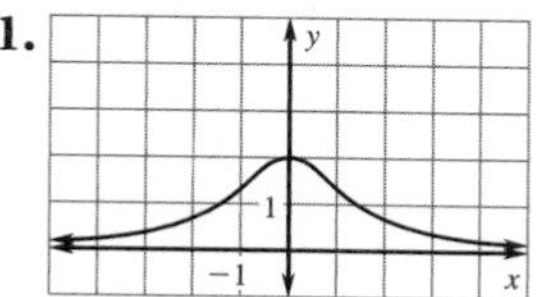

2.

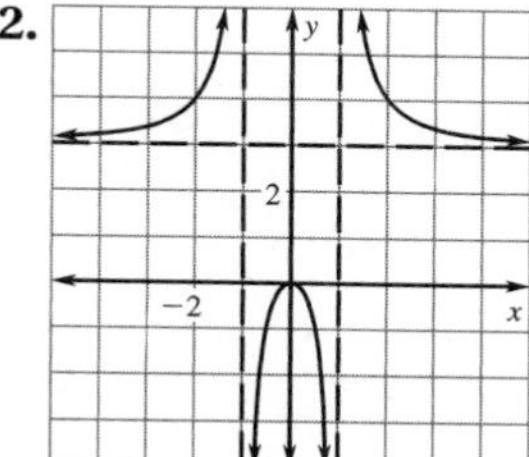

3.

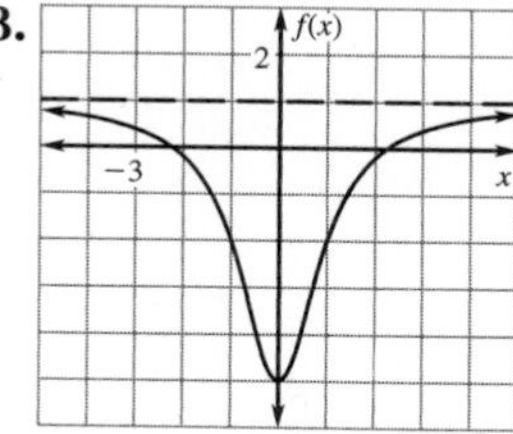

4.

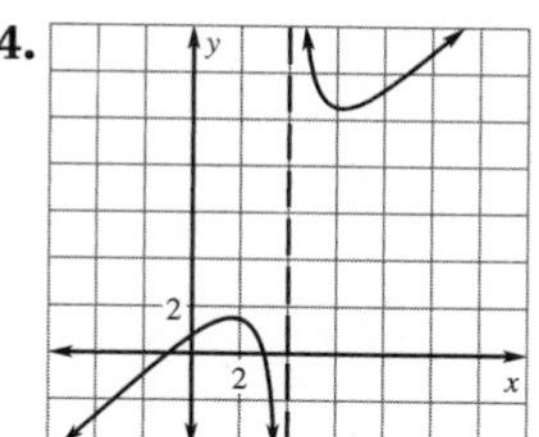

Quiz for Lessons 8.1–8.3 (p. 571)

5. 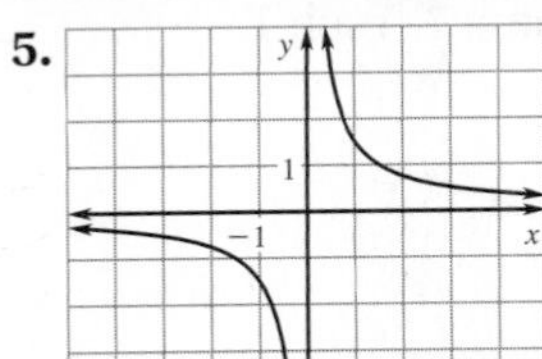

6. 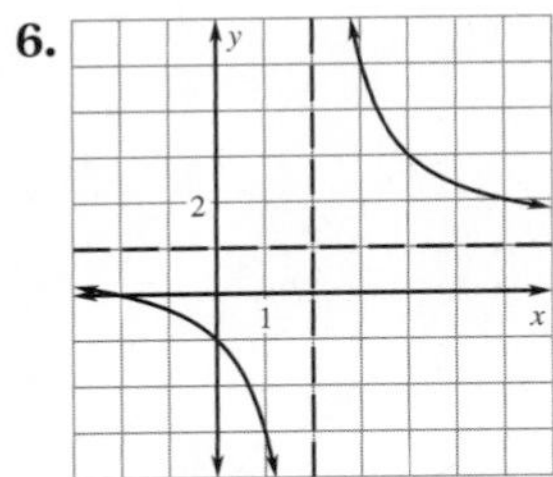

7. 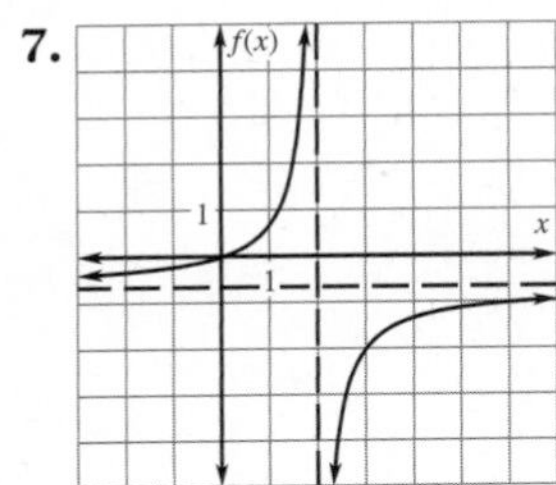

8. 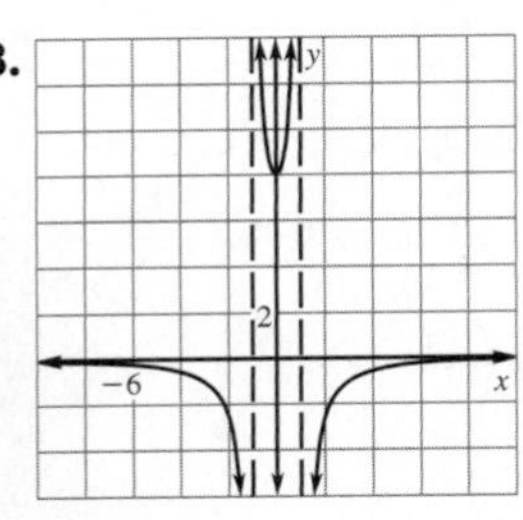

9. 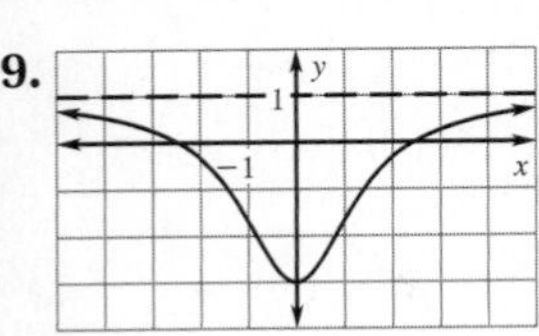

10. 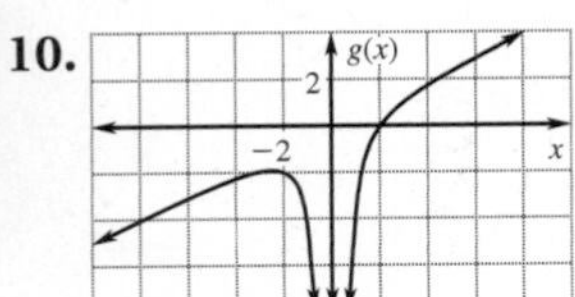

11. 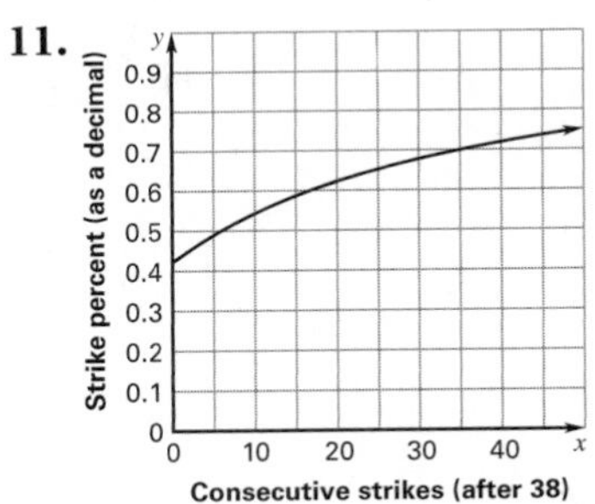

8.5 Problem Solving (pp. 587–588)

44. a. 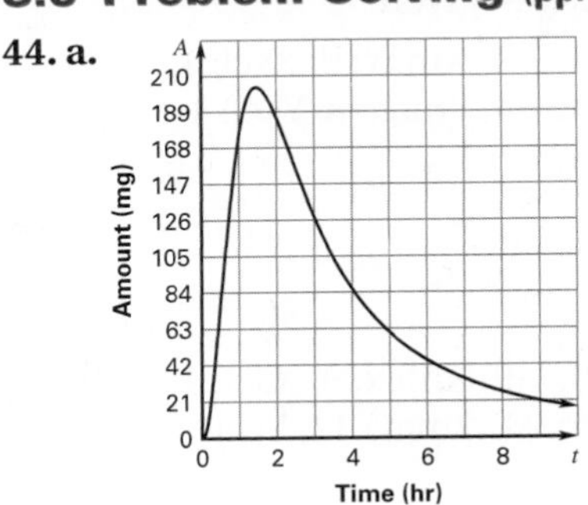

b. $A = \dfrac{391(t-1)^2 + 0.112}{0.218(t-1)^4 + 0.991(t-1)^2 + 1}$

c. $\dfrac{391t^2 + 0.112}{0.218t^4 + 0.99t^2 + 1} + \dfrac{391(t-1)^2 + 0.112}{0.218(t-1)^4 + 0.99(t-1)^2 + 1}$

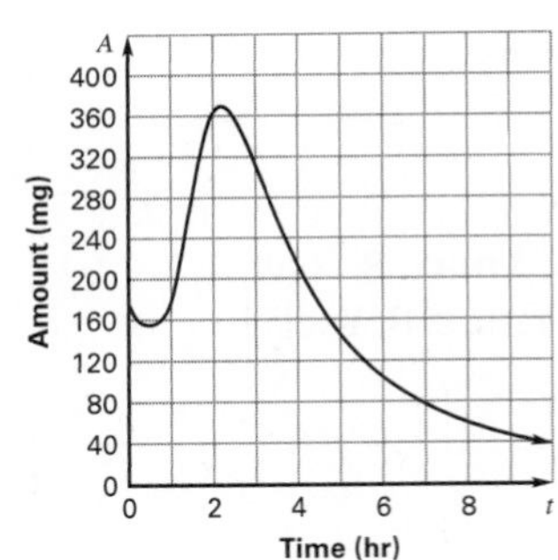

d. about 1 h 13 min

Chapter 9

9.2 Skill Practice (pp. 623–624)

3. 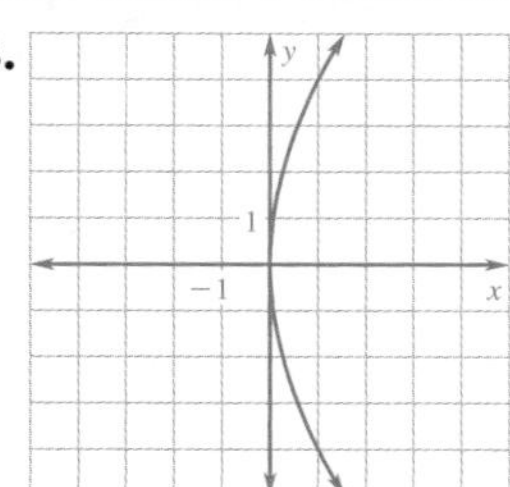

4. 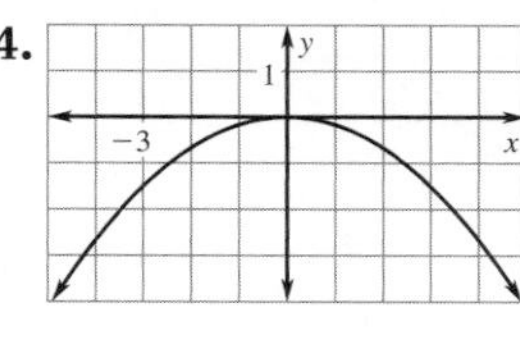

5. 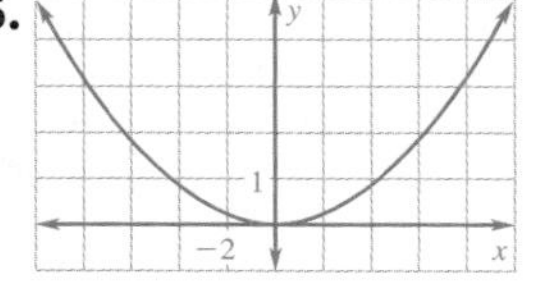

6. 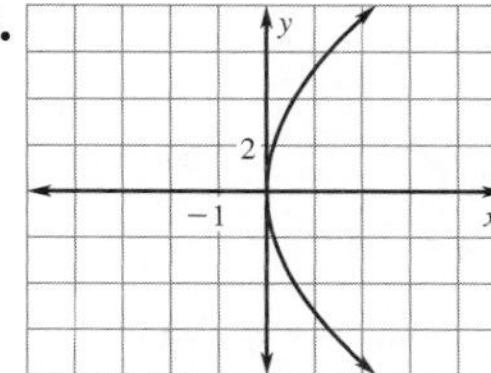

7. 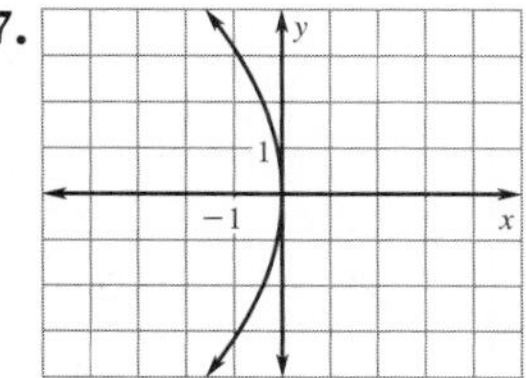

8. 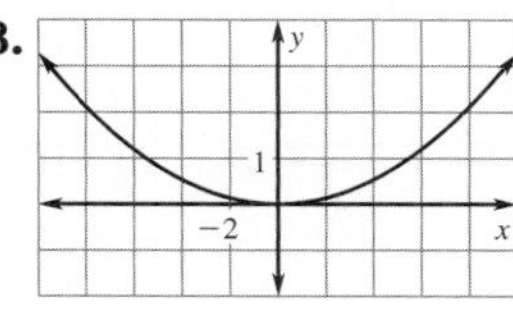

9. 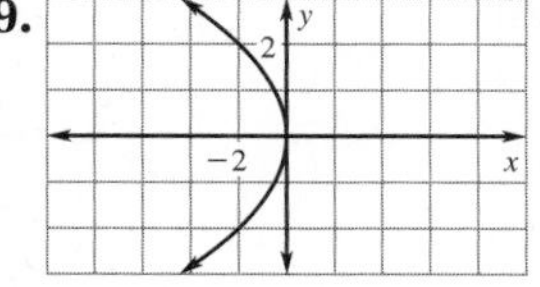

10. 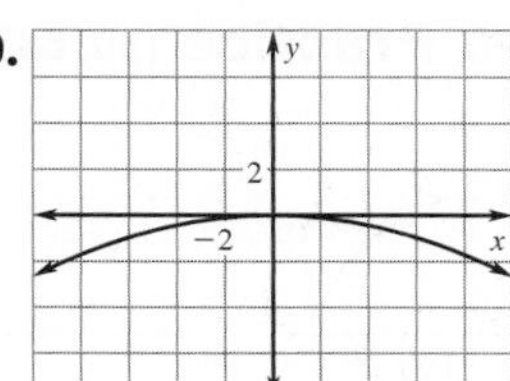

11. 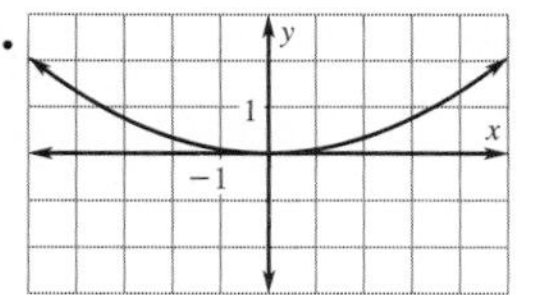

12. 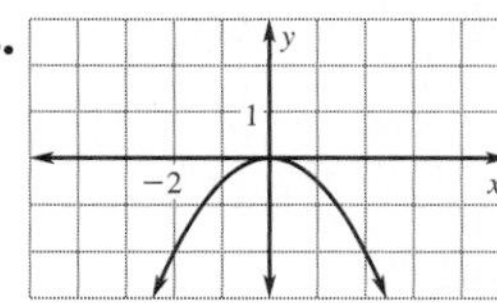

13. 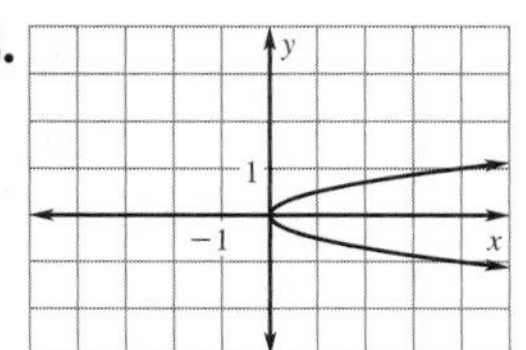

14. 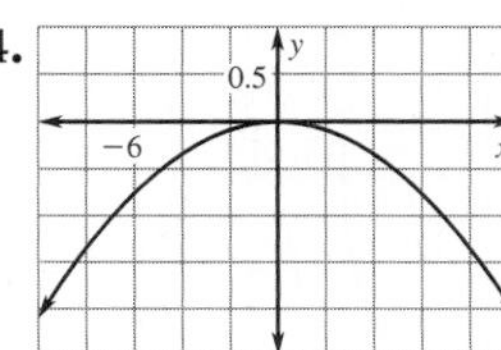

15. 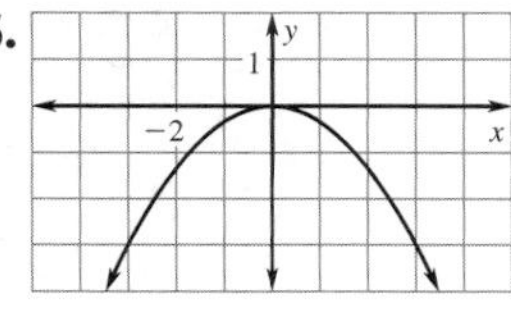

16. 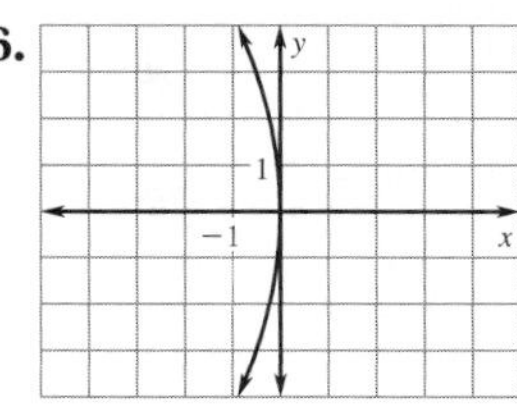

17. 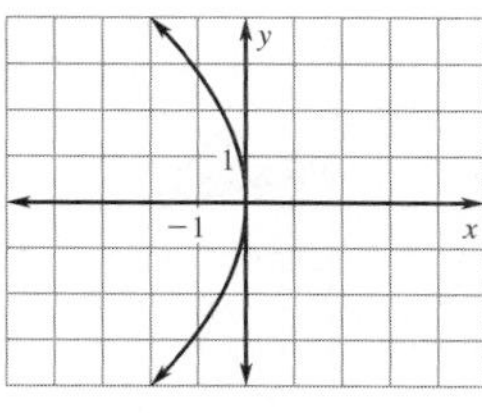

18. 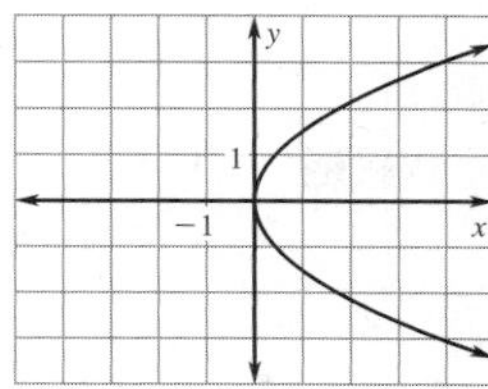

19. 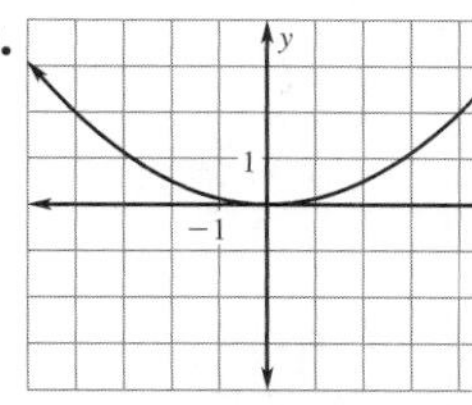

20. 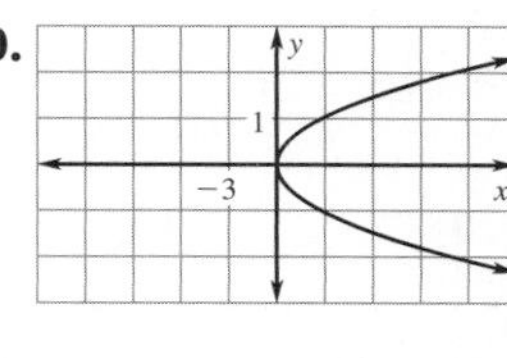

21. 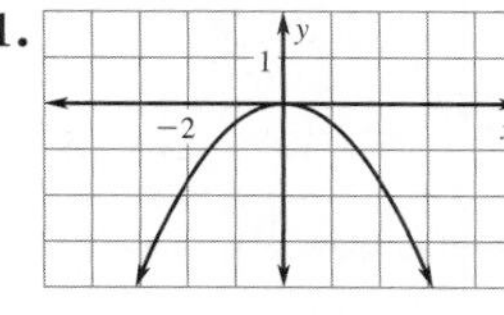

22. 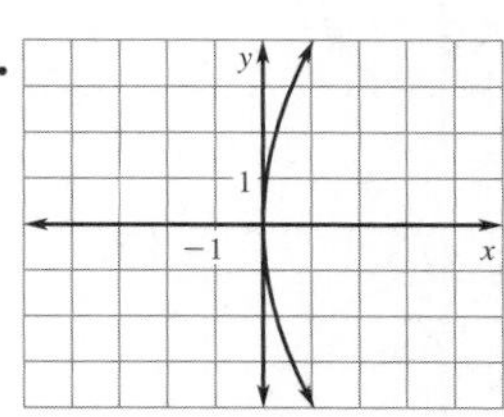

54. *Sample answer:* distance from focus $=$
$\sqrt{(x-0)^2+(y-p)^2}=\sqrt{x^2+y^2-2py+p^2}$;
distance from directrix $=\sqrt{(x-x)^2+(y-(-p))^2}=$
$\sqrt{y^2+2py+p^2}$; $\sqrt{x^2+y^2-2py+p^2}=\sqrt{y^2+2py+p^2}$;
$x^2+y^2-2py+p^2=y^2+2py+p^2$; $x^2=4py$

9.2 Problem Solving (pp. 624–625)

57. a. 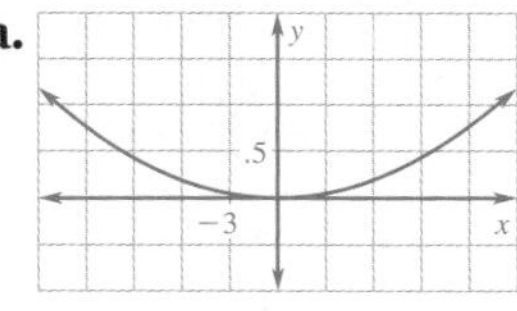

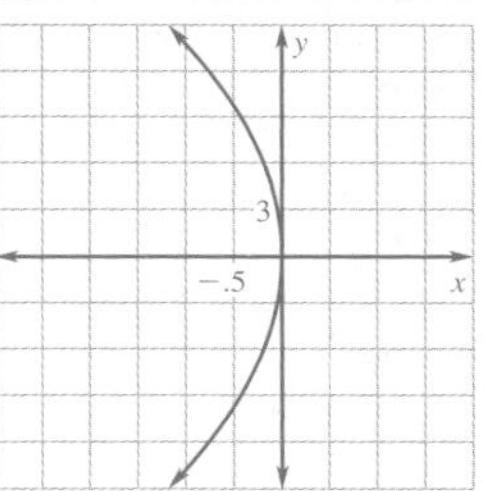

9.3 Skill Practice (pp. 629–630)

9. 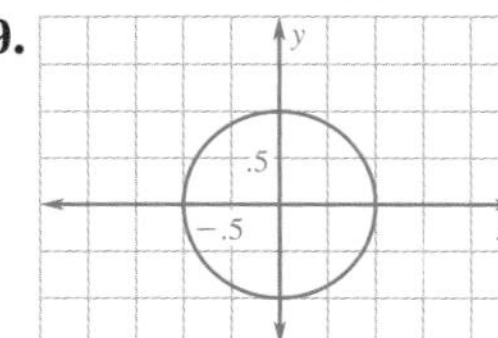

10. 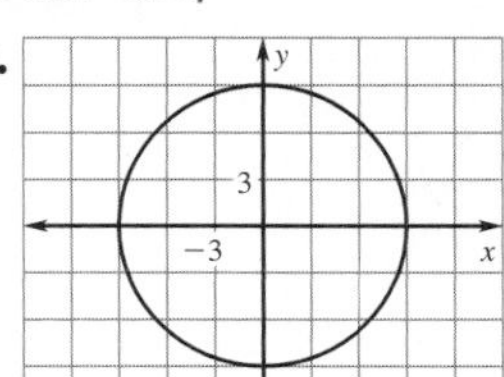

11.
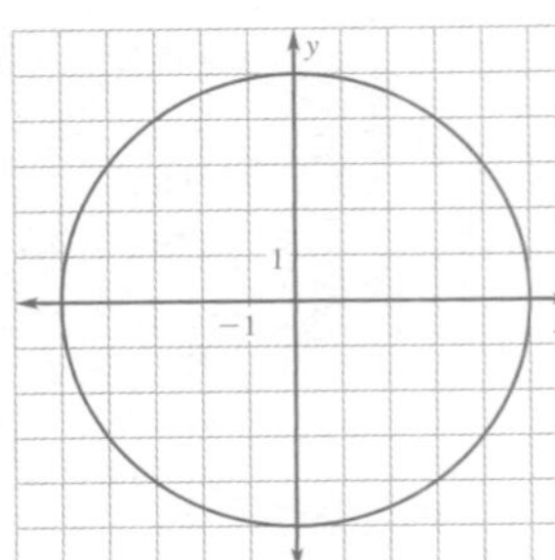

12.
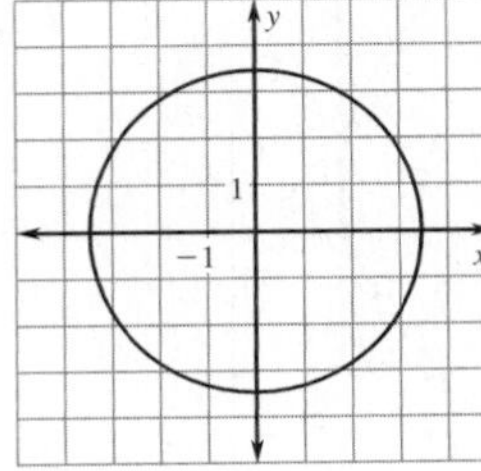

13.
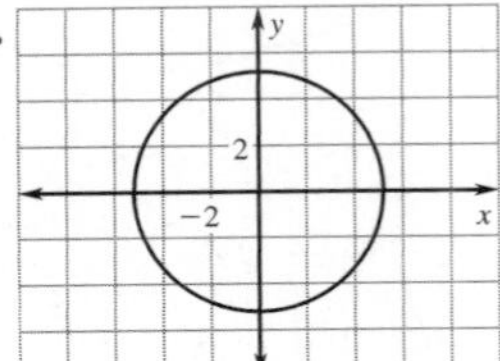

14.
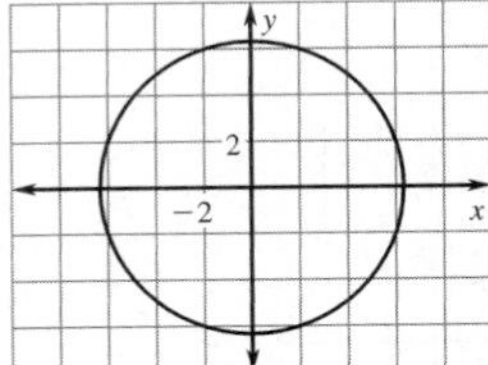

15.
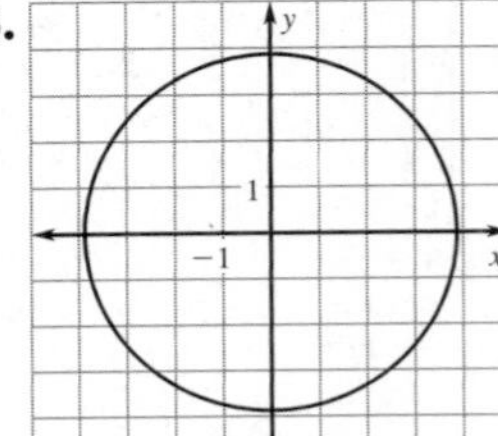

16.
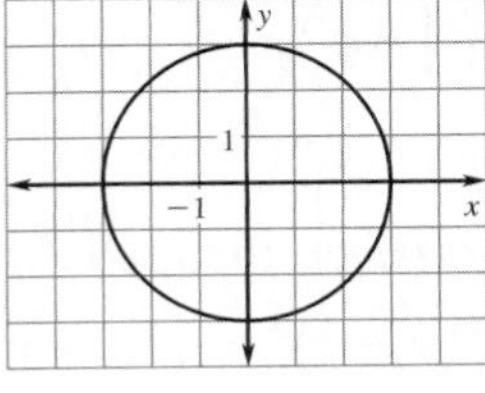

17.
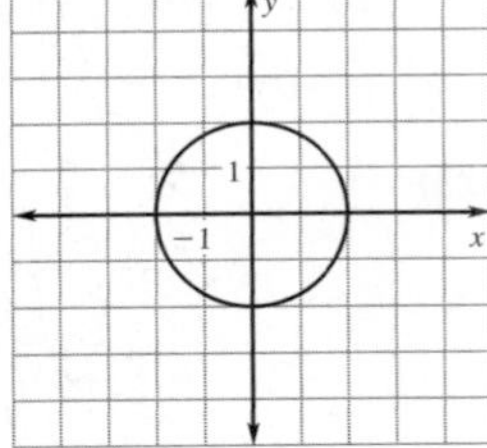

18.
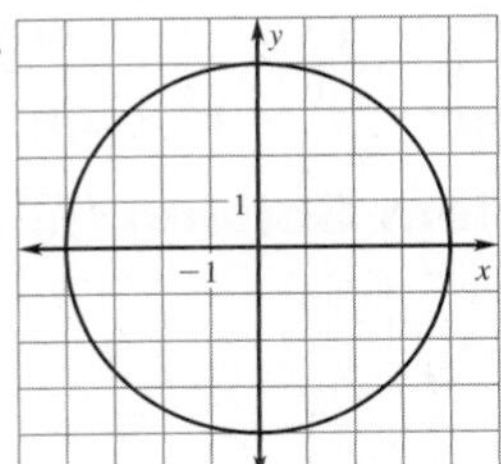

19.
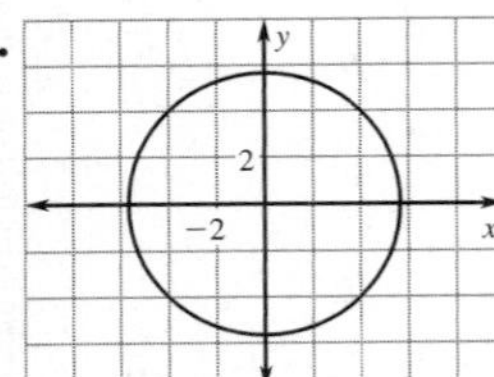

20.
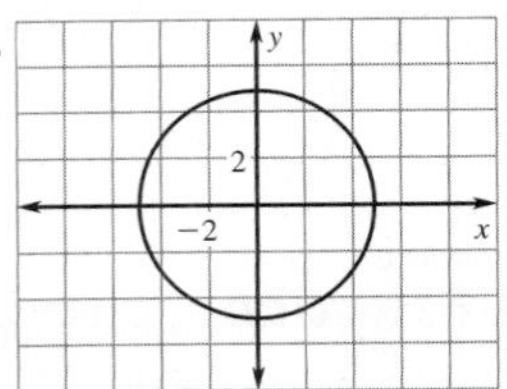

Quiz for Lessons 9.1–9.3 (p. 632)

13.
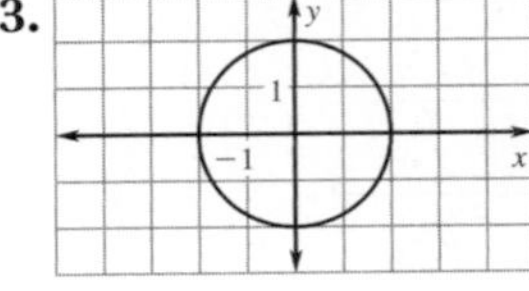

14.
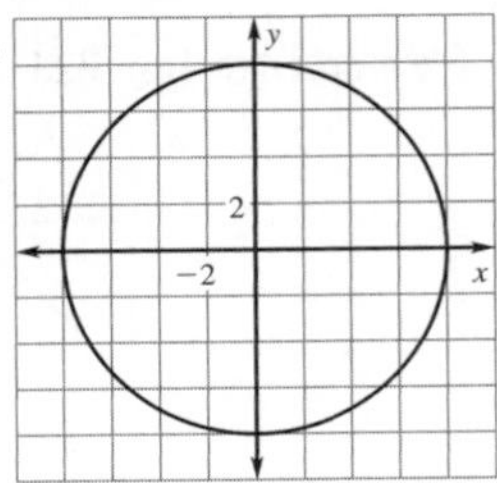

15.
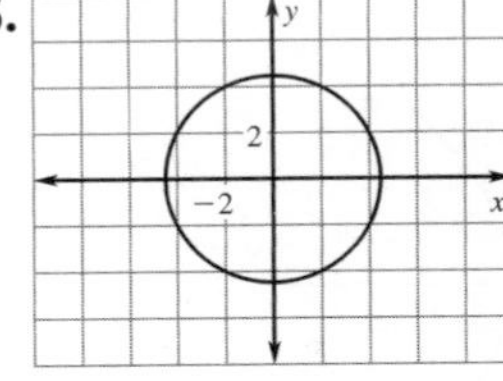

16.
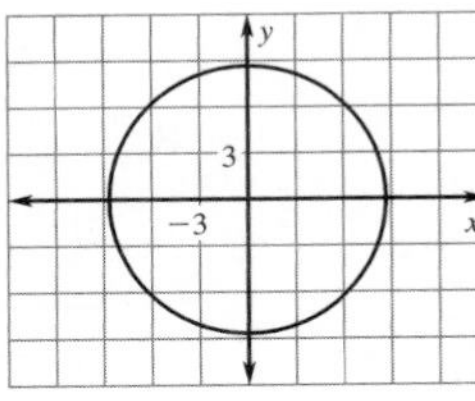

17.
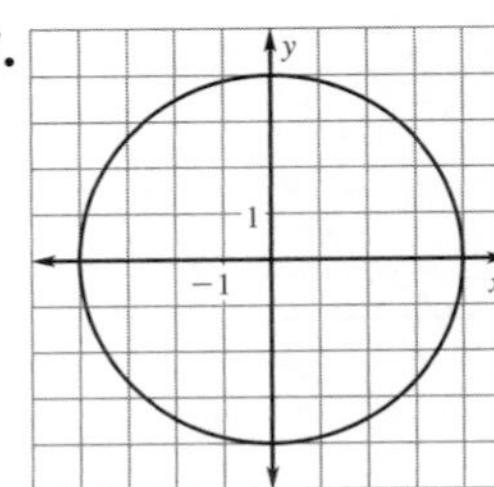

18.
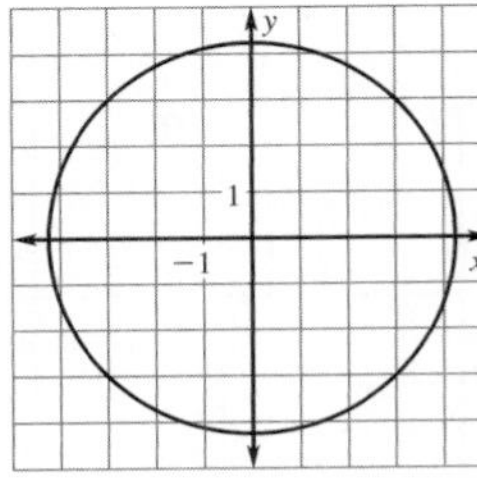

9.4 Guided Practice (pp. 635–636)

1.
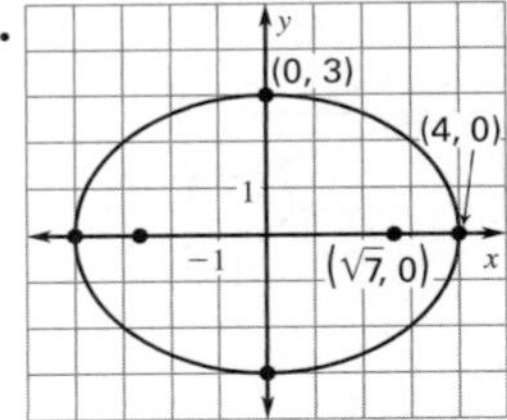

2.
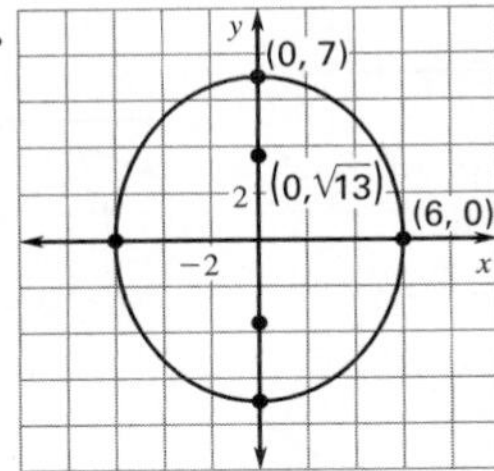

3.
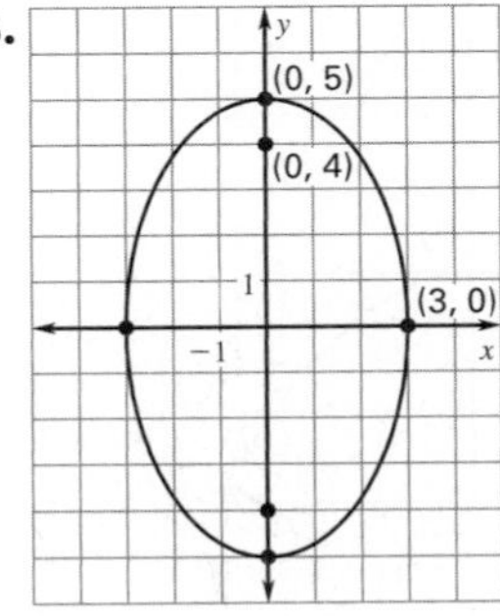

9.4 Skill Practice (pp. 637–638)

3.

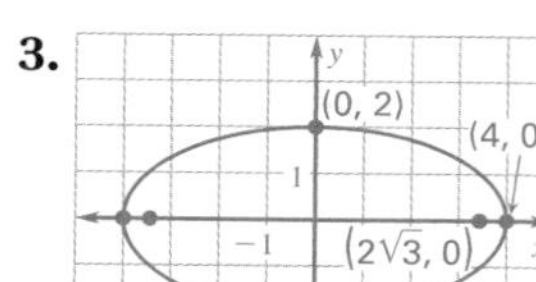

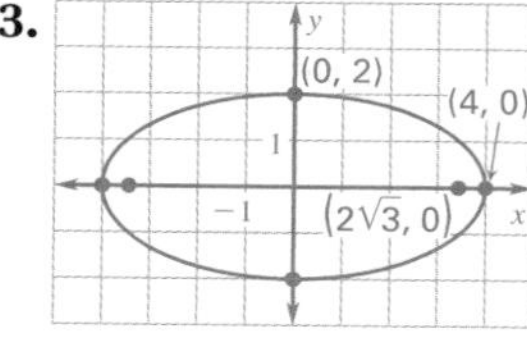

$(\pm 4, 0)$, $(0, \pm 2)$, $(\pm 2\sqrt{3}, 0)$

4.

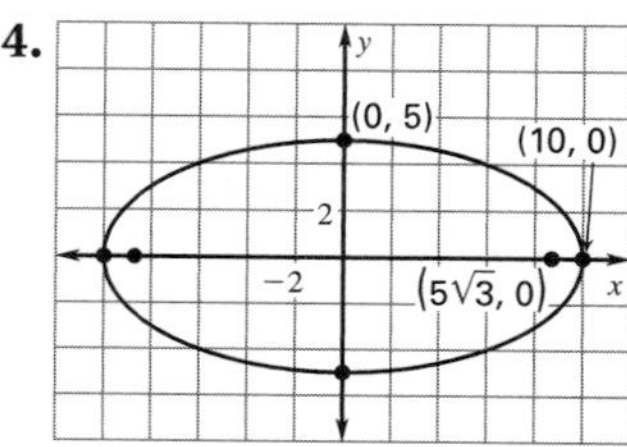

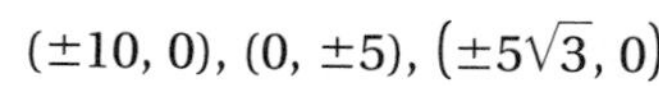

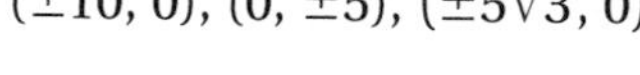

$(\pm 10, 0)$, $(0, \pm 5)$, $(\pm 5\sqrt{3}, 0)$

5.

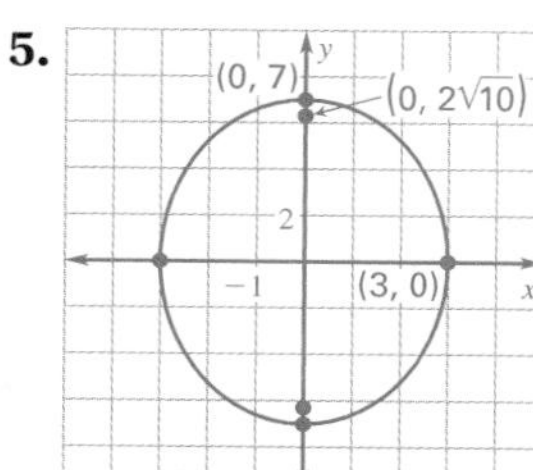

$(0, \pm 7)$, $(\pm 3, 0)$, $(0, \pm 2\sqrt{10})$

6.

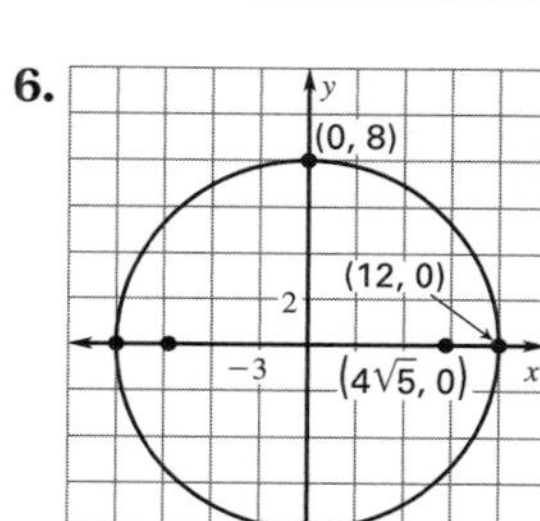

$(\pm 12, 0)$, $(0, \pm 8)$, $(\pm 4\sqrt{5}, 0)$

7.

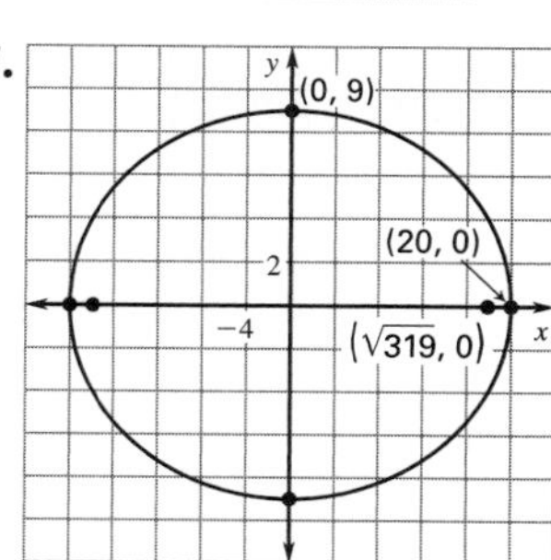

$(\pm 20, 0)$, $(0, \pm 9)$, $(\pm\sqrt{319}, 0)$

8.

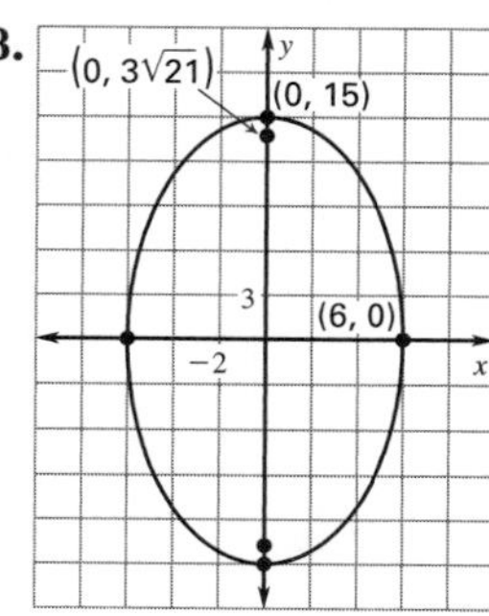

$(0, \pm 15)$, $(\pm 6, 0)$, $(0, \pm 3\sqrt{21})$

9.

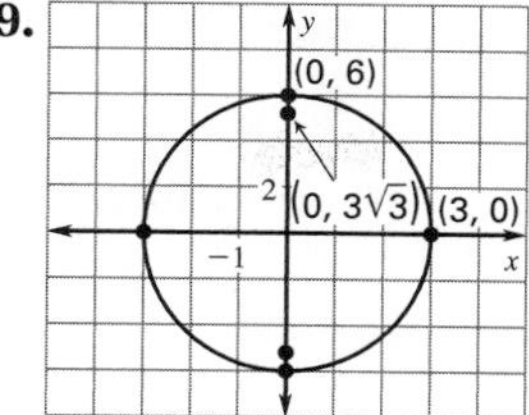

$(0, \pm 6)$, $(\pm 3, 0)$, $(0, \pm 3\sqrt{3})$

10.

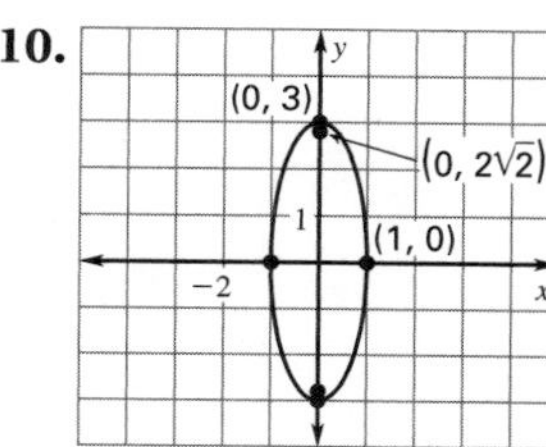

$(0, \pm 3)$, $(\pm 1, 0)$, $(0, \pm 2\sqrt{2})$

11.

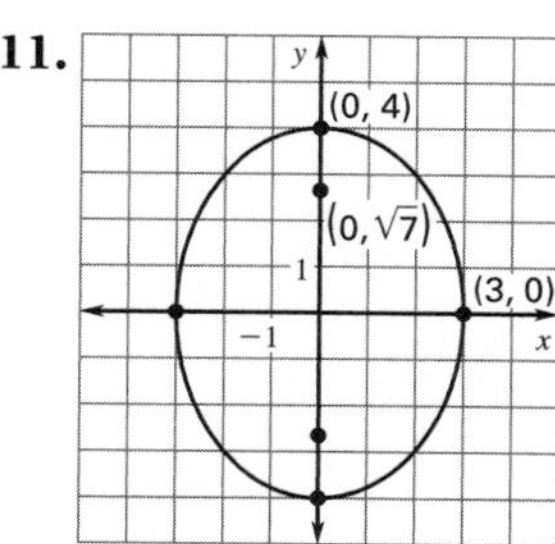

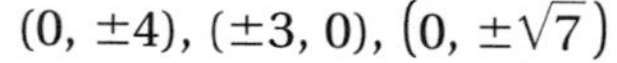

$(0, \pm 4)$, $(\pm 3, 0)$, $(0, \pm\sqrt{7})$

12.

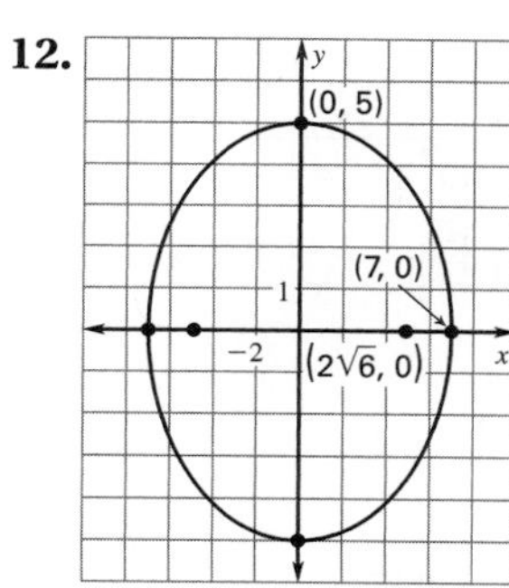

$(\pm 7, 0)$, $(0, \pm 5)$, $(\pm 2\sqrt{6}, 0)$

13.

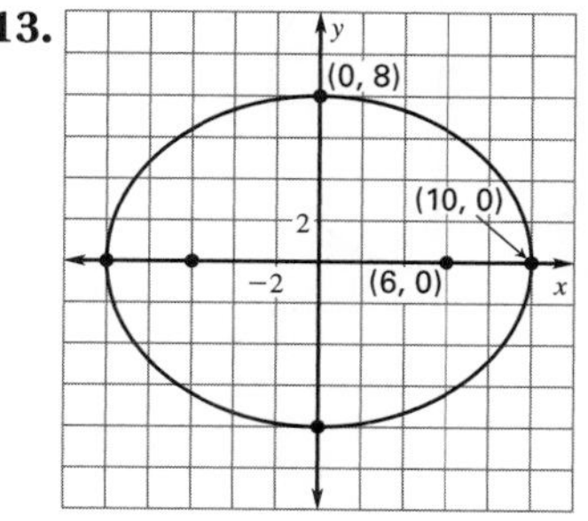

$(\pm 10, 0)$, $(0, \pm 8)$, $(\pm 6, 0)$

14.

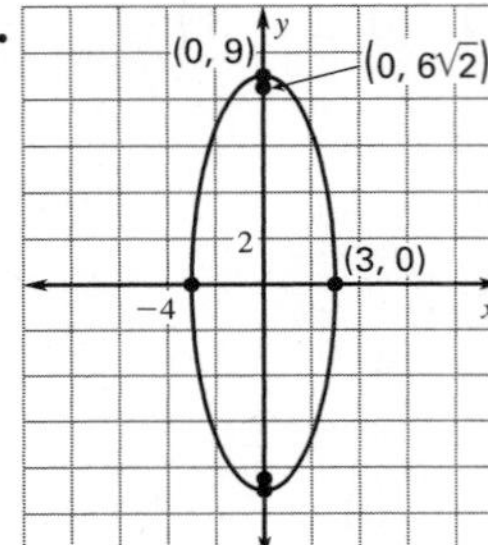

$(0, \pm 9)$, $(\pm 3, 0)$, $(0, \pm 6\sqrt{2})$

36.

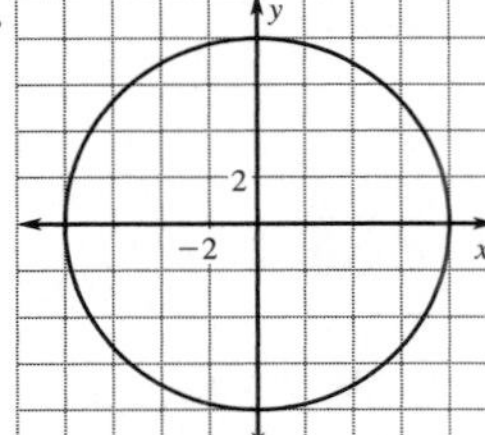

37.

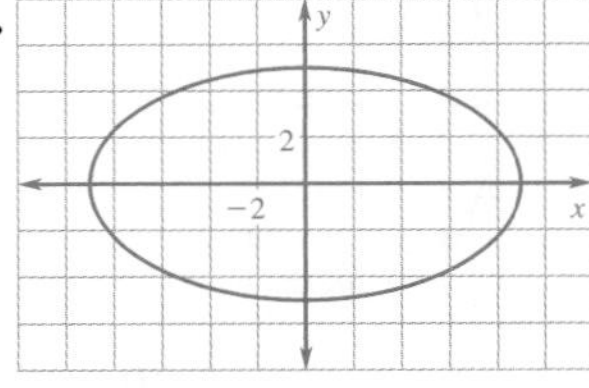

38.

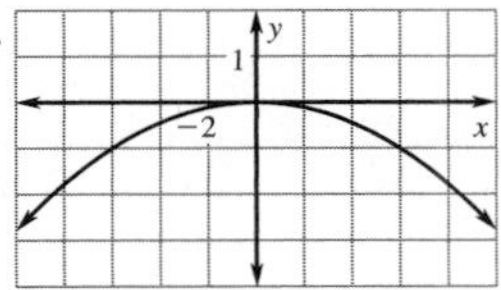

39.

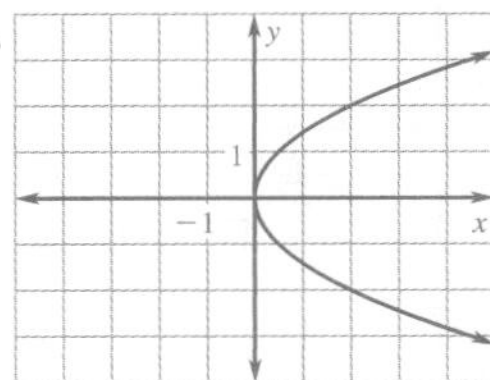

40.

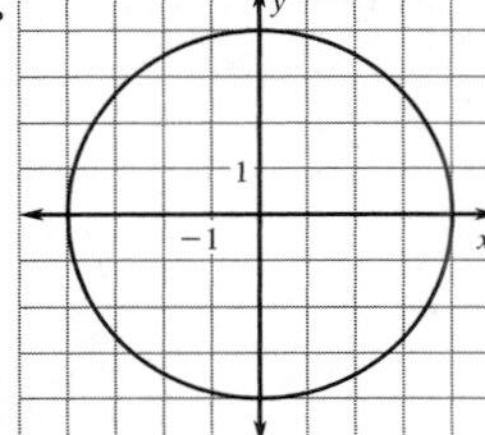

41.

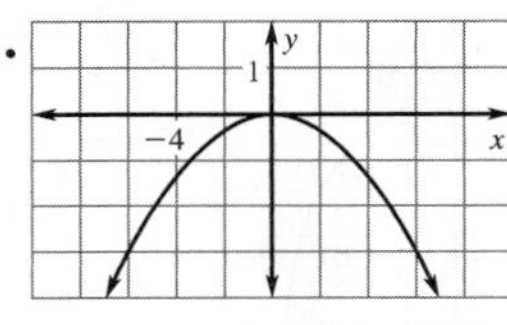

42.

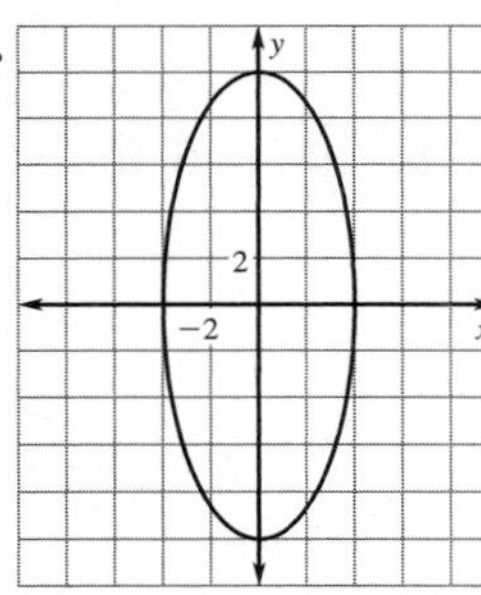

43.

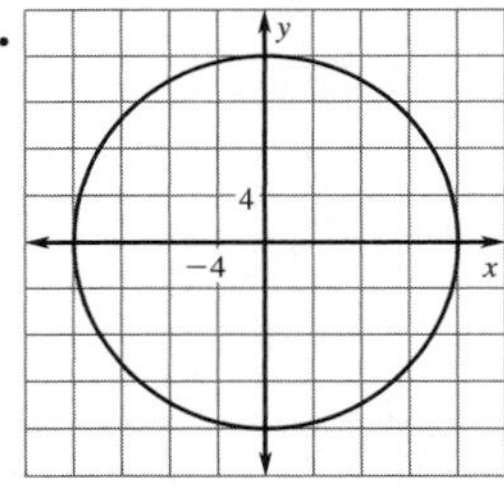

44.

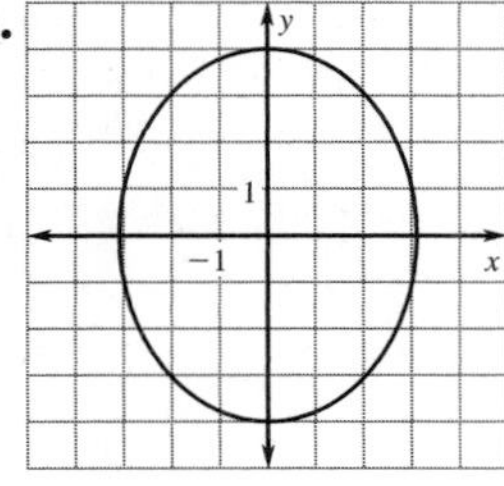

9.5 Guided Practice (p. 644)

1.

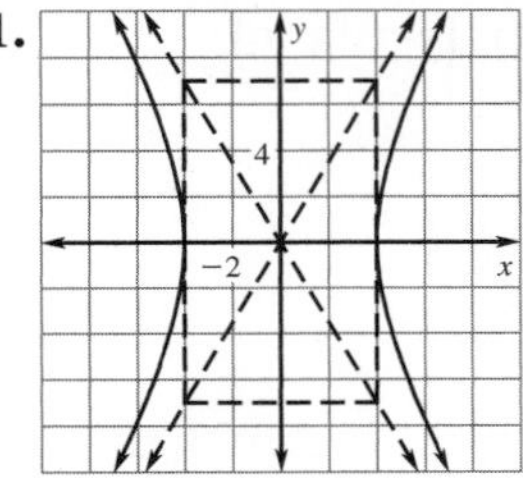

2.

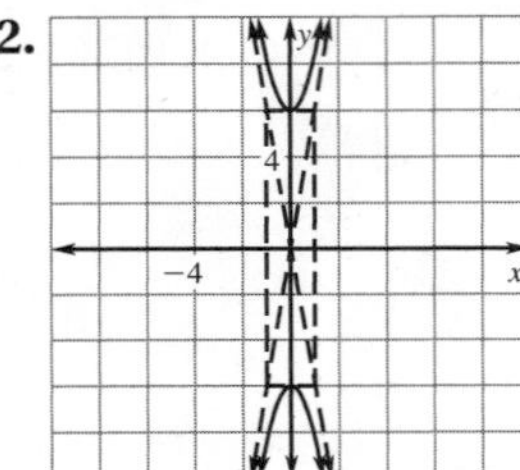

3.

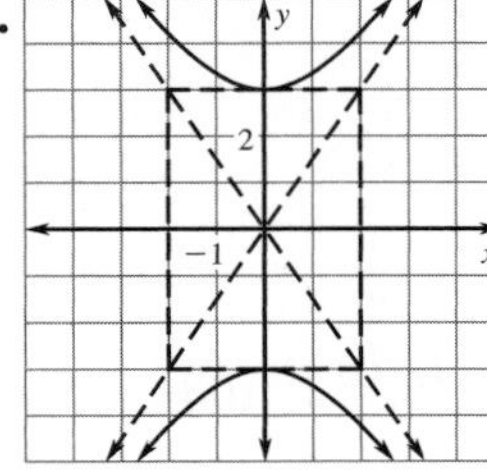

9.5 Skill Practice (pp. 645–646)

3.

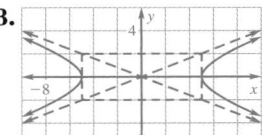

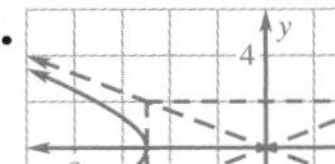

$(\pm 5, 0)$, $(\pm\sqrt{29}, 0)$, $y = \pm\frac{2}{5}x$

4.

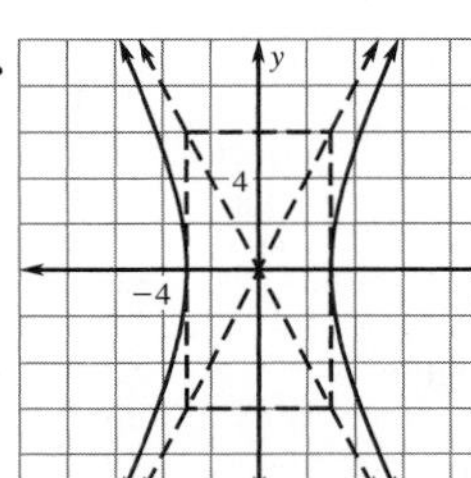

$(\pm 3, 0)$, $(\pm 3\sqrt{5}, 0)$, $y = \pm 2x$

5.

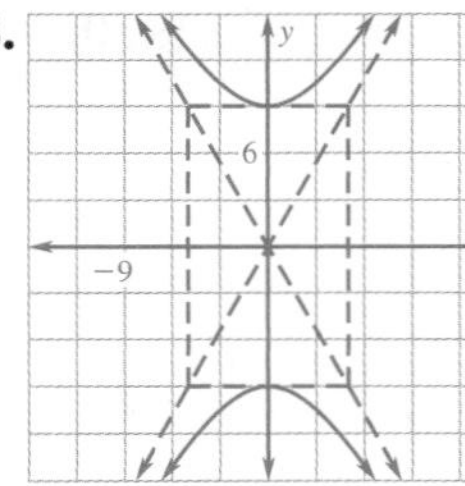

$(0, \pm 9)$, $(0, \pm\sqrt{106})$, $y = \pm\frac{9}{5}x$

6.

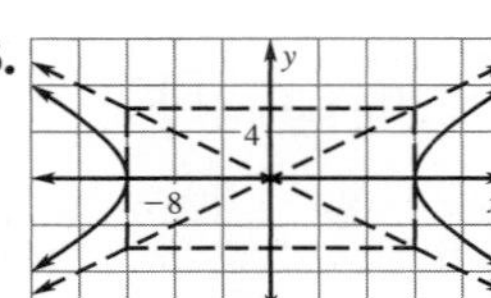

$(\pm 12, 0)$, $(\pm 6\sqrt{5}, 0)$, $y = \pm\frac{1}{2}x$

7. 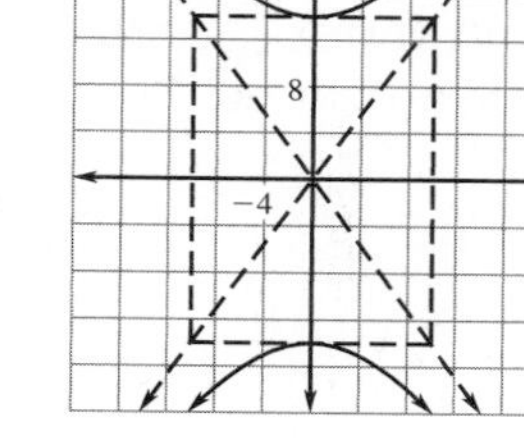

$(0, \pm 14), \left(0, \pm 2\sqrt{74}\right), y = \pm\frac{7}{5}x$

8. 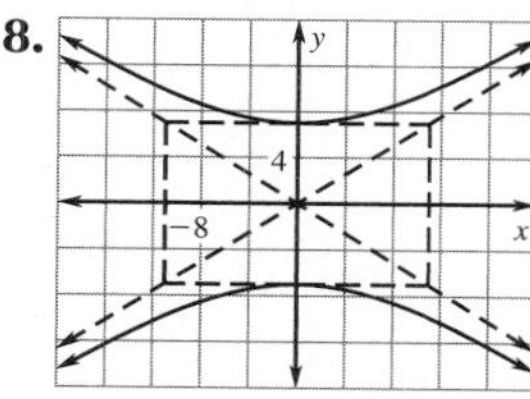

$(0, \pm 7), \left(0, \pm\sqrt{170}\right), y = \pm\frac{7}{11}x$

9. 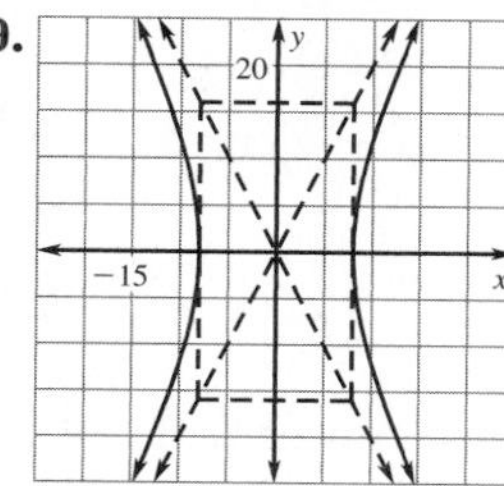

$(\pm 8, 0), \left(\pm 8\sqrt{5}, 0\right), y = \pm 2x$

10. 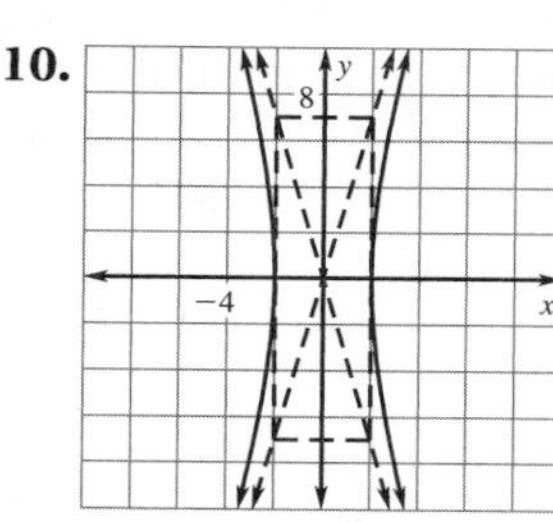

$(\pm 2, 0), \left(\pm\sqrt{53}, 0\right), y = \pm\frac{7}{2}x$

11. 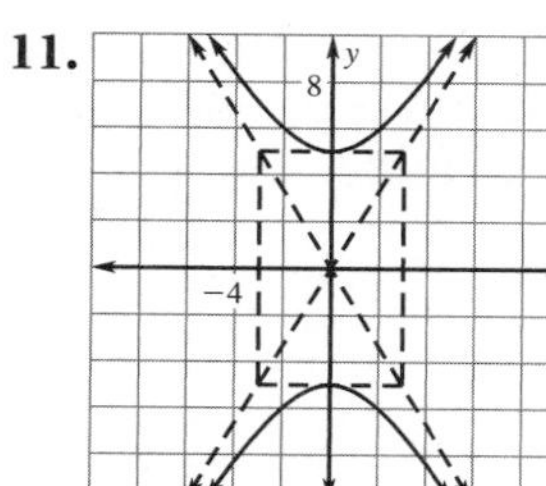

$(0, \pm 5), \left(0, \pm\sqrt{34}\right), y = \pm\frac{5}{3}x$

12. 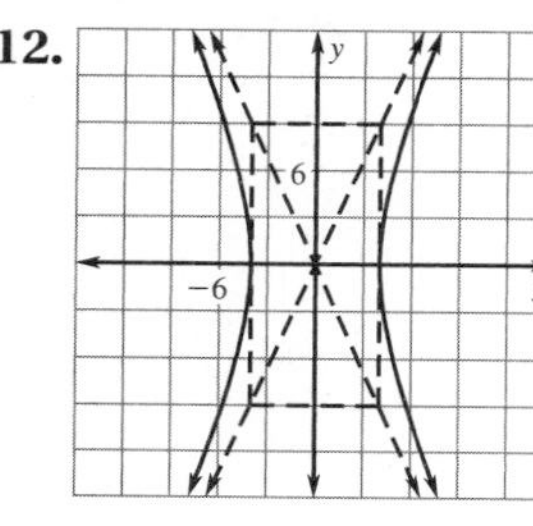

$(\pm 4, 0), \left(\pm\sqrt{97}, 0\right), y = \pm\frac{9}{4}x$

13. 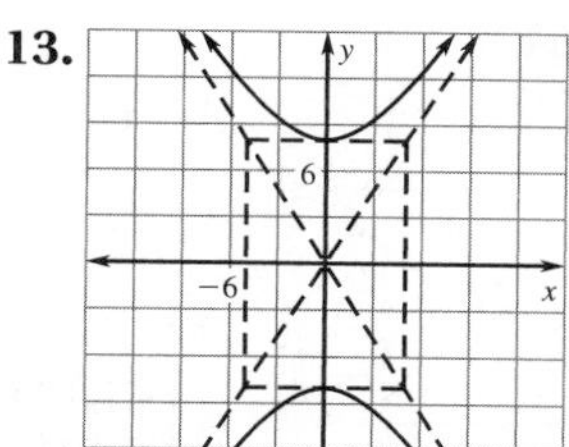

$(0, \pm 8), \left(0, \pm\sqrt{89}\right), y = \pm\frac{8}{5}x$

14. 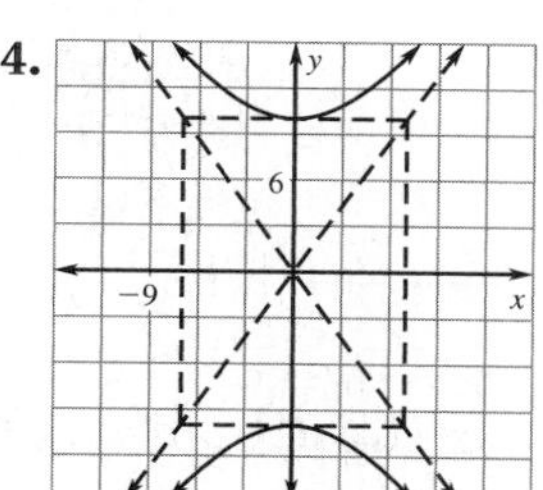

$(0, \pm 10), \left(0, \pm\sqrt{149}\right), y = \pm\frac{10}{7}x$

Quiz for Lessons 9.4–9.5 (p. 648)

1. 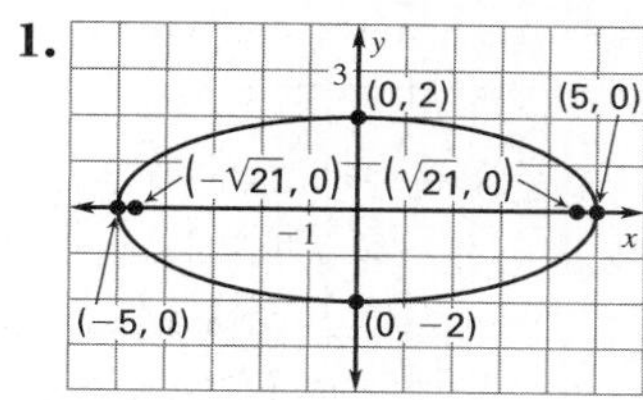

2. 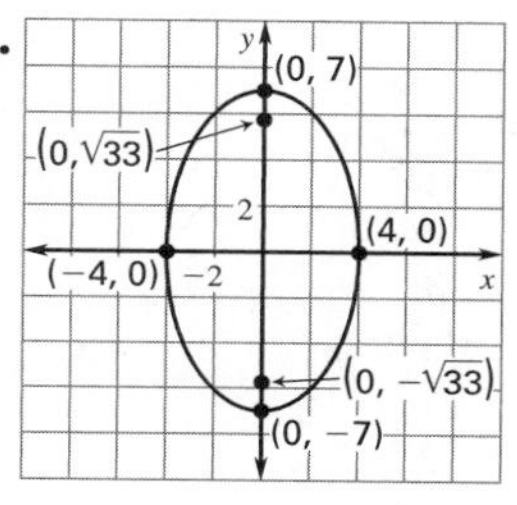

3. 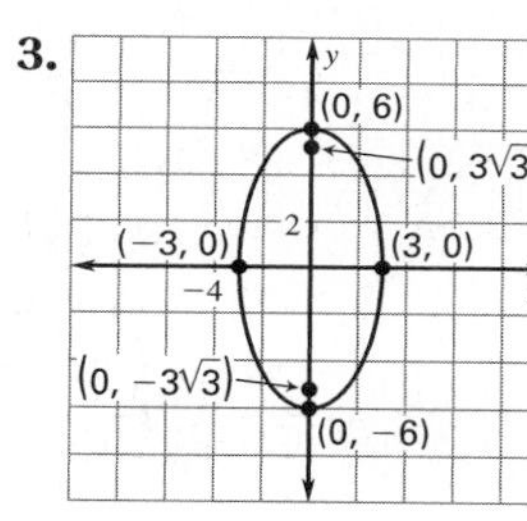

7. 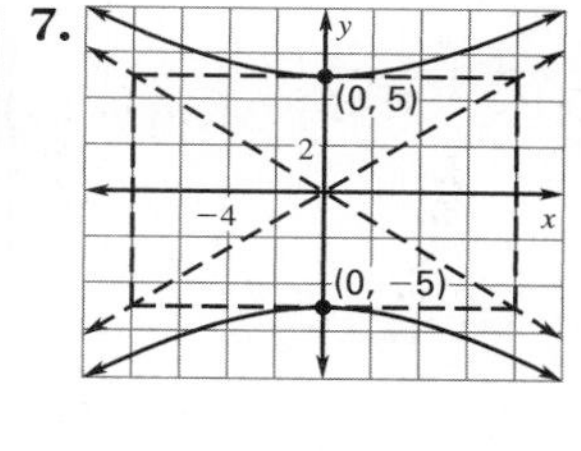

8. 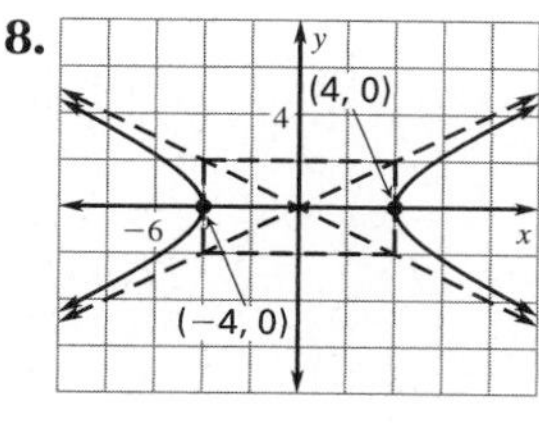

9. 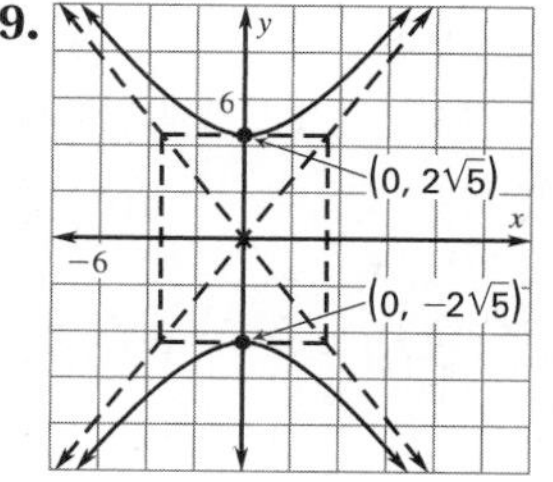

ADDITIONAL ANSWERS

9.6 Guided Practice (pp. 651–654)

1. 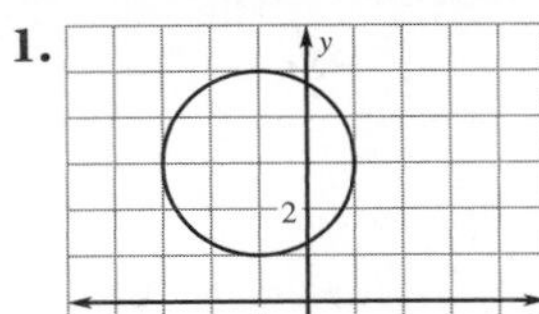

2. 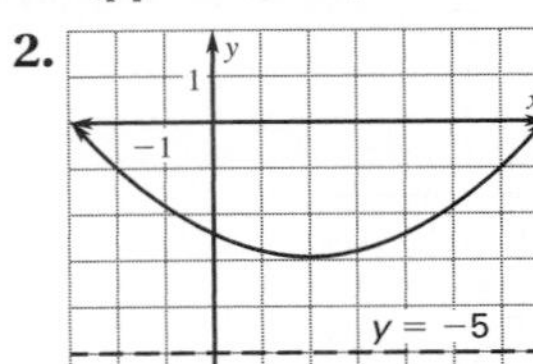

3. 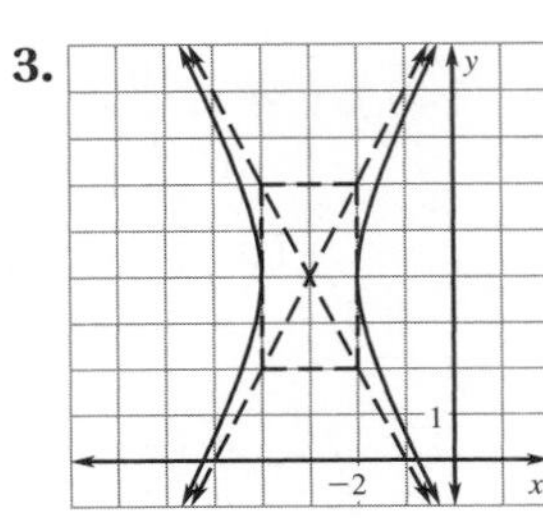

4. 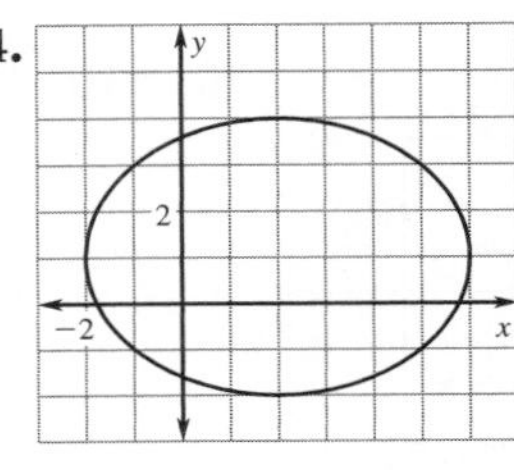

10. 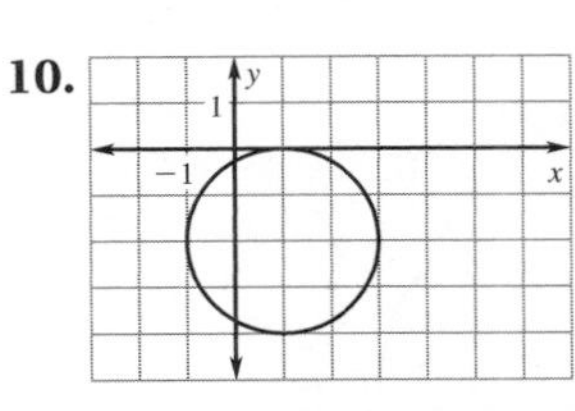

11. 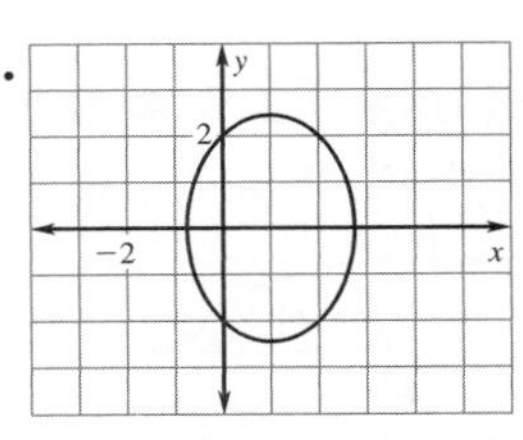

12. 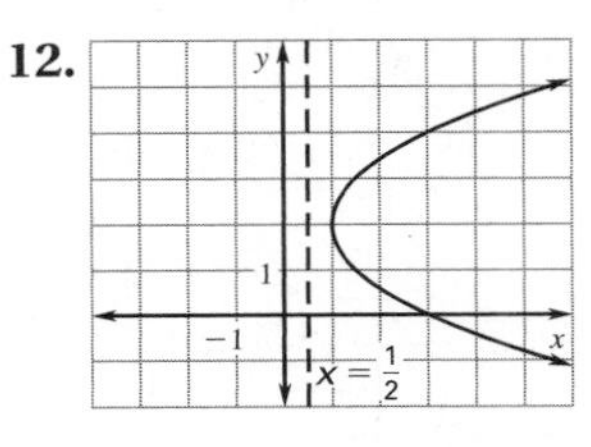

13. 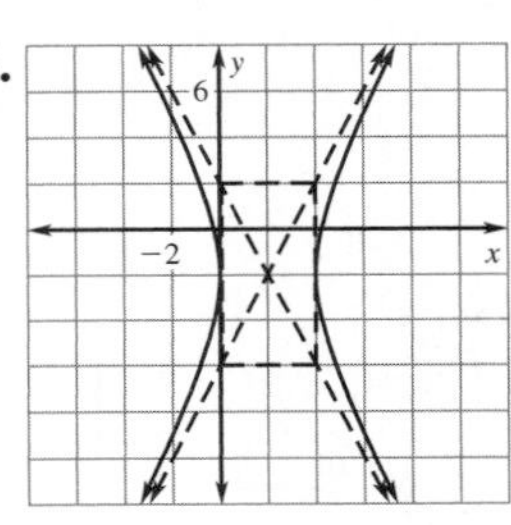

9.6 Skill Practice (pp. 655–656)

3. 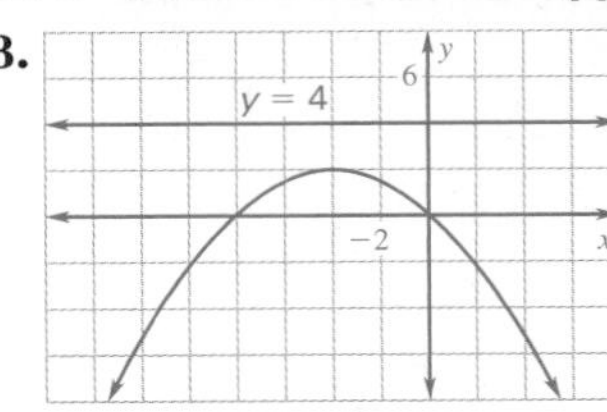

parabola with vertex $(-4, 2)$, focus $(-4, 0)$, and directrix $y = 4$

4. 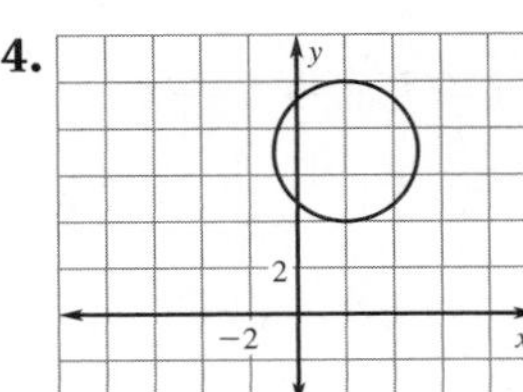

circle with center $(2, 7)$ and radius 3

5. 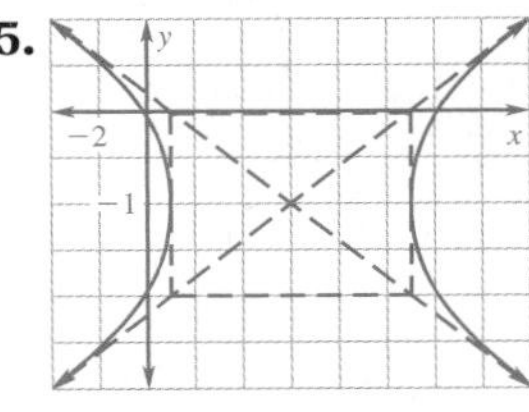

hyperbola with center $(6, -1)$, vertices $(11, -1)$ and $(1, -1)$, asymptotes $y = \frac{1}{5}x - \frac{11}{5}$ and $y = -\frac{1}{5}x + \frac{1}{5}$

6. 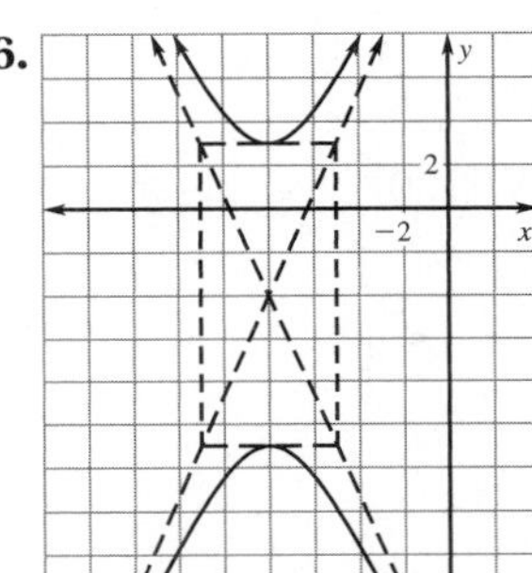

hyperbola with center $(-8, -4)$, vertices $(-8, -3)$ and $(-8, -11)$, asymptotes $y = \frac{7}{3}x + \frac{44}{3}$ and $y = -\frac{7}{3}x - \frac{68}{3}$

7. 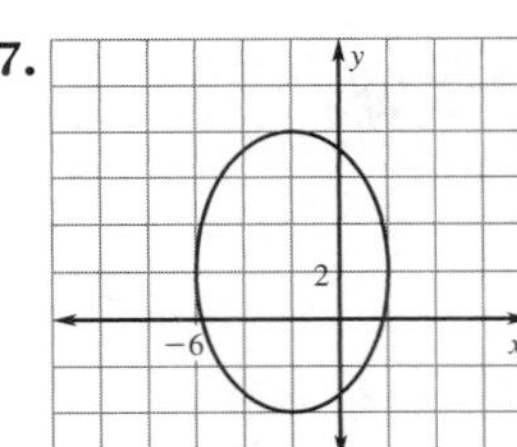

ellipse with center $(-2, 2)$, vertices $(-2, 8)$ and $(-2, -4)$, co-vertices $(2, 2)$ and $(-6, 2)$

8. 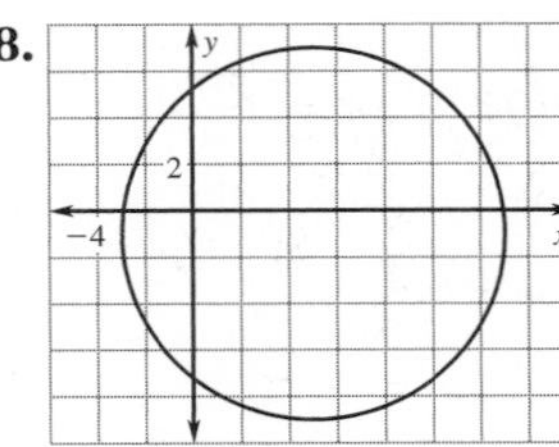

circle with center $(5, -1)$ and radius 8

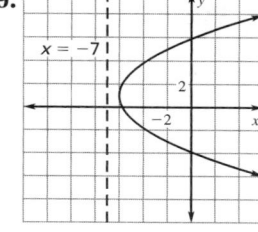

9. parabola with vertex $(-6, 1)$, focus $(-5, 1)$, and directrix $x = -7$

10. 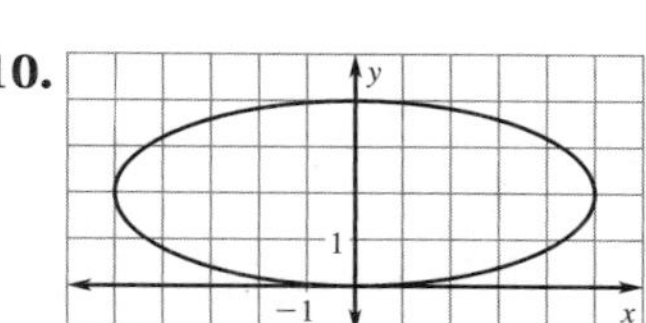

ellipse with center $(0, 2)$, vertices $(5, 2)$ and $(-5, 2)$, and co-vertices $(0, 0)$ and $(0, 4)$

11. 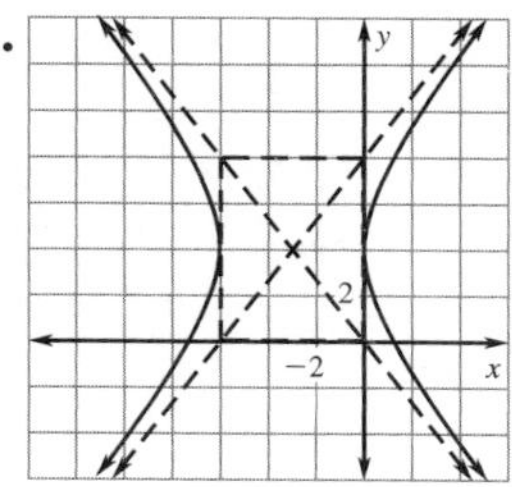

hyperbola with center $(-3, 4)$, vertices $(0, 4)$ and $(-6, 4)$, and asymptotes $y = \frac{4}{3}x + 8$ and $y = -\frac{4}{3}x$

37. circle, $(x - 7)^2 + (y + 2)^2 = 64$;

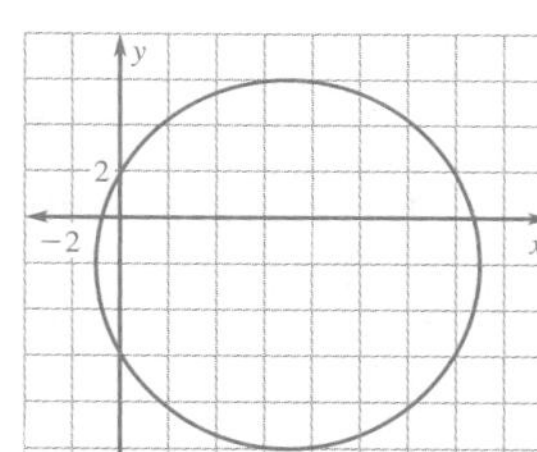

38. ellipse, $\frac{(x - 5)^2}{4} + (y + 2)^2 = 1$;

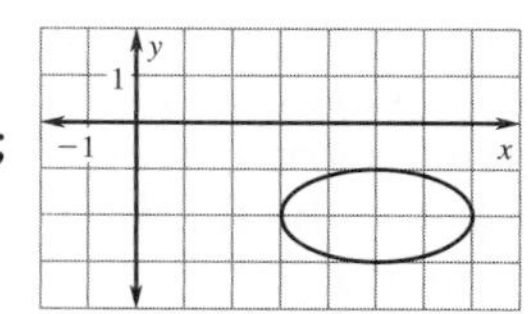

39. parabola, $(x - 8)^2 = 8(y - 2)$;

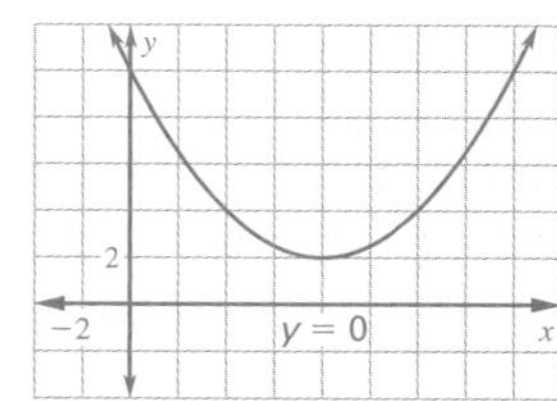

40. hyperbola, $(y - 3)^2 - \frac{(x - 4)^2}{9} = 1$;

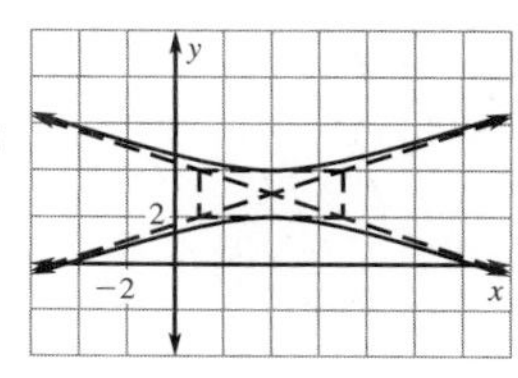

41. ellipse, $\frac{(x - 2)^2}{4} + \frac{(y - 3)^2}{9} = 1$;

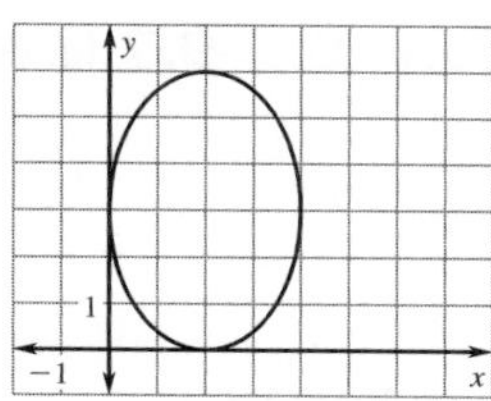

42. parabola, $(y + 7)^2 = -16(x - 1)$;

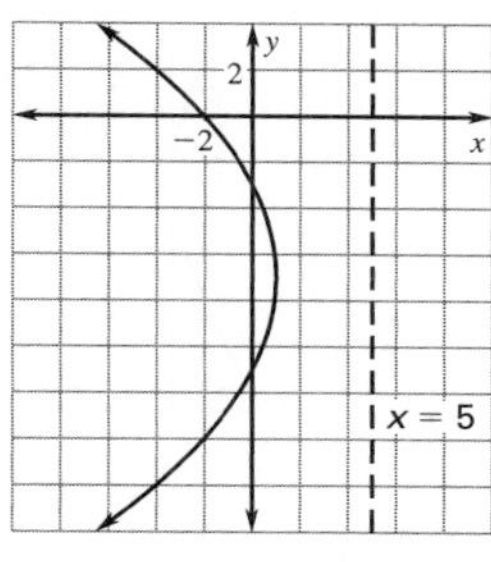

43. circle, $(x + 8)^2 + (y - 4)^2 = 64$;

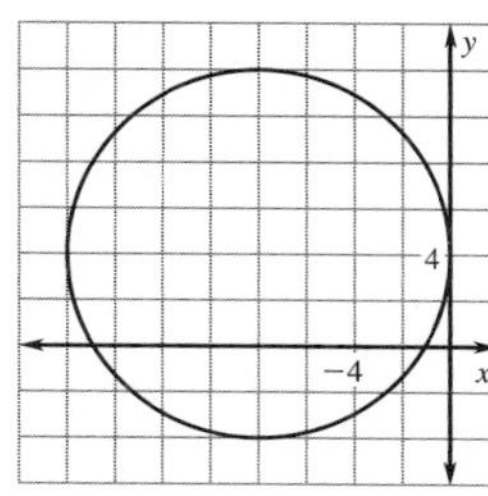

44. hyperbola, $\frac{(x + 4)^2}{4} - (y + 3)^2 = 1$;

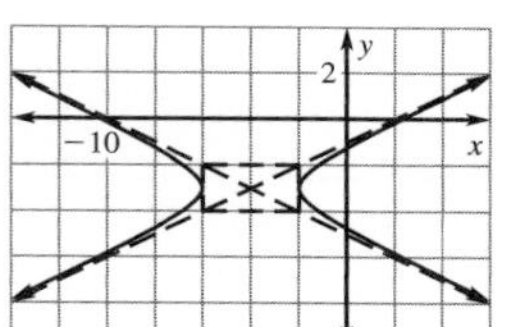

Quiz for Lessons 9.6–9.7 (p. 664)

3. $\dfrac{\left(x - \frac{3}{2}\right)^2}{\frac{9}{4}} - \dfrac{(y - 1)^2}{18} = 1$

4. hyperbola,
$\dfrac{(x - 2)^2}{4} - \dfrac{(y + 4)^2}{9} = 1$;

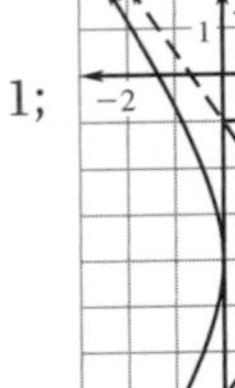

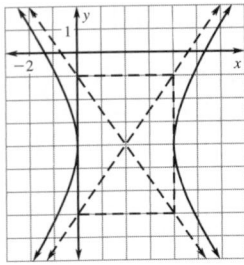

5. circle,
$(x + 2)^2 + (y - 6)^2 = 169$;

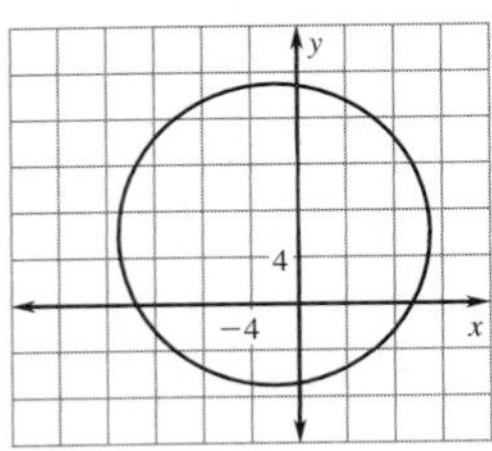

6. parabola,
$(x + 3)^2 = y - 7$;

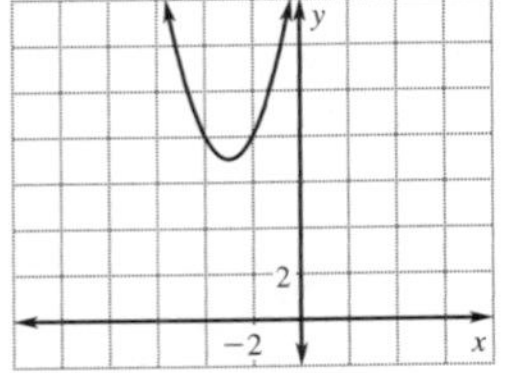

7. ellipse,
$\dfrac{(x + 5)^2}{\frac{165}{4}} + \dfrac{(y + 1)^2}{11} = 1$;

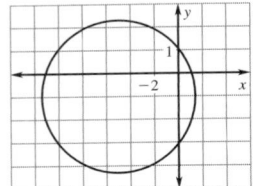

14. $x^2 + y^2 = 10^2$, $(x - 20)^2 + (y - 15)^2 = 15^2$, (8, 6); yes; since the radius of the two circles are 10 and 15 and the distance between the radar stations is 25, there is only one point of intersection for the two circles and therefore one location for the ship.

Chapter Test (p. 673) **24.** ellipse, $\dfrac{(x - 3)^2}{4} + (y - 2)^2 = 1$ **25.** circle, $(x + 4)^2 + (y + 6)^2 = 49$ **26.** hyperbola, $\dfrac{(x - 5)^2}{9} - \dfrac{y^2}{4} = 1$ **27.** parabola, $(y - 8)^2 = 12(x + 2)$ **28.** ellipse, $\dfrac{(x + 1)^2}{4} + \dfrac{(y - 3)^2}{25} = 1$ **29.** hyperbola, $\dfrac{(y + 7)^2}{16} - (x - 2)^2 = 1$

Chapter 10

10.1 Skill Practice (pp. 686–687)

3.

4.

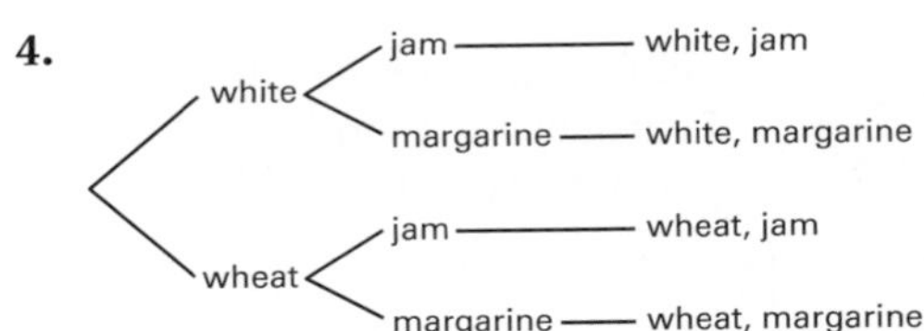

5.

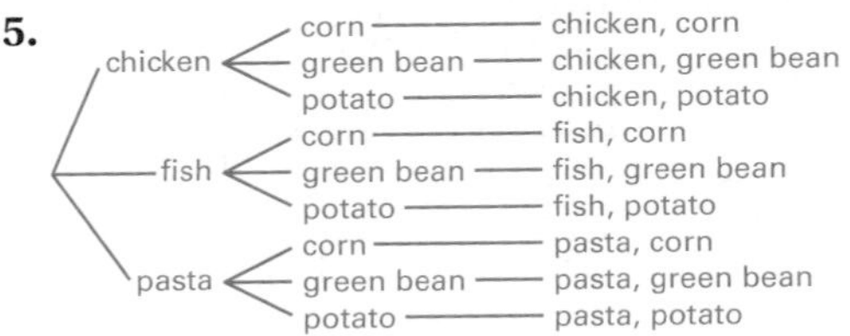

6.

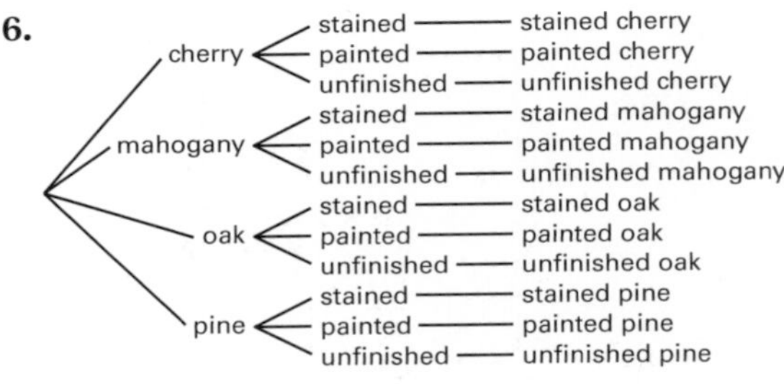

57. To find the number of permutations of n distinct objects, the first event has n ways of occurring, the second event has $(n - 1)$ ways of occurring since one of the n objects was used for the first event, the third event has $(n - 2)$ ways of occurring since one more of the n objects was used for the second, and so on until you reach the last event which only has 1 way of occurring. The fundamental counting principle indicates that to find the number of ways that all the events can happen, multiply each of the number of ways that the individual events can occur. For n distinct objects it would be $n \cdot (n - 1) \cdot (n - 2) \cdot \ldots \cdot 1$, which is the same as $n!$.

10.2 Skill Practice (pp. 694–695)

42. ${}_nC_0 = \frac{n!}{(n-0)! \cdot 0!} = \frac{n!}{n! \cdot 1} = \frac{n!}{n!} = 1$ **43.** ${}_nC_n = \frac{n!}{(n-n)! \cdot n!} = \frac{n!}{0! \cdot n!} = \frac{n!}{n! \cdot 1} = \frac{n!}{n!} = 1$ **44.** ${}_nC_r \cdot {}_rC_m = \frac{n!}{(n-r)! \cdot r!} \cdot \frac{r!}{(r-m)! \cdot m!} = \frac{n!}{(n-r)! \cdot (r-m)! \cdot m!}$; ${}_nC_m \cdot {}_{n-m}C_{r-m} = \frac{n!}{(n-m)! \cdot m!} \cdot \frac{(n-m)!}{[(n-m)-(r-m)]! \cdot (r-m)!} = \frac{n!}{(n-r)! \cdot (r-m)! \cdot m!}$

45. ${}_nC_1 = \frac{n!}{(n-1)! \cdot 1!} = \frac{n!}{(n-1)!}$; ${}_nP_1 = \frac{n!}{(n-1)!}$

46. ${}_nC_r = \frac{n!}{(n-r)! \cdot r!}$; ${}_nC_{n-r} = \frac{n!}{[n-(n-r)]! \cdot (n-r)!} = \frac{n!}{r! \cdot (n-r)!} = \frac{n!}{(n-r)! \cdot r!}$ **47.** ${}_{n+1}C_r = \frac{(n+1)!}{[(n+1)-r]! \cdot r!} = \frac{(n+1)!}{(n+1-r)! \cdot r!}$; ${}_nC_r + {}_nC_{r-1} = \frac{n!}{(n-r)! \cdot r!} + \frac{n!}{[n-(r-1)]! \cdot (r-1)!} = \frac{n!}{(n-r)! \cdot r!} + \frac{n!}{(n-r+1)! \cdot (r-1)!} = \frac{n! \cdot (n-r+1)}{(n-r+1) \cdot (n-r)! \cdot r!} + \frac{n!r}{(n-r+1)! \cdot r \cdot (r-1)!} = \frac{n! \cdot (n-r+1)}{(n-r+1)! \cdot r!} + \frac{n! \cdot r}{(n-r+1)! \cdot r} = \frac{n! \cdot (n-r+1) + n! \cdot r}{(n-r+1)! \cdot r!} = \frac{n! \cdot (n-r+1+r)}{(n-r+1)! \cdot r!} = \frac{n! \cdot (n+1)}{(n-r+1)! \cdot r!} = \frac{(n+1)!}{(n+1-r)! \cdot r!}$

10.6 Guided Practice (pp. 725–727)

1.

x(sum)	2	3	4	5	6	7	8
P(x)	$\frac{1}{16}$	$\frac{1}{8}$	$\frac{3}{16}$	$\frac{1}{4}$	$\frac{3}{16}$	$\frac{1}{8}$	$\frac{1}{16}$

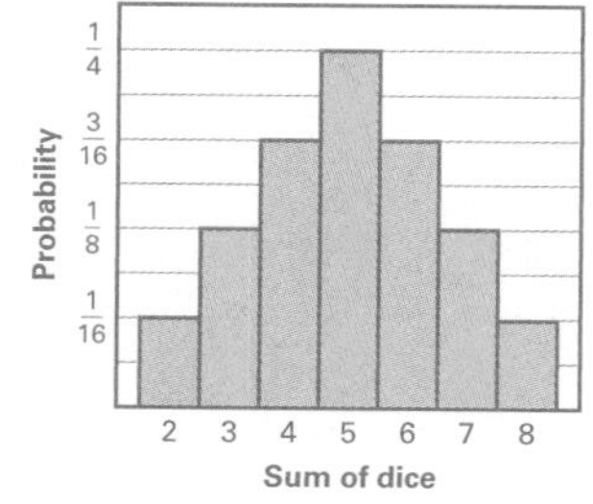

10.6 Skill Practice (pp. 727–729)

3.

x(value)	1	2	3
P(x)	$\frac{1}{2}$	$\frac{3}{10}$	$\frac{1}{5}$

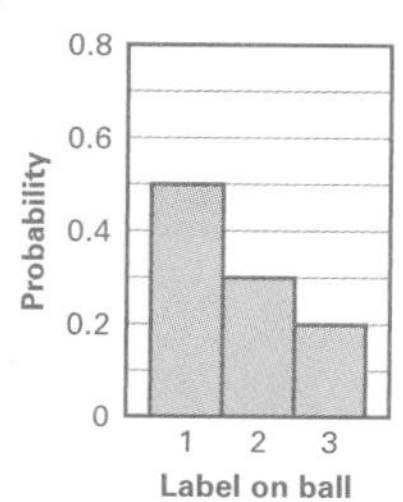

4.

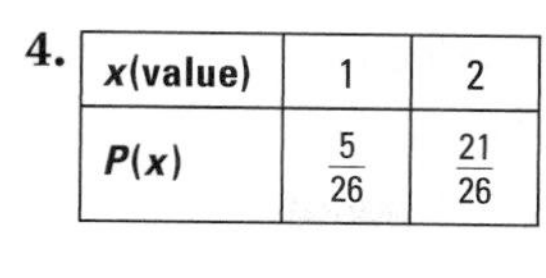

x(value)	1	2
P(x)	$\frac{5}{26}$	$\frac{21}{26}$

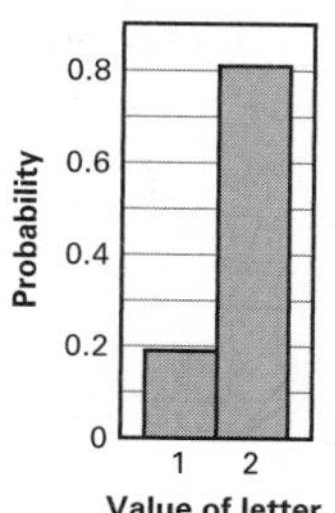

5.

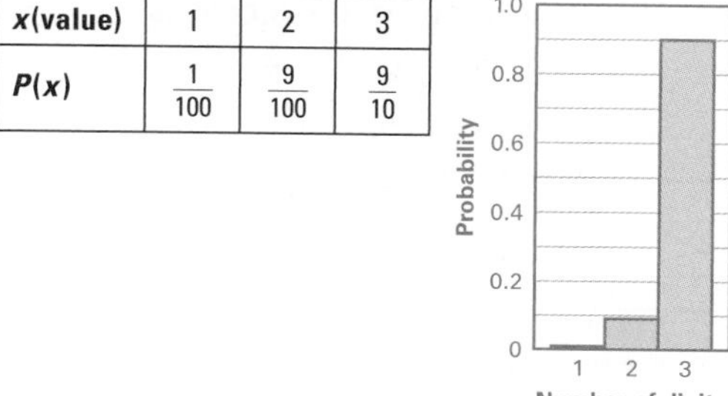

x(value)	1	2	3
P(x)	$\frac{1}{100}$	$\frac{9}{100}$	$\frac{9}{10}$

33. skewed; 1 success

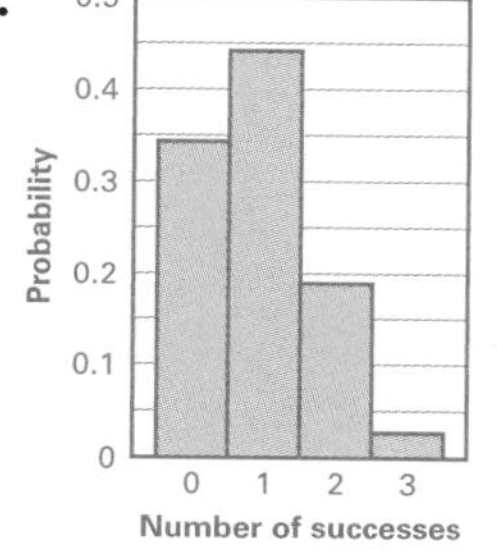

34. symmetric; 3 successes

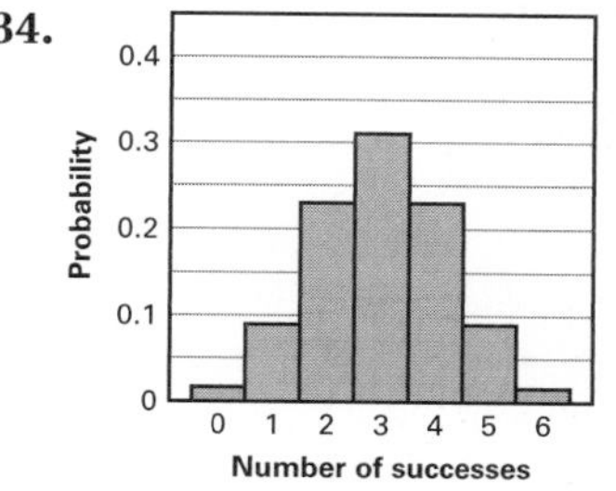

35. skewed; 0 successes

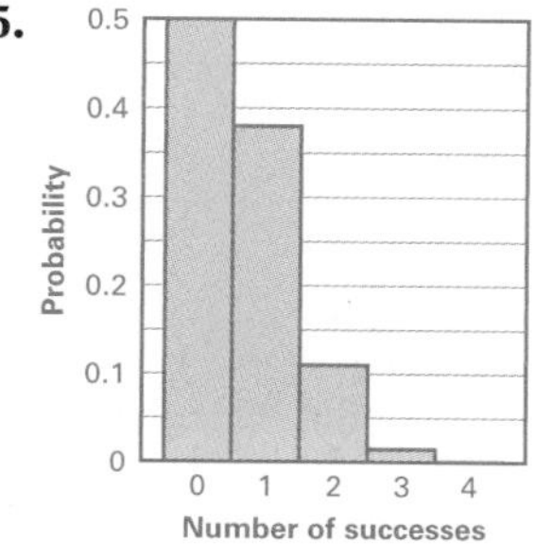

ADDITIONAL ANSWERS

36.

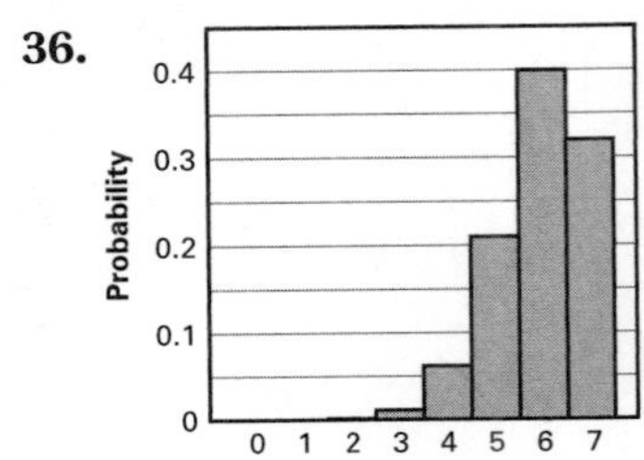
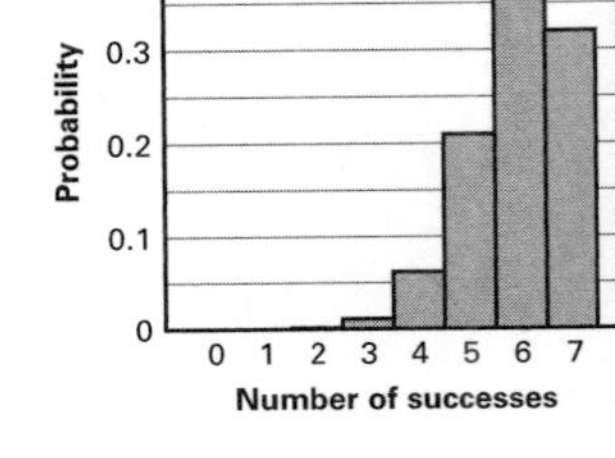

skewed; 6 successes

37.

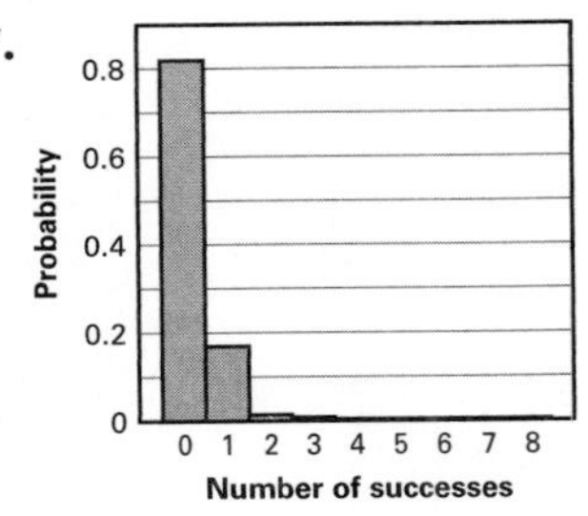

skewed; 0 successes

38.

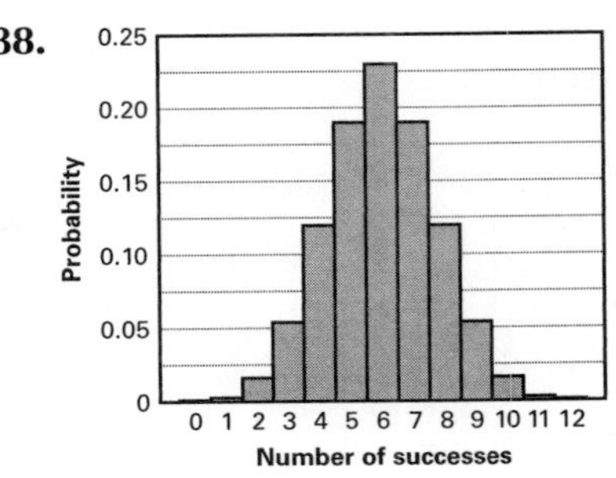

symmetric; 6 successes

10.6 Problem Solving (pp. 729–730)

48. c.

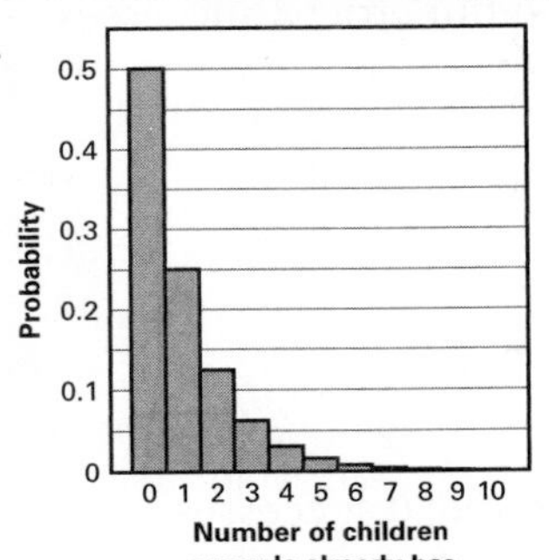

Quiz for Lessons 10.5–10.6 (p. 730)

8.

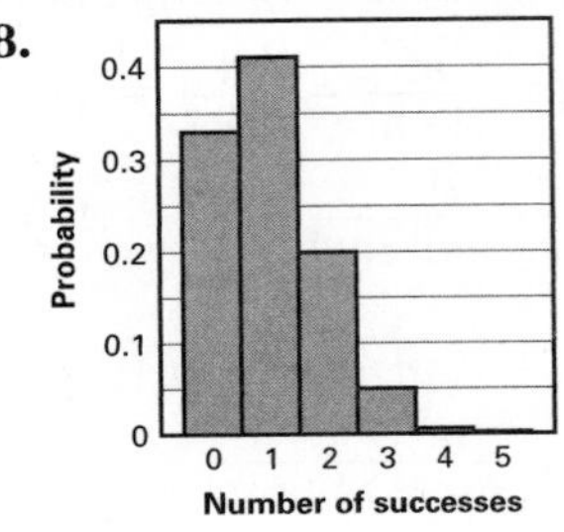

9.

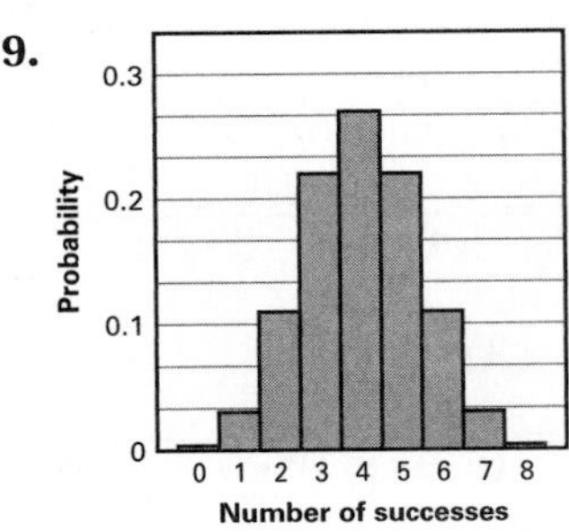

10.

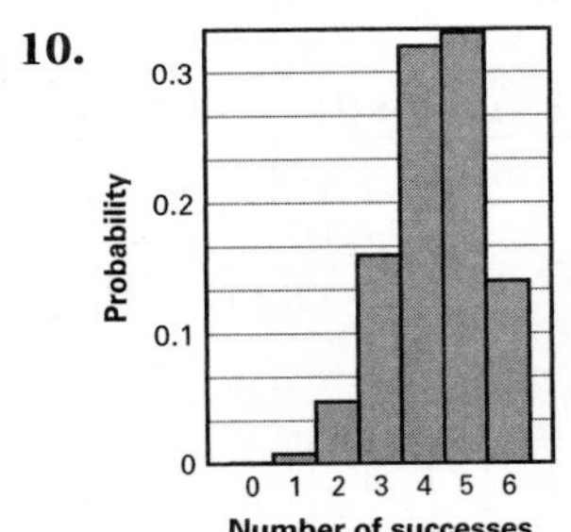

Chapter 11

11.4 Problem Solving (pp. 770–771)

33.

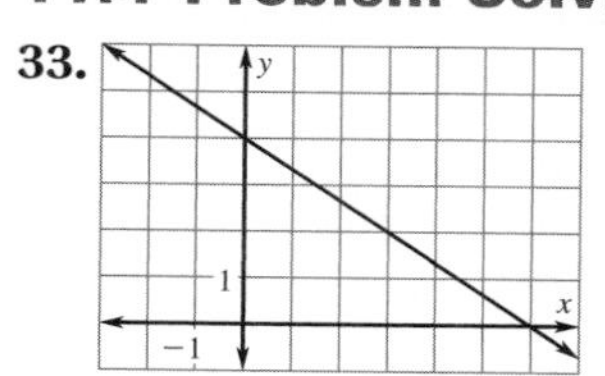

34.

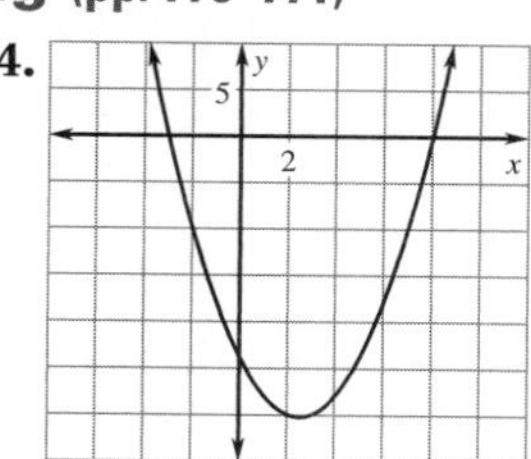

35.

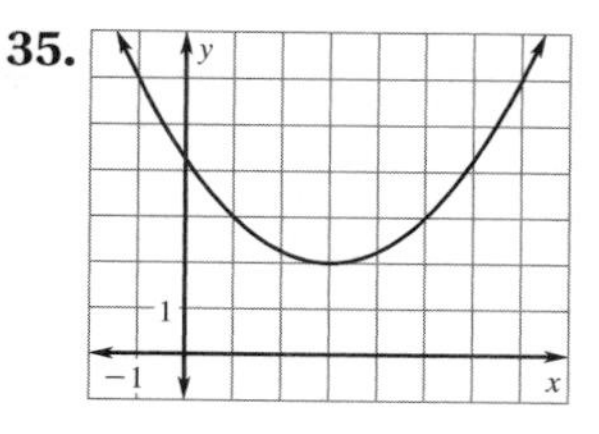

36.

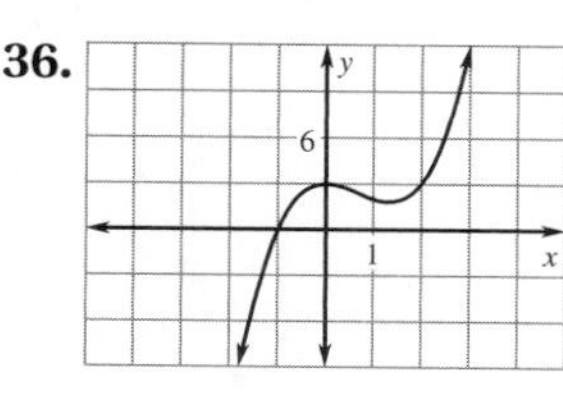

37.

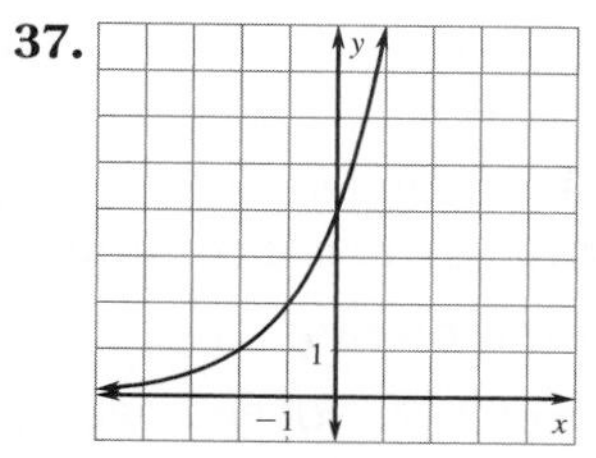

38.

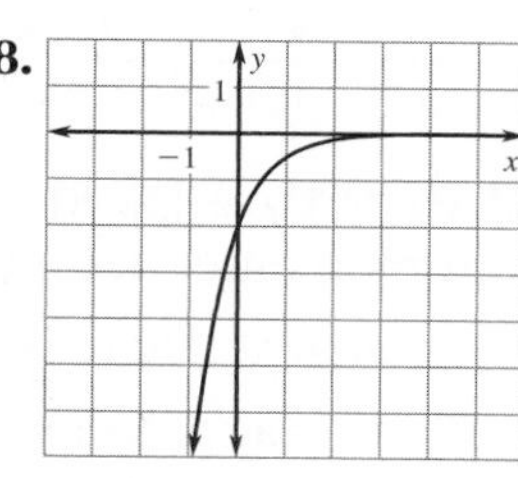

Extension (p. 773) **3–6.** Sample answers are given. **3.** Many patients may answer untruthfully because their dentist is asking the question. The information should be collected anonymously. **4.** This is a leading question. The use of the word *mistake* imparts the question writer's opinion into the question. Respondents may think a "yes" response means they are not in favor of the town government. **5.** The question assumes that the respondent is familiar with the facts of the case. Any presentation of the facts (as interpreted by the pollster) may be biased as well. It might be best then to ask the question as given only to those who reply affirmatively to the question, "Are you familiar with the facts of the Carter case?" **6.** The question assumes that the respondent knows all the candidates' platforms and supports one. You could provide a list of key issues, each with all the candidates' positions given, and ask respondents to check which positions they support.

Chapter 12

12.1 Skill Practice (pp. 798–799)

28.

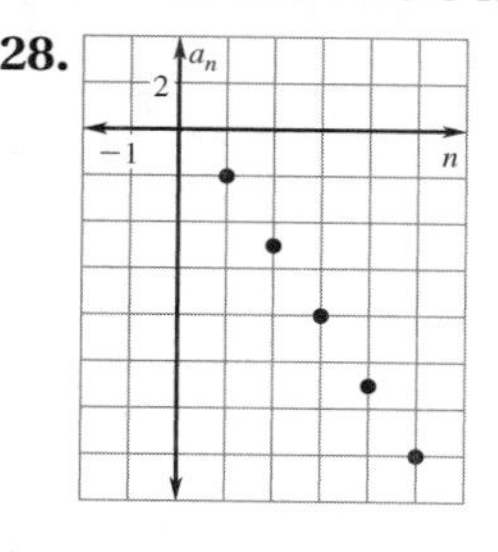

29.

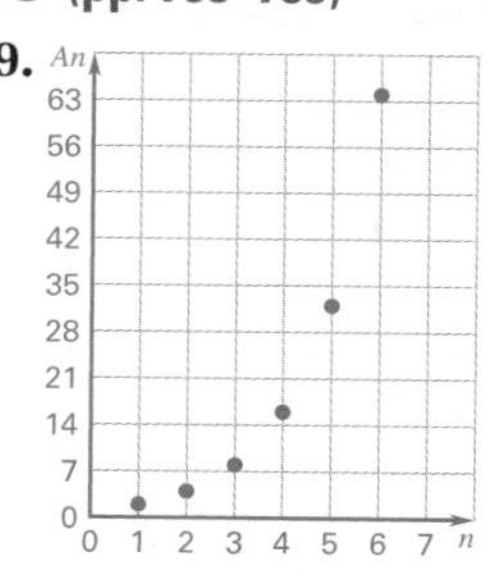

30.

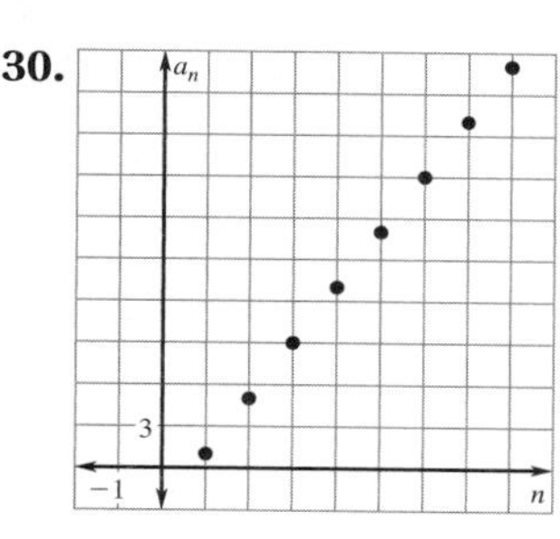

31.

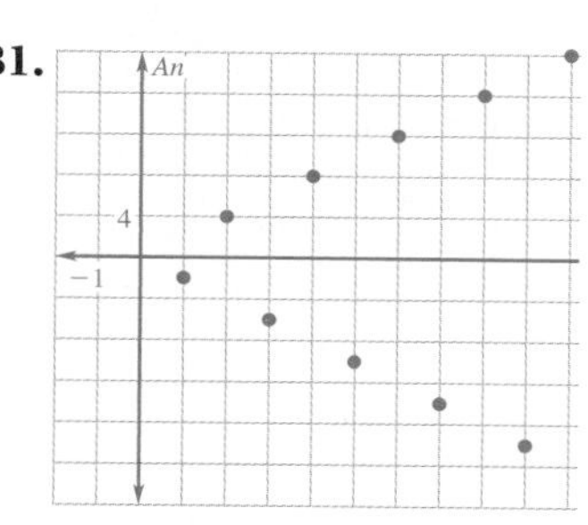

32. **33.**

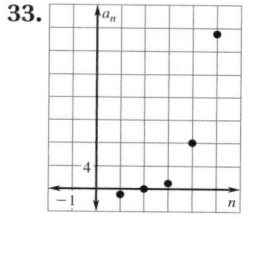

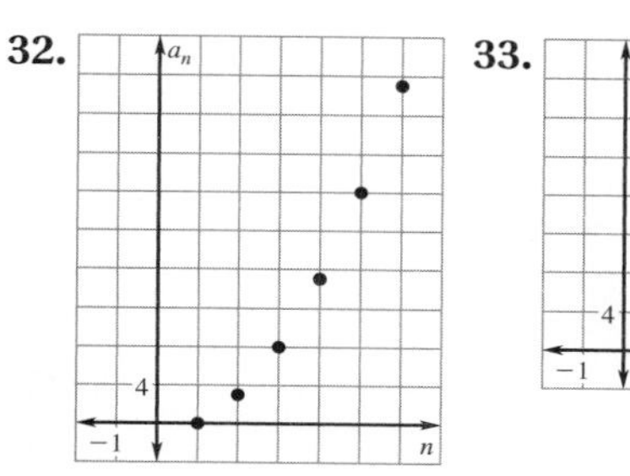

34. **35.**

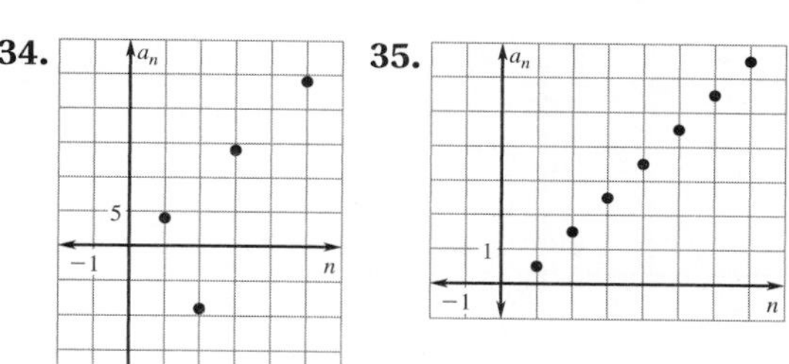

36.

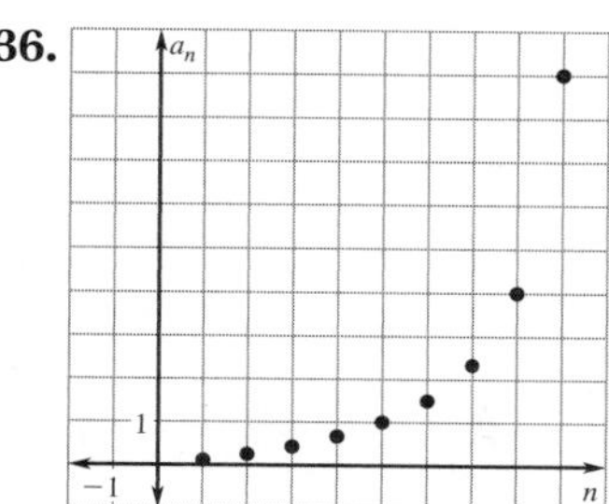

12.1 Graphing Calculator Activity (p. 801)

1. b.

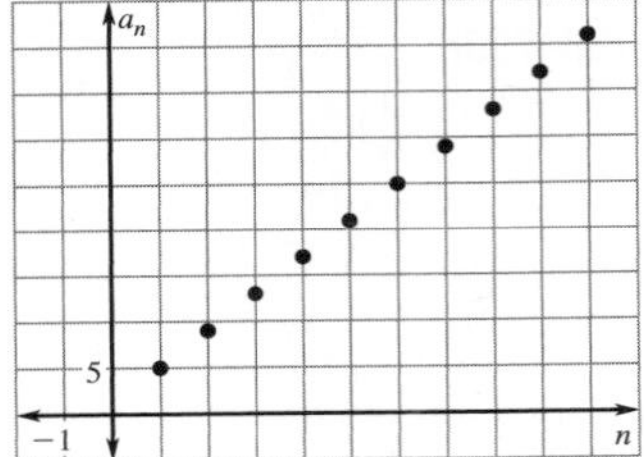

2. b.

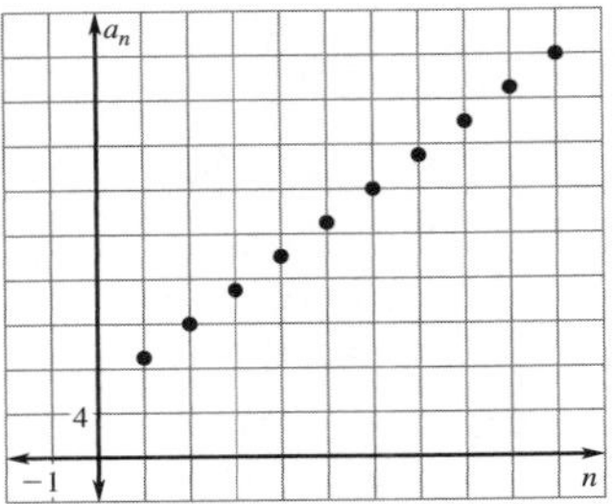

3. b.

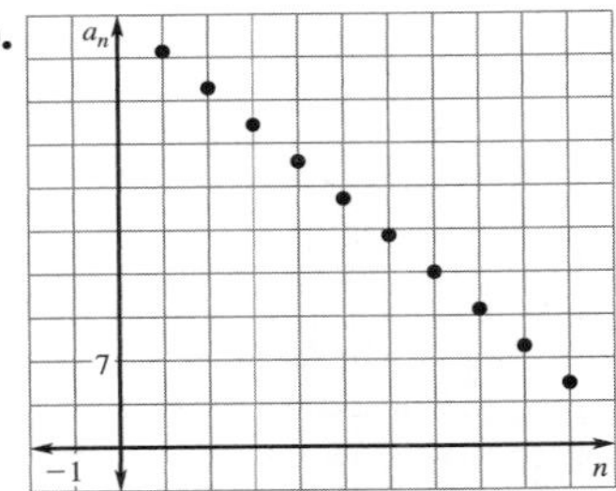

4. b.

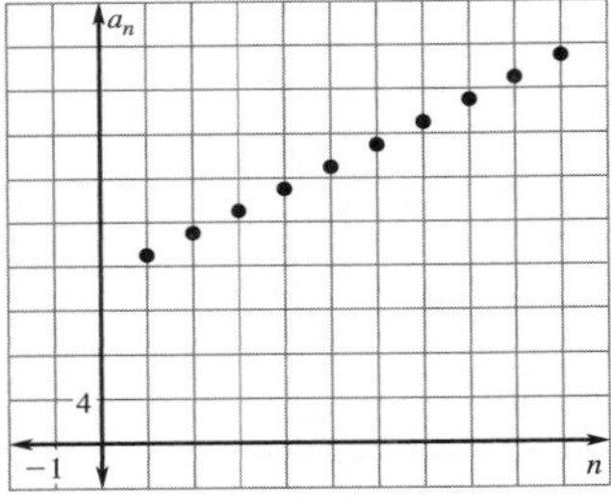

5. b.

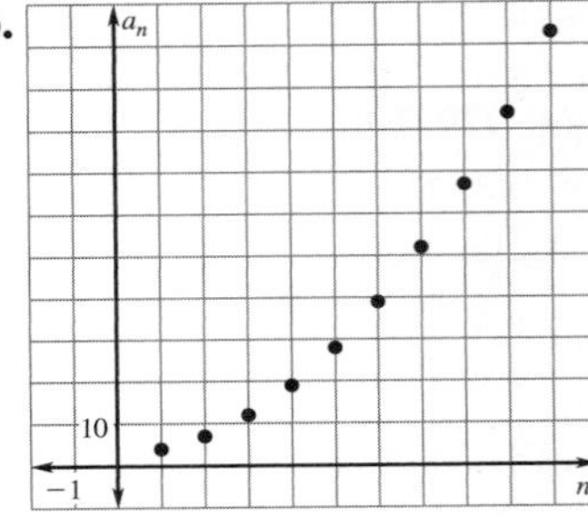

6. b.

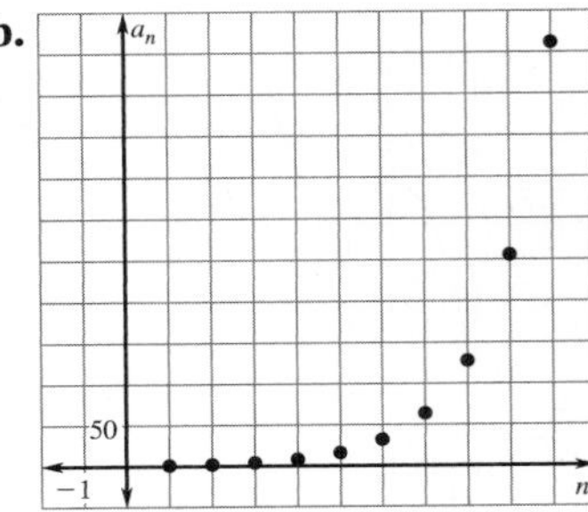

12.3 Skill Practice (pp. 814–815) **3.** Not geometric; there is no common ratio. **4.** Geometric; there is a common ratio of 4. **5.** Geometric; there is a common ratio of $\frac{1}{6}$. **6.** Geometric; there is a common ratio of 2. **7.** Not geometric; there is no common ratio. **8.** Not geometric; there is no common ratio. **9.** Geometric; there is a common ratio of $\frac{1}{2}$. **10.** Not geometric; there is no common ratio. **11.** Geometric; there is a common ratio of −3. **12.** Geometric; there is a common ratio of 3. **13.** Not geometric; there is no common ratio. **14.** Not geometric; there is no common ratio.

12.4 Guided Practice (pp. 821–822)

1.

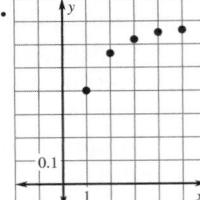

12.4 Skill Practice (pp. 823–824)

3. $S_1 = 0.5$, $S_2 \approx 0.67$, $S_3 \approx 0.72$, $S_4 \approx 0.74$, $S_5 \approx 0.75$;

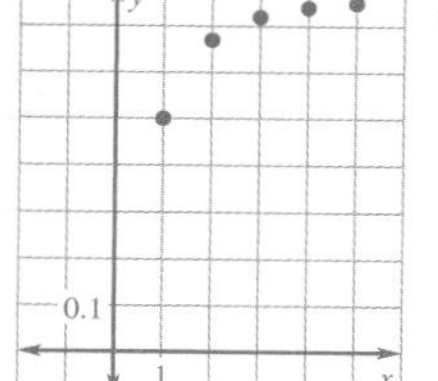

S_n appears to be approaching 0.75.

4. $S_1 = 0.67$, $S_2 = 1$, $S_3 \approx 1.17$, $S_4 = 1.25$, $S_5 \approx 1.29$;

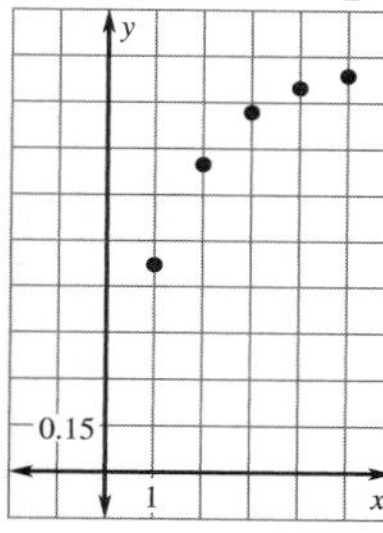

S_n appears to be approaching 1.3.

5. $S_1 = 4$, $S_2 = 6.4$, $S_3 = 7.84$, $S_4 \approx 8.71$, $S_5 \approx 9.22$;

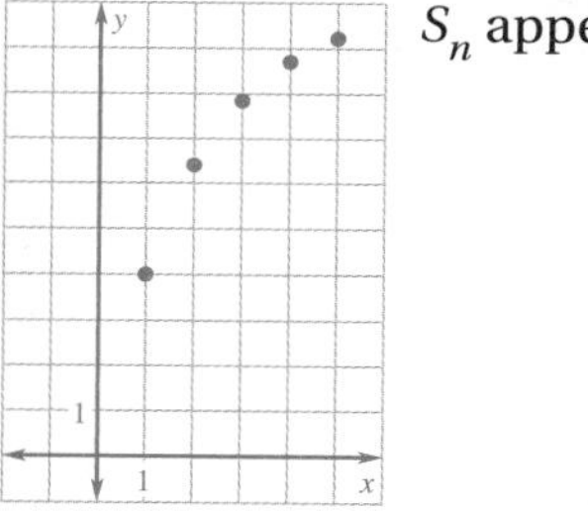

S_n appears to be approaching 10.

6. $S_1 = 0.25$, $S_2 = 1.5$, $S_3 = 7.75$, $S_4 = 39$, $S_5 = 195.25$;

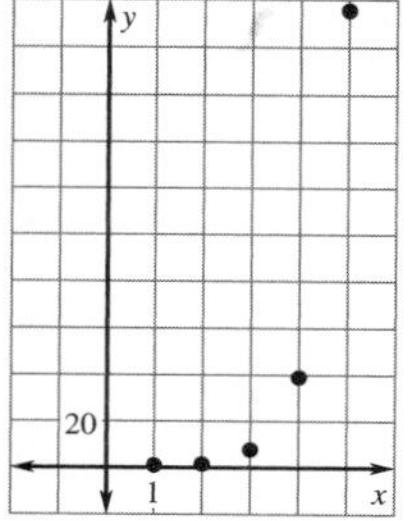

S_n continues to increase.

Extension (p. 837)

1. Basis Step: Check that the formula works for $n = 1$.
$2(1) - 1 = 1^2 \rightarrow 1 = 1$ ✓
Inductive Step: Assume that
$1 + 3 + 5 + \ldots + (2k - 1) = k^2$.
Show that $1 + 3 + 5 + \ldots + (2k - 1) + (2(k + 1) - 1)$
$= (k + 1)^2$.
$1 + 3 + 5 + \ldots + (2k - 1) + (2(k + 1) - 1)$
$= k^2 + (2(k + 1) - 1)$
$= k^2 + 2k + 2 - 1$
$= k^2 + 2k + 1$
$= (k + 1)^2$ ✓

2. Basis Step: Check that the formula works for $n = 1$.
$1^2 = \frac{1(1 + 1)(2 \cdot 1 + 1)}{6} \rightarrow 1 = 1$ ✓
Inductive Step: Assume that
$1 + 4 + 9 + \ldots + k^2 = \frac{k(k + 1)(2k + 1)}{6}$.
Show that $1 + 4 + 9 + \ldots + k^2 + (k + 1)^2$
$= \frac{(k + 1)[(k + 1) + 1][2(k + 1) + 1]}{6}$.
$1 + 4 + 9 + \ldots + k^2 + (k + 1)^2$
$= \frac{k(k + 1)(2k + 1)}{6} + (k + 1)^2$
$= \frac{k(k + 1)(2k + 1) + 6(k + 1)^2}{6}$
$= \frac{k(k + 1)(2k + 1) + 6(k + 1)(k + 1)}{6}$
$= \frac{(k + 1)[k(2k + 1) + 6(k + 1)]}{6}$
$= \frac{(k + 1)(2k^2 + k + 6k + 6)}{6}$
$= \frac{(k + 1)(2k^2 + 7k + 6)}{6}$
$= \frac{(k + 1)(k + 2)(2k + 3)}{6}$
$= \frac{(k + 1)[(k + 1) + 1][2(k + 1) + 1]}{6}$ ✓

3. Basis Step: Check that the formula works for $n = 1$.
$2^{1 - 1} = 2^1 - 1 \rightarrow 2^0 = 2 - 1 \rightarrow 1 = 1$ ✓
Inductive Step: Assume that
$1 + 2 + 2^2 + 2^3 + \ldots + 2^{k - 1} = 2^k - 1$.
Show that $1 + 2 + 2^2 + 2^3 + \ldots + 2^{k - 1} + 2^{(k - 1) - 1}$
$= 2^{k + 1} - 1$.
$1 + 2 + 2^2 + 2^3 + \ldots + 2^{k - 1} + 2^{(k - 1) - 1}$
$= (2^k - 1) + 2^{(k + 1) - 1}$
$= 2^k - 1 + 2^k$
$= 2(2^k) - 1$
$= 2^{k + 1} - 1$ ✓

4. **Basis Step:** Check that the formula works for $n = 1$.

$a_1 \cdot r^{1-1} = a_1\left(\frac{1-r^1}{1-r}\right) \to a_1 r^0 = a_1 \cdot 1 \to a_1 \cdot 1 = a_1 \cdot 1$ ✓

Inductive Step: Assume that $\sum a_1 \cdot r^{k-1} = a_1\left(\frac{1-r^k}{1-r}\right)$.

Show that $\sum a_1 \cdot r^{k+1-1} = a_1\left(\frac{1-r^{k+1}}{1-r}\right)$.

$\sum (a_1 \cdot r^{k-1}) + a_1 \cdot r^{k+1-1}$

$= a_1\left(\frac{1-r^k}{1-r}\right) + a_1 \cdot r^{k+1-1}$

$= a_1\left(\frac{1-r^k}{1-r}\right) + a_1 \cdot r^k$

$= a_1\left[\left(\frac{1-r^k}{1-r}\right) + r^k\right]$

$= a_1\left(\frac{1-r^k+r^k(1-r)}{1-r}\right)$

$= a_1\left(\frac{1-r^k+r^k-r^{k+1}}{1-r}\right)$

$= a_1\left(\frac{1-r^{k+1}}{1-r}\right)$ ✓

5. **Basis Step:** Check that the formula works for $n = 1$.

$\frac{1}{1(1+1)} = \frac{1}{1+1} \to \frac{1}{1(2)} = \frac{1}{2}$ ✓

Inductive Step: Assume that

$\frac{1}{1(2)} + \frac{1}{2(3)} + \frac{1}{3(4)} + \dots + \frac{1}{k(k+1)} = \frac{k}{k+1}$.

Show that $\frac{1}{1(2)} + \frac{1}{2(3)} + \frac{1}{3(4)} + \dots + \frac{1}{k(k+1)} + \frac{1}{(k+1)[(k+1)+1]} = \frac{k+1}{(k+1)+1}$.

$\frac{1}{1(2)} + \frac{1}{2(3)} + \frac{1}{3(4)} + \dots + \frac{1}{k(k+1)} + \frac{1}{(k+1)[(k+1)+1]}$

$= \frac{k}{k+1} + \frac{1}{(k+1)(k+2)}$

$= \frac{k(k+2)}{(k+1)(k+2)} + \frac{1}{(k+1)(k+2)}$

$= \frac{k^2+2k+1}{(k+1)(k+2)}$

$= \frac{(k+1)(k+1)}{(k+1)(k+2)}$

$= \frac{k+1}{k+2}$

$= \frac{k+1}{(k+1)+1}$ ✓

6. **Basis Step:** Check that the formula works for $n = 1$.

$(2 \cdot 1)^2 = \frac{2 \cdot 1(1+1)(2 \cdot 1+1)}{3} \to 4 = \frac{2(2)(3)}{3} \to$

$4 = \frac{12}{3} \to 4 = 4$ ✓

Inductive Step: Assume that

$4 + 16 + 36 + \dots + (2k)^2 = \frac{2k(k+1)(2k+1)}{3}$.

Show that $4 + 16 + 36 + \dots + (2k)^2 + [2(k+1)]^2$

$= \frac{2(k+1)[(k+1)+1][2(k+1)+1]}{3}$.

$4 + 16 + 36 + \dots + (2k)^2 + [2(k+1)]^2$

$= \frac{2k(k+1)(2k+1)}{3} + [2(k+1)]^2$

$= \frac{2k(k+1)(2k+1)}{3} + \frac{3[2(k+1)]^2}{3}$

$= \frac{2k(k+1)(2k+1) + 2(2k+2)^2}{3}$

$= \frac{2k(k+1)(2k+1) + 3[4(k^2+2k+1)]}{3}$

$= \frac{2k(k+1)(2k+1) + 12(k+1)^2}{3}$

$= \frac{2k(k+1)[k(2k+1) + 6(k+1)]}{3}$

$= \frac{2(k+1)(2k^2+k+6k+6)}{3}$

$= \frac{2(k+1)(2k^2+7k+6)}{3}$

$= \frac{2(k+1)(k+2)(2k+3)}{3}$

$= \frac{2(k+1)[(k+1)+1]2(k+1)+1]}{3}$ ✓

7. A recursive formula for the nth hexagonal number is $H_n = H_{n-1} + 4n - 3$.

Basis Step: Check that the formula works for $n = 1$.

$H_1 = 1(2(1) - 1) \to 1 = 1(2 - 1) \to 1 = 1$ ✓

Inductive Step: Assume that $H_k = k(2k - 1)$.

Show that $H_{k+1} = (k+1)[2(k+1) - 1]$.

$H_{k+1} = H_{(k+1)-1} + 4(k+1) - 3$

$= H_k + 4(k+1) - 3$

$= k(2k-1) + 4(k+1) - 3$

$= 2k^2 - k + 4k + 4 - 3$

$= 2k^2 + 3k + 1$

$= (k+1)(2k+1)$

$= (k+1)[2(k+1) - 1]$ ✓

ADDITIONAL ANSWERS

Chapter 13

13.1 Skill Practice (pp. 856–857) **3.** $\sin \theta = \frac{12}{13}$, $\cos \theta = \frac{5}{13}$, $\tan \theta = \frac{12}{5}$, $\csc \theta = \frac{13}{12}$, $\sec \theta = \frac{13}{5}$, $\cot \theta = \frac{5}{12}$ **4.** $\sin \theta = \frac{3\sqrt{73}}{73}$, $\cos \theta = \frac{8\sqrt{73}}{73}$, $\tan \theta = \frac{3}{8}$, $\csc \theta = \frac{\sqrt{73}}{3}$, $\sec \theta = \frac{\sqrt{73}}{8}$, $\cot \theta = \frac{8}{3}$ **5.** $\sin \theta = \frac{8}{11}$, $\cos \theta = \frac{\sqrt{57}}{11}$, $\tan \theta = \frac{8\sqrt{57}}{57}$, $\csc \theta = \frac{11}{8}$, $\sec \theta = \frac{11\sqrt{57}}{57}$, $\cot \theta = \frac{\sqrt{57}}{8}$ **6.** $\sin \theta = \frac{7}{15}$, $\cos \theta = \frac{4\sqrt{11}}{15}$, $\tan \theta = \frac{7\sqrt{11}}{44}$, $\csc \theta = \frac{15}{7}$, $\sec \theta = \frac{15\sqrt{11}}{44}$, $\cot \theta = \frac{4\sqrt{11}}{7}$ **7.** $\sin \theta = \frac{\sqrt{115}}{14}$, $\cos \theta = \frac{9}{14}$, $\tan \theta = \frac{\sqrt{115}}{9}$, $\csc \theta = \frac{14\sqrt{115}}{115}$, $\sec \theta = \frac{14}{9}$, $\cot \theta = \frac{9\sqrt{115}}{115}$ **8.** $\sin \theta = \frac{\sqrt{17}}{17}$, $\cos \theta = \frac{4\sqrt{17}}{17}$, $\tan \theta = \frac{1}{4}$, $\csc \theta = \sqrt{17}$, $\sec \theta = \frac{\sqrt{17}}{4}$, $\cot \theta = 4$ **29. b.** A regular n-gon inscribed in a circle can be divided into n identical triangles, each with side lengths of 1. The angle formed by the two radii of the circle, $\angle A$, has a measure of $\left(\frac{360}{n}\right)^\circ$. When the altitude of the triangle is drawn, $\angle A$ is divided in half so the measure of each half-angle is $\left(\frac{180}{n}\right)^\circ$. The length of the bottom leg of the right triangle is $\sin\left(\frac{180}{n}\right)^\circ$, which is half of one side of the the n-gon. To find the perimeter of the n-gon, n(the number of large triangles) must be multiplied by $2 \cdot \sin\left(\frac{180}{n}\right)^\circ$ (the length of one side of the n-gon), so $P = 2n \cdot \sin\left(\frac{180}{n}\right)^\circ$.

13.3 Skill Practice (pp. 870–871) **3.** $\sin \theta = \frac{15}{17}$, $\cos \theta = \frac{8}{17}$, $\tan \theta = \frac{15}{8}$, $\csc \theta = \frac{17}{15}$, $\sec \theta = \frac{17}{8}$, $\cot \theta = \frac{8}{15}$ **4.** $\sin \theta = \frac{4}{5}$, $\cos \theta = -\frac{3}{5}$, $\tan \theta = -\frac{4}{3}$, $\csc \theta = \frac{5}{4}$, $\sec \theta = -\frac{5}{3}$, $\cot \theta = -\frac{3}{4}$ **5.** $\sin \theta = -\frac{24}{25}$, $\cos \theta = -\frac{7}{25}$, $\tan \theta = \frac{24}{7}$, $\csc \theta = -\frac{25}{24}$, $\sec \theta = -\frac{25}{7}$, $\cot \theta = \frac{7}{24}$ **6.** $\sin \theta = -\frac{12}{13}$, $\cos \theta = \frac{5}{13}$, $\tan \theta = -\frac{12}{5}$, $\csc \theta = -\frac{13}{12}$, $\sec \theta = \frac{13}{5}$, $\cot \theta = -\frac{5}{12}$ **7.** $\sin \theta = -\frac{\sqrt{2}}{2}$, $\cos \theta = \frac{\sqrt{2}}{2}$, $\tan \theta = -1$, $\csc \theta = -\sqrt{2}$, $\sec \theta = \sqrt{2}$, $\cot \theta = -1$ **8.** $\sin \theta = \frac{3\sqrt{13}}{13}$, $\cos \theta = -\frac{2\sqrt{13}}{13}$, $\tan \theta = -\frac{3}{2}$, $\csc \theta = \frac{\sqrt{13}}{3}$, $\sec \theta = -\frac{\sqrt{13}}{2}$, $\cot \theta = -\frac{2}{3}$ **9.** $\sin \theta = -\frac{5\sqrt{34}}{34}$, $\cos \theta = -\frac{3\sqrt{34}}{34}$, $\tan \theta = \frac{5}{3}$, $\csc \theta = -\frac{\sqrt{34}}{5}$, $\sec \theta = -\frac{\sqrt{34}}{3}$, $\cot \theta = \frac{3}{5}$ **10.** $\sin \theta = -\frac{\sqrt{11}}{6}$, $\cos \theta = \frac{5}{6}$, $\tan \theta = -\frac{\sqrt{11}}{5}$, $\csc \theta = -\frac{6\sqrt{11}}{11}$, $\sec \theta = \frac{6}{5}$, $\cot \theta = -\frac{5\sqrt{11}}{11}$

16. **17.**

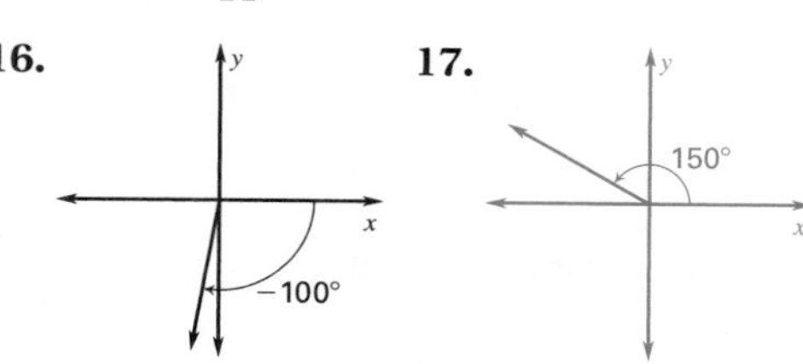

18. **19.**

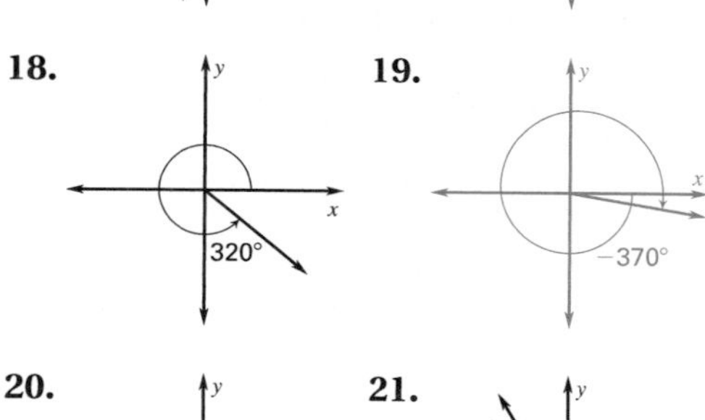

20. **21.**

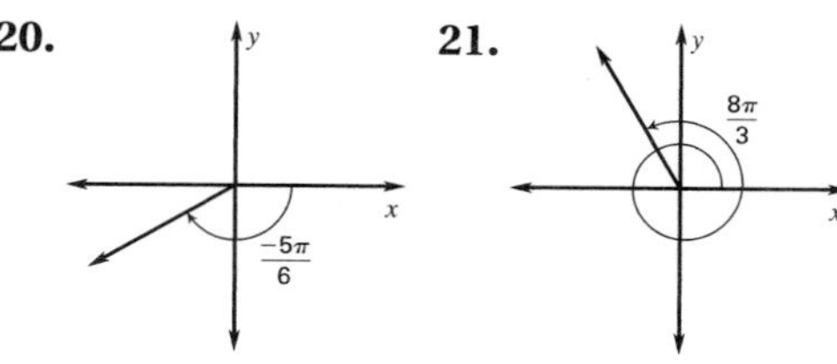

22. **23.**

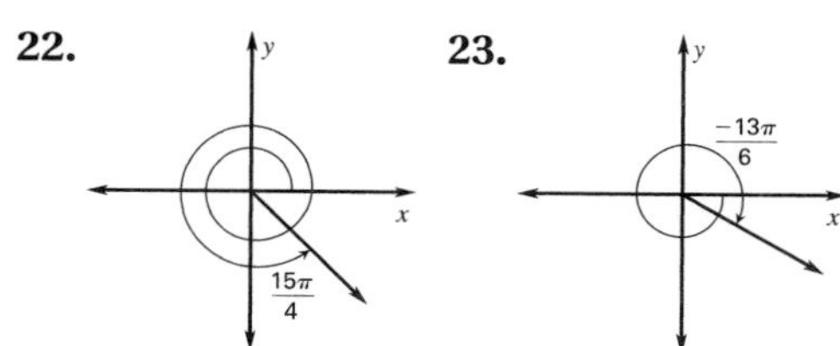

34.
$$\begin{aligned} e^{a+bi} &= e^a(\cos b + i \sin b) \\ \ln (e^{a+bi}) &= \ln [e^a(\cos b + i \sin b)] \\ (a+bi) \ln e &= a \ln e + \ln (\cos b + i \sin b) \\ (a+bi)(1) &= a(1) + \ln (\cos b + i \sin b) \\ a + bi &= a + \ln (\cos b + i \sin b) \\ bi &= \ln (\cos b + i \sin b) \\ e^{bi} &= e^{\ln (\cos b + i \sin b)} \\ e^{bi} &= \cos b + i \sin b \end{aligned}$$

Letting $b = \pi$:

$$\begin{aligned} e^{\pi i} &= \cos \pi + i \sin \pi \\ e^{\pi i} &= -1 + i(0) \\ e^{\pi i} &= -1 \\ e^{\pi i} + 1 &= 0 \end{aligned}$$

13.4 Investigating Algebra Activity (p. 874)

Step 1.

θ	$-\pi$	$-\frac{3\pi}{4}$	$-\frac{\pi}{2}$	$-\frac{\pi}{4}$	0	$\frac{\pi}{4}$	$\frac{\pi}{2}$	$\frac{3\pi}{4}$	π
$f(\theta) = \sin \theta$	0	$-\frac{\sqrt{2}}{2}$	-1	$-\frac{\sqrt{2}}{2}$	0	$\frac{\sqrt{2}}{2}$	1	$\frac{\sqrt{2}}{2}$	0
$g(\theta) = \cos \theta$	-1	$-\frac{\sqrt{2}}{2}$	0	$\frac{\sqrt{2}}{2}$	1	$\frac{\sqrt{2}}{2}$	0	$-\frac{\sqrt{2}}{2}$	-1

Step 2. $-\frac{\sqrt{2}}{2}$ appears more than once for different values of θ. **Step 3.** No; $\frac{\sqrt{2}}{2}$ appears more than once for different values of θ.

Quiz for Lessons 13.3–13.4 (p. 880) **1.** $\sin \theta = -\frac{\sqrt{10}}{10}$, $\cos \theta = \frac{3\sqrt{10}}{10}$, $\tan \theta = -\frac{1}{3}$, $\csc \theta = -\sqrt{10}$, $\sec \theta = \frac{\sqrt{10}}{3}$, $\cot \theta = -3$ **2.** $\sin \theta = \frac{5\sqrt{74}}{74}$, $\cos \theta = -\frac{7\sqrt{74}}{74}$, $\tan \theta = -\frac{5}{7}$, $\csc \theta = \frac{\sqrt{74}}{5}$, $\sec \theta = -\frac{\sqrt{74}}{7}$, $\cot \theta = -\frac{7}{5}$ **3.** $\sin \theta = \frac{2\sqrt{5}}{5}$, $\cos \theta = \frac{\sqrt{5}}{5}$, $\tan \theta = 2$, $\csc \theta = \frac{\sqrt{5}}{2}$, $\sec \theta = \sqrt{5}$, $\cot \theta = \frac{1}{2}$ **4.** $\sin \theta = -\frac{\sqrt{17}}{17}$, $\cos \theta = -\frac{4\sqrt{17}}{17}$, $\tan \theta = \frac{1}{4}$, $\csc \theta = -\sqrt{17}$, $\sec \theta = -\frac{\sqrt{17}}{4}$, $\cot \theta = 4$

13.5 Problem Solving (pp. 887–888) **47. b.** *Sample answer:* Method 1: use the Pythagorean Theorem to find the third side of the triangle (451 m). Now construct a triangle from the top of the cliff to the top of the building and the observer. The angle at the observer is 9° and the angle at the base of the building is 153°. Use the law of sines to find the height of the building. Method 2: Construct a right triangle with the height of the building and the cliff being a leg which measures $300 + x$, the distance from the observer to the base of the cliff being 152.9 meters, and the measure of the angle from the observer to the top of the building is 72°. Now use the sine relationship to solve for x; about 170 m.

13.6 Skill Practice (pp. 892–893) **42.** *Sample answer:* Place $\triangle ABC$ on a coordinate system such that $\overline{AC}$ is on the x-axis with A having coordinates (0, 0), B having coordinates (x, h), and C having coordinates $(b, 0)$. Start by finding the coordinates of B in terms of trigonometric values. Do this by solving the right triangle: $\sin A = \frac{h}{c} \rightarrow h = c \sin A$ and $\cos A = \frac{x}{c} \rightarrow x = c \cos A$. Now use the distance formula to find the length of a: $a^2 = (x - b)^2 + (h - 0)^2$. Substitute the trigonometric ratios for x and h to get $a^2 = (c \cos A - b)^2 + (c \sin A)^2$. Next simplify the right side by evaluating each set of parentheses. Simplifying gives

$$\begin{aligned} a^2 &= c^2 \cos^2 A - 2bc \cos A + b^2 + c^2 \sin^2 A \\ a^2 &= c^2 (\cos^2 A + \sin^2 A) - 2bc \cos A + b^2 \\ a^2 &= b^2 + c^2 (1) - 2bc \cos A \\ a^2 &= b^2 + c^2 - 2bc \cos A \end{aligned}$$

This gives you one formula for the law of cosines. The other two versions can be derived in a similar fashion. If you evaluate the law of cosines with a right triangle, the side opposite the 90° angle would reduce the law of cosines to

$$\begin{aligned} a^2 &= b^2 + c^2 - 2bc \cos 90 \\ a^2 &= b^2 + c^2 - 2bc(0) \\ a^2 &= b^2 + c^2 \end{aligned}$$

which is the Pythagorean theorem.

Chapter 14

14.1 Guided Practice (pp. 909–912)

1.

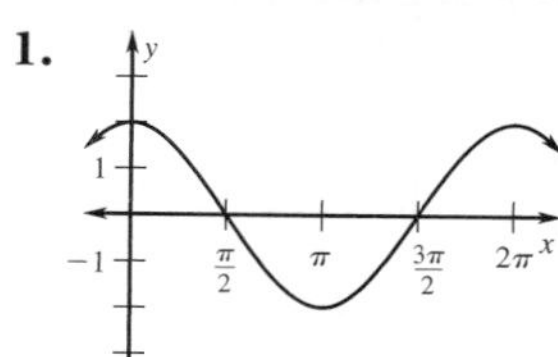

2.

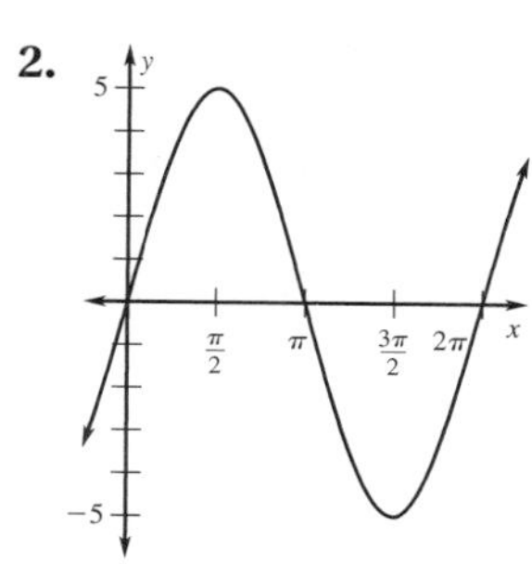

3.

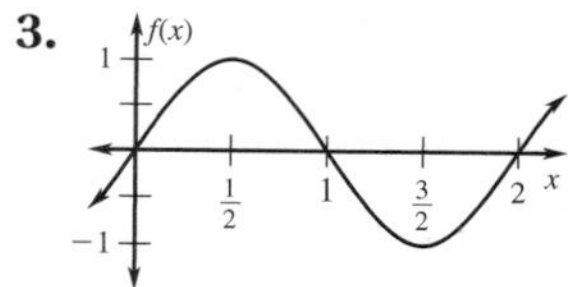

4.

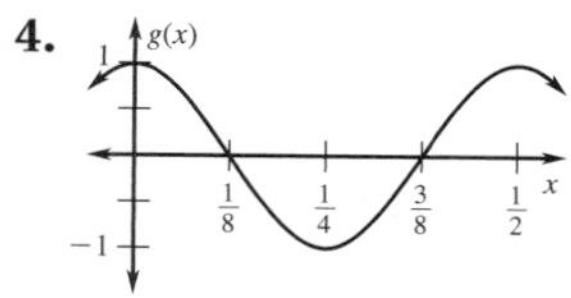

14.1 Skill Practice (pp. 912–913)

6.

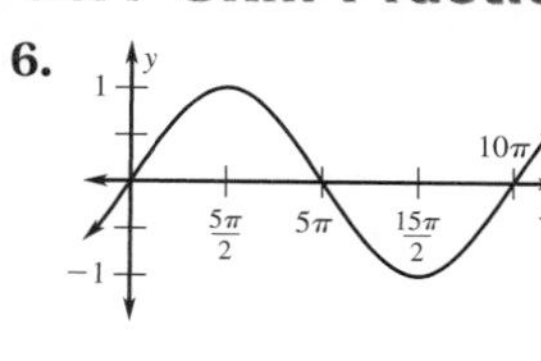

7.

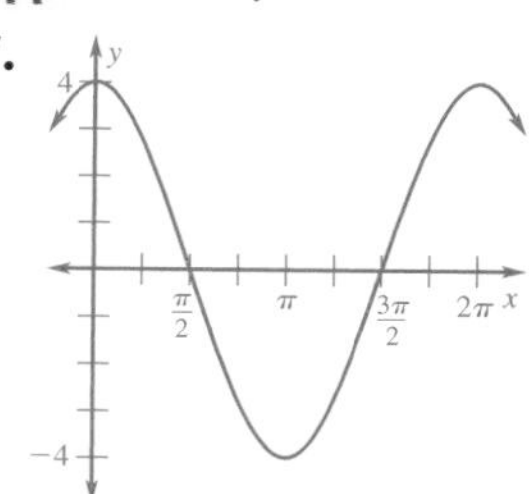

8. 9.

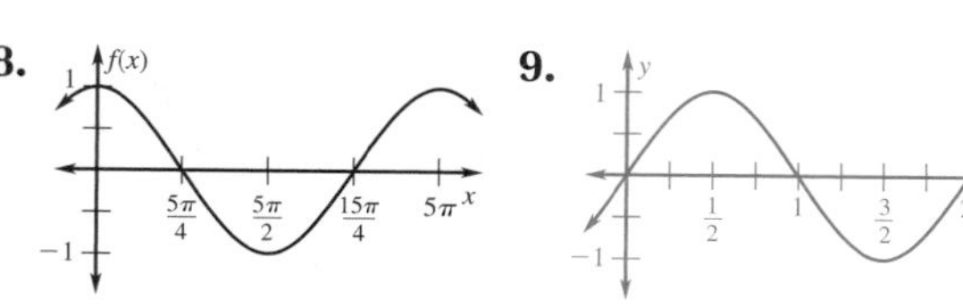

10.

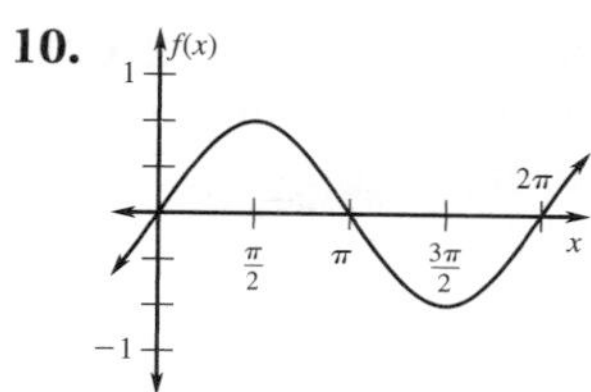

11.

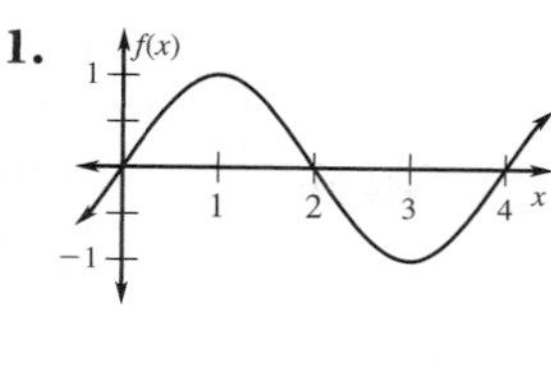

12.

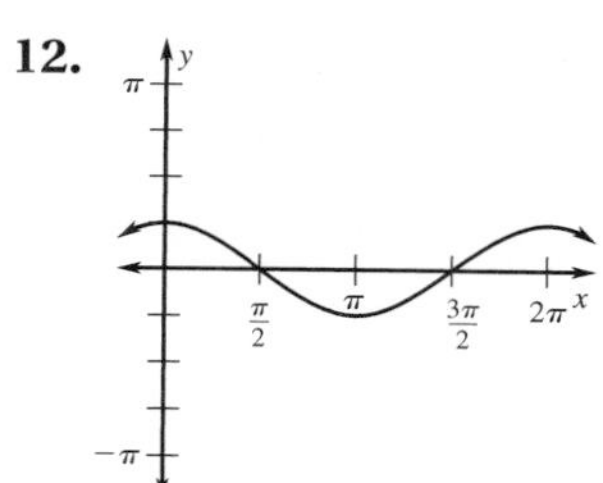

13.

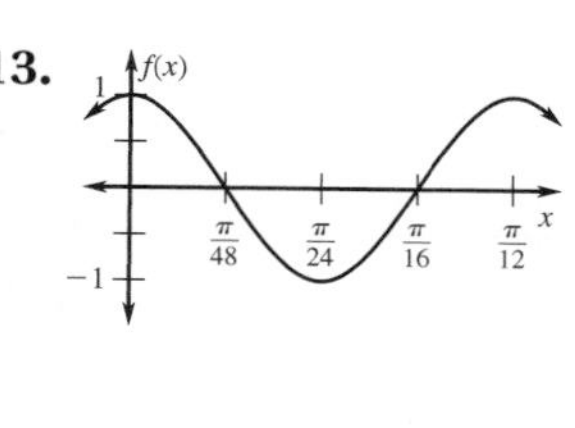

16.

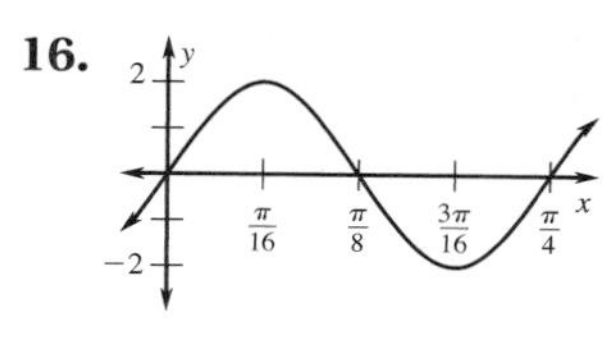

17.

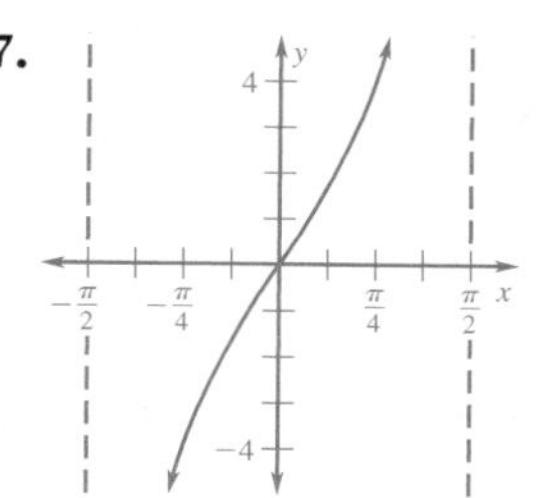

18.

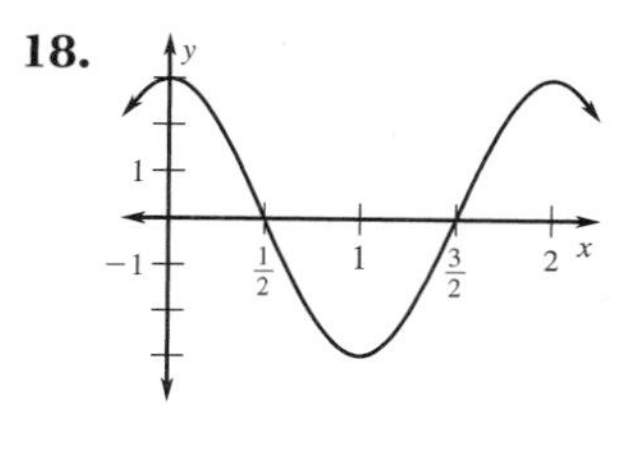

19.

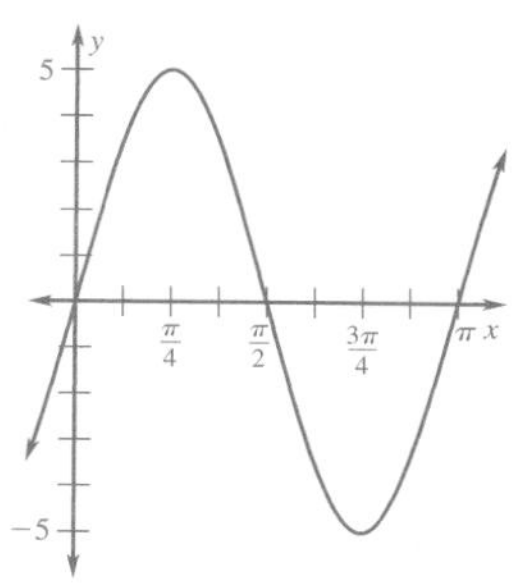

20.

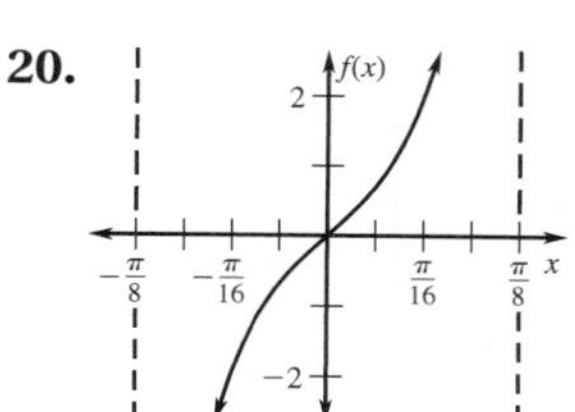

21.

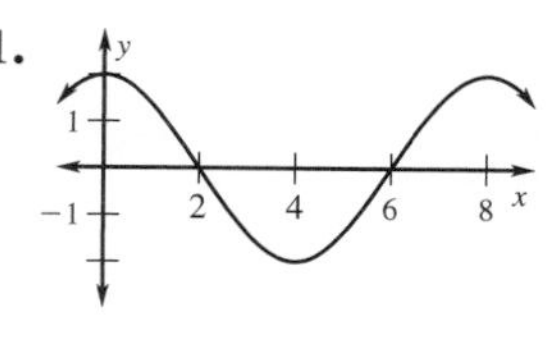

22.

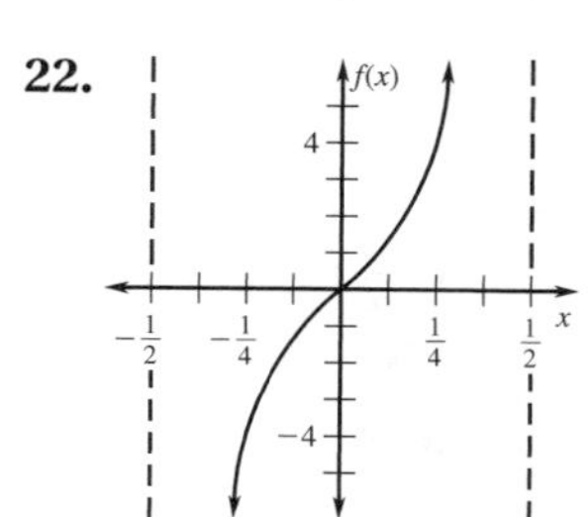

23.

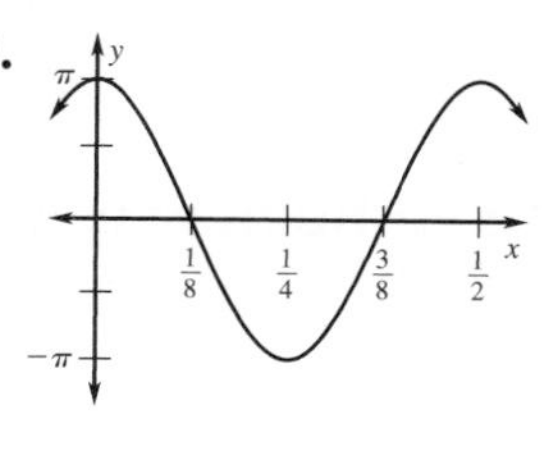

ADDITIONAL ANSWERS

26. 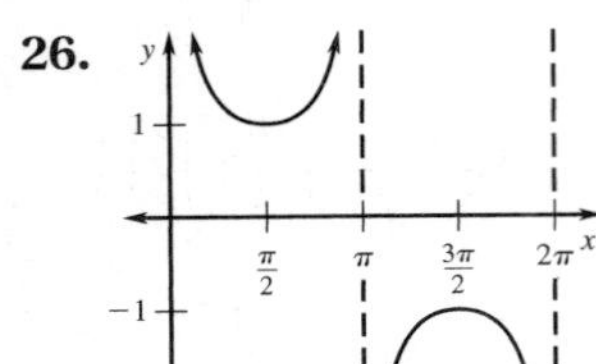

domain: all real numbers except multiples of π, range: all real numbers except $-1 < y < 1$, period: π

27. 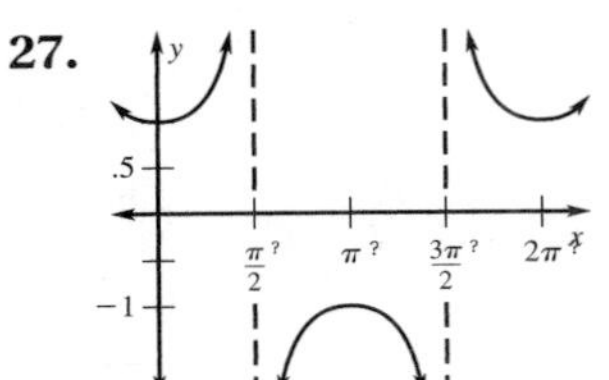

domain: all real numbers except multiples of $\frac{\pi}{2}$, range: all real numbers except $-1 \le y \le 1$, period: 2π

28. 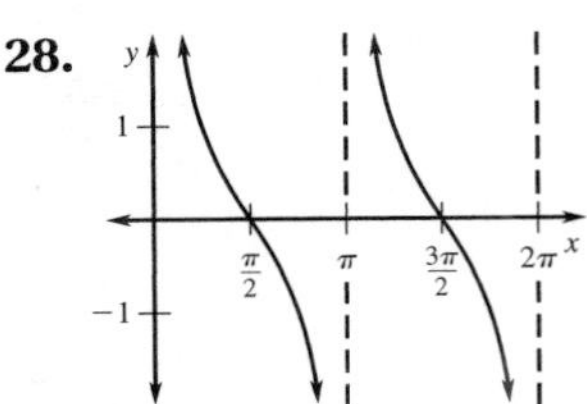

domain: all real numbers except multiples of π, range: all real numbers, period: π

14.1 Problem Solving (pp. 913–914)

32. b. 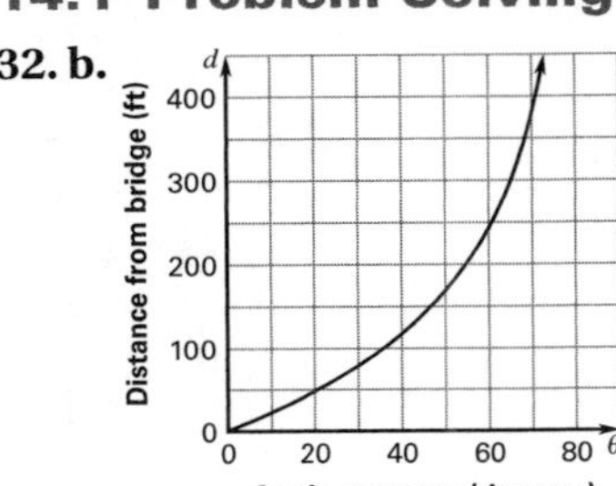

As the angle at which you are looking down at the car increases, the distance between you and the car increases.

c. 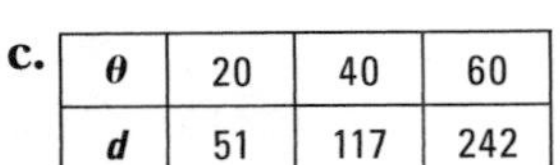

θ	20	40	60
d	51	117	242

33. a. 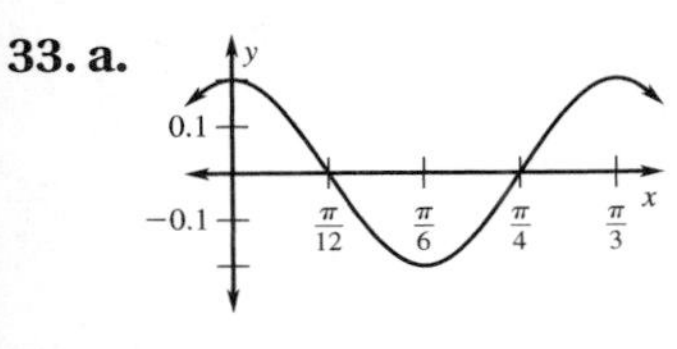

b. 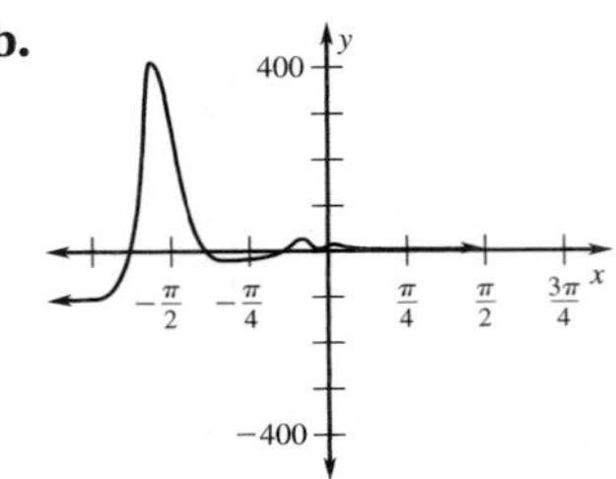

14.1 Mixed Review (p. 914)

34. 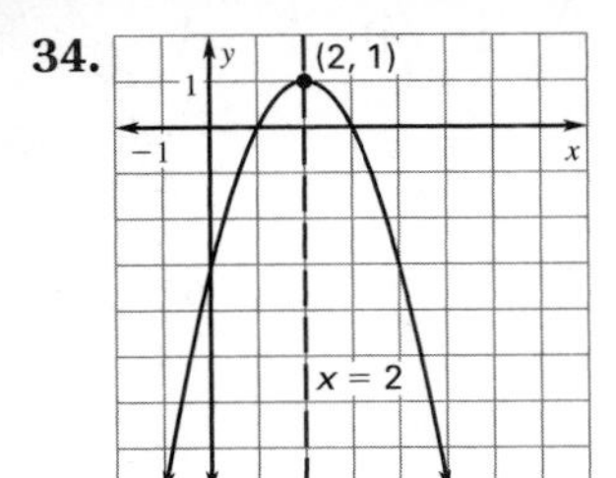

35. 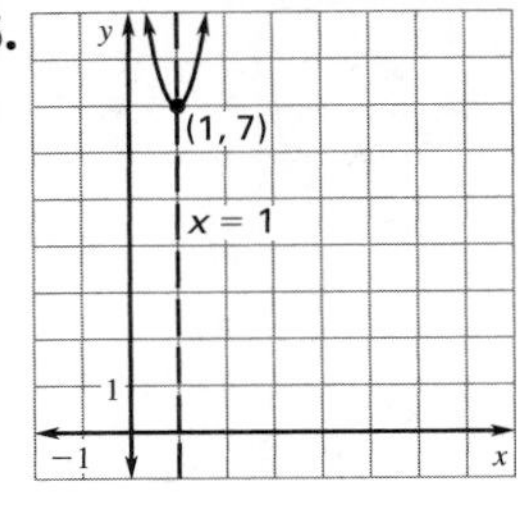

36. 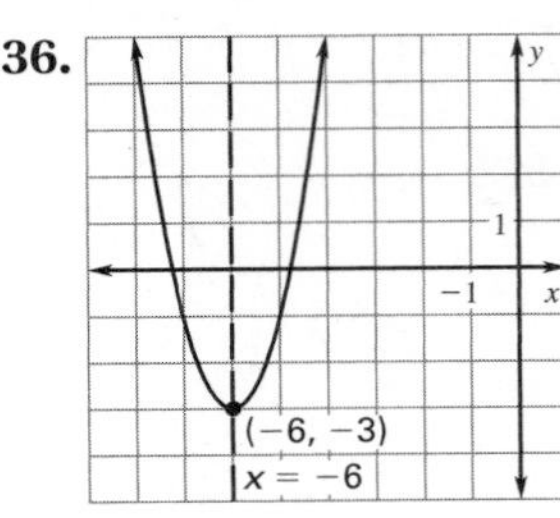

37. 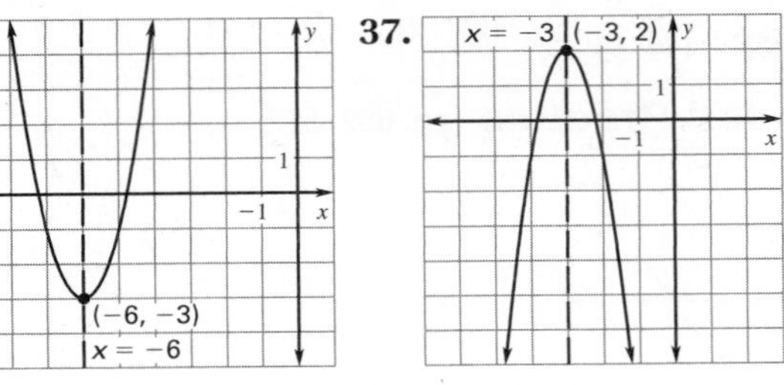

38. 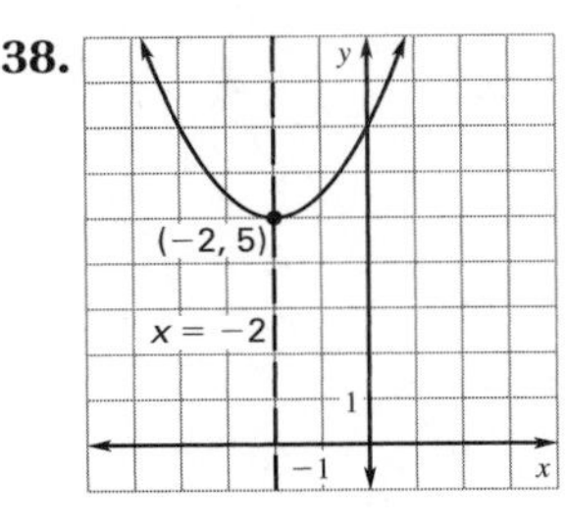

39. 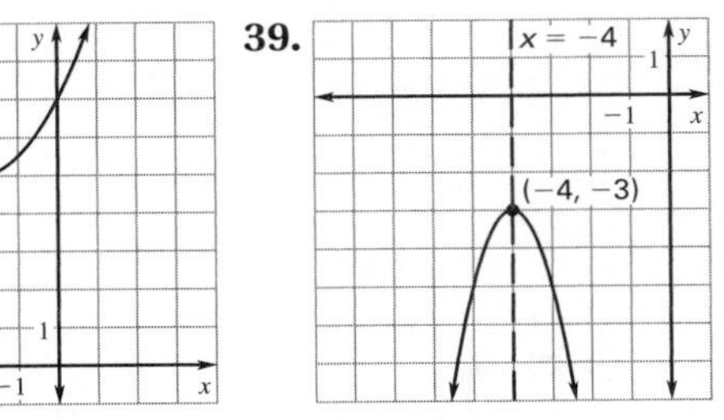

44. 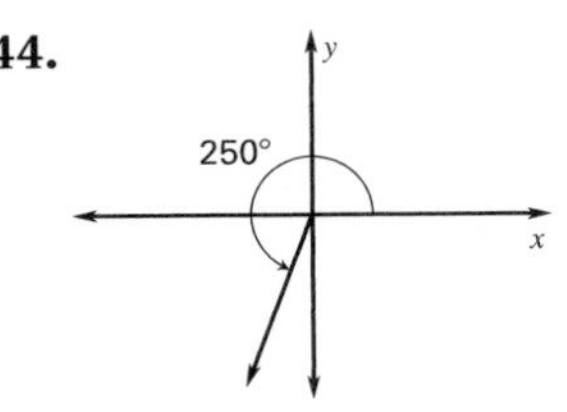

45. 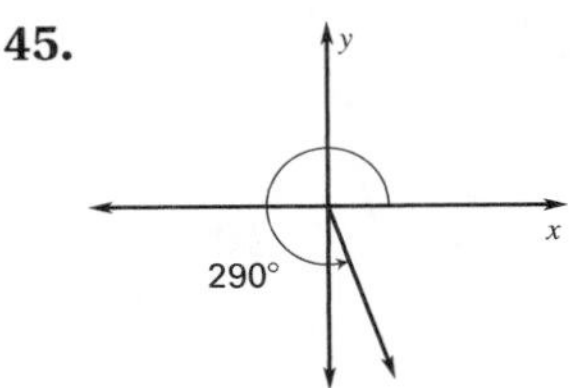

46. 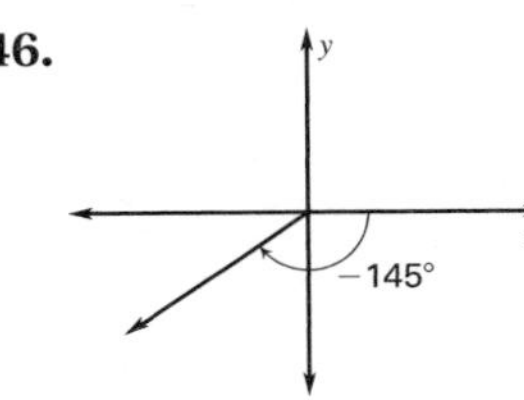

47. 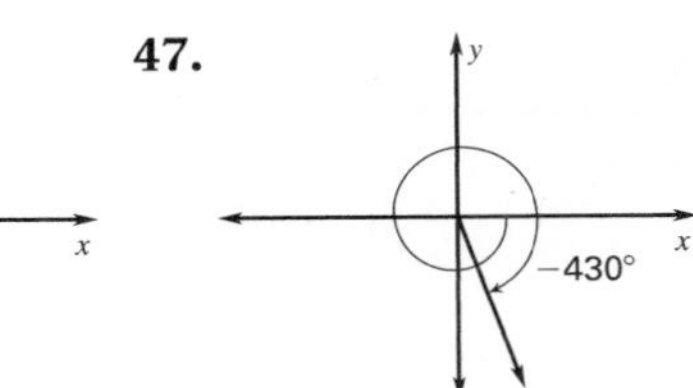

48. 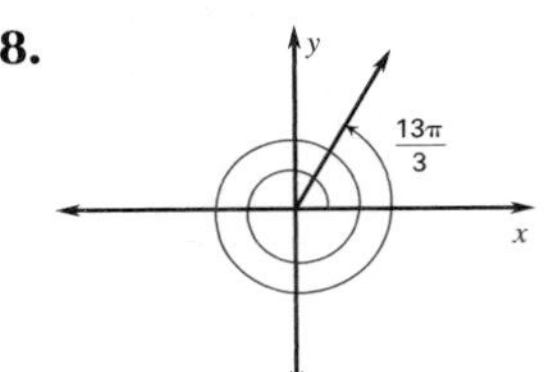

49. 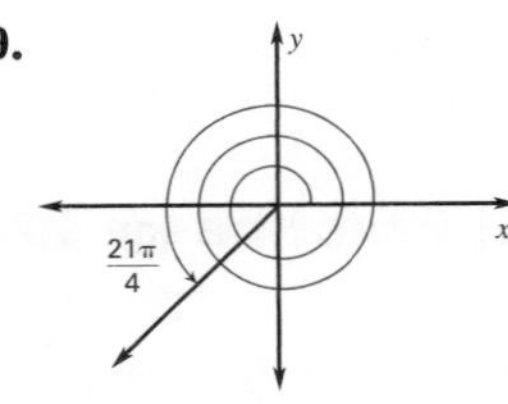

50. 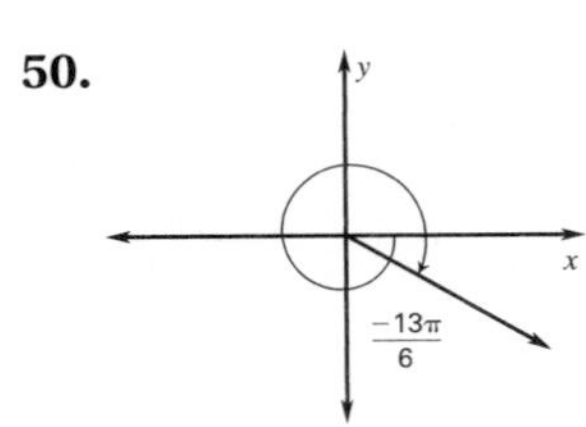

51. 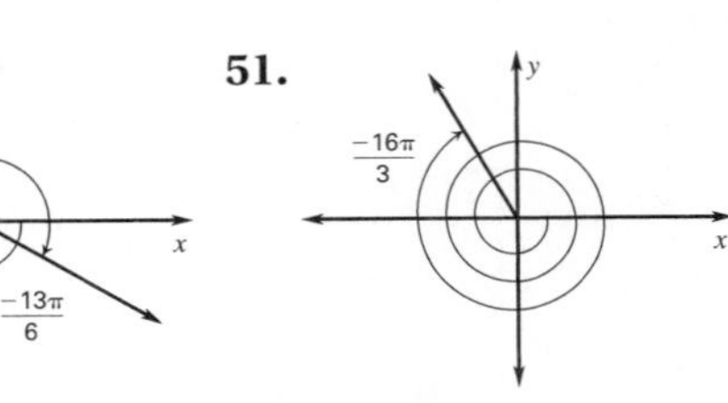

14.2 Skill Practice (pp. 919–921)

9. 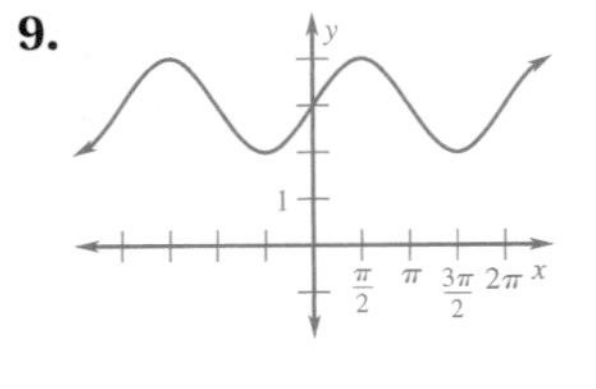

10. 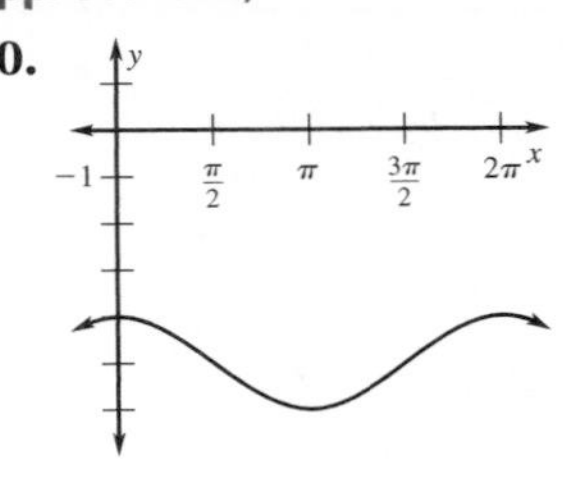

11.

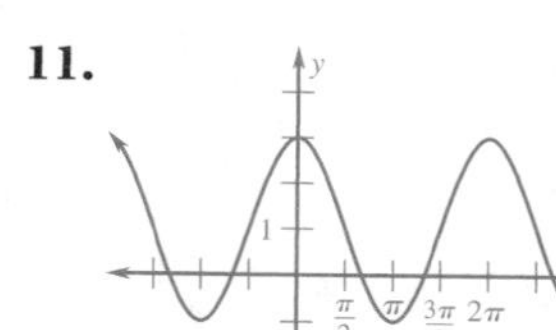

12.

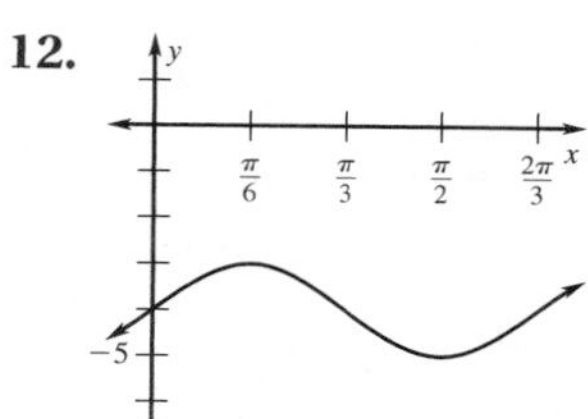

13.

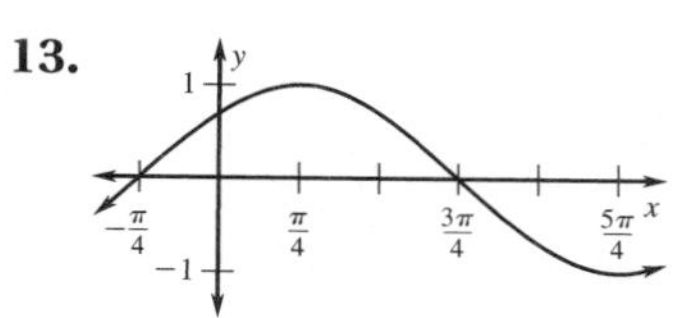

14.

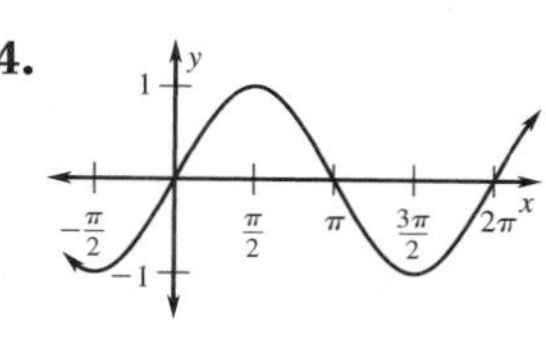

15.

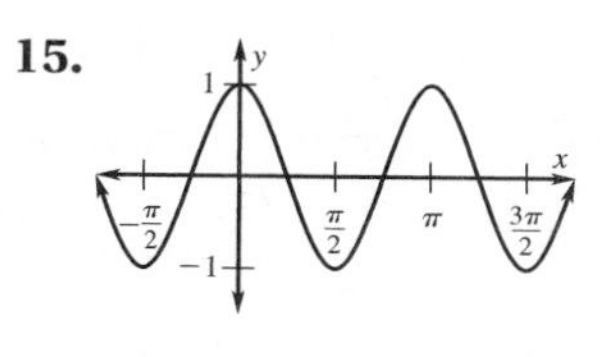

16.

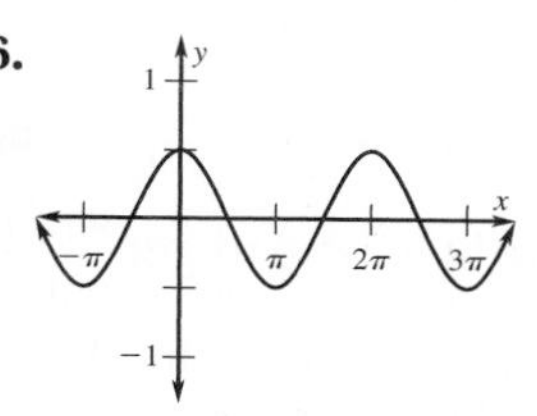

17.

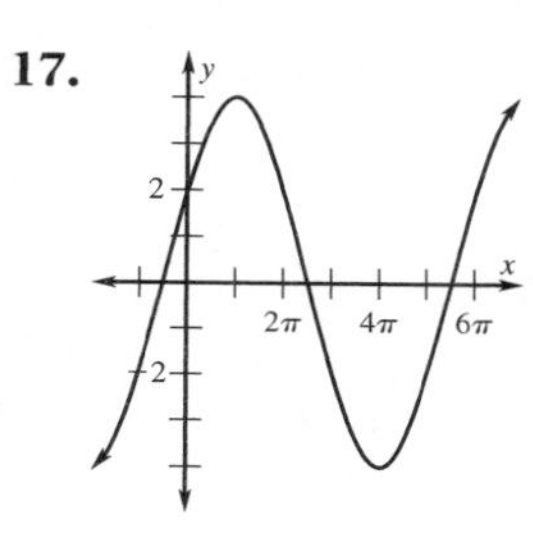

18.

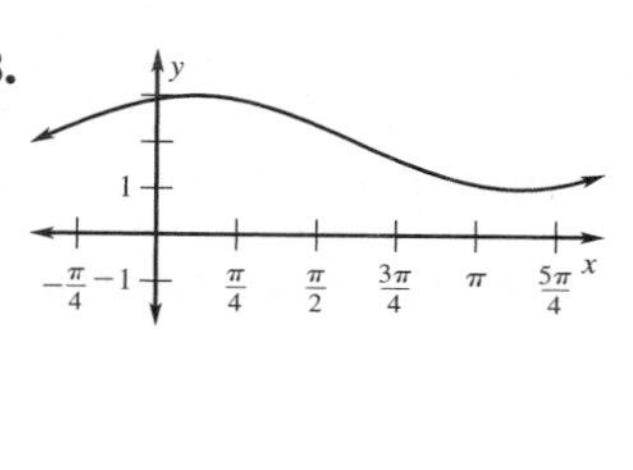

19.

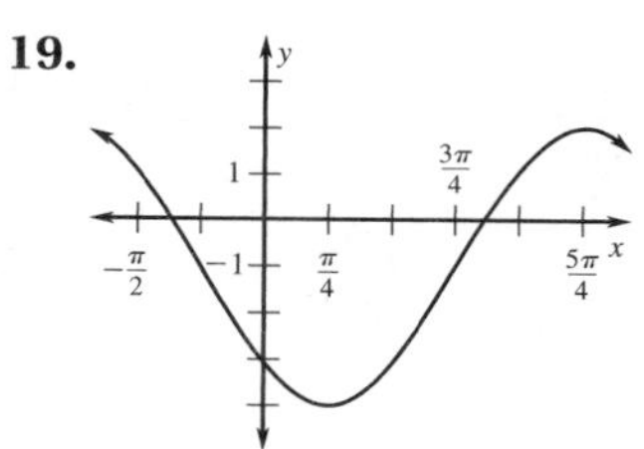

20.

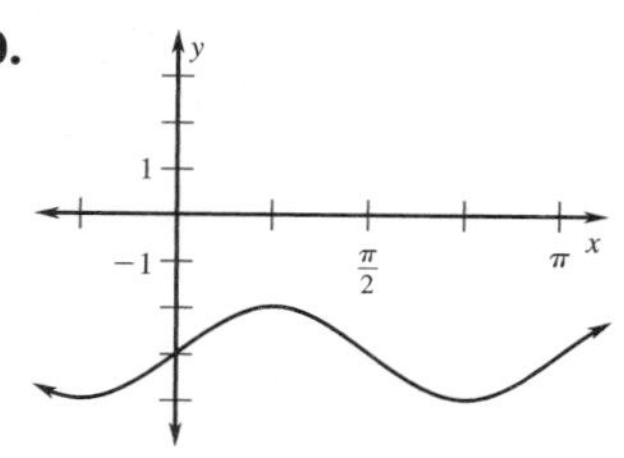

36.

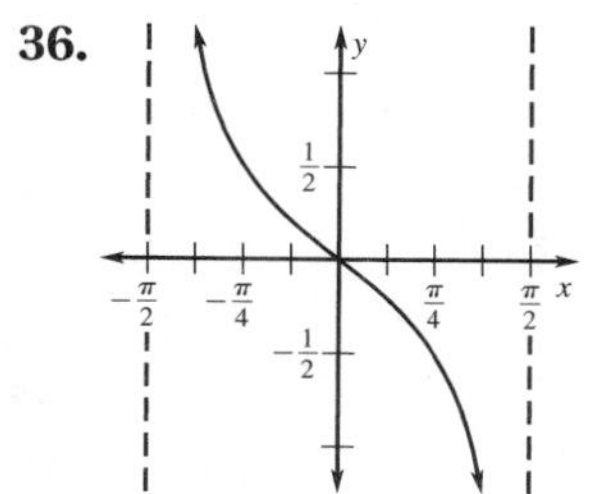

37.

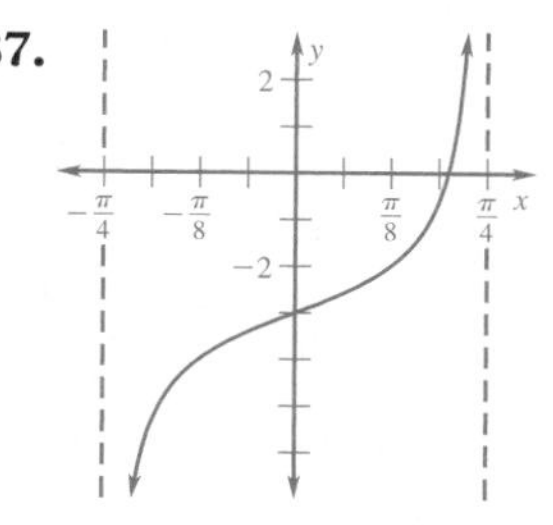

38.

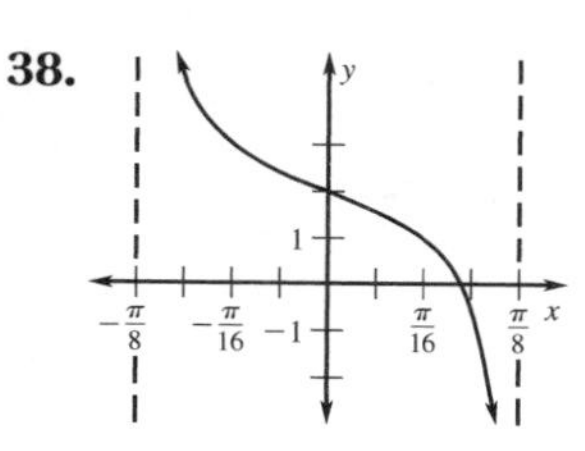

39.

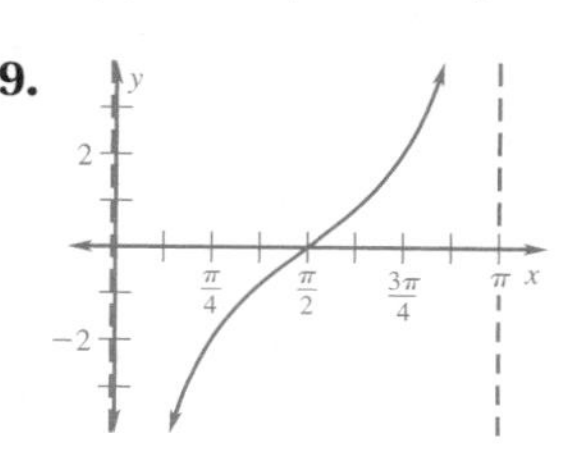

40. **41.**

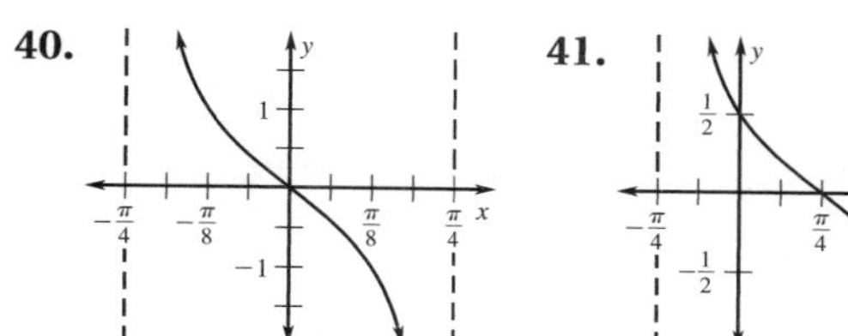

14.2 Problem Solving (pp. 921–922)

54. b.

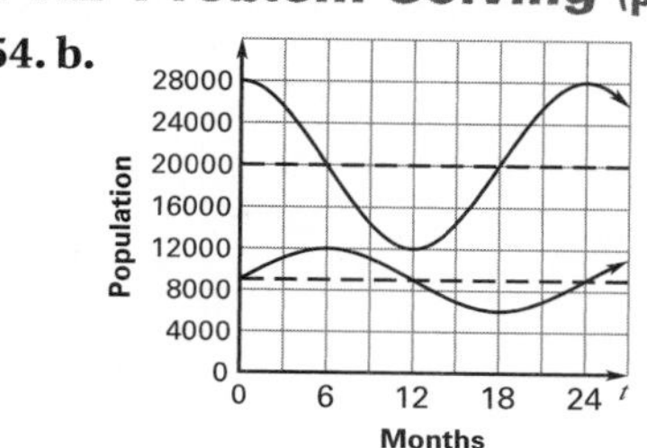

c. When the number of coyotes is at the midline and increasing, the number of rabbits decreases. Once the number of coyotes reaches a maximum and begins to decrease, the number of rabbits decreases to its minimum. At this point, the number of rabbits begins to increase to its midline and the number of coyotes starts to decrease until it reaches its minimum. The number of coyotes then starts to increase as the number of rabbits reaches its maximum.

Quiz for Lessons 14.1–14.2 (p. 922)

7.

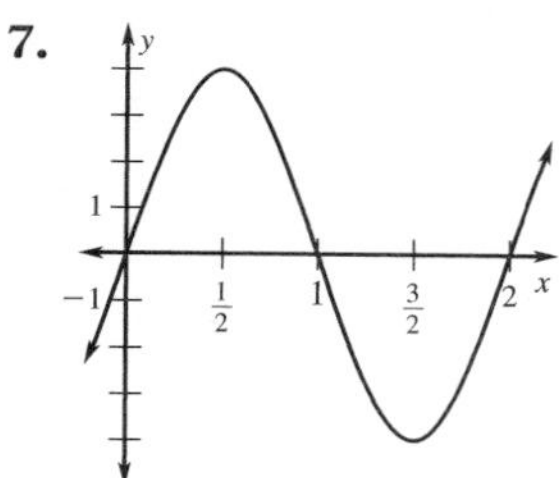

8.

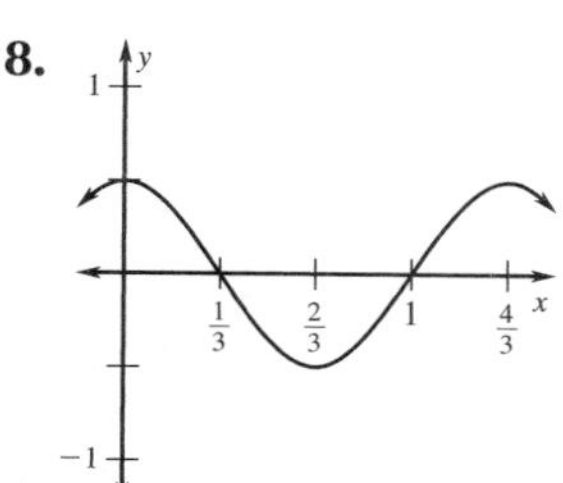

9.

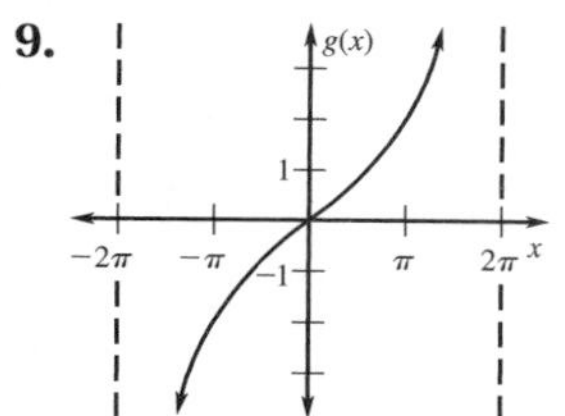

ADDITIONAL ANSWERS

10. 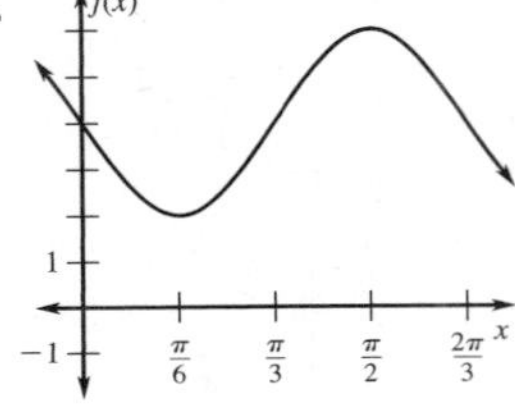

11. 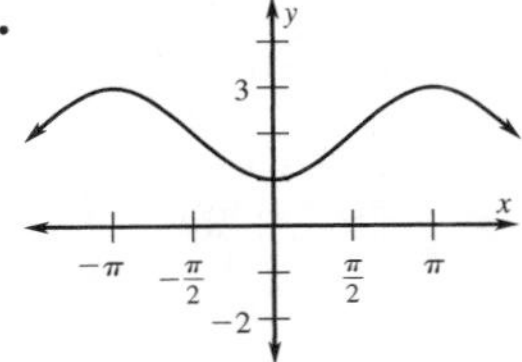

12. 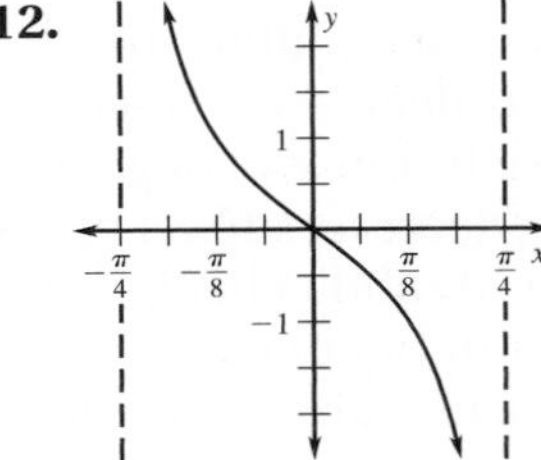

13.

14.3 Skill Practice (pp. 927–928) **3.** $\cos\theta = \frac{2\sqrt{2}}{3}$, $\tan\theta = \frac{\sqrt{2}}{4}$, $\csc\theta = 3$, $\sec\theta = \frac{3\sqrt{2}}{4}$, $\cot\theta = 2\sqrt{2}$
4. $\sin\theta = \frac{3\sqrt{58}}{58}$, $\cos\theta = \frac{7\sqrt{58}}{58}$, $\csc\theta = \frac{\sqrt{58}}{3}$, $\sec\theta = \frac{\sqrt{58}}{7}$, $\cot\theta = \frac{7}{3}$ **5.** $\sin\theta = -\frac{\sqrt{11}}{6}$, $\tan\theta = -\frac{\sqrt{11}}{5}$, $\csc\theta = -\frac{6\sqrt{11}}{11}$, $\sec\theta = \frac{6}{5}$, $\cot\theta = -\frac{5\sqrt{11}}{11}$ **6.** $\cos\theta = -\frac{\sqrt{51}}{10}$, $\tan\theta = \frac{7\sqrt{51}}{51}$, $\csc\theta = -\frac{10}{7}$, $\sec\theta = -\frac{10\sqrt{51}}{51}$, $\cot\theta = \frac{\sqrt{51}}{7}$
7. $\sin\theta = \frac{5\sqrt{29}}{29}$, $\cos\theta = -\frac{2\sqrt{29}}{29}$, $\tan\theta = -\frac{5}{2}$, $\csc\theta = \frac{\sqrt{29}}{5}$, $\sec\theta = -\frac{\sqrt{29}}{2}$ **8.** $\sin\theta = \frac{\sqrt{65}}{9}$, $\cos\theta = -\frac{4}{9}$, $\tan\theta = -\frac{\sqrt{65}}{4}$, $\csc\theta = \frac{9\sqrt{65}}{65}$, $\cot\theta = -\frac{4\sqrt{65}}{65}$ **38.** $\sin^2\theta + \cos^2\theta = 1$, divide everything by $\cos^2\theta$ to get $\frac{\sin^2\theta}{\sin^2\theta} + \frac{\cos^2\theta}{\sin^2\theta} = \frac{1}{\sin^2\theta}$, further simplifying yields the identity $\tan^2\theta + 1 = \sec^2\theta$. Taking the original Pythagorean identity and divide everything by $\sin^2\theta$ you get $\frac{\sin^2\theta}{\sin^2\theta} + \frac{\cos^2\theta}{\sin^2\theta} = \frac{1}{\sin^2\theta}$, which when simplified results in $1 + \cot^2\theta = \csc^2\theta$.

14.3 Problem Solving (pp. 929–930)

39. $\sec x \tan x - \sin x = \frac{1}{\cos x} \cdot \frac{\sin x}{\cos x} - \sin x = \frac{\sin x}{\cos^2 x} - \frac{\sin x \cos^2 x}{\cos^2 x} = \frac{\sin x - \sin x \cos^2 x}{\cos^2 x} = \frac{\sin x(1 - \cos^2 x)}{\cos^2 x} = \frac{\sin x(\sin^2 x)}{\cos^2 x} = \sin x \tan^2 x$

41. b.

c.

θ	0	$\frac{\pi}{4}$	$\frac{\pi}{2}$	$\frac{3\pi}{4}$	π	$\frac{5\pi}{4}$	$\frac{3\pi}{2}$
r	35.6	3.40	1.07	0.634	0.542	0.634	1.07

about 500,000 mi, about 3,310,800,000 mi

ADDITIONAL ANSWERS

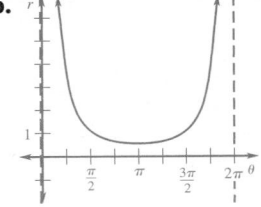

44. a. $\dfrac{n_1}{\sqrt{\cot^2\theta_1 + 1}} = \dfrac{n_2}{\sqrt{\cot^2\theta_2 + 1}}$

$$\frac{n_1}{\sqrt{\csc^2\theta_1}} = \frac{n_2}{\sqrt{\csc^2\theta_2}}$$

$$\frac{n_1}{\csc\theta_1} = \frac{n_2}{\csc\theta_2}$$

$$n_1 \sin\theta_1 = n_2 \sin\theta_2$$

45. a. $\sin^2\theta_2 + \cos^2\theta_2 = \left(\dfrac{n_1}{n_2}\sin\theta_1\right)^2 + \left(\dfrac{n_2}{n_1}\cos\theta_1\right)^2$

$$1 = \frac{n_1^2}{n_2^2}\sin^2\theta_1 + \frac{n_2^2}{n_1^2}\cos^2\theta_1$$

b. $1 = \dfrac{n_1^2}{n_2^2}\sin\theta_1 + \dfrac{n_2^2}{n_1^2}\cos^2\theta_1$

$$\frac{n_2^2}{n_2^2} - \frac{n_1^2}{n_2^2}\sin^2\theta_1 = \frac{n_2^2}{n_1^2}\cos^2\theta_1$$

$$\frac{n_2^2 - n_1^2}{n_2^2}\sin^2\theta_1 = \frac{n_2^2 - n_1^2}{n_1^2}\cos^2\theta_1$$

c. $\dfrac{n_2^2 - n_1^2}{n_2^2}\sin^2\theta_1 = \dfrac{n_2^2 - n_1^2}{n_1^2}\cos^2\theta_1$

$$\left(\frac{n_1^2}{n_2^2 - n_1^2}\right)\left(\frac{n_2^2 - n_1^2}{n_2^2}\right)\left(\frac{\sin^2\theta}{\cos^2\theta}\right) = 1$$

$$\frac{n_1^2}{n_2^2}\tan^2\theta = 1$$

$$\tan^2\theta = \frac{n_2^2}{n_1^2}$$

$$\tan\theta = \frac{n_2}{n_1}$$

$$\theta = \tan^{-1}\left(\frac{n_2}{n_1}\right)$$

14.6 Problem Solving (pp. 953–954)

42. $y_1 + y_2 = A\cos\left(\dfrac{2\pi t}{3} - \dfrac{2\pi x}{5}\right) + A\cos\left(\dfrac{2\pi t}{3} + \dfrac{2\pi x}{5}\right)$

$= A\left(\cos\dfrac{2\pi t}{3}\cos\dfrac{2\pi x}{5} + \sin\dfrac{2\pi t}{3}\sin\dfrac{2\pi x}{5}\right)$

$+ A\left(\cos\dfrac{2\pi t}{3}\cos\dfrac{2\pi x}{5} - \sin\dfrac{2\pi t}{3}\sin\dfrac{2\pi x}{5}\right)$

$= A\cos\dfrac{2\pi t}{3}\cos\dfrac{2\pi x}{5} + A\sin\dfrac{2\pi t}{3}\sin\dfrac{2\pi x}{5}$

$+ A\cos\dfrac{2\pi t}{3}\cos\dfrac{2\pi x}{5} - A\sin\dfrac{2\pi t}{3}\sin\dfrac{2\pi x}{5}$

$= A\cos\dfrac{2\pi t}{3}\cos\dfrac{2\pi x}{5} + A\cos\dfrac{2\pi t}{3}\cos\dfrac{2\pi x}{5}$

$= 2A\cos\dfrac{2\pi t}{3}\cos\dfrac{2\pi x}{5}$

44. b. $y = 5(\sin 2t\cos C + \cos 2t\sin C)$ and substituting in the results from part (a) yields $y = 5\left(\sin 2t \cdot \dfrac{4}{5} + \cos 2t \cdot \dfrac{3}{5}\right)$.

c.

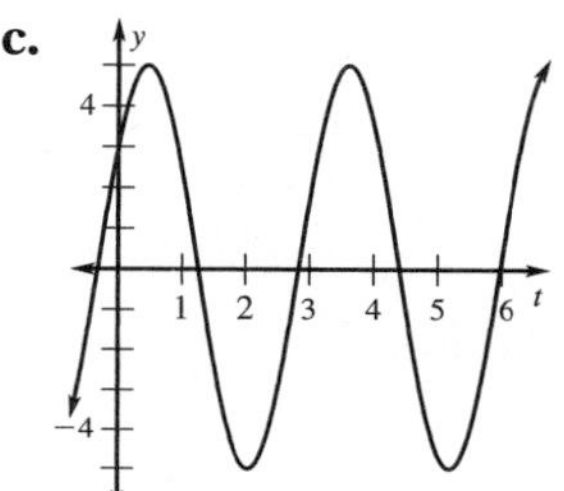

5 in.; this is the maximum distance that the spring gets from the ceiling.

45. $y_1 + y_2 = \cos 960\pi t + \cos 1240\pi t$

$= \cos(1100\pi t - 140\pi t) + \cos(1100\pi t + 140\pi t)$

$= \cos 1100\pi t\cos 140\pi t + \sin 1100\pi t\sin 140\pi t$

$+ \cos 1100\pi t\cos 140\pi t - \sin 1100\pi t\sin 140\pi t$

$= \cos 1100\pi t\cos 140\pi t + \cos 1100\pi t\cos 140\pi t$

$= 2\cos 1100\pi t\cos 140\pi t$

14.7 Problem Solving (pp. 961–962)

54. a. $y = r\ln\left[\tan\left(\dfrac{\frac{\pi}{2} + L}{2}\right)\right] = r\ln\left[\dfrac{1 - \cos\left(\frac{\pi}{2} + L\right)}{\sin\left(\frac{\pi}{2} + L\right)}\right]$

$= r\ln\left[\dfrac{1 - \left(\cos\frac{\pi}{2}\cos L - \sin\frac{\pi}{2}\sin L\right)}{\sin\frac{\pi}{2}\cos L + \cos\frac{\pi}{2}\sin L}\right]$

$= r\ln\left[\dfrac{1 + \sin L}{\cos L}\right]$

Quiz for Lessons 14.6–14.7 (p. 962)

7. $\sqrt{\dfrac{34 - 5\sqrt{34}}{68}}, \sqrt{\dfrac{34 + 5\sqrt{34}}{68}}, \dfrac{\sqrt{34} - 5}{3}$

ADDITIONAL ANSWERS

Extra Practice

Chapter 2 (p. 1011)

29. a–b.

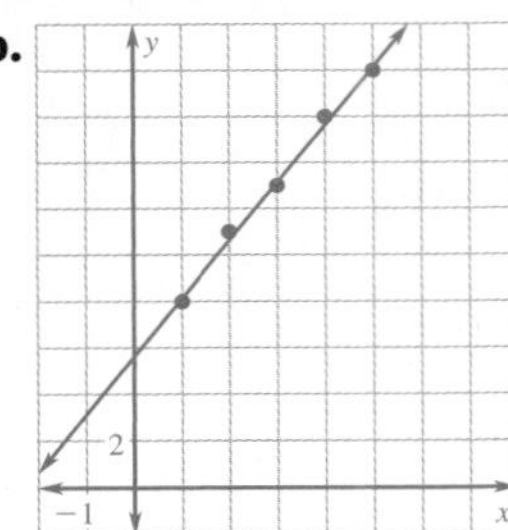

30. a–b.

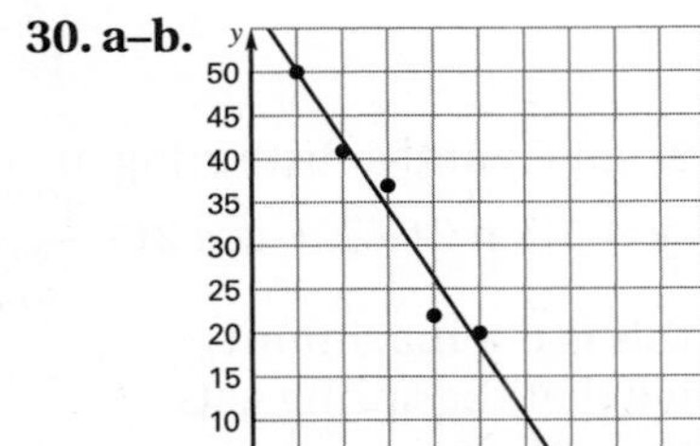

31.

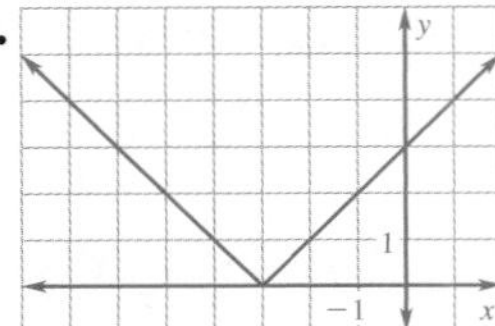

shifted left 3 units

32.

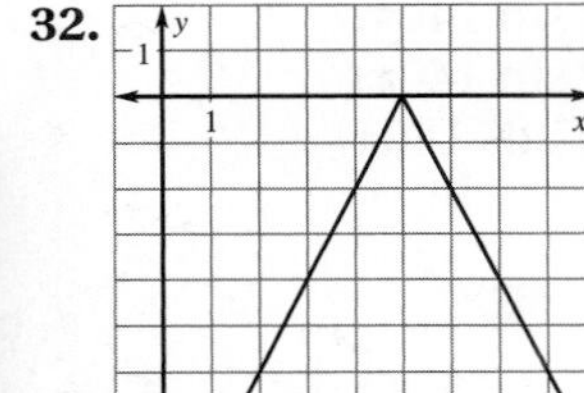

reflected in the x-axis, shifted right 5 units, and stretched vertically by a factor of 2

33.

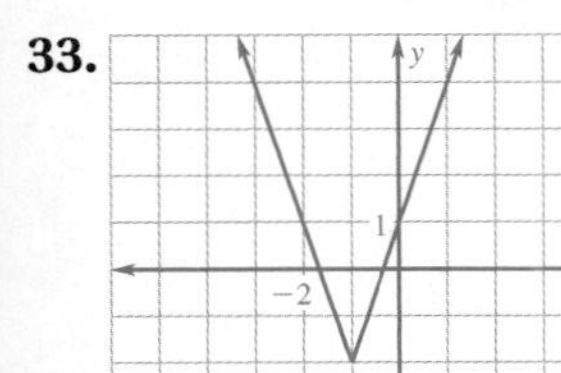

shifted down 2 units, left 1 unit, and stretched vertically by a factor of 3

34.

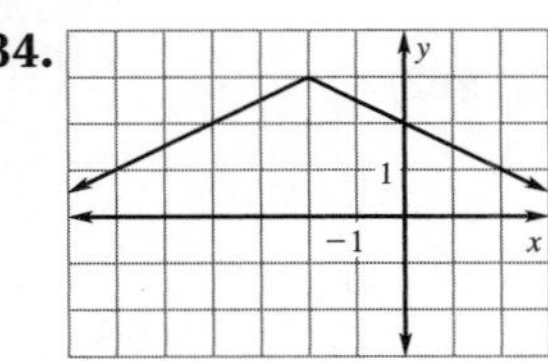

reflected in the x-axis, shifted up 3 units, left 2 units, and shrunk vertically by a factor of $\frac{1}{2}$

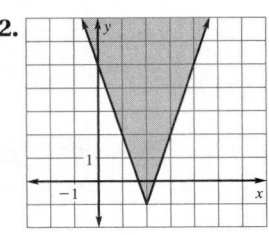

35.

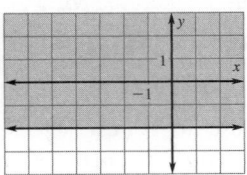

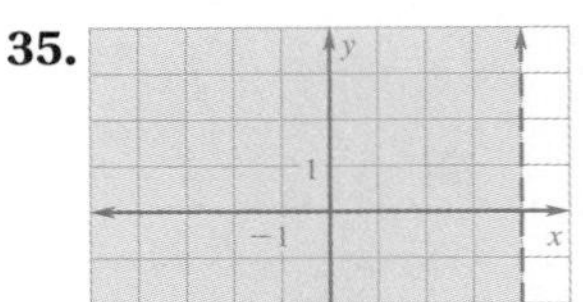

36.

37.

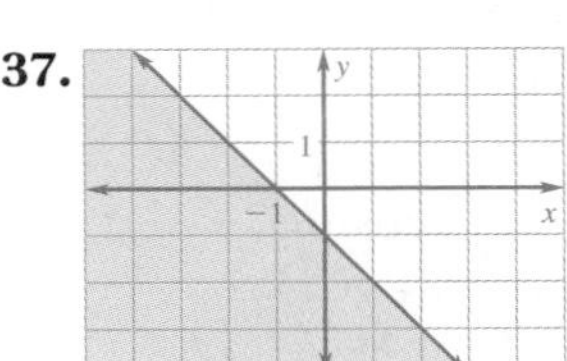

38.

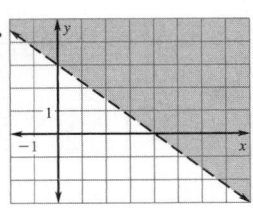

39.

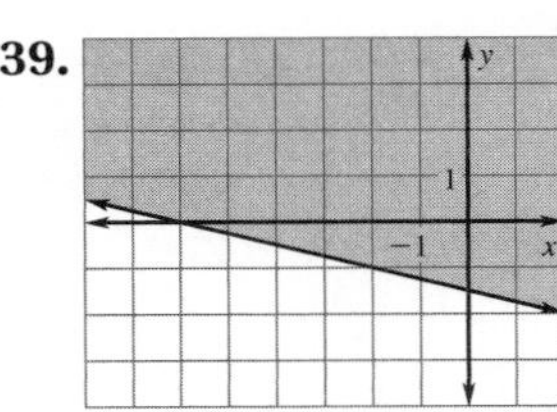

40.

41.

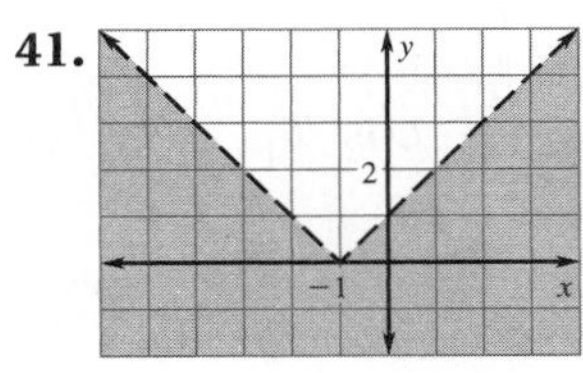

42.

Chapter 6 (p. 1015)

32. $f(g(x)) = 2\left(\frac{1}{2}x + 2\right) - 4 = x + 4 - 4 = x,$

$g(f(x)) = \frac{1}{2}(2x - 4) + 2 = x - 2 + 2 = x$

33. $f(g(x)) = 3\left(\left(\frac{x-1}{3}\right)^{1/2}\right)^2 + 1 = x - 1 + 1 = x,$

$g(f(x)) = \left(\frac{(3x^2 + 1) - 1}{3}\right)^{1/2} = \left(\frac{3x^2}{3}\right)^{1/2} = x$

Chapter 7 (p. 1016)

13.

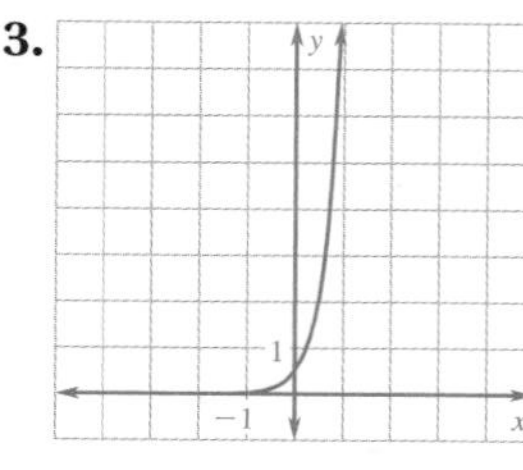

14.

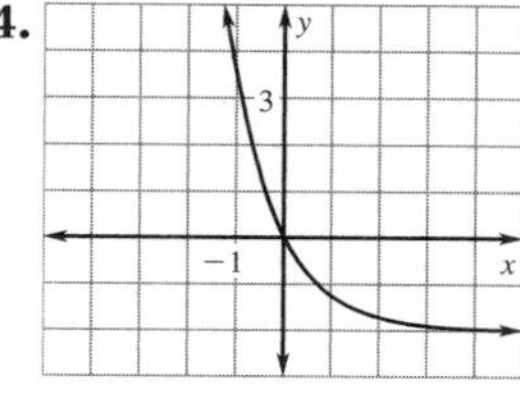

15.

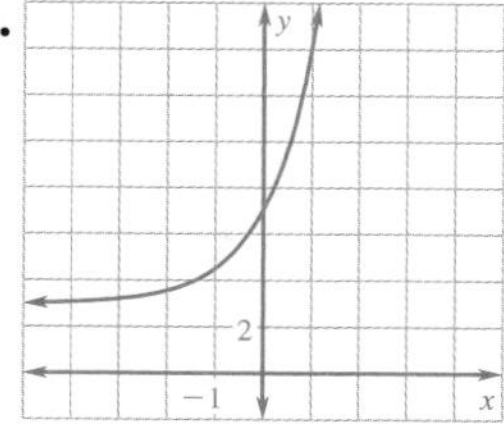

16.

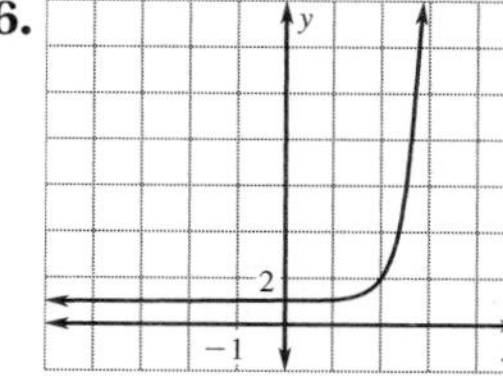

25.

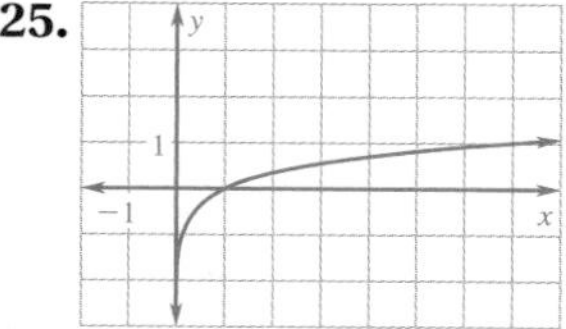

26.

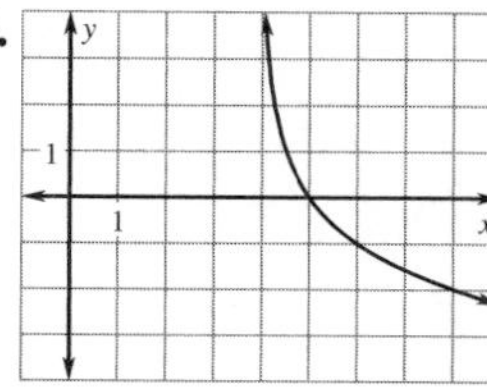

27.

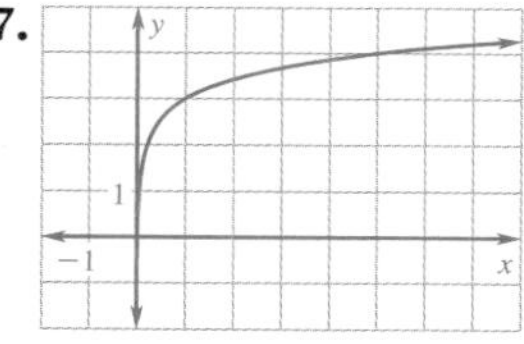

28.

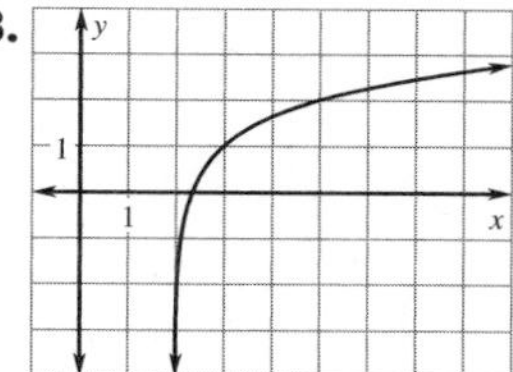

Chapter 9 (p. 1018)

25.

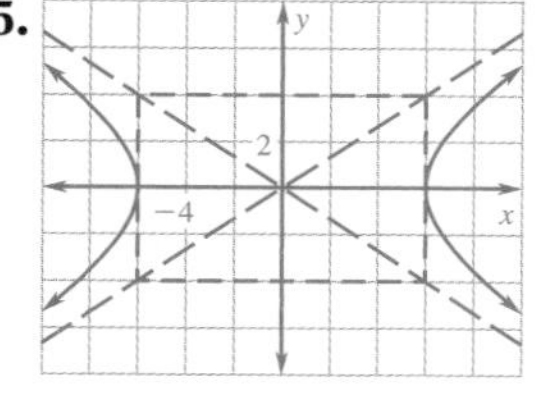

26.

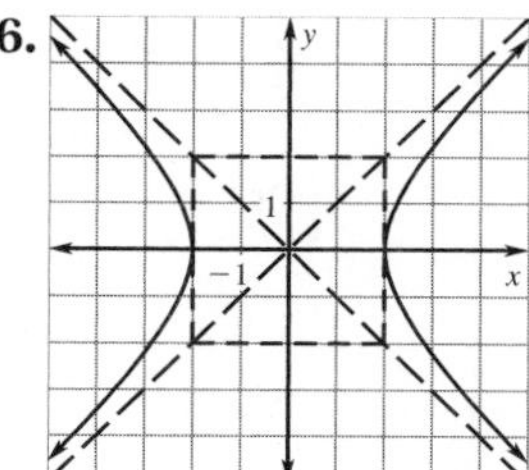

27.

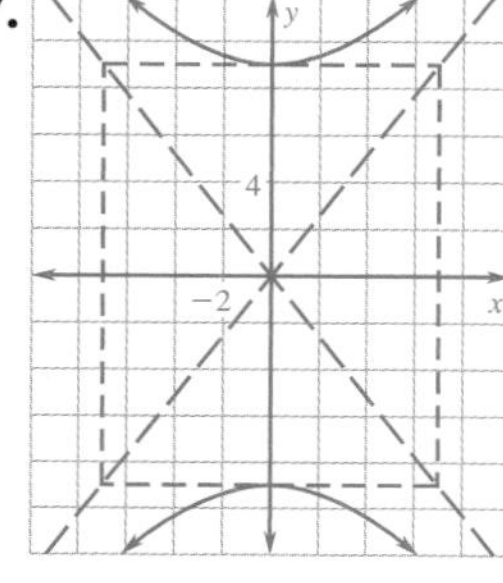

31.

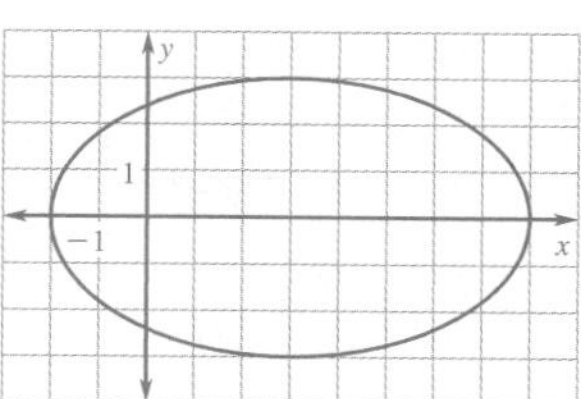

center: (3, 0),
vertices: (−2, 0), (8, 0),
co-vertices: (3, 3), (3, −3),
foci: (−1, 0), (7, 0)

32.

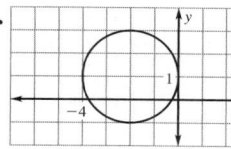

center: (−2, 1), radius: 2

33.

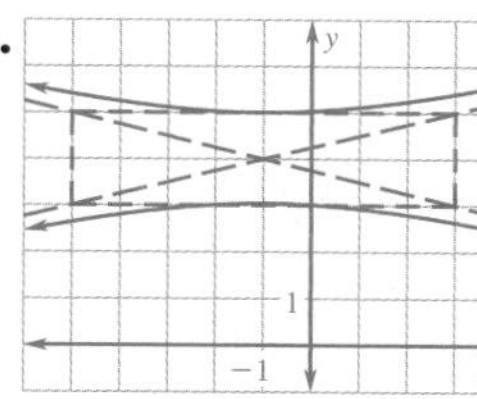

center: (−1, 4),
vertices: (−1, 5), (−1, 3),
foci: $\left(-1, 4 + \sqrt{17}\right), \left(-1, 4 - \sqrt{17}\right)$,
asymptotes: $y = \pm\frac{1}{4}x$

34.

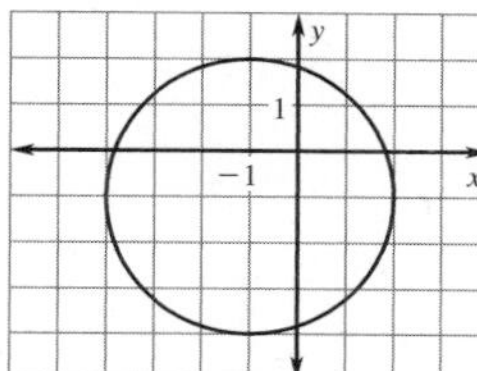

35.

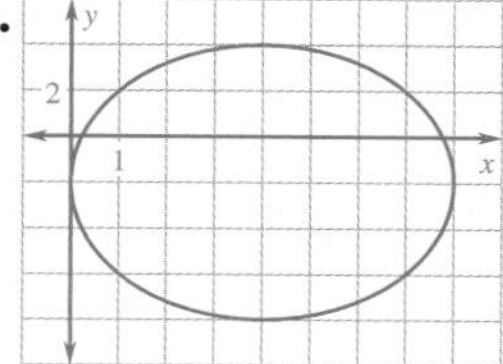

36.

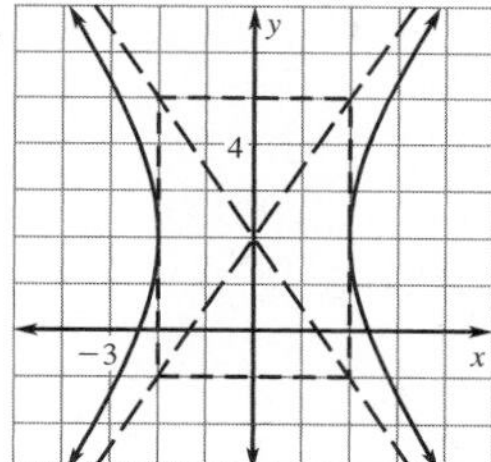

37.

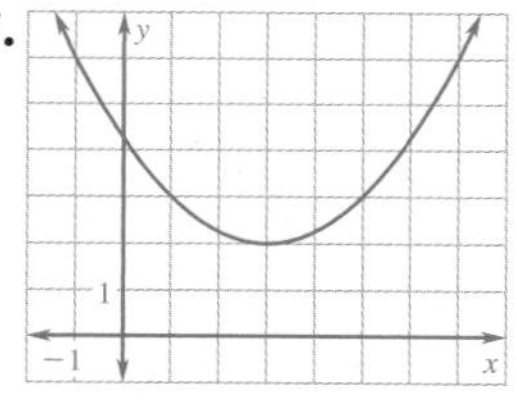

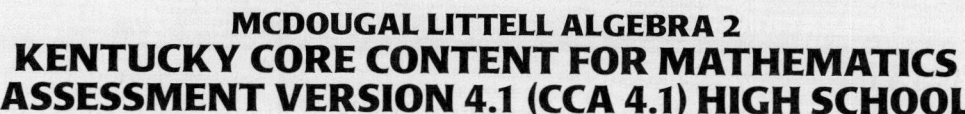

MCDOUGAL LITTELL ALGEBRA 2

KENTUCKY CORE CONTENT FOR MATHEMATICS ASSESSMENT VERSION 4.1 (CCA 4.1) HIGH SCHOOL

Number Properties and Operations

High school students should enter high school with a strong background in rational numbers and numerical operations and expand this to real numbers. This becomes the foundation for algebra and working with algebraic symbols. They understand large and small numbers and their representations, powers and roots. They compare and contrast properties of numbers and number systems and develop strategies to estimate the results of operations on real numbers. Students will use, and understand the limitations of, graphing calculators and computer spreadsheets appropriately as learning tools.

NUMBER SENSE

MA-HS-1.1.1
Students will compare real numbers using order relations (less than, greater than, equal to) and represent problems using real numbers.

PE/TE: *Opportunities to address this standard can be found on the following pages:* 2-3, 6 (#3-10), 8 (#57-59), 16 (Quiz #1-3), 33 (#3), 65 (#1-2), 742 (#3-4), 1010 (#1-3)

MA-HS-1.1.2
Students will demonstrate the relationships between different subsets of the real number system.

PE/TE: 2 (Key Concept)

MA-HS-1.1.3
Students will use scientific notation to express very large or very small quantities.

PE/TE: 331 (Example 2), 333 (#15-23), 334 (#49-50), 369 (#1), 402 (#10), 904 (#1), 982, 1014 (#1-3)

ESTIMATION

MA-HS-1.2.1
Students will estimate solutions to problems with real numbers (including very large and very small quantities) in both real-world and mathematical problems, and use the estimations to check for reasonable computational results.

PE/TE: 91, 96 (Quiz #9), 153, 156 (#3-14), 335 (#53b), 390 (#15-20), 416 (Example 5, Guided Practice 19), 480 (Example 4, Guided Practice 4), 484 (#35b, 36b, 39c), 485 (#41b), 488 (Example 4, Guided Practice 7), 490 (#31c), 491 (#33a, 35c), 494 (Example 4, Guided Practice 9), 497 (#59b), 498 (Quiz #12), 543 (#29b), 557 (#41b), 781, 870 (Example 6, Guided Practice 10), 887 (#44), 904 (#1)

Key:
Bold – State Assessment Content Standard
Italics – Supporting Content Standard
Plain Text – ADP Benchmarks Supporting Content Standard

NUMBER OPERATIONS

MA-HS-1.3.1
Students will solve real-world and mathematical problems to specified accuracy levels by simplifying expressions with real numbers involving addition, subtraction, multiplication, division, absolute value, integer exponents, roots (square, cube) and factorials. DOK 2

PE/TE: 983

MA-HS-1.3.2
Students will:

- **describe and extend arithmetic and geometric sequences;**
- **determine a specific term of a sequence given an explicit formula;**
- **determine an explicit rule for the nth term of an arithmetic sequence and**
- **apply sequences to solve real-world problems.**

DOK 3

PE/TE: 802-804, 805 (Example 6a), 806, 807 (#30-39, 49-51, 62), 808 (#63a, 64, -65a, 66), 809 (#68-69), 810, 813 (Example 6, Guided Practice 8), 814 (#1-14), 815 (#55, 57-58), 816 (#59, 61), 817 (Quiz #1, 3, 5, 13-15), 818 (#2-4, 6), 838 (#2), 839 (Big Idea 1), 841 (Example 12.2, #9-11), 843 (#1-6, 9, 33), 845, 846 (#3-4, 6), 847 (#14), 848 (#41-42), 849 (#51), 1021 (#10-18)

MA-HS-1.3.3
Students will write an explicit rule for the nth term of a geometric sequence.

PE/TE: 811-812, 814 (#15-38), 815 (#39-47, 57a, 58a), 816 (59, 61a), 817 (Quiz #2, 4, 6, 13-16), 818 (#6), 839 (Big Idea 1), 841 (Example 12.3, #17-19), 843 (#10, 33), 844, 846 (#4), 848 (#43), 1021 (#19-21)

MA-HS-1.3.4
Students will recognize and solve problems that can be modeled using a finite geometric series, such as home mortgage problems and other compound interest problems.

PE/TE: 813 (Example 6b), 815 (#57b, 58b), 816 (#61), 817 (#62)

Key:
Bold – State Assessment Content Standard
Italics – Supporting Content Standard
Plain Text – ADP Benchmarks Supporting Content Standard

RATIOS AND PROPORTIONAL REASONING

MA-HS-1.4.1
Students will apply ratios, percents and proportional reasoning to solve real-world problems (e.g., those involving slope and rate, percent of increase and decrease) and will explain how slope determines a rate of change in linear functions representing real-world problems. DOK 2

PE/TE: 5, 7 (#25-48), 8 (#60), 9 (#61-63), 24 (#79-80), 40 (#35), 82 (Example 1), 83 (Guided Practice 1), 85, 87 (#41-45), 88 (#46-49), 111 (#46-47), 148 (#5), 149 (#16), 173 (#42), 202 (#46), 251 (#57), 265 (#70), 274 (#4), 377 (#52), 464 (#1), 491 (#38), 580 (#55), 679 (#47), 680 (#2), 689 (#73), 849 (#47), 1010 (#4-6)

PROPERTIES OF NUMBERS AND OPERATIONS

MA-HS-1.5.1
Students will identify real number properties (commutative properties of addition and multiplication, associative properties of addition and multiplication, distributive property of multiplication over addition and subtraction, identity properties of addition and multiplication and inverse properties of addition and multiplication) when used to justify a given step in simplifying an expression or solving an equation.

PE/TE: 3 (Key Concept), 4 (Example 4, Guided Practice 7-8), 6 (#17-22), 12 (Example 4), 13 (Example 5), 20, 62 (Examples 1.2, 1.3), 65 (#3-4)

MA-HS-1.5.2
Students will use equivalence relations (reflexive, symmetric, transitive).

PE/TE: *Not addressed in this text.*

Key:
Bold – State Assessment Content Standard
Italics – Supporting Content Standard
Plain Text – ADP Benchmarks Supporting Content Standard

CORRELATIONS

Measurement

High school students continue to measure and estimate measurements including fractions and decimals. They use formulas to find surface area and volume. They use U.S. Customary and metric units of measurement. They use the Pythagorean theorem and other right triangle relationships to solve real-world problems.

Measuring Physical Attributes

MA-HS-2.1.1
Students will determine the surface area and volume of right rectangular prisms, pyramids, cylinders, cones and spheres in real-world and mathematical problems. DOK 2

PE/TE: 63 (#31), 65 (#31), 96 (#71), 335 (#53-54), 350 (#48-51), 407 (#29), 427 (#89), 436 (#1), 580 (#51b), 619 (#59), 639 (#54), 780 (#17), 894 (Quiz #15), 922 (#56), 993

MA-HS-2.1.2
Students will describe how a change in one or more dimensions of a geometric figure affects the perimeter, area and volume of the figure. DOK 3

PE/TE: 47 (#62), 332 (Example 5), 335 (#54), 427 (#89c)

MA-HS-2.1.3
Students will apply definitions and properties of right triangle relationships (right triangle trigonometry and the Pythagorean theorem) to determine length and angle measures to solve real-world and mathematical problems. DOK 3

PE/TE: 9 (#64), 40 (#36), 88 (#48), 129 (#44), 138 (#51), 202 (#47), 419 (#68), 513 (#75), 557 (#43), 588 (#46), 625 (#61), 825 (#44), 850 (#4-6), 852-858, 865 (Quiz #1-6), 872 (#42), 873 (#2-3), 877, 878 (#27-29), 879, 880 (Quiz #17), 896 (#2, 6), 897 (Big Ideas 1-2), 898 (Example 13.1, #7), 899 (#17), 901 (#28), 903 (#1), 904 (#3, 5-6), 905 (#12), 906 (#1-3), 995 (Example 2, #4-8), 1022 (#1-10)

MA-HS-2.1.4
Students will apply special right triangles and the converse of the Pythagorean theorem to solve real-world problems.

PE/TE: *Opportunities to address this standard can be found on the following pages:* 995

Systems Of Measurements

MA-HS-2.2.1
Students will continue to apply to both real-world and mathematical problems U.S. customary and metric systems of measurement.

PE/TE: *Found throughout the text. See, for example:* 5, 7 (#26, 28, 30, 31-48), 8 (#60), 9 (#61), 204 (Example 2), 208 (#40-41), 209 (#45), 616 (Example 5), 618 (#47-52), 619 (#53b-53c, 54-55, 59), 622 (Example 3), 624 (#55-56), 625 (#57c, 58-59, 61), 628 (Example 5, Guided Practice 6), 849 (#45, 48), 855, 857 (#30-34), 858 (#35-37), 862 (Example 4, Guided Practice 9), 863 (#32-38), 864 (#51b, 52, 53a, 53c), 865 (#54a, Quiz #11-12), 869 (Example 5), 870 (Example 6, Guided Practice 10-11), 871 (#35, 37), 872 (#38b, 39, 42), 873 (#1-3, 6), 879 (#37, 38b-38c), 880 (#40, 42, Quiz #17), 885 (Example 5), 887 (#43-45), 888 (#47, 49-50), 891 (Example 4), 893 (#44-45, 46a), 894 (#47a, 48, Quiz #15), 895 (Problem, #4-5), 896 (#1, 3-6), 901 (#28, 30), 902, 904 (#1-4), 905 (#10, 16A, 17D), 913 (#29), 981, 1010 (#4-6), A2-A3

Geometry

High school students expand analysis of two-dimensional shapes and three-dimensional shapes. They translate shapes in a coordinate plane. They extend work with congruent and similar figures, including proportionality.

SHAPES AND RELATIONSHIPS

MA-HS-3.1.1
Students will analyze and apply spatial relationships (not using Cartesian coordinates) among points, lines and planes (e.g., betweenness of points, midpoint, segment length, collinear, coplanar, parallel, perpendicular, skew). DOK 2

PE/TE: *Opportunities to address this standard can be found on the following pages:* 99 (Example 3, Guided Practice 5), 102 (#20-26), 145 (#12-13), 148 (#5), 149 (#13), 167 (#65), 258 (#74), 271 (#45), 723 (#43)

MA-HS-3.1.2
Students will use spatial relationships to prove basic theorems.

PE/TE: *Not addressed in this text.*

MA-HS-3.1.3
Students will analyze and apply angle relationships (e.g., linear pairs, vertical, complementary, supplementary, corresponding and alternate interior angles) in real-world and mathematical problems. DOK 2

PE/TE: 32 (#41), 335 (#56), 522 (#63), 595 (#40), 962 (#57), 994

MA-HS-3.1.4
Students will use angle relationships to prove basic theorems.

PE/TE: *Not addressed in this text.*

MA-HS-3.1.5
Students will classify and apply properties of two-dimensional geometric figures (e.g., number of sides, vertices, length of sides, sum of interior and exterior angle measures). DOK 2

PE/TE: 58 (#84), 59 (#7), 104 (#60), 498 (#64), 595 (#40), 657 (#55), 771 (#34), 850 (#10-12)

MA-HS-3.1.6
Students will know the definitions and basic properties of a circle and will use them to prove basic theorems and solve problems.

PE/TE: 352 (#66), 992

MA-HS-3.1.7
Students will solve real-world and mathematical problems by applying properties of triangles (e.g., Triangle Sum theorem and Isosceles Triangle theorems). DOK 2

PE/TE: 96 (#70), 158 (#42), 995

Key:
Bold – State Assessment Content Standard
Italics – Supporting Content Standard
Plain Text – ADP Benchmarks Supporting Content Standard

Shapes and Relationships *(cont.)*

MA-HS-3.1.8
Students will use the properties of triangles to prove basic theorems.

PE/TE: *Not addressed in this text.*

MA-HS-3.1.9
Students will classify and apply properties of three-dimensional geometric figures. DOK 2

PE/TE: 209 (#48), 557 (#44)

MA-HS-3.1.10
Students will describe the intersection of a plane with a three-dimensional figure.

PE/TE: *Not addressed in this text.*

MA-HS-3.1.11
Students will visualize solids and surfaces in three-dimensional space when given two-dimensional representations (e.g., nets, multiple views) and create two-dimensional representations for the surfaces of three-dimensional objects.

PE/TE: 947 (#30)

MA-HS-3.1.12
Students will apply the concepts of congruence and similarity to solve real-world and mathematical problems. DOK 3

PE/TE: 16 (#65), 451 (#42), 755 (#27)

MA-HS-3.1.13
Students will prove triangles congruent and similar.

PE/TE: *Not addressed in this text.*

Transformations of Shapes

MA-HS-3.2.1
Students will identify and describe properties of and apply geometric transformations within a plane to solve real-world and mathematical problems. DOK 3

PE/TE: 491 (#37), 930 (#47), 988-989

Key:
Bold – State Assessment Content Standard
Italics – Supporting Content Standard
Plain Text – ADP Benchmarks Supporting Content Standard

COORDINATE GEOMETRY

MA-HS-3.3.1
Students will apply algebraic concepts and graphing in the coordinate plane to analyze and solve problems (e.g., finding the final coordinates for a specified polygon, midpoints, betweenness of points, parallel and perpendicular lines, the distance between two points, the slope of a segment). DOK 2

PE/TE: 82-88, 96 (Quiz #4-5), 142 (Example 2.2, #8-11), 145 (#4-7), 149 (#10), 185 (#49-50), 204 (Key Concept, Example 2, Guided Practice 4), 208 (#40-41), 209 (#45-46), 230 (#8), 231 (#16), 232 (#42), 291 (#69), 427 (#91), 614-619, 632 (#71, Quiz #1-6), 669 (Example 9.1, #5-8), 674-675, 677 (#8, 13), 678 (#34-36), 679 (#45), 704 (#44-45), 749 (#33), 800 (#70), 809 (#70), 858 (#39), 894 (#50), 914 (#35), 988-989, 1011 (#5-10), 1018 (#1-4)

FOUNDATIONAL STATEMENTS

MA-HS-3.4.1
Students will identify definitions, axioms and theorems, explain the necessity for them and give examples of them.

PE/TE: *Not addressed in this text.*

MA-HS-3.4.2
Students will recognize that there are geometries, other than Euclidean geometry, in which the parallel postulate is not true.

PE/TE: *Opportunities to address this standard can be found on the following pages:* A5-A6

MA-HS-3.4.3
Students will be able to perform constructions such as a line parallel to a given line through a point not on the line, the perpendicular bisector of a line segment and the bisector of an angle.

PE/TE: *Not addressed in this text.*

Key:
Bold – State Assessment Content Standard
Italics – Supporting Content Standard
Plain Text – ADP Benchmarks Supporting Content Standard

CORRELATIONS

Data Analysis and Probability

High school students extend data representations, interpretations and conclusions. They describe data distributions in multiple ways and connect data gathering issues with data interpretation issues. They relate curve of best fit with two-variable data and determine line of best fit for a given set of data. They distinguish between combinations and permutations and compare and contrast theoretical and experimental probability.

Data Representations

MA-HS-4.1.1
Students will analyze and make inferences from a set of data with no more than two variables, and will analyze problems for the use and misuse of data representations. DOK 3

PE/TE: 113, 114 (Guided Practice 1-3), 117 (#3-6), 744-749, 750, 756, 757-762, 763-765, 783, 784, 785 (Example 11.3, #12-17), 787 (#1-12), 849 (#50), A12-A13, A18-A19

MA-HS-4.1.2
Students will construct data displays for data with no more than two variables. DOK 2

PE/TE: 112 (#1), 115, 118 (#10-15), 119 (#27b, 28a-28b), 139 (#6A), 143 (Example 2.6), 774 (Explore), 775-777, 778 (#3-4), 779 (#12, 13a), 781, 786 (Example 11.5, #23), 791 (#15A), 1007 (#12-14), 1011 (#29-30), A18-A19, A24-A25

MA-HS-4.1.3
Students will represent real-world data using matrices and will use matrix addition, subtraction, multiplication (with matrices no larger than 2 × 2) and scalar multiplication to solve real-world problems.

PE/TE: 189, 192, 194 (#5), 198, 200 (#37-39), 201, 202 (#44), 225 (#28)

Key:
Bold – State Assessment Content Standard
Italics – Supporting Content Standard
Plain Text – ADP Benchmarks Supporting Content Standard

CHARACTERISTICS OF DATA SETS

MA-HS-4.2.1
Students will describe and compare data distributions and make inferences from the data based on the shapes of graphs, measures of center (mean, median, mode) and measures of spread (range, standard deviation). DOK 2

PE/TE: 113-114, 117 (#2-9), 118 (#21, 23), 119 (#28), 120 (#29), 727 (Example 5, Guided Practice 5), 728 (#33-39), 730 (#48), 731, 733 (Big Idea 3), 742 (#2), 744-749, 750, 755 (Quiz #1-7), 756, 782 (#7), 783 (Big Idea 1), 784 (Example 11.1, #4-8), 787 (#1-3), 789 (Problem 2, #1-2), 790 (#1-2, 6, 9), 791 (#11-12, 14), 848 (#31-36), 849 (#50), 922 (#57), 1005, 1020 (#1-10), A8 (Example 2, #5)

MA-HS-4.2.2
Students will know the characteristics of the Gaussian normal distribution (bell-shaped curve).

PE/TE: 757-762, 763-765, 780 (Quiz #1-3), 783 (Big Idea 2), 785 (Example 11.3, #12-17), 787 (#4-6, 12), 1020 (#11-13)

MA-HS-4.2.3
Students will:

- **identify an appropriate curve of best fit (linear, quadratic, exponential) for a set of two-variable data;**
- **determine a line of best fit equation for a set of linear two-variable data and**
- **apply a line of best fit to make predictions within and beyond a given set of two-variable data.**

DOK 3

PE/TE: 112, 115-116, 117 (Guided Practice 4), 118 (#10-20, 22), 119 (24-27), 231 (#15), 143 (Example 2.6, #23), 145 (#18-19, 27), 233 (#46), 774, 775-780, 781, 782 (#1, 3), 786 (Example 11.5, #23), 787 (#14), 789 (#3), 790 (#8), 791 (#15), 1011 (#29-30), 1020 (#24-25)

MA-HS-4.2.4
Students will recognize when arguments based on data confuse correlation and causation.

PE/TE: A24-A25

Key:
Bold – State Assessment Content Standard
Italics – Supporting Content Standard
Plain Text – ADP Benchmarks Supporting Content Standard

CORRELATIONS

Experiments And Samples

MA-HS-4.3.1
Students will recognize potential for bias resulting from the misuse of sampling methods (e.g., non-random sampling, polling only a specific group of people, using limited or extremely small sample sizes) and explain why these samples can lead to inaccurate inferences. DOK 2

PE/TE: 766-767, 769 (#3-5), 770 (#28), 782 (#2, 4, 6), 783 (Big Idea 3), 788, 1020 (#14-23)

MA-HS-4.3.2
Students will design simple experiments or investigations to collect data to answer questions of interest.

PE/TE: 772-773

MA-HS-4.3.3
Students will explain the differences between randomized experiments and observational studies.

PE/TE: *Opportunities to address this standard can be found on the following pages:* 766-770

Key:
Bold – State Assessment Content Standard
Italics – Supporting Content Standard
Plain Text – ADP Benchmarks Supporting Content Standard

PROBABILITY

MA-HS-4.4.1
Students will:

- **determine theoretical and experimental (from given data) probabilities;**
- **make predictions and draw inferences from probabilities;**
- **compare theoretical and experimental probabilities and**
- **determine probabilities involving replacement and non-replacement.**

DOK 3

PE/TE: 698, 699 (Example 2, Guided Practice 1-3), 700 (Key Concept, Example 4, Guided Practice 6), 701 (#2-10), 702 (#11-19, 26, 28-32), 703 (#38, 40), 704 (#42-43), 705 (#4), 713 (Quiz #1-6, 15), 719 (Example 5, Guided Practice 5-6), 722 (#26-32), 730 (Quiz #1-3), 732 (#1, 4), 735 (Example 10.3, #15-19), 736 (Example 10.5, #23-25), 737 (#13-16, 26), 739 (Problem 2, #2), 740 (#1), 741 (#10, 15), 742 (#1), 742 (#5-8), 809 (#71), 1019 (#21-22, 33-39), A14-A15, A16-A17, A20 (Example 1b), A21 (#1b, 1c)

MA-HS-4.4.2
Students will recognize and identify the differences between combinations and permutations and use them to count discrete quantities.

PE/TE: 684-685, 686 (Example 6, Guided Practice 8-10), 687 (#30-57, 61), 688 (#64-68), 689 (#69-71), 690, 694 (#2-18), 695 (#38-47), 696, 697 (#53, Quiz #3-10, 16), 705 (#1, 3, 5-6), 734 (Example 10.1), 735 (#5-9, 14), 737 (#1-8, 27), 739 (#1), 740 (#3-4), 741 (#14), 755 (#26), 849 (#49), 1019 (#1-4, 9-12)

MA-HS-4.4.3
Students will represent probabilities in multiple ways, such as fractions, decimals, percentages and geometric area models.

PE/TE: 698-704, 705 (#2, 4), 706, 707-713, 714, 717-723, 724-725, 726 (Example 4b, Guided Practice 4), 727 (#3-5), 728 (#6-31, 39), 729 (#43-45, 46b, 47), 730 (#48b, Quiz #1-11), 732, 735 (Example 10.3, #15-19), 736, 737 (#13-26, 28-30), 738, 739 (Problem 2, #2), 740 (#1, 5), 741 (#12-13, 15A), 742 (#5-8), 1019 (#21-39), A14-A15, A16-A17, A20 (Example 1b), A21 (#1b, 1c)

MA-HS-4.4.4
Students will explain how the law of large numbers can be applied in simple examples.

PE/TE: 714 (#4), A17 (Key Concept, #7)

Key:
Bold – State Assessment Content Standard
Italics – Supporting Content Standard
Plain Text – ADP Benchmarks Supporting Content Standard

CORRELATIONS

Algebraic Thinking

High school students extend analysis and use of functions and focus on linear, quadratic, absolute value and exponential functions. They explore parametric changes on graphs of functions. They use rules and properties to simplify algebraic expressions. They combine simple rational expressions and combine simple polynomial expressions. They factor polynomial expressions and quadratics of the form $1x^2 + bx + c$.

Patterns, Relations and Functions

MA-HS-5.1.1
Students will identify multiple representations (tables, graphs, equations) of functions (linear, quadratic, absolute value, exponential) in real-world or mathematical problems. DOK 2

PE/TE: 73-75, 76 (Example 6, Guided Practice 7), 77 (#10-33), 78, 79 (#48-50), 80-81, 89-96, 97, 98-104, 105, 106, 107-111, 115-116, 117 (Guided Practice 4), 118 (#10-20) 119, 120 (#29, Quiz #1-15), 121-122, 123-129, 130-131, 138 (Quiz #1-6), 139 (#1), 140, 141 (Example 2.1, #5-7), 142 (Example 2.3, #12-15, Example 2.4, #16-18), 143, 144 (Example 2.7, #24-27), 145 (#8-20, 25-27), 146-147, 148 (#1-2, 6), 149 (#10, 12-13, 15-16), 158 (#41), 232 (#20-25, 29-30), 233 (#44), 236-243, 244, 245-251, 265 (Quiz #1-6), 308, 309-315, 317 (Big Idea 1), 318 (Example 4.1, #5-7), 319 (Example 4.2, #8-14), 322 (Example 4.10, #45-48), 323 (#1-3, 28-30, 32), 337, 338 (Guided Practice 1-3), 339-340, 341 (Guided Practice 9-12, #3-8), 342 (#38-50), 343, 344 (#58-60, 62), 352 (#65, Quiz #9-11), 369 (#2), 393-399, 401 (Big Idea 1), 403 (Example 5.2, #13-15), 406 (Example 5.9, #41), 407 (#5-7, 23-26, 28-29), 434 (#49), 451 (#41), 475 (#53, 56-57), 478-485, 486-491, 498 (Quiz #1-3), 506 (#2), 528, 529-530, 531 (Guided Practice 1-4), 533 (#3-14), 535 (#33), 536 (Quiz #10-12), 537 (#4), 538 (Big Ideas 1, 3), 539 (Example 7.1, #6-9), 540 (Example 7.2, #10-12), 542 (Example 7.7, #35-37), 543 (#1-6, 25), 563 (#44), 609 (Problem 2, #2), 730 (#50), 749 (#34), 800 (#69), 848 (#1-12), 849 (#44), 865 (#55), 937 (#46), 1010 (#31-32), 1011 (#11-28), 1016 (#1-8), A22-A23

MA-HS-5.1.2
Students will identify, relate and apply representations (graphs, equations, tables) of a piecewise function (such as long distance telephone rates) from mathematical or real-world information.

PE/TE: 130-131

MA-HS-5.1.3
Students will demonstrate how equations and graphs are models of the relationship between two real-world quantities (e.g., the relationship between degrees Celsius and degrees Fahrenheit).

PE/TE: 44 (Example 7, Guided Practice 13), 91 (Example 3, Guided Practice 10), 94 (#59-62), 95, 96 (Quiz #9), 108, 109 (Guided Practice 5-6), 110 (#38-41), 111 (#44-45), 143 (#22), 145 (#26), 233 (#44-46), 239 (Example 5), 242, 247 (Example 4, Guided Practice 8), 250 (#51-53), 262 (Example 7, Guided Practice 22), 270 (#38-39), 295, 298, 327 (#17), 396 (Example 4), 398 (#26-28), 399 (Quiz #13), 447 (Example 3, Guided Practice 5), 450 (#35-37), 480 (Example 4), 484 (#35-36, 39-40), 485 (#41-42), 500 (Example 4), 501 (Guided Practice 9), 504 (#58-59), 552 (Example 3), 553, 556 (#37-40), 560 (Example 4), 562 (#39), 570, 571 (#36)

PATTERNS, RELATIONS AND FUNCTIONS *(cont.)*

MA-HS-5.1.4
Students will recognize and solve problems that can be modeled using an exponential function, such as compound interest problems.

PE/TE: 480-481, 483 (#28-30), 484, 485 (#41-44), 488 (Example 4, Guided Practice 7-8), 489 (#26), 490 (#30-32), 491 (#33-36), 506 (#1, 3), 530 (Example 2), 531 (Guided Practice 4), 532 (Example 5), 533 (Guided Practice 9), 534 (#31), 535, 536 (#36, Quiz #16), 537 (#2-5), 543 (#27-29), 544, 545 (Problem 2, #1, 3), 546 (#1-2, 6, 8, 10-11), 547 (#16-18), 679 (#48)

MA-HS-5.1.5
Students will:

- **determine if a relation is a function;**
- **determine the domain and range of a function (linear and quadratic);**
- **determine the slope and intercepts of a linear function;**
- **determine the maximum, minimum, and intercepts (roots/zeros) of a quadratic function and**
- **evaluate a function written in function notation for a specified rational number.**

DOK 2

PE/TE: 73, 74 (Example 3, Guided Practice 3), 75 (Example 5, Guided Practice 5-6), 76 (Example 6, Guided Practice 7), 77 (#9-24), 78, 79 (#48-50), 106 (#2), 130 (Example 1), 131 (#1-4, 8), 140 (Big Idea 1), 141 (Example 2.1, #5-7), 145 (#1-3), 148 (#1, 5, 8), 149 (#11-12), 167 (#64, 66), 193 (#37), 202 (#46), 232 (#16-19, 29-30), 233 (#44), 238 (Key Concept), 239, 241 (#33-38), 242 (#55-57), 243 (#61), 244, 246 (Key Concept), 247 (Guided Practice #5-7), 249 (#13-21, 33-41), 250 (#51, 53b), 251 (#55), 253 (Key Concept), 254 (Example 3, Key Vocabulary), 255 (Example 5, Guided Practice 10-12, #1), 256 (#41, 44-57), 257 (#63), 258 (#73), 265 (Quiz #13), 282 (#78), 316 (#1), 319 (Example 4.2), 325 (#2), 326 (#1, 4), 327 (#12-13, 16-17), 368 (#48), 445 (#52), 459 (#63), 472 (#2, 11), 476 (#1-2), 513 (#76), 546 (#10), 595 (#39), 619 (#58), 723 (#43), 792 (#1-2), 872 (#43), 880 (#41), 937 (#47), 1011 (#1-10), 1013 (#25-28)

MA-HS-5.1.6
Students will find the domain and range for absolute value functions.

PE/TE: *Opportunities to address this standard can be found on the following pages:* 121-122, 123-129, 138 (Quiz #1-6), 144 (Example 2.7, #24-27)

MA-HS-5.1.7
Students will apply and use direct and inverse variation to solve real-world and mathematical problems.

PE/TE: 107-111, 120 (Quiz #7-14), 139 (#3), 140 (Big Idea 3), 143 (Example 2.5, #19-22), 148 (#7), 233 (#45), 548 (#2, 4-6), 550, 551-553, 555 (#1-23), 556 (#37-39), 571 (Quiz #1-4), 572 (#2-4), 603 (Example 8.1, #6-9), 607 (#1-6), 611 (#11), 678 (#28-30), 848 (#17-20), 1017 (#1-8)

Key:
Bold – State Assessment Content Standard
Italics – Supporting Content Standard
Plain Text – ADP Benchmarks Supporting Content Standard

CORRELATIONS

PATTERNS, RELATIONS AND FUNCTIONS *(cont.)*

MA-HS-5.1.8
Students will identify the changes and explain how changes in parameters affect graphs of functions (linear, quadratic, absolute value, exponential) (e.g., compare $y = x^2$, $y = 2x^2$, $y = (x - 4)^2$, and $y = x^2 + 3$). DOK 2

PE/TE: 89 (Example 1), 90 (Guided Practice 1-3), 93 (#3-8), 97, 121-122, 123-124, 125 (Example 3, Guided Practice 1-3), 126, 127 (#3-14, 21-26, 28), 128 (#32-34), 138 (Quiz #1-3), 144 (Example 2.7, #24-26), 145 (#20), 236-237, 240 (#7-18), 392 (#46), 478 (Key Concept), 479 (Example 3), 485 (#45), 522 (#62), 539 (Example 7.1), 540 (Example 7.2), 749 (#32), 817 (#64), 1011 (#31-34)

VARIABLES, EXPRESSIONS AND OPERATIONS

MA-HS-5.2.1
Students will apply order of operations, real number properties (identity, inverse, commutative, associative, distributive, closure) and rules of exponents (integer) to simplify algebraic expressions. DOK 1

PE/TE: 12, 13 (Example 5, Guided Practice 15), 14 (#25-32, 34-36, 43-51), 16 (Quiz #10-12), 60 (Big Idea 1), 61 (Example 1.1, #9), 62 (Example 1.2, #10-16), 65 (#7-12), 129 (#43), 232 (#1-3), 330 (Key Concept), 331 (Example 3), 332 (Example 4), 333 (Guided Practice 5-8, #24-36), 334 (#37-39), 352 (Quiz #5-8), 377 (#53), 402 (Example 5.1, #7-8, 11-12), 411 (#9), 412 (#4-6), 419 (#67), 434 (#48), 474 (#31-34), 639 (#55), 1010 (#10-15), 1014 (#4-7)

MA-HS-5.2.2
Students will evaluate polynomial and rational expressions and expressions containing radicals and absolute values at specified values of their variables.

PE/TE: 11 (Examples 2-3, Guided Practice 4-7), 13 (Example 5, Guided Practice 15), 14 (#16-24, 34-42), 15 (#57-58, 60-62), 16 (#63, Quiz #7-9, 13), 17 (#7-12), 40 (#5-8), 70 (#3-6), 762 (#37), 1010 (#7-9)

MA-HS-5.2.3
Students will:

- **add, subtract and multiply polynomial expressions;**
- **factor polynomial expressions using the greatest common monomial factor and**
- **factor quadratic polynomials of the form $ax^2 + bx + c$, when $a = 1$ and b and c are integers.**

DOK 2

PE/TE: 252-253, 255 (#3-14), 256 (#15-23), 323 (#4-9), 346-352, 353 (Example 1), 354 (Guided Practice 1-2), 356 (#3-8), 403 (Example 5.3, #17-20), 407 (#8-11), 474 (#35-37), 548 (#7-12), 580 (#54), 608, 609 (#1), 680 (#7-9), 1013 (#13-16), 1014 (#12-14)

Key:
Bold – State Assessment Content Standard
Italics – Supporting Content Standard
Plain Text – ADP Benchmarks Supporting Content Standard

VARIABLES, EXPRESSIONS AND OPERATIONS *(cont.)*

MA-HS-5.2.4

Students will factor quadratic polynomials, such as perfect square trinomials and quadratic polynomials of the form $ax^2 + bx + c$ when $a \neq 1$ and b and c are integers.

PE/TE: 252-253, 255 (#3-14), 256 (#15-23), 323 (#4-9), 548 (#7-8, 10-11), 1013 (#13-16)

MA-HS-5.2.5

Students will add, subtract, multiply and divide simple rational expressions with monomial first-degree denominators and integer numerators (e.g., $\frac{3}{5x} + \frac{4}{3y}$; $\frac{9}{2a} - \frac{-7}{4b}$; $\frac{3}{-5x} \times \frac{-4}{7y}$; $\frac{5}{2c} \div \frac{9}{-11d}$), and will express the results in simplified form. DOK 1

PE/TE: 582 (Example 1a, Guided Practice 1), 586 (#3, 16)

EQUATIONS AND INEQUALITIES

MA-HS-5.3.1

Students will model, solve and graph first degree, single variable equations and inequalities, including absolute value, based in real-world and mathematical problems and graph the solutions on a number line. DOK 2

PE/TE: 18-24, 25, 32 (#42), 33 (#1, 4-6), 34-39, 40 (#34, Quiz #1-4, 11-12), 41-47, 48-49, 50, 51-58, 59 (#1-5, 7), 60 (Big Idea 3), 62 (Example 1.3, #17-24), 63 (Example 1.5, #32-33), 64, 65 (#13-15, 19-27), 66-67, 68 (#2-4, 6), 69, 70 (#7-9), 88 (#51), 209 (#47), 217 (#52), 232 (#4-15), 299 (#75), 316 (#2), 344 (#61), 427 (#92), 475 (#52), 625 (#62), 664 (#47), 678 (#1-2, 41), 713 (#51), 730 (#51), 792 (#4-9), 833 (#49), 954 (#47), 1010 (#16-24, 32-53)

MA-HS-5.3.2

Students will solve for a specified variable in a multivariable equation.

PE/TE: 26-32, 40 (#5-8), 63 (Example 1.4, #25-31), 65 (#16-18), 70 (#10-12), 233 (#43), 327 (#9), 412 (#7-9)

MA-HS-5.3.3

Students will model, solve and graph first degree, two-variable equations and inequalities in real-world and mathematical problems. DOK 2

PE/TE: 74 (Key Concept), 75 (Example 4, Guided Practice 4), 77 (#25-33), 78 (#47), 89-96, 97, 98-104, 105, 106 (#1, 3, 5-7), 107-111, 112, 113-120, 121-122, 123-129, 130-131, 132-138, 139 (#2, 5-6), 140 (Big Idea 2), 142 (Example 2.3, #12-15), 143 (#22), 144 (Example 2.7, #24-27, Example 2.8, #31-34), 145 (#8-11, 21-24), 146, 149 (#15), 150 (#1-11), 158 (#41), 232 (#20-28), 233 (#44-45), 243 (#63), 271 (#44-45), 274 (#4, 7), 282 (#78), 291 (#70), 307 (#78), 315 (#53-54), 316 (#7), 344 (#62), 352 (#65), 434 (#49), 451 (#41), 459 (#64), 464 (#3), 474 (#1-6, 13, 15), 475 (#53), 536 (#38), 563 (#44), 595 (#39), 610 (#7), 664 (#46), 678 (#10), 679 (#42), 730 (#50), 749 (#34), 780 (#16), 800 (#69-70), 848 (#1-3), 849 (#44), 865 (#55), 894 (#50), 937 (#46), 1011 (#11-28, 31-42)

EQUATIONS AND INEQUALITIES *(cont.)*

MA-HS-5.3.4
Students will model, solve and graph systems of two linear equations in real-world and mathematical problems. DOK 3

PE/TE: 152, 153-158, 159, 160-167, 186, 205, 207 (Guided Practice 5-6), 208 (#29-31, 42), 212 (Example 4), 213 (Guided Practice 8-10), 215 (#25-34), 216 (#45-46), 217 (#53, Quiz #8-13), 221 (Big Ideas 1-2), 222 (Example 3.1, #4-6), 223 (Example 3.2, #7-10), 226 (Example 3.8, #33-35), 227 (#1-4, 9-11, 27-31), 228, 230 (#2, 7), 231 (#11), 232 (#31-32), 258 (#74), 299 (#76), 368 (#47), 386 (#66), 399 (#31), 445 (#53), 474 (#22-23), 475 (#54), 588 (#47), 612 (#11-13), 632 (#70), 679 (#43), 697 (#54), 792 (#10-12), 817 (#63), 1012 (#1-8, 27-28, 35-38)

MA-HS-5.3.5
Students will write, graph, and solve systems of two linear inequalities based on real-world or mathematical problems and interpret the solution.

PE/TE: 168-173, 193 (Quiz #1-6), 221 (Big Idea 2), 223 (Example 3.3, #11-13), 227 (#5-8), 230 (#3), 233 (#47), 1012 (#9-10)

MA-HS-5.3.6
Students will model, solve and graph quadratic equations in real-world and mathematical problems. DOK 2

PE/TE: 236-237, 238 (Example 3, Guided Practice 4-6), 240 (7-32), 241 (#44-52), 242 (#55-56, 59), 243 (#60), 245-247, 249 (#3-23), 250 (#43-48), 253 (Key Concept), 254, 256 (#24-43), 257 (#59-62, 65-67), 258 (#68-72), 261-262, 263 (#32-40), 264 (#50-58, 62-64, 66), 265 (Quiz #1-3, 7-12), 267 (Example 3), 268, 269 (Example 5, Guided Practice 20), 270 (#22-39), 271 (#41-42), 272-273, 274 (#5), 284 (Example 1), 285 (Guided Practice 1-3, Example 3), 286, 288 (#3-12, 22-38), 289 (#52-57, 61), 290 (#66-67), 291 (Quiz #1-6), 292-299, 315 (Quiz #1-3), 316 (#1, 3, 5), 317 (Big Idea 2), 318 (Example 4.1, #5-7), 319, 320 (Example 4.4, #22-24, Example 4.5, #25-28), 321 (Example 4.7, #35-37, Example 4.8, #38-41), 323 (#1-3, 10-15, 19-24), 324-325, 326 (#2-8), 327 (#15-17), 369 (#5), 399 (#32), 474 (#28-30), 475 (#56-57), 476 (#10-12), 612 (#4-10), 678 (#3-4), 679 (#46), 689 (#72), 723 (#44), 771 (#33), 848 (#4-6), 858 (#38), 1013 (#1-12, 17-20, 33-36, 41-48, 53-55)

Key:
Bold – State Assessment Content Standard
Italics – Supporting Content Standard
Plain Text – ADP Benchmarks Supporting Content Standard

KENTUCKY PROGRAM OF STUDIES (POS) HIGH SCHOOL

Big Idea: Number Properties and Operations

High school students should enter high school with a strong background in rational numbers and numerical operations and expand this to real numbers. Solving quadratic equations produces a working knowledge of complex numbers. This becomes the foundation for algebra and working with algebraic symbols. They understand large and small numbers and their representations, powers and roots. They compare and contrast properties of numbers and number systems and develop strategies to estimate the results of operations on real numbers. Students will use and understand the limitations of, graphing calculators and computer spreadsheets appropriately as learning tools.

Academic Expectations

2.7 Students understand number concepts and use numbers appropriately and accurately.

2.8 Students understand various mathematical procedures and use them appropriately and accurately.

2.12 Students understand mathematical structure concepts including the properties and logic of various mathematical systems.

HIGH SCHOOL ENDURING KNOWLEDGE – Understandings

MA-HS-NPO-U-1

Students will understand that numbers, ways of representing numbers, relationships among numbers and number systems are means of representing real-world quantities.

PE/TE: *Opportunities to address this standard can be found on the following pages:* 2-9, 978-979, 980, 982

MA-HS-NPO-U-2

Students will understand that meanings of and relationships among operations provide tools necessary to solve realistic problems encountered in everyday life and problems encountered in mathematical situations.

PE/TE: 18-24, 33 (#2, 4-5, 7B), 34-40, 42-47, 51-58, 59 (#1, 2, 4-5, 8), 62 (Example 1.3, #17-24), 64, 65 (#13-15, 19-27, 29-30), 252-258, 259-265, 267 (Example 3), 268 (Example 4, Guided Practice 17-19), 269 (Example 5, Guided Practice 20), 270 (#22-39), 271 (#40-43), 275, 279 (#3-11), 284-291, 320 (Example 4.4, #22-24, Example 4.5, #25-28), 321 (Example 4.7, #35-37, Example 4.8, #38-41), 323 (#10-15, 19-24), 452-459, 464 (#2, 5), 468 (Example 6.6, #30-32), 469 (#34-36), 589-595, 606, 607 (#25-27), 1010 (#16-24, 33-53), 1013 (#17-20, 33-36, 41-48), 1017 (#33-36)

High School Enduring Knowledge – Understandings *(cont.)*

MA-HS-NPO-U-3
Students will understand that computing fluently and accurately with real numbers and making reasonable estimates increases the ability to solve realistic problems encountered in everyday life.

PE/TE: 5, 7 (#25-48), 8 (#57a, 60a-60b), 9 (#61a, 62), 11 (Example 3), 13 (Example 5), 15 (#57-58, 60, 61d, 62), 16 (#63, Quiz #13), 33 (#1), 65 (#28), 977 (Example 2, #24-31), 981, 983 (Example, #17-24)

MA-HS-NPO-U-4
Students will understand that problem solving and connections with other content areas require a strong sense of number, including applications of absolute value (magnitude) and the ordering of numbers.

PE/TE: *Found throughout the text. See, for example:* 8, 9 (#61-62), 15 (#57-62), 16 (#63), 34-40, 57, 58 (#81-82), 94 (#59-62), 103 (#50-54), 104 (#55-58), 105, 172 (#34-36), 173 (#37-40), 208 (#40-42), 209 (#43-46), 242, 243 (#60-61), 257 (#65-67), 258 (#68-72), 270 (#38-39), 271 (#40-43), 298, 299 (#73-74), 334 (#49-50), 335 (#51-54), 358, 359 (#63-65), 367 (#41-42), 368 (#43-46), 376, 377 (#51), 426, 427 (#89-90), 444, 450 (#35-37), 451 (#38-40), 457 (#56), 458, 484, 485 (#41-44), 504 (#58-59), 505 (#60-63), 594, 595 (#38), 630 (#62-63), 631, 632 (#69), 753 (#18), 754, 755 (#24-25), 893 (#43-46), 945 (#23-25), 946

MA-HS-NPO-U-5
Students will understand that proportional reasoning is a tool for modeling and solving problems encountered in everyday situations.

PE/TE: 601 (#1), 689 (#73)

HIGH SCHOOL SKILLS AND CONCEPTS – Number Sense

MA-HS-NPO-S-NS1
Students will compare real numbers using order relations.

PE/TE: *Opportunities to address this standard can be found on the following pages:* 2-3, 6 (#3-10), 8 (#57-59), 33 (#3), 742 (#3-4)

MA-HS-NPO-S-NS2
Students will locate the position of a real number on the number line, find its distance from the origin (absolute value/magnitude) and find the distance between two numbers on the number line (the absolute value of their difference).

PE/TE: 2 (Example 1), 3 (Guided Practice 1), 6 (#3-8), 7 (#56), 16 (Quiz #1-3), 51 (Key Vocabulary), 742 (#3-4), 1010 (#1-3)

MA-HS-NPO-S-NS3
Students will determine the relative position on the number line of real numbers, including very large and very small numbers, and the relative magnitude of numbers expressed in fractional form, in decimal form, as roots or in scientific notation.

PE/TE: 2 (Example 1), 3 (Guided Practice 1), 6 (#3-8), 7 (#56), 16 (Quiz #1-3), 742 (#3-4), 1010 (#1-3)

MA-HS-NPO-S-NS4
Students will explore vectors and matrices as systems that have some of the properties of the real number system.

PE/TE: 188 (Concept Summary)

MA-HS-NPO-S-NS5
Students will compare and contrast number systems, including complex numbers as solutions to quadratic equations that do not have real solutions.

PE/TE: 2 (Key Concept), 276 (Complex Numbers), 279 (#2)

High School Skills and Concepts – Estimation

MA-HS-NPO-S-E1
Students will use calculators appropriately and regularly make estimations without a calculator to detect potential errors.

PE/TE: *Opportunities to address this standard can be found on the following pages:* 975, 976, 977, 978-979, 982, 983

MA-HS-NPO-S-E2
Students will estimate solutions to problems with real numbers (including very large and very small quantities) in both realistic and mathematical situations.

PE/TE: 335 (#53), 557 (#41b), 904 (#1a)

MA-HS-NPO-S-E3
Students will establish and apply benchmarks for real numbers in context.

PE/TE: *Opportunities to address this standard can be found on the following pages:* 976

High School Skills and Concepts – Number Operations

MA-HS-NPO-S-NO1
Students will add, subtract, multiply and divide real numbers.

PE/TE: 975, 979 (Example, #46-69)

MA-HS-NPO-S-NO2
Students will add, subtract and multiply complex numbers.

PE/TE: 276-277, 278 (Guided Practice 10-12), 279 (#12-20), 280 (#21-27), 291 (Quiz #7-10), 317 (Big Idea 3), 320 (Example 4.6), 321 (#29-33), 323 (#16-17), 327 (#10), 1013 (#37-38)

MA-HS-NPO-S-NO3
Students will multiply and divide numbers expressed in scientific notation.

PE/TE: 331 (Example 2, Guided Practice 4), 333 (#15-23), 334 (#49), 369 (#1), 1014 (#1-3)

MA-HS-NPO-S-NO4
Students will apply absolute value, integer exponents, roots and factorials to solve problems.

PE/TE: 10, 11 (Guided Practice 1-3), 55 (#3-8), 60 (Big Idea 1), 330-335, 352 (Quiz #1-4), 402 (#5-6, 9-10), 414, 415 (Guided Practice 1-4), 417 (#15-21, 24, 28-29), 421 (Example 3), 422, 424 (#15-41), 427 (Quiz #9-10, 12), 466 (Example 6.1a, #10-11, 14-15), 467 (Example 6.2a, #16), 469 (#3-4, 7-12), 684-689, 690-691, 694 (#3-18), 697 (Quiz #3-10), 734 (Example 10.1), 735 (#5-9, 14), 737 (#1-8, 27), 1015 (#1-3, 14-17, 19), 1019 (#5-16)

HIGH SCHOOL SKILLS AND CONCEPTS – Number Operations *(cont.)*

MA-HS-NPO-S-NO5
Students will determine a specific term of a sequence given an explicit formula.

PE/TE: 794, 798 (#3-14), 799 (#63), 801, 843(#5-8)

MA-HS-NPO-S-NO6
Students will describe and extend arithmetic and geometric sequences.

PE/TE: 802, 806 (#3-11, 23-28), 839 (Big Idea 1), 843 (#1-12), 846 (#3), 847(#8, 10-13)

MA-HS-NPO-S-NO7
Students will determine an explicit rule for the *n*th term of an arithmetic sequence

PE/TE: 803-804, 805 (Example 6), 806 (#12-29), 807 (#30-39), 808 (#63-66), 817 (Quiz #10-12), 841 (Example 12.2, #9-11), 843 (#9, 11), 845, 846 (#6), 847 (#14), 849 (#51), 1021 (#10-18)

MA-HS-NPO-S-NO8
Students will apply sequences and arithmetic and geometric series to solve realistic problems.

PE/TE: 795 (Example 3, Guided Practice 5), 799 (#63-64), 800, 805 (Example 6, Guided Practice 6), 808-809, 813 (Example 6, Guided Practice 8), 815 (#57-58), 816, 817 (#62, Quiz #16), 818, 838 (#3-6), 843 (#32-33), 846 (#1, 4-5)

MA-HS-NPO-S-NO9
Students will solve realistic problems to a specified degree of accuracy.

PE/TE: 273 (#10), 418 (#62), 983 (Example, #17-24)

MA-HS-NPO-S-NO10
Students will judge the effects of multiplication, division and computing powers and roots on the magnitudes of quantities.

PE/TE: *Opportunities to address this standard can be found on the following pages:* 10, 414-415, 975

MA-HS-NPO-S-NO11
Students will develop an understanding of the properties and representations for the addition and multiplication of vectors and matrices.

PE/TE: 187-193, 194, 195-202, 217 (Quiz #1-4), 220, 221 (Big Idea 3), 224 (Example 3.5), 225, 227 (#15-22), 475 (#55), 1012 (#17-22)

MA-HS-NPO-S-NO12
Students will develop fluency in operations with real numbers and matrices, using mental computation or paper-and-pencil calculations for simple cases and calculators and/or computers for more-complicated cases.

PE/TE: 10, 11 (Guided Practice 1-3), 13 (#4-15), 60 (Big Idea 1), 187-193, 194, 195-202, 217 (Quiz #1-4), 220, 221 (Big Idea 3), 224 (Example 3.5), 225, 227 (#15-22), 975, 977, 979 (Example, #46-69)

MA-HS-NPO-S-NO13
Students will use concrete, pictorial and abstract models to develop and/or generalize a procedure.

PE/TE: 258 (#68), 283, 284 (Key Concept), 285 (Example 2)

CORRELATIONS

HIGH SCHOOL SKILLS AND CONCEPTS – Ratios and Proportional Reasoning

MA-HS-NPO-S-RP1
Students will calculate and apply ratios, proportions, rates and percentages to solve problems.

PE/TE: 5, 7 (#25-48), 9 (#61-62), 24 (#79), 40 (#35), 85, 87 (41-45), 88 (#46-49), 108 (Example 3), 109 (Guided Practice 6), 111 (#47), 173 (#42), 265 (#70), 491 (#38), 580 (#55), 872 (#41), 977, 980, 1010 (#4-6)

MA-HS-NPO-S-RP2
Students will translate real-world proportional relationships into mathematical expressions and vice versa.

PE/TE: 291 (#70), 689 (#73)

MA-HS-NPO-S-RP3
Students will represent slope graphically, numerically and symbolically and relate it to a graph of an equation based on a realistic situation.

PE/TE: 82-88, 94 (#60), 95 (#68b), 142 (Example 2.2, #8-11), 145 (#4-7), 258 (#73), 1011 (#5-8)

HIGH SCHOOL SKILLS AND CONCEPTS – Properties of Numbers and Operations

MA-HS-NPO-S-PNO1
Students will identify and apply real number properties.

PE/TE: 3-4, 6 (#11-22, 24), 12 (Example 4), 13 (Example 5), 16 (Quiz #4-6), 20, 28 (Example 4), 61 (Example 1.1, #7-9), 62 (Examples 1.2-1.3), 65 (#3-4), 202 (#46), 253 (Key Concept), 254, 255 (Example 5, Guided Practice 10-12), 256 (#24-57), 257, 258 (#68-72), 265 (#7-9), 317 (Big Idea 2), 319 (Example 4.3, 15-21), 323 (#10-15), 1033

MA-HS-NPO-S-PNO2
Students will use equivalence relations of real numbers to solve problems.

PE/TE: 18-24, 26-32, 40 (Quiz #1-8), 42-43, 44 (Example 7, Guided Practice 9-13), 45 (#22-51), 46 (#52-53, 56), 47 (#59-60), 60 (Big Idea 3), 62 (Example 1.3, #17-24), 62 (Example 1.4, #25-31), 64 (Example 1.6, #34-40), 65 (#13-21, 31), 1010 (#16-30, 33-41)

MA-HS-NPO-S-PNO3
Students will compare and contrast the number systems according to their properties.

PE/TE: 2, 18, 188, 197, 253, 266, 420, 465, 1033, 1034

MA-HS-NPO-S-PNO4
Students will justify the solution steps in simplifying expressions or solving an equation.

PE/TE: 11 (Examples 2-3), 12 (Example 4), 13 (Example 5), 18-20, 34-36, 254, 261, 267 (Example 3), 268 (Example 4), 269 (Example 5), 285 (Example 3), 286 (Examples 4-5), 287 (Examples 6-7), 292-293, 295 (Example 5), 319 (Example 4.3), 320 (Examples 4.4-4.6), 321 (Examples 4.7-4.8), 452 (Example 1), 453 (Examples 2-3), 454 (Examples 4-5), 455 (Example 6), 468 (Example 6.6), 515 (Example 1), 516 (Examples 2-3), 517 (Examples 4-5), 518 (Example 6), 519 (Example 7), 589, 590 (Examples 3-4), 591 (Example 5), 592 (Example 6), 606 (Example 8.6)

Big Idea: Measurement

High school students continue to measure and estimate measurements including fractions and decimals. They use formulas to find surface area and volume. They use U.S. Customary and metric units of measurement. They use the Pythagorean theorem and other right triangle relationships to solve realistic problems.

Academic Expectations

2.9 Students understand space and dimensionality concepts and use them appropriately and accurately.

2.10 Students understand measurement concepts and use measurements appropriately and accurately.

HIGH SCHOOL ENDURING KNOWLEDGE – Understandings

MA-HS-M-U-1

Students will understand that measurable attributes of objects and the units, systems and processes of measurement are powerful tools for making sense of the world around them.

PE/TE: *Found throughout the text. See, for example:* 5, 7 (#25-48), 8 (#60), 9 (#61), 31 (#33-34), 32 (#35-36), 34-36, 37 (#3-6), 38 (#24-27), 39 (#29-30, 32-33), 40 (#34, 36), 44 (Example 7, Guided Practice 13), 46 (#54-55), 47 (#57-58), 54, 55 (Guided Practice 13), 57, 58 (#81-82, Quiz #14), 59 (#1-3, 8), 62 (#24), 63 (Example 1.5, #32-33), 85 (Example 5, Guided Practice 13), 87 (#45), 88 (#46, 48-49), 334 (#49-50), 335 (#51, 53), 373 (Example 4, Guided Practice 7), 376 (#45-46), 426 (#83-85), 450 (#35-36), 475 (#58), 563 (#42), 567 (Example 4, Guided Practice 5), 570 (#32-33), 618 (#47-52), 622 (Example 3), 623 (Guided Practice 9), 891 (Example 4), 893 (#44-46), 896 (#1, 4-6), 901 (#28, 30), 961 (#50), A2-A3

MA-HS-M-U-2

Students will understand that numerical values associated with measurements of physical quantities must be assigned units of measurement or dimensions.

PE/TE: *Found throughout the text. See, for example:* 31 (#33-34), 32 (#36), 33 (#5), 35 (Guided Practice 3), 39 (#29-30, 33), 40 (#34, 36), 54, 55 (Guided Practice 13), 57 (#74, 76-77), 58 (Quiz #14), 59 (#2, 8), 62 (#24), 85 (Example 5, Guided Practice 13), 88 (#46, 48), 334 (#49-50), 335 (#51, 53), 373 (Example 4, Guided Practice 7), 376 (#45-46), 426 (#83, 85), 450 (#36b), 475 (#58), 567 (Example 4, Guided Practice 5), 570 (#33), 622 (Example 3), 624 (#55), 625 (#57-59, 61), 631 (#65, 67), 636 (Example 3, Guided Practice 8), 638 (#48-49), 639 (#50), 644 (Example 3, Guided Practice 6), 891 (Example 4), 893 (#44-46), 895 (Problem, #4-5), 896 (#1, 4-6), 901 (#28, 30), 961 (#50), A2-A3

MA-HS-M-U-3

Students will understand that measurements are determined by using appropriate techniques, tools, formulas and degree of accuracy needed for the situation.

PE/TE: 991, 992, 993

High School Skills and Concepts – Measuring Physical Attributes

MA-HS-M-S-MPA1
Students will apply units of measurements of physical quantities correctly in expressions, equations and problem solutions that involve measurement.

PE/TE: *Found throughout the text. See, for example:* 31 (#33-34), 32 (#36), 33 (#5), 35 (Guided Practice 3), 39 (#29-30, 33), 40 (#34, 36), 54, 55 (Guided Practice 13), 57 (#74, 76-77), 58 (Quiz #14), 59 (#2, 8), 62 (#24), 85 (Example 5, Guided Practice 13), 88 (#46, 48), 334 (#49-50), 335 (#51, 53), 373 (Example 4, Guided Practice 7), 376 (#45-46), 426 (#83, 85), 450 (#36b), 475 (#58), 567 (Example 4, Guided Practice 5), 570 (#33), 622 (Example 3), 623 (Guided Practice 9), 624 (#55-56), 625 (#57-59, 61), 631 (#67), 636 (Example 3, Guided Practice 8), 638 (#48-49), 639 (#50), 644 (Example 3, Guided Practice 8), 891 (Example 4), 893 (#44-46), 895 (Problem, #4-5), 896 (#1, 4-6), 901 (#28, 30), 961 (#50)

MA-HS-M-S-MPA2
Students will analyze precision, accuracy and approximate error in measurement situations.

PE/TE: *Not addressed in this text.*

MA-HS-M-S-MPA3
Students will determine the surface area and volume of right rectangular prisms, pyramids, cylinders, cones and spheres in realistic problems.

PE/TE: 96 (#71), 332 (Example 5), 335 (#53), 386 (#67), 427 (#89), 436 (#1), 639 (#54), 780 (#17), 922 (#56)

MA-HS-M-S-MPA4
Students will describe how change in one or more dimensions of a geometric figure or object affects the perimeter, circumference, area and/or volume of the figure or object.

PE/TE: 332 (Example 5), 335 (#54)

MA-HS-M-S-MPA5
Students will explore the relationships between the right triangle trigonometric functions, using technology (e.g., graphing calculator) as appropriate.

PE/TE: 852-858, 865 (Quiz #1-6), 872 (#42), 873 (#2-3), 897 (Big Idea 1), 898 (Example 13.1, #6-7), 901(#1-3, 28, 30), 903 (#1), 904 (#3), 1022 (#1-10)

MA-HS-M-S-MPA6
Students will apply definitions and properties of right triangle relationships (basic right triangle trigonometry and the Pythagorean theorem) to determine length and angle measures to solve realistic problems.

PE/TE: 40 (#36), 88 (#48), 138 (#51), 202 (#47), 419 (#68), 464 (#6), 625 (#61), 833 (#50), 855, 857 (#30-34), 858 (#35-37), 877 (Example 4, Guided Practice 14), 879, 880 (#40, Quiz #17), 898 (#7), 899 (#17), 901 (#28), 903 (#1), 904 (#3)

MA-HS-M-S-MPA7
Students will apply special right triangles and the converse of the Pythagorean theorem to solve realistic problems.

PE/TE: *Opportunities to address this standard can be found on the following page:* 995

HIGH SCHOOL SKILLS AND CONCEPTS – Measuring Physical Attributes *(cont.)*

MA-HS-M-S-MPA8
Students will explore periodic real-world phenomena, using technology (e.g., graphing calculator) as appropriate.

PE/TE: 910 (Example 3), 911 (Guided Practice 9), 913 (#29-30), 914 (#31-33), 916 (Example 3), 918 (Example 6), 919 (Guided Practice 7), 921 (#50-53), 922 (#54-55, Quiz #13), 969 (#23)

HIGH SCHOOL SKILLS AND CONCEPTS – Systems of Measurement

MA-HS-M-S-SM1
Students will convert a measurement using one unit of measurement to another unit of measurement given the relationship between the units (e.g., miles per hour to feet per second, °F to °C).

PE/TE: 5 (Examples 5-6, Guided Practice 11-14), 7 (#31-48), 8 (#60), 9 (#61-62), 981

MA-HS-M-S-SM2
Students will apply to both real world and mathematical situations U.S. Customary and metric systems of measurement.

PE/TE: *Found throughout the text. See, for example:* 31 (#33-34), 32 (#36), 33 (#5), 35 (Guided Practice 3), 39 (#29-30, 33), 40 (#34, 36), 54, 55 (Guided Practice 13), 57 (#74, 76-77), 58 (Quiz #14), 59 (#2, 8), 62 (#24), 85 (Example 5, Guided Practice 13), 88 (#46, 48), 334 (#49-50), 335 (#51, 53), 373 (Example 4, Guided Practice 7), 376 (#45-46), 426 (#83, 85), 450 (#36b), 475 (#58, 60), 567 (Example 4, Guided Practice 5), 570 (#33), 622 (Example 3), 623 (Guided Practice 9), 624 (#55), 625 (#57-59, 61), 631 (#67), 636 (Example 3, Guided Practice 8), 638 (#48-49), 639 (#50), 644 (Example 3, Guided Practice 6), 891 (Example 4), 893 (#44-46), 895 (Problem, #4-5), 896 (#1, 4-6), 901 (#28, 30), 961 (#50)

MA-HS-M-S-SM3
Students will make decisions about units and scales that are appropriate for problem solving situations involving measurement.

PE/TE: A2 (Example 1), A3 (#1-4)

MA-HS-M-S-SM4
Students will use unit analysis to check measurement computations.

PE/TE: 5, 7 (#25-30), 34 (Example 1)

MA-HS-M-S-SM5
Students will compare and contrast the use of U.S. Customary and metric systems of measurement.

PE/TE: A2 (Measurement Systems), A3 (Conversions, Example 3, #11)

Big Idea: Geometry

High school students expand analysis of two-dimensional figures and three-dimensional objects. They translate figures in a coordinate plane. They extend work with congruent and similar figures, including proportionality.

Academic Expectations

2.9 Students understand space and dimensionality concepts and use them appropriately and accurately.

2.10 Students understand measurement concepts and use them appropriately and accurately.

2.12 Students understand mathematical structure concepts including the properties and logic of various mathematical systems.

HIGH SCHOOL ENDURING KNOWLEDGE – Understandings

MA-HS-G-U-1

Students will understand that characteristics and properties of two-dimensional figures and three-dimensional objects describe the world and are used to develop mathematical arguments about geometric relationships and to evaluate the arguments of others.

PE/TE: *Opportunities to address this standard can be found on the following pages:* 991, 992, 993, 1032

MA-HS-G-U-2

Students will understand that representational systems, including coordinate geometry, are means for specifying locations and describing spatial relationships and are organizers for making sense of the world around them.

PE/TE: 987, 988-989

MA-HS-G-U-3

Students will understand that transformations and symmetry are used to analyze real-world situations (e.g., art, nature, construction and scientific exploration).

PE/TE: *Opportunities to address this standard can be found on the following pages:* 988-989, 990

MA-HS-G-U-4

Students will understand that similarity of figures and scale factors are used to analyze and solve problems.

PE/TE: 16 (#65), 47 (#62), 307 (#79), 451 (#42), 755 (#27)

MA-HS-G-U-5

Students will understand that visualization, spatial reasoning and geometric relationships model real-world situations.

PE/TE: *Found throughout the text. See, for example:* 24 (#78), 31 (#33-34), 32 (#36, 38-39), 47 (#62), 85 (Example 5, Guided Practice 13), 88 (#47-48), 108 (Example 3), 109 (Guided Practice 6), 137 (#48), 173 (#42), 204 (Example 2), 208 (#40-41), 209 (#45-46), 232 (#42), 257 (#65-67), 258 (#69-72), 261 (Example 6), 264 (#62-63, 66), 265 (#67), 274 (#1, 6), 290 (#67), 291 (#68), 298 (#72), 351 (#62), 356 (Example 6, Guided Practice 11), 358 (#58-62), 359 (#63, 67), 360, 361 (#8-9), 373 (Example 4, Guided Practice 7), 376 (#45-46), 386 (#65), 389 (Example 3, Guided Practice 5), 391 (#39-40)

HIGH SCHOOL SKILLS AND CONCEPTS – Shapes and Relationships

MA-HS-G-S-SR1
Students will identify and apply the definitions, properties and theorems about line segments, rays and angles and use them to prove theorems in Euclidean geometry, solve problems and perform basic geometric constructions using a straight edge and a compass.

PE/TE: *Not addressed in this text.*

MA-HS-G-S-SR2
Students will identify and apply properties and theorems about parallel and perpendicular lines and use them to prove theorems and to perform constructions.

PE/TE: *Not addressed in this text.*

MA-HS-G-S-SR3
Students will analyze and apply angle relationships (e.g., linear pairs, vertical, complementary, supplementary, corresponding and alternate interior angles) in real-world or mathematical situations.

PE/TE: 32 (#41), 522 (#63), 595 (#40), 962 (#57), 994

MA-HS-G-S-SR4
Students will use the definitions, properties and theorems about congruent and similar triangles and other figures to prove additional theorems and apply these to solve real-world problems.

PE/TE: *Opportunities to address this standard can be found on the following pages:* 996-997

MA-HS-G-S-SR5
Students will use the definitions and basic properties of a circle (e.g., arcs, chords, central angles, inscribed angles) to prove basic theorems and solve problems.

PE/TE: *Not addressed in this text.*

MA-HS-G-S-SR6
Students will analyze and apply spatial relationships (not using Cartesian coordinates) among points, lines and planes (e.g., "betweenness" of points, midpoint, segment length, collinear, coplanar, parallel, perpendicular, skew).

PE/TE: 148 (#5), 149 (#13), 299 (#75)

MA-HS-G-S-SR7
Students will classify, determine attributes of, analyze and apply properties of two-dimensional geometric figures and three-dimensional objects.

PE/TE: 58 (#84), 59 (#7), 104 (#60), 185 (#50), 209 (#48), 299 (#75), 498 (#64), 557 (#44), 595 (#40), 614 (Example 2), 615 (Guided Practice 2), 617 (#22-30), 657 (#55), 771 (#34), 850 (#10-12)

MA-HS-G-S-SR8
Students will describe the intersection of lines, planes and solids and visualize three-dimensional objects and spaces from different perspectives and analyze their cross sections.

PE/TE: 178, 649, 657 (#53)

CORRELATIONS

High School Skills and Concepts – Shapes and Relationships *(cont.)*

MA-HS-G-S-SR9

Students will classify and apply properties of three-dimensional geometric figures.

PE/TE: 209 (#48), 557 (#44)

MA-HS-G-S-SR10

Students will visualize solids and surfaces in three-dimensional space when given two-dimensional representations and create two-dimensional representations for the surfaces of three-dimensional objects.

PE/TE: 178, 649, 657 (#53), 947 (#30)

MA-HS-G-S-SR11

Students will draw and construct representations of two-dimensional figures and three-dimensional objects using a variety of tools.

PE/TE: 881

MA-HS-G-S-SR12

Students will use geometric models and ideas to gain insights into and answer questions in other areas of mathematics and into other disciplines and areas of interest, such as art and architecture.

PE/TE: *Found throughout the text. See, for example:* 23 (#73), 24 (#74, 78), 31 (#33-34), 32 (#36, 38-39), 78 (#44-45), 108 (Example 2), 109 (Guided Practice 5), 204 (Example 2), 208 (#40-41), 209 (#45-46), 232 (#42), 254 (Example 4, Guided Practice 9), 257 (#65-67), 258 (#68-70, 72), 261 (Example 6), 264 (#62-63, 66), 283, 284 (Key Concept), 285 (Example 2) 290 (#67), 291 (#68), 298 (#72), 319 (#21), 334 (#49), 335 (#51-54), 351 (#62), 358 (#60, 62), 359 (#65, 67), 360, 361 (#8-10), 373 (Example 4, Guided Practice 7), 376 (#45-46), 377 (#51), 386 (#65), 389 (Example 3, Guided Practice 5), 392 (#42, 44), 399 (#29-30), 404 (#24), 419 (#65), 427 (#89, Quiz #15), 569 (#31), 570 (#32), 571 (#36), 574 (Example 2, Guided Practice 7), 578 (#21-22), 579 (#47-48), 580 (#51-53), 594 (#37), 616 (Example 5), 618 (#47-52), 619 (#53-56), 622 (Example 3), 623 (Guided Practice 9), 624 (#55-56), 625 (#57-59), 631 (#65-67), 632 (#69), 636 (Example 3, Guided Practice 8), 638 (#48-49), 639 (#50-53), 640, 644 (Example 3, Guided Practice 6), 646 (#38-39), 647, 649, 657 (#53), 663 (#41, 43), 664 (#45), 673 (#33), 701 (Example 5, Guided Practice 7), 703 (#34-37, 39), 737 (#28), 799 (#63), 809 (#68), 837 (#7), 855, 857 (#30-34), 858 (#35-37), 862 (Example 4, Guided Practice 9), 864, 865 (#54, Quiz #12), 1019 (#23-25)

MA-HS-G-S-SR13

Students will explore geometry to make and test conjectures using geometric tools and technology.

PE/TE: 881

High School Skills and Concepts – Transformations of Shapes

MA-HS-G-S-TS1

Students will understand and represent transformations within a plane (translations, reflections, rotations and dilations) of figures by using sketches, coordinates, vectors, function notation, matrices and technology.

PE/TE: 202 (#45), 291 (#69), 491 (#37), 930 (#47), 988-989

MA-HS-G-S-TS2

Students will use various representations, including electronic displays, to understand the effects of simple transformations within a plane and compositions of transformations.

PE/TE: *Opportunities to address this standard can be found on the following pages:* 988-989

HIGH SCHOOL SKILLS AND CONCEPTS – Coordinate Geometry

MA-HS-G-S-CG1
Students will express the intuitive concept of the "slant" of a line as slope, use the coordinates of two points on a line to determine its slope and use slope to express the parallelism and perpendicularity of lines.

PE/TE: 82-88, 96 (Quiz #4-5), 142 (Example 2.2, #8-11), 145 (#4-7), 147 (#1), 148 (#8), 149 (#11, 13), 167 (#65), 232 (#16-19), 271 (#45), 315 (#54), 344 (#62), 427 (#91), 723 (#43), 894 (#50), 1011 (#5-10)

MA-HS-G-S-CG2
Students will describe a line by a linear equation.

PE/TE: 98-104, 105, 106 (#7), 120 (Quiz #1-6), 138 (#50), 140 (Big Idea 3), 142 (Example 2.4, #16-18), 145 (#12-13), 1011 (#19-24)

MA-HS-G-S-CG3
Students will find the distance between two points using their coordinates and the Pythagorean theorem or the distance formula.

PE/TE: 614, 615 (Guided Practice 1-2), 617 (#3-18, 20-30), 618 (#47-52), 619 (#53), 632 (#71, Quiz #1-6), 669 (Example 9.1, #5-8), 673 (#1-6), 674, 677 (#13), 678 (#34-36), 749 (#32), 914 (#35), 1018 (#1-4)

MA-HS-G-S-CG4
Students will find the equation of a circle given its center and radius; given the equation of a circle, find its center and radius.

PE/TE: 626, 627 (Example 2, Guided Practice 1-4), 629 (#9-30), 632 (Quiz #13-18), 670 (Example 9.3, #15-20), 677 (#14), 1018 (#9-16)

MA-HS-G-S-CG5
Students will find the midpoint of a segment when the coordinates of the endpoints are identified.

PE/TE: 615 (Key Concept, Example 3), 616 (Guided Practice 3-5), 617 (#3-17, 19), 632 (Quiz #1-6), 648 (#46), 669 (Example 9.1, #5-7), 673 (#1-6), 677 (#8B), 678 (#34-36), 704 (#45), 1018 (#1-4)

MA-HS-G-S-CG6
Students will use Cartesian coordinates and other coordinate systems (e.g., navigational, polar, spherical systems) to analyze geometric situations.

PE/TE: 185 (#49-50), 204 (Example 2, Guided Practice 4), 208 (#40), 209 (#45-46), 614 (Example 2), 615 (Guided Practice 2), 617 (#22-30), 679 (#45), 704 (#44), 809 (#70), 858 (#35, 39), 872 (#38), A4-A6

MA-HS-G-S-CG7
Students will investigate conjectures and solve problems involving two-dimensional figures and three-dimensional objects represented graphically.

PE/TE: 129 (#39), 614 (Example 2), 615 (Guided Practice 2), 616 (Example 5, Guided Practice 6), 617 (#22-30), 619 (#53)

HIGH SCHOOL SKILLS AND CONCEPTS – Coordinate Geometry *(cont.)*

MA-HS-G-S-CG8
Students will use a variety of technological tools to explore and test conjectures about slope, midpoints and other geometric ideas that can be expressed using the Cartesian plane.

PE/TE: *Opportunities to address this standard can be found on the following pages:* 82-88, 614-619

HIGH SCHOOL SKILLS AND CONCEPTS – Foundational Statements

MA-HS-G-S-FS1
Students will identify, explain the necessity of and give examples of definitions, axioms and theorems.

PE/TE: *Not addressed in this text.*

MA-HS-G-S-FS2
Students will explore geometries other than Euclidean geometry, in which the parallel postulate is not true.

PE/TE: *Opportunities to address this standard can be found on the following pages:* A5-A6

MA-HS-G-S-FS3
Students will establish the validity of geometric conjectures using deduction, prove theorems and critique arguments made by others.

PE/TE: *Opportunities to address this standard can be found on the following pages:* 1000-1001

MA-HS-G-S-FS4
Students will perform constructions such as a line parallel to a given line through a point not on the line, the perpendicular bisector of a line segment and the bisector of an angle.

PE/TE: *Not addressed in this text.*

Big Idea: Data Analysis and Probability

High school students extend data representations, interpretations and conclusions. They describe data distributions in multiple ways and connect data gathering issues with data interpretation issues. They relate curve of best fit with two-variable data and determine line of best fit for a given set of data. They distinguish between combinations and permutations and compare and contrast theoretical and experimental probability.

Academic Expectations

2.8 Students understand various mathematical procedures and use them appropriately and accurately.

2.13 Students understand and appropriately use statistics and probability.

HIGH SCHOOL ENDURING KNOWLEDGE – Understandings

MA-HS-DAP-U-1

Students will understand that quantitative literacy is a necessary tool to be an intelligent consumer and citizen.

PE/TE: 7 (#28), 16 (Quiz #13), 23 (#68-72), 40 (Quiz #11-12), 48-49, 68 (#1, 5-6), 103 (#50, 53-54), 111 (#46-47), 155 (Example 4, Guided Practice 7), 157 (#35, 37-38), 185 (#46-47), 223 (#10), 230 (#4, 9), 316 (#2), 431 (Example 6, Guided Practice 13), 433 (#45), 679 (#42, 47), 688 (#63), 703 (#38), 737 (#27), 771 (#29), 773 (#2, 6)

MA-HS-DAP-U-2

Students will understand that data analysis requires developing a plan for collecting, organizing and analyzing data in order to make decisions.

PE/TE: 766-771, 772-773, 780 (#4-7), 782 (#2, 5-6), 783 (Big Idea 3), 786 (Example 11.4, #18-22), 787 (#13), 788, 790 (#7), 1008-1009, 1020 (#14-23)

MA-HS-DAP-U-3

Students will understand that graphical and numerical techniques can be used to study patterns and analyze data.

PE/TE: 744-749, 750, 751-755, 756, 757-762, 768, 769 (Example 5, Guided Practice 3), 770, 771 (#29-32), 775-780, 781, 783 (Big Ideas 1-2), 784 (Example 11.1, #4-8), 785 (Example 11.3, #12-17), 786, 787, 1005, 1006-1007, 1020, A18-A19

High School Enduring Knowledge – Understandings *(cont.)*

MA-HS-DAP-U-4
Students will understand that the choice of data display can affect the visual message communicated.

PE/TE: *Opportunities to address this standard can be found on the following pages:* 1006-1007

MA-HS-DAP-U-5
Students will understand that inferences and predictions from data are used to make critical and informed decisions.

PE/TE: 116 (Example 4), 117 (Guided Practice 4b-4c), 119 (#26, 27c), 139 (#6C), 777 (Guided Practice 3), 791 (#15D)

MA-HS-DAP-U-6
Students will understand that probability can be used to make decisions or predictions or to draw conclusions.

PE/TE: 704 (#42c), 723 (#41c)

High School Skills and Concepts – Data Representations

MA-HS-DAP-S-DR1
Students will be familiar with the definitions of measurement data and categorical data, univariate and bivariate data and the term variable.

PE/TE: *Opportunities to address this standard can be found on the following pages:* 112, 113-120, 143 (Example 2.6, #23), 724, 1006-1007, 1008-1009

MA-HS-DAP-S-DR2
Students will apply histograms, parallel box plots and scatterplots to display data.

PE/TE: 112, 113-120, 143 (Example 2.6, #23), 888 (#51), 1008 (Example c), 1009 (#5), A18, A19 (#2), A24-A25

MA-HS-DAP-S-DR3
Students will display the distribution, analyze patterns and describe relationships in paired data for univariate measurement data.

PE/TE: 1006-1007, 1008-1009

MA-HS-DAP-S-DR4
Students will display a scatterplot and describe its shape for bivariate data.

PE/TE: 112, 113-115, 117 (#2-9), 118 (#10-15, 19-23), 119 (#24-25, 27-28), 143 (Example 2.6, #23), 311, 314 (#48-50), 774, 775-780, 781, 786 (Example 11.5, #23), 787 (#14), 790 (#8), A18, A19 (#2), A24-A25

HIGH SCHOOL SKILLS AND CONCEPTS – Data Representations *(cont.)*

MA-HS-DAP-S-DR5
Students will display and discuss bivariate data where at least one variable is categorical.

PE/TE: 1006 (Examples 1-2), 1007 (#6-14)

MA-HS-DAP-S-DR6
Students will organize and display data using appropriate methods (e.g., spreadsheets and graphing calculators) to detect patterns and departures from patterns.

PE/TE: 116 (Example 5), 117 (Guided Practice 4), 118 (#19-20), 119 (#24-25), 311, 314 (#48-49), 774, 775-780, 781, 786 (Example 11.5, #23), 787 (#14), A18-A19, A24-A25

MA-HS-DAP-S-DR7
Students will identify and explain misleading uses of data displays.

PE/TE: A12-A13

HIGH SCHOOL SKILLS AND CONCEPTS – Characteristics of Data Sets

MA-HS-DAP-S-CDS1
Students will understand the distinction between a statistic and a parameter.

PE/TE: A7, A8 (#1-4)

MA-HS-DAP-S-CDS2
Students will describe the shape and select and calculate summary statistics for univariate measurement data, using technological tools as necessary.

PE/TE: 727 (Example 5, Guided Practice 5), 728 (#33-39), 742 (#2), 744-749, 750, 755 (Quiz #1-7), 756 (#1-3, 5-6), 783 (Big Idea 1), 784 (Example 11.1, #4-8), 787 (#1-3), 790 (#1-2, 6, 9), 791 (#12, 14), 848 (#31-36), 849 (#50), 1005, 1020 (#1-6), A8 (Example 2, #5)

MA-HS-DAP-S-CDS3
Students will recognize how linear transformations of univariate data affect shape, center and spread.

PE/TE: 751-755, 756 (#4, 7), 783 (Big Idea 1), 785 (Example 11.2, #9-11), 787 (#1-3), 791 (#11), 1020 (#7-10)

MA-HS-DAP-S-CDS4
Students will determine regression coefficients, regression equations and correlation coefficients for bivariate data using technological tools.

PE/TE: 114 (Example 2, Guided Practice 1-3), 116 (Example 5), 117 (Guided Practice 4c), 118 (#19-20, 22), 119

HIGH SCHOOL SKILLS AND CONCEPTS – Characteristics of Data Sets *(cont.)*

MA-HS-DAP-S-CDS5
Students will apply line-of-best fit equations for a set of two-variable data to make predictions.

PE/TE: 116 (Example 4), 117 (Guided Practice 4b), 119 (#27c), 139 (#6), 233 (#46), 475 (#53), 791 (#15)

MA-HS-DAP-S-CDS6
Students will collect, organize and display bivariate data and use a curve of best fit as a model to make predictions.

PE/TE: 308, 311, 314 (#48-50), 774, 775-780, 781, 782 (#1, 3), 786 (Example 11.5, #23), 787 (#14), 1020 (#24-25), A18, A19 (#2), A24-A25

MA-HS-DAP-S-CDS7
Students will identify trends in bivariate data and find functions that model the data or transform the data, so that they can be modeled.

PE/TE: 115-116, 118 (#10-16, 19-20), 119, 120 (Quiz #15), 139 (#6), 143 (Example 2.6, #23), 145 (#27), 149 (#15), 308, 311, 314 (#48-50), 774, 775-780, 781, 782 (#1, 3), 786 (Example 11.5, #23), 787 (#14), 789 (#3), 1011 (#29-30), 1020 (#24-25)

MA-HS-DAP-S-CDS8
Students will understand how simple statistics reflect the values of population parameters and use sampling distributions as the basis for informal inference.

PE/TE: A7-A8

MA-HS-DAP-S-CDS9
Students will explore how basic statistical techniques monitor process characteristics in the workplace.

PE/TE: A8 (Example 2, #5)

MA-HS-DAP-S-CDS10
Students will compare data sets using graphs and summary statistics.

PE/TE: 744 (Example 1), 745 (Example 2), 749 (#30), 791 (#14), 849 (#50)

MA-HS-DAP-S-CDS11
Students will know the characteristics of the Gaussian normal distribution (*bell-shaped curve*).

PE/TE: 757-762, 763-765, 780 (Quiz #1-3), 782 (#7), 783 (Big Idea 2), 785 (Example 11.3, #12-17), 787 (#4-12), 789 (Problem 2, #1), 790 (#3-5), 791 (#10, 13), 1020 (#11-13)

MA-HS-DAP-S-CDS12
Students will evaluate reports based on data published in the media by considering the source of the data, the design of the study and the way the data are displayed and analyzed.

PE/TE: A9-A11

MA-HS-DAP-S-CDS13
Students will identify and explain misleading uses of data.

PE/TE: A12-A13

HIGH SCHOOL SKILLS AND CONCEPTS – Experiments and Samples

MA-HS-DAP-S-ES1
Students will understand and explain the differences among various kinds of studies (e.g., randomized experiments and observational studies) and which types of inferences can be legitimately be drawn from each.

PE/TE: *Opportunities to address this standard can be found on the following pages:* 766-767, 769 (#3-5), 770 (#28), 772-774, 783 (Big Idea 3)

MA-HS-DAP-S-ES2
Students will know the characteristics of well-designed studies, including the role of randomization in surveys and experiments.

PE/TE: *Opportunities to address this standard can be found on the following pages:* 766-767, 769 (#3-5), 770 (#28), 772-774, 783 (Big Idea 3)

MA-HS-DAP-S-ES3
Students will use simulations to explore the variability of sample statistics from a known population and to construct sampling distributions.

PE/TE: A14-A15

MA-HS-DAP-S-ES4
Students will evaluate published reports that are based on interpretations of data by examining the design of the study, the appropriateness of the data analysis and the validity of the conclusions.

PE/TE: A9-A11

MA-HS-DAP-S-ES5
Students will explain the impact of sampling methods, bias and the phrasing of questions asked during data collection and the conclusions that can be justified.

PE/TE: 766-767, 769 (#3-5), 772-773

MA-HS-DAP-S-ES6
Students will design and conduct simple experiments or investigations to collect data to answer student-generated questions.

PE/TE: *Opportunities to address this standard can be found on the following pages:* 772-773

HIGH SCHOOL SKILLS AND CONCEPTS – Probability

MA-HS-DAP-S-P1
Students will design and conduct probability simulations and interpret the results.

PE/TE: 714, A14, A15 (#1-3)

MA-HS-DAP-S-P2
Students will apply the concepts of sample space and probability distribution to construct sample spaces and distributions in simple cases.

PE/TE: 724 (Example 1), 725 (Guided Practice 1), 726 (Example 3), 727 (#3-5), 728 (#33-38), 729 (#46a, 47c), 730 (#48c, Quiz #8-10), 731, A15 (Example 2, #3b)

MA-HS-DAP-S-P3
Students will design simulations to construct empirical probability distributions and report/interpret the results.

PE/TE: A14, A15 (#1-3)

MA-HS-DAP-S-P4
Students will compute and interpret the expected value of random variables in simple cases.

PE/TE: A21 (Example 2, #1c, 2c)

MA-HS-DAP-S-P5
Students will apply the concepts of conditional probability and independent events and be able to compute those probabilities.

PE/TE: 717-723, 730 (Quiz #4-7), 732 (#1-3), 733 (Big Idea 2), 736 (Example 10.5, #23-25), 737 (#20), 739 (Problem 2), 849 (#49), 1019 (#33-35)

MA-HS-DAP-S-P6
Students will compute the probability of a compound event.

PE/TE: 707-713, 732 (#5-6), 736 (Example 10.4, #20-22), 737 (#29), 740 (#5), 741 (#9, 12), 762 (#38), 848 (#28-30), 1019 (#26-32)

MA-HS-DAP-S-P7
Students will explain how probability quantifies the likelihood that an event occurs in terms of numbers.

PE/TE: 698 (Key Vocabulary), 742 (#1)

MA-HS-DAP-S-P8
Students will explain how the relative frequency of a specified outcome of an event can be used to estimate the probability of the outcome.

PE/TE: 700 (Key Concept, Example 4, Guided Practice 6), 702 (#28-32), 735 (#19), A20-A21

MA-HS-DAP-S-P9
Students will explain how the law of large numbers can be applied in simple examples.

PE/TE: A17 (Key Concept, #7)

HIGH SCHOOL SKILLS AND CONCEPTS – Probability *(cont.)*

MA-HS-DAP-S-P10
Students will determine and compare theoretical and experimental probabilities.

PE/TE: 698, 700 (Key Concept, Example 4, Guided Practice 6), 701 (#2-10), 702 (#11-19, 26, 28-32), 703 (#38, 40), 704 (#42-43), 705 (#4), 713 (Quiz #1-6), 735 (Example 10.3, #15-19), 737 (#13-16), 738, 740 (#1-4), 741 (#10, 15), 742 (#5-8), 809 (#71), 1019 (#21-25), A16, A17 (#1-6), A20 (Example 1b), A21 (#1b, 2b)

MA-HS-DAP-S-P11
Students will determine the probability of an event and the probability of its complement.

PE/TE: 709, 710 (#16-19, 25), 712 (#44), 736 (#21-22)

MA-HS-DAP-S-P12
Students will make predictions and draw inferences from probabilities and apply probability concepts to practical situations to make informed decisions.

PE/TE: *Opportunities to address this standard can be found on the following pages:* 698-704, 707-713, 717-723

MA-HS-DAP-S-P13
Students will determine probabilities involving replacement and non-replacement.

PE/TE: 719 (Example 5, Guided Practice 5-6), 722 (#26-32), 730 (Quiz #1-3), 736 (Example 10.5, #23-25), 865 (#56), 1019 (#33-35)

MA-HS-DAP-S-P14
Students will recognize and identify the differences between combinations and permutations and use them to count discrete quantities.

PE/TE: 684-685, 686 (Example 6, Guided Practice 8-10), 687 (#30-57, 61), 688 (#64-68), 689 (#69-71), 690, 694 (#2-18), 695 (#38-47), 696, 697 (#53, Quiz #3-10, 16), 705 (#1, 3, 5-6), 734 (Example 10.1), 735 (#5-9, 14), 737 (#1-8, 27), 739 (#1), 740 (#2-3, 6), 741 (#9, 14), 755 (#26), 1019 (#1-16)

MA-HS-DAP-S-P15
Students will represent probabilities in multiple ways (e.g., fractions, decimals, percentages, geometric area models).

PE/TE: 698-704, 706, 707-713, 714, 717-723, 724-730, 731, 732, 735 (Example 10.3, #15-19), 736, 737 (#13-26, 28-30), 738, 739 (Problem 2, #2), 740 (#1, 5), 741 (#12-13, 15A), 742 (#5-8), 1019 (#21-39), A14-A15, A16, A17 (#1-6), A20 (Example 1b), A21 (#1b, 2b)

Big Idea: Algebraic Thinking

High school students extend analysis and use of functions and focus on linear, quadratic, absolute value and exponential functions. They explore parametric changes on graphs of functions. They use rules and properties to simplify algebraic expressions. They combine simple rational expressions and simple polynomial expressions. They factor polynomial expressions and quadratics of the form $1x^2 + bx + c$.

Academic Expectations

2.7 Students understand number concepts and use numbers appropriately and accurately.
2.8 Students understand various mathematical procedures and use them appropriately and accurately.
2.11 Students understand mathematical change concepts and use them appropriately and accurately.
2.12 Students understand mathematical structure concepts including the properties and logic of various mathematical systems.

HIGH SCHOOL ENDURING KNOWLEDGE – Understandings

MA-HS-AT-U-1
Students will understand that patterns, relations and functions are tools that help explain or predict real-world phenomena.

PE/TE: 76 (Example 6, Guided Practice 7), 78 (#46-47), 79 (48-51), 113 (Example 1), 115 (Example 3), 116, 117 (Guided Practice 4), 119, 120 (#29, Quiz #15), 125 (Example 4), 126 (Guided Practice 4), 128 (#36-38), 129 (#39-42), 131 (#8), 144 (#27), 145 (#25-27), 239 (Example 5, Guided Practice 8), 242, 243 (#60-61), 246 (Example 2, Guided Practice 4), 247 (Example 4, Guided Practice 8), 250 (#51-53), 251 (#54-56), 307 (#78), 311 (Example 4, Guided Practice 7), 314, 315 (#51), 322 (#48), 323 (#32), 340 (Example 6), 341 (Guided Practice 12), 343 (#54-57), 344 (#58-60), 348 (Example 6, Guided Practice 6), 351, 352 (#64), 365 (Example 6, Guided Practice 9), 367 (#41-42), 368 (#43-46), 376 (#48-50), 383 (Example 6, Guided Practice 12), 385 (#59-62), 386 (#63-65), 389 (Example 3, Guided Practice 5), 391 (#39-40), 396, 398 (#26-28), 399 (#13), 403 (#16), 405 (#38), 429 (Example 3, Guided Practice 7), 431 (Example 6, Guided Practice 13), 433 (#43-45), 434 (#46), 439 (Example 3, Guided Practice 4), 441 (Example 6), 442 (Example 7, Guided Practice 11), 444, 445 (Quiz #19), 447 (Example 3, Guided Practice 5), 450 (#35-37), 451 (#38-39), 453 (Example 2, Guided Practice 4), 457 (#56), 458, 460-461, 469 (#37-38), 475 (#57), 480 (Example 4, Guided Practice 4-5), 481, 484, 485 (#41-44), 488 (Example 4, Guided Practice 7-8), 489 (#26), 490 (#30-32), 491 (#33-36), 494 (Example 4, Guided Practice 9), 495 (Example 5, Guided Practice 10-11), 497, 498 (#61-62), 500 (Example 4), 501 (Guided Practice 9), 504 (#58-59), 505 (#60-63), 509 (Example 5, Guided Practice 11), 511 (#62-63), 512, 513 (#74, Quiz #20), 516 (Example 3), 519 (Example 7, Guided Practice 11), 521, 522 (#60-61), 524, 525 (Method 2, #9, 11-13), 530 (Example 2), 531 (Guided Practice 4), 532 (Example 5), 533 (Guided Practice 9), 534 (#31), 535, 536 (#36, Quiz #16), 539 (#9), 540 (#16), 541 (#24), 542 (#38), 543 (#27-29), 560 (Example 4), 561 (Guided Practice 7), 562 (#37-39), 563 (#40-42), 567 (Example 4, Guided Practice 5),

HIGH SCHOOL ENDURING KNOWLEDGE – Understandings *(cont.)*

569 (#31), 570, 571 (#36, Quiz #11), 592 (Example 6, Guided Practice 11), 595 (#38), 596-597, 607 (#29), 795 (Example 3, Guided Practice 5), 800 (#65-67), 808, 809 (#68-69), 813 (Example 6, Guided Practice 8), 815 (#57-58), 816, 817 (#62, Quiz #16), 829 (Example 4, Guided Practice 10), 832, 833 (#48, Quiz #19), 834-835, 841 (#16), 842 (#38), 843 (#33), 869 (Example 5), 870 (Example 6, Guided Practice 10-11), 871 (#35-37), 872 (#38-40), 877 (Example 4, Guided Practice 14), 879, 880 (#40, Quiz #17), 899 (#17), 901 (#28-30), 910 (Example 3), 911 (Guided Practice 9), 913 (#29-30), 914 (#31-33), 916 (Example 3), 918 (Example 6), 919 (Guided Practice 7), 921 (#50-53), 922 (#54-55, Quiz #13), 929 (#41), 932 (Example 3), 933 (Guided Practice 3), 936 (#41-42), 937 (#43-44), 938-939, 942 (Example 2, Guided Practice 3), 943 (Example 3, Guided Practice 4), 945 (#23-25), 946, 947 (Quiz #12), 969 (#23-34)

MA-HS-AT-U-2

Students will understand that there are relationships between and among patterns and functions, their representations and their properties.

PE/TE: 89-96, 97, 121-122, 123-129, 130-131, 140 (Big Ideas 2-3), 142 (Example 2.3, #12-15), 144 (Example 2.7, #24-27), 145 (#8-11), 236-243, 245-251, 265 (Quiz #1-6), 308, 317 (Big Idea 1), 318 (Example 4.1, #5-7), 319 (Example 4.2, #8-14), 323 (#1-3), 336, 337, 338 (Guided Practice 1-3), 339 (Key Concept, Example 4, Guided Practice 8), 340, 341 (Guided Practice 9-12, #2-8), 342 (#24-51), 343 (#53, 55-57), 344 (#58-60), 387-392, 393 (Example 1), 394 (Key Concept), 395-396, 397 (#3-5, 18-21), 398 (#25-28), 399 (Quiz #7-10, 13), 401 (Big Ideas 1, 3), 403 (Example 5.2, #13-16), 406, 407 (#5-7, 19-26, 28-29), 437, 438-444, 445 (#51, Quiz #9-18), 446-451, 459 (Quiz #1-6), 465 (Big Ideas 2-3), 467 (Example 6.4, #24-26), 468 (Example 6.5, #27-29), 469 (#25-33, 37-38), 478-480, 482 (#3-25), 483 (#26-30, 32), 484 (#35-36, 39-40), 485 (#41-42), 486-491, 493 (Key Concept, Example 3), 494 (Example 4, Guided Practice 6-9), 495 (#2), 496 (#31-50), 497 (#59-60), 498 (#62, Quiz #1-3, 8-11), 501 (Example 6, Guided Practice 14-15), 502, 503 (Example 8, Guided Practice 16-18), 504 (#37-53), 505 (#60-63), 506 (#2, 5), 513 (Quiz #5-7), 514, 529, 530 (Example 2), 531 (Guided Practice 1-3, Example 4, Guided Practice 5-8), 532, 533 (#3-14), 534 (#15-29, 31), 535, 536 (#36, Quiz #10-15), 537 (#2, 4), 538 (Big Ideas 1, 3), 539 (Example 7.1, #6-8), 540 (Example 7.2, #10-12, Example 7.3, #13-15), 541 (#21-23), 542 (Example 7.7, #35-38), 543 (#1-9, 13-15, 25-27, 29), 551-557, 558-563, 564, 565-571, 572 (#4, 6-7), 602 (Big Idea 1), 603 (Example 8.1, #6-9), 604, 607 (#1-12, 28-29), 679 (#49), 908-914, 915-922, 941-947, 964 (Big Idea 1), 965 (Example 14.1, #6-9), 966 (Example 14.2, #10-15), 967 (Example 14.5, #24-25), 969 (#1-11, 23-24), 1011 (#11-28, 31-34), 1013 (#1-12, 53-55), 1014 (#8-11, 31-32), 1015 (#34-47), 1016 (#1-8, 13-16, 25-28, 46-53), 1017 (#1-4, 9-16), 1023 (#1-10, 24-25)

High School Enduring Knowledge – Understandings *(cont.)*

MA-HS-AT-U-3

Students will understand that algebra represents mathematical situations and structures for analysis and problem solving.

PE/TE: *Found throughout the text. See, for example:* 11 (Example 3, Guided Practice 7), 13 (Example 5, Guided Practice 15), 15 (#57-62), 16 (#63, Quiz #13), 20 (Example 5), 21 (Guided Practice 11), 23 (#68-73), 24, 29 (Example 5, Guided Practice 14-15), 32 (#35-38), 33, 34-39, 40 (Quiz #11-12), 42 (Example 3), 44 (Example 7, Guided Practice 13), 46, 47 (#57-60), 54 (Example 6), 55 (Guided Practice 13), 57, 58 (#81-82, Quiz #13-14), 59 (#2-3, 8), 62 (#16, 23-24), 63 (Example 1.5, #32-33), 64 (#40, 47), 65 (#28-30), 66-67, 68, 76 (Example 6, Guided Practice 7), 78 (#46-47), 79 (#48-50), 113 (Example 1), 115 (Example 3), 116, 117 (Guided Practice 4), 119, 120 (#29, Quiz #15), 125 (Example 4), 126 (Guided Practice 4), 128 (#36-38), 129 (#39-42), 131 (#8), 144 (#27), 145 (#25-27), 239 (Example 5, Guided Practice 8), 242, 243 (#60-61), 246 (Example 2, Guided Practice 4), 247 (Example 4, Guided Practice 8), 250 (#51-53), 251 (#54-56), 311 (Example 4, Guided Practice 7), 314, 315 (#51), 322 (#48), 323 (#32), 340 (Example 6), 341 (Guided Practice 12), 343 (#54-57), 344 (#58-60), 348 (Example 6, Guided Practice 6), 351, 352 (#64), 365 (Example 6, Guided Practice 9), 367 (#41-42), 368 (#43-46), 376 (#48-50), 383 (Example 6, Guided Practice 12), 385 (#59-62), 386 (#63-65), 389 (Example 3, Guided Practice 5), 391 (#39-40), 392 (#41-44), 396, 398 (#26-28), 399 (Quiz #13), 403 (#16), 405 (#38), 429 (Example 3, Guided Practice 7), 431 (Example 6, Guided Practice 13), 433 (#43-45), 434 (#46), 439 (Example 3, Guided Practice 4), 441 (Example 6), 442 (Example 7, Guided Practice 11), 444, 445 (Quiz #19), 447 (Example 3, Guided Practice 5), 450 (#35-37), 451 (#38-39), 453 (Example 2, Guided Practice 4), 457 (#56), 458, 460-461, 469 (#37-38), 475 (#57), 480 (Example 4, Guided Practice 4-5), 481, 484, 485 (#41-44), 488 (Example 4, Guided Practice 7-8), 489 (#26), 490 (#30-32), 491 (#33-36), 494 (Example 4, Guided Practice 9), 495 (Example 5, Guided Practice 10-11), 497, 498 (#61-62, Quiz #12-13), 500 (Example 4), 501 (Guided Practice 9), 504 (#58-59), 505 (#60-63), 509 (Example 5, Guided Practice 11), 511 (#62-63), 512, 513 (#74, Quiz #20), 516 (Example 3), 519 (Example 7, Guided Practice 11), 521, 522 (#60-61), 524, 525 (Method 2, #9, 11-13), 530 (Example 2), 531 (Guided Practice 4), 532 (Example 5), 533 (Guided Practice 9), 534 (#31), 535, 536 (#36, Quiz #16), 539 (#9), 540 (#16), 541 (#24), 542 (#38), 543 (#27-29), 560 (Example 4), 561 (Guided Practice 7), 562 (#37-39), 563 (#40-42), 567 (Example 4, Guided Practice 5), 569 (#31), 570, 571 (#36, Quiz #11), 592 (Example 6, Guided Practice 11), 595 (#38), 596-597, 607 (#29), 795 (Example 3, Guided Practice 5), 800 (#65-67), 808, 809 (#68-69), 813 (Example 6, Guided Practice 8), 815 (#57-58), 816, 817 (#62, Quiz #16), 829 (Example 4, Guided Practice 10), 832, 833 (#48, Quiz #19), 834-835, 841 (#16), 842 (#38), 843 (#33), 869 (Example 5), 870 (Example 6, Guided Practice 10-11), 871 (#35-37), 872 (#38-40), 877 (Example 4, Guided Practice 14), 879, 880 (#40, Quiz #17), 899 (#17), 901 (#28-30), 910 (Example 3), 911 (Guided Practice 9), 913 (#29-30), 914 (#31-33), 916 (Example 3), 918 (Example 6), 919 (Guided Practice 7), 921 (#50-53), 922 (#54-55, Quiz #13), 929 (#41), 932 (Example 3), 933 (Guided Practice 3), 936 (#41-42), 937 (#43-44), 938-939, 942 (Example 2, Guided Practice 3), 943 (Example 3, Guided Practice 4), 945 (#23-25), 946, 947 (Quiz #12), 969 (#23-34)

HIGH SCHOOL ENDURING KNOWLEDGE – Understandings *(cont.)*

MA-HS-AT-U-4
Students will understand that real-world situations can be represented using mathematical models to analyze quantitative relationships.

PE/TE: *Found throughout the text. See, for example:* 11 (Example 2-3, Guided Practice 7), 13 (Example 5, Guided Practice 15), 15 (#58-62), 16 (#63, Quiz #13), 20 (Example 5), 21 (Guided Practice 11), 23 (#72-73), 24 (#74), 32 (#37), 33 (#6-7), 34-39, 40 (Quiz #11-12), 42 (Example 3), 44 (Example 7, Guided Practice 13), 46, 47 (#57-60), 54 (Example 6), 55 (Guided Practice 13), 57, 58 (#81-82, Quiz #13-14), 59 (#2-3, 8), 62 (#16, 23-24), 63 (Example 1.5, #32-33), 64 (#40, 47), 65 (#28-30), 66-67, 68, 81 (#5-9), 95 (#67), 100 (Example 5, Guided Practice 9), 101 (Example 6, Guided Practice 10), 103 (#50-54), 104 (#55-58), 105 (#2-5), 106 (#1, 5-6), 108, 109 (Guided Practice 5-6), 110 (#38-41), 111 (#44-45), 115 (Example 3), 116, 117 (Guided Practice 4), 119, 120 (Quiz #15), 125 (Example 4), 126 (Guided Practice 4), 128 (#38), 129 (#39, 41), 134 (Example 4), 135 (Guided Practice 11), 137, 138 (Quiz #10), 139 (#1, 5-6), 144 (#27), 145 (#25-27), 147 (#2), 148 (#2, 5), 149 (#15), 239 (Example 5, Guided Practice 8), 242 (#55-56, 58), 243 (#60-61), 250 (#51-53), 251 (#54-56), 262 (Example 7, Guided Practice 22), 265 (#67), 268, 269 (Example 5, Guided Practice 20), 270 (#38), 271 (#40-41), 274 (#7), 311 (Example 4, Guided Practice 7), 314, 319 (#21), 322 (#48), 323 (#32), 396, 398 (#26-28), 399 (Quiz #13), 405 (#38), 407 (#28-29), 439 (Example 3, Guided Practice 4), 441 (Example 6), 442 (Example 7, Guided Practice 11), 444, 451 (#39), 469 (#37-38), 480, 483 (#28-30), 484 (#39-40), 485 (#41-42), 488, 490 (#31-32), 491 (#36), 530, 532 (Example 5), 533 (Example 6, Guided Practice 9), 534 (#31), 535, 536 (#36), 537 (#4), 542 (#38), 543 (#27, 29), 546 (#1), 547 (#17-18), 552 (Example 3, Guided Practice 7), 553 (Example 4, Guided Practice 8), 556 (#37-40), 557 (#41), 560 (Example 4), 561 (Guided Practice 7), 562 (#37-38), 564 (#9), 567 (Example 4, Guided Practice 5), 569 (#31), 570 (#32), 571 (#36, Quiz #11), 572 (#6), 606 (#36), 607 (#28-29), 611 (#13), 775-780, 781, 782 (#1, 3), 910 (Example 3), 911 (Guided Practice 9), 913 (#30), 914 (#31-33), 942 (Example 2, Guided Practice 3), 943, 945 (#23-25), 946, 947 (Quiz #12), 969 (#23-24)

MA-HS-AT-U-5
Students will understand that functions are used to analyze change in various contexts and model real-world phenomena.

PE/TE: 76 (Example 6, Guided Practice 7), 78 (#46-47), 79 (#48, 50), 81 (Example 2, #5-9), 91 (Example 3, Guided Practice 10), 94 (#59-62), 95, 96 (Quiz #9), 100 (Example 5, Guided Practice 9), 103 (#50-54), 104 (#55-58), 105 (#2-5), 106 (#1, 4-6), 108, 109 (Guided Practice 5-6), 110 (#38-41), 111 (#44-45), 112, 115 (Example 3), 116, 117 (Guided Practice 4), 119, 120 (Quiz #15), 125 (Example 4), 126 (Guided Practice 4), 128 (#36-38), 129 (#39-42), 139 (#1, 3-6), 143 (#22), 144 (#27), 145 (#25-27), 146, 147 (#2), 148 (#2, 4-5), 149 (#15-16), 239 (Example 5, Guided Practice 8), 242, 243 (#60-63), 250 (#51-53), 251 (#54-56), 262 (Example 7, Guided Practice 22), 265 (#67), 268, 269 (Example 5, Guided Practice 20), 270 (#38-39), 271 (#40-43), 272-273, 274 (#1-4, 6-7), 311 (Example 4, Guided Practice 7), 314, 319 (#21), 322 (#48), 323 (#32), 340 (Example 6), 341 (Guided Practice 12), 343 (#54-57), 344 (#58-60), 369 (#5-6), 396, 398 (#26-28), 399 (Quiz #13), 403 (#16), 405 (#38), 407 (#28-29), 408-409, 410 (#1, 3, 5),

411 (#8), 439 (Example 3, Guided Practice 4), 441 (Example 6), 442 (Example 7, Guided Practice 11), 444, 447 (Example 3, Guided Practice 5), 450 (#35-37), 451 (#38-39), 469 (#37-38), 480, 481 (Example 5, Guided Practice 6), 483 (#28-30), 484, 485 (#41-45), 488, 490 (#30-32), 491 (#33-36), 530, 532 (Example 5), 533 (Example 6, Guided Practice 9), 534 (#31), 535, 536 (#36, Quiz #16), 537 (#4-5), 540 (#16), 542 (#38), 543 (#27-29), 546 (#1, 6), 547 (#17-19), 552 (Example 3, Guided Practice 7), 553 (Example 4, Guided Practice 8), 556 (#37-40), 557 (#41), 560 (Example 4), 561 (Guided Practice 7), 562 (#37-39), 563 (#40-42), 564 (#9), 567 (Example 4, Guided Practice 5), 569 (#31), 570 (#32-35), 571 (#36, Quiz #11), 572 (#6), 606 (#36), 607 (#28-30), 611 (#13-14), 775-780, 781, 782 (#1, 3), 910 (Example 3), 911 (Guided Practice 9), 913 (#30), 914 (#31-33), 942 (Example 2, Guided Practice 3), 943, 945 (#23-25), 946, 947 (Quiz #12), 969 (#23-24)

MA-HS-AT-U-6
Students will understand that functions can be written in words, in a symbolic sentence or in a table or graph.

PE/TE: 89-96, 97, 121-122, 123-129, 130-131, 140 (Big Ideas 2-3), 142 (Example 2.3, #12-15), 144 (Example 2.7, #24-27), 145 (#8-11, 20), 236-243, 245-251, 265 (#1-6), 308, 317 (Big Idea 1), 318 (Example 4.1, #5-7), 319 (Example 4.2, #8-14), 323 (#1-3), 336, 337, 338 (Guided Practice 1-3), 339 (Key Concept, Example 4, Guided Practice 8), 340, 341 (Guided Practice 9-12, #2-8), 342 (#24-51), 343 (#53, 55-57), 344 (#58-60), 387-392, 393 (Example 1), 394 (Key Concept), 395-396, 397 (#3-5, 18-21), 398 (#25-28), 399 (Quiz #7-10, 13), 401 (Big Ideas 1, 3), 403 (Example 5.2, #13-16), 406, 407 (#5-7, 19-26, 28-29), 437, 438-444, 445 (#51, Quiz #9-18), 446-451, 459 (Quiz #1-6), 465 (Big Ideas 2-3), 467 (Example 6.4, #24-26), 468 (Example 6.5, #27-29), 469 (#25-33, 37-38), 478-480, 482 (#3-25), 483 (#26-30, 32), 484 (#35-36, 39-40), 485 (#41-42), 486-491, 493 (Key Concept, Example 3), 494 (Example 4, Guided Practice 6-9), 495 (#2), 496 (#31-50), 497 (#59-60), 498 (#62, Quiz #1-3, 8-11), 501 (Example 6, Guided Practice 14-15), 502, 503 (Example 8, Guided Practice 16-18), 504 (#37-53), 505 (#60-63), 506 (#2, 5), 513 (Quiz #5-7), 514, 529, 530 (Example 2), 531 (Guided Practice 1-3, Example 4, Guided Practice 5-7), 532, 533 (#3-14), 534 (#15-29, 31), 535, 536 (#36, Quiz #10-15), 537 (#2, 4), 538 (Big Ideas 1, 3), 539 (Example 7.1, #6-8), 540 (Example 7.2, #10-12, Example 7.3, #13-15), 541 (#21-23), 542 (Example 7.7, #35-38), 543 (#1-9, 13-15, 25-27, 29), 551-557, 558-563, 564, 565-571, 572 (#4, 6-7), 602 (Big Idea 1), 603 (Example 8.1, #6-9), 604, 607 (#1-12, 28-29), 679 (#49), 908-914, 915-922, 941-947, 964 (Big Idea 1), 965 (Example 14.1, #6-9), 966 (Example 14.2, #10-15), 967 (Example 14.5, #24-25), 969 (#1-11, 23-24), 1011 (#11-28, 31-34), 1013 (#1-12, 53-55), 1014 (#8-11, 31-32), 1015 (#34-47), 1016 (#1-8, 13-16, 25-28, 46-53), 1017 (#1-4, 9-16), 1023 (#1-10, 24-25)

HIGH SCHOOL SKILLS AND CONCEPTS – Patterns, Relations and Functions

MA-HS-AT-S-PRF1
Students will use explicitly-defined or recursively defined functions to generalize patterns.

PE/TE: 37 (#11-15), 38 (#22-23, 27), 39 (#28), 40 (Quiz #9-10), 107-111, 112, 113-120, 143, 145 (#14-19, 27), 311, 314 (#48-50), 322 (#48), 323 (#32), 396, 397 (#18-21), 398 (#25-28), 399 (Quiz #13), 406 (Example 5.9, #41), 774, 775-780, 781, 786 (Example 11.5, #23), 787 (#14), 803, 804 (Example 4, Guided Practice 2-4), 806 (#12-29), 807 (#30-39, 62), 808 (#63-66), 809 (#68-69), 810 (Key Concept), 811, 812 (Example 4, Guided Practice 4-6), 814 (#15-39), 815 (#39-47, 57-58), 816, 817 (Quiz #1-6, 10-16), 826 (#2-3), 828-829, 831 (#13-23, 34-39), 832 (#43-45, 47), 833 (#48, Quiz #10-12), 838 (#2, 7), 839 (Big Ideas 1, 3), 841 (Example 12.2, #9-11, 16, Example 12.3, #17-19), 842 (Example 12.5, #35-38), 843 (#9-12, 25-28, 33), 844, 846 (#2), 847 (#15), 848 (#41-43), 1021 (#10-21, 33-35)

MA-HS-AT-S-PRF2
Students will understand relations and functions and use various representations for them.

PE/TE: *Found throughout the text. See, for example:* 72-79, 80-81, 89-96, 97, 98-104, 105, 107-111, 121-122, 123-129, 130-131, 140, 141 (Example 2.1, #5-7), 142 (Example 2.3, #12-15, Example 2.4, #16-18), 143 (Example 2.5, #19-22), 145 (#1-2, 8-17, 20, 25-27), 236-238, 239 (Example 5, Guided Practice 8), 240 (#1, 3-32), 241 (#43-52), 242 (#55-56, 59), 243 (#60), 245-251, 265 (#67, Quiz #1-6), 270 (#38), 271 (#41), 272-273, 287 (Example 6, Guided Practice 13-15), 289 (#41-49), 290 (#64-67), 291 (Quiz #13-18), 297 (#63-65), 309-315, 317 (Big Idea 1), 318 (Example 4.1, #5-7), 319 (Example 4.2, #8-14), 322 (Example 4.10, #45-48), 323 (#1-3, 28-30), 340, 341 (Guided Practice 9-12), 342 (#38-50), 343 (#55-57), 344 (#58-60), 352 (Quiz #16), 356 (Example 6, Guided Practice 11), 358 (#60), 360-361, 368 (#44), 369 (#2), 376 (#49-50), 386 (#64), 387-392, 393-399, 401 (Big Ideas 1, 3), 403 (Example 5.2, #13-16), 406, 407 (#5-7, 23-24, 29), 446-451, 459 (Quiz #1-6), 465 (Big Idea 3), 468 (Example 6.5, #27-29), 469 (#31-33), 478-485, 486-491, 493 (Key Concept, Example 3), 494 (Example 4, Guided Practice 6-9), 495 (#2), 496 (#31-51), 497 (#59-60), 498 (Quiz #1-3, 8-12), 502, 503 (Example 8, Guided Practice 16-18), 504 (#45-53), 505 (#62-63), 513 (Quiz #5-7), 514, 529, 530 (Example 2), 531-532, 533 (#3-14), 534 (#15-26, 31), 535, 536 (#36, Quiz #10-15), 538 (Big Ideas 1, 3), 539 (Example 7.1, #6-8), 540, 541 (#21-23), 542 (Example 7.7, #35-38), 543 (#1-9, 13-15, 25-27, 29), 558-563, 564, 565-571, 589 (Example 2), 590 (Guided Practice 4), 594 (#34-35), 602 (Big Idea 1), 604, 606 (#36), 607 (#7-12, 28-29), 775-780, 781, 786 (Example 11.5, #23), 787 (#14), 908-914, 915-922, 941-947, 964 (Big Idea 1), 965 (Example 14.1, #6-9), 966 (Example 14.2, #10-15), 967 (Example 14.5, #24-25), 969 (#1-6, 10-11, 23-24), 1011 (#1-4, 11-34), 1013 (#1-12, 53-55), 1014 (#8-11, 31-32), 1015 (#40-47), 1016 (#1-8, 13-16, 25-28, 46-53), 1017 (#9-16), 1020 (#24-25), 1023 (#1-10, 24-25), A22-A23

HIGH SCHOOL SKILLS AND CONCEPTS – Patterns, Relations and Functions *(cont.)*

MA-HS-AT-S-PRF3

Students will analyze functions by investigating rates of change, intercepts, zeros, asymptotes and local and global behavior.

PE/TE: 82-88, 89-96, 120 (#31), 254 (Key Vocabulary), 255 (Example 5, Guided Practice 10-12), 256 (#44-56), 257 (#63), 339, 342 (#25-37), 344 (#58), 369 (#3), 379 (Example 1, Guided Practice 2), 380 (Example 2, Guided Practice 3-4), 379-386, 387-392, 399 (Quiz #1-2), 400 (#1, 4), 401 (Big Idea 3), 405 (Example 5.6, #33-34), 406 (Example 5.8, #39-40), 407 (#17-18, 23-24), 410 (#2, 4), 411 (#11-12, 14), 459 (#63), 478 (Key Concept), 479 (Example 3), 483 (#32), 486 (Key Concept), 487 (Example 3), 490 (#27), 539 (Example 7.1), 540 (Example 7.2), 610 (#2, 5-6), 1013 (#25-28), 1014 (#23-30)

MA-HS-AT-S-PRF4

Students will transform functions (e.g., arithmetically combining, composing and inverting commonly used functions), using technology on more complicated symbolic expressions.

PE/TE: 428-434, 435, 436 (#3, 5), 437, 438-445, 465 (Big Idea 2), 467 (Example 6.3, #20-23, Example 6.4, #24-26), 469 (#17-30), 474 (#42-51), 1015 (#24-31, 34-39)

MA-HS-AT-S-PRF5

Students will understand and compare the properties of classes of functions (e.g., absolute value, step, exponential, polynomial, rational, logarithmic, periodic).

PE/TE: 80-81, 121-122, 123-129, 130-131, 140 (Big Idea 2), 144 (Example 2.7, #24-27), 446-451, 465 (Big Idea 3), 468 (Example 6.5, #27-29), 469 (#31-33), 478-485, 486-491, 492-498, 499-505, 507-513, 514, 538 (Big Ideas 1, 3), 539 (Example 7.1, #6-9), 540-541, 543 (#1-15, 27), 558-563, 564, 565-571, 602 (Big Idea 1), 604, 607 (#7-12), 678 (#22-24)

MA-HS-AT-S-PRF6

Students will interpret representations of functions of two variables.

PE/TE: *Found throughout the text. See, for example:* 72-79, 80-81, 89-96, 97, 98-104, 105, 107-111, 121-122, 123-129, 130-131, 140, 141 (Example 2.1, #5-7), 142 (Example 2.3, #12-15, Example 2.4, #16-18), 143 (Example 2.5, #19-22), 145 (#1-2, 8-17, 20, 25-27), 236-237, 238 (Example 3, Guided Practice 4-6), 239 (Example 5, Guided Practice 8), 240 (#1, 3-32), 241 (#43-52), 242 (#55-56, 59), 243 (#60), 245-251, 265 (#67, Quiz #1-6), 270 (#38), 271 (#41), 272-273, 287 (Example 6, Guided Practice 13-15), 289 (#41-49), 290 (#64-67), 291 (Quiz #13-18), 297 (#63-65), 309-315, 317 (Big Idea 1), 318 (Example 4.1, #5-7), 319 (Example 4.2, #8-14), 322 (Example 4.10, #45-48), 323 (#1-3, 28-30), 340, 341 (Guided Practice 9-12), 342 (#38-50), 343 (#55-57), 344 (#58-60), 352 (Quiz #16), 356 (Example 6, Guided Practice 11), 358 (#60), 360-361, 368 (#44), 369 (#2), 376 (#49-50), 386 (#64), 387-392, 393-399, 401 (Big Ideas 1, 3), 403 (Example 5.2, #13-16), 406, 407 (#5-7, 23-24, 29), 446-451, 459 (Quiz #1-6), 465 (Big Idea 3), 468 (Example 6.5, #27-29), 469 (#31-33), 478-485, 486-491, 493 (Key Concept, Example 3), 494 (Example 4, Guided Practice 6-9), 495 (#2), 496 (#31-51), 497 (#59-60), 498 (Quiz #1-3, 8-12), 502, 503 (Example 8, Guided Practice 16-18), 504 (#45-53),

HIGH SCHOOL SKILLS AND CONCEPTS – Patterns, Relations and Functions *(cont.)*

505 (#62-63), 513 (Quiz #5-7), 514, 529, 530 (Example 2), 531-532, 533 (#3-14), 534 (#15-26, 31), 535, 536 (#36, Quiz #10-15), 538 (Big Ideas 1, 3), 539 (Example 7.1, #6-8), 540, 541 (#21-23), 542 (Example 7.7, #35-38), 543 (#1-9, 13-15, 25-27, 29), 558-563, 564, 565-571, 589 (Example 2), 590 (Guided Practice 4), 594 (#34-35), 602 (Big Idea 1), 604, 606 (#36), 607 (#7-12, 28-29), 775-780, 781, 786 (Example 11.5, #23), 787 (#14), 908-914, 915-922, 941-947, 964 (Big Idea 1), 965 (Example 14.1, #6-9), 966 (Example 14.2, #10-15), 967 (Example 14.5, #24-25), 969 (#1-6, 10-11, 23-24), 1011 (#1-4, 11-34), 1013 (#1-12, 53-55), 1014 (#8-11, 31-32), 1015 (#40-47), 1016 (#1-8, 13-16, 25-28, 46-53), 1017 (#9-16), 1020 (#24-25), 1023 (#1-10, 24-25)

MA-HS-AT-S-PRF7
Students will use a variety of symbolic representations, including recursive and parametric equations, for functions and relations.

PE/TE: 37 (#11-15), 38 (#19-20, 22-23, 27), 39 (#28), 40 (Quiz #9-10), 107-111, 112, 113-120, 143, 145 (#14-19, 27), 311, 314 (#48-50), 322 (#48), 323 (#32), 396, 397 (#18-21), 398 (#25-28), 399 (Quiz #13), 406 (Example 5.9, #41), 410 (#6), 563 (#44), 774, 775-780, 781, 786 (Example 11.5, #23), 787 (#14), 803, 804 (Example 4, Guided Practice 2-4), 806 (#12-29), 807 (#30-39, 62), 808 (#63-66), 809 (#68-69), 810 (Key Concept), 811, 812 (Example 4, Guided Practice 4-6), 814 (#15-38), 815 (#39-47, 57-58), 816, 817 (Quiz #1-6, 10-16), 827 (Key Concept), 828-829, 831 (#13-23, 34-39), 832 (#43-45, 47), 833 (#48, Quiz #10-12), 839 (Big Ideas 1, 3), 841 (Example 12.2, #9-11, 16, Example 12.3, #17-19), 842 (Example 12.5, #35-38), 843 (#9-12, 25-28, 33), A22-A23

MA-HS-AT-S-PRF8
Students will identify essential quantitative relationships in a situation and determine the class or classes of functions that might model the relationship.

PE/TE: 115-116, 118 (#10-16, 19-20), 119, 120 (Quiz #15), 139 (#6), 143 (Example 2.6, #23), 145 (#27), 149 (#15), 308, 311, 314 (#48-50), 774, 775-780, 781, 782 (#1, 3), 786 (Example 11.5, #23), 787 (#14), 789 (#3), 1011 (#29-30), 1020 (#24-25)

MA-HS-AT-S-PRF9
Students will determine whether a relationship given in symbolic or graphical form is a function.

PE/TE: 73 (Key Concept), 74 (Example 3, Guided Practice 3), 77 (#21-24), 78 (#42-43), 128 (#33), 140 (Big Idea 1), 148 (#1), 232 (#29-30)

CORRELATIONS

High School Skills and Concepts – Patterns, Relations and Functions *(cont.)*

MA-HS-AT-S-PRF10

Students will determine the domain of a function represented in either symbolic or graphical form.

PE/TE: 78 (#46-47), 79 (#48), 81 (Example 2, #5-9), 96 (Quiz #9), 391 (#34-37), 446, 447 (Example 2, Guided Practice 1-4), 448 (Examples 4-5), 449 (Guided Practice 6-11, #3-8, 10-25), 450 (#28-33, 37), 459 (Quiz #1-6), 464 (#4), 468 (Example 6.5, #27-29), 469 (#31-33), 476 (#4-6), 478 (Key Concept), 479 (Example 3, Guided Practice 1-3), 482 (#15-23), 484 (#36, 39), 487 (Example 3), 488 (Guided Practice 4-6), 489 (#16-24), 493 (Example 3), 494 (Guided Practice 6-8), 496 (#42-50), 498 (Quiz #1-3, 8-12), 503 (Example 8, Guided Practice 16-18), 504 (#45-53), 513 (Quiz #5-7), 539 (Example 7.1, #6-8), 540 (Example 7.2, #10-12), 543 (#1-9, 13-15), 558-559, 560 (Example 3), 561 (Guided Practice 4-6, #3-22), 562 (#27-34), 565 (Example 1), 604 (Example 8.2, #10-12), 607 (#7-9), 611 (#10), 792 (#1, 13-15), 1015 (#40-47), 1016 (#1-8, 13-16, 25-28), 1017 (#9-12)

MA-HS-AT-S-PRF11

Students will understand functional notation and evaluate a function at a specified point in its domain.

PE/TE: 75 (Example 5, Guided Practice 5-6), 78 (#34-39), 130 (Example 2), 131 (#1-4), 141 (#7), 145 (#3), 149 (#14), 338 (Example 2, Guided Practice 4-5, Example 3), 341 (#9-23), 445 (#52), 472 (#2)

MA-HS-AT-S-PRF12

Students will combine functions by addition, subtraction, multiplication and compositions.

PE/TE: 428-434, 435, 436 (#3, 5), 445 (Quiz #1-8, 19), 465 (Big Idea 2), 467 (Example 6.3, #20-23), 469 (#17-24), 474 (#42-45), 792 (#3, 13-15), 1015 (#24-31)

MA-HS-AT-S-PRF13

Students will graph linear, absolute value, quadratic and exponential functions and identify their key characteristics.

PE/TE: 89-96, 97, 103 (#53), 104 (#57), 107 (Example 1, Guided Practice 1-4), 109 (#3-10), 121-122, 123-124, 125 (Example 3, Guided Practice 1-3), 126, 127 (#3-14, 21-27), 128 (#31, 36-37), 129 (#40-41), 130 (Example 2), 131 (#5-7, 9-10), 140 (Big Idea 2), 142 (Example 2.3, #12-15), 144 (Example 2.7, #24-26), 145 (#8-11, 20), 150 (#3-5), 236-243, 244, 245-251, 265 (Quiz #1-3), 292 (Example 1), 293 (Example 2, 3), 294 (Key Concept), 299 (#73), 317 (Big Idea 1), 318 (Example 4.1, #5-7), 319 (Example 4.2, #8-13), 323 (#1-3), 328 (#4-6), 478-480, 482 (#3-24), 483 (#26), 484 (#35-36, 39-40), 485 (#41-42), 486-488, 489 (#7-24), 490 (#27, 31), 491 (#33-35), 498 (Quiz #1-3, 8-11), 538 (Big Idea 1), 539 (Example 7.1, #6-8), 540 (Example 7.2, #10-12), 543 (#1-9), 544, 546 (#3, 11), 612 (#4-7), 1011 (#11-18, 31-34), 1013 (#1-8), 1016 (#1-8)

HIGH SCHOOL SKILLS AND CONCEPTS – Patterns, Relations and Functions *(cont.)*

MA-HS-AT-S-PRF14
Students will recognize and solve problems that can be modeled using linear, absolute value, quadratic or exponential functions.

PE/TE: 91 (Example 3, Guided Practice 3), 94 (#59-62), 95 (#64-68), 100 (Example 5, Guided Practice 9), 101 (Example 6, Guided Practice 10), 103 (#50-54), 104 (#55-58), 105 (#2-5), 106 (#5-6), 107-111, 112, 115-116, 117 (Guided Practice 4), 119, 120 (Quiz #15), 125 (Examples 3-4), 126 (Guided Practice 4), 128 (#36-38), 129 (#39-42), 131 (#8), 139 (#1), 143 (Example 2.6), 144 (#27), 145 (#25-27), 239 (Example 5, Guided Practice 8), 241 (#41-42), 242, 243 (#60-61, 63), 246 (Example 2, Guided Practice 4), 247 (Example 4, Guided Practice 8), 250 (#51-53), 251 (#54-56), 254 (Example 4, Guided Practice 9), 256 (#42-43), 257 (#65-67), 258 (#68-72), 261 (Example 6), 262 (Example 7, Guided Practice 22), 264 (#62-66), 265 (#67, Quiz #13), 268, 269 (Example 5, Guided Practice 20), 270 (#38-39), 271 (#40-43), 272-273, 274 (#1-4, 6-7), 287 (Example 7, Guided Practice 16), 289 (#39-40), 290 (#64-67), 295, 298, 299 (#73-74), 311, 314, 315 (#51, 53, Quiz #13), 319 (#14), 321 (#41), 322 (#48), 323 (#31-32), 480 (Example 4, Guided Practice 4), 481, 482 (#25), 483 (#28-31), 484, 485 (#41-44), 488 (Example 4, Guided Practice 7-8), 489 (#26), 490 (#30-32), 491 (#33-36), 543 (#27), 546 (#2, 8), 547 (#17-18), 730 (#50), 775-780, 781, 787 (#14), 849 (#47), 954 (#46)

MA-HS-AT-S-PRF15
Students will extend the ideas of transformations and parametric changes of linear function, such as vertical and horizontal shifts, to transformations of non-linear functions.

PE/TE: 121-122, 123-124, 125 (Example 3, Guided Practice 1-3), 126, 127 (#3-14, 21-26, 28), 128 (#32-34), 138 (Quiz #1-3), 144 (Example 2.7, #24-26), 145 (#20), 236-237, 240 (#7-18), 392 (#46), 478 (Key Concept), 479 (Example 3), 485 (#45), 522 (#62), 539 (Example 7.1), 540 (Example 7.2), 749 (#32), 817 (#64), 1011 (#31-34)

MA-HS-AT-S-PRF16
Students will see the patterns in arithmetic and geometric sequences using recursion.

PE/TE: 826, 827-833, 834-835, 839 (Big Idea 3), 842 (Example 12.5), 843 (#25-28), 1021 (#33-35)

MA-HS-AT-S-PRF17
Students will see patterns in other sequences (e.g., quadratic, cubic).

PE/TE: 795 (Example 3, Guided Practice 5)

MA-HS-AT-S-PRF18
Students will relate the patterns in arithmetic sequences to linear functions.

PE/TE: 803-804, 806 (#12-29), 807 (#30-39, 49-51), 808 (#63a, 64, 65a), 817 (Quiz #10-12), 841 (Example 12.2, #9-11, 16), 843 (#9, 12), 1021 (#10-15)

HIGH SCHOOL SKILLS AND CONCEPTS – Patterns, Relations and Functions *(cont.)*

MA-HS-AT-S-PRF19
Students will relate the patterns in geometric sequences to exponential functions.

PE/TE: 811-812, 814 (#15-38), 815 (#39-47, 57a, 58a), 816 (#59a, 60, 61a), 817 (Quiz #13-16), 818 (#6B), 841 (#17-19), 843 (#10), 846 (#4), 1021 (#19-21)

MA-HS-AT-S-PRF20
Students will solve problems that have direct or inverse relationships for any variable.

PE/TE: 108 (Example 2), 109 (Guided Practice 5, #11-16, 24-29), 110 (#38-39), 120 (Quiz #11-14), 139 (#3), 143 (Example 2.5, #19-22), 145 (#14-17), 146, 233 (#45), 548 (#4-6), 551 (Example 2), 552 (Guided Practice 4-7), 553, 555 (#12-19), 556 (#37-39), 571 (Quiz #1-4), 572 (#2-3), 603 (Example 8.1, #6-9), 607 (#1-6), 611 (#11), 848 (#17-20), 1011 (#25-28), 1017 (#1-4)

HIGH SCHOOL SKILLS AND CONCEPTS – Variables, Expressions and Operations

MA-HS-AT-S-VEO1
Students will write expressions, equations, inequalities and relations in equivalent forms.

PE/TE: 12 (Example 4, Guided Practice 9-14), 14 (#25-32, 43-51), 16 (Quiz #10-12), 26-32, 40 (Quiz #5-8), 51-58, 62 (Example 1.2, #10-16), 63 (Example 1.4, #25-31), 65 (#7-12, 16-18), 129 (#43), 248 (Examples 5-6, Guided Practice 9-16), 249 (#24-32), 252-253, 255 (Example 5, Guided Practice 10-12, #3-14), 256 (#15-23, 44-55), 259-260, 263 (#3-31), 264 (#59-61), 265 (Quiz #4-6), 317 (Big Idea 1), 323 (#4-9), 328 (#7-9), 331 (Example 3), 332 (Example 4), 333 (Guided Practice 5-8, #24-36), 334 (#37-39), 352 (Quiz #5-8), 353-354, 355 (Example 4, Guided Practice 5-7), 356 (#3-9), 357 (#10-29, 42-50, 54-57), 402 (Example 5.1, #7-8, 11-12), 404 (Example 5.4, #21-23, 407 (#1-4, 14-16), 411 (#9), 412 (#4-9), 419 (#67), 423, 425 (#43-59, 69-81), 427 (Quiz #11, 13-14), 467 (Example 6.2b, #18-19), 469 (#13-16), 472 (#6, 12-13), 473 (#19), 474 (#31-34, 39-41), 492 (Example 1c), 493 (Guided Practice 4), 495 (#5, 7-8, 10-16), 496 (#17-18), 498 (Quiz #5-7), 499, 501 (Example 5b, Guided Practice 10-12), 503 (#3-6), 504 (#28-36), 508 (Example 2, Guided Practice 5), 510 (#15-43), 513 (Quiz #8-11, 13, 15), 541 (Example 7.5, #25-30), 548 (#7-9), 580 (#54), 678 (#37-40), 1010 (#10-15), 1013 (#13-16, 25-28), 1014 (#4-7), 1015 (#20-23), 1016 (#10-12, 21, 23, 29-35)

MA-HS-AT-S-VEO2
Students will use symbolic algebra to represent and explain mathematical relationships.

PE/TE: *Found throughout the text. See, for example:* 11 (Example 3, Guided Practice 7), 13 (Example 5, Guided Practice 15), 15 (#58-62), 16 (#63, Quiz #13), 20 (Example 5), 21 (Guided Practice 11), 23 (#72-73), 24 (#74), 32 (#37), 33 (#6-7), 34-39, 40 (Quiz #11-12), 42 (Example 3), 44 (Example 7, Guided Practice 13), 46, 47 (#57-60), 54 (Example 6), 55 (Guided Practice 13), 57, 58 (#81-82, Quiz #13-14), 59 (#2-3, 8), 62 (#16, 23-24), 63 (Example 1.5, #32-33), 64 (#40, 47), 65 (#28), 66-67, 68, 81 (#5-9), 95 (#67), 100 (Example 5, Guided Practice 9), 101 (Example 6, Guided Practice 10), 103 (#50-54), 104 (#55-58), 105 (#2-5), 106 (#1, 5-6), 108,

HIGH SCHOOL SKILLS AND CONCEPTS – Variables, Expressions and Operations *(cont.)*

109 (Guided Practice 5-6), 110 (#38-41), 111 (#44-45), 115 (Example 3), 116, 117 (Guided Practice 4), 119, 120 (Quiz #15), 125 (Example 4), 126 (Guided Practice 4), 128 (#38), 129 (#39, 41), 134 (Example 4), 135 (Guided Practice 11), 137, 138 (Quiz #10), 139 (#1, 5-6), 144 (#27), 145 (#25-27), 147 (#2), 148 (#2, 5), 149 (#15), 239 (Example 5, Guided Practice 8), 242 (#55-56, 58), 243 (#61-62), 250 (#51-53), 251 (#54-56), 262 (Example 7, Guided Practice 22), 265 (#67), 268, 269 (Example 5, Guided Practice 20), 270 (#38), 271 (#40-41), 274 (#7), 311 (Example 4), 314, 319 (#21), 322 (#48), 323 (#32), 396, 398 (#26-28), 399 (Quiz #13), 405 (#38), 407 (#28-29), 439 (Example 3, Guided Practice 4), 441 (Example 6), 442 (Example 7, Guided Practice 11), 444, 451 (#39), 469 (#37-38), 480, 483 (#28-30), 484 (#39-40), 485 (#41-42), 488, 490 (#31-32), 491 (#36), 530, 531 (Guided Practice 4), 532 (Example 5), 533 (Example 6, Guided Practice 9), 534 (#31), 535, 536 (#36), 537 (#4), 542 (#38), 543 (#27, 29), 546 (#1), 547 (#17-18), 552 (Example 3, Guided Practice 7), 553 (Example 4, Guided Practice 8), 556 (#37-40), 557 (#41), 560 (Example 4), 561 (Guided Practice 7), 562 (#37-38), 564 (#9), 567 (Example 4, Guided Practice 5), 569 (#31), 570 (#32), 571 (#36, Quiz #11), 572 (#6), 606 (#36), 607 (#28-29), 611 (#13), 775-780, 781, 782 (#1, 3), 910 (Example 3), 911 (Guided Practice 9), 913 (#30), 914 (#31-32), 942 (Example 2, Guided Practice 3), 943, 945 (#23-25), 946, 947 (Quiz #12), 969 (#23-24)

MA-HS-AT-S-VEO3
Students will use symbolic expressions, including iterative and recursive forms, to represent relationships among various contexts.

PE/TE: 11 (Example 3, Guided Practice 7), 13 (Example 5, Guided Practice 15), 15 (#58-62), 16 (#63, Quiz #13), 62 (#16), 65 (#28), 984

MA-HS-AT-S-VEO4
Students will judge the meaning, utility and reasonableness of the results of symbol manipulations, including those carried out using technology.

PE/TE: 157 (#38c), 158 (#39b), 166 (#60d), 184 (#45b), 186 (#6C), 254 (Example 4, Guided Practice 9), 261 (Example 6), 269 (Example 5, Guided Practice 20), 286 (Example 5), 290 (#67b), 295 (Example 5, Guided Practice 10), 356 (Example 6, Guided Practice 11), 359 (#63), 434 (#46c), 484 (#40b), 491 (#33b), 560 (Example 4), 592 (Example 6, Guided Practice 11)

MA-HS-AT-S-VEO5
Students will understand the properties of integer exponents and roots and apply these properties to simplify algebraic expressions.

PE/TE: 330 (Key Concept), 331 (Example 3), 332, 333 (Guided Practice 5-8, #24-36), 334 (#37-38), 352 (Quiz #5-8), 377 (#53), 402 (Example 5.1, #7-8, 11-12), 407 (#1-4), 411 (#9), 412 (#4-6), 421 (Key Concept), 423 (Examples 6-7, Guided Practice 10-11), 425 (#45, 48-50, 52-59), 427 (Quiz #13-14), 434 (#48), 467 (#19), 469 (#13-16), 472 (#13), 473 (#19), 474 (#31-34), 1014 (#4-7), 1015 (#20-23)

High School Skills and Concepts – Variables, Expressions and Operations *(cont.)*

MA-HS-AT-S-VEO6

Students will add, subtract and multiply polynomials.

PE/TE: 346-352, 403 (Example 5.3, #17-20), 407 (#8-11), 474 (#35-37), 548 (#10-12), 1014 (#12-14)

MA-HS-AT-S-VEO7

Students will divide a polynomial by a first-degree polynomial.

PE/TE: 363 (Example 2, Guided Practice 2, Example 3), 364 (Guided Practice 3-4), 366 (#3-6, 11-20), 377 (Quiz #8), 404 (Example 5.5, #27-28), 407 (#12), 1014 (#21-22)

MA-HS-AT-S-VEO8

Students will factor polynomials by removing the greatest common factor.

PE/TE: 260 (Example 4, Guided Practice 13-18), 263 (#1, 22-31), 353 (Example 1), 354 (Guided Practice 1-3), 356 (#3-9), 404 (Example 5.4c, #22), 678 (#16), 353, 356 (#3-8), 1014 (#15)

MA-HS-AT-S-VEO9

Students will factor quadratic polynomials.

PE/TE: 252-253, 255 (#3-14), 256 (#15-23), 259-260, 263 (#1, 3-31), 323 (#4-9), 328 (#7-9), 548 (#7), 678 (#16-17), 1013 (#13-16, 21-24)

MA-HS-AT-S-VEO10

Students will determine when an expression is undefined.

PE/TE: *Opportunities to address this standard can be found on the following pages:* 428 (Key Concept), 429 (Example 2c, Guided Practice 6), 430 (Example 5d), 431 (Guided Practice 12), 432 (#12-19, 28-35), 445 (Quiz #1-8), 469 (#17-24), 558-563, 564, 565-571, 576 (Key Concept, Example 6), 577 (Example 7, Guided Practice 11-12), 578 (#34-43), 579 (#44-46), 581, 582-585, 586 (#3-8, 16-30), 587 (#31-40), 595 (Quiz #1-7), 602 (Big Ideas 1-2), 604-605, 607 (#17-24), 1015 (#24-31), 1017 (#17-32)

MA-HS-AT-S-VEO11

Students will add, subtract, multiply, divide and simplify rational expressions.

PE/TE: 573-580, 581, 582-588, 595 (Quiz #1-7), 601 (#3-4), 602 (Big Idea 2), 605, 607 (#17-24), 678 (#31-33), 1017 (#17-32)

MA-HS-AT-S-VEO12

Students will evaluate polynomial and rational expressions and expressions containing radicals and absolute values at specified values of their variables.

PE/TE: 10 (Example 2, Guided Practice 4-6), 14 (#16-24, 37-42), 16 (Quiz #7-9), 17 (#7-12), 65 (#5-6), 1010 (#7-9)

HIGH SCHOOL SKILLS AND CONCEPTS – Equations and Inequalities

MA-HS-AT-S-EI1
Students will write equivalent forms of equations, inequalities and systems of equations and inequalities and solve them with fluency—mentally or with paper and pencil in simple cases and using technology in all cases.

PE/TE: 18-24, 25, 26-32, 33 (#1, 4-6), 34-39, 40 (#34, Quiz #1-4), 41-47, 48-49, 50, 51-58, 59 (#1-5, 7), 60 (Big Idea 3), 62 (Example 1.3, #17-24), 63 (Example 1.4, #25-31), 64, 65 (#13-18, 19-27), 66-67, 68 (#2-4, 6), 69, 70 (#7-12), 88 (#51), 152, 153-158, 159, 160-167, 177, 178-185, 186, 193 (Quiz #7-9, 14), 205-,206, 207 (Guided Practice 5-7), 208 (#29-37, 42), 209 (#47), 213 (Example 5, Guided Practice 11), 215 (#35-40), 216 (#48), 217 (#52-53), 221 (Big Idea 1-2), 222 (Example 3.1, #4-6), 223 (Example 3.2, #7-10), 224 (Example 3.4, #14-17), 227 (#1-4, 9-14, 22, 31), 228, 230 (#2, 7), 231 (#11), 232 (#4-15, 31-33), 233 (#43), 236-237, 238 (Example 3, Guided Practice 4-6) 240 (#7-32), 241 (#44-52), 242 (#55-56, 59), 243 (#60), 245-247, 249 (#3-23), 250 (#43-48), 253 (Key Concept), 254, 256 (#24-43), 257 (#59-62, 65-67), 258 (#68-72, 74), 261-262, 263 (#32-40), 264 (#50-58, 62-64, 66), 265 (Quiz #1-3, 7-12), 267 (Example 3), 268, 269 (Example 5, Guided Practice 20), 270 (#22-39), 271 (#41-42), 272-273, 274 (#5), 284 (Example 1), 285 (Guided Practice 1-3, Example 3), 286, 288 (#3-12, 22-38), 289 (#52-27, 61), 290 (#66-67), 291 (Quiz #1-6), 292-299, 315 (Quiz #1-3), 316 (#1-3, 5), 317 (Big Idea 2), 318 (Example 4.1, #5-7), 319, 320 (Example 4.4, #22-24, Example 4.5, #25-28), 321 (Example 4.7, #35-37, Example 4.8, #38-41), 323 (#1-3, 10-15, 19-24), 324-325, 326 (#2-8), 327 (#9, 15-17), 344 (#61), 368 (#47), 369 (#5), 386 (#66), 399 (#31-32), 412 (#7-9), 427 (#92), 445 (#53), 474 (#22-24, 28-30), 475 (#54, 56-57), 476 (#10-12), 588 (#47), 612 (#4-13), 625 (#62), 632 (#70), 664 (#47), 678 (#1-4, 41), 679 (#43, 46), 689 (#72), 697 (#54), 713 (#51), 723 (#44), 730 (#51), 771 (#33), 792 (#4-12), 833 (#49), 848 (#4-6), 858 (#38), 954 (#47), 1010 (#25-53), 1012 (#1-8, 13-16, 27-28, 35-38), 1013 (#1-12, 17-20, 33-36, 41-48, 53-55)

MA-HS-AT-S-EI2
Students will draw reasonable conclusions about a situation being modeled.

PE/TE: 271 (#42b), 306 (#74d), 433 (#45c), 458 (#60c), 505 (#62d), 563 (#40b, 41c), 570 (#35d), 647 (#42d)

High School Skills and Concepts – Equations and Inequalities *(cont.)*

MA-HS-AT-S-EI3

Students will solve one-variable equations and inequalities using manipulatives, symbols, procedures and graphing, including graphing the solution set on a number line.

PE/TE: 18-24, 25, 32 (#42), 33 (#1, 4-6), 34-39, 40 (#34, Quiz #1-4), 41-47, 48-49, 50, 51-58, 59 (#1-5, 7), 60 (Big Idea 3), 62 (Example 1.3, #17-24), 64, 65 (#13-15, 19-27), 66-67, 68 (#2-4, 6), 69, 70 (#7-9), 209 (#47), 217 (#52), 232 (#4-15), 253 (Key Concept), 254, 256 (#24-43), 257 (#59-62, 65-67), 258 (#68-72), 261-262, 263 (#32-40), 264 (#50-58, 62-64, 66), 265 (Quiz #7-12), 267 (Example 3), 268, 269 (Example 5, Guided Practice 20), 270 (#22-39), 271 (#41-42), 272-273, 274 (#5), 284 (Example 1), 285 (Guided Practice 1-3, Example 3), 286, 288 (#3-12, 22-38), 289 (#52-57, 61), 290 (#66-67), 291 (Quiz #1-6), 292-299, 315 (Quiz #1-3), 316 (#1-2, 3, 5), 317 (Big Idea 2), 319 (Example 4.3, #15-21), 320 (Example 4.4, #22-24, Example 4.5, #25-28), 321 (Example 4.7, #35-37, Example 4.8, #38-41), 323 (#10-15, 19-24), 324, 344 (#61), 355 (Example 5, Guided Practice 8-10), 356 (Example 6, Guided Practice 11), 357 (#32-41), 358, 399 (#32), 404 (#24), 427 (#92), 452-459, 460-461, 462-463, 468 (Example 6.6, #30-32), 469 (#34-36), 471 (Problem 2, #1), 473 (#14), 474 (#7-12), 475 (#52), 515-522, 523-525, 526-527, 536 (Quiz #1-9), 542 (Example 7.6, #32-34), 543 (#22-24), 547 (#12-13, 15), 589-595, 596-597, 598-600, 606, 607 (#25-27), 611 (#9), 612 (#8-10), 625 (#62), 664 (#47), 678 (#1-9, 41), 713 (#51), 723 (#44), 730 (#51), 771 (#33), 792 (#4-9), 833 (#49), 954 (#47), 1010 (#16-24, 33-53), 1013 (#17-20, 33-36, 41-52), 1015 (#48-56), 1016 (#40-45), 1017 (#33-36)

MA-HS-AT-S-EI4

Students will solve linear equations and inequalities in one variable including those involving the absolute value of a linear function.

PE/TE: 18-24, 25, 32 (#42), 33 (#1, 4-6), 34-39, 40 (#34, Quiz #1-4), 41-47, 48-49, 50, 51-58, 59 (#1-5, 7), 60 (Big Idea 3), 62 (Example 1.3, #17-24), 63 (Example 1.5, #32-33), 64, 65 (#13-15, 19-30), 66-67, 68 (#2-4, 6), 69, 70 (#7-9), 150 (#6-8), 173 (#41), 209 (#47), 217 (#52), 232 (#4-15), 234 (#11-14), 344 (#61), 427 (#92), 474 (#7-8), 664 (#47), 678 (#1-2, 41), 730 (#51), 792 (#4-9), 833 (#49), 954 (#47), 1010 (#16-24, 33-53)

MA-HS-AT-S-EI5

Students will solve an equation involving several variables for one variable in terms of the others.

PE/TE: 26-32, 40 (Quiz #5-8), 63 (Example 1.4, #25-31), 65 (#16-18), 70 (#10-12), 233 (#43), 327 (#9), 412 (#7-9), 1010 (#25-30)

MA-HS-AT-S-EI6

Students will solve systems of two linear equations in two variables.

PE/TE: 152, 153-158, 159, 160-167, 186, 205, 207 (Guided Practice 5-6), 208 (#29-31, 42), 217 (#53), 221 (Big Ideas 1-2), 222 (Example 3.1, #4-6), 223 (Example 3.2, #7-10), 227 (#1-4, 9-11, 31), 228, 230 (#2, 7), 231 (#11), 232 (#31-33), 258 (#74), 299 (#76), 368 (#47), 386 (#66), 399 (#31), 445 (#53), 474 (#22-24), 475 (#54), 588 (#47), 612 (#11-13), 632 (#70), 679 (#43), 697 (#54), 792 (#10-12), 817 (#63), 1012 (#1-8, 27-28, 35-38)

HIGH SCHOOL SKILLS AND CONCEPTS – Equations and Inequalities *(cont.)*

MA-HS-AT-S-EI7
Students will solve systems of three linear equations in three variables.

PE/TE: 178-185, 193 (Quiz #7-9, 14), 206, 207 (Guided Practice 7), 208 (#32-37), 213 (Example 5, Guided Practice 11), 215 (#35-40, 44), 216 (#48), 224 (Example 3.4, #14-17), 227 (#12-14, 32), 229 (#1), 231 (#13), 1012 (#13-16)

MA-HS-AT-S-EI8
Students will solve quadratic equations in one variable.

PE/TE: 253 (Key Concept), 254, 256 (#24-43), 257 (#59-62, 65-67), 258 (#68-72), 261-262, 263 (#32-40), 264 (#50-58, 62-64, 66), 265 (Quiz #7-12), 267 (Example 3), 268 (Example 4, Guided Practice 17-19), 269 (Example 5, Guided Practice 20), 270 (#22-39), 271 (#41-42), 272-273, 274 (#6), 284 (Example 1), 285 (Guided Practice 1-3, Example 3), 286, 288 (#3-12, 22-38), 289 (#52-27), 290 (#66-67), 291 (Quiz #1-6), 292-299, 316 (#1, 3, 5), 317 (Big Idea 2), 319 (Example 4.3, #15-21), 320 (Example 4.4, #22-24, Example 4.5, #25-28), 321 (Example 4.7, #35-37, Example 4.8, #38-41), 323 (#10-15, 19-24), 324, 399 (#32), 474 (#9-10), 612 (#8-10), 678 (#3-4), 723 (#44), 771 (#33), 1013 (#17-20, 33-36, 41-48)

MA-HS-AT-S-EI9
Students will approximate and interpret rates of change from graphical and numerical data.

PE/TE: 82-88, 96 (Quiz #4-5), 106 (#4), 142 (Example 2.2, #8-11), 145 (#4-7), 146, 149 (#11, 16), 1011 (#5-10)

MA-HS-AT-S-EI10
Students will graph a linear equation and demonstrate that it has a constant rate of change.

PE/TE: 89-96, 97, 142 (Example 2.3, #12-15), 145 (#8-11), 232 (#20-22), 474 (#13), 536 (#38), 1011 (#11-18)

MA-HS-AT-S-EI11
Students will relate the coefficients of a linear equation and the slope and x- and y-intercepts of its graph.

PE/TE: 89-96, 98-100, 101 (#3-17), 102 (#18-39), 103 (#46, 50-51), 104 (#55-56, 58), 105, 106 (#1-4, 7), 142 (Example 2.3, #12-15, Example 2.4, #16-18), 145 (#8-13), 147, 149 (#10, 12-13), 167 (#64, 66), 193 (#37), 258 (#74), 368 (#48), 595 (#39), 648 (#45), 749 (#32), 800 (#70), 872 (#43), 880 (#41), 937 (#47), 1011 (#11-24)

MA-HS-AT-S-EI12
Students will relate a solution of a system of two linear equations in two variables and the graphs of the corresponding lines.

PE/TE: 153-158, 159, 167 (Quiz #1-3), 221 (Big Idea 1), 222 (Example 3.1, #4-6), 227 (#1-4), 1012 (#1-4)

CORRELATIONS

HIGH SCHOOL SKILLS AND CONCEPTS – Equations and Inequalities *(cont.)*

MA-HS-AT-S-EI13
Students will graph the solution set of a linear inequality and identify whether the solution set is an open or closed half-plane.

PE/TE: 132-138, 139 (#2), 140 (Big Idea 2), 144 (Example 2.8, #28-34), 150 (#9-11), 232 (#26-28), 271 (#44), 1011 (#35-42)

MA-HS-AT-S-EI14
Students will graph the solution set of a system of two or three linear inequalities.

PE/TE: 168-173, 174-176, 221 (Big Idea 2), 223 (Example 3.3, #11-13), 227 (#5-8), 233 (#47), 1012 (#9-12)

MA-HS-AT-S-EI15
Students will read information and draw conclusions from graphs and identify properties of a graph that provide useful information about the original problem.

PE/TE: 91, 94 (#59, 61-62), 95 (#64-66, 68), 96 (Quiz #9), 128 (#36-38), 129 (#40, 41c), 131 (#8b), 134 (Example 4), 137 (#44-45, 47), 144 (#27), 155 (Example 4, Guided Practice 7), 157 (#38b), 158 (#39c), 159 (#7-8), 170, 172 (#35), 173 (#37c, 39c), 175 (Example 1), 176 (#7-9), 239 (Example 5, Guided Practice 8), 242, 243 (#60-61), 246 (Example 2), 247 (Example 4, Guided Practice 8), 250 (#51-53), 251 (#54-55), 319 (#14), 326 (#6-7), 389 (Example 3, Guided Practice 5), 391 (#39-40), 392 (#41-43), 447 (Example 3, Guided Practice 5), 450 (#35-36), 451 (#38), 480 (Example 4, Guided Practice 4), 484 (#35b, 36b, 39c), 485 (#41b, 42d), 488 (Example 4, Guided Practice 7), 490 (#30, 31c), 491 (#33a, 34c, 35c), 494 (Example 4, Guided Practice 9), 497 (#59b, 60c), 560 (Example 4), 562 (#37-38, 39b), 563 (#40b, 41c), 564 (#9), 567 (Example 4, Guided Practice 5), 570 (#33b, 34b-34c, 35), 571 (Quiz #11)

MA-HS-AT-S-EI16
Students will graph a quadratic function and understand the relationship between its real zeros and the x-intercepts of the graph.

PE/TE: 236-243, 244, 245-251, 265 (Quiz #1-3), 318 (Example 4.1, #5-7), 319 (Example 4.2, #8-14), 323 (#1-3), 326 (#1), 327 (#13), 328 (#1-3), 335 (#55), 411 (#14), 474 (#16-17), 612 (#4-7), 619 (#58), 1013 (#1-8)

MA-HS-AT-S-EI17
Students will write and solve linear sentences, describing real-world situations by using and relating formulas, tables, graphs and equations.

PE/TE: 19 (Example 2, Guided Practice 4), 20 (Example 5), 21 (Guided Practice 11), 23 (#68-73), 24 (#74-78), 29, 31 (#33-34), 32 (#35-39), 33 (#1-2, 4-7), 34, 35 (Example 2), 36, 37 (#3-15), 38 (#24-26), 39 (#29-33), 40 (#34, Quiz #11-12), 62 (#23-34), 63 (#31, Example 1.5, #32-33), 65 (#28-31), 68 (#4-7), 69 (#8-9), 100 (Example 5, Guided Practice 9), 101 (Example 6, Guided Practice 10), 103 (#50-54), 104 (#55-59), 108 (Example 3), 109 (Guided Practice 6), 110 (#38-41), 111 (#42-45), 115-116, 117 (Guided Practice 4), 119, 120 (Quiz #15), 139 (#6), 143 (#22), 145 (#25-27), 148 (#2), 149 (#15), 451 (#41)

HIGH SCHOOL SKILLS AND CONCEPTS – Equations and Inequalities *(cont.)*

MA-HS-AT-S-EI18
Students will recognize and solve problems that can be modeled using a linear equation in one variable, a quadratic equation or a system of linear equations.

PE/TE: 19 (Example 2, Guided Practice 4), 20 (Example 5), 21 (Guided Practice 11), 23 (#68-73), 24 (#74c, 75-78), 47 (#61), 58 (#83), 59 (#1, 4-8), 62 (#23-24), 65 (#29), 155 (Example 4, Guided Practice 7), 157 (#35-38), 158 (#39-40), 159 (#7-8), 162, 163 (Guided Practice 4), 165 (#55-56), 166, 167 (Quiz #13), 181, 184, 185 (#46-48), 186 (#1-3), 206 (Example 4), 208 (#42), 209 (#43-44), 213 (Example 5, Guided Practice 11), 215 (#43-44), 216 (#45-48), 217 (#51), 220 (#5), 223 (#10), 224 (#17), 227 (#32), 254 (Example 4, Guided Practice 9), 256 (#42-43), 257 (#65-67), 258 (#68-72), 261 (Example 6), 262 (Example 7, Guided Practice 22), 264 (#62-66), 265 (#67, Quiz #13), 269 (Example 5, Guided Practice 20), 270 (#38-39), 271 (#40-43), 272-273, 290 (#64-67), 295, 298, 299 (#73-74, 76), 321 (#41), 323 (#31), 344 (#61), 368 (#47), 369 (#4), 399 (#32), 475 (#52), 563 (#43), 678 (#41)

MA-HS-AT-S-EI19
Students will use the skills learned to solve linear equations and inequalities to solve numerically, graphically or symbolically non-linear equations (e.g., absolute value, quadratic, exponential equations).

PE/TE: 51-53, 54 (Example 5), 55 (Guided Practice 10-12, #3-39), 56, 58 (Quiz #7-12), 60 (Big Idea 3), 64 (Example 1.7, #41-47), 65 (#22-27), 254 (Example 3, Guided Practice 9), 256 (#24-40), 261 (Example 5), 262 (Guided Practice 19-21), 263 (#32-40), 264 (#53-58), 267 (Example 3), 268 (Example 4, Guided Practice #17-19), 270 (#22-34), 275, 279 (#3-11), 284, 285 (Guided Practice 1-3, Example 3), 286, 288 (#22-34), 289 (#50-57), 291 (Quiz #1-6), 319 (Example 4.3, #15-21), 320 (Example 4.4, #22-24, Example 4.5, #25-28), 321 (Example 4.7, #35-37), 323 (#10-15, 19-21), 355 (Example 5, Guided Practice 8-10), 356 (Example 6, Guided Practice 11), 357 (#32-41), 452-459, 460-461, 468 (Example 6.6, #30-32), 469 (#34-36), 471 (Problem 2, #1), 473 (#14, 20), 474 (#8-12), 515-522, 523-525, 542 (Example 7.6, #32-34), 543 (#22-24), 547 (#12-13, 15), 589-595, 596-597, 606, 607 (#25-27), 611 (#9), 612 (#8-10), 678 (#2-9), 848 (#3-10), 1010 (#42-53), 1013 (#17-20, 33-36, 41-44), 1015 (#48-56), 1016 (#40-45), 1017 (#33-36)

MA-HS-AT-S-EI20
Students will use graphing technology to explore the meaning of quadratic equations with complex solutions.

PE/TE: 293 (Example 3)